THE OFFICIAL REGISTRY AND CHECKLIST — ROSA

Published by
International Cultivar Registration Authority — Rosa
Shreveport, LA

This book presents information obtained from American Rose Society registration files, past editions of *Modern Roses* and various publications and industry sources. Every effort has been made to give reliable data and information, but the publisher cannot assume responsibility for the validity of all materials or for the consequences of their use. The absence of ™ or ® symbols in this publication should not be regarded as an indication that these words, designations, or names are not trademarks.

This list includes all registration data through August 2008.

Please send all corrections to:

>Chairman, ARS Registration Committee
>American Rose Society
>P.O. Box 30,000
>Shreveport, Louisiana 71130-0030

Copyright © by the American Rose Society, 2009

No part of this publication may be reproduced or transmitted in any form or by any means electronic or mechanical without written permission from the publisher.

On Our Cover: 'Wekcryland' ('Cadillac DeVille', 'Marguerite Bourgeoys', Moonstone™) HT, w, 1998, Carruth, Tom; flowers ivory white with a fine, delicate pink edging, 4½-5 in., full, high-centered, borne singly, slight fragrance; recurrent; foliage large, medium green, dull; prickles moderate; upright, medium (120-160 cm.) growth; PP11384; [Crystalline™ × 'Lynn Anderson']; intr. 1998. See page 787. Photo by Cliff Orent. Rose grown by Hal Reynolds.

TABLE OF CONTENTS

Introduction 5
Key to Entries 6
A 7
B 52
C 98
D 151
E 189
F 209
G 237
H 271
I 306
J 316
K 352
L 379
M 423
N 534
O 545
P 555
Q 610
R 612
S 657
T 730
U 766
V 769
W 781
X 811
Y 811
Z 816

INTRODUCTION

In 1955, the American Rose Society was appointed by the Commission for Nomenclature and Cultivar Registration, a part of the International Society for Horticultural Science, as the International Registration Authority — Rosa (IRAR). In the years since, the name of the Authority has changed to the International Cultivar Registration Authority — Rosa (ICRA), and the duties have changed and expanded. The overall goals of the ICRA system are to assure "the stability and fixity of cultivated plant nomenclature"[1] and to "prevent duplicated uses of cultivar and Group epithets within a defined denomination class (usually a genus)"[1]. The ICRA system is a voluntary one, and its success depends on the cooperation and coordination of all those involved with the creation, marketing, and documentation of new plants. This is especially important with today's widespread use of the World Wide Web, where incorrect data can be distributed globally with the click of a mouse button.

The ICRA scheme operates under the International Code of Nomenclature for Cultivated Plants[2] (ICNCP), which provides a comprehensive set of rules for naming cultivated plants, as well as outlining the functions of the individual ICRA. In addition to registering cultivar epithets and ensuring their formal establishment, an ICRA is obligated to:

- Publish full lists of all cultivars and cultivar-group epithets in the denomination class (i.e., international registers and checklists)
- Maintain records, in as great a detail as is practical, of the origin, characteristics and history of each cultivar and cultivar-group in the denomination class

It is important to note that these two functions apply to all cultivars within the denomination class, not just those for which the ICRA has received an application for registration. In effect, the publication of registers and checklists and the maintenance of a comprehensive database establish each ICRA, according to the ISHS, as the official source of data for the cultivars within its area of responsibility.

This publication, *The Official Registry and Checklist — Rosa*, will be published regularly in order to fulfill the responsibilities of ICRA — Rosa. Formerly, the publication of a registry and checklist took a more encyclopedic approach (the *Modern Roses* series), attempting to appeal not only to breeders, nurserymen and botanists, but also to rose society members, hobbyists and exhibitors. Unfortunately, it became an impossible task for one volume, and the American Rose Society made the decision to publish *Modern Roses 12*[3] as a separate work.

The Official Registry and Checklist — Rosa, in order to meet the listing requirements set forth in the ICNCP, shall:

- Include epithets of ALL cultivars in the genus Rosa, whether or not they are registered, and regardless of whether they are still in cultivation. Even those cultivars which are confidently thought to be extinct are included, since the epithets are often of historical importance.
- Include all known synonyms, including trade designations, translations, and transliterations, that have been used for a given cultivar. In cases where such synonyms exist, the detailed cultivar entry is listed under the earliest accepted epithet, and all other names are listed parenthetically following it (as well as being cross-referenced).
- Include epithets which are not acceptable for registration but are in commercial use.
- Include duplicate epithets, indicating precedence of establishment where known.

The Official Registry and Checklist — Rosa does not attempt to identify or distinguish, by typography or other means, those names which have special meaning to a national, regional or local rose organizations or publications.

---

[1] *ISHS Commission Nomenclature and Cultivar Registration*. International Society for Horticultural Science, 2008. < http://www.ishs.org/sci/icra.htm >

[2] *International Code of Nomenclature for Cultivated Plants, 7th edition*. C.D. Brickell (Commission Chairman), B.R. Baum, W.L.A. Hetterscheid, A.C. Leslie, J. McNeill, P. Trehane, F. Vrugtman, J.H. Wiersema (eds.), 2004.

[3] *Modern Roses 12*. Phillip Schorr, Marily Young (eds.), 2004.

KEY TO ENTRIES

The format for a typical entry relies on the positional placement of specific data and certain typographical conventions. Not all entries will contain all elements of data.

Cultivar epithet[1], (synonyms[1]), horticultural class, color class, registration year[2], breeder; bud description; sepal description; flower description, including detailed color information, size, petal count, form, bloom habit, and fragrance; bloom frequency; foliage description; stem description, prickle description, growth habit; hip description; hardiness; patent number; parentage; year of introduction[3]

[1] All acceptable epithets are enclosed in single quotes.

[2] If 1955 or later, a year indicated in this position identifies a cultivar for which a registration application has been received by the ICRA and approved.

[3] Year of introduction is approximate (first known to the ICRA) and should not be assumed to be the first introduction.

EXAMPLES

1. 'AC William-Booth' ('William Booth', 'William-Booth') HKor, mr, 1999, Agriculture et Agroalimentaire Canada, Ogilvie; bud pointed; flowers medium red, reverse medium pink, 2 in., single, flat, borne in large clusters, slight to moderate fragrance; foliage medium size, dark green, semi-glossy; prickles moderate, long, concave, green touched red; arching, tall growth; hips round, abundant, shiny orange-red; very hardy; PP11629; [(R. kordesii × Max Graf O.P.) × ('Arthur Bell' × 'Applejack')]

   This cultivar is listed under its accepted epithet and includes two synonyms which are also acceptable according to the ICNCP. The cultivar is formally registered.

2. 'A Whiter Shade of Pale' HT, w, Pearce; flowers white with a touch of pink shading, large, dbl., high-centered, borne mostly singly, intense fragrance; recurrent; foliage semi-glossy; medium (3-4 ft.) growth; intr. 2006

   The only known epithet for this cultivar is acceptable under the ICNCP. The cultivar is not formally registered.

3. A Caen la Paix® HT, m, Orard, Joseph; intr. 1994

   The only known epithet for this cultivar is not acceptable under the ICNCP because it is a trademark; the epithet is not enclosed in single quotes. The cultivar is not formally registered. (For a complete specification of acceptability of epithets, please see the ICNCP.)

4. 'Abbé Berlèze' HGal, w, before 1845, Baumann; flowers white, shaded flesh, dbl.
   'Abbé Berlèze' HP, dp, Guillot et Fils; [sport of 'Géant des Batailles']; intr. 1864

   The epithet is acceptable under the ICNCP, although use has been duplicated. Entries are listed in order of precedence and the earliest use is treated as registered.

—A—

'À Balais' -- See 'Comtesse de Chamoïs'

'À Bois Brun' HMult, mp, 1849, Vibert; flowers carminy pink, petals notched, often with a line in the middle, full, borne in clusters

'À Bordures' -- See 'Comtesse de Chamoïs'

'À Bouquets' -- See 'Argentée'

'À Boutons Renversés' -- See 'Boursault Rose'

A Caen la Paix® HT, m, Orard, Joseph; intr. 1994

'A Capella' HT, mr, 1984, Stoddard, Louis; flowers large, 35 petals, borne singly, slight fragrance; foliage large, medium green, matte; upright growth; ['Command Performance' × 'Tiffany']

'À Coeur Jaune' ('Blanche à Coeur Jaune', 'Blanche') A, w, about 1810, Descemet; flowers white with yellow center

'A Country Woman' HT, dr, Zary; intr. 1997

'À Douze Pétales' -- See 'À Fleurs Presque Simples'

'À Feuille de Chêne' ('Grandidentata', 'Ilicifolia', 'Quercifolia') C, mp, before 1811, Trianon; bud round; flowers rose pink, medium, very full, borne in clusters of 5-7; foliage oval, close-set, deeply toothed; prickles few, weak

'À Feuilles Bipinnées' -- See R. centifolia bipinnata

'À Feuilles Cloquées' -- See 'Bullata'

'À Feuilles Crénelées' ('Crenata') C, lp, before 1804, Dupont; flowers delicate pink, small, full, borne in small clusters, moderate fragrance; foliage rounded, very deeply dentate; prickles small, almost straight

'À Feuilles Crépues' -- See 'Bullata'

'À Feuilles Crispées' -- See R. centifolia bipinnata

'À Feuilles de Bengale' Misc OGR, before 1815, Descemet; hybrid canina

'À Feuilles de Céleri' -- See R. centifolia bipinnata

'À Feuilles de Chanvre' -- See 'Cymbaefolia'

'À Feuilles de Chanvre' ('Cannabina') C, lp, before 1811; flowers pinkish white, dbl.; foliage long, slender, pointed, serrate

'À Feuilles de Chou' -- See 'Bullata'

'À Feuilles de Fraxinelle' Misc OGR, before 1815, Descemet; hybrid canina

'À Feuilles de Frêne' -- See 'Turneps'

'À Feuilles de Groseillier' -- See R. centifolia bipinnata

'À Feuilles de Pêcher' ('Persicifolia') A, w, before 1817, Pelletier; flowers medium, full; foliage pointed, regularly dentate; possibly synonymous with 'Cymbaefolia'

'À Feuilles de Persil' -- See R. centifolia bipinnata

'À Feuilles d'Ormé' HGal, lp, before 1820, Descemet

'À Feuilles Gaufrées' -- See 'Bullata'

'À Fleur d'Anémone' -- See 'De La Flèche'

'À Fleur Double' -- See 'La Moderne'

'À Fleur d'un Rouge Pâle' -- See 'Agathe Incarnata'

'À Fleurs d'Anémone' -- See 'Anémone'

'À Fleurs de Rose Tremier de la Chine' C, dp, before 1828, Pelletier; flowers rosy crimson, edged and mottled with blush, large, dbl., cupped; prickles few, gray; growth upright

'À Fleurs Doubles' -- See 'Plena'

'À Fleurs Doubles' -- See 'Petite Hessoise'

'À Fleurs Doubles' -- See 'Double White'

'À Fleurs Doubles Violettes' C, m, from France; flowers violet purple, medium, full, moderate fragrance

'À Fleurs Doubles Violettes' Ch, m, before 1818

'A Fleurs Gigantesques' HGal, mp, 1813; flowers rich deep pink, large, very dbl.; bushy growth

'À Fleurs Marbrée' -- See 'Marmorea'

'À Fleurs Panachées' -- See 'Variegata'

'À Fleurs Presque Simples' ('À Douze Pétales', 'À Sept Pétales') C, mp, 1807, Charpentier; flowers small, 5-7 petals; foliage small, light green; prickles slightly hooked; growth upright, small (15-20 in.); hips small, elongate, red

'À Fleurs Roses' -- See 'Elisa'

'À Fleurs Roses de Laffay' HSem, Laffay, M.

'À Fleurs Rouges Doubles' -- See 'Red Damask'

'À Fleurs Simples' C, mp, before 1804, Dupont; flowers rose pink, medium, single to semi-dbl.

'A. Geoffrey de St Hilaire' HP, mr, 1878, Verdier; flowers medium, dbl.; tall growth

'À Grand Cramoisi' ('Grand Cramoisi de Trianon') HGal, m, before 1818, Trianon; flowers very dark purple, semi-dbl.

'À Gros Cul' -- See R. × francofurtana

'À Longs Pédoncule' M, lp, 1854, Robert; bud pale green, mossy, long peduncles; flowers pink, flushed lilac, many petaled, 6 cm., dbl., globular, borne in clusters of 20-25; foliage small, round, soft green; vigorous growth

'A Midsummer Nights Dream' -- See 'Rawroyal'

'A Night in June' HT, or, 1935, Elmer's Nursery; flowers coral-red, very large, dbl.; foliage leathery; vigorous, bushy growth; [sport of 'Evening Star']

'À Odeur de Noisette' -- See 'Thisbé'

'À Odeur de Punaise' -- See 'Le Rire Niais'

'À Odeur Ingrate' -- See 'Le Rire Niais'

'À Pedoncules Courbées' HGal, lp, before 1829, Coquerel; flowers flesh pink

'À Pétale Teinté de Rose' -- See R. × damascena subalba

'À Pétales Variés' -- See R. × damascena versicolor

'À Petites Fleurs' -- See 'Enfant de France'

'A Royal Bride' -- See 'Tanlopo'

'À Sept Pétales' -- See 'À Fleurs Presque Simples'

'A Shropshire Lad' -- See 'Ausled'

'A Thousand Cranes' -- See 'Senbatsuru'

'À Tiges sans Épines' -- See 'Inermis'

'A True Gentleman' -- See 'Worcalorie'

'A Whiter Shade of Pale' HT, w, Pearce; flowers white with a touch of pink shading, large, dbl., high-centered, borne mostly singly, intense fragrance; recurrent; foliage semi-glossy; medium (3-4 ft.) growth; intr. 2006

'A. Boquet' -- See 'A. Bouquet'

'A. Bouquet' ('A. Boquet') T, w, 1873, Liabaud; flowers white, striped, large, full, borne in small clusters; probably extinct

'A. Denis' HT, my, 1935, Böhm, J.; flowers lemon-yellow, streaked carmine, large, dbl.; ['Gorgeous' × 'Marion Cran']

'A. Drawiel' HP, dr, 1887, Lévêque; flowers large, dbl.

'A. Dvorak' ('Antonín Dvorák') HT, op, 1933, Böhm, J.; flowers light pinkish orange, open, large, dbl.; foliage glossy, dark; bushy growth; ['Mme Butterfly' × 'Gorgeous']

'A. G. A. Rappard' ('A. G. A. Ridder van Rappard') HT, op, 1934, Buisman, G. A. H.; flowers salmon, verging on Neyron pink, well-shaped, dbl., slight fragrance; foliage glossy, bright green; vigorous, bushy growth

'A. G. A. Ridder van Rappard' -- See 'A. G. A. Rappard'

'A. G. Furness' HT, mr, 1941, Clark, A.; flowers rich red; semi-climbing growth; ['Sensation' × unknown]

'A. H. Kirk' HT, op; flowers salmon pink with carmine, large, dbl.

'A. J. Herwig' -- See 'Arend Herwig'

'A. K. Mishra' HT, w, Pushpanjali; flowers large, milky white with broad petals, well formed; vigorous, hardy growth; intr. 1997

'A. K. Williams' -- See 'Alfred K. Williams'

'A. M. Ampère' HP, dr, 1881, Liabaud; ['Lion des Combats' × unknown]

'A. MacKenzie' ('Alexander MacKenzie') S, rb, 1985, Svejda, Felicitas; bud ovoid; flowers medium dbl., reverse lighter, 3 in., 45 petals, cupped, borne in clusters of 6-12; repeat bloom; foliage yellow-green, glossy, leathery; prickles purple; upright growth; [Queen Elizabeth® × ('Red Dawn' × 'Suzanne')]; intr. 1985

'A. N. W. B. Rose' HT, w, 1933, Buisman, G. A. H.; flowers white, tinted yellow, open, large, dbl.; very vigorous growth; ['Frau Karl Druschki' × 'Souv. de Claudius Pernet']

'A. R. S. Centennial' -- See 'Savars'

'A. W. Jessep' HT, dp, 1952, Clark, A.; flowers rich cerise-pink, large, 38 petals, vigorous growth

'Aachener Dom' -- See 'Meicapinal'

'Aafje Heynis' HT, mr, 1964, Buisman, G. A. H.; flowers bright red, well-shaped, large; foliage glossy, light green; vigorous, upright growth; ['Prima Ballerina'

× 'Salvo']

'Aaland' S, dp

'Aalrise' ('Niagara Sunrise') Min, dy, 2001, Aalbers, Jamie; flowers 1½-2 in., full, borne mostly solitary, no fragrance; foliage medium size, medium green, semi-glossy; prickles ¼ in., straight, numerous; growth upright, medium (8-10 in.); garden decorative, containers; [seedling × 'Lavjune']; intr. 2001

Aalsmeer Gold® ('Bekola') HT, dy, 1978, Kordes; bud long, pointed; flowers deep yellow, 23 petals, high-centered, borne singly, slight fragrance; foliage glossy; vigorous, upright, bushy growth; PP4421; ['Berolina' × seedling]

'Aaron Dean' -- See 'Kenlimon'

'Aasha' HT, mr, Datta; flowers rose red, non-fading, classic; long stems; intr. 2003

'Aasmeer' HT, ob; flowers peachish-orange with yellow tones

'Aba Saheb' HT, ob, Chiplunkar; flowers show splashes and streaks of paler orange on both sides of the broad petals, full, high-centered; [sport of 'Modern Art']; intr. 1993

'Abailard' ('Abeilard') HGal, lp, before 1826, Sommesson; flowers delicate pink, medium, very dbl.

'Abaillard' HGal, lp, 1845, Robert; flowers light pink and dark pink, marbled, medium, very dbl.

'Abasanta' HT, dp, 1956, Motose; bud pointed, cerise; flowers carmine, occasionally streaked white, large, dbl., moderate fragrance; foliage dark; compact growth; PP1527; ['Red Columbia' × ('Red Columbia' × 'Tausendschön sport')]

'Abba Dabba' Min, mr, 1980, Lyon; bud long, pointed; flowers 38 petals, borne 1-5 per cluster, slight fragrance; foliage small, medium green; prickles tiny, curved; compact, bushy growth; ['Red Can Can' × seedling]; intr. 1980

Abbaye de Cluny™ -- See 'Meibrinpay'

Abbaye de Valsaintes® HT, mp, Dorieux; flowers medium pink in heart, outer petals fading lighter, large , double, crumpled, intense old rose, lily of the valley, and grapefruit fragrance; recurrent; vigorous growth; intr. 2006

'Abbé André Reitter' HT, lp, 1901, Welter; flowers light flesh pink, large, full, slight fragrance

'Abbé Berlèze' HGal, w, before 1845, Baumann; flowers white, shaded flesh, dbl.

'Abbé Berlèze' HP, dp, Guillot et Fils; [sport of 'Géant des Batailles']; intr. 1864

'Abbé Bramerel' HP, dr, 1871, Guillot et Fils; flowers large, dbl.; ['Géant des Batailles' × unknown]

'Abbé de la Haye' HT, mp, Bourbin; flowers bright pink, large, full; intr. 1855

'Abbé de la Haye' B, mp, 1854, Robert; flowers glowing pink, large, full

'Abbé Garroute' T, pb, 1902, Bonnaire; flowers coppery yellow and carmine pink, petals edged pink, large, full, intense fragrance; probably extinct

'Abbé Girardin' B, mp, 1881, Bernaix, A.; flowers carmine-pink, center darker, large, dbl.; ['Louise Odier' × 'Hermosa']

'Abbé Giraudier' HP, mr, 1869, Levet; flowers cherry red, very large, dbl.; ['Géant des Batailles' × 'Victor Verdier']

'Abbé Lemire' HT, dr, Orard; intr. 1997

'Abbé Millot' HT, lp, 1900, Corboeuf; flowers silvery pink, large, dbl.

'Abbé Miolan' Ch, m, 1839; flowers purple, striped white, dbl.

'Abbé Reynaud' HP, m, 1863, Guillot

'Abbé Vénière' HP, mp, 1867, Guillot; flowers shining pink, medium, semi-dbl. to dbl.; recurrent

'Abbeyfield Gold' -- See 'Korquelda'

'Abbeyfield Rose' -- See 'Cocbrose'

'Abbotswood' S, mp, 1954, Hilling; flowers lighter at edges, medium, semi-dbl.; growth habit similar to R. canina; [chance hybrid of R. canina × unknown]

'Abby's Angel' -- See 'Welabb'

'Abd-el-Kader' HP, pb, 1861, Verdier, E.; flowers carmine, tinted dark purple, semi-dbl.

'Abdul-Hamid' -- See 'S. M. I. Abdul-Hamid'

'Abeilard' -- See 'Abailard'

'Abel Carrière' HP, dr, 1875, Verdier, E.; flowers velvety crimson, brighter center, large, 45 petals; ['Baron de Bonstetten' × seedling]

'Abel Grand' -- See 'Abel Grant'

'Abel Grant' ('Abel Grand') HP, lp, 1866, Damaizin; flowers silky whitish-pink, streaked lighter silver, large, dbl., intense fragrance; medium growth; ['Jules Margottin' × unknown]

'Abelzieds' HRg, mp, Rieksta, Dr. Dz.; flowers large, semi-dbl., slight fragrance; growth medium; [R. rugosa alba × 'Poulsen's Pink']; intr. 1957

Abendglut™ -- See 'Poulcs001'

'Abendröte' HP, op, 1919, Ebeling; flowers light coral-red; compact growth; ['Frau Karl Druschki' × 'Juliet']

Aberdeen™ -- See 'Poulshine'

'Aberdeen Celebration' -- See 'Cocmystery'

'Aberdonian' F, rb, 1976, Cocker; flowers golden bronze and scarlet, large, 20 petals, slight fragrance; foliage glossy; [('Evelyn Fison' × 'Manx Queen') × ('Sabine' × 'Circus')]

Aberlady™ -- See 'Tuckaberlady'

'Abhaya' -- See 'Magic Medley'

'Abhisarika' HT, rb, 1976; bud long, pointed; flowers red stripes on yellow background, 2½-3 in., 48 petals, high-centered; free blooming; foliage glossy, yellowish; vigorous growth; [induced sport of 'Kiss of Fire']; intr. 1975

'Abhishek' Gr, rb, IARI; flowers streaks and splashes of yellow and white on broad, crimson red petals; very floriferous; [sport of 'Jantar Mantar']; intr. 2003

'Abiding Faith' HT, dp, 1954, Montose; bud semi-ovoid; flowers deep rose-pink, 4-5 in., 20-35 petals, intense fragrance; vigorous, upright growth; PP1323; [sport of 'La France' × ('Senator' × 'Florex')]

'Abiding Faith, Climbing' Cl HT, dp, 1957, Motose

'Abigail Adams Rose' HMult, mp, Lowe, Mike; flowers fade to white, medium, semi-dbl., borne in small to large clusters, moderate fragrance; reliable repeat; growth low, spreading; groundcover; [R. multiflora nana × 'Sweet Chariot']; intr. 2005

Abigaile® F, pb, Tantau; intr. 1988

'Abington Park Northampton ' HT, op, 1997, Jones, L.J.; flowers very dbl., 41 petals, borne in small clusters; foliage medium size, medium green; some prickles; bushy, medium (3 ft.) growth; ['Cynthia Brooke' × 'Little Darling']

'Ablaze' MinFl, ob, 2007, Read, Allan; flowers 6 cm., semi-dbl., borne in small clusters; foliage small, medium green, semi-glossy; prickles small, straight, brown, moderate; growth upright, short (65 cm.); [('Orange Honey' × unknown) × 'Rise 'n' Shine']; intr. 2007

Able™ -- See 'Tuckable'

'Abol' HT, w, 1927, Evans; flowers ivory-white tinted blush, large, dbl.

'Abondant' Pol, mp, 1914, Turbat; flowers medium-large, dbl.

'Abondante' -- See 'Belle Couronnée'

About Face™ -- See 'Wekosupalz'

'Abracadabra' -- See 'Jacbute'

Abracadabra® HT, rb; flowers deep red/brown petals with lemon yellow stripes; intr. 2002

Abraham Darby® -- See 'Auscot'

'Abraham Zimmerman' HP, mr, 1879, Lévêque; flowers large, dbl.

'Abraxas' S, dr, VEG; flowers medium-large, dbl.; intr. 1973

'Abricot' HT, ab, 1929, Barbier; flowers apricot and coral-salmon, reverse coral-red; ['Mrs Aaron Ward' × 'Jean C.N. Forestier']

'Abricotée' ('Fanny Dupuis') T, ab, 1843, Dupuis; flowers apricot, margins flesh, dbl., cupped

'Absent Friends' F, ab, Dickson; flowers peach, reverse yellow, fading to pink, full, rosette, borne in large clusters, moderate fragrance; recurrent; foliage small, dark green, glossy; vigorous, bushy (100 cm.) growth; intr. 2006

Absolute™ -- See 'Poulrouge'

'Absolute Hit' (Absolute™, Orange Paillette™) MinFl, or, Poulsen; flowers orange-red, 5-8 cm., dbl., no fragrance; growth bushy, 40-60 cm.; intr. 1996

Absolutely™ -- See 'Savalute'

'Abu' HT, dp, VEG; flowers large, dbl.

'Abundance' F, mp, 1976, Gandy, Douglas L.; flowers 4½ in., 30 petals, slight fragrance; foliage dark; low, bushy growth; [seedling × 'Firecracker']; intr.

1974

'Abundancia' -- See 'Mary Hayley Bell'

'Aburae' ('Oil Painting') HT, yb, Ota; intr. 1988

'Abyssinian Rose' -- See 'St John's Rose'

'AC De Montarville' ('De Montarville') HKor, mp, 1999, Agriculture et Agroalimentaire Canada; flowers medium pink, reverse light pink, 3 in., dbl.; foliage small, blue-green, dull; few prickles; compact, medium growth; PP11635; [((Queen Elizabeth® × 'Arthur Bell') × (R. × kordesii × seedling)) × ('Red Pinocchio' × ('Joanna Hill' × R. spinosissima altaica))]

'AC Marie Victorin' ('Marie-Victorin') HKor, pb, 1999, Agriculture et Agroalimentaire Canada; flowers medium pink-yellow, reverse pink-yellow, 3 in., full, borne in small clusters; foliage medium size, light green, semi-glossy; few prickles; arching, medium (1½ m.) growth; PP11650; ['Arthur Bell' × (R. × kordesii × Max Graf O.P.)]

'AC William-Booth' ('William Booth', 'William-Booth') HKor, mr, 1999, Agriculture et Agroalimentaire Canada, Ogilvie; bud pointed; flowers medium red, reverse medium pink, 2 in., single, flat, borne in large clusters, slight to moderate fragrance; foliage medium size, dark green, semi-glossy; prickles moderate, long, concave, green touched red; arching, tall growth; hips round, abundant, shiny orange-red; very hardy; PP11629; [(R. kordesii × Max Graf O.P.) × ('Arthur Bell' × 'Applejack')]

Academy® -- See 'Macgutsy'

Acadia™ -- See 'Trelleborg'

'Acadia Sunrise' -- See 'Bairise'

'Acadian' Ch, dp, 1987, James, John; flowers deep, bright pink, medium, 5 petals, intense fragrance; foliage small, medium green, matte; prickles fine; upright, bushy, hardy growth; [R. nitida × R. chinensis semperflorens]; intr. 1986

Acapella® -- See 'Tanallepa'

'Acapulco' -- See 'Dicblender'

'Acapulco' F, yb, 1962, Von Abrams; bud pointed; flowers yellow and light orange, often flushed pink, medium, 30-40 petals, cupped, borne in clusters; foliage dark, glossy; bushy, compact growth; [seedling × 'Masquerade']; intr. 1962

'Acapulco Sunset' -- See 'Twoaebi'

'Acaritha' HRg, Wartz

Accademia® HT, dp, Barni; bud globular, deep pink-violet; flowers very double , deep cup, rosette, strong fragrance; foliage medium size, dark green; 80 - 100 cm. growth; intr. 2006

'Accent' F, mr, 1976, Warriner, William A.; bud ovoid; flowers cardinal-red, 2-2½ in., 25 petals, flat, slight fragrance; foliage small, dark, leathery; bushy, compact growth; PP3994; ['Marlena' × seedling]; intr. 1977

'Accidentally' HT, ob, Suga, M.; flowers orange-red with light yellow reverse, 12 cm., 30 petals, high-centered, borne mostly solitary, slight fragrance; foliage purplish-green; prickles sparse, concaved; growth upright, low; ['Lamplighter' × Piccadilly®]; intr. 1988

'Acclaim' -- See 'Jacaim'

'Accolade' HT, rb, 1981, Dawson, George; bud ovoid; flowers bright red, shaded darker, 48 petals, high-centered, borne mostly singly, slight fragrance; foliage dark, matte; prickles hooked, brown; vigorous growth; [('Daily Sketch' × 'Charles Mallerin') × Peter Frankenfeld®]; intr. 1979

'Accord' F, ab, 1969, Mason, P.; flowers apricot-peach, reverse carmine, well-formed, high-centered, borne in clusters, moderate fragrance; foliage dark; bushy growth; ['Circus' × seedling]; intr. 1965

'Ace of Diamonds' -- See 'Briace'

'Ace of Hearts' -- See 'Korred'

'Ace of Hearts' -- See 'Herz As'

'Acervate' Pol, mp, 1934, Miers

Acey Deucy™ -- See 'Savathree'

'Achan' HT, yb, Suga, M.; flowers light yellow, edged deep pink, 15 cm., high-centered, slight fragrance; foliage large, brownish-green; growth upright; ['Lady X' × 'Red Lion']

'Achanta' Gr, dr, Viraraghavan, M.S. Viru; intr. 1987

'Achantha' Gr, dr, Viraraghavan, M.S. Viru; intr. 1987

'Achievement' HWich, dp, 1925, English; flowers deep rose pink shaded coral, small, full; foliage variegated; [sport of 'Dorcas']

'Achille' Pol, mp, Guinoisseau; flowers medium-large, semi-dbl.; intr. 1836

'Achille' ('Belle Italienne', 'Louis XVI', 'Superbe Brune') HGal, dr, before 1810, possibly Miellez; flowers deep velvety purple-red, 4 in., dbl.; prickles numerous, fairly hooked

'Achille Cesbron' HP, mr, 1894, Rousset; flowers very large, dbl.; ['Mme Eugène Frémy' × unknown]

'Achille Gonod' HP, mr, 1864, Gonod; flowers large, dbl.; ['Jules Margottin' × unknown]

'Acidalie' B, w, 1833, Rousseau; flowers white with blush center, large, dbl., globular; recurrent bloom; vigorous growth

'Acqua Cheta' HT, rb, 1962, Giacomasso; flowers magenta-red, reverse silvery, 50 petals; foliage dark; compact growth; ['Crimson Glory' × 'Peace']

'Acropolis' S, r, Meilland; flowers pink bronze, reverse lighter, dbl., cupped, borne in clusters; free-flowering; growth to 50-70 cm.; intr. 2002

'Actrice' HT, rb, 1966, Verschuren, A.; bud ovoid; flowers red and light pink, large, dbl.; foliage dark; ['Tzigane' × 'Kordes Perfecta']

'Ada Perry' Min, op, 1978, Bennett, Dee; bud ovoid; flowers soft coral-orange, medium, 40 petals, high-centered, slight fragrance; foliage dark; vigorous, upright growth; ['Little Darling' × ('Coral Treasure' × unknown)]

Adabaluc® ('Scented Whisper') F, ab, Adam; intr. 2000

'Adabaring' ('Grand Huit, Climbing', Grimpant Le Grand Huit®, 'Le Grand Huit, Climbing', 'Red Flame') Cl HT, dr, Adam; intr. 2004

'Adabel' ('Belles and Beaus') S, rb, 1987, Adams, Dr. Neil D.; flowers red-white bicolor, floribunda type, medium, dbl., high-centered; foliage medium size, dark green, glossy, disease-resistant; upright, moderately hardy growth; ['Little Darling' × seedling]

'Adabicpoint' HT, rb, Adam, Michel; intr. 2005

'Adabiterse' HT, rb, Adam; intr. 2006

'Adablarop' HT, w, Adam; intr. 2004

'Adabourgrud' ('Gladis') S, mp, Adam; intr. 2004

'Adabuco' F, m, Adam; intr. 2004

'Adabumon' Pol, ob, Adam

'Adaburi' (Dame de L'Etoile®) F, w, Adam, M.; intr. 1994

'Adacecmar' LCl, mp, Adam; intr. 2001

'Adacecu' S, mp, Adam; intr. 1998

'Adacentapo' S, dp, Adam; intr. 1997

'Adacokro' HT, rb, Adam; intr. 2006

'Adacorhuit' HT, yb, Adam; intr. 2003

'Adacrema' HT, dp, Adam

'Adadisres' ('Disraeli') S, mr, 1987, Adams, Dr. Neil D.; flowers medium, full, no fragrance; foliage large, dark green, glossy; upright, bushy, tall, broad growth; ['Hamburger Phoenix' × seedling]

'Adaelseize' HT, yb, Adam; intr. 2007

'Adaexlya' ('Fragrant Alizée') HT, pb, Adam; intr. 2003

'Adafero' HT, yb, Adam, Michel; intr. 2005

'Adafetap' S, mp, Adam; intr. 1995

'Adaflash' F, or, Adam, Micheldbl.; intr. 2004

'Adafucomy' HT, ob, Adam; intr. 2005

'Adafunhup' HT, ab, Adam; intr. 2006

Adaghaki® HT, rb, Adam; intr. 2002

Adagio® -- See 'Cocquamber'

'Adagio' HT, dr, 1979, Lens, Louis; bud very long, pointed; flowers blood-red, 3½-4 in., 28-35 petals, globular; foliage dark; vigorous, bushy growth; [seedling × 'Uncle Walter']; intr. 1971

'Adaharlu' F, dy, Adam; intr. 2003

'Adahoriv' F, op, Adamdouble; intr. 2006

'Adahuin' (Velvet Alibi®) HT, dr, Adam, M.; intr. 1996

'Adair Roche' HT, pb, 1968, McGredy, Sam IV; flowers deep pink, reverse silver, well-formed, large, 30 petals; foliage glossy; ['Paddy McGredy' × ('Femina' × unknown)]

'Adajan' ('Jan's Wedding Bouquet', 'Jan's Wedding') S, yb, 1993, Adams, Dr. Neil D.; flowers 2-2½ in., dbl., borne in large and medium clusters; foliage medium size, dark green, semi-glossy; some prickles; tall (6 ft.), bushy growth; winter hardy; ['Dornroschen' × 'Lichtkonigin

Lucia']; intr. 1993
'Adalécob' HT, ob, Adam
'Adalegour' ('Copacabana') HT, rb, Adam; intr. 2004
'Adalyakces' ('Julia') HT, rb, Adam; intr. 2002
'Adam' ('President') T, mp, 1833, Adam; flowers rich rosy-salmon, more yellow inside, 7-9 cm., semi-dbl. to dbl., globular, strong tea fragrance; [possibly 'Hume's Blush' × 'Rose Edouard']
'Adam Messerich' B, mr, 1920, Lambert, P.; flowers rose-red, semi-dbl., cupped, intense raspberry fragrance; recurrent bloom; foliage glossy, light; vigorous, bushy growth; ['Frau Oberhofgärtner Singer' × ('Louise Odier' × 'Louis Philippe (Ch)')]
'Adam Paul' HP, lp, 1852, Laffay; flowers very large, full, globular, moderate fragrance
'Adam Rackles' T, pb, 1905, Rommel; flowers marbled and spackled pink, very large, full, slight fragrance; [sport of 'Mme Caroline Testout']
Adamelie® HT, yb, Adam; intr. 2006
'Adamibros' Min, w, Adam; intr. 2006
'Adamona' (Santiago®) F, mr, Adam
'Adamonbu' (Montauban de Bretagne®) F, w, Adam
'Adamonmar' F, dp, Adam; intr. 1993
Adam's Smile™ -- See 'Savarend'
'Adanacpar' HT, mp, Adam; intr. 2002
'Adanuamn' (Parfum d'Armor®) HT, mp, Adam, M.; intr. 1992
'Adapanco' F, dp, Adam; intr. 2006
'Adapolred' F, mr, Adam, Michel; intr. 2005
'Adaporba' S, lp, Adam; intr. 2006
'Adaquethom' F, dp, Adam; intr. 2000
'Adarocona' HT, lp, Adam; intr. 2004
'Adaromaq' HEg, mr, Adamsingle; intr. 2006
'Adasilthé' HT, pb, Adam; intr. 2000
'Adasnow' ('Snow Bear') S, w, 1993, Adams, Dr. Neil D.; flowers 3-3¼ in., dbl., borne in clusters of 3-5; foliage medium size, dark green, semi-glossy; some prickles; upright (4 ft.) growth; ['Dornroschen' × 'Rosanna']; intr. 1993
Adassili® HT, lp; intr. 2000
'Adasun' ('Summer Sun') LCl, my, 1993, Adams, Dr. Neil D.; flowers medium, dbl., borne in large clusters; repeat bloom; foliage medium size, dark green, semi-glossy; some prickles; tall (6 ft.), spreading growth; hardy; ['Prairie Princess' × 'Lichtkonigin Lucia']; intr. 1993
'Adasundi' S, yb, Adam; intr. 2003
'Adatapora' ('Bourgogne No. 2') S, mr, Adam, M.; intr. 1996
'Adaterhuit' HT, rb, Adam; intr. 2002
'Adatonysil' ('Rose d'Or de Montreux') F, dy, Adam, M.
'Adavorjap' HT, op, Adam; intr. 2008
'Adayakshor' F, m, Adam; intr. 1995
'Adazombar' Min, op, Adam; intr. 1997
'Added Touch' -- See 'Loyad'
'Addo Heritage' -- See 'Pouldotage'
'Adecapma' F, dp, Adam; intr. 2001

'Adecohuit' HT, yb, Adam; intr. 2000
'Adecosil' HT, dp, Adam, M.; intr. 1997
Adela® -- See 'Fegama'
'Adela' HT, lp, Kordes; flowers porcelain pink, dbl., high-centered, no fragrance; stems long; growth vigorous, tall; intr. 2001
'Adelaide' -- See 'Adelaide Hoodless'
'Adélaïde Bougère' B, m, 1852, Bougère; flowers velvety purple, shaded darker, large, full; possibly synonymous with 'Adèle Bougère'
'Adélaïde de Meynot' HP, mp, 1882, Gonod; flowers bright cerise pink, rounded petals, large, moderate centifolia fragrance; quite remontant; numerous prickles; stems very dark green; growth upright
'Adélaïde d'Orléans' ('Princesse Adélaïde d'Orléans') HSem, w, 1826, Jacques; bud small, dark pink; flowers pale rose, fading to cream/white, yellow stamens, 6-7 cm., semi-dbl., loosely cupped, borne in clusters; non-recurrent; lax, sprawling, vigorous (15 ft.) growth; [R. sempervirens × 'Parson's Pink']
'Adelaide d'Orléans' HP, mp, 1861, Robert; flowers medium pink, shaded lilac
'Adelaïde Dufresnois' ('Adèle Dufresnoy', 'Mme Dufresnois') HP, dp, 1876, Robert; flowers dark pink with flesh pink, aging to white, very large, full; ['Anna Alexieff' × unknown]
'Adelaïde Fontaine' B, mp, 1856, Fontaine
'Adelaide Hoodless' ('Adelaide') S, dp, 1973, Marshall, H.H.; bud ovoid; flowers light red, medium, semi-dbl., slight fragrance; repeat bloom; foliage glossy; vigorous, bushy growth; ['Fire King' × ('J. W. Fargo' × 'Assiniboine')]; intr. 1975
'Adelaide Lee' Min, pb, 1986, Stoddard, Louis; flowers white with red petal edges, 1 in., 25 petals, urn-shaped, borne singly; foliage medium green, matte; prickles few, green, straight; upright growth; ['Gene Boerner' × Magic Carrousel®]
'Adélaïde Moullé' HWich, pb, 1902, Barbier; flowers lilac-pink, center carmine, 4 cm., dbl., borne in clusters; midseason bloom; foliage oval, slightly pointed, reflexed, smooth; prickles numerous, straight, slender, very sharp, dark brown; [R. wichurana × 'Souv. de Catherine Guillot']
'Adelaide Pavié' -- See 'Adèle Pavié'
'Adelaide Tonight' -- See 'Tomdel'
'Adèle' HGal, mp, before 1814, Descemet; flowers medium, full
'Adèle' P, dp, Prévost; flowers glowing deep pink, medium to large; intr. about 1830
'Adèle' HT, dy, 1935, Lens; flowers clear gold, base deeper; ['Roselandia' × 'Clarice Goodacre']; intr. 1935
'Adèle Bernard' N, w; flowers white with salmon pink, full
'Adèle Bougère' HT, dr, 1852, Robert; flowers velvety dark purple, full

'Adèle Courtoisé' HGal, dp, before 1842; flowers rosy red, small, very dbl.
'Adèle Crofton' HT, yb, 1928, Dickson, A.; flowers yellow overlaid scarlet-orange, dbl.
'Adèle de Bellabre' T, pb, 1888, Ducher fils; flowers coppery pink to reddish-peach, large, full; probably extinct
'Adèle Descemet' HGal, Descemet, M.
'Adèle Dufresnoy' -- See 'Adelaïde Dufresnois'
Adele Duttweiler™ -- See 'Royal Dane'
'Adele Frey' Cl HT, dp, 1911, Walter; flowers large, very dbl.
'Adèle Gérard' HGal, lp; flowers light pink, aging to white, large, full
'Adèle Heu' HGal, m, 1816, Vibert; flowers purple-pink with white shadings, medium large, dbl., moderate fragrance
'Adèle Mauzé' ('Rose de Trianon Double') P, lp, 1847, Vibert; flowers rose pink, medium to large, full
'Adèle Pavie' M, lp, 1850, Vibert; flowers flesh white to pink, medium, 8 cm., dbl., rosette, moderate fragrance
'Adèle Pavié' ('Adelaide Pavié', 'Mme Loiseleur') N, lp, 1857, Moreau & Robert; flowers light pink, center crimson, shaded white, often yellow at base,; ['Lamarque' × unknown]; possibly synonymous with 'Mme Deslongchamps', from Lévêque, 1850
'Adèle Pradel' -- See 'Mme Bravy'
'Adèle Prévost' HGal, lp, before 1836; flowers blush, center pink, large, dbl.; vigorous, upright growth
'Adele Searll' S, ab, Kordes; flowers apricot-pink, heavy, 100 petals, borne in large clusters, moderate sweet fragrance; growth semi-prostrate, compact, spreading; intr. 1999
'Adéline' C, pb, 1830, Vibert; flowers vivid rose, paler toward edge, dbl.; foliage dark; compact, branching growth
'Adeline' M, dp; bud well mossed; flowers lilac-rose, 2 in., dbl.; foliage light green; compact, well-branched growth
'Adeline Genée' F, my, 1967, Harkness; bud plump; flowers 4 in., 50 petals, borne in clusters; foliage glossy; low, bushy growth; ['Paddy McGredy' × seedling]
'Adesmano' HT, pb, Adam; intr. 2002
Adesmano® HT, pb, Adam
'Adharman' ('Commandant Cousteau', 'Grand Huit', 'Grande Classe', 'Le Grand Huit') HT, dr, Adam, M.; intr. 1993
'Adharos' HT, lp, Adam, M.; intr. 1995
'Adiantifolia' HRg, mp, 1907, Cochet-Cochet; foliage ferny
'Adieu de Bordier' HGal, mr; flowers vivid red, very dbl.
'Aditya' HT, dy, K&S; flowers long lasting, deep yellow, dbl., broad; intr. 1990
'Admirable' -- See 'Searodney'
'Admirable' ('Carmosina', 'L'Admirable', 'Superbissima', 'Mirabilis', 'Chremesina Scintilland', 'Multiplex', 'Couleur de Sang') HGal, mr, before 1787; flowers scarlet red, full; prickles numerous,

short; from Holland
'Admirable de Lille' -- See 'Orphise'
'Admirable Panachée' -- See 'Comte Foy'
'Admiral' -- See 'WAVES'
'Admiral' -- See 'Sea Rodney'
'Admiral' HT, mr, Tantau; intr. 2002
'Admiral de Rigny' ('Admiral Rigney', 'Eugène Pirolle') N, mp, before 1844; growth dwarf
'Admiral Dewey' HT, mr, 1899, Taylor; flowers rich creamy rose, shaded with gold-yellow and peach, large, dbl.; [sport of 'Mme Caroline Testout']
'Admiral la Peyrouse' -- See 'La Peyrouse'
'Admiral Rigney' -- See 'Admiral de Rigny'
'Admiral Rodney' HT, pb, 1974, Trew, C.; flowers pale rose-pink, reverse deeper, 4-4½ in., 45 petals, intense fragrance; foliage large, glossy, dark; vigorous growth; intr. 1973
'Admiral Schley' HT, r, 1901, Cook, J.W.; flowers red; ['Col. Joffé' × 'Général Jacqueminot']
'Admiral Ward' HT, rb, 1915, Pernet-Ducher; flowers crimson-red, shaded fiery red and velvety purple, large, dbl., globular; [seedling × 'Château de Clos Vougeot']
'Admiration' -- See 'Rosa Zwerg'
'Admiration' HT, rb, 1922, McGredy; flowers cream, shaded vermilion, pointed, large, dbl.; foliage light green; moderately bushy growth
Admired Miranda® -- See 'Ausmira'
'Adolf Deegen' HT, pb, 1935, Böhm, J.; flowers rosy pink with fiery streaks, large; ['Ophelia' × 'Wilhelm Kordes']
'Adolf Grille' F, dp, 1940, Kordes; bud pointed, ovoid; flowers scarlet-carmine, 4-5 in., 25 petals, cupped, borne in clusters, slight fragrance; foliage leathery, dark, wrinkled; vigorous, bushy, compact growth; PP475; ['Dance of Joy' × ('Cathrine Kordes' × 'E. G. Hill')]
Adolf Horstmann® ('Adolph Horstmann') HT, yb, 1973, Kordes, R.; flowers deep yellow-orange with pink overtones, 5 in., dbl., high-centered; foliage glossy; vigorous, upright growth; PP3414; ['Colour Wonder' × 'Dr. A. J. Verhage']; intr. 1972
'Adolf Kärger' HT, my, 1918, Kordes, H.; bud long; flowers golden yellow, fading lighter in full sun, very large, full; foliage large, dark green; ['Cissie Easlea' × 'Sunburst']
'Adolf Koschel' HT, ab, 1918, Kordes, H.; bud long, pointed; flowers light orange yellow, nuanced red, large, very full, borne mostly solitary, moderate fragrance; foliage medium size, leathery, bronzy green; ['Harry Kirk' × 'Louise Catherine Breslau']
'Adolf Papeleu' F, w, RvS-Melle; ['Maizières' × 'Maria Mathilde']; intr. 1996
'Adolph Gude' HT, pb, 1941, Gude; flowers rose-pink, reverse darker, 5½-6 in., 30 petals, high-centered, moderate fragrance; very vigorous growth; PP462; [sport of 'Red Radiance']
'Adolph Horstmann' -- See 'Adolf Horstmann'
'Adolphe Brogniard' HP, mp, 1868, Margottin; flowers carmine pink, large, full
'Adolphe Noblet' HP, dp, Ledechaux
'Adonis' HGal, dp, before 1814, Descemet; flowers bright pinky red, flat
'Adonis' HGal, lp; flowers flesh pink, medium, full; possibly from Vibert; intr. before 1829
'Adonis' HP, m, Verdier, V.; flowers light violet-pink, large, full; intr. 1835
'Adonis' HT, ly, Bees; flowers ivory-yellow, shaded lemon, dbl., moderate fragrance; ['Sunburst' × 'American Beauty']; intr. 1921
'Adora' Pol, mp, 1936, Beckwith; bud deep flame-pink; flowers rose-pink, dbl.; vigorous, dwarf growth
'Adora' HT, op, Kasturi; flowers luminous coral to deep vermilion, well formed; long stems; intr. 1986
'Adorable' HT, lp, 1930, Eichholz; flowers flesh-pink; [sport of 'Columbia']
'Adoration' ('Ile de France') HT, op, 1940, Gaujard; bud long, pointed; flowers bright salmon, 5 in., 22 petals, moderate fragrance; foliage leathery; vigorous, bushy growth; PP453; [('Mme Joseph Perraud' × seedling) × seedling]
'Adorn' Min, pb, 1986, McDaniel, Earl; flowers medium pink blending lighter, reverse medium pink, 30 petals, high-centered, urn-shaped, borne singly; foliage medium size, dark, semi-glossy; prickles slender, light; medium, upright, bushy growth; [seedling × seedling]
'Adriadne' -- See 'Ariane'
'Adrian' F, Camprubi, C.
'Adrian Bailey' F, op, 1978, Bailey; bud globular; flowers orange-scarlet, large, 28 petals; foliage glossy; bushy, upright growth; ['Fragrant Cloud' × 'Evelyn Fison']
'Adrian Reverchon' HMult, mp, 1909, Lambert; flowers bright pink with white blaze, fading almost to white, 5-6 cm., single, borne in large clusters; autumn repeat
'Adriana' HT, ab; flowers pale cream deepening to creamy caramel, large, dbl., classic, moderate spicy fragrance; recurrent; foliage dark green, disease-resistant; well-branched, medium (30 in.) growth; intr. 2000
'Adriana Top Model' F, ab, Laperrière; flowers apricot, slight fragrance; growth compact; intr. 2005
'Adrie Stokman' HT, mp, 1948, Stokman; flowers darker pink than Briarcliff; ['Parel van Aalsmeer' × unknown]
'Adrien de Montebello' HP, dp, 1868, Margottin; flowers silky dark pink, medium, full
'Adrien Marx' HP, mr, 1866, Granger; flowers cherry red, large, full
Adrien Mercer® ('Dorache') F, rb, Dorieux; intr. before 1990
'Adrien Schmitt' HP, mr, 1889, Schmitt
'Adrienne Berman' HT, mr, 1996, Poole, Lionel; flowers very large, spiraled, with thick-textured petals, full, borne mostly singly, moderate fragrance; foliage large, dark green, semi-glossy; some prickles; upright, medium growth; [('Precious Platinum' × 'Silver Jubilee') × 'Cardiff Bay']; intr. 1997
'Adrienne Christophe' N, ab, 1869, Guillot; flowers coppery apricot yellow, shaded peach pink, sometimes deep yellow, very dbl.; foliage smooth, pale green; prickles long, sharp, brown
'Adrienne de Cardoville' B, lp, 1864, Guillot père; flowers light rosy crimson, large, full, cupped to globular; growth branching
'Adrienne Leal' F, dp, 1965, Leal; bud ovoid; flowers deep pink to soft mauve, medium, dbl.; foliage dark, leathery; vigorous, upright growth; [sport of 'Roundelay']
'Adrienne Martin' HT, dp, 1930, Buatois; flowers carmine, base yellow, very dbl., cupped; foliage glossy, dark; vigorous, bushy, low growth; ['Recuerdo de Angel Peluffo' × 'The Queen Alexandra Rose']
Advance+ HT, w, Voom, Lex; flowers white with greenish tint, double, high-centered, borne mostly singly; recurrent; stems very long; [sport of 'Avalanche']; intr. 2007
'Advance' HT, rb, 1940, LeGrice; flowers orange-flame, shaded cerise, reverse cerise, large, dbl.; foliage leathery, dark; long, strong stems; vigorous, bushy growth; ['Comtesse Vandal' × 'Mrs Sam McGredy']
'Advance Guard' -- See 'Wilhelm Teetzmann'
'Adventure' -- See 'Aventure'
Adventure™ -- See 'Poulpal021(N)'
Adventure® HT, pb, Spek; flowers blush with pink edges and greenish guard petals, very large, full, high-centered, borne mostly singly; good repeat; stems long; florist rose; intr. 2003
'Adventure Palace' (Adventure™) Min, dr, Poulsen; flowers dark red, 2 in., dbl. to full, cupped, no fragrance; foliage dark green, glossy; bushy, low (40-60 cm.) growth; intr. 2005
'Adversity' MinFl, w, 2005, Goldstein, Jack J.; flowers white, reverse light yellow, 1¼ in., full, borne mostly solitary, moderate fragrance; foliage medium size, medium green, matte; prickles few, ¼ in., triangular, green; bushy, medium growth; [sport of 'Soroptimist International']; intr. 2005
'Advocate' HT, mr, 1928, Dickson, A.; flowers crimson-scarlet, dbl.
'Æbleblomst' HMsk, lp, Petersen; intr. 1955
'Aegeria' -- See 'Egeria'
'Aëlita' S, w, 1952, Shtanko, E.E.; flowers white tinted green, large, 50 petals;

foliage glossy; vigorous growth; ['New Dawn' × unknown]
'Aennchen Müller' -- See 'Ännchen Müller'
'Aennchen von Tharau' ('Ännchen von Tharau') HMult, w, 1886, Geschwind, R.; flowers creamy mother-of-pearl, darker at center, 7 cm., very dbl., borne in small clusters, moderate sweet fragrance; foliage glaucous; prickles moderate; ['an Alba' × 'an arvensis hybrid']
'Aenne Burda' HT, mr, 1973, Kordes; flowers blood-red, large, dbl., high-centered; foliage large, glossy; vigorous, upright, bushy growth
'Aenne Kreis' HT, ab, 1930, Kreis; flowers orange-yellow, reverse lighter, well-formed, dbl.; vigorous, branching growth; [sport of 'Wilhelm Kordes']
'Aetna' -- See 'Etna'
Affection™ MinFl, mr, Poulsen; flowers medium red, 5-8 cm., semi-dbl., no fragrance; foliage dark; growth bushy, 20-40 cm.; intr. 2005
'Affirm' ('McMillan's Pink') HT, mp, 1998, McMillan, Thomas G.; flowers high center, medium pink, 4 in., very dbl., high-centered, borne mostly singly or small clusters; foliage medium size, medium green, dull; numerous prickles; low, spreading growth; [seedling × seedling]; intr. 1998
'Aflame' F, op, 1954, LeGrice; flowers orange-strawberry, 4 in., semi-dbl., borne in clusters; foliage dark, glossy; vigorous, low, spreading growth; [('Poulsen's Pink' × 'Ellinor LeGrice') × 'Mrs Pierre S. duPont']
'Africa Star' HT, m, 1965, West; flowers 3½-4 in., 65 petals; foliage coppery; bushy growth
African Dawn® HT, pb, Schreurs; intr. 2004
'African Queen' -- See 'Taneliet'
'African Rose' HT, dp; flowers rich pink, large, intense fragrance; robust growth
'African Sunset' -- See 'Jacpik'
'African Sunset' HT, ab, 1966, Herholdt, J.A.; flowers apricot-orange, pointed, 4½ in., dbl.; free growth; ['Sutter's Gold' × 'Chantré']
'After Dark' -- See 'Ponark'
'After Glow' -- See 'JOHilmar'
After Midnight™ -- See 'Kinnight'
'Afterglow' HT, ab, 1930, Joseph H. Hill, Co.; flowers apricot-yellow, dbl., intense fragrance; PP9; [seedling × 'Souv. de Claudius Pernet']
'Afterglow' ('Sam Buff') HT, ob, LeGrice; bud long, pointed, orange; flowers golden yellow, reverse golden orange, large, dbl., slight fragrance; foliage bluish green, glossy; long stems; vigorous, bushy growth; [sport of 'Mrs Sam McGredy']; intr. 1938
'Afterglow' S, pb, Williams, J.B.; intr. 2004
'Afternoon Delight' -- See 'Jolaft'
'Afternoon Delight' -- See 'Kormamtiza'
'Agar' HGal, dp, before 1836, Laffay; flowers bright cherry pink
'Agar' HGal, pb, Vibert; flowers dark rose, spotted, medium, dbl., quartered, borne in clusters of 3-4, slight to moderate fragrance; foliage thick, clear green, large; numerous prickles; intr. 1843
'Agar' B, lp, Robert; flowers flesh pink, overlaid with salmon pink, aging to lilac, large; intr. 1853
'Agar' HT, w, Brassac; intr. 1910
'Agate Pourpre' HT, mr, 1967, Delbard-Chabert; flowers currant-red, 5-6 in., dbl., cupped; intermittent bloom; foliage dark, serrated; ['Impeccable' × 'Rome Glory']; intr. 1965
'Agatha' -- See 'Francfort Agathé'
'Agatha Christie' -- See 'Ramira'
'Agatha Christie' F, dp, 1966, Buisman, G. A. H.; bud ovoid; flowers pink-red, dbl., borne in clusters; foliage dark; compact growth
'Agatha Francofurtana' -- See 'Francfort Agathé'
'Agathe à Dix Coeurs' HGal, m, before 1836, Lahaye; flowers lilac pink, edges lighter and spotted, medium
'Agathe à Feuilles Glauques' HGal, dp, before 1836, Noisette, E.; flowers medium, full
'Agathe Admirable' HGal, mp, about 1860, Miellez
'Agathe Agréable' D, mp, before 1814, Descemet
'Agathe Agréable' HGal, mp, Miellez; intr. about 1860
'Agathe Amédée' -- See 'Amédée'
'Agathe Amusante' HGal, mp, about 1860, Miellez
'Agathe Anaïs' HGal, m, 1819, Vibert; flowers dark lilac pink, often marbled, full, semi-globular; Agathe group
'Agathe Anna' HGal, mp, before 1840, Vétillard; flowers bright pink
'Agathe Athala' HGal, op, before 1840, Garilland; flowers aurora-pink
'Agathe Bécourt' HGal, about 1860, Baumann
'Agathe Carnée' -- See 'Agathe Incarnata'
'Agathe Couronnée' -- See 'Marie-Louise'
'Agathe de Pelletier' -- See 'Fleur de Pelletier'
'Agathe Fatime' ('Fatime') HGal, dp, before 1815, Descemet, M.; flowers carmine at center, tinted with mauve on the edges, with a central button, medium, very dbl., flat, quartered, borne singly or in pairs, slight fragrance; foliage medium green, elliptical, with 5-7 leaflets; Agathe group
'Agathe Incarnata' ('À Fleur d'un Rouge Pâle', 'Agathe Marie-Louise', 'Pink Agatha', 'Pallidior', 'Jolie Rose Pierret', 'Flamande', 'Duchesse d'Angoulême', 'De Flandre', 'De Bruxelles', 'Carné', 'Blanda', 'Agathe Carnée', R. gallica agatha incarnate, 'Blässe Niederländisch) HGal, lp, before 1811; sepals long; flowers silvery blush pink, small eye at center, medium, very dbl., quartered, flat, borne in small clusters, intense fragrance; foliage dark green, lightly serrated; numerous prickles; growth habit intermediate between the Gallicas and the Damasks; Agathe group; probably a hybrid of Gallica and Damask, from Holland
'Agathe Majesteuse' -- See 'Aimable Rouge'
'Agathe Marie-Louise' -- See 'Agathe Incarnata'
'Agathe Nabonnand' -- See 'Mme Agathe Nabonnand'
'Agathe Nouvelle' -- See 'Héloïse'
'Agathe Rose' -- See 'Marie-Louise'
'Agathe Royale' -- See 'Royale'
'Agathoïde' HP, pb, 1860, Lebreton; flowers light pink with red tints, large, full
'Age Tendre' HT, dp, 1966, Croix, P.; bud long, pointed; flowers rose, large, dbl., high-centered; strong stems; vigorous growth; [Queen Elizabeth® × 'Spartan']
'Agemy' HT, ob
'Agemy Sport' HT, dy
Agéna® -- See 'Delcus'
'Agénor' HGal, m, 1832, Vibert; flowers reddish-purple, medium, dbl.
'Agkon' HT, dp, Agel
'Aglaé Adanson' HGal, m, 1823, Vibert; flowers lilac pink, spotted with white, very large, dbl., cupped
'Aglaia' C, lp, before 1811, possibly Descemet; bud pink, pointed; flowers pink shading to lilac mixed with white, petals fluted, 2½ in., full, moderate fragrance; foliage slender, delicate
'Aglaia' ('Yellow Rambler') HMult, ly, 1896, Schmitt; flowers straw-yellow to white, small, semi-dbl. to dbl., cupped, borne in very large clusters, moderate fragrance; seldom repeats; foliage glossy; vigorous growth; [R. multiflora × 'Rêve d'Or']; intr. 1896
'Agnes' HRg, my, 1900, Saunders; flowers pale amber, center deeper, open, dbl., moderate fragrance; profuse, non-recurrent bloom; foliage light green, glossy, rugose; short stems; vigorous (6 ft.), bushy growth; very hardy; [R. rugosa × R. foetida persiana]; intr. 1922
'Agnès Ageron' HT, mr, 1958, Arles; flowers cerise-red, reverse tinted currant-red, well-formed; very vigorous growth; ['Mme Méha Sabatier' × 'Léonce Colombier']
'Agnes Barclay' HT, yb, 1927, Clark, A.; flowers yellow and reddish-salmon
Agnes Bernauer® -- See 'Kornauer'
'Agnes De Puy' HT, dp, 1930, De Puy; flowers geranium-red veined gold, large, 22 petals, high-centered; long stems; very vigorous growth; hardy; ['Lady Battersea' × ('Honeymoon' × 'Mme Butterfly')]
'Agnes Emily Carman' HRg, mr, 1898, Carman; flowers bright crimson, large, dbl.; some repeat bloom; foliage large, rugose; vigorous (5 ft.) growth; possibly

R. rugosa × 'Harison's Yellow'

'Agnes Glover'   HT, dr, 1924, Chaplin Bros.; flowers deep velvety crimson; ['Admiral Ward' × 'George Dickson']

'Agnes Kruse'   F, dr, 1936, Tantau; flowers velvety red, fiery, large; vigorous growth; ['Mme Edouard Herriot' × 'Eblouissant']

'Agnes Laura Blackburn'   F, yb, 1990, Cants of Colchester, Ltd.; bud pointed; flowers bicolor yellow, medium, 5 petals, borne in sprays; ['City of Portsmouth' × seedling]; intr. 1989

'Agnes Lucké'   HT, pb, 1960, Armbrust; bud long, pointed; flowers cerise-pink, reverse whitish pink, large to medium size, 50 petals, high-centered, moderate fragrance; foliage leathery; vigorous, upright growth; ['Happiness' × 'Peace, Climbing']; intr. 1959

'Agnes Marguerite'   HT, or, 1953; flowers reddish-orange, shaded apricot; foliage glossy

'Agnes My Oh!' -- See 'Levfamagnes'

'Agnes Roggen'   HT, pb, 1926, Leenders, M.; flowers pale pink, reverse carmine, dbl.

'Agnes Schilliger'   S, pb, Guillot-Massad; flowers full; intr. 2003

'Agnes und Bertha' ('Kala Agneta') HMult, lp, 1926, Bruder Alfons; bud dark pink; flowers small, single to semi-dbl., borne in large clusters; ['Tausendschön' × 'Dorothy Perkins']

'Agnes Winchel'   HT, pb, 1989, Winchel, Joseph F.; bud pointed; flowers light pink with deep pink border, medium, 28 petals, high-centered, borne singly, slight fruity fragrance; foliage medium size, dark green, semi-glossy; prickles slightly hooked, medium, green; upright, medium growth; hips globular, medium, orange; PP7826; ['Dorothy Anne' × seedling]; intr. 1990

'Agni'   HT, or, or, G&L; flowers deep orange-red with blackish sheen, high-centered, long stems; intr. 1985

'Agnihotri'   HT, dp, Kasturi; flowers large, rose red with lighter overtones at petal edges; intr. 1981

'Agra'   HRg, lp, Riekstra; flowers large, loosely petaled, slight fragrance; growth to 1¼ m. tall and wide; intr. 1949

'Agreement'   F, pb, 1971, LeGrice; flowers deep glowing pink, base golden, 3 in., 30 petals, high-centered, foliage glossy, bright green; tall, very free growth

'Agrippina' -- See 'Cramoisi Supérieur'

'Agrippina, Climbing' -- See 'Cramoisi Supérieur, Climbing'

'Aguigolden' ('Westminster 50th Anniversary') HT, mr, 2007, Aguilar, Sergio; flowers medium red, reverse lighter, fading to dark pink, 5 in., dbl., borne mostly solitary; foliage medium size, dark green, semi-glossy; prickles medium, hooked, moderate; growth upright, compact, medium (4 ft.); cutting, garden decoration; ['Elizabeth Taylor' × 'New Zealand']; intr. 2007

'Agulily' ('Kieran's Rose') MinFl, yb, 2006, Aguilar, Sergio; flowers yellow with red edges, reverse white, 1½ in., single, borne mostly solitary; foliage large, medium green, glossy, disease-resistant; prickles small, hooked downward, few; growth upright, medium (24-30 in.); small specimen; border; cut flower; ['Elizabeth Taylor' × Playboy®]; intr. 2006

'Ah Mow'   T, lp, Hay

'Ahalya'   F, lp, Kasturi; flowers pale pink; continuous bloom; compact growth; [sport of 'Summer Snow']; intr. 1969

'Ahimsa' ('Orient Silk') HT, my, 1996, Viraraghavan, M.S. Viru; bud golden; flowers large, clear yellow with darker centers, 5 in., full, borne mostly singly, moderate fragrance; foliage large, medium green, semi-glossy; no prickles; upright, medium (3 ft.) growth; ['Mme Charles Sauvage' × seedling]; intr. 1996

'Ahlin'   F, ob, 1980, Fong; bud ovoid; flowers orange, 15 petals, high-centered, borne 4-6 per cluster, slight fragrance; foliage large, leathery; prickles hooked, upright growth; [seedling × 'Little Darling']

'Ahoi'   F, or, 1964, Tantau, Math.; bud urn shaped; flowers bright orange-red, dbl., borne in clusters; low, bushy growth

'Aïcha'   HSpn, dy, 1966, Petersen; bud long, pointed; flowers deep yellow, large, semi-dbl.; foliage light green; vigorous, bushy growth; ['Souv. de Jacques Verschuren' × 'Guldtop']

'Aïda'   HT, mr, 1957, Mansuino, Dr. Ada; bud urn shaped; flowers clear rose-red, 5 in., 25 petals, cupped, intense fragrance; foliage leathery; vigorous, upright, symmetrical growth; PP1639; ['Crimson Glory' × 'Signora']; intr. 1956

'Aigle Brun' ('Altissima', 'La Très Haute') HGal, dr, before 1811; bud pointed; flowers blackish velvety bright crimson, 2½ in., semi-dbl.; few prickles

'Aigle Noir' ('Maheca Nova') HGal, dr, 1818, Godefroy (possibly Descemet); flowers velvety purple, medium, dbl.

'Aigle Rouge' -- See 'La Belle Sultane'

'Aiglon'   HT, rb, 1961, Gaujard; bud long, pointed; flowers coppery red, reverse yellow, large, 38 petals; foliage glossy, light green; vigorous, upright growth; ['Viola' × ('Opera' × unknown)]

'Aila Korhonen'   HSpn, pb, Rautio, Pirjo; flowers shades of soft lilac pink, aging lilac-red, center yellow aging white, 7-8 cm, semi-double, borne in clusters, slight fragrance; prickles many, needle shaped; hips flattened; intr. 2000

'Aileen'   F, ab, 1976, Wood; flowers light apricot, peach blended, large, dbl., moderate fragrance; upright, free growth; [sport of 'Elizabeth of Glamis']

'Aimable Amie'   HGal, dp, before 1818, Trianon; flowers medium, dbl.

'Aimable Beauté' -- See 'L'Aimable Beauté'

'Aimable Eléonore'   C, dp, before 1828, Coquerel; flowers medium, full

'Aimable Emma' -- See 'Belle Hélène'

'Aimable Henriette'   HGal, mp; flowers carmine, medium

'Aimable Pourpre'   HGal, dr, before 1811; bud round, flattened; flowers purple black, 3 in., semi-dbl., moderate fragrance; foliage elongated, finely dentate; from Holland

'Aimable Rouge' ('Agathe Majesteuse', 'Royal Virgin Rose', 'Le Triomphe', 'Boule d'Hortensia') HGal, dp, 1819-1820, Vibert; flowers pink with hints of mauve, medium, very dbl., quartered, flat, borne mostly solitary, moderate fragrance; foliage small, clear green, round to eliptical; growth bushy, medium (1¼ m.); possibly synonymous with 'Aimable Rose'

'Aimable Rouge'   HGal, mp, Godefroy; flowers pink, edges whitish, medium, full, dahlia-like; intr. before 1845

'Aimable Sophie' -- See 'Belle Hélène'

Aimé Jacquet®   HT, ab, Dorieux; flowers apricot-orange, fading pink, dbl., high-centered, slight fragrance; foliage glossy, broad; low to medium growth; intr. 2005

'Aimé Plantier' -- See 'Safrano'

'Aimée Cochet'   HT, lp

'Aimée Desprez'   N, m, about 1830, Desprez; flowers violet, center whitish pink, small, full

'Aimée Vibert Scandens' -- See 'Aimée Vibert, Climbing'

'Aimée Vibert' ('Nivea', 'Repens') N, w, 1828, Vibert; bud pinking; flowers pure white, 5 cm., dbl., rosette, borne in small to medium clusters, strong musky fragrance; recurrent bloom; foliage semi-evergreen; nearly thornless; vigorous growth; ['Champneys' Pink Cluster' × a double form of *R. sempervirens*]

'Aimée Vibert, Climbing' ('Aimée Vibert Scandens') N, w, 1841, Curtis

'Aimée Vibert Jaune' -- See 'Mme Brunner'

'Ain't Misbehavin'' -- See 'Seabla'

Ain't She Sweet™ -- See 'Wekfrag'

'Air France' -- See 'Meifinaro'

'Air France'   HT, dr, 1964, Asseretto, A.; flowers red to cherry-red, medium, dbl., cupped, moderate fragrance; vigorous, bushy growth; PP2120; RULED EXTINCT 9/82 ARM; [seedling × 'Poinsettia']; intr. 1958

'Air France Meillandina' -- See 'Meifinaro'

'Airain' -- See 'Châtelet'

'Airborne'   F, dp, 1949, Leenders, M.; flowers deep pink, large, dbl.; vigorous growth; ['Donald Prior' × 'Rosamunde']

'Aishwarya' ('Queen Aishwarya') HT, dr, Kasturi & Sriram; flowers dark, velvety crimson with a blackish sheen, high-centered, moderate fragrance; recurrent; intr. 2001

'Aisling'   F, w, 1966, Slattery; flowers ivory-cream, 4 in., dbl.; foliage small, glossy; very vigorous growth; [Queen Elizabeth® × Allgold®]

'Ajaccio' HT, mr, Croix, P.; intr. 1968
'Ajanta' HT, m, 1979, Takur; bud tapered; flowers 5-5½ in., 35-40 petals, high-centered, moderate spicy fragrance; foliage large, glossy; bushy growth; [('Lady X' × unknown) × 'Memoriam']; intr. 1978
'Aka Tombo' Min, rb
'Akane Fuji' ('Fujiyama Rose') HRg, dp, Komatsu
'Akash' HT, m, Ghosh; flowers lilac pink, satiny petals, high-centered; intr. 1998
'Akash Sundari' HT, m, Pal, Dr. B.P.; flowers lilac pink with deep red flushes on outer petals, high-centered; intr. 1982
'Akashdeep' F, or, Chiplunkar; flowers bright pomegranate red, semi-dbl., borne in clusters; intr. 1992
'Akashi' S, lp
'Akatsuki' ('Daybreak') HT, mr, Hiroshima; intr. 2005
'Akebono' ('Daybreak') HT, yb, Kawai; flowers light yellow flushed carmine, high pointed, 15 cm., 40-50 petals, high-centered, borne mostly solitary, moderate fruity, sourish fragrance; foliage large, thick, dark green, glossy; prickles pointing downward, underside concave; growth vigorous, upright, tall; ['Ethel Sanday' × 'Narzisse']; intr. 1964
'Akemi' F, or, 1977, Keisei Rose Nurseries, Inc.; bud ovoid; flowers, 2-2½ in., 33 petals, cupped, slight fragrance; foliage dark; vigorous, upright growth; [(Sarabande® × 'Hawaii') × (Sarabande® × 'Ruby Lips')]
'Akito' F, w, 1973, Tantau, Math.; bud ovoid; flowers, dbl., borne in clusters; foliage medium size, medium green; upright, bushy growth; ['Zorina' × 'Nordia']
'Akito' HT, w, Tantau; flowers clear white, medium to large, dbl., high-centered, borne mostly singly; recurrent; stems medium to long; florist rose; intr. 1998
'Akogare' HT, pb, Hiroshima; intr. 1998
'Aksel Olsen' Misc OGR, mp, Gustavsson; [R. helenae × unknown]; very close in appearance and growth to R. helenae, its parent.; intr. 1998
'Alabama' HT, pb, 1976, Weeks; bud long, pointed; flowers deep pink, reverse near white, 3½-4 in., 25 petals, high-centered, moderate tea fragrance; foliage dark, leathery; upright growth; PP4008; ['Mexicana' × 'Tiffany']
'Alabaster' HT, w, 1963, Wyant; flowers, 5 in., 70-80 petals, high-centered, moderate fragrance; moderate, upright growth; ['Blanche Mallerin' × 'McGredy's Ivory']; intr. 1961
'Alabaster' HT, w, Tantau; intr. 2002
'Aladdin' -- See 'Sunalad'
Aladdin ™ -- See 'Poulac007'
'Aladdin' F, mr, 1965, Verbeek; bud ovoid; flowers red, very dbl., borne in clusters; foliage dark; numerous prickles; ['Miracle' × 'Edith Piaf']
'Aladdin Palace' (Aladdin ™) MinFl, ab, Poulsen; flowers apricot blend, 5-8 cm.,
25 petals, slight wild rose fragrance; foliage dark; growth bushy, 40-60 cm.; PP15794; intr. 2002
'Aladdins Dream' -- See 'Twolad'
Aladin® Min, ob
'Alain' F, mr, 1948, Meilland, F.; bud ovoid; flowers bright carmine-red, semi-dbl., borne in clusters; foliage glossy, dark; upright, bushy growth; [('Guineé' × 'Skyrocket') × Orange Triumph®]
'Alain, Climbing' Cl F, mr, 1957, Roth; flowers scarlet, small , semi-dbl., borne in small clusters
'Alain Blanchard' HGal, m, 1839, Vibert; flowers purplish-crimson, becoming mottled giving a spotted look, semi-dbl., cupped, moderate fragrance; foliage medium green; vigorous, medium growth; [probably R. centifolia × R. gallica]; could be classified as a Centifolia, as it is probably a hybrid; possibly bred by Coquerel, and distributed by Vibert
'Alain Blanchard Panachée' HGal, pb; flowers identical to its parent, but with fewer petals and stripes instead of spots; [sport of 'Alain Blanchard']
'Alain Souchon' -- See 'Meikarouz'
'Alamein' F, mr, 1963, McGredy, Sam IV; flowers scarlet, 3 in., 10 petals, flat, borne in clusters; foliage dark; vigorous, bushy growth; ['Spartan' × Queen Elizabeth®]
'Alamode' -- See 'Broala'
'Alan Butterworth' -- See 'Rawgeel'
'Alan Sandys' -- See 'Tomaln'
'Alan Tew' HT, op, McGredy; flowers deep salmon, large, dbl., high-centered, moderate fragrance; free-flowering; foliage glossy, leathery; growth medium; intr. 2003
'Alan Titchmarsh' ('Huntington Rose') S, dp, Austin, David; bud rounded; flowers very full, globular, moderate warm Old Rose fragrance; recurrent; slightly arching (4 ft.) growth; intr. 2006
'Alanna Holloway' HT, dr, 1974, Holloway; flowers ovoid; foliage glossy, leathery; very vigorous growth; [sport of 'Uncle Walter']
'Alaska' HT, w, 1949, Meilland, F.; flowers ivory-white, well-formed, large, 50 petals; vigorous, upright growth; ['Peace' × 'Blanche Mallerin']
'Alaska' S, lp, Radler, William; flowers light pink fading to near white , single , flat , borne in small clusters, intense from foliage, none from bloom sweetbriar fragrance; recurrent; foliage medium to dark green; 40 inch growth; ['Radtee' × 'Radral']; intr. 2008
'Alaska Centennial' Gr, dr, 1967, Morey, Dr. Dennison; bud long, pointed; flowers dark blood-red-scarlet, 3½-5 in., dbl., high-centered; foliage dark, leathery, glossy; vigorous, upright growth; ['Siren' × 'Avon']; intr. 1967
'Alastair McEwan' -- See 'Rawslam'
'Alba' -- See 'Fausse Unique'
'Alba' ('Blanche Double') C, w, before 1775; flowers pure white, large, full
'Alba Bifera' A, w, 1843, Augeul; flowers lilac white, 5-6 cm., very full; some repeat
'Alba Carnea' HP, lp, 1867, Touvais
'Alba Flore Multiplici' -- See 'Pompon Blanc'
'Alba Foliacea' A, w, 1824
Alba Garcia® -- See 'Festro'
'Alba Maxima' ('Bonnie Prince Charlie's Rose', 'The Jacobite Rose', 'Great Double White', 'Maxima', R. alba anglica minor, R. × alba var. florepleno, R. × alba maxima) A, w, before 1867; flowers similar to Maiden's Blush, but center creamy, with a faint buff tinge on opening, aging to pure white, 4 in., dbl, flat, borne in clusters of 2-6, moderate fragrance; non-recurrent; foliage clear gray-green; growth to 6-8 ft.; a natural sport of R. × alba semi-plena, but with more petals
Alba Meidiland™ -- See 'Meiflopan'
'Alba Meillandécor' -- See 'Meiflopan'
Alba Meillandina® -- See 'Meinabron'
'Alba Minima' A, mp, Scarman; intr. 1997
'Alba Mutabilis' HP, 1865, Verdier; flowers delicate pink, clouded with deeper pink; sometimes classed as M
'Alba Odorata' (R. × bracteata alba odorata, R. × microphylla alba odorata) HBc, w, 1834, Mariani; flowers yellowish-white, anthers yellow, large, full, flat, moderate fragrance; foliage 5-7 oval leaflets, glossy; prickles straight, large; stems wood greenish-purple; [R. bracteata × R. roxburghii]; often confused with Maria Leonida
'Alba Regalis' -- See 'Great Maiden's Blush'
'Alba Rosea' -- See 'Celestial'
'Alba Rosea' -- See 'Beauté Tendre'
'Alba Rosea' -- See 'Mme Bravy'
'Alba Rubifolia' HWich, w, 1901, Van Fleet; flowers large, dbl., moderate fragrance; foliage glossy, evergreen; growth creeping
'Alba Semi-plena' ('Alba Suavelons', R. × alba suaveolens, 'Vierge', 'Suavelons', R. incarnata, R. × alba semi-plena, R. × alba nivea, 'Duplex', 'Semi-Plena') A, w, before 1754; flowers medium, showing yellow stamens, 8-12 petals, strong fragrance; non-recurrent; foliage glaucous, gray-green; prickles strong, few; growth upright, large (12-15 ft.); large crop of red hips in fall
'Alba Simplex' HBc, w; flowers single; [R. bracteata × unknown]
'Alba Suaveolens' -- See 'Alba Semi-plena'
'Albania' Min, Dot, Simon; intr. 1991
'Albast' HT, op, 1928, Van Rossem; bud ovoid; flowers salmon-pink, open, large, dbl.; foliage bronze, glossy; vigorous growth; ['Morgenglans' × 'Mrs Wemyss Quin']
'Albatross' HT, w, 1908, Paul, W.; flowers white, shaded pink, large, full
'Albatross' HWich, w; intr. 1988

'Albella' ('Sara', Piacenza™) HT, pb, 2005, Alberici, Marc; flowers pink blend, reverse light pink, 10-12 cm., very full, borne in large clusters, intense fragrance; foliage large, light green, glossy, blackspot-resistant; prickles normal, straight,; growth upright, bushy, tall (more than 1 m.); garden decoration; [Allgold® × Yves Piaget®]; intr. 2006

'Albéric Barbier' HWich, w, 1900, Barbier; bud small, yellow; flowers creamy white, center yellow, 8 cm., dbl., borne singly or in small clusters, moderate fruity, sweet fragrance; non-recurrent; foliage glossy, dark; vigorous growth; [R. wichurana × 'Shirley Hibberd']

Alberich® -- See 'Happy'

'Albert' F, op, 1962, Jones; flowers orange salmon, 50 petals, high-centered, borne in clusters; foliage glossy, bronze; vigorous, bushy, compact growth

'Albert Durand' T, lp, 1906, Schwartz; flowers light carmine pink, shaded flesh white, center darker carmine, large, full; ['Luciole' × 'André Schwartz']

'Albert Dureau' ('Mons Albert Dureau') HP, dr, 1869, Vigneron; flowers shining dark red, shaded scarlet, large

'Albert Edward' S, ly, 1970, Hillier; flowers creamy yellow, 1½-2 in., 5 petals, moderate fragrance; vigorous growth; [R. spinosissima altaica × R. hugonis]; intr. 1961

'Albert Fourès' T, rb, 1899, Bonnaire; flowers brick red with golden yellow, large, full

'Albert-Georg Pluta Rose' F, mr, Tantau, Math.; flowers luminous red, large, dbl.; intr. 1986

'Albert Gilles' HT, op, 1943, Mallerin, C.; flowers pink tinted coral; ['Julien Potin' × 'Mme Joseph Perraud']

'Albert Hoffmann' T, ly, 1904, Welter; flowers very large, dbl., intense fragrance; ['Souv de Catherine Guillot' × 'Maman Cochet']

'Albert la Blotais' HP, dr, 1881, Moreau et Robert

'Albert la Blotais, Climbing' Cl HP, mr, 1888, Pernet Père; flowers deep pink to light red, 11 cm., very dbl., flat, strong fragrance; ['Gloire de Dijon' × 'Général Jacqueminot']

'Albert Maumené' S, or, 1934, Sauvageot, H.; bud large, pointed, ovoid, copper-red; flowers carrot-red shaded copper, semi-dbl., cupped; recurrent; foliage glossy, dark; growth very vigorous, bushy, open; ['Mme Edouard Herriot' × R. hugonis]

'Albert Pagé' -- See 'Albert Payé'

'Albert Payé' ('Albert Pagé') HP, lp, 1873, Touvais; flowers flesh-pink, large; vigorous growth

'Albert Pike' HT, dp, 1926, Vestal; flowers glowing cerise, flushed peach at times; [sport of 'Columbia']

'Albert Poyet' LCl, pb, Eve, A.; flowers cherry pink, cream at center, aging to crimson with light pink, 4 in., dbl., borne in small clusters, slight fragrance; intr. 1979

'Albert Stopford' T, lp, 1898, Nabonnand; bud long; sepals large; flowers dark crimson rose, large, full, borne mostly solitary, moderate fragrance; foliage large; prickles strong, numerous; growth vigorous; ['Général Schablikine' × 'Papa Gontier']

'Albert Weedall' -- See 'Scrivleo'

'Alberta' F, dp, 1995, Fleming, Joyce L.; flowers large, 10 petals, flat, borne in small clusters, slight fragrance; foliage medium size, dark green, semi-glossy; some prickles; growth compact, spreading, medium; ['Carefree Beauty' × 'Red Hot']

'Alberta Hunter' F, ly, 1985, French, Richard; flowers red stamens, large, 25 petals, cupped, borne singly; foliage medium size, dark, semi-glossy; prickles small, straight, red; medium, upright, bushy growth; hips small, globular, dull orange; ['Eleanor Perenyi' × 'Lillian Gish']

'Albertan' S, mp, 1962, Erskine; flowers bright pink, 15-18 petals; ['Athabasca' × unknown]

'Albertina Sisulu' S, w, Dickson; intr. 2004

'Albertine' HWich, op, 1921, Barbier; bud ovoid; flowers light salmon pink, tinted yellow, darker reverse, aging to light pink, 7-9 cm., semi-dbl. to dbl., cupped, borne in small clusters, moderate fragrance; non-recurrent; foliage dark green, glossy; prickles numerous, large; vigorous growth; [R. wichurana × 'Mrs Arthur Robert Waddell']

'Alberto N. Calamet' HT, mp, 1909, Soupert & Notting; flowers flesh pink, large, full

'Alberton Amor' -- See 'Ludsportiana'

'Albgiovi' ('Roberta') HT, lp, 2005, Alberici, Marc; flowers light pink, reverse more light, 7-10 cm., single, borne mostly solitary; prickles normal, brown, numerous; growth to 100 cm.; garden decorative; ['Nil Bleu' × Abraham Darby®]; intr. 2007

'Albinia' S, op, Poulsen; intr. 1996

'Albion' HP, pb, 1870, Liabaud; flowers scarlet red, shaded orange, large, full, spherical

'Albion' HT, mp, Poulsen, Niels D.; flowers large, dbl., urn-shaped, borne singly, slight fragrance; foliage semi-glossy; bushy growth; ['Frileuse' × seedling]; intr. 1969

'Albion' S, w, Skinner; bud cream; flowers dbl.; recurrent bloom; foliage leaflets small, firm, dark; growth to 4 ft.; hardy; [sport of R. laxa hybrid]

'Albo Pleno' -- See 'Pompon Blanc'

'Albrecht Dürer' ('Albrecht Dürer Rose') S, ob, Tantau; flowers orange to apricot, large, very full, intense fragrance; bushy growth starting with second year; intr. 2003

'Albrecht Dürer Rose' -- See 'Albrecht Dürer'

'Albunda' ('I Have A Dream') F, ob, 2005, Alberici, Marc; flowers yellow peach, reverse white cream, 10 cm., dbl., borne in small clusters, slight fragrance; foliage medium size, medium green, matte; prickles normal, numerous; growth bushy, medium (80 cm.); hedging; [Henri Matisse™ × 'Mutabilis']; intr. 2007

'Albuquerque Enchantment' -- See 'Moralbuque'

'Alcantara' -- See 'Red Flower Carpet'

'Alcazar' F, or, 1961, Gaujard; bud pointed; flowers coppery red, 3 in., 18 petals; foliage glossy, bronze; bushy growth; ['Jolie Princesse' × ('Opera' × 'Miss France')]

'Alcha' S, mp

'Alchemist' -- See 'Alchymist'

'Alchymist' ('Alchemist') S, ab, 1956, Kordes; bud ovoid; flowers yellow shaded orange, pink and red, large, very dbl.; heavy, non-recurrent bloom; foliage glossy, bronze; vigorous, upright (6 ft.) growth; ['Golden Glow' × R. rubiginosa hybrid]

'Alcide Vigneron' ('Alice Vigneron') HP, mp, 1862, Vigneron; flowers large, full

'Alcime' HGal, m, 1845, Vibert; flowers very dark violet, medium, dbl.

'Alcime' M, mr, Robert & Moreau; flowers purple-red, 8-10 cm., borne in large clusters; intr. 1861

'Alcine' HGal, dp, 1834, Vibert; flowers deep rosy pink, spotted white, edged lilac-blush, large, dbl., cupped; vigorous, upright growth

'Alcmaria' F, mr, Verbeek; flowers blood red, large, dbl.; intr. 1971

'Alconbury' -- See 'Talalconbury'

'Aldégonde' -- See 'Rouge Formidable'

'Alden Biesen' -- See 'LLX8964'

'Alderley Park' F, mp, Fryer; flowers porcelain pink, large, double, low-centered, moderate fragrance; recurrent; vigorous, spreading, bushy (3 ft.) growth; intr. 2007

Alea® F, dp, Noack; flowers bright pink, 2 in., double, loose, borne in clusters; recurrent; foliage medium green, glossy; compact (2 ft.) growth; intr. 2007

'Alec and Paul' -- See 'Worcarter'

'Alec Rose' F, or, 1969, McGredy, Sam IV; flowers scarlet, well-formed, borne in trusses; free growth; ['Hassan' × 'John Church']

'Alecia Carol' -- See 'Mancarol'

Alec's Red® HT, mr, 1971, Cocker, A. M.; flowers deep, bright crimson, 6 in., 45 petals, moderate fragrance; foliage matte, green; vigorous, upright growth; PP3056; ['Fragrant Cloud' × 'Dame de Coeur']; intr. 1970

Alec's Red, Climbing® Cl HT, mr, 1976, Harkness; flowers dbl., borne singly or in small clusters; [sport of 'Alec's Red']

'Alector Cramoisi' ('Major') HGal, dr, before 1811, Dupont; flowers velvety crimson red, large, dbl., moderate fragrance

'Aleene' -- See 'Gelal'
'Alegria' F, ob; intr. 2001
'Alegrias' F, rb, 1981, Rose Barni; bud globular; flowers medium yellow, reverse orange-red, 23 petals, cupped, borne 3-6 per cluster, no fragrance; foliage medium size, glossy; prickles straight, reddish-green; upright, bushy growth; [seedling × ('Charleston' × unknown)]; intr. 1978
Alejandra Conde® -- See 'Fegosa'
'Alena' Gr, ob, 1970, Raffel; flowers orange, large, dbl., cupped; foliage large, glossy, dark; vigorous, upright, bushy growth; [seedling × 'Tropicana']
'Alessa' LCl, mr, Jensen; intr. 1988
'Aletha' -- See 'Dwaaletha'
'Aletha June' -- See 'Moealetha'
'Alex Brackstone' -- See 'Rawstone'
'Alex C. Collie' -- See 'Cococrust'
'Alex Dickson' -- See 'Mme Pulliat'
'Alexa' -- See 'Moealexa'
Alexander® ('Alexandra') HT, or, 1972, Harkness, R.; bud pointed; flowers bright vermilion-red, 5 in., 25 petals, high-centered, slight fragrance; foliage glossy; tall, vigorous growth; ['Tropicana' × ('Ann Elizabeth' × Allgold®)]
'Alexander Emslie' HT, dr, 1918, Dickson, A.; flowers deep crimson, base slightly white, large, full, moderate fragrance
'Alexander Hill Gray' ('Yellow Cochet', 'Yellow Maman Cochet') T, dy, 1911, Dickson, A.; flowers deep lemon-yellow, aging deeper, large; vigorous growth
'Alexander Laquemont' -- See 'Alexandre Laquement'
'Alexander MacKenzie' -- See 'A. MacKenzie'
'Alexander Marghiloman' HT, w, 1928, Mühle; flowers cream-white, center salmon; ['Harry Kirk' × unknown]
'Alexander Milne' -- See 'Lavmilne'
'Alexander von Humboldt' HKor, mr, 1960, Kordes, R.; flowers fiery blood red, occasionally flecked white, medium, dbl., rosette, borne in large clusters, slight fragrance; foliage glossy; vigorous (9-12 ft.) growth; [R. × kordesii × 'Cleopatra']
'Alexandra' -- See 'Korbaxand'
Alexandra™ -- See 'Princess Alexandra'
'Alexandra' -- See 'Alexander'
'Alexandra' ('The Alexandra') T, op, 1900, Paul, W.; flowers light salmon-pink, with golden-orange centers and apricot-bronze shading, large, dbl., slight fragrance
Alexandra® HT, ly, Kordes; flowers pale yellow, dbl., high-centered, slight fragrance; stems 80 cm.; Florist rose; intr. 2003
'Alexandra Kordana' Min, ab, Kordes; flowers bronzy apricot with pink tones on reverse, 3 -4 cm., dbl., cupped , borne mostly singly, recurrent; growth height 50 cm.; [sport of 'Vanilla Kordana']; container rose
'Alexandra Leek' F, ob, 1995, Fleming, Joyce; flowers soft orange, medium, single, borne in small clusters, moderate fragrance; foliage medium size, medium green, semi-glossy; some prickles; growth upright, bushy, tall; ['Masquerade' × 'Mrs John Laing']
'Alexandra Rose' -- See 'Ausday'
'Alexandre Chomer' HP, m, 1875, Liabaud; flowers velvety pruple, nuanced violet, large, full; prickles irregular, reddish
'Alexandre Damaizin' HP, mp, 1861, Damaizin
'Alexandre Dumas' D, lp, Fankhauser; flowers very dbl., cupped, borne in clusters, intense damask fragrance; abundant, non-recurrent bloom; foliage small, light green, glossy, leathery; vigorous, upright (6-8 ft.) growth; ['Ma Perkins' × R. damascena versicolor]; intr. 1969
'Alexandre Dumas' HP, dr, 1861, Margottin; flowers velvety maroon, striped poppy, large, full
'Alexandre Dupont' HP, dr, 1892, Liabaud; flowers dark, velvety red, very large, dbl.; ['Triomphe de l'Exposition' × unknown]
'Alexandre Dutitre' HP, lp, 1878, Lévêque; flowers light bright pink, large, full; very remontant
'Alexandre Fontaine' HP, dp, 1860, Fontaine
'Alexandre Girault' HWich, pb, 1909, Barbier; bud rose-pink; flowers carmine-red, base salmon, reverse lighter, 6-7 cm., dbl., borne in small clusters, moderate fragrance; non-recurrent; foliage dark green, glossy; vigorous growth; [R. wichurana × 'Papa Gontier']
'Alexandre Laquement' ('Alexander Laquemont') HGal, m, before 1885; flowers violet spotted with red
'Alexandre Trémouillet' HWich, dp, 1903, Barbier; flowers blush white, tinted with rose and salmon center, 8-9 cm., dbl., borne in large clusters; foliage dark green, oval, glossy, heavily dentate; prickles numerous, upright; [R. wichurana × 'Souv de Catherine Guillot']
'Alexandre von Humboldt' HP, lp, 1869, Verdier, E.; flowers silvery pink, shaded carmine, large, full
'Alexandria Rose' -- See 'Wilalex'
Alexandria's Rose™ -- See 'Micalex'
'Alexandrine Bachmeteff' HP, mr, 1852, Margottin
'Alexandrine Chapuis' HT, my, 1935, Vially; bud long, pointed, yellow, shaded carmine; flowers well-formed, large, dbl.; foliage bright green; ['Feu Joseph Looymans' × seedling]
'Alexandrine de Belfroy' HP, op, 1859, Fontaine
'Alexia' -- See 'Canlot'
'Alexia Wilson' F, ob, 1972, Horner, C. P.; flowers cream veined orange; [sport of 'Elizabeth of Glamis']
'Alexis' -- See 'Harlexis'
'Alexis Lepère' HP, mr, 1875, Vigneron; flowers very large, dbl.
Alexis+ HT, ly, Voom, Lex; flowers cream, double, high-centered, borne mostly singly; recurrent; stems long; florist rose
'Alezane' HT, ab, 1935, Pahissa; bud urn shaped, reddish brown; flowers deep apricot, large, dbl., cupped, moderate fruity fragrance; foliage glossy, bronze, dark; very vigorous growth; PP116; ['Angèle Pernet' × 'Comtesse de Castilleja']
'Alezane' F, ob, Dorieux; flowers bright orange with yellow at petal base, medium, semi-dbl.; intr. 1986
Alfabia® ('Coral Flower Carpet') S, op, Noack; flowers coral, lighter reverse, 3 cm., 5-10 petals, cupped, flattening when open, borne in large sprays; recurrent; foliage dark green, glossy; prickles moderate, 5 mm., curved slightly downward; compact (3-4 ft.) growth; PP14441; ['Korsami' × seedling]; intr. 2002
Alfalfa® -- See 'Bagalf'
Alfi™ -- See 'Poulfi'
'Alfie Luv' -- See 'Talalf'
'Alfieri' HGal, m, 1833, Vibert; flowers lilac-pink, medium, dbl.
'Alfred A. Buckwell' HT, mr, 1952, Buckwell; flowers red, 3 in., 30 petals, high-centered; foliage dark, leathery; vigorous growth; ['Hector Deane' × 'Betty Uprichard']
'Alfred Colomb' HP, dp, 1865, Lacharme, F.; flowers strawberry-red, reflexes crimson-carmine, large, 45 petals, high-centered, intense fragrance; recurrent bloom; growth dense; ['Général Jacqueminot' × unknown]
'Alfred de Dalmas' ('Mousseline') M, lp, 1855, Laffay, M.; bud rose-colored; flowers light pink with blush edges, of poor quality, small, dbl., borne in corymbs; some recurrent bloom; very prickly; vigorous, straggling growth
'Alfred de Rougemont' HP, dr, 1863, Lacharme, F.; flowers crimson-magenta, well-formed, very large, dbl.; vigorous, upright growth; ['Général Jacqueminot' × unknown]
'Alfred Dietrich' HMult, rb, Mertens; flowers carmine with white stripes, dbl., slight fragrance; intr. 1980
'Alfred K. Williams' ('A. K. Williams') HP, mr, 1877, Schwartz, J.; flowers carmine-red, changing to magenta; [sport of 'Général Jacqueminot']
'Alfred Leveau' ('Mme Alfred Leveau', 'Mons Alfred Leveau') HP, mp, 1880, Vigneron; flowers carmine-rose, aging lighter, large, full, borne mostly solitary; foliage dark green; prickles few, chestnut brown; growth upright
'Alfred Newton' HT, yb, 1959, Kemp, M.L.; flowers pale yellow edged crimson, 5 in., 35-40 petals, high-centered; foliage dark; vigorous growth; ['Moonbeam' × 'Karl Herbst']
'Alfred Pétot' HT, dr, 1935, Buatois; bud elongated; flowers crimson, well-formed, large, dbl.; foliage dark; strong stems;

very vigorous growth; ['Jeanne Excoffier' × 'Yves Druhen']

'Alfred Sisley® S, ob, Delbard; flowers orange and pink stripes with yellow reverse, full, slight fragrance; free-flowering; growth to 80 cm.; intr. 2005

'Alfred W. Mellersh' HT, op, 1918, Paul, W.; flowers salmon-yellow, shaded rose, center amber

'Alfredo Moreira da Silva' HT, yb, 1946, Mallerin, C.; bud long, pointed; flowers golden yellow tinted coral, large, semi-dbl.; foliage dark; very vigorous, upright growth; ['Dr. Kirk' × 'Peace']

'Alfresco' -- See 'Chewcorpink'

'Alger' HT, op, 1943, Gaujard; bud pointed; flowers clear pink, reverse salmon-pink, very large, dbl.; foliage leathery; vigorous growth

'Algonquin' S, pb, 1928, Central Exp. Farm; flowers purplish rose, center white, large, single, flat; non-recurrent; foliage dull, yellow-green; very vigorous (10 ft.) growth; hips large, bottle-shaped, red; hardy; [R. rubrifolia × (R. rugosa hybrid × unknown)]

'Alhambra' HT, rb, Tantau; flowers bright red with yellow base, large, double, high-centered, borne mostly singly; recurrent; stems long (60-80 cm.)

'Ali-Baba' F, or, 1963, Croix, P.; flowers large, 15-20 petals, borne in clusters; [('Corail' × Baccará®) × seedling]

'Ali Pacha Chériff' ('Aly Pacha Chérif') HP, mr, 1886, Lévêque, P.; flowers vermilion red, tinted blackish purple, large, full

'Alibi' F, w, 1961, deRuiter; flowers well-formed, 3-4 in., 30 petals; vigorous growth; ['Kaiserin Auguste Viktoria' × 'Pink Fragrance']

Alicante™ MinFl, dp, Poulsen; flowers deep pink to light red, 5-8 cm., dbl., no fragrance; foliage dark; growth bushy, 20-40 cm.; intr. 2004

'Alice' HT, lp, Allender, Robert William; bud long; flowers light pink, darker center, 45 petals, high-centered, borne singly, no fragrance; shy bloom; foliage large; prickles long, red; spreading (to about 4 ft.) growth; ['Royal Highness' × 'Christian Dior']; intr. 1978

'Alice' A, w, about 1830, Parmentier; flowers white shaded flesh, medium, full

'Alice' Pol, mp, Spek; flowers pink, fringed, borne in large clusters; RULED EXTINCT 11/80 ARM; ['Echo' × 'Orléans Rose']; intr. 1923

'Alice' S, pb, Wright, Percy H.; flowers dbl.; RULED EXTINCT 11/80 ARM; hybrid macounii; intr. 1935

'Alice Aldrich' HRg, lp, 1901, Lovett, J.T.; flowers clear, bright pink, large, dbl.; repeat bloom; [R. rugosa × 'Colonel de Sansal, or Caroline de Sansal']

'Alice Amos' F, pb, 1922, Spek; bud long, pointed; flowers cerise, white eye, single, borne in clusters on strong stem; very vigorous growth; [Tip-Top® × seedling]

'Alice Bracegirdle' HT, w, 2001, Bracegirdle, A.J.; flowers 5 in., full, high-centered, borne mostly solitary; foliage large, medium green, matte; prickles medium, straight, few; growth upright, medium (3½ ft.); exhibition; [sport of 'Sunderland Supreme']

'Alice Chamrion' Pol, lp, 1908, Dubreuil; flowers flesh pink

'Alice Cory Wright' HT, dp, 1910, Paul, W.; flowers large, full

'Alice de Rothschild' HT, w, 1920, Gemen & Bourg; flowers creamy white with pink reflections, center darker

'Alice Dureau' -- See 'Mme Alice Dureau'

'Alice Faye' -- See 'Seaodd'

'Alice Fontaine' -- See 'Emotion'

'Alice Furon' HT, w

'Alice Garnier' -- See 'Mme Alice Garnier'

'Alice Grahame' HT, w, 1903, Dickson, A.; flowers ivory white, tinted salmon, very large, very dbl., moderate fragrance

'Alice Gray' -- See 'Scandens'

'Alice Hamilton' Ch, dr, 1903, Nabonnand; bud long; flowers velvety crimson red, dbl., slight sweet fragrance; foliage dark green; ['Bengale Nabonnand' × 'Parsons' Pink China']

'Alice Harding' HT, my, 1937, Mallerin, C.; bud ovoid; flowers golden yellow, large, dbl., moderate fragrance; foliage glossy, dark; vigorous growth; PP202; ['Souv. de Claudius Pernet' × 'Mrs Pierre S. duPont']

'Alice Hoffmann' Ch, rb, 1897, Hoffmann; flowers pink, touched cherry

'Alice Jarrett' -- See 'Evejaunty'

'Alice Kaempff' HT, pb, 1921, Felberg-Leclerc; bud medium, long-pointed, pink with a light violet tint; flowers silvery rose-pink, center coppery yellow, large, dbl., globular, moderate fragrance; foliage medium size, glossy; ['General MacArthur' × 'Radiance']

'Alice King' Cl F, mr, 1988, Harrison, G.; flowers medium, luminous red, aging lighter, small, 40-50 petals, borne in sprays; foliage light green, glossy; prickles small, medium red; vigorous, slight perpetual growth; [Dublin Bay® × seedling]

'Alice Lee' -- See 'Talali'

'Alice Lemon' HT, w, 1912, Hill, E. G.

'Alice Leroi' M, pb, 1842, Vibert; bud well-mossed; flowers lilac-blush shaded rose, center deep rose, very large, dbl.; vigorous growth

'Alice Lindsell' HT, lp, 1902, Dickson, A.; flowers creamy white with a pink center, large, dbl., high-centered

'Alice Manley' HT, my, 1959, Joseph H. Hill, Co.; bud long, pointed; flowers mimosa-yellow, 3½-4 in., 45-50 petals, high-centered, slight fragrance; foliage leathery; vigorous, upright, bushy growth; PP1546; [seedling × 'Golden Rapture']; intr. 1958

'Alice Marion Whyte' HT, lp, 1932, Evans; flowers soft pink, fading pure white

'Alice Mavis' S, lp, Peden, G.H.; intr. 1994

'Alice of Ingleside' HT, 1910, Briggs

'Alice Pat' F, rb, 1982, Jerabek, Paul E.; bud ovoid; flowers red shading to white, reverse white shaded pink, 38 petals, flat, borne 1-6 per cluster, slight fragrance; foliage dark, glossy; prickles slightly hooked, reddish-tan; upright, short growth; [seedling × seedling]

'Alice Springs' LCl, lp, Peden; flowers cupped, cupped, moderate fragrance

'Alice Stern' HT, w, 1926, Gillot, F.; bud long, pointed; flowers white, center cream, sometimes salmon, large, 30-40 petals; foliage dark, bronze; vigorous, bushy growth; ['Grange Colombe' × 'Sunburst']

'Alice Vena' HGal, m, before 1867; flowers plum-purple, large, borne in clusters

'Alice Vibert' C, mr, 1855, Robert; flowers bright rose red, medium, full, globular

'Alice Vigneron' -- See 'Alcide Vigneron'

'Alice Wieman' Pol, dp, 1970, Bodley; flowers pink, open, small, dbl., moderate fragrance; continuous bloom; growth moderate, bushy; PP2893; [seedling × 'Rita Sammons']

'Alicia' -- See 'Gelali'

'Alicia' HT, pb, 1972, Lees; flowers rose-pink, edged cream, large, 36 petals; foliage dark; vigorous growth; ['Golden Scepter' × 'Ena Harkness']

'Alicia Courage' HT, pb, Courage; flowers pink with shades changing with weather, dbl., high-centered, moderate fragrance; growth medium; intr. 2002

'Alicja' LCl

'Alida' HT, mr, 1938, Lens; bud long, pointed; flowers well-formed, very dbl.; foliage bright; vigorous, bushy growth; ['Charles P. Kilham' × 'E.G. Hill']

'Alida Lovett' HWich, lp, 1905, Van Fleet; bud long, pointed; flowers shell-pink, base shaded sulfur, 7-8 cm., dbl., borne in clusters of 3-10; non-recurrent; foliage glossy; vigorous, climbing growth; [R. wichurana × 'Souv de President Carnot']

'Alie Dool' -- See 'Rawgecko'

Aliena™ -- See 'Tuckaliena'

'Aliénor d'Aquitaine' ('Eleanor of Aquitaine') HGal, mr, Rautio; intr. 1999

'Aliette' HT, 1958, Arles; flowers salmon-pink tinted orange, well-formed; vigorous, bushy growth; ['Pres. Herbert Hoover' × 'Signora']

'Alika' ('Gallica Grandiflora', 'Grandiflora', R. gallica grandiflora) HGal, mr, 1906; flowers brilliant red with no purple, many stamens, petalage variable, large, semi-dbl., moderate fragrance; vigorous growth; brought to the U.S. from St. Petersburg, Russia, by Prof. N. E. Hansen

'Alina' HT, w, Tantau; intr. 2003

'Aline' HGal, lp, 1816, Vibert; flowers flesh pink, medium, full

'Aline' Ch, m, Laffay; flowers purple, centers white, small, dbl.; intr. 1836

'Aline' P, w, Vibert; flowers white, shaded flesh pink, medium, full; intr. 1846

'Aline' HT, or, Astolat Nursery; flowers peach, compact, 4 in., 22 petals, moderate fragrance; foliage dark; vigorous growth; [sport of 'Picture']; intr. 1950

'Aline' Min, or, Laperrière; intr. 1994

'Aline Rozey' N, lp, 1884, Schwartz; sometimes classed as HP

'Aline Sisley' T, dr, 1874, Guillot fils; flowers red to purplish rose or violet/crimson, large, dbl.; foliage yellowish green; growth vigorous, semi-climbing

'Alinka' HT, ob, Kordes; intr. 1985

'Alisha' -- See 'Spoday'

'Alison' -- See 'Coclibee'

'Alison' LCl, dp, McAllister; flowers vibrant pink, dbl.; dark green foliage; [sport of 'Dublin Bay']; intr. 2001

'Alison 2000' F, ob, Pfl-Kontor; flowers gold/orange blend, medium; bushy, compact growth; intr. 2000

'Alison Brown' HT, dp, 1993, Brown, Mrs. Ann; flowers deep pink, 3-3½ in., full, borne mostly singly, some small clusters, intense fragrance; foliage medium size, dark green, semi-glossy; some prickles; medium (125 cm.), bushy growth; [sport of 'Ena Harkness']; intr. 1993

'Alison Pitt' -- See 'Sarmemory'

'Alison Wheatcroft' F, ab, 1959, Wheatcroft Bros.; flowers apricot flushed crimson; [sport of 'Circus']

'Alistair Sheridan' -- See 'Pearich'

'Alister Clark' F, lp, 1999, Newman, Laurie; flowers 3-3½ in., full, borne in small clusters, intense fragrance; foliage small, dark green, glossy; prickles moderate; spreading, medium (3 ft.) growth; [sport of 'Marjory Palmer']; intr. 1990

'Alister Clark's Pink' HT, lp, Clark, A.

'Alister Stella Gray' ('Golden Rambler') N, ly, 1894, Gray, A.H.; bud long, pointed; flowers pale yellow, center orange, fading to white, 6-7 cm., dbl., borne in small clusters, moderate fragrance; recurrent bloom; foliage small, glossy; vigorous, climbing growth; ['William Allen Richardson' × 'Mme Pierre Guillot']

'Alister's Gift™ -- See 'Virmanipuri'

'Alix' -- See 'Diadême de Flore'

'Alix Roussel' T, yb, 1908, Gamon; flowers yellow with salmon center, large, full

All Ablaze™ -- See 'Weksamsou'

'All-American Bride' -- See 'Wilbrid'

'All-American Magic' Gr, rb, Meilland; flowers striped with various shades of red, pink, cream and white , 3-3.5 in., 35 petals, pompon , borne in clusters of 4 - 15, slight raspberry fragrance; recurrent; foliage medium green, glossy; bushy (4 - 5.5 ft.) growth; intr. 2008

'All Gold' -- See 'Allgold'

'All In One' -- See 'Meilider'

All That Jazz™ -- See 'Twoadvance'

'All the Rage' S, ab, Lim, Ping; bud coral; flowers apricot with yellow center, single to semi-double , flat, no fragrance; medium (2.5 - 4 ft.) growth ; winter hardy ; PPAF; intr. 2008

'Allalujah' -- See 'Alleluia'

'Allamand-Ho' S, pb, 1985, Buck, Dr. Griffith J.; bud ovoid; flowers pink and yellow blend, petals edged ruby red, color intensifying with age, 38 petals, cupped, borne in clusters of 1-6, moderate sweet fragrance; repeat bloom; foliage dark, leathery, semi-glossy; prickles awl-like, red-brown; erect, bushy growth; hardy; [('Hawkeye Belle' × 'Prairie Star') × 'lobelle']

'Allambie' ('Allumbie') HT, Donovan, R.

'Allanson Rose' HT, or, Kordes; flowers bright vermilion intensifying to burnt orange in the sun, medium, dbl., high-centered, borne one to a stem and candelabras; free-flowering; foliage glossy green; growth medium, neat, upright; intr. 2001

'Allard' (R. xanthina slingerii) Misc OGR, dy; flowers chrome-yellow, dbl.; from the Botanic Gardens, Lyon, France; a form or hybrid of R. xanthina

'Allegeo '80' -- See 'Meifikalif'

'Allegra' -- See 'Ardjoy'

'Allégresse' HT, mr, 1952, Robichon; flowers red, becoming lighter, well-formed, very dbl.; strong stems; vigorous, upright growth; ['Fantaisie' × 'Sensation']

'Allegretto' HT, or, 1979, Huber; bud long, pointed; flowers 4 in., 14-17 petals, slight fragrance; foliage leathery; upright growth; ['Fragrant Cloud' × 'Sutter's Gold']; intr. 1975

Allegro® HT, or, 1962, Meilland, Alain A.; flowers 3½-4½ in., 30 petals, high-centered, slight fragrance; foliage leathery, glossy; vigorous, bushy growth; PP2358; [('Happiness' × 'Independence') × 'Soraya']; intr. 1962

Allegro® HT, mr, Richardier; intr. 1999

Allegro Symphonie® Min, ob, Meilland; flowers orange and yellow bicolor, color deepening, dbl.; intr. 2004

'Alleluia' -- See 'Delatur'

'Alleluia' Cl Pol, Cazzaniga, F. G.; intr. 1960

'Alleluia' ('Allalujah') HT, ab, Delbard; greenhouse cut flower; sold only in Australia; intr. 2003

'Allen Box' Pol, lp, 1928, Box, S.

'Allen Brundrett' HT, dr, Brundrett; intr. 1994

'Allen Chandler' Cl HT, mr, 1923, Chandler; bud long, pointed; flowers brilliant crimson, large, semi-dbl., borne 3-4 per cluster; recurrent bloom; foliage dark, leathery, glossy; vigorous, pillar growth; ['Hugh Dickson' × unknown]

'Allen's Fragrant Pillar' Cl HT, rb, 1931, Allen; bud long, pointed; flowers cerise, base flushed yellow, 4 in., dbl., open, borne mostly solitary, moderate fragrance; recurrent bloom; foliage glossy, bronze; long, strong stems; moderate climbing growth; ['Paul's Lemon Pillar' × 'Souv. de Claudius Denoyel']

'Allen's Golden Climber' LCl, ob, 1933, Allen; flowers dark yellow, reverse orange, 3½-4 in., dbl.; non-recurrent; foliage glossy

'Allen's Jubilee' -- See 'Jubilee'

Allgold® ('All Gold') F, my, 1957, LeGrice; flowers bright buttercup-yellow, 3 in., 15-22 petals, borne singly and in large trusses, slight fragrance; foliage small, glossy, dark; vigorous growth; PP1665; ['Goldilocks' × 'Ellinor LeGrice']

'Allgold, Climbing' ('Grimpant All Gold', Grimpant Allgold®) Cl F, my, 1965, Gandy, Douglas L.; [sport of 'Allgold']; intr. 1961

'Alliance' -- See 'Meibleri'

'Alliance' F, dp, 1966, Delforge; bud ovoid; flowers light red and deep pink, large, dbl.; foliage soft; strong stems; very vigorous, bushy growth; ['Rosita' × Queen Elizabeth®]

Alliance® ('Keimateo') HT, rb, Keisei; flowers medium red, white reverse; intr. 2002

'Alliance Franco-Russe' T, my, 1899, Goinard; bud long; flowers tea-yellow, shading to salmon towards the center, large, dbl.; foliage large, bright green

'Allie' -- See 'Geled'

'Allison Sweetie' Gr, mr, 1978, Miller, F.; bud long, pointed, oval; flowers 3-3½ in., 21-25 petals, high-centered, moderate fragrance; foliage large, glossy, dark; tall, vigorous growth; ['Tropicana' × Mister Lincoln®]

'Alliswell' HT, w, 1956, Motose; bud ovoid; flowers white overcast pink, center cameo-pink, 5-6 in., 50-60 petals, peony-like, moderate fragrance; vigorous, bushy growth; PP1480; ['Neige Parfum' × ('Charlotte Armstrong' × 'Blanche Mallerin')]

Allotria® F, or, 1959, Tantau, Math.; flowers orange-scarlet, 3 in., dbl., flat, borne in large clusters; foliage dark, glossy; vigorous growth; ['Fanal' × ('Cinnabar' × unknown)]; intr. 1958

'Allspice' HT, my, 1976, Armstrong, D.L.; bud ovoid, pointed, deep yellow; flowers 4½ in., 35 petals, moderate honey and tea rose fragrance; foliage large, olive-green; vigorous, upright, bushy growth; PP4301; ['Buccaneer' × 'Peace']; intr. 1977

'Allumbie' -- See 'Allambie'

'Allure' HT, pb, 1950, Swim, H.C.; bud long, pointed, carmine-rose; flowers Neyron rose, base yellow, 5-6 in., 28-30 petals, high-centered, slight fragrance; foliage leathery, glossy, light green; very vigorous, upright growth; PP886; ['Mrs Pierre S. duPont' × 'Charlotte Armstrong']

'Alluring' -- See 'Sealure'

'Allux Symphony' -- See 'Auslett'

'Alma' F, dr, Riethmuller; flowers dark crimson, dbl., borne in large clusters; dwarf growth; [Orange Triumph® × 'Eutin']

'Alma' ('Alma Blue') HT, m; intr. 1980

'Alma-atinskaj Aromatnaja' HT, m, Besschetnowa; flowers large, very dbl.; intr. 1959

'Alma Bierbauer' S, op, Williams, J. Benjamin; flowers salmon pink with yellow eye and pink stamens, single; intr. 1997

'Alma Blue' -- See 'Alma'

'Alma June Seville' -- See 'Rawville'

'Alma Mater' HT, lp, 1929, Good & Reese; flowers lighter in color; [sport of 'Columbia']

'Almandet' HT, mp, Croix; intr. 1966

'Almirante Américo Tomás' ('Miramar') HT, rb, 1955, Moreira da Silva; flowers geranium-red, reverse old-gold, large, dbl.; very vigorous growth; ['Sultane' × 'Peace']

'Almond Glory' -- See 'Zipalm'

'Almondeen' -- See 'Arofrap'

'Almost Perfect' -- See 'Welmost'

'Almost Sunset' HT, yb, Zary

'Almost Wild Cerise' S, lp; intr. 2005

'Almost Wild Embers' S, or; intr. 2005

'Almost Wild Yellow' S, my; intr. 2005

'Alnwick Castle' -- See 'Ausgrab'

'Aloerin' ('Erin Alonso') Min, my, 2003, Alonso, Peter G. Jr.; flowers full, high-centered, borne mostly solitary, no fragrance; foliage medium size, dark green, semi-glossy; prickles 3/8 in., sharp, green to brown, moderate; growth upright, tall (36-48 in.); garden decoration, exhibition; [sport of 'Bees Knees']; intr. 2002

Aloha® -- See 'Korwesrug'

'Aloha' Cl HT, mp, 1949, Boerner; bud ovoid; flowers rose-pink, reverse deeper, large, 58 petals, cupped, moderate fragrance; recurrent bloom; foliage leathery, dark; vigorous, pillar (8-10 ft.) growth; PP948; ['Mercedes Gallart' × 'New Dawn']

Aloha® ('Kordes' Rose Aloha') HT, yb, Kordes; flowers yellow with slight reddish margin, medium, double, high-centered, borne mostly singly; recurrent; stems 60 cm; greenhouse rose; intr. 1999

'Aloha' HT, dy, McGredy; flowers golden yellow, dbl., classical; growth medium to tall; intr. 2000

'Aloha Hawaii' -- See 'Korwesrug'

'Alois Jirásek' HT, ob, 1931, Böhm, J.; bud long, pointed; flowers dark orange, tinted brownish yellow, large, dbl.; foliage glossy; vigorous growth; ['Mme Butterfly' × 'Mrs George Shawyer']

'Alojosh' (Josh Alonso™) Min, op, 2006, Alonso, Peter G., Jr.; flowers orange/pink blend, reverse yellow, 2-3 in., full, high-centered, borne mostly solitary; foliage medium size, dark green, semi-glossy; prickles average, sharp, green to brown, numerous; growth upright, tall (36-48 in.); [sport of 'Bee's Knees']; intr. 2007

'Alolinda' (Melinda Alonso™) MinFl, ab, 2007, Alonso, Peter G., Jr.; flowers larger and showier than parent; form more well-defined, 3 in., full, borne mostly solitary; foliage medium, medium green, matte; prickles small, pointed, brown, moderate; growth upright, tall (4-5 ft.): exhibition; [sport of 'Jean Kenneally']; intr. 2007

'Alopiña' ('Piña Colada') Min, ly, 2005, Alonso, Peter G., Jr.; flowers creamy light yellow, 2½ in., full, high-centered, borne mostly solitary, slight fragrance; foliage medium size, medium green, matte; prickles few, small, pointed, reddish brown; growth upright, tall (3 to 4 ft.): exhibition; ['Olympic Gold' × 'Olympic Gold']; intr. 2005

'Alorobin' (Robin Alonso™) MinFl, dr, 2005, Peter G. Alonso Jr.; flowers deep red, reverse medium red, over 3 in., full, borne mostly solitary; foliage large, dark green, semi-glossy; prickles ½ cm., curved, brown, moderate; growth compact, medium; exhibition; [sport of 'Caliente']; intr. 2007

'Alouette' ('Lark') Pol, op, 1971, Delforge; bud long, pointed; flowers salmon-orange, medium, semi-dbl., cupped; profuse, continuous bloom; foliage leathery; vigorous, bushy growth; ['Ambassadeur Baert' × seedling]

'Aloysia Kaiser' S, my, 1937, Lambert, P.; bud ochre-yellow; flowers reddish bright yellow, round, large, dbl., borne in clusters; seasonal bloom; vigorous growth; ['Miss G. Mesman' × 'Belle Doria']

'Alpaïde de Rotalier' ('Alphaïde de Rotallier') HP, lp, 1863, Campy; flowers transparent light pink, large, full

'Alpenfee' HSet, lp, before 1890, Geschwind, R.; flowers dbl., borne in clusters, no fragrance; probably R. setigera × a Hybrid Perpetual

'Alpenglühen' -- See 'Alpine Glow'

Alpenglühen® S, mr, Tantau; flowers bright signal-red with yellow stamens, borne in clusters; foliage fresh green, glossy; growth low and spreading, maximum 2 ft.; intr. 2004

'Alpengrüss' F, Noack, Werner; intr. 1974

Alpenkonigin® F, mr

'Alpha' -- See 'Meinastur'

'Alpha Meidiland' -- See 'Meirameca'

'Alpha Moe' -- See 'Moealpha'

'Alphaïde de Rotallier' -- See 'Alpaïde de Rotalier'

'Alphée' HT, pb, Croix, P.; flowers pink with silver reverse; intr. 1972

'Alphonse Belin' HP, mr, 1863, Gautreau; flowers cherry red, large, full

'Alphonse Damaizin' HP, mr, 1861, Damaizin

'Alphonse Daudet' -- See 'Meirouve'

'Alphonse de Lamartine' HP, lp, 1853, Ducher; flowers rosy blush, medium, dbl.; moderate growth

'Alphonse Fontaine' HP, mp, 1868, Fontaine; flowers carmine, shaded cherry red, large, full

'Alphonse Karr' HP, dr, 1845, Portemer

'Alphonse Karr' HP, lp, Feuillet; flowers bright pink, edges lighter, large, very full; intr. 1855

'Alphonse Karr' T, m, Nabonnand, G.; flowers crimson-purple, center lighter, large, dbl.; ['Duchess of Edinburgh' × unknown]; intr. 1879

'Alphonse Maille' HCh, dr, 1825, Boutigny; flowers dark purple-red, full

'Alphonse Maille' HCh, mr, Laffay; flowers bright carmine, shaded purple; intr. before 1838

'Alphonse Soupert' HP, mp, 1883, Lacharme, F.; flowers rose pink, large, dbl., moderate fragrance; numerous prickles; ['Jules Margottin' × unknown]

'Alphonse Troussard' HT, 1951, Buatois

'Alpin' LCl, or, 1964, Combe; flowers bright orange-red, 3 in., dbl., borne singly or in small clusters; recurrent bloom; foliage dark, glossy; vigorous growth; ['Spectacular' × 'Toujours']; intr. 1960

'Alpine' HT, my, 1954, Grillo; bud long, pointed; flowers clear yellow, open, 5½ in., 30 petals; foliage leathery; vigorous, upright growth; [sport of 'Sunnymount']

'Alpine Glow' ('Alpenglühen') F, or, 1954, Tantau, Math.; bud deep orange-red; flowers vermilion-red, 3-4 in., 28 petals, cupped, borne in clusters of 4-10, moderate fragrance; foliage glossy; vigorous, bushy growth; PP1395; ['Cinnabar' × ('Cinnabar' × 'Käthe Duvigneau')]; intr. 1954

'Alpine Gold' Min, dy; growth short

'Alpine Rock' HT, w

Alpine Sunset® HT, ab, 1975, Cants of Colchester, Ltd.; flowers peach-pink, apricot reverse, 7-8 in., 30 petals, moderate fragrance; foliage glossy, medium green; vigorous, upright growth; ['Dr. A.J. Verhage' × 'Irish Gold']; intr. 1973

'Alsace' -- See 'Pektarampe'

'Alsace' HT, op, 1946, Meilland, F.; flowers salmon-pink, base gold, 6 in., dbl., foliage dark; free growth; ['Peace' × 'Mme Joseph Perraud']

'Alsace-Lorraine' HP, dr, 1879, Duval; flowers dark velvety red, large

'Alsterufer' ('Zwerg Teplitz') HT, dr, 1909, Lambert, P.; flowers medium large, dbl., intense fragrance

'Alt-marburg' S, lp, Weihrauch; flowers large, dbl.; intr. 1979

'Alt-Rothenburg' HT, dp, 1939, Burkhardt; flowers large, dbl.

'Alt Wien' HT, pb, 1968, Prinz; flowers carmine-rose, 4 in., dbl.; foliage dark, glossy; compact growth; [sport of 'Queen of Bermuda']; intr. 1965

'Altaica' Sp, w

'Altair' ('Baralt') S, pb, Barni; flowers light pink with salmon tones, dbl., rosette, borne in clusters of 8 to 10, slight fragrance; continuous; foliage small to medium size, medium green; growth vigorous, fast grower, 50-70 cm.; groundcover; [Frine® × seedling]

'Altalaris' S, w, 1941, Skinner; bud large, pointed; flowers white, sometimes flushed pink, single, open; abundant, non-recurrent bloom; foliage leathery; numerous prickles; vigorous, bushy, growth; hips apple-shaped, bright red; [*R. spinosissima altaica* × *R. acicularis*]

'Alte Liebe' HT, or, Berger, A.; flowers large, dbl.; intr. 1974

'Alte Liebe' F, op, W. Kordes Söhne; flowers salmon-orange and pink, medium large, dbl.; intr. 1983

'Altenburg' F, or, Berger, A.; flowers medium large, dbl.; intr. 1977

'Alter Ego' HT, pb, Nirp; flowers hot pink with golden reverse; intr. 2003

'Altesse' -- See 'Meidinro'

Altesse® HT, ab, Richardier; flowers yellow and copper, dbl.; growth compact, uniform, medium (3 ft.); intr. 1999

Altesse® F, lp, Meilland; flowers light buff-colored pink, dbl., high-centered; greenhouse rose; intr. 2004

'Altesse' HT, dp, 1950, Meilland, F.; bud ovoid; flowers strawberry-red, large, 35-40 petals, globular; vigorous, upright growth; ['Vercors' × 'Léonce Colombier']

'Altesse 75' HT, Meilland, L.; intr. 1975

'Althea' HT, mr, 1930, Pemberton; flowers glowing crimson, moderate damask fragrance

'Altissima' -- See 'Aigle Brun'

Altissimo® ('Altus', 'Sublimely Single') LCl, mr, 1966, Delbard-Chabert; flowers blood-red, 4-5 in., 7 petals, cupped, borne singly or in small clusters; repeat bloom; foliage dark, serrated; tall growth; ['Ténor' × seedling]

'Altmärker' HT, yb, 1908, Türke; flowers ochre-yellow tinted garnet, large, dbl.; vigorous growth; ['Kaiserin Auguste Viktoria' × 'Luciole']

'Alto' -- See 'Poulpar'

Alto Parade™ ('Alto') MinFl, ab, Poulsen; flowers apricot blend, 5-8 cm., dbl., slight wild rose fragrance; bushy (20-40 cm.) growth; intr. 2004

'Altonia' (natural variation of *R. setigera*), mp; flowers brilliant pink, single to semi-dbl.

'Altrusa' Min, ob, Eagle; intr. 1998

'Altus' -- See 'Altissimo'

'Alupka' N, w, before 1900; flowers medium large, dbl., moderate fragrance; [sport of 'Maréchal Niel']; possibly synonymous with 'White Marechal Niel' or 'Mme Hoste'

'Alvares Cabral' F, mr, Moreira da Silva; flowers bright red; ['Pinocchio' × 'Alain']

'Always' HT, dr, 1958, Leon, Charles F., Sr.; bud long, pointed; flowers dark cardinal-red, 6 in., 28 petals, moderate fragrance; foliage leathery; vigorous growth; PP1692; [('Charlotte Armstrong' × 'Applause') × 'Ena Harkness']

'Always A Lady' -- See 'Tinlady'

'Always a Smile' -- See 'Horjaffa'

'Always Love You' -- See 'Umsalllovu'

Always Mine™ -- See 'Devsiem'

'Always Special' Min, dr, Benardella; growth medium; intr. 2001

'Alwyn's Favourite' -- See 'Webcoquette'

'Aly Pacha Chérif' -- See 'Ali Pacha Chériff'

'Ama' F, or, 1955, Kordes; bud ovoid; flowers deep orange-scarlet, large, dbl., high-centered, borne in clusters (up to 20); foliage dark, glossy, leathery; vigorous, bushy growth; ['Obergärtner Wiebicke' × 'Independence']

'Amabile' HT, ob, Teranishi; intr. 2005

'Amabilis' HGal, m, before 1845; flowers purple, streaked lilac, full, slight fragrance

'Amabilis' T, mp, Robert; intr. about 1850

'Amabilis' T, mp, Touvais; flowers shining pink, large, full; intr. 1856

'Amabilis' T, mp, Lartay; flowers large, full; intr. 1857

Amada+ HT, dr, Voom, Lex; flowers large, double, high-centered, borne mostly singly; recurrent; stems medium to long; florist rose

Amadeus® -- See 'Korlabriax'

Amadeus® S, rb, Barni, V.; flowers red with yellow center, small, semi-double, flat, borne in clusters; once-bloomer; foliage small; vigorous, bushy, spreading growth; intr. 1991

'Amadine' P, mp

'Amadis' ('Crimson Boursault') Bslt, dr, 1829, Laffay, M.; flowers deep crimson-purple, usually striped with white, 6-7 cm., semi-dbl., cupped, borne in small clusters; very early; non-remontant; foliage thin, pale; thornless; stems young wood whitish green, old wood red-brown; vigorous, upright growth; excellent pillar; [*R. chinensis* × *R. pendulina*]

'Amaevelina' ('Evelina') Min, lp, 1992, Mansuino, Dr. Andrea; flowers large, full, borne mostly singly, no fragrance; foliage medium size, medium green, semi-glossy; medium (100-150 cm.), bushy growth; ['Rosa Maria' × 'seedling (pink 078)']; intr. 1990

'Amaglia' LCl, w; intr. 1980

'Amalfi' Pol, dy, 1971, Delforge; bud long, pointed; flowers deep yellow to salmon-pink, small, dbl., cupped; abundant, continuous bloom; foliage small, dark; vigorous, bushy growth

Amalia™ -- See 'Meicauf'

'Amalia' HT, pb, Meilland; flowers two-toned deep pink; intr. 2006

'Amalia Jung' HT, mr, 1934, Leenders, M.; flowers crimson-red, large, dbl.; foliage glossy, cedar-green; vigorous growth; ['Mrs Henry Winnett' × 'Lady Helen Maglona']

'Amalie de Greiff' HT, pb, 1912, Lambert, P.; flowers brick-rose, center salmon and orange-yellow, large, dbl., moderate fragrance; ['Herrin von Lieser' × 'Mme Mélanie Soupert']

'Amalinda' HT, mr

'Amami' HT, op, 1927, Easlea; flowers peach-pink, overlarge, 12-15 petals; foliage light; very vigorous growth

'Amanda' -- See 'Amruda'

'Amanda' F, my, 1979, Bees; bud globular; flowers large, 25 petals, high-centered, slight fragrance; foliage small, light green; upright growth; ['Arthur Bell' × Zambra®]

'Amanda' F, ob, Noack, Werner; intr. 1979

'Amanda Ivy' -- See 'Worcars'

'Amanda Justine' -- See 'Majlaq'

'Amanda Kay' -- See 'Jusamanda'

Amanda Marciel™ -- See 'Devnina'

'Amanda Patenaude' -- See 'Amanda Patenotte'

'Amanda Patenotte' ('Amanda Patenaude') P, mp, 1845, Vibert; flowers pale rose, large, full, globular; foliage medium size, light green; few prickles; roses sold as Amanda Patenaude in the U.S. in recent years are almost certainly Joasine Hanet

'Amandine' HP, dp, 1846, Vibert; flowers large, full

Amandine Chanel® S, pb, Guillot-Massad; flowers raspberry pink, reverse white, borne in clusters of 5 - 7; growth to 1 m.; intr. 2005

'Amanecer' HT, Dot, Pedro

'Amanogawa' ('Milky Way') F, ly, Suzuki; intr. 1956

'Amara' -- See 'Gauhari'

'Amarancha' F, ab

'Amarante' Pol, mr, Barbier; flowers dark crimson, sometimes striped white, borne in clusters of 25-70; intr. 1916

'Amarante' B, dr, Page; flowers carmine purple with cherry red, medium, full, cupped; intr. 1859

'Amarante' HGal, dr; flowers dark amaranthe-purple, medium, full; intr. before 1845

'Amarante' Ch, dr, before 1836, Laffay; flowers dark crimson, medium, full

Amaretto® LCl, w, Kordes; flowers cream with light pink tones in center, 8 cm., dbl., high-centered, borne singly and in small clusters, moderate fruity fragrance; recurrent; strong (8 ft.) growth; intr. 2006

'Amarillo' HT, dy, 1961, Von Abrams; bud pointed; flowers deep yellow, 5 in., 30 petals; foliage leathery, light green; vigorous, upright growth; ['Buccaneer' × 'Lowell Thomas']; intr. 1961

'Amarillo' F, dy, Select Roses, B.V.; intr. 1994

Amarula Profusion™ F, ab, Kordes; intr. 2007

'Amateur André Fourcaud' HT, lp, 1903, Puyravaud; bud very long; flowers light pink, reverse darker, very large, dbl., high-centered, moderate fragrance; ['Mme Caroline Testout' × unknown]

'Amateur E. Biron' HT, op, 1928, Biron; flowers shrimp-pink, center tinted copper, reverse old-rose, camellia-like

'Amateur Lopes' HG, 1905, Cayeux; ['Mme Berard' × *R. gigantea*]

'Amateur Teyssier' HT, w

'Amatsu-Otome' ('Heavenly Maiden') HT, yb, Teranishi, K.; flowers golden yellow, edged deep orange, 4½-5 in., 48 petals, high-centered, borne mostly solitary, slight fragrance; foliage small, semi-glossy; vigorous, compact growth; ['Chrysler Imperial' × 'Doreen']; intr. 1960

'Amatsu-Otome, Cl' Cl HT, yb; intr. 1967

'Amaury Fonseca' Pol, w, 1914, Soupert & Notting; flowers white, suffused light pink in fall, well-formed

Amazing™ -- See 'Poulac014(N)'

'Amazing Grace' -- See 'Cocgrand'

'Amazing Grace' HT, mp, 1973, Anderson's Rose Nurseries; flowers rich pink, high pointed, 5 in., 43 petals; [Carina® × 'Mischief']

'Amazing Grace '07' HT, w, 2007, Chapman, Bruce; flowers 9 cm., full, borne mostly solitary; foliage large, dark green, glossy; prickles medium, hooked, brown, few; growth upright, tall (1½ m.); garden decoration; ['White Spray' × 'Aotearoa']; intr. 2007

'Amazing Palace' (Amazing™) MinFl, ab, Poulsen; bud pointed ovoid; flowers blend of apricot with orange and orange-red tones, 5-8 cm., 30-35 petals, deep cup , borne singly and in small clusters, slight fragrance; recurrent; foliage dark, glossy; prickles numerous, 10 mm, deeply concave; bushy, 40-60 cm. growth; PP15895; intr. 2004

'Amazing!' HT, w, Scheurs; intr. 2006

'Amazon' ('Apollo Tribute') F, ob, Christensen, Jack E.; flowers orange bronze, large, well-formed, borne in neat clusters; intr. 1992

'Amazon Lady' -- See 'Jachon'

'Amazone' T, my, 1872, Ducher; flowers yellow, reverse veined rose, well-formed; ['Safrano' × unknown]

'Amazone' LCl, mr, Delforge; flowers bright red; [sport of 'Spectacular']; intr. 1961

Amazone™ F, mr, de Ruiter, G.

'Ambasciatore Marco Fracisci' T, lp

'Ambassadeur Baert' F, op, 1964, Delforge; flowers salmon; foliage bronze; low, compact growth; ['Sumatra' × seedling]

'Ambassadeur Nemry' F, dp, 1949, Leenders, M.; flowers deep rose-pink, reverse salmon-carmine, large, dbl.; vigorous growth

'Ambassador' -- See 'Meibigoud'

Ambassador® -- See 'Meinuzeten'

'Ambassador' HT, ob, 1930, Premier Rose Gardens; bud long, pointed; flowers bronze-salmon, large, dbl., moderate fragrance; foliage leathery, dark; vigorous, bushy growth; PP11; ['Mme Butterfly' × 'Souv. de Claudius Pernet']

Amber™ -- See 'Poultrav'

Amber® HT, yb, Spek; flowers deep yellow with pink tips, 9-10 cm., 35-40 petals, high-centered, borne mostly singly; recurrent; prickles moderate; stems long (60-80 cm.); intr. 2006

'Amber' HT, my, Jordan, B.L.; flowers amber-yellow; RULED EXTINCT; [sport of 'Ophelia']

'Amber' Cl Pol, ly, 1908, Paul, W.; flowers pale straw yellow, single; early; low growth; RULED EXTINCT; ['Jersey Beauty' × unknown]

'Amber Abundance' -- See 'Harfizz'

'Amber Beauty' F, pb, 1962, Leenders, J.; flowers pink tinted brown, dbl.; ['Goldilocks' × 'Lavender Pinocchio']

Amber Cloud™ -- See 'Vircloud'

Amber Cover™ (Taos™) S, ab, Olesen; bud ovate; flowers yellow-orange to apricot, 6 cm., 18-22 petals, open cup, borne in clusters of 5 - 15, slight honey fragrance; recurrent; foliage dark green, semi-glossy; prickles several, 4-7 mm., deeply concave, ocher; compact, bushy (2 ft.) growth; PP13292; ['Amber Hit' × Aspen™]; intr. 2001

Amber Flash™ -- See 'Wildak'

'Amber Flush' -- See 'Devotion'

'Amber Gem' -- See 'Moramber'

'Amber Glo' -- See 'Amber Glow'

'Amber Glow' ('Amber Glo') LCl, ab, Nieuwesteeg; flowers apricot-yellow, dbl., slight rose fragrance; constant; growth to 2 × 2 m., low, vigorous; intr. 2004

'Amber Gold' HT, dy, 1962, Moro; bud ovoid; flowers deep golden yellow, 5-5½ in., 40-45 petals, cupped, moderate fragrance; foliage leathery; vigorous, upright growth; PP2301; ['Golden Rapture' × 'Golden Scepter']; intr. 1962

'Amber Hit' (Amber™) MinFl, ab, Poulsen; flowers orange and orange blend with tones of other hues, 5-8 cm., 25 petals, slight wild rose fragrance; growth bushy, 40-60 cm.; intr. 2000

'Amber Honey' HT, ab

'Amber Kordana' Min, ab, Kordes; flowers amber yellow with pink tones as it ages, semi-dbl., opens quickly to flat, borne mostly singly; recurrent; foliage dark green; compact growth; container rose

'Amber Light' -- See 'Amberlight'

'Amber Nectar' -- See 'Mehamber'

Amber Panarosa™ S, ab; intr. 2004

Amber Queen® -- See 'Harroony'

'Amber Ribbon' -- See 'Zipamb'

'Amber Rose' -- See 'Parks' Yellow Tea-Scented China'

'Amber Sands' Min, ab, 1985, Hardgrove, Donald & Mary; flowers large, 35 petals, high-centered, slight fragrance; foliage medium size, medium green, semi-glossy; upright, bushy growth; ['Fragrant Cloud' × 'Poker Chip']; intr. 1984

'Amber Spire' S, ab, Kordes; intr. 1995

'Amber Star' -- See 'Manstar'

'Amber Star' -- See 'Jacob van Ruysdael'

'Amber Sun' -- See 'Mansun'

'Amber Sun' ('Sonne des Allgäus') S, ab, Kordes; bud small, elongated, orange-yellow; flowers copper yellow, fading to cream yellow, 2 in., semi-dbl., cupped, borne in clusters of 5 - 8, moderate fragrance; free-flowering; foliage medium size, dark green, very glossy; bushy (50 × 60 cm.) growth; intr. 2006

'Amber Sunset' -- See 'Manamsun'

Amber Waves™ -- See 'Jacamque'

Amberglo™ -- See 'Minapco'

'Amberlight' -- See 'Cocbamber'

'Amberlight' ('Amber Light') F, yb, 1961, LeGrice; flowers clear amber, 3½-4 in., dbl., borne in open clusters, intense fruity fragrance; vigorous, upright, bushy growth; PP2197; [(seedling × 'Lavender Pinocchio') × 'Marcel Bourgouin']; intr. 1961

'Ambiance' -- See 'Nirpnufdeu'

'Ambiance' -- See 'Lenborata'

Ambiance™ -- See 'Bensiete'

'Ambiance' HT, lp, 1955, Delforge; bud long, pink, passing to cream; ['Comtesse Vandal' × 'Pres. Macia']

Ambiente® HT, ly, Noack; bud rounded, greenish white; flowers cream white with yellowish center, 4 in. , dbl., high-centered, borne singly and in small clusters, slight fragrance; recurrent; foliage dark green, medium size, slightly glossy; growth robust, low (70 × 40 cm.), bushy; intr. 2002

'Ambossfunken' ('Anvil Sparks') HT, rb, 1961, Meyer; flowers coral-red streaked golden yellow, well-formed, large, 33 petals; bushy growth

Ambra® F, ob, 1983, Rose Barni-Pistoia; flowers deep large, 20 petals, cupped, borne in clusters of 3-5, slight fragrance; foliage medium size, brownish-green, glossy; prickles reddish; upright, bushy growth; [seedling × seedling]; intr. 1982

'Ambre' HT, ob, 1956, Gaujard; bud ovoid; flowers brilliant orange and yellow, very large, dbl., moderate fragrance; foliage glossy, dark; very vigorous, bushy growth; ['Peace' × seedling]

'Ambre Solaire' Pol, pb, 1966, Ebben; bud ovoid; flowers red, pink and yellow, dbl., borne in clusters; foliage dark; ['Masquerade' × seedling]

'Ambridge Rose' -- See 'Auswonder'

'Ambrogio Maggi' HP, mr, 1879, Pernet fils; flowers bright rose pink, very large, dbl., globular; very remontant; foliage light green; growth upright, vigorous; ['John Hopper' × unknown]

'Ambroise Paré' HGal, m, 1846, Vibert; flowers rose-purple, tinted carmine with mottling of pale lilac grey tones in cool, moist weather, dbl., rosette

'Ambroise Verschaffelt' HP, dr, 1858, Vindrin; flowers violet-red, large, full

'Ambrosia' -- See 'Sunambro'

'Ambrosia' F, ob, 1962, Dickson, Patrick; flowers amber, 2½-3 in., 7-10 petals, flat, borne in large clusters; foliage dark; vigorous, bushy growth; [seedling × 'Shepherd's Delight']

'Amdo' HRg, mp, 1927, Hansen, N.E.; flowers medium, 16 petals, borne in clusters of 7-10; non-recurrent; ['Tetonkaha' × 'La Mélusine']

'Amédée' ('Agathe Amédée') HGal, mp, 1827, Desportes; Agathe group

'Amédée de Langlois' B, m, 1872, Vigneron; flowers dark, velvety purple,

medium, full, borne in small clusters
'Amédée Philibert' HP, m, 1879, Lévêque; flowers purple and red
Amefica® HT, yb, Tantau; intr. 2002
Amelia™ -- See 'Poulen011(N)'
'Amélia' -- See 'Belle Rosine'
'Amélia' A, mp, 1823, Vibert, J. P.; sepals foliaceous, persistent; flowers bright pink, anthers deep yellow, large, semi-dbl. to dbl., borne in clusters of 4-6, moderate fragrance; non-recurrent; foliage arching, simply serrate, gray-green, pointed-elliptical; prickles sparse, uneven, needle-like; hips large, oval
'Amelia Anderson' T, pb
'Amelia Barter' HT, mr, 1965, Barter; flowers bright scarlet tinted silvery, 5½ in., dbl.; foliage dark, glossy; [Queen Elizabeth® × 'Claude']
'Amelia Earhart' ('Président Charles Hain') HT, yb, 1932, Reymond; flowers golden yellow, center flushed pink, large, dbl., intense fragrance; vigorous growth; PP63; ['Souv. de Claudius Pernet' × ('Louise Catherine Breslau' × 'Paul Neyron')]
'Amelia Fleming' F, mp, 1995, Fleming, Joyce L.; flowers medium pink with pink tones, prominent stamens, medium, 5 petals, borne in clusters, moderate fragrance; foliage medium size, medium green, matte; upright (120-140 cm.) growth; ['Marchenland' × Bambula®]; intr. 1994
'Amelia Louise' Min, mp, 1994, Haynes, F.; flowers small, full, borne mostly singly, slight fragrance; foliage small, medium green, semi-glossy; few prickles; low, bushy growth; [seedling × seedling]; intr. 1993
'Amelia Renaissance' (Amelia™) S, ab, Poulsen; flowers apricot blend, 10-15 cm., dbl., moderate fragrance; growth bushy, 100-150 cm.; PP15167; intr. 2002
'Amelia Rey Colaco' F, Moreira da Silva, A.; intr. 1960
'Amélie de Bethune' HT, rb, 1923, Pernet-Ducher; flowers coral-red shaded carmine, medium, dbl.
'Amélie de Mansfield' HGal, mp, before 1842; flowers vivid pink, medium, dbl.
'Amélie de Marsilly' A, lp, 1818, Vibert; flowers light flesh pink, globular
'Amélie d'Orléans' HGal, dp, 1825, Cartier; flowers large, semi-dbl.
'Amelie Fristel' HT, yb, Adam; flowers yellow, outer petals turning orange and pink, dbl., high-centered; recurrent; foliage dark green; robust (3-4 ft.) growth; intr. 2006
'Amélie Gravereaux' HRg, mr, 1903, Gravereaux; bud ovoid; flowers medium red, fading to purplish, 10 cm., semi-dbl. to dbl., strong sweet fragrance; recurrent bloom; foliage dark, rugose; numerous prickles; vigorous, spiny growth; [('Général Jacqueminot' × 'Maréchal Niel') × 'Conrad Ferdinand Meyer']
'Amélie Hoste' HP, lp, 1874, Gonod; flowers flesh pink, reverse darker, large, full
'America' -- See 'Hill's America'
'America' N, ly, 1859, Page, G.; flowers light yellow-white with cream, tints of flesh pink, full; ['Solfaterre' × 'Safrano']
'America' HRg, mr, Paul, W. / Harvard University Gardens; flowers bright crimson, large, semi-dbl.; hips long, red, ovate; intr. 1895
'America' ('Walsh's Rambler') HMult, mp, Walsh; flowers pink, center white, 3-3½ cm., single, borne in large clusters (often to 75); [R. wichurana × R. multiflora]; sometimes classed as HWich. intr. 1915
America™ LCl, op, Warriner, William A.; bud ovoid, pointed; flowers salmon, reverse lighter, imbricated, 3½-4½ in., 43 petals, borne singly and in small clusters, intense fragrance; foliage large, medium green; climbing (10-12 ft.) growth; PP3682; ['Fragrant Cloud' × 'Tradition']; intr. 1976
'American Banner' N, pb, 1879, Cartwright; flowers carmine striped white, small, semi-dbl., intense fragrance; probably extinct; [sport of 'Bon Silène']
'American Beauty' ('Mme Ferdinand Jamin') HP, dp, 1875, Lédéchaux; bud globular; flowers large, 50 petals, cupped, intense fragrance; sometimes recurrent bloom; vigorous growth; intr. 1886
'American Beauty, Climbing' HWich, dp, 1909, Farrell; flowers deep rose-pink, 7-8 cm., dbl., cupped, borne in small clusters, moderate damask fragrance; non-recurrent; foliage glossy; growth to 12-15 ft.; [(R. wichurana × Marion Dingee) × 'American Beauty']
'American Belle' HP, mp, 1893, Burton; [sport of 'American Beauty']
'American Classic' ('America's Classic') HT, dr, 1994, Winchel, Joseph F.; flowers dbl., borne mostly singly; foliage large, medium green, matte; some prickles; tall, upright growth; [seedling × seedling]; intr. 1997
'American Dawn' HT, rb, 1976, Warriner, William A.; bud ovoid; flowers rose-red, base white, 4-5 in., 30 petals, high-centered, slight fragrance; foliage glossy, dark; upright growth; PP3666; ['Personality' × seedling]
American Dream™ -- See 'Winbur'
American Fantasy™ -- See 'Twofan'
'American Flagship' HT, mr, 1946, Lammerts, Dr. Walter; bud urn-shaped; flowers bright scarlet, 3½-4½ in., 15 petals, slight spicy fragrance; foliage leathery; vigorous, upright, bushy growth; PP676; ['Crimson Glory' × 'Crimson Glory']
'American Girl' HT, mr, 1929, Maton; flowers large, dbl., high-centered; foliage leathery, dark; long stems; vigorous growth; [sport of 'Hollywood']
'American Glory' -- See 'Twoadmire'
American Heritage® HT, yb, 1965, Lammerts, Dr. Walter; bud long, pointed; flowers ivory and salmon blend, becoming salmon, large, dbl., high-centered; foliage dark, leathery; tall growth; PP2687; [Queen Elizabeth® × 'Yellow Perfection']
'American Heritage, Climbing' Cl HT, yb, 1973, Arora, Bal Raj; buds long pointed; flowers cream with pink edges, large, high-centered, borne mostly singly; foliage leathery, light green; [sport of 'American Heritage']; intr. 1971
American Hero™ HT, mr, Zary; flowers scarlet red, 4-6 cm., 35-40 petals, slight sweet fragrance; foliage glossy; stems long, nearly thornless; growth 5 × 4 ft.; PPRR; intr. 2002
'American Home' HT, dr, 1960, Morey, Dr. Dennison; bud ovoid; flowers 4½ in., 30 petals, cupped, intense fragrance; foliage leathery, vigorous, upright growth; PP2096; ['Chrysler Imperial' × 'New Yorker']; intr. 1960
'American Honor' -- See 'Twohonor'
'American Independence' -- See 'Meifinaro'
'American Legion' -- See 'Legion'
'American Pillar' HWich, pb, 1902, Van Fleet; flowers carmine-pink, white eye, golden stamens, 5-6 cm., single, borne in clusters of 10-20; non-recurrent; foliage large, dark green, glossy; vigorous (15-20 ft.) growth; hips red; [(R. wichurana × R. setigera) × red Hybrid Perpetual]; intr. 1908
'American Pride' HT, w, 1928, Grillo; bud long, pointed; flowers pure white, outside petals occasionally tinted pink, 4½ in., 35 petals, moderate fragrance; foliage leathery; very vigorous growth; PP49; RULED EXTINCT 2/79 ARM; [sport of 'Grillodale']
'American Pride' HT, dr, 1978, Warriner, William A.; bud pointed, ovoid; flowers dark velvety red, 4-5 in., 33 petals, high-centered; foliage large, dark; tall, upright growth; PP4139; intr. 1974
American Rose Centennial™ -- See 'Savars'
'American Roseate' HEg, dp, about 1840, Prince Nursery; flowers bright rose, semi-dbl.; vigorous growth
'American Seedling' HT, dp, 1904, Bissot; flowers dark rose pink, reverse darker; ['Chatenay' × 'Liberty']
'American Shakira' -- See 'Playrose'
'American Spirit' -- See 'Jactred'
'American White' HEg, w, about 1840, Prince Nursery; flowers creamy white, semi-dbl.; vigorous growth
'Americana' HT, mr, 1961, Boerner; bud ovoid; flowers bright red, 5½ in., 28 petals, high-centered, moderate fragrance; foliage leathery; vigorous, upright growth; PP2058; [('Poinsettia' × unknown) × 'New Yorker']; intr. 1961
America's Choice™ -- See 'Poulander'
'America's Classic' -- See 'American Classic'
'America's Junior Miss' ('Junior Miss') F, lp, 1964, Boerner; bud ovoid; flowers

soft coral-pink, medium, dbl., moderate fragrance; foliage glossy; vigorous, bushy growth; PP2541; ['Seventeen' × ('Demure' × unknown)]; intr. 1964

Amerlock® S, op; flowers coral and rose, dbl., borne in small clusters; remontant; intr. 1979

'Ames 5' ('Ames Climber') HMult, mp, 1932, Maney; flowers good size, borne in clusters; non-recurrent; thornless; stems red in winter; very vigorous growth; very hardy; [*R. blanda* × *R. multiflora*]

'Ames 6' HMult, mp; [*R. blanda* × *R. multiflora*]

'Ames Climber' -- See 'Ames 5'

'Amethyst' HT, m, Urban, J.; flowers violet-pink, large, dbl.; intr. 1978

'Améthyste' HMult, m, 1911, Nonin; flowers violet-crimson, streaked with white, small, very dbl., borne in large trusses; non-recurrent; foliage glossy; stems long, arching; either a sport of 'Non Plus Ultra' or 'Non Plus Ultra' × *R. multiflora*

'Amethyste' HT, m, Christensen

Ametista® HT, m, Barni, V.; buds long, tapering; flowers strong, non-fading color, large, dbl., moderate fragrance; growth vigorous, 80-100 cm.; intr. 1985

Amherst™ (Bright Cover™) S, w, Poulsen; flowers white, small, no fragrance; foliage dark; growth broad, bushy, 60-100 cm.; PP16128; intr. 2003

'Ami Aminta' ('Aminta') HGal, before 1814, Descemet

'Ami Charmet' HP, dp, 1900, Dubreuil; flowers satiny China-rose pink, thick-petaled, very large, very dbl., camellia-like, borne in small clusters, moderate Gallica fragrance

'Ami Chenault' HT, Moreira da Silva, A.

Ami Clement® F, dp, Pineau; flowers bright cherry pink, medium, dbl.; intr. 1977

'Ami des Jardins' -- See 'Finale'

'Ami Desvignes' HT, mr, 1954, Privat; flowers base of petals veined coral, petals waved, large, semi-dbl.; foliage glossy; vigorous growth

'Ami Dietrich' HT, Moreira da Silva, A.

'Ami F. Mayery' HT, mr, 1938, Denoyel, Mme.; bud long, pointed, vermilion-red; flowers poppy-red, very large, dbl., cupped; foliage dark; stiff stems; vigorous growth; ['Huguette Vincent' × seedling]

'Ami L. Cretté' HT, rb, 1931, Chambard, C.; bud long, pointed, coppery oriental red; flowers crimson-red, reverse light coral-rose and yellow, medium to large, semi-dbl., cupped, moderate fragrance; foliage dark; very vigorous, bushy growth

'Ami Léon Chenault' F, mr, 1929, Nonin; flowers dark garnet, slightly striated white, borne in clusters; [sport of 'Lafayette']

'Ami Léon Pin' HT, ly, 1947, Gaujard; bud long, pointed; flowers pale yellow, reverse pink, very large, dbl.; foliage dark; very vigorous growth

'Ami Martin' HP, or, 1906, Chédane-Guinoisseau; flowers vermilion orange-red, very large, very dbl.

'Ami Poncet' T, pb, 1903, Toussaint; flowers bright pink, edged light violet with salmon pink, very large, full; ['Papa Gontier' × unknown]

'Ami Quinard' HT, dr, 1927, Gaujard; bud long, pointed; flowers blackish garnet and coppery scarlet, medium, 17 petals, cupped, moderate fragrance; foliage leathery; vigorous growth; ['Mme Méha Sabatier' × ('Mrs Edward Powell' × *R. foetida bicolor*)]; possibly Mallerin instead of Gaujard; intr. 1930

'Ami René Badel' F, mr, 1961, Arles; bud pointed; flowers carthamus-red, 36 petals, high-centered; foliage bronze; ['Belle Créole' × ('Gloire du Midi' × 'Paul Crampel')]

'Amica' HT, 1969, Cazzaniga, F. G.; flowers cinnabar-red, large, moderate fragrance; foliage light green; PP2827; ['Coup de Foudre' × 'Lampo']; intr. 1966

Amie™ -- See 'Poulen008(N)'

'Amie Renaissance' ('Melany', Amie™) S, lp, Poulsen; bud ovoid; flowers light pink with slight orange and yellow tints, 8-10 cm., 65 petals, deep cup, borne mostly singly, moderate floral fragrance; upright, bushy (100-150 cm.) growth; PP15158; [seedling × 'Clair Renaissance']; intr. 2002

'Amiga Mia' S, mp, 1978, Buck, Dr. Griffith J.; bud ovoid, pointed; flowers empire-rose, 4-5 in., 30 petals, high-centered, moderate fragrance; foliage large, dark, leathery; vigorous, upright, bushy growth; [Queen Elizabeth® × 'Prairie Princess']

'Amigo' F, mr, 1951, Whisler; bud short, pointed; flowers currant-red, 3-3½ in., 17-20 petals, cupped, moderate spicy fragrance; foliage leathery; upright, bushy growth; PP1042; ['World's Fair' × 'Adolf Grille']

'Amigo Roger Sucret' F, Dot, Simon; intr. 1970

'Aminta' -- See 'Ami Aminta'

'Amiral Cécile' HP, m, 1850, Debeaumont; flowers purple-violet, medium to large, full, moderate fragrance

'Amiral Courbet' HP, mr, 1884, Dubreuil; bud oval; flowers bright carmine red with magenta tints, full, cupped; foliage pale green, matte; prickles scattered

'Amiral Gravina' HP, m, 1860, Moreau et Robert; flowers blackish purple, shaded with scarlet

'Amiral Nelson' HP, lp, 1859, Ducher; flowers light carmine pink, large, dbl.

'Amirose' F, yb, Delbard; flowers yellow with vermilion, dbl., borne in small clusters; intr. 1980

'Amistad Sincera' ('Sincera') HT, w, 1963, Camprubi, C.; bud ovoid; flowers pure white, 4-4½ in., 55 petals, high-centered to cupped, borne mostly singly, slight to moderate tea fragrance; recurrent; foliage large, dark green, leathery; prickles several, reddish-brown; vigorous, well-branched growth; PP2055; ['Alaska' × 'Virgo']; intr. 1963

'Amitié' HT, ob, 1951, Mallerin, C.; flowers coppery orange-yellow, well-shaped, large, dbl.; vigorous, branching growth; ['Mandalay' × 'Schéhérazade']

'Amitié' HGal, pb; sometimes classed as D

'Amleger' HT, mr, 1973, Molina; flowers blood-red to cardinal-red, imbricated, 4½ in., 40 petals, cupped, slight tea fragrance; foliage dark, leathery; vigorous growth; [sport of 'Baccará']; intr. 1972

'Amma' HT, w, Ghosh; flowers light lemon yellow to pure white, high-centered, moderate fragrance; intr. 2006

Ammerland® S, my, Noack, Werner; intr. 1986

'Ammonit' F, mp, Scholle; bud scrolled; flowers large, coral-rose, white eye, pink stamens, cupped, borne in cluster-flowering, intense damask fragrance; intr. 1974

Amor™ -- See 'Poulhi016(N)'

'Amor' F, mp, 1958, deRuiter; bud pointed; flowers clear pink, medium, 22 petals; vigorous, bushy growth; [('Golden Rapture' × 'floribunda seedling') × ('Golden Rapture' × 'Floribunda seedling')]; intr. 1957

'Amor Hit' (Amor™) Min, dr, Olesen; bud globular; flowers dark red, reverse darker, 1-1½ in., very full, cupped, borne in clusters, very slight fragrance; recurrent; foliage dark green, glossy; prickles numerous, variable lenght, concave; vigorous, bushy (2 ft.) growth; PP15812; [seedling × seedling]; intr. 2003

'Amore' F, mp, 1957, Riethmuller; flowers rosy pink, reverse lighter, medium, dbl.; foliage semi-glossy; moderate growth; [Orange Triumph® × 'Spring Song']

Amore® HT, rb, Kordes; flowers small, dark red with yellow reverse; [sport of 'Frisco']; greenhouse rose

'Amore Kordana' Min, dr, Kordes; flowers dbl.; container rose

Amoretta® -- See 'Amoru'

'Amorette' -- See 'Amoru'

'Amoretto' -- See 'Korpastato'

'Amorosa' HT, w, Kordes; flowers white, tinted pink, 4½ in., 30 petals, high-centered; intr. 1995

'Amorosa' F, my, Fryer; flowers pale gold; intr. 2005

'Amorosa' F, Moreira da Silva, A.

'Amorous' -- See 'Jacarina'

'Amoru' ('Amorette', Amoretta®, 'Snowdrop') Min, w, 1980, deRuiter; bud long, pointed ovoid; flowers white, ivory center, 2 in., 50 petals, flat, borne 10-15 per cluster, slight fragrance; recurrent; foliage light, mid-green, leathery; prickles long, narrow, hooked slightly downward, red to brown; stems medium, slender; short, dense, bushy growth; patio; PP4493; ['Rosy Jewel' × 'Zorina']; intr. 1979

'Amour Ardent' -- See 'Burning Love'

'Amourette' Ch, mp; flowers rose-pink, edged lighter, large, pointed, petals recurving; foliage dark; stems red

'Amoureuse' HT, ab, 1960, Gaujard; flowers coppery yellow, large, 34 petals, borne singly; foliage large, medium green; ['Peace' × (Rose Gaujard® × unknown)]

'Amours de Saverne' F, rb, Sauvageot; flowers velvety red, silver reverse, dbl.; intr. 1999

'Ampère' HT, or, 1937, Meilland, F.; flowers nasturtium-red, edges lighter, reverse orange-yellow, very large, dbl.; foliage bright green; ['Charles P. Kilham' × 'Condesa de Sástago']

'Amruda' ('Amanda', 'Red Ace') Min, dr, 1982, deRuiter; flowers medium, 20 petals, slight fragrance; foliage small, medium green, semi-glossy; bushy growth; [Scarletta® × seedling]; intr. 1977

'Amstelveen' -- See 'Meipopul'

Amsterdam® F, or, 1976, Verschuren, Ted; bud ovoid; flowers clear orange-red, 2½ in., 12-15 petals; foliage glossy, brown-red; vigorous growth; [Europeana® × Parkdirektor Riggers®]; intr. 1972

Amsterdam+ F, op, Perfecta Plant; flowers salmon pink, double, high-centered, borne mostly singly; recurrent; stems medium to long; florist rose

'Amulett' HT, mr, 1932, Tantau; bud ovoid; flowers fiery red, very dbl., high-centered, moderate fragrance; foliage dark, glossy; vigorous, bushy growth; ['Mrs Henry Winnett' × 'Johanniszauber']

Amulett® Min, pb, Tantau; flowers rich pink, very dbl.; foliage medium green; wide, bushy (20 in.). growth; intr. 1991

'Amurensis' (form of R. blanda carpohispida), mp; flowers large, semi-dbl.; prickles sparsely armed; stems wood red; tall growth

'Amy' F, mp, 1954, Von Abrams; bud ovoid; flowers carmine-rose, 2½-3 in., 38 petals, high-centered, borne in loose clusters, moderate fragrance; foliage leathery; compact, dwarf growth; PP1455; ['Show Girl' × 'Fashion']; intr. 1954

Amy Brown® -- See 'Harkushi'

'Amy Donelan' -- See 'Rawlavlan'

'Amy Elizabeth' -- See 'Worcarry'

Amy Grant™ -- See 'Tuckamy'

'Amy Johnson' LCl, mp, 1931, Clark, A.; bud ovoid; flowers lighter pink at edges, large, dbl., cupped, moderate fragrance; recurrent; foliage wrinkled; vigorous (12-15 ft.) growth; ['Souv. de Gustave Prat' × unknown]

'Amy Rebecca' Min, dy, 1986, Jolly, Marie; flowers deep yellow, small, 38 petals, high-centered, borne usually singly, slight fragrance; foliage small, medium green, semi-glossy; prickles small, brown; medium, upright growth; ['Rise 'n' Shine' × 'Summer Butter']; intr. 1987

'Amy Robsart' HEg, dp, 1894, Penzance; flowers deep rose, center white, large, semi-dbl., moderate fragrance; summer bloom; foliage fragrant; vigorous growth; [R. rubiginosa × hybrid perpetual or bourbon]

'Amy Sis' Min; intr. 1999

'Amy Vanderbilt' F, m, 1956, Boerner; bud globular; flowers lavender-lilac, 3 in., 70 petals, cupped, borne in pyramidal clusters, moderate fragrance; foliage dark, glossy; upright, bushy growth; PP1585; [('Lavender Pinocchio' × unknown) × 'Lavender Pinocchio']; intr. 1956

'Amy's Delight' Min, mp, 1981, Williams, Ernest D.; bud ovoid; flowers clear medium pink, opening imbricated, 60 petals, borne usually singly, no fragrance; foliage small, medium green, very glossy; prickles straight, tan; compact, bushy growth; ['Little Darling' × 'Little Chief']; intr. 1980

'Amy's Delight' F, pb, Williams, J. B.; flowers shades of light pink to orange-red, semi-dbl., borne in clusters, moderate fragrance; abundant; intr. 2001

'Ana de Cuevas' -- See 'Femiento'

'Ana Olga Steppuhn' HT, ob, Vidal

Anabell® -- See 'Korbell'

'Anabelle' Min, mr, Benardella

'Anacréon' HGal, mp, 1828, Vibert; flowers carmine-pink, medium large, very dbl.

'Anadia' -- See 'Meirameca'

'Anaïs' HSpn, dp, 1823, Bizard

'Anaïs Charles' -- See 'Charles-Anaïs'

'Anaïs Ségalas' ('Anna Ségales') HGal, pb, 1837, Vibert; flowers rosy crimson, edged rosy lilac, expanded, large, dbl., borne singly or in clusters of 2-5, moderate fragrance; foliage clear green, elliptical to round, with 3 leaflets; numerous prickles; branching growth; maybe be from Parmentier, introduced by Vibert; sometimes classified as C

'Anaïse' B, mp; flowers medium large, dbl.

'Anant' HT, pb, Chiplunkar; intr. 1991

'Ananya' HT, pb, Ghosh; flowers light pink and cream, changing to deep pink with petal tips cerise, well formed; intr. 1998

'Anastasia' HT, w, 1981, Greff, N.P.; bud ovoid, pointed; flowers 30 petals, high-centered, borne usually singly, no fragrance; recurrent; foliage large, dark; prickles bronze, turning brown with age; vigorous, dense growth; ['John F. Kennedy' × Pascali®]; intr. 1980

'Anathalie Chantrier' HP, w, 1854, Cherpin; flowers white, edges shaded carmine, medium, full, semi-globular

'Anatole' HGal, mr, 1827, Noisette

'Anatole de Montesquieu' N, m, before 1835, Jacques; flowers violet-purple, medium, full

'Anatole de Montesquieu' HSem, w, Van Houtte; bud pink; flowers small, dbl., borne in large, open clusters of 10-30, moderate musk fragrance; intr. before 1852

'Ancelin' HGal, dp, 1829, Noisette, E.; flowers deep rose, very large, dbl., borne in clusters of 5-7; foliage rounded, slightly dentate; prickles numerous, hooked; [R. turbinata × unknown]; a variety of R. francofurtana

Ancestry™ -- See 'Jayanc'

'Anchieta' HT, (Brazil)

'Anci Böhm' -- See 'Anci Böhmova'

'Anci Böhmova' ('Anci Böhm') HMult, mp, 1929, Böhm, J.; bud medium, globular; flowers deep violet pink, large, full, globular, borne in large clusters; foliage small, sparse, gray-green, soft; [sport of 'Marietta Silva Tarouca']

'Ancienne' -- See 'Shailer's White Moss'

'Ancienne Pivoine' -- See 'Bourbon'

'Ancient Art' Min, op, 1985, Hardgrove, Donald L.; flowers orange-pink blend, yellow reverse, medium, dbl., slight fragrance; foliage medium size, medium green, matte; upright, bushy growth; ['Rise 'n' Shine' × 'Picnic']

'Anda' -- See 'Lenda'

Andalusien® -- See 'Kordalu'

'Andante' HT, mr, Laperrière; flowers large, 40 petals; foliage bronze; vigorous, bushy growth; intr. 1962

'Andante' S, op, 1964, Buck, Dr. Griffith J.; bud ovoid, pointed; flowers light salmon-pink, medium, dbl., cupped, slight fragrance; repeat bloom; foliage dark, bronze, leathery; vigorous (5-6 ft.), upright, arching growth; ['Sea of Fire' × ('Josef Rothmund' × R. laxa)]; intr. 1962

'Andeli' HT, rb, 1976, Swim, H.C. & Ellis, A.E.; bud long, pointed to urn-shaped

'Andenken an Alma de l'Aigle' ('Andenken an Alma de l'Aigle Ilsabella', 'Isabella', 'Souv d'Alma de l'Aigle') HMsk, lp, 1948, Kordes; flowers light pink, blush at the base, 9 cm., full, moderate fragrance

'Andenken an Alma de l'Aigle Ilsabella' -- See 'Andenken an Alma de l'Aigle'

'Andenken an Breslau' HWich, mr, 1913, Kiese; flowers carmine-red, 5-6 cm., dbl., borne in large clusters; foliage small, glossy

'Andenken an Franz Heinsohn' F, dr, 1985, Poulsen, S.; flowers medium, dbl., urn-shaped, borne in clusters, slight fragrance; upright, bushy growth; ['D.T. Poulsen' × seedling]; intr. 1938

'Andenken an Gartendirektor Siebert' HMult, pb, 1923, Kiese; flowers carmine-rose, with yellow, borne in clusters; ['Eisenach' × 'polyantha seedling']

'Andenken an Gustav Frahm' -- See 'Gustav Frahm'

'Andenken an Hermann Thiess' F, or, Krause; flowers medium large, semi-dbl.; intr. 1959

'Andenken an J. Diering' Cl HT, 1902, Hinner, W.

'Andenken an Johannes Gehlhaar' HT, w,

1925, Gehlhaar; flowers large, dbl.
'Andenken an Kricker Hahn' S, Weihrauch; intr. 1995
'Andenken an Moritz von Fröhlich' HT, mr, 1905, Hinner, W.; flowers carmine red, large, dbl.; ['Mme Caroline Testout' × possibly 'Princesse de Béarn']
'Andersen's Yellow' HT, my, 1985, Walter, J.C.; flowers large, dbl., slight fragrance; foliage medium size, dark, semi-glossy; [Queen Elizabeth® × seedling]; intr. 1984
'Andersonii' (R. × andersonii, R. canina andersonii) S, mp, 1935; flowers bright pink, 2-2½ in., single, borne in clusters of 4-6; early summer; growth vigorous, branching (4-5 ft.); [chance hybrid of R. canina × possibly R. arvensis]
'Anderson's Double Lady's Blush' HSpn, ly, about 1810, Anderson, George
'Andgeo' ('Georgie Anderson') F, ob, 1982, Anderson's Rose Nurseries; flowers shades of orange, medium, dbl.; foliage medium size, dark, semi-glossy; upright growth; [Elizabeth of Glamis® × seedling]
'Andglo' ('Glowing Embers') F, yb, 1982, Anderson's Rose Nurseries; flowers yellow, red reverse, medium, 35 petals, slight fragrance; foliage medium size, medium green, glossy; bushy growth; ['Manx Queen' × 'Daily Sketch']
'Andie MacDowell' MinFl, or, 2003, Williams, Michael C.; flowers medium orange, reverse lighter, 2½ in., dbl., borne in large clusters, no fragrance; foliage large, dark green, matte; prickles ¼ in., pointed down; growth upright, tall (2½ ft.); garden, exhibition, cutting; [unknown × unknown]; intr. 2004
'Andmac' ('Whisky Mac, Climbing', 'Whisky, Climbing') Cl HT, yb, 1984, Anderson's Rose Nurseries; [sport of 'Whisky Mac']; intr. 1985
'Andorra' HT, ab, 1976, Kordes; bud long, pointed; flowers large, 24 petals, high-centered, intense fragrance; foliage glossy, dark; vigorous, upright, bushy growth; ['Dr. A.J. Verhage' × seedling]; intr. 1973
'Andour' ('Our Love') HT, yb, 1984, Anderson's Rose Nurseries; flowers yellow-orange; [sport of 'Doris Tysterman']
'Andpai' ('Paisley Anniversary') F, dr, 1987, Anderson's Rose Nurseries; flowers medium, dbl.; foliage medium size, dark green, glossy; upright growth; ['Michele' × 'Smiling Through']
'Andpin' ('Pink Ice') F, w, 1984, Anderson's Rose Nurseries; flowers white with deep pink petal edges, medium, 20 petals, no fragrance; foliage medium size, light green, semi-glossy; bushy (2 ft.) growth; [seedling × 'Iceberg']
'André Brichet' F, w, DVP Melle; flowers large, dbl, borne in clusters, moderate fragrance; foliage dense, disease-resistant; ['Melrose' × Mary Rose®]; intr. 2001
André Brunel® S, mp, Panozzo, Bernard;
flowers stable pink, 3½ in., full, pompon, intense fragrance; vigorous (3-4 ft.) growth; intr. 2006
'André Chénier' HP, m, 1851, Robert; flowers dark violet, medium, full, globular
'André de Garnier des Garets' HT, pb, 1899, Buatois; flowers bright pink, shaded coppery yellow, medium; ['Luciole' × 'Ophirie']
'André Du Pont' -- See 'Rouge Formidable'
'André Durand' HP, lp, 1871, Schwartz
'Andre Eve' HT, pb, Adam; flowers various shades of pink to rosy apricot, 4 in., double, high-centered, slight fragrance; recurrent; growth strong, 80-120 cm.; intr. 2002
'André Fresnoy' HP, rb, 1869, Pernet; flowers shining red, shaded deep purple, very large, full, globular; ['Victor Verdier' × unknown]
'André Gamon' HT, mp, 1908, Pernet-Ducher; flowers carmine
'André le Nôtre' -- See 'Meiceppus'
'André le Nôtre, Climbing' Cl HT, mp, Meilland; flowers deeper in center, outer petals fading, full, cupped, moderate old rose fragrance; foliage disease-resistant; 7+ ft. growth; intr. 2006
'André le Troquer' HT, ob, 1946, Mallerin, C.; flowers orange shading to apricot, 5 in., 30 petals, cupped; foliage very dark; very vigorous, upright growth
'André Leroy' HP, lp, 1860, Pradel; intr. 1860
'André Leroy d'Angers' HP, mr, 1866, Trouillard; bud dark violet; flowers crimson, shaded with violet, often ill-formed, large, dbl.; vigorous growth
'André Louis' HMult, w, 1920, Tanne; flowers white, center flesh-pink, full, borne in clusters of 4-5; sometimes classed as HWich
'André Pernet' HT, mr, 1956, Gaujard; bud long; flowers red, becoming lighter at center and purplish on outer petals, dbl.; foliage dark; very vigorous growth; ['Peace' × ('Mme Elie Dupraz' × unknown)]
'André Schwartz' HT, mr, Tantau; flowers clear red, dbl., high-centered; recurrent; medium growth; intr. 2003
'André Schwartz' T, mr, 1882, Schwartz, J.; flowers crimson, sometimes striped white
Andrea™ -- See 'Poulpar034(N)'
'Andrea' HT, ob; intr. 1968
'Andrea' Min, pb, 1978, Moore, Ralph S.; bud pointed; flowers deep pink, silver reverse, 1½ in., 20 petals, high-centered; foliage dark; vigorous, bushy, spreading growth; ['Little Darling' × unknown]; intr. 1978
'Andrea Jane' HT, pb, McGredy; flowers large, edged red, suffusing to pink; intr. 2003
'Andrea Jones' -- See 'Rawmolax'
'Andrea Muraglia' -- See 'Frau Betty Hartmann'
'Andrea Parade' (Andrea™) MinFl, m, Poulsen; flowers lavender and purple, 5-8 cm., dbl., no fragrance; foliage dark; growth bushy, 20-40 cm.; intr. 2004
'Andrea Stelzer' -- See 'Korfachrit'
'Andreas Höfer' HMult, mr, 1911, Kiese; flowers brilliant blood-red, small, full, borne in clusters of up to 30; foliage somber green; thornless; growth vigorous (3 m.); ['Tausendschön' × unknown]
'Andrée Joubert' HT, op, 1952, Mallerin, C.; bud very long, dark orange-coral; flowers pastel salmon, large; ['Soeur Thérèse' × 'Duquesa de Peñaranda']
'Andrée Lenoble' Pol, dp, 1915, Turbat; flowers unfading rose or red
'Andrée Palthey' HT, mr, 1946, Gaujard; bud long, pointed; flowers bright red, large, very dbl.; foliage bronze; vigorous growth; ['Mme Joseph Perraud' × seedling]
'Andrée Perrier' HT, ob, 1932, Chambard, C.; bud long; flowers orange-yellow, shaded carmine, very large, dbl., cupped; ['Souv. de F. Bohé' × seedling]
'Andrée Roux' HT, rb, 1927, Pernet-Ducher; flowers coral-red, tipped carmine, reverse yellow
'Andrée Sauvager' HT, yb, 1935, Mallerin, C.; flowers light orange-yellow, large, dbl.
'Andrée-Sophie Girard' F, mr, 1958, Arles; flowers currant-red, edged silvery, dbl.; ['Alain' × 'Independence']
'Andrée Vanderschrick' HWich, w, 1935, Buatois; bud greenish; flowers opening well, small, very dbl., borne in clusters; profuse seasonal bloom; foliage dark; very vigorous, climbing growth
'Andres Battle' HT, dr, 1951, Camprubi, C.; bud long, pointed; flowers crimson, large, dbl., high-centered; strong stems; vigorous growth; ['Comtesse Vandal' × 'Sensation']
'Andrew Barton Patterson' HT, ob, Allender, Robert William; intr. 1999
'Andrew's Comfort' S, ly; flowers light yellow, dbl., borne on every branch and stem; continuous bloom; growth neat, densely branched shrublet, 70 cm.; intr. 1996
'Andrewsii' M, mp, 1807; flowers soft blush tinted lavender pink with chartreuse stamens
'Androi' ('Royal Mail') F, rb, 1985, Anderson's Rose Nurseries; flowers red with yellow petal edges, small, 20 petals, no fragrance; foliage small, medium green, glossy; upright, bushy growth; [seedling × 'Manx Queen']; intr. 1986
Andromeda™ -- See 'Poulpah025(N)'
'Andromeda' HT, pb, Ghosh; buds long; flowers medium pink with lighter reverse, large, full; free-flowering; strong growth; intr. 1998
Andromeda® ('Barvir') S, dp, Barni; flowers rose carmine, large, semi-dbl., moderate fruity fragrance; continuous; foliage medium size, shiny; growth to

50-70 cm.; groundcover; intr. 2003

'Andromeda Hit' (Andromeda™) MinFl, w, Poulsen; flowers white, 5-8 cm., dbl., slight fragrance; foliage dark; growth bushy, 20-40 cm.; intr. 2004

'Andros' ('Rosy Cheeks, Climbing') Cl HT, rb, 1984, Anderson's Rose Nurseries; intr. 1985

'Androy' ('Royal Touch') F, rb, 1983, Anderson's Rose Nurseries; flowers red, reverse silver, medium, 20 petals; foliage medium size, medium green, semi-glossy; upright growth; [Orange Sensation® × Elizabeth of Glamis®]

'Andshy' ('Shy Maiden') F, rb, 1984, Anderson's Rose Nurseries; flowers white with red petal edges, large, 35 petals; foliage medium size, light green, glossy; bushy growth; ['Iceberg' × 'Iceberg']

'Andsun' ('Sunshine Princess') F, yb, 1983, Anderson's Rose Nurseries; flowers medium, 20 petals; foliage medium size, medium green, semi-glossy; bushy growth

'Andulka' HT, op, 1935, Brada, Dr.; bud long, pointed; flowers pink to salmon-pink, large, dbl.; vigorous, bushy growth

'Andwee' ('Wee Topper') Min, mr, 1988, Anderson's Rose Nurseries; flowers small, dbl.; foliage small, light green, semi-glossy; bushy growth; [sport of 'Starina']

'Andwel' ('Welcome Home') F, mr, 1984, Anderson's Rose Nurseries; flowers 20 petals; foliage medium size, light green, semi-glossy; upright growth; [Orange Sensation® × 'Michelle']

'Andwit' ('With Love') HT, yb, 1983, Anderson's Rose Nurseries; flowers yellow, petal edges pink; foliage medium size, medium green, semi-glossy; upright growth; ['Irish Gold' × 'Daily Sketch']

'Andy Gray' -- See 'Rawblob'

'Anémone' -- See 'De La Flèche'

'Anémone' -- See 'Provins Renoncule'

'Anémone' ('À Fleurs d'Anémone', 'Mousseux Anémone') M, mp, 1844, Mauget; flowers even crimson, center petals curling, 6 cm., dbl., cupped

'Anemone' ('Anemone Rose', 'Sinica Anemone', *R.* × *anemonoides*, 'Anemonenrose', 'Anemonoides', 'Pink Cherokee') S, lp, 1896, Geschwind/Schmidt; flowers silver pink, petals shell-shaped, 4 in., 5 petals, moderate fragrance; spring bloom, then scattered bloom; foliage glossy; vigorous, bushy growth; [*R. laevigata* × *R. odorata*]

'Anémone Ancienne' -- See 'Ornement de la Nature'

'Anémone Argentée' HGal, m, before 1826, Barrier; flowers violet-purple; Agathe group

'Anemone Rose' -- See 'Anemone'

'Anemonenrose' -- See 'Anemone'

'Anemonoides' -- See 'Anemone'

'Anemonoides' C, mr, 1814, Poilpre

'Anette' F, Noack, Werner; intr. 1978

'Angara' HT, rb, 1983, Gupta, Dr. M.N. & Shukla, R.; flowers dark red with hues of orange; [sport of 'Montezuma']

'Ange Divin' MinFl, op, Lens; flowers salmon pink, very dbl., rosette; very floriferous; red tips on foliage; growth to 20-30 cm.; intr. 1994

Angel™ -- See 'Devite'

Angel Bells® HT, rb, 1964, Herholdt, J.A.; flowers ivory, flushed orange and red, well-formed, large, dbl., borne singly; foliage dark, glossy; bushy growth; ['Peace' × 'Rina Herholdt']

'Angel Cream' F, w, 1989, Ravi, Professor N.; bud broadly ovate; flowers creamy white, turning pure white; [sport of 'Angel Face']

'Angel Darling' Min, m, 1976, Moore, Ralph S.; flowers lavender, 1½ in., 10 petals, slight fragrance; foliage leathery; vigorous growth; PP4070; ['Little Chief' × 'Angel Face']

'Angel Delight' HT, ab, 1977, Fryers Nursery, Ltd.; flowers peach shaded salmon and apricot buff, full, high-centered; [sport of 'Femina']; intr. 1976

'Angel Dust' Min, w, 1978, Bennett, Dee; bud ovoid; flowers small, 18-20 petals, high-centered; foliage dark; vigorous, upright, spreading growth; [Magic Carrousel® × Magic Carrousel®]

'Angel Eve' -- See 'Poulit'

'Angel Eyes' Min, dp, 1979, Lyon; bud ovoid; flowers spinel-red, 1 in., 10 petals, slight fragrance; foliage small; very compact, bushy growth; intr. 1978

'Angel Face' F, m, 1968, Swim & Weeks; bud pointed; flowers deep mauve-lavender, petal edges blushed ruby, 3½-4 in., 25-30 petals, high-centered, borne in large clusters, intense strongly citrus fragrance; foliage dark, leathery, glossy; vigorous, upright, bushy growth; PP2792; [('Circus' × 'Lavender Pinocchio') × 'Sterling Silver']

'Angel Face, Climbing' Cl F, m, Haight (also Ruston, 1996); flowers ruffled, lavender-mauve, borne in best on old wood, intense fragrance; growth to 10-12 ft.; intr. 1981

'Angel Gates' HSem, pb

'Angel Girl' HT, pb, 1973, Wyant; flowers peach-pink; [sport of 'Bel Ange']

'Angel Guiméra' HT, my, 1926, Dot, Pedro; bud long, pointed; flowers amber-yellow, medium, dbl.; foliage large, thick; ['Frau Karl Druschki' × 'Souv. de Claudius Pernet']

'Angel Pink' -- See 'Morgel'

'Angel Wings' HT, yb, 1959, Lindquist; bud ovoid; flowers yellow, shading to white, edged pink, 3½-4 in., 23 petals, cupped, moderate fragrance; foliage leathery; upright growth; PP1865; ['Golden Rapture' × 'Girona']; intr. 1958

'Angel Wings' ('Michaela') Min, mp, J&P; flowers rose pink, double, high-centered, then cupped; compact growth; intr. 2007

'Angela' -- See 'Jaccream'

Angela® -- See 'Korday'

'Angela' F, yb, 1958, Kordes; flowers golden yellow shaded crimson, 2½ in., 28 petals, borne in trusses of 15-20, slight fragrance; very free bloom; foliage glossy, dark; vigorous, upright growth; ['Masquerade' × 'Golden Scepter']; intr. 1957

'Angela Daffey' Min, lp, Hannemann, F.; intr. 1989

'Angela Davis' -- See 'Lioang'

'Angela Lansbury' -- See 'Twoangel'

'Angela Marie' HT, lp, 2000, Ohlson, John; flowers light pink, reverse lighter, 4 in., full, high-centered, borne mostly solitary, slight fragrance; foliage medium size, medium green, semi-glossy; numerous prickles; growth compact, medium (5 ft.); ['First Prize' × seedling]; intr. 2001

'Angela Merici' HT, w, Lens, Louis; bud very elegant; flowers white with reflections of pink at the center, moderate fragrance; foliage dark green; growth to 60-80 cm.; intr. 1987

Angela Rippon® -- See 'Ocaru'

'Angela Rose Taylor' ('Angela's Rose') F, pb, 2004, Smith, Keith; flowers semi-dbl., borne in large clusters, intense fragrance; foliage medium size, medium green, semi-glossy; prickles 1½ cm., normal; growth upright, tall (2 m.); garden decorative; hedging; [('Hannah Gordon' × 'Raspberry Ice') × unknown]; intr. 2001

'Angela's Choice' F, pb, 1972, Gobbee, W.D.; flowers light pink, reverse deep pink, 3 in., 15 petals; foliage matte; vigorous, upright growth; ['Dainty Maid' × 'Anna Wheatcroft']

'Angela's Rose' -- See 'Angela Rose Taylor'

'Angèle' D, lp, before 1846; flowers light carmine pink, very large, very dbl.

'Angèle' HT, w, Vestal; bud ovoid; flowers creamy white, large, dbl., borne in clusters, moderate fragrance; foliage leathery; long stems; vigorous, bushy growth; [seedling × 'Kaiserin Auguste Viktoria']; intr. 1933

'Angèle d'Arnex' HT, mp, 1912, Bernaix fils; flowers China pink with silvery lavender reflections, large, full

'Angèle Fontaine' HP, lp, 1877, Fontaine; flowers medium to large, full

'Angèle Pernet' HT, ob, 1924, Pernet-Ducher; bud ovoid; flowers reddish-orange shaded yellow, large, dbl., globular, moderate fruity fragrance; foliage dark, bronze, leathery; vigorous, bushy growth; ['Bénédicte Seguin' × 'hybrid tea seedling']

Angelglo™ -- See 'Minaco'

'Angelica' -- See 'Korday'

Angelica Renae™ -- See 'Welangel'

Angelika® ('Volki') F, dp; flowers small, deep pink, dbl., high-centered; greenhouse rose; intr. 1993

'Angelina' S, pb, 1976, Cocker; flowers rose-pink, white eye and reverse, 3 in., 11 petals, borne in clusters; foliage matte, light green; bushy, spreading growth; [('Tropicana' × 'Carine') × ('Cläre Grammerstorf' × 'Frühlingsmorgen')]; intr. 1976

'Angelina Lauro' -- See 'Angeline Lauro'

'Angeline Lauro' ('Angelina Lauro') HT, or, 1970, Lens; flowers medium, dbl.; foliage dark; intr. 1968

Angelique® -- See 'Korangeli'

'Angélique' HGal, mr, about 1820, Descemet; flowers medium red, center brighter, large, very full

'Angelique' F, op, Swim, H.C.; bud ovoid; flowers coral-pink to salmon-pink, open, 2½-3 in., 20-25 petals, borne in clusters, slight fragrance; vigorous, spreading growth; PP1390; ['World's Fair' × 'Pinocchio']; intr. 1961

'Angélique Quétier' M, m, 1839, Quétier; bud well mossed; flowers violet-rose, large, very dbl., cupped

'Angelis' HT, w, 1960, Dot, Pedro; bud long; flowers , 8-10 petals; upright, bushy growth; ['Virgo' × 'Ibiza']

Angelita® -- See 'Macangel'

'Angelita Ruaix' HT, ob, 1940, Dot, Pedro; flowers orange-yellow, large, dbl., high-centered; foliage glossy, dark; very vigorous growth; ['Duquesa de Peñaranda' × 'Pres. Herbert Hoover']

'Angelo Sgaravatti' HT; intr. 1981

'Angels' -- See 'Worchapter'

'Angel's Angel' -- See 'Casang'

'Angel's Blush' -- See 'Wilgene'

'Angel's Blush' -- See 'Micangel'

'Angels Mateu' HT, ab, 1934, Dot, Pedro; bud ovoid; flowers salmon, overlaid gold, large, 40 petals, globular, moderate blackberry fragrance; foliage dark; vigorous, bushy growth; PP174; ['Magdalena de Nubiola' × 'Duquesa de Peñaranda']

'Angelsie' (Lady Elsie May™) S, op, 2001, Noack, Reinhard; flowers semi-dbl., with 1-3 petaloids in center, 3-4 in., 10-11 petals, borne in clusters and large sprays, moderate rose fragrance; continuous; foliage dark green, glossy; prickles medium, hooked downward, green when young, few; growth upright, dense, bushy (3 ft.); landscape; disease-resistant; PP15763; [Repandia® × Gruss an Angeln®]; intr. 2002

'Angelus' HT, w, 1921, Lemon; flowers white, center cream, large, 40-45 petals, moderate fragrance; foliage leathery, dark; vigorous growth; ['Columbia' × ('Ophelia' × unknown)]

'Angelus, Climbing' Cl HT, w, 1933, Dixie Rose Nursery; flowers large, full, moderate fragrance; [sport of 'Angelus']

'Angelus' HT, ob, Gaujard; flowers orange, well-formed; intr. 1980

'Angers-Rose' Pol, mp, 1912, Delaunay

'Angie' -- See 'Lovblend'

'Angie Heatwole' MinFl, mp, 1996, Heatwole, Robert E.; flowers medium, dbl., borne in small clusters, slight fragrance; foliage medium size, medium green, semi-glossy; few prickles; medium, upright growth; [seedling × Dreamer™]

Angkor® -- See 'Deltrac'

'Angle' -- See 'Rose Angle'

'Anglica Minor' A, w; flowers center muddled, dbl.; foliage dark gray-green; dwarf growth

'Angola' F, dr, Moreira da Silva; [seedling × 'Alain']

'Angora' HT

'Angus MacNeil' F, op, 1967, Vincent; flowers salmon-pink and cream, well-formed, borne in clusters; foliage dark; free growth; ['The Optimist' × 'Ma Perkins']

'Anibal David' HT, my, 1961, Moreira da Silva

'Anicet Bourgeois' HP, mr, 1881, Moreau & Robert; flowers bright cherry red, large, full, cupped; ['Senateur Vaisse' × 'Mme Victor Verdier']

'Anicka' Pol, dr, 1940, Valàsek; flowers small, dbl.

Anika® ('Anikall') HT, dy, Haschke; flowers golden-yellow, dbl., high-centered, borne mostly singly, slight fragrance; recurrent; foliage dark green, glossy; stems long, strong; strong, upright, branching growth; intr. 1987

'Anikall' -- See 'Anika'

'Animating' -- See 'Bengale Animée'

Animo™ F, yb, 1962, deRuiter; flowers yellow, becoming copper-red, open, 2½ in., semi-dbl., borne in clusters; bushy growth; ['Masquerade' × 'Beauté']

'Anirvan' HT, rb, Ghosh; flowers bright scarlet with silvery reverse, large, well formed, moderate fragrance; free-flowering; intr. 2001

'Anisley Dickson' -- See 'Dickimono'

'Anita' F, pb, Swim, H.C. & Christensen, J.E.; bud ovoid, pointed; flowers large, 43 petals, borne in clusters of 3-7, slight tea fragrance; foliage large, glossy; prickles medium; medium growth; ['Rumba' × 'Marmalade']; intr. 1982

'Anita' F, mp, 1965, de Ruiter; bud ovoid; flowers medium, very dbl., borne in clusters; foliage dark green

Anita Charles™ -- See 'Mornita'

'Anita Charles, Climbing' Cl Min, op, Vidal

'Anita M.' -- See 'Chewscotch'

'Anita Pereire' S, w, Orard; flowers single; ['Anisley Dickson' × R. wichurana]; intr. 1996

'Anita Russell' -- See 'Jalanita'

'Anita Stahmer' F, dp, 1976, Kordes; bud long, pointed; flowers deep pink, 2½ in., 27 petals, high-centered, slight fragrance; foliage soft; vigorous, upright, bushy growth; [sport of 'Zorina']

'Anitra Louisa' -- See 'Rawanitra'

'Anja' -- See 'Korkompo'

'Anjani' Pol, rb, Kasturi; flowers red with prominent white eye, borne in large sprays; intr. 1970

Anjou® -- See 'Kornicken'

Anjou™ -- See 'Poulac004(N)'

Anjou Festival® F, mr, Pineau; intr. 1982

'Anjou Palace' (Anjou™, Sweet Chariot™) S, mr, Poulsen; flowers medium red, 8-10 cm., 25 petals, no fragrance; foliage dark; growth bushy, 40-60 cm.; PP15507; intr. 2002

'Ankara' HT, op, 1940, Meilland, F.; flowers salmon-orange, center coppery, very large, dbl., cupped; foliage leathery; vigorous, upright growth; ['Joanna Hill' × 'Mme Joseph Perraud']

Anke Schwarz® HT, mr, Hetzel; intr. 1993

'Ankori' ('Kordes' Rose Angelique', Angelique®) HT, ob, 1985, Kordes; flowers bright vermilion orange, well-formed, large, 40 petals; foliage medium size, medium green, matte; bushy growth; PP5012; ['Mercedes' × seedling]; intr. 1980

'Ann' -- See 'Ausfete'

'Ann Aberconway' F, ab, 1976, Mattock; flowers apricot-orange, 3 in., 20 petals; foliage dark, leathery; ['Arthur Bell' × seedling]

'Ann Barter' HT, mr, 1962, Barter; flowers cerise, 5 in., 18 petals; foliage dark; vigorous growth; ['Peace' × 'Ena Harkness']

Ann Cox Chambers™ -- See 'Wekanchaco'

'Ann Delforge' HT, ob

'Ann Elizabeth' F, mp, 1962, Norman; flowers clear rose-pink, large, 15 petals, borne in open clusters; foliage glossy; vigorous, quite tall growth; intr. 1962

'Ann Elizabeth Vear' -- See 'Rawbamb'

'Ann Endt' HRg, dr, 1979, Nobbs; bud long-sepaled; flowers medium, 5 petals, moderate cinnamon fragrance; foliage small, soft; [R. rugosa × R. foliolosa]; intr. 1978

'Ann Factor' HT, ab, 1974, Ellis & Swim; bud ovoid; flowers pastel apricot, large, very dbl., high-centered, intense fragrance; foliage large, glossy, bronze, leathery; vigorous, bushy growth; PP3670; ['Duet' × 'Jack O'Lantern']; intr. 1975

'Ann Henderson' F, r; flowers coppery red-orange, coffee, bronze, medium, dbl., borne in clusters, moderate fragrance; repeats freely; foliage glossy, bronze green; growth rounded, medium (3 × 2 ft.); intr. 2004

'Ann Holbrook' Min, yb, 1982, Dobbs, Annette E.; bud globular; flowers yellow-pink blend, small, dbl., slight fragrance; foliage small, medium green, glossy; spreading growth; ['Patricia Scranton' × 'Little Darling']

'Ann Kercher' HT, dp; flowers variable form, small

'Ann Moore' -- See 'Morberg'

'Ann Reilly' -- See 'Balann'

Anna® -- See 'Pekcougel'

'Anna' -- See 'My Lady Kensington'

'Anna' S, op, Carlsson-Nilsson; flowers color lighter toward petal edges, dbl.

'Anna Aguilera' F, Dot, Simon; intr. 1972

'Anna Alexieff' HP, mr, 1858, Margottin; flowers rose pink, large, dbl., cupped, borne in clusters of 3; medium, upright growth

'Anna Babkina' HT, ob, Dorieux; flowers coppery orange, spiral; foliage dark green, healthy; squat (60 - 70 cm) growth; intr. 2007

'Anna Caroline Maxwell' -- See 'Permax'

'Anna Chartron' T, w, 1896, Schwartz, Vve.; flowers white shaded carmine on the edges, center darker, large, full; ['Kaiserin Auguste Viktoria' × 'Luciole']

'Anna de Diesbach' ('Anna Von Diesbach', 'Glory of Paris', 'Gloire de Paris') HP, dp, 1858, Lacharme, F.; bud long, pointed; flowers deep pink, center darker, 5-6 in., 40 petals, cupped, intense fragrance; vigorous, tall growth; ['La Reine' × unknown]

'Anna de Melun' HP, dp, 1849, Vibert; flowers medium, full

'Anna de Noailles' HT, dr, 1941, Gaujard; flowers crimson-red, medium, semi-dbl., high-centered; very vigorous, bushy growth; ['Étoile de Hollande' × seedling]

Anna Fendi® HT, ab, Barni; flowers intense apricot in the heart, fading to cream at the petal edges, large, dbl., moderate fragrance; growth to 90-100 cm.; intr. 2004

Anna Ford® -- See 'Harpiccolo'

'Anna Fugier' HT, w, 1903, Bonnaire; flowers white, center salmon pink, very large, very full

'Anna Hartmannová' HT, w, 1933, Brada, Dr.; flowers cream-white, very dbl.; [sport of 'Frau Luise Kiese']

'Anna Jane' -- See 'Horquaff'

'Anna Jung' T, mp, 1903, Nabonnand; flowers bright pink with salmon tints, center coppery, very large, semi-dbl., moderate fresh fragrance; foliage very large, dark green

'Anna Katherine' -- See 'Ortana'

'Anna Leese' -- See 'Wekscemala'

'Anna Livia' -- See 'Kormetter'

'Anna Louisa' F, lp, 1967, deRuiter; flowers soft pink, 2½ in., dbl., borne in large clusters; vigorous, low, bushy growth; ['Highlight' × 'Valeta']

'Anna Maria de Montravel' -- See 'Anne-Marie de Montravel'

'Anna Marie' -- See 'Anne Marie'

Anna Marie™ -- See 'Ricanna'

'Anna Marie' HP, 1928, Alfons

'Anna Marie' HT, dp, 1948, Ohlhus; bud ovoid; flowers rosy pink, 5 in., 40-70 petals, high-centered, intense fragrance; foliage leathery, dark; vigorous, upright growth; PP935; ['Soeur Thérèse' × ('Duquesa de Peñaranda' × 'Mrs Pierre S. duPont')]

'Anna-Marie Côte' -- See 'Anne-Marie Côte'

'Anna Milam' -- See 'Moeanna'

'Anna Müller-Idserda' F, mp, 1966, Buisman, G. A. H.; bud ovoid; flowers pink, medium, dbl.; foliage dark; ['Duet' × 'Juliette E. van Beuningen']

'Anna Neagle' HT, rb, 1937, McGredy; flowers bright currant-red, base sunflower-yellow, dbl.; foliage dark; free, branching growth

'Anna Olivier' T, pb, 1872, Ducher; flowers yellowish-flesh, shaded salmon, reverse rose, well-formed, large, dbl.; vigorous growth

'Anna Olivier, Climbing' Cl T, yb; flowers golden pink, large, full

'Anna Pavlova' HT, lp, Beales, Peter; flowers delicate pink, darker at base, large, dbl., globular, intense sweet fragrance; intr. 1981

'Anna Poulsen' -- See 'Anne-Mette Poulsen'

'Anna Rübsamen' HWich, mp, 1904, Weigand, C.; flowers clear pink, aging lighter, 4 cm., dbl., borne in compact clusters; vigorous growth

'Anna Saheb' HT, pb, Chiplunkar; intr. 1993

'Anna Scharsach' HP, mp, 1890, Geschwind, R.; flowers large, dbl.; ['Baronne Adolphe de Rothschild' × 'Mme Lauriol de Barney']

'Anna Ségales' -- See 'Anaïs Ségalas'

'Anna Soupert' HT, yb, 1934, Soupert, G.; flowers yellow, center orange, very large, cactus-dahlia form, dbl.; foliage bronze, dark; dwarf growth; ['Sunburst' × 'Prince de Bulgarie']

'Anna Stave' HT, w, 1973, Curtis, E.C.; bud ovoid; flowers white, tipped pink, medium, dbl., high-centered; foliage dark, soft; moderate, upright growth; ['Pink Parfait' × 'Kordes' Perfecta']; intr. 1973

'Anna-Toki' Min, pb, 2000, Hamilton, Noel; flowers salmon pink, reverse silver white, medium, very full, borne in large clusters, slight fragrance; foliage medium size, dark green, glossy, disease-resistant; few prickles; growth spreading, low (24 in.); containers, borders; [seedling × seedling]; intr. 2000

'Anna Vena' Pol, dr, Zyla; flowers medium, dbl.; intr. 1972

'Anna Von Diesbach' -- See 'Anna de Diesbach'

'Anna Watkins' ('Anne Watkins') HT, ab, 1963; flowers deep cream shaded yellow, reverse apricot, well-shaped, 5 in., 30 petals; foliage dark, glossy; vigorous, upright growth; ['Ena Harkness' × 'Grand'mère Jenny']; intr. 1963

'Anna Wheatcroft' -- See 'Anne Wheatcroft'

'Anna Yung' T, dp, Nabonnand; intr. 1904

'Anna Zinkeisen' -- See 'Harquhling'

'Annabella' HT, dy, 1940, Grillo; flowers light buff-gold, 5 in., 55 petals, moderate fragrance; RULED EXTINCT 5/83 ARM; [sport of 'Joanna Hill']

Annabella® HT, my, Rose Barni-Pistoia; bud ovoid; flowers deeply cupped, medium, 35 petals, cupped, borne singly, no fragrance; foliage medium size, dark, matte; prickles straight, light yellow; upright growth; ['Ambassador' × seedling]; intr. 1983

'Annabelle' -- See 'Korbell'

'Annabelle Kolle' F, dp, Hetzel; intr. 1993

'Annan's Orchard' M, dp

Annapolis™ (Soft Cover™) S, dp, Poulsen; flowers deep pink to light red, small, dbl., cupped, borne in clusters, very slight fragrance; recurrent; foliage dark green, glossy; bushy, low (40-60 cm.) growth; intr. 2005

'Annapurna' -- See 'Virwhite'

Annapurna® HT, w, Dorieux; flowers pure white, double, cupped, intense fragrance; recurrent; vigorous, robust growth; intr. 2000

'Annaroy' HT, pb, 1951, Shepherd; bud ovoid; flowers pink with slight salmon undertone, imbricated, 110 petals; foliage glossy; ['Pink Princess' × 'Los Angeles']

'Annchen Muller' -- See 'Ännchen Müller'

'Ännchen Müller' ('Aennchen Müller', 'Annchen Muller', 'Anny Muller') Pol, dp, 1907, Schmidt, J.C.; flowers warm rose, fading, large, dbl., cupped, borne in clusters; foliage glossy; vigorous, bushy growth; ['Crimson Rambler' × 'Georges Pernet']

'Ännchen von Tharau' -- See 'Aennchen von Tharau'

'Anne' HT, mr, 1925, Pemberton; flowers cherry-red, large, dbl., globular, moderate damask fragrance; foliage leathery; vigorous, bushy, compact growth

Anne Aymone® -- See 'Doralp'

Anne-Aymone Giscard d'Estaing® ('Giscard d'Estaing', Anne Aymone®) F, w, Dorieux; flowers single; intr. 1993

'Anne Béluze' -- See 'Mme Anne Béluze'

'Anne Boleyn' -- See 'Ausecret'

Anne Cocker® F, op, 1971, Cocker, A.; flowers vermilion, 2½ in., 36 petals; foliage glossy, light to medium green; vigorous, upright growth; ['Highlight' × 'Colour Wonder']; intr. 1970

'Anne Colle' ('Ludsponelle') HT, pb, Ludwig; intr. 2003

'Anne Dakin' LCl, pb, Holmes; flowers coral pink, medium, dbl., borne in small clsuters, slight fragrance; foliage glossy; intr. 1974

'Anne de Boleyn' S, lp, 1829, Girardon; bud pointed, long; flowers large, with delicate green pip, 3 in., semi-dbl., borne mostly solitary; foliage finely dentate, widely set; prickles numerous, straight, unequal; ['Grosse Mohnkopfs Rose' × unknown]

Anne de Bretagne® -- See 'Meituraphar'

'Anne de Bretagne' Ch, mp, before 1836, Laffay; flowers bright pink, medium, dbl.

'Anne de Bretagne' HP, lp, Vibert; flowers flesh pink, large, full; intr. 1849

'Anne de Bretagne' HT, Bahaut; intr. 1906

'Anne Diamond' -- See 'Landia'

'Anne d'Ornano' HT, m, 1967, Gaujard; bud long, pointed; flowers bright purple-crimson, very large, dbl.; foliage dark, leathery; vigorous, bushy growth; ['John S. Armstrong' × Rose Gaujard®]

'Anne Elizabeth' HT, lp, Thomas, Dr. A.S.; intr. 1979

'Anne Farnworth' HT, rb, 1964, Court; flowers like parent, in sunset shades; [sport of 'Tzigane']

'Anne Graber' F, dp, 2008, Jerabek, Paul; flowers light red with wavy petals, large, 4-7 cm., dbl., borne in large clusters; foliage medium-size, medium green, semi-glossy; prickles medium, perpendicular to slightly down-angled, red-green to tan, moderate; growth upright, tall (4-5 ft.); [unknown × unknown]; intr. 2010

'Anne Gregg' HT, ab, 1994; flowers moderately large, 3-3½ in., dbl.; foliage large, dark green, matte; some prickles; medium (80 cm.), upright growth; [sport of 'Diorama']; intr. 1994

'Anne Hall' HRg, mp, Johnson; intr. 2002

Anne Harkness® -- See 'Harkaramel'

'Anne Hathaway' -- See 'Harbrite'

'Anne Hering' -- See 'Moeanne'

'Anne Jackson' LCl, dp, 1973, Jackson, J.R.; flowers cerise, medium, 30-35 petals, cupped; foliage glossy, bronze; vigorous growth; [sport of 'Spectacular']

'Anne Kercher' -- See 'Simjezbel'

'Anne Laferrère' HP, dr, 1916, Nabonnand, C.; flowers deep velvety blood-red; vigorous growth

'Anne Laure' ('Marraine', 'Mme Helmut Kohl') S, dr, 1996, Guillot-Massad; flowers bright, blood red with golden stamens, single; growth to 4 ft.; intr. 1996

'Anne Letts' HT, pb, 1954, Letts; flowers rose-pink, reverse silvery, pointed, 4½ in., 28 petals, moderate fragrance; foliage glossy; bushy growth; ['Peace' × 'Charles Gregory']

'Anne Leygues' T, lp, 1905, Nabonnand, P.&C.; flowers flesh-pink; ['Gén. Schablikine' × 'Comtesse Bardi']

'Anne Lorentz' HT, lp, Spek; intr. 2005

'Anne Marie' -- See 'Meifour'

'Anne Marie' ('Anna Marie') HSet, dp, 1843, Feast; flowers pale rose, large, dbl., borne in clusters

'Anne-Marie Côte' ('Anna-Marie Côte') N, w, 1875, Guillot; flowers pure white, sometimes tinted pink, medium, full, globular, borne in small clusters; foliage dark green; prickles long, straight

'Anne-Marie de Montravel' ('Anna Maria de Montravel') Pol, w, 1879, Rambaux; flowers pure white, of irregular form when fully open, sometimes showing stamens, 1½ in., dbl., moderate lily-of-the-valley fragrance; foliage dark green above, grayish beneath, glossy, 3-5 leaflets; prickles very few; dwarf, compact growth; ['dbl.-flowered multiflora' × 'Mme de Tartas']

'Anne Marie Laing' -- See 'Jospink'

'Anne-Marie Milliat' HT, w, 1939, Gaujard; bud very long; flowers large, very dbl.; very vigorous growth

'Anne Marie Soupert' HT, op, 1904, Soupert & Notting; flowers glossy carmine-salmon, very large, full; ['Mme Edmé Metz' × 'Mme Jules Grolez']

Anne Marie Trechslin® -- See 'Meifour'

'Anne Marie Treschlin, Climbing' Cl HT, ap,

'Anne McDonald' F, pb, 1992, Spriggs, Ian Raymond; flowers rose pink and creamy yellow, classical, 3¼ in., 30 petals, high-centered, borne in clusters of 10-30; foliage medium green, glossy; medium to tall (1-3 m.), upright growth; ['Granada' × 'Kordes' Perfecta']; intr. 1991

'Anne-Mette Poulsen' ('Anna Poulsen', 'Anne Poulsen') F, mr, 1935, Poulsen, S.; bud long, pointed; flowers bright crimson-red, darkening, large, dbl., borne in clusters, moderate fragrance; vigorous growth; PP182; ['Ingar Olsson' × seedling]; intr. 1935

'Anne Morrow Lindbergh' -- See 'Jacyap'

'Anne no Omoide' -- See 'Souv d'Anne Frank'

'Anne of Geierstein' HEg, dr, 1894, Penzance; flowers deep crimson, medium, single, moderate fragrance; summer bloom; foliage fragrant; vigorous growth; hips bright scarlet; [R. rubiginosa × hybrid perpetual or bourbon]

'Anne Poulsen' -- See 'Anne-Mette Poulsen'

'Anne Scranton' F, lp, 1971, Dobbs, Annette E.; bud ovoid; flowers light pink, center flesh-white, medium, dbl.; foliage leathery; vigorous, upright growth; [Queen Elizabeth® × 'Katherine T. Marshall']

'Anne Vanderbilt' HT, or, 1941, Brownell; bud pointed; flowers reddish-orange, open, 4-5 in., 28 petals, intense fragrance; foliage leathery, glossy; very vigorous, bushy growth; PP504; [seedling × 'Stargold']

'Anne Watkins' -- See 'Anna Watkins'

'Anne Wheatcroft' ('Anna Wheatcroft') F, or, 1960, Tantau, Math.; flowers light vermilion, gold stamens, 4 in., single, borne in clusters, slight fragrance; foliage dark, glossy; vigorous growth; [('Cinnabar' × unknown) × seedling]; intr. 1960

'Anneka' -- See 'Harronver'

'Anneke Doorenbos' F, pb, 1956, Doorenbos; flowers silver-pink, reverse darker; [sport of 'Buisman's Triumph']

'Anneke Koster' Pol, dr, 1927, Koster, D.A.; flowers deep red; [sport of 'Greta Kluis']

'Anneli' -- See 'Seaanne'

'Anneli van Rooyen' HT, pb, Interplant; flowers creamy white with coral pink edges, double, high-centered; floriferous; medium, compact growth

'Annelies' HMsk, lp, Lens; flowers small, light pink, rosette, borne in pyramidal clusters, slight fragrance; growth to 125-150 cm.; intr. 2001

'Anneliese' HT, dr, Miessler, Herbert; intr. 1971

'Anneliese' HT, lp, Wänninger, Franz; flowers light pink to white, large, semi-dbl.; intr. 1990

'Anneliesse Rothenberger' -- See 'Miss Harp'

Annelise Border™ S, mr, Poulsen; flowers medium red, small, no fragrance; foliage dark; growth tall (100-150 cm.), bushy; intr. 1998

'Annemarie Jacobs' HT, dy, 1910, Jacobs; flowers dark golden yellow, shaded red, medium to large, full, moderate fragrance

'Annemarie van Onsem' F, mr, 1971, Institute of Ornamental Plant Growing; bud ovoid; flowers vivid red, open, medium, semi-dbl.; foliage large, glossy, dark; very vigorous, upright, bushy growth; ['Circus' × 'Korona']

'Annerose' ('Annirose') F, or, Croix; flowers medium size, slow opening, long lasting, dbl., slight fragrance; young foliage reddish, turning dark green, glossy; growth to 50-70 cm.; intr. 1976

'Anne's Delight' Min, dp, 1982, Williams, Ernest D.; bud pointed; flowers 40 petals, high-centered, borne usually singly, slight fragrance; foliage small, dark, glossy; prickles long, thin; upright, bushy growth; ['Little Darling' × 'Over the Rainbow']; intr. 1981

'Annette' HT, op, 1952, Swim, H.C.; bud long, pointed; flowers salmon-pink, 4-4½ in., 20-25 petals, high-centered; foliage glossy, leathery, dark; vigorous, compact growth; ['Charlotte Armstrong' × 'Contrast']

Annette™ ('Annette Hit') MinFl, mp, Olesen; flowers dbl., borne mostly solitary, slight fragrance; foliage dark green, glossy; growth bushy, low (40-60 cm.); PP12762; intr. 1998

'Annette Dobbs' -- See 'Mornet'

'Annette Elizabeth' LCl, lp, Stewart, L.; [Clair Matin® × 'Wedding Day']; intr. 1992

'Annette Gatward' HT, ab, 1954, Gatward; flowers peach, large, dbl.; foliage light green; upright growth; ['Mrs Charles Lamplough' × 'Barbara Richards']

'Annette Gravereaux' HT, my, 1929, Leenders, M.; bud large, ovoid; flowers lemon-yellow, shaded orange, very large, dbl.; foliage medium size, dark green; growth upright; ['Mev. C. van Marwijk Kooy' × 'Golden Emblem']

'Annette Hit' -- See 'Poulhilda'

'Anni Jebens' HT, dy, 1932, Kordes; bud large, long, pointed, golden yellow; flowers blood-red, reverse golden yellow, dbl., high-centered; foliage leathery, glossy, bronze; bushy, dwarf growth; ['Charles P. Kilham' × 'Mev. G.A. van Rossem']

'Anni Welter' M, mp, 1906, Welter; flowers large, full, moderate fragrance; ['Crested Moss' × 'La France']

'Annick' F, or, Fryer; flowers large, orange scarlet, dbl., borne singly and in trusses, moderate fragrance; foliage dense, lush; growth vigorous (90 cm.); intr. 2002

'Annie' -- See 'Bosrexever'

'Annie' -- See 'Dewdrop'

'Annie Beaufais' F, or, deRuiter; intr. 1962

'Annie Besant' HT, w, 1910, Nabonnand; flowers flesh to cream with peach tints; growth upright

'Annie Brandt' HT, op, 1932, Mallerin, C.; bud long, pointed; flowers pink tinted coral, open, large, semi-dbl.; foliage leathery, glossy; very vigorous, bushy growth; ['Mrs Pierre S. duPont' × 'Colette Clément']

'Annie Burgess' HP, lp, 1926, Burgess, S.W.; flowers pale pink, borne in clusters; early bloom; ['Lyon Rose' × 'Frau Karl Druschki']

'Annie Cook' T, rb, 1888, Cook, J.W.; flowers blush-tinted; probably extinct; [sport of 'Bon Silène']

'Annie Crawford' ('Miss Annie Crawford') HP, mp, 1915, Hall; flowers bright pink, very large, 30-35 petals, high-centered; recurrent bloom; vigorous growth

'Annie de Metz' HT, or, 1932, Mallerin, C.; bud large; flowers dbl., high-centered; ['Golden Emblem' × (R. foetida bicolor × unknown)]

'Annie Drevet' HT, rb, 1939, Caron, B.; bud long, yellow; flowers fiery red, reverse yellow, large, semi-dbl., cupped; foliage leathery, glossy, dark; vigorous growth; ['Charles P. Kilham' × ('Kitchener of Khartoum' × 'Mari Dot')]; intr. 1939

'Annie Dupeyrat' HT, op, 1935, Mallerin, C.; bud ovoid; flowers very large, dbl.; foliage leathery; bushy growth; ['Mrs T. Hillas' × 'Elvira Aramayo']

'Annie East' -- See 'Bosrexever'

'Annie Girardot' ('Kripalli') HT, Kriloff, Michel; intr. 1979

'Annie Laurie' -- See 'Annie Laurie McDowell'

'Annie Laurie' -- See 'Sarannla'

'Annie Laurie' ('Double Mme Butterfly') HT, pb, 1918, Stuppy Floral Co.; bud long, pointed; flowers flesh-pink, base yellow, large, dbl., cupped; foliage glossy; very vigorous growth; [sport of 'Ophelia']

'Annie Laurie McDowell' ('Annie Laurie') LCl, mp, Rupert; intr. 2001

'Annie Laxton' HP, mp, 1869, Laxton

'Annie M. G. Schmidt' S, lp; flowers borne in clusters; intr. 2001

'Annie Nell' -- See 'Ponnell'

'Annie R. Mitchell' -- See 'Mormitchell'

'Annie Vibert' N, w, before 1871, Vibert; flowers pink on opening, then white, medium, moderate fragrance; foliage glossy; stems long, arching; growth to (12 ft.)

'Annie Wood' -- See 'Mlle Annie Wood'

'Annie's Song' F, lp, Spriggs, Ian Raymond; intr. 1990

'Annique' S, dr, Kordes; flowers have white streak on five outer petals, double, globular, borne singly and in small clusters; recurrent; moderate growth; intr. 2008

'Annirose' -- See 'Annerose'

'Anniversarie de Willemse' HT, pb; flowers striped; intr. 2003

'Anniversary' -- See 'Mattlace'

'Anniversary' HT, my, 1961, Byrum, Roy L.; bud ovoid; flowers yellow, 4-5 in., 55-60 petals, high-centered, moderate fragrance; foliage leathery, dark; strong stems; vigorous, upright growth; PP2084; RULED EXTINCT 5/81 ARM; ['Mary Jo' × 'Lamplighter']

'Anniversary' HT, dr, 1981, Hoy, Lowel L.; bud long, pointed; flowers 23 petals, high-centered, borne 1-3 per cluster, moderate fragrance; foliage medium to large; prickles hooked down; upright growth; PP4986; ['Love Affair' × seedling]

'Anniversary Fukuyama' HT, ob, Hiroshima; intr. 2007

'Ann's Rose' -- See 'Judann'

'Ann's Wedding' HT, my, 1976, Rosemount Nursery; flowers very full, 4 in., 40 petals, moderate fragrance; foliage glossy, dark; free growth; [sport of 'Whisky Mac']

'Annulet' Pol, lp, 1935, Miers, A.

'Anny' Min, w, 1949, Dot, Pedro; long, leafy sepals; flowers pale pink fading white, micro-mini, ½ in., 30 petals; growth to 6 in; ['Rouletii' × 'Perla de Montserrat']

'Anny Brandt' HT, yb, 1951, Mallerin, C.; bud pointed; flowers creamy yellow, edges and reverse tinted lilac, petals waved, dbl.; vigorous growth

Anny Duperey® S, my, Meilland; flowers golden yellow, fading toward white, 85 petals, cupped to rosette, borne in clusters, moderate fragrance; recurrent; foliage dense; bushy (80 - 110 cm.) growth; intr. 2006

'Anny Muller' -- See 'Ännchen Müller'

'Anomalia' B, mp, 1838, Bizard; flowers medium, full

'Another Chance' HT, w, 1994, Heyes, Alex; flowers medium, full, borne mostly singly, slight fragrance; foliage medium to large, medium green, matte; some prickles; medium-tall, bushy growth; ['Mount Shasta' × 'Saffron']; intr. 1996

'Anri' HT, yb, 1997, Otsuki, Hironaka; flowers 4½ in., very dbl.; foliage large, dark green, glossy; few prickles; bushy, upright, medium (180cm.) growth; ['Mme. Sachi' × 'Yarna']

'Ans' Min, dr, Benardella, Frank A.; bud pointed; flowers shapely, burgundy wine-colored, borne on long stems, slight fragrance; foliage glossy; growth vigorous, tall; intr. 1990

'Anson Jones' S, yb, 2005, Shoup, George Michael; flowers semi-dbl., borne mostly solitary, moderate fragrance; remontant; foliage large, dark green, semi-glossy; prickles moderate; growth upright, tall (5-6 ft.); hedge; [('Carefree Beauty' × 'Carefree Beauty') × 'Mrs Oakely Fisher']; intr. 2000

'Antares' -- See 'Bartares'

'Anthea' HT, yb, 1949, Bees; flowers pale yellow flushed rose, compact, 4-5 in., 20-25 petals; foliage dark; vigorous growth; ['McGredy's Yellow' × 'Phyllis Gold']

'Anthea Fortescue' -- See 'Peashine'

'Anthea Turner' HT, yb, 1997, Thomas, D.; flowers very dbl., 41 petals; foliage medium size, dark green, semi-glossy; few prickles; compact, medium growth; ['Alec's Red' × 'Harry Wheatcroft']

'Anthéor' HT, ab, 1948, Meilland, F.; bud long, furled; flowers reddish-apricot, dbl.; [('Joanna Hill' × 'Duquesa de Peñaranda') × ('Charles P. Kilham' × 'Mme Joseph Perraud')]

'Anthéros' HP, mp, 1839, Lepage; flowers large, flat

'Anthony' S, lp, 2006, Beales, Amanda; flowers small, full, borne in large clusters; foliage medium size, dark green, glossy; prickles average, straight, numerous; growth bushy, short (1 m.); [Armada® × Centenaire de Lourdes®]; intr. 2002

'Anthony Meilland' -- See 'Meitalbaz'

'Anticipation' ('Altesse', 'Rodin') HT, rb, 1990, Meilland; flowers red with silver/white reverse, medium, 35 petals, high-centered, borne singly, slight fragrance; foliage medium size, medium green, semi-glossy; bushy growth; [seedling × seedling]; intr. 1991

Antico Amore® HT, mp, Barni, V.; flowers pink with apricot tinge, color holds, dbl., cupped, intense fragrance; growth to 90-100 cm.; intr. 1988

Antigone® HT, yb, 1969, Gaujard; bud pointed; flowers yellow shaded red, large, dbl.; foliage light green, soft; vigorous, upright growth; [Rose Gaujard® × Guitare®]

'Antigua' -- See 'Antigua Kordana'

'Antigua' HT, ab, 1974, Warriner, William A.; bud ovoid; flowers large, dbl., high-centered, slight fragrance; foliage leathery; vigorous, upright, bushy growth; PP3431; ['South Seas' × 'Golden Masterpiece']

'Antigua Kordana' ('Antigua') Min, pb, Kordes; bud ovoid; flowers light pink with deeper pink tones in center, 6 cm., 40-45 petals, cupped to flat, borne mostly singly, no fragrance; recurrent; foliage dark green, glossy; prickles numerous, 4-6 mm., triangular, elongated; upright (10 in.), bushy growth; containers; PP14902; [seedling × seedling]; intr. 2002

'Antike' F, yb, W. Kordes Söhne; flowers reddish-yellow, medium, dbl.; intr. 1966

Antike 89® -- See 'Kordalen'

'Antike Kordana' Min, lp, Kordes; flowers pale pink with deeper center, dbl.; container rose

'Antinea' HT, op, 1934, Gaujard; flowers

salmon-orange, base yellow, very large, dbl.; foliage glossy; very vigorous, bushy growth; ['Julien Potin' × seedling]

'Antiope' HGal, pb, before 1815, Descemet; flowers pink with purple, medium, full

'Antique' F, rb, 1967, Kordes; flowers crimson and gold, borne in clusters; bushy growth; ['Honeymoon' × 'Circus']

'Antique 89' -- See 'Kordalen'

'Antique Abundance' -- See 'Harverag'

'Antique Artistry' S, ab, Clements, John; flowers apricot-peach, 4 in., 95 petals, old-fashioned; foliage serrated, matte green; growth vigorous, compact (4 × 3 ft.); intr. 2000

'Antique Brass' HT, ab, Zary, K.; PP11617; intr. 1999

'Antique Gold' -- See 'Lavtique'

'Antique Lace' F, mp, 1991, Strahle, B. Glen; bud ovoid; flowers medium pink, light pink center, medium, 25-35 petals, urn-shaped; foliage medium size, dark green, semi-glossy; bushy, medium growth; [seedling × 'Little Cameo']; intr. 1990

'Antique Nostalgia' -- See 'Taneiglat'

Antique Rose™ -- See 'Morcara'

'Antique Silk' -- See 'Korampa'

'Antique Tapestry' -- See 'Cletape'

'Antique Velvet' Min, dr, 1993, Jobson, Daniel J.; flowers velvety dark red, large, dbl., borne in large clusters; foliage large, medium green, semi-glossy; few prickles; patio, tall, upright, bushy growth; ['Valerie Joanne' × (Party Girl™ × 'Pillow Talk')]; intr. 1993

'Antoine Alléon' HP, 1872, Damaizin; flowers bright cherry red, center crimson, large, full

'Antoine Devert' T, w, 1880, Gonod; flowers white, tinted flesh and sulfur yellow, reverse salmon pink, large, full, cupped, moderate fragrance

'Antoine Ducher' HP, rb, 1866, Ducher; flowers violet-red, large; ['Mme Domage' × unknown]

'Antoine Mermet' T, dp

'Antoine Mouton' HP, mp, 1874, Levet; flowers deep rose, tinged with lilac, reverse silvery, large, full; foliage very serrated; few prickles; ['La Reine' × unknown]

'Antoine Noailly' HT, mr, 1958, Croix, P.; bud long; flowers clear red, scalloped petals; [seedling × 'Mme G. Forest-Colcombet']

'Antoine Quihou' HP, m, 1880, Verdier, E.; flowers velvety purple, large, full, moderate fragrance

'Antoine Rivoire' HT, lp, 1895, Pernet-Ducher; bud ovoid; flowers light pink shaded darker, imbricated, dbl.; foliage dark; vigorous growth; ['Dr. Grill' × 'Lady Mary Fitzwilliam']

'Antoine Schurz' HP, lp, 1890, Geschwind, R.; flowers flesh-white, very large, very dbl., cupped, quartered, moderate centifolia fragrance

'Antoine Verdier' HP, pb, 1871, Jamain, H.; flowers pink, shaded muddy lilac, dbl.

'Antoine Weber' T, mp, 1899, Weber; flowers soft, rosy flesh-pink, center lighter, large, dbl.

'Antoinette' -- See 'Koriganta'

'Antoinette' HT, ab, Patterson; bud long, pointed; flowers open, medium size, dbl., moderate fragrance; foliage large, glossy, leathery; vigorous, upright growth; [Queen Elizabeth® × 'Peace']; intr. 1968

'Antoinette' ('Victoria') A, w, before 1826, Descemet; flowers pure white, full, globular, moderate fragrance

'Antoinette Bouvagne' T, w, 1842, Béluze; flowers flesh white, large, full

'Antoinette Cuillerat' Ch, w, 1897, Buatois; flowers bright white with coppery sulphur yellow base, lightly edged with carmine/violet; probably extinct

'Antoinette Durieu' T, dy, 1890, Godard; ['Mme Caro' × unknown]

'Antoinette Massard' N, mr, 1913, Nabonnand; flowers bright carmine-red, shaded vermilion, dbl.

'Antonella' HT, mp, 1964, Mondial Roses; bud globular; flowers camellia-pink, 5 in., dbl., high-centered; strong stems; vigorous growth

'Antonella Fineschi' F, yb, Fineschi, G.; flowers medium yellow, shading to soft pink on petal edges as petals open, double, low-centered; intr. 1985

'Antonelliana' HT, ob, 1952, Giacomasso; flowers orange and deep yellow tipped, well-formed, dbl.; foliage glossy; vigorous growth; ['Gaiezza' × 'Margaret McGredy']

'Antonia' F, w, 1980, Bazeley, B.L.; bud long, pointed; flowers blushed white, palest pink flush, well-formed, dbl., borne in large clusters, slight fragrance; vigorous, bushy, low growth; [sport of 'Tantau's Tip Top']; intr. 1979

'Antonia d'Ormois' -- See 'Antonine d'Ormois'

'Antonia Pahissa' HT, ob, 1935, Pahissa; bud long, pointed; flowers rich orange, large, dbl., cupped; foliage glossy, dark; long stems; very vigorous, bushy growth

Antonia Ridge® -- See 'Meiparadon'

'Antonietta Ingegnoli' Pol, pb, 1923, Ingegnoli; flowers golden pink, opening in two distinct tones on same plant, dbl.; [R. wichurana × R. chinensis]

'Antonín Dvorák' -- See 'A. Dvorak'

'Antonine d'Ormois' ('Antonia d'Ormois') HGal, lp, 1835, Vibert; flowers blush, fading at edge, small eye at center, petals recurved at the edge, small to medium, dbl., cupped, quartered, borne in clusters of 2-3; foliage dark green, small, pointed; prickles moderate

'Antonine Verdier' HT, lp, 1872, Jamain; flowers light carmine, large, full

'Antonio Rolleri de Peluffo' HT, dr, 1926, Soupert & Notting; bud large, ovoid; flowers brilliant red, center darker, very large, dbl., borne mostly solitary, moderate fragrance; ['Gen. MacArthur' × 'Mme Edouard Herriot']

'Antoon van Dijk' S, dp, DVP Melle; ['Maizières' × seedling]; intr. 2000

'Antopp' (Golden Opportunity™) Gr, dy, 1996, Perry, Anthony; bud urn-shaped; flowers golden yellow, light golden yellow, dbl., borne in small clusters, slight fragrance; foliage medium size, medium green, semi-glossy; some prickles; medium growth; ['Broadway' × Delta Gold™]; intr. 1995

'Anurag' HT, pb, 1981, Division of Vegetable Crops and Floriculture; bud long, pointed; flowers Tyrian rose, 54 petals, high-centered, borne singly, intense fragrance; free-flowering; foliage large, smooth, light green; prickles hooked, brown; upright, bushy growth; ['Sweet Afton' × 'Gulzar']; intr. 1980

'Anurupa' HT, mp, Friends Rosery; intr. 1997

Anuschka® -- See 'Tankanusch'

Anuschka® HT, dp, Tantau; intr. 2004

'Anusheh' -- See 'Payable'

'Anusuya' HT, m, Chakraborty, Dr. K.; flowers purple pink, large, dbl., high-centered, moderate sweet fragrance; intr. 1995

'Anvil Sparks' -- See 'Ambossfunken'

'Anvil Sparks, Climbing' Cl HT, ob

'Anydale' -- See 'Liogeorge'

'Anytime' ('Tick-Tock') Min, op, 1974, McGredy, Sam IV; flowers salmon-orange, purplish eye, ½-1 in., 12 petals, moderate fragrance; foliage dark; ['New Penny' × Elizabeth of Glamis®]; also registered as Tick Tock, 1974; intr. 1973

'Anzac' HT, op, 1943, Howard, F.H.; flowers azalea-pink with coppery scarlet sheen, 5 in., 42-50 petals, camellia-like, moderate fruity fragrance; foliage leathery; long stems; very vigorous, upright, compact growth; PP636; ['Miss Rowena Thom' × seedling]

'Aoraki' -- See 'Socmount'

'Aorangi' HT, w, Sandbrook; flowers white, of elegant form; growth medium to tall; intr. 1995

'Aorangi' F, w, 1980, Murray, Nola; bud pointed; flowers cream, 3 in., 41 petals, high-centered, slight fragrance; foliage large; upright growth; ['Arthur Bell' × 'Red Devil']

'Aotearoa-New Zealand' -- See 'Macgenev'

'Aozora' ('Blue Sky') HT, m, 1973, Suzuki, Seizo; flowers deep lilac-blue, large, dbl., high-centered; foliage large, leathery; vigorous, upright growth; [('Sterling Silver' × unknown) × seedling]; intr. 1973

'Apache' S, yb, 1961, Von Abrams; bud ovoid, flushed red; flowers medium to buff-yellow, 5-6 in., 60 petals; foliage leathery; vigorous (5-6 ft.), spreading, open growth; ['Fred Howard' × 'Buc-

caneer']; intr. 1961
'Apache'® HT, op, Kordes; flowers bright pink-orange, medium, dbl., high-centered, borne mostly singly; recurrent; stems average 24 in.; florist rose; intr. 2005

'Apache Belle' HT, rb, 1968, Sitton; bud ovoid; flowers orange-red, 5 in., very dbl., slight fragrance; foliage glossy; vigorous, upright, compact growth; PP2847; [sport of 'The Alamo']

'Apache Princess' -- See 'Twomin'

'Apache Tears' F, rb, 1972, Pikiewicz; flowers cream to creamy pink, petals edged red, medium, dbl., high-centered, slight fragrance; foliage large, light; vigorous, bushy growth; ['Karl Herbst' × 'China Doll']; intr. 1971

'Apache Wells' F, yb, 1971, Williams, J. Benjamin; bud ovoid; flowers canary-yellow, washed pink, medium-small, dbl., high-centered; foliage leathery; vigorous, bushy growth; ['Circus' × 'The Optimist']

'Apachi' -- See 'Tai-Gong'

'Apart' ('Apart Pavement') HRg, m, Uhl, J.; flowers mauve blend, dbl.; prolific fruit; intr. 1981

'Apart Pavement' -- See 'Apart'

'Aparte' -- See 'Spartan'

'Apeles Mestres' Cl HP, dy, 1931, Dot, Pedro; flowers sunflower-yellow, large, dbl., globular, moderate fragrance; occasional repeat; foliage dark, glossy; vigorous, climbing growth; ['Frau Karl Druschki' × 'Souv. de Claudius Pernet']

'Apéritif' -- See 'Macwairar'

'Apéritif' F, pb, 1973, Boerner; bud ovoid; flowers ivory, petals edged rose-pink, medium, dbl., high-centered, slight fragrance; foliage leathery; vigorous, upright, bushy growth; PP3118; [seedling × 'Starbright']; intr. 1972

'Apfelblüte' Pol, lp, 1907, Wirtz & Eicke; flowers light pink-white, small, dbl.; ['Mme Norbert Levavasseur' × unknown]

'Apfelblüte' S, w, Noack, Werner; flowers light pink-white, medium, semi-dbl.; intr. 1991

'Aphrodite' HT, or, 1928, Easlea; bud long, pointed; flowers coral-red, shaded gold, large, semi-dbl.; foliage dark, glossy; vigorous, bushy growth; ['Hortulanus Budde' × 'Toison d'Or']

'Aphrodite, Climbing' Cl HT, or, 1933, Hillock

Aphrodite® ('Foundation') HT, ab, Tantau; intr. 2003

Apogée® -- See 'Delbaf'

'Apolline' B, mp, 1848, Verdier, V.; flowers bright rose-pink, large, full, cupped; ['Pierre de St. Cyr' × unknown]

Apollo™ -- See 'Poulpollo'

'Apollo' HT, dy, 1941, Armstrong, J.A.; flowers golden yellow; [sport of 'Mme Joseph Perraud']

'Apollo, Climbing' ('Apollo XI') Cl HT, my, Leenders; bud reddish; intr. 1970

Apollo® HT, my, 1971, Armstrong, D.L.; bud long, pointed; flowers soft sunshine yellow, large, dbl., moderate fragrance; foliage large, glossy, dark, leathery; vigorous, upright, bushy growth; PP3322; ['High Time' × 'Imperial Gold']

'Apollo Parade' (Apollo™) Min, ab, Poulsen; flowers apricot blend, medium, semi-dbl., no fragrance; growth narrow, bushy, 20-40 cm.; PP11539; intr. 1998

'Apollo Tribute' -- See 'Jacap'

'Apollo XI' -- See 'Apollo, Climbing'

'Apollon' -- See 'Superbe Cramoisie'

Apoman® HT, yb, Adam

'Apotheker Franz Hahne' S, op, 1919, Müller, Dr. F.; flowers salmon-rose on orange-yellow ground, large, full, moderate fragrance

'Apotheker Georg Höfer' HT, or, 1900, Welter; flowers coppery-red, very large, very dbl.

'Apotheker George Höfer, Climbing' Cl HT, or, 1941, Vogel, M.; flowers very large, dbl.; [sport of 'Apotheker George Höfer']

'Apotheose' F, yb, 1963, Delforge; flowers Indian yellow edged red, becoming garnet-red; vigorous growth; ['Arc-en-Ciel' × seedling]

'Appassionata' -- See 'La Passionata'

'Appeal' HT, mp, 1959, Fletcher; flowers clean pink, dbl., intense fragrance; long stems; vigorous, bushy growth; ['Ena Harkness' × 'Treasure']; intr. 1957

'Applause' -- See 'Harxever'

'Applause' -- See 'Savapple'

'Applause' HT, dp, 1949, Swim, H.C.; bud long, pointed; flowers light red, 4-4½ in., 50 petals, high-centered, slight fragrance; foliage leathery, dark; vigorous, upright, bushy growth; PP829; ['Contrast' × 'Charlotte Armstrong']

'Apple Blossom' HMult, lp, 1890, Dawson; ['Dawson' × R. multiflora]; possibly the same as the 1932 version from Burbank

'Apple Blossom' HT, mp, Cooling; intr. 1906

'Apple Blossom' Pol, lp, Schultheis; intr. 1908

'Apple Blossom' HMult, lp, Burbank; flowers light pink, center lighter, petals crinkled, semi-dbl., borne in huge clusters; vigorous growth; PP65; q-r; ['Dawson' × R. multiflora]; possibly bred by Dawson about 1890, and introduced by Stark Bros., in 1932

'Apple Blossom Flower Carpet ' -- See 'Noamel'

'Apple Seed' S, mp, Keihan; intr. 2000

'Appleblossom' S, lp, 1963, Skinner; flowers apple blossom-pink, dbl., cupped; recurrent bloom; bushy (2 ft.) growth

'Appleblossom' ('Apple Blossom Flower Carpet ', 'Mareva', 'Sommermelodie') S, mp, Noack, Werner; flowers soft pink, 4 cm., semi-dbl., cupped, borne in clusters, slight fragrance; recurrent; growth low (2 × 3 ft.), bushy; groundcover; PP10239; intr. 1997

'Appleblossom Festival' S, pb, Williams, J. Benjamin; intr. 1999

'Appledore' F, lp, 1965, Allen, E.M.; flowers medium, 24 petals, moderate fragrance; foliage glossy; vigorous growth; ['Karl Herbst' × 'Pink Charming']

'Applejack' S, pb, 1973, Buck, Dr. Griffith J.; bud small, long, pointed, ovoid; flowers Neyron rose, stippled crimson, large, semi-dbl., intense fragrance; repeat bloom; foliage leathery; vigorous, upright, bushy growth; ['Goldbusch' × ('Josef Rothmund' × R. laxa)]

'Appleton's Limelight' HT, dy, 1934, Appleton; bud long, pointed; flowers deep golden yellow, open, large, semi-dbl.; foliage leathery, glossy; vigorous, bushy growth; [sport of 'Lady Forteviot']

'Appreciation' HT, mr, 1971, Gregory; flowers light red shading crimson, pointed, 4 in., 27 petals; foliage glossy; vigorous growth; [Queen Elizabeth® × seedling]

'Apps Rose' -- See 'Koralogen'

'Apricot Abundance' -- See 'Harfracas'

'Apricot Angel' HT, ab; intr. 1999

'Apricot Beauty' S, ab, Rendu; intr. 1980

Apricot Bells® -- See 'Lentrichin'

'Apricot Brandy' F, ab, 1970; flowers apricot, base yellow, 4 in., 22 petals, slight fragrance; foliage bronze-green; intr. 1972

'Apricot Brandy' Min, ab, Benardella; growth tall; intr. 1996

'Apricot Candy' HT, ab; flowers strong apricot pink in center, fading to pale pink on outer petals, full, low-centered, moderate fragrance; intr. 2007

'Apricot Castle' -- See 'Poulkalm'

Apricot Charm™ -- See 'Minaeco'

'Apricot China' F, mr; intr. 1996

Apricot Clementine® Min, ab, Tantau; flowers long lasting, bright apricot; growth compact, vigorous; intr. 2002

'Apricot Cottage Rose' -- See 'Poulave'

'Apricot Crème' Min, ab, 1989, Bell, Douglas & Judy; bud pointed; flowers light apricot, edges cream, reverse apricot to cream; [sport of 'Yellow Doll, Climbing']; intr. 1989

'Apricot Dawn' HT, ab, 1938, Wyant; flowers apricot, base yellow; [sport of 'Golden Dawn']

'Apricot Delicious' Min, ab, Welsh; intr. 1996

'Apricot Delight' -- See 'Attlight'

'Apricot Delight' HT, ab, Delbard; bud long bud; flowers rich, deep apricot with broad petals, dbl., slight fragrance; growth medium; intr. 1978

'Apricot Doll' -- See 'Lavdoll'

'Apricot Garland' -- See 'Horcoherent'

'Apricot Gem' F, ab, Delbard-Chabert; flowers dbl.; intr. 1978

'Apricot Glow' LCl, ab, 1936, Brownell; flowers apricot, turning apricot-pink, 7 cm., dbl., borne in large trusses, intense fragrance; non-recurrent; foliage very glossy; numerous prickles; long stems; very vigorous (20 ft.) growth; PP200;

[('Emily Gray' × 'Dr. W. Van Fleet') × 'Jacotte']; intr. 1936

Apricot Hit® ('Poulamb') Min, ab

'Apricot Ice' F, ab, Dickson; flowers light pastel apricot, darker in center, dbl., borne in clusters of 5 - 30, slight fragrance; growth slightly arching, bushy, vigorous, 3 ft.; intr. 2003

'Apricot Impressionist' LCl, ab, Clements, John; bud apricot bronze; flowers 4-5 in., 50 petals, moderate fragrance; recurrent; free standing (6-7 ft.) or supported (9-12 ft.) growth; PPAF; intr. 2006

'Apricot Kisses' -- See 'Geacot'

'Apricot Medinette' -- See 'Poulcot'

'Apricot Midinette' -- See 'Poulcot'

'Apricot Mikado' F, ab, Tantau; flowers blooms small to medium , borne in sprays; recurrent; stems moderate (40 - 60 cm.); Florist rose

'Apricot Mist' -- See 'Socspo'

Apricot Mist™ -- See 'Savamist'

'Apricot Moon' F, ab, Lowery/Eisen; flowers deep apricot-yellow, very dbl., intense anise, myrrh fragrance; [sport of 'Moonsprite']; intr. 1995

Apricot Multirosa® S, ab, J&P; low, spreading, groundcover growth

'Apricot Nectar' F, ab, 1965, Boerner; bud ovoid; flowers pink-apricot, base golden, 4-4½ in., dbl., cupped, intense fruity fragrance; foliage glossy, dark; vigorous, bushy growth; PP2594; [seedling × 'Spartan']; intr. 1965

'Apricot Nectar, Climbing' Cl F, ab

'Apricot Nectar - Dawson's Selection' HT, ab, Dawson; larger form of Apricot Nectar; intr. 2002

'Apricot Panarosa' S, ab, Kordes; intr. 2004

'Apricot Parfait' -- See 'Aussaucer'

'Apricot Parfait' HT, ab, 1976, Warriner, William A.; bud ovoid; flowers apricot-pink blend, 4 in., 53 petals, high-centered, slight fragrance; foliage large, dark; upright growth; [seedling × 'South Seas']

Apricot Passion™ -- See 'Jacpinap'

'Apricot Perfection' -- See 'Cleperf'

'Apricot Prince' -- See 'Gingersnap'

'Apricot Profusion' F, ab, Kordes; bud slender, pointed, apricot colored; flowers deep cream-apricot, semi-dbl., open, borne in clusters; continuous bloom; foliage glossy; growth short, spreading, densely branched

'Apricot Queen' HT, ab, 1940, Howard, F.H.; bud pointed; flowers salmon-pink, base apricot-orange, large, 45 petals; foliage leathery; very vigorous, bushy growth; PP464; ['Mrs J.D. Eisele' × 'Glowing Sunset']

'Apricot Queen, Climbing' Cl HT, ab, 1950, Maranda

'Apricot Queen' ('Interfrico') S, ab, Interplant; intr. 1999

'Apricot Queen Elizabeth' ('Queen Elizabeth Abricot') Gr, ab, Verschuren; flowers apricot yellow aging to buff and pale orange; intr. 1980

'Apricot Silk' ('Orange Silk') HT, ob, 1965, Gregory, C.; flowers coppery orange, double , high-centered, borne several together; foliage deep green, glossy; ['Souv de Jacques Verschuren' × unknown]

'Apricot Sky' LCl, ab, Barni; flowers yellow cream and apricot, very dbl., cupped; growth to 8-20 ft.; intr. 2004

'Apricot Spice' -- See 'Sanspic'

'Apricot Summer' -- See 'Korpapiro'

'Apricot Sunblaze' -- See 'Savamark'

Apricot Sunblaze™ -- See 'Meifruije'

'Apricot Surprise' S, ab

'Apricot Twist' -- See 'Morbrown'

'Apricot Wine' F, ab, 1980, Slack; flowers burnt apricot, 12 petals, foliage dark, glossy; low, compact growth; [Allgold® × seedling]; intr. 1978

'Apriheart' Min, ab, 1984, Hardgrove, Donald L.; bud small; flowers light apricot, center deeper, small, dbl., borne singly, intense fragrance; foliage small, medium green, semi-glossy; prickles very few; bushy growth; ['Picnic' × 'Rise 'n' Shine']; intr. 1983

Aprikola® -- See 'Kororbe'

'April' -- See 'Horsorbello'

'April' HT, dy, Schreurs; greenhouse rose; intr. 2002

'April Fool's Day' -- See 'Gregsil'

'April Hamer' HT, pb, 1983, Bell, Ronald J.; flowers shell pink with bright pink edges, large, 40 petals, high-centered; foliage dark; vigorous, upright growth; ['Mount Shasta' × 'Prima Ballerina']; intr. 1998

April in Paris™ -- See 'Jacprize'

'April Love' S, mp, Clements, John; flowers soft, sweet pink, 4-5 cm., very full, cupped, heavy fruity, myrrh fragrance; profuse bloom; foliage rich, dark green; growth spreading (4-5. × 4-5 ft.); intr. 2004

'April Moon' S, my, 1985, Buck, Dr. Griffith J.; bud small; flowers lemon yellow, 28 petals, cupped, borne 5-10 per cluster, moderate sweet fragrance; repeat bloom; foliage dark, leathery; prickles awl-like, tan; erect, short, bushy growth; hardy; ['Serendipity' × ('Tickled Pink' × 'Maytime')]; intr. 1984

'April Moore' -- See 'Liosanz'

'Aprilia' HT, dp, 1937, Cazzaniga, F. G.; bud ovoid; flowers old-rose, open, very large, dbl.; foliage leathery; vigorous, upright growth

'Aprutina' F, Borgatti, G.; intr. 1969

'Apsara' F, op, 1970, Pal, Dr. B.P.; bud ovoid; flowers salmon-pink, open, medium, semi-dbl.; foliage glossy; vigorous, upright, open growth; RULED EXTINCT 3/84 ARM; intr. 1966

'Apsara' HT, pb, 1984, Pal, Dr. B. P.; flowers flesh pink with salmon shadings, strong fragrance; foliage medium size, leathery, round; stems long, uniform; growth upright; ['Sonia' × 'Sabine']; intr. 1983

'Aptos' -- See 'Letrob'

'Aqua' HT, mp, Schreurs; intr. 2004

'Aquarelle' F, dy, 1979, Lens; bud ovoid; flowers open, 2 in., 18-25 petals, flat, moderate fruity fragrance; foliage dark; very vigorous growth; ['Gold Strike' × 'Golden Garnette']; intr. 1969

'Aquarelle' HT, yb, Tantau; intr. 2002

'Aquarelle' HT, r, Croix

'Aquarius' Gr, pb, 1970, Armstrong, D.L.; bud ovoid; flowers medium pink blend, medium, dbl., high-centered, slight fragrance; foliage large, leathery; vigorous, upright, bushy growth; PP3128; [('Charlotte Armstrong' × 'Contrast') × ('Fandango' × ('World's Fair' × 'Floradora'))]; intr. 1971

'Aquarius' HT, dp, Tantau; intr. 2002

'Aquarius' Min, rb, Burston; intr. 2004

'Aquilla Bright' HT, ob, 1988, Lea, R.F.G.; flowers medium, full, slight fragrance; foliage medium size, medium green, semi-glossy; upright growth; ['Sunblest' × 'Matador']

Aquitaine™ -- See 'Poulnoz'

'Ara Pacis' HT, w, 1955, Giacomasso; bud tubular, well formed; flowers ivory-white edged reddish-purple, very large, 50 petals; foliage glossy, bright green; long stems; vigorous growth; ['Peace' × 'Marguerite Chambard']

'Arabella' HT, dp, 1918, Schilling/Tantau; flowers crimson-pink, pointed, large, full, moderate fragrance; vigorous growth; [sport of 'Mme Caroline Testout']

'Arabella' F, rb, Benny, David; flowers bright red with white reverse, dbl, borne in trusses

'Arabella's Rambler' lp, Scarman; intr. 2001

'Arabesque' -- See 'Interstreep'

'Arabesque' F, lp, 1978, Sanday, John; bud pointed; flowers soft pink, 3 in., 10 petals; vigorous growth; [('Gavotte' × 'Tropicana') × 'Tropicana']

'Arabesque' F, Christensen; intr. 1988

Arabia® F, ob, Tantau; intr. 1986

Arabia® HT, r, Tantau; possibly synonymous with 'Tanibara'; intr. 1999

'Arabian Nights' F, op, 1963, McGredy, Sam IV; flowers light salmon-orange, well-formed, 4½ in., 25 petals; vigorous growth; ['Spartan' × 'Beauté']; intr. 1963

'Araby' Gr, lp, 1973, Thomson; bud long, pointed; flowers light orchid-pink, center white, open, large, dbl.; foliage large, glossy, dark, leathery; vigorous, upright growth; ['Honey Chile' × 'Rose Merk']

'Araceli Leyva' HT, op, 1940, Dot, Pedro; bud long, pointed; flowers rose-salmon, large, dbl., cupped; foliage leathery; strong stems; vigorous, upright growth; ['Mme Butterfly' × 'Comtesse Vandal']

'Arahina' Min, dy; intr. 2001

'Arakan' F, lp, 1968, Harkness; flowers dbl., borne in trusses; ['Pink Parfait' × 'Ivory Fashion']

'Aramis' F, dr, Laperrière; flowers bright scarlet, 3 in., semi-dbl., borne in clusters of 7-8; foliage dark; very bushy, compact growth; ['Bel Ami' × ('Java' × 'Alain')]

'Aramis' HGal, pb, 1845, Vibert; flowers white striped with deep rose pink, medium, full, cupped

'Aramis' B, dp, Boyau; flowers dark pink, shaded light pink, medium, dbl.; intr. 1849

'Arashiyama' ('Kyoto 1200', 'YKH 501') HT, w, 1997, Kameyama, Yasushi; flowers large, 41 petals; foliage medium size, medium green, glossy; some prickles; medium (1-2m.) growth; ['Garden Party' × Pristine®]

'Aratama' ('Uncut Gem') HT, yb, Takahashi, Takeshi; bud pointed; flowers apricot-yellow, edged scarlet, lighter reverse, petals reflexed, 6 in., 30 petals, high-centered, slight fragrance; foliage glossy, light green, with long, narrow leaflets; stems slender; growth upright; ['Kordes' Perfecta' × ('Garden Party' × 'Christian Dior')]; intr. 1976

'Aravali Princess' HT, op, Pal, Dr. B.P.; intr. 1987

'Arbelle' -- See 'Gaurama'

'ARC Angel' -- See 'Fryorst'

'Arc de Triomphe' -- See 'Jacale'

'Arc de Triomphe' HT, yb, 1955, Buyl Frères; bud globular; flowers yellow-copper, large, dbl., moderate fragrance; foliage glossy, olive-green; upright growth; RULED EXTINCT 1/86

'Arc-en-Ciel' F, pb, 1961, Delforge; flowers rich yellow to salmon-pink, carmine and crimson, 65-70 petals, borne in tight clusters; foliage dark; growth moderate; ['Masquerade'] × 'Maria Delforge']

'Arcade' Min, mr, Spooner, Raymond A.; intr. 1996

'Arcadia' HWich, dr, 1913, Walsh; flowers crimson-scarlet, 3 cm., dbl., rosette, borne in small clusters; very vigorous growth

'Arcadia' HT, rb, 1938, Gaujard; bud ovoid; flowers reddish-copper, very large, dbl.; foliage glossy; long stems; vigorous growth

'Arcadia' F, mp, Noack; intr. 2004

'Arcadian' -- See 'Macnewye'

'Arcanto' -- See 'Bararc'

'Arcanum' -- See 'Tuckarc'

'Arcata Light Yellow Wichurana' -- See 'Weisse New Dawn'

'Arc-en-Ciel' HT, rb, Teranishi; flowers striped; intr. 2006

'Arch. Reventós' HT, ab, 1935, Leenders, M.; bud ovoid, apricot; flowers cream-yellow, large, dbl.; foliage glossy, dark; vigorous, bushy growth

'Arch. Reventós, Climbing' Cl HT, Leenders, M.

'Archange' LCl, mr; intr. 2004

'Archangel' S, lp, 1980, Hawker, U.; flowers delicate pink, frilled, large, 9-10 petals, slight fragrance; foliage light green; tall growth; ['Little Darling' × 'Gypsy Moth']

'Archbishop Desmond Tutu' S, mr, Kordes; bud pointed; flowers sparkling reed, double, globular; recurrent; foliage glossy; loosely branched, neat proportions, medium growth; intr. 2008

'Archduchess Charlotte' Ch, dp, 1976, Earing, F.E.; bud pointed; flowers intense deep solid pink, 2½-3 in., 76 petals, cupped, moderate fragrance; profuse bloom early summer; foliage glossy, smooth; climbing growth; [sport of 'Archduke Charles']; intr. 1975

'Archduke Charles' ('Archiduc Charles') Ch, rb, before 1837, Laffay, M.; flowers rose with paler edges, aging to rich crimson, dbl.; moderate growth

'Archévêque' -- See 'La Provence'

'Archiduc Charles' -- See 'Belle Hélène'

'Archiduc Charles' -- See 'Archduke Charles'

'Archiduc Joseph' T, pb, 1892, Nabonnand, G.; flowers purplish pink, center flesh-pink; vigorous growth; ['Mme Lombard' × unknown]

'Archiduchesse Elisabeth d'Autriche' HP, mp, 1881, Moreau et Robert; flowers rose-pink, dbl.

'Archiduchesse Elisabeth-Marie' Pol, ly, 1898, Soupert & Notting; flowers canary-yellow fading white, imbricated, medium, dbl.; vigorous growth; ['Mignonette' × 'Luciole']

'Archiduchesse Maria Immaculata' T, mr, 1887, Soupert & Notting

'Archiduchesse Marie-Dorothée Amélie' -- See 'Erzherzogin Marie Dorothea'

'Archiduchesse Marie Marguerite' HT, dp, 1889, Balogh; flowers large, full; ['Général Jacqueminot' × 'Mme Falcot']

'Archiduchesse Thérèse-Isabelle' T, w, 1834, Barbot; flowers white, tinted yellow at center, large, full

'Archie Gray' HT, dr, 1920, Dickson, H.; flowers deep crimson, shaded scarlet, dbl.

'Archimède' T, mp, Robert; flowers pink, shaded chamois, center darker, very large, full, globular; intr. 1855

'Archimède' HP, w, 1852, Laffay; flowers light lilac-white, very large, full, cupped

'Arctic Emerald' S, w, 1982, James, John; bud globular, pointed; flowers white, with yellow-green center, small to medium, 12 petals, borne 1-5 per cluster; repeat bloom; foliage small, light green; low, compact growth; ['Thérèse Bugnet' × Europeana®]; intr. 1978

'Arctic Flame' HT, mr, 1957, Brownell; bud medium, pointed; flowers bright crimson red, 5 in., 50-60 petals, high-centered, borne singly and in small clusters, moderate tea fragrance; free-flowering; foliage medium size, dark green; prickles several; stems long, stiff; vigorous (4 ft.), bushy growth; winter hardy ; PP1432; [('Queen o' the Lakes' × 'Pink Princess') × 'Mirandy']; intr. 1956

'Arctic Glow' S, rb, 1982, James, John; bud globular, pointed; flowers scarlet shading to white center, large, 28 petals, borne singly; repeat bloom; foliage dark, rough; compact growth; ['Pike's Peak' × 'Show Girl']; intr. 1978

'Arctic Pink' F, lp, 1966, Smith, E.; flowers pink fading lighter, 3 in., cupped, borne in trusses; vigorous growth; [sport of 'Dearest']

Arctic Snow™ -- See 'Minlco'

'Arctic Sunrise' -- See 'Bararcsun'

'Arctica' HT, w, Tantau; intr. 2006

'Ardarkness' ('Nightmoss') M, m, 2001, Barden, Paul; flowers deep royal purple, medium purple reverse, yellow stamens, large, full, flat, borne in small clusters, intense earthy, smoky rose scent fragrance; spring only; foliage medium size, dark green, matte; prickles ¼ in., straight, needle-shaped, brown; growth spreading, arching, medium (5 ft.); specimen, back of border; ['Nuits de Young' × 'Tuscany Superb']; intr. 2001

'Ardelle' HT, w, 1955, Eddie, H.M.; bud long, pointed; flowers creamy white, 5 in., 72 petals, high-centered, moderate fragrance; foliage glossy; very vigorous, compact growth; PP2042; ['Mrs Charles Lamplough' × 'Peace']

'Ardellen' ('Ellen Tofflemire') HGal, m, 2001, Barden, Paul; flowers mauve/purple blend, 3-3½ in., very full, borne in small clusters, moderate fragrance; early summer; foliage medium size, medium green (bright green when young), matte, crinkled; prickles ¼ in., straight, brown, moderate; growth upright, short (3-4 ft.); hedging, specimen; ['Tuscany Superb' × 'Othello']

'Ardennes' -- See 'Interpeel'

'Ardente' Cl F, op, Moreira da Silva; flowers salmon and orange; [seedling × 'Alain']

'Ardestiny' ('Golden Buddha') HBc, ob, 2005, Barden, Paul; flowers gold-orange, 3½ in., very full, borne in small clusters, intense fruity fragrance; generous rebloom in big flushes; foliage medium size, dark green, glossy; prickles ½ in., straight, green-tan, moderate; growth very compact, dense, short (2½ ft.); small shrub, containers; [June Laver™ × 'Out of Yesteryear']; intr. 2006

'Ardfang' ('Won Fang Yon') T, or, 2007, Barden, Paul; flowers light red/coral, reverse coral/pink, darkening to red in sunlight, 3½ in., very full, borne in small clusters; foliage medium, medium green, semi-glossy; prickles ½ in., curved, brown, few; growth bushy, somewhat V-shaped, tall (4-7 ft.); specimen, cutting; may not be winter-hardy; ['Avandel' × 'Mons. Tillier']; intr. 2008

'Ardfara' ('Fara Shimbo', 'Nightmoss #1') M, m, 2007, Barden, Paul; flowers deep purple, reverse medium purple, 2½-3 in., semi-dbl., borne in small clusters; spring-blooming; foliage medium size, dark green, matte; prickles ¼ in., straight, brown, numerous; growth bushy, suckering, medium (3-5 ft.); very hardy; ['Nuits de Young' × 'Tuscany Superb']; intr. 2003

'Ardgoldeneyes' ('Marianne') HGal, ab,

2004, Barden, Paul; flowers apricot/ gold, reverse pale apricot, 3½ in., very full, borne in small clusters, intense fragrance; spring-blooming, non-recurrent; foliage medium size, dark green, glossy; prickles ½ in., curved; growth upright, arching, tall (5-7 ft.); specimen, small climber; ['Duchesse de Montebello' × Abraham Darby®]; intr. 2005

'Ardjeri' ('Jeri Jennings') HMsk, yb, 2007, Barden, Paul; flowers yellow-orange, reverse paler yellow-orange, 1¾ in., very full, borne in large clusters; foliage medium size, medium green, semi-glossy; prickles ¼ in., curved, tan, few; bushy, arching growth habit, medium (4-7 ft.); specimen, containers; [Joycie™ × Trier®]; intr. 2007

'Ardjoy' ('Allegra') HGal, mp, 2003, Barden, Paul; flowers medium pink, reverse light pink, 3½-4 in., very full, borne in small clusters, intense fragrance; once blooming, for four to six weeks in Spring; foliage large, dark green, matte; prickles ¼ to ½ in., curved, reddish, few; bushy, arching growth, medium (5-6 ft.); ['Duchesse de Montebello' × 'St Swithun']; intr. 2004

'Ardkernel' ('Mel Hulse') M, m, 2001, Barden, Paul; bud moderately mossed and scented of balsam; flowers dark crimson/mauve, medium crimson/ magenta reverse, large, full, borne in large clusters, slight fragrance; medium size, medium green, young leaves bright green, semi-glossy; prickles ¼ - ½ in., straight, red and straw color, numerous; growth bushy, medium (2-3 ft tall × 2-3 ft. wide); specimen, containers; ['Scarlet Moss' × The Prince™]

'Ardlinds' ('Lindsay's Rose') Min, w, 2003, Barden, Paul; flowers white, light yellow, reverse white, light yellow, 1½ in., very full, borne in large clusters; foliage medium size, dark green, semi-glossy; prickles 1/3 in., straight, reddish, moderate; growth bushy, medium (12-18 in.); exhibition, cutting, specimen; [('Poker Chip' × 'Poker Chip') × Loving Touch™]; intr. 2002

'Ardluna' ('Umbra') HGal, m, 2008, Barden, Paul; flowers lavender/deep purple, reverse paler lavender, 4 in., very full, borne in small clusters; non-remontant; foliage medium, dark green, semi-glossy; prickles 6-7 mm., slightly curved, tan, numerous; growth upright, tall (5-7 ft.); small climber; ['Tuscany Superb' × 'William Lobb']; intr. 2008

'Ardmarbré' ('Song of the Stars') HGal, m, 2004, Barden, Paul; flowers dark purple with paler spots, reverse light mauve, 3 in., 30 petals, shallow cup, borne in small clusters, moderate fragrance; spring-blooming, non-recurrent; foliage small, dark green, matte; prickles ¼ in., straight; growth bushy, some suckering, medium (4-5 ft.); specimen, border shrub; ['Alain Blanchard' × 'Alain Blanchard']; intr. 2005

'Ardmarcrest' ('Crested Damask') D, mp, 2004, Barden, Paul; flowers medium warm pink, reverse darker pink, 3½ in., very full, borne in small clusters, intense fragrance; late spring bloom; foliage medium size, medium green, semi-glossy, blackspot-resistant; prickles ½ in., curved, brown-red; upright, arching growth, tall (5-7 ft.); specimen; ['Marbrée' × 'Crested Jewel']; intr. 2005

'Ardmizkernel' ('Loan Hulse') M, dr, 2003, Barden, Paul; buds heavily mossed; flowers dark crimson-red, reverse medium crimson-red, 3 in., dbl., borne in small clusters; foliage medium size, dark green, semi-glossy; prickles 3/8 in., straight, some hooked, tan and green, numerous; growth upright, medium (3-4 ft.); feature shrub, back of border; ['Scarlet Moss' × The Prince™]

'Ardnan' ('Hettie') LCl, w, 2004, Barden, Paul; flowers white, soft amber, reverse white, cream, 3½ in., very full, borne in large clusters, moderate green apple fragrance; remontant; foliage medium size, dark green, semi-glossy; prickles ½ in., curved, brown, moderate; lax, arching growth, medium (6-8 ft.); small climber, shrub; ['Bonica 82' × Abraham Darby®]; intr. 2004

'Ardoisée' -- See 'Busard Triomphant'

'Ardoisée de Lyon' HP, m, 1858, Damaizin; flowers violet-rose, very large, full, quartered; foliage dark green; vigorous growth

'Ardoliva' ('Barbara Oliva') M, m, 2004, Barden, Paul; flowers violet-purple blend, reverse paler violet, 4 in., very full, borne in small clusters, intense fragrance; spring-blooming only; foliage medium size, dark green, matte; prickles ¼ in., mostly straight; growth bushy, arching canes when mature, medium (4-7 ft.); borders; ['unidentified centifolia/moss' × 'self']; intr. 2005

'Ardolly' ('Dolly's Forever Rose') S, rb, 2006, Barden, Paul; bud slightly mossy; flowers vermilion-red, reverse medium yellow, 2½-3 in., dbl., borne in small clusters; foliage medium size, dark green, glossy; prickles ¼ in., slightly curved, brown, numerous; growth bushy, medium (3-4 ft.); specimen, borders, containers; [(('Little Darling' × 'Lemon Delight') × 'Angel Face') × 'Scarlet Moss']; intr. 2007

'Ardon' HWich, mp, 1925, Turbat; flowers bright Neyron rose, stained white, 5-6 cm., very full, borne in pyramidal clusters of 30-40; foliage small, glossy; nearly thornless

'Ardore' HT, mr, 1974, Calvino; bud ovoid, globular; flowers orient red, large, dbl., cupped, moderate fragrance; foliage large, dark, leathery; very vigorous, upright, bushy growth; PP2814; [seedling × 'Ninfa']

'Ardorisha' ('Oshun') S, ab, 2004, Barden, Paul; flowers apricot-orange, reverse lighter apricot, 4 in., very full, borne in small clusters, intense rose and citrus fragrance; foliage medium size, dark green, glossy, very disease-resistant; prickles ½ in., hooked, brown, moderate; growth bushy, medium (4 to 7 ft.); specimen, middle border, small climber; [Abraham Darby® × Abraham Darby®]; holds its color well in hot weather; intr. 2004

'Ardour' ('Joyce Barden') S, ly, 1999, Barden, Paul; flowers 4 in., full, borne in small clusters, intense fragrance; foliage medium size, dark green, dull, light green when new; moderate, outer shoots mostly thornless; upright, spreading, medium (5-6 ft.) growth; ['Sweet Juliet' × 'Souv de la Malmaison']

'Ardraco' ('Dragon's Blood') S, r, 2005, Barden, Paul; flowers deep orange/ purple, reverse Chinese red, 3½ in., dbl., borne in small clusters; foliage medium size, dark green, semi-glossy, new growth deep plum; prickles moderate, 1/3 in., hooked, deep red; growth bushy, arching canes with age, medium (5 × 5 ft.); specimen, borders; [(('Little Darling' × 'Yellow Magic') × 'Grandmother's Hat') × 'Brown Velvet']; intr. 2007

'Ardresden' ('Connie Lohn') Min, lp, 2003, Barden, Paul; buds mossed; flowers very small, 1 in., dbl., borne in large clusters; foliage small, medium green, semi-glossy; prickles 1/8 to ¼ in., straight, mossy; growth compact, short (12 in.); specimen, containers, borders; ['Dresden Doll' × 'Dresden Doll']; intr. 2003

'Ards Beauty' -- See 'Dicjoy'

'Ards Pillar' HT, mr, 1903, Dickson, A.; flowers velvety crimson, large, semi-dbl., cupped

'Ards Rambler' Cl HT, or, 1908, Dickson, A.; flowers orange-red, dbl., intense fragrance

'Ards Rover' Cl HP, dr, 1898, Dickson, A.; flowers crimson, shaded maroon, large, dbl.; sometimes recurrent bloom; pillar growth

'Ardshine' ('October Moon') F, ab, 2005, Barden, Paul; flowers apricot-orange, reverse lighter apricot, 3 in., very full, borne in small clusters; foliage medium size, medium green, semi-glossy; prickles ½ in., curved, green/tan, moderate; growth bushy, somewhat upright but very full, medium (3-4 ft.); ['Rise 'N' Shine' × 'It's Showtime']; intr. 2006

'Ardspell74' ('Incantation') S, pb, 2007, Barden, Paul; flowers deep raspberry pink, reverse white, 3 in., semi-dbl., borne in large clusters, moderate pleasant, clove-like fragrance; foliage medium, dark green, glossy, disease-resistant; prickles ¼ in., curved, green/ brown, few; growth bushy, wider than tall, medium (3-4 ft.); specimen, containers; ['Condoleezza' × 'Scarlet Moss']; prolific bloom; intr. 2008

'Ardtuscoth' ('Gallicandy') HGal, mp, 2003, Barden, Paul; flowers medium pink, reverse darker pink, 3-3½ in., full, borne in small clusters, moderate fragrance; Spring blooming only, over a three to six week period; foliage medium size, medium green, Semi-glossy; prickles ¼-½ in., straight, brownish, moderate; growth spreading, thicket-forming, medium (5 ft.), somewhat wider; ['Tuscany Superb' × 'Othello']; intr. 2004

'Ardwesternstar' ('Lang Havey', 'Unconditional Love') Min, dr, 2003, Barden, Paul; bud mossy, balsam/lemon scented; flowers deep red, reverse medium red, 1½ in., very full, borne in large clusters; foliage medium size, medium green, glossy; prickles moderate, ¼ in., straight, reddish; growth upright, tall (up to 24 in.); bedding, pots; ['Sequoia Ruby' × 'Scarlet Moss']; intr. 2004

'Ardyes' ('Oui') Min, dr, 2005, Barden, Paul; flowers deep red, reverse medium pink-red, ½ in., semi-dbl., borne in small clusters, no fragrance; foliage small, dark green, semi-glossy; prickles 1/16 in., straight; growth compact, very bushy, short, 8 in; specimen, containers; ['Oakington Ruby' × 'Little Chief']; intr. 2006

'Arejay' -- See 'Kirrad'

'Arena 91' HT, dp, Dey, S. C.; flowers large, full, well formed; intr. 1991

'Arena 92' HT, dp, Dey, S. C.; flowers very large, well formed

'Arena 93' F, yb, Dey, S.C.; flowers deep yellow changing to pink and deepening to red, borne in well-placed clusters; intr. 1993

'Arena 94' F, mr, Dey, S. C.; flowers velvety red, borne in large clusters; growth vigorous; intr. 1994

'Arena 95' HT, w, Dey, S. C.; flowers white with petal edges purple, large, well formed; intr. 1995

'Arena's Dream' F, ly, Kordes; flowers medium, 25-30 petals, high-centered, foliage very disease-resistant; growth tall, bushy; PP11355; [sport of 'Dream']; intr. 1998

'Arend Herwig' ('A. J. Herwig') F, ob, 1966, Buisman, G. A. H.; bud ovoid; flowers orange-red, medium, dbl.; foliage dark; ['Korona' × Heureux Anniversaire®]

'Arethusa' Ch, yb, 1903, Paul, W.; flowers yellow, tinted apricot, borne in small clusters, moderate fresh fragrance; foliage glossy, somewhat sparse; growth medium (3 × 3 ft.)

'Argental' HT, w, Croix

'Argentée' ('À Bouquets', 'Elongata') D, lp, before 1811; flowers satiny flesh pink, medium, borne in clusters of 5-20; foliage oval, pointed; numerous prickles

'Argentina' F, ab, 1941, Leenders, M.; flowers reddish-apricot, semi-dbl.; ['Mev. Nathalie Nypels' × 'Orange Glory']

'Argentine Cramon' -- See 'Mlle Argentine Cramon'

'Argosy' HT, op, 1938, Clark, A.; flowers salmon, flushed pink, dbl.; long stems; ['Souv. de Gustave Prat' × seedling]

'Argovia' HT, pb, Huber; flowers strong pink with yellow in center; intr. 1998

'Argyle' HT, w, 1921, Dobbie; flowers creamy yellow to pure white, large, full; vigorous growth; ['Mme Caroline Testout' × 'Marquise de Sinéty']

'Argyll' HT, ly, 1918, Dobbie; flowers light yellow, fading to white, large, full; ['Mme Caroline Testout' × 'Marquise de Sinéty']

'Aria' F, op, 1957, deRuiter; flowers salmon shaded pink, large, dbl.; bushy growth; ['Duchess of Rutland' × 'Fashion']

'Ariadne' -- See 'Ariane'

'Ariadne' Ch, rb, 1918, Paul, W.; flowers bright crimson, center shaded yellow

'Ariake' ('Dawn') HT, w, 1978, Teranishi, K.; bud globular; flowers ivory, 5 in., 47-50 petals, cupped, moderate fragrance; foliage light green; vigorous, upright growth; [('Lady X' × 'Garden Party') × seedling]; intr. 1976

'Ariana d'Algier' -- See 'Complicata'

'Ariane' A, w, 1818, Vibert; not the same as Vibert's HGal Ariane

'Ariane' ('Adriadne', 'Ariadne') HGal, m, Vibert; flowers light purple-pink, medium, full; not the same as Vibert's Alba Ariane; intr. 1818

'Ariane de Vibert' HGal, dp, about 1835, Vibert; flowers very large, very full; perhaps synonymous with Ariadne

Arianna® HT, pb, 1968, Meilland, Louisette; flowers carmine-rose suffused coral, large, 35 petals, high-centered, slight fragrance; foliage dark, leathery; vigorous, upright, open growth; ['Charlotte Armstrong' × ('Peace' × 'Michèle Meilland')]

'Arianna' HT, w, Meilland

'Aribau' HT, mr, 1936, Dot, Pedro; bud long, pointed; flowers brilliant red, large, dbl.; foliage glossy; long stems; very vigorous growth; ['Kitchener of Khartoum' × 'Director Rubió']

'Aridhra' HT, pb, K & S; flowers cream to pale pink, full, well shaped; [sport of 'Raja Surendra Singh of Nalagarh']; intr. 2003

'Ariel' HT, my, Bees; flowers golden yellow, streaked crimson, large, dbl., globular, moderate fragrance; foliage dark; long stems; vigorous, bushy growth; ['Mme Edouard Herriot' × 'Natalie Boettner']; intr. 1921

'Ariel' Cl T, pb, 1910, Paul; flowers coppery golden yellow over pink

'Arielle' ('Damas Monstrueux') P, lp, 1845, Vibert; flowers lilac-pink, small, full; sometimes classed as HP

Arielle® (Cosima®) HT, mp, Tantau; intr. 2001

Arielle Dombasle® LCl, yb, Meilland; flowers salmon yellow, reverse yellow, 3 in., semi-dbl.; intr. 1991

'Aries' F, mr, Burston; intr. 2004

Arifa® F, rb, Tantau; florist rose

'Arioso' -- See 'Meimucas'

'Arioso' -- See 'Meihud'

'Ariste' HT, my, Jones; bud very pointed, deep yellow; flowers light yellow, medium, 5 petals, moderate fragrance; foliage dark, leathery; vigorous, bushy growth; ['Joanna Hill' × 'Souv. de Mme Boullet']; intr. 1960

'Aristide' -- See 'Mlle Aristide'

'Aristide' HSpn, mp, from Scotland

'Aristide Briand' HWich, m, 1928, Penny; flowers mauve-pink, reverse lighter, medium, semi-dbl., borne in clusters of 10-15, moderate fragrance; some repeat; ['Yseult Guillot' × unknown]

'Aristide Dupuy' HP, dp, 1866, Trouillard or Touvais; flowers slatey violet bordered bright pink, large, dbl.

'Aristobule' M, dp, 1849, Foulard; flowers dark rose with touches of clear rose, dbl.

Aristocrat™ -- See 'Savarist'

'Aristocrat' HT, w, Chakraborty, Dr. K.; flowers creamy white with deep pink at petal edges, well-formed; very vigorous growth; intr. 2003

'Aristocrat' HT, pb, 1949, Holmes, M.A.; bud long, pointed; flowers clear light pink, reverse darker, 4½-5 in., 28-35 petals, high-centered, moderate fragrance; foliage leathery, dark; very vigorous, upright growth; PP903; [sport of 'Pink Delight']

'Aristote' HGal, pb; a variety of R. francofurtana

'Arizona' ('Tocade') Gr, ob, 1974, Weeks; bud urn-shaped; flowers golden bronze to orangy yellow, medium, 25-30 petals, high-centered, borne singly, intense sweet fragrance; foliage glossy, dark, leathery; long, cutting length stems; vigorous, upright, bushy growth; PP3568; [(('Fred Howard' × 'Golden Scepter') × 'Golden Rapture') × (('Fred Howard' × 'Golden Scepter') × 'Golden Rapture')]; intr. 1975

'Arizona Sunset' Min, yb, 1985, Jolly, Nelson F.; flowers light yellow, flushed orange-red, medium, 20 petals, cupped; foliage small, medium green, semi-glossy; prickles slanted downward; bushy, spreading growth; PP6559; [('Orange Sweetheart' × 'Zinger') × Party Girl™]

'Arjun' HT, or, 1981, Division of Vegetable Crops and Floriculture; bud long, pointed; flowers 35 petals, cupped, borne singly or 8 per cluster, slight fragrance; foliage large, smooth; prickles hooked; tall, upright growth; ['Blithe Spirit' × 'Montezuma']; intr. 1980

'Arkansas' HT, or, 1980, Weeks; bud ovoid, pointed; flowers paprika red-orange, 48 petals, urn-shaped, borne singly or 2-4 per cluster, slight spicy fragrance; foliage leathery; prickles long, oval-based, hooked downward; upright, vigorous growth; PP4700; [seedling × seedling]

'Arkansas Sunshine' F, my, 1965, Jones; flowers golden yellow, 30 petals, cupped, borne in clusters; foliage dark, leathery;

vigorous, bushy growth; ['Goldilocks' × seedling]; intr. 1962

'Arkavathi' F, dp, Kasturi; intr. 1971

'Arkle' HT, or, 1978, Hughes Roses; bud cupped; flowers dark tangerine, 4 in., 45-50 petals, cupped, intense fragrance; foliage glossy; vigorous growth; [sport of 'Whisky Mac']

'Arlene Francis' HT, my, 1958, Boerner; bud long, pointed; flowers golden buttery yellow, 5 in., 25-30 petals, high-centered, borne mostly singly, intense sweet licorice fragrance; foliage dark, glossy; vigorous growth, upright, medium sized; PP1684; [('Eclipse' × unknown) × 'Golden Scepter']; intr. 1957

'Arlequin' -- See 'Pourpre Marbrée'

'Arlequin' HGal, rb, before 1821, Vibert; flowers crimson marbled with pink, medium, full

Arlequin® HT, ob, Meilland; flowers yellow ocher, suffused orange , 40 petals, cupped to flat, slight fragrance; strong, moderate growth; intr. 2007

'Arlequin' HT, ob, Gaujard; flowers orange-yellow and coppery red, very large, dbl., globular, moderate fragrance; foliage dark, glossy; bushy growth; intr. 1945

'Arlequin' HGal, dr, Paillard; flowers red with violet-purple, marbled crimson, medium, full; intr. 1837

'Arlequin' HP, rb, Taillandier; intr. 1872

'Arles' -- See 'Fernand Arles'

'Arles Dufour' HP, m, 1863, Liabaud

'Arlette' -- See 'Poulske'

'Arm-Roy Beauty' HT, mr, 1945, Armacost & Royston; very vigorous, tall growth; PP647; [sport of 'Better Times']

Armada® -- See 'Haruseful'

'Armagh' HT, ab, 1950, McGredy, Sam IV; flowers creamy pink, apricot and buff, pointed, large, 49 petals; foliage dark; free growth; ['Sam McGredy' × 'Admiration']

Armani™ ('Armani Hit') S, mp, Poulsen; flowers medium pink, 8-10 cm., semi-dbl., no fragrance; foliage dark; growth bushy, 20-40 cm.; intr. 2005

'Armani Hit' -- See 'Poulpah031(N)'

'Armaq' Gr, pb, 1970, Armstrong, D.L.; bud ovoid; intr. 1971

'Arménie' HT, ab, 1936, Buatois; bud purple-garnet; flowers blood-red, shaded, large, very dbl.; very vigorous, bushy growth; ['Rhea Reid' × 'Yves Druhen']

'Armide' P, mp, Vibert; flowers pink with salmon reflections, large, full, cupped; intr. 1847

'Armide' HSem, mp; flowers medium, dbl.; intr. before 1845

'Armide' N, mp, Laffay; flowers pink, aging to lilac, medium, lightly dbl.; intr. before 1836

'Armide' A, lp, 1818, Vibert; flowers flesh with pale edges, medium, very dbl., borne in clusters, moderate fragrance; non-recurrent; foliage acutely serrated, veined, medium green; growth bushy, shrubby, 3 ft.; winter hardy, tolerates part shade

'Armide' HP, mp, Margottin; intr. 1858

'Armilla' -- See 'Cherry-Vanilla'

'Arminda' HT, op, 1956, Camprubi, C.; bud ovoid; flowers bright pink tinted coral, large, very dbl., globular; foliage glossy; strong stems; vigorous growth; ['Peace' × 'Symphonie']

'Armlu' Gr, lp, 1966, Armstrong, D.L. & Swim, H. C.; bud long, pointed

'Armma' HT, w, 1965, Armstrong, D.L. & Swim, H. C.

'Armolo' HT, my, 1971, Armstrong, D.L.; bud long, pointed

'Armonia' HT, mr, 1951, Cazzaniga, F. G.; bud long, pointed; flowers bright red, dbl., high-centered; foliage dark, leathery; long stems; very vigorous, upright growth

Armorique™ -- See 'Poulaps'

'Armosa' -- See 'Hermosa'

'Armoton' -- See 'San Antonio'

Arnaud Delbard® -- See 'Deltep'

'Arndt' LCl, lp, 1913, Lambert, P.; bud yellowish red; flowers pale salmony pink to medium, 4-5 cm., semi-dbl. to dbl., borne in clusters of 10-20; recurrent bloom; foliage dark; half-climbing growth; ['Hélène' × 'Gustav Grünewald']

'Arnelda Mae' Min, lp, 1983, Pencil, Paul S.; bud small; flowers small, 30 petals, high-centered, borne singly and in clusters up to 7; foliage small, light green, matte; bushy growth; ['Sheri Anne' × seedling]

'Arnhem Glory' HT, dr, 1959, Verschuren; flowers deep velvety red, large; vigorous growth

'Arnold Greensitt' -- See 'Nostarn'

'Arnold Rose' ('Arnoldiana', R. × arnoldiana) HRg, mr, 1914, Dawson; flowers reddish-purple, semi-dbl.; some recurrent bloom; vigorous growth; [R. rugosa × 'Général Jacqueminot']

'Arnoldiana' -- See 'Arnold Rose'

'Aroall' HT, my, 1976, Armstrong, D.L.; bud ovoid, pointed, deep yellow; intr. 1977

'Aroart' HT, dr, 1982, Swim, H.C. & Christensen, J.E.; bud ovoid, pointed; intr. 1982

'Arobipy' ('Nursing Centenary', Crystalline™, 'Valerie Swane') HT, w, 1987, Christensen, Jack & Carruth, Tom; bud medium, pointed ovoid; flowers pure white, 5-5½ in., 30-35 petals, high-centered, cupped, borne usually singly, some small clusters, moderate spicy or sweet tea fragrance; recurrent; foliage medium size, medium green, semi-glossy; prickles normal, long, hooked downward, light green-tan; upright, bushy, tall growth; hips globose, large, orange; PP6714; [Bridal Pink™ × (Blue Nile® × ('Ivory Tower' × 'Angel Face'))]; intr. 1986

'Aroblaveet' ('Centenary College') HT, dr, 1983, Christensen, Jack E.; flowers deep red, large, 35 petals, intense fragrance; foliage large, medium green, matte; vigorous, upright, tall growth; ['Angel Face' × 'Typhoo Tea']; intr. 1982

'Arobri' Min, ab, 1979, Christensen, Jack E.; bud ovoid, pointed; intr. 1978

'Arobrisp' ('Tuxedo') HT, dr, 1989, Christensen, Jack E.; bud ovoid; flowers large, 45 petals, urn-shaped, borne singly; foliage medium size, medium green, semi-glossy; prickles broad, hooked downward, red-brown; upright growth; ['Portland Trailblazer' × 'Olympiad']; intr. 1988

'Arocad' (Brandy™) HT, ab, 1981, Swim, H.C. & Christensen, J.E.; bud long, pointed; flowers deep apricot, 5 in., 25-30 petals, high-centered, borne mostly singly, slight tea fragrance; foliage large, dark green; prickles straight; vigorous, medium growth; PP5168; ['First Prize' × 'Dr. A. J. Verhage']

'Arocant' ('Spring Fever') HT, ob, 1985, Christensen, Jack E.; flowers apricot, pink and orange blend, large, 35 petals; foliage large, dark, semi-glossy; ['Gingersnap' × Brandy™]

'Arocharm' ('Young at Heart', Origami™) F, pb, 1987, Christensen, Jack & Carruth, Tom; flowers clear, soft pink, outstanding form, medium, 25 petals, high-centered, borne usually singly, moderate spicy fragrance; foliage medium size, medium green, semi-glossy; prickles normal, light green-tan; upright, bushy, medium growth; ['Coquette' × 'Zorina']; intr. 1986

'Arocher' (Mon Cheri™) HT, rb, 1981, Christensen, Jack E.; bud ovoid, pointed; flowers medium pink, suffusing to near yellow at base, aging to dark, 38 petals, slight spicy fragrance; foliage semi-glossy, medium green; prickles short; upright, medium growth; PP5156; [('White Satin' × 'Bewitched') × Double Delight™ ®]

'Aroclidd' ('Grimpant Double Delight', Double Delight, Climbing®) Cl HT, rb, 1983, Christensen, Jack E.; flowers creamy white, broadly edged with crimson, 14-16 cm., borne mostly on second year wood, intense fragrance; intermittent flowering after spring flush; strong (8-10 ft.) growth; PP5155; [sport of 'Double Delight']; intr. 1985

'Arocomu' (Patsy Cline™) HT, m, 1983, Christensen, Jack E.; flowers light lavender, petals edged ruby lavender, large, 35 petals, high-centered, intense fragrance; foliage medium size, dark, matte; upright, bushy growth; PP5556; ['Angel Face' × Double Delight™ ®]

'Arocore' ('Sunset Strip', Rodeo Drive™) HT, mr, 1987, Christensen, Jack E.; flowers bright deep red, large, 32 petals, high-centered, borne usually singly; foliage medium to large, medium green, semi-glossy; prickles many attenuated, medium, reddish aging light brown; bushy, medium growth; fruit not observed; PP6813; ['Merci' × Pharaoh®];

intr. 1986

'Arocruby' ('Park Place') F, rb, Christensen, Jack E.; intr. 1987

'Aroder' HT, dr, 1972, Armstrong, D.L.

'Arodi' Min, mp, 1977, Christensen, Jack E.; bud mossy; intr. 1978

'Arodousna' ('Paris Pink', Givenchy™) HT, rb, 1986, Christensen, Jack E.; flowers pink, blushed red, reverse pink, yellow base, 30 petals, high-centered, borne in sprays, intense spicy fragrance; foliage medium size, dark; prickles medium, brown, hooked; medium, upright, bushy growth; no fruit; ['Gingersnap' × Double Delight™®]; intr. 1985

'Arofeigel' HT, lp, 1983, Feigel, John R.; intr. 1982

'Arofiric' (Fire 'n' Ice™) F, rb, 1987, Christensen, Jack & Carruth, Tom; flowers red, reverse white, fading purplish-red, medium, 40 petals, high-centered, borne mostly singly; foliage medium size, dark green, glossy, very attractive, pointed; upright, bushy, tall growth; no fruit; ['Bluhwunder' × 'Love']; intr. 1985

'Arofrap' ('Almondeen') HT, pb, 1983, Christensen, Jack E.; buds pointed; flowers almond and pink blend, large, dbl.; foliage large, medium green, semi-glossy; upright, bushy growth; PP5704; ['Angel Face' × 'First Prize']; intr. 1984

'Arofrichee' ('Pink Lemonade') HT, yb, 1983, Christensen, Jack E.; flowers yellow turning bright pink, well-formed, large, 35 petals, moderate fragrance; foliage large, medium green, semi-glossy; upright, bushy growth; ['Friendship' × 'Rosy Cheeks']; intr. 1986

'Arofuto' ('City of Warwick', Grand Marshall™) HT, mr, 1989, Christensen, Jack E.; bud ovoid, pointed; flowers large, 35 petals, high-centered, borne usually singly; foliage medium size, medium green, semi-glossy; prickles hooked, medium, red to brown; upright, bushy, medium growth; ['Futura' × 'Olympiad']; intr. 1989

'Aroglofy' (Bugle Boy™) F, dy, 1989, Christensen, Jack E.; bud ovoid, pointed; flowers deep yellow, good substance, medium, 35 petals, cupped, borne in sprays of 5-6, slight tea fragrance; foliage medium size, medium green, very glossy; prickles hooked slightly downward, medium, red to tan; bushy, medium growth; fruit unknown; ['Sunsprite' × (('Katherine Loker' × unknown) × 'Gingersnap')]; intr. 1988

'Aroglor' ('Governor's Lady Gloria') HT, m, 1983, Christensen, Jack E.; flowers pastel mauve, well-formed, large, 35 petals, intense fragrance; foliage large, medium green, matte; growth upright, bushy; ['Sweet Afton' × Blue Nile®]

'Arogobi' ('Fool's Gold') Min, ob, 1984, Christensen, Jack E.; flowers gold, reverse bronze, well-formed, small, 20 petals, slight fragrance; foliage medium size, dark, semi-glossy; upright growth; [Cricket™ × 'Dr. A. J. Verhage']

'Arograju' ('Plum Crazy') HT, m, 1985, Christensen, Jack E.; flowers deep lavender, well-formed, large, 35 petals, moderate fragrance; foliage medium size, dark, matte; bushy growth; [('Ivory Tower' × 'Angel Face') × Blue Nile®]

'Arogresh' ('Emerald Mist', 'Mint Julep') HT, w, 1983, Christensen, Jack E.; flowers pale green and pink blend, large, 35 petals; foliage medium size, medium green, semi-glossy; upright growth; ['White Masterpiece' × Queen Elizabeth®]; intr. 1983

'Arogrewod' ('Silverado') HT, m, 1986, Christensen, Jack E.; bud long, pointed ovoid; flowers soft silvery lavender blushed ruby, reverse creamy white, 4½-5 in., 28-34 petals, high-centered, borne singly or in clusters of 2 or 3, slight fruity fragrance; foliage medium size, dark green, matte; prickles large, hooked slightly downward; stems average, strong; medium, bushy growth; hips globular to pear-shaped, orange; PP6861; [('Ivory Tower' × 'Angel Face') × 'Paradise']; intr. 1987

'Aroha' -- See 'Murha'

'Arohaiclo' (Olé, Climbing™) Cl Gr, or, 1982, Haight, George S. & Swim, H.C.; PP5213; [sport of 'Olé']

'Arojechs' F, rb, 1980, Swim, H.C. & Christensen, J.E.; bud ovoid; intr. 1983

'Aroket' (Cricket™) Min, ob, 1978, Christensen, Jack E.; bud ovoid; flowers light orange to yellow, 1-1½ in., 25 petals, globular, slight fragrance; foliage dark; upright, bushy growth; PP4663; ['Anytime' × 'Katherine Loker']

'Arokonic' HT, dr

'Arokr' F, my, 1978, Swim, H.C. & Christensen, J.E.; bud pointed; intr. 1979

'Arokris' ('Golden Wedding Anniversary', 'Noces d'Or') F, dy, Bear Creek Gardens; intr. 1990

'Arokunce' ('Inferno') HT, ob, 1983, Christensen, Jack E.; flowers well-formed, large, slight fragrance; foliage medium size, dark, semi-glossy; upright, bushy growth; PP5558; ['Zorina' × Yankee Doodle®]; intr. 1982

'Arolala' ('Azure Sea') HT, m, 1983, Christensen, Jack E.; flowers silvery lavender, petals edged ruby, deeper reverse, well-formed, large, 30 petals; foliage large, dark, matte; upright, bushy growth; PP5693; [('Angel Face' × 'First Prize') × 'Lady X']

'Arolaqueli' ('Starlight', Lagerfeld™) Gr, m, 1983, Christensen, Jack E.; flowers silvery lavender, 4-5 in., 30 petals, high-centered, borne in sprays of 5-15, intense fragrance; foliage medium size, medium green, matte; prickles medium, light brown, hooked downward; tall, upright, bushy growth; hips large, globular, orange; [Blue Nile® × ('Ivory Tower' × 'Angel Face')]; intr. 1986

'Arolemo' ('Lanvin™) HT, ly, 1986, Christensen, Jack E.; flowers 30 petals, high-centered, borne in sprays of 3-5, moderate fragrance; foliage medium size, dark green tinted red, semi-glossy; prickles medium, straight, light brown to red; medium, upright bushy growth; no fruit; [seedling × 'Katherine Loker']; intr. 1985

'Arolical' ('Blue Ribbon') HT, m, Christensen, Jack E.; bud ovoid; flowers medium lavender, 5-6 in., 35-40 petals, borne mostly singly, intense sweet citrus-blossom fragrance; foliage large, medium green, semi-glossy; upright growth; PP6000; [('Angel Face' × 'First Prize') × Blue Nile®]; intr. 1986

'Arolyme' (Sundial™) HT, my, 1987, Christensen, Jack E.; flowers medium, bright yellow, medium, 30 petals, high-centered, borne usually singly, slight spicy fragrance; foliage medium size, medium green, glossy; prickles numerous, normal, small and large, light green-tan; upright, bushy, medium growth; no fruit; [('Golden Wave' × (American Heritage® × 'First Prize')) × (('Camelot' × 'First Prize') × Yankee Doodle®)]; intr. 1986

'Aroma' HT, mr, 1931, Cant, B. R.; bud ovoid; flowers crimson, large, dbl.; vigorous, bushy growth

Aromatherapy™ -- See 'Jachonew'

'Aromatic' HT, pb; flowers blend of light and medium pinks, cupped, borne in clusters, intense fragrance; intr. 1970

'Aromiclea' (Voodoo™) HT, ob, 1984, Christensen, Jack E.; bud pointed; flowers salmon, yellow, orange and pink blend, 5-6 in., 30-35 petals, high-centered, borne mostly singly, can have 2 - 3 per cluster, intense rich, sweet fragrance; recurrent; foliage medium size, dark green, very glossy; prickles numerous, short, hooked slightly downward; stems long, strong; upright, bushy, tall growth; hips ovoid to globular, yellow; PP6121; [(('Camelot' × 'First Prize') × 'Typhoo Tea') × 'Lolita']; intr. 1986

'Aromikeh' (Hotline™) Min, mr, 1981, Christensen, Jack E.; bud ovoid, pointed, lightly mossed; flowers bright medium red, mini-moss, 22 petals, high-centered, borne usually singly, moderate moss fragrance; foliage medium green; prickles straight, thin; compact (12 in.) growth; PP5672; [Honest Abe™ × Trumpeter®]; intr. 1984

'Aromontelib' ('Harry Wheatcroft, Climbing') Cl HT, yb, 1981, Mungia, Fred A., Sr.; bud pointed

'Aron' Min, dr, 1977, Christensen, Jack E.; bud mossy; intr. 1978

'Aronance' -- See 'First Lady Nancy'

'Aronemo' Min, ly, 1977, Sudol, Julia; bud mossy

'Aronesuf' F, dy, 1988, Christensen, Jack E.; intr. 1988

'Aronewp' (New Peace™) HT, yb, 1988, Christensen, Jack E.; flowers yellow-cream with bright red margins aging larger red margin, 48-52 petals, high-centered; foliage medium size, medium green, matte; prickles pointed, small, dark tan; upright, medium growth; ['Gingersnap' × Young Quinn®]; intr. 1988

'Aropiclu' ('Dream Cloud') S, pb, 1985, Christensen, Jack E.; flowers light to dark salmon-pink, 20 petals, borne in large pyramidal clusters, slight fragrance; foliage medium size, long, narrow, medium green, matte; spreading, bushy, semi-pendulous growth; PP5998; ['Zorina' × 'Gartendirektor Otto Linne']; intr. 1985

'Aroplumi' Gr, m, Christensen, Jack E.; bud long, ovoid; intr. 1990

'Aroprawn' ('Helen Boehm') Min, lp, 1982, Christensen, Jack E.; flowers soft pink, small, 20 petals, high-centered; foliage small, medium green, semi-glossy; upright, bushy growth; PP5397; [Foxy Lady™ × 'Deep Purple']; intr. 1983

'Aroraju' ('Lady Glencora', 'Orange Juice') F, ob, 1986, Christensen, Jack E.; flowers clear orange, 33 petals, high-centered, borne in sprays of 3-5; prickles long, red; medium, upright, bushy growth; hips ovoid, medium, orange-red; ['Katherine Loker' × 'Gingersnap']

'Arorasp' (Sunspray™) Min, dy, 1980, Christensen, Jack E.; bud ovoid, long, pointed; flowers bright deep yellow, 1½ in., 12-18 petals, cupped, borne singly or several per cluster, slight tea fragrance; recurrent; foliage semi-glossy, dark green; prickles few, medium to long, almost straight; stems long, strong; vigorous, upright growth; hips globular, smooth, orange; PP5035; ['Gingersnap' × Magic Carrousel®]; intr. 1981

'Aroreroy' ('Royal Delight', Royal Success™) HT, mr, 1987, Christensen & Carruth, Tom; flowers large, 30 petals, high-centered, borne usually singly; foliage medium size, medium green, semi-glossy; prickles normal, light green to tan; upright, bushy, tall growth; fruit not observed; PP6910; ['Red Success' × 'Royalty']; intr. 1986

'Aroresas' (Scarlett O'Hara™) Gr, mr, 1987, Christensen, Jack & Carruth, Tom; flowers medium, 35 petals, high-centered, borne usually singly; foliage medium size, medium green, semi-glossy; nearly thornless; upright, tall growth; ['Red Success' × 'Mary DeVor']; intr. 1986

'Aroshrel' ('Michelle Joy') HT, op, Bear Creek Gardens

'Aroshrim' (Foxy Lady™) Min, op, 1980, Christensen, Jack E.; bud ovoid, pointed; flowers salmon and creamy blend, imbricated, 1½ in., 25 petals; foliage small; tall, vigorous, bushy growth; PP4762; ['Gingersnap' × Magic Carrousel®]

'Arosia' HT, mp, Noack, Werner; intr. 1998

'Arosilha' (Silk Hat™) HT, m, 1986, Christensen, Jack E.; flowers red purple, cream reverse, large, 45 petals, high-centered, borne usually singly, moderate damask fragrance; foliage large, medium green, matte; medium, upright, bushy growth; no fruit; ['Ivory Tower' × ('Night 'n' Day' × 'Plain Talk')]; intr. 1985

'Arosnap' ('Apricot Prince', 'Prince Abricot') F, ob, 1977, Delbard, G., & Chabert, A.; bud long, pointed

'Arostal' ('Quicksilver') HT, m, 1986, Christensen, Jack E.; flowers pale lavender gray, large, 25 petals, high-centered, borne singly, moderate fragrance; foliage large, dark, matte; prickles medium, yellow-gray; tall, upright, bushy growth; [Blue Nile® × Brandy™]; intr. 1985

'Arosumo' ('Morning Sun') HT, my, Christensen, Jack E.; intr. 1983

'Arotigy' ('Cherry Gold', Polo Club™) HT, yb, 1987, Christensen, Jack E.; flowers yellow bordered red, fading cream with pink edges, dbl., high-centered; foliage medium size, dark green, semi-glossy; prickles straight, small, few, greenish to light brown; upright, bushy, tall growth; fruit not observed; PP6758; ['Gingersnap' × Young Quinn®]; intr. 1986

'Arotrusim' (Bloomin' Easy™) S, mr, 1988, Christensen, Jack E.; flowers clear, bright red, medium, 22-25 petals, urn-shaped, borne singly, moderate tea fragrance; repeat bloom; foliage large, medium green, glossy; prickles hooked slightly downward, medium, red; upright, bushy, medium growth; hips round, medium size, bright red-orange; PP7157; [Trumpeter® × 'Simplicity']; intr. 1987

'Arovidil' ('Little Red Devil') Min, mr, 1980, Christensen, Jack E.; bud ovoid, pointed; flowers imbricated, 1½ in., 44 petals, borne 1 - 8 per cluster; foliage small, semi-glossy, irregularly serrated; prickles small, narrow; vigorous, bushy, fairly tall growth; ['Gingersnap' × Magic Carrousel®]

'Arovulc' ('Harlequin', 'Miss Liberty', 'Miss Liberté') HT, ob, 1984, Christensen, Jack E.; bud medium to large, pointed, ovoid; flowers coral-orange to dusty deep red, well-formed, 4½-5½ in., 35 petals, high-centered, borne usually singly, sometimes 2 or 3 in cluster; foliage large, dark, semi-glossy; prickles straight to hooked slightly downward; upright, bushy, medium growth; PP6151; [('Camelot' × 'First Prize') × 'Gingersnap']

'Arovule' ('Harlequin', 'Miss Liberty', 'Miss Liberté') HT, ob, 1984, Christensen, Jack E.; bud medium to large, pointed, ovoid

'Arowago' ('Showoff') HT, rb, 1986, Christensen, Jack E.; flowers velvety brilliant red, reverse silvery blend, large, 35 petals; foliage large, dark, semi-glossy; upright, bushy growth; ['Typhoo Tea' × 'Snowfire']

'Arowedye' (Candlelight™) HT, dy, 1982, Christensen, J.E. & Swim, H.C.; bud ovoid, pointed; flowers deep yellow, spiraled, 30 petals, borne mostly singly; foliage large, semi-glossy; prickles large-based; medium-tall, upright, branching growth; PP5398; ['Shirley Laugharn' × ('Bewitched' × King's Ransom®)]

'Arowhif' (White Lightnin'™) Gr, w, 1979, Swim, H.C. & Christensen, J.E.; bud ovoid, pointed; flowers clear white, ruffled, 3½-4 in., 30 petals, high-centered, borne in small clusters, intense citrus fragrance; recurrent; foliage glossy, medium green; prickles few, short, straight to hooked slightly downward, brown; upright, bushy growth; PP4670; ['Angel Face' × 'Misty']; intr. 1980

'Arowillip' ('Strawberry Fayre') MinFl, rb; intr. 1991

'Aroyefel' (Haiku™) F, my, 1987, Christensen, Jack & Carruth, Tom; flowers medium, 38 petals, high-centered, borne usually singly or in sprays of 2-3; foliage medium size, dark green, glossy; prickles normal, light green to tan; upright, bushy, medium growth; no fruit; [Bridal Pink™ × Sunspray™]; intr. 1986

'Aroyol' Min, my, 1979, Christensen, Jack E.; bud ovoid, pointed

'Aroyqueli' ('Centurian Gold', Gold Medal®, 'Golden Medal') Gr, my, 1981, Christensen, Jack E.; bud ovoid, long, pointed; flowers deep golden yellow sometimes flushed orange, 4½-5 in., 30-35 petals, high-centered, borne mostly singly, slight fruity fragrance; foliage large, dark; tall, upright, bushy growth; PP5177; ['Yellow Pages' × ('Granada' × 'Garden Party')]

'Aroyumi' ('Ferris Wheel') Min, yb, 1984, Christensen, Jack E.; flowers yellow, turning pink, orange and red (striped), medium, 20 petals; foliage small, dark, semi-glossy; bushy growth; PP5703; ['Golden Angel' × Cricket™]

'Arpége' HT, Dorieux, Francois; intr. 1978

'Arpege' HT, Boerner, E. S.; PP2237

'Arpeggio' F, dp, 1961, Von Abrams; bud pointed; flowers light pink, 3 in., 12-18 petals, borne in clusters; foliage dark, glossy; vigorous, compact growth; intr. 1961

'Arras' Pol, mr, 1924, Turbat; flowers crimson-red; [sport of 'Triomphe Orléanais']

'Arrillaga' HP, lp, 1929, Schoener; flowers light pink, base golden, large, 50 petals, moderate fragrance; vigorous growth; [('a centifolia' × 'Mrs John Laing') × 'Frau Karl Druschki']

'Arrogance' HT, pb, 1978, Poulsen, Niels D.; flowers coral-pink, 4 in., 25 petals, slight fragrance; foliage dark, leathery; compact growth; ['Mischief' × 'John S. Armstrong']; intr. 1970

'Arromanches' F, op, Eve, A.; repeats well in fall; growth vigorous, 80-100 cm.; intr. 1975

Arrow™ -- See 'Poulypso'

Arrow Folies® F, m, J&P; flowers light ruby purple striped with white, dbl., borne in sprays; PP15082; greenhouse rose; intr. 2004

'Arrow Hit' -- See 'Poulypso'

'Arrow Patiohit' -- See 'Poulypso'
'Arrowtown' LCl, dy, Martin; buds apricot; flowers large, deep golden yellow; growth to 12-14 ft.; intr. 1982
'Art Deco' -- See 'LLX8739'
'Artama' HT, yb, 1978, Takahashi, Takeshi; bud pointed; flowers 25 petals, high-centered; foliage light green, pointed, glossy; few prickles; sturdy growth; ['Kordes' Perfecta' × ('Garden Party' × 'Christian Dior')]
'Artek' HT, dr, 1939, Kosteckij; flowers dark, velvety red, medium, dbl.
Artemis® HT, w, Tantau; flowers creamy white, large, full, high-centered, flat top, borne mostly singly; recurrent; stems medium (40 - 70 cm); Florist rose; intr. 2003
'Artémise' HP, dp, 1851, Robert
'Artful Dodger' -- See 'Sabbelief'
'Arthur Bell' F, my, 1965, McGredy, Sam IV; flowers golden yellow fading to creamy yellow, large, 15 petals, intense sweet fragrance; foliage heavily veined; vigorous growth, medium to tall; ['Cläre Grammerstorf' × Piccadilly®]
'Arthur Bell, Climbing' Cl F, my, 1976, Pearce, C.A.; intr. 1979
'Arthur Cook' HT, dr, 1924, McGredy; bud long, pointed; flowers deep crimson, large, dbl.; foliage light, glossy; long, strong stems; vigorous, bushy, compact growth
Arthur Cox™ -- See 'Jayart'
'Arthur de Sansal' P, m, 1855, Cochet; flowers rich crimson-purple, fully damask-like, medium, dbl., cupped, intense fragrance; growth small, twiggy; ['Géant des Batailles' × unknown]; sometimes classed as HP
'Arthur Hillier' HMoy, dp, 1970, Hillier; flowers rose-crimson, 2½-3 in., 5 petals, slight fragrance; repeat bloom; vigorous growth; [R. macrophylla × R. moyesii]; intr. 1961
'Arthur J. Taylor' HT, dr, 1947, Wheatcroft Bros.; flowers large, dbl.
'Arthur Merrill' -- See 'Hormerry'
'Arthur Oger' HP, m, 1875, Oger; flowers purple/pink, very large, dbl.; ['Gloire de Ducher' × unknown]
'Arthur R. Goodwin' HT, or, 1909, Pernet-Ducher; flowers coppery orange-red, passing to salmon-pink, medium to large, full; [seedling × 'Soleil d'Or']
'Arthur R. Goodwin, Climbing' Cl HT, or
'Arthur Scargill' Min, mr, 1985, Thompson, M.L.; [sport of 'Amruda']
'Arthur Schulte' HT, rb, 1987, Williams, J. Benjamin; flowers cherry to blood red with ivory white at base of petals, large, 43 petals, high-centered, borne singly and in sprays of 1-3, moderate damask fragrance; foliage large, dark green, semi-glossy, disease-resistant; prickles medium-large, light green-bronze; upright, bushy, medium, very vigorous, some interbranching growth; hips rounded, medium size, pumpkin-orange; [('Colorama' × unknown) ×

'Chrysler Imperial']; intr. 1986
'Arthur Vesey' HT, mr; intr. 2005
'Arthur Weidling' HP, dp, 1932, Vogel; flowers large, full, moderate fragrance; [sport of 'Pride of Reigate']
'Arthur Wood' -- See 'Gelart'
'Arthur Young' M, m, 1863, Portemer fils; flowers dark velvety purple, large, full, cupped; recurrent bloom; vigorous growth
'Artic Circle' HT, w, 2007, Edwards, Eddie, & Phelps, Ethan; flowers white with deep pink edging, 5 in., dbl., high-centered, borne mostly solitary; foliage medium green, glossy; few prickles; growth upright, to 5 ft.; ['Pop Warner' × seedling]; intr. 2007
'Artica' HT, w, Tantau; intr. 2006
'Artista' HT, pb, Delbard; flowers medium size, pink striped and painted yellow and white, dbl., no fragrance; growth compact, vigorous; intr. 2001
'Artista Panarosa' -- See 'Maurice Utrillo'
Artiste® F, w, Dorieux; flowers white with scarlet border; heavy bloomer; vigorous growth; intr. 1986
'Artiste' HT, my, 1965, Jones, J. A.; bud long, pointed, deep yellow; flowers single, borne singly and several together; foliage dark green, leathery, few prickles; growth vigorous, bushy; ['Joanna Hill' × 'Souv de Mme Boullet']; intr. 1960
'Artistic' F, ob, 1971, LeGrice; flowers orange, fading red, pointed, 2 in., 10-15 petals, moderate fragrance; foliage small
'Artistic Licence' -- See 'Guesmarble'
Artistry™ -- See 'Jacirst'
'Arturo Toscanini' -- See 'Meilucre'
'Aruba' -- See 'Specawijk'
'Aruba-Caribe' HT, pb, 1967, Boerner; bud ovoid; flowers rose-pink and ivory, 5 in., 38 petals, high-centered, intense fruity fragrance; foliage leathery; vigorous, upright growth; PP2779; [('Diamond Jubilee' × unknown) × ('Fashion' × unknown)]
'Aruna' HT, or, 1970, Pal, Dr. B.P.; flowers bright orange-scarlet, medium, dbl., cupped; foliage glossy; bushy, compact growth; ['Independence' × seedling]; intr. 1968
'Arunima' F, dp, 1976, IARI; bud ovoid; flowers deep pink, 2 in., 50 petals, foliage glossy; vigorous, bushy, compact growth; ['Frolic' × seedling]; intr. 1975
Arusha® HT, mp; flowers 3 in., 30-35 petals; stems 50 - 70 cm length; greenhouse rose; intr. 2004
'Arva Leany' A, w, 1911, Geschwind; flowers cream yellow with a delicate carmine tint, large, full, moderate fragrance; growth upright, semi-climbing
'As de Coeur' -- See 'Herz As'
'Asaborake' ('Dawn') HT, dy, 1984, Ota, Kaichiro; flowers deep yellow, sometimes tipped pink, large, 30 petals, high-centered, slight fragrance; foliage medium green, semi-glossy; bushy,

upright growth; [('Golden Scepter' × 'Narziisse') × 'Kordes' Perfecta']; intr. 1979
'Asagumo' ('Morning Cloud', 'Oriental Dawn') HT, yb, 1973, Suzuki, Seizo; bud ovoid; flowers large, dbl., cupped; foliage glossy, dark; vigorous, upright growth; [('Peace' × unknown) × ('Charleston' × unknown)]
'Asahi' ('Morning Sun') HT, yb, Sugiura, S.; flowers pale yellow, striped pink, 16 cm., 30-50 petals, high-centered, borne mostly solitary; ['Ethel Sanday' × 'Peace']; intr. 1973
'Asalav' ('Crystal Lavender') Min, m; intr. 1985
'Asam Rose' HT, dp, Asami; intr. 1994
'Asasblue' Min, m; intr. 1986
'Asatsuyu' ('Morning Dew') HT, ab, Onodera, T.; flowers pale beige, tinted glossy yellow, 10 cm., 15 petals, borne mostly solitary; foliage dark green, leathery; growth bushy; ['Sterling Silver' × seedling]; intr. 1969
'Asbach' F, or, 1960, Leenders, M.; ['Ambassadeur Nemry' × 'Cinnabar']
'Aschenbrödel' Pol, 1903, Lambert, P.; flowers rose with salmon, small, dbl.; bushy, dwarf growth; ['Petite Léonie' × R. foetida bicolor]
'Aschermittwoch' ('Ash Wednesday') LCl, w, 1955, Kordes; bud silvery gray; flowers silver-gray white, large, dbl., borne in large trusses; vigorous growth
'Aschersoniana' (R. × aschersoniana) S, m, 1880, Münden; flowers bright, light purple, very numerous, small; numerous prickles; growth to 6 ft.; [R. blanda × R. chinensis]
'Ascot' F, ab, 1962, Dickson, Patrick; flowers salmon-coral, 4 in., 18 petals, borne in clusters; low growth; ['Brownie' × seedling]
'Ascot Bonnet' -- See 'Helbonnet'
'Ascot Jubilee' HT, lp, Welsh, Eric
'Asepala' M, w, 1840, Foulard/Verdier; flowers white, shaded flesh, sometimes edged rose, petal edges curled, small, dbl.; compact, erect growth
'Ash Wednesday' -- See 'Aschermittwoch'
'Asha' HT, pb, Agarwal; flowers salmon pink with yellow reverse, large, exhibition, moderate fragrance; intr. 1968
'Ashgrove Jubilee' -- See 'Welco'
'Ashlesha' Gr, op, K & S; flowers soft coral apricot, well formed; growth similar to Prima Donna; [sport of 'Prima Donna']; intr. 2003
Ashley™ S, ly, John Clements; flowers soft yellow, 4 in., 20 petals, cupped, borne in clusters, intense sweet fragrance; foliage light green; growth sturdy, upright, 4 × 3 ft.; PPAF; intr. 2002
'Ashley Marie' -- See 'Judmarie'
'Ashley's Surprise' Min, m, King; flowers 2-3 in., moderate fragrance; growth tall (2-3 ft.); intr. 1997
'Ashlin Rose' HT, dp, 2007, Martin,

Dale E.; flowers large, 5 in., full, high-centered, borne mostly solitary; foliage large, dark green, semi-glossy; prickles medium, downward hooked, light green when new, moderate; growth upright, medium (3-4 ft.); [seedling × 'First Prize']; intr. 2007

'Ashram' ('Bora Bora', 'King David') HT, r, Tantau; flowers copper brown orange, dbl., moderate fruity fragrance; growth strong growing; intr. 1998

'Ashton' -- See 'Welton'

'Ashwini '89' HT, dr, K&S; flowers crimson with deep velvety black overtones, large, full; intr. 1989

'Asja' HT, or, McGredy, Sam IV; intr. 1998

'Ask Maureen' -- See 'Worcorridor'

'Askari' -- See 'Jackari'

'Asmodée' HGal, mr, 1849, Vibert; flowers rosy crimson, large, dbl.

'Aspasia' -- See 'Aspasie'

'Aspasie' ('Aspasia', 'Stéphanie') HGal, lp, 1819, Vibert; Parkman (p202), Hibberd (p247) say Touvais

Aspen™ (Chitina™, Gold Magic Carpet™, Golden Plover™, Gwent™, Sun Cover™) S, my, 1996, Olesen, Pernille & Mogens N.; flowers dbl., borne in small clusters, slight fragrance; foliage medium size, dark green, semi-glossy; few prickles; low (14-16 in.), spreading growth; PP9637; intr. 1995

'Aspen Snow' HT, w; intr. 2002

'Aspirant Marcel Rouyer' HT, ab, 1919, Pernet-Ducher; bud long, pointed; flowers apricot, tinted salmon-flesh, veined yellow, large, dbl.; foliage glossy, bronze; long, strong stems; very vigorous growth; ['Sunburst' × seedling]

'Aspirant Marcel Rouyer, Climbing' Cl HT, ab, 1934, Brenier, E.C.

'Aspirin' -- See 'Taniripsa'

'Aspirin-Rose' -- See 'Taniripsa'

'Assemblage de Beauté(s)' ('Rouge Éblouissant') HGal, dr, 1823, Delaâge; flowers brilliant crimson, with a small button at center, medium, dbl., slight fragrance; foliage thick, somber green; few prickles; erect growth

'Assiniboine' S, dp, 1968, Marshall, H.H.; flowers purplish red, large to medium, semi-dbl., slight fragrance; intermittent bloom; foliage glossy; weak stems; vigorous growth; ['Donald Prior' × R. arkansana]; originally registered as hybrid suffulta; intr. 1962

Asso di Cuori® -- See 'Korred'

'Asso di Cuori, Climbing' Cl HT, dr, Barni; intr. after 1983

'Asso Francesco Baracca' HT, pb, 1936, Giacomasso; bud long; flowers golden salmon, center deeper, well-formed, dbl.; long stems; vigorous growth; ['Julien Potin' × seedling]

'Asta von Parpat' ('Asta von Parpat') HMult, m, 1909, Geschwind, R.; bud fat; flowers carmine pink to light purple, lighter edges and reverse, 4-5 cm., dbl., flat, quartered, borne in small clusters, slight sweet fragrance; repeats well; foliage glaucous, tinted blue, sometimes edged red; prickles large; ['De La Grifferaie' × 'a hybrid perpetual or bourbon']

'Asta von Parpat' -- See 'Asta von Parpart'

Asterix® -- See 'Lenpon'

'Astolat Charm' HT, pb, 1951, Astolat Nursery; flowers flesh-pink, base apricot, 4 in., 30 petals; foliage dark; vigorous growth; [sport of 'McGredy's Salmon']

'Astor Perry' -- See 'Burastor'

'Astoria' HT, ob, 1963, Delforge; bud pointed; flowers bright orange shaded coral; foliage bronze, glossy; ['Opera' × 'Demoiselle']

'Astra' -- See 'Ruizesac'

'Astra' -- See 'Benstar'

Astra™ -- See 'Wilsma'

'Astra' HT, lp, 1890, Geschwind; flowers flesh pink, sometimes edged lighter, large, full, cupped, borne mostly solitary

'Astra Desmond' LCl, yb

'Astral' HT, dp, 1976, Bees; flowers deep rose-pink, low-centered, 4 in., 24 petals, intense fragrance; recurrent; foliage glossy, dark; vigorous growth; ['Tropicana' × 'Pink Favorite']

'Astral' LCl, dr, Croix; flowers deep crimson, large; intr. 1983

'Astre Brillant' HGal, mp

Astrea® Min, m, Barni, V.; intr. 1985

'Astrée' A, mp; flowers pink, changing to delicate lilac blush, very large, very dbl., globular; growth branching; intr. before 1842

'Astrée' HT, pb, Croix, P.; flowers medium pink, reverse shaded orange, large, dbl., intense fragrance; ['Peace' × 'Blanche Mallerin']; intr. 1956

'Astrée' Ch, w, 1836, Laffay; flowers pure white, full; intr. 1836

'Astrée, Climbing' Cl HT, op, Croix, P.; flowers apricot, edged pink, large, flat; intr. 1960

'Astrid Gräfin von Hardenberg' ('Gräfin von Hardenberg') S, m, Tantau; flowers warm, intense Bordeaux-red with violet in the center, medium, full, cupped, almost quartered, borne in clusters, intense fragrance; recurrent; loose, arching (to 4-5 ft.) growth; intr. 2002

Astrid Lindgren™ ('Dream Sequence', Charentes™, Egon Schiele™, Macabo™) S, lp, Poulsen; bud medium pink; flowers light pink, 10-15 cm., dbl., borne in clusters, slight raspberry fragrance; foliage dark, glossy; growth bushy, 6-8 ft.; intr. 1991

'Astrid Späth' -- See 'Frau Astrid Späth'

'Astrid Späth Striped' F, rb, 1933; flowers soft pink and white with bright carmine striping, slight fragrance; free-flowering; growth to 3 ft.; [sport of 'Frau Astrid Späth']

'Astroïde' F, rb; intr. 2004

'Astrolabe' HMult, mr, 1825, Garilland

Astronomia® S, lp, Meilland; flowers blush, fading to white, single, flat, borne in clusters; recurrent; foliage dark green; growth height 2 ft.; intr. 2007

'Astrorose' HT, mr, 1970, Porter; bud long, pointed; flowers cardinal-red to crimson, medium, dbl., moderate fragrance; foliage large, dark, bronze, leathery; vigorous growth; ['Helene Schoen' × 'Chrysler Imperial']; intr. 1971

'Asturias' F, rb, 1956, Dot, M.; flowers red, reverse carmine, large, 40 petals, borne in corymbs; foliage glossy; strong stems; very vigorous growth; ['Méphisto' × 'Coralín']

'Asuka' HT, lp, Kono, Y.; flowers 15 cm., 45 petals, high-centered, moderate fragrance; foliage thick, semi-glossy; growth very vigorous; [Queen Elizabeth® × 'Minuet']; intr. 1974

'Asuka Otome' S, pb, 2001, Simizu, Jungi; flowers light pink with deep pink edge, small, single, slight fragrance; foliage small, medium green, matte; growth bushy; ['Azumino' × 'Azumino']

'Asun Galindez de Chapa' HT, pb, 1923, Ketten Bros.; flowers salmon-pink, reverse darker, base yellow; ['Mons. Paul Lédé' × 'Jacques Vincent']

'Atago' HT, or, Keihan Gardening Co.; flowers orange-red, greenish-yellow at base, reverse pink, petals slightly reflexed, 13 cm., 40-50 petals, well-formed, borne mostly solitary, slight fragrance; foliage semi-glossy, thick, usually with 7 leaflets; prickles few, concaved; growth vigorous; ['Hawaii' × ('Super Star' × 'Christian Dior')]; intr. 1984

'Atalanta' LCl, 1927, Williams, A.; bud coppery pink; flowers flesh-pink, dbl.; ['Paul Ploton' × 'William Allen Richardson']

'Atalante' F, mr, 1958, Buyl Frères; flowers geranium-red, large; very vigorous growth

'Atalante' HT, rb, Adam; intr. 2002

'Atar Gull' HP, mp, 1858, Avoux / Crozy; flowers bright pink, medium

'Atara' HT, rb, 1985, Nevo, Motke; flowers medium red, flecked and striped near white, reverse near white with red; [sport of 'Suspense']; intr. 1974

'Atco Royale' F, my, Fryer, Gareth; flowers large, pale amber, dbl., borne singly and in clusters, moderate fragrance; foliage bright green, dense; intr. 1994

Atena® ('Barten') HT, dy

'Athabasca' Sp, dp, 1930; flowers deep pink, 15-20 petals; non-recurrent; very vigorous growth; hardy; a R. macounii variant, found growing at Vilna, Alberta, Canada, about 1930

'Athalie' -- See 'Fanny Bias'

'Athalie' P, lp, 1851, Robert; flowers flesh pink, medium, full, cupped

'Athalin' ('Général Athalin') B, mr, 1830, Jacques; flowers cherry-red, large, cupped

'Athanase Coquerel' B, m, 1853, Pradel;

flowers reddish-violet, medium, full
'Athelin'   HGal
'Athena' -- See 'Rühkor'
'Athene' -- See 'Bencreberg'
'Athene'   HT, lp, 1976, Murray & Hawken; bud green; flowers porcelain-pink, base yolk-yellow, 5½ in., 37 petals, intense apple fragrance; foliage large; moderate, bushy growth; ['Peace' × 'Diamond Jubilee']; intr. 1975
'Atherton'   HT, my, 1980, Perry, Astor; bud long, pointed; flowers 35 petals, urn-shaped, borne 1-3 per cluster, moderate fruity fragrance; foliage medium size, matte; prickles small, recurved; medium growth; [seedling × 'Sunblest']; intr. 1981
'Athlete'   HT, rb, 1965, Barter; flowers nasturtium-red shaded gold, medium, 16 petals, slight fragrance; foliage light green; bushy growth; ['Tzigane' × 'Claude']
'Athlone'   F, yb, 1965, McGredy, Sam IV; flowers cream edged orange-scarlet, open, borne in clusters; foliage small, dark; free growth; ['Circus' × 'Cinnabar']
'Atholl Grant' -- See 'Rawblight'
Athos®   F, ob, 1965, Laperrière; flowers bright orange, large, 28 petals; foliage dark; bushy growth; ['Coup de Foudre' × 'Soleil']
'Athybecca'   HT, op, Athy, M.; intr. 2006
'Athybrow'   F, ab, Athy, Mike; bud pinky red; intr. 2004
'Athydoug'   HT, ab, Athy; bud reddish apricot; intr. 2004
'Athylight'   F, ly, Athy; intr. 2006
'Athyspoon'   HT, m, Athy
'Atida' -- See 'Saublim'
'Atida'   HT, dr, 1941, Sauvageot, H.; flowers velvety dark scarlet, well-formed, quite large, semi-dbl., moderate fragrance; very vigorous growth; ['Mme Van de Voorde' × 'Dance of Joy']
'Atida 93'   HT, Sauvageot, H.; intr. 1993
'Atkins Beauty' -- See 'Savacent'
'Atlanta' -- See 'Wekdoclem'
'Atlanta'   Min, mp, deRuiter; intr. 1992
Atlantic® ('Gaval') Gr, or, 1956, Gaujard; flowers medium, semi-dbl., slight fragrance; foliage glossy, dark; ['Peace' × seedling]
'Atlantic City' -- See 'Jollmea'
'Atlantic Star' -- See 'Fryworld'
'Atlantida'   HT, op, 1939, Pahissa; flowers coppery salmon, shaded peach; vigorous growth
Atlantis™ -- See 'Poulsiana'
'Atlantis'   F, m, 1970, Harkness, R.; flowers deep mauve, 3 in., 5 petals, moderate fragrance; foliage glossy, purple tinted; [Orangeade® × 'Lilac Charm']; intr. 1969
'Atlantis Palace' (Atlantis™) F, dy, Poulsen; flowers deep yellow, 5-8 cm., dbl., slight wild rose fragrance; foliage dark; growth bushy, 40-60 cm.; PP11638; intr. 1998
Atlas® -- See 'Delkort'

'Atocha Gold' -- See 'Pongold'
'Atoll' -- See 'Meibystar'
'Atoll'   F, my, Richardier; intr. 2002
'Atoll 99'   LCl, Meilland; intr. 1999
'Atom Bomb' -- See 'Atombombe'
'Atombombe' ('Atom Bomb', 'Atomflash', 'Velvet Robe') HEg, mr, 1953, Kordes; bud pointed; flowers deep scarlet-orange, 2½ in., 28 petals, borne in clusters; very vigorous growth; ['Obergärtner Wiebicke' × 'Independence']
'Atomflash' -- See 'Atombombe'
'Atomic White'   HT, ly, 1948, Brownell; bud long, pointed; flowers white, center tinted yellow, large, dbl., high-centered, moderate fragrance; vigorous, bushy growth; ['Pink Princess' × 'Shades of Autumn']
'Atropurpurea' -- See 'Subnigra'
'Atropurpurea' (R. × rugosa atropurpurea) HRg, mr, 1899, Paul; flowers carmine-crimson, single, borne in clusters; early summer, vigorous (3-5 ft.) growth; [R. rugosa × R. × damascena]
'Atropurpurea'   Pol, m, Levavasseur; flowers purple-red; ['Mme Norbert Levavasseur' × 'Perle des Rouges']; intr. 1910
'Attache'   HT, m; intr. 2001
'Attar of Roses'   HT, w, 1936, Cant, B. R.; bud globular; flowers creamy white, edged pink, dbl., cupped; foliage glossy, bronze; long, strong stems; vigorous, bushy, compact growth
'Attbright'   F, mr, Attfield; intr. 2003
'Attila'   A, dp; flowers deep pink, large, semi-dbl., cupped
'Attire'   HT, ob, Ghosh; buds long; flowers orange blended pink, large, dbl.; intr. 1999
'Attleborough' -- See 'Beaat'
'Attlight' ('Apricot Delight') HT, ab, Attfield-dbl.; intr. 1999
'Attraction'   HT, lp, 1886, Dubreuil; bud ovoid; flowers light carmine, nuanced China pink, paler edging, full; foliage matte
'Attraction'   HT, yb, Dickson, A.; flowers yellow and orange, dbl., globular, slight fragrance; foliage glossy, bronze; dwarf, bushy growth; intr. 1931
Attractive Cover™ (Baton Rouge™) S, dr, Poulsen; flowers dark red, 5-8 cm., slight wild rose fragrance; foliage dark; growth flat, bushy, 40-60 cm.; PP13270; intr. 2000
Attraktion®   F, op, 1963, Tantau, Math.; bud long, pointed; flowers salmon-copper, reverse golden yellow, dbl., borne in large clusters; foliage glossy, dark; vigorous, bushy growth
'Aubade'   HT, ob, 1963, Verbeek; flowers yellow-orange, medium, dbl.; foliage dark; ['Docteur Valois' × seedling]
'Auberge de l'Ill' -- See 'Evelill'
'Aubrey Cobden'   HT, my, 1948, Mee; flowers clear yellow, medium, 30 petals; foliage glossy, stems red; free growth; ['Oswald Sieper' × seedling]
'Auckland Metro' -- See 'Macbucpal'

Audace® -- See 'Bucbi'
'Audie Murphy'   HT, mr, 1957, Lammerts, Dr. Walter; bud long, pointed, crimson; flowers 4½-5½ in., 20 petals, high-centered, moderate spicy fragrance; foliage semi-glossy, dark, bronze; vigorous, upright, bushy growth; PP1558; ['Charlotte Armstrong' × 'Grande Duchesse Charlotte']; intr. 1956
'Audine'   HT, lp, 1950, Gatward; flowers shell-pink, reflexed, 22 petals, high-centered; foliage dark; vigorous, upright growth; ['Percy Izzard' × 'William Moore']
'Audobon' -- See 'Audubon'
'Audrey'   HT, dr, 1922, Paul, W.; flowers deep crimson, well-formed, high-centered
'Audrey Gardner' -- See 'Peaspecial'
'Audrey Harrison'   Cl HT, ab, 1971, Harrison; flowers pale apricot, 4 in., semi-dbl., intense fragrance; free bloom, early; foliage glossy, dark; [sport of 'Shot Silk']; intr. 1969
'Audrey Hepburn' -- See 'Twoadore'
'Audrey Marie'   F, mr, 1994, Dobbs, Annette E.; flowers medium red, medium, full, borne mostly singly, slight fragrance; foliage medium size, medium green, semi-glossy; some prickles; low (2½ ft.), bushy growth; ['Tamanga' × 'Anne Scranton']; intr. 1994
'Audrey McCormack' -- See 'Kenobsess'
'Audrey Mieklejohn'   HT, my, Delbard
'Audrey Stell'   HT, pb, 1937, Stell; flowers soft strawberry-pink, reverse sulfur-yellow, semi-dbl., full; foliage light; long, strong stems; vigorous, bushy growth; [sport of 'Soeur Thérèse']
Audrey Wilcox® -- See 'Frywilrey'
'Audrey's Rose' -- See 'Ripaud'
'Audubon' ('Audobon') S, mr; flowers 5 petals, no fragrance; growth to 3-4 ft.; intr. 2005
'Augie Boy' -- See 'Renboy'
'August Kordes' -- See 'Lafayette'
'August Noack'   HT, dr, 1928, Kordes; bud long, pointed; flowers deep scarlet, open, large, dbl., high-centered; foliage bronze, dark; vigorous, bushy growth; [sport of 'Columbia']
'August Noack, Climbing'   Cl HT, dr, 1935, Lens
'August Seebauer' ('The Queen Mother') F, dp, 1944, Kordes; bud long, pointed; flowers deep rose-pink, large, dbl., high-centered, borne in clusters; foliage glossy; vigorous growth; ['Break o' Day (HT)' × 'Else Poulsen']
'Augusta' -- See 'Pouldava'
'Augusta' -- See 'Solfaterre'
'Augusta'   HRg, lp, 1953, Wright, Percy H.; flowers flat, intense fragrance
Augusta Luise® ('Fox-Trot', 'Hayley Westenra', 'Rachel') S, pb, Tantau; flowers large, pink to peach, dbl., intense fruity fragrance; foliage dark green; medium growth; intr. 2000
'Auguste Barbier'   HWich, mp, 1900, Barbier; flowers medium pink to mauve;

['L'Idéal' × *R. wichurana*]

'Auguste Buchner' HP, m, 1880, Lévêque; flowers velvety dark purple, shaded scarlet, large, full, slight fragrance

'Auguste Chaplain' HP, mr, 1921, Tanne; flowers large, dbl.

'Auguste Comte' T, mp, 1896, Soupert & Notting; flowers outer petals carmine red, center flesh pink, large, dbl.; foliage dark green; ['Marie Van Houtte' × 'Mme Lombard']

'Auguste Delobel' LCl, mr, 1924, Turbat; flowers carmine, large white eye, yellow stamens, borne in clusters

'Auguste Finon' HMult, yb, 1923, Turbat; flowers golden yellow passing to coppery and salmon, borne in clusters; ['Goldfinch' × seedling]

'Auguste Gervais' HWich, ab, 1918, Barbier; flowers coppery yellow and salmon, fading white, 4-5 in., semi-dbl., borne in clusters, moderate fragrance; seasonal bloom; very vigorous, climbing growth; [*R. wichurana* × 'Le Progrès']

'Auguste Guinoisseau' HP, dr, 1853, Guinoisseau

'Auguste Kordes' ('Lafayette, Climbing') Cl F, mr, 1928, Kordes; flowers light scarlet, borne in clusters; fine seasonal bloom, later intermittent; vigorous, climbing growth; [sport of 'Lafayette']

'Auguste Mie' ('Mme Rival') HP, mp, 1851, Laffay; flowers glossy pink, silvery reverse, large, very full, globular; prickles numerous, straight; [sport of 'La Reine']

'Auguste Neumann' HP, mr, 1869, Verdier, V.; flowers poppy red, shaded fiery red, sometimes marbled white, large, full

'Auguste Oger' T, pb, 1855, Oger; flowers rose pink with copper tints, large, very full, globular

Auguste Renoir® -- See 'Meitoifar'

'Auguste Rigotard' HP, mr, 1871, Schwartz

'Auguste Rivière' -- See 'Souv d'Auguste Rivière'

'Auguste Rivière' T, yb, 1853, Lacharme

'Auguste Roussel' LCl, pb, 1913, Barbier; flowers salmon-pink to flesh-pink, well-formed, petals undulated, large, semi-dbl., borne in clusters of 5-12; seasonal bloom; very vigorous, climbing growth; [*R. macrophylla* × 'Papa Gontier']

'Auguste Vacher' T, yb, 1853, Lacharme; flowers yellow, shaded copper, medium, full

'Auguste Vermare' HT, or, 1958, Arles; bud pointed; flowers coral-red; vigorous, upright growth; ['Comtesse Vandal' × seedling]

'Auguste Victoria' S, dy; intr. 1999

'Augustine Bertin' HGal, dp, 1818, Vibert

'Augustine Guinoisseau' ('Mlle Augustine Guinoisseau', 'White La France') HT, lp, 1889, Guinoisseau fils; flowers white, tinted light flesh, large, full; [sport of 'La France']

'Augustine Halem' HT, dp, 1891, Guillot, J. B.; flowers carmine rose, shaded with purple, medium, full, globular

'Augustine Margat' B, mp; flowers bright pink, reverse lighter, medium, very full, cupped

'Augustine Pourprée' -- See 'Marie-Louise'

'Augustus Hartmann' HT, dp, 1914, Cant, B. R.; flowers Tyrian rose, large, dbl., slight fragrance; foliage rich green, leathery; vigorous growth

'Augustus Hartmann, Climbing' Cl HT, Fineschi, G.; intr. 1980

'Augustus Stone' HT, ab, 1999, Poole, Lionel; flowers light apricot/amber, resist bad weather, 4-4½ in., full, borne in small clusters, moderate fragrance; foliage medium size, dark green, dull; some prickles; bushy, medium (3 ft.) growth; ['Gavotte' × 'Pot of Gold']; intr. 2000

'Auld Lang Syne' HT, ob, 1957, Motose; bud ovoid; flowers orange edged pale orange-yellow, 4 in., 35-45 petals, moderate fruity fragrance; bushy growth; PP1500; ['Tawny Gold' × ('Talisman' × 'Tawny Gold')]

'Aunt Belle's Tea' T, pb

'Aunt Gerry' HT, ly, 1992, Sheldon, John & Jennifer; flowers golden yellow, 3-3½ in., 35 petals, slight spicy fragrance; foliage medium size, medium green, semi-glossy; prickly peduncle; medium (90-120 cm.), upright, very vigorous growth; [sport of 'Lanvin']; intr. 1992

'Aunt Harriet' HWich, rb, 1918, Van Fleet; flowers scarlet-crimson, white eye, yellow stamens, semi-dbl.; vigorous growth; ['Apolline' × *R. wichurana*]

'Aunt Honey' S, mp, 1985, Buck, Dr. Griffith J.; bud large, ovoid; flowers large, rose-pink shading lighter toward outer petals, 4-5 in., 36-42 petals, high-centered, borne 5-10 per cluster, moderate damask fragrance; repeat bloom; foliage medium size, dark olive-green; prickles awl-like, tan; erect, short, bushy growth; hardy; ['Music Maker' × 'Habanera']; intr. 1984

'Aunt Lucy' S, w, Williams, J.B.; buds amber yellow; flowers ivory with yellow stamens, single; foliage dark green; growth upright, vigorous; intr. 2003

'Aunt Rosie' -- See 'Majlynlinto'

'Aunt Ruth' LCl, pb, 1995, Jerabek; flowers streaked medium pink, white eye, reverse white streaked pink, 3 in., semi-dbl., borne in small and large clusters, slight fragrance; foliage medium size, medium green, semi-glossy; few prickles; growth bushy, spreading

'Auntie Louise' -- See 'Jalouise'

'Aunty Dora' F, m, 1970, Deamer; flowers magenta, semi-dbl., borne in trusses; low growth; ['Dearest' × 'Lilac Charm']

'Aunty Lil' -- See 'Kenmasnia'

'Aurea' -- See 'Aureus'

'Aurea' HT, yb, 1948, Dot; flowers yellow, reverse red, well-formed, moderate fruity fragrance; foliage glossy; vigorous growth

'Aurea' HT, dy, Meilland; intr. 1987

'Aureate' HT, ob, 1932, Dickson, A.; flowers orange and scarlet to yellow, large, dbl., moderate fragrance; foliage bronze; vigorous, bushy growth

'Aurelia Capdevila' HT, pb, 1933, Dot, Pedro; flowers pink, base salmon; foliage dark; vigorous growth

'Aurelia Liffa' HSet, mr, 1886, Geschwind, R.; flowers carmine with magenta tints, 4-6 cm., dbl., borne in small clusters, slight fragrance; numerous prickles; growth tall (3-4 m.), upright; very winter hardy; [*R. setigera* × 'Marie Baumann']

'Aurelia Weddle' HT, or, Weddle, Von C.; flowers 65 petals, exhibition; heat tolerant; intr. 1995

'Aurélien Igoult' HMult, m, 1924, Igoult; flowers bluish-violet, shaded reddish, medium, semi-dbl.; vigorous, climbing growth; ['Veilchenblau' × seedling]

'Aureola' HT, my, 1934, Böhm, J.; flowers golden yellow; [sport of 'Mev. G.A. van Rossem']

'Auréole' HT, ob, 1951, Gaujard; bud large; flowers orange-yellow, semi-dbl.; foliage glossy, dark; very vigorous growth

'Aureus' ('Aurea') T, yb, 1873, Ducher; flowers coppery yellow, medium, full

'Auria' ('Femme Actuelle') HT, mr, Richardier; flowers clear red, very dbl., moderate citrus fragrance; growth to 70-100 cm.; intr. 1999

'Auriol' Pol, rb, 1930, Alderton

'Auriu de Cluj' F, yb, Wagner, S.; flowers flat, 15 petals, slight fragrance; foliage medium size, light green, glossy; intr. 1984

'Aurora' -- See 'Celestial'

'Aurora' HT, op, 1898, Paul, W.; bud very long; flowers salmon towards center, paler edges, large, full; foliage dark green

'Aurora' HT, mp, Niehof; flowers carnation-pink, center shaded darker, large; intr. 1908

'Aurora' HMsk, ly, Pemberton; flowers yellow, passing to creamy white, medium, single, borne in small clusters, moderate fragrance; ['Danaë' × 'Miriam']; intr. 1928

'Aurora' F, op, Leenders, M.; flowers salmon-pink tinted golden yellow and orange, dbl., moderate fragrance; ['Mev. Nathalie Nypels' × seedling]; intr. 1941

'Aurora' HKor, ob, Kordes; flowers orange-yellow outside, pinker within, large, dbl., borne in small clusters; non-recurrent; foliage dark green, glossy; vigorous growth; very hardy; intr. 1956

'Aurora' (variety of *R. acicularis*), mr; flowers have wide, thick petals, 5 petals, borne singly; non-remontant; foliage red and purple in fall; prickles to the end of the branch

'Aurora' HT, mr, Strnad

'Aurora' F, my

'Aurora Boreal' HT, rb, 1935, Munné, B.; flowers geranium, shaded fiery red, semi-dbl.; foliage dark; very vigorous growth; ['Étoile de Hollande' × ('Ville de Paris' × 'Sensation')]

'Aurora-Hime' ('Princess Aurora') HT, or, Mikami, K.; flowers orange-vermilion, reverse creamy white, long lasting, petals reflexed, 14-15 cm., 60 petals, high-centered, borne mostly solitary, intense fragrance; foliage medium size, medium green, matte, narrow; prickles horizontal, sparse; growth upright; [sport of 'Red Queen']; intr. 2001

'Aurore' -- See 'Celestial'

'Aurore' HP, pb, Touvais; flowers pink over copper, edged red, large, full; intr. 1860

'Aurore' T, ly, Touvais; flowers yellowish white, center golden, large, full; intr. 1871

'Aurore' Ch, yb, Widow Schwartz; flowers yellow passing to salmon-pink, loose; recurrent bloom; ['Mme Laurette Messimy' × unknown]; intr. 1897

'Aurore' HT, pb, Capiago; flowers pink, base yellow, dbl., moderate fragrance; vigorous growth; intr. 1936

'Aurore' F, or

'Aurore' N, lp, 1836, Laffay; flowers dawn-pink, edges flesh pink, small, semi-dbl.

'Aurore Boréale' HP, mr, 1865, Oger; flowers large, full; remontant

'Aurore de Guide' B, dr, 1849, Thomas; flowers red, shaded violet, full, globular

Aurore de Jacques-Marie® S, yb, Guillot-Massad; flowers white and pale yellow, fading pink, borne in small clusters; growth compact; intr. 2001

'Aurore d'Enghien' HGal, m, about 1830, Parmentier; flowers bright dawn pink, medium, full

'Aurore d'Espagne' HT, pb, 1966, Dot; bud long, pointed; flowers salmon-pink to nankeen yellow, medium, semi-dbl., cupped; vigorous growth; [Zambra® × Queen Elizabeth®]

'Aurore du Matin' HP, mr, 1867, Rolland; flowers light red, reverse silvery, large, dbl., intense fragrance

'Aurore Lassalle' S, mp, Gilet; intr. 2005

'Aurore Sand' LCl, pb, 1964, Robichon; flowers two-tone soft pink and copper, 5 in., dbl., moderate fragrance; recurrent bloom; vigorous growth; ['Mme Moisans' × 'Odette Joyeux']

'Ausap' (Queen Nefertiti®) S, ab, Austin, David; intr. 1988

'Ausbaker' ('Teasing Georgia') S, yb, 1998, Austin, David; flowers deep yellow in center, paler yellow on outer petals, large, very dbl., cupped, borne mostly singly, moderate tea rose fragrance; good repeat; foliage medium size, semi-glossy, disease-resistant; few prickles; branching, strong, graceful, medium (3½ ft.) growth; [Charles Austin® × seedling]; intr. 1998

'Ausband' ('Buttercup', Buttercup 98™) S, dy, 2000, Austin, David; flowers golden yellow, upper petals fade to deep pink, reverse apricot, 9 cm., dbl., borne in small clusters; foliage medium size, medium green, dull; few prickles; branching, medium (4 ft.) growth; [Graham Thomas® × seedling]; intr. 1998

'Ausbeam' ('Moonbeam') S, ab, 1992, Austin, David; flowers apricot yellow, medium, semi-dbl., borne in small clusters, intense fragrance; foliage medium size, light green, semi-glossy; some prickles; medium (39 in.), bushy growth; intr. 1983

'Ausbecks' ('Bishop's Castle') S, mp, 2006, Austin, David; flowers 6½ cm., very full, borne in small clusters; foliage medium size, dark green, matte; prickles medium, hooked downward, medium red, moderate; growth bushy, vigorous, medium (120 cm.); garden decorative; [seedling × seedling]; intr. 2006

'Ausbells' (Bow Bells™) S, dp, 1994, Austin, David; flowers deep pink, medium, dbl., borne in large clusters, moderate fragrance; foliage medium size, medium green, semi-glossy; some prickles; upright, bushy (47 in.) growth; [seedling × Graham Thomas®]; intr. 1991

'Ausbernard' ('Munstead Wood') S, dr, 2008, David Austin Roses, Ltd.; flowers 9½ cm., very full, borne in small clusters; foliage medium, medium green, matte; prickles medium, linear, orange, numerous; growth bushy, short (90 cm.); garden decorative; ['red English-type shrub' × 'pink English-type shrub']; intr. 2008

'Ausbilda' ('Lochinvar') S, lp, 2005; flowers light pink, reverse light pink, 6 cm., very full, borne in small clusters, intense fragrance; foliage medium size, medium green, semi-glossy; prickles medium, deeply concave; growth bushy, branching, short (70 cm.); garden decorative; ['seedling (light yellow species type)' × 'seedling (light pink species type)']; intr. 2002

'Ausbite' ('Spirit of Freedom') S, lp, 2005; bud globular; flowers very full, cupped, borne in clusters of up to 15, intense myrrh fragrance; recurrent; foliage medium size, dark green, semi-glossy; prickles medium, concave; stems strong; growth bushy, branching, tall (5-6 ft.); garden decorative; hips cupped, green; PP14973; ['seedling (pink English type shrub)' × Abraham Darby®]; intr. 2002

'Ausbloom' ('Dark Lady', 'The Dark Lady') S, dr, 1994, Austin, David; bud long, pointed, globular; flowers dark ruby red, 3-3½ in., very full, cupped, flattens, borne singly and in small clusters, moderate fragrance; recurrent; foliage medium size, dark green, semi-glossy; prickles some, medium, hooked downward; stems 12 - 18 in.; medium (3 ft.), upright, bushy growth; PP8677; [Mary Rose® × Prospero®]; intr. 1991

'Ausblossom' ('Peach Blossom') S, lp, 1994, Austin, David; flowers blush pink, medium, semi-dbl., borne in large clusters, slight fragrance; foliage medium size, medium green, semi-glossy; some prickles; bushy, spreading (4 ft.) growth; ['The Prioress' × Mary Rose®]; intr. 1990

'Ausblush' ('Open Field', Heritage®, 'Roberta') S, lp, 1985, Austin, David; flowers medium, full, cupped, intense fragrance; recurrent bloom; foliage small, dark, semi-glossy; upright, bushy growth; [seedling × ('Iceberg' × unknown)]; intr. 1984

'Ausbonny' ('Wildeve') S, pb, 2004; flowers medium pink, touched apricot, in center, outer petals and reverse lighter, 7½ cm., very full, cupped, rosette, borne in small clusters, slight fresh fragrance; foliage large, dark green, semi-glossy; prickles medium, deeply concave; bushy, medium (100 cm.), arching growth; garden decorative; ['seedling (medium pink English-type shrub)' × 'Golden Celebration']; intr. 2003

'Ausbord' S, mp, Austin, David; bud oval, pointed; intr. 1986

'Ausbosky' (Hyde Hall™) S, pb, 2004; flowers very full, borne in small clusters; foliage large, medium green, matte; prickles medium, hooked downward; growth bushy, dense, vigorous, branching, tall (175 cm.); ['seedling (white English-type shrub)' × 'seedling (medium pink shrub)']; intr. 2004

'Ausbottle' ('Cordelia') S, mp, 2001, Austin, David; flowers semi-dbl., borne in small clusters, moderate fragrance; foliage medium size, dark green, matte, disease-resistant; prickles medium, hooked downward, few; growth upright, medium (105 cm.); garden decorative; [seedling × seedling]; intr. 2000

'Ausbreak' (Jayne Austin™) S, my, 1993, Austin, David; flowers old fashioned, medium, 110-130 petals, borne in small clusters, intense fragrance; foliage medium size, dark green, semi-glossy; few prickles; medium (43 in.), upright growth; PP8682; [Graham Thomas® × 'Tamora']; intr. 1990

'Ausbred' (Bredon®) S, ab, 1985, Austin, David; flowers medium, dbl.; repeat bloom; foliage small, light green, matte; upright growth; ['Wife of Bath' × Lilian Austin®]; intr. 1984

'Ausbrid' ('Mayor of Casterbridge') S, lp, 1997, Austin, David; flowers very dbl., 90 petals, old-fashioned, borne in small clusters; foliage medium size, light green, leathery; some prickles; upright, medium (3½ × 2½ ft.)growth

'Ausbrother' ('Lady Emma Hamilton') S, ob, 2006; bud dark red with dashes of orange; flowers tangerine orange, reverse yellow-orange, 8½ cm., very full, cupped, borne in small clusters; recurrent; foliage medium size, medium green, matte; prickles medium, deeply concave, dark red, moderate; growth bushy, vigorous, medium (120 cm.); garden decoration; [seedling × seedling]; intr. 2005

'Ausbuff' ('Schloss Glücksburg', English Garden®) S, ab, 1991, Austin, David; flowers soft apricot yellow, very large, very dbl., cupped, intense fragrance; foliage clear green; bushy, vigorous growth; PP7214; [Lilian Austin® × (seedling × 'Iceberg')]; intr. 1988

'Ausburn' ('Robbie Burns') S, lp, 1987, Austin, David; flowers light pink, white center, small, 5 petals, moderate fragrance; foliage small, medium green, matte; bushy, strong (5 ft.) growth; hips large, mahogany; ['Wife of Bath' × *R. pimpinellifolia*]; intr. 1985

'Ausburton' ('Emily') S, lp, 1994, Austin, David; flowers pale pink, 3-3½ in., very dbl., borne in small clusters, moderate fragrance; foliage medium size, medium green, semi-glossy; numerous prickles; upright, bushy (30 in.) growth; PP8838; ['The Prioress' × Mary Rose®]; intr. 1992

'Ausbury' S, mp, 1969, Austin, David

'Ausca' ('White Bianca', Fair Bianca®) S, w, 1983, Austin, David; flowers light yellow to white, very dbl., quartered, moderate fragrance; foliage medium size, light green, semi-glossy; upright, medium growth; hardy

'Auscam' ('Marinette') S, mp, 1997, Austin, David; bud pointed; flowers lighten with age, large, semi-dbl., flat, borne singly or in small clusters, slight myrrh fragrance; foliage medium size, medium green, semi-glossy; prickles few to some; bushy, medium growth; [Lucetta® × 'Red Coat']

'Auscanary' ('Malvern Hills') LCl, yb, 2001, Austin, David; flowers 4¾-6 cm., full, borne in large clusters; foliage medium size, medium green, semi-glossy, disease-resistant; prickles medium, deeply concave, few; growth upright, sprawling, tall (3 m.); garden, decorative; [seedling × seedling]; intr. 2000

'Auscanterbury' S, mp, 1969, Austin, David

'Auscat' (Winchester Cathedral®) S, w, 1995, Austin, David; flowers white, with a tendency to revert to pink, 2-2¾ in., very dbl., cupped, borne in small clusters, moderate sweet fragrance; recurrent; foliage medium size, medium green, semi-glossy; some prickles; medium (4 ft.), upright, bushy growth; PP8141; [sport of 'Mary Rose']; intr. 1988

'Auscent' (John Clare™) S, dp, 1997, Austin, David; flowers deep pink to light crimson, medium, 110-130 petals, borne in small clusters; foliage medium size, dark green, semi-glossy; few prickles; upright, medium (4 ft.) growth; ['Wife of Bath' × seedling]; intr. 1994

'Auschar' ('Charity', Charity 97™) S, yb, 2000, Austin, David; flowers apricot-yellow, 3 in., very full, borne in small clusters, intense fragrance; foliage medium size, dark green, glossy; prickles moderate; upright, bushy, medium (3 ft.) growth; PP11483; [Graham Thomas® × seedling]; intr. 1997

'Auschesnut' ('St Alban') S, my, 2004; flowers medium yellow, reverse light yellow, 6½ cm., very full, borne in small clusters, slight fragrance; foliage medium size, dark green, semi-glossy; prickles medium, hooked downward; growth bushy, narrow / branching, medium (4 ft.); garden decorative; ['Ausgold' × 'seedling (medium pink English-type shrub)']; intr. 2003

'Auschild' (Fisherman's Friend®) S, dr, 1987, Austin, David; flowers deep crimson, reverse lighter, fading crimson-purple, large, very dbl., cupped, intense damask fragrance; repeat bloom; foliage medium size, dark green, semi-glossy; prickles broad, straight, large, red-brown; bushy growth; no fruit; [Lilian Austin® × The Squire®]

'Auschool' ('Blythe Spirit') S, my, 2000, Austin, David; flowers soft yellow, 2¼ in., 51 petals, loose, borne in large sprays, moderate musk fragrance; foliage bright green, matte; bushy growth; intr. 1999

'Ausclough' S, dp, Austin, David; intr. 1983

'Ausclub' ('Kathryn Morley') S, lp, 1995, Austin, David; flowers pale pink, 3-3½ in., very dbl., cupped, borne in small clusters, moderate fragrance; foliage medium size, dark green, glosssy; numerous prickles; tall (5-6 ft.), bushy growth; PP8814; [Mary Rose® × Chaucer®]; intr. 1990

'Auscoat' ('Red Coat') F, mr, 1981, Austin, David; bud pointed; intr. 1973

'Auscomp' ('Happy Child') S, my, 1994, Austin, David; flowers bright yellow, 3-3½ in., very dbl., borne in small clusters; foliage medium size, medium green, glossy; some prickles; medium (39 in.), bushy growth; PP9007; [seedling × Hero®]; intr. 1993

'Auscon' S, mp, 1981, Austin, David; bud globular; intr. 1970

'Auscook' ('Heather Austin') S, dp, 1997, Austin, David; flowers deep, dusky pink, 5-6 cm., 50 petals, borne in small clusters, moderate clove fragrance; foliage medium size, medium green, semi-glossy; some prickles; upright to bushy, medium (3x2½ ft.) growth; PP10618

'Auscot' ('Candy Rain', Abraham Darby®) S, ab, 1991, Austin, David; bud rounded, dark pink base with yellow; flowers pink peach-apricot, 3-4 in., very dbl., cupped, quartered, intense fragrance; foliage dark green, shiny; vigorous, bushy, angular growth; PP7215; ['Yellow Cushion' × 'Aloha']; intr. 1985

'Auscountry' ('Country Living') S, lp, 1994, Austin, David; flowers pale pink, 3-3½ in., very dbl., borne in small clusters; foliage medium size, medium green, semi-glossy; some prickles; upright, bushy (41 in.) growth; ['Wife of Bath' × Graham Thomas®]; intr. 1991

'Auscress' ('Cressida') S, ab, 1992, Austin, David; flowers apricot peach, 3-3½ in., very dbl., borne in small clusters; foliage small, light green, semi-glossy; some prickles; tall (70 in.), upright growth; intr. 1983

'Auscrim' ('L. D. Braithwaite', 'Leonard Dudley Braithwaite') S, dr, 1993, Austin, David; flowers bright red, 3-3½ in., very dbl., informal, borne in small clusters, intense fragrance; foliage medium size, dark green, semi-glossy; some prickles; growth medium (110 cm.), bushy; PP8154; [Mary Rose® × The Squire®]; intr. 1988

'Auscross' ('Windflower') S, lp, 1997, Austin, David; flowers soft lilac-pink, medium, double, cupped, borne in small clusters, moderate Old Rose, apple and cinnamon fragrance; recurrent; foliage medium size, medium green, semi-glossy, disease-resistant; stems wiry; bushy, medium (120 cm.) growth; very disease resistant; intr. 1994

'Auscrystal' ('James Galway') S, lp, 2001, Austin, David; flowers very full, borne in small clusters, moderate fragrance; foliage large, medium green, semi-glossy, disease-resistant; prickles medium, hooked downward, few; growth upright, tall (1¼ m.); garden decoration; PP13918; ['AUSblush' × seedling]; intr. 2000

'Auscup' (Ellen®) S, ab, 1986, Austin, David; flowers old rose form, large, dbl., intense fragrance; foliage large, medium green, semi-glossy; bushy growth; intr. 1984

'Ausdapple' ('English Dawn') S, lp, Austin, David; intr. 1983

'Ausday' ('Alexandra Rose', 'The Alexandra Rose') S, pb, 1994, Austin, David; flowers coppery pink, medium, 5 petals, borne in large clusters; foliage medium size, medium green, semi-glossy; few prickles; bushy, compact (51 in.) growth; ['Shropshire Lass' × Heritage®]; intr. 1992

'Ausdecorum' ('Darcey Bussell') S, rb, 2006, Austin, David; flowers deep crimson with mauve tints , 10 cm., very full, cupped, then rosette , borne in small clusters; recurrent; foliage medium size, medium green, matte; prickles medium, concave, curved inward, red, moderate; growth bushy, vigorous, medium (90 - 120 cm.); garden decorative; [seedling × seedling]; intr. 2006

'Ausdimindo' ('Bibi Maizoon', Bibi Mezoon®) S, dp, 1995, Austin, David; flowers have cabbage rose form early, opening to cupped, rich pink, 7 cm., 41 petals, cupped, borne in small clusters, moderate fragrance; medium size, dark green, semi-glossy foliage; some prickles; strong, arching growth; 4 × 4 ft.; intr. 1989

'Ausdir' ('Tradescant') S, dr, 1994, Austin, David; bud short, pointed ovoid; flowers very dark purplish-red, 2½ in., very full, cupped, then rosette, borne in small clusters, moderate sweet fragrance; recurrent; foliage medium size, dark green, semi-glossy; prickles some, medium, straight to hooked downward; stems long; bushy, spreading growth; PP9009; [Prospero® × seedling]; intr. 1993

'Ausdoctor' (Doctor Jackson™) S, mr, 1992, Austin, David; flowers scarlet, golden stamens, medium, 5 petals, borne mostly singly, no fragrance; foliage medium size, medium green, semi-glossy; few prickles; medium (120 cm.), spreading growth; intr. 1987

'Ausdor' ('Mrs Doreen Pike') HRg, mp, 1994, Austin, David; flowers medium, very dbl., borne in large clusters; foliage small, light green, semi-glossy; numerous prickles; medium (35 in.), bushy, spreading, compact growth; ['Martin Frobisher' × 'Roseraie de l'Hay']; intr. 1993

'Ausdove' ('Dove', 'Dovedale', 'The Dove') S, lp, 1986, Austin, David; flowers medium, dbl.; foliage medium size, dark, semi-glossy; spreading growth; ['Wife of Bath' × ('Iceberg' × unknown)]; intr. 1984

'Ausdrawn' (The Generous Gardener™) S, lp, 2004; flowers soft pink in center, very pale on outer petals, 6 cm., very full, cupped, borne in small clusters, intense fragrance; recurrent; foliage large, dark green, glossy; prickles medium, concave; growth bushy, arching, tall (150 cm.); garden decorative; ['Sharifa Asma' × 'seedling (unnamed pink English-type shrub)']; intr. 2002

'Ausecret' ('Anne Boleyn') S, lp, 2000, Austin, David; flowers soft warm pink, 3 in., 110 petals, rosette; foliage shiny, disease-resistant; almost thornless; arching growth; intr. 1999

'Auselle' (Belle Story®) S, lp, 1985, Austin, David; flowers light pink, yellow stamens, large, 35 petals, cupped, intense fragrance; foliage medium size, medium green, semi-glossy; bushy growth; PP7213; [(Chaucer® × 'Parade') × ('The Prioress' × 'Iceberg')]; intr. 1984

'Ausemi' ('English Apricot', Lucetta®) S, ab, 1992, Austin, David; flowers pale peach, 5¼ in., semi-dbl. to dbl., borne in small clusters, moderate fragrance; foliage medium size, medium green, semi-glossy; some prickles; medium (47 in.), spreading growth; intr. 1983

'Ausencart' ('Ben Britten', 'Benjamin Britten') S, or, 2002, Austin, David; flowers very dbl., cupped, borne in small clusters, intense fragrance; foliage medium size, dark green, semi-glossy; prickles medium, deep concave, red/brown, moderate; growth bushy, medium (120 cm.); garden decorative; ['Ausfather' × 'pink English-type shrub']; intr. 2001

'Ausfar' ('Dr Herbert Gray') S, lp, 1998, Austin, David; flowers clear light pink, reverse medium pink, large, 75-80 petals, cupped, borne in small clusters; foliage small, dark green, glossy; few prickles; spreading, medium (3 ft.) growth; [Heritage® × seedling]; intr. 1998

'Ausfather' S, ab, 1981, Austin, David; bud globular; intr. 1973

'Ausfete' ('Ann') S, mp, 1998, Austin, David; flowers 2½ in., single, borne in clusters; foliage medium size, medium green, semi-glossy; prickles moderate; bushy, medium (3 ft.) growth; intr. 1997

'Ausfin' ('Financial Times Centenary') S, dp, 1994, Austin, David; flowers deep pink, 3-3½ in., very dbl., borne in small clusters; foliage medium size, dark green, semi-glossy; some prickles; medium (43 in.), upright, bushy growth; PP8142; intr. 1988

'Ausfire' ('Morning Mist 96', 'Morning Mist') S, pb, 1997, Austin, David; flowers coppery red, 4 in., 5 petals, borne in small clusters; foliage large, light green, leathery; prickles moderate; attractive, shrubby, spreading, tall (4½x4ft.) growth; intr. 1996

'Ausfirst' ('Constanze Spry') S, lp, 1961, Austin, David; intr. 1961

'Ausfudge' ('Rose of Picardy') S, mr, 2004; flowers single, borne in small clusters, slight fragrance; foliage medium size, medium green, matte; prickles medium, concave curved inward; growth compact, narrow bushy, vigorous, medium (100 cm.); garden decorative; ['seedling (deep pink English-type shrub)' × 'seedling (deep pink English-type shrub)']; intr. 2004

'Ausglisten' ('The Cottage Rose') S, mp, Austin, David; intr. 1991

'Ausglobe' ('Brother Cadfael') S, mp, 1995, Austin, David; flowers rich pink, 45 petals, cupped, intense old rose fragrance; foliage dark green; prickles few thorns; straight stems; strong, bushy growth; PP8681; intr. 1990

'Ausgold' ('Golden Celebration') S, dy, 1993, Austin, David; flowers old fashioned, 3-3½ in., 55-75 petals, borne in small clusters, intense fragrance; foliage large, dark green, semi-glossy; some prickles; medium (120 cm.), bushy growth; PP8688; [Charles Austin® × Abraham Darby®]; intr. 1992

'Ausgrab' ('Alnwick Castle', 'The Alnwick Rose') S, pb, 2002, Austin, David; flowers dusty apricot-pink, 7 cm., very dbl., cupped, borne in small clusters, no fragrance; foliage medium size, medium green, semi-glossy, leathery, smooth; prickles medium, concave, brown, moderate; growth bushy, medium (120 cm.); garden decorative; [seedling × 'Ausgold']; intr. 2001

'Ausguard' ('Portmeirion') S, dp, 2000, Austin, David; flowers very full, shallow cupped, borne singly or in small clusters, strong old rose fragrance; foliage medium size, dark green, semi-glossy, disease-resistant; numerous prickles; spreading, low (3 ft.) growth; ['Ausblush' × 'seedling (pink English shrub)']; intr. 1999

'Ausham' ('Geoff Hamilton') S, mp, 1998, Austin, David; flowers rounded, 3-4 in., 108 petals, borne in small clusters, moderate fragrance; foliage medium size, medium green, semi-glossy, good disease resistance; prickles moderate; sturdy, compact, upright, medium (4 ft.) growth; PP11421; [Heritage® × seedling]; intr. 1997

'Aushedge' ('Wild Edric') S, dp, 2006, Austin, David; flowers deep pink with shades of purple and mauve, yellow stamens, 9½ cm., double, cupped, borne in small clusters, intense fragrance; recurrent; foliage medium size, dark green, matte; prickles numerous, medium to large, linear, light green; growth bushy, vigorous, medium (120 cm.); garden decorative, hedging; [seedling × seedling]; intr. 2005

'Aushero' (Hero®) S, mp, 1983, Austin, David; flowers glistening medium pink, large, 20 petals, cupped, intense fragrance; foliage medium size, medium green, semi-glossy; spreading growth; ['The Prioress' × seedling]; intr. 1982

'Aushomer' ('Windermere') S, w, 2006, Austin, David; flowers 7½ cm., very full, borne in small clusters; foliage medium size, dark green, matte; prickles medium, concave, curved inward, medium red, few; growth compact, medium (100 cm.); garden decorative; [seedling × seedling]; intr. 2006

'Aushouse' (Harlow Carr™) S, mp, 2004; flowers very full, borne in small clusters, intense fragrance; foliage medium size, medium green, semi-glossy; prickles medium, concave curved inward,; growth bushy, vigorous, branching, medium (125 cm.); garden decorative; ['seedling (white English-type shrub)' × 'Ausman']; intr. 2004

'Aushunter' (Jubilee Celebration™) S, pb, 2004; flowers pink blend & light yellow, reverse pink blend, 8-9 cm., very full, borne in small clusters, intense fruity fragrance; foliage medium size, dark green, semi-glossy; prickles medium, deeply concave; growth bushy, broad, vigorous (120 cm.); garden decorative; ['Ausgold' × 'seedling (medium yellow English-type shrub)']; intr. 2002

'Ausimple' ('Skylark') S, mp, 2008, David Austin Roses, Ltd.; flowers 9 cm., very full, borne in small clusters; foliage medium, dark green, semi-glossy; prickles medium, hooked downward, brown, moderate; growth bushy, short (90 cm.); garden decorative; ['English-type shrub' × 'English-type shrub']; intr. 2008

'Ausintense' ('Wisley') S, dp, 2004, Austin, David; flowers 6½ cm., very full, borne in small clusters, moderate fragrance;

foliage large, dark green, semi-glossy; prickles medium, hooked downward; growth bushy, vigorous, medium (125 cm.); garden decorative; ['seedling (apricot English type shrub)' × 'Golden Celebration']; intr. 2004

'Ausjac' ('Jacquenetta') S, ab, Austin, David; intr. 1983

'Ausjake' ('Miss Alice') S, lp, 2001, Austin, David; flowers 7-8½ cm., very full, borne mostly solitary, moderate fragrance; foliage small, light green, matte, disease-resistant; prickles medium, hooked downward, numerous; growth compact, medium (1 m.); garden decorative; [Mary Rose® × seedling]; intr. 2000

'Ausjameson' S, ab, Austin, David; intr. 2006

'Ausjess' ('Pretty Jessica') S, dp, 1992, Austin, David; flowers medium, very full, cupped, borne in small clusters, intense old rose fragrance; free-flowering; foliage medium size, dark green, semi-glossy; some prickles; low (65 cm.), bushy growth; ['Wife of Bath' × seedling]; intr. 1983

'Ausjive' ('Huntington Rose') S, dp, Austin, David; bud roundedvery full; intr. 2006

'Ausjo' ('England's Rose (Germany)', 'Jude the Obscure') S, my, 1997, Austin, David; flowers large, 55-70 petals, globular, borne singly or in small clusters, intense fragrance; foliage medium size, medium green, semi-glossy; some prickles; bushy, medium growth; PP10757; [Abraham Darby® × Windrush®]; intr. 1995

'Ausjolly' ('Mary Magdalene') S, pb, 1998, Austin, David; flowers soft pink shaded apricot, 4 in., 100-110 petals, borne in small clusters, intense myrrh fragrance; foliage medium size, medium green, dull; prickles moderate; spreading, medium (3 ft.) growth; [seedling × seedling]; intr. 1998

'Ausjump' ('Christopher Marlowe') S, or, 2004; flowers orange-red, reverse yellow blend & orange-red, 7½ cm., very full, borne in small clusters, moderate fragrance; foliage medium size, dark green, semi-glossy; prickles medium, deeply concave; growth bushy, branching, short (90 cm.); garden decorative; PP14943; ['seedling (medium pink shrub)' × 'Golden Celebration']; intr. 2002

'Ausjuno' ('Immortal Juno') S, dp, 1992, Austin, David; flowers deep pink, 3-3½ in., very dbl., borne in small clusters, intense fragrance; foliage medium size, medium green, semi-glossy; some prickles; tall (59 in.), upright growth; intr. 1982

'Auskeppy' ('Grace') S, ab, 2002, Austin, David; flowers apricot-yellow, fading to white, 7 cm., very dbl., rosette, borne in large clusters, intense fragrance; foliage medium size, light green, semi-glossy; prickles short, concave, brown/red, few; growth bushy, medium (120 cm.); garden decorative; ['Sweet Juliet' × 'yellow english-type shrub']; intr. 2001

'Ausky' ('Mistress Quickly') S, mp, 1997, Austin, David; flowers petals informally arranged, small, 90-100 petals, borne in very large clusters; foliage small to medium size, medium green, semi-glossy; few prickles; bushy, medium growth; disease resistant; PP10617; ['Blush Noisette' × 'Martin Frobisher']; intr. 1998

'Ausland' ('Scepter'd Isle') S, lp, 1997, Austin, David; bud short, pointed ovoid; flowers soft pink, 4 in., 45 petals, cupped, borne in small clusters, intense myrrh fragrance; good repeat; foliage medium size, dark green, semi-glossy; prickles some, medium, hooked downward; narrow, bushy (4 ft.) growth; PP10969; [seedling × Heritage®]; intr. 1996

'Auslea' (Leander®) S, ab, 1983, Austin, David; flowers small, very dbl., flat, borne in clusters; foliage medium size, medium green, semi-glossy; spreading growth; [Charles Austin® × seedling]; intr. 1982

'Ausleaf' ('Autumn Leaves', English Elegance®) S, ob, 1986, Austin, David; flowers large, dbl., moderate fragrance; foliage medium size, medium green, semi-glossy; upright growth; PP7557

'Auslean' ('Cymbaline', 'Cymbeline') S, lp, 1983, Austin, David; flowers medium, dbl., intense fragrance; foliage medium size, medium green, semi-glossy; spreading growth; [seedling × Lilian Austin®]; intr. 1982

'Ausleap' ('Sweet Juliet') S, ab, 1994, Austin, David; bud rounded with long cuspidate apex; flowers apricot-yellow, fading lighter, medium, 90 petals, cupped, borne singly and in small clusters, moderate sweet, fruity fragrance; recurrent; foliage medium size, medium green, semi-glossy; prickles some, 9 mm., reddish; upright, bushy (39 in.) growth; PP8153; [Graham Thomas® × Admired Miranda®]; intr. 1989

'Ausled' ('A Shropshire Lad') S, yb, 1997, Austin, David; flowers very dbl., 100 petals, rosette, borne in small clusters; foliage medium size, medium green, semi-glossy; prickles moderate; bushy, medium (5 × 4 ft.)growth; PP10607; intr. 1996

'Auslett' ('Allux Symphony', 'Symphony') S, ly, 1994, Austin, David; flowers soft yellow, deeper in center, 3-4 in., very dbl., rosette, borne in small clusters, slight spicy fragrance; recurrent; foliage medium size, light green, glossy; medium (120 cm.), upright, bushy growth; ['The Friar' × 'Yellow Cushion']; intr. 1986

'Auslevel' ('Glamis Castle') S, w, 1994, Austin, David; flowers medium, very dbl., cupped, borne in small clusters, intense myrrh fragrance; foliage medium size, medium green, semi-glossy; numerous prickles; medium (100 cm.), bushy growth; PP8765; [Graham Thomas® × Mary Rose®]; intr. 1992

'Auslian' (Warwick Castle®) S, dp, 1992, Austin, David; flowers rose pink, 3-3½ in., very full, rosette, borne in small clusters, moderate Bourbon fragrance; recurrent; foliage small, medium green, matte; some prickles; stems slender, arching; low (75 cm.), spreading growth; [The Reeve® × Lilian Austin®]; intr. 1986

'Auslight' ('Claire', Claire Rose®) S, mp, 1991, Austin, David; flowers very large, full, cupped, intense fragrance; foliage clear green; bushy, vigorous growth; [Charles Austin® × (seedling × 'Iceberg')]; intr. 1988

'Auslilac' ('Old Lilac', Lilac Rose™) S, pb, 1994, Austin, David; flowers lilac pink, 3-3½ in., very dbl., borne in small clusters; foliage medium size, medium green, semi-glossy; some prickles; upright (90 cm.) growth; PP8837; [seedling × Hero®]; intr. 1990

'Ausling' ('Ausyel') S, ly, 1981, Austin, David; intr. 1979

'Auslo' (Othello®) S, mr, 1991, Austin, David; bud medium, broad with flat top; flowers clear red, fading to purple-red, 4-5 in., 78 petals, cupped, borne usually singly, intense old rose fragrance; recurrent; foliage dark green, semi-glossy; prickles many large thorns; vigorous, bushy growth; PP7212; [Lilian Austin® × The Squire®]; intr. 1989

'Auslofty' ('Port Sunlight') S, ab, 2008, David Austin Roses, Ltd.; flowers 9 cm., single, borne mostly solitary; prickles medium, hooked downward, orange, few; growth vigorous (150 cm.); garden decorative; ['pink English-type shrub' × 'yellow English-type shrub']; intr. 2008

'Auslot' ('Sophy's Rose') S, rb, 1999, Austin, David; bud short, pointed ovoid; flowers red-purple, 3½ in., 82 petals, cupped, domed, borne singly and in small clusters, moderate light tea fragrance; recurrent; foliage medium size, medium green, semi-glossy; prickles moderate, medium to short, hooked downward; strong, bushy, vigorous, medium (3½ ft.) growth; PP11422; [Prospero® × seedling]; intr. 1997

'Ausmak' ('Eglantyne Jebb', 'Eglantyne', 'Masako') S, lp, 1994, Austin, David; flowers light, delicate pink, 3-3½ in., very dbl., cupped, borne in small clusters; foliage medium size, medium green, matte; some prickles; medium (115-130 cm.), bushy growth; PP9526; [seedling × Mary Rose®]; intr. 1994

'Ausman' (The Countryman®) S, mp, 1987, Austin, David; bud oval; flowers greyish-rose, 6-8 cm., 40 petals, rosette, borne singly and in sprays of 3-5, intense damask fragrance; repeat bloom; foliage medium size, medium green, matte; prickles hooked, small, downward pointing, pale; spreading, bushy, medium growth; hips ovoid, medium, red; PP7556; [Lilian Austin® × 'Comte de Chambord']

'Ausmary' ('Country Marilou', 'Pink River', Mary Rose®) S, mp, 1983, Austin, David; flowers large, very dbl., cupped; recurrent bloom; foliage medium size, medium-green, matte; upright, bushy growth; [seedling × 'The Friar']

'Ausmas' ('English Yellow', 'Graham Stuart Thomas', Graham Thomas®, 'Lemon Parady') S, dy, 1983, Austin, David; flowers rich deep yellow, medium, 35 petals, cupped, intense fragrance; recurrent bloom; foliage small, dark, glossy; bushy growth; [seedling × (Charles Austin® × ('Iceberg' × unknown))]

'Ausmash' ('Heavenly Rosalind') S, pb, 1997, Austin, David; flowers wild-rose effect, medium, 5 petals, borne in small clusters; foliage medium size, dark green, dull, leathery; upright, bushy, medium growth; intr. 1995

'Ausmerchant' ('Princess Alexandra of Kent') S, mp, 2008, David Austin Roses, Ltd.; flowers 11 cm., very full, borne in small clusters; foliage medium, medium green, matte; prickles medium, hooked downward, brown, moderate; growth bushy, medium (100 cm.); garden decorative; ['crimson English-type shrub' × 'crimson English-type shrub']; intr. 2008

'Ausmian' (Charmian®) S, mp, 1983, Austin, David; flowers large, dbl.; foliage medium size, medium green, semi-glossy; spreading growth; [seedling × Lilian Austin®]; intr. 1982

'Ausmira' (Admired Miranda®) S, lp, 1983, Austin, David; flowers opening flat, then reflexing, large, dbl., flat; foliage medium size, medium green, semi-glossy; upright growth; ['The Friar' × 'The Friar']; intr. 1983

'Ausmit' ('St Cecilia') S, lp, 1987, Austin, David; flowers pale buff yellow, fading cream, medium, 40 petals, cupped, borne usually singly, moderate myrrh fragrance; repeat bloom; foliage small, medium green, matte; bushy, low, medium growth; no fruit; PP8157; [seedling × seedling]

'Ausmol' (Molineux™) S, dy, 1994, Austin, David; bud pointed ovoid and globular; flowers 7 cm., 110-120 petals, rosette, borne in clusters, slight fragrance; recurrent; foliage large, leathery; prickles few, medium, hooked downward, vigorous (3 ft.) growth; PP9524; [Graham Thomas® × seedling]

'Ausmoon' ('Pegasus') S, ly, 1997, Austin, David; flowers large, camelia-like, 110 petals, borne in small clusters, intense rich tea-rose fragrance; foliage large, dark green, semi-glossy, leathery; few prickles; bushy, branching, medium growth; PP9705; [Graham Thomas® × Pascali®]; intr. 1995

'Ausmound' S, pb, 1981, Austin, David; bud globular; intr. 1973

'Ausmove' ('Tess of the d'Urbervilles') S, dr, 1999, Austin, David; flowers dark, crimson red, large, very dbl., cupped, borne in small clusters, moderate fragrance; foliage large, dark green, semi-glossy; numerous prickles; branching, medium (3 ft.) growth; [The Squire® × seedling]; intr. 1998

'Ausmum' (Pat Austin™) S, ob, 1997, Austin, David; bud pointed, ovoid; flowers bright copper inside, paler outside, 3½-4½ in., 50 petals, borne in small clusters, moderate fragrance; foliage large, dark green, glossy; prickles some, long to medium, slighty hooked downward; branching, rounded, medium growth; PP9527; [Graham Thomas® × Abraham Darby®]

'Ausmurr' (Hilda Murrell®) S, mp, 1986, Austin, David; flowers old rose form, large, full, flat, intense fragrance; few blooms after spring flush; foliage large, medium green, matte; strong, upright, bushy (4 ft.) growth; [seedling × ('Parade' × Chaucer®)]; intr. 1984

'Ausnetting' ('Corvedale') S, pb, 2002, Austin, David; flowers dusty rose pink, 7 cm., dbl., cupped, borne in small clusters, moderate fragrance; foliage large, medium green, semi-glossy; prickles medium, deep concave, brown, few; growth bushy, medium (150 cm.); garden decorative; [Charles Rennie Mackintosh® × 'deep red English-type shrub']; intr. 2001

'Ausnun' S, w, Austin, David; intr. 1987

'Ausoil' ('Troilus') S, ab, 1992, Austin, David; flowers creamy apricot to honey-buff, 3-3½ in., very full, cupped, borne in large clusters, intense sweet fragrance; recurrent; foliage large, dark green, semi-glossy; some prickles; medium (110 cm.), upright growth; [('Duchesse de Montebello' × Chaucer®) × Charles Austin®]; intr. 1983

'Ausold' (Trevor Griffiths™) S, dp, 1997, Austin, David; flowers dusky pink, large, very full, loose to flat, borne in small clusters, intense oaky claret fragrance; recurrent; foliage medium size, dark green, dull, rough texture; some prickles; upright, spreading, medium (105 cm.) growth; ['Wife of Bath' × Hero®]; intr. 1994

'Ausome' ('Rose-Marie', 'White Heritage') S, w, 2003, Austin, David; flowers very full, borne in small clusters, intense fragrance; foliage medium size, dark green, semi-glossy; prickles few, 9 mm., concave, curved inwards; upright growth; garden decorative; [sport of 'Heritage']; intr. 2003

'Ausonius' HMsk, pb, 1932, Lambert, P.; buds oval, yellow-red; flowers yellowish-pink, center white, medium, semi-dbl., borne in pyramidal trusses of 20-50, moderate fragrance; free, recurrent bloom; foliage leathery; semi-climbing, bushy growth; [('Chamisso' × 'Léonie Lamesch') × ('Geheimrat Dr. Mittweg' × Tip-Top®)]

'Ausoran' (Scarborough Fair™) S, lp, 2004; flowers soft pink, golden stamens, 5½ cm., semi-dbl. to dbl., globular to cupped, borne in small clusters, moderate old rose to musk fragrance; recurrent; foliage medium size, dark green, matte; prickles medium, concave, curved inward; growth bushy, narrow, branching, short (75 cm.); garden decorative; ['seedling (medium yellow English type shrub)' × 'seedling (light pink English type shrub)']; intr. 2003

'Ausorts' (Mortimer Sackler™) S, lp, 2004; flowers very full, borne in small clusters, moderate fragrance; foliage large, dark green, semi-glossy; prickles medium, concave; growth upright, vigorous, branching, tall (5 ft.); garden decorative; ['Lillian Austin' × 'seedling (apricot English-type shrub)']; intr. 2002

'Auspale' S, lp, Austin, David; bud short, slightly pointed ovoid; intr. 1992

'Auspalette' ('Sister Elizabeth') S, mp, 2006, Austin, David; flowers 8 cm., very full, borne in small clusters; foliage medium size, medium green, matte; prickles medium, concave, curved inward, red, numerous; growth compact, bushy, short (80 cm.); garden decorative; PPAF; [seedling × seedling]; intr. 2006

'Auspeet' ('Charles Darwin') S, my, 2002, Austin, David; flowers very dbl., borne in small clusters, moderate fragrance; foliage medium size, medium green, semi-glossy; prickles medium, hooked downwards, brown, few; growth bushy, branching, medium (1 m.); garden decorative; PP13992; ['peachy pink english-type shrub' × 'yellow english-type shrub']; intr. 2001

'Ausperd' (Perdita®) S, ab, 1992, Austin, David; flowers blush apricot, large, very full, borne in small clusters, intense fragrance; foliage medium size, medium green, semi-glossy; some prickles; medium (100 cm.), bushy growth; ['The Friar' × (seedling × 'Iceberg')]; intr. 1983

'Auspero' (Prospero®) S, dr, 1983, Austin, David; flowers large, full, flat, rosette, intense fragrance; good repeat; foliage medium size, dark green, matte; weak, upright (3 ft.) growth; PP9008; ['The Knight' × seedling]; intr. 1982

'Auspishus' ('Janet') S, pb, 2004; flowers very full, borne in small clusters, slight fragrance; foliage large, dark green, semi-glossy; prickles medium, deeply concave; growth bushy, broad, vigorous, medium (120 cm.); garden decorative; ['Ausgold' × 'seedling (medium pink English-type shrub)']; intr. 2003

'Auspoly' ('Charlotte', 'Elgin Festival') S, ly, 1994, Austin, David; flowers soft yellow, 3-3½ in., very dbl., borne in small clusters; foliage medium size, medium green, semi-glossy; few prickles; medium (100 cm.), upright, bushy growth; [seedling × Graham Thomas®]; intr. 1993

'Auspom' ('Snow Goose') S, w, 1997, Austin, David; bud creamy, pink-tipped, pointed; flowers white with very narrow petals, 1-2 in., full, pompon, borne in small clusters, slight sweet, musk fragrance; good repeat; foliage small, dark green, smooth; few prickles; bushy (8-10 ft.) growth; tall shrub or short climber; intr. 1997

'Ausport' ('Wise Portia') S, m, 1983, Austin, David; flowers rich magenta, large, dbl., intense fragrance; foliage medium size, dark, semi-glossy; bushy growth; ['The Knight' × seedling]

'Auspot' ('Potter & Moore') S, mp, Austin, David; intr. 1988

'Ausprima' ('Sir Edward Elgar') S, mr, 1995, Austin, David; flowers cerise-crimson, medium, very dbl., cupped, borne mostly singly; foliage medium size, medium green, semi-glossy; numerous prickles; medium (75 cm.), upright, bushy, compact growth; [Mary Rose® × The Squire®]; intr. 1992

'Ausprior' ('Claire Austin') S, w, 2008, David Austin Roses, Ltd.; flowers 9 cm., single, borne mostly solitary; prickles medium, hooked downward, orange, moderate; growth , , , 135 cm., Garden Decorative; ['yellow English-type shrub' × 'pink English-type shrub']; intr. 2008

'Ausquest' ('City of Timaru', 'Crocus Rose', 'Emanuel') S, w, 2001, Austin, David; flowers very full, borne in small clusters, moderate fragrance; foliage medium size, medium green, semi-glossy, disease-resistant; prickles medium, slightly hooked downward, moderate; growth bushy, medium (1¼ m.); garden decorative; PP14092; [seedling × 'Golden Celebration']; intr. 2000

'Ausquire' S, dr, 1981, Austin, David; bud globular; intr. 1976

'Ausrace' ('England's Rose', 'Ludlow Castle') S, w, 2000, Austin, David; flowers pale apricot in center, fading to cream, rounded, 3 in., 118 petals, rounded, borne in small clusters, moderate tea fragrance; foliage slightly glossy, dark green; bushy growth; PP13299; ['seedling (pink English shrub)' × 'seedling (yellow English shrub)']; intr. 1999

'Ausram' ('Francine Austin') S, w, 1994, Austin, David; flowers 1½ in., very dbl., borne in large clusters; foliage small, medium green, semi-glossy; some prickles; groundcover; bushy, spreading (90 cm.) growth; PP8156; ['Alister Stella Gray' × 'Ballerina']; intr. 1988

'Ausreef' ('Sharifa Asma', 'Sharifa') S, lp, 1995, Austin, David; bud rounded; flowers blush pink, fading to almost white on outer petals, 3-4 in., 90 petals, cupped, then rosette, borne singly and in small clusters, moderate fruity (white grapes and mulberry) fragrance; recurrent; foliage dark green, semi-glossy; numerous prickles; bushy, upright (3 ft.) growth; hips none ; PP8143; [Mary Rose® × Admired Miranda®]; intr. 1989

'Ausreeve' S, dp, 1981, Austin, David; bud globular; intr. 1973

'Ausrelate' ('Lichfield Angel') S, w, 2006, Austin, David; flowers white with apricot tones, reverse light yellow, 8½ cm., very full, cupped rosette , borne in small clusters; recurrent; foliage medium size, dark green, semi-glossy; prickles medium, concave, curved inward, medium red, few; growth bushy, vigorous, medium (120 cm.); garden decorative; [seedling × seedling]; intr. 2006

'Ausren' (Charles Rennie Mackintosh®) S, pb, 1994, Austin, David; flowers lilac pink, medium, very dbl., borne in small clusters; reliable repeat; foliage medium size, dark green, matte; growth medium (110 cm.), bushy; PP8155; intr. 1988

'Ausrimini' ('Strawberry Hill') S, lp, 2006, Austin, David; flowers rose pink, paling to lighter pink on the outer petals , 9 cm., very full, cupped rosette , borne in small clusters; recurrent; foliage medium size, dark green, glossy; prickles medium, concave, curved inward, dark red, moderate; growth bushy, vigorous, medium (120 cm.); garden decorative; [seedling × seedling]; intr. 2006

'Ausromeo' ('Love Surprise', 'New William Shakespeare', 'William Shakespeare 2000') S, mr, 2001, Austin, David; bud pointed ovoid; flowers velvety crimson, changing to deep purple-red, 10-11 cm., very full, cupped, borne singly and in small clusters, intense Old Rose fragrance; recurrent; foliage medium size, medium green, matte; prickles moderate, 10 mm., hooked downward, dark red-purple; stems strong; growth bushy, medium (105 cm.); garden, decorative; hips none ; PP13993; [seedling × 'The Dark Lady']; intr. 2000

'Ausron' ('Lordly Oberon') S, lp, 1983, Austin, David; flowers large, very dbl., cupped; foliage large, medium green, matte; upright growth; [Chaucer® × seedling]; intr. 1982

'Ausrover' ('Tea Clipper') S, ab, 2006, Austin, David; flowers 9 cm., very full, borne in small clusters; foliage medium size, dark green, matte; prickles medium, concave, curved inward, yellow blend, few; growth bushy, vigorous, medium (120 cm.); garden decorative; [seedling × seedling]; intr. 2006

'Ausroyal' ('Love Surprise', William Shakespeare®) S, dr, 1987, Austin, David; flowers deep crimson-purple, fading rich purple, small, dbl., rosette, borne in sprays of 3 - 7, intense damask fragrance; repeat bloom; foliage large, dark green, semi-glossy; prickles broad based, straight, medium, red; upright, tall growth; no fruit; [The Squire® × Mary Rose®]; intr. 1987

'Ausrumba' ('Gentle Hermione') S, lp, 2006, Austin, David; flowers 9½ cm., very full, borne in small clusters; foliage medium size, dark green, matte; prickles medium, concave, curved inward, dark red, moderate; growth bushy, vigorous, medium (120 cm.); garden decorative; [seedling × seedling]; intr. 2005

'Ausrush' (Windrush®) S, ly, 1985, Austin, David; flowers soft yellow, large, semi-dbl., shallow cup, intense spicy musk fragrance; recurrent; foliage medium size, light green, matte; vigorous, branching growth; [seedling × ('Canterbury' × 'Golden Wings')]; intr. 1984

'Aussal' ('Radio Times') S, mp, 1997, Austin, David; bud pointed ovoid, globular; flowers rich, clear pink, 2½-3 in., 95-110 petals, flat, borne in small clusters, intense fragrance; foliage medium size, medium green, semi-glossy; prickles numerous, straight or slightly hooked; bushy, speading, low (75 cm.) growth; PP9525; [seedling × seedling]; intr. 1994

'Aussaucer' ('Apricot Parfait', 'Evelyn') S, ab, 1992, Austin, David; flowers very dbl., old-fashioned, rosette, borne in small clusters; foliage medium size, medium green, semi-glossy; some prickles; medium (110 cm.), upright, bushy growth; PP8680; [Graham Thomas® × 'Austamora']; intr. 1991

'Aussemi' ('Herbalist', The Herbalist™) S, dp, 1994, Austin, David; flowers deep pink, medium, semi-dbl., borne in small clusters, slight fragrance; foliage medium size, medium green, semi-glossy; some prickles; medium (90 cm.), bushy, spreading growth; [seedling × 'Louise Odier']; intr. 1991

'Aussnow' ('Mountain Snow') HWich, w, 1986, Austin, David; flowers dbl., 20 petals, borne in large clusters; foliage large, dark, semi-glossy; vigorous (to 20 ft.) growth; intr. 1985

'Ausspry' (Sir Walter Raleigh™) S, mp, 1994, Austin, David; bud medium, ovate pointed; flowers warm medium pink, 4 in., very dbl., flat cup, borne mostly singly or in small clusters, intense fragrance; recurrent; foliage medium size, medium green, semi-glossy; prickles few, slightly recurved, brown; medium (4 ft.), upright, bushy growth; PP7213; [Lilian Austin® × Chaucer®]; intr. 1985

'Austamora' ('Tamora') S, ab, 1992, Austin, David; flowers apricot yellow, 3-4 in., very dbl., cupped, borne in small clusters, intense unusual myrrh fragrance; recurrent; foliage small, dark green, semi-glossy; some prickles; medium (90 cm.), bushy growth; [Chaucer® × 'Conrad Ferdinand Meyer']; intr. 1983

'Austango' ('Summer Song') S, ob, 2006, Austin, David; bud rounded; flowers burnt orange, 9½ cm., very full, globular, then cupped, borne in small clusters, intense fragrance; foliage medium size, dark green, semi-glossy; prickles moderate, medium, concave, curved inward, red; growth upright, bushy, medium (120 cm.); garden decorative; [seedling × seedling]; intr. 2005

'Austania' ('Proud Titania') S, w, 1983,

Austin, David; flowers white with apricot blush, large, 35 petals, flat, rosette, intense fragrance; recurrent; foliage small, medium green, semi-glossy; growth upright, medium; [seedling × seedling]

'Austew' S, lp, Austin, David; bud small; intr. 2006

'Austiger' ('Queen of Sweden') S, lp, 2004; flowers very full, cupped, borne in small clusters, slight myrrh fragrance; foliage medium size, medium green, matte; prickles medium, hooked downward; growth upright, narrow, medium (3½ ft.); garden decorative; ['seedling (medium pink English type shrub)' × 'Auspoly']; intr. 2004

'Austijus' (The Ingenious Mr Fairchild™) S, pb, 2004; flowers lavender pink, reverse lighter mauve, 7 cm., very full, borne in small clusters, moderate fragrance; foliage medium size, dark green, semi-glossy; prickles medium, deeply concave; growth bushy, broad, branching, medium (120 cm.); garden decorative; ['seedling (medium pink English-type shrub)' × 'seedling (medium pink English-type shrub)']; intr. 2003

'Austilly' ('The Mayflower') S, pb, 2002, Austin, David; flowers very dbl., borne in small clusters, moderate fragrance; foliage medium size, dark green, matte, leathery; prickles few, medium, concave; growth bushy, upright, medium (120 cm.); garden decorative; ['peachy-pink English-type shrub' × 'yellow English-type shrub']; intr. 2001

'Austin Jace' Min, m, 2005, Ellerman, Gigi; flowers mauve, reverse mauve, small, full, borne mostly solitary; foliage medium size, medium green, matte; prickles average, slight curve, few; growth bushy, medium; [sport of 'Black Jade']; intr. 2005

'Austop' ('Barbara Austin') S, lp, 1999, Austin, David; flowers 3-4 in., 73 petals, borne mostly singly, moderate fragrance; foliage medium size, medium green, semi-glossy, good disease-resistant; prickles moderate; upright, medium (4 ft.) growth; PP11423; [Fair Bianca® × seedling]; intr. 1997

'Austough' (Rosemoor™) S, lp, 2004; flowers very full, borne in small clusters, intense fragrance; foliage medium size, dark green, semi-glossy; prickles medium, linear; growth bushy, narrow, vigorous, medium (100 cm.); garden decorative; ['Sharifa Asma' × 'light pink modern shrub seedling']; intr. 2004

Austragold® HT, my, McGredy, Sam IV; flowers non-fading yellow; stems strong; growth medium; intr. 1980

'Austral' HT, Bees; intr. 1976

'Australia Fair' -- See 'Tombosa'

'Australia Felix' HT, pb, 1919, Clark, A.; bud small, globular; flowers pink and silver shaded lavender, semi-dbl., cupped, intense fragrance; foliage dark, glossy; vigorous, bushy growth; ['Jersey Beauty' × 'La France']; May be extinct. Rose sold under this name by most is really Mrs. R. M Finch, a polyantha.

'Australian Beauty' Cl HP, mr, 1907, Kerslake; flowers crimson, moderate fragrance; ['President' × 'Lord Macaulay']

'Australian Bicentennial' HT, lp, Bell, Ronald J.; ['Daily Sketch' × 'Red Planet']; intr. 1987

'Australian Centenary of Federation' -- See 'Korvegata'

'Australian Centre Gold' -- See 'Savacent'

Australian Gold® ('Mona Lisa') F, ab, 1981, Kordes; bud ovoid; flowers apricot-peach, 20 petals, borne 5 per cluster, moderate fragrance; foliage dark, leathery; prickles red; bushy growth

'Australian Sunrise' -- See 'Irsnar'

'Australia's Olympic Gold Rose Rose' -- See 'Wekblagab'

'Australie' HT, dp, 1907, Kerslake; flowers large, dbl.

'Austream' ('Rushing Stream') S, w, 1997, Austin, David; flowers single, borne in large clusters, slight clove fragrance; foliage large, light green, glossy; few prickles; broad, bushy, medium (1½ ft.) growth; intr. 1986

'Austriaca' -- See 'Rosier d'Amour'

'Austriana' -- See 'Tananaistrua'

'Austwist' ('The Shepherdess') S, ab, 2006, Austin, David; flowers rich apricot-pink, fading to pale apricot on outer petals, 7 cm., very full, deeply cupped, borne in small clusters, moderate fruity fragrance; recurrent; foliage medium size, dark green, semi-glossy; prickles few, medium, deeply concave, light green; growth upright, medium (100 cm.); garden decorative; [seedling × seedling]; intr. 2005

'Ausuel' (Emanuel®) S, ab, 1992, Austin, David; flowers apricot-pink, opening rosette, 3-3½ in., dbl., flat, borne in small clusters; foliage small, medium green, semi-glossy; some prickles; medium (43 in.), bushy growth; [(Chaucer® × 'Parade') × (seedling × 'Iceberg')]; intr. 1985

'Ausufo' ('Comtes des Champagne', 'Coniston') S, yb, 2002, Austin, David; flowers medium yellow fading to white, 7 cm., semi-dbl., borne in small clusters, moderate fragrance; foliage medium size, medium green, semi-glossy, leathery, smooth, disease-resistant; prickles medium, deep concave, red, few; growth bushy, medium (120 cm.); garden decorative; ['pink English-type shrub' × 'Tamora']; intr. 2001

'Ausvelvet' S, dr, Austin, David; bud long, globular, cuspidate apex; intr. 1990

'Ausverse' ('Falstaff') S, dr, 2000, Austin, David; flowers dark crimson changing to rich purple, large, 105 petals, cupped, borne in small clusters; foliage medium size, medium green, semi-glossy; numerous prickles; vigorous, upright, bushy (3½ ft.) growth; PP13315; ['seedling (red English shrub)' × 'seedling (pink English shrub)']; intr. 1999

'Ausvolume' ('Lady of Megginch') S, dp, 2006, Austin, David; flowers 10½ cm., very full, borne in small clusters; foliage medium size, dark green, matte; prickles small, concave, curved inward, light green, moderate; growth bushy, vigorous, medium (120 cm.); garden decorative; [seedling × seedling]; intr. 2006

'Auswalker' ('Gartenarchitekt Günther Schulze') S, my, Austin, David; bud globular, pointed ovoid; intr. 1993

'Ausway' ('Noble Antony') S, mr, 1997, Austin, David; flowers deep magenta, deeply domed, outer petals recurve, large, 85-90 petals, borne singly or in small clusters, moderate fragrance; foliage medium size, dark green, semi-glossy; some prickles; bushy, medium, growth; PP10779; [seedling × seedling]; intr. 1995

'Auswebb' (Mary Webb®) S, ab, 1986, Austin, David; flowers very large, dbl., cupped, intense fragrance; foliage large, light green, matte; bushy growth; [seedling × Chinatown®]; intr. 1984

'Auswen' (Wenlock®) S, mr, 1985, Austin, David; flowers crimson, 5 in., very full, cupped, intense Old Rose & citrus fragrance; recurrent; foliage large, dark, semi-glossy; vigorous, bushy growth; shrub or low climber; ['The Knight' × 'Glastonbury']; intr. 1984

'Auswest' (Carding Mill™) S, ab, 2004; flowers apricot, reverse yellow blend, 7½ cm., very full, borne in small clusters, moderate fragrance; foliage medium size, medium green, semi-glossy; prickles medium, hooked downward; growth bushy, vigorous, medium (120 cm.); garden decorative; ['Ausland' × 'seedling (yellow English type shrub)']; intr. 2004

'Auswhite' ('Swan') S, w, 1987, Austin, David; flowers white, tinged buff, reverse white, large, very dbl., rosette, borne usually singly or in small clusters, moderate fruity fragrance; repeat bloom; foliage large, light green, semi-glossy; prickles few, hooked, medium, brownish-red; upright, tall growth; no fruit; PP7564; [Charles Austin® × (seedling × 'Iceberg')]; intr. 1987

'Auswife' ('Wife of Bath') S, pb, 1969, Austin, David

'Auswill' ('William Morris') S, ab, 1999, Austin, David; flowers apricot blend, reverse light pink, large, 120 petals, cupped, quartered, borne in small clusters, intense fragrance; recurrent; foliage medium size, dark green, glossy; prickles moderate; branching, medium (5 × 4 ft.) growth; [Abraham Darby® × seedling]; intr. 1998

'Auswine' S, m, 1967, Austin, David; intr. 1967

'Auswing' ('Wild Flower', 'Wildflower') S, ly, 1994, Austin, David; flowers pale yellow, 1½ in., 5 petals, shallow cup, borne mostly singly, slight fragrance; recurrent; foliage small, light green, semi-glossy; some prickles; low (2 ft.), bushy, spreading growth; ['Canterbury' × seedling]; intr. 1986

'Auswinter' ('Crown Princess Margareta') S, ab, 2000, Austin, David; flowers bright apricot orange, 3 in., very dbl., cupped, borne in small clusters, intense fruity fragrance; foliage medium size, bronze when young, semi-glossy; almost thornless; strong, arching growth to 1½ m.; PP13484; ['seedling (apricot English shrub)' × Abraham Darby®]; intr. 1999

'Auswith' ('St Swithun') S, lp, 1994, Austin, David; flowers pale pink, large, very dbl., borne in small clusters, moderate fragrance; foliage medium size, medium green, semi-glossy; some prickles; medium (4-5 ft.), bushy growth; PP9010; [Mary Rose® × seedling]; intr. 1993

'Auswonder' ('Ambridge Rose') S, ab, 1994, Austin, David; flowers apricot-pink, 2½-3 in., very dbl., cupped, borne in small clusters; foliage medium size, dark green, semi-glossy; some prickles; small (2½ ft.), bushy growth; PP8679; [Charles Austin® × seedling]; intr. 1990

'Ausyel' -- See 'Yellow Charles Austin'

'Autocrat' HT, pb, 1925, Beckwith; flowers ochre to flesh-pink, reverse prawn-red, large

'Autograph' HT, pb, 2000, Mattia, John; flowers deep pink, reverse light pink, striped white, 4½ in., very full, high-centered, borne mostly singly, slight fragrance; foliage medium size, medium green, semi-glossy; prickles moderate; growth upright, medium (4-5 ft.); [sport of 'Signature']; intr. 2003

'Autumn' HT, ob, 1928, Coddington; bud deep burnt orange; flowers burnt-orange, streaked red, medium, 20-25 petals, cupped, moderate fragrance; foliage dark, glossy; ['Sensation' × 'Souv. de Claudius Pernet']

'Autumn, Climbing' Cl HT, ob, 1951, deVor, W.L.

'Autumn Bliss' -- See 'Welbliss'

'Autumn Bouquet' S, mp, 1948, Jacobus; bud long, pointed; flowers carmine-rose-pink, large, dbl.; recurrent bloom; foliage leathery; vigorous, upright, compact growth; ['New Dawn' × 'Crimson Glory']

'Autumn Colours' F, ab, Poulsen; bud orange red; flowers apricot gold with brown tones, small to medium, double, borne in large clusters, slight fragrance; recurrent; foliage dark green, glossy; neat, bushy growth; intr. 2007

'Autumn Damask' -- See 'Quatre Saisons Continue'

'Autumn Dawn' -- See 'Briautumn'

'Autumn Days' F, ob

'Autumn Delight' HMsk, w, 1933, Bentall; flowers white with red stamens, large, single, borne in large clusters, moderate fragrance

'Autumn Dusk' Gr, pb, 1976, Buck, Dr. Griffith J.; bud ovoid, pointed; flowers pale Tyrian rose and white, 3½-4½ in., 33 petals, high-centered; foliage leathery; upright, bushy growth; ['Music Maker' × ('Dornröschen' × 'Peace')]; intr. 1975

'Autumn Fire' -- See 'Moranium'

'Autumn Fire' -- See 'Herbstfeuer'

'Autumn Flame' HT, ob, 1953, Thomson; bud long, pointed; flowers orange-yellow tinted red, 4 in., 35-40 petals, cupped; foliage dark, leathery; upright, bushy, compact growth; ['Ednah Thomas' × 'Autumn']

'Autumn Frost' -- See 'Litlin'

'Autumn Glow' HT, ob, 1979, Anderson's Rose Nurseries; bud pear shaped; flowers yellow-orange, 5 in., 55 petals, high-centered, slight fragrance; foliage small; bushy growth; [Pascali® × 'Bayadère']; intr. 1978

'Autumn Gold' HT, yb, 1975, Weeks; bud pointed; flowers brown-butterscotch-yellow, 3½-4 in., 42 petals, globular, moderate fragrance; foliage glossy, dark, leathery; tall, upright growth; PP3710; [seedling × seedling]; intr. 1974

'Autumn Hues' F, ob, 1962, Von Abrams; bud pointed; flowers orange, yellow and scarlet, 3-3½ in., 35 petals, high-centered, borne in clusters; foliage glossy; upright growth; ['Pinocchio' × 'Fred Edmunds']

'Autumn Kiss' -- See 'Walkiss'

'Autumn Leaves' -- See 'Ausleaf'

'Autumn Magic' -- See 'Foutum'

'Autumn Moon' -- See 'Shugetsu'

'Autumn Queen' ('Vice-President Curtis') HT, ob, 1933, Vestal; bud long, pointed; flowers burnt-orange, pink, gold, open, semi-dbl.; foliage leathery, bronze; vigorous, bushy growth

'Autumn Shades' Min, lp, Hannemann, F.; ['Silver Jubilee' × 'Oz Gold']; intr. 1997

'Autumn Song' -- See 'Jacment'

'Autumn Spice' -- See 'Silorbright'

'Autumn Splendor' -- See 'Micautumn'

'Autumn Spray' F, yb, 1964, Norman; flowers gold edged red, 3 in., 40 petals, flat; foliage glossy; ['Masquerade' × 'Isobel Harkness']

Autumn Sunblaze™ -- See 'Meiferjac'

'Autumn Sunlight' LCl, or, 1965, Gregory; flowers orange-vermilion, medium, 30 petals, semi-globular, borne in small clusters, moderate fragrance; foliage glossy, bright green; ['Spectacular' × 'Goldilocks, Climbing']

Autumn Sunset™ S, ab, 1987, Lowe, Malcolm; flowers medium apricot, with touches of orange and golden yellow, fading lighter, 20 petals, cupped, intense fruity fragrance; repeat bloom; foliage medium size, medium green, glossy, disease-resistant; prickles curved, medium, red; bushy, tall, climbing growth; hips round, medium, orange; [sport of 'Westerland']; intr. 1988

'Autumn Tints' HT, yb, 1914, Cant, B. R.; flowers coppery-pink with yellow, medium, dbl.

'Aux Cent Écus' -- See 'Belle Laure'

'Auzou' -- See 'Couture'

'Ava Rose' F, yb, McCann, Sean; flowers light yellow, flushed pink, semi-dbl., moderate fragrance; recurrent; medium (3-5 ft.) growth; [Playboy® × unknown]

'Avalanch II' ('Avalanche II') S, w, Williams, J. Benjamin; groundcover; spreading growth; intr. 1998

Avalanche+ HT, w, Voom, Lex; flowers clear white , double, high-centered, borne mostly singly; recurrent; stems long; florist rose; intr. 2004

'Avalanche' HT, w, 1922, Lippiatt; flowers creamy white, center deeper, dbl.

'Avalanche' HT, w, Chambard, C.; bud long; flowers large; foliage slightly bronze; vigorous, bushy, compact growth; intr. 1936

'Avalanche' F, w, Warriner, William A.; bud cream color; flowers cream changing to white, borne in clusters; growth vigorous, medium; intr. 1991

Avalanche Rose® -- See 'Delaval'

Avalanche Rose® S, mp, Delbard; flowers single; intr. 2002

'Avalanche II' -- See 'Avalanch II'

'Avalon' HT, ab, 1935, Western Rose Co.; bud ovoid; flowers apricot-yellow, center deeper, very large, dbl., globular; foliage glossy, bronze; vigorous, bushy growth; [sport of 'Duchess of Atholl']

Avance® S, mp, 1999, Barni, V.; flowers medium size, strong color, dbl., borne in large clusters; blooms all season; growth compact (40-60 cm.); intr. 1999

'Avandel' Min, yb, 1977, Moore, Ralph S.; bud long, pointed; flowers pink-yellow blend, 1-1½ in., 23 petals, cupped to flat, moderate fruity fragrance; foliage medium to dark green, leathery; upright, bushy growth; PP4366; ['Little Darling' × 'New Penny']

'Avant-Garde' HT, rb, Delbard; flowers striped; intr. 2003

'Avant Garde' HT, m, Schreurs, P.N.J.; flowers pale lilac with deeper edges, pointed petals, large, dbl., high-centered, borne mostly singly, slight fragrance; repeats in flushes; foliage dark green; few prickles; intr. 2005

'Avanti' -- See 'Jacsay'

'Avanti' HT, rb, Teranishi; flowers single; intr. 1966

Ave Maria® -- See 'Korav'

'Ave Maria' Pol, w, 1933, Bohm; growth compact, low (24-32 in.); [sport of 'Ulster']

'Ave Maria' HT, w, Brownell; flowers pure white, well-formed, 4-6 in., dbl.; vigorous, bushy growth; RULED EXTINCT 12/85; [seedling × 'Break o' Day, Climbing']; intr. 1957

'Ave Maria' HT, op; intr. 1972

'Avebury' LCl, lp, McLeod, J.; intr. 1995

'Avenant' -- See 'Belle Biblis'

'Avenir' ('L'Avenir') B, mp, 1858, Lartay; flowers bright pink, center darker, large, full

'Avenir' ('L'Avenir') HWich, lp, Corboeuf; flowers whitish pink, 3-4 cm., semi-dbl., borne in large clusters; intr. 1910

'Avenir' HT, Godin; intr. 1980

'Aventure' ('Adventure') HT, or, 1964, Croix, P.; flowers large, 55 petals, high-centered, slight fragrance; foliage leathery, glossy; vigorous, upright, bushy growth; PP2500; [('Corail' × Baccará®) × seedling]; intr. 1965

'Aventure No. 2' -- See 'Cropal'

'Avenue's Red' -- See 'Koriet'

'Aveu' HT, dp, Croix; flowers large, dbl.

'Aviateur Blériot' HWich, yb, 1910, Fauque; flowers pale orange-yellow, fading white, 6-7 cm., 34 petals, borne in clusters, moderate magnolia fragrance; non-recurrent; foliage small, glossy, dark green; vigorous, climbing growth; [R. wichurana × 'William Allen Richardson']

'Aviateur Michel Mahieu' HT, mp, 1912, Soupert & Notting; flowers coral-red, center brighter, large, dbl., intense fragrance; ['Mme Mélanie Soupert' × 'Lady Ashtown']

'Aviator Parmentier' HT, op, 1941, Verschuren-Pechtold; bud long, pointed; flowers peach-pink to orange, 4-4½ in., 30-35 petals, high-centered; foliage glossy; very vigorous growth; PP445; [seedling × 'Briarcliff']

'Avignon' F, my, 1974, Cants of Colchester, Ltd.; flowers dbl., 23 petals; foliage light, glossy; vigorous growth; [Zambra® × Allgold®]

'Aviora' HT, mr, 1960, Verbeek; flowers clear red, 40 petals; foliage glossy, dark; very large growth; ['Happiness' × seedling]

'Avô Albina' HT, rb, 1956, Moreira da Silva; flowers crimson, reverse silvery, large, high-centered; very vigorous growth; ['Peace' × 'Crimson Glory']

'Avô Alfredo' HT, rb, 1956, Moreira da Silva; flowers spectrum-red, reverse carmine; [seedling × 'Independence']

'Avoca' HT, mr, 1907, Dickson, A.; flowers crimson-scarlet, large, dbl., high-centered; very vigorous growth

'Avocat Duvivier' HP, m, 1875, Lévêque; flowers dbl.; ['Général Jacqueminot' × unknown]

'Avocat L. Lambert' HP, mp, 1884, Besson; flowers silky pink, center white, large, full

'Avocet' -- See 'Harpluto'

Avon™ -- See 'Niagara'

Avon® HT, dr, 1961, Morey, Dr. Dennison; bud ovoid; flowers 4½-5½ in., 23 petals, high-centered, intense fragrance; foliage leathery; vigorous, upright growth; PP2154; ['Nocturne' × 'Chrysler Imperial']; intr. 1961

'Avon, Climbing' Cl HT, dr, 1975, Kumar, S.

'Avril Elizabeth Home' -- See 'Korravreli'

'Avril Sherwood' F, my, 1976, Sherwood; bud ovoid; flowers golden yellow fading to buttercup-yellow, 3-3½ in., 18 petals, slight fragrance; foliage glossy, dark, leathery; upright growth; ['Pink Parfait' × Allgold®]; intr. 1975

'Awakening' -- See 'Probuzeni'

'Award' HT, mr, 1953, Taylor, C.A.; flowers velvety red; foliage very glossy, dark; short stems; vigorous growth; ['Will Rogers' × 'Mme Henri Guillot']

'Awareness' ('Lady Aberdeen') HT, dp, Fryer, Gareth; flowers bright pink, full, high-centered, borne singly and in clusters; recurrent; vigorous, medium growth; intr. 1997

'Awayuki' S, w

'Axeline' LCl, mp

'Axelle' HT, Gaujard; intr. 1964

'Aya' HT, m, Yasuda; flowers purple, 12 cm., 25 petals, high-centered, borne mostly solitary, intense fragrance; foliage matte; numerous prickles; growth upright, bushy, medium (110-130 cm.); garden decoration; ['Madame Violet' × 'Intrigue']; intr. 1994

Ayako™ -- See 'Malmiya'

'Ayanishiki' -- See 'Mini Wings'

'Ayaori' F, rb

'Ayez' -- See 'Spectabilis'

'Aylsham' S, dp, 1948, Wright, Percy H.; bud ovoid; flowers deep pink, large, dbl.; non-recurrent; foliage light green, glossy; vigorous (to 5 ft.) growth; ['Hansa' × R. nitida]

'Ayrshire Queen' ('Reine des Ayrshire') Ayr, dr, 1835, Rivers; flowers purplish crimson, large, semi-dbl.; ['Blush Ayrshire' × 'Tuscany']

'Ayrshire Rose' ('Ayrshirea', R. arvensis ayreshirea) Misc OGR, pb, 1790; buds rosy pink; flowers medium size, white, dbl.; heavy spring bloom; non-recurrent; strong growth to 5-7 m.

'Ayrshire Splendens' -- See 'Splendens'

'Ayrshirea' -- See 'Ayrshire Rose'

'Azafran' HT, my, Meilland; flowers saffron yellow, dbl., exhibition; greenhouse rose; intr. 2004

'Azalea Rose' Pol, mp, 1940, Griffing Nursery; flowers bright rose-pink, resemble azaleas; [sport of 'Ellen Poulsen']

'Azeez' F, op, 1969, Pal, Dr. B.P.; bud pointed; flowers coral-pink, reverse lighter, medium, dbl., high-centered; foliage leathery; upright, compact growth; intr. 1965

'Azelda' HT, op, 1963, Matthews; bud long, pointed; flowers coral-rose, dbl., cupped; foliage glossy, light green; long stems; vigorous, upright growth; [Queen Elizabeth® × 'Rosenelfe']

'Aztec' HT, or, 1957, Swim, H.C.; bud long, pointed; flowers scarlet-orange, 4-5 in., 25 petals, high-centered, moderate fragrance; foliage glossy, leathery; vigorous, spreading growth; PP1648; ['Charlotte Armstrong' × seedling]; intr. 1957

'Aztec Gold' Gr, dy, Winchel, J.; flowers golden yellow, dbl., very slight fragrance; foliage glossy; stems sturdy; tall growth; intr. 2006

'Azubis' -- See 'Indigoletta'

'Azubis' LCl, m, van den Laak; flowers large, lilac, intense fragrance; growth to 10 ft.; intr. 1981

'Azulabria' -- See 'Ruiblun'

'Azumino' Cl Min, rb, Onodera; flowers single; intr. 1983

'Azur' F, m, 1979, Lens; bud ovoid; flowers deep lavender-mauve, pointed, 2½-3 in., 15 petals, intense fragrance; foliage dark reddish-green; vigorous, compact, bushy growth; ['Sterling Silver' × ('Gold Strike' × 'Golden Garnette')]; intr. 1967

'Azure Sea' -- See 'Arolala'

'Azusa' Min, mr, Takatori

— B —

B. C.™ -- See 'Kinbee'

'B. S. Bhatcharji' HT, my, 1933, Dickson, A.; flowers buttercup-yellow, well-formed, large; foliage glossy, dark; vigorous growth

'B. W. Price' HT, mp, 1943, McGredy; bud long, pointed; flowers cerise-pink, open, large, 6-8 petals; foliage soft; vigorous, upright, bushy growth; ['Night' × 'Mme Butterfly']

'Babe' Pol, pb, Hazelwood; intr. 1958

'Babe' Min, mp, Lougheed; intr. 2004

'Babe Ruth' HT, op, 1950, Howard, F.H.; bud ovoid; flowers coral, reverse rose-coral, 4-4½ in., 35-40 petals, cupped, moderate fragrance; foliage leathery, glossy, bronze; vigorous, upright growth; PP996; ['Los Angeles' × seedling]

'Babet' -- See 'Babette'

'Babette' M, lp, 1836, Miellez; flowers flesh pink, medium, full

'Babette' ('Babet') D, lp; flowers flesh pink, medium, full; intr. before 1838

'Babette' HWich, mr, Walsh; flowers carmine-red, 4 cm., semi-dbl. to dbl., borne in large clusters; non-recurrent; foliage glossy; Ruled extinct 1970 ARA; intr. 1906

'Babette' F, m, Gaujard; flowers lavender-pink, small, single, cupped, slight fragrance; foliage leathery, small; vigorous, bushy growth; [seedling × 'Eminence']; intr. 1970

'Babette' ('Babette Stutzer') HT, op, Kordes; flowers medium size, salmon pink, dbl., exhibition, no fragrance; stems medium; growth tall (2 m.); intr. 1999

'Babette Stutzer' -- See 'Babette'

'Babs' ('Coton Gold') HT, dy, 1984, Babb, J.T.; flowers glowing yellow; [sport of 'Whisky Mac'

'Babt Deitz' Pol, or, 1924, Opdebeeck; flowers oriental red, edged salmon, dbl.

'Baby Abel Chatenay' Pol, op, 1914, Altmüller; flowers salmon pink, medium, full

'Baby Alan' Pol, mp, 1930, Kessler; flowers shining pink, very dbl., daisy-like, borne in clusters

'Baby Alberic' Pol, ly, 1932, Chaplin Bros.; bud yellow; flowers creamy white, small, dbl.; recurrent bloom; vigorous growth

'Baby Allan' Pol, mp, 1930, Kessler; flowers glossy pink, small, very full

Baby Ashley™ -- See 'Kinash'

Baby Austin™ -- See 'Morbaby'

Baby Baccará® Min, or, 1965, Meilland, Alain A.; flowers orange-scarlet, 1½ in., dbl.; foliage dark; ['Callisto' × 'Perla de Alcañada']

Baby Baccara® Min, mr, Meilland; flowers dbl., borne in clusters; growth compact (40-45 cm.); intr. 2002

'Baby Ballerina' Min, pb, Villegas; flowers deep pink lightening to white near the center, 5 petals, borne in clusters; spreading growth, 2 ft. high by 4-5 ft. wide; intr. 1997

'Baby Bath' Pol, mp, Robinson; flowers tiny, rosette, borne in tight clusters, moderate sweet fragrance; good repeat; very dwarf, compact growth; intr. 1989

'Baby Betsy McCall' Min, lp, 1960, Morey, Dr. Dennison; flowers micro-mini, 1 in., 20 petals, cupped, moderate fragrance; foliage leathery, light green; vigorous, dwarf, compact (8 in.) growth; PP1984; ['Cécile Brünner' × 'Rosy Jewel']; intr. 1960

'Baby Bettina' -- See 'Meidacinu'

'Baby Betty' Pol, mp, 1929, Burbage Nursery; bud ovoid, yellow, tinged red; flowers pink, base lighter, small, dbl., cupped; abundant, recurrent bloom; foliage leathery, dark, bronze; vigorous, compact, bushy growth; ['Eblouissant' × 'Comtesse du Cayla']

'Baby Bio' F, dy, 1977, Smith, E.; flowers deep golden yellow, patio, 3 in., 28 petals; foliage glossy; ['Golden Treasure' × seedling]

'Baby Blanket' -- See 'Korfullwind'

'Baby Blaze' ('Lunds Jubiläum') F, mr, 1954, Kordes, W.; bud ovoid; flowers cherry-red, white eye, 3 in., 33 petals, cupped, borne in clusters of 10-25, moderate fragrance; foliage light, glossy; vigorous, bushy, compact growth; PP1362; ['World's Fair' × 'Hamburg']; intr. 1954

Baby Bloomer™ -- See 'Jacseboy'

'Baby Boomer' -- See 'Benminn'

'Baby Bunting' Min, dp, 1953, deVink, J.; flowers deep pink, 1½ in., 20 petals; ['Ellen Poulsen' × 'Tom Thumb']

'Baby Cakes' -- See 'Talbaby'

'Baby Carnaval' -- See 'Tanbakede'

'Baby Carnival' -- See 'Tanbakede'

'Baby Carol' Min, rb, Kakujitsu-en; flowers single; intr. 1987

'Baby Caroline Louise' Min, w, 1998, Barker, S.J.L.; bud tall; flowers white, slight lemon center, white reverse, opening flat, 2 in., very dbl., high-centered, borne in small, well-formed clusters; foliage medium size, medium green, semi-glossy; prickles moderate; tall, bushy growth; [Sexy Rexy® × Laura Ford®]

'Baby Cécile Brunner' -- See 'Morcebru'

'Baby Château' ('Baby Vougeot', 'Château') F, mr, 1936, Kordes; bud ovoid, crimson; flowers red shaded garnet, large, dbl.; foliage glossy, bronze; very vigorous, bushy growth; ['Aroma' × ('Eva' × 'Ami Quinard')]

'Baby Cheryl' Min, lp, 1965, Williams, Ernest D.; bud pointed; flowers light pink, reverse lighter, micro-mini, small, dbl., moderate spicy fragrance; foliage leathery; vigorous, dwarf growth; ['Spring Song' × seedling]

'Baby Chicks' Min, my

'Baby Claire' Min, pb, 2001, Sproul, James A.; bud pointed; flowers white to light pink, edged in darker pink, medium, 25-35 petals, high-centered, borne in small clusters, slight fragrance; foliage medium size, medium green, semi-glossy; prickles medium, few; growth compact, bushy, medium (24-30 in.); exhibition, garden decorative; ['Fairhope' × Hot Tamale™]; intr. 2001

'Baby Crimson' -- See 'Perla de Alcañada'

'Baby Darling' Min, ab, 1964, Moore, Ralph S.; bud pointed; flowers apricot-orange, small, 20 petals; dwarf, bushy (12 in.) growth; PP2682; ['Little Darling' × 'Magic Wand']; intr. 1964

'Baby Darling, Climbing' Cl Min, ab, 1973, Trauger, F.; buds small, long pointed; flowers orange-apricot softening to peach pink, small, dbl, open, borne singly and several together; [sport of 'Baby Darling']; intr. 1972

Baby Diana™ -- See 'Savadi'

'Baby Dioressence' Min, m; growth short

'Baby Doll' -- See 'Tip-Top'

'Baby Dominic' -- See 'Judnic'

'Baby Donnie' Min, mr; flowers scarlet-crimson, very long lasting, single, borne in clusters; growth dwarf; intr. 1972

'Baby Dorothy' -- See 'Maman Levavasseur'

Baby Eclipse™ -- See 'Morecli'

'Baby Elegance' Pol, ab, 1912, Hobbies; flowers pale yellow-orange, single

'Baby Face' Min, lp, Laver, Keith G.; bud tapered; flowers light pink, very small, 35 petals, borne in large sprays, slight fragrance; foliage small, light green, matte; compact growth; ['Popcorn' × 'Popcorn']; intr. 1982

'Baby Farbenkönigin' Pol, dp, 1914, Altmüller; flowers medium

'Baby Faurax' Pol, m, 1924, Lille, L.; flowers violet, small, dbl., borne in large clusters; dwarf growth

'Baby Fifty-Fifty' Min, ob; flowers orange with lemon yellow stripes, double, rosette; good repeat; intr. 2007

'Baby Garnette' Min, mr, 1962, Morey, Dr. Dennison; flowers blood-red, small, dbl.; foliage dark; vigorous (10-12 in.), compact growth; ['Red Imp' × 'Sparkler']

'Baby Girl' Min, yb, Clements, John; flowers butter yellow shading to bronzy copper., 1½ in., 5 petals; Profusion; foliage shiny, leathery, dark green; growth to 2½ × 2 ft.; intr. 2001

'Baby Gloria' Pol, or, 1936, Böhm, J.; flowers salmon-red, larger than parent; very dwarf (6-8 in.) growth; [sport of 'Gloria Mundi']

'Baby Gold' -- See 'Baby Gold Star'

'Baby Gold Star' ('Baby Gold', 'Estrellita de Oro') Min, dy, 1940, Dot, Pedro; bud pointed; flowers golden yellow, 14 petals, slight fragrance; foliage small, soft; PP407; ['Eduardo Toda' × 'Rouletii']

'Baby Gold Star, Climbing' Cl Min, dy, 1965, Williams, Ernest D.; intr. 1964

Baby Grand™ -- See 'Poulit'

'Baby Herriot' -- See 'Étoile Luisante'

'Baby Jack' Min, w, Benardella; flowers white, adding pink tones in heat, dbl.; [sport of 'Figurine']; intr. 1999

'Baby Jane Clare' -- See 'Mordelahanty'

'Baby Jayne' ('Fairy Hedge', 'Pixie Hedge') Cl Min, mp, 1959, Moore, Ralph S.; flowers soft pink, very small, 45 petals, borne in clusters; foliage small, glossy; growth to 3-4 ft.; ['Violette' × 'Zee']; intr. 1957

Baby Katie™ Min, pb, 1979, Saville, F. Harmon; bud ovoid, pointed; flowers cream and pink blend, small, 28 petals, high-centered, slight fragrance; foliage matte, green; vigorous, compact, bushy growth; PP4471; ['Sheri Anne' × 'Watercolor']; intr. 1978

'Baby Lilian' Min; flowers begonia-rose, base tinted orange-yellow, rather large for the class, dbl.; foliage small, light, glossy; vigorous (12-15 in.) growth

Baby Love® Min, lp, Barni; flowers clear pink, dbl.; compact (30-35 cm.) growth; intr. 1992

Baby Love™ Min, dy, 1992, Scrivens, Len; bud small, pointed; flowers buttercup yellow, medium, 5 petals, borne mostly singly, slight licorice fragrance; foliage small, medium green, semi-glossy; some prickles; compact (3 ft.) growth; [('Sweet Magic' × seedling) × (miniature seedling × R. davida elongata seedling)]; intr. 1992

'Baby Luke' S, pb, 2005, Cockerham, John E.; flowers pink and yellow blend, reverse pink blend, aging to all-pink, 3-3½ in., single, borne mostly solitary; foliage medium size, medium green, semi-glossy; prickles varied, blade, numerous; growth upright, medium (3 ft); informal hedges, garden decoration; ['Sheer Bliss' × Gizmo™]; intr. 2005

'Baby Lyon Rose' Pol, rb, 1916, Turbat; flowers coral-rose, shaded chrome-yellow or shrimp-red, dbl.

'Baby Maria' Min, dp

'Baby Mascarade' -- See 'Tanbakede'

'Baby Maskarade' -- See 'Tanbakede'

'Baby Maskerade' ('Baby Carnaval', 'Baby Mascarade', 'Baby Maskarade', 'Baby Carnival', Baby Masquerade®)

Min, rb, 1956, Tantau, Math.; bud ovoid; flowers yellow aging red, 1 in., 23 petals, slight fruity fragrance; foliage leathery; vigorous, compact (8 in. tall) growth; PP1580; ['Tom Thumb' × 'Masquerade']; intr. 1956

Baby Masquerade® -- See 'Tanbakede'

'Baby Masquerade, Climbing' Cl Min, rb, 1976, Sykes, R.O.; intr. 1974

'Baby Mermaid' -- See 'Happenstance'

'Baby Michael' -- See 'Jusmichael'

'Baby Mine' Pol, my, 1929, Moore, Ralph S.; flowers sulfur to butter-yellow; ['Cécile Brunner, Climbing' × unknown]

'Baby Ophelia' Min, lp, 1961, Moore, Ralph S.; bud pointed; flowers soft pink, 1 in., 33 petals, moderate fragrance; foliage glossy; vigorous, bushy (8-12 in.) growth; [(R. wichurana × Floradora) × 'Little Buckaroo']; intr. 1961

'Baby Orange Triumph' Min, or; flowers small, dbl.

Baby Paradise™ -- See 'Meifovett'

'Baby Peace' Min, yb, 1962, De Mott & Johnson, G.E.; bud urn shaped; flowers ivory-yellow tipped pink, ½-1 in., 50-55 petals, slight fragrance; very vigorous growth; PP2201; [sport of 'Peace']

'Baby Pinocchio' Min, pb, 1967, Moore, Ralph S.; bud ovoid; flowers salmon-pink blend, small, dbl., moderate fragrance; foliage glossy, leathery; vigorous, bushy growth; PP2967; ['Golden Glow' × 'Little Buckaroo']

'Baby Rambler' -- See 'Chewramb'

'Baby Rambler, Climbing' -- See 'Miss G. Mesman'

'Baby Ria' -- See 'Jayrea'

Baby Romantica® HT, yb, Meilland; flowers ocher yellow with pink edges, dbl.; greenhouse rose; intr. 2004

'Baby Rosamunde' Pol, mp, 1930, Kessler; flowers rose-pink, semi-dbl.

'Baby Secret' ('Baby's Secret') Min, w, Bridges, Dennis A.; flowers long, slender, white with salmon pink edges, dbl., exhibition; foliage glossy, dark green; stems long; growth slightly spreading; PPRR; intr. 1997

'Baby Shannon' -- See 'Denshan'

'Baby Sunbeam' LCl, ab, 1934, Burbank; flowers light apricot, passing to cream-yellow, large yellow center, borne in large clusters; foliage bronze; very vigorous growth

'Baby Sunrise' -- See 'Macparlez'

'Baby Sylvia' F, op, 1960, Fryers Nursery, Ltd.; flowers flesh-salmon-pink, 3 in., 25-30 petals; very vigorous growth; ['Lady Sylvia' × seedling]; intr. 1959

'Baby Talisman' -- See 'Presumida'

'Baby Talk' F, m, 1980, Weeks; bud small, ovoid, pointed; flowers dusty mauve-pink, patio, 26 petals, borne mostly singly, moderate tea fragrance; foliage small to medium size, moderately thin; low to medium, compact, dense growth; PP4713; ['Plain Talk' × 'Angel Face']

'Baby Tausendschön' -- See 'Echo'

'Baby Tom' -- See 'Boseyeball'

'Baby Typhoon' Min, ab, 1988, Halevi, A.M.; flowers bright, clear apricot, center golden-yellow, medium, 35-40 petals, high-centered, borne singly or in sprays of 3-5, moderate damask fragrance; foliage medium size, dark green, semi-glossy; prickles pointed, large, straw; bushy, spreading, tall growth; [sport of 'Gold Coin']

'Baby Vougeot' -- See 'Baby Château'

'Babyface' -- See 'Rawril'

Babyflor® -- See 'Tanrolfy'

'Babylon' HT, op, 1976, Bees; flowers deep coral-pink, low-centered, 5 in., 36 petals; foliage glossy, dark; moderately vigorous growth; ['Tropicana' × 'Pink Favorite']

'Baby's Blush' Ch, mp, Scarman; intr. 1995

'Baby's Secret' -- See 'Bribaby'

'Bacardi' HT, ob, 1987, Weeks, O.L.; flowers uniform iridescent coral-orange, fading lighter, small, 30 petals, high-centered, borne singly, slight fruity fragrance; foliage medium size, medium green, semi-glossy; prickles straight, small, reddish; upright, medium growth; PP6862; [seedling × 'self']

Baccará® ('Baccarat', 'Jacqueline') HT, or, 1962, Meilland, F.; bud globular, medium; flowers geranium red, 3 in., 75 petals, cupped, opening flat, borne mostly singly; foliage dark green, leathery; bushy, upright growth; PP1367; ['Happiness' × 'Independence']; intr. 1954

Baccará, Climbing® Cl HT, or, 1965, Meilland

'Baccara Blanca' Min, w

'Baccarat' -- See 'Meger'

'Bacchante' HGal, dr, before 1811; flowers wine red, very dbl., moderate fragrance; foliage yellow-green, very dentate

'Bacchus' HP, mp, 1855, Paul, W.; flowers bright carmine, medium, full

'Bacchus' HT, dp, Dickson, A.; flowers cherry-pink, medium, 25 petals, moderate fragrance; vigorous growth; intr. 1951

'Bacchus' HP, mr, Paul, G.; flowers shining scarlet, shaded with glowing chestnut-brown, medium to large, full; intr. 1896

'Back Home' -- See 'Gelback'

'Bad Bergzabern' HT, mr, Hetzel; intr. 1993

'Bad Birnbach' -- See 'Korpancom'

'Bad Ems' S, mp, Schultheis; intr. 1990

Bad Füssing® -- See 'Korbad'

'Bad Homburg' HT, ab, Eichelmann; intr. 1995

'Bad Langensalza' F, pb, 1954, Berger, W.; flowers carmine-pink, large, dbl.

'Bad Nauheim' -- See 'National Trust'

'Bad Naukeim' -- See 'National Trust'

'Bad Neuenahr' HKor, mr, 1958, Kordes, W.; bud ovoid; flowers deep crimson, 4 in., 50 petals, cupped, borne in clusters (to 15), moderate fragrance; foliage dark green, glossy, leathery; vigorous (6 ft.) growth

'Bad Pyrmont' F, or, 1976, Kordes; bud pointed; flowers 4 in., 40 petals, high-centered; abundant bloom; foliage dark, soft; vigorous, upright, bushy growth; ['Duftwolke' × seedling]

Bad Salzuflen® F, mp

Bad Wörishofen® ('Gruss an Wörishofen') F, mr, 1976, Kordes, W.; bud ovoid; flowers 2½ in., 18 petals, cupped, slight fragrance; foliage dark, soft; vigorous, bushy growth; [Sarabande® × 'Marlena']; intr. 1972

'Bad Wörishofen 2005' -- See 'Emely Vigorosa'

'Baden-Baden' HT, dr, 1952, Kordes; flowers deep crimson, large, dbl.; foliage dark, leathery; vigorous, upright growth; ['Poinsettia' × 'Crimson Glory']

Badener Gold® F, ob, McGredy, Sam IV; intr. 1974

'Badia' HT, Mansuino, Dr. Andrea

'Badinage' HT, op, 1951, Gaujard; flowers salmon-pink flushed coppery, 4-4½ in., 30 petals; foliage leathery, dark; vigorous growth; ['Peace' × seedling]

'Badner Traberchampion' HT, lp

'Baedonthorp' HT, w, 2000, Baer, Rich; flowers white, shading to light pink at edge, 5 in., full, high-centered, borne mostly singly, slight fragrance; foliage large, dark green, semi-glossy; prickles moderate; growth upright, medium (4-5 ft.); [sport of 'Signature']; intr. 2002

'Bagalf' (Alfalfa®) Pol, m, 2007, Bagnasco, John; flowers medium, dbl., borne in large clusters; foliage medium green, semi-glossy; few prickles; growth spreading, short, cascading; good for hanging baskets; [Wild Dancer™ × 'China Doll']

'Bagatelle' HMult, w, 1908, Soupert & Notting; flowers white, washed very delicate pink, 4 cm., full, borne in large clusters; ['Turner's Crimson Rambler' × 'Mignonette']

'Bagatelle' HT, mr, Gaujard; bud large, oval; flowers bright red, very dbl., moderate fragrance; foliage leathery; very vigorous, bushy growth; intr. 1943

'Bagcott' (Cotton Candy®) Pol, lp, 2007, Bagnasco, John; flowers medium, full, borne in small clusters; foliage medium green, semi-glossy; few prickles; growth compact, medium; ['Gourmet Popcorn' × 'Marie Pavie']

'Bagdad' HT, or, 1953, Swim, H.C.; bud ovoid to urn shape; flowers nasturtium-red to orange, becoming cupped, 4½ in., 48-55 petals, high-centered, intense fragrance; foliage glossy; very vigorous, bushy growth; PP1291; ['Charlotte Armstrong' × 'Signora']

'Bagdar' (Darla®) Min, lp, 2007, Bagnasco, John; flowers small, semi-dbl., borne mostly solitary; foliage medium green, semi-glossy; prickles moderate; growth compact, short; [Gizmo™ × 'Bagcott']

'Bagheera' -- See 'Korgera'

'Bagliore' HT, mr, 1955, Aicardi, D.; flowers crimson-red; stiff stems; very vigorous growth

'Bagmallow' (Marshmallow Fluff®) Pol, w, 2007, Bagnasco, John; flowers medium, full, borne in small clusters; foliage medium green, semi-glossy; few prickles; growth compact, medium; ['Gourmet Popcorn' × 'Marie Pavie']

'Bagspank' (Spanky®) Pol, mp, 2007, Bagnasco, John; flowers medium, dbl., borne in large clusters; foliage medium green, semi-glossy; few prickles; growth spreading, cascading, short; hanging baskets; [Wild Dancer™ × 'China Doll']

'Bahama' F, dr, 1968, Soenderhousen; flowers semi-dbl.; vigorous, low growth; ['Fidélio' × 'Hanne']

'Bahia' F, ob, 1973, Lammerts, Dr. Walter; bud ovoid; flowers orange, medium, dbl., cupped, moderate spicy fragrance; foliage glossy, dark, leathery; vigorous, upright, bushy growth; PP3525; ['Rumba' × 'Tropicana']; intr. 1974

'Bahrs Lieveling' F, mr, 1950, Leenders, M.; flowers velvety crimson-red; ['Donald Prior' × Orange Triumph®]

'Baiall' S, dp, Ping Lim; intr. 2005

'Baicer' S, pb, Lim, Ping; intr. 2006

'Baicker' S, mr, Lim, P, & Twomey, J.; intr. 2004

'Baicream' ('Garden Art Macy's Pride') S, w, Lim; P. and Twomey; J.; bud lemon yellow, slim; intr. 2003

'Baieam' ('DayDream') S, m, 2004, Lim, Ping; flowers fuchsia pink, reverse deeper fuchsia pink, small, 10 petals, borne in large clusters; foliage small, dark green, glossy; prickles ¼ cm., awl; growth compact, medium (2 ft.); garden decoration, containers; PP15736; [Lavender Dream® × 'Henry Kelsey']; intr. 2004

'Baiena' S, pb, Zuzek, Kathy; intr. 2008

'Baieye' ('Garden Jubilee Golden Eye') S, rb, Ping Lim; intr. 2004

'Baiface' ('Garden Jubilee Funny Face') S, pb, Lim, P, & Twomey, J.; intr. 2004

'Baifairy' ('Garden Path Mystic Fairy') S, mr, Bailey; intr. 2004

'Baifree' ('Dreaming Free') S, m, 2001, Lim, Ping; flowers deep mauve, reverse lighter mauve, 2½ in., single, borne in large clusters, slight fragrance; foliage medium size, medium green, semi-glossy, disease-resistant; few prickles; growth spreading, low (2-3 ft.); garden, groundcover; [seedling × 'Ballerina']; intr. 2002

'Baigirl' S, dp, Lim, Ping; bud round, deep pink; intr. 2008

'Baihero' S, mr, Bailey; bud red; intr. 2003

'Baiief' ('Little Mischief Garden Path') S, pb, Ping Lim; intr. 2004

'Baiine' S, my, Lim, Ping; bud slender; intr. 2004

'Baiing' ('Garden Art Grandma's Blessing') S, dp, Lim, Ping; intr. 2004

'Baikye' ('Garden Jubilee Sierra Skye') HT, mr, Ping Lim; bud round to oval; intr. 2004

'Bailando' HT, lp, Tantau; intr. 2001

'Bailey's Red' -- See 'Karen Poulsen'

'Bailgance' HT, dr, Twomey, Jerry; intr. 1996

'Baince' Gr, ab, Lim, Ping; intr. 2007

'Bainder' (Garden Jubilee Hot Wonder™) S, mr, Lim, P, & Twomey, J.; intr. 2004

'Baingo' ('Garden Art Last Tango') S, mr, Ping Lim; intr. 2004

'Bainial' F, dy, Lim, Pingdouble; intr. 2008

'Baioad' S, dy, Lim, Ping; intr. 2007

'Baioist' ('Garden Art Orange Impressionist') S, ob, Lim, P, & Twomey, J.; intr. 2004

'Baiole' S, lp, Zuzek, Kathy; intr. 2008

'Baioon' S, ly, Ping Lim; intr. 2004

'Baipeace' ('Orient Express', Love and Peace™, 'Pullman Orient Express') HT, yb, 2001, Twomey, Jerry, and Lim, Ping; flowers golden yellow with pink edge, 5 in., full, high-centered, borne mostly solitary, slight fragrance; foliage medium size, dark green, glossy, disease-resistant; prickles moderate; growth upright, medium (4-5 ft.), garden, cutting; PP14731; [seedling × 'Peace']; intr. 2002

'Baipeach' HT, ob, Lim, Ping; intr. 2006

'Baipome' ('Garden Path Pink Gnome') S, pb; bud pink; intr. 2004

'Baiprez' F, yb, Lim, Ping; bud pointed; intr. 2006

'Bairage' S, ab, Lim, Ping; bud coral; intr. 2008

'Bairift' S, w, Lim, Ping; intr. 2007

'Bairise' ('Acadia Sunrise') F, or, 2001, Twomey, Jerry, and Lim, Ping; flowers rich orange, 4½ in., dbl., high-centered, borne mostly solitary, slight fragrance; foliage medium size, dark green, glossy; prickles moderate; growth upright, compact (4 ft.); garden decoration; [seedling × seedling]; intr. 2002

'Bairls' S, dp, Lim, Pink; intr. 2007

'Baiset' ('Garden Path Sunrise Sunset') S, pb, Ping Lim; bud medium, pointed; intr. 2004

'Baisist' S, op, Lim, P, & Twomey, J.; bud medium, rounded; intr. 2004

'Baisme' Gr, mp, Lim, Ping; intr. 2006

'Baista' S, pb, Ping Lim; intr. 2007

'Baisuhe' F, mr, Lim, Ping; bud medium, pointed; intr. 2008

'Baisven' S, m, Zuzek; intr. 2008

'Baitime' LCl, mr, Lim, Ping; intr. 2007

'Baition' S, dp, Lim, Ping; intr. 2006

'Baitouch' ('Elegant Touch') HT, pb, 2001, Twomey, Jerry, and Lim, Ping; flowers deeper pink, reverse lighter pink, 5 in., dbl., high-centered, borne mostly solitary; foliage medium size, dark green, glossy; prickles moderate; growth upright, low (3-4 ft.); garden; [seedling × Sheer Elegance™]; intr. 2002

'Baitown' S, mr, Lim, Ping; intr. 2005

'Baiurst' S, dy, Lim, Ping; intr. 2007

'Bajazzo' HT, rb, 1961, Kordes, R.; flowers velvety blood-red, reverse white, well-formed, large; vigorous, upright growth

'Bakels' F, Gaujard; intr. 1980

'Bakewell Scots Briar' HSpn, ly

Bakker's Newcomer® HT, m

'Bakker's Orange' HT, ob, Bakker; flowers bright orange, dbl., high-centered, moderate soft fragrance

'Baktaf' ('Taffy') Min, yb, 1988, Baker, Larry; flowers soft, pastel butter yellow, tipped light pink, reverse pure pink, 33 petals, high-centered; foliage small, medium green, matte; prickles nearly straight, small, light brown; growth bushy, low, compact, full; [seedling × seedling]

'Baladin' F, Combe, M.

'Balaji' HT, ob, Patil, B.K.; intr. 1998

'Balalaika' F, dr, 1978, Hubner; bud ovoid; flowers blood-red, dbl.; foliage glossy; low, bushy growth

'Balann' ('Ann Reilly') F, mp, 2004, Ballin, Don; flowers satiny, reverse slightly duller, 2½-3 in., very full, borne mostly solitary, no fragrance; foliage medium size, semi-glossy; prickles small to medium, slightly curved down; growth compact, medium; garden decoration; [sport of 'Olympiad']; intr. 2005

'Balcon' LCl, or, 1962, Combe; bud ovoid; flowers geranium-red, open, 3 in., dbl.; foliage dark, glossy; very vigorous growth; ['Spectacular' × unknown]; intr. 1960

'Balder' S, mr, Carlsson-Nilsson; intr. 2001

Baldo™ -- See 'Moebaldo'

'Baldock Festival' -- See 'Golden Friendship'

'Balduin' -- See 'Sleepy'

'Balduin' ('Helen Gould') HT, pb, 1896, Lambert, P.; flowers pink, edged darker, large, dbl.; vigorous growth; ['Charles Darwin' × 'Marie van Houtte']; intr. 1901

'Balduinus' HT, r, DVP Melle; ['Floirzel' × 'Ingrid Bergman']; intr. 2000

'Baléares' HT, w, 1957, Dot, Simon; bud pointed; flowers base and reverse of petals white suffused carmine, deeper at edges, 35 petals; foliage dark, glossy; stiff stems; upright growth; ['Peace' × 'Flambee']

'Balets' ('Just Peachy') HT, pb, 2006, Ballin, Don; flowers peach pink, reverse lighter, yellow petal hinge, 3½-4 in., full, borne mostly solitary; foliage medium size, medium green, semi-glossy; prickles large, sligley curved, light green, moderate; growth upright, tall (6-7 ft.); exhibition; [sport of 'European Touch']; intr. 2007

'Bali' Pol, 1960, Leenders, J.; flowers orange-yellow, open, large, 6 petals; foliage glossy, light green; bushy growth; ['Masquerade' × 'Golden Rain']

'Bali-Hi' HT, mp, 1960, Lowe; flowers peach-pink to shell-pink, medium, high-centered, moderate fragrance;

foliage glossy; vigorous, upright growth; intr. 1959

'Balinese' HT, m, 1963, Boerner; bud ovoid; flowers brown and lavender tones, 4½-5 in., 35-40 petals, cupped, intense fruity fragrance; foliage glossy; vigorous, upright growth; PP2300; ['Grey Pearl' × 'Brownie']; intr. 1963

'Balizys' ('Catherine Graham') HT, pb, 2007, Ballin, Don; flowers light pink, darker at center, greenish-yellow petal hinge, 4-5 in., full, borne mostly solitary; foliage large, medium green, semi-glossy; prickles small to medium, slightly hooked angled down, light green; growth upright, tall (5-6 ft.); garden decoration, exhibition; [sport of 'Izy']

'Baljit' HT, dp, 1980, Lucknow; bud pointed; flowers spirea-red, open but full, 5 in., 30-40 petals; long-lasting, profuse bloom; foliage dark, leathery; free growth; [sport of 'Velsheda']; intr. 1979

'Balkan Star' HT, m, Tapanchev; flowers large, dark pink to mauve, dbl., slight fragrance; intr. 1997

'Ball of Snow' N, w, 1887, Henderson

'Ballade' -- See 'Tanedallab'

'Ballade' F, op, 1960, deRuiter; flowers deep orange-salmon, well-formed, 25 petals, borne in clusters; bushy growth; ['Signal Red' × 'polyantha seedling']

'Ballady' C, lp, 1934, Perrot; flowers large, dbl.

'Ballerina, Climbing' -- See 'Reaclibal'

'Ballerina' F, my, Leenders, M.; flowers naples yellow, large, dbl., moderate fragrance; intr. 1941

Ballerina™ Min, lp; flowers small, full, cupped, very slight fragrance; foliage dark green, glossy; bushy, low (20-40 cm.) growth; intr. 1996

'Ballerina' HT, lp, Kordes; flowers medium size, soft pink, dbl., high-centered; stems 60 cm length; greenhouse rose; intr. 2001

'Ballerina' HMsk, mp, 1937, Bentall; flowers bright soft pink, white eye, small, single, borne in very large clusters; vigorous (3 ft.) growth

'Ballerina × R. filipes' S, pb, Lens; bud pointed; flowers bright pink with white eye, fading white, single, borne in large clusters; once blooming; arching, tall (to 10 ft.) growth; intr. after 1980

'Ballerine' HT, w, 1955, Buyl Frères; bud long; flowers satiny snow-white, open, medium, dbl.; foliage glossy; vigorous, bushy growth

'Ballet' HT, ab, 1947, Boerner; bud long, pointed; flowers buff-apricot, 4½ in., 30 petals, high-centered; foliage dark green, wrinkled; growth vigorous, upright; PP800; name released for re-use (MR 6); [seedling × 'Orange Nassau']

Ballet® HT, dp, 1959, Kordes, R.; flowers deep pink, 5 in., 52 petals, slight fragrance; foliage gray-green; vigorous, bushy growth; ['Florex' × 'Karl Herbst']

'Ballet, Climbing' Cl HT, op, 1962, Kordes

'Ballet' ('New Ballet') HT, dp, Kordes; bud round; flowers strong, stable pink, medium to large, dbl., high-centered; stems length 60 cm; florist rose; intr. 1999

'Ballila' HT, mr, 1935, Bräuer; flowers medium, dbl.

'Ballindalloch Castle' -- See 'Cocneel'

'Balmain Climber' LCl, lp; flowers single

'Balparty' ('Rose Odyssey 2000') HT, w, 1999, Ballin, Don & Paula; flowers cream with pink edge, 4-5 in., full, high-centered, borne mostly singly, moderate fragrance; foliage medium to large, medium to dark green, semi-glossy; prickles moderate; upright, bushy, medium (3½-4½ ft.) growth; PP11091; [sport of 'Garden Party']; intr. 1999

'Balrihus' ('Misty Twilight') HT, mp, 2004, Ballin, Don; flowers medium, 24-26 petals, borne mostly solitary, no fragrance; foliage medium size, medium green, semi-glossy; prickles medium, curved, moderate; growth compact to slightly spreading, medium; [sport of 'Rina Hugo']; intr. 2003

'Baltik' F, m, VEG; flowers violet, large, dbl.

'Baltimore' HT, lp, 1898, Cook, J.W.; flowers blush tinted; ['Mme Antoine Rivoire' × 'Lady Mary Fitzwilliam']

'Baltimore Beauty' LCl, ly, 1927, Schluter; flowers buff-yellow, fading white, semi-dbl., borne in clusters; long, strong stems

'Baltimore Belle' ('Belle de Baltimore') HSet, lp, 1843, Feast; flowers pale blush to rose-white, small to medium, very dbl., borne in clusters of 6-12, moderate fragrance; non-recurrent; vigorous growth; [R. setigera × probably a Noisette]

'Balusiana' HGal, m, about 1845, from Austria; flowers lilac purple with silvery gray reflections

'Balwant' HT, ab, Phadtare; flowers non-fading apricot; [sport of 'Christian Dior']

'Bambey' HT, mr, 1980, Perry, Astor; bud long, pointed; flowers 60 petals, high-centered, intense fruity fragrance; foliage matte; prickles small, recurved; medium growth; [('Fragrant Cloud' × 'Peace') × Alec's Red®]; intr. 1981

'Bambi' -- See 'Delmistri'

'Bambi' F, mp, 1962, Watkins Roses; flowers bright pink, 2 in., 24 petals, borne in clusters; foliage dark; vigorous, bushy, low growth; ['The Optimist' × 'Korona']

'Bambi' F, mp, 1962, Von Abrams; bud pointed; flowers light apricot-pink, 3 in., 20 petals, cupped, borne in clusters; foliage glossy; vigorous, bushy, compact growth; intr. 1962

'Bambina' F, w, 1962, Moreira da Silva; bud yellow; flowers large, semi-dbl., borne in clusters; [seedling × 'Virgo']

'Bambino' -- See 'Savabino'

'Bambino' Min, mp, 1953, Dot, Pedro; [sport of 'Perla de Alcañada']

'Bambino' Min, mp, Noack; flowers single; intr. 2005

Bambolina® Min, pb

Bambula® F, op, 1971, Tantau, Math.; flowers 5 in., 28 petals, slight fragrance; foliage glossy, dark; intr. 1970

'Banana Split' -- See 'Gelba'

'Banana Split' -- See 'Zipban'

'Banana Splits' -- See 'Rawsplits'

'Banaras Dawn' HT, ab, 1979, Saxena; bud tapered; flowers apricot-buff, 4½ in., 30 petals, high-centered, intense fruity fragrance; foliage glossy, light green; vigorous growth; intr. 1977

'Banater Rose' HT, w, 1927, Mühle; flowers cream-white, center orange-yellow, dbl.; ['Harry Kirk' × unknown]

'Banbridge' F, pb, 1967, McGredy, Sam IV; flowers rose-red and yellow, well-shaped, 3 in., borne in clusters; ['Mme Léon Cuny' × 'Cläre Grammerstorf']

'Banbridge, Climbing' ClF, pb; intr. 1978

'Banco' HT, op, 1956, Laperrière; flowers salmon-pink becoming gold tinted, well-formed, large, 50 petals; foliage bright green; vigorous, upright growth; ['Peace' × seedling]

Banco 86® HT, dy, Laperrière; flowers intense yellow, 35 petals; intr. 1986

'Bandeau de Soliman' -- See 'Charles X'

'Banestu' HGal, m, about 1845, Calvert

Bangalore™ ('Bangalore Palace') S, mp, Poulsen; flowers soft medium pink, outer petals lighten, 8-10 cm., dbl., slight fragrance; foliage dark green, glossy; broad, bushy (40-60 cm.) growth; intr. 2004

'Bangalore Palace' -- See 'Poulpal019(N)'

'Bangor' F, or, 1972, Dickson, A.; flowers geranium-lake, ovate, large, 24 petals; foliage leathery; free growth; ['Jubilant' × 'Marlena']

'Bangor Cathedral' -- See 'Kirmelody'

Bangsbo™ -- See 'Poulrine'

'Banjaran' F, yb, 1970, Pal, Dr. B.P.; flowers gold and orange-red, small, dbl., cupped, borne in clusters, slight fragrance; foliage leathery; vigorous, upright, compact growth; intr. 1969

'Banjo' HT, lp, Tantau; intr. 2002

'Banksiaeflora' HSem, w; flowers white with cream center, small, very dbl.

'Banner' HT, pb, 1951, Raffel; flowers deep pink, striped white, moderate fragrance; PP1071; [sport of 'Charlotte Armstrong']

'Banquet' F, w, Noack; intr. 2002

Banquise™ -- See 'Lapruni'

'Banshee' S, mp, 1928, Origin unknown; flowers pink, troubled by balling, of poor texture, very dbl., moderate fragrance; non-recurrent

Bantry Bay® LCl, mp, 1967, McGredy, Sam IV; flowers soft pink, reverse bright pink, 4 in., semi-dbl. to dbl., borne in small clusters; foliage large, semi-glossy; ['New Dawn' × 'Korona']

Banzai™ -- See 'Meilimona'

'Banzai' HT, rb, 1961, Meilland, Mrs.

Marie-Louise; bud ovoid; flowers red, pink and cream blend, large, 30 petals, high-centered, slight fragrance; foliage leathery, dark; vigorous, bushy growth; PP2142; ['Radar' × 'Caprice (Meilland)']; intr. 1961

'Banzai '76' -- See 'Meilimona'

'Banzai 83' -- See 'Meizalitaf'

'Baptiste Desportes' ('Mme Baptiste Desportes') HP, mr, Trouillard; flowers large, full; good repeat

'Baptiste Lafaye' Pol, dp, 1910, Puyravaud; flowers carmine-pink, medium, dbl.

'Bar-le-Duc' HMult, mr, 1907, Soupert & Notting; flowers brick red to carmine, reverse carmine & copper, large, full; ['Souv. de Pierre Notting' × 'Crimson Rambler']

'Bar4470' F, mr, Barni, Anna; intr. 2005

'Baracc' HT, dp, Barni; bud globular, deep pink-violetvery double; intr. 2006

'Barafne' ('Dafne') S, pb, Barni, V.; intr. 1995

'Baraguay' HGal, lp, 1819, Hardy; flowers ashy-pink; foliage nearly thornless

'Barakura' -- See 'Beajap'

'Baralt' -- See 'Altair'

'Baramad' S, rb, Barni, V.; intr. 1991

'Baranam' HT, mp, Barni, V.; intr. 1988

'Barand' ('Barvir') S, dp, Barni; intr. 2003

'Barapp' -- See 'La Passionata'

'Bararc' ('Arcanto') S, mp, Barni, V.; intr. 1995

'Bararcsun' ('Arctic Sunrise') Min, w, 1990, Barrett, F.H.; bud pointed; flowers small, 30 petals, flat, borne in sprays of 40-60, no fragrance; foliage small, medium green, glossy; prickles long, thin, small, pale tan; spreading, low growth; no fruit; [Snow Carpet® × 'Tranquillity']; intr. 1989

'Barasd' -- See 'Rapsodia'

'Barash' F, ob, Barni; intr. 2000

'Barba Blue' -- See 'Barbe Blue'

'Barbab' Min, lp, Barni; intr. 1992

'Barbara' HT, rb, 1923, Paul, W.; flowers bright red, base yellow, reverse pale yellow, very large, semi-dbl.

'Barbara' HT, yb, Gaujard; flowers amber-yellow lightly flushed pink, 5 in., 20 petals, high-centered; foliage dark; very vigorous growth; intr. 1962

'Barbara Allen' S, w, Williams, J. Benjamin; flowers ivory with pink washing on petal edges, semi-dbl.; spreading growth; intr. 1999

'Barbara Austin' -- See 'Austop'

Barbara Bush™ -- See 'Jacbush'

'Barbara Carrera' F, op, Beales, Peter; flowers bright orange salmon, softening with age, dbl., slight fragrance; foliage matte, dark green; growth short; intr. 1994

'Barbara Dawson' HT, lp, Dawson; ['Mount Shasta' × 'Saffron']; intr. 1987

'Barbara Frietchie' HT, dp, 1960, Silva; bud long, pointed; flowers rose-red, open, large, dbl.; vigorous, upright growth; ['Heart's Desire' × 'The Chief']; intr. 1959

'Barbara Hauenstein' HT, mp, Poulsen; flowers large, dbl.; intr. 1957

Barbara Hendricks® HT, ab, Dorieux; flowers luminous apricot with pink tones , double, cupped; intr. 1998

'Barbara Joyce' Min, mr, 1999, Jolly, Betty J.; flowers 1½ in., 41 petals, borne in small clusters; foliage medium size, dark green, resistant, semi-glossy; few prickles; upright, medium (16 in.) growth; [Miss Dovey™ × Kristin™]

Barbara Mandrell™ -- See 'Kinbarb'

'Barbara Mason' HT, my, 1947, Moss; bud pointed; flowers medium, semi-dbl., high-centered; foliage glossy, vigorous, upright growth; ['Eclipse' × 'Luis Brinas']

'Barbara Meyer' Gr, or, 1971, Meyer, H.M.; bud ovoid; flowers medium, very dbl., high-centered; foliage glossy, dark; vigorous, upright growth; [Queen Elizabeth® × 'Tropicana']

'Barbara Oliva' -- See 'Ardoliva'

'Barbara Richards' HT, yb, 1930, Dickson, A.; flowers yellow, reverse flushed pink, very large, dbl.; stems weak necks; vigorous, bushy growth

'Barbara Robinson' HT, w, 1925, Dickson, A.; bud long, pointed; flowers creamy white, large, dbl., high-centered

'Barbara Straus' HT, dr, 1978, Schwartz, Ernest W.; bud long, pointed; flowers 22 petals, borne singly; foliage glossy; spreading, upright growth; [Mister Lincoln® × unknown]

'Barbara Ward' HT, mr, 1931, Ward, F.B.; flowers crimson-scarlet, large, 42 petals; vigorous growth; ['Royal Red' × 'Columbia']

'Barbara Windsor' F, op, Gandy; flowers salmon pink, double, high-centered to cupped, borne in large clusters, moderate fragrance; recurrent; foliage medium green; 30 - 40 inch growth; intr. 2008

'Barbararosa' LCl, lp, Worl; flowers soft lilac pink fading to blush pink, single to semi-dbl., moderate fragrance; abundant bloomer; growth vigorous; intr. 1980

'Barbara's Rose' HBc, yb; flowers single; intr. 1992

'Barbarella' Min, pb, 1983, Rose Barni-Pistoia; flowers deep pink, reverse creamy yellow, small, 20 petals, slight fragrance; foliage small, dark, matte; bushy growth; [seedling × seedling]; intr. 1981

'Barbarina' F, yb, Berger, A.; flowers large, dbl.; intr. 1965

'Barbarossa' HP, m, 1906, Welter; flowers carmine-purple, large, 55 petals; vigorous growth; [('Frau Karl Druschki' × 'Captain Hayward') × 'Princesse de Béarn']

'Barbe Blue' ('Barba Blue') HT, m

'Barbea' ('Beatrice') HT, lp, Barni, V.; intr. 1995

'Barbelvi' -- See 'Bellavista'

'Barbeque' F, mr, 1961, Dickson, Patrick; flowers rich red, 4 in., 30 petals, flat, borne in large clusters; foliage dark; vigorous, upright, bushy growth; [seedling × Lilli Marleen®]; intr. 1961

'Barbetod' -- See 'Bella di Todi'

Barbie® -- See 'Jacmobli'

'Barbie' F, mp, 1976, Swim, H.C. & Ellis, A.E.; bud pointed, ovoid; flowers sweetheart, 2½ in., 35-40 petals, slight fragrance; foliage small, glossy; upright growth; PP4723; ['Escort' × 'Jazz Fest']; intr. 1977

Barbie Dazzler™ -- See 'Wilbard'

'Barbra Streisand' -- See 'Wekquaneze'

'Barbrio' Min, yb, Barni, V.; bud globular; intr. 2007

'Barby' -- See 'Koraby'

'Barby Kordana' Min, mp, Kordes; flowers full; container rose

'Barcaik' LCl, rb, Barni, V.; intr. 1994

'Barcarolle' HT, mr, 1959, Laperrière; flowers crimson tinted geranium-red, large, 50 petals; vigorous, bushy growth; ['Paulette' × 'Tonnerre']

'Barcast' (Castor®) S, lp, Barni, V.; intr. 1987

'Barcelona' HT, dr, 1932, Kordes; bud long, pointed; flowers crimson, large, 75 petals, moderate spicy fragrance; foliage dark; vigorous growth; [('Sensation' × 'Templar') × 'Lord Charlemont']

Barcelona 95® -- See 'Fecasa'

'Barcora' ('Corallina') MinFl, ob, Barni, V.; intr. 1993

'Barcupu' HT, lp, Barni; intr. 2001

'Bardem' F, yb, Barni; bud large buds; intr. 2003

'Bardern' F, ob, Barni, V.; bud golden yellow; intr. 1996

'Bardion' F, yb, Barni; intr. 2003

'Bardon' (Donna Marella Agnelli®) HT, lp, Barni, V.dbl.; intr. 1988

'Bardord' ('Dorada') HT, ab, Barni, V.; intr. 1998

'Bardorg' ('Newbury Angel') Min, yb, 1993, Barrett, F.H.; flowers open yellow turning to pale orange, medium, full, borne in large clusters, no fragrance; foliage small, medium green, matte; some prickles; low (40 cm.), bushy growth; [Freegold® × 'Orange Honey']; intr. 1993

'Bardou Job' B, dr, 1887, Nabonnand, G.; flowers crimson, shaded blackish, semi-dbl.; vigorous, semi-climbing growth; ['Gloire des Rosomanes' × 'Général Jacqueminot']

'Baremoz' ('Emozione') HT, ab, Barni, V.; intr. 1999

'Baremp' -- See 'Maia'

'Barenic' ('Berenice') S, pb, Barni, V.; intr. 1993

'Barfed' S, ab, Barni; buds light pink; intr. 2005

'Barfeel' (Feeling®) F, lp, Barni, V.; intr. 1994

'Barfen' HT, ab, Barni; intr. 2004

'Barfine' -- See 'Roseto Carla Fineschi'

'Barfiob' ('Fiocco Bianco') F, w, Barni,

V.; intr. 1988
'Barflam' S, dr, Barni, V.; intr. 1993
'Barflor' (Florita®) MinFl, dp, Barni, V.; intr. 1994
'Barforev' F, dy, Barni; intr. 2004
'Barfort' Min, op, Barni, V.; intr. 1999
'Barfra' -- See 'Frasquita'
'Barfrei' S, lp, Barni; intr. 1999
'Barfri' (Frine®) S, mp, Barni, V.; intr. 1992
'Barfunn' ('Funny Girl') F, ob, Barni, V.; intr. 1998
'Bargai' (Gaia®) MinFl, pb, Barni, V.; intr. 1993
'Bargal' S, w, Barni; intr. 2004
'Barger' ('Ranger') S, mr, Barni, V.; intr. 1996
'Bargis' F, op, Barni; intr. 2003
'Bargold' (Golden Dance®) F, my, Barni, V.; intr. 1991
'Bargui' F, dr, Barni; intr. 2005
'Barhop' ('Hot Point Spire') HT, mr, Barni, V.; intr. 1999
'Barillet' -- See 'Mons Barillet-Deschamps'
'Barillet' M, mr, 1850, Verdier, V.; flowers dark carmine, large, dbl., cupped
'Barimp' (Impulse®) HT, mr, Barni, V.; intr. 1990
'Barinas' (Rinascimento®) S, pb, Barni, V.; intr. 1989
'Barinc' LCl, mp, Barni; intr. 2006
'Baringo' HT, dp; flowers 9 cm., 30-35 petals; greenhouse rose; intr. 2004
'Barire' F, lp, Barni, Enrico; intr. 2000
'Barise' LCl, lp, Barni; intr. 2006
'Baritzia' ('Letizia') HT, w, Kordes; intr. 1996
'Barjon' ('Jocelyne Pardo') F, dy, Barni
'Barjou' S, dy, Barni, V.; intr. 1999
Barkarole® -- See 'Tanelorak'
'Barkel' HT, pb, Barni, V.; intr. 1991
'Barkhatnaia Krasavitsa' ('Velvet Beauty') HT, dr, 1938, Gubonen; flowers velvety red, medium, semi-dbl., cupped; foliage dark; low growth
'Barlar' ('La Rossa') F, mr, Barni, V.; intr. 1999
'Barleo' (Eleonora®) LCl, dy, Barni, V.
'Barlev' (Rita Levi Montalcini®) F, ab, Barni, V.; intr. 1991
'Barley Gold' -- See 'Tanolgnil'
'Barley Sugar' Cl Min, my, Peden, R.; intr. 1995
'Barlio' F, w, Barni; intr. 2004
'Barliz' (Liza®) MinFl, mr, Barni, V.; intr. 1993
'Barlow' HP, dp, 1860, Ducher
'Barluc' ('Lucy') Min, ob, Barni, V.; intr. 1992
'Barludo' HT, mp, Barni; intr. 2000
'Barmar' (Marina Marini®) HT, dr, Barni, V.; intr. 1992
'Barmast' -- See 'Dorabella'
'Barmega' HT, mr; intr. 2005
'Barmeri' (Meridiana®) HT, op, Barni, V.; intr. 1994
'Barmezz' -- See 'Brunella'
'Barmiss' ('Rosita Missoni') HT, yb, Barni, V.; intr. 1999

'Barmiz' ('Mizar') S, dy, Barni, V.; intr. 1999
'Barmut' -- See 'Ornella Muti'
'Barn Dance' S, op, 1975, Buck, Dr. Griffith J.; bud ovoid, long, pointed; flowers light salmon-pink, 2½-3½ in., 23 petals, cupped; foliage light to dark, leathery; ['Tickled Pink' × 'Prairie Princess']
'Barna' HT, dp, Ghosh; flowers florescent deep pink with violet tinge, well formed; free-flowering; intr. 2001
'Barnard's Magic Day' -- See 'Horcointreau'
'Barnec' (Mirella®) HT, pb, Barni, V.; intr. 1986
'Barnerio' -- See 'Orione'
'Barni' HT, ob; intr. 2004
'Báró Natália Majthényi' HSet, m, 1889, Geschwind; flowers violet-purple, tinted ash gray; ['Souv. de President Lincoln' × 'Mme Lauriol de Barny']
'Barock' -- See 'Tankorab'
'Barock' S, yb, Tantau; flowers yellow to light yellow cream, very dbl., slight fragrance; heavy bloomer; foliage dark, very glossy; growth to 200-250 cm.; intr. 2000
Barockes Bischofszell® S, rb; flowers bright red with white reverse, dbl., high-centered; intr. 2006
'Baroly' ('Olympus') S, rb, Barni, V.; intr. 1998
'Baron Adolphe de Rothschild' ('Baron de Rothschild') HP, m, 1862, Lacharme
'Baron Alexandre de Vrints' HP, pb, 1880, Gonod; flowers dark pink, striped with red over white, full, moderate fragrance; ['Mme de Tartas' × unknown]
'Baron Chaurand' HP, mr, 1869, Liabaud; flowers velvety scarlet, deep grenadine in center, large, full, cupped; prickles straight, very strong at base; growth upright; possibly a seedling of 'Mons Bonçenne'
'Baron Cuvier' HGal, pb; flowers pink over violet-red, large, full
'Baron de Bastrop' -- See 'Pontrop'
'Baron de Bonstetten' HP, dr, 1871, Liabaud; flowers dark velvety crimson, large, 80 petals, moderate fragrance; sometimes recurrent bloom; vigorous, compact growth; ['Général Jacqueminot' × 'Géant des Batailles']
'Baron de Gossard' -- See 'Le Pérou'
'Baron de Gossard' HP, m, Gravereaux
'Baron de Maynard' -- See 'Baronne de Maynard'
'Baron de Rothschild' -- See 'Baron Adolphe de Rothschild'
'Baron de Rothschild' ('Le Baron de Rothschild') HP, m, 1862, Guillot; flowers dark carmine, shaded violet, aging to amaranth, large, full, moderate fragrance
'Baron de St. Triviers' T, pb, 1882, Nabonnand; flowers flesh-pink, shaded to copper, large, semi-dbl., moderate fragrance; few prickles; growth vigorous; ['Isabelle Nabonnand' × unknown]
'Baron de Wassenaër' M, dp, 1854, Verdier, V.; flowers light crimson, dbl., cupped, borne in clusters; some repeat; vigorous growth
'Baron de Wolseley' HP, 1882, Verdier, E.; flowers velvety bright crimson with flame tints, large, full; foliage oval-rounded, serrated, delicate green; prickles numerous, short, pink; stems reddish-green; growth upright
'Baron Elisi de St Albert' -- See 'Gabriel Fournier'
'Baron Elisi de St Albert' HP, dr, 1893, Widow Schwartz; flowers violet-red, aging to lilac-red, very large, full
'Baron Ernest Leroy' HP, dp, 1875, Garçon
'Baron G. B. Gonella' ('Baron J. B. Gonella', 'Baronne Gonella', 'Baron J. G. Gonella') B, pb, 1859, Guillot Père; flowers medium-dark pink, large, full, some quartering, moderate fragrance; ['Louise Odier' × unknown]
'Baron Giraud de l'Ain' -- See 'Baron Girod de l'Ain'
'Baron Girod de l'Ain' ('Baron Giraud de l'Ain', 'Princesse Christine von Salm') HP, rb, 1897, Reverchon; flowers bright red, petals edged white, dbl., slight fragrance; [sport of 'Eugène Furst']
'Baron Girod de l'Ain Striped Sport'
'Baron Haussmann' HP, mr, 1867, Lévêque; flowers light red, large, very dbl.
'Baron Heckeren de Wassenaer' ('Mme Eugene Cavaignac') HP, mp, 1852, Margottin; flowers bright pink, large, full
'Baron J. B. Gonella' -- See 'Baron G. B. Gonella'
'Baron J. G. Gonella' -- See 'Baron G. B. Gonella'
'Baron Jacques Riston' HT, op, 1936, Ketten Bros.; bud long, pointed; flowers salmon-pink, well-shaped, large, 45-50 petals; very vigorous growth; ['Mme Butterfly' × ('Rev. David R. Williamson' × 'Gorgeous')]
'Baron Lassus de St Geniez' HP, mp, Granger; flowers large, dbl.
Baron Meillandina® -- See 'Meitifran'
'Baron N. de Rothschild' HP, mp, 1882, Lévêque; flowers bright carmine, large, full
'Baron Nathaniel de Rothschild' HP, mr, 1882, Lévêque; flowers bright crimson red, large, full; foliage dark green
'Baron Palm' HT, mr, 1913, Lambert, P.; flowers velvety red with deep yellowish-red and vermilion reflections, large, dbl., cupped, moderate fragrance; ['Étoile de France' × 'Mme Ravary']
'Baron Peletan de Kinkelin' ('Baronne Peletan') HP, dr, 1864, Granger; flowers large, dbl.
'Baron Sunblaze' -- See 'Meitifran'
'Baron Taylor' HP, mr, 1880, Dugat; flowers light red, large, dbl.; [sport of 'John Hopper']
'Baron T'Kind de Roodenbecke' HP, m, 1897, Lévêque; flowers shaded purple
'Baronesa de Ovilar' HT, 1935, Munné,

B.; flowers carmine tinted yellow, very large, dbl.; foliage dark; strong stems; very vigorous growth; ['Sensation' × 'Souv. de Claudius Pernet']

'Baroness Henrietta Snoy' -- See 'Baronne Henriette de Snoy'

'Baroness Krayenhoff' HT, pb, 1931, Buisman, G. A. H.; flowers peach-pink, center orange, very large, dbl.; foliage light green; long stems; vigorous, compact growth; ['Mrs Henry Bowles' × 'Lady Roundway']

'Baroness Rothschild' ('Baronne Adolphe de Rothschild', 'Mme la Baronne de Rothschild') HP, lp, 1867, Pernet Père; flowers very soft rose, tinted white, large, 40 petals, cupped; some recurrent bloom; vigorous, erect growth; [sport of 'Souv. de la Reine d'Angleterre']

Baronesse® HT, or, Tantau; flowers red-orange, double, high-centered, borne mostly singly; recurrent; stems long; medium tall growth; intr. 1989

'Baronesse A. van Hövell tôt Westerflier' HT, m, 1933, Leenders, M.; flowers carmine-purple, base yellow, large, dbl.; foliage bronze; very vigorous, bushy growth

'Baronesse H. von Geyr' HT, pb, 1928, Leenders, M.; flowers pale flesh and vermilion-red, dbl.; [('Farbenkonigin' × 'Juliet') × 'Sunburst']

'Baronesse M. van Tuyll van Serooskerken' HT, pb, 1922, Leenders, M.; flowers rose and lilac-white, base apricot, semi-dbl.; ['Jonkheer J.L. Mock' × 'Mme Mélanie Soupert']

'Baronesse Manon' F, mp, 1938, Poulsen, S.; flowers clear pink, firm petals, 3 in.; foliage glossy, holly-like; vigorous, bushy growth; ['Else Poulsen' × 'Dame Edith Helen']; intr. 1952

'Baronesse S. H. W. van Dedem' HT, yb, 1923, Leenders, M.; flowers yellow and coppery, open, large, semi-dbl.; foliage dark, glossy; vigorous, bushy growth

'Baronesse von Ittersum' ('Jkvr D. Baroness von Ittersum') HMult, rb, 1910, Leenders, M.; flowers light crimson, shaded deeper, medium, semi-dbl., borne in clusters; free, non-recurrent bloom; foliage dark, glossy; vigorous, climbing (15 ft.) growth; ['Crimson Rambler' × 'Mme Laurette Messimy']

'Baronin Anna von Lüttwitz' HMult, lp, 1909, Walter; flowers cream-pink, 3½ cm., dbl., borne in large clusters, moderate musky fragrance; non-recurrent; ['Euphrosine' × 'Rösel Dach']

'Baronin von Adelebsen' S, mr, 1938, Vogel, M.; flowers medium, single

'Baronne' F, dp, Select; flowers 9 cm., 30-40 petals, high-centered; stems 50 - 70 cm; greenhouse rose; intr. 2003

'Baronne Ada' T, w, 1897, Soupert & Notting; flowers cream with chrome yellow center, large, full, globular, intense fragrance; ['Mme Lonbard' × 'Rêve d'Or']

'Baronne Adolphe de Rothschild' -- See 'Baroness Rothschild'

'Baronne Berge' -- See 'Mme la Baronne Berge'

'Baronne C. Rochetaillée' T, op, 1900, Dubreuil; flowers sulfur yellow, tinted salmon, large to very large, full, moderate fragrance

'Baronne Charles de Gargan' Cl T, ly, 1893, Soupert & Notting; flowers light daffodil yellow, center darker, large, full, moderate fragrance; ['Mme Barthélemy Levet' × 'Socrate']

'Baronne Charles d'Huart' HT, pb, 1910, Ketten Bros.; flowers lilac-rose suffused white, reflexed, dbl.; ['Pharisaer' × seedling]

'Baronne Daumesnil' B, mp, 1863, Thomas; flowers shining pink

'Baronne de Beauverger' HP, mr, 1867, Gautreau or Cochet; flowers cherry red

'Baronne de Hoffmann' T, rb, 1887, Nabonnand; flowers coppery, shaded red, large, dbl.

'Baronne de Maynard' ('Baron de Maynard') N, w, 1865, Lacharme, F.; flowers white, edges tinged pink, medium, full, cupped, borne in small clusters; moderately vigorous growth; ['Mlle Blanche Lafitte' × 'Sapho']; sometimes classed as B

'Baronne de Medem' HP, mr, 1876, Verdier, E.; flowers bright carmine cerise-red, large, full, globular

'Baronne de Nervo' S, Delbard-Chabert; intr. 1969

'Baronne de Noirmont' ('Baronne Noirmont') B, mp, 1861, Granger; flowers purplish-pink, medium, full, cupped, borne in small clusters, moderate violet fragrance; sometimes classed as HP

'Baronne de Prailly' HP, mr, 1871, Liabaud, J.; flowers bright red, large, very full, globular; ['Victor Verdier' × unknown]

'Baronne de Rothschild, Climbing' -- See 'Meigrisosar'

'Baronne de St Didier' HP, mr, 1886, Leveque, P.; flowers crimson red, sometimes shaded lilac and purple, often edged white, very large, full

'Baronne de Savigny' T, mp, 1854, Desprez; flowers pink, center darker, large, full

'Baronne de Schorlemmer' HT, mp, Lens, Louis; flowers large, dbl.; intr. 1985

'Baronne de Stael' HGal, ob, 1820, Vibert; flowers salmon-pink, open, large, dbl.; vigorous, branching growth

'Baronne de Vivario' Pol, w, 1925, Soupert & Notting; flowers dbl., borne in clusters; ['Orléans Rose' × 'Jeanny Soupert']

'Baronne d'Ivry' HGal, w; flowers yellowish-white, aging to red, medium, very full, globular

Baronne Edmond de Rothschild, Climbing® -- See 'Meigrisosar'

Baronne Edmond de Rothschild® HT, rb, 1970, Meilland; flowers ruby-red, whitish reverse, large, 40 petals, high-centered, intense fragrance; foliage glossy, leathery; vigorous growth (90-100 cm.); [(Baccará® × 'Crimson King') × 'Peace']; intr. 1968

'Baronne Finaz' HT, mp, 1962, Gaujard; flowers bright pink, large, 35 petals, moderate fragrance; foliage glossy, dark; long stems; very vigorous, upright growth; [('Peace' × unknown) × 'Opera']

'Baronne G. Chandon' -- See 'Socrate'

'Baronne G. de Noirmont' HT, pb, 1891, Cochet; bud rounded; flowers flesh pink with salmon, fading to blush white, large, full; foliage light green; prickles few, strong, reddish; growth upright

'Baronne Gonella' -- See 'Baron G. B. Gonella'

'Baronne Gustave de St Paul' HP, lp, 1894, Glantenet; flowers pale pink with silvery tints, 4½ in., dbl.

'Baronne Hallez de Claparède' HP, dr, 1849, Lebougre

'Baronne Haussmann' ('Mme Haussmann') HP, mr, 1867, Verdier, E.

'Baronne Henriette de Loew' ('Therese Welter') T, w, 1888, Nabonnand, G.; flowers pinkish white, center yellow, dbl.

'Baronne Henriette de Snoy' ('Baroness Henrietta Snoy', 'Henrietta de Snoy') T, pb, 1897, Bernaix, A.; flowers flesh, reverse carmine-pink, well-formed, 9-10 cm., dbl., flat, borne in small clusters, slight fragrance; reliable repeat; vigorous growth; ['Gloire de Dijon' × 'Mme Lombard']

'Baronne Jard-Panvillers' HP, mp, 1880, Duval; flowers bright pink, large, full

'Baronne Louise Uxkull' HP, pb, 1871, Guillot; flowers bright flesh pink with carmine, very large, full

'Baronne Maurice de Graviers' HP, rb, 1866, Verdier, E.; flowers intense cerise red, tinted and shaded pink and carmine, reverse whitish, medium, full

'Baronne Nathalie de Rothschild' ('Baronne Nathaniel de Rothschild') HP, lp, 1885, Pernet Père; flowers bright pink with silvery shadings, very large, very dbl., globular, moderate fragrance; growth upright; ['Baronne Adolphe de Rothschild' × unknown]

'Baronne Nathaniel de Rothschild' -- See 'Baronne Nathalie de Rothschild'

'Baronne Noirmont' -- See 'Baronne de Noirmont'

'Baronne Peletan' -- See 'Baron Peletan de Kinkelin'

'Baronne Presval' HP, dp

'Baronne Prévost' HP, mp, before 1841, Desprez; flowers rose-pink, shading lighter, large, dbl., flat, moderate fragrance; recurrent bloom; vigorous, erect growth

'Baronne Prévost, Climbing' Cl HP, mp

'Baronne Surcouf' S, mp, Briant; intr. 1989

'Baronne Vitat' HP, mp, 1873, Liabaud;

flowers very large, full, globular
'Baroque' ('Baroque Floorshow') S, m, Harkness; flowers magenta with small white eye and yellow stamens, semi-dbl.; growth low and spreading (2 × 3½ ft.); intr. 1995
'Baroque Floorshow' -- See 'Baroque'
'Barorp' Min, m, Barni, V.; intr. 1985
'Barossa Dream' -- See 'Sunauck'
'Barottoc' HT, ab, Barni, Enrico; intr. 2000
'Barout' ('Handout', 'Tranquility') HT, ab, 1983, Barrett, F.H.; flowers pale apricot, peach and yellow blend, 35 petals, borne mostly singly; foliage medium size, dark, glossy; upright growth; ['Whisky Mac' × 'Pink Favorite']; intr. 1982
'Barpess' -- See 'La Favorita'
'Barpipp' MinFl, pb, Barni, V.; intr. 1995
'Barpoll' (Pollux®) S, mr, Barni, V.; intr. 1987
'Barpolv' LCl, w, Barni; intr. 2006
'Barprett' ('Pretty Pink') HWich, dp, Barni, V.; intr. 1992
'Barprimo' S, ly, Barni, V.; intr. 1995
'Barpris' (Primo Sole®) HT, my, Barni, V.; intr. 1987
'Barred' (Red Sea®) F, dr, Barni, V.; intr. 1990
'Barrez' ('Carezza') HT, op, Barni, V.; buds elegant; intr. 1996
'Barrian' ('Brian') MinFl, mr, Barni, V.; intr. 1995
'Barricade' ('Combar') LCl, mr, Combe, C.; flowers vermilion/orange, medium to large, dbl., borne in small clusters, no fragrance; intr. 1968
'Barrie' F, pb, 1973, Schloen, J.; bud ovoid; flowers salmon-pink, medium, dbl., cupped; free bloom; foliage glossy, light; ['Sumatra' × 'Fashion']
'Barrom' F, or, Barni, Enrico; intr. 2000
'Barros' (Rosellana®) F, mp, Barni, V.
'Barry Fearn' -- See 'Korschwama'
'Barry Stephens' -- See 'Horcabellero'
'Barsan' ('Sans Souci') F, w, Barni, V.; intr. 1996
'Barsav' ('Mafalda di Savoia') F, op, Barni, V.; intr. 1999
'Barser' ('Serenata') HT, op, Barni, V.; intr. 1998
'Barshiflo' ('Snowgoose') F, w, 1986, Barrett, F.H.; flowers small, 20 petals, borne in clusters; foliage medium size, medium green, semi-glossy; upright growth; ['Seaspray' × 'Iceberg']
'Barsib' (Sibilla®) HT, dr, Barni, V.; intr. 1987
'Barsido' F, dy, Barni; intr. 2003
'Barsilv' -- See 'Silver Queen'
'Barsin' -- See 'Talia'
'Barsor' ('Eros') HT, ob, Barni, V.; intr. 1990
'Barspot' F, mr, Barni; bud globular; intr. 2007
'Barstel' F, dy, Barni, V.; intr. 1999
'Barsup' S, w, Barni; intr. 2003
'Barsus' F, pb, Barni, V.; intr. 1993
'Bartam' HT, op, Barni; intr. 2004
'Bartares' ('Antares') S, pb, Barni, V.; intr. 1996
'Barten' -- See 'Atena'
'Barteo' HT, mr, Barni; bud globular; intr. 2003
'Barter's Pink' HT, ob, 1965, Barter; flowers bright coral-pink, deeply veined, 4 in., dbl., slight fragrance; foliage light green; vigorous, bushy growth; [Queen Elizabeth® × 'Claude']
'Barthélemy Joubert' HP, mr, 1877, Moreau et Robert; flowers bright cerise red, large, full
'Bartra' F, yb, Barni; intr. 2004
'Bartral' S, ab, Barni; intr. 2004
'Bartusc' HT, mr, Barni, V.; intr. 1993
'Barunka' F, op, Urban, J.; flowers salmon-pink, large, very dbl.; intr. 1983
'Barvan' S, mp, 1999, Barni, V.; intr. 1999
'Barvar' HT, yb, Barni; bud long, narrow; intr. 2007
'Barvelv' LCl, mr, Barni, V.; intr. 1998
'Barvir' -- See 'Andromeda'
'Barwast' HT, op, Barni, V.
'Barwrock' LCl, w, Barni, V.; intr. 1996
'Barzos' -- See 'Tersicore'
'Bashful' ('Giesebrecht') Pol, pb, 1958, deRuiter; flowers reddish-pink, white eye, small, single, borne in trusses; bushy, compact growth; intr. 1955
'Basier' HT, w, 1955, Mallerin, C.; flowers pearly white, edges tinted pink, 3 in., 40 petals, high-centered, moderate fragrance; vigorous growth; ['Mme Joseph Perraud' × 'Independence']; intr. 1954
'Basildon Belle' F, or, 1965, Maarse, G.; flowers vermilion; [sport of 'Anna Wheatcroft']; intr. 1964
'Basildon Bond' -- See 'Harjosine'
'Basilika' HT, op, VEG; flowers salmon-pink, large, dbl.
Bassino® -- See 'Kormixal'
'Bastei' S, or, Schmadlak, Dr.; flowers deep orange shaded burnt umber, very dbl., flat, then recurved, no fragrance; intr. 1973
'Bastogne' HT, or, Grandes Roseraies; flowers vermilion, shaded darker, well-formed; foliage dark; very vigorous growth
'Basye's Amphidiploid' S, mp, Basye, Dr. Robert; flowers medium, single; prickles very numerous; growth very large; [R. moschata abysinnica × R. rugosa rubra]; intr. 1955
'Basye's Blueberry' S, mp, Basye, Robert; intr. 1982
'Basye's Legacy' S, mp, Basye; flowers small, medium to dark pink, 5 petals, borne in small clusters, moderate fragrance; may repeat if kept deadheaded; growth spreading; can be used as a climber; intr. 2002
'Basye's Myrrh-Scented Rose' S, lp, Basye, Robert; intr. 1980
'Basye's Purple Rose' S, m, Basye, Robert; flowers large, velvety purple with gold stamens, single, moderate fruity fragrance; rough, sparse foliage; growth thick, erect, with prickly canes; [R. rugosa × R. foliolosa]; intr. 1968
'Basye's Thornless' -- See 'Commander Gillette'
Bataclan® S, dy, Tantau; intr. 2005
'Batamy' ('Little Amy') Min, yb, 2004; flowers yellow blend, reverse red blend, 4 cm., dbl., borne in large clusters; foliage small, medium green, semi-glossy; prickles small; growth bushy, short (25 cm.); garden decoration, exhibition; [sport of 'Amber Sunset']; intr. 2004
'Batmercury' ('Freddie Mercury') HT, my, 1994, Stainthorpe, Eric; flowers medium, full, borne mostly singly, moderate fragrance; foliage large, dark green, glossy; some prickles; medium, bushy growth; [sport of 'Tina Turner']; intr. 1994
Baton Rouge™ -- See 'Poulattra'
'Batsybil' ('Dr Sybil Johnson') HT, dr, 1993, Stainthorpe, Eric; flowers medium, full, borne mostly singly, moderate fragrance; foliage medium size, medium green, semi-glossy; some prickles; medium (85 cm.), upright growth; ['Tropicana' × 'Prima Ballerina']; intr. 1994
Battersby Beauty' -- See 'Horbatbeaut'
'Battle of Britain' HT, yb, 1970, Gandy, Douglas L.; flowers yellow-orange, medium, 30 petals; ['Miss Ireland' × 'Summer Sunshine']
'Battmurdina' ('Murdina Lowe') F, pb, 2004; flowers pink blend, 2 in., dbl., borne in small clusters, slight fragrance; foliage light green, semi-glossy; growth upright, medium (2½ ft.); garden; ['Elsie Warren' × 'Tina Turner']; intr. 2005
'Battoo' ('Myra') HT, pb, 1992, Stainthorpe, Avril E.; flowers medium, dbl., borne in small clusters; foliage medium size, dark green, glossy; numerous prickles; medium (75 cm.), bushy growth; [Matangi® × 'Mood Music']; sometimes classed as a floribunda, but registered as HT; intr. 1990
'Bavaria' -- See 'Kormun'
Bavaria München™ -- See 'Poulkalm'
'Bavarian Girl' -- See 'Korleen'
'Bavarian Gold' -- See 'Tanyab'
'Baviera d'Oro' -- See 'Tanyab'
'Baxter Beauty' T, ab, 1938, Clark, A.; flowers light yellow to sulphur overlaid outside with light salmon pink; [sport of 'Lorraine Lee']
Bay ™ -- See 'Poulcot003'
'Bay Cottage' (Bay ™) S, dp, Poulsen; flowers deep pink, small, single, borne in clusters, no fragrance; foliage dark; growth broad, bushy, 40-60 cm.; intr. 2004
'Bay Glow' Min, yb
'Bay of Bengal' HT, m, Ghosh; flowers silver lilac with deeper petal edges and veins, dbl.; intr. 2001
'Bayadère' HT, ab, 1954, Mallerin, C.; flowers salmon-pink to canary yellow, tinted pink, large, 52 petals, high-centered; foliage dark, bronze; vigorous, bushy growth; [R.M.S. Queen Mary × seedling]; intr. 1954
Bayerngold® ('Bavarian Gold', 'Baviera

d'Oro', 'Goldbay') F, my, Tantau; flowers clear yellow, medium, dbl., high-centered; foliage glossy; compact, low (40-50 cm.) growth; very winter hardy; among the healthiest of the yellows; intr. 1990

Bayernland™ -- See 'Poulrijk'

Bayernland Cover™ -- See 'Poulrijk'

'Bayerntraum' HT, mp, Cocker; intr. 1999

'Bayreuth' S, rb, W. Kordes Söhne; flowers medium, dbl., moderate fragrance; intr. 1965

Be-Bop™ -- See 'Weksacsoul'

'Be Glad' HT, rb, 1988, McMillan, Thomas G.; flowers white changing to red, reverse white, aging deep pink, medium, 25-30 petals, high-centered, moderate fruity fragrance; foliage medium size, dark green, glossy; prickles normal; upright, medium growth; no fruit; ['Paradise' × 'Color Magic']

'Be My Valentine' HT, mr, Williams, J.B.; flowers velvet red; intr. 2003

'Bea Wallace' -- See 'Burbeawall'

'Beaagile' ('Joan Beales') S, dr, 2006, Beales, Amanda; flowers semi-dbl., borne in large clusters; foliage medium size, dark green, matte; prickles average, straight, moderate; growth upright, medium (1-1½ m.); containers, hedges; ['Henry Kelsey' × 'Souvenir du Docteur Jamain']; intr. 2004

'Beaarty' ('Kitty's Rose') S, lp, 2006, Beales, Amanda; flowers 8 cm., dbl., borne in large clusters; foliage small; prickles average, hooked, few; growth bushy, short (60 cm.); landscape, containers; [Centenaire de Lourdes® × City of London®]; intr. 2003

'Beaat' ('Attleborough') LCl, mr, 2006, Beales, Amanda; flowers medium red, reverse medium red, 10 cm., full, borne in large clusters; foliage medium size, medium green, glossy; prickles average, curved down, moderate; growth bushy, tall (3-4 m.), climbing; ['Paul's Scarlet Climber' × Parkdirektor Riggers®]; intr. 2001

'Beabimbo' ('St Ethelburga') S, lp, 2006, Beales, Amanda; flowers soft pink, 15 cm., very full, cupped, borne in large clusters, intense clove fragrance; free-flowering; foliage medium green, semi-glossy; prickles average, hooked, moderate; growth bushy, medium (4 ft.); containers, hedging; intr. 2003

'Beabliss' ('Bliss') S, dp, 2006, Beales, Amanda; flowers deep pink, reverse deep pink, 10 cm., very full, borne in small clusters; foliage medium size, medium green, matte; prickles average, straight, moderate; growth bushy, short (60 cm.); containers, landscape; ['Comte de Chambord' × Centenaire de Lourdes®]; intr. 2000

'Beacake' ('Nelson's Pride') S, w, 2006, Beales, Amanda; flowers dbl., borne mostly solitary; foliage medium size, dark green, semi-glossy; prickles medium, curved downwards, moderate; growth bushy, short (1 m.); landscape, containers; ['Bonica' × 'Maigold']; intr. 2005

'Beacarol' ('Our Beth') S, lp, 2006, Beales, Amanda; flowers full, borne in small clusters; foliage medium green, semi-glossy; prickles average, hooked, moderate; growth bushy, medium (4 ft.); landscape, containers; ['Louise Odier' × 'English Miss']; intr. 2006

'Beacath' ('Norwich Cathedral') HT, my, 1997, Beales, Peter; flowers full, borne mostly singly, intense fragrance; foliage medium size, medium green, leathery, semi-glossy; some prickles; upright, low (3 ft.)growth; [sport of 'Diamond Jubilee']; intr. 1996

Beach® HT, r, Tantau; flowers medium size, tan/yellow, dbl.; heavy bloomer; greenhouse rose; intr. 2001

'Beach Baby' F, ob, Benny, David; flowers warm orange to salmon, borne in large trusses; growth medium; intr. 2005

'Beach Boy' Min, my, 1982, Williams, Ernest D.; bud pointed; flowers golden buff, 48 petals, high-centered, borne usually singly, slight fragrance; foliage small, dark, slightly glossy; prickles short, tan; upright, bushy growth; ['Tom Brown' × seedling]; intr. 1981

'Beach Girl' HT, ab, Dorieux; flowers peach-apricot and yellow, dbl., high-centered, slight fragrance; growth to 4-5 ft.; intr. 1998

'Beachcomber' -- See 'Maclapaz'

'Beacon' HT, mr, 1952, Swim, H.C.; flowers cerise-red, medium, 60-70 petals, high-centered, slight fragrance; growth vigorous, bushy, upright; PP938; registration refused because of similarity to The Beacon

'Beacon Belle' Ayr, lp, 1919, Farquhar; flowers flesh passing to white, small, dbl., borne in clusters, moderate fragrance; ['Orléans Rose' × ('Katharina Zeimet' × R. arvensis)]

'Beacon Lodge' HT, dr, 1976, Ellick; flowers deep red, 4-5 in., 40-45 petals; foliage glossy, dark; very vigorous growth; ['Chopin' × 'Ena Harkness']

'Beacon View' HT, mr, 1977, Ellick, C. W.; flowers dbl., borne several together and in trusses; foliage large, long, pointed, medium green, semi-glossy; growth very vigorous; ['Karl Herbst' × 'Lathom Park']

'Beacost' ('Festive Jewel') S, pb, 2006, Beales, Amanda; flowers full, borne in large clusters; foliage medium size, medium green, semi-glossy; prickles average, straight, few; growth bushy, medium (1½ m.); shrub, small climber, hedging; ['Aloha' × 'Comte de Chambord']; intr. 2004

'Beacream' ('Countess of Wessex') S, w, 2006, Beales, Amanda; flowers full, borne in large clusters; foliage medium size, dark green,; prickles average, hooked, moderate; growth upright, medium (1½ m.); garden decoration, containers, hedging; ['Bonica' × 'Maigold']; intr. 2006

'Beadaffy' ('Sir John Mills') LCl, mp, 2006, Beales, Amanda; flowers glowing pink, outer edges fading lighter, 10 cm., full, hybrid tea, borne mostly solitary, moderate fragrance; recurrent; foliage medium size, dark green, glossy; prickles average, hooked, moderate; growth upright, medium (2½ m.); small climber for walls, fences, obelisks; [Armada® × Westerland®]; intr. 2005

'Beadick' ('Fragrant Vision') S, mr, 2006, Beales, Amanda; flowers plum red, 8 cm., full, borne in small clusters; foliage medium size, dark green, matte; prickles hooked, moderate; growth bushy, medium (1¼ m.); landscape, containers; ['Roundelay' × 'Crimson Glory']; intr. 2005

'Beadix' ('Dixieland Linda') Cl HT, ab, 1997, Beales, Peter; flowers very dbl., 41 petals, borne in small clusters; foliage medium size, dark green, glossy; upright, medium (8-10ft.)growth; [sport of 'Aloha']; intr. 1996

'Beadonald' ('Ivor's Rose') S, rb, 2006, Beales, Amanda; flowers medium red, reverse dark pink, 10 cm., very full, borne in large clusters; foliage light green, semi-glossy; prickles average, straight, few; growth upright, short (1 m.); garden decoration, hedging; ['Bonica' × 'Roundelay']; intr. 2004

'Beadrum' ('Gardener's Joy') S, ab, 2006, Beales, Amanda; flowers semi-dbl., borne in large clusters; foliage medium size, dark green, glossy; prickles average, straight, moderate; growth upright, medium (1½ m.); landscape, small climber; ['Centennaire de Lourdes' × 'Maigold']; intr. 2005

'Beaexam' ('Colby School') F, lp, 2006, Beales, Amanda; flowers creamy white to blush pink, deeper in center, medium, dbl, cushion-like, borne mostly solitary, slight fragrance; foliage medium green, glossy; prickles straight, few; bushy, compact, low growth; ['Bonica' × 'Great Ormond Street']; intr. 2005

'Beahor' ('Horatio Nelson') S, mp, 1998, Beales, Peter; flowers clear pink, outer petals lighter, 41-50 petals, cupped, then rosette, borne in small clusters; recurrent; foliage medium size, medium green, glossy; prickles moderate; compact (3 ft.) growth; [Centenaire de Lourdes® × 'Aloha']; intr. 1997

'Beajap' ('Barakura') S, lp, 2006, Beales, Amanda; flowers small, dbl., borne in large clusters; foliage small, light green, semi-glossy; prickles small, straight, few; growth spreading, short (60 cm.); groundcover, containers; ['Bonica' × 'Rambling Rector']; intr. 1998

'Beajil' ('Jill Dando') S, rb, 2000, Beales, Peter; flowers red blend, reverse softer, 4 in., semi-dbl., very cupped, open, borne in small clusters, slight fragrance;

foliage large, dark green, semi-glossy; prickles moderate; upright, medium (4 ft.) growth; [Armada® × 'Maigold']; intr. 1999

'Beamac' ('Macmillan Nurse') S, w, 1998, Beales, Peter; flowers white, 41-50 petals, borne in large clusters; foliage medium size, dark green, glossy; prickles moderate; compact, 3 ft growth; ['Bonica' × 'Maigold']; intr. 1998

'Bean Rock' HT, op, McGredy; flowers large, rich salmon pink, dbl., exhibition; growth medium; intr. 2001

'Beapaul' ('Sir Paul Smith') LCl, ab, 2006, Beales, Amanda; flowers full, borne in large clusters; foliage medium size, medium green, semi-glossy; prickles large, hooked, moderate; growth spreading, medium (2-3 m.); ['Louise Odier' × 'Aloha']; intr. 2006

'Beapaw' ('Paws') S, mp, 1999, Beales, Peter; flowers 4 in., very dbl., borne mostly singly, intense fragrance; foliage medium size, medium green, dull; numerous prickles; bushy, medium (2½ × 2 ft.) growth; ['Silver Jubilee' × Constance Spry®]; intr. 1999

'Beatrice' -- See 'Barbea'

'Beatrice' F, dp, McGredy, Sam IV; flowers deep rose pink, dbl., borne in large sprays, slight fragrance; ['Paddy McGredy' × ('Kordes' Perfecta' × 'Montezuma')]; intr. 1968

'Beatrice' HT, mp, 1908, Paul, W.; flowers dark carnation pink tinted scarlet-vermilion, very large, very full

'Beatrice Berkeley' HT, rb, Fitzhardinge

'Beatrice Boeke' HT, dp, 1966, Buisman, G. A. H.; bud ovoid; flowers pink-red, large, dbl.; ['Montezuma' × 'Detroiter']

'Beatrice Jennings' -- See 'Rawjen'

'Beatrice McGregor' HT, dr, 1938, Clark, A.; flowers large, dbl.; ['Sensation' × seedling]

'Beatrice Samzin' F, mp, Scholle, E.; flowers large, very dbl.; intr. 1970

'Béatrix' B, mr, 1865, Cherpin; flowers bright carmine red, medium to large, full, cupped, borne in small clusters; nearly thornless; growth upright; ['Louise Odier' × unknown]

'Beatrix, Comtesse de Buisseret' ('Comtesse Beatrix de Buisseret') HT, mp, 1900, Soupert & Notting; flowers silver rose, aging to rosy carmine red, very large, dbl., moderate fragrance

'Beatwe' ('Twenty-Fifth') F, dr, 1997, Beales, Peter; flowers deep red, golden yellow stamens, 2½ in., semi-dbl., shallow cup to flat, borne in large clusters, slight fragrance; foliage medium size, dark green, semi-glossy; some prickles; growth compact, low (2ft.); ['Redbreast' × 'Pearl Drift']; intr. 1996

'Beau Carmin' Ch, pb, before 1810, Descemet; flowers velvety carmine, shaded purple, medium, full

'Beau Cramoisi Royal' -- See 'Cramoisi Royal'

'Beau Narcisse' HGal, m, before 1828, Miellez; flowers purple, striped, medium, full, cupped

'Beau Rose' Misc OGR, mp

'Beau Rose Primaplant' Pol, dp, Vlaeminck; flowers large, dbl.; intr. 1963

'Beaucaire' Pol, rb, 1937, Grandes Roseraies; flowers edges chamois-pink, center coppery yellow, reverse coppery-red, dbl.; vigorous, dwarf growth

'Beaujolais' HT, dr, Select; flowers 10 cm., 40 petals, high-centered; stems 60 - 80 cm long; greenhouse rose; intr. 2003

'Beaujolais' HT, mr, 1932, Croibier; flowers crimson-carmine, very large, dbl., globular; very vigorous growth; ['Hadley' × 'Laurent Carle']

'Beaulieu' -- See 'Tanzahde'

'Beaulieu' -- See 'Dicobey'

'Beaulieu' HP, 1883, Moreau et Robert

'Beaulieu Abbey' F, ab, 1964, Cobley; flowers creamy yellow suffused pink, well-formed, 4 in., dbl.; foliage dark, glossy, leathery; vigorous growth; ['Masquerade' × 'Docteur Valois']

'Beauregard' LCl, Croix, P.; intr. 1972

'Beauté' HT, ab, 1953, Mallerin, C.; bud long; flowers light apricot, well-formed, large, dbl.; vigorous growth; ['Mme Joseph Perraud' × seedling]; intr. 1954

'Beauté d'Automne' Pol, dp, 1918, Turbat; flowers bright rose-pink, dbl., borne in clusters of 50-70; ['Phyllis' × seedling]

'Beauté de Billard' HMult, mr, before 1855, Billard; flowers glowing scarlet, full

'Beauté de France' HT, w, 1920, Toussaint Mille Fils; flowers creamy white to pure white, inside yellow, dbl., moderate fragrance; ['Mme Mélanie Soupert' × 'Kaiserin Auguste Viktoria']

'Beauté de France' HT, rb, Gaujard; bud long, pointed; flowers brick flushed coppery, medium, dbl., moderate fragrance; foliage leathery, dark; upright growth; [('Comtesse Vandal' × seedling) × seedling]; intr. 1952

'Beauté de la Malmaison' HGal, dr, before 1885; flowers deep red, marbled with violet, medium, full

'Beauté de l'Europe' T, op, 1881, Gonod; flowers light orange-pink, yellow base, large, dbl., intense fragrance; few prickles; ['Gloire de Dijon' × unknown]

'Beauté de Lyon' -- See 'Beauté Inconstante'

'Beauté de Lyon' HP, or, 1910, Pernet-Ducher; flowers coral-red, tinted yellow, large, dbl., globular, moderate fragrance; foliage brilliant green; prickles very large, red; ['Soleil d'Or' × seedling]

'Beauté de Roulers' HP, mp, 1860, de Cock

'Beauté de Versailles' -- See 'Georges Cuvier'

'Beaute Francaise' HP, mr, 1862, Lartay

'Beauté Incomparable' D, mr, 1860, Miellez

'Beauté Inconstante' ('Beauté de Lyon') T, ob, 1892, Pernet-Ducher; flowers orange to coppery red, shaded carmine and yellow, highly variable, 9-10 cm., semi-dbl. to dbl., moderate fragrance; vigorous growth; ['Safrano' × 'Earl of Eldon']; sometimes classed as a Noisette

'Beauté Insurmontable' ('Lyre de Flore', 'Panachée Superbe', 'Phoenix') HGal, dp, before 1811; flowers plumed deep pink and delicate pink and purple ground, small, dbl.; from Holland

'Beauté Lyonnaise' HT, w, 1895, Pernet-Ducher; flowers white tinted pale yellow, large; ['Baronne Adolphe de Rothschild' × unknown]

'Beauté Orléanaise' HWich, w, 1919, Turbat; bud salmon red; flowers white to flesh-pink, 4 cm., dbl., borne in small to medium clusters; foliage small, dark green, glossy

'Beauté Rare' -- See 'Sapho'

'Beauté Renommée' HGal, mr, before 1811; flowers red with purple tones to medium, 2 in., full; from Holland

'Beauté Riante' HGal, dp, before 1836, Calvert; flowers dark pink, aging to red, edges lighter, small to medium

Beauté Spatiale® -- See 'Deldrop'

'Beauté Superbe Agathée' ('Pétronille') HGal, lp, before 1811; bud pointed; flowers small, very dbl., borne in small clusters, moderate fragrance; Agathe group

'Beauté Suprême' C, m, before 1846; flowers dark purple with bluish carmine, full

'Beauté Surprenante' HGal, w, before 1820, Descemet/Vibert; flowers white, with a pink heart, medium; possibly synonymous with 'Beauté Suprême'

'Beauté Tendre' ('Rouge Rayé') HGal, dp, before 1810, Dupont; flowers deep pink, vinous white beneath, veined darker red above, large, very dbl.

'Beauté Tendre' ('Alba Rosea', 'Enfant de France', 'Regia') A, lp, possibly Vibert; flowers pale rose, nearly white edges, very large, full; intr. before 1813

'Beauté Touchante' HGal, mr, before 1813, Miellez

'Beauté Virginale' ('Carnea Virginalis', 'Virginale', 'La Virginale') D, w, before 1811, Descemet; bud pointed, delicate pink; flowers blush white, medium, full, borne in clusters of 3-4; foliage oval, deeply toothed, ashy green

'Beautiful Black' HP, dr

'Beautiful Bride' -- See 'Lenmacra'

'Beautiful Britain' -- See 'Dicfire'

'Beautiful Carpet' -- See 'Wiltshire'

'Beautiful Doll' Min, mp, 1982, Jolly, Betty J.; flowers 25 petals, high-centered, borne singly and in small clusters; foliage small, dark, semi-glossy; bushy, spreading growth; [seedling × 'Zinger']

'Beautiful Dreamer' -- See 'Summer Dream'

'Beautiful Dreamer' F, ob, 1976, Herholdt, J.A.; flowers orange to sunset-gold, pointed, 2-2½ in., 35 petals, slight fragrance; foliage glossy; [seedling × seedling]; intr. 1977

'Beautiful Fukuyama' HT, or, Hiroshima; intr. 1986

'Beautiful Nature' S, pb; intr. 1999

'Beautiful Sunday' Min, mr, 1977, Takatori, Yoshiho; bud ovoid; flowers bright geranium-red, small, 60 petals, cupped; foliage glossy, dark, leathery; compact, bushy growth; ['Camelot' × ('Camelot' × unknown)]

'Beautiful Sunrise' -- See 'Bostimebide'

'Beauty' HT, mr, 1931, Ward, F.B.; flowers american beauty red, but darker, very large, dbl.; long stems; vigorous growth; [('Crusader' × 'Premier') × 'American Beauty']

Beauty™ Min, mr, Olesen; flowers dbl., 25-30 petals, no fragrance; foliage dark green, glossy; growth narrow, bushy, very low (20-40 cm.); intr. 1996

'Beauty by Oger' HT, pb, Select; flowers medium pink with outer petals turning darker as they open, 11 cm., 40 petals, high-centered; stems 60 - 80 cm long; intr. 2003

'Beauty Cream' F, w, 1956, Verschuren; flowers cream, large; foliage dark; vigorous, upright growth

'Beauty Fairy' LCl, dp

'Beauty Festival' -- See 'Beauty of Festival'

'Beauty from Within' HT, ob, Orard; flowers deep golden center with pink edges on the outer petals, takes on an orange hue as, dbl., high-centered, then cupped; foliage dark green; straight stems; growth vigorous, upright, medium; intr. 2002

'Beauty of Badgen' HT, lp, 1924, French, A.

'Beauty of Beeston' HP, dr, 1882, Frettingham; flowers velvety crimson, small, full

'Beauty of Brisbane' Pol, pb, 1932, Perrot; [sport of 'Goldlachs']

'Beauty of Dropmore' S, w, 1956, Skinner; flowers dbl.; non-recurrent; bushy, erect growth; [R. spinosissima altaica × R. spinosissima cultivar]

'Beauty of England' HP, dp

'Beauty of Festival' ('Beauty Festival') HT, Klimenko, V. N.; intr. 1955

'Beauty of Glazenwood' -- See 'Fortune's Double Yellow'

'Beauty of Glenhurst' Ch, dp, Morley; flowers 5-7 cm.; growth semi-climbing (10 ft.); ['Parsons' Pink China' × unknown]; intr. 1983

'Beauty of Greenmount' ('Beauty of Greenwood') N, dp, 1854, Pentland; flowers cherry pink with rose red shades, full

'Beauty of Greenwood' -- See 'Beauty of Greenmount'

'Beauty of Hurst' LCl, w, 1926, Hicks; flowers creamy buff, dbl.; foliage dark; very vigorous growth

'Beauty of Leafland' HSpn, pb, Erskine; flowers blend of pale pink and pale yellow, almost creamy white, 25-30 petals, intense fragrance; non-remontant; ['Butterball' × 'Haidee']

'Beauty of New South Wales' Pol, rb, 1931, Knight, G.; flowers bright crimson, center white, small, single, borne in clusters of 20; bushy, dwarf growth; ['Orléans Rose' × 'Alice Amos']

'Beauty of Rosemawr' T, pb, 1903, Van Fleet/Conard & Jones; flowers carmine rose veined vermilion and white, medium, dbl., slight fragrance; growth medium (3 × 2 ft.)

'Beauty of Stapleford' HT, rb, 1879, Bennett; flowers red and violet, well-formed, large, no fragrance; moderate growth; ['Mme Bravy' × 'Comtesse d'Oxford']; very prone to mildew

'Beauty of the Prairies' -- See 'Queen of the Prairies'

'Beauty of the Thames' HP, mp, 1876, Walker; flowers bright carmine, large, full

'Beauty of Waltham' HP, mr, 1862, Paul, W.; flowers rosy crimson, large, dbl.; recurrent bloom; vigorous growth; ['Général Jacqueminot' × unknown]

'Beauty of Westerham' HP, mr, 1864, Cattell

'Beauty Queen' -- See 'Canmiss'

'Beauty Secret' Min, mr, 1965, Moore, Ralph S.; bud pointed; flowers cardinal-red, 1½ in., dbl., high-centered; foliage small, glossy, leathery; vigorous, bushy growth; ['Little Darling' × 'Magic Wand']

'Beauty Show' -- See 'Shobha'

'Beauty Star' -- See 'Frystar'

'Beauty Temple' HT, w, Chakraborty, Dr K.; flowers pure white, large; intr. 2005

Beautyglo™ -- See 'Minwco'

'Beauty's Blush' HRg, dp, 1955, Univ. of Saskatchewan; flowers deep pink, becoming lighter, dbl.; non-recurrent; vigorous (6 ft.) growth; hardy onthe Canadian prairies; ['Tetonkaha' × 'Pink Pearl']

'Beayar' ('Yardley Baroque') HT, ly, 1999, Beales, Peter; flowers soft, primrose yellow, 4½ in., full, cupped, borne mostly singly, moderate fragrance; recurrent; foliage medium size, dark green, semi-glossy; numerous prickles; upright, medium (2-3 ft.) growth; [sport of 'Alpine Sunset']; intr. 1997

'Bébé Blanc' Pol, w, 1922, Turbat; flowers dbl., borne in large clusters; dwarf growth

'Bébé Fleuri' Ch, mp, 1906, Dubreuil; flowers small, occasionally striped, semi-dbl.

'Bébé Leroux' Pol, w, 1901, Soupert; flowers medium, in trusses of 20-40; compact growth; ['Mignonette' × 'Archiduchesse Elisabeth-Marie']

Bebe Lune® F, my, Delbard; flowers yellow-gold, large , double, shallow cup; recurrent; compact, well-branched growth; intr. 1965

'Becca Godman' F, pb, Wells; intr. 1998

'Becker's Ideal' -- See 'Ideal'

'Beckett's Single' HGal, mp, Quest-Ritson

'Becky' HT, dp, 1925, Beckwith; flowers glowing rose-pink, single; vigorous growth

'Becky Adams' -- See 'Moebecky'

Bedazzled™ -- See 'Jachotta'

'Bedazzler' S, mr; intr. 2003

'Bedchild' ('Pudsey Bear') HT, dy, Chessum, Paul; intr. 1996

'Bedford Belle' HT, mr, 1884, Laxton; flowers reddish-white, large, very full, cupped; foliage bluish green; ['Gloire de Dijon' × 'Souv du Comte de Cavour']

'Bedford Crimson' HT, dr, 1926, Laxton Bros.; flowers velvety crimson, well-formed, 40 petals; ['Richmond' × 'Château de Clos Vougeot']

'Bedfordia' HT, pb, 1931, Laxton Bros.; flowers pink, outer petals lighter, center salmon, 52 petals; vigorous growth

'Bedfranc' F, pb, Chessum; intr. 2001

'Bedjust' ('Karina Eloise') F, dr, 2004, Paul Chessum Roses; flowers deep red, reverse lighter red, 5 cm., dbl., borne in small clusters; foliage medium size, dark green, semi-glossy; prickles small, dark green, moderate; growth compact, medium (75 cm.); bedding, containers; intr. 2004

'Bedone' MinFl, mp, Chessum, Paul; intr. 1995

'Bedont' F, ab, Harkness; flowers light apricot, 4 in., 20-25 petals, spiral, moderate fragrance; recurrent; foliage dark green, glossy; vigorous, compact, upright (3-4 ft.) growth; intr. 2006

'Bedqueen' ('Gracious Queen') HT, dy, 2001, Chessum, Paul; flowers medium, full, borne mostly solitary, moderate fragrance; foliage medium size, medium green, semi-glossy; prickles medium, hooked, few; growth compact, medium (90 cm.); beds, borders, containers; intr. 2001

'Bedrich Smetana' HT, w, 1933, Böhm, J.; flowers pearly white, open, very large, semi-dbl.; vigorous, bushy growth; ['Modesty' × 'Ophelia']

'Bedsinker' ('New Scotland Yard') LCl, mr, 2004, Paul Chessum Roses; flowers semi-dbl., borne in small clusters, slight fragrance; foliage medium size, medium green, semi-glossy; prickles small; growth vigorous (10 ft.); climber; [seedling × seedling]; intr. 2004

'Bedswap' MinFl, w, Chessum, Paul; intr. 1997

'Beebop' ('Cleo') HT, lp, 1981, Bees; flowers soft light pink, 37 petals, high-centered, borne singly and in pairs, slight fragrance; foliage light green, semi-matte; prickles red; strong, bushy growth; ['Kordes' Perfecta' × 'Prima Ballerina']

'Beehive Gold' -- See 'Goldfinch'

'Beehive Gold' Min, dy; flowers smallish, pure golden, non-fading; growth medium

'Beejes' ('Jessie Mathews') HT, yb,

1982, Bees; flowers light yellow, petals edged pink, medium, 35 petals; foliage medium size, light green, semi-glossy; bushy growth; ['Ernest H. Morse' × 'Rosenella']

'Beelah' ('Tallulah') HT, yb, 1983, Bees; flowers gold with deep pink petal edges, large, 20 petals, cupped; foliage medium size, dark, semi-glossy; bushy growth; ['Astral' × Piccadilly®]

'Beeril' ('Cyril Fletcher') HT, w, 1983, Bees; flowers creamy white, large, 35 petals, cabbage-like; foliage medium size, dark, semi-glossy; upright, bushy growth; ['Fragrant Cloud' × 'Whisky Mac']

'Bee's Balm' S, mp, J. B. Williams; flowers ruffled, single, slight fragrance; growth to 4 × 4 ft.; intr. 2005

'Bee's Frolic' S, lp, 1980, Dawnay, Mrs. E.; bud small, pointed; flowers 14 petals, borne 2-3 per cluster, intense fragrance; repeat bloom; foliage medium size, matte; prickles small; upright, strong growth; ['Schneezwerg' × Clair Matin®]; intr. 1976

Bees Knees™ -- See 'Jackee'

'Bee's Landing' S, op, J. B. Williams; intr. 2005

'Beesian' F, my, 1979, Bees; bud globular

'Beeval' ('Vale of Clwyd') F, pb, 1983, Bees; flowers yellow, pink petal edges, medium, dbl.; foliage large, medium green, glossy; upright growth; [Handel® × 'Arthur Bell']

'Beginnings' S, pb, Williams, J.B.; flowers silvery pink, center lighter, showy stamens, single, flat, borne in clusters, slight fragrance; recurrent; growth to 4 ft.; intr. 2006

'Begonia' HT, op; flowers frilled and crimped petals, moderate fragrance; long stems; medium growth

Behold™ -- See 'Savahold'

'Bekola' -- See 'Aalsmeer Gold'

'Bel-Air' HT, dr, Swane; intr. 1986

'Bel Ami' -- See 'Philippe'

Bel Ami® F, mr, 1958, Laperrière; flowers large, dbl., borne in clusters of 7-8; bushy growth; ['Michèle Meilland' × 'Tonnerre']

'Bel Ange' ('Bella Epoca', 'Rosa Stern', 'Belle Epoque', 'Belle Ange') HT, mp, 1962, Lens; flowers soft pink, reverse darker, 4½ in., 35 petals, moderate fragrance; foliage dark; vigorous growth; PP2579; [('Independence' × 'Papillon Rose') × ('Charlotte Armstrong' × 'Floradora')]; intr. 1965

'Bel Ange, Climbing' Cl HT, mp, Ruston, D.; [sport of 'Bel Ange']; intr. 1970

'Bel Canto' HT, or, 1964, Mondial Roses; flowers bright geranium-red, well-formed; foliage coppery; upright growth

'Bel Esprit' -- See 'LLX8792'

'Bela Portuguesa' -- See 'Belle Portugaise'

'Belami' -- See 'Korprill'

'Belami' -- See 'Korterschi'

'Belbrio' HT, m, Bell, Laurie; bud long, elegant

'Belcharm' ('Bell Charmer') Min, ob, 1992, Bell, Charles E., Jr.; flowers distinctive soft orange with light yellow petal base and reverse, large, full, slight fragrance; foliage medium size, medium green, semi-glossy; some prickles; medium (45-55 cm.), upright, bushy growth; [('Cherish' × 'Avandel') × seedling]; intr. 1993

'Belcur' HT, ly, Bell, Laurie

'Belfast Belle' -- See 'Dicrobot'

'Belfield (from Bermuda)' -- See 'Slater's Crimson China'

'Belfre' Min, w, Bell; bud slender, pointed buds; intr. 1996

Belgian Lace® -- See 'Lenloro'

'Belgic Blush' -- See 'Blush Belgiques'

'Belgic Provence' -- See 'Blush Belgiques'

'Belgic Rose' -- See 'Blush Belgiques'

'Belgica' HT, dr, 1929, Buyl Frères; flowers crimson-red, shaded garnet, large, very dbl.; vigorous growth

'Belgica Flore Rubricante' -- See 'Blush Belgiques'

'Belgica Rubra' -- See 'Rouge de Belgique'

'Belgol' Min, dy, Bell, Laurie

'Beliff' F, lp, Bell, Laurie

'Belinda' -- See 'Tanbeedee'

'Belinda' HMsk, mp, 1936, Bentall; flowers soft pink, medium, semi-dbl., borne in very large, erect trusses, moderate fragrance; vigorous (4-6 ft.) growth; a good hedge or pillar rose

'Belinda's Dream' ('Belinda's Rose') S, mp, 1992, Basye, Robert; flowers 3¼-4¼ in., very full, borne in small clusters, moderate fruity, raspberry fragrance; repeat bloom; foliage medium size, medium green, matte; medium (5 × 4 ft.), bushy growth; ['Jersey Beauty' × 'Tiffany']; intr. 1989

'Belinda's Rose' -- See 'Belinda's Dream'

'Bélisaire' D, lp, before 1829; flowers pale or flesh pink, medium, very dbl., borne in small clusters; foliage pale green, regularly toothed; prickles numerous, uneven, enlarged at base

'Belkanto' LCl, mr, Noack; intr. 2005

'Bell Charmer' -- See 'Belcharm'

'Bell Ringer' Min, dp, 1989, Bell, Charles E., Jr.; flowers deep pink, silver at base, small, 34 petals, slight fruity fragrance; foliage medium size, medium green, semi-glossy; upright, bushy growth; [('Fragrant Cloud' × 'Avandel') × 'Bonny']; intr. 1989

'Bella' -- See 'Devsmooth'

Bella™ -- See 'Pouljill'

'Bella' T, w, 1890, California Nursery Co.; bud pointed; flowers large; probably extinct

Bella Christina™ -- See 'Manbella'

'Bella di Monza' -- See 'Belle de Monza'

'Bella di Todi' ('Barbetod') HT, dy, Barni; flowers yellow with apricot tones, outer petals lighter, 10-12 cm., very dbl., quartered, Intense fragrance; foliage medium size, dark green; growth to 80-100 cm. [seedling × Antico Amore®]; intr. 2000

'Bella Diana' -- See 'Mandiana'

'Bella Donna' D, lp, before 1848; flowers soft lilac-pink, large, with a small center eye, very dbl., flat, strong fragrance; foliage pale green

'Bella Donna' F, mr, Verbeek; bud ovoid; flowers bright red medium, dbl., borne in clusters; foliage dark; [(Baccará® × unknown) × 'Miracle']; intr. 1964

'Bella Epoca' -- See 'Bel Ange'

'Bella Minijet' Min, ab, Meilland

'Bella Multiflora' HMult, mp, Uhl, J.; flowers large, borne in sprays; few prickles; arching growth; intr. 1994

'Bella Nitida' S, mp, Uhl, J.; flowers large; medium growth; very hardy; intr. 1994

'Bella Notte' S, dr, Hiroshima; groundcover; spreading growth; intr. 2002

'Bella Renaissance' ('Belle Renaissance', Child of Achievement™, Bella™) S, my; flowers medium yellow, 8-10 cm., very dbl., borne in clusters, moderate fragrance; free-flowering; foliage dark, leathery; growth bushy, 3 × 4 ft.; PP12522; intr. 1995

'Bella'roma' -- See 'Jacfrepu'

'Bella Roma' -- See 'Jacfrepu'

Bella Rosa® -- See 'Korwonder'

'Bella Via' -- See 'Zipvia'

Bella Vita+ HT, w, Voom, Lex; flowers white with pink edge, double, high-centered, borne mostly singly; recurrent; stems medium to long; florist rose; intr. 2005

Bella Weiss® ('White Bella Rosa') F, w, Kordes; flowers white version of Bella Rosa, no fragrance; growth to 60 cm.high × 40 cm.wide; [sport of 'Bella Rosa']; intr. 1989

'Bellard' HGal, lp, Before 1842; flowers beautifully shaped, translucent shade of pink, light and bright, very dbl., moderate fragrance

Bellavista® ('Barbelvi') LCl, lp, Barni; bud elongated; flowers pastel pink, double, borne 5 - 7 per cluster, moderate fragrance; foliage large, dark green; tall (250 - 600 cm.) growth; intr. 2006

'Belle' -- See 'Marbel'

Belle™ -- See 'Poulviol'

'Belle Adélaide' HGal, dp, Miellez; flowers cerise-red, very dbl., flat

'Belle Aimable' ('Pale Rouge Panaché') HGal, rb, before 1811; flowers pale red plumed white, small, dbl.; from Holland

'Belle Allemand' T, lp, 1841, Beluze, J.; flowers flesh pink, shaded rose pink, large, semi-dbl. to dbl.

'Belle Alliance' -- See 'Tricolore'

'Belle Americaine' HP, dp, 1837, Boll, Daniel

'Belle Amour' A, lp, before 1867; flowers soft pink with salmon tones, prominent yellow stamens, semi-dbl., moderate myrrh fragrance; growth to 5-6 ft.; found at a convent at Elboeuf, Normandy, in the 1940's, but undoubtedly a much older variety; sometimes classed as D

'Belle Ange' -- See 'Bel Ange'

'Belle Angevin' -- See 'Calypso'

'Belle Anglaise' HT, dy; intr. 1995

'Belle Anglaise' HP, mp, 1856, Ducher

'Belle Aspasie' T, m, Coquerel; flowers vivid velvety purple, very large, semi-dbl.; intr. before 1836

'Belle Aspasie' N, dp, Laffay; flowers medium, full; intr. before 1836

'Belle au Bois Dormant' S, pb, Kordes; flowers pink with salmon, full, some fragrance; growth vigorous, 100-120 cm.; intr. 1960

'Belle Auguste' ('La Belle Augusta') D, lp, before 1824, Descemet/Vibert; flowers blush pink changing to nearly white, large, full

'Belle Aurore' -- See 'Celestial'

'Belle Aurore' ('Poniatowska') A, lp, about 1815, Descemet; flowers light pink, tinted lilac

'Belle Aurore' HGal, lp, Vibert; flowers flesh pink with lilac tints, large, full; sometimes classed as A; intr. before 1836

'Belle Biblis' ('Avenant') HGal, m, 1815, Descemet, M.; flowers deep flesh pink, changing paler, large, dbl., moderate fragrance; growth erect

'Belle Blanca' HG, w; flowers large, semi-dbl.; [probably a 'Belle Portugaise' sport]

'Belle Blonde' HT, my, 1955, Meilland, F.; flowers yellow, center darker, well-formed; foliage glossy; bushy growth; ['Peace' × 'Lorraine']

'Belle Bourbon' -- See 'Rouge Formidable'

'Belle Brun' HGal, dr, before 1811; flowers velvety violet purple, large, semi-dbl.; ['Aigle Brun' × unknown]

'Belle Camille' HGal, pb, before 1820, Descemet; flowers lilac pink, aging to red, medium

'Belle Cerise' HGal, mr, about 1810, Descemet

'Belle Champenoise' HT, my, Orard; intr. 1997

'Belle Chartronnaise' HGal, m; flowers violet purple, full

'Belle Chartronnaise' T, pb, 1861, Lartay; flowers vivid pink with canary yellow

'Belle Clementine' A, lp, before 1845; flowers mottled flesh-color; mottling in the blooms suggests R. alba × R. gallica

'Belle Coquette' S, mp; groundcover; spreading growth; intr. 1999

'Belle Couronnée' ('Abondante', 'Bifera Coronata', 'Cels', 'Celsiana', 'Incarnata Maxima', 'La Coquette', 'Rose de Van Huysum', 'Van Huysum') D, lp, before 1817; flowers silky pale pink, petals crinkled, with golden stamens, 4 in., semi-dbl., borne in cluster of 3-4, moderate fragrance; non-recurrent; foliage oval, smooth, grayish-green, reverse lighter, fragrant; vigorous, upright (4-5 ft.) growth; from Holland; introduced to France by Cels

'Belle Créole' F, rb, 1958, Arles; flowers variegated red and brick-red, borne in clusters; foliage dark; vigorous, upright growth; [('Gruss an Teplitz' × 'Independence') × ('Floradora' × 'Independence')]

'Belle Cuivrée' HT, or, 1924, Pernet-Ducher; flowers coral-red, shaded coppery yellow, medium, semi-dbl.

'Belle Danielle' -- See 'Frydabble'

'Belle d'Aulnay' HGal, mp, before 1824, Barrier; flowers full, moderate fragrance; sometimes attributed to Prévost

'Belle d'Auteuil' D, dp, before 1826, Prévost (?); flowers rosy lilac, large, full, globular; foliage short, round; prickles short; growth branching, robust

'Belle d'Automne' HT, Ducher, Ch.; intr. 1969

'Belle de Baltimore' -- See 'Baltimore Belle'

'Belle de Bordeaux' ('Gloire de Bordeaux') T, pb, 1861, Lartay (possibly Bernède); flowers pink with crimson center, large, dbl.; vigorous growth; ['Gloire de Dijon' × unknown]

'Belle de Bourg-la-Reine' HP, mp, 1859, Margottin; flowers large, full

'Belle de Crécy' HGal, m, 1829, Roeser (introduced by Hardy); sepals leafy; flowers cerise and purple, becoming lavender-gray, center green, medium, very dbl., flat, quartered, borne in small clusters; foliage dark green elongated, irregularly dentate; prickles numerous, dark brown, slightly hooked; stems slender; growth upright; sometimes classed as HCh

'Belle de Dom' -- See 'Masdomo'

'Belle de Florence' -- See 'Belle de Monza'

'Belle de Fontenay' HGal, mr, before 1828, Boutigny; flowers glowing cherry red, edges lighter pink, medium, very full

'Belle de Hesse' -- See 'Illustre'

'Belle de Juin' F, Croix, P.; intr. 1974

'Belle de la Carnière' HT, lp, Ducher, Fabien; flowers pale pink, large, double, high-centered, borne mostly singly, slight fragrance; good repeat; few prickles; 4 ft. growth; intr. 2007

'Belle de Lille' -- See 'Calypso'

'Belle de Londres' -- See 'Compassion'

'Belle de Marly' HGal, dp; flowers bright rose, shaded violet, large, dbl.

'Belle de Monza' ('Bella di Monza', 'Belle de Florence') Ch, mr, about 1825, Villaresi/Noisette; flowers light cherry red to light purple, medium, semi-dbl., cupped, borne in large clusters; re-introduced by Vibert about 1840

'Belle de Normandy' HP, mp, about 1890, California Nursery Co; flowers clear rose, shaded with rosy carmine and lilac, very large

'Belle de Parme' F, mp, 1962, Arles; flowers lilac-mauve; low, spreading growth; [('Lafayette' × ('Gruss an Teplitz' × 'Independence')) × R. rugosa rubra]

'Belle de Provins' HT, dr, 1954, Robichon; flowers velvety dark red, well-formed, large, dbl.; vigorous growth; ['Crimson Glory' × 'E.G. Hill']

Belle de Regnie® S, mr, Dorieux; flowers crimson red, large, double, cupped to flat; intr. 2004

'Belle de Remalard' HMult, pb, d'Andlau; flowers small, bright pink with a whiter heart, borne in large sprays; one blooming in the spring only; growth vigorous and spreading, 5-6 m.; hips small, red; found growing from seed in garden by Mme d'Andlau at Rémelard; intr. 1998

'Belle de Ségur' A, lp, before 1828, Lelieur; flowers soft rosy flesh, edges blush, dbl., cupped; foliage dark; vigorous, upright growth

'Belle de Stors' ('Favorite Purple', 'Pourpre Favorite') HGal, m, about 1836, Lahaye; flowers purple pink, medium, full

'Belle de Trianon' P, lp, before 1826, Prévost

'Belle de Vaucresson' HGal, lp, before 1840, Dubourg or Prévost; flowers flesh pink, medium, very full

'Belle de Vernier' HCh, pb, before 1827, from Douai; flowers rosy crimson, marbled with dark purplish slate, medium, full, cupped; possibly synonymous with 'Belle Violette' and/or 'De Vergnies'

'Belle de Vilmorin' -- See 'Unique Carnée'

'Belle de Yèbles' ('Belle de Zelbes') HGal, mr, before 1835, Desprez; flowers bright red

'Belle de Zelbes' -- See 'Belle de Yèbles'

'Belle des Jardins' HGal, m, 1872, Guillot et Fils; flowers purplish violet-red, striped lilac and white, with a button center, dbl., cupped, borne singly or in small clusters, strong fragrance; foliage medium green, elliptical; prickles moderate; vigorous growth; ['La Rubanée' × unknown]

'Belle des Massifs' HP, mp, 1862; flowers bright carmine, dbl.

'Belle des Neiges' HT, w; intr. 2005

Belle d'Espinouse® S, rb, Guillot-Massad; intr. 2006

'Belle Dijonnaise' -- See 'Zéphirine Drouhin'

'Belle Doria' HGal, pb, before 1847, Parmentier; flowers lilac, spotted and striped with white, carmine center, small to medium, full, cupped

'Belle d'Orléans' HP, m, 1851, Vigneron; flowers lilac pink

'Belle d'Orléans' N, w, Conard & Jones; flowers white, sometimes tinted rose, small, borne in large clusters; remontant; growth semi-climbing; intr. 1902

'Belle d'Orléans' LCl, or, Robichon; flowers reddish-crimson, 4½-5 in., dbl., borne in large clusters; recurrent bloom; foliage glossy; vigorous growth; [seedling × 'Independence']; intr. 1958

'Belle du Printemps' HP, pb, 1863,

The Official Registry and Checklist — Rosa 65

Damaizin; flowers carmine, striped with darker carmine, large, dbl.

Belle du Seigneur® ('The Midlands Rose') HT, ab, Delbard; flowers large, coppered ocher two tone, holds well when open, dbl., high-centered; growth vigorous; intr. 2002

'Belle Egarée' -- See 'Mme Charles Damé'

'Belle Elisa' -- See 'Elisa'

'Belle Emilie d'Arlon' HGal, lp, 1839, David; flowers flesh pink, shaded white, large, full

'Belle Epoque' -- See 'Fryyaboo'

'Belle Epoque' -- See 'Bel Ange'

Belle Epoque® HT, pb, Christensen; flowers pink with bronze tones, large , double, high-centered; recurrent; attractive, compact growth; intr. 2003

'Belle Époque' ('Royale') HT, pb, 1965, Kriloff, Michel; flowers fuchsia-pink, reverse creamy, 6 in., 40 petals, moderate fragrance; foliage glossy; vigorous, upright growth; ['Peace' × 'Independence']; intr. 1963

'Belle Estelle' ('Charpentier', 'Estelle') HSpn, lp, before 1820, Vibert; flowers flesh pink, medium, semi-dbl., borne in clusters; sometimes repeats in autumn; possibly synonymous with 'Jenny', Dupont, before 1810

'Belle Étoile' Gr, my, 1961, Lens; bud long, pointed; flowers golden yellow, well-formed, 25 petals, borne in clusters of 5-7; long stems; vigorous, upright growth; ['Joanna Hill' × 'Tawny Gold']

'Belle Fabert' P, dp, before 1825, Fabert; flowers rosy crimson, sometimes tinted with purple, very large, full, globular

'Belle Flamande' -- See 'Marie-Louise'

'Belle Fleur' -- See 'Damas Violacé'

'Belle Fleur d'Anjou' T, lp, 1873, Touvais; flowers shining flesh pink, very large, full

'Belle Flore' HGal, dr, before 1813, Descemet; flowers velvety violet crimson, darker at center, large, very dbl., moderate fragrance

'Belle Florentine' HGal, mp, before 1829, Boutigny; flowers large, full

'Belle Galathée' HGal, w, before 1813, Descemet; flowers flesh white

'Belle Hébé' HGal, mp, Laffay; flowers bright pink, flesh center, large; Agathe group; intr. about 1835

'Belle Hébé' Ch, lp, before 1815, Descemet; flowers vivid flesh pink, center darker, medium, full

'Belle Hélène' T, lp; flowers light flesh pink shaded over white, large, full

'Belle Hélène' Ch, w, Laffay; intr. about 1835

'Belle Hélène' ('Aimable Emma', 'Archiduc Charles', 'Aimable Sophie') HGal, m, before 1818, Descemet; flowers delicate blush pink, large, very dbl., cupped

'Belle Hélène' C, mp, Boutigny; flowers large, full; intr. before 1829

'Belle Hélène' HGal, dr, Vibert; flowers intense purple, nuanced violet, medium, very full; intr. about 1830

'Belle Henriette' M, lp, about 1830, Vibert

'Belle Henriette' HP, dr; flowers dark red, medium, full

'Belle Herminie' ('Ponctuée', 'Punctata') HGal, m, 1819, Coquerel; flowers bright purple-pink, spotted white, medium, semi-dbl.

'Belle Hit' (Belle™) MinFl, lp, Poulsen; flowers light pink, 5-8 cm., dbl., slight wild rose fragrance; foliage dark; growth bushy, 20-40 cm.; intr. 2005

'Belle Isidore' Ch, mp; flowers bright carmine, shaded flesh pink, medium, full

'Belle Isis' HGal, lp, 1845, Parmentier; flowers flesh-pink, lighter at edges, with a central button, dbl., quartered, borne singly or in clusters of 2-3; foliage small, light green, rounded, coarsely toothed; numerous prickles; Agathe group

'Belle Italienne' -- See 'Achille'

'Belle Ivryenne' HP, dp, 1891, Lévêque; flowers large, dbl.

'Belle Jardinière' HP, lp, 1853, Avoux & Crozy

'Belle Junon' -- See 'Junon'

'Belle Laure' ('Aux Cent Écus', 'Belle Laure No. 1') HSpn, w, 1817, Dupont/Vibert; flowers white, spotted purple at center, 2-2½ in., single; prickles straight, unequal, mixed with bristles

'Belle Laure' HGal, mr, Miellez; intr. about 1850

'Belle Laure No. 1' -- See 'Belle Laure'

'Belle Laure II' HSpn, w, Descemet/Vibert; flowers marbled white and purplish pink, 2-3 in., single; foliage ovate simply dentate; prickles very numerous, dense, fine, unequal, almost straight; hips oval-globular, brown-black; intr. 1818

'Belle Laure III' HSpn, w, Vibert; flowers white, marbeld with purple-pink; intr. about 1830

'Belle Laure IV' HSpn, m, Vibert; flowers vivid purple, shaded white, reverse lilac; intr. about 1830

'Belle Léonide' C, 1823, Bizard

'Belle Léopoldine' HGal, mp, before 1829, Boutigny

'Belle Lilette' HT, mr, 1926, Gemen & Bourg; flowers carmine-red, very large, dbl.

'Belle Loire' S, Croix, P.

'Belle Lucile' HGal, before 1810, Descemet

'Belle Lyonnaise' -- See 'Fürst Bismarck'

'Belle Lyonnaise' HP, mp, 1854, Lacharme

'Belle Lyonnaise' Cl T, ly, Levet, F.; flowers canary yellow, fading white, 10-11 cm., dbl., loosely quartered, borne mostly solitary, moderate fragrance; prickles large; vigorous, climbing growth; ['Gloire de Dijon' × unknown]; intr. 1869

'Belle Mâconnaise' T, mp, 1870, Ducher; flowers large, full

'Belle Marie' -- See 'La Belle Marie'

'Belle Marseillaise' -- See 'Fellemberg'

'Belle Mathilde' -- See 'La Belle Mathilde'

Belle Meillandina® -- See 'Meidanego'

'Belle Mignonne' ('Petite Louise') HGal, lp, before 1819, Prévost; flowers light pink, inner petals often rayed white, small, dbl.

'Belle Nanon' B, dp, 1872, Lartay; flowers carmine

'Belle Nantaise' HT, w, 1901, Bahaud; flowers white tinted salmon pink, very large, full, moderate fragrance; ['Mme Caroline Testout' × 'Viscountesse Folkestone']

'Belle Ninon' ('La Belle Ninon') HGal, m, before 1821, Boutigny; flowers dark lilac, edges lighter, medium, full, semi-globular

'Belle Noisette' -- See R. × noisettiana

'Belle Normande' HP, w, Oger; flowers silvery rose; [sport of 'La Reine']

'Belle Octavie' T, mp, before 1845; flowers tender pink, edges lighter, reverse flesh pink to white, large, full

'Belle Octavie' HGal, mp; flowers medium, full

'Belle of Berlin' -- See 'Tanireb'

'Belle of Portugal' -- See 'Belle Portugaise'

'Belle of Punjab' F, mp, 1969, Pal, Dr. B.P.; bud ovoid; flowers warm salmon pink, 52 petals, high-centered, borne singly and in clusters; foliage dark, glossy; very vigorous, compact growth; ['Montezuma' × 'Flamenco']; originally registered as HT; re-registered 1980 as F; intr. 1965

'Belle of Tasmania' F, or, 1968, Holloway; bud pointed; flowers velvety scarlet, center darker, medium, dbl., high-centered; foliage glossy; vigorous, tall, compact growth; ['Korona' × 'Étoile de Hollande']

'Belle Olympe' HGal, mr, before 1820, Descemet

'Belle Orléanaise' HT, mp, 1902, Corboeuf; ['Mme Caroline Testout' × 'Mme Abel Chatenay']

'Belle Parade' HGal, m, before 1811; flowers carnation-cerise, with lilac tints, large, very dbl., borne in clusters of 6-8; foliage oval, dentate; few prickles; from Holland

'Belle Perle' w, Delbard

'Belle Poitevine' HRg, mp, 1894, Bruant; bud long, pointed; flowers rose-pink to magenta-pink, large, semi-dbl., slight sweet fragrance; recurrent bloom; foliage dark, rugose; vigorous (3½-4 ft.), bushy growth; ['Regeliana' × unknown]

'Belle Portugaise' ('Bela Portuguesa', 'Belle of Portugal') HG, lp, 1903, Cayeux, H.; bud very long, pointed (to 4 in.); flowers light flesh-pink, slightly darker reverse, 4-6 in., semi-dbl., slight damask/tea fragrance; long spring bloom; foliage long, narrow, light green; very vigorous (20 ft.) growth; not hardy north; ['Souv de Mme Léonie Viennot' × R. gigantea]

'Belle Pourpre' HGal, m, before 1813, from Holland; flowers dark violet purple

'Belle Pourpre Violette' -- See 'Belle Violette Foncé'

'Belle Renaissance' -- See 'Pouljill'

'Belle Rose' HP, mp, 1864, Touvais; flowers bright pink, very large, full

'Belle Rosine' ('Amélia', 'Cerise') S, dp, before 1820, Descemet; flowers bright cerise pink, large, dbl., borne in clusters; foliage very villose beneath; prickles very hooked; stems crooked; hybrid turbinata

'Belle Rosine' HGal, dp, Vibert; flowers deep pink, edged lighter, open, large, dbl.; erect growth; intr. 1829 or 1830

Belle Rouge™ HT, dr, 1956, Delbard-Chabert; flowers dark velvety red becoming carmine-purple, large; [('Happiness' × unknown) × 'Impeccable']

'Belle Rouge' HT, dr, Delbard; flowers firm petaled, velvet red, dbl., high-centered, no fragrance; growth tall, grows easily; PP9915; intr. 1999

'Belle Rubine' -- See 'La Rubanée'

'Belle sans Flatterie' HGal, m, before 1806; flowers lilac-pink, lighter on the edges, heavily veined, with a center button, medium, very dbl., quartered, flat, borne usually solitary; foliage oblong, dark green; prickles very few; from Holland

'Belle sans Pareille' HGal, mp, before 1845, in Brussels; flowers shining carmine, aging to lilac, striped violet, globular, slight fragrance

'Belle Siebrecht, Climbing' -- See 'Mrs W. J. Grant, Climbing'

'Belle Siebrecht' -- See 'Mrs W. J. Grant'

'Belle Splendens' HGal, before 1820, Descemet

'Belle Stéphanie' D, m, about 1825, Boutigny; flowers lilac pink, medium, full

Belle Story® -- See 'Auselle'

'Belle Suisse' HT, mr, 1936, Heizmann, E.; flowers large, dbl.

'Belle Sultane' -- See 'La Belle Sultane'

'Belle Sunblaze' -- See 'Meidanego'

'Belle Symphonie' ('Carefree Days') Min, mp, Meilland; intr. 1997

'Belle Ternaux' HGal, m, about 1825, Boutigny; flowers purple, shaded violet, small to medium, full

'Belle Thérèse' -- See 'Maiden's Blush'

'Belle Vichysoise' ('Cornélie') N, lp, 1895, Lévêque; flowers pink or pinkish white, small, very dbl., borne in clusters of 20-50; very vigorous growth; may have originally been introduced as Cornélie (Moreau-Robert, 1858)

'Belle Victorine' C, lp, before 1815, Descemet; flowers flesh pink, center darker, edges lighter, medium, full

'Belle Villageoise' -- See 'Panachée Pleine'

'Belle Violette' HCh, m, before 1830, De Vergnies; flowers bright violet, medium, full; possibly synonymous with 'Belle de Vernier 'and/or 'De Vergnies'

'Belle Violette Foncé' ('Belle Pourpre Violette') HGal, m, before 1815, Descemet

'Belle Virginie' HGal, m, about 1814; flowers violet pink, medium, full; from Sèvres

'Belle Yvrienne' HP, rb, 1890, Lévêque; flowers brilliant red, shaded white and carmine, very large, very full

'Belles and Beaus' -- See 'Adabel'

Bellevue® ('Jarlina') HT, yb, 1978, Poulsen, Niels D.; flowers dark yellow and apricot, edged red, 6 in., 23 petals; foliage glossy, leathery; vigorous, upright growth; [('Tropicana' × Piccadilly®) × 'Fru Jarl']; intr. 1976

'Bellina' F, op, 1959, Von Abrams; flowers shrimp-pink, 2-2½ in., 40 petals, high-centered, borne in large clusters, moderate fragrance; foliage glossy; low, compact growth; PP1915; ['Pinocchio' × ('Fashion' × Orange Triumph®)]; intr. 1958

Bellisima® -- See 'Sunlampo'

'Bellissima' -- See 'Zipbell'

Bellissima® HT, my, Laperrière; flowers pale yellow at the center, darker edges, dbl.; intr. 1991

'Bellona' F, my, 1975, Kordes, R.; bud ovoid; flowers golden yellow, pointed, 3 in., 27 petals, slight fragrance; foliage light; very vigorous, upright growth; PP3790; ['New Day' × 'Minigold']; intr. 1976

'Bellotte' HGal, mp, before 1826, Vibert; flowers crimson pink, medium

'Belmont' HCh, lp, 1846, Vibert; flowers flesh, tinted pink, moderate Tea fragrance

'Beloved' -- See 'Jacolman'

'Beloved' HT, w, 1978, Hill, E.H.; bud tinted pink; flowers reflexing, 6-7 in., 33-35 petals; foliage glossy; [sport of 'Memoriam']

'Belrub' Min, dr, Bell, Laurie

'Beltoro' Min, ob, Bell, Laurie

'Beltral' S, mr, Bell, Laurie

'Beltsecs' Min, dp, Bell

'Béluze' B, mr, about 1840, Béluze; flowers cherry red, medium, full

'Belvedere' -- See 'Princesse Marie'

'Belvédère' F, dr, 1928, Kiese; flowers velvety dark red, large, dbl.; vigorous, dwarf growth; ['Eblouissant' × 'Château de Clos Vougeot']

'Belvédère' HT, dr, Delforge; flowers large, deep red. large petals, moderate fragrance; ['Reine Elisabeth' × 'Christopher Stone']; intr. 1955

Belvedere® S, ob, Tantau; flowers orange-peach, large, long-lasting, very dbl., slight fragrance; foliage dark green, glossy; growth strong grower; intr. 2002

'Belvedere Park' -- See 'Lecbelpa'

'Belvel' Cl Min, dr, Bell; intr. 2003

'Belyeld' HT, dy, Bell

'Ben Arthur Davis' HT, yb, 1935, Bostick; flowers yellow, reverse pinkish gold, dbl., cupped; foliage leathery, glossy, dark; bushy growth; [sport of 'Edith Nellie Perkins']

'Ben Britten' -- See 'Ausencart'

'Ben Cant' HP, dr, 1901, Cant, B. R.; flowers crimson, center darker, very large, 25 petals, high-centered, intense fragrance; vigorous growth; ['Suzanne-Marie Rodocanachi' × 'Victor Hugo']

'Ben Chaplin' HT, w, 2003, Chaplin, Mrs. Mavis; flowers medium red, changing to purple, large, single, borne mostly solitary, no fragrance; foliage medium size, medium green, matte; prickles 10mm., straight; growth upright, medium (60 cm.); [sport of 'Lincolnshire Poacher']; intr. 2003

'Ben-Hur' Gr, mr, 1960, Lammerts, Dr. Walter; bud long, pointed; flowers crimson, 4-5 in., 23 petals, high-centered, moderate fragrance; foliage leathery, glossy; vigorous growth; PP2066; ['Charlotte Armstrong' × ('Charlotte Armstrong' × 'Floradora')]

'Ben Stad' ('Rev. Floris Ferwerda') LCl, pb, 1925, Undritz; flowers pink, center yellow, edged white, reverse flesh-pink; ['Silver Moon' × 'Mme Jules Grolez']

'Benable' Min, w, Benardella, Frank

'Benalav' (Lavender Jade™) Min, m, 1987, Benardella, Frank A.; flowers lavender-white bicolor-mauve blend, large, 32-35 petals, high-centered, borne usually singly, intense damask fragrance; foliage medium size, dark green, semi-glossy; prickles short, straight; growth upright, tall; PP6517; ['Rise 'n' Shine' × 'Laguna']; intr. 1987

'Benapri' F, yb, Benardella, Frank; intr. 2001

'Benardella's Pearl' -- See 'Bencherry'

'Benarka' Min, r, Benardella, Frank

'Benbaas' ('Solar Flair') MinFl, yb, 2004, Benardella, Frank; flowers yellow with red edges, 2-2½ in., full, high-centered, borne mostly solitary, slight fragrance; foliage medium size, dark green, glossy; prickles ¼ in. long, pointed down; growth upright, medium (2-2½ ft.); exhibition;cut flowers;decorative; ['Antique Gold' × 'Brett's Rose']; intr. 2005

'Benblack' (Black Jade™) Min, dr, 1985, Benardella, Frank A.; bud near black; flowers deep red, 1-1½ in., 35 petals, high-centered, borne singly, no fragrance; foliage medium size, dark, semi-glossy; upright growth; PP5925; ['Sheri Anne' × 'Laguna']

'Benbra' Min, ab, Benardella; intr. 1996

'Benbret' ('Brett's Rose', 'Chinaberry', Sunswept™) Min, yb, 2008, Benardella, Frank A.; intr. 2008

'Benbret' Min, yb, Benardella, Frank

'Benbrett' ('Brett's Rose', 'Chinaberry', Sunswept™) Min, yb, 2008, Benardella, Frank A.; flowers dark yellow edged red, reverse yellow, 1½ in., full, borne mostly solitary; foliage large, dark green, glossy; prickles moderate; growth compact, well-branched, medium (18 in.); gardens decoration, exhibition, patio, containers, cutting; [June Laver™ × Kristin™]; intr. 2008

'Benburgun' Min, dr, Benardella, Frank A.; bud pointed; intr. 1990

'Bencamelia' ('Roedean') HT, pb, Benardella, Frank A.; intr. 1993

'Bencham' Min, ab, Benardella, Frank; intr. 1996

'Bencharm' ('Charmer') Min, w, 2004, Benardella, Frank; flowers ivory with pink at base, reverse ivory and pink, 1½-1¾ in., dbl., borne mostly solitary, slight fragrance; foliage medium size, medium green, semi-glossy; prickles ¼ to 3/8 in., pointed slightly down; growth upright, well-branched, medium (18 in.); garden decoration, cutting; intr. 2004

'Bencherry' ('Benardella's Pearl', 'Jilly Jewel', 'Pearl') Min, mp, 2003, Benardella, Frank; intr. 1996

'Bencincuenta' (Bonfire™) Min, rb, 2006, Benardella, Frank; flowers bright red with lighter reverse, medium, full, hybrid tea, borne singly and in sprays; foliage medium size, dark green, matte; prickles 3/8-¼ in., top angled down; bottom curved, very light green; growth upright, well branched; vigorous, medium (24-30 in.); garden decoration; ['Ruby' × 'Timeless']; intr. 2007

'Bencolo' Min, w, Benardella, Frank; intr. 2001

'Bencrazy' Min, yb, Benardella, Frank; intr. 2008

'Bencreberg' ('Athene') HT, w, Benardella, Frank A.; bud long, pointed; intr. 1996

'Benday' (Old Glory™) Min, mr, 1988, Benardella, Frank A.; flowers bright post office red, aging blood-red to crimson, 1½-2 in., 23-25 petals, high-centered, borne singly and in small clusters; foliage medium size, medium green, semi-glossy; prickles long, thin, curved downward, gray-red; mini-flora upright, tall, vigorous growth; PP5658; ['Rise 'n' Shine' × 'Harmonie']; intr. 1988

'Bendiez' ('My Sweetie', Caliente™) Min, dr, 2005, Benardella, Frank A; flowers dark red, reverse medium red, 2 in., full, borne mostly solitary, moderate fragrance; foliage medium size, dark green, semi-glossy, disease-resistant; prickles ¼ in., slight curved and angled down, moderate; growth upright, bushy, medium (2 × 2 ft.); exhibition, garden decorative; hardy; ['Ruby' × 'Timeless']; intr. 2004

'Bendigold' F, or, 1978, Murley, J.J.; bud globular; flowers 3 in., dbl., moderate fragrance; foliage glossy, bronze; vigorous, upright growth; ['Rumba' × 'Redgold']; intr. 1979

'Bénédicte Seguin' HT, ob, 1918, Pernet-Ducher; flowers ochre, shaded coppery orange, large, dbl., moderate fragrance

'Benedictus XV' HT, w, 1917, Leenders, M.; bud large, long-pointed; flowers white, center toned rose-salmon, large, dbl., borne mostly solitary, moderate fragrance; ['Jonkheer J.L. Mock' × 'Marquise de Sinéty']

'Benedikt Roezl' HRg, lp, 1925, Berger, V.; flowers light carmine-rose, large, very dbl.; foliage rugosa-like, vigorous, very bushy growth; [(R. rugosa × unknown) × 'La France']

'Benelux' F, dr, 1949, Leenders, M.; flowers crimson-red, semi-dbl.; ['Donald Prior' × 'Rosamunde']

'Benelux Star' HT, yb, 1997, RvS-Melle; flowers 4 in., 37 petals, cupped, moderate fragrance; foliage matte; strong grower growth; intr. 1997

'Benevolence' -- See 'Sanolence'

'Benfebu' ('Merlot', 'Sparkle Berry') Min, rb, 2001, Benardella, Frank; flowers dark red, white washed reverse, 2 in., dbl., borne mostly singly or in small clusters, slight fragrance; foliage large, dark green, semi-glossy; prickles ¼ in., angled down, few; growth upright, medium (24-30 in.); exhibition, specimen, containers, cutting; PP16483; [Kristin™ × seedling]; intr. 2002

'Benfig' Min, w, Benardella, Frank A.; buds delicately colored; intr. 1991

'Bengal Centifolia' Ch, pb, 1804, Noisette

'Bengal Cramoisi Double' -- See 'Sanguinea'

'Bengal Crimson' -- See 'Sanguinea'

'Bengal Rose' -- See 'Slater's Crimson China'

Bengal Tiger™ -- See 'Krabentiger'

'Bengale à Grandes Feuilles' -- See 'Bengale Centfeuilles'

'Bengale Animée' ('Animating', 'Bengale Animée des Anglais') Ch, mp, before 1817, from England; flowers lilac pink, small

'Bengale Animée des Anglais' -- See 'Bengale Animée'

'Bengale Centfeuilles' ('Bengale à Grandes Feuilles', 'Bengale Centifolia', 'Bengale Œillet') Ch, pb, 1804, Noisette; flowers pink bordered with deep wine pink, medium, full, borne in small clusters; foliage large, dark green, elongated, flat, slightly toothed; numerous prickles; stems upright

'Bengale Centifolia' -- See 'Bengale Centfeuilles'

'Bengale Cerise' Ch, mr

'Bengale Cypress' -- See 'Calypso'

'Bengale d'Automne' Ch, dp, 1825, Laffay, M. (possibly Cartier); flowers deep rose, paler at the petal bases, large, moderate sweet, with a hint of pepper fragrance

'Bengale Gontier' Cl HCh, dp; flowers pink, with carmine tones and violet veins through the petals, 7 cm., dbl., borne in clusters; vigorous, tall (10-15 ft.) growth

'Bengale Hollandaise' -- See 'Maheca'

'Bengale Nabonnand' Ch, dr, 1886, Nabonnand; flowers very dark velvety purplish red, with tints of copper and yellow

'Bengale Noire' -- See 'Pourpre Foncé'

'Bengale Noisette' -- See R. × noisettiana

'Bengale Œillet' -- See 'Bengale Centfeuilles'

'Bengale Pourpre' -- See 'Pourpre'

'Bengale Rouge' HCh, dr; flowers small, dark red to purple, semi-dbl.; blooms from spring through autumn; possibly synonymous with 'Rose du Bengale'/'Sanguinea'; intr. about 1781

'Bengale Rouge' Ch, mr, 1955, Gaujard; bud ovoid; flowers bright carmine-red, open, very large; recurrent bloom; foliage abundant; very vigorous growth; ['Gruss an Teplitz' × seedling]

'Bengale Sanguinaire' Ch, mr, 1838, Desprez; flowers crimson, petals concave, small, very dbl.

'Bengale Violet' -- See 'Reversa'

'Bengali' Ch, dp, 1913, Nonin; flowers medium, full, slight fragrance

Bengali® F, or, Kordes; bud ovoid; flowers red-orange, medium, dbl.; foliage dark; ['Dacapo' × seedling]; intr. 1969

'Bengee' (Gee Gee™) Min, ly, 1987, Benardella, Frank A.; flowers medium yellow, fading lighter, loose, small, 20-25 petals, cupped, borne usually singly, slight fruity fragrance; foliage medium size, light green, matte, edges toothed; prickles pointed, beige; upright, bushy, medium growth; no fruit; PP6783; ['Rise 'n' Shine' × 'Patricia']; intr. 1987

'Bengt M. Schalin' HKor, dp, 1956, Kordes; flowers rose-red, semi-dbl., borne in clusters (up to 10), slight fragrance; non-recurrent; foliage light green, leathery, glossy; very vigorous growth; [R. × kordesii × 'Eos']

'Benhile' ('Hilde') Min, rb, 1999, Benardella, Frank A.; flowers white with red washing, reverse ivory, 1½-2 in., dbl., borne mostly singly, moderate fragrance; foliage medium size, dark green, glossy; few prickles; bushy, medium (12-18 in.) growth; PP14533; ['Figurine' × Kristin™]

'Beni-Kanoko' ('Red Fawn', 'Stefanie Gachot') HT, rb, Tagashira, K.; flowers red, striped white, petals slightly reflexed, 13 cm., cupped, slight fragrance; foliage narrow, matte; growth bushy; ['Chrysler Imperial' × ('Barcelona' × 'Purple Tiger')]; intr. 1994

'Benidah' Min, op, Benardella, Frank

'Benihime' ('Red Princess') Min, mr; intr. 1992

'Benilli' F, mp; flowers french pink, 45 petals, high-centered; recurrent; PPAF; intr. 2008

'Benimbro' ('Imbroglio') Min, yb, Benardella, Frank A.; intr. 1990

'Beniowa' ('Pinnacle') F, rb, 2004, Benardella, Frank; flowers scarlet red, reverse silver, 2 in., semi-dbl., borne in small clusters, slight fragrance; foliage medium size, medium green, semi-glossy; prickles small, recurved; compact, medium growth; garden; ['Ivory Beauty' × 'Kristen']; intr. 2004

'Beniowski' HGal, m, before 1836, Co-

querel; flowers purple, medium, full
'Benita' -- See 'Dicquarrel'
'Benita' -- See 'Benita Stripe'
'Benita Stripe' ('Benita') Min, rb, Benardella, Frank; flowers striped; intr. 1992
'Benjamin Britten' -- See 'Ausencart'
'Benjamin Drouet' HP, dr, 1878, Verdier, E.; flowers intense purplish red, brightened with fiery red, very large, full, borne in small clusters; foliage large, ovate, deeply toothed; prickles numerous, large, brownish green; growth vigorous
'Benjamin Franklin' HT, lp, 1969, Von Abrams; bud ovoid; flowers dawn-pink, large, 55 petals, high-centered; foliage dark, leathery; upright growth; intr. 1970
'Benjen' (Jennifer™) Min, pb, 1985, Benardella, Frank A.; flowers light pink, white reverse, small, 35 petals, high-centered, intense fragrance; foliage medium size, dark, semi-glossy; bushy, spreading growth; PP5857; [Party Girl™ × 'Laguna']
'Benjim' (Jim Dandy™) Min, rb, 1989, Benardella, Frank A.; bud pointed; flowers medium red, reverse yellow flushed red, aging lighter, medium, high-centered, slight spicy fragrance; foliage medium size, medium green, semi-glossy; no prickles; upright, bushy, medium growth; no fruit; PP7166; ['Rise 'n' Shine' × Marina®]; intr. 1989
'Benkey' HT, ltami, B.; intr. 1969
'Benkricl' (Kristin, Climbing™) Cl Min, rb, 2008, Benardella, Frank A.; flowers white edged with red, reverse lighter, 1½ in., full, borne mostly solitary; foliage large, dark green, glossy; prickles small, downward curved, dark brown, moderate; growth upright, tall (5-8 ft.); climber, pillar, accent rose; [sport of 'Kristin']; intr. 2008
'Benlavscent' ('Moon River') Min, m, Benardella, Frank A.; intr. 1997
'Benlexa' (Magenta Mystique™) Min, m, 2004, Benardella, Frank A.; flowers mauve & magenta, reverse mauve, 1¾-2 in., very full, borne singly and in small clusters, moderate fragrance; foliage medium size, dark green, glossy; prickles 1/8 in., triangular; apex hooked down,; growth upright, well branched, medium (18-24 in.); garden decoration, exhibition; [seedling × Kristin™]; intr. 2005
'Benmable' Min, ob, Benardella, Frank; intr. 1999
'Benmable' Min, rb, Benardella, Frank; intr. 1996
'Benmagic' ('Pirouette', Kristin™) Min, rb, 1992, Benardella, Frank A.; flowers white/red bicolor, do not open beyond 1/2 open stage, 1½ in., 27-30 petals, high-centered, borne singly, no fragrance; foliage large, dark green, semi-glossy; upright, bushy, medium growth; PP8603; ['DICmickey' × 'Tinseltown']; intr. 1993
'Benmay' Min, ob, Benardella, Frank; intr. 2001
'Benmech' Min, op, Benardella, Frank; intr. 1999
'Benmfig' ('Benardella's Pearl', 'Jilly Jewel', 'Pearl') Min, mp, 2003, Benardella, Frank; flowers light pink, flushed darker, reverse soft pink, medium, dbl., borne mostly solitary, moderate fragrance; foliage medium size, dark green, semi-glossy; prickles medium, thin, slight downward angle, moderate; growth upright, spreading, bushy, tall (30 in.); cutting, garden decorative; ['Figurine' × 'Kristen']; intr. 1996
'Benmgolf' Min, dp, Benardella, Frank; intr. 1999
'Benmhot' Min, yb, Benardella, Frank
'Benmil' ('Dr B. Benacerraf') Min, pb, 1988, Miller, F.
'Benminn' ('Baby Boomer') Min, mp, 2003, Benardella, Frank; flowers medium pink, reverse lighter pink, 1½ in., dbl., borne mostly solitary; foliage medium size, medium green, semi-glossy; prickles 3/16 in., angled slightly down, few; growth upright, spreading, bushy, tall (28-36 in.); garden decorative, cutting; PP14894; ['Ivory Beauty' × Kristin™]; intr. 2002
'Benmjaz' Min, pb, Benardella, Frank
'Benmjul' ('Berry Patch', 'Ruby') Min, dr, 2002, Benardella, Frank; flowers dark red, medium red reverse, 1½-2 in., dbl., borne mostly solitary, slight fragrance; foliage medium size, dark green, semi-glossy; prickles 5/16 in., slightly angled down, moderate; growth upright, medium (24-30 in.); containers, cutting, exhibition; ['Jennifer' × Kristin™]; intr. 2002
'Benmoon' Min, m, Benardella, Frank; intr. 1992
'Benmyolg' Min, dy, Benardella, Frank; bud golden yellow; intr. 1999
'Bennett's Seedling' ('Thoresbyana') Ayr, w, 1840, Bennett; bud pink; flowers pale pink, fading to white, 5 cm., semi-dbl. to dbl., borne in large clusters, strong musky fragrance; raised by Bennett, the gardener for Lord Manners at Thoresby
'Bennewhampshire' Min, yb, Benardella, Frank; intr. 2001
'Bennovecientos' (Power Point™) MinFl, mr, 2007, Benardella, Frank; flowers 2-2½ in., very full, high-centered, borne mostly solitary; foliage large, medium green, matte; prickles straight, slightly hooked at top, brown, moderate; growth upright, spreading (30-36 × 36 in.); exhibition, cutting, garden decoration; ['Ruby' × 'Timeless']; intr. 2008
'Benocho' (Double Take™) MinFl, rb, 2008, Benardella, Frank A.; flowers red blend, reverse white, edged red, 1¾-2¼ in., dbl., high-centered, borne mostly solitary; foliage medium, dark green, semi-glossy; prickles less than ¼ in., curved/angled down, red becoming tan, few; growth upright, very well branched, medium (20-30 in.);patio, containers, cut flowers; ['Baby Boomer' × 'Timeless']; good substance; flower dries well; intr. 2008
'Benoist Pernin' ('Benoît Pernin') HP, mp, 1889, Myard; flowers bright velvety pink; [sport of 'Duchess of Edinburgh']
'Benoit Cornet' HP, mr, 1868, Cornet/Ducher; flowers poppy red
'Benoit Friart' HT, m, 1985, Rijksstation Voor Sierplantenteelt; flowers rosy lilac, medium, 47 petals, flat, borne singly and in clusters of up to 7, intense fragrance; foliage matte; upright growth; ['Fragrant Cloud' × 'Astrée']; intr. 1978
'Benoît Pernin' -- See 'Benoist Pernin'
Benoni '75™ -- See 'Pouloni'
'Benorchid' ('Orchid Lace') Min, m, Benardella, Frank A.; intr. 1995
'Benpete' ('Liberty Bell') MinFl, rb, 2003, Benardella, Frank; flowers dark red with white eye, reverse white, large, full, borne mostly solitary; foliage medium size, dark green, semi-glossy; prickles ¼ - 3/8 in., curved slightly down; growth upright, bushy, tall; exhibition, cutting, garden decoration; intr. 2003
'Benpico' ('Picotee') Min, rb, 2003, Benardella, Frank; flowers white with red edges, reverse white, 1½ in., 20-25 petals, borne singly and in small clusters; foliage small, medium green, semi-glossy; prickles 3/16 - 7/16 in., trianglular, sometimes hooked down,; growth upright, bushy, medium (18-24 in.); exhibition, cut flower, decorative; PP16817; [seedling × 'Ruby']; intr. 2004
'Benraar' HT, rb, Benardella, Frank A.; bud small, ovoid; intr. 1995
'Benrad' (Radiant™) Min, or, 1988, Benardella, Frank A.; bud medium, pointed, ovoid; flowers brilliant orange-red, 1¾ in., 23-27 petals, high-centered, then flat, borne singly, moderate spicy fragrance; foliage large, dark green, semi-glossy; prickles long, thin, straight, pointed slightly downward, gray-red; stems long, straight; upright, vigorous (18-30 in.) growth; no fruit; PP6569; ['Sheri Anne' × 'Sheri Anne']; intr. 1988
'Benrave' (Focal Point™) MinFl, pb, 2008, Benardella, Frank A.; flowers outer petals deep pink, inner petals lighter apricot-pink, medium, 2½-3 in., full, borne mostly solitary; foliage medium, dark green, glossy; prickles 4-5 mm., sharply slanted downward, tan, few; growth upright, medium (2-3 ft.); patio, containers, cutting, garden decoration; [unknown × unknown]; intr. 2008
'Benros' (Rosie™) Min, pb, 1987, Benardella, Frank A.; bud medium, pointed; flowers cream with pink edges, 1¼ in., 30-33 petals, high-centered, borne singly and in sprays, slight fragrance; recurrent; foliage medium size, medium green, semi-glossy; prickles long, thin, straight, angled slightly downward; upright, bushy, medium (14-16 in.) growth;

fruit not observed; PP6508; ['Rise 'n' Shine' × ('Sheri Anne' × 'Laguna')]; intr. 1987

'Benrye' (Flawless™) MinFl, mp, 2008, Benardella, Frank A.; flowers 5-8 cm., dbl., high-centered, blooms borne mostly solitary; foliage large, dark green, semi-glossy; prickles 2-8 mm., deltoid, angled down, red, becoming brown, numerous; growth upright, tall (75-120 cm.); exhibition, patio, containers, cut flowers; [unknown × unknown]; slow to open and long lasting with excellent substance; intr. 2008

'Ben's Gold' HT, dy, Williams, J. Benjamin; flowers semi-dbl., star-shaped; intr. 1996

'Ben's Pink Cluster' S, pb, J. B. Williams; flowers red buds opening to pink clusters; intr. 2004

'Benseah' ('Show Stopper', Showstopper™) MinFl, ab, 2007, Benardella, Frank; flowers peach/apricot, reverse lighter, 1½-2 in., very full, high-centered, borne mostly solitary; foliage large, dark green, semi-glossy; prickles hooked, brown, moderate; growth upright, tall (36 in.); exhibition, cutting, garden decoration; [Lorena® × 'Baby Boomer']; intr. 2008

'Bensho' Min, m, Benardella, Frank

'Bensiete' (Ambiance™) MinFl, ab, 2008, Benardella, Frank A.; flowers peach blend, reverse lighter, 2½ in., very full, high-centered, borne mostly solitary or in small clusters; foliage medium, dark green, matte; prickles 2-9 mm., deltoid, angled down, reddish-brown to tan, moderate; growth upright, medium (24-36 in.); exhibition, cut flower, containers; [seedling × 'Timeless']; intr. 2008

'Benson and Hedges' -- See 'Macgem'

Benson and Hedges Gold® -- See 'Macgem'

'Benson & Hedges Special' -- See 'Macshana'

'Benstar' ('Astra', 'The Soroptimist Rose', 'Soroptimist International', 'Little Star Rose') Min, pb, 1995, Benardella, Frank A.; flowers shrimp pink and ivory, opening to star shape, large, very dbl., high-centered, borne singly and in clusters, slight fragrance; recurrent; foliage large, dark green, glossy; no prickles; tall (24in.), upright, bushy growth; [Party Girl™ × Rosie™]

'Benswee' Min, dr, Benardella, Frank

'Benswise' (Dejá Blu™) MinFl, m, 2008, Benardella, Frank A.; flowers 2-2½ in., dbl., borne mostly solitary or in small clusters; fast repeat; foliage medium, dark green, glossy, very disease-resistant; no prickles; growth upright, compact, well-branched, medium (20-36 in.); exhibition, cut flower, containers; ['Ivory Beauty' × 'Laguna']; intr. 2008

'Bentall's Scarlet' HT, or, 1935, Bentall; flowers bright scarlet; very vigorous growth

Bente® HT, op; greenhouse rose; intr. 2004

'Bentem' ('Rosetime') Min, dr, 1990, Benardella, Frank A.; flowers medium red, brushed with dark red, upright, medium, full, slight fragrance; foliage medium size, medium green, matte; upright growth; ['Rise 'n' Shine' × Black Jade™]; intr. 1989

'Bentexa' Min, dr, Benardella; intr. 2001

'Bentintot' ('Tiny Tot') Min, ab, Benardella, Frank A.; intr. 1990

'Bentveld' HT, op, 1932, Posthuma; flowers carmine-orange, edges lighter than parent; vigorous growth; [sport of 'Charles P. Kilham']

'Benuno' (Leading Lady™) MinFl, w, 2006, Benardella, Frank; flowers white with pink, reverse white, long-lasting, 2¾-3 in., dbl., borne mostly solitary; foliage medium size, medium green, glossy, disease-resistant; prickles moderate, ¼ in., angled and curved down, medium orange-brown; growth upright, well branched, medium (3 × 2 ft.); cutting, garden decoration; [seedling × 'Timeless']; intr. 2007

Benvenuto® LCl, mr, 1967, Meilland; flowers rose-red, medium, semi-dbl., borne in small clusters; recurrent bloom; prickles numerous, short; vigorous, climbing growth; [('Alain' × 'Guinée') × Cocktail®]

'Benwfig' Min, w, Benardella; intr. 1999

'Benwise' HT, m, Benardella, Frank; intr. 2003

'Bérangère' M, lp, 1849, Vibert; flowers delicate pink, large, dbl.

Berbow™ ('Oxbow') Min, or, 1997, Berg, David H.; flowers medium, dbl., borne mostly singly; foliage medium size, medium green, dull; compact, medium (12-15in.) growth; ['Luis Desamero' × Rainbow's End™]

'Berbut' ('Butter 'n' Sugar') Min, w, 1994, Berg, David H.; flowers vary from white to yellow shading to white, large, very dbl., borne mostly singly; foliage medium size, medium green, semi-glossy; few prickles; low (15-18 in.), spreading growth; [Klima™ × ('Intrigue' × 'Poker Chip')]

'Berceau Impérial' HP, mp, 1856, Vigneron; flowers bright pink, moderate fragrance

'Berceuse' HT, my, 1950, Robichon; bud globular, yellow; flowers chamois, very large, very dbl.; foliage leathery; very vigorous, upright growth; ['Signora' × 'Mrs Pierre S. duPont']

'Berendina' -- See 'Pimprenelle'

'Berenice' -- See 'Barenic'

'Bérénice' -- See 'Commonwealth Glory'

'Bérénice' HGal, lp, Racine; flowers light bright pink, medium, full, borne in small clusters; intr. before 1829

'Bérénice' Ch, m, Laffay; flowers light whitish-lilac, small, very full, globular; intr. before 1836

'Bérénice' HGal, rb, 1818, Vibert; flowers rose and crimson, shaded with slate, large, dbl., globular; pendulous growth

'Bérénice' F, dr, Croix, P.; flowers luminous red; intr. 1979

'Berenice Neville' -- See 'Kirbell'

'Bergers Erfolg' HRg, mr, 1925, Berger, V.; flowers fire-red with yellow stamens, 3-4 in., single, borne in clusters; occasionally recurrent bloom; foliage dark; very vigorous, bushy growth; [(R. rugosa × unknown) × 'Richmond']

'Bergers Koralle' F, op, Berger, W.; flowers dark salmon-pink, large, dbl.; intr. 1956

'Bergers Morgenröte' S, lp, Berger, W.; flowers creamy pink, medium, dbl.; intr. 1959

'Bergers Roma' HT, rb, Berger, W.; flowers large, dbl.; intr. 1965

'Bergesloh' Pol, mr, 1929, Vogel, M.; flowers carmine-red, small, dbl.

'Bergfeuer' F, Leenders, J.; intr. 1959

'Bergfeuer Superior' F, Leenders, J.; intr. 1968

'Bergme' ('Gabrielle', Gabriella®) F, mr, 1977, Berggren; bud ovoid; flowers 3 in., 33 petals, cupped; foliage glossy; vigorous, bushy growth; PP4452

'Bergrat Otto Berger' HT, w, 1924, Berger, V.; flowers creamy white to sulfur, center deeper, dbl.; ['Pharisaer' × 'Prince de Bulgarie']

Bering™ -- See 'Poulberin'

'Bering Renaissance' (Bering™, Eleanor™) S, m, Poulsen; flowers mauve, 10-15 cm., dbl., intense fragrance; foliage dark; growth bushy, 100-150 cm.; intr. 1997

'Berkeley' -- See 'Jacient'

Berkeley Beauty™ -- See 'Morberk'

'Berkshire' -- See 'Korpinka'

Berleburg™ ('Berleburg Castle', Bewitched™, Memory Lane™, Jasper™, Herrenchiemsee™, Cuyahoga™, 'Fuchsia Pink Castle') F, dp, Poulsen; flowers 8-10 cm., 25 petals, no fragrance; foliage dark; growth bushy, 60-100 cm.; PP12904; intr. 1996

'Berleburg Castle' -- See 'Poulbella'

'Berlei' ('Leila') Min, ob, 1995, Berg, David H.; flowers light orange with yellow reverse, 1½ in., full, borne mostly singly, slight fragrance; foliage medium size, medium green, semi-glossy; some prickles; medium (15 in.), upright growth; ['Arizona Sunset' × June Laver™]

'Berlengas' HT, Moreira da Silva, A.

'Berlin' S, ob, 1949, Kordes; bud long, pointed; flowers orange-scarlet, center golden, large, single, borne in large clusters; repeat bloom; foliage leathery, dark; prickles large; very vigorous, upright growth; ['Eva' × 'Peace']

'Berlin Beauty' HT, lp

Berliner Luft® ('Jura') F, ob, Hauser; flowers orange-yellow, large, dbl., high-centered, borne in small clusters, slight fragrance; bushy, vigorous (80-100 cm.) growth; intr. 1985

'Berlitz' S, mr; intr. 2001

'Bermer Stadtmusikanten' S, lp; intr. 2000

'Bermina, Cl.' Cl F, ly, Ruston; flowers plae yellow, fading almost to white, full, moderate fragrance

'Bermuda Pink' HT, lp, 1975, Golik; bud ovoid; flowers flesh-pink, 4-5 in., 35-40 petals, globular, slight rose fragrance; foliage glossy, light; compact, moderate growth; ['Queen of Bermuda' × 'Montezuma']; intr. 1974

'Bermuda Yellow Mutabilis' HCh, ly, 2004, Watlington, Ronica; flowers light yellow, shaded pink towards petal edges, large, single

'Bermuda's Emmie Gray' Ch, rb; discovered in Bermuda

'Bermudiana' HT, mp, 1966, Boerner; bud ovoid; flowers 5-6 in., 35-60 petals, high-centered, moderate fragrance; foliage leathery; vigorous, upright growth; PP2578; [('Golden Masterpiece' × unknown) × ('Golden Masterpiece' × unknown)]

Bern® HT, dp, 1979, Huber; bud long, pointed; flowers deep pink, shallow, 4 in., 24 petals, intense spicy fragrance; foliage dark, leathery; spreading growth; ['Crimson Glory' × 'Lilac Charm']; intr. 1975

'Bernadette' HT, lp, 1964, Kelly; flowers large, dbl., high-centered; foliage dark, leathery; vigorous, bushy growth; [sport of 'Peace']

'Bernadette' HT, w, Dorieux; flowers pure white, moderate fragrance; intr. 1976

Bernadette Chirac® -- See 'Delbéchir'

'Bernadette Lafont' S, dp, Sauvageto; flowers rose-fuchsia, very dbl., quartered, cupped; intr. 2004

'Bernaix, Climbing' Cl HT, dr, 1935, Shamburger, C.S.; [sport of 'Souv. d'Alexandre Bernaix']

'Bernalene' -- See 'Korcountry'

'Bernalia' S, mp, 1965, Bernal; flowers pink, center white, small, semi-dbl., borne in clusters, moderate fragrance; recurrent bloom; foliage bright green; vigorous growth; ['Mosqueta' × 'Cecilia']

'Bernard' ('Mme Ferray', 'Pompon Perpetual') P, op, 1836, unknown; flowers salmon-pink, medium, full, cupped; growth small; [sport of 'Rose du Roi']

'Bernard Buffet' HT, dp, Gaujard; flowers pink cyclamen rose, exhibition, slight fragrance; growth very bushy; intr. 2003

'Bernard Palissy' B, mp, 1847, Vibert; flowers bright pink, striped garnet red, large, full, globular

'Bernard Palissy' HP, mp, Margottin; flowers bright carmine, very large, very full; intr. 1863

Bernard Pivot™ F, dy, Orard; flowers bright yellow, dbl.; compact, strong growth; intr. 2002

'Bernard Verlot' HP, rb, 1874, Verdier, E.; flowers red-scarlet, center violet, full

'Bernd Clüver' F, mp, 1974, Reinold; bud pointed; flowers 2½-3 in., moderate fruity fragrance; moderate, upright growth; ['Nordia' × 'Sans Souci']

'Bernd Weigel Rose' F, mp, Tantau; flowers strong pink in center, fading to pale pink on the outer petals, dbl., borne in clusters; intr. 2004

Bernensis® S, mr, Meilland; flowers bright red, dbl.; good repeat; dark green, small foliage; growth to 40-60 cm.; groundcover; intr. 1994

'Bernhard Daneke Rose' -- See 'Tanweieke'

'Bernice' HT, mp, 1927, Pemberton; flowers carmine-pink on yellow base, semi-dbl., moderate fragrance

'Bernice' Pol, mp, Nicolas; bud ovoid; flowers brilliant cerise-pink, small, dbl., globular, borne in clusters, intense fragrance; recurrent bloom; foliage glossy, light; dwarf growth; PP285; ['Baby Tausendschön' × 'Gloria Mundi']; intr. 1937

'Bernice Cooper' -- See 'Liobern'

Bernina® F, w, deRuiter; flowers white, medium, full, slight fragrance; intr. 1979

'Bernina, Climbing' Cl F, w

'Bernor' (Norwich Sweetheart™) Min, mr, 2002, Berg, David; flowers medium, dbl., borne mostly solitary, moderate fragrance; foliage medium size, medium green, matte; growth upright, medium; garden, exhibition; ['Radiant' × 'Jilly Jewel']; intr. 2002

Bernora™ ('Nora') Min, yb, 1997, Berg, David H.; flowers medium, dbl., borne mostly singly; foliage medium size, medium green, dull; upright, tall (15-18in.) growth; [Rainbow's End™ × 'Leila']

Bernstein® -- See 'Taneitber'

'Bernstein' ('Tesco Bernstein') Pol, yb, VEG (S) Baumschulen Dresden; flowers dark yellow and copper, medium, dbl.; intr. 1972

Bernstein-Rose® (Bernstein®) F, dy, Tantau; flowers large, warm amber-yellow, very dbl., moderate fresh herb fragrance; growth to 50-60 cm.; intr. 1987

Bernstorff™ F, mp, Olesen; bud broad based ovoid; flowers medium pink, 8 cm., 75-80 petals, rosette, borne in clusters of up to 7, slight floral fragrance; recurrent; foliage dark; prickles numerous, 6 mm., linear to hooked; bushy (60-100 cm.) growth; PP15161; [seedling × Queen Margrethe™]; intr. 2003

'Berolina' -- See 'Selfridges'

'Berolina' F, my, 1976, Kordes; bud long, pointed; flowers 24 petals, high-centered, slight fragrance; foliage dark, soft; vigorous, upright growth; ['Mabella' × seedling]

'Berpar' ('Wintonbury Parish') Min, w, 1988, Berg, David H.; flowers white with top third of petal light red, medium, 14 petals, high-centered, borne usually singly; foliage medium size, medium green, semi-glossy; prickles curved, large, light greenish-white; upright, medium growth; PP6843; ['Poker Chip' × 'Lady X']

Berries 'n' Cream™ -- See 'Poulclimb'

'Berry Berry Grape' Min, m, King; intr. 1997

'Berry Berry Red' -- See 'Talber'

'Berry Patch' -- See 'Benmjul'

'Bersagliera' HT, dp, 1960, Luigi; bud globular; flowers crimson, phlox-pink and fuchsia-pink, medium, dbl.; strong stems; vigorous growth

'Bert Hinkler' Pol, dp, 1928, Harrison, A.

'Bert Mulley' -- See 'Edna Walling'

'Bertha' S, lp, 1946, Wright, Percy H.; flowers delicate pink, very large, single, borne like hollyhock flowers; non-recurrent; erect stems; growth to 8 ft.; [(R. rugosa × hybrid perpetual) × (R. multiflora × R. blanda)]

'Bertha Aikman' HT, op, 1977, Simpson, J.W.; bud high pointed; flowers two-toned salmon-pink, 4 in., 45 petals, moderate fragrance; foliage matte; moderate, slightly spreading growth; ['Gypsy Moth' × 'Percy Thrower']

'Bertha Gorst' HT, mr, 1933, Beckwith; flowers crimson-cerise, base gold, veined bronze, very large, dbl.; foliage bronze; [sport of 'Autumn']

'Bertha Kiese' ('Frau Berthe Kiese') HT, my, 1913, Jacobs; flowers medium, semi-dbl.; ['Kaiserin Auguste Vlktoria' × 'Undine']

'Bertha Turner' HT, op, 1925, Pemberton; flowers salmon-peach

'Bertha von Suttner' HT, ly, 1918, Verschuren; flowers light yellow with copper tints, medium, dbl.

'Berthe Baron' HP, lp, 1869, Baron-Veillard; flowers delicate rose shaded with white, large, dbl.; ['Jules Margottin' × unknown]

'Berthe de Sansal' HP, mp, about 1850, de Sansal, Desprez, or Jamain; flowers medium, full

'Berthe du Mesnil de Mont Chauvau' HP, lp, 1876, Jamain, H.; flowers light silvery rose pink, center lighter, medium, dbl.

'Berthe Gaulis' HT, rb, 1909, Bernaix fils; flowers light red over China pink, center darker, very large, full, moderate fragrance

'Berthe Lévêque' -- See 'Mlle Berthe Lévêque'

'Berthe Mallerin' HT, or, 1960, Mallerin, C.; flowers red tinted orange, dbl.; strong stems; vigorous growth

'Berthet' HGal, m, before 1827, Cartier; flowers violet

'Berti Gimpel' HP, mp, 1913, Altmüller; flowers large, semi-dbl.; ['Frau Karl Druschki' × 'Fisher Holmes']

'Bertin' N, mp, about 1836, Bertin; flowers fresh pink, aging to purple pink, large, full

'Bertram' -- See 'Sneezy'

'Bertram Park' ('Coquette') HT, mr, 1928, Burbage Nursery; flowers rosy crimson, base yellow, single, slight fragrance; ['Eblouissant' × 'Mme Edouard Herriot']

Bertrand Amoussou® HT, dr, Reuter; flowers double, cupped, slight fragrance; good repeat; foliage disease resistant; low (70-80 cm.), rounded growth; intr. 2008

'Berwick' HSpn, pb; flowers rose shading to white at edges, large, semi-dbl.; growth low

'Beryl' T, dy, 1897, Dickson; bud long; flowers deep golden yellow, shaded reddish, small, dbl., strong fragrance

'Beryl Ainger' HT, w, 1955; flowers cream, base golden yellow; [sport of 'The Doctor']

'Beryl Bach' -- See 'Hartesia'

'Beryl Formby' HT, yb, 1948, Fryers Nursery, Ltd.; flowers golden yellow shaded crimson, 36-40 petals; foliage glossy; bushy growth; [sport of 'McGredy's Sunset']

'Beryl Formby, Climbing' Cl HT, yb, 1956, Letts

'Beryl Joyce' HT, ob, Tantau; intr. 2006

'Beryl Wearmouth' F, mp, 1974, Harkness; flowers 4½ in., 19 petals; foliage light green, matte; [('Ann Elizabeth' × Orange Sensation®) × 'Sea Pearl']

'Besançon' HT, op, Sauvageot; flowers rose-salmon, reverse carmine, 50-60 petals; growth to 80-90 cm.; intr. 1973

'Beslan' HT, mp, 2004, Ryan, Max; flowers medium pink, reverse white, 7½ cm., very full, borne mostly solitary, slight fragrance; recurrent; foliage medium size, dark green,; prickles moderate, moderate,; stems long; growth compact, bushy; exhibition; ['Virgo' × Signature®]; intr. 2002

'Bess Lovett' HWich, dp, 1915, Van Fleet; flowers light red, 7-8 cm., dbl., cupped, borne in clusters of 10-20, moderate fragrance; foliage dark green, glossy; vigorous, climbing growth; [R. wichurana × 'Souv du Président Carnot']

'Bessie Brown' HT, ly, 1899, Dickson, A.; flowers yellowish-white, large, very dbl.; foliage light, leathery, glossy

'Bessie Chaplin' HT, mp, 1921, Chaplin Bros.; flowers bright pink, center deeper, very dbl.; ['Lady Pirrie' × 'Gorgeous']

'Bessie Johnson' HP, lp, 1873, Curtis; flowers light flesh pink, large, very dbl., globular; [sport of 'Abel Grand']

'Bessie Johnson, Climbing' Cl HP, dp, 1878, Paul, G.

'Bessie Lee' Pol

'Bessy' S, ob, Interplant; bud small, roundish; flowers gold-orange to apricot, medium size; foliage dark green, glossy; growth to 40-60 cm.; intr. 1998

'Best Friend' -- See 'Meisionver'

'Best Friend' -- See 'Morfriend'

'Best Friends' -- See 'Brifriends'

'Best of 04' -- See 'Welbest'

Best of Friends™ (Kaj Munk™) HT, my, Poulsen; flowers medium yellow, 8-10 cm., 25 petals, borne one to a stem, slight fragrance; foliage dark, glossy; growth bushy, 60-100 cm.

'Best Regards, Climbing' Cl HT, pb, 1940, Elmer, C.A.; PP1002

'Best Regards' HT, pb, 1944, Morris; flowers pink bicolor, 6-7 in., 50-60 petals, dahlia-like, moderate fragrance; foliage leathery, dark; very vigorous, compact growth; PP652; ['Soeur Thérèse' × 'Signora']

'Best Wishes, Climbing' ('Curiosity, Climbing') Cl HT, rb, Chessum, Paul; flowers red with gold reverse; variegated foliage; intr. 1996

'Best Wishes' Min, dp, Delbard; intr. 2001

'Best Wishes' HT, dp, 1960, Fisher, G.; bud long, pointed; flowers currant-red, 5½-6 in., 25-35 petals, high-centered, moderate fragrance; foliage leathery; strong stems; very vigorous growth; PP1937; intr. 1959

'Beta' HT, pb, 2007, Chapman, Bruce; flowers full, borne mostly solitary; foliage medium size, dark green, glossy; prickles medium, hooked, brown, few; growth upright, medium (1½ m.); garden decoration; ['Kardinal' × St Patrick™]; intr. 2007

'Betahat' ('Malahat') HT, rb, 1988, Betts, John; flowers scarlet, reverse white, fading slightly, medium, very dbl., high-centered, borne usually singly, intense fragrance; foliage medium size, red-brown to dark green, glossy; bushy, vigorous growth; hips round, medium, brown; [Pristine® × 'Shockling Blue']; intr. 1988

'Betano Beach' F, rb, 1966, Fankhauser; bud long, pointed; flowers light salmon-pink, reverse scarlet and burnt crimson, medium, dbl., high-centered; foliage glossy, dark, leathery; vigorous, upright growth; ['Ma Perkins' × 'Detroiter']

'Beth' F, ly, 1968, O'Connell; flowers buff-yellow; [sport of 'Elizabeth of Glamis']; intr. 1966

'Beth' HSpn, lp, Mertens; flowers single; intr. 1973

'Bethany Grace' -- See 'Pixbeth'

'Bethany Helena' HT, pb, 1997, Poole, Lionel; flowers large, very dbl., borne mostly singly; foliage large, dark green, semi-glossy; upright, medium growth; ['Tom Foster' × 'Gavotte']

'Betinho' HT, rb, 1958, Moreira da Silva; flowers velvety red and brown; ['Charles Mallerin' × 'Monte Carlo']

'Betsat' ('Black Satin') HT, dr, 1988, Betts, John; flowers 30 petals, high-centered, borne singly, slight fragrance; foliage medium size, dark green, semi-glossy; prickles few, pointed slightly down, small, light brown; upright, medium growth; hips rounded, medium size, red; [Folklore® × 'Loving Memory']; intr. 1987

'Betsie Jane' HT, ab, 1977, Tresise; bud long, pointed; flowers soft apricot-pink, large, dbl., moderate fragrance; foliage light green; tall, vigorous growth; [sport of 'Bewitched']; intr. 1976

'Betsue' ('Sue Betts') F, or, 1988, Betts, John; flowers long lasting color, large, dbl., cupped, borne in sprays of 65-120, moderate fragrance; foliage medium size, medium green, semi-glossy; prickles sharp, thin, brown; bushy, low growth; hips round, red; [sport of 'Europeana']; intr. 1987

'Betsy' -- See 'Houbetsy'

'Betsy Jane' -- See 'Crlbetsy'

'Betsy McCall' F, op, 1956, Boerner; bud ovoid; flowers shrimp-pink, open, 3-3½ in., 25-30 petals, borne in large clusters, moderate fragrance; foliage glossy; vigorous, bushy growth; PP1603; [seedling × 'Fashion']

'Betsy Murchison' -- See 'Desbet'

'Betsy Ross' -- See 'La Passionata'

'Betsy Ross' HT, ob, 1931, Samtmann Bros.; flowers like parent but marked russet-orange; [sport of 'Talisman']

'Betsy Taaffe' S, ab, Taaffe; [sport of 'Abraham Darby']; intr. 1996

'Betsy van Nes' Pol, mr, 1914, van Ryn; flowers pure bright red, unusually large, semi-dbl.; [sport of 'Mrs W. H. Cutbush']

'Bette Irene' S, ab, 1987, Schneider, Peter; flowers apricot, reverse deeper, fading light pink, imbricated, medium, 9 petals, moderate fragrance; repeat bloom; foliage medium size, dark green, matte; prickles awl-like, medium, brown; upright, medium-tall growth; hips rounded, medium size, ornamental, bright red; ['Dairy Maid' × seedling]

'Bettelstudent' Pol, dp, 1909, Lambert; flowers dark carmine; ['Euphrosyne' × 'Sunset']

'Better Half' HT, pb, Tagashira, K.; flowers deep pink, salmon pink at base, 15-16 cm., 30 petals, high-centered, borne mostly solitary, slight fragrance; foliage reddish-green, semi-glossy; growth spreading; [Gold Medal® × 'Karl Herbst']

'Better Homes & Gardens' HT, pb, 1976, Warriner, William A.; bud ovoid; flowers rose, ivory reverse, 3-3½ in., 38 petals, high-centered, slight fragrance; foliage glossy, dark; medium-tall, upright growth; PP3956; ['Tropicana' × 'Peace']; intr. 1975

Better Homes & Gardens Diamond Jubilee™ -- See 'Winbilee'

'Better Times' HT, mr, 1934, Joseph H. Hill, Co.; flowers cerise, large, dbl., high-centered, slight fragrance; foliage dark, leathery; very vigorous, compact growth; PP23; [sport of 'Briarcliff']

'Better Times, Climbing' Cl HT, mr, 1937, Parmentier, J.

'Bettie Herholdt' -- See 'Betty Herholdt'

Bettina® HT, op, 1953, Meilland, F.; flowers salmon-orange, veined, well-formed, 4 in., 37 petals, moderate fragrance; foliage dark, glossy, bronze; vigorous growth; ['Peace' × ('Mme Joseph Perraud' × 'Demain')]

Bettina, Climbing® (Grimpant Bettina®) Cl HT, op, 1959, Meilland, F.; flowers salmon pink at center, buff yellow at edges, large, moderate fragrance; intr. 1958

'Bettina '78' -- See 'Meibrico'

'Bett's Cardinal Spirit' F, dr, 1999, Walters, Betty & Richard; flowers cardinal red, 4½ in., dbl., borne in small clusters; foliage medium size, medium green, semi-glossy; few prickles; upright, medium (3 ft.) growth; ['High Spirit' × ('Moody Blues' × Melina®)]

'Bett's Christine' HT, mp, 2008, Walters, Betty & Richard; flowers cerise pink, reverse lighter, large, very full, borne mostly solitary; foliage large, dark green, glossy; prickles medium, hooked, moderate; growth upright, tall (2 m.); garden decoration, exhibition; [sport of 'Olympic Torch']; intr. 2000

'Bett's Lemon Cream' F, ly, 2003, Walters, Betty and Richard; flowers full, borne in small clusters; foliage medium size, dark green, matte; prickles medium, hooked; growth upright, tall (1 m.); garden, exhibition; ['Mt. Hood' × Casino®]; intr. 1995

'Bett's Little Gem' Min, mp, 1996, Walters, Betty & Richard; flowers medium pink with white ring around stamens, full, open, cupped, slight fragrance; foliage medium size, light green, semi-glossy; few prickles; upright, medium growth; ['Pink Petticoat' × unknown]

'Bett's Little Rhapsody' -- See 'Waltrap'

'Bett's Pink Lace' Min, pb, 1996, Walters, Betty & Richard; flowers white with pink edge, changing to salmon pink, full, borne singly and in small clusters, intense fragrance; foliage medium size, dark green, glossy; few prickles; compact, low growth; ['Pink Petticoat' × seedling]

'Bett's Snow Dancer' F, w, 1999, Walters, Betty & Richard; bud hint of green, opening to white; flowers outer edge white with cream center, numerous golden stamens, 4½ in., full, borne in large clusters; foliage medium size, medium green, semi-glossy; some prickles; compact, medium (4 ft.) growth; ['Mt Hood' × 'Aorangi']

'Bett's White Delight' Min, w, 1992, Walters, Betty & Richard; flowers creamy white opening to pure white, rosette, 2½ in., 58-86 petals, borne in clusters of 5; foliage medium to dark green, matte; tall, compact growth; ['Pink Petticoat' × seedling]

'Bett's White Sensation' F, w, 2003, Walters, Betty and Richard; flowers white to cream, 8 cm., very full, borne in large clusters; foliage medium size, dark green, matte; prickles medium, hooked; growth upright, tall (1-2 m.); garden, exhibition; ['Mt Hood' × 'Aorangi']; intr. 1995

'Bett's Winter Holly' Min, or, 2003, Walters, Betty and Richard; flowers very full, borne in small clusters; foliage small, dark green, glossy; prickles ½ cm., narrow; growth upright, tall (18 in.); garden; [Winter Magic™ × Irresistible™]; intr. 1999

'Betty' HT, pb, 1905, Dickson, A.; flowers coppery rose, shaded yellow, large, dbl.; very vigorous growth

'Betty, Climbing' Cl HT, pb, 1926, Hohman

'Betty' HT, dr, Priestly, J.L.; flowers dark red, 9 cm., dbl., slight fragrance; medium size, light green, dull foliage; prickles moderate; compact, medium growth (3 ft.); ['Satellite' × 'Ena Harkness']; intr. 2000

'Betty Alden' Cl Pol, lp, 1919, Farquhar; flowers appleblossom-pink passing to white, single; ['Orléans Rose' × ('Katharina Zeimet' × R. arvensis hybrid)]

'Betty Baum' HT, lp, 1927, Baum; flowers delicate pink, base yellow, dbl.; [sport of 'Premier']

Betty Bee™ -- See 'Blabee'

'Betty Berkeley' T, mr, 1904, Bernaix, A.; bud long, ovoid; flowers bright red, medium, dbl.

'Betty Bland' S, dp, 1925, Skinner; flowers deep rose, fading pink, center deeper, dbl.; non-recurrent bloom; foliage rich green, soft; stems twigs ruby-red; vigorous (6 ft.), bushy growth; very hardy; [R. blanda × hybrid perpetual]

'Betty Blossom' HWich, mp, 1900, Dawson; flowers clear rose-pink, semi-dbl., borne in loose clusters; growth vigorous; pillar or bush; [R. wichurana × 'Mrs W. J. Grant']

Betty Boop™ -- See 'Wekplapic'

'Betty Cuthbert' HT, or, 1964, Palmer; bud long, pointed; flowers medium, very dbl.; foliage soft, glossy; very vigorous, upright growth; [sport of 'Roundelay']

'Betty Driver' -- See 'Gandri'

'Betty Free' F, mp, 1950, LeGrice; bud pointed; flowers Neyron rose, 25 petals, borne in clusters; vigorous growth; [sport of 'Fortschritt']

'Betty Grace Clark' HT, ob, 1933, Clarke Bros.; flowers orange-yellow, reverse streaked red, high-centered; vigorous, bushy growth; [sport of 'Marie Adélaide']

'Betty Harkness' ('Glowing Abundance') F, ob, Harkness; flowers deep tangerine, 4 in., 24 petals, high-centered, moderate orange/clove fragrance; recurrent; foliage dark green, glossy; moderate (3 ft.) growth; intr. 1998

'Betty Herholdt' ('Bettie Herholdt', 'Messagere') HT, w, 1978, Herholdt, J.A.; bud pointed; flowers ivory-white, 5½ in., 50 petals, moderate fragrance; vigorous growth; PP3923; [('White Swan' × seedling) × Pascali®]

'Betty Hulton' HT, dy, 1923, Dickson, A.; flowers deep saffron-yellow, dbl.

Betty Lou™ -- See 'Ricbetty'

'Betty May Wood' HT, ab, 1970, Wood; flowers apricot to buff, reverse coral-salmon, well-formed, 30 petals; foliage light green; free growth; [sport of 'Mischief']

'Betty Morse' HT, mr, 1950, Kordes; bud long, pointed; flowers 4 in., 25 petals; foliage olive-green; vigorous growth; ['Crimson Glory' × ('Crimson Glory' × 'Cathrine Kordes')]

'Betty Neuss' HT, mp, 1974, Dawson, George; bud small, long, pointed; flowers pure pink, medium, dbl., slight fragrance; foliage small; very vigorous, upright growth; intr. 1973

'Betty O' -- See 'Welosb'

'Betty Paul' HT, mp, 1988, Warner, A.J.; flowers medium pink blend, medium, 20-25 petals, high-centered, borne usually singly or in sprays; foliage medium size, medium green, semi-glossy, disease-resistant; prickles straight, medium, light brown; upright, medium, tall growth; hips ovoid, small, yellow-orange; [Queen Elizabeth® × ('Tiffany' × 'Tropicana')]

'Betty Pearson' HT, w, 1929, Burbage Nursery; flowers cream, center apricot, petals shell-shaped, large

'Betty Prior, Climbing' -- See 'Cooprior'

'Betty Prior' F, mp, 1935, Prior; bud ovoid, dark carmine; flowers carmine-pink, 5 petals, cupped, borne in clusters, moderate fragrance; vigorous, bushy growth; PP340; ['Kirsten Poulsen' × seedling]; intr. 1938

'Betty Sheriff' LCl, w, Sheriff

'Betty Stielow' HT, dp, 1928, Stielow Bros.; flowers dark pink, almost red at times, dbl.; [sport of 'Premier']

'Betty Sutor' HT, pb, 1929, McGredy; flowers pale pink, veined rose, reverse rosy, large, dbl.; foliage light, glossy; vigorous, bushy growth

'Betty Uprichard' HT, ab, 1922, Dickson, A.; bud long, pointed; flowers delicate salmon-pink, reverse carmine with coppery sheen, large, 20 petals, high-centered, intense fragrance; foliage large, light bronze green, leathery, glossy; very vigorous, tall growth

'Betty Uprichard, Climbing' Cl HT, ab, 1936, Krause

'Betty White' ('André le Nôtre') HT, pb, Meilland Intl.; flowers light pink, darker toward center, large, 60-65 petals, cupped; foliage semi-glossy; growth to 90-110 cm.; PP13897; intr. 2001

'Betty Will' S, pb, 1963, Erskine; flowers bright pink, lighter reverse, 35 petals; recurrent; foliage dark, leathery; some large prickles; red canes; tall growth; very hardy; ['George Will' × 'Betty Bland']

'Betty Wilson' -- See 'Sheriscent'

Betty Wright™ -- See 'Burbet'

'Betty's Baby' -- See 'Judbaby'

Betty's Pride® Min, rb

'Betzel's Pink' HT, op, 1955, Betzel; bud long; flowers coral-pink, 5 in., 55-60 petals, high-centered; foliage leathery, glossy; strong stems; vigorous, bushy growth; [sport of 'Pres. Herbert Hoover']; intr. 1955

'Beulah Belle' S, mp, Rupert; flowers

dbl., sometimes quartered, borne in along arching canes, strong fragrance; occasional repeat; foliage greyish-green; growth 7-8 ft.; good for pegging; intr. 2001

'Bev Dobson' LCl, pb, 2000, Jerabek, Paul; flowers white with pink edge, 3 in., dbl., borne in small clusters, moderate fragrance; foliage medium size, medium green, semi-glossy, reddish when young; prickles moderate; growth climbing, spreading; intr. 2001

'Beverley Anne' Ch, mr, 1987, Nobbs, Kenneth J.; flowers red-purple, open, 21 petals, flat, borne in sprays of 3-7, slight fragrance; foliage pivoted, serrated; no prickles; semi-dwarf growth; [seedling × seedling]

'Beverley Stoop' -- See 'Jaydon'

Beverly® ('Perfume Passion') HT, pb, Kordes; flowers soft pink, petal edges deeper pink , 4 in., full, high-centered, borne mostly singly, intense fragrance; recurrent; erect, upright growth; intr. 2008

'Beverly-Ann' -- See 'Horcojones'

'Beverly Hills' -- See 'Delmator'

'Beverly Jayne' S, lp, 1999, Jones, L.J.; flowers center deep pink, outer light pink, 1¼ in., 41 petals, borne in large clusters; foliage small, light green, dull; few prickles; upright, bushy, medium (3 ft.) growth; [Angela Rippon® × 'New Dawn']

'Beverly Kordana' Min, op, Kordes; flowers coral pink, dbl.; container rose

'Beverly Nicols' HT, op, 1939, Burbage Nursery; flowers cream, reverse salmon, well-formed, large, high-centered; vigorous growth

'Beverly Watson' HT, w, Kordes; bud creamy white; flowers white with a delicate tan tint, full, cupped, slight fragrance; free-flowering; long, firm stems; tall growth; intr. 1997

Bewitched™ -- See 'Poulbella'

'Bewitched' HT, mp, 1967, Lammerts, Dr. Walter; bud urn shaped; flowers cotton candy pink, 5 in., 27-30 petals, high-centered, borne singly, moderate damask fragrance; foliage large, apple green, glossy; new stems and foliage is red; vigorous, medium, rounded growth; PP2755; [Queen Elizabeth® × 'Tawny Gold']

'Bewitched, Climbing' Cl HT, mp; intr. 1989

'Bezkit' ('Miss Kitty') HT, w, 2007, Belendez, Kitty; flowers 4½ in., very full, blooms borne mostly solitary; foliage medium size, dark green, semi-glossy; prickles 3/8 in., triangular, curved downward, pinkish-beige, few; growth upright, tall (6 ft.); [sport of 'Cajun Moon']; intr. 2007

'Bezruc' HT, mr, 1938, Böhm, J.; flowers large, dbl.

'Bhagmati' F, mr, 1979, Viraraghavan, M.S. Viru; bud ovoid; flowers 2½-3 in., 15-20 petals, cupped, slight fragrance; foliage glossy, light green; dwarf, vigorous, bushy growth; ['Charleston' × (('Roman Holiday' × 'Flamenco') × 'Goldgleam')]; intr. 1977

'Bhanu' HT, yb, K&S; flowers cream to yellow with pink, full, well formed, moderate fragrance; intr. 1990

'Bharami' -- See 'Bharani'

'Bharani' ('Bharami') Min, m, 1984, Kasturi; flowers small, mauve with white eye, semi-dbl.; foliage small, light green, matte; upright growth; [seedling × seedling]; intr. 1973

'Bhargav' HT, op, K&S; flowers coral pink, dbl., classic, slight tea fragrance; intr. 1993

'Bhavani' HT, op, Kasturi; flowers salmon orange to vermilion, spiral; intr. 1986

'Bhim' HT, dr, 1970, IARI; bud long, pointed; flowers scarlet-red, open, large, very dbl.; abundant, intermittent bloom; vigorous, upright growth; ['Charles Mallerin' × 'Delhi Princess']

'Bi-Centennial Rose' -- See 'The Australian Bicentennial'

'Bianca' HT, w, 1913, Paul, W.; bud long, pointed; flowers pale peach tinted pink- and violet, center shaded rose, medium, dbl.; RULED EXTINCT 3/83 ARM

'Bianca' HT, w, 1927, Pemberton; flowers white, sometimes lightly flushed cream or pink, well-formed, dbl., moderate fragrance; RULED EXTINCT 3/83 ARM

Bianca® HT, w, Kuhn; bud slim bud; flowers clean white, large, slight fragrance; dark green leaves; growth upright, strong; intr. 1987

Bianca™ Min, w, Olesen; flowers dbl., 25-30 petals, borne mostly solitary, moderate fragrance; foliage medium green, semi-glossy; growth bushy, very low (20-40 cm.); intr. 1996

Bianca® HT, w, Preesman; intr. 2007

'Bianca Camelia' HT, w, 1933, San Remo Exp. Sta.; bud ovoid, pointed; flowers snow-white, center light blush-yellow, very large, 23-25 petals; foliage light green; very vigorous, upright growth; ['Nuntius Pacelli' × 'Sachsengruss']

'Bianca Candy' HT, lp, Preesman; flowers soft pink

'Bianca Parade' Min, w, Poulsen; flowers white, medium, dbl., moderate fragrance; growth bushy, 20-40 cm.; intr. 1996

'Biancaneve' S, w, Mansuino; intr. 1961

'Bianco' -- See 'Cocblanco'

'Biarritz' S, yb, Huber; flowers light yellow with light reddish edge, double, slight, fruity fragrance; foliage dark green; strong (120 - 130 cm.) growth; intr. 2006

'Bibi Maizoon' -- See 'Ausdimindo'

Bibi Mezoon® -- See 'Ausdimindo'

Bibiché® -- See 'Dorflo'

'Bibiché, Climbing' Cl F, ob, Dorieux, Francois; intr. 1980

'Bicentenaire de George Sand' S, mp, Gilet; intr. 2005

Bicentenaire de Guillot® S, dp, Guillot; free-flowering; foliage dense, healthy; growth vigorous; intr. 2004

'Bicentennial' F, rb, 1973, Meyer, C.; flowers deep pink and red blend, medium, dbl., high-centered, slight fragrance; foliage leathery; vigorous, upright, bushy growth; PP3802; intr. 1975

'Bichette' HT, mp, 1970, Verschuren, A.; flowers Persian rose, large, 20-25 petals; foliage dark, leathery; vigorous, upright growth; ['Diamond Jubilee' × seedling]; intr. 1968

Bico™ Min, yb, Poulsen Roser; intr. 2000

'Bicolette' HT, rb, Tschanz, E.; flowers rusty red with cream reverse, dbl., high-centered; recurrent; intr. 1980

'Bicolor' M, pb, 1855, Lacharme; flowers pink, spotted with violet, medium, dbl.; some repeat

'Bicolore' HP, w, 1877, Oger; flowers white with pink edge, aging to frosty pink, full, flat

'Bicolore Incomparable' HP, pb, 1861, Touvais; flowers deep pink, darker at center, striped with lighter pink, medium, full; sometimes classed as HGal or M

'Bicolore Nana' HSpn, w, Smith; flowers cream, flecked with carmine, medium, single; growth dwarf

'Bicolour' HT, rb; intr. 2004

'Biddulph Grange' ('Dark Eyes', 'Rosentanz') S, rb, Fryer, Gareth; flowers velvety bright red with white base and reverse, semi-dbl., borne in large trusses, slight fragrance; bushy (3-4 ft.) growth; intr. 1988

'Biddy' Min, pb, Benardella, Frank; flowers soft pink with creamy yellow in the heart, 54 petals; good repeat; foliage medium green; growth bushy, 35 cm.

'Biedermeier' HT, pb, Tantau; flowers white with pink edges, large, very dbl., borne in sprays; greenhouse rose; intr. 2002

'Biedermeier' Min, rb, Tantau; flowers cherry red and creamy white, globular; 40 cm. growth; intr. 2006

Biedermeier Garden® HT, pb, Tantau; flowers white with strong pink edges, full, high-centered, borne singly or in small clusters, moderate fragrance; good repeat; compact, bushy growth; intr. 2006

'Bien-Aimée' ('La Bien Aimé') HGal, mr, before 1845; flowers shining fiery red, full, moderate fragrance

'Bienkie' -- See 'Korsisten'

'Bienvenu' Gr, ob, 1969, Swim & Weeks; bud long, pointed; flowers reddish-orange, large, 70 petals, high-centered, intense fragrance; foliage leathery, matte; vigorous, upright growth; PP3007; ['Camelot' × ('Montezuma' × 'War Dance')]

'Bienvêtu' -- See 'Mons Gustave Bienvêtu'

'Bifera Coronata' -- See 'Belle Couronnée'

'Bifera Italica' ('Henriette') HGal, lp, before

1811, from Italy; bud pointed; flowers medium, dbl., borne in clusters; foliage light green; few prickles

'Big and Beautiful' -- See 'Tinbab'

'Big Apple'   HT, mr, 1984, Weeks, O.L.; flowers large, dbl., moderate fragrance; foliage large, medium green, matte to semi-glossy; upright, spreading growth; [Mister Lincoln® × ('Suspense' × King's Ransom®)]; intr. 1984

Big Apple®   HT, pb, Jackson & Perkins; bud ivory; flowers rose pink with carmine petal edges, large, dbl., exhibition, intense fragrance; strong growth, 100-120 cm.; intr. 2003

'Big Apricot'   HT, ab, Wells; intr. 2006

Big Bang®   F, or, 1981, Barni-Pistoia, Rose; bud pointed; flowers deep orange-red, shallow-cupped, 13 petals, cupped, borne 5-10 per cluster, no fragrance; foliage matte, light green; prickles reddish-green; bushy growth; [Sarabande® × (Sarabande® × unknown)]; intr. 1980

'Big Ben'   HT, dr, 1964, Gandy, Douglas L.; flowers well-formed, 5-6 in.; foliage dark; tall growth; ['Ena Harkness' × 'Charles Mallerin']

'Big Bowie'   S, ob, J. B. Williams; flowers apricot and orange blend, dbl., moderate fragrance; repeats well; growth strong grower to 5 ft.; intr. 2005

'Big Chief' ('Portland Trailblazer') HT, dr, 1976, Dickson, A.; bud pointed, ovoid; flowers crimson, 5½ in., 20-30 petals, high-centered, borne singly, slight fragrance; foliage large, matte, brittle; prickles few, short, hooked downward, brown; growth vigorous, very upright; PP4222; ['Ernest H. Morse' × 'Red Planet']; intr. 1975

Big Daddy® -- See 'Macchome'

'Big Duke' ('Duke Wayne') HT, dp, 1991, Weddle, Von C.; bud pointed; flowers deep pink, silvery pink reverse, large, dbl., high-centered, borne usually singly, moderate fruity fragrance; foliage large, medium green, semi-glossy; upright, tall growth; ['The Duke' × seedling]

'Big Fruitilia' -- See 'Koreledas'

'Big Jack Charlton'   HT, w, 1994, Poole, Lionel; flowers ivory, pale pink edge, 3-3½ in., full, borne mostly singly, slight fragrance; foliage large, dark green, glossy; some prickles; medium (85 cm.), upright growth; ['Gavotte' × 'Queen Esther']; intr. 1995

'Big Jim Larkin' -- See 'Sealark'

'Big John' -- See 'Steteaw'

'Big John' -- See 'Galleria'

'Big John'   Min, mr, 1980, Williams, Ernest D.; bud pointed; flowers deep medium red, base yellow, 1-1½ in., 42 petals, high-centered; foliage small, glossy, bronze; upright, bushy growth; PP4754; ['Starburst' × 'Over the Rainbow']; intr. 1979

'Big Pink' -- See 'Mr Ernest Holmes'

'Big Pink'   HT, lp, Hiroshima Rose Nursery; flowers bright pastel pink, large, 30-35 petals, borne mostly solitary, slight fragrance; foliage large, thick, roundish; stems thick; intr. 1985

'Big Purple' -- See 'Stebigpu'

'Big Red'   HT, dr, 1967, Meilland, Mrs. Marie-Louise; bud pointed; flowers 4½-6 in., 52 petals, high-centered, slight fragrance; foliage leathery; vigorous, upright, bushy growth; PP2693; ['Chrysler Imperial' × seedling]

'Big Red'   HT, mr, Edwards, Eddie; flowers 5 -6 in., full, high-centered, borne mostly singly, moderate fragrance; recurrent; foliage large, dark green, glossy ; prickles moderate; upright, tall growth; [Veterans' Honor™ × 'Unnamed seedling']; intr. 2007

'Big Splash'   Cl HT, rb, 1969, Armstrong, D.L.; bud pointed; flowers flame-red, reverse lighter, base yellow, large, dbl., high-centered, moderate fragrance; foliage glossy, leathery; vigorous, climbing (8-10 ft.) growth; PP3076; ['Buccaneer' × 'Bravo']

'Big Spring Belle' -- See 'Carbelle'

'Big Time'   HT, dp; flowers dbl., exhibition, borne mostly one to a stem; intr. 2001

'Biggi'   HT, yb, 1976, Kordes; bud ovoid; flowers 4½ in., 27 petals, high-centered, moderate fragrance; intermittent bloom; foliage glossy, dark; vigorous, upright growth; ['Dr. A.J. Verhage' × seedling]; intr. 1975

'Bigleaf Panarosa'   HRg, pb, Moore, Ralph; flowers show faint stripes; intr. 2008

'Bignonia'   N, yb, 1874, Levet; flowers golden orange, full

'Bigoudi'   Min, rb, Meilland; flowers red and yellow striped, medium, dbl.; growth to 40-45 cm.; intr. 2001

'Bihanga'   HT, ob, Ghosh; flowers flower orange with pink blend, reverse golden yellow, large, dbl., high-centered; intr. 2001

'Bijarre' -- See 'Francfort Agathé'

'Bijou'   MinFl, pb, Lens, Louis; intr. 1991

Bijou®   S, dy, Barni, V.; flowers creamy yellow, small, borne in large sprays, covering the plant; growth low, spreading, 40-60 cm.; intr. 1999

'Bijou'   Pol, lp, 1932, deRuiter; flowers old rose

'Bijou de Couasnon'   HP, dr, 1886, Vigneron; flowers intense velvety red, large, full; growth upright; ['Charles Lefebvre' × unknown]

'Bijou de Lyon'   HMult, w, 1882, Schwartz; flowers small, full, borne in clusters

'Bijou de Royat-les-Bains'   Ch, mp, 1891, Veysset; flowers medium pink, marbled with carmine medium, dbl.; ['Hermosa' × unknown]

'Bijou des Amateurs'   HGal, dr, before 1830, Jacquemet-Bonnefont; flowers dark cerise, medium to large, full

'Bijou des Prairies' -- See 'Gem of the Prairies'

'Bijou d'Or' -- See 'Tanledolg'

'Bijou Superior'   Pol, lp, deRuiter; flowers have more lasting color; [sport of 'Bijou']

'Bikini Red'   HT, mr, 1976, Golik; bud ovoid; flowers rose-red, tinged white, ruffled, 5 in., 40 petals, moderate fruity fragrance; foliage glossy, dark; ['Queen of Bermuda' × 'Peace']; intr. 1974

'Bila Junior Miss'   HT, w, Strnad

'Bilfan' ('Jack's Fantasy') Min, yb, 1987, Bilson, Jack M., Jr. & Bilson, Jack M. III; flowers yellow blushed with orange-red from edge, reverse medium yellow, 21 petals, high-centered, slight fragrance; foliage medium size, medium green, semi-glossy; prickles few, beige slightly sloped downward; upright, bushy, medium growth; no fruit; ['Little Darling' × 'Over the Rainbow']

'Bilice' (Phoebe's Choice™) Min, pb, 1987, Bilson, Jack M., Jr. & Bilson, Jack M. III; flowers pink, edges yellow, pink softens, white edges, dbl., high-centered; foliage medium size, medium green, glossy; prickles reddish-green ,sloped downwards; upright, bushy growth; hips round, light orange and green; ['Little Darling' × 'Over the Rainbow']

'Bilitis'   F, or, 1978, Gaujard; flowers vermilion-red, center yellow; ['Tabarin' × 'Golden Slippers']; intr. 1969

'Bill Beaumont'   F, mr, 1983, Fryer, Gareth; flowers crimson, 20 petals, slight fragrance; foliage medium size, medium green, matte; bushy growth; ['Evelyn Fison' × 'Redgold']; intr. 1982

'Bill Cone' -- See 'Micone'

'Bill Daisey'   HT, mr, J. B. Williams; intr. 2005

'Bill Grant'   S, w, Clements, John; flowers white with gold stamens., 1 in., 5 petals, borne in clusters; free-flowering; foliage medium green, glossy; bushy (3-4 ft.), arching growth; intr. 2001

'Bill Heath' -- See 'Liopearl'

'Bill Hunt'   HT, op, 1976, Blakemore; flowers deep coral, medium, 30 petals; foliage glossy; fairly vigorous growth; ['Mischief' × 'Serenade']

'Bill Slim' -- See 'Harquito'

'Bill Temple'   HT, w, 1976, Harkness; flowers cream, 5-6 in., 30 petals, slight fragrance; foliage glossy, dark; ['Crimson Halo' × Piccadilly®]

Bill Warriner™ -- See 'Jacsur'

'Billard'   HP, op, before 1845, Billard; flowers bright peach-pink, large, very full, moderate fragrance

'Billard et Barré'   Cl T, my, 1898, Pernet-Ducher; flowers deep buff, edges lighter, 9 cm., dbl., strong tea fragrance; ['Mlle Alice Furon' × 'Duchesse d'Auerstädt']

'Billie and Lew'   HWich, m, Nobbs; intr. 1995

'Billie Teas' -- See 'Hootea'

'Billionaire'   HT, mr, 1973, Warriner, William A.; bud ovoid, long, pointed; flowers large, dbl., high-centered, slight fragrance; foliage leathery; vigorous, upright growth; PP3381; ['Fragrant Cloud' × 'Proud Land']

'Billy'   S, rb, Hauser; intr. 1993

The Official Registry and Checklist — Rosa

'Billy Boiler' Cl HT, mr, 1927, Clark, A.; flowers glowing red, semi-dbl.; vigorous, tall growth; ['Black Boy' × unknown]

'Billy Boy' -- See 'Morboy'

'Billy Boy' HT, my, 1926, McGredy; flowers sunflower-yellow,, semi-dbl.; ['Golden Emblem' × 'Christine']

'Billy Fury' -- See 'Worarm'

Billy Graham™ -- See 'Jacgray'

'Bilpat' ('Naughty Patricia') Min, pb, 1989, Bilson, Jack M., Jr. & Bilson, Jack M. III; flowers medium pink, edges blush, outer petals quill, large, 29 petals, high-centered, borne usually singly and in clusters of 3-5, slight fruity fragrance; foliage large, medium green, matte; prickles slight downward slope, reddish-tan; upright, tall growth; hips globular, medium, green blotched with orange-red; ['Rise 'n' Shine' × 'Redgold']

Bimboro® HT, dr, 1979, W. Kordes Söhne; bud globular; flowers 3-3½ in., 46 petals, high-centered, moderate fragrance; foliage glossy; vigorous, bushy, upright growth; [seedling × 'Kardinal']

'Binapani' HT, w, Dey, S. C.; flowers large, pastel cream with shades at petal edges, dbl.; floriferous

'Bing Crosby' HT, ob, 1980, Weeks; bud ovoid; flowers strong clear orange, 5 in., 40-45 petals, cupped, borne mostly singly, slight light spice fragrance; foliage medium size, heavy, leathery, wrinkled, dark; prickles long hooked downward; long stems; vigorous, upright, bushy growth; PP4695; [seedling × 'First Prize']

'Bingo' ('Dyna') HT, dr, 1956, Robichon; bud pointed; flowers cardinal-red, 4-5 in., 55 petals, high-centered, intense fragrance; foliage glossy; upright growth; PP1392; [(('Hadley' × unknown) × 'Ami Quinard') × 'Crimson Glory']; intr. 1955

Bingo Meidiland® -- See 'Meipotal'

Bingo Meillandecor® -- See 'Meipotal'

'Bingo Queen' -- See 'Tinqueen'

'Biola Centennial' -- See 'Sprobiolacentennial'

'Bionic Beauty' HT, lp, Meilland; flowers soft shell pink , full; recurrent; foliage dark green, glossy ; stems long ; 5 ft. growth; intr. 2007

'Bipinnata' -- See R. centifolia bipinnata

'Bipontina' S, mr, Huber; intr. 1988

Bipontina 650® S, pb, Huber; flowers bright pink with white eye, semi-dbl., flat, borne in large sprays; very willing bloomer; light green foliage; tall (150 cm.) and spreading growth; intr. 2002

'Bir-Hackeim' HT, mr, 1946, Mallerin, C.; bud long, pointed; flowers fiery red, open, semi-dbl., cupped; very vigorous, upright, bushy growth

'Bird of Fire' -- See 'Taybird'

'Birdie Blye' HMult, mp, 1904, Van Fleet; bud long, pointed, carmine; flowers rose-pink, 7-8 cm., dbl., cupped, borne in small clusters; recurrent bloom; foliage light green; vigorous (4-5 ft.) growth; ['Helene' × 'Bon Silene']

'Birdsong' LCl, mp, 1991, Seward, Grace; flowers small, semi-dbl., borne in very large clusters, moderate fragrance; foliage small to medium size, medium green, semi-glossy; few prickles; tall (300+ cm.), spreading, large, rambling growth; [seedling × seedling]

'Birdy' HT, rb, Tantau; flowers red with yellow center and reverse, medium, dbl., cupped, borne mostly singly; recurrent; stems moderate; greenhouse rose; intr. 1997

'Birendranath' HT, pb, Chakraborthy, Dr K.; flowers cream white with pronounced raspberry color blend, dbl., high-centered, moderate fragrance

'Birgitta' HT, dr, 1961, de Boer; bud ovoid; flowers large, dbl.

'Birgitte de Villenfagne' HMsk, pb

'Birichina' F, (Italy)

'Birmingham Boerner' F, w, 1976, Schoepfle; flowers light flesh-pink turning white; [sport of 'Gene Boerner']

'Birmingham Post' F, dp, 1968, Watkins Roses; flowers deep pink, large, dbl.; foliage leathery; vigorous growth; [Queen Elizabeth® × 'Wendy Cussons']

'Birthday Boy' F, m, Tantau; intr. 2005

'Birthday Candle' HT, rb, Teranishi; intr. 2003

'Birthday Girl' -- See 'Meilasso'

'Birthday Party' Min, mp, 1979, Strawn; bud ovoid; flowers pink, 1½-2 in., 28 petals, high-centered, moderate fragrance; foliage dark; upright, spreading growth; PP4637; [Attraktion® × 'Sheri Anne']

'Birthday Present' Cl HT, dr, 1950, Toogood; bud ovoid; flowers dark velvet red, 20 petals, high-centered, intense fragrance; non-recurrent; foliage dark, leathery; vigorous, climbing growth; ['Guineé' × 'Rouge Mallerin']

'Birthday Wishes' -- See 'Guesdelay'

'Birthday Wishes' -- See 'Shrimp Hit'

'Biscay' Min, mp, 1989, Bridges, Dennis A.; bud ovoid; flowers medium pink, reverse slightly darker, medium, 26 petals, high-centered, borne usually singly, slight fragrance; foliage medium size, medium green, semi-glossy; prickles slightly downward pointed, medium, deep pink; upright, medium growth; ['Summer Spice' × seedling]; intr. 1989

'Bischof Dr Korum' HT, pb, 1921, Lambert, P.; flowers yellowish-rose, dbl., moderate fragrance; ['Frau Karl Druschki' × 'Laurent Carle']; sometimes classed as HP

'Bischofsstadt Paderborn' ('Fire Pillar', 'Paderborn') S, or, 1964, Kordes, R.; flowers cinnabar-scarlet, semi-dbl., saucer-shaped; vigorous (3-4 ft.), bushy growth

Bischofzell® HT, rb, Huber; intr. 2005

'Biscof' ('Sadler') Min, op, 1983, Bischoff, Francis J.; flowers orange pink, small, 43 petals, high-centered; foliage medium green, matte; upright growth; ['Faberge' × 'Darling Flame']

'Bisfra' ('Penny Annie') Min, lp, 1984, Bischoff, Francis J.; flowers small, 35 petals, high-centered, no fragrance; foliage medium size, medium green, matte; bushy growth; ['Little Darling' × seedling]

'Bishop Darlington' HMsk, ab, 1926, Thomas; bud ovoid; flowers cream to flesh-pink, with yellow glow, 10-11 cm., 17 petals, cupped, borne in small clusters, moderate fruity fragrance; recurrent bloom; foliage bronze, soft; semi-climbing growth; ['Aviateur Bleriot' × 'Moonlight']; intr. 1928

'Bishop Elphinstone' -- See 'Cocjolly'

'Bishop of Sherwood' HT, op, 1977, Bracegirdle; flowers pale salmon flushed pink, 5 in., 34 petals, intense fragrance; vigorous, upright growth; ['Mischief' × ('Wendy Cussons' × 'Peace')]

'Bishop's Castle' -- See 'Ausbecks'

'Bishop's Paul Neyron' HP, mp, Ruston?; flowers similar to Paul Neyron; seedling from Paul Neyron

'Bishop's Rambler' HWich, dr, Scarman; intr. 1996

'Bishop's Rose' C, pb; vigorous (to 5 ft.) growth; [apparently R. gallica × R. centifolia]

'Bisjen' Min, rb, 1981, Bischoff, Francis J.; bud ovoid

'Bismar' (Marty's Triumph™) Min, op, 1985, Bischoff, Francis J.; flowers bright coral pink, white reverse, small, 28 petals, high-centered, borne singly; foliage medium size, dark, semi-glossy; prickles pale green, straight; upright, bushy growth; PP6099; ['Little Darling' × seedling]

'Bisred' (JuJu™) Min, rb, 1996, Bischoff, Francis J.; flowers dark red with a little white at base, slow opening, medium, full, exhibition, borne in small clusters, no fragrance; foliage medium size, dark green, glossy; few prickles; upright, bushy, medium growth; ['Little Darling' × Black Jade™]; intr. 1997

'Bisyel' ('Lida O') Min, my, 1997, Bischoff, Francis J.; flowers very dbl., borne in small clusters; foliage medium size, medium green, semi-glossy; medium (23 cm.) compact growth; [Party Girl™ × 'Miss Dovie']

'Bit o' Gold' Min, dy, 1982, Williams, Ernest D.; bud ovoid; flowers deep yellow, imbricated petals, very small, 40 petals, moderate fragrance; foliage small, dark, semi-glossy; compact, bushy growth; PP5306; [seedling × 'Golden Angel']; intr. 1981

'Bit o' Magic' Min, pb, 1980, Williams, Ernest D.; bud pointed; flowers deep pink, reverse nearly white, micro-mini, 1 in., 50 petals, high-centered; foliage small, dark, glossy; compact, spreading growth; PP4729; ['Over the Rainbow' × 'Over the Rainbow']; intr. 1979

'Bit o' Spring' Min, pb, 1981, Williams, Ernest D.; bud long, pointed; flowers medium buffy pink, reverse lighter yellow-pink, 45 petals, high-centered, borne usually singly, moderate fragrance; foliage deep green, matte; prickles thin, tan curved down; upright, bushy growth; ['Tom Brown' × 'Golden Angel']; intr. 1980

'Bit o' Sunshine' ('Little Bit o' Sunshine') Min, dy, 1956, Moore, Ralph S.; flowers bright buttercup-yellow, 1½ in., 18-20 petals, moderate fragrance; bushy (12-14 in.), compact growth; PP1631; ['Copper Glow' × 'Zee']

'Bit of Honey' Min, dy, 1980, Vastine, Gilbert; flowers 48 petals; [sport of 'Sunnydew']

'Bit of Paradise' Min, m; intr. 1999

'Bitten Clausen' -- See 'Scented Memory'

'Biva' HT, pb, Ghosh; flowers large, pale pink turning deeper, dbl., high-centered, intense tea fragrance; intr. 2001

'Bizarre' HGal, m, before 1836, Calvert; flowers dark purple/pink, aging to dark purple, small to medium, full

'Bizarre Changeant' -- See 'Pourpre Marbrée'

'Bizarre Marbrée' HGal, rb, before 1848; flowers red, marbled with white

'Bizarre Triomphant(e)' -- See 'Busard Triomphant'

'Blå Måndag' -- See 'Tannacht'

'Blabee' (Betty Bee™) Min, pb, 1984, Blazey, Daniel; flowers pink, white reverse, small, dbl., high-centered, no fragrance; foliage small, medium green, semi-glossy; compact, bushy growth; PP5448; ['Little Darling' × 'Toy Clown']; intr. 1983

'Blaby Courier' HT, mr, 1956, Verschuren; bud deep crimson; flowers vivid scarlet; strong stems

'Blaby Jubilee' -- See 'Dries Verschuren'

'Blaby's Monarch' HT, lp, 1960, Verschuren; flowers rose-pink, 5-6 in., 40 petals, high-centered; foliage light green; vigorous growth; ['Briarcliff' × seedling]; intr. 1960

'Black Baccara' -- See 'Meidebenne'

Black Beauty® -- See 'Black Beauty 99'

'Black Beauty' HT, dr, 1976, Delbard; flowers garnet-red, large, dbl., slight fragrance; bushy growth; [('Gloire de Rome' × 'Impeccable') × Papa Meilland®]; intr. 1973

'Black Beauty' HT, dr, Hiroshima; intr. 1994

'Black Beauty 99' (Black Beauty®) F, rb, Kordes; flowers small, blackish red with yellow reverse, dbl., high-centered; PP11185; [sport of 'Frisco']; greenhouse rose; intr. 1999

'Black Bess' F, dr, 1939, Kordes; bud long, pointed; flowers blackish crimson, semi-dbl., high-centered, borne in clusters; foliage dark, bronze; vigorous, bushy growth; ['Dance of Joy' × 'Crimson Glory']

'Black Bourbon' B, dr

'Black Boy' ('Blackboy') LCl, dr, 1919, Clark, A.; flowers very dark red, petals satiny, 3 in., semi-dbl., moderate fragrance; foliage sparse, wrinkled, light; vigorous growth; ['Étoile de France' × 'Bardou Job']

'Black Boy' M, dr, Kordes; bud ovoid, lightly mossed; flowers deep crimson, large, very dbl., intense fragrance; non-recurrent; foliage light green, leathery; vigorous, upright, bushy growth; ['World's Fair' × 'Nuits de Young']; intr. 1958

'Black Butterfly' -- See 'Kurocho'

Black Cherry™ -- See 'Jacreflo'

'Black Delight' HT, dr, G&L; flowers deep, blackish red, dbl., well formed; free-flowering; intr. 1985

'Black Fire' Pol, dr, 1971, Delforge; bud ovoid; flowers open, medium, dbl., slight fragrance; foliage dark, soft; vigorous, bushy growth; ['Red Favorite' × seedling]

'Black Garnet' HT, dr, 1980, Weeks; bud ovoid, pointed; flowers dark, black-red, velvety, 5½ in., 50-55 petals, high-centered, borne singly or 2-3 per cluster, slight tea fragrance; foliage medium to large, moderately leathery, dark grayish-green; prickles short to medium, hooked downward; bushy, upright, branching growth; PP4738; [Mister Lincoln® × 'Mexicana']

'Black Gold' -- See 'Cleblack'

'Black Heart' Min, dr, 2006, Hopper, Nancy; flowers velvety dark red, 2 in., single, borne mostly solitary; foliage medium size, medium green, semi-glossy; growth bushy, medium (15 in.); ['Scarlet Moss' × Black Jade™]; intr. 2006

'Black Ice' F, dr, 1972, Gandy, Douglas L.; flowers 4 in., 24 petals, slight fragrance; foliage glossy, dark; [('Iceberg' × Europeana®) × 'Megiddo']

Black Jack™ -- See 'Minkco'

Black Jade™ -- See 'Benblack'

'Black Knight' HT, dr, 1934, Hillock; flowers crimson shaded blackish, 30-35 petals, moderate fragrance; foliage glossy, dark; vigorous growth; PP159; ['Ami Quinard' × 'Château de Clos Vougeot']

Black Lady® -- See 'Tanblady'

'Black Madonna' -- See 'Korschwama'

'Black Magic' -- See 'Tankalcig'

'Black Magic' -- See 'Socred'

'Black Magic' Cl HT, dr, 1953, Hamilton; flowers blackish crimson, medium, dbl., intense fragrance; occasional repeat bloom; ['Guineé' × unknown]

'Black Moss' -- See 'Nuits de Young'

Black Night® HT, dr, 1979, Huber; bud long; flowers 4 in., 26 petals; foliage dark, leathery; vigorous, upright growth; ['Fragrant Cloud' × Pharaoh®]; intr. 1975

'Black Opal' HT, dr, 1957, Ulrick, L.W.; flowers dark velvety red; ['Mirandy' × 'Tassin']

'Black Pearl' -- See 'Kuroshinju'

'Black Pearl' -- See 'Delurt'

'Black Prince' HP, dr, 1866, Paul, W.; flowers dark crimson shaded black, large, dbl., cupped; recurrent bloom; vigorous growth; ['Pierre Notting' × unknown]

'Black Ruby' LCl, mr

'Black Ruby' HT, dr, 1970, Delbard-Chabert; flowers center crimson, large, 40 petals, cupped; tall growth; ['Rome Glory' × 'Impeccable']; intr. 1965

'Black Sapphire' -- See 'Lavsaph'

'Black Satin' -- See 'Betsat'

'Black Shadow' HT, dr; intr. 2005

'Black Swan' HT, dr, Asami; intr. 1988

'Black Tarquin' Cl HT, dr, 1955, Eacott; flowers dark crimson-maroon; vigorous growth; ['Honour Bright' × 'Guinee']

'Black Tea' HT, r, 1986, Okamoto, K.; flowers brown, 32 petals, urn-shaped, borne usually singly, slight fragrance; foliage medium size, dark, semi-glossy; prickles deep brown, hooked; medium, bushy growth; ['Hawaii' × ('Aztec' × ('Goldilocks' × 'Fashion'))]; intr. 1973

'Black Velvet' -- See 'Schwarzer Samt'

'Black Velvet' HT, dr, 1960, Morey, Dr. Dennison; bud ovoid; flowers 5-5½ in., 28 petals, high-centered, intense fragrance; foliage leathery, dark; vigorous, upright growth; PP2182; ['New Yorker' × 'Happiness']; intr. 1960

'Blackberry Blossom' Pol, w, Semple; intr. 1980

'Blackberry Nip' -- See 'Somnip'

'Blackboy' -- See 'Black Boy'

'Blackout' HT, r, 2007, Edwards, Eddie and Phelps, Ethan; flowers large, full, high-centered, borne mostly solitary; foliage large, dark green, semi-glossy; few prickles; growth upright, to 6 ft.; ['Marilyn Wellan' × 'Black Magic']; intr. 2007

'Bladud' HP, pb, 1896, Cooling; flowers dark carnation, becoming coppery pink, edged silvery white, large, full, globular

'Blairii No. 1' HCh, mp, 1845, Blair; flowers bright rose, sometimes tinged red, large, semi-dbl., cupped, intense fragrance; branching growth; liable to injury from severe cold; [a China (probably 'Parks' Yellow Tea-scented China') × a hardy rose (possibly 'Tuscany')]

'Blairii No. 2' HCh, lp, 1845, Blair; flowers rosy blush, large, dbl., moderate fragrance; blooms over a long period; vigorous (up to 15 ft hardy); [a China (probably 'Parks' Yellow Tea-scented China') × a hardy rose (probably 'Tuscany')]

'Blairii No. 3' HCh, mp, 1845, Blair

'Blake Hedrick' HT, mr, 2004, Edwards, Eddie & Phelps, Ethan; flowers full, borne mostly solitary, slight fragrance; foliage medium size, dark green, glossy; prickles small; upright, medium (5 ft.) growth; exhibition; [Veterans' Honor™ × 'Hot Princess']; intr. 2005

'Blakeney's Red' HT, mr, 1962, Blakeney; bud long, pointed; flowers currant-red, base yellow, 5 in., 45 petals, high-centered; foliage leathery; moderate, bushy growth; ['Karl Herbst' × 'Peace']; intr. 1962

'Blanc à Fleurs Doubles' -- See 'Pompon

Blanc'
'Blanc à Fleurs Pleines' -- See 'Plena'
'Blanc Carné' -- See 'Shailer's White Moss'
'Blanc de Vibert' ('Blanche-Vibert') P, w, 1847, Vibert; flowers small white, full of petals, dbl., moderate damask perfume fragrance; sometimes recurrent bloom; foliage light green; slender and upright growth
'Blanc Dot' -- See 'Blanche Dot'
'Blanc Double de Coubert' HRg, w, 1892, Cochet-Cochet; bud pleasing; flowers half-open white, fairly large, semi-dbl. to dbl., intense even at night fragrance; repeat bloom; foliage very rugose; vigorous (5-7 ft.) growth; [R. rugosa × 'Sombreuil']
'Blanc Lafayette' -- See 'Dagmar Späth'
'Blanc Meillandécor' -- See 'Meicoublan'
'Blanc Ordinaire' -- See 'Plena'
'Blanc Parfait' -- See 'Pompon Blanc Parfait'
'Blanc Pierre de Ronsard' -- See 'Meiviowit'
'Blanc Pur' Misc OGR, w, 1827, Mauget; flowers pure white, large, dbl., borne in large clusters, moderate fragrance; prickles large
'Blanc Queen Elizabeth' -- See 'White Queen Elizabeth'
Blanca™ -- See 'Poulra017(N)'
'Blanca' F, w, 1966, Lens; flowers pure white, large, dbl., borne in clusters, slight fragrance; vigorous growth; ['Purpurine' × ('Papillon Rose' × 'Sterling Silver')]
'Blanca Parade' (Blanca™) MInFl, w, Poulsen; flowers white, 5-8 cm., dbl., no fragrance; foliage dark; growth bushy, 20-40 cm.; PP15084; intr. 2001
'Blanche' -- See 'Shailer's White Moss'
'Blanche' -- See 'À Coeur Jaune'
'Blanche à Coeur Jaune' -- See 'À Coeur Jaune'
'Blanche Amiet' HT, op, 1921, Turbat; flowers coppery salmon, passing to clear rose
'Blanche Anglaise' -- See 'White Bath'
Blanche Cascade® ('Cascade Blanche') S, w, Delbard; bud white with pink edge; flowers very white, semi-dbl., flat, borne in clusters, slight citronnelle fragrance; almost constant bloom; growth to 50-100 cm.; intr. 2000
Blanche Colombe® ('Ice Cool') LCl, w, Delbard; bud tinted lemon; flowers pure white, 3½-4 in., dbl., borne mostly solitary; vigorous growth; intr. 1995
'Blanche Comète' -- See 'Deloblan'
'Blanche de Bath' -- See 'White Bath'
'Blanche de Beaulieu' HP, w, 1850, Margottin; flowers white, shaded pink, full, cupped
'Blanche de Belgique' ('Blanche Superbe') A, w, before 1848; sepals long; flowers pure white, center tinted sulphur, stamens visible, very large, semi-dbl. to dbl., borne in clusters of 3-4, moderate fragrance; foliage somber grey-green, deeply dentate; tall, arching growth

'Blanche de Bernède' HP, w, 1852, Bernède; flowers pure white, large, full
'Blanche de Castille' -- See 'Jacfabco'
'Blanche de Méru' HP, w, 1869, Verdier, C.; flowers lightly blushing white, aging to pure white, large, full, borne in small clusters; ['Jules Margottin' × unknown]
'Blanche de Portemer' HP, lp, 1851, Portemer; flowers flesh white, large, full
'Blanche de Soleville' T, w, 1854, Pradel; flowers white, shaded cherry red, large, full
'Blanche d'Italie' M, w, about 1835, Prévost; flowers medium, dbl., moderate fragrance
'Blanche d'Orléans' N, w; flowers pure white, large, full
'Blanche Dot' ('Blanc Dot') HT, w, 1962, Dot, Pedro; flowers snow-white, well-formed, large, 33 petals; ['White Knight' × 'Virgo']
'Blanche Double' -- See 'Alba'
'Blanche du Roi' -- See 'Célina Dubos'
'Blanche Duranthon' -- See 'Mme Lucien Duranthon'
'Blanche Frowein' HMult, yb, 1916, Leenders, M.; flowers coppery yellow, 5-6 cm., full; remontant
'Blanche Lafitte' -- See 'Mlle Blanche Lafitte'
'Blanche Mallerin' HT, w, 1941, Mallerin, C.; bud long, pointed; flowers pure white, 4 in., 33 petals, high-centered; foliage leathery, glossy; vigorous growth; PP594; ['Edith Krause' × 'White Briarcliff']
'Blanche Messigny' HT, ly, 1923, Gillot, F.; flowers creamy yellow, large, 45 petals; vigorous, bushy growth
'Blanche Moreau' ('Blanche Roberts') M, w, 1880, Moreau et Robert; bud well mossed; flowers pure white, large, dbl., borne in clusters, moderate fragrance; some repeat bloom; lax growth; ['Comtesse de Murinais' × 'Perpetual White Moss']
'Blanche Mousseuse' -- See 'White Bath'
'Blanche Nabonnand' T, w, 1883, Nabonnand, G.; flowers creamy white tinged lemon or flesh, dbl., globular
'Blanche Neige' -- See 'Maccarpe'
'Blanche Neige' ('Koster Blanc', 'Snövit') Pol, w, 1929, Koster
'Blanche Nouvelle' -- See 'White Bath'
'Blanche Odorante' HT, w, 1952, Caron, B.; bud very long, pointed; flowers purest white, large, very dbl.; vigorous growth; ['Pole Nord' × 'Neige Parfum']
Blanche Pasca® -- See 'Pascali'
'Blanche Rebatel' ('Mlle Blanche Rebatel') Pol, pb, 1889, Bernaix, A.; flowers carmine and white
'Blanche Roberts' -- See 'Blanche Moreau'
'Blanche Semi-Double' HSpn, w, before 1819; flowers semi-dbl.
'Blanche Simon' M, w, 1862, Moreau et Robert; flowers white, green pip at center, large, dbl.
'Blanche Simple' HGal, w

'Blanche Superbe' -- See 'Blanche de Belgique'
'Blanche Unique' -- See 'White Provence'
'Blanche-Vibert' -- See 'Blanc de Vibert'
'Blanche Wimer' Min, pb, 1986, Shaw, Dr. John; flowers light yellow and pink blend, 66 petals, cupped, borne usually singly, slight fruity fragrance; foliage medium size, medium green, semi-glossy; prickles slightly hooked, reddish-green; tall, upright growth; no fruit; ['Pink Petticoat' × seedling]
'Blanchefleur' C, w, 1835, Vibert; sepals long; flowers white tinted blush, medium, dbl., cupped and quartered, borne in clusters of 4-8, intense fragrance; foliage gray-green, oblong-pointed; prickles moderate; broad, vigorous growth
'Blanda' -- See 'Agathe Incarnata'
'Blanda Egreta' HMult, mp, 1926, Bruder Alfons; flowers single; nearly thornless; [sport of 'Tausendschön']
'Blandford Rose' (R. parviflora provincialis) HGal, mp, about 1791
'Blandine Choupette' HT, rb; flowers white with red edges, double, high-centered, intense fragrance; recurrent; moderate growth; intr. 2000
'Blanik' F, dr, Vecera, L.; flowers medium, dbl.; intr. 1964
'Blarney' Cl HT, mp, 1934, Howard Rose Co.; flowers pink, base apricot, dbl.; recurrent bloom; foliage leathery, dark; vigorous, climbing growth; [sport of 'Irish Charm']
'Blässe Niederlandische Rose' -- See 'Agathe Incarnata'
Blastoff™ -- See 'Morflash'
'Blatenskà Kràlovna' ('Königin von Blatna') HWich, mp, 1937, Böhm, J.; flowers dbl.
'Blatná' HT, dr, 1927, Böhm, J.; flowers velvety dark red, dbl.; dwarf growth; ['Lieutenant Chauré' × 'Oskar Cordel']
'Blaue Adria' HT, mr; intr. 2002
'Blauwe Donau' ('Blue Danube') F, m, 1975, Verschuren, Ted; bud ovoid; flowers open, 3 in., 10-12 petals, intense fragrance; foliage glossy; bushy growth; [Orangeade® × 'Sterling Silver']; intr. 1973
'Blaydon Races' F, yb, 1976, Wood; flowers scarlet shading to yellow, 2½ in.; foliage glossy, dark, leathery; vigorous, tall, upright growth; ['Bobby Shafto' × ('Arthur Bell' × Piccadilly®)]
'Blaze' LCl, mr, 1932, Kallay; flowers bright scarlet, 2-3 in., 20-25 petals, cupped, borne in large clusters; recurrent bloom; foliage leathery, dark; very vigorous, climbing growth; PP10; distributed as 'Paul's Scarlet Climber' × 'Gruss an Teplitz', but may be a sport of the former
'Blaze Away' F, or, 1979, Sanday, John; bud pointed; flowers scarlet-vermilion, large, 7 petals; vigorous, bushy growth; [('Karl Herbst' × 'Crimson Glory') × Sarabande®]

'Blaze Improved' -- See 'Demokracie'

'Blaze of Glory' LCl, ob, Zary, Keith; bud pointed ovoid; flowers bright coral/orange/red, 4 in., 25 petals, cupped, slight musk fragrance; recurrent; foliage dark green, glossy; vigorous (12-14 ft.) growth; PP17791; [Dream Weaver™ × Dynamite™]; intr. 2004

'Blaze Superier' -- See 'Demokracie'

'Blazing Lights' HT, ob, K&S; intr. 1995

'Bleak House' HRg, dp, Irvine, Susan; flowers rich, clear pink , 5 cm., semidouble, flat, moderate sweet fragrance; recurrent; 4 ft. × 4 ft. growth; Seedling discovered in Susan Irvine's garden; intr. 1995

'Blebar' ('Wagbi') F, ob, 1981, Barrett, F.H.; bud pointed; flowers orange-pink, 20 petals, hybrid tea, opening flat, borne 3 - 5 per cluster, moderate fragrance; free-flowering; foliage large, dark green; prickles large, red; vigorous, upright growth

'Blenheim' -- See 'Tanmurse'

'Bles Bridges' HT, dr, Kordes; flowers dark red, slow to open, good petal substance, 3-4 in., 28-33 petals, exhibition, no fragrance; dark green, glossy foliage; short stems; growth to 3-4 ft.; intr. 1996

'Blésine' -- See 'Blessings'

'Blesma Soul' HT, lp, 1981, Anderson's Rose Nurseries; bud long, pointed; flowers 36 petals, borne singly or in small clusters, intense fragrance; foliage light green; prickles large based, reddish-brown; upright growth; [Pascali® × 'Fragrant Cloud']; intr. 1982

'Bless My Time' Gr, lp, 1983, Orr, Rudolph F.; flowers clear light pink, veins sometimes darker; [sport of Queen Elizabeth®]

'Blessed Child' S, pb; intr. 2008

'Blessed Event' -- See 'Lavfun'

'Blessings, Climbing' Cl HT, op, Gregory; flowers salmon, fading to soft pink, dbl., high-centered; foliage dark green; strong growth, 8 ft. and greater; intr. 1972

Blessings® ('Blésine') HT, op, 1967, Gregory; flowers medium coral-salmon, large, 30 petals, high-centered, moderate fragrance; [Queen Elizabeth® × seedling]; intr. 1968

'Blestogil' ('St John Ogilvie') S, pb, 1982, Ogilvie, W.D.; intr. 1986

'Bleu' -- See 'Busard Triomphant'

'Bleu Céleste' -- See 'Celestial'

'Bleu Magenta' -- See 'Bleu Violette'

'Bleu Violette' ('Bleu Magenta') HMult, m, 1900, Van Houtte; flowers dark crimson-purple, sometimes flecked white, 6-7 cm., dbl., flat, borne in medium clusters, moderate fragrance; foliage dark; nearly thornless; ['Turner's Crimson Rambler' × unknown]; French origin; 'Bleu Violette' probably has precedence as correct name

'Blickfang' F, dr, VEG; flowers reddish-violet, large, very dbl.

'Bliss' -- See 'Beabliss'

'Blithe Spirit' HT, lp, 1964, Armstrong, D. L. & Swim, H. C.; flowers medium, dbl., slight fragrance; foliage leathery; vigorous, spreading, upright growth; PP2653; ['Fandango' × seedling]; intr. 1964

'Blizzard' -- See 'Jacdrift'

'Bloemfontein' -- See 'Kortrolle'

'Blöhm & Voss' F, or; flowers bright orange-scarlet good trusses

Blois™ S, w, Olesen; bud pointed ovoid; flowers pure white, 4 cm., 25 petals, high-centered, then flat, borne in clusters of 3 - 7, slight floral fragrance; free-flowering; foliage semi-glossy; prickles few, 8 mm., hooked downward; upright (3 ft.), bushy growth; PP15810; [Bernina® × seedling]; intr. 2003

'Blonde Bombshell' F, my, 1995, Bees of Chester; flowers medium yellow, fading to pale yellow with pink edging, full, borne in small clusters, slight fragrance; medium size, dark green, glossy foliage; numerous prickles; growth strong, bushy, upright grower to 3 ft.; intr. 1995

'Blondie' -- See 'Lapdil'

'Blondie' -- See 'Jacliy'

'Blondine' HT, lp, 1954, Grillo; bud pointed, globular; flowers blush-pink, 4 in., 60 petals; foliage leathery; upright growth; [sport of 'Catalina']

'Blondine' Cl HT, w, Arles; flowers pearl-white, well-formed, large; foliage clear green; vigorous growth; ['Comtesse Vandal, Climbing' × 'Michèle Meilland, Climbing']

'Blood' -- See 'Hector'

'Blood d'Angleterre' -- See 'Hector'

'Blood-red China Rose' -- See 'Sanguinea'

'Bloodstone' HT, or, 1951, McGredy, Sam IV; flowers large, 24 petals, high-centered; foliage dark, coppery green; vigorous growth; ['The Queen Alexandra Rose' × 'Lord Charlemont']

'Bloomer Girl' -- See 'Tingirl'

'Bloomerick' HGal, m, before 1845, Calvert; flowers light lilac pink, aging lighter, medium, full

Bloomfest™ -- See 'Judfest'

'Bloomfield Abundance' ('Shrub Cecile Brunner') F, lp, 1920, Thomas; flowers light salmon-pink, dbl.; foliage glossy, dark; bushy growth; ['Sylvia (rambler, Paul, 1912)' × 'Dorothy Page-Roberts']

'Bloomfield Acrobat' HT, dp, 1929, Thomas; flowers full, moderate fragrance; ['Mme Abel Chatenay' × 'Mme Butterfly']

'Bloomfield Beauty' HT, op, 1929, Thomas; flowers carmine-orange, large, full, moderate fragrance; ['Bloomfield Exquisite' × 'Hoosier Beauty']

'Bloomfield Beverly' HT, or, 1924, Thomas; flowers orange-crimson, dbl.; vigorous growth; ['Mary, Countess of Ilchester' × 'Mme Edouard Herriot']

'Bloomfield Brilliant' LCl, op, 1931, Thomas; flowers light salmon with orange glow, large, 18 petals; vigorous growth; ['Mme Abel Chatenay' × 'Kitty Kininmonth']

'Bloomfield Comet' HMsk, op, 1924, Thomas; bud long, pointed, reddish orange; flowers orange, base yellow, large, 5 petals; foliage sparse, light bronze, soft; ['Duchess of Wellington' × 'Danaë']

'Bloomfield Completeness' HMsk, ab, 1931, Thomas; flowers deep orange-yellow, dbl., moderate fragrance; continuous; ['Bloomfield Perfection' × 'Mme Butterfly']

'Bloomfield Courage' HWich, rb, 1925, Thomas; flowers dark velvety red, center white, prominent yellow stamens, 3 cm., single, borne in medium to large clusters, no fragrance; non-recurrent; foliage dark; few prickles; vigorous, climbing or pillar (20 ft.) growth; hips small, red

'Bloomfield Culmination' HMsk, pb, 1924, Thomas; bud long, pointed; flowers rose-pink, center white, 3 in., single; recurrent bloom; foliage leathery; moderately vigorous growth; ['Sheila Wilson' × 'Danaë']

'Bloomfield Dainty' HMsk, my, 1924, Thomas; bud long, pointed, deep orange; flowers clear canary-yellow, 2 in., single, moderate fragrance; foliage glossy; moderately vigorous growth; ['Danaë' × 'Mme Edouard Herriot']

'Bloomfield Dawn' HMsk, pb, 1931, Thomas; bud long, slender, rose-pink; flowers light pink, base yellow, reverse deep pink, large, semi-dbl.; long, strong stems; ['a climbing rose' × 'Bloomfield Progress']

'Bloomfield Decoration' HMsk, pb, 1925, Thomas; flowers cerise-pink, center white, prominent golden stamens, open, single; foliage glossy; ['Sylvia' × 'Arndt']; intr. 1927

'Bloomfield Discovery' HMsk, pb, 1925, Thomas; flowers pink, reverse darker, large, single; foliage dark; moderately vigorous growth; ['Danaë' × ('Frau Karl Druschki' × 'Mme Caroline Testout')]

'Bloomfield Dream' T, pb, 1924, Thomas; flowers medium pink with saffron yellow, reverse pink with wine-red, dbl., moderate fragrance; ['Rêve d'Or' × unknown]

'Bloomfield Endurance' -- See 'W. Freeland Kendrick'

'Bloomfield Experiment' Cl HP, my, 1929, Thomas; flowers citron yellow, full, slight fragrance; ['Frau Karl Druschki' × 'Frau Ida Münch']

'Bloomfield Exquisite' Cl HT, mp, 1924, Thomas; flowers clear pink, dbl.; recurrent bloom; vigorous growth; ['Gloire de Dijon' × 'Gruss an Teplitz']

'Bloomfield Fascination' HMsk, ly, 1924, Thomas; flowers light canary yellow, small, dbl.; foliage rich bronze green, soft; ['Danaë' × 'Mme Laurette Messimy']

'Bloomfield Favorite' HMsk, w, 1924, Thomas; bud deep salmon; flowers pinkish cream, 1½ in., dbl.; ['Debutante' × 'Moonlight']; sometimes classed as

HWich
'Bloomfield Flame' HT, rb, 1930, Thomas; bud long, pointed, flame-red; flowers crimson-flame, center orange-yellow, large, 22 petals, moderate spicy fragrance; foliage leathery, glossy, dark bronze; vigorous, bushy growth; ['Louise Crette' × 'Mme Charles Lutaud']
'Bloomfield Giant' HT, op, 1929, Thomas; flowers silvery salmon pink, large, very full, moderate fragrance; ['Mme Abel Chatenay' × 'Mme Butterfly']
'Bloomfield Gipsy' T, ob, 1929, Thomas; flowers shining orange, full; ['Rêve d'Or' × 'Rosomane Narcisse Thomas']
'Bloomfield Gold' T, ob, 1929, Thomas; flowers coppery orange; ['Gloire de Dijon' × 'Rosomane Narcisse Thomas']
'Bloomfield Improvement' -- See 'Ednah Thomas'
'Bloomfield Loveliness' -- See 'Sophie Thomas'
'Bloomfield Lustre' LCl, op, 1931, Thomas; flowers salmon-pink, base yellow, dbl.; ['Hortulanus Budde' × 'Souv. de Mme Léonie Viennot']
'Bloomfield Magic' LCl, op, 1924, Thomas; flowers light salmon to cream, flat; moderately vigorous growth; ['Gloire de Dijon' × 'Frau Berta Gurtler']
'Bloomfield Mystery' LCl, lp, 1924, Thomas; flowers silver-pink, tinged yellow, 2 in., flat; moderately vigorous growth; ['Blanche Frowein' × 'Bloomfield Abundance']
'Bloomfield Perfection' HMsk, w, 1925, Thomas; bud ovoid, orange and pink; flowers cream-yellow suffused lilac, large, dbl.; recurrent bloom; ['Danaë' × 'Bloomfield Abundance']; intr. 1927
'Bloomfield Perpetual' HP, w, 1920, Thomas; flowers resembling R. laevigata, single; ['Iceberg' × 'Frau Karl Druschki']
'Bloomfield Progress' HT, mr, 1920, Thomas; flowers glowing red, dbl.; vigorous growth; ['Mary, Countess of Ilchester' × 'General MacArthur']
'Bloomfield Quakeress' Cl T, ly, 1931, Thomas; flowers small, semi-dbl.; free recurrent bloom; foliage glossy, light; long stems; vigorous growth; ['Safrano' × unknown]
'Bloomfield Rocket' LCl, dp, 1925, Thomas; flowers dark pink, center lighter, very large, single; very vigorous (6-8 ft.) growth; ['Mme Caroline Testout' × 'Ulrich Brunner Fils']
'Bloomfield Ruby' Cl HT, mr, 1929, Thomas; flowers ruby red, large; ['Hortulanus Budde' × 'Souv de Mme Leonie Viennot']
'Bloomfield Star' Cl Pol, ob, 1929, Thomas; flowers orange with canary yellow
'Bloomfield Success' HT, ob, 1929, Thomas; flowers orange with canary yellow to creamy yellow, shaded lilac, dbl., moderate fragrance; ['Laurette Messimy' × 'Danae']

'Bloomfield Vanity' HFt, or, 1929, Thomas; flowers coral-red, large; ['Rêve d'Or' × 'Lutea hybrid']
'Bloomfield Velvet' Cl HT, mr, 1929, Thomas; flowers large, full, moderate fragrance; ['Crimson Queen' × 'Kitty Kininmonth']
'Bloomfield Victory' HWich, lp, 1929, Thomas; flowers light flesh pink, tinted darker pink, slight fragrance; ['Aviateur Blériot' × 'Yvonne Rabier']
'Bloomfield Volcano' HFt, mr, 1929, Thomas; flowers dark fiery red, large, semi-dbl.; ['Louise Crettè' × 'The Queen Alexandra Rose']
Bloomin' Easy™ -- See 'Arotrusim'
'Bloomin' Pretty' LCl, w, Williams, J. Benjamin; flowers white with pale pink paint, semi-dbl.; intr. 1999
'Blooming Carpet' -- See 'Noatraum'
'Blooming Marvelous' Min, dp
'Bloomsday' F, ob, 1981, McCann, Sean; flowers orange, marked brown, reverse deep gold, 28 petals, loose , borne in clusters of 4-5, moderate fragrance; foliage matte, green; prickles straight, red-brown; vigorous, upright growth; ['Belinda' × ('Maxi' × 'Joyfulness')]
'Bloomtown' -- See 'Talblo'
'Blossom' HT, pb, 1925, Beckwith; flowers red over peach-pink, reverse pinkish yellow
'Blossom Blanket' -- See 'Dicwhynot'
'Blossom Hill' F, ob, 1957, Kordes; flowers orange, 2½ in., 10 petals, cupped, borne in clusters; foliage dark, glossy; vigorous, upright, bushy growth
'Blossom Magic' -- See 'Meimanoir'
'Blossomtime' LCl, mp, 1951, O'Neal; bud pointed; flowers pink, reverse deeper, 4 in., 38 petals, high-centered, borne in small clusters, intense fragrance; repeat bloom; tall shrub or moderate climbing (6-7 ft.) growth; PP1240; ['New Dawn' × 'a hybrid tea']
'Blue Angel' -- See 'Renangel'
Blue Bajou® ('Blue Bayou', 'Blue-Bijou') F, m, Kordes; flowers silvery lilac to lavender blue with large, rounded petals, dbl., rounded, slight fragrance; dark green, glossy foliage; opens like a water lily; intr. 1993
'Blue Bajou, Climbing' ClF, m, Ichibashi; intr. 1998
'Blue Bayou' -- See 'Blue Bajou'
Blue Bell™ ('Blue Bells', Bluebell®, Martinez®) HT, rb, Meilland; bud conical, large; flowers currant red with magenta reverse, 4-5 in., 20-25 petals, cupped, borne mostly singly, no fragrance; good repeat; foliage medium size, medium green, semi-glossy; numerous prickles; erect (4-5 ft.) growth; PP10948; ['Livia' × ('White Success' × Candia™)]; greenhouse rose; intr. 1997
'Blue Bells' -- See 'Meinalpir'
'Blue-Bijou' -- See 'Blue Bajou'
'Blue Bird' F, m, Dey, S. C.; flowers blue-violet, borne in large clusters; [sport of 'Fraternity'; intr. 1989

'Blue Bird' HT, Poulsen
'Blue Boy' M, m, 1959, Kordes; bud ovoid; flowers deep reddish-violet, large, dbl., high-centered, intense fragrance; non-recurrent; foliage light green, glossy; vigorous (3 ft.), upright, bushy growth; ['Louis Grimmard' × 'Independence']; intr. 1958
'Blue Boy' S, m, Interplant; groundcover; spreading growth; intr. 2001
'Blue Boy' HT, m
'Blue Carpet' -- See 'Harquillypond'
'Blue Chateau' HT, m, 1999, Teranishi, K.; flowers pale violet, 50 petals, high-centered; growth to 4 ft.; ['Madame Violet' × seedling]; intr. 1994
'Blue Chip' -- See 'Jacave'
'Blue Cupido' Min, m, deRuiter; PP9735; intr. 2003
'Blue Curiosa' HT, m, Pouw; PP10918; originally a greenhouse rose.; intr. 1997
'Blue Danube' -- See 'Blauwe Donau'
'Blue Delight' HT, m, Kasturi; flowers orchid mauve, dbl., intense fragrance; intr. 1980
'Blue Diamond' HT, m, 1963, Lens; flowers lavender, 4 in., 35 petals; foliage dark, coppery; vigorous, compact, bushy growth; ['Purpurine' × ('Purpurine' × 'Royal Tan')]
'Blue Fairy' S, m, Kordes; flowers lavender, semi-dbl., borne in clusters; intr. 2004
'Blue For You' -- See 'Pejamblu'
'Blue Friendship' S, m, Verschuren; flowers small, semi-dbl.; repeats well; groundcover; spreading growth; intr. 1984
'Blue Girl, Climbing' -- See 'Kölner Karneval, Climbing'
'Blue Girl' -- See 'Cologne Carnival'
'Blue Glow' HT, m, 1983, Cattermole, R.F.; bud pointed; flowers pinkish-mauve, 45 petals, high-centered, borne singly and 3-5 per cluster, slight fragrance; foliage light green; prickles light brown, triangular; upright, branching growth; ['Silent Night' × Blue Moon®]
'Blue Heaven' ('My Blue Heaven') HT, m, 1971, Whisler, D.; bud ovoid; flowers large, dbl., high-centered, intense fragrance; foliage large, glossy; vigorous, upright growth; PP3818; [('Sterling Silver' × 'Simone') × 'Song of Paris']; patent application says parentage is Simone × Sterling Silver
'Blue Ice' -- See 'Lavchip'
'Blue Jay' F, m
Blue Lady® LCl, m, Moore; intr. 2007
'Blue Light' HT, m, Ito, R.; flowers mauve-pink, reverse deeper, 13 cm., 25 petals, high-centered, borne mostly solitary, intense fragrance; foliage large, dark green, semi-glossy; prickles pointing slightly downward, moderate; growth tall; ['Madame Violet' × 'Lady Luck']; intr. 1995
'Blue Magenta' HT, m; intr. 2002
'Blue Magic' HT, m, Dot, Pedro; intr.

1955
'Blue Magic' Min, m; intr. 1986
'Blue Margrethe' HWich, m; from Germany
'Blue Mist' Min, m, 1975, Moore, Ralph S.; bud short, rounded; flowers soft pink to lavender, micro-mini, small, 23 petals, intense fragrance; foliage soft; vigorous, bushy, rounded growth; [seedling × seedling]; intr. 1970
'Blue Monday, Climbing' -- See 'Blue Moon, Climbing'
'Blue Monday' -- See 'Tannacht'
Blue Moon® ('Blå Måndag', 'Blue Monday', 'Mainzer Fastnacht', 'Sissi') HT, m, 1965, Tantau, Math.; bud long, pointed; flowers lilac, 4 in., 40 petals, intense fragrance; vigorous growth; [('Sterling Silver' × unknown) × seedling]; intr. 1964
'Blue Moon, Climbing' ('Blue Monday, Climbing', 'Sissi, Climbing', 'Mainzer Fastnacht, Climbing') Cl HT, m, 1981, Mungia (also Jackson, 1978); flowers lilac mauve, 12 cm., dbl., strong fragrance; PP5049; [sport of 'Blue Moon']
Blue Nile® -- See 'Delnible'
'Blue Ocean' HT, m, Hande, Dr Y. K.; flowers light mauve with deeper edges, dbl., high-centered; intr. 1983
'Blue Ovation' Min, m, deRuiter; intr. 2000
Blue Parfum® -- See 'Tanfifum'
'Blue Perfume' -- See 'Tanfifum'
'Blue Peter' -- See 'Ruiblun'
'Blue Rambler' -- See 'Veilchenblau'
'Blue Ribbon' -- See 'Arolical'
'Blue River' HT, m, 1974, Kordes; bud long, pointed; flowers mauve-magenta, large, dbl., cupped, intense fragrance; foliage glossy; vigorous, upright growth; RULED EXTINCT 6/84 ARM; ['Mainzer Fastnacht' × 'Silver Star']; intr. 1973
Blue River® -- See 'Korsicht'
'Blue Rosalie' -- See 'Veilchenblau'
'Blue Skies' -- See 'Bucblu'
'Blue Sky' ('Cel Blau') HT, m, Dot; flowers lavender, high-centered, moderate fragrance; intr. 1982
'Blue Sky' -- See 'Aozora'
'Blue Star, Climbing' Cl HT, m, 1963, Thompson, M.L.; flowers lavender-blue, small, dbl., flat, borne in clusters, slight fragrance; profuse, non-recurrent bloom; foliage glossy; vigorous (8 ft.) growth; PP2448
'Blue Star' LCl, m, Clements, John; flowers old fashioned style, lavender and purple, 3 in., 50 petals, cupped, intense expensive perfume fragrance; blue-green foliage; growth to 8-10 ft.; intr. 2003
'Blue Time' HT, m, Teranishi; intr. 2005
'Blue Violet' HT, m, Perry; intr. 1981
'Blue Work' HT, m
Bluebell® -- See 'Meinalpir'
Blueberry Hill™ -- See 'Wekcryplag'
Blueblood™ -- See 'Lavblu'
'Bluenette' -- See 'Ruiblun'
Blues™ LCl, mp, Poulsen; flowers medium pink, 5-8 cm., 25 petals, no fragrance; foliage dark; growth bushy, 100-150 cm.; intr. 2004
Bluesette® -- See 'Lenmau'
'Bluewunder' -- See 'Flower Power'
'Blühendes Barock' F, mp, Noack, Werner; intr. 1997
Blühwunder® -- See 'Flower Power'
'Blumen Dankert' HMult, mp, 1904, Kiese; flowers carmine-pink, 3½ cm., dbl., borne in large clusters, no fragrance; few prickles; growth vigorous, upright (3 m.)
'Blumenschmidt' T, yb, 1906, Schmidt, J.C.; flowers primrose-yellow, outer petals rose-pink, full; [sport of 'Mlle Franziska Kruger']
'Blumenschmidt's Elfenkönigin' HT, w, 1939, Weigand, C.; flowers ivory-white, center orange, very large, dbl., high-centered, moderate lily-of-the-valley fragrance; long, strong stems; bushy, dwarf growth; ['Ophelia' × 'Julien Potin']
'Blumenschmidts Sonntagskind' F, mp, 1945, Vonholdt; flowers medium, dbl.
'Blush' M, m, before 1838, Hooker; flowers lilac blush, medium, dbl.; foliage very dense; growth erect
Blush™ Min, mp, Olesen; flowers dbl., 25-30 petals, no fragrance; foliage medium green, semi-glossy; growth bushy, very low (20-40 cm.); intr. 2000
'Blush' HT, ob, Pressman; flowers 35 petals, borne mostly singly; recurrent; upright growth; intr. 2007
'Blush Baby' Min, Pearce, C.A.; intr. 1986
'Blush Belgic' -- See 'Blush Belgiques'
'Blush Belgiques' ('Belgic Blush', 'Belgica Flore Rubricante', 'Blush Belgic', 'La Grande Belgique', 'Belgic Provence', 'Belgic Rose') A, lp; flowers blush pink, large, dbl.
'Blush Boursault' -- See 'Calypso'
'Blush China' HCh, lp, 1903, Cant, B. R.; flowers medium, semi-dbl.
'Blush Damask' ('Blush Gallica') D, lp, before 1806; flowers center rose, shading to pale blush on outside petals, small, dbl., quartered, moderate fragrance; non-recurrent; foliage dark green, elliptical, with 5-7 leaflets
'Blush Flower Circus' F, lp, Kordes; flowers pale pink, full, cupped, borne in clusters; recurrent; foliage dark green; short growth; intr. 2008
'Blush Gallica' -- See 'Blush Damask'
'Blush Hip' ('New Blush Hip') A, lp, before 1846; flowers delicate soft pink, green eye, medium, dbl., flat, borne singly and in clusters of 3-6; foliage gray-green, deeply dentate; growth vigorous, branching; a form of Cuisse de Nymphe, according to G.S. Thomas
'Blush Knock Out' -- See 'Radyod'
'Blush Maman Cochet' -- See 'William R. Smith'
'Blush Monthly' -- See 'Old Pink Daily'
'Blush Moss' M, lp, before 1854; flowers blush, center pinkish when first open, well-mossed, large, dbl., cupped; moderate branching growth
'Blush Musk' -- See 'Fraser's Pink Musk'
'Blush Noisette' ('Flesh-Coloured Noisette') N, w, before 1817, Noisette; bud crimson; flowers pinkish white, tinted lilac, edges lighter, 4 cm., cupped, borne in large, upright clusters, moderate fragrance; recurrent; foliage dark; nearly thornless; stems reddish; growth vigorous (8-10 ft.); ['Champneys' Pink Cluster' × unknown]
'Blush o' Dawn' -- See 'Flush o' Dawn'
Blush of Success™ F, pb, Poulsen; flowers pink blend, 5-8 cm., dbl., no fragrance; growth bushy, 60-100 cm.; PP15053; intr. 2003
'Blush Queen' HT, lp, 1924, Cant, F.; flowers blush-pink, dbl.
'Blush Rambler' HMult, lp, 1903, Cant, B. R.; flowers blush-pink, pale at the center, 4 cm., semi-dbl., cupped, borne in large clusters; non-recurrent; vigorous, climbing (10-12 ft.) growth; ['Crimson Rambler' × 'The Garland']
Blushing Akito® HT, lp, Tantau; flowers soft pink, medium to large, double, high-centered, borne mostly singly; recurrent; foliage dark green, glossy; stems moderate to long; [sport of 'Akito']; florist rose; intr. 2007
'Blushing Beauty' -- See 'Dykpink'
'Blushing Beauty' LCl, lp, 1934, Burbank; flowers three-toned shell-pink, very large; very vigorous growth
'Blushing Blue' -- See 'Renblue'
'Blushing Bride' HT, W, 1930, Joseph H. Hill, Co.; flowers white tinged pink, large, dbl., intense fragrance; vigorous growth; RULED EXTINCT 5/90; ['Mme Butterfly' × 'Premier']
Blushing Bride™ F, lp, Harkness; intr. 1998
'Blushing Bride' HT, w, 1918, Dickson, H.; flowers white, center blush, dbl.; RULED EXTINCT 5/90
'Blushing Bride' -- See 'Greblub'
'Blushing Cheeks' HT, mp, Dickson; intr. 1970
'Blushing Dawn' -- See 'Weeblush'
'Blushing Groom' -- See 'Seagru'
'Blushing Jewel' Min, lp, 1959, Morey, Dr. Dennison; bud ovoid; flowers blush-pink, overcast rose-pink, open, ½-¾ in., 45-50 petals, moderate fragrance; low, compact growth; PP1906; ['Dick Koster' × 'Tom Thumb']; intr. 1958
'Blushing June' -- See 'Lecblu'
Blushing Knock Out™ ('Blush Knock Out', 'Blushing Knockout') S, lp, Bell, John; flowers light pink aging to shell pink, medium, single, cupped to flat, borne singly and in small clusters, no fragrance; free-flowering; foliage mossy green with blue hues; prickles mostly on lower portions of canes; compact (2-3 ft.), spreading growth; PP14700; [sport of 'Knock Out']; intr. 2004
'Blushing Knockout' -- See 'Radyod'
'Blushing Lucy' HWich, lp, 1938, Wil-

liams, A.; flowers pale pink with a white eye, semi-dbl., borne in large clusters; profuse, late bloom; foliage glossy; growth vigorous

'Blushing Maid' -- See 'Mackepa'

'Blushing Panarosa' S, lp, Delbard; intr. 2004

'Blushing Pink Iceberg' -- See 'Pink Iceberg'

'Blushing Queen' ('Queen Elizabeth Blush') Gr, w, 1976, Baker, Larry; bud pointed; flowers near white, center blush-pink, 38-40 petals, high-centered; vigorous, upright growth; [sport of Queen Elizabeth®]

'Blushing Rose' -- See 'Coy Colleen'

Blushing Yuki™ -- See 'Virsilver'

'Blutpurpurne Rose' -- See 'Sanguineo-Purpurea Simplex'

'Blythe Spirit' -- See 'Auschool'

'Bo' HT, op, Pekmez, Paul; intr. 1997

'Bo-Peep' ('Bopeep') Min, mp, 1950, deVink; bud ovoid, pointed; flowers rose-pink, micro-mini, very small, 28 petals, cupped, slight fragrance; foliage small, glossy; bushy, dwarf (5-8 in.) growth; PP976; ['Cécile Brunner' × 'Tom Thumb']

'Boadicea' T, mp, 1901, Paul, W.; flowers creamy pink edged with rose, large, dbl., moderate fragrance; growth vigorous

'Boardwalk' HT, pb, 2004, Edwards, Eddie & Phelps, Ethan; flowers pink blend, reverse pink blend, 4-5 in, full, borne mostly solitary; foliage dark green, semi-glossy; prickles small, hooked,; growth upright, medium; exhibition; ['White Success' × 'Hot Princess']; intr. 2005

'Bob & Linda' -- See 'Silfairknerr'

'Bob Collard' F, mr, 1987, Turley, V.G.; flowers very luminous, brilliant red, reverse deeper red, medium, 11 petals, cupped, borne singly or in sprays of 5-10, slight fruity fragrance; foliage medium size, medium green, glossy; upright, bushy, medium growth; hips round, cupped, average, red; ['Happiness' × 'Copenhagen']

'Bob Davison' HP, mr, before 1910, Dickson, A.; bud large; flowers glossy scarlet, shaded crimson, large, very full

'Bob Fleming' F, w, Fleming; intr. 2004

'Bob Greaves' -- See 'Fryzippy'

'Bob Hope' HT, mr, 1966, Kordes, R.; bud urn-shaped; flowers scarlet red, 6 in., 35-40 petals, high-centered, borne mostly singly, intense damask fragrance; foliage dark, leathery; vigorous, tall, upright growth; PP2734; ['Friedrich Schwartz' × 'Kordes' Perfecta']

'Bob Kennedy' HT, Ingegnoli

'Bob Thomas' -- See 'Webwarm'

'Bob Woolley' HT, ab, 1970, Sanday, John; flowers peach-pink, reverse lemon, 5 in., 60 petals, slight fragrance; foliage matte, green; ['Gavotte' × 'Golden Scepter']

'Bobbie B' -- See 'Worcamp'

'Bobbie Darlene' HT, lp, 2001, Caruthers, Carlton & Bobbie; flowers medium to large, full, high-centered, borne mostly solitary, slight fragrance; foliage medium size, medium green, semi-glossy; growth upright, medium; garden decorative, exhibition; [sport of 'Touch of Class']; intr. 2004

'Bobbie James' HWich, w, 1970, Thomas, G. S.; flowers creamy white, 2 in., 7-9 petals, cupped, borne in large clusters, intense fragrance; foliage large, glossy; vigorous growth; intr. 1961

'Bobbie Lucas' F, op, 1967, McGredy, Sam IV; flowers deep salmon-orange, well-formed, large, borne in clusters; foliage dark; ['Margot Fonteyn' × Elizabeth of Glamis®]

'Bobbie Robbie' -- See 'Souv de J. Chabert'

'Bobbie Vesely' -- See 'Resbobie'

'Bobbink White Climber' LCl, w, 1951, Jacobus; flowers creamy yellow to pure white, 3 in., 45-50 petals, moderate fragrance; recurrent bloom; foliage dark, glossy; vigorous, climbing growth; PP1163; ['Dream Girl' × seedling]

'Bobby Charlton' HT, pb, 1975, Fryer, Gareth; flowers deep pink, reverse silver, well-formed, 6 in., 38 petals, moderate spicy fragrance; foliage dark, leathery; ['Royal Highness' × 'Prima Ballerina']; intr. 1974

'Bobby Dazzler' ('Rosella') F, ab, 1972, Harkness; flowers blush, shaded rich apricot, 3 in., 50 petals, slight fragrance; foliage small, matte; [('Vera Dalton' × 'Highlight') × ('Ann Elizabeth' × 'Circus')]

'Bobby Shafto' HT, my, 1967, Wood; [sport of 'Piccadilly']

'Bobino' F, mr; flowers bright scarlet red

'Bobo' HT, mr, 1980, Perry, Astor; bud long; flowers 30 petals, urn-shaped, borne singly, intense fruity fragrance; intr. 1981

'Bobolink' Min, dp, 1960, Moore, Ralph S.; flowers rose-pink, base near white, 1-1½ in., 50 petals, slight fruity fragrance; foliage leathery, glossy; vigorous, bushy (18 in.) growth; PP2009; [(R. wichurana × Floradora) × ('Oakington Ruby' × 'Floradora')]; intr. 1959

'Bobo's Rose' -- See 'Rawfling'

'Bobravka' S, op, Urban, J.; flowers dark orange-pink with red tones, medium, dbl.; intr. 1975

'Bobrinski' -- See 'Comte de Bobrinsky'

'Bob's Peach' -- See 'Webbread'

'Bocca Negra' HMult, dr, 1910, Dubreuil; flowers purple-crimson, center white, 3-5 cm., cupped, borne in medium to large clusters, moderate musky fragrance; vigorous growth

'Boccaccio' F, or, 1965, Verschuren, A.; flowers bright scarlet-red, large, 30-40 petals, borne in clusters; foliage glossy; vigorous, upright growth; ['Atombombe' × seedling]; intr. 1963

'Boccace' HP, dp, 1859, Moreau et Robert; flowers bright carmine, large, full; foliage dark, rough

'Bocher' HT, pb, 1990, Rodgers, Shafner R.; flowers very dbl.; foliage medium size, medium green, matte; upright growth; ['Prima Ballerina' × Alec's Red®]

'Bocrogosnif' ('Sniffer') HRg, m, 2004, Bock, Chuck; flowers beet purple with white eye and white streaks, 4 in., semi-dbl., borne in small clusters, intense clove fragrance; remontant; foliage medium size, dark green, glossy, disease-resistant; prickles straight; growth bushy, wide, dense, short (33 in.); landscape, borders; hips red; hardy; ['hybrid rugosa seedling' × 'miniature seedling']; intr. 2006

'Bocrugostre' ('Streaker') HRg, m, 2004, Bock, Chuck; flowers frosted orchid, reverse orchid, streaked, white eye, 4½ in., dbl., borne in small clusters, intense clove fragrance; recurrent; foliage large, dark green, semi-glossy; prickles straight; bushy, wide, dense growth; landscape, borders; hips orange-red; winter hardy; ['hybrid rugosa seedling' × 'miniature seedling']

'Bodhisatva' -- See 'Virsplash'

Boeing® HT, w; flowers 10 cm., 30-35 petals, high-centered; greenhouse rose; intr. 2004

'Bohemia' HT, mp, 1928, Böhm, J.; flowers pure rose-pink, semi-dbl.; ['Mrs Franklin Dennison' × ('Mrs Henry Morse' × unknown)]

'Bohémienne' HT, or, 1954, Mallerin, C.; flowers 45 petals; bushy growth

'Böhm Junior' HT, dp, 1935, Böhm, J.; flowers carmine-red, dbl.; foliage glossy; bushy growth; ['Laurent Carle' × ('Paul's Scarlet Climber' × 'Ethel Somerset')]

'Böhm Senior' HT, mr, 1938, Böhm, J.; flowers large, dbl.

'Böhmorose' HT, mp, 1935, Böhm, J.; flowers rosy carmine to light rose-pink, very large, dbl.; foliage glossy, dark; very vigorous growth; ['Gen. MacArthur' × 'Laurent Carle']

'Böhmova Azurovà' HP, m, 1934, Böhm, J.; flowers dark violet-pink, large, dbl.

'Böhmova Popelka' Pol, dr, 1934, Böhm, J.; flowers dark blood-red; foliage curiously variegated

'Böhm's Climber' Cl HT, mr, before 1935, Böhm, J.; flowers light to medium crimson, medium, dbl., moderate fragrance

'Böhm's Triumph' HT, dr, 1934, Böhm, J.; flowers very large, semi-dbl., high-centered; foliage dark; vigorous, bushy growth; ['Vaterland' × 'Lord Charlemont']

'Boieldieu' HP, mr, 1877; flowers cherry red, very large; ['Jules Margottin' × 'Baronne Prévost']; intr. 1877

'Boileau' HP, mp, 1883, Moreau-Robert; flowers satiny pink, large, full, cupped; ['Victor Verdier' × unknown]

'Bojangles' F, ob, Bell; short growth; intr. 2001

'Bojangles' -- See 'Jacsun'

'Boksburg Fantasia' -- See 'Kornitzel'

'Bolchoï' ('Madam Speaker') HT, rb; flowers yellow gold, bordered with strong red, 45 petals, intense fragrance; good repeat bloom; dark green, leathery foliage; growth to 3-5 ft.; intr. 1996

Bold Seduction® F, pb; flowers ivory cream with deep pink edges, semi-double to double, cupped, slight fragrance; recurrent; 1 meter growth; [sport of 'Seduction']; intr. 2007

Bolero™ LCl, w, Olesen; flowers white, 8-10 cm., 14 petals, slight wild rose fragrance; foliage dark; growth bushy, 200-300 cm.; PP12683; intr. 1999

Bolero® HT, w, Meilland; flowers dbl., high-centered, borne mostly singly; recurrent; florist rose; intr. 1998

'Bolero' HT, Pironti, N.; intr. 1963

'Boléro' HT, rb, 1937, Gaujard; flowers nasturtium-red and gold, dbl.; foliage leathery; long stems; very vigorous, bushy growth

'Boléro' F, ob, Buyl Frères; bud pointed; flowers orange, large, dbl.; very vigorous growth; intr. 1958

Bolero™ -- See 'Meidelweis'

'Bolero 2004' -- See 'Meidelweis'

Bolivar™ -- See 'Marbol'

'Bombon' Min, Dot, Simon; intr. 1967

'Bon Accord' HT, pb, 1967, Anderson's Rose Nurseries; flowers pink shaded silver, high-pointed, 4½ in.; foliage glossy; ['Prima Ballerina' × 'Percy Thrower']; intr. 1967

'Bon-Bon' F, pb, 1973, Warriner, William A.; bud ovoid; flowers deep rose-pink, reverse white, large, semi-dbl., slight fragrance; foliage dark; vigorous, bushy growth; PP3555; [Bridal Pink™ × seedling]; intr. 1974

'Bon Chance' -- See 'Mike's Old-Fashioned Pink'

'Bon Silène' ('Goubault') T, dp, before 1837, Hardy; bud well-formed; flowers deep rose, large, dbl., moderate fragrance; recurrent bloom; vigorous growth

'Bon Silène Blanc' ('White Bon Silène') T, ly, 1885, Morat; flowers pale yellow to creamy white, large; [sport of 'Bon Silène']

'Bon Voyage' -- See 'Voeux de Bonheur'

'Bon007' S, mp, Bond; intr. 2002

'Bona Weillschott' HT, rb, 1889, Soupert & Notting; flowers vermilion pink, center orange-red, large, full, moderate fragrance; ['Bon Silène' × 'Marie Baumann']

Bonanza® HT, ab, Kordes; flowers apricot with pink on outer petals, medium; [sport of 'Sioux']; intr. 2002

'Bonanza' HT, yb, 1957, Verbeek; flowers yellow shaded red, slight fragrance; foliage dark; vigorous growth

Bonanza® -- See 'Kormarie'

'Bonanza Kordana' Min, ab, Kordes; flowers apricot-pink, full; container rose

'Bonapart' -- See 'Korpancom'

'Bonavista' HRg, lp, 1978, Svedja, Felicitas; bud ovoid; flowers open, 2 in., 20 petals, intense fragrance; abundant, repeat bloom; foliage yellow-green; upright, bushy growth; ['Schneezwerg' × Nemesis™]

Bonbon™ -- See 'Poulbon'

'Bonbon Hit' (Bonbon™) MinFl, yb, Poulsen; flowers yellow blend, 5-8 cm., semi-dbl., slight wild rose fragrance; foliage dark; growth bushy, 40-60 cm.; intr. 1992

'Bonbori' LCl, ob, 1977, Suzuki; flowers orange, with apricot yellow reverse; ['Golden Slippers' × (Joseph's Coat® × 'Circus')]; intr. 1973

'Bond Street' HT, op, 1965, McGredy, Sam IV; flowers deep salmon-pink, 4½ in., 75 petals; ['Radar' × Queen Elizabeth®]

'Boneyard Yellow' F, my; intr. 1996

'Bonfire' HWich, mr, 1928, Turbat; flowers brilliant scarlet red, lighter reverse to medium, 4-5 cm., dbl., rosette, borne in clusters of 20-25; foliage light green, small, glossy; very vigorous growth; ['Turner's Crimson Rambler' × R. wichurana]

Bonfire® F, ob, J&P; intr. 2006

'Bonfire' -- See 'Bonfire Night'

Bonfire™ -- See 'Bencincuenta'

Bonfire Night® ('Bonfire') F, rb, 1972, McGredy, Sam IV; flowers red, shaded yellow-orange, large, 19 petals, globular, slight fragrance; foliage matte; ['Tiki' × 'Variety Club']; intr. 1971

'Bonfire of Artec' HT

'Bonhomme' -- See 'Lavhomme'

Bonica® F, or, 1959, Meilland, F.; flowers scarlet, 70 petals, high-centered, borne in clusters, slight fragrance; foliage dark, leathery; vigorous, bushy growth; PP1673; [('Alain' × 'Independence') × Moulin Rouge®]

'Bonica, Climbing' ('Bonica 82, Climbing', 'Canibo') S, mp; intr. 1994

Bonica™® -- See 'Meidomonac'

'Bonica 82, Climbing -- See 'Bonica, Climbing'

Bonica '82® -- See 'Meidomonac'

'Bonica Meidiland' -- See 'Meidomonac'

'Bonita' LCl, dr, 1958, Knight, A.T.; flowers crimson, medium, 15 petals, borne in clusters of 3-8; foliage dark, glossy; vigorous (10-15 ft.) growth

Bonita™ -- See 'Poulen009(N)'

'Bonita Renaissance' (Bonita™, The St. Edmund's Rose™) S, pb, Olesen; bud pointed ovoid; flowers mainly soft pink with some yellow-orange tones when first opening, 4 in., 45 petals, rosette, borne in clusters of 5 or 6, intense sweet fragrance; recurrent; foliage medium to dark green, glossy; prickles moderate, 6 mm., concave, tan to brown; bushy (100-150 cm.) growth; PP15887; [seedling × 'Clair Renaissance']; intr. 2001

'Bonjour' Gr, mr, 1965, Gaujard; flowers bright red, medium, dbl.; foliage leathery; very vigorous, bushy growth; ['Mignonne' × 'Miss Universe']

'Bonmoon' -- See 'Virmoon'

'Bonn' HMsk, or, 1950, Kordes; flowers orange-scarlet, 4 in., 25 petals, borne in trusses of 10, moderate musk fragrance; foliage glossy; upright, bushy (4-5 ft.) growth; ['Hamburg' × 'Independence']

'Bonne Chere' S, rb, 1986, James, John; flowers bright velvet red, creamy eye, large, 5 petals, borne in large clusters, slight fragrance; repeat blooming; foliage medium size, dark, leathery; vigorous, arching (to 4 ft.) growth; [(R. nutkana × Baronne Prevost) × 'Alika']; intr. 1985

'Bonne Fête' HT, or, 1960, Delbard-Chabert; bud long, pointed; flowers orange-coral, large, 25-30 petals; foliage leathery, glossy; strong stems; vigorous, bushy growth; ['Independence' × 'Barcelona']

'Bonne Geneviève' ('La Bonne Geneviève') HCh, m, 1826, Chevrier/Laffay; flowers bright purple, center garnet, large, full

'Bonne Nouvelle' -- See 'Good News'

'Bonne Nuit, Climbing' Cl HT, dr, 1964, Kashimoto

'Bonne Nuit' HT, dr, 1968, Combe; bud pointed; flowers blackish red, medium, dbl., high-centered, moderate fragrance; foliage sparse, glossy; bushy growth; intr. 1966

'Bonnie' S, dp, 1956, Wright, Percy H.; growth similar to Aylsham but taller and more rapid and vigorous; ['Hansa' × R. nitida]

'Bonnie Anne' HT, pb, 1976, MacLeod; flowers pink, reverse yellow and pink, 3-3½ in., 30 petals, moderate fragrance; foliage large, dark, glossy; ['Prima Ballerina' × 'Wendy Cussons']

'Bonnie Belle' HWich, mp, 1911, Walsh; flowers rose pink, lighter towards edges, 5 cm., single, borne in medium to large clusters; foliage glossy; growth to 8-10 ft.

'Bonnie Bess' HT, op, 1929, Dale; flowers deep coral-pink, suffused copper, dbl.; ['Wilhelm Kordes' × ('Crusader' × 'Sunburst')]

'Bonnie Doone' Cl HT, yb, 1941, Clark, A.; [('City of Little Rock' × unknown) × seedling]

'Bonnie Hamilton' F, or, 1976, Cocker; flowers vermilion-red, well-formed, 2½ in., 26 petals, slight fragrance; foliage dark; [Anne Cocker® × Allgold®]

'Bonnie Jack' -- See 'Tinshoultz'

'Bonnie Jane' Pol, dp; intr. 2000

'Bonnie Jean' HT, rb, 1933, Archer; flowers carmine-cerise, base white, large, single; vigorous growth

'Bonnie Maid' F, pb, 1951, LeGrice; flowers silvery pink reverse deep pink, 3 in., 17 petals, borne in clusters of 5-8; foliage leathery, dark; vigorous, bushy growth

'Bonnie Pink' F, lp, 1964, Boerner; bud ovoid; flowers geranium-pink overcast begonia-rose, with upright center petals, 4½ in., 35-40 petals, high-centered,

moderate fragrance; foliage glossy; vigorous, upright growth; PP2411; [('White Garnette' × unknown) × 'Hawaii']
'Bonnie Prince' HMult, w, 1916, Cook, T.N.; bud small, pointed; flowers white, center tinged yellow, medium, dbl., cupped, borne in medium clusters, moderate fragrance; foliage medium size, glossy, thick; excellent pillar growth; hips round, 1/2 in., red; ['White Tausendschön' × 'Wichurana seedling']; intr. 1924
'Bonnie Prince Charlie' HT, mr, 1960, Cuthbert; bud pointed; flowers bright red, well-formed, dbl.
'Bonnie Prince Charlie's Rose' -- See 'Alba Maxima'
'Bonnie Rosalie' -- See 'Ripbon'
'Bonnie Scotland' HT, dp, 1976, Anderson's Rose Nurseries; flowers light red, 5 in., 43 petals, high-centered, intense damask fragrance; foliage glossy; ['Wendy Cussons' × 'Percy Thrower']
Bonnie Sky™ -- See 'Tucksky'
'Bonny' Min, mp, 1975, Kordes; flowers deep pink, lighter reverse, dbl., globular, slight fragrance; foliage small, light, wrinkled; dwarf growth; ['Zorina' × seedling]; intr. 1974
Bonny® LCl, lp, Kordes; bud small, deep pink; flowers pure pink, 5 cm., borne in large clusters; profuse spring bloom, non-recurrent; medium green, glossy foliage; vigorous growth to 10 ft.; intr. 1998
'Bonny Kordana' Min, dp, Kordes; flowers soft, deep pink, full; container rose; intr. 2005
'Bonsoir' HT, mp, 1967, Dickson, A.; bud ovoid; flowers peach-pink, 6 in., dbl., intense fragrance; foliage glossy; intr. 1968
'Bonza' F, op, Bell; intr. 2001
'Booful' HT, dr, 2000, Priestly, J.L.; flowers full; foliage medium size, light green, dull; prickles moderate; growth compact, medium (3 ft.); [sport of 'Delsatel']
Boogie-Woogie™ LCl, mp, Poulsen; flowers medium pink, 8-10 cm., dbl., slight wild rose fragrance; foliage reddish green; growth bushy, 100-150 cm.; PP15102; intr. 2002
'Booker T. Washington' HMult, dr, 1930, Turbat; flowers deep maroon, borne in clusters
'Boomerang' -- See 'Spoboom'
'Booyol' ('Rachel') S, mp, 1984, Booth, Mrs. Rachel Y.; flowers medium, 35 petals, slight delicate fragrance; foliage medium size, medium green, matte; upright growth
'Bopeep' -- See 'Bo-Peep'
'Bora Bora' -- See 'Tanmarsa'
'Bordeaux' HMult, mr, 1908, Soupert & Notting; flowers wine-red, 3½ cm., dbl., borne in large clusters, slight fragrance; non-recurrent; very vigorous growth; ['Crimson Rambler' × 'Mlle Blanche Rebatel']
Bordeaux ™ -- See 'Poulac016(N)'

'Bordeaux des Dames' -- See 'Petite de Hollande'
'Bordeaux Kordana' Min, or, Kordes; flowers orangey-red, small, dbl., cupped, borne singly and in small clusters; compact, small growth; container rose; intr. 1998
'Bordeaux Kordana' Min, dr, Kordes; flowers small, full, cupped to flat, borne mostly singly; recurrent; foliage dark green; compact growth; container rose; intr. 2005
Bordeaux Mikado® F, dr, Tantau; florist spray rose; intr. 2006
'Bordeaux Palace' (Bordeaux ™) MinFl, mr, Poulsen; flowers medium red, 5-8 cm., 25 petals, no fragrance; foliage dark; growth narrow, bushy, 40-60 cm.; PP15874; intr. 2004
'Border Beauty' F, mr, 1958, deRuiter; flowers bright scarlet, 2-2½ in., semi-dbl., borne in very large trusses (10-12 in); foliage dark, glossy; vigorous, upright growth; ['floribunda seedling' × 'Signal Red']; intr. 1957
'Border Coral' F, op, 1958, deRuiter; flowers coral-salmon, 2-2½ in., semi-dbl., borne in trusses; foliage dark, glossy; vigorous, spreading growth; ['Signal Red' × 'Fashion']; intr. 1957
'Border Coral, Climbing' Cl F, op, 1965, Sanday, J.
'Border Gem' F, pb, 1961, Morey, Dr. Dennison; bud ovoid; flowers geranium-pink, center light salmon-orange, 2½-3 in., 20 petals, borne in clusters, moderate fragrance; foliage leathery; compact, low growth; PP2059; [('Navajo' × 'Golden Dawn') × 'Pinocchio']; intr. 1961
'Border Gold' F, dy, 1966, Morey, Dr. Dennison; bud ovoid; flowers medium to deep yellow, very dbl.; foliage dark, leathery; vigorous, low, bushy growth; [Allgold® × 'Pigmy Gold']
'Border King' ('Roi des Bordures') Pol, mr, 1952, deRuiter; flowers bright strawberry-red, small large truss, 16 petals; foliage dark, glossy; very vigorous growth
'Border King, Climbing' Cl Pol, mr, 1960, Gregory
'Border Princess' F, op, 1951, Verschuren-Pechtold; flowers coral-pink shaded orange, reflexed, 3 in., 22 petals, high-centered; foliage light, glossy; vigorous growth
'Border Queen' ('Reine des Bordures') F, op, 1951, deRuiter; flowers salmon-pink, center paler, reverse darker truss, 2½ in., 9 petals; foliage leathery, olive-green; vigorous, compact growth
'Borderer' Pol, pb, 1918, Clark, A.; flowers salmon, fawn and pink, semi-dbl.; dwarf, spreading growth; ['Jersey Beauty' × unknown]
'Bordura de Nea' F, w, Wagner, S.; bud short; flowers small to medium sized, white-pink, 8 petals, flat, borne in clusters, slight fragrance; foliage small, semi-glossy, medium green; [Bonica

'82® × 'Incandescent']; intr. 1995
'Bordure' Pol, mp, 1911, Barbier; flowers carmine-pink, small, dbl.; ['Universal Favorite' × unknown]
'Bordure Blanche' -- See 'Delbobla'
Bordure Camaïeu® F, ob, Delbard; buds orange-yellow; flowers have tones of orange and yellow, turning pink as they age, semi-dbl., flat, borne in clusters; growth to 50-100 cm.; intr. 2002
Bordure d'Or® -- See 'Delbojaune'
'Bordure Magenta' F, dp, Delbard; flowers magenta, borne in large clusters; growth to 50-60 cm.; intr. 2004
Bordure Nacrée® -- See 'Delcrouf'
Bordure Rose® -- See 'Strawberry Ice'
'Bordure Rose Number 2' F, mp, Delbard; growth low, dense, vigorous; intr. 1993
Bordure Vermillon® -- See 'Delbover'
Bordure Vive® -- See 'Delboviv'
Bordurella® F, pb
'Borealis' HKor, w, 1980, James, John; bud globular, pointed; flowers 27 petals, high-centered, borne singly, moderate sweet fragrance; repeat bloom; foliage shiny; prickles gray; bushy growth; ['Blanche Mallerin' × 'Leverkusen']
'Born Again' -- See 'Renaissance'
'Born Free' Min, or, 1978, Moore, Ralph S.; bud long, pointed; flowers brilliant orange-red, 1½ in., 20 petals; foliage dark; bushy, upright growth; PP4454; ['Red Pinocchio' × 'Little Chief']
Borsalino® S, mr, Interplant; intr. 1987
Borussia™ -- See 'Poulspan'
'Boryana' HT, dr, 1985, Staikov, Prof. Dr. V.; flowers large, 55 petals; foliage dark, glossy; vigorous, upright growth; ['Tallyho' × 'Spartan']; intr. 1977
'Bosaceball' ('Jim Larkin') F, dr, 2000, Bossom, Bill; flowers small, semi-dbl., hydrangea-shaped, borne in large clusters, no fragrance; foliage medium size, medium green, glossy; few prickles; bushy, low (2½ ft) growth; ['Red Ace' × 'Ballerina']; intr. 2000
'Bosadson' ('Louisa Jane Morris') LCl, dr, 1997, Bossom, W.E.; flowers frilly, medium, dbl.; foliage medium size, medium green, semi-glossy; some prickles; climbing (15 ft.) growth; ['Admiral Rodney' × 'Evelyn Fison']
'Bosanncoat' ('Country Garden') Cl F, dp, 1996, Bossom, W.E.; flowers bright pink, white center, 4 in., 8-14 petals, borne in large clusters; foliage medium size, light green, glossy; few prickles; spreading, climbing, tall (15 ft.) growth; [Anne Harkness® × seedling]
'Bosanne' ('Capel Manor College', 'Middlesex County') F, op, 1991, Bossom, W.E.; bud pointed; flowers golden peach, medium, 10 petals, flat, borne in sprays of 20-36; foliage medium size, medium green, glossy; tall, upright, very vigorous growth; [Anne Harkness® × 'Greensleeves']
'Bosanneves' ('Enfield in Bloom') F, my, 1996, Bossom, W.E.; flowers deep yellow, reddish tinge to petal edge,

reverse lighter yellow, large, full, slight fragrance; foliage large, medium green, semi-glossy; prickles moderate; upright, tall (115 cm.) growth; [Anne Harkness® × 'Greensleeves']

'Bosarthric' ('Caring For You', 'Together For Ever') Cl F, pb, 1997, Bossom, W.E.; flowers large, 41 petals, borne in small clusters; foliage medium size, medium green, semi-glossy; some prickles; climbing (15 ft.) growth; ['English Miss' × 'Summer Wine']

'Bosbigsouth' ('Lady Yvonne') F, lp, 1999, Bossom, W.E.; flowers large, dbl., borne in small clusters; foliage medium size, medium green, semi-glossy; prickles moderate; medium (3 ft.) growth; ['Southampton' × seedling]

'Boscherry' ('Darling Diane') F, pb, 1995, Bossom, W.E.; flowers lavender pink blend, 3-3½ in., full, slight fragrance; foliage large, dark green, semi-glossy; tall, upright growth; ['Champagne Cocktail' × seedling]

'Boscherrydrift' ('Deborah Devonshire') F, pb, 1997, Bossom, W.E.; flowers very dbl., 41 petals, old-fashioned, borne in small clusters; foliage medium size, dark green, glossy; few prickles; bushy, medium (90 cm.) growth; ['Pearl Drift' × 'CherryAde']

Boscobel™ -- See 'Kinbosco'

'Bosconpea' ('Fab', 'Lady of Hertford') F, pb, 1997, Bossom, W.E.; flowers semi-dbl., 8-14 petals, borne in small clusters, slight fragrance; foliage small, medium green, glossy; few prickles; upright, tall (120 cm.) growth; ['Conversation' × 'Pearl Drift']

'Bosdonford' ('Sue Watkins') F, mp, 2002, Bossom; flowers medium pink, reverse lighter, 2½ in., semi-dbl., borne in small clusters, slight fragrance; foliage small, medium green, semi-glossy; prickles moderate, ¼ in., slender, pointed, triangular; growth bushy, medium (2½ ft.); garden decorative, containers; [City of London® × Anna Ford®]

'Boseladnee' ('Linda Mary') F, dr, 1996, Bossom, W.E.; flowers dark red, silver reverse, 3¼ in., dbl., borne in small clusters; foliage medium size, dark green, semi-glossy; few prickles; bushy, medium (70 cm.) growth; ['Guineé' × 'Glad Tidings']

'Boselftay' ('Connie Crook', 'My Dad') F, mr, 1997, Bossom, W.E.; flowers large, very dbl., borne in large clusters; foliage large, dark green, glossy; few prickles; upright, tall (120 cm.) growth; [seedling × 'Selfridges']

'Bosemwine' ('Mrs Cecily McMullen') Cl F, dp, 1995, Bossom, W.E.; flowers salmon pink, 2¾ in., very dbl., borne in small clusters; foliage large, medium green, semi-glossy; few prickles; tall, spreading (10 × 10 ft.), climbing growth; ['English Miss' × 'Summer Wine']

'Boseyeball' ('Baby Tom') S, mr, 1997, Bossom, W.E.; flowers single, single, borne in small clusters; foliage small, light green, glossy; few prickles; spreading, medium (60 cm.) growth; [Eyepaint® × 'Ballerina']

'Boseyesouth' ('Elke Fair') LCl, ab, 2000, Bossom, Bill; flowers peach, straw reverse, red edge, frilly petals, 2¾ in., single, borne in large clusters; foliage large, medium green, semi-glossy; prickles moderate; climbing, spreading, tall (8 × 8 ft.) growth; ['Southampton' × Eyepaint®]; intr. 2000

'Bosfordlish' ('Kerry Anne') Min, ab, 2000, Bossom, Bill; flowers dbl., borne in small clusters; foliage small, dark green, semi-glossy; prickles moderate; growth upright, medium (3 ft.); containers; [Laura Ford® × 'English Miss']

'Bosgreen' ('Peppermint Ice') F, w, 1992, Bossom, W.E.; flowers creamy greenish white, 3¼ in., 10 petals, cupped, borne singly and in sprays of 3 - 5; foliage medium size, medium green, semi-glossy; upright, medium growth; [Anne Harkness® × 'Greensleeves']; intr. 1991

'Boshipeacon' ('Emily Victoria') F, op, 1994, Bossom, W.E.; flowers salmon pink, medium, very dbl., borne in small clusters; foliage medium size, medium green, semi-glossy; some prickles; low to medium (60 cm.), bushy, compact growth; ['Conservation' × ('Pearl Drift' × Highfield®)]

'Bosholsex' ('Carole Lovett') F, r, 2000, Bossom, Bill; flowers russet, medium, dbl., borne in small clusters; foliage medium green, semi-glossy; prickles moderate; upright growth to 3 ft.; ['Edith Holden' × Sexy Rexy®]; intr. 2000

'Boshotearl' ('Lady Barbara Bossom') F, lp, 1997, Bossom, W.E.; flowers frilly, 4 in., very dbl., borne in small clusters; foliage medium size, light green, glossy; some prickles; upright, tall (90cm.) growth; ['Savoy Hotel' × 'Pearl Drift']

'Bosiljurika' ('Preservation') F, mr, 1995, Bossom, W.E.; flowers bright red, large, very full, borne in small clusters, slight fragrance; foliage medium size, medium green, glossy; some prickles; medium, upright growth; ['Silver Jubilee' × 'Paprika']

'Boskathrex' ('My Grandma') F, mp, 2002, Bossom, Bill; flowers very full, borne in small clusters, slight fragrance; foliage medium size, dark green, glossy; prickles 3/8 in., slender, slightly curved, moderate; growth upright, tall (3½ ft.); garden decorative, containers; [Sexy Rexy® × ('Kathlene's Rose' × seedling)]

'Boslauramber' ('Good Morning Sunshine') Min, dy, 1998, Bossom, W.E.; flowers golden yellow, 2½ in., very dbl., borne mostly singly; foliage small, dark green, semi-glossy; numerous prickles; low, compact growth; [Laura Ford® × 'Forever Amber']

'Boslorvet' ('Sharon Anne') F, ob, 1993, Bossom, W.E.; flowers orange salmon, medium, dbl., borne in large clusters; foliage large, medium green, semi-glossy; few prickles; tall to medium (120 cm.), upright growth; ['Sharon Lorraine' × 'Brown Velvet']; intr. 1993

'Boslovebell' ('Our Baby') Min, pb, 2002, Bossom, Bill; flowers very full, borne in small clusters, intense fragrance; foliage small, medium green, matte; prickles very small, very few; growth upright, medium (2 ft.); garden decorative, containers; ['seedling 3692' × 'seedling LMXTLXABXIS']

'Bosneech' ('William Stubbs') S, dr, 1996, Bossom, W.E.; flowers 3¼ in., dbl., borne in small clusters; early flowering (may); foliage small, medium green, glossy; prickles moderate; spreading (10 × 12 ft.) growth; [seedling × 'Guinee']

'Bosom Buddy' HT, or, Wells; intr. 1992

'Bosor' ('Jessie Patricia') F, ob, 2000, Bossom, Bill; flowers orange, reverse gold, 8 cm., semi-dbl., borne in small clusters, slight fragrance; foliage medium size, medium green, semi-glossy; few prickles; upright, medium (70 cm.) growth; [Sexy Rexy® × 'Edith Holden']; intr. 2001

'Bospardon' ('Nancy Bennett') F, m, 1998, Bossom, W.E.; flowers lavender pink, 2¾ in., dbl., borne in small clusters; foliage large, dark green, semi-glossy; prickles moderate; tall, spreading growth; [City of London® × 'Paprika']

'Bospeabay' ('Tender Loving Care') F, mp, 1993, Bossom, W.E.; flowers medium pink, 4 in., 20 petals, borne in large clusters; foliage medium size, dark green, semi-glossy; some prickles; medium to tall (90 cm.), upright growth; ['Pearl Drift' × (Dublin Bay® × seedling)]; intr. 1995

'Bosrexch' ('Tender Love') F, lp, 1997, Bossom, W.E.; flowers very dbl., 41 petals, high-centered, borne in large clusters, no fragrance; foliage medium size, light green, glossy; some prickles; growth upright, medium (90 cm.); [Sexy Rexy® × seedling]

'Bosrexcity' ('Frances Perry') F, w, 1995, Bossom, W.E.; flowers 7+ cm., full, borne in small clusters, moderate fragrance; foliage medium size, medium green, semi-glossy; some prickles; low, bushy growth; [Sexy Rexy® × City of London®]

'Bosrexever' ('Annie East', 'Annie') S, ly, 1998, Bossom, W.E.; flowers cream yellow, 3 in., 8-14 petals, borne in large clusters; foliage large, dark green, semi-glossy; prickles moderate; spreading, medium growth; [Sexy Rexy® × 'Forever Amber']

'Bosrexeye' ('Irene Smith') F, or, 1998, Bossom, W.E.; flowers coral with lighter reverse, 2¾ in., very dbl., borne in large clusters; foliage medium size, dark green, glossy; prickles moderate; bushy, medium growth; [Sexy Rexy® × Eyepaint®]

'Bosrexfolk' ('Our Son') MinFl, mr, 2001,

Bossom, Bill; flowers 2 in., dbl., borne in small clusters, moderate fragrance; foliage small, dark green, semi-glossy; prickles ¼ in., moderate; growth compact, bushy (20 in.); garden decorative, containers; [Sexy Rexy® × 'Suffolk']

'Bosrexfor' ('Chloe of Childerly') F, or, 2002, Bossom, Bill; flowers large, semi-dbl., borne in small clusters, slight fragrance; foliage dark green, semi-glossy; prickles 3/8 in., triangular, moderate; growth upright, medium (3 ft.); garden decorative; [Sexy Rexy® × 'Forever Amber']

'Bosrexhold' ('Sean and Joan') F, ob, 2000, Bossom, Bill; flowers orange, reverse lighter, large, dbl., borne in small clusters, slight fragrance; foliage medium size, dark green, glossy; prickles moderate; upright (4½ ft.) growth; [Sexy Rexy® × 'Edith Holden']

'Bosrexsplender' ('My Sweet Girl') F, m, 2001, Bossom, Bill; flowers large, dbl., borne mostly solitary, moderate fragrance; foliage medium size, dark green, semi-glossy; prickles 5/16 in., pointed, moderate; growth upright, bushy, medium (2½ ft.); garden decorative; ['Purple Splendour' × Sexy Rexy®]

'Bossa Nova' HT, dy, 1964, McGredy, Sam IV; flowers deep golden yellow, 4 in., 28 petals, high-centered; foliage dark; ['Leverkusen' × 'Buccaneer']

Bossa Nova™ ('My Ouma', Land Brandenburg™, The Faun™, Meine Oma™, Granny™, My Granny™) F, mp, Olesen; flowers flower light on edges, deeper in heart, 5-8 cm., full, borne in clusters; recurrent; foliage dark, glossy; growth bushy, 100-150 cm.; PP12523; [seedling × 'The Fairy']; intr. 1996

'Bosseedgard' ('My Grandad') F, ab, 2002, Bossom, Bill; flowers dbl., borne in small clusters, slight fragrance; foliage medium size, medium green, semi-glossy; prickles ¼ in., triangular, moderate; growth upright, medium (2½ ft.); garden decorative, containers; [seedling × seedling]

'Bossexeye' F, mr, Bossom, W.E.; intr. 1999

'Bossexpaint' ('Margaret Chessum') F, dp, 2000, Bossom, Bill; flowers deep pink, white reverse, no fragrance; foliage light green, semi-glossy; growth bushy, medium (3½ ft.); [Sexy Rexy® × Eyepaint®]; intr. 2000

'Bossexwonder' ('Olive Elsie') F, lp, 2000, Bossom, Bill; flowers , 80 petals, borne in small clusters, moderate fragrance; foliage foliate large, medium green, semi-glossy; prickles moderate; upright, medium (3½ ft.) growth; [Sexy Rexy® × 'Wonder of Woolies']

'Bossiljubnew' ('Forever Eve') HT, m, 2002, Bossom, Bill; flowers medium, dbl., borne in small clusters, slight fragrance; foliage medium size, medium green, semi-glossy; prickles 3/8 in., pointed, straight, moderate; growth upright, medium (3 ft.); garden decorative; ['Silver Jubilee' × News®]

'Bossuet' HP, mr, about 1836, Vibert; flowers cherry red with vivid carmine, large, full, cupped

'Bossuet' HGal, mr; flowers scarlet, edges darker; intr. before 1846

Bossuet, Aigle de Meaux® HT, m, J&P; intr. 2005

'Bossufrex' ('Our Daughter') MinFl, mp, 2001, Bossom, Bill; flowers 2¼ in., very full, rosette, borne in small clusters, intense fragrance; foliage small, dark green, semi-glossy; prickles ¼ in., hooked down, moderate; growth compact, low (20 in.); garden decorative, containers; [Sexy Rexy® × 'Suffolk']

'Bostimebide' ('Beautiful Sunrise') LCl, pb, 2000, Bossom, W.E.; flowers salmon with yellow center, light pink reverse, 5 cm., semi-dbl., borne in large clusters, slight fragrance; foliage small, medium green, semi-glossy, disease-resistant; prickles small, straight, few; growth spreading, tall (3 m.); walls, fences, pergolas; ['Phyllis Bide' × ('Anytime' × ('Liverpool Echo' × (Flamenca × R. bella)))]; intr. 2001

'Boston' HT, mp, 1917, Montgomery Co.; flowers dbl.; ['Mrs George Shawyer' × seedling]

'Boston Beauty' Pol, mp, 1919, Farquhar; flowers clear pink, dbl.; ['Orléans Rose' × ('Katharina Zeimet' × 'Old Ayrshire rose')]

'Boston Rambler' -- See 'Farquhar'

'Bosum Buddy' -- See 'Welbud'

'Botanica' -- See 'Tombot'

'Botaniste Abrial' -- See 'Lowell Thomas'

'Botaniste Henri Grimm' F, my, 1958, Gaujard, R.; flowers golden to straw-yellow, becoming pink tinted, large, borne in clusters; vigorous growth; ['Goldilocks' × 'Fashion']

'Botany Bay' HT, rb, J&P?; flowers deep coral-red with a cream center, dbl., slight fragrance; medium growth; possibly from 1988; intr. 1988

Botero® ('Duftfestival', 'Sir Donald Bradman') HT, mr; flowers very dbl., high-centered; growth to 100-120 cm.; intr. 2002

'Bottanix' F, or, McGredy; flowers bright orange-red, borne in clusters; mid-green foliage; intr. 2003

Botticelli® F, mp, Meilland; flowers , 50-55 petals, well-formed, borne in clusters; good repeat; growth compact (70-80 cm.)

'Botzaris' D, w, before 1856; flowers creamy white, medium size, very dbl., flat, quartered; non-recurrent; foliage light green; growth to 4 × 3 ft., vase-shaped

'Boudoir' -- See 'Clebou'

'Boudoir' ('Paul Fromont') HT, pb, 1942, Meilland, F.; flowers Tyrian rose, reverse white, large, 50 petals, high-centered; foliage leathery; vigorous, upright, bushy growth; ['Ampere' × ('Charles P. Kilham' × 'Margaret McGredy')]

'Bougainville' N, pb, 1822, Cochet/Vibert; bud crimson-purple, round; flowers pink in center, becoming paler and tinged with lilac at the base, 4 cm., very dbl., cupped, borne in large clusters, slight fragrance; foliage narrow, glossy; numerous prickles

'Bougère' ('Clotilde') T, op, 1832, Bougère; flowers deep salmon, shaded bronze, large, full, cupped; growth vigorous; probably extinct

'Bougère' -- See 'Clotilde'

'Boula de Nanteuil' ('Boule de Nanteuil', 'Comte Boula de Nanteuil', 'Comte de Nanteuil') HGal, m, 1834, Roeser; flowers crimson purple, center sometimes fiery crimson, reverse silvery, large, dbl., irregularly quartered, borne in clusters of 2-4, moderate fragrance; foliage medium green, elliptical, deeply toothed; prickles very thin; branching growth; named after the Boula family from the region of Crécy

'Boule d'Abricot' S, ab, Verschuren; flowers apricot pink, large , very full, globular, borne singly, moderate fragrance; recurrent; medium (3 - 4 ft.), bushy growth; intr. 2008

'Boule de Nanteuil' -- See 'Boula de Nanteuil'

'Boule de Neige' ('Snowball') B, w, 1867, Lacharme, F.; flowers pure white, compact, dbl., moderate fragrance; occasional recurrent bloom; foliage dark; ['Mlle Blanche Lafitte' × 'Sappho (Damask Perpetual)']; sometimes classified as N

'Boule de Neige' -- See 'Globe Hip'

'Boule d'Hortensia' -- See 'Aimable Rouge'

'Boule Hortensia' -- See 'Majestueuse'

Boulie's Dream™ -- See 'Wilfolk'

'Boulie's Favorite' S, mp, Williams, J.B.; intr. 2004

'Bountiful' F, pb, 1972, LeGrice; flowers strawberry-salmon, reverse deeper, 3 in., 33 petals, high-centered; foliage small; tall, erect growth; ['Vesper' × seedling]

'Bountiful Abundance' S, op; flowers dainty coral pink, dbl., borne in clusters; blooms all season; prostrate ground-cover growth; intr. 2000

'Bounty' HT, w, Select; flowers pure white, 9 cm., very full, high-centered, borne mostly singly; recurrent; stems long; florist rose; intr. 2005

'Bouquet' ('Lied', 'Siegeslied') F, dp, 1940, Tantau; flowers deep pink, 33 petals, cupped; foliage dark, leathery; vigorous, bushy, compact growth; ['Ingar Olsson' × 'Heidekind']

'Bouquet Blanc' N, w, before 1845, Vibert; flowers small, full

'Bouquet Blanc' HP, w, Robert; flowers white, aging to flesh pink, medium, dbl., globular; intr. 1856

'Bouquet Blanc' Pol, w, Corrard; flowers pure white with some yellow towards center, medium, dbl.; intr. 1914

'Bouquet Charmant' HSet, lp, about 1810, Descemet

'Bouquet Charmant' ('Bouquet Superbe', 'Pâle Rouge Superbe', 'Vénus Mère') HGal, mp; flowers vivid pink, large, dbl., moderate fragrance; from Holland; intr. before 1845

'Bouquet de Flore' ('Bouquet des Fleurs') B, mr, 1839, Bizard; flowers light carmine red, very large, dbl., cupped; foliage dark green

'Bouquet de la Mariée' -- See 'Bouquet de Marie'

'Bouquet de Marie' ('Bouquet de la Mariée') N, w, 1858, Damaizin; flowers light greenish-white, fading to pure white, 6 cm., dbl., borne in small clusters; foliage light green; prickles numerous, short

'Bouquet de Mühlenbeck' HGal, about 1860, Baumann

'Bouquet de Neige' Pol, w, 1900, Vilin; flowers bright white, medium, dbl., borne in clusters of 20-30

'Bouquet de Venus' ('Bouquet Rose de Vénus') HGal, lp, before 1819; bud elongate; flowers silky flesh pink, mixed with touches of white, large buttoned center, small, very dbl., pompon; foliage light green, round; prickles moderate; stems slender, yellowish; growth small, compact; Agathe group; Lerouge claims to have received it from Malmaison

'Bouquet des Fleurs' -- See 'Bouquet de Flore'

'Bouquet d'Or' N, yb, 1872, Ducher; flowers buff yellow, center coppery salmon, large, 9 cm., dbl., cupped, moderate fragrance; ['Gloire de Dijon' × unknown]

'Bouquet d'Or' HT, ly, Lippiatt; flowers light golden yellow, well-formed, medium, full, moderate fragrance; vigorous growth; intr. 1922

'Bouquet d'Otto' HGal, before 1860, Baumann

'Bouquet Fait' -- See 'Len 1'

Bouquet Parfait® -- See 'Lenbofa'

'Bouquet Parfait' -- See 'Royale'

'Bouquet Rose' HWich, mp, 1912, Theunis/Eindhoven; flowers rose pink to lilac-white, reverse lighter, small, 1½-2 in., full, borne in medium clusters; ['Turner's Crimson Rambler' × 'Ernst Grandpierre']

'Bouquet Rose' Pol, lp, Granger-Gaucher; flowers flesh-pink to peach-pink with darker pink, small, full, borne in clusters of 30-40; intr. 1928

'Bouquet Rose de Vénus' -- See 'Bouquet de Venus'

'Bouquet Rouge' F, mr, 1963, Arles; flowers large, 45 petals, borne in clusters of 14-16; vigorous growth; [('Gruss an Teplitz' × 'Independence') × ('Independence' × 'Floradora')]

'Bouquet Superbe' -- See 'Bouquet Charmant'

'Bouquet Tout Fait' -- See 'Red Damask'

'Bouquet Tout Fait' N, w, before 1836, Laffay, M.; sepals long, foliolate; flowers creamy white, 3-4 cm., semi-dbl., borne in large clusters; repeats well

Bouquet Vanille® ('Peaches') S, ab, Delbard; intr. 1993

'Bouquetterie' Min, mr; flowers bright red, borne in clusters; free-flowering

'Bourbon' ('Ancienne Pivoine', 'Formosa', 'Visqueuse', 'Rose Mauve', 'Pivoine', 'Mauve', 'Malvina', 'Inermis Sub Albo Violacea', 'Des Alpes sans Épines', 'Jéricho') HGal, pb, before 1811; bud delicate pink, pointed; flowers striped and mottled with pink and a pale ground, medium, semi-dbl., moderate fragrance

'Bourbon Jacques' -- See 'Rosier de Bourgon'

'Bourbon Queen' -- See 'Reine des Iles-Bourbons'

'Bourbon Rose' (R. borboniana, R. canina burboniana, 'Rose Edward', 'The Bourbon Jacques') B, dp, 1817; flowers pink, red or purple, 3 in., semi-dbl., borne solitary or in few-flowered clusters, moderate applesauce fragrance; some repeat; foliage large, thick, edged purplish-red when young, with 5-7 leaflets; stems bright green with purple shading; growth compact, vigorous; brought to France from Réunion (Ile de Bourbon); probably R. chinensis × 'Quâtre Saisons'

Bourgogne® S, pb, Interplant; flowers strong, medium pink, grading to almost white at the petal base, 4 cm., single, shallow cup, no fragrance; non-remontant; foliage dark green; bushy, arching (150 cm.) growth; hips long; intr. 1983

'Bourgogne No. 2' -- See 'Adatapora'

Bournonville™ -- See 'Pink Fizz'

'Boursault Rose' ('À Boutons Renversés', R. boursaulti, R. reclinata, R. × lheritierana, R. boursaultii, 'Lheritieranea', R. boursaultiana) Bslt, mp, about 1810; flowers pink to purple, often showing a white stripe, semi-dbl., nodding, in corymbs; non-recurrent; foliage medium size, bright green, deeply serrated; stems long, flexible, reddish-purple; climbing to 12 ft. growth; subglobose, smooth fruit; very hardy; [probably R. pendulina × a China (possibly R. chinensis)]; possibly bred in 1810 by Cugnot and sent to the garden of Henri Boursault

'Bouton d'Or' T, dy, 1867, Guillot; flowers dark golden yellow, reverse whitish yellow, very full; ['Canari' × unknown]

'Boutonniere' HT, op, 1940, Lammerts, Dr. Walter; flowers salmon-pink, 3 in., 40-50 petals; foliage dark, glossy, bronze; vigorous, bushy, compact growth; PP454; ['Lulu' × 'Mrs Sam McGredy']

'Boutons d'Unique' HSpn, mp, 1821, Cartier

'Bouzloudja' HT, mr, 1985, Staikov, Prof. Dr. V.; flowers large, 40 petals, slight fragrance; foliage dark, glossy; vigorous, bushy growth; ['Sarah Arnot' × 'Rina Herholdt']; intr. 1974

Bow Bells™ -- See 'Ausbells'

'Bowie Pink' S, mp

'Bowie Pink Lady' HT, lp, Williams, J. Benjamin; bud dark pink; flowers soft pink with hint of lemon at heart, high-centered; intr. 1995

'Bowie White Patio' Min, w, Williams, J. Benjamin

'Bowie Yellow Blush' Gr, ly, Williams, J.B.; intr. 2004

'Bowie Yellow Patio' MinFl, my, Williams, J. Benjamin; flowers high-centered, high-centered; intr. 1995

'Bowled Over' -- See 'Tanolgnil'

'Boy Crazy' -- See 'Dicrevival'

Boy O Boy™ -- See 'Dicuniform'

'Boy Scout' ('Scout') HT, or, 1946, Duehrsen; bud long, pointed; flowers flame, large, dbl., high-centered; foliage dark, glossy; very vigorous, upright, bushy growth; ['Joanna Hill' × 'Olympiad']

Boys' Brigade® -- See 'Cocdinkum'

'Bozena Nemcová' HT, dp, 1931, Böhm, J.; flowers pure dark pink, very large, dbl., cupped; foliage bronze, thick; strong stems; vigorous growth; ['Sylvia' × 'Priscilla']

'Brad' HT, ab, 1999, Poole, Lionel; flowers 5½ in., full, borne mostly singly, moderate fragrance; foliage medium size, medium green, dull; few prickles; bushy, medium (3 ft.) growth; ['Gavotte' × 'Ravenswood']

'Bradgate' HT, yb, 1971, Worth; flowers yellow and deep red bicolor, pointed, 4-5 in., 27 petals, slight fragrance; foliage dark; free growth; [sport of 'Piccadilly']; intr. 1970

Bradley Craig® -- See 'Macstewar'

'Bradova Germania' HFt, op, 1932, Brada, Dr.; flowers coppery-pink, large, semi-dbl.

'Bradova Lososova Druschki' HP, op, 1937, Brada, Dr.; flowers salmon-pink, large

'Bradwardine' -- See 'Rose Bradwardine'

'Braham Datt' HT, lp, 2005, Shastri, N.V.; flowers light pink, reverse light pink, 4½ in., full, borne mostly solitary, moderate fragrance; foliage medium size, medium green, semi-glossy; prickles medium, crooked; growth compact, medium (3½ ft.); ['Sahasradhara' × Pristine®]; intr. 1996

'Braine l'Alleud' HT, Delforge, H.; intr. 1984

'Braiswick Beatuy' HMult, pb, 1912, Cant, F.; flowers silky pink, base bronze-pink, center tinted scarlet, moderate fragrance

'Braiswick Charm' HWich, ob, 1914, Cant, F.; flowers orange-yellow, edges almost white, borne in clusters; foliage dark, glossy, leathery; long, strong stems; very vigorous growth

'Braiswick Fairy' HMult, dp, 1912, Cant, F.; flowers darp pink, aging lighter, semi-dbl.

'Braiswick Gem' HMult, my, 1912, Cant, F.; flowers nankeen yellow, moderate fragrance

'Bramble Bear' Min, ab, Benardella, Frank; intr. 1997

'Brandenburg' HT, or, 1965, Kordes, R.; flowers deep salmon, reverse darker, 5 in., 40 petals, high-centered; vigorous, upright growth; PP2810; [('Spartan' × 'Prima Ballerina') × 'Karl Herbst']

'Brandenburg Gate' -- See 'Jacgate'

'Brandon' LCl, mr, 1964, Combe; bud long, pointed; flowers dark carmine-red, large, dbl., borne mostly solitary; very free, recurrent bloom; vigorous growth

'Brandon's Dream' -- See 'Weldream'

'Brandy, Climbing' Cl HT, ab, Swane; [sport of 'Brandy']; intr. 1994

Brandy™ -- See 'Arocad'

'Brandy Butter' HT, ob, 1980, Northfield, G.; bud long, pointed; flowers pale gold, 28 petals, high-centered, borne 4-5 per cluster, moderate fragrance; foliage mid-green; prickles thick, triangular-shaped; tall, upright growth; ['Fred Gibson' × 'Royal Gold']

Brandy Snap™ -- See 'Dicqueue'

'Brandyglow' ('Vanessa Belinda') F, yb, 1993, Bracegirdle, A.J.; flowers yellow blend, 3-3½ in., dbl., borne in small clusters; foliage medium size, dark green, glossy; some prickles; medium (100 cm.), bushy growth; ['Champagne Cocktail' × ('Glenfiddich' × Priscilla Burton®)]; intr. 1993

'Brandypink' ('Ronald George Kent') F, mp, 1992, Bracegirdle, A.J.; flowers 3-3½ in., dbl., borne in small clusters; foliage large, dark green, semi-glossy; few prickles; medium (86 cm.), bushy growth; ['Pink Favorite' × 'Piccasso']

'Brandysnap' -- See 'Dicqueue'

'Brandywine' HT, ly, 1941, Thompson's, J.H., Sons; bud long, pointed; flowers buff-yellow, 4-5 in., 25-30 petals, slight fragrance; foliage olive-green, leathery; very vigorous, upright growth; PP530; [seedling × 'Souvenir']

'Brasero' F, mr, Kordes; flowers large; intr. 1978

'Brasier' ('Brazier') HT, mr, 1937, Mallerin, C.; flowers flame-scarlet, large, dbl.; foliage glossy; very vigorous, bushy growth; ['Charles P. Kilham' × seedling]

'Brasilia' HT, rb, 1967, McGredy, Sam IV; flowers scarlet, reverse gold, 4 in., dbl., slight fragrance; PP3071; ['Kordes Perfecta' × Piccadilly®]; intr. 1968

Brass Band™ -- See 'Jaccofl'

'Brass Monkey' ('Top Brass') LCl, ab, Harkness; flowers peach-apricot, changing to amber, dbl., cupped, dahlia-like; moderate growth; intr. 1998

'Brass Ring' -- See 'Dicgrow'

'Bratowin' ('George Armer') HT, dp, 1993, Bracegirdle, A.J.; flowers deep pink, medium, dbl., high-centered, borne mostly singly, slight fragrance; foliage medium size, bronze-red, matte; some prickles; medium (12 cm.), upright growth; ['Gavotte' × 'First Prize']; intr. 1993

Braunwald® S, w

'Brautzauber' F, w, Noack; bud light rose; flowers white, some pink tones in cool weather, 4 cm., semi-double, shallow cup, borne in clusters; recurrent; foliage medium to dark green, glossy; intr. 2001

'Bravado' -- See 'Jacro'

'Brave Heart' -- See 'Horbondsmile'

'Brave Patriot' S, mr, 2003, Buck; flowers single, borne in small clusters, moderate fragrance; foliage medium size, dark green, semi-glossy; prickles ¼ in., straight, moderate; growth upright, tall (6 ft.); hedge or specimen shrub; [sport of 'Maytime']; intr. 2002

'Braveheart' -- See 'Clebravo'

'Braveheart' -- See 'Cocjabby'

'Bravo' HT, mr, 1951, Swim, H.C.; bud ovoid; flowers cardinal-red, 4-5 in., 35 petals, high-centered, borne in clusters, slight fragrance; foliage leathery; vigorous, upright, moderately bushy growth; PP983; ['World's Fair' × 'Mirandy']

Bravo™ ('Bravo Parade') Min, mr, Poulsen; flowers medium red, medium, dbl., no fragrance; foliage dark; growth bushy, 20-40 cm.; PP10629; intr. 1998

'Bravo Parade' -- See 'Poulbao'

'Braz Ornelas' HT, Moreira da Silva, A.

'Brazerade' LCl, mr

'Brazier' -- See 'Brasier'

'Brazil' HT, rb, 1947, Caron, B.; bud long, pointed; flowers saturn-red, reverse saffron-yellow, well-shaped, dbl.; foliage light green

'Bread 'n' Butter' -- See 'Tinbutt'

'Break o' Dawn' -- See 'Minfco'

'Break o' Day, Climbing' Cl HT, ob, 1944, Brownell; flowers pale pink, apricot at center, large, full; PP696

'Break o' Day' Pol, pb, 1937, Archer; flowers copper-pink, center yellow, fading to shell-pink, semi-dbl., cupped, borne in clusters; recurrent bloom; vigorous growth

'Break o' Day' ('Delta') HT, ob, Brownell; flowers orange shades, large, 50 petals, intense fragrance; vigorous growth; [seedling × 'Glenn Dale']; intr. 1939

'Breakaway' Min, mr, 1981, Lyon, Lyndon; bud ovoid, pointed; flowers 23 petals, borne singly, slight fragrance; foliage small, medium green; prickles straight, tiny, brownish-green; compact, upright, bushy growth; ['Dandy Lyon' × seedling]; intr. 1980

'Breath of Heaven' -- See 'Hamari'

'Breath of Life' -- See 'Harquanne'

'Breath of Spring' -- See 'Brispring'

'Breathless' -- See 'Jacchry'

'Breathtaking' HT, my; flowers crisp, rich yellow, 4 in., 30 petals, old-fashioned form, moderate fruity/tea fragrance; bright, lime green foliage; growth to 4 × 3 ft.; intr. 2003

'Breathtaking' -- See 'Leobretak'

Bredon® -- See 'Ausbred'

Breeze™ -- See 'Poulbrez'

'Breeze Hill' HWich, ab, 1926, Van Fleet; flowers flesh tinted apricot, center rose, paling, 3 in., 55 petals, cupped, borne in clusters, moderate fragrance; non-recurrent; foliage small, round matte; growth bushy, heavy canes; [R. wichurana × 'Beauté de Lyon']

'Breeze Parade' (Breeze™) Min, ab, Poulsen; flowers apricot blend, medium, dbl., no fragrance; growth bushy, 20-40 cm.; PP13426

Breezy™ -- See 'Savabrez'

'Bregina' F, or, 1965, deRuiter; flowers vermilion-red; [sport of 'Mandrina']

'Breid' MinFl, rb, 2007, Kenny, David; intr. 2007

Bremer Stadtmusikanten® -- See 'Korterschi'

'Brenda' HEg, lp, 1894, Penzance; flowers peach-blossom-pink, single; foliage fragrant; very vigorous growth

'Brenda Ann' HT, dy, 1975, Watts; flowers amber-yellow, 5 in., 37 petals, slight fragrance; foliage glossy, tinted bronze; vigorous, tall, upright growth; [sport of 'Piccadilly']; intr. 1973

'Brenda Burg' -- See 'Cleswan'

'Brenda Colvin' LCl, lp, 1970, Colvin; flowers apple-blossom pink, 1 in., 5 petals, borne in trusses, strong sweet-musk fragrance; foliage dark, glossy; very vigorous growth

'Brenda Lee' Min, yb, 1991, Williams, Michael C.; bud pointed; flowers red edge to yellow base, small, 20 petals, urn-shaped; foliage small, medium green, semi-glossy; bushy, low, compact growth; ['Rise 'n' Shine' × Rainbow's End™]; intr. 1991

'Brenda Mowery' -- See 'Jasmow'

'Brenda of Tasmania' F, w, 1971, Holloway; bud ovoid; flowers white, center pink, large, dbl., cupped; foliage large, glossy; upright, bushy growth; [sport of Queen Elizabeth®]

'Brendan Maguire' -- See 'Kengirl'

'Brenda's Cosmic Dancer' -- See 'Worcaddie'

'Brenda's Fragrance' HT, pb, 1967, Smith, W.H.; flowers cerise edged white, high-centered; foliage leathery; vigorous growth; ['Lieutenant Chaure' × 'Hector Deane']

'Brennende Liebe' -- See 'Burning Love'

'Brennpunkt' F, mr, Haenchen, E.; intr. 1972

'Brennus' ('Brutus', 'Queen Victoria', 'St. Brennus') HCh, dp, 1830, Laffay, M.; flowers deep red, shaded with violet, large, full, flat; sometimes classes as B

'Brentwood Style' -- See 'Horcohutton'

'Bresilienne' Pol, dr, 1971, Delforge; bud long, pointed; flowers deep red, medium, dbl., cupped; foliage bronze, leathery; vigorous, dwarf, bushy growth; ['Red Favorite' × 'Ena Harkness']

'Brett's Rose' Min, yb, Benardella, Frank; intr. 2001

'Brett's Rose' -- See 'Benbrett'

'Brewood Belle' LCl, mr, Scarman; intr.

1996
'Briace' ('Ace of Diamonds') Min, mr, 1998, Bridges, Dennis A.; flowers bright medium red, good substance, 1-1½ in., full, high-centered, borne mostly singly and small clusters, intense fragrance; foliage small, dark green, semi-glossy; few prickles; stems strong; bushy, spreading, medium growth; Disease resistant; intr. 1998

'Briador' HT, op

'Brian' -- See 'Barrian'

'Brian Donn' -- See 'Tindonn'

'Brian Lee' -- See 'Tinlee'

'Brian Rix' ('The Mencap Rose') S, mp, Harkness; flowers lilac pin, intense fragrance; growth to 100 cm.; intr. 1999

'Briana's Rose' F, lp; intr. 2001

'Briancouf' S, mp, Briant; intr. 1989

'Briand-Paneuropa' HT, mp, 1931, Böhm, J.; flowers carmine-rose, base yellow, very large, dbl.; vigorous growth; ['Franklin' × 'Willowmere']

'Brianna' -- See 'Devcarlos'

'Brian's Song' S, op, 1978, Smith, R.L.; flowers 4 in., 35 petals, high-centered, moderate fragrance; intermittent bloom; foliage large, glossy, dark; ['Independence' × 'Pike's Peak']

Briant Hill® Min, ob, Poulsen; flowers bright orange, small, rosette, borne singly and in clusters; recurrent; intr. 1994

'Briarcliff' HT, pb, 1926, Pierson, P.M.; flowers center deep rose-pink, outer petals lighter; [sport of 'Columbia']

'Briarcliff, Climbing' Cl HT, pb, 1929, Parmentier, J.

'Briarcliff Brilliance' HT, dp, 1932, Pierson, P.M.; flowers rose to rose-red, large, dbl.; vigorous growth; PP33; [sport of 'Briarcliff']

'Briarcliff Supreme' HT, pb, 1947, Hinner, P.; bud long, pointed; flowers briarcliff pink, very large, dbl.; foliage dark; very vigorous, upright growth; [sport of 'Briarcliff']

'Briautumn' ('Autumn Dawn') Min, op, 1999, Bridges, Dennis A.; flowers orange-pink, reverse slightly lighter, 1¼ in., dbl.; foliage medium size, dark green, semi-glossy; prickles moderate; spreading, medium (2 ft.) growth; [Carrot Top™ × unknown]; intr. 2000

'Bribaby' ('Baby's Secret') Min, w, Bridges, Dennis A.; intr. 1997

'Bribeam' ('Moonbeam') MinFl, pb, 2008, Bridges, Dennis; flowers medium pink, reverse white, medium, 2 in., dbl., borne mostly solitary; foliage medium, medium green, semi-glossy; prickles ¼ in., sharp, slightly downward, tan, moderate; growth upright, tall (36-44 in.); garden decoration; ['Dr John Dickman' × unknown]

'Briben' ('Dr Jack Bender') HT, pb, 1993, Bridges, Dennis A.; flowers pink and white, 3-3½ in., full, borne in flowers borne mostly singly; foliage medium size, dark green, semi-glossy; numerous prickles; bushy, spreading (120 cm.) growth; ['Lady X' × 'Flaming Beauty']; intr. 1993

'Bribolt' ('Thunderbolt') HT, pb, 1991, Bridges, Dennis A.; bud ovoid; flowers pink blend, white reverse, color intensifies with age, medium, 45 petals, urn-shaped, borne singly, slight fragrance; foliage medium size, dark green, matte; bushy, medium growth; ['Lady X' × 'Flaming Beauty']; intr. 1990

'Bricharm' ('Southern Charm') Min, yb, 1992, Bridges, Dennis A.; flowers shades of light yellow and pink, pink intensifying with sun, large, 25-40 petals; foliage large, medium green, semi-glossy; no prickles; medium (40-45 cm.), upright, bushy, slightly spreading growth; [Baby Katie™ × unknown]

'Bricharm' MinFl, ab, Bridges, Dennis; intr. 2002

'Brichat' ('Chit Chat') Min, my, 1999, Bridges, Dennis A.; flowers ¾ in., full, borne mostly singly, no fragrance; foliage medium size, dark green, semi-glossy; few prickles; compact, bushy, medium (18-20 in.) growth; ['Cal Poly' × unknown]

'Bricindy' ('Sassy Cindy') MinFl, rb, 2006, Bridges, Dennis; flowers bright red, reverse light yellow to white, 2 in., full, high-centered, borne mostly solitary, slight fragrance; recurrent; foliage medium size, dark green, semi-glossy; prickles moderate, ¼ in., sharp, pointed slightly downward, tan; upright, tall (28-36 in.) growth: exhibition, containers, garden decorative; ['Purple Dawn' × 'Trickster']; intr. 2005

'Bricky' HT, r, Delbard; flowers brick orange, adding brown tones as it ages, dbl., high-centered, borne mostly singly, moderate fragrance; recurrent; medium growth; intr. 2005

'Briclass' ('Carolina Classic') HT, pb, 1992, Bridges, Dennis A.; flowers medium pink edged deeper pink, 3-3½ in., very dbl., borne mostly singly; foliage medium size, medium green, matte; few prickles; medium (90-100 cm.), upright growth; ['Just Lucky' × 'Flaming Beauty']

'Bricos' ('Cosmic') Min, ob, 1997, Bridges, Dennis A.; flowers light to medium orange with light yellow reverse, medium, full, borne in small clusters, slight fragrance; foliage large, medium green, semi-glossy; upright (24-26 in.), bushy growth

Bridal Blush™ -- See 'Twoblush'

'Bridal Bouquet' HT, w, 1976, Ormerod; flowers 3-4 in., 23 petals; foliage matte, green; vigorous, compact growth; [sport of 'Lady Sylvia']

'Bridal Delight' HT, lp, Day; [sport of 'Bridal White']

'Bridal Meillandina' -- See 'Meilmera'

Bridal Pink™ F, mp, 1967, Boerner; bud ovoid, pointed, long; flowers large, pink blended with cream, 30-35 petals, high-centered, borne in small clusters or singly, moderate spicy fragrance; foliage leathery; vigorous, upright, bushy growth; PP2851; [('Summertime' × unknown) × ('Spartan' × unknown)]

'Bridal Robe' HT, w, 1955, McGredy, Sam IV; flowers ivory-white, high-pointed, 4 in., 54 petals, moderate fragrance; foliage glossy, olive-green; vigorous growth; ['McGredy's Pink' × 'Mrs Charles Lamplough']

Bridal Shower™ -- See 'Jactafl'

'Bridal Shower' -- See 'Devblush'

'Bridal Sonia' HT, pb, Okawa, K.; flowers pink, reverse pale purplish-pink; [sport of 'Sonia']; intr. 1985

Bridal Sunblaze® -- See 'Meilmera'

'Bridal Veil' F, ly, 1954, Boerner; bud ovoid, cream; flowers white overcast seafoam-yellow, open, 2½ in., 75-80 petals, borne in clusters, intense fragrance; vigorous, bushy growth; PP1347; [('Pinocchio' × unknown) × 'Pigmy Gold']; intr. 1954

'Bridal White' ('Tricia') F, w, 1972, Warriner, W. A.; buds medium, long pointed; flowers white with ivory overcast, medium, dbl., high-centered, borne singly and several together, slight fragrance; PP3235; [sport of 'Bridal Pink']; intr. 1972

'Bridal Wreath' HWich, 1909, Manda

'Bridancer' ('Fancy Dancer') MinFl, w, 2002, Bridges, Dennis; flowers white edged pink, 2¼ in., dbl., borne mostly solitary, no fragrance; foliage medium size, medium green, matte; prickles ¼ in., curved down, moderate; growth compact, medium (2½ ft.); PPAF; ['Trickster' × unknown]; intr. 2002

'Bridawn' ('Purple Dawn') MinFl, m, 1991, Bridges, Dennis A.; flowers velvety mauve, long-lasting, 1½ in., 25 petals, high-centered, borne usually singly or in sprays of 5 - 7, slight fragrance; foliage medium size, dark green, semi-glossy; upright, tall growth; [Party Girl™ × unknown]; intr. 1991

'Bride' -- See 'Fryyearn'

'Bride' -- See 'Hanayome'

'Bride, Climbing' -- See 'Ruth Vestal'

'Bride of Abydos' -- See 'La Fiancée d'Abydos'

'Bride of Colmar' Gr, mr, Williams, J.B.; flowers bright red, fading to light pink with age, single, flat; recurrent; foliage dark green; growth to 4 ft.; intr. 2004

'Bride of Lille' -- See 'Triomphe de Lille'

'Bride's Blush' HT, w, 1923, Amling Co.; flowers creamy white, at times blush-pink, 6 petals; [sport of 'Columbia']

'Bride's Dream' -- See 'Koroyness'

'Bride's Maid' F, dp, Ghosh; intr. 2001

'Bride's Maid' w

'Bride's White' F, w, 1970, Mansuino, Q.; flowers pure white, small, dbl., cupped; vigorous, upright, bushy growth; PP2833; intr. 1968

'Bridesmaid' ('The Hughes') T, lp, 1893, Moore; flowers clear silvery pink; [sport of 'Catherine Mermet']; like its parent except in color

'Bridesmaid, Climbing' Cl T, lp, 1897, Dingee & Conard; flowers clear rose-pink with crimson shading, 10-12 cm.; [sport of 'Bridesmaid']

'Bridge of Sighs' LCl, ab, Harkness; flowers amber to rich, deep apricot, petals drop cleanly, 3-4 in., 18 petals, slight fragrance; rapid repeat; growth to 10 ft., with pliable canes; intr. 2001

'Bridget' -- See 'Clebridge'

'Bridget' -- See 'Koreibei'

'Bridget' HT, op, 1947, Fletcher; bud long, pointed; flowers brilliant orange-scarlet, base bright golden yellow, 4-5 in., 35-40 petals, flat; foliage glossy, bright green; ['Mrs Henry Bowles' × 'Phyllis Gold']

'Bridget Mary' ('Mrs V.A.Treloar') S, dp, 2006, Treloar, R.V.; flowers full, borne in small clusters; foliage medium size, medium green, matte; prickles 5 mm., hooked, brown, moderate; growth bushy, medium (1 m.); [sport of 'Mary Rose']; intr. 2007

'Bridget's Joy' HT, lp, 1997, Johnstone, Leonard E.; flowers very dbl., borne mostly singly; foliage medium size, medium green, semi-glossy; compact, medium (140cm.) growth; [sport of 'Coral Fiesta']

'Bridgwater Pride' F, op, 1982, Sanday, John; flowers rich salmon, medium, 20 petals; foliage medium size, dark, semi-glossy; bushy, compact growth; ['Vera Dalton' × Allgold®]

'Bridixie' ('Dixieland') Min, rb, 1992, Bridges, Dennis A.; flowers in shades of vibrant pink, red and white intensifying with sun, large, dbl., high-centered; foliage medium size, medium green, semi-glossy; no prickles; tall (50-60 cm.), upright growth; [Fancy Pants™ × seedling]; intr. 1992

'Bridoah' ('Shenandoah') MinFl, dr, 2006, Bridges, Dennis A.; flowers dark red, reverse lighter, 2¼ in., dbl, high-centered, borne mostly solitary, moderate slightly sweet fragrance; recurrent; foliage medium size, dark green, semi-glossy, disease-resistant; prickles moderate, ¼ in., curved slightly downward, tan; growth upright, medium (24-28 in.); garden, exhibition, containers, cutting; ['Dr. John Dickman' × Miss Flippins™]; intr. 2006

'Bridream' ('Christine's Dream') HT, rb, 2002, Bridges, Dennis; flowers medium red, reverse pink-white, medium, full, borne mostly solitary, moderate fragrance; foliage medium size, dark green, semi-glossy; prickles moderate; growth vigorous, upright, medium (4½-5½ ft.); garden, exhibition, cutting; ['King of Hearts' × 'Thriller']; intr. 2002

'Brie-Rose' T, 1913, Boulanger; [sport of 'Mme Bérard']

'Brifire' ('Gabriel's Fire') Min, rb, 1991, Bridges, Dennis A.; bud pointed; flowers creamy light yellow turning red, 2 in., 20-22 petals, high-centered, borne usually singly, intense fragrance; foliage medium size, medium green, semi-glossy; bushy, spreading, medium growth; [Sachet™ × unknown]; intr. 1991

'Briflip' ('Flip Flop') Min, mp, 2003, Bridges, Dennis; flowers deep coral pink, reverse lighter, 1 in., full, borne in small clusters; foliage medium size, dark green, Semi-glossy; prickles small, sharpe curved down, tan, moderate; growth bushy, slightly spreading, medium (20-24 in.); garden decoration; [sport of 'Ace of Diamonds']; intr. 2003

'Brifont' ('Fontana') MinFl, ab, 2001, Bridges, Dennis; flowers 2¼ in., dbl., borne mostly solitary; foliage medium size, dark green, semi-glossy; prickles ¼ in., sharp, straight, moderate; growth upright, medium (3 ft.); garden decorative, exhibition, cutting; ['Purple Dawn' × unknown]; intr. 2002

'Brifree' ('Freemont') HT, w, 1994, Bridges, Dennis A.; flowers near white blushed with salmon, 3-3½ in., very dbl., borne mostly singly; foliage large, dark green, semi-glossy; some prickles; tall, upright growth; ['Thriller' × 'Tiki']; intr. 1994

'Brifriends' ('Best Friends') Min, ob, 2001, Bridges, Dennis; flowers reverse yellow, 1½ in., dbl., borne mostly solitary, slight fragrance; foliage medium size, dark green, semi-glossy; prickles ¼ in., downward curved, moderate; growth compact, bushy, low (16-18 in.); garden, container, border, cutting; [Hot Tamale™ × unknown]; intr. 2002

'Brigadeiro França Borges' F, or, 1960, Moreira da Silva; flowers bright orange-red; ['Independence' × seedling]

Brigadoon™ -- See 'Jacpal'

'Brigarold' HT, mr, Briant; intr. 2001

'Brigarold' (Roland Garros®) HT, mr, Briant; intr. 1989

'Brigaunt' ('Gauntlet') Min, dr, 1991, Bridges, Dennis A.; bud ovoid; flowers dark red, lighter reverse, lightens slightly with age, medium, 20-22 petals, high-centered, slight fragrance; foliage large, medium green, semi-glossy; spreading, medium growth; ['Kitty Hawk' × seedling]; intr. 1990

'Brigentle' ('Gentleman's Agreement') MinFl, mr, 1998, Bridges, Dennis A.; bud long, slender; flowers medium red, excellent substance, 1-1½ in., full, high-centered, borne mostly singly, no fragrance; foliage large, medium green, semi-glossy; few prickles; tall, upright, bushy growth; Disease resistant; ['Purple Dawn' × unknown]; intr. 1998

'Bright Angel' S, yb, 1978, Smith, R.L.; bud ovoid; flowers light yellow, edged pink, 4 in., 48 petals, high-centered, intense fragrance; intermittent bloom; foliage large, glossy, dark; vigorous, bushy growth; ['Dornroschen' × 'Golden Wings']

'Bright Beam' Gr, pb, 1974, Fuller; bud ovoid; flowers cream, edged pink, large, dbl., cupped, moderate fragrance; profuse, intermittent bloom; foliage glossy, dark; very vigorous, upright growth; ['Peace' × 'Little Darling']; intr. 1972

'Bright Beauty' HT, or, Delbard

'Bright Boy' HT, mr, 1948, Clark, A.; flowers brilliant red

'Bright Carpet' -- See 'Hertfordshire'

Bright Cover™ -- See 'Poultn003'

'Bright Day' -- See 'Chewvermillion'

'Bright Delight' F, yb, 2005, McMillan, Thomas; flowers dark yellow with pink highlights, reverse dark yellow, 2½ in., full, borne in small clusters, no fragrance; foliage small, dark green, glossy; prickles medium, triangular, few; growth compact, short (2½ ft.); garden decorative; ['Yellow Flurette' × Rainbow's End™]; intr. 2006

'Bright Eyes' F, yb, 1948, Duehrsen; bud ovoid; flowers light yellow to primrose, medium, large truss, 25 petals, slight fragrance; foliage leathery, glossy, dark; dwarf growth; PP880; RULED EXTINCT 6/83 ARM; ['Joanna Hill' × ('Heidekind' × 'Betty Uprichard')]

'Bright Eyes' -- See 'Sanmar'

'Bright Eyes' -- See 'Dicreason'

'Bright Fire' Cl HT, dr, 1977, Pearce; flowers crimson, shaded darker, 4½ in., 15 petals, slight fragrance; foliage glossy, dark; free growth; [Parkdirektor Riggers® × 'Guinee']; originally registered as LCl

'Bright Fire' ('Brightfire', 'Peaxi') LCl, or, Pearce; buds urn shaped, pointed; flowers bright orange-vermillion, 5-6 in., 40 petals; foliage dark green and leathery; growth to 10-12 ft.; intr. 1997

'Bright Future' LCl, ob, Kirkham; intr. 2008

'Bright Garbs' F, or, 1978, Hardikar, Dr. M.N.; bud pointed; flowers 2½ in., 12 petals, moderate fragrance; foliage large; dwarf growth; [Orangeade® × seedling]

'Bright Ideas' -- See 'Horcoffdrop'

'Bright Jewel' Min, pb; bud pointed; flowers rose-pink, white center, very small, semi-dbl., borne in clusters; low, compact growth

'Bright Lights' -- See 'Kseelite'

'Bright Meadow' -- See 'Yasnaya Poliana'

'Bright Melody' S, mr, 1985, Buck, Dr. Griffith J.; bud ovoid, pointed; flowers large, 30 petals, cupped, borne 1-10 per cluster, slight fragrance; repeat bloom; foliage medium-large,dark olive green, leathery; prickles awl-like, tan; erect, bushy growth; ['Carefree Beauty' × ('Herz As' × 'Cuthbert Grant')]; intr. 1984

'Bright Minijet' Min, dp, Meilland

'Bright Morning' HT, my, 1958, Ratcliffe; flowers golden yellow

'Bright Pink Iceberg' -- See 'Probril'

'Bright Red' Pol, dr, 1938, deRuiter; flowers velvety dark red, dbl., borne in large clusters; bushy growth

'Bright Sight' -- See 'Judbright'

'Bright Smile, Climbing' Cl F, my, Vidal;

intr. after 1981
Bright Smile® -- See 'Dicdance'
'Bright Spark' -- See 'Centenaire de Lourdes Rouge'
'Bright Spark'   Min, rb; flowers red and gold
'Bright Star'   S, or, Williams, J. Benjamin; flowers single; intr. 1999
'Bright Wings' ('Gitane') HT, op, 1942, Mallerin, C.; bud long, pointed, rosy orange; flowers centers orange shading to pink, large, 22 petals, cupped, moderate fruity fragrance; foliage bronze; strong stems; vigorous, bushy growth; ['Mme Arthaud' × 'Annie Drevet']
'Brightfire' -- See 'Bright Fire'
'Brightness' HT, rb, 1959, Fryers Nursery, Ltd.; bud long, pointed; flowers scarlet, reverse golden yellow, merging to orange, 4½-5½ in., 28-35 petals, high-centered, intense fragrance; foliage leathery, glossy; bushy, moderately vigorous growth; PP1917; [sport of 'Doreen']; intr. 1958
'Brightness of Cheshunt'   HP, mr, 1881, Paul, G.; flowers shining brick red, full; ['Duke of Edinburgh' × unknown]
'Brighton Beauty'   T, mr, 1891, Bragg
'Brighton Cardinals' -- See 'Welcard'
'Brightside'   Min, or, 1975, Moore, Ralph S.; flowers 1 in., 25 petals, high-centered, moderate fragrance; foliage small, matte; upright, bushy growth; ['Persian Princess' × 'Persian Princess']; intr. 1974
'Brigitte'   HT, ob, Asami, H.; flowers bright orange red, reverse pale yellowish-pink, greenish-yellow at base of petals, 12 cm., 25-29 petals, borne mostly solitary, slight fragrance; foliage dark green, glossy, often with 7 leaflets; prickles concave; growth tall, upright, moderately bushy; ['Yasaka' × Prominent®]; intr. 1984
Brigitte Bardot®   HT, rb, Orard; flowers red striped with white, dbl.; growth to 100 cm.; intr. 2002
'Brigitte de Landsvreugd' HMult, w, Mertens; flowers semi-dbl., borne in large clusters; intr. 1988
'Brigitte de Villenfagne' -- See 'Lenamo'
Brigitte Fossey® HT, ab, Dorieux; flowers amber pink, double; intr. 1999
'Brigitte Jourdan'   F, or, 1962, Arles; bud ovoid; flowers pomegranate-red, large, dbl., globular, slight fragrance; foliage dark, glossy; vigorous, bushy growth; ['Belle Créole' × 'Independence']; intr. 1960
'Brigran' ('Grand Romance') HT, mp, 1991, Bridges, Dennis A.; bud ovoid; flowers medium pink, reverse slightly lighter, aging slightly lighter, medium, 50 petals, urn-shaped, borne singly, moderate fragrance; foliage medium size, dark green, semi-glossy; upright, medium growth; ['Lady X' × 'Wini Edmunds']; intr. 1990
'Briheart' ('Hearts A'Fire') Min, dr, 1996, Bridges, Dennis A.; flowers velvety, 1¼ in., single, borne mostly singly; foliage medium size, dark green, glossy, disease-resistant; prickles moderate; strong, upright growth; [Merrimac™ × seedling]; intr. 1996
'Briice' ('Ice Breaker') HT, lp, 1994, Bridges, Dennis A.; flowers medium, dbl., borne mostly singly; foliage medium size, medium green, semi-glossy; some prickles; tall, upright growth; ['Thriller' × 'Just Lucky']; intr. 1994
'Briincog' (Incognito™) Min, m, 1995, Bridges, Dennis A.; flowers mauve blend with yellow reverse, medium, dbl., borne mostly singly; foliage medium size, dark green, semi-glossy; few prickles; tall (30-34 in.), upright, bushy growth; PP9932; [Jean Kenneally™ × Twilight Trail™]; intr. 1995
'Brijes' ('Jeslyn') Min, ly, 2000, Bridges, Dennis A.; flowers light yellow, 2 in., dbl., exhibition, borne mostly singly, slight fragrance; foliage medium size, dark green, glossy; few prickles; stems long, straight; upright, vigorous, hardy, tall (26-30 in.) growth; ['Fairhope' × unknown]; intr. 2001
'Brijup' ('Jupiter') MinFl, m, 2008, Bridges, Dennis; flowers purple, reverse lighter, large, 2 in., full, borne mostly solitary; foliage medium, medium green, semi-glossy; prickles ¼ in., sharp, slightly downward, light tan, few; growth upright, tall (36-44 in.); garden decoration, cutting, exhibition; ['Dr John Dickman' × unknown]
'Briking' ('King's Mountain') Min, dy, 2004, Bridges, Dennis; flowers 1¼ in., dbl., borne mostly solitary, slight fragrance; foliage medium size, medium green, semi-glossy; prickles ¼ in., curved slightly downward; growth compact, medium (26-30 in.); container, garden, cutting, exhibition; ['Doris Morgan' × unknown]; intr. 2005
'Briletjui' (Juillet®) S, rb, Briant; intr. 1989
'Brilight' ('Lighten Up') Min, ly, 2000, Bridges, Dennis A.; flowers 1½ in., full, borne mostly singly; foliage medium size, medium green, semi-glossy; upright, bushy (26-30 in.) growth; [Loving Touch™ × unknown]; intr. 2001
'Brillant' HT, mr, 1952, W. Kordes Söhne; flowers somewhat large, semi-dbl., moderate fragrance
'Brillant' -- See 'Korbisch'
'Brillante' ('Rose Brillante') HGal, mp, about 1810, Descemet; flowers bright pink, large, full
'Brilliance'   F, or, 1959, Boerner; bud ovoid; flowers coral, 2 in., 50 petals, cupped, moderate fragrance; foliage glossy; compact growth; PP1799; [seedling × 'Independence']; intr. 1959
'Brilliancy' HT, or, 1936, LeGrice; flowers brilliant scarlet, dbl.; foliage leathery; short stems; bushy growth; ['Étoile de Hollande' × 'Daily Mail Scented Rose']
'Brilliant' -- See 'Detroiter'
'Brilliant Betty' -- See 'Wisbril'
Brilliant Cover™ -- See 'Poulterp'
'Brilliant Echo' Pol, mp, 1927, Western Rose Co.; flowers rosy pink; [sport of 'Echo']
'Brilliant Flower Circus' F, ob, Kordes; flowers brilliant orange, 2.5 in., full, cupped, borne in clusters, slight sweet fragrance; recurrent; moderate (30 - 40 in), compact growth; intr. 2007
Brilliant Hit™ -- See 'Poultop'
'Brilliant King' F, mr, 1961, Leenders, J.; flowers bright red, shallow, 4 in., 32 petals, cupped; ['Cocorico' × 'Orange Delight']
'Brilliant Light' -- See 'Kagayaki'
'Brilliant Meillandina' -- See 'Meiranoga'
Brilliant Pink Iceberg™ -- See 'Probril'
'Brilliant Red' HT, mr, 1938, Lens; bud very long, pointed; flowers brilliant red, well-formed, very large, dbl.; foliage bright green; vigorous, bushy growth; ['Charles P. Kilham' × 'Étoile de Hollande']
'Brilliant Rosamini' Min; intr. 2000
'Brilliant Sea-duction' -- See 'Just Brilliant'
'Brilliant Star' F, mr, 1965, Watkins Roses; flowers bright red, center shaded yellow, 2½-3 in., 12-20 petals, borne in clusters; foliage glossy; vigorous growth; ['Masquerade' × 'Dickson's Flame']
'Brilliant Vigorosa' -- See 'Korgazell'
'Briman' ('Manteo') Min, mp, 1993, Bridges, Dennis A.; flowers medium, dbl., borne mostly singly; foliage small, medium green, semi-glossy; some prickles; tall (55-60 cm.), upright, bushy growth; ['Rise 'n' Shine' × seedling]; intr. 1993
'Briman'   MinFl, m, Bridges, Dennis; intr. 2003
'Brimark' ('Remarkable') F, pb, 2004, Bridges, Dennis A.; flowers shades of pink with white and a little yellow, reverse lighter, 3½ in., full, borne in small clusters, slight fragrance; foliage medium size, dark green, semi-glossy; prickles 1/8 to 7/16 in., slight curve pointing slightly; growth bushy, medium, vigorous (4 ft); garden, exhibition, cutting; ['Tiki' × 'Mixed pollen']; intr. 2005
'Brimolly' ('Molly') Min, mp, 2006, Bridges, Dennis A.; flowers medium pink, reverse slightly lighter, 1½ in., full, borne mostly solitary; foliage medium size, dark green, semi-glossy; prickles moderate, ¼ in., straight, tan; growth compact, medium (22-24 in.); garden decoration, containers, exhibition, cutting; ['Sam Trivett' × unknown]; intr. 2006
'Brimoon' -- See 'Brirose'
'Brimorgan' ('Doris Morgan') Min, dp, 2003, Bridges, Dennis; flowers 1 in., dbl., borne mostly solitary, moderate fragrance; foliage medium size, medium green, semi-glossy; prickles ¼ in., straight, moderate; growth upright, bushy, tall (28-32 in.); garden, exhibition, cutting; ['Jennifer' × unknown];

intr. 2003

'Brindis' LCl, rb, 1962, Dot, Simon; flowers geranium-red, center light yellow to medium, 2-2½ in., single, borne in small clusters, no fragrance; foliage dark; vigorous growth; ['Orange Triumph, Climbing' × ('Phyllis Bide' × Baccará®)]

Brinessa® HT, pb, Delforge; flowers different shades of pink, 10 cm., very dbl., high-centered, intense fragrance; dark green, glossy, leathery foliage; strong stems; erect, upright growth to 80 cm.; intr. 1985

'Briney' ('Whitney') Min, w, 1994, Bridges, Dennis A.; bud blush pink; flowers near white with a hint of pink, medium, dbl., vase-shaped, borne mostly singly or in small clusters, moderate fragrance; foliage small, medium green, semi-glossy; few prickles; medium (38 cm.), upright, spreading growth; ['Jennifer' × unknown]; intr. 1994

'Brinight' ('Night Out') F, pb, 2004, Bridges, Dennis A.; flowers deep pink with a little white at base of petals, reverse slightly lighter, 3½ in., dbl., high-centered, borne mostly solitary, slight fragrance; foliage medium size, dark green, semi-glossy, disease-resistant; prickles ¼ in., pointed, curving downward; growth upright, medium (3½ ft.); garden, exhibition, cut flower; [Signature® × 'Doris Morgan']; intr. 2005

Briosa® Min, yb, Barni, V.; bud globular; flowers yellow, orange and pink, very double, borne in clusters of 3 - 5, moderate fragrance; foliage small; compact (40 - 45 cm.) growth; intr. 2007

'Briricky' ('Ricky Hendrick') MinFl, dr, 2006, Bridges, Dennis A.; flowers dark red, reverse slightly lighter, 2¼ in., full, high-centered, borne mostly solitary; recurrent; foliage medium size, dark green, semi-glossy, disease-resistant; prickles moderate, ¼ in., straight, slightly pointing down, light tan; growth spreading, medium (24-30 in.); garden, exhibition, containers; ['Jennifer' × Miss Flippins™]; intr. 2006

'Brirose' ('Brimoon', 'Moonlight and Roses') Min, m, 1998, Bridges, Dennis A.; flowers light lavender with rosy edges, with darker lavender and lavender overlay, 2-2½ in., full, high-centered, borne mostly singly; foliage medium size, dark green, glossy; some prickles; bushy, upright growth; PP11531; [seedling × unknown]; intr. 1998

'Brisbane Blush' F, pb, Long, P.; [('Golden Slippers' × 'Lavendula') × 'Prima Ballerina']; intr. 1993

Brise Parfum® LCl, lp, Barni; flowers soft pink, fading toward white, 3 cm., double, rosette, borne in large, spike-shaped clusters, intense fragrance; foliage medium to small; 250 - 400 cm. growth; intr. 2006

'Brise Parfumée' F, mr, 1950, Truffaut, G.; bud pointed; flowers dbl., borne in clusters; foliage glossy, bronze; numerous prickles; stems bark and twigs reddish brown; very vigorous growth; ['Böhm's Triumph' × 'Baby Chateau']

'Briseflu' ('Rosenzauber') S, w, Briant; intr. 1989

'Brisiness' ('Riviere de Diamant') Min, w, Briant; intr. 1990

'Brisis' ('Sis') Min, w, 1998, Bridges, Dennis A.; flowers delicate white with a hint of pink, firm substance, 1½ in., dbl., high-centered, borne mostly singly, slight fragrance; recurrent; foliage small, medium green, semi-glossy; few prickles; stems long; strong, bushy, slightly spreading growth; disease resistant; [Party Girl™ × 'Cape Hatteras']; intr. 1998

'Brispring' ('Breath of Spring') Min, my, 2001, Bridges, Dennis; flowers 1⅞ in., dbl., borne mostly solitary; foliage large, dark green, semi-glossy; prickles 3/8 in., straight, moderate; growth upright, tall (2½ ft.); garden decorative, containers, cutting; PPAF; [('Summer Sunset' × seedling) × unknown]; intr. 2002

'Bristar' ('Starship') MinFl, yb, 2002, Bridges, Dennis; flowers yellow blushed with coral, reverse yellow, 2½ in., full, high-centered, borne mostly solitary, no fragrance; recurrent; foliage medium size, medium green, semi-glossy; prickles ¼ in., pointed, slight downward curve, moderate; growth upright, tall (2½-3 ft.); garden, exhibition, containers, cutting; ['Summer Sunset' × unknown]; intr. 2003

'Bristep' ('Steppin' Out') HT, mp, 1995, Bridges, Dennis A.; flowers clear pink, large, 30-35 petals, high-centered, borne mostly singly, moderate fragrance; recurrent; foliage medium size, dark green, semi-glossy; few prickles; medium (4½ ft.), bushy growth; ['Kardinal' × 'Thriller']; intr. 1995

'Bristly Cushion' ('White Balconia') S, w, Kordes; flowers pure white; low, spreading growth; subject to powdery mildew; intr. 2007

'Bristol' HT, rb, 1968, Sanday, John; flowers bright crimson, reverse lighter, large, dbl.; foliage dark; compact growth; ['Gavotte' × 'Tropicana']

'Bristol Post' HT, op, 1972, Sanday, John; flowers pale salmon-pink, base orange, pointed, 4½ in., 29 petals; foliage slightly glossy, dark; upright growth; ['Vera Dalton' × 'Parasol']

'Brisun' ('Summer Sunset') Min, yb, 1993, Bridges, Dennis A.; flowers bright yellow with salmon pink shading, medium, dbl., high-centered, borne mostly solitary; foliage small, medium green, semi-glossy; some prickles; medium (45 cm.), bushy, compact growth; [Fancy Pants™ × seedling]; intr. 1993

'Brisuzy' ('Suzy') Min, mp, 1991, Bridges, Dennis A.; bud pointed; flowers medium pink, near white at base blending to light pink, lightens slightly with age, medium, 38-40 petals, high-centered, borne singly or in sprays of 3 - 5, slight fragrance; foliage medium size, dark green, semi-glossy; bushy, medium growth; PP7738; [Party Girl™ × seedling]; intr. 1991

'Britannia' HT, Dobbie; intr. 1916

'Britannia' ('Britannica') Pol, rb, 1929, Burbage Nursery; flowers crimson, center white, small, single, borne in clusters of 30-40; recurrent bloom; foliage small, leathery, light; compact, bushy growth; ['Coral Cluster' × 'Eblouissant']

'Britannia' ('Rochemenier Village') HT, ob, Fryer, Gareth; flowers apricot and gold, changing to nectarine and orange as it opens, dbl., high-centered, borne profusely, moderate fragrance; growth free branching, medium (75 cm.); intr. 1998

'Britannica' -- See 'Britannia'

'Brite Blue' HT, m; flowers of blue mauve with deep lavender shades and a red purple finish, intense fragrance; florist rose; intr. 1984

'Brite Eyes' LCl, pb, Radler; flowers medium pink with white eye and yellow stamens, 7-10 petals, shallow cup, borne in clusters, moderate fragrance; recurrent; foliage disease-resistant; compact (6-8 ft.) growth; intr. 2006

Brite Lites® -- See 'Hartanna'

'Britestripe' -- See 'Clebrite'

'Britestripes' -- See 'Clebrite'

'Britide' ('Tidewater') MinFl, w, 1991, Bridges, Dennis A.; bud pointed; flowers ivory white with slight pink tints, 2½ in., 30-36 petals, high-centered, borne usually singly, moderate fruity fragrance; recurrent; foliage medium size, medium green, matte; prickles few, flat, 5 mm.; stems long; bushy, spreading, medium growth; hips globular, 1.5-2 cm., green with medium orange shades; PP8531; ['Jennifer' × unknown]; intr. 1991

'British Columbia Centennial' HT, pb, 1972, Boerner; bud ovoid; flowers light rose-pink, reverse white, large, dbl., high-centered, slight fragrance; foliage leathery; vigorous growth; ['Pink Masterpiece' × seedling]

'British Queen' HT, w, 1912, McGredy; flowers creamy white, center flushed, large, dbl., high-centered; foliage light green, soft; long, weak stems; bushy growth

'Britrick' ('Trickster') Min, rb, 1995, Bridges, Dennis A.; bud medium; flowers red with pale pink to white reverse, medium, 28-32 petals, high-centered, borne mostly singly, moderate fruity fragrance; recurrent; foliage small, medium green, semi-glossy; prickles moderate, medium length; medium (18 in.), slightly spreading growth; hips globular, medium green; PP9931; ['Jennifer' × 'Red Beauty']; intr. 1995

'Brittany Noel' S, w, J. B. Williams; flowers dbl., pompon, borne in clusters of pure white blooms; groundcover; spreading growth to 2 ft.; intr. 2005

'Brittany's Glowing Star' -- See 'Manstar'

'Brity' ('Tycoon') HT, mr, 1997, Bridges,

Dennis A.; flowers very dbl., 41 petals, borne mostly singly; foliage medium size, dark green, semi-glossy; medium (4ft.) upright, bushy growth; ['Kardinal' × 'Thriller']

'Briyoung' ('Forever Young') Min, pb, 1997, Bridges, Dennis A.; flowers full, 1½ in., very dbl., borne mostly singly; foliage medium size, dark green, semi-glossy; low (12-14 in.), compact growth; ['Trickster' × unknown]

'Brno' HT, ob, 1933, Böhm, J.; flowers maroon, orange, gold, open, large, semi-dbl.; foliage glossy; vigorous, bushy growth; ['Souv. de George Beckwith' × 'Rosemary']

'Broadcaster' Gr, or, 1971, Perry, Anthony; bud ovoid; flowers medium, dbl., slight fragrance; foliage dark; vigorous growth; [Queen Elizabeth® × 'Circus']; intr. 1969

'Broadlands' -- See 'Sonnenschirm'

'Broadway' LCl, ab, Clark, A.; flowers apricot, large, single, flat; spring-blooming; healthy evergreen foliage; some references say introduction date is 1933; no support found for this date

Broadway™ -- See 'Burway'

'Broala' ('Alamode') Min, w, 1997, Brown, Ted; flowers medium, single, borne in small clusters; foliage medium size, dark green, glossy; bushy, medium (2½ ft.) growth; ['Esprit' × Party Girl™]

'Brobunt' ('Snow Bunting') S, w, 2000, Brown, Ted; flowers white with pale pink center, 2½ in., full, borne in large clusters, slight fragrance; foliage medium size, dark green, glossy; few prickles; bushy, low (4 ft.) growth; ['Meidomonac' × seedling]

'Broburn' ('Burning Ember') LCl, rb, 2000, Brown, Ted; flowers cream, center fading to medium red petal edges, reverse cream, frilled edges, 3½ in., 8-14 petals, borne in small clusters; foliage medium size, medium green, semi-glossy; prickles moderate; climbing, upright, medium (8-10 ft.) growth; ['Esprit' × Night Light™]; intr. 2000

'Brocade' ('Jeune Fille') HT, pb, 1960, Combe; bud ovoid; flowers soft rose, base cream-white, 4-5 in., 54 petals, cupped, moderate fragrance; foliage leathery; vigorous, upright growth; PP1856; ['Charlotte Armstrong' × 'Baiser']

'Brocade' S, w, Williams, J. Benjamin; flowers ivory with mauve tint, dbl.; intr. 1998

'Brocake' ('Cheese Cake') Min, w, 1997, Brown, Ted; flowers medium, dbl., borne mostly singly; foliage medium size, dark green, glossy; bushy, medium (5 ft.) growth; ['Esprit' × seedling]

'Brocap' ('Polar Cap') MinFl, w, 2004, Brown, Ted; flowers white, green tinge, reverse white, 2¼ in., dbl., borne mostly solitary, slight fragrance; foliage medium size, dark green, matte; prickles very small, pointed; growth upright, tall (30 in.); exhibition; ['Luis Desamero' × 'Radiant (Min)']; intr. 2005

'Brocarp' ('Fragrant Carpet') Min, dp, 1997, Brown, Ted; flowers medium, dbl., borne in small clusters, intense fragrance; foliage medium size, dark green, semi-glossy; spreading (2 × 5 ft.) growth; [seedling × seedling]

'Brocéliande' HT, rb, Adam; flowers fuchsia with lilac, ivory, and yellow stripes, dbl.; intr. 2002

'Broclann' ('LeAnn Rimes, Climbing') Cl HT, pb, 2007, Brown, Ted; flowers medium, full, borne mostly solitary; prickles moderate; growth climbing, tall (15 ft.); [sport of 'LeAnn Rimes']; intr. 2007

'Brocor' ('Corinne') F, ab, 1997, Brown, Ted; flowers medium, dbl., borne in small clusters; foliage medium size, dark green, glossy; bushy, medium (30 in.) growth; ['Esprit' × 'Indian Summer']

'Brodan' ('Danielle') Min, mp, 1997, Brown, Ted; flowers medium pink, fading to light pink, 1½ in., full, borne in small clusters, intense fragrance; foliage medium size, medium green, semi-glossy; bushy, medium (18 in.) growth; ['Esprit' × seedling]

'Brodream' ('Canadian Dream') F, m, 1997, Brown, Ted; flowers single, 3 in., single, borne in small clusters; foliage medium size, dark green, glossy; upright, tall (4½ × 6ft.)growth; ['Nymphenburg' × seedling]

'Broemp' ('Red Emperor') F, dr, 1997, Brown, Ted; flowers large, dbl., borne in small clusters; foliage medium size, dark green, glossy; spreading, low (2ft.) growth; ['Esprit' × seedling]

'Brofox' ('Foxtrot') F, ob, 1997, Brown, Ted; flowers medium, single, borne mostly singly; foliage medium size, burgundy turning dark green, glossy; spreading, low (1ft.) growth; ['Esprit' × 'Stretch Johnson']

'Brogar' ('Red Garter') F, rb, 1997, Brown, Ted; flowers medium, single, borne in small clusters; foliage medium size, dark red turning dark green, glossy; upright, medium (4 ft.) growth; ['Esprit' × 'Stretch Johnson']

'Brogold' ('Going for Gold') HT, my, 2004, Brown, Ted; flowers medium yellow, reverse medium yellow, 5 in., dbl., borne mostly solitary; foliage medium size, medium green, semi-glossy, red when new; prickles medium, hooked; growth upright, medium (4-5 ft.); garden decoration, exhibition; [seedling × seedling]; intr. 2005

'Brög's Canina' (strain of R. canina), lp; almost thornless; vigorous growth; in use as an understock

'Broham' ('Hambleden') F, pb, 2000, Brown, Ted; flowers medium pink fading to yellow center, slightly deeper pink reverse, frilled outer, 4½ in., 8-14 petals, borne in small clusters, slight fragrance; foliage large, dark green, semi-glossy; prickles moderate; upright, medium (4½ ft.) growth; ['Esprit' × Night Light™]

'Brohan' ('Hannah Brown') Min, dp, 2004, Brown, Ted; flowers deep pink, reverse deep pink, 1½ in., dbl., borne mostly solitary, moderate fragrance; foliage medium size, dark green, matte; prickles small, pointed,; growth upright, medium (2 ft.); exhibition; garden decorative; ['Luis Desamero' × Shadow Dancer™]; intr. 2005

'Broheart' ('Heartstrings') Min, mr, 1997, Brown, Ted; flowers large, opening to old-fashioned form, 41 petals, borne in small clusters; foliage medium size, dark green, dull; bushy, medium (16 in.) growth; ['Esprit' × seedling]

'Brojoy' ('Kayli Joy') Min, yb, 2004, Brown, Ted; flowers light yellow/pink edging, reverse light yellow, 1½ in., dbl., borne mostly solitary; foliage medium size, dark green, matte; prickles small, pointed,; growth upright, medium (2 ft.); exhibition; garden decorative; ['Luis Desamero' × Hot Tamale™]; intr. 2005

'Brokat' HT, r, Tantau; intr. 2003

'Brolife' ('Night Life') S, op, 2000, Brown, Ted; flowers orange pink, reverse lighter, 3½ in., dbl., borne in small clusters, slight fragrance; foliage medium size, medium green, semi-glossy; few prickles; upright, medium (5-6 ft.) growth; ['Esprit' × seedling]

'Bromal' ('Malcolm Scott') F, mr, 2000, Brown, Ted; flowers large, full, borne in small clusters, slight fragrance; foliage large, dark green, semi-glossy; few prickles; growth upright, medium (3 ft.); ['Esprit' × 'Rosana']

'Broman' ('Music Man') Min, ob, 1997, Brown, Ted; flowers medium, dbl., borne mostly singly; foliage medium size, medium green, semi-glossy; upright, tall (20-24in.)growth; ['Esprit' × seedling]

'Bronew' ('New Antique') Min, lp, 1997, Brown, Ted; flowers large, very dbl., borne in small clusters; foliage medium size, dark green, semi-glossy; growth bushy, tall (30 in.)

Bronze™ Min, ob, Olesen; flowers dbl., 25-30 petals, no fragrance; foliage dark green, glossy; growth bushy, very low (20-40 cm.); PP11500

'Bronze Baby' -- See 'Peaxanthous'

'Bronze Beauty' F, ob, 1975, Warriner, William A.; bud ovoid-pointed; flowers golden yellow to orange-yellow, open, 4 in., 27 petals, slight fragrance; foliage large, leathery; vigorous growth; ['Electra' × 'Woburn Abbey']; intr. 1974

'Bronze Bedder' HT, yb, 1920, Paul, W.; flowers bronzy yellow, large, single

'Bronze Masterpiece' HT, ab, 1960, Boerner; bud long; flowers bronze-apricot, becoming orange-yellow, 5½-6 in., 48 petals, high-centered, moderate fragrance; foliage leathery, glossy; vigorous, upright growth; PP2000; ['Golden Masterpiece' × 'Kate Smith']; intr. 1960

Bronze Star™ -- See 'Wezaprt'

'Bronze Sunset' HT, ab, 2001, Coiner,

Jim; flowers medium, semi-dbl., borne in small clusters, no fragrance; foliage medium size, light green, matte; prickles 1/16 in., few; growth compact, medium; garden decorative; [seedling × seedling]

'Brook' -- See 'Seseragi'

'Brook Song' S, my, 1985, Buck, Dr. Griffith J.; flowers imbricated form, large, 40 petals, borne singly and in clusters of up to 8; repeat bloom; foliage leathery, dark; prickles awl-like, tan; erect growth; hardy; ['Prairie Star' × 'Tom Brown']; intr. 1984

'Brookdale Giant White' -- See 'Jackman's White'

'Brooks' Red' HT, mr, 2000, Brooks, Warren; flowers medium red, reverse blushing red to yellow, 5 in., full, high-centered, exhibition, borne mostly singly, slight fragrance; good repeat; foliage large, dark green, semi-glossy; prickles moderate; long, strong stems; growth upright, tall (5 ft.); intr. 2000

'Brookville' HT, ly, 1942, Brookville Nursery; flowers cream-yellow; [sport of 'Leonard Barron']

'Broomfield Novelty' -- See 'Margaret Anderson'

'Broper' ('Persistence') LCl, mp, 2000, Brown, Ted; flowers dbl., borne in small clusters; foliage medium size, dark green, semi-glossy; prickles moderate; growth upright, climbing, tall (9 ft.); ['Esprit' × 'Meg']

'Bropre' ('Du Pré Tell') S, pb, 2001, Brown, Ted; flowers blush pink to light pink with deeper petal edges, light pink reverse, mauve, 4½ in., semi-dbl., borne in small clusters, moderate fragrance; foliage medium size, dark green, glossy; prickles small, hooked, moderate in number; growth upright (4-6 ft.); garden decorative; [sport of 'Jacqueline du Pré']

'Brorasp' ('Raspberry Bouquet') S, rb, 2006, Brown, Ted; flowers red, reverse cream, 4 in., full, borne in large clusters, strong raspberry fragrance; foliage medium size, medium green, semi-glossy; prickles small, hooked, brown, moderate; growth upright, bushy, tall (4-6 ft.); exhibition, garden decorative; ['Lydia (Kordes)' × 'Cocktail (Meimick)']; intr. 2006

'Broreal' ('Reality') LCl, mp, 2000, Brown, Ted; flowers medium pink, reverse lighter, 3½ in., full, borne in small clusters, moderate fragrance; foliage medium size, dark green, glossy, very thick, rubbery; prickles moderate; growth spreading, medium (6-8 ft.); ['Esprit' × seedling]

'Broroy' ('Viceroy') Gr, dp, 1997, Brown, Ted; flowers medium, dbl., borne in large clusters; foliage medium size, dark green, glossy; growth upright, medium (4½ ft.); ['Esprit' × 'Harmonie']

'Brosay' ('Rothsay') F, or, 2000, Brown, Ted; flowers bright orange-red, 3½ in., dbl., borne in small clusters, slight fragrance; foliage medium size, dark green, semi-glossy; few prickles; bushy, medium (3 ft.) growth; ['Royal Occasion' × seedling]

'Broser' ('Serenity') S, lp, 2000, Brown, Ted; flowers semi-dbl., borne in large clusters, moderate fragrance; foliage large, dark green, dull; prickles moderate; growth upright, tall (6-7 ft.); ['Esprit' × seedling]

'Brospark' ('Sparkling Fire') F, mr, 2000, Brown, Ted; flowers very bright red, 4 in., semi-dbl., borne in large clusters, slight fragrance; foliage medium size, medium green, semi-glossy; numerous prickles; upright, medium (4 ft.) growth; ['Esprit' × 'Stretch Johnson']

'Brosun' ('Harvest Sun') F, ob, 1997, Brown, Ted; flowers large, 8-14 petals, borne in large clusters (8-10), moderate fragrance; foliage medium size, dark green, glossy; growth upright, tall (4½ ft.); ['Esprit' × Mountbatten®]

'Brother Cadfael' -- See 'Ausglobe'

Brother John™ F, ab; flowers apricot in center, fading to blush pink on outer petals, full, rosette; intr. 2004

'Brother Sun' Gr, my, 1998, Fleming, Joyce L.; flowers medium yellow, deeper color at base, flattened top, long lasting, 2½-3 in., 41-50 petals, borne mostly singly, moderate fragrance; foliage medium size, medium green, dull; prickles moderate; compact, upright growth; [Goldener Olymp® × Australian Gold®]; intr. 1997

'Brother Wilfred' HT, mp, 1976, Wood; [sport of 'Alec's Red']

'Brothers Grimm Fairy Tales' -- See 'Korassenet'

'Browave' ('Tidal Wave') S, pb, 2004, Brown, Ted; flowers pink, yellow, cream, and orange, reverse cream with pink edges, 4 in., dbl., borne in large clusters, slight fragrance; foliage medium size, medium green, semi-glossy; prickles medium, slightly hooked; growth upright, medium (6½ ft.); garden decorative; ['Nymphenberg' × seedling]; intr. 2005

Brown County Splendor™ -- See 'Wilkbsp'

'Brown Study' F, r, 1999, Jerabek, Paul E.; flowers russet, turning brown, darker at edges, 2¾ in., dbl., borne singly and in small clusters; foliage medium size, dark green, semi-glossy; prickles moderate; spreading, medium (3 ft.) growth; intr. 1998

'Brown Sugar' -- See 'Talbro'

'Brown Velvet' -- See 'Macultra'

'Brownell Yellow Rambler' ('Yellow Rambler') HMult, my, 1942, Brownell; flowers petals recurved, dbl., borne in more open clusters than Dorothy Perkins, slight fragrance; [('Emily Gray' × 'Ghislaine de Feligonde') × 'Golden Glow']

'Brownell's Everblooming Pillar No. 73' -- See 'Scarlet Sensation'

'Brownie' F, r, 1960, Boerner; bud ovoid, tan shades, edged pinkish; flowers brownish tan, reverse yellow, 3½-4 in., 38 petals, cupped, borne in small clusters, moderate fragrance; foliage leathery; vigorous, upright, bushy growth; PP1720; [('Lavender Pinocchio' × unknown) × 'Grey Pearl']; intr. 1959

'Brownlow Hill Rambler' -- See 'Mme Alice Garnier'

'Browsholme Rose' Ayr, w, 1900

'Brundrette Centenary' S, dp

Brunella® ('Barmezz') Min, mr

'Brunette' HGal, Descemet; intr. about 1810

'Brunette' F, yb, 1979, Lens; bud ovoid; flowers amber-yellow to orange, 1½-2½ in., 25 petals, cupped; foliage glossy; [('Purpurine') × ('Lavender Pinocchio' × 'Fillette')) × ('Gold Strike' × 'Golden Garnette')]; intr. 1970

'Bruno Perpoint' S, mp, Guillot-Massad; intr. 1998

'Bruno, Golden Boy' -- See 'Horoldbruno'

'Brunonii Himalayica' -- See 'Paul's Himalayan Musk Rambler'

Bruocsella® -- See 'Lenbru'

'Brushstrokes' -- See 'Guescolour'

'Brutus' -- See 'Brennus'

'Bruun' F, Delforge, H.; intr. 1995

'Bruxelles' -- See 'Lenbru'

'Bryan' -- See 'Gelyan'

'Bryan' LCl, my, Mekdeci; intr. 1993

'Bryan Freidel Pink Tea' T, w

Bryce Canyon™ -- See 'Pouldrik'

'Brymom' ('Dyllan's Mom') MinFl, rb, 2001, Bryan Epstein; flowers red/orange/yellow, yellow/red reverse, 2 in., dbl., high-centered, borne mostly solitary, slight fragrance; foliage large, dark green, matte; growth upright, tall (3-4 ft.); garden decorative, exhibition; ['Fireworks' × Perfect Moment™]

'Brymore Jubilee' HT, my, 2002, Poole, Lionel; flowers full, high-centered, borne mostly solitary, slight fragrance; foliage medium size, dark green, glossy; prickles medium, triangular, moderate; growth upright, bushy, vigorous, medium; exhibition, bedding; ['Tom Foster' × 'Ravenswood Village']; intr. 2002

'Brypink' ('My Pink') HT, pb, 2001, Bryan Epstein; flowers petals pink with white edge, reverse lighter, 2½ in., very full, high-centered, borne mostly solitary, slight fragrance; foliage medium size, dark green, semi-glossy; growth upright, tall (6-7 ft.); garden decorative, exhibition; ['Duchess' × 'First Prize']

'Brypurple' ('Purple Pleasure') HT, m, 2001, Bryan Epstein; flowers mauve with darker edge, reverse lighter, 3-4 in., dbl., high-centered, borne mostly solitary, moderate fragrance; foliage medium size, medium green, semi-glossy; growth upright, medium (5 ft.); garden decorative, exhibition; ['Fragrant Plum' × 'Blue Bird']

'Brysun' ('Sunsational') HT, yb, 2001, Epstein, Bryan; flowers yellow with white edges, reverse lighter, 4-4½ in., full, high-centered, borne mostly solitary, moderate fragrance; foliage dark green, semi-glossy; growth upright, medium (5 ft.); garden decorative, exhibition; [sport of 'Veldfire']

'Bryte White' HT, w

'BS Red' HT, dr, Sugimoto, M.; flowers dark crimson, petals slightly reflexed, large, 25-29 petals; prickles concave, numerous; growth tall, upright; ['Marjorie Anderson' × (Uwe Seeler® × 'Cara Mia')]; intr. 1983

'Bubble Bath' HMsk, lp, Matson; flowers soft pink, dbl., borne in clusters; growth large, cascading shrub, can be trained as a climber; ['Kathleen' × 'Climbing Cecile Brunner']; intr. 1980

'Bubble Gum' -- See 'Busugum'

'Bubble Gum Mega Brite' Min, mp, J&P; PP11299; intr. 2000

'Bubbles' -- See 'Frybubbly'

'Bubbles' -- See 'Zipbub'

Bubikopf® -- See 'Tankobi'

'Bucaroo' -- See 'Simon Estes'

'Bucbi' ('Katy Road Pink', Audace®, Carefree Beauty™) S, mp, 1979, Buck, Dr. Griffith J.; bud ovoid, long, pointed; flowers light rose, 4½ in., 15-20 petals, moderate fragrance; repeat bloom; foliage olive-green, smooth; vigorous, upright, spreading growth; PP4225; [seedling × 'Prairie Princess']; intr. 1977

'Bucblu' ('Blue Skies') HT, m, 1983, Buck, Dr. Griffith J.; flowers large, 35 petals, moderate fragrance; foliage large, semi-glossy; upright, bushy growth; PP5756; [((('Sterling Silver' × 'Intermezzo') × ('Sterling Silver' × 'Simone')) × ('Music Maker' × (Blue Moon® × 'Tom Brown'))]; intr. 1984

'Buccaneer' Gr, my, 1952, Swim, H.C.; bud urn-shaped; flowers buttercup-yellow, 3-3½ in., 30 petals, cupped, moderate fragrance; foliage dark, leathery; vigorous, upright, tall growth; PP1119; ['Golden Rapture' × ('Max Krause' × 'Capt. Thomas')]

'Buckaroo' -- See 'Simon Estes'

'Buckeye Belle' S, pb, 1956, Garwood; bud globular; flowers pale to deep pink, open, 1½ in., 15 petals, borne in compact clusters; abundant, recurrent bloom; foliage dark; vigorous, upright, bushy growth; [R. hugonis × seedling]

Buck's Fizz™ -- See 'Poulgav'

'Bucred' S, rb, Buck; intr. 2005

'Bucroo' ('Bucaroo', 'Buckaroo') S, mp, 2006, Buck, Dr. Griffith J.; intr. 2003

'Bud Meyers' -- See 'Seabud'

'Budapest' HT, ab

'Budatetini' T, ob, Mark; intr. 1960

'Buenos Aires' F, r, 1957, Silva; flowers burnt brick to dark red-ochre, dbl.; low growth; ['Mme Henri Guillot' × 'Pinocchio']

'Buff Beauty' HMsk, ab, 1939, Bentall, Ann; flowers apricot-yellow, 4 in., 50 petals, borne in clusters of 8-12, moderate fragrance; foliage large, medium green, semi-glossy; vigorous (to 6 ft.) growth; ['William Allen Richardson' × unknown]

'Buff King' LCl, ab, 1939, Horvath; bud ovoid, deep amber; flowers amber and buff, large, cupped; foliage glaucous green; long, strong stems; very vigorous (10-12 ft.) growth

'Buffalo' HRg, dp, Uhl, J.; intr. 1989

'Buffalo-Bill' HP, lp, 1889, Verdier, E.; flowers very light pink, large, full, flat

'Buffalo Bill' -- See 'Macyoumis'

'Buffalo Gal' ('Foxi Pavement', 'Foxi', 'Foxy Pavement', 'Luberon') HRg, dp, Uhl, J.; flowers lavender-pink, dbl., loose, borne in clusters, intense fragrance; foliage large, light green, wrinkled, shiny; growth upright, 3-4 ft.; intr. 1989

'Buffon' HGal, m, Vibert; flowers purple-violet, large, full, slight fragrance; intr. 1836

'Buffon' HP, mr, Guillot; flowers velvety scarlet, medium, full; intr. 1859

'Buffon' ('Joséphine', 'Rose Buffon') P, lp, before 1821; flowers pale rose-flesh, large, plump, Centifolia-like, very dbl.; often described as a Damask Perpetual

Buffy™ -- See 'Kinbuff'

'Buffy Sainte-Marie' -- See 'Manclassic'

Bugatti® HT, m, W. Kordes Söhne; bud urceolate; flowers magenta-purple, 10 cm., 50-55 petals, cupped, borne mostly singly, slight fragrance; recurrent; foliage large, dark green, glossy; prickles numerous, 8-10 mm., hooked downward; stems 70 cm; vigorous, upright growth; PP14176; [seedling × seedling]; florist rose; intr. 2002

Bugle Boy -- See 'Aroglofy'

'Buisman's Glory' F, mr, 1952, Buisman, G. A. H.; flowers currant-red, open, medium, single; foliage light green; ['Karen Poulsen' × 'Sangerhausen']

'Buisman's Gold' F, dy

'Buisman's Triumph' F, mp, 1952, Buisman, G. A. H.; flowers bright pink, becoming lighter, large, 13 petals; foliage dark; vigorous growth; ['Käthe Duvigneau' × 'Cinnabar']

'Buisson Ardent' Gr, mr, 1956, Gaujard; flowers bright red, medium; foliage dark; ['Peace' × seedling]

'Buisson d'Or' HFt, my, 1928, Barbier; flowers canary-yellow, dbl.; good seasonal bloom; growth to 3-5 ft.; ['Mme Edouard Herriot' × 'Harison's Yellow']

'Bukala' LCl, ob

Bukavu -- See 'LLX9001'

'Bullata' ('À Feuilles Cloquées', 'À Feuilles de Chou', 'Rose à Feuilles de Laitue', R. × centifolia bullata, 'Monstrueuse', 'À Feuilles Crépues', 'À Feuilles Gaufrées') C, mp, 1809; flowers deep rose, vary large, 3 in., very dbl., globular, borne mostly singly or in clusters on long, slender peduncles, intense fragrance; summer bloom; foliage very large, thick, and crinkled like lettuce; becoming bronze-tinted in late summer

'Bullmeg' ('Meghan's Arrival') F, mr, 1995, Bull, Derek Gordon; flowers small, full, borne in large clusters; foliage medium size, light green, glossy; some prickles; upright, bushy, medium (1 m.) growth; [Doris Tysterman® × unknown]; intr. 1986

'Bull's Eye' HT, dr; flowers 11 cm., 30-40 petals, high-centered; greenhouse rose; intr. 2002

'Bull's Red' -- See 'Macroro'

'Bundesrat Häberlin' HFt, yb, 1940, Soupert & Notting; flowers medium, dbl.

'Bundle of Joy' -- See 'Socmagic'

'Bunker Hill' HT, dp, 1949, Fisher, G.; bud pointed; flowers rose-red, large, 25-40 petals, high-centered, intense fragrance; foliage leathery, dark; very vigorous, bushy growth; PP997; ['Rome Glory' × 'Better Times']

Bunny Hop -- See 'Jacclip'

'Bunte Frau Astrid Späth' Pol, lp, 1940, Vogel, M.; flowers light pink with red, medium, semi-dbl.

'Bunte Provinrose' -- See 'Variegata'

'Bunter Kobold' MinFl, yb, Dickson, Patrick; intr. 1995

'Buralp' (National Velvet™) HT, dr, 1988, Burks, Larry; flowers dark, deep velvet red, medium, 35 petals, urn-shaped, borne usually singly; foliage large, medium green, semi-glossy; prickles recurved, average, dark; upright, tall growth; hips globular, average, orange; PP7236; ['Poinsettia' × National Beauty™]; intr. 1990

'Burapward' ('Dreamward') HT, yb, 1996, Perry, Astor; flowers light yellow with pink blush, 4½ in., dbl., borne mostly singly; prickles moderate; ['Peace' × 'Granada']; intr. 1997

'Burastor' ('Astor Perry') HT, dy, 2004, Astor Perry; flowers full, borne mostly solitary, moderate fragrance; foliage medium size, dark green, semi-glossy; prickles average, recurved; growth upright, medium; garden decorative; ['Irish Gold' × 'Voo Doo']; intr. 2005

'Burbank' T, pb, 1900, Burbank; flowers light pink and crimson, 3-3½ in., dbl.; foliage glossy; Hermosa × Bon Silene seedling

'Burbeawall' ('Bea Wallace') HT, dr, 2007, Burks, Larry; flowers deep red, reverse medium red, 5 in., full, borne mostly solitary; foliage medium size, dark green, semi-glossy; prickles average, recurved, green/brown, moderate; growth upright, tall (60 in.); garden decorative, exhibition; [seedling × seedling]; intr. 2007

'Burbet' (Betty Wright™) Gr, m, 1988, Burks, Larry; flowers lilac-mauve, darker at tips, aging lighter lilac, semi-dbl., cupped, urn-shaped, slight fruity fragrance; foliage medium size, medium green, matte; prickles slight recurved, average, brown; bushy, medium growth; hips globular, average, orange-yellow; ['Angel Face' × seedling]

'Burbrahmvidya' ('Just Simon', 'Simply

Irresistible') HT, w, 1996, Datt, Braham; flowers white with pink tones, reverse cream with pink tones, medium, dbl., borne in small clusters, moderate fragrance; foliage medium size, medium green, semi-glossy; few prickles; upright, medium (4½ ft.) growth; ['First Prize' × 'Garden Party']

'Burbrindley' ('Katie Crocker') F, or, Burrows, Steven; intr. 1995

'Burcen' (Redlands Century™) HT, or, 1988, Perry, Anthony; flowers medium orange-red, aging slightly lighter, medium, semi-dbl., urn-shaped; foliage medium size, medium green, semi-glossy; prickles average, yellow-green; upright, medium growth; hips globular, small, orange; [World Peace™ × 'Command Performance']; intr. 1988

'Burcharlotte' ('Charlotte's Rose') F, ab, 2006, Burks, Larry; flowers pastel apricot, reverse pink to apricot, 3 in., semi-dbl., borne in small clusters; foliage medium size, medium green, semi-glossy; prickles average, slightly recurved, brown to dark tan, moderate; growth compact, medium (24-36 in.); garden decorative; [seedling × seedling]; intr. 2006

'Burcoy' ('Rosemary McCoy') HT, pb, 2004, Larry Burks; flowers pink blend, reverse pink, medium, full, borne mostly solitary, slight fragrance; foliage medium size, dark green, semi-glossy; prickles average, curve, few; upright, medium (60 in.) growth; garden; [seedling × seedling]; intr. 2004

'Burdancer' (Cloud Dancer™) Gr, w, 1995, Burks, Larry; flowers white blend, dbl., borne in small clusters; foliage medium size, medium green, semi-glossy; few prickles; upright, medium growth; ['White Queen Elizabeth' × unknown]; intr. 1995

'Burdel' (Delta Gold™) HT, yb, 1988, Perry, Anthony; flowers red and yellow blend, reverse red-yellow, medium, 35 petals, urn-shaped, slight fragrance; foliage medium size, dark green, glossy; prickles slight recurved, average, dark; strong stems; bushy, medium growth; hips round, average, orange; ['Arizona' × World Peace™]; intr. 1989

'Buret' T, m, about 1860, Buret; flowers bluish-red with violet, sometimes edged white, full, globular

'Bureuro' ('Europeana, Climbing') Cl F, dr, 1986, Burks, Joe J.; [sport of 'Europeana']; intr. 1987

'Burforyou' ('Forever Young') HT, yb, 2004, Burks, Larry; flowers full, borne mostly solitary; foliage medium size, medium green, semi-glossy; prickles average, recurved; growth upright, medium (60 in.); garden decorative; [Voodoo™ × unknown]; intr. 2004

'Burg Baden' LCl, mp, Kordes; flowers pale crimson, medium, single, borne in large clusters; intr. 1955

'Burgemeester Berger' HT, lp, 1934, Leenders Bros.; flowers soft pink, marked white; vigorous growth; [sport of 'Dame Edith Helen']

'Burgemeester Sandberg' HT, op, 1920, Van Rossem; flowers silvery pink, shaded coral-rose-pink, dbl.; ['Pharisaer' × 'Lady Alice Stanley']

'Burgemeester van Oppen' HT, my, 1939, Leenders, M.; flowers golden yellow; ['Golden Ophelia' × 'Pardinas Bonet']

'Bürgermeister Christen' HT, dp, 1911, Bernaix, A.; flowers large, dbl.; ['Mme Caroline Testout' × 'Fisher-Holmes']

'Burgess Pink' Min, mp
'Burgess Red' Min, mr
'Burgess Yellow' Min, my
Burghausen® -- See 'Koronto'
Burgund® -- See 'Korgund'
'Burgund '81' -- See 'Korgund '81'
'Burgundiaca' -- See 'Petite de Hollande'
'Burgundian Rose' -- See 'Pompon de Bourgogne'

'Burgundy' HT, mr, 1939, H&S; flowers wine-red broad, evenly arranged petals, dbl.; very vigorous growth; ['Vaterland' × seedling]

'Burgundy Ice' -- See 'Burgundy Iceberg'
'Burgundy Iceberg' ('Burgundy Ice', 'Prose', 'Purple Iceberg') F, m, Weatherly, Lilia; bud pointed to somewhat ovoid; flowers deep purple-red, lighter reverse, with velvety texture, 3-4 in., 25-30 petals, somewhat cupped, borne in clusters, slight honey fragrance; recurrent; foliage semi-glossy; prickles very few, medium, straight, angled slightly downward; bushy, medium (3 ft.) growth; hips obovate to ovoid ; PP16198; [sport of 'Brilliant Pink Iceberg']; intr. 2003

'Burgundy Popwell' HT, w, 2006, Popwell, Larry G., Sr; flowers white/pink edges, reverse white/pink edges, 2¾ in., full, borne mostly solitary; foliage medium size, medium green, semi-glossy; prickles moderate; growth bushy, up to 5 ft.; [Crystalline™ × 'Love']; intr. 2006

'Burgundy Queen' -- See 'Wiljame'
'Burgundy Rose' -- See 'Pompon de Bourgogne'
'Burgundy Trail' Cl Min, dr

'Burjes' ('Jesse's Jewels') HT, mp, 1996, Burks, Larry; flowers , 6-14 petals, borne mostly singly; foliage medium size, medium green, dull; few prickles; upright, medium growth; [(unknown × 'Pink Apache Belle') × unknown]

'Burke' P, m, 1860, Moreau & Robert; flowers slatey lilac

'Burkhard' -- See 'Grumpy'
'Burkhardt' -- See 'Grumpy'

Burlington™ (Red Fairy™, Velvet Cover™) S, dr, Olesen; bud short, globular; flowers dark red, 1½-2 in., 40-50 petals, cupped, borne in large clusters, slight floral fragrance; recurrent; foliage dark green, matte; prickles numerous, 4-5 mm, slightly concave, tan; broad, bushy (2 ft.) growth; PP12563; [seedling × seedling]; intr. 1995

'Burlov' (Pure Love™) HT, w, 1988, Perry, Anthony; bud medium, pointed; flowers 4½ in., 35-40 petals, cupped, borne singly, slight fragrance; recurrent; foliage medium size, dark green, semi-glossy; prickles slight recurved, average, brown-green; upright, medium growth; hips globular, average, grey-red; PP6781; [Queen Elizabeth® × World Peace™]; intr. 1987

'Burma Star' F, ab, 1975, Cocker; flowers light apricot yellow, large, 22 petals, moderate fragrance; foliage large, glossy; ['Arthur Bell' × 'Manx Queen']; intr. 1974

'Burnaby' ('Gold Heart', 'Golden Heart') HT, w, 1954, Eddie; flowers creamy white, 4-6 in., 56 petals, high-centered, slight fragrance; foliage dark, glossy; vigorous, bushy growth; PP1314; ['Phyllis Gold' × 'Pres. Herbert Hoover']

'Burnet Irish Marbled' -- See 'Irish Rich Marbled'

Burning Desire™ -- See 'Jacladin'
'Burning Desire' HT, ab, Delbard; intr. 2001

'Burning Ember' -- See 'Broburn'
'Burning Glow' -- See 'Burning Gold'
'Burning Gold' ('Burning Glow') F, ob, Poulsen; bud deep orange-red buds; flowers bright orange; vigorous growth; intr. 1990

'Burning Love' ('Amour Ardent', 'Brennende Liebe') F, mr, 1956, Tantau, Math.; flowers scarlet, 4 in., 22 petals, borne in trusses of 3-5, moderate fragrance; foliage dark, glossy; vigorous, bushy growth; ['Fanal' × 'Crimson Glory']; intr. 1956

'Burning Sky' -- See 'Wezeip'
'Burnleigh' F, lp; intr. 1999

'Burnt Orange' F, ob, 1976, Hamilton; flowers deep orange; [sport of 'Woburn Abbey']; intr. 1973

'Burred' ('Theodore Roosevelt') HT, dr, 1987, Burks, Larry; flowers deep red, fading slightly lighter, medium, 6-14 petals, high-centered, borne singly; foliage large, medium green, semi-glossy; prickles average, light yellow-green; upright, tall growth; hips globular, large, dark red; [sport of 'Alamo']; intr. 1986

'Burr's Multiflora' (clone of R. multiflora); growth vigorous; used as understock; used for understock

'Burseptdawn' ('September Dawn') HT, dy, 2007, Burks, Larry; flowers golden yellow, reverse deep yellow, medium, 4½ in., full, borne mostly solitary; foliage medium size, dark green, semi-glossy; prickles average, slightly recurved, brownish green, moderate; growth upright, medium (50 in.); garden decoration; [unknown × unknown]; intr. 2007

'Burspec' ('Good Luck') F, w, Burston; intr. 1996

'Bursrtpara' ('Tropical Paradise') HT, ob, 1996, Rodgers, Shafter R.; flowers orange blend, reverse orange blend with yellow gold, 4½ in., dbl., high-centered, borne mostly singly, moderate fragrance; recurrent; foliage large, dark green, glossy; few prickles; upright, tall (5 ft.) growth; ['South Seas' × 'First Prize']

'Burstein' ('Super Derby') HT, op, 1983, Burks, Joe J.; intr. 1982

'Burstol' ('Vivian Vivio Stolaruk') HT, rb, 2004, Burks, Larry; flowers red blend, pastel at base, reverse pink blend, 5 in., full, borne mostly solitary, slight fragrance; foliage medium size, medium green, semi-glossy; prickles average, curved; upright, medium (5 ft.) growth; garden decoration; [seedling × ('King of Hearts' × unknown)]; intr. 2004

'Burwah' Cl HT, dp, 1953, Ulrick, L.W.; flowers deep rose-pink, large, dbl., cupped; very vigorous climbing growth; ['Editor McFarland' × 'Black Boy (Cl HT)']

'Burway' (Broadway™) HT, yb, 1985, Perry, Anthony; bud pointed; flowers golden yellow, blended orange-pink, well-formed, 4-4½ in., 30-35 petals, high-centered, borne singly, moderate spice and damask fragrance; foliage medium to large, dark, semi-glossy; upright growth, moderately tall; PP5827; [('First Prize' × 'Gold Glow') × 'Sutter's Gold']; intr. 1986

'Burwin' (Double Perfection™) HT, rb, 1988, Winchel, Joseph F.; flowers red, reverse white, aging darker red, reverse cream, 4½ in., dbl., high-centered, borne singly, slight fragrance; recurrent; foliage medium size, dark green, semi-glossy; prickles average, slightly recurved, medium size, brown; bushy, upright, medium growth; hips round, average, orange; PP6705; [('My Dream' × 'First Prize') × seedling]

'Burwinladhom' (Ladies Home Journal®) HT, m, 1998, Winchel, Joseph F.; flowers pinkish mauve, medium, 8-14 petals, borne mostly singly; foliage medium size, medium green, semi-glossy; few prickles; upright, medium (4½-5 ft.) growth; [unknown × unknown]; intr. 1998

'Burwintradhom' (Traditional Home®) HT, m, 1998, Winchel, Joseph F.; flowers pinkish, high-centered, 4 in., dbl., high-centered, borne mostly singly; foliage medium size, dark green, semi-glossy; prickles moderate; growth upright, medium (5 ft.); [unknown × unknown]; intr. 1998

'Burworpe' (World Peace™) HT, pb, 1987, Perry, Anthony; flowers pink blend suffused with cream, tips of petals tinged dark pink, large, 30-35 petals, high-centered, moderate fruity fragrance; foliage large, medium green, semi-glossy, disease-resistant; prickles average; upright, tall growth; hips globular, orange; ['First Prize' × 'Gold Glow']; intr. 1991

'Buryear' ('New Year, Climbing') Cl Gr, ob, 1995, Burks, Joe J.; flowers spanish orange, medium, semi-dbl., borne in small clusters, slight fragrance; foliage medium size, medium green, glossy; some prickles; spreading, tall growth; [sport of 'New Year']; intr. 1995

'Buryellow' ('Yellow Blaze', Sun Flare, Climbing™) Cl F, my, 1987, Burks, Joe J.; flowers medium yellow, fading lighter, large, 20 petals, cupped, borne in sprays of 3-5, slight licorice fragrance; recurrent; foliage medium size, medium green, semi-glossy; prickles short, yellow-green, slightly curved; spreading, tall (14 ft.) growth; hips globular, medium, orange-red; PP6509; [sport of 'Sun Flare']; intr. 1987

'Busard Triomphant' ('Ardoisée', 'Mahaeca de Dupont', 'Rose Bleu', 'Violette Bronzée', 'Pourpre Ardoisée', 'Bleu', 'Bizarre Triomphant(e)', 'Charles de Mills') HGal, dr, before 1790; flowers dark, velvety violet-crimson, medium, very dbl., flat, regularly quartered, slight fragrance; foliage elliptical, dark green; few prickles; from Holland

'Busbugum' ('Bubble Gum') Min, pb, 1999, Buster, Larry S.; flowers pink, reverse ivory, 1¼ in., dbl., borne mostly singly; foliage medium size, medium green, semi-glossy; prickles moderate; upright, tall (2 ft.) growth; ['Garden State' × seedling]; intr. 1998

'Bush Baby' -- See 'Peanob'

'Bush Fire' HWich, mr, 1917, Clark, A.; flowers bright crimson, yellow zone around center, small, very large, dbl.

'Bush Garden Climber' LCl, op, Thomas

'Bush Walk' HRg, dr; intr. 2001

'Bushfire' -- See 'Poulbufi'

'Bushu' HT, ob, 1985, Yasuda, Yuji; bud ovoid; flowers orange-red, reverse lighter, large, 35 petals, high-centered, no fragrance; foliage medium size, dark, semi-glossy; prickles slanted downward; tall, vigorous, upright growth; [Dolce Vita® × Roklea®]

'Bushveld Dawn' -- See 'Meimainger'

'Busimel' ('Simply Elegant') Min, m, 1993, Buster, Larry S.; flowers light lavender inside with darker reverse, large, full, borne mostly singly; foliage medium size, medium green, matte; some prickles; upright, compact (50 cm.) growth; ['Lady X' × 'Winsome']; intr. 1993

'Busmalou' ('Mary Louise') MinFl, m, 1996, Buster, Larry S.; flowers red lavender, lighter lavender reverse, full, borne mostly singly, moderate fragrance; foliage medium green, dull; prickles moderate; upright, tall growth; ['Lady X' × 'Winsome']; intr. 1996

'Bustev' ('Stevie') Min, w, 1992, Buster, Larry S.; flowers 3 cm., 53 petals, borne mostly singly; foliage small, medium green, matte; some prickles; low (42 cm.), upright, compact growth; ['Frau Karl Druschki' × 'miniature seedling']

'Busy' Min, dp

'Busy Bee' -- See 'Savabusy'

'Busy Bee' -- See 'Korpancom'

'Busy Lizzie' F, mp, 1971, Harkness; flowers pink, 2 in., 12 petals; foliage glossy, dark; [('Pink Parfait' × 'Masquerade') × 'Dearest']; intr. 1970

'Busybody' HT, dy, 1929, Clark, A.; flowers rich chrome-yellow, small; ['Georges Schwartz' × 'Lena']

'Buta' HT, w, Cant, B. R.; flowers pure white, well-formed

Butter Cream™ -- See 'Marbutter'

'Butter 'n' Sugar' -- See 'Berbut'

'Butterball' S, ly, 1950, Skinner; flowers creamy yellow, single; non-recurrent; foliage small; prickly, arching branches; growth spinosissima type; 6 ft.; hips large, rounded, reddish

'Buttercream' -- See 'Ripbutter'

'Buttercream' -- See 'Jacworro'

'Buttercup' -- See 'Ausband'

'Buttercup' HT, my, Dobbie; flowers buttercup-yellow, well-formed, semi-dbl., cupped, moderate fruity fragrance; vigorous growth; intr. 1930

'Buttercup' HT, ab, Towill; flowers apricot-yellow to golden-yellow, medium, dbl., cupped, moderate fragrance; intr. 1929

'Buttercup' HWich, my, 1909, Paul, W.; bud light orange; flowers bright yellow, fading to lemon and cream, small to medium, single to semi-dbl., borne in large clusters; foliage small, dark green, glossy; few prickles; growth vigorous, climbing

Buttercup 98™ -- See 'Ausband'

'Buttercurls' S, dy, Delbard ?; intr. 2003

'Butterflies' -- See 'Mekkada'

'Butterflies' -- See 'Intermug'

'Butterflies' LCl, rb

Butterflies Cover™ -- See 'Poulbut'

'Butterflies of Gold' HT, my, 1939, Brownell; ['Mrs Arthur Curtiss James' × unknown]

Butterfly® HT, rb, Herholdt; bud pointed buds; flowers cream changing to red with sun exposure, flat

'Butterfly Glow' HT, or, 1969, Barter; flowers vermilion, large, 20 petals; foliage dark; free growth; ['Centre Court' × 'Carla']

'Butterfly Kisses' -- See 'Gelfly'

'Butterfly Kisses' LCl, ob, Pallek; flowers blend of orange, yellow and coral, double, high-centered; intr. 2008

'Butterfly Papilio' -- See 'Motylek'

'Butterfly Wings' F, pb, 1977, Gobbee, W.D.; flowers ivory, petals edged pink, 4-4½ in., 12 petals, flat, borne in clusters, moderate fragrance; foliage large; ['Dainty Maid' × 'Peace']; intr. 1976

'Buttermere' HWich, yb, 1932, Chaplin Bros.; flowers creamy yellow flushed pink, 6 cm., semi-dbl., borne in large trusses, moderate fragrance; foliage glossy; numerous prickles; vigorous, erect growth

'Buttermilk Sky' -- See 'Seabutt'

'Buttermint' -- See 'Morsnop'

'Butterscotch' HT, yb, 1942, Joseph H. Hill, Co.; bud long, pointed; flowers lemon-chrome, reverse pale orange-yellow, 4½-5½ in., 28 petals, slight fragrance; foliage leathery, glossy, dark; upright, compact growth; PP613; ['Souv. de Claudius Pernet' × R.M.S. Queen Mary]; intr. 1946

'Butterscotch' -- See 'Jactan'

'Butterscotch Dream' Min, op; intr. 2005

'Buttons' Min, w, 1981, Lemrow, Dr. Maynard W.; bud globular; flowers 35 petals, borne singly, no fragrance; foliage very tiny, smooth; no prickles; compact growth; [seedling × seedling]

'Buttons' -- See 'Dicmickey'

Buttons 'n' Bows™ ('Felicity II', Teeny WeenyN) Min, dp, 1981, Poulsen Roser APS; bud small; flowers deep pink, reflexing at maturity, 28 petals, high-centered and cupped, borne singly and in sprays, moderate fruity fragrance; recurrent; prickles straight; compact, upright growth; PP4939; [Mini-Poul® × 'Harriet Poulsen']; intr. 1980

'Buxom Beauty' -- See 'Korbilant'

'Buzby' F, or, 1978, Plumpton, E.; flowers light vermilion, conical, 1½ in., 11 petals, slight fragrance; dwarf, compact, upright growth; ['Irish Mist' × Topsi®]

'Buzzy's White Seedling' N, w

'By Appointment' -- See 'Harvolute'

'By Design' -- See 'Lavsign'

'By Joe' Min, w, 1990, Gatty, Joseph; bud pointed; flowers ivory white, 25 petals, high-centered, borne singly; foliage medium size, dark green, matte; upright, bushy, tall growth; ['Pink Petticoat' × 'Pink Petticoat']; intr. 1990

'Byakuya' ('White Night') HT, ly, Keihan Gardening Co.; flowers pale yellow, 14 cm., 50 petals, borne mostly solitary; foliage bronze, glossy; growth spreading; [seedling × 'Garden Party']; intr. 1971

'Byala Valentina' Gr, w, 1986, Staikov, Prof. Dr. V.; flowers creamy white, large, 25 petals, slight delicate fragrance; foliage dark, glossy; vigorous, upright growth; [Queen Elizabeth® × seedling]; intr. 1974

'Byrbradby' (Mary Bradby™) HT, op, 1999, Byrnes, Robert; flowers unusual orange and russet, reverse salmon, ruffled petals, 3 in., dbl., borne mostly singly; foliage medium size, dark green, semi-glossy, disease-resistant; few prickles; upright, medium (5 ft.) growth; hardy; [Queen Elizabeth® × Taboo™]; intr. 1999

'Byrlynne' (Lynne Elizabeth™) S, pb, 1999, Byrnes, Robert; flowers light pink, reverse medium pink, 4 in., dbl., borne mostly singly; foliage medium size, medium green, semi-glossy, disease-resistant; few prickles; spreading, bushy, medium (4½ ft.) growth; winter hardy; ['Carefree Beauty' × 'Carefree Beauty']; intr. 1999

'Byrneumann' ('Dr Elizabeth Neumann') HT, lp, 2001, Byrnes, Robert L.; flowers light pink, blush pink reverse, 4 in., full, high-centered, borne mostly solitary, intense fragrance; foliage medium green, semi-glossy, disease-resistant; few prickles; growth upright, medium; ['Morden Centennial' × unknown]; intr. 2001

'Byroldfashion' (Old Fashioned Romance™) S, dp, 2001, Byrnes, Robert L.; flowers large, full, borne in small clusters, no fragrance; foliage medium green, semi-glossy; prickles moderate; growth bushy, tall; ['Illusion' × 'Illusion']; intr. 2001

'Byrpeachy' (Everything's Peachy™) Gr, pb, 2001, Byrnes, Robert L.; flowers pink/peach, medium pink reverse, large, dbl., borne mostly solitary, slight fragrance; foliage medium green; few prickles; growth upright, medium; [sport of Queen Elizabeth®]; intr. 2001

'Byrsherrill' (Sherrill Anne™) S, pb, 1999, Byrnes, Robert; flowers blush pink, reverse medium pink, 4 in., 41 petals; foliage medium size, medium green, semi-glossy; few prickles; upright, medium (4-5 ft.) growth; ['Country Dancer' × 'Country Dancer']; intr. 1999

'Byrstarting' (Starting Over™) Gr, pb, 2001, Byrnes, Robert L.; flowers silvery pink, mauve/pink reverse, some striping, large, dbl., borne mostly solitary, moderate fragrance; foliage medium green, semi-glossy; few prickles; growth upright, medium; specimen; very disease resistant and hardy.; ['Country Dancer' × 'Fragrant Plum']; intr. 2001

'Byryesteryear' (Thoughts of Yesteryear™) S, lp, 2001, Byrnes, Robert L.; flowers blush pink, light pink and peach reverse, 3 in., full, borne in small clusters, moderate fragrance; foliage medium green, semi-glossy; few prickles; bushy, medium growth; [sport of 'Goldbusch']; intr. 2001

— C —

'C. A. Fletcher' HT, dp, 1947, Fletcher; flowers clear rose-crimson, well-formed, 5-6 in., 35-40 petals; vigorous growth; ['May Wettern' × 'Mrs Henry Bowles']

'C. Chambard' HT, 1934, Bel; flowers deep yellow, reverse tinted red, dbl., cupped; foliage dark; vigorous growth

'C. F. Worth' -- See 'Mme Charles Frédéric Worth'

'C. Gaudefroy' N, dp, 1901, Bonnaire; flowers carmine pink, center brick red, medium

'C. H. Middleton' HT, dr, 1939, Cant, B. R.; flowers dark crimson, large, very dbl., high-centered; foliage glossy; long stems; vigorous, bushy growth

'C. S. R.' HP, 1934, Böhm, J.; flowers white with pink striping, large, dbl.

'C. V. Haworth' HT, dr, 1917, Dickson, A.; flowers intense black-scarlet with rich crimson, with massive shell-shaped petals; vigorous growth

'C. V. Haworth, Climbing' Cl HT, dr, 1932, Cant, F.

'C. W. Cowan' ('Improved Marquise Litta de Breteuil') HT, mr, 1912, Dickson, A.; bud short, pointed; flowers warm carmine-cerise, large, dbl., rather flat, moderate fragrance

'C. W. S.' -- See 'Canadian White Star'

Caballero® HT, dr, Tantau; flowers large, double, high-centered, borne mostly singly; recurrent; stems long; Florist rose; intr. 2001

Cabana™ -- See 'Jacepirt'

Cabaret® -- See 'Laped'

'Cabaret' F, or, 1964, deRuiter; flowers vermilion-salmon, 2½ in., 35-40 petals, camellia-like, borne in clusters; vigorous, upright growth; RULED EXTINCT 6/83 ARM; ['Dacapo' × 'floribunda seedling']; intr. 1963

'Cabaret' -- See 'Jacaret'

'Cabbage Rose' Gerard ('Cent Feuilles', 'Rose à Cent Feuilles', 'Rose of Rove', 'Rose of Rhone', 'Rose of Provence', 'Rose de Batavie', 'Rose Chou de Hollande', R. gallica centifolia, R. × centifolia, R. batavica, 'Common Centifolia', 'Chou', R. provincialis) C, mp, before 1596; flowers rose pink, outer petals larger and lighter, 3 in., very dbl., globular, borne singly or in clusters, moderate fragrance; summer blooming; foliage egg-shaped, pointed, usually with 5 leaflets; prickles moderate, uneven, scythe-shaped; growth branching, tall (5 ft.); hips almost round, rare; mentioned as early as about 410 B.C. by Herodotus

'Cacaphony' HT, op, 1975, Golik; flowers pink tinged orange, 4 in., 28 petals, moderate fruity fragrance; foliage glossy, dark; [Baccará® × Golden Showers®]; intr. 1974

Cachet™ -- See 'Tuckach'

'Cacilda Backer' ('Casilda Becker') HT, ab; from Brazil

'Cacophony' Min, rb; flowers white with irregular stripes, dots and patches of red, no fragrance; growth compact, shrubby, spreading plant; intr. 2000

Cactus Blanc® -- See 'Deltrob'

'Caddy' HT, my, 1943, Meilland, F.; bud large, well formed, yellow; vigorous growth; ['Soeur Thérèse' × 'Prof. Deaux']

'Cadenza' LCl, dr, 1967, Armstrong, D.L.; bud ovoid; flowers dark scarlet, 2½-3 in., dbl., slightly cupped, borne in clusters; recurrent bloom; foliage glossy, dark, leathery; compact, moderate growth; PP2915; ['New Dawn' × 'Embers, Climbing']

'Cadette' F, ab, 1979, Lens, Louis; bud pointed; flowers pastel pink-apricot, 2 in., 35 petals, cupped, moderate fruity fragrance; foliage glossy, dark; vigorous, upright growth; ['Poupee' × 'Fillette']; intr. 1971

'Cadillac' -- See 'Korveril'

Cadillac™ F, or, Olesen; bud pointed ovoid; flowers orange-red, reverse slightly lighter, 5-5.5 cm., 30-35 petals, shallow cup, borne typically in clusters of 5, slight wild rose fragrance; recurrent; foliage dark green, glossy; prickles numerous, 5 mm, concave; moderate, upright to bushy (60-100 cm.) growth; PP15819; ['seedling' × Tobago®]; intr. 2003

'Cadillac DeVille' -- See 'Wekcryland'

Cadiz™ F, my, Poulsen; flowers medium yellow, 5-8 cm., 25 petals, no fragrance; foliage dark; growth bushy, 60-100 cm.; intr. 2005

'Cæcilie Scharsach' HP, lp, 1887, Geschwind, R.; flowers flesh white fading to white, large, very dbl., intense fragrance; ['Jules Margottin' × unknown]

'Caesar' -- See 'Varbole'

'Caesar's Rose' -- See 'Judsar'

'Café' F, r, 1956, Kordes; flowers coffee-with-cream color, very dbl., flat, borne in clusters; foliage olive-green; vigorous growth; [('Golden Glow' × R. kordesii) × 'Lavender Pinocchio']

'Café Olé' -- See 'Morolé'

'Cafougnette' HT, op, 1956, Dorieux; flowers soft orange-salmon, reverse carmine-red, open, well-shaped; foliage dark; strong stems; ['Happiness' × 'Peace']

'Cagul' HT, op, Moreira da Silva, A.; flowers salmon-orange and pink, large, very dbl.; intr. 1971

'Cahto Maid' S, lp

'Caid' Pol, ob, 1971, Delforge; bud ovoid; flowers orange, medium, dbl.; repeat bloom; foliage leathery; vigorous, bushy growth; [Orangeade® × seedling]

'Cairngorm' F, ob, 1974, Cocker; flowers tangerine and gold, 2½ in., 25 petals, slight fragrance; foliage glossy, dark; upright growth; [Anne Cocker® × 'Arthur Bell']; intr. 1971

'Caitlin' -- See 'Tracait'

Caitlin May™ -- See 'Jaycai'

'Cajun Dancer' -- See 'Talcaj'

'Cajun Firelight' HT, or, 2001, Edwards, Eddie; flowers 4½-5 in., full, borne mostly solitary, moderate fragrance; foliage medium size, dark green, glossy; prickles rounded, few; growth upright, tall (5-6 ft.); garden decorative, exhibition; [seedling × seedling]; intr. 2001

Cajun Moon™ -- See 'Wekonine'

'Cajun Pearl' HT, lp, 2003, Edwards, Eddie; flowers reverse light pearl pink, 5½ in., full, borne mostly solitary; foliage medium size, dark green, glossy; growth upright, medium (5 ft.); exhibition; [Cajun Moon™ × 'Fantasy']; intr. 2003

'Cajun Queen' -- See 'Deidre Hall'

'Cajun Signature' HT, w, 2004, Meyer, Larry & Doris; flowers white with raspberry edges, reverse white with lighter edge, 4½-5 in., full, borne mostly solitary; foliage large, dark green, semi-glossy; prickles 3/8 in., slightly hooked; growth bushy, tall (3½-5 ft.); garden decoration, exhibition; [sport of 'Jacnor']; intr. 2004

'Cajun Spice' HT, or, McMillan, Thomas G.; flowers lustrous orange-red, dbl., high-centered; intr. 1996

'Cajun Spice, Climbing' Cl HT, or; flowers large, vermilion, full; growth sturdy, vigorous plant; [sport of 'Cajun Spice']; intr. 2003

'Cajun Spice' -- See 'Talspi'

'Cajun Sunrise' HT, pb, 2000, Edwards, Eddie; flowers pink yellow, 4-4½ in., full, high-centered, borne mostly singly, slight fragrance; foliage medium size, medium green, semi-glossy; few prickles; growth upright, medium (4-5 ft.); [Crystalline™ × 'Elegant Beauty']; intr. 2001

'Cal Poly' -- See 'Morpoly'

'Cal Poly, Cl' Cl Min, my, Moore, Ralph; intr. 2000

Calapuno® S, dy, Noack; flowers creamy gold, 8 cm., dbl., cupped, slight fragrance; recurrent; growth to 4-5 ft.; intr. 2005

'Calay' -- See 'Trobelle'

'Calcutta 300' HT, pb, V&B; flowers large, bright pink with stripes and patches of white, broad petals, dbl.; free-flowering; [sport of 'Taj Mahal']; intr. 1994

'Caldwell Pink' -- See 'Pink Pet'

'Caldwell Pink Cl.' -- See 'Pink Pet, Climbing'

'Caledonia, Climbing' Cl HT, w, 1936, Bel; flowers ivory-white, full; fairly good rebloom

'Caledonia' HT, w, 1928, Dobbie; bud long, pointed; flowers large, 25 petals, high-centered; foliage leathery, dark; vigorous growth; RULED EXTINCT 7/83 ARM

Caledonia™ -- See 'Tuckscotland'

'Caledonian' HT, ly, 1983, Mayle, W.J.; flowers creamy yellow, large, dbl.; foliage medium size, medium green, semi-glossy; bushy growth; ['Kordes' Perfecta' × 'Irish Gold']

'Calgary' HT, mr, Twomey, Jerry; intr. 1997

'Calgold' Min, dy, 1977, Moore, Ralph S.; bud pointed; flowers deep clear yellow, 1½ in., 23 petals, slight fragrance; foliage small to medium size, glossy; bushy growth; PP4230; ['Golden Glow (Brownell)' × 'Peachy White']

'Calibra' -- See 'Korcrisett'

'Calibra Kordana' Min, ob, Kordes; flowers orange, full; container rose

'Calico' HT, pb, 1976, Weeks; flowers pink, yellow reverse, 3½-4 in., dbl., globular, slight tea fragrance; foliage dark; vigorous, upright to spreading growth; PP4006; [seedling × 'Granada']

'Calico Doll' Min, ob, 1979, Saville, F. Harmon; bud ovoid, pointed; flowers orange, striped yellow, 1-1½ in., 18 petals, cupped; foliage dark; compact growth; ['Rise 'n' Shine' × 'Glenfiddich']

'Calico Star' F, yb, 1978, Fong; bud ovoid; flowers golden yellow, edged red, 4 in., 25-30 petals, high-centered, slight fragrance; upright growth; ['Circus' × 'Lavender Girl']; intr. 1976

'Caliente' F, dr, 1974, Warriner, William A.; bud ovoid-pointed; flowers deep pure red, medium, dbl., high-centered, slight fragrance; foliage large, leathery; very vigorous, bushy growth; PP3595; [seedling × seedling]

Caliente™ -- See 'Bendiez'

'California' HP, mp, 1905, California Nursery Co.; flowers bright rosy pink

'California, Climbing' Cl HT, ob, 1953, Howard, A.P.; PP1136

'California' HT, ob, Howard, F.H.; bud long, pointed; flowers ruddy orange, reverse overlaid pink, 5-6 in., 30 petals, moderate fruity fragrance; foliage leathery, glossy; vigorous, bushy, spreading growth; PP449; ['Miss Rowena Thom' × 'Lady Fortevoit']; intr. 1940

'California' HT, ob, 1916, H&S; flowers deep orange, base golden yellow, large, full, moderate fragrance; intr. 1916

'California Beauty' HT, my, 1926, Pacific Rose Co.

'California Beauty' HT, dp, Proietti; bud long, pointed to ovoid; flowers deep bright pink, very large, dbl.; foliage leathery, dark; vigorous growth; PP333; ['Dame Edith Helen' × 'Hollywood']; intr. 1935

'California Blonde' -- See 'Renblonde'

'California Centennial' HT, dr, 1949, Howard, F.H.; bud long, pointed; flowers 3½-4 in., 28 petals, high-centered, intense fragrance; foliage leathery, bronze; vigorous, upright growth; PP953; ['Tango' × 'Mauna Loa']

'California Dreaming' -- See 'Renove'

'California Girl' -- See 'Renirl'

'California Glory' -- See 'Ortcal'

'California Gold' Pol, ab, 1934, Smith, J.; flowers orange-yellow, dbl., globular, borne in clusters; foliage leathery, light; long stems; very vigorous, bushy growth; [sport of 'Gloria Mundi']

'California Heart' -- See 'Tinheart'

'California Sun' -- See 'Rensun'

'California Surf' -- See 'Renurf'

'California's Favorite' HT, op, 1949, Raffel; bud long, pointed; flowers light salmon-pink, base yellow, large; foliage soft; vigorous, bushy growth; [sport of 'Stockton Beauty']

'Caline' HT, op, 1958, Ducher, Ch.; flowers soft geranium-red, medium, 33 petals; foliage clear green; vigorous, upright growth

'Calizia' S, op, Noack; intr. 2006

'Callie Liane' -- See 'Poncal'

Calliope® S, mp, Barni, V.; intr. 1985

'Calliope' ('Apricot Abundance') F, ab, Harkness; flowers apricot in center fading to light pink on outer petals, dbl., borne in large clusters, moderate fragrance; good rebloom; upright growth to 3 × 2 ft.; intr. 1998

'Calliope' HP, mp, Moreau & Robert; flowers bright silky pink, center darker, large, full; intr. 1879

'Calliope' HP, pb, 1853; flowers cherry-carmine, center white, medium, very full; possibly from Boyau

'Callista' -- See 'Ripcal'

'Callisto' HMsk, my, 1920, Pemberton; flowers golden yellow, small, rosette, borne in clusters; recurrent bloom; foliage dark green; growth branching, bushy, 3-4 ft.; ['William Allen Richardson' × 'William Allen Richardson']

'Callum's Glow' -- See 'Mansun'

'Calocarpa' (R. × calocarpa, R. × rugosa calocarpa) HRg, mp, 1894, Bruant; flowers rose-colored, 4-4½ in., single; hips abundant, scarlet, shiny; [R. rugosa × 'Parsons' Pink China']

'Calumet' -- See 'Socapan'

'Calvert' -- See 'Globe Hip'

Calypso™ -- See 'Poulclimb'

'Calypso' HGal, Descemet; intr. about 1810

'Calypso' ('Belle Angevin', 'Fleurette', 'White Boursault', 'Florida', 'De l'Ile', 'Cypris', 'Blush Boursault', 'Bengale Cypress', 'Belle de Lille', 'Rose de la Floride') Bslt, pb, before 1824, Noisette; flowers blush, center deep flesh, very large, tending to ball, pendulous, very dbl., globular, borne in small clusters; foliage remains longer than other boursaults; thornless; pendulous growth; apparently a hybrid of Red Boursault and R. odorata; credited to various breeders, including Noisette and Vilmorin

'Calypso' D, lp, Vibert; flowers rosy blush with paler edges, large, dbl., cupped; intr. about 1825

'Calypso' F, or, Boerner; bud globular; flowers orange-red, reverse red, loose, 3-3½ in., 18 petals, cupped, borne in large, pyramidal trusses, intense damask fragrance; foliage dark, leathery; vigorous, bushy growth; PP1624; ['Geranium Red' × 'Fashion']; intr. 1957

'Calypso' ('Tanosyl') HT, pb, Tantau; flowers light salmon-pink, shaded cerise pink, large, dbl., exhibition, moderate Damask and fruit fragrance; dark, glossy foliage; intr. 1988

'Calypso' -- See 'Calypso Petite'

'Calypso Dancer' F, ob, Jalbert, Brad; flowers soft orange with yellow base, double, cupped, borne in clusters

'Calypso Hit' ('Arrow Hit', 'Arrow Patiohit', Arrow™) MinFl, dr, Poulsen; flowers dark red, 5-8 cm., dbl., no fragrance; foliage dark; growth bushy, 40-60 cm.; PP11541; intr. 1998

'Calypso Petite' ('Calypso') C, mp, before 1820, Descemet; flowers bright crimson, very large, very dbl., borne in large clusters

'Camaieu' ('Camaieux') HGal, m, 1830, Gendron; flowers white and pale rosy purple, striped, with a small button at center, small, dbl., flat, rosette, borne singly or in clusters of 2-3, moderate fragrance; foliage small, thick, dark green; prickles small; vigorous, rather dwarf growth; intr. 1830

'Camaieux' F, rb

'Camaieux' -- See 'Camaieu'

'Camaieux Fimbriata' HGal, m, Bell; intr. 1980

'Camaieux Reversion' HGal, m, Robinson; flowers rich rose purple subdued with an overlay of pink, moderate fragrance; sport of 'Camaieux' (or reversion); intr. 1985

'Camalpha' F, lp, Benny; intr. 1998

Camara® -- See 'Delcama'

'Camargue' -- See 'Chewoz'

'Camay' HT, dp, 1959, Fletcher; flowers deep rose-pink to carmine, 5 in., 40 petals; foliage light green; vigorous growth; ['Ena Harkness' × 'C.A. Fletcher']

'Cambabe' F, ob, Benny, David; intr. 2005

'Cambeta' LCl, pb, Benny, David; intr. 2004

'Cambrai' HFt, yb, 1920, Smith; flowers light orange-yellow, medium, dbl.; [sport of 'Mme Edouard Herriot']

'Cambria' S, lp

Cambridge™ (Lavender Cover™) S, m, Poulsen; bud short, ovoid; flowers mauve, 5 cm., semi-dbl. to dbl., cupped, borne in clusters, slight wild rose fragrance; recurrent; foliage dark green, glossy; growth broad, bushy, 60-100 cm.; PP12520; [seedling × 'Dorus Rijkers']; intr. 1997

'Cambridgeshire' -- See 'Carpet of Color'

'Camcream' HT, ly, Benny, David; intr. 2004

'Camden' -- See 'Houcam'

'Camdo' HT, w, Benny

'Cameleon' F, yb, Verschuren, A.; flowers yellow, pink and orange, 22-27 petals, borne in large clusters, intense fragrance; foliage dark, glossy, upright, compact, bushy, symmetrical growth; ['Masquerade' × seedling]; intr. 1961

'Caméléon' Ch, pb, from Angers; flowers rose pink, shaded and striped with carmine

'Caméléon' Ch, mr, about 1827, Desprez; flowers crimson

'Caméléon' T, pb, Laffay; flowers pink, shaded carmine, medium, full, cupped, moderate fragrance; intr. about 1830

'Camélia' HT, or, 1948, Heizmann & Co.; bud pointed; flowers fiery vermilion-red, medium, semi-dbl., cupped; foliage glossy, dark; vigorous, bushy growth; ['Vainqueur' × ('Charles P. Kilham' × 'Katharine Pechtold')]

'Camelia' F, dp, 1953, Klyn; flowers cerise-pink, medium, borne in clusters; strong stems; moderate growth; ['Pinocchio' × seedling]

'Camélia Rose' Ch, lp, about 1830, Prévost; flowers bright rosy pink, shaded lilac, medium, dbl., cupped; foliage dark green; sometimes classed as N

'Cameliarose' F, lp, 1960, Croix, P.; flowers soft pink, camellia-like; very free bloom, especially in autumn; upright growth; ['Mme Joseph Perraud' × 'Incendie']

'Camella' -- See 'Camilla'

'Camelot' Gr, op, 1965, Swim & Weeks; bud ovoid; flowers shrimp-pink, 3½-4 in., 48 petals, cupped, borne in clusters, moderate spicy fragrance; foliage leathery, glossy, dark; vigorous, tall growth; PP2371; ['Circus' × Queen Elizabeth®]

'Camelot, Climbing' Cl Gr, op; intr. after 1965

'Cameo' Pol, op, 1932, deRuiter; flowers salmon-pink, turning soft orange-pink; [sport of 'Orléans Rose']

'Cameo, Climbing' -- See 'Pink Cameo'

'Cameo Cream' -- See 'Meipierar'

'Cameo Perfume' -- See 'Renaissance'

'Cameo Queen' Min, pb, 1986, Bridges, Dennis A.; flowers light pink, reverse blends of pink, mini-flora, 34 petals, high-centered, borne usually singly; foliage large, medium green, semi-glossy; prickles medium, long, light; medium, bushy growth; [Heartland™ × seedling]

'Cameo Superior' Pol, mp, deRuiter; flowers have more lasting color; [sport of 'Cameo']

Cameron Bohls™ -- See 'Ponbohls'

Camilla™ -- See 'Poulra022(N)'

'Camilla' ('Camella') HT, ab; intr. 2000

'Camilla' HT, dp, 1954, Aicardi, D.; bud ovoid; flowers strawberry-red, loosely formed, large, 30-36 petals; very vigorous growth; ['Fiamma' × 'Talisman']

'Camilla Parade' (Camilla™) MinFl, w, Poulsen; flowers white with faint pink cast, 2 in., 70 petals, high-centered, borne mostly singly, slight floral fragrance; recurrent; foliage dark green, glossy; prickles moderate, 4 mm; stems 6 in.; bushy, compact (20-40 cm.) growth; PP15142; ['Patricia Kordana' × 'Peach Parade']; intr. 2002

'Camilla Sunsation' -- See 'Korfibi'

'Camille' -- See 'Jacfruit'

'Camille Bernardin' HP, rb, 1865, Gautreau; flowers red with white, very large, dbl., intense fragrance; ['Général Jacqueminot' × unknown]

'Camille Bouland' A, lp, before 1826, Prévost; flowers delicate rose, medium, very dbl., globular

'Camille Pissarro' ('Rainbow Nation') F, yb, Delbard, Georges; flowers yellow, striped and shaded with red, pink, orange and white, dbl.; dark green foliage; intr. 1996

'Camille Raoux' -- See 'Camille Roux'

'Camille Rose' S, mp, 2006, Jerabek, Paul; flowers very full, borne in small clusters; foliage dark green, semi-glossy; prickles medium, straight, red, moderate; growth upright, bushy, wide and tall (5-6 ft.); hedging; [unknown × unknown]; intr. 2007

'Camille Roux' ('Camille Raoux') T, mr, 1885, Nabonnand; flowers bright red, pinkish at petal edges, large, full, globular; prickles large, few; growth vigorous, bushy

'Camillo Schneider' HT, mr, 1922, Kordes; flowers clear blood-red, dbl.; ['Lieutenant Chauré' × 'Comte G. de Rochemur']

Camisole™ -- See 'Jacnereb'

'Cammaid' F, dy, Benny, David

'Camoëns' HT, mp, 1881, Schwartz, J.; flowers bright rose, center shaded yellow, very large, full, moderate fragrance; foliage semi-glossy, bronzed; prickles strong, widely-spaced; moderately vigorous growth; ['Antoine Verdier' × unknown]

'Camp David' HT, dr, Tantau; flowers very dark red, dbl., high-centered, intense fragrance; growth small, sturdy, compact plant; intr. 1984

'Campanela' -- See 'Deltrut'

Campanile® -- See 'Deltrut'

'Campfire' -- See 'Wilcamp'

'Campfire' Cl Pol, or, 1956, Fryers Nursery, Ltd.; flowers orange-scarlet, small, rosette, borne in clusters; vigorous (6-8 ft.) growth; [sport of 'Cameo']

'Campfire Arteka' -- See 'Kostior Arteka'

'Campfire Girl' HT, op, 1946, Duehrsen; bud long, pointed; flowers deep salmon, large, dbl., high-centered; foliage dark, leathery; vigorous, upright, bushy growth; ['Joanna Hill' × 'Gruss an Aachen']

'Camphill Glory' -- See 'Harkreme'

'Campina' HT, lp, 1937, Lens; bud long; flowers flesh-pink; very vigorous growth; ['Comtesse Vandal' × 'White Briarcliff']

'Camping' Pol, pb, 1967, Grabczewski; flowers deep lavender-pink with white eye, small, single, globular, borne in large clusters; foliage small, olive-green; low, bushy growth; [sport of 'Paul Crampel']

'Camprize' F, dy, Benny, David

'Camrio' F, rb, Benny, David

'Camrose' S, mp, Twomey, Jerry; intr. 1998

'Camsun' F, yb, Benny, David

'Camuzet' HCh, m, before 1829, Camuzet; flowers dark purple

'Camuzet Carné' HCh, op, 1829, Camuzet; flowers peach-pink aging to flesh white, large, full

'Can-Can' -- See 'Legglow'

'Canadian Belle' T, ab, 1907, Conard & Jones; flowers creamy-buff with deep apricot center, shaded with rose and amber, moderate fragrance

'Canadian Centennial' F, or, 1965, Boerner; bud ovoid; flowers coral-red, medium, dbl., cupped, moderate fragrance; foliage glossy; vigorous, upright, compact growth; PP2628; [('Pinocchio' × unknown) × 'Spartan']

'Canadian Dream' -- See 'Brodream'

'Canadian Jubilee' HT, op, 1927, Dunlop; flowers Indian red to pink, base orange, dbl.; ['Priscilla' × 'Commonwealth']

'Canadian Northlight' HT, dp, 1984, Mander, George; flowers large, 28 petals, high-centered, borne in clusters of 6-9, light fragrance; foliage medium green, leathery; prickles dark red; spreading growth; [('Fragrant Cloud' × 'Diamond Jubilee') × 'Super Sun']

'Canadian Sunset' -- See 'Wilcan'

Canadian White Star® ('C. W. S.', 'Dr Wolfgang Pöschl') HT, w, 1980, Mander, George; flowers opening to multi-pointed star, 43 petals, high-centered, borne singly; foliage dark, leathery, glossy; prickles slightly hooked; vigorous, upright growth; PP5852; ['Blanche Mallerin' × Pascali®]; intr. 1985

'Canadiana' -- See 'Imperial Gold'

'Canana' ('Lady Donaldson', 'Mary Donaldson') HT, mp, 1984, Cants of Colchester, Ltd.; flowers medium salmon-pink, medium, dbl., high-centered, intense fragrance; foliage large, dark, glossy; upright growth; ['Kathleen O'Rourke' × seedling]

'Canari' ('Canarie', 'Canary') T, my, 1852, Guillot Père; bud small, well formed; flowers canary-yellow; growth rather weak

'Canari' T, my, 1852, Guillot père; flowers canary yellow, medium, full, borne in small clusters

'Canarias' HT, mr, 1964, Dot, Pedro; flowers bright red, large

'Canarie' -- See 'Canari'

'Canarienvogel' ('Sunset Glow') Pol, 1903, Welter; flowers saffron-yellow and amber-yellow stained pink and purple, semi-dbl.; strong stems; vigorous growth; ['Étoile de Mai' × 'Souv. de Catherine Guillot']

'Canarina' ; intr. 1965

'Canary' -- See 'Canari'

'Canary' -- See 'Tancary'

'Canary' HT, ly, 1929, Dickson, A.; bud golden yellow, edges flushed; flowers light yellow, deepening, spiral, high-centered; branching growth

'Canary' Min, my, Letts; flowers primuline-yellow, semi-dbl., star-shaped; intr. 1955

'Canary Bird' (R. xanthina spontanea) S, dy, 1907; flowers golden yellow, aging to cream, medium, 5 petals; hips blackish-purple; originally thought to be a form of R. xanthina, but more probably a hybrid of R. xanthina × R. hugonis or R. pimpinellifolia; intr. 1911

'Canary Charm' HT, my, 1969, Knight, G.; flowers very large, dbl., high-centered; foliage dark, leathery; free growth; [sport of 'Wiener Charme']

Canary Diamond™ -- See 'Wezcanary'

'Canasta, Climbing' Cl HT, mr; intr. after 1966

'Canasta' HT, mr, 1966, Gaujard; bud long, pointed; flowers bright red, large, dbl., high-centered; very vigorous, upright growth; ['Karl Herbst' × 'Miss Universe']

'Canberra' Pol, op, Knight, G.; flowers salmon-coral-pink; [sport of 'Gloria Mundi']; intr. 1935

'Canberra' HT, op, 1927, Burbage Nursery; flowers carmine, reverse buff at base, shading to salmon-pink; ['Donald MacDonald' × 'The Queen Alexandra Rose']

'Canberra' HT, mp, Harrison; flowers very dbl.; intr. 1928

'Canberra Rose' -- See 'Tomfed'

'Cancan' ('Diorette', 'Jelfax') F, ob, 1969, Jelly; bud short, pointed; flowers mandarin-red, small, dbl., moderate spicy fragrance; foliage leathery; PP2902

'CanCan' -- See 'Legglow'

'Cancan Swirl' -- See 'Seaaffi'

'Cancer' F, w, Burston; intr. 2004

Cancun™ -- See 'Wekibertaz'

Candelabra™ -- See 'Jaccinqo'

Candella® -- See 'Macspeego'

Candeur® -- See 'Delcande'

'Candeur Lyonnaise' HP, w, 1913, Croibier; bud long, pointed; flowers white, sometimes tinted pale yellow, large, dbl.; very vigorous growth; ['Frau Karl Druschki' × unknown]

Candia™ -- See 'Meibiranda'

Candia Meillandecor® S, mr, Meilland; flowers medium red with small white eye, single, flat, borne in clusters; recurrent; low (70 - 80 cm.), mounding growth; intr. 2007

'Candice' -- See 'Zipcan'

'Candid' HT, w, Delbard

'Candid Prophyta' HT, ab, de Ruiter; PP10531

'Candida' HT, yb, 1964, Leenders, J.; flowers creamy yellow, center salmon, well-formed; ['Tawny Gold' × 'Golden Scepter']

'Candide' Ch, w; flowers pure white, medium, full; intr. before 1936

'Candide' ('Gold Star', Disque d'Or®, 'Goldina', Point du Jour®) HT, dy, Cants of Colchester, Ltd.; intr. 1983

'Candide' HP, w, Touvais; flowers flesh-white, medium, full

'Candide' B, m, Robert & Moreau; flowers lilac, medium, full

'Candide' A, w, Vibert; flowers white, tinged with fawn, medium, full; intr. about 1825

'Candide' HGal, w, 1820, Vibert; flowers nearly white, small to medium, full

'Candide' HT, Gaujard; intr. 1970

Candide™ -- See 'Poulgav'

'Candle in the Wind' ('The Princess') S, ob, McGredy; flowers oriental orange-red with fine brush strokes of white, 4 in., 9 petals; foliage rich green; growth upright, 4 × 2½ ft.

'Candle Light' Cl Min, yb, Warner, Chris; intr. 1995

'Candleflame' Min, yb, 1956, Moore, Ralph S.; bud slender; flowers red, yellow and orange, 5 petals; foliage leathery; vigorous (10 in.), bushy growth; [('Soeur Thérèse' × 'Julien Potin') × ('Eblouissant' × 'Zee')]

'Candleglow' HT, yb, 1951, Whisler; bud long, pointed; flowers yellow washed shrimp-pink, 5-6 in., 38 petals, cupped, slight fragrance; foliage glossy, dark; vigorous, upright growth; PP1199; ['Golden Rapture' × (seedling × 'Joanna Hill')]

Candlelight™ -- See 'Arowedye'

'Candlelight' HT, my, 1932, Horvath; flowers yellow, deeper in hot weather, large, dbl., high-centered, moderate fragrance; foliage glossy; bushy growth; RULED EXTINCT 9/81 ARM; ['Souv. de Claudius Pernet' × 'Mme Butterfly']

Candlelight® S, dy, Tantau; flowers unfading deep yellow, full, cupped, intense fragrance; long, strong stems; intr. 2002

'Candoodle' ('Lady Rachel') F, w, Cants of Colchester, Ltd.; intr. 1990

'Candy' HT, ob, 1950, Brownell; bud long, pointed; flowers apricot-orange, medium, dbl., high-centered, moderate fragrance; vigorous, upright, compact, bushy growth; ['Pink Princess' × 'Shades of Autumn']

'Candy Apple' Gr, mr, 1975, Weeks, O.L.; bud ovoid; flowers bright apple red, 5 in., 40-45 petals, cupped, borne in small clusters, slight tea fragrance; foliage matte, olive-green; upright, medium, bushy growth; PP3748; ['Jack O'Lantern' × (seedling × 'El Capitan')]; intr. 1975

'Candy Cane' Cl Min, pb, 1959, Moore, Ralph S.; flowers deep pink, striped white, 1½ in., 13 petals, borne in loose clusters; vigorous, upright (to 4 ft.) growth; PP1951; [seedling × 'Zee']; intr. 1958

Candy Corn™ -- See 'Talcan'

Candy Cover™ -- See 'Poulbico'

'Candy Cream' HT, pb, Ghosh; flowers large, cream white with tips of petals and edges cerise pink, full; intr. 1999

'Candy Favourite' HT, pb, 1970, Heath, W.L.; flowers carmine, striped pale rose, 4½-5 in., 25 petals, slight fragrance; foliage very glossy; vigorous growth; [sport of 'Pink Favorite']

'Candy Flo' HT, rb

'Candy Floss' F, lp, 1960, Fryers Nursery, Ltd.; flowers bright pink, 3 in., 40 petals, rosette, borne in large clusters, slight fragrance; very vigorous growth; ['Lilibet' × seedling]; intr. 1959

Candy Girl® HT, or, Tantau; flowers small to medium, double, high-centered, borne mostly singly; good repeat; stems medium; Florist rose; intr. 2007

Candy Land™ -- See 'Wekrosopela'

Candy Mountain™ -- See 'Jacchari'

'Candy Oh! Vivid Red' S, mr, Zlesak, David; flowers candy apple red, single, shallow cup to flat, borne in clusters; recurrent; foliage light to medium green, disease-resistant; dense, mounded (3 - 4 ft.) growth; hardy; intr. 2008

'Candy Pink' Min, lp, 1969, Moore, Ralph S.; bud ovoid; flowers small, dbl.; foliage small, leathery; vigorous, dwarf, bushy growth; [(R. wichurana × Floradora) × ('Oakington Ruby' × 'Floradora')]

'Candy Rain' -- See 'Auscot'

Candy Rose® -- See 'Meiranovi'

'Candy Stick' -- See 'Candystick'

'Candy Stripe' ('Candystripe') HT, pb, 1963, McCummings; flowers dusty pink streaked (striped) lighter; PP2278; [sport of 'Pink Peace']; intr. 1964

Candy Sunblaze™ -- See 'Meidanclar'

'Candy Tower' HT, op

'Candyfloss' Min, dp; intr. 2005

'Candystick' ('Candy Stick', 'Red-n-White Glory') HT, pb, 1976, Williams, J. Benjamin; flowers deep pink striped white; [sport of 'Better Times']; intr. 1975

'Candystripe' -- See 'Candy Stripe'

'Caneghem' -- See 'Kanegem'

'Canibo' -- See 'Bonica, Climbing'

'Canicule' -- See 'Sonnenschirm'

'Canigó' HT, w, 1927, Dot, Pedro; flowers dbl.; ['Antoine Rivoire' × 'Mme Ravary']

'Canlish' ('St Helena', Union-Rose St Helena®) F, mp, 1983, Cants of Colchester, Ltd.; flowers medium lilac pink, medium, 20 petals, cupped, slight fragrance; free-flowering; foliage medium size, medium green, semi-glossy; upright, compact growth; ['Jubilant' × 'Prima Ballerina']

'Canlloyd' ('Lloyds of London') F, ob, Cants of Colchester, Ltd.; intr. 1991

'Canlot' ('Alexia') F, pb, 1983, Cants of Colchester, Ltd.; flowers cream blended pink, medium, 20 petals, moderate fragrance; foliage medium size, medium green, semi-glossy; upright growth; ['Jubilant' × seedling]; intr. 1984

'Canmiss' ('Beauty Queen') F, mp, 1983, Cants of Colchester, Ltd.; flowers medium, dbl., intense fragrance; foliage large, dark, glossy; ['English Miss' × seedling]

'Cannabina' -- See 'À Feuilles de Chanvre'

'Cannes Festival' -- See 'Meilicafal'

'Cannes Festival' HT, yb, 1951, Meilland, F.; flowers Indian yellow veined amber, pointed, 4 in., 35 petals; foliage dark; vigorous, upright, branching growth; ['Peace' × 'Prinses Beatrix']

'Cannes Festival 83' ('Cannes Festival') HT, yb, Meilland, Alain A.; flowers Indian-yellow, edged with orange, large, dbl.; intr. 1983

'Cannes La Coquette' HT, op, 1877, Nabonnand

'Canonvale' HSpn, m; flowers white to blush pink with lilac at petal base, medium, semi-dbl., borne in clusters, strong sweet fragrance; growth small, compact (1 m.); hips small, round, black

'Canoodling' -- See 'Seaoodle'

'Canrem' ('Sally's Rose') HT, pb, 1994, Cants of Colchester, Ltd.; flowers pale pink and cream, shaded apricot, medium, dbl., high-centered, slight fragrance; foliage reddish when young, maturing to dark green, glossy; numerous prickles; short (60 cm.), bushy growth; [Amber Queen® × Remember Me®]; intr. 1994

'Cansend' ('Colchester Beauty') F, dp, 1992, Pawsey, P.R.; flowers candy pink, medium, 6-14 petals, borne mostly singly; foliage medium size, dark green, semi-glossy; some prickles; medium (60-80 cm.), bushy growth; ['English Miss' × seedling]; intr. 1989

'Cansit' ('Jenny's Rose') F, lp, Cants of Colchester, Ltd.; intr. 1996

'Canson' ('Dame Wendy') F, mp, Cants of Colchester, Ltd.; intr. 1991

'Cantab' S, dp, 1927, Hurst; bud long, pointed; flowers deep pink, base white, prominent yellow stamens, large, single, saucer-shaped; non-recurrent; foliage dark, 7-9 leaflets; growth to 6-8 ft.; [R. nutkana × 'Red-Letter Day']

'Cantabile' S, lp, 1964, Buck, Dr. Griffith J.; bud ovoid; flowers light camellia-rose shaded darker, medium, 25 petals, moderate fragrance; repeat bloom; foliage leathery, bronze; vigorous, upright (5 ft.) growth; ['Harmonie' × ('Josef Rothmund' × R. laxa)]; intr. 1962

'Cantabrigiensis' (R. × cantabrigiensis, 'The Cambridge Rose') S, ly, 1935; flowers cream to pale yellow, 2¼ in., single; [R. hugonis × R. sericea]; introduced by Cambridge Botanic Garden

'Cantapek' mp, Cant; intr. 1987

Cantario® F, mr, Noack; flowers bright red, 3 cm., semi-double, cupped, borne in clusters; recurrent; foliage dark green, glossy; compact (60 cm.) growth; intr. 2007

'Cantate' F, ob, 1959, van de Water; flowers orange; [sport of 'Red Favorite']

'Canterbury' -- See 'Perpetually Yours'

'Canterbury' -- See 'Scoop Jackson'

'Canterbury' S, mp, 1969, Austin, David; flowers rose-pink, medium, 12 petals; repeat bloom; [('Monique' × Constance Spry®) × seedling]

'Canterbury Pride' -- See 'Reycantpri'

'Cantilena Bohemica' HT, dp, Havel; flowers carmine-pink, large, very dbl.; intr. 1977

'Cantilena Moravica' HT, yb, Havel; intr. 1981

Canyon Cupido® Min, yb, de Ruiter; PP10818; intr. 2002

Canyonlands™ ('Shrimp Pink Castle', Solliden™, Fascination™, Fredensborg™, Schloss Herrenchiemsee™) F, op, Poulsen; flowers orange pink, 8-10 cm., dbl., no fragrance; foliage dark; growth bushy, 60-100 cm.; intr. 1996

'Canzonetta' F, or, 1953, San Remo Exp. Sta.; bud ovoid, cardinal-red; flowers orange-red, reverse yellow suffused red, open, large, 10-12 petals, borne in clusters of 25-40; foliage dark, glossy, leathery; vigorous, bushy growth; ['Lawrence Johnston' × 'Fashion']

Canzonetta® F, or, Noack; flowers bright red, 4 cm., semi-double, shallow cup, borne in clusters; recurrent; foliage medium to dark green, glossy; compact (40 - 50 cm.) growth; intr. 2005

Cap Diamant® -- See 'Darpellerin'

Cap Horn® Gr, or, Dorieux; flowers bright salmon fire red, large, double; heavy bloomer; vigorous, tall growth; intr. 2000

'Cap Horn, Climbing' (Grimpant Cap Horn®) Cl Gr, or, Dorieux; flowers luminous fire red; intr. 2005

Cap Nord® F, pb, Harkness; intr. France

'Cape Cod' -- See 'Poulfan'

'Cape Coral' HT, ab, 1964, Boerner; bud ovoid; flowers orange-coral, 5 in., 50-55 wavy petals, cupped, moderate fragrance; foliage leathery, glossy, veined red; long, strong stems; vigorous, bushy growth; PP2400; ['Spartan' × 'Golden Masterpiece']; intr. 1964

Cape Diamond® -- See 'Darpellerin'

'Cape Hatteras'   Min, w, 1988, Bridges, Dennis A.; flowers medium, 40 petals, high-centered, borne singly, slight spicy fragrance; foliage medium size, dark green, glossy; prickles long, pointed, medium pink-tan; upright, medium, vigorous growth; ['Rise 'n' Shine' × seedling]

'Cape Horn'   S, pb; flowers ivory white with pink and red edges, semi-dbl.; growth to 4 ft.

'Capel Manor College' -- See 'Bosanne'

'Capeline'   LCl, mp, 1967, Hémeray-Aubert; flowers Tyrian rose, semi-dbl., high-centered; recurrent bloom; foliage leathery; vigorous growth; ['Etendard' × 'Diane d'Urfe']

'Capella' -- See 'Meirilocra'

'Caper'   F, dr, 1976, Warriner, William A.; bud long, pointed; flowers open, 2-2½ in., 25 petals, slight fragrance; foliage dark; upright growth; PP3937; [seedling × 'Mary DeVor']

'Capflare' ('Solar Flare', 'Solarflare', 'Solar Flash', 'Solarflash') HT, or, 1996, Pallek, Otto; flowers bright vermilion, vibrant dark orange, with dark petal edge, medium to large, full, borne mostly singly; foliage medium size, dark green, semi-glossy; prickles some to numerous; medium to low (2½-3 ft.), compact growth; [seedling × 'Hot Pewter']; intr. 1995

'Capistrano'   HT, mp, 1949, Morris; bud ovoid; flowers bright pink, 6 in., 36 petals, globular, moderate fragrance; foliage leathery; vigorous, upright growth; PP922

'Capistrano, Climbing'   Cl HT, mp, 1952, Germain's

'Capitaine Basroger'   M, rb, 1890, Moreau et Robert; flowers bright carmine-red, shaded purple, large, dbl.; very vigorous, almost climbing growth

'Capitaine Dyel de Graville'   B, pb, 1905, Boutigny; flowers pink with darker center, very large, very dbl.; very remontant; [sport of 'Souv de la Malmaison']

'Capitaine Georges Dessirier'   HT, dr, 1919, Pernet-Ducher; bud large, globular; flowers dark velvety red, shaded crimson, large, dbl., borne mostly solitary, moderate fragrance; ['Château de Clos Vougeot' × unknown]

'Capitaine John Ingram' ('Captain Ingram') M, m, 1855, Laffay, M.; bud well mossed; flowers variously described as dark purple, velvety crimson and reddish-purple, dbl., moderate fragrance; vigorous growth

'Capitaine Jouen'   HP, mr, 1900, Boutigny; flowers vivid crimson, very large, dbl.; ['Eugene Furst' × 'Triomphe de l'Exposition']

'Capitaine Lamure'   HP, m, 1870, Levet

'Capitaine Lefort'   T, dp, 1888, Bonnaire; bud long, large; flowers purplish rose, reverse paler, 5-5½ in.; ['Socrate' × 'Catherine Mermet']

'Capitaine Millet'   T, mr, 1901, Ketten Bros.; flowers bright red, reverse purplish, base golden, large, dbl.; ['Général Schablikine' × 'Mme A. Etienne']

'Capitaine Paul'   HP, 1867, Boyau

'Capitaine Peillon'   HP, m, 1893, Liabaud; flowers purple-pink, large, dbl.

'Capitaine Rénard' ('Rose du Roi Strié') P, pb, before 1843; flowers pale flesh pink, striped with crimson, large, very full

'Capitaine Rognat'   HP, mr, 1864, Guillot; flowers glowing scarlet, large, full, cupped

'Capitaine Sissolet'   B, mp, before 1841; flowers rosy lilac, large, very dbl., cupped; vigorous, branching growth; from France; sometimes classed as HCh, HP, or N

'Capitaine Soupa'   HT, dp, 1902, Laperrière; flowers carmine-pink, very large, dbl.; ['Mme Caroline Testout' × 'Victor Verdier']

'Capitaine Soupa, Climbing'   Cl HT, dp, 1938, Vogel, M.; flowers carmine-pink, large, dbl.; [sport of 'Capitaine Soupa']

'Capitaine Williams' ('Captain Williams') HGal, dr, before 1843; flowers deep carmine red, medium, very dbl., moderate fragrance

'Capitalia'   HT, Ansaloni

Capitole® -- See 'Lapovi'

Capitoule™ -- See 'Poulac009(N)'

'Capitoule Palace' (Capitoule™) MinFl, dr, Poulsen; flowers dark red, 5-8 cm., dbl., slight wild rose fragrance; foliage dark; growth bushy, 40-60 cm.; PP15645; intr. 2002

'Capmina' ('Conservancy Rose') F, mp, 1996, Pallek, Ruth; flowers vibrant pink, some variation, not solid pink, long lasting, 1½ in., 30 petals; foliage medium size, medium green, glossy, disease-resistant; some prickles; medium (20 in.), bushy growth; intr. 1995

'Caporosso'   HRg, mr, Mansuino, Q.; intr. 1975

Cappa Magna®   F, mr, 1967, Delbard-Chabert; flowers have yellow stamens and wavy petals, 4 in., 8-10 petals, cupped, borne in clusters of 20-30; foliage dark, glossy, large; upright growth; ['Tenor' × unknown]; intr. 1967

'Cappuccino'   HT, ob, Teranishi; intr. 1998

'Cappuccino'   HT, dy, Tantau; flowers cream-yellow with deeper ocher in center, medium, dbl., high-centered; foliage dark, slightly glossy; few prickles; greenhouse rose; intr. 1999

Cappuccino®   HT, dy, Tantau; flowers creamy white to tan-gold, 8 cm., full, cupped, moderate fruity fragrance; low to moderate growth; intr. 2005

'Capreolata Ruga'   Misc OGR, mp, 1820

'Capri'   F, op, 1960, Fisher, E. G.; bud conical; flowers bright coral, reverse lighter, 3-3½ in., 38 petals, high-centered, borne in small clusters, slight fragrance; foliage bright green, glossy, leathery; vigorous growth; PP1453; ['Fashion' × 'Floradora']; intr. 1960

'Capri'   HT, ab

'Capri Sun' -- See 'Tannus'

'Caprice' -- See 'Meisionver'

'Caprice' -- See 'Meixetal'

'Caprice, Climbing' ('Lady Eve Price, Climbing') Cl HT, or, 1951, Lens

'Caprice'   HT, dp, Meilland; intr. 2004

'Caprice' ('Lady Eve Price') HT, pb, Meilland, F.; bud ovoid; flowers deep pink, reverse cream, large, 24 petals, slight fragrance; foliage dark, leathery; vigorous, upright, bushy growth; ['Peace' × 'Fantastique']; intr. 1948

'Caprice'   HT, or, Leenders, M.; bud long, pointed; flowers orient red and peach-red, large, dbl., slight fragrance; foliage glossy, light; vigorous growth; [seedling × 'Gwyneth Jones']; intr. 1934

'Caprice'   B, mp, 1852, Vivant-Faivre; flowers vivid pink

'Caprice de Meilland' ('Best Friend', 'Caprice') HT, mp, Meilland; flowers pink tinted mauve, large, full, high-centered, strong fruity fragrance; foliage semi-glossy; growth to 100 cm.; intr. 1998

'Caprice des Dames'   HCh, pb, before 1831, Miellez; flowers dark purple/pink, small, flat; foliage oval lanceolate, sharply dentate; growth dwarf (6 in.); Lawrenciana

'Caprice du Zéphyre' -- See 'Marie-Louise'

'Capricious' -- See 'Seacap'

'Capricorn'   F, rb, 1961, Verschuren; flowers scarlet, reverse silver, 2 in., 16 petals, borne in large clusters, slight fragrance; foliage dark, dull, leathery; very vigorous growth; intr. 1961

'Capricorn'   F, w, Burston; intr. 2004

'Capricorne'   HGal, dp, 1819, Miellez; flowers bright pink, medium, full

'Capricornus' ('Rouge Vif') C, mr, before 1811; bud pointed; flowers intense velvety red, 2 in., very dbl.; foliage glaucous green

'Capriole'   F, mp, 1959, Tantau, Math.; bud cherry-red; flowers vivid pink, stamens prominent, medium, semi-dbl., borne in large clusters; foliage dark, semi-glossy; vigorous, dwarf, bushy growth; ['Red Favorite' × 'Fanal']; intr. 1956

'Captain Bligh'   HT, mp, 1939, Fitzhardinge; bud long, pointed; flowers silvery rose, large, very dbl.; foliage leathery, dark; very vigorous growth; ['Gustav Grünerwald' × 'Betty Uprichard']

'Captain Blood'   HT, dr, 1938, Melville Bros.; bud ovoid; flowers scarlet and crimson, dbl., cupped; foliage leathery; vigorous, bushy growth; ['Gen. MacArthur' × 'E.G. Hill']

'Captain Christy'   HT, lp, 1873, Lacharme, F.; flowers soft flesh-pink, center darker, large, 40 petals, globular, slight fragrance; wide, compact growth; ['Victor Verdier' × 'Safrano']

'Captain Christy, Climbing' Cl HT, lp, 1881, Ducher; flowers delicate flesh, deeper in center, large, full, globular, strong fragrance; [sport of 'Captain Christy']

'Capt Christy Mossed' -- See 'Mme Louis Lévêque'

'Captain Christy Panaché' HT, pb, 1896, Letellier; flowers striped white and pink; [sport of 'Captain Christy']

'Captain Cook' F, op, 1976, McGredy, Sam IV; flowers orange-salmon, 4 in., 10 petals, moderate fragrance; foliage glossy; growth medium; ['Irish Mist' × seedling]; intr. 1977

'Captain F. Bald' HT, dr, 1919, Dickson, A.; flowers scarlet-crimson, velvety black sheen, dbl.

'Capt. F. S. Harvey-Cant' HT, pb, 1923, Cant, F.; bud long, pointed; flowers peach-pink, reverse deep pink, very large, dbl.; foliage dark, leathery; vigorous, bushy growth

'Captain George C. Thomas' -- See 'Captain Thomas'

'Captain Glisson' HT, dy, 1935, Joseph H. Hill, Co.; bud long, pointed; flowers dark yellow, edged lighter, large, 28-30 petals, very vigorous, compact growth; PP155; ['Joanna Hill' × 'Sweet Adeline']

'Captain Harry Stebbings' HT, dp, 1980, Stebbings; bud long, pointed; flowers deep pink, 5-6½ in., 43 petals, high-centered, intense fruity fragrance; foliage large, leathery; upright, bushy growth

'Captain Hayward' HP, dp, 1893, Bennett; flowers light crimson, edged lighter, large, 25 petals, high-centered; sparsely recurrent; vigorous growth; hips large, orange; ['Triomphe de l'Exposition' × unknown]

'Captain Hayward, Climbing' Cl HP, dp, 1906, Paul; flowers pinkish-crimson, lighter at edges, 10-12 cm., semi-dbl., cupped, strong fragrance; [sport of 'Captain Hayward']

'Captain Ingram' -- See 'Capitaine John Ingram'

'Captain Kidd' HSet, mr, 1934, Horvath; flowers blood-red, 10 cm., dbl., open, cupped, moderate fragrance; non-recurrent; foliage leathery, dark; prickles long; long, strong stems; very vigorous, climbing or tall pillar growth; [(R. setigera × unknown) × 'Hoosier Beauty']

'Captain Kilbee Stuart' HT, dr, 1922, Dickson, A.; bud long, pointed; flowers scarlet-crimson, very large, dbl.; moderate growth

'Captain Kilby' F, mr, 1955, deRuiter; flowers blood-red, medium, semi-dbl., borne in large trusses, moderate fragrance; foliage glossy, parsley-green; very vigorous growth; intr. 1955

'Captain Philip Green' T, pb, 1899, Nabonnand; bud long; flowers cream with carmine, large, full; prickles strong; growth vigorous; ['Marie Van Houtte' × 'Devoniensis']

'Capt. Robinson' Sp, dp, Robinson, C.H.; flowers 13 petals; non-recurrent; foliage small, dark; few prickles; growth to 1 ft.

'Capt. Ronald Clerk' HT, or, 1923, McGredy; flowers vermilion-scarlet, semi-dbl.

'Capt. Ronald Clerk, Climbing' Cl HT, or, 1935, Austin & McAslan

'Captain Samuel Holland' ('Samuel Holland') S, mr, 1991, Ogilvie, Ian S.; flowers medium, dbl., slight fragrance; foliage medium size, medium green, glossy; spreading, medium growth; [(R. × kordesii × (Red Dawn × Suzanne)) × ((R. × kordesii × Red Dawn × Suzanne) × (Red Dawn × Suzanne))]; intr. 1990

'Captain Sassoon' HT, dr, 1938, Gaujard; flowers dark crimson; vigorous growth

'Captain Scarlet' Cl MinFl, mr; flowers scarlet red, 2 in., semi-dbl., shallow cup, borne in clusters, flowers all the way up the plant; recurrent; foliage dark green, glossy; tall (6-8 ft.) growth

'Captain Thomas' ('Captain George C. Thomas') Cl HT, ly, 1935, Thomas; bud long, pointed; flowers lemon to cream, red stamens, large, single, borne in small clusters, moderate fragrance; recurrent bloom; foliage glossy, light; climbing or pillar (10 ft.) growth; PP393; ['Bloomfield Completeness' × 'Attraction']; intr. 1938

'Captain Watkins' Pol, dp, Heyde, C.W.

'Captain Williams' -- See 'Capitaine Williams'

'Captain Woodward' HP, dp; flowers light red

Captivation™ -- See 'Kincap'

'Captivator' HT, mp, 1942, Joseph H. Hill, Co.; [sport of 'Better Times']

'Capuchonnée' D, mp, 1820, Bozérian

'Capucine Chambard' HFt

'Cara Bella' -- See 'Carabella'

'Cara Mia' ('Danina', 'Natacha', 'Maja Mauser', 'Dearest One') HT, mr, 1969, McDaniel, G.K.; bud ovoid; flowers large, dbl., moderate fragrance; foliage dark; vigorous, upright growth; PP3059

'Cara Mia, Climbing' Cl HT, mr; intr. 1976

'Carabella' ('Cara Bella') F, yb, 1960, Riethmuller; bud pointed, apricot; flowers cream edged pink, open, single, borne in clusters; foliage glossy, light green; moderate, bushy growth; ['Gartendirektor Otto Linne' × seedling]

'Caraibes' HT, Combe, M.; intr. 1970

'Carale' (Cisco™) F, dy, 1993, Strahle, Robert; flowers medium, full, borne in small clusters, slight fragrance; foliage medium size, medium green, glossy; medium (60 cm.), upright growth; ['Escort' × 'Golden Nugget']; intr. 1989

Caramba® HT, rb, 1970, Tantau, Math.; bud pointed; flowers bright red, reverse white, well-formed, large, 45 petals, foliage glossy; upright growth; intr. 1967

'Caramba' S, ob, Evers, Hans-Jurgen; bud rounded; flowers apricot orange, 7 cm., 20 petals, high-centered, borne in small clusters, slight sweet fragrance; recurrent; foliage dark green, leathery; prickles few, 9 mm., hooked downward; vigorous, bushy, flat (2 ft. × 3 ft.) growth; hips none; PP13396; [seedling × seedling]; intr. 2002

'Carambole' -- See 'Varbole'

'Caramel Antike' F, ab, Kordes; flowers honey-yellow to apricot, full, cupped, borne mostly in clusters, moderate fragrance; recurrent; moderate growth; intr. 2005

'Caramel Creme' HT, my, 1980, Weeks, O.L.; bud ovoid; flowers caramel yellow, 30 petals, cupped, borne singly, slight spicy fragrance; foliage finely serrated; prickles long, hooked downward; bushy, moderate growth; PP4706; [('Sunbonnet' × Mister Lincoln®) × 'Oldtimer']

Caramel Kisses™ -- See 'Jacdandy'

Caramella® -- See 'Meinitper'

Caramella® -- See 'Korkinteral'

'Caramella Kordana' Min, ab, Kordes; flowers copper center, outer petals yellow tinged with pink, full; container rose

'Carange' ('Tropical Passion') HT, or, Strahle, B. Glen; intr. 1999

'Caravelle' HT, mr, 1964, Mondial Roses; flowers bright cherry-red, large, dbl., high-centered; strong stems; vigorous, upright growth; ['Better Times' × seedling]

'Carbane' (Hot Spot™) HT, dp, 1993, Strahle, B. Glen; flowers red pink, 3-3½ in., full, borne mostly singly, intense fragrance; foliage large, dark green, semi-glossy; some prickles; upright (90-100 cm.) growth; PP7995; [sport of 'Duchess']; intr. 1990

'Carbelle' ('Big Spring Belle') Min, lp, 2008, Carman, Howard; flowers 2 in., dbl., borne mostly solitary; foliage medium, light green, semi-glossy; few prickles; growth upright, medium (20 in.); containers, garden decoration, exhibition,; [sport of 'Miss Charleston']; intr. 2008

'Carcade' (White Cascade™) HT, w, 1993, Strahle, B. Glen; flowers large, white, 3-3½ in., very dbl., borne mostly singly; foliage medium size, medium green, semi-glossy; some prickles; medium, upright growth; ['Coquette' × 'Jack Frost']; intr. 1984

Carcassonne™ F, ab, Olesen; bud short, pointed, broad-based; flowers apricot-pink, 8 cm., 28-35 petals, deep cup, borne in clusters, slight fragrance; recurrent; foliage glossy, disease-resistant; prickles moderate, 7 mm., hooked downward; bushy (60-100 cm.) growth; PP15232; [seedling × Queen Margrethe™]; intr. 2003

'Cardeal de Rohan' F, dr, 1957, Moreira da Silva; flowers deep red, semi-dbl.

'Cardiff Bay' HT, mr, 1993, Poole, Lionel;

flowers 3-3½ in., full, borne mostly singly, intense fragrance; foliage medium size, red changing to dark green, matte; some prickles; medium (105 cm.), upright growth; [seedling × 'Loving Memory']; intr. 1994

'Cardinal' HT, mr, 1904, Cook, J.W.; flowers deep rich crimson tinted golden at center, medium, full, flat; RULED EXTINCT 12/85 ARM; ['Liberty' × seedling]

Cardinal™ MinFl, dr, Olesen; flowers dbl., borne mostly solitary, slight fragrance; foliage dark green, glossy; growth bushy, low (40-60 cm.)

'Cardinal de Richelieu' ('Cardinal Richelieu', 'Rose van Sian') HGal, m, before 1847, Parmentier; flowers dark purple, small, very dbl., moderate fragrance; foliage elliptical, dark green; few prickles; bushy, compact growth; sometimes classed as HCh

Cardinal Hume® -- See 'Harregale'

'Cardinal Mercier' HT, op, 1930, Lens; flowers salmon-pink tinted orange, very large, full, globular; foliage bronze; vigorous growth

'Cardinal Patrizzi' ('Vainqueur de Solférino') HP, dr, 1857, Trouillard; flowers velvety purplish red tending towards black, edges bright flame, medium, very full; ['Géant des Batailles' × unknown]

'Cardinal Richelieu' -- See 'Cardinal de Richelieu'

Cardinal Song™ -- See 'Meimouslin'

'Cardinale de la Puma' HT, dp, 1938, Leenders, M.; flowers carmine-red, large, semi-dbl.; foliage glossy; vigorous, bushy growth; ['Mgr. Lemmens' × 'Lord Charlemont']

'Cardinals Hat' HT, mr, 1960, Leenders, J.; ['Souv. de Jacques Verschuren' × 'Charles Mallerin']

'Cardinal's Robe' -- See 'Macreno'

Carding Mill™ -- See 'Auswest'

'Cardon' HCh, m, before 1830, Cardon; flowers bright purple, center lighter

'Care 2000' S, pb, 2006, Beales, Amanda; flowers soft pink, reverse pink with salmon highlights, 10 cm., dbl., borne in small clusters; foliage medium size, medium green, semi-glossy; prickles average, straight, moderate; growth bushy, short (1 m.); containers; ['Kathleen Ferrier' × La Sevillana®]; intr. 1999

'Care Deeply' -- See 'Lyoca'

'Carefree' F, dp, 1959, Fletcher; flowers rose bengal, camellia form, medium, 75 petals, borne in clusters; foliage dark; free growth; ['Alain' × 'Pinocchio']

'Carefree Beauty' -- See 'Meipotal'

Carefree Beauty™ -- See 'Bucbi'

'Carefree Celebration' S, op, Radler; flowers deep orange pink, 2.5 inches, 15-18 petals, cupped, borne in clusters, slight fragrance; recurrent; medium to tall (4 - 5 ft.) growth; intr. 2008

'Carefree Days' -- See 'Meirivoui'

'Carefree Delight' -- See 'Meipotal'

Carefree Marvel™ -- See 'Meirameca'

'Carefree Spirit' ('Red Carefree Delight') S, rb, Meilland; flowers deep cherry red with a white eye, single, shallow cup, borne in clusters, slight fragrance; recurrent; foliage glossy, disease resistant; bushy, mounding growth; PPAF; [('Red Max Graf' × Seedling) × (Pink Meidiland® × Immensee®)]; intr. 2006

'Carefree Sunshine' -- See 'Radsun'

'Carefree Tapestry' S, ob; flowers orange and yellow, small, borne in clusters; foliage glossy, green; groundcover; spreading growth; intr. 2003

Carefree Wonder™ -- See 'Meipitac'

'Careless Love' HT, pb, 1955, Conklin; flowers deep pink, streaked (striped) and splashed white; PP1582; [sport of 'Red Radiance']; intr. 1955

'Careless Moment' Min, pb, 1978, Williams, Ernest D.; bud long, pointed; flowers white, lightly edged pink, 1-1½ in., 45 petals, high-centered, moderate fragrance; foliage small; bushy, spreading growth; PP4426; ['Little Darling' × 'Over the Rainbow']; intr. 1977

'Caremo' -- See 'Meitoflapo'

'Caress' HT, yb, 1935, Dickson, A.; flowers pale buttercup yellow, tinted rose, edged salmon-carmine, dbl.; foliage bright green, leathery; vigorous growth

'Carezza' -- See 'Barrez'

'Carfait' (Peach Parfait™) HT, op, 1993, Strahle, B. Glen; flowers pink coral, medium, full, borne mostly singly; foliage medium size, medium green, semi-glossy; few prickles; medium (70-100 cm.), upright growth; ['Indian Pink' × 'Melissa']; intr. 1992

Caribbean™ -- See 'Korbirac'

'Caribbean Dawn' -- See 'Korfeining'

'Caribbean Queen' -- See 'Reneen'

'Caribe' -- See 'Jacibe'

'Caribia, Climbing' ('Harry Wheatcroft, Climbing') Cl HT, yb, 1981, Mungia, Fred A., Sr.; bud pointed; flowers orange vermilion, striped and flecked yellow, large, 20-25 petals, cupped, borne singly with some side buds; foliage large, dark green, waxy; prickles flat, straight; PP4841; [sport of 'Caribia']

'Caribia' -- See 'Harry Wheatcroft'

'Caribia Twist' HT, rb; intr. 2004

'Caribou' HRg, w, 1946, Preston; bud pointed; flowers large, 5 petals, flat, slight fragrance; non-recurrent bloom; foliage glossy, leathery, dark, rugose, scented like sweetbrier; bushy, vigorous growth; ornamental fruit; very hardy; ['Ross Rambler' × ((R. rugosa × R. eglanteria) × seedling)]

'Carike Keuzenkamp' -- See 'Kanegem'

'Carillon' HT, or, 1935, Nicolas; bud long, pointed, scarlet-orange; flowers brilliant flame, paling, large, semi-dbl.; foliage glossy, light; bushy growth; PP136; ['Charles P. Kilham' × 'Mrs Pierre S. duPont']

'Carillon' HT, dy, Moulin-Epinay; bud long, pointed, deep yellow spotted carmine; flowers medium, 30-35 petals; vigorous growth; [('Soeur Thérèse' × 'Orange Nassau') × 'Orange Nassau']; intr. 1953

Carina, Climbing® -- See 'Meichimsar'

Carina® HT, mp, 1963, Meilland, Alain A.; flowers 5 in., 40 petals, high-centered, moderate fragrance; foliage leathery; upright, bushy growth; PP2378; ['White Knight' × ('Happiness' × 'Independence')]; intr. 1963

'Carina Spire' HT, pb, Kordes; flowers silvery pink on inside, strong pink on reverse, dbl., high-centered; good repeat bloom; growth bushy, tall (to 2 m.); intr. 1999

'Carina Superior' HT, w, 1977, Takatori, Yoshiho; bud pointed; flowers white, reverse light pink, 5 in., 35-40 petals, high-centered, moderate fragrance; foliage leathery; upright, bushy growth; [sport of 'Carina']; intr. 1978

'Carine' HT, op, 1911, Dickson, A.; bud long, pointed; flowers orange-carmine tinted buff, well-formed; strong stems; vigorous growth

'Carinella' HT, w, Meilland; intr. 1973

'Caring' Min, dp; flowers deep pink with many yellow stamens, single, flat, borne in clusters; recurrent; compact (24 in.) growth; intr. 2003

'Caring For You' -- See 'Bosarthric'

'Caring For You' -- See 'Coclust'

'Carinita' -- See 'Meivostro'

'Carioca' HT, ab, 1942, Chase; bud long; flowers 4½ in., 25-38 petals, high-centered, slight fragrance; foliage dark, glossy, leathery; vigorous, upright growth; PP532; [sport of 'Talisman']

'Carioca' HT, ob, Lens; bud semi-ovoid; flowers tangerine-orange, large, dbl., globular, moderate fragrance; foliage bright bronze green; long, strong stems; very vigorous growth; ['Rubin' × 'Mme Henri Guillot']; intr. 1951

'Carioca' HT, pb, Teranishi; intr. 1989

'Carissima' HWich, lp, 1905, Walsh; flowers delicate flesh, carnation-like, small, petals quilled, dbl., rosette, borne in large clusters, moderate fragrance; foliage glossy

'Caritas' HT, mp, Urban, J.; flowers large, dbl.; intr. 1970

Caritas™ (Dr Ingrid™, Grenadine™, Dronning Ingrid™) HT, ob, Poulsen; flowers orange and orange blend, 8-10 cm., 25 petals, borne one to a stem, slight fragrance; foliage reddish green; growth bushy, 60-100 cm.; PP13295; intr. 2001

'Carito MacMahon' HT, my, 1934, Dot, Pedro; bud large, ovoid; flowers dbl., cupped; foliage glossy, dark; strong stems; vigorous growth; ['Mrs Pierre S. duPont' × 'Cayetana Stuart']

'Carl Coërs' HP, rb, 1865, Granger; flowers bright red with dark purple, very large, full

'Carl Kempkes' F, dr, 1937, Kordes; bud long, pointed; flowers crimson, open, large, semi-dbl., borne in clusters;

foliage glossy, dark; strong stems; vigorous, bushy growth; ['Dance of Joy' × 'Mary Hart']
'Carl Philip' -- See 'Korpeahn'
'Carl Philip Kristian IV' -- See 'Korpeahn'
'Carl Red'   HT, mr; flowers dbl., high-centered; intr. 1992
'Carla, Climbing'   Cl HT, op, 1970, Riethmuller, F.; buds large, long pointed; flowers soft salmon, large, dbl high-centered, borne singly, moderate fragrance; foliage medium size, dark green, leathery; growth vigorous, climbing; [sport of 'Carla']
'Carla'   S, mr, Erskine; ['Will Alderman' × 'Hansa']; intr. 1963
'Carla'   HT, op, 1963, deRuiter; flowers soft salmon-pink, 3½-5 in., 26 petals, moderate fragrance; foliage dark; vigorous growth; PP2401; [Queen Elizabeth® × 'The Optimist']; intr. 1968
'Carla Ann' -- See 'Horcarla'
'Carla Fineschi' -- See 'Evepro'
'Carlea'   S, mp, 1965, Wright, Percy H.; flowers similar to Victory Year but darker and more abundant; non-recurrent; ['Betty Bland' × unknown]
'Carley' -- See 'Carley Regan'
'Carley Regan'   ('Carley', 'Carley's Rose')   Min, mr, Jalbert; flowers , hybrid tea; growth to 16-18 in.; intr. 2004
'Carley's Rose' -- See 'Carley Regan'
'Carlin's Rhythm'   F, m, 2008, Rupert, Kim L.; flowers 2 in., single, borne mostly solitary; foliage medium, medium green, semi-glossy; prickles 3-4 mm., curved, tan, few; growth bushy, 3-4 ft.; hips marble-sized, yellow; ['Lilac Charm' × 'Basye's Legacy']; intr. 2007
'Carlita' -- See 'Kamchin'
'Carlos Beauty'   (variety of R. acicularis), mp, Erskine; flowers bright pink, 12-15 petals
'Carlos Dawn'   S, dp, Erskine; CRL suggests HAcicularis; intr. 1950?
'Carlos Perpetual'   S, lp, Erskine
'Carlos Red'   S, dr, Erskine
'Carlos Reis'   Cl HT, mr, Moreira da Silva; flowers purplish red; ['Étoile de Hollande, Climbing' × 'Pres. Herbert Hoover']
'Carl's Rose' -- See 'Lemcar'
'Carlsham'   S, mp, 1964, Erskine; flowers rose-pink, large, 25 petals; recurrent bloom; foliage glossy; ['Hansa' × R. nitida]
Carmagnole® -- See 'Delrobla'
'Carmel Bice'   F, pb, 1959, Riethmuller; bud pointed; flowers pink, reverse lighter, semi-dbl., borne in clusters; foliage leathery, glossy; vigorous, upright growth; ['Gartendirektor Otto Linne' × seedling]
'Carmel Sunset' -- See 'Macclosup'
'Carmela'   Min, ob, 1986, Moore, Ralph S.; bud lightly mossed; flowers orange, yellow center, small, 15 petals, borne in sprays of 3-5, slight fragrance; foliage small, light green, matte; prickles small, brownish; medium, bushy, spreading growth; hips small, ovoid to globular, orange; ['Fairy Moss' × 'Yellow Jewel']; intr. 1980
Carmela™ -- See 'Intergeorge'
'Carméline'   S, lp, Guillot-Massad; flowers soft, pale pink, full, cupped form; intr. 2000
'Carmelita'   HT, mr, 1933, Spanbauer; bud ovoid; flowers vivid red, large, dbl., high-centered; foliage dark; very vigorous, bushy growth; PP91; ['Matchless' × 'Milady']
Carmelita™   ('Carmelita Castle', Fredericia™) F, my, Poulsen; flowers medium yellow, 8-10 cm., dbl., no fragrance; foliage dark; growth bushy, 100-150 cm.; intr. 1998
'Carmelita Castle' -- See 'Poullitam'
'Carmen' -- See 'Tanemrac'
Carmen™ -- See 'Sensuous Parade'
'Carmen'   Cl T, lp, 1888, Dubreuil; flowers buff pink at opening, very dbl.; ['Souv de la Malmaison' × unknown]
'Carmen'   HRg, mr, Lambert, P.; flowers crimson, stamens yellow, large, single, borne in clusters; foliage dark; vigorous growth; [R. rugosa rosea × 'Princesse de Béarn']; intr. 1907
'Carmen'   HT, dr, Delforge; flowers deep red, well-formed, large, dbl., intense fragrance; foliage dark; moderate growth; ['Crimson Glory' × seedling]; intr. 1956
'Carmen'   F, mr, Roman, G., and Wagner, S.; flowers light carmine red, small to medium, semi-dbl., borne in clusters; foliage medium to large, dark green, glossy; [Candy Rose® × Yesterday®]; intr. 1999
'Carmen'   HT, dr, Tantau; flowers dark velvet red, dbl., high-centered; few prickles; long stems; greenhouse rose
'Carmen' -- See 'Jaclam'
'Carmen de Bencomo'   HT, Camprubi, C.
'Carmen Miranda'   HT; from Brazil
'Carmen Papandrea'   Min, dp, 1989, Papandrea, John T.; flowers deep pink; [sport of 'Magic Carrousel']
'Carmen Sistachs'   Pol, 1936, Dot, Pedro; flowers rose-pink, base old-gold, dbl., borne in clusters; foliage sparse, small, soft, light; small vigorous, bushy growth
'Carmen Sylva'   HT, yb, 1891, Heydecker; flowers yellowish-white with pink, large, dbl.; ['Baronne Adolphe de Rothschild' × 'Mme Barthélemy Levet']
'Carmen Talón'   HT, dr, 1953, Dot, Pedro; bud oval; flowers velvety dark red, large, 35 petals; strong stems; vigorous growth; ['Charles Mallerin' × 'Satan']
'Carmen Tessier'   HT, dr, 1964, Mondial Roses; bud long, pointed; flowers crimson-red, open, dbl.; foliage leathery; vigorous, bushy growth; [seedling × 'Independence']
'Carmencita'   Min, w, 1954, Camprubi, C.; bud ovoid; flowers pure white, 55 petals; foliage clear green; vigorous growth; ['Lady Sylvia' × 'Perla de Alcañada']
'Carmenetta'   (R. rubrosa, 'Rubrosa') S, lp, 1923, Central Exp. Farm; flowers pale pink, medium, single, borne in clusters; foliage leathery, reddish; growth vigorous(7 ft), spreading (11 ft.); very hardy; [R. rubrifolia × R. rugosa]
'Carmin Brillant'   HGal, mr, before 1813; flowers light purple, carmine in center, medium, very dbl.; from Holland
'Carmin d'Yèbles'   Ch, mr, 1839, Desprez; flowers carmine red, full, cupped, moderate fragrance
'Carmin Velouté'   Ayr, mp; flowers bright carmine pink, very full
'Carmine Button'   Min, dp
'Carmine Panarosa'   S, mr, Delbard; intr. 2004
'Carmine Pillar' -- See 'Paul's Carmine Pillar'
'Carmosina' -- See 'Cramoisie'
'Carmosina' -- See 'Admirable'
'Carmosine' -- See 'Lapmiravi'
'Carnation Rose' -- See 'Great Maiden's Blush'
Carnaval® -- See 'Korfrilla'
Carnaval de Rio® -- See 'Delorfeu'
'Carné' -- See 'Agathe Incarnata'
'Carné' -- See 'Vilmorin'
'Carné' -- See 'Great Maiden's Blush'
'Carnea' -- See 'Unique Carnée'
'Carnea Double' -- See 'Double Carnée'
'Carnea Virginalis' -- See 'Beauté Virginale'
'Carnée' -- See 'Victoria'
'Carnée Double' -- See 'Double Carnée'
'Carnet de Bal'   HT, Dorieux, Francois; intr. 1972
'Carnival' -- See 'Wekwinwin'
'Carnival'   HT, op, 1939, Archer; flowers glowing orange to soft cerise, dbl.; foliage glossy, light; vigorous growth; RULED EXTINCT, 1/88
'Carnival Glass'   Min, ob, 1979, Williams, Ernest D.; bud pointed; flowers yellow-orange blend,, 1-1½ in., 38 petals, slight fragrance; foliage small, glossy, bronze; bushy, spreading growth; [seedling × 'Over the Rainbow']
'Carnival Parade'   Min, yb, 1979, Williams, Ernest D.; bud long, pointed; flowers golden yellow, edged red, 1 in., 45 petals, high-centered, slight fragrance; foliage small, dark, glossy; upright, bushy growth; PP4580; ['Starburst' × 'Over the Rainbow']
'Carnival Queen'   HT, mr, 1965, Armbrust; bud long, pointed; flowers luminous red, large, semi-dbl.; vigorous growth; [('Tassin' × 'Priscilla') × 'Charlotte Armstrong']
'Carol' -- See 'Carol Amling'
'Carol, Climbing' -- See 'Carol Amling, Climbing'
'Carol'   HT, pb, 1964, Herholdt, J.A.; flowers cyclamen-rose, becoming orchid at edge, center apricot, well-formed, 45 petals; no prickles; moderate growth; [Queen Elizabeth® × 'Confidence']
'Carol Amling'   ('Carol', 'Garnette Carol', 'Garnette Pink', 'Garnette') F, mp, 1953,

Amling, C.M. & Beltran; flowers deep rose-pink, edged lighter; PP1126; [sport of 'Garnette']

'Carol Amling, Climbing' ('Carol, Climbing') Cl F, mp

'Carol Ann' -- See 'Peapost'

'Carol Ann' Pol, op, 1940, Kluis; flowers orange-salmon, 1-1½ in., 35-45 petals, cupped, borne in tight clusters; recurrent bloom; dwarf (12 in. or less) growth; PP707; [sport of 'Marianne Kluis Superior']

'Carol Ann' HT, dr, Ohlson; flowers dark red, lighter reverse, 4-5 in., full, high-centered, borne mostly solitary, slight fragrance; foliage large, medium green, semi-glossy; prickles hooked, moderate; growth upright, tall (5-6 ft.); ['First Prize' × Mister Lincoln®]; intr. 2002

'Carol Ann' Min, lp, Welsh

'Carol Burnett' F, ab, Weeks; flowers rich apricot, 0-35 petals, borne in sprays, slight fragrance; recurrent; compact growth; intr. 2008

Carol Burnett™ -- See 'Wekyosotono'

'Carol Howard' HT, mp, 1935, Pfitzer; bud long, pointed; flowers rose-pink, very large, peony-like; foliage dark; vigorous growth

'Carol-Jean' ('Indian Meillandina', 'Indian Sunblaze') Min, dp, 1977, Moore, Ralph S.; bud pointed; flowers deep pink, 1 in., 22 petals, slight fragrance; foliage small to medium size, dark; upright, very bushy growth; PP4277; ['Pinocchio' × 'Little Chief']

'Carol-Joy' HT, mr, Allender, Robert William; intr. 1991

'Carol McLure' -- See 'Worcad'

Carola® S, dp, Noack, Werner; flowers cherry pink shaded salmon-rose with a white eye, large, semi-dbl.; compact growth; intr. 1988

'Carole Anne' HT, my, Thames; flowers chrome yellow, large; free-flowering; intr. 1986

'Carole Bouquet' HT, lp; intr. 2000

'Carole Lovett' -- See 'Bosholsex'

'Carolin' -- See 'Coralin'

'Carolin Reiberl' -- See 'Helreib'

'Carolina Bank' -- See 'Caroline Bank'

'Carolina Budde' HMult, mr, 1913, Leenders; flowers crimson, 6 cm., full, no fragrance; foliage glossy; ['Turner's Crimson Rambler' × 'Léonie Lamesch']

'Carolina Classic' -- See 'Briclass'

Carolina Daza® -- See 'Fepuma'

'Carolina Lady' -- See 'Micarol'

'Carolina Moon' HT, my, 1990, Bridges, Dennis A.; bud pointed; flowers medium yellow, fading slightly, 28 petals, high-centered, borne singly, intense fruity fragrance; foliage medium size, medium green, semi-glossy; prickles pointed slightly downward, medium, deep pink; upright, tall, vigorous growth; ['Just Lucky' × 'Thriller']; intr. 1990

'Carolina Morning' -- See 'Micam'

'Carolina Sunset' LCl, rb, 1990, Jeremias, Lephon L.; bud ovoid; flowers crimson, gold reverse, dbl., cupped, borne in sprays of 3-7; foliage average, dark green, matte; growth upright, tall (10-12 ft.); [seedling × seedling]

'Caroline' ('Caroline de Rosny') T, lp, 1829, Guérin; bud firm, red, ovoid; flowers light pink with yellowish center, medium, full, cupped, borne in small clusters, moderate centifolia fragrance; foliage oval to round; prickles few, small; probably extinct; sometimes classed as N

'Caroline' HT, op, Gaujard; flowers cinnabar-salmon, very large, 70 petals, moderate fragrance; foliage dark, glossy, leathery; very vigorous, bushy growth; ['Peace' × seedling]; intr. 1955

'Caroline Anne' HT, my, Thomas; intr. 1986

'Caroline Bank' ('Carolina Bank') HMult, lp, before 1890, Geschwind, R.; flowers crimson, flecked with white, fading to pink with lilac tints, medium, dbl., flat; ['De La Grifferaie' × 'a hybrid perpetual or bourbon']; sometimes classed as HSet

'Caroline Brian' MinFl, ob; intr. 1997

'Caroline Budde' ('Lien Budde') HMult, dr, 1913, Leenders, M.; flowers crimson-red, large, dbl.; foliage dark; vigorous growth; ['Crimson Rambler' × 'Léonie Lamesch']

'Caroline Clarke' -- See 'Horbondarc'

'Caroline Cook' T, ab, 1871, Cook; ['Safrano' × unknown]

'Caroline d'Angleterre' A, lp, 1822, Calvert; flowers pale pink, small, full, globular; prickles sparse, red, aciculate; stems slender

'Caroline d'Arden' HP, mp, 1888, Dickson, A.; flowers delicate pure pink, very large, dbl., intense fragrance; foliage large; ['Alfred K. Williams' × 'Marie Baumann']

'Caroline Davison' -- See 'Harhester'

'Caroline de Berri' -- See 'Foliacée'

'Caroline de Berry' Ch, w; flowers flesh white, medium, full, cupped

'Caroline de Monaco' -- See 'Meipierar'

'Caroline de Rosny' -- See 'Caroline'

'Caroline de Sansal' HP, mp, 1849, Desprez; flowers pink, center darker, large, dbl., flat; recurrent bloom; vigorous growth; ['Baronne Prévost' × unknown]

'Caroline d'Erard' B, w, 1850, Cochet; flowers flesh white, edges lighter, medium, full

'Caroline Emmons' F, rb, 1962, Boerner; bud ovoid; flowers scarlet-red, large, 55-60 petals, cupped, intense geranium fragrance; foliage leathery; vigorous, upright, bushy growth; PP2130; [('Geranium Red' × 'Fashion') × ('Diamond Jubilee' × 'Fashion')]; intr. 1962

'Caroline Esberg' LCl, mp, 1926, Diener; flowers dull rose, dbl., borne in clusters

'Caroline Hairston' S, ab; flowers large, buff to pink, held above the foliage, double, cupped to flat, some fragrance; remontant; growth large (5-6 ft.); hardy to -10°F; ['Buff Beauty' × Heritage®]; intr. 2004

'Caroline Kaart' HT, op, 1964, Buisman, G. A. H.; flowers salmon-pink veined dark red, large; foliage glossy; upright growth; ['Bayadère' × 'Ballet']

'Caroline Küster' -- See 'Mme Caroline Küster'

'Caroline Louise' -- See 'Seacaro'

'Caroline Maille' C, mp, about 1825, Boutigny; flowers semi-dbl.

'Caroline Marniesse' N, w, 1848, Roeser; bud pink; flowers creamy white, 5 cm., dbl., globular, borne in clusters of 3-9, slight musky fragrance; blooms throughout summer; probably synonymous with 'Duchesse de Grammont'

'Caroline Nicholson' -- See 'Worangle'

'Caroline Oldrey' HT, lp, 1998, Jones, L.J.; flowers pale pink, high-centered, 2½-3 in., 41-45 petals, borne mostly singly; foliage medium size, medium green, semi-glossy; prickles moderate; medium, compact, upright growth; ['Solitaire' × 'Prima Ballerina']; intr. 1997

'Caroline Plumpton' F, dp, 1976, Plumpton, E.; flowers deep Neyron rose, edged lighter, 2½ in., 20-25 petals, slight fragrance; foliage matte, green; very free growth; ['Red Lion' × seedling]

'Caroline Riguet' ('Mlle C. Riguet') B, lp, 1857, Lacharme; flowers whitish pink

'Caroline Schmitt' -- See 'Mme Caroline Schmitt'

'Caroline Ternaux' N, w, about 1840, Laffay; flowers pure white, large, full

'Caroline Testout' -- See 'Mme Caroline Testout'

'Caroline Testout, Climbing' -- See 'Mme Caroline Testout, Climbing'

'Caroline Victoria' HT, w, Harkness; flowers ivory, dbl., high-centered, intense fragrance; moderate growth; intr. 2006

'Carolyn' -- See 'Maccolumb'

'Carolyn' -- See 'Coralin'

'Carolyn Ann' Min, mp, 1985, Hooper, Clint; flowers small, 20 petals; foliage medium size, medium green, semi-glossy; bushy growth; ['Gene Boerner' × Baby Katie™]

'Carolyn Dean' LCl, mp, 1941, Moore, Ralph S.; bud long, pointed; flowers bright pink, 1¾ in., single, borne in clusters; recurrent bloom; foliage glossy; growth to 5 ft.; ['Étoile Luisante' × 'Sierra Snowstorm']

'Carolyn Dianne' F, lp, 1964, Patterson; flowers medium, dbl., moderate fragrance; foliage glossy; vigorous, compact growth; PP2749; ['Ma Perkins' × 'Pinocchio']

'Carolyn Elizabeth' -- See 'Sprocarolyn'

Carolyn's Passion™ -- See 'Wilcapa'

'Caron' F, pb, 1972, Langdale, G.W.T.; flowers white and pink, 3 in., 38 petals, foliage semi-glossy; upright growth; ['Kordes' Perfecta' × 'Saratoga']

'Carosi' HT, Wituszynski, B.; intr. 1969

'Caroubier' HMult, mr, 1912, Nonin;

flowers very bright light crimson-scarlet, medium, single, borne in clusters; early bloom, some repeat; ['Hiawatha' × *R. multiflora*]

'Carouge' HT, dr, 1978, Gaujard; flowers crimson-red, dbl.; ['Marylene' × 'Credo']

'Carousel' ('New Carousel') HT, pb, Kordes; flowers cream with pink to red edges, medium; greenhouse rose; intr. 2002

'Carousel' F, w; intr. 2006

'Carousel Panarosa' -- See 'Oragofe'

'Caroyal' HRg, mr, Erskine

'Carpark Rambler' S, rb; flowers red and yellow, medium, single; spreading, groundcover growth

Carpe Diem+ HT, op, Voom, Lex; flowers orange salmon, double, high-centered, borne mostly singly; recurrent; stems medium; florist rose

'Carpet of Color' ('Cambridgeshire', 'Fun Sunsation') S, rb, Kordes

'Carpet of Gold' HWich, my, 1939, Brownell; bud golden yellow; flowers golden yellow, aging to lemon yellow, 2-3 in., single to semi-dbl.; some repeat; foliage glossy; trailing growth, 12-15 ft.; PP541; [('Emily Gray' × 'Aglaia') × 'Golden Glow']

'Carriage Dorizy' B, m, 1849, Dorizy; flowers bright garnet purple, medium, full

'Carrie Corl' Gr, mr, 1969, Germain's; bud ovoid; flowers large, dbl.; foliage dark, leathery; vigorous growth; [Queen Elizabeth® × ((Queen Elizabeth® × unknown) × 'Happiness')]

'Carrie Jacobs Bond' HT, mp, 1935, Howard, F.H.; bud ovoid; flowers rose-pink, center flushed crimson, large, very dbl., intense fragrance; foliage leathery, dark; long stems; vigorous growth; PP158; ['Premier Supreme' × 'Lady Leslie']

'Carrie Jacobs Bond, Climbing' Cl HT, mp, 1940, H&S

'Carrot Top'™ -- See 'Poultop'

'Carrousel' Gr, mr, 1950, Duehrsen; flowers medium, 20 petals, moderate fragrance; foliage leathery, dark, glossy; vigorous, upright, bushy growth; PP1066; [seedling × 'Margy']

'Carrousel, Climbing' Cl Gr, mr, 1960, Weeks; PP1990; intr. 1959

'Carrousel Maid' Min, rb

'Carry Nation' F, w, 1960, Silva; bud ovoid; flowers white, center cream, small, semi-dbl., globular, borne in clusters, slight fragrance; foliage soft, glossy; vigorous, low growth; ['Pinocchio' × 'Katharina Zeimet']; intr. 1959

Carte Blanche™ -- See 'Meiringa'

'Carte Blanche' F, w; flowers pure white, full; growth to 90-100 cm.; intr. 2000

'Carte d'Or' -- See 'Meirobidor'

'Carte d'Or' ('Dancing Girl', 'Izu no Odoriko') F, my; flowers non-fading bright yellow, dbl., moderate fragrance; growth compact (65-75 cm.); intr. 2002

'Carte Noire' ('Fuego Negro') F, dr, Meilland; flowers black-red; greenhouse rose; intr. 1998

'Carte Rose' F, lp

'Carter' HT, dp, 2002, Ohlson, John; flowers full, borne mostly solitary, intense fragrance; foliage medium size, medium green, semi-glossy; prickles hooked, moderate; growth upright, medium (4-5 ft.); ['First Prize' × 'Intrigue']

'Carthage Rose' -- See 'Summer Damask'

Cartier™ ('Cartier Hit') S, pb, Poulsen; flowers pink blend, 8-10 cm., dbl., slight fragrance; foliage dark; growth bushy, 20-40 cm.; intr. 2004

'Cartier Hit' -- See 'Poulpah029(N)'

Cartoon® F, pb, Spek; flowers pink with green on guard petals, 3 in., 40-45 petals, cupped, borne singly and in sprays; recurrent; prickles moderate; stems long; florist rose; intr. 2005

'Cartwheel' -- See 'Jaccart'

'Caruso' -- See 'Meikarouz'

'Carwhit' ('The Whitgift Rose') HT, pb, 2000, Carlile, Adrian; flowers pink, reverse yellow, 4 in., full, borne mostly singly, moderate fragrance; foliage medium size, medium green, semi-glossy; few prickles; growth upright, medium; [('Lovely Lady' × unknown) × unknown]; intr. 2000

Cary Grant™ -- See 'Meimainger'

'Caryatide' HT, dr, 1955, Buyl Frères; bud long, pointed; flowers semi-dbl.; strong stems; upright growth; ['Hens Verschuren' × 'Poinsettia']

'Caryophyllata' -- See 'Œillet'

'Casa Blanca' -- See 'Casablanca'

'Casa Blanca' LCl, w, 1968, Sima; bud tinged carmine-pink; flowers semi-dbl., flat, borne in clusters; intermittent bloom; foliage medium size, dark green, glossy; vigorous, climbing growth; ['New Dawn' × 'Fashion']

'Casa Loma' S, dp, Hortico; flowers deep pink, large, full, quartered, cupped, moderate fragrance; growth to 5 ft.; intr. 1996

Casablanca® ('Casa Blanca') F, w, Select; flowers intermediate, sweetheart-size; intr. 2003

'Casang' ('Angel's Angel') F, or, 2006, Castillo, Angel; flowers orange-red, reverse pink and red, 4 in., single, borne in small clusters; foliage large, medium green, semi-glossy, disease-resistant; prickles medium, slightly hooked, moderate; growth spreading, medium (24 in.); garden decorative, exhibition; ['Little Darling' × Sarabande®]; intr. 2007

'Casanova' HT, ly, 1964, McGredy, Sam IV; flowers straw-yellow, 6 in., 38 petals, high-centered; [Queen Elizabeth® × 'Kordes' Perfecta']

'Casanova' -- See 'Tatton'

'Cascabel' F, rb, 1957, Dot, Pedro; flowers red, reverse pearly, passing to carmine, 45-50 petals, globular, borne in clusters; foliage glossy; very vigorous, upright, compact growth; ['Méphisto' × 'Perla de Alcañada']

'Cascade' LCl, mr, 1951, Mallerin, C.; flowers bright crimson, with white flecks at center, 2½ in., single to semi-dbl., borne in large clusters; very vigorous growth; ['Holstein' × 'American Pillar']

'Cascade' HT, w, Strahle, B. Glen; PP7382; intr. 1990

Cascade™ (Nordina™) LCl, pb, Poulsen; flowers pink blend, 8-10 cm., slight wild rose fragrance; foliage reddish green; growth bushy, 100-150 cm.; intr. 2000

'Cascade Blanche' -- See 'Blanche Cascade'

'Cascadia' HMsk, lp, 1925, Thomas; flowers blush-pink paling to white, 1 in., 15 petals, borne in clusters, slight fragrance; recurrent bloom; foliage glossy, dark; tall growth; ['Mme d'Arblay' × 'Bloomfield Abundance']

'Cascading White' -- See 'Dicwhynot'

'Cascry' ('Crystal River') Gr, ly, 2006, Castillo, Angel; flowers dbl., borne in small clusters; foliage large, dark green, glossy, disease-resistant; prickles medium, straight, moderate; growth upright, tall (48 in.); garden decorative; exhibition; ['red blend hybrid tea seedling' × 'Golden Unicorn']; intr. 2007

'Casdar' ('Darien') F, dr, 2006, Castillo, Angel; flowers long-lasting, 3 in., very full, old-fashioned, borne in small clusters; foliage medium size, dark green, glossy; prickles medium, slightly hooked, moderate; growth spreading, medium (34 in.); garden decorative, exhibition; ['Fragrant Cloud' × Eyepaint®]; intr. 2007

'Casey's Blush' -- See 'Judblush'

'Cashmere' HT, ab, 1980, Weeks, O.L.; bud pointed; flowers soft apricot, 30 petals, globular, borne singly and 3-5 per cluster, slight spicy fragrance; foliage leathery, dark; prickles long, hooked; vigorous, bushy growth; PP4736; ['Tanya' × 'Jack O'Lantern']

'Casilda Becker' -- See 'Cacilda Backer'

'Casimir Delavigne' P, mr, 1848, Vibert; flowers violet-red and crimson, nuanced lilac, 8-9 cm., full, globular

'Casimir Moullé' ('Mme Casimir Moullé') HWich, pb, 1910, Barbier; flowers purplish pink, reverse silvery pink, 4-5 cm., very dbl., flat, borne in clusters of 20-50; foliage medium green, glossy; [*R. wichurana* × 'Mme Norbert Levavasseur']

Casino® ('Gerbe d'Or') LCl, ly, 1963, McGredy, Sam IV; flowers soft yellow, well-formed, 4½ in., dbl., borne mostly solitary, moderate fragrance; recurrent bloom; foliage dark, glossy; vigorous (10 ft.) growth; [Coral Dawn® × 'Buccaneer']; intr. 1963

'Casino Mama' Min, mp, 2007, Bennett, John; flowers medium, 2 in., full, borne mostly solitary; foliage dark green, matte; few prickles; growth upright, medium (2 ft.); garden decoration, exhibition; ['Fairhope' × Hot Tamale™]; intr. 2007

'Caslon' (Long Island®) HT, rb, 1996, Castillo, Angel; flowers creamy white with red edge, 4 in., full, borne mostly singly, moderate fragrance; foliage medium size, light green, semi-glossy; upright, tall (3-4 ft.) growth; ['Tiki' × 'Color Magic']; intr. 1998

'Casper' -- See 'Magna Charta'

Casque d'Or® -- See 'Delcascor'

'Casred' ('Red Sea') F, dr, 2006, Castillo, Angel; flowers single, borne in large clusters; foliage large, medium green, semi-glossy; prickles medium, slightly hooked, moderate; growth spreading, tall (48 in.); garden decorative; ['pink grandiflora seeding' × 'orange-red Floribunda seedling']; intr. 2007

'Cassandra' F, or, Noack, Werner; intr. 1998

'Cassandra' HT, mr, 1966, Dorieux; flowers cherry,, 4½ in., high-centered; foliage dull, serrated; free growth; [('Karl Herbst' × 'Ena Harkness') × ('Christian Dior' × 'Peace')]

Cassandre® LCl, mr, Meilland; flowers light red aging to rich carmine pink, medium, borne in small clusters, moderate fragrance; growth pillar climber; intr. 1989

'Cassie' -- See 'Snowbelt'

Casta Diva® HT, w, 1983, Rose Barni-Pistoia; flowers large, clear white with cream center, 35 petals, cupped, no fragrance; foliage large, dark, glossy; prickles flat, yellow; upright growth; [Pascali® × seedling]; intr. 1982

'Castanet' F, op, 1960, Boerner; bud ovoid; flowers orange-pink, reverse lighter, large, 45 petals, moderate fragrance; upright, bushy growth; PP1840; ['Chic' × ('Garnette' × unknown)]; intr. 1959

'Castel' -- See 'Delset'

Castella® -- See 'Tanallet'

'Castellana' F; from Italy

Castello® HT, rb, Tantau; flowers dark red with yellow base, medium, double, high-centered, flat top, borne mostly singly; recurrent; stems medium; intr. 2007

'Castera' HT, r, Delbard; flowers orange-red, taking on hues of brown and grey lilac, medium, double, high-centered, borne mostly singly; recurrent; medium height, vigorous growth; intr. 2007

'Castilian' HT, ob, Williams, J. Benjamin; flowers ivory in heart, orange on outer part of petals, spreading toward heart as it ages, dbl., high-centered, intense fragrance; recurrent; stems long; medium (4 ft.) growth; intr. 1996

'Castilian Rose' -- See 'Summer Damask'

'Castle Hill' -- See 'Ziphill'

'Castle Howard Tercentenary' -- See 'Tantasch'

'Castle Hyde' -- See 'Kenpass'

'Castle of Dreams' S, my

'Castle of Mey' -- See 'Coclucid'

Castor® -- See 'Barcast'

Castore® (Castor®) S, lp, Barni, V.; flowers pink with base of petals lighter, semi-dbl., borne in large corymbs, moderate fragrance; spreading, bushy growth to 70-90 cm.; intr. 1987

'Caswin' ('Winter Haven') F, lp, 2006, Castillo, Angel; flowers dbl., borne in large clusters; foliage medium size, medium green, semi-glossy; prickles medium, straight, moderate; growth spreading, medium (34 in.); garden decorative, exhibition; ['Carefree Beauty' × 'orange-red floribunda seedling']; intr. 2007

Catalina™ ('Catalina Palace') S, lp, Poulsen; flowers light pink, 8-10 cm., dbl., no fragrance; foliage dark; growth bushy, 20-40 cm.; intr. 2005

'Catalina' HT, pb, 1939, San Remo Exp. Sta.; bud long, pointed, carmine, reverse salmon; flowers carmine suffused yellow and rose, very large, 23 petals, intense fragrance; foliage dark, glossy; very vigorous growth; ['Pres. Herbert Hoover' × 'Katharine Pechtold']

'Catalina' HT, op, Grillo; bud very long, coral-pink edged old-rose; flowers salmon to shrimp-pink, 4½ in., 25-30 petals, high-centered, moderate fragrance; very vigorous, upright growth; PP1013; [sport of 'Joanna Hill']; intr. 1940

Catalina™ -- See 'Jaccolap'

Catalina Frau© -- See 'Ferama'

'Catalina Palace' -- See 'Poulpal028(N)'

'Catalonia' HT, or, 1933, Dot, Pedro; flowers bright orange-crimson, shaded gold, large, very dbl., globular; foliage dark; bushy growth; [('Shot Silk' × 'Mari Dot') × 'Jean C.N. Forestier']

'Catalunya' -- See 'Gruss an Teplitz, Climbing'

Caterpillar™ -- See 'Poulcat'

'Catharina Klein' HT, pb, 1930, Berger, V.; bud ovoid; flowers bright pink, yellow background, large, very dbl.; foliage rich green; very vigorous growth; ['Mrs Franklin Dennison' × 'Hadley']

'Cathay' F, ly, 1957, Swim, H.C.; flowers 3½-4½ in., 35-40 petals, high-centered, intense fragrance; foliage glossy, leathery; vigorous, compact growth; PP1368; ['Fandango' × 'Pinocchio']

'Cathcart Bedder' HT, op, 1939, Austin & McAslan; flowers salmon-shrimp-pink; foliage bronze; vigorous, bushy growth

'Cathedral' -- See 'Coventry Cathedral'

'Cathedral City' -- See 'Kortanken'

'Cathedral Peak' -- See 'Jacwiht'

'Cathedral Splendour' -- See 'Harbell'

'Catherine and Thomas' -- See 'Worchicken'

'Catherine Anne' Min, w, 1999, Goodall, G. T.; flowers medium, dbl., borne in small clusters; foliage medium size, medium green, semi-glossy; numerous prickles; bushy, tall (3 ft.) growth; ['Rise 'n' Shine' × City of London®]

'Catherine Bell' Cl HP, pb, 1877, Bell & Son

'Catherine Blackburn' Pol, pb, Matthews, W.J.

'Catherine Bonnard' B, dp, 1871, Guillot fils; flowers cerise pink, medium, full; non-remontant; foliage dull green; numerous prickles; sometimes classed as HCh

'Catherine Cookson' -- See 'Noscook'

'Catherine de Würtemberg' M, lp, 1843, Robert; bud well mossed; flowers soft pink, large, very dbl., globular; vigorous growth; sometimes attributed to Vibert

Catherine Deneuve® -- See 'Meipraserpi'

'Catherine Frances' HT, lp, 2001, Jacobs, Mrs. Margaret; flowers pale pink, 14 cm., dbl., borne mostly solitary, intense fragrance; foliage medium size, medium green, glossy; prickles 7 mm., moderate; growth bushy, medium (120 cm.); garden decorative, exhibition; ['Mt. Shasta' × ('Apogee' × 'Ena Harkness')]

'Catherine Ghislaine' D, m, 1885; flowers violet-pink, fading to white, small, semi-dbl., moderate fragrance

'Catherine Graham' -- See 'Balizys'

Catherine Guelda™ -- See 'Zlecatherine'

'Catherine Guillot' ('Michel Bonnet') B, dp, 1860, Guillot fils; flowers carmine-rose, large, dbl.; vigorous growth; ['Louise Odier' × unknown]

Catherine Laborde® HT, yb, Adam; flowers yellow with carmine petal edges , double, high-centered, moderate fragrance; intr. 2007

'Catherine Langeais' HT, mr, 1965, Hémeray-Aubert; flowers carmine-red, well-formed, 46 petals, high-centered; vigorous, upright growth; ['Michèle Meilland' × 'Berthe Mallerin']

'Catherine Marie' HT, mp, 1991, Wambach, Alex A.; bud pointed; flowers medium to shell pink, 26 petals, high-centered, intense fragrance; foliage medium size, medium green, semi-glossy; [Pristine® × 'Captain Harry Stebbings']; intr. 1995

'Catherine McAuley' -- See 'Jacibras'

'Catherine Mermet' T, lp, 1869, Guillot et Fils; bud well-shaped; flowers flesh-pink, edges tinted lilac-pink, large, dbl.; vigorous growth

'Catherine Mermet, Climbing' Cl T, lp, 1913, Cant, F.

'Catherine Nelson' LCl, mp; intr. 2005

'Catherine Pericard' F, Pineau; intr. 1981

'Catherine II' Ch, lp, 1832, Laffay, M.; flowers flesh pink, medium, full

'Catherine Seyton' HEg, lp, 1894, Penzance; flowers soft pink, with prominent yellow stamens, single, moderate fragrance; non-recurrent; foliage fragrant (apple); vigorous growth

'Catherine Soupert' HP, w, 1879, Lacharme, F.; flowers white, washed peach-pink, large, full; ['Jules Margottin' × unknown]

'Catherine von Wurtemburg' M, m, 1843, Robert

'Cathie' HT, m, 1999, Priestly, James L.; flowers mauve, outer petals edges shaded light red, large, full; foliage medium size, dark green, dull; upright, tall

(4 ft.) growth; ['Paradise' × unknown]
'Cathie Irwin' -- See 'Korlowi'
'Cathrine Kordes, Climbing' Cl HT, dr, 1938, Krohn; flowers crimson, reverse lighter, 5 in., dbl., globular
'Cathrine Kordes' HT, dr, 1930, Kordes; bud long, pointed, blood-red, shaded black; flowers dark scarlet, large, dbl.; foliage dark (blood-red when young), leathery; very vigorous growth; [('Mme Caroline Testout' × 'Willowmere') × 'Sensation']
'Cathy Anne' HT, r, 1990, Wilson, George D.; bud pointed; flowers 25 petals, high-centered, borne singly; foliage small, dark green; prickles long, slender, red; long, straight stems; medium growth; ['Judith Morton' × 'Sylvia']
'Catinat' HP, mr, Oger; intr. 1874
'Catinat' HGal, m, 1838, Vibert; flowers violet, spotted with purple, some stamens visible, medium, full, quartered, borne solitary or in pairs, slight fragrance; sometimes attributed to Robert, 1850
'Cato' HMult, lp, 1904, Gratama; bud crimson red; flowers pink-yellow, 2 in., dbl., borne in clusters of 20-25; foliage shallowly dentate, dark green, glossy; prickles small, recurved
'Catorce de Abril' HT, yb, 1932, Padrosa; flowers yellow streaked red
'Catriona Annette' LCl, pb; intr. 2000
Cat's Meow™ -- See 'Desling'
'Cauldron' HT, pb, 1970, Waterhouse Nursery; flowers rose-pink to yellow, 4½ in., 23 petals, moderate fragrance; foliage glossy, dark; RULED EXTINCT 6/83 ARM
'Cauldron' S, mp, 1983, Holliger, Franc; flowers small, 5 petals, slight fragrance; foliage medium size, mid-green, matte; upright growth; [R. rubrifolia × R. nutkana]
'Cauvery' HT, dr, Kasturi; flowers medium, non-fading blackish crimson, ruffled petals, dbl.; intr. 1973
'Cavalcade' F, rb, 1950, Verschuren-Pechtold; bud ovoid; flowers oxblood-red and yellow, changing daily to crimson, carmine and silvery pink, 32 petals, intense fruity fragrance; foliage glossy, dark; vigorous, bushy growth; PP991
'Cavalcade, Climbing' Cl F, rb, 1957, Gandy, Douglas L.
'Cavalier' HT, ob, 1939, Samtmann Bros.; flowers burnt-orange to cream-buff, dbl., moderate fragrance; PP402; [sport of 'Mrs Franklin D. Roosevelt']
'Cavallii' -- See 'Ravellae'
'Cavriglia' HT, Fineschi, G.; intr. 1989
'Cayenne' HT, ob, 1975, Warriner, William A.; bud short, pointed; flowers deep orange, 3-4 in., 38 petals, slight fragrance; upright growth; PP3779; ['South Seas' × seedling]; intr. 1976
'Cayetana Stuart' HT, my, 1931, Dot, Pedro; bud long, pointed; flowers very large, dbl., cupped; foliage dark, glossy; very vigorous, bushy growth; ['Isabel Llorach' × ('Constance' × 'Sunburst')]
'Cechoslavia' HT, w, 1921, Berger, V.; flowers milky white suffused salmon-carmine, center golden yellow, dbl.; ['Pharisaer' × 'Mme Antoine Mari']
'Cecil' HT, my, 1926, Cant, B. R.; flowers golden yellow, 4 in., 5 petals, borne in large clusters; bushy growth
'Cecil, Climbing' Cl HT, my, 1940, Chaffin
'Cecil Earl' S, w, J. B. Williams; flowers 5 petals, slight fragrance; foliage dark green; growth to 4 × 3 ft.; intr. 2005
'Cécile Brünner' -- See 'Mlle Cécile Brünner'
'Cécile Brünner, Climbing' -- See 'Mlle Cécile Brünner, Climbing'
'Cecile Brunner, Everblooming Climbing' ('Cl Cecile Brunner, Continuous Blooming') Cl Pol, lp, Siskiyou; flowers delicate, soft pink, sweetheart size, 2 in., 18 petals, moderate pepper/spice fragrance; vigorous growth, 14-20 ft.; intr. 1996
'Cl Cecile Brunner, Continuous Blooming' -- See 'Cecile Brunner, Everblooming Climbing'
'Cecile Custers' HT, pb, 1914, Leenders, M.; flowers lilac-rose, reverse deep rose-pink,, dbl.; ['Mme Abel Chatenay' × 'Violet Liddell']
'Cecile Lens' ('Lencil') Min, mp
'Cecile Mann' HT, mr, 1939, Clark, A.; vigorous growth; ['Mrs Albert Nash' × seedling]
'Cécile Ratinckx' HT, my, 1924, Vandevelde; flowers coppery yellow, large, full; foliage glossy; ['Louise Catherine Breslau' × 'Mme Edouard Herriot']
'Cécile Verlet' HT, yb, 1926, Walter, L.; flowers yellow, passing to rose-pink; ['Marianna Rolfs' × 'Nordlicht (HT)']
'Cécile Walter' HT, op, 1926, Mallerin, C.; bud long, pointed; flowers coral-pink to coppery pink, base gold, very large, 28 petals, cupped; foliage rich green, leathery; vigorous growth; [('Mme Mélanie Soupert' × 'Mme Edouard Herriot') × seedling]
'Cecilia' S, pb, 1980, James, John; bud globular, pointed; flowers light pink blended darker pink, 25 petals, carnation-like, borne singly, moderate spicy fragrance; foliage small, pointed, glossy; prickles hooked; vigorous, compact, bushy growth; [(R. wichurana × Baronne Prevost) × R. × odorata]
'Cecilia 89' ('Hanib') F, ab, Hannemann, F.; ['Oz Gold' × 'Eye Paint']; intr. 1992
'Cecilio Rodriguez' HT, dr, 1950, Camprubi, C.; bud long, pointed; flowers dark velvety red, large, dbl., high-centered; foliage dark; strong stems; very vigorous growth; ['Tassin' × 'Eugenio d'Ors']
'Cecilitas' Min, lp
'Cecil's Bright Apricot' HT, ab, Godman; intr. 1996
'Cecily Gibson' -- See 'Evebright'
'Cedar Crest College' -- See 'Wilcrest'
'Cedric Adams' HT, dr, 1949, Brownell; bud ovoid; flowers scarlet to carmine, large, dbl., high-centered, moderate fragrance; foliage dark, bronze; vigorous growth; ['Pink Princess' × 'Crimson Glory']
'Cédrika Provencher' -- See 'Wekwinwin'
'Cee Dee Moss' -- See 'Morceedee'
'Ceearcee' HT, ob, Gokhale; intr. 1995
'Cel Blau' -- See 'Blue Sky'
'Celamire' -- See 'Sophie de Bavière'
'Celeb' S, op, McCann, Sean; flowers soft orange pink, 3 in., dbl., slight fragrance; repeatbloom; growth upright, bushy, medium (4-5 ft.); intr. 2004
Celebrate America™ -- See 'Tancressor'
'Celebrate Life' -- See 'Morcelebrate'
'Celebration' -- See 'Cocgrand'
'Celebration' F, op, 1962, Dickson, Patrick; flowers light salmon red with ivory disc, reverse peach, 3 in., 30 petals, cupped, borne in clusters, slight fragrance; foliage light green; vigorous, bushy growth; ['Dickson's Flame' × 'Circus']
'Celebration Days' HT, mp, Thames Valley Rose Growers; flowers shell pink, color deepening at the edges; intr. 1987
'Celebration 2000' -- See 'Horcoffitup'
'Celebrity' ('Lustrous') HT, pb, 1945, E.G. Hill, Co.; bud pointed; flowers pink, base shaded yellow, 6-7 in., 30-35 petals, high-centered, moderate spicy fragrance; foliage leathery, dark; vigorous, bushy growth; PP695; RULED EXTINCT 1/88; ['Golden Rapture' × 'Carmelita']
'Celebrity' HT, dy, 1988, Weeks, O.L.; bud pointed, large; flowers deep yellow, aging clear yellow, 4½-5 in., 30-35 petals, high-centered, borne usually singly, moderate fruity fragrance; foliage large, dark green, glossy; prickles pointed slightly downward, small, yellow-brown; upright, bushy, medium growth; PP7264; [('Sunbonnet' × Mister Lincoln®) × 'Yello Yo Yo']
Celebrity® HT, dr, Select; flowers 11 cm., 30-35 petals, high-centered, borne mostly singly; greenhouse rose; intr. 2003
'Celery-Leaved Rose' -- See R. centifolia bipinnata
'Céleste' -- See 'Celestial'
'Céleste' -- See 'Grand Sultan'
'Céleste Blanche' -- See 'Celestial'
'Celeste Mahley' F, pb, 1974, Byrum; bud long, pointed; flowers medium, dbl., slight fragrance; foliage leathery; vigorous, upright, bushy growth; PP3466; ['Seventeen' × 'Gemini']; intr. 1972
'Celestial' HT, lp, Myers & Samtmann; flowers light pink, edged paler, dbl., moderate fragrance; [sport of 'Premier']; intr. 1924
'Celestial' HSpn, lp; flowers pale flesh, small, dbl., intense fragrance; low growth; [R. rubiginosa × R. spinosissima]; sometimes listed as HEg; intr. about 1854

'Celestial' ('Alba Rosea', 'Nova Coelestis', 'Royale Aurore', 'Celestis', 'Nuancée de Bleu', 'Le Rosier Aurore Poniatowska', 'Erubescens', 'Céleste', 'Bleu Céleste', 'Belle Aurore', *R. damascena aurora*, 'Aurore', 'Aurora', 'Céleste Blanche') A, lp, before 1810; flowers light blush, golden stamens, large, semi-dbl. to dbl., cupped, intense sweet fragrance; non-recurrent; foliage bluish, large, with 5-7 leaflets; vigorous (to 6 ft.) growth; from Holland; possibly introduced to France by Charpentier

'Celestial Star' F, or, 1969, Pal, Dr. B.P.; bud ovoid; flowers dbl., borne in clusters; foliage glossy; vigorous, compact growth; intr. 1965

'Célestine' Ch, w, about 1825, Laffay; flowers pure white, full

'Célestine' HGal, cp, Vibert; intr. before 1836

'Célestine' HP, mp; flowers bright pink, full, cupped; intr. before 1848

'Célestine' D, lp, Coquerel; intr. before 1936

'Celestis' -- See 'Celestial'

'Celia' HT, mp, 1906, Paul, W.; flowers silky pink, large, full

'Celia' HT, mr; intr. 2003

'Celia Walker' F, rb, 1962, Fletcher; flowers cherry-red, reverse silver, 3 in., 15-20 petals, borne in clusters; foliage dark, glossy; vigorous, upright growth; ['Alain' × 'Golden Scepter']; intr. 1962

'Celica' -- See 'Meifota'

'Celientje' HT, ly; intr. 1997

'Célina' ('Céline', 'La Gracieuse', 'Coelina') M, m, before 1843, Hardy; bud heavily mossed; flowers reddish-purple, center occasionally streaked white, large, dbl.

'Celina' ('Sunshine Flower Carpet', 'Yellow Flower Carpet') S, dy, Noack, Werner; bud pointed; flowers lemon yellow, fading as they age, 2 in., 10-15 petals, cupped, borne in large sprays, slight fragrance; free-flowering; foliage medium size, light green, glossy; prickles average, 5 mm., slightly curved down, brown; vigorous (60-80 cm.), spreading, groundcover growth; hips small, round, green with reddish tint; PP10527; [Immensee® × 'Westfalengold']; intr. 1997

'Célina Dubos' ('Blanche du Roi', 'Sélima Dubos', 'Céline Dubois', 'Coelina Dubos', 'Rose du Roi à Fleurs Blanches') D, w, 1849, Dubos; flowers pale pink, nearly white, intense fragrance; sometimes recurrent bloom; [probably a sport of 'Rose du Roi']; Damask Perpetual

'Céline' -- See 'Célina'

'Céline' B, mp, about 1835, Laffay, M.; flowers pale rose, large, dbl., cupped, borne in large clusters; does not repeat; very vigorous growth

'Céline' HCh, m, Robert; flowers carmine-purple; intr. 1855

'Céline Bourdier' P, mr, 1852, Robert; flowers red shaded with lilac, 2½ in., full

'Céline Briant' M, lp, 1853, Robert; flowers 5-6 cm., full, rosette, borne in clusters of 8-12; freely remontant

Céline Delbard® -- See 'Delcélit'

Celine Dion™ -- See 'Wilbakd'

'Céline Dubois' -- See 'Célina Dubos'

'Céline Forestier' ('Liésis', 'Lusiadas') N, ly, 1842, Trouillard; flowers pale yellow, buff, with slight touches of pink, darker at center, 6-8 cm., dbl., frequently quartered, borne singly or in small clusters, moderate fragrance; repeat blooming; foliage dark, glossy; vigorous (to 6 ft.) growth; ['Champneys' Pink Cluster' × 'a tea']; probably re-introduced as 'Lusiadas' by da Costa (Portugal)

'Céline Gonod' B, mr, 1861, Gonod; flowers silvery red, edged bright pink, full, globular

'Célinette Chataigne' B, mp, 1880, Brassac; flowers medium

'Cels' -- See 'Belle Couronnée'

'Cels Multiflora' -- See 'Cels Multiflore'

'Cels Multiflore' ('Cels Multiflora') T, lp, 1836, Hardy/Cels; flowers flesh pink with darker center, medium, full, cupped; very recurrent

'Celsiana' -- See 'Belle Couronnée'

'Celtic Cream' HT, my, Dickson; buds pointed, lime lemon; flowers large, rich golden cream, moderate fragrance; growth medium to tall; intr. 1999

'Celtic Honey' S, ab, Dickson; buds apricot salmon; flowers non-fading honey toned apricot, dbl., exhibition; growth medium to tall; intr. 2000

'Celtic Pride' -- See 'Marjorie Marshall'

'Cendres de Napoléon' B, m, 1841, Béluze; flowers lilac pink with violet, medium, full

'Cendrillon' HT, mp, 1951, Gaujard; bud very large; flowers salmon, dbl.; foliage leathery; very vigorous, upright growth

'Cent Feuilles' -- See 'Cabbage Rose'

'Centenaire de Lourdes, Climbing' Cl F, mp, Delbard; flowers large, dbl.; glossy, dark green foliage; few prickles; growth to 3 m.; intr. 2005

Centenaire de Lourdes® ('Mrs Jones') F, mp, 1958, Delbard, G.; flowers soft rose, 3½-4 in., semi-dbl., borne in clusters of 5-10; vigorous, bushy growth; [('Frau Karl Druschki' × seedling) × seedling]

Centenaire de Lourdes Rouge® ('Bright Spark') F, mr, Delbard; flowers borne in clusters, intense jasmine fragrance; good rebloom; bushy growth, 50-100 cm.; intr. 1992

Centenaire du Tour de France® HT, my, Delbard; intr. 2004

'Centenaire du Vesinet' -- See 'Pironia'

'Centenary' -- See 'Koreledas'

'Centenary College' -- See 'Aroblaveet'

'Centenary of Federation' -- See 'Wekplapic'

'Centennial' HT, ob, 1953, Mallerin, C.; bud ovoid; flowers peach-red, reverse orange-buff, 4-4½ in., 40-45 petals, high-centered, moderate fragrance; foliage rich green; vigorous, bushy growth; PP1384; [seedling × 'Orange Nassau']

'Centennial' Gr, ab, Ping Lim; flowers apricot to light yellow, fading to creamy white, 2½ in., 22 petals, high-centered, borne in clusters; recurrent; foliage bronze tinged; stems long; low (2-3 ft.) growth; intr. 2006

'Centennial Gold' HT, my

'Centennial Miss' Min, dr, 1952, Moore, Ralph S.; flowers deep wine-red, base tinged white, 1 in., 60 petals, moderate fragrance; foliage small, dark, leathery, glossy; no prickles; dwarf (10-12 in.), bushy growth; PP1301; ['Oakington Ruby' × 'Oakington Ruby']

'Centennial Rose' S, dy, Ludwig; intr. 2003

Centennial Star™ -- See 'Meinereau'

'Centennial Sweetheart' Cl F, mr, 1960, Greene; bud globular; flowers bright red, large, 25 petals, borne in large clusters, intense fragrance; foliage glossy, light green; very vigorous growth; PP1871; [sport of 'Alain']; intr. 1959

Center Gold™ ('Atkins Beauty', 'Australian Centre Gold') Min, dy, 1981, Saville, F. Harmon; bud pointed; flowers deep yellow, sometimes near white, 60 petals, high-centered, borne singly or up to 12 per cluster, moderate spicy fragrance; foliage glossy, textured; prickles long, thin, slanted downward; upright, compact growth; PP5141; ['Rise 'n' Shine' × 'Kiskadee']

Centerpiece™ -- See 'Savapiece'

'Centfeuilles Anglais' -- See 'Rubra'

'Centfeuilles de Bordeaux' -- See 'Petite de Hollande'

'Centfeuilles Foliacée' -- See 'Foliacée'

'Centfeuilles Nain' -- See 'Pompon Varin'

'Centfeuilles Roses' -- See 'Centifolia Rosea'

'Centifolia a Fleurs Doubles Violettes' C, m

'Centifolia d'Avranches' -- See 'Duchesse de Grammont'

'Centifolia Foliacea' C, mp, 1810

'Centifolia Minima' -- See 'Rouletii'

'Centifolia Muscosa' ('Common Moss', 'Moss Rose', 'Single Moss', 'Rosier Mousseux', 'Rose Mousseuse Ordinaire', *R. rubra plena spinosissima pedunculo muscosa, R. muscosa multiplex, R. muscosa, R. × centifolia muscosa*, 'Mousseau Ancien', 'Moss Provence Rose', 'Gewohnlich') M, mp, before 1720; sepals, peduncles and calyx glandular, mossy; flowers large, dbl.; [sport of *R. centifolia*]; the presence of 'moss' on the peduncles and calice is highly variable and unstable, and likely to revert; because of the variability, this rose entered commerce under many different names

'Centifolia Rosea' ('Centfeuilles Roses') HP, mp, 1863, Touvais; flowers bright rose, large, cupped; foliage crinkled, light green wood with many red prickles; vigorous growth; ['La Reine' × unknown]

'Centifolia Unica' -- See 'Rubra'
'Centifolia Variegata' -- See 'Variegata'
'Central Park' -- See 'Poulpyg'
'Centre Court' HT, w, 1964, Barter; flowers white, center tan, well-shaped, 4 in., 38 petals; foliage dark; vigorous growth; [Eden Rose® × 'Ena Harkness']
'Centre Stage' -- See 'Chewcreepy'
'Centrex Gold' F, my, 1977, Smith, E.; flowers 3 in., 25 petals, slight fragrance; foliage matte, green; ['Alison Wheatcroft' × Chinatown®]; intr. 1975
'Centro de Lectura' HT, mr, 1959, Dot, M.; flowers crimson, 40 petals; foliage glossy, bright green; long strong stems; vigorous growth; ['Texas Centennial' × 'Peace']
CentrO-Rose® ('Chateau Merlot', 'Red Mirato') S, mr, Tantau; bud pointed ovoid; flowers strong red, 6 cm., 20-22 petals, high-centered, borne in clusters of 6-15, no fragrance; recurrent; fresh green, glossy foliage; prickles 5 mm., hooked downward, brown; compact (2 ft.), bushy, groundcover growth; no hips; PP12190; ['Footloose' × seedling]; intr. 2002
'Centurian Gold' -- See 'Aroyqueli'
Centurio® -- See 'Havop'
'Centurion' F, dr, 1976, Mattock; flowers blood-red, shaded crimson, 3 in., 30 petals, slight fragrance; foliage glossy, dark; ['Evelyn Fison' × seedling]; intr. 1975
'Century Sunset' -- See 'Tansaras'
'Century 21' HT, lp, Morey, Dr. Dennison; bud ovoid; flowers shell-pink, reverse slightly darker, large, dbl., high-centered, moderate fragrance; foliage glossy; vigorous growth; ['Condessa de Sástago' × 'Soeur Thérèse']; intr. 1962
'Century Two' HT, mp, 1971, Armstrong, D.L.; bud long, pointed; flowers large, hot pink, 5 in., 30-35 petals, high-centered, borne singly, moderate damask fragrance; foliage leathery; vigorous, upright, bushy growth; PP3340; ['Charlotte Armstrong' × 'Duet']
'Cera' F, r, DVP Melle; flowers deep pink to light red, dbl., borne in large clusters; recurrent; foliage dark green, disease-resistant; growth to 3 ft.; ['Melglory' × 'Guirlande d'Amour']; intr. 1998
'Ceremony' F, w, 1979, Lens, Louis; bud cupped; flowers pure white, 2½ in., 40-45 petals; foliage leathery; very bushy growth; ['Tiara' × Pascali®]; intr. 1970
'Ceres' T, mp, 1853, Oger; flowers vivid pink, large, full; growth vigorous, climbing
'Ceres' ('Orange Baby', 'Orange Babyflor') Min, or, Tantau; intr. 1994
'Ceres' HT, ob, Spek; flowers deep orange, center salmon, large, full; ['Sunburst' × 'Mme Edmond Rostand']; intr. 1922
'Ceres' HMsk, lp, Pemberton; flowers pale blush, tinted light yellow, stamens bright yellow, semi-dbl.; profuse seasonal bloom; shrub growth; intr. 1914
'Ceres' T, lp, Schwartz; flowers cream, center pink, shaded with China-rose, large, full; intr. 1896
'Cerise' -- See 'Belle Rosine'
'Cerise' Ch, mr, about 1836, Prévost; flowers cherry red
'Cerise' HT, dp, Tantau; flowers deep pink, large, 25 petals, intense fragrance; foliage dark, leathery, vigorous, upright growth; ['Crimson Glory' × 'Sterling']; intr. 1945
'Cerise' S, dp, Delbard
'Cerise' N, pb; flowers bright pink, mixed with cherry and coral-red, large, full, globular
'Cerise Bouquet' S, dp, 1958, Kordes; flowers cerise-crimson, semi-dbl., loose, then flat, moderate fragrance; foliage small, grayish; open, arching growth; [*R. multibracteata* × 'Crimson Glory']; a different rose may have been introduced under this name by Tantau, about 1937, but Kordes confirms this one is theirs
'Cerise d'Angers' Ch, about 1834, from Angers
Cerise Dawn™ -- See 'Devrise'
'Cerise d'Enghien' HGal, mp, about 1830, Parmentier; flowers bright carmine, medium, full
'Cerise d'Orlin' HGal, dp; flowers deep pink, reverse silver, loose, semi-dbl.
'Cerise Flower Circus' F, dp, Kordes; flowers deep pink, reverse lighter, double, borne in clusters; recurrent; short growth; intr. 2008
'Cerise Rouge' S, mr
'Cerise Talisman' HT, dp, 1933, Clarke Bros.; flowers cerise; [sport of 'Talisman']
'Cérisette la Jolie' -- See 'Surpasse Tout'
'Cernousek' HT, Strnad
'Certinia' S, w, Noack; flowers creamy white, occasional rose pink petal edge, 8 cm., dbl., borne in clusters; recurrent; vigorous (5 ft.) growth; intr. 2006
'Cervanek' HT, or, Strnad
'Cervanky' Cl HT, dy, 1935, Böhm, J.; flowers large, dbl.
'Cervantes' S, mr
'Cervena Gloria Dei' HT, mr, Strnad
'Cervena Super Star' HT, dr, Strnad; intr. 1976
'Cervia' -- See 'Kormamtiza'
'Cerys Ann' -- See 'Guescan'
César™ ('Romantic Occasion') S, yb, Meilland; flowers creamy yellow with pink, very large, dbl.; intr. 1993
'César Beccaria' HGal, w, 1855, Robert; flowers white, striped and spotted lilac and pink, large, dbl., flat
'Cesar E. Chavez' -- See 'Jacolman'
'César Jules' B, dp, 1865, Verdier, E.; flowers dark cherry pink, large, full
'Ceská Pohadka' Pol, rb, 1933, Böhm, J.; flowers red, salmon, rose and white, borne in clusters; very vigorous, dwarf growth; [sport of 'Golden Salmon']
'Ceské 'Praci cest'' LCl, Vecera, L.; flowers small, dbl.; prickles large; intr. about 1970
'Césonie' M, dp, Moreau et Robert; flowers carmine-crimson, large, dbl., borne in large clusters; some repeat; compact growth; intr. 1859
'Césonie' P, dp, before 1836, Vibert; flowers dark rose, large, full
'Cestiflora' HSpn, ly; flowers sulfur-yellow; early bloom; foliage finely divided; growth to 3-4 ft.; hips glossy, black
'Cetina' -- See 'Setina'
'Cevennes' -- See 'Korlirus'
Cha Cha® -- See 'Cocarum'
'Chablis' HT, w, 1984, Weeks, O.L.; flowers creamy white, medium-large, dbl., high-centered, slight fragrance; foliage large, medium green, matte; upright growth; [seedling × 'Louisiana']; intr. 1984
'Chacita' F, dr, 1947, Boerner; bud ovoid, globular; flowers deep red, medium, dbl., cupped, borne in clusters; foliage dark, leathery, vigorous, bushy growth; ['Pinocchio' × 'Crimson Glory']
'Chacok' -- See 'Meicloux'
'Chagip' F, mr, 1956, Delbard-Chabert
'Chaim Soutine' HT, pb, Delbard; bud longs, pointed; flowers with variations of deep pink and white on every petal, large, dbl., high-centered, borne mostly singly, no fragrance; growth vigorous, 4-5 ft.; PP11502; intr. 2001
'Chaldean' -- See 'Franfelluv'
'Chalice' HT, ab, 1960, Verschuren, H. A.; bud ovoid, pointed; flowers apricot-yellow, 5½-6 in., 55-60 petals, high-centered, intense fragrance; foliage leathery, glossy, vigorous, upright growth; PP1961; ['Orange Delight' × 'Golden Rapture']; intr. 1959
'Chalice Well' HMult, pb, McLeod, J.; [*R. multiflora* × unknown]; intr. 1995
'Challenge' F, dr, 1962, Fletcher; flowers deep blood-red, 2 in., 20 petals, camellia-like, borne in clusters; foliage dark; bushy, low growth; ['Alain' × 'Pinocchio']; intr. 1962
Challenger™ -- See 'Hilred'
'Challenger' HT, dr, 1938, Cant, B. R.; flowers dark crimson, very large, dbl., high-centered; foliage leathery, dark; long stems; vigorous, bushy growth; RULED EXTINCT, 6/89
'Challis Gold' -- See 'Noschal'
'Chalom' HT, Moreira da Silva, A.
'Chamade' mr, Kriloff; intr. 1977
'Chamba Princess' F, op, 1971, Pal, Dr. B. P.; flowers salmon-pink, open, medium, semi-dbl., slight fragrance; intermittent bloom; foliage leathery; moderate, bushy growth; intr. 1969
'Chambe di Kali' HT, mp, 1984, Pal, Dr. B.P.; flowers large, 22 petals, high-centered, borne singly, slight fragrance; foliage large, dark, glossy; prickles green to brown; medium, compact growth; ['Bewitched' × seedling]; intr. 1983
'Chambord' F, mp, 1960, Delforge; bud pointed; flowers pink, becoming darker, open, large, dbl., borne in clusters; foliage bronze; bushy growth; ['Roque-

brune' × Queen Elizabeth®)]
'Chambord'™ F, my, Poulsen; flowers medium yellow, 8-10 cm., 25 petals, no fragrance; growth bushy, 60-100 cm.; PP16143
'Chameleon' -- See 'Pur Caprice'
'Chameleon' -- See 'Émilie Gonin'
'Chameleon' HT, or, 1918, Dickson, A.; flowers flame, edged cerise; ['Lyon Rose' × unknown]
'Chameleon' Min, yb, Welsh, Eric; ['Wee Beth' × (Starina® × unknown)]; intr. 1995
'Chami' HMsk, mp, 1929, Pemberton; flowers bright rose-pink, stamens yellow, medium, single, intense fragrance; recurrent bloom; bushy growth
'Chami' ('Charmi') HMsk, mp, 1929, Pemberton; flowers light to dark pink, medium, semi-dbl.
'Chamisso' HMult, pb, 1922, Lambert, P.; flowers flesh-pink, center yellowish-white to medium yellow, 5-6 cm., semi-dbl., borne in large clusters, moderate fragrance; profuse, recurrent bloom.; foliage bronze; long stems; vigorous, trailing growth; ['Geheimrat Dr. Mittweg' × Tip-Top®]
'Chamoïs' -- See 'Comtesse de Chamoïs'
'Chamois' C, mp, before 1824, Mme Chamois
'Chamoïs' T, ly, 1869, Ducher; bud deep apricot; flowers fawn yellow, somtimes changing to coppery yellow, medium, semi-dbl.
Chamois Doré® -- See 'LLX8694'
'Champ Weiland' HT, mp, 1915, Weiland & Risch; flowers clear pink; foliage glowing, reddish; [sport of 'Killarney']
'Champagne' -- See 'Korampa'
'Champagne' HT, yb, 1961, Lindquist; bud pointed, ovoid; flowers buff shaded apricot, 4-5 in., 28 petals, high-centered, moderate fragrance; foliage leathery, dark; vigorous, upright, bushy growth; PP2151; ['Charlotte Armstrong' × 'Duquesa de Peñaranda']; intr. 1961
'Champagne Cocktail' -- See 'Horflash'
'Champagne Dream' Min, ab; intr. 2004
'Champagne Moment' -- See 'Korvanaber'
'Champagne on Ice' Min, r, Rasmussen; intr. 2002
'Champagne Patio' Min, ab; intr. 2003
'Champagne Pearl' ('Champagnerperle') F, ab, W. Kordes Söhne; flowers large, apricot cream with a green shade as they age, dbl., borne in large clusters; intr. 1983
'Champagne Time' Min, ab, Benardella, Frank; intr. 1996
Champagner® -- See 'Korampa'
'Champagnerperle' -- See 'Koropti'
'Champion' HT, yb, 1976, Fryer, Gareth; flowers yellow-cream, flushed red and pink, 7-8 in., 50-55 petals, moderate fragrance; foliage large, light; ['Irish Gold' × 'Whisky Mac']; intr. 1976
Champion® F, or, Noack, Werner; intr. 1988
'Champion, Climbing' Cl HT, yb, 1999, Kameyama, Yasushi; flowers yellow-cream, flushed red and pink, 3-3½ in., 50-55 petals, high-centered; foliage large, medium green; climbing (12 ft.) growth; [sport of 'Champion']; intr. 1998
'Champion of the World' ('Mrs de Graw') HP, mp, 1894, Woodhouse; flowers rose-pink, large, dbl.; seasonal bloom; vigorous growth; ['Hermosa' × 'Magna Charta']
'Champlain' HKor, dr, 1983, Svedja, Felicitas; flowers large, bright medium red with darker petal tips, 2½ in., 30 petals, borne in small clusters, slight fragrance; repeat bloom; foliage small, dark yellow-green; prickles straight, yellow-green; bushy growth, 3 ft.; hardy; [(R. × kordesii × seedling) × ('Red Dawn' × 'Suzanne')]; intr. 1983
'Champneyana' -- See 'Champneys' Pink Cluster'
'Champneys' Bengal Rose' Ch, mp, about 1800, Champneys
'Champneys' Pink Cluster' ('Champneyana', 'Champneys' Rose') N, lp, before 1810, Champneys; flowers dbl., borne in large clusters, moderate musky-sweet fragrance; recurrent bloom; moderately vigorous growth; moderately hardy; [R. moschata × 'Parsons' Pink China']
'Champneys' Rose' -- See 'Champneys' Pink Cluster'
'Champs de Mars' HP, pb, 1867, Verdier, E.; flowers carmine, shaded violet, large, full
Champs-Elysées, Climbing® -- See 'Meicarlsar'
Champs-Elysées® HT, dr, 1958, Meilland, F.; flowers rich crimson-red, large, 35 petals, cupped, slight fragrance; vigorous, bushy growth; ['Monique' × 'Happiness']; intr. 1957
'Chancelier d'Angleterre' HGal, mr, before 1836, Calvert; flowers bright red, medium, full
'Chandelle' F, lp, 1958, Lens; flowers light pink, reverse darker, well-formed, medium, dbl., borne in clusters; foliage bronze; vigorous, compact growth; ['Gretel Greul' × ('Lady Sylvia' × 'Fashion')]
'Chanderi' HT, lp, 1968, Singh, R. S.; bud long, pointed; flowers light pink, edged deeper, medium, dbl., high-centered, slight fragrance; foliage soft; moderate, upright, compact growth; ['Peace' × seedling]
'Chandon Rose' HT, pb, Delbard; intr. 2003
'Chandos Beauty' HT, pb; flowers medium pink in center, petals fading to light pink as they open, 40 petals, intense fruity & spicy fragrance; recurrent; growth to 3 ft.; intr. 2005
'Chandrama' F, w, 1981, Division of Vegetable Crops and Floriculture; bud pointed; flowers 25 petals, borne in clusters of 3-6, slight fragrance; foliage dark; prickles straight, brown; spreading growth; ['White Bouquet' × 'Virgo']; intr. 1980
'Chandrika' Min, w, Kasturi; flowers greenish white to pure white, pompon, borne in clusters; intr. 1978
'Chanel' HT, dp, Juneida; intr. 1995
'Chanelle' F, op, 1960, McGredy, Sam IV; flowers peach-pink shaded rose-pink, well-formed, 3 in., 20 petals, borne in clusters, moderate fragrance; foliage dark, glossy, pointed; vigorous, bushy growth; ['Ma Perkins' × ('Fashion' × 'Mrs William Sprott')]; intr. 1959
Change of Heart™ -- See 'Jacwypin'
'Changeante' -- See 'White Provence'
'Changing My Habits' Min, r, 2006, Hopper, Nancy; flowers light tan, aging to mauve, 1¾ in., very full, borne mostly solitary; foliage medium size, medium green, matte; prickles ½ in., tan, few; growth bushy, short (12 in.); [Winter Magic™ × 'Cafe Ole']; intr. 2006
'Chanoine Tuaillon' HT, dp, 1931, Gillot, F.; bud persian red; flowers carmine, very large, dbl., globular; very vigorous growth; ['Betty Uprichard' × 'Lucie Nicolas Meyer']
'Chanson d'Été' -- See 'Summer Song'
'Chant Rose Misato' S, m, Delbard; intr. 2007
'Chantal' HT, w, 1958, Moulin-Epinay; bud long, ovoid; flowers ivory, center yellow, edged carmine, very large, 60 petals; vigorous, bushy, upright growth; ['Mme Charles Sauvage' × 'Carillon']
'Chantal' S, ab, Williams, J.B.; flowers soft apricot-pink with lighter center, golden stamens, semi-dbl., flat, moderate fragrance; recurrent; low (2 ft.) growth; intr. 2006
'Chantal Mérieux' S, mp, Guillot-Massad; flowers very dbl., quartered; growth to ¾ m.; intr. 2000
'Chantana' -- See 'Umschan'
'Chantebrise' LCl, mr, Croix, P.; intr. 1969
'Chanteclerc' F, mr, 1956, Gaujard; flowers bright red, large; foliage bright green; bushy growth; ['Peace' × seedling]
'Chantefleur' F, op, Laperriere, L.; flowers rose-salmon; growth to 60-70 cm.; intr. 1958
Chantelle® HT, ab, Kordes; flowers light apricot, pink tones on reverse, large, dbl., high-centered, borne mostly singly; recurrent; stems long; intr. 2005
'Chanterelle' -- See 'Wardrosa'
'Chantilly' HT, or, 1964, Verschuren, A.; flowers orange to red-lead, 40 petals; foliage glossy, dark; strong stems; vigorous growth; [Baccará® × seedling]
'Chantilly' ('Grandchant') HT, w, Grandiflora Nurseries; intr. 2002
'Chantilly Lace' HT, m, 1979, deVor, Paul F.; bud long; flowers red-purple, 4-5 in., 35 petals, high-centered, intense fragrance; foliage glossy; vigorous growth; PP4665; [Blue Moon® × 'Angel

Face']; intr. 1978
'Chantoli' -- See 'Fryxotic'
'Chantré' HT, ob, 1959, Kordes, R.; bud long, pointed; flowers orange and golden yellow, 5 in., 20-25 petals, high-centered, moderate fragrance; foliage dark, leathery; very vigorous, upright, bushy growth; ['Fred Streeter' × 'Antheor']; intr. 1958
'Chantre, Climbing' Cl HT, ob, 1974, Arora, B. R.; buds large, long pointed; flowers orange and golden yellow, large, very dbl., high-centered, borne singly; foliage medium size, dark green, leathery; growth vigorous, upright (300 cm.); [sport of 'Chantre']; intr. 1973
'Châpeau de Napoléon' -- See 'Crested Moss'
'Chapel Bells' S, lp, Williams, J.B.; flowers delicate pink, semi-dbl., slight fragrance; foliage glossy, dark green.; hardy to -20°F; intr. 2003
'Chapelain d'Arenberg' HGal, mp, before 1847, possibly Parmentier; flowers bright pink, medium
'Chaperon Rouge' F, mr, 1951, Vilmorin-Andrieux; bud globular; flowers velvety crimson, center darker, open, medium, very dbl.; foliage glossy, bronze, dark; vigorous, upright growth; ['Crimson Glory' × ('Baby Chateau' × seedling)]
'Chaplin's Crimson Glow' HWich, rb, 1930, Chaplin Bros.; flowers deep crimson, base white, large, dbl.
'Chaplin's Pink Climber' HWich, mp, 1928, Chaplin Bros.; flowers bright pink, reverse lighter, stamens golden yellow, 6-7 cm., semi-dbl., flat, borne in large clusters; non-recurrent; foliage large, dark green, glossy; very vigorous growth; ['Paul's Scarlet Climber' × 'American Pillar']
'Chaplin's Pink Companion' LCl, lp, 1961, Chaplin, H.J.; flowers silvery pink, 2 in., 22 petals, borne in clusters of up to 30, moderate fragrance; non-recurrent; foliage glossy; vigorous growth; ['Chaplin's Pink Climber' × 'Opéra']
'Chaplin's Triumph' HT, dr, 1936, Chaplin Bros.; bud long, pointed; flowers deep velvety crimson; foliage dark; vigorous growth
'Charade' F, op, 1965, Herholdt, J.A.; flowers coral-cerise tinted salmon, pointed, 3 in., dbl., borne in clusters; foliage glossy; free growth; [Queen Elizabeth® × seedling]
Charade™ F, dr, Joseph H. Hill, Co.; flowers cardinal-red, small, 20-25 petals, high-centered, borne in sprays of 2-5, slight fragrance; foliage medium size, dark green, semi-glossy; prickles straight, medium, lilac; mini flora bushy, profuse growth; PP6669; ['Cindy' × Sassy™]; intr. 1988
'Chardonnay' -- See 'Macrelea'
Charentes™ -- See 'Pouluf'
'Chariot of Roses' Min, dr, 1986, Fischer, C.&H.; flowers 25 petals, borne singly; foliage small, dark, matte; prickles small, nearly straight, reddish; long, pendulous growth; small, globular fruit; [seedling × 'Fairy Moss']
'Chariots of Fire' LCl, dr, Williams, J. Benjamin; free-standing, climbing growth; intr. 1996
'Chariotteer' HT, rb, J.B. Williams; flowers red and white; intr. 2004
'Charisma' -- See 'Peatrophy'
Charisma® F, mr, Zary; intr. 2002
'Charisma, Climbing' Cl F, rb, Katsuri & Sriram; very free flowering; [sport of 'Charisma']; intr. 2004
'Charisma' HT, or, 1974, Meilland; RULED EXTINCT 3/77 ARM; intr. 1977
'Charisma' ('Surprise Party') F, rb, 1977, Jelly, R. G.; bud ovoid; flowers scarlet and yellow, 2-2½ in., 40-50 petals, high-centered, borne in small clusters, slight fruity fragrance; foliage medium size, dark green, glossy, leathery; vigorous, bushy, upright growth; PP4173; ['Gemini' × 'Zorina']
Charismatic™ -- See 'Decmatic'
'Charity' -- See 'Auschar'
'Charity' HT, mr, 1953, Taylor, C.A.; flowers bright velvety red, 5 in., 40-50 petals, high-centered; foliage glossy; vigorous, upright, bushy growth; ['Will Rogers' × 'Mme Henri Guillot']
Charity 97™ -- See 'Auschar'
'Charivari' S, yb, 1971, Kordes, R.; bud ovoid; flowers golden yellow to salmon, large, dbl., cupped; foliage glossy; vigorous, upright, bushy growth; ['Königin der Rosen' × 'Goldrausch']
'Charlemagne' -- See 'Président Dutailly'
'Charlemagne' HP, dp, 1836, Dorisy; flowers bright pink, large, very full; growth to 4 ft.
'Charlemagne' HP, mr, Oger; flowers shining cherry red, large, full, globular; intr. 1863
Charlene® HT, mr, Tantau; flowers brilliant red, large, double, borne mostly singly; recurrent; stems long; intr. 2004
'Charles Albanel' HRg, mr, 1983, Svedja, Felicitas; flowers medium, 20 petals, moderate fragrance; repeat bloom; foliage yellow-green, rugose; prickles straight, gray-green; groundcover; low, spreading growth; ['Souv. de Philemon Cochet' × seedling]; intr. 1983
'Charles-Anaïs' ('Anaïs Charles') C, 1824, Bizard
Charles Austin® S, ab, 1981, Austin, David; bud globular; flowers apricot tinged pink, fading to light pink, rosette, 70 petals, borne singly and in small clusters, moderate fragrance; foliage medium green, dense; prickles hooked, red; vigorous, upright, bushy growth; [Chaucer® × 'Aloha']; intr. 1973
'Charles Aznavour' -- See 'Meibeausai'
'Charles Baltet' HP, mp, 1877, Verdier, E.; flowers bright carmine pink, large, full
'Charles Bonnet' HP, dp, 1884, Bonnet; flowers dark rose, medium, dbl.; repeat bloom
'Charles Cretté' HT, mp, 1917, Chambard, C.; flowers velvety rose, large
'Charles Darwin' -- See 'Auspeet'
'Charles Darwin' HP, mp, 1879, Laxton Bros.; flowers brownish crimson, large; ['Pierre Notting' × 'Mme Julia Daran']
'Charles de Franciosi' T, yb, 1890, Soupert & Notting; bud long, well-formed, red-orange; flowers chrome yellow with salmon, outer petals tinted pink; large, full, rosette, borne mostly solitary; ['Sylphide' × 'Mme Crombez']
Charles de Gaulle® -- See 'Meilanein'
'Charles de Lapisse' ('Mme Charles de Lapisse', 'Mons Charles de Lapisse') HT, lp, 1910, Laroulandie; flowers pale blush-pink, very large, full; [sport of 'Mme Caroline Testout']
'Charles de Legrady' T, dr, 1884, Pernet-Ducher; flowers red, richly shaded with violet crimson, large, full, intense fragrance
'Charles de Mills' -- See 'Busard Triomphant'
Charles de Nervaux® S, ab, Massad; flowers straw yellow with pink tones, very full, cupped, some quartering, moderate lemon, orange, myrrh and tarragon fragrance; foliage dark green, matte; moderate growth; intr. 2008
'Charles Desprez' B, dp, 1831, Desprez; flowers medium, full
'Charles Dickens' HP, mp, 1886, Paul, W.; flowers full
'Charles Dickens' F, op, McGredy, Sam IV; flowers rosy salmon, 3 in., 16 petals, slight fragrance; ['Paddy McGredy' × Elizabeth of Glamis®]; intr. 1970
'Charles Dillon' F, mp, 1971, Wood; flowers soft pink, large, 24 petals, slight fragrance; foliage dark; low, bushy growth; [Orangeade® × Piccadilly®]; intr. 1970
'Charles Dingee' -- See 'William R. Smith'
'Charles Duval' B, mp, 1841, Duval, C.; flowers variable pink, large, full, cupped; growth erect
'Charles Duval' HP, mr, Verdier, E.; flowers scarlet, large, semi-dbl. to dbl., globular; vigorous growth; intr. 1877
'Charles E. Shea' HT, mp, 1917, Hicks; flowers rich pink; [sport of 'Mrs George Shawyer']
'Charles Eyck' F, yb; flowers yellow with red
'Charles F. Warren' HT, mp, 1960, Mee, O.; flowers rose-pink, well-formed, large, 40 petals, moderate fragrance; vigorous growth; ['Wilfred Pickles' × 'Karl Herbst']
'Charles Fargas' HT, pb, 1935, Dot, Pedro; flowers large, dbl.
'Charles Fontaine' HP, dr, 1868, Fontaine; flowers dark red, shaded purple, large, full
'Charles Gater' HP, mr, 1893, Paul; flowers red, 40 petals, globular; vigorous growth
'Charles Getz' HBank, lp, 1871, Cook
'Charles Gregory' HT, ob, 1947, Ver-

schuren; flowers vermilion, shaded gold, well-formed, 22 petals; foliage dark, glossy; vigorous growth

'Charles Gregory, Climbing' Cl HT, ob, 1960, Gregory

'Charles H. Rigg' HT, mr, 1931, Chaplin Bros.; flowers bright red fading to pink, dbl.; large stout, erect stems; vigorous growth

'Charles Hamlet Butler' S, lp, 2002, Andresen, Terry; flowers single, borne mostly solitary, no fragrance; foliage medium size, light green, matte; prickles small, straight, thin, dark green, moderate; growth bushy, medium; [sport of 'Mary Rose']; intr. 2003

'Charles Henry' HT, mr, 1967, Hooney; flowers crimson; foliage dark; vigorous, upright growth; ['Ena Harkness' × 'Lady Sylvia']

'Charles J. Grahame' HT, mr, 1905, Dickson, A.; flowers dazzling scarlet, well-formed, large, dbl., intense fragrance; vigorous growth

'Charles K. Douglas' HT, mr, 1919, Dickson, H.; bud long, pointed; flowers large, 28 petals; foliage dark; vigorous growth

'Charles K. Douglas, Climbing' Cl HT, mr, 1934, Leenders Bros.

'Charles Kuralt' -- See 'Cletraveler'

'Charles Lamb' HP, mr, 1884, Paul, W.; flowers light, glossy cerise-red, large, full

'Charles Lawson' B, dp, 1853; flowers vivid rose, very large, full; prickles unequal, numerous, vigorous, compact growth; introduced by Lawson

'Charles Lee' HP, dp, 1868, Gautreau; flowers dark vermilion, shaded bright scarlet, large, full

'Charles Lefèbvre, Climbing' Cl HP, dr, 1875, Cranston

'Charles Lefèbvre' ('Paul Jamain') HP, dr, 1861, Lacharme, F.; flowers reddish-crimson, shaded purple, large, 70 petals, cupped, moderate fragrance; bloom often recurrent; vigorous, tall growth; ['Général Jacqueminot' × 'Victor Verdier']

'Charles Lemayeux' HGal, dp, before 1885; flowers deep carmine, large, full

'Charles Lemoine' HGal, m, before 1885; flowers velvety purple lilac, medium, full

'Charles Louis' HP, mr, before 1936; flowers bright cherry-crimson, edged lighter, large, very full

'Charles Louis No. 1' HCh, mr, 1840, Foulard/Verdier; bud round; sepals long; flowers deep cherry red, large, full, moderate fragrance; foliage fresh green, purplish when young

'Charles Mallerin' HT, dr, 1951, Meilland, F.; flowers blackish crimson, 6 in., 38 petals, flat, intense fragrance; foliage leathery, dark; vigorous, irregular growth; PP933; [('Rome Glory' × 'Congo') × 'Tassin']

'Charles Mallerin, Climbing' Cl HT, dr, 1960, Balducci & Figli; buds large, shapely; flowers deep, velvet red, intense fragrance; vigorous, loose growth

'Charles Margottin' HP, mr, 1863, Margottin; flowers carmine red, with flame-red at center, very large, full, slightly cupped, moderate fragrance; foliage slightly crimped, dark green; prickles few, small, upright; stems reddish, smooth; ['Jules Margottin' × unknown]

'Charles Martel' HP, dr, Oger; flowers velvety crimson-purple, sometimes with a violet tinge, very large, dbl., globular; remontant; intr. 1876

'Charles Martel' HGal, pb, 1840, Parmentier; flowers slate pink, shaded purple, center carmine, large, full

'Charles Martel' B, mr, Guillot; flowers dark garnet, shaded crimson, medium, full, borne in clusters; intr. 1847

'Charles Métroz' Pol, dp, 1900, Schwartz; flowers China pink tinted salmon pink and carmine, small; foliage bright green, glossy

'Charles Notcutt' -- See 'Korhassi'

'Charles P. Kilham' HT, or, 1926, McGredy; flowers red-orange, fading to lincoln red, well-formed, large, 32 petals; vigorous, bushy growth

'Charles P. Kilham, Climbing' Cl HT, or, 1931, Howard Rose Co. (also Morse, 1934)

'Charles Quint' HGal, m, 1856, Robert; flowers lilac-rose and white, medium, full, globular

'Charles Ravolli' T, dp, Pernet Père; flowers carmine-rose; moderate growth

Charles Rennie Mackintosh® -- See 'Ausren'

'Charles Robin' B, m, 1853, Vigneron; flowers light purple

'Charles Rouillard' HP, lp, 1852, Laffay

'Charles Rovelli' T, rb, 1876, Pernet père; flowers brilliant carmine, changing to silver rose, center and base of petals golden yellow, very full, globular

'Charles Turner' HP, mr, 1868, Verdier, E.; flowers glowing red, very large, full; growth tall

'Charles Turner' HP, mr, Margottin; flowers vivid crimson-vermilion, aging to bright pink, large, dbl., cupped; prickles numerous, dark red; intr. 1869

'Charles XII' B, dp; flowers strong pink with touches of lilac, 5 in., moderate fragrance; growth tall, bushy; intr. 2004

'Charles Verdier' HP, mp, 1867, Guillot; flowers bright pink, edged lighter, very large, full; ['Victor Verdier' × unknown]

'Charles Wagner' HP, mr, 1907, Van Fleet/Conard & Jones; flowers clear bright red, approaching scarlet, large, dbl., borne in clusters of 3-5; foliage dark green; ['Jean Liabaud' × 'Victor Hugo']

'Charles William' HT, pb, 1989, Cattermole, R.F.; bud urn-shaped; flowers carmine rose, reverse lighter, yellow at base, petals pointed, reflexed, 56 petals, no fragrance; foliage matte, medium green, large; prickles light brown; upright, tall growth; ['Bradenburg' × 'Command Performance']

'Charles Wood' HP, rb, 1864, Portemer; flowers red shaded with crimson, reverse white, very large, full

'Charles X' ('Bandeau de Soliman', 'La Napolitaine') HGal, mr, before 1826, Descemet; flowers glossy crimson

'Charleston' F, yb, 1965, Meilland, Alain A.; bud pointed; flowers yellow flushed crimson, becoming crimson, 3 in., 20 petals, borne in clusters, slight fragrance; foliage dark, leathery, glossy; upright, compact growth; ['Masquerade' × ('Radar' × 'Caprice')]

'Charleston, Climbing' Cl F, yb, 1966, Rumsey, R.H. (also Keisei, 1978); flowers yellow with red edges; intr. 1966

'Charleston' HP, mp

'Charleston 88' -- See 'Meirestif'

Charlie™ -- See 'Kincha'

'Charlie Brown' -- See 'Morcharlie'

'Charlie Chaplin' HT, ab, Tschanz, E.; intr. 1989

'Charlie Dimmock' -- See 'Tanallepa'

'Charlie McCarthy' Pol, w, 1955, Wiseman; bud creamy white; flowers pure white, 1½-2 in., 28 petals, borne in clusters, moderate fragrance; foliage glossy, leathery, dark; dwarf, compact growth; ['Mrs Dudley Fulton' × 'Mermaid']; intr. 1955

'Charlie Perkins' HT, dr, 1970, Zombory; bud long, pointed; flowers overlaid black, large, semi-dbl.; foliage large, glossy, dark, bronze, leathery; very vigorous, upright, bushy growth; ['Carrousel' × 'Circus']

'Charlie's Aunt' HT, pb, 1965, McGredy, Sam IV; flowers cream, heavily suffused rose, high-pointed, 5 in., 65 petals; foliage dark; ['Golden Masterpiece' × 'Karl Herbst']

'Charlies Rose' -- See 'Tanallepa'

'Charlie's Uncle' HT, rb, 1976, Haynes; flowers cream, suffused carmine, 5-6 in., 40 petals, high-centered, slight fragrance; foliage large, leathery; [sport of 'Charlie's Aunt']; intr. 1975

'Charlotte' -- See 'Tanettola'

'Charlotte' -- See 'Auspoly'

'Charlotte' LCl, Zampini, P.; PP2284

'Charlotte' HT, op, 1941, Duehrsen; bud long, pointed; flowers salmon-pink and coral, base gold, dbl., high-centered; foliage glossy; vigorous, bushy growth; ['Joanna Hill' × 'Golden Dawn']

'Charlotte Anne' F, m, 1993, Blankenship, Paul; flowers lavender, medium, 5 petals, borne in small clusters; foliage medium size, dark green, glossy; some prickles; medium, spreading growth; [sport of 'Playgirl']; intr. 1994

'Charlotte Armstrong' HT, dp, 1940, Lammerts, Dr. Walter; bud long, pointed, blood-red; flowers deep pink to cerise, 3-4 in., 35 petals, moderate fragrance; foliage dark, leathery; vigorous, compact growth; PP455; ['Soeur Thérèse' ×

'Crimson Glory']
'Charlotte Armstrong, Climbing' Cl HT, dp, 1942, Morris; bud long, pointed; flowers deep pink, moderate fragrance; PP523; intr. 1942
'Charlotte Brownell' HT, yb, Brownell, H.C.; flowers buff with chrome yellow center and pink tint on edges, 4-5 in., dbl., high-centered; growth to 3-4 ft.; very winter hardy; PP3374
'Charlotte Chevalier' HT, dy, 1916, Chambard, C.; flowers dark canary-yellow; [sport of 'Arthur R. Goodwin']
'Charlotte Corday' HP, dr, 1864, Joubert
'Charlotte de Lacharme' HGal, pb, before 1824, Vibert; flowers purple-pink plumed and spotted with white and pale pink, medium, dbl.
'Charlotte E. van Dedem' HT, my, 1937, Buisman, G. A. H.; bud long, pointed; flowers large, semi-dbl.; foliage glossy; vigorous growth; ['Roselandia' × 'Ville de Paris']
'Charlotte Elizabeth' Gr, dp, 1965, Norman; flowers deep rose-pink, 3-4 in., 26 petals, high-centered, borne in clusters; foliage glossy
'Charlotte Gillemot' HT, pb, 1894, Guillot; flowers milk white with salmon and rose pink, large, full, moderate fragrance
'Charlotte Ives' F, pb, 1965, Warren; bud globular; flowers rose-pink, center light yellow, open, medium, single, borne in clusters; compact, upright, bushy growth; ['Ma Perkins' × Rose Gaujard®]
Charlotte Jan™ -- See 'Wilsent'
'Charlotte Kemp' HWich, m, Nobbs; intr. 1997
'Charlotte Klemm' ('Sirena', 'Sirene', 'Sisena') Ch, or, 1905, Türke; flowers red shaded orange, medium, semi-dbl.; probably extinct; ['Alfred Colomb' × 'Cramoisi Supérieur']
'Charlotte Mackensen' HMult, mr, 1938, Vogel, M.; flowers carmine red with silvery reverse, 7-8 cm., dbl., borne in tight clusters
'Charlotte Maertz' Pol, mr, 1913, Altmüller; flowers red with silvery reflections
'Charlotte Marie' S, pb, 1998, Fleming, Joyce L.; flowers pale pink, light at the base, pale reverse, 3 in., single, borne in small clusters; foliage medium size, narrow, dark green, semi-glossy; prickles moderate; low, compact, upright growth; ['Marchenland' × R. virginiana]; intr. 1997
'Charlotte Pate' HT, yb, 1971, MacLeod; bud globular; flowers pink, yellow reverse, large, 25 petals; foliage medium size, medium green, glossy; ['Wendy Cussons' × 'Golden Sun']
Charlotte Rampling® ('Thomas Barton') HT, mr, Meilland; flowers velvety red, large, 80 petals, moderate fragrance; growth to 70-80 cm.; intr. 1988
'Charlotte Rose Elson' -- See 'Worcandle'

'Charlotte Searle' -- See 'Kornends'
'Charlotte Séguier' HP, lp, 1849, Béluze; flowers flesh pink, tinted lilac at edges, large, full; very remontant
'Charlotte von Rathlef' HWich, dp, 1936, Vogel, M.; flowers deep pink, lighter at edges, small, very dbl., borne in small clusters; non-recurrent; foliage leathery, dark; vigorous, climbing growth; ['Fragezeichen' × 'American Pillar']
'Charlotte Wheatcroft' F, mr, 1959, Wheatcroft Bros.; flowers bright scarlet, large, single, borne in large trusses; foliage dark, glossy; vigorous, tall growth; intr. 1958
'Charlotte Wierel' Pol, w, 1926, Walter, L.; flowers cream-white, center bright rose-pink; vigorous growth; ['Bebe Leroux' × 'Helene Videnz']
'Charlottenhof' S, mr, 1938, Vogel, M.; flowers medium, dbl.
'Charlotte's Rose' -- See 'Burcharlotte'
Charlye Rivel® -- See 'Fekusa'
'Charm' -- See 'Charme'
'Charm' HT, op, 1920, Paul, W.; bud reddish orange, shaded pink and copper; flowers coppery yellow
'Charm Bracelet' -- See 'Jacfog'
'Charm of Paris' HT, mp, 1965, Tantau, Math.; flowers pink, large, 48 petals; vigorous growth; ['Prima Ballerina' × 'Montezuma']
Charma® S, mr, J&P; intr. 2006
'Charmaine' Pol, mp, 1929, Burbage Nursery; flowers pink tinged salmon, open, dbl., borne in sprays; recurrent bloom; foliage bright, glossy; long stems; very vigorous, bushy growth; ['Evelyn Thornton' × unknown]
Charmant® -- See 'Korzimko'
'Charmant' HT, ab, Kordes; flowers creamy apricot with green tints on some petal edges, large, dbl., high-centered, borne mostly singly; recurrent; stems long; upright growth; intr. 2005
Charmant® -- See 'Korpeligo'
'Charmant Blanc' HT, w, Kubokawa; intr. 2007
'Charmant Isidore' HGal, m, before 1829, Boutigny; flowers lilac
'Charme' ('Charm', 'Germania') HT, dp, 1930; bud long, pointed; flowers cherry-red, large, dbl.; foliage glossy; vigorous growth
'Charme d'Amour' -- See 'Liebeszauber'
'Charme de Paris' F, ob, Delbard, Georges; flowers salmon-orange with rose-salmon reverse, dbl.; intr. 1979
'Charme de Vienne' -- See 'Vienna Charm'
'Charmed' MinFl, ab, Bridges, Dennis; flowers 2¼ in., dbl., borne mostly solitary, slight fragrance; prickles 3/8 in., straight, pointing slightly down, few; growth upright, tall (2½-3 ft.); garden decorative, exhibition, cutting; PPAF; ['Purple Dawn' × unknown]; intr. 2002
'Charmente' HT, lp, 1979, Huber; bud globular; flowers 4 in., 42 petals; foliage bright green, leathery; upright, spreading

growth; ['Fragrant Cloud' × 'Ena Harkness']; intr. 1975
'Charmer' -- See 'Bencharm'
'Charmer' HT, lp, 1923, Schoener; flowers silvery pink; [('Pharisaer' × unknown) × 'Joseph Hill']
'Charmer' HT, lp, Dickson, A.; flowers light pink, center Neyron pink, shaded with salmon-orange, base yellow, aging to pink, large, dbl., high-centered, moderate fragrance; foliage leathery; vigorous, free branching growth; intr. 1934
'Charmglo' Min, pb, 1981, Williams, Ernest D.; bud long, pointed; flowers creamy white painted deep pink, reverse lighter, 35 petals, high-centered, borne usually singly, slight fragrance; foliage small, medium to dark green, slightly matte; prickles long, thin, brown, curved down; bushy, compact growth; [seedling × 'Over the Rainbow']; intr. 1980
'Charmi' -- See 'Chami'
Charmian® -- See 'Ausmian'
Charming™ -- See 'Poulhappy'
'Charming' HT, mp, 1922, Van Rossem; flowers salmon-pink, reverse coral-pink, semi-dbl.; ['Alexander Hill Gray' × 'Mme Edouard Herriot']
Charming Bells™ -- See 'Poulcat'
Charming Cover™ (Manhattan™, Schwarzwaldfeuer™) S, mr, Olesen; bud pointed-ovoid; flowers medium red with orange overtones, 5 cm., 14-16 petals, shallow cup, borne in large panicles, very slight fragrance; recurrent; foliage dark green, glossy; prickles moderate, linear to deeply concave, tan; bushy, compact (80 cm.) growth; PP12681; [seedling × seedling]; intr. 2000
Charming Diana™ -- See 'Twodi'
'Charming Maid' F, ob, 1953, LeGrice; bud orange-salmon; flowers salmon, base golden, 4-4½ in., 5-6 petals, borne in trusses, moderate fragrance; foliage dark, glossy; PP2209; ['Dainty Maid' × 'Mrs Sam McGredy']
'Charming Parade' (Charming™) Min, or, Poulsen; flowers orange-red, medium, semi-dbl., no fragrance; foliage dark; growth bushy, 20-40 cm.
'Charming Princess' HT, yb, 1926, Hancock; flowers deep yellow, edged vermilion large, dbl.; foliage dark; vigorous growth; [sport of 'The Queen Alexandra Rose']
'Charming Rosamini' -- See 'Ruicharo'
'Charming Rose' HT, lp
'Charming Unique' HT, mp, deRuiter; PP11175
'Charming Vienna' -- See 'Vienna Charm'
Charmwell Pretty Girl™ HT, lp, Davidson, Harvey; flowers light pink with deeper center, double, high-centered; prickles many; medium growth; intr. 2007
'Charpentier' -- See 'Belle Estelle'
'Charter 700' F, my, Fryer, Gareth; flowers bright yellow, large, dbl., exhibition, borne in well-spaced clusters; good rebloom; growth upright to 2 ft.; intr.

1993

'Chartreuse' HT, my, 1940, Mallerin, C.; bud long; flowers canary-yellow, dbl.; foliage glossy; bushy growth; ['Soeur Thérèse' × 'Angels Mateu']

'Chartreuse' -- See 'Macyefre'

'Chartreuse de Parme' -- See 'Delviola'

'Charugandha' HT, mr, 1974, IARI; buds large, long, pointed; flowers velvety crimson-red, very large, dbl, high-centered, borne singly and several together; foliage medium size, green, soft; growth vigorous, upright (90 cm.); ['Delhi Princess' × 'Eiffel Tower']

'Chase Beauty' HT, dr, 1947, Chase; bud long; flowers rich dark red, 5½ in., 35-45 petals, high-centered, slight fragrance; foliage dark; very vigorous, tall growth; PP870; [sport of 'Better Times']

Chasin' Rainbows™ -- See 'Savachase'

'Chastity' Cl HT, w, 1924, Cant, F.; flowers pure white, base lemon, 3½-4 in., dbl., high-centered, borne in small to medium clusters; non-recurrent bloom; foliage light, glossy; vigorous growth

'Chastleton' HP, lp, 1800; flowers large, very dbl.

'Château' -- See 'Baby Château'

Château Angelus™ -- See 'Poulaps'

'Chateau Canon' -- See 'Macghovie'

Château d'Amboise® -- See 'Delrouvel'

'Château de Bagnols' F, lp, Orard; intr. 1997

'Château de Beauregard' F, yb, Sauvageot; flowers creamy white with pale yellow centers and cerise edges, dbl.; intr. 2000

'Château de Chenonceaux' ('Chenonceaux', 'Galioca') HT, mp, 1978, Gaujard; flowers brilliant pink, large, 45 petals; tall growth; ['Americana' × Queen Elizabeth®]; intr. 1973

'Château de Clos Vougeot' HT, dr, 1908, Pernet-Ducher; flowers deep velvety red, 75 petals, intense damask fragrance; foliage dark, leathery; sprawling growth

'Château de Clos Vougeot, Climbing' Cl HT, dr, 1920, Morse; bud very large; flowers deep velvety red, turning darker with age, 10-12 cm., full, peony-shaped; foliage leathery, glossy; [sport of 'Château de Clos Vougeot']

'Château de Filain' F, op, Sauvageot; flowers rose-salmon, dbl.; intr. 1994

'Château de Gros-Bois' N, dy, 1909, Laperrière; flowers golden yellow, semi-dbl.; recurrent; ['Mme Pierre Cochet' × unknown]

'Château de la Juvénie' S, lp, 1901, Gravereaux; flowers soft, pale pink, small; non-recurrent; pillar growth to 2½ m.

'Château de Namur' HGal, pb, before 1842; flowers very dark violet, striped white, crimson center, medium, full; possibly from Quétier, but more probably from Parmentier

'Château de Vaire' ('Vaire') S, dr, 1934, Sauvageot, H.; flowers deep velvety red, large, dbl., cupped; non-recurrent; foliage bronze, dark; bushy (3½-6½ ft.) growth; moderately hardy; ['Charles K. Douglas' × R. macrophylla]

Château de Vaumarcus® S, op; flowers orange-nasturtium pink, medium, dbl., classic hybrid tea form, slight fragrance; floriferous; growth to 5 ft.; intr. 2000

Château de Versailles® -- See 'Delricos'

'Château des Bergeries' T, ly, 1886, Widow Lédéchaux; bud large; flowers pale canary yellow, darker at center, large, very full, globular

Château du Rivau® -- See 'Everive'

'Château Frontenac' S, dp; flowers purplish-crimson, very full, open wide, moderate licorice/myrrh fragrance; recurrent; tall, spreading growth; intr. 1996

'Château la Croix' HT, ab, Dorieux; flowers pastel apricot, large; vigorous growth; intr. 1995

'Château La Salle' HT, yb, 1966, Morey, Dr. Dennison; bud long, pointed; flowers buff-yellow, large, dbl., high-centered, intense fragrance; foliage dark, leathery; vigorous, bushy, compact growth; PP2947; ['Joanna Hill' × 'Ellinor LeGrice']

'Château Laroche Perganson' HT, mr, Meilland; flowers dbl.; intr. 2005

'Château Luegg' -- See 'Schloss Luegg'

'Chateau Merlot' -- See 'Tanoronez'

Chateau Montrose™ -- See 'Poulkini'

'Chateau Pavie' -- See 'Poulduce'

'Château Pelles' HT, lp, 1927, Mühle; bud cream-white; flowers soft pink, shaded salmon, dbl.; ['Harry Kirk' × unknown]

'Châteauroux' F, or, Croix, P.; intr. 1989

'Châtelaine' F, op, 1960, Lens; bud pointed; flowers coral overcast salmon, well-formed, 3 in., 32 petals, borne in small clusters, moderate fragrance; foliage glossy, coppery; vigorous growth; [('Peace' × seedling) × 'Fashion']; intr. 1957

'Châtelaine de Lullier' -- See 'Rendez-Vous'

'Châtelaine de Lullier' HT, mr, Meilland; flowers carmine-red, large, dbl.; intr. 1987

'Châtelet' ('Airain') HT, mp, 1952, Moulin-Epinay; bud globular, coral; flowers pink heavily tinted salmon, medium, very dbl.; ['Yvonne Plassat' × seedling]

'Châtillon Rambler' HWich, mp, 1913, Nonin; flowers salmon-pink, 3 cm., semi-dbl., cupped, borne in large clusters; growth to 15-20 ft.; ['Dorothy Perkins' × 'Turner's Crimson Rambler']

'Châtillon Rose' Pol, mp, 1923, Nonin; flowers bright pink, semi-dbl., cupped, borne in large clusters; foliage glossy; bushy (1-2 ft. growth; ['Orléans Rose' × seedling]

'Chatillon White' -- See 'White Chatillon'

'Chatsworth' -- See 'Tanotax'

Chattem Centennial™ Min, or, 1979, Jolly, Betty J.; bud ovoid; flowers medium, 38 petals, cupped, slight fruity fragrance; upright, bushy growth; PP4564; [Orange Sensation® × 'Zinger']

'Chattem Centennial, Climbing' Cl Min, or, 1991, Jolly, Marie; bud ovoid; flowers orange-red, aging light orange, medium, 38 petals, cupped, loose, borne usually singly or in sprays of 3-5, slight fruity fragrance; foliage medium size, light green, matte; tall (4-6 ft.) growth; [sport of 'Chattem Centennial']; intr. 1991

'Chatter' F, mr, 1947, Boerner; flowers velvety bright crimson, 14 petals, cupped, borne in large clusters, moderate fragrance; bushy, compact growth; PP739; ['World's Fair' × 'Betty Prior']

'Chatter, Climbing' Cl F, mr, 1960, Schmidt, K.; flowers light red, medium, semi-dbl., moderate fragrance

'Chatterbox' F, ob, 1973, Sanday, John; flowers bright orange-vermilion, rosette, 2 in., 16 petals; foliage glossy; dwarf growth; [Sarabande® × 'Circus']

'Chattooga' -- See 'Mictooga'

Chaucer® S, mp, 1981, Austin, David; bud globular; flowers rose pink in center, paling toward edges, full, cupped, borne singly and in small clusters, intense fragrance; foliage medium green; prickles slightly hooked, red; vigorous, upright, bushy growth; PP10618; [seedling × Constance Spry®]; intr. 1970

'Chaumant' -- See 'Maclocker'

'Cheaky Monkey' Min, dp, Jalbert; intr. 2005

'Checkers' -- See 'Pixchek'

Checkmate™ -- See 'Tuckmate'

'Chédane-Guinoisseau' -- See 'Mons Chédane-Guinoisseau'

Cheek to Cheek™ ('Salsa') LCl, w, Poulsen; flowers white with pink tinge, 5-8 cm., full, cupped, borne mostly in clusters, very slight fragrance; recurrent; foliage dark green, glossy; bushy, tall (150-200 cm.) growth; intr. 2002

'Cheer' ('Freude') F, mp, 1941, Kordes; flowers deep rose-pink, open, 4 in., semi-dbl., borne in clusters, moderate fragrance; foliage leathery; vigorous, upright growth; ['Dance of Joy' × 'Golden Rapture']

'Cheer Up' -- See 'Tincheer'

'Cheerful' HT, ob, 1915, McGredy; flowers orange-flame, base yellow, very large, dbl.; foliage rich green, glossy

'Cheerful Charlie' -- See 'Cocquimmer'

'Cheerful Days' HT, dy, Bell; intr. 2001

'Cheerfully Pink' F, op, 2001, Coiner, Jim; flowers medium pink, pink blend reverse, 2½ in., semi-dbl., borne in large clusters, no fragrance; foliage medium size, medium green, semi-glossy; prickles small, regular, moderate; growth bushy, tall (4 ft.); [seedling × seedling]

'Cheerfulness' F, op, 1981, Everitt, Derrick; flowers orange, pink and yellow blend, 8 petals, borne 10 per cluster; foliage small; prickles small, brown; compact growth; [seedling × seedling]

'Cheergirl' HT, or; intr. 2007

'Cheerie' -- See 'Chérie'

'Cheerio' -- See 'Chérie'

'Cheerio' -- See 'Playboy'

'Cheerio' F, dp, 1937, Archer; flowers carmine-cerise, large, semi-dbl., cupped, borne in clusters, slight fragrance; vigorous, compact growth

'Cheerio' ('Planten un Blomen') F, mp, Kordes; flowers clear mallow-pink, shading to Tyrian rose, reverse rose-madder, semi-dbl., cupped, slight fragrance; foliage leathery; vigorous, bushy growth; ['Holstein' × 'Sapho']; intr. 1940

Cheerleader™ -- See 'Morcheer'

Cheers™ -- See 'Savalot'

'Cheers' -- See 'Kanpai'

'Cheers To You' S, yb; growth to 3-4 ft.; intr. 2001

'Cheery Chatter' -- See 'Lyoter'

'Cheese Cake' -- See 'Brocake'

Chelsea™ -- See 'Ortsea'

'Chelsea' -- See 'Morsea'

'Chelsea' HT, mr, 1950, LeGrice; flowers carmine shaded orient red, 4 in., dbl.; vigorous, compact growth; RULED EXTINCT 6/86

'Chelsea Belle' -- See 'Talchelsea'

'Chelsea Brittlyn' Min, mp, 2006, Smith, Joseph and Brenda; flowers full, borne mostly solitary; foliage medium size, dark green, semi-glossy; prickles small, tan/red, moderate; growth compact, medium (30 in.); [sport of 'Aristocrat']; intr. 2007

'Chelsea Gold' -- See 'Lanwool'

Chelsea Morning™ -- See 'Jacnewpu'

'Chelsea Pensioner' -- See 'Mattche'

'Chénédolé' HCh, or, about 1840, Thierry; flowers crimson, small, dbl., cupped, moderate fragrance; very prickly; vigorous, upright growth

'Chénier' HCh, mp, about 1825, Laffay; flowers bright pink

'Chenonceaux' -- See 'Château de Chenonceaux'

'Cheré Michelle' Min, op, 1986, Jolly, Marie; flowers white with coral pink petal edges, small, 30 petals, high-centered; foliage medium size, medium green, semi-glossy; prickles small, cream to light brown, hooked downward; medium, upright growth; hips medium, globular, orange-green; ['Sheri Anne' × Anita Charles™]; intr. 1987

'Chérie' N, dp, about 1825, Laffay; flowers pink over cherry-red; may be synonymous with the Noisette 'Cerise'

'Chérie' D, mp, Miellez; intr. 1860

'Chérie' ('Cheerie', 'Cheerio') F, mp, Morse; flowers bright rose-pink, small, dbl., cupped, borne in clusters, moderate fragrance; foliage leathery; vigorous, bushy growth; [sport of 'Else Poulsen']; intr. 1931

'Chérie' F, ob, Gaujard; bud long; flowers bright orange, reverse coppery, well-formed, dbl.; intr. 1964

Cherie® S, dp; flowers single; intr. 2002

'Chérie' D, mp, about 1860, Miellez

'Cherish' -- See 'Jacsal'

'Cherokee' HT, mr; flowers bright red, round, dbl.; intr. 2004

'Cherokee Fire' -- See 'Lyoch'

Cherries 'n' Cream -- See 'Jachanpa'

'Cherries 'n' Cream' Min, rb, King; intr. 1997

'Cherries Jubilee' -- See 'Clecherry'

Cherry™ -- See 'Poulhyr'

'Cherry, Climbing' Cl HT, pb, 1934, Savage Nursery

'Cherry' HT, pb, 1928, McGredy; flowers brilliant carmine-pink flushed yellow, lower half yellow, large, dbl., high-centered; vigorous, bushy growth

'Cherry Blossom' F, mp, 1964, Verschuren, A.; bud orient red; flowers rose-pink to camellia-pink, 26 petals, borne in clusters; foliage glossy, dark; compact growth; ['Fashion' × seedling]

'Cherry Blossom Clam' -- See 'Sakura-gai'

'Cherry Blossom Haze' -- See 'Sakura-Gasumi'

'Cherry Blossom Viewing on the River' -- See 'Hanami-Gawa'

'Cherry Bomb' -- See 'Jolcher'

Cherry Brandy® HT, ob, 1965, Tantau, Math.; flowers orange, 5 in., 30 petals; foliage dark, glossy, leathery; very vigorous, upright growth

Cherry Brandy® HT, ab, Tantau; flowers peachy apricot, large, double, borne mostly singly; recurrent; stems long; Florist rose; intr. 2004

'Cherry Brandy '85' -- See 'Tanryrandy'

'Cherry Charm' LCl, pb, 1976, MacLeod; flowers deep pink, reverse silver pink, 5 in., 25 petals; non-recurrent; foliage dark; ['Norwich Salmon' × ('seedling sport' × 'Peeping Tom')]

'Cherry Cheerful' Pol, rb, 1995, Jobson, Daniel J.; flowers cherry red with white shadings, small, 6-14 petals, borne in large clusters; foliage medium size, medium green, glossy; compact, spreading, bushy, medium (3 × 5 ft.) growth

'Cherry Chinks' -- See 'Wettra'

'Cherry Cola' HT, dr

'Cherry Cordial' -- See 'Welcord'

Cherry Cover® -- See 'Poulerry'

'Cherry Cream' Gr, op; flowers creamy white and salmon blend, dbl.; intr. 1995

'Cherry Drop' -- See 'Ripcher'

Cherry Folies® F, rb, Meilland; flowers cherry red with white reverse; greenhouse rose; intr. 2004

Cherry Garland™ LCl, mr, Taschner, Ludwig; flowers cherry red, medium, full, pompon, borne in clusters; foliage glossy; stems long, supple; rapid, tall growth; intr. 2005

'Cherry Gem' Min, mr, Bell; flowers dbl., no fragrance; growth compact (16 in.)

Cherry Girl® ('Leigh Matthews Memorial Rose') HT, mr, Kordes; flowers strong pink, large, dbl.; stems 55 cm.; [sport of 'Cherry Lady']; intr. 2002

'Cherry Glow' -- See 'Sweet Cherry'

'Cherry Glow' Gr, mr, 1959, Swim, H.C.; flowers cherry-red, 3-4 in., 23 petals, cupped, moderate spicy fragrance; foliage leathery, glossy; vigorous, upright growth; PP1490; [('Floradora' × 'First Love']; intr. 1959

'Cherry Gold' -- See 'Arotigy'

'Cherry Hi' -- See 'Morshodot'

'Cherry Jubilee' -- See 'Jacsos'

'Cherry Kordana' Min, mr, Kordes; flowers cherry red

'Cherry Lady' HT, mr, Kordes; intr. 1999

'Cherry Lips' F, dp, Williams, J. Benjamin; flowers fluorescent hot pink, dbl.; profuse; compact growth; intr. 1997

Cherry Magic™ -- See 'Morchermag'

'Cherry Meidiland' -- See 'Meirumour'

'Cherry Meillandecor' -- See 'Meirumour'

'Cherry Page' HT, pb, 1914, Easlea; flowers carmine-pink, base yellow; ['Duchess of Bedford' × 'Le Progres']

'Cherry Parade' (Cherry™) Min, dp, Poulsen; flowers deep pink, medium, dbl., no fragrance; foliage dark; growth bushy, 20-40 cm.; PP12738; intr. 1999

Cherry Parfait™ -- See 'Meisponge'

Cherry Pastel™ -- See 'Wilcher'

'Cherry Pie' HT, dp, 1967, Gaujard; flowers deep rose-pink, 4½ in., dbl., high-centered, slight fragrance; intr. 1965

'Cherry Red' HMoy, mr; flowers rich cherry red; [R. moyesii fargesii × unknown]

'Cherry Ripe' HT, mr, before 1922, Paul, W.

'Cherry Ripe' F, mr, Heers; flowers scarlet, small, 70 petals; intermittent bloom; vigorous growth; [sport of 'Orange Triumph']; intr. 1949

'Cherry-Rose' HT, mp, 1946, Brownell; bud long, pointed; flowers cherry-rose, very large, dbl., high-centered, moderate fragrance; foliage glossy; very vigorous, upright, compact growth; ['Pink Princess' × 'Crimson Glory']

'Cherry Rose' Min, dp

Cherry Sunblaze® -- See 'Meibekarb'

'Cherry-Vanilla' ('Armilla') Gr, pb, 1973, Armstrong, D.L.; bud pointed; flowers pink, center creamy yellow, medium, dbl., cupped, moderate fragrance; foliage dark, leathery; vigorous, upright, bushy growth; PP3440; ['Buccaneer' × 'El Capitan']

'Cherry-Vanilla, Climbing' Cl Gr, pb, Fineschi; flowers lemon yellow, changing to white with deep pink edges, very large, dbl.; intr. about 1990

Cherry Velvet® -- See 'Poultress'

'Cherry Wine' -- See 'Jalwine'

'Cherryade' S, dp, 1961, deRuiter; flowers deep pink, well-formed, 4 in., 40 petals; foliage dark; vigorous, tall growth; ['New Dawn' × 'Red Wonder']

'Cherub' ('Cherubim') HMult, pb, 1923, Clark, A.; flowers pink and salmon, small, semi-dbl., cupped, remontant; foliage rich green, glossy, wrinkled; very vigorous, climbing growth; ['Claire Jacquier' × unknown]; cultivar currently in commerce is probably not correct

'Cherubim' -- See 'Cherub'

'Chervena Ghita' HT, mr, 1986, Staikov, Prof. Dr. V.; flowers bright cerise, large, 75 petals, borne in clusters; foliage dark, glossy; vigorous, upright growth; ['General Stefanik' × 'Peace']; intr. 1974

Cheryl's Delight™ -- See 'Minrco'

'Chesapeake' Min, lp, 1984, Jolly, Nelson F.; flowers small, 50 petals; foliage medium size, medium green, semi-glossy; bushy growth; [('Rise 'n' Shine' × ('Helen Traubel' × 'First Prize')]

'Chesapeake Sunset' F, ob, Williams, J. Benjamin; flowers orange-yellow blend, dbl.; intr. 1999

'Chesdeep' MinFl, pb, Chessum, Paul; intr. 1996

'Cheshire' -- See 'Fryelise'

'Cheshire' ('County of Cheshire') S, mp, Kordes; flowers medium pink in center, outer petals pale pink to white, full, rosette, no fragrance; growth short (2 × 3 ft.), broad; intr. 2001

'Cheshire Cream' F, w, 1976, Holmes, R.; flowers soft buff, becoming cream, 2½ in., 50 petals, moderate spicy fragrance; foliage small, glossy; low growth; [('Anna Wheatcroft' × 'Ivory Fashion') × ('Buff Beauty' × 'Masquerade')]

'Cheshire Lady' HT, pb, 1970, Dale, F.; flowers bright pink to scarlet, large, 30-40 petals; free growth; ['Fragrant Cloud' × 'Gavotte']

'Cheshire Life' HT, or, 1973, Fryer, Gareth; flowers vermilion, 5 in., 36 petals, spiral-shaped, slight fragrance; foliage dark, leathery; ['Prima Ballerina' × 'Princess Michiko']; intr. 1972

'Cheshire Regiment' -- See 'Fryzebedee'

'Cheshunt Hybrid' Cl HT, mr, 1872, Paul; flowers red shaded violet, large, dbl.; vigorous growth; ['Mme de Tartas' × 'Prince Camille de Rohan']; sometimes referred to as the first Hybrid Tea

'Cheshunt Scarlet' HP, mr, before 1902, Paul; flowers scarlet crimson, semi-dbl.

'Chesnut' ('Curiosity, Climbing') Cl HT, rb, Chessum, Paul; intr. 1996

Chess® -- See 'Intertra'

'Chess Man' -- See 'Gelman'

'Chessupremo' ('Golden Hands') MinFl, my, Chessum, Paul; intr. 1995

'Chester' F, my, 1977, Bees; flowers golden yellow, 3 in., 15 petals, slight fragrance; foliage glossy, dark; vigorous growth; ['Arthur Bell' × Zambra®]; intr. 1976

'Chester Cathedral' -- See 'Franshine'

'Chestock' Sp, w, 1986, Chessum, Paul; [sport of 'Pfander's Canina']; strain of R. canina; used as a stem of standard (tree) roses; intr. 1988

'Chevalier Angelo Ferrario' ('Mons le Chevalier Angelo Ferrario') T, dr, 1895, Bernaix; flowers carmine-purple, large, full

'Chevalier Nigra' HP, dr, 1865, Damaizin/Verdier

'Chevreul' M, mp, 1887, Moreau et Robert; flowers salmon-pink, well mossed; large fruit, colorful in fall

'Chevreuse' -- See 'Korplavi'

'Chévrier' -- See 'Miralda'

'Chevy Chase' HMult, dr, 1939, Hansen, N.J.; flowers dark crimson, small, 65 petals, borne in clusters of 10-20, moderate fragrance; non-recurrent; foliage soft, light green, wrinkled; vigorous, climbing (to 15 ft.) growth; PP443; [R. soulieana × 'Eblouissant']

'Chewability' LCl, dy, Warner; intr. 2008

'Chewadmore' Cl Min, lp, Warner; intr. 2001

'Chewallop' ('Rocketeer', 'Rosalie Coral', 'Rosilia') Cl Min, ob, 1992, Warner, Chris; bud short, pointed ovoid; flowers bright coral-orange, reverse yellow, 1-1½ in., 20 petals, flat, quilled, borne in large clusters, slight fragrance; recurrent; foliage small, medium green, glossy; prickles few, hooked downward; medium (175-190 cm.), bushy growth; PP9013; [(Elizabeth of Glamis® × (Galway Bay® × 'Sutter's Gold')) × Anna Ford®]; intr. 1991

'Chewalma' HT, ab, Warner; intr. 2006

'Chewapri' ('Patio Charm') Cl Min, ab, Warner, Chris; intr. 1994

'Chewarvel' ('King Tut', Laura Ford®, 'Normandie') Cl Min, my, 1990, Warner, Chris; bud pointed; flowers medium yellow, reverse lighter yellow, aging pink, 2 in., 22 petals, high-centered, borne in small clusters, slight fruity fragrance; foliage small, light green, glossy; prickles straight, small, infrequent, light brown; upright, bushy, tall growth (7 ft.); round, large, average fruit; PP9012; [Anna Ford® × (Elizabeth of Glamis® × (Galway Bay® × 'Sutter's Gold'))]; intr. 1990

'Chewaze' ('Pillar Box', 'Wardlip') F, or, 1987, Warner, Chris; flowers vivid vermilion, medium, dbl.; foliage medium size, medium green, semi-glossy; upright growth; [Alexander® × (Galway Bay® × Elizabeth of Glamis®)]; intr. 1986

'Chewba' -- See 'Lady Barbara'

'Chewbeaut' ('Donald Davis') F, or, 1992, Warner, Chris; flowers vermilion, medium, dbl., borne in small clusters; foliage medium size, medium green, semi-glossy; few prickles; medium (90 cm.), upright growth; [Anne Harkness® × 'Beautiful Britain']

'Chewcorpink' ('Alfresco', 'Dame de Montsoreau') LCl, pb, 2000, Warner, Chris; flowers salmon blended with yellow, reverse pink, 4 in., 24 petals, borne in small clusters, moderate sweet fragrance; foliage medium size, dark green, semi-glossy; few prickles; growth climbing, upright, spreading, tall (9-10 ft.); walls, fences, pergolas; ['Mary Sumner' × 'Summer Wine']; intr. 2001

'Chewcreepy' ('Centre Stage', 'Mini Love') S, lp, 2000, Warner, Chris; flowers light pink with paler reverse, small, single, borne in clusters, slight fragrance; foliage small, medium green, glossy; prickles small, curved, moderate in number; growth spreading, very low; groundcover; ['Eyeopener' × (R. luciae × Laura Ashley)]

'Chewcrest' Cl Min, w, Warner, Chris; intr. 1997

'Chewdainty' ('Gilt Edged') Cl Min, yb, Warner, Chris; intr. 1997

'Chewdor' ('Lady Penelope') LCl, op, 1998, Warner, Chris; flowers salmon pink, pink reverse, 2½-3 in., full, pompon, borne in small clusters; repeats well; foliage medium size, medium green, glossy; few prickles; spreading, medium (8 ft.) growth; [Laura Ford® × 'Royal Baby']; intr. 1998

'Chewell' ('Iris Webb') F, r, 1988, Warner, Chris; flowers tan, fading to slate gray, medium, dbl.; foliage medium size, dark green, semi-glossy; bushy growth; ['Southampton' × ('Belinda' × (Elizabeth of Glamis® × '(Galway Bay × Sutters Gold)'))]; intr. 1990

'Chewglorious' ('Love Knot') Cl Min, mr, 1999, Warner, Chris; flowers crimson, reverse light red, 2½ in., dbl., borne in small clusters; foliage small, medium green, glossy; few prickles; upright, tall (6 ft.) growth; [Laura Ford® × 'Ingrid Bergman']; intr. 2000

'Chewgoldtop' (Scent From Above™) LCl, my, 2005, Warner, Christopher H. ; bud long, pointed ovoid; flowers golden yellow, 10 cm., 25-30 petals, high-centered, borne in small clusters of 3 - 5, moderate spicy fragrance; recurrent; foliage medium size, dark green, glossy; prickles 6-8 mm., hooked slightly downward, greyed-yellow, moderate; growth upright, branching and vigorous, tall (3-4 m.); climber; PP17126; [Laura Ford® × 'Amanda']; intr. 2005

'Chewground' ('Fragrant Spreader', 'Oso Easy') S, m, Warner, Chris; bud lanceolate; intr. 2002

'Chewharla' ('Laura Ashley', 'Perigord') Cl Min, m, 1990, Warner, Chris; bud pointed; flowers lilac-mauve pink, reverse pink, aging same, loose, small, single, moderate fruity fragrance; foliage small, medium green, semi-glossy; prickles hooked, small, brown; spreading, low growth; hips oval, small, red; [Marjorie Fair® × 'Nozomi']; intr. 1990

'Chewily' ('Cottage Garden', 'Pink Cottage', 'Mix 'n' Match') S, mp, 1999, Warner, Chris; bud short, furled; flowers pastel pearl pink with golden boss of stamens, 1½-2 in., 10-15 petals, borne in large clusters; foliage medium size, dark green, quilted; medium, rounded, slight spreading growth; ['Seaspray' × (R. sinowilsonii × Marjorie Fair®)]

'Chewizz' ('Warm Welcome') Cl Min, or, 1992, Warner, Chris; bud pointed; flowers orange vermilion, yellow base, 1½ in., 10 petals, opens quickly to flat, borne singly and in medium clusters, moderate spicy fragrance; recurrent;

foliage small, dark green (red when young), semi-glossy; prickles few, pointed slightly downward, brown; tall (200+ cm.), upright growth; PP9356; [(Elizabeth of Glamis® × (Galway Bay® × 'Sutter's Gold')) × Anna Ford®]; intr. 1990

'Chewlahit' S, w, Warner; intr. 2007

'Chewlarmoll' ('Summer Time', 'Summertime') Cl Min, ly, 2003, Warner, Chris; flowers lemon with cream rim, reverse pale yellow, medium, dbl., borne singly and in clusters, no fragrance; free-flowering; foliage small, medium green, semi-glossy, very disease-resistant; prickles moderate; growth upright, tall (7-8 ft.); garden decorative; [Laura Ford® × 'Golden Future']; intr. 2005

'Chewlegacy' ('Edith Holden', 'The Edwardian Lady', 'Edwardian Lady') F, r, 1988, Warner, Chris; flowers russet-brown with yellow center, reverse slightly paler, aging slate grey, 15 petals, shallow cup, slight fragrance; free-flowering; foliage medium size, medium green, glossy; prickles very few; upright, tall, robust growth; hips rounded, small, orange; ['Belinda' × (Elizabeth of Glamis® × (Galway Bay® × 'Sutter's Gold'))]; intr. 1988

'Chewmaytime' S, ob, Warner, Chris; intr. 2006

'Chewoz' ('Camargue', 'Telford's Promise') S, ob, 1992, Warner, Chris; flowers coppery salmon, small, semi-dbl., borne in large clusters; foliage small, medium green, glossy; few prickles; spreading (60 cm.) growth; ['Mary Sumner' × 'Nozomi']; intr. 1990

'Chewpan' ('Peter Pan') Min, mr, 1997, Warner, Chris; flowers bright red, dull red reverse; foliage small, medium green, glossy; bushy, low (10-12 cm.) growth; ['Eyeopener' × seedling]

'Chewpatyel' S, dy, Warner; bud pointed, ovoid; intr. 2005

'Chewpeachdell' ('What a Peach') S, ab, 2000, Warner, Chris; bud pointed, ovoid; flowers clear apricot, retaining color well, 5-6 cm., 26-32 petals, cupped, borne in small clusters, slight tea fragrance; free-flowering; foliage small, dark green, glossy; prickles numerous, 5-10 mm, straight, angled down, brown; stems new shoots dark red; growth very upright, bushy, tall (140-180 cm.); garden decoration; hips globular to urn-shaped, orange; PP15287; [Laura Ford® × 'Sweet Magic']; intr. 2002

'Chewpearl' ('Star Performer', Pink Above All™) Cl Min, mp, 1999, Warner, Chris; bud obovate; flowers satin pink, reverse medium pink, 4 cm., 20-25 petals, borne in small clusters, slight sweet fragrance; recurrent; foliage small, medium green, glossy; prickles few, curved; upright, tall (7 ft.) growth; for walls, fences, pillars; hips globular ; PP13877; [Laura Ford® × 'Congratulations']; intr. 1999

'Chewpechette' ('Evening Light') S, pb, 2002, Warner, Chris; flowers light peach, pale pink reverse, 2 in., dbl., borne in small clusters, moderate fragrance; foliage small, medium green, glossy; prickles small, straight; growth spreading, tall (7 ft.); fences, walls, pillars; [Laura Ford® × ('Mary Sumner' × 'Kiskadee')]; intr. 2003

'Chewpiwite' Cl Min, ly, Warner, Chris; intr. 1995

'Chewpixcel' ('Open Arms') Cl Pol, lp, 1995, Warner, Chris; bud peach; flowers shell pink, small, semi-dbl., borne in large clusters, moderate fragrance; foliage small, dark green, glossy; few prickles; spreading, medium growth; PPAF; ['Mary Sumner' × 'Laura Ashley']

'Chewpobey' ('Pathfinder') S, or, 1995, Warner, Chris & Barbara; flowers vermillion, yellow eye, small, semi-dbl., borne in large clusters, slight fragrance; foliage small, medium green, glossy; few prickles; spreading, low growth; patio, groundcover; [('Little Darling' × Anna Ford®) × 'Eyeopener']; intr. 1996

'Chewpope' ('Gloriana 97', 'Gloriana', 'Sugar Plum') Cl Min, m, 1997, Warner, Chris; flowers dbl., high-centered, borne in small clusters; foliage medium size, medium green, semi-glossy; upright, tall (7 ft.) growth; [Laura Ford® × 'Big Purple']

'Chewramb' ('Baby Rambler', 'Little Rambler') Cl Min, lp, 1994, Warner, Chris; flowers pale pink, 1½ in., full, borne in large clusters, intense fragrance; foliage small, dark green, semi-glossy; few prickles; tall (7 × 7 ft.), bushy, spreading growth; [('Mlle Cecile Brunner' × 'Baby Faurax') × (Marjorie Fair® × 'Nozomi')]; intr. 1995

'Chewscotch' ('Anita M.') S, op, 2004, Warner, Chris; flowers peach pink, reverse light pink, 7-8 cm., dbl., borne in small clusters, moderate fragrance; repeat flowering; foliage small, medium green, semi-glossy; prickles small, straight; growth bushy, medium (4 ft.); garden decorative; [Laura Ford® × ('Lichtkonigin Lucia' × ('Angelina' × ('Flamenca' × R. bella)))]; pimpinellifolia-type; intr. 2004

'Chewsea' ('Nice Day', 'Patio Queen') Cl Min, op, 1992, Warner, Chris; flowers salmon pink, medium, dbl., moderate fragrance; foliage small, bronze turning medium green, glossy; few prickles; upright (200 cm.), bushy, climbing growth; ['Seaspray' × 'Warm Welcome']; intr. 1993

'Chewsofree' ClMin, dy, Warner; intr. 2003

'Chewsos' ('Society Special') Min, ob, 1996, Warner, Chris; flowers yellow with red reverse, small, full, borne in small clusters; foliage small, medium green, semi-glossy; few prickles; upright, bushy, tall growth; [Laura Ford® × Anne Harkness®]; intr. 1997

'Chewsunbeam' ('Good as Gold') Cl Min, dy, 1994, Warner, Chris; flowers small, dbl., high-centered, borne in small clusters, moderate fragrance; foliage small, light green, semi-glossy; some prickles; tall (7 ft.), upright growth; [Anne Harkness® × Laura Ford®]; intr. 1995

'Chewsunford' ('Golden Handshake') Cl Min, dy, 1996, Warner, Chris; flowers clear bright yellow, small, dbl., borne in small clusters; foliage small, light green, glossy; few prickles; upright, bushy, tall growth; ['Pam Ayres' × Laura Ford®]; intr. 1997

'Chewtingle' S, yb, Warner; intr. 2005

'Chewvermillion' ('Bright Day') Cl Min, rb, 2002, Warner, Chris; flowers dbl., borne in small clusters, slight fragrance; foliage medium green, glossy; prickles small, straight, few; growth upright, tall (6 ft.); fences, walls, pillars; intr. 2003

'Cheyenne' Cl HT, lp, 1962, Von Abrams; bud long, pointed; flowers light pink, coral-pink at base, 4-5 in., 30-40 petals, high-centered, slight fragrance; foliage leathery; vigorous (6-7 ft.) growth; RULED EXTINCT 1/85 ARM; [Queen Elizabeth® × seedling]; intr. 1962

'Cheyenne' -- See 'Spochey'

'Cheyenne Frontier' HT, w, 1972, Adams, M.R.; bud large; flowers white, slowly changing to red, medium, dbl., high-centered, slight fragrance; foliage large, glossy, dark; moderate, upright growth; [('Charlotte Armstrong' × 'Vogue') × 'Peace']

'Chez Vito' HT, mr, 1973, Meilland; bud ovoid; flowers medium red, reverse lighter, medium, dbl., high-centered, moderate fragrance; foliage large, leathery; vigorous, upright, bushy growth; ['Paris-Match' × (Baccará® × 'Happiness')]

'Chi Dan Hóng Xîn' HCh, mr, from China

'Chi lo Sà?' HT, yb, 1965, Fratelli Giacomasso; flowers yellow suffused red; [('Peace' × 'Fiaba') × seedling]

'Chi Long Han Zhu' -- See 'White Pearl in Red Dragon's Mouth'

'Chianti' S, m, 1967, Austin, David; flowers purplish maroon, semi-dbl., borne in small clusters, moderate fragrance; repeat bloom; foliage dark, glossy; vigorous growth; ['Dusky Maiden' × 'Tuscany']; intr. 1967

'Chianti' F, dy, Select; intr. 2003

'Chiarastella' HT, rb, 1948, Fratelli Giacomasso; flowers rose-red and yellow bicolor, well-formed, large, dbl.; foliage glossy; strong stems; vigorous growth; ['Julien Potin' × 'Mme G. Forest-Colcombet']

'Chibi' F, Shinoda, D. S. & Umeda, G. Y.; PP3840

'Chic' F, pb, 1953, Boerner; bud ovoid; flowers geranium-pink, 2½ in., 68 petals, cupped, borne in clusters, moderate fragrance; vigorous, branching growth; PP1286; [('Pinocchio' × unknown) × 'Fashion']

Chic™ -- See 'Poulra018(N)'

'Chic Folies' F, dp, Meilland; flowers magenta pink, dbl.; florist rose; intr. 2004

'Chic Parade' (Chic™) MinFl, lp, Poulsen; flowers light pink, 5-8 cm., dbl., no fragrance; foliage dark; growth bushy, 20-40 cm.; PP15405; intr. 2001

'Chic Parisien' F, op, 1956, Delbard-Chabert; flowers coral-pink, center darker, well-formed, dbl., borne in clusters of 4-8; foliage dark; vigorous growth

'Chica' HT, lp, Kordes; intr. 1998

'Chica Kordana' -- See 'Chica Kordana Mini Brite'

Chica Kordana Mini Brite® ('Chica Kordana') Min, dp, Kordes; bud long, pointed ovoid; flowers 1¾ in., 40-45 petals, high-centered, flattens, borne singly and in small clusters, no fragrance; free-flowering; foliage leathery, glossy; prickles few, short, hooked downward; stems strong; vigorous, upright (20-22 in.), compact growth; PP11154; ['Korialie' × seedling]; intr. 1998

'Chicago' HT, m, 1928, Aldous; flowers soft mauve-pink, dbl.; [sport of 'Premier']

Chicago Peace® HT, pb, 1962, Johnston; flowers phlox-pink, base canary-yellow, 5-5½ in., 50-60 petals, cupped, borne mostly singly, slight fragrance; recurrent; foliage large, dark green, leathery, glossy; tall growth; PP2037; [sport of 'Peace']

'Chicago Peace, Climbing' Cl HT, pb, Brundrett; [sport of 'Chicago Peace']; intr. 1978

'Chichi Rose' F, op

'Chick-A-Dee, Climbing' -- See 'Morclchick'

'Chick-a-dee' -- See 'Morchick'

'Chidori' -- See 'Ryokkoh'

'Chief' -- See 'The Chief'

'Chief Justice Holmes' Cl HT, dr, 1935, Schoener; flowers very dark red; ['Jules Margottin' × 'Château de Clos Vougeot']

'Chief Seattle' HT, yb, 1951, Swim, H.C.; bud conical; flowers buff and old-gold, center shrimp-red, 4-5 in., 55 petals, high-centered, moderate fragrance; foliage glossy; tall growth; PP1030; ['Charlotte Armstrong' × 'Signora']

'Chieftain' HT, rb, 1936, Montgomery Co.; bud ovoid; flowers brilliant red, base yellow, large, dbl., high-centered; foliage leathery, dark; vigorous growth; PP150; ['Hadley' × 'Talisman']

'Chiffon' HT, lp, 1940, Grillo; flowers blush-pink, tinted light lavender,, 5½ in., 30 petals; [sport of 'Regina Elena']

Chihuly™ -- See 'Wekscemala'

'Chikugo' HT, pb, Kubota, O.; flowers pink, reverse pale yellowish-pink; [sport of 'Fortuna']; intr. 1988

'Chikuho' HT, yb, Fujimoto, Y.; flowers pale yellow, edges dark rose-red, with color spreading to base in mesh patterns; [sport of 'Peace']; intr. 1974

Child of Achievement™ -- See 'Pouljill'

'Child of France' -- See 'Enfant de France'

'Childhood Memories' -- See 'FeRho'

'Childling' ('Grand Cels', 'Prolifère', 'Prolifera', 'La Digittaire', 'La Variable') C, mp, before 1759; sepals long; flowers large; foliage similar to R. × centifolia; frequently showing proliferation

'Childs' Jewel' HT, yb, 1902, Childs; flowers varying from dark copper-yellow to lighter, or vermilion with apricot yellow, medium, dbl.; [sport of 'Killarney']

Child's Play™ -- See 'Savachild'

Chili Clementine® Min, rb, Tantau; flowers light red with orange markings, double, rosette , borne in clusters; recurrent; foliage susceptible to mildew; upright (50 cm.) growth; intr. 2005

'Chili Pepper' -- See 'Gelpep'

Chili Pepper® F, mr, Select; intr. 2003

'Chilicothe' ('Elegans') HMult, mp, about 1840, Feast; flowers dbl.

'Chill Out' -- See 'Gelout'

'Chilterns' -- See 'Kortemma'

'Chimène' -- See 'Sue Hipkin'

Chimo® -- See 'Intercher'

'Chin Chin' -- See 'Promise'

'Chin Chin China' Ch, ly, 1909, Hobbies; [sport of 'Mme Eugene Résal']

'China Belle' HCh, pb, 1980, James, John; bud ovoid; flowers light and medium pink blend with yellow, dbl., cupped, borne 5-7 per cluster, slight fruity fragrance; foliage glossy; prickles curved, red; short stems; compact, bushy, upright growth; [(('Doubloons' × 'Holiday') × 'Slater's Crimson China']

'China Doll' Pol, mp, 1946, Lammerts, Dr. Walter; bud pointed; flowers China-rose, base mimosa-yellow, 1-2 in., 24 petals, cupped, borne in large trusses, slight tea fragrance; foliage leathery, with mostly 5 leaflets (similar to Pinkie); dwarf (18 in.), bushy growth; PP678; ['Mrs Dudley Fulton' × 'Tom Thumb']

'China Doll, Climbing' ('Weeping China Doll') Cl Pol, mp, 1978, Weeks; flowers bright pink, 5 cm., dbl., borne several to a stem on laterals from climbing canes, slight tea to spicy fragrance; recurrent; foliage glossy; prickles very few, short, hooked downward; vigorous, tall (4 - 6 ft.) growth; PP4323; [sport of 'China Doll']; intr. 1977

China Girl® F, my, Tantau; flowers strong lemon yellow, 4 in., very full, cupped, borne in clusters, slight fragrance; good repeat; strong, compact (2-3 ft.) growth; intr. 2006

'China Sunrise' -- See 'Zhang Zuo Shuang'

'Chinaberry' Min, yb, Benardella, Frank

'Chinaberry' -- See 'Benbrett'

Chinatown® ('Ville de Chine') F, dy, 1965, Poulsen, Niels D.; flowers yellow, sometimes edged pink, 4 in., dbl., borne in clusters, intense fragrance; foliage dark; vigorous, tall, bushy growth; ['Columbine' × 'Cläre Grammerstorf']

'Chinatown Moss' M, rb

'Chinese Lantern' -- See 'Fouchin'

'Chinese Monthly Rose' -- See 'Slater's Crimson China'

'Chinese Puzzle' -- See 'Gelpuzzle'

'Chingari' F, yb, 1976, Pal, Dr. B.P.; bud pointed; flowers aureolin to currant-red, open, 3 in., 17 petals; foliage glossy; vigorous, bushy, compact growth; ['Charleston' × seedling]; intr. 1975

'Chipie' -- See 'Poubicarbe'

'Chipmonk' -- See 'Pixichip'

'Chipmunk' -- See 'Pixichip'

Chippendale® S, ob, Tantau; flowers deep orange, outer petals lighter, 4 in., full, cupped, intense fragrance; good repeat; foliage dark green, glossy; strong (80-100 cm.) growth; intr. 2006

'Chipper' Min, ab, 1966, Meilland, Alain A.; bud ovoid; flowers salmon-pink, small, dbl., slight fragrance; foliage glossy, leathery; vigorous, dwarf growth; PP2764; [((('Dany Robin' × unknown) × 'Fire King') × 'Perla de Montserrat']

'Chippewa' S, mp, Central Exp. Farm; flowers rose-pink, semi-dbl., borne in clusters; foliage leathery, bronze

'Chiquita' LCl, op, 1938, Moore, Ralph S.; flowers orange-yellow to coppery orange and salmon-pink, base yellow; RULED EXTINCT 1/88; ['Sierra Snowstorm' × 'Étoile Luisante']

Chiquita™ -- See 'Morkita'

'Chiquito' F, or, de Ruiter; intr. 1977

Chiraz® HT, pb, 1986, Kriloff, Michel; flowers creamy white, flushed pink, petals edged carmine red, large; foliage dark; dense growth; ['Kordes' Perfecta' × 'Peace']

Chireno™ -- See 'Ponreno'

'Chiripa' F, mr, 1957, de Dot, G.F.; bud pointed; flowers red, reverse carmine, 26 petals, borne in clusters of 3-5; foliage bright green; upright, compact growth; ['Radar' × ('Rosalia Riviera' × 'Independence')]

'Chit Chat' -- See 'Brichat'

'Chitchor' F, pb, 1974, Pal, Dr. B.P.; buds medium, pointed; flowers white suffused with pink, medium, dbl, open, borne several together; foliage light green, soft; growth very vigorous, bushy (95 cm.); ['Pink Parfait' × unknown]; intr. 1972

Chitina™ -- See 'Poulurt'

'Chitra' HT, ob, IARI; flowers tangerine orange with white stripes; free-flowering; [sport of 'Janina']; intr. 1995

'Chitralekha' HT, or, 1974, IARI; buds large, long pointed; flowers ruby-red to signal-red, large, dbl, high-centered, borne singly, slight tea fragrance; foliage medium size, soft; growth vigorous, bushy (65 cm.); ['Montezuma' × 'Baccara']; intr. 1972

'Chitrarajini' HT, pb, Kasturi; flowers ivory with a tinge of pink, becoming deeper rose red, dbl., high-centered; intr. 1985

'Chitwan' HT, my, 1973, Indian Agri. Research Institute; buds large, long pointed; flowers primrose-yellow, large, very dbl., high-centered, borne mostly singly; foliage medium size, light green, soft; growth vigorous, compact, bushy; ['Western Sun' × 'Golden Splendor']

Chivalry® -- See 'Macpow'

'Chiyo' HT, dp, 1976, Ota, Saku; bud long, pointed; flowers deep pink, 4-4½ in., 25 petals, high-centered, slight fruity fragrance; foliage glossy, medium to dark green; vigorous, upright growth; ['Karl Herbst' × 'Chrysler Imperial']; intr. 1975

'Chloe' -- See 'Pazstar'

Chloe™ -- See 'Poulen003(N)'

'Chloe of Childerly' -- See 'Bosrexfor'

'Chloe Renaissance' (Chloe™, Hjemmetrosen™) S, lp, Poulsen; flowers light pink, 10-15 cm., dbl., intense fragrance; foliage dark; growth bushy, 100-150 cm.; PP15467; intr. 2001

Chloe's Star™ -- See 'Pazstar'

'Chloris' A, lp, before 1820, Descemet; flowers soft pink, many-petaled, reflexing with a button eye, medium, dbl., borne in clusters of 4-6, slight fragrance; foliage dark, leathery, bluish-green; very few prickles; vigorous (to 4-5 ft.) growth

'Chloris' HT, mr, Geschwind; flowers light purple-crimson, very large, full; intr. 1890

'Chobee' F, mr, 1993, Giles, Diann; flowers medium, full, borne mostly singly, slight fragrance; foliage medium size, medium green, matte; few prickles; medium, bushy growth; [seedling × 'Congratulations']; intr. 1993

'Chocolan' S, ab, Kordes; intr. 2007

'Chocolate Prince' -- See 'Terracotta'

'Chocolate Ruffles' F, r; intr. 2005

'Choir of Angels' F, yb; flowers yellow with petal edges turning orange, red and pink, double; foliage glossy; 36 in. growth

'Choo-Choo Centennial' Min, lp, 1980, Jolly, Betty J.; bud ovoid; flowers light pink, edged darker, reverse white, small, 68 petals, high-centered, borne in clusters, slight fragrance; foliage matte, light green; prickles straight; compact, bushy growth; PP4849; ['Rise 'n' Shine' × 'Grand Opera']

'Choo-Choo's Baby' Min, rb, 1981, Jolly, Betty J.; bud urn-shaped; flowers red, shaded to yellow at base, 26 petals, flat, borne singly and in pairs, slight fragrance; foliage tiny, light green; no prickles; low, branching, dense growth; ['Watercolor' × ('Watercolor' × unknown)]; intr. 1980

'Chopin' -- See 'Fréderic Chopin'

'Chopin' HT, mr, 1968, Ellick; flowers 4-6 in., 38 petals; foliage medium to light green; vigorous growth; ['Montezuma' × 'Christian Dior']

'Chorale' S, lp, 1978, Buck, Dr. Griffith J.; bud ovoid, pointed; flowers pale pink, large, 48 petals, high-centered; foliage dark, leathery; vigorous, upright, bushy growth; [('Ruth Hewitt' × Queen Elizabeth®) × ('Morning Stars' × 'Suzanne')]

'Chorus, Climbing' -- See 'Meijulitasar'

Chorus® -- See 'Meimoré'

'Chorus Girl' F, or, 1970, Robinson, H.; flowers vermilion, 3 in., 16 petals, high-centered; foliage dark, coppery; ['Highlight' × seedling]

'Chorus Line' -- See 'Jacdaz'

'Chot Pestitele' HP, mp, 1932, Böhm, J.; bud oblong; flowers rose-pink, 6 in., 22 petals, flat; foliage glossy; [sport of 'Frau Karl Druschki']

'Chota' F, or, 1976, Sheen; flowers light vermilion, large, 50 petals, slight fragrance; foliage small, semi-glossy; moderately low growth; ['Violet Carson' × 'Korona']

'Chou' -- See 'Cabbage Rose'

'Chouette' Pol, dr, 1969, Delforge; bud ovoid; flowers dark fire-red, large, dbl.; foliage dark, soft; vigorous, bushy growth; [Atlantic® × seedling]

'Chowan' HT, ob, 1995, Perry, Astor; flowers 4¾ in., full, high-centered, borne mostly singly, moderate fragrance; recurrent; foliage large, medium green, dull; some prickles; tall (160 cm.), upright growth; [Folklore® × 'Hot Pewter']; intr. 1995

'Chremesina Scintilland' -- See 'Admirable'

'Chricinn' HT, pb, Christensen; intr. 2003

'Chris' -- See 'Kirsan'

Chris Evert™ -- See 'Wekjuvoo'

'Chris Jolly' MinFl, or, 1985, Jolly, Nelson F.; flowers medium, 40 petals, high-centered, slight fragrance; foliage medium size, medium green, semi-glossy; upright, bushy growth; [('Orange Sweetheart' × 'Zinger') × 'Rise 'n' Shine']

'Chris Rabe' F, w, 2002, Chaney, William E.; flowers , borne in small clusters, slight fragrance; foliage small, medium green, semi-glossy; prickles small, thin, curved downward, green, moderate; growth compact, short; ['floribunda seedling' × 'miniature seedling']

'Chrisgobro' ('Joshua Bradley') HT, yb, 1998, Christensen, Jack E.; flowers deep gold, bronze reverse, strong substance, 3-3½ in., dbl., borne mostly singly; foliage medium size, dark green, dull; prickles moderate, medium, hooked; upright, medium growth; [('Gingersnap' × Brandy™) × 'Caramel Creme']; intr. 1999

'Chrisgood' ('Rainbow Warrior', Modern Magic™) F, ob, 2001, Christensen, Jack; flowers orange with red stripes, 4 in., dbl., borne in small clusters, no fragrance; foliage medium size, medium green, glossy; prickles moderate; growth compact, medium (4 ft.); PP14936; [Voodoo™ × 'Tiger Tail']; intr. 2001

'Chrisjevans' ('Vivacious Dianne') HT, or, 1990, Christensen, Jack E.; flowers medium, 33 petals; foliage medium size, medium green, semi-glossy; upright, bushy growth; [Voodoo™ × 'Hello Dolly']; intr. 1989

'Chriss and Dianni' Sp, w; growth used as understock; clone of R. multiflora

'Chrissie MacKellar' HT, op, 1913, Dickson, A.; bud crimson-carmine on deep madder; flowers orange-pink, reverse deeply zoned orange, semi-dbl.

'Christa' -- See 'Pixsta'

Christel von der Post® -- See 'Korpora'

Christian™ ('Metset') F, m; PPAF; intr. 2000

'Christian Curle' HWich, lp, 1910, Cocker; flowers flesh-pink, small, full; [sport of 'Dorothy Perkins']

'Christian Dior' HT, mr, 1959, Meilland, F.; bud ovoid, pointed; flowers clear true red, 4-4½ in., 45-50 petals, high-centered, borne mostly singly, slight soft spice fragrance; foliage leathery, glossy; long stems; vigorous, upright, bushy growth; PP1943; [('Independence' × 'Happiness') × ('Peace' × 'Happiness')]; intr. 1958

'Christian Dior, Climbing' Cl HT, mr, 1966, Chang, Chi-Shiang

'Christian Püttner' HP, m, 1862, Oger; flowers bright purple, shaded pomegranate, large, full

'Christian Schultheis' S, pb, Schultheis; flowers deep pink, paler reverse, large, very dbl., cupped; dark green, glossy foliage; strong growth to 5 ft. tall and wide; intr. 2000

'Christiana Wood' HT, mr, 1979, Wood, J.; bud ovoid, upright, bushy growth; [sport of 'Tropicana']; intr. 1975

'Christiane Horbiger' F, w

'Christina' HT, pb, 1959, Crouch; flowers pink, reverse currant red, dbl.; very vigorous growth; RULED EXTINCT 12/85 ARM; ['Granat' × 'Radiance']

'Christina' HT, pb, 1986, Staikov, Prof. Dr. V., Kalaydjieve & Chorbadjiiski; flowers deep pink, reverse light pink, large, 45 petals; foliage leathery, glossy; vigorous, upright growth; ['Rina Herholdt' × seedling]; intr. 1977

'Christina' -- See 'Selstar'

'Christina Atherton' -- See 'Macsev'

'Christina Nilsson' ('Mme Boutin') HP, mr, 1861, Jamain; flowers cerise red, very large, full, cupped; ['Général Jacqueminot' × unknown]

'Christine' -- See 'Clealta'

Christine® HT, ab, Kordes

'Christine' HT, dy, 1918, McGredy; flowers deep golden yellow, small, moderate fragrance; foliage dark, glossy

'Christine, Climbing' Cl HT, dy, 1936, Willink; flowers golden-yellow, small, dbl.; growth to 15 ft.

'Christine' S, ab; intr. 2001

'Christine de Noué' -- See 'Mlle Christine de Noué'

'Christine Gandy' F, dp, 1959, deRuiter; flowers deep pink, 3 in., semi-dbl., borne in small clusters, moderate fragrance; foliage dark; vigorous growth; ['polyantha seedling' × 'Fashion']; intr. 1958

'Christine Hélène' ly; flowers light yellow, fading to creamy white, yellow stamens, semi-double, shallow cup to flat, borne in clusters, slight fragrance; recurrent; foliage matte, dark green; thin, supple canes (to 10 ft.) growth; Chance seedling found by Christine Melle; intr. 2007

'Christine Horbiger' -- See 'Foster's Wellington Cup'

'Christine Lanson' HT, ob

'Christine Marina' -- See 'Seacancan'

'Christine Prior' HT, rb, 1924, McGredy; flowers deep rosy red, flushed yellow and peach, base yellow, semi-dbl.

'Christine Todd Whitmann' HT, lp, Moorestown; [sport of 'Gold Glow']; intr. about 1992

'Christine Weinert' Min, or, 1976, Moore, Ralph S.; flowers brilliant scarlet, shaded deeper, flat to rounded, 1 in., 25 petals, moderate fragrance; foliage small, leathery; upright, bushy growth; PP4030; [('Little Darling' × 'Eleanor') × ('Little Darling' × 'Eleanor')]

'Christine Wright' HWich, mp, 1909, Farrell; flowers wild-rose-pink, fading to pale, silvery pink, 7-9 cm., semi-dbl., cupped, borne singly and in small clusters, moderate fragrance; foliage glossy; long stems; growth to 12-15 ft.; [(R. wichurana × Marion Dingee) × 'Mme Caroline Testout']

'Christine Wunderlich' HT, op, 1934, Wunderlich; flowers yellowish-orange-pink, large; very vigorous growth; [sport of 'Golden Ophelia']

'Christine's Dream' -- See 'Bridream'

'Christingle' -- See 'Harvalex'

'Christmas Beauty' HT, dr, 1942, Krowka; flowers darker red than parent, 4½-5 in., 25-30 petals, moderate fragrance; foliage blue-green, leathery; vigorous growth; PP743; [sport of 'Better Times']

'Christmas Card' -- See 'Rescard'

'Christmas Cheer' HT, mr, 1957, Joseph H. Hill, Co.; bud long, pointed; flowers cherry-red, 4½-5½ in., 45-50 petals, high-centered, slight fragrance; foliage dark, leathery; vigorous, upright growth; PP1468; ['Sister Kenny' × 'Happiness']

'Christmas Red' HT, mr, 1948, Brownell; bud large, long, pointed; flowers spectrum-red, open, dbl., moderate fragrance; foliage glossy; bushy, dwarf growth; ['Pink Princess' × 'Crimson Glory']

Christmas Snow™ HMult, w, Clements, John; flowers pure white, 2½ in., 60 petals, cupped, borne in large clusters; non-recurrent; rich green foliage; vigorous, climbing growth, 14 ft.; PPAF; intr. 2000

'Christobel' HT, ab, 1937, Croibier; flowers apricot-yellow shaded salmon, very large, dbl.; foliage glossy; very vigorous, bushy growth; ['Frau Karl Druschki' × 'Mme Butterfly']

'Christoph Colombus' -- See 'Meinronsse'

'Christoph Weigand' HT, lp, 1928, Weigand, C.; flowers very large, dbl., high-centered; foliage rich green, wrinkled; vigorous growth; ['Frau Karl Druschki' × 'Souv. de Claudius Pernet']

'Christophe Colomb' -- See 'Cristoforo Colombo'

'Christophe Colomb' -- See 'Meinronsse'

'Christophe Colomb, Cl.' ('Christophe Colomb, Gpt.') Cl HT, or, Meilland; flowers much like the bush form, large, dbl.; dark green foliage; growth to 2 m. and more

'Christophe Colombe' P, m, 1854, Robert; flowers amaranth purple, darker at center, 11-13 cm., full, flat

'Christophe Colomb, Gpt.' -- See 'Meironssesar'

Christophe Combejean® Gr, rb, Guillot-Massad; bud pointed; flowers red, striped yellow which fades to white, borne in clusters of 5 - 7; intr. 2005

'Christopher' -- See 'Cocopher'

'Christopher' -- See 'Tinchris'

Christopher Columbus™ -- See 'Poulbico'

'Christopher Columbus' -- See 'Meinronsse'

'Christopher Marlowe' -- See 'Ausjump'

'Christopher Milton' HT, dp, 1967, Martin, W.A.; bud long, pointed, light red; flowers medium pink, edged lighter, large, dbl., high-centered; foliage dark, glossy; very vigorous, upright growth; [sport of 'Christian Dior']

'Christopher Popwell' HT, dr, 2006, Popwell, Larry G., Sr; flowers large, semi-dbl., borne mostly solitary; foliage medium size, medium green, semi-glossy; prickles moderate; growth bushy, 30 in.; [Altissimo® × 'Love']; intr. 2006

'Christopher Stone' HT, mr, 1935, Robinson, H.; bud long, pointed; flowers large, 30 petals, moderate damask fragrance; foliage bright green; vigorous growth; intr. 1935

'Christopher Stone, Climbing' ('John Christopher') Cl HT, mr, 1942, Marsh's Nursery; flowers intense red-scarlet flowers with maroon-scarlet flush to outer petals, 5 in., semi-dbl.; PP626; on the market as John Christopher for a time, in error

'Chromatella' ('Cloth of Gold') N, ly, 1843, Coquereau; flowers creamy white, center yellow, large, very dbl., globular, quartered, moderate fragrance; vigorous, climbing growth; ['Lamarque × unknown]

'Chrysandra' S, dp, Weihrauch; flowers carmine-pink, large, semi-dbl.; intr. 1983

'Chrysler' Min, pb, Benardella, Frank; intr. 2003

'Chrysler Imperial, Climbing' ('Grimpant Chrysler Imperial') Cl HT, dr, 1958, Begonia, P.B.; flowers dark red, velvety, very dbl., intense fragrance; PP1528; [sport of 'Chrysler Imperial']; intr. 1956

'Chrysler Imperial' HT, dr, 1952, Lammerts, Dr. Walter; bud long, pointed; flowers deep red, velvety, 4½-5 in., 45-50 petals, high-centered, borne singly, intense fragrance; foliage dark, semi-glossy; vigorous, compact growth; PP1167; ['Charlotte Armstrong' × 'Mirandy']

'Chrystelle' -- See 'Godialing'

'Chryzia' HT, dp, 1970, Wyant; bud long, pointed; flowers light red, large, dbl.; vigorous, upright, bushy growth; ['Chrysler Imperial' × 'Lady Zia']

'Chuckles' F, dp, 1955, Shepherd; bud long, pointed; flowers deep pink, white eye, large, 11 petals, borne in large clusters, moderate fragrance; foliage dark, leathery; vigorous, bushy growth; PP1608; [('Jean Lafitte' × 'New Dawn') × Orange Triumph®]; intr. 1955

'Chula Vista' -- See 'Tinchula'

'Chumki' HT, pb, Ghosh; flowers creamy pink with outer edges and reverse of deeper pink, well formed; intr. 2001

'Chunga' -- See 'Morpapplay'

'Church Mouse' -- See 'Foumouse'

Ciak® LCl, rb, Barni, V.; flowers red with golden yellow halo in center, single, borne in clusters, no fragrance; growth to 8-20 ft.; intr. 1994

'Ciana Rose' -- See 'Seacia'

'Ciao' S, or, Hiroshima; groundcover; spreading growth; intr. 2002

'Cibles' HRg, mr, 1893, Kaufmann; flowers bright red, base yellow, medium, single; vigorous, upright growth; [R. rugosa rubra × 'Perle de Lyon']

'Cicely Lascelles' Cl HT, op, 1932, Clark, A.; flowers pink shaded salmon, reverse darker, 12 cm., semi-dbl.; recurrent; growth very vigorous; pillar; ['Frau Oberhofgartner Singer' × 'Scorcher']

'Cicely O'Rorke' Cl HT, mp, 1937, Clark, A.; flowers pink, shaded salmon, large, semi-dbl., cupped; recurrent bloom; long stems; very vigorous, climbing or pillar growth; ['Souv. de Gustave Prat' × seedling]

Cicely Phippen Marks™ -- See 'Wilcipks'

'Cidade de Lisboa' LCl, pb, 1939, Moreira da Silva; bud long, pointed; flowers salmon-pink, edged yellow, large, semi-dbl., high-centered; long stems; vigorous growth; ['Belle Portugaise' × 'Mme Edouard Herriot']

'Cider Cup' -- See 'Dicladida'

Ciel Bleu® HT, m, Dot, Simon; intr. 1982

'Cilly Michel' HT, or, 1928, Felberg-Leclerc; flowers nasturtium-red, large, dbl.; ['Mme Mélanie Soupert' × 'Felbergs Rosa Druschki']

Cimarosa® -- See 'LLX8698'

'Cimarron' HT, pb, 1938, Hillock; bud spiraled, almost red; flowers ruffled, salmon, reverse deep pink; vigorous, compact growth; ['Nellie E. Hillock' × 'Golden Dawn']

'Cina' HT, ob, 1978, Gaujard; bud full; flowers brilliant coral, flushed salmon; foliage large; ['Premiere Ballerine' ×

'Femina']; intr. 1973

Cinco de Mayo™ -- See 'Wekcobeju'

'Cinderella' HWich, dp, Walsh; flowers deep pink, petal tips quilled, small, dbl., borne in large clusters; free, non-recurrent bloom; vigorous growth; intr. 1909

'Cinderella' Min, w, deVink; flowers satiny white tinged pale flesh, very small, 1 in., 55 petals, moderate spicy fragrance; no prickles; upright growth; PP1051; ['Cécile Brunner' × 'Tom Thumb']; intr. 1953

'Cinderella, Climbing' Cl Min, w, 1975, Sequoia Nursery; intr. 1975

'Cinderella' HT, op, Kordes; flowers salmon-pink, double , high-centered; [sport of 'Calibra']; intr. 1995

'Cinderella' Min, m, Schuurman; flowers deep vibrant mauve, dbl.; growth medium to tall; intr. 1999

Cinderella® HT, mp, Kordes; flowers medium pink, turning lighter as it opens, large, full, high-centered, borne mostly singly; recurrent; prickles nearly absent; stems long; intr. 2006

'Cinderella' N, pb, 1859, Page; flowers salmon-pink to carmine-pink

Cinderella® -- See 'Korfobalt'

'Cinderella' -- See 'Kormixsosia'

'Cinderella Freelander' ('Cinderella', 'Ruth Bell Graham Rose') HT, lp, Kordes; flowers light pink with hint of yellow in heart , double, high-centered; intr. 2003

'Cinderella Gold' -- See 'Morcingold'

'Cinderella Kordana' Min, mp, Kordes; flowers soft pink, full, high-centered to cupped; container rose; intr. 2005

'Cinderella's Midnight Rose' HT, mp, 1978, Bernard; flowers rich pink, 4-5 in., slight fragrance; foliage glossy; vigorous growth

'Cindy' -- See 'Meitinor'

'Cindy' -- See 'Harzippee'

Cindy™ -- See 'Minaaco'

'Cindy de Meilland' ('Cindy') F, pb, Meilland; flowers pale pink edged with dark pink; greenhouse rose; intr. 1997

'Cineraire' Ch, rb, 1970, Lambert; flowers rich red, center white, very small, 5 petals, cupped, borne in trusses; intr. before 1964

'Cinerama' HT, pb, 1966, Herholdt, J.A.; flowers salmon, reverse buff-yellow, pointed, 4½-5 in.; vigorous growth; [seedling × 'Tzigane']

'Cineraria' Pol, rb, 1909, Lambert; flowers light red, center white, small, single

'Cineraria' Pol, m, Leenders, M.; flowers carmine-purple, center white, open, large, semi-dbl., slight fragrance; foliage soft; vigorous, bushy growth; ['Miss Edith Cavell' × Tip-Top®]; intr. 1934

'Cingallegra' HT, yb, 1958, Cazzaniga, F. G.; bud well shaped; flowers lemon-yellow, edged pinkish, dbl.; long, strong stems; ['Golden Scepter' × 'Crimson Glory']

'Cinnabar' ('Tantau's Triumph') F, or, 1945, Tantau; bud small, globular; flowers vermilion to scarlet, semi-dbl., cupped, borne in clusters, slight fragrance; recurrent; foliage leathery; bushy, upright growth; ['Baby Chateau' × R. roxburghii]

'Cinnabar Improved' ('Verbesserte Tantau's Triumph') F, or, 1951, Tantau; flowers orange-scarlet, semi-dbl., borne in trusses; [('Cinnabar' × 'Kathe Duvigneau') × 'Cinnabar']

Cinnamon Delight™ -- See 'Minicin'

Cinnamon Girl™ -- See 'Jacpehot'

Cinnamon Toast™ -- See 'Savacin'

Cinnamon Twist™ -- See 'Jacoutra'

'Cinzia' ; intr. 1996

'Cioccofiore' Min, r, Meilland; intr. 2004

'Circé' M, pb, 1855, Robert; flowers delicate pink spotted with white, 4-6 cm., full, flat; some repeat

'Circe' HT, lp, 1916, Paul, W.; flowers whitish-pink shaded with carmine, base deep yellow, large, dbl.

'Circé' -- See 'Gaumova'

'Circus' ('Circus 99') HT, yb, Kordes; flowers medium, intense yellow with red on petal tips, full, high-centered, borne mostly singly; greenhouse rose

'Circus' F, yb, 1956, Swim, H.C.; bud urn-shaped; flowers yellow marked pink, salmon and scarlet, 2½-3 in., 45-58 petals, high-centered, borne in large, ruffled clusters, moderate tea to spicy fragrance; foliage semi-glossy, leathery; bushy growth; PP1382; ['Fandango' × 'Pinocchio']; intr. 1956

'Circus, Climbing' Cl F, yb, 1961, House; PP2074

'Circus Clown' -- See 'Morpico'

'Circus Clown' -- See 'Send in the Clowns'

'Circus Days' Gr, rb, William, J.B.; flowers ivory white edged red, ruffled, dbl.; intr. 2003

Circus Knie® HT, yb, 1979, Huber; bud long, pointed; flowers 3½-4 in., 32-38 petals, cupped, slight fragrance; foliage dark, leathery; [Moulin Rouge® × 'Peace']; intr. 1975

'Circus Minijet' Min, yb, Meilland; intr. 2003

'Circus 99' -- See 'Korlumara'

'Circus Parade' F, yb, 1964, Begonia, F.B. & DeVor, P.; flowers yellow-orange overlaid with crimson which spreads down petals, redder than Circus; growth more vigorous than Circus; PP2150; [sport of 'Circus']; intr. 1963

Cisco™ -- See 'Carale'

'Cissie' Min, mp, 1979, Bennett, Dee; bud long, pointed; flowers 1 in., 18-20 petals, high-centered, borne singly, slight fragrance; foliage dark green with touches of red and bronze on edges; prickles small, thin; bushy, upright growth; PP4730; ['Gene Boerner' × 'Elfinesque']

'Cissie Easlea' HT, my, 1913, Pernet-Ducher; bud oval, pale buff; flowers clear saffron yellow, with carmine center, large, full, globular; foliage green-bronze; few prickles; ['Melanie Soupert' × 'Rayon d'Or']

'Citation' Gr, dr, 1986, Hoy, Lowel L.; flowers dark red, reverse lighter, 35 petals, high-centered, borne in sprays of 2-3; foliage large, dark, semi-glossy; prickles short, lilac, hooked downward; medium, bushy growth; hips globular, light orange; [seedling × seedling]; intr. 1982

'Citrina' HT, dy

'Citron' HT, ly, 1942, Gaujard; flowers buff, shaded copper, 28 petals, cupped; foliage reddish; vigorous growth; ['Julien Potin' × seedling]

'Citron-Fraise' -- See 'Delcifra'

Citronella® -- See 'Sunsien'

'Citronella' F, ly, 1946, Leenders, M.; flowers lemon-yellow, 15 petals, globular, borne in clusters; foliage glossy; branching growth; ['Mev. Nathalie Nypels' × 'Donald Prior']

'Citrus Candy' -- See 'Gelcan'

Citrus Splash™ -- See 'Jaczorba'

Citrus Tease™ -- See 'Jacpolpa'

'City Girl' -- See 'Harzorba'

'City Lights' -- See 'Poulgan'

'City Livery' ('Honor Elizabeth') F, my, Harkness; flowers full, borne in clusters; growth to 3 ft.; PPAF; intr. 2001

'City of Adelaide' -- See 'Meichoiju'

'City of Alexandria' -- See 'Wilalex'

'City of Auckland' -- See 'Mactane'

'City of Bath' HT, pb, 1976, Sanday, John; flowers deep candy-pink, reverse lighter, 4 in., 55 petals, moderate fragrance; foliage matte, green; ['Gavotte' × 'Buccaneer']; intr. 1969

City of Belfast® F, or, 1968, McGredy, Sam IV; flowers bright red, dbl., cupped, borne in trusses; foliage glossy; PP3070; ['Evelyn Fison' × ('Circus' × 'Korona')]

'City of Benalla' HT, op, 1983, Dawson, George; bud globular, pointed; flowers carmine, opening with outer petals paling, inner petals coral, dbl., high-centered; foliage dark, dense, glossy; prickles brown, hooked down; vigorous, tall growth; ['My Choice' × 'Extravaganza']

'City of Birmingham' -- See 'Korholst'

'City of Bradford' -- See 'Harrotang'

'City of Cardiff' HT, rb, 1992, Poole, Lionel; flowers 3-3½ in., very dbl., borne mostly singly; foliage medium size, medium green, matte; some prickles; medium, upright growth; ['Lady Sylvia' × Chicago Peace®]; intr. 1993

'City of Carlsbad' -- See 'Wektorcent'

'City of Christchurch' -- See 'Macoffer'

'City of Dunedin' -- See 'Reycidun'

'City of Gisborne' HT, op, 1968, Appleyard; bud long, pointed; flowers pink shaded orange-yellow, large, semi-dbl., high-centered; foliage glossy; vigorous, upright growth; ['Prima Ballerina' × 'Prima Ballerina']

'City of Glasgow' HT, ab, 1970, Haynes; flowers apricot, suffused pink; [sport of 'Femina']

'City of Gloucester' HT, dy, 1970, Sanday, John; flowers saffron-yellow shaded gold, large, dbl., high-centered; vigorous growth; ['Gavotte' × 'Buccaneer']; intr. 1970

'City of Goulburn' F, yb, Swane; flowers blend of yellow, copper and gold, dbl., cupped; growth to 3-4 ft.; intr. 1995

'City of Hamilton' F, ob, 1972, Dickson, A.; flowers orange and gold, large, dbl.; foliage dull; free growth; ['Innisfree' × Elizabeth of Glamis®]

'City of Harvey' HWich, op, 1944, Wiseman; flowers pink tinted orange, small, semi-dbl., cupped, borne in clusters; profuse bloom, not repeated; foliage dark, glossy; growth to 12 ft.; [R. wichurana × 'Orléans Rose']

'City of Hereford' HT, mp, 1967, LeGrice; flowers carmine-pink, pointed,, 6 in.; foliage dark; ['Wellworth' × 'Spartan']

'City of Ichalkaranji' HT, pb, Chiplunkar; intr. 1989

'City of Invercargill' -- See 'Reyinver'

'City of Joy' HT, dr, Chakroborty; flowers velvety crimson red, full; intr. 2003

'City of Kingston' F, or, 1973, Schloen, J.; bud ovoid; flowers medium, very dbl., globular; foliage dark, leathery; moderate, bushy growth; ['Malibu' × 'Independence']

'City of Leeds' F, op, 1966, McGredy, Sam IV; flowers salmon, 4½ in., 19 petals, borne in clusters, slight fragrance; foliage dark; ['Evelyn Fison' × ('Spartan' × 'Red Favorite')]

'City of Little Rock' HT, mp, 1924, E.G. Hill, Co.; flowers hydrangea-pink, open, semi-dbl.; vigorous growth

City of London® -- See 'Harukfore'

'City of Manchester' -- See 'Nosman'

'City of Newcastle' HT, yb, 1976, Wood; flowers yellow, tinged salmon-orange, 5 in., 35 petals; foliage semi-glossy; vigorous, tall, upright growth; ['Arthur Bell' × 'Mischief']

'City of Newcastle Bicentennary' -- See 'Jacopper'

'City of Norwich' HT, mr, 1949, Kordes; bud ovoid; flowers scarlet-crimson, well-formed, 6 in., 35 petals; foliage leathery; ['Crimson Glory' × ('Crimson Glory' × 'Cathrine Kordes')]

'City of Nottingham' F, or, 1962, deRuiter; flowers orange-scarlet, 2½ in., 30-40 petals, rosette, borne in clusters; foliage dark; vigorous, bushy, compact growth; [seedling × Moulin Rouge®]

'City of Oelde' S, mp, 2006, Beales, Amanda; flowers semi-dbl., borne in small clusters; foliage medium size, dark green, semi-glossy; prickles average, straight, few; growth bushy, 1¼ m.; ['Bonica' × 'Maigold']; intr. 2002

'City of Panjim' HT, pb, Kasturi; flowers pink and off-white; intr. 1972

'City of Pilsen' -- See 'Plzen'

'City of Portland' F, mr, 1977, Takatori, Yoshiho; bud pointed; flowers geranium-red, base primrose-yellow, 2½-3½ in., 5 petals; foliage glossy; very free growth; [seedling × (Cocktail® × unknown)]

'City of Portland' -- See 'Mme Caroline Testout'

'City of Portsmouth' F, ob, 1976, Cants of Colchester, Ltd.; flowers copper, 3-4 in., 25 petals, moderate fragrance; foliage bronze; tall growth

'City of Pretoria' -- See 'Korseubel'

'City of Sails' LCl, mp, Matthews; intr. 2000

'City of San Diego' -- See 'Wekrera'

City of San Francisco™ -- See 'Weksanpoly'

'City of Sheffield' -- See 'Nosshef'

'City of Springfield' F, rb, 1989, Pencil, Paul S.; flowers non-fading, medium, 34 petals, borne in sprays of 6-10; bushy, hardy growth; ['Pink Parfait' × 'Roman Holiday']

'City of Timaru' -- See 'Ausquest'

'City of Wangaratta' HT, mr, Dawson; intr. 1985

'City of Warwick' -- See 'Arofuto'

'City of Welland' HT, yb, Kordes; flowers dbl.; foliage deep green, glossy; upright growth; intr. 1996

'City of Windsor' HT, ob; intr. 1999

'City of Windsor' -- See 'Kormiach'

'City of Worcester' HT, mr, 1983, Scrivens, L.; flowers large, 35 petals, high-centered, moderate fragrance; foliage medium size, medium green, matte; ['Red Planet' × ('Ena Harkness' × 'Fragrant Cloud')]

'City of York' -- See 'Direktor Benschop'

'Ciudad de Oviedo' C, mp, before 1932; flowers single; from Spain

'Clair' -- See 'Poulsyng'

'Clair de Lune' HT, m, 1967, Gaujard; bud pointed; flowers large, dbl.; foliage leathery; vigorous, upright growth; ['Eminence' × 'Viola']

Clair Matin® ('Grimpant Clair Matin') LCl, mp, 1962, Meilland, Mrs. Marie-Louise; bud pointed; flowers , 15 petals, cupped, borne in rounded clusters, moderate sweetbriar fragrance; foliage dark, leathery; vigorous (10-12 ft.), well-branched growth; PP2186; ['Fashion' × (('Independence' × Orange Triumph®) × 'Phyllis Bide')]; intr. 1960

'Clair Renaissance' ('Clair', 'Liliana') S, lp, Olesen; flowers light pink, 8-10 cm., full, intense fragrance; foliage dark; growth bushy, 100-150 cm.; intr. 1995

'Claire' HMult, mp, before 1866; flowers carmine pink, cupped

'Claire' HT, pb, Dawson; intr. 1987

'Claire' -- See 'Auslight'

'Claire Austin' -- See 'Ausprior'

'Claire Carnot' N, yb, 1873, Guillot; flowers yellow, bordered with white and carmine rose, medium, full, cupped, borne in small clusters

Claire Chazal® HT, w, Adam; flowers white with bright pink edges, dbl., globular, slight fragrance; moderate (80-100 cm.) growth; intr. 2006

'Claire Desmet' HT, my, 1932, Buatois; flowers golden yellow, very dbl., cupped; foliage leathery, bronze; long, strong stems; vigorous, bushy growth; ['Margaret Dickson Hamill' × 'Souv. de Claudius Pernet']

'Claire d'Olban' HGal, dp, 1825, Vibert; flowers deep pink with pale edges, medium, full; numerous prickles

'Claire-France' HT, mp, 1964, Mondial Roses; bud pointed; flowers clear pink, large, 40 petals, high-centered; foliage glossy; vigorous, upright growth

'Claire Godard' T, w, 1894, Godard; flowers pure white, large, full

'Claire Jacquier' ('Mlle Claire Jacquier') N, ly, 1888, Bernaix, A.; flowers yellow, fading to creamy yellow, 3 cm., semi-dbl., borne in clusters of 5-10, moderate musky fragrance; occasional autumn repeat; very vigorous growth; [possibly R. multiflora × Tea rose]

'Claire Jolly' -- See 'Lenadeba'

'Claire Laberge' HRg, mp, 2001, Fleming, Joyce; flowers medium pink with lighter pink reverse, 5-6 cm., borne in small clusters, intense fragrance; continuous; foliage medium size, medium green, semi-glossy; prickles 1½ cm., numerous; growth bushy, medium (5 ft.); hedging, specimen; hardy, disease-resistant, ['Jens Munk' × 'Scabrosa']; intr. 2001

'Claire Rayner' -- See 'Macpandem'

Claire Rose® -- See 'Auslight'

'Claire Scotland' -- See 'Cocdimity'

'Claire's Dream' -- See 'Guesideal'

'Clairette' HT, mp, Croix, P.; intr. 1974

'Clanwilliam' HT, op

'Clara' -- See 'Resclara'

Clara® -- See 'Fesato'

'Clara' F, lp, Barni; flowers pastel pink, dbl., borne in small clusters, intense fragrance; recurrent bloom; bronzy foliage; growth to 2½-3 ft.; intr. 2004

Clara™ -- See 'Poulpar036(N)'

'Clara Barton' HT, ab, 1898, Van Fleet; flowers delicate amber pink, 3-3½ in., dbl., moderate fragrance; ['American Beauty' × 'Clotilde Soupert']

'Clara Bow' Cl HT, yb, 1927, Padella Rose Co.; flowers yellow stained crimson, dbl., growth to 12-15 ft.; [sport of 'Golden Emblem']

'Clara Cochet' HP, lp, 1886, Lacharme, F.; flowers light pink, center brighter pink, very large, dbl., globular; ['Jules Margottin' × unknown]

'Clara Curtis' HT, my, 1922, Dickson, A.; flowers rich golden yellow, very dbl.

'Clara d'Arcis' -- See 'Mme Clara d'Arcis'

'Clara Eileen' -- See 'Rawchinme'

'Clara Granato' F, mr

'Clara Munger' LCl, m, Munger; flowers lavender

'Clara Parade' (Clara™) MinFl, w, Poulsen; flowers white, 5-8 cm., dbl., no fragrance; growth bushy, 20-40 cm.; intr. 2004

'Clara Sylvain' ('Lady Warrender') T, w, 1838; flowers pure white with cream, large, full

'Clara Watson' HT, w, 1894, Prince; flowers mother-of-pearl white, center peach, dbl.

'Clara's Surprise' -- See 'Kirwim'

'Clare' HT, pb, 1972, MacLeod; flowers cream, edged rose-pink, 5½ in., 35 petals, high-centered; foliage large, medium green, semi-glossy; vigorous, tall growth; ['Ethel Sanday' × Rose Gaujard®]

'Clare de Escofet' HT, w, 1920, Easlea; flowers delicate flesh-white, very large, dbl.

'Cläre Grammerstorf' F, dy, 1957, Kordes; bud ovoid; flowers large, dbl., high-centered; foliage leathery, glossy; vigorous, bushy growth; ['Harmonie' × (R. rubiginosa × unknown)]

'Clare Helen' HT, lp, 1985, Owen, Fred; [sport of 'Gail Borden']

'Clarence House' LCl, w, 2006, Beales, Amanda; flowers light yellow, reverse white, 10 cm., very full, borne in small clusters; foliage medium size, dark green, glossy; prickles average, straight, moderate; growth upright, spreading, medium (3-4 m.), climbing; ['City of York' × 'Aloha']; intr. 2000

'Claret' Min, m, 1978, Saville, F. Harmon; bud short, pointed; flowers 1 in., 48 petals, cupped; very compact, spreading. growth; ['Little Chief' × 'Little Chief']; intr. 1977

'Claret' HT, dr, Fryer; bud large, almost black; flowers velvety, dark crimson, dbl., high-centered, borne in trusses, moderate fragrance; recurrent; bushy, medium (3 ft.) growth; intr. 2005

'Claret Cup' Min, rb, 1962, Riethmuller; bud globular; flowers dark red, white eye, small, dbl., borne in clusters, moderate fragrance; foliage leathery, dark; vigorous, bushy, compact growth; ['Spring Song (min)' × 'Eutin']; intr. 1962

'Clarice Goodacre' HT, w, 1916, Dickson, A.; bud pointed; flowers ivory-white, shaded chrome, dbl., high-centered; foliage dark, soft; vigorous, bushy growth

'Clarice Weston Flower Maker' -- See 'Framak'

Clarice Wood™ -- See 'Jayclar'

'Claridge' -- See 'Peklipink'

'Clarinda' -- See 'Cocsummery'

'Clarion Call' F, op, 1995, Fleming, Joyce L.; flowers orange-pink with red-salmon hues, medium, 6-14 petals, borne singly and in clusters of up to 5, slight fragrance; foliage medium size, medium green, matte; bushy (to 75 cm.) growth; ['Canadian Centennial' × 'Traumerei']; intr. 1994

Clarissa® -- See 'Harprocrustes'

'Clarissa Dana' HT, pb, 1933, Nicolas; flowers brilliant pink with amber glow, large, dbl., high-centered; vigorous growth; [(a hybrid tea × 'La France') × 'Marechal Niel']

'Clarita' ('Atoll') HT, or, 1972, Meilland; flowers vermilion, 5 in., 30-35 petals, high-centered, slight fragrance; foliage dark; very vigorous, upright growth; ['Tropicana' × (Zambra® × 'Romantica')]; intr. 1971

'Clarity' F, w, 1993, Jobson, Daniel J.; flowers white with cream center, medium, dbl., borne in small clusters; foliage large, dark green, glossy; some large prickles; medium, upright, bushy growth; [Pristine® × (Party Girl™ × 'Laureate')]; intr. 1993

'Clark Ochre Seedling' Cl HT, dy, Clark

'Clark Pink' Cl HT, mp, Clark

'Clarke's Multiflora' Sp, w; thornless; growth used as understock; clone of R. multiflora; used for understock

'Clark's Tea' HT, mr

'Class Act' -- See 'Jacare'

Class of '73™ -- See 'Tuc30reunion'

'Classic' HT, dp, Kasturi & Sriram; flowers large, deep rose pink, intense fragrance; vigorous growth; intr. 1997

'Classic Beauty' HT, pb, 1994, Winchel, Joseph F.; flowers cream and dark pink blend with yellow base, 3-3½ in., dbl., borne mostly singly; foliage medium size, medium green, matte; some prickles; medium, bushy growth; intr. 1997

'Classic Chic' Min, ob, 1986, McDaniel, Earl; flowers orange, 35 petals, high-centered, borne usually singly; foliage medium size, dark, semi-glossy; prickles few, slender; medium, upright growth; [seedling × seedling]

Classic Duet® HT, mp, Kordes; flowers medium, full, high-centered, borne mostly singly; recurrent; stems moderately long; [sport of 'Duett']; intr. 2005

'Classic Fruitilia' F, mr, Kordes; flowers single; recurrent; foliage medium, glossy; growth 80 cm. height; hips round

'Classic Love' -- See 'Lyocl'

'Classic Orange' Min, ob, Spooner, Ray; flowers bright orange , double, high-centered; medium to tall growth; intr. 1997

Classic Sunblaze® -- See 'Meipinjid'

'Classic Touch' HT, lp, 1991, Hefner, John; flowers large, full, borne mostly singly; foliage large, medium green, semi-glossy; tall, upright growth; [sport of 'Touch of Class']; intr. 1993

'Classic Woman' -- See 'Meigroupy'

'Classical Velvet' -- See 'Johillstar'

Classie Lassie™ Gr, pb, 1990, Winchel, Joseph F.; bud pointed; flowers ivory-pink, with salmon pink edges, aging to salmon, 25-30 petals, high-centered, oval-shaped, moderate fruity fragrance; foliage medium size, medium green, glossy, disease-resistant; prickles average, brown-green, slightly recurved; bushy, medium growth; [Touch of Class™ × seedling]; intr. 1991

Classy™ -- See 'Hilrap'

'Classy' -- See 'Tracla'

'Classy Carol' HT, pb, Delaney, Larry; flowers white blushed salmon, 4-6 in., 30 petals, decorative, borne one to a stem, slight fragrance; dark green glossy foliage; stems long and straight; well behaved, 4-5 ft. growth; intr. 2005

'Classy Lady' HT, ab; intr. 2005

'Claude' HT, mr, 1950, Mallerin, C.; flowers bright orient red, 6-7 in., 35 petals; foliage glossy, dark; vigorous, upright growth; [('Comtesse Vandal' × 'Brazier') × seedling]

'Claude Bernard' HP, dp, 1878, Liabaud; flowers large, full, globular; ['Jules Margottin' × unknown]

Claude Brasseur® ('Meibriacus') HT, m, Meilland; flowers lavender, large, double, high-centered; foliage dark green, semi-glossy; moderate growth; intr. 2007

'Claude Henry McLean' S, dr, Gawron; intr. 1995

'Claude Jacquet' HP, dr, 1892, Liabaud; flowers dark red/purple, very large, dbl.

'Claude Levet' ('Mons Claude Levet') HP, mr, 1872, Levet

'Claude Million' HP, dr, 1863, Verdier, E.; flowers scarlet-crimson, touched with rose and violet, velvety, large, full, cupped

Claude Monet® -- See 'Jacdesa'

'Claude Petit' HT, mp, 1936, Buatois; flowers soft salmon-pink, stamens yellow, very dbl., high-centered; vigorous growth; ['Mlle Marie Mascuraud' × 'Beauté de Lyon']

'Claude Rabbé' HWich, dp, 1941, Buatois; flowers carmine-pink, 7 cm., borne in clusters of 6-10

'Claude's Cracker' -- See 'Rawcrack'

'Claudia' -- See 'Meiyacom'

'Claudia' F, pb, 1959, Broadley; flowers deep cherry-coral, dbl.; vigorous growth; ['Ma Perkins' × 'Geranium Red']

Claudia™ -- See 'Poulra004(N)'

'Claudia Augusta' ('Claudie Augustin') N, w, 1856, Damaizin; flowers white with cream center, large, full; foliage dark green

'Claudia Cardinale' S, my, Guillot-Massad; flowers warm yellow-amber, incurving, full, globular, domed form, moderate fragrance; glossy foliage; growth to 5 ft.; intr. 1997

'Claudia Parade' (Claudia™) MinFl, lp, Poulsen; flowers light pink, 5-8 cm., dbl., no fragrance; foliage dark; growth bushy, 20-40 cm.; PP13454; intr. 2000

'Claudie Augustin' -- See 'Claudia Augusta'

'Claudine' A, w, 1823, Vibert; sepals foliaceous; flowers medium, semi-dbl.

'Claudius' HT, rb, 1910, Cant, B.; flowers glowing fire red with salmon pink, large, full

'Claudius Levet' T, pb, 1886, Levet; flowers carmine rose, salmon center, large, full

'Claudy Chapel' HT, yb, 1930, Beaumez; flowers deep yellow and coppery, to salmon-pink, large, dbl.; vigorous growth

'Claus Groth' ('Klaus Groth') HSpn, ob,

1951, Tantau; flowers salmon-orange shaded apricot-yellow, large, dbl., intense spinosissima fragrance; foliage dark; vigorous, bushy (5 ft.) growth; large fruit; [R.M.S. Queen Mary × R. spinosissima]

'Claysnow' (Snowballet®) S, w, 1977, Clayworth; intr. 1977

'Clealta' ('Christine') S, ob, Clements, John K.; intr. 1998

'Cleamour' ('Glamour Girl') MinFl, rb, Clements, John K.; intr. 1992

'Cleaprimp' LCl, ab, Clements, John; bud apricot bronze; intr. 2006

'Clear Moon' HT, my, 2007, Otsuki, Hironaka; flowers 13 cm., dbl., borne mostly solitary; foliage medium size, medium green, semi-glossy; growth upright, medium; cutting; ['Kamakura' × ('Golden Heart' × 'Hoshizukuyo')]; intr. 2007

'Clear Oceans' HT, w; flowers medium, full, high-centered; intr. 2001

'Cleartfull' S, ob, Clements, John; bud long and pointed; intr. 2003

'Cleartul' S, ab, Clements, John; intr. 2000

'Cleballet' S, mp, Clements, John; intr. 2000

'Clebeau' ('Golden Beauty', 'Golden Girls') Min, yb, 1992, Clements, John K.; flowers gold, edged copper and pink, medium, full, high-centered, borne mostly singly; foliage small, dark green, glossy; few prickles; medium (12-15 in.), bushy, spreading growth; [seedling × seedling]; intr. 1990

'Clebig' S, mp, Clements, John; intr. 2004

'Clebktea' S, or, John Clements; intr. 2003

'Cleblack' ('Black Gold') Min, dr, Clements, John K.; intr. 1996

'Clebliss' S, lp, Clements, John; intr. 2000

'Cleblusta' LCl, m, Clements, John; intr. 2003

'Clebou' ('Boudoir') S, pb, Clements, John K.; intr. 1995

'Clebravo' ('Braveheart') S, dr, Clements, John K.; intr. 1998

'Clebridge' ('Bridget') HMsk, ab, Clements, John K.; intr. 1996

'Clebrite' ('Britestripe', 'Britestripes') Min, rb, 1991, Clements, John K.; flowers soft pink, striped bright red, medium, full, borne in small clusters, no fragrance; foliage small, medium green, semi-glossy; some prickles; medium (30 cm.), bushy, compact growth; [Pinstripe™ × seedling]; intr. 1990

'Clebronze' S, op, Clements, John; intr. 2004

'Clebuxom' S, lp, Clements, John; intr. 2004

'Clecarmen' S, mr, Clements, John; intr. 2002

'Clecats' S, mp, Clements, John K.; intr. 1996

'Clecham' ('Pink Champagne') S, mp, Clements, John K.; intr. 1995

'Clecharisma' S, mp, Clements, John; intr. 2000

'Clecherry' ('Cherries Jubilee') HWich, mr, Clements, John K.; intr. 1999

'Cleclown' ('Circus Clown') HWich, mp, Clements, John; intr. 1997

'Cleconcert' ('Regina Louise') S, lp, 1999, Clements, John K.; intr. 1999

'Clecopperstar' MinFl, ob, Clements, John; intr. 2007

'Clecupcake' -- See 'It's Magic'

'Cledan' ('Dancing in the Wind') HMsk, pb, Clements, John K.; intr. 1995

'Cledare' ('Virginia Dare') MinFl, w, Clements, John K.

'Cledijon' S, ab, Clements, John; intr. 2007

'Cledrag' ('Dragon's Eye', 'Eye of the Dragon', 'The Dragon's Eye') HCh, dr, 1992, Clements, John K.; flowers medium, very dbl., high-centered, borne mostly singly; foliage small, dark green, semi-glossy; some prickles; medium (70 cm.), bushy, compact growth; [seedling × seedling]; intr. 1991

'Cledream' HWich , lp, Clements, John; intr. 2006

'Cleegypt' S, dp, Clements, John; intr. 2000

'Cleexpert' S, mr, Clements, John; intr. 2000

'Clefire' ('Firestorm') Min, or, 1991, Clements, John K.; flowers fiery oriental lacquer orange-red, medium, very full, high-centered, borne mostly singly, no fragrance; foliage small, medium green, semi-glossy; few prickles; medium (35 cm.), bushy, spreading growth; [seedling × seedling]; intr. 1991

'Clefriendship' S, w, Clements, John; intr. 2001

'Clefrosty' HMult , w, Clements, John; intr. 2000

'Clegem' HMult, mr, Clements, John; intr. 2000

'Cleglobe' S, dy, Clements, John; intr. 2005

'Clego' S, pb, Clements, John; intr. 2002

'Clegran' ('Grandma's Lace') S, lp, 1994, Clements, John K.; flowers pale pink, medium, full, borne in clusters, moderate fragrance; foliage medium size, medium green, semi-glossy; medium, spreading growth; [Sexy Rexy® × Trier®]

'Clegreengate' S, yb, Clements, John; intr. 2008

'Cleheat' ('Good Ol' Summertime') S, ly, Clements, John K.; intr. 1997

'Clehelp' ('Helping Hands') S, mr, Clements, John K.

'Clehon' ('Honey Mini-Delite') Min, w, 1991, Clements, John K.; flowers honey cream, medium, full, borne in small clusters, no fragrance; foliage small, medium green, matte; few prickles; low (25 cm.), bushy, compact growth; [seedling × seedling]; intr. 1991

'Clehonor' ('Ora Kingsley') S, dr, Clements, John K.; intr. 1999

'Clehope' S, ly, John Clements; intr. 2002

'Clehope' S, rb, Clements, John; intr. 2003

'Clehtclassic' S, op, Clements, John; intr. 2008

'Cleice' ('Ice Crystal') Min, w, 1991, Clements, John K.; flowers crystal white, micro-mini, very full, high-centered, borne in small clusters, no fragrance; foliage small, medium green, semi-glossy; some prickles; micro-mini; low (20 cm.), bushy, compact growth; [seedling × 'Baby Betsy McCall']; intr. 1989

'Cleirish' S, dr, Clements, John; intr. 2000

'Clejoan' (Joan Fontaine™) S, w, Clements, John K.; bud soft, flesh pink; intr. 1996

'Clejoy' S, mp, Clements, John; intr. 2005

'Clekate' ('Kateryna') S, mp, Clements, John K.; intr. 1996

'Clekiss' ('Strawberry Kiss') Min, rb, 1991, Clements, John K.; flowers white edged red, medium, dbl., high-centered, borne mostly singly, no fragrance; foliage small, light green, semi-glossy; some prickles; medium (35 cm.), upright, bushy growth; [seedling × seedling]; intr. 1989

'Clelady' ('Fancy Lady') Min, pb, 1991, Clements, John K.; flowers ivory white, edged bright pink and blushed pink, medium, very full, high-centered, borne mostly singly, no fragrance; foliage small, dark green, glossy; few prickles; tall (50 cm.), upright growth; [seedling × seedling]; intr. 1990

'Cleland' ('Landscape Splendor') HWich, w, Clements, John K.; intr. 1996

'Clelight' ('Little Lighthouse') Min, rb, 1991, Clements, John K.; flowers bright red with yellow to white eye, medium, single, high-centered, borne in small clusters, no fragrance; foliage small, medium green, semi-glossy; some prickles; low (18 cm.), bushy, spreading, compact growth; groundcover; ['Robin Red Breast' × Little Artist®]; intr. 1992

'Clelight' S, op, Clements, John; intr. 2001

'Clelips' ('Lipstick 'n' Lace') Min, rb, 1991, Clements, John K.; flowers cream, shaded lipstick red, large, full, high-centered, borne in small clusters, moderate fragrance; foliage medium size, medium green, matte; no prickles; medium (30 cm.), upright, compact growth; [seedling × seedling]; intr. 1992

'Clelock' ('Turlock High') Min, my, 1991, Clements, John K.; flowers bright yellow, small, full, borne mostly singly, intense fragrance; recurrent; foliage small, dark green, semi-glossy; some prickles; medium (40 cm.), upright, bushy growth; ['Rise 'n' Shine' × seedling]; intr. 1992

'Clelou' ('Louise Clements') S, ob, Clements, John K.; intr. 1996

'Clelovsng' S, lp, Clements, John; intr. 2004

'Clematis' HWich, rb, 1924, Turbat; flowers dark red, prominent white eye, 2 cm., single, borne in clusters of 40-50, no fragrance; foliage small, glossy; vigorous, climbing growth

'Clémence Beaugrand' -- See 'Mme Clémence Beauregard'

'Clémence Isaure' HGal, dp, about 1835, Vibert; flowers deep pink, center crimson, large, full

'Clémence Isaure' HP, op, Robert; flowers salmon pink, medium, full, globular; intr. 1851

'Clémence Isaure' (R. cretica sabina) HEg, pb, Trattinnick; flowers pink over white, medium, single

'Clémence Joigneaux' HP, mr, 1861, Liabaud; flowers bright red, tinted with lilac, very large, full

'Clémence Lartay' HP, mr, 1860, Lartay

'Clémence Raoux' HP, mp, 1869, Granger; flowers bright pink, shaded silvery pink, large, full, quartered, moderate fragrance; foliage dark green, glossy; prickles straight, flat

'Clémence Robert' M, mp, 1863, Robert et Moreau; bud heavily mossed; flowers bright pink, 9-11 cm., full, borne in clusters; sometimes recurrent bloom

'Clement' ('Commitment') LCl, dr, Clements, John K.; intr. 1995

'Clément Marot' HP, m, 1860, Oger

'Clément Nabonnand' T, yb, 1877, Nabonnand

'Clément Pacaud' HT, dp, 1916, Chambard, C.; flowers brilliant carmine, large, full

'Clementina' HT, pb, 1961, Dot, Pedro; flowers carmine and rosy white bicolor; ['Grand Gala' × 'Vicky Marfá']

'Clementina Carbonieri' T, yb, 1913, Bonfiglio, A.; bud long, reddish-yellow; flowers light violet pink, medium, full; growth medium (3 × 2 ft.); ['Kaiserin Auguste Viktoria' × 'Souv de Catherine Guillot']

'Clementine' ('Showdown') Min, ob, Tantau; flowers apricot-orange, dbl., borne in clusters; dark green foliage

'Clémentine' HT, w, Wagner; flowers cream-white, petals edged with pink, medium, full; ['Kaiserin Auguste Viktoria' × 'Fragezeichen']; intr. 1928

'Clémentine' HGal, mp, Vibert; intr. 1818

'Clémentine' ('Janet's Pride', 'Rose Jay') HEg, pb, about 1810, Descemet; flowers white with carmine red edges, with striped, medium, semi-dbl.; foliage darker green, glossy; hips dark red, very large, flattened cone-shaped; synonymous with Janet's Pride, as reintroduced by W. Paul

'Clémentine Duval' B, mp, 1847, Laffay, M.; flowers bright rose, cupped; sometimes classed as HP

'Clémentine Séringe' HP, mp, 1840, Wood; flowers rose-pink, dbl.

'Clemist' ('Will-o'-the-Wisp') MinFl, pb, Clements, John K.; intr. 1998

'Clemom' S, op, Clements, John; intr. 2000

'Clemulti' S, lp, Clements, John; intr. 2004

'Cleo' -- See 'Beebop'

'Cleojo' S, ob, Clements, John; intr. 2005

'Cleonagh Ann' -- See 'Horcleann'

'Cleopatra' HP, mp, 1857, Oger; flowers glowing pink

'Cleopatra' T, pb, Bennett; flowers flesh colour shaded with rose, large, full; intr. 1889

'Cleopatra' ('Kleopatra') HT, rb, Kordes; flowers scarlet, reverse old-gold, well-formed, medium, 45 petals, moderate fragrance; foliage dark, glossy; vigorous growth; [('Walter Bentley' × 'Condesa de Sástago') × 'Golden Scepter']; intr. 1955

'Cleopatra' -- See 'Korverpea'

'Cleora' Min, mp, 1976, Dobbs; bud globular; flowers medium pink, reverse darker, 1½ in., 50 petals, flat; foliage small, light, leathery; vigorous growth; ['Fairy Moss' × 'Fairy Moss']; intr. 1977

'Cleorleans' S, dp, John Clements; intr. 2005

'Cléosthène' HP, m, before 1866; flowers lilac pink, very large, full

'Clepainter' LCl, yb, Clements, John; intr. 2000

'Clepchsilk' LCl, op, Clements, John; intr. 2004

'Clepeach' ('Peach Silks') Min, ab, 1991, Clements, John K.; flowers rich peach, medium, dbl., borne in small clusters, no fragrance; foliage small, dark green, glossy; few prickles; tall (50 cm.), upright growth; [seedling × seedling]; intr. 1991

'Clepeachy' S, pb, Clements, John; intr. 2004

'Cleperf' ('Apricot Perfection') Min, ab, 1992, Clements, John K.; flowers soft apricot, small, dbl., high-centered, borne mostly singly, slight fragrance; foliage small, medium green, matte; some prickles; tall (50 cm.), upright, bushy growth; ['My Louisa' × seedling]; intr. 1990

'Cleperf' S, lp, Clements, John; intr. 2003

'Clepoetry' S, dy, Clements, John; intr. 2003

'Clepurp' ('Color Purple') Min, m, 1991, Clements, John K.; flowers rich deep purple, medium, very dbl., borne mostly singly, moderate fragrance; foliage medium size, dark green, holly-like, glossy; few prickles; low (25 cm.), spreading, compact growth; ['Angel Face' × seedling]; intr. 1990

'Clequeen' S, mp, Clements, John; intr. 2003

'Clerain' ('Oregon Rainbow') Min, yb, 1991, Clements, John K.; bud high-pointed; flowers golden yellow, shaded and edged red, medium, full, high-centered, no fragrance; foliage small, dark green, semi-glossy; medium (40 cm.), bushy growth; [seedling × seedling]; intr. 1991

'Clerhoda' S, lp, Clements, John; intr. 2002

'Cleruff' ('Ruffles 'n' Flourishes') S, rb, 1994, Clements, John K.; flowers violet red and gold, medium, dbl., borne in small clusters; foliage medium size, reddish green, glossy; few prickles; low (18 in.), upright, bushy growth; [Sexy Rexy® × 'Whistle Stop']; intr. 1994

'Clescrub' ('Patriot Flame', 'Scudbuster') Min, or, 1991, Clements, John K.; flowers intense rocket flame orange, medium, very full, high-centered, borne mostly singly, slight fragrance; foliage small, dark green, semi-glossy; some prickles; medium (35 cm.), upright growth; [seedling × seedling]; intr. 1992

'Cleshir' ('Sweet Shirley') Min, mp, 1991, Clements, John K.; flowers medium pink, lighter reverse, medium, dbl., high-centered, borne mostly singly, slight fragrance; foliage small, medium green, semi-glossy; some prickles; bushy (40 cm.), spreading growth; ['Tweedle Dee' × seedling]; intr. 1991

'Clesmile' S, pb, Clements, John; intr. 2002

'Clesnob' ('Snowblush') Min, rb, 1991, Clements, John K.; intr. 1992

'Clesnow' ('Snowblush') Min, rb, 1991, Clements, John K.; flowers purest white, edges red, medium, very full, high-centered, borne mostly singly, no fragrance; foliage medium green, matte; some prickles; tall (50 cm.), upright growth; ['Minuette' × seedling]; intr. 1992

'Clespirit' ('Laura Clements') S, dp, Clements, John K.; intr. 1999

'Clesruby' MinFl, rb, Clements, John; intr. 1996

'Clestormy' S, m, Clements, John; intr. 2002

'Clestyle' S, pb, John Clements; intr. 2005

'Clesunshine' S, ab, Clements, John; intr. 2002

'Cleswan' ('Brenda Burg') S, ob, Clements, John K.; intr. 1999

'Cletape' ('Antique Tapestry') Min, rb, 1991, Clements, John K.; flowers burgundy and gold, large, dbl., high-centered, borne mostly singly, slight fragrance; foliage medium size, dark green, semi-glossy; few prickles; medium (40 cm.), upright growth; ['Redgold' × seedling]; intr. 1990

'Cletess' ('Tess') Min, lp, 1991, Clements, John K.; flowers flesh pink, medium, semi-dbl., high-centered, borne mostly singly, no fragrance; foliage small, medium green, semi-glossy; few prickles; medium (30 cm.), bushy growth; [Cupcake™ × seedling]; intr. 1992

'Cletest' ('Tess') Min, lp, 1991, Clements, John K.; intr. 1992

'Clethor' S, mp, Clements, John; intr.

'Cletig' ('Tiger Stripes') Min, yb, 1992, Clements, John K.; flowers unusual striped color combination, yellow, striped orange, medium, full, no fragrance; foliage small, medium green, semi-glossy; few prickles; low (25 cm.), bushy, compact growth; [seedling × seedling]; intr. 1991

'Cletivoli'   S, ab, Clements, John; intr. 2000

'Cletrail'   S, op, Clements, John; intr. 2004

'Cletraveler' ('Charles Kuralt') S, mp, Clements, John K.; intr. 1999

'Cletwin' ('Twin Pinks') Min, pb, 1991, Clements, John K.; flowers two-tone pink, medium, dbl., high-centered, borne in small clusters, slight fragrance; foliage small, medium green, semi-glossy; some prickles; low (30 cm.), bushy, compact growth; [seedling × seedling]; intr. 1991

'Cleveland Bouquet'   HT, op, 1940, Horvath; flowers shrimp-pink with salmon-pink undertone, open, semi-dbl.

'Cleveland I'   HT, yb, 1916, Dickson, A.; flowers coppery yellow

'Cleveland II' ('Mrs Dunlop Best') HT, pb, 1916, Dickson, H.; bud long; flowers antique pink, shaded reddish-copper, base copper-yellow, large, full, high-centered, moderate fragrance

'Clever Gretel'   S, pb, Kordes; intr. 2003

'Clewedding' ('Morning Has Broken') S, my, Clements, John K.; intr. 1996

'Clewine'   S, m, Clements, John; intr. 2000

'Clewonder'   S, pb, Clements, John K.; intr. 1997

'Clewonder'   Min, yb, Clements, John; intr. 2001

'Clezap'   LCl, pb, Clements, John; intr. 2002

'Clezap'   S, mr, Clements, John; intr. 2006

'Cliché' -- See 'Frywhoppa'

'Cliff Richard' ('Sir Cliff Richard') F, pb, Van Geest; flowers medium pink, silver reverse; foliage glossy, mid-green; upright growth, 4-5 ft.; intr. 1993

'Clifford'

'Clifford'   HT, ly; intr. 2007

'Clifford' -- See 'Worahat'

'Cliffs of Dover' -- See 'Poulemb'

Cliffs of Dover Cover™ -- See 'Poulemb'

'Clifton Moss' -- See 'White Bath'

'Climentina'   HT, mp, 1955, Klimenko, V. N.; flowers rosy pink, large; ['Independence' × 'Peace']

'Clinora' ('Landora, Climbing', 'Sunblest, Climbing') Cl HT, dy, 1979, Orard, Joseph (also Tantau, 1978, NR); bud pointed; flowers pure, dark yellow, large, intense fragrance; [sport of 'Sunblest']; intr. 1978

'Clio'   HGal, mr, before 1820, Descemet; flowers carmation red

'Clio'   HP, lp, Paul, W.; flowers flesh, large, very dbl., globular, borne in clusters, moderate fragrance; seasonal bloom; foliage rich green; vigorous growth; intr. 1894

'Clio'   HT, or, Gaujard; flowers luminous Indian red, large

'Clitus'   Ch, m, 1853, Bernède; flowers purple-pink aging to carmine, large, full

'Clive Beck'   HT, yb, Kordes; flowers sand yellow with coral pink edges, large, dbl., high-centered, no fragrance; long stems; upright growth, 7 ft.; intr. 2001

'Clive Lloyd'   HT, dp

Clivia® -- See 'Kortag'

'Clo-Clo' -- See 'Pekatan'

Clochemerle® -- See 'Delpétri'

'Clodagh McGredy'   HT, ab, McGredy; flowers soft golden amber, ruffled petals, dbl., moderate fragrance; matte foliage; compact (2½ ft.), bushy growth; intr. 2001

'Cloris Adriana'   HT, dp, 1997, Poole, Lionel; flowers high-centered, large, 41 petals, borne mostly singly; foliage large, dark green, dull; some prickles; spreading, bushy, medium growth; [Blue Moon® × 'Gavotte']

'Clos de la Pellerie' -- See 'Delclopel'

'Clos Fleuri'   S, Delbard-Chabert; intr. 1970

Clos Fleuri Bicolore™ -- See 'Delrula'

Clos Fleuri Blanc® -- See 'Delblan'

Clos Fleuri Champagne® F, ab, Delbard; flowers medium, honey-champagne with some pink petal edges, dbl., high-centered, slight fragrance fragrance; recurrent bloom; growth to 2 ft.; intr. 1990

'Clos Fleuri d'Or'   F, ob, Delbard; flowers orange and gold shades, dbl., borne in clusters; growth to 2 ft.; intr. 1990

Clos Fleuri Jaune® -- See 'Deljaune'

Clos Fleuri Rose® -- See 'Delpomp'

'Clos Fleuri Rose No. 2' ('Pink Ribbon') F, mp, Delbard; flowers pure rose pink, full; low growth; intr. 1994

Clos Fleuri Rouge® -- See 'Delecla'

'Clos Fleuri Vermilion'   F, or, Delbard; flowers bright vermilion, semi-dbl. to dbl., cupped to open, borne in clusters of 5 to 10; recurrent; foliage dark bronzy green, glossy; growth to 2-3 ft.; intr. 2005

Clos Vougeot® -- See 'Delific'

'Close to You'   HT, ly; flowers medium, intense lemony fragrance; robust growth; intr. 2006

'Close Up' -- See 'Macclosup'

'Closer to Heaven' -- See 'Morheaven'

'Clotaria' ('Red Gruss an Coburg') HT, mr, 1936, San Remo Exp. Sta.; flowers bright fuchsia-red, well-formed, medium, 26-28 petals; foliage dark, glossy; vigorous, upright, bushy growth; ['Gruss an Coburg' × 'J. C. Thornton']

'Cloth of Gold' -- See 'Chromatella'

'Clothilde' HGal, lp, 1867, Coquerel

'Clothilde Roland'   HP, mr, 1867, Roland; flowers cherry red, large, full

'Clothilde Sigrist'   T, mp, 1907, Bidaud; flowers pink, striped darker pink, large, full

'Clothilde Soupert'   T, mp, 1883, Levet; flowers carmine-pink, large, very full; ['Gloire de Dijon' × unknown]

'Clotilde' ('Bougère') T, mp, 1867, Roland; flowers medium pink with violet pink, very large, full

'Clotilde' -- See 'Bougère'

'Clotilde Soupert' ('Mme Hardy du Thé', 'Mme Melon du Thé') Pol, w, 1890, Soupert & Notting; flowers pearly white, center soft rose-pink, large, very dbl., borne in clusters, moderate fragrance; foliage rich green, soft; bushy (10-20 in.) growth; ['Mignonette' × 'Mme Damaizin']

'Clotilde Soupert, Climbing'   Cl Pol, w, 1896, Berckmans, P.J., Co. (also Dingee & Conard, 1901); flowers , borne in small clusters, moderate tea fragrance; good repeat

Cloud Dancer™ -- See 'Burdancer'

'Cloud Nine'   S, w, Williams, J. Benjamin; flowers white touched with apricot, moderate fragrance; intr. 1999

'Cloud Nine'   HT, mp, Fryer; flowers bright, glowing pink, large, dbl., classically structured, moderate fragrance; growth to 110 cm.; intr. 2004

'Cloud Nine' -- See 'Jaclite'

'Cloud No. 9' -- See 'Tanmauve'

'Cloudland'   HT, m, 1994, Perry, Astor; flowers 3-3½ in., full, moderate fragrance; foliage large, medium green, matte; upright (150 cm.) growth; [Blue Moon® × 'Paradise']; intr. 1995

'Clouseau' -- See 'Talclouseau'

'Clove Scented Musk'   Misc OGR, w

'Clovelly'   HT, dp, 1924, Hicks; flowers carmine-pink, well-formed; vigorous growth

'Cloverdene' -- See 'Herclov'

'Clovis'   HP, m, 1868, Ledéchaux; flowers purple-pink

'Club'   F, mr, 1957, Gaujard; flowers bright red, open, medium, single; foliage glossy, bronze; very vigorous, bushy growth; ['Peace' × ('Opera' × unknown)]

'Clubrose Lulu' -- See 'Lulu'

'Clubrose Lydia' -- See 'Lydia'

'Clubrose Scala' ('Scala') F, rb, 1973, Kordes; flowers blood-red and orange, medium, dbl., globular, slight fragrance; foliage glossy, dark, leathery, bronze; vigorous, upright, bushy growth; ['Marlena' × seedling]

'Clydebank Centenary' -- See 'Cocdazzle'

'Clytemnestra'   HMsk, op, 1915, Pemberton; bud copper; flowers salmon-chamois, ruffled, small, 18-20 petals, borne in clusters, moderate fragrance; recurrent bloom; foliage leathery, dark; bushy (3-4 ft.), spreading growth; [Trier® × 'Liberty']

'Cnos X'   HT, my, 1957, Bronisze (Poland) State Nursery; flowers golden yellow tinged copper; vigorous growth; [Bettina® × unknown]

'Coachman'   F, mr, Williams, J.B.; flowers cherry-red, outer petals lighter, dbl., pompon, borne in clusters; recurrent; foliage glossy; intr. 1996

'Coalite Flame' HT, or, 1976, Dickson, A.; flowers 5 in., 60 petals, moderate fragrance; foliage large, matte; ['Fragrant Cloud' × 'Red Planet']; intr. 1974

'Coby Fankhauser' HT, my, 1971, Fankhauser; flowers buttercup-yellow, large, dbl., high-centered; foliage leathery; vigorous, upright, bushy growth; ['John S. Bloomfield' × 'Elizabeth Fankhauser']

'Cocabel' ('Little Jewel') Min, dp, 1980, Cocker, James; flowers deep pink, 34 petals, borne 6-12 per cluster; foliage small, glossy, dark; prickles straight; growth low, compact; containers; ['Wee Man' × 'Belinda']

'Cocabest' (Wee Jock®) Min, mr, 1980, Cocker, James; bud pointed; flowers small, 50 petals, borne 9 - 15 per cluster; recurrent; foliage small, fairly glossy, medium green; prickles red; low, compact growth; ['National Trust' × 'Wee Man']

'Cocacert' ('Vital Spark') F, ab, 1982, Cocker, James; flowers gold, flushed coral, medium, 35 petals; foliage medium size, medium green, semi-glossy; bushy growth; [(Anne Cocker® × ('Sabine' × 'Circus')) × 'Yellow Pages']

'Cocadilly' ('The Coxswain') HT, pb, 1984, Cocker, Alexander M.; flowers cream and pink blend, large, 35 petals, intense fragrance; foliage medium size, medium green, semi-glossy; bushy growth; [('Tropicana' × 'Ballet') × 'Silver Jubilee']; intr. 1985

'Cocagold' HT, my, Cocker, James

'Cocamond' ('Dainty Dinah') Min, op, 1982, Cocker, James; flowers medium salmon-pink, patio, small, semi-dbl., slight fragrance; foliage small, medium green, semi-glossy; bushy growth; [Anne Cocker® × 'Wee Man']; intr. 1981

'Cocanelia' ('Pink Posy') Min, m, 1983, Cocker, James; flowers lilac, small, dbl., moderate fragrance; foliage dark, matte; bushy growth; [Trier® × 'New Penny']

'Cocapeer' ('Sweetheart') HT, mp, 1980, Cocker, James; bud ovoid; flowers rose pink, yellow base, 52 petals, imbricated, borne singly, moderate fragrance; recurrent; foliage large, medium green, semi-glossy; vigorous, upright (2½ ft.) growth; [Peer Gynt® × ('Fragrant Cloud' × Gay Gordons®)]

'Cocaquil' ('Cock A Doo') F, dr, Cocker; intr. 1984

'Cocarde' -- See 'Majestueuse'

'Cocarde' ('Mutabilis') A, mp, about 1810, Descemet; flowers bright pink, edges lighter

'Cocarde Jacobée' HGal, mr, 1824, in Brussels

'Cocarde Jaune' HT, pb, 1933, Ketten Bros.; bud large, long, pointed, reddish salmon; flowers yellowish-salmon, base yellow, reverse coral-red, dbl., cupped; foliage dark; vigorous, bushy growth; ['Diana' × 'Marie Adélaïde']

'Cocarde Pâle' HGal, lp, before 1813, Pradel, H.; flowers bright, light pink, edges lighter

'Cocarde Rouge' HGal, mp, about 1825, Vibert; flowers bright glowing pink

'Cocarde Royale' -- See 'Grand Monarche'

'Cocared' ('Roddy MacMillan') HT, ab, 1982, Cocker, James; flowers large, 35 petals; foliage medium size, medium green, semi-glossy; bushy growth; [('Fragrant Cloud' × Postillion®) × 'Wisbech Gold']

'Cocarum' (Cha Cha®) Min, ob, 1983, Cocker, James; flowers orange-red with yellow eye, dbl., slight fragrance; foliage small, medium green, semi-glossy; bushy growth; [('Wee Man' × 'Manx Queen') × 'Darling Flame']; intr. 1983

'Cocason' ('Sunset Song') HT, ab, 1980, Cocker, James; bud pointed; flowers golden amber, medium, 46 petals, hybrid tea, borne 1 - 5 per cluster, slight fragrance; free-flowering; foliage large, glossy, light olive green; prickles beak-shaped, red-brown; upright growth; [('Sabine' × 'Circus') × 'Sunblest']; intr. 1981

'Cocathes' ('Crathes Castle') F, mp, 1980, Cocker, James; flowers 18 petals, borne 12-15 per cluster; foliage large, dark, glossy; prickles triangular; rounded, bushy growth; ['Dreamland' × Topsi®]

'Cocavoter' ('Sweet Nell') F, ob, 1984, Cocker, Alexander M.; flowers medium orange, large, 35 petals; foliage medium size, medium green, semi-glossy; upright growth; [Anne Cocker® × ('Mischief' × ('(Sabine × Circus)' × '(Tropicana × Circus)')]; intr. 1984

'Cocbaden' ('Doctor Dick') HT, op, 1986, Cocker, James & Sons; flowers orange-coral, large, dbl., high-centered, slight fragrance; foliage large, medium green, matte; upright growth; ['Fragrant Cloud' × Corso®]

'Cocbamber' ('Amberlight', 'Fyvie Castle') HT, pb, 1985, Cocker, Alexander M.; flowers light apricot, amber and pink blend, well-formed, large, 35 petals; foliage large, medium green, semi-glossy; upright growth; [('Sunblest' × ('Sabine' × 'Dr. A.J. Verhage')) × 'Silver Jubilee']

'Cocbay' ('May Lyon') HT, mp, 1983, Cocker, James; flowers large, 35 petals; foliage large, medium green, glossy; bushy growth; [((Anne Cocker® × 'Arthur Bell') × 'National Trust') × 'Silver Jubilee']; intr. 1983

'Cocblanco' ('Bianco') Min, w, 1983, Cocker, James; flowers patio, small, 35 petals; foliage medium size, medium green, semi-glossy; bushy growth; ['Darling Flame' × 'Jack Frost']

'Cocbonne' ('Ena Baxter') HT, or, 1990, Cocker, James & Sons; bud pointed; flowers salmon pink, reverse salmon red, medium, 26 petals, high-centered, borne in sprays of 5-9, slight fragrance; foliage large, medium green, glossy; prickles triangular, average, green; bushy, medium growth; hips urn-shaped, large, brown; ['HARkrispin' × 'Silver Jubilee']; intr. 1989

'Cocbrose' ('Abbeyfield Rose') HT, dp, 1984, Cocker, A.; flowers rose red, large, 35 petals, slight fragrance; foliage medium size, medium green, semi-glossy; bushy growth; ['National Trust' × 'Silver Jubilee']; intr. 1985

'Coccages' ('Country Heritage', 'Our Jubilee') HT, ob, 1986, Cocker, James & Sons; flowers medium, 20 petals; foliage medium size, medium green, semi-glossy; upright growth; ['Yellow Pages' × 'Silver Jubilee']

'Coccastle' ('My Everything') F, or, 2006, Cocker, A. G.; flowers salmon vermilion, reverse lighter, 2½ in., dbl., cupped, borne in large clusters, slight fragrance; foliage medium size, medium green, glossy; prickles moderate, 9 mm., straight; growth bushy, medium (2½ ft.); garden decoration; ['Fyvie Castle' × 'Beautiful Britain']; intr. 2006

'Cocceleste' ('Rosabell') MinFl, mp, 1988, Cocker, James & Sons; flowers medium, incurving petals, dbl., cupped, borne in clusters, slight fragrance; foliage medium size, medium green, semi-glossy; bushy (15 in.) growth; patio; [('National Trust' × 'Wee Man') × 'Darling Flame']; intr. 1986

'Coccharm' HT, my, Cocker; intr. 2008

'Coccinea' HMult, pb, Legris; bud round, fat; flowers varied, white, pink, and scarlet, 2½-3 in., full, borne in clusters of up to 30; not recurrent; sometimes attributed to Van Houtte; intr. 1843

'Coccinea' T, m, Cels; flowers dark purple, medium, full; intr. about 1840

'Coccinea' HBc, dr, before 1835

'Coccinée Superbe' -- See 'Le Vingt-Neuf Juillet'

'Coccinelle' LCl, or, 1956, Buyl Frères; flowers bright geranium-red

'Cocclare' ('Ray of Sunshine') S, my, 1990, Cocker, James & Sons; bud pointed; flowers clear, bright yellow, small, 15 petals, cupped, borne in sprays of 3 - 9, slight spicy fragrance; foliage small, dark green, glossy; prickles small, green; bushy, low growth; hips round, small, green; ['Sunsprite' × ('Cläre Grammerstorf' × 'Fruhlingsmorgen')]; intr. 1988

'Cocclarion' ('Laura Anne') HT, op, 1992, Cocker, James; flowers pink flushed orange, 3-3½ in., full, borne in large clusters, moderate fragrance; foliage large, medium green, glossy; some prickles; growth bushy (75 cm.); [(('Sabine' × 'Circus') × 'Maxi') × 'Harriny']; intr. 1990

'Coccopna' ('Coppa Nob') F, op, Cocker; intr. 1982

'Coccord' ('Little Prince') Min, or, 1983, Cocker, James; flowers orange-red, yellow eye, small, semi-dbl.; foliage medium size, medium green, semi-glossy; growth upright, bushy; containers, patio; ['Darling Flame' × ('National Trust' × 'Wee Man')]; intr. 1983

'Coccrazy' ('Gingernut') F, r, 1989, Cocker, James & Sons; flowers medium, 43 petals, moderate fragrance; foliage small, medium green, semi-glossy; patio; bushy growth; [('Sabine' × 'Circus') × 'Darling Flame']; intr. 1989

'Cocdana' ('Fulton MacKay', 'Maribel', 'Senteur des Iles') HT, yb, 1989, Cocker, James; flowers large, 20 petals, moderate fragrance; foliage large, medium green, glossy; bushy growth; ['Silver Jubilee' × 'Jana']; intr. 1989

'Cocdandy' ('Royal Volunteer') HT, ob, 1988, Cocker, James & Sons; flowers orange-red and yellow blended, medium, full; foliage medium size, light green, semi-glossy; upright growth; ['Yellow Pages' × Alexander®]

'Cocdapple' ('Scottish Special') Min, lp, 1985, Cocker, Ann G.; flowers patio, large, semi-dbl.; foliage small, medium green, semi-glossy; bushy growth; ['Wee Man' × 'Darling Flame']

'Cocdarlee' ('Coral Reef') Min, op, 1985, Cocker, Ann G.; flowers orange, patio, medium, semi-dbl., slight fragrance; foliage small, medium green, glossy; bushy growth; [('Darling Flame' × 'St. Albans') × 'Silver Jubilee']

'Cocdazzle' ('Clydebank Centenary') F, or, 1988, Cocker, James & Sons; flowers orange-vermilion red, medium, 15-25 fimbriated petals; foliage medium size, medium green, matte; upright growth; [(('Highlight' × 'Colour Wonder') × (Parkdirektor Riggers® × Piccadilly®)) × 'Darling Flame']

'Cocdestin' ('Rose d'Amour', Remember Me®) HT, ob, 1984, Cocker; flowers orange and yellow blend, large, 20 petals, high-centered; foliage small, dark, glossy; bushy, spreading growth; ['Anne Letts' × ('Dainty Maid' × 'Pink Favorite')]

'Cocdimity' ('Claire Scotland') Min, ab, 1992, Cocker, James; flowers light apricot-pink, large, dbl., borne in small clusters; foliage medium size, medium green, semi-glossy; some prickles; patio; low (50-80 cm.), bushy growth; [('National Trust' × 'Wee Man') × 'Darling Flame']; intr. 1990

'Cocdimple' ('Conservation') Min, pb, 1986, Cocker, James & Sons; flowers medium, semi-dbl., slight fragrance; foliage small, light green, semi-glossy; bushy growth; [(('Sabine' × 'Circus') × 'Maxi') × 'Darling Flame']

'Cocdinkum' (Boys' Brigade®) Min, mr, 1984, Cocker, Ann G.; flowers medium, patio, 5 petals, borne in clusters, no fragrance; foliage small, medium green, semi-glossy; bushy growth; [('Darling Flame' × 'Saint Alban') × ('Little Flirt' × 'Marlena')]; intr. 1984

'Cocember' ('Roxburghe Rose') HT, or, Cockerdbl.; intr. 1991

'Cocflag' ('Highland Laddie') Min, mr, 1990, Cocker, James & Sons; bud pointed; flowers scarlet red, medium, 19 petals, cupped, borne in sprays of 5-11, slight fragrance; foliage medium size, medium green, glossy; prickles medium, green; upright growth; hips urn-shaped, medium, brown; ['National Trust' × 'Dainty Dinah']; intr. 1989

'Cocfoster' ('Regal Red') S, mr, Cocker; intr. 1988

'Cocglen' (Honey Bunch®) F, yb, 1990, Cocker, James & Sons; bud ovoid; flowers yellow with salmon-red, reverse yellow, aging honey-yellow, 45 petals, cupped, moderate fragrance; foliage small, dark green, glossy; prickles small, green; patio; bushy, low growth; hips round, small, green; [(('Sabine' × 'Circus') × 'Maxi') × Bright Smile®]; intr. 1989

'Cocgold' ('Dania', 'Roche du Theil', 'Top Rose', 'Toprose') F, dy, 1992, Cocker, James; flowers bright yellow, 3-3½ in., full, cupped to flat, borne in clusters, slight fragrance; recurrent; foliage large, medium green, glossy; some prickles; medium (75 cm.), upright growth; [((Chinatown® × 'Golden Masterpiece') × Adolf Horstmann®) × 'Yellow Pages']; intr. 1991

'Cocgrand' ('Amazing Grace', 'Celebration', 'Myriam') HT, lp, 1992, Cocker, James; flowers 3-3½ in., very dbl., borne mostly singly; foliage large, medium green, semi-glossy; some prickles; medium (75 cm.), upright growth; ['Typhoo Tea' × 'Grandpa Dickson']; intr. 1990

'Cocharod' ('Shirley Spain') F, mr, 1993, Cocker; flowers glowing russet red, medium, dbl., borne in small clusters; foliage medium size, dark green, glossy; some prickles; medium, compact growth; [seedling × 'Roddy McMillan']; intr. 1992

'Cochello' ('Hello') Min, mr, 1992, Cocker, James; flowers crimson with white eye, large, 6-14 petals, borne in large clusters; foliage medium size, medium green, semi-glossy; some prickles; patio; medium (50-80 cm.), bushy growth; ['Darling Flame' × seedling]; intr. 1990

'Cochineal Glory, Climbing' Cl HT, mr, 1945, Vogel, M.; flowers large, semi-dbl.

'Cochineal Glory' HT, mr, 1937, Leenders, M.; bud pointed; flowers open, large, semi-dbl.; vigorous, bushy growth

'Cochuster' ('Ohshima Rose') HT, or, 1992, Cocker, James; flowers medium, full, borne mostly singly, moderate fragrance; foliage medium size, medium green, matte; some prickles; tall (1 m.), upright growth; [('National Trust' × Alexander®) × 'Red Planet']; intr. 1991

'Cocjabby' ('Braveheart', 'Gordon's College') F, op, 1992, James Cocker & Sons, Ltd.; flowers coral salmon, 3-3½ in., full, borne in large clusters, moderate fragrance; foliage large, dark green, glossy, purplish when young; some prickles; medium, upright growth; ['Abbeyfield Rose' × 'Roddy McMillan']

'Cocjojo' ('The Audrey Hepburn Rose') F, ob, Cocker; intr. 1993

'Cocjolly' ('Bishop Elphinstone') F, dr, 1993, Cocker, James; flowers crimson, medium, full, borne in large clusters, slight fragrance; foliage large, dark green, semi-glossy; some prickles; tall (3 ft.), upright growth; [seedling × ('Tropicana' × 'Baccara')]; intr. 1994

'Cock A Doo' -- See 'Cocaquil'

'Cockadoo' ('Cock A Doo') F, dr, Cocker; intr. 1984

'Cockle Shells' -- See 'Leocok'

Cocktail® S, rb, 1958, Meilland, F.; bud pointed; flowers geranium red, base primrose yellow, 2½ in., 5 petals, borne in clusters, slight spicy fragrance; foliage leathery, glossy; vigorous, semi-climbing growth; shrub or hedge; PP1821; [('Independence' × Orange Triumph®) × 'Phyllis Bide']; intr. 1957

'Cocktail '80' HT, my, Meilland, Mrs. Marie-Louise; bud elongated; flowers 5 in., 20 petals, high-centered; foliage dark; very vigorous growth; intr. 1977

'Coclager' ('William Quarrier') F, ab, 1997, Cocker, Ann G.; flowers medium, very dbl., borne in large clusters; foliage medium size, light green, dull; some prickles; compact, tall (2½-3ft.) growth; ['Silver Jubilee' × 'Geraldine']

'Coclament' ('Hope 98', 'Hope') F, mr, 1998, Cocker, Ann G.; flowers sparkling geranium red, lighter reverse, frilly petals, 1-1½ in., dbl., borne in large clusters; foliage small, medium size, glossy; prickles moderate, small, slightly hooked; compact, low, bushy growth; [Memento® × 'Evelyn Fison']; intr. 1998

'Coclands' ('Scotland's Trust') HT, lp, 1992, Cocker, James & Sons; flowers light pink, silver reverse, moderately well-shaped, medium, dbl.; foliage medium size, medium green, matte; some prickles; medium (16-20 cm.), upright growth; ['Sunblest' × 'Prima Ballerina']

'Coclent' ('Lady MacRobert') F, ab, 1993, Cocker; flowers light apricot, medium, dbl., borne in large clusters; foliage medium size, light green, semi-glossy; some prickles; medium (2½ ft.), upright, compact growth; ['Clydebank Centenary' × seedling]; intr. 1993

'Coclibee' ('Alison') F, op, 1996, Cocker, James & Sons; flowers peach salmon, 3-3½ in., borne in large clusters; foliage medium size, medium green, glossy; some prickles; medium, upright, bushy growth; ['Silver Jubilee' × ('Sabine' × 'Circus')]; intr. 1995

'Coclion' ('Press and Journal') HT, op, Cocker; intr. 1997

'Coclistine' ('Princess Nobuko') HT, mp, 2001, Cocker, A.G.; flowers medium pink, reverse lighter pink, 2½ in., dbl., high-centered, borne mostly solitary, moderate fragrance; foliage large, medium green, semi-glossy; prickles 9 mm., straight, moderate; upright, tall (3 ft.) growth; garden, decorative; [Pristine® × 'National Trust']; intr. 2002

'Coclucid' ('Castle of Mey') F, ob, 1992, Cocker, James; flowers orange gold, medium, dbl., borne in small clusters; foliage medium size, dark green, semi-glossy; some prickles; medium, bushy growth; [Anne Cocker® × ('Yellow Pages' × 'Silver Jubilee')]

'Coclust' ('Caring For You') HT, lp, 2000, Cocker, A.G.; flowers large, light pink, full, high-centered, borne mostly singly; foliage large, medium green, glossy; prickles moderate; upright, tall growth; [Pristine® × 'National Trust']; intr. 2000

'Cocmarris' ('Wee Cracker') F, or, 1996, Cocker, James & Sons; flowers orange vermilion, medium, dbl., borne in large clusters, slight fragrance; recurrent; foliage small, medium green, semi-glossy; some prickles; low (46-60 cm.), bushy, compact growth; ['Len Turner' × 'Jean Thomson Harris']; intr. 1995

'Cocmystery' ('Aberdeen Celebration') F, ob, Cocker; intr. 1994

'Cocnanne' ('Friend for Life') F, pb, 1993, Cocker; flowers pink, medium, 6-14 petals, borne in large clusters; foliage medium size, dark green, glossy; some prickles; medium (2½ ft.), bushy, compact growth; [seedling × (Anne Cocker® × 'Silver Jubilee')]; intr. 1994

'Cocneel' ('Ballindalloch Castle') F, dp, 1997, Cocker, Ann G.; flowers medium, very dbl., borne in large clusters; foliage medium size, medium green, glossy; some prickles; bushy, medium (2½ ft.) growth; [(Anne Cocker® × 'Maxi') × 'Silver Jubilee']; intr. 1996

'Cocnest' ('Constance Fettes') F, ab, 1993, Cocker; flowers medium, full, borne in small clusters, moderate fragrance; foliage medium size, medium green, glossy; some prickles; medium (2½ ft.), upright, bushy growth; [('Fragrant Cloud' × Alexander®) × 'Sunblest']; intr. 1993

'Cocnilly' ('Ray of Hope') F, mr, Cocker; intr. 1996

'Coco' -- See 'Korferse'

'Coco' F, yb, 1976, Fryer; flowers deep golden yellow with orange-pink, 3 in., 20-25 petals, borne in small clusters; foliage glossy; [Pernille Poulsen™ × 'Redgold']; intr. 1975

Coco® Min, op, Kordes; flowers salmon orange to salmon pink, with yellow stamens, 3 cm., single, shallow cup, borne in clusters; recurrent; compact (40 cm.) growth; intr. 2007

Coco™ Min, ob, Poulsen; flowers orange and orange blend, medium, dbl., no fragrance; growth bushy, 20-40 cm.; PP15083; intr. 2002

'Cococircus' ('Good Live') HT, op, Cocker; intr. 2001

'Cococrust' ('Alex C. Collie') F, mr, Cocker; intr. 1996

'Coconut Ice' -- See 'Horlovesong'

'Coconut Ice' HT, pb, 1991, Walker, D.R.; bud large, pointed; flowers pink blend with mauve shadings, medium, full, high-centered, borne 1-3 per stem, slight fragrance; foliage medium green, semi-glossy; tall, vigorous growth; [Alexander® × 'Vol de Nuit']

'Cocopher' ('Christopher') HT, mr, Cocker; intr. 1993

'Cocoplan' ('Where The Heart Is') HT, dp, 2002, Cocker, Anne G.; bud long; flowers cerise pink, 2½ in., full, borne mostly solitary, moderate fragrance; foliage large, medium green, glossy; prickles moderate, 9 mm., straight; growth bushy, tall (2½-3 ft.); garden decorative; ['National Trust' × 'Silver Jubilee']; intr. 2002

'Cocoray' ('Innocence 96') F, ab, 1997, Cocker, Ann G.; flowers small, 8-14 petals, borne in small clusters; foliage small, medium green, glossy; few prickles; bushy, low (2½ ft.) growth; ['Clydebank Centenary' × 'Ray of Sunshine']

'Cocorico' F, or, 1951, Meilland, F.; bud pointed; flowers geranium-red, 3 in., 8 petals, borne in clusters, moderate spicy fragrance; foliage glossy, bright; vigorous, upright, bushy growth; PP1193; ['Alain' × Orange Triumph®]; intr. 1951

'Cocorico, Climbing' Cl F, or, 1964, Ruston, D.

Cocorico® ('Birthday Girl', 'The Karnival') F, pb, Meilland; flowers ivory with rose-carmine edges, semi-dbl., cupped, borne in clusters; recurrent; foliage dark green, glossy, thick; medium growth

'Cocorona' ('Heartbeat 96', 'Heartbeat') F, ab, 1997, Cocker, Ann G.; flowers medium, dbl.; foliage medium size, medium green, glossy; some prickles; upright, medium (2½ ft.) growth

'Cocosimber' ('President Heidar Aliyev') HT, rb, 1998, Cocker, Ann G.; flowers vibrant salmon red, lighter reverse, 2-2½ in., 41 petals, borne singly or in large clusters; foliage large, dark green, glossy; prickles moderate, medium, slightly hooked; upright, medium growth; ['Silver Jubilee' × Remember Me®]; intr. 1999

'Cocotte' HT, mp, 1957, Gaujard; flowers bright salmon, large, dbl., moderate fragrance; foliage bronze; upright growth; ['Peace' × ('Fashion' × 'Vogue')]

'Cocover' ('Gwen Mayor') HT, ab, Cocker, Ann G.; flowers large, very dbl., borne mostly singly or in large clusters, moderate fragrance; foliage medium size, dark green, glossy; some prickles; bushy, upright, medium (2½ ft.)growth; ['Silver Jubilee' × Remember Me®]; intr. 1997

'Cocquamber' ('Home of Time', Adagio®) HT, r, 1998, Cocker, Ann G.; flowers cinnamon red with bronze shading, lighter reverse, 2 in., very dbl., borne mostly singly; foliage medium size, dark green, glossy; prickles moderate, medium, slightly hooked; upright, medium (2½ ft.) growth; [('Sabine' × 'Circus') × Amber Queen®]; intr. 1998

'Cocquation' ('Hi Society') F, lp, 1999, Cocker, A.; flowers lilac pink, reverse lighter, 1 in., dbl., borne in large clusters; foliage small, light green, glossy; prickles moderate; upright, bushy, medium (2-2½ ft.) growth; ['Conservation' × ('Chanelle' × ('Golden Masterpiece' × Adolf Horstmann®))]; intr. 1999

'Cocquetrum' ('Rose 2,000', 'Rose Two Thousand') F, op, 1998, Cocker, Ann G.; flowers coral vermilion, lighter reverse, ½-1½ in., 8-14 petals, borne in large clusters; foliage medium size, dark green, glossy; prickles moderate amount, small, slightly hooked; bushy, low, rounded growth; [Trumpeter® × 'Clydebank Centenary']; intr. 1998

'Cocquimmer' ('Cheerful Charlie') F, mr, 2004, Cocker, A.G.; flowers semi-dbl., borne in small clusters; foliage medium size, medium green, glossy; prickles 6 mm., straight,; growth compact, medium (2-2½ ft.); garden decorative; ['Drummer Boy' × 'Abbeyfield Rose']; slight swirling of petals; intr. 2004

'Cocquiriam' ('White Gold 98', 'White Gold') F, w, 1998, Cocker, Ann G.; flowers white with golden yellow center, opens wide and flat, 3 in., full, borne in large clusters, moderate fragrance; foliage large, medium green, semi-glossy; prickles moderate, medium, slightly hooked; tall, bushy growth; [Morning Jewel® × 'Myriam']; intr. 1998

'Cocredward' ('Marguerite Anne') F, lp, 1997, Cocker, Ann G.; flowers medium, full, borne in large clusters, moderate fragrance; foliage medium size, dark green, glossy; bushy, broad, medium (2½ ft.) growth; ['Anisley Dickson' × 'Roddy McMillan']

'Cocringer' ('Lorna') F, dp, 2003, Cocker, A.G.; flowers rich rose pink, 3 in., dbl., borne in large clusters; foliage medium size, dark green, glossy; prickles 9 mm., straight, moderate; growth bushy, medium (2½ ft.); garden decorative; ['Ginger Nut' × Memento®]; intr. 2003

'Cocrocket' ('Dorothy') F, ab, 2004, Cocker, A.G.; flowers apricot, reverse lighter, 2½ in., dbl., borne in large clusters, slight fragrance; foliage medium size, medium green, glossy; prickles 6 mm., straight; growth upright, medium (2½-3 ft.); garden decorative; ['Gingernut' × seedling]; intr. 2004

'Cocshimmer' ('Shining Light') F, ab, 2000, Cocker, A.G.; flowers apricot, reverse golden, 1 in., dbl., cupped, borne in large clusters, slight fragrance; free-flowering; foliage small, medium green, glossy; prickles moderate; growth bushy, medium (2 ft.); patio; ['Prima Ballerina' × 'Ohshima Rose']; intr. 2000

'Cocslightly' ('Eleanor Annelise') F, pb, 2002, Cocker, Anne G.; flowers peach pink, lighter reverse, 2 in., dbl., borne in large clusters, moderate fragrance; foliage medium size, very dark green, very glossy; prickles 9 mm., straight, moderate; growth upright, medium (2½ ft.); garden decorative; [Fragrant Delight® × 'Clydebank Centenary']; intr. 2002

'Cocsummery' ('Clarinda') F, mr, 2001, Cocker, A.G.; flowers medium, semi-dbl., borne in large clusters, slight fragrance; foliage medium size, dark green, glossy; prickles 6 mm., straight, moderate; growth bushy, medium (2-2½ ft.); garden decorative; ['Drummer Boy' × Playboy®]; intr. 2002

'Coctail' ('Elizabeth') F, dp, 2004, Cocker, A.G.; flowers rose pink, 1½ in., full, borne in large clusters; foliage small, medium green, glossy; prickles 6 mm., straight,; growth compact, bushy, short (2 ft.); garden decorative, containers; ['Claire Scotland' × 'Princess Alice']; intr. 2004

'Coctarlotte' ('Heart of Gold') HT, ab, 2003, Cocker, A.G.; flowers ripe peach, reverse lighter, 3 in., full, borne mostly solitary; foliage large, dark green, glossy; prickles 9 mm., straight, moderate; growth upright, medium (30-36 in.); garden decorative; ['Queen Charlotte' × 'Shirley Spain']; intr. 2003

'Cocty' HT, rb, 1972, Cocker

'Cocupland' ('Jean') F, pb, 2004, Cocker, A.G.; flowers peach pink, reverse lighter, 1½-2 in., semi-dbl., borne in large clusters; foliage small, medium green, glossy; prickles 6 mm., straight,; growth compact, bushy, short (2 ft.); garden decorative, containers; ['Claire Scotland' × Pristine®]; intr. 2004

'Cocuseful' ('Dazzling Delight') F, op, 2004, Cocker, A.G.; flowers deep salmon, reverse lighter, 2½ in., dbl., borne in large clusters, slight fragrance; foliage medium size, medium green, glossy; prickles 6 mm., straight; growth bushy, medium, garden decorative; ['Anisley Dickson' × Pristine®]; intr. 2004

'Cocwarble' F, ab, Cocker; intr. 2008

'Cocweaver' ('Sunsplash') F, ab, 2001, Cocker, A.G.; flowers light apricot, reverse cream, medium, full, quartered, borne in small clusters, moderate sweet fragrance; foliage medium size, dark green, glossy, deeply veined; prickles moderate, 6 mm., straight; growth compact, bushy, medium (2-2½ ft.); garden, decorative; ['Indian Summer' × seedling]; deeply veined leaves; intr. 2003

'Cocyearn' ('Mellow Yellow') F, yb, 2004, Cocker, A.G.; flowers golden, reverse lighter, 2½-3 in., full, borne in large clusters, moderate fragrance; foliage large, medium green, glossy; prickles 6 mm., straight; growth upright, tall (2½-3 ft.); garden decorative; ['Princess Alice' × ('Sunblest' × 'Fyvie Castle')]; intr. 2004

'Coczero' ('Iris') HT, op, 2006, Cocker, A. G.; flowers coral pink, 2½ in., full, cupped, borne singly and in large clusters; recurrent; foliage large, dark green, glossy; prickles moderate, 9 mm., straight; growth upright, bushy, medium (2½-3 ft.); garden decoration; ['Sheila's Perfume' × 'Gordon's College']; intr. 2006

'Coczodiac' ('With All My Love') HT, or, 2005, Cocker, A.G.; flowers orange/salmon/vermilion, large, very full, borne mostly solitary, slight fragrance; foliage medium size, dark green, glossy; prickles 9 mm., straight; growth upright, bushy, medium (2½-3 ft.); garden decoration; ['Fragrant Cloud' × 'Christopher']; intr. 2005

'Coczorose' F, ab, Cocker; intr. 2005

Coed™ F, my, 1971, Jelly; bud short, pointed; flowers medium, dbl., high-centered, slight fragrance; foliage dark, leathery; vigorous, upright growth; PP3166; ['Golden Garnette' × seedling]

'Coelina' -- See 'Célina'

'Coelina Dubos' -- See 'Célina Dubos'

'Coeur Aimable' HGal, m, about 1860, Miellez; flowers crimson-purple, medium, full

'Coeur d'Alene' HRg, mp; intr. 1996

'Coeur d'Amour' -- See 'Red Devil'

'Coeur de Lion' HP, mp, 1867, Paul, W.; flowers shining pink with light pink, large, dbl.

Coeur Farouche® -- See 'Delfrei'

'Coeur Noir' HGal, dr, about 1860, Miellez

'Coeur Tendre' D, dp, about 1860, Miellez

Coffee Bean™ -- See 'Wekdoudou'

'Coffee Country' -- See 'Virbrown'

'Coffee Fruitilia' -- See 'Kordwarul'

'Coffee Ovation' Min, r, de Ruiter; intr. 2000

'Cogamo' ('My Love') LCl, pb, 1996, Coggiatti, Stelvio; flowers phlox pink, reverse coral pink, cream pink at base, 4½ in., full, borne mostly singly, moderate fragrance; foliage medium size, dark green, semi-glossy to glossy; few prickles; growth spreading, tall (300 cm.); ['Caprice' × 'Peace, Climbing']; intr. 1996

'Cognac' F, ab, 1959, Tantau, Math.; flowers apricot, reverse darker, stamens dark amber, large, dbl., borne in small clusters; foliage glossy, dark olive-green; moderate growth; ['Alpine Glow' × 'Mrs Pierre S. duPont']; intr. 1956

'Cognac, Climbing' Cl F, ab, 1962, Kordes

'Coimbra' HT, dp, 1953, Moreira da Silva; flowers cerise-pink, large, dbl., high-centered; ['Heinrich Wendland' × 'Crimson Glory']

'Coistor' (Hailstorm™) S, w, 1999, Coiner, Jim; flowers 1 in., semi-dbl., borne in large clusters; foliage small, medium green, dull; prickles moderate; upright, tall (3 ft.) growth; PP13676; [seedling × seedling]; intr. 2000

Colbert® -- See 'Delcolb'

'Colby School' -- See 'Beaexam'

'Colcestria' Cl HT, pb, 1916, Cant, B. R.; flowers rose to silver-pink, reverse darker, petals reflexed, 4-5 in., dbl., borne singly or in small clusters, intense damask fragrance; foliage light

Colchester™ -- See 'Randers'

'Colchester Beauty' -- See 'Cansend'

'Colchester Castle' F, ab, Poulsen; intr. 2005

'Colchester Evening Gazette' -- See 'Colchester Gazette'

'Colchester Gazette' ('Colchester Evening Gazette') F, mr, 1972, Cants of Colchester, Ltd.; flowers bright red, 2 in., 40-50 petals, rosette, slight fragrance; foliage light; very free growth; ['Evelyn Fison' × 'Etendard']

'Coleraine' HT, lp, 1971, McGredy, Sam IV; flowers pale pink, large, 49 petals, high-centered, slight fragrance; foliage light; free growth; ['Paddy McGredy' × ('Mme Léon Cuny' × 'Columbine')]; intr. 1970

'Cole's Pink Lafayette' F, mp, 1930, Cole Nursery Co.; flowers rose-pink, semi-dbl.; [sport of 'Lafayette']

'Cole's Settlement' S, w, 2006, Shoup, George Michael; flowers single, borne in small clusters, moderate fragrance; remontant; foliage large, medium green, semi-glossy; few prickles; growth bushy, tall, (6 ft.); hedging; [(('Carefree Beauty' × Heritage®) × 'Bayse's Blueberry') × Heritage®]; intr. 1998

'Coletta Montanelli' HT, dy, 1976, Kordes; bud globular; flowers deep yellow, 4 in., 32 petals, high-centered, slight fragrance; foliage dark, soft; vigorous, upright, bushy growth; [seedling × Peer Gynt®]; intr. 1975

'Colette' N, pb, 1932, Schwartz, A.; flowers nankeen yellow at center, shaded salmon-pink, large; foliage glossy, light; very vigorous growth; RULED EXTINCT 7/90; ['William Allen Richardson' × 'Mme Laurette Messimy']

'Colette' -- See 'Jaccol'

Colette™ -- See 'Meiroupis'

'Colette Berges' HT, mr, 1940, Dot, Pedro; flowers crimson, medium, 45 petals, high-centered, moderate damask fragrance; vigorous growth; ['Red Columbia' × 'Ami Quinard']

'Colette Clément' HT, ob, 1932, Mallerin, C.; flowers reddish-orange, medium, semi-dbl.; foliage glossy, dark; vigorous growth; [(('Mme Mélanie Soupert' × 'Mme Edouard Herriot') × ('Mrs Edward Powell' × R. foetida bicolor)]

'Colette Jelot' F, yb, 1942, Meilland, F.; flowers amber-yellow shaded currant-red, open, medium, semi-dbl., borne in clusters; foliage soft; dwarf growth; ['Ampere' × ('Charles P. Kilham' × ('Charles P. Kilham' × 'Capucine Chambard'))]

'Colette Pappin Glynn' -- See 'Seaco-

lette'
'Colfragrasar' ('Nuage Parfumé, Climbing') Cl HT, or, 1974, Collin, W.C.
'Colibre' -- See 'Meimal'
Colibre 79® ('Colibre 80', 'Star Trail') Min, ob, Meilland; flowers golden yellow, edged and veined orange; intr. 1979
'Colibre 80' -- See 'Meidanover'
'Colibri' HMult, rb, before 1855; flowers violet, center scarlet, small to medium, full; growth vigorous, climbing
'Colibri' Pol, ly, Lille; flowers soft yellow, fading; intr. 1898
'Colibri' ('Colibre') Min, ob, Meilland, F.; bud ovoid; flowers bright orange-yellow, small, dbl., borne in clusters, slight fragrance; foliage glossy; bushy growth; ['Goldilocks' × 'Perla de Montserrat']; intr. 1958
'Colibri Meillandina' Min, ob, Meilland; flowers coppery ocher , 45 petals, cupped; recurrent; foliage bright green; 30 - 40 cm. growth; intr. 2008
'Colin Kelly' HT, dp, 1945, Krebs; bud pointed; flowers cerise-red, very large, dbl., intense fragrance; foliage leathery; upright, bushy growth; PP752; ['E.G. Hill' × 'The Queen Alexandra Rose']
'Colin Kelly, Climbing' Cl HT, dp, Marsh's Nursery
'Colinda' -- See 'Jacredi'
'Colin's Fubar' -- See 'Seafubar'
'Colin's Salmon' HT, op, Bell, Ronald J.; [sport of 'Bel Ange']; intr. 1970
'Colisée' ('Colysée') F, mr, 1965, Gaujard; bud pointed; flowers coppery pink, open, medium, semi-dbl.; foliage dark, glossy; very vigorous, bushy growth; [Atlantic® × 'Circus']
'Colleen' HT, mp, 1914, McGredy; bud high pointed; flowers bright rose shaded rose-pink, large, dbl.; vigorous growth
'Colleen' HT, pb, Kordes; flowers large, creamy white and pink blend, dbl.; medium to tall growth; intr. 1994
'Colleen Little' -- See 'Leecal'
Colleen Mary™ -- See 'Meikentuk'
'Colleen Moore' HT, dr, 1944, Joseph H. Hill, Co.; flowers velvety carmine, open, 4-4½ in., dbl., intense fragrance; foliage leathery, dark; strong stems; vigorous, upright growth; PP582; [(('De Luxe' × 'Senior') × 'Premier') × 'Chieftain']
'College Avenue Columbia' HT, dp
'College Avenue #10' -- See 'Heinrich Wendland'
'Collegiate 110' -- See 'Dicknowall'
'Collegiate Pride' HT, mr, Bell; intr. 1989
'Cologne' -- See 'Macsupbow'
'Cologne' -- See 'Köln am Rhein'
'Cologne Carnival' ('Blue Girl', 'Kölner Karneval') HT, m, 1965, Kordes, R.; flowers silvery lilac-lavender, 5½ in., 35-40 petals, high-centered, borne singly, moderate lightly fruity fragrance; foliage large, deep green; vigorous, bushy growth; intr. 1964
'Coloma's Gold' Min, yb, Fischer; [sport of 'Work of Art']; intr. 1998
'Colombe' HT, Croix, P.; intr. 1976

Colombina® HT, pb, Barni, V.; flowers white with deep pink edges which spread with age, dbl., high-centered, borne mostly singly, no fragrance; few prickles; growth to 3 ft.; intr. 1985
'Colombine' -- See 'Columbine'
'Colonel Campbell Watson' HT, mp, 1936, Bees; bud pointed; flowers salmon-pink, dbl., high-centered; foliage soft; long stems; vigorous growth; ['Joan Howarth' × 'Portadown']
'Colonel Combe' B, m, 1856, Pradel; flowers lilac pink, globular, moderate fragrance
'Colonel Dazier' HT, w, 1927, Ketten Bros.; flowers rosy white, reverse bright rose, base golden yellow, dbl.; ['Le Progrés' × 'Jonkheer J.L. Mock']
'Colonel de Rougemont' HP, pb, 1853, Lacharme
'Colonel de Sansal' HP, mr, 1875, Jamain, H.; flowers velvety carmine shaded deep carmine, large, full
'Colonel Félix Breton' HP, rb, 1883, Schwartz; flowers velvety grenadine red at center, outer petals violet, amaranth reverse, large, full, borne singly or in small clusters; foliage light green; prickles moderate, red, slightly hooked
'Colonel Foissy' HP, mp, 1849, Margottin; sepals often foliaceous; flowers bright cherry-cerise, medium, dbl., borne in clusters of 5-10; foliage dark green, irregularly dentate; prickles very numerous, reddish
'Colonel Gravereaux' HT, op, 1940, Mallerin, C.; flowers salmon-coral, reverse yellow; strong stems; vigorous, upright growth
'Colonel Joffé' T, mr, 1893, Liabaud; flowers purplish red, petals wrinkled, flat
'Colonel Leclerc' HT, mp, 1909, Pernet-Ducher; flowers Tyrian pink, dbl.; ['Mme Caroline Testout' × 'Horace Vernet']
'Colonel Lindbergh' Pol, op, 1928, Kromhout; flowers salmon-orange; [sport of 'Juliana Rose']
'Colonel Nicolas Meyer' HT, mr, 1934, Sauvageot, H.; bud pointed; flowers brilliant velvety red, open, dbl.; foliage leathery; strong stems; vigorous, bushy growth; ['La Maréchale Petain' × 'Edouard Mignot']
'Colonel Oswald Fitzgerald' HT, dr, 1917, Dickson, A.; flowers dark velvety crimson, well-formed, dbl.; vigorous, branching growth
'Colonel R. S. Williamson' HT, lp, 1907, Dickson, A.; flowers white, center deep blush, large, dbl., high-centered; foliage glossy, dark; vigorous, open growth
'Colonel R. S. Williamson, Climbing' Cl HT, w, 1920, Dingee & Conard; [sport of 'Colonel R. S. Williamson']
'Colonel Robert Lefort' M, dr, 1864, Verdier, E.; flowers purple-red
'Colonel Sharman-Crawford' HT, mr, 1933, Dickson, A.; flowers rich velvety crimson, large, dbl., high-centered; foliage leathery; long, strong stems;

vigorous, bushy growth
'Colonel Souflot' HP, mr, 1862, Vigneron
'Colonel Svec' -- See 'Plukovnik Svec'
'Colonel Tillier' B, m; flowers lilac pink, medium, full
Colonia® -- See 'Meilider'
'Colonial Days' -- See 'Gelcol'
'Colonial White' -- See 'Sombreuil'
'Color Burst' -- See 'Twocherish'
'Color Carnival' -- See 'Colour Carnival'
'Color Girl' F, pb, 1966, Fuller; bud ovoid; flowers whitish, edged red, medium, dbl., high-centered; foliage dark, leathery; bushy, low growth; ['Little Darling' × 'Cocorico']
'Color-Guard' -- See 'Kejgard'
'Color Guard' -- See 'Jolcol'
'Color Magic' HT, pb, 1977, Warriner, William A.; bud long; flowers pale salmon blushing pink, 5 in., 25-30 petals, flat, borne singly, intense fruity fragrance; foliage large, dark green; upright growth; PP3998; [seedling × 'Spellbinder']; intr. 1978
'Color Me Pink' HT, pb; bud pointed, ovoid; flowers pink with cream reverse, 5 in., 40 petals, cupped, borne singly and in small clusters, moderate tea fragrance; foliage dark green, glossy; growth to 5-6 ft.; PPAF; [Touch of Class™® × unknown]; intr. 2007
'Color Purple' -- See 'Clepurp'
'Color Purple' -- See 'Jalpurple'
'Color Wonder' Min, yb, Clements, John; flowers bright yellow, changing to wine purple, 1¼ in., 5 petals; continuous bloom; bushy growth, 2½-3 ft high, 2 ft wide; intr. 2001
'Colorado' HT, Combe, M.; intr. 1970
'Colorado' F, mp, Select Roses, B.V.
'Colorama' ('Colourama', 'Dr R. Maag') HT, rb, 1968, Meilland, Mrs. Marie-Louise; bud ovoid; flowers red with yellow reverse, large, dbl., cupped, moderate fragrance; foliage very glossy; vigorous, upright, bushy growth; PP2862; ['Suspense' × 'Confidence']
'Coloranja' -- See 'Mustang'
'Colorbreak' -- See 'Macultra'
'Colorburst' ('Color Burst') Gr, dp, Twomey, Jerry; flowers borne in small clusters; good repeat; PP10113; intr. 1995
'Coloso' HT, mp, 1962, Dot, Simon; flowers 50 petals; very vigorous growth; ['Chrysler Imperial' × ('Peace' × Queen Elizabeth®)]
'Colossal' -- See 'Meiclosal'
'Colossal Meidiland' ('Colossal') S, mr, Meilland; flowers bright red, medium size, dbl., borne in clusters; recurrent bloom; intr. 2000
Colossus™ -- See 'Persus'
Colour™ -- See 'Poulrolyt'
'Colour Carnival' ('Color Carnival') F, yb, 1962, LeGrice; flowers primrose-yellow edged pink, well-formed, 3 in., 50 petals, borne in clusters; vigorous, low, bushy growth; intr. 1962
'Colour Glow' F, ob, 1971, Butter; flow-

ers orange, reddening to flame, large, 36 petals, globular, slight fragrance; vigorous growth; ['Tropicana' × 'Masquerade']; intr. 1969

'Colour Harmony'   HT, pb, Ghosh; intr. 1998

'Colour Hit' -- See 'Poulrolyt'

'Colour Magic'   MinFl, pb; intr. 1999

'Colour Parade' ('Colour Hit', Colour™, 'Colour Patiohit') MinFl, or, Poulsen; bud long, pointed, ovoid; flowers orange-red, 5 cm., 25-35 petals, borne usually in small clusters, very slight fragrance; recurrent; foliage dark green, glossy; prickles average, 3-4 mm., straight; bushy, compact (20-40 cm.) growth; PP13138; [seedling × 'Charming Parade']; intr. 1998

'Colour Parade' -- See 'Lavcoat'

'Colour Patiohit' -- See 'Poulrolyt'

'Colour Sergeant'   F, or, 1972, Harkness; flowers 4 in., 20 petals; foliage glossy; [Queen Elizabeth® × ('Ann Elizabeth' × 'Circus')]; intr. 1970

'Colour Wonder'   HT, pb, Dey, S. C.; flowers large, creamy ivory to apricot-pink to light red; intr. 2000

'Colour Wonder' ('Königin der Rosen', 'Queen of Roses', 'Reine des Roses') HT, ob, 1964, Kordes, R.; bud ovoid; flowers orange-coral, reverse cream, large, 50 petals, slight fragrance; recurrent; foliage glossy, bronze; prickles numerous, large; vigorous, bushy growth; ['Kordes' Perfecta' × 'Tropicana']; intr. 1964

'Colourama' -- See 'Meirigalu'

'Colourbox'   F, yb, Benardella, Frank; intr. 2001

'Coluche'   F, mr; flowers luminous red, dbl., borne in large clusters; recurrent; foliage semi-glossy; growth to 60-80 cm.; intr. 2002

'Columbia'   HWich, mp, 1903, Hooper Bro. & Thomas; non-recurrent; moderately vigorous growth; [seedling × 'Mme Caroline Testout']

'Columbia'   HT, mp, E.G. Hill, Co.; bud long, pointed; flowers glistening rose-pink, large, 65 petals, intense fragrance; foliage dark; vigorous growth; ['Ophelia' × 'Mrs George Shawyer']; intr. 1916

'Columbia, Climbing' ('Columbian Climber') Cl HT, mp, 1920, Totty (also Hill (1920), Vestal (1923), and Lens); bud very large, long-pointed; flowers pink changing to brighter pink, large, very full; [sport of 'Columbia']

'Columbian Climber' -- See 'Columbia, Climbing'

'Columbine' ('Colombine') F, yb, 1956, Poulsen, S.; flowers creamy yellow tinged pink, well-formed, borne in open clusters; foliage glossy; vigorous growth; ['Danish Gold' × 'Frensham']

Columbine™ -- See 'Poulra001(N)'

'Columbine Parade' (Columbine™, Monica™) MinFl, lp, Poulsen; flowers light pink, 5-8 cm., dbl., no fragrance; foliage dark; growth bushy, 20-40 cm.; PP13487; intr. 2000

Columbus™ -- See 'Wekuz'

'Columbus Queen'   HT, pb, 1962, Armstrong, D.L., & Swim, H. C.; bud ovoid, pointed; flowers light pink, reverse darker, 4 in., 24-30 petals, high-centered, slight fragrance; foliage leathery, dark; vigorous, upright growth; PP2170; ['La Jolla' × seedling]; intr. 1962

'Columella' ('Colmelle') HGal, dr, 1841, Vibert; flowers rich rosy crimson, often shaded violet, medium, full, cupped

'Columelle'   HGal, m, 1860, Moreau et Robert; flowers lilac-pink center, lighter at edges, very full; sometimes classed as D

'Columelle' -- See 'Columella'

'Colysée' -- See 'Colisée'

'Comanche'   Gr, or, 1968, Swim & Weeks; bud pointed; flowers bright, medium, dbl., high-centered; foliage leathery; vigorous, upright, bushy growth; PP2855; ['Spartan' × ('Carrousel' × 'Happiness')]

'Combar' -- See 'Barricade'

'Come Lei'   HT, Giacomasso; intr. 1968

'Comedie'   F, Combe, M.; intr. 1977

'Comedy' -- See 'Gelco'

'Comendador Nogueira da Silva'   HT, rb, 1961, Moreira da Silva; flowers dark red, reverse silvery; ['Confidence' × 'Independence']

'Comet'   Cl F, pb, 1934, Mesman; flowers flesh pink, shaded salmon-yellow, large, very dbl., slight fragrance; foliage leathery; short, strong stems; [sport of 'Gruss an Aachen']

Comet Tail™   F, m, Zary; flowers striped

'Comice de Seine-et-Marne'   Ch, mr, 1842, Desprez; flowers scarlet, shaded carmine, full, cupped

'Comice de Tarn-et-Garonne'   B, mr, 1852, Pradel; flowers carmine red, medium, full, intense fragrance

'Command Performance'   HT, or, 1970, Lindquist; bud ovoid; flowers medium, dbl., high-centered, intense fragrance; foliage leathery; vigorous, tall, bushy growth; PP3063; ['Tropicana' × 'Hawaii']

'Commandant Beaurepaire' ('Panachée d'Angers') HP, pb, 1875, Moreau-Robert; flowers intense rose pink, striped purple and violet, spotted white, large, dbl., cupped; occasional repeat; foliage light green; prickles spiny; vigorous growth; originally put in commerce under this name and classified as HGal; later renamed Panachée d'Angers and reclassed after some remontancy was noted

'Commandant Cousteau' -- See 'Adharman'

'Commandant Cousteau, Climbing' ('Grand Huit, Climbing', Grimpant Le Grand Huit®, 'Le Grand Huit, Climbing', 'Red Flame') Cl HT, dr, Adam; flowers velvety dark red, dbl., moderate fragrance; recurrent; foliage dark green to reddish green; vigorous (10 ft.) growth; [sport of 'Commandant Cousteau']; intr. 2004

'Commandant Félix Faure'   HP, mr, 1901, Boutigny; flowers light crimson-red, tinted vermilion, 25 petals, cupped; vigorous, upright growth

'Commandant L. Bartre'   HT, rb, 1920, Schwartz, A.; flowers dark carmine-red, tinted brilliant pink, dbl.; vigorous growth; ['Lady Ashtown' × 'Louis van Houtte']

'Commandant Letourneux'   HT, dp, 1903, Bahaud; flowers carmine-pink, very large, very dbl.; [sport of 'Joséphine Marot']

'Commandant Mansuy'   HP, mr, 1869, Vigneron; flowers fire-red, large, full

'Commandant Marchand'   T, my, 1900, Puyravaud; flowers yellow, center darker, petals edged cream, large, full, moderate fragrance; ['Gloire de Dijon' × unknown]

'Commandatore Francesco Ingegnoli'   Cl HT, or, 1923, Ingegnoli; flowers geranium-red

'Commander Gillette' ('Basye's Thornless') S, mp; flowers single; some repeat; thornless; [R. carolina alba × 'Hugh Dickson']; intr. before 1990

'Com. Sukumar Da'   HT, lp, Pushpanjali; flowers ivory pink, moderate fragrance; intr. 1997

'Commandeur Jules Gravereaux'   HP, mr, 1908, Croibier; bud pointed; flowers dazzling red, center shaded maroon, large, peony-like, dbl.; vigorous growth; ['Frau Karl Druschki' × 'Liberty']

'Commandeur Jules Gravereaux, Climbing'   Cl HP, mr, 1925, Belouet

'Commando'   HT, op, 1945, Howard, F.H.; bud long, pointed; flowers orange-buff, suffused pink, 5 in., 30-35 petals, camellia-like, moderate fragrance; foliage leathery, glossy; upright, bushy growth; PP702; ['Mrs J.D. Eisele' × 'Glowing Sunset']

'Commitment' -- See 'Clement'

'Common Blush China' -- See 'Old Pink Daily'

'Common Centifolia' -- See 'Cabbage Rose'

'Common China' -- See 'Old Pink Daily'

'Common Monthly' -- See 'Old Pink Daily'

'Common Moss' -- See 'Centifolia Muscosa'

'Common Pink China' ('Blush Monthly', 'Monthly Rose', 'Pallida', 'Common Monthly', 'Common China', 'Common Blush China') Ch, mp, 1751, Parsons; flowers two-tone pink, semi-dbl., borne in loose sprays; dependably recurrent; vigorous, upright growth

'Common Pompon' -- See R. × centifolia pomponia

'Common Purple Boursault' -- See 'Reversa'

'Common Red China' -- See 'Slater's Crimson China'

'Commonwealth'   HT, dp, 1923, Montgomery Co.; bud pointed; flowers deep pink, large, dbl., moderate fragrance; foliage leathery, rich green; ['Ophelia' × seedling]

'Commonwealth' ('Herzblut') F, pb, Kordes; flowers crimson with white eye, 10 petals, borne in clusters, slight fragrance; foliage leathery; ['Col. Nicolas Meyer' × 'Holstein']; intr. 1948

'Commonwealth Glory' ('Bérénice') HT, ab, Harkness; flowers large, peach-apricot in center, outer petals pearly pink to ivory, 7 in., 30-35 petals, high-centered, borne mostly singly, moderate fruity fragrance; recurrent; foliage glossy; stems long; upright (3-5 ft.) growth; intr. 1998

'Communique' S, pb, Williams, J.B.; flowers soft pink with ivory center, semi-dbl., flat, moderate fragrance; recurrent; growth to 3 ft.; intr. 2006

'Communis' -- See 'Centifolia Muscosa'

'Community Banquet' HT, lp, 2007, Bell, Ron; flowers large, 10 cm., full, borne mostly solitary; foliage medium size, dark green, semi-glossy; prickles medium, hooked, brown, few; growth upright, medium (1½ m.); garden decorative; [('Daily Sketch' × unknown) × 'Red Planet']; intr. 2007

'Compactilla' HSpn, ly; flowers small, creamy ivory with yellow stamens, single

Compassion® ('Belle de Londres') LCl, op, 1973, Harkness; flowers salmon pink shaded apricot, large, 36 petals, borne singly or in small clusters, moderate sweet fragrance; foliage large, dark; prickles large, reddish; medium, bushy growth; ['White Cockade' × 'Prima Ballerina']

'Compassionate Friend' -- See 'Harzodiac'

'Compassionate Friends' -- See 'Walfriends'

'Complicata' ('Ariana d'Algier', *R. gallica complicata*) HGal, pb; flowers deep pink, white eye, yellow stamens, large, single; rampant (to 6 ft.) growth; probably *R. gallica* × *R. canina*

'Compostelle' S, w, Harkness; flowers ivory with pink tones in center, double, cupped, borne in clusters, moderate spice & fruit fragrance; recurrent; moderate (60 - 70 cm.) growth; intr. 2008

'Comptoir des Bourbons' B, mp

'Comrade' HT, mr, 1948, Dickson, A.; flowers scarlet-crimson, well-formed, medium

'Comsan' (Cosmos®) HT, w, Combe; intr. 1993

'Comsor' (Schwarze Rose®) HT, dr, 1973, Combe; intr. 1971

'Comte Adrien de Germiny' HP, mp, 1881, Lévêque; flowers bright rose pink, large, full; very remontant; foliage dark green; ['Jules Margottin' × unknown]

'Comte Alphonse de Serenyi' HP, pb, 1865, Touvais; flowers bright carmine, shaded purple and garnet, large, full

'Comte Amédé de Foras' T, pb, 1900, Gamon; flowers China pink shaded with saffron, full, moderate sweet fragrance; ['Luciole' × 'G. Nabonnand']

'Comte Bobrinsky' -- See 'Comte de Bobrinsky'

'Comte Boula de Nanteuil' -- See 'Boula de Nanteuil'

'Comte Cavour' ('Comte de Cavour') HP, pb, Liabaud; intr. 1859

'Comte Cavour' HP, mp, 1856, Vigneron; flowers bright pink, large, full, moderate fragrance

'Comte Chandon' T, my, 1894, Soupert & Notting; flowers outer petals light yellow, center bright chrome yellow, large, full; ['Lutea Flora' × 'Coquette de Lyon']

'Comte Charles d'Harcourt' HP, mr, 1897, Lévêque; flowers bright carmine red, large, full; foliage dark green

'Comte de Beaufort' HP, m, 1858, Boyau; flowers purple, shaded darker, medium, full

'Comte de Bobrinsky' ('Bobrinski', 'Count Bawbrinzki', 'Comte Bobrinsky') HCh, dp, 1849, Marest; flowers carmine-pink, medium, dbl.; sometimes classed as HP

'Comte de Boubert' Ch, lp, before 1855; flowers bright pink, shaded flesh pink, large, full

'Comte de Cavour' -- See 'Comte Cavour'

'Comte de Chambord' P, pb, about 1860, Moreau-Robert; flowers pink tinted lilac, very dbl., flat, intense fragrance; vigorous, erect growth; confused in commerce with Mme Boll

'Comte de Colbert' -- See 'Comtesse de Colbert'

'Comte de Falloux' HP, dp, 1863, Trouillard or Standish; flowers crimson-pink; intr. 1863

'Comte de Flandres' HP, dr, 1881, Lévêque, P.; flowers velvety blackish purple red, shaded carmine, very large, full; foliage brownish-green; ['Mme Victor Verdier' × unknown]

'Comte de Grassin' HP, dp, 1890, Corboeuf; flowers dark pink, shaded carmine, large, full; ['General Jacqueminot' × 'La France']

'Comte de Grivel' T, ly, 1871, Levet; flowers straw yellow, dbl.

'Comte de Montalivet' HP, 1846, Mondeville

'Comte de Montessier' HP, mp, 1852, Berger

'Comte de Montijo' B, m, 1855, Fontaine; flowers velvety dark purple, shaded violet, full

'Comte de Mortemart' HP, mp, 1880, Margottin fils; flowers clear pink, very large, full, intense fragrance

'Comte de Murinais' HGal, dr; flowers slate-red, marbled, large

'Comte de Nanteuil' HGal, pb, Quétier; flowers bright rose with crimson edges, sometimes with a green center, large, dbl., cupped; vigorous growth; ['Boule de Nanteuil' × unknown]; intr. 1852

'Comte de Nanteuil' -- See 'Boula de Nanteuil'

'Comte de Paris' HP, m, Laffay, M.; flowers purplish pink, very large, full, cupped; very remontant; growth erect; intr. 1839

'Comte de Paris' T, lp, 1839, Hardy; flowers very large, full, moderate fragrance

'Comte de Paris' HP, dp, Verdier, E.; flowers pink over cherry, large, full; intr. 1864

'Comte de Paris' HP, rb, Lévêque; flowers poppy red, shaded with bright purple and crimson, large, full; intr. 1886

'Comte de Raimbaud' -- See 'Comte Raimbaud'

'Comte de Sembui' -- See 'Jean Ducher'

'Comte de Taverna' T, ly, 1872, Ducher; flowers whitish yellow, darker at center, large, very full

'Comte de Thun-Hohenstein' -- See 'Comte Frédéric de Thun-Hohenstein'

'Comte de Torres' Cl HT, op, 1906, Schwartz, A.; flowers coppery salmon-pink, large, dbl., borne in small to medium clusters; prickles large; ['Kaiserin Auguste Viktoria' × 'Mme Bérard']

'Comte d'Epremesnil' HRg, m, 1882, Nabonnand; flowers violet-pink, large, semi-dbl.

'Comte d'Eu' B, mr, 1844, Lacharme

'Comte F. de Chavagnac, Climbing' Cl HT, op, 1929, Siret-Pernet; flowers orange pink, rosy carmine at center, medium, full; foliage light green; nearly thornless; ['Antoine Rivoire' × 'Zéphirine Drouhin']

'Comte F. de Chavagnac' HT, mp, before 1929; flowers peach-blossom-pink, center rosy carmine; ['Antoine Rivoire' × 'Zéphirine Drouhin']

'Comte Florimond de Bergeyck' HP, rb, 1879, Soupert & Notting; flowers pink-brick, tinted orange-red, large, very full

'Comte Foy' ('Comte Foy de Rouen') HGal, lp, 1827, Lecomte; flowers pale rose, aging lilac, whitish-violet at edges, very large, dbl., cupped, borne singly or in clusters of 2-3, slight fragrance; foliage small, round, light green; no prickles

'Comte Foy' ('Admirable Panachée') HGal, rb; flowers white, striped red

'Comte Foy de Rouen' -- See 'Comte Foy'

'Comte Frédéric de Thun-Hohenstein' ('Comte de Thun-Hohenstein') HP, dr, 1880, Lévêque; flowers deep reddish-crimson, tinted carmine, large, full, moderate fragrance; foliage large, dark green; prickles numerous, small, white

'Comte G. de Rochemur' HT, 1911, Schwartz, A.; flowers bright scarlet, large, dbl.; ['Xavier Olibo' × 'Gruss an Teplitz']

'Comte G. de Roquette-Buisson' T, mp, 1887, Nabonnand; flowers bright pink, large, very full, moderate fragrance; ['Reine Maria Pia' × unknown]

'Comte Galatine' HT, pb, 1901, Brauer;

flowers dark flesh pink, shaded yellow-red, reverse carmine

'Comte H. de Choiseul' HFt, op, 1894, Pernet-Ducher; flowers salmon-orange, salmon-pink at center, shaded yellow at base, large, full; ['Lady Mary Fitzwilliam' × 'Souv de Mme Levet']

'Comte Henri Rignon' HT, yb, 1885, Pernet-Ducher; flowers coppery yellow with salmon pink center, large to very large, full, cupped; ['Baronne Adolphe de Rothschild' × 'Ma Capucine']

'Comte Horace de Choiseul' HP, mr, 1879, Lévêque; flowers fiery vermilion with scarlet, velvety, large, full, moderate fragrance

'Comte Lelieur' ('Lee's Crimson Perpetual', 'Rose Lelieur', 'Rose du Roi', *R. paestana*) P, mr, about 1819, Souchet or Ecoffé; flowers bright red shaded violet, large, semi-dbl., intense fragrance; remontant bloom; foliage clear green, slightly fluted; vigorous growth; cultivar widely sold under this name may be misidentified

'Comte Litta' HP, rb, 1866, Verdier, E.; flowers velvety scarlet, shaded grenadine-violet, large, full

'Comte Odart' HP, mr, 1850, Dupuy-Jamain; flowers bright red, aging to violet, 8-9 cm., full, quartered; foliage rounded, dark green; prickles nearly straight, deep maroon, numerous; stems short, brown-green

'Comte Raimbaud' ('Comte de Raimbaud') HP, mr, 1867, Rolland; flowers crimson, large, dbl.

'Comte Raoul Chandon' HP, rb, 1896, Lévêque; flowers vermilion tinted with brown, large, full

'Comte-Robert' -- See 'Maurice Bernardin'

'Comteri' LCl, ab, Combe, M.; intr. 1976

'Comtes des Champagne' -- See 'Ausufo'

Comtessa® HT, ly, Tantau; flowers cream colored, large, full, cupped to flat, intense fragrance; heavy bloomer; intr. 2007

'Comtesse Alban de Villeneuve' T, pb, 1881, Nabonnand; flowers coppery pink, shaded scarlet, full; growth vigorous

'Comtesse Anna Thun' T, yb, 1887, Soupert & Notting; flowers golden orange-yellow, large, full, cupped, intense fragrance; ['Sylphide' × 'Mme Camille']

'Comtesse Anne de Bruce' HT, pb, 1937, Mallerin, C.; bud pointed; flowers coppery pink to nasturtium-red, very large, semi-dbl., cupped; foliage glossy; very vigorous growth; ['Charles P. Kilham' × ('Mrs Pierre S. duPont' × (*R. foetida bicolor* × unknown))]

'Comtesse Antonia Migazzi' HP, mp, 1889, Benkö, Dr.; flowers silvery rose, large, full; [sport of 'Mabel Morrison']

'Comtesse Barbantane' -- See 'Comtesse de Barbantane'

'Comtesse Bardi' ('Comtesse de Bardi') T, yb, 1896, Soupert & Notting; flowers dull reddish-yellow, center coral-red with gold tints, large, dbl., moderate fragrance; ['Rêve d'Or' × 'Mme Lombard']

'Comtesse Bardi' T, yb, Nabonnand; flowers canary-yellow, center fawn, edges shaded carmine, large, dbl.; ['Safrano' × 'Château des Bergeries']; intr. 1900

'Comtesse Beatrix de Buisseret' -- See 'Beatrix, Comtesse de Buisseret'

'Comtesse Bertrand de Blacas' HP, mp, 1888, Verdier, E.; flowers soft bright rose, large, full, globular, cupped; foliage very large, light green, elliptical, irregularly serrated; prickles few, straight, pink; growth erect

'Comtesse Branicka' HP, lp, 1888, Lévêque; flowers delicate silvery pink, large, dbl.

Comtesse Brigitte Chandon-Moet® HT, ab, Dorieux; flowers champagne with salmon tints, large; intr. 1996

Comtesse Brigitte de la Roche Foucauld® S, pb, Dorieux; flowers deep pink, striped white, petals notched, large, intense fragrance; flexible (4 - 5 ft.) growth; intr. 2001

'Comtesse Cahen d'Anvers' HP, mp, 1885, Lédéchaux; flowers deep pink, large, dbl., globular, moderate fragrance; foliage dark green; growth upright; ['La Reine' × unknown]

'Comtesse Cécile de Chabrillant' HP, pb, 1858, Marest; flowers satiny pink, silvery reverse, medium, dbl., globular; foliage dark, leathery; prickles numerous small, dark; ['Jules Margottin' × unknown]

'Comtesse Cécile de Forton' Cl T, pb, 1916, Nabonnand, G.; flowers rose-peach, very large, dbl.

'Comtesse d'Alcantara' -- See 'Kribatis'

'Comtesse d'Ansembourg' HT, ly, 1918, Leenders, M.; flowers yellowish-white, dbl.; ['Étoile de France' × 'Marquise de Sinéty']

'Comtesse de Baillet' HGal, w, 1827, from Courtray

'Comtesse de Barbantane' ('Comtesse Barbantane') B, lp, 1858, Guillot Père; flowers blush, shaded with rose, large, full, cupped, borne in small clusters; ['Reine des Ile-Bourbons' × unknown]; sometimes classed as HP

'Comtesse de Bardi' -- See 'Comtesse Bardi'

'Comtesse de Bouchard' -- See 'Comtesse de Bouchaud'

'Comtesse de Bouchaud' ('Comtesse de Bouchard') N, my, 1890, Guillot et Fils; flowers saffron yellow, very large

'Comtesse de Bresson' HP, lp, 1873, Guinoiseau, B.; flowers bright pink, petal edges white, large, dbl.; ['Jules Margottin' × unknown]

'Comtesse de Brossard' T, my, 1862, Oger; flowers canary yellow, medium, full

'Comtesse de Camondo' -- See 'Mme la Comtesse de Camondo'

'Comtesse de Caserta' ('Mme la Comtesse de Caserta') T, mr, 1877, Nabonnand, G.; flowers coppery-red, large

'Comtesse de Cassagne' HT, op, 1919, Guillot, M.; flowers coppery rose, shaded bright rose, sometimes entirely yellow, large, dbl., moderate fragrance

'Comtesse de Castilleja' HT, op, 1926, Chambard, M.; bud orange; flowers coral, cupped; foliage dark; strong stems; very vigorous growth; [('Mme Edouard Herriot' × 'Juliet') × seedling]

'Comtesse de Chabrillant Blanche' -- See 'Mme Lefrançois'

'Comtesse de Chamoïs' ('À Balais', 'À Bordures', 'Chamoïs', 'Fasciculée', 'Fastigiata', 'Rose Bordée de Blanc') C, mp, about 1810, Descemet; flowers small, full, semi-globular; foliage large, oval-rounded; growth vertical

'Comtesse de Chaponnay' HG, lp, 1924, Nabonnand, P.; flowers creamy pink, center bright salmon-pink, very large, full, cupped, strong fragrance; [*R. gigantea* × 'Mme Hoste']

'Comtesse de Choiseul' -- See 'Mlle Marie Rady'

'Comtesse de Colbert' ('Comte de Colbert') B, m, about 1846, from Angers; flowers purple, medium, full

'Comtesse de Coursy' HP, dp, 1862, Lévêque; flowers pink over red

'Comtesse de Coutard' HCh, mp, 1829, Noisette, E.; flowers large, very dbl., borne in clusters of 5-7; foliage elongate, glabrous, lightly dentate; prickles numerous, unequal

'Comtesse de Falloux' HP, mp, 1867, Trouillard; flowers pink, nuanced mauve, very large, very full

'Comtesse de Flandres' HP, lp, 1878, Verdier, E.; flowers light silvery pink, center bright pink, large, dbl., cupped; foliage delicate green, deeply toothed; few prickles; growth upright

'Comtesse de Fresnel' N, m, before 1835, Prévost; flowers lilac pink, with dark pink-purple, medium, full

'Comtesse de Fressinet de Bellanger' HP, lp, 1885, Lévêque; flowers flesh pink, very large, full; foliage light green

'Comtesse de Frigneuse' T, my, 1885, Guillot et Fils; flowers large, dbl.; ['Mme Damaizin' × unknown]

'Comtesse de Galard-Béarn' N, ly, 1893, Bernaix, A.; flowers light yellow with pink tones, 7-9 cm., dbl., strong tea fragrance

'Comtesse de Greffulhe' HP, pb, 1896, Lévêque; flowers carmine, shaded fiery red with dark purple, large, full

'Comtesse de Jaucourt' -- See 'Mme la Comtesse de Jaucourt'

'Comtesse de la Morandière' HT, op, 1929, Chambard, C.; flowers shrimp-pink, reverse coral-red, dbl.

'Comtesse de Labarthe' -- See 'Duchesse de Brabant'

'Comtesse de Lacépède' ('Comtesse Lacépède') HGal, lp, 1840, Duval/Verdier; flowers silvery blush, center sometimes rosy, large, dbl.; moderate growth; sometimes classed as HCh

'Comtesse de Leusse'   T, mp, 1878, Nabonnand; flowers large, soft medium pink, dbl.

'Comtesse de Ludre'   HP, mr, 1879, Verdier; flowers carmine, edged white, very large, full, cupped, strong fragrance

'Comtesse de Marnes'   HP, pb, 1854, Desprez; flowers lilac pink, shaded dark crimson, large, full

'Comtesse de Martel'   HT, mp, 1939, Meilland, F.; flowers carnation-pink, center coppery, very large; very vigorous growth; ['Charles P. Kilham' × 'Margaret McGredy']

'Comtesse de Medina Coeli' ('Duchesse de Medina Coeli') HP, mr, 1864, Marest; flowers glowing red, large, full

'Comtesse de Murinais'   HGal, lp, 1843, Robert; flowers large, full

'Comtesse de Murinais' ('White Moss') M, w, Vibert; flowers flesh, opening white, large, dbl., moderate fragrance; non-recurrent; growth to 4-5 ft.; intr. 1843

'Comtesse de Nadaillac'   T, ab, before 1910, Guillot; flowers coppery yellow, centers salmon

'Comtesse de Noë'   M, m, 1846, Portemer; flowers shining purple-carmine, shaded dark lilac, medium, very full; remontant

'Comtesse de Noghera'   T, op, 1902, Nabonnand; flowers light salmon-pink, very large, very dbl.; ['Reine Emma des Pays-Bas' × 'Paul Nabonnand']

'Comtesse de Palikao'   HP, lp, 1865, Pernet; flowers flesh pink, shaded white, large, full

'Comtesse de Panisse'   T, pb, before 1910; flowers rosy buff, shaded with carmine and violet; large, full

'Comtesse de Paris'   HP, pb, 1864, Verdier, E.; flowers bright pink, petal edges tinted white, reflexed, 10-12 cm., full, globular; foliage dark green; ['Victor Verdier' × unknown]; re-released by Lévêque in 1882

'Comtesse de Paris'   HT, dy, Briant; intr. 1993

'Comtesse de Polignac'   HP, dr, 1862, Granger; flowers poppy red, velvety, tinted flame, and purple, medium, dbl.

Comtesse de Provence™ -- See 'Meibacus'

'Comtesse de Rességuier'   B, mp, 1842, Béluze; flowers silver pink, medium, full, cupped

'Comtesse de Rocquigny'   B, lp, 1874, Vaurin; flowers white, tinted with rosy salmon, medium, full, globular

'Comtesse de Roquette-Buisson'   HP, lp, 1888, Lévêque; flowers light pink, tinted both darker and lighter, very large; foliage very large, light green

'Comtesse de Rosemond-Chabeau de Lussay'   T, op, 1887, Chauvry; flowers salmon pink, center bright pink over coppery yellow base, reverse China pink, large, full

'Comtesse de Saxe'   T, w, 1904, Soupert & Notting; flowers porcelain white, tinted yellow, large, very full, moderate fragrance; ['Leonie Osterrieth' × 'Souv de Mme Eugene Verdier']

'Comtesse de Seguier'   HP, mr, 1848, Verdier, V.

'Comtesse de Séguier'   HP, mr, 1861, Samson; flowers bright red

'Comtesse de Ségur' ('Comtesse Panarosa', 'Tendresse') S, mp, Delbard; flowers light rose pink, petals dahlia-like, very dbl., moderate rose & raspberry fragrance; intr. 1994

'Comtesse de Ségur'   C, lp, 1848, Verdier, V.; flowers pale flesh, medium, full

'Comtesse de Serenye'   HP, lp, 1874, Lacharme, F.; flowers soft pink, very large, full; foliage dark green, regularly dentate; prickles flattened, hooked; ['La Reine' × unknown]

'Comtesse de Turenne'   HP, lp, 1853, Oger; flowers flesh pink, lilac centered

'Comtesse de Turenne'   HP, lp, Verdier, E.; flowers flesh pink, large, full; foliage dark green; intr. 1867

'Comtesse de Vallier'   HP, 1866, Damaizin

'Comtesse de Vezins' -- See 'Vicomtesse de Vezins'

'Comtesse de Vitzthum'   T, my, 1890, Soupert & Notting; flowers light yellow outer petals, bright yellow center, large, full

'Comtesse de Woronzoff' -- See 'Regulus'

'Comtesse Diana' -- See 'Hellux'

'Comtesse Doria'   M, m, 1854, Portemer fils; flowers purple-pink, shaded salmon, heavily mossed

'Comtesse d'Orléans'   HP, w, 1854, Descemet; flowers lilac-flesh-white, medium, full

'Comtesse d'Oxford' ('Countess of Oxford') HP, mr, 1869, Guillot Père; flowers bright velvety carmine red, sometimes with violet tones, large, dbl., globular, moderate fragrance; recurrent bloom; ['Victor Verdier' × unknown]

Comtesse du Barry® ('Golden Border') F, ly, Verschuren; flowers light sulpher yellow, 5-6 cm., 50-60 petals, borne in large clusters; growth to 60 cm.; intr. 1993

'Comtesse du Cayla'   Ch, ob, 1902, Guillot, P.; flowers nasturtium-red, tinted orange,, semi-dbl., flat, moderate fragrance; recurrent bloom; foliage dark, glossy; vigorous growth; [('Rival de Pæstum' × 'Mme Falcot') × 'Mme Falcot']

'Comtesse Duchatel'   HP, m, 1842, Laffay; flowers purple pink, medium to large, very full, cupped

'Comtesse Dusy'   T, w, 1893, Soupert & Notting; bud long; flowers large, full, moderate fragrance

'Comtesse Emmeline de Guigné'   T, pb, 1903, Nabonnand; bud long, ovoid, coppery carmine; flowers delicate flesh-pink, coppery center, very large, full; foliage dark green; growth bushy, vigorous; ['Papa Gontier' × 'Comtesse Festetics Hamilton']

'Comtesse Eva Starhemberg'   T, yb, 1890, Soupert & Notting; bud long; flowers cream yellow, center chromeochre, edge of outer petals tinted pink, large, full; ['Étendard de Jeanne d'Arc' × 'Sylphide']

'Comtesse Eva Starhemberg, Climbing' Cl T, yb, 1917, Glen St. Mary Nurs.; [sport of 'Comtesse Eva Starhemberg']

'Comtesse Festétics Hamilton'   T, pb, 1892, Nabonnand; bud long, elegant; flowers carmine red with coppery tints in center, large, full, borne mostly solitary; foliage very large, wavy, dark green; prickles numerous, strong; growth vigorous

'Comtesse Fressinet de Belanger'   HP, mp, 1886, Lévêque; flowers rose

'Comtesse Georges de Roquette-Buisson' N, my, 1885, Nabonnand; flowers bright yellow, fading to cream, medium, dbl., globular

'Comtesse Georges de Roquette-Buisson' HP, mp, Lévêque; intr. 1899

'Comtesse Hélène Mier'   HP, lp, 1876, Soupert & Notting; flowers light satiny pink, tinted darker, large, full

'Comtesse Henrietta Combes'   HP, pb, 1881, Schwartz, J.; flowers satin-rose with silvery reflections, full, centifolia-like; very remontant

'Comtesse Horace de Choiseul'   T, pb, 1886, Lévêque; flowers dark pink, shaded coppery yellow, large, full

'Comtesse Icy Hardegg'   HT, dp, 1911, Soupert & Notting; flowers carmine, large, dbl.; ['Mrs W.J. Grant' × 'Liberty']

'Comtesse Jeanne de Flandre' -- See 'Meisolroz'

'Comtesse Julie de Schulenburg'   HP, dr, 1889, Soupert & Notting; flowers red with purple, dark velvety brown at center, large, full, rosette, moderate fragrance

'Comtesse Julie Hunyady'   T, yb, 1888, Soupert & Notting; flowers yellow shaded greenish, edged with pink, large, full

'Comtesse Lacépède' -- See 'Comtesse de Lacépède'

'Comtesse Lily Kinsky'   T, w, 1895, Soupert & Notting; flowers pearly white with yellowish tint in center, full; ['Marie Van Houtte' × 'Victor Pulliat']

'Comtesse Louise de Kergorlay'   HP, m, 1860, Touvais; flowers bright purple, large, full

'Comtesse Maggi Starzunska'   T, pb, 1911, Nabonnand

'Comtesse Maria Cristina Pes'   HT, mp, 1911, Bernaix fils; flowers glowing China pink, large, full

'Comtesse Marie de Bourges' ('Vicomtesse Marie de Bourges') HP, mp, 1853, Cherpin; flowers glowing carmine pink, center garnet, large, full

'Comtesse Mélanie de Pourtales'   HT, w, 1914, Walter; flowers creamy white,

outer petals shaded red; ['Frau Karl Druschki' × 'Mme Ravary']
'Comtesse Moens de Fernig'   HT, dr, 1961, Verbeek; flowers wine-red, 25 petals; vigorous growth; ['Poinsettia' × seedling]
'Comtesse Molé'   Ch, mp, before 1866; flowers bright pink, shaded grenadine, very large, full, cupped
'Comtesse Nathalie de Kleist'   HP, op, 1881, Soupert & Notting
'Comtesse O'Gorman'   T, pb, Nabonnand; flowers China pink, golden yellow at base, medium, dbl., moderate fragrance; ['Baron de St. Triviers' × unknown]; intr. 1892
'Comtesse O'Gorman'   HP, rb, 1888, Lévêque; flowers red and violet, large, full; foliage glaucous green
'Comtesse Olivier de Lorgeril'   T, op, 1901, Bernaix; flowers peach pink shaded capucine-yellow, reverse light coppery red, large, full
'Comtesse Ouwaroff' -- See 'Duchesse de Brabant'
'Comtesse Panarosa' -- See 'Deltendre'
'Comtesse Prozor'   HG, pb, 1922, Nabonnand, P.; flowers salmon-rose, reverse coral-red; [R. gigantea × 'Comtesse de Bouchaud']
'Comtesse Renée de Béarn'   HP, dr, 1896, Lévêque, P.; flowers carmine, brightened with blackish purple, tinted flame, large, full; foliage glaucous green
'Comtesse Renée de Mortemart'   T, w, 1893, Godard; flowers creamy white, golden at base, large, full, moderate fragrance
'Comtesse Riza du Parc'   T, mp, 1876, Schwartz, J.; flowers rose to carmine, large, dbl., globular; ['Comtesse de Labarthe' × unknown]
'Comtesse Sophie Torby'   T, ob, 1902, Nabonnand; flowers peachy-red with orange shading, intense fragrance; ['Reine Emma des Pays-Bas' × 'Archiduc Joseph']
'Comtesse Vaillant'   HP, m, 1854, Margottin; flowers light violet, sometimes shaded dark violet, large, full
'Comtesse Vally de Serenye'   HP, 1875, Fontaine
'Comtesse Vandal' ('Comtesse Vandale', 'Countess Vandal')   HT, pb, 1932, Leenders, M.; flowers salmon-pink, reverse coppery pink, large, 30 petals, high-centered, moderate fragrance; foliage leathery; bushy growth; PP38; [('Ophelia' × 'Mrs Aaron Ward') × 'Souv. de Claudius Pernet']
'Comtesse Vandal, Climbing' ('Comtesse Vandale, Climbing', 'Countess Vandal, Climbing', 'Grimpant Comtesse Vandal')   Cl HT, op, 1936, J&P; flowers bright crimson, interior chamois, very large, full, moderate fragrance; [sport of 'Comtesse Vandal']
'Comtesse Vandale, Climbing' -- See 'Comtesse Vandal, Climbing'
'Comtesse Vandale' -- See 'Comtesse Vandal'

Concert™ -- See 'Poulclimb'
Concertino® -- See 'Meibinosor'
Concertino™ -- See 'Meiglusor'
'Concerto' ('Concerto 94', 'Starstruck')   S, ab, Meilland; flowers light ochre pink; growth to 100 cm.; PP7390; intr. 1994
'Concerto'   F, mr, 1953, Meilland, F.; PP1244; ['Alain' × 'Floradora']
'Concerto, Climbing' ('Mecertsar')   Cl F, mr, 1970, Truffant, G.; [sport of 'Concerto']; intr. 1968
'Concerto 94' -- See 'Meirolour'
'Conch Shell Climber'   LCl, pb, 2006, Starnes, John A., Jr.; flowers shell pink, 2½-3 in., very full, borne mostly solitary, slight apple/tea fragrance; very remontant; foliage medium size, medium green, semi-glossy, disease-resistant; prickles ¼ in., sharply curved, light brown, moderate; growth upright, climbing, medium (8-12 ft.); pillar/climber; ['wichurana rambler' × 'Sunflare']; intr. 2006
'Conchita'   Pol, op, 1935, Jordan, H.; flowers clear salmon, dbl., cupped, borne in clusters; foliage glossy; vigorous growth; intr. 1935
'Concorde'   F, pb, Meilland; flowers carmine pink with yellow heart, 3½-4 in.; growth to 30 in.; intr. 1995
'Concorde' -- See 'Forever Yours'
'Concorde 92'   HT, dy, Meilland, Alain A.; flowers large, dark lemon yellow, loose; intr. 1992
'Concordia'   HT, mp, 1924, Brix; flowers glowing pink, edged silver-pink, semi-dbl., moderate fragrance
'Concordia'   HT, rb, Giacomasso; flowers red, reverse deep yellow, well-formed, dbl., moderate fragrance; vigorous growth; ['Charles P. Kilham' × 'Crimson Glory']; intr. 1946
'Condesa da Foz' -- See 'Rêve d'Or'
Condesa de Barcelona® -- See 'Feodase'
'Condesa de Benahavis'   HT, mp, 1949, La Florida; flowers salmon-pink, well-formed; ['Étoile de Hollande' × 'Sensation']
'Condesa de Glimes'   F, pb, Bofill; flowers begonia-pink, center ochre-yellow, single
'Condesa de Mayalde'   HT, rb, 1956, Dot, Pedro; bud pointed; flowers white edged carmine, 30 petals, high-centered; foliage glossy; compact, upright growth; ['Peace' × 'Flambee']
'Condesa de Mayalde, Climbing'   Cl HT, w, 1964, Samuels
'Condesa de Munter'   HT, or, 1932, Munné, B.; flowers geranium-red, tinted orange-yellow, large, semi-dbl., cupped; long, strong stems; vigorous growth; ['Souv. de Josefina Plà' × 'Souv. de Claudius Pernet']
'Condesa de Saldanha'   HT, ob, 1961, Munné, M.; flowers reddish-orange, mottled yellow, large, 45 petals; vigorous growth

'Condesa de Sástago'   HT, pb, 1932, Dot, Pedro; bud ovoid; flowers deep pink, reverse yellow, large, 55 petals, cupped, moderate fragrance; foliage glossy, dark; vigorous, tall growth; [('Souv. de Claudius Pernet' × 'Maréchal Foch') × 'Margaret McGredy']
'Condesa de Sástago, Climbing'   Cl HT, pb, 1936, Vestal; flowers oriental red and yellow, large, full, moderate fragrance; [sport of 'Condesa de Sástago']
'Condesa de Villarrea'   HT, mr, 1960, Dot, M.; flowers crimson, reverse cardinal-red, large, 35 petals; long, stiff stems; vigorous growth; ['Chrysler Imperial' × 'Texas Centennial']
'Conditorum' (R. gallica conditorum, 'Tidbit Rose')   HGal, dp; flowers deep pink to red-pink, large, semi-dbl.; recorded in 1900, but undoubtedly a very old form; perhaps identical with Parkinson's Hungarian Rose
'Condoleezza' -- See 'Morharmony'
'Conestoga'   S, w, 1946, Preston; bud ovoid; flowers open, 2 in., 30 petals, borne in clusters; non-recurrent; foliage soft, sparse, small; upright, vigorous growth; hardy; ['Betty Bland' × seedling]
'Confection' -- See 'Jacute'
'Confederation'   HT, mp, 1964, Golik; flowers compact, large, 70 petals; foliage dark, glossy; moderate, vigorous growth; ['Queen o' the Lakes' × 'Serenade']
'Conference 63'   HT, dr, 1965, Quentin; flowers deep crimson, 4½ in., dbl.; foliage light green; tall growth
'Confetti'   F, rb, 1980, Swim, H.C. & Christensen, J.E.; bud ovoid; flowers deep yellow, aging orange-red, 18-25 petals, high-centered, borne 3-7 per cluster, slight tea fragrance; foliage medium green; prickles hooked downward; upright growth; PP5399; ['Jack O'Lantern' × 'Zorina']; intr. 1983
'Confetti' -- See 'Konfetti'
Confidence™ -- See 'Meigafor'
'Confidence'   HT, pb, 1951, Meilland, F.; bud ovoid; flowers pearly light pink to yellow blend, large, 28-38 petals, high-centered, moderate fragrance; foliage dark, leathery, vigorous, upright, bushy growth; PP1192; ['Peace' × 'Michèle Meilland']; intr. 1951
'Confidence, Climbing'   Cl HT, pb, 1961, Hendrickx
'Confusion'   S, mp, Croix; flowers large, semi-double, borne in clusters; recurrent; foliage glossy; compact, shrubby (2 m.) growth; intr. 2003
Conga®   HT, my, Tantau; flowers golden-yellow, medium, dbl., high-centered, borne mostly singly; recurrent; stems long; florist rose; intr. 2000
'Congo'   HT, dr, 1943, Meilland, F.; bud long, pointed; flowers velvety maroon, open, medium, dbl.; foliage leathery, bronze; bushy, dwarf growth; ['Admiral Ward' × 'Lemania']
'Congolaise'   HT, dr, Tantau; flowers

The Official Registry and Checklist — Rosa   139

velvety dark red, well-formed, large, dbl.; vigorous growth

'Congratulations' -- See 'Korlift'

'Congratulations' -- See 'Kotobuki'

'Coniston' -- See 'Ausufo'

'Connie' Min, dy, 1991, Jerabek, Paul E.; bud pointed; flowers dark yellow fading to light yellow, 11 petals, flat, borne singly or in small clusters, slight fragrance; foliage medium size, dark green, glossy; bushy, medium (36 cm.), very dense growth; [unknown × unknown]

'Connie Crook' -- See 'Boselftay'

'Connie Lohn' -- See 'Ardresden'

'Connie Mack' F, dr, 1952, Duehrsen; flowers dark velvety crimson, medium, 25 petals, borne in clusters, slight fragrance; foliage glossy, dark; vigorous growth; PP1062; [seedling × 'Margy']

'Connie's Choice' -- See 'Paul Potter'

'Connoisseur' S, m, William, J.B.; buds tall, elegant; flowers purple-burgundy with pink stripes, borne in large clusters; foliage glossy; intr. 2003

'Conqueror' HT, ly, 1929, Chaplin Bros.; flowers saffron-yellow, fading pale yellow, 15 petals; vigorous, bushy growth

'Conqueror's Gold' -- See 'Hartwiz'

'Conquest' -- See 'Harbrill'

'Conquete' HT, Combe, M.; intr. 1967

'Conquistador' LCl, mr, Pineau; flowers vermilion, 3 in., semi-dbl., moderate fragrance; foliage glossy; intr. 1983

'Conquistador' LCl, mr, Fryer; flowers velvety red, dbl.; growth to 10-12 ft.; intr. 2005

'Conrad Ferdinand Meyer' HRg, lp, 1899, Müller, Dr. F.; flowers silver pink, large, dbl., cupped, borne in clusters, intense fragrance; repeat bloom; foliage leathery; vigorous (8-10 ft.), good pillar rose, bushy growth; [*R. rugosa* × 'Gloire de Dijon']

'Conrad Hilton' F, my, 1962, Shepherd; bud ovoid; flowers golden yellow, outer petals sometimes white, 2½ in., 30-45 petals, flat, moderate fragrance; foliage leathery, dark, glossy, crinkled; very vigorous, upright, bushy growth; PP1828; [('Dupontii' × 'Pinocchio') × ('Goldilocks' × 'Feu Pernet-Ducher')]; intr. 1962

'Conrad O'Neal' S, dp, 1968, O'Neal; bud ovoid; flowers deep pink, medium, very dbl., intense fragrance; foliage dark, glossy; vigorous, upright growth; [('Blossomtime' × unknown) × 'Don Juan']; intr. 1966

'Conrad's Crimson' S, rb, 1972, Eacott; flowers crimson, shaded purple, 3 in., 30 petals, flat; early bloom; foliage light green to bronze; ['Sweet Sultan' × 'Conrad F. Meyer']

'Conservation' -- See 'Cocdimple'

'Conservency Rose' -- See 'Capmina'

'Consolata' HT, yb, 1936, Capiago; bud pointed; flowers yellow and coppery nasturtium-red; foliage bronze; long, strong stems

'Conspicuous' HT, mr, 1930, Dickson, A.; flowers glowing scarlet, very large, dbl.; vigorous growth; intr. 1932

'Constance, Climbing' Cl HT, my, 1927, Pacific Rose Co.

'Constance' HT, my, 1915, Pernet-Ducher; flowers yellow to golden yellow, medium, dbl., high-centered; foliage rich green, glossy; bushy growth; ['Rayon d'Or' × unknown]

'Constance des Hollandaises' -- See 'My Lady Kensington'

'Constance Casson' HT, pb, 1920, Cant, B. R.; flowers carmine, flushed apricot, dbl.; ['Queen Mary' × 'Gorgeous']

'Constance Fettes' -- See 'Cocnest'

'Constance Finn' ('Windsor Castle') F, lp, Harkness; flowers very dbl., moderate fragrance; recurrent; upright, vase shaped growth to 3 ft; intr. 1997

'Constance Morley' HT, ob, 1982, Gregory, C. & Sons, Ltd.; flowers orange-gold tinged red, diffused center, 39 petals, borne singly, slight fragrance; foliage dark, glossy; prickles elongated, orange; spreading, bushy growth; [Piccadilly® × seedling]; intr. 1981

Constance Spry® ('Constanze Spry') S, lp, 1961, Austin, David; flowers rose pink, 5 in., 55-70 petals, cupped, borne in clusters, moderate myrrh fragrance; foliage dark; vigorous (5-6 ft.) growth; ['Belle Isis' × 'Dainty Maid']; intr. 1961

'Constant Lusseau' HP, mp, 1864, Trouillard; flowers bright carmine, shaded violet, medium, full

'Constantia' HT, mp, 1960, Herholdt, J.A.; bud pointed; flowers Neyron rose, well-formed, 4-4½ in., 40 petals; moderate growth; [Baccará® × Grace de Monaco®]

'Constanza' HT, ob, 1967, Tantau, Math.; bud pointed; flowers orange, well-formed, large, 25-30 petals; foliage dark, glossy; upright, bushy growth

'Constanze' -- See 'Tanzecon'

'Constanze' -- See 'Tanagosh'

'Constanze Spry' -- See 'Constance Spry'

'Constellation' -- See 'Savacon'

'Constellation' HT, ob, 1949, Gaujard; bud long, pointed; flowers coppery orange, well-formed, very large; very vigorous, erect growth; ['Peace' × seedling]

'Constellation' LCl, ab; flowers cream and apricot, moderate fragrance; growth to 8-10 ft.; intr. 1999

'Constellation' HT, m, Harkness; intr. 2007

Consul M. Mezin' HT, Verbeek

'Contempo' F, ob, 1970, Armstrong, D.L.; bud ovoid; flowers orange blending to gold, medium, dbl., high-centered, moderate fragrance; foliage light, leathery; vigorous, bushy growth; PP3102; ['Spartan' × ('Goldilocks' × ('Fandango' × 'Pinocchio'))]; intr. 1971

'Contentment' HT, pb, 1956, Boerner; bud globular; flowers soft pink suffused yellow, 5½ in., 65-70 petals, high-centered, intense fragrance; foliage glossy, leathery; vigorous, upright growth; PP1644; [(seedling × 'Lilette Mallerin') × 'Orange Delight']

'Contessa' -- See 'Jacris'

'Contessa Cecilia Lurani' HT, dp, 1902, Brauer; flowers deep pink with salmon red, large to very large, full, moderate fragrance; ['Kaiserin Auguste Viktoria' × 'Principessa di Napoli']

'Contessa Mona Bismark' Gr

'Contiki' HT, ab, 2004, Wilke, William; flowers apricot, pink, and cream, reverse light pink, 4½-5½ in., dbl., borne mostly solitary, slight fragrance; foliage medium size, medium green, semi-glossy; prickles ¼ in., curved downwards; growth bushy, medium (4-5 ft.); garden, exhibition; [unknown × unknown]

'Continental' HT, mr, 1966, Lammerts, Dr. Walter; bud ovoid; flowers cardinal-red, large, dbl., moderate fruity fragrance; foliage leathery; vigorous, upright growth; PP2751; [Baccará® × 'Yuletide']

'Continued Friendship' F, ab, Harkness; flowers apricot, deeper in center, full, globular, borne in clusters of up to 7, slight fragrance; recurrent; bushy (3 ft.) growth; intr. 2008

'Continued Friendship' -- See 'Jacbelgo'

'Contrast' HT, pb, 1937, H&S; flowers China-pink and bronze, reverse white and bronze, large, dbl., high-centered, moderate fragrance; foliage leathery, glossy; very vigorous, bushy, compact growth; [seedling × 'Talisman']

'Contribute' HT, my, Dawson; intr. 1977

Conundrum™ -- See 'Tuckpuzzle'

'Convivial' -- See 'Seavivial'

'Conway Jones' HT, 1913, Dickson

'Cookie' LCl, or, Meilland; flowers scarlet red-orange, dbl.; growth climbing (2½ m.); intr. 2001

'Cool Breeze' HT, lp, Spek; bud large; flowers soft, delicate pink, full, high-centered; intr. 2002

'Cool Dude' -- See 'Rendude'

'Cool Water' HT, w, Schreurs; intr. 2004

'Cool Wave' -- See 'Zipcool'

'Coolidge' -- See 'I. X. L.'

'Coolness' F, w, 1959, Boerner; bud ovoid, cream; flowers 2½-3 in., 55-60 petals, moderate fragrance; foliage leathery, glossy; vigorous, bushy, compact growth; [('Glacier' × unknown) × ('Starlite' × unknown)]; intr. 1959

Coon Carnival® -- See 'Korcoon'

'Cooperi' -- See 'Cooper's Burmese'

'Cooperoo Emblem' Pol, m, Harrison,

'Cooper's Burmese' ('Cooperi', 'Gigantea Cooperi', *R.* × *cooperi*) HG, w, 1927; flowers near white, large, single; foliage glossy; vigorous (to 20 ft.) growth; [possibly a natural hybrid of *R. gigantea* × *R. laevigata*; collected as seed from Burma by Roland Cooper]

'Cooplo' ('Lolo') HT, rb, 2000, Cooper, Ralph D.; flowers cherry red, reverse silver white, 4-5 in., full, high-centered, borne mostly singly, slight fragrance; foliage medium size, dark green, semi-glossy; prickles moderate; growth spreading, medium (5-6 ft.); [seedling × seedling]; intr. 2001

'Cooprior' ('Betty Prior, Climbing') Cl F, mp, 1995, Cooper, Donell; flowers medium carmine pink, medium, 5 petals, borne in small clusters; foliage large, medium green, dull; some prickles; upright, spreading, medium growth; [sport of 'Betty Prior']; intr. 1997

'Cooran' F, dp, 1953, Ulrick, L.W.; bud long, pointed; flowers deep rose-pink, very large, dbl., borne in clusters; very vigorous growth; ['Mrs Tom Henderson' × 'Ming Toy']

'Coorg' -- See 'Virbrown'

'Cooroy' F, mp, 1953, Ulrick, L.W.; flowers rose-pink, very dbl., high-centered, borne in clusters; ['Mrs Tom Henderson' × 'Mrs Tom Henderson']

'Coosyl' ('My Own') Min, rb, 1984, Cook, Sylven S.; flowers red, yellow center, small, 5 petals, moderate fragrance; foliage medium size, medium green, semi-glossy; [('Scarlet Knight' × 'Soeur Therese') × 'Willie Winkie']; intr. 1977

'Coosyn' ('Golden Penny') LCl, yb, 1984, Cook, Sylven S.; flowers gold, reverse creamy, dbl., intense lemon fragrance; foliage medium size, medium green, semi-glossy; upright growth (7-8 ft.); [Queen Elizabeth® × 'Scarlet Knight']; intr. 1981

'Copacabana' LCl, or, 1966, Dorieux; flowers vermilion, tinted brown, large, 40 petals, globular, borne in small clusters; foliage dark green; ['Coup de Foudre' × unknown]

Copacabana® F, ob, Dorieux; flowers orange with copper tints, aging darker , semi-double, cupped, borne in clusters; recurrent; early foliage red; strong growth; intr. 1995

'Copacabana' -- See 'Macha Méril'

'Copenhagen' ('København') Cl HT, mr, 1964, Poulsen, Niels D.; flowers scarlet, 5 in., dbl., borne in small clusters, moderate fragrance; foliage large, coppery dark green; vigorous growth; ['Hakuun' × 'Ena Harkness']

'Copia' F, mr, 1964, Mondial Roses; flowers bright cardinal-red, large, semi-dbl.; vigorous, bushy growth; [('Independence' × seedling) × 'Tour de France']

'Coppa Nob' -- See 'Coccopna'

'Coppélia' HT, ob, 1952, Meilland, F.; flowers rosy shades, deepening to orange, medium, 28 petals, cupped; foliage leathery; vigorous, upright growth; ['Peace' × 'Europa']

'Coppelia' S, dp, Kordes

'Coppélia 76' -- See 'Meigurami'

'Copper Arch' -- See 'Korhurtlen'

'Copper Climber' LCl, op, 1938, Burbank; bud pointed, coppery; flowers glowing coppery salmon, edged pink, large; PP266

'Copper Coronet' HT, ab, 1987, Strange, J.F.; flowers coppery amber, reverse blush pink, fading amber and cream, large, 60 petals, high-centered, slight fragrance; foliage medium size, medium green, semi-glossy, upright, medium growth; ['Ginger Rogers' × 'Royal Highness']

'Copper Crown' -- See 'Wilcrown'

'Copper Delight' F, ob, 1956, LeGrice; flowers clear orange, large, 14 petals, borne in large clusters; foliage olive-green; vigorous, upright, bushy growth; ['Goldilocks' × 'Ellinor LeGrice']

'Copper Gem' HT, ab, Cocker; flowers rich copper; strong stems; medium growth; intr. 1984

'Copper Glow' LCl, ob, 1940, Brownell; flowers coppery yellow, 4 in., 27 petals, intense fragrance; seasonal bloom; foliage dark green, glossy; vigorous, climbing (20 ft.), open habit growth; PP458; ['Golden Glow' × 'Break o' Day']

'Copper Kettle' F, ob, 1978, Williams, J. Benjamin; bud elongated, tangerine; flowers brilliant copper-orange and yellow, 2½-3½ in., 28 petals, high-centered, moderate fragrance; foliage glossy, dark bronze green; upright growth; hardy to -20°F; [Queen Elizabeth® × 'Golden Slippers']

'Copper King' -- See 'Hercop'

'Copper Luster' HT, op, 1945, Roberts; flowers coppery pink, loosely, large, 23 petals, cupped, slight fragrance; foliage glossy, bronze; vigorous, upright growth; PP641; ['Better Times' × 'Orange Nassau']

'Copper Nugget' HT, op, 1942, Lammerts, Dr. Walter; bud ovoid to urn shaped; flowers orange-salmon, small, 50-60 petals, high-centered; foliage leathery, glossy, dark; strong stems; dwarf, bushy growth; ['Charles P. Kilham' × 'Captain Thomas']

'Copper Pot' F, ob, 1968, Dickson, A.; flowers orange-yellow, deeper reverse, large, 15 petals, borne in trusses; foliage glossy, bronze; tall growth; [seedling × 'Golden Scepter']

'Copper Ruffles' Min, or, 1983, Dobbs, Annette E.; flowers small, dbl., high-centered, slight fragrance; foliage small, medium-green, semi-glossy; upright growth; ['Anytime' × 'Sheri Anne']; intr. 1982

Copper Star™ MinFl, ob, Clements, John; flowers bronzy copper, 2½ in., single, flat, star-shaped, moderate fresh fragrance; recurrent; foliage small, dark green; bushy, compact (30 in.) growth; intr. 2007

Copper Sunset™ -- See 'Savacop'

'Copperkins' HT, ob, 1957, Ratcliffe; bud long, pointed, dark orange-flame; flowers orange, well-formed, 25 petals, intense fruity fragrance; foliage glossy, vigorous growth; ['Mme Henri Guillot' × 'Golden Scepter']

'Coppers Grand' S, mr; intr. 1997

'Coppertone' -- See 'Oldtimer'

'Coppery Heart' S, yb, 1958, Gaujard; flowers coppery yellow shaded red, large, dbl.; repeat bloom; foliage dark, glossy; long stems; very vigorous growth; ['Peace' × 'Conrad Ferdinand Meyer']

'Copy Cat' -- See 'Morcat'

'Coq de Roche' HT, dr, 1945, Meilland, F.; flowers blood-red, large, very dbl.; very vigorous growth; ['Duquesa de Peñaranda' × 'J. B. Meilland']

'Coquellicot' HT, or, 1942, Meilland, F.; flowers orange-red with gold, medium, semi-dbl.

'Coquette' HT, lp, 1929, Dobbie; flowers pale flesh-pink, well-formed, slight fragrance; vigorous growth

'Coquette' Pol, mr, Geary; flowers bright vermilion, base yellowish, large; ['Éblouissant' × 'Mme Edouard Herriot']; intr. 1929

'Coquette' HT, w, Warriner, William A.; bud long; flowers 4 in., 30-35 petals, high-centered, slight fragrance; foliage light green, reddish underneath; upright growth; PP4019; [seedling × seedling]; intr. 1976

'Coquette' -- See 'Bertram Park'

'Coquette Bordelaise' ('Panachée de Bordeaux', 'Paul Neyron Panachée') HP, pb, 1896, Duprat; flowers dark pink with white stripes, very large, dbl.; [sport of 'Mme Georges Desse']

'Coquette de Lyon' HP, lp, 1859, Lacharme, F.; flowers flesh-pink

'Coquette de Lyon' ('La Coquette de Lyon') T, ly, Ducher; flowers canary-yellow, medium size; intr. 1872

'Coquette de Melun' B, lp, Varengot; flowers flesh pink, medium, full

'Coquette des Alpes' B, w, 1867, Lacharme, F.; flowers white tinged blush, medium to large, dbl., semi-cupped; very remontant; vigorous growth; ['Mlle Blanche Lafitte' × 'Sappho (Damask Perpetual)']

'Coquette des Blanches' B, w, 1871, Lacharme, F.; bud fat; flowers white, lightly washed pink, 10 cm., dbl., cupped, moderate fragrance; vigorous growth; ['Mlle Blanche Lafitte' × 'Sappho (Damask Perpetual)']; sometimes classified as N

'Coquina' HWich, pb, 1909, Walsh; flowers rose-pink fading lighter, base creamy white, single, cupped, borne in large clusters, moderate fragrance; foliage dark, almost evergreen; stems long, strong; very vigorous (20-24 ft.) growth

'Cora' HGal, m, 1827, Lecomte or Savoureux; flowers velvety purple-violet, shaded red, small, dbl., borne in clusters of 3-4; prickles scattered, fine; growth erect, small

'Cora' HP, mp, Touvais or Guillot; flowers bright pink, medium; ['Général Jacqueminot' × unknown]; intr. 1859

'Cora' Ch, yb, Schwartz; flowers yellow and orange, shaded carmine, medium, full; intr. 1899

'Cora à Pétales Variés' yb, before 1819; flowers yellowish-pink, large

'Cora L. Barton' N, 1840, Buist; ['Lamarque' × unknown]

'Cora Marie' -- See 'Korlimit'

'Corail' LCl, pb, 1931, Schwartz, A.; flowers light peach-blossom-pink, reverse coral-pink and carmine, opening well, dbl.; recurrent bloom; foliage bright, glossy; very vigorous growth; ['William Allen Richardson' × 'Orléans Rose']

Coral® -- See 'Feloma'

'Coral' HT, pb, 1931, Dickson, A.; flowers bright coral, base buttercup-yellow, dbl., globular; wiry erect stems; vigorous growth

Coral™ Min, rb, Olesen; flowers dbl., 25-30 petals, borne mostly solitary, no fragrance; foliage dark green, glossy; intr. 1996

'Coral' LCl, mp; foliage massive; vigorous, climbing growth; half-hardy; [R. sinowilsonii × seedling]

'Coral 'n' Gold' -- See 'Mancoral'

'Coral Anne Griffiths' HT, mp, 1979, Henson; bud very tight; flowers 72 petals, moderate fragrance; foliage glossy, dark; very large (6 in.) very vigorous growth; [sport of 'Red Devil']; intr. 1978

'Coral Bay' HT, op, 1972, Swim & Weeks; bud ovoid; flowers silvery coral-orange, medium, dbl., cupped, moderate fragrance; foliage glossy, leathery; vigorous growth; PP3243; [seedling × seedling]; intr. 1971

'Coral Beauty' Pol, mp, 1941, deRuiter; flowers spinel-pink, 1½ in., dbl., flat, borne in clusters; vigorous, branching growth; PP746; [sport of 'Orléans Rose']

'Coral Belle' F, ob, 1962, Jelly; bud pointed, ovoid; flowers vermilion, 1½-2½ in., 45 petals, high-centered; foliage leathery; strong stems; vigorous, upright growth; ['Stoplite' × 'Orange Sweetheart']; intr. 1962

'Coral Bells' Pol, op, J&P; flowers coral pink, medium, dbl.; intr. 1962

Coral Border™ -- See 'Poulalo'

'Coral Button' Min, op

'Coral Cameo' -- See 'Morcalyn'

'Coral Carpet' MinFl, mp, Williams, J. Benjamin; flowers coral pink to light pink; groundcover; spreading growth; intr. 1997

'Coral Cascade' F, or, 1980, James, John; flowers coral-red, 50-75 petals, globular, borne singly or 3-5 per cluster, slight carnation fragrance; foliage opens russet, turning dark green, glossy; prickles reddish-gray; vigorous, compact, bushy growth; ['Van Bergen' × sport of 'Pink Hat']

'Coral Chateau' HT, op, Teranishi; intr. 1998

'Coral Cluster' Pol, op, 1920, Murrell, R.; flowers coral-pink; [sport of 'Orléans Rose']

'Coral Cover' S, op; groundcover; spreading growth; intr. 2002

'Coral Creeper' LCl, dp, 1938, Brownell; bud deep red; flowers coral to light pink, 3 in., semi-dbl., borne singly or in small clusters, strong musky fragrance; foliage dark green, glossy, leathery; numerous prickles; upright stems; very vigorous growth; [('Dr. W. Van Fleet' × 'Emily Gray') × 'Jacotte']

'Coral Crown' F, or, 1960, Von Abrams; flowers coral-red, 3 in., 35 petals, high-centered, borne in clusters, moderate fragrance; foliage glossy; low, compact growth; PP1991; ['Else Poulsen' × ('Fashion' × Orange Triumph®)]; intr. 1959

'Coral Cup' Pol, op, 1936, B&A; flowers soft coral, very dbl., cupped, borne in clusters; profuse, repeated bloom; very vigorous, bushy growth; [sport of 'Gloria Mundi']

'Coral Cushion' S, op; intr. 2004

Coral Dawn® LCl, mp, 1952, Boerner; bud ovoid; flowers coral pink, aging to rose pink, lighter edges, 6-8 cm., 30-35 petals, cupped, borne singly or in small clusters, moderate fragrance; remontant; foliage wide, dark green, glossy; vigorous (8-12 ft.) growth; PP1117; [('New Dawn' × unknown) × seedling]

'Coral Delight' Gr, op, Hiroshima; [sport of 'Cream Delight']; intr. 2001

'Coral Destiny' HT, op, 1983, Perry, Anthony; flowers medium coral pink, large, 35 petals, slight fragrance; foliage medium green, semi-glossy; upright growth; ['Joanna Hill' × Queen Elizabeth®]; intr. 1984

'Coral Drift' S, op; flowers, 20-25 petals, slight to none fragrance; low, groundcover growth; intr. 2006

'Coral Drops' HMoy, op, before 1927; flowers pale coral-pink, single; non-recurrent

'Coral Fairy' -- See 'Morcofair'

'Coral Fantasy' -- See 'Lyoco'

Coral Fiesta® ('Maria Teresa de Esteban', 'Mme Teresa Estaban') HT, or, 1983, Dot, Simon; flowers large, 45 petals, cupped, no fragrance; foliage large, dark, matte; prickles light yellow; bushy growth; [seedling × seedling]

'Coral Fiesta, Climbing' Cl HT, or, Barni; flowers coral and vermilion, growth to 10-25 ft.; intr. after 1983

'Coral Floc' F, or, Dot

'Coral Flower Carpet' -- See 'Noala'

Coral Gables™ -- See 'Poulalo'

'Coral Galaxy' F, op, Zary

'Coral Gem' F, pb, 1959, Boerner; bud ovoid; flowers light coral-pink, open, 2½ in., 40-45 petals, cupped, borne in clusters, moderate fruity fragrance; foliage leathery, dark; vigorous, bushy growth; PP1797; [(('Pinocchio' × 'Mrs Sam McGredy, Climbing') × ('Pinocchio' × 'Mrs Sam McGredy, Climbing')) × 'Fashion']; intr. 1959

'Coral Glow' LCl, op, 1964, Croix, P.; flowers salmon-pink, borne in clusters; ['Spectacular' × seedling]

Coral Hush™ -- See 'Jacmpiad'

'Coral Ice' -- See 'Interice'

'Coral Island' Min, op

Coral Meidiland™ -- See 'Meipopul'

Coral Midinette™ -- See 'Salmo'

'Coral Mist' HT, op, 1966, Patterson; bud ovoid; flowers coral-pink, dbl., high-centered; foliage glossy, light green; vigorous, bushy, open growth; ['Spartan' × 'Good News']

Coral Pagode™ MinFl, pb, Poulsen; flowers pink blend, 5-8 cm., dbl., borne in clusters, no fragrance; foliage dark; cascading growth, hanging basket type; PP13593; intr. 2000

Coral Palace™ -- See 'Pouldron'

'Coral Panarosa' S, op, Kordes; flowers large, coral, full, no fragrance; growth tall (2 m.), thick; intr. 2001

'Coral Pastel' MinFl, op, Williams, J.B.; intr. 2003

'Coral Pillar' Cl HT, mr, 1945, Lammerts, Dr. Walter; flowers geranium-pink, large, dbl., high-centered; foliage glossy, dark; very vigorous, upright growth; ['Crimson Glory' × 'Captain Thomas']

'Coral Princess' F, ob, 1966, Boerner; bud ovoid; flowers coral-orange, large, 25 petals, cupped, moderate fragrance; foliage leathery; vigorous, bushy growth; PP2635; [(('Fashion' × unknown) × ('Garnette' × unknown)) × 'Spartan']

'Coral Prophyta' HT, op, de Ruiter

'Coral Queen' HT, or, 1928, Reeves; flowers coral-red, large, dbl., cupped; foliage dark, glossy; long, strong stems; vigorous, bushy growth; [sport of 'The Queen Alexandra Rose']

'Coral Queen Elizabeth' F, op, 1966, Gregory; flowers coral-salmon, 3 in., dbl., borne in clusters; foliage glossy; very vigorous growth; [Queen Elizabeth® × seedling]

'Coral Reef' HT, mp, 1948, Joseph H. Hill, Co.; bud long, pointed; flowers pink, medium, 25-30 petals, moderate fragrance; foliage leathery, wrinkled, dark; vigorous, upright, bushy growth; PP839; ['Joanna Hill' × R.M.S. Queen Mary]

'Coral Reef' -- See 'Cocdarlee'

'Coral Reef' -- See 'Jalreef'

'Coral Rosamini' Min, op

'Coral Sand' -- See 'Rensand'

'Coral Satin' LCl, op, 1960, Zombory; bud ovoid; flowers coral pink, reverse lighter, 3½-4 in., 25 petals, high-centered, borne in small clusters, moderate fragrance; foliage dark green, glossy; numerous prickles; vigorous (6-8 ft.) growth; PP2098; ['New Dawn' × 'Fashion']; intr. 1960

'Coral Sea' -- See 'Jaccogel'

'Coral Sea' HT, dp, 1942, Joseph H. Hill, Co.; bud globular, old-rose; flowers light red, large, 40-45 petals, high-centered; foliage leathery, dark; long, strong stems; vigorous, upright, much branched growth; ['Katharine Pechtold' × R.M.S. Queen Mary]

'Coral Silk' F, op, 1972, Gregory; flowers coral and peach, 3 in., 18 petals, flat;

foliage glossy, dark; very free growth
'Coral Spire' -- See 'Korkragor'
Coral Sprite™ -- See 'Jacoral'
'Coral Star' HT, op, 1967, Robinson, H.; flowers coral-pink, well-formed, medium; vigorous, upright growth; ['Tropicana' × 'Stella']
'Coral Sunblaze' Min, op, Meilland; bud ovoid; flowers soft coral pink, 2 in., 65-110 petals, flat cupped, borne singly and in small clusters, no fragrance; free-flowering; foliage dark green, semi-glossy; prickles sharply pointed, 6 mm., yellow-green; bushy (2 ft.), spreading growth; PP15500; [('Parador' × Swany Mimi®) × 'Air France']; intr. 2004
'Coral Sunset' ('Coucher de Soleil') HT, or, 1965, Boerner; bud ovoid; flowers coral-red, large, dbl., moderate fragrance; foliage dark, leathery; vigorous growth; PP2569; [('Garnette' × unknown) × 'Hawaii']; intr. 1964
'Coral Treasure' Min, ob, 1972, Moore, Ralph S.; bud ovoid; flowers coral-orange, medium, dbl.; foliage glossy, leathery; dwarf, bushy growth; [seedling × 'Little Buckaroo']; intr. 1971
'Coral White' HT, w, Ota, K.; flowers white, shaded pale pink, 13 cm., 30 petals, high-centered, slight fragrance; foliage roundish, dark green; prickles medium size, straight; growth bushy; ['Miss Ireland' × 'Izayoi']; intr. 1989
'CoralGlo' F, op, 1960, Boerner; bud ovoid; flowers orange-rose, large, 42 petals, cupped, slight fragrance; foliage bronze; bushy growth; PP1830; ['Independence' × 'Fashion']; intr. 1960
'Corali' LCl, rb, 1931, Dot, Pedro; flowers coral-red to rosy salmon; profuse seasonal bloom; foliage bright green; vigorous growth
'Coralie' D, lp, before 1848; flowers soft pink, lighter at edges, medium, very dbl., cupped; foliage grayish-green, small; vigorous growth
'Coralie' M, lp, Miellez; flowers flesh, well-formed, medium, dbl.; intr. about 1860
'Coralie' HMult, pb, Paul, W.; bud coral; flowers coral-red to deep pink, 6-7 cm., dbl.; non-recurrent; foliage glossy, vigorous growth; ['Hiawatha' × 'Lyon Rose']; intr. 1919
'Coralin' ('Carolin', 'Carolyn', 'Karolyn') Min, or, 1955, Dot, M.; flowers coral-red, 40 petals; low, compact growth; ['Méphisto' × 'Perla de Alcañada']
'Coralín Superb' Min, dr, 1958, Will; [sport of 'Coralín']
'Coraline' S, mp, Tschanz, Gisèle; flowers pure pink, large, full; floriferous; growth to 3 ft.; intr. 2003
'Coraline' LCl, ab, Eve, Andre; flowers salmon-apricot, 15-20 petals; heavy spring bloom, then recurrent; growth to 2-4 m.; intr. 1976
'Coralita' LCl, or, 1964, Zombory; bud ovoid, deep red; flowers orange-coral, 4 in., 40-45 petals, moderate fragrance; foliage dark, leathery; vigorous (6-8 ft.) growth; PP2531; [('New Dawn' × 'Geranium Red') × 'Fashion']
'Coralitos' -- See 'Suncor'
'Corallina' -- See 'Barcora'
'Corallina' T, rb, 1900, Paul, W.; flowers coppery red, large, dbl.
'Corallina, Climbing' Cl T, mp, 1930, Neisser; flowers carmine with vermilion
'Coralline' Pol, or, 1938, Smith, J.; flowers borne in very large clusters; profuse, repeated bloom; very rampant growth; ['Gloria Mundi' × 'Golden Salmon Superieur']
'Corallovy Surprise' HT, Klimenko, V. N.; intr. 1982
'Corbeille Royale' HT, mp, 1956, Buyl Frères; bud globular; flowers salmon-pink, dbl.; vigorous, upright growth
'Cordelia' HT, ab, 1976, LeGrice; flowers peach shaded deeper, pointed, 4-4½ in., 20 petals, moderate fragrance; foliage dark; tall growth; intr. 1975
'Cordelia' -- See 'Ausbottle'
'Cordelia de Grey' S, dp, 1995, de Grey, Cordelia; flowers deep, bright pink with white eye, golden stamens, 2 in., 5 petals, borne in small clusters, slight fragrance; foliage small, dark green, dull; numerous prickles; medium, upright growth, arching canes
'Cordial' HT, mp, 1961, Verbeek; bud ovoid; flowers pink, medium, dbl., borne in clusters; foliage dark; ['Satisfaction' × seedling]
Cordoba™ S, or, Poulsen; flowers orange-red, 5-8 cm., full, classic hybrid tea form, very slight fragrance; foliage dark green, glossy; bushy (60-100 cm.) growth; intr. 2005
'Cordon Bleu' -- See 'Harubasil'
'Cordon Rouge' LCl, or, Combe; flowers vermilion, 3 in., dbl.; intr. 1970
Cordula® -- See 'Kortri'
'Cored' HT, mr, 1971, Cocker, A. M.; intr. 1970
'Corehead' HT, mr, 1960, Dicksons of Hawlmark; flowers bright crimson; ['Ena Harkness' × 'Hazel Alexander']
'Corimbosa' -- See 'Red Damask'
'Corina' -- See 'Jacvep'
'Corinium' F, m, 1970, Cooper; flowers mauvish pink, 3 in., 48-50 petals, full rosette; foliage semi-glossy; [sport of 'Alamein']
'Corinna' T, pb, 1893, Paul, W.; bud long; flowers flesh pink, shaded with rose and tinted with coppery-gold, medium, dbl.
'Corinne' -- See 'Brocor'
'Corinne's Choice' -- See 'Wemcor'
'Corky' -- See 'Zipcork'
'Corlia' HT, or, 1921, Bees; flowers terracotta; moderate growth
'Corne Herholdt' F, pb
'Cornelia' HT, pb, 1919, Scott, R.; flowers light pink, base orange, dbl.; ['Ophelia' × 'Mrs Aaron Ward']
'Cornelia' HMsk, pb, 1925, Pemberton; flowers strawberry flushed yellow, small, dbl., rosette, borne in flattish sprays; recurrent bloom; foliage dark bronze, leathery, glossy; very vigorous growth
Cornelia™ -- See 'Poulhi019(N)'
'Cornelia Cook' ('Cornélie Koch', 'Mlle Denise de Reverseau') T, w, 1855, Cook; flowers creamy white, tinged lemon-yellow and flesh, well-formed, dbl., moderate fragrance; vigorous growth; ['Devoniensis' × unknown]
'Cornelia Hit' ('Cornelia Patiohit', Cornelia™) MinFl, my, Poulsen; flowers medium yellow, 5-8 cm., full, cupped, borne mostly singly, no fragrance; recurrent; foliage dark green, glossy; growth bushy, 20-40 cm.; intr. 2003
'Cornelia Patiohit' -- See 'Poulhi019(N)'
'Cornélie' -- See 'Belle Vichysoise'
'Cornélie Koch' -- See 'Cornelia Cook'
'Cornelis Timmermans' HT, pb, 1919, Timmermans; flowers clear pink, edged deep yellow, very large, dbl., moderate fragrance; ['Pharisaer' × 'Le Progres']
'Corner' HT, pb, 1945, Wyant; bud pointed; flowers cerise, base yellow, reverse yellow washed pink, 4½ in., 20 petals; foliage leathery, glossy, dark; vigorous, bushy growth; ['Soeur Thérèse' × seedling]
'Cornet' ('Rose Cornet') HP, m, 1845, Lacharme, F.; flowers rose tinted with purple, very large, very dbl., cupped, moderate centifolia fragrance; vigorous, branching growth
Cornsilk™ -- See 'Savasilk'
'Corob' F, dr, 1970, Cocker
'Corolle' LCl, mr, 1962, Dot, Simon; flowers semi-dbl., 12 petals, slight fragrance; foliage glossy; vigorous growth; ['Spectacular' × Cocktail®]
'Corona de Oro' -- See 'Gold Crown'
'Coronado, Climbing' Cl HT, Ansaloni
'Coronado' HT, rb, 1961, Von Abrams; bud long, pointed; flowers red, reverse yellow, 5-6 in., 40 petals, high-centered, moderate fragrance; foliage glossy, dark; vigorous, upright growth; PP2162; [('Multnomah' × 'Peace') × ('Multnomah' × 'Peace')]; intr. 1960
'Coronation' HWich, rb, 1911, Turner; flowers red, lightly striped white, small, semi-dbl., rosette, borne in clusters
'Coronation' HP, mp, Dickson, H.; flowers flesh, shaded bright shrimp-pink, well-formed, large, 50 petals, moderate fragrance; recurrent bloom; stems smooth wood; vigorous growth; intr. 1913
'Coronation' -- See 'Harbella'
'Coronation Gold' HT, yb, 1954, Cox; flowers golden yellow flushed crimson, large, intense damask fragrance; foliage glossy; vigorous growth; RULED EXTINCT 1980; ['Signora' × 'Peace']
'Coronation Gold' ('Maja Oetker') F, ab, 1978, Cocker, A.; bud globular; flowers golden yellow to apricot, 4 in., 27 petals; foliage glossy, vigorous, upright growth; [('Sabine' × 'Circus') × (Anne Cocker® × 'Arthur Bell')]
'Coroneola' -- See 'Double White'
'Coronet' HT, lp, 1897, Dingee-Conard; bud deep carmine; flowers silvery carna-

tion pink, very large, full, round; ['Paul Neyron' × 'Bon Silène']

'Coronet' Pol, yb, Paul, W.; flowers yellow tinted pink; intr. 1912

'Coronet' F, dr, deRuiter; flowers deep crimson, 3 in., 17 petals, borne in clusters; foliage dark, glossy; vigorous, upright growth; ['Independence' × 'Red Wonder']; intr. 1957

'Coronet Supreme' HT, mp, 1955, Jelly; bud short, pointed; flowers rose-pink, 4-5 in., 45-65 petals, moderate fragrance; foliage dark, glossy; very vigorous, upright growth; PP1374; [seedling × 'Golden Rapture']

'Corp de Ballet' F, dp, Hiroshima; intr. 2004

'Corporal Johann Nagy' HSet, dp, 1890, Geschwind, R.; bud fat; flowers crimson and violet, 6-7 cm., dbl.; foliage rounded, tinged purple when young; ['De La Grifferaie' × 'a hybrid perpetual or bourbon']

'Corpus Christi' HT, dr, 1985, Weeks, O.L.; flowers large, 35 petals; foliage large, medium green, semi-glossy; upright, bushy, spreading growth; PP5854; [seedling × 'Night Time']

'Corrida' Gr, Delbard-Chabert; intr. 1969

'Corrie' HT, dp, Kordes; flowers hot pink, large, long lasting, double, high-centered, borne mostly singly; recurrent; foliage leathery ; prickles normal; upright, medium growth; intr. 2006

'Corrie Koster' Pol, dp, 1923, Koster, M.; flowers light coral-red, opening to deep pink, semi-dbl., borne in clusters; [sport of 'Juliana-Roos']

'Corroboree' HT, m, 1969, Fankhauser; bud long, pointed; flowers lilac-mauve, open, very large, dbl., intense damask fragrance; foliage glossy; vigorous, upright growth; [Baccará® × 'My Choice']

'Corry' HT, or, Kordes; intr. 1978

'Corsage' F, w, 1965, Belden; flowers small, semi-dbl., globular, borne in clusters; foliage soft; vigorous, bushy growth; ['Blanche Mallerin' × 'White Swan']

'Corsage' MinFl, w, Williams, J.B.; flowers white with faint pink tint in center, dbl., globular, slight fragrance; intr. 2004

'Corsair' -- See 'Sanroc'

'Corsaire' HT, Combe, M.; intr. 1974

'Corsica' F, pb, 1964, Verschuren, A.; flowers salmon-pink edged dark pink to red, 20 petals; foliage dark, glossy; vigorous, bushy growth

Corso® HT, ob, 1976, Cocker; flowers coppery orange,, 4½ in., 33 petals; foliage glossy, dark; [Anne Cocker® × 'Dr. A. J. Verhage']

'Corso Fleuri' F, dr, 1956, Mondial Roses; flowers scarlet-red, petals waved, semi-dbl.; dwarf, compact growth; [sport of 'Red Favorite']

'Cortège' LCl, ab, Combe, M.; flowers pale orange, fading to soft apricot, 3 in., borne singly or in small clusters; intr. 1976

'Corvedale' -- See 'Ausnetting'

Corvette™ HT, or, Kordes; flowers large, bright orange-red, dbl., high-centered; PP11189; greenhouse rose; intr. 1997

'Coryana' (R. × coryana, R. macrophylla coryana) S, mp, 1926, Hurst, C.C.; flowers rich pink, 2½ in., single; few prickles; tall (8 ft.), shrub growth; [R. macrophylla × R. roxburghii]

'Corylus' S, mp, 1988, LeRougetel, Hazel; flowers open, medium, single, borne usually singly or in sprays of 2-4, slight fragrance; foliage medium size, dark green, deep veined; prickles small, light brown; bushy growth; hips round, medium, scarlet; [R. nitida × R. rugosa rubra]; intr. 1988

Cosetta® F, ob, 1985, Bartolomeo, Embriaco; flowers light orange, reverse deeper with reddish shadings, medium, 30 petals, no fragrance; foliage medium size, dark, matte; ['Zorina' × 'Sole di San Remo']; intr. 1984

'Cosette' -- See 'Harquillypond'

Cosima® HT, ob, Tantau; flowers soft orange, large, full, high-centered, borne mostly singly; recurrent; prickles very few to none; stems medium; intr. 2004

Cosima® -- See 'Tancofeuma'

Cosima® -- See 'Tanelleira'

'Cosimo Ridolfi' HGal, m, 1842, Vibert; flowers old-rose to lilac, spotted crimson, medium, full, cupped; foliage soft green; compact growth

'Cosmic' -- See 'Bricos'

'Cosmo' HMsk, lp, Robinson; flowers creamy blush, frilly, 2 in.; intr. 2000

'Cosmopoliet' -- See 'Cosmopolitan'

'Cosmopolit' -- See 'Cosmopolitan'

'Cosmopolitan' ('Cosmopoliet', 'Cosmopolit') F, mp, 1955, Buisman, G. A. H.; flowers borne in large clusters; bushy growth; ['Silberlachs' × seedling]

Cosmos® -- See 'Comsan'

Cosmos™ LCl, lp, Olesen; bud broad based; flowers light pink, 5 cm., 50-55 petals, rosette, borne in large clusters, flowers evenly top to bottom, slight fragrance; recurrent; foliage dark green, glossy; prickles numerous, 5 mm., hooked downward; growth broad, bushy, 200-300 cm.; PP15482; ['Red Paillette' × seedling]; intr. 2002

'Costa Dorada' HT, Dot; intr. 1967

'Cote d'Azur' HT, m; intr. 1998

Côte Jardins® ('Orapent') F, mp, Orard; intr. 2001

'Cote Rotie' -- See 'Grand Amour'

Cotillion™ -- See 'Jacshok'

'Cotillion' F, yb, 1969, Byrum, Roy L.; bud ovoid; flowers yellow, edged pink, medium, high-centered, slight fragrance; foliage leathery; vigorous, upright growth; PP2978; ['Rumba' × 'Golden Garnette']; intr. 1967

'Cotlands Rose' -- See 'Micautumn'

'Coton Gold' -- See 'Babs'

'Cotorrita Real' Pol, pb, 1931, Padrosa; flowers white, rose and yellow, small, very dbl., globular, borne in clusters; profuse, repeated bloom; vigorous growth

'Cotswold Charm' HT, dp, 1967, Bennett, V.G.T.; flowers magenta, high-centered; foliage dark, leathery; moderate growth; [('Ophelia' × unknown) × 'William Moore']

'Cotswold Gold' -- See 'Jaycot'

'Cotswold Sunset' -- See 'Jaysun'

'Cottage Dream' -- See 'Pink Fire'

'Cottage Garden' -- See 'Chewily'

'Cottage Garden' -- See 'Haryamber'

Cottage Maid™ ('Odense City', Devon™, Jade™, Odense By-Rose™, Borussia™) S, my, Poulsen; flowers medium yellow, 8-10 cm., semi-dbl., borne in large clusters, slight wild rose fragrance; recurrent bloom; foliage dark; growth broad, bushy, 100-150 cm.; intr. 1990

'Cottage Maid' -- See 'Perle des Panachées'

'Cottage Pink' HMult, mp; flowers single

'Cottage Rose' ('The Cottage Rose') S, mp, Austin, David; flowers warm pink, medium, very full, borne in large clusters, moderate fragrance; foliage medium size, medium green, semi-glossy; numerous prickles; medium (40 in.), upright, bushy growth; [Mary Rose® × 'Wife of Bath']; intr. 1991

'Cottage Rose' S, mp; groundcover; spreading growth; intr. 2002

'Cottage White' HMult, w; flowers single

'Cotton Candy' HWich, mp, 1952, Moore, Ralph S.; bud well-formed; flowers 2½ in., very dbl., borne in clusters; foliage very glossy, turning to autumn colors; vigorous (10-15 ft.) growth; [R. wichurana × seedling (floribunda with R. multibracteata ancestry)]

Cotton Candy® -- See 'Bagcott'

'Cotton Top' F, w, 1960, Joseph H. Hill, Co.; bud short, pointed; flowers 2-3 in., 45-50 petals, flat, slight fragrance; foliage leathery; vigorous, upright, well-branched growth; PP1886; [seedling × 'White Butterfly']; intr. 1962

'Cottontail' -- See 'Tintail'

'Coucher de Soleil' -- See 'Coral Sunset'

Coucou® F, dy, Dorieux; flowers pure yellow; 80 cm. growth; intr. 1982

'Cougar' -- See 'Moecougar'

'Cougava' S, mp, Courage, R.full; intr. 2001

'Couglow' HT, yb, Courage; intr. 2001

'Couleur de Brennus' HGal, mr, before 1857; flowers medium, dbl.; slender, shrubby growth

'Couleur de Chair' -- See 'Vilmorin'

'Couleur de Feu' C, or, before 1908; flowers fiery orange, medium, full

'Couleur de Sang' -- See 'Admirable'

'Count Bawbrinzki' -- See 'Comte de Bobrinsky'

'Countenance' HT, mr, Williams, J.B.; flowers scarlet red, full, cupped, quartered, moderate fragrance; growth to 4 ft.; intr. 2005

'Countess Bertha' -- See 'Duchesse de Brabant'
'Countess Cadogan' HT, lp, 1978, Buss; bud long, pointed; flowers 4½ in., 40-45 petals, high-centered; foliage light green, leathery; very vigorous, upright growth; [sport of 'Carlita']
Countess Celeste™ -- See 'Pouldron'
'Countess Clanwilliam' HT, mr, 1915, Dickson, H.; flowers pinkish cherry-red, dbl., high-centered; foliage rich green; bushy growth
'Countess M. H. Chotek' -- See 'Gräfin Marie Henriette Chotek'
'Countess Mary' Cl HT, mp, 1933, Dixie Rose Nursery; [sport of 'Mary, Countess of Ilchester']
'Countess Mary of Ilchester' -- See 'Mary, Countess of Ilchester'
'Countess of Annesley' HT, pb, 1905, Dickson, A.; flowers flesh pink with salmon, medium, moderate fragrance
'Countess of Caledon' HT, lp, 1897, Dickson, A.; flowers blush pink, center darker, large
'Countess of Dalkeith' F, rb, 1958, Dobbie; flowers vermilion flushed orange, very dbl., intense fragrance; vigorous growth; [sport of 'Fashion']; intr. 1957
'Countess of Derby' HT, w, 1906, Dickson, A.; flowers creamy white with pink tints, large, dbl.
'Countess of Elgin' HT, op, 1925, Ferguson; flowers salmon-pink, reverse deep rose-pink; vigorous growth; [sport of 'Mme Edouard Herriot']
'Countess of Glasgow' HSpn, dr, before 1817, from England
'Countess of Gosford' HT, op, 1906, McGredy; flowers salmon-pink, long pointed, large, dbl.
'Countess of Ilchester' -- See 'Mary, Countess of Ilchester'
'Countess of Lieven' Ayr, w; flowers creamy white, medium, semi-dbl., cupped
'Countess of Lonsdale' HT, dy, 1919, Dickson, H.; flowers dbl.
'Countess of Oxford' -- See 'Comtesse d'Oxford'
'Countess of Pembroke' HT, pb; flowers pink shaded darker, large, very dbl.; vigorous growth
'Countess of Roseberry' HP, mr, 1879, Postans; flowers carmine red, large, full, cupped; foliage dark green; few prickles; ['Victor Verdier' × unknown]
'Countess of Shaftesbury' HT, pb, 1912, Dickson, H.; flowers silvery carmine, edged pearl pink, large, full
'Countess of Stradbroke' Cl HT, dr, 1928, Clark, A.; bud ovoid; flowers dark glowing crimson, well-shaped, very large, dbl., globular, borne singly or in small clusters, intense fragrance; free, recurrent bloom; foliage rich green, wrinkled; vigorous growth; ['Walter C. Clark' × unknown]
'Countess of Warwick' HT, my, 1919, Easlea; flowers lemon-yellow, edged pink, large, dbl.; foliage dark olive green
'Countess of Wessex' -- See 'Beacream'
'Countess Sonja' -- See 'Korfeimot'
'Countess Vandal, Climbing' -- See 'Comtesse Vandal, Climbing'
'Countess Vandal' -- See 'Comtesse Vandal'
'Country Dancer' S, dp, 1972, Buck, Dr. Griffith J.; bud ovoid; flowers rose-red, large, dbl., moderate fragrance; repeat bloom; foliage large, glossy, dark, leathery; vigorous, dwarf, upright, bushy growth; ['Prairie Princess' × 'Johannes Boettner']; intr. 1973
'Country Doctor' HT, lp, 1952, Brownell; bud long, pointed to ovoid; flowers silvery pink, large, dbl., high-centered, moderate fragrance; foliage glossy; vigorous, bushy growth; ['Pink Princess' × 'Crimson Glory']
'Country Fair' -- See 'Harbanner'
'Country Garden' -- See 'Bosanncoat'
'Country Girl' -- See 'Wilcgir'
'Country Girl' F, mr, 1960, Temmerman; bud ovoid; flowers geranium-red, medium, dbl.; vigorous growth; ['Independence' × 'Salmon Perfection']; intr. 1958
'Country Girl, Climbing' Cl F, mr, 1962, Buyl Frères
'Country Gold' -- See 'Sommermond'
'Country Heritage' -- See 'Coccages'
'Country Joy' -- See 'Morcojo'
'Country Lady' -- See 'Hartsam'
'Country Lass' -- See 'Korfullwind'
'Country Life' -- See 'Harzap'
'Country Living' -- See 'Auscountry'
'Country Maid' F, lp, 1972, Whartons Roses; low, compact growth; [sport of 'Tip Top']; intr. 1971
'Country Marilou' -- See 'Ausmary'
'Country Morning' -- See 'Flomor'
'Country Music' -- See 'Harcheer'
'Country Music' S, dp, 1972, Buck, Dr. Griffith J.; bud ovoid; flowers Neyron rose, large, dbl., moderate fragrance; intermittent bloom; foliage large, leathery; vigorous, dwarf, upright, bushy growth; ['Paddy McGredy' × (('World's Fair' × 'Floradora') × 'Applejack')]; intr. 1973
'Country Pride' LCl, ab
'Country Prince' -- See 'Royal Bassino'
'Country Song' -- See 'Korconta'
'Country Song' S, lp, 1985, Buck, Dr. Griffith J.; bud ovoid; flowers large, 28 petals, cupped, borne 1-5 per cluster, moderate myrrh fragrance; repeat bloom; foliage leathery, dark; prickles awl-like, brown; erect, bushy growth; hardy; ['Carefree Beauty' × 'The Yeoman']; intr. 1984
'Country Time' F, my, J&P; flowers creamy yellow, 25-30 petals, hybrid tea, borne in clusters, moderate spicy fragrance; recurrent; foliage dark green; few prickles; vigorous, compact (3.5 ft.) growth; intr. 2008
'Countryman' S, pb, 1978, Buck, Dr. Griffith J.; bud ovoid, pointed; flowers light rose-bengal, 4-5 in., 25-30 petals, cupped, moderate fragrance; foliage large, dark, leathery; vigorous, upright, spreading, bushy growth; [('Improved Lafayette' × 'Independence') × 'Maytime']
'Countryside Rose' S, ab; intr. 2004
'Countrywoman' HT, my, 1978, Dawson, George; bud globular; flowers lemon-yellow, medium, dbl.; foliage leathery; bushy growth; [seedling × 'Peace']
'County Fair' F, mp, 1960, Swim, H.C.; bud ovoid, pointed; flowers medium to dark pink, fading much lighter, 2½-3 in., 8-10 petals, flat, borne in clusters, slight fragrance; foliage leathery, dark, semi-glossy; vigorous, bushy growth; PP1897; ['Frolic' × 'Pink Bountiful']; intr. 1960
'County Fair, Climbing' Cl F, mp; intr. 1989
'County Girl' -- See 'Horalcamstrip'
'County of Cheshire' -- See 'Cheshire'
'Coup de Coeur' ('Home Sweet Home') LCl, mr, Maillard
'Coup de Foudre' F, or, 1956, Hémeray-Aubert; bud well-formed; flowers fiery red, cupped; foliage glossy, bronze; vigorous growth; [('Peace' × 'Independence') × 'Oiseau de Feu']
'Coup de Foudre, Climbing' Cl F, Fineschi, G.; intr. 1976
'Coupe d'Hébé' B, dp, 1840, Laffay, M.; flowers deep pink, waxy texture, large, very dbl., cupped; foliage glossy; vigorous, erect growth; ['Bourbon' × R. chinensis hybrid]
'Coupe d'Or' HWich, my, 1930, Barbier; flowers canary-yellow, aging lighter, 2 in., dbl., cupped, moderate fragrance; foliage rich green, leathery, glossy; vigorous, climbing or trailing growth; ['Jacotte' × unknown]
'Coupe d'Or' -- See 'Gold Cup'
'Courage' -- See 'Meicairma'
'Courage' HT, rb, Mallerin, C.; flowers red tinted yellow, open, very large, dbl., slight fragrance; vigorous, bushy growth; [seedling × 'Brazier']; intr. 1941
Courage™ ('Roy Castle Rose') HT, dr, Poulsen; flowers dark red, lighter reverse, 10-15 cm., full, high-centered, borne one to a stem, slight fragrance; recurrent; foliage matte; bushy (3-4 ft.) growth; intr. 1998
'Courage' HT, dr, 1923, McGredy; flowers deep brilliant maroon-crimson, very large, dbl., high-centered, intense fragrance; foliage rich green, leathery; bushy, dwarf growth
'Courageous' -- See 'Madrigal'
'Courageous Indira' HT, ob, Chandrakant More; flowers orange vermilion with white stripes and streaks; intr. 1991
'Courave' S, mr, Courage; intr. 2002
'Courier' HG, pb, 1930, Clark, A.; bud pale pink; flowers pink on white ground, 8-9 cm., dbl., borne in small clusters; foliage large; vigorous, climbing growth; [R. gigantea × 'Archiduc Joseph']
'Couronne de Salomon' HGal, dp, before

1819; flowers very intense pink, large, very dbl., flat; growth upright

'Couronne de Vibert'   HCh, mp, 1825, Bizard

'Couronne d'Or' -- See 'Gold Crown'

'Couronne Impériale'   HGal, m, about 1810, Descemet; flowers light violet, becoming purple, shaded lighter, large, full

'Couronnée'   HGal, m, about 1811; flowers light violet, large

'Court Jester'   F, ob, 1980, Cants of Colchester, Ltd.; flowers orange, reverse yellow, high-centered, borne 5-7 per cluster, slight fragrance; foliage mid-green, glossy; prickles large, hooked, red-brown; tall, upright growth

'Courtin'   HGal, lp, 1824, Cartier; flowers flesh pink

'Courtisane'   HT, or, Gaujard; flowers large, dbl.; intr. 1965

'Courtney' -- See 'Gelcourt'

'Courtney Carol' -- See 'Horpriceless'

'Courtney Page'   HT, dr, 1922, McGredy; flowers velvety dark scarlet-crimson, dbl.

Courtoisie® -- See 'Delcourt'

'Courtosie des Relais et Châteaux' -- See 'Delcourt'

'Courtship'   HT, mp, 1955, Shepherd; bud conical; flowers cerise-pink, reverse lighter, 4-5 in., 28 petals, high-centered; foliage dark; vigorous, bushy growth; PP1511; ['Mme Henri Guillot' × 'Peace']; intr. 1955

Courvoisier®   F, dy, 1971, McGredy, Sam IV; flowers large, 49 petals, high-centered, intense fragrance; foliage glossy, dark; [Elizabeth of Glamis® × 'Casanova']

'Cousaint'   HT, dy, Courage; intr. 2001

'Cousin Essie'   S, w, 1996, Robertson, Myrtle; flowers 1½ in., 8-14 petals, moderate fragrance; foliage medium size, medium green, semi-glossy; few prickles; spreading, bushy, tall, (6 ft.) growth; ['Honeyflow' × unknown]; intr. 1988

'Cousun'   HT, my, Courage; intr. 2002

'Couture'   ('Auzou') HCh, m, about 1825, Cartier; flowers bright violet

'Cova da Iria'   HT, rb, 1963, Moreira da Silva; flowers light red, reverse gold; [seedling × 'Crimson Glory']

'Covent Garden' -- See 'Cream Abundance'

'Covent Garden'   HT, rb, 1919, Cant, B. R.; flowers rich deep crimson flushed plum-black on reverse; foliage leathery, glossy; vigorous growth

'Coventrian'   F, dp, 1962, Robinson, H.; flowers ruby-cerise, well-formed, 3-3½ in., 30 petals, borne in large clusters; foliage dark, glossy; vigorous, bushy growth; ['Highlight' × seedling]

'Coventry Cathedral'   ('Cathedral', 'Houston') F, ab, 1973, McGredy, Sam IV; flowers apricot shading salmon, 4-5 in., 22-25 petals, borne in small clusters, slight anise fragrance; foliage glossy, olive-green; growth bushy, medium, compact; PP3524; ['Little Darling' × ('Goldilocks' × 'Irish Mist')]; intr. 1972

'Cover Girl'   HT, ob, 1960, Von Abrams; bud long, pointed; flowers orange, copper and gold, 5 in., 28-35 petals, high-centered, slight fragrance; foliage glossy, dark; upright, bushy growth; PP2020; ['Sutter's Gold' × ('Mme Henri Guillot' × seedling)]; intr. 1959

'Cowichan Super'   Cl HT, op, 1976, Meier, V. C.; flowers orange-salmon, 5 in., 30-35 petals, intense fragrance; bloom repeats; foliage glossy; tall, very vigorous growth; intr. 1975

'Cowli' ('Lisa') HT, dp, 1989, Cowper, Mrs. Maree; intr. 1989

'Cowra Rose'   Gr, mp, J&P; intr. 2000

'Cox's Pink Polyantha'   Pol, mp

'Cox's Red Polyantha'   Pol, mr

'Coy Colleen'   ('Blushing Rose') HT, w, 1953, McGredy, Sam IV; bud pointed, rosy white; flowers milky white, well-formed, borne in clusters; foliage glossy; vigorous growth; [('Modesty' × 'Portadown Glory') × 'Phyllis Gold']

'Cracker'   ('Cracker, Climbing') HWich, mr, 1920, Clark, A.; flowers bright red with prominent stamens, 7-8 cm., single; sometimes classed as HG

'Cracker, Climbing' -- See 'Cracker'

'Crackerjack' -- See 'Poulcrack'

'Crackerjack'   F, rb, 1960, Fryers Nursery, Ltd.; flowers scarlet flushed yellow, 20 petals, borne in clusters, moderate fragrance; free growth; ['Fashion' × 'Masquerade']; intr. 1959

Crackling Fire™ -- See 'Jacorg'

'Craig Christie'   F, dr, 2006, Paul Chessum Roses; flowers dbl., borne in small clusters, slight fragrance; foliage medium size, medium green, glossy; prickles large, long, red, few; growth compact, medium (24 in.); bedding, containers; [seedling × seedling]; intr. 2005

'Craighall Climbing Rose'   Ayr, w, 1828; flowers dbl.; possibly a natural hybrid between R. arvensis and a form of R. alba

'Craigweil'   HT, pb, 1929, Hicks; flowers silvery cerise-pink, reverse deeper, dbl.; strong stems; vigorous growth; ['Mme Abel Chatenay' × unknown]

'Cramoisi' -- See 'Tinwell Moss'

'Cramoisi' -- See 'Pompon de Bourgogne'

'Cramoisi' -- See 'Rubra'

'Cramoisi Brillant' -- See 'Temple d'Apollon'

'Cramoisi de Meaux' -- See 'Little Gem'

'Cramoisi des Alpes' ('Grand Corneille') HGal, mr, before 1829, Trébucien; flowers bright purplish red, dbl.; heavy, non-recurrent bloom

'Cramoisi Éblouissant'   Ch, dr, 1839, possibly Laffay; flowers medium, dbl.

'Cramoisi Foncé Velouté'   M, dr; flowers deep velvety crimson

'Cramoisi Incomparable' -- See 'Velours Pourpre'

'Cramoisi Majeur' -- See 'Hector'

'Cramoisi Picoté'   HGal, rb, 1834, Vibert; flowers crimson, streaked and mottled (striped & spotted) darker, 2 in., very dbl., moderate fragrance

'Cramoisi Royal' ('Beau Cramoisi Royal') HGal, about 1810, Descemet

'Cramoisi Simple'   HWich, rb, 1901, Barbier; flowers deep crimson red with white center, 4 cm., single to semi-dbl., borne in large, upright panicles; foliage light green, glossy; prickles moderate, pink, large; [R. wichurana rubra × 'Turner's Crimson Rambler']

'Cramoisi Supérieur' ('Agrippina', 'Lady Brisbane', 'Queen of Scarlet') Ch, mr, 1832, Coquereau; flowers crimson-red, small, dbl., cupped, borne in large clusters; recurrent bloom; vigorous growth

'Cramoisi Supérieur, Climbing' ('Agrippina, Climbing', 'Lady Brisbane, Climbing', 'Mme Couturier-Mention') Cl Ch, mr, 1885, Couturier; flowers crimson, medium, semi-dbl., cupped; ['Cramoisi Supéieur' × unknown]; possibly the same as 'Mme Couturier-Mention' or 'Rev. James Sprunt'

'Cramoisie' ('Carmosina', 'Crimson-Coloured Provins Rose') HGal, dr, before 1791; flowers crimson-red, turning to purple, medium, dbl.

'Cramoisie Éblouissante' ('L'Infante d'Espagne') HGal, dr, before 1811, from Holland; flowers crimson purple, very dbl.; foliage long, very dentate; prickles numerous, small, flexible

'Cramoisie Triomphante' ('La Plus Élégante', 'Superbe') HGal, dp, before 1811, from Holland; flowers crimson, plumed with lighter pink, small, moderate fragrance

'Cranbrook'   Pol, m, 1921, Matthews, W.J.

'Crane' -- See 'Tan Cho'

'Crane Viewing' -- See 'Tsurumi 90'

'Crarae'   HT, yb, 1986, McKirdy, J.M.; flowers deep yellow marked with scarlet, large, 35 petals, slight fragrance; foliage medium size, dark, glossy; bushy growth; [Piccadilly® × 'Fred Gibson']; intr. 1981

'Crathes Castle' -- See 'Cocathes'

'Crazy Dottie' -- See 'Seadot'

'Crazy For You' -- See 'Wekroalt'

'Crazy Horse'   HT, rb, Delbard; flowers basic white, striped, dotted and flecked with red, medium, dbl., no fragrance; numerous prickles; growth relatively compact and dense; PP10621; intr. 2001

'Crazy One' ('High Perfume') HT, rb, Delbard; flowers striped; intr. 2006

'Crazy Quilt' -- See 'Mortrip'

'Crazy Spire'   HT, or; flowers striped and spotted orange-red and yellow, dbl., high-centered, no fragrance; growth upright and slightly arching, 6 ft.; intr. 1995

'Creakes Rose'   F, lp; intr. 2007

'Cream Abundance' ('Covent Garden',

'Creme Abundance') F, w; flowers creamy color, 3½-4 in., 50 petals, borne in clusters that cover the bush; repeats well; foliage dark green; growth rounded (3 × 3 ft.); intr. 1999

'Cream Chica Kordana' Min, lp, Kordes; [sport of 'Chica Kordana']; container rose

'Cream Cracker' HT, w, 1979, Murray, Nola; bud pointed; flowers cream, high-centered, 4½ in., 38 petals, borne singly, intense apple fragrance; foliage large, matte; often thornless; bushy growth; ['Columbine' × 'Iceberg']

'Cream Cracker' HT, lp, 1933, Dickson, A.; flowers creamy buff, reverse shaded salmon, large, dbl., vigorous growth; RULED EXTINCT 10/78 ARM

'Cream Delight' HT, ab, Douglas; flowers cream, centered apricot; [sport of 'Nitouche']; intr. 1987

'Cream Delight' -- See 'Suncredel'

'Cream Dream' -- See 'Koromtar'

'Cream Flower Circus' F, ly, Kordes; flowers light amber, full, cupped, borne in clusters, moderate floral fragrance; recurrent; short growth; intr. 2008

'Cream Gold' Min, my, 1978, Moore, Ralph S.; bud long, pointed; flowers dbl., 38 petals, high-centered; compact, spreading growth; ['Golden Glow' × seedling]

'Cream Midinette' Min, w, Pearce; intr. 2003

'Cream Peach' F, w, 1976, Sheridan; flowers cream, edged pink, 3-4 in., 15-20 petals, slight fragrance; foliage large, glossy; very free growth; ['Paddy McGredy' × seedling]

Cream Prophyta™ HT, w, de Ruiter

'Cream Puff' MinFl, pb, 1981, Bennett, Dee; bud ovoid; flowers cream blushed pink, 18 petals, borne singly or in clusters of 3, moderate fragrance; foliage dark, semi-glossy; prickles long; spreading, bushy growth; PP5458; ['Little Darling' × 'Elfinesque']

'Cream Puff, Climbing' Cl Min, pb, Trimper, K.; [sport of 'Cream Puff']; intr. 1996

'Cream Silk' Min, w; intr. 2005

'Cream Sunsation' -- See 'Korgatine'

'Cream Trip' HRg, w, Bell; prickles very few; intr. 2001

'Creamsicle' Min, yb, Benardella, Frank; intr. 2007

'Credo' HT, mr, 1965, Gaujard; flowers purplish red, medium, dbl., high-centered; foliage leathery; vigorous, upright growth; ['Eminence' × 'John S. Armstrong']

'Cree' S, lp, 1932, Central Exp. Farm; flowers pale pink fading to white, large, single; early bloom, non-recurrent; foliage glossy, bright green; bushy growth; [R. rugosa albo-plena × R. spinosissima hispida]

'Creeping Everbloom' LCl, mr, 1939, Brownell; flowers 4 in., 30 petals, borne in clusters, moderate fragrance; recurrent bloom; growth to 3 ft.; ['Frederick S. Peck' × ('Général Jacqueminot' × 'Dr. W. Van Fleet')]

'Creepy' -- See 'Morpapplay'

'Creina Murland' HT, dy, 1934, Dickson, A.; flowers sunflower-yellow, deepening, dbl.; foliage glossy; very vigorous growth

'Crême' S, lp, 1895, Geschwind, R.; flowers pale yellowish-pink, 4-5 cm., semi-dbl., borne in clusters of 10-15, strong musk fragrance; good autumn repeat; numerous prickles; very hardy; [(R. canina × a Tea) × (R. canina × a Bourbon)]

'Creme Abundance' -- See 'Cream Abundance'

'Crème Anglais' ('Ganang') LCl, ly, Gandy; flowers soft yellow, dbl., borne in trusses; recurrent bloom; foliage pale green, plentiful; growth to 12-14 ft.; intr. 2004

'Crème Brulée' S, pb, Gandy; flowers peach tinted copper, large, semi-dbl.; recurrent bloom; foliage glossy; growth to 12-15 ft.; intr. 2004

'Crème Brulee' S, ly; flowers large, soft yellow, self-cleaning, dbl.; recurrent bloom; groundcover; spreading (24 × 36 in.) growth; intr. 2005

'Créme Caramel' -- See 'Pure Gold'

'Crème de la Crème' -- See 'Gancre'

'Creme de la Creme' HT, ly, Tantau; flowers large, double, flat topped, borne mostly singly; recurrent; stems medium to long; Florist rose; intr. 2006

'Crème Glacée' -- See 'Lavcreme'

'Creme Tausendschön' HMult, w

'Crenata' -- See 'À Feuilles Crénelées'

'Créole' HT, dr, 1962, Gaujard; bud long, pointed; flowers purplish, red base coppery, large, dbl.; foliage dark, glossy; very vigorous, bushy growth; ['Peace' × 'Josephine Bruce']

Crêpe de Chine® -- See 'Deltop'

'Crepe Myrtle' ('Harold Ickes') F, mr, 1937, Dixie Rose Nursery; growth to 5 ft.; [sport of 'Permanent Wave']

'Crepe Rose' -- See 'Paul Perras'

'Crepe Suzette' -- See 'Trasuz'

'Crépuscolo' HT, ob, 1955, Aicardi, D.; flowers copper, pointed, dbl.; strong stems; upright growth; ['Julien Potin' × 'Sensation']

'Crépuscule' N, ab, 1904, Dubreuil; flowers copper orange, fading to apricot-yellow, 8-9 cm., semi-dbl., borne in small clusters, intense sweet, musky fragrance; tall growth

'Crescendo' HT, rb; flowers bright red, base touched with white, well-formed, large, dbl.; tall growth

Crescendo® ('Noacres') F, mp, Noack; flowers 10 cm., full, cupped, quartered, borne in clusters; recurrent; foliage medium green, glossy; vigorous (80 - 90 cm) growth; intr. 2004

Crescent Moon™ -- See 'Moecrescent'

'Cresset' Gr, mr, 1961, Francis Hastings; bud long, pointed; flowers scarlet, semi-dbl., high-centered, borne in clusters, moderate fragrance; foliage leathery, glossy, dark; vigorous, bushy growth; [Queen Elizabeth® × 'Cocorico']; intr. 1961

'Cressida' -- See 'Auscress'

'Crested Damask' -- See 'Ardmarcrest'

'Crested Jewel' M, mp, 1971, Moore, Ralph S.; bud long, pointed, mossed like Crested Moss; flowers bright rose-pink, medium, semi-dbl., high-centered; foliage leathery; vigorous growth; ['Little Darling' × 'Crested Moss']

'Crested Marvel' F, dp, Moore; sepals long, fern-like, fluffy, much like those of Chapeau de Napoleon; flowers semi-dbl., borne in dense clusters, moderate fragrance; compact, medium growth; intr. 2005

'Crested Moss' ('Châpeau de Napoléon', 'Cristata', R. centifolia muscosa cristata, 'Crispé Mousseux', 'Crested Provins', 'Crested Provence', R. centifolia cristata) C, mp, 1827, Kirche/Roblin/Vibert; very heavily mossed, with 2 pairs of sepals joined and the 3rd separate; flowers rosy pink, medium to large, very full; probably a seedling of R. centifolia, rather than a sport; discovered by Kirche in the ruins of an old villa near Fribourg, Switzerland, then sent to Robbin and put in commerce by Vibert

'Crested Provence' -- See 'Crested Moss'

'Crested Provins' -- See 'Crested Moss'

'Crested Sweetheart' -- See 'Morsweet'

'Cri-Cri' ('Cricri', 'Gavolda') Min, ob, 1959, Meilland, F.; flowers salmon shaded coral, small, dbl.; foliage leathery; dwarf, very bushy growth; [('Alain' × 'Independence') × 'Perla de Alcañada']; intr. 1958

Cricket™ -- See 'Aroket'

'Cricket Cl.' Cl Min, ob

'Cricks' -- See 'Yorkshire Provence'

'Cricri' -- See 'Meicri'

'Crignon de Montigny' ('Monthyon', 'Montigny') HGal, dr, before 1842; flowers violet red, medium, full

'Crimean Night' HT, dr, USSR

'Crimewatch Rose' F, my; intr. 2006

'Crimson' -- See 'Tinwell Moss'

Crimson™ Min, dr, Poulsen; intr. 2000

'Crimson Beauty' HT, dr, LeGrice; flowers red, shaded scarlet and maroon, large, dbl., intense fragrance; foliage leathery, vigorous growth; ['Daily Mail Scented Rose' × 'Étoile de Hollande']; intr. 1935

'Crimson Beauty' HT, dr, 1930, Dingee & Conard; flowers crimson, dbl.; very vigorous growth; ['Hoosier Beauty' × 'Crimson Champion']

'Crimson Bedder' ('Souv de Louis Van Houtte') HP, mr, 1874, Cranston; flowers bright grenadine, large, dbl.

'Crimson Bedder' HMult, mp, Cooling; flowers single; intr. 1896

'Crimson Blush' -- See 'Sieson'

Crimson Bouquet™ -- See 'Korbeteilich'

The Official Registry and Checklist — Rosa

'Crimson Boursault' -- See 'Amadis'
'Crimson Brocade'   HT, dr, 1962, Robinson, H.; flowers bright scarlet-crimson, large, high-centered; strong stems; vigorous growth
'Crimson Cascade' -- See 'Fryclimbdown'
'Crimson Champion'   HT, dr, 1916, Cook, J.W.; flowers velvety crimson-red, dbl.; dwarf growth; ['Étoile de France' × seedling]
'Crimson Chatenay'   HT, dr, 1915, Merryweather; ['Mme Abel Chatenay' × 'Leuchtfeuer (HCh)']
'Crimson China Rose' -- See 'Slater's Crimson China'
'Crimson-Coloured Provins Rose' -- See 'Cramoisie'
'Crimson Conquest'   HWich, dr, 1931, Chaplin Bros.; flowers scarlet crimson, 2½ in., semi-dbl., borne in small clusters, moderate fruity fragrance; foliage large, glossy; vigorous growth; [sport of 'Red-Letter Day']
'Crimson Crown'   HT, mr, 1905, Dickson, A.; flowers red, middle yellowish-white, medium, semi-dbl.
'Crimson Damask'   ('Turner's Crimson Damask') D, dr, 1901, Turner; flowers crimson, semi-dbl.
'Crimson Dawn'   F, rb, 1970, Ellick; flowers crimson to carmine, 3½-4½ in., 20 petals; foliage dark; vigorous growth; [('Anne Poulsen' × 'Dainty Maid') × ('Bonn' × 'Opera')]
'Crimson Delight' -- See 'Johillgolf'
'Crimson Descant'   LCl, mr, 1972, Cants of Colchester, Ltd.; flowers crimson, 5 in., 30 petals, borne singly and in small clusters; foliage dark green, glossy; [Dortmund® × 'Etendard']
'Crimson Diamond'   HT, dr, 1947, Lammerts, Dr. Walter; bud long, pointed; flowers crimson-red, open, large, 35-40 petals; bushy growth; ['Crimson Glory' × 'Charlotte Armstrong']
'Crimson Duke'   HT, mr, 1963, Meilland, Alain A.; bud ovoid; flowers crimson, 4-5 in., 45-55 petals, high-centered, moderate fragrance; foliage leathery, dark; vigorous, upright, bushy growth; PP2348; [('Happiness' × 'Independence') × 'Peace']; intr. 1963
'Crimson Elegance' -- See 'Leocrel'
'Crimson Emblem'   HT, dr, 1916, McGredy; flowers brilliant crimson-scarlet, large, dbl., cupped; vigorous growth
'Crimson Erecta'   HT, 1954, Cazzaniga, F. G.
'Crimson Fire'   S, mr; flowers bright red with bright yellow center, single, flat; free-flowering; foliage glossy, medium green; mounding growth to 3 ft.; hips bright orange-red; intr. 2005
'Crimson Flame'   F, rb; flowers striped, 20 petals, slight to none fragrance; intr. 2007
'Crimson Floorshow'   S, dr, Harkness; flowers bright crimson, opening to show golden stamens, 2¾ in., dbl.; foliage leathery, dark green; mounding, spreading growth (2½ × 4 ft.); intr. 1999
'Crimson Fragrance'   HT, dr, 1980, Wright, R. & Sons; bud long, slender; flowers 38 petals, borne singly, intense fragrance; foliage slender, mid-green; prickles reddish-bronze; branching, upright growth; ['Fragrant Cloud' × seedling]
'Crimson Gem'   ('Flammette') Min, dr, 1974, deRuiter; bud ovoid; flowers deep red, medium, very dbl., cupped; foliage bronze, soft; vigorous, bushy growth; ['Lillan' × 'polyantha seedling']
'Crimson Globe'   M, dr, 1890, Paul, W.; flowers deep crimson, large, dbl., globular; vigorous growth
'Crimson Globe' -- See 'Dr Rocques'
'Crimson Glory'   HT, dr, 1935, Kordes; bud long, pointed; flowers deep velvety crimson, 5 in., 30-35 petals, cupped, borne mostly singly, intense damask fragrance; foliage leathery; vigorous, bushy, spreading growth; PP105; ['Cathrine Kordes' × 'W.E. Chaplin']
'Crimson Glory, Climbing'   ('Grimpant Crimson Glory') Cl HT, dr, 1942, Millar (also Richardson, 1944, J&P, 1946); flowers richer crimson than bush form, 10-12 cm., intense fragrance; PP736; intr. 1941
'Crimson Glow'   Pol, dr, Lammerts; flowers oxblood-red, semi-dbl., cupped, intense fragrance; foliage glossy, dark; vigorous, upright growth; ['Night' × 'Mrs Dudley Fulton']; intr. 1945
'Crimson Glow'   HWich, mr, 1930, Chaplin; flowers glowing carmine, semi-dbl.; ['Paul's Scarlet Climber' × 'American Pillar']
'Crimson Glow' -- See 'Our Princess'
'Crimson Grandiflora'   HMult, mr, 1912, Ghys; flowers purple red, 6 cm., full, borne in large clusters; very late spring bloom
'Crimson Halo'   HT, dr, 1964, Park; flowers deep rose-red, 5 in., 30 petals, globular; vigorous growth; ['Karl Herbst' × 'Crimson Glory']
'Crimson King'   ('Liebesglut') HT, dr, 1943, Kordes; bud ovoid, long, pointed; flowers deep velvety crimson, large, dbl., high-centered, intense damask fragrance; foliage leathery; vigorous, bushy growth; ['Crimson Glory' × 'Kardinal']
'Crimson Knight'   S, mr, Williams, J.B.; flowers crimson, borne in masses, moderate fragrance; intr. 1997
'Crimson Knight Mega Brite'   Min, dr, Walden; PP11158; intr. 1999
Crimson Lace™ -- See 'Jacezz'
'Crimson Mme Desprez'   B, dr; flowers crimson, large, cupped
'Crimson Masse' -- See 'Liberté'
'Crimson Medinette' -- See 'Poulcrim'
Crimson Meidiland® -- See 'Meiouscki'
Crimson Meidiland™ -- See 'Meizerbil'
Crimson Meillandecor® (Crimson Meidiland®) S, dr; flowers luminous red, dbl., borne in small clusters; growth to 90-120 cm.; intr. 1996
'Crimson Minijet'   Min, dr, Meilland
Crimson Minuetto™ -- See 'Meibarco'
'Crimson Moos' -- See 'Tinwell Moss'
'Crimson Moss' -- See 'Tinwell Moss'
'Crimson Moss de Meaux' -- See 'Little Gem'
'Crimson Orléans'   Pol, dr, 1922, Koster, M. (also Laxton, 1923); [sport of 'Orléans Rose']
Crimson Pillar™ -- See 'Meifulcen'
'Crimson Promise' -- See 'Springpromise'
'Crimson Queen'   HP, dr, 1890, Paul; flowers velvety crimson, shaded with fiery red and maroon, very large, globular
'Crimson Queen'   HT, dr, Montgomery, A.; flowers rich crimson, turning blue with age, very large, dbl., globular, intense fragrance; vigorous growth; [('Liberty' × 'Richmond') × 'Gen. MacArthur']; intr. 1912
'Crimson Rambler'   ('Shi Tz-mei', 'Soukara-Ibara', 'Ten Sisters', 'Turner's Crimson Rambler') HMult, mr, 1893, Turner; flowers bright crimson, fading toward blue, 3½-4 cm., semi-dbl. to dbl., borne in pyramidal corymbs, no fragrance; heavy, non-recurrent bloom; foliage light, leathery, glossy, disposed to mildew; very vigorous, climbing (15-24 ft.) growth; intr. 1893
'Crimson Rambler Remontant' -- See 'Flower of Fairfield'
'Crimson Rosamini'   Min, mr
'Crimson Rosette'   F, dr, 1948, Krebs; bud small, ovoid; flowers dark crimson, rosette, 1-1½ in., 30 petals, borne in clusters, slight fragrance; foliage leathery, dark; vigorous, bushy, dwarf growth; PP901
'Crimson Shower'   HWich, mr, 1951, Norman; flowers clear crimson, lighter reverse, 1¼ in., 20 petals, pompon, borne in loose clusters; foliage small, dark green, glossy; vigorous (10 ft.) growth; ['Excelsa' × unknown]
Crimson Sky™   LCl, mr, Meilland; flowers bright red, large , 28-35 petals, cupped, borne in clusters, slight to none fragrance; recurrent; foliage dark green; 8 - 12 ft. growth; PPAF; [Cappa Magna® × 'Ulmer Munster']; intr. 2007
'Crimson Spire' -- See 'Kormiach'
'Crimson Star' -- See 'Dencrim'
'Crimson Superb' -- See 'Mogador'
'Crimson Tide' -- See 'Macmota'
'Crimson Velvet'   F, dr; flowers medium, single
'Crimson Volunteer'   S, dr, Williams, J.B.; flowers velvet red, borne mostly one to a stem; intr. 2002
'Crimson Wave'   ('Imperator') F, mr, 1972, Meilland; flowers cardinal-red, shaded cherry, 4-5 in., 25-30 petals, slight apple fragrance; foliage large, semi-matte, dark; vigorous, upright growth; [Zambra® × (Sarabande® × ('Goldilocks' × 'Fashion'))]
'Crinkles' -- See 'Frocrin'
'Crinoline'   LCl, or, 1967, Hémeray-

Aubert; flowers semi-dbl., cupped; recurrent bloom; foliage bronze; vigorous, climbing growth; ['Diane d'Urfe' × 'Étendard']
Criollo® F, dp, Noack; flowers carmine pink, 6 cm., semi-double, shallow cup, borne in clusters; recurrent; foliage dark green, glossy; compact (40 - 50 cm.) growth; intr. 2005
'Crispata' HRg, lp, 1902, Kiese; flowers light carmine, single
'Crispé Mousseux' -- See 'Crested Moss'
'Crispin-Morwenna' -- See 'Harkitten'
'Crissy' Min, ob, 1979, Strawn; bud pointed; flowers deep bright coral, 1½-2 in., 20-25 petals, slight fragrance; foliage dark; PP4638; ['Liverpool Echo' × 'Sheri Anne']
'Cristal' HT, ob, 1937, Gaujard; bud long, pointed; flowers orange-yellow, large, dbl.; foliage leathery, light; vigorous, bushy growth; ['Julien Potin' × seedling]
'Cristata' -- See 'Crested Moss'
'Cristel Palace' -- See 'Poulrek'
'Cristian' -- See 'Metset'
'Cristin Cira' Gr, op, 1996, Vanderkruk, William; flowers orange, yellow, salmon blend, dbl., borne in small clusters, slight fragrance; foliage large, medium green, semi-glossy; some prickles; upright, medium growth; intr. 1995
'Cristina' HT, Zandri, R.; intr. 1972
'Cristina Vidal' F, my, Vidal
'Cristobal Colon' -- See 'Meinronsse'
'Cristoforo Colombo' ('Christophe Colombo') HT, yb, 1953, Aicardi, D.; bud long; flowers reddish-yellow, reverse tinged pink, large, 25-35 petals; foliage glossy; long stems; very vigorous growth; RULED EXTINCT 4/92; ['Julien Potin' × 'Frau Karl Druschki']
'Cristoforo Colombo' -- See 'Meinronsse'
'Criterion' HT, dp, 1966, deRuiter; flowers rose-red, 5 in., dbl., high-centered, moderate fragrance; recurrent; foliage dark; vigorous, tall growth; [('Independence' × 'Signal Red') × 'Peace']
'Criterion, Cl.' Cl HT, mr, Gressard; intr. 1978
'Crlbetsy' ('Betsy Jane') S, pb, 2004, Carle, Mary C.; flowers medium pink with white base, yellow stamens, 1 in., 5 petals, borne in clusters of 24-36, slight fragrance; quick repeat; foliage medium size, dark green, semi-glossy; small, hooked, brown, no prickle; growth spreading, medium (3-3½ ft.); garden; hips ruby; ['Climbing Rainbow's End' × unknown]; intr. 2004
'Crlsimple' (Simple Splendor™) Min, yb, 2003, Carle, Mary C.; flowers med. yellow with crimson edges, fading to pink, yellow stamens, 2 in., single, flat, wavy petals, borne solitary and in small clusters, slight fragrance; recurrent; foliage medium size, medium green, semi-glossy; prickles medium, hooked, green, few; growth upright, medium (18 in.); garden, exhibition; [sport of 'Autumn Splendor']; intr. 2003
'Crobourg' HT, my, Croix; intr. 2005
'Crock O' Gold' HT, my, 1970, Anderson's Rose Nurseries; flowers clear golden yellow, 4½ in., 30-35 petals, high-centered; [sport of 'Beauté']
'Crocus Rose' -- See 'Ausquest'
'Croft Original' HT, RB, 1972, Cocker; flowers old-gold and red, 5 in., 30 petals, moderate fragrance; foliage light
'Croix Blanche' HT, w, Croix, P.; flowers dbl., borne singly and in small clusters; intr. 1984
'Croix d'Honneur' HGal, mr, about 1830, Prévost; flowers bright red, small, full
'Croix d'Honneur' ('La Croix d'Honneur') HCh, w, Dorisy; flowers flesh white, reverse pink, large, dbl.; intr. 1852
'Croix d'Or' HT, my, Croix; flowers golden yellow, 4 in.; intr. 1985
'Croix d'Or, Climbing' Cl HT, my, Croix, P.
'Croix Mauve' S, m, Croix, P.; intr. 2004
'Croix Verte' -- See 'Rose Verte'
'Cromwell School' Misc OGR, rb
'Cropal' ('Aventure No. 2') HT, ob, Croix
'Crowd Pleaser' -- See 'Wekchrisg'
'Crown' -- See 'Louis-Philippe'
'Crown Jewel' F, or, 1965, Boerner; flowers bright orange-red, medium, dbl., borne in clusters, moderate fragrance; foliage dark, leathery; moderate growth; PP2590; ['Pink Bountiful' × 'Spartan']
'Crown of Gold' HT, yb, 1937, Duehrsen; bud pointed; flowers deep gold, edged lemon-yellow, large, dbl., high-centered; foliage light green, leathery, vigorous growth; [seedling × 'Joanna Hill']
'Crown of Jewels' -- See 'Little Beauty'
'Crown Prince' HP, rb, 1880, Paul & Son; flowers reddish-crimson tinged with purple; ['Duke of Edinburgh' × unknown]
'Crown Princess Margareta' -- See 'Auswinter'
Crown Princess Mary™ -- See 'Tomroyal'
Crowning Glory™ -- See 'Dicyardstick'
'Crucenia' -- See 'Hot Pewter'
'Crumble Bar' F, ab, LeGrice; flowers in shades of copper, apricot and old gold, medium size, 50-60 petals, borne in clusters; moderate rebloom; relatively low growth; intr. 1982
'Crusader' HT, dr, 1920, Montgomery Co.; flowers crimson-red, center brighter, large, 65 petals; foliage leathery, rich green; vigorous growth
'Crystal' Min, pb, 1985, Bridges, Dennis A.; flowers light pink, deep pink reverse, small, 35 petals, high-centered; foliage large, dark, glossy; bushy growth; ['Zinger' × seedling]
Crystal™ ('Cristel Palace', 'Crystal Palace') F, lp, Poulsen Roser APS; flowers creamy pink, 8-10 cm., dbl., slight wild rose fragrance; foliage dark; growth bushy, 40-60 cm.; intr. 1996
'Crystal Brook' HWich, pb, Sutherland; flowers single; intr. 1994
'Crystal Fairy' Pol, w, Spek; flowers snowy with touches of soft pink blush; low, spreading growth; PPAF; intr. 2001
'Crystal Lavender' -- See 'Lavender Crystal'
'Crystal Palace' -- See 'Poulrek'
'Crystal River' -- See 'Cascry'
'Crystal Star' Min, w, 1994, Muha, Julius; flowers medium, full, borne mostly singly and in small clusters, slight fragrance; foliage small, medium green, semi-glossy; some prickles; medium growth; ['Pink Petticoat' × 'Tooth of Time']; intr. 1994
'Crystal White' HT, w, 1965, Boerner; flowers clear white, large, dbl., high-centered, moderate fragrance; foliage leathery, moderate, bushy growth; PP2553; ['Princess White' × 'White Queen']
Crystalline™ -- See 'Arobipy'
'Crystal's Double Dark Red' HT, dr
'Csárdás' F, op, Berger, W.; flowers luminous orange-pink, large, dbl.; intr. 1965
'Csl Cerveny Kriz' Pol, mr, 1928, Böhm, J.; flowers small, dbl.
'Csl Legie' Cl HT, dr, 1933, Böhm, J.; flowers dark scarlet, dbl.
'Cuba' HT, rb, 1926, Pernet-Ducher; flowers cardinal-red, tinted yellow, fading quickly, large, semi-dbl., globular, intense fragrance; foliage dark, bronze; very vigorous growth
Cubana® -- See 'Korpatetof'
'Cuddle Up' -- See 'Tincuddle'
'Cuddles' Min, op, 1978, Schwartz, Ernest W.; bud ovoid; flowers deep coral-pink, 1-1½ in., 55-60 petals, high-centered, slight fragrance; compact growth; PP4291; ['Zorina' × seedling]
'Cuisse de Nymphe' -- See 'Great Maiden's Blush'
'Cuisse de Nymphe à Ovaire Lisse' -- See 'Maiden's Blush'
'Cuisse de Nymphe Émue' -- See 'Maiden's Blush'
'Cuisse de Nymphe Grande' -- See 'Great Maiden's Blush'
'Culverbrae' S, dr, 1972, Gobbee, W.D.; flowers crimson-purple, 3½-4 in., 58 petals, intense fragrance; some repeat bloom; foliage light; vigorous growth; ['Scabrosa' × 'Francine']
Cum Laude+ HT, op, Voom, Lex; flowers soft orange pink, double, high-centered, borne mostly singly; recurrent; stems medium; [sport of 'Talea']; florist rose
'Cumba Meillandina, Climbing' Cl Min, ob, Meilland; intr. 2003
Cumba Meillandina® -- See 'Meineyta'
'Cumbaya' HT, r, Meilland; flowers dusty orange-red with tan at base of petals, dbl., high-centered, borne mostly singly; recurrent; intr. 2005
Cumbaya® S, pb, Meilland; flowers pink with white eye, yellow stamens, medium, single, borne in large clusters; growth low, spreading (50 cm.); intr. 2000
'Cumberland' LCl, mr, Harkness; intr.

2008
'Cumberland' -- See 'Rubra'
'Cumberland Belle' ('La Poilu', 'Le Poilu') Cl M, lp, 1900, Dreer; flowers silvery pink, well mossed, small, very dbl.; [sport of 'Princesse Adélaide']
'Cunningham Lady Banks' S, ly, 1900
'Cunningham West Climber' N, ly, 1900
'Cup Final' -- See 'Macsingap'
'Cup of Joy' -- See 'Newgreg'
Cupcake™ Min, mp, 1981, Spies, Mark C.; bud ovoid; flowers clear medium pink, long lasting, 60 petals, high-centered, borne 1-5 per cluster, no fragrance; foliage glossy; no prickles; compact, bushy growth; PP4835; ['Gene Boerner' × ('Gay Princess' × 'Yellow Jewel')]
'Cupid' Cl HT, lp, 1915, Cant, B. R.; flowers glowing flesh, tinted peach, 4-5 in., single, borne in small clusters, moderate fragrance; non-recurrent; foliage large, light green; vigorous, pillar growth; hips large, orange, pear-shaped
'Cupid in the Garden' S, ab, Dickson; flowers peach with pink tones, 5.5 cm., 12 petals, borne in clusters of 7 - 30, slight fragrance; somewhat slow repeat; foliage medium, medium green, glossy; prickles few, medium; growth height 110 cm.; intr. 2007
Cupido® F, dr, Spek; flowers 9 cm., 30-35 petals, borne mostly singly; recurrent; stems long; intr. 2006
'Cupido' Min, lp, Maarse, G.; flowers shell-pink; growth to 6 in.
'Cupidon' F, dr, 1966, Gaujard; flowers brilliant crimson, small, semi-dbl., cupped; foliage leathery; vigorous, bushy growth; ['Chanteclerc' × 'Red Favorite']
'Cupid's Beauty' Min, ob, 1979, Williams, Ernest D.; bud long, pointed; flowers light orange and cream, 1½ in., 40-45 petals, high-centered, moderate fragrance; foliage small, dark; compact, spreading growth; PP4581; [seedling × 'Over the Rainbow']; intr. 1978
'Cupid's Charm' F, pb, 1964, Fuller; bud pointed; flowers salmon-pink, medium, 22 petals; vigorous, bushy growth; ['Little Darling' × 'First Love']
'Cupid's Heart' HT, rb; intr. 1997
'Cupid's Mark' Min, pb; intr. 2005
'Cupie Doll' -- See 'Tincupie'
'Curbal' ('Little Ballerina') Min, pb, 1988, Curtis, Thad; flowers white flushed pink, medium, 34-40 petals, high-centered, urn-shaped, borne singly; foliage medium size, medium green, semi-glossy; no prickles; growth bushy, medium; no fruit; ['Little Darling' × 'Little Pioneer']; intr. 1988
'Curé de Charentay' HP, dr, 1867, Ducher; flowers dark garnet purple, very large, full
'Curiace' T, yb, 1860, Bernède; flowers yellowish-white, edged pink, medium, full
'Curiosa, Climbing' Cl F, op

'Curiosa' -- See 'My Girl'
'Curiosity, Climbing -- See 'Best Wishes, Climbing'
'Curiosity' HT, rb, 1972, Cocker; flowers scarlet, reverse gold, 4 in., 35 petals, cupped; foliage variegated, green and white; [sport of 'Cleopatra']
'Curlem' ('Lemon Fluff') Min, my, 1985, Curtis, Thad; flowers small, 20 petals, high-centered, borne singly and in clusters; foliage small, medium green, matte; upright, bushy growth; [(seedling × 'Rise 'n' Shine') × 'Summer Butter']; intr. 1986
'Curly Locks' Min, lp, 1954, Robinson, T.; flowers soft pink; dwarf, compact growth
'Curly Pink' HT, mp, 1948, Brownell; bud long, pointed, rose-red; flowers 3½-5 in., dbl., moderate fragrance; foliage glossy, dark; vigorous, compact growth; PP842; ['Pink Princess' × 'Crimson Glory']
'Curmist' ('Mister Otis') Min, mr, 1985, Curtis, Thad; flowers small, 35 petals, high-centered, borne singly, no fragrance; foliage small, medium green, matte; upright, bushy growth; ['Rise 'n' Shine' × 'Fire Princess']; intr. 1986
'Curneer' ('Little Pioneer') Min, mr, 1985, Curtis, Thad; flowers gold stamens, small, 35 petals, high-centered, borne singly and in clusters, moderate fragrance; foliage small to medium size, medium green, matte; upright, bushy growth; [('Rise 'n' Shine' × 'Summer Butter') × 'Sheri Anne']; intr. 1986
'CurrentAffair' Min, dr, 1991, Gruenbauer, Richard; flowers red, reverse red with yellow, ages dark pink, medium, 80 petals, cupped, no fragrance; foliage medium size, dark green, semi-glossy; upright, medium growth; ['Red Ace' × seedling]; intr. 1993
'Curtain Call' HT, dp, 1978, Weeks; bud pointed; flowers cherry-red, 4-5 in., 32-35 petals, high-centered, slight fragrance; foliage dark, leathery; vigorous, growth; PP4282; ['First Prize' × seedling]
'Curtis Yellow' HT, my, 1974, Curtis, E.C.; flowers clear yellow, large, dbl., high-centered, moderate fragrance; foliage light, leathery; vigorous, upright growth; ['Golden Scepter' × 'Miss Hillcrest']; intr. 1973
'Curtoy' ('Toy Soldier') Min, rb, 1985, Curtis, Thad; flowers red-white blend, medium, 20 petals; foliage medium size, medium green, semi-glossy; bushy growth; ['Pink Parfait' × 'Over the Rainbow']
'Cute' HT, ob, Shirakawa, T.; flowers bright orange, reverse bright red, 11 cm., 30 petals, borne mostly solitary, moderate fragrance; foliage dark green, semi-glossy, often with 7 leaflets; prickles concave, numerous; growth upright, medium; [seedling × Prominent®]; intr. 1985
'Cuthbert Grant' ('Manitoba Centennial Rose') S, dr, 1967, Marshall, H.H.; bud ovoid; flowers deep purplish red, large, semi-dbl., cupped, slight fragrance; intermittent bloom; foliage glossy; vigorous, bushy growth; [('Crimson Glory' × 'Assiniboine') × 'Assiniboine']; originally registered as hybrid suffulta

'Cutie' Min, mp, 1952, Moore, Ralph S.; bud pointed; flowers clear pink, base white, 1 in., 16 petals, flat, slight fragrance; foliage small, glossy, bright green; prickles very few; dwarf (10 in.), bushy growth; PP1302; ['Dancing Doll' × 'Oakington Ruby']
'Cutie' Min, w, Tantau; intr. 2006
'Cutie Pie' -- See 'Renpie'
'Cuwaert' HT, Delforge, H.; intr. 1992
Cuyahoga™ -- See 'Poulbella'
'Cybele' HT, or, Kriloff; intr. 1973
Cybelle® S, m, Guillot-Massad; flowers bright reddish-purple, full, cupped, borne in clusters of 3-5; dark, glossy foliage; growth to 4 ft.; intr. 2000
Cyclamen® -- See 'Orafuna'
'Cyclamen' F, mp, 1959, Delbard-Chabert; bud long; flowers 3 in., semi-dbl., borne in sprays of 4-6; vigorous, bushy growth; [(('Frau Karl Druschki' × unknown) × (Orange Triumph® × unknown)) × ((Orange Triumph® × unknown) × 'Tonnerre')]
'Cyclamen La Sevillana' – See 'Orfuna'
'Cyclamen Meillandecor' -- See 'Meipelta'
Cycloon® F, mr, Interplant; intr. 2006
'Cyclope' Pol, m, 1909, Dubreuil; flowers velvety carmine purple, lined white, with pale yellow stamens, borne in clusters of 10-20; ['Mme Norbert Levavasseur' × unknown]
'Cygne Blanc' -- See 'White Swan'
'Cygne Noir' HT, dr
'Cymbaefolia' ('À Feuilles de Chanvre', R. alba staxon cymbaefolia, R. cannabifolia, R. cymbifolia) A, w, 1807, Flobert/Pelletier; flowers matte white, small, semi-dbl. to dbl., borne in clusters; foliage whitish and cottony beneath, simple, elongate; nearly thornless; possibly synonymous with 'À Feuilles de Pêcher'
'Cymbaline' -- See 'Auslean'
'Cymbeline' -- See 'Auslean'
'Cynosure' HT, rb, 1978, Hardikar, Dr. M.N.; bud ovoid; flowers red, striped pink, 4½ in., 50 petals, intense fragrance; foliage glossy, soft; vigorous, upright growth; ['Scarlet Knight' × 'Festival Beauty']; intr. 1973
'Cynthia' HT, my, 1909, Paul, W.; flowers citron-yellow, tinted white, very large, full
'Cynthia' HT, mr, Verschuren-Pechtold; flowers rich oriental red, dbl.; intr. 1934
'Cynthia' ('Chanterelle') HT, dp, Warriner, William A.; bud long; flowers deep pink, 5 in., 35 petals, high-centered, moderate fragrance; foliage large, matte, light; tall, upright growth; PP3838; [seedling × 'Bob Hope']; intr. 1976
'Cynthia Ann Parker' HT, w, 1929,

Vestal; flowers white tinged yellow or cream, dbl.

'Cynthia Brooke' HT, yb, 1943, McGredy; flowers empire yellow, reverse light salmon, 4 in., 45 petals, globular, moderate fruity fragrance; foliage leathery, dark; moderate, compact, bushy growth; PP551; [('Le Progres' × ('Mme Mélanie Soupert' × 'Le Progres')]

'Cynthia E. Hollis' HMult, lp, Dawson; flowers pale pink, dbl.; foliage small, glossy

'Cynthia Forde' -- See 'Miss Cynthia Forde'

'Cynthia Westcott' F, mp, Williams, J. Benjamin; flowers medium pink fading to ivory pink, 4 in., moderate fragrance; growth to 3 ft.; intr. 1997

'Cynthie I' HGal, lp, before 1820, Descemet, M.; flowers pale rose, circumference almost blush, large, dbl., cupped; erect, moderate growth

'Cynthie II' HGal, m, before 1820, Descemet/Vibert; flowers lilac-garnet, aging to purple-violet, reverse creamy white, large, full, cupped

'Cyprienne' Pol, mr, 1969, Delforge; bud ovoid; flowers light brilliant red, large, dbl.; abundant, continuous bloom; foliage glossy, light; moderate, bushy growth; ['Sumatra' × 'Fashion']

'Cypris' -- See 'Calypso'

'Cyrano' HT, rb, 1954, Gaujard; flowers bright red shaded purple, large, dbl.; long stems; very vigorous, upright growth; [('Opera' × seedling) × seedling]

Cyrano de Bergerac® -- See 'Meivanery'

'Cyril Fletcher' -- See 'Beeril'

'Cyril Gully' HT, lp, 2002, Poole, Lionel; flowers full, high-centered, borne mostly solitary, slight fragrance; foliage medium size, medium green, semi-glossy; prickles medium, slightly hooked, moderate; growth upright, bushy, vigorous, medium (1 m.); garden, exhibition; [('Hazel Rose' × 'Cardiff Bay') × 'New Zealand']; intr. 2003

'Cystic Fibrosis' -- See 'Tomfib'

'Czardas' HT, rb, 1956, Delforge; flowers red, becoming pink; vigorous growth; ['Tango' × seedling]

— D —

'D. Ana Guedes' HT, ob, 1938, Moreira da Silva; bud ovoid; flowers orange and salmon-pink, veined yellow, large, dbl., cupped; foliage soft; vigorous, bushy growth; ['Angèle Pernet' × 'Mme Méha Sabatier']

'D. Angelica Pereira da Rosa' HT, pb, 1936, Moreira da Silva; flowers pink, shaded golden orange, reverse red, open, very large, dbl.; foliage light; ['Angèle Pernet' × 'Edith Nellie Perkins']

'D. D. Ruaux' -- See 'Doryeco'

'D. H. Lawrence' -- See 'Roslaw'

'D. Laura Pinto d'Azevedo' HT, pb, 1936, Moreira da Silva; flowers shrimp-pink, center coral-red, base orange-yellow, very large, dbl., high-centered; foliage light, soft; ['Pink Pearl' × 'Constance']

'D. Malvina Loureiro' F, Moreira da Silva, A.

'D. Maria Antonia Pacheco' HT, mp, 1935, Moreira da Silva; flowers deep carmine-pink, well-formed, large, dbl.; foliage rich green, glossy; vigorous growth; ['Mme Butterfly' × 'Johanniszauber']

'D. Maria do Carmo de Fragoso Carmona' HT, pb, 1939, Moreira da Silva; bud long, pointed; flowers flesh-pink, edged yellow, large, dbl., high-centered; foliage glossy; long stems; vigorous growth; ['Charles P. Kilham' × 'Souv. de Claudius Pernet']

'D. Maria José de Melo' HT, op, Moreira da Silva; flowers salmon-pink

'D. Maria Navarro' HT, rb, 1962, Moreira da Silva; flowers carmine; ['First Love' × 'Paramount']

'D. Silvia Ferreira' HT, ob, Moreira da Silva; flowers salmon and red, reverse old-gold

'D. T. Poulsen' F, mr, 1930, Poulsen, S.; flowers bright blood-red, open, semi-dbl.; foliage dark, leathery; bushy growth; ['Orléans Rose' × 'Vesuvius']

'D. T. Poulsen Improved' F, mr, 1940, Van der Vis; bud small, globular, blood-red; flowers solid cherry-red, open, 30-35 petals; foliage leathery, wrinkled, dark; short, strong stems; vigorous, compact, bushy growth

'Dab' HT, ab, 1985, Bridges, Dennis A.; flowers apricot center, pink reverse, petals tipped deep pink, large, 35 petals, high-centered, no fragrance; foliage large, dark, glossy; bushy growth; ['Lady X' × 'Flaming Beauty']; intr. 1985

'Dacapo' F, op, 1961, deRuiter; flowers deep salmon-pink, 3-4 in., 28 petals, borne in clusters, slight fragrance; vigorous, compact, bushy growth; ['Fashion' × 'floribunda seedling']

Dacapo™ ('Merengue') LCl, mr, Olesen; bud pointed ovoid, broad base; flowers medium red, 2 in., 25-30 petals, rosette, borne in large clusters, very slight fragrance; recurrent; foliage dark green, glossy; prickles numerous, 10 mm., hooked downward; bushy (150-200 cm.) growth; PP16502; [Bassino® × seedling]; intr. 2004

'Daddies Girl' HT, yb, 1963, McTeer, Gilbert; flowers milky white flushed pink, base golden, 5-6 in., 40 petals; foliage dark; vigorous, spreading growth; ['McGredy's Ivory' × 'Peace']

'Daddy Anstey' -- See 'Rawsolbab'

'Daddy's Girls' F, ab; flowers orangey-apricot, full; intr. 2006

'Daddy's Pink' A, lp

'Dad's Promise'

Dady® F, mp, 1978, Gaujard; ['Mignonne' × seedling]; intr. 1975

'Dafne' -- See 'Barafne'

'Dagenham Show' F, ob, 1976, Warley Rose Gardens; flowers salmon-orange, large, 25 petals; foliage matte; bushy growth; [Elizabeth of Glamis® × seedling]

'Dagmar' F, mr, Urban, J.

Dagmar Hastrup® ('Frau Dagmar Hartopp', 'Frau Dagmar Hastrup', 'Fru Dagmar Hartopp', 'Fru Dagmar Hastrup') HRg, lp, 1914, Hastrup; flowers silvery pink, 5 petals; foliage crinkled, rich green; low growth; [R. rugosa × unknown]; intr. about 1914

'Dagmar Späth' ('Blanc Lafayette', 'White Lafayette') F, w, 1936, Wirtz & Eicke; flowers white, edge flushed pink, fading pure white; [sport of 'Lafayette']

'Dagmar Späth, Climbing' Cl F, w, 1940, Buisman, G. A. H.; also Howard Rose Co., 1943, Huber, 1961

'D'Aguesseau' HGal, mr, 1836, Parmentier or Vibert; flowers crimson at center, shaded purple-mauve on the edges, aging to violet, with a small center button, small, dbl., flat, borne singly or in clusters of 2-3, moderate fragrance; foliage thick, medium green; few prickles; compact, erect growth

'Dahlila' F, yb, 1962, Leenders, J.; flowers yellow, becoming red; ['Golden Perfume' × 'Peace']

'Daichi Mao' HT, mp, Teranishi; intr. 2004

Daidala® F, m, 1976, Kordes; bud ovoid; flowers 4 in., 35 petals, high-centered, slight fragrance; foliage dark, soft; vigorous, upright, bushy growth; [seedling × 'Silver Star']; intr. 1975

'Daily Express' -- See 'Frychambi'

'Daily Herald' HT, yb, 1942, Robinson, T.; bud pointed; flowers yellowish-orange, 4-5 in., dbl., cupped; foliage glossy, dark; vigorous, upright growth

'Daily Mail Rose' -- See 'Mme Édouard Herriot'

'Daily Mail Rose, Climbing' -- See 'Mme Édouard Herriot, Climbing'

'Daily Mail Scented Rose' HT, rb, 1927, Archer; flowers crimson, shaded maroon and vermilion, reverse dark crimson, petals imbricated, intense damask fragrance; ['Château de Clos Vougeot' × 'Kitchener of Khartoum']

'Daily Mail Scented Rose, Climbing' Cl HT, rb, 1930, Archer

'Daily Post' -- See 'Frytrooper'

'Daily Sketch' F, pb, 1961, McGredy, Sam IV; flowers petals silver, edged deep pink, well-formed, large, 46 petals, borne in clusters, moderate fragrance; foliage dark; vigorous, bushy growth; ['Ma Perkins' × 'Grand Gala']; intr. 1961

'Daily Telegraph' -- See 'Peahigh'

'Daimonji' HT, or, 1986, Shibata, T.; flowers large, 48 petals, high-centered, borne usually singly, slight fragrance; foliage medium size, dark; medium, bushy growth; [seedling × ('Miss Ireland' × 'Polynesian Sunset')]; intr. 1981

'Dainty' T, yb, 1902, Paul; flowers primrose yellow, edged & tipped with carmine, large, borne in clusters

'Dainty' HT, pb, Dickson, H.; flowers rosy

apricot, tinted cherry-pink, edges and reverse deeper pink, dbl., moderate fragrance; intr. 1922

'Dainty' Pol, op, deRuiter; flowers salmon-pink, cupped; intr. 1931

'Dainty Bess' HT, lp, 1925, Archer; flowers soft rose-pink, very distinct maroon stamens, broad, fimbriated petals, 5 in., single, borne in clusters of 5-9, moderate tea fragrance; foliage leathery, dark green; vigorous growth; ['Ophelia' × 'Kitchener of Khartoum']

'Dainty Bess, Climbing' Cl HT, lp, 1935, van Barneveld; flowers pale lilac pink, darker reverse, prominent maroon stamens, large, single; [sport of 'Dainty Bell']

'Dainty Bouquet' -- See 'Lavfuhr'

'Dainty Dawn' Pol, mp, 1931, Knight, G.; flowers cerise-pink to mauve, semi-dbl., cupped, borne in clusters; foliage bronze; ['Amaury Fonseca' × 'Annchen Müller']

'Dainty Delight' Cl HT, mp, 1949, Duehrsen; bud ovoid; flowers darker pink than Dainty Bess, medium, semi-dbl., globular, borne in clusters; foliage glossy; vigorous (6-8 ft.) growth; ['Ednah Thomas' × 'Dainty Bess']

'Dainty Dinah' -- See 'Cocamond'

'Dainty Double Pink Cushion Rose' -- See 'The Fairy'

'Dainty Lady' HT, mp, 1959, Peden, G.H.; bud long, pointed; flowers pink, medium, dbl., high-centered, moderate fragrance; foliage leathery; vigorous, upright, compact growth; [('Girona' × 'Pres. Herbert Hoover') × 'Michèle Meilland']

'Dainty Lady' F, op, Fryers Nursery, Ltd.; flowers coppery salmon-pink, well-formed, borne in clusters; moderate growth; ['Baby Sylvia' × seedling]; intr. 1963

'Dainty Maid' F, pb, 1940, LeGrice; bud pointed, cerise; flowers silvery pink, reverse carmine, single, borne in clusters; foliage leathery, dark; vigorous, compact, bushy growth; ['D.T. Poulsen' × seedling]

'Dainty Ruffles' S, w, Lougheed, Larry; flowers white with some pink tints, 15-20 petals; intr. 2007

'Dainty Star' F, mr, 1973, Khanna, K. R., & Lata, P.; buds medium, pointed; flowers light crimson, medium, semi-dbl., open, borne mostly singly; foliage medium size, dark green, soft; few prickles; growth very vigorous, upright, open; ['Dusky Maiden' × 'Docteur Valois']

'Dainty Superior' Pol, op, deRuiter; flowers have more lasting color; [sport of 'Dainty']

'Dairy Maid' F, ly, 1957, LeGrice; bud yellow, splashed carmine; flowers cream, fading white, large, 5 petals, borne in large clusters; foliage glossy; vigorous growth; PP1792; [('Poulsen's Pink' × 'Ellinor LeGrice') × 'Mrs Pierre S. duPont']

'Daisy' HT, mp, 1898, Dickson, A.; flowers silvery carnation pink, large, full, moderate fragrance

'Daisy' HT, ob, Hicks; flowers orange-flamed; [sport of 'Mme Edouard Herriot']; intr. 1923

'Daisy Brasileir' HMult, rb, 1918, Turbat; flowers bright red and purple-red, anthers yellow, 3 cm., single, borne in clusters of 30; foliage dark green; hips orange-red

'Daisy Bud' HT, pb, 1933, Dickson, A.; bud well shaped; flowers rosy pink, shaded carmine and silver, large, moderate fragrance

'Daisy Doll' Min, pb, 1977, Lyon; bud long, pointed; flowers rose-pink, open, 1½ in., 20-25 petals; foliage tiny; compact, upright growth; ['Little Amy' × seedling]

'Daisy Dumas' HT, rb, 1965, White, T. Howland; flowers bright red, reverse gold edged red, medium, dbl., slight fragrance; foliage dark; bushy growth; [seedling × ('Tzigane' × seedling)]; intr. 1962

'Daisy Hill' S, lp, about 1906, Smith; flowers pale silvery blush, suffused with peach, medium, single, moderate fragrance; growth to 8 ft.; abundant fruit; [R. waitziana macrantha × R. chinensis]

'Daisy Hillary' F, op, 1963, Mell; bud pointed; flowers salmon-pink, large, dbl., high-centered, borne in clusters; foliage leathery, vigorous, bushy growth; [sport of 'Spartan']

'Daisy Kordana' Min, lp, Kordes; flowers soft pink, dbl., container rose

'Daisy Lane' -- See 'Seadai'

'Daisy Mae' HT, dy, 1987, Stoddard, Louis; flowers deep yellow, reverse medium yellow, large, 6 petals, flat, borne singly; foliage large, dark green, semi-glossy; prickles large, red down-curved, fading gray-tan; upright, tall growth; hips round to ovoid, russet-yellow; [Golden Showers® × 'Golden Sun']

'Daisy May Rogers' HMsk, w, 1996, Muia, Charlotte R.; flowers 1 in., single, borne in large clusters, slight fragrance; foliage small, medium green, semi-glossy; prickles small, moderate; bushy, spreading, medium (4 × 5 ft.) growth; ['Mozart' × unknown]; intr. 1992

'Daisy Rose' -- See 'Kordaisy'

'Dakar' HT, dy, Interplant; greenhouse rose; intr. 2002

'Dakar' HT, pb, 1932, Gaujard; flowers silvery pink, striped rose-pink, large; long, strong stems; ['Julien Potin' × seedling]

'Dakota' Min, mr, 1991, McGredy, Sam; flowers bright clear red, showing golden stamens, medium, semi-dbl., borne singly or with 2 side buds; foliage small, medium green, semi-glossy; growth bushy (32 cm.); ['Volare' × 'Eyeopener']; intr. 1992

'Dakota' HT, dr; flowers dbl., high-centered, borne one per stems; foliage medium size, dark green, matte

'Dakota Sun' -- See 'Daksun'

'Dakota's Song' -- See 'Daksong'

'Daksong' ('Dakota's Song') S, ab, 2005, Smith, Robert L.; flowers apricot-pink, reverse yellow blend, 3 in., single, borne in small clusters, moderate fragrance; foliage medium size, medium green, semi-glossy; prickles 3/8 in., wide based; growth upright, medium (3½ × 2 ft.); garden; hardy to -30°F; ['Prairie Harvest' × ('Golden Unicorn' × 'Applejack')]

'Daksun' ('Dakota Sun') S, my, 2005, Smith, Robert L.; flowers 4 in., single, borne in small clusters, no fragrance; foliage medium green, glossy; prickles ½ in., wide-based; growth upright, medium (4 × 3 ft.); garden decoration; hardy to -30°F; ['Prairie Harvest' × 'Shrub seedling']

'Dale Farm' F, or, 1975, Smith, E.; flowers vermilion, 3 in., 25 petals, moderate fragrance; foliage dark; vigorous growth; intr. 1973

Dale's Sunrise® -- See 'Kinsun'

'Dalila' HT, rb, 1943, Gaujard; bud long, pointed; flowers brilliant coppery red, large, semi-dbl., moderate fragrance; foliage leathery; vigorous, erect growth; ['Souv. de Claudius Pernet' × seedling]

'Dalila' F, ob, Buyl Frères; flowers orange, dbl.; intr. 1958

'Dallas' HT, rb, 1965, Hunter; flowers crimson-carmine, base primrose-yellow, very large, 40 petals; foliage dark, glossy; vigorous growth; [sport of 'Peace']; intr. 1963

'Dallas' -- See 'Korlimit'

'Dallas Gold' HT, yb, 1987, Winchel, Joseph F.; flowers large, heavy, 25 petals; foliage medium size, dark green, glossy; bushy growth; [seedling × 'Flaming Beauty']; intr. 1987

Dalli Dalli® -- See 'Tanlilida'

'Dalton's Gold' Min, dy, Dickson; buds golden; flowers dbl.; growth medium; intr. 1999

'Dalvey' HT, dp, 1971, MacLeod; flowers deep pink, 5½ in., high-centered; foliage medium size, light green, matte; vigorous growth; ['Peeping Tom' × seedling]

'Dama di Cuori' -- See 'Dame de Coeur'

'Damara' Min, mr, 2006, Hopper, Nancy; flowers bright, velvety red, 2¼ in., dbl., borne mostly solitary; foliage medium green, matte, new growth is reddish; prickles ¼ in., brown, moderate; growth bushy, medium (16 in.); ['red seedling' × 'unnamned red']; intr. 2006

Damaris® HT, ab, Spek; flowers pale, pastel apricot, 11-12 cm., 35-45 petals, high-centered, borne mostly singly; recurrent; prickles moderate; stems long; intr. 2006

'Damas de Yuste' -- See 'Liberty Bell'

'Damas Franklin' D, pb, 1853, Robert; flowers flesh-pink, shading to silver

'Damas Monstrueux' -- See 'Arielle'

'Damas Mousseux' -- See 'Tinwell Moss'

'Damas Violacé' ('Belle Fleur', 'La Divinité') D, m, 1820, Godefroy; flowers pale flesh pink with purple-violet, medium, very full; few prickles

'Damascena Petala Variegata' -- See *R. × damascena versicolor*

'Damask Monthly' -- See 'Quatre Saisons Continue'

'Damask Rose' -- See 'Summer Damask'

'Dame Blanche' HWich, w, 1923, Turbat; flowers greenish white, stamens yellow, single, borne in clusters; non-recurrent bloom; vigorous growth

'Dame Blanche' ('White Lady') HT, w, Mühle; flowers white tinged green, dbl., moderate fragrance; ['Stadtrat Glaser' × unknown]; intr. 1927

'Dame Cath' -- See 'Machilver'

'Dame Catherine' HT, dy, 1937, Cant, B. R.; bud ovoid; flowers golden yellow, large, dbl., high-centered; foliage glossy; long stems; vigorous, bushy growth

'Dame de Coeur' ('Dama di Cuori', 'Red Peace', 'Herz-Dame', 'Queen of Hearts') HT, mr, 1959, Lens; flowers cherry-red, large, dbl., moderate fragrance; foliage dark, glossy; vigorous growth; ['Peace' × 'Independence']; intr. 1958

'Dame de Coeur, Climbing' Cl HT, mr, 1985, Mungia, Fred A., Sr.; upright growth, 8-10 ft.; PP4876; [sport of 'Dame de Coeur']; intr. 1984

'Dame de Köbenhavn' -- See 'Poulusa'

Dame de L'Etoile® -- See 'Adaburi'

'Dame de Montsoreau' -- See 'Chewcorpink'

'Dame Edith Helen' HT, mp, 1926, Dickson, A.; flowers glowing pink, very large, full, cupped, moderate fragrance; not very free bloom; foliage leathery; long, strong stems; vigorous, bushy growth; ['Mrs John Laing' × 'a Pernetiana']

'Dame Edith Helen, Climbing' Cl HT, mp, 1930, H&S; flowers dark pink, very large, very full; [sport of 'Dame Edith Helen']

'Dame Elisabeth Murdoch' -- See 'Korwarpeel'

'Dame Joyce Frankland' -- See 'Hornewgram'

'Dame Kazuko' HT, dr, Takahashi, T.; flowers purplish-crimson, petals slightly reflexed, 14 cm., 30-32 petals, high-centered, slight fragrance; foliage dark green, large; prickles pointing slightly downward, moderate; growth bushy; ['Royal Highness' × 'Big Chief']; intr. 1993

'Dame of Sark' F, ob, 1976, Harkness; flowers orange flushed red, reverse yellow, 4½ in., 33 petals; foliage large, dark; [('Pink Parfait' × 'Masquerade') × 'Tablers' Choice']

'Dame Prudence' S, lp, 1969, Austin, David; flowers soft pink, reverse lighter, medium, 65 petals, flat; ['Ivory Fashion' × (Constance Spry® × 'Ma Perkins')]

'Dame Roma' -- See 'Tomrom'

'Dame Vera Lynn' -- See 'Peamax'

'Dame Wendy' -- See 'Canson'

'Dames de Chenonceau' S, lp, Delbard; flowers very dbl., intense rose, orange and apricot fragrance; intr. 2002

'Dames Patronesses d'Orléans' HP, dr, 1877, Vigneron; flowers crimson red, large

'Damien's Amulet' T, lp

'Damon Runyon' HT, mr, 1955, Duehrsen; bud ovoid; flowers crimson, 4-5½ in., 50 petals, high-centered, moderate fragrance; foliage glossy, coppery green; vigorous, upright, bushy growth; PP1441; ['Major Shelley' × 'Heart's Desire']; intr. 1954

'Dan Poncet' ('Poncet') S, pb, Massad-Guillot; flowers small, chubby, crimson pink, pointed petals, some fragrance; foliage dark green; growth bushy, 70 cm.; intr. 2000

'Dan Rafter' -- See 'Kensoixnu'

'Dana' HT, mp, 1982, Swim, H.C. & Ellis, A.E.; bud long, pointed; flowers 38 petals, spiraled, formal, borne singly, sometimes 3 per cluster, slight carnation fragrance; foliage large, semi-glossy; prickles long, straight; tall, upright, bushy growth; PP4707; ['White Satin' × 'Bewitched']

'Danaé' HGal, lp, 1854, Robert; flowers flesh pink, shaded violet, medium, full

'Danaé' HP, pb, 1865, Touvais; flowers translucent pink, shaded cherry red, large, full

'Danaë' HMsk, ly, 1913, Pemberton; flowers pale buff-yellow, fading white, semi-dbl. to dbl., borne in clusters; recurrent bloom; growth to 6 ft.; ['reputedly Trier' × 'Gloire de Chedane-Guinoiseau']

'Danara' Min, rb, 2006, Hopper, Nancy; flowers blended dark red and mauve, reverse red, 3½ in., full, borne mostly solitary; foliage medium size, medium green, semi-glossy; prickles ¼ in., yellow, few; growth bushy, medium (16 in.); ['single red mini' × 'Sweet Chariot']; intr. 2007

'Dance of Joy' F, mr, 1931, Sauvageot, H.; flowers vivid scarlet-crimson, large, dbl.; foliage dark; vigorous growth; ['Paul's Scarlet Climber' × seedling]

'Dance of Joy 95' -- See 'Saudero'

'Dance of Spring' -- See 'Harunomai'

'Dancer' Min, m; intr. 2005

'Dancing Butterflies' LCl, ab

'Dancing Dawn' -- See 'Webrut'

'Dancing Doll' Cl F, dp, 1952, Moore, Ralph S.; bud small, pointed; flowers deep rose-pink, 10-14 petals, cupped, borne in clusters; profuse, repeated bloom; foliage leathery, glossy; vigorous, climbing or spreading (10 ft.) growth; ['Étoile Luisante' × seedling]

'Dancing Fairies' S, dp, DeVor; flowers deep, velvet pink with prominent golden stamens, 2 in., 15 petals, open, borne in dense clusters, no fragrance; glossy green foliage; wiry, curved stems; growth that of a broad floribunda; intr. 2002

'Dancing Fan' -- See 'Maiogi'

'Dancing Fire' -- See 'Gelfire'

Dancing Flame™ -- See 'Tuckflame'

'Dancing Girl' -- See 'Meidresia'

'Dancing in the Wind' -- See 'Cledan'

'Dancing Pink' -- See 'Hendan'

'Dancing Queen' HT, pb, Tantau; flowers pink with green edge; intr. 2004

'Dancing Queen' LCl, mp, Fryer; flowers bright pink, dbl., high-centered; recurrent bloom; foliage dark green; vigorous growth, 2-3 m.; intr. 2005

'Dancing Silk' HT, op, 1966, Barter; flowers coral-pink, reflexed, 5 in.; foliage light green; vigorous growth; ['Ena Harkness' × 'McGredy's Yellow']

'Dancing Team' F, ab, Takatori

'Dandee' Min, dr, 1983, Meredith, E.A. & Rovinski, M.E.; bud globular; flowers 35 petals, flat, borne singly; foliage medium size, dark, semi-glossy; upright growth; [seedling × 'Libby']

'Dandenong' MinFl, or; flowers rich orange-red, large, exhibition; strong growth; intr. 1987

'Dandy' Pol, op, 1945, Wiseman; flowers light orange-pink, small, semi-dbl., cupped; profuse, non-recurrent bloom; foliage wrinkled, glossy, dark; very vigorous growth; ['Gloria Mundi' × 'unidentified species rose']

'Dandy Dick' F, mp, 1967, Harkness; flowers well-formed, large, 25 petals, borne in clusters, moderate spicy fragrance; foliage light; ['Pink Parfait' × 'Red Dandy']

'Dandy Lyon' Min, dy, 1979, Lyon; bud long, pointed; flowers buttercup-yellow, 2 in., 30 petals, moderate fragrance; foliage small, dark, glossy; compact, bushy growth; [seedling × 'Sunspot']; intr. 1978

Dani® HT, or, Kordes; flowers medium size, luminous orange-red, dbl.; growth strong, medium

'Dania' -- See 'Cocgold'

'Danica' -- See 'Noarda'

'Daniel' HT, dr, Williams, J. Benjamin; flowers large, high-centered, intense fragrance; intr. 1995

'Daniel' HT, rb, 1943, Mallerin, C.; bud long, pointed; flowers capucine-red on golden yellow base, dbl., cupped; foliage dark, glossy; vigorous, bushy growth

'Daniel Boon' ('The Gathering') S, dr, Williams, J.B.; flowers large flowered dark red.; intr. 2004

'Daniel Boone' HT, dr, Morey, Dr. Dennison; flowers dusky red, large, dbl., globular; vigorous growth

Daniel Gélin® -- See 'Harquince'

'Daniel Greenway' -- See 'Lovauction'

'Daniel Lacombe' HMult, yb, 1885, Allard; flowers yellow washed pink, 5-6 cm., dbl., flat, borne in large clusters; some autumn repeat; almost thornless; growth vigorous, arching (6-7 m.); [*R. multiflora* × 'Margarita']

'Daniel Lesueur' HRg, ly, 1908, Gravereaux; bud salmon-pink to coppery pink; flowers large, dbl., cupped; foliage medium size, elliptical, not rugose; [('Pierre Notting' × 'Safrano') × *R. rugosa*]

'Daniel Philip' F, mr, 1999, Fleming, Joyce L.; flowers 1¼-1½ in., semi-dbl., borne in small clusters; foliage small, medium green, semi-glossy, disease-resistant; prickles moderate; upright, medium (6 ft.) growth; [('Morden Fireglow' × unknown) × seedling]; intr. 1999

Daniela® -- See 'Korlunta'

'Danielle' -- See 'Brodan'

Danielle® HT, w, Cocker; intr. 1992

'Danielle Darrieux' HT, pb, 1948, Gaujard; bud long, pointed; flowers salmon suffused yellow, reverse salmon-orange-pink, very large, dbl.; very vigorous, bushy growth

'Danielle Robyn' HT, rb, 1971, Hastie; bud globular; flowers pinky red and creamy white bicolor, large, dbl., high-centered; intermittent bloom; foliage glossy, dark; bushy growth; ['Grand Gala' × Western Sun™]

'Danielle Turner' -- See 'Rawdan'

'Danina' -- See 'Cara Mia'

'Daniphyl' HT, mr, 1978, Ellick; flowers mandarin-red, 4-5 in., 45-50 petals; foliage semi-glossy, light; vigorous, upright growth; ['Puccini' × 'Chopin']

Danish™ Min, pb, Olesen; flowers dbl., borne mostly solitary, no fragrance; foliage dark green, glossy; growth bushy, very low (20-40 cm.); PP10809; intr. 1998

'Danish Gold' F, yb, 1949, Poulsen, S.; flowers yellow fading to creamy white, 2½-3 in., 5-9 petals, moderate spicy fragrance; foliage glossy; vigorous, compact growth; PP1133; [('Golden Salmon' × 'Souv. de Claudius Pernet') × 'Julien Potin']

'Danish Pink' F, dp, 1965, Soenderhousen; flowers deep pink, almost full, medium, 2-2½ in., single, borne in large clusters, moderate fruity fragrance; vigorous, tall growth

'Danmark' HT, mp, 1891, Zeiner-Larsen; flowers silvery rose-red, large, dbl., cupped, intense fragrance; [sport or seedling of 'La France']

'Dannenberg' HT, op, 1916, Kiese; flowers coral pink, large, dbl.; ['Gruss an Teplitz' × 'Lyon Rose']

'Dannie's Smile' HT, lp, 1994, Maxheimer, Joanne; flowers medium, full, borne mostly singly; foliage medium size, dark green, matte; some prickles; medium, spreading growth; [sport of 'Elizabeth Taylor']; intr. 1993

'Danny Boy' LCl, or, 1969, McGredy, Sam IV; flowers orange vermilion, fading to salmon pink, large, borne in small clusters, intense fragrance; recurrent bloom; foliage dark; ['Uncle Walter' × 'Milord (HT)']

'Danny Boy' S, dr, Clements, John; flowers rich deep crimson-red showing a distinct mossing effect, 2½ in., 15 petals; foliage rich, dark green.; growth compact (3 × 3½ ft.), shrubby; intr. 2000

'Danny Boy' F, ob, Dickson; flowers rusty orange, dbl., borne singly and in clusters; intr. 2001

'Danny Thomas' Min, or, 1980, Wells, V.W., Jr.; flowers with yellow stamens, 35 petals, borne usually singly, moderate fragrance; foliage dark; prickles straight; compact growth; ['Rose Hills Red' × 'Rose Hills Red']

'Danorang' HT, or, 1973, McDaniel, G. K.; intr. 1972

'Danse Azteque' -- See 'Rigobec 3'

'Danse des Étoiles' -- See 'Godsensor'

Danse des Sylphes® ('Grimpant Danse des Sylphes') LCl, or, 1959, Mallerin, C.; flowers rich red suffused geranium-red, 2½ in., dbl., globular, borne in small clusters; foliage glossy; very vigorous growth; ['Spectacular' × 'Toujours']

'Danse de Feu' ('Mada', 'Spectacular') LCl, or, 1953, Mallerin, C.; bud ovoid; flowers scarlet-red, medium, 33 petals, cupped, borne singly or in small clusters, moderate old rose fragrance; recurrent bloom; foliage glossy, bronze; prickles average, short, straight to hooked downward; vigorous, climbing (8-10 ft.) growth; PP1416; ['Paul's Scarlet Climber' × (R. multiflora × unknown)]; intr. 1953

'Danse du Printemps' LCl, lp, 1954, Combe; flowers light crimson pink, 7-8 cm., semi-dbl. to dbl.; infrequent repeat

'Danubio Azul' HT, m, 1957, Camprubi, C.; flowers lilac, medium, dbl., cupped; upright growth; ['Tristesse' × 'Independence']

Dany Hahn® S, w, Guillot-Massad; flowers white tinged with pink, changing to apricot, quartered, borne in clusters of 4 or 5, moderate spicy, fruity fragrance; 4 ft. growth; intr. 2006

'Danyrose' HT, mp, Croix, P.; intr. 1975

'Danzig' HT, dr, 1940, Tantau; flowers shining dark red, medium, dbl., borne in clusters; upright growth; ['Hadley' × 'Kardinal']

'Danzille' -- See 'Mme Bravy'

'Daphne' HSpn, dp, before 1817, from England; flowers full

'Daphné' HGal, dp, Vibert; flowers rose carmine touched with mauve, medium, dbl., globular; intr. 1819

'Daphné' HCh, dp; flowers vivid pink, medium, full, cupped; intr. 1855

'Daphne' HMsk, lp, Pemberton; flowers blush-pink, small, semi-dbl., borne in clusters, moderate fragrance; vigorous growth; intr. 1912

'Daphne' HT, lp, Dobbie; flowers soft pink, flushed rose, well-formed, dbl., moderate fragrance; intr. 1925

'Daphne Claire Jones' -- See 'Kirjack'

'Daphne Gandy' F, mr, 1952, Leenders, M.; flowers blood-red, 3 in., borne in large trusses; foliage dark; vigorous growth; ['Farida' × 'Crimson Glory']

'Daphnis' HT, mp, 1978, Gaujard; flowers brilliant pink, very large; upright growth; ['Marylène' × 'Mignonne']; intr. 1974

'Dapple Dawn' ('English Dawn') S, lp, Austin, David; flowers soft pink, large, single, slight musk fragrance; growth 5 × 4 ft.; [sport of 'Red Coat']; intr. 1983

'Dara' HT, ob, 1991, Wambach, Alex A.; flowers medium, 30 petals, high-centered, borne usually singly, intense fragrance; foliage medium size, medium green, semi-glossy; upright growth; ['Olympiad' × 'Just Joey']; intr. 1995

'Darby' -- See 'Devcico'

'Darby O'Gill' -- See 'Seadarby'

'Darcelle' -- See 'Spodarc'

'd'Arcet' M, dr, 1851, Robert; flowers scarlet red, medium to large, dbl.

'Darcey Bussell' -- See 'Ausdecorum'

'Dardanelle' HT, mr, 1926, Vestal; flowers cherry-rose, dbl.; foliage wrinkled, dark; bushy growth; ['Premier' × 'Ophelia']

'Darien' -- See 'Casdar'

'Darius' Ch, m, 1827, Laffay; flowers lilac-purple, medium to large, very dbl., slight fragrance

'Darius' HGal, mr; flowers vivid red, large, dbl.

'Dark Boy' HT, dr, 1970, Pal, Dr. B.P.; bud ovoid; flowers velvety dark maroon-red, medium, dbl., slight fragrance; foliage soft; moderate, upright, open growth; ['Nigrette' × seedling]; intr. 1965

'Dark Eyes' -- See 'Frydarkeye'

'Dark Foxi' HRg, m; flowers deep purple-pink, large, shallow cup, moderate fragrance; compact (50 - 60 cm.) growth; intr. 2005

'Dark Lady' -- See 'Ausbloom'

Dark Lulu® HT, dr, Kordes; flowers dark red with cream base, medium, dbl., high-centered, borne mostly singly; recurrent; stems long; [sport of 'Lulu']; intr. 2005

Dark Milva® HT, ob, Tantau; flowers dark orange, large , double, high-centered, borne mostly singly; recurrent; stems medium; [sport of 'Milva']; Florist rose; intr. 2006

'Dark Mirage' -- See 'Seadark'

'Dark Secret' HT, dr, 1937, Amling Co.; flowers large, dbl., globular; foliage leathery; short stems; dwarf growth; ['Radiance' × 'Hollywood']

'Dark Velvet' HT, dr, Ogawa, H.; flowers dark velvety crimson, petals slightly reflexed, large, 32 petals, high-centered, borne mostly solitary, intense fragrance; foliage large, dark green; prickles wide, pointing slightly downward, concave, numerous; growth upright; ['Red Lion' × Papa Meilland®]; intr. 1988

Darla® -- See 'Bagdar'

'Darling' -- See 'Korspatax'

'Darling' HT, lp, 1956, Taylor, C.A.; bud ovoid; flowers large, dbl., moderate fruity fragrance; foliage dark, glossy; vigorous, bushy growth; ['Pink Princess' × 'Charlotte Armstrong']

'Darling' HT, op, Noack, Werner; intr. 1985

'Darling' -- See 'Suncredel'

'Darling Annabelle' HT, w, 1992, Perry, Astor; flowers white with faint pink center, 7-10 cm., full, high-centered, moderate fragrance; foliage large, medium green, matte; growth upright (170 cm.); ['South Seas' × 'Peace']; intr. 1993

'Darling B' -- See 'Horcohesive'

'Darling Diane' -- See 'Boscherry'

'Darling Flame' ('Minuette', 'Minuetto') Min, or, 1971, Meilland; flowers mandarin-red to vermilion-red, yellow anthers, 1½ in., 25 petals, globular, slight fruity fragrance; foliage glossy, dark; vigorous growth; [('Rimosa' × 'Josephine Wheatcroft') × Zambra®]

'Darling Jenny' HT, pb, 1996, Poole, Lionel; flowers deep pink shaded peach, large, full, borne mostly singly, slight fragrance; foliage medium size, dark green, semi-glossy; some prickles; bushy, medium growth; ['Solitaire' × 'Gavotte']; intr. 1997

'Darlow's Enigma' HMsk, w, Darlow; flowers pure white with golden stamens, 1½ in., 5-8 petals, borne in clusters of 50-100, intense sweet, honey fragrance; good rebloom; foliage dark green; growth large, 10 × 10 ft.; [sport of seedling of unknown parentage]; intr. 1995

'Darpellerin' (Cap Diamant®, Cape Diamond®) HKor, mp, 2007, Bedard, Christian; buds mossy, fragrant; flowers even pink, medium, 8-10 cm., full, borne in small clusters; foliage medium, light green, semi-glossy, very disease-resistant; prickles medium, hooked, greenish-beige, few; growth spreading to upright, medium (110-130 cm.); garden decoration; ['Marie Victorin' × 'Louis Jolliet']; intr. 2008

'D'Artagnan' D, dr, 1969, Fankhauser; flowers wine-red, dbl., cupped, borne in clusters, intense damask fragrance; non-recurrent; foliage dark, leathery, wrinkled; vigorous, upright (6 ft.) growth; ['Ma Perkins' × 'York and Lancaster']

D'Artagnan® F, ob, Laperrière

'Darthuizer Orange Fire' -- See 'Interfire'

'Dart's Dash' HRg, dr; flowers large, purple red, dbl., flat, intense sweet fragrance; foliage dark green; few prickles; growth bushy, spreading

'Dart's Defender' S, m, Darthuis; flowers mauve to violet-pink; growth 5 × 5 ft.; intr. 1971

'Dart's Presence' S, or; intr. 2005

Dart's Red Dot® ('Red Dot') S, mr, Interplant; low, spreading growth; intr. 1989

'Darzens' HP, op, 1860, Ducher

'Das Goldene Prag' -- See 'Zlatá Praha'

'Dasher' -- See 'Spodash'

'D'Assas' HP, pb, 1850, Vibert; flowers dark pink, tinged crimson, petals somewhat fringed, medium, dbl.; vigorous, straggling growth

'Datin Melleney' HT, pb, Delbard; buds pointed, pink cream; flowers large, cream with coral edges, coral spreads with exposure to sun, dbl., high-centered; recurrent bloom; growth tall, vigorous; intr. 2002

'Daughter Margaret' -- See 'Nobam'

'Dauntless' HT, pb, 1949, Davis; bud long, pointed; flowers pink, reverse yellow, large, 60 petals, high-centered; foliage leathery, dark; upright growth; ['Crimson Glory' × 'Feu Pernet-Ducher']

'Dauphine, Climbing' Cl F, op, 1959, Gaujard

'Dauphine' F, op, 1955, Gaujard; bud ovoid; flowers pink shaded salmon, open, large, dbl., borne in clusters; very vigorous growth; [seedling × ('Opera' × unknown)]

'Dave Davis' HT, dr, 1965, Davis, C. A.; bud long, pointed; flowers dark velvety red, large, 60 petals, high-centered, intense fragrance; foliage leathery; moderate growth; [seedling × 'Charles Mallerin']

'Dave Hessayon' -- See 'Driscobruce'

'Dave McQueen' -- See 'Lovbonny'

'David Arnot' HT, rb; flowers bright scarlet, reverse old-gold; vigorous growth

David Barber™ S, w; bud white with rose tints; flowers white, dbl., pompon, borne in clusters of 10-12, slight fragrance; recurrent; foliage medium green; stems reddish; low (16 × 48 in.), spreading, groundcover growth; intr. 2005

'David Charles Armstrong' -- See 'Driscogeorge'

'David D. Bernstein' -- See 'Woraston'

'David Dot' Min, Dot, Simon; intr. 1978

'David Fleming' F, mr, 2007, Fleming, Joyce L.; flowers have reflexed petals, good substance, 2 in., dbl., borne in large clusters; remontant; foliage medium, medium green, glossy; prickles triangular, moderate; growth upright, medium; mass plantings; hardy; ['Masquerade' × 'Mrs John Laing']; intr. 2006

'David Gilmore' HT, mr, 1923, Dickson, H.; flowers brilliant scarlet

'David Gold' HT, rb, 1957, Robinson, H.; flowers cherry-cerise tinted golden yellow, 6 in., high-centered, intense fragrance; foliage dark, glossy; very vigorous growth; ['Shot Silk' × 'Peace']

'David Harum' HT, op, 1904, Hill, E. G.; flowers peach pink, very large, very full

'David Leek' F, dp, Fleming, Joyce L.; flowers dark, smoky pink to red, dbl., moderate fragrance; good repeat; growth to 4 ft.; intr. 1996

'David Mace' HT, mr, 2003, Thomas, D.; flowers large, very full, borne mostly solitary; foliage large, dark green, semi-glossy; numerous prickles; growth upright, medium; ['Gavotte' × ('Jan Guest' × 'Red Devil')]; intr. 2003

'David McKee' HT, mr, 1933, Dickson, A.; flowers carmine-red, large, dbl., high-centered; foliage leathery; vigorous, bushy growth

'David O. Dodd' HT, mr, 1926, Vestal; flowers rich crimson flushed scarlet, large, dbl.; foliage glossy; bushy growth

'David O. Dodd, Climbing' Cl HT, mr, 1937, Howard Rose Co.

'David Pradel' T, m, 1851, Pradel; flowers pale rose and lavender, mottled, very large, full, globular, intense fragrance

'David R. Williamson' -- See 'Rev. David R. Williamson'

'David Ruston' HT, pb

'David Thompson' HRg, mr, 1979, Svedja, Felicitas; bud ovoid; flowers with yellow stamens, 2½ in., 25 petals, intense fragrance; upright growth; [('Schneezwerg' × 'Frau Dagmar Hartopp') × seedling]

'David Whitfield' -- See 'Gana'

'David Wilson' HT, ab, 2002, Rawlins, R.; flowers apricot-yellow, orange-yellow reverse, medium, full, borne in small clusters, moderate fragrance; foliage large, medium green, glossy; prickles medium, pointed; growth upright, tall (3 ft.); garden decorative; ['Southampton' × 'Sweet Heart']; intr. 2007

Davidoff® HT, op, Guillot; buds slender, pointed; flowers dbl., borne singly and in clusters; foliage dark green, semi-glossy; intr. 1984

'David's Star' F, w, Horner; intr. 2005

'Davina Jane' HT, ob, 1997, Rawlins, R.; flowers very dbl., borne mostly singly, no fragrance; foliage medium size, medium green, semi-glossy; upright, medium (3 ft.) growth; [Sexy Rexy® × Corso®]

'Davit Dot' S, mr

'Davona' ('Red Splendour') F, dr, 1982, Davies, Gareth; flowers deeper red than Europeana, petals frilled, medium, dbl., borne in clusters, slight fragrance; foliage medium size, dark green, glossy; medium, bushy growth; [sport of 'Europeana']; intr. 1979

'Davy Crockett' F, dr, 1956, deRuiter; flowers large, dbl.; vigorous growth; ['Étoile de Hollande' × 'floribunda seedling']

'Dawn' Cl HT, mp, 1898, Paul, G.; flowers silvery rose pink, semi-dbl.; ['Mme Caroline Testout' × 'Mme Paul']

'Dawn' HT, op, Jelly; bud long, pointed; flowers salmon-pink, base yellow, 5-6 in., 28-36 petals, high-centered, moderate spicy fragrance; vigorous, upright growth; PP1316; intr. 1953

'Dawn' -- See 'Ariake'

'Dawn' -- See 'Asaboraké'

'Dawn Chorus' -- See 'Dicquasar'

Dawn Cover™ S, mr, Poulsen; flowers medium red, 5-8 cm., single, no fragrance; foliage dark; growth bushy, 40-60 cm.; intr. 2005

Dawn Creeper™ -- See 'Wildawn'

'Dawn Fragrance' LCl, op, 1969, Mason, P.G.; flowers salmon-flesh, flushed rose-pink, well-formed, cupped; intermittent bloom; foliage dark, leathery; vigorous growth; ['Blossomtime' × ('Blossomtime' × unknown)]

'Dawn Haggie' HT, op, Kordes; flowers firm-petaled, soft salmon, slow opening, dbl., borne mostly singly, no fragrance; recurrent; sturdy stems; growth medium; intr. 1997

'Dawn Mist' F, pb, 1962, Boerner; bud ovoid; flowers reddish-pink, base yellow, 3 in., 30-35 petals, cupped, intense spicy fragrance; foliage leathery, glossy; vigorous, bushy, compact growth; PP2113; [('Goldilocks' × 'Pinocchio') × 'Vogue']; intr. 1962

'Dawn Pink' F, mp, 1962; bud apricot; flowers pink, rosette form, large, 45-50 petals, borne in clusters, moderate fragrance; foliage light green; vigorous, upright growth; ['Magenta' × 'Ma Perkins']; intr. 1962

'Dawn Sunsation' -- See 'Korfeining'

'Dawn Weller' -- See 'Poulsum'

'Dawnglow' HT, pb, 1937, Burbank; flowers flesh-pink, large, dbl., high-centered, moderate fragrance; PP269

'Dawning, Climbing' LCl, op, 1956, Bennett, H.; flowers salmon-pink; foliage glossy; vigorous growth; ['New Dawn' × 'Margaret McGredy']

'Dawning Moment' HT, ab; flowers 35 petals, slight to none fragrance; intr. 2007

'Dawnlight' F, pb, 1959, Motose; bud ovoid; flowers soft pink, 2-2½ in., 30-35 petals, flat, slight fragrance; foliage leathery, light green; thornless; vigorous, bushy growth; PP1740; ['Summer Snow, Climbing' × 'Summer Snow']; intr. 1958

'Dawns Early Light' HT, w, 1977, Linscott; bud long, palest pink; flowers white, faintly edged pale pink, pointed, long-lasting, 3½-4 in., 6 petals, intense fragrance; foliage light; tall growth; ['Vesuvius' × 'Vesuvius']; intr. 1972

'Dawshadwell' ('Matilda Jones') F, ab, 2007, Dawson, John F.; flowers dbl., borne in small clusters; foliage medium size, medium green, semi-glossy; prickles average, hooked, numerous; growth bushy, medium (3 ft.); [Laura Ford® × 'Fulton Mackay']; intr. 2008

'Dawson' ('Dawsoniana', R. dawsoniana, 'The Dawson Rose') HMult, mp, 1888, Dawson; flowers bright rose-pink with white centers, fading lighter, 3 cm., semi-dbl., borne in clusters of 10-20, moderate fragrance; non-recurrent; vigorous (10-25 ft.) growth; [R. multiflora × 'Général Jacqueminot']

'Dawsoniana' -- See 'Dawson'

'Dawson's Climber' Cl HT, pb, Dawson; intr. 1960

'Dawson's Delight' HT, pb, Dawson; flowers cerise pink with straw yellow reverse, veined pink, dbl., moderate fragrance; tall growth; intr. 1978

'Dawson's Yellow Climber' LCl, my

'Day Break' -- See 'Daybreak'

'Day Breaker' -- See 'Frycentury'

'Day Dream' HT, dp, 1971, Armstrong, D.L.; bud long, pointed; flowers deep pink, large, dbl.; foliage glossy, leathery; vigorous, upright, bushy growth; PP3077; ['Helen Traubel' × 'Tiffany']; intr. 1969

'Day Glow' -- See 'Jacrink'

'Day Is Done' HT, or, 1985, Schneider, Peter; flowers large, 35 petals, high-centered; foliage large, dark, semi-glossy; [Die Welt® × 'Rosalynn Carter']

Day Light® -- See 'Interlight'

'Day of Triumph' ('Rendez-vous') HT, mp, 1956, Meilland, F.; bud ovoid; flowers pink edged lighter, 5½ in., 50-65 petals, cupped, moderate fragrance; foliage leathery; vigorous, upright, bushy growth; PP1358; ['Peace' × 'Europa']; intr. 1953

'Daybreak' HWich, op, 1909, Dawson; flowers deep salmon-pink, borne in clusters; late; [R. wichurana × R. chinensis]

'Daybreak' ('Day Break') HMsk, my, Pemberton; flowers golden yellow, medium, single, moderate fragrance; recurrent bloom; foliage dark; vigorous, bushy growth; [Trier® × 'Liberty']; intr. 1918

'Daybreak' HT, pb, Laxton Bros.; bud large, long, pointed; flowers salmon-pink and yellow, very dbl., high-centered, slight fragrance; foliage leathery; long stems; very vigorous growth; ['Violet Simpson' × 'Ivy May']; intr. 1935

'Daybreak' S, dp, Erskine; flowers deep pink, 25-30 petals, moderate fragrance; non-remontant, but long blooming season; ['Hansa' × R. woodsii]; intr. 1960

'Daybreak' Min, ab; flowers rich apricot-pink; good repeat; growth to 18-24 in.

'Daybreak' -- See 'Akebono'

'Daybreak' -- See 'Rassvet'

'Daybreak' -- See 'Akatsuki'

'Daydream' Min, ab; intr. 2005

'Daydream' Cl HT, lp, Clark, A.; flowers blush pink, shading to a white center, ruffled, large, single to semi-dbl.; growth vigorousd bush or pillar; ['Souvenir de Gustave Prat' × 'Rosy Morn or Gwen Nash']; intr. 1925

'DayDream' -- See 'Baieam'

'Daydream' -- See 'Dicjeep'

'Daylight' HT, pb, 1939, Hansen, N. J.; flowers creamy blush-pink, base yellow, 4 in., very dbl., high-centered; foliage soft; vigorous growth; RULED EXTINCT 4/92 ARM; ['Grange Colombe' × 'Los Angeles']

'Daylight Katy' F, my, 1987, Schneider, Peter; flowers bright yellow, fading slightly paler, medium, 22 petals, urn-shaped, borne in sprays of 3-15; foliage medium size, bronze-green, semi-glossy; prickles pointed, medium, reddish; bushy, low growth; hips round, small, red; [Bright Smile® × (Princess Michael of Kent® × Party Girl™)]

'Daylight's Glow' Min, my, 2006, Hopper, Nancy; flowers 1¾ in., dbl., borne mostly solitary; foliage medium green, matte; prickles ¼ in., tan, few; growth bushy, 10 in.; [sport of 'Tobo']; intr. 2006

'Dayna Sawyer' HT, pb, 2008, Edwards, Eddie, and Phelps, Ethan; flowers white with thin pink edge, medium, 5 in., full, borne mostly solitary; foliage medium, dark green, semi-glossy; nearly thornless; growth bushy, medium (5-6 ft.); [seedling × seedling]; intr. 2008

'Daytona' -- See 'Olijzouc'

'Dazla' HT, rb, 1930, Cant, B. R.; bud long, pointed; flowers orange-scarlet, base and reverse golden yellow, wavy petals, 6 in., semi-dbl.; foliage dark; vigorous growth

'Dazla, Climbing' Cl HT, rb, 1950, Cant, B. R.

Dazzla® -- See 'Wapiti'

'Dazzler' -- See 'Wapiti'

Dazzler™ -- See 'Keldaz'

'Dazzler' -- See 'Genpat'

'Dazzler' Min, pb, Kasturi; flowers dark pink with prominent white eye, borne in large clusters; low growth; intr. 1992

'Dazzler' -- See 'Leonie'

'Dazzling Beauties' Min, ob, Moore, Ralph; flowers blend of yellow, gold, orange and red, dbl., high-centered, borne in large clusters, no fragrance; constant bloom; stems short; vigorous growth, neat rounded shape; intr. 2001

'Dazzling Delight' -- See 'Cocuseful'

'Dazzling Red' HWich, mr, 1914, Manda; flowers ruby red

'De Bordeaux' -- See 'Petite de Hollande'

'De Bruxelles' -- See 'Agathe Incarnata'

'De Candolle' HWich, op, Robichon; bud yellow; flowers deep yellow to salmon yellow, medium, full, borne in clusters of 30-40; [R. wichurana × 'Eugenie Lamesch']; intr. 1913

'De Candolle' HSpn, w, about 1830, Prévost; flowers white, edges marbled pink, sometimes striped, single

'De Candolle' HCh, m, Calvert; flowers violet-purple; intr. about 1845

'De Candolle' M, lp, Portemer fils; flowers soft pink or rose-tinted, large, dbl.; intr. 1857

'De Chartres' ('Nain') HCh, lp, before 1829, Laffay; flowers very small, dbl.; growth dwarf (3-5 in.); Lawrenciana

'De Esmée' HT, lp, deRuiter; intr. 2001

'De Flandre' -- See 'Agathe Incarnata'

'de Fontenelle' ('Fontenelle') M, dp, 1849, Vibert; flowers dark pink, dotted, medium, full

'De Greeff's Jubilee' ('Fellowship') F, dr, 1982, Verschuren, Ted; flowers large, semi-dbl., slight fragrance; foliage medium size, dark, semi-glossy; bushy growth; [Diablotin® × Gisselfeld®]; intr. 1980

'De Hollande' -- See 'Majestueuse'

'De Kat' HT, w, Kordes; bud white with green tinge; flowers white with pink tones in center, double, high-centered, borne mostly singly; recurrent; vigorous growth; intr. 1995

'De La Flèche' ('À Fleur d'Anémone', 'Anémone', R. muscosa anemonflora, 'Sanguinea', 'Scarlet Moss') M, dr, 1824, Lemeunier; flowers purple red, 1½ in., dbl., cupped; foliage reddish when young, dark green, rather small, elongate; prickles numerous, unequal, straight

'De la Grifferaie' HMult, dp, 1845, de Grille/Vibert; flowers carmine to pink, fading almost to white, 8 cm., dbl., round and flat, borne in clusters of 10-15, moderate fragrance; non-recurrent;

foliage large, round, rugose, matte; nearly thornless; growth robust, arching, tall (3 m.); [*R. multiflora platyphylla* × a form of *R. gallica*]

'De la Maître-Ecole' -- See 'Rose de La Maître-Ecole'

'De la Malmaison' HGal, lp, before 1826, Pelletier; flowers medium to large, full; Agathe group

'De la Mothe' HP, mp, 1858, Avoux / Crozy; flowers very large, very full

'De la Reine' -- See 'Regina Dicta'

'De la Reine' -- See 'Reine des Fleurs'

'De l'Ile' -- See 'Calypso'

'De Luxe' HT, rb, 1931, White Bros.; flowers bright velvety scarlet, reverse red, semi-dbl.; [sport of 'Premier']

'De Marienbourg' ('Glauque à Feuille de Pimprenelle', 'Redutea Glauca', 'Redouté', 'Mariaeburgensis') HSpn, w, before 1820, Redouté, H.; flowers whitish, streaked with red points at the tip, medium, single; foliage glaucous, oval; prickles unequal, almost straight

'De Meaux White' -- See 'Rose de Meaux White'

'De Mon Fils' A, mp, before 1815, Descemet

'De Montarville' -- See 'AC De Montarville'

'De Naples' P, about 1810, Descemet

'De Reims' -- See 'Petit St François'

'De Rennes' ('Eremit de Granval') Ch, m, about 1840, Prévost; flowers bright, glowing purple

'De Ruiter's Herald' ('DeRuiter's Herald', 'Herald') Pol, dr, 1949, deRuiter; flowers blood-red, prominent yellow stamens, small, 6 petals, borne in large trusses; foliage glossy, dark; vigorous, bushy growth; [Orange Triumph® × seedling]

'De St Barthélémy' P, m, 1820, Delaâge; flowers violet-purple, aging to deep pink, medium, dbl.

'De Schelfhout' ('Rose Schelfhout') HGal, lp, before 1847, Parmentier; flowers whitish pink, medium, dbl.

'De Tous Mois' ('Perpétuelle de St Ouen') HMsk, w, before 1828

'De Van Eeden' -- See 'L'Obscurité'

'Dean Collins' Gr, dp, 1953, Lammerts, Dr. Walter; bud ovoid, red; flowers deep pink, 4½-5 in., 53 petals, slight fragrance; foliage dark, glossy, leathery; vigorous growth; PP1279; ['Charlotte Armstrong' × 'Floradora']

'Dean Hole' HT, pb, 1904, Dickson, A.; flowers silvery carmine, shaded salmon, very large, dbl., moderate fragrance; [sport of 'Mme Caroline Testout']

'Dean of Windsor' HP, mr, 1878, Turner; flowers vermilion with scarlet, large, full, moderate fragrance

'Deana' -- See 'Worcrank'

'Deane Ross' -- See 'Tomboss'

'Deanna' -- See 'Ponanna'

'Dear Daughter' F, dp; intr. 2005

'Dear Eleanor' -- See 'Gelele'

'Dear Kath' -- See 'Worcrunch'

'Dear One' F, lp, Benny; flowers porcelain pink, high-centered; good repeat; growth medium; intr. 1998

'Dear One' -- See 'Kara'

'Dear Prudence' -- See 'Taldearpru'

'Dearest' F, pb, 1960, Dickson, A.; flowers rosy salmon-pink, gold stamens, well-formed, large, 30 petals, borne in clusters, moderate fragrance; foliage dark, glossy, vigorous, bushy growth; [seedling × 'Spartan']

'Dearest, Climbing' Cl F, pb, Ruston, D.; intr. 1970

'Dearest One' -- See 'Cara Mia'

'Dearly Departed' HT, mr; intr. 2005

'Debbie' Min, yb, 1966, Moore, Ralph S.; flowers yellow, edges becoming pink, small, dbl., moderate fragrance; foliage small, leathery; bushy, low, sometimes semi-climbing growth; PP2911; ['Little Darling' × 'Zee']

'Debbie' S, dp, Poulsen

'Debbie Dawn' F, lp, 1997, Rawlins, R.; flowers medium, dbl., borne in small clusters; foliage medium size, dark green, semi-glossy; upright (2½ ft.) growth; [Margaret Merril® × 'Melrose']

'Debbie-Karen' HT, mp, 1984, Burdett, H.J.; flowers 4½-5½ in., dbl., high-centered, borne singly, slight fragrance; foliage large, light green, semi-glossy; vigorous, upright growth; [seedling × seedling]; intr. 1983

'Debbie Lynn' HT, dr, 1992, Jerabek, Paul E.; flowers dbl., 36 petals, high-centered, urn-shaped, borne usually singly; foliage medium size, dark green, semi-glossy; upright, bushy, medium growth; intr. 1986

'Debbie Thomas' HT, rb, 1996, Thomas, D.; flowers crimson, lighter reverse, large, very dbl., high-centered; foliage medium size, medium green, semi-glossy; numerous prickles; upright, tall growth; ['City of Gloucester' × 'My Joy']; intr. 1992

'Debbie Trinder' -- See 'Worcranberry'

Debidue™ -- See 'Micdeb'

'Debonair' HT, my, 1946, Lammerts, Dr. Walter; bud ovoid; flowers primrose-yellow, 3-4½ in., 28-35 petals, high-centered, moderate fragrance; foliage leathery, glossy, dark; very vigorous, upright, bushy growth; PP677; ['Golden Rapture' × seedling]

'Debonnaire' ('The Pink Professor') S, dp; flowers glowing deep pink, large, very dbl., borne in clusters, strong sweet fragrance; free-flowering; foliage dark green, glossy; growth upright, medium tall; intr. 2004

Deborah® (Play Rose®) S, mp, Meilland; flowers dbl., cupped, borne in small clusters; foliage glossy green; growth to 100-110 cm.; intr. 1990

'Deborah Beggs Moncrief' -- See 'Tiger'

'Deborah Beggs Moncrief' -- See 'Wildeb'

'Deborah Devonshire' -- See 'Boscherrydrift'

Deborah Moncrief™ -- See 'Wildeb'

'Deborah Reilly' -- See 'Liolilac'

'Debra Gaye' -- See 'Tindeb'

'Debrad' ('Royal Baby') F, mr, 1982, Bracegirdle, Derek T.; flowers medium, 20 petals; foliage small, medium green, semi-glossy; upright growth; ['Generosa' × 'Baby Darling']

'Debraf' ('Wendy Pease') HT, yb, 1985, Bracegirdle, Derek T.; flowers medium, 35 petals; foliage medium size, medium green, semi-glossy; upright growth; [John Waterer® × 'Tenerife']; intr. 1986

'Debrah' ('Mary Sheffield') F, mr, 1987, Bracegirdle, Derek T.; flowers medium, dbl., moderate fragrance; foliage small, medium green, glossy; spreading growth; [Doris Tysterman® × 'Admiral Rodney']

'Debraro' ('William Walker') HT, dy, 1985, Bracegirdle, Derek T.; flowers medium, 20 petals, no fragrance; foliage medium size, medium green, semi-glossy; upright growth; [Western Sun™ × 'Circus']; intr. 1984

'Deb's Delight' -- See 'Legsweet'

Debut™ -- See 'Meibarke'

'Debutante' HWich, lp, 1902, Walsh; flowers rose-pink, fading to cameo-pink, small, dbl., rosette, borne in large clusters, moderate sweetbriar fragrance; non-recurrent; foliage dark, glossy; short stems; growth to 6-8 ft.; [*R. wichurana* × 'Baroness Rothschild']

'Debutante' -- See 'Jacinal'

'Decbridled' (Unbridled™) MinFl, yb, 2007, Clemons, David E.; flowers light yellow fading to white, with light pink to salmon edge, medium, 1½ in., dbl., high-centered, borne mostly solitary; foliage medium, medium green, semi-glossy; prickles ¼ in., straight, slightly pointing down, light tan, moderate; growth upright, medium (3 ft. × 2 ft.); garden, exhibition, containers, cutting; [('Rosie O'Donnell' × 'Fairhope') × Conundrum™]; intr. 2008

'Deccan Delight' F, yb, Chiplunkar; flowers yellow to apricot orange, changing to orange and white; [sport of 'Anita']; intr. 1985

'Deccan Deluxe' HT, m, Chiplunkar; flowers pale pink, dbl.; [sport of 'Dr B. P. Pal']; intr. 1988

'Decea Ann' F, ab, 1976, Horsfield; flowers flushed peach-pink, 3½-4 in., 26 petals, intense fragrance; foliage dark, leathery; upright growth; [Queen Elizabeth® × Elizabeth of Glamis®]

'Deception' HT, dp, 1923, Beckwith; flowers deep rose, large

'Decjoy' (Joy™) Min, pb, 2007, Clemons, David E.; flowers white with pink edge, reverse white, 1-1½ in., dbl., borne singly and in sprays; foliage medium size, medium green, matte, disease-resistant; prickles average, angled down, bottom curved, tan, moderate; growth spreading, tall (24-28 in.); garden decoration, exhibition; ['Silverhill' × Kristin™]; intr. 2008

'Declady' (Splendid Lady™) HT, w, 2001, Clemons, David; flowers white with pink edges, reverse white, 4 in., very full, exhibition, borne mostly solitary, slight fragrance; foliage medium size, dark green, semi-glossy; prickles moderate; growth upright, medium; garden decorative; ['Lynn Anderson' × unknown]; intr. 2001

'Déclic' S, m, Croix; flowers lilac pink, 3 in., dbl., borne in large clusters; foliage glossy; intr. 1988

'Decmatic' (Charismatic™) MinFl, rb, 2003, Clemons, David; flowers edged red, white to light yellow base, reverse white, red edge intensifies in bright sun, 1½-2 in., dbl., borne mostly solitary, no fragrance; foliage medium size, medium green, semi-glossy; few prickles; growth upright, tall (24-36 in.); exhibition, garden decoration; [Ruffian™ × Kristin™]; intr. 2004

'Décor' ('Record') LCl, or, 1951, Mallerin, C.; flowers bright scarlet, semi-dbl., borne in clusters; foliage leathery; vigorous growth; [('Love' × 'Paul's Scarlet Climber') × 'Demain']

'Decor Arlequin' -- See 'Meizourayor'

'Decor Rose' -- See 'Meituraphar'

'Décor Terrasse' ClMin, dy, Meilland; intr. 2002

'Décora' C, mp; flowers clear rose, small, very dbl., slight fragrance; intermediate between Rose de Meaux and Spong

'Decorat' -- See 'Dekorat'

'Décoration de Geschwind' -- See 'Geschwind's Orden'

'Decorator' HT, rb, Dickson, A.; flowers brilliant carmine, base orange-yellow; foliage glossy; very vigorous growth; intr. 1936

'Decorator' HT, rb, 1913, Hobbies; bud bright carmine, striped yellow; flowers reddish-yellow, large, semi-dbl.

'Decorator' HT, yb; flowers bright cream yellow, striped glowing red, semi-dbl.; from Brasil; intr. 1914

'Decruf' (Ruffian™) MinFl, op, 2000, Clemons, David E.; flowers orange pink, reverse light pink, 1½ in., dbl., high-centered, borne mostly singly, slight fragrance; foliage medium size, dark green, semi-glossy; prickles moderate; growth upright, medium (24-36 in.); ['Corina' × Child's Play™]; intr. 2003

'Decsure' (Foolish Pleasure™) MinFl, pb, 2003, Clemons, David; flowers medium to dark pink edge with white center, reverse white, 1½-2 in., full, borne solitary, no fragrance; foliage medium size, dark green, glossy; prickles small, few; growth upright, tall (36-48 in.); exhibition and garden/decorative; ['Lynn Anderson' × unknown]; intr. 2004

'Decwhirl' (Whirlaway™) MinFl, w, 2005, Clemons, David E.; flowers pure white, 2 in., full, high-centered, borne mostly solitary, no fragrance; foliage medium size, medium green, semi-glossy; prickles few, small, straight, very thin, light green; stems long; growth upright, tall (36-48 in); exhibition, garden decoration; ['Merlot' × Foolish Pleasure™]; intr. 2006

'Dedication' F, ly, 1968, Harkness; flowers creamy ivory, dbl., borne in trusses; foliage glossy; ['Pink Parfait' × 'Circus']

Dee Bennett™ -- See 'Savadee'

Dee Dee® F, my, Meilland; flowers saffron yellow, dbl., high-centered; greenhouse rose; intr. 1998

'Dee Dee Bridgewater' LCl, mp, Meilland; flowers large, dbl., moderate fragrance; growth to 7 ft.; intr. 2004

'Deep Purple' F, m, 1979, Kordes, R.; bud ovoid, pointed; flowers mauve-pink, imbricated, 3-4 in., 30-45 petals, moderate fragrance; foliage glossy, dark; vigorous, upright, bushy growth; PP4672; ['Zorina' × 'Silver Star']; intr. 1980

'Deep Secret' HT, mr, 1946, Hildebrandt; flowers rich red becoming darker, compact, intense fragrance; PP755; RULED EXTINCT 4/77 ARM; ['Matchless' × seedling]; was never introduced

'Deep Secret' ('Mildred Scheel') HT, dr, 1977, Tantau, Math.; flowers deep crimson, 4 in., 40 petals, intense fragrance; foliage glossy, dark; vigorous, upright, medium growth; intr. 1977

Deep Velvet™ Min, dr, 1981, Jolly, Betty J.; flowers 33 petals, high-centered, urn-shaped, borne singly and 2-3 per cluster, slight fragrance; foliage tiny, medium green; prickles straight; bushy, compact growth; [('Grand Opera' × 'Jimmy Greaves') × Baby Katie™]

'Deepika' F, rb, 1976, IARI; bud pointed; flowers 2 in., 15 petals; free bloom, fairly lasting; foliage glossy, dark; vigorous, upright, open growth; ['Shepherd's Delight' × seedling]; intr. 1975

'Deepshikha' F, mr, 1976, IARI; bud pointed; flowers open, 2½ in., 35 petals, slight tea fragrance; foliage glossy, light; vigorous, compact, bushy growth; ['Sea Pearl' × 'Shola']; intr. 1975

'Déesse' ('Goddess') HT, rb, 1957, Gaujard; bud long, pointed, white; flowers red spreading from outside to center petals, ending crimson, dbl.; vigorous, upright growth; ['Peace' × seedling]

'Déesse Flore' D, lp, 1827, Vibert; flowers blush white, center cerise pink, small to medium, full; growth branching

'Defiance' HT, mr, 1907, Hill, E. G.; flowers rich red, large, full; ['Lady Battersea' × 'Gruss an Teplitz']

'Defiance' HT, dr, Kress; flowers dark velvety red, 5-6 in., dbl., intense fragrance; foliage dark; vigorous growth; ['Gruss an Teplitz' × 'Étoile de France']; intr. 1914

'Deford Bailey' -- See 'Welharp 1999'

'Degenhard' -- See 'Doc'

'DeGrazia's Pink' -- See 'Minhco'

'Deidre Hall' ('Cajun Queen') HT, yb, 2005, Edwards, Eddie & Phelps, Ethan; flowers yellow blend, 5-6 in., full, high-centered, borne in small clusters, no fragrance; foliage large, dark green, glossy; prickles moderate; growth upright, tall, (5-6 ft.); garden, exhibition; [seedling × 'Santa Fe']; intr. 2006

Dejá Blu™ -- See 'Benswise'

'Déjà Vous' Min, ab, 1986, Jolly, Nelson & Marie; bud pointed; flowers light apricot, aging lighter, large, 50 petals, high-centered, borne usually singly, slight fragrance; foliage medium size, medium green, semi-glossy; no prickles; medium, upright, spreading growth; no fruit; [Anita Charles™ × 'Sheri Anne']; intr. 1987

Dekora® HT, mp, Kordes; flowers bright pink to hot pink, medium, dbl., high-centered, borne mostly singly; recurrent; prickles very few; stems long; florist rose; intr. 2005

'Dekorat' ('Decorat') HT, or, 1974, W. Kordes Söhne; intr. 1975

'Del Mar Fair' -- See 'Tindel'

'Delaby' ('Papi Delbard') LCl, ab, Delbard; intr. 1995

'Deladel' (Madame Delbard®, Mme Georges Delbard®) HT, dr, 1985, Delbard, Georges; flowers large, 40 petals, exhibition, no fragrance; foliage large, medium green, semi-glossy; upright growth; PP4391; [('Tropicana' × 'Samourai') × ('Tropicana' × 'Rome Glory' × 'Impeccable'))]; intr. 1980

'Delalac' S, mp, Delbard; intr. 1998

'Delalac' S, pb, Delbard; intr. 2006

'Delambre' P, dp, 1863, Moreau et Robert; flowers carmine, darker at center, edges tinted lilac, dbl., quartered, borne in clusters, moderate sweet fragrance; remontant

'Delamo' ('Towering Rose Magic') HT, m, Delbard; bud deep rosy mauve; intr. 2005

'Delanche' ('Perle Blanche') HT, w, 1985, Delbard, Georges; flowers large, 35 petals, no fragrance; foliage medium size, medium green, semi-glossy; upright, bushy growth; [('Virgo' × 'Peace') × ('Goldilocks' × 'Virgo')]; intr. 1981

Delany Sisters™ -- See 'Wildels'

'Delapo' HT, rb, Delbard; intr. 1997

'Delarle' ('Rose des Cisterciens') S, pb, Delbard; intr. 1998

'Delatur' ('Alleluia', 'Hallelujah') HT, rb, 1982, Delbard, Georges; flowers velvety deep red, silver reverse, large, of heavy substance, 30 petals; foliage deep green, glossy; [(('Impeccable' × Papa Meilland®) × ('Gloire de Rome' × 'Impeccable')) × 'Corrida']

'Delaur' S, lp, Delbard; intr. 2004

'Delav' S, mp, Delbard; intr. 2001

'Delaval' (Avalanche Rose®) F, mr, 1986, Delbard; flowers large, dbl.; vigorous, bushy growth; [('François et Joseph Guy' × ('Sultane' × unknown)) × ('Alain' × 'Étoile de Hollande')]; intr. 1977

'Delbaf' (Apogée®) HT, ob, 1970, Delbard-Chabert; bud ovoid; flowers coppery, large, dbl., cupped, slight fragrance; foliage bronze, glossy; vigorous, upright growth; [(Queen Elizabeth® ×

'Provence') × (('Sultane' × unknown) × 'Mme Joseph Perraud')]; intr. 1966
'Delbara' -- See 'Strawberry Ice'
'Delbard' F, or, Delbard-Chabert; flowers light orange-red, large, dbl.
'Delbard's Orange Climber' -- See 'Delpar'
'Delbéchir' (Bernadette Chirac®) HRg, ab, 1986, Delbard-Chabert; flowers apricot, yellow and orange blend, large, 23 petals, cupped, slight fragrance; foliage rugose; vigorous, bushy growth; [R. rugosa × ('First Edition' × 'Floradora')]; intr. 1979
'Delbir' (Milrose®) F, mp, 1970, Delbard-Chabert; flowers rose pink, semi-dbl., cupped, borne in clusters of 5 - 15; foliage light green, glossy; vigorous, bushy growth; ['Orléans Rose' × ('Francais' × 'Lafayette')]; originally registered as Pol; intr. 1965
'Delblabe' S, dy; intr. 1999
'Delblacrem' w, Delbard
'Delblan' ('Snowy Summit', Clos Fleuri Blanc®) F, w, 1989, Delbard & Chabert; flowers large, 40 petals, slight fragrance; foliage bright; semi-climbing, vigorous growth; [(Milrose® × 'Legion d'Honneur') × Candeur®]; intr. 1988
'Delblatine' ('Peaches') S, ab, Delbard; intr. 1993
'Delblue' (Mamy Blue®) HT, m, 1985, Delbard, Georges; flowers large, 35 petals, high-centered; foliage medium size, dark; few prickles; bushy growth; [(('Holstein' × 'Bayadère') × ('Prelude' × 'St. Exupery')) × seedling]; intr. 1984
'Delbobla' ('Bordure Blanche') F, w, Delbard; intr. 1997
'Delboip' (Lancôme®) HT, dp, 1986, Delbard; flowers deep pink, large, 28 petals, high-centered; vigorous, upright, bushy growth; [('Dr. Albert Schweitzer' × 'Michèle Meilland' × 'Bayadère')) × ('MElmet' × 'Present Filial')]; intr. 1973
'Delbojaune' (Bordure d'Or®) F, my, Delbard
'Delboul' ('Cascade Blanche') S, w, Delbard; bud white with pink edge; intr. 2000
'Delbourbo' (Gloire du Bourbonnais®) Pol, rb, 1988, Delbard-Chabert; flowers center cream, margin carmine, opening turns purple, large, 35-40 petals, no fragrance; foliage bright; good, dwarf growth; [(Milrose® × 'Legion d'Honneur') × (Zambra® × 'Sensation')]
'Delbover' (Bordure Vermillon®) F, rb, Delbard; intr. 1990
'Delboviv' (Bordure Vive®) Pol, mp, Delbard; intr. 1985
'Delbrat' HT, dp, 1969, Delbard, G.; intr. 1969
'Delbre' F, mp, 1959, Delbard-Chabert; bud long
'Delbric' HT, r, Delbard; intr. 2005
'Delbro' (Parthenon®) HT, pb, 1970, Delbard-Chabert; flowers carmine-pink, reverse soft yellow, large, dbl., cupped, moderate fragrance; recurrent; foliage bronze, glossy; vigorous, upright, bushy growth; ['Chic Parisien' × ('Bayadere' × 'Rome Glory')]; intr. 1967
'Delbut' ('Moon Magic', 'YelloGlo') F, dy, 1969, Delbard-Chabertdbl.
'Delcama' (Camara®) HT, or, 1979, Delbard; flowers orange-vermilion, petals recurved, 4-5 in., 33 petals, slight fragrance; PP4332; [(('Chic Parisien' × 'Tropicana') × ('Gloire de Rome' × 'Impeccable')) × ('Tropicana' × 'Samourai')]; intr. 1978
'Delcande' (Candeur®) F, w, 1986, Delbard; flowers large, 30 petals, high-centered, no fragrance; low, upright growth; [(('Robin Hood' × 'Virgo') × ('Frau Karl Druschki' × '(Queen Elizabeth × Provence)')) × ('Virgo' × 'Peace')]; intr. 1978
'Delcap' LCl, mr, 1963, Delbard-Chabert
'Delcapo' F, ob, Delbard; buds orange-yellow; intr. 2002
'Delcart' ('Le Rouge et Le Noir') HT, dr, Delbard; intr. 1973
'Delcascor' (Casque d'Or®) HT, my, 1986, Delbard; flowers well-shaped, 4 in., 30 petals, no fragrance; vigorous, upright, bushy growth; [(Zambra® × 'Jean de la Lune') × ('Michèle Meilland' × 'Tahiti')]; intr. 1979
'Delcélit' (Céline Delbard®) F, ob, 1986, Delbard, G.; flowers salmon, silver reverse, large, 23 petals, cupped, borne in clusters, no fragrance; recurrent; foliage dark green; bushy, rounded growth; [seedling × (Milrose® × 'Legion d'Honneur')]; intr. 1983
'Delchacré' HT, ab, Delbard; intr. 2005
'Delchame' S, lp, Delbard; intr. 2000
'Delchibis' HT, dp, Delbard; intr. 2005
'Delchifrou' ('Heinz Winkler') S, dr, Delbard; intr. 2005
'Delchine' (Shantung®) F, pb, 1989, Delbard & Chabert; flowers mottled pink, cream and red, large, 22 petals, flat; foliage matte; vigorous growth; [('Orléans Rose' × 'Goldilocks') × (Bordure Rose® × unknown)]; intr. 1988
'Delcien' S, w, Delbard; intr. 2004
'Delcifra' ('Citron-Fraise') S, pb, 1998, Delbard; bud yellow
'Delciste' ('Libre Ingenue') S, w, Delbard; intr. 1996
'Delclopel' ('Clos de la Pellerie') HT, or, 1988, Delbard-Chabert; flowers medium vermilion red, long, large, 25-35 petals, slight fragrance; foliage large; good, vigorous, bushy growth; [('Spartan' × Baccará®) × seedling]
'Delcola' ('Infante Marie-Thérèse') F, r, Delbard; intr. 2001
'Delcolb' (Colbert®) HT, pb, 1991, Delbard-Chabert; flowers creamy white, delicately shaded porcelain pink, large, 27-35 petals, cupped, slight fragrance; foliage dark green, flat; bushy (80-100 cm.) growth; [(('Peace' × Bettina®) × ('President Herbert Hoover' × 'Tropicana')) × 'Chateau de Versailles']; intr. 1990
'Delcouro' ('Rose Cascade') LCl, lp, Delbard; intr. 1995
'Delcourt' ('Courtosie des Relais et Châteaux', Courtoisie®) F, ob, 1985, Delbard, Georges; flowers orange, reverse orange blended with yellow, large, 20 petals, moderate fragrance; foliage medium size, medium green; bushy growth; ['Avalanche Rose' × ('Fashion' × unknown)]; intr. 1984
'Delcoussi' F, mp, Delbard; intr. 1993
'Delcraf' ('Louksor', Louqsor®) HT, ab, 1970, Delbard-Chabert; flowers golden coral with base yellow, medium, dbl., globular, borne singly and several together; foliage medium size, glossy; vigorous, bushy growth; ['Dr. Albert Schweitzer' × 'Provence']; intr. 1967
'Delcreme' ('Regine Crespin') F, pb, Delbard; intr. 1990
'Delcril' S, yb, Delbard; intr. 2002
'Delcrip' (Mme Dimitriu®) Pol, mp, 1970, Delbard-Chabert; bud globular; flowers pink tinted lighter, large, dbl., borne in clusters of 5-10; foliage bronze, glossy; vigorous, bushy growth; ['Chic Parisien' × 'Provence']; intr. 1967
'Delcro' ('Moon Magic', 'YelloGlo') F, dy, 1969, Delbard-Chabertdbl.
'Delcrouf' ('Honey Bear', Bordure Nacrée®) Min, ly, 1986, Delbard; flowers creamy light yellow, small, 38 petals, no fragrance; low, bushy growth; [('Orléans Rose' × 'Francois et Joseph Guy') × ('Goldilocks' × 'DELtorche')]; intr. 1973
'Delcuiv' F, yb, Delbard; intr. 1980
'Delcus' (Agéna®) HT, op, 1970, Delbard-Chabert; bud long, pointed; flowers salmon-pink, large, dbl., moderate fragrance; foliage glossy, leathery; vigorous, bushy growth; ['Chic Parisien' × ('Michèle Meilland' × 'Mme Joseph Perraud')]; intr. 1966
'Delcylanc' HT, dp, Delbard; intr. 2005
'Deldal' ('Niagara Pride', Dolce Vita®) HT, op, 1986, Delbard; flowers rosy salmon, large, 37 petals, high-centered, slight fragrance; vigorous, upright, bushy growth; ['Voeux de Bonheur' × ('Chic Parisien' × ('Michele Meilland' × 'Mme Joseph Perraud'))]; intr. 1971
'Delde' F, dr, 1957, Delbard-Chabert
'Deldido' (Fêtes Galantes®) HT, pb, Delbard; intr. 1994
'Deldiore' (Dioressence®) Gr, m, 1985, Delbard, Georges; flowers lavender, well-formed, large, 35 petals, intense fragrance; foliage large, medium green, semi-glossy; bushy growth; [(('Holstein' × 'Bayadère') × 'Prelude') × seedling]; intr. 1984
'Deldog' ('Berendina') S, dy, Delbard; intr. 1997
'Deldra' (Venusic®) HT, my, 1970, Delbard-Chabert; flowers saffron-yellow, medium, dbl., cupped, moderate fragrance; foliage dark, glossy; vigorous, upright, bushy growth; [(Queen Elizabeth® × 'Provence') × ('Mme Joseph

Perraud' × 'Bayadere')]; intr. 1966

'Deldrop' (Beauté Spatiale®) HT, mr, 1970, Delbard-Chabert; flowers velvety red, medium, semi-dbl., high-centered, slight fragrance; foliage bronze, soft; moderate, bushy growth; ['Walko' × 'Impeccable']; intr. 1966

'Delecla' ('Sparkler', Clos Fleuri Rouge®) F, mr, 1989, Delbard & Chabert; flowers medium, 20 petals, flat, slight fragrance; foliage bright; bushy, vigorous growth; ['Orléans Rose' × Queen Elizabeth®]; intr. 1988

'D'Eleganta' -- See 'Kricarlo'

'Delego' HT, dr, Delbard; intr. 1999

'Delegran' ('Grand Age', Grand Siècle®, 'Great Century', 'Greatest Century') HT, pb, 1986, Delbard; flowers creamy pink blend, well-formed, large, 33 petals, cupped, slight fragrance; foliage large; vigorous, bushy, branching growth; [((Queen Elizabeth® × 'Provence') × ('Michele Meilland' × 'Bayadere')) × (('Voeux de Bonheur' × 'MEImet') × ('Peace' × 'Dr. Debat'))]; intr. 1977

'Deleme' S, mp, Delbardsingle; intr. 2002

'Delépi' (Épidor®) HT, dy, 1982, Delbard, Georges; flowers large, 35 petals, slight fragrance; foliage large, medium green, matte; bushy growth; [('Peace' × 'Marcelle Gret') × (Velizy® × 'Jean de la Lune')]; intr. 1981

'Deléri' LCl, lp, Delbardvery dbl.; intr. 1998

'Delexoid' S, m, Delbard; bud pointed; intr. 2002

'Delfat' (Louvre®) HT, ab, 1970, Delbard-Chabert; bud long, pointed; flowers rosy apricot, medium, dbl.; foliage bronze, glossy; moderate, upright growth; ['Souv. de J. Chabert' × ('Walko' × 'Souv. de J. Chabert')]; intr. 1967

'Delfesrou' ('Red Festival', Festival Rouge®) F, dr, 1982, Delbard, Georges; flowers semi-dbl., well-formed, borne in clusters; foliage dark; ['Walko' × ('Happiness' × 'Sonia')]

'Delfib' F, my, Delbard; intr. 1965

'Delfire' MinFl, rb, Delbard; intr. 2005

'Delflip' (Escurial®) HT, mr, 1970, Delbard-Chabert; flowers velvety cardinal-red, medium, semi-dbl., high-centered, slight fragrance; foliage dark, glossy; vigorous, bushy growth; ['Gay Paris' × 'Impeccable']; intr. 1967

'Delflori' (Fluorescent®) F, mr, 1986, Delbard; flowers medium, 33 petals, cupped, no fragrance; glossy foliage; vigorous, bushy, branching growth; [Zambra® × (('DELtorche' × 'Tropicana') × ('Alain' × 'Souv. de J. Chabert'))]; intr. 1977

'Delfloro' ('Bright Spark') F, mr, Delbard; intr. 1992

'Delfocy' S, mp, Delbardfull; intr. 2006

'Delfrei' (Coeur Farouche®) S, m, Delbard; intr. 1993

'Delfri' HT, pb, 1970, Delbard-Chabert; intr. 1965

'Delfror' (Rose du Ciel®) HT, pb, 1970, Delbard-Chabert; flowers cream-white broadly edged carmine-pink, large, dbl., globular; foliage dark, glossy; vigorous, bushy growth; ['Chic Parisien' × ('Michèle Meilland' × 'Bayadere')]; intr. 1966

'Delfumros' HT, pb, Delbard; buds pointed, pink cream; intr. 2002

'Delgap' ('Lido di Roma') HT, yb, 1970, Delbard-Chabert; bud long, pointed; flowers deep yellow, shaded red, large, dbl., high-centered; foliage glossy, leathery; vigorous, upright, bushy growth; [('Chic Parisien' × 'Michele Meilland') × ('Sultane' × 'Mme Joseph Perraud')]

'Delge' ('Mrs Jones') F, mp, 1958, Delbard, G.

'Delgenta' F, dp, Delbard; intr. 2004

'Delgeot' ('Isobel Champion', La Marseillaise®) HT, dr, 1986, Delbard; bud large, ovoid; flowers well-formed, large, 40 petals; vigorous, bushy growth; [(('Rome Glory' × 'Impeccable') × ('Rouge Meilland' × 'Soraya')) × ('MEIsar' × 'Walko')]; intr. 1976

'Delglap' (Puerta del Sol®) Cl HT, my, 1986, Delbard; flowers medium golden yellow, large, 28 petals, borne in small clusters, slight fragrance; foliage deep green, glossy; vigorous, climbing (to 9 ft.) growth; [(Queen Elizabeth® × 'Provence') × ('Michèle Meilland' × 'Bayadere')]; intr. 1971

'Delgo' LCl, or, 1961, Delbard-Chabert

'Delgold' (Lord Gold®) HT, dy, Delbard; intr. 1980

'Delgramat' HT, rb, Delbard; intr. 2003

'Delgramo' F, m, Delbard; flowers dbl.

'Delgranbo' HT, my, Delbard; intr. 2004

'Delgribla' ('Ice Cool') LCl, w, Delbard; bud tinted lemon; intr. 1995

'Delgrim' (Dune®) LCl, my, Delbard; intr. 1993

'Delgrinro' Cl F, mp, Delbard; intr. 2005

'Delgrord' ('Great North', Grand Nord®, Great Nord®) HT, w, 1986, Delbard; flowers large, 28 petals, high-centered, vigorous, bushy growth; [((Queen Elizabeth® × 'Provence') × ('Virgo' × Carina®)) × (('Voeux de Bonheur' × 'Virgo') × ('Virgo' × 'Peace'))]; intr. 1974

'Delgrouge' LCl, dr; intr. 2002

'Delgus' (Prince Tango®) Pol, or, 1970, Delbard-Chabert; bud pointed; flowers mandarin color, open, small, semi-dbl.; foliage bronze, glossy; moderate, bushy growth; [('Orléans Rose' × 'Goldilocks') × ((Orange Triumph® × unknown) × 'Floradora')]

'Delhi Apricot' HT, ab, 1970, Pal, Dr. B.P.; bud pointed; flowers apricot-yellow, medium, dbl., slight fragrance; foliage light green, soft; moderate, bushy growth; intr. 1964

'Delhi Brightness' F, op, 1970, Pal, Dr. B.P.; flowers open, medium, semi-dbl.; foliage glossy; vigorous, upright, bushy growth; intr. 1963

'Delhi Daintiness' F, lp, 1970, Pal, Dr. B.P.; bud pointed; flowers light pink, reverse darker, medium, semi-dbl.; foliage glossy; vigorous, upright, compact growth; intr. 1963

'Delhi Maid' F, ob, 1970, Pal, Dr. B.P.; bud pointed; flowers flame-orange, base gold, open, medium, single; foliage dark, glossy; vigorous, upright, compact growth; intr. 1963

'Delhi Pink Pearl' HMult, lp, 1970, Pal, Dr. B.P.; bud ovoid; flowers pearly pink, open, medium, semi-dbl.; foliage glossy, light green; very vigorous, compact growth; [sport of 'Echo']; intr. 1962

'Delhi Prince' F, dp, 1970, Pal, Dr. B.P.; bud pointed; flowers glowing deep pink, open, medium, semi-dbl., slight fragrance; foliage glossy; vigorous, bushy growth; intr. 1963

'Delhi Princess' F, mp, 1969, Pal, Dr. B.P.; bud ovoid, cerise-red; flowers deep pink, open, large, semi-dbl., borne in clusters, slight fragrance; foliage glossy, bronze; very vigorous, compact growth; intr. 1963

'Delhi Rosette' F, ob, 1970, Pal, Dr. B.P.; bud ovoid; flowers bright orange-scarlet, open, medium, 28 petals; foliage dark, glossy; vigorous, compact growth; intr. 1965

'Delhi Sherbet' F, mp, 1970, Pal, Dr. B.P.; bud ovoid; flowers deep rose-pink, medium, dbl., intense fragrance; foliage glossy; vigorous, bushy, compact growth; ['Gruss an Teplitz' × seedling]; intr. 1963

'Delhi Starlet' Min, ly, 1970, Pal, Dr. B.P.; bud pointed; flowers open, small, semi-dbl., slight musk fragrance; foliage small, glossy; dwarf, compact growth; ['Goudvlinder' × seedling]; intr. 1963

'Delhi Sunshine' HT, yb, 1970, Pal, Dr. B.P.; bud pointed; flowers deep cream, reverse flushed pink, medium, dbl.; foliage light green; bushy, open growth; ['Mme Charles Sauvage' × seedling]; intr. 1963

'Delhi White Pearl' LCl, w, 1969, Pal, Dr. B.P.; bud ovoid; flowers pearly white, dbl., borne in clusters, slight fragrance; repeat bloom; foliage glossy; vigorous growth; ['Prosperity' × seedling]; intr. 1963

Délia® HT, op, Guillot-Massad; flowers coppery pink, dbl., slight wild rose fragrance; foliage disease-resistant; stems flexible; growth shrubby; intr. 2004

'Delic' (Éterna®) HT, lp, 1979, Delbard-Chabert; bud long; flowers light carmine pink, 4-5 in., 28-32 petals; vigorous, upright growth; PP4440; [(('Michèle Meilland' × 'Carla') × ('Dr. Schweitzer' × 'Tropicana')) × (Queen Elizabeth® × 'Provence')]; intr. 1978

'Delicado' HT, op, 1954, Lowe; flowers shell-pink shaded peach, well-shaped, 6 in.; moderate growth

'Delicata' HRg, lp, 1898, Cooling; flowers soft lilac-pink, large, semi-dbl., moderate fragrance; recurrent bloom;

vigorous growth

'Délicate' HGal, mr, before 1827, Dubourg; flowers cherry red with bright lilac

'Delicate Beauty' -- See 'Korlarkon'

'Delicate Lady' HT, w, 2004, Sheldon, John; flowers white with pink at center, aging to pure white, reverse white, 4-6 in., full, borne mostly solitary, moderate fragrance; foliage dark green, semi-glossy; prickles medium, pointed, maroon, aging to green; growth upright, medium (4-6 ft.); exhibition, garden decoration; ['Sheer Bliss' × 'Headliner']; intr. 2004

'Delicate Sunsation' S, w, Kordes ; buds long, pointed; flowers large, deep cream brushed with light pink, dbl.; constant bloom; growth neat, compact, prostrate; intr. 1998

'Delicate Wine' -- See 'Vino Delicado'

Delicia® HRg, dp, Kordes; bud very long, pointed; flowers deep pink, 4 in., dbl., intense sweet fragrance; recurrent; foliage large, dark green, glossy; numerous prickles; vigorous, erect, bushy growth to 7 ft.; intr. 2003

'Delicia' -- See 'Korgatum'

'Délicieuse' HGal, mp, about 1830, Vibert; flowers bright pink, medium, full

'Delicious' HT, yb, 1933, Sauvage; flowers yellow, shaded peach, large, semi-dbl., [sport of 'Los Angeles']

'Delicious' Min, mp, Welsh, Eric; flowers small, full, borne in small clusters, intense fragrance; foliage small, medium green, semi-glossy; few prickles; tall (65-70 cm.), upright, compact growth; ['Avandel' × ((seedling × 'Friesia') × seedling)]; intr. 1994

'Delicious Mood' F, pb, 2008, Yasuda, Yuji; flowers medium, semi-dbl., borne mostly solitary; foliage medium, dark green, matte; prickles medium, moderate; growth upright, medium (1 m.); garden decoration, cutting; ['seeding' × 'Ayaka']; intr. 2008

'Délie Communaudat' HT, yb, 1933, Buatois; flowers Naples yellow, shaded and edged carmine, dbl., cupped, moderate fragrance; foliage leathery; very vigorous, bushy growth; ['Mme Charles Detreaux' × 'Mme Edouard Herriot']

'Delific' ('Red Prolific', Rouge Prolific®, Clos Vougeot®) F, mr, 1986, Delbard-Chabert; flowers medium, 28 petals, no fragrance; bushy growth; [('Alain' × 'Charles Mallerin') × ('Lafayette' × 'Walko')]; intr. 1983

'Delight' HWich, rb, 1904, Walsh; flowers bright carmine, base white, stamens yellow, medium to large, semi-dbl., cupped; foliage glossy; long stems; very vigorous, climbing (15-20 ft.) growth

'Delight' F, dp, intr. 2005

Delight™ ('Delight Hit') MinFl, ab, Olesen

'Delight Hit' -- See 'Poulstigh'

'Delight Smooth Touch' -- See 'Haddel'

'Delightful' HT, pb, 1931, McGredy; flowers rose, base yellow, reverse amber-yellow, large, dbl., high-centered, moderate fragrance; foliage glossy; vigorous growth; ['George Dickson' × unknown]

'Delightful' HT, yb, Brownell; bud pointed; flowers straw-yellow, base shaded red, 4-5 in., 35-50 petals, high-centered, moderate fragrance; upright, compact growth; PP1372; ['Curly Pink' × 'Shades of Autumn']; intr. 1956

'Delightful Kiwi' HT, lp, 1989, Cattermole, R.F.; bud tapering; flowers blush pink aging to creamy pink, medium, 45 petals, urn-shaped, borne singly; foliage light green, large, shiny; prickles light brown, very few; upright, branching growth; ['Silent Night' × ('Prima Ballerina' × 'Irish Mist')]; intr. 1988

'Delightful Lady' HT, lp, 1983, Attfield, B.B.; flowers large, 30-35 petals, high-centered, borne singly in spring, 3-5 per cluster in autumn, slight fragrance; foliage semi-glossy; prickles brown; medium-tall growth; [Pascali® × 'Merry Widow']

'Delightful Pink' F, mp, 1959, Boerner; bud ovoid; flowers pink, medium, 40-45 petals, cupped, borne in clusters, moderate fragrance; vigorous, upright growth; PP1803; ['Chic' × 'Demure']; intr. 1959

Delilah® -- See 'Sundel'

'Delille' M, w, 1852, Robert; flowers blush-white, nicely mossed, semi-dbl.; may repeat

'Delimon' HT, or, Delbard; intr. 1978

'Delindrus' mp, Delbard; intr. 1984

'Delisse' Min, op, Delbard

'Delivour' ('Empress Farah', 'Kaiserin Farah', 'Strawberry Parfait') HT, w, Delbard; intr. 1992

'Deljaber' (Professeur Jean Bernard®) HT, dr, 1990, Delbard & Chabert; bud cupped; flowers very large, 25-30 petals; foliage dark green, abundant; bushy growth; [('Charles Mallerin' × 'Divine') × ('Tropicana' × ('Rome Glory' × 'Impeccable'))]; intr. 1989

'Deljacq' ('La Joconde') HT, or, 1988, Delbard & Chabert; flowers well-shaped, large, 40 petals; upright, vigorous growth; [('Tropicana' × ('Rome Glory' × 'Impeccable')) × ('Spartan' × 'MElger')]

'Deljapal' ('Folio Courtisane') HT, ly, Delbard, Georges; intr. 1996

'Deljape' HT, yb, Dorieux; intr. 2006

'Deljaune' (Clos Fleuri Jaune) F, my, 1989, Delbard & Chabert; flowers yellow, shaded ochre, opening to yellow-amber, large, 18 petals, slight fragrance; foliage bright; semi-climbing, vigorous growth; [('Orléans Rose' × 'Goldilocks') × Parure d'Or®]; intr. 1988

'Deljaunor' ('Desert Spice', France Libre®) HT, ob, 1991; flowers nasturtium orange and coppery, yellow and gold reverse, large, 25-30 petals, cupped, slight fragrance; foliage dark green, glossy; upright growth; [(Zambra® × Orange Sensation®) × (seedling × seedling)]; intr. 1990

'Deljausor' S, yb, Delbard; intr. 2003

'Deljavert' ('Chameleon') S, w, Delbard; intr. 1997

'Deljis' LCl, or, 1956, Delbard-Chabert

'Deljofem' ('Tendresse') HT, pb, 1985, Delbard, Georges; flowers light pink, reverse apricot-pink, large, dbl., high-centered, moderate fragrance; free-flowering; foliage dense; growth to 50-100 cm.; [('Michèle Meilland' × 'Bayadère') × (Grace de Monaco® × 'Present Filial')]; intr. 1980

'Deljonq' ('Jonquille') F, dy, 1982, Delbard, Georges; flowers large, 35 petals; foliage medium size, medium green, matte; bushy growth; [('Peace' × 'Marcelle Gret') × (Velizy® × 'Jean de la Lune')]

'Deljuli' (Julie Delbard®) F, ab, 1986, Delbard; flowers apricot with yellow and orange hues, large, 28 petals, hybrid tea, no fragrance; vigorous, bushy growth; [(Zambra® × (Orange Triumph® × 'Floradora')) × (('Orléans Rose' × 'Goldilocks') × (Bettina® × 'Henri Mallerin'))]; intr. 1976

'Delki' ('Pinocchio') Min, ob, Delbard; intr. 1998

'Delki' Min, yb, Delbard; intr. 2001

'Delkort' (Atlas®) HT, dr, 1970, Delbard-Chabert; bud long, pointed; flowers magenta-red edged darker, large, dbl., cupped; foliage dark, glossy; vigorous, upright, bushy growth; ['Chic Parisien' × 'Provence']; intr. 1966

'Delkri' HT, mr, 1969, Delbard

'Delkrum' HT, mr, 1964, Delbard-Chabert; bud dark purplish

'Della Balfour' ('Desert Glow', 'Renown's Desert Glo', 'Royal Pageant') S, ab, Harkness; flowers golden peach-orange, 4 in., dbl., borne in clusters, slight lemony fragrance; recurrent; foliage dark green, lush; growth to 8 ft.; ['Rosemary Harkness' × 'Elena']; intr. 1994

Della Reese™ -- See 'Wekrorobluni'

'Delludmean' F, ob, Delbard; intr. 2008

'Delmadra' S, mp, Delbard; intr. 2002

'Delmagsa' F, dp, Delbard; bud globular; intr. 1995

'Delmaja' S, dy, Delbard; intr. 2002

'Delmalor' F, or, Delbard; intr. 2005

'Delmanche' ('Maman Chérie') HT, pb, 1982, Delbard, Georges; flowers dbl., borne in clusters; ['Gay Paris' × (Baccará® × 'Impeccable')]

'Delmarou' S, mr, Delbard; intr. 2002

'Delmator' ('Beverly Hills', 'Malicorne') HT, ob, 1982, Delbard, Georges; flowers dark orange, greenhouse variety, borne in clusters; PP5673; [(Zambra® × Orange Sensation®) × (Zambra® × (Orange Triumph® × 'Floradora'))]

'Delmic' Min, yb, Delbard; intr. 2000

'Delmigre' Min, rb, Delbard; intr. 2002

'Delmino' HT, dy, Delbard; intr. 2006

'Delmir' (Parure d'Or®) LCl, yb, 1970, Delbard-Chabert; flowers golden yellow edged orange, medium, semi-dbl., borne in small clusters; repeat bloom; foliage dark, glossy; vigorous, climbing growth; [(Queen Elizabeth® × 'Provence') × ('Sultane' × 'Mme Joseph Perraud')]; intr. 1968

'Delmistri' ('Bambi') Min, rb, Delbard; intr. 1998

'Delmone' F, op, Delbard; intr. 2005

'Delmont' (Obélisque®) LCl, op, 1970, Delbard-Chabert; flowers coppery orange-pink, medium, semi-dbl., globular, borne in large clusters; abundant, intermittent bloom; foliage bronze, glossy; vigorous, climbing growth; ['Spectacular' × ('Orange Triumph® × 'Floradora')]; intr. 1967

'Delmori' HT, pb, Delbard; intr. 2001

'Delmoun' (Sensass Delbard®) Cl HT, mr, 1986, Delbard; flowers bright velvety red, 3 in., 28 petals, cupped, borne in small clusters, no fragrance; foliage dark green, glossy; vigorous, climbing (to 10 ft.) growth; [(('Danse du Feu' × ('Orange Triumph® × 'Floradora')) × ('Tenor' × unknown)]; intr. 1973

'Delmur' ('Altus', 'Sublimely Single') LCl, mr, 1966, Delbard-Chabert

'Delnat' (Mitsouko®) HT, yb, 1983, Delbard, Georges; flowers yellow, petals edged red, large, 50 petals, moderate fruity fragrance; foliage medium size, clear green; prickles bronze-red; dense, bushy growth; [('Michèle Meilland' × 'Chic Parisien') × 'Peace']; intr. 1970

'Delnible' ('Nil Bleu', Blue Nile®) HT, m, 1980, Delbard, Georges; bud ovoid, pointed; flowers deep lavender, 5 in., 28-30 petals, high-centered, borne singly or 2-3 per cluster, intense fruity fragrance; foliage large, olive green; prickles short, hooked downward; tall, upright, spreading growth; PP4671; [('Holstein' × 'Bayadere') × ('Prelude' × 'Saint-Exupery')]; intr. 1977

'Delnnet' Min, dy, Delbard

'Delnolli' ('Tourbillon') F, pb, 1985, Delbard, Georges; flowers deep pink, yellow reverse, large, 20 petals, moderate fragrance; foliage small, medium green, semi-glossy; upright growth; [Zambra® × (('Orléans Rose' × 'Goldilocks') × ('Spartan' × 'Fashion'))]; intr. 1981

'Deloblan' ('Blanche Comète', 'White Comet') HT, w, 1982, Delbard, Georges; flowers dbl., borne in clusters; [('Virgo' × 'Peace') × ('Goldilocks' × 'Virgo')]

'Delocabri' ('The Midlands Rose') HT, ab, Delbard; intr. 2002

'Delocare' Gr, or, Delbard; intr. 2001

'Delodive' ('Pink Ribbon') F, mp, Delbard; intr. 1994

'Deloitte & Touche' -- See 'Koraucher'

'Delolia' S, w, Delbard; intr. 2005

'Delop' (Vatican®) HT, ab, 1970, Delbard-Chabert; bud ovoid; flowers apricot-yellow shaded carmine, medium, dbl., high-centered, slight fragrance; foliage glossy; moderate, bushy growth; ['Grande Premiere' × ('Sultane' × 'Mme Joseph Perraud')]; intr. 1967

'Delopyg' Min, yb, Delbard; intr. 1978

'Delorbo' F, ob, Delbard; bud long, pointed, apricot orange; intr. 2001

'Delore' HT, ly, Kordes; flowers creamy buff shading to light apricot, high-centered, borne singly and in small clusters; growth medium to tall, strong and healthy; [sport of 'Folklore']; intr. 1982

'Delorfeu' (Carnaval de Rio®) F, ob, 1982, Delbard, Georges; flowers orange, dbl., borne in clusters; [(Zambra® × Orange Sensation®) × (Zambra® × (Orange Triumph® × 'Floradora'))]

'Deloro' HT, pb, Delbard; intr. 2003

'Delorvi' ('Puerto del Sol') F, ob, Delbard; intr. 1999

'Delosol' (O Sole Mio®) HT, my, 1985, Delbard, Georges; flowers bright, well-formed, large, 35 petals, borne singly and in clusters of 2 or 3, slight fresh fragrance; foliage medium size, medium green, glossy; growth to over 100 cm.; [('Peace' × 'Marcelle Gret') × (Velizy® × unknown)]; intr. 1984

'Delpabra' S, lp, Delbardvery dbl.; intr. 2002

'Delpapy' F, my, Delbard; intr. 1992

'Delpar' ('Delbard's Orange Climber') LCl, or, 1965, Delbard-Chabert; bud ovoid; intr. 1963

'Delparo' Min, mp, Delbard; intr. 2002

'Delperl' LCl, dr, Delbard; intr. 1994

'Delpétri' (Clochemerle®) HT, mr, 1989, Delbard & Chabert; flowers large, 38 petals, cupped, slight fragrance; foliage matte; vigorous, bushy growth; [seedling × (('Michèle Meilland' × 'Karla') × seedling)]; intr. 1988

'Delphin' HT, m, VEG; flowers violet-pink, large, dbl.; intr. 1980

'Delphine Gaudot' T, w, 1840, Béluze; flowers cream white, medium, full

'Delphine Gay' HP, w, Vibert; intr. 1847

'Delphine Gay' HGal, m, about 1820, Vibert; flowers bright bluish-red, sometimes striped, medium, full

'Delphine Gay' D, w, Vibert; flowers white, shaded flesh pink, medium to large; full; intr. 1823

'Delphiniana' -- See 'Enfant de France'

'Delphinie' ('La Delphinie') M, mp, before 1846; flowers rose pink, small, dbl., cupped

'Delpli' Pol, ob, 1969, Delbard

'Delpo' ('Little Devil') F, mr, 1965, Delbard-Chabert; intr. 1961

'Delpoc' (Diapason®) HT, mp, 1970, Delbard-Chabert; flowers porcelain pink, medium, 40 petals, globular, moderate fragrance; foliage bronze, glossy; very vigorous, bushy growth; ['Chic Parisien' × (('Sultane' × unknown) × 'Mme Joseph Perraud')]; intr. 1966

'Delpomp' ('Pink Ribbon', Clos Fleuri Rose®) F, mp, 1989, Delbard & Chabert; flowers medium, 30 petals, borne in clusters; foliage bright; bushy, vigorous growth; [(Zambra® × Orange Sensation®) × ('Robin Hood' × 'Virgo')]; intr. 1988

'Delposar' ('Diablotin, Climbing', 'Little Devil, Climbing', Grimpant Diablotin®) Cl F, mr, 1986, Delbard; [sport of 'Diablotin']; intr. 1970

'Delpous' ('Fontaine Blue', Fontainebleu®) HT, dp, 1970, Delbard-Chabert; bud long, pointed; flowers magenta-pink, large, dbl., globular, slight fragrance; foliage dark, glossy, leathery; vigorous, bushy growth; ['Dr. Albert Schweitzer' × ('Bayadere' × 'Rome Glory')]; intr. 1967

'Delprat' ('Présence') HT, lp, 1983, Delbard, Georges; flowers pink, lighter reverse, large, 38 petals, slight fruity fragrance; foliage medium size, medium green, matte; upright, bushy growth; ['Dr. Albert Schweitzer' × ('Michèle Meilland' × 'Bayadere')]; intr. 1970

'Delpre' ('Happy Anniversary') Gr, op, 1960, Delbard-Chabert; bud urn-shaped; intr. 1963

Delprima® (Grand Prix®) HT, op, 1970, Delbard-Chabert; intr. 1968

'Delredi' ('Renata Tebaldi') HT, ob, Delbard; intr. 1987

'Delreno' ('Mme Georges Renoard') HT, dy, 1988, Delbard-Chabert; flowers long, large, 35-40 petals, moderate fragrance; foliage clear, matte; upright, vigorous growth; [('Peace' × 'Marcelle Gret') × ('Legion d'Honneur' × unknown)]

'Delreslud' HT, mp, Delbard; bud globular; intr. 2001

'Delribbo' HT, yb, Delbard; bud creamy yellow; intr. 2001

'Delricos' ('Gorgeous George', La Tour d'Argent™, Château de Versailles®, 'Guy Laroche') HT, rb, 1986, Delbard, Georges; flowers brilliant red, silver reverse, large, 30 petals, high-centered, borne mostly singly; foliage medium size, medium green, matte; upright, bushy growth; [seedling × ('Michèle Meilland' × 'Carla')]; intr. 1985

'Delrima' ('Sasa') F, rb, Delbard; intr. 1995

'Delrio' ('Night Flight', 'Vol de Nuit') HT, m, 1983, Delbard, Georges; flowers deep lilac, large, 33 petals, high-centered, borne mostly singly, intense fragrance; recurrent; foliage medium size, light green, matte; prickles bronze-red; bushy growth; [('Holstein' × ('Bayadere' × 'Prelude')) × 'Saint-Exupery']; intr. 1970

'Delrobla' (Carmagnole®) F, w, 1991, Delbard & Chabert; flowers white cream with soft pink, medium, 20-25 petals, cupped, slight fragrance; foliage dark green; bushy (80-100 cm.) growth; [(Milrose® × 'Legion d'Honneur') × (Zambra® × Orange Sensation®)]; intr. 1990

'Delrocarm' F, dr, Delbard; intr. 2006

'Delroceles' (Rose Céleste®) Cl HT, lp, 1986, Delbard; flowers light pink, darker at center, large, 33 petals, cupped, borne in small clusters, moderate fragrance; vigorous, climbing (to 9 ft.) growth; [(Queen Elizabeth® ×

'Provence') × ('Sultane' × 'Mme Joseph Perraud')]; intr. 1979
'Delroli' S, ab, Delbard; bud small, orange; intr. 2003
'Delrona' (Figaro Panarosa™) S, lp, Delbardvery dbl.; intr. 2000
'Delrospiv' S, mp; intr. 2003
'Delrou' S, mr, Delbard; intr. 2004
'Delroue' Min, rb, Delbard
'Delroujan' HT, rb, Delbard, Georges; intr. 1988
'Delrouvel' (Château d'Amboise®) HT, dr, 1989, Delbard & Chabert; flowers dark red, opening bright, long, 23-30 petals; foliage bright; vigorous growth; [('Tropicana' × unknown) × (('Rome Glory' × 'Impeccable') × ('Rouge Meilland' × 'Soraya'))]; intr. 1988
'Delrovrai' HT, mp, Delbard, Georges; intr. 1995
'Delrugro' LCl, mr, Delbardsemi-dbl.; intr. 1998
'Delrula' ('Ville du Perreux', Clos Fleuri Bicolore™) F, pb, 1989, Delbard & Chabert; flowers pink with white and cream, long, large, 28 petals; foliage bright; bushy, vigorous growth; [seedling × (Milrose® × 'Legion d'Honneur')]; intr. 1988
'Delsab' (Royal Ascot®) HT, pb, 1970, Delbard-Chabert; flowers pink, reverse shaded crimson, large, semi-dbl., high-centered; foliage glossy, leathery; vigorous, bushy growth; ['Chic Parisien' × ('Grande Premiere' × ('Sultane' × 'Mme Joseph Perraud')]; intr. 1968
'Delsacre' S, op, Delbard; intr. 2001
'Delsam' F, ob, Delbard, Georges; intr. 1979
'Delsamar' (Légion d'Honneur®) F, mr, 1986, Delbard; flowers well-formed, medium, 55 petals, cupped; low, bushy growth; [('Souv. de J. Chabert' × ('Walko' × 'Souv. de J. Chabert')) × (('Tamango' × 'Gay Paris') × (Zambra® × 'Jean de la Lune'))]; intr. 1974
'Delsamo' (Paris 2000®) HT, dp, 1986, Delbard; flowers deep pink, large, 28 petals, cupped, no fragrance; vigorous, upright, bushy growth; [('DELtorche' × ('Sultane' × 'Mme Joseph Perraud')) × (Queen Elizabeth® × 'Provence')]; intr. 1974
'Delsamour' (Velizy®) HT, ab, 1986, Delbard; flowers well-formed, large, 30 petals, slight fragrance; bushy, branching growth; [(('Peace' × 'Marcelle Gret') × ('Michele Meilland' × 'Tahiti')) × ('Peace' × 'Grand Premiere')]; intr. 1973
'Delsap' F, mr, 1967, Delbard-Chabert; intr. 1967
'Delsatel' ('Satellite') HT, or, 1985, Delbard, Georges; flowers vermilion, medium, 28 petals, high-centered, borne mostly singly, moderate fragrance; good repeat; foliage medium size, medium green, semi-glossy; moderate, bushy growth; [(('Tropicana' × 'Samourai') × ('Tropicana' × '(Rome Glory × Impeccable)')) × 'Granada']; intr. 1982

'Delset' ('Castel', Versailles®) HT, lp, 1970, Delbard-Chabert; bud ovoid; flowers soft pink, medium, dbl., cupped, slight fragrance; recurrent; foliage dark, glossy, leathery; vigorous, upright, bushy growth; [(Queen Elizabeth® × 'Provence') × ('Michèle Meilland' × 'Bayadere')]; intr. 1967
'Delsiel' Gr, dy, Delbardfull; intr. 2001
'Delsire' (Grandessa®, Messire Delbard®) Cl HT, dr, 1986, Delbard; flowers deep crimson red, well-formed, large, 38 petals, borne in small clusters; foliage large; vigorous (to 9 ft.) growth; [('Danse du Feu' × 'Guinee') × (('Tenor' × Fugue®) × ('Delbard's Orange Climber' × 'Gloire de Dijon')]; intr. 1976
'Delsirp' Pol, ob, 1971, Delforge; bud ovoid
'Delsob' ('Puerto Rico', 'Sable Chaud') F, ob, 1974, Delbard; flowers orange, reverse blended with yellow, medium, dbl., cupped, borne in large clusters, slight spicy fragrance; good repeat; foliage small to medium size, bronze, leathery, semi-glossy; prickles medium, hooked downward, brown; vigorous, bushy growth; PP3519; [Zambra® × (Orange Triumph® × 'Floradora')]
'Delsorb' S, pb, Delbard; intr. 1994
'Delsouche' ('Souv de Maurice Chevalier') Gr, dr, 1982, Delbard, Georges; flowers semi-dbl., borne in clusters; [('Walko' × 'Impeccable') × (Papa Meilland® × (Baccará × 'Michele Meilland'))]
'Delstavo' ('Artista Panarosa') F, rb, Delbard; intr. 2003
'Delstribuc' HT, rb, Delbard; intr. 2001
'Delstricol' ('Rainbow Nation') F, yb, Delbard, Georges; intr. 1996
'Delstricycla' HT, pb, Delbard; bud longs, pointed; intr. 2001
'Delstrijor' S, ob, Delbard; intr. 2005
'Delstrimer' S, rb, Delbard; intr. 2002
'Delstriro' HT, rb, Delbard; intr. 2004
'Delstrobla' F, pb, Delbard, Georges; intr. 1996
'Delstror' F, pb, Delbard; intr. 1997
'Delstrorange' S, rb, Delbard
'Delsulan' (Europe 92®) HT, mp, 1989, Delbard & Chabert; flowers pink magenta, long, large, 11 petals, slight fragrance; foliage bright; vigorous, bushy growth; [seedling × ('Michèle Meilland' × 'Karla')]; intr. 1988
'Delsur' F, dr, Delbard; intr. 2001
'Delta' -- See 'Break o' Day'
'Delta Dawn' -- See 'Ivemax'
'Delta Gamma' HT, ly, 1977, Kimbrew-Walter Roses; bud pointed; flowers creamy white, base pale yellow, 4-4½ in., 38 petals, high-centered, moderate spicy fragrance; foliage dark; vigorous, upright, bushy growth; [Queen Elizabeth® × 'Mount Shasta']
Delta Gold™ -- See 'Burdel'
'Delta Queen' HT, mp; intr. 1998
'Deltaf' HT, pb, 1964, Delbard-Chabert
'Deltanga' ('Tango Rose') HT, ob, 1979, Delbard; bud pointed; flowers salmon-orange, large, 35-40 petals; foliage matte green; bushy growth; [(('Belle Rouge' × ('Rome Glory' × 'Gratitude')) × (('Dr. Schweitzer' × 'Tropicana') × ('Ena Harkness' × 'Quebec')]; intr. 1978

'Delteb' F, ob, Delbard; intr. 1985
'Deltendre' ('Comtesse Panarosa', 'Tendresse') S, mp, Delbard; intr. 1994
'Deltep' (Arnaud Delbard®) F, op, 1976, Delbard; bud ovoid, pointed
'Delter' HT, r, Delbard; intr. 2007
'Deltesse' HT, Delbard, Georges; intr. 1990
'Deltil' S, mp, Delbardsemi-dbl.; intr. 2002
'Deltisse' F, pb, Delbard, Georges; intr. 1996
'Deltogo' (Tobago®) F, ab, 1982, Delbard, Georges; flowers yellow apricot, outer petals aging pink, large, 35 petals, cupped, borne in clusters, moderate citrus fragrance; recurrent; foliage medium size, dark green, semi-glossy; vigorous, upright growth; ['Avalanche' × (Zambra® × Orange Sensation®)]; intr. 1981
'Deltop' (Crêpe de Chine®) HT, mr, 1983, Delbard, Georges; flowers large, 20 petals; foliage glossy, clear green, dense; prickles bronze-red; vigorous, upright, bushy growth; ['Joyeux Noel' × ('Rome Glory' × 'Impeccable')]; intr. 1970
'Deltora' S, ob, Delbard; intr. 2001
'Deltos' ('Waltz Time') HT, m, 1960, Delbard-Chabert
'Deltou' F, Delbard, Georges; intr. 1986
'Deltrac' (Angkor®) HT, mr, 1967, Delbard-Chabert; flowers carmine-red, large, dbl., globular; foliage bronze, glossy, leathery; vigorous, bushy growth; ['Belle Rouge' × ('Rome Glory' × 'Gratitude')]
'Deltrap' (Saint-Vincent®) F, mr, Delbard, Georgesdbl.; intr. 1994
'Deltre' HT, mr, 1959, Delbard-Chabert; bud long
'Deltrisang' S, rb, Delbard
'Deltrob' (Cactus Blanc®) Pol, w, 1970, Delbard-Chabert; bud globular; flowers creamy white, small, dbl., cupped, borne in clusters; foliage light green, glossy; moderate, bushy growth; [('Orléans Rose' × 'Orléans Rose') × (('Francais' × 'Lafayette') × ('Orléans Rose' × 'Goldilocks'))]; intr. 1967
'Deltrut' ('Campanela', Campanile®) LCl, dp, 1967, Delbard-Chabert; bud globular; flowers deep magenta-pink, 4 in., dbl., borne singly and in small clusters, moderate fragrance; repeat bloom; foliage glossy, leathery, bronze; vigorous, climbing growth; [(Queen Elizabeth® × 'Provence') × (('Sultane' × unknown) × 'Mme Joseph Perraud')]
'Deltuf' (Grand Prix®) HT, op, 1970, Delbard-Chabert; flowers coral-pink shaded ochre, large, semi-dbl., slight fragrance; foliage glossy, leathery; vigorous, upright, bushy growth; ['Chic Parisien' × ('Grande Premiere' × ('Sultane' × 'Mme Joseph Perraud')]; intr. 1968
'Delup' ('Betsy Ross') HT, dr, 1970, Del-

bard; intr. 1969

'Delurt' ('Black Pearl', Perle Noire®) HT, dr, 1986, Delbard; flowers velvety dark red, well-formed, large, 38 petals; vigorous, bushy growth; [(('Impeccable' × Papa Meilland®) × ('Gloire de Rome' × 'Impeccable')) × (('Rome Glory' × 'Impecable') × ('Charles Mallerin × Gay Paris)' × '(Rouge Meilland × Soraya)'))]; intr. 1975

'Delveen' P, mp, 1930, Alderton

'Delverjaune' ('Nedbank Rose') F, dy, Delbard; buds golden; intr. 1997

'Delviola' ('Chartreuse de Parme') S, m, Delbard, Georges; intr. 1996

'Delvirge' ('Vierge Folle', 'White Beauty') S, w, Delbardsingle; intr. 1998

'Delvor' ('Femme') HT, yb, 1983, Delbard, Georges; flowers ivory yellow, tinted pink, large, 28 petals, slight fragrance; foliage medium size, dark, glossy; prickles bronze-red; upright growth; [('Rome Glory' × 'Bayadere') × (Queen Elizabeth® × 'Provence')]; intr. 1970

'Delwish' Min, dp, Delbard; intr. 2001

'Delzen' ('Zenith') LCl, or, 1985, Delbard, Georges; flowers vermilion, semi-dbl., borne in clusters; climbing (to 8 ft.) growth; [('Spectacular' × ('Tenor' × unknown)) × ('Floradora' × 'Incendie')]; intr. 1982

'Delzinsch' HT, dy, Delbard; intr. 1998

'Demain' HT, mr, 1945, Mallerin, C.; bud pointed; flowers brilliant cardinal-red, reverse saffron-yellow, semi-dbl., cupped; very vigorous, upright growth; ['Mrs Pierre S. duPont' × 'Dr. Kirk']

'Dembrosky' -- See 'Dembrowski'

'Dembrowski' ('Dembrosky', 'Dombrowski') HP, dr, 1849, Vibert; flowers deep crimson-violet; sometimes classed as B

'Demetra' F, yb, Barni; bud large buds; flowers cream clear apricot with deeper tones in center, full, high-centered; repeats quickly; vigorous growth, 2-3 ft.; intr. 2003

Demitasse™ -- See 'Jacmarne'

'Demitasse' -- See 'Demitasse of Pinot'

'Demitasse of Pinot' ('Demitasse') HMsk, m; flowers rich purple-pink, small, very full, borne in broad clusters, slight sweet fragrance; recurrent

'Demoiselle' HT, pb, 1960, Delforge; flowers soft pink becoming darker, open, medium, 25-30 petals; foliage bronze; vigorous, bushy growth; ['Peace' × 'Opera']

'Demokracie' ('Blaze Improved', 'Blaze Superier', 'Imperial Blaze', 'New Blaze') LCl, dr, 1935, Böhm, J.; flowers medium to large, 8 cm., dbl., borne singly or in small clusters, no fragrance; said to be recurrent

'Demon' -- See 'Meidomonac'

'Démone' HT, dr, 1967, Tantau, Math.; bud ovoid; flowers medium, dbl., intense fragrance; foliage dark; intr. 1965

'Demure' F, dp, 1952, Boerner; bud ovoid; flowers rose-pink, 2 in., 52 petals, flat, borne in clusters, moderate fragrance; foliage leathery; vigorous, compact growth; PP1065; ['Garnette' × seedling]

'Denali' HT, w, 2004, Edwards, Eddie & Phelps, Ethan; flowers large, petals very wide, 5-5½ in., full, high-centered, borne mostly solitary, moderate fragrance; recurrent; foliage medium size, dark green, semi-glossy; prickles small, hooked; growth upright, tall (5-6 ft.); exhibition; [Crystalline™ × 'White Success']; intr. 2005

'Dencrim' ('Crimson Star') Min, rb, 2000, Denton, J.A.; flowers crimson red, reverse golden yellow, 4-6 cm., full, high-centered, borne in small clusters; foliage medium size, medium green, semi-glossy; few prickles; growth upright, medium (16-20 in.); exhibition; [(June Laver™ × ('Rubies 'n' Pearls' × unknown)) × 'Glowing Amber']

'Deneb' LCl, dy

'Denexpo' ('Exposé') Min, dp, 2002, Denton, James A.; flowers full, borne mostly solitary, no fragrance; foliage medium size, medium green, semi-glossy; prickles medium, straight, moderate; growth upright, medium (35 cm.); garden decorative, exhibition; [Hot Tamale™ × 'Reiko']

'Denfair' ('Fairqueen') Min, ly, 2002, Denton, James A.; flowers full, borne mostly solitary, no fragrance; foliage medium size, medium green, semi-glossy; prickles medium, straight, moderate; growth upright, medium (40 cm.); garden decorative, exhibition; ['Fairhope' × Behold™]

Denice® ('Spedeni') HT, w, Spek; flowers pure white, 12 cm., 35-40 petals, high-centered, borne mostly singly; recurrent; numerous prickles; stems long; intr. 2005

'Denis Hélye' M, m, Lévis; flowers violet-purple; intr. 1864

'Denis Hélye' HP, mr, Gautreau; flowers rosy crimson; vigorous growth; intr. 1864

'Denise' HT, my, 1955, Buyl Frères; bud oval; flowers citron-yellow, open, large, dbl.; foliage glossy, clear green; vigorous, bushy growth; ['Peace' × 'Brandywine']

Denise™ -- See 'Poulra015(N)'

'Denise-Anne' F, op, 1973, Ellick; flowers blush-pink to orange-apricot, 4 in., 30-35 petals; foliage small, glossy, dark; vigorous growth; [('Memoriam' × Orange Sensation®) × ('Peace' × 'Memoriam')]

'Denise Cassegrain' ('Mme Denise Cassegrain') Pol, w, 1922, Grandes Roseraies; flowers snow-white, very dbl., borne in clusters of 30-40

'Denise Chambard' HT, yb, 1940, Chambard, C.; bud long, carmine-yellow; flowers sulfur-yellow, shaded carmine, large, cupped; foliage bright green; strong stems; vigorous, upright growth

'Denise Dewar' HT, dr, 1968, Trew, C.; flowers crimson, pointed; foliage bronze-green; free growth; ['Isabelle de France' × 'Karl Herbst']

Denise Grey® ('Caprice', 'Make-Up') S, lp, Meilland; flowers clear rose; intr. 1988

'Denise Hale' -- See 'Wamhale'

'Denise Hilling' HMoy, dp

'Denise Lefeuvre' HT, rb, 1930, Chambard, C.; flowers nasturtium-red, center yellow, reverse bright red, large, dbl., cupped; strong stems; very vigorous growth

'Denise McClelland' HT, dr, 1965, Riethmuller; flowers claret-red, large, 30 petals, moderate fragrance; foliage dark, leathery, glossy; vigorous, upright, bushy growth; ['Amy Johnson' × 'New Yorker']; intr. 1964

'Denise Parade' (Denise™) MinFl, w, Olesen; bud pointed ovoid; flowers ivory white, 5-6 cm., 13-15 petals, high-centered, borne mostly singly, very slight fragrance; free-flowering; foliage dark green, matte; few prickles; bushy (20-40 cm.) growth; PP14309; ['Patricia Kordana' × seedling]; container rose; intr. 2001

'Denjo' ('Joanne's Wedding') Min, pb, 2003, Denton, James A; flowers deep pink, reverse white, medium, full, borne mostly solitary, no fragrance; foliage medium size, medium green, semi-glossy; prickles medium, down curved, dark brown, moderate; growth upright, medium (20 in.), garden decorative, exhibition; ['Fairhope' × Kristin™]; intr. 2004

'Denk an Mich' F, mr; flowers geranium red; intr. 2006

'Denman' ('Mandarin Silk') MinFl, ob, 2005, Denton, James A; flowers orange, reverse medium yellow, medium, full, borne mostly solitary, no fragrance; foliage medium size, medium green, semi-glossy; prickles few, medium, downturning, red-brown; growth upright, tall (30in.); exhibition, garden decoration; [Hot Tamale™ × June Laver™]

'Denman' -- See 'Landen'

'Denmar' ('Margaret Denton') MinFl, rb, 2003, Denton, James A.; flowers red/orange, reverse yellow/orange, 2½-3 in., full, borne mostly solitary, no fragrance; foliage medium size, dark green, glossy; prickles small, straight, brown, few; stems long; growth compact, medium (24 in.); patio, exhibition; [June Laver™ × 'Glowing Amber']; intr. 2003

'Denmel' ('Miss Melanie') Min, pb, 2003, Denton, James A; flowers medium pink and white, reverse white, 1½ in., full, borne mostly solitary, no fragrance; foliage medium size, dark green, glossy; prickles medium, down-curved, light brown, few; growth compact, medium (18 in.); garden decoration, exhibition; [Hot Tamale™ × Kristin™]; intr. 2004

'Denny Arter' -- See 'Jasdarter'

'Denny Boy' F, yb, 1949, Marsh; bud small, ovoid; flowers orange-yellow, becoming redder, reverse sulfur-yellow, very dbl., cupped, slight fragrance; very vigorous, bushy, dwarf growth; PP1105; ['Pinocchio' × 'Mrs Erskine Pembroke Thom']

'Denoyel' -- See 'Souv de Claudius Denoyel'

'Denpea' ('Peachy Queen') Min, ab, 2003, Denton, James A.; flowers apricot/pink, reverse apricot, 1¾ in., dbl., borne mostly solitary, no fragrance; foliage medium size, medium green, semi-glossy; prickles small, straight, light brown; growth bushy, medium (20-24 in.); garden decoration, containers; [June Laver™ × 'Reiko']; intr. 2003

'Denpix' ('Pixie Dust') Min, yb, 2003, Denton, James A.; flowers light yellow/pink, reverse light yellow, medium, full, borne mostly solitary, no fragrance; foliage medium green, Semi-glossy; prickles small, straight, light brown, moderate; growth bushy, medium (18-20 in.); garden decoration, exhibition; [Hot Tamale™ × 'Amber Sunset']; intr. 2003

'Densaf' ('Sweet Saffron') Min, my, 2003, Denton, James A.; flowers quilling to star shape, 1¾ in., full, borne mostly solitary, no fragrance; foliage large, dark green, glossy; prickles moderate, small, straight, red brown; upright, medium (20 in.) growth; garden/patio/exhibition; ['Amber Sunset' × 'Louis Desamero']; intr. 2003

'Denshan' ('Baby Shannon') Min, my, 2005, Denton, James A; flowers full, borne mostly solitary, no fragrance; foliage medium size, medium green, semi-glossy; prickles medium, straight, light brown, moderate; growth bushy, medium (24 in.); exhibition, garden decoration; [June Laver™ × Incognito™]

Dentelle® S, mp, Huber; intr. 2005

Dentelle de Bruges® -- See 'LLX8814'

Dentelle de Bruxelles® -- See 'LLX8600'

'Dentelle de Malines' -- See 'LLX8603'

Denver's Dream™ -- See 'Savaden'

'Denyse Ducas' HWich, yb, 1953, Buatois; flowers golden yellow, carmine red exterior, 4½ in.

'Député Debussy' Cl HT, w, 1902, Buatois; flowers flesh white, yellow nub

'Der Krad' HT, dr, 1962, Wyant; bud long, pointed; flowers maroon-red, striped darker, 3½ in., dbl., high-centered; foliage glossy; vigorous, bushy growth; ['Ami Quinard' × 'Crimson Glory']

'Derby' F, or, 1963, Gaujard; bud ovoid; flowers medium, semi-dbl.; foliage light green, soft; very vigorous, bushy growth; ['Miss France' × seedling]

'Derby-Hagen Gmelin Rose' -- See 'Dorient'

'Derbyshire Dawn' -- See 'Worcold'

Derdinger Sommer® F, mp, Hetzel; intr. 1991

'Dereham Pride' Pol, dr, 1932, Norfolk Nursery; flowers darkest crimson; vigorous, dwarf growth; ['Éblouissant' × 'Orange King']

'Derek Nimmo' -- See 'Macwhenu'

'Dernburg' HT, pb, 1916, Krüger; flowers bright rose, shaded coral-red and yellow, large, dbl.; ['Mme Caroline Testout' × 'Souv d'Aimée Terrel des Chênes']

'Derrich Gardner' -- See 'Jaclinber'

'Derrich Gardner, Flame of Fantasy' -- See 'Jacinber'

'DeRuiter's Herald' -- See 'De Ruiter's Herald'

'Des Alpes sans Épines' -- See 'Bourbon'

'Des Peintres' ('Grande Centfeuilles de Hollande', 'Major Multiplex', 'Maxima Multiplex', R. × centifolia maxima, 'Rose des Peintres', 'Souchet', 'Vierge') C, mp, before 1806; flowers red, tending toward scarlet, darker at center, sometimes with faint white stripes, very large, full, cupped, borne in small clusters; foliage very large, dull green, deeply toothed; prickles nearly straight, unequal

'Des Peintres' -- See 'Rubra'

'Des Poêtes' ('Reine des Poêtes') D, mp, about 1825, Cartier

'Desbet' ('Betsy Murchison') HT, dp, Desamero, Luis

'Descanso Dream' -- See 'Wekdesc'

'Descanso Pillar' LCl, pb, 1952, Lammerts, Dr. Walter; bud urn-shaped, carmine to scarlet-red; flowers begonia-rose to deep rose-pink, inside varying to scarlet, 4½-5 in., 33 petals, high-centered, moderate fragrance; recurrent bloom; foliage dark, glossy; growth to 6-7 ft.; PP943; ['Crimson Glory' × 'Captain Thomas']

'Descemet' B, w, Vibert; flowers flesh-white, tinted mauve, medium; intr. 1847

'Descemet' C, mp, before 1820, Descemet; flowers bright pink, changing to pale rose, very large, dbl., cupped; growth branching

'Deschamps' HGal, pb, about 1830, Charpentier or Parmentier; flowers light pink, shaded bright pink, medium, full

'Deschamps' N, mr, Deschamps; flowers cherry-red, 6-7 cm., cupped, borne in small clusters; good repeat; numerous prickles; vigorous growth; possibly synonymous with 'Longworth Rambler'; intr. 1877

'Desdechardo' HT, dp, 1980, Taylor, W.J.; flowers deep pink; [sport of 'Red Lion']

'Desdémona' P, mr, 1841, Vibert; flowers carmine red, medium, dbl.; some autumn repeat

'Desdemona' HT, lp, 1912, Paul, W.; flowers opaque light pink, large, dbl., globular, intense fragrance

'Desert Charm' Min, dr, 1973, Moore, Ralph S.; flowers deep red, medium, dbl., high-centered, slight fragrance; foliage dark, leathery; vigorous, dwarf, bushy growth; PP3654; [Baccará® × 'Magic Wand']

'Desert Dance' F, ob, 1977, Herholdt, J.A.; bud pointed; flowers orange, reverse gold, 3 in., 15-18 petals, cupped,

slight fragrance; foliage glossy; moderately tall growth; ['Impala' × seedling]; intr. 1975

'Desert Dawn' Gr, yb; intr. 1998

'Desert Dream' HT, lp, 1955, McGredy, Sam IV; flowers buff-pink, high pointed, 5 in.; foliage light green; very vigorous growth; [R.M.S. Queen Mary × 'Mrs Sam McGredy']

'Desert Glow' -- See 'Harblend'

'Desert Island' F, ab, Dickson; flowers creamy caramel, outer petals lighter, medium, 32 petals, high-centered, moderate, pleasing fragrance; foliage medium size, medium green, glossy; growth bushy to spreading, 3 ft.; [White Diamond® × 'Apricot Ice']; intr. 2005

'Desert Magic' S, pb, 2005, Singer, Judith A; flowers hot pink to deep smoky russet pink, reverse medium to deep pink, petal edges scalloped, 5½ in., semi-dbl., borne mostly solitary, no fragrance; foliage medium size, dark green, semi-glossy; prickles small, slightly curved, beige to light brown, few; growth medium; ['Sonia' × 'Blue Girl']; intr. 2006

'Desert Orchid' -- See 'Rawsob'

'Desert Peace' -- See 'Meinomad'

'Desert Sands' F, ab, 1977, Bees; flowers deep apricot, 4½ in., 30 petals, intense fragrance; vigorous growth; ['Arthur Bell' × Elizabeth of Glamis®]; intr. 1976

'Desert Song' HT, rb, 1948, Fletcher; flowers glowing reddish-copper, 4-5 in., 40-45 petals, peony-like; foliage glossy, bronze; ['Mrs Sam McGredy' × 'Golden Dawn']

'Desert Spice' -- See 'Deljaunor'

'Desert Storm' Min, op, 1991, Gruenbauer, Richard; bud ovoid; flowers orange in summer, pink in cold weather, medium, dbl., urn-shaped, borne singly; foliage medium size, dark green, semi-glossy; upright, medium growth; ['Libby' × 'Rise 'n' Shine']; intr. 1991

'Desert Storm' S, or, Williams, J. Benjamin; intr. 1997

'Desert Sun' -- See 'Devsleek'

'Desert Sunset' Gr, or, 1962, Booy, H.; bud ovoid; flowers 3-4 in., 10 petals, cupped; foliage glossy; upright growth; ['Floradora' × 'Chrysler Imperial']

'Desfontaines' HGal, mp, about 1825, Cartier; flowers bright carmine, medium, dbl.

'Desgaches' ('Eugène Desgaches') B, mp, 1840, Desgaches; flowers carmine pink, large, full, borne in small clusters; sometimes classed as Ch

'Desgaches' HP, mr, Lacharme; flowers bright red, exterior petals bordered crimson, medium, full; foliage delicate green; prickles numerous, irregular; intr. 1850

'Desgaches' HCh, lp, Gantin; flowers light pink, medium, full, borne in clusters; intr. 1850

'Desi' HT, yb, Rupprecht-Radke; flowers golden yellow with red stripes, large, dbl.; intr. 1964

'Designer Sunset' S, ob; flowers pink, orange, and yellow; growth to 2 ft.; intr. 2003

'Designer's Choice' ('Hi Teen') Gr, yb, 1989, deVor Nursery; bud pointed; flowers yellow marked orange, medium, 30 petals, high-centered, borne usually singly and in small clusters, slight fragrance; foliage medium size, dark green, glossy; prickles slight recurved, small, brown; upright, medium growth; hips ovoid, small, orange; [Prominent® × 'Bengali']; intr. 1989

'Désir' HT, rb, 1945, Gaujard; flowers purplish red, large, dbl.; foliage glossy; very vigorous, bushy growth

'Desire' HT, mr, 1953, Obertello; bud ovoid; flowers cardinal-red, 5 in., 35-45 petals, high-centered, moderate fragrance; foliage dark; upright, compact growth; PP1289; [sport of 'Pink Delight']

'Désiré Bergera' HWich, pb, 1910, Barbier; flowers coppery rose, center brighter, 5-6 cm., dbl., borne in clusters of 2-6, moderate tea fragrance; seasonal bloom; foliage small, dark green, glossy; vigorous growth; [R. wichuraina × 'Aurore']

Desiree® HT, lp, Tantau; flowers large, double, high-centered, borne mostly singly; recurrent; stems long; Florist rose; intr. 2003

'Desireé' S, pb, Clements, John; flowers rich peach with highlights at the center, shading to delicate peach-pink towards edges, 4 in., 20 petals, borne in clusters, intense fruity myrrh fragrance; blooms in abundance; mid-green foliage with reddish, serrated edges; upright growth to 3 ft.; intr. 2004

Desirée® -- See 'Tanerised'

'Désirée Clary' Gr, lp, Guillot-Massad; intr. 2002

'Desirée Fontaine' HP, dr, 1884, Fontaine; flowers deep rich grenadine, tinted with bluish violet, large, full, cupped, borne 4-5 per cluster

'Désirée Parmentier' HGal, lp, before 1841, Parmentier; flowers vivid pink, large, dbl., flat; bushy growth

'Desling' (Cat's Meow™) F, ob, 1996, Desmet, Paul; flowers medium orange, petal base medium yellow, bright orange, buff, large, 29-31 petals, slight fragrance; foliage medium size, dark green, semi-glossy; numerous prickles; growth upright, tall (40 in.); ['Colour Wonder' × unknown]

'Desmarita' ('Marita Lindner') Min, lp, 2006, Desamero, Luis; flowers full, borne in small clusters; foliage small, medium green, semi-glossy; prickles small, straight and tapering, reddish, moderate; growth bushy, medium (24 in.); ['Jilly Jewel' × 'Luis Desamero']; intr. 2006

'Desmond Gatward' HT, mr, 1966, Kemp, M.L.; flowers cerise-crimson, well-formed, 4½ in.; foliage red-bronze; free growth; ['Karl Herbst' × 'Dicksons Red']

'Desmond Johnston' HT, mr, 1927, McGredy; flowers brilliant scarlet, base orange, reverse veined orange, large, dbl., high-centered; foliage rich green, leathery, glossy; short stems; bushy growth

'Desmond Wilcox' F, mr; intr. 2004

'Desmother' ('Sadie') Min, w, Desamero, Luisvery dbl.

'Desparado' F, yb, 1968, Harkness; flowers yellow shaded pink, semi-dbl., borne in trusses; ['Pink Parfait' × 'Masquerade']

'Desperado' HT, rb, Edwards, Eddie & Phelps, Ethan; flowers large, 5-6 in., full, high-centered, borne mostly singly, slight fragrance; recurrent; foliage medium, dark green, glossy; few prickles; upright, tall (5 - 6 ft.) growth; [Veteran's Honor™ × Crystalline™]; intr. 2007

'Desprez' N, op, 1838, Desprez; flowers dawn pink to flesh pink, aging to pink with coppery yellow center, reverse lighter

'Desprez à Fleur Jaunes' -- See 'Jaune Desprez'

'Dessert' F, rb, VEG; flowers red with white, medium, semi-dbl.

'Desspecial' ('Special Effects') F, ob, 2006, Desamero, Luis; flowers orange & white striped, 4½ in., full, borne in small clusters; foliage medium size, dark green, matte; prickles small, straight, reddish, moderate; growth upright, tall (4 ft.); [sport of 'Sentimental']; intr. 2006

'Dessy' F, Williamson

'Destin' HT, mr, Croix, Paul; flowers , 30-40 petals, spiral , blooms early, intense fragrance; good repeat; vigorous growth; intr. 1961

'Destin, Climbing' Cl HT, mr

'Destino' HT, pb, Camprubi, C.; flowers salmon-pink, becoming lilac-pink, well-formed, 45 petals; foliage dark; upright growth

'Destiny' -- See 'Meikiji'

'Destiny' HT, dr, 1935, Beckwith; bud long, pointed, well shaped; flowers rich crimson-scarlet shaded blackish, dbl.; foliage dark, leathery; vigorous, bushy growth

'Destiny's Dream' -- See 'Webten'

'Detroiter' ('Brilliant', 'Schlosser's Brilliant') HT, dr, 1952, Kordes; bud long, pointed; flowers 5½ in., 23 petals, high-centered, moderate fragrance; vigorous, upright, bushy growth; PP1219; ['Poinsettia' × 'Crimson Glory']

'Detroiter, Climbing' ('Schlössers Brilliant, Climbing') Cl HT, dr, 1960

Detty® HT, or, Adam

'Deuil de Colonel Denfert' ('Deuil du Colonel d'Enfer') HP, dr, 1878, Margottin Père; flowers velvety purplish black, large, full

'Deuil de Dr Reynaud' B, dp, 1862, Pradel; flowers deep crimson pink, large, dbl., intense fragrance

'Deuil de Duc d'Orleans' B, m, 1845, Lacharme, F.; flowers deep purple, large, very dbl.; foliage dark green; nearly thornless

'Deuil de Dunois' HP, dr, 1873, Lévêque; flowers blackish-red, dbl.

'Deuil de la Duchesse d'Orléans' B, m, 1858, Pradel; flowers glowing purple

'Deuil de l'Empereur du Mexique' HP, m, 1867, Cordier; flowers dark purple

'Deuil de Paul Fontaine' ('Paul de Fontainne') M, m, 1873, Fontaine; bud somewhat mossy; flowers purple-red, reverse mahogany, full, cupped; repeat bloom; very prickly; vigorous growth

'Deuil du Colonel d'Enfer' -- See 'Deuil de Colonel Denfert'

'Deuil du Maréchal Mortier' ('Maréchal Mortier') HCh, dr, before 1841; flowers velvety maroon purple, sometimes marbled with white, large, full, cupped

'Deuil du Prince Albert' HP, dp, 1862, Lapente; flowers dark carmine, medium, full, globular, moderate fragrance

'Deutsche Hoffnung' HT, yb, 1920, Kiese; flowers salmon-yellow to apricot-yellow; ['Mme Caroline Testout' × 'Grossherzogin Feodora von Sachsen']

Deutsche Welle® F, m, Leenders; intr. 1983

'Deutsches Danzig' Pol, pb, 1935, Lambert, P.; flowers carmine-pink with white, small, single

Deutsches Rosarium Dortmund® -- See 'Rosarium Dortmund'

'Deutschland' HT, yb, 1910, Kiese; flowers cream, opening to golden yellow, faint rose in the center, large; ['Frau Karl Druschki' × 'Soleil d'Or']

'Devabe' ('White Mystery') HT, w, 1984, deVor, Paul F.; [sport of 'Paul's Pink']; intr. 1982

'Devamarillo' (Rainbow Yellow™) Min, ob, 1989, Marciel, Stanley G.; bud pointed, urn-shaped; flowers tangerine orange with yellow base, aging lighter, 48 petals, cupped, borne singly, intense fruity fragrance; free-flowering; foliage medium size, medium green, matte; prickles declining, reddish-brown; bushy, upright, medium growth; PP7638; [seedling × Amber Flash™]

'Devaurora' (Rainbow Sunrise™) Min, ob, 1989, Marciel, Stanley G.; bud pointed; flowers orange with tinge of red, reverse same, 1 in., 15-18 petals, cupped, borne singly, slight spicy fragrance; free-flowering; foliage small, medium green, glossy; prickles sparse, declining, brown; bushy, upright, medium growth; PP6583; [Amber Flash™ × 'Rumba']

'Devbill' ('Sheer Elegance, Climbing') Cl HT, op, 1995, deVor, Bill; flowers pink blend, 3-3½ in., full, slight fragrance; foliage large, dark green, semi-glossy; few prickles; tall (315-345cm.), upright, branching growth; [sport of 'Sheer Elegance']; intr. 1994

'Devblush' ('Bridal Shower') HT, w, deVor;

intr. 1996

'Devcal' ('Victorian Lace') HT, w, 1995, Marciel, Stanley G.; flowers 1½-2½ in., full, borne mostly singly, no fragrance; foliage medium size, medium green, semi-glossy; some prickles; tall (60 in.), upright growth; [seedling × seedling]; intr. 1995

'Devcali' HT, dp, Marciel, Stanley G.; bud slender, tapering; intr. 1989

'Devcarlos' ('Brianna') HT, ly, 1992, Marciel, Stanley G.; flowers canary yellow, 3-3½ in., full, borne mostly singly, moderate fragrance; foliage large, medium green, semi-glossy; few prickles; upright (152 cm.) growth; [(seedling 75062-1 × Excitement™) × (seedling 75062-1 × Cocktail®)]

'Devcico' ('Darby') HT, mp, 1993, Marciel, Stanley G. & Jeanne A.; flowers medium, dbl., borne mostly singly, no fragrance; foliage large, dark green, semi-glossy; some prickles; tall, upright growth; [Dolores™ × Cerise Dawn™]; intr. 1993

'Devclavel' (Rainbow Cerise™) Min, dp, 1989, Marciel, Stanley G.; bud tapering, slender; flowers medium, 39-45 petals, cupped, borne singly, slight fruity fragrance; free-flowering; foliage medium size, dark green, glossy; bushy, medium growth; PP7560; [Scarlet Sunblaze™ × seedling]

'Devdicha' (Rainbow Bliss™) Min, rb, 1990, Marciel, Stanley G.; bud slender, tapering; flowers white with cream inside with red edges, reverse same, medium, 37-45 petals, cupped, borne mostly singly, slight damask fragrance; foliage small, dark green, glossy; prickles declining, brown-orange; upright, low growth; [seedling × Scarlet Sunblaze™]; intr. 1989

'Devdorado' ('Mariko') HT, ly, 1992, Marciel, Stanley G. & Jeanne A.; flowers 3-3½ in., full, borne mostly singly, moderate fragrance; foliage large, dark green, semi-glossy; some prickles; tall (210 cm.), upright growth; [seedling × seedling]

'Deveclipsar' (Rainbow Eclipse™) Min, rb, 1989, Marciel, Stanley G.; bud pointed; flowers crimson-pink edges, center very light whitish-pink, fading to white, medium, 34-40 petals, cupped, borne singly, slight fragrance; foliage small, dark green, glossy; prickles declining, rusty-brown; bushy, medium growth; PP7637; [Scarlet Sunblaze™ × seedling]

'Devfè' S, dp, DeVor; intr. 2002

'Devfrago' ('Fragrant Fantasy') HT, ab, 1992, Marciel, Stanley G. & Jeanne A.; flowers 3-3½ in., dbl., borne mostly singly, intense fragrance; foliage medium size, dark green, matte; few prickles; medium (3-4 ft.), upright growth; ['seedling 80227-20' × 'seedling 82249-1']

'Devhaute' ('Matty') HT, dp, 1994, Marciel, Stanley G. & Jeanne A.; flowers deep pink, 3-3½ in., dbl., borne mostly singly; foliage large, medium green, matte; some prickles; tall (97 cm.), upright growth; [('Happiness' × seedling) × ('Emily Post' × 'Visa')]; intr. 1993

'Devi Gayatri' F, w, Sen; flowers creamy white, borne in clusters; vigorous, shrubby growth; intr. 1992

'Devicio' (Touch of Raspberry™) HT, dp, 1989, Marciel, Stanley G.; bud slender, tapering; flowers deep pink, large, 30 petals, cupped, borne singly, slight fruity fragrance; foliage large, dark green, semi-glossy; prickles declining, light lime green with mauve tinges; upright, tall growth; PP7548; ['Love Affair' × 'Paul's Pink']

'Devienne l'Ami' -- See 'Devienne-Lamy'

'Devienne-Lamy' ('Devienne l'Ami') HP, mr, 1868, Lévêque; flowers deep carmine, large, dbl., cupped, globular

'Deviente' (Rainbow Hot Pink™) Min, dp, 1989, Marciel, Stanley G.; bud long, slightly urn-shaped; flowers deep pink, small, 26 petals, cupped, borne singly, very slight fragrance; free-flowering; foliage small, dark green, semi-glossy; prickles declining, mauve; stems strong, upright; bushy, upright, medium growth; PP7689; [Orange Sunblaze™ × seedling]

'Devil Dancer' HT, mr, 1980, Hawken, Una; bud ovoid; flowers brilliant brick-red, 4 in., 5 petals, slight fragrance; foliage dark; bushy growth; ['Sonora' × Matangi®]

'Devilk' (Sparkling Orange™) HT, rb, 1989, Marciel, Stanley G.; bud tapering; flowers vermilion, reverse scarlet, aging to rose, sweetheart, large, dbl., borne singly, intense musk fragrance; foliage large, dark green, glossy; prickles variation, reddish-brown; upright, tall growth; ['Sonia' × Prominent®]

'Devil's Dance' F, mr

'Devine' (Dolores™) HT, pb, deVor

'Devite' (Angel™) S, w, 1983, deVor, Paul F.; flowers flora-tea, small, 35 petals, slight fragrance; foliage medium size, light green, semi-glossy; upright growth; PP5172; [(Queen Elizabeth® × seedling) × 'Jack Frost']; intr. 1982

'Devlass' HT, w, 1989, Marciel, Stanley G.; bud pointed

'Devlicor' ('Licorice Twist') HT, dy, deVor; intr. 1995

'Devloren' HT, op, 1989, Marciel, Stanley G.; bud slender, tapering

'Devmauve' ('Sonora Sunset') HT, m, deVor; intr. 1995

'Devmenta' (Peppermint Swirl™) HT, rb, 1989, Marciel, Stanley G.; bud slender, tapering; flowers currant red, aging discolors slightly, large,, 30 petals, cupped, slight spicy fragrance; foliage medium size, dark green, semi-glossy; prickles declining, copper brown; upright, tall growth; PP7612; [seedling × seedling]

'Devmesi' (Rainbow Crimson™) Min, dr, 1990, Marciel, Stanley G.; bud slender; flowers deep red, aging discolors slightly, small, 33 petals, cupped, borne singly, slight damask fragrance; foliage medium size, dark green, semi-glossy; prickles declining, slightly dark mauve; upright, low growth; [seedling × seedling]; intr. 1989

'Devmomento' ('Glory') HT, dy, 1993, Marciel, Stanley G. & Jeanne A.; flowers 3-3½ in., full, borne mostly singly, no fragrance; foliage large, dark green, semi-glossy; some prickles; tall (205 cm.), upright growth; ['Capella' × seedling]; intr. 1992

'Devmorada' (Royal Amethyst™) HT, m, 1989, deVor, Paul F.; bud pointed; flowers lavender, large, 32 petals, borne singly, intense fruity fragrance; foliage medium size, medium green, glossy; prickles declining, henna; upright, tall growth; hips globular, tangerine-orange; ['Angel Face' × Blue Moon®]

'Devnina' (Amanda Marciel™) HT, lp, 1989, Marciel, Stanley G.; bud slender and tapering; flowers very delicate pink, large, 26 petals, cupped, borne singly, slight spicy fragrance; foliage medium size, dark green, glossy; no prickles; upright, tall growth; [seedling × 'Pink Puff']

'Devnovia' ('Megan Dolan') HT, mp, 1989, Marciel, Stanley G.; bud urn-shaped; flowers small, sweetheart, 18 petals, cupped, borne singly, slight spicy fragrance; foliage medium size, dark green; prickles declining, copper brown with olive green tinges; upright, tall growth; PP7520; [Angel™ × 'Independence '76']

'Devon' -- See 'Poulrijk'

Devon™ -- See 'Poulspan'

'Devon Maid' LCl, pb, 1977, Warner, Chris; flowers light pink, reverse medium pink, large, 22 petals, borne in clusters of 3-4, moderate fruity fragrance; foliage large, medium green, glossy; prickles large, curved, orange; needs support; vigorous, spreading, tall growth; hips ovoid, orange; [Casino® × Elizabeth of Glamis®]

'Devoniensis, Climbing' ('Magnolia Rose, Climbing') Cl T, w, 1858, Pavitt; bud pink; flowers creamy white, tinted pink or yellow at center, 4 in., full, intense tea fragrance; recurrent; growth large, 10-15 ft; [sport of 'Devoniensis']

'Devoniensis' ('Magnolia Rose', 'Range View Cream Tea') T, w, 1838, Foster; flowers creamy white, center sometimes tinged blush, very large, dbl.; recurrent bloom; very vigorous growth; [probably 'Park's Yellow Tea-Scented China' × 'Smith's Yellow']; intr. 1841

'Devonshire Maid' LCl, mp, Marciel; intr. 1993

'Devoran' HT, yb, Marciel; intr. 1989

'Devoro' (Rainbow Gold™) Min, yb, 1991, Marciel, Stanley G.; bud ovoid; flowers yellow-orange blend, medium, dbl., cupped, then flat, borne in small clusters, slight musk fragrance; foliage small, dark green, semi-glossy; prickles moderate, pointed, thin, declining; upright, medium (54 cm.) growth; PP7914; [Amber Flash™ × 'Rhumba']; intr. 1991

'Devotion' F, pb, 1971, Harkness; flowers light pink, flushed deeper, 4½ in., 32 petals; foliage light; [Orange Sensation® × 'Peace']

'Devotion' ('Amber Flush') HT, ab, IIsink; flowers apricot-orange, dbl.; growth upright, bushy; intr. 2003

'Devotion' F, ab, Dickson; intr. 2004

'Devpajaro' ('Red Satin') HT, mr, 1994, Marciel, Stanley G. & Jeanne A.; flowers 3-3½ in., full, borne mostly singly; foliage large, medium green, matte; few prickles; low (55-60 cm.), upright growth; ['Jacqueline' × Prominent®]; intr. 1993

'Devpresa' (Rainbow Surprise™) Min, ab, 1989, Marciel, Stanley G.; bud slender, tapering; flowers medium coral, reverse light coral, aging pink, 28 petals, cupped, borne singly, slight fruity fragrance; free-flowering; foliage small, dark green, glossy; prickles declining, mauve; bushy, upright, medium growth; PP7558; [Orange Sunblaze™ × seedling]

'Devrico' (Rainbow Stanford™) Min, rb, 1989, Marciel, Stanley G.; bud pointed, slender; flowers bright red, aging discolors to a bright red-orange, medium, 12-15 petals, high-centered, borne singly, slight fruity fragrance; free-flowering; foliage medium size, dark green, glossy; prickles declining, reddish-brown; bushy, compact, medium growth; PP7559; [Candia™ × seedling]

'Devrise' (Cerise Dawn™) HT, dr, 1989, Marciel, Stanley G.; bud urn-shaped; flowers magenta, reverse Tyrian purple, aging without discoloration, large, 30 petals, globular, slight damask fragrance; foliage large, dark green, semi-glossy; prickles declining and well spaced apart, pea green; upright, tall growth; [Carina® × 'Angel Face']

'Devrojo' (Rainbow Red™) Min, mr, 1989, Marciel, Stanley G.; bud pointed; flowers small, 25-28 petals, flat, borne singly, slight spicy fragrance; foliage small, dark green, glossy; prickles declining, brown with orange; bushy, upright, compact, medium growth; PP6584; [Scarlet Sunblaze™ × 'Rumba']

'Devrosado' (Rainbow Pink™) Min, dp, 1989, Marciel, Stanley G.; bud ovoid, pointed; flowers deep pink, petals imbricated, small, 32 petals, high-centered, borne singly, slight spicy fragrance; free-flowering; foliage medium size, dark green, semi-glossy; prickles sparse, declining, purple; bushy, compact, medium growth; PP6875; [seedling × Orange Sunblaze™]

'Devrudi' ('First Light') S, lp, 1998, Stanley/Marciel; bud pointed, dark candy pink; flowers light pink with purple stamens, 3½-4 in., 5-7 petals, borne in clusters, moderate spicy fragrance; foliage dark green; compact, low growth; PP11223; ['Bonica' × 'Ballerina']

'Devsiem' (Always Mine™) HT, dr, 1989, Marciel, Stanley G.; bud pointed, tapering; flowers deep red, large, 39 petals, cupped, borne singly, intense spicy fragrance; foliage large, dark green, glossy; prickles declining, pea green with cinnamon tinges; upright, tall growth; ['Visa' × Sassy™]

'Devsleek' ('Desert Sun') HT, dy, deVor; intr. 1996

'Devsmooth' ('Bella') F, mr, deVor; intr. 1995

'Devsolear' (Goldlite™) Gr, dy, 1989, Marciel, Stanley G.; bud urn-shaped; flowers canary yellow, reverse buttercup yellow, aging no discoloration, dbl., slight musk fragrance; foliage medium size, dark green, semi-glossy; prickles declining, red; upright, tall growth; hips round, average, tangerine-orange; PP7462; [seedling × Excitement™]; intr. 1987

'Devspilio' ('Silver Fox') HT, w, 1992, Marciel, Stanley G. & Jeanne A.; bud medium, pointed, slender; flowers clear white, 3-4 in., 26-30 petals, imbricated, then flat, borne mostly singly, slight fragrance; recurrent; foliage large, dark green, semi-glossy; prickles some, thin, straight, slightly wing-shaped; stems long; tall (210 cm.), upright growth; hips globose ; PP8931; [seedling × seedling]; florist rose; intr. 1994

'Devstar' ('Stardust') HT, w, 1992, Marciel, Stanley G. & Jeanne A.; flowers 3-3½ in., full, borne mostly singly, no fragrance; foliage large, medium green, semi-glossy; some prickles; tall (230 cm.), upright growth; ['Coquette' × 'seedling 64022-39']

'Devstica' (Mystique™) HT, mr, 1989, Marciel, Stanley G.; bud pointed, slender, tapering; flowers bright red, sweetheart, large, 28 petals, cupped, borne singly, intense musk fragrance; foliage large, medium green, semi-glossy; prickles declining, pale red with tinges of green; upright, tall growth; ['Samantha' × 'Royalty']

'Devsunset' HT, yb, deVor; intr. 1995

'Devtinta' ('Obsession') HT, dr, 1990, Marciel, Stanley G.; bud high-centered, pointed; flowers currant red, large, 42 petals, cupped, imbricated, borne singly, moderate fragrance; free-flowering; foliage medium size, medium green, semi-glossy; prickles wing-shaped, reddish tinge; stems strong, upright; upright, tall (200 cm.) growth; hips pear-shaped, green; PP7902; [seedling × seedling]; greenhouse rose

'Devunican' ('Golden Sprite') F, dy, 1992, Marciel, Stanley G. & Jeanne A.; flowers 3-3½ in., dbl., borne mostly singly, slight fragrance; foliage medium size, dark green, matte; some prickles; medium, upright growth; ['Golden Fantasie' × Excitement™]

'Dew Drop' -- See 'Zipdew'

'Dewdrop' ('Annie') HT, ob, 2006, Wilce, David Edward; flowers dbl., borne mostly solitary; foliage medium size, medium green, glossy; prickles moderate; growth upright, 90 cm.; ['Silver Jubilee' × 'Grandpa Dickson']; intr. 2006

'Dewdrop' HT, lp, 1921, McGredy; flowers pale pink to pale rose; RULED EXTINCT 11/91 ARM

'Dewdrop' Pol, dr, Hobbies; flowers dark cherry red, dbl.; intr. 1913

'Dewey' -- See 'Geldew'

'Dezent' HT, ly, VEG; flowers yellowish-white, large, dbl.

'Diablo' S, or, Interplant; flowers single

Diablotin® ('Little Devil') F, mr, 1965, Delbard-Chabert; flowers 2-3 in., 17 petals, borne in small clusters, no fragrance; bushy, compact growth; ['Orléans Rose' × 'Fashion']; intr. 1961

'Diablotin, Climbing' -- See 'Delposar'

'Diabolo' HWich, rb, 1908, Fauque & fils; flowers velvety crimson, white center, golden stamens, 7-8 cm., single to semi-dbl., borne in large clusters, no fragrance; foliage dark green; prickles small, crimson, numerous; [R. wichurana × 'Xavier Olibo']

'Diabolo' F, op, Gaujard; flowers bright salmon, medium, semi-dbl., cupped, slight fragrance; foliage bronze; short stems; very vigorous, bushy growth; ['Jolie Princesse' × ('Alain' × 'Miss France')]; intr. 1959

'Diadeem' -- See 'Tanmeda'

'Diadem' HT, ob, 1922, McGredy; flowers orange-crimson suffused salmon and yellow, very large, dbl., high-centered, moderate fragrance; foliage rich green, leathery, glossy; vigorous, bushy growth

'Diadem' ('Diadeem', 'Royal Bouquet') F, mp, Tantau; flowers dbl., borne in clusters, slight fragrance; foliage medium green; medium to tall growth; intr. 1986

'Diadême de Flore' ('Alix') HGal, m, before 1835, Descemet/Vibert; flowers lilac pink, edges lighter, large

'Diamant' Pol, w, 1908, Robichon; bud conical; flowers sulphur-white, petals fringed and ruffled, large, borne in clusters of 6-12, moderate almond fragrance; [sport of 'Marie Pavie']

Diamant® ('Diamond') F, or, Kordes, R.; bud ovoid; flowers bright orange-scarlet, well-formed, large, 40 petals, borne in clusters, slight fragrance; foliage dark, glossy; vigorous, upright growth; PP2445; intr. 1962

Diamant® -- See 'Korgazell'

'Diamant Rose' -- See 'Lendiro'

'Diamantina' HT, op, 1949, Giacomasso; flowers salmon and rose, large; strong stems; ['Julien Potin' × 'Ophelia']

'Diamond' -- See 'Koreb'

Diamond™ -- See 'Poulyv001'

'Diamond' -- See 'Korgazell'

'Diamond Anniversary' -- See 'Morsixty'

Diamond Border™ -- See 'Pouldiram'

'Diamond Days Forever' F, w, Fryer; flowers white with creamy centers, dbl., high-centered, borne usually in clusters; recurrent; foliage dark green, glossy; medium, bushy growth; intr. 2006

'Diamond Doll' -- See 'Juddoll'

'Diamond Gray' HT, m, Teranishi; intr. 2004

Diamond Head™ (Diamond Border™) S, w, Poulsen; flowers white, 8-10 cm., slight wild rose fragrance; dark foliage; growth bushy, 100-150 cm.; PP12568; intr. 1997

'Diamond Jewel' Min, w, 1959, Morey, Dr. Dennison; bud globular; flowers white, overcast blush-pink, ½-¾ in., 45-50 petals, cupped; compact, low, open growth; PP1908; ['Dick Koster' × 'Tom Thumb']; intr. 1959

'Diamond Jubilee' HT, ly, 1947, Boerner; bud ovoid; flowers buff-yellow, 5-6 in., 28 petals, cupped, moderate fragrance; foliage leathery; upright, compact growth; PP824; ['Marèchal Niel' × 'Feu Pernet-Ducher']

'Diamond Rose' -- See 'Meisponge'

'Diamond Victory' (Diamond™) S, w, Poulsen; flowers white, 8-10 cm., 25 petals, moderate fragrance; foliage dark; growth bushy, 20-40 cm.; PP15889; intr. 2000

'Diamond Wishes' -- See 'Poulhi011(N)'

'Dian' Min, dp, 1958, Moore, Ralph S.; flowers soft red, 1 in., 45 petals, moderate apple fragrance; foliage small, dark, glossy; vigorous (15 in.), bushy growth; PP1808; [(R. wichurana × Floradora) × ('Oakington Ruby' × 'Floradora')]; intr. 1957

'Diana' HP, dp, 1873, Paul

'Diana' HT, mp, Bees; flowers Malmaison pink, very large, dbl., globular, moderate fragrance; vigorous growth; ['Mrs Frank Workman' × 'Sunburst']; intr. 1921

'Diana' Pol, op, Spek; flowers bright orange shaded pink, large, semi-dbl.; intr. 1922

Diana® -- See 'Tandinadi'

'Diana' -- See 'Jacshaq'

'Diana Allen' HT, op, 1939, Clark, A.; flowers salmon-pink, small, dbl.; short stems; bushy, compact growth; ['Mrs Aaron Ward' × seedling]

'Diana Armstrong' HT, dy, 1992, Thompson, Robert; flowers medium, full, borne mostly singly, intense fragrance; foliage medium size, medium green, semi-glossy; some prickles; upright (80 cm.) growth; [seedling × 'Prima Ballerina']; intr. 1993

'Diana Cant' HT, rb, 1928, Cant, B. R.; flowers carmine-red, base flushed orange, dbl.; ['Isobel' × seedling]

'Diana Festival' Min, lp, Laver, Keith G.; intr. 1996

'Diana H. Gupta' -- See 'Jaygup'

'Diana Holman' -- See 'Pejpur'

'Diana Maxwell' HT, ob, 1957, Kemp, M.L.; flowers orange-cerise, high pointed, 5 in., 45 petals; foliage bronze; vigorous growth; ['Ena Harkness' × 'Sam McGredy']

'Diana Menhuin' HT, dy, 1963, LeGrice; flowers deep buttercup-yellow, 5½ in., 30 petals, globular; foliage dark, glossy; vigorous, upright growth; [('Golden Masterpiece' × 'Ellinor LeGrice') × 'Forward']

'Diana Rowden' LCl, op, 1977, Hawker; flowers deep copper-salmon to rose-pink, 5-6 in., 30 petals, intense fragrance; profuse, continuous bloom; foliage large, copper to green; ['Mrs Sam McGredy, Climbing' × 'Red Dandy']

'Diana, Princess of Wales' -- See 'Jacshaq'

'Diane' HT, yb, 1958, Gaujard; flowers clear yellow, center orange-yellow, well-formed, large; vigorous growth; ['Peace' × (seedling × 'Opera')]

'Diane' HT, yb, Dawson, George; intr. 1976

'Diane de Bollvillers' T, w, before 1884, Baumann; flowers cream white, shaded pink, large, very full

'Diane de Broglie' HT, ob, 1929, Chambard, C.; flowers coral-orange, very large, dbl., cupped; foliage dark; strong stems; very vigorous growth

'Diane de Poitiers' HT, dp; flowers pure pink; growth to 3-4 ft.

'Diane d'Urfé' HT, w, 1958, Croix, A.; flowers white, becoming red-edged; vigorous growth; ['Peace' × 'Incendie']

'Dianna Kay' Min, or, 1982, Dobbs, Annette E.; flowers small, 20 petals, no fragrance; foliage small, medium green, semi-glossy; upright growth; ['Anytime' × 'Sheri Anne']

'Dianne Feinstein' HT, yb, 1980, Fong, William P.; bud ovoid; flowers 23 petals, high-centered, borne singly, moderate fragrance; foliage dark; prickles triangular; vigorous, spreading growth; ['McGredy's Yellow' × 'Sutter's Gold']

'Dianthaeflora' -- See 'Œillet'

'Dianthiflora' -- See 'Fimbriata'

'Diany Binny' LCl, w, 1976, Binny; flowers pure white with prominent yellow stamens, 2 in., 5 petals, borne in clusters of 10-20, intense fragrance; foliage gray-green; ['Kiftsgate' × R. rubrifolia (?)]

Diapason® -- See 'Delpoc'

'Diavoletta' ; intr. 1966

'Dic Della' -- See 'Dicdella'

'Dicalow' ('Yellow Ribbon') F, dy, 1977, Dickson, Patrick; flowers deep golden yellow, medium, 23 petals, cupped; foliage medium green, semi-glossy; vigorous, compact, bushy growth; ['Illumination' × 'Stroller']

'Dicalways' HT, yb, Dickson; intr. 2003

'Dicam' ('Coeur d'Amour') HT, mr, 1967, Dickson, A.; bud ovoid; intr. 1970

'Dicappeal' (Lime Sublime™) F, w, 2004, Dickson, Colin; flowers pastel chartreuse-white, long-lasting, 7-9 cm., dbl., borne in small clusters; prolific, slight fragrance; foliage medium size, dark green, glossy; prickles small, almost straight, brown, moderate; growth upright, vigorous, medium (120-140 cm.); garden decoration; [Sexy Rexy® × 'Dawn Chorus']; intr. 2005

'Dicband' ('Springfields') F, ob, 1977, Dickson, A.; flowers orange, red, gold, 3 in., 48 petals, cupped; ['Eurorose' × Anabell®]; intr. 1978

'Dicbar' (Memento®) F, rb, 1978, Dickson, Patrick; bud globular; flowers salmon-red, 3 in., 22 petals, cupped, borne in clusters; free-flowering; foliage sage green; bushy growth; ['Bangor' × Anabell®]

'Dicbee' ('High Summer') F, or, 1978, Dickson, Patrick; bud ovoid; flowers vermilion, 3 in., 26 petals, cupped; foliage large; bushy growth; ['Zorina' × 'Ernest H. Morse']

'Dicblender' ('Acapulco') HT, rb, Dickson, Patrick; intr. 1997

'Dicbo' HT, mp, 1967, Dickson, A.; bud ovoid; intr. 1968

'Dicchange' HT, ab, Dickson; intr. 2001

'Diccheeky' F, ob, Dickson; bud reddish pink; intr. 2004

'Dicdance' (Bright Smile®) F, my, 1980, Dickson, Patrick; bud pointed; flowers empire yellow, convex, small, 15 petals, flat, borne 15 per cluster; foliage dense, mid-green; prickles concave, purple; bushy, medium growth; ['Eurorose' × seedling]; intr. 1981

'Dicdanger' F, dr, Dickson; intr. 2006

'Dicdella' ('Dic Della') HT, dp, Chiplunkar; flowers large, deep pink, full, high-centered; [sport of 'Ace of Hearts']; intr. 1996

'Dicdip' HT, pb, 1985, Dickson, Patrick; flowers large, 32 petals, moderate fragrance; foliage medium size, purple when young; upright, bushy growth; ['Eurorose' × 'Typhoon']; intr. 1974

'Dicdivine' ('Pot o' Gold') HT, my, 1980, Dickson, Patrick; bud pointed; flowers golden yellow, 32 petals, high-centered, open flat, borne singly and in clusters, intense sweet fragrance; recurrent; foliage mid-green with strong purple veins; prickles brown; bushy, medium growth; ['Eurorose' × 'Whisky Mac']

'Dicdomino' F, dp, Dickson; intr. 2005

'Dicdothis' HT, ly, Dickson; intr. 2008

'Dicdrafty' S, ab, Dickson; intr. 2007

'Dicdrum' ('Shona') F, op, 1982, Dickson, Patrick; flowers medium coral pink, 23 petals, borne in clusters, slight fragrance; foliage medium size, medium green, semi-glossy; bushy growth; ['Bangor' × Anabell®]; intr. 1982

'Dicdwarf' Min, dy, Dickson; intr. 2006

Dicdyna® F, my, Dickson; intr. 2008

'Dicecho' ('Forever Together') F, op, Dickson; intr. 2006

'Dicel' ('Queen Elizabeth Rouge', 'Queen of Diamonds') F, or, 1965, Dickson, Patrick; intr. 1962

'Dicelope' F, lp, Dickson; intr. 2005

'Dicemblem' F, ab, Dickson; intr. 2006

'Dicentice' (Gold Cottage Ediparc®) S, dy,

Dickson; intr. 2004
'Dicetch' F, rb, Dickson; intr. 2004
'Dicfate' F, mp, 1985, Dickson, Patrick; flowers medium, 18 petals, slight fragrance; foliage medium size, medium green; upright, bushy growth; [('Futura' × ('Pye Colour' × Prominent®)]; intr. 1975
'Dicfire' ('Beautiful Britain') F, or, 1983, Dickson, Patrick; flowers orange-red, reverse deeper, medium, 20 petals, borne in clusters; foliage medium size, medium green, semi-glossy; upright, bushy growth; ['Red Planet' × 'Eurorose']
'Dicfizz' F, ab, Dickson; intr. 2005
'Dicghost' F, w, Dickson; bud white with pinkish-red flush; intr. 2007
'Dicgottago' F, ly, Dickson; intr. 2007
'Dicgrow' ('Brass Ring', 'Peek a Boo') Min, ob, 1981, Dickson, Patrick; bud pointed; flowers coppery orange, fading to rose pink, patio, dbl., flat, borne in large clusters; foliage small, pointed, glossy; upright, arching growth; PP4991; [Memento® × 'Nozomi']
'Dichimanher' F, ab, Dickson; intr. 2007
'Dichimanher' Min, dr, Dickson; intr. 2008
'Dichirap' F, m, Dickson; intr. 2007
'Dichusk' F, w, Dickson; intr. 2003
'Diciluvit' HT, ly, Dickson; bud creamy gold with slight pink edges; intr. 2008
'Dicinfra' (Disco Dancer®) F, or, 1984, Dickson, Patrick; flowers orange scarlet, medium, semi-dbl.; foliage medium size, medium green, glossy; bushy growth; ['Cathedral' × Memento®]
'Dicjana' ('Peaudouce', Elina®) HT, ly, 1984, Dickson, Patrick; flowers pale yellow to ivory, luminous, 5-5½ in., 30-35 petals, high-centered, borne singly; foliage large, dark, glossy; long stems; vigorous, tall growth; ['Nana Mouskouri' × 'Lolita']; intr. 1985
'Dicjeep' ('Daydream', 'Len Turner') F, rb, 1984, Dickson, Patrick; flowers ivory petals flushed and edged carmine, large, 35 petals; foliage medium size, medium green, glossy; bushy, very compact growth; [Electron® × Eyepaint®]
'Dicjem' ('Freedom') HT, dy, 1984, Dickson, Patrick; flowers chrome yellow, large, 35 petals, high-centered, moderate fragrance; foliage medium size, medium green, glossy; bushy growth; [('Eurorose' × 'Typhoon') × Bright Smile®]
'Dicjoon' ('Leslie's Dream', 'Pantheon', 'Pavarotti') HT, mr, 1984, Dickson, Colin; flowers signal red, 7+ cm., full, borne mostly solitary, slight fragrance; foliage medium size, dark green, glossy; numerous prickles; growth upright, tall (1 m.); garden decoration; ['Bonfire' × 'Typhoon']
'Dicjoy' ('Ards Beauty') F, my, 1984, Dickson, Patrick; bud large; flowers large, 20 petals, high-centered; foliage medium size, medium green, glossy; bushy growth; [('Eurorose' × 'Whisky Mac') × Bright Smile®]; intr. 1986

'Dicjubell' ('Dickson's Jubilee', 'Lovely Lady') HT, mp, 1984, Dickson, Patrick; flowers large, 35 petals, moderate fragrance; foliage medium size, mid-green, glossy; bushy growth; ['Silver Jubilee' × ('Eurorose' × Anabell®)]
'Dick Balfour' S, w; flowers white blush; recurrent bloom; groundcover; spreading growth
'Dick Koster' Pol, dp, 1929, Koster, D.A.; flowers small, deep pink, dbl., cupped, borne in clusters; recurrent bloom; growth mounded, low, spreading; [sport of 'Anneke Koster']
'Dick Koster Fulgens' Pol, dp, 1940, Koster, M.; flowers light red, semi-dbl., borne in clusters; low, compact growth
'Dick Koster Superior' Pol, mr, 1955, Koster, D.A.; flowers rosy red; [sport of 'Dick Koster']
'Dick Lindner' HT, mp; flowers coral pink, dbl., high-centered; growth vigorous, medium; intr. 1996
'Dick Tracy' Min, rb, Dickson
'Dick Wilcox' HT, dr, 1949, Brownell; bud long, pointed to ovoid; flowers rose-red, 4-5½ in., 50-60 petals, high-centered, moderate fragrance; foliage dark; vigorous growth; PP845; ['Pink Princess' × 'Crimson Glory']
'Dickerfuffle' ('Georgie Girl', 'Wishing') F, op, 1984, Dickson, Patrick; flowers medium peachy pink, large, 35 petals, pointed, slight fragrance; foliage medium size, medium green, semi-glossy; bushy growth; ['Silver Jubilee' × Bright Smile®]; intr. 1984
'Dickerry' ('Laughter Lines') F, pb, 1987, Dickson, Patrick; flowers large, semi-dbl.; foliage small, medium green, semi-glossy; bushy growth; [('Pyecolour' × 'Sunday Times') × Eyepaint®]
'Dickimono' ('Anisley Dickson', München Kindl®, 'Münchner Kindl', Dicky®) F, op, 1984, Dickson, Patrick; flowers reddish salmon-pink, reverse lighter, large, 35 petals, slight fragrance; foliage medium size, medium green, glossy; bushy growth; ['Cathedral' × Memento®]; intr. 1983
'Dickindle' F, ly, Dickson, Patrick; intr. 1986
'Dickisser' ('Hi Doll') F, or, Dickson, Patrick; intr. 1995
'Dickitty' ('Old Flame') F, ob, Dickson, Patrick; intr. 1987
'Dicknowall' ('Collegiate 110') F, my, Dickson, Patrick
'Dickooky' (Tall Story®) F, my, 1984, Dickson, Patrick; flowers soft primrose yellow, medium, semi-dbl., shallow cup to flat, borne in clusters; free-flowering; foliage medium size, light green, glossy; low, spreading growth; ['Sunsprite' × Yesterday®]
Dick's Delight™ -- See 'Dicwhistle'
'Dickson's Bouquet' HT, ab, 1938, Dickson, A.; flowers salmon, carmine and apricot, blended saffron, dbl.; long, wiry stems; vigorous growth

'Dickson's Centennial' HT, mr, 1936, Dickson, A.; bud pointed; flowers crimson to scarlet, loosely formed, very large, moderate fragrance; foliage bronze; long, strong stems; vigorous, bushy growth; PP223; intr. 1937
'Dickson's Delight' HT, ob, 1938, Dickson, A.; flowers vivid orange, heavily shaded scarlet-orange; foliage bronze-green; vigorous growth
'Dickson's Flame' F, or, 1959, Dickson, A.; flowers scarlet-flame, large, dbl., borne in trusses, slight fragrance; vigorous growth; [('Independence' × unknown) × 'Nymph']; intr. 1958
'Dickson's Jubilee' -- See 'Dicjubell'
'Dickson's Perfection' HT, pb, 1937, Dickson, A.; flowers shrimp-pink, base orange-yellow, large, dbl.; very vigorous growth
'Dickson's Red' ('Dr F. G. Chandler') HT, dr, 1938, Dickson, A.; flowers velvety crimson-scarlet, large, 18 petals, cupped, intense spicy fragrance; foliage leathery, dark; vigorous, bushy growth; PP376
'Dickson's Wonder' HT, ob, Dickson; intr. 1978
Dicky® -- See 'Dickimono'
'Dicladida' ('Cider Cup') Min, ob, 1987, Dickson, Patrick; flowers medium, dbl.; foliage medium size, medium green, glossy; patio growth; [Memento® × ('Liverpool Echo' × Woman's Own®)]; intr. 1988
'Diclady' (Feu Follet®) MinFl, or, Lens, Louis; intr. 1991
'Diclittle' ('Little Woman') Min, pb, 1987, Dickson, Patrick; flowers soft pink with deeper edges, dbl., classic, moderate fragrance; foliage small, medium green, semi-glossy; patio; tall, bushy growth; [Memento® × ('Liverpool Echo' × Woman's Own®)]; intr. 1986
'Diclulu' ('Gentle Touch') Min, lp, 1987, Dickson, Patrick; flowers moderately small, dbl., slight fragrance; foliage small, medium green, semi-glossy; patio; bushy growth; [('Liverpool Echo' × Woman's Own®) × Memento®]; intr. 1986
'Dicmadder' ('Tangeglow', Star Child®) F, rb, 1987, Dickson, Patrick; flowers small, 6-14 petals; foliage small, medium green, glossy; strong, straight stems; bushy, prolific growth; PP7312; [Eyepaint® × ('Liverpool Echo' × Woman's Own®)]; intr. 1988
'Dicmagic' ('Sweet Magic') Min, ob, 1987, Dickson, Patrick; flowers orange-gold, small, dbl., cupped, borne in clusters, slight sweet fragrance; recurrent; foliage small, medium green, glossy; bushy (15-18 in.) growth; ['Peek A Boo' × Bright Smile®]
'Dicmickey' ('Buttons') Min, or, 1987, Dickson, Patrick; flowers medium, dbl., slight fragrance; foliage small, medium green, glossy; patio; bushy growth;

[('Liverpool Echo' × Woman's Own®) × Memento®]

'Dicmoppet' ('Goldfächer', 'Minilights') S, my, 1987, Dickson, Patrick; flowers small, single to semi-dbl., flat, borne in small clusters; quick repeat; foliage small, dark green, glossy; spreading, compact growth; ['White Spray' × Bright Smile®]; intr. 1988

'Dicmoust' Min, w, Dickson; intr. 2003

'Dicname' ('Peter Goldman') HT, yb, 1987, Dickson, Patrick; flowers medium, full; foliage medium size, medium green, glossy; bushy growth; ['Silver Jubilee' × Bright Smile®]

'Dicnifty' ('Empress Michiko') HT, lp, Dickson, Patrick; intr. 1992

'Dicnorth' ('Harvest Fayre') F, ob, 1990, Dickson, Patrick; flowers medium, 15-24 petals, slight fragrance; foliage medium size, medium green, glossy; bushy growth; [seedling × Bright Smile®]; intr. 1990

'Dicobey' ('Beaulieu', 'Tequila Sunrise') HT, rb, 1989, Dickson, Patrick; flowers deep yellow heavily edged in scarlet red, 4 in., 40 petals, spiral, slight tea fragrance; recurrent; foliage medium size, medium green, glossy; bushy growth; [Bonfire Night® × 'Freedom']; intr. 1989

'Dicodour' ('Fragrant Dream') HT, ab, 1989, Dickson, Patrick; flowers apricot blended orange, large, 20 petals, intense fragrance; foliage large, medium green, glossy; upright growth; [('Eurorose' × 'Typhoon') × 'Bonfire']; intr. 1989

'Dicogle' ('St. Andrews', 'Valentine Heart') F, mp, 1990, Dickson, Patrick; flowers pale pink with hint of lilac, serrated edges, dbl., high-centered, borne in clusters, intense fragrance; recurrent; foliage large, medium green, glossy, purple when young; bushy growth; ['Shona' × 'Pot 'o Gold']; intr. 1990

'Dicomo' ('Tear Drop') Min, w, 1989, Dickson, Patrick; flowers pure white with yellow stamens, small, semi-dbl., flat, borne in clusters, slight fragrance; recurrent; foliage small, medium green, glossy; bushy, compact growth; [Pink Spray® × Bright Smile®]; intr. 1989

'Dicor' ('Red Gold', 'Rouge et Or') F, yb, 1967, Dickson, A.; bud ovoid, pointed; intr. 1971

'Dicorsar' ('Grimpant Rouge et Or', 'Redgold, Climbing', 'Rouge et Or, Climbing') Cl F, yb, 1980, Pekmez, Paul; bud cylindric; flowers borne 3 - 5 per cluster; foliage green, glossy; large growth; [sport of 'Redgold']

'Dicpaint' ('Painted Moon') HT, rb, 1990, Dickson, Patrick; flowers large, 40 petals, cupped; foliage medium size, medium green, semi-glossy; upright, bushy, stocky growth; ['Bonfire' × 'Silver Jubilee']; intr. 1990

'Dicparty' (Party Trick™) F, dp, 1999, Dickson, Colin; flowers cerise pink, 2 in., single, borne in small clusters; foliage small, medium green, glossy; prickles moderate; compact, low (18 in.) growth; ['Robin Redbreast' × seedling]; intr. 1999

'Dicpe' F, ob, 1968, Dickson, A.

'Dicperhaps' ('Quaker Star') Gr, op, 1991, Dickson, Colin; flowers orange with silver reverse, aging to salmon with orange petal edges, large, very full, borne mostly singly, no fragrance; foliage medium size, dark green, glossy; prickles few, straight, small; upright, medium (4 ft.) growth; ['Anisley Dickson' × seedling]; intr. 1991

'Dicplay' ('New Horizon') F, ob, Dickson, Patrick; intr. 1991

'Dicpleasant' ('Ruth Woodward') F, or, 1992, Dickson Nurseries; flowers 3-3½ in., full, borne in small clusters; foliage medium size, medium green, semi-glossy; some prickles; medium, bushy growth; ['Wishing' × seedling]

'Dicquarrel' ('Benita') Gr, my, 1994, Dickson, Colin; flowers saffron yellow, 3 in., full, moderate fragrance; foliage medium size, medium green, semi-glossy; upright (90 cm.) to bushy growth; intr. 1994

'Dicquasar' ('Dawn Chorus') HT, ob, 1994, Dickson, Colin; buds vivid orange; flowers orpiment orange with buttercup yellow at base, medium, dbl., borne in large clusters; foliage medium size, medium to dark green, glossy; some prickles; medium (74 cm.), upright to bushy growth; ['Wishing' × Peer Gynt®]; intr. 1993

'Dicqueen' F, or, 1990, Dickson, Patrick; intr. 1991

'Dicqueue' ('Brandysnap', Brandy Snap™, 'Liz McGrath') HT, ob, 1999, Dickson, Colin; flowers orange/bold, large, full, borne mostly singly, intense fragrance; foliage medium size, medium green, glossy; prickles moderate; upright, medium (30 in.) growth; [seedling × seedling]; intr. 1999

'Dicquiet' ('Gypsy Dancer') S, yb, 1994, Dickson, Patrick; bud small, pointed; flowers hand-painted light yellow with orange and light yellow reverse, medium, 20 petals, borne in clusters, slight citrus fragrance; foliage medium size, dark green, glossy; few prickles; medium (100-110 cm.), bushy growth; PP8900; ['Sweet Magic' × Little Artist®]; intr. 1994

'Dicracer' ('Duchess of York', 'Sarah, Duchess of York', 'Sunseeker') F, or, 1994, Dickson, Colin; flowers mandarin red suffused with sulfur yellow, small, full, borne in small clusters, slight fragrance; foliage medium size, medium green, semi-glossy; some prickles; low (56 cm.), bushy growth; patio; ['Little Prince' × 'Gentle Touch']

'Dicreason' ('Bright Eyes', 'Our Molly') S, mr, 1994, Dickson, Colin; flowers currant red with a silvery white eye, medium, 5 petals, borne in large clusters, no fragrance; foliage medium size, medium green; some prickles; tall (90 cm.), spreading growth; hips orange

'Dicrelax' ('Flair') F, yb, Dickson, Patrick; intr. 1993

'Dicrevival' ('Boy Crazy') S, dp, 1992, Dickson, Patrick; flowers deep pink, petal base has cream colored "half moon", heavy petal substance, medium, dbl.; foliage medium size, dark green, glossy; some prickles; patio; medium (90 cm.), upright, bushy growth; ['Sweet Magic' × 'DICmerlin']; intr. 1992

'Dicrobot' ('Belfast Belle', 'Miranda') HT, dy, 1990, Dickson, Patrick; flowers large, full, slight fragrance; foliage medium size, medium green, semi-glossy; upright, bushy growth; [seedling × 'Pot O' Gold']; intr. 1991

'Dicrocky' ('Explorer', 'Space Invader') S, lp, 1990, Dickson, Patrick; flowers large, full, moderate fragrance; foliage medium size, medium green, semi-glossy; spreading growth; [seedling × 'Temple Bells']

'Dicroyal' ('Princess Royal') HT, ab, 1992, Dickson, Colin; flowers apricot center, outer petals fading lighter, large, full, borne mostly singly, slight fragrance; foliage large, medium green, semi-glossy; numerous prickles; stems very stiff; medium (3 ft.), bushy growth; ['Tequila Sunrise' × seedling]

'Dicsilving' ('Silver Lining, Climbing') Cl HT, pb, 1997, Dickson, Alex; flowers large, very dbl.; foliage medium size, medium green, glossy; numerous prickles; tall, spreading growth, with 10-12 canes ranging in size to 10-20 ft.; [sport of 'Silver Lining']

'Dicstartle' F, ab, Dickson; intr. 1995

'Dicsun' ('Mr Joseph Cyril Bamford') S, dy, Dickson, Patrick; intr. 1993

'Dictalent' ('Just Happy', Shine On™) Min, op, 1999, Dickson, Colin; flowers nasturtium red, reverse azalea pink, 2½ in., dbl., cupped, borne in small clusters; free-flowering; foliage small, medium green, semi-glossy; prickles moderate; compact, low (22 in.) growth; ['Sweet Magic' × seedling]; intr. 1994

'Dictator' (Pure Bliss™) HT, mp, 1999, Dickson, Alex; flowers pale pink, reverse mid-pink, 2¼-2½ in., full, borne mostly singly, moderate fragrance; foliage medium size, medium green, semi-glossy; prickles moderate; patio; upright, medium growth; [Elina® × seedling]; intr. 1994

'Dictech ??' -- See 'Red Cottage'

'Dicticktock' S, yb, Dickson, Patrick; intr. 1994

'Dictino' Min, rb, Dickson; intr. 2004

'Dicumpteen' (Pretty in Pink™) S, lp, 1999, Dickson, Colin; flowers pale pink, 2 in., very dbl., rosette, borne in small clusters, moderate fragrance; foliage medium size, medium green, glossy; few prickles; groundcover; low (24 in.), spreading (4-5 ft.) growth; [seedling ×

'Grouse']; intr. 1994

'Dicuncle' (Wine and Dine™) S, dp, 1999, Dickson, Colin; flowers rose red, ivory white eye, 2¼ in., single, borne in small clusters, moderate fragrance; foliage small, medium green, glossy; numerous prickles; groundcover; spreading, medium (3 ft.) growth; [seedling × seedling]; intr. 1999

'Dicuniform' (Boy O Boy™) S, mr, 1999, Dickson, Colin; flowers 2¾-3 in., semi-dbl.; foliage small, medium green, glossy; prickles moderate; flori-shrub; bushy, spreading (30 in.) growth; ['Little Prince' × 'Eye Opener']; intr. 1996

'Dicuptight' (Tintinara™) HT, or, 1999, Dickson, Colin; flowers poppy red, reverse geranium-lake, 5 in., full, high-centered, borne in small clusters, slight fragrance; recurrent; foliage large, medium green, glossy; prickles moderate; upright, tall (40 in.) growth; ['Melody Maker' × seedling]; intr. 1996

'Dicuseful' Min, dy, Dickson; buds gold-endbl.; intr. 1999

'Dicvanilla' (Happy Ever After™) F, pb, 1999, Dickson, Colin; flowers pale pink/lemon, revers pale pink, 2 in., semi-dbl., borne in large clusters; foliage medium size, light green, semi-glossy; prickles moderate; bushy (33 in.) growth; ['The Fairy' × seedling]; intr. 1997

'Dicvintage' ('Roche Centenary') MinFl, mr, Dickson, Patrick; intr. 1993

'Dicvood' (Glenshane™) S, mr, 1999, Dickson, Colin; flowers 1½ in., semi-dbl., borne in large clusters, no fragrance; foliage medium size, medium green, semi-glossy; few prickles; flori-shrub; spreading, bushy, medium (30 in.) growth; [seedling × Star Child®]; intr. 1997

'Dicvoxpop' Min, dp, Dickson; intr. 2001

'Dicwaffle' (Racy Lady™) HT, w, 1999, Dickson, Colin; flowers creamy white, reverse cream, 4½ in., full, borne mostly singly, moderate fragrance; foliage medium size, dark green, glossy; numerous prickles; upright, medium (3 ft.) growth; ['Solitaire' × Elina®]

'Dicwhatnext' S, rb, Dickson; intr. 2000

'Dicwhistle' (Dick's Delight™) Min, dp, 1999, Dickson, Colin; flowers 1¼ in., full, borne in large clusters; foliage small, dark green, glossy; prickles moderate; patio; compact to spreading, low (24 in.) growth; [seedling × 'The Fairy']; intr. 1999

'Dicwhoops' HT, ly, Dickson; intr. 1999

'Dicwhynot' ('Blossom Blanket', To Mummy™, 'Cascading White', 'Newly Wed') S, w, 2001, Dickson, Colin; bud palest pink; flowers with prominent yellow stamens, 5 cm., dbl., borne in small clusters, moderate apple fragrance; foliage small, medium green, glossy, red when young; prickles small, few; growth spreading, low (60 × 110 cm.); garden decorative; [seedling × 'The Fairy']; intr. 2001

'Dicwillynilly' (Old John™) F, ob, 1999, Dickson, Colin; flowers mid-orange, reverse orange-red, 2½ in., dbl., borne in large clusters, moderate fragrance; foliage medium size, dark green, glossy; prickles moderate; upright, medium (40 in.) growth; ['Sunseeker' × 'New Horizon']; intr. 1999

'Dicwisp' HT, w, Dickson; bud pointed, ovoid; intr. 2003

'Dicwitness' (Irish Eyes™) F, yb, 1999, Dickson, Patrick; flowers mid-yellow/red, reverse mid-red/yellow, 2½ in., full, borne in large clusters; foliage medium size, medium green, semi-glossy; prickles moderate; bushy (30 in.) growth; ['Mr J. C. B.' × 'Gypsy Dancer']; intr. 2000

'Dicwonder' (Marry Me™) Min, mp, 1999, Dickson, Patrick; flowers 2 in., full, borne in small clusters; foliage medium size, dark green, glossy; prickles moderate; growth upright, medium (28 in.); containers, patio; [seedling × 'Cider Cup']; intr. 1998

'Dicwriter' F, yb, Dickson; intr. 1999

'Dicxcalibur' HT, my, Dickson; buds pointed, lime lemon; intr. 1999

'Dicxciting' S, ab, Dickson; buds apricot salmon; intr. 2000

'Dicxcon' F, ob, Dickson; intr. 2001

'Dicxotic' ('Lady Diana', Her Majesty™) F, ab, 2001, Dickson, Colin; flowers apricot/peach/pink, paler reverse, predominately lemon yellow when young, s, 5 cm., very dbl., borne in small clusters, slight fragrance; foliage small, medium green, semi-glossy; prickles medium, moderate; growth bushy, low (70 × 95 cm.); garden decorative; [seedling × 'Interbronzi']; intr. 2001

'Dicxplosion' (Rainbow Magic™) Min, rb, 1999, Dickson, Colin; flowers cerise red, reverse yellow, 1¾ in., semi-dbl., borne in large clusters, slight fragrance; foliage small, medium green, glossy; prickles moderate; spreading, low (2 ft × 3 ft.) growth; patio; ['Sunseeker' × seedling]; intr. 1999

'Dicxtol' ('Dictech ??') S, rb, Dickson, Patrick; intr. 1998

'Dicyardstick' (Crowning Glory™) S, rb, 2001, Dickson, Colin; flowers red with yellow center, 4-5 cm., dbl., borne in large clusters, slight fragrance; foliage medium size, medium green, semy-glossy; prickles medium, few; growth spreading, tall (115 × 140 cm.), vigorous; garden decorative; ['Duchess of York' × 'New Penny']; intr. 2001

'Dicyellmag' Min, my, Dickson; intr. 2004

'Dicyeti' F, ab, Dickson; intr. 2003

'Diczodiac' F, op, Dickson; intr. 2003

'Diczombie' HT, ly, Dickson; intr. 2002

'Diczoobie' S, w, Dickson; intr. 2004

'Diczoom' S, my, Dickson; intr. 2003

'Didot' HSpn, w, from Scotland; flowers blush white

'Die Berühmte' -- See 'Illustre'

'Die Bloemhoffer' HT, w, Kordes; bud pointed, urn shaped; flowers cream, outer petals cream tinted green, dbl., exhibition, no fragrance; growth to 4-5 ft.; intr. 2001

'Die Krone' HT, dy

'Die Mutter von Rosa' HT, lp, 1906, Verschuren; flowers medium, dbl.

'Die Präsidentin' HT, w, 1928, Mühle; flowers marble white, center soft yellow, semi-dbl.; ['Harry Kirk' × unknown]

'Die Rheinpfalz' -- See 'Helrobu'

Die Schöne Tölzerin® S, mp, Schultheis; flowers lasting pink, medium, very dbl., almost quartered; growth broad, upright, 5 ft; intr. 2001

'Die Schonste' HT, w; intr. 1998

'Die Spree' HT, lp, 1907, Nauke; flowers flesh pink, satiny whitish pink in center, large, dbl., moderate fragrance

Die Welt® ('The World', 'World Rose') HT, ob, 1976, Kordes; bud long, pointed; flowers orange, red and yellow blend, 4½ in., 25 petals, high-centered, borne mostly singly, slight fragrance; foliage glossy; vigorous, upright, very tall, bushy growth; [seedling × Peer Gynt®]

'Diekor' ('The World', 'World Rose') HT, ob, 1976, Kordes; bud long, pointed

'Diener's Blue' HMult, m, 1926, Diener; flowers violet, 2 in., dbl., borne in heavy clusters; almost thornless; vigorous growth

'Diener's Rose Understock' HMult, rb, 1932, Diener; bud long; flowers rose-red shaded purple, stamens yellowish, 2 in., 10 petals, borne in clusters; foliage small, notched; climbing or trailing growth; producing much new wood in a season; PP70; ['Veilchenblau' × sport of 'Veilchenblau']

Dieter Müller® S, m, Delbard; flowers rose-lilac, intense fragrance; intr. 2006

'Dieter Wolf' Pol, or, 1978, Buisman, G. A. H.; flowers salmon-orange, semi-dbl.; foliage glossy, dark; vigorous, compact growth; ['Tropicana' × 'Jiminy Cricket']; intr. 1969

Dietlikon® HT, mr, Huber; flowers cherry-red, dbl., high-centered; intr. 2005

Dietrich Woessner® F, w, Huber; flowers creamy white, center tinted yellow in autumn, 6 cm., dbl., borne in clusters of 4-6; new foliage copper red, turning dark green; growth to 2-3½ ft., somewhat irregular; intr. 2001

'Dieudonné' HCh, dr, 1827, Mauget; flowers crimson purple, very small; Lawrenciana

'Different Charm' -- See 'Seacharm'

'Dignity' HT, w, 1940, LeGrice; bud long, pointed; flowers creamy white, dbl.; foliage leathery; vigorous, bushy, compact growth

'Dignity' HT, m, Athy; flowers deep lilac, double, intense fragrance; recurrent; medium growth

'Dignity 2008' -- See 'Worcookie'

'Dikgang Moseneke' S, mr, Kordes; intr. 2002

'Dil-Ki-Rani' HT, lp, Pal, Dr. B.P.; intr.

1985

'Diletta' HT, mr, Barni, V.; flowers large, brilliant geranium red, dbl., high-centered, moderate fragrance; foliage bronzy green; growth vigorous, erect, 3-4 ft; intr. 1985

'Dilly Dilly' -- See 'Tindilly'

'Dilly's Wiederkehr' HFt, 1925, Schwartzbach; flowers large, dbl.

'Dilys Allen' ('Dily's Allen') HT, ob, 1952, Norman; bud long, pointed, ovoid; flowers orange-red, base saffron, 4 in.; foliage glossy, dark bluish green; vigorous, bushy growth; ['Mrs Sam McGredy' × seedling]

'Dily's Allen' -- See 'Dilys Allen'

'Dimity' HT, pb, 1956, Taylor, C.A.; bud ovoid, pointed; flowers ivory to pure white, edged pink, large, dbl., cupped; foliage dark, leathery; upright, bushy growth; ['Peace' × seedling]

'Dimples' F, ly, 1968, LeGrice; flowers canary-yellow to ivory, semi-dbl., borne in trusses; foliage glossy

'Dina Gee' -- See 'Silitalia'

'Dinah' HT, dr, 1920, Paul, W.; flowers deep crimson, shaded darker

'Dinah Shore' HT, dp, 1942, Grillo; flowers cerise-pink, 5 in., 65 petals, globular, intense fragrance; foliage glossy, dark; vigorous, upright growth; PP762; [sport of 'Jewel']

'Dingee & Conard' HP, mr, 1875, Verdier, E.; flowers shining poppy red, large, full, moderate fragrance

'Dinia' my, Vire Aimery

'Dinky' Min, or, 1986, Bridges, Dennis A.; flowers orange-red, reverse orange, 20 petals, urn-shaped, borne usually singly; foliage medium size, medium green, semi-glossy; prickles long, light red; upright growth; ['Sheri Anne' × seedling]

Dinky® HMsk, dp, Velle-Boudolf; flowers pink fuchsia, full, borne in large, pyramidal sprays; recurrent; growth to 4 ft.; intr. 2003

'Dinsmore' -- See 'Mme Charles Wood'

'Diny Hage' HT, dr, 1956, Leenders, M.; flowers crimson-red, large, dbl.; vigorous growth; ['Ambassadeur Nemry' × 'Crimson Glory']

Dionisia® F, yb, Barni; flowers white with yellow in the heart and deep pink edges, semi-dbl., borne in clusters, slight fruity fragrance; growth to 3-4 ft.; intr. 2003

'Diorama' HT, yb, 1965, deRuiter; flowers apricot-yellow, 4½ in., dbl., high-centered; vigorous, upright growth; ['Peace' × 'Beauté']

'Diorama, Climbing' Cl HT, yb; intr. after 1965

Dioressence® -- See 'Deldiore'

'Diorette' -- See 'Cancan'

'Diplomat' HT, dr, 1962, Boerner; bud ovoid; flowers current red edged blood-red, 3½-4 in., 50-55 petals, cupped, moderate fragrance; foliage leathery, dark; vigorous, upright growth; PP2114; [('Poinsettia' × 'Tawny Gold') × 'Detroiter']; intr. 1962

'Diplomatka' F, mr, Klimenko, V. N.; flowers blood red, large, dbl.; intr. 1967

'Diputacion de Tarragona' ('Tarragona') HT, ob, 1970, Dot, Pedro; bud pointed; flowers orange-coral, large, 35 petals, high-centered, moderate fragrance; foliage glossy, bronze; upright, compact growth; [Baccará® × ('Chrysler Imperial' × 'Soraya')]; intr. 1967

'Directeur Alphand' HP, m, 1883, Lévêque; flowers blackish purple, large, dbl.

'Directeur Constantin Bernard' HT, m, 1886, Soupert & Notting; flowers delicate magenta pink on a silvery ground, large, very full; ['Abel Grand' × 'Mlle Adèle Jougant']

'Directeur Donatien Lelievre' F, ob, 1959, Privat; flowers coppery orange, medium, dbl.

'Directeur Guérin' HT, ob, 1935, Gaujard; flowers orange-yellow, center coppery, overlarge, dbl.; foliage light; long stems; very vigorous growth

'Directeur N. Jensen' HP, m, 1883, Verdier, E.; flowers purple/pink, large, dbl.

'Directeur René Gérard' T, yb, 1892, Pelletier; flowers canary yellow, tinted China pink, edges shaded magenta, large, full; ['Mme Falcot' × 'Marquise de Vivens']

'Director Plumecock' -- See 'Président Plumecocq'

'Director Rubió' HT, rb, 1929, Dot, Pedro; flowers magenta-red, very large, semi-dbl.; stiff stems; dwarf, bushy growth; ['O. Junyent' × 'Jean C.N. Forestier']

'Direkteur H. J. Bos' S, pb; flowers large, borne in clusters; recurrent

'Dir. Rijnveld' ('Direkteur Rijnveld') F, or; flowers medium size, bright, semi-dbl.; recurrent; intr. 2001

'Direkteur Rijnveld' -- See 'Dir. Rijnveld'

'Direkteur Rikala' -- See 'Direktor Rikala'

'Direktor Benschop' ('City of York') LCl, w, 1945, Tantau; bud buff yellow; flowers creamy white, small to medium, 15 petals, cupped, borne in clusters of 7-15, moderate fragrance; may repeat; foliage glossy, leathery; vigorous, climbing growth; ['Dorothy Perkins' × 'Professor Gnau']

'Direktor Eric Hjelm' ('Direktor Hjelm') Pol, rb, 1927, Koster, D.A.; flowers red; [sport of 'Prasident Hindenburg']

'Direktor Hjelm' -- See 'Direktor Eric Hjelm'

'Direktor Rebhuhn' HT, ob, 1929, Kordes; flowers orange, center reddish, dbl.; ['Mme Butterfly' × 'Angèle Pernet']

'Direktor Rikala' ('Direkteur Rikala') F, mp, 1934, Koster, D.A.; [sport of 'Lafayette']; possibly synonymous with 'Frau Astrid Späth'

'Direktor Struve' Pol, w, 1924, van Nes; [sport of 'Echo']

Dirigent® ('The Conductor') HMsk, mr, 1959, Tantau, Math.; bud pointed; flowers blood-red, semi-dbl., borne in clusters of up to 28, slight fragrance; recurrent bloom; foliage leathery; vigorous (4 ft.) growth; ['Fanal' × 'Karl Weinhausen']; intr. 1956

'Disco' HT, rb, 1980, Weeks, O.L.; bud medium to long, pointed; flowers medium red, reverse cream, 30 petals, high-centered, borne singly and 2-4 per cluster, slight spicy fragrance; foliage leathery, dark; prickles hooked downward; tall, upright growth; PP4737; ['Sunrise-Sunset' × seedling]

Disco® F, pb, Harkness

Disco Dancer® -- See 'Dicinfra'

'Discovery' Gr, pb, 1959, deRuiter; flowers soft pink shaded apricot, 5-6 in., dbl., intense fragrance; vigorous growth; [('Peace' × 'Christopher Stone') × 'floribunda seedling']; intr. 1958

'Discovery' S, mp, Clements, John; flowers 4 in., 50 petals, deeply cupped, old-fashioned, slight myrrh fragrance; good repeat bloom; foliage lime green; growth upright, dense (3½ ft.); intr. 2004

'Discretion' HT, pb, 1952, Gaujard; flowers salmon-pink shaded copper, large, 28 petals; foliage glossy; ['Peace' × seedling]

'Disguise' F, rb, William, J.B.; bud coral red; flowers creamy white in center, red on outer petals spreading toward center, semi-dbl. to dbl., slight fragrance; growth to 3 ft.; intr. 2006

'Disneyland' -- See 'Jacmouse'

Disneyland Rose® -- See 'Jacmouse'

Dispetto® S, rb, Barni; flowers striped red and white, pattern variable, borne in clusters, slight fragrance; recurrent; foliage large, glossy, vigorous (50-70 cm.), spreading growth; intr. 2006

'Display' F, pb, 1956, Arnot; flowers salmon-pink, becoming cherry-pink, well-formed, 2½ in., 13 petals, borne in large clusters; foliage glossy, bronze-green; very vigorous growth; [Orange Triumph® × 'Golden Scepter']

Disque d'Or® -- See 'Candide'

'Disraeli' -- See 'Adadisres'

'Distant Drums' S, m, 1985, Buck, Dr. Griffith J.; bud ovoid, pointed; flowers rose-purple, imbricated, large, 40 petals, borne singly and in clusters of up to 10, intense myrrh fragrance; repeat bloom; foliage medium-large, dark, leathery; prickles awl-like, brown; vigorous, erect, bushy growth; ['September Song' × 'The Yeoman']; intr. 1984

'Distant Sounds' -- See 'Webpriace'

'Distant Thunder' S, m, Clements, John; flowers lavender-pink with hints of brown and gold (much like Distant Drums), 3½-4 in., 30 petals, strong fruity, myrrh fragrance; foliage reddish-bronze early, aging to deep olive-green, serrated red edges; growth compact (3 × 3 ft.), very bushy plant with foliage to the ground; intr. 2002

'Distinct' F, rb, 1953, Boerner; flowers spectrum-red with white eye, imbricated, small, 25-30 petals, cupped, borne in rounded clusters, moderate fragrance;

foliage glossy; vigorous, compact growth; PP1024; ['Triomphe Orléanais' × 'Mrs Pierre S. duPont']

'Distinction' HT, ab, 1882, Bennett; flowers shaded peach, dbl., cupped; either Mme de St. Joseph × Eugène Verdier, or Mabel Morrison × Devoniensis

'Distinction' F, dp, Turbat; flowers deep rose-pink, center brighter; [sport of 'Lafayette']; intr. 1927

'Distinction, Climbing' Cl F, dp, 1935, Lens, Louis; flowers medium, semi-dbl.

'Ditto' -- See 'Lyodit'

'Diva' HT, dr, 1978, Poulsen; flowers dark velvety red, 6 in., 30 petals, slight fragrance; foliage dark; spreading growth; ['Sonia' × Gisselfeld®]; intr. 1976

'Diva' mp, INRA; intr. 1982

'Diva' HT, dy, Cocker; intr. 1995

'Diversity' HT, rb, K&S; flowers medium, pale salmon base, scarlet and yellow with yellow stripes; intr. 1995

'Dividend' HT, dy, 1931, Clark, A.; flowers rich yellow, dbl., globular; foliage dark; dwarf growth; ['Franz Deegen' × seedling]

'Divine' HT, mr, 1964, Delbard-Chabert; bud dark purplish; flowers cardinal-red, well-formed, large, 45 petals; foliage bright green; strong stems; vigorous, upright growth

'Divine Lady' F, op, 1966, Lens, Louis; flowers salmon-pink suffused brownish, dbl.; very vigorous, dense growth; ['Circus' × Queen Elizabeth®]

'Dixie' HT, op, 1925, Gray, W.R.; flowers salmon-pink, more large, dbl., cupped; [sport of 'Radiance']

'Dixie Belle' HT, lp, 1963, Boerner; bud ovoid, rose-pink; flowers 5-5½ in., 38 petals, cupped, moderate fragrance; foliage leathery; vigorous, upright growth; PP2302; ['Golden Masterpiece' × seedling]; intr. 1963

'Dixie Climber' Cl HT, ob, 1935, Watkins, A.F.; flowers salmon and gold; PP163; [sport of 'Gov. Alfred E. Smith']

Dixie Dazzle™ -- See 'Kindixie'

'Dixie Dream' -- See 'Festival'

'Dixie Holiday' HT, mr, 1968, Garrison; bud long, pointed; flowers medium, dbl., high-centered; foliage bronze, leathery; very vigorous growth; [sport of 'Étoile de Hollande']

'Dixieland' -- See 'Bridixie'

'Dixieland Linda' -- See 'Beadix'

'Dizzy' F, Delforge, H.; intr. 1974

'Dizzy Heights' -- See 'Fryblissful'

'Do-Si-Do' S, mp, 1985, Buck, Dr. Griffith J.; flowers medium lavender-pink, large, cupped, borne 3-10 per cluster, moderate fragrance; repeat bloom; foliage dark olive green, leathery, glossy; prickles awl-like, tan; vigorous, erect, bushy growth; hardy; [('Autumn Dusk' × 'Solitude') × 'Wanderin' Wind']; intr. 1984

'Doamna in Mov' HT, m, Wagner, S.; flowers large, 28 petals, strong fragrance; foliage large, medium green, glossy, healthy; ['Lavendula' × 'Mainzer Fastnacht']; intr. 2003

'Doc' ('Degenhard') Pol, mp, 1958, deRuiter; flowers phlox-pink, small, 15 petals, borne in large trusses; compact growth; ['Robin Hood' × 'polyantha seedling']; intr. 1954

'Docile' F, mp, Eve, A.; buds round; flowers pink with ruffled petals, dbl., borne in clusters of 3-5; growth to 3 ft.; intr. 1995

'Docteur Berthet' B, mr, 1858, Damaizin; flowers shining cherry red with carmine, large, full

'Docteur Brière' B, pb, 1860, Vigneron; flowers cerise pink with yellow stamens, full, cupped, moderate fragrance; intr. 1860

'Docteur F. Debat' -- See 'Doctor F. Debat'

'Docteur Hurta' -- See 'Dr Hurta'

'Docteur Leprestre' ('Docteur Leprêtre') B, dr, 1852, Oger; flowers bright velvety purplish-red, large, full; foliage olive green

'Docteur Leprêtre' -- See 'Docteur Leprestre'

'Docteur Louis Escarras' HT, rb, 1922, Nabonnand, C.; flowers dark salmon-red shaded carmine-pink, 120 petals; ['Constance' × seedling]

'Docteur Marjolin' M, dp, 1860, Robert et Moreau; flowers bright red-pink, 7-9 cm., dbl., very globular

'Docteur Morel' HT, m, 1946, Laperrière; flowers carmine with chrome-yellow reflections, large, 40-45 petals; foliage dark; vigorous, upright growth; ['Edith Nellie Perkins' × 'Pres. Herbert Hoover']

'Docteur Reymont' HMult, w, 1907, Mermet; flowers pure white on pale green base, 3 cm., dbl., borne in medium, pyramidal clusters; numerous prickles; ['Turner's Crimson Rambler' × unknown]

'Docteur Robert Salmont' HT, yb, 1946, Gaujard; bud pointed; flowers capucine and yellow, reverse tinted chrome, base coppery; foliage dark; vigorous growth

'Docteur Valois' HT, rb, 1950, Mallerin, C.; flowers geranium shaded vermilion, reverse yellow, 4 in., semi-dbl.; foliage dark, glossy; vigorous, bushy growth; [('Annie Drevet' × 'Condesa de Sástago') × 'Vive la France']

'Dr A. Hermans' HT, ly, 1906, Verschuren; flowers yellowish-pink, large, very full; ['Rosa Verschuren' × unknown]

'Dr A. I. Petyt' ('Dr Petyt') HT, rb, 1924, Burrell; flowers maroon-crimson shaded scarlet, large, dbl., high-centered; vigorous, bushy growth; [('George Dickson' × unknown) × 'Edward Mawley']

'Dr A. J. Verhage' ('Golden Wave') HT, dy, 1961, Verbeek; flowers large, petals wavy, 22-30 petals, intense fragrance; foliage dark, glossy; vigorous, bushy growth; PP2105; ['Tawny Gold' × (Bacará® × seedling)]; patent issued as Golden Wave; re-registered as Golden Wave, 1968

'Dr A. J. Verhage, Climbing' Cl HT, dy, 1968, Blaby Rose Gardens

'Dr A. S. Thomas' HT, rb, 1951, Clark, A.; bud long, pointed; flowers dark crimson shaded darker, large, 60 petals, high-centered; foliage leathery, dark; vigorous, fairly compact growth

'Dr A. Svehla' HT, rb, 1935, Böhm, J.; flowers dark carmine, very large, dbl.; bushy growth; ['Col. Leclerc' × 'Gen. MacArthur']

'Dr A. von Erlach' HT, pb, 1932, Soupert & Notting; bud nankeen yellow and salmon; flowers pink and straw-yellow, stamens yellow, semi-dbl., cupped; stiff stems; vigorous growth; ['Prince de Bulgarie' × 'Mrs S.K. Rindge']

'Doctor Abrahams' HT, ab, Hallows; intr. 1991

Dr Adam Christman™ -- See 'Wildac'

'Doctor Albert Schweitzer' HT, pb, 1961, Delbard-Chabert; flowers opal-pink, reverse rose-red, well-formed, 5-6 in., 30-35 petals; foliage leathery, glossy; vigorous, upright bushy growth; ['Chic Parisien' × 'Michèle Meilland']

'Dr Andrew Carnegie' HT, pb, 1927, Ferguson, R.C.; flowers light silvery pink, base yellowish; [sport of 'Mrs Henry Morse']; intr. 1930

'Dr Andry' HP, mr, 1864, Verdier, E.; flowers rosy crimson, medium, 45 petals, cupped; foliage glossy; vigorous, upright growth; ['Victor Verdier' × unknown]

'Dr Antonin Joly' HP, op, 1886, Besson; flowers salmon-pink, large, very dbl.; ['Baronne Adolphe de Rothschild' × unknown]

'Dr Arnal' HP, mr, 1848, Roeser

'Dr Auguste Krell' HP, rb, 1877, Verdier, E.; flowers carmine cerise red, shaded purple, whitish reverse, large, full; foliage dark green, finely dentate; prickles numerous, unequal, straight, pink

'Dr Augustin Wibbelt' HT, yb, 1928, Leenders, M.; flowers golden yellow, shaded orange, large, semi-dbl., moderate fragrance; foliage medium size, light green; [sport of 'Los Angeles']

'Dr Augusto de Castro' HT, rb, 1954, Moreira da Silva; flowers bright red, reverse yellow; ['Sultane' × 'Peace']

'Dr B. Benacerraf' -- See 'Milben'

'Dr B. G. Kane' -- See 'Dr Kane'

'Dr B. P. Pal' HT, m, 1981, Division of Vegetable Crops and Floriculture; bud long, pointed; flowers solferino purple, 70 petals, high-centered, borne singly; foliage dark, leathery; prickles straight, brown; upright growth; [seedling × seedling]; intr. 1980

'Dr Baillet' T, m, 1903, Corboeuf; flowers violet with white reflections, striped yellow

'Dr Baillon' HP, dr, 1878, Margottin père; flowers bright crimson, shaded purple, large, full

'Dr Barnardo' F, dr, 1968, Harkness; flowers crimson, large, 30 petals, borne in trusses; upright, bushy growth; ['Vera Dalton' × 'Red Dandy']

'Doctor Behring' -- See 'Dotemibe'

'Dr Belville' Cl HT, ob, 1931, Thomas; flowers orange-crimson, base yellow, open, large, semi-dbl., moderate fragrance; profuse spring bloom, then scattered; very vigorous (12 ft.) growth; ['Barbara' × 'Sunstar']

'Dr Benjamin Pal' HT, mp, IARI; flowers dbl., well formed; intr. 1993

'Dr Berthet' T, mp, 1879, Pernet; flowers bright pink, large, full

'Dr Bharat Ram' HT, ab, IARI; flowers apricot with shades of pink, high-centered; profuse bloom; intr. 2000

'Dr Bob Harvey' -- See 'Winbob'

'Dr Brada's Rosa Druschki' HP, mp, 1934, Brada, Dr.; flowers very large, dbl.

'Dr Branscom' HT, ab, 1947, Danegger; bud pointed; flowers peach-blossom flushed apricot-pink, large, dbl., moderate spicy fragrance; upright growth; [sport of 'Pink Dawn']

'Dr Bretonneau' HP, m, 1858, Trouillard; flowers violet-red, medium, dbl.; ['Géant des Batailles' × unknown]

'Dr Brownell' HT, yb, 1964, Brownell, H.C.; bud long, pointed; flowers buff, center chrome-yellow, 5½ in., 34 petals, high-centered, intense fragrance; foliage glossy, dark; vigorous, upright growth; PP2499; ['Helen Hayes' × 'Peace']; intr. 1964

'Dr Burt' LCl, rb, 1942, Brownell; bud long, pointed; flowers deep red to pink flushed orange, large, 45 petals; non-recurrent; foliage glossy, light; very vigorous, climbing (to 20 ft.), branching growth; ['Coral Creeper' × seedling]

'Dr Carabare' HT, m; flowers purple/pink, large, dbl.

'Dr Carbonaro' HT, pb, 1958, Moreira da Silva; flowers rose, reverse silver; ['Happiness' × 'Grand'mère Jenny']

'Dr Carneiro Pacheco' HT, rb, 1938, Moreira da Silva; flowers carmine, open, large, dbl.; foliage glossy, light; vigorous, bushy growth; ['Mev. G.A. van Rossem' × 'Sir David Davis']

'Dr Cathrall' HT, pb, 1966, Hills; flowers deep pink, reverse lighter, 4½-5 in.; foliage dark, leathery; vigorous growth; [sport of 'Hector Deane']

'Dr Cazeneuve' HT, dr, 1899, Dubreuil; bud deep purple-black; flowers dark velvety crimson, large, dbl.

'Dr Charles T. Beaird' -- See 'Wambeaird'

'Dr D. F. Malan' HT, dr, 1960, Herholdt, J.A.; bud pointed; flowers very dark maroon, large, 45-50 petals; upright growth; ['Happiness' × 'Mirandy']

'Dr Darley' -- See 'Harposter'

'Dr de Chalus' HP, mr, 1871, Touvais; flowers scarlet, center velvety, reverse pink, very large, full

'Dr Debat' -- See 'Doctor F. Debat'

'Doctor Dick' -- See 'Cocbaden'

'Dr Dielthem' HGal, mp, before 1866; flowers bright pink, large, very full

'Doctor Domingo Pereira' Cl T, pb, 1925, de Magalhaes; flowers lilac-rose, center yellow, large, dbl., moderate fragrance

'Doctor Dorothy' F, pb, 1997, Jones, L.J.; flowers medium, 41 petals, borne in small clusters; foliage medium size, medium green, semi-glossy; some prickles; upright, medium (5ft.)growth; ['Jubilee' × 'Little Darling']

'Dr E. M. Mills' S, yb, 1926, Van Fleet; flowers primrose suffused pink, becoming darker, 2-2½ in., semi-dbl., globular; early; foliage small, dark; growth bushy (to 4 ft.); [R. hugonis × 'Radiance']

'Dr Eckener' HRg, pb, 1930, Berger, V.; flowers coppery rose on yellow ground, aging soft pink, large, semi-dbl., cupped; repeat bloom; vigorous (5-6 ft.) growth; ['Golden Emblem' × 'hybrid rugosa']; intr. 1930

'Dr Edvard Benes' HT, rb, 1935, Böhm, J.; flowers red with many white streaks, very large, dbl.; bushy growth; [sport of 'Étoile de France']

'Dr Edward Deacon' HT, ob, 1926, Morse; flowers deep salmon-orange to shrimp-pink, large, dbl., globular; vigorous, bushy growth; ['Mme Edouard Herriot' × 'Gladys Holland']

'Dr Edwin J. Cohn' -- See 'Percohn'

'Dr Eileen O'Neil' F, op, Harkness; growth to 1 m.; intr. 2001

'Doctor Eldon Lyle' Gr, dr, 1968, Mackay; bud pointed; flowers medium, dbl., high-centered, moderate fragrance; foliage soft, bronze; vigorous, compact growth; PP2942; ['President Eisenhower' × 'Suspense']

'Dr Elizabeth Neumann' -- See 'Byrneumann'

'Dr Ernst Mühle' HT, pb, 1928, Mühle; flowers rose-pink, with salmon-white reflex, very large, very dbl.; ['Mme Edmée Metz' × unknown]

'Doctor F. Debat' ('Docteur F. Debat', 'Dr Debat', 'Dr F. Debat', 'La Rosée') HT, pb, 1952, Meilland, F.; bud ovoid, pointed; flowers bright pink tinted coral, 5-6 in., 25-30 petals, high-centered, moderate fragrance; foliage leathery, dark; vigorous, upright growth; PP961; ['Peace' × 'Mrs John Laing']

'Dr F. Débat, Climbing' Cl HT, pb, 1955, Barni, V.; flowers deep pink, lighter at edges, very large

'Dr F. Debat' -- See 'Doctor F. Debat'

'Dr F. G. Chandler' -- See 'Dickson's Red'

'Dr F. L. Skinner' ('Dr Skinner') HSpn, yb, Simonet; flowers amber-yellow-pink, high-centered; growth very tall, almost climbing habit; very hardy; ['Joanna Hill' × R. spinosissima altaica]

'Dr F. Weigand' HT, mr, 1930, Weigand, C.; flowers cherry-red, dbl.; ['Mme Caroline Testout' × 'Hadley']

'Dr Faust' ('Faust') F, yb, 1957, Kordes, R.; flowers golden yellow shaded orange-pink, 2 in., 25 petals, borne in large clusters; foliage dark, glossy; vigorous, bushy growth; ['Masquerade' × 'Golden Scepter']

'Dr Félix Guyon' T, dy, 1901, Mari; flowers dark yellow, center lighter, with shades of orange and apricot, very large, intense fragrance; foliage dark green

'Dr Ferrandiz' HT, ob, Camprubi, C.; flowers deep orange-red; vigorous growth

'Dr Fleming' HT, pb, 1960, Dot, M.; flowers soft pink, flushed crimson, well-formed, 40 petals; vigorous growth; [Queen Elizabeth® × 'Baleares']

'Dr Franco Nogueira' HT, Moreira da Silva, A.

'Dr G. Krüger' HT, dr, 1913, Ulbrich; bud long; flowers carmine and crimson, large, very dbl.; foliage large, dark green; [('Mme Victor Verdier' × ('Mme Caroline Testout' × unknown)) × 'Mme Falcot']

'Dr Gallwey' LCl, w, 1937, Reiter; flowers snow-white, 2 in., single, borne in large clusters; profuse bloom; very vigorous growth

'Dr Gentil' HT, Moreira da Silva, A.

'Dr Georges Leger' HT, mr, 1935, Gebrüder Ketten; flowers blood red, large, dbl., slight fragrance

'Dr Georges Martin' HP, mr, 1908, Vilin; flowers carmine-pink, very large, very dbl.; ['Mme Prosper Laugier' × 'L'Ami E. Daumont']

'Doctor Goldberg' -- See 'Gango'

'Dr Grandvilliers' T, pb, 1893, Perny; bud very long; flowers yellowish-pink with darker pink, medium, dbl., borne in small clusters; prickles numerous, hooked; ['Isabelle Nabonnand' × 'Aureus']

'Doctor Griffith Buck' HT, 1977, Patterson; buds large, globular; flowers , 40-45 petals, high-centered, borne singly and several together in irregular clusters; foliage soft green; growth very vigorous; ['San Francisco' × 'Peace']

'Dr Grill' T, op, 1886, Bonnaire; flowers rose shaded coppery; ['Ophirie' × 'Souv. de Victor Hugo']

'Dr Guarnero' HT, dp, 1958, Moreira da Silva; flowers deep rose, well-formed, large, dbl.; vigorous, bushy growth; ['Happiness' × 'Grand'mère Jenny']

'Dr Guépin' HP, dr, 1872, Moreau & Robert; flowers glowing velvety red, shaded dark violet, large, full, moderate fragrance; ['Duc de Cazes' × unknown]

'Dr Guilherme Pereira da Rosa' HT, mr, 1955, Moreira da Silva; flowers cherry-red, well-formed; moderate growth; ['Charles Mallerin' × 'Lisboa']

'Dr H. E. Rumble' Min, mr, 1982, Hooper, John C.; flowers scarlet red, small, 30 petals, cupped, no fragrance; foliage large, light green; prickles small, brown; vigorous, upright growth; ['Born Free' × Westmont]; intr. 1981

'Dr H. I. Gallagher' HT, yb, 1990, Anderson, Mrs. Etta S.; bud ovoid; flowers yellow with bright pink on petal tips, reverse same, 35-50 petals, high-centered, intense spicy fragrance; foliage medium size, bronze-medium green, semi-glossy heavy, disease-resistant; prickles medium, bronze-green; bushy, medium to tall growth; ['Spellbinder' × 'Irish Gold']; intr. 1989

'Dr Harry Upshall' S, pb, 1993, Fleming, Joyce L.; flowers pink and yellow, center blush, prominent stamens, medium, full, moderate fragrance; non-recurrent; foliage small, medium green, matte; bushy, spreading (2 m.) growth; ['Liverpool Echo' × R. foetida persiana]; intr. 1993

'Dr Heinrich Lumpe' HT, pb, 1928, Berger, V.; flowers light rose-pink, base yellow, large, dbl., high-centered; strong stems; very vigorous, bushy growth; ['Constance' × 'Admiral Ward']

'Dr Helfferich' HT, pb, 1919, Lambert, P.; bud very large, ovoid, rose-orange; flowers rose, center yellowish-orange, edged silvery, very large, dbl., cupped, borne singly or in small clusters, moderate fragrance; foliage medium size, glossy; growth upright; ['Gustav Grunerwald' × 'Mrs Aaron Ward']

'Dr Hénon' HP, w, 1855, Lille

'Dr Henri Neuprez' HWich, ly, 1913, Tanne; flowers canary-yellow to sulfur-white; [R. wichurana × 'Mme Barthelémy Levet']

'Dr Herbert Gray' -- See 'Ausfar'

'Dr Herbert Hawkesworth' HT, dr, 1927, Bees; flowers deep crimson, center almost black

Dr Hermann Schulze-Delitzsch® F, ab, Liebig; flowers creamy yellow to white with darker apricot-orange center, full, low-centered, borne in clusters, moderate fragrance; free-flowering; foliage dark green, glossy; bushy (3-4 ft.) growth; intr. 2000

'Dr Hess von Wichdorf' HT, rb, 1936, Vogel, M.; flowers red, shaded rose-lilac, large, dbl., high-centered; vigorous, bushy growth; [sport of 'Frank W. Dunlop']

'Dr Hoffmann' HT, my, 1904, Welter

'Dr Hogg' HP, dr, 1880, Laxton; flowers deep violet-red, medium, dbl.

'Dr Homi Bhabha' HT, w, 1970, Pal, Dr. B.P.; bud long, pointed; flowers white, center somtimes tinted cream, large, very dbl., high-centered, slight fragrance; foliage leathery; vigorous, upright growth; ['Virgo' × seedling]; intr. 1968

'Dr Homi Bhabha, Climbing' Cl HT, w, 1976, IARI

'Dr Hooker' HP, mr, 1876, Paul, G.; flowers scarlet-carmine, shaded violet, large, full; ['Duke of Edinburgh' × unknown]

'Dr Huas' HT, w, 1903, Corboeuf-Marsault; flowers flesh white, large, full, cupped, moderate fragrance; ['Souv du Président Carnot' × 'Mme Caroline Testout']

'Dr Huey' ('Dr Robert Huey', 'Shafter') HWich, dr, 1914, Thomas; flowers crimson-maroon, anthers light yellow, 2 in., 15 petals, borne in clusters of 3-4; foliage rich green; nearly thornless; ['Ethel' × 'Gruss an Teplitz']; sometimes classed as LCl; intr. 1920

'Dr Hurta' ('Docteur Hurta') HP, m, 1867, Geschwind; flowers purplish pink, large, full, flat

'Dr Ingomar H. Blohm' HP, dr, 1919, Lambert, P.; flowers dark carmine-red, shaded chestnut-brown, large, dbl., intense fragrance

Dr Ingrid™ -- See 'Poulgrena'

'Dr J. Campbell Hall' HT, op, 1905, Dickson, A.; flowers coral pink, white reflections, large, full

'Dr J. G. Fraser' HT, ab, 1926, Easlea; flowers salmon-apricot, suffused vermilion-pink; vigorous growth; ['St. Helena' × 'Muriel Dickson']

'Dr J. H. Nicolas' LCl, mp, 1940, Nicolas; flowers rose-pink, 5 in., 50 petals, globular, borne in clusters of 3-4, moderate fragrance; recurrent bloom; foliage dark, leathery; vigorous, pillar (8 ft.) growth; PP457; ['Charles P. Kilham' × 'Georg Arends']

'Dr Jack Bender' -- See 'Briben'

Doctor Jackson™ -- See 'Ausdoctor'

'Dr Jaime Lopes Dias' HT, mp, 1961, Moreira da Silva; flowers large; ['Confidence' × 'Juno']

'Dr Jamain' HP, mr, 1851, Jamain; flowers bright crimson, fading to pink, full; foliage brownish red when young, glabrous, finely dentate; prickles enlarged at base, very sharp, slightly hooked

'Dr Jo' F, ob; flowers peach apricot, mid-sized., dbl., borne in clusters., moderate fragrance; blooms throughout the season.; well foliaged, lush; growth upright, moderate (3 ft.) grower; intr. 2000

'Dr John Dickman' MinFl, m, Bridges, Dennis; flowers mauve, edged red, reverse mauve, 2 in., dbl., borne mostly solitary; foliage medium size, medium green, semi-glossy; few prickles; growth upright, tall (36 in.); exhibition, cutting, garden; ['Purple Dawn' × unknown]; intr. 2003

'Dr John Snow' HT, w, 1979, Gandy, Douglas L.; flowers creamy white, 5 in., 35 petals, high-centered; foliage light green; tall growth; ['Helen Traubel' × seedling]

'Dr Joseph Drew' HT, yb, 1918, Page; flowers salmon-yellow, suffused pink, large, dbl., moderate fragrance; foliage dark green; ['Mme Mélanie Soupert' × 'Comtesse Icy Hardegg']

'Dr Jules Bouché' -- See 'Mme Jules Bouché'

'Dr Julliard' HP, dr, 1851, Lacharme; flowers garnet purple, shaded carmine, large, full

'Dr K. C. Chan' -- See 'Tinchan'

'Dr Kane' N, my, 1856, Pentland; flowers sulphur yellow, large

'Dr Kane' ('Dr B. G. Kane') HT, mp, Shastri; flowers large, luminous pink, full, high-centered; intr. 1999

'Dr Karel Kramár' HT, dr, 1937, Böhm, J.; flowers large, dbl.

'Dr Kater' Pol, dr, 1925, Struwe; flowers velvety dark red, shaded blackish, small, full; [sport of 'Orléans Rose']

'Dr Kidwai' HT, pb, 1999, Chiplunkar, C. R.; flowers light pink, edges blended magenta, reverse light pink, 3-4 in., full, borne mostly singly; foliage medium size, medium green, semi-glossy; prickles moderate; upright, tall (4-5 ft.) growth; ['Paradise' × ('Paradise' × 'Oklahoma')]; intr. 1998

'Dr Kirk' HT, op, 1940, Mallerin, C.; bud long, pointed; flowers coral, shaded nasturtium-yellow, very large, 35 petals, high-centered; vigorous growth; ['Charles P. Kilham' × R. foetida bicolor hybrid]

'Dr Lande' ('Dr Laude') T, op, 1902, Berger, V.; flowers deep salmon pink, darker in hot weather, large, semi-dbl., moderate fragrance

'Dr Larrey' HP, m, 1866, Moreau & Robert; flowers velvety purple, shaded carmine, medium, full

'Dr Laude' -- See 'Dr Lande'

'Dr Lindley' HP, dp, 1866, Paul, W.; flowers dark carmine, large, full

'Dr Lopez Diaz' HT, Moreira da Silva, A.

'Dr M. Euwe' HT, pb, 1936, Buisman, G. A. H.; bud pointed; flowers salmon, tinted yellow and pink, dbl., intense fragrance; foliage leathery, bronze; bushy growth

'Dr M. S. Randhawa' HT, pb, Pal, Dr. B.P.; flowers large, outside creamy white, inside splashed and edged deep pink, dbl., moderate fragrance; intr. 1989

'Dr Manuel Alves de Castro' HT, rb, Moreira da Silva; flowers red, reverse golden yellow

'Dr Margaretha' F, dr, 1960, Maarse, G.; flowers velvety dark red, medium, dbl., borne in large clusters; vigorous, bushy growth; [('Red Pinocchio' × unknown) × 'Alain']

Dr Margrethe™ -- See 'Poulskov'

'Dr Mark Weston' -- See 'Spowest'

'Dr Martin Luther' S, w, Scholle; buds long, slim; flowers bright white, opening quickly, with golden stamens, dbl., moderate fragrance; recurrent; growth to 5 ft.; intr. 2000

'Dr Marx' ('Marquis d'Ailsa') HP, mr, 1842, Laffay, M.; flowers crimson red, very large, full, cupped; growth erect

'Dr Maximo de Carvalho' HT, dr, 1960, Moreira da Silva; flowers crimson-red; ['Crimson Glory' × 'Charles Mallerin']

'Dr Mazaryk' HP, lp, 1930, Böhm, J.; flowers large, dbl.

'Dr McAlpine' -- See 'Peafirst'

'Dr Mendes Correia' HT, mr, 1938, Moreira da Silva; bud pointed; flowers bright red, very large, dbl.; foliage soft; vigorous, bushy growth; ['Frau Margarete Oppenheim' × 'Hortulanus Budde']

'Dr Mengelberg' F, dr, 1952, Leenders,

M.; flowers deep blood-red, large, semi-dbl.; very vigorous growth

'Dr Merkeley' HSpn, dp, 1924; flowers deep pink, small, dbl., moderate fragrance; non-recurrent; low to medium growth; double pink wild form of *R. pimpinellifolia*; named in honor of Dr. Merkeley, who first grew it in Canada; discovered in eastern Siberia; intr. 1924

'Dr Michael Noble' -- See 'Manmichael'

'Dr Miroslav Tyrs' HP, rb, 1932, Böhm, J.; flowers crimson, shaded darker, very large; [sport of 'Anna de Diesbach']

'Dr Morse' HT, m

'Dr Müller' HFt, op, 1905, Müller, Dr. F.; flowers salmon-pink with touches of red, medium, semi-dbl.

'Dr Müller's Rote' HT, m, 1920, Müller, Dr. F.; flowers purple/pink, medium, dbl., intense fragrance; sometimes classed as HP

'Dr Murphy's Magic Touch' -- See 'Tinmurphy'

'Dr Néran' B, mr, 1856, Bernéde; flowers cherry red

'Dr Nicolas Welter' HT, op, 1912, Soupert & Notting; flowers delicate salmon pink, center darker, very large, dbl., moderate fragrance; ['Mme Mélanie Soupert' × 'Mme Segond Weber']

'Dr Noshir Wadia' HT, rb, 1999, Chiplunkar; flowers bright red, white stripes, reverse light red with stripes, 3-4 in., dbl., borne mostly singly; foliage large, dark green, glossy; numerous prickles; compact, medium (4-5 ft.) growth; [sport of 'Norma']; intr. 1992

'Dr O'Donel Browne' HT, pb, 1908, Dickson, A.; flowers carmine-rose, large, well-formed, dbl.; vigorous growth

'Dr Oliveira Salazar' HT, ob, 1955, Moreira da Silva; flowers salmon and yellow shaded carmine, large, very dbl.; ['Mme Marie Curie' × 'Peace']

'Dr P. G. Purohit' F, pb, Chiplunkar; intr. 2001

'Dr Pasteur' HT, dp, 1887, Moreau-Robert; bud very long, globular; flowers soft rosy crimson, satiny, large, full; foliage dark green

'Dr Paul Menzel' HT, mp, Lucke, G.; flowers carmine-pink, large, dbl.; intr. 1980

'Dr Petyt' -- See 'Dr A. I. Petyt'

'Dr Pouleur' T, rb, 1897, Ketten Bros.; flowers carmine and copper-red, outer petals striped reddish-pink, medium, full, globular, moderate fragrance; growth vigorous; ['Lady Zoë Brougham' × 'Alphonse Karr']

'Dr R. Maag' -- See 'Meirigalu'

'Dr Rafael Duque' HT, rb, 1938, Moreira da Silva; flowers velvety purplish red, large; ['Frau Margarete Oppenheim' × 'Hortulanus Budde']

'Dr Raimont' Pol, mp, 1888, Alégatière; flowers carmine pink, aging to violet pink, darker center, medium, full, moderate fragrance; ['Général Jacquiminot' × unknown]

'Dr Reiner Klimke' F, lp, Noack, Werner; intr. 1988

'Dr Renata Tyrsová' LCl, op, 1937, Böhm, J.; flowers salmon-pink, 4 in., semi-dbl., globular, borne singly or in small clusters, moderate damask fragrance

'Dr Ricaud' Pol, lp, 1907, Corboeuf; flowers salmony flesh on copper ground, large, dbl., borne in large clusters, moderate fragrance; ['White Pet' × unknown]

'Dr Richard Legler' HT, pb; flowers shrimp-pink changing to old-rose and orange, moderate fruity fragrance; moderate growth

'Dr Robert Huey' -- See 'Dr Huey'

'Doctor Robert Korns' ('Aptos') HMsk, ab, Lettunich; flowers small, borne in clusters, no fragrance; recurrent; growth arching, 6 ft; intr. 1996

'Dr Rocques' ('Crimson Globe') B, mp, 1839, Desprez; flowers bright carmine, medium, full, globular

'Dr Rouges' Cl T, rb, 1893, Schwartz; flowers deep coppery-red with orange shading, petals reflexed, 8 cm., dbl., moderate tea fragrance; very remontant

'Dr Ruschpler' ('Duc de Ruschpler') HP, dp, 1856, Ruschpler; flowers silky pink, center brighter, large, full

'Dr S. S. Bhatnagar' F, dr, IARI; intr. 1994

'Dr Scheiner' HT, dr, 1929, Böhm, J.; flowers large, dbl.

'Dr Schnitzler' -- See 'Emin Pascha'

'Dr Scott' (strain of *R. multiflora*), w; foliage mildew-resistant; growth used as understock

'Dr Selma Lagerlof' HRg, mp

'Doctor Sewell' HP, mr, before 1910; flowers crimson, shaded with purple, cupped

'Dr Skinner' -- See 'Dr F. L. Skinner'

'Dr Spitzer' HP, pb, 1862, Geoffre; flowers bright carmine, shaded violet, reverse purple, large, full

'Dr Sybil Johnson' -- See 'Batsybil'

'Dr Tomin' HT, Tagashira, Kazuso; intr. 1990

'Dr Trigo de Negreiros' HT, dr, 1954, Moreira da Silva; bud long, pointed; flowers deep red, large; very vigorous growth; ['Charles Mallerin' × 'Lisboa']

'Dr Troendlin' -- See 'Oberbürgermeister Dr Troendlin'

'Dr Troy Garret' -- See 'Weltroy'

'Dr Valois' HT, 1950, Mallerin, C.

'Dr van de Plassche' Pol, mp, 1968, Buisman, G. A. H.; bud ovoid; flowers pink, medium, semi-dbl.; foliage dark; [Heureux Anniversaire® × Allotria®]

'Dr van Rijn' HT, my, 1952, Leenders, M.; bud ovoid; flowers lemon-yellow, large, dbl., high-centered; foliage light green, glossy; vigorous, bushy growth

'Dr Vazquez' HT, op, 1935, Camprubi, C.; flowers salmon, open, medium, semi-dbl.; foliage glossy; upright growth; ['Duchess of Atholl' × 'Margaret McGredy']

'Dr Vingtrinier' HP, dp, 1863, Fontaine; flowers bright carmine with cherry red, large, full

'Dr W. E. Hadden' HT, rb, 1934, McGredy; flowers raspberry-red, flushed yellow, deepening at base, well-formed; foliage dark; long, strong stems; vigorous growth

'Dr W. Van Fleet' LCl, lp, 1910, Van Fleet; bud pointed; flowers cameo-pink fading flesh-white, 8-10 cm., dbl., moderate fragrance; non-recurrent; foliage dark, glossy; vigorous, climbing (15-20 ft.) growth; [(*R. wichurana* × Safrano) × 'Souv. du Prés. Carnot']

'Dr Wauer' HT, dp, 1902, Brauer; flowers dark carmine, aging lighter, very large, very full, globular

'Dr William Gordon' HP, mp, 1905, Paul, W.; flowers satiny carnation pink, large

'Dr Wolfgang Pöschl' -- See 'Canadian White Star'

'Dr Zamenhof' HWich, rb, 1935, Brada, Dr.; flowers crimson-red, base yellow, 12-14 cm., semi-dbl., loose, borne in small clusters, intense fragrance; very vigorous growth; [*R. wichurana* × seedling]

'Dr Zumel' HT, Kordes, R.

'Doctor's Wife' HT, op, 1967, Von Abrams; bud long, pointed; flowers salmon-pink, large, dbl., high-centered; foliage dark, glossy, leathery; vigorous, upright growth

'Dogflame' ('Heartland Flame') Min, ob, 2007, Dickson, Jack; flowers orange, reverse darker, medium, 1½ in., dbl., borne mostly solitary; foliage medium, dark green, semi-glossy; prickles medium, straight, brown, moderate; growth upright, medium (20-28 in.); [Sun Sprinkles™ × Rainbow's End™]; intr. 2008

'Doglady' ('Heartland Lady') Min, pb, 2000, Dickson, Jack; flowers dbl., borne mostly solitary, slight fragrance; foliage medium size, dark green, semi-glossy; prickles medium, pointed, straight, brown; growth compact, medium (16-20 in.); [seedling × 'Gene Boerner']; intr. 2001

'Dohhawk' (Nighthawk™) Min, mr, 1989, Hardgrove, Donald L.; bud globular, pointed; flowers medium, 22 petals, high-centered, then flat, borne singly and in sprays of 3-5, intense damask fragrance; foliage medium size, medium green; prickles straight, slanted down, medium, reddish-brown; upright, bushy, medium growth; PP7417; ['Quinella' × 'Poker Chip']; intr. 1989

'Doktor Sieber' -- See 'Toniro'

'Dolce Luna' HT, mp, Barni; flowers soft lilac pink, 10 cm., dbl., moderate fragrance; foliage large, medium green; growth erect, 100-120 cm.; ['Mount Shasta' × Rinascimento®]; intr. 2000

Dolce Vita+ HT, w, Voom, Lex; flowers white with fuchsia pink edge, double,

high-centered, borne mostly singly; recurrent; stems long; florist rose
Dolce Vita® -- See 'Deldal'
Dolcezza® S, mp, Barni; flowers dbl.; intr. 1986
'Dollar-Rose' HT, mr, 1936, Tantau, Math.; flowers carmine-red, medium, dbl.
'Dollie B' -- See 'Trobee'
Dolly™ (Springs 75™) F, dp, 1978, Poulsen, Niels D.; flowers 2½-3 in., 20 petals; foliage glossy, dark; bushy growth; [('Nordia' × Queen Elizabeth®) × (seedling × 'Mischief')]; intr. 1975
'Dolly Brownell' F, lp, 1926, Brownell; flowers color same as Dr W van Fleet; ['Dr. W. Van Fleet' × unknown]
'Dolly Darling' HT, mp, 1949, Brownell; bud long, pointed, red; flowers lustrous pink, open, 4-5 in., 20 petals, moderate fragrance; foliage glossy; vigorous, compact growth; PP942; ['Pink Princess' × 'Crimson Glory']
'Dolly Dot' MinFl, dy, J&P; intr. 1998
'Dolly Madison' ('Super-Dupont') HT, dy, 1935, Hillock; flowers golden yellow; vigorous growth; PP326; [(sport of 'Mrs Pierre S. duPont, Climbing' × unknown)]
'Dolly Parton' HT, or, 1985, Winchel, Joseph F.; flowers luminous orange-red, large, 35 petals, borne mostly singly, intense fragrance; foliage large, medium green, semi-glossy; upright growth; PP5608; ['Fragrant Cloud' × 'Oklahoma']; intr. 1984
'Dolly Varden' HRg, ab, 1914, Paul; bud deep yellow; flowers light apricot-pink, base yellow, large, semi-dbl.; recurrent bloom; vigorous growth
'Dolly Varden' Pol, mp, deRuiter; flowers clear pink, dbl.; intr. 1930
'Dolly's Forever Rose' -- See 'Ardolly'
'Dolly's Sister' HT, op, 1989, Taylor, Thomas E.; flowers medium coral-pink; [sport of 'Dolly Parton']; intr. 1989
'Dolly's Sister' Gr, or, Williams, J. Benjamin; flowers large, brilliant orange-red, dbl., high-centered, intense fragrance; intr. 1999
'Dolomiti' HT, ab, 1933, Ingegnoli; bud pointed; flowers flesh, with yellow reflex, very large, dbl.; foliage dark; strong stems; vigorous growth
Dolores™ -- See 'Devine'
Dolores Hope™ -- See 'Wekcrying'
Dolores Marie™ -- See 'Tuckmarie'
'Domaine de Chapuis' S, m, 1901, Roseraie de l'Hay; flowers violet-red; growth tall
Domaine de Charance® HT, mp, Guillot-Massad; flowers clear pink, borne singly and in small clusters; foliage medium green, glossy; growth to 80 cm.; intr. 2005
'Domaine de Courson' ('Gp. Domaine de Courson') LCl, pb, Meilland; flowers pale pink with carmine pink tints, dbl., moderate fragrance; growth vigorous, 8 ft and up; intr. 1995
Domaine de Saint-Jean de Beauregard® S, mp, Delbard; flowers full, pompon, borne in clusters; free-flowering; vigorous (2-3 ft.) growth; intr. 2006
'Dombrowski' -- See 'Dembrowski'
'Dométile Bécar' -- See 'Dometil Beccard'
'Dometil Beccard' ('Dométile Bécar', 'Dometille Baccard', 'Dominic Boccardo') C, pb, before 1853; flowers light pink, striped with white, large, full, cupped, moderate fragrance; possibly synonymous with R. centifolia variegata
'Dometille Baccard' -- See 'Dometil Beccard'
Domila® -- See 'Lapnat'
'Domina' HT, op, 1943, Heizmann, E.; flowers salmon-pink, large, dbl.
'Dominant' HT, op, 1966, Boerner; bud ovoid; flowers salmon-pink, medium, dbl., borne in clusters, slight fragrance; foliage dark; ['Golden Masterpiece' × 'Spartan']; intr. 1964
'Dominator' F, mp, 1961, deRuiter; flowers 3 in., semi-dbl., borne in clusters; vigorous, upright growth; ['New Yorker' × 'The Optimist']
'Domingo' F, dy, Select; intr. 2003
'Dominic Boccardo' -- See 'Dometil Beccard'
'Dominie Sampson' HSpn, lp, before 1848; flowers soft pink, marbled blush, semi-dbl.; very early, non-recurrent; foliage finely divided; dense, shrubby (3-4 ft.) growth; hips glossy, black
'Dominique' Min, lp, 1981, Bennett, Dee; bud ovoid; flowers light peachy pink, 30 petals, high-centered, intense apple fragrance; foliage medium green, arrow-shaped; prickles curved; upright growth; PP5069; [Electron® × 'Little Chief']
'Dominique Daran' HP, m, 1860, Touvais; flowers velvety purple, large, full, cupped
Dominique Loiseau® S, w, Delbard; flowers pure white with golden stamens, moderate fragrance; growth to 2 ft.; intr. 2005
'Domino' -- See 'Tandomo'
'Domino' HT, dr, 1956, Gaujard; bud long, pointed; flowers dark crimson, medium; foliage dark; ['Peace' × seedling]
'Domkapitular Dr Lager' HT, pb, 1903, Lambert, P.; flowers rose and carmine; ['Mme Caroline Testout' × 'Princesse de Bassaraba de Brancovan']
Domstadt Fulda® -- See 'Kortanken'
'Domus Aurea' HT, my, 1940, Aicardi, D.; flowers pure yellow; foliage dark, glossy; strong stems; very vigorous growth; ['Julien Potin' × 'yellow seedling']
'Don Alvarès' ('Don Alvart') B, mp, 1842, Boyau; flowers medium, full
'Don Alvart' -- See 'Don Alvarès'
'Don Bosco' HT, Dorieux, Francois; intr. 1976
'Don Bosco' HT, op, Laperriere, L.; intr. 1989
'Don Bradman' HT, rb, 1938, Wheatcroft Bros.; bud long, shapely; flowers coppery claret, fading to silvery pink, 40-50 petals
Don Cartwright™ ('Donella') F, mr, Jellyman, J. S.; flowers velvety red, medium, dbl, borne in small clusters, slight fragrance; foliage medium size, medium green, semi-glossy; growth upright, compact, medium (2½ ft.); [seedling × ('Tony Jacklin' × 'Andrea')]; intr. 1997
'Don Charlton' HT, pb, 1991, Thompson, Robert; flowers deep rose pink with silver reverse, large, very full, moderate fragrance; foliage large, dark green, glossy; upright growth; ['Silver Jubilee' × (Chicago Peace® × (Doris Tysterman® × unknown))]; intr. 1990
'Don de Guérin' HGal, dp, before 1846; flowers bright rose, sometimes shaded with light purple, large, full
'Don Don' Min, dr, 1977, Williams, Ernest D.; flowers red, reverse blending near white at base, 1-1½ in., 60 petals, moderate fragrance; foliage small, glossy, bronze; upright, bushy growth; [seedling × 'Over the Rainbow']; intr. 1976
'Don José' HT, op, 1922, Clark, A.; flowers salmon-pink, semi-dbl.; ['Archiduc Joseph' × seedling]
'Don Juan' LCl, dr, 1958, Malandrone; bud ovoid; flowers velvety crimson red, 5 in., 30-35 petals, cupped, intense fragrance; recurrent bloom; foliage dark green, glossy, leathery; growth climbing, 12-14 ft; PP1864; [('New Dawn' × unknown) × 'New Yorker']
'Don Marshall' -- See 'Morblack'
'Don Pedro' D, lp, before 1811; flowers delicate blush white-pink, 3 in., dbl., moderate fragrance; foliage elongate, pale green, glaucous; sometimes classed as M
'Don Quichotte' ('Don Quixote') F, rb, 1970, Robichon; flowers cherry-red, base yellow, well-formed, large, dbl., borne in clusters, slight fragrance; foliage glossy, leathery; vigorous, upright growth; ['Charles Gregory' × 'Marcelle Auclair']; intr. 1964
'Don Quixote' -- See 'Don Quichotte'
'Don Rose' HT, pb, 1943, Mallerin, C.; bud long, pointed, carmine-red; flowers coppery pink, open, large, 40 petals, cupped; foliage leathery, bluish green; vigorous, upright, bushy, rather compact growth; ['Soeur Thérèse' × seedling]
'Don Vogt' F, w, 2004, Vogt, Don; flowers small, semi-dbl., borne mostly solitary, slight fragrance; foliage medium size, medium green, matte; prickles small, hooked, none; growth bushy, medium; exhibition, garden decoration; [Blueberry Hill™ × unknown]; intr. 2004
'Doña Clara' HT, m, 1965, Camprubi, C.; bud ovoid; flowers purplish pink, large, 50 petals, high-centered, vigorous growth
'Dona Isaura Alexandrina' HP, 1891, Alexandrino, Domingos
'Doña Maria' ('Donna Maria') HSem, w, 1828, Vibert; flowers white, tinted pink

to medium, 5-6 cm., semi-dbl., flat to cupped, borne in small clusters, moderate musk fragrance; foliage pale green; possibly synonymous with 'Princesse Marie'

'Doña Sol' HGal, w, about 1830, Vibert; probably extinct; not the same as the HGal of the same name, Vibert, 1842

'Doña Sol' HGal, rb, Vibert; flowers currant red, spotted lighter pink or white, medium, very dbl.; supercedes an earlier (Vibert; 1830) white cultivar of the same name; intr. 1842

'Donald Davis' -- See 'Chewbeaut'

'Donald Macdonald' HT, ob, 1916, Dickson, A.; flowers orange-carmine, semi-dbl., borne in clusters; dwarf growth

'Donald Prior' F, mr, 1938, Prior; bud ovoid; flowers bright scarlet flushed crimson, 3 in., 11 petals, cupped, borne in large clusters, moderate fragrance; foliage leathery, dark; vigorous, bushy growth; PP377; [seedling × 'D.T. Poulsen']

'Donald Prior, Climbing' Cl F, mr, Farr

'Donald Thomas Heald' -- See 'Kirsmile'

'Donaldo' HT, rb, 1980, Murray, Nola; bud ovoid; flowers red to pink, shapely, 4 in., 35 petals; foliage large, glossy, dark; tall growth; ['Honey Favorite' × Rose Gaujard®]

'Donatella' -- See 'Granada'

'Donau' ('Donau!') HWich, m, 1913, Praskac; flowers purple-violet, fading to steely blue, 5 cm., semi-dbl., borne in clusters of 20-30, moderate lily-of-the-valley fragrance; foliage large; few prickles; ['Erinnerung an Brod' × R. wichurana rubra]

'Donau!' -- See 'Donau'

Donauprinzessin® F, mp, Noack, Werner; intr. 1994

'Donauwalzer' -- See 'Hartwiz'

'Donauwelle' S, m, Weihrauch; low, spreading growth; intr. 1991

'Doncasterii' (R. doncasterii, R. macrophylla doncasterii) HMoy, dp, 1930, Hurst, C.C.; flowers bright deep pink to light red, 2 in., single; foliage purplish-green; stems plum colored; arching growth (to 6 ft.); hips flagon-shaped, large, red; possibly R. moyesii × R. macrophylla; intr. about 1930

'Donella' -- See 'Don Cartwright'

'Donna Clara' HT, pb, Leenders, M.; flowers buff, reverse strawberry-pink

'Donna Darlin'' -- See 'Windonna'

'Donna Fanny Cavalieri' HT, 1953, San Remo Exp. Sta.

'Donna Faye' Min, lp, 1976, Schwartz, Ernest W.; bud pointed; flowers 1 in., 27 petals, high-centered, moderate fragrance; upright growth; ['Ma Perkins' × 'Baby Betsy McCall']

'Donna Jean' -- See 'Taldon'

'Donna Kordana' Min, dr, Kordes; flowers wine red, full, borne singly and in small clusters; recurrent; compact growth; containers

Donna Marella Agnelli® -- See 'Bardon'

'Donna Margaret' -- See 'Hordonna'

'Donna Maria' -- See 'Donna Marie'

'Donna Maria' -- See 'Doña Maria'

'Donna Marie' ('Donna Maria') HSem, w, 1830, Vibert; flowers pure white, small, very dbl.

'Donna Rose' -- See 'Webgold'

'Donna Silva Carmine' F, dp, Cazzaniga, F. G.; intr. 1974

'Donna's Rambler' w, Scarman; intr. 2001

Donnaway™ -- See 'Poulpah026(N)'

'Donnaway Hit' (Donnaway™) MinFl, ab, Poulsen; flowers apricot blend, 5-8 cm., dbl., slight fragrance; foliage dark; growth bushy, 20-40 cm.; intr. 2004

'Dony Robin' F, op, 1959, Meilland, F.; bud pointed; flowers salmon-pink, open, medium, dbl., borne in clusters, slight fragrance; foliage leathery; vigorous, compact growth; ['Goldilocks' × 'Fashion']; intr. 1958

'Doorenbos Selection' HSpn, dr, Doorenbos; flowers rose-purple, yellow stamens, single; small, fine foliage; growth short, dense

'Dooryard Delight' HT, pb, 1940, Horvath; bud short, pointed, spiraled; flowers light pink, reverse rose-pink, petals sharply pointed, 2½ in., dbl.; recurrent bloom; foliage leathery; vigorous, bushy growth; [R. setigera × 'Lady Alice Stanley']

'Dopey' ('Eberwein') Pol, mr, 1958, deRuiter; flowers crimson-red, small, semi-dbl., borne in trusses; compact growth; ['Robin Hood' × 'polyantha seedling']; intr. 1954

'Dora' HT, or, Gaujard; bud long; flowers brilliant orange-red, dbl.; foliage bronze; [Tanagra® × 'Rubens']; intr. 1975

'Dora' HMult, 1887, Geschwind

'Dora' HT, op, Paul, W.; flowers silvery peach pink, very large, full; intr. 1906

'Dora Delle' -- See 'Taldor'

'Dora Hansen' HT, mp, 1908, Jacobs; bud long, pointed; flowers thulite-pink, open, large, dbl.; ['Mme Caroline Testout' × 'Mme Jules Grolez']

'Dora Stober' HT, w, 1925, Leenders, M.; flowers white shaded yellow, dbl.

'Dorabella' ('Barmast') HT, Barni, V.; intr. 1986

'Dorache' -- See 'Adrien Mercer'

'Dorada' -- See 'Bardord'

'Doralp' ('Giscard d'Estaing', Anne Aymone®) F, w, Dorieuxsingle; intr. 1993

'Doralta' HT, Dorieux, Francois; intr. 1979

'Dorance' S, pb, Dorieux; intr. 2001

'Dorandi' -- See 'Korlette'

'Dorapri' HT, ob, Dorieux; intr. 1988

'Dorastri' ('Hugues Aufray') S, pb, Dorieux; intr. 1996

'Doravig' HT, dr, Dorieux; intr. 2005

'Dorbandina' Gr, w, Dorieux; intr. 2005

'Dorbest' S, lp, Dorieux; intr. 2007

'Dorbin' -- See 'Jericho'

'Dorblan' HT, w, Dorieux; intr. 2000

'Dorcafe' HT, ob, Dorieux; intr. 2000

'Dorcas' HWich, pb, 1922, English; flowers deep rose-pink to coral-pink, base yellow, 3 cm., dbl., borne in large clusters; foliage small, semi-glossy; vigorous growth

'Dorcas' S, pb, 1985, Buck, Dr. Griffith J.; bud ovoid, pointed; flowers light pink, pale yellow blend, flecked deeper pink, 40 petals, cupped, slight fragrance; repeat bloom; foliage dark, leathery; prickles awl-like, tan; erect, bushy growth; hardy; ['Minigold' × 'Freckle Face']; intr. 1984

'Dorcast' F, dy, Dorieux; intr. 1996

'Dorcroix' HT, ab, Dorieux; intr. 1995

'Dordeli' HT, pb, Dorieux; intr. 1987

'Dordie's Rose' -- See 'Worclim'

'Dorecou' HT, op, Dorieuxdouble; intr. 2007

'Doreen' HT, ob, 1951, Robinson, H.; flowers deep golden orange flushed scarlet, well-formed; foliage dark; vigorous growth; ['Lydia' × 'McGredy's Sunset']

'Doreen Farrow' -- See 'Evefury'

'Doreen Johnson' HT, lp, 1977, Dawson, George; bud long, pointed; flowers pale pink, dbl.; foliage large, light; vigorous, bushy growth; [('Great Venture' × 'Fort Vancouver') × 'Memoriam']

'Doreen Thorn' HT, pb, 1934, Cant, F.; flowers deep pink, base yellow, well-shaped, large, dbl.; vigorous growth

'Doreen Wells' F, or, 1970, Watkins Roses; flowers orange-scarlet, 3 in., 25 petals, flat; foliage glossy, dark; low, bushy growth; ['Soraya' × 'Circus']

'Dorepin' LCl, rb, Dorieux; intr. 2005

'Dorfaut' HT, ab, Dorieux; intr. 1996

'Dorflo' (Bibiché®) F, ob, Dorieux, Francois; intr. 1974

'Dorfrag' HT, m, Dorieux; intr. 2005

'Dorfram' HT, ab, Dorieux; intr. 1999

'Dorfree' HT, ob, Dorieux; intr. 2001

'Dorfuri' ('Roseraie de Blois') HT, mr, Dorieux; intr. 1991

'Dorgold' F, dy, Dorieux; intr. 1982

'Dorgran' HT, ab, Dorieux; intr. 1998

'Doriang' HT, dy, Dorieux; intr. 2002

'Doric' F, yb, 1963, LeGrice; flowers golden salmon, large, 40 petals, borne in well-spaced clusters; foliage glossy; vigorous, compact growth; ['Masquerade' × 'Korona']

'Dorienne' HT, mr, 1958, Buyl Frères; bud short; flowers large, 34 petals, cupped; bushy, spreading growth; ['Mrs Nieminen' × seedling]

'Dorient' ('Derby-Hagen Gmelin Rose', 'Melodie Parfumée', Melody Parfumée™, Violette Parfumee®, 'Zulu Royal') Gr, m, 1998, Dorieux, Francois; bud long, pointed ovoid; flowers dark lavender-plum, lighter reverse, 4½ in., 25-30 petals, high-centered, borne in large clusters, intense damask fragrance; recurrent; foliage medium size, dark green, semi-glossy; prickles moderate, straight; stems strong, 14 - 18 in; bushy, upright, 5 ft. growth; PP11014; [Dioressence® × 'Stephens' Big Purple']; intr. 1995

'Dorientsar' ('Violette Parfumee, Climbing', Grimpant Violette Parfumee®) Cl HT, m, Dorieux; intr. 2004
'Dorille' ('Janita Claassen') HT, rb, Dorieux; intr. 2001
'Dorina Neave' HT, pb, 1926, Pemberton; flowers silvery pink, large, dbl., globular; stiff stems; compact growth
'Dorinda' S, pb, Peden, R.; intr. 1998
'Doris' HT, rb, 1939, Spandikow; flowers cerise striped white; PP167; [sport of 'Briarcliff']
'Doris Ann' Min, dr, 1987, Wambach, Alex A.; flowers small, full; foliage small, medium green, matte; [Black Jade™ × 'Tiki']
'Doris Archer' F, rb, 1962; flowers yellow, bronze and red, well-formed, 4 in., 30-35 petals, borne in clusters, moderate fragrance; foliage glossy; vigorous, compact growth; ['Circus' × seedling]; intr. 1962
'Doris Bennett' -- See 'Morben'
'Doris Dickson' HT, ob, 1924, Dickson, S.; flowers orange-cream, veined cherry-red; foliage very dark; stiff, wiry stems; vigorous growth
'Doris Dowman' -- See 'Horsilkarl'
'Doris Downes' LCl, pb, 1932, Clark, A.; flowers pink, aging to pale crimson very large, 11-15 cm., semi-dbl., cupped, intense fragrance; early; nearly thornless; climbing growth; hybrid gigantea
'Doris Findlater' HT, ab, 1936, Dickson, A.; flowers light apricot, reverse flushed reddish-salmon and carmine, dbl.; vigorous growth
'Doris Grace Robinson' HT, w, 1943, Bees; bud pointed; flowers creamy white, well-shaped, large; foliage olive-green; vigorous, upright growth
'Doris Howard' F, mr, 1957, Wheatcroft Bros.; flowers blood-red, borne in large clusters; vigorous, bushy growth
'Doris J. Robertson' HT, lp; flowers whitish-pink, large, dbl.
'Doris Lee' Min, ab, Wells; flowers white with apricot to pink edges, reverse light apricot to white, double, high-centered, borne mostly singly; recurrent; foliage dark green; compact (24 - 36 inches) growth; intr. 2008
'Doris Morgan' -- See 'Brimorgan'
'Doris Norman' F, or, 1959, Norman; flowers bright orange, to open, 2 in., 30 petals, high-centered, borne in small clusters; foliage purplish to dull green; vigorous, bushy growth; ['Paul's Scarlet Climber' × 'Mary']; intr. 1958
'Doris Osborne' HT, mr, 1937, Clark, A.; bud pointed; flowers ruby-cerise, semi-dbl.; bushy growth; ['Mme Abel Chatenay' × seedling]
'Doris Page' HSpn, ly, Page, Doris; flowers creamy yellow, small, single, flat; foliage serrated, fern-like; growth to 3 ft.; intr. 2005
'Doris Pleasance' HT, w, 1979, Brewer; flowers blush-pink to white; [sport of 'Queen Elizabeth']
'Doris Read' -- See 'Kenedel'
'Doris Reese' -- See 'Resgold'
'Doris Ryker' -- See 'Dorus Rijkers'
'Doris Stanbridge' -- See 'Worcabbage'
'Doris Trayler' HT, yb, 1924, McGredy; bud pointed, orange; flowers yellow, reverse flushed crimson and orange, large, dbl., high-centered; foliage light green, leathery, glossy; bushy, dwarf, compact growth
Doris Tysterman® HT, ob, 1976, Tysterman; flowers tangerine and gold, 4-5 in., 28 petals, slight fragrance; foliage glossy; upright growth; [Peer Gynt® × seedling]; intr. 1975
'Doriste' F, w, Dorieux; intr. 1986
'Dorjaor' HT, yb, Dorieux; bud long, pointed; intr. 2004
'Dorjape' HT, yb, Dorieux; intr. 2005
'Dorjure' ('Julien Renouard', 'Portland Rose Festival') HT, rb, 1992, Dorieux, Francois; bud large, ovoid; flowers strawberry red, white reverse, 5 in., 40 petals, high-centered, borne singly, moderate spicy fragrance; foliage large, dark green, glossy; prickles numerous, scattered, slighty recurved; growth tall (5 ft.), upright; PP8278; ['Osiria' × 'Pharaon']; intr. 1992
'Dorkade' HT, dr, Dorieux; intr. 1996
'Dorlain' HT, w, Dorieux; intr. 1996
'Dorlibla' HT, w, Dorieux; intr. 2006
'Dorlina' ('Provence') HT, w, Dorieux; intr. 1996
'Dorma' (Majesté®) HT, op, 1970, Dorieux; bud oval; flowers salmon, large, dbl., moderate fragrance; foliage glossy, leathery; very vigorous, upright growth; ['Radar' × 'Eclipse']; intr. 1966
'Dormagi' HT, rb, Dorieux; intr. 1992
'Dormal' (Rouge Dorieux®) HT, mr, 1970, Dorieux; bud pointed; flowers cherry-red, open, over large, dbl.; foliage dark, glossy, leathery; vigorous, upright growth; [seedling × 'Ena Harkness']; intr. 1967
'Dormelo' HT, rb, Dorieux; intr. 2004
'Dormima' ('Mimie Mathy') F, ab, Dorieux; bud rosy white; intr. 1999
'Dormodesar' (Grimpant Cap Horn®) Cl Gr, or, Dorieux; intr. 2005
'Dornapa' (Flushing Meadow®) HT, rb, Dorieux; intr. 1988
'Dorneye' F, ob, Dorieux; intr. 1995
'Dornice' ('Orange d'Éte') F, rb, Dorieux; intr. 1997
'Dornonde' Gr, or, Dorieux; intr. 2000
'Dornröschen' ('Sleeping Beauty') S, pb, 1960, Kordes, R.; bud well-shaped; flowers salmon to deep pink, reverse yellow, large, dbl., borne in clusters; recurrent bloom; upright, well-branched growth; ['Pike's Peak' × 'Ballet']
Dornröschenschloss Sababurg® -- See 'Kortensei'
'Dorobla' ('Kempton Park') F, rb, Dorieux; intr. 1999
Dorola® -- See 'Macshana'
Dorothe® -- See 'Legga'
Dorothea Furrer® HT, dr
'Dorothea Howard' HT, pb, 1985, Barclay, Hilary M.; flowers light pink, deeper pink reverse, well-formed, large, 30 petals, borne singly, moderate tea fragrance; foliage medium green, glossy; many hooked, brown prickles; ['First Prize' × 'Roundelay']; intr. 1978
'Dorothee Heidorn' Bslt, mp; flowers small, borne in large clusters; recurrent in late summer; growth to 8-12 ft.; reintroduced in 1995
'Dorothy' HT, lp, 1905, Dickson; flowers flesh pink, large, full; ['Mme Caroline Testout' × unknown]
'Dorothy, Climbing' Cl HT, pb, 1935, Bostick; [sport of 'Dorothy Page-Roberts']
'Dorothy' LCl, or; flowers smoky Mandarin orange, large, single; intr. 1997
'Dorothy' -- See 'Cocrocket'
'Dorothy A. Golik' HT, ob, 1976, Golik; bud ovoid; flowers orange to flaming red, 4 in., 35 petals, high-pointed, moderate spicy fragrance; foliage glossy; moderate growth; ['Tropicana' × 'Peace']; intr. 1973
'Dorothy Anderson' HT, lp, 1949, McGredy; flowers large, 33 petals, high-centered; free growth; ['Sam McGredy' × 'George Dickson']
'Dorothy Anne' HT, pb, 1985, Winchel, Joseph F.; flowers white blending to deep pink at edges, large, 35 petals, no fragrance; foliage medium size, dark, semi-glossy; upright growth; PP6100; ['First Prize' × 'Lady X']
'Dorothy Broster' HT, mp, 1978, Ellick; flowers azalea-pink, 5 in., 45 petals, foliage dark; very vigorous growth; [Blue Moon® × 'Karl Herbst']
'Dorothy Dennison' HWich, lp, 1909, Dennison; flowers pale salmon pink, small, full, borne in large clusters; foliage light green, glossy; [sport of 'Dorothy Perkins']
'Dorothy Dix' Pol, mp, 1923, Hicks; flowers rose-pink, borne in clusters
'Dorothy Donnelly' HT, mr, 1997, Poole, Lionel; flowers large, very dbl., borne mostly singly; foliage medium size, dark green, semi-glossy; upright, bushy, medium growth; ['Adrienne Berman' × ('Royal William' × 'Gabi')]
'Dorothy Douglas' HT, rb, 1924, Dobbie; flowers vivid cerise-pink
'Dorothy Drowne' HWich, pb, 1924, Brownell; flowers white to pink, center crimson and scarlet; ['Sodenia' × unknown]
'Dorothy Fowler' HRg, mp, 1938, Skinner; flowers clear pink, well-formed, 3-3½ in., semi-dbl.; non-recurrent; growth to 3 ft.; [R. rugosa × (R. acicularis × R. spinosissima)]
'Dorothy Goodwin' ('Perfect Peace') HT, yb, 1954, Goodwin; flowers yellow tipped cerise-pink, well-formed, 4 in., 32 petals; foliage dark holly-green; vigorous growth; [sport of 'Peace']
'Dorothy Grace' Cl Min, pb, 1986, Dobbs, Annette E.; flowers yellow with pink petal

edges, small, 25 petals, high-centered, borne in sprays of 3-5, no fragrance; foliage small, medium green, semi-glossy; prickles very few, brown, hooked downward; upright, climbing (to 6 ft.) growth; ['Little Darling' × sport of 'Rise 'n' Shine']

'Dorothy Hilda Wood' -- See 'Rawood'

'Dorothy Hodgson' HT, ob, 1930, Cant, F.; flowers orange-cerise, veined darker, well-formed, large; vigorous growth

'Dorothy Howarth' Pol, op, 1921, Bees; flowers coral-pink, tinted salmon, open, dbl., borne in clusters; foliage dark; bushy growth; ['Léonie Lamesch' × 'Annchen Müller']

'Dorothy James' HT, pb, 1939, C-P; flowers peach-pink reverse deep rose; [sport of 'Golden Dawn']

'Dorothy Jeavons' HMult, w, 1912, Bakers; flowers white, lightly shaded yellow; [sport of 'Blush Rambler']

'Dorothy King' HT, rb, 1924, King; flowers scarlet-crimson and maroon, semi-dbl.

'Dorothy Lee' HT, pb, 1929, Morse; flowers silvery shell-pink, base golden yellow, dbl.

'Dorothy Lewis' -- See 'Everedruf'

'Dorothy Lloyd' -- See 'Sherigrey'

'Dorothy Marie' HT, dp, 1935, Scittine; [sport of 'Talisman']

'Dorothy May Cooper' Min, w, 1976, Ellick; flowers pure white, 1-2 in., 25-30 petals; foliage dark; very vigorous growth; [Roulettii × 'Memoriam']

'Dorothy McGredy' HT, rb, 1936, McGredy; flowers deep vermilion, base and reverse yellow, well-shaped; foliage cedar-green; strong stems; vigorous growth

'Dorothy Mollison' HT, dr, 1930, Clark, A.; flowers dark crimson; ['Mrs R.C. Bell' × seedling]

'Dorothy Page-Roberts' HT, pb, 1907, Dickson, A.; flowers coppery pink, suffused yellow, open, very large, dbl.; vigorous growth

'Dorothy Peach' HT, yb, 1957, Robinson, H.; flowers deep yellow flushed pink, 5 in., 37 petals, high-centered, moderate fragrance; foliage dark, glossy; vigorous growth; ['Lydia' × 'Peace']

'Dorothy Peach, Climbing' Cl HT, yb, 1963, Watkins Roses

'Dorothy Perkins' HWich, lp, 1901, Miller; flowers bright carminy pink, lighter reverse, 4-5 cm., dbl., rosette, borne in large clusters, moderate fragrance; foliage small, dark, glossy; very vigorous (10-20 ft.) growth; [R. wichurana × 'Mme Gabriel Luizet']

'Dorothy Ratcliffe' HT, rb, 1910, McGredy; flowers coral-red shaded fawn-yellow; vigorous growth

'Dorothy Rose' -- See 'Jondorose'

'Dorothy Superior' -- See 'Super Dorothy'

'Dorothy Vietor Munger' Gr, op, 2001, Burks, Larry; flowers coral, coral to salmon reverse, 4½ in., full, borne mostly solitary, moderate fragrance; foliage medium size, medium green, semi-glossy; prickles moderate; growth upright, medium; garden decorative; [('Camelot' × unknown) × ('Tropical Paradise' × unknown)]; intr. 2002

'Dorothy Virginia' -- See 'Judvirg'

'Dorothy Wheatcroft' F, mr, 1962, Tantau, Math.; flowers oriental red shaded darker, large, 18 petals, borne in clusters of 13, slight fragrance; foliage bright green; vigorous, bushy growth; intr. 1961

'Dorothy Whitney Wood' HT, op, Fryer, Gareth; intr. 1992

'Dorothy Wilson' F, ob, Beales, Peter; flowers vermilion orange, highlighted with yellow, dbl.; foliage mid-green, healthy; growth tidy and bushy, 2½ ft; intr. 1995

'Dorothy's Gem' S, ab, 2000, Harris, Dorothy; flowers peach, pink and yellow, reverse peach, pink, and white, medium, full, borne in small clusters, moderate fragrance; foliage medium size, medium green, semi-glossy; growth climbing, spreading, tall; [sport of 'Leverkusen']; intr. 1998

'Dorothy's Regal Red' HT, mr, 1984, Jerabek, Paul E.; flowers large, 58 petals, borne in small clusters, intense fragrance; foliage medium dark, glossy; bushy growth

'Dorotka Darling' Min, pb, 1991, Sudol, Julia; flowers pink and cream blend, medium, full, well-formed, borne mostly singly, sometimes in small clusters, slight fragrance; foliage medium size, dark green, semi-glossy, clean and abundant; some prickles; tall (60-80 cm.), upright growth; ['Orange Darling' × unknown]

'Dorouvi' ('Perle du Lac Annecy', 'Perle du Lac') HT, dr, Dorieux; intr. 1992

'Doroxan' HT, ab, Dorieux; intr. 2005

'Dorparf' HT, dp, Dorieux; intr. 2005

'Dorpark' F, rb, Dorieux; intr. 1996

'Korpimp' S, yb, Dorieux; intr. 2007

'Dorpure' HT, ob, Dorieux; intr. 2007

'Dorpurp' (Parc des Princes®) HT, rb, Dorieux; intr. 1990

'Dorris Lee' -- See 'Wellee'

'Dorrit' F, ob, 1970, Sonderhousen; flowers orange-yellow, full, flat, borne in trusses

'Dorroug' S, mr, Dorieux; intr. 2004

'Dorsafr' (Open d'Australie®) HT, yb, Dorieux; intr. 1990

'Dorsand' ('Gaby Morlay') HT, ab, Dorieux; intr. 1994

'Dorsarf' HT, ab, Dorieux; intr. 1998

'D'Orsay Rose' ('Rose d'Orsay') Misc OGR, dp; bud deep pink; long sepals; flowers deep pink, outer petals fading to pale pink receptacle wide, dbl.; summer bloom; foliage leaflets 5-7, leaden green; prickles paired below each leaf; erect growth to 5 ft.

'Dorsexy' F, rb, Dorieux; intr. 2006

'Dorshan' HT, pb, Dorieux; intr. 2000

'Dorsland' -- See 'Meilider'

'Dorster' ('Ressins Etienne Gautier') HT, pb, Dorieux; intr. 1996

'Dortan' F, ab, Dorieux; intr. 1994

'Dortem' ('Tentation') HT, op, 1970, Dorieux; bud pointed; flowers carmine-pink to orange, large, dbl.; foliage glossy; vigorous, upright growth; ['Touggout' × 'Flaminaire']

'Dortiche' ('Marguerite d'Autricho') HT, dr, Dorieux

'Dortive' HT, pb, Dorieux; intr. 1991

Dortmund® HKor, mr, 1955, Kordes' Sohne, W.; bud long, pointed; flowers red, white eye, 11-12 cm., single, open, borne in large clusters, moderate fragrance; recurrent bloom; foliage dark, very glossy; vigorous, climbing growth; hips numerous, orange; [seedling × R. × kordesii]

'Dortmunder Kaiserhain' S, lp, Noack, Werner; flowers medium-large, dbl.; intr. 1995

'Dorto' HT, op, Dorieux; intr. 1974

'Dortomy' Pol, rb, Dorieux; intr. 1992

'Dorus Rijkers' ('Doris Ryker') Pol, op, 1942, Leenders, M.; flowers salmon-pink, dbl., borne in clusters, moderate fragrance; recurrent bloom; foliage light green; vigorous, upright growth

'Dorval' HT, mp, Dorieux; intr. 2006

'Dorvand' F, m, Dorieux; intr. 2007

'Dorvengold' HT, yb, Dorieux; intr. 2000

'Dorvengoldsar' (Grimpant Vendée Globe®) Cl HT, yb, Dorieux; intr. 2005

'Dorvizo' ('Rina Hugo') HT, dp, Dorieux; intr. 1993

'Dorwest' ('Ellen Hamlyn') S, dy, Dorieux

'Doryeco' ('D. D. Ruaux') HT, ob, Dorieux; intr. 1998

'Dospearl' ('Our Coral Pearl') Min, op, 1991, Osburn, Dr. William; flowers coral-salmon-pink, petals quill, large, full, borne mostly singly; foliage medium size, medium green, semi-glossy; prickles few, tan, straight and sharp; medium growth; [sport of 'Minnie Pearl']

'Dot Com' -- See 'Moedotcom'

'Dotcris' Pol, Dot, Simon; intr. 1971

'Dotemibe' ('Doctor Behring') HT, m, 1979, Dot, Simon; bud pointed; flowers red-purple, 4 in., 35 petals, cupped, moderate fragrance; foliage dark; tall, upright growth; ['Amanecer' × 'Tanya']

'Dotflo' F, op, Dot

'Dothan' HT, mp, 1984, Perry, Astor; flowers large, 35 petals, high-centered, slight fragrance; foliage large, medium green, matte; upright growth; ['Koppies' × 'King of Hearts']; intr. 1984

'Dotrames' ('Maria Teresa de Esteban', 'Mme Teresa Estaban') HT, or, 1983, Dot, Simon

'Dotraner' HT, rb, Dot; intr. 1969

'Dotsubebe' ('Galaty') HT, or, 1979, Dot, Simon; flowers 4 in., 32 petals, cupped, intense fragrance; foliage dark; ['Tropicana' × 'Lola Montes']; intr. 1977

'Dotsurodo' ('Simon Dot') HT, or, 1979, Dot, Simon; flowers orange-red, lighter reverse, 5 in., 35 petals, cupped, intense fragrance; foliage dark, upright growth; [Pharaoh® × 'Rose Dot']; intr. 1978

'Dotty' HT, dy, 1931, Towill; flowers bronze-yellow, large, semi-dbl., globular; foliage glossy; long stems; very vigorous growth; ['Souv. de Claudius Pernet' × (*R. foetida bicolor* × unknown)]

'Dotty Bass' HT, dr, 1970, Bass; bud long, pointed; flowers medium, dbl.; foliage dark, leathery; vigorous, upright growth; intr. 1968

'Dotty Louise' S, dr, Rupert; buds slender; flowers satiny dark reddish-purple, borne in clusters of 3, moderate fragrance; recurrent; new growth thornless, at base of older canes; growth to 5 ft.; intr. 2001

'Double' -- See 'Plena'

'Double Blanche' -- See 'Double White Burnet'

'Double Blanche' -- See 'Pompon Blanc'

'Double Blush' -- See 'Victoria'

'Double Blush Burnet' HSpn, pb, before 1821; flowers center blush, fading at edges, reverse white, medium, full; possibly the same as 'Double Carnée', or *R. pinpinellifolia rubra* (Redouté)

'Double Brique' HGal, pb, before 1842; flowers rosy pink, shading silver toward outside, dbl.

'Double Bubble' Min, mp, Zary; PP10929; intr. 1997

'Double Carlos Red' S, dr, Erskine; hybrid acicularis

'Double Carnée' ('Carnea Double', 'Carnée Double', 'Incarnata') HSpn, w, before 1826, Prévost; sepals glabrous; flowers flesh, small, dbl.; numerous prickles; possibly the same as 'Double Blush Burnet'

'Double Cherokee' -- See 'Fortuniana'

'Double Cream' HG, w, 2006, Brichet, Helga; flowers large, full, borne mostly solitary; foliage large, medium green, glossy; prickles moderate; growth rampant, tall; [*R. gigantea* × unknown]; intr. 2006

'Double Dark Marbled' ('Petite Red Scotch') HSpn, rb, Brown; flowers red mottled purple, small, semi-dbl.; early; possibly the same as 'Double Purple'

'Double Date' -- See 'Lavflush'

Double Delight™® HT, rb, 1976, Swim, H.C. & Ellis, A.E.; bud long, pointed to urn-shaped; flowers creamy white becoming strawberry-red, 5½ in., 30-35 petals, high-centered, borne mostly singly, intense spicy fragrance; foliage large, deep green; upright, spreading, bushy growth; PP3847; ['Granada' × 'Garden Party']

Double Delight, Climbing® -- See 'Aroclidd'

'Double Delight Supreme' HT, rb, Chiplunkar; intr. 1993

'Double Else Poulsen' -- See 'Else's Rival'

'Double Feature' ('Lakeland's Pride') Gr, m, 1976, Williams, J. Benjamin; bud pointed; flowers reddish-purple, reverse yellow, 4 in., 28 petals, high-centered, slight damask fragrance; foliage large, dark; vigorous, upright growth; ['Angel Face' × 'Granada']; intr. 1975

'Double Glee' S, mp, Joyce Fleming; intr. 2005

Double Gold™ -- See 'Savadouble'

'Double Happy' -- See 'Sundoha'

'Double Helix' HT, pb, 2005, Shastri, N.V.; flowers pink and cream, 12 cm., very full, borne mostly solitary, intense fragrance; foliage medium size, dark green, matte; prickles medium, crooked; growth bushy, medium (36 in.); garden, exhibition; ['Sheer Bliss' × Cary Grant™]; intr. 1998

'Double Hugonis' (*Hugonis plena, R. hugonis flora pleno*, 'Plenissima') S, ly, before 1932; flowers dbl.

'Double Jaune' -- See 'Multiplex'

'Double Joy' Min, op, 1979, Moore, Ralph S.; bud long, pointed; flowers 1½ in., 35 petals, moderate fragrance; foliage small, matte, green; bushy growth; PP4619; ['Little Darling' × 'New Penny']

Double Knock Out™ -- See 'Radtko'

'Double Mme Butterfly' -- See 'Annie Laurie'

'Double Marbrée' -- See 'Maculata'

'Double Ophelia' HT, lp, 1916, E.G. Hill, Co.; flowers similar to Ophelia, but with twice as many petals; ['Ophelia' × seedling]

'Double Orléans' Pol, mr, 1924, Hicks; flowers rosy crimson, center white; [sport of 'Orléans Rose']

Double Perfection™ -- See 'Burwin'

'Double Pink' ('Double Pink Edine') HSpn, mp, from Scotland

'Double Pink Edine' -- See 'Double Pink'

'Double Pink Killarney' HT, mp, 1910, Scott; flowers large, very dbl.

'Double Pink Memorial Rose' -- See 'Universal Favorite'

'Double Purple' HSpn, rb, before 1820; flowers dark lake, inclining to purple, lighter reverse, 2-2½ in., semi-dbl., cupped; hips black, globular, slightly flattened; possibly synonymous with 'Double Dark Marbled'

'Double Red' -- See 'Rouge'

'Double Red' -- See 'La Belle Distinguée'

'Double Scarlet' HEg, mr; flowers bright rosy red, dbl.; weak growth

'Double Scarlet Sweet Briar' -- See 'La Belle Distinguée'

'Double Scotch White' -- See 'Double White Burnet'

'Double Star' Min, w, 1978, Dobbs, Annette E.; bud ovoid; flowers 10 petals, borne 2-5 per cluster; foliage small, firm, disease-resistant; no prickles; vigorous growth; ['Fairy Moss' × 'Fairy Moss']

Double Take™ -- See 'Benocho'

'Double Talk' F, rb, 1980, Weeks, O.L.; bud ovoid, pointed; flowers medium red, creamy white reverse, petals rolled loosely outward, 48 petals, cupped, slight spicy fragrance; foliage glossy, slightly wrinkled, dark; prickles long, hooked downward; compact growth; PP4710; ['Plain Talk' × 'Suspense']

'Double Time' HT, rb

'Double Treat' -- See 'Mortreat'

'Double Trouble' -- See 'Judtrouble'

'Double White' ('À Fleurs Doubles', 'Coroneola') HMsk, w; flowers dirty white, medium, semi-dbl.; no repeat; prickles numerous, hooked; intr. before 1629

'Double White' HEg, w; flowers flesh-white, dbl.; vigorous growth

'Double White' -- See 'Double White Burnet'

'Double White' -- See 'Elegans'

'Double White Altaica' -- See 'Double White Burnet'

'Double White Burnet' ('Double Blanche', 'Double White', 'Scotch Double White', 'Double White Altaica', 'Double Scotch White', 'Double White Scots') HSpn, w, before 1818; flowers ivory-white, 2-3 in., semi-dbl., intense fragrance; vigorous growth

'Double White Cherokee' Sp, w; flowers semi-dbl.; [sport of *R. laevigata*]

'Double White Killarney' -- See 'Killarney Double White'

'Double White Memorial Rose' -- See 'Manda's Triumph'

'Double White Moss' -- See 'Shailer's White Moss'

'Double White Noisette' -- See 'Plena'

'Double White Scots' -- See 'Double White Burnet'

'Double White Striped Moss' -- See 'Panachée Pleine a Petales Etroites'

'Double Yellow' -- See 'Williams' Double Yellow'

'Double Yellow Scots Rose' -- See 'Williams' Double Yellow'

'Doubloons' HSet, my, 1934, Horvath; bud ovoid, deep saffron-yellow; flowers rich gold, fading to lemon yellow, 5-7 cm., dbl., cupped, borne in large clusters, moderate fragrance; intermittent repeat; foliage glossy; vigorous growth; not dependably hardy; PP152; [(*R. setigera* × *R. wichurana*) × *R. foetida bicolor* hybrid]

'Douce Blanche' HT, w; flowers pure white, large, double, cupped, moderate fragrance; recurrent; foliage dark green, dense; medium growth; intr. 2007

'Douce Symphonie' -- See 'Meibarke'

Douceur Normande® -- See 'Meipopul'

'Douchka' -- See 'Mary DeVor'

'Doué Rambler' HWich, mp, 1921, Begault-Pigné; flowers bright pink, borne in well-filled clusters

'Douglas' ('Douglass') Ch, dr, 1848, Verdier, V.; flowers crimson, medium; vigorous growth; probably extinct

'Douglas Gandy' S, op, Gandy; flowers 4 in., 24 petals, borne in small clusters; recurrent; rich green foliage; growth vigorous, upright, 4-5 ft; [Graham Thomas® × seedling]; intr. 2000

'Douglas MacArthur' HT, pb, 1943, Howard, F.H.; bud long, pointed; flowers

Delft rose, base slightly bronze, 4-4½ in., 24-30 petals, high-centered; foliage leathery; long stems; vigorous, upright, bushy, compact growth; PP581; ['Mrs J.D. Eisele' × 'Glowing Sunset']

'Douglas MacArthur, Climbing' Cl HT, pb, 1949, Howard, F.H.; PP855

'Douglass' -- See 'Douglas'

'Doulce France' F, pb, 1964, Mondial Roses; bud round; flowers clear pink flushed apricot, large, dbl.; vigorous, upright growth; [('Peace' × seedling) × 'Lady Sylvia']

'Dourada' HT, dy, 1957, Moreira da Silva; flowers well-formed, dbl.; very vigorous growth; ['Mme Marie Curie' × 'Julien Potin']

'Doutz' S, lp, Beales, Amanda; intr. 1994

'Doux Parfum' -- See 'Typhoo Tea'

'Dove' -- See 'Ausdove'

'Dove Dale' -- See 'Matdove'

'Dovedale' HT, rb, 1976, Moorhouse & Thornley; flowers cream, petals edged carmine, 5 in., 42 petals; foliage dark; low, bushy growth; ['Fragrant Cloud' × 'Stella']; intr. 1975

'Dovedale' -- See 'Ausdove'

'Downland Cherry' HT, mr, 1954, Ratcliffe; flowers light cerise shaded scarlet, intense spicy fragrance; foliage dark, leathery, dull green; vigorous growth; ['Vanessa' × 'Shot Silk']

'Downland Lustre' HT, yb, 1955, Ratcliffe; bud bronzy gold; flowers maize-yellow, reverse orange, medium, dbl., intense spicy fragrance; compact, bushy growth; ['Vanessa' × 'Shot Silk']

'Downunder' S, dr, Peden, R.

'Doyen Théodore Cornet' HP, mr, 1900, Bénard or Corboeuf; flowers currant red

'Dragon's Blood' -- See 'Ardraco'

'Dragon's Eye' -- See 'Cledrag'

Dragon's Fire™ -- See 'Minifire'

'Drama Queen' -- See 'Wekwinwin'

'Drambuie' HT, rb, 1972, Anderson's Rose Nurseries; flowers orange-red, reverse red, high pointed, 5 in., 28-30 petals, intense fragrance; foliage glossy; vigorous, bushy growth; [sport of 'Whisky Mac']; intr. 1973

'Dream' HT, op, 1938, Dramm; flowers geranium-pink, 4½ in., 50-60 petals, moderate fragrance; strong stems; PP301; [sport of 'Better Times']

Dream™ HT, pb; flowers medium, pastel pink, lightly flushed apricot and salmon, dbl., high-centered, borne mostly singly; recurrent; PP11269; greenhouse rose; intr. 1997

Dream™ ('Dream Palace') S, my, Poulsen; flowers medium yellow, 8-10 cm., dbl., no fragrance; foliage dark; growth bushy, 40-60 cm.; PP13278; intr. 2000

'Dream' F, pb; intr. 2005

'Dream Baby' -- See 'Renbaby'

'Dream Blush' -- See 'Twoat'

'Dream Boat' -- See 'Dreamboat'

'Dream Cloud' -- See 'Aropiclu'

'Dream Come True' HT, ly, 2005, Clark, Linda; flowers medium, full, borne mostly solitary, slight fragrance; foliage medium size, dark green, glossy; prickles moderate; growth upright, medium; [sport of 'Vanilla Perfume']; intr. 2005

Dream Come True™ -- See 'Wekdocpot'

'Dream Dolly' -- See 'Jacpin'

'Dream Dust' F, mp, 1968, Gardner, B.C.; bud pointed; flowers small, dbl., borne in clusters, slight fragrance; foliage leathery; very vigorous, spreading growth; [('Lavender Girl' × unknown) × ('Little Darling' × unknown)]

'Dream Girl' ('Dreamgirl') LCl, pb, 1944, Jacobus; flowers salmon-pink overlaid apricot, large, 55-65 petals, flat, borne in small clusters, intense fragrance; recurrent bloom; foliage dark green, glossy; climbing growth; pillars; PP643; ['Dr. W. Van Fleet' × 'Senora Gari']

'Dream Kid' F, mp, Bell; intr. 2003

'Dream Kordana' Min, mp, Kordes; Pot rose

'Dream Lover' -- See 'Peayetti'

'Dream Lover' -- See 'Renlover'

'Dream On' F, mr, 2000, Delves, P.R.; flowers medium red, reverse lighter, medium size, dbl., borne in small clusters; foliage medium size, medium green, semi-glossy; prickles moderate; growth compact, low; [sport of 'Fryminicot']; intr. 2000

'Dream Orange' -- See 'Twoaebi'

'Dream Palace' -- See 'Poulac003(N)'

'Dream Parade' HT, op, 1938, Hillock; flowers amber in spring, seashell-pink in hot weather, burnt-orange, dbl.; vigorous growth; [sport of 'Condesa de Sástago']

'Dream Pink' -- See 'Twojoan'

'Dream Red' -- See 'Twopaul'

'Dream Ruffles' F, rb; intr. 2002

'Dream Scarlet' -- See 'Twoagain'

'Dream Sequence' -- See 'Pouluf'

'Dream Time' ('Dreamtime') HT, mp, 1977, Bees; flowers 5 in., 38 petals, high-centered; foliage light green; moderately vigorous growth; ['Kordes' Perfecta' × 'Prima Ballerina']

'Dream Time' ('Dreamtime') Min, op, Benardella, Frank; flowers large, coral pink fading to pink, dbl.; growth tall; intr. 1999

'Dream Waltz' F, dr, 1970, Tantau, Math.; flowers large, dbl., borne in trusses; foliage glossy; intr. 1969

Dream Weaver™ -- See 'Jacpicl'

'Dream White' HT, w, Twomey, Jerry; intr. 2004

'Dream Yellow' -- See 'Twoyel'

'Dreamboat' ('Dream Boat') Min, my, 1982, Jolly, Betty J.; flowers medium, 60-70 petals, high-centered, slight fragrance; bushy, spreading growth; ['Rise 'n' Shine' × 'Grand Opera']; intr. 1982

'Dreamboat' HT, lp, Dawson; intr. 1995

'Dreamcatcher' -- See 'Seacatch'

'Dreamcoat' -- See 'Seacoat'

Dreamer™ -- See 'Savadream'

'Dreamgirl' -- See 'Dream Girl'

'Dreamglo' Min, rb, 1979, Williams, Ernest D.; bud long, pointed; flowers white, tipped and blended red, 1 in., 50 petals, high-centered, slight fragrance; foliage small, dark; upright growth; PP4579; ['Little Darling' × 'Little Chief']; intr. 1978

'Dreaming' HWich, lp, Clements, John; flowers blush with large group of golden stamens, 1½ in., single, flat, borne in clusters, moderate sweet/honey fragrance; recurrent; rambling (10-15 ft.) growth; PPAF; intr. 2006

Dreaming™ -- See 'Pouloral'

'Dreaming' -- See 'Reikor'

'Dreaming Free' -- See 'Baifree'

'Dreaming Parade' (Dreaming™) Min, op, Poulsen; flowers coral-red, medium, dbl., no fragrance; foliage dark; growth bushy, 20-40 cm.; intr. 1996

'Dreaming Spires' LCl, dy, 1973, Mattock; flowers bright golden yellow, 3 in., 25 petals, intense fragrance; repeat bloom; foliage dark; [('Arthur Bell' × unknown) × Allgold®]

'Dreamland' -- See 'Resland'

'Dreamland' -- See 'Traumland'

'Dreamrider' -- See 'Minrid'

'Dreams Come True' -- See 'Meivestal'

'Dreamsicle' -- See 'Taldre'

'Dreamtime' -- See 'Dream Time'

'Dreamtime' -- See 'Dream Time'

'Dreamward' -- See 'Burapward'

'Dreamy' -- See 'Tindream'

'Drei Gleichen' HFt, ly; flowers medium, semi-dbl.

'Dreienbrunnen' Pol, mr, Berger, W.; flowers small, dbl.; intr. 1957

'Dresden' ('Mathé Altéry') HT, w, 1961, Robichon; bud ovoid; flowers white lightly suffused pink, 4-5 in., 60 petals, high-centered, intense fragrance; foliage leathery, dark; very vigorous, upright growth; PP1857; ['Ophelia' × 'Cathrine Kordes']; intr. 1961

'Dresden Doll' Min, lp, 1976, Moore, Ralph S.; bud mossy; flowers soft pink, 1½ in., 18 petals, cupped, moderate fragrance; foliage glossy, leathery; low, bushy, compact growth; PP4026; ['Fairy Moss' × 'moss seedling']; intr. 1975

'Dresdner Gelbe No. 79311' F, dy, VEG; flowers medium-large, semi-dbl.

'Dresselhuys' -- See 'Macjocel'

'Dries Verschuren' ('Blaby Jubilee') HT, my, 1963, Verschuren, A.; bud pointed; flowers buttercup-yellow, well-formed, large, 25 petals, moderate fragrance; foliage glossy, bronze; vigorous, upright, bushy growth; ['Golden Rapture' × seedling]; intr. 1961

'Drifter's Escape' F, or, 1971, Greenway; flowers vermilion, 3-3½ in., 10 petals; foliage glossy, reddish when young; [Orangeade® × Orange Sensation®]

'Driscoaust' ('Jo McMath') F, ly, 2001, Driscoll, W.E.; flowers medium, very full, borne in small clusters, slight fragrance; foliage medium size, medium green, semi-glossy; prickles 1 cm., triangular, moderate; growth compact, medium (3-3½ ft.); garden decorative; [Anne Harkness® × 'Robin Redbreast']; intr. 2001

'Driscobert' ('Jackpot 99', 'Jackpot') F, mr, 2000, Driscoll, William E.; flowers medium red, light yellow eye, medium, semi-dbl., borne in small clusters, no fragrance; foliage medium size, medium green, semi-glossy; numerous prickles; compact, medium (18-24 in.) growth; ['Heathers Red' × ('Kiskadee' × ('Liverpool Echo' × ('Flamenco' × R. bella)))]

'Driscobruce' ('Dave Hessayon') HT, mp, 1990, Driscoll, W.E.; flowers full, moderate fragrance; foliage medium size, medium green, glossy; bushy growth; ['Silver Jubilee' × 'Pink Favorite']; intr. 1989

'Driscogeorge' ('David Charles Armstrong') HT, mr, 1992, Driscoll, W.E.; flowers coral-red, 3-3½ in., full, borne mostly singly, slight fragrance; foliage medium size, medium green, semi-glossy; some prickles; tall (106 cm.), upright growth; ['Silver Jubilee' × 'Fragrant Cloud']; intr. 1993

'Drisconun' ('Maud Nunn') F, ly, 1989, Driscoll, W.E.; bud pointed; flowers creamy yellow, aging paler lemon yellow, loose, 16 petals, high-centered, foliage medium green, semi-glossy; prickles green; bushy, medium growth; ['Rise 'n' Shine' × 'Rise 'n' Shine']; intr. 1988

'Driscored' ('Just William') Min, op, 1999, Driscoll, W.E.; flowers salmon pink, reverse pale rose, 2½ in., full, no fragrance; foliage medium size, light green, semi-glossy; few prickles; upright, tall (40 in.) growth; ['Perestroika' × 'Pink Petticoat']

'Driscorob' ('Norah Gabbattass') F, mp, 2000, Driscoll, William E.; flowers medium pink, center lighter, reverse lighter, large, full, borne in small clusters, slight fragrance; foliage medium size, medium green, glossy; prickles moderate; growth upright, tall (120 cm.); [((Minnie Pearl™ × Flower Carpet™) × (Mountbatten® × ('Angelina' × R. bella))) × ('Kiskadee' × ('Liverpool Echo' × ('Flamenco' × R. bella)))]

'Driscoroy' ('Menaka Durga Roy') HT, dr, 1996, Driscoll, W.E.; flowers deep red, full, borne mostly singly, moderate fragrance; foliage medium size, medium green, lighter underside, semi-glossy; few prickles; upright, tall (3 ft.) growth; ['Silver Jubilee' × (('Red Planet' × Blessings®) × ('Parkdirector Riggers' × 'Honey Favorite'))]

'Dronning Alexandrine' HT, dp, 1985, Poulsen, S.; flowers deep pink, medium, dbl., urn-shaped, no fragrance; foliage medium green, semi-glossy; medium, bushy growth; intr. 1926

Dronning Ingrid™ -- See 'Poulgrena'

Dronning Margrethe™ -- See 'Poulskov'

'Dronningen af Danmark' -- See 'Königin von Dänemark'

'Dropmore Yellow' HFt, my, Skinner; [R. foetida × R. spinosissima altaica]

'Drottning Margretha' -- See 'Poulskov'

'Drottning Silvia' -- See 'Meimafris'

Drottningholm™ -- See 'Rosenborg'

'Droujba' F, yb, 1985, Staikov, Prof. Dr. V.; flowers yellow, shaded red, small, 42 petals, cupped, borne in clusters of 5-30, moderate tea fragrance; foliage dark, glossy; bushy growth; ['Masquerade' × 'Rumba']; intr. 1975

'Dru' Min, dy, 1985, Hunt, W. Henry; flowers small, 35 petals, high-centered; foliage medium size, medium green, semi-glossy; upright, bushy growth; intr. 1986

'Drummer Boy' F, mp, 1965, Lammerts, Dr. Walter; bud ovoid; flowers soft carmine-rose, small, dbl., borne in large clusters, slight fragrance; foliage leathery; vigorous, tall growth; PP2722; ['Pinocchio' × Queen Elizabeth®]; intr. 1964

'Drummer Boy' -- See 'Harvacity'

'Drummer Girl' -- See 'Drummergirl'

'Drummergirl' ('Drummer Girl') S, dp; flowers small, single; non-recurrent; CRL says HVirginiana; intr. 2000

'Drummond's Thornless' (R. alpina speciosa) Bslt, mp, before 1846, Drummond; flowers rosy carmine, aging lighter, large, semi-dbl., cupped

'Druschka' HP, dp, Kordes, W.; flowers carmine-pink, large, dbl., slight fragrance; intr. 1932

'Druschki' -- See 'Frau Karl Druschki'

'Druschki Rubra' HP, mr, 1929, Lambert, P.; flowers crimson lightening to scarlet around edges, dbl.; ['Frau Karl Druschki' × 'Luise Lilia']

'Du Luxembourg' N, m, 1829, Hardy; flowers rosy purple, large, full

'Du Maître d'École' -- See 'Rose de La Maître-Ecole'

'Du Pont' -- See 'Rouge Formidable'

'Du Pré Tell' -- See 'Bropre'

'Duarte de Olivera' N, op, 1879, Brassac; flowers salmon rose, coppery at base, 7-8 cm., full, borne in small clusters, moderate tea fragrance; good repeat; ['Ophirie' × 'Rêve d'Or']

'Dublin' HT, mr, 1983, Perry, Astor; flowers large, smoky red, 5 in., 35-40 petals, high-centered, borne mostly singly, intense raspberry fragrance; foliage large, medium green, matte; long, straight stems; upright growth; [(seedling × Mister Lincoln®) × 'Ann Letts']; intr. 1983

Dublin Bay® -- See 'Macdub'

'Dubonnet' Pol, dr, 1959, Jelly; bud small; flowers cardinal-red, dbl., slight fragrance; foliage leathery; vigorous growth; PP1675; [sport of 'Stoplite']; intr. 1958

'Dubourg' HCh, w, 1826, Dubourg; flowers white, shaded lilac-violet, very large

'Duc d'Angoulême' C, dp, 1821, from Holland; flowers vivid rose pink, medium, full

'Duc d'Angoulême' -- See 'Duchesse d'Angoulême'

'Duc d'Angoulême' -- See 'Duchesse d'Angoulême'

'Duc d'Anjou' HP, dr, 1862, Boyau; flowers crimson, shaded with dark red, very large, full; foliage dark green

'Duc d'Arenberg' ('Prince d'Arenberg') HGal, m, before 1836; flowers deep violet rose, edges tending to lilac, large, full, borne in small clusters; growth erect

'Duc d'Audiffret-Pasquier' HP, rb, 1887, Verdier, E.; flowers carmine red with bright purplish hue, center brighter, sometimes bordered white, large, full; foliage somber green, oblong, irregular, deep serration; prickles numerous, unequal, straight, think, yellowish; growth upright

'Duc d'Aumale' B, dp, 1858; flowers bright glowing pink, shaded purple, very large, full

'Duc de Bassano' HP, dp, 1862, Portemer; flowers velvety dark carmine, large, full

'Duc de Bavière' HGal, dp, 1824, in Brussels; flowers large, full

'Duc de Bavière' -- See 'Duchesse d'Angoulême'

'Duc de Beaufort' HGal, pb, about 1825, from Belgium; flowers flesh with violet over carmine, medium, full

'Duc de Berry' ('Roi d'Angleterre') HGal, m, before 1845, Prévost; flowers dark violet purple, medium, full

'Duc de Bordeaux' HGal, pb, 1820, Vibert; flowers rosy lilac, large, dbl.

'Duc de Brabant' C, mp, before 1842; flowers bright pink, medium to large, dbl.; foliage dark green, elongate; prickles numerous, hooked; growth vigorous, tall

'Duc de Bragance' HP, dr, 1886, Verdier, E.; flowers poppy red, shaded violet, large, full, globular, very full, borne in small clusters

'Duc de Cambridge' ('Duke of Cambridge') D, m, before 1841, Laffay; flowers deep purplish rose, edged crimson, large, dbl., flat, regular, moderate fragrance; foliage dark, edged reddish brown when young

'Duc de Cazes' B, m, before 1848; flowers lilac pink, very full, cupped

'Duc de Cazes' Ch, dr, about 1850; flowers velvety dark red-purple, large, full

'Duc de Cazes' HP, m, 1861, Touvais; flowers velvety purple, dbl., cupped; ['Général Jacqueminot' × unknown]

'Duc de Chartres' ('Nouveau Triomphe') D, lp, 1820, Godefroy; flowers medium bright red; intr. 1827

'Duc de Chartres' HCh, mr, Hardy; flowers bright red; intr. 1827

'Duc de Chartres' HP, dr, Verdier, E.; flowers violet purple red tinted crimson, plumed flame and carmine, large, full, borne mostly solitary; foliage rough, dark green; prickles numerous, recurved; intr. 1876

'Duc de Choiseul' C, pb; flowers pale rose colour, with a deep carmine center

'Duc de Constantine' Ayr, mp, 1857, Soupert & Notting; flowers bright lilac-pink, fading to silvery pink, 7-8 cm., full, cupped; non-recurrent

'Duc de Crillon' ('Duc de Grillon') B, mr, 1860, Robert et Moreau; flowers brilliant red, changing to bright rose, large, full, flat

'Duc de Devonshire' HP, mp, Vibert; intr. 1857

'Duc de Devonshire' Ch, pb, 1852, Laffay; flowers lilac pink, striped white, large, full, cupped

'Duc de Fitzjames' HGal, dr, before 1835; flowers very dark crimson, shaded purple; from France

'Duc de Grammont' T, pb, 1825, Laffay

'Duc de Grillon' -- See 'Duc de Crillon'

'Duc de Guiche' ('Sénat Romain') HGal, m, 1821, possibly Sèvres; flowers light reddish-violet, lilac at edges, large, dbl., flat, quartered, borne singly or in clusters of 2-3, moderate fragrance; foliage medium green, elliptical; prickles moderate

'Duc de Magenta' T, ab, 1859, Margottin; flowers flesh shaded fawn, large, dbl.

'Duc de Marlborough' HP, dr, 1884, Lévêque; flowers bright crimson red, large, full; very remontant; foliage dark green

'Duc de Montpensier' HP, dr, 1875, Lévêque; flowers red, tinted crimson and brown, large, dbl., moderate fragrance; prickles hooked

'Duc de Mortemart' HT, dp, 1901, Godard; flowers carmine-pink, tinted bronze, large, full; ['La France de 89' × 'Reine Emma de Pays-Bas']

'Duc de Rohan' -- See 'Duchesse de Rohan'

'Duc de Ruschpler' -- See 'Dr Ruschpler'

'Duc de Sussex' D, lp, before 1841, Laffay; flowers pale pink, center velvety ruby, large, dbl., globular; sometimes classed as HCh

'Duc de Valmy' HGal, m; flowers light purplish rose, marbled purple, large, dbl., cupped

'Duc de Wellington' -- See 'Duke of Wellington'

'Duc d'Enghien' HGal, mr, about 1830, Parmentier; flowers cherry red, shaded dark violet, medium, full

'Duc d'Estrée' -- See 'Henri Lecoq'

'Duc d'Harcourt' HP, mr, 1863, Moreau et Robert; flowers carmine red, outer petals light carmine, large, dbl., borne in small clusters; foliage somber green; prickles long, straight

'Duc d'Orléans' HGal, pb, 1830, Vibert; flowers cherry rose, covered with small white spots, large, dbl., cupped

'Duc d'Orléans' HP, mr, Verdier, E.; flowers vermilion, shaded carmine, large, full; intr. 1888

'Duc d'Ossuna' HP, dr, 1855, Avoux & Crozy

'Duc d'York' ('Rose d'York', 'White Rose of York') A, w, before 1818, Miellez; flowers flesh white, large, dbl.; thornless; stems reddish

'Duc Engelbert d'Arenberg' HT, w, 1899, Soupert & Notting; flowers alabaster white, center flesh pink, very large, full, moderate fragrance; ['Mme Lombard' × 'Belle Siebrecht']

'Duc Meillandina' -- See 'Meipinjid'

'Ducher' Ch, w, 1869, Ducher; bud tinted pink; flowers pure white to medium, 2½-3 in., dbl., flat, borne singly or in small clusters; foliage light green, glossy, narrow; vigorous growth

'Duchess' HT, mp, 1977, Van Veen; bud ovoid; flowers cameo-pink shaded deeper, 4-4½ in., dbl., high-centered, moderate fragrance; foliage glossy, leathery; bushy, upright growth; PP4241; ['White Satin' × seedling]; intr. 1976

'Duchess of Abercorn' HT, pb, 1919, Dickson, H.; flowers creamy white edged bright rose, dbl.

'Duchess of Albany' ('Red La France') HT, dp, 1888, Paul, W.; flowers deep pink, very large, full, globular; [sport of 'La France']

'Duchess of Atholl' HT, ob, 1928, Dobbie; flowers vivid orange, flushed old-rose, large, dbl., cupped; foliage bronze, leathery; vigorous growth

'Duchess of Atholl, Climbing' Cl HT, ob, 1933, Howard Rose Co.

'Duchess of Bedford' HP, mr, 1879, Postans, R.B.; flowers bright medium red, large, dbl., globular; ['Charles Lefebvre' × unknown]

'Duchess of Connaught' HP, dr, 1882, Standish & Noble; flowers crimson red shaded velvety purple-black, large, full, globular, moderate fragrance; growth medium to tall

'Duchess of Connaught' HT, pb, 1879, Bennett; flowers deep silvery pink, large, globular, intense fragrance; growth dwarf; ['Adam' × 'Duchesse de Vallombrosa']

'Duchess of Cornwall' ('The Duchess of Cornwall') HT, op, Tantau; flowers salmon-pink, very full, cupped, moderate fragrance; free-flowering; foliage glossy; intr. 2006

'Duchess of Edinburgh' ('Prince Wasiltchikoff') T, dr, 1874, Nabonnand, G.; flowers crimson, becoming lighter, large, dbl.; moderate growth; ['Souv de David d'Angers' × unknown]

'Duchess of Edinburgh' HP, lp, Dunant, A.; flowers delicate silvery pink, center brighter, large, full; intr. 1874

'Duchess of Fife' HP, lp, 1893, Cocker; flowers delicate silvery pink, large, dbl., cupped, intense fragrance; [sport of 'Countess of Rosebery']

'Duchess of Kent' ('Duchesse de Kent') Ch, w, 1840, possibly Laffay; flowers creamy white, sometimes edged with rose pink, small, full, cupped

'Duchess of Kent' F, dp, Waterhouse, W.P.; flowers rose-Neyron-red, cupped, borne in trusses; low, bushy growth; [sport of 'Katharine Worsley']; intr. 1968

'Duchess of Marlborough' HT, pb, 1922, Nabonnand, P.; flowers brilliant lilac-rose, reverse carmine-crimson, dbl.; [('Jonkheer J.L. Mock' × unknown) × 'Beauté de Lyon']

'Duchess of Montrose' HT, rb, 1929, Dobbie; flowers vermilion-crimson, large

'Duchess of Norfolk' HP, mp, 1853, Margottin; flowers carmine pink, medium, full

'Duchess of Normandy' HT, pb, 1912, Le Cornu; flowers soft salmon-flesh, overlaid yellow, large, dbl., high-centered; vigorous, branching growth; [sport of 'Dean Hole']

'Duchess of Paducah' HT, w, 1971, Williams, J. Benjamin; bud ovoid; flowers white, edge flushed red, large, dbl., high-centered; foliage large, glossy, dark, leathery; vigorous, upright growth; ['Kordes' Perfecta' × 'Peace']

'Duchess of Portland' ('Duchesse de Portland', R. portlandica, 'Rosier de Portland', 'Portland Crimson Monthly Rose', 'The Portland Rose', 'Portland Rose') P, mr, about 1770; flowers bright scarlet, with prominent golden stamens, large, semi-dbl., moderate fragrance; occasional repeat in autumn; foliage clear green; bushy, moderate growth; possibly 'Red Quatre Saisons' × R. gallica officinalis

'Duchess of Rutland' F, dp, 1956, deRuiter; flowers rich carmine-pink, small, semi-dbl., borne on large trusses; vigorous growth

'Duchess of Sutherland' ('Duchesse de Sutherland') HP, lp, 1839, Laffay, M.; flowers rosy pink, large, dbl., moderate fragrance; vigorous growth

'Duchess of Sutherland' HT, pb, Dickson, A.; flowers rose-pink shaded lemon on white base, large, dbl., high-centered, moderate sweetbriar fragrance; foliage glossy, olive-green; vigorous growth; intr. 1912

'Duchess of Wellington' ('Orange Killarney') HT, ly, 1909, Dickson, A.; bud pointed; flowers buff-yellow, deeper toward center, open, large, 17 petals; foliage leathery; long, strong stems; bushy growth

'Duchess of Wellington, Climbing' Cl HT, ly, 1924, Howard Rose Co.

'Duchess of Westminster' HT, pb, 1879, Bennett; flowers satiny pink shaded carmine, large, dbl., slight Tea fragrance; moderate growth; ['Adam' × 'Marquise de Castellane']

'Duchess of Westminster' HT, mp, 1911, Dickson, A.; flowers clear rose-pink, dbl., moderate fragrance

'Duchess of Windsor' -- See 'Permanent Wave'

'Duchess of York' HP, op, 1897, Cocker; flowers salmon pink

'Duchess of York' HT, yb, Dickson, S.; flowers deep golden yellow, center tangerine, very well-formed, large, dbl.; vigorous growth; intr. 1925

'Duchess of York' -- See 'Dicracer'

'Duchesse d'Abrantes' M, lp, 1851, Robert; flowers light pink with dark pink shading, large, dbl., rosette

'Duchesse d'Albe' T, yb, 1903, Lévêque; flowers yellowish-salmon, shaded coppery purple rose, base golden yellow, dbl., globular

'Duchesse d'Angoulême' ('Duc d'Angoulême') HGal, mp, Vibert; flowers translucent pink, lighter on the border, dbl., irregularly quartered, borne in clusters of 3-4; foliage pointed, lanceolate, light green; few prickles; intr. 1835

'Duchesse d'Angoulême' ('Duc d'Angoulême', 'Triomphe de Brabant', 'Duc de Bavière', 'Reine de Prusse') HGal, lp, Miellez; flowers blush-lilac, mottled crimson, medium, dbl., cupped; moderate, upright growth; [probably a gallica × centifolia hybrid]; intr. before 1860

'Duchesse d'Angoulême' -- See 'Agathe Incarnata'

'Duchesse d'Anjou' -- See 'Godzoty'

'Duchesse d'Aoste' HP, mr, 1867, Margottin; flowers rich vivid rose, large, very dbl., flat, moderate fragrance; foliage light green; prickles carmine, laterally flattened, recurved, unequal

'Duchesse d'Arenberg' HGal, m; flowers violet pink, large, full

'Duchesse d'Assuma' -- See 'Duchesse d'Ossuna'

'Duchesse d'Auerstädt' ('Mme la Duchesse d'Auerstädt') N, my, 1888, Bernaix, A.; flowers golden yellow, touched with apricot at center, 11 cm., very full, cupped, borne mostly solitary, moderate tea fragrance; ['Reve d'Or' × unknown]

'Duchesse de Berry' HGal, pb, 1820, Vibert; flowers light pink, shaded carmine, large, semi-dbl.

'Duchesse de Berry' Ch, dp, Mauget; flowers full; intr. 1827

'Duchesse de Brabant' ('Comtesse de Labarthe', 'Comtesse Ouwaroff', 'Countess Bertha', 'Mlle de Labarthe') T, lp, 1857, Bernède; flowers soft rosy pink, large, 45 petals, cupped, intense fragrance; vigorous, spreading growth

'Duchesse de Brabant, Climbing' Cl T, pb, about 1900; flowers pale coral pink, fading to medium pink, darker reverse, strong tea fragrance

'Duchesse de Bragance' HP, mp, 1886, Verdier; flowers delicate satiny pink, tinted brighter pink, very large, dbl.; foliage dark green, oval, irregularly toothed; prickles unequal, short, straight, brown; growth upright

'Duchesse de Bragance' T, my, 1886, Dubreuil; flowers canary-yellow, edges lighter, very large; ['Coquette de Lyon' × unknown]; may be synonymous with Mons Furtado

'Duchesse de Buccleugh' HGal, rb, 1837, Vibert; flowers medium pink, edges tinged lavender, small button at center, large, dbl., cupped, moderate fragrance; foliage elliptical, gray-green, large; nearly thornless; growth vigorous, tall (2 m.)

'Duchesse de Cambacérès' ('Mme de Cambacérès') HP, m, 1854, Fontaine; flowers carmine pink with distinct purplish tones, large, dbl., globular, cupped, borne in large clusters; foliage thick, large, glaucous green, slightly rugose; prickles numerous, gray-brown, unequal, slightly hooked; vigorous growth

'Duchesse de Caylus' ('Penelope Mayo') HP, dp, 1864, Verdier, C.; flowers brilliant carmine-pink, well-formed, large, full, globular, moderate fragrance; moderate growth; ['Alfred Colomb' × unknown]

'Duchesse de Chartres' HP, mp, 1875, Verdier, E.; flowers bright velvety pink, reverse lighter, very large, full

'Duchesse de Coutard' C, lp, before 1885; flowers medium, full; possibly synonymous with 'Comtesse de Coutard'

'Duchesse de Dino' HMult, lp, before 1860, Baumann; flowers flesh white, medium, semi-dbl.

'Duchesse de Dino' HP, dr, Lévêque; flowers blackish crimson, tinted carmine and velvety purple, very large, dbl.; foliage dark green; growth tall; intr. 1889

'Duchesse de Galliera' HP, pb, 1847, Portemer; flowers bright rose shaded flesh, large, dbl., cupped; foliage ovate, mostly serrated; prickles numerous, nearly straight, very sharp, brownish-red

'Duchesse de Galliera' HP, mp, Verdier, E.; flowers rose-pink; intr. 1887

'Duchesse de Germantes' C, lp; intr. 1988

'Duchesse de Grammont' ('Centifolia d'Avranches') D, mp, 1825, Cels

'Duchesse de Grammont' N, w; flowers flesh, small, dbl., borne in small clusters, moderate fragrance; probably synonymous with 'Caroline Marniesse'; intr. before 1838

'Duchesse de Guermantes' M, mp, Morley, Dr B.; intr. 1988

'Duchesse de Kent' -- See 'Duchess of Kent'

'Duchesse de la Mothe-Houdancourt' HT, dp, 1907, Mille-Toussaint; flowers carmine pink shaded vermilion pink, nuanced straw yellow and coppery red, large, dbl., moderate fragrance; ['Mme Abel Chatenay' × 'Maman Cochet']

'Duchesse de la Tremoille' M, dp, Morley, Dr B.; intr. 1988

'Duchesse de Magenta' HP, lp, 1859, Guillot père

'Duchesse de Mecklemburg' T, ly; flowers straw yellow, shaded pink, large, semi-dbl., cupped

'Duchesse de Medina Coeli' -- See 'Comtesse de Medina Coeli'

'Duchesse de Montebello' HGal, lp, 1824-1825, Laffay, M.; flowers pale pink, almost white at edges, with a small center button, small to medium, very dbl., rosette, borne singly or in clusters of 2-3, moderate fragrance; foliage small, rounded, light green; few prickles; erect, compact growth; sometimes classed as HCh

'Duchesse de Montmorency' P, mp, 1844, Lévêque, R.; flowers satiny rose pink, shaded lilac, large, dbl., globular; some autumn repeat

'Duchesse de Montpensier' HP, lp, 1846, Margottin

'Duchesse de Norfolk' B, m, Wood; flowers purple-carmine, large, full, moderate fragrance

'Duchesse de Portland' -- See 'Duchess of Portland'

'Duchesse de Reggio' -- See 'Fanny Bias'

'Duchesse de Rohan' ('Duc de Rohan') HP, pb, before 1867, from France (possibly Lévêque); flowers rosy crimson, margined with lilac, compact, large, dbl.

Duchesse de Savoie® -- See 'Lapbel'

'Duchesse de Sutherland' -- See 'Duchess of Sutherland'

'Duchesse de Talleyrand' HT, yb, 1944, Meilland, F.; bud pointed; flowers egg-yolk-yellow to chrome-yellow, dbl.; well branched growth; ['Mme Joseph Perraud' × 'Fred Edmunds']

'Duchesse de Thuringe' B, w, 1847, Guillot Père; flowers white tinted lilac, large, full, borne in small clusters

'Duchesse de Vallombrosa' HP, ab, 1875, Dunand (Schwartz, J.); flowers flesh shaded rose, large, dbl.; ['Jules Margottin' × unknown]

'Duchesse de Vallombrosa' ('Mme la Duchesse de Vallombrosa') T, rb, Nabonnand; flowers coppery red, very large, full, borne in small clusters; intr. 1879

'Duchesse de Vendome' HT, rb, 1924, Nabonnand, P.; flowers crimson, coppery reflexes, reverse yellow, dbl.; ['Souv. de Gilbert Nabonnand' × 'Juliet']

'Duchesse de Verneuil' M, pb, 1856, Portemer fils; bud heavily mossed; flowers flesh-pink deepening to salmon-pink, camellia-like

'Duchesse d'Istrie' -- See 'William Lobb'

'Duchesse d'Orléans' -- See 'Lustre d'Église'

'Duchesse d'Orléans' -- See 'Jean-Baptiste Casati'

'Duchesse d'Orléans' T, w, Robert; flowers white, shaded flesh pink, center darker, large, very full; intr. about 1860

'Duchesse d'Orléans' HGal, mp, 1821, Laffay, M.

'Duchesse d'Orléans' C, lp, Vibert; intr. 1837

'Duchesse d'Orléans' HP, m, Quétier; flowers carmine-lilac, reverse white, large, very full; [probably a 'La Reine seedling']; intr. 1852

'Duchesse d'Ossuna' ('Duchesse d'Assuma') HP, dp, 1877, Jamain, H.; flowers vermilion rose, large, full

'Duchesse Hedwige d'Arenberg' HT, mp, 1899, Soupert & Notting; flowers silky pink with silvery reflections, center darker, very large, full, moderate fragrance; ['Belle Siebrecht' × 'Mme Caroline Testout']

'Duchesse Marie Salviati' T, ob, 1889, Soupert & Notting; bud long; flowers orange-yellow tinted pink, full, moderate violet fragrance; ['Mme Lombard' × 'Mme Maurice Kuppenheim']

'Ducis' M, lp, 1857, Robert et Moreau; flowers light pink shaded with lilac, 7-8 cm., full, flat, borne in small clusters

'Dudley Cross' -- See 'Mrs Dudley Cross'

'Duet' -- See 'Rendan'

'Duet' HT, mp, 1960, Swim, H.C.; bud ovoid; flowers light pink, reverse dark pink, ruffled, 4 in., 25-30 petals, high-centered, borne singly and in small clusters, slight tea fragrance; foliage leathery, dark green, glossy; vigorous, upright growth; PP1903; ['Fandango' × 'Roundelay']; intr. 1960

'Duet Supreme' HT, pb, 1990, Patterson, William; bud rounded; flowers light to medium pink blend, medium pink reverse, 35 petals, urn-shaped, slight fragrance; foliage medium size, dark green, semi-glossy; [sport of 'Duet']; intr. 1990

Duett® F, or, Noack, Werner; intr. 1982

'Duett' ('New Duet') HT, pb, Kordes; flowers medium, cream colored with touch of pink; intr. 2001

'Duett Kordana' Min, pb, Kordes ; bud between urceolate and ovate; flowers cream with pink, 2 in., 40 petals, cupped, borne mostly singly, no fragrance; recurrent; foliage dark green, matte; prickles moderate, 3-4 mm., triangular, elongated, compact, upright growth; PP15059; [seedling × seedling]; container rose

'Duffey's Delight' HT, dr, 1977, Duffey; bud long, pointed; flowers velvety dark red, 5-6 in., 60 petals, high-centered, slight fragrance; foliage dark; very vigorous, upright growth; [sport of 'Norman Hartnell']; intr. 1976

'Dufresnois' N, lp, 1825, Vibert; flowers flesh-white, small, full

Duftbella® F, dr, 1975, Hetzel; bud ovoid; flowers dark velvet red, center lighter, large, dbl., intense fragrance; vigorous, bushy growth; ['Fragrant Cloud' × ('Monique' × 'Mardi Gras')]; intr. 1973

'Duftendes Weisskirchen' F, mp, Hetzel; intr. 2002

Duftes Berlin® HT, ob, Cocker; intr. 1988

'Duftfestival' -- See 'Meiafone'

'Duftgold' -- See 'Tanduft'

'Duftparadies' F, dr, Hetzel; intr. 1966

'Duftrausch' F, mp, 1972, Tantau, Math.; bud globular; flowers semi-dbl.; foliage soft; upright growth; RULED EXTINCT 4/85 ARM; [unknown × unknown]

Duftrausch® -- See 'Tanschaubud'

'Duftstar' HT, dr, 1976, Kordes; bud long, pointed; flowers 4 in., 24 petals, high-centered, intense fragrance; foliage dark, soft; vigorous, upright growth; [seedling × Papa Meilland®]; intr. 1974

Duftstern® HT, op, Noack, Werner; buds long, cylindrical; flowers coral-orange to orange pink, large petals, dbl., well-formed, moderate fragrance; recurrent; foliage deep, burgundy-colored new growth; intr. 1973

'Duftwolke' ('Fragrant Cloud', 'Nuage Parfumé') HT, or, 1967, Tantau, Math.; bud ovoid; flowers coral-red becoming geranium-red, well-formed, 5 in., 28-35 petals, high-centered, borne mostly singly, intense damask-fruity-spicy-citrus-sharp fragrance; foliage dark, glossy; prickles moderate; vigorous, upright growth; PP2574; [seedling × 'Prima Ballerina']; intr. 1968

'Duftwunder' F, ob, 1972, Hetzel; flowers yellowish-orange, large, very dbl.; moderate, upright growth; ['Fragrant Cloud' × 'Goldmarie']

'Duftzauber' -- See 'Kordu'

'Duftzauber '84' -- See 'Korzaun'

'Dugcream' HT, ab, Douglas; intr. 1987

'Duhamel Dumonceau' HP, mr, 1872, Vilin; flowers bright red, shaded violet at edges, large, dbl., moderate fragrance; sometimes classed as B

'Duiliu Zamfirescu' HT, mr, 1938, Palocsay, R.; flowers large, dbl.

'Duisburg' HT, dp, 1908, Hinner, W.; flowers carmine-pink, large, dbl.

'Dukat' HT, my, Brabec

'Dukat' LCl, my, 1959, Tantau, Math.; bud red-tipped; flowers golden yellow, lighter at edges, 4½ in., dbl., moderate fragrance; foliage glossy, leathery; vigorous (10-16 ft.), upright growth; ['Mrs Pierre S. duPont' × 'Golden Glow']; intr. 1955

'Dukat' -- See 'Rose de Limoux'

'Dukata' Min, ob, 2006, Hopper, Nancy; flowers orange with pink edge, reverse dark orange, 2½ in., semi-dbl., borne mostly solitary; foliage medium size, medium green, semi-glossy; prickles ¼ in., red/tan, moderate; growth bushy, medium (16 in.); [Tobo™ × 'Pierrine']

'Duke Meillandina' -- See 'Meipinjid'

'Duke of Albany' HP, dr, 1882, Paul; flowers vivid crimson when first opening, changing darker as the flowers expand, very large, very full

'Duke of Argyll' HSpn, pb

'Duke of Cambridge' -- See 'Duc de Cambridge'

'Duke of Connaught' HP, rb, 1875, Paul; flowers dark velvety crimson flushed brighter, large, dbl.; vigorous growth

'Duke of Connaught' HT, mr, 1879, Bennett; flowers rose-crimson, very large, with a tendency to ball, dbl.; moderate growth; ['Adam' × 'Louis van Houtte']

'Duke of Edinburgh' HP, dr, 1868, Paul; flowers deep red, large, dbl.; vigorous, erect growth; ['Général Jacqueminot' × unknown]

'Duke of Edinburgh'™ -- See 'The Gold Award Rose'

'Duke of Fife' HP, dr, 1892, Cocker & Sons; flowers deep crimson-scarlet, large, full; [sport of 'Étienne Levet']

'Duke of Normandy' HT, lp, 1921, Jersey Nursery; flowers silvery pink; ['St. Helena' × 'George Dickson']

'Duke of Paducah' HT, rb, 1971, Williams, J. Benjamin; bud ovoid; flowers dark velvety crimson, large, dbl., slight fragrance; foliage large, glossy, dark, leathery; vigorous, bushy growth; ['Grand Gala' × 'Josephine Bruce']

'Duke of Teck' HP, dp, 1880, Paul; flowers deep pink, large, 40 petals, globular, moderate fragrance; vigorous growth; ['Duke of Edinburgh' × unknown]

'Duke of Wellington' ('Duc de Wellington') HP, dr, 1864, Granger; flowers velvety crimson-red, large, dbl., cupped; vigorous growth; ['Lord Macaulay' × unknown]

'Duke of Wellington' -- See 'Rosiériste Jacobs'

'Duke of Windsor' ('Herzog von Windsor') HT, ob, 1968, Tantau, Math.; bud pointed; flowers orange, well-formed, large, 27 petals, intense fragrance; foliage dark, glossy; very vigorous, upright growth; intr. 1967

'Duke of York' Ch, pb, 1894, Paul & Son; flowers rosy-pink and white to crimson, variable

'Duke Sunblaze' -- See 'Meipinjid'

'Duke Wayne' -- See 'Big Duke'

'Dulce Bella' T, op, 1890, Bennett; flowers coppery pink, large, full

'Dulcinea' HT, mr, 1965, Verschuren, A.; flowers oriental red, edged darker, reverse yellow, large, 50-55 petals; foliage dark, glossy; upright, bushy growth; ['Condesa de Sástago' × seedling]; intr. 1963

'Dumbo' F, mr, 1956, Combe; flowers bright cherry-red, very large, semi-dbl.; foliage dark; very vigorous growth; ['Mme G. Forest-Colcombet' × 'Independence']

'Dumnacus' HP, mp, 1880, Moreau & Robert; flowers carmine pink, very large, full, cupped; ['Countess of Oxford' × unknown]

'Dumortier' HGal, pb, before 1843, Parmentier; flowers light red with silvery reflex, medium, very dbl., flat

'Duncan Reade-Hill' HT, ob, 2000, Poole, Lionel; flowers orange, medium, dbl., borne mostly singly, moderate fragrance; foliage medium size, dark green, semi-glossy; prickles moderate; growth upright, bushy, vigorous (3 ft.); ['Golden Splendour' × Doris Tysterman®]

'Duncan's Rose' S, dp, Poulsen; flowers single, borne in clusters, no fragrance; recurrent; foliage glossy; ['Johannesburg

Garden Club' × unknown]; intr. 1998
'Dundee' HSpn, w, before 1832, Austin, R.; flowers white blotched pink, reverse pure white, dbl., cupped; moderate growth
'Dundee Rambler' Ayr, lp, before 1838, Martin; flowers white edged with pale pink, fading to white, 5 cm., dbl., borne in medium clusters, slight sweet, musky fragrance; thought to be R. arvensis × a noisette
Dune® -- See 'Delgrim'
'Dunkelrote Ellen Poulsen' -- See 'Red Ellen Poulsen'
'Dunkelrote Hermose' B, dr, 1899, Geissler; flowers dark carmine red; foliage glossy; ['Reine Marie Henriette' × 'Hermosa']
'Dunkelrote Tausendschön' HMult, dr, 1942, Vogel, M.; flowers dbl., borne in small clusters; ['Tausendschön' × unknown]
'Dunkerque' HT, op, 1940, Laperrière; bud pointed, ovoid; flowers bright pink, slightly coppery, very large, 30 petals; foliage clear olive-green; long, strong stems; vigorous, upright, branching growth; ['Charles P. Kilham' × seedling]
'Dunkirk' HT, mr, 1947, Dickson, A.; flowers rose-red, 4-5 in., 36 petals; foliage glossy
'Dunton Gold' HT, ob, 1966, Dunton Nursery; flowers deep golden yellow-orange and pink tipped, 6 in., high-centered, moderate fragrance; foliage glossy; vigorous growth; [sport of 'Tzigane']
'Dunwich Rose' ('Dunwichiensis') HSpn, ly; flowers soft lemon yellow to white, small, single, borne along arching canes, very early bloomer; fern-like foliage; prickles numerous, bristly; low, spreading, groundcover growth; intr. 1956 or before
'Dunwichiensis' -- See 'Dunwich Rose'
'Duo' F, or, 1955, Gaujard; flowers coppery orange, open, petals fringed, medium, single; foliage dark; very vigorous growth; ['Peace' × seedling]
'Duo Unique' HT, pb, deRuiter; intr. 2001
'Dupetit Thouars' B, mp, 1844, Portemer; flowers bright pink, large, full
'Duplex' ('Pommifère à Fleur Double', R. pomifera duplex, 'Wolley-Dod's Rose') Misc OGR, mp, before 1770; sepals foliaceous; flowers clear pink, medium, semi-dbl., slight fragrance; foliage downy, gray-green; prickles heavy; chance garden hybrid of R. pomifera × unknown
'Duplex' -- See 'Alba Semi-plena'
'Duplex' -- See 'Rose d'Amour'
'Dupont Rose' -- See 'Dupontii'
'Dupontii' ('Dupont Rose', R. freundiana, R. moschata nivea, R. × dupontii, 'Snow-Bush Rose') Misc OGR, w, 1817; flowers blush, aging to creamy white, 3 in., single, perfectly circular shape, borne in small corymbs, slight musk fragrance; early summer; hips large, round, golden-orange; [perhaps descended from R. gallica × R. moschata hybrid]
'Dupuy-Jamain' HP, mr, 1868, Jamain, H.; flowers cerise-red, well-formed, 30 petals; vigorous growth
'Dupuytren' HGal, dr, 1823, Cartier; flowers very bright crimson, black velvet in center, cupped
'Duquesa' -- See 'Turduq'
'Duquesa de Peñaranda' ('Morning Blush') HT, ob, 1931, Dot, Pedro; bud pointed; flowers shades of orange, large, 35 petals, cupped, moderate fragrance; foliage rich green, glossy; vigorous growth; ['Souv. de Claudius Pernet' × 'Rosella']
'Duquesa de Peñaranda, Climbing' Cl HT, ob, 1940, Germain's
'Dura' S, w
'Durban July' -- See 'Durbankor'
'Durbankor' ('Durban July') F, rb, 1982, Kordes, W.
'Durbanville Flame' HT, ab; flowers peach-apricot with orange edges, dbl., exhibition; firm, medium long stems; growth vigorous, tall, 5-6 ft; intr. 2001
'Durgapur Delight' HT, lp, Gupta; flowers flower light porcelain pink; free-flowering; growth vigorous; [sport of 'Montezuma']; intr. 1980
'Durgapur Jubilee' HT, pb, Ghosh; flowers light pink with deeper petal edges, high-centered; intr. 1998
'Durham Pillar' HMult, mr, 1960, Risley; bud globular; flowers rose-red, small, single, cupped, borne in clusters, slight fragrance; free, recurrent boom; foliage dark, leathery, glossy; moderate climbing or trailing growth; ['Chevy Chase' × seedling]; intr. 1958
'Durham Prince Bishops' HT, op, 1991, Thompson, Robert; flowers orange, flushed pink, medium, full, moderate fragrance; foliage large, dark green, glossy; bushy growth; ['Silver Jubilee' × Doris Tysterman®]; intr. 1989
'Dusky Dancer' -- See 'Frytrooper'
'Dusky Maiden' F, dr, 1947, LeGrice; flowers deep crimson scarlet, 3 in., single, borne in trusses, moderate fragrance; foliage dark; vigorous growth; PP2210; [('Daily Mail Scented Rose' × Étoile de Hollande') × 'Else Poulsen']
'Dusky Red' HT, dr, 1974, Wyant; flowers medium red, veined, large, dbl., high-centered, intense fragrance; intermittent bloom; foliage dark, leathery, vigorous, upright, bushy growth; ['Karl Herbst' × 'Big Red']; intr. 1972
'Düsterlohe' ('Düsterlohe I', 'Gloomy Fire') S, dp, about 1931, Kordes; flowers rose-red, 3 in., single to semi-dbl., borne singly and in small clusters; non-recurrent bloom; foliage dark green; vigorous, climbing growth; not dependably hardy; ['Venusta Pendula' × 'Miss C.E. van Rossem']
'Düsterlohe I' -- See 'Düsterlohe'
'Düsterlohe II' S, mr, 1941, Kordes; flowers light red, large, single; hybrid macrantha
'Dusty Pink' F, lp, 1961, Jelly; bud ovoid, long, pointed; flowers 3-3½ in., 50-60 petals, high-centered, moderate fragrance; vigorous, upright growth; PP2164; ['Garnette' × ('Garnette' × unknown)]; intr. 1961
Dusty Pink Folies® F, mp, Meilland; intr. 2006
'Dusty Red' -- See 'Weldust'
'Dusty Rose' Min, m, 1975, Morey, Dr. Dennison; flowers reddish-purple, 1½ in., 40-50 petals, high-centered, moderate spicy fragrance; foliage dark; upright growth; ['Amy Vanderbilt' × 'Cécile Brunner']; intr. 1974
'Dusty Springfield' -- See 'Horluvdust'
'Dutch Bengal' -- See 'Maheca'
Dutch Gold® HT, my, 1977, Wisbech Plant Co.; flowers golden yellow, 6 in., 32-34 petals, moderate fragrance; foliage glossy, dark; vigorous growth; [Peer Gynt® × 'Whisky Mac']; intr. 1978
'Dutch Hedge' HRg, lp, 1958, Nyveldt; flowers small, single; hips orange-red; [(R. rugosa rubra × R. cinnamomea) × R. nitida]
'Dutch Miss' Min, pb, 1987, Bridges, Dennis A.; flowers light pink veining to white base, fading slightly, medium, 22 petals, high-centered, borne singly, slight fragrance; foliage medium size, dark green, glossy; prickles straight, pointed, medium, tan; upright, medium growth; ['Summer Spice' × seedling]
'Dutch Provence' -- See R. centifolia batavica
'Dwaaletha' ('Aletha') Min, yb, 2000, Schramm, Dwayne; flowers yellow, tinged pink, reverse yellow, small, full, borne mostly singly, slight fragrance; foliage small, light green, matte; few prickles; growth spreading, low (8-12 in.); ['Orange Honey' × 'Orange Honey']
'Dwamallory' ('Mallory Marie') F, pb, 2000, Schramm, Dwayne; flowers light pink, reverse medium pink, medium, semi-dbl., borne in small clusters, no fragrance; foliage medium size, medium green, semi-glossy; few prickles; growth upright, medium (2-3 ft.); ['Gene Boerner' × 'Dainty Bess']
'Dwarf Austrian Rose' -- See 'Rosier d'Amour'
'Dwarf Crimson Rambler' -- See 'Mme Norbert Levavasseur'
'Dwarf Fairy' -- See 'Zwergenfee'
'Dwarf King' -- See 'Zwergkönig'
'Dwarf King 78' -- See 'Korkönig'
'Dwarf Pavement' -- See 'Rosa Zwerg'
'Dwarf Queen' -- See 'Queen of the Dwarfs'
'Dwarf Queen '82' -- See 'Korwerk'
'Dwarfking' -- See 'Zwergkönig'
'Dwashirley' ('Shirley Marie') Min, mp, 2000, Schramm, Dwayne; flowers light pink, reverse medium pink, 1½ in., dbl., borne mostly singly, slight fragrance; foliage medium size, light green, semi-

glossy; few prickles; upright, medium (1½-2 ft.) growth; ['Why Not' × 'Why Not']

'Dwasusanne' ('Susanne Marie') F, pb, 2000, Schramm, Dwayne; bud deep pink; flowers medium pink, edged deep pink, reverse deep pink, 2-3 in., full, borne mostly singly, no fragrance; foliage medium size, medium green, semi-glossy; few prickles; upright, medium (2-3 ft.) growth; ['Gene Boerner' × 'Gingersnap']

'd'Yèbles' B, m, about 1830, Desprez; flowers violet-purple, medium, full

'Dyknini' ('Hanini') Min, rb, 1995, Dykstra, Dr. A. Michael; flowers burgundy red stripes serrated by reddish-pink, white throat, 2 in., 5 petals, moderate fruity fragrance; foliage medium size, medium green, semi-glossy; medium (2 ft.), spreading (30in.) growth; PPRR; [Sarabande® × 'Hurdy Gurdy']; intr. 1995

'Dykpink' ('Blushing Beauty') HT, w, 2000, Dykstra, Dr. Michael; flowers white and pink blend, reverse light pink, 4-5 cm., full, exhibition, borne mostly singly, slight fragrance; foliage medium size, medium green, glossy; prickles moderate; growth upright, medium; [Pristine® × Touch of ClassTM®]; intr. 2001

'Dyktick' ('Tickles™) F, pb, 1999, Dykstra, Dr. A. Michael; flowers pink and cream stripes, reverse same, 2½ in., semi-dbl., borne in small clusters, slight fragrance; few prickles; [(Pristine® × 'Typhoo Tea') × 'Hurdy Gurdy']; intr. 2000

'Dyllan's Mom' -- See 'Brymom'

'Dyna' -- See 'Bingo'

Dynamite™ -- See 'Jacsat'

Dynastie™ -- See 'Meipitac'

'Dynastie Piccard' HT, pb, Meilland; flowers light pink with deeper pink edges, dbl., high-centered, borne mostly singly; florist rose; intr. 2002

'Dynasty' HT, mr, Keisei; flowers inner petals tan, outer petals dusty pink, dbl., informal; growth medium, open; intr. 1992

Dynasty™ -- See 'Jacyo'

'Dzambul' HP, mr, 1938, Kosteckij; flowers medium, dbl.

— E —

'E. B. LeGrice' ('Pearl Drift, Climbing') LCl, w, 2001, Kull, Amelita E.; flowers white, light pink reverse, 3 in., semi-dbl., borne in large clusters; foliage large, dark green, glossy; prickles small, slightly hooked, few; growth climbing (12-15 ft.); [sport of 'Pearl Drift']

'E. E. Saskavá' HT, dy, 1933, Böhm, J.; flowers large, dbl.

'E. G. Hill, Climbing' Cl HT, mr, 1942, Marlin

'E. G. Hill' HT, mr, 1929, E.G. Hill, Co.; bud ovoid; flowers dazzling scarlet, well-formed, very large, dbl., intense damask fragrance; vigorous growth

'E. Godfrey Brown' HT, dr, 1919, Dickson, H.; flowers deep reddish-crimson, dbl.

'E. H. Morse' -- See 'Ernest H. Morse'

'E. H. T. Broadwood' HT, 1916, Dickson, H.

'E. I. Farrington' F, mr, 1953, Brownell; flowers cardinal-red to blood-red, turning almost crimson, 3½-4 in., 50-60 petals, high-centered, moderate fragrance; vigorous, spreading growth; PP1404; ['Queen o' the Lakes' × seedling]

'E. J. Baldwin' HT, my, 1952, Robinson, H.; flowers rich golden yellow, high pointed, well-formed, large, 30-40 petals; foliage dark; vigorous, upright, branching growth; ['Phyllis Gold' × seedling]

'E. J. Ludding' HT, pb, 1931, Van Rossem; flowers carmine-pink shaded coral-red and salmon, open, large, dbl.; bushy growth; ['Ophelia' × 'Hill's America']

'E. J. Moller' HT, dr, 1924, Moller; flowers intense red, deepening toward black, dbl.; ['George Dickson' × unknown]

'E. N. Ward' Pol, pb, Kershaw

'E. P. H. Kingma' HT, ab, 1919, Verschuren; flowers apricot and orange-yellow, medium, dbl.; ['Mme Edouard Herriot' × 'Duchess of Wellington']

'E. Pemberton Barnes' HT, pb, 1928, Pemberton; flowers light pink, shaded cerise

'E. V. Lucas' HT, dr, 1934, McGredy; flowers dark velvety crimson, large, semi-dbl., borne in sprays; foliage dark; vigorous, upright, branching growth

'E. Veyrat Hermanos' ('E. Veyrath Hermanos', 'Pillar of Gold') Cl T, pb, 1895, Bernaix, A.; bud long, pointed; flowers apricot and carmine-pink, reflexes violet-rose, 9-10 cm., dbl., borne in small clusters, intense tea fragrance; vigorous growth

'E. Veyrath Hermanos' -- See 'E. Veyrat Hermanos'

'E. Y. Teas' ('Mons E. Y. Teas') HP, mp, 1874, Verdier, E.; flowers bright red, large, full, globular, intense fragrance; ['Alfred Colomb' × unknown]

'Eads' F, pb, 1991, Burks, Larry; flowers pink and yellow, medium, semi-dbl., borne in small clusters, slight fragrance; foliage medium size, medium green, semi-glossy; low, compact growth; [(seedling × 'Pinocchio') × seedling]; intr. 1991

Eagle® -- See 'Haveal'

Eagle Wings® -- See 'Lensim'

'Earl Beatty' HT, dr, 1923, Chaplin Bros.; flowers deep crimson, large, dbl., cupped; bushy growth; ['Hoosier Beauty' × 'George Dickson']

'Earl Godard Bentinck' HT, mr, 1931, Buisman, G. A. H.; flowers red, base orange, large, dbl.; very vigorous growth; ['Pharisaer' × 'Covent Garden']

'Earl Haig' HT, mr, 1921, Dickson, A.; flowers brick-red, large, dbl.; prickles few thorns; vigorous, bushy growth

'Earl of Beaconsfield' -- See 'Lord Beaconsfield'

'Earl of Dufferin' HP, dr, 1887, Dickson, A.; flowers velvety crimson, shaded chestnut-red, very large, 53 petals, globular; vigorous growth

'Earl of Eldon' ('Lord Eldon') N, ob, 1872, Eldon/Coppin; flowers coppery orange, 7 cm., dbl., flat, borne in small clusters, moderate tea fragrance

'Earl of Gosford' HT, dr, 1912, McGredy; flowers dark crimson scarlet, large, dbl., intense fragrance

'Earl of Mexborough' T, mp, 1902, Brauer

'Earl of Pembroke' HP, mr, 1882, Bennett; flowers carmine-red, large, dbl.; ['Marquise de Castellane' × 'Maurice Bernardin']

'Earl of Warwick' HT, lp, 1904, Paul, W.; flowers pale pinkish buff, reverse livid pink, large, dbl.; ['Souv. de S.A. Prince' × 'Mrs W. J. Grant']

'Earldomensis' (R. earldomensis) S, my, 1934, Page; flowers bright yellow; growth to 6 ft.; [R. hugonis × R. omeiensis pteracantha]

'Early Bird' F, mp, 1965, Dickson, Patrick; flowers rose-opal, well-formed, 4 in., dbl.; free growth; ['Circus' × 'Fritz Thiedemann']; intr. 1965

'Early Blush' HRg, pb, Wheen, G.; [R. rugosa × unknown]

'Early Mist' Min, w, 1972, Van de Yssel; flowers cream, 2 in., 25 petals, globular, slight fragrance; foliage dull, light; vigorous growth; intr. 1970

'Early Morn' HT, lp, 1944, Brownell; flowers shell-pink, large, dbl., high-centered, moderate fragrance; foliage glossy; long stems; vigorous growth; [('Dr. W. Van Fleet' × 'Général Jacqueminot') × 'Break o'Day']

'Early Peace' -- See 'Molodost Mira'

'Early Ray' -- See 'Gelray'

'Early Red' HSpn, rb; flowers carmine-red with gold, medium-large, semi-dbl.; [R. pimpinellifolia × 'Claudius Denoyel']

'Early Spring' -- See 'Soshun'

'Earth Song' Gr, dp, 1976, Buck, Dr. Griffith J.; bud long, pointed to urn-shaped; flowers Tyrian red to Tyrian rose, 4-4½ in., 25-30 petals, cupped, moderate fragrance; foliage glossy, dark, leathery; upright, bushy growth; ['Music Maker' × 'Prairie Star']; intr. 1975

Earthquake™ -- See 'Morquake'

'Earthquake, Climbing' -- See 'Morshook'

'Easlea's Golden Rambler' ('Golden Rambler') HWich, yb, 1932, Easlea; flowers rich buff-yellow marked crimson, 4 in., 35 petals, flat, borne singly or in small clusters, moderate fragrance; non-recurrent; foliage leathery, rich olive-green; vigorous, climbing growth; PP114

'East Anglia' HT, mp, 1939, Morse; flowers aurora-pink; [sport of 'Golden Dawn']

'East Europe' F, mp, Urban, J.

Easter™ Min, my, Olesen; flowers dbl., borne mostly solitary, moderate fragrance; foliage dark green, glossy; growth bushy, very low (20-40 cm.)

'Easter Basket'   F, yb, Meilland; flowers soft yellow with petal edges turning pink, ruffled petals, large, semi-double, shallow cup, borne in clusters, slight fragrance; recurrent; foliage medium green; medium, bushy growth; intr. 2007

'Easter Bonnet' ('Super Derby') HT, op, 1983, Burks, Joe J.; [sport of Queen Elizabeth®]; intr. 1982

'Easter Bunny' -- See 'Renbun'

'Easter Morn' -- See 'Easter Morning'

'Easter Morning' ('Easter Morn') Min, w, 1960, Moore, Ralph S.; bud pointed; flowers ivory-white, 1½ in., 60-70 petals; foliage leathery, glossy; vigorous, dwarf (12-16 in.) growth; PP2177; ['Golden Glow' × 'Zee']; intr. 1960

'Easter Parade'   F, yb, 1951, Whisler; bud ovoid, golden yellow; flowers salmon-pink and cerise, reverse yellow, becoming light carmine, 2½-3½ in., 50-55 petals, slight fragrance; foliage dark, glossy, bronze; vigorous, bushy growth; PP1200; ['Sunshine' × 'Herrenhausen']

'Eastern Gem'   T, w, 1905, Conard & Jones; flowers creamy white, shaded light pink and yellow

'Easy' -- See 'Zipeasy'

Easy Cover™ -- See 'Pouleas'

Easy Going™ -- See 'Harflow'

'Easy Orange'   F, ob, 1995, Jobson, Daniel J.; flowers bright orange, medium, full, borne in small clusters, moderate fragrance; foliage medium size, dark green, glossy; numerous prickles; upright, medium growth; [('Valerie Jeanne' × Eyepaint®) × 'Laureate']

'Easy to Cut' -- See 'Lenbefas'

'Easy Vibes' -- See 'Geleasy'

'Ebb Tide'   HT, ab, 1961, Von Abrams; bud long, pointed; flowers light yellowish-pink, 5 in., 28 petals, high-centered; foliage glossy; vigorous, upright, compact growth; [('Sutter's Gold' × seedling) × 'Peace']; intr. 1961

Ebb Tide™ -- See 'Weksmopur'

Ebby™ -- See 'Wilyeld'

'Ebène'   HP, m, 1844, Boyau; flowers violet-purple, medium, full

'Eberhard Jung'   Pol, mr, 1930, Schmitt, L.; flowers small, semi-dbl.

'Eberwein' -- See 'Dopey'

'Éblouissant'   Pol, dr, 1918, Turbat; flowers dazzling deep red, very dbl., globular, borne in clusters, slight fragrance; foliage bronze, glossy; bushy growth; ['Bengale Rose' × 'Cramoisi Superieur']

'Ebony'   Gr, dr, 1960, Von Abrams; bud ovoid; flowers velvety dark red, 3-4 in., 20-30 petals, high-centered, slight fragrance; foliage glossy; vigorous, upright growth; PP2137; ['Carrousel' × 'Charles Mallerin']; intr. 1960

'Eboracum'   LCl, w, 1977, Powell, G.; flowers creamy white, yellow at base, 2½-3 in., 30-35 petals, borne singly and several together, moderate sweet fragrance; reliable repeat; foliage glossy; growth strong; hardy; [Casino® × 'Ice White']

'Écarlate'   HT, mr, 1907, Boytard; flowers brilliant scarlet, somewhat like Grüss an Teplitz, open, small, semi-dbl.; foliage rich green, glossy; vigorous, bushy growth; ['Camoens' × unknown]

Ecco™ ('Ecco Parade') Min, dy, Olesen; flowers dbl., no fragrance; foliage medium green, semi-glossy; growth bushy, very low (20-40 cm.); intr. 2000

'Ecco Parade' -- See 'Poulra008'

'Echizo'   HT, Camprubi, C.

'Echo' ('Baby Tausendschön') Pol, pb, 1914, Lambert, P.; flowers varying (like Tausendschön) from dark pink to almost white, semi-dbl., parti-colored; reliable repeat; growth short, bushy; [sport of 'Tausendschön']; reclassified as Polyantha based on growth habit and historical classification

'Echo'   S, op, Lens, Louis; flowers pink-salmon, dbl., borne in large clusters; vigorous growth, 80-120 cm; intr. 1970

'Eckart Witzigmann'   S, mp, Delbard; flowers soft, tender pink, full, cupped, borne in loose clusters, intense rose, red berries and peach fragrance; recurrent; foliage dark green, glossy; intr. 2007

'Éclair' ('Gärtendirektor Lauche') HP, dr, 1883, Lacharme, F.; flowers very dark red shaded blackish, well-shaped, small, dbl.; tall growth; ['Général Jacqueminot' × unknown]

'Eclair de Jupiter'   N, mr; flowers scarlet, shaded violet, large, dbl.

'Eclair de Jupiter'   HP, mr; flowers rose red, shaded glowing garnet purple, large, full

'Éclaireur'   HP, dr, 1895, Vigneron; flowers dark bright red, exterior petals velvety, large, dbl., cupped, borne mostly solitary, moderate fragrance; very remontant; foliage dark green; ['Duhamel Dumonceau' × unknown]

'Eclaireur'   F, Godin, M.; intr. 1971

Éclat de Haute Bretagne® HT, ab, Adam; flowers rosy apricot, reverse lighter, dbl., globular, intense fragrance; to 70-90 cm. growth; intr. 2006

Eclat de Rire®   S, yb, Dorieux; flowers yellow with salmon tints, turning salmon pink with age, single, flat, borne in broad inflorescences; foliage clear green, glossy; 100 cm. growth; intr. 2007

'Éclatant'   Misc OGR, Vibert; intr. 1825

'Éclatant'   Ch, mp, before 1836, Prévost; bud dark purple; flowers carmine

'Éclatante'   HGal, mr, about 1860, Miellez

'Éclatante'   HP, rb, Guillot; flowers poppy red with purple-violet, medium, full; intr. 1862

'Eclipse' -- See 'Saudora'

'Eclipse, Climbing'   Cl HT, ly

'Eclipse'   HT, ly, 1935, Nicolas; bud remarkably long, pointed, deep gold, with long, narrow,; flowers golden yellow, loose, 28 petals, moderate fragrance; foliage leathery, dark; vigorous, bushy growth; PP172; ['Joanna Hill' × 'Federico Casas']

Ecole de Barbizon® LCl, rb, Dorieux; flowers crimson striped white, semi-double; very floriferous; intr. 2005

'Ecole d'Écully'   HT, op, Laperrière; flowers light salmon with saffron yellow at base, dbl.; intr. 1988

'Ecstasy'   HT, yb, 1935, Dickson, A.; flowers pale yellow shaded bronze and cerise, dbl.; erect, branching growth

'Ecstasy' ('Ekstasse', 'Extase') HT, dr, Kordes; buds large, pointed; flowers crimson, deepening to magenta, full, intense fragrance; nearly thornless flowering stems; growth medium; intr. 1994

'Ed Steer'   HT, mr, 1999, Poole, Lionel; flowers 5 in., full, borne mostly singly, slight fragrance; foliage medium size, dark green, semi-glossy; prickles moderate; upright, medium (30 in.) growth; [('Royal William' × 'Gabi') × 'Adrienne Berman']

'Edda'   LCl, lp, 1929, Lodi; flowers pale pink, slightly darker center, 9-10 cm., very dbl.; ['Reine Marie Henriette' × 'Boncenne']

'Edda'   S, mr, Lundstad; flowers clear rose-red, open, medium, 16 petals, borne in clusters; profuse, repeated bloom; foliage dark, glossy, leathery; vigorous growth; [Lichterloh® × 'Scharlachglut']; intr. 1969

'Eddan' -- See 'Makeddan'

'Eddie'   HT, mr, 2004, Walsh, Richard; flowers medium red with yellow at petal base, 10 cm., full, borne mostly solitary, slight fragrance; foliage medium size, dark green, glossy, bronze when new; prickles medium, pointed; growth upright, tall (2 m.); garden; cutting; ['Living' × Uwe Seeler®]; intr. 2003

'Eddie's Advent'   HT, lp, 1938, Eddie; flowers pale buff, tipped pink, fading almost white, large, dbl., high-centered; foliage leathery; vigorous growth; ['Mrs Sam McGredy' × 'Edith Krause']

'Eddie's Cream'   F, w, 1956, Eddie; flowers cream, large, dbl., borne in clusters, moderate apricot fragrance; vigorous growth; ['Golden Rapture' × 'Lavender Pinocchio']

'Eddie's Crimson'   HMoy, mr, 1956, Eddie; flowers blood-red, 4-5 in., semi-dbl.; non-recurrent; vigorous (9-10 ft.) growth; large, globular fruit; ['Donald Prior' × R. moyesii hybrid]

'Eddie's Jewel'   HMoy, mr, 1962, Eddie; flowers fiery red, semi-dbl.; recurrent bloom; few prickles; stems bark red; vigorous (8-9 ft.) growth; ['Donald Prior' × R. moyesii hybrid]

'Eddie's Multiflora'   Sp; clone of R. multiflora; used for understock

'Edel'   HT, w, 1919, McGredy; flowers ivory-white, passing to pure white, well-formed, very large, dbl.; vigorous growth; ['Frau Karl Druschki' × 'Niphetos']

'Edelweiss'   HP, w, 1925, Dienemann; flowers medium, full; ['Frau Karl

Druschki' × unknown]

Edelweiss™ -- See 'Pouledel'

Eden™ Min, mp, Olesen; flowers dbl., 25-30 petals, no fragrance; foliage medium green, semi-glossy; growth bushy, very low (20-40 cm.); intr. 1996

'Eden' -- See 'Meiviolin'

Eden Climber™ -- See 'Meiviolin'

'Eden Ellen' F, ab, 1985, Schneider, Peter; flowers medium, 35 petals, slight fragrance; foliage medium size, medium green, matte; bushy growth; [seedling × seedling]; intr. 1984

'Eden Folies' -- See 'Meiptipier'

'Eden Romantica' F, pb, Meilland; flowers light orient pink and light green, very full, globular, borne in sprays; PP15501; greenhouse rose; intr. 2004

Eden Rose® HT, dp, 1950, Meilland, F.; bud ovoid; flowers Tyrian rose, 4½ in., 50-60 petals, cupped, intense fragrance; foliage glossy, bright dark green; vigorous, upright growth; PP1149; ['Peace' × 'Signora']; intr. 1950

Eden Rose, Climbing® Cl HT, dp, 1962, Meilland, Alain A.; flowers deep pink, fading to medium pink, lighter reverse, 12-14 cm., strong fragrance

'Eden Rose 85' -- See 'Meiviolin'

'Eden Sungold' F, my, 1977, Herholdt, J.A.; flowers pure yellow, 3 in., 30-35 petals, slight fragrance; semi-dwarf growth; [seedling × seedling]; intr. 1976

'Edgar Andreu' HWich, mr, 1912, Barbier; flowers bright blood-red, streaked white, reverse lighter, 7 cm., dbl., borne in clusters of 7-15; foliage small, dark green, glossy; [*R. wichurana* × 'Cramoisi Supérieur']

'Edgar Blanchard' ('Mons Edg. Blanchard') HT, lp, 1912, Duron; flowers pink shading to white, large, dbl.; ['Frau Karl Druschki' × unknown]

'Edgar Degas' S, rb, Delbard; flowers red irregularly striped yellow and pink, semi-dbl.; foliage dark green, glossy; growth to 2-3 ft.

'Edgar Jolibois' HP, mr, 1883, Verdier, E.; flowers velvety scarlet, shaded with carmine, poppy and violet, large, full

'Edgar M. Burnett' HT, pb, 1914, McGredy; flowers flesh-pink, center dark pink, very large, dbl., moderate fragrance

'Edie Anne' HT, mp; intr. 1997

'Edina' HT, w, Dobbie; flowers white, occasionally flushed pink, well-formed, intense fragrance; foliage bronze red passing togreen; vigorous growth; intr. 1934

'Edina' B, mp, 1849, Boyau; flowers bright pink, medium, full

'Edisto' -- See 'Micedi'

'Edith Bellenden' HEg, mp, 1895, Penzance; flowers pale rose, small, single, borne in clusters; foliage fragrant; vigorous growth; very hardy

'Edith Cavell' HT, ly, 1918, Chaplin Bros.; flowers pale lemon-white, large, dbl.

'Edith Cavell' -- See 'Miss Edith Cavell'

'Edith Clark' HT, mr, 1928, Clark, A.; flowers fiery red, dbl., globular; foliage rich green; dwarf growth; ['Mme Abel Chatenay' × seedling]

Edith de Martinelli® F, op, 1958, Arles; flowers salmon-pink, well-formed; vigorous growth; [('Gruss an Teplitz' × 'Independence') × 'Floradora']

Edith de Martinelli, Climbing® -- See 'Oradit'

'Edith de Murat' B, w, 1858, Ducher; flowers flesh, changing to white, petals somewhat fringed, medium, full

'Edith Dennett' F, op, 1974, Holmes, R.; flowers salmon-pink, 2-3 in., 24-30 petals, rosette, slight fragrance; foliage glossy, dark; free growth; intr. 1973

'Edith d'Ombrain' ('Edith Dombrain') HT, w, 1902, Dickson; flowers white with touches of light pink, large, full

'Edith Dombrain' -- See 'Edith d'Ombrain'

'Edith Felberg' HT, w, 1931, Felberg-Leclerc; flowers cream, center slightly darker, rather, dbl., cupped; foliage leathery; [seedling × 'Souv. de H.A. Verschuren']

'Edith Hayward' Cl HT, lp, 1967, Hayward; flowers pastel pink, large, dbl., high-centered; recurrent bloom; foliage glossy, dark; vigorous growth; ['Fontanelle' × 'Gen. MacArthur']

'Edith Hazelrigg' HT, ob, 1953, Cant, F.; flowers orange-cerise, pointed, 25 petals; foliage dark; vigorous growth

'Edith Holden' -- See 'Chewlegacy'

'Edith Krause' HT, w, 1930, Krause; flowers greenish white, large, 30 petals, high-centered; very vigorous growth; ['Mrs Charles Lamplough' × 'Souv. de H.A. Verschuren']

'Edith Mary Mee' HT, or, 1936, Mee; flowers vivid orient red, flushed orange, base yellow, dbl.; foliage dark, leathery; vigorous, bushy, compact growth

'Edith Nellie Perkins' HT, op, 1928, Dickson, A.; flowers salmon-pink, flushed orange, reverse orange-red, shaded orange, 35-40 petals, moderate fragrance; few prickles; vigorous, bushy growth

'Edith Nellie Perkins, Climbing' Cl HT, op, 1936, H&S; Howard Rose Co.

'Edith Oliver' HT, lp, 1984, Singleton, C.H.; flowers soft light pink, large, 35 petals, borne in clusters of 4, moderate fragrance; foliage medium size, medium green, semi-glossy; prickles brownish-red; bushy growth; ['Pink Parfait' × seedling]; intr. 1980

'Edith Part' HT, pb, 1913, McGredy; flowers rich red, suffused deep salmon and coppery yellow

'Edith Piaf' -- See 'Meinical'

'Edith Piaf' HT, dr, Meilland; flowers dark red, 56 petals, high-centered, intense fruity fragrance

'Edith Piaf' HT, m, 1965, Verbeek; bud ovoid; flowers purple-red, large, dbl., slight fragrance; foliage dark; ['Poinsettia' × (Baccará® × seedling)]; intr. 1962

'Edith Roberts' HT, ab, 1969, Roberts, P.D.; flowers 5 in., high-centered; foliage glossy, dark; [sport of 'Dorothy Peach']

'Edith Schurr' S, yb, 1976, Stanard; bud globular, sulfur-yellow; flowers light yellow, center pink, 5 in., 60 petals, intense damask fragrance; recurrent bloom; foliage glossy; spreading growth; [('Wendy Cussons' × 'Gavotte') × 'Leverkusen']

'Edith Southgate' Cl Min, pb, 1997, Barker, S.J.L.; flowers medium, dbl., borne mostly singly; foliage medium size, medium green, semi-glossy; some prickles; upright, medium (5ft.)growth; [Laura Ford® × 'Admiral Rodney']

'Edith Turner' HP, lp, 1898, Turner; flowers light flesh pink, petals edged white

'Edith Willkie' HT, pb, 1943, Joseph H. Hill, Co.; bud long, pointed; flowers vivid pink, base lemon-chrome, 4½-5 in., 25-30 petals; foliage leathery, dark; vigorous, upright, compact growth; PP500; ['Joanna Hill' × R.M.S. Queen Mary]; intr. 1946

'Edith Yorke' HMult, lp, 1953, Miller, A.I.; flowers light almond-pink, semi-dbl., rosette, borne in trusses; foliage light green; very vigorous growth; ['Havering Rambler' × seedling]

'Editor McFarland' HT, mp, 1931, Mallerin, C.; flowers glowing pink, slightly suffused yellow, large, 30 petals; vigorous, bushy growth; ['Pharisaer' × 'Lallita']

'Editor McFarland, Climbing' Cl HT, mp, 1948, Roseglen Nursery

'Editor Stewart' LCl, rb, 1939, Clark, A.; flowers crimson, sometimes flecked with white, fading to dark purple/pink, large, semi-dbl.; foliage bronze; long stems; growth vigorous; pillar or large bush; hybrid gigantea

'Editor Tommy Cairns' HT, pb, 1991, Winchel, Joseph F.; flowers bright pink, light pink reverse, medium, 32-40 petals, borne mostly singly, slight fragrance; foliage medium size, medium green, semi-glossy; upright, medium growth; [seedling × seedling]

'Edmée Cocteau' -- See 'Mme Edmée Cocteau'

'Edmée et Roger' HT, op, 1903, Ketten Bros.; bud long; flowers flesh, center salmon flesh pink, darker ground, large; ['Safrano' × 'Mme Caroline Testout']

'Edmond Charles-Roux' HT, Dorieux, Francois; intr. 1990

'Edmond de Biauzat' T, op, 1885, Levet; flowers peach, tinted with salmon, large, full

'Edmond Deschayes' -- See 'Edmond Deshayes'

'Edmond Deshayes' ('Edmond Deschayes') HT, ly, 1901, Bernaix, A.; flowers yellowish-white, large, dbl.

'Edmond Duval' HGal, mp, about 1835, Parmentier

'Edmond Proust' HWich, mr, 1903,

Barbier; flowers pale rose and carmine, darker at center, 5-6 cm., very dbl., borne in clusters of 3-6, moderate fragrance; sparse seasonal bloom; foliage glossy; short stems; growth to 5-8 ft.; [*R. wichurana* × 'Souv. de Catherine Guillot']

'Edmond Sablayrolles' T, pb, 1888, Bonnaire; flowers hydrangea pink with peach/yellow, aging to bright carmine pink, large; ['Souv de Victor Hugo' × 'Mme Cusin']

'Edmond Wood' HP, mr, 1875, Verdier, E.; flowers cherry red, reverse carmine, large, full

Edmonton™ (Explosion Border™) S, mp, Poulsen; flowers medium pink with mauve tones, 5-8 cm., semi-dbl. to dbl., cupped, borne in clusters, very slight fragrance; recurrent; foliage dark green, glossy; growth bushy (60-100 cm.); intr. 2005

'Edmund M. Mills' HT, ob, 1927, Hieatt; flowers rosy flame, base deep gold, open, large, semi-dbl.; foliage dark, leathery; very vigorous, upright growth; ['Red Radiance' × 'Padre']

'Edmund Rice' -- See 'Welpin'

'Edna-Chris' F, w, 1978, Ogden; bud pointed; flowers off-white, large, 30 petals, slight fragrance; foliage matte, green; tall, upright growth; [sport of 'Gene Boerner']

'Edna Kaye' HT, lp, 1959, Kemp, M.L.; flowers light pink tinted buff,, 5 in., 56 petals; foliage bronze; free growth; ['Directeur Guerin' × 'Mirandy']

'Edna Marie' -- See 'Mored'

'Edna Mary' F, dp, Horner; intr. 2005

'Edna Walling' ('Bert Mulley') HMult, w, 1940, Clark or Mulley; flowers white to light rose pink, small, single, borne in clusters of 5-20; vigorous, climbing growth

'Edna Wilson' -- See 'Grifed'

'Ednah Thomas' ('Bloomfield Improvement') Cl HT, op, 1931, Thomas; flowers salmon-rose, large, dbl.; recurrent bloom; strong stems; vigorous, climbing growth; ['seedling climber' × 'Bloomfield Progress']

'Edo Bergsma' HT, pb, 1932, Buisman, G. A. H.; bud pointed; flowers bright flesh and peach, large, intense fragrance; ['Capt. F.S. Harvey-Cant' × 'Étoile de Hollande']

'Edon' F, ab, Kordes

'Edouard André' ('Edouard André le Botaniste') HP, dr, 1880, Verdier, E.; flowers red, tinged with purple, large, full; foliage light green, oblong, finely dentate; prickles numerous, irregular, pointed, pink; growth upright

'Edouard André le Botaniste' -- See 'Edouard André'

'Edouard Desfossés' ('Gloire des Brotteaux') B, m, 1840, Renard; flowers bright lilac pink, large, full

'Edouard Dufour' HP, dp, 1877, Lévêque; flowers dark carmine with brown tints, large, full, moderate fragrance; ['Annie Wood' × unknown]

'Edouard Fontaine' HP, mp, 1878, Fontaine; flowers frosty pink, large, full

'Edouard Gautier' T, yb, 1883, Pernet-Ducher; flowers have outer petals white, slightly pink on reverse, interior buff yellow with light pink, full, globular; ['Devoniensis' × unknown]

'Edouard Guillot' HT, op, Guillot-Massad; flowers salmon pink with slight yellow edges, borne in clusters of 3 - 5; foliage medium green, semi-glossy; intr. 2005

'Edouard Hervé' HP, dr, 1884, Verdier, E.; flowers dark currant red, large, full; foliage dark green, oblong, deeply toothed; prickles long, unequal, very sharp

'Edouard Jesse' -- See 'Edward Jesse'

'Edouard Lefort' HP, mr, 1886, Verdier, E.; flowers scarlet-carmine, shaded shining purple, large, very full

'Edouard Mignot' HT, m, 1927, Sauvageot, H.; flowers purplish garnet-red, reverse amaranth, dbl.; bushy growth

'Edouard Morren' HP, dp, 1869, Granger; flowers silky carmine pink, tinted cherry red, very large, full; ['Jules Margottin' × unknown]

'Edouard Morren' -- See 'Edward Morren'

'Édouard Pinaert' ('Edouard Pynaert') HP, dr, 1877, Schwartz; flowers dark currant-red, edged in crimson, large, full, globular; foliage dark green; prickles numerous, slightly curved; growth upright; ['Antoine Ducher' × unknown]

'Edouard Pynaert' -- See 'Édouard Pinaert'

'Edouard Renard' HT, mr, 1933, Dot, Pedro; flowers carmine, base yellow; long, stiff stems

'Edu Meyer' HT, rb, 1904, Lambert

'Eduard Schill' HT, or, 1931, Kordes; flowers brick-red shaded nasturtium-yellow, very large, semi-dbl., cupped; foliage glossy; vigorous growth; ['Charles P. Kilham' × 'Mev. G.A. van Rossem']

'Eduardo Toda' HT, my, 1947, Dot, Pedro; bud pointed; flowers sunflower-yellow; ['Ophelia' × 'Julien Potin']

'Edward Behrens' HT, dr, 1921, Kordes; flowers very dark velvety crimson, very large, dbl.; ['Richmond' × 'Admiral Ward']

'Edward Bohane' HT, or, 1915, Dickson, A.; flowers velvety crimson-orange to scarlet, large, very full, moderate fragrance

'Edward Colston' -- See 'Sancol'

'Edward Hyams' S, yb; collected by Edward Hyams from Sharud in Iran in 1972; hybrid Persica; intr. 1972

'Edward Jesse' ('Edouard Jesse') B, m, about 1840, Laffay; flowers dark purple, shaded crimson, medium, dbl., cupped

'Edward Little Star' -- See 'Hormyboy'

'Edward Mawley' HT, dr, 1911, McGredy; bud almost black; flowers dark crimson, large, 18 petals, high-centered; bushy growth

'Edward Morren' ('Edouard Morren') HP, mr, 1868, Granger; flowers deep cherry-rose, large, dbl., flat; vigorous growth; ['Jules Margottin' × unknown]

'Edward VII' Pol, mp, 1911, Low; flowers clear pink, small; [sport of 'Mme Norbert Levavasseur']

'Edwardian Lady' -- See 'Chewlegacy'

'Edwin F. Smith' HT, 1918, Byrnes

'Edwin Lonsdale' HWich, dy, 1919, Dickson, H.; flowers bright light orange with citron yellow, fading to white, full; [*R. wichurana* × 'Safrano']

'Edwin Markham' HT, mp, 1923, Clarke Bros.; flowers bright rose-pink suffused silvery, dbl.; ['Ophelia' × 'Hoosier Beauty']

'Edwin T. Meredith' HT, ob, 1978, Warriner, William A.; bud ovoid, pointed; flowers coral-pink, 5 in., 30 petals, flat, slight fragrance; bushy, upright growth; PP4648; ['Futura' × 'First Prize']; intr. 1979

'Efekto 21' -- See 'Meitobla'

'Effective' LCl, mr, 1913, Hobbies; bud long; flowers crimson, 4 in., dbl., cupped, borne singly or in small clusters, moderate fragrance; intermittent repeat; very vigorous growth; [('Gen. MacArthur' × unknown) × 'Paul's Carmine Pillar']

'Effekt' HT, rb, 1935, Krause; flowers scarlet-red, reverse flushed golden yellow, large, dbl., cupped; vigorous, bushy growth; ['I Zingari' × seedling]

'Effekt' F, dr, Berger; intr. 1975

'Egalité' F, m, 1946, Leenders, M.; bud pointed; flowers pale lilac-rose, 4 in., 25 petals, borne in trusses; foliage bronze; vigorous, branching growth; ['Irene' × seedling]

'Egas Monitz' HT, Moreira da Silva, A.

'Egeria' ('Aegeria', 'Peach Blossom') HP, lp, 1874, Paul, W.; flowers delicate flesh pink, nuanced carmine and washed with white, large, full, semi-globular; ['Jules Margottin' × unknown]

Egeskov™ (Enduring Spirit™, Lill Lindfors™, Rosehill™) F, mp, 1985, Olesen, Pernille & Mogens N.; bud long, pointed ovoid; flowers bright medium pink, 20 petals, cupped, borne in large clusters, slight fragrance; foliage medium size, light green, glossy; prickles moderate, 4 mm., concave, greyed-orange; bushy growth; PP13835; [Tornado® × Matangi®]; intr. 1982

'Egggina' ('Margina') Pol, w, Martin, John & Gina; intr. 1998

'Eggjulia' HT, r, Martin; intr. 2003

'Eglantine' Pol, dp, 1930, Soupert & Notting; flowers carmine, center white, many yellow stamens, single; small vigorous, dwarf, bushy growth; ['Amaury Fonseca' × 'Rodhatte']

'Eglantine Guillot' -- See 'Mlle Eglantine Guillot'

'Eglantyne' -- See 'Ausmak'

'Eglantyne Jebb' -- See 'Ausmak'

'Egmont Behrens' LCl, dr, Kordes; flowers deep velvet red, maturing to magenta

burgundy, large, dbl., cupped, borne in clusters, moderate fragrance; recurrent; growth tall (10 ft.); intr. 2002
'Egoli' -- See 'Korameget'
Egon Schiele™ -- See 'Pouluf'
'Egyptian Treasure' S, ob, 1974, Gandy, Douglas L.; flowers orange, 4 in., 16 petals, slight fragrance; foliage dark, glossy; [('Coup de Foudre' × 'S'Agaro') × 'Vagabonde']; intr. 1973
'Ehigasa' ('Flower Parasol') F, yb, Keihan; intr. 1974
'Eichsfeldia' HMult, ly, 1925, Bruder Alfons; flowers yellowish-white, 3-4 cm., single, borne in small clusters, moderate musky fragrance; foliage glossy
'Eiffel Tower' ('Eiffelturm', 'Tour Eiffel') HT, mp, 1963, Armstrong, D.L. & Swim, H. C.; bud long, urn-shaped; flowers 3½-5 in., 35 petals, high-centered, intense fragrance; foliage leathery, semi-glossy; vigorous, upright growth; PP2332; ['First Love' × seedling]; intr. 1963
'Eiffel Tower, Climbing' Cl HT, mp, 1970, Laveena Roses; [sport of 'Eiffel Tower']; intr. 1967
'Eiffelturm' -- See 'Eiffel Tower'
'Eiko' ('Glory') HT, yb, 1978, Suzuki, Seizo; bud pointed; flowers yellow and scarlet, pointed., 5-6 in., 30-35 petals; foliage large, glossy, light green; vigorous growth; [('Peace' × 'Charleston') × 'Kagayaki']
'Eileen Bee' -- See 'Lioglow'
'Eileen Boxall' HT, dr, 1948, Boxall; flowers cerise, 5 in., 18 petals; foliage dark; vigorous growth; [sport of 'Betty Uprichard']
'Eileen Dorothea' HT, mr, 1931, Dickson, A.; bud pointed; flowers crimson-scarlet, edged darker, base yellow, dbl., high-centered; foliage deeply serrated; vigorous growth
'Eileen Loow' -- See 'Eileen Low'
'Eileen Louise' HT, mp, 1985, Brown, Harry G.L.S.; [sport of 'Admiral Rodney']
'Eileen Low' ('Eileen Loow') Pol, mp, 1911, Levavasseur; flowers China pink, grading to cream at base of petals, medium, dbl.; ['Mme Norbert Levavasseur' × 'Orléans Rose']
'Eileen Whyte' -- See 'Horeileen'
'Eileen's Rose' -- See 'Horchappy'
'Eisenach' HWich, mr, 1910, Kiese; flowers bright red, small, single, borne in large clusters; very vigorous growth
'Eisprinzessin' HT, pb
'Ekstasse' -- See 'Korazerka'
'Ekta' HGal, mp, 1927, Hansen, N.E.; flowers medium, single to semi-dbl., moderate fragrance; non-recurrent; ['Alika' × 'American Beauty']
'El Areana' HSpn, w, 1911, Geschwind; flowers semi-dbl., borne singly on small stalks; early summer; foliage small, light green, matte; numerous prickles; growth low, compact
'El Capitan' Gr, mr, 1960, Swim, H.C.; flowers cherry to rose-red, 3½-4½ in., 30 petals, high-centered, borne in small clusters, slight fragrance; foliage dark, glossy; vigorous, upright, bushy growth; PP1796; ['Charlotte Armstrong' × 'Floradora']; intr. 1959
'El Capitan, Climbing' Cl Gr, mr, 1963, Armstrong, D.L.; PP2697
'El Catala' Gr, rb, 1981, Buck, Dr. Griffith J.; bud ovoid, pointed; flowers medium red, reverse light pink, 35 petals, cupped, borne 1-8 per cluster, slight fragrance; foliage large, glossy; prickles awl-like; erect, slightly bushy growth; ['Wanderin' Wind' × (('Dornroschen' × 'Peace') × 'Brasilia')]
'El Chocón' HT, dp
'El Cid' HT, or, 1969, Armstrong, D.L.; bud ovoid; flowers orange-red early, becoming more vivid red, 4-4½ in., 30-35 petals, high-centered to cupped, borne usually singly, some small clusters, very slight fragrance; recurrent; foliage medium size, olive green, semi-glossy, soft; prickles numerous, long, hooked slightly downward, yellowish-brown; stems medium, strong; vigorous, upright, bushy growth; PP3075; ['Fandango' × 'Roundelay']
'El Dorado' HT, yb, 1972, Armstrong, D.L.; flowers golden yellow, edged reddish, open, large, dbl., high-centered, intense fragrance; foliage large, glossy, leathery; vigorous, upright growth; PP3348; ['Manitou' × 'Summer Sunshine']
'El Paso' HT, yb, 1988, Ohlson, John; flowers light yellow on outer petals, deep yellow on inner petals, reverse light yellow, dbl., high-centered, borne usually singly, slight spicy fragrance; foliage medium size, medium green, semi-glossy; prickles straight, medium, greenish-brown; bushy, medium, floriferous growth; ['First Prize' × 'Arlene Francis']
'El Toro' -- See 'Uncle Joe'
'Elaina' -- See 'Zipela'
'Elaina Rothman' HT, mp, 2002, Poole, Lionel; flowers full, borne mostly solitary, slight fragrance; foliage medium size, medium green, semi-glossy; prickles medium, long, pointed, medium; growth upright, medium (2½ ft.); garden decorative, exhibition; ['Gavotte' × 'Spirit of the Heath']; intr. 2002
'Elaine' HT, ab, Boerner; bud pointed; flowers 4½ in., 35-45 petals, high-centered, slight fragrance; foliage leathery; very vigorous, upright growth; PP978; ['Eclipse' × R.M.S. Queen Mary]; intr. 1951
'Elaine' HT, yb, 1908, Paul, W.; flowers citron yellow with pink tints, large, full
'Elaine' HT, mp, Robinson, H.; flowers rose-pink, large, very dbl., high-centered, moderate fragrance; ['Mrs A.R. Barraclough' × 'Lady Sylvia']; intr. 1950
'Elaine Frawley' Pol, m, 2000, Weatherly, Lilia; flowers mauve-pink, tinted blue, reverse lighter, 1-2 in., very full, borne in small clusters, slight fragrance; foliage medium size, medium green, matte; few prickles; stems compact, low (less than 3 ft); ['Cornelia' × unknown]; intr. 1996
'Elaine Greffulhe' T, w, 1892, Cochet; flowers bright white, center sulfer yellow, large, very full
'Elaine Holman' HT, pb, 1976, Watson; bud long, pointed; flowers 3½-4 in., 50 petals, high-centered, moderate fragrance; foliage soft; vigorous growth; ['Red Devil' × 'Avon']; intr. 1975
'Elaine Stuart' HT, w, 1932, Edwards; flowers cream, center yellow; long stems; ['Antoine Rivoire' × 'Lillian Moore']
'Elaine White' F, w, 1959, Riethmuller; bud pointed; flowers cream, white and pink, open, small, semi-dbl., borne in clusters; foliage leathery; very vigorous, upright growth; ['Gartendirektor Otto Linne' × seedling]
'Elaine's Choice' F, pb, 1973, Ellick; flowers pale pink-apricot, yellow blend, 5 in., 40 petals, intense fragrance; foliage semi-glossy; vigorous growth; [Orange Sensation® × 'Peace']; intr. 1972
Élan' F, my, Croix, P.; intr. 1960
'Elation' HT, dy, 1974, Warriner, William A.; bud long, pointed; flowers large, dbl.; foliage large, glossy, dark, leathery; vigorous, upright growth; ['Buccaneer' × seedling]
'Elba' HT, dr, 1963, Moreira da Silva; flowers deep red, reverse gold; ['Confidence' × 'Crimson Glory']
'Elbefreude' F, mr, Schmadlak, Dr.; flowers vermilion, large, dbl.; intr. 1983
'Elbeglut' Pol, dr, Schmadlak, Dr.; flowers large, semi-dbl.; intr. 1978
'Elbegold' Pol, dy, Schmadlak, Dr.; flowers golden yellow, medium, dbl.; intr. 1973
'Eldora Harvey' HT, pb, 1930, Harvey; flowers pink, center tinted lavender, reverse dark pink, dbl.; ['Red Radiance' × 'Maman Cochet']
'Eldorado' HT, ob, 1923, H&S; flowers copper, suffused orange and salmon, very large, dbl., moderate fragrance; bushy growth; [seedling × 'Mme Edouard Herriot']
'Eldorado' HT, ob, Tantau; intr. 2004
'Eldorado' -- See 'Jacspri'
'Eleanor' Min, op, 1960, Moore, Ralph S.; bud long, pointed; flowers coral-pink, aging darker, 1 in., 20-30 petals; foliage leathery, glossy; upright, bushy (12 in.), growth; PP2175; [(R. wichurana × Floradora) × (seedling × 'Zee')]; intr. 1960
Eleanor™ -- See 'Poulberin'
'Eleanor Annelise' -- See 'Cocslightly'
'Eleanor Frances' HT, dy, 1971, Green Acres Rose Nursery; flowers deep aureolin-yellow, 5 in., 28 petals; foliage glossy, leathery; vigorous, tall, upright growth; ['Vienna Charm' × seedling]
'Eleanor Henning' HT, op, 1920, Easlea; bud pointed; flowers salmon-pink
'Eleanor of Aquitaine' -- See 'Aliénor d'Aquitaine'

'Eleanor Perenyi' Gr, yb, 1986, French, Richard; flowers yellow flushed apricot, reverse yellow flushed salmon, loose, 25 petals, moderate fruity fragrance; foliage medium size, dark, semi-glossy; prickles very few, hooked, small, red; medium, upright growth; hips small, globular, orange-red; ['America' × 'Sunsong']

'Electra' S, dy, Winchell; flowers dbl., borne in clusters, slight fruity fragrance; free-flowering; growth moderate, much like a floribunda; PPAF; intr. 2006

'Electra' HMult, ly, 1900, Veitch; flowers yellow, fading white, medium, dbl., globular; foliage rich green, glossy; very vigorous, climbing growth; Ruled extinct 1971 ARA; [R. multiflora × 'William Allen Richardson']

'Electra' HT, my, 1971, Boerner; flowers open, large, dbl., slight fragrance; foliage large, glossy, leathery; vigorous, upright growth; PP2979; ['Eclipse' × seedling]; intr. 1970

'Electric Blanket' -- See 'Korpancom'

Electron® -- See 'Mullard Jubilee'

'Elegance' Min, m; recurrent; growth medium

Elegance™ ('Elegance Hit') Min, or, Olesen; bud short, pointed ovoid; flowers orange-red, medium, 25 petals, rosette, borne in clusters of 6-8; recurrent; foliage dark green, glossy; prickles few, 4 mm., hooked, greyed-orange; growth compact, bushy (40-60 cm.); PP15384; [seedling × seedling]; intr. 2003

'Elegance' HWich, my, 1937, Brownell; flowers yellow, fading white at edges, reverse darker, 6 in., 48 petals, moderate fragrance; foliage large, dark green, glossy; prickles broad, red; vigorous growth; ['Glenn Dale' × ('Mary Wallace' × 'Miss Lolita Armour')]

'Elégance' HT, pb, Buyl Frères; bud globular; flowers rose-copper, large, dbl., moderate fragrance; foliage dark, leathery; moderate growth; intr. 1955

'Elegance' -- See 'Meibicmarj'

'Élégance' -- See 'Elegans'

'Elegance Champagne' HT, op, Teranishi; intr. 2005

'Elegance Hit' -- See 'Poulhi014(N)'

'Elegance Ivory' HT, w, Teranishi; intr. 2005

'Elegans' ('Élégance') Bslt, rb; flowers purple and crimson, often striped or spotted white, medium, semi-dbl., borne in very large clusters; probably synonymous with 'Amadis'; intr. before 1844

'Elegans' ('Double White') Ayr, w; flowers semi-dbl., borne in large clusters; very vigorous growth

'Elegans' -- See 'Chilicothe'

'Elegant' -- See 'Korterschi'

'Elegant Beauty' -- See 'Korgatum'

'Elegant Design' -- See 'Mordarcrest'

'Elegant Fairy Tale' -- See 'Korterschi'

'Elegant Lady' -- See 'Mirai'

'Elegant Pearl®' -- See 'Intergant'

'Elegant Pink™' -- See 'Ricpink'

'Elegant Touch' -- See 'Baitouch'

'Eleganta' Min, mr

'Élégante' HMult, mr, Laurentius; flowers cherry red; intr. 1859

'Élégante' HT, ly, Pernet-Ducher; bud pointed; flowers creamy yellow, large, dbl., globular; branching growth; intr. 1918

'Élégante' T, pb, Guillot; flowers China rose, aging to dawn pink, base coppery yellow, medium to large, dbl.; intr. 1882

'Élégante' HMult, lp, Laffay; sepals white over pink; intr. about 1835

'Élégante' HGal, lp, before 1820, Hardy; flowers light pink, very large

'Élégante, Climbing' LCl, w; bud long, slender; flowers white, center creamy yellow; foliage dull; possibly a HMult by Laffay, about 1835

'Élégante' ('L'Élégante') HP, lp, Laffay; flowers large, full; intr. 1847

Eleganza™ HT, lp; flowers creamy pink, 35 petals, classic hybrid tea, slight fragrance; tall growth; PPAF; intr. 2006

'Eleghya' Gr, dr, 1985, Staikov, Prof. Dr. V.; flowers deep blackish-red, 80 petals, cupped, borne in clusters of 2-5; foliage dark; bushy growth; ['Spectacular' × seedling]; intr. 1975

'Elegy' ('Arturo Toscanini') HT, or, 1971, Meilland; flowers vermilion, 5½ in., 30 petals, globular; foliage semi-matte, dark; vigorous growth; [(('Happiness' × 'Independence') × 'Sutter's Gold') × (('Happiness' × 'Independence') × 'Suspense')]

'Elektra' HT, ly, Rupprecht-Radke; flowers yellowish-white, large, dbl.; intr. 1964

'Elektron' -- See 'Mullard Jubilee'

'Elena Castello' HT, pb, 1932, Munné, B.; flowers apricot-yellow to rose, semi-dbl.; vigorous growth; ['Mme Butterfly' × 'Angèle Pernet']

Eleonora® -- See 'Barleo'

'Eleonore' F, Noack, Werner; intr. 1973

'Eléonore Berkeley' HMult, m, 1900; flowers pale mauve-pink; [R. multiflora × 'Mme Luizet']

'Eleta' HT, mp, 1934, Dahlgren; bud pointed; flowers clear rose-pink, large, 65 petals, high-centered; vigorous growth; ['Sensation' × seedling]

'Elettra' HT, op, 1940, Aicardi, D.; flowers copper-pink suffused reddish-yellow, large, dbl., high-centered; foliage leathery; very vigorous growth; ['Julien Potin' × 'Sensation']

'Eleusine' HT, m

'Elf' Min, dr

Elfe® ('L'Alcazar') LCl, w, Tantau; flowers large, ivory with green tint, full, slight fruity fragrance; recurrent; foliage large; growth vigorous, 8-10 ft.; intr. 2001

'Elfe' F, w, 1951, Tantau; bud pointed; flowers white tinted rose, petals shell-shaped, large, borne in clusters, intense fragrance; foliage glossy, dark; vigorous, upright, bushy growth; ruled extinct, ARA 1985; ['Swantje' × 'Hamburg']

Elfe® -- See 'Tanefle'

'Elfe Supreme' F, mp; flowers rose-pink; [sport of 'Rosenelfe']

'Elfenreigen' S, dp, 1939, Krause; flowers deep rose-pink, center brighter, petals shell-shaped large, single; profuse, non-recurrent bloom; foliage reddish orange, later gray-green; very vigorous (5 ft.) growth; ['Daisy Hill' × seedling]; hybrid macrantha

'Elfie's Joy' HT, mp, 1995, Dry, Elfie; flowers medium pink, darker edges, lighter reverse, 5 in., full, borne mostly singly, moderate fragrance; foliage large, medium green, semi-glossy; numerous prickles; upright, medium growth; [sport of 'Sheer Elegance']; intr. 1995

'Elfin' F, or, 1939, Archer; flowers cherry-rose shaded orange-salmon, 4½ in., dbl., borne in clusters; growth low growing; RULED EXTINCT 12/85

Elfin® -- See 'Poulfi'

'Elfin Charm' Min, pb, 1975, Moore, Ralph S.; bud short, pointed; flowers phlox-pink, 1 in., 65 petals, moderate fragrance; foliage small, glossy, leathery; bushy, compact growth; [(R. wichurana × Floradora) × 'Fiesta Gold']; intr. 1974

'Elfinesque' Min, op, 1974, Morey, Dennison; bud pointed; flowers coral-orange to bright pink, small, semi-dbl., slight fragrance; foliage small, glossy, leathery; vigorous, dwarf, upright, bushy growth; [('Little Darling' × unknown) × 'Yellow Bantam']; intr. 1973

'Elfinglo' Min, m, 1978, Williams, Ernest D.; bud ovoid; flowers red-purple, micro-mini, ½ in., 33 petals, cupped, moderate fragrance; foliage small, glossy, compact growth; ['Little Chief' × 'Little Chief']; intr. 1977

'Elfrid' -- See 'Wiltshire'

'Elgin Festival' -- See 'Auspoly'

'Eliane' HT, ab, 1960, Gaujard; flowers bright salmon, well-formed, large, moderate fragrance; foliage dark; vigorous growth; ['Mme Joseph Perraud' × R. foetida bicolor hybrid]; intr. 1959

'Eliane Gillet' -- See 'Maselgi'

'Elias' S, pb, Buck; flowers deep pink with white eye, open; intr. 2005

'Elida' HT, or, 1970, Tantau, Math.; flowers vermilion, large, 30 petals, high-centered, moderate fragrance; foliage dark, glossy; vigorous, branching growth; intr. 1966

'Elie Beauvillain' Cl T, mp, 1887, Beauvillain; flowers buff edges, coppery pink at center, 9-10 cm., dbl., borne in large clusters, moderate tea fragrance; prickles numerous, large; vigorous growth; ['Gloire de Dijon' × 'Ophirie']

'Elie Lambert' HP, mr, 1898, Lambert, E.; flowers bright carmine, large, full, globular

'Elie Morel' HP, m, 1867, Boucharlat

Elina® -- See 'Dicjana'

'Elina-la-Jolie' HGal, mr, before 1815, Descemet

'Elisa' ('À Fleurs Roses', 'Belle Elisa',

'Rosée du Matin', 'Elisa Blanche', 'Nova Incarnata') A, lp, before 1810, Charpentier; flowers delicate pink, lighter at edges, 2-3 in., semi-dbl., borne in clusters of 6-8; foliage large, oval, light green, deeply toothed; prickles straight, very long

Elisa® HT, mp, Rose Barni-Pistoia; flowers large, 40 petals, cupped, no fragrance; foliage large, light green, matte; upright growth; [seedling × Blessings®]; intr. 1981

'Elisa Blanche' -- See 'Elisa'

'Élisa Boëlle' HP, w, 1869, Guillot Père; flowers white, tinted with rose, medium, full, circular, cupped; vigorous growth; ['Mme Récamier' × unknown]

'Elisa Descemet' HGal, lp, about 1810, Descemet; flowers glossy light pink, aging to flesh pink, large

'Elisa Fugier' T, w, 1890, Bonnaire; bud very long; flowers pure white lightly tinted soft yellow at center, very large, very full; ['tea seedling' × 'Niphetos']

'Elisa Mercoeur' HCh, mp, 1842, Vibert; flowers carmine pink, reverse lighter, large, full, cupped

'Elisa Robichon' HWich, mp, 1901, Barbier; flowers salmon-pink, fading pinkish buff, 4-5 cm., semi-dbl., open, borne in clusters of 5-10; some intermittent repeat; foliage dark, glossy; short, strong stems; vigorous, climbing (10 ft.), or trailing growth; [*R. luciae* × 'L'Ideal']

'Elisabeth' HMult, lp, 1926, Bruder Alfons; flowers light, creamy pink, 3 cm., dbl., borne in small clusters, moderate fragrance; nearly thornless; ['Wartburg' × unknown]

'Elisabeth' -- See 'Macel'

'Elisabeth Barnes' HT, op, 1907, Dickson, A.; flowers silky salmon pink, shaded yellow, reverse dark pink with coppery yellow, large, full, moderate fragrance

'Elisabeth Didden' HT, mr, 1918, Leenders, M.; flowers glowing carmine-red and scarlet, semi-dbl.; ['Mme Caroline Testout' × 'General MacArthur']

'Elisabeth Faurax' HT, w, 1937, Meilland, F.; bud pointed; flowers white, lightly shaded ivory, large, very dbl.; long stems; upright growth; ['Caledonia' × 'Mme Jules Bouche']

'Elisabeth Faurax, Climbing' Cl HT, w, 1937, Meilland, F.

'Elisabeth Pollon' -- See 'Wamlilsapol'

'Elisabeth Tschudin' F, mp, Hetzel; intr. 1981

'Elisabeth Vigneron' ('Elise Vigneron') HP, lp, 1865, Vigneron; flowers light pink, darker within, very large, very full; foliage light green; prickles numerous, chestnut; growth upright, vigorous; ['Duchesse de Sutherland' × unknown]

'Elise' HT, w, 1969, Edmunds, F.; [sport of 'Prima Ballerina']

'Elise' -- See 'Elsie'

'Elise Fleury' -- See 'Elyse Flory'

'Elise Heymann' T, yb, 1891, Strassheim; flowers coppery yellow, center peach-pink, reverse chrome yellow; very large, full; ['Mme Lombard' × 'Mont Rosa']

'Elise Lemaire' HP, lp, before 1886; flowers delicate pink, medium; foliage dark green, glossy; nearly thornless

'Elise Noelle' LCl, mr, 1991, Alde, Robert O.; flowers medium, dbl., borne in small clusters, slight fragrance; foliage medium size, medium green, semi-glossy; climbing (10 ft.) growth; [Dublin Bay® × Burgund®]

'Elise Rovella' HGal, mp, before 1842, Roseraie de l'Hay; flowers rosy pink, medium, dbl.; tall growth

'Elise Sauvage' T, yb, 1838, Miellez; flowers orange to yellow, sometimes yellow to white

'Elise Tesch' HT, yb, 1912, Altmüller, Johann; flowers Indian yellow with orange, large, very full; [sport of 'Mme Ravary']

'Elise Vigneron' -- See 'Elisabeth Vigneron'

'Elisio' S, dp, Availishivilli; flowers bright pink, borne in clusters; recurrent; tall growth; intr. 1998

'Eliska Krásnohorská' HP, mp, 1932, Böhm, J.; flowers brilliant pink, large, semi-dbl., high-centered; foliage soft, bronze; bushy growth; ['Capt. Hayward' × 'Una Wallace']

'Elite' HT, yb, 1936, Tantau; bud pointed, red; flowers salmon-pink and yellow blend, very large, dbl., high-centered; foliage leathery, light; upright growth; ['Charles P. Kilham' × 'Pres. Herbert Hoover']; intr. 1941

'Elite' HT, ly, Fryer; flowers deep cream to yellow, small, dbl., high-centered, borne in abundant bloom; recurrent; growth vigorous, 4-5 ft.; intr. 2004

'Eliza' S, mp, 1961, Skinner; flowers clear pale rose, borne in clusters; non-recurrent; foliage dark, bushy, erect (3 ft.) growth

'Eliza' -- See 'Geliza'

Eliza® -- See 'Koraburg'

'Eliza Balcombe' HP, w, 1842, Laffay, M.; sepals very long; flowers white, pale flesh at center; foliage gray-green

'Eliza Kordana' Min, dp, Kordes; compact growth

'Eliza Panarosa' -- See 'Koraburg'

'Eliza Wren' Pol, lp, Williamson; intr. 1997

'Elizabeth' HT, dp, 1911, Cant, B. R.; flowers deep carnation pink at the center, lighter towards edges, large, dbl., moderate fragrance; ['Frau Karl Druschki' × unknown]

'Elizabeth' Pol, mp, Letts; flowers rich salmon, semi-dbl., borne in large clusters; intr. 1937

'Elizabeth' -- See 'Coctail'

'Elizabeth Abler' -- See 'Tinabler'

'Elizabeth Ann' -- See 'Kirbronze'

'Elizabeth Arden' HT, w, 1929, Prince; flowers pure white, dbl.; ['Edith Part' × 'Mrs Herbert Stevens']

'Elizabeth Brow' -- See 'Elizabeth Rowe'

'Elizabeth Casson' F, lp, Harkness; flowers pale pink with lilac tones, borne in large clusters, moderate fruity fragrance; repeats well; growth bushy, robust; intr. 2005

'Elizabeth Cone' HT, lp, 1954, Cone; flowers flesh-pink, well-shaped; vigorous, low growth; [sport of 'Picture']

'Elizabeth Cullen' HT, mr, 1921, Dickson, A.; flowers rich scarlet-crimson, semi-dbl.

'Elizabeth Dorothy' HT, my, Allender, Robert William; intr. 1984

'Elizabeth Fankhauser' HT, op, Fankhauser, D.; bud large, long, pointed; flowers pure porcelain pink, edged deep crimson, very dbl., high-centered, borne singly and several together; foliage dark green, leathery, glossy; growth compact, medium; ['Ma Perkins' × 'Burnaby']; intr. 1965

'Elizabeth Hamlin' LCl, pb, 1987, Nobbs, Kenneth J.; flowers blush pink, fading to white, small, 5 petals, cupped, borne in mass clusters, slight fragrance; foliage medium size, pennate, with 5-7 leaflets; few prickles; rampant growth; [seedling × seedling]; intr. 1986

'Elizabeth Harbour' -- See 'Habone'

Elizabeth Harkness, Climbing® Cl HT, w, 1973, Harkness; flowers pale yellow, fading to buff, 5-6 in.; [sport of 'Elizabeth Harkness']

Elizabeth Harkness® HT, ly, 1969, Harkness; flowers off-white to creamy buff, often with pastel yellow and pink, 28 petals, moderate fragrance; foliage dark; upright, bushy growth; ['Red Dandy' × Piccadilly®]

'Elizabeth Harwood' LCl, lp

'Elizabeth Hassefras' Pol, mp, 1951; flowers buttercup form, glistening rose-pink with many stamens

'Elizabeth Heather Grierson' -- See 'Mattnot'

'Elizabeth Lee' HT, dr, 1935, Chaplin Bros.; flowers dark velvety red, well-shaped

Elizabeth Marie™ -- See 'Greliz'

'Elizabeth Munn' -- See 'Seabet'

Elizabeth Navarro™ -- See 'Marliz'

Elizabeth of Glamis® ('Elisabeth', 'Irish Beauty') F, op, 1964, McGredy, Sam IV; flowers light orange-salmon, 4 in., 35 petals, flat, borne in clusters, intense fragrance; vigorous, compact bushy growth; PP2721; ['Spartan' × 'Highlight']; intr. 1964

'Elizabeth of Goshen' -- See 'Ponshen'

'Elizabeth of York' HT, dp, 1928, Dobbie; bud large, pointed, cerise; flowers cerise-pink, 27 petals, high-centered; foliage dark, glossy; prickles few thorns

'Elizabeth Park Centennial' HT, pb, 2007, Mattia, John P.; flowers pink and white, 5-6 in., dbl., borne mostly solitary; foliage medium size, medium green, semi-glossy; prickles small, hooked, greenish-yellow, few; growth upright, medium (4-5 ft.); ['Pretoria' ×

Signature®]; intr. 2007

'Elizabeth Philp' F, ab, 1977, Philp, J.B. & Son; flowers creamy peach; [sport of 'Liverpool Echo']

'Elizabeth Rowe' ('Elizabeth Brow') M, mp, before 1888; flowers satiny pink, very large, dbl., moderate fragrance

Elizabeth Scholtz™ -- See 'Wilscso'

'Elizabeth Stuart' S, ab, Massad-Guillot; flowers apricot with pink tones, moderate fragrance; foliage glossy; growth shrubby, 1 m.; intr. 2004

'Elizabeth Taylor' HT, dp, 1986, Weddle, Von C.; flowers deep pink with smoky edges, 4½-5 in., 30-35 petals, high-centered, borne usually singly, moderate spicy fragrance; foliage large, dark, semi-glossy; long stems; upright growth; PP6492; ['First Prize' × 'Swarthmore']

'Elizabeth W. Adam' HT, dp, 1926, Adam & Craigmile; flowers pink veined crimson, base yellow, 50 petals

'Elizabeth Zeigler' HWich, dp, 1917, Pierson, A.N.; flowers deep rose-pink; [sport of 'Dorothy Perkins']

'Elka Gaarlandt' Pol, dp, 1966, Buisman, G. A. H.; bud ovoid; flowers medium, dbl., borne in large clusters; foliage dark; ['Hobby' × 'Kathleen Ferrier']

Elke Fair -- See 'Boseyesouth'

'Elke Gönewein' HT, op, Gönewein; flowers bright salmon-pink, dbl., urn-shaped; recurrent; moderate (3-4 ft.) growth; intr. 1974

'Ella Bodendorfer' HMult, w, 1913, Paul; flowers cream white, speckled red with age, full

'Ella Gordon' HP, mr, 1883, Paul, W.; flowers glowing cherry red, large, full, globular; ['Mme Victor Verdier' × unknown]

'Ella Guthrie' HT, mp, 1937, Clark, A.; flowers large, dbl.; vigorous growth; ['Premier' × seedling]

'Ella McClatchy' HMult, mp, 1926, Diener; flowers rose, single, borne in clusters; sometimes recurrent bloom; thornless

'Ella Scott' HWich, dp, 1925, Scott, G.J.; flowers deep rose-pink, approaching red, dbl., borne in clusters of 15-20; prickles few thorns; vigorous, climbing growth; ['Orléans Rose' × seedling]

Ellamae™ -- See 'Savamae'

'Elle' S, dp, 1981, Lundstad, Arne; bud pointed; flowers deep pink, 16 petals, borne 3-5 per cluster, intense fragrance; non-recurrent; foliage light green, 5-7 leaflets; prickles curved gray; vigorous, upright dense growth; ['Schneezwerg' × 'Splendens']; intr. 1980

Elle™ -- See 'Meibderos'

'Elle' -- See 'Nobility'

'Ellen' HT, dp, 1929, Hinner, P.; bud pointed; flowers unvarying dark pink, large, very dbl.; bushy growth; RULED EXTINCT 12/85; [sport of 'Premier']

Ellen® -- See 'Auscup'

'Ellen Drew' HP, lp, 1896, Drew; flowers light silvery pink with peach reflections, large, full; [sport of 'Duchesse de Morny']

'Ellen Griffin' Min, lp, 1988, Hefner, John; flowers medium, dbl.; foliage medium size, medium green, semi-glossy; upright, bushy growth; [Uwe Seeler® × Party Girl™]; intr. 1988

'Ellen Hamlyn' -- See 'Dorwest'

'Ellen Mary' HT, dr, 1963, LeGrice; flowers well-formed, 5 in., 34 petals, moderate fragrance; vigorous, upright growth; ['Wellworth' × 'Independence']

'Ellen Poulsen' Pol, mp, 1911, Poulsen, D.T.; flowers bright cherry-pink, large, dbl., borne in clusters; recurrent bloom; foliage glossy, dark; bushy growth; ['Mme Norbert Levavasseur' × 'Dorothy Perkins']

'Ellen Poulsen Lysrosa' Pol, op, 1938, Poulsen; flowers light salmon-pink, medium, dbl.

'Ellen Poulsen Mork' Pol, dr, 1985, Poulsen, S.; [sport of 'Ellen Poulsen']; intr. 1928

'Ellen Terry' HT, ly, 1925, Chaplin Bros.; flowers soft sulfur-cream, outer petals soft peach, well-shaped; upright, vigorous growth

'Ellen Tofflemire' -- See 'Ardellen'

'Ellen Willmott' HT, lp, 1898, Bernaix, A.; flowers silvery flesh to shell-pink, dbl., cupped; very vigorous growth

'Ellen Willmott' HT, yb, Archer; flowers creamy lemon, flushed rosy pink, large, single; foliage leathery, dark; vigorous, upright growth; ['Dainty Bess' × 'Lady Hillingdon']; intr. 1936

'Ellen Zinnow' HT, my, 1930, Krause; flowers yellow, shaded coppery orange and pink, dbl.; ['Souv. de H.A. Verschuren' × 'Sunstar']

'Ellen's Joy' S, lp, 1990, Buck, Dr. Griffith J.; bud ovoid; flowers light shell pink, aging lighter, medium, 23 petals, cupped, borne singly and in small clusters, moderate fruity fragrance; repeat bloom; foliage medium size, medium green, semi-glossy; prickles awl-like, rusty-green; upright, bushy, spreading, medium, winter hardy growth; hips globular, orange-red; ['Vera Dalton' × ('Dornroschen' × ('Tickled Pink' × 'Applejack'))]; intr. 1991

'Ellesmere' HT, w, 1927, Allen; flowers ivory-white to pure white; prickles few thorns; ['Ophelia' × unknown]

'Elli Hartmann' HT, my, 1913, Welter; flowers yellowish old-gold, dbl.; [('Souv. du Pres. Carnot' × 'Mme Mélanie Soupert') × 'Marechal Niel']

'Elli Knab, Climbing' Cl HT, pb, 1959, Tantau; intr. 1953

'Elli Knab' HT, pb, 1934, Kordes; flowers flesh-cream flushed bright rose, veined vermilion, very large, dbl., high-centered; foliage leathery; upright, very vigorous growth; ['Cathrine Kordes' × 'W.E. Chaplin']

'Ellie Johnson' -- See 'Kenhandon'

'Ellinor LeGrice, Climbing' Cl HT, my, 1959, LeGrice

'Ellinor LeGrice' HT, my, 1949, LeGrice; bud ovoid; flowers 5-5½ in., 50 petals, cupped, moderate fruity fragrance; foliage leathery, glossy, dark; vigorous, upright growth; PP917; ['Mrs Beatty' × 'Yellowcrest']

'Elliot's Clementine' HT, m, Elliot, Charles P.; flowers deep pink with mauve tones, 3½ in., very full, borne mostly solitary, slight fragrance; growth medium, upright, well-branched; intr. 1976

'Ellis Wood' F, yb, 1983, Gateshead Metro. Borough Council; [sport of 'Arthur Bell']

'Elmar Gunsch' F, w, Scholle; flowers white with touch of yellow in center, small, dbl.; growth to 2-3 ft.; intr. 2001

'Elmhurst' HT, pb, 1985, Perry, Astor; flowers large, peachy pastel pink with yellow, 5 in., 30-35 petals, high-centered, borne mostly singly, moderate fruity fragrance; foliage medium size, medium green, matte; upright growth, moderately tall; ['Granada' × Helmut Schmidt®]

'Elmira' HRg, mr, 1978, Svedja, Felicitas; bud ovoid; flowers bright red, open, 1½-2 in., 25 petals, intense fragrance; foliage yellow-green; upright, bushy growth; ['Schneezwerg' × 'Old Blush']; intr. 1977

'Elmshorn' S, dp, 1951, Kordes; flowers deep pink, pompom type, 1 in., 20 petals, cupped, borne in large trusses (to 40); recurrent bloom; foliage glossy, wrinkled, light green; ['Hamburg' × 'Verdun']

'Elna' HMult, lp, Petersen; intr. 1964

'Elna Noack' Pol, or, Schmid, P.; flowers orange-red, medium, semi-dbl.; intr. 1960

'Elnar Tonning' HT, dp, 1926, Gyllin; flowers fuller and darker; [sport of 'Ophelia']

'Elodea' -- See 'Fegima'

Elodie Gossuin® S, dp, Massad; flowers very full, cupped, some quartering, moderate fruity fragrance; recurrent; moderate (80 cm.) growth; intr. 2008

'Eloira' -- See 'Variora'

'Eloise' MinFl, mp, 2003, Fleming, Joyce L.; flowers medium, dbl., borne in small clusters; foliage medium size, medium green, semi-glossy, disease-resistant; growth spreading, open, medium (to 24 in.); hanging baskets, rock gardens; ['Alberta' × Lavender Dream®]; intr. 2003

'Eloise' HT, op, Kirkham; flowers salmon orange, double, high-centered, slight fragrance; recurrent; foliage large, semi-glossy; strong, upright growth; intr. 2007

'Éloïse' -- See 'Héloïse'

'Elongata' -- See 'Argentée'

'Eloquence' -- See 'Jacsil'

'Elouise' -- See 'Héloïse'

Elsa® S, ab, Huber; flowers blooms large, moderate fruity fragrance; foliage rich green, glossy; stems strong; upright (200 cm.) growth; intr. 2007

'Elsa Arnot' HT, pb, 1960, Arnot; flowers

golden yellow shaded pink and cerise,, 4 in., 32 petals; foliage glossy; vigorous, upright growth; ['Ena Harkness' × 'Peace']; intr. 1959

'Elsa Knoll'   HT, op, 1968, Morey, Dr. Dennison; flowers shrimp-pink, large, 30 petals, high-centered, intense fragrance; foliage dark, glossy, leathery; vigorous, upright growth; ['First Love' × 'Castanet']; intr. 1966

'Elsbeth'   F, lp, 1963, deRuiter; flowers soft pink, dbl., borne in clusters; foliage dark; [sport of 'Valeta']

'Elsbeth Meyer'   Pol, dr, 1940, Vogel, M.; flowers medium, semi-dbl.

'Else'   HT, mr, 1929, Vogel, M.; flowers medium, dbl.

'Else Chaplin'   Pol, dp, 1937, Chaplin Bros.; flowers deep rich pink, semi-dbl., borne in large trusses; vigorous growth

'Else Kreis' -- See 'Frau Elise Kreis'

'Else Poulsen'   ('Joan Anderson') F, mp, 1924, Poulsen, S.; flowers bright rose-pink, 2 in., 10 petals, borne in clusters; foliage dark, bronze, glossy; vigorous, bushy growth; ['Orléans Rose' × 'Red Star']

'Else Poulsen, Climbing'   Cl F, mp, 1932, Ley

'Else Poulsen Meldugsfri'   F, mp, 1986, Poulsen, S.; [sport of 'Else Poulsen']; intr. 1937

'Else Poulsen Morkrod'   F, dr, 1985, Poulsen, S.; [sport of 'Else Poulsen']; intr. 1934

'Else's Rival'   ('Double Else Poulsen') F, mr, 1938, Boer Bros.; flowers carmine red, more, dbl.; healthier growth than parent; [sport of 'Else Poulsen']

'Elsie'   ('Elise') HWich, lp, 1910, Paul, W.; flowers flesh pink with deeper centers, 4 cm., full, rosette, borne in clusters of 10-30; foliage glossy

'Elsie'   LCl, lp, Chaplin Bros.; flowers soft pink, single; foliage dark, glossy; very vigorous growth; intr. 1934

'Elsie Allen'   HT, lp, 1972, Allen, L.C.; flowers pale pink, medium, dbl., high-centered, slight fragrance; vigorous, bushy growth; [sport of 'Montezuma']; intr. 1971

'Elsie Beckwith'   HT, mp, 1922, Beckwith; flowers rich rosy pink, center deeper, large, dbl., high-centered; foliage dark, shaded red, leathery; upright growth; [('Ophelia' × unknown) × 'Mev. Dora van Tets']

'Elsie Boldick'   Min, mr, 1978, Dobbs, Annette E.; bud ovoid, mossy; flowers single, borne 1-5 per cluster; foliage small, soft; growth to 15 in.; ['Fairy Moss' × 'Fairy Moss']

'Elsie de Radt' -- See 'Korquelda'

'Elsie Devy'   F, m, 1967, Fankhauser; bud ovoid; flowers soft lavender-pink, reverse mauve-pink, dbl., high-centered; foliage light green, leathery; very vigorous, upright, bushy growth; ['Ma Perkins' × 'Detroiter']

'Elsie May'   LCl, mp, Hamilton; intr. 1992

'Elsie Melton'   ('Picture Perfect') HT, pb, 1991, Wambach, Alex A.; bud pointed; flowers large, dbl., high-centered, borne usually singly, moderate fruity fragrance; foliage large, dark green, semi-glossy; upright, tall growth; [Pristine® × 'King of Hearts']; intr. 1990

'Elsie Warren' -- See 'Milsweet'

'Elsie Wright'   F, dr, 1983, Cattermole, R.F.; bud long, pointed; flowers large, 15 petals, borne usually singly, sometimes 3 per cluster, intense damask fragrance; foliage medium size, medium green, glossy; prickles light brown; upright growth; ['Crimson Glory' × 'Crimson Glory']

'Elsiemae'   Min, op, 1986, Dobbs, Annette E.; flowers light coral pink, 25 petals, high-centered, borne in sprays of 2-4; foliage medium size, medium green, semi-glossy; prickles very few straight, light brown; tall, bushy growth; ['Anne Scranton' × 'Patricia Scranton']

'Elsinore'   ('Helsingör') F, mr, 1958, Lindquist; flowers bright scarlet, semi-dbl., borne in large, open clusters; ['Floradora' × 'Pinocchio']; intr. 1957

'Elusive'   F, pb, 1993, Jobson, Daniel J.; flowers soft pink/cream blend, medium, dbl., borne in small clusters; foliage medium size, dark green, semi-glossy; some prickles; medium, upright, bushy growth; [(Party Girl™ × 'Laureate') × 'Ivory Fashion']; intr. 1993

Elveshörn® -- See 'Korbindu'

'Elvira'   HEg, lp; flowers flesh, medium, semi-dbl.; vigorous growth

'Elvira' -- See 'Varelvi'

'Elvira Aramayo'   HT, mr, 1922, Looymans; flowers Indian red, petals curling lengthwise, medium, semi-dbl.; bushy growth; ['Feu Joseph Looymans' × ('Leslie Holland' × 'Rayon d'Or')]

'Elvira Aramayo, Climbing'   Cl HT, mr, 1933, Ingegnoli; flowers copper-orange-red, medium, semi-dbl., moderate fragrance; [sport of 'Elvira Aramayo']

'Elvire' -- See 'Poniatowsky'

'Elvire Popesco'   HT, my, 1949, Gaujard; bud long, pointed; flowers golden yellow, large, 25 petals; foliage bronze; very vigorous, upright growth; ['Comtesse Vandal' × seedling]

'Elvis'   Min, mr, 1979, Wells, V.W., Jr.; bud pointed, ovoid; flowers medium red, base white, 1 in., 60-70 petals, high-centered, borne singly and in clusters of 5, slight tea fragrance; recurrent; foliage dark green, glossy; prickles several, long, nearly straight; vigorous (14-16 in.) growth; PP4760; ['Judy Fischer' × seedling]; intr. 1978

'Elvis'   HT, w, Adam; flowers ivory washed with pink, large, very dbl.; intr. 2004

'Elvis' -- See 'Miss Elvis'

Elwina®   Min, or

'Elyse Flory'   ('Elise Fleury') Ch, lp, 1852, Guillot père; flowers bright pink, paling at edges, medium to large, full

Elysée™   S, lp, Poulsen; flowers light pink, 5-8 cm., full, slight fragrance; foliage dark; growth bushy, 60-100 cm.; PP15859; intr. 2003

Elysium®   F, op, 1961, Kordes, R.; bud pointed; flowers salmon-pink, well-formed, large, 35 petals, cupped, moderate fragrance; foliage glossy; vigorous, tall, growth

'Emaline Rouge'   HT, dr, 1938, Hofmann; flowers deep red; PP286; [sport of 'Better Times']

'Emanuel' -- See 'Ausquest'

Emanuel® -- See 'Ausuel'

Emanuelle+   HT, ab, Voom, Lex; flowers pale, creamy apricot, double, high-centered, borne mostly singly; recurrent; stems medium to long; florist rose

'Embajador Lequerica'   HT, pb, 1962, La Florida; bud pointed; flowers strawberry-pink, reverse Indian yellow at base passing to brick red at edge, 30 petals; vigorous growth

'Embassy'   HT, yb, 1967, Sanday, John; flowers light gold veined and edged carmine, pointed, large, dbl.; foliage glossy; ['Gavotte' × ('Magenta' × 'Golden Scepter')]

'Embassy Regal'   HT, pb, 1976, Sanday, John; flowers cream overlaid peach-pink, 5 in., 30 petals, moderate fragrance; [('Gavotte' × 'Ethel Sanday') × ('Crimson Glory' × seedling)]

'Ember' -- See 'Savember'

'Emberglow'   HT, mp, 1935, Grillo; flowers rich salmon-pink, 5 in., 50 petals; foliage leathery; long stems; vigorous growth; [sport of 'Souvenir']

'Embers'   F, mr, 1953, Swim, H.C.; bud ovoid; flowers scarlet, 2½-3 in., 23 petals, high-centered, borne in clusters, moderate spicy fragrance; foliage dark, semi-glossy; vigorous, bushy, compact growth; PP1178; ['World's Fair' × 'Floradora']

'Embers'   S, yb, Delbard

Emblem™   HT, my, 1981, Warriner, William A.; flowers 25 petals, high-centered, borne singly, no fragrance; foliage glossy, dark; prickles straight, long, light green; upright growth; PP4847; [seedling × 'Sunshine']

'Embrace'   Pol, lp, 1974, Byrum; flowers medium, very dbl., high-centered, slight fragrance; foliage leathery; vigorous, upright, bushy growth; PP3468; ['Seventeen' × 'Jack Frost']; intr. 1972

'Embrasement'   F, mr, 1956, Delbard-Chabert; flowers fiery red, dbl., borne in clusters of 8-12; foliage bronze; vigorous growth

'Embruixada' -- See 'Violetera'

'Emden'   HP, dp, 1915, Schmidt; flowers large, full; ['Frau Karl Druschki' × 'Veluwezoom']

'Emélie Fontaine'   HP, pb, 1881, Fontaine; flowers bright carmine with fiery purple, large, very full

'Emely'   HT, w, Kordes; flowers large, off-white, dbl., moderate fragrance; healthy,

The Official Registry and Checklist — Rosa   197

robust growth; intr. 1998
'Emely 2000' HT, w, Kordes; intr. 2002
'Emely Kordana' -- See 'Vanilla'
'Emely Vigorosa' ('Bad Wörishofen 2005', 'Pink Emely') F, dp, Kordes; flowers carmine-pink, 7 cm., semi-dbl., shallow cup, borne in large clusters, slight fragrance; recurrent; foliage dark green, semi-glossy, dense; upright (2 ft.), bushy growth; intr. 2006
Emera® -- See 'Noatraum'
'Emera Pavement' -- See 'Noatraum'
Emerald™ -- See 'Poulpah030(N)'
'Emerald Dream' F, w, 1976, Williams, J. Benjamin; bud pointed, light to apple green; flowers white to ivory, center green, 1½-2 in., 12 petals, flat, loosely cupped, slight fruity fragrance; foliage dull, very dark, leathery; low, compact growth; ['Pinafore' × 'Ivory Fashion']; intr. 1975
'Emerald Hit' (Emerald™) MinFl, w, Poulsen; flowers white, 5-8 cm., dbl., no fragrance; growth bushy, 20-40 cm.; intr. 2004
'Emerald Mist' -- See 'Arogresh'
'Emerance' HGal, w, before 1910; flowers cream, centers pale lemon, medium, full
'Emeraude d'Or' HT, yb, 1967, Delbard-Chabert; flowers yellow suffused carmine-pink, petals serrated, 5 in.; vigorous growth; ['Sultane' × Queen Elizabeth®]; intr. 1965
'Emerickrose' HMult, lp, 1922, Bruder Alfons; flowers light pink, white center to medium, 5 cm., dbl., borne in medium clusters, moderate fragrance; ['Tausendschön' × unknown]
'Emi' ('Smile') F, ob, Keisei; flowers orange blend with grey tones; intr. 2005
'Emil Kruisius' F, my, 1943, Tantau; bud long, pointed; flowers large, 25-30 petals, borne in clusters; foliage glossy, light green; vigorous, bushy growth; ['Golden Rapture' × ('Johanna Tantau' × 'Eugenie Lamesch')]
Emil Nolde® S, dy, Tantau; flowers intense yellow, large, dbl., cupped, borne in free blooming, moderate fragrance; recurrent; foliage medium green, glossy; growth to 3-4 ft.; intr. 2002
'Émile Audusson' T, 1842, Audusson
'Emile Bardiaux' HP, 1889, Lévêque, P.; flowers bright carmine red, tinted poppy and deep violet, large, full; foliage dark green, very large; ['Mme Isaac Pereire' × unknown]
'Émile Charles' HT, or, 1922, Bernaix, P.; flowers coral-red, medium, full; [sport of 'Mme Edouard Herriot']
'Emile Courtier' ('Emilie Courtier') B, mp, 1837, Portemer; bud round; flowers lilac pink, medium, full, flat, borne in clusters of 4-5; foliage dark green, deeply dentate; prickles short, red, numerous
'Emile Cramon' HT, or, 1937, Chambard, C.; bud pointed; flowers coppery carmine, stamens chrome-yellow, very large; foliage dull green; very vigorous growth
'Émile Debroise' -- See 'Jaczorba'
'Émile Fortépaule' HWich, w, 1902, Barbier; flowers white, flushed salmon, 5-7 cm., dbl., globular, borne in large clusters, moderate tea rose fragrance; foliage dark green, oval-oblong, regularly dentate; prickles hooked, red; vigorous growth; [R. wichurana × 'Souv. de Catherine Guillot']
'Emile J. Le Duc' HT, mr, 1931, Le Duc; flowers scarlet-crimson, larger and stronger than the parent; PP45; [sport of 'Scott's Columbia']
'Emile Nérini' HWich, dp, 1911, Nonin; flowers carmine-pink with white, 5 cm., semi-dbl., borne in medium clusters; foliage large; few prickles; ['Turner's Crimson Rambler' × 'Dorothy Perkins']
'Emilia Plantier' N, ly, 1878, Schwartz; flowers light coppery yellow, medium large to large, dbl., moderate fragrance; foliage glossy
'Emilia Rose Burke' -- See 'Worcreate'
'Emilie' M, w, before 1885, Roseraie de l'Hay; flowers small, folded center, full
'Emilie Courtier' -- See 'Emile Courtier'
'Émilie Dupuy' ('Mme Émilie Dupuy') Cl T, op, 1870, Levet; flowers light coppery-pink, fading to cream, large, dbl., moderate fragrance; ['Mme Flacot' × 'Gloire de Dijon']
'Émilie Gonin' ('Chameleon') T, w, 1896, Guillot; flowers ivory white, tinted with orange and fawn, edged with bright carmine, very large, full, moderate fragrance
'Emilie Hausburg' HP, m, 1868, Lévêque; flowers lilac-rose, large, dbl.
'Emilie Plantier' B, mp, about 1845, Plantier; flowers bright pink, large, full
'Emilie Verachter' HGal, mp, 1840, Parmentier; flowers medium, full, quartered; foliage small; few prickles; growth upright; hips rounded
Emilien Guillot® S, or, Guillot-Massad; flowers bright orange-red, 5 in., full, cupped; continuous bloom; foliage dark green; intr. 2001
Emilo Feliu® -- See 'Fesodios'
'Emily' HT, lp, 1949, Baines; flowers soft pink, 5-6 in., 40 petals, moderate fragrance; foliage dark; vigorous, upright growth; ['Mme Butterfly' × 'Mrs Henry Bowles']
'Emily' -- See 'Ausburton'
'Emily Carr' S, mr, semi-dbl., Ag Canada; flowers bright red, semi-dbl., shallow cup to flat, mild fragrance; foliage dark green; growth compact (2 ft.); winter hardy to -40°F; intr. 2007
'Emily Dodd' HT, w, 1927, Dickson, A.; flowers milk-white, center cream, large, dbl.
'Emily Gray' HWich, dy, 1917, Williams, A.; flowers deep golden buff, stamens yellow, 6-7 cm., 25 petals, cupped, borne in small clusters, moderate tea fragrance; non-recurrent; foliage large, very glossy, dark, bronze-green; vigorous, climbing growth; ['Jersey Beauty' × 'Comtesse du Cayla']
'Emily Hough' -- See 'Houemily'
'Emily Laxton' HP, mr, 1878, Laxton; bud globular, pointed; flowers rich cherry-rose, large, full; ['Jules Margottin' × unknown]
'Emily Louise' -- See 'Harwilla'
'Emily Post' ('Omega') HT, mp, 1975, Byrum; flowers soft medium pink, 3½-4 in., 48 petals, high-centered, moderate fragrance; upright, bushy growth; PP3749; ['Eternal Sun' × Carina®]; intr. 1974
'Emily Rhodes' LCl, mp, 1937, Clark, A.; flowers vermilion pink, large, semi-dbl. to dbl., cupped, moderate fragrance; reliable repeat; vigorous, climbing or pillar growth; ['Golden Ophelia' × 'Zephirine Drouhin']
'Emily Victoria' -- See 'Boshipeacon'
'Emily's Rose' Cl Min, lp, Warner; flowers soft pink, dbl.; intr. 2001
'Emin Pascha' ('Dr Schnitzler') HT, dp, 1894, Drögemüller; flowers deep carmine, rose shaded crimson, 11 cm., dbl.; some autumn repeat; ['Gloire de Dijon' × 'Louis Van Houtte']
Emina™ -- See 'Virbright'
Éminence® HT, m, 1962, Gaujard; flowers lavender, large, 40 petals, intense fragrance; foliage leathery, light green; vigorous, upright growth; PP2455; ['Peace' × ('Viola' × seedling)]; intr. 1965
'Eminence' F, mr, Kordes, R.; bud large, ovoid, scarlet; flowers scarlet red, chromium yellow at base, 4-4½ in., 40-45 petals, high-centered, borne singly and several together in irregular clusters, slight fragrance; foliage medium size, medium green, leathery, glossy; prickles medium, hooked downward, moderate
'Éminence, Climbing' Cl HT, m, Gaujard; [sport of 'Éminence']; intr. 1972
'Emir' HT, rb, 1960, Verbeek; flowers yellow with orange-red, 6 in., 45 petals; foliage glossy; free growth; [seedling × 'Peace']
'Emjay Skiba' Min, mp, 1990, Skiba, Norman A.; bud pointed; flowers medium pink, outer petals lighter, large, 45 petals, high-centered, borne usually singly, moderate fruity fragrance; foliage large, dark green, edged red, semi-glossy; prickles sharp, pointed slightly downward, light green; bushy, tall growth; hips round, dark green-orange; ['Sonia' × 'Pink Petticoat']
'Emma' F, dp, 1980, Pearce, C.A.; flowers deep pink, 70 petals, borne 6-10 per clusters; foliage dark, glossy; prickles large; upright, branching growth; ['Chanelle' × 'Prima Ballerina']
'Emma' (Emma de Meilland®) HT, lp, Meilland; flowers off-white with a pink tip, full, classic form; PP12499; intr. 1996
'Emma Agnes' HT, ob; intr. 2004
'Emma Brady' -- See 'Webelina'
'Emma Carter' F, mp, 2004, Paul Ches-

sum Roses; flowers semi-dbl., borne in small clusters, slight fragrance; foliage medium size, dark green, semi-glossy; growth upright, tall (100 cm.); beds, borders, hedges; [seedling × seedling]; intr. 2004

'Emma Clare' HMult, pb; intr. 1994

Emma de Meilland® -- See 'Meileyet'

'Emma Grace' -- See 'Welgrace 0656'

'Emma Jane' F, op, 1970, Sanday, John; flowers salmon-pink, base orange, 3 in., 16 petals; ['Vera Dalton' × ('Masquerade' × ('Independence' × unknown))]

'Emma Kate' -- See 'Jayemm'

'Emma May' -- See 'Sherisilver'

'Emma Mitchell' -- See 'Horharpdos'

'Emma Vidal' HT, dy, Vidal

'Emma Vidal, Climbing' Cl HT, dy, Vidal

'Emma Wallace O'Flaherty' -- See 'Worcavity'

'Emma Wright' HT, op, 1918, McGredy; flowers orange shaded salmon, large, semi-dbl., moderate fragrance; foliage rich green, glossy; dwarf growth

'Emma Wright, Climbing' Cl HT, op, 1932, Cant, F.

'Emmanuella de Mouchy' HG, mp, 1922, Nabonnand, P.; bud long, pale pink; flowers delicate transparent rose-pink, very large, semi-dbl., borne singly or in small clusters, intense fragrance; [R. gigantea × 'Lady Waterlow.']

'Emmanuelle' w, Pineau; intr. 1981

'Emmanuelle' -- See 'Peamight'

'Emmeline' HCh, w, before 1829, Boutigny; flowers flesh white, edges tinted violet, cupped

'Emmeline' HP, lp, Vibert; flowers light flesh pink, edged lilac; intr. about 1830

'Emmeline' M, w, Robert & Moreau; flowers pure white, petals curly, 2½ in., full, rosette, borne in small clusters; intr. 1859

'Emmeline' HT, my, 1921, Paul, W.; bud pure deep yellow; flowers lemon-yellow

'Emmeline' -- See 'Madeline'

'Emmeloord' Pol, or, 1973, Buisman, G. A. H.; bud cupped; flowers semi-dbl., round; foliage glossy, dark; [Olala® × 'Finale']

'Emmerdale' F, mp, 1984, Greensitt, J.A.; flowers medium, 35 petals, moderate fragrance; foliage medium size, medium green, semi-glossy; bushy growth; [seedling × 'Pink Parfait']; intr. 1983

'Emmie Koster' Pol, dr, 1956, Koster, D.A.; flowers deep red; [sport of 'Dick Koster']

Emmy® Min, op, Barni, V.; flowers coral-salmon, dbl., high-centered; growth to 14-16 in.; intr. 1993

'Emotion' B, w, 1862, Guillot père; flowers white, touched with pink, medium, full

'Emotion' ('Alice Fontaine') B, op, Fontaine; flowers light salmon-pink, slightly domed, moderate fragrance; recurrent; stems smooth; intr. 1879

'Emotion' F, dp

'Emotion' -- See 'President Kekkonen'

Emotion™ -- See 'Poulruk'

'Emotion Parade' (Emotion™) Min, dp, Poulsen; flowers deep pink, medium, dbl., no fragrance; foliage dark; growth bushy, 20-40 cm.; intr. 1997

'Emozione' -- See 'Baremoz'

'Empereur' HGal, dr, before 1810; flowers dark red with lilac

'Empereur de Russie' HGal, m, about 1840, Prévost; flowers lilac pink, medium to large, full

'Empereur du Brésil' HP, rb, 1880, Soupert & Notting; flowers violet-brown with magenta over varnished red, shaded carmine, very large, very full, globular

'Empereur du Maroc' HP, dr, 1858, Guinoiseau, B.; flowers crimson, tinged purple, very distinct, small, 40 petals, moderate fragrance; low, compact growth; ['Geant des Batailles' × unknown]

'Empereur Napoléon III' HP, dr, 1855, Granger

'Empereur Nicolas II' T, dr, 1903, Lévêque; bud large, long; flowers dark rich crimson, flamed with scarlet, very large, full; foliage dark green

'Emperor' ('The PTA News Centenary') HT, yb, McGredy; flowers cream with deeper golden yellow in the center, large, dbl., high-centered; recurrent; foliage large, glossy; bushy, vigorous growth; ['Solitaire' × 'New Zealand']; intr. 1999

'Emperor' HT, dr, Kuramoto, H.; bud urn shaped; flowers rose-red becoming darker, 3-3½ in., 35-45 petals, high-centered, intense fragrance; foliage glossy; vigorous, compact growth; PP1813; [sport of 'Pink Delight']; intr. 1958

'Emperor' HP, dr, 1883, Paul, W.; flowers very dark red, nearly blackish, small, full

'Emperor' -- See 'Jacrette'

'Empire Granger' HT, mr, 1970, Morey, Dr. Dennison; bud long, pointed; flowers velvety blood-red, very large, dbl.; foliage large, glossy, dark, bronze, leathery; very vigorous, upright, bushy growth; ['Rose Bowl' × 'Hallmark']

'Empire Queen' HT, mr, 1925, Easlea; flowers brilliant cerise, large, dbl.; upright growth; ['Cherry Page' × 'Vanessa']

'Empire State' HT, mr, 1934, Nicolas; bud pointed; flowers velvety scarlet, base golden yellow, large, dbl., high-centered; foliage leathery; vigorous growth

Empreinte® HT, m, Dorieux; flowers violet-purple-red, dbl., cupped, intense fragrance; growth 100-120 cm.; intr. 2005

'Empress' HT, dr, 1933, Chaplin Bros.; flowers dark cerise and red, well-formed; vigorous, upright growth; [('Ophelia' × unknown) × seedling]

'Empress Alexandra' -- See 'Empress Alexandra of Russia'

'Empress Alexandra of Russia' ('Empress Alexandra') T, rb, 1897, Paul, W.; flowers carmine red, tinted with orange and tipped with fiery red, large, full, globular, intense fragrance

'Empress Eugénie' -- See 'Impératrice Eugénie'

'Empress Farah' -- See 'Delivour'

'Empress Josephine' -- See 'Impératrice Joséphine'

'Empress Marie of Russia' -- See 'Impératrice Maria Féodorowna de Russie'

'Empress Michiko' -- See 'Dicnifty'

'Empress of China' Cl Ch, mp, 1896, Jackson; flowers soft dark red, aging to light pink, 6 cm., semi-dbl. to dbl., slight fruity fragrance; foliage small; few prickles

'Empress of India' HP, dr, 1876, Laxton; flowers velvety crimson and purple, medium, globular, moderate fragrance; foliage dark green; ['Triomphe des Beaux-Arts' × unknown]

'Emsie Girl' -- See 'Wilcgir'

'Ena Baxter' -- See 'Cocbonne'

'Ena Gladstone' HT, dp, 1936, Chaplin Bros.; flowers carmine-pink, base yellow, well-shaped, large

'Ena Harkness, Climbing' ('Grimpant Ena Harkness') Cl HT, mr, 1954, Gurteen & Ritson (also Murrell, 1954); flowers bright crimson, 12-13 cm., intense fragrance; [sport of 'Ena Harkness']

'Ena Harkness' HT, mr, 1946, Norman; flowers large, dbl., high-centered; foliage leathery; vigorous, upright growth; ['Crimson Glory' × 'Southport']; intr. 1946

'Enchanted' ('Amazon Lady') HT, mp, J&P; intr. 1995

'Enchanted Autumn' Gr, ob, 1976, Buck, Dr. Griffith J.; bud ovoid, pointed; flowers orange, 4-4½ in., 33 petals, cupped; foliage glossy, dark, coppery; upright, bushy growth; [(Queen Elizabeth® × 'Ruth Hewitt') × 'Whisky']; intr. 1975

Enchanted Evening™ -- See 'Jacperby'

'Enchanter' HT, dp, 1903, Cook, J.W.; flowers deep pink, large, full; ['Mme Caroline Testout' × 'Mlle Alice Furon']

'Enchanting Days' HRg, dr, Bell; flowers claret wine color with prominent yellow stamens, semi-dbl.; compact growth; intr. 2001

'Enchantment' HT, pb, 1946, E.G. Hill, Co.; bud long, pointed; flowers shell-pink, base yellow, 6 in., 35 petals, slight fragrance; foliage leathery; vigorous, upright growth; PP737; [R.M.S. Queen Mary × 'Eternal Youth']

'Enchantment' -- See 'Sanka'

Enchantment™ -- See 'Poulskov'

'Enchantress' T, w, 1896, Paul & Son; flowers cream white

'Enchantress' T, mp, Cook, J.W.; flowers rose-pink; intr. 1904

'Enchantress' HRg, dr; flowers velvety blood-red, very dbl.; extra strong and hardy; intr. before 1940

'Enchantress' -- See 'L'Enchantresse'

'Encore' F, mp, 1958, Von Abrams; bud pointed; flowers creamy pink, reverse rose-pink, 3 in., 10-14 petals, cupped, borne in large clusters, slight spicy fragrance; foliage glossy; vigorous, upright, bushy growth; PP1662; ['Else Poulsen' × 'Captain Thomas']; intr. 1958

'Encore' -- See 'Jacore'

'Endearment'   HT, op, 1989, Taylor, Thomas E.; bud pointed; flowers creamy pink, reverse coral pink, large, 10 petals, borne usually singly, slight sweet fragrance; foliage large, medium green, matte; prickles straight, medium, light brown; upright, tall growth; no fruit; ['Gladiator' × 'First Prize']; intr. 1989

'Endeavour' -- See 'Talend'

Endless Dream™ -- See 'Twodream'

'Endless Love' -- See 'Lyoss'

'Endless Summer' -- See 'Renmer'

'Endless Summer' -- See 'Tokonatsu'

'Endless Tale'   Cl HT, my, 1956, Motose; bud ovoid, deep yellow; flowers amber-yellow, outer petals creamy, 6-7 in., 30-35 petals; abundant, intermittent bloom; foliage leathery; vigorous (20+ ft.) growth; ['Lestra Hibberd, Climbing' × sport of 'Lestra Hibbard']

'Endora' -- See 'Zipend'

'Enduring Love'   HT, yb, Pallek, Karl; flowers peachy apricot , double, moderate fragrance; recurrent; 5 ft. growth; intr. 1998

Enduring Spirit™ -- See 'Poulrohill'

'Enemy of War'   HT, pb, 1987, Hardikar, Dr. M.N.; flowers open, 50-60 petals, slight fragrance; foliage large, dark green, glossy, leathery; prickles beak-shaped, light green to deep brown; very vigorous, profuse growth; ['Festival Beauty' × 'Gynosure']; intr. 1986

'Enfant d'Ajaccio' -- See 'Souv d'Anselme'

'Enfant de France'   HP, rb, Lartay; flowers red-violet, edges whitish, very large, very dbl., moderate fragrance; intr. 1860

'Enfant de France' ('Enfant de France de Bruxelles')   HGal, lp, from Brussels; flowers flesh pink, small to medium, full; Agathe group; possibly a sub-variety of 'Marie-Louise'; intr. before 1824

'Enfant de France' ('À Petites Fleurs', 'Child of France', 'Delphiniana', 'Grand-Dauphin', 'Le Grand Dauphin', 'Le Jeune Roi Dauphin', 'L'Enfant de France', 'Roi de Rome', *R. gallica agatha delphiniana*)   HGal, m, about 1802, from Holland; bud round; flowers carminy crimson with light purple, medium, full, pompon; foliage dark green, small, oblong ovate; prickles numerous, small, unequal, almost straight; hips pyriform, red; Agathe group

'Enfant de France' -- See 'Beauté Tendre'

'Enfant de France de Bruxelles' -- See 'Enfant de France'

'Enfant de la Libarde'   N, my, 1904, Chauvry

'Enfant de Lyon' -- See 'Narcisse'

'Enfant d'Orléans'   Pol, m, 1929, Turbat; flowers Neyron rose, tinted purple, fading lighter, borne in clusters

'Enfant Trouvé' ('L'Enfant Trouvé')   T, mp, 1861, Lartay

'Enfield in Bloom' -- See 'Bosanneves'

'Engagement'   Gr, op, 1969, Patterson; bud globular; flowers coral-pink, large, dbl., high-centered; foliage dark, leathery; vigorous, bushy growth; ['Ma Perkins' × 'Montezuma']; intr. 1968

'Engagement'   HT, lp, Tantau; flowers very large, dbl., high-centered; stems very long; greenhouse rose; intr. 2003

'Engelmann's Quest'   S, my, 2005, Shoup, George Michael; flowers single, borne in small clusters, slight fragrance; remontant; foliage medium size, dark green, semi-glossy; prickles moderate; growth compact, medium (3-4 ft.); containers, borders; hips small; hardy to -20°F; [('The Fairy' × *R. wichurana*) × 'Baby Love']; intr. 2000

'Enghien'   HT, ob, RvS-Melle; ['Silver Jubilee' × seedling]; intr. 1991

'Eng. D. José de Mendia'   HT, mp, Moreira da Silva; flowers rosy salmon

'Eng. Duarte Pacheco'   HT, dr, 1938, Moreira da Silva; flowers blackish crimson, large, very dbl., cupped; dwarf growth; ['Hadley' × 'Presidente Carmona']

'Eng. Pereira Caldas'   HT, mp, 1954, Moreira da Silva; flowers salmon-pink, base yellow

'Eng. Pulido Garcia'   HT, yb, 1961, Moreira da Silva; flowers yellow stained pink; ['Grand'mere Jenny' × 'Michèle Meilland']

'Eng. Vitória Pires'   HT, dr, 1954, Moreira da Silva; flowers velvety dark red

'England's Glory' ('Gloire d'Angleterre')   HT, lp, 1904, Wood; flowers flesh-pink with a rosy center, large, dbl.; [('Gloire de Dijon' × 'Mrs W. J. Grant') × unknown]

'England's Rose' -- See 'Ausrace'

'England's Rose (Germany)' -- See 'Ausjo'

'Englemann's Quest'   S, dy; flowers Yellow, single, Yes fragrance; Repeat bloom.; growth to 3-4 ft.; intr. 2004

'English Apricot' -- See 'Ausemi'

'English Courtyard' -- See 'Rawsolly'

'English Dawn' -- See 'Ausdapple'

English Elegance® -- See 'Ausleaf'

'English Estates'   HT, yb, 1992, Thompson, Robert; flowers deep yellow edged red, medium, full, borne mostly singly, intense fragrance; foliage medium size, dark green, glossy; some prickles; upright (80 cm.) growth; ['Whisky Mac' × 'Catherine Cookson']; intr. 1991

English Eyes®   F, w, Spek; flowers 9 cm., 55-65 petals, high-centered, borne mostly singly; recurrent; thornless; stems medium to long; florist rose; intr. 2006

English Garden® -- See 'Ausbuff'

'English Hedge'   HRg, mp, 1959, Nyveldt; flowers pink, small, single; hips red; [(*R. rugosa rubra* × *R. cinnamomea*) × *R. nitida*]

'English Holiday'   F, yb, 1976, Harkness; flowers yellow, blended with salmon,, 4 in., 33 petals, moderate fragrance; foliage large, glossy; ['Bobby Dazzler' × 'Goldbonnet']; intr. 1977

'English Lavender'   Min, m, Bell; flowers deep lavender, moderate fragrance; short growth

'English Miss'   F, lp, 1977, Cants of Colchester, Ltd.; flowers pale pink, 2½ in., 60 petals, borne in clusters, intense fragrance; foliage dark purple to dark green; ['Dearest' × 'The Optimist']

English Perfume™ -- See 'Jaclewt'

'English Porcelain' -- See 'Morporc'

English Sachet™ -- See 'Jacolfa'

'English Sonnet' -- See 'Harverag'

'English Violet'   S, dp, Austin, David

'English Wedding Day' -- See 'Wedding Day'

'English Yellow' -- See 'Ausmas'

'Enhance' -- See 'Sandaya'

'Enid'   Pol, lp, 1936, Prior; flowers pale pink, borne in clusters; foliage light; upright growth

Enigma™   HT, rb, deRuiter

'Enigma Variation'   S, mp; flowers pure pink, outer petals lighter, very full, cupped, quartered, moderate fragrance; recurrent; [sport of 'Sir Edward Elgar']; intr. 2006

'Enjoy' -- See 'Lavjoy'

'Ennio Morlotti'   F, mp, 1976, Cazzaniga, F. G.; bud globular; flowers clear pink, 2½-3 in., 35 petals, high-centered, intense fragrance; foliage glossy; vigorous, upright growth; ['Fashion' × Queen Elizabeth®]; intr. 1973

'Enric Palau'   HT, m, Dot

Ensa de Rennes®   HT, dp, Adam, M.; intr. 1997

Ensemble®   HT, rb, Spek; flowers white with broad red edges, 4 in., 30-35 petals, high-centered, borne mostly singly; recurrent; few prickles; stems long; florist rose; intr. 2006

'Entente Cordiale'   HT, yb, 1908, Guillot, P.; flowers nasturtium-red, base yellow. large, dbl., loose, borne in small clusters; ['Mme Caroline Testout' × 'Soleil d'Or']

'Entente Cordiale'   HT, w, Pernet-Ducher; flowers creamy white, tinged carmine at edges; ['Mme Abel Chatenay' × 'Kaiserin Auguste Viktoria']; intr. 1909

'Enterprise'   F, pb, 1958, Kordes; flowers deep pink edged peach, 2 in., 20 petals, borne in large clusters, moderate fragrance; foliage dark, glossy, vigorous; upright, bushy growth; ['Masquerade' × seedling]; intr. 1956

'Enver Pascha'   HT, lp, 1916, Kiese; flowers fleshy white, outside soft pink, dbl.

'Envy'   HT, w, Zary; buds green; PP11633; intr. 1999

'Enzo Fumagalli'   F, mp, 1966, Cazzaniga, F. G.; bud globular; flowers salmon-pink, medium, very dbl.; abundant, intermittent bloom; foliage glossy; vigorous, bushy growth; ['Mount Shasta' × 'Papillon Rose']

'Eos'   (*R. eglanteria eos*) HMoy, rb, 1950, Ruys; bud ovoid; flowers sunset-red becoming brighter, center light pink, semi-dbl., cupped, borne in small clusters; non-recurrent; foliage leathery, glossy; shrub or pillar (to 6 ft.) growth; [*R. moyesii* × 'Magnifica']

'Epic' F, mp, 1989, Cattermole, R.F.; bud tapering; flowers medium, dbl., flat, borne in sprays of 3-6, moderate spicy fragrance; foliage bronze to dark green, glossy; prickles brown; upright, bushy growth; ['Silent Night' × 'Irish Mist']

Épidor® -- See 'Delépi'

'Epinal' F, Croix, P.; intr. 1994

'Épineux de la Chine' -- See 'Fortuniana'

'Epoca' -- See 'Len 2'

'Epoca Mondadori' -- See 'Len 2'

'Eponine' HMsk, w, before 1835; flowers medium, dbl., cupped, borne in large clusters, moderate fragrance

'Éponine' HGal, m, before 1829, Coquerel; flowers slatey lilac pink, shaded red, medium, very full

'Epos' Pol, mr, 1971, Delforge; bud ovoid; flowers medium, semi-dbl., cupped; foliage bronze, leathery; vigorous, upright growth; ['Tommy Bright' × seedling]

Equinox™ -- See 'Tucknox'

'Erato' HMult, dp, 1937, Tantau; bud pointed; flowers small, semi-dbl., borne in medium clusters; foliage glossy; long stems; very vigorous climbing growth; [('Ophelia' × *R. multiflora*) × 'Florex']

'Erbprinzessin Leopold von Anhalt' HT, ly, 1933, Behrens; flowers whitish-yellow, large, dbl.

'Eremit de Granval' -- See 'De Rennes'

Erfordia® F, dr, Matthews; flowers warm, bright dark red, medium, double, cupped, borne in clusters of 3 - 7, no fragrance; recurrent; foliage dark green, glossy; robust (70 - 90 cm.) growth

'Erfurt' HMsk, pb, 1939, Kordes; bud long, pointed; flowers medium pink, yellow toward base, large, semi-dbl., borne in clusters, intense musk fragrance; recurrent bloom; foliage leathery, wrinkled, bronze; vigorous (5-6 ft.), trailing, bushy growth; ['Eva' × 'Reveil Dijonnais']

'Eric' F, mr, 1965, Hémeray-Aubert; bud ovoid; flowers medium, semi-dbl., cupped; foliage dark, glossy, leathery; vigorous growth; ['Alain' × 'Coup de Foudre']

'Eric B. Mee' HT, mr, 1937, Mee; flowers vivid cerise, well-shaped, small

'Eric Green' -- See 'Rawsoltan'

'Eric Hobbis' HT, pb, 1966, Sanday, John; flowers pink, reverse peach, 4½ in., high-centered; low growth; ['Gavotte' × 'Peace']

'Eric Holroyd' HT, mr, 1925, Chaplin Bros.; flowers bright scarlet, base shaded gold

'Eric Louw' HT, mr, 1964, Herholdt, J.A.; bud pointed; flowers cyclamen-red, well-formed, 35-40 petals; foliage leathery, glossy; strong stems; vigorous, bushy growth; [Queen Elizabeth® × 'Confidence']

'Eric Tabarly' ('Grimpant Eric Tabarly', 'Red Eden', 'Red Eden Rose', 'Red Pierre') LCl, dr, Meilland; bud medium, ovoid; flowers crimson, 4½ in., 95-100 petals, cupped, borne in small clusters, intense fragrance; recurrent; foliage medium to dark green, semi-glossy; prickles average, 5 mm. or more, hooked slightly downward; growth to 7 ft. and more; hips pitcher shaped, 3 cm. in diameter, olive green with orange shadings; PP15052; ['Cappa Magna seedling' × Ulmer Münster®]; intr. 2003

'Eric The Red' Min, mr, Welsh

'Eric von Melnibonée' S, op, Weihrauch; flowers yellowish salmon-pink, large, dbl.; intr. 1983

'Erica' F, or, 1964, Herholdt, J.A.; flowers orange-scarlet, frilled, semi-dbl., borne in large clusters; [seedling × 'Montezuma']

'Erica' -- See 'Interop'

'Erica Herholdt' F, or, Herholdt, J.A.; flowers large, semi-dbl.; intr. 1964

'Erich Frahm' F, mr, 1939, Kordes; bud long, pointed, yellowish red; flowers carmine-scarlet, center yellow, petals shell-shaped, open, borne in umbels of up to 20; foliage dark, glossy, leathery; vigorous growth, very branching.; ['Dance of Joy' × 'Mary Hart']

'Eric's Choice' -- See 'Webtweed'

'Erie' S, lp, 1946, Preston; flowers pale pink, 5 petals, borne in clusters; very free, non-recurrent bloom; foliage dark, fragrant (sweetbriar); vigorous, spreading growth; hips bottle-shaped, bright red; hardy

'Erie Treasure' HRg, w, Wedrick; flowers blush to white, dbl.; recurrent bloom; foliage wrinkled; vigorous (6 ft.), bushy growth; ['Souv. de Pierre Leperdrieux' × 'Nova Zembla']

'Erik Hjelm' HT, op, 1929, Kordes; flowers pure salmon-pink, very dbl.; ['Lieutenant Chaure' × 'Sachsengruss']

'Erika' HT, mp, Asami; intr. 1990

'Erika My Love' Min, my, 1993, Armstrong, James L.; flowers yellow with white tips, 2-3 in., 25-30 petals, borne mostly singly; foliage medium green, semi-glossy; some prickles; tall (72 cm.), upright growth; ['Rise 'n' Shine' × seedling]

'Erika Pluhar' HT, dr

'Erika Teschendorff' HT, mr, 1949, Berger, V.; bud long, pointed; flowers fiery scarlet, open, very large, dbl., globular; foliage glossy, dark; very vigorous, upright growth

'Erikonig' HMult, m, 1886, Geschwind, R.

'Erin Alonso' -- See 'Aloerin'

'Erin Elise' -- See 'Jayerel'

'Erin Fleming' LCl, mp, 1997, Fleming, Joyce L.; flowers medium to deep pink, medium size, 41 petals, borne singly and in large clusters, up to 15 buds per cluster, moderate fragrance; foliage medium size, dark green, glossy; upright, tall growth; ['Sunsation' × 'Henry Kelsey']; intr. 1995

'Erinnerung an Brod' ('Souv de Brod') HSet, rb, 1886, Geschwind, R.; flowers cerise through crimson to purple, paler at center, 8 cm., dbl., quartered, flat, moderate fragrance; very remontant; [(*R. setigera* × unknown) × 'Génie de Châteaubriand']; sometimes classed as HP

'Erinnerung an Brod × Belle Siebrecht' LCl, m, 1930, Krüger

'Erinnerung an Schloss Scharfenstein' HT, m, 1892, Geschwind, R.; flowers purple/pink, large, dbl., intense fragrance

'Erlkönig' -- See 'Roi des Aunes'

'Erna' HWich, pb, 1929, Vogel, M.; flowers pale salmon pink, reverse darker, 4 cm., dbl., borne in small clusters; foliage dark green, glossy

'Erna Baltzer' HT, my, 1954, Leenders, M.; flowers golden yellow, medium; vigorous growth; ['Tawny Gold' × 'Gaudia']

'Erna Doris' -- See 'Lendori'

'Erna Grootendorst' F, dr, 1938, Grootendorst, R.; flowers deep velvety crimson, large, semi-dbl.; foliage glossy, dark; bushy growth; ['Bergers Erfolg' × 'Gloria Mundi']

'Erna Teschendorff' Pol, mr, 1911, Teschendorff; flowers strawberry-red, open, small, semi-dbl.; foliage rich green, soft; bushy growth; [sport of 'Mme Norbert Levavasseur']

'Ernest Bonçenne' HP, mp, 1868, Cherpin/Liabaud; flowers bright pink, edges and reverse lighter pink, medium, full

'Ernest H. Morse' ('E. H. Morse', 'Souv de Ernest H. Morse') HT, mr, 1965, Kordes; flowers turkey-red, 4 in., 30 petals, intense fragrance; foliage leathery; vigorous growth; intr. 1964

'Ernest H. Morse, Climbing' Cl HT, mr; intr. after 1964

'Ernest Laurent' HT, lp, 1914, Viaud-Bruant; flowers whitish pink, large, dbl., moderate fragrance

'Ernest May' HT, Seale; intr. 2003

'Ernest Metz' T, mp, 1888, Guillot, J. B.; flowers rose-pink, center darker, large, dbl.

'Ernest Morel' HP, dr, 1898, Cochet, P.; flowers bright garnet-red, full; growth tall; ['Général Jacqueminot' × unknown]

'Ernest Prince' HP, mr, 1881, Ducher; flowers light red, darker at center, reverse silvery, very large, full, globular; foliage dark green; numerous prickles; growth upright; ['Antoine Ducher' × unknown]

'Ernestine Cosme' HWich, rb, 1926, Turbat; flowers brilliant red, with large white eye, single, borne in clusters of 75; numerous prickles; very vigorous, climbing growth

'Ernestine de Barante' HP, mp, 1843, Lacharme

'Ernest's Blue' HT, m, LeGrice; flowers full, high-centered, moderate fragrance; very long stems; compact, strong, medium growth; intr. 1990

'Ernie' -- See 'Tinernie'

'Ernie Pyle' HT, mp, 1946, Boerner; bud long, pointed; flowers deep rose-pink, reverse deeper, 4½-5 in., 35-40 petals, cupped, intense fragrance; foliage leathery; vigorous, upright, bushy growth; PP673; [(('Royal Red' × 'Talisman') × 'red seedling') × ('Talisman' × 'Nutneyron')]

'Ernistine Audio' D, m, before 1842, Audio; flowers bluish pink, full, moderate fragrance

'Ernnst Hempel' HT, lp, 1907, Mietzsch; flowers large, full

'Ernst Dechant' HWich, w, 1928, Vogel, M.; flowers white with yellow tints, small, semi-dbl., borne in small clusters

Ernst G. Dörell® HMult, dp, 1887, Geschwind, R.; flowers carmine, 3-4 cm., dbl., cupped

'Ernst Grandpierre' HWich, w, 1902, Weigand, C.; flowers pale cream, base yellow, 5-6 cm., dbl., open, borne in large clusters; sparse bloom; foliage light, glossy; growth to 8-10 ft.; [R. wichurana × 'Perle des Jardins']

'Eroica' ('Eroika', 'Erotica', Erotika®) HT, dr, 1968, Tantau, Math.; bud ovoid; flowers velvety dark red, well-formed, large, 33 petals, intense fragrance; foliage dark, glossy; vigorous, upright growth; intr. 1969

'Eroika' -- See 'Eroica'

'Eros' F, dp, 1955, Maarse, G.; flowers deep rosy pink shaded brick-red, base yellow; dwarf, compact growth; ['Pinocchio' × unknown]

'Eros' -- See 'Barsor'

'Erotica' -- See 'Eroica'

Erotika® -- See 'Eroica'

'Erskine' (form of R. blanda), mp, Hansen, N.E.

'Erubescens' -- See 'Celestial'

'Eruption' HT, mr, 1934, Van Rossem; flowers fiery scarlet-red, large, semi-dbl.; foliage sea-green; bushy growth; ['Red-Letter Day' × 'Columbia']

'Erwin Hüttmann' HWich, dp, 1941, Krause; flowers rose-red, medium, dbl., intense fragrance

'Erzherzog Franz Ferdinand' ('Louis Lévêque') T, pb, 1892, Soupert & Notting; flowers peach-red on yellow, peony-like, reverse often striped magenta red, large, full, cupped

'Erzherzogin Marie Dorothea' ('Archiduchesse Marie-Dorothée Amélie') HT, yb, 1892, Balogh; flowers yellowish rose-red, large, very full; ['Mme Falcot' × 'Général Jacqueminot']

'Esa' HT, pb, Ghosh; flowers pastel pink with rich, deeper center, very full, well formed; intr. 2001

'Esbank' HT, mp, 1916, Dobbie

'Escada' -- See 'Tanadac'

'Escalade' Cl HT, mr, 1962, Combe; bud pointed; flowers carmine, large, high-centered; vigorous growth; ['Spectacular' × 'Charlotte Armstrong']

Escapade® F, m, 1967, Harkness; flowers magenta-rose, center white, 3 in., 12 petals, borne in clusters; foliage glossy, light green; ['Pink Parfait' × 'Baby Faurax']

'Escimo' -- See 'Korcilmo'

'Escimo' -- See 'Silver Ghost'

'Escimo Kordana' Min, w, Kordes; flowers full; container rose

'Esco Rose' F, Gregory, C.

'Escort' F, dr, 1963, Swim & Weeks; bud pointed to urn-shaped; flowers small to medium, 30 petals, high-centered; foliage dark, leathery; vigorous, bushy growth; PP2436; ['Spartan' × 'Garnette']

'Escultor Clará' HT, m, 1956, Dot, Pedro; bud pointed; flowers purple-garnet, reverse magenta, large, 30 petals, high-centered, moderate fragrance; foliage dark, glossy; very vigorous, upright, compact growth; ['Lilette Mallerin' × 'Floradora']

Escurial® -- See 'Delflip'

'Eskil' HT, yb, 1939, Ringdahl; flowers light yellow overlaid red and orange; PP353; [sport of 'Mrs Franklin D. Roosevelt']

Eskimo® ('Escimo') F, w, Kordes; flowers small, dbl., high-centered; PP8580; greenhouse rose; intr. 1991

'Esmae Lilly' -- See 'Worcomputer'

'Esmé' HT, w, 1920, Cant, B. R.; flowers cream-white, edged rosy carmine, dbl.; ['Mme Edouard Herriot' × seedling]

'Esme Euvrard' -- See 'Korelgas'

'Esmeralda' A, lp, 1847, Verdier; flowers delicate flesh, margins white, medium, full

'Esmeralda' ('La Esmeralda') HP, mp, Fontaine; flowers bright pink; intr. 1862

'Esmeralda' HT, w, Geschwind; flowers flesh white, aging to lilac pink, large, full; intr. 1888

'Esmeralda' F, dp, Riethmuller; flowers deep rose-pink, reverse lighter, small, dbl., borne in very large clusters, moderate fragrance; vigorous growth; ['Gartendirector Otto Linne' × seedling]; intr. 1957

Esmeralda® -- See 'Kormalda'

'Esmeralda Kordana' Min, dp, Kordes; bud pointed ovoid; flowers hot pink , 2 in. , 34 -38 petals, high-centered, borne singly, slight fragrance; recurrent; foliage dark green, glossy ; prickles some, 6 mm., linear; vigorous, upright (16 in.), bushy growth ; PP15716; ['Korlusma' × Vanilla Kordana®]; container rose

'Esmond Jones' HRg, mp; flowers deep magenta pink, 3 in., semi-double, flat, moderate sweet fragrance; recurrent; foliage dark green, fairly narrow; bushy (5 ft.) growth; hips rounded; intr. 2006

'Especially for You' -- See 'Fryworthy'

'Espérance' HT, lp, deRuiter; PP14663; intr. 2001

'Espérance' T, 1905, Dubourdieu/Chauvry

'Esperanto' HT, my, 1932, Böhm, J.; flowers pure yellow, very large, 60 petals, globular; [sport of 'Miss Lolita Armour']

'Esperanto Jubileo' -- See 'Sanrozo'

'Espéranza' F, mr, 1966, Delforge; bud ovoid; flowers bright red, large, dbl., borne in clusters; foliage dark, bronze, leathery, glossy; upright growth; ['Donald Prior' × 'Reverence']; originally registered as Pol

'Esplanade' HT, dr, 1961, Verbeek; flowers 40 petals; foliage glossy growth; ['Soraya' × seedling]

'Espoir' HT, pb, 1947, Lens; bud long, pointed; flowers pink, center light salmon-pink, large, 35 petals, slight fragrance; abundant bloom; foliage soft; bushy growth; RULED EXTINCT 6/83; ['Charles P. Kilham' × 'Neville Chamberlain']

'Espoir' F, op, 1958, Combe; flowers rich salmon, 4½ in., 50 petals, rosette, moderate fragrance; vigorous, low, bushy growth; RULED EXTINCT 6/83 ARM; [('Oiseau de Feu' × 'Fashion') × ('Independence' × seedling)]

'Espoir' HT, mr, Meilland; flowers velvety red, large, 35 petals; foliage matte; intr. 1981

'Espoir' -- See 'Interbec'

'Espresso' F, r, Spek; flowers light russet, deeper reverse, 9 cm., 25-30 petals, high-centered, borne mostly singly; recurrent; few prickles; stems long; intr. 2005

'Espresso' HT, dr, Teranishi; intr. 2005

'Esprit' F, or, GPG; intr. 1985

'Esprit' HT, mp, Kordes; intr. 2002

Esprit® -- See 'Korholst'

'Esprit Kordana' Min, mp, Kordes; Pot rose

'Essence' HT, op, deRuiter; intr. 2001

'Essence, Climbing' Cl HT, dr, 1938, Western Rose Co.

'Essence' HT, dr, 1930, Cant, B. R.; bud pointed; flowers rich scarlet-crimson, becoming bluish, outer petals slightly fimbriated, cupped, moderate damask fragrance

Essex™ -- See 'Poulnoz'

'Essie Lee' -- See 'Judlee'

'Estafette' F, dr, 1964, Delforge; flowers open, 2½-3 in., semi-dbl., borne in clusters; foliage dark, glossy, vigorous growth; ['Alain' × 'Elmshorn']; intr. 1962

'Estelle' HGal, mp, before 1810; flowers flesh pink, medium, very dbl., intense fragrance

Estelle™ ('Ian Thorpe', Estelle de Meilland®) HT, r, Olij, Huibert W; flowers ochre shaded with brown, creamy yellow on reverse, dbl., high-centered, borne mostly singly, slight fragrance; foliage dark bronze-green, glossy; growth upright (5 ft.); PP10844; intr. 1997

'Estelle' HT, op, Croix

'Estelle' -- See 'Belle Estelle'

Estelle de Meilland® -- See 'Olijbrau'

'Estelle Pradel' -- See 'Esther Pradel'

Estepona™ -- See 'Poulpah028(N)'

'Estepona Hit' (Estepona™) MinFl, ob, Poulsen; flowers orange blend, 5-8 cm.,

dbl., no fragrance; foliage dark; growth bushy, 20-40 cm.; intr. 2004
'Esterel' -- See 'Koriver'
'Esther' ('Grande Esther') HGal, pb, 1845, Vibert; flowers blush pink petals overlaid magenta, pompon, moderate sweet, spicy fragrance; basal canes nearly smooth; possibly synonymous with 'Duchesse d'Oldenburg', Calvert, about 1845
'Esther' F, ob, San Remo Exp. Sta.; bud pointed, turkey-red; flowers golden orange, reverse lighter, open, large, 7-8 petals, borne in clusters; foliage glossy, bright green; long stems; very vigorous, bushy growth; ['Cocorico' × 'Canzonetta']; intr. 1954
'Esther' ('Our Esther') HT, lp, Kordes; flowers light pink, medium, dbl., high-centered, borne mostly singly; recurrent; stems 50 cm.; [sport of 'Escimo']; florist rose; intr. 1999
'Esther Ellen' F, ob, Ford, Albert; intr. 2005
'Esther Geldenhuys' -- See 'Korskipei'
'Esther Jasik' -- See 'Zipest'
'Esther Jerabek' F, mp, 1979, Jerabek, Paul E.; flowers 18 petals; spreading growth; [sport of 'The Fairy']
'Esther O'Farim' -- See 'Matador'
Esther Peiro® -- See 'Febasa'
'Esther Pradel' ('Estelle Pradel') T, ab, 1860, Pradel; bud pure white; flowers chamois, aging to salmon, medium, full; foliage large, dark green, glossy
'Esther Rantzen' F, ob, 1982, Dwight, Robert & Sons; flowers medium, semi-dbl., moderate fruity fragrance; foliage medium size, medium green, semi-glossy; upright, bushy growth; ['Spartan' × Orangeade®]
Esther's Baby® -- See 'Harkinder'
'Estima' S, lp, Noack; low, spreading, groundcover growth; intr. 1998
'Estima' Min, op
'Estralia' -- See 'Pixie Pearl'
'Estralita' -- See 'Pixie Pearl'
'Estrellita de Oro' -- See 'Baby Gold Star'
'Estru' F, lp, 1976, deRuiter; flowers patio, 1½ in., 50 petals; foliage small, glossy, dark; low, compact growth; ['Rosy Jewel' × 'floribunda seedling']; intr. 1975
'Étain' HWich, op, 1953, Cant, F.; flowers salmon-pink, 5-6 cm., borne in large clusters; foliage small, glossy, dark green, almost evergreen; very vigorous growth
'Été Parfumé' -- See 'Typhoo Tea'
'Étendard' ('New Dawn Rouge', 'Red New Dawn') HWich, mr, 1956, Robichon; flowers scarlet red, 8 cm., dbl., borne in small clusters, moderate fragrance; recurrent bloom; foliage very glossy, leathery; vigorous growth; ['New Dawn' × seedling]
'Étendard de Jeanne d'Arc' ('Jeanne d'Arc') N, w, 1882, Garçon/Margottin; flowers creamy white changing to pure white, 9-10 cm., full, moderate fragrance; ['Gloire de Dijon' × unknown]; sometimes classified as a T
'Étendard de Lyon' HP, mr, 1885, Gonod; flowers glossy peony red with metallic reflections, large, full
'Étendard de Marengo' ('Standard of Marengo') HP, mr, 1848, Armand, Étienne; flowers dark scarlet with carmine, large, very full, cupped
Éterna® -- See 'Delic'
'Eterna Giovanezza' -- See 'Eternal Youth'
'Eternal' HT, ob, Delbard; intr. 2003
'Eternal Flame' ('Everblooming Pillar No. 12') LCl, ob, 1955, Brownell; flowers light orange, 3-4 in., 12-19 petals, moderate fragrance; upright, climbing growth; PP1439; [seedling × 'Queen o' the Lakes']
'Eternal Flame' F, ob, Interplant; intr. 1992
Eternal Flame™ HT, my, Meilland; bud medium yellow; flowers soft yellow, lightening as they open, large, 25 petals, high-centered, borne mostly singly, intense citrus fragrance; recurrent; foliage dark green; stems long; tall, upright growth; intr. 2007
'Eternal Flame' -- See 'Korassenet'
'Eternal Sun' HT, or, 1966, Joseph H. Hill, Co.; bud ovoid; flowers vermilion, large, dbl., high-centered, slight fragrance; foliage dark, leathery; vigorous, upright, bushy growth; PP2689; [seedling × 'Jacqueline (HT)']
'Eternal Youth' ('Eterna Giovanezza', 'Jeunesse Éternelle') HT, lp, 1937, Aicardi, D.; bud long, pointed; flowers light pink, heavily suffused orange-salmon, 4-5 in., 50 petals, cupped, intense fragrance; recurrent; foliage abundant, large, leathery; stems long, strong; vigorous, upright, bushy growth; PP332; ['Dame Edith Helen' × 'Julien Potin']
'Eternally' HT, rb, Hiroshima; intr. 1997
'Eternally Yours' -- See 'Macspeego'
'Eternité' F, mr, 1947, Gaujard; flowers scarlet, 4-5 in., 25 petals; foliage dark; very free growth; ['Mme Joseph Perraud' × 'Holstein']
'Eternity' -- See 'Twoetern'
'Ethel' HWich, lp, 1912, Turner; flowers flesh-pink, small, semi-dbl., borne in large clusters; foliage glossy; vigorous growth; ['Dorothy Perkins' × unknown]
'Ethel Austin' -- See 'Frymestin'
'Ethel Brownlow' ('Miss Ethel Brownlow') T, op, 1887, Dickson, A.; flowers salmon pink, large; foliage glossy
'Ethel Chaplin' HT, my, 1926, Chaplin Bros.; flowers soft lemon-yellow, dbl.
'Ethel Dawson' HT, rb, Dawson, George; [Red Meillandina® × seedling]; intr. before 1987
'Ethel Dickson' HT, dp, 1917, Dickson, H.; flowers deep salmon-rose with silvery flesh reflexes, large, dbl.
'Ethel James' HT, dp, 1921, McGredy; flowers softer carmine-red than Isobel, flushed orange-scarlet, center yellow, 5 petals; bushy growth
'Ethel Kennedy' HT, ab, Takatori, Y.; flowers amber with reddish-edges, petals wavy and slightly reflexed, 13-15 cm., 30-35 petals, high-centered, borne singly and in small clusters, intense fragrance; foliage light green, acuminate; growth upright; ['Hawaii' × seedling]; intr. 1975
'Ethel Malcolm' HT, w, 1909, McGredy; flowers ivory-white, very large; vigorous growth
Ethel Orr™ -- See 'Minamco'
'Ethel Sanday' HT, yb, 1954, Mee; flowers yellow flushed apricot, well-formed, 4-5 in., 34 petals, slight fragrance; foliage dark; vigorous, upright growth; ['Rex Anderson' × 'Audrey Cobden']
'Ethel Sloman' HT, mr, 1966, Fankhauser; bud ovoid; flowers crimson, very dbl.; foliage leathery; compact, bushy growth; [Baccará® × 'My Choice']
'Ethel Somerset' HT, mp, 1921, Dickson, A.; bud pointed; flowers shrimp-pink, large, dbl., high-centered, intense fragrance; vigorous, branching growth
'Ethel Utter' LCl, my, Wilber; bud cherry-red; flowers dbl.
'Ethical' F, rb, Dawson; intr. 1995
'Étienette Desbrosses' D, about 1828, from Angers
'Étienne Dubois' HP, dr, 1873, Damaizin; flowers deep velvety crimson, large, dbl.
'Étienne Levet' HP, mr, 1871, Levet Père; flowers carmine-red, large, 70 petals; sometimes recurrent bloom; vigorous, erect growth; ['Victor Verdier' × unknown]
'Étienne Levet, Climbing' Cl HP, mp; [sport of 'Étienne Levet']
'Étienne Rebeillard' HT, pb, 1924, Pernet-Ducher; flowers flesh-pink, suffused golden, semi-dbl.
'Étincelante' HT, dr, 1913, Chambard, C.; flowers brilliant red, tinted purple, large, dbl., moderate fragrance; ['Gruss an Teplitz' × 'Étoile de France']
'Étincelle' HT, or, 1958, Moulin; flowers bright red tinted orange, medium, 40-45 petals, low, bushy growth; ['Crimson Glory' × seedling]
'Etna' F, ob; intr. 2005
'Etna' Ch, dp, 1825, Laffay; flowers vivid pink, becoming fiery crimson, medium, very full
'Etna' ('Aetna') M, dr, Vibert; flowers crimson shaded purple, large, very mossy, very dbl., cupped, moderate fragrance; intr. 1845
'Etna' HT, dr, Looymans; flowers deep crimson-maroon, semi-dbl.; ['Red-Letter Day' × 'H.V. Machin']; intr. 1924
Etna™ -- See 'Poulpar031(N)'
'Etna Parade' (Etna™) Min, or, Poulsen; flowers orange-red, medium, dbl., no fragrance; growth bushy, 20-40 cm.; intr. 2004
'Étoile d'Alaï' HMsk, mr, 1946, Meilland, F.; flowers brilliant red, prominent golden stamens, medium, very dbl.; repeat

bloom; bushy growth; ['Skyrocket' × unknown]

'Étoile de Belgique'   HT, mr, 1946, Lens; flowers brilliant red, very large, dbl., slight fragrance; foliage bronze; vigorous, bushy growth; ['Charles P. Kilham' × 'Étoile de Hollande']

'Étoile de Belgique'   HT, mr, Buyl Frères; bud ovoid; flowers geranium-red, large, dbl.; bushy, spreading growth; ['Independence' × 'Happiness']; intr. 1956

'Étoile de Bologne' -- See 'Stella di Bologna'

'Étoile de Feu'   HT, op, 1921, Pernet-Ducher; flowers salmon-pink and coral-red, large, dbl., globular; foliage bronze; vigorous, bushy, branching growth

'Étoile de Feu, Climbing'   Cl HT, ob, 1930, H&S

'Étoile de France'   HT, dr, 1904, Pernet-Ducher; bud pointed; flowers dark rose-red, center cerise, medium to small, dbl., cupped; bushy growth; ['Mme Abel Chatenay' × 'Fisher Holmes']

'Étoile de France, Climbing'   Cl HT, dr, 1915, Howard Rose Co.

'Étoile de Hollande'   HT, mr, 1919, Verschuren; flowers bright red, very large, 35-40 petals, cupped, intense damask fragrance; foliage soft; growth moderate (to 3 ft.), branching; ['Gen. MacArthur' × 'Hadley']

'Étoile de Hollande, Climbing' ('Grimpant Étoile de Hollande') Cl HT, mr, 1931, Leenders, M.; flowers rich velvet crimson, very large, dbl., cupped, intense old rose fragrance; [sport of 'Étoile de Hollande']

'Étoile de la Malmaison'   A, lp, before 1844; flowers flesh, fading to French white, medium to large, full, cupped; foliage dark, dull green, thick; growth erect

'Étoile de Lyon' ('Monroe St. Yellow Tea') T, my, 1881, Guillot fils; bud large, full; flowers golden yellow, fading to ivory, 8-10 cm., dbl., moderate fragrance; sparse intermittent bloom; foliage soft; short, weak stems; bushy growth; ['Mme Charles' × unknown]

'Étoile de Mai'   Pol, ly, 1893, Gamon; flowers sulfur-white, small, dbl.; vigorous growth

'Étoile de Poitevine'   HT, rb, 1910, Bruant; flowers velvety red, striped pink and white; ['Étoile de France' × unknown]

'Étoile de Portugal'   HG, dp, 1903, Cayeux, H.; flowers rose-red to salmon, large, dbl., loose; [R. gigantea × 'Reine Marie Henriette']

'Étoile d'Or'   Pol, ly, 1889, Dubreuil; flowers small

'Étoile d'Or'   HT, yb, Pernet-Ducher; flowers golden yellow, reverse shaded orange, large, semi-dbl., intense fragrance; upright, bushy growth; intr. 1931

'Étoile du Berger'   B, w, 1841, Béluze; flowers flesh white, medium, full

'Étoile du Matin'   B, dp, 1851, Bernède; flowers pink aging to violet, medium, full

'Étoile du Nord'   HP, mr, 1854, Fontaine; flowers bright cherry red, shaded garnet purple, medium, full, globular

'Étoile du Nord'   HP, dr, Bernède; intr. 1859

'Étoile Luisante' ('Baby Herriot') Pol, mr, 1918, Turbat; bud pointed; flowers cerise-red, shaded coppery, semi-dbl., high-centered, borne in clusters; foliage bronze, glossy; prickles few thorns; long stems; bushy growth

'Etoile Rouge' ('Pekminou') Min, rb

'Etrusca'   HT, ob, Barni; bud globous; flowers soft orange, fading to bright apricot, full, cupped, then pompon, moderate fragrance; recurrent; foliage bronze red when young, then dark green; moderate (80-100 cm.) growth; intr. 2006

'Etty van Best'   HT, ly, 1934, Buisman, G. A. H.; flowers white, shaded yellow, dbl.; foliage leathery; vigorous growth; ['Pharisaer' × 'Souv. de H.A. Verschuren']

'Etude'   LCl, dp, 1965, Gregory; bud coral; flowers deep peachy rose-pink, 8 cm., semi-dbl., borne in clusters, moderate fragrance; recurrent bloom; foliage glossy, light green; ['Spectacular' × 'New Dawn']

'Etude'   HT, yb, Hiroshima; intr. 2005

'Eucharis'   HGal, dp, before 1820, Descemet, M. (?); flowers bright rose, edged lighter, large, dbl.

'Eudoxia' -- See 'Eudoxie'

'Eudoxie'   HGal, dp, Descemet; flowers dark rose; intr. before 1820

'Eudoxie' ('Eudoxia')   D, mp; flowers vivid rose, reverse lilac-pink, large, dbl., cupped; numerous prickles; growth branching, vigorous; possibly synonymous with the HGal of the same name; intr. before 1848

'Eudoxie'   N, dy, Léon-Lille; flowers copper-yellow, edges whitish, medium, full, globular; intr. 1852

'Eugène Appert'   HP, dr, 1860, Trouillard; flowers velvety crimson-maroon, medium, full; [sport of 'Géant des Batailles']

'Eugène Barbier'   HP, dy, 1920, Barbier; flowers brilliant canary-yellow, shaded coppery golden yellow, dbl., globular; prickles few thorns; upright growth; ['Frau Karl Druschki' × 'Rayon d'Or']

'Eugène Boullet'   HT, dr, 1909, Pernet-Ducher; flowers crimson-red, shaded carmine, large, dbl., globular, borne mostly solitary; foliage bronze green; vigorous growth; ['Liberty' × 'Étoile de France']

'Eugène Bourgeois' -- See 'René Denis'

'Eugène Bréon'   B, op, 1847, Paillet; flowers salmon pink with flesh, large, full

'Eugène de Beauharnais' ('Prince Eugène') Ch, dr, 1838, Hardy; flowers purple, large, dbl., moderate fragrance

'Eugène de Luxembourg' -- See 'Prince Eugène de Beauharnais'

'Eugène de Savoie'   M, mr, 1860, Moreau et Robert; flowers bright red, shaded, 10-12 cm., dbl., flat; some repeat

'Eugène Desgaches' -- See 'Desgaches'

'Eugène d'Orléans'   HSem, lp, before 1829, Jacques; flowers delicate pink, 2 in., dbl., borne in small clusters; foliage oval, glabrous, glossy, leathery; prickles few, red, nearly straight; stems thick, reddish, creeping

'Eugène E. Marlitt' ('Mme Eugène Marlitt') B, mr, 1900, Geschwind, R.; flowers bright carmine shaded scarlet, large, dbl.; few prickles; vigorous growth

'Eugène Fürst' ('General Korolkow') HP, dr, 1875, Soupert & Notting; flowers crimson-red, shaded purple, large, dbl., globular; recurrent bloom; ['Baron de Bonstetten' × unknown]

'Eugène Jacquet'   HWich, mr, 1916, Turbat; flowers cherry-red, dbl., borne in clusters; very early bloom; foliage bright green; vigorous, symmetrical growth; ['red wichurana hybrid' × 'Multiflora hybrid (pink)']

'Eugène Janvier'   HGal, dp; flowers dark pink, paling to lilac, medium, dbl.

'Eugene Jardine'   N, w, 1898, Conard & Jones; flowers pure white, large, full, moderate fragrance

'Eugène Maille'   HGal, mp, about 1825, Boutigny; flowers bright pink, very large, full

'Eugène Picard'   HT, op, 1938, Sauvageot, H.; flowers light coppery-pink with red tints, large, very dbl.

'Eugène Pirolle' -- See 'Admiral de Rigny'

'Eugène Transon'   LCl, or, 1926, Barbier; flowers orange and copper, reverse orange-red, shaded, borne in clusters; vigorous, climbing growth; ['Mme Bérard' × 'Constance']

'Eugène Vavin'   HP, mr, 1869, Duval; flowers shining cherry red, shaded scarlet, large, full

'Eugène Verdier'   HP, m, 1863, Guillot fils; flowers rich dark violet, large, full; ['Victor Verdier' × unknown]

'Eugène Verdier'   M, dp, Verdier, E.; flowers crimson or light red, center deeper, well-formed, very dbl., moderate fragrance; intr. 1872

'Eugenia'   HT, rb, 1920, Collier; flowers coral-red to prawn-red, flecked or striped yellow, dbl.; [sport of 'Mme Edouard Herriot']

'Eugénie Boullet' -- See 'Mme Eugénie Boullet'

'Eugénie Bourgeois'   T, w, 1897, Bourgeois; flowers silky cream-white, center apricot, large, full; ['Mme Bérard' × unknown]

'Eugénie Buatois'   Pol, 1904, Buatois

'Eugénie Chamusseau'   C, dp

'Eugénie de Guinoisseau' -- See 'Eugénie Guinoisseau'

'Eugénie Guinoisseau'   B, mp, 1860, Guinoisseau; flowers bright pink, shaded flesh white, medium, very full

'Eugénie Guinoisseau' ('Eugénie de Guinoisseau') M, mr, Bertrand-Guinoiseau; flowers reddish-cerise, changing to reddish-violet, 8-10 cm., dbl.; some repeat; foliage dark green, oval, pointed, finely dentate; prickles numerous, red; vigorous growth; intr. 1864

'Eugénie Guinoisseau × Nuits de Young' M, dr, Dechant; flowers magenta red, brown tones in autumn, medium, dbl., cupped; recurrent; upright (5 ft.), strong growth; intr. 1938

'Eugénie Jauvin' -- See 'Mme Roussel'

'Eugénie Lamesch' Pol, yb, 1899, Lambert, P.; flowers ochre-yellow and bright yellow, shaded pink, dbl., borne in clusters, moderate fragrance; foliage glossy; dwarf, compact growth; ['Aglaia' × 'William Allen Richardson']

'Eugénie Lebrun' HP, dr, 1860, Fontaine; flowers amaranth red, shaded brown, large, full

'Eugenio d'Ors' HT, dr, 1946, Camprubi, C.; flowers oxblood-red, large, dbl.; ['Sensation' × 'Margaret McGredy']

'Eugenio Fojo' HT, mr, 1953, Dot, Pedro; bud pointed; flowers vermilion-red, well-formed, large, 35 petals; vigorous, bushy growth; ['Texas Centennial' × 'Carlos Fargas']

'Eughien' ('Pearly Shores') HT, ab, (EUGhien)

'Eulalia' HT, mp, 1934, Verschuren-Pechtold; flowers pink, lighter toward base, large, dbl.; vigorous growth

'Eulalia Berridge' Pol, lp; flowers medium, dbl.

'Eulalia de la Falconnière' B, dr, 1854, Dorizy; flowers dark red, edges lighter, large, full

'Eulalie Lebrun' HGal, w, 1845, Vibert; flowers white, striped with rose and lilac, medium, dbl.; sometimes classed as C

'Eumundi' F, w, 1953, Ulrick, L.W.; flowers pure white, very dbl., cupped; foliage light green; vigorous, bushy growth; ['Yvonne Rabier' × 'Baby Alberic']

'Euphémie' B, lp, 1847, Vibert; flowers delicate rose, 7 cm., full

'Euphoria' ('Peachy Creeper') S, ob, Interplant; flowers bright orange with yellow center and golden eye, 1½ in., semi-dbl., cupped, borne usually in clusters; free-flowering; foliage dense, medium green, glossy; low (6-12 in.), spreading (3-5 ft.) growth; groundcover; intr. 1997

'Euphrates' -- See 'Harunique'

'Euphrosine' HCh, mp, 1826, Vibert

'Euphrosine' ('L'Elégante') HGal, dp, Prévost; flowers vivid pink or dark carmine, medium, full; intr. about 1835

'Euphrosine' N, yb; flowers light pink with yellow, large, full, cupped; intr. before 1866

'Euphrosine l'Élégante' C, dp, before 1811, Descemet; bud long; flowers dark rose pink, 2-3 in., borne in large clusters

'Euphrosyne' ('Pink Rambler') HMult, mp, 1895, Schmitt; flowers pure pink, 3-4 cm., single to semi-dbl., borne in large clusters, moderate fragrance; non-recurrent; very vigorous growth; [*R. multiflora* × 'Mignonette']

'Eureka' HT, mp, 1914, Hobbies; flowers bright rose

'Eureka' S, w, Wright, Percy H.; flowers pure white, small, semi-dbl., borne in clusters; intended for trial as a hardy understock; [probably 'Betty Bland' × 'Ames 5']; intr. 1956

'Eureka' F, ab; flowers golden, apricot yellow, 4 in., dbl., borne in clusters of 3-5, slight fragrance; good repeat; foliage glossy; growth to 3½ ft.; PP15712; intr. 2003

'Euro 92' F, dr, RvS-Melle; ['Windekind' × 'Patricia']; intr. 1989

'Eurogroot' (Sunny Sky™) F, ob, Kordes/Grootendorst; bud pointed; intr. 1991

'Europa' HT, mp, 1928, Keessen; flowers bright pink; [sport of 'Columbia']

'Europa' -- See 'Kortexung'

'Europas Rosengarten' -- See 'Heleuro'

'Europawelle Saar' HT, op, Meilland; flowers salmon-pink, large, dbl.; intr. 1985

Europe 92® -- See 'Delsulan'

'Europe Sensation' F, or

'European Touch' HT, ab, Von Koss; bud elongated, edged with pink; flowers dbl., high-centered, borne singly, no fragrance; foliage large, dark green, matte; long, straight stems; very tall (5-6 ft.), upright, vigorous growth; intr. 1997

Europeana® F, dr, 1964, deRuiter; flowers dark velvety crimson, 3 in., 25-30 petals, rosette, borne in large, heavy clusters, slight tea fragrance; foliage bronze-green to dark green; vigorous growth; PP2540; ['Ruth Leuwerik' × 'Rosemary Rose']; intr. 1963

'Europeana, Climbing' -- See 'Bureuro'

'Eurorose' F, yb, 1974, Dickson, A.; flowers yellow-ochre, flushed fire-red, large, 25 petals, globular; ['Zorina' × 'Redgold']; intr. 1973

'Eurorose' -- See 'Eurorose 2000'

'Eurorose 2000' ('Eurorose') LCl, pb, Croix, P.; intr. 2001

Eurosong® -- See 'Lenoran'

Eurostar™ -- See 'Poulreb'

'Eurovision' HT, dr, 1961, Delforge; flowers 4 in., 30 petals; foliage dark; vigorous, bushy growth; ['Miss France' × 'Rosita']

'Euroway' -- See 'Helway'

Euryanthe® S, mp

'Eurydice' HSet, pb, 1886, Geschwind, R.; flowers carmine flesh; [*R. setigera* × 'Louise Odier']

'Eustace' HT, w, Robinson; flowers large, ivory-cream with blush pink edges, high-centered; ['Reve d'Or seedling']; intr. 1989

'Eustacia' -- See 'Seaeus'

'Euterpe' HMult, ly, 1937, Tantau; bud pointed; flowers semi-dbl., open, borne in medium clusters; foliage glossy; long stems; very vigorous, climbing growth; [('Ophelia' × *R. multiflora*) × 'Florex']

'Eutin' ('Hoosier Glory') F, dr, 1940, Kordes; bud globular, pointed; flowers glowing carmine-red, dbl., cupped, borne in clusters; foliage leathery, glossy, dark; vigorous growth; ['Eva' × 'Solarium']

'Eutin, Climbing' Cl F, dr, 1957, Lindquist; PP1531; [sport of 'Eutin']

'Eva' HMsk, rb, 1933, Kordes; bud pointed; flowers carmine-red, center white, large, semi-dbl., borne in large clusters, moderate fragrance; intermittent bloom; very vigorous growth; ['Robin Hood (HMsk)' × 'J. C. Thornton']

'Eva Corinne' HSet, lp, about 1846, Pierce; bud reddish; flowers light flesh, 3-4 cm., dbl., globular, borne in clusters of 10-20; non-recurrent; foliage medium size, somewhat rugose; prickles purplish; growth very erect

'Eva de Grossouvre' HT, mp, 1908, Guillot; flowers salmon-pink, large, full, globular; ['Mrs W. J. Grant' × unknown]

'Eva Eakins' HT, or, 1926, McGredy; flowers scarlet-carmine, flushed orange, base bright yellow, small, dbl., high-centered; foliage leathery; bushy growth

Eva Gabor™ -- See 'Poultal'

'Eva Knott' HT, ob, 1957, Mee; flowers coppery orange, well-formed, 35 petals; vigorous growth; ['Ethel Sanday' × 'Mrs Sam McGredy']

'Eva Schubert' -- See 'Frau Eva Schubert'

'Eva Simone' F, op, Michler, K. H.; flowers dbl.; intr. 1992

'Eva Teschendorff' Pol, w, 1923, Grunewald; flowers greenish-white, aging to pure white, medium, full, slight fragrance; [sport of 'Echo']; reclassified as Polyantha based on parentage, growth habit and historical classification

'Eva Teschendorff, Climbing' Cl Pol, w, 1926, Opdebeeck (also Teschendorff, 1932); flowers creamy white, small, full; [sport of 'Eva Teschendorff']

'Evaline' Pol, lp, 1920, Prosser; flowers light pink, edged brighter, petals quilled, small, dbl., borne in clusters, moderate fragrance; bushy growth; ['Orléans Rose' × 'Rayon d'Or']

'Evangeline' HWich, pb, 1906, Walsh; flowers rosy white, veined cameo-pink, 2 in., single, borne in large clusters, moderate fragrance; late seasonal bloom; foliage dark, leathery; long stems; very vigorous, climbimg (12-15 ft.) growth; [*R. wichurana* × 'Turner's Crimson Rambler']

'Evangeline' T, w, Krider Nursery; bud deep pink; flowers creamy white, edged blush-pink, medium, dbl., moderate fragrance; almost thornless; vigorous, spreading growth; [sport of 'Mrs Dudley Cross']; intr. 1951

'Evangeline Bruce' F, yb, 1971, Dickson, A.; flowers yellow, flushed pink, well-formed, 4½ in., 24 petals; foliage light; ['Colour Wonder' × 'Sea Pearl']

'Evasion' F, Hendricks; intr. 1972

'Eve' HT, ob, 1959, Gaujard; bud long, pointed; flowers coral-red shaded yellow, very large, dbl., moderate fragrance; foliage glossy; vigorous growth; intr. 1959

'Eve Allen' HT, rb, 1964, Allen, E.M.; flowers crimson, reverse and base saffron-yellow, 5 in., 26 petals; foliage dark, glossy; vigorous growth; ['Karl Herbst' × 'Gay Crusader']

'Evebeau' LCl, rb, Eve; intr. 2006

'Eveber' S, dp, Eve; intr. 2001

'Eveblanc' S, w, Eve, André; intr. 2005

'Evebordo' HMult, dr, Eve; intr. 2000

'Evebright' ('Cecily Gibson', 'Lady Cecily Gibson') F, rb, 1991, Everitt, Derrick; bud ovoid; flowers currant red, yellow base, medium, 35 petals, cupped, borne in sprays of 3-6, slight to moderate fragrance; foliage medium to large, dark green, glossy; bushy, medium to tall growth; ['Southampton' × (('Arthur Bell' × 'Maigold') × 'Glenfiddich')]; intr. 1990

'Evechant' F, op, Eve, A.; intr. 1980

'Evecoin' F, mp, Eve, A.; buds round; intr. 1995

'Evefrandore' ('Frances Louise') Gr, ob, 2002, Everitt, Derrick; flowers rich salmon pink, cream reverse, medium, full, borne in small clusters, moderate fragrance; foliage medium size, medium green, semi-glossy; prickles medium, slightly hooked, moderate; growth upright, medium to tall (1 m.); garden decorative; ['Golden Future' × (('Mary Sumner' × ('L'Oreal Trophy × Edith Holden')) × ('Mary Sumner × (Korp × Southampton))' × 'Edith Holden'))]

'Evefrenzy' ('Forever Zaidee') HT, mr, 2002, Everitt, Derrick; flowers scarlet red, 10 cm., full, borne mostly solitary or small clusters, slight fragrance; foliage medium size, dark green, semi-glossy; prickles medium, hooked, moderate; growth upright, medium (80-100 cm.); garden decorative; [('L'Oreal Trophy' × 'Edith Holden') × ('Mary Sumner' × ('Silver Jubilee' × 'L'Oreal Trophy'))]

'Evefury' ('Doreen Farrow') Gr, ob, 2003, Everitt, Derrick; flowers orange-vermilion, reverse paler, large, full, borne in small clusters, moderate fragrance; medium size, medium green, semi-glossy foliage; prickles medium, hooked; growth upright, tall (3 ft.); garden decorative; ['Solitaire' × ('Mary Sumner' × ('L'Oreal Trophy' × 'Edith Holden'))]; intr. 2004

'Evegaytime' ('Kantha Selvon') F, ob, 1999, Everitt, Derrick; flowers light orange, reverse cream yellow, 3-3½ in., full, borne singly and in small clusters, slight fragrance; foliage medium size, medium green, glossy; prickles moderate; upright, medium (2½ ft.) growth; ['Pot O'Gold' × ('Mary Sumner' × ('Glenfiddich' × '(Arthur Bell × Maigold)'))]

'Eveglitter' ('Katiroy') F, ob, 2001, Everitt, Derrick; flowers pale tangerine with red edging, medium, dbl., borne in small clusters, slight fragrance; foliage medium size, medium green, semi-glossy; prickles medium, straight, moderate; growth compact, low to medium (2-3½ ft.); [(R. virginiana × (Mary Sumner × Typhoon)) × Remember Me®]

'Evegold' ('Lynne's Gold') F, yb, 2001, Everitt, Derrick; flowers deep yellow, red edgings to petals, medium, dbl., borne in small clusters, slight fragrance; foliage medium size, dark green, glossy; prickles medium, hooked, moderate; growth upright, bushy, medium (3-3½ ft.); garden decorative; [('Mary Sumner' × ('L'Oreal Trophy' × 'Edith Holden')) × ('Mary Sumner' × '((Southampton × Korp)' × 'Edith Holden'))]

'Evehorgold' ('The Sandylands Rose') F, yb, 2007, Everitt, Derrick; flowers deep yellow, reverse cream, 3 in., dbl., borne in small clusters; foliage medium, dark green, semi-glossy; prickles medium, straight, moderate; growth upright, bushy, medium (2½ ft.); garden decorative; ['Golden Future' × (seedling × 'New Zealand')]; intr. 2007

'Evejaunty' ('Alice Jarrett') F, ob, 1999, Everitt, Derrick; flowers orange, reverse cream yellow, 3-3½ in., full, borne in small clusters, slight fragrance; foliage medium size, medium green, semi-glossy; prickles moderate; upright, tall (3-3½ ft.) growth; [('Mary Sumner' × ('L'Oreal Trophy' × 'Edith Holden')) × 'Friendship']

'Evejava' Pol, dp, Eve, A.full; intr. 1994

'Eveka' Min, pb, 2006, Hopper, Nancy; flowers pink/white blend, 2 in., full, borne mostly solitary; foliage medium green, matte; prickles ¼ in., reddish, few; growth upright, medium (16 in.); ['pink seedling' × unknown]; intr. 2006

'Eveleine' ('Lady Madeleine') F, ob, 1993, Everitt, Derrick; flowers tangerine, paler reverse, medium, dbl., borne singly and in small clusters; foliage medium size, medium green, semi-glossy; some prickles; medium (30 cm.), upright growth; [(Pristine® × 'Edith Holden') × ('L'Oreal Trophy' × 'Edith Holden')]

'Evelien' -- See 'Interlien'

'Evelill' ('Auberge de l'Ill') S, pb, 2002, Eve; flowers pale pink, 3-4 cm., dbl., pompons, borne in large sprays, slight fragrance; repeats well; foliage medium size, medium green, glossy; prickles moderate; growth low, spreading, bushy (40-50 cm.); ['Beauce' × seedling]; intr. 2003

'Evelina' -- See 'Amaevelina'

'Eveline Turner' HP, mp, 1876, Verdier, E.; flowers bright shining pink, very large, full

'Evelora' ('Miss Lorraine') Gr, mp, 2002, Eve, André; flowers dbl., borne in small clusters, slight fragrance; foliage medium size, medium green, semi-glossy; prickles moderate; growth upright, medium (80 cm.); [seedling × 'Versailles']; intr. 2001

'Evelsac' ('La Belle Alsacienne') S, dp, 2002, Eve; flowers velvety pink-crimson with purplish reflections, dbl., tangled OGR form, intense fragrance; vigorous (5 ft.) growth; intr. 2001

'Evelyn' Min, dp, Agel

'Evelyn' HT, mp, 1918, Paul, W.; flowers salmon, shaded and edged rose, base yellow, imbricated, large, dbl.; RULED EXTINCT 1/92; [sport of 'Ophelia']

'Evelyn' -- See 'Aussaucer'

'Evelyn Buchan' HT, pb, 1959, Riethmuller; flowers pink tinted yellow,, 3-4 in., 23 petals, high-centered; foliage leathery, dark; vigorous, upright growth; ['Luis Brinas' × 'Crimson Glory']

'Evelyn Dauntessey' HT, pb, 1909, McGredy; flowers salmon stained carmine-rose; moderately vigorous growth

'Evelyn Ellice' F, lp, 1966, Ellice; flowers light pink, becoming white, pointed, 3 in., borne in clusters; foliage light green; vigorous growth; [sport of Queen Elizabeth®]

'Evelyn Fison' ('Irish Wonder') F, mr, 1962, McGredy, Sam IV; flowers scarlet, 3 in., dbl., borne in broad clusters; foliage dark, glossy; compact, bushy growth; PP2424; [Moulin Rouge® × 'Korona']; intr. 1962

'Evelyn Grace' -- See 'Horavme'

'Evelyn Hough' HT, lp

'Evelyn Lauder' -- See 'Wekvosuimp'

'Evelyn May' HT, dp, 1932, Edward; flowers vermilion-pink, 65 petals; free growth; ['Lady Alice Stanley' × 'Edith Part']

'Evelyn May' S, op, Beales, Peter; flowers yellow blend, reverse orange pink, 15 cm., dbl., borne in large clusters; foliage large, dark green, semi-glossy; prickles average, straight, moderate; growth upright, medium (1 m.); shrubs, hedging; [Elizabeth of Glamis® × 'Arthur Bell']; registration rejected due to duplication of name with existing registration; intr. 2000

'Evelyn Murland' HT, pb, 1923, Dickson, A.; flowers salmon-pink and carmine, veined yellow, reverse veined pink, dbl.

'Evelyn Redfern' F, mr, 2003, Fleming, Joyce; flowers 2½ in., 16-18 petals, borne in clusters of 3-12, moderate fragrance; recurrent; foliage medium size, medium green, matte, disease-resistant; prickles 3/16 in., light brown; growth medium (30 in.); ['Morden Fireglow' × 'Bonica']; intr. 2002

Evelyn Rogers™ -- See 'Minarco'

'Evelyn Taylor' F, ob

'Evelyn Tebbutt' -- See 'Lovalady'

'Evelyn Thornton' Pol, mp, 1919, Bees; flowers shell-pink deepening to salmon and lemon shaded orange, open, dbl.; foliage leathery, glossy, dark bronze; bushy growth; ['Léonie Lamesch' × 'Mrs W. H. Cutbush']

Evelyne Dheliat® HT, pb, Sauvageot; intr. 2007

'Evemas' ('Monte Cristo') S, mr, 2002, Eve, André; flowers strawberry red, semi-dbl., borne in small clusters; foliage medium green, semi-glossy; prickles moderate; growth upright, tall (100-120 cm.); intr. 2001

'Evemont' S, lp, Eve; intr. 1972

'Evening Fire' -- See 'Frofire'

'Evening Glow' HT, r, 1960, Armbrust; bud long, pointed; flowers buff, large, 35 petals, moderate fragrance; foliage leathery; moderate growth; ['Charlotte Armstrong' × 'Narzisse']; intr. 1959

'Evening Light' -- See 'Chewpechette'

'Evening Light' -- See 'Tarde Gris'

'Evening Mist' F, m, 2007, Martin, Dale E.; bud lavender, flushed with tawny yellow at base; flowers warm lilac, aging to cool gray, ruffled when open, each petal having a small, pointed tip, golden stamens, medium, 4 in., semi-dbl., borne in small clusters; foliage medium, medium green, semi-glossy; prickles small, pointed, slanted down, light green when new, few; growth upright, slightly spreading, medium (2.5-3 ft.); ['Angel Face' × Blue Moon®]

'Evening News' HT, my, 1927, Letts; flowers apricot-yellow veined rose, base deep buttercup-yellow, open, dbl.; foliage glossy, rich green; vigorous, bushy growth; [sport of 'Mme Edouard Herriot']

'Evening Queen' -- See 'Hadevening'

'Evening Sentinel' -- See 'Fryevenest'

'Evening Shadows' -- See 'Miceven'

'Evening Sky' HT, ob, 1939, Moore, Ralph S.; flowers orange, tipped scarlet, base yellow, 2½-3 in., 6-8 ruffled petals; foliage bluish green; vigorous growth; ['Talisman' × unknown]

'Evening Star' HT, my, 1919, Morse; flowers golden yellow, shaded apricot, large, dbl., slight fragrance; bushy growth; [sport of 'Mme Edouard Herriot']

Evening Star® F, w, 1973, Warriner, William A.; flowers white, base shading pale yellow, large, dbl., high-centered, slight fragrance; foliage large, dark, leathery; vigorous, upright, bushy growth; PP3432; name approved for re-use, ARA 1973; ['White Masterpiece' × 'Saratoga']; intr. 1974

'Evening Star' -- See 'Ichibanboshi'

'Evening Telegraph' HT, dy, 1976, Haynes; [sport of 'Whisky Mac']

'Evensong' HT, op, 1963, Arnot; flowers rosy salmon, well-formed, 5 in., 25 petals; foliage dark; vigorous growth; ['Ena Harkness' × 'Sutter's Gold']; intr. 1963

'Eventail' HT, yb, 1989, Kono, Yoshito; bud ovoid; flowers light yellow to pink, medium, 50 petals, borne singly; foliage medium size, semi-glossy, slightly denticulated; prickles downward-pointed, reddish-purple; upright, tall growth; ['Sonia' × 'Miyabi']

'Eventide' HT, dr, 1948, Toogood; bud ovoid; flowers dark velvety red, open, medium, dbl.; foliage wrinkled, soft; moderate growth; [('Crimson Glory' × unknown) × 'Rouge Mallerin']

'Evepi' ('Villa Rosa') LCl, dp, 2002, Eve, André; flowers deep pink, lighter reverse, medium, dbl., borne in small clusters, slight fragrance; recurrent; foliage medium size, medium green, glossy; prickles moderate; tall (4-5 m.) growth; intr. 2004

'Evepilk' ('Mary Pilkington') F, pb, 1993, Everitt, Derrick; flowers peach, quickly paling to light pink, creamy yellow reverse, medium, dbl., moderate fragrance; foliage medium size, dark green, semi-glossy; some prickles; tall (80-90 cm.), bushy growth; ['Mary Sumner' × Remember Me®]

'Eveprest' F, mr, Eve, A.; intr. 1974

'Evepro' ('Carla Fineschi') LCl, rb, Andre, Guy; flowers carmine red, reverse silvery red, 4-5 cm., semi-dbl., borne in large clusters, slight fragrance; good repeat; foliage medium size, medium green, semi-glossy; prickles moderate to numerous; growth to 2½-3 m.; [('Étendard' × unknown) × 'Don Quichotte']; intr. 2002

'Évêque de Nîmes' HP, mr, 1856, Plantier/Damaizin

'Ever Ready' LCl, mr, 1976, MacLeod; flowers bright crimson, 3 in., 32 petals; recurrent bloom; foliage large, medium green, matte; ['Aloha' × 'Étoile de Hollande']

'Everbloom' Cl Pol, dp, 1939, Archer; flowers deep pink, single, borne in clusters; recurrent bloom; foliage glossy; growth to 3-6 ft. first year, 8-10 ft. in about 3 years; ['Phyllis Bide' × unknown]

'Everblooming Dr W. Van Fleet' -- See 'New Dawn'

'Everblooming Jack Rose' -- See 'Richmond'

'Everblooming Pillar No. 3' ('White Cap') Cl HT, w, Brownell; bud medium, pointed; flowers nearly pure white, 3½-4 in., 60 petals, high-centered, then open, borne both singly and in small clusters, moderate fragrance; recurrent; prickles several; stems long, stiff; upright, tall growth; PP1273; ['wichurana seedling' × 'Break o' Day, Climbing']; intr. 1954

'Everblooming Pillar No. 12' -- See 'Eternal Flame'

'Everblooming Pillar No. 73' -- See 'Scarlet Sensation'

'Everblooming Pillar No. 82' -- See 'Show Garden'

'Everblooming Pillar No. 83' -- See 'Salmon Arctic'

'Everblooming Pillar No. 84' -- See 'Golden Arctic'

'Everblooming Pillar No. 122' LCl, yb, 1954, Brownell; flowers light yellow and orange, 3½-4½ in., 90 petals, moderate fragrance; growth like a hybrid tea, followed by 4-5 ft. canes; PP1263; [seedling × 'Break o' Day, Climbing']

'Everblooming Pillar No. 126' LCl, mp, 1955, Brownell; flowers pink, base yellow, 3½-4½ in., 35-50 petals, moderate fragrance; bushy, upright growth; PP1425; [seedling × 'Queen o' the Lakes']

'Everblooming Pillar No. 214' LCl, my, 1954, Brownell; flowers amber-yellow, large, 75 petals; growth like a hybrid tea, followed by 4-5 ft. canes; PP1296; [seedling × 'Break o' Day, Climbing']

'Everblooming Pillar No. 340' LCl, pb, 1957, Brownell; flowers pink and yellow, 4½-5 in., 35-40 petals, high-centered, moderate fragrance; growth like a hybrid tea, followed by longer canes.; PP1606; ['Queen o' the Lakes' × 'Scarlet Sensation']

'Everdream' HT, my, 1956, Motose; bud ovoid; flowers canary-yellow, 4-5 in., 35-40 petals; bushy growth; ['Souv. de Claudius Pernet' × 'Kaiserin Auguste Viktoria']

'Everedruf' ('Dorothy Lewis') HT, dr, 2001, Everitt, Derrick; flowers dark red shaded russet, varying with weather conditions, 10 cm., full, borne in small clusters, slight fragrance; foliage medium size, dark green, semi-glossy; prickles small, slightly hooked, moderate; growth upright, low to medium (75-90 cm.); garden decorative; [(('L'Oreal Trophy' × 'Edith Holden') × ('Mary Sumner' × (Silver Jubilee × L'Oreal Trophy')) × ('Mary Sumner' × ('L'Oreal Trophy' × 'Edith Holden'))]

'Everest' HP, w, 1927, Easlea; flowers cream-white, center tinted green-lemon, very large, 38 petals, high-centered, moderate fragrance; foliage light; low, spreading growth; ['Candeur Lyonnaise' × 'Mme Caristie Martel']

'Everest Double Fragrance' F, lp, 1980, Beales, Peter; bud pointed; flowers 25 petals, borne 3-7 per cluster; foliage dark, heavily veined; prickles large; tall, upright growth; ['Dearest' × Elizabeth of Glamis®]; intr. 1979

'Everglades' (Shenandoah™, Søren Kanne™) F, op, 1999, Poulsen; flowers salmon-orange, 8-10 cm., semi-dbl. to dbl., cupped, very slight fragrance; foliage reddish green; bushy, tall (100-150 cm.) growth; intr. 1996

'Everglo' Min, or, Laver, Keith G.; intr. 1998

'Everglow' ('Poulglow') F, ob

'Evergold' LCl, my, Kordes; flowers medium; foliage dark green, glossy; intr. 1966

'Evergreen Gem' HWich, w, 1899, Horvath; bud buff; flowers buff-yellow, 2-3 in., dbl., borne in clusters, moderate sweetbriar fragrance; foliage almost evergreen; vigorous, climbing or trailing growth; [R. wichurana × 'Maréchal Niel']

Evergreen Gene™ -- See 'Virgene'

'Everive' (Château du Rivau®) HMult, w, Eve; flowers with yellow stamens,

3-4 cm., single, borne in broad sprays, slight fragrance; non-recurrent; foliage large, dark green, semi-glossy; prickles moderate; vigorous growth to 5-8 m.; intr. 2004

'Everlasting Love' -- See 'Graelove'

'Evermore' -- See 'Meipotal'

'Evero' ('Roville') LCl, mp, 2002, Eve, André; flowers carmine pink, silvery reverse, 8 cm., single, borne in large clusters, slight fragrance; recurrent; foliage medium size, medium green, matte; prickles moderate; growth tall (4-5 m.), climbing; [Red Parfum® × 'Phyllis Bide']

'Evert Regterschot' F, mr, 1965, Buisman, G. A. H.; bud ovoid; flowers bright red, medium, semi-dbl.; foliage dark; ['Korona' × seedling]

'Evert van Dyk' HT, mp, 1931, Van Rossem; flowers rose-pink tinted salmon, large, dbl., high-centered; foliage dark; long stems; bushy growth; ['Ophelia' × 'Hill's America']

Everything's Peachy™ -- See 'Byrpeachy'

'Evesafia' Pol, op, Eve, A.; intr. 1997

'Evesaine' F, yb, Eve, A.; intr. 1992

'Evesilvergold' ('Noreen Mackey') HT, my, 2001, Everitt, Derrick; flowers chrome yellow, 10-12 cm., full, borne mostly solitary, slight fragrance; foliage small, medium green, glossy; prickles medium, hooked, moderate; growth upright, medium (90 cm.); ['Silver Jubilee' × ('Arthur Bell' × 'Maigold')]

'Evesylva' Pol, mp, Eve; intr. 1968

'Evghenya' F, op, 1985, Staikov, Prof. Dr. V.; flowers coral-orange, darker petal edges, base cream, large, 75 petals, borne in clusters of 3-12; foliage dark, glossy; vigorous growth; ['Highlight' × 'Masquerade']; intr. 1975

'Evian Cachat' HT, mp, 1939, Chambard, C.; flowers bright pink, center copper salmon, very large, dbl., cupped; vigorous growth

'Evie' -- See 'Worchild'

'Evita' -- See 'Poulvita'

'Evita' -- See 'Tanlarpost'

'Evita Bezuidenhout' -- See 'Jacblar'

'Evodia' HMult, lp, 1925, Bruder Alfons; flowers whitish pink, small, dbl., borne in medium clusters, moderate fragrance; nearly thornless

'Evolution' F, pb, Olij, Huibert; flowers white, edged pink, 4-5 in., high-centered; ['Laminuette' × 'Nicole']; intr. 1995

'Evrard Ketten' HT, m, 1920, Ketten Bros.; flowers bright unshaded carmine-purple, dbl.; ['Farbenkonigin' × 'Ruhm de Gartenwelt']

'Évratin' -- See 'Evratina'

'Evratina' ('Évratin', 'Muscade Rouge') A, dp, 1809, Bosc; flowers flesh tinted pale red, medium, dbl., borne in large clusters; foliage dark green, oblong, simply dentate; prickles few, straight, short

'Ex Albo Inermis Violacea' HGal, m, before 1814, Descemet; flowers lilac white

'Exadelphé' T, my, 1885, Nabonnand; flowers canary yellow, fading to creamy white, large, full, intense fragrance

'Excalibur' F, mr, 1967, Harkness, J.; flowers scarlet, 2½ in., 14 petals, borne in clusters, slight fragrance; foliage dark, glossy; bushy growth; ['Vera Dalton' × 'Woburn Abbey']

'Excellence' HT, mr, Weeks, O.L.; flowers deep, rich red , 35 petals, high-centered, borne mostly singly, moderate fragrance; recurrent; foliage large, leathery, dark green ; stems strong; intr. 2004

'Excellens' ('Excelsior') Pol, pb, 1913, Levavasseur; flowers pink washed white, edged carmine, borne in small clusters; nearly thornless

Excellent™ S, mr, Tantau; intr. 2003

'Excellent' Min, dy, Olesen; flowers dbl., borne mostly solitary, slight fragrance; foliage dark green, glossy; growth bushy, low (40-60 cm.)

'Excellenz Kuntze' S, ly, 1909, Lambert, P.; flowers creamy yellow, small, dbl., borne in large clusters; foliage dark, glossy; vigorous, upright growth; ['Aglaia' × 'Souv. de Catherine Guillot']

'Excellenz M. Schmidt-Metzler' HT, w, 1910, Lambert, P.; flowers large, dbl.; ['Frau Karl Druschki' × 'Franz Deegen']

'Excellenz von Schubert' Pol, dp, 1909, Lambert, P.; flowers dark carmine-rose, small, dbl., borne in clusters; late; foliage dark; vigorous growth; ['Mme Norbert Levavasseur' × 'Frau Karl Druschki']

'Excelsa' ('Red Dorothy Perkins') HWich, mr, 1909, Walsh; flowers intense crimson-maroon, tips of petals tinged scarlet, small, dbl., cupped, borne in clusters of 30-40; non-recurrent; foliage rich green, glossy; vigorous, climbing (12-18 ft.) growth

'Excelsa Superior' -- See 'Super Excelsa'

'Excelsior' F, mp, 1959, Buisman, G. A. H.; flowers salmon, borne in clusters; foliage dark; vigorous, upright growth; ['Pinocchio' × 'Mrs Henri Daendels']

'Excelsior' -- See 'Excellens'

'Exception' -- See 'Märchenland'

'Excite' -- See 'Gelex'

Excitement™ -- See 'Hilco'

Exciting® HT, pb; bud conical; flowers pink, mottled near edges, with lighter reverse, 4 in., 50-55 petals, high-centered, borne mostly singly; good repeat; foliage dark green, semi-glossy; prickles moderate; growth erect (5 ft.); PP14064; [Lorena® × Laser™]; greenhouse rose; intr. 2002

'Exciting' S, lp, Harkness; flowers soft pastel pink to white, 3½ in., dbl., slight fruity/rose fragrance; foliage shiny, medium green; growth vigorous and spreading, 4-5 × 4-5 ft.; PPAF; intr. 2005

'Exciting' -- See 'Roter Stern'

'Exhibitionist!' -- See 'Jalexhibit'

'Exita' HT, mr, 1962, Meilland; flowers pelargonium red, dbl., borne singly and in small clusters; numerous prickles

'Exodus' -- See 'Godusex'

'Exotic' HT, McGredy, Sam IV; intr. 1995

Exotic® -- See 'Fryxotic'

'Exotic Beauty' -- See 'Leoexbeau'

'Exotic Treat' -- See 'Morshack'

'Exotica' ('Puy du Fou') HT, ob, Meilland; bud conical, large; flowers ochre and orange-yellow, 5-6 in., 36 petals, high-centered, borne mostly singly, no fragrance; good repeat; foliage medium green, semi-glossy; prickles medium; growth erect, tall; PP11731; [('Golden Emblem' × 'Pareo ') × ('Lovely Girl' × Marina®)]; greenhouse rose; intr. 1999

Exploit® -- See 'Meilider'

'Explorer' -- See 'Dicrocky'

'Explorer's Dream' -- See 'Micexplore'

Explosion Border™ -- See 'Poultc012'

'Expo 64' F, Tschanz, E.; intr. 1964

'Exposé' -- See 'Denexpo'

'Exposition de Brie' -- See 'Maurice Bernardin'

'Exposition de Provins' HP, mr, 1895, Cochet-Cochet; flowers velvety red, large, full; ['Triomphe de l'Exposition' × unknown]

'Exposition de Toulouse' HP, mr, 1873, Brassac; flowers bright cherry, shaded carmine

'Express' LCl, dp, VEG; flowers carmine-pink, 4 in., dbl., borne singly or in small clusters, slight fragrance; [Queen Elizabeth® × 'Gurss an Heidelberg']

'Expression' HT, ob, Williams, J.B.; flowers unusual orange, reverse slightly darker, dbl., moderate fragrance; recurrent; growth to 4 ft.; intr. 2006

'Expressions' HT, pb, Winchel. Joseph; flowers mdium pink with deeper pink edges, 35 petals, high-centered, borne mostly singly, slight fragrance; recurrent; foliage large, dark green; intr. 2006

'Exquisite' HT, rb, 1899, Paul, W.; bud large, long; flowers bright crimson shaded magenta, large, full, globular

'Exquisite' HT, ly, Therkildsen; flowers creamy yellow, dbl., slight fragrance; intr. 1918

'Exquisite' HMult, op, Praskac; flowers salmon pink, shaded red, very small, full; ['Dorothy Perkins' × 'Rubin']; intr. 1926

'Exquisite' HT, lp, 1979, Leon, Charles F., Sr.; bud long, pointed; flowers 5½-6 in., 30 petals, high-centered, moderate fragrance; vigorous, upright growth; ['Memoriam' × (('Blanche Mallerin' × 'Peace') × ('Peace' × 'Virgo'))]

'Extase' HT, dr, 1956, Delforge; bud long, dark red; vigorous growth; ['E.G. Hill' × seedling]

'Extase' -- See 'Korazerka'

'Extasis' LCl, dr, 1963, Dot, Simon; flowers red, shaded darker, 5 petals, borne in clusters; vigorous growth; ['Spectacular' × Cocktail®]

'Extravaganza' F, pb, 1974, Dawson, George; bud ovoid; flowers pink, base cream, medium, dbl.; foliage leathery; vigorous, bushy growth; ['Stella' × ('Sabrina' × Golden Giant®)]

Extravaganza™ HT, ab, Poulsen; bud long, pointed ovoid; flowers light apricot, 8 cm., 40 petals, high-centered, borne singly and in small clusters, slight floral fragrance; recurrent; prickles numerous, 9 mm., hooked downward; growth bushy, upright (100-150 cm.); PP15453; [seedling × 'Tivoli Gardens']; intr. 2003

'Exuberance' S, mr, Williams, J.B.; flowers bright red, semi-dbl. to dbl., rosette, moderate fragrance; recurrent; foliage reddish-green, matte; growth to 4 ft.; intr. 2006

'Eydie' Min, w, 1982, Hooper, John C.; flowers white with pink blush, fading to white, small, 50 petals, borne in clusters, moderate tea fragrance; foliage medium green, purple, when young; prickles beige; vigorous, bushy growth; ['Janna' × seedling]; intr. 1981

Eye Appeal® -- See 'Interpeel'

'Eye Liner' HT, dr, 1966, Armbrust; bud long, pointed; flowers blood red, medium, semi-dbl., high-centered; foliage dark, leathery; vigorous, upright growth; [Queen Elizabeth® × 'Montezuma']

'Eye of the Dragon' -- See 'Cledrag'

'Eye Paint' -- See 'Maceye'

'Eyecatcher' F, pb, 1977, Cants of Colchester, Ltd.; flowers pink flushed apricot, reverse silvery cream, 2½ in., 22 petals, moderate fragrance; foliage glossy, light; ['Arthur Bell' × Pernille Poulsen™]; intr. 1976

'Eyeopener' -- See 'Interop'

Eyepaint® -- See 'Maceye'

'Eyriés' HCh, m, about 1845, Calvert; flowers bright light purple, medium to large, full

'Ezzy' ('NH NH #1') HMult, lp, Lowe; flowers single, borne in large clusters, moderate fragrance; non-recurrent; intr. 2001

— F —

'F. Cambó' HT, mr, 1933, Dot, Pedro; flowers carmine, large, dbl., cupped; foliage glossy; dwarf growth; ['Li Bures' × 'Florence L. Izzard']

'F. Cuixart' ('Francesca de Cuixart') HT, rb, 1960, Dot, Simon; bud ovoid; flowers lincoln red, reverse fuchsine-red, open, large, 40 petals; foliage glossy, bronze; long stems; vigorous, compact growth; [Baccará® × 'Golden Masterpiece']

'F. Ferrer' LCl, dr, 1940, Pahissa; bud long, pointed; flowers dark velvety red, open, large; somewhat recurrent bloom; foliage leathery; vigorous, climbing growth

F. Green® HT, w, Preesman; flowers greenish; intr. 2007

'F. J. Grootendorst' ('Grootendorst Red', 'Grootendorst', 'Nelkenrose') HRg, mr, 1915, de Goey; flowers bright red, edges serrated like a carnation, small, dbl., borne in clusters of up to 20, slight fragrance; recurrent bloom; foliage small, leathery, wrinkled, dark; growth vigorous, bushy (6 ft.); [R. rugosa rubra × 'Mme Norbert Levavasseur']

'F. J. Lindheimer' S, yb, 2006, Shoup, George Micheal; flowers dbl., borne in small clusters, moderate fragrance; very remontant; foliage medium size, medium green, matte, uniquely recurved, few prickles; growth upright, medium (3-4 ft.); containers, hedges; hardy to -20°F; [(('Carefree Beauty' × 'Bayse's Blueberry') × ('Carefree Beauty' × 'Bayse's Blueberry')) × 'Rise n Shine']; intr. 2000

'F. K. Druschkii' -- See 'Frau Karl Druschki'

F. Katom® Gr, op, McGredy, Sam IV; intr. 1982

'F. L. de Voogd' HT, yb, 1920, Timmermans; flowers clear reddish-yellow, semi-dbl.; ['Mme Mélanie Soupert' × 'Mme Jenny Gillemot']

'F. L. Segers' T, pb, 1898, Ketten Bros.; bud long on strong peduncle; flowers carmine-scarlet with yellowish-pink, creamy white around the edge, large, very full, cupped, moderate fragrance; ['Safrano' × 'Adam']

F. Lilac® HT, m, Preesman; flowers lilac; intr. 2007

'F. M. Vokes' HT, my, 1927, Hicks; flowers yellow, passing to cream, semi-dbl.; ['Ophelia' × unknown]

'F. P. Merritt' Cl HT, dr, 1951, Merritt; flowers bright fiery crimson, 5 in., 50-60 petals, high-centered, intense fragrance; foliage glossy; very long stems; very vigorous, climbing (12 ft.) growth; PP856; [sport of 'Hoosier Beauty']

'F. R. M. Undritz' -- See 'Gen. John Pershing'

'F. R. Patzer' HT, pb, 1909, Dickson, A.; flowers creamy buff, reverse warm pink, large, dbl.; branching growth

F. Ruby Red® HT, mr, Preesman; intr. 2007

'F. W. Alesworth' ('Fred W. Alesworth') HT, dr, 1954, Robinson, H.; flowers deep crimson, well-shaped, large; foliage dark; vigorous growth; ['Poinsettia' × 'Crimson Glory']

'F. W. Lowe' HT, ab, 1936, Lowe; flowers rich orange-yellow, well-shaped; foliage glossy; vigorous growth

'F. W. Mee' -- See 'Fred W. Mee'

F. White® HT, w, Preesman; intr. 2007

'Fab' -- See 'Bosconpea'

'Fab at Fifty' -- See 'Woraunt'

'Fabergé' F, pb, 1969, Boerner; bud ovoid; flowers light peach-pink, reverse tinted yellow, large, dbl., high-centered, slight fragrance; foliage dark, leathery; vigorous, dense, bushy growth; PP2886; [seedling × 'Zorina']

'Fabienne' F, mp, 1958, Arles; flowers reddish-salmon, small, 35 petals; foliage clear green; bushy, low growth; [Orange Triumph® × ('Independence' × 'Floradora')]

'Fabiola' -- See 'Queen Fabiola'

'Fabros' ('Petite Rosamund') C, lp, 2003, Boutin, Fred; flowers streaked lavender-pink on white, reverse fainter streaks of lavender-pink, 1¾ in., very full, borne mostly solitary, no fragrance; foliage small, medium green, matte; prickles very small, 1/8 in., thin, slightly recurved, light brown; growth upright, compact, short (24 in.); specimen or hedge; ['Pompon de Bourgogne' × 'Ferdinand Pichard']; very similar in character and size to Pompon de Bourgogne; intr. 2003

Fabulous!™ -- See 'Jacrex'

'Fabvier' ('Général Fabvier') Ch, mr, 1832, Laffay, M.; flowers crimson-scarlet, often striped white, very showy, medium, semi-dbl.; recurrent bloom

'Facade' HT, mp, 1970, Fankhauser; flowers apricot-pink, very large, 60 petals, high-centered; foliage glossy, dark, leathery; vigorous, upright growth; ['Elizabeth Fankhauser' × 'Royal Highness']

'Fackel' HT, dr, 1937, Krause; flowers crimson-red, shaded blackish, very dbl., cupped; compact growth; ['Vaterland' × 'Barcelona']

'Faïence' HT, op, 1935, Van Rossem; flowers peach and apricot, reverse pure yellow, large, 45 petals, cupped; foliage leathery; vigorous, bushy growth; ['Charles P. Kilham' × 'Julien Potin']; intr. 1937

'Faint Heart' HT, w, 1980, Pavlick, Mike; flowers cream edged light pink, 25 petals, high-centered, borne 1-3 per cluster; foliage mid to dark, leathery, semi-glossy; prickles straight; medium, branching growth; ['Hawaii' × seedling]

Fair™ MinFl, mp, Olesen; flowers dbl., borne mostly solitary, slight fragrance; foliage dark green, glossy; growth bushy, low (40-60 cm.); PP10727; intr. 1996

Fair Bianca® -- See 'Ausca'

'Fair Dinkum' F, op, 1966, Small; flowers peach-salmon, 3-4 in., borne in clusters, moderate fragrance; foliage glossy; RULED EXTINCT 6/83 ARM; [Queen Elizabeth® × 'Circus']

'Fair Dinkum' -- See 'Tindink'

'Fair Eva' -- See 'Seaeva'

'Fair Genie' -- See 'Lavmoth'

'Fair Lady' HT, ab, 1959, Boerner; bud ovoid to pointed; flowers buff overcast pink, 4½ in., 50 petals, high-centered, intense fragrance; foliage glossy; vigorous, upright growth; PP1900; ['Golden Masterpiece' × 'Tawny Gold']; intr. 1959

Fair Lady® HT, w; flowers creamy white with red edges on outer petals that darken with age, double , urn-shaped , borne mostly singly; recurrent; foliage dark green, glossy; moderate (3 ft.) growth; intr. 2000

'Fair Maid' HT, mp, 1940, Peirce; flowers bright rose to strawberry-pink, changing to deep pink, 4-5 in., 60-75 petals, intense fragrance; foliage light green; vigorous, upright growth; PP438; [sport of 'Talisman']

'Fair Marjorie' Pol, lp, 1952, Armstrong, P.M.; bud ovoid, bright pink; flowers blush-pink, lighter in sun, medium, semi-dbl., cupped; vigorous, bushy growth; ['Katharina Zeimet' × unknown]

'Fair Molly' -- See 'Morfairpol'

'Fair Opal' -- See 'Fire Opal'

Fair Play® -- See 'Interfair'

'Fair Pol' Min, Moore, R. E.; intr. 1985

'Fair Princess' S, mr, Williams, J. Benjamin; intr. 1999

'Fairest Cape' S, ab, Kordes; intr. 2003

'Fairest of Fair' Min, ly, 1982, Bennett, Dee; flowers medium yellow, 15-18 petals, high-centered, borne singly or 3-5 per cluster, slight tea fragrance; foliage small, medium green; very compact, low growth; PP5260; ['Sunbonnet' × 'Rise 'n' Shine']

'Fairfield Blaze' LCl, mr; intr. 1962

'Fairfield Pink Cluster' HMult, lp, Lowe; flowers dbl., open, borne in large clusters, moderate fragrance; non-recurrent; intr. 2003

'Fairhope' -- See 'Talfairhope'

'Fairlane' Min, yb, 1980, Schwartz, Ernest W.; flowers near white flushed pink and yellow, 20 petals, high-centered, urn-shaped, borne 1-5 per cluster; foliage glossy, medium green, deeply serrated; prickles slanted downward; compact, bushy growth; PP4711; ['Charlie McCarthy' × seedling]; intr. 1981

'Fairlie Rede' HT, op, 1937, Clark, A.; flowers salmon, flushed fawn, large, dbl.; vigorous growth; ['Mrs E. Willis' × seedling]

'Fairlight' F, op, 1964, Robinson, H.; flowers coppery salmon to flame, well-formed, large, dbl., borne in clusters; foliage coppery bronze; ['Joybells' × seedling]

'Fairmount Memory' -- See 'Jasfair'

'Fairqueen' -- See 'Denfair'

'Fairy' HMult, w, 1909, Paul, W.; flowers pure white, large, single; somewhat remontant

'Fairy' -- See 'The Fairy'

'Fairy Ambiance' HT, yb, Adam, Michel; flowers golden yellow, edged orange-pink, star-shaped, dbl.; intr. 2005

'Fairy Castle' -- See 'Kortensei'

'Fairy Changeling' -- See 'Harnumerous'

'Fairy Cluster' F, mp, 1935, Archer; flowers rose-pink, single, borne in clusters; foliage glossy; long stems; very vigorous growth; ['Dainty Bess' × 'Ideal']

'Fairy Crystal' Pol, w, 1980, Harkness, R., & Co., Ltd.; bud squat; flowers 22 petals, cupped, borne several per cluster; foliage small, dark, glossy; prickles slender, dark; short, bushy growth; ['The Fairy' × Yesterday®]

'Fairy Damsel' -- See 'Harneatly'

Fairy Dance® -- See 'Harward'

'Fairy Dancer' Pol, pb

'Fairy Dancers' HT, ab, 1969, Cocker; flowers buff-pink, small, dbl.; low, spreading growth; ['Wendy Cussons' × 'Diamond Jubilee']

'Fairy Floss' Min, mp, Hannemann, F.; ['Sweet Chariot' × seedling]; intr. 1992

'Fairy Frolic' Pol, pb; flowers small, rosy pink with white reverse, very dbl.; hips numerous

'Fairy Gold' -- See 'Frygoldie'

'Fairy Hedge' -- See 'Baby Jayne'

Fairy Lights™ -- See 'Niagara'

'Fairy Like' -- See 'Harnimble'

'Fairy Magic' Min, mp, 1979, Moore, Ralph S.; bud mossy, long, pointed; flowers semi-dbl., 10-15 petals, moderate fragrance; foliage small, glossy, bushy, upright growth; ['Fairy Moss' × 'miniature moss seedling']

'Fairy Maid' -- See 'Harlassie'

Fairy Meidiland™ -- See 'Meiklutz'

'Fairy Moon' -- See 'Warbler'

'Fairy Moss' Min, mp, 1969, Moore, Ralph S.; bud mossy; flowers semi-dbl.; foliage mini-moss, small, light green, leathery; vigorous, bushy, dwarf growth; PP3083; [('Pinocchio' × 'William Lobb') × 'New Penny']

'Fairy Pompons' -- See 'Trapom'

Fairy Prince® -- See 'Harnougette'

'Fairy Princess' Cl Min, lp, 1955, Moore, Ralph S.; bud pointed, salmon-apricot; flowers 1 in., very dbl., borne in clusters; foliage small, fern-like; growth to 2½ ft.; ['Eblouissant' × 'Zee']

'Fairy Princess' -- See 'Lilibet'

'Fairy Queen' T, yb, 1902, Paul, W.; flowers fawn yellow, shaded cherry pink with cream white reflections, medium, full

'Fairy Queen' F, lp, Williams, J. Benjamin; bud ovoid; flowers bluish pink, center coral-pink, small, dbl., high-centered, moderate fragrance; foliage small, glossy, bronze; very vigorous, bushy growth; ['The Fairy' × Queen Elizabeth®]; intr. 1972

'Fairy Queen' ('The Fairy Queen') Pol, mr, Vurens; flowers crimson red, 3 cm., dbl., rosette, borne in clusters, dense, no fragrance; recurrent; foliage dark green; PPAF; [sport of 'The Fairy']; intr. 1998

'Fairy Queen' -- See 'Rosalie'

'Fairy Red' -- See 'Harneatly'

'Fairy Red 92' S, mr, Liebig; flowers scarlet, medium size, semi-dbl., borne in large clusters; recurrent; foliage dark green, glossy; bushy, spreading (12-20 in.) growth; intr. 1992

'Fairy Ring' -- See 'Harnicely'

'Fairy Rose' -- See 'The Fairy'

'Fairy Shell' Min, mp; intr. 2001

'Fairy Snow' Pol, w, 1979, Harkness; bud squat; flowers medium, 20-25 petals, cupped; low, bushy growth; ['The Fairy' × Yesterday®]

'Fairy Snow' -- See 'Holfairy'

'Fairy Tale' S, lp, 1960, Thomson; bud ovoid; flowers open, small, dbl.; foliage dark, glossy; very vigorous, upright (6 ft.) growth; Ruled extinct, 3/93 ARM; ['The Fairy' × 'Goldilocks']

'Fairy Tale' ('Little Diane') Min, lp, J&P; flowers rosy pink, borne singly and in clusters; intr. 1994

'Fairy Tale' F, mp

'Fairy-Tale' -- See 'Keiren'

'Fairy Tale Queen' -- See 'Koroyness'

'Fairy Tale Red' F, mr

Fairyland® -- See 'Harlayalong'

'Faith' HT, r, Grayco; [sport of 'Amatsu Otome']; intr. 2000

'Faith' -- See 'Horfaiwil'

Faith Whittlesey™ -- See 'Virwhite'

'Faithful' F, mr, Harkness; flowers deep cherry red, dbl.; continuous bloom; bushy, compact (30 in.) growth; intr. 1998

'Faithful' F, rb, 1964, Latham; flowers crimson edged white, becoming velvety crimson, well-shaped, semi-dbl.; foliage small, light green; vigorous growth; ['Dusky Maiden' × 'Tabarin']

'Faithful Companion' -- See 'Geaaura'

'Faithful Friend' HT, ab, Dickson; flowers of warm golden apricot; foliage rich, glossy; growth medium; intr. 2001

'Faivre d'Arcier' HT, mp, 1901, Schwartz; flowers carmine, edged lilac pink, large, full, globular, moderate fragrance

'Faja Lobbi' HT, mr, 1963, Leenders, J.; flowers bright red; vigorous growth; [Queen Elizabeth® × 'Florence Mary Morse']

'Fakir' -- See 'Meicloux'

'Fakir's Delight' -- See 'Morfakir'

'Falbala' ('Falbalas') HT, mp, 1948, Gaujard; bud long; flowers brilliant salmon; foliage glossy, dark; erect growth

'Falbalas' -- See 'Falbala'

'Falcon' F, lp, Dot, Simon; flowers delicate pink, shaded with light yellow at base, semi-dbl.; intr. 1989

'Falcon' LCl, dr, Kordes; intr. 1998

'Falkland' HSpn, w, before 1930, possibly from Ireland; flowers pale pink to nearly white, medium, semi-dbl.; low, bushy growth

Fall Festival™ -- See 'Lavfal'

'Fall Splendor' -- See 'Minidor'

'Falla' HT, or, Asami, H.; flowers dark orange-red, petals slightly reflexed, 10 cm., 25-29 petals, cupped, borne mostly solitary, slight fragrance; foliage dark green, semi-glossy, usually with 7 leaflets; prickles straight, numerous; growth upright, not very bushy; ['Red Bingo' × seedling]; intr. 1985

Falling in Love™ -- See 'Wekmoomar'

'False River Beauty' Min, mp, 2000, Picard, Ancil; flowers medium pink, reverse white, 1¼-1½ in., full, borne mostly singly; foliage medium size, dark green, semi-glossy; few prickles; upright, spreading, tall (24-30 in.) growth; winter hardy; [sport of 'Over the Rainbow']; intr. 2001

'Falstaff' -- See 'Ausverse'

'Fama' F, dy, Cocker; intr. 1986

'Fama' HT, rb, 1942, Dot, Pedro; flowers amber and red, large, 25-30 petals,

cupped; foliage soft, light green; short stems; vigorous, upright, bushy growth
Fame!™ -- See 'Jaczor'
Fame™ -- See 'Poultory'
'Fame Parade' (Fame™) Min, dr, Poulsen; flowers dark red, medium, dbl., slight wild rose fragrance; foliage dark; growth narrow, bushy, 20-40 cm.; intr. 1996
'Family Life' F, my, Harkness; flowers pure yellow; free-flowering; compact, medium growth; intr. 2003
'Famosa' HT, mp, 1964, Leenders, J.; flowers pink, well-formed; ['Tallyho' × 'Flamingo']
Famosa® S, mr, Noack; intr. 2003
'Famous Cliff' -- See 'Yaroslavna'
'Fan Fare '81' HT, ob, 1981, Byrum, Roy L.; bud short, pointed; flowers 23 petals, high-centered, borne singly, slight rose fragrance; foliage medium to large; prickles straight, short, broad-based; vigorous growth; PP4631; ['Cotillion' × 'Hoosier Gold']
'Fan Mail' F, dy, 1974, Boerner; bud long, pointed; flowers open, medium, dbl., moderate fragrance; foliage large, leathery; very vigorous, bushy growth; ['Spanish Sun' × seedling]
'Fanal' F, mr, 1946, Tantau; flowers large, 20 petals, borne in clusters of 10 - 15, moderate fragrance; foliage dark, glossy; upright growth; [('Johanna Tantau' × 'Heidekind') × 'Hamburg']
'Fancy' HT, mr, 1928, Van Rossem; flowers peach shaded cherry-red, base yellow, open, semi-dbl.; ['Souv. de Claudius Pernet' × 'Gen. Smuts']
'Fancy' F, ob; intr. 2001
Fancy™ -- See 'Poulfancy'
'Fancy Amazone' HT, rb; PP11171
'Fancy Beauty' F, or; flowers orange-red, yellow reverse, semi-dbl.; intr. 1999
'Fancy Dancer' -- See 'Bridancer'
'Fancy Free' HT, pb, 1922, Clark, A.; flowers pink, center white, semi-dbl.; dwarf growth; ['Gustav Grunerwald' × seedling]
'Fancy Hit' (Fancy™) MinFl, or, Poulsen; flowers orange-red, 5-8 cm., dbl., no fragrance; foliage dark; growth narrow, bushy, 40-60 cm.; intr. 1994
'Fancy Lace' HT, mp, 1967, Patterson; bud ovoid; flowers pink tipped silver, large, dbl., high-centered, moderate fragrance; foliage glossy; very vigorous, upright growth; PP2989; [seedling × Queen Elizabeth®]
'Fancy Lady' -- See 'Clelady'
Fancy Pants™ -- See 'Kinfancy'
'Fancy Potluck' -- See 'Lavfan'
'Fancy Princess' -- See 'Otohime'
'Fancy Talk' F, pb, 1965, Swim & Weeks; bud urn-shaped; flowers pink tinted orange, small, dbl., high-centered, borne in clusters, slight fragrance; foliage leathery; vigorous, bushy, low growth; PP2602; ['Spartan' × 'Garnette']
'Fancy That' Min, pb, 1989, Jolly, Marie; bud pointed; flowers different shades of pink, reverse pink-yellow blend, medium, 68 petals, high-centered, slight spicy fragrance; foliage medium size, medium green, semi-glossy; no prickles; upright, spreading, medium, vigorous growth; hips globular, green-brown; ['Rise 'n' Shine' × Rainbow's End™]
'Fandango' HT, mr, 1950, Swim, H.C.; bud ovoid, turkey-red, base yellow; flowers orange-red, 3½-4½ in., 16-25 petals, open, moderate fragrance; foliage leathery, glossy, dark; vigorous, upright, bushy growth; PP894; ['Charlotte Armstrong' × seedling]
Fandango® LCl, pb; flowers medium to light pink, 9 cm., semi-dbl., rosette, borne in small clusters; growth to 7 ft. and up; intr. 1989
'Fanely Revoil' HT, or, 1962, Orard, Joseph; flowers cerise-red, reverse tinted orange, well-formed; long stems; ['Michèle Meilland' × seedling]
Fanette® -- See 'Lapcal'
'Fanfan' F, or, 1956, Gaujard; flowers coppery orange, small; foliage small; ['Eternite' × seedling]
'Fanfare' F, pb, 1956, Swim, H.C.; bud urn shaped; flowers orange and salmon to pink, open, 3-4 in., 20-30 petals, cupped, borne in large clusters, moderate spicy fragrance; foliage glossy, leathery; very vigorous, spreading growth; PP1385; ['Fandango' × 'Pinocchio']
'Fanion' -- See 'Puregold'
'Fanny' A, pb, before 1848; flowers salmon blush, large, full
'Fanny' HT, mr, Lens; flowers bright red; vigorous growth; ['Hadley' × 'Mrs Henry Winnett']; intr. 1935
Fanny Ardant® HT, lp, Adam; flowers light pink with deeper center, full, low-centered; vigorous (80-100 cm.) growth; intr. 2004
'Fanny Bias' ('Athalie', 'Duchesse de Reggio') HGal, mp, before 1811, Descemet; flowers blush, center rosy, edges whitish, 3 in., full, moderate fragrance; erect, bushy growth
'Fanny Blankers-Koen' ('Luxembourg') HT, ob, 1949, Verschuren-Pechtold; bud long, pointed; flowers orange-yellow, flushed and veined red, large, 16 petals; foliage glossy; very vigorous, upright, bushy growth; ['Talisman' × seedling]
'Fanny Boydt' T, w, before 1844, Burel, Adolphe; flowers white, center cream, medium, full
'Fanny Bullivant' HT, dr, 1941, Clark, A.; [sport of 'The Rajah']
'Fanny Dupuis' -- See 'Abricotée'
'Fanny Elssler' HGal, mp, 1835, Vibert; flowers bright pink with minute pale spots, very full, moderate fragrance; named after the Viennese ballet dancer, Franziska Elssler (1810-1884)
'Fanny Oppenheimer' HT, mr, 1923, McGredy; flowers brilliant cardinal, shaded gold
'Fanny Parissot' -- See 'Fanny Pavetot'
'Fanny Pavetot' ('Fanny Parissot') HGal, mp, 1819; flowers large, very dbl., moderate fragrance
'Fanny Rousseau' A, lp, 1817, Vibert; flowers flesh pink, medium, semi-dbl.
'Fanny-Sommesson' A, lp, before 1826, Vibert; flowers light pink, fadeing to flesh white, large, very dbl.; nearly thornless; growth erect
'Fanny's La France' HT, dp; flowers large, deep pink, same as La France; recurrent; vigorous growth; may be sport of La France
'Fano' S, mp; flowers single
'Fantaisie' HT, r, 1948, Gaujard; flowers coppery-salmon, base yellow; foliage dark; vigorous growth
'Fantan' F, or, Gaujard; flowers soft tan overlaid on cream, small, dbl., slight fragrance; recurrent; intr. 1956
'Fantan' HT, r, 1959, Meilland, F.; bud urn-shaped; flowers burnt-orange to yellow-ochre, large, 48 petals, cupped, slight fragrance; foliage leathery; moderate growth; PP1913; [('Pigalle' × 'Prelude') × ('Pigalle' × 'Prelude')]
Fantasi™ -- See 'Kinfanta'
'Fantasia, Climbing' Cl HT, my, 1956, Mell
'Fantasia' HT, dp
'Fantasia' HT, ab, Kordes; intr. 1998
'Fantasia' HT, my, 1943, Dickson, A.; bud long, pointed; flowers golden to lighter yellow, open, medium, 30-35 petals, intense fragrance; foliage glossy; strong stems; vigorous, bushy, compact growth; PP590; RULED EXTINCT; [seedling × 'Lord Lonsdale']
'Fantasia' ('Fantazia') HT, pb, 1974, Kordes; bud ovoid; flowers cherry pink with cream reverse, globular, borne in clusters of 3-5, moderate fragrance; foliage leathery; vigorous, well-branched, medium growth; ['Silver Star' × 'Tradition']; flora-tea; intr. 1974
Fantasia Mondiale™ HT, ab, Kordes; flowers apricot, salmon pink on petal edges, 4 in. , full, high-centered, no fragrance; recurrent; medium (100 cm.) growth; [sport of 'Mondiale']; intr. 2006
'Fantasque' -- See 'Fantastique'
'Fantastique' ('Fantasque') HT, yb, 1943, Meilland, F.; flowers yellow, heavily edged carmine, 2½-3 in., 38 petals, cupped, moderate spicy fragrance; foliage dark, leathery, glossy; vigorous, compact growth; PP574; ['Ampere' × ('Charles P. Kilham' × ('Charles P. Kilham' × 'Capucine Chambard'))]
'Fantasy' HT, rb, 1945, Wyant; bud long, pointed; flowers cerise, reverse yellow ashed pink, open, 4½ in., 9-11 petals; foliage leathery, glossy; slender stems; very vigorous, upright growth; RULED EXTINCT 1/86 ARM; ['Soeur Thérèse' × seedling]
'Fantasy' Min, pb; flowers large, cream edged cerise, semi-dbl.; medium growth
'Fantasy' -- See 'Jacpow'
Fantasy™ -- See 'Pouldyb'
'Fantasy Hit' (Fantasy™) MinFl, dr,

Poulsen; flowers dark red, 5-8 cm., semi-dbl., no fragrance; foliage dark; growth bushy, 40-60 cm.; intr. 1993

'Fantasy Queen' HT, mp, J&P; flowers clear pink, double, high-centered, borne mostly singly; recurrent; growth medium height; intr. 2007

'Fantazia' -- See 'Korfan'

'Fantin-Latour' C, lp, before 1900; flowers blush with a small yellow-green eye, dbl., flat to cupped, borne in clusters of 4-6, moderate fragrance; foliage dark green, broad, elliptical; prickles moderate; vigorous, bushy growth (5-6 ft.)

'Far Side' F, ob, 1989, Stoddard, Louis; bud ovoid, pointed; flowers orange-vermilion, yellow center, small, 5 petals, borne in sprays of up to 20, moderate spicy fragrance; foliage large, medium green, glossy, smooth; prickles straight, medium, stout, pink to brown; upright, spreading, tall growth; hips globular, medium, vermilion; [('Sunsprite' × ('Many Moons' × 'Maigold')) × Eyepaint®]; intr. 1990

'Fara Shimbo' -- See 'Ardfara'

'Farah' HT, yb, 1961, Gaujard; flowers coppery yellow, large, dbl.; foliage glossy; long stems; very vigorous, bushy growth; ['Peace' × 'Georges Chesnel']

'Farandole' F, mr, 1959, Meilland, Mrs. Marie-Louise; bud oval; flowers vermilion, open, medium, 25 petals, borne in large clusters; foliage leathery; vigorous, well branched growth (70-80 cm.); [('Goldilocks' × Moulin Rouge®) × ('Goldilocks' × 'Fashion')]

Farandole® F, or, Meilland; flowers Indian orange bordered red, borne in clusters; foliage dense, medium green; growth to 30 in.; intr. 2000

'Farbenkönigin' ('Queen of Colors', 'Reine des Couleurs') HT, mr, 1902, Hinner, W.; flowers bright carmine, overlaid with silvery gloss, deeper at base, large, dbl., moderate fragrance; ['Grand-Duc Adolphe de Luxembourg' × 'La France']

'Farbenspiel' F, rb, 1962, von Engelsen, A. J.; flowers pink edged red, dbl., intense fragrance; foliage dark; bushy, compact growth; ['Pinocchio' × 'Masquerade']; originally registered as Pol

'Farfadet' F, or, 1955, Combe; flowers semi-dbl.; very upright growth; ['Méphisto' × 'Incendie']

'Faria' -- See 'Olijkroet'

'Farida' F, dp, 1941, Leenders, M.; flowers deep rose-pink, semi-dbl.; [seedling × 'Permanent Wave']

Farinet® S, yb; intr. 2003

'Farny Wurlitzer' HT, mr, 1970, Cadey; bud long, pointed; flowers large, dbl., intense fragrance; foliage dark, glossy; vigorous, upright growth; ['Poinsettia' × 'Charlotte Armstrong']; intr. 1968

'Farouche' -- See 'Richotale'

'Farquhar' ('Boston Rambler', 'The Farquhar Rose') HWich, mp, 1903, Dawson; flowers bright clear pink, carnation-like, resembling Lady Gay, 3 cm., dbl., borne in large clusters; late; foliage glossy; prickles long; vigorous, climbing growth; [*R. wichurana* × 'Crimson Rambler']

'Fasciculée' -- See 'Comtesse de Chamoïs'

'Fascinating' HT, yb, 1960, Fisher, G.; bud long, pointed; flowers rose-opal suffused yellow, 4½ in., 25 petals, high-centered, moderate fragrance; foliage leathery, glossy, dark; upright, bushy growth; PP1945; ['Peace' × 'Orange Nassau']; intr. 1961

'Fascination' HT, pb, 1927, Chaplin Bros.; flowers rosy cerise, shaded yellow, moderate fragrance; foliage dark, glossy; vigorous growth; RULED EXTINCT 2/81

'Fascination' HT, op, 1981, Warriner, William A.; bud nearly globular; flowers orange and rose blend, 55 petals, high-centered, borne usually singly, no fragrance; foliage very large, semi-glossy; prickles long-based, hooked down; upright, heavy branching growth; PP4461; [seedling × 'Spellbinder']; intr. 1982

'Fascination' -- See 'Miwaku'

Fascination™ -- See 'Poulmax'

'Fashion' F, pb, 1949, Boerner; bud ovoid, deep peach; flowers lively coral-peach, 3-3½ in., 23 petals, borne in clusters, moderate fragrance; vigorous, bushy growth; PP789; ['Pinocchio' × 'Crimson Glory']

Fashion™ ('Fashion Hit') S, dr, Poulsen; flowers dark red, 8-10 cm., dbl., no fragrance; foliage reddish green; growth narrow, bushy, 20-40 cm.; not synonymous with either of the other Poulsen Fashions; intr. 2005

'Fashion' ('Fashion Parade') Min, mp, Poulsen; flowers dbl., moderate wild rose fragrance; foliage dark, glossy; growth bushy, low (20-40 cm.); not a duplicate with the rose of the same name from 1998; intr. 1996

'Fashion, Climbing' Cl F, pb, 1951, Boerner (also Mattock, 1955); PP1057

Fashion™ -- See 'Poulyn'

'Fashion Doll' F, mp, Bell, Laurie; flowers coral pink; free blooming; healthy, bushy, medium growth; intr. 2001

'Fashion Flame' Min, op, 1977, Moore, Ralph S.; bud ovoid, pointed; flowers coral-orange, 1-1½ in., 35 petals, high-centered, slight fragrance; foliage large, leathery; bushy growth; PP4365; ['Little Darling' × 'Fire Princess']

'Fashion Hit' -- See 'Poulpah035'

'Fashion Parade' (Fashion™) Min, mp, Poulsen; flowers light red or dark pink, less than 5 cm., dbl., slight fragrance; growth bushy, 20-40 cm.; PP11544; not synonymous with the 1996 Poulsen Fashion; intr. 1998

'Fashion Parade' -- See 'Poulion'

'Fashion Statement' S, pb, John Clements; flowers white center blending to crisp pink toward the edges, 3 in., 8-12 petals, moderate sweet/honey fragrance; foliage dense; growth bushy, 3½ × 3 ft.; PPAF; intr. 2005

'Fashionette' F, pb, 1959, Boerner; bud pointed to ovoid, coral; flowers pinkish coral, 3 in., 35-40 petals, cupped, borne in irregular clusters, moderate fragrance; foliage glossy; vigorous, upright growth; PP1563; ['Goldilocks' × 'Fashion']; intr. 1958

'Fashionette, Climbing' Cl F, pb, 1962, Noack, Werner

'Fassadenzauber' LCl, lp, Noack, Werner; intr. 1997

'Fastigiata' -- See 'Comtesse de Chamoïs'

'Fat 'n' Sassy' -- See 'Tinsassy'

'Fat Tuesday' -- See 'Talfat'

'Fata Morgana' T, mp, 1893, Drögemüller; flowers silky pink, often shaded flesh pink, large, full; ['Niphetos' × 'Mme Lombard']

'Fata Morgana' F, ob, Kordes, R.; flowers orange-yellow, open, 2½ in., 28 petals, borne in large trusses, slight fragrance; foliage leathery, glossy; vigorous, upright growth; ['Masquerade' × seedling]; intr. 1957

'Father Christmas' -- See 'Talchris'

'Father's Day' -- See 'Vatertag'

'Fatima' HT, ob, 1955, Gaujard; bud long, pointed; flowers orange, reverse bright golden yellow, very large; vigorous growth; [('Opera' × unknown) × seedling]

'Fatima '67' HT, Moreira da Silva, A.; intr. 1967

'Fatime' -- See 'Agathe Fatime'

'Fatinitza' HT, op, Berger, W.; flowers yellowish salmon-pink, medium, dbl.; intr. 1956

'Fatinitza' HMult, pb, 1886, Geschwind; flowers varying light pink, sometimes striped white, 7 cm., semi-dbl., borne in medium clusters; a complex hybrid of Multiflora and Ayrshire

'Fausse Unique' ('Alba', 'Provins Blanc') D, w, before 1818; flowers white, flesh center, large, full

Faust, Climbing' Cl F, yb, 1963, deRuiter

'Faust' -- See 'Dr Faust'

'Faust' -- See 'Scarlano'

'Favori' -- See 'Len 3'

Favorita™ HT, op, 1954, Boerner; bud ovoid, burnt-orange; flowers salmon overcast orange, 5½-6 in., 48 petals, moderate fragrance; foliage dark; vigorous growth; PP1340; ['hybrid tea seedling' × 'Serenade']; intr. 1954

'Favorite' -- See 'Len 3'

'Favorite Dream' -- See 'Twofavor'

'Favorite Purple' -- See 'Belle de Stors'

Favourite™ -- See 'Poululv'

'Favourite Hit' ('Good Wishes', Favourite™) MinFl, ab, Poulsen; bud broad based, pointed ovoid; flowers light peach, 5 cm., 20 petals, open cup, borne in small clusters, slight floral fragrance; recurrent; foliage dark green, glossy;

prickles moderate, 5 mm., greyed-red, concave; bushy, compact (40-60 cm.) growth; PP15183; [Mini-Poul® × seedling]; intr. 2002

'Favourite Rosamini' -- See 'Ruifarol'

'Fay' S, pb, 1997, Robert, David; flowers medium, dbl., borne mostly singly; foliage medium size, light green, semi-glossy; few prickles; growth upright, medium (36 in.); ['Cecile Brunner' × 'Zéphirine Drouhin']

'Fay Euphemia Evelyn Benson Gibson Cullen' -- See 'Worcontrast'

'Fay Morris' HT, mp, 2000, Poole, Lionel; flowers medium pink, 5½-6 in., very full, exhibition, borne mostly singly; repeats quickly; foliage large, dark green, glossy; few prickles; upright, bushy, very vigorous, tall (4 ft.) growth; ['Gavotte' × ('Solitaire' × 'Mischief')]; intr. 2001

'Fayanne' F, pb, 1953, Pinchbeck; flowers deep rose-pink, reverse lighter, 2 in., 55 petals, globular, slight fragrance; foliage leathery; dwarf, bushy growth; PP1232; [sport of 'Garnette']

'Faye Reynolds' -- See 'Reyfaye'

'Fay's Folly' HT, ob, Kordes; buds pointed, urn-shaped, warm tangerine orange; flowers warm tangerine orange fading to cream at the edges, dbl., no fragrance; recurrent; compact, dense, medium (4 ft.) growth; intr. 2002

'Fazcanne' ('Red France') HT, mr, Fazari, Evelyne; bud long, pointed ovoid; intr. 1999

'Fear Naught' F, dp, 1969, Harkness, R.; flowers deep pink, dbl., slight fragrance; [Queen Elizabeth® × 'Ena Harkness']; intr. 1968

'Febama' (Iberflora 95®) HT, mr, Roses Noves Ferrer, S L

'Febasa' (Esther Peiro®) F, or, Roses Noves Ferrer, S L

'Febesa' HT, lp, Ferrer; intr. 1999

'Febesa' (Vanessa Campello®) Gr, lp, Roses Noves Ferrer, S L

'Febima' (Infanta Pilar™) HT, dp, 2001, Ferrer, Fco.; flowers dbl., borne mostly solitary, slight fragrance; foliage dark green, matte; [Zambra® × 'Frisko']; intr. 1995

'Februc' ('American Shakira') HT, dp, Ferrer; intr. 2004

'Fecasa' (Barcelona 95®) HT, w, Roses Noves Ferrer, S L

'Fecirco' HT, Ferrer, F.; intr. 1987

'Federation' LCl, op, 1938, Horvath; bud pointed; flowers rosy pink, orange undertone, large, 24-36 wavy petals, cupped, intense fragrance; foliage leathery, glossy, dark; long, strong stems; very vigorous climbing (12-14 ft.) growth; PP287; ['Mrs F. F. Prentiss' × 'Director Rubió']

'Federico Casas' ('Federico Cassio') HT, op, 1931, Dot, Pedro; flowers coppery pink and orange, open, very large, semi-dbl.; foliage dark; vigorous, bushy growth; [seedling × 'Eugene Barbier']

'Federico Casas, Climbing' Cl HT, op, 1937, Stell

Federico Garcia Lorca® -- See 'Feticos'

'Fedra' F, mr, 1963, Giacomasso; flowers brick-red, dbl.; vigorous growth; [('Fiamma' × 'Independence') × seedling]; intr. 1958

Fedra® S, ab, Barni; buds light pink; flowers soft apricot with outer petals lighter, dbl., rosette, borne in clusters; recurrent; growth to 4-5 ft.; intr. 2005

'Fedugia' (Marta Salvador®) HT, Ferrer, F.; intr. 1988

'Fee' F, or, 1963, Kordes, R.; flowers orange, large, dbl.; strong, wiry stems; moderate growth

'Fee' ('Pink Pearl') HT, lp, Martens; flowers pearly-pink; intr. 1989

'Fée Clochette' Min, mp, Delbard; intr. 2002

'Fée des Champs' Pol, op, 1965, Dot; flowers salmon-orange, 20-25 petals; foliage bronze; low growth; [Queen Elizabeth® × Zambra®]

'Fée des Neiges' -- See 'Iceberg'

'Fée des Neiges, Climbing' -- See 'Iceberg, Climbing'

'Fée Opale' N, ly, 1899, Bruant; flowers light yellow with pearly white, large, full

Feeling® -- See 'LLX8882'

Feeling® -- See 'Barfeel'

'Féerie' HT, ob, 1938, Gaujard; flowers coppery red, reverse orange-yellow, open, semi-dbl.; long stems; vigorous, erect growth

'Féerie' -- See 'The Fairy'

'Fegama' (Adela®) HT, pb, Viveros Fco. Ferrer, S L; intr. 1991

'Fegima' ('Elodea') HT, ly, Roses Noves Ferrer, S L

'Fegosa' (Alejandra Conde®) Min, dr, Viveros Fco. Ferrer, S L

Feisty™ -- See 'Jacrenim'

'Fekusa' (Charlye Rivel®) HT, dr, Roses Noves Ferrer, S L

'Felberg's Rosa Druschki' HP, mp, 1929, Felberg-Leclerc; flowers bright rose-pink, large, 25 petals; ['Frau Karl Druschki' × 'Farbenkonigin']

'Feliae Regis' HT, pb, Delbard; intr. 2003

'Felicia' HMsk, pb, 1928, Pemberton; flowers pink fading to blush and partly white, large, branching panicles, semi-dbl., moderate musk fragrance; pillar or shrub growth; ['Trier' × 'Ophelia']

'Felicia Teichmann' -- See 'Korciate'

'Félicie' ('Petite Renoncule Violette', 'Sultane Favorite') HGal, m, 1820, Vibert; flowers deep magenta to violet, small, dbl., ranunculus-shaped, moderate fragrance; foliage small; Agathe group; foliage suggests it may be a hybrid China

'Félicien David' HP, m, 1872, Verdier, E.; flowers deep rose tinged with purple, large, very full

Felicitas® -- See 'Korberis'

'Félicité Bohain' ('Félicité Bohan') M, dp, before 1866, from France; flowers vivid pink or bright rose, pronounced button eye, large, very full, globular to cupped, moderate fragrance

'Félicité Bohan' -- See 'Félicité Bohain'

'Félicité et Perpétue' -- See 'Félicité-Perpétue'

'Félicité Hardy' ('Mme Hardy') D, w, 1832, Hardy; bud large, round, pink outside; sepals long, foliaceous at top; flowers pure white, occasionally tinged flesh-pink, petals incurved at center, green pip, 8 cm., very dbl., cupped, opening flat, borne in small clusters, intense fragrance; foliage medium green, slightly pubescent underneath, regularly dentate, large; prickles numerous, uneven; stems light green; growth erect, vigorous

'Félicité Parmentier' A, lp, before 1841, Parmentier; flowers soft flesh-pink, aging to creamy white, petals reflexing, with a small yellow-green eye, very dbl., flat, intense fragrance; foliage gray-green, very dentate; prickles brown; vigorous, compact growth; according to François Joyaux, this rose should not be called simply 'Félicité', as it is listed in Parmentier's catalog as Félicité Parmentier

'Félicité-Perpétue' ('Félicité et Perpétue') HSem, w, 1828, Jacques; flowers pale flesh changing to white, 3-4 cm., very dbl., globular, opening flat, borne in large clusters, strong musk fragrance; foliage almost evergreen; very vigorous growth; [thought to be R. sempervirens × a Noisette, or maybe 'Parson's Pink China']; intr. 1829

'Felicity' HT, mp, 1919, Clarke Bros.; flowers rose-pink suffused silvery, large, 50-60 petals; foliage dark; vigorous, branching growth; ['Ophelia' × 'Hoosier Beauty']

'Felicity II' -- See 'Poulteeny'

'Felicity Kendal' -- See 'Lanken'

'Felidaé' S, ab, Schultheis; flowers large, apricot center with cream outer petals, very full, moderate fragrance; foliage dark green, glossy, resistant; bushy (4 ft.) growth; intr. 2002

'Felix Brix' HT, pb, 1921, Brix; flowers soft rose, suffused yellow, passing to salmon-rose, semi-dbl.; ['Natalie Boettner' × 'Old Gold']

'Felix Dorizy' B, dr, 1852, Dorizy; flowers dark scarlet, medium, full

'Félix Généro' HP, m, 1866, Damaizin

'Felix Laporte' HT, m, 1928, Buatois; flowers blackish velvety purple tinged garnet, dbl., cupped; foliage dark, leathery, glossy; vigorous, bushy growth; ['Yves Druhen' × 'Mme Edouard Herriot']

'Felix Leclerc' S, dp, Ag Canada; flowers bright pink with yellow stamens, semi-dbl., shallow cup to flat, borne in small clusters; growth tall; shrub or small climber; second in new Canadian Artist series; intr. 2007

'Félix Mousset' HP, m, 1884, Verdier, E.; flowers deep intense purplish pink, large, full; foliage rounded, dark green,

regularly toothed; prickles unequal, short, straight, pink; growth upright
'Fellemberg' ('Belle Marseillaise', 'Fellenberg') Ch, mr, before 1835, Fellemberg; bud crimson; flowers dark carmine, fading to mauve pink, 6 cm., 36 petals, cupped, borne in small clusters, moderate sweet fragrance; recurrent; foliage small, bluish-green; vigorous, spreading growth
'Fellemberg' -- See 'Fellemberg'
'Fellini' -- See 'Interdain'
'Fellowship' -- See 'Harwelcome'
'Fellowship' -- See 'Yu-Ai'
'Fellowship' -- See 'De Greeff's Jubilee'
'Feloma' (Coral®) HT, dy, Roses Noves Ferrer, S L
'Feloma' -- See 'Yellow Coral'
'Femental' (Juli de Sala®) Gr, or, Roses Noves Ferrer, S L
'Femiento' ('Ana de Cuevas') HT, yb, Viveros Fco. Ferrer, S L
'Femina' HT, lp, 1957, Poulsen, S.; flowers soft pink, large, dbl.; vigorous growth
'Femina' HT, op, Gaujard; bud long, pointed; flowers salmon-pink, large, dbl., moderate fragrance; foliage leathery; vigorous, upright growth; PP2586; ['Fernand Arles' × 'Mignonne']; intr. 1963
Feminine™ ('Feminine Hit') Min, pb, Olesen; bud pointed ovoid; flowers medium pink, reverse darker, outer petals lighter, 1½ in., 30 petals, cupped, borne singly and in small clusters, very slight fragrance; recurrent; foliage dark green, glossy; prickles moderate, 6 mm., hooked downward; bushy, compact (30-40 cm.) growth; PP15473; [seedling × seedling]; container rose; intr. 2003
'Feminine Hit' -- See 'Poulhi015(N)'
'Femme' -- See 'Delvor'
'Femme Actuelle' -- See 'Richzone'
'Femnet' -- See 'Pekaledon'
'Fen Queen' F, lp, 1963, Sharman; flowers pale flesh, large, 25 petals; foliage light green; vigorous, upright growth; [Queen Elizabeth® × 'unknown hybrid tea']
'Fen Zhuang Lou' -- See 'Fun Jwan Lo'
'Fénelon' Ch, m, 1835, Laffay (possibly Desprez); flowers purple-violet, medium, full, globular
'Fénelon' HP, mp, Rousseau; flowers bright carmine, medium; intr. 1852
'Fenja' HSpn, mp, Petersen; flowers bright pink, medium size, single; non-remontant; growth to 8 ft.; hips large, elongated, flask-shaped, orange-red; sometimes considered HMoy, or HDavidii; intr. 1965
'Fennet' HT, rb, Laperrière; buds ovoid; flowers red with white reverse, high-centered; intr. 1985
'Fennica' -- See 'Runatru'
'Feodase' (Condesa de Barcelona®) HT, yb, Viveros Fco. Ferrer, S L
'Feprogo' (Lourdes Arroyo®) HT, yb, Viveros Fco. Ferrer, S L
'Fepuma' (Carolina Daza®) HT, my, Viveros Fco. Ferrer, S L
'Ferama' (Catalina Frau®) HT, lp, Viveros Fco. Ferrer, S L
'Ferdin-Chaffolte' -- See 'Ferdinand Chaffolte'
'Ferdinand' HP, mr, 1852, Bernède; flowers poppy red, shaded carmine, medium, full; ['Géant des Batailles' × unknown]
'Ferdinand Batel' HT, yb, 1896, Pernet-Ducher; flowers variable, from rosy flesh to nankeen orange, medium, dbl.
'Ferdinand Chaffolte' ('Ferdin-Chaffolte') HP, mr, 1879, Pernet fils; flowers brilliant red, outer petals shaded violet, very large, very dbl., cupped, borne mostly solitary, moderate fragrance; foliage somber green; growth upright
'Ferdinand de Buck' ('Feu de Buck') HGal, mp, before 1842; flowers brilliant pink, medium, dbl.
'Ferdinand de Lesseps' -- See 'Maurice Bernardin'
'Ferdinand Deppe' HP, m, 1852, Laffay
'Ferdinand Jamin' HP, mr, 1888, Lévêque; flowers vermilion-red, full; foliage dark glaucous green
'Ferdinand Jamin' HT, op, Pernet-Ducher; bud long, pointed; flowers carmine pink nuanced salmon, large, full, globular; foliage bronzy green; intr. 1896
'Ferdinand Lecomte' HT, mp, 1909, Robichon; flowers China pink, center darker, large, full, moderate fragrance
'Ferdinand Pichard' HP, rb, 1921, Tanne; flowers streaked (striped) pink and scarlet, yellow stamens, 25 petals; recurrent bloom; vigorous, tall growth
'Ferdinand Roussel' HWich, m, 1902, Barbier; flowers purple/pink to light red, 3-4 cm., dbl., borne in medium clusters; foliage medium size, oval, glossy; prickles numerous, straight, long and narrow; [R. wichurana × 'Luciole']
'Ferdinando Dukei' HT, yb; flowers orange-yellow with red, large, semi-dbl.
FerdyTM® -- See 'Keitoli'
Ferecha® ('Iris') HT, rb, Viveros Fco. Ferrer, S L
'Fergie' -- See 'Ganfer'
'Fergus Games' S, op, Williams, J. Benjamin; flowers light salmon pink, dbl.; growth to 3 × 4 ft.; intr. 1999
'FeRho' ('Childhood Memories') LCl, mp, Fergusson; intr. 1997
'Feria' HT, op, 1970, Meilland; flowers coral suffused pink, large, dbl., globular, moderate fragrance; foliage leathery; upright growth; [('Grand Gala' × 'Premier Bal') × 'Love Song']; intr. 1968
'Féria' ('Faria') HT, yb, Olij, Huibert; flowers pale yellow edged orange-red, dbl., high-centered; greenhouse rose; intr. 1996
Ferline® HT, mr, Laperrière; intr. 1984
'Fern Kemp' HRg, lp, 1918, Kemp, J.A.; flowers delicate pink, 4 in., semi-dbl.; vigorous growth; hardy; ['Conrad Ferdinand Meyer' × 'Frau Karl Druschki']
'Fern Roehrs' LCl, mp, 1943, Graf; flowers same as parent but much more dbl.; PP606; [sport of 'Paul's Scarlet Climber']
'Fernand Arles' ('Arles') HT, op, 1949, Gaujard; bud long, pointed; flowers orange-salmon shaded red, very large, dbl.; foliage bronze; very vigorous, bushy growth; ['Mme Joseph Perraud' × seedling]
'Fernand Gignac' -- See 'Wekosunkora'
'Fernand Majorel' F, Gaujard; intr. 1975
'Fernand Point' HT, rb, 1964, Orard, Joseph; flowers crimson-red, reverse flesh-pink, base yellow; foliage glossy; ['Peace' × seedling]
'Fernand Rabier' HWich, dr, 1918, Turbat; flowers pure deep scarlet, 3 cm., semi-dbl. to dbl., borne in clusters of 40-50, slight fragrance; vigorous, climbing or trailer growth; ['Delight' × unknown]
'Fernand Tanne' LCl, dy, 1920, Tanne; flowers deep yellow to cream-yellow, 7 cm., dbl., quartered, borne in clusters of 5-10, intense Tea fragrance; vigorous growth
'Fernanda' HT, (Brazil)
'Fernande Krier' HWich, pb, 1925, Walter, L.; flowers peach-pink, occasionally margined red, fading to white, medium, semi-dbl.; [sport of 'Excelsa']
'Fernande Lumay' HT, ab, 1922, Buatois; flowers apricot-nankeen-yellow, edged milk-white, dbl.; ['Mrs Aaron Ward' × seedling]
'Fernandel' -- See 'Mme Fernandel'
'Ferniehurst' HT, pb, 1912, Dickson; flowers coppery carnation pink, large, full, cupped, moderate fragrance
'Fernielea' HT, ab, 1926, Adam & Craigmile; flowers apricot, center deeper
'Fern's Rose' F, my; flowers creamy yellow, double, borne in large clusters, moderate fragrance; recurrent; medium (3 ft.) growth; intr. 2006
'Ferox' A, w, before 1844; flowers flesh white, medium, very dbl.; foliage pointed, yellowish-green; prickles very numerous
'Ferrin' -- See 'Tuckferrin'
'Ferris Wheel' -- See 'Aroyumi'
'Ferrugineux du Luxembourg' ('Luxembourg') M, mr, before 1834, Hardy; flowers bright crimson red, medium, full, flat
'Ferry Porsche' HT, mr, 1976, W. Kordes Söhne; bud long, pointed; flowers 34 petals, high-centered, borne singly and in small clusters, slight fragrance; foliage large, dark, soft; vigorous, upright growth; ['Tropicana' × 'Americana']; intr. 1971
'Fertry' ('The Didgemere Rose') S, my, 1998, Ferguson, B.; flowers medium yellow, 2½-3 in., full, borne mostly singly, moderate fragrance; recurrent; foliage medium size, medium green, dull; prickles small, slightly hooked; upright, low (3-4ft.) growth; ['Sunsprite' × Trier®]; intr. 1998
'Fervid' F, or, 1960, LeGrice; flowers

scarlet-orange, 3 in., single, borne in clusters; foliage glossy, dark; vigorous, upright growth; ['Pimpernell' × 'Korona']

'Fesaru' (Neus®) HT, w, Viveros Fco. Ferrer, S L

'Fesato' (Clara®) Min, op, Viveros Fco. Ferrer, S L; intr. 1986

'Fesodios' (Emilo Feliu®) HT, op, Viveros Fco. Ferrer, S L

'Festival' ('Dixie Dream') HT, mr, 1943, Dixie Rose Nursery; flowers rich red, very dbl., moderate fragrance; entirely prickle free; PP545; RULED EXTINCT, 8/93 ARM; ['E.G. Hill' × unknown]; intr. 1945

'Festival, Climbing' Cl HT, mr, 1945, Watkins, A.F.; flowers large, globular, intense fragrance; free, intermittent bloom; foliage glossy; thornless; very vigorous, climbing growth; hardy in South; PP687; [sport of 'E.G. Hill']

'Festival' -- See 'Matsuri'

'Festival' -- See 'Kordialo'

'Festival Beauty' -- See 'Krasavitza Festivalia'

Festival des Jardins de Chaumont® S, ab, Guillot-Massad; flowers rosy apricot, outer petals fading, full, cupped; recurrent; foliage dark green; moderate growth; intr. 2007

'Festival Fanfare' ('St John Ogilvie') S, pb, 1982, Ogilvie, W.D.; flowers dark orange-pink with paler stripes which become nearly white, 3 in., semi-dbl., borne in large clusters; tall, broad growth; [sport of 'Fred Loads']; intr. 1986

'Festival Lady' F, r; flowers terracotta to golden brown, borne in clusters; recurrent; bushy, compact growth; intr. 2008

'Festival Meidiland' -- See 'Rote Woge'

'Festival Music' -- See 'Kagura'

Festival Pink™ -- See 'Rupfespin'

'Festival Queen' HT, lp, 1969, Lindquist; bud long, pointed; flowers light pink, edged deeper, well-formed, high-centered, slight fragrance; foliage dark, leathery; upright, compact growth; intr. 1968

Festival Rouge® -- See 'Delfesrou'

'Festive' Pol, dr, 1976, Jelly; bud short, pointed; flowers 3-3½ in., 30 petals, high-centered, slight sweetbriar fragrance; repeat bloom; foliage parsley-green; vigorous, upright growth; PP3914; [Baccará® × seedling]; patent issued as F; intr. 1975

'Festive Jewel' -- See 'Beacost'

'Festivity' -- See 'Lenor'

'Festro' (Alba Garcia®) HT, w, Viveros Fco. Ferrer, S L

'Fesuma' (Gloria Ferrer®) HT, w, Viveros Fco. Ferrer, S L

'Fesun' HT, my, Meillanddbl.; intr. 2004

'Fête des Mère, Climbing' -- See 'Mothersday, Climbing'

'Fête des Mères' -- See 'Mothersday'

'Fête des Pères' -- See 'Vatertag'

'Fête des Pères, Climbing' -- See 'Vatertag, Climbing'

Fêtes Galantes® -- See 'Deldido'

'Fétiche' F, mr, 1962, Delforge; flowers coral-red, center white, open, 2 in., 12 petals, borne in clusters; foliage dark; moderate, bushy growth; ['Philippe' × 'Tabarin']

'Feticos' (Federico Garcia Lorca®) HT, ab, Viveros Fco. Ferrer, S L

'Fetino' (Venus™) Min, yb, 2001, Ferrer, Fco.; flowers cream yellow, 2 cm., very dbl., borne mostly solitary, slight fragrance; foliage dark green; ['Yellow Meillandina' × seedling]; intr. 2001

'Fetosa' (Rosella™) S, dp, 2001, Ferrer, Fco.; flowers single, borne in small clusters, slight fragrance; foliage medium green; growth medium (1 m.); ['Heideschnee' × 'Purple Rain']; intr. 2000

'Fetrone' (Rocio Elias®) HT, m, Viveros Fco. Ferrer, S L

'Fetural' (Lucia Cotarelo®) Min, op, Viveros Fco. Ferrer, S L

'Fetzer Syrah Rose' -- See 'Harextra'

'Feu Amoureux' HGal, m, before 1811; bud round; flowers deep wine purple, large, dbl., no fragrance; foliage long, finely dentate, unequal in size; prickles numerous, broad-based, red

'Feu d'Artifice' ('Fireworks, Climbing') LCl, yb, 1935, Mallerin, C.; bud long, pointed, nasturtium-red; flowers yellow, tinted nasturtium-red, 4 in., semi-dbl., open, borne in clusters, slight fragrance; non-recurrent; foliage dark green, glossy; long stems; vigorous, climbing (over 8 ft.) growth; [R. foetida hybrid × 'Colette Clément']; intr. 1939

'Feu d'Artifice' -- See 'Magneet'

'Feu de Bengale' F, lp, 1951, Gaujard, R.; flowers pearl-pink, large, dbl., cupped; foliage glossy; vigorous growth; [Orange Triumph® × seedling]

'Feu de Buck' -- See 'Ferdinand de Buck'

'Feu de Camp' -- See 'Lagerfeuer'

'Feu de Joie' F, mr, 1951, Gaujard, R.; flowers carmine-red, large, dbl., borne in clusters; foliage dark, glossy; vigorous growth; [Orange Triumph® × seedling]

'Feu de Joie' S, or, Croix; intr. 2005

'Feu de Saint-Jean' Pol, dr, 1951, Gaujard, R.; flowers blackish red, small, semi-dbl., borne in clusters; foliage dark, glossy; vigorous, bushy growth; [Orange Triumph® × seedling]

'Feu de Vesta' ('Vesta') HGal, mr, before 1829, Coquerel; flowers velvety, light bright crimson, large, dbl.

'Feu d'Enfer' F, or, 1958, Gaujard, R.; flowers large, dbl.; upright, well branched growth; [Orange Triumph® × seedling]

'Feu du Ciel' Pol, ob, 1951, Gaujard, R.; flowers clear orange, small, semi-dbl., borne in clusters; foliage glossy; vigorous, bushy growth; [Orange Triumph® × seedling]

'Feu Follet' F, mp, 1953, Gaujard, R.; flowers salmon, cupped; vigorous growth

Feu Follet® -- See 'Diclady'

'Feu Joseph Looymans' HT, ob, 1921, Looymans; flowers orange-yellow, large, dbl., cupped; foliage leathery; weak stems; vigorous growth; ['Sunburst' × 'Rayon d'Or']

'Feu Joseph Looymans, Climbing' Cl HT, ob, 1935, Western Rose Co.; flowers apricot, edged buff, 4½-5 in., semi-dbl., cupped

'Feu Magique' F, mr, 1956, Buyl Frères; flowers cherry-red, 18 petals; vigorous growth; ['Independence' × 'Signal Red']

'Feu Pernet-Ducher' HT, my, 1935, Mallerin, C.; flowers bright yellow, center apricot, large, dbl., moderate fruity fragrance; foliage leathery, dark; vigorous, branching growth; PP103; ['Julien Potin' × 'Margaret McGredy']

'Feu Rouge' F, mr, 1959, Tantau, Math.; bud ovoid; flowers open, large, semi-dbl., slight fragrance; foliage glossy; vigorous growth; ['Red Favorite' × 'Fanal']; intr. 1956

'Feudor' HT, yb, 1963, Croix, P.; flowers golden yellow shaded vermilion; foliage bright green; vigorous growth; ['Peace' × Baccará®]

'Feuerball' HT, mr, 1965, Tantau, Math.; bud globular; flowers red lead color, well-formed, large, 25-30 petals; foliage glossy; very vigorous, bushy growth

'Feuerfunken' S, or, GPG Bad Langensalza; flowers large, dbl.; intr. 1979

'Feuerland' F, or, 1978, W. Kordes Söhne; bud ovoid; flowers 2½ in., 25 petals, cupped, slight fragrance; very vigorous, upright growth; ['Kathe Duvigneau' × Topsi®]; intr. 1977

'Feuermeer' ('Sea of Fire') F, or, 1954, Kordes; flowers orange-scarlet, 3 in., semi-dbl., open wide, borne in small clusters, slight fragrance; recurrent; foliage dark, leathery; vigorous, upright, bushy growth; [('Baby Chateau' × 'Else Poulsen') × 'Independence']; intr. 1954

'Feuerreiter' ('Fire-Rider') F, mr, 1968, Haenchen, E.; bud long, pointed; flowers open, large, semi-dbl., borne in clusters; foliage dark, leathery; very vigorous, upright growth; ['Alain' × 'Oskar Scheerer']

'Feuerschein' ('Krause's Rote Joseph Guy') F, mr, 1930, Krause; flowers brilliant red, not turning blue, dbl.; foliage dark; bushy growth; [sport of 'Lafayette']

'Feuerschein, Climbing' Cl F, mr, 1936, Krause

'Feuersturm' F, or, Verschuren; flowers medium

'Feuertaufe' Pol, GPG Bad Langensalza; flowers dbl.; intr. 1980

Feuerwerk® -- See 'Magneet'

'Feuerzauber' Ch, mr, 1913

Feuerzauber® -- See 'Korber'

'Feunon Rouge' HGal, mr, before 1811; bud elongate; flowers medium, very dbl., moderate fragrance; foliage oval, very dentate, pointed; Agathe group

'Feurio' F, or, 1956, Kordes, R.; bud ovoid;

flowers scarlet-red, 2½ in., 30 petals, cupped, borne in clusters, moderate fragrance; foliage glossy, light green; vigorous, low, bushy growth; PP1778; ['Rudolph Timm' × 'Independence']; intr. 1957

'Feurio, Climbing'   Cl F, or, 1963, Kordes

'Fever' -- See 'Peafever'

'Fevrusa' (Papa Falcon™) Min, w, 2001, Ferrer, Fco.; flowers very dbl., borne mostly solitary, no fragrance; foliage medium green; ['FE-84113' × 'Orange M']

'Feybell' ('Rebell') HT, ob, 1973, Kordes; flowers dark orange, large, dbl., high-centered, intense fragrance; foliage leathery; vigorous, upright growth; ['Brandenburg' × seedling]; intr. 1971

'Fiaba' HT, rb, 1963, Giacomasso; flowers bright red tipped yellow; foliage dark, glossy; very vigorous growth; [('Fiamma' × 'Sovrana') × seedling]

'Fialawn' ('Wood Lawn') HT, mp, 1985, Fiamingo, Joe; flowers clear medium pink; [sport of 'Fontainebleau']

'Fialopi' ('Loads of Pink') F, mp, 1991, Fiamingo, Joe; flowers medium, semi-dbl., borne in large clusters, moderate fragrance; foliage medium green, semi-glossy, disease-resistant; some prickles; growth tall, upright, very vigorous; [sport of 'Fred Loads']

'Fiametta' Min, dp; flowers sparkling pink; free-flowering

'Fiametta' F, dr, 1962, Leenders, J.; flowers velvety red, center yellow; moderate growth; ['Karl Weinhausen' × 'Goldilocks']

'Fiamma' F, or, 1948, Aicardi, D.; flowers vermilion, borne in clusters; vigorous growth; ['Paul's Scarlet Climber' × ('Talisman' × unknown)]

'Fiamma Nera' HMult, w, about 1938, possibly from Yugoslavia; flowers white with a touch of yellow at center, 5 cm., semi-dbl., borne in clusters of 10-30

'Fiammetta' HG, ab, 1922, Nabonnand, P.; flowers warm amber-yellow, streaked yellow, single, intense fragrance; vigorous, climbing growth; [R. gigantea × 'Margaret Molyneux']

'Fiançailles de la Princesse Stéphanie et de l'Archiduc Rodolphe' ('Princesse Stéphanie', 'Stéphanie et Rodolphe') N, ob, 1880, Levet; flowers orange salmon yellow, medium, full, borne in small clusters; foliage dark green; prickles long, hooked

'Ficksburg' F, ob, Delbard; flowers cream with petal edges turning salmon, then orange, dbl., no fragrance; recurrent; vigorous, medium to tall growth; intr. 1994

Fiddler's Gold™ -- See 'Minzco'

Fidélio® F, or, Meilland, Alain A.; bud long, pointed; flowers medium, 35 petals, high-centered, slight fragrance; foliage leathery; vigorous, upright growth; [('Radar' × 'Caprice') × 'Fire King']; intr. 1964

'Fidélio' F, ab, 1961, Horstmann; bud long, pointed, rosy red; flowers dbl., borne in large clusters; vigorous growth

'Fidelity' HT, mr, 1962, Abrams, Von; bud long, pointed; flowers large, dbl., high-centered; foliage glossy; tall growth; RULED EXTINCT 7/80 ARM; ['Crimson Glory' × 'Peace']

'Fidelity' -- See 'Scoop Jackson'

'Fides' HT, ly, Urban, J.; flowers large, dbl.; intr. 1970

Fidibus® HT, rb, Kordes; flowers small, red with yellow stripes, dbl., high-centered; stems length 16 in; greenhouse rose; intr. 2002

'Fidji' HT, yb; flowers striped; intr. 2001

'Field Marshal' Cl Ch, mr, before 1910, Paul; flowers velvety blood-crimson

Field of Dreams™ -- See 'Umsafield'

'Field of Woods' -- See 'Rhode Island Red'

'Fieldfare' S, rb, Delbard; flowers red with yellow eye, medium size, 10 petals; recurrent; foliage bronzy-green; vigorous (3 ft.) growth; intr. 1989

'Fields of the Wood' -- See 'Rhode Island Red'

Fiery™ -- See 'Poulfiry'

Fiery Hit® ('Loving Wishes', Fiery™) MinFl, ob, Poulsen; flowers orange and orange blend, 5-8 cm., semi-dbl., no fragrance; foliage reddish green; growth bushy, 40-60 cm.; PP12484

'Fiery Star' -- See 'Umsfire'

'Fiery Sunblaze' -- See 'Meineyta'

'Fiery Sunsation' -- See 'Kortemma'

'Fiesta' HT, rb, 1940, Hansen, C.B.; bud ovoid; flowers vermilion, splashed bright yellow, large, dbl., moderate fragrance; foliage glossy, dark; vigorous, bushy, compact growth; PP389; [sport of 'The Queen Alexandra Rose']

Fiesta+ HT, yb, Voom, Lex; flowers yellow with broad pink stripes, double, high-centered, borne mostly singly; recurrent; stems long; [sport of 'King Kong']; florist rose

'Fiesta' S, pb, Ping Lim; flowers deep pink and white stripes, touch of yellow in center, 1.5-3 in., 40 petals; recurrent; foliage dark green, glossy; medium (2 - 4 ft.) growth; PPAF; intr. 2007

'Fiesta' -- See 'Macfirinlin'

Fiesta™ -- See 'Poulesta'

'Fiesta Brava' Min, or, 1956, Dot, M.; flowers geranium-red, 14 petals, borne in clusters; foliage glossy; vigorous, upright, bushy growth; ['Méphisto' × 'Perla de Alcañada']

'Fiesta Charm' F, Schloen, P.

'Fiesta Clown' -- See 'Lavclo'

'Fiesta Flame' F, mr, 1978, Sanday, John; bud pointed; flowers intense scarlet, 3 in., 15 petals; low, bushy growth; [Sarabande® × 'Ena Harkness']

Fiesta Flamenco® S, mr, NIRP; intr. 2003

'Fiesta Gold' Min, yb, 1971, Moore, Ralph S.; bud long, pointed; flowers yellow orange, small, dbl., cupped, slight fragrance; foliage small, glossy, light, leathery; vigorous, dwarf, upright, bushy growth; PP3331; ['Golden Glow' × 'Magic Wand']; intr. 1970

Fiesta Parade® (Fiesta™) Min, dp, Poulsen; bud pointed ovoid; flowers deep lavender-pink, medium, 55-65 petals, high-centered, borne in small clusters; prolific, very slight fragrance; recurrent; foliage dark green, glossy; prickles average, 3-4 mm., linear to hooked slightly downward; bushy, compact (25-35 cm.) growth; PP11509; [sport of 'Purple Parade']; intr. 1999

'Fiesta Ruby' Min, mr, 1977, Moore, Ralph S.; bud ovoid, pointed; flowers 1 in., 40 petals, high-centered, slight fragrance; foliage dark; bushy, compact growth; PP4368; ['Red Pinocchio' × 'Little Chief']

Fiesta Time™ -- See 'Mingco'

'Fièvre d'Or' -- See 'Korbi'

'Fifi' -- See 'Henfif'

'Fifth Avenue' HT, dp, 1948, Johnson, W.E.; bud large, ovoid; flowers grenadine-pink, dbl., high-centered, moderate fragrance; vigorous growth; PP777; [sport of 'Orange Nassau']

'5th Avenue' -- See 'Sutton Place'

'Fifty Fifty' F, ob; flowers striped; intr. 2002

'Figaro' HT, dr, 1954, Lens; flowers velvety scarlet, 4½ in., 26 petals; vigorous growth; [('Crimson Glory' × 'Grande Duchesse Charlotte') × 'New Yorker']

Figaro Panarosa™ -- See 'Delrona'

'Figment' F, m, 1998, Rawlins, R.; flowers purple, overlaid with bright magenta in fresh flower, dark magenta reverse, 4 in., very dbl., borne in small clusters; foliage medium size, medium green, semi-glossy; prickles moderate; upright, medium (2½ ft.) growth; ['Len Turner' × Remember Me®]

'Figurine' HT, pb, 1952, Lens; flowers China pink, 25 petals, moderate fragrance; foliage bluish green; vigorous growth; ['Soeur Thérèse' × seedling]

Figurine™ Min, w, Benardella, Frank A.; buds delicately colored; flowers ivory white tinged pink, large, dbl., well-formed, borne mostly singly, some in small clusters; foliage medium size, dark green, matte; few prickles; long stems suitable for cutting; medium (40-50 cm.), upright, bushy growth; PP8020; ['Rise 'n' Shine' × 'Laguna']; intr. 1991

'Fiji' Gr, or, 1965, Schwartz, Ernest W.; bud ovoid; flowers bright orange-red, medium, dbl., cupped; vigorous, upright growth; [Queen Elizabeth® × seedling]; intr. 1964

Fil d'Ariane® -- See 'Lenfil'

'Fil des Saisons' S, m, Lens; flowers deep lavender pink, yellow stamens, 4-5 cm., single, borne in large clusters, intense fragrance; recurrent; foliage small, clear green, glossy; low, spreading (16 × 32 in.) growth; intr. 2004

'Filagree Pillar' LCl, dp, 1962, Riethmuller; bud ovoid; flowers Tyrian rose, heavily veined, reverse lighter, 50 petals; foliage glossy, bronze; strong stems; vigorous, upright (to 5 ft.) growth; ['Titian' × 'Sterling']; intr. 1962

'Fillette' F, mp, 1965, Lens; bud ovoid; flowers dbl., borne in clusters; foliage dark; ['Circus' × 'Papillon Rose']

'Filomena' F, dy, 2007, Mallari, Hermes B.; flowers very full, 80+ petals, borne in small clusters; foliage medium size, dark green, glossy; prickles ½ cm., thin, triangular, tan, few; growth bushy, upright, compact; [sport of 'Korresia']

'Fimbriata' ('Dianthiflora', 'Phoebe's Frilled Pink', *R. fimbriata*) HRg, lp, 1891, Morlet; flowers medium, petals carnation-like, fringed & serrated, dbl., borne in clusters of 15-25, intense fragrance; foliage glossy above, glaucous beneath; growth compact (5 ft.); [*R. rugosa* × 'Mme Alfred Carrière']

'Fimbriata à Pétales Frangés' -- See 'Serratipetala'

'Finale' ('Ami des Jardins') F, op, 1964, Kordes, R.; flowers salmon-rose, well-formed, large, 21 petals, borne in clusters; foliage light green; low, compact growth; ['Nordlicht' × 'Meteor (F)']

'Financial Times Centenary' -- See 'Ausfin'

'Fine Fare' HT, or, 1978, Bees; bud pointed; flowers vermilion, rounded, 4 in., 40 petals; foliage dark; moderately vigorous, upright growth; ['Fragrant Cloud' × 'Mildred Reynolds']

'Fine Gold' -- See 'Weegold'

'Fine Touch' -- See 'Lyofin'

'Finesse' Min, my, 1984, Hardgrove, Donald L.; flowers small, dbl., high-centered, borne 1-3 per stem, no fragrance; foliage small, medium green, semi-glossy; bushy, spreading growth; ['Picnic' × 'Rise 'n' Shine']; intr. 1983

'Finest Hour' -- See 'Micfinest'

'Fingerpaint' -- See 'Morfing'

'Finkenrech' F, mp, Michler, K. H.; flowers dbl.; intr. 1989

'Finlandia' Pol, op, 1969, Kraats; flowers orange-salmon; [sport of 'Greta Kluis']

Finnstar® -- See 'Rufin'

'Finstar' -- See 'Rufin'

'Fintona' HT, w, Brundrett; intr. 1997

'Fiocco Bianco' -- See 'Barfiob'

'Fiona' -- See 'Korfi'

Fiona® -- See 'Meibeluxen'

Fiona Gelin® S, ab, Guillot-Massad; flowers soft coppery pink to warm apricot, 60 petals, cupped, moderate fruity fragrance; recurrent; foliage dark green, glossy; vigorous (100 cm.) growth; intr. 2007

'Fiona Ivin' HT, dr, 2002, Poole, Lionel; flowers full, high-centered, borne mostly solitary; foliage dark green, semi-glossy; prickles medium, long, pointed, triangular, moderate; growth upright, bushy, medium (1 m.); garden, exhibition; ['New Zealand' × 'Royal William']; intr. 2004

'Fiona Lynch' -- See 'Kenicma'

Fiona Old™ -- See 'Poulfio'

'Fiona Parade' (Fiona Old™) Min, rb, Poulsen; flowers red blend, medium, dbl.; foliage dark; growth bushy, 20-40 cm.; PP11594; intr. 1998

'Fiona Ravenscroft' HT, Tebbin, N.H.; intr. 1972

'Fiona Stanley' HT, ab; intr. 2005

'Fiona's Affection' F, pb, 2001, Rosenberg, Ronald; flowers large, full, borne mostly solitary, slight fragrance; foliage medium size, medium green, semi-glossy; prickles 3/8 in., slightly curved, numerous; growth bushy, tall (4 ft.); [Honor™ × Affection™]

'Fiona's Delight' HT, op, 2001, Rosenberg, Ronald J.; flowers large, medium orange-pink, large, full, borne mostly solitary, moderate fragrance; foliage medium size, medium green, semi-glossy; prickles medium, moderate; growth upright, medium (3½ ft.); garden decorative; [Honor™ × 'Cherish']

'Fiona's Honor' HT, pb, 2005, Rosenberg, Ronald J; flowers full, borne mostly solitary, no fragrance; foliage medium size, dark green, semi-glossy; prickles few, 3/8 in., slightly curved; growth upright, medium (2½ ft.); garden decoration; [sport of Honor™]; intr. 2006

'Fiona's Wish' HT, rb, Meilland; flowers cherry red, cream reverse, dbl., moderate fragrance; medium growth; intr. 2001

'Fionia' HWich, lp, 1985, Poulsen, D.T.; flowers light pink to rose, small, borne in clusters; foliage dark, glossy; vigorous growth; ['Mme Norbert Levavasseur' × 'Dorothy Perkins']; intr. 1914

'Fiord' -- See 'Meicauf'

'Fiorella' -- See 'Meicapula'

'Fiorella '82' -- See 'Meicapula'

'Fiorona' F, Mati

Fire 'n' Ice™ -- See 'Arofiric'

'Fire and Peace' HT, ob, Williams, J. B. ; bud deep red-orange; flowers orange-yellow with red edges, aging red, full, moderate fragrance; foliage dark, leathery, semi-glossy; intr. 2005

'Fire Bird' F, rb, 1992, Strange, J.F.; flowers vermilion, pale yellow center, medium, 6-14 petals, borne in large clusters; foliage medium size, dark green, leathery; some prickles; medium (70 cm.), upright growth; ['Avocet' × 'Evelyn Fison']

'Fire Bird' -- See 'Oiseau de Feu'

'Fire Chief' HT, mr, 1942, Jacobus; bud long, pointed; flowers flame-red, large, 24-28 petals, high-centered; foliage glossy; very vigorous, bushy growth; ['Crimson Glory' × 'Ami Quinard']

'Fire Dance' HT, mr, 1951, Verschuren; bud very long, ovoid; flowers brilliant velvety scarlet, 4-6 in., 25-35 petals, globular, slight fragrance; foliage glossy, light green; upright, moderately vigorous growth; PP1019; [('Ulrich Brunner Fils' × 'Westfield Star') × ('Chieftain' × 'Better Times')]

'Fire Flame' F, or, 1958, Morse; flowers scarlet, center orange, 4 in., single; moderate growth

Fire Fox™ -- See 'Navaho'

'Fire Impact' F, or, Hiroshima; intr. 2006

'Fire King' F, or, 1959, Meilland; bud ovoid; flowers fiery scarlet, 2½ in., 48 petals, high-centered, borne in clusters, moderate musk fragrance; foliage dark, leathery; vigorous, upright, bushy growth; PP1758; [Moulin Rouge® × 'Fashion']; intr. 1958

'Fire King' HT, or, Meilland; flowers geranium red, dbl.; PP11748; greenhouse rose; intr. 1999

'Fire Magic' -- See 'Korber'

Fire Meidiland™ S, mr, Meilland; bud conical, small; flowers fire engine red, 2½-3 in., 30 petals, cupped, opens flat, borne in small clusters; free-flowering; foliage medium size, dark green, glossy; prickles medium; growth mounding; groundcover; PP11583; [(Rote Max Graf® × 'Fiona') × Red Meidiland™]; intr. 1999

'Fire Opal' ('Fair Opal') F, or, 1959, Boerner; bud ovoid; flowers reddish orange-scarlet, reverse lighter, medium, 20-25 petals, cupped, borne in clusters, moderate fragrance; foliage glossy; vigorous, open growth; ['Goldilocks' × orange Polyantha]; intr. 1954

'Fire Pillar' -- See 'Bischofsstadt Paderborn'

'Fire Princess' Min, or, 1969, Moore, Ralph S.; flowers small, dbl.; foliage small, glossy, leathery; vigorous, bushy growth; PP3084; [Baccará® × 'Eleanor']

'Fire Queen' F, dr, 1967, VonAbrams; bud ovoid; flowers bright red, medium, dbl., borne in clusters; foliage dark, glossy; vigorous, bushy growth; ['Fusilier' × ('Carrousel' × 'Queen o' the Lakes')]; intr. 1963

'Fire-Rider' -- See 'Feuerreiter'

'Fire Robe' Gr, rb

'Fire Signal' -- See 'Signalfeuer'

'Fire Sky' HT, mr, 1952, Silva; bud long, pointed; flowers large, cupped; foliage dark, glossy; vigorous growth; ['Gen. MacArthur' × 'Étoile de Hollande']

Fire Star® (Firestar®) LCl, mr, Barni; flowers bright red, dbl., borne in clusters of 5-7, moderate fragrance; recurrent; rapid, tall (16-22 ft.) growth; intr. 1994

'Fire Storm' HT, yb, Kono, Y.; flowers yellow, edged red, petals reflexed, 14 cm., 20-25 petals, borne mostly solitary, slight fragrance; foliage semmi-glossy; growth vigorous, upright; ['Christian Dior' × 'Garden Party']; intr. 1974

'Fireball' Pol, or, 1931, deRuiter; flowers glowing reddish-orange; foliage dark, glossy

'Fireball' HT, ob, Tantau; flowers salmon-orange to vermilion, large, dbl., well formed; intr. 1994

'Firebeam' F, rb, 1960, Fryers Nursery, Ltd.; flowers yellow, flame, orange and crimson, 2½ in., 14 petals, borne in clusters; foliage glossy; vigorous growth; ['Masquerade' × seedling]

'Firebird' F, ob, 1960, Watkins Roses; flowers bright orange, base golden yellow, 2½-3 in., 12-18 petals, borne in clusters; foliage glossy, light green; vigorous, upright growth; RULED EXTINCT 4/92; ['Masquerade' × 'Mme Henri Guillot']

Firebird® HT, rb, Kordes; flowers bright red and yellow blend, medium, full, cupped, borne moslty singly; recurrent; stems long; florist rose; intr. 2005

'Firebrand' HP, mr, 1874, Labruyère/Paul, W.; flowers bright crimson, sometimes shaded maroon, very large, full

'Firebrand' HT, or, Cant, B. R.; flowers bright scarlet; [sport of 'Flamingo']; intr. 1938

'Firebrand, Climbing' Cl HT, or, 1953, Raffel

'Fireburst' -- See 'Tworight'

'Firecracker' F, mr, 1956, Boerner; flowers scarlet, base yellow, 4½ in., 14 petals, borne in clusters, moderate fragrance; foliage leathery, light green; dwarf, bushy growth; PP1629; [('Pinocchio' × unknown) × ('Numa Fay' × unknown)]; intr. 1956

'Firecracker' S, mr, Lim, P, & Twomey, J.; flowers bright red, 3 in., single; recurrent; foliage medium green; growth compact (2 ft.), upright; PP15737; intr. 2004

'Firecrest' F, mr, 1964, LeGrice; flowers 3 in., 35 petals, borne in clusters; vigorous, low growth; PP2856; [('Cinnabar' × 'Marjorie LeGrice') × 'Pimpernell']

'Firecrest, Climbing' Cl F, mr, 1969, LeGrice; intr. 1969

'Firedance' -- See 'Judfire'

'Firedragon' HT, mr, 1923, Clark, A.; flowers fiery red, dbl.

'Firefall' Cl Min, dr, 1979, Moore, Ralph S.; bud short; flowers 1½ in., 43 petals, flat, borne in clusters; foliage small, glossy; trailing, arching growth; PP4717; [Dortmund® × 'Little Chief']; intr. 1980

Firefighter™ -- See 'Oradal'

'Fireflame' F, mr, 1954, Boerner; bud ovoid; flowers carmine, 2½-3 in., 65-70 petals, borne in pyramidal clusters, moderate fragrance; vigorous growth; PP1379; ['Chatter' × 'Red Pinocchio']; intr. 1954

'Fireflash' HT, yb, 1960, LeGrice; flowers golden yellow splashed scarlet, well-formed, 4½ in., 25-30 petals; foliage glossy; upright growth; ['Marjorie LeGrice' × seedling]

'Firefly' F, yb, 1978, Joliffe; bud slightly pointed; flowers medium yellow, large, 22 petals, cupped, slight fragrance; foliage dark; upright growth; [sport of 'Contempo']

'Firefly' -- See 'Macfrabro'

'Firefly' -- See 'Holstein'

'Fireglow' Pol, or, 1929, Wezelenburg; flowers brilliant vermilion-red, shaded orange, single, borne in clusters; dwarf, compact growth; [sport of 'Orange King']

'Fireglow, Climbing' Cl Pol, or, 1950, Guillot, M.

'Firelight' HT, or, 1971, Kordes, R.; flowers large, dbl., high-centered, moderate fragrance; foliage large, light, leathery; vigorous, upright growth; PP3078; ['Detroiter' × 'Orange Delbard']

'Fireside' HT, yb, 1977, Lindquist; bud ovoid; flowers yellow, white, red, imbricated, 5½-6 in., 35 petals, slight fragrance; foliage large, glossy, dark; vigorous, bushy growth; PP4283; ['Kordes' Perfecta' × 'Belle Blonde']

Firestar® -- See 'Selbar 0152'

'Firestorm' Min, mr, Pearce; intr. 2001

'Firestorm' -- See 'Clefire'

'Firetail' Cl Min, rb, Peden, G.H.

'Fireworks' MinFl, rb, Delbard; flowers red with white stripes and streaks, dbl.; intr. 2005

'Fireworks, Climbing' -- See 'Feu d'Artifice'

'Fireworks' -- See 'Magneet'

Fireworks™ -- See 'Savafire'

'Firlefanz' S, yb, GPG Bad Langensalza; flowers golden yellow plus carmine-red, medium, dbl.; intr. 1968

'Firmament' HT, dr, 1978, Gaujard; flowers vermilion-crimson, large, dbl.; foliage bronze; ['Chrysler Imperial' × 'Credo']; intr. 1971

'Firminio Huet' HT, dr, 1909, Soupert & Notting; flowers fiery dark carmine red, large, full, globular; ['American Beauty' × 'Richmond']

First™ -- See 'Poulrang'

'First Affair' -- See 'Jacvoo'

'First Blush' Pol, mp, 1967, Delbard-Chabert; flowers phlox-pink, 3 in., cupped, borne in clusters; intermittent bloom; foliage dull, light green; moderate growth; ['Francais' × 'Orléans Rose']; intr. 1965

'First Blush' -- See 'Meizincaro'

'First Born' -- See 'Gilfleur'

'First Choice' F, or, 1959, Morse; flowers fiery orange-scarlet, center yellow, in trusses, 5 in., 7 petals, moderate fragrance; tall, spreading growth; ['Masquerade' × 'Sultane']; intr. 1958

'First Choice' -- See 'Welchoice 0377'

'First Class' Gr, w, Certified; flowers large, pure white; intr. 1993

'First Class' HT, ab; intr. 2004

'First Class' -- See 'Jacare'

'First Edition' (Arnaud Delbard®) F, op, 1976, Delbard; bud ovoid, pointed; flowers luminous coral, shaded orange, 2-2½ in., 28 petals, slight tea fragrance; foliage glossy, light; upright growth; PP3647; [(Zambra® × ('Orléans Rose' × 'Goldilocks')) × ((Orange Triumph® × unknown) × 'Floradora')]

First Edition® HT, or, Select; flowers 9 cm., 40 petals, pompon; greenhouse rose; intr. 2003

'First Enterprise' Gr, mr, Williams, J.B.; flowers large, deep pink to brilliant red, ruffled and quilled, very dbl., old fashioned; foliage clean; intr. 2003

'First Federal' HT, pb, 1964, Boerner; bud ovoid; flowers geranium-pink tinted scarlet, 5-5½ in., 35-40 petals, high-centered, intense rose geranium fragrance; strong stems; vigorous, upright growth; PP2402; [('Radiance' × 'Pageant') × ('Diamond Jubilee' × unknown)]; intr. 1963

'First Federal Gold' HT, dy, 1967, Boerner; bud ovoid; flowers gold and yellow, large, dbl., high-centered, moderate fragrance; foliage glossy, leathery; vigorous, upright growth; PP2729; [('Golden Masterpiece' × unknown) × ('Golden Masterpiece' × unknown)]

'First Federal's Renaissance' HT, mp, 1979, Warriner, William A.; bud long, pointed; flowers medium pink, tinted lighter, 5-7 in., 23 petals, slight fragrance; very early bloom; foliage large; compact growth; PP4459; [seedling × 'First Prize']; intr. 1980

'First Flight' -- See 'Perflight'

'First Gold' ('Isabel', Satin Touch™) HT, dy, Kordes; buds elongated, sharply pointed; flowers large, strong yellow, petals curl into points, dbl., high-centered, star-shaped, slight spicy fragrance; recurrent; foliage glossy green; no prickles on stems; stems long; vigorous, medium growth

'First Great Western' -- See 'Muriel Robin'

'First Hit' (First™) Min, or, Poulsen; flowers bright orange-red, medium, dbl., slight wild rose fragrance; recurrent; foliage dark; growth bushy, 40-60 cm.; intr. 1995

'First Kiss' -- See 'Jacling'

'First Lady' HT, dp, 1961, Swim, H.C.; bud ovoid; flowers rose madder to phlox-pink, 3½-4½ in., 18-22 petals, cupped, slight fragrance; foliage leathery, dark, semi-glossy; very vigorous, upright growth; PP1893; ['First Love' × 'Roundelay']; intr. 1961

'First Lady, Climbing' Cl HT, dp, 1964, Burr, C.R.

'First Lady' HT, pb, Tantau; flowers deep pink with lighter reverse, 8 cm., very full, cupped; recurrent; vigorous (4-5 ft.), large, broad growth, arching canes; intr. 2006

'First Lady' -- See 'Tanrif'

'First Lady Nancy' ('Aronance') HT, yb, 1981, Swim, H.C. & Christensen, J.E.; bud ovoid, long, pointed; flowers light yellow tinged light pink, 36 petals, formal, spiraled, borne singly, slight tea fragrance; foliage semi-glossy, medium; prickles medium; medium, upright, bushy growth; PP5295; [American Heritage® × 'First Prize']

'First Light' -- See 'Devrudi'

'First Love' ('Premier Amour') HT, lp, 1951, Swim, H.C.; bud long, pointed; flowers 2½-3½ in., 25 petals, slight fragrance; foliage leathery, light green; moderately bushy growth; PP921; ['Charlotte Armstrong' × 'Show Girl']

'First National Gold'   Min, dy, 1978, Saville, F. Harmon; bud pointed; flowers 1-1½ in., 38-42 petals, high-centered, slight fragrance; foliage small; compact, upright growth; ['Rise 'n' Shine' × 'Yellow Jewel']; intr. 1976

'First National Silver'   Min, w, 1978, Saville, F. Harmon; bud ovate; flowers very dbl., 50-55 petals, flat, slight fragrance; foliage small, very glossy; compact, spreading growth; ['Charlie McCarthy' × 'Little Chief']

'First Offering'   F, dr, 1976, Viraraghavan, M.S. Viru; bud ovoid; flowers 2½ in., 15 petals, globular, open, moderate fragrance; profuse, very lasting bloom; foliage large, glossy, bronze, reddish brown when young; vigorous, dwarf, bushy growth; [seedling × 'Samba']; intr. 1975

'First Prize'   HT, pb, 1970, Boerner; bud long, pointed; flowers rose-pink, center blended with old ivory, 5½-6 in., 25-30 petals, high-centered, borne singly, moderate tea fragrance; foliage large, dark green, leathery; long, stout stems; vigorous, upright growth; PP2774; [(Enchantment × unknown) × ('Golden Masterpiece' × unknown)]

'First Prize, Climbing'   Cl HT, pb, 1974, Reasoner; flowers magnolia pink, lighter at center, very large (up to 20 cm.), slight fragrance; very vigorous, climbing growth; PP3539; [sport of 'First Prize']; intr. 1976

First Red® -- See 'Pekcoujenny'

'First Rose Convention'   HT, dr, 1980, Hardikar, Dr. M.N.; bud globular; flowers dark crimson, 48 petals, cupped, borne singly, no fragrance; foliage red when young, turning dark green; prickles hooked, pale cream; vigorous, upright growth; ['Flaming Peace' × 'Helen Traubel']; intr. 1978

'Firstar' -- See 'Jacary'

'Fisher & Holmes' -- See 'Fisher Holmes'

'Fisher Holmes' ('Fisher & Holmes') HP, dr, 1865, Verdier, E.; bud long, pointed; flowers deep red, well-formed, large, 30 petals; recurrent bloom; upright growth; [probably 'Maurice Bernardin' seedling]

Fisherman's Friend® -- See 'Auschild'

'Fishpond Pebbles'   S, w, Kordes; flowers off-white, borne in tight clusters, no fragrance; foliage deep green, glossy; vigorous, speading (3 × 6 ft.) growth; intr. 2001

'Fismelody'   Min, ab, Fischer; intr. 1998

'Fitzhugh's Diamond' -- See 'Welhugh's'

'Five-Colored Rose' -- See 'Fortune's Five-colored Rose'

'Five-Roses Rose' -- See 'Jacopper'

'Flag of the Union'   T, pb, before 1882, Hallock & Thorpe; [sport of 'Bon Silène']

'Flair'   HT, op, 1951, Verschuren-Pechtold; bud ovoid; flowers coral-blush, 3½-4½ in., 30-35 petals, high-centered; vigorous growth; PP1038; ['Lady Sylvia' × seedling]

'Flair'   HT, rb, Cummings, Peter E.; bud pointed; flowers medium red to dark red, reverse lighter, medium, dbl., high-centered, borne singly, slight fragrance; foliage medium size, dark green, semi-glossy; prickles curved, hooked, reddish-brown, sparse; upright, medium growth; hips obovate, 1 in., green with red splotch; [Pristine® × 'Ink Spots']; intr. 1991

Flair™ ('Flair Parade') Min, op, Olesen; PP13109; not the same as Flair/Poulpar040, 2005; intr. 2000

'Flair' -- See 'Dicrelax'

Flair™ -- See 'Poulpar040(N)'

'Flair Parade' (Flair™) Min, mp, Poulsen; flowers medium pink, dbl., no fragrance; foliage dark; growth bushy, 20-40 cm.; not the same as Flair/Poulra003, 2000; intr. 2005

'Flair Parade' -- See 'Poulra003'

'Flamande' -- See 'Agathe Incarnata'

'Flambeau'   HT, mr, 1940, Nicolas; bud pointed; flowers crimson shaded scarlet, open, large, dbl.; foliage glossy; strong stems; vigorous, bushy, open growth; PP374; ['Royal Red' × 'Johanniszauber']

'Flambée'   F, or, 1954, Mallerin, C.; flowers medium, 25-30 petals, borne in clusters of 5-6; foliage reddish to bronze; upright, bushy growth

'Flambo'   HT, or, Kordes; intr. 1993

'Flamboyance' -- See 'Meinronsse'

'Flamboyant'   Pol, mr, 1931, Turbat; flowers bright scarlet, aging to crimson-carmine, large, dbl., borne in clusters; foliage glossy; dwarf growth

'Flamboyant'   F, mr, Croix, P.; flowers bright red; vigorous growth; ['Holstein' × 'Incendie']; intr. before 1965

'Flamboyante'   HGal, mr, before 1815, Descemet

'Flamboyante'   B, mr, Vivant-Faivre; flowers bright crimson, medium, full; intr. 1852

'Flamboyante'   HGal, m, Godefroy; flowers bluish dark purple, center crimson, small to medium, full; intr. about 1820

'Flame'   HMult, op, 1912, Turner; flowers bright salmon-pink, semi-dbl., borne in large clusters; foliage dark, glossy; very vigorous, compact growth; ['Crimson Rambler' × unknown]

Flame Bouquet™ -- See 'Lavfire'

'Flame Dance' -- See 'Korflata'

'Flame Dancer' -- See 'Hardancer'

Flame Meillandina®   Min, yb, Meilland; flowers yellow with carmine red on the outer petal edges, 4-5 cm., 70 petals; recurrent; compact, bushy (12 in.) growth; intr. 2006

'Flame of Fantasy' ('Derrich Gardner') HT, rb, J&P; flowers medium, dark velvet red with silver reverse; recurrent; healthy, medium growth; intr. 2001

'Flame of Fire'   HT, ob, 1917, McGredy; flowers orange-flame, open, large, dbl.; bushy growth

'Flame of Hope'   MinFl, mr; intr. 2007

'Flame of Love'   HT, mr, 1950, Hieatt; flowers single

'Flame of the East' -- See 'Plamya Vostoka'

'Flameburst'   F, dr, 1961, Brownell, H.C.; bud pointed; flowers crimson, center yellow, 2 in., single, borne in clusters, slight fragrance; foliage dark, glossy; very vigorous growth; PP2304; ['Nearly Wild' × 'hybrid tea seedling']

'Flameche'   F, or

'Flameglo'   Min, yb, 1982, Williams, Ernest D.; flowers deep yellow to orange-red, reverse deep yellow, small, dbl., slight fragrance; foliage small, dark, glossy; upright, bushy growth; PP5176; ['Starburst' × 'Over the Rainbow']; intr. 1981

Flamenco™ (Northern Lights™) LCl, mp, Poulsen; flowers medium pink, 10-15 cm., 25 petals, old-fashioned, no fragrance; foliage dark; growth bushy, 200-300 cm.; PP12468; intr. 1998

'Flamenco' ('Jacpetex') F, yb, Zary, Keith

'Flamenco'   F, lp, 1960, McGredy, Sam IV; flowers light salmon-pink, large, 21 petals, borne in clusters; foliage dark; ['Cinnabar' × 'Spartan']; intr. 1960

'Flamenco'   HT, yb; intr. 2004

'Flamendr'   HT, dp, Urban, J.; flowers large, dbl.; intr. 1969

'Flames 'n' Sparks' -- See 'Ludsporcoma'

'Flametta'   Min, mp

'Flamina'   F, my, 1964, Mondial Roses; bud pointed, flushed red; flowers golden yellow, large, dbl.; foliage clear green; very vigorous, upright, bushy growth; [('Faust' × 'Peace') × seedling]

'Flaminaire' ('Montagny') HT, ob, 1960, Dorieux; bud globular; flowers orange-flame, medium, semi-dbl.; foliage dark, glossy; vigorous, bushy growth; ['Eclipse' × 'Independence']; intr. 1960

Flaming™ MinFl, ob, Olesen; flowers dbl., borne mostly solitary, slight fragrance; foliage dark green, glossy; growth bushy, low (40-60 cm.); PP14390; intr. 2001

'Flaming Arrow'   F, or, 1965, Schwartz, Ernest W.; bud long, pointed; flowers bright orange-red, medium, dbl.; foliage glossy; vigorous, upright growth; ['Montezuma' × 'Nadine']; intr. 1965

'Flaming Beauty'   HT, rb, 1979, Winchel, Joseph F.; flowers yellow and red-orange, 4 in., 35 petals, high-centered, slight fragrance; foliage matte, green; bushy growth; PP4620; ['First Prize' × Piccadilly®]

'Flaming Heart' -- See 'Umsflame'

'Flaming June' ('Mrs A. Hudig') Pol, or, 1931, Cutbush; flowers bright orange-scarlet; vigorous growth

'Flaming Peace' -- See 'Kronenbourg'

'Flaming Potluck' -- See 'Lavflame'

'Flaming Rosamini' -- See 'Ruiflami'

'Flaming Ruby'   F, dr, 1963, Hennessey; flowers deep ruby-red, 3 in., 60 petals, borne in clusters; foliage dark, reddish green, small; vigorous growth; [(('Eva' × 'Eva') × 'Guinee') × 'Guinee']

Flaming Star® S, dr, Barni, V.; flowers flaming red, semi-dbl., borne in clusters; recurrent; foliage dark green, abundant; spreading, low (2 ft.) growth; intr. 1993

'Flaming Sunset' HT, ob, 1948, Eddie; flowers deep orange, reverse lighter; foliage light bronze; [sport of 'McGredy's Sunset']

'Flaming Sunset, Climbing' Cl HT, ob, 1956, Mattock

'Flaming Torch' F, op; intr. 1999

'Flamingo' HT, dp, 1929, Dickson, A.; flowers bright geranium-red to rosy cerise, dbl., high-centered, spiraled, intense fragrance; vigorous growth

'Flamingo' HRg, mp, Howard, F.H.; bud pointed; flowers rich pink, large, 5 petals, cupped, borne in clusters; recurrent bloom; foliage glossy, gray-green; vigorous (3 ft.) growth; [R. rugosa × 'White Wings']; intr. 1956

'Flamingo' F, mp, Buyl Frères; flowers rose; long, strong stems; very vigorous growth; intr. 1958

'Flamingo' F, op, Horstmann; bud long, pointed; flowers deep scarlet-pink, open, 30 petals, borne in clusters; vigorous, upright growth; intr. 1961

Flamingo™ MinFl, mp, Olesen; flowers dbl., 25-30 petals, borne mostly solitary, slight fragrance; foliage medium green, semi-glossy; growth bushy, low (40-60 cm.); intr. 1999

'Flamingo' HT, mp, Kordes; intr. 2002

Flamingo® -- See 'Korflüg'

'Flamingo' -- See 'Herfla'

'Flamingo Meidiland' ('Comtesse Jeanne de Flandre', 'Sandra Kim', 'Heidepark', 'Sandra') S, mp, Meilland; flowers medium, semi-dbl., borne in clusters, no fragrance; modest growth; intr. 1990

'Flamingo Queen' Gr, dp, 1973, Chan; flowers deep pink; [sport of Queen Elizabeth®]; intr. 1972

'Flammèche' F, ob, 1959, Combe; flowers bright orange, medium, dbl., borne in clusters, bushy, vigorous (2 ft.) growth

'Flammenmeer' -- See 'Poulsha'

'Flammenrose' HT, ob, 1921, Türke; bud striped orange and yellow; flowers bright orange-yellow, medium, 16 petals; ['Mrs Joseph Hill' × 'Mme Edouard Herriot']

'Flammenspiel' S, mp, 1975, Kordes; bud ovoid; flowers salmon-pink, dbl.; foliage large, leathery, dark; vigorous, upright growth; [Peer Gynt® × seedling]; intr. 1974

Flammentanz® ('Flame Dance') HEg, mr, 1955, Kordes' Söhne, W.; flowers crimson, 9 cm., dbl., cupped, borne in clusters, moderate fragrance; non-recurrent; foliage dark, leathery, matte; very vigorous (10-15 ft.) growth; [R. rubiginosa hybrid × R. × kordesii]

'Flammentour' S, mr, Meilland

'Flammette' -- See 'Crimson Gem'

'Flanders Field' -- See 'Horflan'

'Flandria' Pol, mr, 1966, Delforge; bud ovoid; flowers open, semi-dbl.; foliage dark, glossy; bushy growth

'Flapper' F, lp, 1998, Bennett, Frank David; flowers light pink, slightly curled petals, 3 in., 5-7 petals, borne in small clusters; foliage medium size, dark green, semi-glossy; prickles few, medium sized, straight; compact, medium (5 ft.) growth; [sport of 'Permanent Wave']

'Flare' HT, mr, Meilland; flowers light red; intr. 2006

'Flash' LCl, rb, 1938, Hatton; bud ovoid, yellow suffused scarlet; flowers orange-scarlet, reverse and center yellow, 4 in., dbl., cupped; long blooming season; foliage leathery, glossy, bronze; pillar (6-8 ft.), compact growth; PP396; ['Rosella (Cl HT)' × 'Margaret McGredy']

'Flash' F, ob, Barni; flowers brilliant coral-orange deepening to red-vermilion, 5-6 cm., dbl., high-centered, moderate fragrance; foliage medium size, bronze green; vigorous (2-3 ft.) growth; [Rita Levi Montalcini® × seedling]; intr. 2000

'Flash' -- See 'Rosemary Gandy'

'Flash' -- See 'Lenana'

Flash Baccara® HT, dp, Meilland; flowers hot fuchsia pink, full, high-centered, greenhouse rose; intr. 2004

'Flash Back' ('Orchid Splendour') HT, m, Tantau; flowers dark mauve, double, cupped, moderate fragrance; growth medium height

'Flash Meidiland' -- See 'Meistocko'

'Flashback' HT, pb, Kordes; flowers pink and cream blend, large, full, high-centered, borne mostly singly; recurrent; stems long; florist rose; intr. 2005

Flashdance™ LCl, dy, Poulsen; flowers deep yellow, small, 25 petals, slight wild rose fragrance; foliage dark; growth broad, bushy, 150-200 cm.; PP15502; intr. 2002

'Flashdance' -- See 'Poulflash'

'Flashfire' -- See 'Leefir'

Flashlight® S, mp, Noack; flowers bright pink, outer petals fading lighter, 4 in., full, cupped, borne in clusters, slight fragrance; recurrent; foliage light green; loosely upright (4 ft.) growth; intr. 2007

'Flashlight' F, or, 1976, LeGrice; flowers orange-scarlet, 3-3½ in., 28 petals, moderate fragrance; foliage large, bronze; tall growth; ['Vesper' × seedling]; intr. 1974

'Flashlight' S, or, Bell; flowers cerise-orange-red; free-flowering; spreading, groundcover growth; intr. 2001

'Flauce' HT, rb

'Flavescens' HSpn, ly; flowers pale lemon, rounded; very hardy

'Flavescens' -- See 'Parks' Yellow Tea-Scented China'

'Flavia' HGal, about 1810, Descemet

'Flavia' HCh, dr, Laffay; flowers dark cherry red, medium, full; intr. about 1825

'Flavia' -- See 'Interette'

'Flavien Budillon' T, lp, 1885, Nabonnand; flowers pale flesh, large, globular, intense fragrance; very remontant

Flawless™ -- See 'Benrye'

'Fleet Street' HT, dp, 1973, McGredy, Sam IV; flowers deep rose pink, well-formed, 6 in., 40 petals, intense fragrance; foliage large, dark, leathery; ['Flaming Peace' × 'Prima Ballerina']; intr. 1972

'Fleetwood' F, ob, 1990, Bridges, Dennis A.; bud pointed; flowers bright orange, reverse lighter, aging darker on outer petals, 32 petals, high-centered, slight fruity fragrance; foliage medium size, dark green, glossy; prickles straight, medium pink; bushy, medium, vigorous growth; ['Little Darling' × Orangeade®]; intr. 1990

'Flemington ' ('Flemington Racecourse') F, dp, 2007, Chapman, Bruce; flowers 7 cm., dbl., blooms borne in small clusters; foliage medium size, dark green, glossy; prickles small, hooked, brown, few; growth upright, medium (1¼ m.); garden decoration; ['First Prize' × Sexy Rexy®]; intr. 2007

'Flemington Racecourse' -- See 'Flemington'

'Flesh-Coloured Noisette' -- See 'Blush Noisette'

'Flesh Taito' F, ob, 1988, Kikuchi, Rikichi; flowers yellow at base to vermilion, reverse orange flushed with pink, 25-30 petals, cupped; foliage medium size, dark green, undulated; prickles ordinary, green; bushy, medium growth; ['Masquerade' × 'Matador']; intr. 1989

'Fleur Cowles' F, ly, 1972, Gregory; flowers cream, center buff, 3 in., 35 petals, moderate spicy fragrance; foliage glossy, dark; ['Pink Parfait' × unknown]

'Fleur d'Amour' S, ab, Austin, David; intr. 1998

'Fleur de France' HT, my, 1944, Gaujard; flowers capucine and yellow, medium, semi-dbl., globular; foliage glossy; vigorous, dwarf growth

'Fleur de Pelletier' ('Agathe de Pelletier', 'Rose de Pelletier', 'Pelletier', 'Léandre') HGal, dp, before 1824, Pelletier; flowers cherry edged slatey red, medium, very dbl.

'Fleur de Vénus' Ch, w, before 1813, Descemet; flowers flesh white, center light carmine, medium, full, globular; sometimes attributed to Laffay, 1835

Fleurette® -- See 'Interette'

'Fleurette' -- See 'Calypso'

Fleurop® -- See 'Kortexung'

'Flicker' F, ab

'Fliegerheld Boelcke' HT, my, 1920, Schmidt, J.C.; flowers nankeen yellow, shaded reddish-yellow; ['Mme Caroline Testout' × 'Sunburst']

'Fliegerheld Öhring' HT, or, 1919, Kiese; flowers red-orange, medium, dbl.

'Flighty' F, m, 1969, Trew, C.; bud cherry-red; flowers light mauve, medium, semi-dbl., borne in trusses; foliage dark;

free growth; [Orangeade® × 'Sterling Silver']
'Flimo' F, lp, Poulsen; intr. 1990
'Flinders' -- See 'Tomfair'
'Flip Flop' -- See 'Briflip'
'Flipper' HT, or, 1978, Gaujard; bud long, pointed; flowers large; foliage large; [Tanagra® × 'John S. Armstrong']; intr. 1973
'Flirt' F, mr, 1952, Brownell; bud pointed; flowers bright cherry-red, reverse yellow, medium, 35-40 petals, borne in clusters, moderate fragrance; foliage glossy, dark; vigorous, upright growth; PP1122; ['Pink Princess' × 'Shades of Autumn']
'Flirt' F, dp, Kordes/Koopmann; flowers bright, hot pink, semi-dbl., shallow cup, borne in large clusters; recurrent; foliage dark green, glossy; medium (100 cm.) growth; [sport of 'Sommerwind']; discovered by local grower Koopmann, who brought it to Kordes; intr. 2000
'Flirt' -- See 'Korvondra'
'Flirt Kordana' Min, mp, Kordes; flowers dbl., rosette; container rose; intr. 2000
'Flirtation' HT, pb, 1953, Shepherd; bud pointed; flowers begonia-rose, reverse lemon to deep yellow, 5-6 in., 30 petals, high-centered, moderate fragrance; foliage dark, leathery; strong stems; vigorous, bushy, compact growth; PP1373; ['Fiesta' × 'Peace']
Flirtatious™ -- See 'Jactwist'
Flirting™ -- See 'Poulac011(N)'
'Flirting Palace' (Flirting™) MinFl, mr, Olesen; bud pointed-ovoid with broadened base; flowers 2 in., full, shallow cup, borne in clusters, slight fragrance; recurrent; foliage dark green, glossy; prickles numerous, 8 mm., concave; bushy, compact (40-60 cm.) growth; PP15821; intr. 2003
'Floating Candle' HT, ob, Williams, J. B.; flowers orange with peach and gold undertones at petal base, semi-dbl. , cupped to flat, moderate fragrance; recurrent; growth to 4 ft.; intr. 2006
'Floating Cloud' -- See 'Ukigumo'
'Flocon de Neige' ('Snowflake') Ch, w, 1898, Lille; flowers pure white, small, very full, borne in large pyramidal clusters; recurrent; growth to 2 ft.; sometimes classed as Pol; possibly ['Clothilde Soupert' × 'Pâquerette']
'Floello' ('Hello There') Min, w, 1987, Florac, Marilyn; flowers white, light yellow tints in center, good petal retention, small, 108 petals, cupped, borne usually singly, no fragrance; foliage small, medium green, matte; prickles tan, very few; bushy, low growth; ['Care Deeply' × 'Red Can Can']
'Flohih' ('High Hope') Min, or, 1985, Florac, Marilyn; flowers bright orange-red, small, 45 petals, cupped, borne singly and in clusters; foliage medium size, light, glossy; vigorous, upright growth; ['Young Love' × 'Little Chief']; intr. 1984
'Flomor' ('Country Morning') Min, yb, 1986, Florac, Marilyn; flowers light yellow, blended pink, dbl., high-centered, borne singly, moderate spicy fragrance; foliage medium size, medium green, semi-glossy; prickles small, reddish; medium, upright growth; ['Avandel' × 'Young Love']
'Flomyst' ('Sweet Mystery') Min, ob, 1987, Florac, Marilyn; flowers deep orange fading to pink, medium, 90 petals, cupped, borne usually singly, moderate damask fragrance; foliage medium size, dark green, semi-glossy; prickles few, green; bushy, medium growth; ['Care Deeply' × 'Red Can Can']
'Flon' ('Gloire des Perpetuelles', 'La Mienne') D, mr, 1845, Vibert; flowers bright red; very free bloom, occasionally repeated
'Floper' ('Per Chance') Min, op, 1985, Florac, Marilyn; flowers orange-red fading bright pink, small, 5 petals, borne singly and in small clusters, moderate fragrance; foliage small, dark, matte; bushy growth; ['Red Can Can' × 'Care Deeply']
'Flor de Torino 61' HT, w, 1961, Moreira da Silva; flowers white edged violet-pink; ['Monte Carlo' × 'Michèle Meilland']
'Flora' HT, op, 1957, Maarse, G.; flowers pink tinted salmon, large, dbl., intense fragrance; vigorous, upright growth; ['Independence' × 'Charlotte Armstrong']
'Flora' -- See 'Flore'
'Flora Bama' -- See 'Talflora'
Flora Danica™ -- See 'Poulrim'
'Flora MacLeod' LCl, lp, 1971, MacLeod; flowers pale rose-pink, 4½ in., 50 petals, intense fragrance; non-recurrent; foliage large, medium green, matte; vigorous growth; ['New Dawn' × 'Shot Silk, Climbing']
'Flora McIvor' HEg, pb, 1894, Penzance; flowers rosy pink, veined, white center, yellow stamens, small, single to semi-dbl.; summer bloom; foliage very fragrant (and flowers); vigorous growth; [R. rubiginosa × hybrid perpetual or bourbon]
'Flora Mitten' -- See 'Miss Flora Mitten'
Flora Romantica® -- See 'Meichavrin'
'Florabelle' F, op, 1964, Schwartz, Ernest W.; flowers soft salmon-pink, large, 33 petals, globular; foliage soft; vigorous, bushy growth; ['Ma Perkins' × seedling]
'Floradora, Climbing' Cl F, or, 1951, Shamburger, P.; PP1054
'Floradora' F, or, 1944, Tantau; bud globular; flowers cinnabar-red, 2 in., 25 petals, cupped, borne in sprays of 6-12, slight fragrance; foliage leathery, glossy; upright, bushy growth; ['Baby Chateau' × R. roxburghii]
'Floral Choice' F, ab, Fryer, Gareth; intr. 1982
'Floral Dance' Cl HT, or, 1955, Homan; flowers orange-cerise; very vigorous, climbing growth; ['Souv de Mme Boullet, Climbing' × 'Crimson Glory']
Floral Fairy Tale™ -- See 'Kormamtiza'
'Floralie' T, w, 1838, Coquereau; flowers flesh white, medium, cupped
'Floralies Valenciennoises' LCl, mr, 1955, Dorieux; bud long, pointed; flowers currant-red, large, semi-dbl.; vigorous growth; ['Matador' × 'Soliel d'Orient']
'Floranje' F, or; flowers 3 in., 23 petals, flat; foliage dense dark green; strong grower growth; [R. fedtschenkoana × Burghausen®]; intr. 1990
'Floranne' Min, my, 1996, Pratt, Florence; flowers medium yellow, fades in sun to white, color better in partial shade, large, single; foliage medium size, medium green, semi-glossy; some prickles; upright (30 cm.) growth; [sport of 'Crazy Dottie']
'Flore' ('Flora') HSem, m, about 1830, Jacques; bud crimson; flowers lilac-pink, center deeper, 6-7 cm., dbl., semi-globular, borne in small, loose clusters, moderate musk fragrance; seasonal bloom; [(R. sempervirens × R. arvensis) × 'Parson's Pink']
'Flore Berthelot' Pol, my, 1921, Turbat; flowers clear lemon-yellow, passing to white, borne in clusters
'Flore Magno' -- See 'Foliacée'
'Flore Pallido' -- See 'Vilmorin'
'Flore Pleno' -- See 'Plena'
'Floréal' HT, op, Gaujard; bud pointed; flowers coral-pink tinted yellow, medium, dbl., cupped, moderate fragrance; foliage dark, glossy; vigorous growth; intr. 1944
'Floréal' Pol, pb, 1923, Turbat; flowers flesh and rose-pink, dbl., slight fragrance; ['Orléans Rose' × 'Yvonne Rabier']
'Florence' HT, w, Dorieux; bud long; flowers pure white, large; intr. 1961
'Florence' HT, lp, 1921, Paul, W.; flowers silvery pink
'Florence' -- See 'Kornagent'
'Florence Arthaud' F, op, Adam; intr. 2003
'Florence Chenoweth' ('Yellow Herriot') HT, yb, 1918, Chenoweth; flowers yellow, shaded coral-red; [sport of 'Mme Edouard Herriot']
'Florence Daley' -- See 'Worclementine'
'Florence Delattre' -- See 'Masflodel'
'Florence Ducher' B, mp, Ducher; flowers clear pink, large, dbl., pompon, moderate fragrance; recurrent; growth to 10 ft.; intr. 2005
'Florence Edith Coulthwaite' HT, ly, 1908, Dickson, A.; flowers deep cream, stippled with bright rose, large, dbl., moderate fragrance; foliage deep green, glossy
'Florence Edna' HT, lp, 1985, Owen, Fred; [sport of 'Princesse']
'Florence Ethel Read' -- See 'Worcupboard'
'Florence Forrester' HT, w, 1914, McGredy; flowers white tinged lemon, large, dbl.
'Florence Haswell Veitch' Cl HT, dr, 1911,

The Official Registry and Checklist — Rosa 221

Paul, W.; flowers bright scarlet, shaded black, large, dbl.; vigorous growth; ['Mme Emile Metz' × 'Victor Hugo']

'Florence L. Izzard'   HT, dy, 1923, McGredy; bud pointed; flowers bright deep golden yellow, large, dbl., high-centered; foliage dark, bronze, leathery, glossy; very vigorous, bushy growth

'Florence Lorraine'   F, ab, 1974, Middlebrooks; bud ovoid; flowers dark apricot, large, very dbl., high-centered; moderate fragrance; foliage glossy, dark, leathery, wrinkled; very vigorous, upright, bushy growth; ['Royal Highness' × ('Hawaii' × 'Helen Traubel')]; intr. 1973

'Florence Lydia'   S, ab, 1999, Jones, L.J.; flowers apricot with tint of pink, fading to cream, 2 in., borne in large clusters; foliage medium size, medium green, glossy; prickles moderate; upright, tall (6 ft.) growth; ['Burma Star' × 'Admiral Rodney']

'Florence Mary'   HT, dy, 1964, Morse; flowers deep yellow-ochre, well-formed, large; bushy growth; [sport of 'Doreen']

'Florence Mary Morse, Climbing'   Cl F, mr

'Florence Mary Morse'   F, mr, 1951, Kordes; flowers copper-scarlet, 3 in., 15 petals, borne in large trusses; foliage dark, glossy; ['Baby Chateau' × 'Magnifica']

'Florence Mayer'   HT, w, 1998, Singer, Steven; flowers white and pink blend, reverse white, 4-6 in., very dbl., high-centered, borne mostly singly; foliage medium size, medium green, semi-glossy; prickles moderate, large, hooked downward; upright, tall growth; exhibition; ['Great Scott' × 'Headliner']; intr. 1998

'Florence Nightingale' -- See 'Ganflo'

'Florence Paul'   HP, mr, 1886, Paul, W.; flowers scarlet-crimson, shaded with rose, petals recurved, large, full

'Florence Pemberton'   HT, w, 1903, Dickson, A.; flowers creamy white, suffused pink, large, dbl., high-centered; foliage rich green, leathery; vigorous growth

'Florence Rambler'   HWich, lp

'Florence Russ'   HT, Russ

'Florentia'   HT, ob, 1941, Giacomasso; flowers deep orange, well-shaped, large; vigorous, bushy, compact growth; ['Julien Potin' × seedling]

'Florentina'   F, pb, 1938, Leenders, M.; flowers hydrangea-pink, reverse rose-red, large, single; foliage leathery, dark; long stems; very vigorous growth; [seedling × 'Permanent Wave']

'Florentina'   (Kordes' Rose Florentina®) HT, dr, Kordes; bud large, long, pointed; flowers dark blood red, dbl., high-centered, moderate fragrance; foliage leathery, dark green; vigorous growth; ['Liebeszauber' × 'Brandenberg']; intr. 1973

'Florescence'   F, ob; flowers dbl., high-centered, moderate fragrance; foliage glossy

'Florescent Fuschia'   Gr, mr, 2001, Coiner, Jim; flowers medium red with white stripe on reverse, medium, dbl., borne in large clusters, no fragrance; foliage medium size, dark green, glossy; prickles small, angular, moderate; growth spreading, medium (40 in.); garden decorative; [seedling × seedling]; intr. 2001

'Florett'   F, op, GPG Bad Langensalza; flowers large, dbl.; intr. 1983

'Florex'   HT, op, 1927, Geiger; bud pointed; flowers deep coral-salmon, suffused orange-carmine, large, dbl., high-centered; foliage leathery, glossy, dark; long stems; very vigorous growth; ['Mme Butterfly' × 'Premier']

Flori®   F, ob

'Floriade'   Gr, ob, 1963, van der Schilden; bud urn shaped; flowers bright orange-scarlet, 4 in., dbl., high-centered to open; long, strong stems; vigorous growth; PP2109; [sport of 'Montezuma']; intr. 1963

'Florian' -- See 'Meilaur'

'Florian, Climbing' -- See 'Meilaursar'

'Floribunda'   Pol, lp, 1885, Dubreuil; flowers pale rose, medium, very dbl., borne in large clusters, moderate fragrance

'Floricel'   HT, or, 1957, Dot, Pedro; bud pointed; flowers red and salmon, large, 25 petals, high-centered; foliage dark, glossy; strong stems; upright, compact growth; ['Carito MacMahon' × 'Luis Brinas']

'Florida'   F, my, Select; intr. 2003

Florida® -- See 'Macamster'

'Florida' -- See 'Calypso'

'Florida International' -- See 'Foxflorin'

'Florida Red'   HT, mr, 1964, Hennessey; flowers rich red, 5 in., 60 petals; vigorous growth

'Florida Sun' -- See 'Gelfla'

'Florida von Scharbeutz'   F, ob, 1957, Kordes, R.; flowers orange-yellow shaded coppery, very large, dbl., high-centered, borne in large clusters; foliage dark, glossy; vigorous, bushy growth; ['Golden Scepter' × ('Munchen' × 'Peace')]

'Florimel'   F, mp, 1959, Fryers Nursery, Ltd.; flowers silvery pink to deep rose-pink, well-formed, borne in clusters; foliage glossy; vigorous growth; ['Pinocchio' × seedling]; intr. 1958

'Florinda Norman Thompson'   HT, pb, 1920, Dickson, A.; flowers delicate rose on lemon, base deeper, dbl.

'Florine'   HT, Gaujard; intr. 1981

Florita® -- See 'Barflor'

'Florizel'   HT, ab, RvS-Melle; flowers 36 petals, flat; growth strong

'Floron'   HT, ab, 1948, Camprubi, C.; flowers Indian yellow-orange, inside lighter, very large, dbl., high-centered, slight fragrance; upright growth; ['Comtesse Vandal' × 'Pilar Landecho']

'Florrie Joyce'   F, dp, Riethmuller; flowers cherry-pink, 43 petals, borne in large clusters; bushy growth; ['Gartendirektor Otto Linne' × 'Borderer']

'Flosar'   ('Fresh Start') Min, mp, 1986, Florac, Marilyn; flowers bright medium pink, dbl., globular, borne usually singly, no fragrance; foliage small, medium green, semi-glossy; prickles small, red; low, bushy growth; ['Avandel' × 'Little Chief']

'Flosof'   ('Soft Steps') Min, pb, 1986, Florac, Marilyn; flowers creamy, petal edges pink, medium, 33 petals, cupped, borne singly; foliage medium size, medium green, semi-glossy; prickles small, reddish; tall, upright growth; ['Avandel' × unknown]

'Flossie' -- See 'Horfloss'

'Flower Basket' -- See 'Seabasket'

'Flower Basket' -- See 'Hanakago'

Flower Carpet™   ('Blooming Carpet', Emera®, 'Emera Pavement', Heidetraum™, 'Pink Flower Carpet') S, dp, 1989, Noack, Werner; bud globular; flowers deep pink, reverse lighter, small, profuse, 15 petals, cupped, borne in sprays, slight fragrance; foliage small, dark green, glossy, disease-resistant; prickles crooked, dark; vigorous, hardy, low, spreading growth; hips globular, small, light red; PP7282; [Immensee® × 'Amanda']; intr. 1990

'Flower Carpet Blanc' -- See 'White Flower Carpet'

'Flower Carpet Gold' -- See 'Noalesa'

'Flower Carpet Red' -- See 'Noafeuer'

'Flower Carpet Yellow'   ('Flower Carpet Gold', 'Loredo', 'Suneva') S, dy, Noack; flowers bright yellow, 1½ in., dbl., loose, borne in clusters, slight fragrance; good repeat; upright (2 ft.) growth; PP13869; intr. 2003

'Flower Child' -- See 'Horflower'

'Flower Festival'   F, pb; intr. 2006

'Flower Garland' -- See 'Guirlande Fleurie'

Flower Girl™ -- See 'Fryyeoman'

'Flower Girl' -- See 'Sea Pearl'

'Flower Haze' -- See 'Hana-Gasumi'

'Flower of Fairfield'   ('Crimson Rambler Remontant', 'Immerblühender Crimson Rambler') HMult, mr, 1909, Ludorf; flowers bright crimson red, 3 cm., semi-dbl., no fragrance; sometimes recurrent bloom; [sport of 'Crimson Rambler']

'Flower-Of-The-Month'   HT, mp, Lone Star Nursery; bud large, long, pointed; flowers full, 35-40 petals, borne mostly singly, moderate fragrance; foliage dark green, glossy; growth very vigorous, upright, compact (3 ft.); [sport of 'Etoile de Hollande']; intr. 1963

'Flower Parasol' -- See 'Ehigasa'

'Flower Power'   ('Bluewunder', Blühwunder®, 'Ponderosa') F, mp, Kordes; flowers clear salmon-pink, medium, open, borne in clusters, intense sweet fragrance; continuous bloom; foliage bronzy green, turning dark green, glossy; neat, vigorous, rounded-off (5-6 ft.) growth; intr. 1995

'Flower Power' -- See 'Frycassia'

'Flower Show'   HT, rb, 1980, Bees; bud

ovoid, pointed; flowers scarlet, yellow reverse, 25 petals, borne 3-4 per cluster, moderate fragrance; foliage mid-green, semi-matte; prickles dark red; vigorous, upright growth; ['Fragrant Cloud' × 'Tropicana']

'Flower Show' -- See 'Ginger Rogers'

'Flower World' HT, or, 1979, Warriner, William A.; bud pointed, oval; flowers 4 in., 20-30 petals, high-centered; foliage dark, leathery; tall growth; PP4576; [Baccará® × 'South Seas']; intr. 1980

'Flowin' ('Pink Winks') Min, mp, 1987, Florac, Marilyn; flowers small, 13 petals, urn-shaped, borne usually singly, no fragrance; foliage small, medium green, matte; bushy, low growth; ['Baby Betsy McCall' × 'Red Can Can']

'Fluffly Ruffles' -- See 'Fluffy Ruffles'

'Fluffy' -- See 'Interflu'

'Fluffy Cloud' Pol, w, 2007, Tolmasoff, Jan & William; flowers 1¾ in., semi-dbl., borne in large clusters; foliage medium size, dark green, semi-glossy, disease-resistant; prickles small, dark red, moderate; growth bushy, short (20-24 in.); borders, containers, cutting; [unknown × unknown]; intr. 2004

'Fluffy Ruffles' ('Fluffly Ruffles') F, pb, 1935, H&S; flowers silver-pink, reverse deeper rose, semi-dbl., cupped, borne in clusters; foliage leathery; vigorous growth; ['Miss Rowena Thom' × seedling]

Fluorescent® -- See 'Delflori'

'Fluorette' F, or, 1979, Lens, Louis; bud pointed; flowers salmon-orange, 3-3½ in., 22 petals, cupped, slight fragrance; vigorous, upright, bushy growth; [('Panache' × 'Soprano') × 'Coloranja']; intr. 1971

'Flush o' Dawn' ('Blush o' Dawn') HT, lp, 1900, Walsh; flowers light pink changing to white, large, dbl.; vigorous, upright growth; ['Margaret Dickson' × 'Mme de Sombreuil']

Flushing Meadow® -- See 'Dornapa'

Flutterbye™ -- See 'Wekplasol'

Flying Colors™ -- See 'Savapaint'

'Flying Colours' LCl, dp, 1922, Clark, A.; flowers deep cherry pink, white at base, lighter reverse, large, single to semi-dbl.; foliage light, leathery, glossy; very vigorous, compact growth; ruled extinct ARA 1983; hybrid gigantea

'Flying Doctor' HT, or; intr. 2005

'Flying Tata' HT, dr, 1984, Hardikar, Dr. M.N.; bud ovoid; flowers 45 petals, high-centered, borne singly, moderate fragrance; foliage medium size, dark, glossy; vigorous, upright growth; ['Scarlet Knight' × 'Cynosure']; intr. 1983

Foc de Tabara™ F, mr, Wagner, S.; bud small, ovoid; flowers velvety red, 33 petals, cupped, slight fragrance; foliage medium green, leathery, glossy; ['Paprika' × 'Coup de Foudre']; intr. 1970

Focal Point™ -- See 'Benrave'

'Focus' ('Showtime') Gr, op, Noack, Werner; bud rounded, orange-red; flowers salmon-orange, 8-9 cm., dbl., high-centered; recurrent; foliage dark green, very glossy; upright, bushy (70 cm.) growth; intr. 1997

'Focus' -- See 'Lenpac'

'Foggy Day' -- See 'Jusfoggy'

'Foliacée' ('Caroline de Berri', 'Flore Magno', 'Centfeuilles Foliacée') C, mp, before 1808, from Holland; sepals foliaceous, lanceolate; flowers light rose, very large, dbl., globular, borne mostly solitary; often showing proliferation; sometimes attributed to Vibert, with a date of before 1836

'Folie de Bonaparte' D, mr, about 1810, from Belgium

'Folie d'Espagne' F, yb, 1965, Soenderhousen; flowers yellow, orange and scarlet, 2 in., 20 petals, flat, borne in clusters; foliage dark, glossy

'Folies-Bergère' HT, yb, 1948, Gaujard; flowers yellow shaded coppery, large, dbl.; foliage leathery, light green; very vigorous, erect growth; ['Souv. de Claudius Pernet' × seedling]

'Folio Courtisane' -- See 'Folle Courtisane'

'Folio Variegata' -- See R. × damascena versicolor

'Foljani' HT, ab, Herholdt; bud pointed, golden; intr. 1989

'Folk Dance' -- See 'Juddance'

'Folk Song' S, pb, 1964, Von Abrams; flowers light pink, reverse darker, medium, dbl.; recurrent bloom; foliage glossy; vigorous (3-4 ft.), compact growth

'Folkestone' F, dr, 1936, Archer; flowers semi-dbl., borne in clusters; foliage dark; bushy, spreading growth

Folklore® HT, ob, 1976, Kordes; bud long, pointed; flowers orange, reverse lighter, 4½ in., 44 petals, high-centered, intense fragrance; foliage glossy; very tall and vigorous, upright, bushy growth; ['Fragrant Cloud' × seedling]; intr. 1975

'Folksinger' S, yb, 1985, Buck, Dr. Griffith J.; flowers yellow flushed with dark peach, large, 28 petals, slightly cupped, borne in clusters of 1-15, moderate fragrance; repeat bloom; foliage leathery, glossy, coppery mid-green; prickles awl-like, tan; upright, bushy growth; hardy; ['Carefree Beauty' × 'Sunsprite']; intr. 1984

'Folle Courtisane' ('Folio Courtisane') HT, ly, Delbard, Georges; intr. 1996

'Folletto' F, or, Borgatti, G.; flowers semi-dbl.; intr. 1961

'Fond Memories' Min, ob, Kirkam; flowers ginger-orange, fading to pale apricot, dainty, dbl.; recurrent; foliage glossy; growth to 18 in.; intr. 1999

'Fond Memories' F, pb, McGredy; flowers pale pink, fading to white, edged with pink; medium growth; intr. 1999

'Fond Thoughts' -- See 'Kortensei'

'Fondant Cascade' F, mp, 1996, Bees; flowers mid-pink fading to pale pink, bright yellow stamens, 1½ in., 26 petals, borne in large clusters, slight fragrance; foliage medium size, medium green, glossy; some prickles; spreading, medium (20 in.) growth; patio, containers; intr. 1995

Fondly™ -- See 'Hilset'

'Fontaine' -- See 'Fountain'

'Fontaine Blue' -- See 'Delpous'

'Fontaine des Loups' HMult, w, Louette, I.; flowers small, white, borne in large clusters, moderate fragrance; non-remontant; large, rambler-type (13-17 ft.) growth; ['The Garland' × unknown]; intr. 2000

Fontainebleu® -- See 'Delpous'

'Fontana' -- See 'Brifont'

'Fontanelle' HT, my, 1927, E.G. Hill, Co.; flowers lemon-yellow, center gold, very large, dbl.; foliage leathery; vigorous growth; ['Souv. de Claudius Pernet' × 'Columbia']

'Fontanelle, Climbing' Cl HT, my, 1935, Johns

'Fontenelle' HGal, dr, before 1829, Trébucien; flowers dark wine-red to purple-pink, medium to large, full

'Fontenelle' HP, mr, Moreau et Robert; flowers bright carmine, dotted with red, very large, dbl., borne in clusters, intense fragrance; vigorous, growth; intr. 1877

'Fontenelle' -- See 'de Fontenelle'

Foolish Pleasure™ -- See 'Decsure'

'Fool's Gold' -- See 'Arogobi'

'Footloose' -- See 'Tanotax'

'For Ever Yours' S, mp, Gear; flowers medium pink, dbl., cupped; low, spreading (80 × 80 cm.) growth; intr. 2001

'For Keeps' Gr, lp, Hortico; bud light pink; flowers delicate pink with almost-white outer petals, slight fragrance; foliage clean, disease-resistant; intr. 2003

'For You' HT, mp, Teranishi; intr. 1997

'For You' F, w, 1999, Yasuda, Yuji; flowers white, deep pink on petal edge, 2½ in., 30 petals; foliage medium green; compact, low (75 cm.) growth; ['Majorca' × 'Sweet Memory']

'For You' -- See 'Para Ti'

'For You Dad' -- See 'Jondad'

'For You, With Love' F, op, Fryer; flowers soft orange, large, dbl., borne in clusters of several, moderate fragrance; good repeat; foliage dark green; neat, compact growth; intr. 2004

Forbidden™ -- See 'Minibid'

Fordham Rose™ -- See 'Wilford'

'Forest Fire' -- See 'Leofire'

'Forest Queen' F, dp; intr. 1997

'Forever' HT, dr, Armstrong; flowers non-fading crimson red, large; intr. 1978

'Forever Amber' F, ob, 1976, Bees; flowers golden amber, suffused fiery orange, 4 in., 15 petals, flat, intense fragrance; foliage dark, leathery; vigorous growth; ['Arthur Bell' × Elizabeth of Glamis®]; intr. 1975

'Forever Amber, Climbing' Cl F, ob; found at the Huntington Botanical Gardens

'Forever Eve' -- See 'Bossiljubnew'

'Forever Free' -- See 'Horbritesea'

'Forever Friends' -- See 'Horkedgeree'
'Forever Friends' -- See 'Meioffic'
'Forever, Michael Jon' Gr, mp, 2001, Jerabek, Paul; flowers medium pink with lighter edge, medium, very full, borne in small clusters, moderate fragrance; foliage medium size, medium green, semi-glossy; prickles 3/8 in., curved downwards, moderate; growth upright, medium (4 ft.); garden decorative, cutting; [unknown × unknown]; intr. 2004
'Forever Mine' -- See 'Renmine'
'Forever Royal' -- See 'Franmite'
'Forever Scarlet' HT, pb, 1986, Epperson, Richard G.; flowers deep pink, reverse lighter, large, 80 petals, high-centered, borne singly, moderate spicy fragrance; prickles bright red; tall, upright growth; globular fruit; ['Wini Edmunds' × Mister Lincoln®]; intr. 1976
'Forever Together' -- See 'Together Forever'
'Forever Yellow' F, dy, Barni; flowers intense, clear, yellow gold; fast, continuous rebloom; compact (40-60 cm.) growth; intr. 2004
'Forever Young' -- See 'Briyoung'
'Forever Young' -- See 'Burforyou'
'Forever Young' -- See 'Jacimgol'
'Forever Yours' ('Concorde') HT, dr, 1964, Jelly; bud long, pointed; flowers cardinal-red, 4-5 in., 38 petals, high-centered, moderate spicy fragrance; vigorous, upright growth; PP2443; ['Yuletide' × seedling]; intr. 1964
'Forever Zaidee' -- See 'Evefrenzy'
'Forevermore' -- See 'Lyofor'
'Forez Rose' F, mr, 1964, Croix, P.; flowers geranium-red, becoming old-rose, semi-dbl., borne in clusters; vigorous growth; ['Sumatra' × 'Antoine Noailly']
'Forget Me Not' HT, my, Cocker; flowers lemon yellow , double, high-centered, borne both singly and in clusters; recurrent; foliage dark green, very glossy; strong, upright (2 - 2.5 ft.) growth; ['Marguerite Anne' × Amber Queen®]; intr. 2008
'Forgotten Dreams' HT, mr, 1981, Bracegirdle, Derek T.; bud pointed; flowers cardinal red, 24 petals, borne singly and in trusses of 3-5; foliage medium green, semi-glossy; prickles straight, red-brown; vigorous, bushy growth; ['Fragrant Cloud' × 'Teneriffe']
'Formby Favourite' HT, or, Wright, R. & Sons; flowers orange-scarlet on golden yellow; [sport of 'McGredy's Sunset']; said to be identical with Flaming Sunset
'Formby Show' HT, mr, 1987, Dwight, Robert & Sons; flowers medium, full, slight fragrance; foliage medium size, dark green, semi-glossy; upright growth; ['Fragrant Cloud' × 'Elida']; intr. 1986
'Formosa' -- See 'Bourbon'
'Fornarina' HGal, dr, 1826, Vétillart; flowers blackish-purple, medium; color description from Rosetum Gallicum, Descemet, 1828

'Fornarina' HGal, pb, Vibert; flowers deep rose, marbled white, medium, full, cupped; intr. 1841
'Fornarina' M, dp, Moreau et Robert; flowers deep carmine-pink, medium, 6-8 cm., full, rosette, flat; some repeat; dwarf growth; intr. 1862
'Forst' HT, or, 1937, Krause; flowers fiery scarlet red, well-formed, very large; vigorous growth; ['Essence' × 'Fritz Schrodter']
'Forstmeisters Heim' HSet, mp, 1887, Geschwind, R.; flowers dark pink, tinted purple, silvery pink at center, reverse lighter, medium, dbl., borne in medium clusters, no fragrance; ['a Bourbon' × 'a Boursault']
'Forsythe' HT, dp, 1970, Verbeek; flowers Venetian pink, carmine-rose,, 4½-5 in., 45-50 petals, high-centered, intense fragrance; foliage glossy, dark, leathery; upright growth; PP3112; ['Miracle' × 'Dr. A. J. Verhage']
'Fort Knox' HT, dy, 1956, Howard, A. P.; bud ovoid; flowers clear yellow, 3½-4½ in., 20 petals, intense fragrance; foliage dark, leathery, vigorous, upright, open growth; PP1525; [seedling × 'Ville de Paris']; intr. 1956
'Fort Vancouver' HT, mp, 1957, Swim, H.C.; bud long, pointed; flowers well-formed, 5-6 in., 42 petals, intense damask fragrance; foliage leathery; vigorous growth; PP994; ['Charlotte Armstrong' × 'Times Square']; intr. 1956
Fortissima® -- See 'Lenabavi'
'Fortissimo' S, mr, GPG Bad Langensalza; flowers large, dbl.; intr. 1974
'Fortschritt' ('Progress') F, yb, 1933, Kordes; flowers yellow-pink, open, large, semi-dbl., borne in clusters, slight fragrance; foliage glossy, light; vigorous, bushy growth; ['Mrs Pierre S. duPont' × 'Gloria Mundi']
'Fortuna' ('The New Riviera Rose') T, ab, 1902, Paul, W.; flowers apricot, outer petals lightly tinted red, large
'Fortuna' HT, mp, Pemberton; flowers rose-pink becoming lighter, many golden anthers, 25 petals, moderate fruity fragrance; dwarf, bushy growth; ['Lady Pirrie' × 'Nur Mahal']; ruled extinct 1985 but exists at Roseto Fineschi; intr. 1927
Fortuna® -- See 'Kortuna'
Fortuna® -- See 'Koratomi'
'Fortuna Vigorosa' -- See 'Koratomi'
'Fortune' HT, yb, 1951, Watkins Roses; flowers gold shaded peach, 4 in., 60 petals; foliage glossy; vigorous growth; RULED EXTINCT 12/85; [sport of 'Phyllis Gold']
'Fortune' Gr, pb, 2008, Cavanaugh, Jim; flowers large, 4-5 in., full, borne in small clusters; foliage medium, medium green, semi-glossy; prickles medium, pointed, medium green, moderate; growth bushy, tall (5-6 ft.); garden decoration; [sport of 'Fame!']
'Fortuné Besson' -- See 'Georg Arends'
'Fortune Cookie' -- See 'Savacook'

'Fortune Teller' -- See 'Jacheir'
'Fortuneana' -- See 'Fortuniana'
'Fortunée Besson' -- See 'Mme Fortuné Besson'
Fortunella® Min, op, Barni, V.; flowers orange pink, dbl.; recurrent; growth to 30-35 cm.; intr. 1999
'Fortune's Double Yellow' ('Beauty of Glazenwood', R. odorata pseudindica, 'Wang-Jang-Ve', R. pseudindica, R. fortuniana, R. fortuneana, R. chinensis pseudindica, 'Gold of Ophir', 'San Rafael Rose') Misc OGR, yb, 1845; flowers salmon-yellow, outside tinged red, 7-8 cm., dbl., loose, borne in small clusters, moderate sweet fragrance; non-recurrent; discovered in a garden in Ningpo, China, by Robert Fortune; similar to the Noisettes in certain characteristics
'Fortune's Five-colored Rose' ('Five-Colored Rose', 'Smith's Parish') T, w, 1844, Fortune; bud red-tinged; flowers creamy white tinged with pale blush, fading to white, large, dbl.; foliage light green; vigorous growth
'Fortuniana' ('Double Cherokee', 'Épineux de la Chine', 'Fortuneana', 'La Chinoise', R. fortuneana, R. × fortuniana) Misc OGR, w, 1840; flowers blush white, 6 cm., dbl.; foliage dark green, glossy; prickles few, short, thick; climbing growth; [supposedly R. banksiae × R. laevigata]
'Forty Heroes' F, dy, Lim, Ping; flowers double, hybrid tea, borne in large clusters, slight fruity fragrance; recurrent; intr. 2008
'Forty-niner, Climbing' Cl HT, rb, 1952, Moffet; flowers crimson, reverse yellow, large; PP1094
'Forty-niner' HT, rb, 1949, Swim, H.C.; bud long, pointed; flowers medium red, reverse yellow, 3½-4 in., 33 petals; foliage leathery, glossy, dark; vigorous, upright, compact growth; PP792; ['Contrast' × 'Charlotte Armstrong']
'Forum' Pol, mr, 1969, Delforge; flowers bright red, open, large, dbl.; foliage light green, glossy; vigorous, upright growth; ['Veronique' × ('Independence' × unknown)]
Forum® HT, my, McGredy; intr. 2001
'Forward' HT, my, 1962, LeGrice; flowers clear primrose-yellow, large, dbl.; upright growth; ['Ethel Sanday' × 'Peace']
'Forward March' HT, mp, 1934, Wolfe; bud pointed, bright old-rose; flowers bright rose-pink, becoming lighter, large, dbl.; foliage dark, bronze, leathery, glossy; long stems; very vigorous, bushy growth; PP134; [sport of 'Better Times']
'Fosse Way' HT, mp, 1980, Langdale, G.W.T.; bud long; flowers rose pink, paler reverse, 38 petals, high-centered, borne singly and several to a cluster; foliage matte, light green; prickles hooked; vigorous, tall, upright growth; ['Colour Wonder' × 'Prima Ballerina']
'Foster's Melbourne Cup' -- See 'Mac-

mouhoo'

'Foster's Ruby Glow' -- See 'Webdesire'

'Foster's Wellington Cup' ('Christine Horbiger', 'Foster's Melbourne Cup', 'Mount Hood', 'Mt Hood') HT, w, 1989, McGredy, Sam IV; bud medium, ovoid; flowers creamy white, medium, 40-48 petals, borne in sprays of 6 - 10, moderate old rose fragrance; foliage large, medium green, semi-glossy; prickles medium, curved downward, wide at base; bushy growth; PP9095; [Sexy Rexy® × 'Pot O'Gold']; intr. 1991

'Foucheaux' ('Rose Foucheaux') HGal, mr, before 1846; flowers velvety carmine, medium, full

'Fouchin' ('Chinese Lantern') Min, rb, 1987, Jacobs, Betty A.; flowers handpainted red, yellow and white, reverse light pink, fading red and white, 15 petals, slight spicy fragrance; foliage medium size, medium green, red when young, glossy; bushy, spreading, medium growth; hips round, medium, red-orange; ['Avandel' × 'Old Master']; intr. 1986

'Foumad' (Summer Madness™) Min, my, 1987, Jacobs, Betty A.; flowers medium golden yellow, gold stamens, fading white, deeper in cool weather, petals reflexed, 20-25 petals, high-centered, slight fruity tea fragrance; foliage medium medium green matte; prickles long, red to light brown; bushy, medium growth; hips round, small, orange-red; [Party Girl™ × 'Sun Flare']

'Foumagic' (Winter Magic™) Min, m, 1986, Jacobs, Betty A.; flowers light lavender-gray, golden stamens, large, 30 petals, cupped, borne usually singly or in small sprays, moderate citrus tea fragrance; recurrent; foliage medium size, medium green, semi-glossy; prickles medium, slender, straight, red; medium, upright, bushy growth; hips medium, globular, orange-red; ['Rise 'n' Shine' × Blue Nile®]

'Foumande' ('Mandarin Delight') Min, ob, 1990, Jacobs, Betty A.; bud pointed; flowers soft, light mandarin orange, reverse lighter, aging peach in cooler weather, dbl., high-centered; foliage medium size, medium green, semi-glossy; prickles needle, medium, red to tan; bushy, medium growth; no fruit; [Party Girl™ × 'Gingersnap']; intr. 1989

'Foumich' ('Michel Cholet') Min, ab, 2000, Jacobs, Betty; flowers dark rich apricot, medium to large, dbl. to full, high-centered, borne singly or in small clusters, slight fragrance; foliage medium size, dark green, semi-glossy; few prickles; growth upright, bushy, medium (2½ ft.); ['Prima Donna' × 'San Jose Sunshine']; intr. 2001

'Foumouse' ('Church Mouse') Min, r, 1989, Jacobs, Betty A.; bud pointed; flowers tan-brown, with yellow at base, aging light lavender-brown, 20 petals, moderate sweet fragrance; foliage large, medium green, matte; prickles slightly declining, small, red to tan; low, bushy, compact growth; no fruit; ['Angel Face' × 'Plum Duffy']; intr. 1989

'Foundation' -- See 'Tanetidor'

'Founder's Dream' S, my, J. B. Williams; flowers bright yellow, medium, dbl., cabbage-like, moderate fragrance; recurrent; foliage dark green; growth to 4 ft.; intr. 2005

'Founder's Pride' -- See 'Micpride'

'Fountain' ('Fontaine', Red Prince®) HT, mr, 1971, Tantau, Math.; flowers crimson, 5 in., 35 petals, cupped, intense fragrance; foliage dark, glossy; intr. 1970

'Fountain of Beauty' HT, ab, 1975, Golik; bud ovoid; flowers creamy to salmon, 3-4 in., 100 petals; foliage leathery; moderate growth; [seedling × 'Colour Wonder']; intr. 1974

Fountain Square™ HT, w, 1985, Humenick, Muriel F.; flowers clear white, 5-5½ in., 25-30 petals, high-centered, borne singly; foliage large, dark green, semi-glossy; tall growth; PP6805; [sport of 'Pristine']; intr. 1986

'Four Cheers' HT, ob, 1989, Stoddard, Louis; bud ovoid; flowers soft orange with yellow center, medium, 30 petals, high-centered, urn-shaped, borne usually singly, slight fragrance; foliage medium size, medium green, glossy, smooth, leathery; prickles falcate, moderate, stout, maroon to ivory; spreading, medium growth; hips globular, medium, orange; ['Daisy Mae' × 'First Prize']

'Four Inch Heels' -- See 'Jasheels'

Fourth of July™ -- See 'Wekroalt'

'Fousun' ('San Jose Sunshine') Min, dy, 1991, Jacobs, Betty A.; bud pointed; flowers deep golden yellow, aging light yellow with orange highlights, medium, 25-30 petals, high-centered, borne usually singly or in sprays of up to 10, slight fruity to tea fragrance; foliage medium size, medium green, matte; bushy, spreading, medium to tall growth; [('Rise 'n' Shine' × 'Redgold') × Summer Madness™]; intr. 1991

'Foutell' ('Show 'n' Tell') Min, ob, 1988, Jacobs, Betty A.; bud long, pointed; flowers bright, velvety orange-red, white border, reverse white, 1¾ in., 25-30 petals, high-centered, borne singly and in loose sprays, slight spicy fragrance; free-flowering; foliage medium size, medium green, semi-glossy, disease-resistant; prickles moderate, light brown; stems slender, wiry; spreading, tall growth; hips ball-shaped, orange to russet; PP7375; ['Rocky™ × (Matangi® × 'Honey Hill')]

'Foutouch' ('Touch-Up') Min, pb, 1990, Jacobs, Betty A.; bud pointed; flowers medium pink with cream border, reverse cream, hand-painted, 30 petals, high-centered, moderate tea fragrance; foliage medium size, medium green, matte; prickles straight, large, red to tan; growth upright, bushy, tall; hips round, medium, russet-orange; ['Scarlet Knight' × (Matangi® × 'Honey Hill')]; intr. 1989

'Foutum' ('Autumn Magic') Min, ob, 1987, Jacobs, Betty A.; very long and feathery sepals; flowers bright golden-orange, with red at petal tips, reverse yellow, fading to red, 35 petals, high-centered; foliage medium size, dark green, semi-glossy; prickles very few; bushy, medium growth; no fruit; ['Confetti' × Anita Charles™]

'Foutwist' ('Lemon Twist') Min, dy, 1989, Jacobs, Betty A.; bud pointed; flowers medium, 25 petals, high-centered, borne usually singly and in sprays of up to 3, slight tea fragrance; foliage medium size, medium green, glossy; prickles slightly declining, long, red to brown; bushy, medium growth; PP7450; [Gold Badge™ × 'Great Day']

'Fox-Trot' -- See 'Tangust'

'Foxfire' HT, mr, 1990, Stoddard, Louis; bud pointed; flowers 30 petals, high-centered, borne singly; foliage medium size, medium green, glossy; prickles straight, green; upright, tall growth; [seedling × 'First Prize']; intr. 1991

'Foxflorin' ('Florida International') Min, ab, 1997, Fox, Tillie; flowers medium, 30-35 petals, high-centered, borne mostly singly; foliage medium size, medium green, semi-glossy; upright, spreading, medium to tall (1½-2 ft.) growth; exhibition; ['Pierrine' × (Loving Touch™ × seedling)]

'Foxi' -- See 'Uhlwe'

'Foxi Pavement' -- See 'Uhlwe'

'Foxtrot' -- See 'Brofox'

'Foxy' S, yb, Peden, R.

Foxy Lady™ -- See 'Aroshrim'

'Foxy Pavement' -- See 'Uhlwe'

'Fr. Lad. Rieger' HT, mr, 1939, Böhm, J.; flowers large, dbl.

'Fragezeichen' HWich, mp, 1910, Böttner; flowers shining pink, 8 cm., 25 petals, globular, borne in small clusters, no fragrance; foliage large, glossy; vigorous growth; very hardy; ['Dorothy Perkins' × 'Marie Baumann']

'Fragola' HT, mr, Croix, P.; intr. about 1980

'Fragrance' HT, dr, 1924, Chaplin Bros.; flowers deep crimson, high pointed, large, dbl., moderate fragrance; vigorous growth; ['Hoosier Beauty' × 'George Dickson']

'Fragrance' HT, dp, Lammerts, Dr. Walter; bud long, pointed; flowers carmine to rose-madder, large, dbl., high-centered, intense fragrance; foliage bronze, leathery; vigorous, tall, compact growth; PP2493; ['Charlotte Armstrong' × 'Merry Widow']; intr. 1964

'Fragrant Air' F, rb, 1977, Pearce, C.A.; flowers red changing to magenta-pink, 2½ in., 20 petals; foliage dark

'Fragrant Alizée' -- See 'Reflets de Saint Malo'

Fragrant Apricot™ -- See 'Jacgrant'

'Fragrant Beauty' S, dp, 1950, Jacobus; bud ovoid; flowers carmine, large, 22 petals, cupped, intense spicy fragrance; profuse, repeated bloom; foliage glossy; very vigorous (4-5 ft.), upright, compact growth; [('Pharisaer' × 'Conrad Ferdinand Meyer') × 'Crimson Glory']

'Fragrant Beauty' HT, mr, Ghosh; flowers large, bright scarlet crimson, well formed, moderate fragrance; intr. 1980

'Fragrant Bouquet' HT, lp, 1922, H&S; flowers shell-pink, base yellow, large, 30-35 petals, intense fragrance

'Fragrant Carpet' -- See 'Brocarp'

'Fragrant Charm' -- See 'Kordu'

'Fragrant Charm 84' -- See 'Korzaun'

'Fragrant Cloud, Climbing' ('Nuage Parfumé, Climbing') Cl HT, or, 1974, Collin, W.C.; flowers orange vermilion, large, strong fragrance; [sport of 'Fragrant Cloud']

'Fragrant Cloud' -- See 'Tanellis'

Fragrant Delight® (Wisbech Rose Fragrant Delight®) F, op, 1977, Wisbech Plant Co.; flowers light orange-salmon, reverse deeper, 3 in., 22 petals, intense fragrance; foliage glossy, reddish; ['Chanelle' × 'Whisky Mac']; intr. 1978

'Fragrant Dream' -- See 'Dicodour'

'Fragrant Dream' -- See 'Yumeka'

'Fragrant Fantasy' -- See 'Devfrago'

'Fragrant Glory' HT, dp, 1950, Cobley; bud dark red; flowers deep cyclamen-pink, 6 in., 36 petals, high-centered; strong stems; vigorous growth; ['Phyllis Gold' × 'Crimson Glory']

'Fragrant Gold' -- See 'Tanduft'

'Fragrant Hour' HT, op, 1973, McGredy, Sam IV; flowers bronze-pink, high-pointed, 4½ in., 35 petals, intense fragrance; foliage light; ['Arthur Bell' × ('Spartan' × 'Grand Gala')]

Fragrant Keepsake™ -- See 'Jacfrens'

Fragrant Lace™ -- See 'Jacsee'

'Fragrant Lady' HT, mp, 1991, Perry, Anthony; bud ovoid; flowers medium, semi-dbl., cupped, urn-shaped, borne usually singly, intense fruity fragrance; foliage medium size, dark green, semi-glossy; upright, medium growth; [Queen Elizabeth® × 'Broadway']; intr. 1991

'Fragrant Lady' -- See 'Meiniacin'

'Fragrant Lavendar' -- See 'Velvet Mist'

Fragrant Lavender Simplicity™ -- See 'Jacshlav'

Fragrant Love® HT, mr, 1981, Barni; bud globular, pointed; flowers medium purplish red, 45 petals, cupped, borne 1-3 per cluster, intense fragrance; foliage large, deep green, matte; prickles curved reddish; upright growth; ['Chrysler Imperial' × seedling]; intr. 1979

'Fragrant Masterpiece' S, lp, Clements, John; flowers blush pink, 4-5 in., 100 petals, intense sweet, fruity/lilac/rose fragrance; blooms continuously; 4 × 3 ft. growth; resembles 'Maiden's Blush', but larger; intr. 2002

'Fragrant Mauve' HT, m, Dey, S. C.; flowers large, purple, intense fragrance; intr. 1999

'Fragrant Memories' -- See 'Korpastato'

'Fragrant Memory' -- See 'Jacdis'

'Fragrant Minijet' Min, my, Meilland

'Fragrant Mist' -- See 'Smitsblanc'

'Fragrant Moon' MinFl, my, Rickard, Vernon; flowers medium yellow, lighter at the petal edges, 3 in., semi-dbl., moderate fragrance; foliage dark green, glossy; upright, tall (36 in.) growth; intr. 2005

'Fragrant Morning' -- See 'Renmorning'

'Fragrant Obsession' -- See 'Renfragobses'

'Fragrant Pink Talisman' HT, pb, 1938, Moore, Ralph S.; flowers pink shades, slightly larger than Talisman, 18 petals, intense fragrance; ['Talisman' × unknown]

'Fragrant Plum' Gr, m, Christensen, Jack E.; bud long, ovoid; flowers light lavender blushing purple, smoky edges, 4-4½ in., 20-25 petals, high-centered, borne singly and in large clusters, intense fruity fragrance; tall, upright growth; [Shocking Blue® × (Blue Nile® × ('Ivory Tower' × 'Angel Face'))]; intr. 1990

'Fragrant Queen' HT, op, Williams, J.B.; flowers coral pink, dbl., high-centered, intense fragrance; intr. 1995

Fragrant Rhapsody™ -- See 'Jactrig'

'Fragrant Spreader' -- See 'Scented Carpet'

'Fragrant Star' F, my, 1975, Northfield, G. H.; flowers , 25-30 petals, borne in trusses; foliage medium size, medium green, matte; growth upright; ['Masquerade' × 'Golden Scepter']; intr. 1973

'Fragrant Star' N, w, Tolmosoff; recurrent; 5 - 6 ft. growth; intr. 2005

'Fragrant Sunrise' -- See 'Hawaiian Fragrant Sunrise'

'Fragrant Surprise' -- See 'Harverag'

'Fragrant Treasure' -- See 'Koki'

'Fragrant Vision' -- See 'Beadick'

Fragrant Wave™ -- See 'Jaczeeze'

'Fraîcheur' -- See 'La Fraîcheur'

'Fraîcheur' HT, lp, 1942, Meilland, F.; bud long, pointed; flowers soft pink tinted pearl-white, medium, semi-dbl., cupped; foliage leathery, light green; vigorous, bushy growth; ['Joanna Hill' × unknown]

'Framak' ('Clarice Weston Flower Maker') HT, lp, 2006, Cowlishaw, Frank; flowers light pink, shaded fawn, reverse light pink and fawn blend, petal edges serrated, 3 in., dbl., borne mostly solitary; foliage medium size, medium green, semi-glossy; prickles up to 8mm., straight, green/brown, moderate; growth upright (2 ft.); garden decorative; [Alexander® × 'Forever Royal']; intr. 2008

'Franblue' F, m, Cowlishaw, Frank; intr. 1992

'Franburst' ('Uppingham School') HT, dy, 1999, Cowlishaw, Frank; flowers golden yellow, reverse yellow, 4 in., full, borne in large clusters; foliage medium size, dark green, glossy; prickles moderate; upright, medium (to 5 ft.) growth; ['Ann Harkness' × ('Diamond Jubilee' × 'Picadilly')]

'Franca' F, pb, 1961, Moreira da Silva; flowers pink and yellow; ['Confidence' × seedling]

'Français' F, op, 1951, Mallerin, C.; flowers bright pink tinted orange, semi-dbl., borne in clusters; vigorous growth; ['Holstein' × Orange Triumph®]

'France Bleu' F, m, Adam; intr. 2004

France de Berville® S, dp, Eve; flowers deep pink, single to semi-dbl., flat; non-recurrent; bushy, compact (5-6 ft.) growth; hips luminous red, already colored in July; intr. 2001

'France et Russie' HT, dp, 1900, Bégault-Pigné; flowers carmine pink, edged silver, large, very full; ['La France' × unknown]

'France Info' S, yb, Delbard; flowers yellow, bordered with carmine, very full, moderate fruity, spicy fragrance; vigorous (80 cm.) growth; intr. 2002

'France Inter' HT, mr, 1969, Delbard; flowers magenta-red, ovoid, 4-5 in., 35-45 petals; [('Rome Glory' × 'La Vaudoise') × 'Divine']

France Libre® -- See 'Deljaunor'

'Frances Ashton' HT, mp, 1937, DePuy; bud pointed; flowers carmine, stamens wine-colored, large, 5 petals; foliage leathery; vigorous growth; ['Lady Battersea' × 'Hawlmark Crimson']

'Frances Audrey' S, dr; intr. 2007

'Frances Bloxam' HP, op, 1892, Paul, G.; flowers salmon pink, medium, dbl.; sometimes classed as HCh

'Frances E. Willard' ('President Cleveland') T, w, 1899, Good & Reese; flowers white with greenish tints, camellia-like, large, moderate fragrance; growth tall, almost climbing; ['Marie Guillot' × 'Coquette de Lyon']

'Frances Gaunt' HT, ab, 1918, Dickson, A.; flowers apricot to salmon-yellow, large, semi-dbl., cupped; foliage glossy; vigorous, branching growth

'Frances Gaunt, Climbing' Cl HT, ab, 1934, Cazzaniga, F. G.

'Frances Louise' -- See 'Evefrandore'

'Frances Neale' HT, mr, 1994, Kirkham, Gordon Wilson; flowers medium red, moderately large, 3-3½ in., dbl., borne in small clusters; foliage large, dark green, semi-glossy; few prickles; low, bushy growth; ['Invincible' × 'Red Dandy']; intr. 1995

'Frances Perry' -- See 'Bosrexcity'

'Frances Phoebe' ('Francis Phoebe') HT, w, LeGrice; intr. 1979

'Francesca' HMsk, ab, 1922, Pemberton; flowers copper orange to apricot, medium, single to semi-dbl., borne in large sprays; recurrent bloom; foliage leathery; long stems; vigorous (5-6 ft.) growth; ['Danaë' × 'Sunburst']

'Francesca de Cuixart' -- See 'F. Cuixart'

'Francesch Matheu' HT, ob, 1940, Dot, Pedro; bud long, pointed; flowers rich golden orange, large, dbl., cupped; foliage glossy, dark; strong stems; very vigorous, upright growth; ['Luis Brinas' × 'Catalonia']

'Francesco Dona' -- See 'Himmelsauge'

'Francesco Ingegnoli' HMult, rb, 1888, Bernaix; flowers bright carmine red, edged white, semi-dbl.

'Francesco La Scola' HT, or, 1934, Ketten Bros.; flowers bright orange-red, edged Nilsson pink, large, semi-dbl., slight fragrance; early; foliage holly-green; vigorous growth; ['Hortulanus Budde' × 'Cuba']

'Francette Giraud' F, op, 1961, Arles; flowers bright salmon-pink, dbl., borne in clusters; foliage dark; vigorous growth; ['Aloha' × ('Gloire du Midi' × Edith de Martinelli®)]

'Francfort Agathé' ('Agatha Francofurtana', 'Agatha', 'Bijarre', *R. gallica agatha*) HGal, lp, before 1827; bud large, flat; flowers pale pink mixed with white, inner petals concave, 3 in., dbl., flat; Agathe group

'Francia' HT, Dorieux, Francois; intr. 1982

'Francibel' ('Tonia') HT, m, 1992, Franklin-Smith, Roger; flowers light lavender/mauve with deeper tones (silvery lavender) at edges, 3-3½ in., full, intense fragrance; foliage medium size, medium green, matte; some prickles; upright (175-180 cm.), vigorous growth; [Lagerfeld™ × Remember Me®]; intr. 1995

'Francie Simms' HT, mp, 1926, Dickson, A.; flowers rose-pink, marked carmine, base buttercup yellow, dbl

'Francine' HT, rb, 1961, Kriloff, Michel; bud pointed; flowers crimson, reverse silvery, 6 in., 30-35 petals; foliage glossy; vigorous, bushy growth; intr. 1961

'Francine' HMsk, w

'Francine Austin' -- See 'Ausram'

Francine Contier® HT, my, 1979, Lens, Louis; bud long, pointed; flowers canary-yellow, 3½-4½ in., 40-45 petals, high-centered, slight fragrance; foliage glossy, dark; very vigorous growth; [Peer Gynt® × 'Thalia']; intr. 1977

Francine Royneau® F, dy, Guillot-Massad; flowers luminous yellow, single; growth to 1 m.; intr. 2003

'Francis' HMult, rb, 1908, Fauque et fils; flowers bright red, white center, fading to pale pink, 4-5 cm., single to semi-dbl., borne in clusters of 25-50; foliage large, dark green; [*R. wichurana rubra* × 'Turner's Crimson Rambler']; sometimes attributed to Barbier

'Francis' HWich, mp, Hauser; flowers rose-pink, dbl.; [*R. wichuraiana* hybrid × 'Crimson Rambler']; intr. 1933

'Francis B. Hayes' B, mr, 1892, May; flowers scarlet

Francis Blaise® S, pb, Guillot-Massad; flowers dark pink changing to bright yellow, full, cupped, moderate fragrance; intr. 2000

'Francis Dubreuil' ('François Dubreuil') T, dr, 1894, Dubreuil; bud long; flowers velvety crimson, medium, dbl., moderate sweet fragrance

'Francis E. Lester' HMsk, w, 1946, Lester Rose Gardens; flowers white edged pink, 2 in., single, borne in clusters of 25-30, strong fruity fragrance; infrequent repeat; very vigorous (8-10 ft.) growth; very hardy; ['Kathleen' × unknown]

Francis Jammes® F, ab, Horner; flowers pink apricot, very full, borne in clusters; recurrent; 80 cm. growth; intr. 2007

'Francis King' HT, dy

'Francis Moreau' HT, ob

'Francis Perry' F, w; intr. 2005

'Francis Phoebe' -- See 'Frances Phoebe'

'Francis Scott Key' HT, pb, 1913, Cook, J.W.; flowers deep pink, reverse lighter, very large, dbl., high-centered; foliage dark, leathery, glossy; long, strong stems; very vigorous growth; ['Radiance' × seedling]

'Francis Scott Key, Climbing' Cl HT, pb

'Francisca Krüger' -- See 'Mlle Franziska Krüger'

'Francisca Pries' T, pb, 1888, Pries/Ketten Bros.; flowers pink striped salmon, medium, full, cupped, moderate fragrance; growth vigorous

'Francisco Curbera' HT, pb, 1923, Dot, Pedro; flowers salmon-pink and yellow, well-formed, very dbl.; vigorous growth

'Francisque Barillot' HP, mr, 1873, Damaizin; flowers cherry red with scarlet reflections, shaded darker, large, full, globular

'Francita' HT, dp, 1967, Dervaes, Dr Coninck; flowers light red, medium, very dbl., slight fragrance; foliage dark; [(('Dame Edith Helen' × Baccará®) × Baccará®) × 'Comtesse Vandal']

'Francofurtana' ('À Gros Cul', *R. gallica splendens*, *R. germanica*, *R. inermis*, 'Splendens', 'Frankfurt', 'Francofurtensis', *R. turbinata*, *R. campanulata*) Misc OGR, m, maybe before 1629; bud protrusive, rounded; flowers purple, 2-3 in., semi-dbl.; summer bloom; foliage oval, villose beneath; prickles few, recurved; growth to 6 ft.; hips turbinate; [probably *R. cinnamomea* × *R. gallica*]

'Francofurtensis' – See Francofurtana

'François Allard' HT, yb, 1927, Felberg-Leclerc; flowers creamy yellow, reverse salmon-pink, dbl.; ['Mme Mélanie Soupert' × 'Mme Segond Weber']

'François Arago' HP, dr, 1858, Trouillard; flowers velvety-maroon, shaded with fiery red, medium, dbl.; [sport of 'Géant des Batailles']

'François Bollez' -- See 'Mme François Bolley'

'François Coppée' HP, dr, 1895, Lédéchaux; flowers dark crimson, large, dbl.; ['Victor Verdier' × unknown]

'François Courtin' HP, rb, 1873, Verdier, E.; flowers cherry purple, edged white, reverse pink

'François Crousse' Cl T, mr, 1900, Guillot, P.; flowers cerise-crimson shaded darker, 10 cm., dbl., globular, moderate fragrance; vigorous growth

'François de Salignac' M, mp, 1854, Robert; flowers amaranthe, shaded pink, large, full, rosette; vigorous growth

'François Dubois' HP, dp, 1866, Damaizin; flowers shining pink, aging to red, large, full

'François Dubreuil' -- See 'Francis Dubreuil'

'François Fontaine' ('Rose de Puebla', 'Sénateur Favre') HP, mr, 1867, Fontaine; flowers fiery red with vermilion, medium, full, globular

'François Foucard' HWich, my, 1900, Barbier; flowers lemon-yellow, fading to white, 5-6 cm., semi-dbl., quartered, borne in clusters, slight fragrance; very vigorous growth; ['L'Idéal' × *R. wichurana*]

'François Foucquier' HGal, dp, before 1885; flowers bright crimson, very large, full

'François Gaujard' HT, dr, Gaujard; flowers dark, velvety red; foliage glossy and healthy; intr. 2002

'François Gaulain' HP, dr, 1878, Schwartz; flowers deep purplish crimson, large, full; foliage dark green; nearly thornless; growth upright

'François Guillot' HWich, w, 1907, Barbier; bud long, yellowish-white; flowers milk-white, 8-10 cm., semi-dbl. to dbl., globular, borne singly or in small clusters; foliage dark green, glossy; vigorous (15-18 ft.) growth; [*R. wichurana* × 'Mme Laurette Messimy']

'François Herincq' HP, mr, 1878, Verdier, E.; flowers bright poppy red, medium, full, globular, moderate fragrance

'François I' -- See 'François Premier'

'François Juranville' HWich, op, 1906, Barbier; flowers bright salmon-pink, base yellow, quite distinct, 7 cm., semi-dbl., borne in small clusters, moderate fruity fragrance; foliage small, dark green, glossy; very vigorous growth; [*R. wichurana* × 'Mme Laurette Messimy']

'Francois Krige' -- See 'Korharment'

'François Lacharme' HP, mr, 1861, Verdier

'François Laplanche' HT, w, 1934, Buatois; flowers flesh-white on yellow ground, veined and edged carmine, large, dbl., cupped; foliage leathery; bushy growth; ['Mme Charles Detreaux' × 'Mme Edouard Herriot']

'François Levet' HP, dp, 1880, Levet, A.; flowers cherry-rose, well-formed; very remontant; foliage light green; prickles short, straight; ['Anna de Diesbach' × unknown]

'François Louvat' HP, pb, 1861, Touvais; flowers carmine pink, shaded lilac pink, large, full, globular

Francois Mauriac® -- See 'Tatton'

'François Michelon' HP, m, 1871, Levet, A.; flowers deep rose tinged lilac, large, dbl., globular; foliage somewhat wrinkled; upright growth; ['La Reine' × unknown]

'François Olin' HP, dp, 1881, Ducher; flowers cerise red marbled with pure white, large, full, camellia-like, borne in small clusters; foliage dark green; numerous prickles; growth upright

'François Poisson' HWich, ly, 1902, Barbier; bud lemon yellow; flowers pale sulfur-yellow, center shaded orange, passing to white, 4-5 cm., dbl., borne in clusters; foliage dark green, glossy; prickles wide, red; growth upright, vigorous; [R. wichurana × 'William Allen Richardson']

'François Premier' ('François I') HP, mr, 1859, Trouillard; ['Géant des Batailles' × unknown]

François Rabelais™ -- See 'Meinusian'

'François Treyve' HP, mr, 1866, Liabaud

'Françoise Blondeau' HT, op, 1938, Mallerin, C.; flowers coral, large, dbl.; foliage dark; very vigorous growth; ['Charles P. Kilham' × 'Colette Clément']

'Francoise Drion' -- See 'Lenraba'

'Franfelluv' ('Chaldean') HT, yb, 2002, Cowlishaw, Frank; flowers yellow with orange reverse, 5 in., full, borne mostly solitary, slight fragrance; foliage medium green, semi-glossy; prickles moderate, up to 10 mm., curved and hooked; growth upright, medium (3 ft.); bedding; ['Fellowship' × 'Summer Love']

'Frank Chapman' HT, yb, 1937, Cant, F.; flowers yellowish-orange, medium, dbl.

'Frank Leddy' -- See 'Frans Leddy'

'Frank Macmillan' HT, dr, 1978, Scrivens; flowers crimson-red, 4 in., 26 petals; foliage semi-glossy; moderately vigorous, spreading growth; [('Uncle Walter' × ('Ena Harkness' × 'Fragrant Cloud')]

'Frank Michael' -- See 'Taneidol'

'Frank Naylor' S, rb, 1977, Harkness; flowers dark red, yellowish eye, 1½ in., 5 petals, borne several together and in trusses, moderate musky fragrance; foliage small, plum shaded; [((Orange Sensation® × Allgold®) × ('(Little Lady × Lilac Charm)' × '(Blue Moon × Magenta)')) × (('Cläre Grammerstorf × Fruhlingsmorgen)' × '(Little Lady × Lilac Charm)') × (('Blue Moon × Magenta)' × '(Cläre Grammerstorf × Frühlingsmorgen)'))]; intr. 1978

'Frank Neave' HT, ly, 1928, Morse; flowers pale mustard-yellow, dbl.

'Frank Penn' HT, pb, 1971, Clayworth; bud long, pointed; flowers cerise, reverse pink, large, dbl.; foliage dark, leathery; very vigorous, upright growth; ['Wendy Cussons' × 'Lys Assia']

'Frank Reader' HT, my, 1927, Verschuren; flowers lemon-yellow, center apricot, fairly, large, dbl., high-centered; strong stems; vigorous growth; ['Golden Ophelia' × 'Souv. de H.A. Verschuren']

'Frank Serpa' Gr, op, 1960, Serpa; bud pointed; flowers pink tinted salmon, large, dbl., cupped; foliage leathery, glossy, dark; very vigorous growth; ['Pres. Macia' × unknown]

'Frank W. Dunlop' HT, dp, 1920, Dunlop; flowers deep bright rose-pink, large, 45 petals, high-centered; ['Mrs Charles E. Russell' × 'Mrs George Shawyer']

'Frank W. Dunlop, Climbing' Cl HT, dp, 1933, Dixie Rose Nursery

Frankenland® -- See 'Tankenfram'

'Frankfort Agathé' HGal, dp; flowers cerise

'Frankfurt' HT, dr, 1909, Böttner; flowers large, full

'Frankfurt' -- See R. × francofurtana

'Frankfurt am Main' F, mr, 1963, Boerner; flowers blood-red shaded scarlet, well-formed, 2½-3 in., 25 petals, borne in clusters, slight fragrance; foliage dark; bushy, upright growth

'Frankie' F, pb, 2001, Hastings, Mr. and Mrs. Frank; flowers light mauve with pink edges, deep pink reverse, 4 in., single, borne mostly solitary, slight fragrance; foliage medium size, dark green, semi-glossy; prickles ¼ in., curved down, moderate; growth bushy, medium (4 ft.); garden decorative, exhibition; [Altissimo® × unknown]; intr. 2005

'Frankish' -- See 'Worclimate'

'Franklin' HT, op, 1918, Pernet-Ducher; flowers salmon, shaded yellowish-salmon, dbl.

'Franklin D. Roosevelt' HT, mr, 1939, McClung; flowers bright red fading to rose-purple, medium, 26 petals, cupped, intense fragrance; foliage glossy, dark; bush and semi-climbing growth; PP511; [sport of 'Betty Uprichard']

'Franklin Engelmann' F, dr, 1970, Dickson, A.; flowers bright scarlet, pointed, very large, 36 petals, borne in trusses; vigorous growth; ['Heidelberg' × ('Detroiter' × seedling)]

Frankly Scarlet™ -- See 'Jacrepin'

'Frank's Climber' LCl, ob, Raffel; flowers orange (salmon to apricot-orange) with yellow eye, stamens red with yellow, semi-dbl. to dbl., open

'Franlac' ('Road to Freedom') HT, m, 1995, Cowlishaw, Frank; flowers lilac, gold stamens, medium, dbl.; foliage medium size, medium green, glossy; low (15-20 in.),bushy, compact growth; [seedling × 'Lilac Charm']; intr. 1996

'Franluv' ('Summer Love') F, ab, 1985, Cowlishaw, Frank; flowers light apricot, large, 27 petals, hybrid tea, borne in clusters of 5 - 10, moderate spicy fragrance; foliage large, dark, semi-glossy; upright growth; ['Pink Parfait' × 'Cynthia Brooke']; intr. 1986

'Franmilro' ('Lovebird') MinFl, mp, Cowlishaw, Frank; intr. 1998

'Franmite' ('Forever Royal') F, m, 2001, Cowlishaw, Frank R.; flowers dark purple, reverse lighter purple, 2 in., semi-dbl., borne in large clusters, slight fragrance; foliage medium size, dark green, glossy; prickles ¼ in., curved and hooked, few; growth upright, tall (3½ ft.); garden/decorative; [(International Herald Tribune® × seedling) × seedling]; intr. 2001

'Franriser' ('Sky High') LCl, mp, 2001, Cowlishaw, Frank; flowers medium, dbl., borne in large clusters, moderate fragrance; foliage medium size, medium green, semi-glossy; prickles medium, sharp, moderate; growth upright, tall (2½ m.); garden decorative; intr. 2001

'Frans Hals' S, mp, Williams, J. Benjamin; flowers soft pink, petals have some quilling, single to semi-dbl., flat, moderate fragrance; intr. 1997

'Frans Leddy' ('Frank Leddy') Pol, op, 1927, Kersbergen; flowers light orange-red, turning pink, small, dbl.; [sport of 'Kersbergen']

'Frans Post' S, ob, J. B. Williams; intr. 2005

'Franshine' ('Chester Cathedral') HT, ab, 1991, Cowlishaw, Frank; bud pointed; flowers light apricot, reverse cream to very light gold, medium, dbl., high-centered, borne usually singly, slight fragrance; foliage medium size, dark green, glossy; low, bushy growth; ['Honey Favorite' × Piccadilly®]

'Franski' ('Odyssey') F, m, 2001, Cowlishaw; flowers mauve with prominent yellow stamens, 3 in., single, borne in large clusters, intense fragrance; foliage medium size, light green, glossy; prickles medium, pointed, moderate; growth bushy, medium (30 in.); garden decorative; ['Summer Wine' × seedling]; intr. 2001

'Fransmoov' ('With Thanks') HT, yb, 1995, Cowlishaw, Frank; flowers deep pink, yellow eye and reverse, medium, full, high-centered, then flattens, borne in clusters, moderate fragrance; recurrent; foliage medium size, medium green, glossy; medium (2-3 ft.), upright growth; [('Southampton' × Prominent®) × 'Summer Love']; intr. 1996

'Frantasia' ('Rhapsody in Blue') S, m, 1999, Cowlishaw, Frank; flowers dark purple/blue, reverse lighter, 2½ in., semi-dbl., borne in large clusters, intense fragrance; foliage medium size, light green, glossy; prickles moderate; upright, semi-climbing, tall (6-8 ft.) growth; ['Summer Wine' × seedling]; intr. 2000

'Frantier' ('Maureen Lipman') Min, pb, Cowlishaw, Frank

'Frantisek Valàsek' Pol, dr, 1930, Valàsek; flowers small, dbl.

'Frantonia' Min, ob, Gönewein; flowers orange with yellow eye, semi-dbl., flat, moderate fragrance; recurrent; 30-35 cm. growth; [sport of 'Little Artist']; intr. 1996

'Franwekpink' LCl, mp, Cowlishaw; intr. 2003

'Franwekpurp' LCl, m, Cowlishaw; intr. 2002

'Franwekwhit' LCl, w, Cowlishaw; intr. 2003

'Franz Deegen' ('Friedrich Harms', 'Yellow

Kaiserin Auguste Viktoria') HT, my, 1901, Hinner, W.; flowers soft yellow to golden yellow, large, dbl.; ['Kaiserin Auguste Viktoria' × unknown]

'Franz Degen Junion' N, w, before 1900; [sport of 'Maréchal Niel']

'Franz Grümmer' HT, or, 1927, Maass; flowers coral-red, dbl.; ['Mme Abel Chatenay' × 'Château de Clos Vougeot']

'Franz Lizst' HGal, mr, Rautio; growth 1 meter height; intr. 2000

'Fraser McLay' HT, mr, 1974, Dawson, George; bud ovoid; flowers glossy medium red, medium, dbl.; foliage glossy, leathery; bushy growth; ['Grand Gala' × 'Suspense']

'Fraser's Pink Musk' ('Blush Musk', *R. fraseri*) N, lp, 1818, Fraser; flowers blush, medium, semi-dbl., cupped, borne in large clusters, intense fragrance

Frasquita® ('Barfra') F, op, Barni; intr. 1982

'Frasunpatch' F, ob, Franko; intr. 2008

'Fratelli Ingegnoli' HMult, pb, 1889, Bernaix; flowers pink with white

'Fraternité' F, pb, 1946, Leenders, M.; flowers Neyron rose, reverse pale lilac-rose, 3 in., 25 petals, globular, borne in clusters, slight fragrance; foliage bronze; vigorous growth; ['Florentina' × 'World's Fair']

'Fraternity' F, m, Dey, S. C.; flowers purple with lilac stripes, borne in large trusses; recurrent; intr. 1987

'Frau A. von Brauer' HWich, lp, 1913, Lambert, P.; flowers white, aging to pink, 3-4 cm., very dbl., borne in clusters, moderate fragrance; ['Farquhar' × 'Schneewittchen']

'Frau A. Weidling' S, mp, 1930, Vogel, M.; flowers small, semi-dbl.

'Frau Ada Rehfeld' Pol, pb,]1914, Altmüller; flowers dark flesh pink, center golden, reverse darker, large, full

'Frau Adolf Anders' HT, 1937, Anders, Adolf

'Frau Albert Fischer' HWich, w, 1906, Weigand; flowers white with whitish pink, very large, full

'Frau Albert Hochstrasser' HWich, lp, 1908, Weigand, C.; bud golden yellow; flowers yellow, changing to white, 5-7 cm., dbl., borne in medium clusters, intense fragrance; intermittent repeat; foliage glossy; prickles numerous, very large

'Frau Alexander Weiss' Pol, yb, 1909, Lambert, P.; flowers light yellow with pink, small, dbl.; ['Petite Léonie' × 'Lutea Bicolore']

'Frau Anna Lautz' HT, mr, 1911, Kiese; flowers large, dbl.

'Frau Anna Pasquay' Pol, dp, 1909, Walter; flowers deep pink, small, dbl.; [Trier® × 'Mme Norbert Levavasseur']

'Frau Anny Beaufays' ('Mrs Annie Beaufays') F, mr, 1962, deRuiter; bud ovoid; flowers salmon-red, semi-dbl., borne in clusters; low growth; intr. 1962

'Frau Astrid Späth' ('Astrid Späth') F, dp, 1930, Späth; flowers clear carmine-rose, medium size, semi-dbl.; recurrent; [sport of 'Lafayette']; possibly synonymous with 'Direktor Rikala'

'Frau Astrid Späth, Climbing' Cl F, dp, 1935, Lens

'Frau Berta Gürtler' HMult, lp, 1913, Gurtler; flowers light silky pink, dbl.

'Frau Bertha Kiese' HT, my, 1914, Kiese; flowers pure golden yellow, dbl.; ['Kaiserin Auguste Viktoria' × 'Undine']

'Frau Berthe Kiese' -- See 'Bertha Kiese'

'Frau Betty Hartmann' ('Andrea Muraglia') HT, pb, 1901, Brauer; flowers flesh pink, aging to salmon with rose

'Frau Bürgermeister Kirschstein' HT, dp, 1906, Jacobs; flowers medium, semi-dbl.; ['Luciole' × 'Mrs W. J. Grant']

'Frau Cecilie Walter' Pol, ly, 1904, Lambert, P.; flowers small, dbl., intense fragrance; ['Aglaia' × 'Kleiner Alfred']

'Frau Charlotte Gieseler' Pol, dp, 1939, Vogel, M.; flowers medium, dbl.

'Frau Dagmar Hartopp' -- See 'Dagmar Hastrup'

'Frau Dagmar Hastrup' -- See 'Dagmar Hastrup'

'Frau Dagmar Hastrup Geel' -- See 'Moryelrug'

'Frau Direktor Anni Hartmann' HT, ly, 1933, Brada, Dr.; flowers medium, very dbl.

'Frau Dr Erreth' F, dy, 1915, Geduldig; flowers deep golden yellow, passing to white, dbl., borne in clusters; branching growth; ['Gruss an Aachen' × 'Mrs Aaron Ward']

'Frau Dr Hooftmann' Cl Pol, lp, 1935, Buisman, G. A. H.; flowers large, dbl.

'Frau Dr Krüger' HT, op, 1919, Kiese; flowers cream-salmon on golden ground; ['Baronne Henriette de Loew' × 'Mme Caroline Testout']

'Frau Dr Schricker' HCh, rb, 1927, Felberg-Leclerc; flowers fiery carmine and coppery-red, large, dbl., intense fragrance; dwarf growth; ['Gruss an Teplitz' × 'Souv. de Mme Eugene Verdier']; sometimes classed as B

'Frau E. Weigand' ('Frau Elisabeth Weigand') HT, yb, 1928, Weigand, C.; flowers canary-yellow, large, 70 petals, high-centered; foliage dark, leathery; strong stems; ['Mme Caroline Testout' × 'Souv. de Claudius Pernet']

'Frau Eduard Bethge' HT, dr, 1930, Felberg-Leclerc; flowers dark crimson and velvety blood-red, large, dbl.; foliage light; ['Hadley' × 'Admiral Ward']

'Frau Elisabeth Balzer' HT, w, 1933, Balzer; flowers white, base orange-yellow, reverse bright flesh-pink, pointed; vigorous growth; [sport of 'Mrs Henry Morse']

'Frau Elisabeth Fisher' HFt, dy, 1930, Fisher & Schulz; flowers medium, dbl.

'Frau Elisabeth Münch' Pol, mr, 1921, Münch & Haufe; flowers scarlet-cherry-red, with deeper reflexes; [sport of 'Orléans Rose']

'Frau Elisabeth Sprenger' HT, dy, 1937, Wirtz & Eicke; flowers medium, dbl.

'Frau Elisabeth Weigand' -- See 'Frau E. Weigand'

'Frau Elise Kreis' ('Else Kreis') Pol, mp, 1913, Kreis; flowers bright carmine, 5 cm., borne in large clusters; [seedling or sport of 'Annchen Müller']

'Frau Emma Sasse' HT, lp, 1908, Plog; flowers large, dbl.; ['Mrs W. J. Grant' × 'Paul Neyron']

'Frau Emmy Hammann' HT, yb, 1923, Weigand, C.; flowers reddish lemon-yellow shaded sunflower-yellow, dbl.; ['Mme Caroline Testout' × 'Mme Hoste']

'Frau Ernst Fischer' HT, op, 1909, Hinner

'Frau Eva Schubert' ('Eva Schubert', 'Gela Tepelmann') HWich, mp, 1937, Tepelmann; flowers small, semi-dbl., borne in tight clusters; remontant

'Frau Felberg-Leclerc' HT, my, 1921, Felberg-Leclerc; flowers pure golden yellow, medium, dbl., cupped, borne mostly solitary; foliage leathery, bronze-green; [sport of 'Louise Catherine Breslau']

'Frau Felix Tonnar' HT, mp, 1924, Leenders, M.; flowers bright rose, base coppery orange, semi-dbl.; ['Mme Mélanie Soupert' × 'Mme Annette Aynard']

'Frau Franziska Krüger' -- See 'Mlle Franziska Krüger'

'Frau Fritz Pelzer' HT, or, 1927, Leenders, M.; flowers reddish crimson-orange, dbl.; ['Mme Edouard Herriot' × 'Edward Mawley']

'Frau Geheimrat Dr Staub' Cl HT, dr, 1908, Lambert, P.; flowers large, dbl.; ['Mrs W. J. Grant' × 'Duke of Edinburgh']

'Frau Geheimrat Späth' S, lp, 1941, Tepelmann; flowers large, dbl.

'Frau Geheimrat Von Boch' ('Mme Von Boch') T, w, 1898, Lambert; bud large, long; flowers cream, with carmine on reverse of outer petals, large, full, intense fragrance; ['Princesse Alice de Monaco' × 'Duchesse Marie Salviati']

'Frau Georg von Simson' HMult, mp, 1909, Walter; flowers rose, fading to white, 5-6 cm., semi-dbl., borne in large clusters, slight fragrance; non-recurrent; nearly thornless; vigorous growth; ['Helene' × 'Rosel Dach']

'Frau H. Dentler' HT, w, 1905, Dentler; flowers glossy porcelain white, striped pink, moderate fragrance; ['Mme Caroline Testout' × unknown]

'Frau Hedwig Koschel' Pol, w, 1921, Münch & Haufe; flowers white, slightly shaded yellow, edges tinted rose-pink, dbl.; [sport of 'Ellen Poulsen']

'Frau Hedwig Wagner' HT, mp, 1919, Krüger; flowers dbl.; ['Enchantress' × 'Mrs W. J. Grant']

'Frau Helene Kühn' HT, w, 1938, Vogel, M.; flowers medium, dbl.

'Frau Helene Videnz' ('Helene Videnz') HMult, lp, 1904, Lambert, P.; flowers salmon pink to medium, 3-4 cm., semi-dbl. to dbl., cupped, borne in medium to large clusters, moderate musky fragrance; few prickles; growth to 3 m.; [('Euphrosyne' × 'Princesse Alice de Monaco') × 'Louis-Philippe']

'Frau Hugo Lauster'   HT, dy, 1932, Lauster; flowers deep canary-yellow, edged lighter, well-formed, dbl.; vigorous growth

'Frau Ida Münch'   HT, ly, 1919, Beschnidt; flowers light golden yellow, center deeper, dbl.; ['Frau Karl Druschki' × 'Billard et Barré']

'Frau J. Reiter'   HT, w, 1904, Welter; flowers pure white, sometimes with coppery tints, very large, very full, cupped; ['Mlle Augustine Guinoisseau' × ('Viscountess Folkestone' × 'Kaiserin Auguste Viktoria')]

'Frau Jenny Wienke'   HT, mr, Berger, W.; flowers large, dbl.; intr. 1958

'Frau Karl Brass'   HT, pb, 1913, Brass & Hartmann; flowers deep pink with butter yellow, center darker yellow, salmon reflections; [sport of 'Lyon Rose']

'Frau Karl Druschki'   ('Druschki', 'Mme Charles Druschki', 'White American Beauty', 'Snow Queen', 'Snedronningen', 'Schneekönigen', 'F. K. Druschkii', 'Reine des Neiges') HP, w, 1901, Lambert, P.; bud pointed, tinged carmine-pink; flowers snow-white, center sometimes blush-pink, large, 35 petals, no fragrance; reliably remontant; foliage dark green; vigorous growth; ['Merveille de Lyon' × 'Mme Caroline Testout']

'Frau Karl Druschki, Climbing'   ('Grimpant Reine des Neiges', 'Reine des Neiges, Climbing', 'Snow Queen, Climbing') Cl HP, w, 1906, Lawrenson; flowers dbl., slight fragrance; [sport of 'Frau Karl Druschki']

'Frau Karl Smid' -- See 'Mme Gustave Metz'

'Frau Käte Schmid'   HMult, mp, 1931, Vogel, M.; flowers bright pink, fading to silvery pink, darker reverse, 7 cm., semi-dbl., cupped, opening flat, borne in clusters of 5-10; foliage light green, glossy; ['Fragezeichen' × 'Tausendschön']

'Frau Liesel Brauer'   HWich, mp, 1938, Thönges; flowers semi-dbl., cupped, borne in small to medium clusters, slight fragrance

'Frau Lieselotte Weber'   Pol, 1938, Vogel, M.

'Frau Lilla Rautenstrauch'   ('Frau Lita Rautenstrauch') HT, w, 1902, Lambert; bud coppery orange; flowers creamy white, apricot-orange in center, large, very full, high-centered; ['Mme Caroline Testout' × 'Goldquelle']

'Frau Lina Strassheim'   HMult, op, 1907, Strassheim; flowers reddish salmon-pink, fading to light pink, 3½ cm., semi-dbl., borne in clusters of 5-15; numerous prickles; ['Crimson Rambler' × unknown]

'Frau Lita Rautenstrauch' -- See 'Frau Lilla Rautenstrauch'

'Frau Luise Kiese'   ('Luise Kiese') HT, ly, 1921, Kiese; flowers ivory-yellow, sometimes clear yellow, very dbl.

'Frau Luise Lindecke'   HT, dr, 1928, Lindecke; flowers deep claret-red, sometimes crimson, dbl.; [sport of 'Columbia']

'Frau Margarete Oppenheim'   HT, rb, 1928, Felberg-Leclerc; flowers intense carmine-red shaded brick-red and yellow, semi-dbl.; ['Hortulanus Budde' × 'Souv. de Claudius Pernet']

'Frau Maria Rüdt'   S, lp, Tagashira, Kazuso; flowers medium-large, dbl.; intr. 1994

'Frau Marie Brockhues'   HT, w, 1913, Brass & Hartmann; flowers pure white, center tinted cherry red; [sport of 'Mme Segond Weber']

'Frau Marie Bromme'   Pol, dr, 1928, Wirtz & Eicke; flowers bright dark red; [sport of 'Dr. Kater']

'Frau Marie Weinbach'   HWich, w, 1906, Weigand, C.; flowers dbl., borne in medium clusters, moderate fragrance; foliage dark green, glossy

'Frau Martha Schmidt'   HT, mr, 1923, Kiese; flowers carmine-red, dbl.; ['Paula Clegg' × 'Edward Mawley']

'Frau Math. Noehl'   HT, my, 1913, Welter; flowers lemon-yellow, dbl.; ['Kaiserin Auguste Viktoria' × 'Mme Ravary']

'Frau Mathilde Bätz'   HT, w, 1929, Felberg-Leclerc; flowers pure white, stamens yellow, dbl.; [seedling × 'Ophelia']

'Frau Mélanie Niedieck'   HT, dy, 1916, Leenders, M.; flowers vivid lemon-yellow, dbl.; ['Mme Jenny Gillemot' × 'Prince de Bulgarie']

'Frau Minka Rödiger'   HT, yb, Berger, W.; flowers yellow to light yellow with orange highlights, large, dbl.; intr. 1959

'Frau O. Plegg'   B, dr, 1909, Nabonnand; flowers medium, dbl., intense fragrance

'Frau Oberhofgärtner Schulze'   Pol, mp, 1909, Lambert, P.; flowers small, dbl.; ['Euphrosyne' × 'Mrs W. J. Grant']

'Frau Oberhofgärtner Singer'   HT, pb, 1908, Lambert, P.; flowers soft pink edged white, large, very full, moderate fragrance; ['Jules Margottin' × 'Mme Eugenie Boullet']

'Frau Oberpräsident von Grothe'   HT, op, 1920, Löbner; flowers rose-orange streaked carmine; ['Richmond' × 'Farbenkonigin']

'Frau Peter Lambert'   HT, op, 1902, Welter; flowers pink shading to salmon, large, full, moderate fragrance; [('Kaiserin Auguste Viktoria' × 'Mme Caroline Testout') × 'Mme Abel Chatenay']

'Frau Philipp Siesmayer'   HT, yb, 1908, Lambert; flowers yellow, suffused with pink; ['Mme Caroline Testout' × 'Erzherzogin Marie Dorothea']

'Frau Professor Baranov'   Pol, rb, 1947, Vogel, M.; flowers salmon-red, medium, semi-dbl.

'Frau Professor Gnau'   HT, w, 1925, Kiese; flowers creamy white, large, semi-dbl.

'Frau Professor Grischko'   S, mr, 1947, Vogel, M.; flowers medium, semi-dbl.

'Frau Robert Türke'   HT, dr, 1928, Türke; flowers dark crimson, very dbl.; foliage dark, glossy; long stems; vigorous growth; ['Hadley' × 'Hugh Dickson']

'Frau Rudolf Schmidt'   Pol, dr, 1919, Schmidt, R.; flowers dark ruby-red without objectionable blue shades; very dwarf growth; [sport of 'Jessie']

'Frau Sophie Meyerholz'   S, mp, 1942, Vogel, M.; flowers medium, dbl.

'Frau Therese Lang'   HT, dp, 1910, Welter; flowers large, very dbl.; ['Mme Caroline Testout' × 'Johanna Sebus']

'Fräulein Oktavia Hesse'   HWich, ly, 1910, Hesse; flowers yellowish-white, center deeper, 6-7 cm., dbl., borne in small clusters, moderate fragrance; recurrent bloom; foliage glossy, light green; stems flexible, light green; vigorous, climbing growth; [R. wichurana × 'Kaiserin Auguste Viktoria']

'Fraxinifolia' -- See 'Turneps'

'Frazier Annesley'   HT, dp, 1935, McGredy; bud pointed; flowers carmine, base golden yellow, dbl., high-centered; foliage glossy, bronze; very vigorous growth

'Frechdachs' -- See 'Mehnan'

'Freckle Face'   S, pb, 1976, Buck, Dr. Griffith J.; bud ovoid; flowers light spirea-red, striped dark spirea, 3½-4 in., 23 petals, moderate clove fragrance; foliage coppery, leathery; bushy, spreading growth; [('Vera Dalton' × 'Dornroschen') × (('World's Fair' × 'Floradora') × 'Applejack')]; intr. 1975

'Freckle Face' -- See 'Welfreck'

'Freckles'   S, pb, 1976, Buck, Dr. Griffith J.; bud ovoid, pointed to urn-shaped; flowers light scarlet, flushed yellow, 4-4½ in., 28 petals, cupped; foliage dark, coppery, leathery; upright, bushy growth; ['Tickled Pink' × 'Country Music']; intr. 1975

'Fred Birch'   HT, my, 1995, Poole, Lionel; intr. 1997

'Fred Cramphorn'   ('Manola', 'Samoa') HT, or, 1961, Kriloff, Michel; flowers rose-opal, fringed, 5-6 in., dbl., cupped; foliage dark, glossy; vigorous, upright, bushy growth; PP2258; ['Peace' × Baccará®]; intr. 1961

'Fred Edmunds'   ('L'Arlésienne') HT, ob, 1943, Meilland, F.; bud long, pointed; flowers coppery orange,, 5-5½ in., 25 petals, cupped, intense spicy fragrance; foliage leathery, glossy; bushy, open habit growth; PP731; ['Duquesa de Peñaranda' × 'Marie-Claire']

'Fred Edmunds, Climbing'   Cl HT, ob, 1989, Weeks, O.L.; [sport of 'Fred Edmunds']; intr. 1977

'Fred Fairbrother'   HT, dp, 1976, Sanday, John; flowers bright cerise, 4-5 in., 40 petals, moderate fragrance; foliage semi-glossy; [('Gavotte' × 'Tropicana') × 'Fragrant Cloud']; intr. 1974

'Fred Gibson'   HT, ab, 1966, Sanday,

John; flowers apricot suffused gold, 5 in., 30 petals; foliage dark; tall, vigorous growth; ['Gavotte' × 'Buccaneer']

'Fred Hollows Vision' F, w; [sport of 'Mary McKillop']; intr. 1996

'Fred Howard, Climbing' Cl HT, yb, 1954, Howard, A.P.; PP1417

'Fred Howard' HT, yb, 1952, Howard, F.H.; bud long; flowers golden orange shaded pink, 4 in., 55 petals, high-centered, slight fragrance; vigorous, upright growth; PP1006; ['Pearl Harbor' × seedling]

'Fred J. Harrison' HT, mr, 1924, Dickson, A.; flowers cardinal-red shaded crimson, dbl.

'Fred Loads' S, or, 1967, Holmes, R.A.; flowers vermilion-orange, 3 in., single, borne in clusters, moderate fragrance; foliage glossy; vigorous, tall growth; ['Dorothy Wheatcroft' × Orange Sensation®]; intr. 1968

'Fred Owen' HT, dy, 1985, Owen, Fred; [sport of 'Jan Guest']

'Fred Streeter' HMoy, dp, 1951, Jackman; flowers deep cerise-pink, medium, single, borne in clusters (up to 3); upright, branching growth

'Fred Streeter' HT, my, Kordes; bud pointed; flowers clear yellow, 4 in., 48 petals, moderate fragrance; foliage dark; vigorous growth; ['Luis Brinas' × 'Golden Scepter']; intr. 1955

'Fred W. Alesworth' -- See 'F. W. Alesworth'

'Fred W. Mee' ('F. W. Mee') HT, mr, 1960, Mee; flowers scarlet-cerise, 30 petals, high-centered, intense fragrance; vigorous, upright growth; ['Karl Herbst' × 'The Doctor']

'Fred Walker' HT, mp, 1935, McGredy; flowers glowing pink, base coppery orange, large, dbl., high-centered; foliage soft, light; vigorous growth

'Fredagh of Bellinchamp' ('Swany River') HT, w, 1982, Herholdt, J.A.; flowers large, dbl., moderate fragrance; foliage medium size, dark, semi-glossy; upright growth; [Pascali® × seedling]

'Freddie Mercury' -- See 'Batmercury'

'Freddy' -- See 'Peaproof'

Fredensborg™ -- See 'Poulmax'

'Fredensgedächtnispark Hiroshima' F, dy; intr. 1998

'Frédéric Bihorel' HP, dr, 1865, Damaizin; flowers violet red, center carmine, large, full

'Frédéric Chopin' ('Chopin', 'Frederyk Chopin') HT, ly, Zyla; flowers yellow-ivory, large, full, moderate fragrance; recurrent; foliage rich green; growth to 4 ft.; intr. 1990

'Frédéric Lerr' HT, pb, 1950, Sauvageot, H.; flowers carmine-red, reverse lighter, large, dbl., high-centered, dbl. bronze; very vigorous growth; ['Crimson Glory' × ('Mrs Pierre S. duPont' × 'Signora')]

Frederic Mistral™ -- See 'Meitebros'

'Frederic Schneider II' HP, dp, 1885, Ludovic; flowers deep pink with red, large, dbl.

'Frédéric Soulié' ('Frédéric Soullier') M , rb, 1854, Laffay, M.; flowers carmine-red with purple striping, large, dbl.

'Frédéric Soullier' -- See 'Frédéric Soulié'

'Frédéric II de Prusse' ('Frederick the Second') HCh, m, 1847, Verdier, V.; flowers rich crimson-purple, medium, dbl., moderate fragrance; vigorous growth; sometimes classed as B; intr. 1847

'Frédéric Wood' HP, mr, 1874, Verdier, E.; flowers shining cherry red, shaded poppy red, large, full

'Frédéric Worth' -- See 'Mme Charles Frédéric Worth'

'Frederica' HT, mr; flowers deep crimson, 5 in., 30 petals; foliage dark, glossy; vigorous growth

Fredericia™ -- See 'Poullitam'

'Frederick Keeling' -- See 'Weblove'

'Frederick R. M. Undritz' -- See 'Gen. John Pershing'

'Frederick S. Peck' LCl, dp, 1938, Brownell; flowers deep grenadine-pink, center more yellow, 4 in., semi-dbl., borne in clusters of 2-8, moderate fragrance; foliage dark green, glossy; slightly arched stems; PP419; ['hybrid creeper' × 'Mrs Arthur Curtiss James']

'Frederick the Second' -- See 'Frédéric II de Prusse'

'Fredericksbergrosen' F, dp, 1985, Poulsen, S.; flowers deep pink, medium, 5 petals, cupped, no fragrance; foliage medium size, medium green, semi-glossy; vigorous, bushy growth; ['Orléans Rose' × seedling]; intr. 1942

'Frederico Cassio' -- See 'Federico Casas'

'Frederik Mey' F, op, Eve, A.; flowers coral-pink, dbl., high-centered, borne in clusters of 3-6; recurrent, better in fall; growth to 3 ft.; intr. 1980

Frederiksborg™ -- See 'Pouldrik'

'Frederyk Chopin' -- See 'Frédéric Chopin'

'Fredica' S, w, 1978, INRA; bud oval; flowers medium, 5 petals, cupped; thornless; very vigorous, bushy, upright growth; PP4463; ['Indica Major' × 'Multiflora Inermis']; used for understock; intr. 1974

'Fredrik Hellstrand' HRg, pb, 2005, Verghese-Borg, Helena; flowers dark pink at center, lighter towards edges, 8 cm., very full, borne in small clusters; foliage medium size, medium green, semi-glossy; prickles 4 mm., narrow, straight, green, moderate; growth bushy, medium (120 cm.); hedging, specimen; ['Louis Bugnet' × unknown]; intr. 2005

'Free As Air' -- See 'Mehbronze'

'Free Gold' HT, my, 1948, Brownell; bud long, pointed; flowers yellow, open, large, dbl., high-centered, moderate fragrance; foliage glossy; bushy, dwarf growth; RULED EXTINCT 5/83 ARM; ['Pink Princess' × 'Shades of Autumn']

Free Gold® -- See 'Macfreego'

'Free Spirit' F, op, Fryer; flowers salmon pink, dbl., globular, borne in clusters; free-flowering; foliage disease-resistant; bushy, speading growth; intr. 2006

'Free Spirit' -- See 'Pixiree'

'Freedom' ('White American Beauty, Climbing') LCl, w, 1918, Undritz; flowers white, center yellow, open, 4 in., 75 petals, high-centered, slight fragrance; foliage dark, bronze, glossy; long, strong stems; very vigorous, climbing growth; RULED EXTINCT 3/84 ARM; ['Silver Moon' × 'Kaiserin Auguste Viktoria']

Freedom® -- See 'Dicjem'

'Freedom USA' -- See 'Twofree'

'Freedom's Ring' LCl, rb, 1994, Dykstra, Dr. A. Michael; flowers red and white striped, small, semi-dbl., borne in small clusters; foliage medium size, medium green, matte; some prickles; medium, bushy, spreading growth; ['Stars 'n' Stripes' × 'Paradise']; intr. 1994

Freegold® -- See 'Macfreego'

'Freeleigh' HT, my, 1956, LeGrice; flowers buttercup-yellow, well-shaped, small, dbl.; foliage glossy, light green; vigorous growth; ['Kingcup' × 'Golden Scepter']

'Freemont' -- See 'Brifree'

'Freestar' HT, or; intr. 2003

'Freestew' ('R. B. Stewart') HT, or, 2005, French, Bryan; flowers deep orange-red with small yellow center, yellow stamens, reverse lighter, 4 in., dbl., borne mostly solitary, intense spice fragrance; foliage medium size, semi-glossy; prickles moderate, ¼ in., slight curve downward, yellow-green; growth upright, medium (28-32 in.); garden, cutting; not heat tolerant; ['Playboy' × 'Vannie']; intr. 2006

'Fregate' HT, lp, Delbard; flowers large, dbl.; intr. 1979

'Freia' HT, ab, 1936, Tantau; flowers sun-yellow tinted orange, base orange, open, large, dbl.; foliage leathery, glossy; vigorous, bushy growth; ['Ville de Paris' × 'Rev. F. Page-Roberts']

'Freia' S, lp, Barni; flowers 6-7 cm., semi-dbl., slight fragrance; foliage medium size, light green; growth to 4 ft.; [seedling × Rita Levi Montalcini®]; intr. 1999

'Freiamt' HT, mp, Huber; flowers rose-pink with tints of salmon, dbl., high-centered, moderate spicy fragrance; foliage matte; strong, upright (70 cm.) growth; intr. 1995

'Freiburg II' HT, pb, 1917, Krüger; bud long, pointed; flowers silver-rose, reverse bright apricot-pink, large, dbl.; ['Dr. G. Kruger' × 'Frau Karl Druschki']

'Freiburg II, Climbing' Cl HT, pb, 1958, Lindecke; intr. 1953

'Freifrau Ida von Schubert' HT, dr, 1912, Lambert, P.; flowers dark crimson-red, medium, dbl., moderate fragrance; ['Oskar Cordel' × 'Frau Peter Lambert']

'Freifrau von Marschall' HWich, mp, 1913, Lambert, P.; flowers fresh pink, 3-4 cm., dbl., borne in immense, loose clusters;

mid-season bloom; nearly thornless; vigorous (8-12 ft.) growth; ['Farquhar' × 'Schneewittchen']

'Freiheitsglocke' -- See 'Liberty Bell'

'Freiherr von Marschall' T, mr, 1903, Lambert, P.; bud pointed; flowers large, dbl.; foliage blood-red when young; vigorous growth; ['Princesse Alice de Monaco' × 'Rose d'Evian']

Freisinger Morgenröte® -- See 'Kormarter'

'Freja' S, mp, Carlsson-Nilsson; flowers pink to salmon, cupped, borne in large clusters; recurrent; vigorous (7-10 ft.) growth; intr. 2001

'Frejivesix' dp, INRA; intr. 1978

'French Can Can' HT, pb, 1956, Buyl Frères; bud well formed; flowers pink, reverse yellow, large, dbl.; vigorous, bushy growth

'French Cancan' -- See 'Tourbillon'

'French Lace' F, w, 1981, Warriner, William A.; bud pointed; flowers ivory, pastel apricot to white, 4½ in., 30-35 petals, high-centered, borne in small clusters, slight fruity fragrance; foliage small, dark; prickles small; bushy growth; PP4848; ['Dr. A.J. Verhage' × Bridal Pink™]; intr. 1980

'French Liberty' -- See 'Meijette'

'French Panarosa' S, w, Delbard; intr. 2004

French Perfume™ -- See 'Keibian'

'French Vanilla' Gr, w, 1987, Thomson, R.; flowers white and faint pink, fading white, medium, dbl., high-centered, borne usually singly, moderate fragrance; foliage medium size, dark green, matte; prickles few, moderate, brown; spreading growth; no fruit; ['Araby' × 'Royal Highness']; intr. 1984

'French Vanilla' HT, w; intr. 1999

'Frénésie' LCl, Combe, M.; flowers deep vermilion, reverse lighter, fading to orange, slight fragrance; intr. 1965

'Frensham' F, dr, 1946, Norman; flowers deep scarlet, 15 petals, borne in large trusses; vigorous growth; ['floribunda seedling' × 'Crimson Glory']; intr. 1946

'Frensham, Climbing' Cl F, dr, Bennett, J.A.; intr. 1958

'Frensham's Companion' F, dp, 1952, Morse; flowers cerise, loosely formed, medium, 18 petals, borne in trusses; very free growth; [sport of 'Frensham']

'Frenzy' (Prince Igor®) F, rb, 1971, Meilland; flowers nasturtium-red, reverse yellow, rounded, 2 in., 25 petals, moderate fruity fragrance; foliage matte; vigorous, bushy growth; [(Sarabande® × 'Dany Robin') × Zambra®]; intr. 1970

'Frére Marie Pierre' HP, mp, 1891, Bernaix; flowers China pink fading to blush, 11 cm., very dbl., cupped, borne mostly solitary; growth upright

'Frero' mp, INRA; intr. 1982

Fresco® F, ob, 1968, deRuiter; flowers orange, reverse golden yellow, well-formed, 3 in., slight fragrance; foliage dark, glossy; vigorous, bushy growth; ['Metropole' × Orange Sensation®]

'Fresh Cream' HT, w, Kordes; flowers creamy white with hint of apricot in center, dbl., high-centered; strong, medium to tall growth; intr. 1991

'Fresh Cream' Min, w, Bell; bud slender, pointed buds; flowers creamy white, dbl., high-centered; tall growth; intr. 1996

'Fresh Hit' -- See 'Poulfre'

'Fresh Pink' Min, lp, 1963, Moore, Ralph S.; bud ovoid; flowers light pink tipped salmon, 25 petals, cupped, borne in clusters, slight fragrance; foliage leathery, glossy; vigorous, bushy growth; PP2525; [(R. wichurana × Floradora) × 'Little Buckaroo']; intr. 1962

'Fresh Pink' Min, mp, McGredy, Sam IV; intr. 1987

'Fresh Point' LCl, pb, Barni; flowers cream changing to pink as they open and mature, 8 cm., 12-15 petals, borne in clusters; foliage medium to large, dark green; tall (8 ft and up) growth; ['Altair' × seedling]

'Fresh Snow' -- See 'Shin-Setsu'

'Fresh Start' -- See 'Flosar'

'Freshie' -- See 'Macsweetwa'

Freude® ('Decorat') HT, or, 1974, W. Kordes Söhne; flowers vermilion and gold blend, 4 in., dbl., high-centered; recurrent; foliage dark green, dense, leathery; vigorous, bushy, upright growth; ['Fragrant Cloud' × Peer Gynt®]; intr. 1975

'Freude' -- See 'Cheer'

'Freudenfeuer' Pol, mr, 1918, Kiese; flowers bright red; moderate growth

'Freudentanz' F, mr, 1975, Hetzel; bud pointed; flowers bright red, reverse flamed red, medium, intense fragrance; foliage glossy; vigorous, upright, bushy growth; ['Fragrant Cloud' × 'Goldmarie']; intr. 1973

'Freund Pilz' HT, mr, 1930, Schildmann; flowers carmine-red, medium, dbl.

'Frevan' ('Vannie') F, dp, 2000, French, Bryan; flowers dark pink, reverse slightly lighter, 3 in., semi-dbl., borne singly or in clusters of 3-4, slight fragrance; recurrent; foliage medium size, dark green, semi-glossy; prickles moderate, brown-red; growth upright, medium (3-4 ft.)

'Freya' S, pb, 1910, Geschwind, R.; flowers 4-5 cm., single to semi-dbl., borne in small clusters, no fragrance; hybrid canina

'Freya' HT, dp, Leenders, M.; flowers carmine-red, large, dbl.; vigorous growth; [seedling × 'Étoile de Hollande']; intr. 1956

'Friction Lights' -- See 'Horlights'

'Friday's Child' -- See 'Horabi'

'Fridolin' Min, yb; flowers yellow with orange edges, orange spreading down the petals as it ages, dbl., cupped, then open, borne in clusters; recurrent

'Fridolin Bunnert' T, mr, 1888, Bernaix; flowers carmine, shaded vermilion-amaranth, medium, full

'Frieda Krause' HT, or, 1935, Krause; flowers orange-scarlet-red, large, dbl., high-centered; foliage leathery, dark; very vigorous, bushy growth; ['I Zingari' × seedling]

'Friedlanderiana' HGal, mp; flowers bright rose-pink, single; non-recurrent; [R. gallica × R. canina]

'Friedrich Albert Krupp' -- See 'Friedrich Alfred Krupp'

'Friedrich Alfred Krupp' ('Friedrich Albert Krupp') HT, op, 1903, Welter; flowers yellowish salmon-pink, large, very dbl.

'Friedrich Harms' -- See 'Franz Deegen'

'Friedrich Heyer' S, ob, 1956, Tantau, Math.; flowers bright orange, large, 10 petals, borne in large clusters, moderate fragrance; foliage dark, glossy, leathery; vigorous, upright growth

'Friedrich Schwarz' HT, dr, 1952, Kordes; flowers crimson, large, 30 petals, cupped, foliage dark; very tall, branching growth; ['Poinsettia' × ('Crimson Glory' × 'Lord Charlemont')]

'Friedrich von Schiller' HP, dr, 1881, Mietzsch; flowers crimson shaded with violet, medium, very full

'Friedrich Wörlein' F, dy, 1973, Kordes; bud globular; flowers golden yellow, large, dbl., moderate fragrance; foliage dark; vigorous, upright, bushy growth; ['Clare Grammerstorf' × 'Golden Masterpiece']; intr. 1963

'Friedricharah' -- See 'Friedrichsruh'

'Friedrichsruh' ('Friedricharah') HT, dr, 1908, Türke; flowers dark crimson, shaded black, turning blue, open, large, dbl.; foliage dark, glossy; bushy, open growth; ['Princesse de Bearn' × 'Francis Dubreuil']

'Friend for Life' -- See 'Cocnanne'

'Friend of Heart' HT, pb, 1986, Hardikar, Dr. M.N.; flowers large, 30 petals, high-centered, borne singly, slight fragrance; foliage medium size, dark, glossy; prickles deep brown; upright growth; [('Festival Beauty' × 'Scarlet Knight') × ('Festival Beauty' × 'Scarlet Knight')]; intr. 1985

'Friend of Peace' HT, yb, 1987, Hardikar, Dr. M.N.; flowers , 20-22 petals, globular, intense fragrance; foliage large, dark green, glossy, leathery; prickles crescent, light brown; upright, open growth; [('Scarlet Knight' × 'Festival Beauty') × 'Festival Beauty']; intr. 1986

'Friend Sonia' HT, pb, Okawa, K.; flowers pale pink, yellow at petal base, reverse darker pink; [sport of 'Sonia']; intr. 1985

'Friendenspark Hiroshima' F, dy, Niebourg ?; intr. 1998

'Friends Forever' S, dp, Lowe; flowers fuchsia pink, old fashioned, full, quartered; recurrent; hips disease resistant (6 ft) growth; intr. 2001

'Friends of Benalla Gardens' Pol, w, Sutherland; intr. 1996

'Friendship' HT, dp, 1937, Amling Co.; bud pointed; flowers dark red, semi-dbl., high-centered, intense fragrance; foliage glossy; vigorous growth; RULED EXTINCT 9/77; ['Templar' × 'Talisman']

'Friendship' HT, dr, 1938, Dickson, A.; flowers bright strawberry-red, with bright scarlet undertone, very large, dbl.; very vigorous growth; RULED EXTINCT 9/77

'Friendship' HT, rb, Meilland; flowers medium red, buttercup yellow reverse, dbl.; greenhouse rose; intr. 2004

'Friendship' -- See 'Horcohabit'

Friendship™ -- See 'Linrick'

'Friendship' -- See 'Havipip'

Friesensöhne® -- See 'Tansenfrie'

'Friesia' -- See 'Korresia'

'Friesia, Climbing' -- See 'Sunsprite, Climbing'

'Frigg' S, m, 1969, Lundstad; flowers small, 15 petals, flat, borne in clusters; free, recurrent boom; foliage small, rich green; low growth; ['Schneezwerg' × *R. nitida*]

'Frileuse' Gr, mp, 1985, Poulsen, Niels D.; flowers large, dbl., urn-shaped, slight fragrance; foliage large, light green, glossy; tall, upright, bushy growth; [Queen Elizabeth® × 'Baronesse Manon']; intr. 1966

'Frills' HT, op, 1950, Moss; flowers deep salmon-pink becoming lighter, petals scalloped, large; compact, bushy growth

'Frillseeker' S, mr, George; flowers light red, petals frilled, borne in large clusters; long stems; tall growth; intr. 2003

'Frilly Dilly' MinFl, lp, Cocker; flowers soft pink, medium, dahlia-like, borne in small clusters, no fragrance; compact, very low growth; intr. 1986

'Frilly Dilly' -- See 'Murfri'

'Frimousse' F, op, 1959, Vilmorin-Andrieux; flowers orange-pink, base yellow, medium, single, borne in clusters; vigorous, very bushy growth; ['Masquerade' × unknown]

'Friné' HT, dr, 1961, Dot, Simon; flowers crimson suffused strawberry-red, well-formed, 35 petals; vigorous growth; ['Lila Vidri' × ('Soraya' × 'Vigoro')]

Frine® -- See 'Barfri'

'Fringette' Min, dp, 1964, Moore, Ralph S.; flowers deep pink, white center, small, 25 petals; low (8 in.), compact growth; PP2718; [seedling × 'Magic Wand']

'Friquet' T, mp, 1903, Croibier; flowers bright carmine, center petals streaked white, large, full

Frisco® -- See 'Korflapei'

'Frisco City' F, dr; flowers dark cherry red with prominent yellow stamens; foliage glossy; strong, medium growth

'Frisco Kordana' Min, dy, Kordes; flowers deep yellow center, outer petals paler, full; container rose

'Frisette' F, or, 1964, Mondial Roses; flowers bright scarlet, open, semi-dbl., borne in clusters; growth vigorous, low to medium; [seedling × 'Concerto']

'Frisky' HT, mr, 1960, Wyant; flowers velvety red, open, large, 50 petals, moderate fragrance; foliage dark, glossy; vigorous, bushy growth; ['Charlotte Armstrong' × 'Chrysler Imperial']; intr. 1959

Frisson Frais® -- See 'LLX8740'

'Fritz Hegar' Pol, dr, 1930, Schmitt-Eltville; flowers medium, semi-dbl.

'Fritz Höger' HT, dr, 1934, Kordes; bud pointed; flowers pure crimson, large, dbl., high-centered; foliage leathery, dark; very vigorous growth; [('Hadley' × 'Comte G. de Rochemur') × 'Cathrine Kordes']

'Fritz Maydt' HT, w, 1925, Leenders, M.; flowers coppery flesh-white; ['Mev. C. van Marwijk Kooy' × 'Marquise de Sinéty']

'Fritz Nobis' S, pb, 1940, Kordes; bud long, pointed, light red; flowers white, reverse reddish salmon-pink, large, dbl., high-centered, borne in clusters, intense fragrance; non-recurrent; foliage glossy, leathery; vigorous growth; ['Joanna Hill' × 'Magnifica']

'Fritz Reuter' HMult, pb, 1913, Lambert; flowers carmine, yellow at center, violet pink towards edges, medium, full, moderate fragrance

'Fritz Schrödter' HT, dr, 1928, Mühle; flowers brilliant dark scarlet, large, dbl.; foliage bronze, soft; vigorous, bushy growth; ['Hortulanus Budde' × unknown]

'Fritz Thiedemann' HT, or, 1961, Tantau, Math.; bud pointed; flowers brick-red, well-shaped, 4 in., 36 petals, moderate fragrance; foliage dark; bushy growth; [(Horstmann's Jubilaumsrose × unknown) × ('Alpine Glow' × unknown)]; intr. 1960

'Fritz Thiedemann, Climbing' Cl HT, or, 1961, Kordes

'Fritz Walter' -- See 'Helfriwa'

'Fritzi' -- See 'Heltzi'

'Friuli' HT, ab, 1933, Ingegnoli; flowers amber-yellow, large, cupped; vigorous growth

'Frivole' F, mr, 1958, Buyl Frères; flowers geranium-red, very dbl.; vigorous, low growth; ['Independence' × 'Country Girl']

'Frivolité' HT, or, 1956, Dot, Pedro; flowers scarlet shaded orange and salmon, large, 50 petals; vigorous, compact growth; ['Peace' × 'Catalonia']

'Frivolous' -- See 'Minfriv'

'Frivolous Pink' HT, ab, 2001, Coiner, Jim; flowers pink with apricot, pink blend reverse, large, full, borne in small clusters, moderate fragrance; foliage medium size, medium green, semi-glossy; growth compact, medium (36 in.); garden decorative; PP15638; [seedling × seedling]

'Frocrin' ('Crinkles') Min, w, 1990, Frock, Marshall J.; bud ovoid; flowers white, aging with flecks of red, slow to fade, crinkled center, 60 petals, high-centered, slight fragrance; foliage medium size, dark green, semi-glossy; prickles straight, short, red; upright, bushy, medium growth; fruit not observed; ['Rise 'n' Shine' × seedling]

'Frofire' ('Evening Fire') Min, rb, 1995, Frock, Marshall J.; flowers red, pink reverse, medium, dbl., borne mostly singly, moderate fragrance; foliage medium size, medium green, semi-glossy; some prickles; bushy growth; [Black Jade™ × 'Pierrine']

Frohsinn® F, ab, 1961, Tantau, Math.; bud pointed; flowers apricot, cream and pink blend, large, 20 petals, cupped, borne in large clusters, slight fragrance; foliage glossy; vigorous, bushy growth; [Horstmann's Jubilaumsrose × 'Circus']

'Frohsinn 82' -- See 'Tansinnroh'

'Froissard' -- See 'Mrs Standish'

'Frojean' ('Jeannine Michelle') Min, dy, 1989, Frock, Marshall J.; bud pointed; flowers deep gold-yellow, aging to pale yellow, medium, 30 petals, high-centered, borne usually singly, moderate fruity fragrance; foliage medium size, medium green, semi-glossy; prickles straight, tan; upright, bushy, medium, hardy growth; fruit not observed; ['Rise 'n' Shine' × seedling]

'Frolic' F, pb, Dawson; intr. 1995

'Frolic' F, mp, 1953, Swim, H.C.; flowers bright pink, 2½ in., 21 petals, borne in large sprays, slight fragrance; vigorous, bushy growth; PP1179; ['World's Fair' × 'Pinocchio']

'Fromite' ('White Mite') Min, w, 1991, Frock, Marshall J.; flowers small (micro-mini), full, slight fragrance; foliage small, medium green, semi-glossy; upright growth; [Baby Katie™ × seedling]

Frondeuse® S, pb

'Froneen' ('Jeannine') Min, lp, 1992, Frock, Marshall J.; flowers light pink aging to white with a few red spots, similar to Royal Highness, 1½-1¾ in., 30 petals, high-centered; foliage medium size, medium green, semi-glossy; medium (40-50 cm.), upright growth; [Baby Katie™ × seedling]

'Fronorm' ('Norma Margaret') Min, pb, 1990, Frock, Marshall J.; bud pointed; flowers pink, blending with copper shading, reverse white with pink, 30 petals, high-centered, moderate fragrance; foliage medium size, medium green, semi-glossy; prickles straight, medium, brown; upright, medium growth; fruit not observed; [Baby Katie™ × seedling]

'Front 'n' Center' -- See 'Savafront'

Front Page™ -- See 'Winpage'

'Front Page' -- See 'Hartwiz'

'Frontenac' S, dp, 1992, Ogilvie, Ian S.; flowers dbl., borne in small clusters; foliage medium size, dark green, glossy; some prickles; medium (100 cm.), upright growth; very winter hardy; PP9210; [((Queen Elizabeth® × 'Arthur Bell') × ('Simonet Red' × 'Von Scharnhorst')) × ((*R.* × *kordesii* (Red Dawn × Suzanne)) × ((Red Dawn × Suzanne) × (Red Dawn

× Suzanne)))]; intr. 1992
'Frontier Twirl' S, pb, 1985, Buck, Dr. Griffith J.; flowers pink-yellow blend, large, 25 petals, cupped, borne 1-8 per cluster, moderate fragrance; recurrent; foliage leathery, medium size, bronze green; prickles awl-like, tan; erect, bushy growth; hardy; ['Sevilliana' × 'Just Joey']; intr. 1984
'Frostfire' Min, mr, 1963, Moore, Ralph S.; flowers red, sometimes flecked white, 1 in., 30 petals; foliage dark, glossy; bushy, compact (12-14 in.) growth; [((R. wichurana × Floradora) × seedling) × 'Little Buckaroo']; intr. 1963
'Frosty' Min, w, 1955, Moore, Ralph S.; bud ovoid, pale pink; flowers clear white, very small, 45 petals, borne in clusters of 3 - 10 or more, moderate honeysuckle fragrance; foliage glossy; vigorous (12-14 in.), compact, spreading growth; PP1412; [(R. wichurana × seedling) × (R. wichurana × seedling)]; intr. 1953
Frosty ™ -- See 'Poulezy'
'Frosty Morning' -- See 'Horfrost'
Frosty Paillette™ -- See 'Poulezy'
'Frosty Parade' (Frosty Paillette™, Frosty ™) Min, w, Poulsen; flowers white, medium, slight wild rose fragrance; foliage dark; growth narrow, bushy, 20-40 cm.; PP10737; intr. 1998
'Frothy' Min, w, McGredy, Sam IV; intr. 1992
'Frou Frou' HT, ob, Hiroshima; intr. 2001
'Froufrou' HT, yb, 1955, Moulin-Epinay; flowers chamois-yellow, center carmine, large, very dbl.; vigorous, bushy growth; ['Mme Joseph Perraud' × 'Yvonne Plassat']
'Frou-Frou' HT, rb, 1957, Laperrière; flowers crimson, reverse carmine-pink, large, 25 petals; moderate growth; ['Comtesse Vandal' × seedling]
'Froy' F, or, 1973, Lundstad; bud ovoid; flowers open, medium, semi-dbl., slight fragrance; foliage glossy, dark; bushy growth; ['Traumland' × 'Poulsen's Pink']; intr. 1972
'Fru Dagmar Hartopp' -- See 'Dagmar Hastrup'
'Fru Dagmar Hastrup' -- See 'Dagmar Hastrup'
'Fru Gerda Helmuus' HT, op, 1935, Poulsen, D.T.; flowers light orange-pink, large, semi-dbl.
'Fru Inge Poulsen' -- See 'Mrs Inge Poulsen'
'Fru Johanne Poulsen' HT, mp, 1924, Poulsen, S.; flowers bright pink, well-formed; vigorous growth; ['Margrethe Moller' × unknown]
'Fru Julie Poulsen' -- See 'Poulsen's Delight'
'Fru Xenia Jacobsen' HT, dr, 1925, Poulsen, S.; flowers deep red, well-shaped, dbl.; vigorous growth; ['Étoile de France' × 'Richmond']
'Frühlingsanfang' ('Spring Beginning') HSpn, w, 1950, Kordes; bud long, pointed; flowers ivory-white, 4 in., single; intermittent bloom; foliage leathery; very vigorous, bushy (9 ft.) growth; ['Joanna Hill' × R. spinosissima altaica]
'Frühlingsduft' ('Spring Fragrance') HSpn, pb, 1949, Kordes; bud ovoid, golden yellow; flowers lemon-yellow with light pink, very large, dbl., high-centered, intense Marechal Niel fragrance; non-recurrent; foliage large, leathery; very vigorous, upright, bushy growth; ['Joanna Hill' × R. spinosissima altaica]
Frühlingsgold® ('Spring Gold') HSpn, my, 1937, Kordes; bud pointed, nasturtium-red; flowers creamy yellow, 3 in., single; non-recurrent; foliage large, light, soft, wrinkled; very vigorous, bushy growth; ['Joanna Hill' × R. spinosissima hispida]
'Frühlingsmorgen' ('Spring Morning') HSpn, pb, 1940, Kordes; flowers cherry-pink at edges, center soft yellow, stamens maroon, medium, single; occasionally recurrent bloom; foliage dark; free growth (6 ft.); hips large, red; [('E.G. Hill' × 'Cathrine Kordes') × R. spinosissima altaica]
'Frühlingsschnee' ('Spring Snow') HSpn, w, 1956, Kordes; bud ovoid; flowers snow-white, very large, single, slight fragrance; foliage leathery, wrinkled, light green; very vigorous, upright growth; ['Golden Glow' × R. spinosissima altaica]
'Frühlingsstunde' HSpn, lp, 1942, Kordes; flowers whitish pink, medium, semi-dbl.
'Frühlingstag' HSpn, my, 1949, Kordes; bud ovoid; flowers golden yellow, large, semi-dbl., borne in small clusters, moderate fragrance; profuse non-recurrent bloom; foliage leathery; numerous prickles; growth to 5 ft.; ['McGredy's Wonder' × 'Frühlingsgold']
'Frühlingszauber' ('Spring Charm') HSpn, mp, 1940, Kordes; flowers pink, very large, single; non-recurrent; foliage dark; vigorous (7 ft.) growth; hips large, dark red; [('E.G. Hill' × 'Cathrine Kordes') × R. spinosissima altaica]
'Fruit Buffet' F, yb
Fruité® ('Fruitee') F, ob, Meilland, L.; flowers multiple shades of orange and red, medium, full, slight fruity fragrance; intr. 1984
'Fruite' HT, yb, Meilland; flowers striped; intr. 2003
'Fruitee' -- See 'Meifructoz'
'Fryaffair' ('Sightsaver') HT, lp, Fryer, Gareth; intr. 1997
'Fryatlanta' F, ob; intr. 2000
'Frybingo' ('Lady Aberdeen') HT, dp, Fryer, Gareth; intr. 1997
'Frybizzy' LCl, mp, Fryer; intr. 2001
'Fryblissful' ('Dizzy Heights') LCl, mr, 1999, Fryer, Gareth; flowers bright red, reverse same, 5-5½ in., dbl., borne in large clusters, slight fragrance; foliage medium size, dark green, semi-glossy; prickles moderate; upright, tall (7-10 ft.) growth; intr. 2000
'Frybountiful' ('Phab Gold') F, dy, Fryer, Gareth; intr. 1998
'Frybright' ('Razzle Dazzle') F, ob, Fryer, Gareth; intr. 1997
'Frybubbly' ('Bubbles') Min, mp, Fryer, Gareth; intr. 1998
'Frycalm' ('Rochemenier Village') HT, ob, Fryer, Gareth; intr. 1998
'Frycassia' ('Flower Power') MinFl, ob, Fryer, Gareth; intr. 1998
'Frycentury' ('Day Breaker') F, ab, 2003, Fryer, Gareth; flowers medium, pastel peach with yellow, 4 in., 30-35 petals, borne singly and in small clusters; foliage medium size, dark green, glossy; prickles large, almost straight, light brown to green, none; growth bushy, medium; exhibition, cutting garden decoration; PP15334; ['Silver Jubilee' × ('Pensioners Voice' × 'Cheshire Life')]; intr. 2004
'Frychambi' ('Daily Express') HT, ab, Fryer, Gareth; intr. 1986
'Frycharm' ('Reta Elizabeth Lindsay') HT, dy, Fryer, Gareth; intr. 1998
'Fryclimbdown' ('Crimson Cascade') LCl, dr, Fryer, Gareth; intr. 1991
'Frydabble' ('Belle Danielle') F, dp, Fryer; intr. 2000
'Frydarkeye' ('Dark Eyes', 'Rosentanz') S, rb, Fryer, Gareth; intr. 1988
'Frydesire' HT, ab; intr. 2000
'Frydisco' HT, ab, Fryer; intr. 2003
'Frydishy' HT, ob, Fryers; intr. 2006
'Frydivine' HT, ly, Fryer; intr. 2004
'Frydrama' HT, ab, Fryer; intr. 2002
'Fryeager' ('John Willan', 'Princess Charming') HT, mp, 2001, Fryer, Gareth; flowers satin pink, 12-15 cm., full, high-centered, borne mostly solitary; foliage large, medium green, semi-glossy; prickles moderate; growth bushy, tall (110 cm.); garden decorative; intr. 2002
'Fryelectric' HT, ob, Fryer; intr. 2002
'Fryelise' ('Cheshire') HT, my, 1999, Fryer, Gareth; flowers golden honey yellow, large, dbl., borne in small clusters, moderate fragrance; foliage large, dark green, semi-glossy; prickles moderate; upright, medium (3 ft.) growth; intr. 1999
'Fryentice' ('Casanova', Francois Mauriac®) F, ob, Fryer; intr. 2001
'Fryer's Orange' HT, ab, 1934, Fryers Nursery, Ltd.; flowers orange-yellow; [sport of 'Mrs Sam McGredy']
'Fryessex' Min, ob, Fryer; intr. 2005
'Fryevenest' ('Evening Sentinel') F, ob, Fryer, Gareth; intr. 1986
'Fryextra' HT, mp, Fryer; intr. 2004
'Fryfandango' LCl, mr, Fryer; intr. 2004
'Fryfantasy' HT, ob, Fryer; intr. 2004
'Fryfelma' HT, mp, Fryer; intr. 2002
'Fryferwi' F, ly, Fryer; intr. 2007
'Fryfestoon' LCl, mp, Fryer; intr. 2005
'Fryfixit' F, ab, Fryer; intr. 2001
'Fryflash' F, my; intr. 2002
'Fryflorida' HT, dy, Fryer; intr. 2004
'Fryfocus' LCl, mr, Fryer; intr. 2005

'Fryfrenzy' F, or, Fryer; intr. 2002
'Frygladiator' F, mp, Fryer; intr. 2007
'Fryglitzy' ('The Rotarian', 'Voeux de Bonheur') HT, yb, Fryer; intr. 2004
'Frygoldie' ('Fairy Gold') Min, dy, Fryer, Gareth; intr. 1992
'Frygolly' F, r, Fryer; intr. 2003
'Frygran' ('Johnnie Walker') HT, ab, 1983, Fryers Nursery, Ltd.; flowers buff apricot, well-formed, large, 20 petals; foliage medium size, medium green, matte; vigorous, bushy growth; ['Sunblest' × ('Arthur Bell' × 'Belle Blonde')]
'Frygroovy' HT, w, Fryer; intr. 2006
'Fryhearty' HT, ab, Fryer's; intr. 2007
'Fryhoncho' F, r, Fryer; intr. 2004
'Fryhunky' F, mp, Fryer; intr. 2007
'Fryjak' F, mr, Fryer; intr. 2006
'Fryjam' ('The Flower Arranger') F, ab, 1984, Fryers Nursery, Ltd.; bud large; flowers peach, well-formed, semi-dbl., borne in trusses; foliage large, dark, glossy; upright growth; [seedling × seedling]
'Fryjangle' F, ob, Fryer; intr. 2004
'Fryjasso' ('Inner Wheel') F, pb, 1984, Fryers Nursery, Ltd.; flowers carmine edged rose pink, large, 22 petals; foliage medium size, dark red, matte; bushy growth; ['Pink Parfait' × 'Picasso']
'Fryjess' F, w, Fryer; intr. 2006
'Fryjess' F, op, Fryer; intr. 2006
'Fryjingo' ('The Lady') HT, yb, 1986, Fryer, Gareth; flowers honey yellow, petals edged salmon, well-formed, large, 35 petals, high-centered, borne singly and in clusters, slight fragrance; recurrent; foliage medium size, medium green, semi-glossy; upright growth; ['Pink Parfait' × 'Redgold']; intr. 1985
'Fryjolly' HT, op, Fryer; intr. 2006
'Frykeen' F, ab, Fryer; intr. 2007
'Frykeyno' F, my, Fryer; intr. 2006
'Frykookie' F, dy, Fryer; intr. 2006
'Frykristal' HT, dr, Fryer; bud large, almost black; intr. 2005
'Frylucy' F, mp, Fryer; intr. 2009
'Frymartor' ('Nuit d'Èté') HT, mr, Fryer, Gareth; intr. 1993
'Frymaxicot' ('Beautiful Dreamer', 'Sweet Memories') F, ab, Fryer, Gareth; bud globular; intr. 1990
'Frymestin' ('Ethel Austin') F, dp, 1984, Fryers Nursery, Ltd.; flowers deep pink with lighter pink center, large, 20 petals, high-centered, moderate fragrance; recurrent; foliage large, medium green, semi-glossy; upright growth; ['Pink Parfait' × 'Redgold']
'Fryminicot' ('Sweet Dream') F, ab, 1988, Fryers Nursery, Ltd.; flowers peach-apricot, medium, dbl., globular, borne in clusters, moderate fragrance; free-flowering; foliage medium size, medium green, semi-glossy; low (18-24 in.), bushy growth; [seedling × seedling]
'Fryminiles' ('Lesley Anne') Min, op, 1987, Fryer, Gareth; flowers pale peach-pink, pale yellow base, fading slightly paler, large, 45 petals, cupped; foliage medium size, light green, matte; prickles thin, small, pointed, light brown; upright growth; hips oval, orange-red; [seedling × seedling]
'Fryministar' ('Top Marks') Min, or, Fryer, Gareth
'Frymoody' HT, lp, Fryer; intr. 2007
'Fryorst' ('ARC Angel') HT, ob, Fryer, Gareth; intr. 1996
'Fryosa' F, my, Fryer; intr. 2005
'Fryperdee' ('Velours Parfumé', 'Velvet Fragrance') HT, dr, 1989, Fryers Nursery, Ltd.; flowers deep, velvety crimson, 4½ in., 25 petals, high-centered, intense raspberry/clove fragrance; recurrent; foliage large, dark green, semi-glossy; upright (4½ ft.) growth; [seedling × seedling]; intr. 1988
'Fryprincess' ('Julie Cussons') F, ob, Fryer, Gareth; intr. 1988
'Fryrelax' ('Michelle Wright') F, ab, Fryer, Gareth; intr. 1989
'Fryrhapsody' ('Langdale Chase') F, ab, Fryer, Gareth; intr. 1990
'Fryromeo' ('Scent-Sation') HT, ob, Fryer, Gareth; intr. 1998
'Fryshrewby' HT, dr, Fryer, Gareth; intr. 1988
'Frystar' ('Beauty Star', 'Liverpool Remembers') HT, or, 1992, Fryer, Gareth; flowers vermilion, 3-3½ in., full, borne mostly singly; foliage medium size, medium green, glossy; numerous prickles; tall (240 cm.), upright growth; PP7989; [Corso® × seedling]; intr. 1991
'Frystassi' ('Rosaletta') Min, pb, Fryer, Gareth; intr. 1988
'Frysweetie' ('Mary Gammon') Min, op, Fryer, Gareth; intr. 1993
'Frytango' ('The Observer') HT, ab, Fryer, Gareth; intr. 1992
'Frytranquil' ('Golden Moments') HT, dy, Fryer, Gareth; intr. 1991
'Frytrooper' ('Daily Post', Raven™, 'Liverpool Daily Post', 'Karla', 'Dusky Dancer') S, dr, 1999, Fryer, Gareth; flowers deep velvety red, golden stamens, 1¼-1½ in., 20-25 petals, borne in very large clusters; foliage small, dark green, glossy; prickles moderate; upright, bushy, medium (3-4 ft.) growth; PP9211; [Lavaglut® × (('Anytime' × 'Liverpool Echo') × ('New Penny' × unknown))]; intr. 1992
'Fryvivacious' ('Julie Andrews') F, op, Fryer, Gareth; intr. 1992
'Frywango' HT, dy, Fryer; intr. 2007
'Frywhoppa' ('Cliché') HT, pb, 2001, Gareth Fryer; flowers medium pink, light yellow reverse, 5 in., full, borne mostly solitary; foliage medium size, dark green, glossy; prickles ½ in., straight, few; growth upright, tall (5-6 ft.); garden decorative, exhibition, cutting; ['Grandpa Dickson' × 'Sweetheart']; vigorous; prefers warmer climates; intr. 2002
'Frywilrey' ('Audrey Wilcox®) HT, rb, 1987, Fryers Nursery, Ltd.; flowers cerise red and silver cream, full, intense fragrance; foliage large, dark green, glossy; [Alpine Sunset® × 'Whisky Mac']; intr. 1985
'Frywinner' F, my, Fryer, Gareth; intr. 1994
'Fryworld' ('Atlantic Star') F, op, Fryer, Gareth; intr. 1993
'Fryworthy' ('Especially for You') HT, my, Fryer, Gareth; intr. 1996
'Fryxotic' ('Chantoli', Exotic®, Jolie Môme®, Sunset Celebration™, 'Warm Wishes') HT, ab, 1999, Fryer, Gareth; bud pointed to ovoid; flowers creamy apricot/amber blend, 4½-5 in., 35-40 petals, high-centered, borne mostly singly, moderate fruity fragrance; recurrent; foliage large, medium green, semi-glossy; prickles moderate, long, straight; stems strong, medium; upright, bushy, medium (3½-4 ft.) growth; hips very round to globular, smooth ; PP9718; ['Pot O'Gold' × seedling]; intr. 1994
'Fryxquisite' Min, mp, Fryer, Gareth; intr. 1994
'Fryyaboo' ('Belle Epoque') HT, ab, Fryer, Gareth; intr. 1994
'Fryyat' ('Good Morning') HT, ab, Fryer, Gareth; intr. 1995
'Fryyearn' ('Bride') HT, lp, Fryer, Gareth; intr. 1995
'Fryyeh' F, ob, Fryer, Gareth; intr. 1994
'Fryyeoman' (Flower Girl™) S, lp, 1999, Fryer, Gareth; bud short, ovoid; flowers soft pink fading to light pink centers, 1-1½ in., 8-15 petals, borne in very large clusters, slightly pendulous, slight apple fragrance; foliage medium size, light green, matte; few prickles; long, slender, arching stems; spreading, bushy, medium (4-5 ft.) growth; PP13268; ['Amruda' × 'Fairy Snow']; intr. 2000
'Fryyippee' ('Rosie Larkin') S, m, Fryer, Gareth; intr. 1993
'Fryyoung' ('Special Occasion') HT, ab, Fryer, Gareth; intr. 1995
'Fryzebedee' ('Cheshire Regiment') HT, ab, Fryer, Gareth
'Fryzippy' ('Bob Greaves') F, ob, Fryer, Gareth; intr. 1998
'Fuchsia' HGal, m
Fuchsia Meidiland™ -- See 'Meipelta'
Fuchsia Meillandecor® -- See 'Meipelta'
Fuchsia Minuetto™ -- See 'Meirosfon'
Fuchsia Pink Castle' -- See 'Poulbella'
Fuchsia Sunblaze' -- See 'Meirulex'
'Fuchsine Guy' F, m, 1930, Leenders, M.; flowers lilac-purple, open, large, semi-dbl., borne in clusters; foliage rich green; bushy growth; [sport of 'Lafayette']
'Fuëgo' F, or, 1964, Arles; bud pointed; flowers Chinese vermilion, medium, 30 petals, open, borne in clusters, slight fragrance; ['Aloha' × 'Gabychette']
'Fuego Negro' -- See 'Meilouzou'
Fuggerstadt Augsburg® -- See 'Kortreu'
'Fugitive' F, yb, 1969, Pal, Dr. B.P.; bud pointed; flowers apricot-yellow, becoming lighter, open, semi-dbl., borne in clusters; foliage glossy, bronze; vigorous, bushy growth; ['Mrs Oakley Fisher' × unknown]; intr. 1965
Fugue® LCl, dr, 1959, Meilland, Mrs.

Marie-Louise; bud globular; flowers medium, 30 petals, borne in small clusters; foliage leathery, glossy; vigorous growth; ['Alain' × 'Guinee']; intr. 1958

'Fujimai' HT, m, 2006, Yasuda, Yuji; flowers full, borne mostly solitary; foliage medium size, dark green, matte; prickles medium, moderate; growth upright, medium (1 m.); cutting; garden; ['Madame Violet' × seedling]; intr. 2006

'Fujimino' HT, w, Yasuda, Y.; flowers white, edges shaded darker pink, petals slightly reflexed, 11 cm., 24 petals, borne mostly solitary; foliage semi-glossy; prickles moderate; growth upright, medium; ['Madame Violet' × 'Cheerio']; intr. 1992

'Fujimusume' ('Wisteria Maiden') HT, dp, Keihan; intr. 1999

'Fujinami' ('Waves of Wisteria') HT, m, Onodera, T.; flowers pale mauve, 12 cm., 10 petals, borne mostly solitary, slight fragrance; foliage roundish, light green; [Blue Moon® × 'Sterling Silver']; intr. 1968

'Fujiyama Rose' -- See 'Akane Fuji'

'Fujizakura' Min, mp, 1997, Ohtsuki, Hironaka; flowers small, single; foliage small, medium green, semi-glossy; some prickles; spreading, low (20cm.) growth; ['Azumino' × 'Azumino']

'Fukuyama' HT, op, 1989, Tagashira, Kazuso; bud pointed; flowers salmon-pink, aging dark, large, 35 petals, high-centered, slight fragrance; foliage red aging dark green, matte, ovoid; prickles red to dark green; upright, tall growth; hips round, yellow-blend; [Pristine® × 'Takao']; intr. 1988

'Fulgens' HGal, dp, about 1830, Vibert; flowers vivid bright pink, medium, semi-dbl.

'Fulgens' HSpn, m; flowers lilac-pink, semi-dbl.; early bloom; growth to 3-4 ft.; hips glossy, black; intr. before 1940

'Fulgens' -- See 'Malton'

'Fulgorie' HP, mp, before 1840, from Angers; flowers carmine pink, edged lilac, very large, full

Fulgurante® -- See 'Waroujo'

Full House® HT, w, Tantau; flowers white with thin red edge, large, double, high-centered, borne mostly singly; recurrent; stems medium to long; florist rose; intr. 2004

'Full Moon' -- See 'Springmoon'

Full Moon Rising™ -- See 'Meivanery'

'Full Sail' -- See 'Maclanoflon'

'Fullcream' HT, ly, 1960, LeGrice; flowers creamy yellow, well-formed, 5-7 in., 28 petals, intense honey fragrance; foliage glossy; vigorous, low growth; PP2060; ['Wellworth' × 'Diamond Jubilee']; intr. 1959

'Fullerton Centennial' -- See 'Pixifull'

'Fulsteve' ('Steve Silverthorne') HT, pb, 1991, Fulgham, Mary; flowers white with pink blushing, large, full, borne mostly singly, slight fragrance; foliage large, medium green, semi-glossy; medium, upright growth; ['Dorothy Anne' × 'Headliner']

'Fulton MacKay' -- See 'Cocdana'

'Fulvia' HT, dp, 1950, Gaujard; flowers pink tinted carmine, medium, dbl.; foliage leathery, light green; vigorous, bushy growth; ['Mme Joseph Perraud' × 'Mme Elie Dupraz']

Fun™ Min, dp, Poulsen Roser; flowers very small, dbl.; PP10628; intr. 1995

'Fun Fair' F, yb; intr. 2006

'Fun Jwan Lo' ('Fen Zhuang Lou', 'Indica Major', 'Odorata 22449') S, w, before 1811; flowers white, center pale pink to medium, 6-7 cm., dbl., borne in clusters; very vigorous growth; not hardy; discovered in a garden in Pautung Fu, Chihli province, by Frank N. Meyer and sent to the U.S.D.A. for use as understock

'Fun Sunsation' -- See 'Korhaugen'

'Funchal' HT, Moreira da Silva, A.

'Funkenmariechen' F, yb, 1975, Kordes; flowers yellow, red, dbl., globular, slight fragrance; foliage glossy; upright, bushy growth; [seedling × 'Samba']; intr. 1973

Funkuhr® -- See 'Korport'

'Funny Face' Min, rb, 1982, Jolly, Betty J.; flowers white, petals edged red, aging red, medium, 35 petals, slight fragrance; foliage small, medium green, semi-glossy; upright, bushy growth; ['Avandel' × 'Zinger']

'Funny Face' ('Garden Jubilee Funny Face') S, pb, Lim, P, & Twomey, J.; flowers pink and white painted, 4 in., semi-dbl.; prolific; foliage very clean, disease-resistant.; compact, rounded, upright (3 ft.) growth; PP15753; intr. 2004

'Funny Girl' -- See 'Barfunn'

'Funny Girl' -- See 'Jacfun'

'Fur Elise' -- See 'Ripelise'

'Fure-Daiko' ('Piñata', 'Village Festival') LCl, yb, 1973, Suzuki, Seizo; bud short, ovoid, vermilion; flowers yellow with vermilion overlay, changing to vermilion over most of petal, 3 in., 25-30 petals, borne in clusters, moderate fragrance; foliage large, glossy, dark; vigorous, climbing growth; PP3996; [(('Goldilocks' × unknown) × Sarabande®) × (Golden Giant® × unknown)]; intr. 1974

'Furia' HT, op, Combe, M.; intr. 1968

'Furisode' HT, mp, Teranishi, K.; flowers 7-8 cm., 30 petals, cupped, borne in clusters of 3-5, intense fragrance; foliage dark green, semi-glossy; growth very vigorous (2-3 m.); [Queen Elizabeth® × seedling]; intr. 1968

'Furore' HT, or, 1965, Verbeek; flowers scarlet, medium, very dbl.; foliage dark; [(Baccará® × seedling) × 'Miracle']

'Fürst Bismarck' ('Belle Lyonnaise') T, dy, 1886, Drögemüller; flowers golden yellow, large, very dbl., moderate fruity fragrance; ['Gloire de Dijon' × unknown (probably selfed)]

'Fürst Leopold IV zu Schaumburg-Lippe' HP, dr, 1918, Kiese; flowers large, dbl.

'Fürst Niclot' -- See 'Kaiser Wilhelm II'

'Fürst Bismarck' T, mr, 1887, Drögemüller; flowers China pink to cerise pink, fading lighter, large, very dbl.; ['Gloire de Dijon' × 'Comtesse d'Oxford']

'Fürstin Bülow' T, pb, 1908, Brauer; flowers yellow-pink with gold reflections, shaded violet, medium, full, moderate fragrance

'Fürstin Hohenzollern' -- See 'Fürstin Infantin von Hohenzollern'

'Fürstin Infantin von Hohenzollern' ('Fürstin Hohenzollern', 'Fürstin von Hohenzollern Infantin') T, m, 1898, Brauer, P.; flowers purple rose, center yellowish-salmon, medium, dbl.; ['Mlle la Comtesse de Leusse' × 'Marie Van Houtte']

'Fürstin Maria Hatzfeldt' HT, dr, 1927, Boden; flowers bright dark red, dbl.; ['Gen. MacArthur' × seedling]

'Fürstin von Hohenzollern Infantin' -- See 'Fürstin Infantin von Hohenzollern'

'Fürstin von Pless' HRg, w, 1911, Lambert, P.; flowers white with lemon center, very large, full, cupped, borne mostly singly or in small clusters, moderate fragrance; foliage lush; upright, medium (5 ft.) growth; ['Mme Caroline Testout' × 'Conrad Ferdinand Meyer']

'Furusato' ('Home') HT, mp, Keihan; intr. 1970

'Fushimi' HT, pb, Keihan; flowers pink with a green edge; intr. 1987

'Fushimi, Climbing' Cl HT, pb, Keihan; intr. 1992

'Fushino' HT, lp, 1985, Ota, Kaichiro; flowers large, 45 petals, high-centered, no fragrance; foliage medium green; vigorous, spreading growth; ['Utage' × 'Anne Letts']; intr. 1980

'Fusilier' ('Grenadier', 'Red Soldier') F, or, 1958, Morey, Dr. Dennison; bud globular; flowers orange-scarlet, 3-3½ in., 40 petals, borne in heavy clusters, slight fragrance; foliage dark, glossy, leathery; vigorous growth; PP1709; ['Red Pinocchio' × 'Floradora']; intr. 1957

'Fusion' T, yb, 1901, Croibier; flowers dark chamois-yellow, petals edged safron-yellow, medium to large, full; ['Mme Eugene Verdier' × unknown]

'Futtaker Schlingrose' HMult, dr, about 1900, Geschwind, R.; flowers velvety dark red, 4-5 cm., slight fragrance; foliage dark green, smooth; ['De La Grifferaie' × 'a hybrid perpetual or bourbon']

'Futura' -- See 'Koroketto'

'Futura' -- See 'Future'

'Future' ('Futura') HT, or, 1974, Warriner, W. A.; buds large, pointed; flowers vermilion, large, dbl, cupped, borne singly; foliage large, dark green, leathery; numerous prickles; growth very vigorous, upright, well-branched; PP3569; [seedling × seedling]; intr. 1975

'Future Award' -- See 'Jacsto'

'Fuxiana' HT, Dot, Simon; intr. 1979

'Fuyuume-no-ko' ('Tohbai-no-ko') Ch,

mp
'Fuzzy Navel' -- See 'Winter Sunset'
'Fuzzy Wuzzy Red ' M, mr, Moore, Ralph ; bud bright red, mossy buds; flowers bright red, 1½ in.; recurrent; foliage dark green, glossy; compact, low (18 in.) growth; ['Scarlet Moss' × 'Scarlet Moss']; intr. 2004
'Fyfield Princess' F, my, 1994, Shuttleworth, F.I.; flowers medium, dbl., borne in large clusters; foliage medium size, medium green, semi-glossy; numerous prickles; medium (4 ft.), upright growth; [sport of 'Southampton']; intr. 1994
'Fygi' HT, dr, deRuiter
'Fyvie Castle' -- See 'Cocbamber'

— G —

'G. Amédée Hammond' HT, ab, 1915, Dickson, A.; flowers apricot-yellow on ivory yellow, dbl.
'G. F. Veronica' HMult, ly, 1900, Demitrovisi; bud peachy pink; flowers creamy yellow, 3-4 cm., semi-dbl., borne in small to medium clusters, moderate fragrance
'G. Forest-Colcombet' -- See 'Mme G. Forest-Colcombet'
'G. H. Davison' HT, mr, 1988, Davison, G.H.; flowers medium, well-defined red, large, 45 petals, high-centered, borne singly and in clusters of up to 3; foliage large, dark green, semi-glossy; prickles normal, large, red; upright growth; hips oval, large, green; [seedling × seedling]; intr. 1990
'G. I. Joe' HT, dp, 1943, Parmentier, J.; bud long, pointed; flowers rose-red to deep rose-pink, large, very dbl., moderate fragrance; foliage leathery, dark; vigorous growth; PP603; [sport of 'Red Better Times']
'G. K. Rose' HT, rb, Chiplunkar; flowers crimson with white/cream reverse and base, large, full; intr. 1989
'G. Nabonnand' -- See 'Gilbert Nabonnand'
'G. P. & J. Baker' -- See 'Harrango'
'G. W. Peart' HT, mr, 1948, Toogood; bud ovoid; flowers medium, very dbl.; foliage leathery, dark; moderate, bushy growth; [('Guineé' × unknown) × 'Rouge Mallerin']
'G. W. Watkins' HT, lp, 1890, Williams, A.
'Gaard um Titzebierg' HMsk, pb, Lens; flowers bright, reddish-pink with white centers, fading to lilac pink, semi-dbl., shallow cup to flat, borne in clusters, moderate multiflora fragrance; recurrent; upright (4 ft.), arching growth; hips small, orange; intr. 2006
'Gabi' ('Gabrielle') Gr, or, 1988, Poole, Lionel; flowers very bright orange-red, fading to lighter orange, 24 petals, high-centered, moderate fragrance; foliage medium size, dark green, glossy; prickles fairly flat, small, dark brown; bushy, medium growth; hips rounded, small, light brown-green; ['Pink Favorite' × 'Red Dandy']
'Gabina' HGal, m, about 1845, Calvert; flowers light purple, medium, very full
'Gabriel Fournier' ('Baron Elisi de St Albert') HP, dr, 1877, Levet; flowers dark cherry red, large, full, slight fragrance; ['Jules Margottin' × 'Victor Verdier']
'Gabriel Lombart' HT, w, 1932, Buatois; flowers flesh-white to cream-white, very large, dbl., cupped; vigorous, bushy growth; ['Dr. A. Hermans' × 'Rayon d'Or']
'Gabriel Noyelle' ('Gabrielle Noyelle') M, ab, 1933, Buatois; bud ovoid; flowers apricot, dbl., cupped; recurrent bloom; foliage leathery; very vigorous growth; ['Salet' × 'Souv de Mme Kreuger']
'Gabriela Sabatini' -- See 'Wilsab'
Gabriele Gebauer® F, ly, Kordes; intr. 2007
'Gabriella' ('Kordes' Rose Gabriella') F, mr, Kordes; flowers dbl.; PP4452; intr. 1977
Gabriella® -- See 'Bergme'
'Gabrielle' HCh, lp, before 1829, Coquerel; flowers flesh pink, edges lighter, large, full
'Gabrielle' -- See 'Bergme'
'Gabrielle' -- See 'Gabi'
'Gabrielle d'Estrées' A, lp, 1819, Vibert; flowers flesh pink, becoming white, medium to large, full; foliage bullate, glaucous
'Gabrielle Noyelle' -- See 'Gabriel Noyelle'
'Gabrielle Privat' Pol, mp, 1931, Barthelemy-Privat; flowers brilliant carmine-pink, semi-dbl., borne in pyramidal corymbs of 30-50; continuous flowering; bushy (1 × 1 ft.) growth
'Gabrielle Privat Rouge' -- See 'Rote Gabrielle Privat'
'Gabriel's Fire' -- See 'Brifire'
Gaby Cover™ -- See 'Poulans'
'Gaby Morlay' -- See 'Dorsand'
'Gabychette' F, rb, 1960, Arles; bud ovoid; flowers reddish-salmon, base sulfur-yellow, reverse white to rosy white, dbl., high-centered; foliage glossy, light green; low growth; ['Floradora' × 'Pioupiou']; intr. 1960
'Gacta' HT, or, 1969, Gaujard; bud long, pointed
'Gaegui' F, ob, 1963, Gaujard; bud ovoid
'Gaesca' HT, dp, Gaujard
'Gaëtano Gonsoli' -- See 'Gonsoli Gaëtano'
Gaia® -- See 'Bargai'
'Gaiata' HT, yb, 1956, Moreira da Silva; flowers Indian yellow shaded pink; ['Boudoir' × 'Peace']
'Gaiety' HT, ob, 1926, E.G. Hill, Co.); bud pointed; flowers orange, Indian red and silver, large, dbl., cupped; foliage light, glossy; vigorous, branching growth; ['Mme Butterfly' × 'Souv. de Claudius Pernet']
'Gaiety' HT, op, Archer; flowers salmon-pink flushed yellow, moderate fragrance; vigorous growth; perhaps from McGredy; intr. 1930
'Gaiezza' HT, ob, 1940, Giacomasso; flowers orange touched red, center yellow; ['Julien Potin' × 'Mme G. Forest-Colcombet']
'Gail' -- See 'Tingail'
'Gail Borden' HT, pb, 1958, Kordes; bud ovoid; flowers deep rose-pink, reverse overcast cream, 5½ in., 53 petals, high-centered, moderate fragrance; foliage dark, glossy, leathery; vigorous, upright growth; PP1618; [R.M.S. Queen Mary × 'Viktoria Adelheid']; intr. 1957
'Gail Borden, Climbing' Cl HT, pb, 1960; flowers coral, fading to pink, reverse white, 5-6 in., very dbl., moderate fragrance; intr. 1960
'Gaillarde Marbrée' -- See 'Noire Couronnée'
'Gainesville Garnet' LCl, dr, 2006, John A. Starnes Jr.; flowers red, reverse magenta red, 4-5 in., very full, borne in small clusters; very remontant; foliage medium size, medium green, semi-glossy, disease-free; prickles medium, slightly curved, brown, moderate; growth upright, vigorous climber, tall (8-12 ft.); pillar/climber; ['hybrid wichurana' × unknown]; intr. 2006
'Gainsborough' ('Viscountesse Folkestone, Climbing') Cl HT, lp, 1903, Good & Reese; flowers flesh-pink, almost white, large, dbl.; long stems; vigorous growth; [sport of 'Viscountess Folkestone']
'Gaisu' F, dr, 1968, Gaujard; bud pointed
'Gala' F, pb, 1975, Jelly; bud short, pointed; flowers light pink, 3-3½ in., 28-34 petals, high-centered, slight spicy fragrance; vigorous, upright, free growth; PP3774; ['seedling No. 19-64 ps' × 'Seventeen']; intr. 1973
'Gala' -- See 'Savagala'
'Gala Charles Aznavour' -- See 'Meisazy'
'Gala Day' F, or, 1966, Watkins Roses; flowers vermilion-scarlet, pointed, 4 in.; foliage light green; free, upright growth; [Queen Elizabeth® × 'Dickson's Flame']
'Gala Gold' -- See 'Lavchro'
'Gala Ribbon' S, mr; flowers bright crimson red, spiraling, moderate fragrance; recurrent; strong growth, can be trained as medium climber
'Gala Sunrise' -- See 'Gelrise'
'Galah' HT, mp, 1956, Riethmuller; flowers carmine-pink, base lighter, large, semi-dbl., borne in clusters
'Galahad' HT, w, 1986, Kriloff, Michel; flowers very large, dbl., moderate anise fragrance; foliage medium green, semi-glossy; ['Micaela' × 'Lara']
'Galatea' HMsk, yb, 1914, Pemberton; flowers stone-color, edged pink, small rosette, borne in clusters; recurrent bloom
Galatea® S, w, Barni; recurrent; spreading, low (16-20 in.) growth; intr. 2004
'Galatée' HGal, lp, before 1828, Dubourg;

flowers flesh pink, petals very thin, very dbl.
'Galaty' -- See 'Dotsubebe'
'Galaxie'   Ch, w, 1827, Vétillard; flowers white, center cream, medium, full
'Galaxy'   HWich, dp, 1906, Walsh; flowers bright carmine; vigorous growth
'Galaxy' -- See 'Meihuterb'
Galaxy™ -- See 'Morgal'
'Galaxy Glow' ('Cloud No. 9')   HT, m, Tantau; flowers silvery mauve , double, high-centered, moderate fragrance; tall growth
'Galejade'   S, op, Reuter; intr. 1997
'Galia'   HT, lp, 1966, Betzel; flowers light pink, center darker, large, very dbl.; foliage dark, leathery; very vigorous, upright growth; RULED EXTINCT; 4/81/ARM
Galia® -- See 'Meitinirol'
'Galileo' ('Hilda Heinemann', 'Mme H. Heinemann')   HT, mr, 1971, Meilland; flowers currant-red to cherry-red, 5 in., 30 petals, globular; foliage large, glossy; vigorous, upright growth; ['Ma Fille' × 'Love Song']
'Galina'   HT, mr, Cocker; flowers large, dbl.; intr. 1979
'Galina'   F, ab, VEG; flowers apricot and yellow, medium, dbl.
'Galioca' -- See 'Château de Chenonceaux'
'Gallagher'   F, rb, 1980, Murray, Nola; bud pointed; flowers cream, edged crimson, shapely, 2½ in., 41 petals, moderate fruity fragrance; foliage leathery; bushy growth
'Gallande'   HSemp, mp, about 1830, Jacques; flowers dbl.
'Gallant'   F, mr, 1968, Dickson, A.; flowers scarlet, 3-3½ in., dbl., borne in clusters; foliage glossy; ['Tropicana' × 'Barbecue']
'Gallantry'   HT, pb, Delbard
'Galleria' ('Big John')   HRg, mr, 1990, Weddle, Von C.; bud ovoid; flowers medium watermelon pink, reverse silvery pink, large, 13 petals, high-centered, borne in sprays of 3-5, moderate spicy, fruity fragrance; foliage large, dark green, glossy; prickles straight, medium, light green to pink; bushy, tall (8 ft.) growth; hips round, small, green-yellow; ['The Duke' × 'Hansa']; intr. 1990
'Galleria Borghese'   HT, w, 1954, Giacomasso; flowers flesh streaked coral, very large; foliage glossy; strong stems; ['Peace' × 'Crimson Glory']
'Galli-Curci'   HT, my, 1924, Kinsman; flowers golden yellow; [sport of 'Columbia']
'Gallica Alba' ('Rosea')   HGal, w, before 1811; bud elongate; flowers blush white, dbl., moderate fragrance; foliage pointed, medium size, finely dentate; prickles numerous, slender, straight
'Gallica Alba Flore Plena'   HGal, w, before 1811; flowers white tinted pink, very dbl.
'Gallica Grandiflora' -- See 'Alika'
'Gallica Macrantha' (R. × waitziana macrantha, R. gallica macrantha, R. macrantha)   Misc OGR, w, before 1750; flowers flushed rose at first, changing to nearly white; said to be a cross of R. canina and R. gallica, but more probably R. gallica × R. alba
'Gallica Maheca' -- See 'La Belle Sultane'
'Gallica Vermilion'   HGal, about 1823, from Angers; flowers rose pink, very full
'Gallicandy' -- See 'Ardtuscoth'
'Gallique Nouvelle'   HGal, mp
'Gallivarda' ('Galsar')   HT, rb, 1978, W. Kordes Söhne; bud long, pointed; flowers red, yellow reverse, 4½ in., 34 petals, high-centered, slight fragrance; foliage glossy; vigorous, upright growth; ['Colour Wonder' × Wiener Charme®]; intr. 1977
'Galsar' -- See 'Gallivarda'
Galway Bay®   LCl, op, 1966, McGredy, Sam IV; flowers salmon-pink, reverse darker, 3½-4 in., 20 petals, borne in small clusters; foliage medium green, glossy; vigorous (9-12 ft.) growth; ['Gruss an Heidelberg' × Queen Elizabeth®]
'Gambler' -- See 'Gellov'
'Gamin de Paris'   F, dr, 1964, Mondial Roses; flowers dark blood-red, large, dbl., borne in large clusters; vigorous, upright growth; [(Orange Triumph® × 'Paprika') × seedling]
'Gamine'   F, op, 1961, Kriloff, Michel; flowers salmon-pink, medium, dbl.; vigorous growth; ['Eclipse' × Baccará®]; intr. 1961
'Gamma'   HT, pb, 1978, Gaujard; bud pointed; flowers pink, suffused vermilion, intense fragrance; foliage large; ['Jouvencelle' × American Heritage®]; intr. 1972
'Gamon's Climbing Grolez' -- See 'Mme Jules Grolez, Climbing'
'Gamon's Thornless'   Misc OGR, mp; form of R. canina; used for understock
'Gamusin'   HT, r, 1960, Dot, Pedro; flowers cinnamon to pale pink, 25 petals; vigorous, spreading growth; ['Grey Pearl' × ('Lila Vidri' × 'Prelude')]
'Gana' ('David Whitfield')   F, mp, Gandy; intr. 1991
'Ganang' -- See 'Crème Anglais'
'Ganbru'   S, pb, Gandy; intr. 2004
'Gancre' ('Crème de la Crème')   LCl, w, Gandy; intr. 1998
'Gandri' ('Betty Driver')   F, pb, 1982, Gandy, Douglas L.; flowers pale peach and gold blend, yellow stamens, patio, large, semi-dbl.; foliage medium size, light green, semi-glossy; low, bushy growth; [seedling × Topsi®]
'Ganfer' ('Fergie')   F, ob, 1987, Gandy, Douglas L.; flowers orange-buff and ginger with shell pink edges, 40 petals, hybrid tea form, borne in well-spaced clusters; foliage medium size, medium green, semi-glossy, disease-resistant; short, compact growth; frost-proof; [seedling × 'Copper Pot']; intr. 1988
'Ganflo' ('Florence Nightingale')   S, w, 1990, Gandy, Douglas L.; bud pointed; flowers glowing white, flushed buff, reverse tinged pink, aging to white, 32 petals, moderate spicy fragrance; foliage medium size, medium green, semi-glossy; prickles very pointed, fawn; spreading, medium growth; hips rounded, green; ['Morgengruss' × seedling]; intr. 1989
'Ganga'   HT, dy, 1970, Division of Vegetable Crops and Floriculture; flowers deep golden yellow, medium, dbl., high-centered, moderate tea fragrance; profuse, intermittent bloom; vigorous, upright growth; ['Sabina' × unknown]
Ganges Mist™ -- See 'Viralliance'
'Gango' ('Doctor Goldberg')   HT, my, 1990, Gandy, Douglas L.; flowers large, golden yellow, full, intense fragrance; foliage large, dark green, matte; upright growth; [Royal Dane™ × Dutch Gold®]; intr. 1989
'Ganhol' ('Moriah')   HT, ob, 1984, Holtzman, Arnold; flowers creamy yellow, orange reverse, large, 35 petals, intense fragrance; foliage large, dark, matte; bushy growth; ['Fragrant Cloud' × seedling]; intr. 1983
'Ganjil' ('Jill's Rose')   F, op, Gandy; intr. 1998
'Ganleon'   F, op, Gandy; intr. 2008
'Ganspa' ('Spangles')   F, lp, 1994, Gandy, Douglas L.; flowers pale pink, speckled, medium, dbl., borne in large clusters, moderate musk fragrance; foliage medium size, light green, semi-glossy; numerous prickles; medium, upright, compact growth; ['Florence Nightingale' × 'Silver Jubilee']; intr. 1995
'Ganymed'   F, dr, 1976, Kordes; bud pointed; flowers 2½ in., 32 petals, cupped, slight fragrance; foliage glossy; vigorous, upright, bushy growth; [Europeana® × seedling]; intr. 1975
'Gardejäger Gratzfeld'   Cl Pol, dp, 1940, Gratzfeld; flowers carmine-red, 6 cm., dbl., borne singly or in small clusters, slight fragrance; vigorous growth; [sport of 'Rödhätte']
'Garden and Home'   S, ab, Delbard; buds round, pink; flowers apricot and gold in center, fading to light pink to white outer petals, full, cupped, borne in small clusters, moderate fruity, spicy fragrance; foliage deep green, slightly frilly; informal (4-5 ft.) growth; intr. 2001
'Garden Art Grandma's Blessing' -- See 'Grandma's Blessing'
'Garden Art Last Tango' -- See 'Last Tango'
'Garden Art Macy's Pride' -- See 'Baicream'
'Garden Art Orange Impressionist' -- See 'Orange Impressionist'
'Garden Beauty'   F, ab; intr. 2002
Garden Blanket™ -- See 'Jacgron'
'Garden City' -- See 'Harkover'
'Garden Club'   HT, Mansuino
'Garden Delight'   F, dp, 1957, Norman;

flowers deep rose-pink, rosette form, 3½-4 in., 34 petals, borne in clusters, moderate fragrance; vigorous, branching growth; intr. 1956

'Garden Gem'   HT, lp, 1930, Dingee & Conard; flowers satiny pink, dbl.; very vigorous growth; ['Mrs E.T. Stotesbury' × 'Hill's America']

'Garden Glow'   HT, op, 1937, Cant, B. R.; flowers scarlet, base copper, dbl.; foliage glossy, bronze; very vigorous, bushy growth

'Garden Jubilee Funny Face' -- See 'Funny Face'

'Garden Jubilee Golden Eye' -- See 'Golden Eye'

Garden Jubilee Hot Wonder™ -- See 'Hot Wonder'

'Garden Jubilee Sierra Skye' -- See 'Sierra Skye'

'Garden Magic' -- See 'Gartenzauber'

'Garden News'   HT, dr, 1962, Verschuren; bud pointed; flowers dark crimson-scarlet, large, 32 petals; foliage dull, dark, leathery; strong stems; moderate growth; ['New Yorker' × 'Étoile de Hollande']; intr. 1962

Garden News™ -- See 'Poulrim'

Garden of Roses®   F, w, Kordes; flowers cream with a pastel pink center, 7 cm., very full, rosette, borne in clusters, slight fragrance; recurrent; compact, upright (50 cm.) growth; intr. 2007

Garden Party®   HT, w, 1960, Swim, H.C.; bud urn-shaped; flowers pale yellow to white, often tinged light pink, 4-5 in., 28 petals, high-centered, slight fragrance; foliage large, medium green, semi-glossy; vigorous, bushy, well-branched growth; PP1814; ['Charlotte Armstrong' × 'Peace']; intr. 1959

'Garden Party, Climbing'   Cl HT, w, 1964, Itami Rose Nursery

'Garden Party' -- See 'Kormollis'

'Garden Path Mystic Fairy' -- See 'Mystic Fairy'

'Garden Path Pink Gnome' -- See 'Pink Gnome'

'Garden Path Sunrise Sunset' -- See 'Sunrise Sunset'

'Garden Pavilion Roos'   HT, op; flowers large, orange-vermilion, dbl., high-centered, borne mostly singly, no fragrance; recurrent; tall, vigorous growth; intr. 1998

'Garden Pearl'   HT, w, Tejganga; intr. 1992

'Garden Perfume' ('Paradisea') HT, pb, Kordes; buds egg shaped; flowers blend of magenta and deep pink, large, long lasting, dbl., intense fragrance; intr. 1988

'Garden Princess'   F, my, 1961, Leenders, J.; flowers yellow, becoming lighter, semi-dbl.; growth moderate; ['Goldilocks' × 'Lavender Pinocchio']

'Garden Queen'   HT, op, 1960, Leenders, J.; flowers pink to salmon, 4 in., dbl.; vigorous growth; ['Ambassadeur Nemry' × 'Tawny Gold']

'Garden State'   Gr, mp, 1965, Meilland, Alain A.; bud ovoid, pointed; flowers rose-pink, 3½-4 in., 42 petals, moderate fragrance; foliage leathery; vigorous, tall, bushy growth; PP2349; [('Happiness' × 'Independence') × 'White Knight']; intr. 1965

'Garden State II'   Gr, or, Williams, J. Benjamin; intr. 1997

Garden Sun™ -- See 'Meivaleir'

'Garden Supreme'   F, ob, 1965, Jones; flowers orange blend shaded reddish, medium, 32 petals, borne in clusters; foliage leathery, bronze; low, vigorous growth; intr. 1958

'Gardener's Joy' -- See 'Beadrum'

'Gardeners' Sunday'   F, my, 1976, Harkness; flowers 3 in., 20 petals, moderate fragrance; foliage bright green; [('Pink Parfait' × 'Masquerade') × 'Arthur Bell']; intr. 1975

'Gardenia'   HT, w, 1898, Soupert & Notting; bud long; flowers gardenia white, large, full, moderate fragrance; ['Comtesse Dusy' × 'Mlle Hélène Cambier']

'Gardenia'   HWich, w, 1899, Horvath/Manda, W.A.; bud pointed, yellow; flowers creamy white, center yellow, 6-7 cm., dbl., quartered, borne in small sprays; sparse repeat; foliage small, dark, glossy; short, strong stems; very vigorous growth; [R. wichurana × 'Perle des Jardins']

'Gardeniaeflora'   HMult, w, 1901, Benary; flowers pure white, medium, semi-dbl., borne in large clusters; early bloom

'Garden's Glory' ('Pink Mme Plantier') HMult, mp, 1905, Conard & Jones; flowers clear rose pink, large, dbl., borne in clusters; almost thornless; ['Dawson' × 'Clotilde Soupert']

'Gardens of the World' -- See 'Jaccoeur'

'Gardners Glory'   LCl, dy, Warner; flowers golden yellow, double, moderate fragrance; recurrent; vigorous (2 - 3 m.) growth; intr. 2008

'Gardner's Pleasure' -- See 'Korstesgli'

'Gardorty' ('Rock Creek') S, rb, 2007, Garhart, Michael; flowers red with white eye, reverse red, small, 2½ in., single, borne in large clusters; foliage small, dark green, glossy; prickles small, hooked, light brown, few; growth bushy, short (24 in.); bedding, containers; hips numerous, bright orange; [Dortmund® × 'Circus']

'Gareth Davies'   HT, mr, 1997, Poole, Lionel; flowers large, very dbl., borne mostly singly; foliage medium size, dark green, semi-glossy; upright, bushy, tall growth; ['Crimson Glory' × 'Loving Memory']

'Garhenry' ('Henry's Blend') S, m, 2008, Kuska, Henry; flowers violet, 2 in., single, borne in small clusters; very early blooming; non-remontant; foliage medium, dark green, matte, very disease-resistant; prickles very tiny, soft, straight, grey, numerous; growth bushy, medium (4 ft.); specimen, fall color, hedges, hips; hips dark; ['Rosa acicularis nipponensis' × 'R15']; intr. 2009

'Garibaldi'   B, rb, Pradel; flowers cerise red, shaded with lilac, large, full; intr. 1860

'Garibaldi'   B, dp, 1859, Damaizin; flowers rosy lilac

'Garisenda'   HWich, pb, 1911, Bonfiglio, A.; flowers clear rose-pink, tinted silvery, 6-7 cm., dbl., quartered, borne in clusters of 3-8; [R. wichurana × 'Souv. de la Malmaison']; sometimes sold as Souv de la Malmaison, Climbing

'Garland's Gold' -- See 'Horrespire'

'Garlion' ('Roar!') F, dy, 2008, Garhart, Michael; flowers caramel-gold, reverse gold, not fading in the heat, 3 in., dbl., high-centered, borne in small clusters; foliage medium, dark green, glossy; prickles small, straight, dark brown, few; growth upright, medium (3 ft.); bedding, cutting, exhibition; ['Princess Alice' × 'Freedom']; intr. 2008

'Garnet Climber'   HWich, mr, 1907, Van Fleet; [R. wichurana × 'Lucullus']

Garnet Crest™ -- See 'Virpicotee'

'Garnette' ('Garnette Red', 'Red Garnette') F, dr, 1951, Tantau; flowers garnet-red, base light lemon-yellow, small, 50 petals, slight fragrance; foliage leathery, dark; bushy growth; [('Rosenelfe' × 'Eva') × 'Heros']; greenhouse rose

'Garnette, Climbing'   Cl F, dr, 1954, Soria; PP1505

'Garnette' -- See 'Carol Amling'

'Garnette Apricot'   Pol, ab; free blooming; compact growth

'Garnette Carol' -- See 'Carol Amling'

'Garnette Pink' -- See 'Carol Amling'

'Garnette Red' -- See 'Garnette'

'Garnette Rose'   Pol, dp

'Garnette Supreme'   F, dp, 1954, Boerner; bud ovoid; flowers carmine, 2½-3 in., 35-40 petals, cupped, moderate fragrance; foliage glossy, bronze; vigorous, upright, compact growth; PP1318; [('Yellow Pinocchio' × unknown) × 'Garnette']

'Garnette White'   Pol, w; flowers full; abundant bloom; very compact growth

'Garnette Yellow'   Pol, my

'Garnia'   F, dp, 1971, Butter; flowers deep pink, 4½ in., 48 petals, intense fragrance; foliage matte, green; moderately vigorous growth; ['Lady Sylvia' × 'Garnette']; intr. 1970

'Garninja' ('Shadow Ninja') F, or, 2007, Garhart, Michael; flowers orange-red blended russet, reverse brick red, medium, 3 in., semi-dbl., borne in large clusters; foliage large, dark green, glossy; prickles small, curved, brown, few; growth upright, medium (4 ft.); cutting, garden decoration, exhibition; ['H.C. Andersen' × Playboy®); cool weather brings out orange and russet tones; hot weather brings out red tones with very dark edges; intr. 2009

'Garo'   LCl, dr, 1987, Garelja, Anita; flowers blackish-red, large, 48 petals, high-centered, borne singly and in clusters of up to 5, slight fragrance; foliage red turning dark green, semi-glossy; prickles large, brown; upright growth; ['Uncle Walter' × seedling]; intr. 1978

'Garrose' ('Rose Gold') HT, op, 2007, Garhart, Michael; flowers coral pink, reverse golden yellow, large, 5 in., full, borne mostly solitary; foliage medium, medium green, semi-glossy; prickles small, straight, brown, few; growth upright, tall (5-6 ft.); bedding, exhibition, cutting; ['Solitaire' × Touch of ClassTM®]; intr. 2009

'Garry Brown' -- See 'Mehbrown'

'Garry Moore' -- See 'Kenposh'

'Garry Paul Kirkman' F, w, 2004, Paul Chessum Roses; flowers dbl., borne in small clusters, slight fragrance; foliage medium size, medium green, semi-glossy; growth compact, medium (80 cm.); beds, borders; [seedling × seedling]; intr. 2004

'Garry Woodward' -- See 'Webpass'

'Gartenarchitekt Günther Schulze' -- See 'The Pilgrim'

Gartenblut® HT, dr, Noack, Werner; flowers 5 in., full; good repeat; growth to 80-100 cm.; intr. 1986

'Gartendirektor Glocker' F, or, 1957, Kordes; bud ovoid; flowers cinnabar-red, large, very dbl., borne in clusters; foliage glossy, leathery; vigorous, bushy growth; ['Obergärtner Wiebicke' × 'Independence']

'Gartendirektor Hartrath' HT, lp, 1911, Leenders; flowers light, satiny salmon pink

'Gartendirektor Julius Schutze' HT, pb, 1920, Kiese; flowers pale rosy pink and peach-blossom-pink, 4 in., full, moderate fragrance; ['Mme Jules Gravereaux' × 'Pharisaer']

'Gärtendirektor Lauche' -- See 'Éclair'

'Gartendirektor Nose' HT, dr, 1930, Kordes; bud pointed; flowers dark crimson, large, dbl., high-centered; foliage dark, glossy; vigorous, bushy growth; ['Royal Red' × 'Templar']

'Gartendirektor Otto Linne' S, dp, 1934, Lambert, P.; flowers dark carmine-pink, edged darker, base yellowish-white, medium, dbl., borne in clusters of up to 30; foliage leathery, light green; long strong stems; vigorous, bushy growth; ['Robin Hood (HMsk)' × 'Rudolph Kluis']

'Gartenfee' S, dp, Bergman; flowers deep rose-pink fading to soft pink, semi-dbl., borne in pyramidal clusters; recurrent; bushy growth; intr. 1987

'Gartengold' HT, dy, Noack, Werner; intr. 1984

'Gartenstadt Liegnitz' HMult, m, 1910, Lambert, P.; flowers violet/red, 5-6 cm., semi-dbl., borne in small to medium clusters; non-recurrent; ['Frau Helene Videnz' × 'Dr. Andry']

'Gartenstolz' HT, op, Noack, Werner; intr. 1974

'Gartenstolz' F, op, 1945, Tantau; flowers rose tinted salmon, large, 8-10 petals, borne in clusters of 12-15; foliage leathery, light green; vigorous, upright, bushy growth; ['Swantje' × 'Hamburg']

'Gartenträume' S, mp, Tantau; flowers medium pink with lilac tints, 4 in., full, cupped, borne in small clusters, intense fragrance; recurrent; foliage medium green; compact (90-140 cm.), bushy growth; intr. 2006

'Gartenzauber' ('Garden Magic', 'Magie des Jardins') F, 1965, Kordes, R.; flowers blood-red, tinted cinnabar-red, well-formed, large; low growth; RULED EXTINCT 6/81 ARM; intr. 1963

Gartenzauber® -- See 'Kornacho'

'Gartenzauber '84' -- See 'Kornacho'

'Gärtnerfreude' ('Kordes' Gärtnerfreude') Pol, or, W. Kordes Söhne; flowers medium, dbl.; intr. 1965

Gärtnerfreude® -- See 'Korstesgli'

'Garvey' HT, pb, 1961, McGredy, Sam IV; flowers light geranium, reverse pale red, 6 in., 30 petals, globular; foliage dark, leathery; strong stems; vigorous, upright growth; ['McGredy's Yellow' × 'Karl Herbst']; intr. 1961

'Gary Karr' HT, ly, 2001, Burks, Larry; flowers 4 in., dbl., borne in small clusters, slight fragrance; foliage medium size, medium green, matte; prickles average, curved, few; growth medium (5 ft.); garden decorative; [seedling × ('Gold Glow' × unknown)]; intr. 2001

'Gary Lineker' -- See 'Pearobin'

'Gary Michael ' -- See 'Jalgary'

'Gary Player' ('Goliath') HT, ob, 1979, Herholdt, J.A.; flowers orange-vermilion, 4-4½ in., 35 petals, high-centered; foliage glossy, dark; vigorous growth; ['Jolie Madame' × seedling]; intr. 1970

'Gary Wernett' HT, op, 1986, French, Richard; flowers medium coral pink, large, petals wavy, dbl., high-centered to cupped, borne usually singly, moderate fragrance; foliage medium size, medium green, matte; prickles medium, triangular, light red; bushy growth; rare to full term fruit; ['Helen Traubel' × 'Helen Traubel']; intr. 1985

'Gaspard Monge' C, m, 1854, Robert; flowers light pink with lilac, 9-10 cm., dbl., globular, intense fragrance; some speculation that this may be a HCh, since the stems are too smooth for a centifolia

'Gaspard Monge' HP, mr, Moreau & Robert; flowers crimson, tinted lilac, large, full, globular; intr. 1874

'Gaston Bonnier' HT, rb, 1910, Daniel/Laperrière; flowers silvery flesh-red, center dawn pink over ocher, large, full; ['Antoine Rivoire' × unknown]

'Gaston Chandon' Cl HT, pb, 1884, Schwartz; flowers light pink with coppery highlights, medium, dbl.; very remontant; ['Gloire de Dijon' × unknown]

'Gaston Lenôtre' -- See 'Greta'

'Gaston Lesieur' HWich, dp, 1915, Turbat; flowers carmine-pink, medium, dbl., flat, borne in clusters of 10-15

'Gaston Lévêque' HP, mr, 1878, Lévêque; flowers bright carmine to fiery vermilion, shaded brownish red, very large, full

'Gateshead Festival' HT, op, 1990, Thompson, Robert; flowers glowing orange flushed salmon with gold at base of petals, full, intense fragrance; foliage large, dark green, glossy; bushy growth; [Doris Tysterman® × 'Silver Jubilee']; intr. 1989

'Gaubiroc' (Pénélope®) HT, op, 1985, Gaujard, Jean; flowers medium salmon pink, well-formed, large, 35 petals, moderate fragrance; foliage large, medium green, semi-glossy; upright growth; [('Americana' × unknown) × 'Chenonceaux']; intr. 1980

'Gaucova' (Junon®) HT, or, 1979, Gaujard; bud full; flowers dbl., 45 petals; foliage large, brownish; bushy growth; [Tanagra® × 'Dora']; intr. 1978

'Gaudi' HT, Dot

'Gaudia' F, mp, 1946, Leenders, M.; flowers rose-pink, base gold and salmon, 4 in., 15 petals, borne in clusters; foliage bright green edged red; vigorous, tall growth; ['Florentina' × 'Talisman']

'Gaudino' HT, ob, 1987, Gaujard, Jean; intr. 1980

'Gaufrarner' ('Odeon') HT, op, 1979, Gaujard; bud globular; flowers coral-pink, 3 in., 50 petals, globular, moderate fragrance; foliage large, dark; vigorous growth; [('Chateau de Chenonceaux' × 'Mignonne') × 'Americana']; intr. 1977

'Gauhari' ('Amara') HT, pb, Gaujard; intr. 1980

'Gauhti' HT, yb, 1969, Gaujard; bud pointed

'Gaujard 985' HT, mr, Gaujard; flowers large, dbl.; intr. 1974

'Gaulimor' ('Hermione') HT, op, 1982, Gaujard, Jean; flowers deep salmon, large, 35 petals, moderate fragrance; foliage large, dark, glossy; upright, bushy growth; [Rose Gaujard® × 'Colour Wonder']; intr. 1981

'Gaumo' HT, rb, 1958, Gaujard; bud small to medium, ovoid to globular; intr. 1964

'Gaumova' ('Circé') F, or, 1979, Gaujard; bud long; flowers brilliant orange-red,, 1½-2 in., 16 petals; foliage large, dark; vigorous, compact growth; [Guitare® × Prominent®]

'Gauntlet' -- See 'Brigaunt'

'Gaura' F, ob, Gaujard; bud long; intr. 1957

'Gaurama' ('Arbelle') F, or, Gaujard

'Gauseca' HT, pb, 1981, Gaujard, Jean; bud long; intr. 1979

'Gautara' (Simone Merieux®) HT, rb, 1982, Gaujard; intr. 1981

'Gautira' (Molitor®) HT, or, 1982, Gaujard, Jean; flowers deep orange-red, large, 35 petals, moderate fragrance; foliage medium size, dark, semi-glossy; ['Junon' × Tanagra®]; intr. 1980

'Gauvila' ('Renee Columb') HT, rb, Gaujard; intr. 1979

'Gauvitor' HT, mr, 1978, Gaujard; intr.

'Gauzeca' HT, pb, 1981, Gaujard, Jean; bud long; intr. 1979

'Gauzimi' ('Lisima') HT, mr, Gaujard

'Gauzine' F, mp, 1978, Gaujard; intr. 1975

'Gauzomi' F, or, 1981, Gaujard, Jean; intr. 1979

'Gavá' Cl HT, or, 1934, Munné, B.; flowers oriental red shaded rose-pink, base yellow, 3 in., dbl., cupped, intense fragrance; foliage leathery; very vigorous, climbing growth; ['Souv. de Claudius Denoyel' × 'Souv. de Claudius Pernet']

'Gaval' -- See 'Atlantic'

'Gavina' HT, w, Dot; flowers pure white

Gavnø™ -- See 'Poulgav'

'Gavolda' -- See 'Meicri'

'Gavotte' HT, pb, 1963, Sanday, John; flowers pink, reverse light yellow, 5 in., 45 petals; foliage dark; vigorous, upright growth; ['Ethel Sanday' × 'Lady Sylvia']

'Gavroche' F, ob, 1963, Robichon; flowers orange, center yellow, large; vigorous, bushy growth

'Gavroche' -- See 'Meiriental'

'Gaxence' HT, m, 1962, Gaujard; intr. 1965

'Gay Crusader' HT, rb, 1948, Robinson, H.; flowers red fading to pink, reverse deep yellow, large, high-centered; foliage dark; ['Phyllis Gold' × 'Catalonia']

'Gay Dawn' HT, op, 1956, Taylor, C.A.; bud pointed; flowers large, dbl., cupped, moderate spicy fragrance; foliage dark, semi-glossy; very vigorous, upright growth; ['Eclipse' × 'Mme Henri Guillot']

'Gay Debutante' HT, pb, 1960, Curtis, R.F.; flowers light pink, base yellow, very large, 40-45 petals, cupped, slight fragrance; foliage leathery, glossy; vigorous, upright growth; PP1750; [sport of 'Peace']; intr. 1961

'Gay Dicky' F, ob, 1956, Verschuren-Pechtold; flowers tangerine-orange; moderate growth

'Gay Gold' HT, my, 1973, Lowe; flowers 5½ in., 30 petals; foliage glossy; [King's Ransom® × Piccadilly®]

Gay Gordons® HT, yb, 1969, Cocker; flowers orange-yellow and red, dbl.; foliage dark, glossy; bushy, rather low growth; ['Belle Blonde' × 'Karl Herbst']

'Gay Gypsy' HT, dr, 1949, Crane; flowers long, pointed; flowers oxblood-red shades maroon, open, 4½-5 in., 15-20 petals, cupped, slight fragrance; foliage leathery; vigorous, upright, bushy growth; PP783; [sport of 'Charles K. Douglas']

'Gay Heart' F, mp, 1951, Boerner; bud ovoid; flowers bright pink, large, 25 petals, high-centered, borne in large clusters, moderate fragrance; foliage leathery; vigorous, upright growth; PP1026; ['Joanna Hill' × 'World's Fair']

'Gay Jewel' Min, lp, 1959, Morey, Dr. Dennison; bud globular; flowers light rose-pink, ½ in., 35-40 petals, cupped, moderate fragrance; foliage glossy; compact (6-8 in.) growth; ['Dick Koster' × 'Tom Thumb']; intr. 1959

'Gay Lady' HT, mr, 1953, Swim, H.C.; bud ovoid; flowers currant-red, open, 3½-4½ in., 20-28 petals, moderate spicy fragrance; foliage dark, leathery, glossy; very vigorous, upright growth; PP719; ['Charlotte Armstrong' × Piccadilly®]

'Gay Lyric' HT, mp, 1971, Fankhauser; flowers rose-pink, large, very dbl., high-centered; foliage glossy, dark, leathery; vigorous, upright growth; ['Royal Highness' × 'Elizabeth Fankhauser']

'Gay Maid' F, or, 1969, Gregory; flowers red suffused orange-pink, 26 petals, globular, borne in trusses; foliage light green; very vigorous growth; ['Masquerade' × unknown]

'Gay Mood' LCl, dp, 1940, Lammerts, Dr. Walter; bud large, ovoid to urn shaped, rose-red; flowers deep rose-pink, open, dbl.; profuse, repeated bloom; foliage glossy, dark; very vigorous, climbing growth; ['Joanna Hill' × 'Sanguinaire']

'Gay Nineties' Cl F, mr, 1955, Sima; bud ovoid; flowers rose-red, 2-2½ in., 65 petals, borne in clusters of 5-8, intense fragrance; foliage leathery, glossy; vigorous, pillar (8 ft.) growth; PP1354; [('New Dawn' × 'Red Ripples') × 'Red Ripples']

'Gay Paris' HT, mr, 1962, Delbard-Chabert; bud long; flowers bright crimson, well-formed, large, dbl., moderate fragrance; foliage bright green; vigorous growth; [('Floradora' × 'Barcelona') × ('Charles Mallerin' × 'Tonnerre')]; intr. 1960

'Gay Princess' F, lp, 1967, Boerner; bud ovoid; flowers blush-pink, large, dbl., cupped, borne in clusters, moderate fragrance; foliage leathery; vigorous, upright, bushy growth; PP2763; ['Spartan' × 'The Farmer's Wife']

'Gay Vista' S, lp, 1957, Riethmuller; flowers cerise-pink with white eye, single, borne in large clusters; repeat bloom; growth to 3½ ft

'Gayathri' HT, dp, K&S; flowers rich rose pink, lasting, dbl., high-centered; recurrent; strong growth; intr. 2004

'Gaybar' HT, yb, Gaujard; intr. 1962

'Gaye Babe' HWich, pb, 2000, Huxley, Ian; buds squat but pointed; flowers pale blush pink, reverse blush pink, prominent yellow stamens, 3 in., semi-dbl., cupped, borne in small clusters; remontant; foliage medium size, dark green, semi-glossy, disease-resistant; prickles moderate; rambling, spreading, medium (5 ft.) growth; ['New Dawn' × unknown]; intr. 1994

'Gayle' F, w, J&P; PP11634; intr. 2000

'Gayness' HT, Reithmuller; intr. 1955

'Gaytime' F, rb, 1966, Armstrong, D.L.; bud ovoid, pointed; flowers red and yellow, large, dbl., cupped, slight fragrance; foliage dark, glossy, leathery; vigorous, bushy, compact growth; PP2704; [seedling × 'Circus']

'Gazella' HGal, dp, before 1906

'Gazelle' HGal, lp, before 1843; flowers delicate rose, large

'G'Day -- See 'Tinhat'

'Ge Korsten' -- See 'Hergeko'

'Geaalto' S, mp, Gear; intr. 2001

'Geaaura' ('Faithful Companion', 'Precious Child') S, my, 1999, Gear, Ian Robert; flowers medium, dbl., borne in small clusters; foliage medium size, dark green, semi-glossy; prickles moderate; spreading (4 ft.) growth; ['Hokey Pokey' × Patio Princess™]

'Geaaward' ('The Wedding Rose') S, w, 1999, Gear, Ian Robert; flowers medium, inner petals tinged lemon to white, outer petals white, very dbl., somewhat quartered, borne in small clusters, slight fragrance; free-flowering; foliage dark blue/green, semi-glossy; prickles moderate; upright, compact, bushy, medium (3 ft.) growth; [Enchantment × 'English Miss']; intr. 1999

'Geacot' ('Apricot Kisses') S, ab, 1999, Gear, Ian Robert; flowers dark apricot, aging to pale apricot, 2½ in., full, borne in small clusters, slight fruity fragrance; foliage medium size, medium green, new growth purple-red, semi-glossy; prickles moderate; spreading, bushy, medium (4-5 ft.) growth; patio climber; [Laura Ford® × seedling]

'Géant des Batailles' ('Giant of Battles') HP, mr, 1846, Nérard; flowers deep fiery crimson, medium, 85 petals, intense fragrance; moderately vigorous growth

'Géant des Batailles a Fleurs Roses' HP, dp, 1868, Carré; flowers large, full

Gebrüder Grimm® -- See 'Korassenet'

'Gedenke Mein' HMult, w, 1912, Paul, J; flowers white, shaded flesh pink, semi-dbl.; [R. arvensis × 'Crimson Rambler']

'Gedge's Glory' HT, op, 1998, Webster, Robert; flowers pale orange, salmon pink reverse, 3-4 in., very dbl., borne mostly singly; foliage medium size, dark green, glossy; prickles moderate, medium, straight; low, compact growth; ['Dave Hessayon' × Remember Me®]

'Gee Dee' HT, mr, Dawson; intr. 1979

Gee Gee™ -- See 'Bengee'

'Gee Whiz' S, yb, 1985, Buck, Dr. Griffith J.; flowers yellow tinted orange-red, 23 petals, cupped, borne 1-10 per cluster, moderate sweet fragrance; repeat bloom; foliage medium size, leathery, dark olive green; prickles needle-like, brown; low, bushy, free-branching growth; hardy; ['Gingersnap' × 'Sevilliana']; intr. 1984

'Geelove' ('I Love You') HT, mr, 1996, Bees of Chester; flowers bright red, large, full, borne mostly singly; foliage medium size, dark green, semi-glossy; some prickles; upright, medium growth; intr. 1995

'Geepeop' ('The People's Princess') F, mp, 1997, Bees; flowers very dbl., borne in small clusters; foliage medium size, medium green, semi-glossy; upright, medium growth; [seedling × seedling]; intr. 1997

'Geestraw' ('Strawberries and Cream') Min, yb, 1996, Bees of Chester; flowers light yellow, pink and red striped, small, full, borne in small clusters, slight fragrance; foliage small, medium green, semi-glossy; some prickles; compact, medium (50-70 cm.) growth; [seedling × seedling]; intr. 1995

'Geheimrat Doctor Mittweg' S, pb, 1909, Lambert, P.; flowers rose-red, center yellowish-white, large, borne in large clusters; recurrent bloom; foliage dark; vigorous, bushy growth; ['Mme Norbert Levavasseur' × Trier®]

'Geheimrat Duisberg, Climbing' -- See 'Golden Rapture, Climbing'

'Geheimrat Duisberg' -- See 'Golden Rapture'

'Geheimrat Richard Willstätter' HT, ab, 1931, Felberg-Leclerc; flowers apricot-yellow, veined carmine-red, stamens yellow, large, semi-dbl.; foliage bright, thick; vigorous growth; ['Constance' × 'Admiral Ward']

'Geisha' HMult, rb, 1913, Geschwind, R.; flowers scarlet crimson, with white streaks on center petals, 8-10 cm., full, cupped, borne in clusters; ['De La Grifferaie' × 'a hybrid perpetual or bourbon']

'Geisha' HT, ob, Van Rossem; bud orange, marked coral-red; flowers golden yellow, sometimes striped red, medium to large, borne in small clusters, slight fragrance; foliage medium size, dark green, glossy; [sport of 'Mme Edouard Herriot']; intr. 1920

Geisha® F, ab, Tantau; flowers apricot-orange, 8 cm., dbl., cupped, borne in clusters, slight fragrance; free-flowering; foliage fresh green, durable; bushy (50-80 cm.), arching growth; intr. 2006

Geisha® -- See 'Pink Elizabeth Arden'

'Geisha Girl' F, my, 1964, McGredy, Sam IV; flowers large, 25 petals, borne in clusters; foliage long, pointed; tall growth; ['Gold Cup' × 'McGredy's Yellow']

'Gekko' ('Moonlight') HT, my, Keisei; intr. 1999

'Gela Gnau' HT, ab, 1926, Leenders, M.; flowers amber-yellow, reverse apricot, dbl.

'Gela Tepelmann' -- See 'Frau Eva Schubert'

'Gelal' ('Aleene') Min, mp, 2001, Giles, Diann; flowers medium, full, borne mostly solitary, no fragrance; foliage medium size, medium green, matte; prickles small, straight, few; growth upright, medium; garden decorative, exhibition; [seedling × seedling]; intr. 2001

'Gelali' ('Alicia') HT, pb, 2000, Giles, Diann; flowers full, borne mostly singly, no fragrance; foliage medium size, light green, matte; prickles moderate; growth bushy, medium (4 ft.); ['Vera Dalton' × 'Tiffany']

'Gelance' ('Turbulance') F, rb, 1999, Giles, Diann; flowers large, single, borne in small clusters; foliage medium size, light green, glossy; prickles moderate; bushy, medium growth; ['Pink Favorite' × Scentimental™]; intr. 1999

'Gelangel' ('Silver Angel') F, m, 1998, Giles, Diann; flowers light silver mauve, dbl., borne in small clusters; foliage medium green, semi-glossy; bushy, medium (3 ft.) growth; [sport of 'Angel Face']; intr. 1996

'Gelart' ('Arthur Wood') Min, dr, 2000, Giles, Diann; flowers medium, full, high-centered, borne mostly singly, no fragrance; foliage small, dark green, semi-glossy; prickles moderate; growth compact, medium

'Gelba' ('Banana Split') S, yb, 2001, Giles, Diann; flowers striped, 4 in., full, borne mostly solitary, intense fragrance; foliage medium size, medium green, semi-glossy; prickles medium, straight, few; growth upright, compact, medium (3½ ft.); garden decorative; [Queen Margrethe™ × Scentimental™]; intr. 2001

'Gelback' ('Back Home') HT, ly, 1995, Giles, Diann; flowers 2½-4 in., full, borne mostly singly, intense fragrance; foliage medium size, light green, semi-glossy; few prickles; medium, spreading growth; ['Dr A.J. Verhage' × Midas Touch™]; intr. 1995

'Gelbe' ('Maybe Baby') Min, pb, 2000, Giles, Diann; flowers medium, dbl., high-centered, borne in small clusters, no fragrance; foliage medium size, medium green, matte; few prickles; growth upright, medium

'Gelbe Dagmar Hastrup' -- See 'Moryelrug'

'Gelbe Florida von Scharbeutz' F

'Gelbe Holstein' ('Yellow Holstein') F, ly, 1951, Kordes; bud long, pointed; flowers yellow paling to lemon, 3 in., 20 petals, borne in large clusters; foliage glossy, light green; vigorous, upright, bushy growth; [('Eva' × 'Viscountess Charlemont') × 'Sunmist']

'Gelbe Pharisäer' HT, my, 1927, Hinner, W.; flowers clear yellow, center deeper; ['Pharisaer' × 'Mrs Aaron Ward']

'Gelbe The Fairy' -- See 'Poulfair'

Gelber Engel® -- See 'Korgosumo'

'Gelber Kobold' MinFl, dy; intr. 1996

'Gelberg' ('Sandy Lundberg') Min, w, 2000, Giles, Diann; flowers medium, full, high-centered, borne singly and in small clusters, no fragrance; foliage medium size, medium green, matte; few prickles; upright, medium (2½ ft.) growth; [Party Girl™ × seedling]

'Gelbird' ('Red Bird') LCl, mr, 1997, Giles, Diann; flowers medium, very dbl., borne mostly singly; foliage medium size, medium green, semi-glossy; spreading, medium (6-8 ft.) growth; ['Crepe de Chine' × 'Kardinal']

'Gelburn' ('Sunburnt') F, ob, 1997, Giles, Diann; flowers small, dbl., borne in small clusters; foliage medium size, medium green, semi-glossy; spreading, medium (3½ ft.) growth; ['Dalton' × unknown]

'Gelcan' ('Citrus Candy') Min, ob, 2000, Giles, Diann; flowers orange, medium size, full, exhibition, borne mostly singly, no fragrance; foliage medium size, medium green, dull; prickles moderate; upright, medium growth; ['Little Darling' × Rainbow's End™]; intr. 2000

'Gelco' ('Comedy') MinFl, yb, 2000, Giles, Diann; flowers medium size, yellow blend, full, borne in small clusters, no fragrance; foliage medium size, medium green, dull; few prickles; upright, medium growth; ['Little Darling' × Rainbow's End™]; intr. 2000

'Gelcol' ('Colonial Days') S, dr, 2002, Giles, Diann; flowers large, very dbl., borne mostly solitary; foliage medium size, medium green, matte; prickles small, straight; growth upright, medium; garden decorative; ['Fishermen's Friend' × 'Squire']; intr. 2000

'Gelcourt' ('Courtney') Min, rb, 1999, Giles, Diann; flowers red, reverse gold, 1½ in., dbl., borne in small clusters; foliage medium size, dark green, glossy; numerous prickles; spreading, low (1½ ft.) growth; ['Princess Celest' × Rainbow's End™]; intr. 1999

'Geldavis' ('Ken Davis') HT, pb, 1998, Davis, Ken; flowers light pink with darker edges, medium size, dbl., borne mostly singly; foliage medium size, light green, dull; prickles medium; upright, medium (4 ft.) growth; [sport of 'Bride's Dream']; intr. 1995

'Gelday' ('Sunday China') S, mp, 1997, Giles, Kevin; flowers , borne in large clusters; foliage small, medium green, dull; compact, low (2½ ft.)growth; ['Champney's Pink Cluster' × seedling]

'Geldew' ('Dewey') F, dr, 2001, Giles, Diann; flowers medium, dbl., borne in small clusters, no fragrance; foliage large, dark green, matte; prickles medium, straight, moderate; growth bushy, medium; garden decorative; ['Vera Dalton' × 'Red Simplicity']; intr. 1999

'Geleasy' ('Easy Vibes') F, op, 1999, Giles, Diann; flowers medium, dbl., borne in small clusters; foliage medium size, dark green, glossy; few prickles; compact, medium growth; ['Sun Flare' × 'Easy Living']; intr. 1998

'Geled' ('Allie') S, mp, 2000, Giles, Diann; flowers medium, full, borne mostly singly, no fragrance; foliage medium size, medium green, matte; prickles moderate; growth upright, tall; [sport of 'Auscrim']

'Gelele' ('Dear Eleanor') Min, lp, 1999, Giles, Diann; flowers dbl., borne mostly singly; foliage medium size, dark green, dull; few prickles; upright, medium growth; [Party Girl™ × 'Snow Bride']; intr. 1999

'Geletta' ('Meletta') Min, ob, 2000, Giles,

Diann; flowers apricot, medium, dbl., high-centered, borne mostly singly, slight fragrance; foliage medium size, dark green, semi-glossy; growth compact, medium

'Gelex' ('Excite') HT, dp, 2000, Giles, Diann; flowers deep pink, large, single, borne mostly singly, no fragrance; foliage small, medium green, semi-glossy; numerous prickles; spreading, medium growth; intr. 2000

'Gelfire' ('Dancing Fire') HT, ob, 2000, Giles, Diann; flowers orange, 5 in., full, exhibition, borne mostly singly; foliage large, medium green, semi-glossy; numerous prickles; upright, medium growth; [sport of 'Soaring Wings']; intr. 2000

'Gelfla' ('Florida Sun') F, my, 1997, Giles, Diann; flowers small, very dbl., borne in small clusters; foliage small, medium green, glossy; compact (2½-3ft.) growth; ['Sun Flare' × unknown]

'Gelfly' ('Butterfly Kisses') F, my, 1999, Giles, Diann; flowers medium, single, borne in small clusters; foliage medium size, medium green, semi-glossy; few prickles; upright, spreading, medium growth; ['Sun Flare' × 'Summer Snow']; intr. 1999

'Gelglen' ('Glen Myrie') HT, ab, 2000, Giles, Diann; flowers apricot, medium, dbl., borne mostly singly; foliage medium size, medium green, glossy; few prickles; upright, medium growth; [sport of 'Lady Beauty']; intr. 1999

'Gelgood' ('Good Vibes') F, mp, 1999, Giles, Diann; flowers medium, dbl., borne in large clusters; foliage medium size, medium green, glossy; few prickles; compact, medium growth; ['Sun Flare' × 'Simplicity']; intr. 1999

'Gelgrape' ('Grape Delight') Min, m, 1999, Giles, Diann; flowers small, semi-dbl., borne in small clusters; foliage medium size, medium green, semi-glossy; numerous prickles; compact, low (1½ ft.) growth; [Lavender Sweetheart™ × 'Herbie']; intr. 1999

'Geliza' ('Eliza') F, w, 2002, Giles, Diann; flowers medium, single, borne in small clusters; foliage medium size, light green, semi-glossy; prickles medium, straight, few; growth compact, medium; garden decoration, exhibition; [sport of 'Charlotte Anne']; intr. 2001

'Geljam' ('Jamie's Love') HT, mr, 1999, Giles, Diann; flowers medium, full, borne mostly singly; foliage medium size, dark green, dull; few prickles; upright, medium growth; ['Vera Dalton' × 'Special Merit']; intr. 1999

'Geljean' ('Melba Jean') Min, dp, 2001, Giles, Diann; flowers small, dbl., borne in small clusters, slight fragrance; foliage small, dark green, matte; prickles large, straight, few; growth upright, low; garden decorative, exhibition; [seedling × seedling]; intr. 2001

'Geljig' ('Jigs') F, or, 2001, Giles, Diann; flowers large, dbl., borne in small clusters, slight fragrance; foliage medium size, dark green, matte; prickles medium, slightly curved, few; growth upright, low; garden decorative; ['Vera Dalton' × 'Bing Crosby']; intr. 1999

'Gelken' ('Kenny's Rose') HT, mr, 1996, Giles, Kenneth; flowers 3-3½ in., full, borne mostly singly, moderate fragrance; foliage medium size, dark green, semi-glossy; some prickles; medium, spreading, sprawling growth; ['Swarthmore' × Mister Lincoln®]; intr. 1995

'Gella' ('Laura') MinFl, rb, 2001, Giles, Diann; flowers medium, full, borne in small clusters, no fragrance; foliage medium size, medium green, matte; prickles mixed size, straight, numerous; growth upright, tall; garden decorative, exhibition; [seedling × seedling]; intr. 2001

'Gellando' ('Rose Magic') Min, rb, 1999, Giles, Diann; flowers white and red edge, white reverse, medium, full, borne in small clusters; foliage medium size, dark green, semi-glossy; few prickles; upright, medium growth; ['Little Darling' × 'Kristen']; intr. 1999

'Gellert' HMult, w, 1917, Lambert

'Gellite' ('Tiffany Lite') MinFl, w, 1998, Giles, Diann; flowers large, white, dbl., borne in small clusters, slight fragrance; foliage medium size, medium green, semi-glossy; growth upright, bushy (3-4 ft.); [sport of 'Tiffany Lynn']; intr. 1997

'Gellov' ('Gambler') HT, w, 1995, Gimer, Louis; flowers large, full, borne mostly singly; foliage large, medium green, semi-glossy; few prickles; tall (5 ft.), upright growth; [Grace de Monaco® × seedling]; intr. 1995

'Gellynn' ('Sierra Lynn') HT, rb, 1999, Giles, Diann; flowers medium, full, borne mostly singly; foliage medium size, dark green, semi-glossy; few prickles; upright, medium (4-5 ft.) growth; ['Vera Dalton' × 'Paradise']; intr. 1999

'Gelmad' ('Madison') Min, pb, 2000, Giles, Diann; flowers medium, high-centered, borne mostly singly, slight fragrance; foliage small, dark green, semi-glossy; numerous prickles; growth upright, low; [seedling × seedling]

'Gelmagic' ('Magic Baby') F, pb, 1997, Giles, Diann; flowers medium, very dbl., borne mostly singly, no fragrance; foliage medium size, medium green, dull; growth upright, medium (3½ ft.).

'Gelman' ('Chess Man') Min, mr, 1997, Giles, Kevin; flowers medium, very dbl., borne mostly singly; foliage medium size, dark green, dull; upright, medium (3 ft.) growth; ['Chrysler Imperail' × unknown]

'Gelmar' ('Marvie') Min, mr, 1995, Giles, Diann; flowers medium red, small, full, borne mostly singly; foliage small, medium green, semi-glossy; some prickles; medium, upright growth; ['Winsome' × seedling]; intr. 1995

'Gelmaud' ('Mary Maud') Min, mp, 1999, Giles, Diann; flowers medium, dbl., borne in small clusters; foliage medium size, medium green, semi-glossy; prickles moderate; upright, medium growth; ['Little Darling' × unknown]; intr. 1999

'Gelmiss' ('Miss Mary') HT, dp, 1996, Miller, Carol; flowers deep pink, 3-3½ in., full, no fragrance; foliage large, medium green, matte; few prickles; tall (5 ft.), upright growth; [sport of 'Big Ben']; intr. 1995

'Gelmoon' ('South Moon') S, w, 1998, Giles, Diann; flowers pure white, yellow stamens, full, borne in large clusters, intense fragrance; foliage medium size, medium green, semi-glossy; upright, medium (4 ft.) growth; [sport of 'Belle Story']; intr. 1997

'Gelora' ('Oliver Orange') Min, ob, 2000, Giles, Diann; flowers orange, reverse blending white, medium, full, borne mostly singly, no fragrance; foliage medium size, medium green, matte; few prickles; growth spreading, medium; [seedling × seedling]

'Gelout' ('Chill Out') Min, m, 1999, Giles, Diann; flowers large, dbl., borne mostly singly; foliage large, medium green, semi-glossy; few prickles; upright, tall growth; [Lavender Sweetheart™ × 'Herbie']; intr. 1999

'Gelpam' ('Pam's Passion') HT, ob, 1999, Giles, Diann; flowers medium, full, borne mostly singly; foliage dark green, semi-glossy; few prickles; upright, medium growth; ['Vera Dalton' × unknown]; intr. 1999

'Gelpeach' ('Just Peachy') HT, op, 1997, Giles, Diann; flowers small, dbl., borne mostly singly; foliage medium size, dark green, glossy; upright, medium growth; ['Vera Dalton' × unknown]

'Gelpep' ('Chili Pepper') Min, or, 1997, Giles, Diann; flowers medium, very dbl., borne in small clusters; foliage large, dark green, glossy; bushy, medium (1½-2 ft.)growth; ['Vera Dalton' × unknown]

'Gelpop' ('Hot Poppy') Min, or, 2001, Giles, Diann; flowers medium, dbl., borne mostly solitary, slight fragrance; foliage large, medium green, matte; prickles small, straight, few; growth upright, low; garden decorative, exhibition; [seedling × seedling]; intr. 1999

'Gelpuzzle' ('Chinese Puzzle') MinFl, rb, 1999, Giles, Diann; flowers small, dbl., borne in large clusters; foliage small, dark green, glossy; numerous prickles; climbing, tall growth; ['Vera Dalton' × 'Roller Coaster']; intr. 1999

'Gelray' ('Early Ray') HT, dy, 2001, Giles, Diann; flowers large, dbl., borne mostly solitary, moderate fragrance; foliage medium size, dark green, matte; prickles medium, straight, few; growth upright, low; garden decorative; ['Dr. A.J. Verhage' × 'Stroke o' Luck']; intr. 1999

'Gelred' ('Redneck Girl') Min, op, 1995, Giles, Diann; flowers orange pink with white base, full; foliage small, dark green, semi-glossy; few prickles; spreading growth; intr. 1995

'Gelria' F, pb, Verbeek; flowers dark pink, yellow reverse; intr. 1974

'Gelrise' ('Gala Sunrise') F, rb, 1997, Giles, Diann; flowers medium, very dbl., borne in small clusters; foliage medium size, dark green, dull; upright, medium (3½ ft.) growth; ['Vera Dalton' × Rainbow's End™]

'Gelrite' ('Right Bright', 'Rite Brite') F, my, 1996, Giles, Diann; flowers 1½ in., full, slight fragrance; foliage small, medium green, matte; few prickles; low (3½ ft.), spreading, compact growth; ['Sun Flare' × 'Rise 'n' Shine']; intr. 1995

'Gelrus' ('White Russian') HT, w, 2000, Giles, Diann; flowers medium, dbl., high-centered, borne mostly singly, moderate fragrance; foliage medium size, medium green, matte; prickles moderate; upright, tall (5 ft.) growth; ['Sheer Bliss' × unknown]

'Gelryals' ('Shirley A. Ryals') F, pb, 2000, Giles, Diann; flowers medium, dbl., high-centered, borne in small clusters, no fragrance; foliage medium size, medium green, semi-glossy; few prickles; compact, medium (4 ft.) growth; ['Sun Flare' × 'Simplicity']; intr. 2000

'Gelshan' ('Shannie') Min, pb, 1997, Giles, Diann; flowers medium, very dbl., borne mostly singly; foliage medium size, medium green, semi-glossy; upright, medium (2½ ft.) growth; ['Little Darling' × Magic Carrousel®]

'Gelskies' ('Morning Skies') Min, ab, 1997, Giles, Diann; flowers medium, very dbl., borne mostly singly; foliage medium size, medium green, dull; upright, low (1½ ft.) growth; ['Little Darling' × Rainbow's End™]

'Gelsol' ('Solar Sensation') HT, ob, 2000, Giles, Diann; flowers large, full, borne mostly singly, no fragrance; foliage dark green, semi-glossy; numerous prickles; upright, medium (4 ft.) growth; ['Vera Dalton' × unknown]

'Gelsom' ('Jennie Sommer') S, rb, 2001, Giles, Diann; flowers striped, large, semi-dbl., borne in small clusters, moderate fragrance; foliage medium size, light green, matte; prickles medium, straight, few; growth spreading, tall; garden decorative; [seedling × Scentimental™]; intr. 2001

'Gelsue' ('Linda Sue') Min, my, 2001, Giles, Diann; flowers medium, dbl., borne mostly solitary, no fragrance; foliage medium size, dark green, matte; growth upright, medium; garden decorative; ['Rise 'n' Shine' × 'Early Ray']; intr. 2001

'Gelsweet' ('Sweet Vibes') F, lp, 1999, Giles, Diann; flowers medium, dbl., borne in small clusters; foliage medium size, medium green, glossy; few prickles; compact, medium growth; ['Sun Flare' × 'Simplicity']; intr. 1999

'Geltan' ('Mango Tango') MinFl, ab, 2000, Giles, Diann; flowers medium, dbl., borne mostly singly, no fragrance; foliage medium size, medium green, semi-glossy; few prickles; growth upright, medium; [New Year® × 'miniature seedling']; intr. 2000

'Geltan' MinFl, yb, 2002, Giles, Diann; intr. 2001

'Geltendorf' HT, ob, Croix; intr. 1971

'Geltra' ('Traci') Min, w, 2001, Giles, Diann; flowers white with pink edge, medium, full, borne in large clusters, slight fragrance; foliage medium size, dark green, glossy; prickles few, medium, curved; growth spreading, medium; garden decorative; [seedling × seedling]; intr. 2001

'Geltwo' ('Two Thumbs Up') HT, ab, 1999, Giles, Diann; flowers 5 in., full, borne mostly singly; foliage medium size, medium green, dull; few prickles; upright, medium (5 ft.) growth; ['South Seas' × St Patrick™]

'Gelwin' ('Winter Princess') Min, w, 1997, Giles, Diann; flowers medium, dbl., borne in small clusters; foliage medium size, medium green, semi-glossy; upright, medium (2½ ft.) growth; ['Little Darling' × unknown]

'Gelyan' ('Bryan') F, ob, 2001, Giles, Diann; flowers orange and white, 3 in., dbl., borne in large clusters, slight fragrance; foliage medium size, medium green, glossy; prickles small, straight, numerous; growth spreading, medium; garden decorative, exhibition; [Queen Margrethe™ × Betty Boop™]; intr. 2001

'Gem' HT, mp, 1960, Walker; bud long, pointed; flowers deep soft pink, medium, semi-dbl., high-centered; foliage soft; vigorous, upright growth; ['Ena Harkness' × 'Mme Butterfly']

'Gem of the Prairies' ('Bijou des Prairies') HSet, dp, 1865, Burgess, A.; flowers rosy red, occasionally blotched white, darker at center, 6-7 cm., full, flat, borne in large clusters; non-recurrent; vigorous growth; ['Queen of the Prairies' × 'Mme Laffay']

Gem o' the Rockies™ -- See 'Savorockies'

'Gemini' Pol, ob, 1967, Joseph H. Hill, Co.; bud pointed; flowers orange, small, dbl., high-centered, slight fragrance; foliage dark, glossy; vigorous, upright, bushy growth; PP2728; [seedling × 'Rumba']

'Gemini' ('The Twins') HT, my, Burston; flowers clear yellow with thin pink petal edges, dbl., globular; foliage dark green, glossy; growth to 70 cm.; intr. 2004

Gemini™ -- See 'Jacnepal'

'Gemma' F, mp, Harkness; flowers bright mid-pink, medium, dbl., borne in large clusters, slight fragrance; free-flowering; foliage glossy, disease-resistant green; growth to 4 × 3 ft.; intr. 2003

'Gemma Louise' F, mp, 2008, Heath, William L.; flowers upper silvery pink, reverse lighter, small, 2½ in., dbl., borne in small clusters; foliage medium, medium green, semi-glossy, with distinctive dark edges; prickles medium, narrow, hooked down, red-brown when young; growth upright, medium (4 ft.); garden decoration, cut flowers; sets hips readily; ['Silver Jubilee' × 'Bride']; intr. 2008

'Gemma Rouge' S, dr; groundcover; spreading growth; intr. 2003

'Gemstone' HT, mp, 1978, J&B Roses; bud high-centered; flowers 4½-5 in., 28 petals, high-centered; foliage matte; vigorous, upright growth; ['Helen Traubel' × 'Swarthmore']

'Gen. John Pershing' ('F. R. M. Undritz', 'Frederick R. M. Undritz') LCl, dp, 1917, Undritz; flowers large, 53 petals; vigorous, climbing growth; ['Dr. W. Van Fleet' × 'Mrs W. J. Grant']

'Gendee' S, w, Genesis

'Gene Boerner' F, mp, 1968, Boerner; bud ovoid; flowers deep pink, medium, 35 petals, high-centered; foliage glossy; vigorous, upright growth; PP2885; ['Ginger' × ('Ma Perkins' × 'Garnette Supreme')]

'Gene Jones' -- See 'Wilgene'

'Gene Sandberg' -- See 'Resand'

'Gene Tierney' S, dy, Guillot-Massad; flowers amber yellow, full, cupped, borne in clusters, moderate myrrh fragrance; recurrent; tall growth; intr. 2000

'Generaal Smuts' HT, mr, 1922, Van Rossem; flowers cherry-red, shaded deep coral-red, dbl.; ['Gen. MacArthur' × 'Mme Edouard Herriot']

'Generaal Snijders' ('General Snyders') HT, dp, 1917, Leenders, M.; flowers deep carmine shaded coral-red, large, dbl., intense fragrance; ['Mme Mélanie Soupert' × 'George C. Waud']

'Général Allard' B, dp, 1835, Laffay, M.; flowers bright pink, medium, full, globular; growth branching, small; sometimes classed as Ch

'Général Appert' HP, dr, 1884, Schwartz; flowers velvety blackish purple red, large, full; quite remontant; ['Souv de William Wood' × unknown]

'Général Athalin' -- See 'Athalin'

'Général Baron Berge' HP, mr, 1892, Pernet Père; flowers red, center occasionally striped white, large, 50 petals; erect, vigorous growth

'General Barral' HP, m, 1867, Damaizin; flowers violet pink, medium, full

'Général Bedeau' HP, pb, 1851, Margottin; flowers pink and red, large, dbl.

'Général Bernard' HP, pb, before 1845; flowers carmine, shaded dull violet, full, globular

'Général Berthelot' HT, dp, 1926, Walter, L.; flowers dark pink, slightly streaked white, dbl.; ['J.B. Clark' × 'Farbenkonigin']

'General Browne' HSpn, w, about 1860; flowers blush-white, fading pure white, quilled, dbl., moderate fragrance; foliage dark; twiggy, prickly growth

'General Bülow' HGal, mp, before 1845; flowers carmine, edges darker with violet tones, full

'Général Canrobert' B, mr, about 1860, Pradel; flowers shining crimson, large, full

'Général Cavaignac' HP, mr, 1849, Margottin; flowers shining cherry red, large, full

'General Cavaignac' HP, mr, 1848, Foulard; flowers vary from deep red to pinky red depending upon weather, dbl.; slow to establish

'Général Clerc' M, dr, 1845, Laffay, M.; flowers slaty purple-red, medium, full

'Général D. Mertchansky' T, mp, 1890, Nabonnand; flowers rosy flesh, petals somewhat imbricated, large, full; prickles moderate; stems reddish; growth very vigorous

'Général Daumesnil' HCh, m; flowers violet purple with lilac, full

'Général de Castellane' HP, mr, 1851, Guillot père

'Général de la Martinière' HP, rb, 1869, De Sansal; flowers wine red, center glossy crimson pink, outer petals lilac pink, very large, full

'Général de Lamoricière' HCh, m, before 1866; flowers lilac pink, medium, full

'Général de Tartas' -- See 'Général Tartas'

'Général de Vaulgrenant' HT, dp, 1926, Walter, L.; flowers rose-pink, very dbl.; ['Mme Henriette Schissele' × 'Mme Adele Gance']

'Général Désaix' HGal, dp, before 1829, Boutigny; flowers bright dark pink, edges lighter, medium, full

'Général Désaix' HP, mr, Moreau et Robert; flowers fiery red, shaded poppy, large, full; intr. 1867

'Général d'Hautpoul' HP, mr, 1864, Verdier, E.; flowers bright scarlet, medium, dbl.

'Général Dinot' -- See 'Général Drouot'

'General Domingos de Oliveira' HT, ab, 1939, Moreira da Silva; flowers yellow-apricot tinted flesh-pink, large, dbl., cupped; foliage glossy; dwarf growth; ['Frank Reader' × 'Golden Gleam']

'General Don' HT, pb, 1919, Le Cornu; flowers strawberry tinted coppery, base golden yellow, dbl.; ['Mme Mélanie Soupert' × 'Louise Catherine Breslau']

'Général Donadieu' HGal, mr, before 1835; flowers purplish red, compact, very dbl.

'Général Drouot' ('Général Dinot') M, m, 1847, Vibert; flowers grenadine-purple, becoming currant red, medium, dbl.; not very remontant; foliage dark, tinted brown; prickles numerous, flat at base, straight; vigorous growth

'Général Duc d'Aumale' HP, dr, 1875, Verdier, E.; flowers dark cerise red, large, dbl.

'Général Fabvier' -- See 'Fabvier'

'Général Fetter' HT, m, 1922, Walter, L.; flowers carmine-purple, glossy, very dbl.; ['Jonkheer J.L. Mock' × 'Luise Lilia']

'Général Forey' HP, dr, 1859, Moreau & Robert; flowers wine red, large, full, cupped; ['Triomphe de l'Exposition' × unknown]

'Général Foy' D, dp, 1825, Boutigny; flowers deep brilliant pink to light red, lighter edges, small to medium, very dbl.

'Général Foy' HGal, mr, Pelletier; flowers ruby red, outer petals lighter, very large, full, flat, borne in small clusters; intr. 1827

'Général Foy' HGal, m, Vibert; flowers purple, spotted with dark violet, medium, full; intr. 1845

'Général Galliéni' T, rb, 1899, Nabonnand, G.; flowers coppery red, cupped, moderate fragrance; recurrent; vigorous growth; ['Souv. de Therese Levet' × 'Reine Emma des Pays-Bas']

'General Gordon' T, w, 1885, Bennett; flowers pure white, medium, dbl.

'Général Grant' HP, mr, 1869, Verdier, E.; flowers scarlet, shaded dark carmine, large, full

'Général Guisan' HT, dr, 1945, Heizmann, E.; flowers large, dbl.

'Général Hoche' B, mp; flowers bright pink, medium, very full, cupped

'Général Hudelet' HP, pb, 1852, Crousse; flowers light pink, center cherry red, large, full

'General Jack' -- See 'Général Jacqueminot'

'Général Jacqueminot' HCh, dr, 1846, Laffay

'Général Jacqueminot' ('General Jack', 'Jack Rose', 'La Brillante', 'Mrs Cleveland', 'Richard Smith', 'Triomphe d'Amiens') HP, rb, 1853, Roussel; bud scarlet-crimson; flowers dark red, whitish reverse, 27 petals, intense fragrance; recurrent bloom; foliage rich green; long, strong stems; vigorous, bushy growth; [probable seedling of 'Gloire des Rosomanes']

'Général Kléber' M, mp, 1856, Robert; bud well mossed; flowers pink tinted lilac, large, full, moderate fragrance; non-recurrent; foliage apple green; vigorous, upright (4 ft.) growth

'Général Kléber' HP, mr, Boyau; flowers bright red, shaded dark carmine, large, full; very remontant; intr. 1872

'General Korolkow' -- See 'Eugène Fürst'

'Général Labutère' Ch, mp

'Général Lamarque' -- See 'Lamarque'

'General MacArthur' HT, dp, 1905, E.G. Hill Co.; flowers rose-red, 20 petals, intense damask fragrance; foliage leathery

'General MacArthur, Climbing' Cl HT, dp, 1923, Dickson, H.; flowers bright carmine pink, large, semi-dbl.; [sport of 'General MacArthur']

'Général Miloradowitsch' HP, mr, 1869, Louvat or Lévêque; flowers red, shaded carmine, very large, full

'Général Moreau' HGal, m, before 1885, Moreau, F.; flowers purple pink, medium, full

'Général Négrier' HP, mp, 1851, Portemer; flowers bright pink, large, full

'General Robert E. Lee' T, my, 1896, Good & Reese; bud deep orange-yellow; flowers canary-yellow

'Général Schablikine' ('Vestey's Pink Tea') T, op, 1878, Nabonnand, G.; flowers deep pink with coppery overtones, full, flat; vigorous, medium (3 ft.) growth

'Général Simpson' HP, mp, 1854, Lacharme; flowers rose pink with lilac reflections, medium, full

'Général Simpson' HP, mp, Ducher; flowers bright carmine, medium, very full; intr. 1857

'General Snyders' -- See 'Generaal Snijders'

'General Stefánik' ('Krásná Azurea') HP, m, 1933, Böhm, J.; flowers violet blue; [seedling or sport of 'La Brillante']

'General-Superior Arnold Janssen' HT, dp, 1912, Leenders, M.; bud pointed; flowers deep rose-pink, veined darker, reverse much darker, large, dbl.; ['Farbenkonigin' × 'Gen. MacArthur']

'General-Superior Arnold Janssen, Climbing' Cl HT, dp, 1931, Böhm, J.; flowers deep rose-red, large, full; [sport of 'General-Superior Arnold Janssen']

'Général Tartas' ('Général de Tartas') T, dp, 1860, Bernède; flowers deep rose, large, dbl.

'Général Testard' ('Général Tétard') HWich, rb, 1918, Pajotin-Chédane; flowers red, center white, 6 cm., semi-dbl., borne in large clusters; foliage small, glossy

'Général Tétard' -- See 'Général Testard'

'General Th. Peschkoff' HT, pb, 1909, Ketten, Gebrüder; flowers salmon red, fading to Hermosa pink, center yellow, very large, dbl., moderate fragrance; ['Mme Ravary' × 'Étoile de France']

'General Vaidya' HT, ab, More, Chandrakant; [sport of 'Freude']

'Général Valazé' T, w, before 1835, Dubourg; flowers flesh white, center brighter pink, large, full

'General von Bothnia-Andreæ' HP, mr, 1900, Verschuren; flowers carmine-red, very large, dbl.; ['Victor Verdier' × seedling]

'General von Moltke' HP, rb, 1873, Bell; flowers bright red, shaded scarlet orange, large, full; ['Charles Léfèbvre' × unknown]

'Général Washington' T, mr, 1855, Page

'Général Washington' HP, dr, Granger; flowers deep crimson, reflexes maroon, large, very dbl., flat, moderate fragrance; occasionally recurrent bloom; moderate growth; [sport of 'Triomphe de l'Exposition']; intr. 1860

'Générale Marie Raiewsky' HP, pb, 1911, Ketten Bros.; flowers pink with dark yellow, large, dbl.; ['Frau Karl Druschki' × 'Fisher Holmes']

'Generalin Isenbart' HT, pb, 1915, Lambert, P.; flowers coppery-pink with dark yellow, large, dbl.; ['Triumph' × 'E. Veyrat Hermanos']

'Generaloberst von Kluck' HT, dp, 1917, Lambert, P.; flowers carmine-pink, large, dbl.; ['Frau Geheimrat Dr. Staub' × 'Germanica']

'Generosa' -- See 'Mansuino Rose'

'Generosity' HT, ob, 1983, Northfield, G.; flowers cream with orange center, large, 35 petals, moderate fragrance; foliage large, dark, matte; bushy growth; ['Fred Gibson' × 'Lady Elgin']

Generosity™ S, op, Clements, John; flowers peachy pink, darkening toward the center, 4 inches, 45 petals, intense fruity/myrrh fragrance; recurrent; foliage medium green; 4 ft. × 4 ft. growth; intr. 2008

'Genesis' Min, m, 1991, Jolly, Marie; bud ovoid; flowers lavender, reverse white, 2 in., 45 petals, borne singly, moderate fragrance; foliage medium size, medium green, semi-glossy; upright growth; [Lavender Jade™ × 'Angel Face']; intr. 1992

'Genève' HT, or, 1944, Meilland, F.; bud long; flowers salmon-carmine and capucine-red, high pointed, dbl.; vigorous growth; ['Charles P. Kilham' × 'Mme Joseph Perraud']

'Geneve' -- See Monrose+

Genevieve™ -- See 'Savagen'

'Genevieve' -- See 'Meiroupis'

'Geneviève Genest' -- See 'Mrs Sam McGredy, Climbing'

'Geneviève le Goaster' HT, w, 1923, Carrette; flowers white, center pale rose, base salmon-rose

Geneviève Orsi® F, lp, Jackson & Perkins; flowers soft, rosy pink, changing to honey color , full, cupped, slight fragrance; recurrent; foliage dark green; even (80 cm.) growth; intr. 2007

'Genevieve Rose' S, ob, Peden, R.; intr. 1998

'Génie de Châteaubriand' HP, dr, 1852, Oudin; flowers bishop's violet, with scarlet reflections and tinted black violet, 4 in., rosette, borne in clusters of 2-4; foliage dark green above, silvery beneath, ovate, lightly serrated; prickles down-hooked, reddish when young, small; growth upright

'Genius Mendel' HT, mr, 1935, Böhm, J.; bud pointed; flowers light fiery red to pure red, large, dbl., high-centered; foliage glossy; bushy growth; ['Mrs Henry Winnett' × 'Sir David Davis']

'Genpat' ('Dazzler') MinFl, op, Genesis; intr. 1995

'Genpen' ('Prince Regent') S, m, Genesis

'Genpink' ('King William') S, dp, Genesis

'Genruby' ('King Richard') S, m, Genesis

'Gensuar' -- See 'Top of the Bill'

'Gentil' -- See 'Les Trois Mages'

'Gentil Bernard' D, 1825, Bizard

'Gentiliana' -- See 'Polyantha Grandiflora'

'Gentle' F, op, 1960, Lens; flowers salmon-pink, well-formed, 2½-3 in., 26 petals, borne in clusters; vigorous, compact, bushy growth; ['Independence' × ('Lady Sylvia' × 'Fashion')]

'Gentle Annie' -- See 'Seaannie'

'Gentle Clown' -- See 'Hartopper'

Gentle Cover™ -- See 'Poullen'

Gentle Giant™ -- See 'Wekrigoyelo'

'Gentle Hermione' -- See 'Ausrumba'

'Gentle Kiss' -- See 'Hartbrad'

'Gentle Lady' HT, lp, 1975, Fuller; bud slender, long, pointed; flowers large, 35 petals, cupped, intense fragrance; foliage matte, dark, leathery; upright, bushy growth; ['Tiffany' × 'Michèle Meilland']

'Gentle Maid' -- See 'Harvilac'

'Gentle Persuasion' S, yb, 1985, Buck, Dr. Griffith J.; flowers yellow tinted orange, medium-large, 28 petals, cupped, borne 1-5 per cluster; repeat bloom; foliage large, leathery, semi-glossy, dark olive green; prickles awl-like, tan; vigorous, bushy, erect growth; hardy; ['Carefree Beauty' × 'Oregold']; intr. 1984

'Gentle Touch' -- See 'Diclulu'

'Gentleman's Agreement' -- See 'Brigentle'

'Genval' HT, mp, 1963, Delforge; flowers cyclamen-pink; foliage bronze, dull; vigorous growth; ['Rosita' × 'Margaret']

'Genwine' ('King Henry') S, dp, Genesis

'Geoff Boycott' F, w, 1976, McGredy, Sam IV; flowers large, 35 petals, slight fragrance; foliage dark; ['Ice White' × Tip-Top®]; intr. 1974

'Geoff Hamilton' -- See 'Ausham'

'Geoffrey Henslow' HT, mr, 1912, Dickson, A.; flowers very dbl.

'Geohel' S, dy, Zilligen, George D.; intr. 2004

'Geordie Lad' -- See 'Horkorblush'

'Georg Ahrends' -- See 'Georg Arends'

'Georg Arends' ('Fortuné Besson', 'Georg Ahrends') HP, mp, 1910, Hinner, W.; flowers soft pink, large, 25 petals, intense fragrance; vigorous growth; ['Frau Karl Druschki' × 'La France']

'Georg Geuder' HT, op, 1931, Schmidt, I. C.; flowers dark salmon-pink, medium, dbl.

'George Armer' -- See 'Bratowin'

'George Baker' HP, dp, 1881, Paul & Son; flowers cerise, very dbl.

'George Best' Min, dr, Dickson; intr. 2008

George Burns™ -- See 'Wekcalroc'

'George Burns Centennial' -- See 'Wekcalroc'

'George C. Waud' HT, mp, 1908, Dickson, A.; flowers rose, veined darker, 4½ in., dbl., high-centered, intense fragrance; bushy growth

'George Dakin' HT, pb, 1927, Burbage Nursery; flowers silvery pink, flushed apricot, reverse orange to apricot, dbl., high-centered; foliage glossy, bronze; vigorous, bushy growth; ['Ophelia' × 'Mrs Henry Morse']

'George Dickson' HT, mr, 1912, Dickson, A.; flowers large crimson, 36 petals, borne on weak stems, moderate fragrance

'George Dickson, Climbing' Cl HT, mr, 1949, Woodward; [sport of 'George Dickson']

'George Elger' ('Yellow Baby Rambler') Pol, my, 1912, Turbat; bud small, golden yellow; flowers coppery yellow to clear yellow, very dbl., borne in large clusters; foliage small, dark, soft; bushy, dwarf growth

'George Elliot' HT, op, 1970, Wills; flowers shrimp-pink, 4-5 in., 35 petals, foliage bronze; ['Highlight' × 'Dorothy Peach']

'George Fox' HT, or, 1939, Savage Nursery; flowers orange-vermilion, medium, globular; foliage glossy; compact growth; ['Charles P. Kilham' × 'Lady Forteviot']

'George Geary' HT, yb, 1953, Geary; flowers golden yellow flushed vermilion, high pointed, 4 in.; foliage dark, bronze; vigorous growth; ['Gwyneth Jones' × seedling]

'George Geuder' HT, yb, 1931, Schmidt, J.C.; flowers salmon-pink and bright carmine on yellow ground; vigorous growth

'George H. Mackereth' HT, dr, 1924, Dickson, A.; flowers crimson shaded velvety maroon, dbl.

'George Heers' HT, pb, 1961, Langbecker; flowers rich pink, touched apricot and yellow

'George Howarth' HT, dp, 1928, Bees; flowers bright carmine, dbl.; ['Gorgeous' × 'The Queen Alexandra Rose']

'George IV' -- See 'Rivers' George IV'

'George Laing Paul' HT, mr, 1904, S&H; ['Mme Caroline Testout' × 'Fisher-Holmes']

'George Peabody' Ch, m, 1857, Pentland; flowers bright garnet-purple, large, full; ['Joseph Paul' × unknown]

'George R. Hill' HT, w, 1991, Varney, Eric; flowers 45 petals; foliage large, dark green; vigorous growth; [sport of 'Admiral Rodney']; intr. 1991

'George Rimmer' HT, dr, 2001, Poole, Lionel; flowers 5½ in., full, high-centered, borne mostly solitary, slight fragrance; foliage large, dark green, semi-glossy; prickles medium, hooked down, moderate; growth upright, bushy, medium (1 m.), vigorous; exhibition, bedding; [('Royal William' × 'Gabi') × 'New Zealand']; intr. 2002

'George Sand' HP, mp, 1909, Roseraie de l'Hay; flowers flesh pink

'George Sand' -- See 'Lunelle'

'George Thomas' HT, w, 1972, Ellick; flowers pure white, tinged pink, 6-8 in., 40 petals, moderate fragrance; foliage dark; vigorous growth; ['Ena Harkness' × 'Memoriam']; intr. 1975

'George Vancouver' S, mr, Ogilvie, Ian S.; flowers 24 petals, flat, borne singly and in clusters; good repeat; lush, disease-resistant foliage; open, arching (3 × 4 ft.) growth; PP10009; intr. 1994

'George Will' HRg, dp, 1939, Skinner; flowers deep pink, 3 in., dbl., flat, borne in clusters, moderate clove fragrance; all-summer bloom; foliage rugose; stems slender branches; growth to 3-4 ft.; [(*R. rugosa* × *R. acicularis*) × unknown]

'Georgen' Min, mr, NIRP Intl.full; intr. 2007

Georgeous™ -- See 'Intergeorge'

'Georges Cain' ('Mons Georges Cain') HRg, dr, 1909, Gravereaux; flowers crimson with purple, large, dbl.; very vigorous growth; ['Souv. de Pierre Notting' × *R. rugosa*]

'Georges Cassagne' Gr, mr, Croix; intr. 1980

'Georges Chesnel' HT, dy, 1935, Pernet-Ducher; bud pointed; flowers deep golden yellow, veined copper, dbl.; foliage glossy; [('Julien Potin' × unknown) × 'Étoile d'Or']

'George's Choice' F, mr, 1978, Ellick; bud small, ovoid; flowers currant red, 35-40 petals, moderate fragrance; compact, bushy growth; ['Evelyn Fison' × 'Tabarin']; intr. 1979

'Georges Clemenceau' HT, ob, 1919, Lévêque; flowers bright orange, shaded umber and carmine, large, very full; [sport of 'Mme Edouard Herriot']

'Georges Cuvier' ('Beauté de Versailles') B, dp, 1842, Souchet; flowers bright cerise, shaded pink, large, full, cupped; foliage very dark green; prickles straight, flattened at base; growth vigorous

'Georges d'Amboise' HP, mr, 1853, Boyau; flowers bright rose red, large, full, globular

'Georges de Cadonel' ('Georges de Cadoudal', 'Mons Georges de Cadoudal') B, lp, 1904, Schwartz; flowers bright pink nuanced carmine on coppery ground, large, very full, globular, moderate fragrance; recurrent; foliage purplish green; short stems; arching growth; sometimes classed as Cl T

'Georges de Cadoudal' -- See 'Georges de Cadonel'

'Georges Denjean' F, yb, Guillot-Massad; flowers saffron yellow, lightly edged with pink, center orange, borne in clusters, moderate fragrance; intr. 2005

Georges Denjean® S, ob, Guillot-Massad; intr. 2006

Georges Dubœuf® -- See 'Jacinber'

'Georges Dupont' B, mp, 1856, Lartay; flowers carmine

'Georges Farber' T, dr, 1889, Bernaix; bud longly oval, conical; flowers outer petals velvety purple, thick, veined and reticulated with fiery red, medium; foliage bright green; growth medium

'Georges Hamonière' HT, dr, 1937, Moulin; flowers medium, dbl.

'Georges Moreau' HP, mr, 1880, Moreau-Robert; flowers bright satiny red, tinted vermilion, very large, globular; nearly thornless; ['Paul Neyron' × unknown]

'Georges Paquel' HT, my, 1934, Leenders, M.; flowers saffron-yellow, large, dbl.; vigorous, bushy growth; [seedling × 'Souv. de Claudius Pernet']

'Georges Paul' HP, mr, 1863, Verdier, E.; flowers bright velvety red, 8-10 cm., full, borne in clusters of 6-8

'Georges Perdoux' HT, pb, 1927, Barbier; flowers reddish-pink tinted coppery red, dbl.

'Georges Pernet' Pol, mp, 1887, Pernet-Ducher; flowers bright peach-pink; ['Mignonette' × unknown]

'George's Pride' -- See 'Manpride'

'Georges Prince' HP, mr, 1863, Verdier, E.; flowers bright red, shaded dark pink, medium, full

'Georges Rousset' HP, mr, 1893, Rousset; flowers light silky red, reverse pink, very large, full

'Georges Schwartz' T, my, 1899, Schwartz, Vve.; flowers canary-yellow; ['Kaiserin Auguste Viktoria' × 'Souv. de Mme Levet']

'Georges Schwartz, Climbing' Cl HT, my, 1917, Knight, G.

Georges Truffaut® HT, dr, Dorieux; flowers dark, velvety red, edges turning black , double , high-centered, borne singly and in small clusters; intr. 1996

'Georges Vibert' HGal, rb, 1853, Robert; flowers purplish red, streaked carmine, small eye at center, medium to large, dbl., flat rosette, borne in clusters of 3, moderate fragrance; foliage medium green, small, elliptical; prickles moderate

Georgette® Min, mp, 1981, Bennett, Dee; bud ovoid; flowers medium pink, veined darker, 30 petals, high-centered, slight fragrance; foliage medium green, dense; prickles straight; upright, compact, bushy growth; PP5070; [Electron® × 'Little Chief']

'Georgette' -- See 'Koracona'

'Georgette' -- See 'Interorge'

'Georgette and Valentine' HT, w, 1911, Bernaix fils; flowers white, touched with flesh pink, aging to salmon pink, large, full, cupped

'Georgeus' Min, mp; intr. 1998

'Georgia' HT, ab, 1980, Weeks, O.L.; bud short, pointed; flowers peach-apricot blend, 5½-6 in., 53-55 petals, borne singly, moderate tea fragrance; foliage large, glossy, leathery; prickles long, hooked downward; tall, upright growth; PP4712; ['Arizona' × seedling]

'Georgia Belle' -- See 'Talgeorgia'

'Georgianna Doan' HT, pb, 1942, Joseph H. Hill, Co.; bud long, pointed; flowers two-tone pink, medium, 25-30 petals, high-centered, intense fragrance; foliage leathery, wrinkled, dark; vigorous, upright, much branched growth; PP513; ['Ophelia' × seedling]

'Georgia's Life' -- See 'Horgeorgia'

'Georgie Anderson' -- See 'Andgeo'

'Georgie Bee' -- See 'Silbixlar'

'Georgie Girl' -- See 'Dickerfuffle'

'Gerald Hardy' HT, mr, 1936, Dickson, A.; bud pointed; flowers bright scarlet-red, spiral, large, dbl.; strong, erect stems; bushy growth

'Geraldine' HT, mp, 1924, Chaplin Bros.; flowers buff, shaded pink, dbl., moderate fragrance; RULED EXTINCT 11/82 ARM; ['Antoine Rivoire' × 'Marie Adélaide']

'Geraldine' -- See 'Peahaze'

'Geraldine Ferraro' HT, lp, Zary, Keith; bud pointed; flowers soft pink , double , high-centered, moderate anise fragrance; PPAF; intr. 2007

'Geraldine Hicks' HT, ab, 1950, Hicks; flowers bronze-yellow; [sport of 'William Moore']

'Geranium' HMoy, mr, 1938, Royal Hort. Soc.; flowers almost scarlet, 2 in., single, borne in clusters (up to 5) borne along length of laterals; non-recurrent; upright (8-10 ft.), compact growth; hips crimson

'Geranium' -- See 'Independence'

'Geranium Primaplant' Pol, mr, Vlaeminck; flowers medium, semi-dbl.; intr. 1964

'Geranium Red' F, or, 1947, Boerner; flowers bright geranium red, 4 in., 50 petals, globular, borne in clusters, intense geranium fragrance; foliage dark, glossy; bushy growth; PP811; ['Crimson Glory' × seedling]

'Gerard ter Borch' S, dp, Williams, J. Benjamin; flowers dbl., moderate fragrance; free-flowering; intr. 1997

'Gerbe de Roses' HP, m, 1847, Laffay; flowers rosy lilac, medium, dbl., borne in small clusters; foliage dark green; prickles short, flattened; sometimes attributed to Vibert

'Gerbe d'Or' -- See 'Macca'

'Gerbe Rose' HWich, lp, 1904, Fauque; flowers delicate pink, 8 cm., dbl., cupped, borne in small clusters; some autumn repeat; foliage glossy, large, almost evergreen; nearly thornless; vigorous growth; [*R. wichurana* × 'Baroness Rothschild']

'Gerda Henkel' HT, dr, 1964, Tantau, Math.; flowers deep blood-red, large, dbl.; foliage dark, leathery; strong stems; vigorous, upright growth; ['New Yorker' × 'Prima Ballerina']

'Gerda Hnatyshyn' -- See 'Jalgerda'

'Gerdo' F, lp; PP4982; flora-tea; intr. 1986

'Germaine' HT, w, 1926, Chambard, C.; flowers creamy white, center salmon; [seedling × 'Sunburst']

'Germaine Chenault' HT, lp, 1910, Guillot; flowers cream-pink with darker edges, large, dbl.; ['Killarney' × 'Rosomane Gravereaux']

'Germaine de Marest' T, w, 1892, Guillot; flowers cream white, shaded salmon pink, large, full

'Germaine Lacroix' HMult, w, 1912, Dubreuil; ['Crimson Rambler' × unknown]

'Germaine Laroulandie'   HT, yb, 1908, Chauvry; flowers yellow, shaded apricot and cream, large, full
'Germaine Rossiaud'   HT, op, 1915, Chambard; flowers salmon pink, aging to white, very large, full; ['Antoine Rivoire' × 'Mélanie Soupert']
'Germain's Centennial'   HT, Lammerts; PP3203
'Germanea'   HT, dp, 1929, Ravenberg; flowers deep shining rose-pink, well-formed, very large, dbl.; [sport of 'Columbia']
'Germania' -- See 'Charme'
'Germania' -- See 'Gloire de Ducher'
'Germania-Africana' -- See 'Kortechna'
'Germanica'   HRg, mp, 1890, Müller; flowers rose pink, single
'Germanica'   HRg, rb, Mueller, F.; flowers dark red-violet, 3 in., full; hips large, round, with persistent spidery sepals, orange-red; intr. 1900
'Germiston Gold, Climbing'   Cl HT, dy, Malanseuns; blooms freely all season; intr. 1992
'Germiston Gold' -- See 'Kortake'
'Gero'   F, rb, Scholle, E.; flowers pink and red, medium, dbl.; intr. 1984
'Gert Potgieter'   HT, 1968, Gowie; foliage light green; vigorous growth
Gertrud®   F, dr
'Gertrud Huck'   HT, dp, 1932, Huck; bud pointed; flowers flamingo-red, large, dbl., cupped; foliage leathery, bronze; vigorous growth; [sport of 'Wilhelm Kordes']
'Gertrud Kiese'   HCh, mr, 1918, Kiese; flowers scarlet-vermilion, shaded dark red, medium, full; ['Gruss an Teplitz' × 'Cramoisi Supérieur']
'Gertrud Schweitzer'   HT, ob, 1973, Kordes; bud long, pointed; flowers apricot-orange, large, dbl., cupped; foliage glossy, dark; ['Colour Wonder' × seedling]
'Gertrud Westphal'   F, or, 1951, Kordes; flowers orange-scarlet, 3 in., 5-7 petals; foliage glossy, dark reddish green; dwarf, bushy, much branched growth; ['Baby Chateau' × 'Obergärtner Wiebicke']
'Gertrud Westphal, Climbing'   Cl F, or, 1961, Buisman, G. A. H.
'Gertrude'   HT, lp, 1903, Dickson, A.; flowers flesh pink; [sport of 'Countess of Caledon']
'Gertrude Bernard'   HGal, mr, 1827, Noisette
'Gertrude Gregory'   HT, my, 1957, Gregory; flowers bright golden yellow; [sport of 'Lady Belper']
Gertrude Jekyll®   S, mp, Austin, David; bud oval, pointed; flowers deep pink with yellow base , 11 cm, very full, slightly flattened cup , borne mostly singly, moderate old rose fragrance; recurrent; foliage dark green, matte; tall (4 - 5 ft.), strong, shrubby growth ; PP7220; [seedling × 'Comte de Chambord']; intr. 1986

'Gertrude Raffel'   F, dp, 1957, Raffel; flowers pink, center rosy, well-formed, 2-3 in., 15-20 petals, borne in large clusters; foliage dark; vigorous, bushy growth; intr. 1956
'Gertrude Reutener'   F, dp, 1954, Leenders, M.; flowers crimson-pink; vigorous growth
'Gertrude Shilling'   HT, dy, 1988, Poole, Lionel; flowers bright, deep yellow, aging paler, large, 52 petals, urn-shaped, decorative, moderate fruity fragrance; foliage large, medium green, matte; prickles broad, fairly flat, large, dark brown; upright, tall, vigorous, good basal growth; ['Golden Splendour' × Peer Gynt®]; intr. 1989
'Geschwind's Gilda'   HMult, dr, 1887, Geschwind, R.; bud round, small; flowers reddish-violet at center, pale pink at edges, 5-6 cm., very full, moderate fragrance; foliage pale green, rounded; ['De La Grifferaie' × 'a hybrid perpetual or bourbon']
'Geschwind's Gorgeous'   Cl HT, mr, 1916, Geschwind, R.; flowers light red, 3 in., semi-dbl., borne in small clusters
'Geschwind's Most Beautiful' -- See 'Geschwind's Schönste'
'Geschwind's Nordlandrose' ('Geschwind's Northern Rose', 'Nordlandrose', 'Northland Rose') HSet, lp, 1884, Geschwind, R.; flowers medium, very full, borne in clusters of 3-5, no fragrance; recurrent; ['De La Grifferaie' × 'a hybrid perpetual or bourbon']; sometimes classed as HMult
'Geschwind's Nordlandrose II'   HSet, mr, 1928, Geschwind, R.; flowers cherry red, lighter reverse, dbl., cupped, strong musk fragrance; foliage large, bright green; few prickles; sometimes classed as HMult
'Geschwind's Northern Rose' -- See 'Geschwind's Nordlandrose'
'Geschwind's Orden' ('Décoration de Geschwind') HMult, m, 1886, Geschwind, R.; bud fat; flowers bright violet pink, white edges, medium, very full, cupped and quartered, borne in small clusters, moderate fragrance; non-recurrent; foliage slightly rugose; [R. rugosa × R. multiflora, or R. multiflora cultivar]
'Geschwind's Schönste' ('Geschwind's Most Beautiful') HMult, mr, 1900, Geschwind, R.; flowers very bright crimson, 6 cm., full, cupped, borne in clusters of 6-10; non-recurrent; ['De La Grifferaie' × 'a hybrid perpetual or bourbon']
'Geschwind's Unermüdliche' -- See 'Unermüdliche'
'Geschwister Scholl'   Pol, w, GPG Bad Langensalza; flowers medium, dbl.; intr. 1974
'Gessel'   HT, Pironti, N.
Getano®   S, rb, Noack; flowers bright red with yellow eye, 8-10 cm., semi-double, shallow cup, borne in clusters; recurrent; foliage dark green, glossy, reddish when young; bushy, upright (5 ft.) growth; intr. 2007

Gettysburg™ -- See 'Poulen001'
'Gewohnliche Moss Rose' -- See 'Centifolia Muscosa'
'Ghergana'   Gr, dr, 1985, Staikov, Prof. Dr. V.; flowers deep blackish-red, large, 55 petals, cupped, borne in clusters of 2-5, moderate tea fragrance; foliage dark; vigorous, upright growth; ['Spectacular' × seedling]; intr. 1974
'Ghislaine de Féligonde'   HMult, ly, 1916, Turbat; bud bright yellow/orange; flowers yellowish-white tinted flesh, small, dbl., cupped, borne in clusters of 10-20, moderate fragrance; some autumn repeat; few prickles; vigorous, climbing (8-10 ft.) growth; ['Goldfinch' × 'multiflora seedling']
'Ghislaine Feuerwerk'   HMult, op, Ruf, Werner; flowers salmon pink with yellow base, small, dbl., cupped, borne in large clusters, slight tea fragrance; occasional repeat; prickles very few; vigorous, arching (180-250 cm.) growth; [sport of 'Ghislaine de Feligonde']
Ghita™ -- See 'Poulren013'
'Ghita Renaissance' ('Mum in a Million', Millie™, Ghita™) S, mp, Olesen; bud urceolate; flowers medium pink, fading to pale pink on outer petals as it opens, 8 cm., 50 petals, cupped to flat, borne in clusters of 5-10, moderate fragrance; recurrent; foliage semi-glossy; prickles moderate, 5 mm., hooked downward, greyed-red; growth narrow, bushy (100-150 cm.); PP16541; ['Clair Renaissance' × seedling]
'Gi Gi'   Min, pb, Benardella, Frank; intr. 1999
Giana®   F, dr
'Gianlauro'   MinFl, Zandri, R.; intr. 1978
'Giant of Battles' -- See 'Géant des Batailles'
Giant Pink® -- See 'LLX8775'
'Giant Samantha'   HT, mr; flowers large; [sport of 'Samantha']; intr. 2005
'Gibby'   HT, dp, 1977, Prof. F. Roses; bud ovoid, pointed; flowers carmine-pink, 4½ in., 50 petals, high-centered; foliage dull, dark, leathery; vigorous, upright, bushy growth; [sport of 'Christian Dior']
'Gideon Lincecum'   S, w, 2006, Shoup, George Micheal; flowers single, borne in small clusters, moderate fragrance; remontant; foliage large, dark green, semi-glossy; few prickles; growth bushy, tall (4-6 ft.); hedging; hips large; [(('Carefree Beauty' × 'Basye's Blueberry') × ('Carefree Beauty' × 'Basye's Blueberry')) × 'Mrs Oakely Fisher']; intr. 2000
'Gideux'   S, my; flowers soft yellow, large, dbl., cupped, slight fragrance; free-flowering; growth to 2 ft.; intr. 1998
'Gidget'   Min, op, 1976, Moore, Ralph S.; bud pointed; flowers coral-pink to coral-red, 1 in., informal, slight fragrance; foliage small, glossy; vigorous, bushy growth; [(R. wichurana × Floradora) × 'Fire Princess']; intr. 1975
'Giesebrecht' -- See 'Bashful'

'Gift Basket' HT, rb, Delbard, Georges; flowers scarlet with yellow reverse, high-centered; intr. 1988

'Gift of Grace' HT, pb; intr. 2006

'Gift of Life' -- See 'Harelan'

'Gift of Time' Min, w, Thomson; flowers double, slight fragrance; low growth; intr. 2002

'Gigantea Blanc' LCl, w, 1889, Colett; flowers golden white with yellow center, very large; sometimes classed as HGig

'Gigantea Cooperi' -- See 'Cooper's Burmese'

'Gigantesque' ('Thé a Fleur Gigantesque') T, lp, 1835, Hardy/Sylvain-Péan; flowers flesh pink, shaded with rose, 5 in., full; foliage glossy; prickles strong, few, reddish; growth horizontally spreading; probably extinct; ['Parks' Yellow' × unknown]

'Gigantèsque' T, dp, 1845, Odier; flowers deep pink

'Giggles' -- See 'Kingig'

'Giggles' -- See 'Lyogi'

'Gigi' HT, mp, 1960, Verschuren; flowers rose-pink, reverse brighter, large, dbl., moderate fragrance; foliage light green; long, strong stems; vigorous growth; ['The Doctor' × seedling]; intr. 1959

'Gigliola' ; intr. 1969

'Gigolette' F, rb, 1953, Gaujard; bud ovoid; flowers yellow and red bicolor, medium, semi-dbl., borne in clusters; foliage leathery, light green; vigorous growth

'Gil Blas' HGal, pb, before 1843; flowers light pink, spotted, lighter at edges, large, dbl.; strong, upright (4-5 ft.) growth

'Gil Blas' HSpn, dp; flowers light red; intr. before 1848

'Gilbert Bécaud' -- See 'Meiridorio'

'Gilbert F. Levy' F, mr, 1958, Combe; flowers currant-red, dbl.; very vigorous growth; [Moulin Rouge® × 'Oiseau de Feu']

'Gilbert Nabonnand' ('G. Nabonnand') T, op, 1888, Nabonnand; bud very long, clear rose; flowers pale rose shaded with yellow, large, semi-dbl., moderate fragrance

'Gilberte Routurier' T, w, 1908, Chauvry; flowers cream white, center coppery pink, base golden yellow, large, very full, moderate fragrance

'Gilda' HMult, m, 1887, Geschwind; flowers wine red, medium, full; strong, upright, overhanging (10 ft.) growth

'Gilda' HT, ab, 1936, Towill; bud long, pointed; flowers pure orange-yellow, large, dbl.; foliage leathery, dark; vigorous growth; PP282; RULED EXTINCT 3/87; ['Souv. de Claudius Pernet' × ('Lady Hillingdon' × 'Harry Kirk')]

'Gilda' -- See 'Peahigh'

'Gilfleur' ('First Born') HT, pb, 1993, Gilmore, T.O.; flowers pink/peach, hold well for cutting, 47 petals, borne mostly singly; foliage medium size, dark green, glossy; some prickles; tall (80-90 cm.), upright growth; ['Silver Jubilee' × 'Tahiti']; intr. 1993

'Giliane' F, mp, Sauvageot; flowers Neyron pink, petals ruffled, dbl., borne in large clusters; intr. 2004

'Gillian' HT, op, 1959, Verschuren; bud long, pointed; flowers soft coral-pink; foliage bronze; ['Michèle Meilland' × 'Mme Butterfly']; intr. 1958

'Gillian Dawn ' HT, mr, 1997, Robinson, Kenneth G.; flowers medium, very dbl., borne mostly singly; foliage medium size, medium green, semi-glossy; spreading, medium (24in.) growth

'Gillian Levy' -- See 'Rawgoljub'

'Gilmore' HT, ly, Select Roses, B.V.

'Gilt Edged' -- See 'Chewdainty'

'Gin Fizz' -- See 'Meiromar'

'Gin no suzu' -- See 'Silver Bell'

'Gina' F, dr, 1960, Kriloff, Michel; flowers velvety dark crimson, 6 petals, borne in large clusters, slight fragrance; foliage glossy; vigorous, upright growth; ['Alain' × 'Independence']; intr. 1960

'Gina' F, dr, Kordes; intr. 1978

'Gina Kordana' Min, mr, Kordes; flowers cherry red, full; container rose

Gina Lollobrigida® -- See 'Meilivar'

'Gina Louise' -- See 'Trobgina'

Gina's Rose™ -- See 'Morgina'

'Ginette' HT, op, 1924, Buatois; flowers salmony maize-yellow, dbl.; ['Paul Monnier' × 'Souv. de Claudius Pernet']

'Ginger' F, or, 1962, Boerner; bud ovoid; flowers orange-vermilion, 4 in., 28 petals, cupped, borne in irregular clusters, moderate fragrance; foliage leathery; vigorous, compact, bushy growth; PP2293; [('Garnette' × unknown) × 'Spartan']; intr. 1962

'Ginger Hill' HT, w, (HILcap); flowers white with blush pink center, petals créped, dbl., high-centered; intr. 1999

'Ginger Meggs' F, ob, Tantau; intr. 1962

'Ginger Rogers' ('Flower Show', 'Salmon Charm') HT, op, 1969, McGredy, Sam IV; flowers salmon pink, dbl., loose, borne singly, moderate fragrance; foliage medium size, light green; ['Super Star' × 'Miss Ireland']

'Ginger Sylabub' LCl, ab, Harkness; flowers amber/ginger, large, 70 petals, intense fragrance; vigorous (10-12 ft.) growth; intr. 2001

'Ginger Toddler' -- See 'Peavesta'

Gingerbread Man™ -- See 'Poulxas'

'Gingernut' -- See 'Coccrazy'

'Gingersnap' ('Apricot Prince', 'Prince Abricot') F, ob, 1977, Delbard, G., & Chabert, A.; bud long, pointed; flowers pure orange, imbricated to ruffled, 4 in., 30-35 petals, borne in small clusters, slight fragrance; foliage dark green; vigorous, upright, bushy growth; PP4330; [(Zambra® × (Orange Triumph® × 'Floradora')) × ('Jean de la Lune' × ('Spartan' × 'Mandrina'))]

'Gingia' HT, w, 1984, Fumagalli, Niso; flowers large, 35 petals, intense fragrance; foliage large, light green, glossy; bushy growth; [seedling × seedling]

'Ginny' Min, rb, 1981, Bischoff, Francis J.; bud ovoid; flowers white edged medium red, yellow at hinge, yellow stamens, small, 45 petals, high-centered; foliage dark, leathery, reddish tinge on new growth; prickles straight red; upright, compact growth; PP5275; ['Little Darling' × 'Toy Clown']

'Ginny-Lou' -- See 'Trobinka'

'Ginrei' ('Silver Peak') F, w, Keisei; intr. 1990

'Ginseikei' ('Silver World') F, w, Keisei; intr. 1997

'Ginsky' F, pb, 1983, Barker & Wood; flowers light salmon pink opening to pale pink to cream; [sport of 'Liverpool Echo']

'Ginza Komachi' Cl Min, pb, 1985, Kono, Yoshito; bud globular; flowers deep pink, white eye, yellow stamens, small, 5 petals, borne in clusters, slight fragrance; foliage medium green, glossy; prickles numerous, hooked; vigorous growth; ['Nozomi' × seedling]

'Gioia' -- See 'Peace'

'Gioia, Climbing' -- See 'Peace, Climbing'

'Gioiello' Min, my, 1985, Bartolomeo, Embriaco; flowers small, 20 petals, no fragrance; foliage small, dark, matte; ['Zorina' × 'Sole di San Remo']; intr. 1984

'Gion' Cl Min, pb, 1979, Onodera, Toru F.; bud rounded; flowers 1 in., 5 petals, flat; non-recurrent; foliage tiny, leathery; bushy, climbing growth; ['Nozomi' × seedling]

'Giovane' HT, op, 1970, Dot, Simon; bud pointed; flowers salmon-orange, large, 28 petals, high-centered, moderate fragrance; foliage glossy, bronze; dense growth; [Queen Elizabeth® × 'Orient']; intr. 1965

'Giovanezza' HT, rb, 1933, Ingegnoli; flowers geranium-red, reverse cream-white, edged lighter; vigorous growth

'Giovanni Paolo II' HT, McEntire, J.; intr. 1984

'Gipsy' HT, dr, 1931, Van Rossem; flowers medium, dbl.

'Gipsy Blood' -- See 'Zigeunerblut'

'Gipsy Boy' -- See 'Zigeunerknabe'

'Gipsy Jewel' Min, dp, Moore, Ralph S.; intr. 1975

'Gipsy Lass' ('Gypsy Lass') HT, mr, 1932, Dickson, A.; flowers scarlet-crimson shaded blackish, dbl., globular; long, willowy stems; bushy growth

'Gipsy Love' HT, or, 1964, Delbard-Chabert; flowers orange-vermilion, 4 in., 25 petals; vigorous growth; ['Chic Parisien' × 'Fashion']

'Gipsy Maid' F, dp, 1955, LeGrice; flowers carmine-scarlet, base golden, single, borne in small clusters of 3 or more, moderate sweetbriar fragrance; foliage olive-green

'Giranu Czecheti' Pol, op, Madarsko;

The Official Registry and Checklist — Rosa 249

flowers medium, semi-dbl.; intr. 1955

'Girasol' HT, my, 1945, Dot, Pedro; bud oval; flowers sunflower-yellow, 25-30 petals; foliage dark, glossy; upright, compact growth; ['Joanna Hill' × 'Carito MacMahon']

'Girija' HT, dr, Friends Rosery; flowers crimson-red, high-centered; intr. 1989

'Girl Friend' -- See 'Podruga'

'Girl Guide' HT, dr, Peden; intr. 2002

'Girl Guide' F, op

'Girl Scout' F, my, 1961, Boerner; bud ovoid; flowers golden yellow, 3½-4 in., 50 petals, cupped, moderate fragrance; foliage leathery, glossy; vigorous, medium tall growth; PP2090; ['Gold Cup' × 'Pigmy Gold']; intr. 1960

'Girlie' Pol, dr, 1923, Wezelenburg; flowers bright scarlet-crimson; bushy growth; [sport of 'Orléans Rose']

'Girlie Folies' F, my, Meilland; flowers Egyptian yellow, dbl., borne in clusters; greenhouse rose; intr. 2004

'Girls' Brigade' -- See 'Harbanjo'

'Girona' HT, pb, 1936, Dot, Pedro; flowers soft red and yellow, well-formed, large, 30 petals, high-centered, intense damask fragrance; foliage bright green; vigorous, spreading growth; ['Li Bures' × 'Talisman']; intr. 1939

'Gisborne 2000' HT, dy, Matthews; flowers strong yellow, dbl., moderate lemon fragrance; early to flower and repeats well; vigorous, strong, upright (1 m.) growth; intr. 2000

'Giscard d'Estaing' -- See 'Doralp'

'Gisela' F, op, 1965, Verschuren, A.; flowers salmon-pink, base straw-yellow, 56 petals, borne in clusters; foliage dark, glossy, bronze; upright, bushy, compact growth; ['Masquerade' × 'Pinocchio']; originally registered as Pol; intr. 1963

'Gisèle Alday' HT, mp, 1933, Mallerin, C.; bud pointed; flowers bright rose-pink tinted flesh, large, semi-dbl., cupped; foliage glossy, dark; vigorous growth; ['Mrs Pierre S. duPont' × 'Lallita']

Gisella® F, op, Barni; flowers coral rose, 5-6 cm., dbl., high-centered, slight fragrance; foliage medium to large, dark green; growth to 40-60 cm.; [Ambra® × Venere®]; intr. 2003

'Giselle' HGal, mp, 1843, Vibert; flowers rose, spotted, medium

'Giselle' -- See 'Juselle'

Giselle Folies® F, op, Meilland; flowers soft orange-pink, reverse darker, full, cupped, low-centered, borne in sprays; recurrent; florist rose; intr. 2005

Gisselfeld® HT, dr, 1978, Poulsen, Niels D.; flowers 4-4½ in., 17-20 petals, moderate fragrance; foliage dark, leathery; upright growth; [('Tropicana' × 'Champs-Elysees') × 'Furore']; intr. 1972

'Gitane' -- See 'Bright Wings'

Gites de France® ('Hagenbecks Tierpark') LCl, dp, Meilland; flowers bengal pink, borne in large clusters; robust (7 ft.+) growth; intr. 1994

'Gitta Grummer' -- See 'Korsee'

'Gitte' ('Peach Melba') HT, ab, 1979, W. Kordes Söhne; bud long, pointed; flowers apricot-pink blend, 4 in., 33 petals, high-centered, intense fragrance; foliage dark; vigorous, upright, bushy growth; [('Fragrant Cloud' × Peer Gynt®) × (('Dr. A. J. Verhage' × 'Colour Wonder') × 'Zorina')]

'Giuletta' B, lp, 1859, Laurentius; flowers white to light flesh pink, button center, medium, flat, borne in large clusters; foliage large, dark green; arching growth

'Giuliana Borgatti' HT, w, 1936, Borgatti, G.; flowers white, center shaded rose and salmon, very well-formed, large, dbl.; foliage dark ivy-green; vigorous growth; ['Ophelia' × 'Ville de Paris']

'Giuseppe Motta' HT, lp, 1936, Heizmann, E.; flowers large, semi-dbl.

'Giuseppina Papandrea' Min, pb, 1989, Papandrea, John T.; flowers cerise, reverse lighter; [sport of 'Petite Folie']

'Giuseppina Saragat' HT, w

'Givaro' F, w, Van Gampelaere, J.; ['Graaf van Vlaanderen' × 'Golden Wings']; intr. 2008

'Give Life' -- See 'Horkestrel'

Givenchy™ -- See 'Arodousna'

'Giverny' HMult, w; intr. 2003

Gizmo™ -- See 'Wekcatlart'

'Glacier' F, w, 1952, Boerner; bud ovoid; flowers white, slightly overcast yellow,, 4½ in., 28 petals, cupped, moderate fragrance; foliage glossy, dark; vigorous, upright growth; PP1025; ['white hybrid tea seedling' × 'Summer Snow']

Glacier™ (Gråsten™) F, w, Poulsen; flowers 8-10 cm., dbl.; growth bushy, 100-150 cm.; intr. 1996

'Glacier Magic' -- See 'Taniripsa'

'Glad Eye' -- See 'Seaglad'

'Glad Tidings' -- See 'Tantide'

'Gladiador' Cl HT, dp, 1954, Dot, Pedro; bud pointed; flowers carmine, very large, dbl.; vigorous growth; ['Texas Centennial' × 'Guinée']

'Gladiator' LCl, mr, 1956, Malandrone, M.; bud ovoid; flowers rose-red, 4½-5 in., 35 petals, high-centered, moderate fragrance; foliage dark, leathery; vigorous (10-12 ft.) growth; PP1524; ['Charlotte Armstrong' × ('Pink Delight' × 'New Dawn')]; intr. 1955

'Gladiator' -- See 'Uncle Joe'

'Gladis' -- See 'Gladys'

'Gladness' F, pb, 1959, Fletcher; bud pointed; flowers light pink edged darker, large, 25 petals, borne in clusters; foliage dark, glossy; upright growth; ['Sunny Maid' × 'Cinnabar']

'Gladsome' HMult, mp, 1937, Clark; flowers delicate light pink, white center, 3 cm., single, borne in large clusters; non-recurrent; growth tall hedge rose

'Gladys' ('Gladis') S, mp, Adam; flowers bright pink, dbl., globular, to rosette; recurrent; low, spreading growth; intr. 2004

'Gladys Benskin' HT, op, 1929, Dickson, A.; flowers rose-cerise, shaded orange, base deeper orange, large, dbl., high-centered; vigorous growth

'Gladys Harkness' HT, op, 1900, Dickson, A.; flowers deep salmon pink, silvery pink reflections, very large, dbl., cupped, intense fragrance

'Gladys Holland' HT, lp, 1917, McGredy; flowers light pink, shaded buff, very large, dbl., moderate fragrance

'Gladys Moncrieff' HT, yb, 1982, Jack, J.; flowers golden yellow to apricot, flushed rose red at petal tips; [sport of 'Granada']; intr. 1981

'Gladys Quine' -- See 'Worable'

'Gladys Saavedra' HT, mp, 1922, Nabonnand, P.; flowers rosy peach-blossom-pink, dbl.; ['Mme Abel Chatenay' × 'Jonkheer J.L. Mock']

'Gladys Tweedie' HT, dr, 1950, Toogood; bud long, pointed; flowers crimson, 5 in., 30-35 petals, high-centered; foliage wrinkled; very vigorous, bushy growth; ['Crimson Glory' × 'William Orr']

'Glaive' HT, pb, 1951, Clark, A.; bud long, pointed; flowers cream, center tipped pink, small, 25 petals, high-centered; foliage glossy; vigorous, bushy, compact growth

'Glamis Castle' -- See 'Auslevel'

'Glamorgan' -- See 'Thoom'

'Glamorous' Min, or, 1980, Williams, Ernest D.; bud pointed; flowers orange-red, base yellow, 1-1½ in., 35 petals, high-centered, slight fragrance; foliage small, glossy, bronze-green; bushy, spreading growth; ['Starburst' × 'Over the Rainbow']; intr. 1979

'Glamour' HT, op, 1939, Leenders, M.; bud long, ovoid; flowers salmon-pink, large, dbl.; vigorous growth; ['Comtesse Vandal' × 'Pres. Macia']

Glamour™ HT, mp, Poulsen; bud pointed ovoid, broad base; flowers 4 in., 26-30 petals, high-centered, borne mostly singly, moderate floral fragrance; recurrent; foliage dark green, glossy; prickles several, 6 mm., hooked downward; growth bushy (60-100 cm.); PP15383; [seedling × Sexy Rexy®]; intr. 2003

'Glamour Girl' HT, op, 1942, Joseph H. Hill, Co.; bud pointed, light jasper-red; flowers light salmon, open, 4-5 in., 45-50 petals; foliage dark, leathery; strong stems; very vigorous, upright, much branched growth; PP526; ['Captain Glisson' × 'Justine']

'Glamour Girl' HT, yb, Ghosh; flowers deep yellow flushed red and pink with deeper veins, dbl.; intr. 1998

'Glamour Girl' -- See 'Cleamour'

'Glanlin' ('Lincoln Cathedral', 'Sarong') HT, ob, 1986, Langdale, G.W.T.; flowers outer petals pink, inner ones orange, yellow reverse, large, 28 petals; foliage medium size, medium green glossy; prickles numerous, reddish; bushy growth; ['Silver Jubilee' × Royal Dane™]; intr. 1985

'Glanmusic' ('Sir Neville Marriner') F, pb, 1997, Langdale, G.W.T.; flowers camelia pink, medium, very full, high-centered, borne mostly singly or in small clusters; foliage medium size, medium green, semi-glossy; few prickles; upright, medium (3 × 2 ft.) growth; [seedling × Painted Doll™]

'Glauque à Feuille de Pimprenelle' -- See 'De Marienbourg'

'Glareabit' ('Lincolnshire Poacher') HT, yb, 1992, Langdale, G.W.T.; flowers yellow flushed apricot and pink, 3-3½ in., full, borne mostly singly; foliage medium size, medium green, semi-glossy; some prickles; medium (80-100 cm.), bushy growth; ['Silver Jubilee' × 'Woman and Home']; intr. 1993

'Glarona' HT, w, 1922, Krüger; flowers creamy flesh, center rose, 4 in., borne singly or in small clusters; foliage broad, rounded

'Glastonbury' S, rb, 1981, Austin, David; bud globular; flowers dark crimson to deep purple, 55 petals, borne singly and in clusters of up to 5; repeat bloom; foliage medium green, sparse; prickles hooked, red; weak, spreading growth; ['The Knight' × seedling]; intr. 1974

'Glauca Nova' ('Rosa glauca Nova') S, lp; flowers pastel pink, single, cupped, moderate fragrance; growth to 150-200 cm.; very winter hardy

'Gleam' HRg, w, Erskine; intr. 1999

'Gleaming' F, dy, 1959, LeGrice; flowers deep lemon-yellow, 4 in., 6-8 petals, borne in trusses, intense fragrance; foliage dark; very free growth; ['Goldilocks' × 'Golden Scepter']; intr. 1958

'Glee' S, mr, 2007, Fleming, Joyce L.; flowers have prominent yellow stamens, good substance, small, 1½-2 in., single, borne in small clusters; good repeat; foliage medium, medium green, matte; prickles 2-3 mm., triangular, few; growth upright, short (12 in.); borders, containers; ['Red Hot' × 'Lavender Friendship']; intr. 2006

'Glen Almond' HT, pb, 1972, Wallace; flowers pale orient pink, 3½-4 in., 30 petals; foliage glossy, leathery; free growth; [Pascali® × 'Happy Event']

'Glen Artney' HT, dr, 1972, Wallace; flowers beet-root-purple, 3½-4 in., 40 petals, slight fragrance; vigorous growth; [Baccará® × 'Sterling Silver']

'Glen Myrie' -- See 'Gelglen'

'Glenara' LCl, dp, 1951, Clark, A.; bud long, pointed; flowers deep rosy pink, fading lighter, 9-10 cm., 18 petals; very remontant; foliage leathery; vigorous, upright bush or pillar growth; hybrid gigantea

'Glenara No. 14' Cl HT, pb, Clark, Alister

'Glenda Marie' -- See 'Sitpretty'

Glendora® ('Glendore') HT, ab, Kordes; flowers flower soft pink and honey yellow, with cream colored edges, 4 in., dbl., borne singly and in small clusters, intense fragrance; recurrent; foliage large, medium green, glossy; upright, vigorous (3 ft.) growth; ['Harmonie' × unknown]; intr. 1995

'Glendora' -- See 'Johasine Hanet'

'Glendore' -- See 'Korhuba'

'Glenfiddich' F, dy, 1976, Cocker; flowers amber-gold, 4 in., 25 petals, moderate fragrance; foliage glossy, dark; ['Arthur Bell' × ('Sabine' × 'Circus')]

'Glengarry' F, or, 1969, Cocker; flowers vermilion, large, 32 petals; foliage semi-glossy; compact, bushy growth; ['Evelyn Fison' × 'Wendy Cussons']

'Gleniti Gold' HT, dy, 1983, Bone, John, & Son; flowers very deep yellow; [sport of 'Lady Mandeville']; intr. 1973

'Glenn Dale' HWich, ly, 1927, Van Fleet; bud small, lemon yellow; flowers lemon, fading to white, 7-8 cm., 40 petals, borne in clusters (to 20); foliage dark, leathery; vigorous (10 ft.) growth; [R. wichurana × possibly 'Isabella Sprunt']

'Glenora' F, w

Glenshane™ -- See 'Dicvood'

'Glenys Stewart' HT, dp, 1968, Kemp, M.L.; flowers deep rose-pink, dbl.; moderate bloom; moderate growth; ['Montezuma' × 'Pink Favorite']

'Gletscher' F, m, 1955, Kordes; bud ovoid; flowers pale lilac, large, dbl., high-centered, borne in large trusses; foliage glossy; vigorous, upright, bushy growth; [seedling × 'Lavender Pinocchio']

Gletscherfee® ('Global Rose') S, w, Kordes; intr. 1991

'Glimmer' Min, rb, 1989, Bridges, Dennis A.; bud pointed; flowers bright, medium red, yellow at base, reverse slightly darker, 24 petals, high-centered, slight fragrance; foliage medium size, medium green, semi-glossy; prickles slightly downward pointed, medium, red; upright, medium growth; [Party Girl™ × seedling]; intr. 1989

Glitter® HT, w, Spek; flowers white with green tints on guard petals, 4 in., 30-35 petals, high-centered, borne mostly singly; recurrent; few prickles; stems long; intr. 2005

'Glitter' -- See 'Kagayaki'

'Glitters' Cl HT, mp, 1934, Smith, J.; bud pointed; flowers brilliant pink, base orange, open, very large, dbl., globular; recurrent bloom; foliage leathery; long stems; very vigorous growth; ['Mrs W.J. Grant' × 'Mrs Sam McGredy']

'Gloaming' HT, pb, 1935, Nicolas; bud pointed; flowers luminous pink suffused salmon, reverse lighter, open, very large, 36 petals, intense fragrance; foliage leathery, dark; vigorous, bushy growth; PP137; ['Charles P. Kilham' × 'Mrs Pierre S. duPont']

'Global Beauty' HT, dy, Tantau; flowers very large, dbl., intense fragrance; early bloomer; good repeat; healthy (3-4 ft.) growth; intr. 2003

'Global Rose' F, pb, Kordes; flowers pink, with yellow and green shading, borne in large clusters, no fragrance; wide, compact growth; intr. 1999

'Global Rose' -- See 'Kordomal'

'Globe' F, mr, 1956, Tantau, Math.; flowers blood-red, 2 in., 20 petals, cupped, borne in clusters; foliage dark; vigorous, bushy, compact growth; ['Fanal' × 'Red Favorite']

'Globe Blanc' -- See 'Globe Hip'

'Globe Hip' ('Boule de Neige', 'Calvert', 'Globe Blanc', 'Globe White Hip') C, w, before 1826, Lee; flowers creamy white, medium, full, globular; growth erect

'Globe White Hip' -- See 'Globe Hip'

'Globe Yellow' HFt, my, before 1846, from Italy; flowers bright lemon yellow, large, full, globular

'Globuleuse' M, mp, 1825, Vibert; flowers bright carmine, aging to lilac-flesh, medium, full, globular

'Gloira Dei-mutace' HT, mr, Lorenc

'Gloire d'Angers' HP, m, 1846, Boyau; flowers bright, glowing medium purple, velvety

'Gloire d'Angleterre' -- See 'England's Glory'

'Gloire d'Antibes' HT, dr, 1938, Mallerin, C.; flowers large, dbl.

'Gloire de Bordeaux' -- See 'Belle de Bordeaux'

'Gloire de Bourg-la-Reine' HP, mr, 1879, Margottin; flowers brilliant scarlet red, large, full

'Gloire de Bruxelles' -- See 'Gloire de l'Exposition de Bruxelles'

'Gloire de Charpennes' Pol, mr, 1898, Lille; flowers carmine-red, small, dbl.

'Gloire de Châtillon' -- See 'Mme Masson'

'Gloire de Chédane-Guinoisseau' HP, mr, 1907, Chedane-Pajotin; flowers bright crimson-red, well-formed, large, 40 petals, cupped, moderate fragrance; occasionally recurrent bloom; foliage dark, soft; vigorous growth; ['Gloire de Ducher' × unknown]

'Gloire de Cibeins' HT, or, 1958, Arles; flowers deep vermilion-red, well-formed, 30 petals; long stems; vigorous growth; ['Mme Méha Sabatier' × 'Léonce Colombier']

'Gloire de Colmar' HGal, dr, before 1910

'Gloire de Deventer' T, ly, 1897, Soupert & Notting; flowers light yellow with pink tints, large, dbl.; ['Devoniensis' × 'Distinction']

'Gloire de Dijon' ('Old Glory') Cl T, op, 1853, Jacotot; flowers rich buff-pink shaded orange toward center, 10 cm., dbl., flat, moderate fragrance; very vigorous, climbing growth; [thought to be an unknown Tea, or possibly 'Desprez à Fleur Jaune' × 'Souv. de la Malmaison']

'Gloire de Dijon à Fleur Rouges' -- See 'Reine Marie Henriette'

'Gloire de Ducher' ('Germania') HP, dr, 1865, Ducher; flowers very large, dbl.; occasional recurrent bloom

'Gloire de France' HGal, lp, 1828, Bizard; flowers pale lilac pink, lighter at edges, very large, very dbl., flat, quartered, borne singly or in clusters of 2-3, intense fragrance; non-remontant; foliage soft, gray-green; bushy, low growth

'Gloire de France' HP, pb, Margottin; flowers carmine, shaded vivid crimson, large, full; intr. 1853

'Gloire de France' HT, or, Gaujard; flowers orange-red variegated copper, well-formed, large, dbl.; vigorous growth; intr. 1946

'Gloire de Guérin' HP, dp, 1833, Guérin; flowers deep carmine, medium, full, cupped; ['Malton' × unknown]

'Gloire de Guilan' D, lp, Hilling; flowers clear pink, center incurved, semi-dbl. to dbl., quartered, intense fragrance; spring bloom; foliage light green; prickles small, curved; sprawling shrub (4-5 ft.) growth; probably very old; re-introduced by Lindsay/Hilling in 1949; intr. 1949

'Gloire de Hollande, Climbing' Cl HT, dr; flowers large, dbl.

'Gloire de Hollande' HT, dr, 1918, Verschuren; flowers glowing blood-red, large, very full, moderate fragrance; ['General MacArthur' × 'Hadley']

'Gloire de la Brie' HT, mr, Grandes Roseraies; bud long; flowers bright red, large

'Gloire de l'Exposition de Bruxelles' ('Gloire de Bruxelles') HP, m, 1889, Soupert & Notting; flowers very dark, velvety crimson-purple, large, 60 petals; vigorous, upright growth; ['Souv. de William Wood' × 'Lord Macaulay']

'Gloire de Libourne' T, dy, 1887, Beauvillain; flowers dark canary yellow, shaded apricot, large, very full; ['Perle de Lyon' × unknown]

'Gloire de Margottin' HP, dr, 1887, Margottin; flowers large, 60 petals, globular; occasional recurrent bloom

'Gloire de Mezel' M, mp; flowers pale rose, very large

'Gloire de Montplaisir' HP, mr, 1866, Gonod; flowers bright red

'Gloire de Paris' -- See 'Anna de Diesbach'

'Gloire de Rome' -- See 'Rome Glory'

'Gloire de Santenay' HP, m, 1859, Ducher; flowers dark purple, large, full, globular; ['Général Jacqueminot' × unknown]

'Gloire de Thalwitz' -- See 'Ruhm von Thalwitz'

'Gloire de Toulouse' HP, mr, 1883, Brassac; flowers shining red, petals edged carmine, very large, very full

'Gloire de Vitry' HP, mp, 1854, Masson; flowers bright pink, large, globular; ['La Reine' × unknown]

'Gloire des Anciens' -- See 'Interglo'

'Gloire des Belges' HT, dp, 1916, Chambard, C.; flowers vivid carmine

'Gloire des Blanches' T, w, 1904, Vigneron; flowers pure white, very large, full, globular; ['Niphetos' × 'Grossherzogin Mathilde']

'Gloire des Brotteaux' -- See 'Edouard Desfossés'

'Gloire des Héllènes' -- See 'La Nubienne'

'Gloire des Jardins' -- See 'La Gloire des Jardins'

'Gloire des Lawranceanas' Min, dr, 1837; flowers dark crimson; dwarf growth

'Gloire des Mousseuses' ('Gloire des Mousseux', 'Glory of Mosses') M, mp, 1852, Laffay; bud heavily mossed; flowers clear bright pink, center deeper, petals imbricated, large, dbl., borne in clusters; foliage light green; vigorous growth

'Gloire des Mousseux' -- See 'Gloire des Mousseuses'

'Gloire des Perpetuelles' -- See 'Flon'

'Gloire des Polyantha' Pol, mp, 1887, Guillot et Fils; flowers bright pink, well-shaped, small, dbl., borne in large clusters; dwarf (50 cm.) growth; ['Mignonette' × unknown]

'Gloire des Rosomanes' ('Ragged Robin', 'Red Robin') Ch, mr, 1825, Vibert; flowers glowing crimson, very large, semi-dbl., borne in large clusters, moderate fragrance; repeat bloom; vigorous growth; sometimes classed as B

'Gloire d'Olivet' B, lp, 1886, Vigneron; bud long; flowers delicate lilac-flesh, large, full, globular; prickles numerous, chestnut-colored

'Gloire d'Orient' M, dr, 1856, Béluze; flowers deep red, spotted, medium, full; some repeat

'Gloire d'Orléans' HP, mp, 1879, Boitard; flowers carmine pink, large, full

'Gloire d'Orléans' Pol, mr, Levavasseur; flowers small, dbl., borne in numerous terminal panicles; foliage dark green; intr. 1912

'Gloire du Beaujolais' HT, Delbard, Georges; intr. 1990

'Gloire du Bouchet' HP, mr, 1885, de la Rocheterie/Cochet; flowers crimson, slightly tinted purple, very large, full, cupped; foliage wide, sharply dentate; prickles numerous, small and medium; growth upright; grown from seeds collected by Pignard at Bouchet, the estate of Mons. de La Rocheterie

Gloire du Bourbonnais® -- See 'Delbourbo'

'Gloire du Midi' Pol, or, 1932, deRuiter; flowers brilliant orange-scarlet, small, dbl., borne in clusters; good repeat; vigorous, compact (18 in.) growth; PP270; [sport of 'Gloria Mundi']

'Gloire du Midi Superior' Pol, or, deRuiter; flowers like parent with more lasting color; [sport of 'Gloire du Midi']

'Gloire du Sacré-Coeur' HP, lp, 1864, Pernet; flowers flesh pink, shaded carmine, large, full

'Gloire d'Un Enfant d'Hiram' HP, mr, 1899, Vilin; flowers bright red; ['Ulrich Brunner fils' × unknown]

'Gloire Lyonnaise' HP, w, 1885, Guillot et Fils; flowers white with trace of yellow at center, very large, 84 petals, cupped; foliage leathery; very vigorous, bushy growth; not very hardy; ['Baroness Rothschild' × 'Mme Falcot']

'Gloomy Fire' -- See 'Düsterlohe'

'Gloria' HT, dr, 1922, Paul, W.; flowers brilliant scarlet-crimson, dbl.

'Gloria' -- See 'Horglo'

Gloria™ -- See 'Poulac018(N)'

'Gloria d'Autunno' HT, 1952, Cazzaniga, F. G.

'Gloria de Grado' HT, mp, 1950, La Florida; flowers pink, tinted carmine, globular; foliage bright green; ['Mari Dot' × 'Comtesse Vandal']

'Gloria Dei' -- See 'Peace'

'Gloria Dei, Climbing' -- See 'Peace, Climbing'

'Gloria del Llobregat' HT, or, 1940, Camprubi, C.; flowers strawberry-red to vermilion, large, dbl., cupped; foliage glossy; very vigorous growth; ['Sensation' × 'Margaret McGredy']

'Gloria di Milano' HT, Ingegnoli

'Gloria di Roma, Climbing' Cl HT, mr, Fineschi; flowers scarlet, very large; intr. about 1990

'Gloria di Roma' -- See 'Rome Glory'

'Gloria di Venezia' HT, or, Kordes, R.

'Gloria Dot' Min, Dot, Simon; intr. 1986

'Gloria Ellen' HT, pb, 2007, Edwards, Eddie and Phelps, Ethan; flowers 5 in., full, borne mostly solitary; foliage medium, medium green, semi-glossy; few prickles; growth upright, medium (5-6 ft.); [seedling × seedling]; intr. 2008

Gloria Ferrer® -- See 'Fesuma'

'Gloria Mundi' Pol, or, 1929, deRuiter; flowers striking orange-scarlet, dbl., borne in clusters; foliage light, glossy; vigorous, bushy growth; [sport of 'Superb']

'Gloria Mundi, Climbing' ('Prinses van Oranje, Climbing') Cl Pol, or, 1933, de Ruiter (Lens, 1934, Howard, 1943); flowers orange-scarlet, dbl., borne in large clusters, no fragrance

'Gloria Mundi Superior' Pol, or, deRuiter; flowers like parent with more lasting color; [sport of 'Gloria Mundi']

'Gloria Nigrorum' HGal, m, before 1845, Calvert; flowers dark violet-purple

'Gloria Palace' (Gloria™) MinFl, lp, Olesen; bud broad based ovoid; flowers light pink, 5 cm., 80 petals, deep cup, borne mostly singly, slight fragrance; recurrent; foliage dark green, matte; prickles numerous, 6 mm., greyed-yellow, hooked downwards; bushy, upright (40-60 cm.) growth; PP15150; ['Pernille Hit' × seedling]; container plant; intr. 2003

'Gloria Solis' HT, my, 1949, Giacomasso; flowers well-formed, 4-5 in.; foliage dark, glossy; vigorous growth; ['Ville de Paris' × 'Max Krause']

'Gloriana' HT, my, 1936, Hillock; flowers intense lemon-yellow in heat, deep gold with cerise markings, 35 petals, cupped; foliage leathery, glossy, dark; vigorous, compact growth; ['Condesa de Sástago' × 'Condesa de Sástago']

'Gloriana' -- See 'Chewpope'
'Gloriana 97' -- See 'Chewpope'
'Gloriette' N, lp, Vibert; flowers flesh, brighter pink center, small, full; nearly thornless; possibly synonymous with either Centifolia or HGal of the same name; intr. 1836
'Gloriette' C, lp, Robert; flowers flesh pink, 6-8 cm., full; listed by some sources as HCh; intr. 1854
'Gloriette' HGal, op; flowers salmon pink, large, full; intr. before 1885
'Gloriette' S, op, Cocker; intr. 1979
'Gloriette' Min, rb
'Glorified La France' HT, lp, 1916, Cook, J.W.; flowers silvery pink, deeper than La France, 92 petals, slight fragrance; ['Frau Karl Druschki' × 'Mrs Charles E. Russell']
'Gloriglo' Min, ob, 1977, Williams, Ernest D.; bud pointed; flowers orange, yellow reverse, 1 in., 45 petals, high-centered, slight fragrance; foliage small, glossy, bronze; upright, bushy growth; PP4305; [seedling × 'Over the Rainbow']; intr. 1976
'Glorimontana' F, or, deRuiter; flowers medium, dbl.; intr. 1974
'Glorio' HT, mr, 1923, E.G. Hill, Co.; flowers scarlet-cerise, dbl.; ['Premier' × 'Primrose']
'Gloriosa' HT, w, 1920, Kiese; flowers ivory-white, base yellow; ['Kaiserin Auguste Viktoria' × 'Pharisaer']
'Glorious' ('Glorius') HT, my, Interplant; flowers clear medium yellow, dbl.; free-flowering; foliage medium green, glossy; strong, healthy (4-5 ft.) growth; intr. 2001
'Glorious' F, dp, 1947, Duehrsen; bud pointed; flowers salmon scarlet, shaded orange, open, medium, large trusses, 15-17 petals, 4½ in., slight fragrance; foliage leathery, dark; vigorous, upright growth; PP879; RULED EXTINCT 7/84 ARM; [('Betty Uprichard' × 'Heidekind') × 'Heidekind']
'Glorious' -- See 'Leoglo'
'Glorious Easter' HT, op, 1965, Howard, P.J.; bud ovoid; flowers salmon, medium, dbl., high-centered; foliage leathery; moderate, bushy growth; [seedling × 'Penelope']
'Glorious Hass' -- See 'Sprohass'
'Glorious Pernet' HT, r, 1928, Myers & Samtmann; flowers copper, center orange; [sport of 'Souv. de Claudius Pernet']
'Glorious Sunset' Pol, rb, 1931, Allen; flowers bronze, suffused red, small, semi-dbl., borne in clusters; foliage small, thick; vigorous growth; [sport of 'Mariposa']
'Glorius' -- See 'Interictira'
'Glory' -- See 'Eiko'
'Glory' -- See 'Devmomento'
'Glory Be' -- See 'Savabe'
'Glory Days' -- See 'Jaccor'
'Glory of Battala' Min, pb, Mandal, G.S.; flowers pink with white reverse; free-flowering; [sport of 'Don Don']; intr. 2004
'Glory of California' LCl, ly, 1935, Schoener; flowers large, dbl., moderate fragrance; hybrid gigantea
'Glory of Ceylon' F, op, 1967, Harkness, R.; flowers orange-yellow blended pink, 14 petals, borne in clusters, moderate fragrance; foliage dark, glossy; ['Vera Dalton' × 'Masquerade']
'Glory of Cheshunt' HP, dr, 1880, Paul & Son; flowers rich crimson, cupped; vigorous growth; ['Charles Lefebvre' × unknown]
'Glory of Edsell' -- See 'Glory of Edzell'
'Glory of Edzell' ('Glory of Edsell') HSpn, pb, before 1900; flowers bright cherry pink with a white eye, small, single, borne singly on short laterals; non-recurrent; foliage small, dull green, matte; prickles numerous, small; growth bushy, arching (to 6 ft.)
'Glory of Hurst' Pol, mr, 1921, Hicks; flowers cherry-red, semi-dbl., borne in clusters; foliage small, leathery, glossy, rich green; dwarf growth; ['Orléans Rose' × 'Jessie']
'Glory of Mosses' -- See 'Gloire des Mousseuses'
'Glory of Paris' -- See 'Anna de Diesbach'
'Glory of Rome' -- See 'Rome Glory'
'Glory of Seale' S, ab, Seale
'Glory of Surrey' HT, my, 1935, Ley; flowers golden yellow, semi-dbl.; fairly vigorous growth
'Glory of Waltham' HP, dr, 1865, Vigneron; flowers crimson, very large, very dbl.; vigorous, climbing or pillar growth; ['Souv de Leveson-Gower' × unknown]
'Glossy' HT, pb, Select; flowers light pink with petal edges and veins darker pink, 4½ in., 30-40 petals, exhibition, borne mostly singly; stems 24 - 32 in; greenhouse rose; intr. 2003
'Glow In The Dark' F, rb, Williams, J.B.; flowers deep rose with some white streaking in the middle of petals, aging to dark velvet, moderate fragrance; foliage dark, glossy; vigorous growth; intr. 2003
'Glow Worm' HT, or, 1919, Easlea; flowers scarlet, suffused coppery orange, semi-dbl.
Glowing™ HT, my, Poulsen; flowers medium yellow, 8 cm., 30 petals, cupped, borne mostly singly, moderate fragrance; recurrent; foliage matte; prickles some, 8 mm., convex, greyed-yellow; narrow, upright, bushy (60-100 cm.) growth; PP15385; [seedling × 'The Lady']; intr. 2003
'Glowing Abundance' -- See 'Betty Harkness'
'Glowing Achievement' -- See 'Tanelliv'
'Glowing Amber' -- See 'Manglow'
'Glowing Carmine' HT, dp, 1936, H&S; flowers carmine, large, dbl., globular; foliage leathery, vigorous, open growth; ['Miss Rowena Thom' × seedling]
'Glowing Carpet' -- See 'Morpapplay'
'Glowing Cushion' -- See 'Interreflet'
'Glowing Embers' -- See 'Andglo'
Glowing Peace™ -- See 'Meizoele'
'Glowing Petals' -- See 'Manpetals'
'Glowing Pink' S, mp; flowers small, full, globular, to rosette, borne in clusters; compact (50 cm.) growth; intr. 2006
'Glowing Ruby' F, mr, J&P; intr. 2001
'Glowing Sunset' ('Wilhelm Breder') HT, ob, 1933, Kordes; bud long, pointed; flowers orange shaded yellow and pink, very large, dbl., high-centered, intense fragrance; foliage leathery, glossy, dark; vigorous growth; PP104; ['Fontanelle' × 'Julien Potin']
'Glowing Velvet' HT, dr, 1977, Pasley; flowers deep crimson to scarlet, 4 in., 25 petals, intense fragrance; bloom repeats quickly; foliage dark; intr. 1975
'Glowing With Pride' Min, ob, 2006, Hopper, Nancy; flowers velvety bright orange, reverse white, 2½ in., dbl., borne mostly solitary; foliage medium green, semi-glossy; prickles ¼ in., tan, few; growth bushy, short (10 in.); ['Orange You Happy' × seedling]; intr. 2006
Glowry™ -- See 'Kinglow'
'Glücksburg' ('Rosarium Glücksburg') S, yb, Jensen; flowers copper gold to whitish yellow; intr. 1989
'Glückskette' S, dy; intr. 2006
'Glückskind' HT, dp, 1935, Berger; flowers deep pink, well-formed, large, moderate fragrance
'Glückskind' F, dr, Leenders, M.; flowers dark crimson, medium, semi-dbl., moderate fragrance; very vigorous growth; intr. 1952
'Glücksstern' S, w, Schultheis; flowers clean white, large, very full, cupped, moderate fragrance; upright, bushy (4 × 4 ft.) growth; intr. 2005
'Glyndyfrdwy' HT, mp, 1977, Ellick; flowers Neyron rose, 4-5 in., 35 petals, moderate fragrance; foliage large, light; very vigorous growth; ['Gavotte' × 'George Thomas']; intr. 1978
'Glynis Bryan' Min, pb, 1997, Jones, L.J.; flowers medium, dbl., borne in large clusters, no fragrance; foliage small, medium green, semi-glossy; some prickles; growth spreading, tall; [Party Girl™ × 'Sheri Anne']
'G'Mundi's Rose' -- See 'Rawdawn'
'Gneisenau' HMult, w, 1924, Lambert, P.; bud pale pink; flowers snow-white, stamens yellow, 8 cm., semi-dbl., cupped, borne in clusters of 5-15, moderate fragrance; non-recurrent; foliage dark; prickles numerous, large; growth to 5-6 ft.; ['Schneelicht' × ('Killarney' × 'Veilchenblau')]
'Gnom' F, op, Berger, W.; flowers salmon-orange and pink, medium, dbl.; intr. 1957
'Gnome' Pol, ly, 1936, Leenders, M.; flowers cream-yellow, large, dbl.; foliage leathery, light; short stems; bushy, dwarf growth; [seedling × 'Mev. Nathalie

Nypels']

'Gnome World' ('Jumpin' Jack') F, op, J&P; flowers coral-salmon, semi-dbl., flat, borne in clusters, no fragrance; good rebloom; foliage brown-red on new growth; compact growth

'Godavari' HT, or, Kasturi; flowers vibrant vermilion; intr. 1987

'Goddess' -- See 'Déesse'

'Godescalcus Vulf de Sapprothe' S, lp, Scholle, E.; flowers small, semi-dbl.; intr. 1984

'Godeurpan' F, ob, 1979, Godin, M.; bud ovoid

Godewind® S, mr, Kordes; flowers single; intr. 1992

'Godfrey Winn' HT, m, 1968, Dot, Pedro; flowers purplish, dbl., globular, intense fragrance; free-flowering

'Godfrey's Red Petite' HT, dr, 1969, Godfrey; flowers deep red, medium, 15 petals, slight fragrance; foliage dark; free growth; [Baccará® × 'Audie Murphy']

'Godialing' ('Chrystelle') HT, or, 1979, Godin, M.; bud oval; flowers deep, large, 30-35 petals, cupped; foliage dark; [('Lady Zia' × Wizo®) × 'Silver Lining']; intr. 1975

'Godilofter' ('Maman Pineau') HT, dr, 1979, Godin, M.; bud pointed; flowers dark red-purple, 3-3½ in., 26-28 petals, cupped; foliage bronze; vigorous growth; ['Maryse Kriloff' × 'Uncle Walter']; intr. 1976

'Godomeve' Min, mp

'Godrache' ('Grand Duche') HT, m, 1979, Godin, M.; bud ovoid; flowers 3-3½ in., 25 petals, cupped, slight fragrance; foliage dark; vigorous growth; [American Heritage® × (seedling × 'Blue Girl')]; intr. 1973

'Godsensor' ('Danse des Étoiles') F, or, 1979, Godin, M.; bud ovoid; flowers red-orange, deep, 2½ in., 15-18 petals, cupped; foliage light green; [Orangeade® × Orange Sensation®]; intr. 1973

'Godstowe Girl' HT, mr, Harkness; flowers clear red, dbl., high-centered; medium (3 ft.) growth; intr. 2001

'Godusex' ('Exodus') Gr, mp, 1979, Godin, M.; bud ovoid; flowers 3 in., 50-52 petals, cupped; foliage glossy, dark; ['Kordes Perfecta' × 'Kalinka']; intr. 1974

'Godzoty' ('Duchesse d'Anjou') HT, mr, 1979, Godin, M.; bud pointed; flowers crimson-red, 3-3½ in., cupped, slight fragrance; foliage dark; vigorous growth; [Wizo® × 'Soraya']; intr. 1976

'Goedele' HT, lp, RvS-Melle; intr. 1998

'Goethe' M, m, 1911, Lambert, P.; bud heavily mossed; flowers very dark crimson/magenta, with prominent yellow stamens, 4 cm., single to semi-dbl., open, moderate fragrance; non-recurrent; foliage blue-green, rough; numerous prickles; stems new wood bright red; very vigorous growth; [R. multiflora × a moss rose]; possibly Geschwind rather than Lambert

'Going for Gold' -- See 'Brogold'

'Golconda' HT, ly, 1970, Pal, Dr. B.P.; bud ovoid; flowers pale yellow, center deep apricot, large, dbl., cupped, intense fragrance; foliage leathery; moderate, bushy, compact growth; ['Mme Charles Sauvage' × unknown]; intr. 1968

'Gold' -- See 'Kogane'

'Gold 'n' Flame' Min, rb, 1981, Williams, Ernest D.; bud long, pointed; flowers medium red, deep golden yellow reverse, 33 petals, cupped, borne singly, slight fragrance; foliage dark, glossy; prickles very thin, long, tan, curved down; upright, bushy growth; [seedling × 'Over the Rainbow']; intr. 1980

'Gold 'n' Honey' HT, yb, 1976, Leon, Charles F., Sr.; bud long, pointed; flowers yellow and peach, edged rose, 5-6 in., 28 petals, high-centered; vigorous, upright, bushy growth; ['Helen Traubel' × (seedling × 'Ulster Monarch')]

Gold Badge, Climbing™ ('Gold Bunny, Climbing', 'Rimosa, Climbing', 'Grimpant Rimosa') Cl F, my, Meilland; flowers citron yellow, dbl.; intr. 1991

Gold Badge™ -- See 'Meigronuri'

'Gold Blaze' Min, yb, 1980, Lyon; bud ovoid; flowers yellow, dipped red, 23 petals, borne singly or several together, intense fragrance; foliage small, glossy, deep green; prickles tiny, straight; growth compact, upright; [seedling × seedling]; intr. 1979

'Gold Blush' -- See 'Jasoblush'

'Gold Britannia' HT, my

'Gold Bunny, Climbing' -- See 'Meigronurisar'

Gold Bunny® -- See 'Meigronuri'

'Gold Coast' -- See 'Golden Pride'

'Gold Coin' Min, dy, 1967, Moore, Ralph S.; flowers buttercup-yellow, small, dbl., moderate fragrance; vigorous, bushy growth; PP2921; ['Golden Glow (LCl)' × 'Magic Wand']

'Gold Cottage' (Gold Cottage Ediparc®) S, dy, Dickson; flowers golden yellow, borne in clusters; growth to 4-5 ft.; intr. 2004

Gold Cottage Ediparc® -- See 'Dicentice'

'Gold Country' -- See 'Seagold'

'Gold Crest' -- See 'Golden Crest'

'Gold Crown' ('Corona de Oro', 'Gold Krone', 'Goldkrone', 'Couronne d'Or') HT, dy, 1960, Kordes, R.; flowers golden yellow, well-formed, 5 in., 35 petals, moderate fragrance; foliage leathery, dark; vigorous, upright growth; ['Peace' × 'Golden Scepter']; intr. 1960

'Gold Cup' ('Coupe d'Or') F, dy, 1958, Boerner; bud pointed; flowers golden yellow, 4 in., 28 petals, borne in clusters, moderate fragrance; foliage dark, glossy; bushy growth; PP1683; [('Goldilocks' × unknown) × ('King Midas' × unknown)]; intr. 1957

'Gold Dame' HT, dy, 1929, Dobbie; flowers deep golden yellow, semi-dbl.; foliage dark, glossy; vigorous, bushy growth

'Gold Dollar' HT, dy, 1970, Herholdt, J.A.; flowers large, 35 petals, slight fragrance; foliage glossy; vigorous growth; [seedling × 'Weiner Charme']; intr. 1971

'Gold Dot' HT, my, 1963, Dot, Simon; flowers large, 25 petals; vigorous, upright growth; [Queen Elizabeth® × 'Peace']

'Gold Dust' F, dy, Benny, David; flowers brilliant glowing golden yellow; foliage dark green, glossy

'Gold Dust' -- See 'Jacyepat'

'Gold Fantasy' Min, dy; intr. 1998

'Gold Fever' -- See 'Macparlez'

'Gold Fever' -- See 'Morfever'

'Gold Fountain' -- See 'Tanellelog'

'Gold Glow' ('Goldglow') HT, dy, 1960, Perry, Anthony; flowers bright yellow, 3½-4 in., 100 petals, moderate fragrance; foliage leathery, dark, glossy; vigorous, upright growth; PP2089; ['Fred Howard' × 'Sutter's Gold']; intr. 1959

'Gold Glow, Climbing' Cl HT, dy, 1964, Burr, C.R.

'Gold Glow Bronze Sport' HT, yb, Robinson; flowers amber-apricot to bronze; [sport of 'Gold Glow']; intr. 1986

'Gold Heart' -- See 'Macyelkil'

'Gold Heart' -- See 'Burnaby'

'Gold Krone' -- See 'Gold Crown'

'Gold Leaf' F, dy, Tantau; intr. 1998

'Gold Link' Min, dy, Bell, Laurie; flowers rich golden yellow; free-flowering; medium growth

'Gold Magic' F, dy, 1991, Christensen, Jack E.; flowers golden yellow, medium, dbl., borne in large clusters; foliage medium size, dark green, glossy; bushy, medium growth; [Gold Badge™ × 'Friesensohne']; intr. 1991

Gold Magic Carpet™ -- See 'Poulurt'

Gold Medal® -- See 'Aroyqueli'

'Gold Mine' HT, my, 1925, Joseph H. Hill, Co.; flowers Indian yellow paling toward edges, base deep orange, dbl., intense fragrance; ruled extinct, ARA 1985; ['Golden Rule' × 'Mrs Aaron Ward']

Gold Mine™ Min, dy, 1984, Laver, Keith G.; buds; flowers chrome yellow, small, 20 petals, no fragrance; foliage medium size, medium green, semi-glossy; bushy growth; ['Rise 'n' Shine' × yellow seedling]; intr. 1984

'Gold Mist' F, Swim, H. C.; PP1368

Gold Moon® -- See 'Havoon'

'Gold Nugget' F, dy, 1972, Patterson; flowers bright yellow, medium, dbl., high-centered; foliage glossy, abundant; vigorous, upright growth

'Gold of Ophir' -- See 'Fortune's Double Yellow'

'Gold Patio' MinFl, dy; intr. 1997

'Gold Pin' Min, dy, 1976, Mattock; flowers bright golden yellow, 1 in., 18 petals, slight fragrance; foliage bronze; intr. 1974

'Gold Pique' Min, my, 1978, Lyon; bud pointed; flowers dbl., 36 petals, moderate fragrance; foliage small, dark; compact, bushy growth; [seedling × 'Yellow Jewel']; intr. 1977

'Gold Reef'™ -- See 'Pouldom'
'Gold Roje' -- See 'Gold Rojie'
'Gold Rojie' ('Gold Roje') Min, dy; flowers intense yellow, 1-1½ in., dbl., rosette, slight fragrance; good rebloom; growth compact, moderately tall; from Japan, may be Asami, 1980
'Gold Rush' ('Goldrush') LCl, yb, 1941, Duehrsen; flowers gold, fading to lemon, 3 in., 24 petals, high-centered, borne in clusters, moderate fragrance; not dependably recurrent; foliage glossy, ivy-green; vigorous, climbing growth
'Gold Rush' F, ab, Zary, Keith; flowers apricot, outer petals fading light pink , double, cupped, borne in clusters, slight fragrance; recurrent; intr. 2008
'Gold Rush' S, dy
'Gold Spray' F, my, 1971, Delforge; flowers medium, dbl.; foliage soft; moderate, bushy growth; ['Philippe' × 'Spek's Yellow']
'Gold Star' Min, yb; flowers yellow and gold, globular, borne in clusters; recurrent; foliage dark green, glossy; medium (50 cm.) growth
'Gold Star' HT, yb, 1933, Vestal; bud pointed, orange; flowers golden yellow shaded orange, large, dbl.; foliage glossy, bronze, leathery; very vigorous growth; RULED EXTINCT 6/83 ARM; ['Souv. de Claudius Pernet' × 'Talisman']
'Gold Star' -- See 'Candide'
'Gold Star' -- See 'Tantern'
'Gold Strike' F, my, 1956, Swim, H.C.; bud urn shaped; flowers lemon-yellow, 2-2½ in., 30-35 petals, high-centered, borne in rounded clusters, moderate fragrance; foliage leathery; vigorous, bushy, compact growth; PP1435; ['Goldilocks' × 'Pinocchio']; intr. 1955
Gold Strike® -- See 'Sunluck'
Gold Sweetheart™ -- See 'Wilgosh'
Gold Symphonie® -- See 'Meitoleil'
'Gold Symphonie 2002' -- See 'Meiskaille'
'Gold Top' LCl, dy, 1976, Pearce; flowers golden yellow, 5½ in., 25 petals, moderate fragrance; foliage large, light matte green; free growth; intr. 1978
'Gold Topaz' -- See 'Korgo'
'Goldbay' -- See 'Tanyab'
Goldbeet® F, dy, Noack, Werner; intr. 1974
'Goldbonnet' S, my, 1973, Harkness; flowers 4 in., 13 petals; foliage large, glossy; [('Ann Elizabeth' × Allgold®) × Golden Showers®]
'Goldbusch' HEg, my, 1956, Kordes; bud long, pointed; flowers yellow, becoming lighter, large, semi-dbl., borne in clusters (up to 20); foliage leathery, glossy, light green; very vigorous, upright, bushy growth
'Golddigger' HT, dy, 1963, Verschuren, A.; flowers dark saffron-yellow, large, 50-55 petals, slight spicy fragrance; foliage glossy, bronze; upright growth; ['Marcelle Gret' × 'Dries Verschuren']

'Golddorf Seppenrade' S, dy, Scholle, E.; flowers light, clear yellow, tinted gold inside the petals, large, dbl., tulip-shaped, moderate fragrance; foliage deep green tinted olive green, glossy; intr. 1969
'Golddust' HT, my, 1963, Delforge; flowers golden yellow; foliage clear green; vigorous growth; ['Brandywine' × seedling]
'Goldelse' HT, ob, 1900, Hinner, W.; bud large; flowers golden orange, medium; ['Kaiserin Auguste Viktoria' × unknown]
Goldelse® -- See 'Tanolgnil'
Golden™ -- See 'Poulgold'
'Golden Afternoon' HT, ab, Pal, Dr. B.P.; flowers golden apricot-orange, moderate fragrance; intr. 1984
'Golden Age' -- See 'Resage'
'Golden Altai' HSpn, ly, 1943, Wright, Percy H.; flowers cream to pale yellow, single; non-recurrent; very hardy; [R. spinosissima altaica × 'Harison's Yellow']
Golden Amazone™ HT, dy; flowers dbl., high-centered; PP12615; florist rose
'Golden Angel' ('Moore's Yellow') Min, dy, 1975, Moore, Ralph S.; bud short, pointed; flowers 1 in., 65 petals, moderate fragrance; foliage matte; bushy, compact growth; PP4028; ['Golden Glow' × ('Little Darling' × 'Peachy White')]
'Golden Anniversary' HT, dy, 1948, Mordigan Evergreen Nursery; bud ovoid; flowers 4½-5 in., 50-60 petals, high-centered, intense fragrance; foliage leathery; vigorous, upright, bushy growth; PP806; RULED EXTINCT 9/82 ARM; [sport of 'Good News']
'Golden Anniversary' MinFl, my; flowers golden yellow; growth to 2 ft.; intr. 1997
'Golden Anniversary' -- See 'Jacary'
'Golden Arch' LCl, dy; flowers clear, deep yellow, large, dbl., borne in large clusters, no fragrance; stems supple, bending under weight of blooms; arching (7 × 10 ft.) growth, can be trained over arches; intr. 2000
Golden Arches® Min, dy
'Golden Arctic' ('Everblooming Pillar No. 84') LCl, yb, 1954, Brownell; flowers yellow to orange, 3½-4 in., 38 petals, moderate fragrance; growth like a hybrid tea, followed by 4-5 ft. canes; PP1262; [seedling × 'Free Gold']
'Golden Autumn' HT, dy, Klimenko, V. N.; flowers large, dbl.; intr. 1955
'Golden Bay' S, yb, 1980, Murray, Nola; bud ovoid; flowers deep buff-yellow, shapely, large, 40 petals, slight fragrance; foliage large; spreading, bushy growth; [('Tropicana' × 'Sabine') × 'Zitronenfalter']
'Golden Bear' Min, dy; intr. 2002
'Golden Beauty' HT, ab, 1937, Van Rossem; bud very long; flowers orange buff-yellow, stamens golden, large, semi-dbl.; foliage clear green, glossy; vigorous, bushy growth
'Golden Beauty' -- See 'Clebeau'
'Golden Beryl' -- See 'Manberyl'

'Golden Bettina' HT, yb, Ruston, D.; [sport of 'Bettina']
'Golden Biotech' HT, yb, Shastri, Dr N.V.; flowers golden yellow with pink flush; intr. 1998
'Golden Blush' A, ab, Sievers; intr. 1988
'Golden Border' -- See 'Havobog'
Golden Bounty™ -- See 'Jacsuyel'
'Golden Bouquet' F, dy; flowers golden yellow; free-flowering; strong growth; intr. 1999
'Golden Bouquet' -- See 'Vanda Beauty'
'Golden Boy' HT, dy, 1964, McGredy, Sam IV; flowers deep yellow, very, 5½ in., 35 petals, high-centered; foliage long, pointed; moderate growth; ['Golden Masterpiece' × 'Belle Blonde']
'Golden Buddha' -- See 'Ardestiny'
'Golden Butterfly' HT, ab, 1920, Therkildsen; flowers apricot-yellow, shaded carmine, dbl.; ['Old Gold' × unknown]
'Golden Butterfly' -- See 'Goudvlinder'
'Golden California' HT, dy, 1966, Howard, P.J.; flowers golden, large, dbl., cupped; foliage bronze, leathery, glossy; tall, bushy growth; [sport of 'California']
'Golden Cascade' LCl, my, 1964, Morey, Dr. Dennison; bud ovoid; flowers chrome-yellow, 4½-5 in., 25-30 petals, cupped, moderate fruity fragrance; foliage leathery; vigorous (10-12 ft.) growth; PP2199; [('Capt. Thomas' × 'Joanna Hill') × 'Lydia']; intr. 1962
'Golden Celebration' -- See 'Ausgold'
'Golden Century' Cl Min, ob, 1977, Moore, Ralph S.; bud pointed; flowers cadmium-orange to nasturtium-red, 1½-2 in., 35 petals, intense fragrance; foliage glossy, leathery; moderate climber growth; [(R. wichurana × Floradora) × ('Soeur Thérèse' × unnamed miniature)]; intr. 1978
'Golden Chain' -- See 'Rêve d'Or'
'Golden Chalice' HT, dy, 1960, Boerner; bud ovoid; flowers clear yellow, open, 4 in., 40-45 petals, moderate fragrance; foliage glossy; vigorous, upright growth; PP1958; [('Starlite' × 'Snow White') × 'Golden Masterpiece']; intr. 1959
'Golden Chappy' S, dy, Interplant; intr. 2007
'Golden Charm' HT, dy, 1933, Groshens & Morrison; [sport of 'Talisman']
'Golden Charm, Climbing' Cl HT, dy, 1948
'Golden Chateau' HT, dy, Teranishi; intr. 1998
'Golden Chersonese' S, my, 1967, Allen, E.F.; flowers 1½-2 in., single, borne singly at each node; early; foliage leaflets 7-9; vigorous growth; [R. ecae × 'Canary Bird']
'Golden Choice' HT, my, 1967, Bardill Nursery; flowers lemon-yellow; [sport of 'My Choice']
'Golden City' HT, my, 1922, Lippiatt; bud golden yellow; flowers light buff; ['Rayon d'Or' × 'Frau Karl Druschki']
'Golden Climber' -- See 'Mrs Arthur Curtiss James'

'Golden Coach' -- See 'Zipgold'
'Golden Colonel'   F, ob
'Golden Comet'   HT, yb, 1937, Burbank; bud long, pointed; flowers yellow and pink, open, large, semi-dbl., intense fragrance; foliage dark, leathery; vigorous growth; PP235
'Golden Conquest' -- See 'Meirevolt'
'Golden Coronet'   F, my, 1969, Morey, Dr. Dennison; flowers medium, dbl., high-centered, slight fragrance; foliage glossy, leathery; vigorous, compact growth; [('Lydia' × 'Golden Scepter') × 'Isobel Harkness']
Golden Cover™ -- See 'Poulgode'
'Golden Crest' ('Gold Crest') Cl HT, my, 1948, Archer; flowers pure yellow, 3-4 in., dbl., moderate fragrance; good repeat; foliage glossy, dark; climbing (6 ft.) growth; pillars
'Golden Curls' -- See 'Hamdra'
Golden Dance® -- See 'Bargold'
'Golden Dawn'   HT, my, 1929, Grant; bud yellow, flushed pink; flowers well-formed, 45 petals; low, spreading growth; ['Elegante' × 'Ethel Somerset']
'Golden Dawn, Climbing'   Cl HT, my, 1935, Armstrong, J.A. (Knight, 1937, and Le Grice, 1947); bud deep yellow; flowers pale yellow, very full; PP243
'Golden Day'   HT, my, 1931, Bentley; flowers bright golden yellow, center deeper, larger and fuller; vigorous growth; [sport of 'Independence Day']
'Golden Days' -- See 'Ruggolda'
'Golden Delight'   F, my, 1956, LeGrice; flowers canary-yellow, 3 in., 58 petals; foliage dark, glossy; dwarf growth; ['Goldilocks' × 'Ellinor LeGrice']
'Golden Delight, Climbing'   Cl F, my
'Golden Diamond'   HT, dy, 1943, Verschuren; flowers large, 30 petals; foliage leathery, dark; strong stems; vigorous, upright, compact growth
'Golden Dream' ('Goldener Traum') HRg, my, 1932, Türke; bud pointed, streaked red; flowers pure yellow, large, dbl.; recurrent bloom; very vigorous (6½ ft.) growth; ['Turke's Rugosa Sämling' × 'Constance']
'Golden Drop'   HT, dy, 1939, Clark, A.; flowers rich yellow, small, semi-dbl., borne in clusters; tall growth; ['Mme Mascuraud' × seedling]
Golden Eagle™ -- See 'Wekblagab'
Golden Earing™ -- See 'Wilgold'
Golden Earring®   HT, ly, Spek; flowers pale yellow, 11 cm., 30-35 petals, high-centered, borne mostly singly; recurrent; few prickles; stems long; florist rose; intr. 2006
'Golden Elegance'   HT, dy, Wagner, S.; bud long; flowers large, 30 petals, high-centered, borne singly or in clusters of 3-7, slight fragrance; foliage large, dark green, glossy; [sport of 'Ambassador']; intr. 1995
'Golden Emblem, Climbing'   Cl HT, my, 1927, Armstrong Nursery
'Golden Emblem'   HT, my, 1917, McGredy; bud yellow, splashed and shaded red; flowers canary-yellow, well-formed, large, dbl.; foliage dark, glossy, leathery; vigorous growth; ['Mme Mélanie Soupert' × 'Constance']
'Golden Emblem' -- See 'Jacgold'
'Golden Empire'   HT, ob, 1957, Silva; flowers orange, dbl.; foliage leathery, glossy; ['Orange Everglow' × 'Golden Emblem']
'Golden Evolution'   F, dy; intr. 1999
'Golden Eye' ('Garden Jubilee Golden Eye') S, rb, Ping Lim; flowers bright red-orange with golden eye, 2 in., 7-10 petals, borne in clusters; foliage deep green; growth to 2-3½ ft.; PP16612; intr. 2004
Golden Eye Cover™ -- See 'Poultc014'
'Golden Fairy'   Pol, ly, 1889, Bennett; flowers clear buff, yellow and white; dwarf growth
'Golden Fairy Tale' -- See 'Korquelda'
'Golden Fancy' -- See 'Tanolgnil'
'Golden Fanfare'   F, ab, Harkness; intr. 2008
'Golden Fanfare' -- See 'Worbloom'
'Golden Fantasie' (Joan Brickhill®) HT, my, 1972, Byrum; flowers large, semi-dbl., high-centered, intense fragrance; foliage large, dark, leathery; vigorous, upright, bushy growth; PP3272; ['Dr. A.J. Verhage' × 'Anniversary']; intr. 1971
'Golden Fashion'   HT, dy, NIRP; intr. 2003
'Golden Fiction'   F, my, 1958, Spek; free growth; ['Yellow Pinocchio' × 'Moonbeam']
'Golden Fiesta'   S, my, Roman, G., and Wagner, S.; flowers intense lemon-yellow, medium to large, 30 petals, borne in clusters, moderate fragrance; foliage medium to large, light green, glossy; [Candy Rose® × Allgold®]; intr. 2000
'Golden Fire' -- See 'Korhitom'
'Golden Fish'   Min, dy; flowers deep yellow flushed with orange; intr. 1999
Golden Flame® -- See 'Lapam'
'Golden Fleece' ('Toison d'Or') F, my, 1956, Boerner; bud ovoid; flowers buff-yellow, 4½ in., 38 petals, cupped, borne in clusters (to 20), intense fragrance; foliage leathery; vigorous, bushy growth; PP1512; ['Diamond Jubilee' × 'Yellow Sweetheart']; intr. 1955
'Golden Flipper'   F, dy
'Golden Flush'   F, dy, Interplant; intr. 2006
'Golden Folies' -- See 'Meispreyo'
'Golden Fox'   MinFl, dy, Warner, Chris; intr. 1997
'Golden Freelander'   HT, my, Kordes; flowers golden yellow in center, fading as the petals open, large, double, high-centered, borne mostly singly; recurrent; foliage dark green; few prickles; stems medium; intr. 2006
'Golden Friendship' ('Baldock Festival') HT, my, Harkness; flowers golden amber with outer petals ivory, reverse flushed golden amber, dbl., exhibition; tall, erect growth; intr. 1992
'Golden Frills'   HT, my, 1936, B&A; flowers rich golden yellow, dbl., cupped; foliage glossy, wrinkled; [sport of 'Feu Joseph Looymans']
'Golden Future' -- See 'Horanymoll'
'Golden Galaxy' -- See 'Jacyesp'
'Golden Gardens' -- See 'Morgogard'
'Golden Garnette'   F, dy, 1960, Boerner; bud ovoid; flowers golden yellow, edged lighter, 3-4 in., 33 petals, cupped, borne in clusters, intense fruity fragrance; foliage leathery, dark, glossy; vigorous, upright, bushy growth; PP1898; [(('Goldilocks' × unknown) × seedling) × 'Tawny Gold']; intr. 1960
'Golden Gate'   T, w, 1891, Dingee & Conard; bud pointed; flowers cream-white, anthers golden yellow, very large, dbl., cupped, moderate fragrance; foliage bright green; vigorous growth; name re-leased for re-use, ARA 1971; ['Safrano' × 'Cornelie Koch']
'Golden Gate'   HT, my, 1971, Warriner, William A.; bud ovoid; flowers large, dbl., high-centered, slight fragrance; foliage large, glossy; vigorous, upright, bushy growth; PP3080; ['South Seas' × King's Ransom®]; intr. 1972
'Golden Gate'   LCl, dy, Kordes; flowers golden yellow, changing to pure yellow, large, dbl., borne in clusters of 5 to 10, moderate fruity fragrance; recurrent; foliage large, dark green, matte, dense; bushy, upright (8 ft+) growth; intr. 2005
'Golden Gate'   HT, dy, Kordes; flowers intense, lasting yellow, medium, dbl., high-centered, borne mostly singly; florist rose
'Golden Gem'   HT, my, 1916, Towill; flowers golden yellow; ['Lady Hillingdon' × 'Harry Kirk']
'Golden Giant, Climbing'   Cl HT, dy, 1970, Laveena Roses; [sport of 'Golden Giant']; intr. 1967
Golden Giant® -- See 'Korbi'
'Golden Girl'   Gr, my, 1960, Meilland; bud pointed; flowers golden yellow, 4-4½ in., 45 petals, high-centered, moderate fragrance; foliage leathery, light green; upright, vigorous, bushy growth; PP1912; [('Joanna Hill' × 'Eclipse') × 'Michèle Meilland']; intr. 1959
'Golden Girls' ('Forever Young', 'Queen Wilhelmina') F, dy, Zary, Keith; buds pointed, amber-copper; flowers copper-yellow, petals ruffled, dbl., borne in large clusters; free-flowering; dark green, glossy foliage; medium to tall (5 ft.) growth; intr. 2000
'Golden Girls' -- See 'Clebeau'
'Golden Glamour'   F, my, 1951, Boerner; bud pointed; flowers large, 25 petals, high-centered, moderate fragrance; foliage glossy; vigorous, upright, bushy growth; PP1039; ['Joanna Hill' × ('Mrs Pierre S. duPont' × 'Amelia Earhart')]
'Golden Gleam'   HT, my, 1926, McGredy; flowers buttercup-yellow, outer petals streaked, 25 petals, slight fruity fra-

grance; foliage dark

Golden Globe™   S, dy, Clements, John; flowers large, sometimes quartered, golden yellow, 5 in., 100 petals, old-fashioned, slight fresh fragrance; PPAF; intr. 2005

'Golden Globe'   Min, dy

'Golden Glory'   HT, dy, 1931, Dobbie; flowers deep golden yellow, large, dbl., intense fragrance

'Golden Gloves'   F, dy, Bear Creek Gardens; intr. 1991

'Golden Glow'   HT, ab, 1918, Chaplin Bros.; flowers apricot, shaded bronzy orange; [sport of 'Mme Edouard Herriot']

'Golden Glow'   HWich, my, Brownell; bud pointed; flowers 3½-5 in., dbl., high-centered, borne in small, moderate tea fragrance; non-recurrent; foliage large, dark green, glossy; very vigorous, climbing (20 ft.) growth; PP263; ['Glenn Dale' × ('Mary Wallace' × unknown)]; intr. 1937

'Golden Grand'   Gr, dy, Williams, J.B.; flowers golden, dbl., borne in large clusters; intr. 2004

'Golden Gruss an Aachen' ('Goldene Gruss an Aachen') F, ob, 1935, Kordes; bud pointed, red; flowers golden orange, sometimes shaded reddish, very large, dbl., high-centered; foliage glossy; bushy growth; ['Mme Butterfly' × 'Gloria Mundi']

Golden Halo™ -- See 'Savahalo'

'Golden Hands' -- See 'Chessupremo'

'Golden Handshake' -- See 'Chewsunford'

'Golden Harvest'   HT, dy, 1943, Mallerin, C.; flowers clear yellow, 4½ in., 35 petals, high-centered, moderate fragrance; foliage leathery, glossy, bronze; vigorous growth; PP729; ['McGredy's Ivory' × seedling]

'Golden Haze'   HT, yb, 1965, Verschuren, H.A.M.; bud ovoid; flowers light golden yellow, large, dbl., moderate fragrance; foliage glossy; vigorous growth; PP2609; ['Peace' × 'Golden Rapture']

'Golden Heart'   HT, dy, Tantau; intr. 1991

'Golden Heart' -- See 'Burnaby'

'Golden Heritage'   HT, my, 1973, Herholdt, J.A.; flowers canary-yellow, pointed, large, 25 petals, moderate tea fragrance; bushy growth; ['Golden Masterpiece' × seedling]; intr. 1974

'Golden Hit' ('Golden™) MinFl, dy, Poulsen; flowers deep yellow, 5-8 cm., semi-dbl., slight wild rose fragrance; foliage dark; growth bushy, 40-60 cm.; intr. 1996

Golden Holstein® ('Goldyla', 'Surprise') F, dy, Kordes; flowers bright, clear yellow, wavy petals, semi-dbl., borne in large clusters; recurrent; foliage dark green, glossy; upright, medium to tall growth; intr. 1989

'Golden Hope' -- See 'Mehpic'

'Golden Horizon' -- See 'Morhorizon'

'Golden Hour'   HT, ob, 1952, Howard, P.J.; bud ovoid; flowers golden yellow, reverse orange, 4-5 in., 45-55 petals, high-centered, intense fragrance; foliage leathery, glossy; very vigorous, upright growth; PP1009; ['Los Angeles' × 'California']

Golden Iceberg™ -- See 'Hadice'

'Golden Ideal'   HT, dy, 1939, Lens; bud long, pointed; flowers brilliant chrome-yellow, large, dbl.; vigorous growth; ['Roselandia' × 'Joanna Hill']

'Golden Jet' -- See 'Tantasch'

'Golden Jewel' (Goldjuwel®) HT, dy, 1960, Tantau, Math.; flowers golden yellow, 3 in., dbl., borne in clusters of up to 10, moderate fragrance; foliage dark, glossy; vigorous, bushy growth; ['Goldilocks' × ('Masquerade' × unknown)]; intr. 1959

'Golden Jewel' ('Bijou d'Or', 'Peter Mac Gold Jewel', Goldjuwel®) Min, dy, Tantau; flowers unfading golden yellow, dbl., high-centered; free blooming; foliage dark green, glossy; bushy, compact (18 in.) growth; intr. 1995

'Golden Jubilee'   F, my, 1948, Jacobus; bud ovoid; flowers golden yellow, becoming buff and chrome, 3 in., dbl., borne in clusters; foliage glossy, dark; vigorous, bushy, compact growth; [('Mary Wallace' × 'Talisman') × 'Mrs Pierre S. duPont']

'Golden Jubilee'   HT, my, Cocker, James; flowers 29 petals, high-centered, moderate tea fragrance; foliage large, matte green, glossy; prickles narrow, red-brown; [Peer Gynt® × Gay Gordons®]

Golden Julia™ -- See 'Rupgoljul'

'Golden King'   HRg, ly, 1935, Beckwith; flowers pale yellow, semi-dbl.; [sport of 'Dr. Eckener']

'Golden Kiss'   HT, yb, Dickson; flowers golden yellow with pink edges, large, full, high-centered, borne singly and in clusters of up to 5; bushy, upright (3 ft.) growth; intr. 2003

'Golden Lace'   F, dy, 1962, Von Abrams; bud pointed; flowers 3 in., 28 petals, high-centered, borne in clusters, moderate fragrance; foliage glossy; vigorous, upright growth; ['Goldilocks' × ('Golden Scepter' × 'Encore')]; intr. 1962

'Golden Lady'   HT, dy, McGredy; bud egg-shaped, large; flowers golden yellow, full, intense fragrance; foliage dark green, glossy; strong, upright (70 cm.) growth; intr. 2000

'Golden Leader'   HT, ab, 1961, Leenders, J.; flowers apricot; ['Tawny Gold' × seedling]

'Golden Leopard'   F, my, 1976, Takatori, Yoshiho; bud pointed; flowers daffodil-yellow, 2 in., 18-25 petals, high-centered; foliage glossy, leathery; low, compact growth; [('Golden Slippers' × unknown) × ('Golden Slippers' × unknown)]

'Golden Light'   LCl, ob, 1939, Nicolas; bud pointed; flowers orange-apricot to buff, edged pink, open, large, dbl.; foliage glossy, dark; strong stems; vigorous, climbing growth

'Golden Lion'   HSet, my, 1944, Horvath; flowers clear golden yellow, open, cupped, borne in clusters; non-recurrent; foliage light, glossy; growth to 8-10 ft.

'Golden Lotus Walk' -- See 'Kinrenpo'

'Golden Lustre'   HT, ab, 1964, Boerner; bud ovoid; flowers bronze-apricot overcast yellow, 5 in., 60-65 petals, cupped, moderate fragrance; foliage leathery; moderate growth; PP2442; ['Kate Smith' × 'Tanya']; intr. 1964

'Golden Mme Segond Weber'   HT, op, 1923, Soupert & Notting; flowers salmon, center yellow, dbl.; ['Mme Segond Weber' × 'Primrose']

'Golden Main' ('Golden Romance', 'Golmain', 'Goldenes Mainz') HT, dy, 1933, Kordes; bud golden yellow striped red; flowers golden yellow, large, dbl., cupped, intense fragrance; foliage glossy; very vigorous, bushy growth; PP254; ['Fontanelle' × 'Julien Potin']

'Golden Masterpiece'   HT, my, 1954, Boerner; bud long, pointed; flowers golden yellow, very large, 30-35 petals, high-centered, borne singly, moderate licorice fragrance; foliage very glossy; vigorous, upright growth; PP1284; ['Mandalay' × 'Golden Scepter']

'Golden Masterpiece, Climbing'   Cl HT, my, 1957, Valdrez; PP1660

Golden Medaillon® -- See 'Kornanze'

Golden Medaillon® -- See 'Korikon'

'Golden Medal' -- See 'Aroyqueli'

'Golden Medallion'   HT, my, 1977, Permenter; bud long, pointed; flowers medium golden yellow, loosely imbricated, 7-8 in., 40-50 petals, slight fragrance; foliage large, light; upright growth; PP4086; [sport of 'Medallion']; intr. 1974

'Golden Meillandina' -- See 'Rise 'n' Shine'

'Golden Melody' -- See 'Irene Churruca'

'Golden Memories'   HT, dy, 1965, Ravine; bud long, pointed, canary-yellow tinted coppery; flowers deep canary-yellow, to open, 5-6 in., 28-32 petals, high-centered, moderate spicy fragrance; foliage glossy; vigorous, upright growth; PP2205; [sport of 'Golden Rapture']

'Golden Memories'   F, dy, Kordes; flowers golden yellow, small, semi-dbl., borne in large trusses; recurrent; foliage glossy, disease-resistant; growth to 3 ft.; intr. 2004

'Golden Midinette'   Cl Min, my; flowers clear yellow, borne in clusters on main branches and side stems, no fragrance; recurrent; arching, tall (5 ft.) growth; intr. 2000

'Golden Mimi' ('Golden Folies', 'Mimi Golden') F, my, Meilland; flowers lemon yellow, edges brushed pink at times, dbl., borne in sprays; florist rose; intr. 1998

'Golden Mist'   LCl, Bailey, Dorothy J.; PP4011

'Golden Moments' -- See 'Frytranquil'

Golden Monica® -- See 'Tangolca'
'Golden Morning' -- See 'Judgold'
'Golden Moss' M, my, 1932, Dot, Pedro; bud globular, peach-yellow, sepals well mossed; flowers tawny yellow, large, 37 petals, borne in clusters of 3-5, moderate fragrance; scanty bloom; no repeat; foliage almost rugose; vigorous growth; ['Frau Karl Druschki' × ('Souv. de Claudius Pernet' × 'Blanche Moreau')]
'Golden Mozart' S, my, Verschuren; flowers lemon yellow; recurrent; upright, then arching (2½ ft.) growth; intr. 1986
'Golden Mrs Sam McGredy' -- See 'Golden Sam McGredy'
Golden Nugget™ ('Sorbet') HT, my, Meilland; buds large, conical, lemon yellow; flowers intense, lasting yellow, 5½ in, 35 petals, cupped, borne mostly singly, no fragrance; good repeat; foliage dark green, glossy, disease-resistant; prickles moderate; erect (2-3 ft.) growth; PP9262; ['Lovely Girl' × (Emblem™ × 'Texas')]; intr. 1996
'Golden Nugget' Min, dy
'Golden Nuggets' -- See 'Yellow Fleurette'
'Golden Oldie' ('Golden Oldies') HT, dy, Fryer; flowers golden yellow, 4 in., 40 petals, borne evenly on a neat bush; early to flower, quick to repeat; growth to 3½ × 3 ft.; intr. 2001
'Golden Oldie' S, dy, Kordes; intr. 2003
'Golden Oldie' -- See 'Macgolold'
'Golden Oldies' -- See 'Golden Oldie'
'Golden Ophelia' HT, my, 1918, Cant, B. R.; flowers golden yellow in center, paling slightly on outer petals, medium, dbl.; foliage glossy; vigorous growth; ['Ophelia' × 'Mrs Aaron Ward']
'Golden Ophelia, Climbing' Cl HT, my, 1924, Hage
Golden Opportunity™ -- See 'Antopp'
'Golden Orange Climber' LCl, ob, 1937, Brownell; flowers orange to orange-scarlet, often overlaid golden yellow, 5 in., semi-dbl.; vigorous, climbing growth; PP96; [sport of 'Mrs Arthur Curtiss James']
'Golden Oriole' ('Shepherd's Oriole') T, dy, 1905, Shepherd; flowers deep saffron-yellow, small, very dbl.
'Golden Pamela' HT, yb, 1969, Wheatley; bud ovoid; flowers yellow-apricot and pink, large, dbl., cupped; foliage large, glossy; vigorous, upright growth; [sport of 'Wellworth']
'Golden Pavillion' -- See 'Kinkaku'
'Golden Peace' HT, my, 1970, LeGrice; flowers canary-yellow, large, 45 petals, high-centered, moderate fragrance; foliage dark, dull; very vigorous, tall growth; intr. 1961
'Golden Pearl' HT, my, 1967, Warmerdam; flowers large, single; foliage dark; free growth
'Golden Penny' Min, my
'Golden Penny' -- See 'Coosyn'
'Golden Perfection' Pol, my, 1937, Leenders, M.; flowers golden yellow, small, dbl.; bushy, dwarf growth
'Golden Perfume' F, my, 1960, Leenders, J.; flowers orange-yellow becoming golden yellow, large, 50 petals, borne in clusters, moderate fragrance; foliage dark, glossy, leathery; vigorous, bushy growth; ['Goldilocks' × 'Fashion']; intr. 1958
'Golden Pernet' -- See 'Julien Potin'
'Golden Perraud' HT, my, 1946, Lens; bud long, pointed, well formed; flowers brilliant golden yellow, large, dbl.; foliage glossy; vigorous growth; [sport of 'Mme Joseph Perraud']
'Golden Pheasant' ('Goldfasan') F, ob, 1951, Kordes; flowers orange and gold, imbricated, 4 in., 40 petals; foliage glossy; low, compact growth; ['Pres. Ferier' × 'Dr. Debat']
'Golden Phoenix' -- See 'Nakbet'
Golden Piccolo™ -- See 'Poultex'
'Golden Picture' HT, yb, 1967, Handover, P.&R.; flowers light yellow tinged pink, medium; foliage leathery; upright growth; [('Picture' × unknown) × 'Marcelle Gret']
Golden Pillar™ LCl, my, Meilland; flowers large, loose, golden yellow, non-fading, 4 in., 30-35 petals; foliage medium size, deep green, glossy; intr. 1999
'Golden Pirrie' HT, ly, 1921, Collin/Dobbie; flowers yellowish-white; [sport of 'Lady Pirrie']
'Golden Pixie' Min, my, 1985, Hardgrove, Donald L.; flowers medium golden yellow, medium, 60 petals; foliage small, medium green, semi-glossy; vigorous, upright, bushy growth; ['Yellow Pages' × 'Rise 'n' Shine']
'Golden Planet' HT, yb, Teranishi; intr. 2004
Golden Plover™ -- See 'Poulurt'
'Golden Poly' Pol, my, Leenders, M.; bud yellow with red lines; flowers golden yellow to yellowish-white, open, large, semi-dbl.; foliage light, glossy; bushy, dwarf growth; intr. 1935
'Golden Poly' Pol, yb, 1931, Pahissa; flowers pure yellow, edged carmine, dbl., globular; dwarf growth; ['Angèle Pernet' × 'Orange King']
'Golden Pride' ('Gold Coast') Gr, my, 1957, Robinson, H.; bud ovoid; flowers clear yellow, overcast buff-yellow, 4 in., 25-30 petals, cupped; foliage leathery, glossy; vigorous, upright growth; PP1790; ['Pinocchio' × 'Peace']
'Golden Prince' ('Kabuki') HT, dy, 1970, Meilland, Mrs. Marie-Louise; buds medium, long pointed; flowers Indian yellow, medium, dbl, open, borne singly, slight fragrance; foliage dark green, glossy, disease-resistant; growth vigorous, upright, bushy, medium; PP2949; [('Monte Carlo' × Bettina®) × ('Peace' × 'Soraya')]; registrations published under both Golden Prince and Kabuki, ARA 1970
'Golden Princess' S, yb, 1985, Buck, Dr. Griffith J.; bud ovoid, pointed; flowers yellow, petals edged deep pink, large, 33 petals, cupped, borne singly and in clusters of up to 5, moderate fragrance; repeat bloom; foliage medium size, olive green, semi-glossy; prickles large, hooked, tan; upright, bushy growth; hardy; ['Hawkeye Belle' × ('Roundelay' × 'Country Music')]; intr. 1984
'Golden Promise' F, dy, deRuiter; flowers bright yellow; free-flowering; large, bushy growth; blooms said to look much like Sunsprite; intr. 1972
'Golden Promise' -- See 'Lavluv'
'Golden Pyramid' LCl, my, 1939, Brownell; flowers large, semi-dbl.; free seasonal bloom; vigorous, pyramidal (to 5-6 ft.) growth
'Golden Queen' N, dy, 1904, Paul; flowers dark golden yellow, shaded coppery orange, large, full; growth vigorous, climbing
'Golden Queen' HT, dy, Hill; intr. 1912
'Golden Queen' HT, my, Chambard, C.; bud gold, slightly marked carmine; flowers golden yellow, large, dbl.; foliage glossy; very vigorous, bushy growth; intr. 1937
'Golden Queen' -- See 'Korgitte'
'Golden Quill' F, dy, Harkness; intr. 2002
'Golden Rain' ('Goldregen') F, my, 1951, Tantau; flowers golden yellow, well-formed, large, 20 petals, borne in clusters of 10-15; foliage glossy; upright, bushy growth; ['Swantje' × 'G. Bentheim']
'Golden Rambler' -- See 'Easlea's Golden Rambler'
'Golden Rambler' -- See 'Alister Stella Gray'
'Golden Rapture' ('Geheimrat Duisberg') HT, dy, 1933, Kordes; bud pointed; flowers golden yellow, very large, 40 petals; foliage glossy; vigorous growth; ['Rapture' × 'Julien Potin']; intr. 1934
'Golden Rapture, Climbing' ('Geheimrat Duisberg, Climbing') Cl HT, dy, 1941, Swim, H.C. (also Knackfuss, 1954); flowers deep yellow, fading to lemon, 5 in.; PP508
'Golden Rapture No. 5' HT, my, Krieter; bud ovoid; flowers clear yellow, 5 in., 25 petals, high-centered, intense fragrance; foliage dark, leathery; vigorous growth; PP1413; [sport of 'Golden Rapture']
'Golden Reef' F, dy
'Golden Revelry' HT, my, 1952, McGredy, Sam IV; flowers golden yellow, 21 petals, high-centered; foliage glossy, bright green; ['Phyllis Gold' × 'Blossom']
'Golden Rider' -- See 'Goldener Reiter'
'Golden River' LCl, dy
'Golden Romance' -- See 'Golden Main'
'Golden Rosamini' Min, dy, Ilsink; intr. 1990
'Golden Ruffels' HT, my, 1954, Brownell; bud long, pointed; flowers golden yellow, medium, dbl., moderate fragrance; upright growth; [sport of 'Orange Ruffels']
'Golden Rule' HT, my, 1918, E.G. Hill,

Co.; flowers clear yellow, dbl.; [('Ophelia' × unknown) × 'Sunburst']

'Golden Salmon' ('Goldlachs') Pol, ob, 1926, deRuiter; flowers pure orange, large, borne in huge trusses; vigorous, bushy growth; [sport of 'Superb']

'Golden Salmon Improved' -- See 'Golden Salmon Supérieur'

'Golden Salmon Supérieur' ('Golden Salmon Improved') Pol, ob, 1929, deRuiter; flowers scarlet to orange, small, semi-dbl., borne in large clusters; good repeat; [sport of 'Golden Salmon']

'Golden Salute' HT, dy, 1963, Boerner; bud ovoid; flowers golden yellow, 5-5½ in., 33 petals, cupped, moderate fragrance; foliage leathery, glossy; vigorous, moderately tall growth; PP2303; [('Diamond Jubilee' × unknown) × 'Golden Masterpiece']; intr. 1963

'Golden Sam McGredy' ('Golden Mrs Sam McGredy') HT, yb, 1935, Lens; flowers chrome-yellow, reverse salmon with chrome; [sport of 'Mrs Sam McGredy']

'Golden Sástago' HT, dy, 1938, Dot, Pedro; flowers clear yellow, large, dbl., globular; foliage soft; vigorous growth; [sport of 'Condesa de Sástago']

'Golden Scepter' ('Spek's Yellow') HT, dy, 1950, Verschuren-Pechtold; bud pointed; flowers deep yellow, 4½ in., 35 petals, high-centered, moderate fragrance; foliage leathery, glossy; vigorous, upright growth; PP910; ['Golden Rapture' × seedling]

'Golden Scepter, Climbing' -- See 'Spek's Yellow, Climbing'

'Golden Séverine' HT, dy, 1929, Morse; flowers deep golden yellow

'Golden Sheen' F, my, 1966, Swim & Weeks; bud urn shaped; flowers yellow, edged lighter, dbl., high-centered, borne in clusters; foliage leathery; moderate, upright, bushy growth; PP2727; ['Ophelia' × 'Circus']

'Golden Sheila' F, my, Horner; intr. 2006

'Golden Shot' F, dy, 1976, Martin, J.; flowers golden yellow, 4 in., 24 petals, slight fragrance; foliage dark; [seedling × Allgold®]; intr. 1973

Golden Showers® LCl, my, 1957, Lammerts, Dr. Walter; bud long, pointed; flowers daffodil-yellow, open quickly, loose, 4 in., 25-28 petals, high-centered, borne singly and in clusters, moderate sweet fragrance; recurrent bloom; foliage medium size, medium green, glossy; vigorous, pillar or climbing (6-10 ft.) growth; PP1557; ['Charlotte Armstrong' × 'Captain Thomas']; intr. 1956

'Golden Signora' HT, my, 1954, Lowe; flowers golden veined orange, large, 30 petals; foliage glossy; vigorous growth; [sport of 'Signora']

'Golden Silence' -- See 'Rensilen'

'Golden Slippers' ('Orange Slippers') F, yb, 1961, Von Abrams; bud pointed; flowers yellow flushed vermilion, center golden yellow, 3 in., 23 petals, high-centered, borne in clusters, moderate fragrance; foliage leathery, glossy; vigorous, compact, low growth; PP2244; ['Goldilocks' × seedling]; intr. 1961

'Golden Smiles' F, my, Fryer; flowers golden-yellow, dbl., low-centered, borne in clusters; recurrent`; foliage dark green; bushy growth; intr. 2006

'Golden Song' Cl Min, yb, 1981, Williams, Ernest D.; bud long, pointed; flowers golden yellow, petals edged pink, 35 petals, high-centered, borne usually singly, moderate fragrance; foliage small, medium to dark, glossy; prickles long, thin, tan; upright (to about 5 ft.) growth; ['Little Darling' × 'Golden Angel']; intr. 1980

'Golden Spire' -- See 'Koramgis'

'Golden Splendor' HT, dy, 1965, Jones; bud long, pointed; flowers golden yellow, 5 in., 30 petals, high-centered; foliage glossy; vigorous, tall growth; intr. 1960

'Golden Splendour' HT, my, 1965, Kordes; flowers clear light yellow, large, 40 petals, moderate fragrance; ['Buccaneer' × 'Golden Sun']; intr. 1962

'Golden Spray' HT, my, 1917, Dickson, H.; flowers clear lemon-yellow, huge mass of prominent anthers, semi-dbl., borne in long, arching sprays

'Golden Sprite' -- See 'Devunican'

'Golden Star' HT, dy, 1976, Lowe; flowers full, 4-4½ in., 32 petals, slight fragrance; foliage dark; free growth; [sport of 'Whisky Mac']; intr. 1974

'Golden Star' -- See 'Tantern'

'Golden Starlite' -- See 'Sorraya'

'Golden State' HT, dy, 1937, Meilland, F.; flowers golden yellow, large, dbl., cupped; foliage leathery, glossy; vigorous growth; PP303; ['Souv. de Claudius Pernet' × ('Charles P. Kilham' × seedling)]; intr. 1938

'Golden Summers' -- See 'Korport'

'Golden Sun' -- See 'Goldene Sonne'

'Golden Sunblaze' -- See 'Rise 'n' Shine'

Golden Sunblaze™ -- See 'Meicupag'

'Golden Sunburst' HT, yb, 1969, Schneeberg; bud ovoid; flowers cadmium-orange and saffron-yellow, large, dbl., intense fragrance; foliage dark, glossy; vigorous, bushy growth; PP2708; [sport of 'Golden Wave']; intr. 1967

'Golden Sunset' LCl, my, 1934, Burbank; flowers golden yellow, often tipped orange-red, large, dbl., cupped; foliage glossy; long stems; vigorous growth; PP66

'Golden Sunshine' HT, my, 1964, Brownell, H.C.; bud pointed, ovoid, chrome-yellow splashed red; flowers canary-yellow, 5 in., 50 petals, high-centered; vigorous, upright growth; ['Helen Hayes' × 'Golden Masterpiece']; intr. 1964

'Golden Surprise' F, my, 1979, Hamilton; [sport of 'Woburn Abbey']

'Golden Symphony' -- See 'Meitoleil'

'Golden Talisman' HT, my, 1931, E.G. Hill, Co.; PP20; [sport of 'Talisman']

'Golden Talisman, Climbing' Cl HT, my, 1935, Elmer's Nursery; [sport of 'Talisman']

'Golden Thoughts' -- See 'McGredy's Orange'

Golden Threshold™ -- See 'Virhold'

'Golden Times' F, my, Kordes, R.; PP4044

'Golden Times' HT, my, 1971, Cocker; flowers lemon-yellow, 4-5 in., 40 petals, slight fragrance; foliage glossy; ['Fragrant Cloud' × 'Golden Splendour']; intr. 1970

'Golden Times' -- See 'Kortime'

Golden Token™ -- See 'Minitok'

'Golden Topas' -- See 'Mantopas'

'Golden Touch' -- See 'Tanmirsch'

Golden Tower® HT, dy, Tantau; flowers warm cream to dark yellow, sometimes with thin red petal edges, 14 cm., dbl., classic hybrid tea, borne mostly singly, moderate fragrance; recurrent; stems long; growth to 4-5 ft.; intr. 2005

'Golden Treasure, Climbing' Cl F, my, 1977, Pearson; intr. 1976

'Golden Treasure' ('Goldschatz') F, my, 1966, Tantau, Math.; bud pointed; flowers golden yellow, large, dbl., borne in cluster (up to 30); foliage dark, glossy; bushy, upright growth; intr. 1965

'Golden Tribute' F, dy, Horner; flowers deep golden yellow, dbl., moderate fragrance; free-flowering; short to medium growth; intr. 1997

'Golden Trust' MinFl, yb; flowers yellow with light pink edge, 2 in., dbl., borne in large clusters, slight fragrance; free flowering all season; foliage mid-green, abundant; growth upright (2 × 1 ft.); intr. 2001

'Golden Tzigane' HT, ob, 1961, Gregory; flowers orange; [sport of 'Tzigane']

'Golden Unicorn' S, yb, 1985, Buck, Dr. Griffith J.; flowers yellow, petals edged orange-red, large, 28 petals, cupped, borne 1-8 per cluster, moderate fragrance; repeat bloom; foliage dark olive green, leathery; prickles awl-like, tan; vigorous, upright, bushy, spreading growth; hardy; ['Paloma Blanca' × ('Carefree Beauty' × 'Antike')]; intr. 1984

'Golden Vale' S, y, Sutherland, P; ['Primula' × unknown]; intr. 2000

'Golden Van Rossem' HT, dy, 1937, Lens; flowers chrome yellow; [sport of 'Mev. G.A. van Rossem']

'Golden Vandal' HT, dy, 1935, Lens; flowers chrome yellow; [sport of 'Comtesse Vandal']

'Golden Vision' LCl, my, 1922, Clark, A.; flowers pale creamy yellow, fading nearly white, 7 cm., semi-dbl., moderate fragrance; supposedly Maréchal Niel × R. gigantea

'Golden Wave' Gr, dy, Williams, J.B.; flowers bright golden yellow, dbl., star shaped.; foliage dark green.; hardy to -20°F; intr. 2003

'Golden Wave' -- See 'Dr A. J. Verhage'

'Golden Wedding' HT, my, 1938, Krebs;

bud pointed, yellow tinted crimson; flowers clear yellow, 5 in., dbl.; foliage leathery, dark; growth vigorous; ['Souv. de H.A. Verschuren' × 'yellow seedling']

'Golden Wedding' ('Golden Wedding Anniversary', 'Noces d'Or') F, dy, Bear Creek Gardens; flowers deep golden yellow, large, dbl., high-centered, borne in clusters; free-flowering; foliage glossy, disease-resistant; growth vigorous, compact (3 ft.); intr. 1990

'Golden Wedding Anniversary' -- See 'Golden Wedding'

'Golden Wedding Celebration' F, my; flowers unfading yellow, dbl., high-centered, borne in masses of blooms, slight fragrance; foliage disease-resistant; tough (3 ft.) growth; intr. 2005

'Golden West' HT, my, 1936, Stocking; bud pointed; flowers golden yellow, open, large, semi-dbl.; foliage dark, leathery, glossy; vigorous, bushy, spreading growth; [sport of 'Duchess of York']

'Golden Wings' S, ly, 1953, Shepherd; bud long, pointed; flowers sulfur-yellow, prominent amber stamens, 4-5 in., single, slight fragrance; recurrent bloom; growth vigorous, bushy, to 4 ft.; very hardy; PP1419; [(R. spinosissima × unknown) × 'Soeur Thérèse']

'Golden Wishes' -- See 'Sun Hit'

'Golden Wonder' HT, yb, Gandy, Douglas L.; flowers lemon-yellow, edged red, 4-5 in., 36-40 petals, high-centered, moderate fragrance; foliage dark; ['Miss Ireland' × 'Princess']; intr. 1974

'Golden Wonder' HT, ab, 1936, Gunn; flowers golden apricot suffused pink, medium, full, globular, moderate fragrance; foliage olive-green; vigorous growth

'Golden Wonders 99' -- See 'Rawana'

Golden Years® -- See 'Harween'

Golden Zest™ -- See 'Jacbelgo'

'Goldendale' HT, my, 1956, Grillo; bud long, pointed; flowers golden yellow, 5 in., 50 petals; [sport of 'Annabella']

'Goldene Aue' F, dy, GPG Bad Langensalza; flowers large, dbl.; intr. 1964

'Goldene Druschki' HP, my, 1936, Lambert, P.; bud pointed; flowers golden yellow, edged lighter turning creamy yellow in hot weather, cupped; foliage leathery, dark; very vigorous growth; ['Frau Karl Druschki' × 'Friedrich Harms']

'Goldene Gruss an Aachen' -- See 'Golden Gruss an Aachen'

'Goldene Johanna Tantau' ('Wheatcroft's Golden Polyantha') F, my, 1945, Tantau; bud ovoid; flowers clear golden yellow, large, single, cupped, borne in clusters; foliage glossy, dark; compact, bushy growth; ['Golden Rapture' × ('Johanna Tantau' × 'Eugenie Lamesch')]

'Goldene Sonne' ('Golden Sun') HT, my, 1957, Kordes, R.; bud long, pointed; flowers golden yellow, 5 in., dbl., high-centered; foliage glossy; upright, bushy growth; [('Walter Bentley' × 'Condesa de Sástago') × 'Golden Scepter']

'Goldener Adler' F, my, 1967, Verschuren, A.; bud ovoid; flowers golden yellow, medium, semi-dbl., borne in clusters; foliage light green; [Allgold® × seedling]; intr. 1965

Goldener Olymp® -- See 'Korschnuppe'

'Goldener Reiter' ('Golden Rider') F, my, 1970, Haenchen, E.; flowers golden yellow, large, 25 petals, cupped, intense fragrance; foliage dark; vigorous, upright growth; ['Circus' × Golden Giant®]; intr. 1969

Goldener Sommer 83® F, my, Noack, Werner; flowers large, dbl.; intr. 1983

'Goldenes Herz' HT, dy, 1974, Kordes; bud ovoid; flowers medium, dbl., cupped, moderate fragrance; foliage glossy, dark, leathery; vigorous, upright, bushy growth; ['Dr. A.J. Verhage' × seedling]; intr. 1975

'Goldenes Mainz' Pol, yb, 1927, Kröger; flowers orange yellow, large, semi-dbl., moderate fragrance

'Goldenes Mainz' -- See 'Golden Main'

'Goldenes Prag' HT, GPG Bad Langensalza; flowers dbl.; intr. 1966

'Goldenes Zweibrücken' F, dy, Huber; flowers warm golden yellow; intr. 2005

'Goldfächer' -- See 'Dicmoppet'

'Goldfasan' -- See 'Golden Pheasant'

'Goldfassade' LCl, my, Baum; flowers golden yellow, outer petals lighter and with pink tint, 4 in., dbl., intense fragrance; recurrent; foliage dark green, glossy; growth to 7-13 ft.; intr. 1967

'Goldfever' HT, dy; flowers golden yellow, large, 35-40 petals, borne mostly singly; recurrent; stems 16 - 24 in; florist rose; intr. 2004

'Goldfinch' HMult, ly, 1907, Paul; flowers yellow, aging white, 4 cm., semi-dbl., borne in clusters of up to 25; non-recurrent; foliage small, wrinkled, glossy; vigorous, climbing growth; ['Helene' × unknown]

'Goldfinch' ('Beehive Gold') S, my, Interplant; intr. 1994

Goldfinger® ('William David') F, dy, 1990, Pearce, C.A.; flowers medium, dbl., borne in small clusters, slight fragrance; foliage medium size, dark green, glossy; some prickles; low (40 cm.), compact growth; intr. 1990

'Goldgleam' F, my, 1965, LeGrice; flowers 3½-4 in., 18 petals, borne in small clusters, intense fragrance; foliage dark, glossy; growth moderate; PP2673; ['Gleaming' × Allgold®]

'Goldglow' -- See 'Gold Glow'

'Goldhaube' S, dy; intr. 2004

'Goldi' HT, dy, Kordes; intr. 2006

'Goldie' F, my, 1959, Boerner; bud ovoid; flowers golden yellow, edged lighter, 4 in., 25-30 petals, moderate fragrance; foliage leathery, vigorous, upright bushy growth; PP1764; ['Goldilocks' × 'Pigmy Gold']; intr. 1958

'Goldie' -- See 'Macarom'

'Goldie Locks' -- See 'Goldilocks'

Goldika® HT, ob, Cocker; intr. 1986

'Goldilocks' ('Goldie Locks') F, my, 1945, Boerner; flowers deep yellow, fading to cream, large, 45 petals, globular, borne in clusters, moderate fragrance; foliage leathery, glossy, vigorous, bushy growth; PP672; [seedling × 'Doubloons']

'Goldilocks, Climbing' Cl F, my, 1951, Caluya; PP1090

'Goldilocks' -- See 'Sunlock'

'Goldina' -- See 'Candide'

Goldjuwel® -- See 'Tanledolg'

Goldjuwel® -- See 'Golden Jewel'

'Goldkrone' -- See 'Gold Crown'

'Goldlachs' -- See 'Golden Salmon'

Goldlite™ -- See 'Devsolear'

'Goldmarie' F, dy, 1959, Kordes, R.; flowers orange-gold, very large, semi-dbl., borne in clusters, intense fragrance; foliage glossy; very vigorous, upright, bushy growth; ruled extinct ARA 1984; ['Masquerade' × 'Golden Main']; intr. 1958

'Goldmarie, Climbing' -- See 'Korkuma'

'Goldmarie' -- See 'Korfalt'

Goldmarie Nirp® -- See 'Korfalt'

'Goldmoss' F, my, 1973, Moore, Ralph S.; bud long, pointed; flowers clear yellow, medium, dbl., intense fragrance; foliage light, leathery; vigorous, dwarf, bushy growth; PP3562; ['Rumba' × 'moss hybrid']

'Goldpin' Min, dy, Ilsink; intr. 1998

'Goldpoint' -- See 'Jacpo'

'Goldquelle' T, ob, 1899, Lambert; flowers reddish golden-yellow, medium, dbl., strong fragrance; ['Kaiserin Auguste Viktoria' × 'Mme Eugène Verdier']

'Goldquelle' S, my, Tantau, Math.; bud ovoid; flowers pure golden yellow, large, dbl., borne in clusters, slight fragrance; recurrent bloom; foliage leathery; strong stems; upright (4 ft.) growth; intr. 1965

'Goldquelle 88' ('Gold Fountain') F, dy, Tantau, Math.; flowers golden yellow, medium, dbl.; quick repeat; foliage dark green, glossy; intr. 1988

'Goldrausch' ('Fièvre d'Or', Golden Giant®) HT, dy, 1965, Kordes, R.; flowers rich golden yellow, well-formed, 5 in., 45 petals, moderate fragrance; foliage dark; vigorous, tall growth

'Goldregen' LCl, my, Noack; flowers lemon yellow, frilly, 4 in., dbl.; recurrent; foliage dark green, glossy; vigorous (7 ft.) growth; intr. 1985

'Goldregen' -- See 'Golden Rain'

Goldrush® Ht, dy, Tantau; flowers medium, double, high-centered, borne mostly singly; recurrent; stems medium; florist rose; intr. 2005

'Goldrush' -- See 'Gold Rush'

'Goldschatz' -- See 'Tantasch'

'Goldschatz' -- See 'Golden Treasure'

'Goldschmied' F, dy, VEG (S) Baumschulen Dresden; flowers dbl., slight fragrance

'Goldsmith' -- See 'Korbelma'

'Goldstadt Pforzheim' -- See 'Helpforz'
'Goldstar' ('Gold Star', Disque d'Or®, 'Goldina', Point du Jour®) HT, dy, Cants of Colchester, Ltd.; flowers medium, 35 petals, slight fragrance; foliage small, light green, matte; upright growth; ['Yellow Pages' × 'Dr. A. J. Verhage']; intr. 1983
Goldstein® F, ob, Cocker; intr. 1983
Goldstern® ('Gold Star', 'Golden Star', 'Stella Dorata') HKor, my, 1966, Tantau, Math.; bud long, pointed; flowers golden yellow, 5 in., borne in clusters; recurrent bloom; foliage glossy; vigorous, bushy (7-8 ft.) growth
'Goldstrike' HT, yb, Perry, Astor; intr. 1997
'Goldstück' S, my, Tantau, Math.; bud long, pointed, flowers golden yellow, large, borne in clusters, intense fragrance; abundant, non-recurrent bloom; vigorous, upright, bushy growth; intr. 1963
'Goldstück' F, my, 1965, Verschuren, A.; flowers lemon-yellow, 40-55 petals, borne in clusters; foliage glossy, dark; vigorous, upright growth; ['Goldilocks' × seedling]; intr. 1961
Goldtopas® ('Gold Topaz') F, my, 1963, Kordes, R.; bud ovoid; flowers amber-yellow, large, dbl., cupped, borne in clusters of up to 10; foliage glossy; vigorous, bushy growth
Goldy® HT, dy, Kordes; flowers golden yellow, medium, full, high-centered, borne mostly singly; stems 2 ft; florist rose.; intr. 2003
'Goldy' -- See 'Korgold'
'Goldy' -- See 'Korbeen'
'Goldy Kordana Mini Brite' Min, my, Kordes; bud long pointed, ovoid; flowers yellow, 1½ in., 35-40 petals, borne mostly singly, no fragrance; continuous; foliage small, glossy; prickles few, small, straight to hooked; vigorous, compact, upright (24 in.) growth; PP11188; [sport of 'Vanilla Kordana Mini Brite']; intr. 1997
'Goldyla' -- See 'Kortikel'
'Golestan' -- See 'Meisadina'
'Golf' S, w, Wageningen; flowers clear white with yellow stamens, 1½ in., single, no fragrance; moderate (3 × 3 ft.) growth; intr. 1993
'Golfe-Juan' HP, mr, 1872, Nabonnand; flowers ruby red, very large, full
'Goliath' ('Maxima') C, lp, 1829, Girardon; sepals non-foliaceous; flowers light rosy pink, touched with violet, large, very full, globular, borne in clusters of 2-3; foliage oblong, large; prickles very fine, numerous
'Goliath' HP, mp, Trouillard; flowers large, full; intr. 1861
'Goliath' -- See 'Gary Player'
'Golmain' -- See 'Golden Main'
'Gomathi' HT, mp, Kasturi; flowers flesh pink, edges darker, dbl., high-centered, intr. 1987
'Gomery' HT, yb, DVP Melle; flowers 4½ in., 28 petals; foliage matte; strong grower growth; ['Frederik Chopin' × 'Mme Butterfly']; intr. 1999
'Gondul' F, mr, 1969, Lundstad; flowers cardinal-red, open, medium, 18 petals, borne in clusters; foliage dark, glossy; vigorous growth; [Lichterloh® × 'Lumina']
Gone Fishin'™ -- See 'Savafish'
'Gonsoli Gaëtano' ('Gaëtano Gonsoli') HP, mp, 1874, Pernet père; flowers satiny rose, large, dbl., borne in small clusters
'Gonzalve' HGal, mr, 1835, Vibert; flowers violet red, medium, full, globular
Good 'n Plenty™ -- See 'Jacmound'
'Good as Gold' -- See 'Chewsunbeam'
'Good Cheer' HT, dp, 1937, Amling Co.; bud pointed; flowers cerise, open, dbl.; long, strong stems; very vigorous growth; ['Talisman' × 'Templar']
'Good Companion' F, mr, 1970, Dickson, A.; flowers rich red, large, 30 petals, flat, borne in trusses, moderate fragrance; foliage dark; vigorous growth; intr. 1961
'Good Day Sunshine' -- See 'Talgoo'
'Good Golly' F, ab; intr. 2006
'Good Life' F, or, 1971, McGredy, Sam IV; flowers 2 in., 30 petals, high-centered, slight fragrance; free growth; [Elizabeth of Glamis® × 'John Church']; intr. 1970
'Good Life' ('Good Live') HT, op, Cocker; flowers copper salmon, tinged with orange, large, dbl., high-centered, moderate spicy fragrance; dark green, glossy foliage; growth vigorous, upright (4 × 3 ft.); [('Sabine' × 'Circus') × 'Dr. A. J. Verhage']; intr. 2001
'Good Live' -- See 'Good Life'
'Good Luck' -- See 'Burspec'
'Good Luck' -- See 'Sobhag'
'Good Morning' HT, w, 1935, Kaucher; flowers white, reverse faintly tinged pink, very large, dbl.; foliage leathery; long, strong stems; very vigorous, bushy growth; PP121; [sport of 'Premier Supreme']
'Good Morning' -- See 'The Cheshire Regiment'
Good Morning America™ -- See 'Savagood'
'Good Morning Sunshine' -- See 'Boslauramber'
'Good Neighbor' HT, ob, 1960, Warriner, William A.; flowers burnt-orange, reverse golden, large, dbl., intense fragrance; foliage dark; vigorous, upright growth; ['Fred Howard' × seedling]; intr. 1958
'Good News' F, my; intr. 1992
'Good News' ('Bonne Nouvelle') HT, pb, 1940, Meilland, F.; flowers silvery pink, center tinged apricot, 5-6 in., 50 petals, globular, moderate fragrance; vigorous, bushy growth; PP426; [('Radiance' × 'Souv. de Claudius Pernet') × ('Joanna Hill' × 'Comtesse Vandal')]
'Good News 95' F, mp, Chessum; intr. 1995
'Good Ol' Summertime' -- See 'Cleheat'
'Good Old Summertime' ('Good Ol' Summertime') S, ly, Clements, John K.; flowers soft, warm yellow, 4 in., 35 petals, intense spicy-myrrh fragrance; free-flowering; foliage mid-green; bushy (4 × 3½ ft.) growth; intr. 1997
'Good Samaritan' -- See 'Jactourn'
'Good Show' -- See 'Jacmeen'
'Good Times' HT, pb, 1978, Williams, J. Benjamin; bud ovoid, pointed; flowers ivory to light pink with deep pink edging, 5-5½ in., 56 petals, cupped, slight fragrance; foliage large, glossy; compact, upright growth; [Pink Peace® × 'Peace']; intr. 1977
'Good Vibes' -- See 'Gelgood'
'Good Wishes' -- See 'Poululv'
'Gooiland' HT, mp, 1922, Van Rossem; flowers clear rose-pink, reverse dark coral-rose, dbl.; [('Sunburst' × unknown) × 'Red-Letter Day']
'Gooiland Beauty' HT, ab, 1924, Van Rossem; flowers clear golden orange, open, large, semi-dbl.; foliage dark, leathery; vigorous, bushy growth; ['Sunburst' × 'Golden Emblem']
'Gooiland Glory' HT, or, 1925, Van Rossem; flowers cherry-red shaded coral-red, medium, semi-dbl.; ['General MacArthur' × 'Mme Edouard Herriot']
'Goose Fair' -- See 'Meipopul'
'Gopika' F, op, 1971, Singh, R. S.; flowers light salmon-pink, medium, dbl., globular, slight fragrance; foliage glossy; vigorous, bushy growth; ['Marlena' × unknown]; intr. 1969
'Gordon Drake' F, dp, 1956, Williams, G.A.; flowers cerise-pink, dbl., borne in large clusters; very vigorous growth; [sport of 'Eutin']
'Gordon Eddie' HT, ab, 1949, Eddie; flowers deep apricot, edged lighter, very large, 40 petals, high-centered, moderate fragrance; foliage leathery, glossy; very vigorous, bushy growth; PP1000; ['Royal Visit' × 'Cynthia Brooke']
'Gordon Snell' F, yb, Dickson; flowers pale yellow, flushed with pink and red, dbl., borne in clusters; compact growth; intr. 1999
'Gordon's College' -- See 'Cocjabby'
'Gorgeous' HT, op, 1915, Dickson, H.; flowers deep orange-yellow, veined copper, well-formed, large, dbl., moderate fragrance; foliage rich, green, soft; bushy, open growth
'Gorgeous' HT, mp, Franc; flowers rose-pink, 5 in., 18-20 petals, high-centered, moderate fragrance; foliage leathery; vigorous growth; PP1598; [sport of 'Pink Delight']; intr. 1956
'Gorgeous George' -- See 'Delricos'
'Gorhappy' ('Happy Wanderer', 'Happy, Climbing') Cl Pol, mr, 2000, Gordon, Barbara A. K.; flowers medium currant-red, 1-1¼ in., dbl., borne in large clusters, no fragrance; prolific; foliage medium size, medium to dark green, glossy; numerous prickles; vigorous, upright, tall (10-12 ft.) growth; [sport of

The Official Registry and Checklist — Rosa 261

'Happy']; an earlier, non-registered, apparently identical, sport was introduced in Europe before 1969
'Gosh' S, lp, 2000, Cox, Roy; flowers light pink, reverse deep pink, 1½ in., single, borne in large clusters; foliage medium size, dark green, semi-glossy; few prickles; growth bushy, tall (4 ft.); ['Mlle Cécile Brunner, Cl.' × 'Ballerina']
'Göteborg' -- See 'Korpinrob'
'Gotenborgs Posten' -- See 'Korlanum'
'Gotenhafen' F, mp, 1940, Tantau; flowers pure bright rose, medium, 12-15 petals; vigorous, well branched growth; ['Mev. Nathalie Nypels' × 'Kardinal']
'Gotha' ('Gotha IV') HT, op, 1932, Krause; flowers brownish yellow passing to apricot; [('Souv. de H.A. Verschuren' × 'Sunset') × 'Mev. G.A. van Rossem']
'Gotha IV' -- See 'Gotha'
'Gottfried Keller' HFt, ab, 1894, Müller, Dr. F.; flowers orange yellow to coppery pink, medium, single to semi-dbl., moderate fragrance; [('Mme Bérard' × R. foetida persian') × (('Pierre Notting' × 'Mme Bérard') × R. foetida persiana)]
'Goubault' -- See 'Bon Silène'
'Goudvlinder' ('Golden Butterfly') HT, ab, 1926, Van Rossem; flowers orange-yellow, small, 12 petals; foliage glossy, brownish red; vigorous, bushy growth; ['Lady Hillingdon' × 'Souv. de Claudius Pernet']
'Goulburnian' F, mp, 2005, Ryan, Max; flowers medium, semi-dbl., borne in small clusters, no fragrance; foliage medium size, medium green, glossy, leathery; prickles large, hooked, few; growth spreading, vigorous, medium (1 m.); garden decoration, exhibition; ['Sparrieshoop' × seedling]; semi-double; foliage leathery; vigorous; intr. 2002
'Gourdault' B, m, 1859, Guillot Père; flowers rich purple, medium to large, full
'Gourmet Pheasant' S, dp; flowers deep pink to light red, single, borne in clusters; recurrent; growth spreading, fast growing (2 × 8 ft.); groundcover; intr. 1995
'Gourmet Popcorn' -- See 'Weopop'
'Governador Braga da Cruz' HT, ly, 1954, Moreira da Silva; very vigorous growth; ['Peace' × seedling]
'Governor Alfred E. Smith' HT, yb, 1933, Denoyel, Vve.; flowers blend of buff, terra-cotta, gold and salmon, large, dbl., high-centered; foliage glossy; vigorous growth; PP62; ['Souv. de F. Bohé seedling' × seedling]
'Governor Mark Hatfield' Gr, dr, 1962, Von Abrams; bud pointed; flowers rich red, large, 40 petals, high-centered, slight fragrance; foliage leathery; vigorous, upright growth; ['Carrousel' × 'Charles Mallerin']
'Governor Phillip' Cl HT, mr, 1939, Fitzhardinge; flowers ruby-red, flushed darker, open, large, very dbl.; foliage leathery, glossy, dark, bronze; long stems; vigorous, climbing growth; [('Ophelia' × unknown) × 'Black Boy']

'Governor Rosellini' Gr, mr, 1959, Lindquist; flowers rose-red, 3-4 in., 30 petals, high-centered, moderate raspberry fragrance; foliage dark, leathery; vigorous, upright growth; PP1873; ['Baby Chateau' × 'Tiffany']; intr. 1958
'Governor's Lady Gloria' -- See 'Aroglor'
'Gowan Brae' S, pb, 2005, Cant, Heather; flowers very full, borne in small clusters, slight fragrance; foliage large, medium green, matte, dark red when new; prickles medium, pointed, few; growth upright, tall (1½ m.); landscape; [Leander® × unknown]; intr. 2004
'Gowirichs Traum' Pol, dp
'Gowrishankar' HT, pb, Mandal, G.S.; flowers soft pink with violet tinge; free-flowering; [sport of 'Carmousine']; intr. 2004
'Goya' F, w, 1976, Bees; flowers cream, 30 petals, high-centered, borne in trusses; foliage dark green, heavy; vigorous growth; ['Mildred Reynolds' × 'Arthur Bell']
'Graaf van Vlaanderen' S, w, DVP Melle; ['Mev. Nathalie Nypels' × Yesterday®]; intr. 1993
'Graaff-Reinet' -- See 'Kormate'
'Grace' HRg, 1923, Saunders; flowers amber, center apricot, open, very dbl., moderate fragrance; foliage wrinkled; bushy (5-6 ft.) growth; RULED EXTINCT; [R. rugosa × 'Harison's Yellow']
'Grace' -- See 'Auskeppy'
'Grace Abounding' F, w, 1968, Harkness; flowers ivory, semi-dbl., borne in trusses, moderate musk fragrance; foliage glossy; ['Pink Parfait' × 'Penelope']
'Grace Amazing' -- See 'Sprograce'
'Grace Darling' T, w, 1885, Bennett; flowers cream-white shaded golden, large, dbl., globular; vigorous growth; sometimes classed as HT
Grace de Monaco® HT, lp, 1958, Meilland, F.; flowers light rose-pink, well-formed, large, dbl., intense fragrance; foliage leathery; vigorous, bushy growth; ['Peace' × 'Michèle Meilland']
'Grace Donnelly' -- See 'Horlexstrip'
'Grace Haslam' HT, ob, Fryers Nursery, Ltd.; flowers orange to carmine; ['Scarlet Glory' × 'Mrs Sam McGredy']
'Grace Kelly' -- See 'Meimagarmic'
'Grace Kimmins' F, mr, 1972, Gobbee, W.D.; flowers crimson, 3 in., 28 petals; foliage glossy; vigorous, bushy growth; ['Dainty Maid' × 'Red Dandy']
'Grace Molyneux' HT, ab, 1909, Dickson, A.; flowers creamy apricot, center flesh, large, dbl.
'Grace Moore' ('Paul Holtge') HT, mr, 1948, Kordes; bud ovoid; flowers crimson-red, large, dbl., cupped; foliage leathery, dark olive-green; vigorous, bushy growth; ['Kardinal' × 'Crimson Glory']
'Grace Noll Crowell' HT, pb, 1929, Vestal; flowers rose-pink, base slightly shaded cream, large, dbl., high-centered; foliage soft, light; vigorous, bushy growth
'Grace Note' S, pb, 1985, Buck, Dr.

Griffith J.; bud ovoid, pointed; flowers medium pink, freckled red, imbricated, large, 38 petals, borne 3 - 8 per cluster, moderate fragrance; repeat bloom; foliage large, leathery, dark green; prickles awl-like, tan; vigorous, erect, bushy growth; hardy; [('Tiki' × 'Marigold') × 'Freckle Face']; intr. 1984
'Grace Seward' -- See 'Tingrace'
'Grace Sharington' -- See 'Mangrace'
'Grace Thomson' HMult, rb, 1909, Paul, W.; flowers red over white, full
'Grace Wayman' Cl HT, mp, 1936, Wayman; flowers pink, very large, dbl.; foliage leathery; vigorous, climbing (10 ft.) growth
'Grace Wood' Min, my, 1993, Giles, Diann; flowers full, borne in small clusters, no fragrance; foliage small, medium green, matte; few prickles; medium, compact growth; ['Sun Flare' × 'Rise 'n' Shine']; intr. 1992
'Graceful' S, ly, 1966, Smith, W.H.; flowers yellow fading to cream, well-formed, 4 in., dbl.; foliage glossy; vigorous, bushy growth; ['Paul's Lemon Pillar' × 'Marcelle Gret']
'Graceland' -- See 'Kirscot'
'Graceland' -- See 'Jacel'
'Gracie Allen' -- See 'Wekcryreg'
'Gracie Fields' HT, dy, 1937, Letts; flowers vivid buttercup-yellow, moderate sweetbriar fragrance; foliage glossy; vigorous growth
'Gracieuse' -- See 'Gracilis'
'Gracieuse' -- See 'Graziella'
'Gracilis' Bslt, mr, 1796, Wood/Shailer; flowers cherry shaded lilac-blush, medium, semi-dbl., cupped; foliage dark; prickles large, long; vigorous, slender, branching growth; apparently a cross between an early Boursault and R. arvensis
'Gracilis' HCh, mp, Hardy; flowers vivid pink, medium, full; intr. before 1820
'Gracilis' HGal, w, Vibert; flowers white, flesh center, full, flat; intr. about 1830
'Gracilis' ('Gracieuse', 'Minor Prolific') M, dp, Prévost; flowers deep pink, well mossed, small, dbl., globular; non-remontant; foliage large, glossy, vigorous growth; good as a standard; intr. about 1835
'Gracilis' HSet, mp, Prince Nursery; flowers pink to rose, very dbl., borne in clusters; intr. 1841
'Graciosa' HT, w, 1957, Moreira da Silva; flowers white edged rose, well-formed; very vigorous growth; ['Branca' × 'Peace']
Graciosa® LCl, w, Noack; flowers white with touch of pastel pink, 4 in., dbl., loose, intense fragrance; free-flowering; vigorous (10 ft.) growth; intr. 2002
'Gracious Lady' HT, pb, 1965, Robinson, H.; bud ovoid; flowers peach-pink, base apricot, large, dbl., high-centered, moderate fragrance; foliage glossy, dark; vigorous, bushy growth; PP2582; [(('Peace' × unknown) × 'Gail Borden')

× ('Dorothy Peach' × unknown)]
'Gracious Queen' -- See 'Michelangelo'
'Gracious Queen' -- See 'Bedqueen'
'Graciously Pink' S, mp; growth to 2 ft.; intr. 2003
'Graduation Day' -- See 'Jalgrad'
'Graelove' ('Everlasting Love', Millennium®) F, mr, Grant, Doug; flowers large, scarlet, 2¾ in., dbl., borne in small clusters; foliage medium size, dark green, glossy, new growth is red; some prickles; medium (80-100 cm.), bushy growth; ['Molly McGredy' × Satchmo®]; intr. 1998
'Graeme Douglas' -- See 'Macpiopi'
'Graf Fritz Metternich' HP, dr, 1896, Soupert & Notting; flowers velvety brownish red, shaded black, center cardinal red, large, full, intense fragrance; ['Sultan of Zanzibar' × 'Thomas Mills']
'Graf Fritz Schwerin' HT, mr, 1916, Lambert; flowers large, single; ['General MacArthur' × 'Goldelse']
'Graf Fritz von Hochberg' HT, op, 1905, Lambert, P.; buds almond shaped; flowers yellowish salmon pink, large, dbl., moderate fragrance; ['Mme Caroline Testout' × 'Goldquelle']
Graf Lennart® -- See 'Meisoyris'
'Graf Silva Tarouca' HT, dp, 1916, Lambert, P.; flowers carmine-red, very large, dbl.; very vigorous growth; ['Étoile de France' × 'Lady Mary Fitzwilliam']
'Graf Zeppelin' HMult, dp, 1910, Böhm; flowers light red to bright pink, aging lighter, medium, semi-dbl., borne in large clusters; very free bloom; vigorous (6-8 ft.) growth; [sport of 'Non Plus Ultra']
'Gräfin Ada Bredow' HMult, lp, 1909, Walter; flowers whitish pink, 2-2½ cm., semi-dbl., borne in large clusters; non-recurrent; ['Thalia' × 'Rösel Dach']
'Gräfin Chotek' HMult, lp, 1911, Kiese; bud peach pink; flowers luminous apple blossom pink; ['Tausendschön' × 'Mignonnette']
'Grafin Esterhazy' Ch, dp, Geschwind, R.
'Gräfin Hardenberg' S, dp, 1938, Vogel, M.; flowers carmine-pink, medium, semi-dbl.
'Gräfin Marie Henriette Chotek' ('Countess M. H. Chotek', 'Marie Henriette Gräfin Chotek') HMult, mr, 1911, Lambert, P.; flowers bright red, medium, dbl., borne in very large clusters, moderate fragrance; non-recurrent; ['Farquhar' × 'Richmond']
'Gräfin Minnie Schaffgotsch' HT, w, 1928, Mühle; flowers cream-white, center pink, very dbl.; ['Clio' × 'hybrid tea seedling']
Gräfin Sonja® -- See 'Korfeimot'
'Gräfin von Hardenberg' -- See 'Astrid Gräfin von Hardenberg'
'Grafton Pillar' LCl, mr, 1960, Risley; bud globular; flowers bright red, small, dbl., borne in clusters; slight fragrance; free, recurrent boom; foliage wrinkled; moderate growth; ['second generation Skinner's Rambler' × 'Gruss an Aachen']; intr. 1958

'Graham' HT, dr, 1961, Kriloff, Michel; flowers deep crimson-scarlet, large, 35-40 petals, high-centered; foliage glossy; long stems; vigorous, upright growth; ['Eclipse' × seedling]; intr. 1960
'Graham Stuart Thomas' -- See 'Ausmas'
Graham Thomas® -- See 'Ausmas'
'Graham Thomas Musk' -- See 'Graham Thomas Old Musk'
'Graham Thomas Old Musk' ('Graham Thomas Musk') HMsk, w
Grain de Beauté® Min, mp; flowers small, semi-dbl., borne in clusters; free-flowering; compact, low (40-50 cm.) growth; intr. 2004
Graines d'Or® HT, dy, Dorieux; flowers strong yellow with orange tints , large , double, urn-shaped; intr. 2002
'Gran Parada' ('Grande Parade') F, my, 1970, Dot, Simon; flowers yellow, becoming reddish, open, medium, 25 petals; foliage glossy; vigorous, upright, compact growth; ['Gold Dot' × (Queen Elizabeth® × Zambra®)]; intr. 1967
'Granada' HT, dr, 1955, Delforge; flowers deep red, borne in clusters; ['Opera' × 'The Doctor']
'Granada' ('Donatella') HT, rb, Lindquist; bud urn-shaped, medum; flowers multicolor with shades of rose Bengal, buttercup at base, reverse much lighter, 4-5 in., 18-25 petals, open, borne singly, moderate tea fragrance; foliage foliate leathery, slightly holly-like; vigorous, upright growth; PP2214; ['Tiffany' × 'Cavalcade']; intr. 1963
'Granada, Climbing' Cl HT, rb, 1969, Swim & Weeks; flowers yellow at center, edged red, large, semi-dbl.; intr. 1964
'Granada Sunset' HT, ob, Rupert; flowers red, orange and apricot flecked with cascade of cream and pink, dbl., intense fragrance; [sport of 'Granada']; identical to Granada except for color; intr. about 1997
'Granadina' ('Grenadine') Min, mr, 1956, Dot, Pedro; flowers oxblood-red, small, 30 petals, globular; foliage dark; low, upright growth; ['Granate' × 'Coralín']
'Granat' HT, dr, 1937, Krause; flowers blackish red, well-formed; very vigorous growth; ['Barcelona' × 'Château de Clos Vougeot']
'Granate' Min, dr, 1947, Dot, Pedro; flowers velvety oxblood-red, often streaked white, small; nearly thornless; growth short (6-8 in.); ['Merveille des Rouges' × 'Pompon de Paris']
'Granatina' HT, dp, Cazzaniga, F. G.; intr. 1964
Grand™ ('Grand Palace') S, dr, Poulsen; flowers dark red, 8-10 cm., dbl., no fragrance; foliage dark; growth bushy, 40-60 cm.; PP11610; intr. 1998
'Grand Age' -- See 'Delegran'
'Grand Amore' HT, dr, Kordes; intr. 1968
'Grand Amour' ('Cote Rotie') HT, mr, 1956, Delbard-Chabert; flowers bright red, large
'Grand Amour' -- See 'True Love'
'Grand Apollon' HGal, m, 1824, in Brussels; flowers violet, very large, full
'Grand Bercam' C, dp, before 1826, possibly Prévost; flowers medium to large, semi-dbl.
'Grand Blue' HT, m, Hiroshima; intr. 1996
'Grand Canary' HT, my, 1934, Lowman; flowers dbl., high-centered; foliage glossy; vigorous, compact growth; PP130; [sport of 'Token']
'Grand Canyon'™ (Riberhus') F, op, Poulsen; bud pointed ovoid; flowers 2½-3 in., 18-22 petals, flat, borne singly or in small clusters, no fragrance; recurrent; foliage dark, glossy; prickles moderate, concave, slight downward curve; bushy, vigorous (100-150 cm.) growth; PP12902; [seedling × Sexy Rexy®]; intr. 1998
'Grand Canyon' S, dy, 1951, Whisler; bud long, pointed, chrome-yellow; flowers yellow, salmon and copper, turning to crimson, open, medium; recurrent bloom; foliage glossy, bronze; very vigorous (6 ft.), arching growth; ['Herrenhausen' × 'Golden Rapture']
'Grand Cels' -- See 'Childling'
'Grand Château' -- See 'Tanelorak'
'Grand Condé' -- See 'Rouge Formidable'
'Grand Corneille' -- See 'Cramoisi des Alpes'
'Grand Cramoisi de Trianon' -- See 'À Grand Cramoisi'
'Grand Cramoisi de Vibert' HGal, mr, about 1818, Vibert; flowers light crimson red, medium, full
'Grand-Dauphin' -- See 'Enfant de France'
'Grand-Duc Adolphe de Luxembourg' HT, rb, 1892, Soupert & Notting; flowers brick-red, reverse carmine, large, dbl.; weak stems; moderate growth; ['Triomphe de la Terre des Roses' × 'Mme Loeben Sels']
'Grand-Duc Alexis' HP, mr, 1892, Lévêque; flowers blood red, tinted purple and light vermilion, large, dbl.; foliage large
'Grand-Duc Henri' F, op, Lens; flowers salmon-orange, full, borne in clusters; foliage dark green; growth to 60-80 cm.; intr. 2001
'Grand Duc Héritier de Luxembourg' -- See 'Mlle Franziska Krüger'
'Grand-Duc Pierre de Russie' T, pb, 1895, Perny/Cochet; flowers rose pink veined darker pink, aging to salmon, very large
'Grand Duche' -- See 'Godrache'
'Grand Duchess Hilda' -- See 'Grossherzogin Mathilde'
'Grand Duchess Victoria Melita' -- See 'Grossherzogin Viktoria Melitta von Hessen'
'Grand Edouard' -- See 'La Souveraine'
Grand Finale™ -- See 'Jacpihi'

Grand Gala™ HT, rb, 1954, Meilland, F.; bud globular; flowers rose-red, reverse white suffused pink, 4½-5 in., 45-60 petals, high-centered, slight fragrance; foliage leathery; vigorous, bushy growth; PP1489; ['Peace' × 'Independence']; intr. 1954

'Grand Gala, Climbing' Cl HT, rb, 1961, Yamate

'Grand Gala' HT, mr, Meilland; bud conical, medium; flowers strawberry-red, 4 in., 40 petals, high-centered, borne mostly singly; good repeat bloom; foliage dark green, glossy; prickles few, small; growth erect, moderate (2-3 ft.); PP9309; [('Edith Piaf' × 'Visa') × ('Meiduitra' × 'Madelon')]; florist rose; intr. 1995

Grand Hotel® (Hotel Royal®) LCl, mr, 1972, McGredy, Sam IV; flowers scarlet, darker at petal tips, 4 in., dbl., high-centered, borne singly or in small clusters; repeat bloom; foliage dark green, glossy

'Grand Huit' -- See 'Adharman'

'Grand Huit, Climbing' -- See 'Commandant Cousteau, Climbing'

Grand Impression™ -- See 'Jaclion'

'Grand Ivory' HT, w

'Grand Lady' HT, mp, 1968, Patterson; bud ovoid; flowers pink, center lighter, large, dbl., high-centered; foliage leathery; vigorous, upright, bushy growth; ['Ma Perkins' × 'Peace']

Grand Marshall™ -- See 'Arofuto'

'Grand Masterpiece' HT, mr, 1978, Warriner, William A.; bud ovoid, pointed; flowers 5 in., dbl., high-centered; tall, upright growth; PP4767; [seedling × 'Tonight']

'Grand Mogul' HT, w, 1970, Delbard-Chabert; flowers creamy white, large, 33 petals, high-centered, moderate fragrance; growth moderate; ['Sultane' × 'Chic Parisien']; intr. 1965

'Grand Mogul' -- See 'Jean Soupert'

'Grand Monarche' ('Cocarde Royale') HGal, lp, before 1818, from Holland; flowers pale pink, shaded carmine-cerise, very large, full

'Grand Napoléon' HGal, m, 1809, Sevale & Haghen; flowers intense violet, large, very dbl.

Grand Nord® -- See 'Delgrord'

'Grand Occasion' ('Grande Premiere') HT, pb, 1971, Delbard; flowers rosy coral shaded yellow, edged carmine, 3 in., 30 petals, intense fragrance; foliage glossy, light; vigorous growth; ['Comtesse Vandal' × 'Mme Henri Guillot']; intr. 1970

'Grand Opening' Min, rb, 1991, Gruenbauer, Richard; bud ovoid; flowers orange-red showing yellow eye, red reverse, ages pale red, eye turns white, medium, 35 petals, high-centered, moderate fruity fragrance; foliage medium size, dark green, semi-glossy; upright, medium growth; ['Poker Chip' × 'Zinger']; intr. 1993

'Grand Opera' HT, pb, 1964, Schwartz, Ernest W.; bud long, pointed; flowers cream edged pink, becoming pink, 4-5 in., 40 petals, high-centered, moderate fragrance; foliage leathery; vigorous, bushy growth; ['Masquerade' × 'Peace']; intr. 1964

'Grand Palace' -- See 'Poulgrad'

'Grand Palais de Laeken' ('Palais de Laeken') HGal, lp, 1824; flowers bright light pink, medium, full; from Laeken, Holland

'Grand Parcours' -- See 'New Dawning'

'Grand-Père Lottin' HWich, op, 1918, Lottin; flowers salmony flesh-pink, center brighter, very dbl., borne in clusters; ['Lady Godiva' × 'Mrs W. H. Cutbush']

'Grande Pompadour' -- See 'Pourpre Charmant'

'Grand Prix' ('Jealous Joey') F, ab, Matthews; flowers apricot peach, full, OGR, intense fragrance; free-flowering; medium growth; intr. 1999

'Grand Prix' HT, dr, Select; flowers dark red, 4½ in., 35-40 petals, high-centered, borne mostly singly; recurrent; stem length 28 - 40 in; florist rose

Grand Prix® -- See 'Deltuf'

'Grand Prize' HT, rb, 1935, Kistler; flowers petals red, white and spotted, very large, dbl., cupped, intense fragrance; foliage leathery; very vigorous growth; PP183; [sport of 'Red Radiance']

Grand Prize™ -- See 'Jacbeau'

'Grand Romance' -- See 'Brigran'

Grand Siècle® -- See 'Delegran'

'Grand Slam' HT, mr, 1963, Armstrong, D.L. & Swim, H. C.; bud urn-shaped; flowers cherry to rose-red, 4 in., 28 petals, high-centered, slight fragrance; foliage leathery, dark, semi-glossy; vigorous, upright, spreading growth; PP2187; ['Charlotte Armstrong' × 'Montezuma']; intr. 1963

'Grand Slam' HT, my, Select Roses BV; florist rose; intr. 2003

'Grand St. Francis' -- See 'Lustre d'Église'

'Grand Sultan' ('Céleste', 'Grand Turban') HGal, lp, before 1820, Descemet; flowers delicate flesh pink, large, very full; foliage light green

'Grand Sultan' -- See 'Le Grand Sultan'

'Grand Trianon' HT, Truffaut, G.; intr. 1967

'Grand Turban' -- See 'Grand Sultan'

'Grandad' HT, dr; flowers dbl., cupped; foliage glossy; growth to 2 × 2 ft.; intr. 2005

'Grandchant' -- See 'Chantilly'

'Grandchild' Min, mp, 1987, Garelja, Anita; flowers clear, medium pink, small, 40 petals, high-centered, borne 3-15 per cluster, moderate sweet fragrance; foliage long, narrow, dense, reddish to medium green; prickles hooked, gray-brown; bushy, shrub-like, tall growth; [('Cécile Brunner' × unknown) × ('Cécile Brunner' × unknown)]

'Grande Agathe' -- See 'Henriette'

'Grande Agathe Nouvelle' -- See 'Héloïse'

'Grande Amore' HT, dr, Kordes; intr. 1968

Grande Amore® ('My Valentine', 'Walter Sisulu') HT, mr, Kordes; bud pointed, red; flowers shining dark red, 4 in., full, high-centered, borne usually singly, moderate fragrance; recurrent; foliage medium size, dark green, slightly glossy; stems strong; growth bushy, well-branched, upright; intr. 2005

'Grande Amore' HT, mr, Kordes; flowers brilliant red, velvety, large, full, high-centered, borne mostly singly; recurrent; stems long; intr. 2007

'Grande Bichonne' HGal, mr, about 1815, Descemet

'Grande Brique' HGal, dp, before 1811; flowers dark wine pink, very large, dbl.

'Grande Brune' -- See 'Nouveau Monde'

'Grande Centfeuilles de Hollande' -- See 'Des Peintres'

'Grande Classe' -- See 'Adharman'

'Grande Cuisse de Nymphe' -- See 'Great Maiden's Blush'

'Grande Duchesse Charlotte' HT, mr, 1942, Ketten Bros.; bud long, pointed; flowers tomato-red, shaded geranium-red, cactus form, 5-5½ in., 25 petals, slight fragrance; foliage glossy, dark; vigorous, bushy growth; PP774

'Grande Duchesse de Luxembourg' -- See 'Marie Adélaïde'

'Grande Duchesse Olga' -- See 'Kaiserin Auguste Viktoria'

'Grande esther' -- See 'Esther'

'Grande et Belle' HGal, dp, before 1811; flowers deep purple pink; from Holland

'Grande Henriette' -- See 'L'Enchantresse'

'Grande Maculée' HGal, m, before 1829, Coquerel; flowers purple, large, semi-dbl.

'Grande Parade' -- See 'Gran Parada'

'Grande Première' HT, yb, 1959, Delbard-Chabert; bud long, pointed; flowers yellow edged pink, large, 38 petals; foliage bright green, glossy; upright, bushy growth; ['Comtesse Vandal' × 'Mme Henri Guillot']

'Grande Premiere' -- See 'Grand Occasion'

'Grande Renoncule Violette' C, mp, before 1885; flowers dull pink, shading to violet, medium, dbl.

'Grande Rouge' F, dr, 1973, Tantau, Math.; bud ovoid; flowers medium, dbl.; foliage soft; upright, bushy growth; [unknown × unknown]

'Grande Sultane' -- See 'Le Grand Sultan'

'Grande Violette Claire' HGal, m, about 1811; flowers pale violet, very large, semi-dbl.

'Grande, Violette, et Belle' -- See 'Roxelane'

Grande Walzer® HT, rb, 1981, Kordes, W.; bud ovoid; flowers deep orange-red, reverse deep yellow, 35 petals, cupped, borne singly, slight fragrance;

foliage rather small, light green, glossy; prickles curved, light yellow; upright growth; intr. 1978

'Grande-Duchesse Maria Teresa' F, dp, Lens; flowers deep pink with golden stamens, 8 cm. , double , cupped, borne in clusters, some singly, moderate fragrance; recurrent; moderate (3 ft.) growth; intr. 2008

'Grandee' -- See 'Machomai'

Grandessa® -- See 'Delsire'

'Grandesse Royale' -- See 'Lustre d'Église'

'Grandesse Royale' -- See 'Grosse Mohnkopfs Rose'

'Grandesse Royale' -- See 'Great Royal'

'Grandeur' HT, dp, 1954, Grillo; bud long, pointed; flowers cerise-red, 4 in., 70 petals, high-centered, moderate fragrance; foliage leathery; very vigorous, upright growth; [sport of 'Joyance']

'Grandeur' HT, mr, Mallerin, C.; flowers vermilion-red, medium, 25 petals; moderate, bushy growth; intr. before 1965

'Grandeur of Cheshunt' HP, mr, 1883, Paul, G.; flowers bright carmine, tinted pink, very large, full; quite remontant

'Grandeur Royale' -- See 'Great Royal'

'Grandezza' HT, mp, 1962, Herholdt, J.A.; bud spiral, pointed; flowers peach-blossom-pink, well-formed, large, dbl.; moderate, bushy growth; ['Monique' × 'Radar']

'Grandhotel' -- See 'Macdub'

'Grandidentata' -- See 'À Feuille de Chêne'

'Grandidier' HGal, m, 1826, Dubourg; flowers carmine-violet

'Grandiflora' -- See 'Alika'

'Grandioso' HT, mr, 1961, Verbeek; flowers cherry-red, 5 in., 30-40 petals; foliage dark; [('Happiness' × 'Satisfaction') × ('Poinsettia' × 'Happiness')]

'Grandissima' -- See 'Louis-Philippe'

'Grandma' F, mp; intr. 2005

'Grandma' F, my; flowers bright yellow, dbl., borne in clusters, moderate fragrance; recurrent; foliage dark green, glossy; growth to 80 cm.; intr. 2006

'Grandma Allison' HT, op, 2008, Mallory, Ron; flowers orange-pink, reverse white to pink, aging darker, medium, 4-5 in., very full, high-centered, borne mostly solitary; foliage medium, medium green, semi-glossy; prickles ¼ in., hooked, beige, moderate; growth upright, tall (5-6 ft.); garden decoration, exhibition; [Artistry™ × seedling]

'Grandma's Baby' ('Grandmaw's Baby') Min, lp, Wells, V.; flowers pale pink to white, medium, dbl., high-centered, borne mostly singly, very slight fragrance; recurrent; foliage medium size, medium green, matte; vigorous growth

'Grandma's Blessing' ('Garden Art Grandma's Blessing') S, dp, Lim, Ping; flowers dusty pink, 3-4 in., 25-30 petals; foliage dark green; growth symmetrical, vase-shaped, small (18 in.); PP16993; intr. 2004

'Grandma's Girl' Min, ab; intr. 2005

'Grandma's Lace' -- See 'Clegran'

'Grandma's Pink' -- See 'Morbouquet'

'Grandma's Violet' HT, m

'Grandmaster' HMsk, ab, 1954, Kordes; bud long, pointed; flowers apricot shaded lemon and pink, 10 petals, borne in clusters; recurrent bloom; foliage light green; bushy growth; ['Sangerhausen' × 'Sunmist']

'Grandmaw's Baby' -- See 'Grandma's Baby'

'Grandmaw's Girl' -- See 'Welgirl'

'Grand'mère Jenny' HT, yb, 1950, Meilland, F.; flowers apricot-yellow, edged and suffused pink, 4-4½ in., 30 petals, high-centered, moderate fragrance; foliage dark, glossy; vigorous growth; PP1148; ['Peace' × ('Julien Potin' × 'Sensation')]; intr. 1950

'Grand'mère Jenny, Climbing' ('Grimpant Grand'mère Jenny') Cl HT, yb, 1959, Meilland, F.; flowers apricot yellow with light crimson tints, 12-13 cm.; intr. 1958

'Grandmom Schmidt' T, pb, 2004, Delahanty, James; flowers light pink, reverse medium pink, 2-2½ in., dbl., borne in small clusters, no fragrance; foliage medium size, light green, matte; prickles small, curved backwards, primarily on leaf stem, not canes; growth spreading, medium (4 ft.); specimen; [sport of 'Smith's Parish' ('Fortune's Five Color Rose')]; intr. 2004

'Grandpa Alex' -- See 'Renal'

'Grandpa Dan' -- See 'Respad'

'Grandpa Dickson' ('Irish Gold') HT, my, 1966, Dickson, A.; bud ovoid; flowers 7 in., 33 petals, high-centered, moderate fragrance; foliage dark, glossy, leathery; vigorous, upright, bushy growth; PP2769; [('Kordes' Perfecta' × 'Governador Braga da Cruz') × Piccadilly®]

'Grandpa Dickson, Climbing' Cl HT, my; flowers large

'Grandpa Ray' -- See 'Respar'

'Grandpa Toni' -- See 'Respat'

'Grandpa's Delight' F, ob, 1984, Pawsey, Roger; flowers orange-red, yellow center and stamens, medium, semi-dbl.; foliage medium size, medium green, glossy; bushy growth; ['Living Fire' × seedling]

'Grandrenai' HT, ab; intr. 2002

'Grange Briar'   (strain of R. canina), lp; growth vigorous; once used as understock

'Grange Colombe' HT, w, 1912, Guillot, P.; bud pointed; flowers cream-white, center yellow, large, dbl., cupped; vigorous growth; ['Mme Caroline Testout' × 'Lady Ashtown']

'Grannie's Bonnet' -- See 'Sixth Sense'

'Grannie's Rose' S, mp; flowers clear pink, semi-dbl., borne in clusters of 5-7, intense fragrance; non-recurrent

Granny™ -- See 'Pouloma'

'Granny Beryl' -- See 'Jaygra'

'Granny Grimmetts' HP, dr, Hilling; flowers dark purple-red, often streaked white, 3 in., semi-dbl. to dbl., borne singly and in small clusters, moderate fragrance; some autumn repeat; intr. 1955

'Granny's Delight' S, dp, Poulsen; intr. 2004

'Granny's Favourite' MinFl, op; flowers butterscotch; growth to 2 ft.

'Grape Delight' -- See 'Gelgrape'

'Grapeade' Cl Min, m; intr. 1979

'Grassland Meander' F, ob, Delbard; intr. 2008

Gråsten™ -- See 'Poulfeld'

'Gratia' HT, w, 1934, Leenders, M.; bud pointed; flowers creamy white, large, semi-dbl., high-centered; foliage leathery, dark; vigorous growth; [seedling × 'Pius XI']

'Gratitude' HT, rb, 1962, Delbard-Chabert; bud ovoid; flowers reddish-orange, 3-3½ in., 25-35 petals, slight fragrance; foliage leathery, dark, glossy; vigorous, upright, bushy growth; ['Impeccable' × 'Incendie']; intr. 1960

'Gratulation' F, GPG Bad Langensalza; intr. 1985

'Graulhié' HMult, w, before 1872, Van Houtte; flowers white, reverse light pink, very small, dbl., cupped

Graves de Vayres® HMult, dr, Eve; flowers show shades of red, 8 cm., single to semi-dbl., flat; recurrent; broad (4-5 ft.), shrubby growth, or up to 10 ft. as a climber; intr. 2000

'Gravin D'Alcantara' HT, dr, 1985, Rijksstation Voor Sierplantenteelt; flowers well-formed, 28 petals, cupped, borne singly and in clusters of up to 7; foliage matte, dark; prickles red; upright growth; ['Montezuma' × 'Forever Yours']; intr. 1982

Gravin Michel d'Ursel® -- See 'LLX8779'

'Grazia' HT, op, 1941, Giacomasso; flowers salmon-pink, center darker, very large; foliage bright green; long stems; ['Julien Potin' × 'Mme G. Forest-Colcombet']

'Graziella' ('Gracieuse') HP, mp, 1850, Thomas

'Graziella' HP, lp, Robert & Moreau; flowers flesh pink, very large, full, moderate fragrance; intr. 1879

'Graziella' HMult, w, Geschwind; flowers flesh pink over white; growth vigorous, climbing; intr. 1889

'Graziella' T, lp, Dubreuil; flowers cream-white, center shaded flesh pink, reverse white, very large, very full; intr. 1893

'Graziella' F, ob, Gaujard, R.; bud globular; flowers orange, open, medium, dbl., borne in clusters, slight fragrance; foliage glossy, light green; vigorous, bushy growth; ['Feu Follet' × seedling]; intr. 1960

'Great Century' -- See 'Delegran'

'Great Day' -- See 'Minbco'

'Great Days' HT, lp, ex-Japan; buds pointed, elongated; flowers delicate pink, full; free-flowering

'Great Double White' -- See 'Alba Maxima'

'Great Expectations' -- See 'Jacdal'
'Great Expectations' -- See 'Mackalves'
'Great Expectations' -- See 'Lanican'
'Great Maiden's Blush' ('Alba Regalis', 'La Virginale', R. rubicans, R. incarnata, R. carnea, R. × alba var. rubicunda, R. × alba regalis, R. × alba incarnata, Maiden's Blush, 'Loyalist', 'La Séduisante', 'La Royale', 'Incarnata Major', 'Grande Cuisse de Nymphe', ') A, w, before 1754; bud round; flowers white, tinged pink, petals slightly recurved, 3 in., dbl., globular, borne in clusters of 10-12, intense fragrance; foliage dark green, egg-shaped, pointed; prickles long, slightly hooked; growth branching, tall (5 ft.)
'Great News' F, m, 1976, LeGrice; flowers plum-purple, reverse silver,, 4 in., 33 petals, intense fragrance; foliage large, olive-green; moderate growth; [Rose Gaujard® × 'City of Hereford']; intr. 1973
Great Nord® -- See 'Delgrord'
'Great North' -- See 'Delgrord'
'Great North Eastern Rose' ('Pure Abundace', 'Sir Galahad') F, w, Harkness; flowers pure white, medium, very dbl., borne in large clusters, strong sweet fragrance; repeats quickly; dark green, glossy foliage; vigorous, upright (3 ft × 1 ft.) growth; intr. 2001
'Great Ormond Street' F, my, Beales, Peter; flowers golden yellow, aging to creamy white, dbl., borne in clusters, moderate fragrance; foliage semi-glossy; growth to 2-3 ft.; intr. 1991
'Great Phoebus' -- See 'Hingreat'
'Great Rosarians of the World' HT, ab, 2008, Edwards, Eddie; flowers medium, 4-5 in., full, borne mostly solitary; foliage medium green, semi-glossy; prickles moderate; growth upright, medium (5 ft.); [seedling × seedling]; intr. 2009
'Great Royal' ('Grandesse Royale', 'Grandeur Royale', 'Hortensia', 'Pivoine des Hollandais', 'Regalis') HGal, lp, before 1813, from England; flowers light lilac-rose, globular, borne in clusters of 3-4; foliage thick, rugose; prickles unequal; possibly synonymous with 'Aimable Rouge'
'Great Scott' HT, mp, 1991, Ballin, Don & Paula; peduncles slightly pubescent; flowers large, very full, high-centered; foliage large, medium green, matte; prickles light green with some red, large, hooked down; growth upright (4 ft.), bushy; exhibition; [sport of 'Cleo']
'Great Splash' Min, pb, Bell; flowers striped
'Great Venture' HT, yb, 1971, Dawson, George; bud long, pointed; flowers orange-yellow, flushed pink, medium, dbl., intense fragrance; foliage large, leathery; vigorous, upright growth; ['Daily Sketch' × 'Suspense']; intr. 1970
'Great Wall' S, dp, Ping Lim; flowers blend of red and warm pink, 4 in., semi-dbl., shallow cup to flat; recurrent; foliage starts red and slowly turns to dark green; vigorous (3 ft.) growth; intr. 2005
'Great Western' B, m, 1840, Laffay, M.; flowers purplish maroon, large, dbl.; blooms mostly in early summer; vigorous growth
'Greater Hastings' HT, mp, 1957, Francis
'Greatest Century' -- See 'Delegran'
'Greatheart' HT, op, 1921, Rosenbluth; flowers pale flesh, shaded salmon, center deeper, dbl.; [sport of 'Mrs Walter Easlea']
'Grebetoven' ('Moonlight Sonata') F, w, 2003, Greenwood, Chris; flowers full, borne mostly solitary, intense fragrance; foliage medium size, medium green, matte; prickles medium, straight or slightly hooked, greenish; bushy (4-5 ft.) growth; ['Sheila's Perfume' × 'Silverado']; intr. 2003
'Greblub' ('Blushing Bride') HT, w, 1990, Greenwood, Chris; flowers moderately large, dbl., intense fragrance; foliage large, dark green, semi-glossy; upright, bushy growth; [sport of 'Silverado']
'Greeliz' ('Turn of the Century') F, lp, 1997, Sealand Nurseries, Ltd.; flowers medium, dbl., borne in small clusters; foliage medium size, semi-glossy; some prickles; upright, medium (2-2½ ft.) growth; [Elizabeth of Glamis® × seedling]
'Green Bubbles' Min, w, 1979, Lyon; bud ovoid; flowers light green, 1 in., 12 petals, slight fragrance; foliage tiny; very compact, bushy growth; intr. 1978
'Green Diamond' Min, w, 1975, Moore, Ralph S.; bud pointed, dusty pink; flowers white to soft green, ½ in., 25 petals, cupped; foliage small, leathery; growth upright, bushy; ['polyantha seedling' × 'Sheri Anne']
'Green Dynasty' HT, w; flowers stark white, turning pale greenish-white, large, high-centered, moderate fragrance; recurrent; intr. about 1990
'Green Fire' F, dy, 1959, Swim, H.C.; bud ovoid, pointed; flowers 3 in., 13 petals, flat, borne in clusters, slight fragrance; foliage semi-glossy; vigorous, bushy growth; PP1776; ['Goldilocks' × seedling]; intr. 1958
'Green Ice' Min, w, 1971, Moore, Ralph S.; bud pointed; flowers white to soft green, small, dbl.; foliage small, glossy, leathery; vigorous, dwarf, bushy growth; [(R. wichurana × Floradora) × 'Jet Trail']
'Green Light' -- See 'Ryokkoh'
'Green Planet' HT, w, Spek; flowers yellow with a distinct green tone, dbl.; intr. 2003
'Green Rose' ('La Rose Vert de Chine', 'The Green Rose', R. viridiflora, R. chinensis viridiflora, R. monstrosa) Ch, w, before 1856, Bambridge & Harrison; flowers green, often touched with bronze, with narrow leaf-like petals, 1½-2 in., dbl.; recurrent bloom; medium, upright growth; [probably a sport of 'Parson's Pink China']; known to be in cultivation as early as 1743; some variations with slight red or pink coloration to some petals known to exist
Green Snake® -- See 'Lenwich'
Green Tea® HT, w, Tantau; flowers white with greenish tint, large, double, high-centered, borne mostly singly; recurrent; stems medium to long; florist rose; intr. 2006
'Greenalls Glory' -- See 'Kirmac'
'Greenmantle' HEg, rb, 1895, Penzance; flowers bright rosy red, white eye, golden stamens, single; foliage richly fragrant; very vigorous, tall growth
'Greensleeves' -- See 'Harlenten'
'Greentae' ('Hightae') F, pb, 1988, Greenfield, Mrs. P.L.; flowers clear, medium pink outer petals, deeper in color at the heart, 45-50 petals, high-centered, intense fragrance; foliage small, bronze aging to medium green, glossy; prickles long, curved slightly downward, red; low, bushy, free-flowering growth; ['Duet' × Regensberg®]; intr. 1988
'Greer Garson' HT, pb, 1943, Denoyel, Vve.; bud pointed; flowers begonia-rose, 5 in., 35 petals, high-centered, slight fragrance; foliage leathery, dark; vigorous, tall, bushy growth; PP781
'Greet Koster' Pol, op, 1933, Koster, D.A.; flowers deep pink, shaded salmon, globular, borne in small clusters; recurrent; [sport of 'Margo Koster']
'Greetings' ('Gruss an Berlin') HT, mr, 1965, Kordes, R.; bud ovoid; flowers pure red, 5½ in., 40 petals, high-centered, slight fragrance; foliage dark, glossy; vigorous, upright, bushy growth; intr. 1964
Greetings™ -- See 'Jacdreco'
'Greetings from Alma-Aty' -- See 'Privet iz Alma-Aty'
'Greetje Hennekens' Pol, mr, Loose; flowers carmine-red, medium, semi-dbl.; intr. 1957
'Grefairlynn' (Poopsie™) MinFl, w, 2003, Greenwood, Chris; flowers white with light pink picotee edging, 1-2 in., full, borne in small clusters, no fragrance; foliage medium green, matte; prickles small, straight, greenish red, moderate; upright, tall (3-4 ft.) growth; [Stainless Steel™ × 'Lynn Anderson']
'Greg Chappell' HT, ab; buds deep golden; flowers rich apricot; growth short; intr. 1984
'Greg Moore -- See 'Horgreg'
'Gregart' ('Never Forgotten') HT, mr, 1997, Sealand Nurseries, Ltd.; flowers medium, very dbl., borne in small clusters, moderate fragrance; foliage medium size, dark green; some prickles; growth compact, medium (2-2½ ft.)
'Grégor Mendel' F, op, 1955, Maarse, G.; flowers coral-pink shaded yellow and carmine, dbl.; vigorous growth; ['Pinocchio' × unknown]
'Gregsil' ('April Fool's Day') HT, lp, 1997,

Gregory, C.; flowers medium, very dbl., borne in small clusters, moderate fragrance; foliage medium size, medium green, semi-glossy; some prickles; growth bushy, medium (2½-3 ft.); [sport of 'Silver Jubilee']

'Grejo' w, Gressard; intr. 1987

'Greliz' (Elizabeth Marie™) HT, rb, 2007, Greenwood, Chris; flowers bright red, reverse white, 4-5 in., dbl., borne mostly solitary; foliage medium green, semi-glossy; prickles ¼ in., hooked downward, green, moderate; growth upright; [Stainless Steel™ × 'Rosie O'Donnell']

'Grelovie' (Leah June™) HT, pb, 2007, Greenwood, Chris; flowers medium pink, reverse creamy white, 4-5 in., full, borne mostly solitary; foliage medium green, semi-glossy; prickles ¼ in., slightly hooked downward, green, moderate; growth upright, medium; cutting, exhibition, garden; [Stainless Steel™ × 'Rosie O'Donnell']; intr. 2007

'Greluv' ('Vernon Love') HP, mp, 2001, Greenwood, Chris; bud large; flowers old-fashioned, dusky pink, light pink reverse, 5-6 in., very full, borne mostly solitary, moderate fragrance; foliage large, dark green, semi-glossy; prickles few, medium, hooked downward, green; growth bushy, tall (5-6 ft.); garden decorative, exhibition; [Baronne Edmond de Rothschild® × 'Silverado']

'Grem' HT, yb, 1950, Meilland, F.; intr. 1950

'Gremlin' S, mr, Kordes; flowers bright cherry-red, reverse cream and yellow; growth healthy, compact plant; intr. 2002

'Gremsar' ('Grimpant Grand'mère Jenny') Cl HT, yb, 1959, Meilland, F.; intr. 1958

'Grenadier' HT, mr, 1930, Dickson, A.; flowers brilliant currant-red shaded scarlet, dbl., cupped; foliage rich green, leathery, glossy; vigorous, bushy growth

'Grenadier' -- See 'Fusilier'

Grenadine™ -- See 'Poulgrena'

'Grenadine' -- See 'Granadina'

'Grenewgov' (The Governator™) MinFl, or, 2003, Greenwood, Chris; flowers brilliant orange-red, long-lasting, 2-3 in., full, high-centered, borne mostly solitary, no fragrance; recurrent; foliage medium green, matte; prickles medium, slightly hooked downward, pale amber; growth compact, medium (1-2 ft.); garden decoration, exhibition; ['Silverado' × 'Ingrid Bergman']; intr. 2004

'Grenoble, Climbing' Cl HT, mr, 1939, Western Rose Co.

'Grenoble' -- See 'Ville de Grenoble'

'Grerickie' (Rickie-Tickie™) MinFl, or, 2003, Greenwood, Chris; flowers bright orange fading to pink, medium, single, borne mostly solitary, no fragrance; foliage medium size, dark green, semi-glossy; prickles medium, slightly curved upward, light greenish yellow; upright, medium (2-3 ft.) growth; [Sunset Celebration™ × 'First Prize']

'Greta' ('Gaston Lenôtre') F, w, Briant; intr. 1995

'Greta Fey' HWich, lp, 1909, Strassheim; flowers creamy pink, small, semi-dbl., borne in clusters

'Greta Kluis' Pol, mr, 1916, Kluis & Koning; flowers carmine-red; [sport of 'Echo']

'Greta Kluis Superior' Pol, mr, 1928, Kluis; flowers deep carmine-red; [sport of 'Tausendschön']

'Gretag' ('Terrell Anne') F, lp, 1991, Greenwood, Chris; bud ovoid; flowers medium, full, high-centered, borne in small clusters, slight fragrance; foliage medium size, medium green, glossy; some prickles; medium (90 cm.), upright growth; [sport of 'Gene Boerner']

'Grete Bermbach' HT, pb, 1925, Leenders Bros.; flowers silvery flesh, center rose, sometimes shaded yellow orange, dbl.; ['Mrs Aaron Ward' × 'Pharisaer']

'Grete Schickendanz' HT, Kordes, R.; intr. 1987

'Grete Schreiber' Pol, mp, 1916, Altmüller; flowers medium, full

'Gretel Greul' HT, mr, 1939, Greul; [sport of 'Rote Rapture']

'Gretelein' HFt, lp, 1933, Schmitt, K.; flowers large, semi-dbl.

'Grethe Poulsen' Pol, dp, 1928, Poulsen, S.; flowers light cherry-red, base yellow, semi-dbl.; early; dwarf, well branched growth; ['Ellen Poulsen' × 'Mme Laurette Messimy']

'Gretoots' ('Tootsie') F, pb, 1991, Greenwood, Chris; flowers deep pink painted white, reverse mostly white, aging with a slight fading of pink, medium, 20 petals, loose, borne in sprays of 5 - 7, slight fragrance; foliage medium size, dark green, glossy, disease-resistant; upright, bushy, rounded, medium growth; ['Angel Face' × 'Old Master']; intr. 1991

'Gretta' -- See 'Spogret'

'Grevilii' ('Grevillea', 'Roxburghiana') HMult, w, before 1828; flowers single

'Grevillea' -- See 'Grevilii'

'Grevillia Rose' -- See 'Seven Sisters'

'Grevinde Rose Danneskjold Samsöe' HT, dr, 1914, Poulsen, D.T.; bud dark velvety red; flowers scarlet

'Grevinde Sylvia Knuth' HWich, w, 1913, Poulsen, D.T.; bud yellow; flowers white, center yellow, 3 cm., semi-dbl., borne in clusters of 8-10; foliage narrow, glossy

'Grey Dawn' F, m, 1976, LeGrice; flowers gray, reverse flushed pink and gold, 3-4 in., 45 petals, moderate fragrance; foliage glossy; bushy growth; ['Brownie' × News®]; intr. 1975

'Grey Kollege' -- See 'Jacolman'

'Grey Pearl' ('The Mouse') HT, m, 1945, McGredy; bud ovoid; flowers lavender-gray, shaded olive and tan, 4-4½ in., 43 petals, high-centered, moderate fragrance; foliage glossy; vigorous growth; PP680; [('Mrs Charles Lamplough' × seedling) × ('Sir David Davis' × 'Southport')]

'Grey Pearl, Climbing' Cl HT, m, 1951, Caluya; PP1089

'Gribaldo Nicola' T, w, 1891, Soupert & Notting; flowers white with touches of yellow, 11-12 cm., dbl., moderate fragrance; very remontant; foliage large, rounded; vigorous (8 ft × 6 ft.) growth; ['Bouquet d'Or' × 'La Sylphide']

'Grido' F, or, Pironti, N.; flowers semi-dbl.; intr. 1972

'Grifed' ('Edna Wilson') HT, my, 1983, Griffiths, Trevor; flowers large, dbl., moderate fragrance; foliage glossy; upright, vigorous growth; [sport of 'Beauté']; intr. 1973

'Griff's Red' S, mr, 2001, Buck, Dr. Griffith J.; bud clear ruby red; flowers clear ruby red, large, full, borne mostly solitary, moderate fragrance; foliage medium size, medium green, semi-glossy; prickles moderate; growth upright, medium (45-50 cm.); ['Amiga Mia' × 'Music Maker']; intr. 2002

'Grillodale' HT, lp, 1926, Grillo; flowers light pink, center deeper, 4½ in., 50 petals; foliage dark; [sport of 'Mme Butterfly']

Grimaldi® F, pb, Delbard; flowers deep pink striped and splashed with lighter pink and white, semi-dbl., loose, borne in clusters; intr. 1997

'Grimbeert' HT, Delforge, H.; intr. 1995

'Grimm' LCl, pb, 1932, Lambert, P.; flowers apple-blossom-pink, center white, stamens golden, edges fluted, single; non-recurrent; vigorous growth; [('Hiawatha' × Altmarker) × ('Mme Leon Pain' × 'Marquise de Sinéty')]

'Grimpant All Gold' -- See 'Allgold, Climbing'

Grimpant Allgold® -- See 'Allgold, Climbing'

'Grimpant Baronne de Rothschild' -- See 'Meigrisosar'

Grimpant Bettina® -- See 'Mepalsar'

Grimpant Cap Horn® -- See 'Dormodesar'

Grimpant Carina® -- See 'Meichimsar'

'Grimpant Chrysler Imperial' -- See 'Chrysler Imperial, Climbing'

'Grimpant Clair Matin' -- See 'Meimont'

'Grimpant Comtesse Vandal' -- See 'Comtesse Vandal, Climbing'

'Grimpant Crimson Glory' -- See 'Crimson Glory, Climbing'

'Grimpant Danse des Sylphes' -- See 'Malcair'

'Grimpant Delbard' ('Delbard's Orange Climber') LCl, or, 1965, Delbard-Chabert; bud ovoid; flowers medium, dbl., high-centered, borne in small clusters; repeat bloom; foliage dark, glossy, leathery; vigorous, climbing, well branched growth; PP2573; ['Spectacular' × ('Rome Glory' × 'La Vaudoise')]; intr. 1963

Grimpant Diablotin® -- See 'Delposar'

'Gp. Domaine de Courson' -- See 'Meidrimy'

'Grimpant Double Delight' -- See 'Aroclidd'

'Grimpant Ena Harkness' -- See 'Ena Harkness, Climbing'

'Grimpant Eric Tabarly' -- See 'Meidrason'

'Grimpant Étoile de Hollande' -- See 'Étoile de Hollande, Climbing'

Grimpant Exploit® -- See 'Meilider'

'Grimpant Grand'mère Jenny' -- See 'Gremsar'

Grimpant Le Grand Huit® -- See 'Commandant Cousteau, Climbing'

Grimpant Lilli Marleen® -- See 'Peklimasar'

'Grimpant Marie Claire' -- See 'Marie Claire, Climbing'

'Grimpant Michael Jones' -- See 'Michael Jones'

'Grimpant Michèle Meilland' -- See 'Michèle Meilland, Climbing'

'Grimpant Mrs Herbert Stevens' -- See 'Mrs Herbert Stevens, Climbing'

'Grimpant Opera' -- See 'Opera, Climbing'

Grimpant Orange Meillandina® -- See 'Meijikatarsar'

Grimpant Papa Meilland® -- See 'Papa Meilland, Climbing'

'Grimpant Pierre Bonnard' -- See 'Pierre Bonnard'

Grimpant Pierre de Ronsard® -- See 'Meiviolin'

'Grimpant Queen Elizabeth' -- See 'Queen Elizabeth, Climbing'

'Grimpant Reine des Neiges' -- See 'Frau Karl Druschki, Climbing'

'Grimpant Rimosa' -- See 'Meigronurisar'

Grimpant Rose Gaujard® -- See 'Rose Gaujard, Climbing'

'Grimpant Rouge et Or' -- See 'Dicorsar'

'Grimpant Roxane' -- See 'Roxane, Climbing'

Grimpant Sonia Meilland® -- See 'Sonia, Climbing'

Grimpant Soraya® -- See 'Soraya, Climbing'

'Grimpant Sutter's Gold' -- See 'Sutter's Gold, Climbing'

'Grimpant Tiffany' -- See 'Tiffany, Climbing'

Grimpant Vendée Globe® -- See 'Vendée Globe, Climbing'

Grimpant Violette Parfumee® -- See 'Melodie Parfumée, Climbing'

Gripsholm™ -- See 'Poullug'

'Grisbi' ('Sunlight') HT, my, 1958, Meilland, F.; bud ovoid with conspicuous neck; flowers canary yellow, fading to light yellow, 4 in., 43-48 petals, high-centered to cupped, borne usually singly, moderate tea fragrance; recurrent; foliage medium size, leathery; prickles numerous, medium, straight; stems medium; vigorous, upright, bushy growth; hips ovoid, smooth, green; PP1576; [('Eclipse' × 'Ophelia') × 'Monte Carlo']; intr. 1956

'Grisbi' F, my, Meilland; bud conical; flowers yellow, petal edges turning white, 6-7 cm., 18-20 petals, cupped, borne usually singly, no fragrance; recurrent; foliage dark green, semi-matte; prickles average, small, tan; erect (4-5 ft.) growth; PP7313; ['Sonia' × 'Golden Times']; greenhouse rose; intr. 1989

'Grisbi' F, my, Richardier; flowers clear yellow, large, full, moderate anise fragrance; growth to 110-120 cm.; intr. 1999

'Grisbi, Climbing' -- See 'Sunlight, Climbing'

'Griseldis' LCl, mp, 1895, Geschwind, R.; flowers dark pink, darker at center, fading to light pink, 8-9 cm., semi-dbl., flat, borne in clusters of 1-6, no fragrance; some autumn repeat; [(R. canina × a Hybrid Tea) × (R. canina × a Bourbon)]; hybrid canina

'Griseldis' F, w, Select Roses, B.V.

'Grootendorst' -- See 'F. J. Grootendorst'

'Grootendorst Magenta' HRg, m, Vidal

'Grootendorst Pink' -- See 'Pink Grootendorst'

'Grootendorst Red' -- See 'F. J. Grootendorst'

'Grootendorst Supreme' HRg, dr, 1936, Grootendorst, F.J.; flowers deeper crimson-red, small, full; [sport of 'F.J. Grootendorst']

'Gros Choux d'Hollande' ('Grosse Hollande') C, lp, before 1820; flowers soft rose-pink, medium, dbl., intense fragrance; foliage doubly dentate; vigorous growth

'Gros Pompon' -- See 'Petite de Hollande'

'Gros Provins Panaché' -- See 'Provins Panaché'

'Grosse Cerise' HGal, mr, before 1810, Dupont

'Grosse Hollande' -- See 'Gros Choux d'Hollande'

'Grosse Mohnkopfs Rose' ('Grandesse Royale', 'Tête de Pavot', 'Rose Pavot', 'Poppy Rose', 'Papaverina Major', 'Pavot') S, dp, before 1799, Schwarzkopf; flowers bright rose, 3 in., dbl.; foliage oval-acuminate, finely dentate, villose beneath; few prickles

'Grossherzog Ernst Ludwig von Hesse' ('Red Maréchal Niel') Cl HT, mp, 1888, Müller, Dr. F.; flowers silvery carmine, very large, very dbl., intense fragrance; ['Pierre Notting' × 'Maréchal Niel']

'Grossherzog Friedrich von Baden' HT, mp, 1908, Lambert, P.; flowers carmine rose pink, medium, dbl., intense fragrance; ['Mme Caroline Testout' × 'Meta']

'Grossherzog Wilhelm Ernst von Sachsen' HT, dp, 1915, Welter; flowers bright scarlet with carmine rose, large, dbl., intense fragrance; ['Mme Mélanie Soupert' × 'Lyon Rose']

'Grossherzogin Alexandra' HT, w, 1904, Jacobs; flowers yellowish-white, large, full; ['Merveille de Lyon' × 'Kaiserin Auguste Viktoria']

'Grossherzogin Eleonore von Hessen' HMult, m, 1907, Strassheim; flowers dark violet-red, fading to crimson, 3 cm., dbl., borne in small to medium clusters, no fragrance; ['a multiflora' × 'Turner's Crimson Rambler']

'Grossherzogin Feodora von Sachsen' HT, w, 1914, Kiese; flowers creamy white, base deep yellow; ['Frau Karl Druschki' × 'Kaiserin Auguste Viktoria']

'Grossherzogin Josefine Schararolle' HT, lp, Lens, Louis; flowers medium-large, dbl.; intr. 1989

'Grossherzogin Mathilde' ('Grand Duchess Hilda') T, w, 1869, Vogler; flowers white, tinged green, large, dbl.; [sport of 'Bougère']

'Grossherzogin Mathilde' -- See 'Princesse Olympie'

'Grossherzogin Viktoria Melitta von Hessen' ('Grand Duchess Victoria Melita') HT, w, 1897, Lambert; flowers cream with a yellow center, very large, full, borne mostly solitary; foliage large; ['Safrano' × 'Mme Caroline Testout']

'Grossmütterchen' HCh, mp, Weihrauch; flowers large, very dbl.; intr. 1983

'Ground Zero' -- See 'Welhonor'

'Grouse' -- See 'Korimro'

'Grouse 2000' -- See 'Kortraste'

Grove™ -- See 'Grove Cottage'

'Grove Cottage' ('Grove'™) S, dp, Poulsen; flowers deep pink to light red, less than 2 in., single, shallow cup, borne in clusters, very slight fragrance; recurrent; foliage dark green, glossy; flat, bushy (40-60 cm.) growth; intr. 2004

'Grugakind' Pol, op; flowers small, dbl.

'Grulit' ('Littlest Spartan') Min, rb, 1992, Gruenbauer, Richard; flowers medium red and yellow, 1 in., 22-30 petals, borne mostly singly, no fragrance; foliage medium size, medium green, semi-glossy; some prickles; growth low (20-30 cm.),upright, bushy; ['Red Ace' × seedling]

'Grumpy' ('Burkhard', 'Burkhardt') Pol, mp, 1956, deRuiter; flowers pink, small, dbl., borne in long trusses

'Gruppenkönigin' F, pb, 1935, Kordes, H.; flowers deep bicolor pink, very large, dbl.; foliage light, leathery; vigorous, bushy growth; ['Gruss an Aachen' × 'Mme Edouard Herriot']

'Gruss an Aachen' ('Salut d'Aix la Chapelle') F, lp, 1909, Geduldig; bud orange-red and yellow; flowers flesh-pink fading to creamy white, 3-3½ in., 40-45 petals, borne in clusters, slight sweet fragrance; foliage rich green, leathery; slender stems, will nod; dwarf growth; ['Frau Karl Druschki' × 'Franz Deegen']

'Gruss an Aachen, Climbing' Cl F, lp, 1937, Kordes; flowers ivory-white, enriched with apricot-pink, large, full; [sport of 'Gruss an Aachen']

'Gruss an Aachen Superior' HT, lp, 1942, Leenders; flowers blush white, large, full; presumably a sport of 'Gruss an Aachen'

Gruss an Angeln® HT, mr, Clausen;

intr. 1986

'Gruss an Baden-Baden' Cl Min, mr, Warner; flowers shining, warm ruby red; intr. 2000

Gruss an Bayern® -- See 'Kormun'

'Gruss an Berlin' -- See 'Greetings'

'Gruss an Breinegg' HMult, dp, 1925, Bruder Alfons; flowers light reddish-violet, fading almost white, small, single, borne in medium clusters

'Gruss an Coburg' HT, ab, 1927, Felberg-Leclerc; flowers apricot-yellow, reverse coppery pink, large, full, globular, intense fragrance; foliage bronze; vigorous growth; ['Alice Kaempff' × 'Souv. de Claudius Pernet']

'Gruss an Dresden' HT, mr, 1913, Türke; flowers fiery red; ['Princesse de Bearn' × unknown]

'Gruss an Föhr' HFt, yb, 1930, Riewers; flowers medium, semi-dbl.

'Gruss an Freundorf' HWich, dr, 1913, Praskac; flowers dark velvety crimson, center whitish, stamens bright yellow, 4-5 cm., semi-dbl., borne in clusters; foliage small, glossy; numerous prickles; [R. wichurana rubra × 'Crimson Rambler']

'Gruss an Friedberg' N, dy, 1902, Rogmanns; flowers pale yellow with golden center, medium to large, dbl., moderate fragrance; [sport of 'Duarte de Oliveira']

'Gruss an Germershausen' HMult, rb, 1926, Bruder Alfons; flowers crimson red, white center, 2-3 cm., single, borne in very large clusters; foliage medium green, somewhat glossy

'Gruss an Hannover' HMult, op, 1938, Lahmann; flowers orange pink, 6 cm., dbl.; vigorous, upright (10-13 ft.) growth

'Gruss an Heidelberg' -- See 'Korbe'

'Gruss an Koblenz' LCl, mr, 1963, Kordes, R.; flowers bright scarlet, 3 in., 20 petals, borne in clusters (up to 10); recurrent bloom; vigorous growth

'Gruss an Lorrach' F, Hetzel, K.; intr. 1983

'Gruss an Maiengrun' F, or, Huber; intr. 1986

'Gruss an Munchen' F, Tantau, Math.; intr. 1962

'Gruss an Naumburg' HT, rb, 1928, Muller, J.F.; flowers medium, dbl.

'Gruss an Oldenburg' S, yb, Weihrauch; intr. 1995

'Gruss an Rengsdorf' S, mp, 1920, Boden-Kurtscheid; flowers medium, single; very hardy; hybrid canina

'Gruss an Sangerhausen' HT, mr, 1904, Müller, Dr. F.; flowers brilliant scarlet, center crimson, very large, dbl., moderate fragrance; ['Pierre Notting' × 'Safrano']

'Gruss an Steinfurth' F, my, 1961, Leenders, J.; flowers open, 21 petals, cupped, borne in large clusters (to 15); moderate growth; ['Goldilocks' × 'Masquerade']

'Gruss an Stuttgart' F, mr, 1976, Hetzel; bud ovoid; flowers velvety red, medium, dbl.; vigorous, bushy growth; [(Carina® × seedling) × 'Sans Souci']

'Gruss an Teplitz' ('Virginia R. Coxe') HCh, mr, 1894, Geschwind, R.; bud small, ovoid; flowers dark velvety scarlet, medium, 33 petals, borne on short, weak stems, intense spicy fragrance; recurrent bloom; foliage dark, young growth bronze-red; short, weak stems; vigorous (6 ft.), bushy growth; good for hedges; [(('Sir Joseph Paxton' × 'Fellenberg') × 'Papa Gontier') × 'Gloire des Rosomanes']

'Gruss an Teplitz, Climbing' ('Catalunya', 'Virginia R. Coxe, Climbing') Cl HCh, mr, 1911, Storrs & Harrison Co. (also Nonin, 1919); flowers crimson, 5-7 cm., cupped, borne in small clusters; [sport of 'Gurss an Teplitz']

'Gruss an Weimar' HP, pb, 1919, Kiese; flowers pink on yellowish ground, very large, full; ['Frau Karl Druschki' × 'Lyon Rose']

'Gruss an Wörishofen' -- See 'Bad Wörishofen'

'Gruss an Zabern' HMult, w, 1903, Lambert, P.; flowers full, borne in large clusters, intense spicy-sweet fragrance; numerous prickles; growth vigorous, climbing (4-5 m.); ['Euphrosine' × 'Mme Ocker Ferencz']

'Gruss an Zweibrücken' HT, mr, 1915, Lambert, P.; flowers large, dbl.; ['Charles Gater' × 'Mme Caroline Testout']

'Gruss aus Alma-aty' HT, Sushkov, K. L.; intr. 1958

'Gruss aus Pallien' HP, rb, 1900, Welter; bud long; flowers bright fiery red with purple center, cupped, moderate fragrance; ['Baronne Adolphe de Rothschild' × 'Princesse de Béarn']

'Gruss vom Westerwald' HT, op, 1914, Kettenbeil; flowers medium, dbl.; ['Mme Caroline Testout' × 'Mme Ravary']

'Gruss von Tannenhof' HMult, w, 1913, Friedrich; flowers bright white, 3 cm., dbl., borne in large clusters

'Guadalajara' -- See 'Macdeepo'

'Guadalupe Volunteer' -- See 'Hrgvolunteer'

'Guadalupe's Love' HT, w, 1997, Price, Kathleen M.; flowers ruffled, medium, very dbl., borne mostly singly; foliage medium size, medium green, semi-glossy; upright, medium (2½ to 3ft.) growth; [sport of 'Bewitched']

'Guardian Angel' F, ab; flowers soft orange-buff with yellow stamens, double, open, moderate fragrance; recurrent; sturdy (3 ft.) growth; intr. 2007

'Guardsman' HT, or, 1937, Archer; flowers bright scarlet, base yellow, large, dbl.; foliage glossy; vigorous, compact growth; [seedling × 'Shot Silk']

'Gudhem' -- See 'Gudhemsrosen'

'Gudhemsrosen' ('Gudhem') A, w; flowers pure white, large, single, borne in early blooming; plentiful bloom; growth to 5 ft.; unknown origin and date

'Guenille' -- See 'Œillet'

'Guernsey Gold' -- See 'Trobguern'

'Guernsey Love' -- See 'Troblove'

'Guerreiro' Cl F, dr, Moreira da Silva; [seedling × 'Alain']

'Guescan' ('Cerys Ann') HT, yb, 1997, Guest, M.M.; flowers medium, very dbl., borne mostly singly; foliage large, dark green, glossy; some prickles; bushy, medium (30 in.)growth; ['Fulton Mackay' × 'Freedom']

'Guescolour' ('Brushstrokes') F, yb, 1999, Guest, M.M.; flowers yellow and red striped, reverse paler, large, full, borne in small clusters; foliage medium size, dark green, glossy; few prickles; upright, medium (28 in.) growth; [seedling × 'Solitaire']; intr. 1999

'Guesdelay' ('Birthday Wishes') HT, rb, 1997, Guest, M.M.; flowers large, very dbl., borne mostly singly; foliage large, dark green, glossy; some prickles; upright, medium (30in.) growth; ['Fragrant Cloud' × 'Honey Favourite']

'Guesgenus' ('Ted Allen') HT, ly, 1997, Guest, M.M.; flowers medium, dbl., borne mostly singly; foliage medium size, medium green, dull; some prickles; upright, medium (28 in.) growth; ['Manx Queen' × ('Manx Queen' × R. bella)]

'Guesideal' ('Claire's Dream') HT, mr, 2001, Guest, M.; flowers 4-5 in., full, borne mostly solitary, moderate fragrance; foliage large, dark green (red when young), glossy; prickles up to ½ in., hooked, moderate; growth upright, tall (40 in.); garden decorative, exhibition; ['Gordon's College' × 'Red Planet']; intr. 2002

'Guesimage' ('Mum's Blessing') F, w, 2007, Guest, M.; flowers cream, medium, full, borne in small clusters; foliage medium, light green, matte, very healthy, blackspot-resistant; prickles 12 mm., hooked, moderate; growth bushy, medium (26 in.); garden decoration; ['Ted Allen' × ('Baby Love' × seedling)]; intr. 2008

'Gueslaylow' ('Moonglow') S, w, 2004, Guest, M.; flowers white to pink, reverse white, 3 in., full, borne in large clusters, moderate fragrance; foliage medium size, dark green, glossy; prickles up to ½ in., hooked,; growth spreading, medium (30 in.), groundcover; [('Morgengruss' × 'Baby Love') × Flower Carpet™]; intr. 2006

'Guesmarble' ('Artistic Licence') HT, rb, 2007, Guest, M.; flowers red with variable yellow stripes, 4½ in., full, borne mostly solitary; foliage medium size, dark green, glossy; prickles ½ in., hooked, moderate; growth upright, tall (40 in.); garden decoration, exhibition; [seedling × 'Red Planet']; intr. 2007

'Guesoverlay' ('Ivory Castle') LCl, w, 2007, Guest, M.; flowers ivory to cream, up to 4 in., full, borne in small clusters; foliage medium size, dark green, semi-glossy;

prickles ½ in, hooked, moderate; growth upright, tall (up to 8 ft.); garden decoration; [Westerland® × ('Morgengruss' × 'Baby Love')]; intr. 2008

'Guestall' ('Just Reward') Cl HT, ob, 1994, Guest, M.M.; flowers orange, 3-3½ in., dbl., borne mostly singly; foliage medium size, medium green, glossy; some prickles; tall (6-8 ft.), upright growth; ['Basildon Bond' × Alexander®]; intr. 1994

'Guglielmo Betto' S, dp; intr. 2001

'Guglielmo Marconi' HT, w, 1934, Giacomasso; flowers almost white, tinted flesh; ['Ophelia' × 'Elisabeth Faurax']

'Guglielmo Marconi' -- See 'Harbleep'

'Guiding Spirit' -- See 'Harwolave'

Guido A. Zäch® HT, rb, Huber; flowers bright red with golden-yellow reverse, full; intr. 2005

'Guildfordian' HT, w; flowers pale cream; thornless; long stems; medium growth

'Guillaume' ('Puerto del Sol') F, ob, Delbard; flowers bright orange with yellow reverse, dbl., cupped, borne in large clusters; recurrent; growth vigorous (3 ft.); intr. 1999

'Guillaume Gillemot' HP, dp, 1880, Schwartz; flowers carmine pink with pale silvery reflections, very large, full, globular

'Guillaume Kaempff' HT, dr, 1931, Felberg-Leclerc; flowers dark crimson-red, edged blackish, large, dbl.; foliage thick; vigorous growth; ['Hadley' × 'Admiral Ward']

'Guillaume Tell' HGal, lp, before 1835, from Angers; flowers bright light pink, large, full, globular

'Guimiru' HT, op, Guillot; buds slender, pointeddbl.; intr. 1984

'Guinea Gold' HT, ab, 1945, Joseph H. Hill, Co.; bud long, pointed, buff-yellow; flowers apricot-yellow, open, dbl.; foliage dark, leathery; strong stems; vigorous, upright, much branched growth; PP600; ['Joanna Hill' × 'Golden Rapture']

'Guinée' Cl HT, dr, 1938, Mallerin, C.; bud pointed; flowers velvety blackish garnet, sometimes mottled scarlet, 3-3½ in., dbl., borne in small clusters, intense fragrance; occasional repeat; foliage leathery; growth to 6½-9 ft.; ['Souv. de Claudius Denoyel' × 'Ami Quinard']

'Guinevere' HT, mp, 1967, Harkness; flowers 4½ in., 40 petals; foliage glossy; ['Red Dandy' × 'Peace']

Guinevere™ -- See 'Harbadge'

'Guinguette' F, pb, 1958, Gaujard, R.; flowers pink edged darker, well-formed, cupped; vigorous growth; ['Alain' × 'Feu de Joie']

'Guirime' HT, op, Guillot; intr. 1984

'Guirlande d'Amour' -- See 'Lenalbi'

'Guirlande Diamand' LCl, w; flowers small, single, borne in clusters; spring bloomer; foliage smooth, glossy; growth vigorous (4-6 m.) climbing, or used as groundcover; [unknown × unknown]; seedling found growing at nursery

'Guirlande Fleurie' ('Flower Garland') LCl, mr, 1970, Robichon; bud ovoid; flowers bright red, large, semi-dbl., cupped, borne in large clusters; foliage leathery; very vigorous, climbing growth; ['Valenciennes' × 'Paul's Scarlet Climber']

'Guiseppe Motta' HT, pb, 1936, Heizmann, E.; bud long; flowers flesh-pink, reverse red and yellow, large, semi-dbl., intense fresh, fruity fragrance; recurrent; vigorous growth

Guitare® F, ob, 1963, Gaujard; bud ovoid; flowers gold and orange-red blend, medium, dbl.; foliage light green, leathery; vigorous, bushy growth; ['Vendome' × 'Golden Slippers']

'Guitare, Climbing' Cl F, ob, Kasturi; flowers brilliant orange pink; [sport of 'Guitare']; intr. 1974

Guizzo Rosso® F, dr, Barni; flowers intense red, semi-dbl.; constant bloom; foliage glossy, healthy; moderate (80-100 cm.) growth; intr. 2005

'Gulab Angree Nashik' -- See 'Rose City of Nashik'

'Gulab-E-Pal' HT, m, 1986, Hardikar, Dr. M.N.; flowers mauve, blended with yellow, 70 petals, high-centered, borne singly, moderate fragrance; foliage medium size, light green; prickles brown; upright growth; ['Festival Beauty' × ('Scarlet Knight' × 'Festival Beauty')]; intr. 1985

'Guldtop' HSpn, dy; [R. spinosissima × unknown]

'Gulf Breeze' -- See 'Talgul'

'Gulgong Gold' HT, yb

'Gull Dagmar' -- See 'Moryelrug'

'Gulletta' -- See 'Rugul'

'Gulliver's Glow' S, mr, 1954, Gulliver; flowers bright red, small, dbl., borne in very large clusters; thornless; bushy growth; very hardy; ['Hiawatha' × (R. maximowicziana pilosa × Tausendschon)]

'Gulnare' HT, my, 1918, Poulsen, D.T.; flowers golden yellow

'Gulzar' HT, dr, 1971, IARI; buds medium, pointed; flowers deep magenta-red, satiny, dbl., high-centered, borne singly and several together; foliage medium size, light green, leathery; growth vigorous, bushy

'Gumdrop' -- See 'Jacgum'

'Guna' HRg, mr, Rieksta; flowers bright, light red, semi-dbl., loose, moderate fragrance; bushy, tall (4-5 ft. tall and wide) growth; winter hardy; intr. 1980

'Gundis Rose' HT, mr, Kordes; flowers velvety red, 8 cm., double, high-centered, borne singly and several together, no fragrance; recurrent; foliage dark green, glossy; stems long, thick; growth upright, well-branched; intr. 2007

'Gundy' F, dp, 1967, Schloen, P.; bud ovoid; flowers deep rose-pink, semi-dbl., cupped, borne in clusters, slight fragrance; foliage dark; vigorous, upright growth; intr. 1966

'Gunnels Ros' -- See 'Meirisouru'

'Gunner's Mate' S, rb, Dickson; intr. 2000

'Gunsei' Cl F, pb, 1987, Kikuchi, Rikichi; flowers white flushed pink on fringe, 13-15 petals, cupped, borne in large clusters; foliage 7 leaflet, green; no prickles; vigorous, upright growth; [seedling × 'Summer Snow']; intr. 1988

'Gunston Hall' HT, mr, 1929, U.S. Dept. of Agric.; flowers scarlet-crimson; [seedling × 'Hoosier Beauty']

'Guo Se Tian Xiang' Ch, mr

'Gurney Benham' HT, my, 1935, Cant, B. R.; flowers buttercup-yellow, large, dbl., cupped; foliage glossy, bronze; vigorous, bushy growth; [sport of 'Lady Forteviot']

'Gurney Hill' HT, mr, 1924, E.G. Hill, Co.; flowers pure red, dbl.

'Gussie' Min, pb, 1980, Lorenzen, Frederick; bud ovoid; flowers medium red, reverse pale pink and silver, 90 petals, high-centered, borne singly, slight fragrance; foliage green, leathery; few prickles; bushy, dwarf growth; [seedling × seedling]

'Gustav Frahm' ('Andenken an Gustav Frahm') F, mr, 1959, Kordes; flowers crimson-scarlet, 3 in., 25 petals, flat, borne in large clusters; foliage light, glossy; vigorous, upright growth; ['Fanal' × 'Ama']; 1960 Annual lists registered name as Gustav Frahm

'Gustav Grünerwald' HT, pb, 1903, Lambert, P.; flowers carmine-pink, center yellow, large, full, cupped; ['Safrano' × 'Mme Caroline Testout']

'Gustav Sobry' HT, yb, 1902, Welter; flowers golden yellow and red, large; ['Kaiserin Auguste Viktoria' × 'Comte Chandon']

'Gustave Bonnet' N, w, 1864, Lacharme; flowers pure white, aging to whitish pink, shaded carmine, medium to large, full

'Gustave Coraux' HP, m, 1856, Robert

Gustave Courbet® -- See 'Saubord'

'Gustave Piganeau' HP, mr, 1889, Pernet-Ducher; flowers bright carmine, very large, dbl., cupped; growth moderate

'Gustave Régis' HT, ly, 1890, Pernet-Ducher; flowers creamy yellow, large, semi-dbl.; [possibly a seedling of 'Mlle Blanche Durrschmidt']

'Gustave Révilliod' HP, mp, 1876, Schwartz; flowers pink, tinted dark red at center, purplish at edges, large, full; foliage medium size, thick, dark green, semi-glossy; prickles small, arched, green; ['Victor Verdier' × unknown]

'Gustave Rousseau' HP, m, 1862, Fargeton; flowers violet with fiery red edges, large, full

'Gustave Thierry' HP, dp, 1881, Oger; flowers bright cherry red fading to lilac pink, full, globular

'Gustel Löbner' HT, w, 1927, Löbner; flowers large, dbl.

'Gustel Mayer' Pol, mr, 1909, Lambert, P.; flowers light red, middle yellow, small, dbl.; ['Turner's Crimson Rambler'

× ('Mme Pierre Cochet' × 'Dunkelrote Hermosa')]
Gute Besserung™ -- See 'Pouldron'
'Gütersloh' S, rb, Noack; flowers magenta tinted with crimson and white at the petal bases, dbl., cupped; arching growth; intr. 1969
Gutersloh 85® S, mr
Guy de Maupassant™ -- See 'Meisocrat'
'Guy Fawkes' F, yb, 1976, Cadle's Roses; flowers yellow center, reverse shading scarlet, large, 15 petals, intense fragrance; foliage glossy; ['My Choice' × 'Masquerade']; intr. 1975
'Guy-Guy' F, ab, 1966, Fankhauser; flowers apricot and pink, edged crimson, small, dbl.; foliage dark, glossy, leathery; low, compact growth; [('Circus' × 'Circus') × ('Circus' × 'Circus')]
'Guy Laroche' -- See 'Delricos'
'Guy Savoy' S, rb, Delbard; flowers deep red striped with rosy white, moderate fruity, aromatic fragrance; vigorous growth; intr. 2002
'Guy's Gold' HT, dy, Harkness; intr. 2008
'Guyscliffe' -- See 'Lindliffe'
'Gwen Fagan' -- See 'Poulgewfa'
'Gwen Marie' F, rb, 1964, Robins; flowers dark red, center light cream, open, large, semi-dbl.; foliage soft; tall growth; ['Dainty Bess' × unknown]
'Gwen Mayor' -- See 'Cocover'
'Gwen Nash' Cl HT, pb, 1920, Clark, A.; flowers rich pink, center white, 4-5 in., semi-dbl., cupped; reliable repeat; foliage glaucous, wrinkled; vigorous, climbing growth; ['Rosy Morn' × 'Scorcher']
'Gwen Swane' -- See 'Macwhaka'
'Gwendoline Collins' HT, mr, 1937, Clark, A.; flowers cerise shaded cherry, large, dbl., globular; vigorous, bushy growth
Gwent™ -- See 'Poulurt'
'Gwyneth' HT, ly, Chaplin Bros.; flowers canary-yellow, without shading; ['Willowmere' × 'Mrs Wemyss Quin']; intr. 1928
'Gwyneth' Pol, ly, 1923, Woosman; flowers pale yellow, tinted lemon, changing to nearly white, open, medium, semi-dbl., borne in clusters, moderate musk fragrance; foliage light, leathery; bushy growth; [('Trier' × 'Rayon d'Or') × ('Gottfried Keller' × 'Entente Cordiale')]
'Gwyneth Jones' HT, op, 1925, McGredy; bud pointed; flowers brilliant carmine-orange, medium, semi-dbl., open; foliage light, leathery; vigorous, bushy growth
'Gwynne Carr' HT, lp, 1924, Dickson, A.; flowers silvery pink shaded lilac-rose, dbl.
'Gwynne Carr, Climbing' Cl HT, lp, 1934, Easlea
'Gyldenorange' F, ob, 1985, Poulsen, S.; flowers golden orange, fades to light yellow, large, dbl., no fragrance; foliage medium size, medium green, semi-glossy; medium growth; ['Poulsen's Yellow' × seedling]; intr. 1952

'Gympie' F, pb, 1953, Ulrick, L.W.; flowers white and pink, very dbl., borne in clusters; foliage light green; vigorous, bushy growth; ['Yvonne Rabier' × Tip-Top®]
'Gympie Beauty' F, dr, 1962, Dunstan; flowers deep red, borne in clusters
'Gypsy' HT, or, 1972, Swim & Weeks; bud ovoid; flowers fiery orange-red, large, dbl., slight fragrance; foliage large, glossy, leathery; vigorous, upright, bushy growth; PP3163; [(('Happiness' × 'Chrysler Imperial') × 'El Capitan') × 'Comanche']
'Gypsy' -- See 'Kiboh'
'Gypsy Boy' -- See 'Zigeunerknabe'
'Gypsy Bride' Gr, w
'Gypsy Carnival' -- See 'Kiboh'
'Gypsy Curiosa' HT, ob, deRuiter
'Gypsy Dancer' -- See 'Dicquiet'
'Gypsy Fire' F, rb, Williams, J.B.; flowers red and white striped; dark, glossy foliage; growth upright; intr. 2003
'Gypsy Fire' -- See 'Morglo'
'Gypsy Jewel' Min, dp, 1975, Moore, Ralph S.; flowers deep rose-pink, 1½ in., 50 petals, high-centered; foliage dark, leathery; vigorous growth; PP3940; ['Little Darling' × 'Little Buckaroo']
'Gypsy Jubilee' Gr, yb
'Gypsy Lady' Gr, mp; flowers dbl., cup and saucer; intr. 1995
'Gypsy Lantern' S, rb, Williams, J.B.; flowers red, pink and white stripes.; intr. 2003
'Gypsy Lass' -- See 'Gipsy Lass'
'Gypsy Leonidas' HT, ob, Meilland; flowers orange-red, cream yellow reverse, dbl., high-centered; florist rose; intr. 2002
'Gypsy Minijet' -- See 'Meimagul'
'Gypsy Moth' F, op, 1970, Tantau, Math.; flowers salmon, 35 petals, exhibition, borne in clusters; foliage glossy; intr. 1968
'Gypsy Queen' HMult, mr, 1929, Moore, Ralph S.; flowers crimson, small, dbl., borne in clusters; vigorous, climbing growth; ['Crimson Rambler' × unknown]
'Gypsy Song' HT, pb
Gypsy Sunblaze™ -- See 'Meimagul'
'Gypsy's Wine Cup' F, mr, 1968, Austin, David; flowers deep crimson, borne in trusses; foliage dark; low, bushy growth; ['Highlight' × unknown]
'Gyrene' S, mr, 1987, James, John; flowers bright, medium red, large, dbl.; repeat bloom; foliage medium size, medium green, matte, disease-resistant; upright, bushy, branching, vigorous, hardy growth; ['Arctic Glow' × (('Pink Hat' × R. arkansana) × R. arkansana)]; intr. 1987
'Gzlaty Dech' HT, ob, 1936, Böhm, J.; bud long, pointed; flowers orange-yellow, brown, red and gold shadings, large, semi-dbl., cupped; foliage glossy, light; vigorous growth; ['Admiration' × 'Talisman']

— H —
'H. Armytage Moore' HT, dp, 1908, Dickson
H. C. Andersen™ -- See 'Poulander'
'H. C. Valeton' HT, yb, 1926, Verschuren; flowers golden yellow overspread with rose, large; strong stems; vigorous growth; ['Golden Ophelia' × 'Aspirant Marcel Rouyer']
'H. C. Young' HT, op, 1934, Austin & McAslan; bud pointed; flowers shrimp-pink, deepening to salmon, base yellow; strong stems; vigorous growth
'H. Chaubert' HT, op, 1928, Barbier; flowers coppery salmon, open, semi-dbl., borne in clusters; foliage rich green, glossy; bushy growth; ['Mrs Aaron Ward' × seedling]
'H. D. M. Barton' HT, dr, 1917, Dickson, A.; flowers deep velvety crimson, large, dbl.; bushy growth
'H. E. Richardson' HT, mr, 1913, Dickson, A.; flowers dazzling crimson, large, dbl., high-centered; vigorous growth
'H. F. Alexander' LCl, ab, 1952, Wilber; flowers very large, 30-40 petals; foliage glossy; very long stems; tall, climbing growth; ['Duquesa de Peñaranda' × 'Ruth Alexander']
'H. F. Eilers' HT, mr, 1914, Lambert, P.; bud very long; flowers carmine and reddish terra-cotta, very large, dbl., borne mostly solitary, moderate fragrance; ['Gustav Grünerwald' × 'Luise Lilia']
'H. G. Hastings' -- See 'Harry G. Hastings'
'H. P. Pinkerton' HT, mr, 1915, Dickson, H.; flowers glossy scarlet with velvety crmison, large, full
'H. Plantagenet Comte d'Anjou' T, mp, 1892, Tesnier; flowers brilliant China rose, with deeper shadings
'H. V. Machin' ('H. Vessey Machin') HT, dr, 1914, Dickson, A.; flowers very dark scarlet-crimson, very large, dbl., globular; foliage glaucous beech-green
'H. V. Machin, Climbing' Cl HT, dr, 1919, Dickson, H. (also H&S, 1922); bud large; flowers crimson red, very large, full; [sport of 'H. V. Machin']
'H. Vessey Machin' -- See 'H. V. Machin'
'Haaksbergen' F, my, 1961, Buisman, G. A. H.; flowers bright yellow, medium, semi-dbl., borne in clusters; foliage dark; moderate growth; ['Mrs Pierre S. duPont' × 'King Boreas']
'Habanera' S, dr, 1976, Buck, Dr. Griffith J.; bud ovoid, pointed; flowers dark cardinal-red edged lighter, shallow-cupped, 4-4½ in., 33 petals, cupped; repeat bloom; foliage leathery; upright, bushy growth; [('Vera Dalton' × 'Dornroschen') × (('World's Fair' × 'Floradora') × 'Applejack')]; intr. 1975
'Habitat for Humanity' -- See 'Jacergma'
'Habitat for Humanity 2003' F, ob; PP14803; intr. 2003
'Habitat for Humanity 2004' ('Habitat for Humanity Rose') S, ly, J&P; bud pointed, ovoid; flowers large, graceful,

light yellow, 4 in., 50 petals, strong spicy fragrance; foliage semi-glossy, dark green; growth to 4 ft.; hardy; PPAF; intr. 2004

'Habitat for Humanity Rose' -- See 'Jacmirab'

'Habone' ('Elizabeth Harbour') HT, pb, 1986, Harbour, E.R.; bud pointed; flowers light pink, dark pink reverse, 3 in., 30 petals, borne singly, slight fragrance; foliage medium size, medium green, semi-glossy; upright (3 ft.), bushy growth; [Elizabeth of Glamis® × 'dark red hybrid tea seedling']; intr. 1985

'Hacienda' -- See 'Oradal'

'Hackeburg' ('Hakeburg') HMult, pb, 1912, Kiese; flowers soft lilac-pink, center white, 4 cm., full, borne in very large clusters, slight fragrance; nearly thornless; vigorous, climbing growth; possibly a 'Tausendschön' seedling

'Hada del Amor' F, mp

'Hadangel' ('Smooth Angel') HT, ab, 1986, Davidson, Harvey D.; bud medium, globular; flowers apricot blending to cream at edges, 5 in., 36-48 petals, cupped, borne mostly singly, intense fruity fragrance; recurrent; foliage medium size, medium green, matte; no prickles; medium (1 m.), bushy, spreading growth; no fruit; PP6146; ['Smooth Sailing' × 'Royal Flush']

'Hadango' (Olde Tango™) HT, ob, 1996, Davidson, Harvey D.; flowers orange, old fashioned, 3¼-3½ in., very dbl., flat, borne mostly singly, moderate pine fragrance; foliage medium size, medium green, glossy; prickles moderate; bushy (80-90 cm.) growth; ['Shining Ruby' × 'The World']; intr. 1996

'Hadbal' (Smooth Ballerina™) F, lp, 2006, Davidson, Harvey; bud ovoid; flowers light pink with slight white stripe, reverse light pink, 8-9 cm., 48-52 petals, globular, borne in small clusters, moderate fragrance; rapid repeat; foliage medium size, medium green, matte; growth upright, medium (1¼ m.); garden; hips round, olive green with orange tints; PP15662; ['Pink Empress' × (Blue Moon® × 'Roller Coaster')]; intr. 2006

'Hadcoral' ('Shining Coral') HT, pb, 1992, Davidson, Harvey D.; flowers coral pink, 4 in., 22-24 petals, cupped, borne singly and in small clusters, moderate fruity fragrance; foliage large, dark green, very glossy; medium, bushy growth; ['Shining Ruby' × ('Honey Favorite' × ('Little Darling' × 'Traviata'))]; intr. 1992

'Hadcup' ('Smooth Buttercup', Smooth Touch™) F, dy, 2003, Davidson, Harvey; bud ovoid; flowers deep butter yellow, ruffled petals, 2½-3½ in., 24-26 petals, globular, borne in clusters of 3 - 14, moderate fragrance; fast repeat; foliage medium size, medium green, matte; upright (2½ ft.), medium growth; garden; hips few, round, orange; PP16014; ['Kika' × (('Basildon Bond' × 'Arthur Bell') × Midas Touch™)]; intr. 2003

'Haddel' ('Delight Smooth Touch', Smooth Delight™) HT, op, 2006, Davidson, Harvey; bud ovoid; flowers peach, 11-12 cm., 34-36 petals, globular, borne mostly solitary, moderate fragrance; recurrent; foliage medium green, glossy; growth upright, medium (1¼ m.); garden; hips none ; PP15907; ['yellow HT seedling' × 'Smooth Sailing']; intr. 2006

'Hadden's Variety' S, m, 1948, Hilling; flowers rosy purple, single, borne several together; non-recurrent; foliage small, gray-green; [R. willmottiae × unknown]

'Haddington' HGal, m; flowers dark purple/pink, small to medium, semi-dbl.

'Hadempress' ('Pink Empress') HT, mp, 1991, Davidson, Harvey D.; flowers clean medium pink, large, 32-36 petals, high-centered, borne usually singly or sprays of 1 - 3, moderate fruity fragrance; foliage medium size, medium green, glossy; bushy, medium growth; ['Smooth Sailing' × Medallion®]; intr. 1991

'Hadevening' ('Evening Queen') HT, m, 1995, Davidson, Harvey D.; flowers slight red on edge of petals with aging, 3-3½ in., full, borne in small clusters, intense fragrance; foliage medium size, medium green, matte; medium (3 ft.) bushy growth; ['Blue Ribbon' × 'Great News']; intr. 1994

'Hadflare' ('Shining Flare') HT, or, 1992, Davidson, Harvey D.; bud ovoid; flowers 4½ in., 22-26 petals, cupped, borne in sprays, slight fruity fragrance; foliage medium size, dark green, very glossy; prickles sharp pointed, slight downward curvature; bushy, upright, medium growth; PP8911; ['Shining Ruby' × ('Smooth Sailing' × 'Futura')]; intr. 1992

'Hadfling' (Olde Romance™) HT, mp, 1993, Davidson, Harvey D.; flowers light pink, 7 cm., very full, borne mostly singly; foliage large, dark green, glossy; some prickles; growth tall (5-6 ft.), upright; ['Smooth Sailing' × 'Promise']; intr. 1994

'Hadfra' HT, lp, Davidson, Harvey; intr. 2007

'Hadice' (Golden Iceberg™) F, yb, 2006, Davidson, Harvey; flowers yellow and white, 8-9 cm., dbl., borne in large clusters; foliage medium size, medium green, semi-glossy, disease-resistant; few prickles; growth compact, medium (1 m.); garden; ['Sun Flare' × 'Sun Flare']; intr. 2006

'Hadlace' ('Olde Lace') HT, ly, 1993, Davidson, Harvey D.; flowers 3-3½ in., very dbl.; foliage large, dark green, glossy; some prickles; medium (3-4 ft.), bushy growth; ['Pink Favorite' × ('Polly' × 'Peace')]; intr. 1994

'Hadlady' ('Smooth Lady') HT, mp, 1986, Davidson, Harvey D.; bud slender, tapering; flowers open fast, 4-4½ in., 21-26 petals, high-centered, to loose, borne in clusters of 1-3, moderate spicy fragrance; foliage large, medium green, very glossy; no prickles; tall (5 ft.), upright, bushy growth; hips medium, globular, orange; PP6147; ['Smooth Sailing' × (('Polly' × 'Peace') × 'Circus')]

'Hadley' HT, mr, 1914, Montgomery Co.; flowers rich crimson, well-formed, very large, dbl.; foliage rich green; vigorous growth; [('Liberty' × 'Richmond') × 'Gen. MacArthur']

'Hadley, Climbing' Cl HT, mr, 1927, Heizmann; flowers dark crimson, large, dbl.; [sport of 'Hadley']

'Hadley Elatior' HT, mr, 1927, Teschendorff; [sport of 'Hadley']

'Hadmelody' ('Smooth Melody') F, rb, 1990, Davidson, Harvey D.; bud ovoid, pointed; flowers red with white center, white reverse with red on outer edge, aging darker, 3½ in., 26 petals, cupped to flat, borne in small clusters, intense fruity fragrance; fast repeat; foliage medium size, dark green, semi-glossy; thornless; growth vigorous, upright (3-4 ft.); hips round, rarely sets seed; PP7729; ['Royal Flush' × 'Smooth Lady']; intr. 1979

'Hadmoo' ('Moonlight Smooth Touch', Smooth Moonlight™) HT, m, 2006, Davidson, Harvey; bud ovoid; flowers lavender-pink, aging lavender, 10-12 cm., 36-40 petals, globular, borne mostly solitary, intense Damask fragrance; rapid repeat; foliage medium size, dark green, glossy; growth compact, medium (1 m.); garden decoration; hips round, 1 in., olive green with orange tones; PP15667; ['Smooth Perfume' × 'Blue Boy']; intr. 2006

'Hadness' ('Smooth Princess') HT, w, 2000, Davidson, Harvey; flowers full, borne mostly singly, moderate fragrance; foliage medium size, medium green, semi-glossy; thornless; growth upright, medium to tall (1½ m.); [('Smooth Sailing' × (Blue Moon® × 'Roller Coaster')) × 'Kika']; intr. 2002

'Hadperfume' ('Smooth Perfume') HT, lp, 1990, Davidson, Harvey D.; bud pointed, ovoid, large; flowers cream to light pink, very light mauve on edge, 5 in., 28-30 petals, cupped, open fast, borne singly and in small clusters, intense damask fragrance; recurrent; foliage medium size, medium green, semi-glossy; thornless, upright, bushy, medium (3-4 ft.) growth; hips rounded, flat base; PP7728; [('Smooth Sailing' × Medallion®) × Blue Moon®]; intr. 1979

'Hadpleasure' ('Pink Treasure') HT, mp, 1995, Davidson, Harvey D.; flowers 4½ in., full, borne mostly singly, moderate fragrance; foliage large, medium green, semi-glossy; some prickles; upright, medium (110 cm.) growth; ['Smooth Sailing' × 'Red Planet']; intr. 1995

'Hadprettie' ('Velvet Lady') HT, dr, 1995, Davidson, Harvey; flowers very dark, velvet red, 5 petals, borne in small clusters; foliage medium size, dark green, very glossy; numerous prickles; spreading, medium growth; ['Shining Ruby' × 'Precious Platinum']; intr. 1995

'Hadprince' ('Smooth Prince') HT, mr, 1990, Davidson, Harvey D.; bud ovoid to globular, large; flowers , 26-28 petals, cupped, flat center, urn-shaped, usually borne singly, slight fruity fragrance; good repeat; foliage medium size, medium green, semi-glossy; thornless; vigorous, upright (4 ft.) growth; hips oblong, rarely sets seed; PP7706; ['Smooth Sailing' × 'Old Smoothie']; intr. 1979

'Hadque' (Smooth Queen™) HT, yb, 2006, Davidson, Harvey; bud ovoid; flowers yellow, shaded pink, 12 cm., 34-36 petals, globular, borne mostly solitary, intense fragrance; recurrent; foliage medium size, dark green, semi-glossy; growth upright, medium (1¼ m.); garden; hips none ; PP17482; ['Kika' × Remember Me®]; intr. 2006

'Hadrom' HT, mp, 1996, Davidson, Harvey; intr. 1996

'Hadromance' (Smooth Romance™) HT, w, 1992, Davidson, Harvey D.; flowers cream with tinge of pink in center, 4¾ in., 42-45 petals, urn-shaped, borne usually singly, moderate fragrance; fast repeat; foliage medium size, medium green, glossy; thornless; stems straight, upright; upright, bushy, tall growth; hips will not set seed ; ['Smooth Sailing' × 'Portrait']; intr. 1991

'Hadromeo' ('Olde Romeo') HT, dr, 1993, Davidson, Harvey D.; bud ovoid; flowers ruffled, 3-4 in., 38-40 petals, globular, opening flat, borne mostly singly, intense old rose fragrance; foliage medium size, medium green, matte; prickles numerous, straight, downward pointing; medium (4 ft.), upright growth; PP9404; ['Smooth Sailing' × ('Old Smoothie' × '((Polly × Peace) × 'Simon Bolivar'))]; intr. 1994

'Hadruby' ('Shining Ruby') HT, mr, 1992, Davidson, Harvey D.; flowers medium red, fading to blue, 5½ in., 24-26 petals, cupped, borne in sprays, moderate spicy fragrance; foliage large, dark green, very glossy; bushy, medium growth; ['Pink Favorite' × 'Simon Bolivar']; intr. 1992

'Hadsatin' ('Smooth Satin') HT, mp, 1993, Davidson, Harvey D.; bud ovoid; flowers light to medium pink, reverse slightly darker, 4½ in., 35-40 petals, globular, borne mostly singly, moderate fragrance; recurrent; foliage large, medium green, glossy; nearly thornless; medium (4 ft.), upright, bushy growth; hips does not set seed ; PP8910; ['Smooth Lady' × 'Smooth Sailing']

'Hadsno' (Smooth Snowflake™) HT, w, 2006, Davidson, Harvey; flowers 9-10 cm., full, borne mostly solitary, moderate fragrance; foliage medium size, medium green, matte; growth compact, medium (1 m.); garden decoration; ['Kika' × ('Singin' in the Rain' × 'Joro')]; intr. 2006

'Hadsun' ('Western Sunlight') HT, ab, 1990, Davidson, Harvey D.; bud pointed; flowers apricot-orange, aging to yellow, large, 31 petals, high-centered, borne usually singly, slight fruity fragrance; foliage medium size, dark green, glossy, serrated; prickles hooked downward, light brown; upright, medium growth; hips inverted, orange; does not set seed readily; PP7442; [(('Honey Favorite' × 'Irish Mist') × ('San Francisco' × 'Prima Ballerina')) × 'Just Joey']; intr. 1990

'Hadswee' (Olde Sweetheart™) HT, lp, 1996, Davidson, Harvey D.; flowers light pink, with large, raspberry-colored stamens, large, single; foliage medium size, medium green, glossy; prickles moderate; upright, medium (100 cm.) growth; ['Smooth Sailing' × 'Red Planet']; intr. 1997

'Hadtreasure' ('White Treasure') HT, w, 1995, Davidson, Harvey D.; flowers white, slight cast of light yellow in center, 4¾ in., full, borne mostly singly, moderate fragrance; foliage large, dark green, semi-glossy; few prickles; upright, medium (100 cm.) growth; ['Smooth Sailing' × 'Sunset Jubilee']; intr. 1995

'Hadvelvet' ('Smooth Velvet') HT, dr, 1986, Davidson, Harvey D.; bud pointed ovoid; flowers velvety dark red, 5 in., 38-42 petals, cupped, borne usually singly, slight damask fragrance; recurrent; foliage large, light green, matte; tall (7-8 ft.), upright growth; hips medium, globular, orange; PP6152; ['Smooth Lady' × 'Red Devil']

Haendel® -- See 'Macha'

Hafiz® HT, mp; flowers eglantine rose-salmon, carmine reverse, dbl.; growth ti 70-80 cm.; intr. 1970

Hafnia™ F, op, Olesen; bud broad based ovoid; flowers medium orange-pink, 2½ in., 50 petals, open cup, borne in small clusters, very slight fragrance; recurrent; foliage dark green, glossy; prickles few, 4 mm., hooked downward, greyed-red; bushy, upright (60-100 cm.) growth; PP15875; ['Fredericksborg' × seedling]; intr. 2003

'Hagenbecks Tierpark' -- See 'Meiwaton'

'Hagoromo' ('Heavenly Robe') LCl, op, 1973, Suzuki, Seizo; bud ovoid; flowers silvery coral-pink, 10-11 cm., dbl., high-centered, borne singly or in small clusters, moderate fragrance; free, intermittent bloom; foliage dark green, glossy; vigorous, climbing growth; [('Aztec' × unknown) × ('New Dawn' × unknown)]; intr. 1970

'Haidee' S, pb, 1953, Skinner; flowers clear pink, center cream, large, dbl., cupped; non-recurrent; foliage small, dark; sometimes very prickly; stems wood red; growth to 6 ft.; hips large, dark red; [R. laxa × (R. spinosissima × unknown)]

Haiku™ -- See 'Aroyefel'

'Haileybury' HP, mr, 1896, Paul, G.; flowers crimson cerise, large, very full, moderate fragrance

Hailstorm™ -- See 'Coistor'

'Hair Ornament' -- See 'Kamikazari'

'Haïsha' HT, yb, 1947, Meilland, F.; flowers gold, edges suffused carmine, 6 in., 60 petals; foliage leathery, glossy, dark; upright growth; ['Peace' × 'Fantastique']

'Haitian Belle' LCl, mp

'Hakata Kanoko' Min, rb, 1999, Yamazaki, Kazuko; flowers medium red with white eye, 3¾ in., 5 petals, borne in large clusters; foliage small, medium green, disease-resistant; bushy, very compact (6-10 in.) growth; intr. 1995

'Hakeburg' -- See 'Hackeburg'

'Hakkoda' HT, pb, 1986, Kodoya, Y.; flowers white, pink petal edges, large, 40 petals, high-centered, intense fragrance; foliage medium green, semi-glossy; prickles broad, curved downward; bushy growth; ['Lady X' × 'Izayoi']; intr. 1983

'Hakucho' ('Swan') HT, w, Keisei; intr. 1989

'Hakuhoh' HT, w, 1999, Hayashi, Shunzo; bud pale cream, turning white; flowers 6 in., 40 petals, high-centered; foliage medium green; growth to 4½ ft.; ['White Prince' × 'Bridal Robe']; intr. 1989

'Hakusyu' HT, w, 1999, Ohtsuki, Hironaka; flowers white, center coral pink, 5½-6 in., full; foliage medium size, medium green; some prickles; upright, bushy, medium (4½-5 ft.) growth; ['Sizunomai' × 'Hoshizukuyo']

'Hakuun' ('White Cloud') F, w, 1978, Poulsen, Niels D.; bud small; flowers creamy white, patio, 2 in., 15 petals, slight fragrance; foliage light green; low, compact, bushy growth; [seedling × ('Pinocchio' × 'Pinocchio')]

'Hakuya' ('Night of the Midnight Sun') HT, w, Keihan; intr. 1971

'Halali' F, dp, 1959, Tantau, Math.; flowers deep pink, large, semi-dbl., borne in clusters; foliage leathery, dense; vigorous (5-6 ft.), spreading growth; ['Marchenland' × 'Peace']; intr. 1956

'Halarious' HT, Clark, A.; intr. 1935

'Halcyon Days' -- See 'Korparesni'

'Haleakala' -- See 'Manhale'

'Haleigh Joy' HT, dp, J. B. Williams; flowers solid pink, moderate fragrance; growth to 4 ft.; intr. 2005

'Half Time' HT, rb, 1976, Weeks; bud pointed; flowers cherry-red, reverse and base yellow, 3½-4 in., 40 petals, cupped, high-centered , borne singly and in small clusters, moderate tea fragrance; recurrent; foliage dark green, reverse light yellow-green, wrinkled; prickles numerous, medium to long, hooked slightly downward, brown ; stems strong; upright, vigorous growth; PP4007; [(('Fandango' × 'Roundelay') × ('Happiness' × 'Tiffany')) × 'Peace']

'Halka' HT, lp, 1988, Bracegirdle, Derek T.; flowers white blush pink, reverse white-silver, large, 30 petals, high-centered, borne in sprays, moderate damask fragrance; foliage medium size,

medium green, glossy; prickles straight, medium, red; upright, medium growth; ['Red Queen' × 'Peace']
'Hall of Flowers' -- See 'Mormint'
'Hallandsåsen' HRg; probably from Sweden
'Halle' HT, ob, Fryer; flowers bright orange, gold reverse, large, dbl., borne both singly and in clusters, moderate fragrance; very free flowering; foliage resistant, dark green; growth medium; intr. 2002
'Hallelujah!' -- See 'Radbrich'
'Hallelujah' -- See 'Delatur'
'Halley's Comet' F, mr, 1986, Rearsby Roses, Ltd.; flowers medium, 20 petals; foliage medium size, medium green, semi-glossy; [sport of 'Tip Top']
'Hallmark' HT, mr, 1966, Morey, Dennison H., Jr.; bud ovoid; flowers large, 28 petals, cupped, moderate fragrance; foliage glossy; PP2645; ['Independence' × 'Chrysler Imperial']
'Halloween' HT, yb, 1969, Howard, A.P.; flowers deep yellow, tipped scarlet, large, 65 petals, intense fragrance; foliage glossy, dark, leathery; vigorous, upright growth; PP2523; [('Peace' × 'Fred Howard') × seedling]; intr. 1962
'Halloween' HT, pb; intr. 2002
'Halo' HT, w, 1957, Lens; bud ovoid, seafoam-green; flowers 4½-5 in., 25 petals, high-centered, moderate fragrance; foliage leathery; vigorous, upright growth; PP1530; ['Lady Sylvia' × ('Virgo' × 'White Briarcliff')]; intr. 1956
'Halo Dolly' -- See 'Morwategye'
Halo Fire® -- See 'Morhalfire'
'Halo Glory' -- See 'Morglory'
'Halo Gold' Min, yb, Ralph Moore; flowers single; intr. 2005
'Halo Karol' -- See 'Moreyes'
Halo Rainbow® -- See 'Morrainbow'
'Halo Star' -- See 'Moranyface'
Halo Sunrise® Min, yb, Moore, Ralph; flowers bright yellow with a red halo at base of petals, 1-1½ in., 8-10 petals; fast repeat; growth to 12-18 in.; intr. 1997
'Halo Sunset' -- See 'Morsunset'
'Halo Sweetie' -- See 'Morsweetie'
Halo Today® -- See 'Mortoday'
'Hamari' ('Breath of Heaven') S, mr, 2000, Hamilton, Noel; flowers cerise red, reverse lighter, medium size, 70 petals, exhibition, borne mostly singly; foliage medium size, medium green, semi-glossy; prickles moderate; upright growth, 4½ ft.; [('Heavenly Scent' × seedling) × seedling]; intr. 2002
'Hambleden' -- See 'Broham'
'Hamburg' S, dr, 1935, Kordes; bud pointed; flowers glowing crimson, very large, semi-dbl., borne in clusters; recurrent bloom; foliage large, leathery, glossy; vigorous growth; ['Eva' × 'Daily Mail Scented Rose']
'Hamburg Girl' -- See 'Korpalud'
Hamburger Deern® -- See 'Korpalud'
'Hamburger Phoenix' (Hamburger Phönix®) HKor, mr, 1956, Kordes; bud long, pointed, bronze-black; flowers blood red, 7-8 cm., borne in small clusters; repeat bloom; foliage dark, glossy; vigorous, climbing or trailer growth; hips large, orange; [R. kordesii × seedling]
Hamburger Phönix® -- See 'Hamburger Phoenix'
'Hamburg's Love' F, dy, 1976, Timmerman's Roses; flowers 3 in., 28 petals, intense fragrance; foliage glossy; compact growth; ['Fragrant Cloud' × 'Manx Queen']; intr. 1974
'Hamdra' ('Golden Curls') F, yb, 2000, Hamilton, Noel; flowers gold fading to cream, medium, dbl., borne in small clusters, no fragrance; foliage medium size, medium green, semi-glossy, disease-resistant; prickles moderate; compact, medium (22 × 10 in.) growth; [seedling × seedling]; intr. 2000
'Hamera' ('Memories') Min, pb, 2000, Hamilton, Noel; flowers light pink, base lemon, reverse lighter, medium, full, high-centered, borne in small clusters, no fragrance; foliage medium size, medium green, glossy; few prickles; growth compact, medium (11 in.); [seedling × seedling]
'Hamish' -- See 'Simhaha'
'Hamlet' F, mr, Harkness; flowers rosy red to currant red, dbl., rosette, borne in clusters, moderate fragrance; foliage dark green, glossy, resistant; growth to 70-80 cm.; intr. 1999
'Hammerberg' S, m
Hammershus™ ('Perfect Day') F, w, Poulsen; flowers white with light apricot in the heart, 8-10 cm., full, no fragrance; foliage dark green, glossy; bushy, medium (60-100 cm.) growth; intr. 2001
'Hampshire' -- See 'Korhamp'
'Hampshire' -- See 'Korverlandus'
'Hampton' (Hampton Palace®) MinFl, w, Poulsen; flowers white, 8-10 cm., dbl., slight wild rose fragrance; foliage dark; growth broad, bushy, 40-60 cm.; PP10729; intr. 1996
Hampton Palace® -- See 'Poulgret'
'Hana-Busa' F, or, 1986, Suzuki, Seizo; bud ovoid; flowers 18 petals, flat, borne 6-10 per cluster; prickles straight; bushy growth; [Sarabande® × ('Rumba' × 'Olympic Torch')]; intr. 1981
'Hana-Gasumi' ('Flower Haze') F, w, 1986, Suzuki, Seizo; flowers soft white, aging pink, 13 petals, flat, borne 6 - 12 per cluster, moderate fragrance; foliage dark, semi-glossy; prickles small, hooked, slanted downward; bushy growth; [Europeana® × ('Myo-joh' × 'Fidélio')]; intr. 1985
'Hana-Gasumi, Climbing' Cl F, w, Itamu; [sport of 'Hana-Gasumi']; intr. after 1985
'Hana-Kurenai' HT, pb, 1986, Ohata, Hatsuo; bud ovoid; flowers light pink, flushed yellow, reverse deeper, 33 petals, high-centered, borne singly and in small clusters, slight fragrance; foliage medium size, medium green, glossy; prickles few, sickle-shaped; vigorous, upright growth; ['Big Red' × 'Star Queen']; intr. 1980
'Hanabi' -- See 'Wekroalt'
Hanae Mory' HT, Delbard, Georges; intr. 1990
'Hanagasa' F, or, 1978, Suzuki, Seizo; bud globular; flowers vermilion, 4-4½ in., 23 petals, cupped, foliage large, light green; vigorous growth; [('Hawaii' × seedling) × 'Miss Ireland']; intr. 1979
'Hanaguruma' HT, yb, 1977, Teranishi, K.; bud globular; flowers 6½-7 in., 58 petals, high-centered, slight fragrance; foliage light green; upright growth; ['Kordes' Perfecta' × ('Kordes' Perfecta × American Heritage®)]; intr. 1974
'Hanakagari' HT, ob, Keisei; intr. 1997
'Hanakago' ('Flower Basket') F, or, 1973, Suzuki, Seizo; bud ovoid; flowers deep salmon-vermilion, medium, dbl., cupped, moderate fragrance; foliage glossy, dark; vigorous, bushy growth; [(Sarabande® × unknown) × ('Rondo' × unknown)]; intr. 1972
'Hanami-Gawa' ('Cherry Blossom Viewing on the River') Cl Min, op, 1986, Suzuki, Seizo; flowers soft salmon-pink, shaded orange, small, 23 petals, borne 6 - 10 per cluster, moderate fragrance; foliage dark, semi-glossy; prickles small, curved, slanted downward; vigorous, very bushy growth; [seedling × Petite Folie®]; intr. 1986
'Hanamori' F, rb, 1977, Teranishi, K.; bud circular; flowers 2½ in., 20-25 petals, high-centered, foliage glossy, dark; bushy growth; [('Tropicana' × 'Karl Herbst') × 'Lydia']
'Hanatirusato' Min, dp, 1999, Yamazaki, Kazuko; flowers brilliant rose, 1½ in., 70 petals, flat, borne 2-5 per cluster; foliage medium size, medium green; vigorous, bushy, compact (8 in.) growth; [seedling × Red Minimo™]; intr. 1996
'Hanayome' ('Bride') HT, lp, Keihan; intr. 1970
'Hanayoshino' Min, mp; intr. 2001
'Hanayuzen' Min, dy, 1999, Yamazaki, Kzauko; flowers deep golden yellow, sometimes flushed orange, 1½ in., 45 petals, high-centered; foliage medium size, dark green; very vigorous, upright, bush, compact (12 in.) growth; ['Himetatibana' × 'Hanahotaru']; intr. 1996
'Hanbau' HRg, op, Baum; intr. 1991
'Hand in Hand' -- See 'Haraztec'
Handel® ('Händel', Haendel®) LCl, rb, 1965, McGredy, Sam IV; flowers cream edged red, large, 22-30 petals, slight honey fragrance; recurrent bloom, on both old and new wood; foliage glossy, olive-green; climbing growth; ['Columbine' × 'Gruss an Heidelberg']
'Händel' -- See 'Macha'
'Handel's Largo' -- See 'Largo d'Haendel'
'Handout' -- See 'Barout'
'Handsom Red' HT, mr, 1954, Brownell; flowers spectrum-red, 4-5 in., 45 petals, high-centered, moderate fragrance;

upright, bushy growth; PP1182; [('Pink Princess' × 'Mirandy') × 'Queen o' the Lakes']

'Handy Andy' HT, ab, 1965, McGredy, Sam IV; flowers apricot edged pink, 4 in.; free growth; ['Kordes' Perfecta' × Piccadilly®]

'Hanib' -- See 'Cecilia 89'

'Hanini' -- See 'Dyknini'

'Hanka' HT, ly; flowers creamy yellow, very large, dbl.

'Hanky Panky' -- See 'Wektorcent'

'Hanky Panky' -- See 'Tinpanky'

'Hannah Brown' -- See 'Brohan'

'Hannah Gordon' -- See 'Korweiso'

'Hannah Hansen' HWich, m, Nobbs; intr. 1997

'Hannah Hauxwell' F, op, 1991, Battersby Roses; flowers deep salmon, small, full, slight fragrance; foliage small, medium green, matte; bushy growth; [seedling × seedling]

'Hannah Rose Timings' HT, dp, 2004, Poole, Lionel; flowers deep pink, reverse deep pink, 4½-5 in., full, borne mostly solitary; foliage medium size, dark green, semi-glossy; prickles medium, hooked; growth upright, bushy, medium (3 ft.); garden, bedding, borders; [('Hazel Rose' × 'Cardiff Bay') × 'Fiona Ivin']; intr. 2005

Hannah Ruby™ -- See 'Zlehanruby'

'Hanne' HT, mr, 1959, Soenderhousen; flowers scarlet-crimson, medium to large, dbl., high-centered; foliage leathery; upright growth; ['Ena Harkness' × 'Peace']

'Hanne Dänomik' HT, mr; flowers large, dbl.

'Hanneli Rupert' -- See 'Korsebue'

'Hannes' -- See 'Rose Hannes'

'Hannover' -- See 'Messestadt Hannover'

'Hannover's Weisse' -- See 'Noahan'

'Hans' HT, w, 1970, IARI; flowers open, large, semi-dbl.; foliage glossy, light; vigorous, upright growth; ['Message' × 'Virgo']

'Hans Berger' HT, mr, Berger, W.; flowers carmine-red, large, dbl.; intr. 1958

'Hans Billert' HT, mr, 1928, Billert; flowers brilliant red, very dbl.; ['Laurent Carle' × 'Richmond']

'Hans Christian Andersen' -- See 'Poulander'

'Hans Erni' F, op, Meilland; bud small, pointed; flowers salmon-orange to salmon-pink, moderate fragrance; rounded (2 ft.) growth; intr. 1992

'Hans Haubold' HT, mp, 1942, Vogel, M.; flowers large, dbl.

'Hans Mackart' HP, rb, 1884, Verdier, E.; flowers bright deep geranium red, outer petals tinted carmine purple, dbl.

'Hans Memling' HT, op, J. B. Williams; flowers salmon orange, dbl., moderate fragrance; foliage dark green; intr. 2005

'Hans Rathgeb' HT, dp, Huber; flowers intense wine red, dbl.; intr. 2005

'Hans Rosenthal' -- See 'Révolution Française'

'Hans Schmid' HWich, dp, 1934, Vogel, M.; flowers deep pink, rather well-formed to medium, 4-5 cm., dbl., globular, borne in medium clusters; foliage large, vigorous, climbing growth; ['Fragezeichen' × 'American Pillar']

'Hansa' HRg, mr, 1905, Schaum & Van Tol; flowers mauvy-red, large, dbl., intense clove-rose fragrance; recurrent bloom; short, weak stems; vigorous growth; hips large, red; hardy

Hansa-Park® ('Hanza Park') S, m, Kordes; flowers lavender-pink, 3-4 in., dbl., slight fragrance; free-flowering; vigorous (5-7 ft.) growth; intr. 1994

Hansaland® -- See 'Korhassi'

Hanseat® S, mp, 1961, Tantau, Math.; flowers rose-pink, center lighter, medium, 5 petals, cupped; vigorous (6 ft.) growth

Hanseat® HT, pb, Tantau; flowers varying shades of deep lavender-pink, medium to large, double, high-centered, borne mostly singly; recurrent; thornless; stems long; vigorous growth; florist rose; intr. 2007

'Hansen's Red Hedge' S, mr

'Hansestadt Bremen' F, op, 1959, Kordes, R.; bud ovoid, crimson; flowers deep salmon and reddish-pink, large, 47 petals, borne in clusters (up to 10), moderate fragrance; foliage leathery; very vigorous, bushy growth; ['Ama' × 'Fanal']; intr. 1958

'Hansestadt Lübeck' ('Lübeck') F, mr, 1965, Kordes, R.; flowers large, dbl., slight fragrance; foliage dark; vigorous, tall growth

'Hansette' S, mr, 1938, Wright, Percy H.; flowers red, semi-dbl.; non-recurrent; ['Hansa' × R. rubrifolia]

'Hanuhi' -- See 'Scarlet Pavement'

'Hanza Park' -- See 'Hansa-Park'

'Hap Renshaw' -- See 'Renhap'

'Happenstance' ('Baby Mermaid') HBc, ly, 1950, Buss; flowers pale yellow, small, short-lived, single; foliage small, dark green, glossy; prickles thorns large, hooked; growth low, prostrate ground cover; up to 15 ft.; [sport of 'Mermaid']

'Happiness' ('Rim', 'Rouge Meilland') HT, mr, 1954, Meilland, F.; bud long, pointed; flowers 5-6 in., 38 petals, high-centered, slight fragrance; upright, vigorous growth; PP911; [('Rome Glory' × 'Tassin') × ('Charles P. Kilham' × ('Charles P. Kilham' × 'Capucine Chambard'))]; intr. 1949

'Happiness, Climbing' ('Rouge Meilland, Climbing') Cl HT, mr, 1954, Meilland, F.

'Happy' (Alberich®) Pol, mr, 1957, deRuiter; flowers currant-red, very small, semi-dbl., borne in large trusses; foliage dark, glossy; vigorous, compact (12-15 in.) growth; ['Robin Hood' × ('Katharina Zeimet' × unknown)]; registered as a Floribunda; intr. 1954

'Happy, Climbing' -- See 'Gorhappy'

'Happy Anniversary' HT, ob, Catt, Graeme Charles; flowers deep orange, full, exhibition, borne mostly singly, moderate fragrance; stems long, upright; [sport of 'Kardinal']; intr. 2000

'Happy Anniversary' F, pb, Chessum; flowers salmon pink, borne in clusters, moderate fragrance; recurrent; tall (1 m.) growth; intr. 2001

'Happy Anniversary' -- See 'Strawberry Ice'

'Happy Anniversary' -- See 'Heureux Anniversaire'

'Happy Birthday' HT, dp, 1964, Howard, P.J.; bud ovoid; flowers deep rose, large, 25 petals, high-centered, intense fragrance; foliage leathery; vigorous, upright growth; PP2281; ['Peace' × 'The Doctor']

'Happy Birthday' MinFl, w; flowers cream, borne in flushes, slight fragrance; good repeat; foliage light green, glossy; growth to 1-2 ft.; intr. 1997

'Happy Butt' HT, ab, 1995, Carlson, Wm.; flowers open apricot, deepening to pink as bloom ages, 7+ cm., very full, borne mostly singly, moderate fragrance; foliage medium-size, medium green, semi-glossy; some prickles; growth upright, tall; ['Nantucket' × Medallion®]

'Happy Chappy' S, yb, Ilsink; bud pointed, ovoid; flowers bright orange, pink, and yellow, 1 in., single, flat, light fragrance; continuous; foliage dark green, glossy, disease-resistant; growth mounded, spreading, medium (24 in.); groundcover; intr. 1999

'Happy Child' -- See 'Auscomp'

'Happy Day' ('The Queen's London Child') S, dp, Harkness; flowers, 70 petals, cupped, old-fashioned; profuse; growth compact, bushy (2½ × 2½ ft.); PPAF; intr. 2004

'Happy Day' -- See 'Simpalno'

'Happy Days' HT, or, 1932, Amling, M.C.; bud pointed; flowers geranium-red, open, large, dbl.; foliage dark, long stems; very vigorous growth; PP144; RULED EXTINCT 4/87; [sport of 'Briarcliff']

'Happy Days' HT, dr, 1962, Herholdt, J.A.; bud pointed; flowers oxblood-red, 3-3½ in., dbl., high-centered; long stems; vigorous growth; RULED EXTINCT 4/87; ['Exciting' × 'Grand Gala']

'Happy Days' -- See 'Macseatri'

'Happy Daze' S, mp, Eagle; intr. 1995

'Happy Event' F, pb, 1964, Dickson, Patrick; flowers light chrome-yellow, flushed rose-opal, 3 in., 12 petals, borne in clusters; foliage glossy; growth moderate; [('Karl Herbst' × 'Masquerade') × Rose Gaujard®]

Happy Ever After™ -- See 'Dicvanilla'

Happy Face™ -- See 'Savaface'

'Happy Go Lucky' -- See 'Sunhap'

Happy Go Lucky™ -- See 'Savaluck'

'Happy Hour' F, yb, Delbard; flowers blending of bright yellow, orange and red splashes; growth tall; intr. 2003

Happy Hour® HT, mr, Spek; flowers velvet red, 4 in., 35-40 petals, high-centered, borne mostly singly; recurrent; prickles moderate; stems long; florist rose; intr. 2004

Happy Hour™ -- See 'Savanhour'

'Happy Memories' S, pb, 2006, Beales, Amanda; flowers small, full, borne in large clusters; foliage small, dark green, glossy; few prickles; growth bushy, short (60 cm.); containers, garden decoration; [Centenaire de Lourdes® × 'Bonica']; flowers blended cherry red, pink and white; intr. 2001

'Happy Minijet' Min, mr, Meilland

'Happy Red' F, or, 1960, Leenders, J.; flowers bright brick-red, single, borne in clusters; foliage glossy; moderate growth; ['Red Favorite' × 'Cocorico']

'Happy Retirement' -- See 'Tantoras'

'Happy Talk' F, mr, 1974, Weeks; flowers cherry-red, small, dbl., slight fragrance; foliage glossy, dark; vigorous, upright, bushy growth; PP3559; ['Escort' × 'Orange Garnet']; intr. 1973

'Happy Thought' Min, op, 1978, Moore, Ralph S.; bud pointed; flowers pink blended with coral and yellow, 40 petals; foliage small, glossy; vigorous, bushy growth; PP4479; [(*R. wichurana* × Floradora) × 'Sheri Anne']

Happy Thoughts™ -- See 'Savagrand'

'Happy Time' Cl Min, rb, 1975, Moore, Ralph S.; bud short, pointed; flowers yellow overlaid red, 1 in., 35 petals, slight fragrance; foliage small, glossy, leathery; climbing growth; [(*R. wichurana* × Floradora) × ('Golden Glow' × 'Zee')]; intr. 1974

'Happy Times' MinFl, mp, Chessum, Paul; growth to 18 in.; intr. 1995

'Happy Trails' -- See 'Jaccasp'

Happy Wanderer® F, mr, 1972, McGredy, Sam IV; flowers scarlet, medium, slight fragrance; free-flowering; growth medium; [seedling × 'Marlene']; intr. 1974

'Happy Wanderer' -- See 'Gorhappy'

'Happy Wedding Bells' HT, w, 1970, Morey, Dr. Dennison; bud long, pointed; flowers large, 52 petals, high-centered, moderate spicy fragrance; foliage leathery; vigorous, upright growth; ['White Swan' × 'Virgo']; intr. 1966

'Har Tabor' HT, pb, Fischel; flowers dbl.; intr. 1972

'Haramity' F, my, Harkness; intr. 2000

'Haravis' ('Tower Bridge') HT, mr, Harkness; intr. 1995

'Haraztec' ('Hand in Hand') MinFl, or, Harkness; intr. 1994

'Harbabble' ('Sunset Boulevard') F, op, intr. 1997

'Harbadge' ('Lady Guinevere', Guinevere™, Louisa Stone™) F, ab, 2001, Harkness New Roses Ltd.; flowers 8 cm., full, borne in large clusters; foliage large, dark green, glossy; growth spreading, medium (80 cm.); garden decorative; PP13184; ['Harroony' × 'Harwanted']

'Harbanjo' ('Girls' Brigade') F, or, 1993, Harkness; flowers vermilion, orange-red reverse, aging orange-red, 2 in., 28 petals; foliage small, dark green, glossy; bushy, low growth; [Sexy Rexy® × Anna Ford®]; intr. 1993

'Harbanner' ('Country Fair') S, lp, Harkness; intr. 1998

'Harbar' ('Sporting Duo') F, ob, Harkness, R.; intr. 1995

'Harbaroque' ('Baroque Floorshow') S, m, Harkness; intr. 1995

'Harbell' ('Cathedral Splendour') F, op, Harkness, R.; intr. 1995

'Harbella' ('Coronation', 'Peacekeeper', 'United Nations Rose') F, pb, 1994, Harkness; flowers orange/pink blend, yellowing with age, 3½ in., 30 petals, borne 7 - 10 per cluster, slight spicy fragrance; foliage medium size, light green, glossy; bushy, medium growth; ['Dame of Sark' × Bright Smile®]; intr. 1996

'Harbilbo' ('St John') F, w, 1994, Harkness; flowers medium, dbl., borne in small clusters, slight fragrance; foliage medium size, medium green, glossy; few prickles; low (60 cm.), bushy, spreading growth; ['Prima' × 'Grace Abounding']; intr. 1994

'Harbinger' LCl, lp, 1923, Clark, A.; bud pointed; flowers soft pink, 12 cm., single; foliage light; vigorous, climbing growth; hybrid gigantea

'Harbinger' ('Julie Youell') HT, or, Harkness; intr. 1994

'Harbingo' ('House Beautiful') MinFl, my, Harknessdbl.; intr. 1995

'Harbleep' ('Guglielmo Marconi') F, op, Harkness; intr. 1996

'Harblend' ('Desert Glow', 'Renown's Desert Glo', 'Royal Pageant') S, ab, Harkness; intr. 1994

'Harbloom' F, pb, Harkness; intr. France

'Harbonny' ('Royal Anniversary', 'Ruby Anniversary') F, mr, 1993, Harkness; flowers crimson, yellow base, reverse mid-pink, aging dark red, 2½ in., 24 petals, slight fruity fragrance; foliage small, dark green, glossy; bushy, low growth; ['Intrigue' × Anna Ford®]; intr. 1992

'Harboul' ('Pink Pirouette') MinFl, mp, Harkness; intr. 1998

'Harbrill' ('Conquest') F, my, 1994, Harkness; flowers large, 30 petals, borne in sprays of 7-10, slight spicy fragrance; foliage medium size, light green, glossy; bushy, medium growth; ['Dame of Sark' × Bright Smile®]; intr. 1994

'Harbrite' ('Anne Hathaway', 'Mrs Iris Clow') F, lp, 1993, Harkness; flowers blush pink, light pink reverse, paling to near white, loose, 28 petals, cupped, moderate spicy fragrance; foliage large, dark green, glossy; upright, medium growth; [Memento® × 'Princess Alice']; intr. 1994

'Harbusy' F, mp, 1971, Harkness; intr. 1970

'Harcandour' S, lp, Harkness; intr. 2007

'Harcheer' ('Country Music') S, pb, Harkness; intr. 1998

'Harchutzpah' ('June Whitfield') HT, ob, Harkness, R.dbl.; intr. 1995

'Harclarity' F, lp, Harkness; intr. 1994

'Harclue' ('Bérénice') HT, ab, Harkness; intr. 1998

'Harcogent' ('St Christopher') HT, dy, Harkness, R.; intr. 1996

'Harcomp' (Highfield®) LCl, ly, 1979, Harkness; bud pointed; flowers primrose yellow, 39 petals, round, borne in clusters of 1 - 3, moderate sweet fragrance; good repeat; foliage dark green; prickles hooked; upright, free branching growth; [sport of 'Compassion']; intr. 1980

'Harcross' ('Humanity') MinFl, dr, Harkness; intr. 1995

'Hardancer' ('Flame Dancer') F, ob, 1986, Harkness; flowers orange, red reverse, medium, dbl., cupped, moderate fragrance; foliage dense; prickles large; medium, bushy growth; [Orange Sensation® × 'Alison Wheatcroft']; intr. 1976

'Hardeed' HT, w, Harkness; intr. 1997

'Hardeluxe' ('Lilian Baylis') F, ly, Harkness, R.; intr. 1996

'Hardenier' ('Celtic Pride') S, ab, Harkness; intr. 1996

'Hardimple' ('World Class') F, ab, Harkness; intr. 1996

'Hardinkum' ('Princesse de Galles', 'The Princess of Wales') F, w, Harkness; intr. 1997

'Hardish' MinFl, yb; intr. 2001

'Hardolly' ('Tambourine') F, ob; intr. 1998

'Hardrama' F, mr, Harkness; intr. 1999

'Hardwell' ('Penny Lane') LCl, ab, Harkness; intr. 1998

'Hardy Ottawa' S, m; intr. 2003

'Hareast' ('Rising Star') F, mr, Harkness, R.; intr. 1995

'Hareasy' ('Pure Abundance', 'Sir Galahad') F, w, Harkness; intr. 2001

'Harebb' S, w; intr. 2001

'Hareco' ('Nipper') S, mr, Harkness, R.; intr. 1997

'Hareden' ('Windsor Castle') F, lp, Harknessvery dbl.; intr. 1997

'Haredge' Min, or; intr. 1999

'Harelan' ('Gift of Life', 'Poetry in Motion') HT, yb, 1999, Harkness; flowers mid yellow-pink, reverse yellow, 4 in., full, borne mostly singly, moderate fragrance; foliage large, medium green, glossy; numerous prickles; bushy, medium (40 in.) growth; ['Dr Darley' × Elina®]; intr. 1996

'Harelite' ('Wheel Horse Classic') F, dr, Harkness; intr. 1996

'Harencens' ('Miss Dior') S, ab, Harkness; intr. 1998

'Harencore' ('Pride of England') HT, mr, Harkness; intr. 1998

'Harentente' ('Peter Cottrell', 'Sunny Spring', 'Sunshine Abundance') F, yb; intr. 1999

'Harentrap' ('Lottum Abundance', 'Salmon Abundance') F, mp; intr. 1998

'Harenvoy' HT, dy, Harkness; intr. 2008

'Haressay' F, mr, Harkness; intr. 1998
'Harette' ('Glowing Abundance') F, ob, Harkness; intr. 1998
'Hareverso' ('Spirit Abundance') F, or, Harkness; intr. 1998
'Harewood' -- See 'Satina'
'Harexclaim' ('Irish Hope') F, ly; intr. 1998
'Harextra' ('Courageous', 'Fetzer Syrah Rose') S, dr; intr. 1998
'Harfab' MinFl, dy, Harkness; intr. 1998
'Harfable' ('Canterbury') LCl, my, Harkness; intr. 1999
'Harfacey' F, yb, Harkness; intr. 2001
'Harfang des Neiges' HRg, w
'Harfervour' F, mr, Harkness; intr. 1999
'Harfizz' ('Amber Abundance') F, ab, Harkness; intr. 1999
'Harflax' ('Covent Garden', 'Creme Abundance') F, w; intr. 1999
'Harfleet' ('Snow Cap') Min, w; intr. 1999
'Harfling' F, lp, Harkness; intr. 1998
'Harflipper' ('The Mencap Rose') S, mp, Harkness; intr. 1999
'Harfloorshow' ('Purple Floorshow') S, m, Harkness
'Harflow' (Easy Going™) F, yb, 1999, Harkness; flowers deep gold apricot, overlaid with peach when fresh, 3½-4 in., 26-30 petals, borne in small clusters, moderate fruity fragrance; foliage large, very bright, light green, glossy; numerous prickles; upright, bushy, medium (3-3½ ft.) growth; PP10478; [sport of 'Livin' Easy']; intr. 1999
'Harfond' (Queen of Hearts™) S, mr, 2001, Harkness New Roses, Ltd.; flowers very full, borne in small clusters, intense fragrance; foliage medium size, dark green, glossy; prickles medium, hooked downwards, moderate; bushy, tall (100 cm.) growth; garden decoration; ['KORphean' × 'HARmusky']; intr. 2001
'Harforay' ('The Pink Professor') S, dp; intr. 2004
'Harforey' S, op, Harkness; intr. 2003
'Harfortran' S, ob, Harkness; intr. 2002
'Harforum' S, ab, Harkness; intr. 1999
'Harfracas' ('Apricot Abundance') F, ab, Harkness; intr. 1998
'Harfrisky' ('Pearl Abundance') F, lp, Harkness; intr. 2004
'Harfrothy' F, op; intr. 1999
'Harfully' S, yb; intr. 1999
'Harfurore' HT, mr, Harkness; intr. 2001
'Hargalaxy' ('Harglisser (withdrawn)') F, dp, Harkness; intr. 1999
'Hargalore' HT, my; intr. 2003
'Hargladly' F, my, Harkness; intr. 2003
'Harglamour' S, dr, Harkness; intr. 1999
'Harglisser (withdrawn)' -- See 'Sir Lancelot'
'Harglitter' S, pb; intr. 1999
'Harglobe' F, my, Harkness; intr. 1999
'Harglow' LCl, ab, Harkness; intr. 2001
'Harglowing' LCl, ab, Harkness; intr. 2001
'Hargrace' F, pb, Harkness; bud pointed ovoid; intr. 2006
'Harhandour' F, dp, Harkness; intr. 2002
'Harhappen' ('Créme Caramel', 'The Sir Steven Redgrave Rose', 'Steve Redgrave') S, my; intr. 2002
'Harhefty' (Mimi Fariña™) HT, yb, 2008, Harkness New Roses; flowers pastel yellow blended with pink, large, 12-14 cm., dbl., borne mostly solitary; foliage large, dark green, glossy; prickles average, almost straight, beige, few; growth upright, medium (90-120 cm.); garden decoration; [Livin' Easy™ × 'LeAnn Rimes']; intr. 2006
'Harhelga' F, ab, Harkness; intr. 2006
'Harhero' ('Honor Elizabeth') F, my, Harknessfull; intr. 2001
'Harhero' ('Red Ballerina', 'Red Yesterday') S, rb, 1977, Harkness; intr. 1978
'Harhester' ('Caroline Davison') F, op, 1980, Harkness, R., & Co., Ltd.; flowers medium salmon-pink, mini-flora, small, 16 petals, borne in small clusters; foliage small, dark reddish-green; prickles straight, dark green; low, bushy growth; ['Tip Top' × 'Kim']; intr. 1979
'Harhilt' ('Melba') LCl, mp; intr. 2002
'Harholding' ('Prince's Trust') LCl, mr; intr. 2002
'Haris ' HSpn, mp, Erskine; flowers semidbl. to dbl., cupped; non-remontant; growth tall grower; very hardy; ['Harison's Yellow' × unknown]
'Harisonii' -- See 'Harison's Yellow'
'Harisonii No. 1' HFt, ly, before 1846, from England; flowers pale golden yellow, tinged with copper, medium, dbl., cupped
'Harisonii No. 2' HFt, yb, before 1848; flowers buff, center reddish-salmon, medium, dbl., cupped
'Harison's Hardy' HSpn, ly, 1943, Wright, Percy H.; flowers cream, center tinted yellow, semi-dbl.; non-recurrent; very hardy; [R. spinosissima altaica × 'Harison's Yellow']
'Harison's Lemon' HSpn, ly, 1929, Hamblin; flowers clear lemon-yellow, semi-dbl., moderate fragrance; non-recurrent; bushy (5 ft.) growth; ['Harison's Yellow' × unknown]
'Harison's Profuse' HSpn; ['Harison's Yellow' × unknown]
'Harison's Salmon' HSpn, op, 1929, Hamblin; flowers salmon, medium, semi-dbl., globular, moderate fragrance; non-recurrent; foliage small, rich green; ['Harison's Yellow' × unknown]; sometimes classed as HFt
'Harison's Yellow' ('Harisonii', 'Hogg's Yellow', R. foetida harisonii, R. × harisonii, R. lutea hoggii) HFt, dy, about 1824, Harison; flowers bright yellow, yellow stamens, 2 in., semi-dbl., moderate fragrance; non-recurrent; growth upright (6 × 3 ft.); hips almost black, (28); [probably 'Persian Yellow' × R. spinosissima]
'Harjames' ('Xerxes') S, yb, 1990, Harkness, R., & Co., Ltd.; bud pointed; flowers rich yellow with scarlet-red eye at base, reverse yellow, 5 petals, cupped; foliage small, grayish-green, matte; prickles narrow, small, reddish; upright, medium to tall growth; fruit not observed; ['H. persica' × 'Canary Bird']; intr. 1989
'Harjangle' S, yb, Harkness; intr. 2004
'Harjellow' F, my, Harkness; intr. 2005
'Harjelly' F, op, Harkness; intr. 2001
'Harjob' S, my, Harkness; intr. 2004
'Harjojo' S, my, Harkness; intr. 2004
'Harjolina' LCl, ab, Harkness; intr. 2001
'Harjolly' LCl, ab, Harkness; intr. 2001
'Harjoobily' ('Mr E. E. Greenwell') F, op, 1979, Harkness; flowers rosy salmon, 3 in., 18 petals, flat; vigorous, bushy, spreading growth; ['Jove' × 'City of Leeds']; intr. 1978
'Harjosine' ('Basildon Bond') HT, ab, 1980, Harkness, R., & Co., Ltd.; flowers loose form, 27 petals, borne 1-3 per cluster; foliage large, medium green, very glossy; prickles large, straight; medium, upright growth; [('Sabine' × 'Circus') × ('Yellow Cushion' × 'Glory of Ceylon')]
'Harjug' ('Rosetti Stone') F, mp, Harkness; intr. 2004
'Harkamp' S, ob, Harkness; intr. 2005
'Harkantabil' (Marion Harkness®) HT, yb, 1978, Harkness; flowers canary-yellow, flushed orange-red, large, 24 petals; bushy growth; [(('Manx Queen' × 'Prima Ballerina') × ('Chanelle' × Piccadilly®)) × Piccadilly®]; intr. 1979
'Harkaramel' (Anne Harkness®) F, ab, 1978, Harkness; bud globular; flowers deep apricot, dbl., cupped, borne in trusses, slight fragrance; foliage medium green, semi-glossy; vigorous, upright, tall growth; ['Bobby Dazzler' × (('Manx Queen' × 'Prima Ballerina') × ('Chanelle' × Piccadilly®))]; intr. 1980
'Harkicker' F, ab, Harkness; intr. 2006
'Harkimono' ('Songs of Praise', 'Velvet Abundance') F, dr, Harkness; intr. 2005
'Harkinder' (Esther's Baby®) Min, mp, 1979, Harkness; bud pointed; flowers Persian rose, patio, medium, flat; foliage small, glossy; low, spreading growth; [('Vera Dalton' × ('Chanelle' × Piccadilly®)) × 'Little Buckaroo']
'Harking' F, yb, 1977, Harkness; intr. 1978
'Harkish' F, lp, Harkness; intr. 2005
'Harkitten' ('Crispin-Morwenna') Min, or, 1980, Harkness, R., & Co., Ltd.; flowers salmon-red, small, 25 petals, cupped, borne 3-7 per cluster, slight spicy fragrance; foliage small, dark, glossy; prickles reddish; low, spreading growth; [('Vera Dalton' × ('Chanelle' × Piccadilly®)) × 'Little Buckaroo']
'Harklement' ('Sherlock Holmes') S, ab, Harkness; intr. 2006
'Harkness Marigold' F, ob, Harkness, R., & Co., Ltd.; flowers well-formed, 35 petals, borne in clusters, slight fragrance; foliage medium size, medium green, semi-glossy; upright growth; ['Judy Garland' × Anne Harkness®]; intr. 1986
'Harkoral' F, ab, Harkness; intr. 2006

'Harkotur' ('Softly Softly') F, pb, 1977, Harkness; flowers pink and creamy pink, 5 in., 35 petals, hybrid tea, borne several together, slight fragrance; free-flowering; foliage leathery, medium green, large; free and hardy growth; ['White Cockade' × (('Highlight' × 'Colour Wonder') × (Parkdirektor Riggers® × Piccadilly®))]

'Harkover' ('Garden City', Letchworth Garden City®) F, op, 1978, Harkness; flowers medium salmon-pink, 2½ in., 20 petals, moderate spicy fragrance; foliage medium green, semi-glossy; vigorous, bushy growth; [('Sabine' × 'Pineapple Poll') × ('Circus' × 'Mischief')]; intr. 1972

'Harkover' S, w, Harkness; intr. 2008

'Harkreme' ('Camphill Glory') HT, pb, 1980, Harkness, R., & Co., Ltd.; flowers creamy pink, large, 54 petals, high-centered, borne singly, slight fragrance; foliage medium green, matte; numerous prickles; vigorous, branching growth; [Elizabeth Harkness® × 'Kordes' Perfecta']; intr. 1981

'Harkuly' (Margaret Merril®) F, w, 1977, Harkness; flowers blush white, 4 in., 28 petals, high-centered, borne singly and several together, intense fragrance; free-flowering; foliage medium green with slight grayish tint; growth vigorous, rounded (3 ft.); [('Rudolph Timm' × 'Dedication') × Pascali®]

'Harkushi' (Amy Brown®) F, ob, 1978, Harkness; bud ovoid; flowers burnt-orange to fire-red, rounded, 2½-3 in., 28 petals, moderate fruity fragrance; foliage large, dark; low, bushy growth; [Orange Sensation® × (('Highlight' × 'Colour Wonder') × (Parkdirektor Riggers® × Piccadilly®))]

'Harlacal' ('Rachel Bowes Lyon') S, pb, 1980, Harkness, R., & Co., Ltd.; bud fat; flowers peach pink, reverse yellow, 12 petals, flat, borne in large clusters, moderate wild rose fragrance; good repeat; foliage small to medium size, medium green; prickles small, hooked; low, bushy growth; ['Kim' × ((Orange Sensation® × Allgold®) × *R. californica*)]; intr. 1981

'Harlady' ('Susan Daniel') F, ab, Harkness; intr. 2005

'Harlagoon' F, mp, Harkness; intr. 2003

'Harlark' F, ab, Harkness; intr. 2005

'Harlassie' ('Fairy Maid') Pol, lp, 1980, Harkness; bud short, plump; flowers light rose-pink, medium, 20 petals, cupped; foliage glossy; low, bushy growth; ['The Fairy' × Yesterday®]; intr. 1981

'Harlassie' F, my, Harkness; intr. 2005

'Harlayalong' (Fairyland®) Pol, lp, 1980, Harkness; bud short, fat; flowers medium, 24 petals, cupped; foliage glossy; spreading growth; ['The Fairy' × Yesterday®]

'Harlecho' ('Morning Light') LCl, pb, Harkness; intr. 1994

'Harlekijn' F, yb

'Harlekin' -- See 'Korlette'

Harlekin® -- See 'Korlupo'

'Harlenten' ('Greensleeves') F, w, 1980, Harkness; bud pointed, salmon-rose; flowers rosy-green and chartreuse, finishing creamy-mint with pick spots, large, 15 petals, flat; foliage dark green; vigorous, upright growth; [('Rudolph Timm' × 'Arthur Bell') × ((Pascali® × Elizabeth of Glamis®) × ('Sabine' × 'Violette Dot'))]

'Harlequin' HWich, pb, 1935, Cant, F.; flowers half pale pink and half dark red, small, borne in clusters; very vigorous, climbing growth; RULED EXTINCT 12/83; [sport of 'Excelsa']

Harlequin™ -- See 'Korlette'

'Harlequin' -- See 'Arovule'

'Harlevel' HT, mp, Harkness; intr. 2006

'Harlew' F, rb, Petersen, V.; flowers medium red with yellow reverse, dbl. petals; intr. 1973

'Harlex' ('Alexandra') HT, or, 1972, Harkness, R.; bud pointed

'Harlexis' ('Alexis', 'L'Oréal Trophy') HT, ob, 1980, Harkness, R., & Co., Ltd.; flowers orange; [sport of 'Alexander']; intr. 1981

Harley® -- See 'Lenpaga'

'Harlightly' (Princess Michael of Kent®) F, my, 1980, Harkness, R., & Co., Ltd.; flowers large, 38 petals, high-centered, borne singly or in clusters of 2-3, moderate fragrance; foliage medium large, mid-green, glossy; prickles short, thick, red; growth low (2 ft.), bushy; ['Manx Queen' × Alexander®]; intr. 1981

'Harlino' (Sue Ryder®) F, op, 1980, Harkness; bud slim; flowers salmon orange, reverse shaded yellow, 20 petals, cupped, borne in large clusters; free-flowering; foliage medium size, mid-green, semi-glossy; prickles small; vigorous, medium, bushy growth; ['Southampton' × (('Highlight' × 'Colour Wonder') × (Parkdirektor Riggers® × Piccadilly®))]; intr. 1983

'Harlisted' ('The Queen's London Child') S, dp, Harkness; intr. 2004

'Harlittle' Pol, w, 1979, Harkness; bud squat

'Harlow' HT, op, 1969, Cocker; flowers salmon, large, 29 petals; foliage glossy; ['Fragrant Cloud' × 'Melrose']

'Harlow Carr' -- See 'Kirlyl'

Harlow Carr™ -- See 'Aushouse'

'Harlyric' HT, ab, Harkness; intr. 2005

'Harm Saville' -- See 'Wekclauni'

'Harman' F, Adam, M.; intr. 1991

Harman Inermis® F, dp, Adam; relatively thornless; intr. 1991

'Harmantelle' ('Lord Louie', 'Lord Mountbatten', Mountbatten®) F, my, 1980, Harkness, R., & Co., Ltd.; flowers large, 45 petals, cupped, borne singly or several together, moderate fragrance; foliage large, leathery, glossy; prickles numerous, large; upright, dense growth; [Peer Gynt® × ((Anne Cocker® × 'Arthur Bell') × 'Southampton')]; intr. 1982

'Harmark' ('Hiroshima's Children') F, yb, 1985, Harkness, R., & Co., Ltd.; flowers light yellow, petals edged pink, large, 35 petals, high-centered, slight fragrance; foliage medium size, medium green, matte; bushy growth

'Harmatch' HT, dy, Harkness; intr. 2008

'Harmerry' S, ly, Harkness; intr. 2004

'Harmisty' HT, pb; intr. 2005

'Harmode' F, ab, Harkness; intr. 2006

Harmonia™ HT, pb, Dorieux; flowers pale pink to white with bright pink edges slowly spreading down the petals, double, high-centered; intr. 2000

'Harmonia Sub Rosa' HT, pb, Dorieux; intr. 2000

'Harmonie' ('Kordes' Harmonie') S, pb, 1954, Kordes; bud ovoid, light red; flowers pink bicolor, large, borne in clusters; foliage leathery; very vigorous, upright growth; RULED EXTINCT 5/80; [*R. rubiginosa* hybrid × 'Peace']

'Harmonie' ('Krilani') HT, op, Kriloff

Harmonie® -- See 'Kortember'

'Harmonie 92' HT, ab, Vidal; intr. 1992

'Harmonium' Gr, op, Drummond; intr. 1993

'Harmony' Cl HP, ab, 1933, Nicolas; flowers apricot-pink, very large, semi-dbl., high-centered; foliage leathery, dark; strong stems; very vigorous, climbing growth; ['Rosella' × 'Rosella']

Harmony™ ('Harmony Parade') Min, lp, Olesen; flowers light pink, medium, dbl., no fragrance; foliage dark; growth bushy, 20-40 cm.; intr. 1996

'Harmony' -- See 'Kortember'

'Harmony Parade' -- See 'Poulming'

'Harmusky' ('Radox Bouquet', 'Rosika', 'Thornbury Castle') F, mp, 1980, Harkness, R., & Co., Ltd.; flowers soft medium pink, 4 in., 30-50 petals, cupped, borne 1 - 3 per cluster, moderate rose/lilac fragrance; recurrent; foliage large, glossy, medium green; prickles large, dark; upright, rather open growth; [(Alec's Red® × Piccadilly®) × ('Southampton' × ('Clare Grammerstorf' × 'Fruhlingsmorgen'))]

'Harneatly' ('Fairy Damsel', 'Fairy Red') Pol, dr, 1980, Harkness, R., & Co., Ltd.; bud short, plump; flowers medium, 24 petals, cupped, borne in small clusters, slight fragrance; foliage small, dark green, glossy; prickles slender, dark; upright, spreading growth; ['The Fairy' × Yesterday®]

'Harnext' LCl, mr, Harkness; intr. 2008

'Harnicely' ('Fairy Ring') Pol, mp, 1980, Harkness; bud short, plump; flowers rose-pink, 2 in., 20 petals, cupped; foliage glossy; low, bushy growth; ['The Fairy' × Yesterday®]

'Harnimble' ('Fairy Like') Pol, lp, 1980, Harkness; bud short, plump; flowers light rose-pink, small, 20 petals, cupped; foliage small, glossy; low, spreading growth; ['The Fairy' × Yesterday®]

'Harnoble' ('Pacemaker') HT, dp, 1980, Harkness; bud pointed; flowers deep pink, 4 in., 40 petals, borne singly or in clusters of 3, intense fragrance; foliage large, semi-glossy; prickles large, broad, dark; vigorous, upright, bushy growth; ['Red Planet' × 'Wendy Cussons']; intr. 1981

'Harnougette' (Fairy Prince®) Pol, mr, 1980, Harkness; bud short; flowers medium, 25 petals, cupped; foliage glossy; spreading growth; ['The Fairy' × Yesterday®]; intr. 1981

'Harnumerous' ('Fairy Changeling') Pol, mp, 1980, Harkness; bud short, plump; flowers pink, pompon, medium, 22 petals, cupped, slight fragrance; foliage small, dark; recumbent, spreading growth; ['The Fairy' × Yesterday®]; intr. 1981

'Harold Ickes' -- See 'Crepe Myrtle'
'Harold Macmillan' -- See 'Harwestsun'
'Harpace' F, ab, Harkness; intr. 2008
'Harpade' F, m, 1967, Harkness
'Harpal' F, ab, Harkness; intr. 2008
'Harper Adams' F, my; flowers golden yellow with color that holds well, medium, very double, borne evenly in clusters of several together, moderate fragrance; begins early and continues through season; foliage bright green and dense, disease-resistant; growth compact, medium (4 × 2 ft.); intr. 2002

'Harpiccolo' (Anna Ford®) Min, ob, 1980, Harkness; flowers deep salmon-orange, yellow eye, patio, small, 18 petals, borne in large clusters; foliage small, glossy; prickles small; low, bushy growth; ['Southampton' × 'Darling Flame']

'Harpillar' ('Olive') S, mr, 1982, Harkness, R., & Co., Ltd.; flowers large, 36 petals, cupped, borne in clusters, moderate spicy fragrance; foliage large, dark, glossy; prickles dark; branching growth; [(('Vera Dalton' × 'Highlight') × seedling) × Dublin Bay®]

'Harpippin' LCl, ob, 1984, Harkness; flowers pale salmon-red, yellow reverse, 22 petals, borne singly, slight fragrance; foliage medium size, semi-glossy; upright (to 7 ft.) growth; [Royal Dane™ × (('Mischief' × '(Red Dandy × Buccaneer)') × ('Sabine' × 'Circus'))]

'Harpluto' ('Avocet') F, ob, 1983, Harkness, R., & Co., Ltd.; bud pointed; flowers orange edged vermilion, large, semi-dbl., borne in large clusters; foliage dark, glossy; prickles numerous, dark; medium, bushy growth; ['Dame of Sark' × seedling]; intr. 1984

'Harpmeg' (Megan's Melody™) HT, mr, 2003, Harris, Peter G.; flowers medium red, reverse lighter, medium to large, dbl., high-centered, borne mostly solitary, strong fragrance; foliage large, dark green, semi-glossy; prickles large, hooked, moderate; growth upright, tall (4-7 ft.); garden decorative, exhibition; ['Granada' × 'Karl Herbst']; intr. 2004

'Harpooh' ('Ruth Harker') HT, mp, 1981, Harkness, R., & Co., Ltd.; flowers large, 46 petals, borne singly and in small clusters, intense fragrance; foliage large, medium green, matte to semi-glossy; prickles slightly curved, reddish; upright, bushy growth; ['Fragrant Cloud' × Compassion®]

'Harportly' ('Neville Gibson') HT, mp, 1982, Harkness, R., & Co., Ltd.; flowers large, 40 petals, high-centered; foliage large, medium green, semi-glossy; medium, upright growth; ['Red Planet' × (Carina® × Pascali®)]; intr. 1983

'Harposter' ('Dr Darley') HT, mp, 1980, Harkness, R., & Co., Ltd.; flowers rose bengal, 45 petals, globular, borne usually singly; foliage mid-green, semi-glossy; prickles narrow, reddish; upright, bushy growth; ['Red Planet' × (Carina® × Pascali®)]; intr. 1981

'Harprier' ('Tigris') S, yb, 1986, Harkness; flowers yellow, dark red eye, 1 in., dbl., slight fragrance; recurrent; foliage small, light green, variable in shape; prickles gooseberry-like; stems slim; compact, rounded, wiry growth; [Hulthemia persica × Trier®]; intr. 1985

'Harprincely' ('Innoxa Femille') HT, dr, 1981, Harkness, R.; flowers 50 petals, borne singly, sometimes 3 per cluster, slight fragrance; foliage large, semi-glossy; prickles dark; medium, bushy growth; ['Red Planet' × 'Eroica']; intr. 1983

'Harprior' HT, w, Harkness; intr. 2006
'Harprocrustes' (Clarissa®) Min, ab, 1982, Harkness, R., & Co., Ltd.; flowers small, 43 petals, high-centered, borne in large clusters; foliage small, dark, glossy; prickles small; tall, upright growth; ['Southampton' × 'Darling Flame']; intr. 1983

'Harpurl' ('Leigh-Lo') HT, mp, 1980, Harkness; bud pointed; flowers rose-bengal, large, 42 petals, urn-shaped; foliage large; vigorous, upright growth; [Elizabeth Harkness® × 'Red Devil']; intr. 1981

'Harquaker' ('Volunteer') F, yb, 1985, Harkness, R., & Co., Ltd.; flowers washed soft apricot yellow in center, creamy white on edges, large, 35 petals, informal, slight fragrance; recurrent; foliage medium size, light green, glossy; bushy growth; ['Dame of Sark' × 'Silver Jubilee']; intr. 1986

'Harquanne' ('Breath of Life') LCl, ab, 1980, Harkness, R., & Co., Ltd.; bud plump; flowers apricot to apricot-pink, large, 33 petals, borne singly or in small clusters, moderate fragrance; foliage semi-glossy; prickles large, straight, reddish; upright (to 8 ft.) growth; ['Red Dandy' × Alexander®]; intr. 1981

'Harquantum' ('Margaret Isobel Hayes', International Herald Tribune®, 'Violetta', Vioríta®) F, m, 1984, Harkness, R., & Co., Ltd.; flowers violet-purple, small, 20 petals, cupped, borne in trusses, moderate fragrance; foliage medium size, medium green, semi-glossy; low, bushy growth; [seedling × ((Orange Sensation® × Allgold®) × R. californica)]

'Harqueterwife' ('Heart Throb', 'Paul Shirville', 'Saxo') HT, op, 1981, Harkness, R., & Co., Ltd.; flowers light salmon-pink, medium-large, 30 petals, high-centered, borne singly and in clusters of 3, moderate sweet fragrance; foliage large, dark, semi-glossy; prickles large, reddish; medium, bushy growth; [Compassion® × 'Mischief']; intr. 1983

'Harquhling' ('Anna Zinkeisen') S, ly, 1983, Harkness; bud plump; flowers 30 petals, borne in clusters of 3-7, moderate musk fragrance; foliage small, light green, semi-glossy; prickles small; medium, spreading, dense growth; [seedling × 'Frank Naylor']; intr. 1983

'Harquibbler' ('Nigel Hawthorne') S, pb, 1990, Harkness, R., & Co., Ltd.; bud pointed; flowers pale salmon-rose, deep scarlet eye at base, reverse same, 5 petals, cupped, slight spicy fragrance; foliage medium size, medium green, semi-glossy; prickles thin, narrow, variable, dark to light; spreading, low growth; hips plump, small, green, infrequent; ['H. persica' × Harvest Home®]; intr. 1989

'Harquillypond' ('Blue Carpet', 'Cosette') F, mp, 1987, Harkness, R., & Co., Ltd.; flowers dbl., slight fragrance; foliage small, medium green, matte; prickles small, dark; low, spreading growth; patio; [seedling × Esther's Baby®]

'Harquince' ('The Quest', 'Wandering Minstrel', Daniel Gélin®) F, op, 1986, Harkness; flowers pink shaded orange, large, 28 petals, borne in clusters; foliage dark green, glossy; medium, bushy growth; ['Dame of Sark' × 'Silver Jubilee']

'Harquisp' ('John Bradshaw') Min, dp, 1986, Harkness; flowers light rose red, 24 petals, rosette, flat, star-shaped, borne in clusters, slight fragrance; foliage small, semi-glossy; low, bushy growth; [seedling × Esther's Baby®]; intr. 1985

'Harquito' ('Bill Slim') F, op, 1986, Harkness; bud globular; flowers salmon, deep pink reverse, large, 30 petals, borne singly or in clusters, slight fragrance; foliage glossy; bushy, spreading growth; [seedling × 'Silver Jubilee']; intr. 1987

'Harquorgold' ('Rediffusion Gold') F, dy, 1985, Harkness, R., & Co., Ltd.; flowers deep golden yellow, 70 petals, borne in clusters of 3-7; foliage small, light green, matte; prickles small; medium, bushy growth; [(Orange Sensation® × Allgold®) × 'Sunsprite']; intr. 1984

'Harramin' ('Hollie Roffey') Min, mp, 1985, Harkness, R., & Co., Ltd.; flowers small, 35 petals, rosette, borne in clusters; foliage small, pointed, medium green, semi-glossy; spreading growth; [('Tip Top' × ('Manx Queen' × 'Golden Masterpiece')) × 'Darling Flame']; intr. 1986

'Harrango' ('G. P. & J. Baker') F, op, 1982, Harkness, R., & Co., Ltd.; flowers salmon orange, reverse lighter, 36 petals, flat, borne in clusters of 3-11, slight fragrance; foliage dark, glossy; numerous prickles; medium, bushy growth; [('Bobby Dazzler' × seedling) × Marion Harkness®]; intr. 1984

'Harregale' (Cardinal Hume®) S, m, 1984, Harkness, R., & Co., Ltd.; bud pointed; flowers violet-purple, 31 petals, cupped, borne in clusters of 3 or more, moderate musk fragrance; repeat bloom; foliage variable shades of green, matte; prickles small; medium, spreading growth; [(seedling × '('Orange Sensation × Allgold)' × R. californica)) × 'Frank Naylor']

'Harriet' Cl HT, my, 1931, Moore, Ralph S.; flowers golden yellow, edged paler, dbl.; recurrent bloom; foliage bronze; vigorous, climbing (12-15 ft.) growth; [sport of 'Golden Ophelia']

'Harriet A. Easlea' HT, rb, 1922, McGredy; flowers bright carmine, reverse golden yellow, dbl.

'Harriet Elizabeth' S, mp, 1987, James, John; flowers pure medium pink, large, full, borne singly and in clusters, intense fragrance; repeat bloom; foliage medium size, red aging dark green, leathery, disease-resistant; upright, bushy, vigorous, fully hardy growth; ['Paula' × ('Micki' × 'Northlander')]; intr. 1987

'Harriet Miller' HT, pb, 1973, Brownell, H.C.; bud long, pointed; flowers pink, large, very dbl., globular, moderate fragrance; foliage large, glossy; very vigorous, bushy growth; PP3375; ['Helen Hayes' × 'Traviata']; intr. 1972

'Harriet Neese' S, op, 1928, Conyers; flowers coral blended with yellow, base golden yellow, semi-dbl., slight fragrance; abundant non-recurrent bloom; growth bushy (to 4 ft.); ['Ophelia' × 'Harison's Yellow']

'Harriet Nichola' HT, pb, 2002, Poole, Lionel; flowers peach-pink, 5-5½ in., dbl., borne mostly solitary, moderate fragrance; foliage medium size, dark green, matte; prickles medium, lang, hooked downwards, moderate; growth bushy, medium (3 ft.); garden decorative, bedding; ['Selfridges' × 'Mischief']

'Harriet Poulsen' F, mp, 1912, Poulsen, D.T.; flowers apple-blossom-pink, single; vigorous growth; ['Mme Norbert Levavasseur' × 'Dorothy Perkins']

'Harriet Shepherd' Gr, mp, 1983, Shepherd, David; flowers medium, 35 petals, no fragrance; foliage medium size, medium green, holly-like; upright growth; [Queen Elizabeth® × Queen Elizabeth®]; intr. 1982

'Harriet Sheppard' HWich, m, Nobbs; intr. 1997

'Harriny' HT, mp, 1970, LeGrice; flowers clear pink, pointed, large, 40 petals, intense fragrance; foliage dark; ['Pink Favorite' × 'Lively']; intr. 1967

'Harrison Weir' HP, dr, 1880, Turner; ['Charles Lefèbvre' × 'Xavier Olibo']

'Harroffen' ('Rochester Cathedral') S, mp, 1985, Harkness, R., & Co., Ltd.; flowers medium to large, 58 petals, cupped, borne in clusters, moderate fragrance; repeat bloom; foliage medium size, dark, matte; medium, dense, spreading growth; [(seedling × '('Orange Sensation × Allgold)' × R. californica)) × 'Frank Naylor']; intr. 1986

'Harronver' ('Anneka') HT, yb, 1990, Harkness, R., & Co., Ltd.; bud ovoid; flowers high-centered to cupped to reflexed, medium, 45 petals, high-centered, borne usually singly or in sprays of 3-5, moderate fruity fragrance; foliage medium size, medium green, glossy; prickles slightly curved, medium, dark reddish; upright, medium growth; hips ovoid, medium to large, medium green; ['Goldbonnet' × 'Silver Jubilee']

'Harroony' (Amber Queen®) F, ab, 1984, Harkness; bud plump; flowers apricot gold, large, 25-30 petals, cupped, borne in clusters of 3-7, moderate sweet and spicy fragrance; foliage large, copper red to medium green, semi-glossy; prickles reddish; low, compact, bushy growth; disease resistant; PP5582; ['Southampton' × 'Typhoon']

'Harrotang' ('City of Bradford') F, or, 1986, Harkness; flowers small to medium, semi-dbl., cupped, borne in large clusters; foliage dark, semi-glossy; medium, upright growth; [('Manx Queen' × 'Whisky Mac') × (('Highlight' × 'Colour Wonder') × (Parkdirektor Riggers® × Piccadilly®))]

'Harrowbond' ('Rosemary Harkness') HT, op, 1985, Harkness, R., & Co., Ltd.; flowers orange-salmon, orange-yellow reverse, medium-large, 35 petals, intense fragrance; foliage large, dark, semi-glossy; bushy growth; [Compassion® × ('Basildon Bond' × 'Irish Gold')]

Harry® -- See 'Harry Wheatcroft'

'Harry Ashcroft' F, op; intr. 2005

'Harry Campbell' F, dp, 1976, Burnet; bud small, pointed; flowers cerise-pink shading to white, 2½ in., 45 petals, intense wild apple fragrance; foliage dark, leathery; vigorous, bushy growth; intr. 1977

'Harry Edland' F, m, 1976, Harkness; flowers lilac-pink, 4 in., 26 petals, intense fragrance; foliage dark, glossy; [('Lilac Charm' × 'Sterling Silver') × (Blue Moon® × ('Sterling Silver' × 'Africa Star'))]; intr. 1975

'Harry G. Hastings' ('H. G. Hastings') HT, dr, 1965, Von Abrams; flowers large, dbl.; foliage leathery; vigorous growth; ['Gov. Mark Hatfield' × 'Helene Schoen']

'Harry Kirk' T, ly, 1907, Dickson, A.; bud pointed, very long; flowers light sulfuryellow, dbl., open, moderate fragrance; foliage leathery; strong stems; vigrous, bushy growth

'Harry Maasz' S, rb, 1939, Kordes; bud long, pointed; flowers crimson, center white, very large, single, cupped; foliage large, leathery, wrinkled, dark; very vigorous, climbing growth; ['Barcelona' × 'Daisy Hill']; HMacrantha

'Harry Oppenheimer' -- See 'Korabmask'

'Harry Wheatcroft' ('Caribia', Harry®) HT, yb, 1973; flowers yellow striped red, reverse yellow, wide, dbl., moderate fragrance; bushy, vigorous, medium growth; [sport of 'Piccadilly']; intr. 1972

'Harry Wheatcroft, Climbing' -- See 'Aromontelib'

'Harsamy' ('Shire County') HT, op, 1990, R. Harkness & Co., Ltd.; bud ovoid; flowers peach on primrose yellow base, reverse salmon rose on primrose, medium, 33 petals, cupped, borne usually singly, moderate fragrance; foliage medium size, medium green, semi-glossy; prickles recurved, medium, reddish; bushy, medium growth; [Amy Brown® × Bonfire Night®]; intr. 1989

'Harsherry' ('Sheila's Perfume') F, yb, 1982, Sheridan, John; flowers yellow, petals edged red, 4-5 in., 20-25 petals, high-centered, borne mostly singly, intense sweet fragrance; recurrent; foliage medium size, dark green, semi-glossy; medium, bushy growth; [Peer Gynt® × ('Daily Sketch' × ('Paddy McGredy' × 'Prima Ballerina'))]; intr. 1985

'Harsprice' ('Potton Heritage') HT, rb, 1986, Harkness; flowers plum red, reverse straw-yellow, large, 32 petals, high-centered, moderate fragrance; foliage large, dark, glossy; bushy, branching growth; ['Precious Platinum' × 'Dr. A. J. Verhage']; intr. 1987

'Harsuma' ('Rosy Creeper') S, dp, Onodera, Toru F.

'Hartanna' ('Princess Alice', 'Zonta Rose', Brite Lites®) F, my, 1985, Harkness, R., & Co., Ltd.; bud medium, pointed to ovoid; flowers butter yellow, ruffled, 4-4½ in., 28-32 petals, cupped, borne in large clusters, slight fruity fragrance; free-flowering; foliage medium size, medium green, semi-glossy; prickles few, long, almost straight; bushy, upright, medium to tall growth; disease resistant; PP6953; ['Judy Garland' × Anne Harkness®]

'Hartbrad' ('Gentle Kiss') Min, ab, Harkness; intr. 1989

'Hartellody' ('Baldock Festival') HT, my, Harkness; intr. 1992

'Hartesia' ('Beryl Bach') HT, yb, 1985, Harkness, R., & Co., Ltd.; flowers yellow, blended pink, large, 40 petals, moderate fragrance; foliage large, light green, matte; tall, upright growth; ['Sunsprite' × 'Silver Jubilee']

'Hartilion' ('Seafarer') F, or, 1986, Harkness; flowers large, 30 petals, cupped, borne in clusters of 3-5; foliage medium size, dark, glossy; prickles medium, red; medium, bushy growth; hips medium, green; [Amy Brown® × 'Judy Garland']

'Hartillery' ('Reconciliation') HT, ab, Harkness, J.; intr. 1995

'Hartina' -- See 'Kammersanger Terkal'
'Hartoflax' F, ob, Harkness, R., & Co., Ltd.; intr. 1986
'Hartopper' ('Gentle Clown') MinFl, pb, Harkness; intr. 1994
'Hartred' ('Save the Children') F, mr, 1986, Harkness; flowers bright red, patio, dbl., cupped, borne in clusters; foliage dark, semi-glossy; prickles narrow, straight; low, bushy, compact growth; [Amy Brown® × 'Red Sprite']
'Hartsam' ('Country Lady') HT, ob, 1987, Harkness, R., & Co., Ltd.; flowers burnt orange, reverse suffused pale scarlet, fading orange-salmon, 25 petals, slight spicy fragrance; foliage medium size, medium green, semi-glossy; prickles decurved, medium, reddish; bushy, medium, high-shouldered growth; hips ovoid, medium, green; [Alexander® × Bright Smile®]; intr. 1988
'Hartubond' ('Lord Houghton of Sowerby') HT, op, 1990, Harkness, R., & Co., Ltd.; bud pointed; flowers warm, reddish, salmon-pink, reverse deeper, large, high-centered, borne singly, slight spicy fragrance; foliage large, dark green, glossy; prickles broad based, large, reddish; upright, medium growth; fruit not observed; ['Silver Jubilee' × 'Basildon Bond']
'Hartwiz' ('Conqueror's Gold', 'Front Page', 'Donauwalzer') F, yb, 1985, Harkness, R., & Co., Ltd.; flowers yellow, edged orange-red, 18 petals, cupped, borne in clusters of up to 7, slight fragrance; foliage medium size, dark semi-glossy; medium, bushy growth; [Amy Brown® × 'Judy Garland']; intr. 1987
'Haru-Kaze' LCl, op, 1986, Suzuki, Seizo; bud ovoid; flowers salmon yellow to orange-red, 33 petals, borne 6-8 per cluster; foliage dark, glossy; prickles small, curved, slanted downward; bushy, creeping growth; ['Charleston' × 'Dorothy Perkins']; intr. 1986
'Haru-no-umi' Min, pb, 2007, Ohtsuki, Hironaka; flowers pink, aging to white, then green, 4 cm., single, borne in large clusters; foliage medium, medium green, semi-glossy; prickles moderate, moderate, few; growth upright, tall (40-50 cm.); cutting; ['Fujizakura' × 'My Sunshine']; intr. 2006
'Harubasil' ('Cordon Bleu') HT, ab, 1990, Harkness, R., & Co., Ltd.; bud pointed; flowers apricot with begonia pink reverse, deepening to apricot with aging, 20 petals, cupped, moderate fruity fragrance; foliage medium to large, dark green, glossy; prickles recurving, average, reddish; upright, medium growth; ['Basildon Bond' × 'Silver Jubilee']; intr. 1991
'Harubondee' ('Queen Charlotte') HT, op, 1988, Harkness, R., & Co., Ltd.; flowers deep salmon-red, yellow base, reverse pink-red, aging paler, dbl., high-centered; foliage large, dark green, semi-glossy; prickles recurved, medium,

reddish-green; upright, tall growth; hips ovoid, large, green; ['Basildon Bond' × 'Silver Jubilee']; intr. 1989
'Harugasumi' LCl, mp, Itami
'Haruka' F, dp, Hiroshima; intr. 2004
'Harukfore' (City of London®) F, lp, 1987, Harkness, R., & Co., Ltd.; flowers light pink, fading to blush, large, dbl., intense fragrance; foliage medium size, medium green, glossy, ovate to pointed; prickles small, reddish, sparse; bushy growth; ['Radox Bouquet' × Margaret Merril®]; intr. 1988
'Harunique' ('Euphrates') S, pb, 1986, Harkness; flowers pale salmon red, deep pink eye, small, 5 petals, borne in small clusters; foliage small, variable form (usually long and narrow), ligh; prickly; low, spreading growth; [*Hulthemia persica* × seedling]
'Harunomai' ('Dance of Spring') F, mp, Keisei; intr. 1994
'Haruseful' (Armada®) S, mp, 1988, Harkness, R., & Co., Ltd.; flowers medium pink, aging slightly paler, medium, 17 petals, cupped, borne in sprays of up to 12; repeat bloom; foliage medium size, medium green, glossy; prickles slightly recurved, medium green; spreading growth; hips rounded, medium green; ['New Dawn' × 'Silver Jubilee']
'Haruyo' HT, w
'Harvacity' ('Drummer Boy') F, dr, 1987, Harkness, R., & Co., Ltd.; flowers deep, vivid, bright scarlet, fading slightly paler, loose, 15 petals, cupped, slight spicy fragrance; foliage small, medium green, semi-glossy, oval-pointed; prickles fairly straight, small, purplish-red; patio; spreading, low growth; hips ovoid, small, greenish; [('Wee Man' × ('Southampton' × 'Darling Flame')) × 'Red Sprite']
'Harvalex' ('Christingle') F, or, 1985, Harkness, R., & Co., Ltd.; flowers large, 35 petals; foliage medium size, dark, semi-glossy; bushy growth; ['Bobby Dazzler' × Alexander®]; intr. 1987
'Harvander' ('Phoebe') Min, lp, 1990, Harkness, R., & Co., Ltd.; bud pointed; flowers pale rose pink, aging very little, rosette, medium, very dbl., slight fragrance; foliage small, medium green, semi-glossy; prickles needle-like, long, decurved, small, dark green; bushy, low growth; fruit not a noticeable feature; [Clarissa® × (seedling × 'Mozart')]; intr. 1989
'Harvard' HT, dr, 1926, Vestal; bud pointed; flowers deep crimson, open, very large, dbl.; foliage soft, bronze; long stems; ['Hoosier Beauty' × seedling]
'Harvee' ('Phoenix') Min, rb, 1990, Harkness, R., & Co., Ltd.; bud urn-shaped; flowers blood red, with yellow base, aging orange-carm, dbl., slight fragrance; foliage small, medium green, semi-glossy, pointed; prickles narrow, recurved, small, green; bushy, low growth; fruit not a noticeable feature; [Clarissa® × ('Wee Man' × ('Southamp-

ton' × 'Darling Flame'))]; intr. 1989
'Harverag' ('Antique Abundance', 'Lawrence of Arabia', 'Samaritan', 'Renown's Samaritan', 'English Sonnet', 'Fragrant Surprise', 'King Arthur') F, ab, 1989, Harkness; bud ovoid, reddish-apricot; flowers apricot with pink tints, 4 in., very dbl., cupped, borne singly or in small clusters, intense fruity fragrance; foliage medium size, dark green, glossy; prickles moderate; upright, spreading, medium (3 ft.) growth; ['Silver Jubilee' × 'Dr A. J. Verhage']; intr. 1988
'Harvest Belle' F, my; flowers bright, sunny yellow, borne several to a cluster; free-flowering; medium growth
'Harvest Fayre' -- See 'Dicnorth'
'Harvest Festival' HT, ab, 1986, Law, M.J.; flowers light apricot-orange, reverse apricot flushed pink,, 28 petals, urn-shaped, slight fragrance; foliage medium size, medium green, semi-glossy; prickles medium, reddish-brown; tall, bushy growth; hips globular, large, orange-yellow; [Blessings® × 'Sunblest']; intr. 1980
'Harvest Glow' LCl, rb, 1941, Brownell; bud long, pointed, ovoid; flowers red to pink, reverse yellow, large, 60 petals, high-centered; foliage light green; long stems; vigorous, climbing growth; ['Golden Glow' × 'Mercedes Gallart']
Harvest Home® -- See 'Harwesi'
'Harvest Moon' HT, ly, 1938, Cant, B. R.; flowers cream, open, large, single, borne in clusters; foliage leathery, dark; long stems; vigorous, bushy, compact growth
'Harvest Moon' HT, my, Mason, A.L.; bud long, pointed; flowers 4-5 in., 35 petals, slight fragrance; vigorous growth; [sport of 'Whisky']; intr. 1976
'Harvest Moon' F, dy, Clements; flowers deep yellow in heart, fading rapidly as petals open, dbl.; intr. 2004
'Harvest Song' S, pb
'Harvest Sun' -- See 'Brosun'
'Harvest Time' Cl HT, ab, 1939, Thomas; flowers apricot, reverse sometimes pinkish, open, very large, semi-dbl.; free, recurrent boom; foliage leathery, dark; very vigorous, climbing (15-20 ft.) long stems growth; ['Sophie Thomas' × 'Souv. de Claudius Pernet']
'Harvestal' ('Pallas') Min, lp, 1990, Harkness, R., & Co., Ltd.; bud ovoid; flowers light buff pink, paling to buff white, rosette, medium, 60 petals, rosette, borne in sprays of 5 - 17, no fragrance; foliage small, medium green, semi-glossy, pointed, plentiful; prickles narrow, small, dark green; bushy, spreading, low growth; fruit not a noticeable feature; [Clarissa® × 'New Penny']; intr. 1989
'Harvester' HT, pb, 1976, Mayhew; flowers carmine, reverse silver, center lilac, 5 in., 35 petals, intense fragrance; foliage large, matte; ['Wendy Cussons' × 'Kordes' Perfecta']
'Harvilac' ('Gentle Maid') Min, m, Hark-

ness; intr. 1988

'Harvintage' ('Integrity', 'Savoy Hotel', 'Vercors', 'Violette Niestlé') HT, lp, 1987, R. Harkness & Co., Ltd.; flowers light phlox pink, reverse shaded deeper, large, 40 petals, high-centered, borne usually singly, slight fragrance; foliage medium size, dark green, semi-glossy; prickles small, reddish-green, fairly straight, narrow; bushy, medium growth; hips rounded, average, green; ['Silver Jubilee' × Amber Queen®]; intr. 1989

'Harvissa' ('Juliet Ann') Min, ly, Harkness; intr. 1990

'Harvolute' ('By Appointment') F, ab, 1990, Harkness, R., & Co., Ltd.; bud ovoid; flowers pale buff apricot, aging paler, medium, 22 petals, urn-shaped, becoming cupped, slight fragrance; foliage medium size, dark green, semi-glossy; prickles rather narrow, medium, dark reddish-green; upright, medium growth; [Anne Harkness® × Letchworth Garden City®]

'Harvool' ('Muriel') F, mp, 1992, Harkness, R., & Co., Ltd.; flowers small, dbl., borne in large clusters, slight fragrance; foliage small, medium green, semi-glossy; few prickles; low (30 cm.), bushy growth; patio; ['Liverpool Echo' × seedling]; intr. 1991

'Harwaderox' ('Rosy Future') F, dp, 1992, Harkness, R., & Co., Ltd.; flowers carmine, small, dbl., borne in large clusters, moderate fragrance; foliage small, dark green, semi-glossy; few prickles; medium (60 cm.), upright growth; patio; ['Radox Bouquet' × Anna Ford®]; intr. 1991

'Harwanna' (Jacqueline du Pré®) S, w, 1988, Harkness, R., & Co., Ltd.; flowers creamy blush to white, loose, large, 15 petals, cupped, borne singly or in sprays, moderate musk fragrance; recurrent; foliage medium size, dark green, glossy; prickles small, dark; tall, spreading growth; hips oval, medium size, green-orange; ['Radox Bouquet' × 'Maigold']; intr. 1989

'Harwanted' ('Many Happy Returns', 'Prima') S, pb, 1988, Harkness, R., & Co., Ltd.; flowers blush white, reverse blush pink, aging blush to white, large, 18 petals, cupped, moderate fruity fragrance; repeat bloom; foliage medium size, medium green, semi-glossy; prickles straight, small, red; spreading, medium growth; hips round, medium, red; ['Herbstfeuer' × 'Pearl Drift']; intr. 1990

'Harward' (Fairy Dance®) Pol, mr, Harkness; intr. 1980

'Harwazzle' ('Sheer Delight') F, or, 1992, Harkness, R., & Co., Ltd.; flowers vermilion, small, dbl., borne in large clusters, no fragrance; free-flowering; foliage small, light green, semi-glossy; few prickles; low (40 cm.), bushy growth; patio; ['Bobby Dazzler' × 'Little Prince']; intr. 1991

'Harween' (Golden Years®) F, my, 1989, Harkness, R., & Co., Ltd.; bud ovoid; flowers golden yellow, reverse some bronze tint, large, 46 petals, cupped, borne in sprays, slight fruity fragrance; foliage medium size, dark green, semi-glossy; prickles slightly curved, long, thin, greenish-red; bushy, medium growth; fruit not observed; ['Sunblest' × Amber Queen®]; intr. 1990

'Harwelcome' ('Fellowship', Livin' Easy™) F, ob, 1992, Harkness; bud ovoid, short; flowers frilly, orange-apricot, 4-4½ in., 25-30 petals, borne in clusters, moderate sweet and citrus fragrance; foliage medium size, medium green, semi-glossy; rounded, medium growth; PP9161; ['Southampton' × Remember Me®]

'Harwellington' ('High Sheriff') HT, or, 1992, Harkness, R., & Co., Ltd.; flowers medium, dbl., borne in small clusters; foliage large, dark green, glossy; few prickles; tall (95 cm.), upright growth; [seedling × 'Silver Jubilee']

'Harwesi' (Harvest Home®) HRg, mp, 1978, Rock, Mrs. W.E.; bud pointed; flowers mauve-pink, 4½ in., 14 petals, cupped, slight fragrance; abundant early bloom, then sporadic; foliage light green, wrinkled; bushy growth; [R. rugosa scabrosa × unknown]; intr. 1979

'Harwestsun' ('Harold Macmillan') F, or, 1988, Harkness, R., & Co., Ltd.; flowers medium, 18 petals, cupped, borne in sprays of 3 - 7; foliage medium size, medium green, glossy, abundant; prickles broad, medium, green; bushy, medium growth; hips rounded, medium size, green; ['Avocet' × Remember Me®]; intr. 1989

'Harwex' ('Spirit of Pentax') F, or, 1990, Harkness, R., & Co., Ltd.; bud pointed; flowers bright red, bright orange-red reverse, aging deeper, to roan, medium, 21 petals, high-centered to rounded, borne in clusters of 3 - 7, slight fragrance; recurrent; foliage small to medium size, dark green, glossy; prickles straight, narrow, small to medium, medium green; upright, medium growth; [Alexander® × Remember Me®]

'Harwharry' ('Malcolm Sargent', 'Natascha') HT, mr, 1987, Harkness, R., & Co., Ltd.; flowers shining, bright crimson, medium, 25 petals, urn shaped, loose, borne usually singly, slight spicy fragrance; foliage medium size, dark green, glossy; prickles pointed, narrow, small, reddish-green; bushy, medium growth; hips rounded, medium, green; ['Herbstfeuer' × Trumpeter®]; intr. 1988

'Harwicklow' ('Royal Ballgown', 'The Fisherman's Cot') F, op, 1991, Harkness, R., & Co., Ltd.; bud pointed; flowers light salmon pink, aging to deeper pink, 3-4 in., 28 petals, cupped, borne in sprays of 3 - 9, moderate sweet, slightly pungent fragrance; recurrent; foliage small to medium size, dark green, semi-glossy;

upright (3 ft.), spreading growth; ['Radox Bouquet' × Anna Ford®]

'Harwigwam' ('Indian Summer') Cl Min, op; intr. 1991

'Harwilla' ('Emily Louise') MinFl, dy, Harkness; intr. 1990

'Harwinner' ('Pandora') Min, w, 1990, Harkness, R., & Co., Ltd.; bud ovoid; flowers ivory, medium, 100 petals, rosette, borne in sprays of 3 - 15, slight fragrance; foliage small, medium green, semi-glossy; prickles thin, small, reddish; bushy, spreading, low, compact growth; fruit not a noticeable feature; [Clarissa® × 'Darling Flame']; intr. 1989

'Harwoey' HT, ab, Harkness

'Harwolave' ('Guiding Spirit') Min, dp, 1989, Harkness, R., & Co., Ltd.; bud ovoid; flowers deep pink, reverse lighter, medium, dbl., flat, borne is sprays of 3 - 9; foliage small, dark green, semi-glossy; prickles needle-like, very small; low, bushy growth; [(Blue Moon® × seedling) × 'Little Prince']; intr. 1989

'Harwonder' ('Pride of Maldon') F, ob, 1990, Harkness, R., & Co., Ltd.; bud pointed; flowers bright reddish-orange, light orange-yellow reverse, darkening, 10 petals, cupped; foliage medium size, dark green, glossy; prickles straight or slightly curved, medium to small, green; bushy, medium growth; ['Southampton' × 'Wandering Minstrel']; intr. 1991

'Harwood' F, dp, Harkness; flowers , high-centered, borne in small clusters, intense fragrance; medium (3 ft.) growth; intr. 2002

'Harwotnext' ('Sheila MacQueen') F, w, 1988, R. Harkness & Co., Ltd.; flowers chartreuse green with apricot tint at certain seasons, medium, 24 petals, cupped, borne in sprays of 3 - 9, slight peppery fragrance; foliage medium size, medium green, semi-glossy; prickles broad, straight, green; upright, medium growth; hips rounded, medium, green; ['Greensleeves' × Letchworth Garden City®]; intr. 1988

'Harxaglen' ('Top Brass') LCl, ab, Harkness; intr. 1998

'Harxample' ('Velvia') F, mr, 1992, Harkness, R., & Co., Ltd.; flowers 3-3½ in., full, borne in small clusters, slight fragrance; recurrent; foliage medium size, dark green, semi-glossy; some prickles; medium, bushy growth; ['Dr. Darley' × Trumpeter®]; intr. 1991

'Harxampton' ('Remembrance', 'Scarlet Abundance') F, mr, 1992, Harkness, R., & Co., Ltd.; flowers scarlet, large, 32 petals, cupped, borne in sprays of 5-7, slight fragrance; foliage dark green, glossy; bushy growth; [Trumpeter® × 'Southampton']

'Harxever' ('Applause') F, op, Harkness; intr. 1996

'Haryamber' ('Cottage Garden') Min, ob, 1992, Harkness, R., & Co., Ltd.; flowers deep, rich orange, large, full, borne in large clusters; foliage small, dark green, glossy; some prickles; low (60 cm.), upright growth; [Clarissa® × Amber Queen®]

'Haryearn' ('Lady Mitchell') HT, mr, 1990, Harkness, R., & Co., Ltd.; bud pointed; flowers deep rose-red, reverse to rose-red, paling with age, 50 petals, cupped; foliage medium size, medium green, semi-glossy; prickles slightly declining, medium, green; bushy, low to medium growth; ['Dr. Darley' × 'Silver Jubilee']; intr. 1991

'Haryen' ('Mary Jean') HT, ab, 1990, Harkness, R., & Co., Ltd.; bud ovoid to pointed; flowers large, 37 petals, cupped, borne usually singly, moderate sweet fragrance; foliage medium to large, oval, medium green, semi-glossy; prickles slightly decurved, medium, green; bushy, medium growth; ['Dr. Darley' × Amber Queen®]; intr. 1991

'Haryoricks' ('Midsummer Night's Dream') F, ob, Harkness; intr. 1991

'Haryup' ('High Hopes') LCl, mp, 1994, Harkness; flowers , 32 petals, borne singly or in small clusters, moderate spicy fragrance; foliage medium size, medium green, semi-glossy; upright, tall, climbing growth; [Compassion® × 'Congratulations']; intr. 1992

'Harzap' ('Country Life') F, op, Harkness; intr. 1998

'Harzart' ('Born Again', 'Cameo Perfume') HT, lp; intr. 1994

'Harzazz' ('Chimène', 'Lady Jane Grey', 'Sweet Lady', 'Sweet Revelation') HT, ab, Harkness; intr. 1997

'Harzeal' ('Mrs Octavia Hill', 'Octavia Hill') F, mp, 1993, Harkness; flowers 3¼ in., 75 petals, borne in sprays of 3-5, moderate damask fragrance; foliage medium size, dark green, semi-glossy; medium, bushy growth; [Armada® × Compassion®]; intr. 1994

'Harzelt' ('Hector Berlioz') HT, or, Harkness; intr. 1998

'Harzest' ('Saga Holiday') F, ob, 1993, Harkness; flowers orange, orange-pink reverse, 4 in., 28 petals, high-centered, loose, borne in clusters of 3 - 5, slight spicy fragrance; foliage medium size, purplish, glossy; bushy, medium growth; [seedling × Amber Queen®]; intr. 1993

'Harzippee' ('Cindy', 'LeAnn Rimes', 'Perception') HT, pb, 1999, Harkness; flowers rose pink edged ivory yellow, reverse cream, 5 in., full, high-centered, borne mostly singly, intense citrus and rose fragrance; foliage large, dark green, glossy; prickles moderate; upright, tall (4½ ft.) growth; ['Dr Darley' × 'Sweetheart']; intr. 1997

'Harzodiac' ('Compassionate Friend', 'The Compassionate Friends') F, lp, 1993, Harkness; flowers medium pink, lighter at center, reverse light pink, 4 in., 24 petals, borne in sprays of 5-7, moderate fruity fragrance; foliage medium size, medium green, semi-glossy; spreading, low growth; [seedling × Memento®]; intr. 1985

'Harzola' ('L'Aimant', 'Oxford', 'Scented Abundance', 'L'Aimont', 'Victorian Spice') F, lp, 1999, Harkness, Robert & Philip; flowers soft peach pink, old-fashioned, 3½-4 in., very dbl., cupped, borne in large clusters, intense damask fragrance; recurrent; foliage medium size, dark green, glossy; prickles moderate; spreading, mounding, bushy, medium (3½ ft.) growth

'Harzorba' ('City Girl') LCl, pb, 1993; flowers large, light rose pink with primrose base and salmon pink reverse stained yellow, 4¾ in., 12 petals, borne in sprays of 3-5, moderate fruity fragrance; foliage large, dark green, glossy; upright, tall, climbing growth; [Armada® × Compassion®]; intr. 1985

'Harzumber' (Welsh Gold™) HT, ab, Harkness; bud short; intr. 1996

'Hasina' HT, mr, Ghosh; flowers deep cherry red, shapely, dbl., high-centered; intr. 2001

'Hassan' F, mr, 1963, McGredy, Sam IV; flowers scarlet, 4 in., 28 petals; foliage glossy, light green; vigorous, upright growth; ['Tivoli' × 'Independence']

'Hassi-Messaoud' LCl, or, 1961, Hémeray-Aubert; flowers garnet-red shaded orange, 2½-3 in., full, borne in small clusters; abundant, recurrent bloom

'Hat Pin' -- See 'Tinpin'

'Hat Trick' HT, pb, 1992, Lienau, David W.; flowers pink, darker pink petal edges and reverse, natural recurve,, 3-3½ in., very dbl.; foliage medium size, dark green, semi-glossy; few prickles on upper half of stems; medium (90-120 cm.), upright growth; ['First Prize' × seedling]; intr. 1993

'Hatakeyama' HT, dp, 1995, Shimizu, Junji; flowers deep pink, large, full; foliage medium size, dark green, matte; some prickles; medium, upright growth; ['Garden Party' × 'Kolner Karneval']

'Hatchell Brown Tea' T, lp, Clark

'Hatsu Kari' -- See 'Hatsukari'

'Hatsukari' ('Hatsu Kari') HT, pb, 2005, Yasuda, Yuji; flowers pink blend, reverse light pink, 13 cm., full, borne mostly solitary; foliage medium size, dark green, matte; prickles medium; growth compact, short (100 cm.); cutting, containers; ['Paradise' × 'Colorama']; intr. 1994

'Hatsukoi' HT, w

'Hatuzakura' ('Orange Chateau') HT, ab, 1999, Teranishi, K.; flowers apricot-orange, 5½ in., 80 petals, hybrid tea, moderate fragrance; growth to 4 ft.; intr. 1997

'Hauff' HMult, m, 1911, Lambert, P.; flowers reddish-violet, dbl., borne in clusters; recurrent when established; foliage dark, broad; vigorous, climbing growth; ['Aimee Vibert' × 'Crimson Rambler']

'Haumi' (Sweet Mimi®) HT, mp, 1982, Hauser, Victor; flowers large, 20 petals, moderate fragrance; foliage medium size, reddish green, semi-glossy; bushy growth; ['Tropicana' × Elizabeth Harkness®]; intr. 1981

'Hauraki' -- See 'Macwynscar'

'Hauric' (Ricky®) Min, op, Hauser; intr. 1989

'Hauser' HT, my, 1978, Gaujard; flowers yellow-cream, dbl.; vigorous growth; ['Barbara' × Guitare®]; intr. 1975

'Haute Pink' -- See 'Jachop'

'Havam' F, or, 1976, Verschuren, Ted; bud ovoid; intr. 1972

Havana™ ('Havana Hit', 'Sweet Wishes') Min, dr, Poulsen; flowers dark red, medium, less than 2 in., semi-dbl., cupped, no fragrance; bushy (40-60 cm.) growth; intr. 2005

'Havana' HT, pb, 1950, Fisher, G.; flowers salmon-rose, reverse orange-yellow, 5-5½ in., 40 petals, slight fragrance; foliage soft; vigorous, compact growth; PP1109; ['Peace' × 'Orange Nassau']

'Havana Hit' -- See 'Poulpah032(N)'

'Havaps' (Poker®) HT, dp, 1985, Verschuren, Ted; flowers large, 11 petals, cupped, borne in sprays of 6 - 8, intense fragrance; foliage medium size, medium green, semi-glossy; bushy, medium growth; rounded fruit; ['Red Planet' × 'Sonia']

'Haveal' (Eagle®) HT, dr, 1985, Verschuren, Ted; flowers large, 28 petals, cupped, borne in sprays of 3-5, moderate fragrance; foliage large, dark, semi-glossy; bushy, tall growth; [Centurio® × 'Red Planet']; intr. 1984

'Havering' HMsk, mp, 1937, Bentall; flowers China-pink, large, borne in clusters of 4-5; vigorous growth

'Havering Rambler' HMult, mp, 1920, Pemberton; flowers almond-blossom-pink, 3-4 cm., dbl., rosette, borne in large clusters, slight fragrance; long stems; very vigorous growth; [sport of 'Turner's Crimson Rambler']

'Havink' (Pink Ocean®) Cl HT, lp, 1985, Verschuren; flowers salmon pink, fading to pale pink, large, 20 petals, intense fragrance; foliage medium size, medium green semi-glossy; upright (to 7 ft.) growth; ['Pink Showers' × Alexander®]; intr. 1980

'Havipip' ('Friendship') Min, pb, 1985, Verschuren, Ted; bud ovoid; flowers pink and white blend, small, 5-6 petals, borne in sprays of 30-50, no fragrance; foliage medium size, light green, semi-glossy; groundcover; spreading, medium growth; very small fruit; [(Swany® × 'Mozart') × 'Mozart']; intr. 1981

'Havlickova Národni' HP, rb, 1935, Böhm, J.; flowers dark red with white, medium, semi-dbl.

'Havobog' ('Golden Border') F, ly, Verschuren; intr. 1993

'Havoon' (Gold Moon®) Min, dy, 1985, Verschuren, Ted; bud ovoid; flowers small, 15 petals, borne singly, slight fragrance; foliage medium size, medium green, glossy; no prickles; spreading, low growth; [(Aalsmeer Gold® × seedling) × ('Motrea' × 'Golden Times')]; intr. 1984

'Havop' (Centurio®) HT, dr, 1978, Verschuren, Ted; flowers lasting well; moderate, bushy growth; PP3613; [Orangeade® × Baccará®]; intr. 1974

'Havychi' (Sunny Child®) Min, dy, 1985, Verschuren, Ted; flowers small, 8 petals; foliage medium size, light green; no prickles; spreading, low growth; [Gold Bunny® × seedling]

'Hawa Mahal' HT, op, 1977, Harkness; flowers salmon-pink, 5-6 in., 25 petals, moderate fragrance; foliage dark; ['Fragrant Cloud' × 'Kordes' Perfecta']; intr. 1976

'Hawaii' HT, op, J&P; greenhouse rose; intr. 2001

'Hawaii' HT, or, 1960, Boerner; bud long, pointed; flowers orange-coral, 6 in., 33 petals, high-centered, intense fragrance; foliage leathery; vigorous, upright growth; PP1833; ['Golden Masterpiece' × seedling]; intr. 1960

'Hawaiian Admiral' Wyckoff, Gilbert, Wyckoff, Gilbert; intr. 2006

'Hawaiian Beauty' HT, pb, 1993, Wyckoff, Gilbert R.; flowers have salmon pink outer petals, light pink inner petals, slightly darker reverse, 5-5½ in., very full, borne mostly singly, moderate fragrance; foliage medium size, medium green, semi-glossy; few prickles; medium (4½-5 ft.), bushy growth; ['Thriller' × 'Dothan']; intr. 1994

'Hawaiian Belle' Min, pb, 1983, Dobbs, Annette E.; flowers medium pink, aging to pink blend, small, 35 petals, slight fragrance; foliage small, medium green, matte; bushy growth; ['Pink Ribbon' × 'Pink Ribbon']; intr. 1982

'Hawaiian Delight' F, op, 1970, deRuiter; flowers burnt-orange to pink, small, dbl., cupped, slight fragrance; recurrent; foliage dark, leathery; vigorous, bushy growth; PP2799; [Orange Sensation® × 'Circus']; intr. 1968

'Hawaiian Duchess' HT, op, 2002, Wyckoff, Gilbert R.; bud orange-pink with some red; flowers yellow and orange pink, 5½ in., full, borne mostly solitary, intense fragrance; foliage medium size, medium green, semi-glossy; prickles medium, moderate; growth upright, medium (5-6 ft.); garden decorative, exhibition; ['Elsie Melton' × 'Hawaiian King']; intr. 2002

'Hawaiian Fragrance' HT, or, 1994, Wyckoff, Gilbert R.; flowers coral, orange-red, similar to Fragrant Cloud, 5-6 in., full, borne mostly singly, intense fragrance; foliage large, medium size, semi-glossy; some prickles; tall (6+ ft.), upright growth; ['Fragrant Cloud' × 'Captain Harry Stebbings']; intr. 1994

Hawaiian Fragrant Sunrise™ ('Fragrant Sunrise') HT, pb, 2002, Wyckoff, Gilbert R.; flowers yellow with orange/pink, orange/pink reverse, 5-5½ in., full, borne mostly solitary; foliage medium size, medium green, semi-glossy; prickles medium, straight, moderate; growth upright, medium to tall (5-5½ ft.); garden decorative, exhibition; ['Thriller' × 'Hawaiian Queen Martha']; intr. 1998

'Hawaiian King' HT, lp, 1993, Wyckoff, Gilbert R.; flowers 3-3½ in., very dbl., borne mostly singly; foliage medium size, medium to dark green, semi-glossy; some prickles; tall (5-6 ft.), upright growth; ['Peggy Lee' × 'Captain Harry Stebbings']; intr. 1994

'Hawaiian Lady' HT, dp, 1993, Wyckoff, Gilbert R.; flowers deep pink, 3 in., very full, borne mostly singly, moderate fragrance; foliage medium size, medium green, semi-glossy; numerous prickles; medium (5 ft.), upright, bushy growth; ['Peggy Lee' × 'Captain Harry Stebbings']; intr. 1994

'Hawaiian Prince' HT, mr, 2002, Wyckoff, Gilbert R.; flowers fading to light red, 5-6 in., dbl., borne mostly solitary, moderate fragrance; foliage medium size, medium green, semi-glossy; prickles medium, few; growth upright, medium to tall (5-6 ft.); garden decorative, exhibition; ['Thriller' × 'Captain Harry Stebbings']; intr. 1998

'Hawaiian Princess' HT, op, 2002, Wyckoff, Gilbert R.; flowers white with orange-pink, changing with weather, 5 in., full, borne mostly solitary, moderate fragrance; foliage medium size, medium green, semi-glossy; prickles medium, moderate; growth upright, medium (5 ft.); garden decorative, exhibition; ['Elsie Melton' × 'Hawaiian Queen Martha']; intr. 2002

'Hawaiian Punch' HT, Wyckoff, Gilbert; intr. 2007

'Hawaiian Queen Martha' HT, op, 1994, Wyckoff, Gilbert R.; flowers salmon, interspered with light pink on both petal surfaces,, 5½-6 in., very dbl.; foliage medium size, medium green, semi-glossy; some prickles; medium (4 ft.), upright growth; ['Kordes Perfecta' × 'Dothan']; intr. 1995

'Hawaiian Sunrise' Min, rb, 1982, Williams, Ernest D.; bud pointed; flowers red and yellow blend, 40 petals, high-centered, borne usually singly, slight fragrance; foliage small, dense, glossy, bronze; prickles thin, reddish; upright growth; [seedling × 'Over the Rainbow']; intr. 1981

'Hawaiian Sunrise' HT, op, Wyckoff, Gilbert R.; flowers yellow and orange-pink, reverse orange-pink, 5-5½ in., full, borne mostly solitary, intense fragrance; foliage medium size, medium green, semi-glossy; prickles medium, moderate; growth upright, tall (5 ft.); garden, exhibition; ['Thriller' × 'Hawaiian Queen Martha']; intr. 1998

'Hawaiian Sunset' HT, ob, 1962, Swim & Weeks; bud ovoid; flowers orange edged yellow, open,, 4-5½ in., 45-50 petals, moderate fragrance; foliage leathery, glossy; vigorous, upright, well branched growth; PP2143; ['Charlotte Armstrong' × 'Signora']; intr. 1962

'Hawaiian Thrill' HT, pb, 1993, Wyckoff, Gilbert R.; flowers pink, white center, 5½ in., 23-25 petals, borne mostly singly, intense fragrance; foliage medium size, dark green, semi-glossy; some prickles; medium (4½-5 ft.), upright growth; ['Fragrant Cloud' × 'Thriller']; intr. 1994

'Hawkesbury Wonder' S, mp; ['Hebe's Lip' × unknown]

'Hawkeye Belle' S, w, 1975, Buck, Dr. Griffith J.; bud ovoid, pointed; flowers white, tinted azalea-pink, 4-4½ in., 38 petals, high-centered, intense fragrance; foliage large, dark, leathery; vigorous, erect, bushy growth; [(Queen Elizabeth® × 'Pizzicato') × 'Prairie Princess']

'Hawlmark Crimson' HT, mr, 1920, Dickson, A.; bud pointed; flowers crimson-scarlet, semi-dbl.; bushy growth

'Hawlmark Scarlet' HT, mr, 1923, Dickson, A.; flowers brilliant velvety scarlet-crimson

'Haybarb' (Polo Queen™) HT, pb, 2003, Hayes, Cal; flowers pale pink at the base of each petal blending to a very dark pink on the margin, 4-5 in., full, borne mostly solitary; foliage large, dark green, semi-glossy; upright, tall (4-5 ft.) growth; [sport of 'Cajun Moon']

'Haydock Park' F, mr, Fryer; flowers ruby red, dbl., classic hybrid tea, borne in clusters, moderate fragrance; recurrent; foliage dark green, disease-resistant; vigorous (100 cm.) growth; intr. 2006

'Haylee Denise' Min, ly, 2004, McConathy, George D.; flowers full, borne mostly solitary; foliage medium size, dark green, glossy; prickles moderate; growth bushy, medium (18-24 in.); [sport of 'Hot Tamale']; intr. 2004

'Hayley Scott' -- See 'Worcity'

'Hayley Westenra' -- See 'Tangust'

'Hazel Alexander' HT, dr, 1933, Dicksons of Hawlmark; flowers deep red; ['Ophelia' × unknown]

'Hazel McCallion' -- See 'Manhazel'

'Hazel Rose' HT, lp, 1992, Poole, Lionel; flowers 3-3½ in., full, borne singly, slight fragrance; foliage medium size, dark green, semi-glossy; few prickles; medium (120 cm.), upright growth; ['Queen Esther' × 'Selfridges']

'Hazel Woodland' -- See 'Lovbang'

'Hazeldean' HSpn, my, 1948, Wright, Percy H.; flowers large, dbl., moderate fragrance; very hardy (to -60); [R. spinosissima altaica × 'Harison's Yellow']

'Head of Rivers' D, mp

'Headleyensis' (R. headleyensis) S, ly, 1920, Warburg; flowers creamy yellow, single; foliage ferny; vigorous growth; [R. hugonis × R. spinosissima altaica]

'Headline' HT, yb, Dawson; flowers deep yellow blushed carmine, full; growth tall; intr. 1970

'Headliner' -- See 'Jactu'

'Healing Hands'   HT, yb, 1998, Poole, Lionel; flowers pale yellow, edged pink, 5½ in., very dbl., high-centered, borne mostly singly; foliage large, dark green, glossy; some prickles; upright, bushy, medium growth; [('Gavotte' × (Peer Gynt® × 'Golden Splendour')]; intr. 1999

Heart 'n' Soul™ -- See 'Orapaymel'

'Heart 'n' Soul' -- See 'Lavsans'

'Heart of England' -- See 'Pink Silk'

'Heart of Gold'   HMoy, rb, 1926, Van Fleet; flowers crimson-purple, center white, stamens yellow, 4-5 cm., single, open, borne in clusters of 5-15, moderate fragrance; foliage rich green, glossy; vigorous (10 ft.) growth; [(*R. wichurana* × *R. setigera*) × *R. moyesii*]; sometimes classed as HWich

'Heart of Gold'   HT, yb, Ross; flowers yellow changing to red, double, moderate fragrance; growth medium height; intr. 2006

'Heart of Gold' -- See 'Macyelkil'

'Heart of Gold' -- See 'Coctarlotte'

'Heart of Gold' -- See 'Wekdykstra'

Heart O' Gold™ -- See 'Wekdykstra'

'Heart of T. D. K.'   HT, op, 1985, Ogawa, Isamu; bud ovoid; flowers salmon-pink, large, 50 petals, borne singly, slight fragrance; foliage small, light green; prickles heavy hooked; vigorous, upright, tall growth; ['Sunblest' × 'Red Devil']; intr. 1983

'Heart Throb'   F, yb, 1966, Fankhauser; bud urn shaped; flowers deep yellow, edges flushed pink, medium, very dbl., borne in clusters, intense fragrance; foliage dark, glossy; vigorous, bushy growth; RULED EXTINCT 4/82 ARM; [('Circus' × 'Circus') × ('Circus' × 'Circus')]

'Heart Throb' -- See 'Harqueterwife'

'Heart Throb' -- See 'Leonhart'

'Heartache' -- See 'Koreledas'

'Heartbeat'   F, op, 1971, Dickson, Patrick; flowers deep salmon-orange, 4½ in., 26 petals, globular, slight fragrance; foliage small, dull; very free growth; [('Castanet' × 'Castanet') × ('Cornelia' × seedling)]; intr. 1970

'Heartbeat'   HT, mr, Bridges, Dennis A.; bud pointed; flowers medium red, darker outer petals, reverse lighter, medium, 45 petals, high-centered, borne usually singly, slight fruity fragrance; foliage medium size, medium green, semi-glossy; prickles straight, large, pink to yellow; upright growth; ['Thriller' × 'Wild Cherry']; intr. 1990

'Heartbeat' -- See 'Cocorona'

'Heartbeat 96' -- See 'Cocorona'

'Heartbreaker' -- See 'Weksybil'

'Hearth Glow'   F, or, 1968, Von Abrams; bud ovoid; flowers brick-red, medium, dbl., borne in clusters; foliage soft, light green; vigorous, upright growth; ['Red Pinocchio' × ('Carrousel' × 'Queen o' the Lakes')]; intr. 1963

Heartland™   Min, op, 1982, Saville, F. Harmon; bud short, pointed; flowers 38 petals, high-centered, borne in clusters; prickles long, thin; vigorous, upright growth; PP5045; ['Sheri Anne' × 'Watercolor']

'Heartland Flame' -- See 'Dogflame'

'Heartland Lady' -- See 'Doglady'

Heartlight™ -- See 'Kinheart'

'Hearts Afire'   Min, dr, Michigan Bulb; flowers , 15-25 petals, borne mostly singly; recurrent; foliage dark green, glossy; vigorous, upright (12 - 18 in.) growth; [Merrimac™ × Seedling]

'Hearts A'Fire' -- See 'Briheart'

'Heart's Delight'   HT, op, 1933, Hart, L.P.; flowers apricot-coral-orange, veined red, large, very dbl., high-centered; foliage soft; vigorous, open growth; [sport of 'Mrs Beckwith']

'Heart's Desire'   HT, dr, 1942, Howard, F.H.; bud long, pointed; flowers crimson, 4½ in., 30 petals, high-centered, intense damask fragrance; foliage leathery, dark; vigorous, upright growth; PP501; [seedling × 'Crimson Glory']

'Heart's Desire, Climbing'   Cl HT, dr, 1945, Howard, F.H.; PP663

'Heartsong Mini Brite'   Min, dp, Walden, John; bud long, pointed, ovoid; flowers mauve pink, 2-2¼ in., 25-30 petals, borne in clusters of 3 - 5, slight fragrance; recurrent; foliage medium size, matte; prickles moderate, hooked downward; upright, medium (24 in.) growth; PP11144; [(seedling × Red Minimo™) × 'Winsome']; intr. 1998

'Heartsounds' -- See 'Minsounds'

'Heartstrings' -- See 'Broheart'

'Heat Wave'   ('Mme Paula Guisez') F, or, 1959, Swim, H.C.; bud urn-shaped; flowers orange-scarlet, 3½-4½ in., 30 petals, cupped, borne in clusters; foliage dark, semi-glossy, rounded; vigorous, upright, bushy growth; PP1786; [seedling × 'Roundelay']; intr. 1958

Heather™ -- See 'Poulcot007'

'Heather' -- See 'Jaclav'

'Heather Austin' -- See 'Auscook'

'Heather Claire'   HT, ab, 1983, Allender, Robert William; bud long; flowers apricot-pink, 30 petals, borne singly, no fragrance; foliage dark, red reverse; prickles slightly hooked; medium growth; ['Diamond Jubilee' × 'Bonsoir']

'Heather Cottage'   (Heather™) S, mr, Poulsen; flowers medium red, small, single, borne in clusters, very slight fragrance; recurrent; foliage dark green, glossy; broad, bushy (20-40 cm.) growth; intr. 2005

'Heather Elms'   HT, dr, Orard; flowers very dark red, stiff petals, dbl., high-centered, no fragrance; vigorous, tall growth; intr. 1999

'Heather Honey' -- See 'Horsilbee'

'Heather Jenkins'   HT, mp, 1970, Watson; bud globular; flowers pink, reverse darker, medium, dbl., high-centered, slight fragrance; foliage light green, wrinkled; moderate, upright, open growth; ['Charlotte Armstrong' × 'Ballet']; intr. 1968

'Heather Leigh' -- See 'Talheather'

Heather Lenkin™ -- See 'Wekpegjuc'

'Heather Miranda' -- See 'Majlyniment'

'Heather Mist'   Min, m, 2001, Williams, Michael C.; flowers light to medium lavender, reverse same, 1½-2 in., full, borne mostly solitary, slight fragrance; foliage medium size, dark green, semi-glossy; prickles 1/8 to ¼ in., straight, few; growth compact, medium (18-24 in.); garden decorative; [seedling × unknown]

'Heather Muir'   (variety of *R. sericea*), w, 1957; flowers pure white, 3 in., single; blooms over a long period; foliage ferny; hips orange

'Heather Paton'   HT, mr, 1934, Austin & McAslan; flowers carmine, center darker; vigorous growth

'Heather Pudney'   HT, mp, Dawson; intr. 1995

'Heather Sproul' -- See 'Sproheather'

'Heatherby'   S, op, Kordes; intr. 2004

Heaven™ -- See 'Jacfon'

'Heaven Bound'   F, mp, Williams, J. Benjamin; flowers bright pink, old-fashioned, ruffled, dbl.; compact (2½ ft.) growth; intr. 1999

'Heaven on Earth'   ('Avril Elizabeth Home') F, ab, Kordes; flowers thick petals, peach-apricot, large, dbl., cupped, slight spicy fragrance; foliage glossy, dark green; stems strong; growth compact (1½ × 2 m.); PP15253; intr. 2001

'Heaven Scent'   F, op, 1970, Poulsen; flowers salmon, large, 30 petals, borne in trusses, intense fragrance; [Pernille Poulsen™ × 'Isabel de Ortiz']; intr. 1968

'Heaven Scent' -- See 'Wekblunez'

'Heaven Scent Pink' -- See 'Jalpink'

Heavenly Days™ -- See 'Savaday'

'Heavenly Fragrance'   HT, lp, 1963, Hennessey; flowers light pink, reverse darker, well-formed, 5 in., intense fragrance; moderate growth; ['Tiffany' × 'Mme Gregoire Staechelin']

'Heavenly Gold' -- See 'Macyelkil'

'Heavenly Maiden' -- See 'Amatsu-Otome'

'Heavenly Pink'   F, lp, Zary; PP11561; intr. 2001

'Heavenly Pink' -- See 'Lennedi'

'Heavenly Robe' -- See 'Hagoromo'

'Heavenly Rosalind' -- See 'Ausmash'

'Heavenly Scent'   S, mp, 1999, Hamilton, Noel; flowers cerise pink, lighter reverse, large, 58 petals, borne mostly singly and in small clusters, moderate fragrance; foliage medium size, dark green, glossy; prickles moderate; upright, compact, medium (5 ft.) growth

'Heavenly Vision' -- See 'Minivision'

'Heavens Above' -- See 'Webspark'

'Hébé'   HP, mp, Moreau & Robert; flowers pink, shaded white, very large, full; intr. 1883

'Hebe'   F, dp, Leenders, M.; flowers deep

The Official Registry and Checklist — Rosa   285

pink, reverse lighter; intr. 1941

'Hebe' HT, op, Dickson, A.; flowers rosy salmon toned orange and apricot-yellow, high pointed, 6 in., 27 petals, moderate fragrance; foliage glossy, bronze green; vigorous growth; intr. 1949

'Hébé' Ch, mp

'Hébé' D, mp, about 1860, Miellez

'Hebe Camargo' HT, (Brazil)

'Hebe's Lip' ('Margined Hip', R. damascena rubrotincta, 'Rubiginosa', 'Rubrotincta', 'Reine Blanche', R. damascena rubra) HEg, w, before 1846, Lee; flowers creamy white, petals edged pink, wavy, semi-dbl., cupped, moderate fragrance; non-recurrent; vigorous, moderate growth; thought to be R. × damascena × R. rubiginosa hybrid

Heckenfeuer® -- See 'Korrohe'

'Heckengold' F, dy, W. Kordes Söhne; flowers large, dbl.; intr. 1986

'Heckenzauber' -- See 'Macrexy'

'Hector' ('Blood d'Angleterre', 'Blood', 'Cramoisi Majeur', 'Noire', 'Sang', 'Sanguine d'Angleterre') HGal, m, before 1819, from Holland; flowers purple, faintly striped with white, small, dbl., pompon; sometimes attributed to Parmentier, about 1830. It is probable that more than one cultivar was grown under this name.

'Hector Berlioz' -- See 'Harzelt'

'Hector Deane' HT, rb, 1938, McGredy; bud pointed; flowers orange, carmine and salmon-pink, dbl., high-centered, intense fruity fragrance; foliage glossy, dark; vigorous, compact growth; PP361; ['McGredy's Scarlet' × 'Lesley Dudley']

'Hedda Hopper' HT, mp, 1952, Howard, A.P.; bud ovoid; flowers light peach passing to pearly pink, 3½-4 in., 40 petals, globular, moderate fragrance; foliage coppery; very vigorous growth; PP1047; ['Radiance' × seedling]

'Hede' HT, my, 1934, Tantau; flowers pure sunflower-yellow, large, dbl.; foliage dark, leathery; strong stems; vigorous growth; ['Prof. Gnau' × 'Mev. G.A. van Rossem']

'Hedgefire' MinFl, mr, Kordes; very free flowering; sturdy, strong (18 in.) growth; intr. 1983

'Hedgerow Beauty' HRg, m, Bell; flowers mauve pink, moderate fragrance; free-flowering; growth healthy, bushy plant; intr. 2001

'Hedgerow Bonny' S, ly, Mann; intr. 2003

'Hedgerow Toby' HMult, w, Mann; flowers pure white, single, borne in large clusters, moderate fragrance; foliage grey-green; climbing (20 ft.) growth; intr. 2001

'Hedi Grimm' HMsk, w, Lens, Louis; bud white with pink blush; flowers pure white, 3 -4 cm., semi-dbl., shallow cup , borne in large, pyrimidal clusters; recurrent; foliage dense, healthy; growth vigorous, tall (180-250 cm.); large shrub or small climber; hardy to -10°C; named for Hedi Grimm (1910-2003), who was - together with her husband Wernt - the founder of the rose collection in Kassel-Wilhelmshöhe (Germany); intr. 2005

'Hedwig Fulda' Cl Pol, mr, 1934, Leenders Bros.; flowers clear vermilion-red, well-formed, large, dbl., borne in large clusters; foliage bright, dark; long strong stems; vigorous growth; ['Orléans Rose' × 'Farbenkonigin']

'Hedwig Reicher' HT, ly, 1912, Hinner, W.; flowers yellowish-white, darker center, large, very dbl., moderate fragrance

'Heer' HT, lp, 1971, Singh, R. S.; flowers rose-pink, medium, dbl., high-centered, slight fragrance; vigorous, upright growth; ['Picture' × unknown]; intr. 1969

'Hefqueen' (Regine™) Min, pb, 1990, Hefner, John; flowers soft, light pink, silvery-pink reverse, small, 30 petals; foliage medium size, medium green, semi-glossy; bushy growth; ['Little Darling' × Party Girl™]; intr. 1990

'Hei W. Perron' HT, or

'Heian' HT, op, Keihan; intr. 1979

'Heide Simonis' S, pb; flowers medium pink with apricot tones in center , 7 cm , double , cupped , borne in small clusters, intense fragrance; recurrent; foliage medium, medium green; strong, arching, 3 - 5 ft. growth

Heidefee® Pol, dp, Noack, Werner; intr. 1990

'Heidefeuer' ('Flower Carpet Red') F, dr, Noack, Werner; flowers bright red, 2 in., borne in clusters; free-flowering; upright (20-24 in.) growth; PP10084; intr. 1995

'Heidegruss' F, pb, 1937, Tantau; flowers salmon-flesh, base light yellow, large, very dbl., borne in clusters; foliage leathery; vigorous, bushy growth; ['Heidekind' × 'Ophelia']

'Heidekind' HRg, dp, 1931, Berger, V.; flowers brilliant pink shaded copper-red, large, dbl., borne in clusters; foliage thick, rugose; PP78; ['Mev. Nathalie Nypels' × R. rugosa hybrid]

'Heidekind' -- See 'Koriver'

Heidekönigin® -- See 'Kordapt'

'Heidelberg' ('Gruss an Heidelberg') HKor, mr, 1959, Kordes, R.; flowers bright crimson, reverse lighter, 4 in., 32 petals, high-centered, borne singly or in small clusters; foliage glossy, leathery; very vigorous, bushy growth; ['Minna Kordes' × 'Floradora']; intr. 1958

Heidelinde® ('Malverns') F, m, Kordes; flowers medium, golden stamens , open flat , borne in large clusters; recurrent; foliage dark green, glossy, delicate; bushy (70 cm.) growth

'Heidemarie' F, mr, 1945, Tantau; flowers carmine-red, large, 5-7 petals, borne in clusters of 4-6; foliage dark, leathery; vigorous, upright, bushy growth; ['Hamburg' × ('Heros' × 'Heidekind')]

'Heidemarie Plücker' HP, mp, 1940, Westphal; flowers large, very dbl.

'Heidepark' -- See 'Meisolroz'

'Heideröslein' LCl, yb, 1932, Lambert, P.; bud pointed, orange-red; flowers bright yellowish salmon-pink, base sulfur-yellow, 4-5 cm., single, flat, borne in clusters of 10-30, moderate fragrance; recurrent bloom; broad, bushy growth; ['Chamisso' × 'Amalie de Greiff']

'Heideröslein Nozomi' -- See 'Nozomi'

'Heideschnee' -- See 'Korconta'

Heidesommer® -- See 'Korlirus'

Heidetraum™ -- See 'Noatraum'

'Heidezauber' F, dr, 1936, Tantau; flowers large, very dbl., borne in clusters; foliage dark, leathery; bushy growth; ['Heidekind' × 'Johanniszauber']

'Heidi' S, mp, Noack, Werner; intr. 1987

Heidi™ Min, mp, 1977, Christensen, Jack E.; bud mossy; flowers clear medium pink, mini-moss, 1½ in., 35 petals, intense fragrance; foliage glossy; very vigorous, bushy growth; PP4355; ['Fairy Moss' × 'Iceberg']; intr. 1978

Heidi™ -- See 'Poulra002'

'Heidi-Ho' Min, ab, 2006, Sawyer, Rosemary; flowers blended, apricot at edges, yellow at base, petals quilling on open blooms, up to 2 in., full, borne mostly solitary; foliage medium size, medium green, matte; prickles 3/16 in., straight, thin, moderate; growth upright, tall (to 28 in.); garden; exhibition; [sport of 'Rosemary's Dream']; intr. 2007

'Heidi Jayne' HT, dp, 1986, Esser; flowers bright deep pink, large, 32 petals, high-centered, borne mostly singly, moderate fragrance; recurrent; foliage large, light green, glossy; numerous prickles; medium, upright growth; [(Piccadilly® × Queen Elizabeth®) × ('Fragrant Cloud' × seedling)]

'Heidi Kabel' -- See 'Kordiam'

'Heidi Klum' -- See 'Heidi Klum Rose'

Heidi Klum Rose® ('Heidi Klum') F, m, Tantau; flowers blooms violet, large, very full, cupped, intense fragrance; recurrent; foliage medium, matte; low, compact growth; intr. 2006

'Heidi Parade' (Heidi™) MinFl, op, Poulsen; bud short, pointed ovoid; flowers salmon pink, 2-3 in., 25-35 petals, flat, borne mostly in small clusters, very slight fragrance; recurrent; foliage glossy; prickles very few, 2-3 mm., hooked downward, greyed-red; bushy, low (8-16 in.) growth; PP13275; ['Charming Parade' × Vanilla Kordana®]; container plant; intr. 2000

'Heidi Rossin' S, ly

'Heietta' T, m

'Height of Fashion' -- See 'Seaheight'

'Heiich Blanc' LCl, w, Hetzel; intr. 1994

'Heike' -- See 'Korrundum'

'Heimatlos' S, mp, 1931, Lohrberg; bud pointed; flowers rose-pink, single, borne in clusters, intense fragrance; non-recurrent; short stems; vigorous (5-7 ft.), open habit growth; has endured -27; [(R. canina × R. roxburghii) × R. canina]

Heimatmelodie® ('Frank Michael', 'Majora') F, rb, Tantau; flowers red with white reverse; free-flowering; foliage dark green, glossy, healthy; growth to 2½ ft.

'Hein Evers' F, mr, 1959, Tantau, Math.; bud pointed; flowers bright blood-red, open, semi-dbl., borne in clusters, slight fragrance; foliage leathery; vigorous, upright growth; ['Red Favorite' × 'Fanal']; intr. 1957

'Hein Evers, Climbing' Cl F, mr, 1963, Kordes

Hein Mück® S, dr, 1961, Tantau, Math.; flowers velvety blood-red, single, cupped, borne in clusters; vigorous (6 ft.) growth

'Heine' HMult, w, 1912, Lambert, P.; flowers white with dark reddish stamens, 2½-3 cm., dbl., borne in large clusters; remontant; [Trier® × 'Frau Karl Druschki']

'Heinfels' -- See 'Helfels'

Heinrich Blanc® ('Helklewei', 'Super Bianca') LCl, lp, Hetzel; flowers pale pink, fading to white, 2-2½ cm., very dbl., cabbage-shaped, borne in small clusters; intr. 1994

'Heinrich Conrad Söth' S, pb, 1919, Lambert, P.; flowers light rosy red, with white eye, 3 cm., single, borne in large pyramidal clusters, moderate fragrance; recurrent bloom; foliage large, glossy, dark; long, strong stems; very vigorous, bushy growth; ['Geheimrat Dr. Mittweg' × *R. foetida bicolor*]

'Heinrich Eggers' HT, op, 1928, Kordes; flowers orange-copper, often with lighter outer petals, dbl.; upright growth; ['Mrs Charles E. Russell' × 'Mrs Wemyss Quin']

'Heinrich Karsch' Pol, m, 1927, Leenders, M.; flowers violet-rose, small, semi-dbl., borne in clusters, moderate fragrance; free-flowering; upright, medium (2 ft.) growth; ['Orléans Rose' × 'Joan']

'Heinrich Keller' S, ly, 1894, Müller; flowers semi-dbl.

'Heinrich Laurentius' HP, rb, 1863, Verdier

'Heinrich Münch' HP, mp, 1911, Hinner, W.; flowers soft pink, very large, 50 petals, moderate fragrance; occasionally recurrent bloom; very vigorous growth; ['Frau Karl Druschki' × ('Mme Caroline Testout' × 'Mrs W.J. Grant')]

'Heinrich Schultheis' HP, lp, 1882, Bennett; flowers soft pink, well-formed, very large, dbl.; occasionally recurrent bloom; vigorous growth; ['Mabel Morrison' × 'E.Y. Teas']

Heinrich Siesmayer® S, mr, McGredy; flowers fiery red; intr. 2002

'Heinrich Wendland' ('College Avenue #10') HT, mr, 1930, Kordes; flowers nasturtium-red, reverse deep golden yellow, very large, dbl., high-centered, intense fruity fragrance; foliage bronze, leathery, glossy; vigorous growth; ['Charles P. Kilham' × 'Mev. G.A. van Rossem']

'Heinrich Wendland, Climbing' Cl HT, mr, 1937, Stell

'Heinsohn's Record' S, lp, Heinsohn-Wedel

Heinz Erhardt® F, mr, 1962, Kordes, R.; flowers 3 in., 25 petals, borne in clusters (up to 8); foliage coppery; vigorous, bushy growth

'Heinz Treffinger' -- See 'Heltreff'

'Heinz Winkler' -- See 'Hommage à Barbara'

Heinzelmännchen® -- See 'Kornuma'

'Heiress' HT, mp, 1959, Longsdon; bud pointed; flowers clear rose-pink, well-shaped, medium

'Heirloom' HT, m, 1971, Warriner, William A.; bud long, pointed; flowers deep lilac, medium, semi-dbl., intense fragrance; foliage leathery; vigorous, upright growth; PP3234; [seedling × seedling]; intr. 1972

'Heirloom's Golden Rambler' -- See 'Heirloom's Yellow Rambler'

'Heirloom's Yellow Rambler' ('Heirloom's Golden Rambler') HWich, my, Clements, John; flowers soft lemon yellow, 2 in., 15-20 petals, borne in clusters; foliage light green, holly-like; vigorous (10-12 ft.) growth

'Helbonnet' ('Ascot Bonnet') F, m, 2000, Hetzel, Karl; flowers lilac mauve, reverse lilac, 6 cm., dbl., borne in large clusters; foliage medium size, medium green, glossy; few prickles; growth bushy, medium (80-90 cm.); [seedling × seedling]

'Heldengruss' HT, dr, 1920, Kiese; flowers pure deep blood-red, dbl.; ['Étoile de France' × 'Baron Girod de l'Ain']

'Heldoro' ('Dorothy Superior') HWich, mp, Hetzel; intr. 1986

'Helen' HT, pb, 1930, Ferguson, W.; flowers salmon-pink, base shaded yellow, semi-dbl.; vigorous growth; RULED EXTINCT 11/91

'Helen' -- See 'Tinhelen'

'Helen Allen' HT, dr, 1976, Clayworth; flowers velvety red, 3½-4 in., 20 petals, moderate fragrance; upright growth; ['Evelyn Fison' × 'Vagabonde']; intr. 1975

'Helen Antill' Min, ab, 2005, Townson, S.; flowers apricot, 4-5 cm., full, borne in small clusters, slight fragrance; foliage large, medium green, semi-glossy; prickles average, pointed, few; growth bushy, medium (45 cm.); bedding, containers; [sport of 'Gem']; intr. 2002

'Helen Bamber' -- See 'Horoffside'

'Helen Bland' S, mp, 1950, Wright, Percy H.; flowers rose-pink, center deeper, open, medium, semi-dbl., borne several together; profuse non-recurrent bloom; foliage soft; thornless; stems red-brown; vigorous (7-8 ft.), upright growth; ['Betty Bland' × *R. blanda* (St. Hilaire clone)]

'Helen Boehm' -- See 'Aroprawn'

'Helen Chamberlain' HT, yb, 1918, Easlea; flowers creamy yellow to orange-gold, paling on outer petals

'Helen Davis' HT, dr, 1925; flowers large, dbl.

'Helen de Waal' F, op, Kordes; flowers salmon-orange with yellow at the petal base, medium, dbl., high-centered, no fragrance; foliage glossy green, healthy; growth bushy, upright, tall; intr. 1999

'Helen Fox' HT, my, 1928, Buatois; bud pointed, indian yellow; flowers golden yellow, dbl., cupped; foliage bronze; vigorous, bushy growth; ['Mme Mélanie Soupert' × 'Souv. de Claudius Pernet']

'Helen Gambier' -- See 'Mlle Hélène Gambier'

'Helen Good' T, yb, 1907, Good & Reese; bud pointed; flowers delicate yellow suffused pink, edged deeper, dbl.; vigorous growth; [sport of 'Maman Cochet']

'Helen Gould' -- See 'Balduin'

'Helen Gould, Climbing' Cl HT, pb, 1912, Good & Reese; [sport of 'Balduin']

'Helen Hayes' HT, yb, 1956, Brownell; bud long, pointed; flowers yellow splashed orange and pink, 4-5 in., 43 petals, high-centered, moderate fragrance; foliage glossy; very vigorous growth; PP1509; [*R. wichurana* hybrid × 'Sutter's Gold']

Helen Hoffmann™ HT, lp, 2004, Gareffa, N.; flowers solid light pink, 3-4 in., full, borne mostly solitary, moderate fragrance; continuous; foliage medium size, medium green, semi-glossy; prickles small, sharp,; growth upright, short (2 ft.); container; exhibition; cutting; intr. 2004

'Helen Jane Burn' HT, dp, 1999, Poole, Lionel; flowers high-pointed, classic form, 5½-6 in., full, borne mostly singly; foliage medium size, dark green, semi-glossy; some prickles; long stems; upright, bushy, medium (3 ft.) growth; [Blue Moon® × seedling]

'Helen Keller' HP, dp, 1895, Dickson, A.; flowers rosy cerise, petals large, shell-shaped, full; very free bloom

'Helen Keller' HT, pb, Barni, V.; flowers soft pink suffused salmon-pink in heart, large, dbl., high-centered, slight fragrance; vigorous (3 ft.) growth; intr. 1991

'Helen Knight' S, my, Knight; flowers canary yellow, 5 petals, no fragrance; non-recurrent; small foliage; vigorous (7 × 7 ft.) growth; seedling from *R. ecae*; intr. 1970

'Helen Leenders' S, mp, 1924, Leenders, M.; flowers hydrangea-pink, open, large, semi-dbl., borne in clusters; sometimes recurrent bloom; foliage large, rich green; very vigorous (5 ft.), bushy growth; ['Orléans Rose' × *R. foetida bicolor*]

'Helen M. Greig' HT, lp, Dobbie; flowers pastel pink; ['Mrs A.R. Barraclough' × 'Marmion']

'Helen Margaret' -- See 'Horblush'

'Helen Mills' -- See 'Reine Carola de Saxe'

'Helen Naudé' -- See 'Kordiena'

'Helen of Troy' HT, mp, 1956, Stevenson; flowers rose-pink, very dbl., slight spicy fragrance; vigorous, bushy growth;

['Dame Edith Helen' × 'Mrs Henry Morse']
'Helen Paul'   HP, w, 1881, Lacharme; ['Victor Verdier' × 'Sombreuil']
'Helen Rhodes' -- See 'Rawodes'
'Helen Robinson'   HT, mp, Harkness; flowers medium pink in center, fading on outer petals, dbl., high-centered, moderate fragrance; recurrent; growth to 110 cm.; intr. 2006
'Helen Suzman Rose' -- See 'Jacveryp'
'Helen Taft'   HT, 1913, Byrnes
'Helen Taylor'   HT, pb, 1924, Pemberton; flowers rosy salmon, dbl.
'Helen Teresa' -- See 'Jayhel'
'Helen Traubel'   HT, pb, 1951, Swim, H.C.; bud long, pointed; flowers pink to apricot, 5-6 in., 23-30 petals, high-centered, borne singly, moderate fruity fragrance; foliage leathery, matte, green; stems weak necks; tall, vigorous growth; PP1028; ['Charlotte Armstrong' × 'Glowing Sunset']
'Helen Traubel, Climbing'   Cl HT, ab, 1974, Miller, Jack; bud long pointed; flowers pink to apricot, 5-6 in., 20-25 petals, high-centered; foliage leathery, dull green; [sport of 'Helen Traubel']; intr. 1970
'Helen Vincent'   HP, mp, 1907, Dickson, A.; flowers carnation pink with lighter pink reflections, large, full
'Helen Wild'   HT, op, 1959, Kemp, M.L.; flowers orange-pink veined rose-red, 5-6 in., 35 petals, high-centered; foliage light green; free growth; ['Show Girl' × 'Charlotte Armstrong']
Helena™ -- See 'Poulna'
'Helena'   HT, mr, Strnad
'Helena Johanna' -- See 'Palhel'
'Helena Renaissance' -- See 'Poulna'
'Helena Van Vliet'   Pol, lp, 1931, Kersbergen; flowers soft pink tinted salmon, borne in large trusses; vigorous growth; [sport of 'Salmonea']
'Hélène'   HMult, pb, 1897, Lambert, P.; bud deep pink; flowers soft violet-rose, base yellowish-white, medium, semi-dbl., borne in clusters of 5-10; non-recurrent; nearly thornless; vigorous, climbing (12-15 ft.) growth; ['hybrid tea' × ('Aglaia' × 'Crimson Rambler')]
'Helene'   HT, mp, Vecera, L.; flowers large, dbl.
'Hélène Boulter'   HT, mr, 1902, Bernaix fils; flowers silky garnet
'Hélène Dapples'   HT, mr, 1932, Heizmann, E.; bud pointed, dark; flowers glowing crimson-red; vigorous growth; ['Mrs Henry Winnett' × 'Lady Maureen Stewart']
'Hélène de Gerlache' -- See 'LLX7119'
'Hélène de Montbriand'   HT, mr, 1933, Schwartz, A.; flowers deep carmine-red, shaded vermilion, well-formed, large, globular; foliage glossy, dark; vigorous growth; ['Reine Marie Henriette' × 'Laurent Carle']
'Hélène de Roumanie'   HT, rb, 1949, Meilland, F.; flowers red to pink, 5 in., 35 petals, urn-shaped; upright growth; [('Mme Joseph Perraud' × seedling) × (seedling × 'Pres. Herbert Hoover')]
'Helene de Savoie' -- See 'Krinirosy'
'Hélène Duché'   HT, lp, 1921, Buatois; flowers very large, dbl.
'Hélène François'   HT, pb, 1923, Schwartz, A.; flowers salmon-pink shaded coppery red, center salmon-orange tinted, dbl.; ['Mme Edouard Herriot' × 'Viscountess Enfield']
'Hélène Granger'   HMult, pb, 1910, Granger; flowers pink, center copper-yellow to medium, 4 cm., dbl., borne in clusters of 10-15, slight fragrance; foliage large; ['Tea Rambler' × 'Aglaia']
'Hélène Guillot'   HT, pb, 1901, Guillot; flowers pink, tinted orange and yellow
'Helene Leenders'   Pol, mp, Leenders, M.; flowers medium large, very dbl.; medium growth
'Hélène Maréchal' -- See 'LLX8547'
'Hélène Puyravaud'   T, dy, 1893, Puyravaud; bud shaded carmine; flowers dark yellow, aging light yellow, large, full; ['Pactole' × 'Regulus']
'Hélène Robinet'   HT, lp, 1928, Sauvageot, H.; flowers salmon-white, shaded rose, base yellow, dbl.; [seedling × 'Pres. Parmentier']
'Helene Schoen'   HT, mr, 1963, Von Abrams; bud long, pointed; flowers 6 in., 60 petals, high-centered, slight fragrance; foliage leathery, glossy; vigorous, upright growth; ['Multnomah' × 'Charles Mallerin']; intr. 1962
'Hélène Vacaresco'   HT, pb, 1939, Chambard, C.; flowers salmon, shaded copper-carmine, large, cupped; foliage dark
'Hélène Varabrègue'   HT, lp, 1958, Meilland, F.; bud pointed; flowers pale rose, very large, dbl., cupped; foliage leathery; strong stems; vigorous, bushy growth; ['Lorraine' × 'Michèle Meilland']; intr. 1953
'Helene Videnz' -- See 'Frau Helene Videnz'
'Hélène Videnz'   Pol, pb, 1905, Lambert, P.; flowers salmon-pink, dbl., borne in clusters to 75; vigorous growth; ['Euphrosyne' × 'Louis Philippe']
'Hélène Wattine'   HT, ly, 1910, Soupert & Notting; flowers light citron yellow; ['Kaiserin Auguste Viktoria' × 'Le Progrés']
'Helenia'   LCl, my; flowers clear yellow, profuse bloom, slight fragrance; strong growth
'Helenka'   HT, mp, Tesar
'Helen's White Pol'   HMult, w, Diprose; intr. 1993
'Heleuro' ('Europas Rosengarten') F, mp, Hetzel; intr. 1989
'Helexa' ('Excelsa Superior') LCl, mr, Hetzel; intr. 1986
'Helfels' ('Heinfels', 'Super Sparkle') LCl, dr, 1996, Hetzel, Karl; flowers crimson scarlet, 2 in., dbl., borne in large clusters, slight fragrance; reliable repeat; foliage medium size, dark green, glossy; rambling, climbing (300 cm.) growth; intr. 1997
'Helfriwa' ('Fritz Walter') HT, or, Hetzel; intr. 1981
Helga® -- See 'Helgrui'
'Helga'   HT, dp, 1926, Weigand, C.; flowers deep pink to light red, dbl., high-centered, moderate fragrance; bushy (3-4 ft.) growth
'Helga Brichet'   S, lp, 2000; flowers single, borne mostly singly, moderate fragrance; foliage medium grey-green, dull; few prickles; bushy, tall (6 ft.) growth; ['Complicata' × 'Complicata']; intr. 2001
'Helgoland'   F, mr, 1936, Kordes; bud pointed, dark; flowers crimson to carmine, open, very large, semi-dbl., borne in clusters, slight fragrance; foliage leathery, wrinkled, dark; vigorous, bushy growth; ['Else Poulsen' × 'dark crimson hybrid tea seedling']
'Helgoland'   F, mr, Tantau, Math.; bud pointed; flowers copper-red, medium, semi-dbl., slight fragrance; foliage glossy, light; moderate, upright, bushy growth; intr. 1973
'Helgraf'   HT, mp, Hetzel; intr. 1993
'Helgrui' (Helga®) F, w, deRuiter; intr. 1975
'Helilast'   S, m, Hetzel; intr. 1993
'Héliodore Dober'   HGal, mr; flowers deep red edged crimson, quite large, ball-shaped
'Helios'   HT, dy, 1935, Leenders, M.; flowers deep sunflower-yellow, open, semi-dbl.; foliage leathery, light; vigorous, bushy growth
'Helkleger' ('Strombergzauber', 'Super Elfin') LCl, or, 1996, Hetzel, Karl; flowers orange-scarlet, 2 in., dbl., high-centered, loose, borne in large clusters, slight fragrance; recurrent; foliage medium size, dark green, glossy; rambling, medium (300 cm.) growth; intr. 1997
'Helklewei' -- See 'Heinrich Blanc'
'Hella'   Gr, dy, Guillot-Massad; flowers soft ocher yellow, slight fruity fragrance; moderate (3 ft.) growth; intr. 2004
'Hellen Ann'   HT, Tantau, Math.; intr. 1989
'Hello' -- See 'Krimony'
'Hello'   F, mr, Meilland; flowers small, very dbl., borne in small clusters; growth to 50 cm.; intr. 2002
Hello®   S, mr, Meilland; spreading, low (20 in.) growth
'Hello' -- See 'Cochello'
'Hello There' -- See 'Floello'
'Hellux' ('Comtesse Diana') HT, or, Hetzel; intr. 1989
'Helma'   Min, Delforge, H.; intr. 1986
'Helmedia' ('Medialis') HT, mr, Hetzel; intr. 1993
'Helmut Kohl Rose' ('Red Nostalgie') HT, dr, Tantau, Math.; flowers bright, 9-12 cm., full, high-centered; recurrent; foliage glossy; stems strong; robust, moderate (70 - 90 cm.) growth; intr. 1996
Helmut Schmidt® -- See 'Korbelma'

'Héloïse' ('Agathe Nouvelle', 'Éloïse', 'Elouise', 'Grande Agathe Nouvelle', 'Isabelle', 'Nouvelle Héloïse') HGal, lp, 1816, Descemet; sepals long, viscous; flowers flesh pink nuanced purple, medium to large, full; prickles nearly thornless; Agathe group; listed in Vibert's catalogues from 1819 to 1828 and sometimes attributed to him

'Héloïse' ('Maiden's Blush', 'Rougeau Virginale') C, lp; flowers pale rose, small; growth compact; possibly confused with the HGal (Descemet) listed in Vibert's catalogues from 1819-1829; intr. 1818

'Héloïse' HGal, lp, Vibert; flowers blush white to pale pink, nuanced with purplish-pink, full; nearly thornless; intr. 1834

'Héloïse' M, lp, Vibert or Robert; flowers whitish pink to carmine, medium, full; intr. 1845

'Help For Children' -- See 'Worcake'

'Help the Aged' HT, mp, 1987, Bracegirdle, A.J.; flowers clear pink, reverse slightly darker, satin two-tone effect,, 23 petals, high-centered, intense damask fragrance; foliage medium size, light green, semi-glossy; prickles straight, brown, very few; bushy, medium growth; no fruit; ['Mischief' × 'Fragrant Cloud']; intr. 1987

'Helpforz' ('Goldstadt Pforzheim') HT, dy, Hetzel; intr. 1998

'Helping Hand' S, ob; intr. 2004

'Helping Hands' -- See 'Clehelp'

'Helpkids' F, ob, Delbard; flowers striped; intr. 2008

'Helpmekaar Roos' -- See 'Korogesa'

'Helprinzess' ('Rosenprinzessin') Pol, dp, Hetzel; intr. 1993

'Helreg' (Kleine Regina®) Min, dr, Hetzel; intr. 1983

'Helreib' ('Carolin Reiberl') F, dp, Hetzel; intr. 1992

'Helrobu' ('Die Rheinpfalz') F, ob, Hetzel; intr. 1993

'Helsaar' HT, or, Hetzel; intr. 1976

'Helsabine' ('Sabine Ruf') F, mp, Hetzel; intr. 1988

'Helsingör' -- See 'Elsinore'

'Helstrau' F, mp, Hetzel; intr. 1991

'Helsufair' (Super Fairy®) LCl, lp, 1996, Helzel, Karl; flowers delicate pink, 1¼ in., dbl., cupped, borne in large clusters, moderate green apple fragrance; repeat bloom; foliage medium size, medium green, glossy; rambling (300-500 cm.) growth; intr. 1997

'Heltoria' ('Kronprinzessin Victoria') HT, mr, Hetzel, K.dbl.; intr. 1986

'Heltreff' ('Heinz Treffinger') HT, mp, Hetzel; intr. 1998

'Heltzi' ('Fritzi') Pol, mp, Hetzel; intr. 1994

'Helvetia' ('Louis Richard') T, op, 1873, Ducher; flowers coppery salmon, tinged with fawn, large, full, globular

'Helvetia' HEg, w, Fröbel; flowers greenish-white, single, borne in clusters of 5; intr. 1897

'Helvetia' HT, dp, Heizmann, E.; flowers dark carmine, reverse fiery red, large, dbl., moderate fragrance; ['Mme Caroline Testout' × 'Farbenkonigin']; intr. 1911

'Helvétia' -- See 'Mandalay'

'Helvetius' HGal, rb, about 1830, Desprez; flowers red with lilac edges, large, dbl.

'Helway' ('Euroway') HT, mr, Hetzel; intr. 1993

'Helzwerg' ('Lila Zwerg') Min, m, Hetzel; intr. 1998

'Hemaprova' HT, ly, Ghosh; flowers cream to light yellow, large; intr. 2001

'Hemavathy' F, op, Kasturi; flowers salmon-orange with brown overcast, deepening to smokey color; intr. 1975

'Hen Kauffmann' F, mp, 1954, Leenders, M.; flowers rosy pink, dbl.; vigorous growth

'Hendan' ('Dancing Pink') F, dp, 1993, Henson, R.W.; flowers deep pink, 3-3½ in., 6-14 petals, borne in large clusters; foliage medium size, medium green, semi-glossy; some prickles; medium (75 cm.), bushy growth; ['Southampton' × Dortmund®]; intr. 1993

'Henderson' -- See 'Triomphe de la Terre des Roses'

'Henfif' ('Fifi') F, ab, 1993, Henson, R.W.; flowers cream pale peach, 3-3½ in., semi-dbl., borne in large clusters, intense fragrance; foliage large, dark green, glossy; numerous prickles; tall (100 cm.), upright growth; [Lichterloh® × 'Liverpool Echo']; intr. 1993

Henkell Royal® HT, mr, 1964, Kordes, R.; bud long; flowers blood-red, well-formed, large; vigorous, bushy growth

'Hennequin' HGal, dr, about 1830, Desprez; flowers medium, full

'Hennev' ('Nevertheless') F, rb, 1993, Henson, R.W.; flowers orange/red/yellow blend, medium, full, borne in small clusters, moderate fragrance; foliage large, medium green, matte; few prickles; tall (100 cm.), upright growth; [('Silver Jubilee' × Trumpeter®) × Gold Medal®]; intr. 1993

'Henri Barruet' HWich, pb, 1918, Barbier; flowers coppery yellow, opening to pink and tinted white, 7-8 cm., dbl., borne in clusters of 8-15; vigorous, climbing (8 ft.) growth

'Henri Brichard' HT, w, 1891, Bonnaire; flowers bright carmine red shaded salmon pink, white reverse, large, very dbl.; foliage large, bronzy green; growth upright

'Henri Caillaud' LCl, Moreira da Silva, A.

'Henri Coupé' HP, mp, 1916, Barbier; flowers China pink, dbl., moderate fragrance; ['Frau Karl Druschki' × 'Gruss an Teplitz']

'Henri Declinand' LCl, mr, 1934, Mermet; flowers bright magenta-red, quite large, dbl.; foliage dark

'Henri Foucquier' ('Henri Fouquier') HGal, mp, before 1842; flowers rose-pink, darker at center, large, dbl., moderate fragrance; not named from the jounalist/politician Henri Fouquier, but for a hybridizer named Foucquier

'Henri Fouquier' -- See 'Henri Foucquier'

'Henri IV' ('Henry IV') HP, dr, Verdier, V. & C.; flowers bright purple red, shaded violet, large, full; intr. 1862

'Henri IV' D, dp, before 1829, Trébucien; flowers rose pink, 4-5 in., full; foliage ovoid-oblong, pointed, serrate; prickles sparse, short, thick, unequal

'Henri IV' HP, pb, Vibert; flowers lilac pink, center fiery, edges flesh pink, medium, very full; intr. 1847

'Henri Lecoq' T, pb, Ducher; flowers pink, tinted yellow; intr. 1871

'Henri Lecoq' ('Duc d'Estrée) B, dp, 1845, Lacharme

'Henri Lédéchaux' HP, dp, 1868, Lédéchaux

'Henri Linger' LCl, yb, 1928, Barbier; flowers clear yellow-orange, open, semi-dbl.; foliage light, glossy; very vigorous, climbing growth; [R. wichurana × 'Benedicte Seguin']

'Henri Mallerin' -- See 'Rouge Mallerin'

'Henri Mallerin' HT, yb, 1955, Mallerin, C.; bud ovoid; flowers empire-yellow suffused pink, large, 55-70 petals, slight fragrance; foliage leathery, glossy; bushy growth; PP1349; ['Soeur Thérèse' × 'Duquesa de Peñaranda']

'Henri Martin' ('Red Moss') M, mr, 1862, Laffay, M.; bud sparsely mossed; flowers shining crimson, semi-dbl., borne in clusters of 3 - 8, slight fragrance

Henri Matisse™ F, pb, Delbard, Georges; flowers deep pink to medium red with white stripes, large, dbl., no fragrance; free-flowering; vigorous (50-100 cm.) growth; Deltisse is code name when sold for Garden, Delstrobla for cut flower version. They are the same rose.; intr. 1996

'Henri Pauthier' HT, mr, 1933, Sauvageot, H.; flowers bright red, open, large, semi-dbl.; foliage glossy; bushy growth; [seedling × 'Edouard Mignot']

'Henri Puyravaud' B, pb, 1893, Chauvry; flowers salmon pink, shaded carmine, base white, large, full; ['Robusta' × 'Imperatrice Eugénie']

'Henri Quatre' HGal, dp, 1821, Calvert; flowers bright purple pink, large, dbl.

'Henri Salvador' ('Irene') HT, w, Richardier; flowers cream, moderate fragrance; foliage semi-glossy; growth to 80-100 cm.; intr. 1999

'Henri Ward-Beecher' HP, m, 1874, Verdier, E.; flowers purple-violet, large, full

'Henrietta' HT, op, 1917, Merryweather; bud pointed, orange-crimson; flowers soft coral-salmon, open, semi-dbl., moderate fragrance; foliage dark; vigorous growth; ['Alister Stella Gray' × 'Andre Gamon']

'Henrietta' HT, yb, McGredy; intr. 2001

'Henrietta' -- See 'Pouletta'

The Official Registry and Checklist — Rosa 289

'Henrietta de Snoy' -- See 'Baronne Henriette de Snoy'

'Henriette' -- See 'Bifera Italica'

'Henriette' ('Grande Agathe') HGal, mr, before 1810, Dupont; flowers bright cherry red, large, full, borne in clusters of 8-10; Agathe group

'Henriette' HT, or, Dickson, A.; flowers coppery orange-red, large, dbl.; intr. 1916

'Henriette' Ch, m; flowers violet, shaded purple, medium, semi-dbl.

'Henriette Boulogne' -- See 'Quatre Saisons d'Italie'

'Henriette Campan' A, m, before 1830; flowers purplish pink, 2½-3½ in., 70-80 petals; foliage very large, oval, pointed, dark green; prickles few, slender

'Henriette Chandet' HT, op, 1942, Mallerin, C.; bud oval; flowers orange-coral, large, dbl.; foliage glossy; vigorous, bushy growth; ['Rochefort' × 'La Parisienne']

'Henriette Koster' Pol, mr, 1939, Koster, D.A.; [sport of 'Dick Koster']

'Henriette Pechtold' HT, mr, 1946, Verschuren-Pechtold; bud long, pointed; flowers red, reverse salmon-red, large, dbl.; foliage soft; vigorous, bushy growth; ['Briarcliff' × 'Katharine Pechtold']

'Henriette Petit' HP, rb, 1879, Margottin père; flowers red and deep amaranth, large, full

'Henros' Cl F, dp, 1995, Henson, R.W.; flowers rose pink, medium, dbl., borne in small clusters; foliage medium size, medium green, glossy; some prickles; tall (250 cm.), climbing growth; ['Glenfiddich' × Lichterloh®]

'Henry A. Maynadier' T, before 1920, Dingee & Conard

'Henry Bennett' HP, mr, Lacharme; flowers violet-crimson, medium, full; ['Charles Lefebvre' × unknown]; intr. 1875

'Henry Bennett' T, pb, 1872, Levet; flowers light pink with deep sulphur yellow center, medium, full, intense fragrance

'Henry Bierbauer' S, pb, Williams, J.B.; flowers varying shades of pink, white and apricot, semi-dbl., flat, slight fragrance; recurrent; growth to 4 ft.; intr. 2006

Henry Dunant® HT, mr, Meilland; flowers bright red; intr. 2004

'Henry Field' HT, mr, 1948, Brownell; bud ovoid, long, pointed; flowers crimson-red, 5 in., 60 petals, high-centered, moderate fragrance; foliage glossy; vigorous, bushy growth; PP841; ['Pink Princess' × 'Crimson Glory']

Henry Fonda™ -- See 'Jacyes'

'Henry Ford' HT, my, 1927, Deverman; flowers yellow edged salmon-orange, opening to lemon-yellow, semi-dbl., slight fragrance; ['Mme Edouard Herriot' × 'Golden Emblem']

'Henry Ford' HT, mp, Howard, A.P.; bud long; flowers silvery pink, 4-5 in., 30 petals, high-centered, moderate fragrance; vigorous, upright growth; PP1218; ['Pink Dawn, Climbing' × 'The Doctor']; intr. 1954

'Henry IV' -- See 'Henri IV'

'Henry Hudson' HRg, w, 1977, Svedja, Felicitas; bud ovoid; flowers yellow stamens, 2½-3 in., 25 petals, intense fragrance; recurrent bloom; low, bushy growth; intr. 1976

'Henry Irving' Cl HP, dp, 1907, Conard & Jones; flowers light orange-red, medium, semi-dbl.; ['hybrid perpetual seedling' × 'hybrid multiflora seedling']

'Henry Kelsey' HKor, mr, 1984, Svedja, Felicitas; flowers deep red fading to deep pink, 6-7 cm., 28 petals, borne in clusters of 9-18, moderate spicy fragrance; good repeat; foliage glossy; prickles moderate; trailing growth; remontant, very winter hardy; [R. × kordesii hybrid × seedling]

'Henry King Stanford' F, mr, 1975, Sheridan, V.V.; flowers semi-dbl., 15 petals; spreading growth; ['Red Pinocchio' × unknown]; intr. 1973

'Henry Lawson' HT, ob, Allender, Robert William; intr. 1999

'Henry M. Stanley' T, pb, 1891, Dingee & Conard; flowers deep rose, tinged with apricot yellow, bordered with carmine red, very full, moderate fragrance; ['Mme Lombard' × 'Comtesse Riza du Parc']

'Henry Morse' F, dr, 1959, Kordes; flowers deep blood-red shaded scarlet, 3 in., semi-dbl., borne in large trusses; free growth; intr. 1958

'Henry Nevard' HP, dr, 1924, Cant, F.; flowers crimson-scarlet, very large, 30 petals, cupped, intense fragrance; recurrent bloom; foliage dark, leathery; vigorous, bushy growth

'Henry S. Badgery' HT, Johnson

'Henry V' Ch, rb; flowers crimson, center white, cupped

'Henry's Blend' -- See 'Garhenry'

'Henry's Crimson China' -- See R. chinensis spontanea

'Hens Verschuren' HT, mr, 1948, Verschuren; bud long; flowers bright red, very large; ['Mary Hart' × seedling]

Her Majesty™ -- See 'Dicxotic'

'Her Majesty' HP, mp, 1885, Bennett; flowers clear rose, with carmine reflexes toward center, very large, dbl.; occasionally recurrent bloom; very vigorous growth; ['Mabel Morrison' × 'Canari']

'Hera' HT, mr, 1924, Van Rossem; flowers brilliant carmine shaded blood-red, 40 petals; ['Gen. MacArthur' × 'Luise Lilia']

'Herald' -- See 'De Ruiter's Herald'

'Heraldo' Cl HT, m, 1949, Dot, M.; bud long, pointed; flowers purple-pink, large, very dbl.; foliage leathery, dark; ['Guineé' × 'Texas Centennial']

'Herani' HT, pb, 1960, Herholdt, J.A.; bud long, pointed; intr. 1962

'Heraro' HT, w, 1977, Herholdt, J.A.; bud pointed

'Herbalist' -- See 'Aussemi'

'Herbeau' HT, ob, Herholdt; intr. 1986

'Herbemont's Musk Cluster' N, w, Herbemont; flowers pure white, very large, dbl., borne in large clusters; recurrent bloom

'Herbert Brunning' HT, mr, 1940, Clark, A.; flowers brilliant red

'Herbert Wilson' F, w, 1967, Latham; flowers well-formed; foliage light green; ['White Knight' × 'The Optimist']

'Herbic' Gr, rb, 1985, Herholdt, J.A.; intr. 1981

'Herbie' -- See 'Tinherb'

'Herbiz' Min, op; intr. 1987

'Herbstfeuer' ('Autumn Fire') HEg, dr, 1961, Kordes; flowers large, semi-dbl., borne in clusters (up to 5), moderate fragrance; repeat bloom; vigorous (6 ft.) growth; hips large, pear-shaped, reddish-yellow

'Herclov' ('Cloverdene') HT, pb

'Hercop' ('Copper King') HT, dy, 1982, Herholdt, J.A.; flowers copper-gold, large, 35 petals; foliage dark, glossy; upright growth; ['Vienna Charm' × seedling]

'Hercres' ('Summer Crest') HT, dp, 1982, Herholdt, J.A.; flowers deep pink, large, dbl.; foliage medium size, medium green, semi-glossy; ['Miss All-American Beauty' × seedling]

'Hercules' LCl, mp, 1938, Horvath; flowers Dame Edith Helen pink, over large, dbl., cupped, slight fragrance; foliage large, glossy, dark; long stems; very vigorous, climbing growth; PP296; ['Doubloons' × 'Charles P. Kilham']

'Herdame' F, pb

'Herdio' HT, dy, 1970, Herholdt, J.A.; intr. 1971

'Herdominec' HT, dy

'Herero' Gr, rb, 1985, Herholdt, J.A.; flowers yellow, reverse yellow with red overlay, spreading with age, semi-dbl., no fragrance; foliage large, dark, glossy; upright growth; [Angel Bells® × 'Southern Sun']; intr. 1981

'Here's Charlie' HT, pb, 2006, Eddie Edwards; flowers full, high-centered, borne mostly solitary; foliage medium size, medium green; prickles small, moderate; growth upright, medium; exhibition; ['Gemini' × 'Fantasy']; intr. 2006

'Here's Colette' S, pb, 1999, Watson, Thomas L. & Glenda; flowers dark pink, white eye, reverse dark pink, 1½ in., single, borne in large clusters; foliage small, light green, dull; few prickles; spreading, low (3 ft.) growth; [seedling × 'Ballerina']

'Here's Gert' HT, mp, 2004, Edwards, Eddie & Phelps, Ethan; flowers full, exhibition, borne mostly solitary, moderate fragrance; foliage dark green, glossy; upright, tall (6 ft.) growth; exhibition; [Veterans' Honor™ × 'Hot Princess']; intr. 2005

'Here's Ian' -- See 'Judian'

'Here's Sam' HT, mp, 2004, Edwards, Eddie & Phelps, Ethan; flowers full, exhibition, borne mostly solitary, moderate fragrance; foliage large, dark green, glossy; growth upright, tall (6 ft.); exhibition; [Veterans' Honor™ × 'Hot Princess']; intr. 2005

'Herfla' ('Flamingo') HT, pb, 1985, Herholdt, J.A.; flowers light pink, silvery reverse, large, 35 petals, cupped, moderate fragrance; foliage medium green, semi-glossy; upright growth; [seedling × seedling]; intr. 1981

'Herfordia' F, dp, Hempelmann; flowers medium, dbl.; intr. 1993

'Herfsttooi' HT, dr, 1919, Van Rossem; flowers dark crimson, medium, dbl., moderate fragrance; ['General MacArthur' × 'Leuchtfeuer']

'Hergale' HT, pb, 1970, Herholdt, J.A.

'Hergeko' ('Ge Korsten') HT, mr, Herholdt

'Herice' F, w, Hetzel; intr. 2008

'Heriflor' -- See 'Saubaflor'

Heritage® -- See 'Ausblush'

Herkules® S, m, Kordes; flowers varying shades of soft lavender , 9 cm., very full, cupped, intense fragrance; recurrent; bushy (4 ft.) growth; intr. 2007

'Herman Steyn' -- See 'Korfolklori'

'Hermance' HP, lp, 1853, Robert; flowers flesh pink, large, full, globular

'Hermance Louisa de la Rive' T, w, 1882, Nabonnand; bud long; flowers white, with sometimes a pale pink center, large, full

'Hermann Berger' HT, or, GPG Bad Langensalza; flowers large, dbl.; intr. 1982

'Hermann Eggers' HT, or, 1930, Kordes; flowers deep orange-scarlet, very large, dbl., high-centered; foliage dark, leathery; very vigorous growth; [('Pink Pearl' × 'Templar') × 'Florex']

'Hermann Kegel' M, m, 1849, Portemer fils; flowers reddish-violet, sometimes streaked crimson or lilac, medium, dbl., borne mostly solitary; freely remontant; foliage tinted reddish when young, oblong, dentate; growth vigorous, spreading

'Hermann Kiese' HT, yb, 1906, Geduldig; flowers yellow and pink, large, semi-dbl.

'Hermann Lindecke' HT, lp, 1929, Lindecke; flowers whitish pink, reverse salmon-pink large, dbl., high-centered; [sport of 'General-Superior Arnold Janssen']

'Hermann Löns' HT, dp, 1931, Tantau; flowers shining light red, large, single, cupped, borne in clusters; foliage glossy; vigorous growth; ['Ulrich Brunner Fils' × 'Red-Letter Day']

'Hermann Neuhoff' HT, mr, 1923, Neuhoff; flowers uniform blood-red, dbl.; [sport of 'General-Superior Arnold Janssen']

'Hermann Robinow' HT, op, 1918, Lambert, P.; flowers salmon-orange shaded salmon-rose and dark yellow, large, dbl.; vigorous growth; ['Frau Karl Druschki' × 'Lyon Rose']

'Hermann Robinow, Climbing' Cl HT, pb, 1934, Lambert, P.; flowers salmon pink, center orange, large, full, moderate fragrance; [sport of 'Hermann Robinow']

'Hermann Schmidt' LCl, dp, Hetzel; flowers crimson/cherry red, white center, 4-5 cm., semi-dbl., borne in medium to large clusters; reliable repeat; intr. 1986

'Hermann Schönfeld' HT, lp, 1925, Dechan; flowers large, dbl.

'Hermann Teschendorff' HT, rb, 1949, Berger, V.; bud ovoid; flowers copper-red, reverse old-gold, open, very large, dbl., cupped; foliage glossy, dark, bronze; very vigorous, upright growth

'Hermawi' ('Mary Wise') HT, rb, 1982, Herholdt, J.A.; flowers medium red and gold with red reverse, large, 40 petals, no fragrance; foliage medium green, semi-glossy; bushy growth; ['Madelaine' × (seedling × 'Apogee')]

'Hermela' HT, rb, 1964, Herholdt, J.A.

'Hermelia Casas' F, mp, 1956, Dot, Pedro; flowers pearly, reverse carmine, medium, 30 petals, borne in clusters of 3-6; moderate growth; ['Méphisto' × 'Perla de Alcañada']

'Hermen Anglada' HT, w, 1933, Dot, Pedro; bud very large; flowers white tinted pink, single; very vigorous growth

'Hermes' HT, dy, 1935, Teschendorff; flowers large, dbl.

'Hermesy' ('Mystery') HT, rb, 1985, Herholdt, J.A.; flowers light orange-red, edged amber, golden reverse, large, 35 petals; foliage large, medium green semi-glossy; bushy growth; [(seedling × 'Southern Sun') × 'Southern Sun']; intr. 1983

Hermina® S, pb, 1996, Buck, Dr. Griffith J.; flowers red with white reverse, aging Neyron rose with white reverse, dbl., slight fragrance; good repeat; foliage medium size, dark green, semi-glossy; some prickles; upright, bushy, medium growth; hardy to 18-24; [(('Tickled Pink' × 'Prairie Princess') × 'Autumn Dusk') × ('Tickled Pink' × '(Carrousel × (Morning Stars × Suzanne))' × 'Maytime'))]; intr. 1997

'Hermine Madèlé' Pol, w, 1888, Soupert & Notting; flowers creamy white with yellowish reflections, center darker, small, full; ['Mignonette' × 'Marquise de Vivens']

'Hermione' -- See 'Gaulimor'

'Hermitage' -- See 'Saucabou'

'Hermosa, Climbing' -- See 'Setina'

'Hermosa, Climbing' F, pb, 1997, Horner, Heather M.; flowers large, dbl., borne in small clusters; foliage medium size, semi-glossy; some prickles; upright, medium (80cm.) growth; [seedling × seedling]

'Hermosa' ('Armosa', 'Mélanie Lemarié', 'Mme Neumann) Ch, lp, 1834 or before, Marcheseau; bud pointed; flowers light blush-pink, 35 petals, high-centered, moderate fragrance; recurrent bloom; foliage bluish green; small vigorous growth; sometimes classed as B

Hero® -- See 'Aushero'

'Hérodiade' N, yb, 1888, Brassac; flowers chamois yellow, center darker, tinted pink or carmine, medium to large, full; ['Duarte de Oliveira' × unknown]

'Heroïca' HT, dr, 1960, Lens; flowers deep velvety red, becoming lighter, double, slight fragrance; recurrent; vigorous (80 - 100 cm.) growth; ['Rome Glory' × 'Independence']

'Heroine' HT, op, 1935, Krause; bud pointed; flowers salmon-shrimp-pink, large, dbl., high-centered; foliage leathery, dark; very vigorous, bushy growth; ['Wilhelm Kordes' × 'Mrs Atlee']

'Héroïne de Vaucluse' B, mp, 1863, Moreau et Robert; flowers velvety pink, sometimes washed with carmine, large, full, globular

'Héroïque Commandant Marchand' T, yb, 1900, Buatois; flowers nasturtium yellow, shaded fiery carmine, edges lighter, large, very full; ['Laurette Messimy' × 'Ma Capucine']

'Heros' HT, mr, 1933, Tantau; flowers very large, dbl., cupped; foliage leathery, dark; bushy growth; ['Johanniszauber' × 'Étoile de Hollande']

'Herpim' F, op, 1977, Herholdt, J.A.; bud ovoid, pointed; intr. 1972

'Herpot' ('Kristo Pienaar') HT, yb, Herholdt; intr. 1990

Herrenchiemsee™ -- See 'Poulbella'

'Herrenhausen' HMsk, ly, 1938, Kordes; bud ovoid, greenish yellow; flowers light yellow, fading white, red tints in sun, large, dbl., cupped, borne in clusters, moderate pansy fragrance; profuse, intermittent bloom; foliage leathery, glossy, light; long stems; vigorous, bushy growth; ['Eva' × 'Golden Rapture']

'Herrin von Lieser' HT, ly, 1907, Lambert, P.; flowers cream-yellow, center reddish-yellow; ['Frau Karl Druschki' × 'G. Schwartz']

'Herself' F, lp, 1965, Vincent; flowers 4 in., 18 petals, borne in clusters; free growth; ['The Optimist' × Moulin Rouge®]

'Hershey's Red' HT, dr, Williams, J. Benjamin; intr. 1996

'Hertfordshire' ('Bright Carpet', 'Lazy Susan', 'Sandefjord', 'Tommelise') S, dp, Kordes; flowers carmine-pink, yellow stamens, small, single, borne singly and in clusters, very slight fragrance; free-flowering; spreading, vigorous (1½ × 2½ ft.) growth

'Hertfordshire Glory' F, yb, 1971, Harkness; flowers yellow, tinted red, large, 20 petals, slight fragrance; foliage glossy; ['Isobel Harkness' × 'Circus']

'Hertie' ('Bettie Herholdt', 'Messagere') HT, w, 1978, Herholdt, J.A.; bud pointed

'Hertogin van Brabant' S, pb, DVP Melle; [seedling × 'Eclipse']; intr. 2000

'Hertroci' ('Potch Pearl') HT, pb, Herholdt; bud large, pointed, egg shaped

'Herz As' -- See 'Tansaras'

Herz As® ('Ace of Hearts', 'As de Coeur', 'Herz Ass') HT, mr, 1963, Tantau, Math.;

bud long, pointed; flowers pure blood-red, well-formed, large, dbl.; vigorous, upright growth

'Herz As Typ II' ('Herz Ass Typ II') HT, mr, Tantau; flowers blood-red, slight fragrance; intr. 2000

'Herz Ass' -- See 'Tansaras'

'Herz Ass' -- See 'Herz As'

'Herz Ass Typ II' -- See 'Herz As Typ II'

'Herz-Dame' -- See 'Dame de Coeur'

Herz von Luzern® F, op, Huber; flowers intense salmon color, large, graceful, 20-25 petals, slight fragrance; reddish early foliage; bushy, broad, medium (70 cm.) growth; intr. 2001

'Herzblättchen' Pol, dp, 1889, Geschwind, R.; flowers carmine-pink, small, dbl.

'Herzblut' -- See 'Commonwealth'

'Herzensgruss' HT, dr, 1975, Hetzel, Karl; bud pointed; flowers dark velvety red, medium, dbl., intense fragrance; foliage glossy; vigorous, upright, bushy growth; [('Fragrant Cloud' × 'Goldmarie') × 'Red American Beauty']; intr. 1973

'Herzog Friedrich II von Anhalt' HT, lp, 1906, Welter; flowers soft pink; ['Souv. du President Carnot' × 'Mme Jules Grolez']

'Herzog von Windsor' -- See 'Duke of Windsor'

'Herzogin Frederike' S, pb, Noack; flowers salmon-rose with yellow center, 2-2½ in., semi-dbl., borne in clusters; good repeat; growth to 5 ft.

'Herzogin Marie-Antoinette von Mecklembourg' HT, ob, 1910, Jacobs; bud long; flowers pure orange and golden yellow, large, full, moderate fragrance; foliage large

'Herzogin Marie von Coburg-Gotha' T, w, 1903, Welter; flowers pure white, aging to pale yellow, large; ['Mme Carnot' × 'Marie van Houtte']

'Herzogin Viktoria Adelheid von Coburg-Gotha' HT, op, 1905, Welter; flowers coppery carmine-pink, large, dbl.; [('Mme Jules Grolez' × 'Kaiserin Auguste Viktoria') × 'Captain Hayward']

'Herzogin von Calabrien' HT, ly, 1914, Lambert, P.; bud long, pointed; flowers creamy white, with clear sulphur-yellow center, large, semi-dbl., moderate fragrance; ['Frau Karl Druschki' × ('Hofgärtendirektor Graebener' × 'Herrin von Lieser')]

'Hessengruss' HT, dp, 1928, Thönges; flowers deep pink, reverse carmine-rose, dbl.; (sport of 'Laurent Carle')

'Hessenstar' HT, or, 1975, Hetzel; bud ovoid; flowers orange-red to geranium-red, medium, 30-40 petals, moderate fragrance; moderate growth; [Baccará® × 'Prima Ballerina']; intr. 1973

'Hessie Lowe' HT, op, 1956, Lowe; flowers peach-pink, dbl., high-centered; foliage glossy; very vigorous growth

'Hessoise' HEg, mp, before 1811, Schwarzkopf; flowers bright rose, semi-dbl.; as many as 15 HEg hybrids may have been sold under this name

'Hessoise Anémone' -- See 'Zabeth'

'Hessoise Pourpre Double' HEg, m, before 1815, Descemet; flowers purple

'Hester Prynne' F, dr, Robinson; flowers deep, rich crimson, single, borne in clusters, slight fragrance; [Sarabande® × unknown]; intr. 1993

'Hestia' F, or, Arles, F.

'Hestrie Els' HT, dp, Spek; flowers strong pink, double, high-centered, borne mostly singly; recurrent; few prickles; stems long; tall growth; intr. 2006

'Heterophylla' HRg, w, 1899, Cochet-Cochet; flowers semi-dbl., borne in clusters of 5-10; [R. rugosa × R. foetida]

'Hetkora' ('Queen Beatrix', Königin Beatrix®) HT, ob, 1983, Kordes, W.; flowers orange, large, 35 petals, high-centered; foliage medium size, medium green, semi-glossy; upright, bushy growth; [seedling × 'Patricia']

'Hettie' -- See 'Ardnan'

'Hetty Ann' HT, pb, 2000, Poole, Lionel; flowers pink-peach, reverse pink, 4½ in., full, borne in small clusters, moderate fragrance; foliage medium size, medium green, glossy, weather-resistant; few prickles; upright, medium (2½ ft.) growth; ['Selfridges' × seedling (pink HT)]; intr. 2001

'Heure Mauve' HT, m, 1965, Laperrière; flowers lilac-mauve tinted blush, well-formed, 5 in., 35 petals; foliage glossy, bright green; vigorous growth; ['Simone' × 'Prelude']

'Heureka' HT, w, Urban, J.

Heureux Anniversaire® ('Happy Anniversary') Gr, op, 1960, Delbard-Chabert; bud urn-shaped; flowers salmon-orange, 3 in., 28 petals, slight spicy fragrance; foliage glossy; very vigorous, bushy growth; PP2079; [('Incendie' × 'Chic Parisien') × ('Floradora' × 'Independence')]; originally registered as Pol; patent issued as Gr; intr. 1963

'Hewlet-Packard 2000' -- See 'HP 2000'

'Hexham Abbey' F, op, 1976, Wood; flowers salmon-pink, base yellow turning copper, large, intense fragrance; foliage leathery; growth vigorous, low to medium, upright; ['Fairlight' × 'Arthur Bell']

'Hey Paula' HT, yb, 2007, Edwards, Eddie; flowers yellow with pink edging around outer petals, 4½-5 in., full, borne mostly solitary; foliage medium size, medium green, matte; prickles medium, straight, green, few; growth upright, medium; [unknown × unknown]; intr. 2007

'Heywood' -- See 'Kirtyn'

'Hi' -- See 'Moehi'

'Hi' Min, lp, Strawn; flowers pale pink fading white, yellow stamens, tiny, ½ in. or less, 5 petals; good repeat; bushy, very small (6-8 in.) growth; micro-mini

'Hi-de-hi' -- See 'Macanat'

'Hi Doll' -- See 'Dickisser'

'Hi-Fi' F, or, 1959, Gregory; flowers bright orange-scarlet, semi-dbl., borne in clusters; foliage glossy; ['Independence' × unknown]; intr. 1958

'Hi Ho' Cl Min, op, 1965, Moore, Ralph S.; flowers deep pink, small, dbl., borne in clusters; foliage glossy; vigorous, climbimg growth; PP2719; ['Little Darling' × 'Magic Wand']; intr. 1964

'Hi, Neighbor!' Gr, mr, 1981, Buck, Dr. Griffith J.; bud ovoid, pointed, crimson; flowers , 40-45 petals, cupped, borne 1-6 per cluster, moderate sweet fragrance; continuous; foliage leathery, dark green, matte; prickles awl-like; bushy, erect growth; [(Queen Elizabeth® × 'Prairie Princess') × 'Portrait']

'Hi-Ohgi' HT, or, 1986, Suzuki, Seizo; flowers deep orange-red, large, 28 petals, moderate fragrance; foliage dark, semi-glossy; prickles slanted downward; tall, upright growth; ['San Francisco' × ('Montezuma' × 'Peace')]; intr. 1981

'Hi Society' -- See 'Cocquation'

'Hi Teen' -- See 'Designer's Choice'

'Hiawatha' HMult, rb, 1904, Walsh; flowers deep crimson, center white, anthers golden, small, single, cupped, borne in large clusters; foliage rich green, leathery, glossy; very vigorous, climbing (15-20 ft.) growth; ['Crimson Rambler' × 'Paul's Carmine Pillar']

'Hiawatha Recurrent' -- See 'Hiawatha Remontant'

'Hiawatha Remontant' ('Hiawatha Recurrent') Cl Pol, op, 1931, Sauvageot, H.; flowers carmine suffused orange, white eye, 3 cm., borne in medium clusters; intermittent rebloom; foliage small, glossy; long stems; very vigorous, climbing growth; ['Hiawatha' × 'Mme Norbert Levavasseur']; sometimes classed as HMult

'Hibernica' (R. × hibernica) HSpn, lp, 1802; flowers varying shades of pink, 1 in., single, borne in clusters of 3; foliage glaucous green, with 5-7 leaflets; numerous prickles; growth compact, erect; hips sub-globose, bright red; probably R. canina × R. spinosissima; discovered by Templeton near Belfast

Hidalgo® -- See 'Meitulandi'

'Hidcote Gold' HSpn, my, 1948, Hilling; flowers canary-yellow, single, borne several together; non-recurrent; foliage ferny; prickles very large, flattened, wing-like; thought by Graham Stuart Thomas to be R. sericea pteracantha × R. hugonis

'Hidcote Yellow' -- See 'Lawrence Johnston'

'Hide and Seek' F, op, Dickson; flowers coral-pink, metallic sheen to petals, borne in clusters; free-flowering; foliage reddish early, then medium green, glossy; low, rounded growth; intr. 2003

High & Fantasy® HT, pb, Preesman; flowers cerise pink, reverse white streaked pale pink, double, high-centered; recurrent; intr. 2007

'High Ambition' -- See 'Welhigh'

'High Cloud' -- See 'Tindick'

'High Esteem' HT, pb, 1961, Von Abrams; bud pointed; flowers phlox-pink, reverse silvery, 6 in., 43 petals, high-centered, intense fruity fragrance; foliage leathery, light green; vigorous, upright, compact growth; PP2245; [('Charlotte Armstrong' × 'Mme Henri Guillot') × ('Multnomah' × 'Charles Mallerin')]; intr. 1961

'High Fashion' HT, dp, 1972, Patterson; bud ovoid; flowers deep pink, medium, dbl., high-centered; foliage glossy, soft; vigorous, upright growth; [Queen Elizabeth® × 'Peace']

'High Five' -- See 'Sunhifi'

'High Flier' LCl, mr, Fryer; flowers rich, blood red, well-formed, dbl., moderate fragrance; repeats all season; foliage dark green; vigorous growth to 10-12 ft.; intr. 2004

'High Flight' Min, w; intr. 2001

'High Flyer' -- See 'Jacsat'

'High Flying Cathy' F, yb, McCann, Sean; ['Bloomsday' × Julia's Rose®]; intr. 2004

'High Hope' -- See 'Flohih'

'High Hopes' -- See 'Haryup'

High Jinks™ -- See 'Savajinks'

'High Life' -- See 'Sealife'

'High Noon' Cl HT, my, 1946, Lammerts, Dr. Walter; flowers lemon-yellow, 3-4 in., 28 petals, loosely cupped, borne singly or in small clusters, moderate spicy fragrance; foliage leathery, glossy; upright, vigorous, climbing (8 ft.) growth; PP704; ['Soeur Thérèse' × 'Captain Thomas']

'High Perfume' -- See 'Crazy One'

'High Point' -- See 'Molhip'

'High Sheriff' -- See 'Harwellington'

High Society™ -- See 'Jacadyna'

'High Society' HT, mr, 1961, Kordes, R.; flowers bright red, 4 in., 30 petals, high-centered, slight fragrance; bushy growth; intr. 1961

High Spirits™ -- See 'Savaspir'

'High Stepper' -- See 'Morclim'

'High Style' -- See 'Lyohi'

'High Summer' -- See 'Dicbee'

'High Tide' Min, ob, 1986, McDaniel, Earl; flowers orange, yellow reverse, medium, 25 petals, cupped, borne usually singly; foliage small, dark, semi-glossy; few prickles; upright, bushy growth; [seedling × seedling]

'High Time' HT, pb, 1960, Swim, H.C.; bud urn-shaped; flowers claret-rose, reverse gold and pink, 4-5 in., 24 petals, high-centered, intense spicy fragrance; foliage dark, glossy; vigorous, upright growth; PP1809; ['Charlotte Armstrong' × 'Signora']; intr. 1959

'Highdownensis' (R. × highdownensis) HMoy, mr, 1928, Stern, Sir Frederich; flowers bright medium red, fading to lighter centers, single, borne in clusters of 7-9; foliage dark, coppery; prickles colorful; vigorous, bushy (10 × 10 ft.) growth; hips orange-scarlet; [R. moyesii × unknown]

Highfield® -- See 'Harcomp'

Highglow® LCl, mr, Tantau; flowers large, double, moderate fragrance; strong (350 cm.) growth; intr. 2006

'Highland Beauty' F, mr, 1957, deRuiter; flowers rich red, 3 in., semi-dbl., borne in clusters, slight fragrance; foliage dark, glossy; vigorous growth; ['Signal Red' × 'Red Wonder']; intr. 1956

'Highland Charm' F, op, 1957, deRuiter; flowers coral-salmon, large, semi-dbl., borne in large clusters, slight fragrance; foliage leathery; vigorous, bushy growth; ['Duchess of Rutland' × 'Fashion']; intr. 1956

'Highland Dancer' F, rb

'Highland Fling' F, or, 1971, Anderson's Rose Nurseries; flowers orange-scarlet, veined black, 4-4½ in., 22 petals; foliage glossy; ['Dearest' × Elizabeth of Glamis®]

'Highland Glory' F, mr, 1957, deRuiter; flowers crimson-red, 3 in., semi-dbl., borne in large clusters, slight fragrance; foliage coppery; vigorous growth; ['Sidney Peabody' × 'floribunda seedling']; intr. 1956

'Highland Laddie' -- See 'Cocflag'

'Highland Lass' -- See 'Ziphigh'

'Highland Mary' T, 1908, Dingee & Conard

'Highland Park' HT, op, 1942, Mallerin, C.; bud tawny salmon; flowers salmon-pink, open, large, 35 petals; foliage leathery; vigorous, upright, bushy growth; ['E.G. Hill' × 'Mme Henri Guillot']

'Highland Wedding' HT, w, 1971, MacLeod; flowers white, suffused blush, center light gold, 4½ in., 30 petals; foliage large, dark, semi-glossy; vigorous growth; ['Virgo' × Rose Gaujard®]

'Highlands Rose' -- See 'Sealands'

'Highlight' F, ob, 1957, Robinson, H.; flowers orange-scarlet, 2½ in., 24 petals, borne in large clusters; vigorous growth; [seedling × 'Independence']; intr. 1957

'Hightae' -- See 'Greentae'

'Highveld Sun' -- See 'Morpapplay'

'Highway Rose' S, dp, Kordes; intr. 1984

'Highway to the Capital' -- See 'Miyako Oji'

'Higoromo' HT, dr, 1999, Suzuki, Seizo; flowers deep red, 4-5 in., 30-35 petals, flat, slight fragrance; foliage dark green, semi-glossy; growth vigorous (4-5 ft.); ['Duftzauber' × ('Josephine Bruce' × seedling)]; intr. 1990

'Higth Parade' F, pb

'Hikari' F, Suzuki, Seizo; intr. 1969

'Hilaroma' (Secret™) HT, pb, 1992, Tracy, Daniel; bud ovoid; flowers light creamy pink edged with deep pink, 4-4½ in., 30-40 petals, cupped, borne mostly singly, intense sweet and spicy fragrance; recurrent; foliage large, medium green, semi-glossy; prickles some, medium, reddish green; strong stems; tall (120-130 cm.), bushy growth; PP8494; [Pristine® × 'Friendship']; intr. 1994

'Hilcap' HT, w, (HILcap); intr. 1999

'Hilco' (Excitement™) Gr, dy, 1986, Jelly, Robert G.; flowers 20 petals, high-centered, borne usually singly, moderate fragrance; foliage medium size, dark, semi-glossy; no prickles; medium, upright, bushy growth; hips medium, slightly pear-shaped, orange; PP4412; ['Golden Fantasie' × Coed™]; intr. 1985

'Hilcot' HT, ob, Tracy, Sr.; Daniel L.; bud medium, ovoid; intr. 1992

'Hilda' HT, pb, 1928, Cant, B. R.; flowers salmon-pink, reverse orange-carmine, very large, dbl., globular; foliage leathery; long stems; vigorous growth

'Hilda Heinemann' -- See 'Meigalil'

Hilda Murrell® -- See 'Ausmurr'

'Hilda Phillips' HT, dy, 1948, Bees; flowers deep golden yellow, well-shaped, medium; foliage glossy, bronze; [('Aureate' × unknown) × 'Mrs Sam McGredy']

'Hilda Rahn' F, lp, 2002, Read, Allan; flowers full, borne in small clusters, intense fragrance; recurrent; foliage medium size, medium green, semi-glossy; prickles small, pointed, numerous; growth spreading, tall (10 ft.); garden; hardy; ['Spring Song' × unknown]; intr. 2004

'Hilda Richardson' HT, w, 1913, Dickson, A.; flowers milk white, flushed rosy lilac at tips, with prominent golden stamens, small to m, semi-dbl., intense geranium/primrose fragrance

'Hilda Scott' HT, my, 1955, Glassford; flowers butter-yellow, small; ['Lady Hillingdon' × unknown]

'Hilda's Beauty' -- See 'Worcross'

'Hilde' -- See 'Benhile'

'Hilde Apelt' HT, ob, 1927, Leenders, M.; flowers saffron-yellow, dbl.; [seedling × 'Souv. de Claudius Pernet']

'Hilde Steinert' HT, rb, 1926, Leenders, M.; flowers coral-red, reverse reddish-salmon and old-gold, semi-dbl.

'Hildegarde' HT, ob, 1946, Boerner; bud long, pointed; flowers saffron-rose-pink, 5 in., 30-35 petals, high-centered, intense fragrance; foliage leathery; very vigorous, upright growth; PP799; [sport of 'Briarcliff']

'Hildenbrandseck' HRg, mp, 1909, Lambert, P.; flowers shining clear pink, single, borne in clusters; recurrent bloom; vigorous growth; ['Atropurpurea (HRg)' × 'Frau Karl Druschki']

'Hildeputchen' HMult, m, 1922, Bruder Alfons; flowers violet-pink with white, 2-3 cm., single to semi-dbl., moderate fragrance

'Hilgofan' (Joan Brickhill®) HT, my, 1972, Byrum; intr. 1971

'Hilgold' S, my, 1967, Allen, E.F.

Hill ™ -- See 'Poulcot008'

'Hill Cottage' (Hill ™) S, w, Poulsen; flowers white, small, semi-dbl., borne in clusters, no fragrance; foliage dark green, glossy; broad, bushy growth; intr. 2004

'Hill Crest' HT, rb, 1948, Joseph H. Hill, Co.; bud short, pointed, oxblood-red; flowers carmine, 3½-4 in., 50-55 petals, high-centered, moderate fragrance; foliage leathery; very vigorous, upright, compact, tall growth; PP844

'Hill Top' HT, ab, 1942, Joseph H. Hill, Co.; bud long, pointed, light coral-red; flowers buff, 4-5 in., 28 petals, globular, moderate fragrance; foliage leathery, dark, wrinkled; vigorous, upright growth; PP525; ['Joanna Hill' × R.M.S. Queen Mary]; intr. 1946

'Hillary' Min, yb

'Hillary First Lady' -- See 'Lapcli'

'Hillcrest Pillar' S, my, 1930, Hillcrest Gardens; flowers bright yellow, medium, semi-dbl.; pillar (6 ft.) growth; [R. × harisonii × unknown]

'Hillier Rose' (R. × hillieri, R. × pruhoniciana, R. × moyesii hillieri) HMoy, dr, 1920, Hillier; flowers deep red, 2 in., single; growth dense, to 9 ft.; [R. moyesii × R. willmottiae]

'Hill's America' ('America') HT, mp, 1921, E.G. Hill, Co.; flowers rose-pink, 44 petals; ['Premier' × 'Hoosier Beauty']

'Hill's Hillbilly' F, mp, 1947; bud ovoid, red; flowers pink, open, 1-2 in., 5-6 petals, borne in clusters, slight fragrance; foliage leathery, dark; vigorous, upright, bushy growth; PP838; ['Juanita' × 'Mrs R.M. Finch']

'Hill's Victory' HT, rb, 1942, Joseph H. Hill, Co.; bud red; flowers rose-red to rose-pink, 5-6 in., 50-55 petals, slight fragrance; foliage leathery, dark, wrinkled; long, strong stems; vigorous, upright, much branched growth; PP531; ['Chieftain' × 'Sweet Adeline']

'Hilltop' LCl, pb, Huxley, Ian; intr. 1989

'Hilltop Rose' -- See R. collina

'Hilrap' (Classy™) HT, mr, E.G. Hill, Co.; intr. 1992

'Hilraz' ('Lovely Dream') HT, dp

'Hilred' (Challenger™) HT, dr, 1989, Tracy, Daniel; bud ovoid; flowers dark red, reverse medium red, medium, 25 petals, high-centered, urn-shaped, borne in sprays of 2-3, moderate fragrance; foliage medium size, semi-glossy; prickles angled downward, small, orange blend; upright, medium growth; hips pear-shaped, small, orange blend; ['Jacqueline' × seedling]; intr. 1987

'Hilset' (Fondly™) F, lp, 1986, Jelly, Robert G.; flowers medium, 20 petals, high-centered, borne singly and in clusters of 2-4, moderate spicy fragrance; foliage medium size, dark, matte; prickles few, on peduncles; medium upright growth; hips medium, ovoid, orange-red; PP4983; [seedling × seedling]; intr. 1985

'Hiltaco' (Sassy™) F, dr, 1986, Jelly, Robert G.; flowers sweetheart, small, 20 petals, high-centered, borne usually singly; foliage small, medium green, matte; prickles only on peduncle; upright growth; hips small, globular, greyed-red; PP4559; ['Little Leaguer' × 'Mary DeVor']; intr. 1985

'Hiltig' -- See 'Premier'

'Hilton Edward' -- See 'Stiedward'

'Himalayensis' -- See 'Kaiserin des Nordens'

'Himangini' F, w, 1970, Indian Agri. Research Institute; bud ovoid; flowers ivory-white, center light buff, open, medium, dbl.; vigorous, bushy, compact growth; ['Saratoga' × unknown]; intr. 1968

'Himatsuri' HT, dr, 1977, Teranishi, K.; bud circular; flowers 3½-4 in., high-centered; foliage small; upright growth; [('Tropicana' × 'Karl Herbst') × Mainauperle®]; intr. 1973

'Hime' -- See 'Keifupie'

'Himmelsauge' ('Francesco Dona') HSet, m, 1895, Geschwind, R.; flowers dark velvety purple-red, fading to medium pink, occasionally striped with white,, 4-6 cm., very dbl., borne in small to medium clusters; very fragrant; [R. setigera hybrid × R. rugosa rubra plena]

'Himmelsstürmer' HRg, pb, Wänninger, Franz; flowers carmine-pink with white, small, single; intr. 1990

'Hinaarare' F, lp, Keisei; intr. 2001

'Hinamatsuri' ('The Doll's Festival') F, mp

'Hinemoa' F, rb, 1963, Mason, P.G.; flowers buttercup-yellow shading to vermilion, 3-3½ in., 17-20 petals, cupped, borne in clusters; foliage bronze, leathery; upright, bushy growth; ['Circus' × unknown]

'Hingreat' ('Great Phoebus') LCl, ab, 1999, Hintlian, Nancy Sears; bud white, spherical; flowers opening to orange and yellow, with slight pink edge, 5½ in., 41 petals, pompon, borne mostly singly; foliage large, dark green, semi-glossy; prickles moderate; upright, vigorous, medium (8 ft.) growth; [Abraham Darby® × 'Breath of Life']

'Hinrich Gaede' HT, ob, 1931, Kordes; bud pointed, nasturtium-red; flowers orange-yellow tinted nasturtium-yellow, very large, dbl., high-centered, moderate fruity fragrance; foliage glossy, bronze; vigorous growth; ['Lady Margaret Stewart' × 'Charles P. Kilham']

'Hinrich Gaede, Climbing' Cl HT, ob, 1935, Armstrong, J.A.; PP244

'Hinruby' ('Ruby Velvet') F, dr, 1999, Hintlian, Nancy Sears; flowers dark red, turning purple with age, lasts well, 5 in., 41 petals, borne in small clusters; foliage medium size, medium green, semi-glossy; prickles numerous, very large; spreading, medium (4 ft.) growth; ['The Dark Lady' × 'Oklahoma']

'Hinsweet' ('Sweet Ecstasy') S, m, 1999, Hintlian, Nancy Sears; flowers purple-crimson, turning more purple with age, 5 in., 41 petals, borne mostly singly, intense lasting fragrance; foliage large, dark green, semi-glossy; prickles moderate; upright, vigorous, medium (5 ft.) growth; ['The Dark Lady' × 'Oklahoma']

'Hintuscan' ('Tuscan Beauty') HGal, m, 1999, Hintlian, Nancy Sears; flowers red-lavender, aging to near purple, 4-4½ in., 41 petals, borne mostly singly; foliage medium size, medium green, semi-glossy; prickles moderate; spreading, tall (6 ft.) growth; ['Superb Tuscan' × 'Big Purple']

'Hipango' -- See 'Murgo'

'Hipólito Lázaro' LCl, dr, Pahissa; flowers carmine, large

'Hippolyte' HGal, m, Before 1842, Parmentier; flowers purple-violet, small button at center, medium, dbl., quartered, borne singly or in clusters of 2-3, slight fragrance; foliage light green, elliptical; almost thornless; growth vigorous, tall (6 ft.)

'Hippolyte Abraham' HT, mr, 1903, Abraham; flowers cherry red, shaded violet

'Hippolyte Barreau' HT, dr, 1894, Pernet-Ducher; ['Comtesse de Labarthe' × 'Louis van Houtte']

'Hippolyte Flandrin' HP, mp, 1895, Damaizin

'Hippolyte Jamain' B, m, 1856, Pradel; flowers purple, large, full

'Hippolyte Jamain' HP, mp, Faudon; flowers bright carmine pink, very large, full; intr. 1869

'Hippolyte Jamain' HP, dp, Lacharme, F.; flowers carmine-red, well-formed, 38 petals, semi-globular, moderate fragrance; foliage red, when young; vigorous, erect growth; ['Victor Verdier' × unknown]; intr. 1874

'Hippolyte Jamain, Climbing' Cl HP, m, 1887, Paul, G.; [sport of 'Hippolyte Jamain']

'Hippy' HT, yb, Delbard-Chabert; intr. 1971

'Hiroshima' HT, dp

'Hiroshima Appeal' HT, ob, Hiroshima; intr. 1985

'Hiroshima Mind' HT, ob, Harada; intr. 1995

'Hiroshima no Kane' ('The Bells of Hiroshima') HT, rb, Harada; intr. 1994

'Hiroshima Requiem' HT, dr, Hiroshima; intr. 1999

'Hiroshima Spirit' HT, yb, Harada, Toshiyuki; flowers dark yellow with red, large, dbl.; intr. 1991

'Hiroshima's Children' -- See 'Harmark'

'His Majesty' HT, dr, 1909, McGredy; flowers dark crimson shaded deeper, very large, dbl., high-centered; long, strong stems; very vigorous growth

'Hisami' HT, lp, 1988, Harada, Toshiyuki; flowers light cream, flushed crimson at tip, 50 petals, high-centered, borne usually singly, moderate fragrance; foliage medium size, dark green, matte; prickles downward curved, red to light green; upright, medium growth; ['Kordes Perfecta' × 'Christian Dior']

'Hispania' HT, dr, 1938, Pahissa; bud pointed; flowers velvety red, open, overlarge, dbl.; foliage leathery; long, strong stems; very vigorous growth

'Hispanica Moschata Simplex' -- See 'Spanish Musk Rose'

'History' HT, pb, Tantau; flowers deep pink with white reverse, large, slow opening, dbl., slight fragrance; foliage medium green; compact, upright growth; intr. 2003

'Hit Parade' F, ob, 1962, Dickson, Patrick; flowers red, orange and gold, 4 in., 16 petals, borne in clusters; foliage dark; low growth; [('Independence' × seedling) × 'Brownie']; intr. 1962

Hjemmet-rosen™ -- See 'Poulen003(N)'

'Ho-Jun' ('Hoh-Jun', 'Hojun') HT, pb, 1985, Suzuki, Seizo; flowers pink flushed rose-red, 28 petals, cupped, borne in clusters of 2 - 5, intense fragrance; foliage dark, semi-glossy; prickles large; compact growth; ['Granada' × 'Flaming Peace']; intr. 1984

'Ho-No-o-no-nami' ('Wave of Flame', 'Waves of Flame') LCl, or, 1968, Suzuki, Seizo; bud pointed; flowers orange-red, reverse lighter, to open, medium, dbl., high-centered, slight fragrance; foliage glossy, leathery; vigorous, climbing growth; PP3033; ['Spectacular' × 'Aztec']; intr. 1968

'Hoagy Carmichael' -- See 'Mactitir'

Hobby® Min, dp, Tantau; flowers strong pink, large, full, rosette; compact, rounded growth; intr. 2001

'Hobby' F, op, 1959, Tantau, Math.; flowers coral-pink, large, dbl., borne in open clusters; foliage dark; upright, bushy growth; ['Red Favorite' × 'Kathe Duvigneau']; intr. 1955

'Hobby Striped Sport' F, ob; flowers red stripes against the orange- pink; [sport of 'Hobby']; intr. 2003

'Hochsommer' F, dp, 1965, van Engelen, A. J.; flowers dbl., borne in clusters; foliage dark; low growth; [Queen Elizabeth® × seedling]; intr. 1962

'Hockey' S, mr; flowers red with yellow stamens, small, semi-dbl., cupped to flat, borne in clusters; free-flowering; growth low, spreading, groundcover; intr. 2000

'Hocus-Pocus' Gr, or, 1975, Armstrong, D.L.; flowers 4-4½ in., 30 petals, cupped, slight fragrance; foliage large, dark; vigorous, upright growth; PP3972; ['Fandango' × 'Simon Bolivar']

'Hocus Pocus' F, rb, Kordes; flowers deep red with irregular yellow stripes, small; stems 16 inches; intr. 2001

'Hocus Pocus Kordana' Min, rb, Kordes; flowers red, orange and yellow stripes, dbl.; container rose

Hoddy Toddy™ -- See 'Kintoddy'

'Hoffman von Fallersleben' LCl, rb, 1917, Lambert, P.; flowers salmon-red, shaded yellow and ochre, 4 cm., full, borne in clusters of 5-20; sometimes repeats; foliage glossy; vigorous, climbing growth; ['Geheimrat Dr. Mittweg' × Tip-Top®]

'Hoffnung' HT, ob, Huber; intr. 1995

'Hofgartendirektor Graebener' HT, lp, 1899, Lambert, P.; flowers creamy pink, medium, dbl.; ['Mme Caroline Testout' × 'Antoinette Durieu']

'Hofgärtner Kalb' HCh, pb, 1913, Felberg-Leclerc; flowers bright carmine-rose, center yellow, outer petals shaded red, 35 petals, moderate fragrance; vigorous, bushy growth; ['Souv. de Mme Eugène Verdier' × 'Gruss an Teplitz']

'Hoggar' S, Lens, Louis

'Hogg's Yellow' -- See 'Harison's Yellow'

'Hoh-Jun' -- See 'Ho-Jun'

'Hohshun' HT, dr, 1999, Ohkawara, Kiyoshi; flowers velvet deep red, 25-27 petals, high-centered; foliage dark green, half leathery; growth to 5 ft.; ['Charles Mallerin' × 'Mrs Nieminen']; intr. 1971

'Hoimashree' HT, mr, Ghosh; flowers bright scarlet red, large; intr. 2001

'Hojun' -- See 'Ho-Jun'

'Hokey Pokey' Min, ab, 1980, Saville, F. Harmon; bud long, pointed; flowers deep apricot, 28 petals, high-centered, borne singly, slight spicy fragrance; foliage finely serrated; prickles straight; compact, bushy growth; PP4642; ['Rise 'n' Shine' × 'Sheri Anne']

'Hokkaido' HRg, mp; intr. 1988

'Hoku-To' HT, ly, 1986, Suzuki, Seizo; flowers soft buff yellow, 42 petals, high-centered, moderate fragrance; foliage large, light green; vigorous, upright, spreading growth; [('Myoo-Jo' × Chicago Peace®) × King's Ransom®]; intr. 1979

'Holcombe Honey' F, yb, 2001, Bracegirdle, A.J.; flowers medium, dbl., borne in small clusters; foliage medium size, dark green, semi-glossy; prickles medium, slightly hooked, moderate; growth upright, medium (4 ft.); [('Dusky Maiden' × ('Golden Autumn' × Orangeade®)) × (Chinatown® × 'Picasso')]

'Hold Slunci' HP, ly, Blatnà; flowers medium, dbl.; intr. 1956

'Hole in One' -- See 'Horeagle'

'Holfairy' ('Fairy Snow') Pol, w, Holmes; intr. 1991

'Holiday' F, my, 1948, Boerner; bud ovoid, orange-yellow flushed pink; flowers flame-pink, reverse clear yellow, 3-3½ in., semi-dbl., cupped, borne in clusters of 3-10, moderate clove fragrance; foliage glossy; vigorous, bushy, compact growth; PP915; ruled extinct ARA 1983; ['McGredy's Pillar' × 'Pinocchio']

'Holiday' HT, mr, 1983, Strahle, B. Glen; flowers small, 35 petals, slight fragrance; foliage medium green; upright growth; ['Cara Mia' × 'Volare']; intr. 1981

'Holiday Cheer' -- See 'Morliday'

'Holiday Inn' -- See 'Worcharacter'

'Holje' ('Jerusalem') F, w, 1986, Holtzman, Arnold; flowers cream, large, 40 petals, high-centered, borne in sprays of 5-8, moderate fragrance; foliage medium size, light green, matte; upright, bushy growth; hips ovoid, small, green; [(Queen Elizabeth® × seedling) × 'Moriah']; intr. 1987

'Holland Double White Altai' (form of R. spinosissima altaica), w; flowers dbl.; non-recurrent

'Hollandaise' -- See 'Maheca'

'Holländerin' -- See 'Red Favorite'

'Hollandia' Pol, dr; flowers deep red, small, dbl., rosette; intr. before 1958

'Hollandia' HT, mr, 1930, Zijverden; flowers brick-red, shaded copper; [sport of 'Aspirant Marcel Rouyer']

'Hollandica' C, dp; flowers deep pink, veined darker, petals shell-shaped, very dbl., moderate fragrance; growth widely used as an understock, especially for tree roses; probably refers to multiple cultivars; intr. before 1695

'Hollandica' HRg, lp, about 1888; flowers single; nearly thornless; thought to have been raised by J. Spek; selected Dutch clone of R. rugosa, or perhaps a hybrid with Manettii, widely used as an understock, especially for tree roses

'Hollands Rugosa' HRg, mp; flowers medium, single

'Hollie Roffey' -- See 'Harramin'

'Holly Rochelle' HT, dr, 1977, Graham; bud pointed; flowers velvety red, 4 in., 60-70 petals, high-centered, moderate fragrance; very vigorous, upright growth; PP3899; ['Charlotte Armstrong' × 'Scarlet Knight']; intr. 1974

'Hollybank' F, mr, 1966, Hooney; flowers vermilion, 3-3½ in., globular; foliage coppery; upright growth; ['Independence' × 'United Nations']

'Hollywood' HT, rb, 1930, Scittine; bud pointed; flowers dark rose-red, veined darker, dbl., high-centered; foliage dark; long, strong stems; bushy growth; [sport of 'Premier']

'Hollywood' HT, w, Pouw; A. A.; bud ovate; sepals long, foliated; flowers white to yellow-white, petals reflex to points, 4-4½ in., 23 petals, exhibition, borne one to a stem, slight fragrance; recurrent; foliage abundant, medium green, semi-glossy; prickles few, none on top 16. in of stem; narrow, bushy (5 ft.) growth; PP10529; intr. 1998

'Hollywood Beauty' HT, dp, 1929, Pacific Rose Co.; flowers camellia-red, dbl.; [sport of 'Rose Marie']

'Hollywood Star' -- See 'Reshollywood'

'Holoserica' ('Maheck à Fleurs Simples', 'Velvet Rose') HGal, dr, before 1629; flowers deep purple speckled with violet, semi-dbl. to dbl.; foliage ovoid, saw-toothed; few prickles; Holoserica Duplex and Holoserica Multiplex are similar, with varying petalage

'Holoserica Regalis' ('Royale Veloutée') HGal, m, before 1815, Schwarzkopf; flowers purple tending towards black, dbl., moderate fragrance; foliage oval, dentate; prickles short; stems long, slender

'Holstein' -- See 'Korholst'

'Holstein' ('Firefly') F, mr, 1939, Kordes; bud pointed, dark crimson; flowers clear crimson, 4 in., 6 petals, cupped, borne in immense clusters, slight fragrance; foliage leathery, dark, bronze;

very vigorous, bushy growth; PP395; ['Else Poulsen' × ('Dance of Joy' × unknown)]

'Holstein, Climbing'   Cl F, mr, 1947, Kordes, P.

Holsteinperle® -- See 'Kordiam'

'Holstenrose'   HT, mr, 1937, Tantau; flowers scarlet-red, large, dbl., cupped; foliage glossy; vigorous, bushy growth; ['Gen. MacArthur' × 'Amulett']

Holstenstor®   F, op, Meilland; intr. 1990

'Holstentor' -- See 'Meimuide'

'Holt Hewitt'   HT, rb, 1925, Beckwith; flowers rich velvety crimson, flushed and edged scarlet, well-shaped; vigorous, bushy growth

'Holtermann's Gold'   HT, my, Swane; intr. 1989

Holy Toledo™   Min, ab, 1979, Christensen, Jack E.; bud ovoid, pointed; flowers brilliant apricot-orange, reverse yellow-orange, imbricated, 1½-2 in., 28 petals; foliage small, glossy, dark; vigorous, bushy growth; PP4659; ['Gingersnap' × Magic Carrousel®]; intr. 1978

'Homage'   HT, pb, Pal, Dr. B.P.; bud cerise-red; flowers deep, warm pink with outer petals tinged lilac, large, dbl.; intr. 1986

'Homage'   HT, m, Hiroshima; intr. 2005

'Hombre'   Min, pb, 1983, Jolly, Nelson F.; flowers light apricot-pink, reverse light pink, small, dbl., high-centered; foliage small, medium green, semi-glossy; bushy growth; PP5552; ['Humdinger' × 'Rise 'n' Shine']; intr. 1982

'Home' -- See 'Furusato'

'Home & Country' -- See 'Kribatis'

Home and Family™ -- See 'Wekplagneze'

Home & Garden® -- See 'Korgrasotra'

'Home-Coming' -- See 'Michome'

'Home of Time' -- See 'Cocquamber'

Home Run™ -- See 'Wekcisbako'

'Home Run'   HT, pb, 1956, Motose; bud ovoid; flowers rose-bengal, 5 in., 40 petals, high-centered, moderate fragrance; foliage leathery; vigorous growth; PP1537; [sport of 'Pink Delight']

'Home Sweet Home' -- See 'Mailoeur'

'Home Sweet Home'   HT, mp, 1941, Wood & Ingram; flowers rich velvety pink, dbl., moderate damask fragrance; foliage glossy, dark; vigorous growth

'Home Sweet Home, Climbing'   Cl HT, mp; intr. after 1941

'Homeland'   HT, pb, 1951, LeGrice; flowers Neyron rose, base tinted orange, well-formed, 5½-6 in., 50-60 petals; foliage leathery, dark; very free growth; ['red hybrid tea' × 'Guinee']

'Homeland'   HT, ab, Drummond; intr. 1992

'Homenagem Egas Moniz'   HT, mp, 1959, Moreira da Silva; ['Walter' × 'Juno']

'Homenagem Gago Coutinho'   HT, rb, 1959, Moreira da Silva; flowers crimson-red, reverse yellow; ['Confidence' × seedling]

'Homenagem Pinto d'Azevedo'   HT, op, 1959, Moreira da Silva; flowers bright salmon-pink, dbl.; ['Super-Congo' × 'Independence']

'Homère'   T, pb, 1858, Robert et Moreau; flowers pink, center flesh-white, dbl., cupped; vigorous, bushy growth; [possibly a seedling of 'David Pradel']

'Home's Beauty' -- See 'Jaced'

'Home's Choice' -- See 'Jacade'

'Home's Pride' -- See 'Jacary'

'Homestead'   HCh, dr

'Homesteader'   Min, yb, Williams, J.B.; flowers yellow blend with orange heart, quilling petals, HT shaped, borne in masses of blooms; intr. 2003

'Hometown Ards'   F, ab, Dickson; flowers deep cream/buff, medium, double, borne in large clusters; recurrent; foliage dense, dark green, glossy; tall (4 ft.), upright, vigorous growth; intr. 2007

'Hommage à Barbara' ('Heinz Winkler')   S, dr, Delbard; flowers intense red, with tones of velvety black, large, full, cupped; recurrent; intr. 2005

Hommage à Soupert et Notting®   B, dp, Ducher; flowers deep pink with mauve and silver reflections , 120 petals, cupped, quartered, intense fragrance; recurrent; tall (2 - 3 m.) growth; intr. 2007

'Hommage d'Anjou'   HT, or, Minier; flowers coppery-red, large, dbl.; intr. 1965

'Hondo'   HT, yb, 1990, Perry, Astor; flowers medium yellow with red-purple on tips, aging red-purple, large, 33 petals, moderate fragrance; foliage large, dark green, matte; upright growth; ['Irish Gold' × 'Las Vegas']

'Hondo'   HRg, dp; intr. 1988

Honest Abe™   Min, dr, 1977, Christensen, Jack E.; bud mossy; flowers deep velvety crimson-red, mini-moss, 1½ in., 33 petals, slight tea fragrance; foliage glossy; vigorous, bushy growth; PP4356; ['Fairy Moss' × 'Rubinette']; intr. 1978

'Honest Red'   HT, mr, 1991, Wambach, Alex A.; flowers large, full, borne mostly singly, intense fragrance; foliage medium size, dark green, semi-glossy; tall, bushy growth; [seedling × 'Sea Pearl']

'Honey'   F, my, 1955, Marsh; flowers coppery yellow, becoming lemon-yellow, small, semi-dbl.; [sport of 'Smiles']

Honey® ('Trump')   HT, ab, Kordes; flowers honey colored, medium, dbl., cupped, borne mostly singly, moderate fragrance; recurrent; stems long; florist rose; intr. 2005

Honey 'n' Spice™ -- See 'Minagco'

'Honey Bear' -- See 'Delcrouf'

'Honey Bear' -- See 'Pixihon'

Honey Border™ -- See 'Poultc005'

Honey Bouquet™ -- See 'Jacyimp'

'Honey Bun'   F, my, 1974, Ellis & Swim; bud ovoid; flowers medium, dbl., cupped, intense fragrance; foliage dark, leathery; very vigorous, upright, bushy growth; PP3518; ['Gold Strike' × 'Golden Garnette']; intr. 1973

'Honey Bunch'   F, dy, 1971, Watkins Roses; flowers deep gold, shaded peach, long, pointed, 3 in., 20 petals; foliage light; moderate, upright growth; ['Circus' × 'Soraya']

Honey Bunch® -- See 'Cocglen'

'Honey Butter' -- See 'Pixhoney'

'Honey Caramel'   F, my, Interplant; intr. 2007

'Honey Child'   F, ab, Ilsink; flowers apricot orange, dbl., moderate fragrance; free-flowering; medium growth; intr. 1999

'Honey Chile'   F, lp, 1963, Thomson; bud pointed; flowers dbl., cupped, borne in clusters, slight fragrance; foliage leathery; vigorous, upright, bushy growth; ['Fashion' × Queen Elizabeth®]; intr. 1963

'Honey Dew'   F, ab, Dickson; flowers golden apricot, wavy petals, medium; medium growth; intr. 1995

Honey Dijon™ -- See 'Weksprouless'

'Honey Favorite' ('Honey Favourite')   HT, lp, 1962, Von Abrams; flowers light yellowish-pink, base yellow, slight fragrance; good repeat; [sport of 'Pink Favorite']; intr. 1962

'Honey Favourite' -- See 'Honey Favorite'

'Honey Gold'   F, my, 1959, Boerner; bud ovoid; flowers maize-yellow overcast buff-yellow, 3-3½ in., 43 petals, moderate fragrance; foliage dark, glossy; vigorous, bushy growth; PP1535; ['Yellow Pinocchio' × 'Fashion']; intr. 1956

'Honey Hill'   Min, ob, 1981, Lyon; bud ovoid, pointed; flowers orange, 48 petals, high-centered, borne singly or several together, moderate fragrance; foliage medium green, semi-glossy; prickles curved, light brown; vigorous, bushy, upright growth; [seedling × seedling]; intr. 1980

'Honey Kordana' -- See 'Honey Kordana Mini Brite'

'Honey Kordana Mini Brite' ('Honey Kordana')   Min, rb, Kordes, Wilhelm; bud long pointed, ovoid; flowers red with orange-yellow base, 1¾ in., 25-30 petals, borne mostly singly, no fragrance; free-flowering; foliage abundant, small, glossy; prickles few, small, straight; vigorous, compact, upright (18-20 in.) growth; PP11186; [('Joy' × 'Korgiffer') × 'Mandarin']; intr. 1997

'Honey Mini-Delite' -- See 'Clehon'

'Honey Moss'   Min, ly, 1979, Sudol, Julia; bud mossy; flowers near white, toward honey, mini-moss, 1 in., 52 petals, flat, moderate fragrance; foliage dark, leathery; spreading growth; PP4354; ['Fairy Moss' × unknown]

Honey Perfume™ -- See 'Jacarque'

'Honey Rea'   HT, pb, 1973, Concord Floral Co.; bud ovoid; flowers pink, very large, semi-dbl., high-centered; foliage large, dark, leathery; very vigorous, bushy growth

Honeybee™ -- See 'Zlehoney'

'Honeybun' -- See 'Tan98264'

'Honeycomb' Min, ly, 1975, Moore, Ralph S.; flowers soft yellow to near white, 1½ in., 30 petals, high-centered, moderate fragrance; foliage small, glossy, light, leathery; dwarf, bushy growth; [(*R. wichurana* × Floradora) × 'Debbie']; intr. 1974

Honeycup® HT, ab, Pouw; growth vigorous, to 80 cm.; intr. 1990

'Honeyflow' F, pb, 1957, Riethmuller; flowers white edged pink, single, borne in very large clusters, moderate fragrance; foliage glossy; vigorous growth; ['Spring Song (F)' × 'Gartendirektor Otto Linne']

'Honeyglow' F, yb, 1955, LeGrice; flowers lemon-yellow, reverse shaded orange, pointed, 2 in., semi-dbl., borne in clusters; foliage glossy; vigorous growth; ['Goldilocks' × 'Ellinor LeGrice']

'Honeymilk' Min, w, Tantau; flowers milk white with cream yellow center, dbl., borne in clusters; good repeat; compact (16-20 in.) growth; intr. 2002

'Honeymoon' HT, ly, Benny, David; flowers creamy lemon yellow, silky texture, dbl., high-centered; medium to tall growth; intr. 2004

'Honeymoon in England' -- See 'Honigmond'

'Honeypot' S, my, 1969, Austin, David; flowers sulfur-yellow, 4 in., 40-50 petals, cupped; foliage dark, semi-glossy; vigorous growth; ['Honigmond' × Constance Spry®]

'Honeysweet' S, op, 1985, Buck, Dr. Griffith J.; bud medium-large, ovoid, pointed; flowers yellow-red-orange blend, large, 28 petals, cupped, borne 1 - 8 per cluster; repeat bloom; foliage leathery, dark with copper tints; prickles awl-like, brown-tan; bushy, erect growth; hardy; ['Serendipity' × Wiener Charme®]; intr. 1984

'Honeywood' F, ab, Fryer; flowers orange-apricot, non-fading, small to medium, dbl., borne in large clusters, moderate fragrance; free-flowering; foliage dark green, disease-resistant; bushy, tall (3 ft.) growth; intr. 2001

'Hong-Kong' HT, rb, 1962, Dot, Pedro; flowers citron-yellow edged currant-red, becoming red, dbl.; strong stems; bushy growth; ['Soraya' × ('Henri Mallerin' × 'Peace')]

'Honigmond' ('Honeymoon in England') F, my, 1960, Kordes, R.; flowers canary-yellow, 40 petals, rosette, borne in clusters (up to 5); foliage dark, veined; vigorous, upright, bushy growth; ['Clare Grammerstorf' × 'Golden Scepter']

'Honky Tonk' -- See 'Talhon'

'Honoho-No-Nami' LCl, or, Suzuki; flowers semi-dbl.; ['Danse du Feu' × 'Aztec']; intr. 1968

'Honoka' F, w, Keisei; intr. 2005

Honor™ ('Honour', 'Silhouette', Michèle Torr®) HT, w, 1979, Warriner, William A.; bud ovoid, pointed; flowers loose, 5 in., 18-25 petals, borne singly or several together, slight fragrance; foliage large, dark green; upright growth; PP4167; intr. 1980

'Honor Elizabeth' -- See 'City Livery'

'Hon. A. Norton' T, Williams, A.; [sport of 'Mme Lombard']

'Hon. Charlotte Knollys' HT, pb, 1926, Bees; flowers rose, edged lighter, center creamy yellow, dbl.; ['Antoine Rivoire' × 'Willowmere']

'Hon. Edith Gifford' ('Miss Edith Gifford') T, w, 1882, Guillot et Fils; flowers flesh-white tinted rose, large, dbl.; ['Mme Falcot' × 'Perle des Jardins']

'Hon. George Bancroft' HT, rb, 1879, Bennett; flowers red shaded violet-crimson, large, full, intense fragrance; almost thornless; moderate growth; ['Mme de St. Joseph' × 'Lord Macaulay']; rarely opens properly

'Hon. Ina Bingham' HP, mp, 1905, Dickson, A.; flowers pink, stamens golden yellow, large, 23 petals, cupped, intense fragrance; upright growth; sometimes classed as HT

'Hon. Joan Acton' HT, pb, 1950, Marshall, J.; flowers cream edged pink, pointed, very large, 90 petals; foliage bronze-green; hardy; ['Mrs Sam McGredy' × 'Golden Dawn']

'Honorable Ken' F, ob, 1993, Bracegirdle, Derek T.; flowers orange/yellow reverse, medium, full, borne in small clusters, moderate fragrance; foliage medium size, medium green, semi-glossy; some prickles; compact (100 cm.) growth; ['John Lawrence' × 'Zorina']; intr. 1994

'Hon. Lady Lindsay' ('Honorable Lady Lindsay', 'Honorine Lady Lindsay') S, pb, 1939, Hansen, N.J.; flowers pink, reverse darker, 35 petals; recurrent bloom; foliage dark; bushy (3 × 3 ft.) growth; not dependably hardy; ['New Dawn' × 'Rev. F. Page-Roberts']; intr. 1938

'Honorable Lady Lindsay' -- See 'Hon. Lady Lindsay'

'Hon Mrs R. G. Grosvenor' HT, w, 1916, Cant, B. R.; flowers porcelain white, center tinted orange-yellow, medium, full

'Hon. Violet Douglas Pennant' HT, pb, 1927, Bees; flowers blend of cream and rose, dbl.

Honore de Balzac™ -- See 'Meipamin'

'Honorine de Brabant' B, pb; flowers pale lilac-pink, spotted and striped mauve and crimson, dbl., cupped; recurrent bloom; foliage light green; few prickles; vigorous (to 6 ft.) growth

'Honorine Lady Lindsay' -- See 'Hon. Lady Lindsay'

'Honour' -- See 'Jacolite'

'Honour Bright' LCl, dr, 1950, Eacott; flowers brilliant crimson, medium, semi-dbl.; recurrent bloom; foliage bright green; very vigorous (4-6 ft.) growth; [('New Dawn' × 'Allen Chandler') × ('Mrs W. J. Grant, Climbing' × 'Richmond, Climbing')]

'Hoochie Koochie' -- See 'Umskoochie'

'Hoopearl' ('Miss Pearl™') Min, lp, 1991, Hooper, John C.; flowers large, dbl., borne mostly singly, intense spicy fragrance; foliage medium size, medium green, matte; few prickles; tall (80 cm.), upright growth; ['Gene Boerner' × 'Pacesetter']

'Hooray' ('J. C. Hooper') Min, rb, 2001, Hooper, J.C.; flowers white with burgundy red edges, reverse creamy white, 2 in., semi-dbl., borne in small clusters; foliage medium size, medium green, semi-glossy; prickles straight, moderate; growth bushy, medium; garden decorative, exhibition; [seedling × seedling]; intr. 2002

'Hoosier Beauty' HT, rb, 1915, Dorner; bud pointed; flowers glowing crimson shaded darker, large, dbl.; foliage sparse, rich green, glossy; bushy growth; ['Richmond' × 'Château de Clos Vougeot']

'Hoosier Beauty, Climbing' Cl HT, rb, 1918, Western (also W.R. Gray, 1925); flowers crimson, large, full; [sport of 'Hoosier Beauty']

'Hoosier Glory' -- See 'Eutin'

'Hoosier Gold' F, dy, 1975, Byrum; bud ovoid; flowers 2½-3½ in., 30-35 petals, slight fragrance; vigorous growth; PP3544; ['Lydia' × 'Golden Wave']; intr. 1974

'Hoosier Honey' HT, my, 1955, Joseph H. Hill, Co.; bud ovoid; flowers amber-yellow, open, 4½-5 in., 45-50 petals, moderate fragrance; vigorous, upright, bushy growth; PP1336; ['Anzac' × 'Golden Rapture']

'Hoosier Honey' HT, dy, Byrum; bud long, pointed; flowers mimosa-yellow, 4-5 in., 25-30 petals, high-centered, intense fragrance; foliage dark, leathery; vigorous growth; PP4015; [seedling × 'Golden Fantasie']; intr. 1973

'Hoosier Hysteria' S, dr, 1981, Schwartz, Ernest W.; bud ovoid; flowers 45 petals, high-centered, borne singly or in sprays of 5-7; foliage dark, leathery; prickles very few, curved, dark green; vigorous, tall, upright growth; ['Karl Herbst' × 'Simone']; intr. 1979

'Hoot 'n' Holler' -- See 'Morpetti'

'Hoot Owl' -- See 'Morhoot'

'Hootea' ('Billie Teas') Min, dr, 1992, Hooper, John C.; flowers 1½ in., full, borne mostly singly, no fragrance; foliage medium size, medium green, matte; some prickles; medium (38-45 cm.), upright growth; [seedling × Merrimac™]; intr. 1992

'Hope' -- See 'Tomhope'

'Hope' -- See 'Coclament'

'Hope' -- See 'Oracreps'

'Hope' Min, w, 1985, Bridges, Dennis A.; flowers well-formed, small, 35 petals; foliage large, dark, glossy; bushy growth; ['Rise 'n' Shine' × Party Girl™]

'Hope' -- See 'Kiboh'

'Hope 98' -- See 'Coclament'

'Hope And Joy' -- See 'Morhopjo'

'Hope for Humanity' S, dr, 1996, Collicutt,

L.M. & Davidson, C.G.; flowers deep, dark red, 1¾ in., dbl., borne in small clusters; foliage medium size, semi-glossy; prickles moderate; upright, low (56 cm.) growth; [('Prairie Princess' × 'Morden Amorette') × ('Morden Cardinette' × 'K1')]; intr. 1995

'Hopeful' -- See 'Reshope'

'Hopie Girl' -- See 'Reshopie'

'Hopscotch' Min, my, 1979, Christensen, Jack E.; bud ovoid, pointed; flowers golden yellow, imbricated, 1½ in., 28 petals; foliage small; vigorous, bushy growth; PP4664; ['Gingersnap' × Magic Carrousel®]

'Horaardvark' ('Mario Lanza') HT, yb, 1999, Horner, Calvin; flowers medium yellow, edged red, reverse paler yellow, 5 in., full, borne mostly singly, moderate fragrance; foliage medium size, dark green, glossy; prickles moderate; bushy, medium (3 ft.) growth; [Elina® × Remember Me®]; intr. 2000

'Horabi' ('Friday's Child') HT, mr, 1995, Horner, Colin P.; flowers 5 in., full, borne mostly singly, intense fragrance; foliage medium size, medium green, semi-glossy; tall (120 cm.), upright growth; ['Spirit of Youth' × seedling]; intr. 1997

'Horace McFarland' ('Président Nomblot') HT, op, 1944, Mallerin, C.; bud mahogany-red; flowers coppery pink,, 4½-5½ in., 43 petals, high-centered, moderate fruity fragrance; foliage leathery, dark; vigorous, bushy growth; PP730; ['Mme Arthaud' × seedling]; intr. 1944

'Horace Vernet' HP, dr, 1866, Guillot et Fils; flowers velvety purple, shaded dark crimson, large to very large, 40 petals, somewhat globular, intense fragrance; repeat bloom; moderate, erect growth; ['Général Jacqueminot' × unknown]

'Horalcamstrip' ('County Girl') F, op, 1999, Horner, Colin P.; flowers orange, pink cream striped, reverse paler striped, ages more salmon, 4 in., dbl., borne in small clusters; foliage medium size, medium green semi-glossy; prickles moderate; bushy, medium (3 ft.) growth; [Alexander® × ('Southampton' × ('(New Penny × White Pet)' × 'Stars 'n' Stripes'))]; intr. 2001

'Horannfree' F, dy, Horner; intr. 1997

'Horanyfell' ('Mary Summers') F, ob, 2004, Horner, Colin P.; flowers orange, reverse lighter, 9 cm., dbl., borne mostly solitary, moderate fragrance; foliage medium size, dark green, glossy; prickles medium, curved; growth upright, tall (120 cm.); garden decorative; ['Golden Future' × 'Fellowship']; intr. 2006

'Horanyme' ('Kieran Ross Clark') Gr, mr, 1999, Horner, Colin P.; flowers bright scarlet red, reverse paler, 3 in., dbl., borne in small clusters; foliage medium size, dark green, glossy; prickles moderate; upright, tall (4 ft.) growth; [('Anytime' × ('Liverpool Echo' × ('Flamenco' × R. bella))) × Remember Me®]

'Horanymoll' ('Golden Future') LCl, my, 1997, Horner, Colin P.; flowers medium yellow, reverse lighter, fading to lemon, 3-4 in., very dbl., borne in small clusters, moderate fragrance; foliage large, dark green, glossy; upright, medium (9-12ft.) growth; [('Anytime' × ('Liverpool Echo' × ('Flamenco' × R. bella))) × ('Korresia' × 'Kiskadee')]

'Horapsunmolbabe' ('The Care Rose') S, dy, 1999, Horner, Heather M.; flowers buttercup yellow, reverse medium yellow, small, semi-dbl., borne in small clusters; foliage small, medium green, glossy; few prickles; compact, low (2 ft.); patio growth; ['Apricot Sunrise' × ('Golden Future' × 'Baby Love')]

'Horatio Nelson' -- See 'Beahor'

'Horatius Coclès' HGal, mr, before 1828, Miellez; flowers large, full

'Horavme' ('Evelyn Grace') F, ob, 1993, Horner, Heather M.; flowers orange/yellow bicolor, medium, dbl., borne in small clusters; foliage medium size, light green, glossy; some prickles; medium (90 cm.), compact growth; ['Avocet' × Remember Me®]; intr. 1995

'Horbabapapa' ('Ken n Norma') HT, mp, 2002, Horner, Colin P.; flowers medium pink, lighter reverse, 11 cm., full, borne mostly solitary, intense fragrance; foliage medium size, medium green, semi-glossy; prickles medium, curved, moderate; growth bushy, medium (1 m.); garden decorative, exhibition; ['Prima Ballerina' × 'Memoriam']; intr. 2003

'Horbarjeff' ('Taylors Gold') HT, my, 1990, Horner, Heather M.; bud ovoid; flowers do not fade, medium, 48 petals, cupped, borne singly and in sprays of 5; foliage medium size, medium green, semi-glossy; prickles narrow, small, brown; bushy, medium growth; fruit not known; [Prominent® × Helmut Schmidt®]; intr. 1989

'Horbatbeaut' ('Battersby Beauty') HT, ly, 1997, Horner, Calvin; flowers medium, very dbl., borne mostly singly; foliage medium size, light green, semi-glossy; bushy, medium (90 cm.) growth; ['Polar Star' × (Elina® × Remember Me®)]

'Horblush' ('Helen Margaret') HT, w, 1997, Horner, Colin P.; flowers medium, dbl., borne in small clusters; foliage medium size, light green, glossy; growth compact, medium (80 cm.); ['Champagne Cocktail' × Alpine Sunset®]

'Horbondarc' ('Caroline Clarke', 'The Backpackers Rose') HT, op, 1997, Horner, Heather M.; flowers large, full, borne in small clusters, moderate fragrance; foliage medium size, medium green, semi-glossy; some prickles; bushy, medium (90 cm.) growth; [(Prominent® × 'Southampton') × New Year®]

'Horbondpeace' ('Jenny Reilly') F, ob, 2002, Horner, Heather M.; flowers light orange, pale yellow reverse, 7 cm., dbl., borne mostly solitary, moderate fragrance; foliage medium size, medium green, glossy; prickles small, slightly curved, moderate; growth upright, medium (1 m.); garden decorative; [(Prominent® × 'Southampton') × 'Peacekeeper']

'Horbondsmile' ('Brave Heart') F, mp, 1996, Horner, Heather M.; flowers high-pointed, 4 in., dbl., borne in small clusters; foliage large, medium green, semi-glossy; some prickles; medium (100 cm.), upright growth; [(Prominent® × 'Southampton') × Bright Smile®]; intr. 1998

'Horbritesea' ('Forever Free') S, w, 1997, Horner, Colin P.; flowers small, full, borne in large clusters; foliage small, medium green, glossy; some prickles; spreading, low (45 cm.) growth; [(Anna Ford® × 'Little Darling') × 'Sea Foam']

'Horcabellero' ('Barry Stephens') HT, ab, 2000, Horner, Calvin L.; flowers apricot edged red, reverse lighter, 6 in., full, borne mostly singly, moderate fragrance; foliage large, dark green, semi-glossy; prickles moderate; upright, medium (3½ ft.) growth; ['Typhoon' × 'Benson & Hedges Gold']; intr. 2000

'Horcakebread' ('Missing You') F, w, 2000, Horner, Calvin; bud cream; flowers white, reverse cream, 7 cm., dbl., borne in small clusters, moderate fragrance; foliage medium size, medium green, glossy; few prickles; growth bushy, medium (80-90 cm.); ['Sweet Magic' × 'Golden Future']; intr. 2002

'Horcarla' ('Carla Ann') Gr, yb, 2006, Horner, Calvin; flowers yellow/pale peach, reverse pale peach, 3 in., dbl., borne in small clusters; foliage medium size, light green, matte; prickles medium, hooked, green, few; growth upright, tall (5 ft.); garden decorative; [('Rosemary Harkness' × Remember Me®) × 'Friendship']; intr. 2007

'Horcassiopeia' ('Michelle Rosa') HT, w, 2008, Horner, Calvin; flowers white with yellow base, reverse cream with yellow base, 4-4½ in., full, borne mostly solitary; foliage medium, dark green, matte; prickles up to 4 mm., slightly curved, light green, moderate; growth spreading, medium (3½ ft.); garden decorative; [('Leverkusen' × ('Florence Nightingale' × 'Baby Love')) × ('Golden Future' × 'Solitaire')]; intr. 2008

'Horchappy' ('Eileen's Rose') HT, op, 2006, Horner, Colin; flowers salmon pink, reverse salmon pink, 6 cm., dbl., borne in small clusters; foliage medium size, dark green, glossy; prickles up to ½ in., variable pointed, numerous; growth compact, medium (2½-4 ft.); garden decorative; [Pristine® × 'Silver Jubilee']; intr. 2007

'Horcharters' ('Janie Harrison') F, mp, 2004, Horner, Colin P.; flowers pink, yellow center, reverse paler, 6 cm., semi-dbl., borne in small clusters, slight fragrance; foliage medium size, medium green, glossy; prickles small, curved; growth bushy, medium (80 cm.); garden decorative; [('Baby Love' × Amber Queen®) × 'Beverley-Ann']; intr. 2005

'Horcleann' ('Cleonagh Ann') F, mp, 2001, Horner, Colin P.; flowers medium pink, paler reverse, 7 cm., dbl., borne in small clusters, slight fragrance; foliage medium size, medium green, glossy; prickles medium, slightly curved, moderate; growth spreading, medium (1 m.); garden decorative; [Armada® × ((seedling × ('Robin Redbreast' × *R. bella*)) × Remember Me®)]; intr. 2002

'Horcockalorum' ('Rebecca Paul') HT, yb, 1997, Horner, Colin P.; flowers medium, dbl., borne in small clusters; foliage medium size, medium green, semi-glossy; bushy, medium (80 cm.) growth; ['Silver Jubilee' × 'Isobel Derby']

'Horcoed' ('Kathleen Jane') S, mp, 1997, Horner, Colin P.; flowers medium, 41 petals, borne in large clusters; foliage medium size, light green, glossy; growth spreading, medium (4 ft.); ['Bonica' × 'Leverkusen']

'Horcoexist' ('Star Profusion', 'Starry Eyed') S, yb, 1997, Horner, Colin P.; flowers yellow to ivory with deep pink to red edges, reverse yellow, small, single, borne in large clusters, slight fragrance; free-flowering; foliage small, light green, dull; few prickles; spreading, bushy, low (90cm.) growth, can be trained as climber; [(Anna Ford® × 'Little Darling') × (('Sea Foam' × 'Little Darling') × ('Hamburger Phoenix' × 'Prelude'))]

'Horcoff' ('Hospitality') F, rb, 1997, Horner, Colin P.; flowers medium red, reverse gold, 7-8 cm., dbl., borne in small clusters, moderate fragrance; foliage medium size, medium green, glossy; prickles moderate; bushy, medium (100 cm.) growth; [('Champagne Cocktail' × Alpine Sunset®) × (Prominent® × 'Southampton')]

'Horcoffdrop' ('Bright Ideas') LCl, pb, 2003, Horner, Colin P.; flowers pink with white stripes, reverse paler, 8 cm., dbl., borne in large clusters, moderate fragrance; foliage medium size, medium green, glossy; prickles medium, almost straight, moderate; growth upright, medium (2 m.); garden decorative; [Lichterloh® × (Tall Story® × ('Southhampton' × '((New Penny × White Pet) × Stars 'n' Stripes)'))]; intr. 2003

'Horcoffitup' ('Celebration 2000', 'Rabble Rouser') S, dy, 1998, Horner, Colin P.; flowers deep yellow, non-fading, paler reverse, 1½-2 in., semi-dbl., borne in large clusters; foliage small, medium green, very glossy; prickles moderate; bushy, tall growth; [('Anytime' × 'Liverpool Echo') × (('Flamenco' × *R. bella*) × 'Baby Love')]; intr. 1999

'Horcogwheel' ('Pure and Simple') S, w, 2002, Horner, Colin P.; flowers pure white, small, semi-dbl., borne in large clusters, slight fragrance; foliage small, medium green, glossy; prickles small, curved, moderate; growth spreading, low (45 cm.); garden decorative, groundcover; ['Golden Future' × 'Baby Love']; intr. 2002

'Horcohabit' ('Friendship', 'Playmate') F, op, 2001, Horner, Colin P.; flowers orange/pink with light orange reverse, 4½ cm., semi-dbl., borne in large clusters, moderate fragrance; foliage small, medium green, glossy; prickles small, brown, slightly curved, few; growth bushy, medium (80 cm.); garden decorative; intr. 2002

'Horcoherent' ('Apricot Garland', 'Nice 'n' Easy', 'Peachy Cream') S, ab, 2003, Horner, Colin P.; flowers buff/apricot, reverse apricot, 5-6 cm., semi-dbl., borne in large clusters; foliage medium size, medium green, disease-resistant; prickles small, straight, few; growth spreading, medium (50-60 cm.); garden, decorative; PP15982; ['Baby Love' × Flower Carpet™]

'Horcohesive' ('Darling B') LCl, op, 2001, Horner, Colin P.; flowers orange/pink, pale pink reverse, luminescent in bright sunlight, 8 cm., semi-dbl., borne in small clusters, moderate fragrance; foliage medium size, medium green, semi-glossy; prickles medium, curved, moderate; growth upright, tall (3 m.); garden decorative; ['Warm Welcome' × 'Summer Wine']; intr. 2002

'Horcohort' ('Grand Parcours') LCl, lp, Horner; intr. 2001

'Horcohutton' ('Brentwood Style') F, ab, 2002, Horner, Colin P.; flowers apricot, light yellow reverse, 6 cm., dbl., borne in small clusters, slight fragrance; foliage medium size, medium green, semi-glossy; prickles small, curved, moderate; growth bushy, medium (1 m.); garden decorative; ['Warm Welcome' × 'Pretty Lady']; intr. 2003

'Horcointreau' ('Barnard's Magic Day', 'Magic Day') F, w, 2003, Horner, Colin P.; flowers cream-apricot, reverse white, 8 cm., full, borne in small clusters; foliage medium size, medium green, semi-glossy; prickles medium, curved, moderate; growth bushy, medium (80 cm.); garden decorative; ['Bonica' × 'Golden Celebration']; intr. 2003

'Horcojones' ('Beverly-Ann') F, rb, 2000, Horner, Colin; flowers cerise purple, reverse lighter, 7 cm., dbl., borne in small clusters, moderate fragrance; foliage medium size, medium green, semi-glossy; numerous prickles; growth medium (90 cm.); [Anna Ford® × (seedling × (Blessings® × *R. moyesii fargesii*))]; intr. 2003

'Horcopbond' ('Withersfield') F, ob, 2000, Horner, Heather M.; flowers orange, reverse yellow, 8 cm., dbl., slight fragrance; foliage medium size, medium green, semi-glossy; prickles moderate; growth upright, tall (1¼ m.); ['City of Portsmouth' × (Prominent® × 'Southampton')]

'Hordadstar' F, w, Horner; intr. 2005

'Horden Hall' LCl, w, 1928, Conyers; flowers pure white, with long yellow stamens, large, single; [*R. wichurana* × 'Frau Karl Druschki']

'Hordonna' ('Donna Margaret') HT, w, 2000, Horner, Colin P.; flowers white with pink edge, reverse white, large, full, borne mostly singly; foliage medium size, dark green, semi-glossy; few prickles; growth upright, medium (3 ft.); [Pristine® × 'Esmeralda']; intr. 2002

'Hordreamflight' ('The Grace Land Rose') S, mp, 2000, Horner, Colin P.; flowers medium pink, reverse lighter, 5 cm., dbl., borne in large clusters, slight fragrance; foliage small, medium green, semi-glossy; numerous prickles; growth spreading, medium (60 cm.); patio, containers; [('Robin Red Breast' × 'Lichtkonigin Lucia') × 'Pretty Lady']

'Horeagle' ('Hole in One') F, pb, 1997, Horner, Colin P.; flowers small, dbl., borne in small clusters; foliage small, medium green,semi-glossy; some prickles; spreading, medium (90 cm.) growth; [(('Southampton' × 'New Penny') × ('White Pet' × 'Stars 'n' Stripes')) × (('Vester' × seedling) × 'Edith Holden')]

'Horeducate' ('Precious Anya') F, m, 2004, Horner, Colin P.; flowers cerise/purple, reverse lighter, 6 cm., semi-dbl., borne in small clusters, slight fragrance; foliage medium size, dark green, semi-glossy; prickles medium, curved; compact, medium (80 cm.) growth; garden decorative; [seedling × 'Pretty Lady']; intr. 2006

'Horeileen' ('Eileen Whyte') F, op, 2002, Horner, Colin P.; flowers salmon/orange, lighter reverse, 8 cm., dbl., borne in small clusters, moderate fragrance; foliage medium size, medium green, glossy; prickles medium, curved, moderate; growth upright, medium (1 m.); garden decorative; ['Playmate' × ('Buttons' × ('Korp' × 'Southampton'))]; intr. 2006

'Horengland' ('Our Jane') HT, yb, 2001, Horner, Colin P.; flowers yellow tinged red, pale yellow reverse, 7 cm., dbl., borne mostly solitary, moderate fragrance; foliage medium size, medium green, glossy; prickles few, small, curved; stems flexible, upright; growth upright, tall (130 cm.); garden decorative; ['Tynwald' × ('Baby Love' × Amber Queen®)]; intr. 2003

'Horethel' ('Isobel Derby') HT, pb, 1992, Horner, Colin P.; flowers peach pink, reverse lighter pink, aging deeper pink, 5 in., dbl., urn-shaped, moderate fruity fragrance; foliage medium size, medium green, glossy; bushy, medium growth; ['Champagne Cocktail' × (('Honey Favorite' × 'Dr. A. J. Verhage') × 'Pot 'o Gold')]; intr. 1992

'Horfaiwil' ('Faith') HT, my, 1998, Horner, Colin P.; flowers medium yellow, lighter reverse, 4 in., very dbl., borne mostly singly; foliage medium size, medium green, glossy; prickles moderate, medium, curved; upright, tall growth; ['Golden Future' × 'Solitaire']; intr. 2000

'Horflame' ('Middleborough Football Club') F, mr, 1997, Horner, Heather M.; flowers large, dbl., borne in small clusters; foliage medium size, reddish bronze, glossy; some prickles; upright, medium (60 cm.) growth; ['Alpha' × ('Old Master' × 'Southampton')]

'Horflan' ('Flanders Field') F, dp, 1991, Horner, Heather M.; bud ovoid; flowers light red aging slightly lighter, medium, semi-dbl., urn-shaped, loose, borne usually singly or in sprays of 5-9, slight fragrance; foliage medium size, medium green, semi-glossy; medium to tall, upright growth; [Prominent® × 'Southampton']

'Horflash' ('Champagne Cocktail') F, yb, 1983, Horner, Colin P.; flowers pale yellow, flecked and splashed pink, yellow reverse, medium, 20 petals, borne in clusters of 3-5, moderate fragrance; foliage medium size, medium green, glossy; bushy growth; ['Old Master' × 'Southampton']; intr. 1985

'Horflashrob' ('Valeria Sykes') F, rb, 1999, Horner, Colin P.; flowers red splashed white, reverse silver, 2 in., single, borne in small clusters; foliage small, medium green, semi-glossy; few prickles; bushy, low (2 ft.) growth; ['Champagne Cocktail' × 'Robin Redbreast']; intr. 2000

'Horfloss' ('Flossie') F, mp, 1997, Horner, Colin P.; flowers small, dbl., borne in large clusters, moderate fragrance; foliage small, medium green, semi-glossy; some prickles; upright, medium (3 ft.) growth; ['Coral Reef' × (seedling × 'Lichtkonigin Lucia')]

'Horflower' ('Flower Child') Min, op, 1995, Horner, Heather M.; flowers salmon pink, medium, dbl.; foliage small, medium green, semi-glossy; compact, tall (40 cm.) growth; ['Penelope Keith' × Gold Bunny®]; intr. 1997

'Horfrost' ('Frosty Morning') F, w, 1997, Horner, Colin P.; flowers white, cream at base, 3 in., dbl., borne in small clusters; foliage medium size, medium green, semi-glossy; prickles moderate; bushy, medium (100 cm.) growth; [Sexy Rexy® × Princess Michael of Kent®]

'Horgeorgia' ('Georgia's Life') S, w, 2000, Horner, Colin P.; flowers white, reverse very pale cream, aging white, 8 cm., very full, borne in small clusters; foliage medium size, dark green, semi-glossy; prickles moderate; bushy, medium (4 ft.) growth; ['Lichtkonigin Lucia' × 'Bonica']; intr. 2002

'Horglo' ('Gloria') F, m, 2000, Horner, Colin P.; flowers lavender mauve, reverse paler, 7-8 cm., full, borne in small clusters; foliage medium size, medium green, dull; few prickles; compact, low (2 ft.) growth; [(('Over the Rainbow' × 'Baby Faurax') × ('Tassin ' × 'Harriny')) × 'Pretty Lady']; intr. 2002

'Horgoldshel' F, my, Horner; intr. 2006

'Horgreg' ('Greg Moore') S, w, 1996, Horner, Colin P.; flowers cream tinged pink, 2 in., dbl., camellia-like, borne in large clusters; foliage small, grey green, dull; some prickles; medium (100 cm.), spreading growth; ['Bonica' × ('Lichtkonigin Lucia' × seedling)]

'Horharpdos' ('Emma Mitchell') Min, ob, 1992, Horner, Colin P.; flowers orange/vermillion striped white, light orange reverse, aging light orange, 1¼ in., 12 petals, slight fruity fragrance; foliage small, medium green, semi-glossy; bushy, low growth; intr. 1993

'Horharryplus' ('Whitley Bay') F, w, 1989, Horner, Colin P.; bud ovoid; flowers cream with pink splashes, reverse cream, loose, medium, cupped; foliage medium size, medium green, semi-glossy; prickles medium, brown; spreading, medium growth; hips ovoid, medium, yellow; ['Champagne Cocktail' × ('Colour Wonder' × ('Vera Dalton' × 'Vera Dalton × Piccadilly'))]; intr. 1990

'Horhohoho' ('Life Begins at 40') MinFl, w, 2001, Horner, Colin P.; flowers cream, white reverse, small, dbl., borne in large clusters, slight fragrance; foliage small, medium green, glossy; prickles small, curved, moderate; growth compact, low (50 cm.); garden decorative; [Laura Ford® × ('Robin Redbreast' × 'Lichtkonigin Lucia')]; intr. 2002

'Horhoneylove' ('Inner Temple') F, mr, 2000, Horner, Heather M.; flowers medium red, reverse paler, aging to deep pink, 7 cm., dbl., borne in large clusters, slight fragrance; foliage medium size, medium green, semi-glossy; prickles moderate; compact, medium (80 cm.) growth; ['Honey Bunch' × ('Baby Love' × unknown)]; intr. 2002

'Horhunter' F, ab, Horner; intr. 2005

'Horizon' F, or, 1959, Tantau, Math.; bud pointed; flowers geranium-red, open, large, dbl., borne in large clusters, moderate fragrance; foliage leathery; vigorous, upright, bushy growth; ['Crimson Glory' × 'Cinnabar']; intr. 1956

'Horizon 2000' HT, Delbard, Georges; intr. 1990

'Horjack' ('Jack Collier') HT, ob, 1995, Horner, Colin P.; flowers orange blend, 4 in., dbl., borne mostly singly or in small clusters; foliage medium size, medium green, semi-glossy; tall (120 cm.), upright growth; ['Marjorie May' × Remember Me®]; intr. 1997

'Horjaffa' ('Always a Smile') S, ob, 2003, Horner, Colin P.; flowers tangerine, reverse pale orange, 9 cm., dbl., borne in large clusters; foliage large, dark green, glossy; prickles medium, slightly curved, moderate; growth upright, tall (5 ft.); garden decorative; ['Wandering Minstrel' × 'Golden Future']; intr. 2005

'Horjasper' ('Rambling Rosie') LCl, mr, 2007, Horner, Colin; flowers medium red, reverse lighter, 3-4 cm., semi-dbl., borne in large clusters; foliage small, medium green, glossy; prickles small, slightly hooked, green, few; growth spreading, tall (10-12 ft.); walls, pillar, fences; [Super Excelsa® × ('Baby Love' × 'Golden Future')]; intr. 2005

'Horjemma' ('Jemma Giblin') F, my, 1995, Horner, Colin P.; flowers 2½ in., dbl., borne in small clusters, moderate fragrance; foliage medium size, medium green, semi-glossy; medium (50 cm.), bushy growth; ['Gingernut' × 'Amanda']; intr. 1997

'Horjilly' ('Margaret Ann Silverstein') F, ob, 2001, Horner, Colin P.; flowers orange, pale orange reverse, very wavy petals, semi-dbl., borne in small clusters, moderate fragrance; foliage medium size, medium green, semi-glossy; prickles small, curved, few; growth spreading, medium (80 cm.); garden deocrative; [(('Baby Love' × 'Golden Future') × 'L'Oreal Trophy') × L'Oreal Trophy]; intr. 2003

'Horjoy' ('Our Joy') F, pb, 1997, Horner, Heather M.; flowers candy pink, silver reverse, 3 in., dbl., borne in small clusters; foliage medium size, semi-glossy; prickles moderate; upright (80 cm.) growth; [seedling × seedling]; intr. 1997

'Horjurassic' ('Mavis Ballinger') HT, mr, 2001, Horner, Colin P.; flowers medium red, paler reverse, 8 cm., dbl., borne mostly solitary, moderate fragrance; foliage medium size, dark green, semi-glossy; prickles small, curved, moderate; growth compact, medium (90 cm.); garden decorative; ['Coral Reef' × 'Isobel Derby']

'Horkedgeree' ('Forever Friends', 'The Matsukawa Rose') S, w, 2001, Horner, Colin P.; flowers creamy white, 7 cm., dbl., borne in small clusters, moderate fragrance; foliage medium size, dark green, glossy; prickles small, curved, few; growth spreading, medium (130 cm.); garden decorative; intr. 2003

'Horkeepog' ('Inspiration', 'Susan Jellicoe') F, w, 1994, Horner, Calvin; flowers cream/pink blend, 3 in., full, borne singly and in small clusters, intense fragrance; foliage medium size, medium green, semi-glossy; some prickles; medium (100 cm.), upright, bushy growth; ['Keepsake' × 'Pot O'Gold']; intr. 1993

'Horkestrel' ('Give Life') LCl, op, 2004, Horner, Colin P.; flowers orange-pink, reverse lighter, 4-5 in., full, borne in small clusters, moderate fragrance; foliage large, dark green, glossy; prickles large, straight; growth upright, tall (8-10 ft.); garden decorative; ['Rabble Rouser' × 'Pretty Lady']; intr. 2006

'Horkorblush' ('Geordie Lad') HT, r, 1989, Horner, Colin P.; bud ovoid, red; flowers mahogany-red, yellow at base, reverse lighter red, medium, dbl., cupped, moderate fruity fragrance; foliage medium size, medium green, matte; prickles small, light brown; upright, medium growth; hips ovoid, medium size; [Prominent® × ('Champagne Cocktail' × Alpine Sunset®)]; intr. 1990

'Horlexstrip' ('Grace Donnelly') HT, op, 1991, Horner, Colin P.; bud ovoid; flowers pink, orange, yellow striped, medium, dbl., urn-shaped, loose, borne singly or in sprays of 5-9, slight fruity fragrance; foliage medium size, medium green, semi-glossy; bushy, tall growth; [Alexander® × ('Southampton' × (('New Penny × Little White Pet)' × 'Stars 'n' Stripes'))]; intr. 1992

'Horlights' ('Friction Lights') F, yb, 1987, Horner, Colin P.; flowers canary-yellow edged cherry-red, large, dbl.; foliage medium size, medium green, semi-glossy; upright growth; [Alexander® × 'Champagne Cocktail']; intr. 1987

'Horlikorish' ('Jane, Souvenir Du Barbicon') F, dr, 2001, Horner, Colin P.; flowers very dark red, 8 cm., dbl., borne in small clusters, moderate fragrance; foliage medium size, dark green, glossy, reddish when young; prickles medium, brown, curved, moderate; growth upright, medium (1 m.); garden decorative; [(Anna Ford® × (seedling × ('Blessings' × *R. moyesii fargesii*))) × ('Wandering Minstrel' × (Alexander® × ('Southampton' × (seedling × 'Stars 'n' Stripes'))))]

'Horlobrain' ('The Braintree Rose', 'The John Ray Trust Rose') F, dy, 2001, Horner, Heather M.; flowers deep yellow, medium yellow reverse, 8 cm., semi-dbl., borne in small clusters, moderate fragrance; foliage medium size, medium green, glossy; prickles medium brown, curved, moderate; growth upright, tall (110 cm.); garden decorative; [('Buttons' × ('Korp' × 'Southampton')) × 'Pretty Lady']; intr. 2002

'Horlovequeen' ('Mary Campbell') F, ob, 1992, Horner, Heather M.; flowers orange, medium, 6-14 petals, borne in small clusters; foliage medium size, medium green, semi-glossy; some prickles; medium (80 cm.), bushy growth; ['Lovers Meeting' × Amber Queen®]; intr. 1993

'Horlovesong' ('Coconut Ice') LCl, w, 2003, Horner, Colin P.; flowers white suffused with pink, reverse white, 7 cm., full, borne in large clusters, moderate fragrance; foliage medium size, medium green, matte; prickles small, curved, moderate; growth upright, medium (2 m.); garden decorative; ['Leverkusen' × (seedling × Immensee®)]; intr. 2003

'Horluisbond' ('Little Muff') Min, w, 2000, Horner, Heather M.; flowers cream edged pink, reverse cream, 3½ cm., dbl., high-centered, borne in small clusters, moderate fragrance; foliage medium size, medium green, semi-glossy; few prickles; growth bushy, medium (40 cm.); ['Luis Desamero' × (Prominent® × 'Southampton')]; intr. 2001

'Horluvdust' ('Dusty Springfield') F, lp, 2001, Horner, Colin P.; flowers soft light pink, reverse paler, 7 cm., full, borne in small clusters, moderate fragrance; foliage medium size, medium green, semi-glossy; prickles medium, curved, moderate; growth compact, medium (70 cm.); garden decorative; [seedling × 'Matsukawa Rose']; intr. 2003

'Horluvlush' F, ab, Horner; intr. 2007

'Horluvlush' ('Mia-Lucy Rose') F, pb, 2004, Horner, Colin P.; flowers pink-apricot, reverse paler, 4 in., full, borne in small clusters, moderate fragrance; foliage medium size, dark green, glossy; prickles medium, slightly curved; growth bushy, tall (4 ft.); garden decorative; [(('Robin Redbreast' × 'Lichtkonigin Lucia') × Flower Carpet™) × 'Golden Future']; intr. 2007

'Hormarcar' ('Mariah Carey') LCl, w, 2003, Horner, Colin P.; flowers cream edged pink, reverse white, 9 cm., dbl., borne in small clusters, moderate fragrance; foliage medium size, medium green, semi-glossy; prickles medium, curved, moderate; growth upright, medium (2 m.); garden decorative; ['Tynwald' × 'Rhapsody in Blue']; intr. 2004

'Hormartim' ('Margaret Daintry') F, dr, 1988, Horner, Colin P.; flowers crimson-scarlet, large, dbl., borne singly and in clusters; foliage medium size, dark green, glossy; bushy growth; ['Red Planet' × (Blessings® × (Parkdirektor Riggers® × 'Honey Favorite'))]; intr. 1988

'Hormasbrick' ('Whickham Highway') F, r, 1992, Horner, Heather M.; flowers brick red, medium, 6-14 petals, borne in large clusters; foliage medium size, medium green, glossy; some prickles; tall (120 cm.), upright growth; ['Mary Sumner' × (Prominent® × 'Southampton')]; intr. 1993

'Hormemoriam' ('Jim Pugh') HT, pb, 2001, Horner, Calvin L.; flowers medium pink with yellow reverse, medium, dbl., borne mostly solitary, slight fragrance; foliage medium size, dark green, glossy; prickles medium, curved, brown, moderate; growth compact, medium (1 m.); garden decorative; ['Silver Jubilee' × 'Garden Party']; intr. 2004

'Hormemory' ('Vicky I') S, mp, 2001, Horner, Colin P.; flowers dbl., borne in large clusters, moderate fragrance; foliage very large, dark green, very glossy, tough; prickles few, small, curved; growth upright, bushy, tall (160 cm.); garden decorative; [('Baby Love' × Flower Carpet™) × 'Liliana']; intr. 2003

'Hormerry' ('Arthur Merrill') F, mr, 2001, Horner, Heather M.; flowers medium red with paler reverse, 6 cm., dbl., borne in large clusters, slight fragrance; foliage medium size, medium green, glossy; prickles medium, slightly curved, moderate; growth bushy, medium (80 cm.); [Anna Ford® × Black Jade™]; intr. 2001

'Hormeteorie' S, pb, Horner; intr. 2008

'Horminstrel' ('Margaret Hall') HT, pb, 2003, Horner, Colin P.; flowers medium pink/peach, reverse paler, 12 cm., full, borne in small clusters, moderate fragrance; foliage medium size, dark green, glossy; prickles medium, curved, moderate; growth compact, medium (1 m.); garden decorative; ['Wandering Minstrel' × 'Silver Anniversary']; intr. 2003

'Hormislac' ('Ted Gore') F, dp, 1992, Horner, Colin P.; flowers deep pink, medium, full, borne in large clusters; foliage medium size, medium green, semi-glossy; some prickles; medium (80 cm.), bushy growth; ['Miss Ireland' × 'Lilac Charm']; intr. 1993

'Hormonet' ('Ruth Christine') Cl F, pb, 2004, Horner, Colin P.; flowers pink/cream stripes, reverse cream, 3 in., full, borne in large clusters, intense fragrance; foliage medium size, medium green, semi-glossy; prickles medium, curved; growth upright, tall (6-8 ft.); garden decoration; [seedling × 'Summer Wine']; intr. 2007

'Hormum' F, dp, Horner; intr. 2005

'Hormyboy' ('Edward Little Star') F, m, 2001, Horner, Colin P.; flowers mauve with pink stripes, lavender reverse, small, single, borne in small clusters, moderate fragrance; foliage medium size, medium green, matte; prickles moderate, small, curved; growth upright, tall (170 cm.); garden decorative; ['The Painter' × 'Frantasia']; intr. 2006

'Hormyward' F, mp, Horner; intr. 2008

'Horndon Pink' HT, dp, 1963, Barter; flowers old-rose-pink, 4½ in., 60 petals; foliage dark; ['Lady Elgin' × 'Independence']

'Hornewgram' ('Dame Joyce Frankland') HT, my, 1989, Horner, Colin P.; bud globular, greenish-yellow; flowers large, 32 petals, urn-shaped, borne singly, slight fragrance; foliage large, medium green, glossy; prickles straight, medium, light brown; bushy growth; hips ovoid, large, yellow; [('Honey Favorite' × 'Dr. A.J. Verhage') × 'Pot O'Gold']

'Hornothing' ('Thumbs Up') S, yb, 2005, Horner, Colin P.; flowers light yellow, striped pink, reverse paler, 10-12 cm., full, cupped, borne in small clusters, intense fragrance; free-flowering; foliage medium size, medium green, matte; prickles medium, curved, few; growth upright, tall (4-6 ft.); garden decoration; [('Southampton' × (('New Penny × Little White Pet)' × 'Stars 'n' Stripes')) × Graham Thomas®]; intr. 2006

'Hornymph' F, mp, Horner; intr. 2005

'Horodd' ('Oddball') F, rb, 1998, Horner, Colin P.; flowers crimson stripes on buff brown, fading to red stripes on pink, 2½ in., 8-14 petals, borne in small clusters; foliage medium size, medium green, dull; prickles moderate; spreading growth; [(Lichterloh® × (Tall Story® × 'Southampton')) × (('New Penny' × 'White Pet') × 'Stars 'n' Stripes')]; intr.

'Horoffside' ('Helen Bamber', 'St Clare') S, ab, 2005, Horner, Colin P.; flowers buff/apricot, reverse pale yellow, large, full, borne in small clusters, intense fragrance; foliage medium size, medium green, glossy; prickles medium, curved, numerous; growth upright, tall (4-5 ft.); garden decoration; ['Arthur Bell' × 'Perdita']; intr. 2006

'Horoldbruno' ('Bruno, Golden Boy') F, yb, 2004, Horner, Colin P.; flowers amber yellow, reverse deeper, 7 cm., dbl., borne in small clusters, moderate fragrance; foliage medium size, medium green, semi-glossy; prickles medium, curved; upright, tall (5 ft.)growth; garden decorative; [('Golden Future' × 'Baby Love') × 'Beautiful Britain']

'Horoldnewt' ('Newton') F, or, 2004, Horner, Colin P.; flowers orange/edged red, reverse yellow, small, dbl., borne in small clusters, moderate fragrance; foliage small, medium green, semi-glossy; prickles small, curved; growth compact, short (60 cm.); garden decorative; ['Gold Pin' × Easy Going™]

'Horoscope' ('Lucy Locket') F, mp, 2004, Horner, Colin P.; flowers medium pink, reverse lighter, 7 cm., dbl., borne in small clusters, moderate fragrance; foliage medium size, medium green, glossy; prickles small, curved; growth compact, short (60 cm.); garden decorative; ['Tournament of Roses' × seedling]; intr. 2006

'Horoverture' ('Katherine Helen') F, dr, 2004, Horner, Colin P.; flowers dark red, reverse black red, 6 cm., dbl., borne in small clusters; foliage medium size, medium green, semi-glossy; prickles medium, straight; growth compact, medium (80 cm.); garden decorative; [('Phantom' × seedling) × 'Golden Future']; intr. 2006

'Horpaula' ('Paula Nunn') F, dy, 2001, Horner, Colin P.; flowers deep yellow, paler reverse, 8 cm., dbl., borne in large clusters, moderate fragrance; foliage medium size, medium green, semi-glossy; prickles moderate, medium, slightly curved; growth upright, tall (120 cm.); garden decorative; [(seedling × 'Ann Harkness') × 'Freedom']

'Horpekbond' ('Hot Gossip') Min, or, 1998, Horner, Heather M.; flowers luminous orange-red, reverse matt orange, 1½ in., 8-14 petals, borne in small clusters; foliage medium size, medium green, dull; prickles moderate; compact, medium (50 cm.), dwarf-clustered growth; ['Penelope Keith' × (Prominent® × 'Southampton')]; intr. 1998

'Horperfect' ('My Jeannie') F, ob, 2004, Horner,Colin P.; flowers orange, reverse slightly darker, 1½ in., dbl., borne in large clusters, slight fragrance; foliage small, medium green, semi-glossy; prickles small, slightly curved; growth compact, medium (2½ ft.); garden/decorative; [(seedling × Flower Carpet™) × 'Playmate']; intr. 2006

'Horpriceless' ('Courtney Carol') F, ab, 2004, Horner, Colin P.; flowers orange/apricot, reverse pale apricot, 2½ in., dbl., borne in large clusters; foliage medium size, medium green, semi-glossy; prickles small, straight; growth compact, medium (2½-3 ft.); garden decorative; [(Laura Ford® × 'Goldbusch') × 'Margaret Ann Silverstein']; intr. 2007

'Horproper' ('James Woodlock') S, mr, 2004, Horner, Colin P.; flowers medium red, reverse darker, 2½ in., very full, borne in small clusters, no fragrance; foliage medium size, medium green, semi-glossy; prickles small, slightly curved; growth spreading, medium (4 ft.); garden; decorative; [seedling × seedling]; intr. 2005

'Horquaff' ('Anna Jane') F, or, 2006, Horner; flowers dbl., borne in small clusters; foliage medium size, medium green, glossy; prickles small, hooked, brown, numerous; growth upright, medium (3½ ft.); garden decorative; [(('Baby Love' × 'Golden Future') × 'Cocoa') × 'Hot Chocolate']; intr. 2007

'Horquandaldry' ('The Daldry Rose') F, rb, 2006, Horner; flowers red/deep pink with yellow eye, reverse lighter with white veining, 1½ in., semi-dbl., borne in small clusters; foliage medium size, dark green, semi-glossy; prickles large, hooked, deep red, few; growth bushy, medium (3½ ft.); garden decorative; [(seedling × ('Robin Hood' × seedling)) × 'Nice 'n' easy']; intr. 2007

'Horquestion' ('Irene Dean') HT, pb, 2007, Horner; flowers pink/apricot, reverse pale pink, 2½ in., full, borne mostly solitary; foliage medium size, medium green, glossy; prickles medium, narrow, light green, moderate; growth compact, short (2½ ft.); garden decorative; ['Tournament of Roses' × 'Britannia']; intr. 2008

'Horquinine' ('Lucy Caroline') HT, my, 2008, Horner, Heather; flowers 4-4½ in., dbl., borne in small clusters; foliage medium, light green, semi-glossy; prickles 3-4 mm., slightly curved, green, moderate; growth upright, medium (2½-3 ft.); [(Laura Ford® × 'Goldbusch') × 'Britannia']; intr. 2008

'Horradhe' ('Radhe') S, pb, 2000, Horner, Colin P.; flowers deep and light pink with cream stripes, reverse pink and cream, 3½ in., dbl., borne in small clusters, moderate fragrance; foliage medium size, medium green, matte; prickles moderate; spreading, tall (4-5 ft.) growth; [('Wandering Minstrel' × (Alexander® × 'Southampton × ((Little W Pet × New Penny) × Stars 'n' Stripes))')) × 'striped seedling]; intr. 2002

'Horraycar' ('Raymond Carver') S, ab, 2000, Horner, Colin P.; flowers apricot orange, reverse lighter, 11-12 cm., full, borne in small clusters; foliage large, medium green, glossy; prickles moderate; growth climbing, upright, tall (2 m.); hedges, pillars; ['Summer Wine' × 'Lichtkonigin Lucia']; intr. 1999

'Horrespire' ('Garland's Gold') F, ab, 2006, Horner; flowers apricot, reverse pink, 2 in., dbl., borne in small clusters; foliage medium size, light green, semi-glossy; prickles medium, straight, green, moderate; growth compact, short (2 ft.); garden decorative; ['Phab Gold' × 'Margaret Silverstein']; intr. 2007

Horrido® ('Jockey') F, mr, 1963, Tantau, Math.; bud ovoid; flowers pure blood-red, dbl., cupped, borne in large clusters; foliage dark, glossy; bushy, low growth

'Horsaddler' ('Saddler's Gold') F, ab, 1995, Horner, Heather M.; flowers amber gold, 2½ in., dbl., borne in small clusters; foliage medium size, medium green, semi-glossy; medium (50 cm.), bushy growth; ['Gingernut' × Gold Bunny®]; intr. 1997

'Horseekfell' ('Michelle Claire') MinFl, op, 2001, Horner, Heather M.; flowers orange/salmon, paler reverse, 4 cm., dbl., borne in large clusters, slight fragrance; foliage small, light green, glossy; prickles small, straight, moderate; growth compact, medium (40 cm.); garden decorative; ['Sunseeker' × 'Fellowship']

'Horseekship' ('Morag Ross') MinFl, yb, 2001, Horner, Heather M.; flowers peach/yellow, pale yellow reverse, 3½ cm., dbl., borne in large clusters, moderate fragrance; foliage medium size, medium green, glossy; prickles small, curved, moderate; growth compact, medium (60 cm.); garden decorative; ['Sunseeker' × 'Fellowship']

Hørsholm By-Rose™ -- See 'Patio Princess'

'Horsilbee' ('Heather Honey') HT, ab, 1989, Horner, Colin P.; bud ovoid, bronze; flowers apricot yellow, reverse apricot, medium, 25 petals, urn-shaped, borne usually singly, moderate fruity fragrance; foliage medium size, medium green, glossy; prickles small, greenish-brown; bushy, medium growth; hips globular, medium, yellow; ['Silver Jubilee' × ('Honey Favorite' × 'Southampton')]; intr. 1990

'Horsilkarl' ('Doris Dowman') HT, mp, 1997, Horner, Colin P.; flowers large, very dbl., borne mostly singly; foliage large, medium green, glossy; some prickles; compact, medium (3ft.) growth; ['Silver Jubilee' × (seedling × 'Karlsruhe')]

'Horsimkor' ('Rachel Farrant') F, dy, 2001, Horner, Colin P.; flowers buttercup yellow, slightly paler reverse, medium, dbl., borne in small clusters, slight fragrance; foliage medium size, medium green, glossy; prickles medium, curved, moderate; growth compact, medium (110 cm.); garden decorative; ['Simba' × Prominent®]; intr. 2004

'Horsimruby' F, mr, Horner; intr. 2006
'Horsolbond' ('Michele Lemming') F, yb, 2001, Horner, Heather M.; flowers yellow edged with red, paler reverse, 7 cm., dbl., borne in small clusters, moderate fragrance; foliage medium size, medium green, semi-glossy; prickles small, curved, few; growth upright, medium (1 m.); garden decorative; [('Korp' × 'Southampton') × 'Solitaire']
'Horsorbello' ('April') HT, op, 2000, Horner, Colin P.; flowers orange-pink, aging more pink, reverse lighter, 8 cm., dbl., borne mostly singly; foliage medium size, medium green, semi-glossy; prickles moderate; growth bushy, medium (80 cm.); ['Indian Summer' × 'Beautiful Britain']; intr. 2002
'Horstacey' ('Stacey's Star') F, pb, 1996, Horner, Colin P.; flowers blends of pink, short center petals much darker pink, 2½ in., full, flat, borne in clusters, moderate fragrance; foliage small, medium green, semi-glossy; some prickles; low (50 cm.), bushy growth; intr. 1998
'Horstmann's Bergfeuer' F, dr, 1954, Horstmann; flowers dark blood-red, well-formed, very large, dbl., borne in large clusters; moderate growth; ['World's Fair' × 'Independence']
'Horstmann's Jubiläumsrose' F, op, 1954, Tantau, Math.; flowers pink tinted peach, well-formed, large, dbl., borne in clusters of 10-12; foliage glossy, leathery; dwarf growth; ['Golden Rain' × 'Alpine Glow']
'Horstmann's Leuchtfeuer' F, dr, 1954, Tantau, Math.; flowers blood-red, large, dbl., borne in large clusters; moderate growth; ['Red Favorite' × 'Karl Weinhausen']
'Horstmann's Rosenresli' F, w, 1955, Kordes; flowers pure white, large, dbl., borne in clusters, moderate fragrance; bushy growth; ['Rudolph Timm' × 'Lavender Pinocchio']
'Horstmann's Schöne Brünette' HT, or, 1955, Horstmann; flowers coppery brick-red, large, dbl.; strong stems; ['Independence' × 'Hens Verschuren']
'Horsul' ('The Sulgrave Rose') F, ob, 2000, Horner, Colin P.; flowers orange yellow, reverse creamy yellow, 5 cm., single, borne in large clusters, moderate fragrance; foliage medium size, light green, semi-glossy; prickles moderate; bushy, medium (100 cm.) growth; [('Robin Red Breast' × 'Lichtkonigin Lucia') × (seedling × *R. longicuspis*)]
'Horsun' (Playgroup Rose®) F, yb, 1986, Horner, Heather M.; flowers yellow, petals edged red, reverse pale yellow, 25 petals, cupped, borne in sprays, moderate fragrance; foliage medium size, light green, glossy; prickles large, light brown; medium, bushy growth; hips small, globular, orange; [Prominent® × 'Southampton']
'Horsunpegy' ('Marjorie May') F, op, 1993, Horner, Heather M.; flowers orange/pink blend, 3-3½ in., full, borne in small clusters; foliage medium size, medium green, semi-glossy; some prickles; medium (100 cm.), upright growth; ['Playgroup' × Peer Gynt®]; intr. 1995
'Horsunsmile' ('Voice of Thousands') F, yb, 1993, Horner, Heather M.; flowers yellow edged cherry red, medium, dbl., cupped, borne in small clusters; foliage medium size, medium green, semi-glossy; some prickles; medium (80 cm.), bushy growth; ['Playgroup' × Bright Smile®]; intr. 1994
'Hortense de Beauharnais' HGal, pb, 1834, Vibert; flowers rose edged rosy lilac, dbl.
'Hortense Mignard' HP, rb, 1873, Baltet; flowers shining cherry red, reverse flesh pink, full
'Hortense Vernet' M, w, 1861, Moreau et Robert; flowers white shaded rose, large, very dbl., flat, borne in clusters; some repeat; moderate growth
'Hortensia' -- See 'Great Royal'
'Hortensia' T, mp, 1870, Ducher; flowers pink with yellowish reflections, large, very full
Horticolor® -- See 'Lapbal'
'Horticultor Vidal' HT, op, 1952, Dot, Pedro; bud pointed; flowers salmon-pink, large, 35 petals; bushy growth; ['Mme Butterfly' × 'Federico Casas']
'Hortiflora' Pol, mp, 1976, Delforge, S.; bud oval; flowers dbl., 45 petals, slight fragrance; intr. 1974
'Hortropic' ('Sir William Leech', 'William Leech') HT, yb, 1989, Horner, Colin P.; bud ovoid; flowers yellow edged red, reverse light yellow, large, dbl., high-centered, borne usually singly; foliage medium size, medium green, glossy; prickles medium, red; bushy, medium growth; hips ovoid, large, orange; [Royal Dane™ × Piccadilly®]; intr. 1989
'Hortulanus Albert Fiet' HT, ab, 1919, Leenders, M.; flowers apricot and lilacrose, center coppery orange, dbl.; ['Mme Mélanie Soupert' × 'Mons. Paul Lédé']
'Hortulanus Budde' HT, mr, 1919, Verschuren; bud pointed; flowers dark velvet, shaded yellow at center, large, dbl., moderate fragrance; foliage dark; vigorous growth; ['Gen. MacArthur' × 'Mme Edouard Herriot']
'Hortulanus Fiet' HT, w, 1919, Verschuren; bud pointed; flowers deep and light cream, open, very large, dbl.; foliage sparse, glossy, dark; vigorous growth; ['Cissie Easlea' × 'Golden Star']
'Hortus Tolosanus' T, w, 1881, Brassac; flowers pure white, center light yellow, large, very full, moderate fragrance
'Hortyard' ('Olga Rippon') F, m, 1992, Horner, Colin P.; flowers purple/mauve, loose, 2½ in., dbl., borne in sprays of 5-9, slight spicy fragrance; foliage medium size, medium green, semi-glossy; bushy, low growth; [Sexy Rexy® × (('INTermezzo' × 'Baby Faurax') × ('Tassin' × seedling))]
'Horvalkath' ('Valerie Kathleen') F, yb, 1997, Horner, Colin P.; flowers medium, dbl., borne in small clusters; foliage large, dark green, glossy; some prickles; bushy, medium (2½ ft.) growth; [('Silver Jubilee' × 'Pink Favorite') × Amber Queen®]
'Horwander' ('Wanderer') S, mp, 1997, Horner, Colin P.; flowers medium pink, reverse lighter, 3-4 cm., semi-dbl., globular, borne in large clusters, slight fragrance; recurrent; foliage small, dark green, semi-glossy; spreading, low (50-60cm.) growth; ['Sea Foam' × 'Eyeopener']
'Horwingfel' ('Winged Fellowship') F, or, 1989, Horner, Heather M.; bud ovoid; flowers vermillion orange, reverse lighter, medium, 28 petals, urn-shaped; foliage medium size, medium green, matte; prickles small, brown; bushy, medium growth; hips globular, medium, red-orange; [Guitare® × Prominent®]; intr. 1989
'Hoshikage' ('Star Dust') HT, m, Hiroshima; intr. 2000
'Hoshizukuyo' HT, w, 1991, Ohtsuki, Hironaka; bud pointed; flowers ivory, large, 35-40 petals, high-centered, borne usually singly, intense fruity fragrance; foliage medium size, light green, semi-glossy; medium, upright growth; [('Izayoi' × 'Sodori-Hime') × 'White Success']
'Hospitality' -- See 'Horcoff'
'Hostess' F, op, 1960, Lens; flowers pink tinted salmon, open, large, semi-dbl., borne in clusters; vigorous, upright growth; ['Papillon Rose' × ('Cinnabar' × 'Alain')]
'Hostess Gisela' F, dp, 1975, Hetzel; bud ovoid; flowers medium, dbl., intense fragrance; foliage very glossy; vigorous, upright, bushy growth; [Sympathie® × 'Dr. A. J. Verhage]; intr. 1973
Hot™ -- See 'Poulpar038(N)'
'Hot 'n' Spicy, Climbing' Cl F, or; PP16707; intr. 2001
'Hot 'n' Spicy' -- See 'Macsoda'
'Hot Chile' -- See 'Macbunber'
'Hot Chocolate' -- See 'Wekpaltlez'
'Hot Chocolate' F, r, Simpson; flowers sienna-red, 30 petals, moderate fragrance; foliage semi-glossy; intr. 1986
Hot Cocoa™ -- See 'Wekpaltlez'
'Hot Diggity' S, or, Delbard; intr. 2002
'Hot Fire' -- See 'Interbricor'
'Hot Gossip' -- See 'Horpekbond'
'Hot Gossip' Min, or, Zary, Dr. Keith; intr. 1997
'Hot Jazz' HT, rb; bud Large, elegant and pointed.; flowers Opens slowly to golden rose with red edges. Good vase life.; intr. 2002
Hot Lady® HT, dp, Tantau; flowers hot pink, large , double, high-centered, borne mostly singly; recurrent; stems medium to long; florist rose; intr. 2003
'Hot Lips' HT, or, Dickson
'Hot Lips' -- See 'Tinlips'
'Hot Pants' -- See 'Simhopan'

'Hot Parade' (Hot™) MinFl, dp, Poulsen; flowers deep pink, 5-8 cm., dbl., no fragrance; foliage dark; growth bushy, 20-40 cm.; intr. 2005

'Hot Pewter' ('Crucenia') HT, or, 1981, Harkness, R.; flowers brilliant orange-red, 41 petals, high-centered, borne usually singly; foliage large, mid-green, semi-glossy; prickles broad, dark; bushy growth; [Alec's Red® × 'Red Dandy']; intr. 1978

Hot Pink Folies® F, dp, Meilland; intr. 2004

'Hot Pink Pastel' -- See 'Wilpksh'

'Hot Point' ('Hot Point Spire') HT, mr, Barni, V.; flowers dark cherry red, long lasting, dbl., high-centered, no fragrance; good repeat; foliage dark green, disease-resistant; vigorous, tall growth; intr. 1999

'Hot Point Spire' -- See 'Hot Point'

'Hot Poppy' -- See 'Gelpop'

'Hot Princess' HT, dp; flowers hot pink, medium, dbl., high-centered, borne mostly singly; recurrent; foliage large, dark green; intr. 2000

'Hot Romance' HT, ob; flowers dbl., high-centered, no fragrance; intr. 2002

'Hot Shot' ('Hotshot') Min, or, 1982, Bennett, Dee; flowers vibrant vermilion, medium, 28 petals, high-centered, slight fragrance; foliage small, medium green; upright, bushy growth; PP5259; ['Futura' × 'Orange Honey']

Hot Spot™ -- See 'Carbane'

'Hot Stuff' Min, mr, 1979, Lyon; bud pointed; flowers turkey-red, 1 in., 10 petals, slight fragrance; foliage tiny; very compact, bushy growth; intr. 1978

'Hot Stuff' Min, ob, Jones, K.; flowers orange and scarlet, dbl.; [sport of 'Pandemonium']; intr. 2004

Hot Tamale™ -- See 'Jacpoy'

Hot To Trot™ -- See 'Moehot'

'Hot Wonder' (Garden Jubilee Hot Wonder™) S, mr, Lim, P, & Twomey, J.; flowers hot pink, flourescent, 3 in., 25 petals; flowers all season long.; foliage glossy green; growth short, upright (3 ft.) stature; PP15740; intr. 2004

'Hotarugawa' HT, my, 2005, Ohtsuki, Hiromaka; flowers full, borne mostly solitary, moderate fragrance; foliage medium size, medium green, glossy; prickles 7 mm., moderate; upright, medium (120 cm.) growth; garden; ['Kamakura' × 'Hoshizukuyo']

'Hotel California' HT, my, Orard; flowers yellow color lasts, opens fast in heat., 30 petals, high centered, slight. fragrance; foliage dark, shiny green, resistant.; stems strong; upright, slightly spreading (4-6 ft.) growth; intr. 2001

'Hotel Hershey' Gr, or, 1976, Williams, J. Benjamin; bud long, pointed to urn-shaped; flowers salmon orange-red, 4-4½ in., dbl., high-centered, slight fragrance; foliage dark, leathery; upright growth; PP4138; [Queen Elizabeth® × 'Comanche']; intr. 1977

Hotel Royal® -- See 'Mactel'

'Hôtesse de France' HT, dr, 1962, Hémeray-Aubert; flowers velvety deep red, medium, cupped; foliage bronze; ['Soraya' × seedling]

Hotline™ -- See 'Aromikeh'

'Hotmagic' S, pb, 2005, Singer, Judith A; intr. 2006

'Hotshot' -- See 'Hot Shot'

'Hotspur' F, or, 1963, McGredy, Sam IV; flowers orange-salmon, 3 in., 24 petals, high-centered, borne in clusters; ['Independence' × 'Spartan']; intr. 1962

'Houbetsy' ('Betsy') Min, ob, 2003, Hough, Robin; flowers full, borne mostly solitary; foliage medium size, medium green, semi-glossy; prickles medium, slightly curved down, moderate; growth upright, medium (18-24 in.); exhibition; [sport of 'Pierrine']; intr. 2002

'Houcam' ('Camden') MinFl, m, 2002, Hough, Robin; flowers red with mauve tinge, fading to pink with mauve, 1½-2 in., dbl., high-centered, borne mostly solitary, slight fragrance; foliage large, medium green, glossy; prickles long, straight, moderate; growth upright, tall (3 ft.); exhibition; [Black Jade™ × 'Mollycita']

'Houemily' ('Emily Hough') HT, lp, 1991, Hough, Robin; flowers white, blushing pink toward center, more pink in cooler weather, large, dbl., high-centered, borne mostly singly, slight fragrance; foliage large, medium green, semi-glossy; some prickles; medium, upright growth; [sport of 'Touch of Class']; intr. 1993

'Houkitty' ('Kitty-Lew') Min, yb, 2001, Hough, Robin; flowers yellow with pink edges, reverse lighter, 1¼ in., single, borne mostly solitary, slight fragrance; foliage medium size, medium green, semi-glossy; prickles long, straight, moderate; growth compact, medium (18 in.); [Phyllis Shackelford™ × Oriental Simplex™]; intr. 2001

'Houlucy' ('Little Lucy') Min, rb, 2002, Hough, Robin; bud yellow; flowers bright velvety red with yellow eye, reverse yellow, 1¼-1½ in., single, borne usually solitary, slight fragrance; foliage medium size, medium green, semi-glossy; prickles medium, straight, moderate; growth compact, medium (18 in.); [Phyllis Shackelford™ × Oriental Simplex™]

'Houmoll' ('Mollycita') Min, dp, 2001, Hough, Robin; flowers deep hot pink with bright yellow stamens, 1½-1¾ in., single, borne mostly solitary, no fragrance; foliage medium size, medium green, semi-glossy; prickles medium, straight, moderate; growth upright, medium (18 in.); [June Laver™ × After Midnight™]; intr. 2001

'Houmom' ('Mo Mama') F, ab, 2001, Hough, Robin; flowers peach blend, lighter reverse, 2-2¼ in., full, exhibition, borne mostly solitary, slight fragrance; foliage medium size, medium green, semi-glossy; prickles small, straight,

very few; growth upright, tall (24 to 30 in.); ['Joyfulness' × 'Linville']; intr. 2001

'House Beautiful' -- See 'Harbingo'

'House of York' HT, w, Williams, J. Benjamin; flowers creamy white, large, high-centered, moderate fragrance; intr. 1998

'Houstill' ('Ray Still') MinFl, mr, 2001, Hough, Robin; flowers velvety red , 1¾ in., dbl., exhibition, borne mostly solitary, slight fragrance; foliage large, dark green, semi-glossy; prickles medium, straight, moderate; growth bushy, tall (24-30 in.); [seedling × Halo Today®]; intr. 2001

'Houston' -- See 'Coventry Cathedral'

'Houston' HT, dy, 1980, Weeks, O.L.; bud ovoid; flowers deep bright yellow, 38 petals, high-centered, borne singly or 3 - 4 per cluster, moderate tea fragrance; foliage leathery, wrinkled, dark; prickles long, hooked downward; vigorous, upright growth; PP4687; ['Summer Sunshine' × seedling]

'Houstonian' Gr, dr, 1962, Patterson; bud ovoid; flowers 4 in., 35 petals; foliage leathery, glossy, bronze; vigorous, upright, tall growth; ['Carrousel' × seedling]; intr. 1962

'Hovyn de Tronchère' T, rb, 1899, Puyravaud; flowers red with orange depths, bordered silver; ['Regulus' × unknown]

'Howard and Sara' -- See 'Silsarjo'

'Howard Florey' -- See 'Tomflo'

'Howard Jerabek' S, mp, 1979, Jerabek, Paul E.; flowers pearl-pink, 100 petals, moderate apple-blossom fragrance; foliage large, glossy; vigorous growth

'Howard Morrison' -- See 'Maccrackle'

'HP 2000' ('Hewlett-Packard 2000') HT, ab, Kordes; bud pointed, urn shaped; flowers deep peach-apricot, large, full, exhibition, intense fragrance; recurrent; growth vigorous, medium high, neat

'HRGpet' HGal, dp, 2006, Hulse, Merrill

'Hrgvolunteer' ('Guadalupe Volunteer') HMsk, w, 2003, Hulse, Merrill; flowers very full, borne in large clusters, intense fragrance; foliage medium size, medium green, semi-glossy, 5-7 leaflets, disease-free; prickles 5/16, falcate, reddish-brown, moderate; growth spreading, climbs when supported, tall (more than 30 ft.)

'Hubar' HT, dr, 1979, Huber; bud long; intr. 1975

'Hubar 2003-1' S, mp, Huber, R.semi-dbl.; intr. 2005

'Hubicka' HT, pb, 1935, Böhm, J.; flowers alabaster-white, sometimes rosy, base yellow, very large, dbl.; foliage dark; bushy growth; [sport of 'Grete Bermbach']

'Huckleberry' HT, mr, Bell, Laurie; intr. 2001

'Hudson' HT, mp, Mallerin, C.; flowers pale rose, well-shaped; foliage glossy

'Huette's Dainty Florrie' Min, lp, 1980, Schwartz, Ernest W.; flowers 24 petals, moderate fragrance; foliage dark green edged dark red; prickles dark red; upright, bushy growth; ['Sweet and Low' × 'Mary Marshall']; intr. 1979

'Hugh Dickson' HP, mr, 1905, Dickson, H.; flowers very large, 38 petals, high-centered, intense fragrance; recurrent bloom; vigorous growth; ['Lord Bacon' × 'Gruss an Teplitz']

'Hugh Ringold' HT, Gregory, C.

'Hugh Watson' HP, op, 1905, Dickson, A.; flowers deep pink tinged salmon and silver-pink, very large, 24 petals, flat; vigorous growth

'Hugo Maweroff' HMult, dp, 1910, Soupert & Notting; flowers carmine-pink, edges lighter, white center, 5 cm., semi-dbl. to dbl., borne in medium clusters, slight fragrance; foliage large, light green; ['Turner's Crimson Rambler' × 'Mrs W. H. Cutbush']

'Hugo Piller' HT, ab, 1927, Leenders, M.; flowers flesh-white, center pale ecru; [sport of 'Ophelia']

'Hugo Roller' T, yb, 1907, Paul, W.; flowers lemon-yellow, edged and suffused crimson, well-formed, dbl.; foliage small, rich green; weak stems; compact, bushy growth

'Hugo Roller, Climbing' Cl T, yb, 1932, Rogers; [sport of 'Hugo Roller']

'Hugo Schlösser' HT, op, 1955, Kordes; bud long, pointed; flowers salmon-pink, very large, dbl., high-centered; foliage leathery; strong stems; very vigorous, upright, bushy growth; ['World's Fair' × 'Peace']

'Hugonis plena' -- See 'Double Hugonis'

Hugs 'n' Kisses™ -- See 'Jaciraps'

'Huguenot 300' F, ob, Delbard; flowers salmon-orange, dbl., high-centered, borne in large clusters, no fragrance; good repeat; new foliage red; vigorous, tall (4-5 ft.) growth; needs support in spring to hold up the large sprays.; intr. 1985

'Hugues Aufray' -- See 'Dorastri'

'Huguette' Min, op; flowers shrimp-pink shaded salmon

'Huguette Despiney' ('Mme Huguette Despiney') HWich, yb, 1911, Girin; flowers light buff-yellow, edged red, small, very dbl., borne in large clusters; vigorous growth; [sport of 'Marco']

'Huguette Duflos' HT, op, 1937, Lille; bud pointed, dark pink; flowers satiny pink, touched salmon, large, 30-40 petals; foliage dark; vigorous, bushy growth; ['Betty Uprichard' × seedling]

'Huguette Vincent' HT, op, 1921, Chambard, C.; flowers brilliant velvety geranium-red, semi-dbl.; [('Mrs Edward Powell' × unknown) × 'Willowmere']

'Hula Girl' Min, ob, 1976, Williams, Ernest D.; bud long, pointed; flowers bright orange, 1 in., 45 petals, moderate fruity fragrance; foliage small, glossy, embossed; bushy growth; PP4091; ['Miss Hillcrest' × 'Mabel Dot']

'Hula Hoop' HT, pb, 1960, Freud; flowers striped bright pink and red; RULED EXTINCT 11/90

'Hula Hoop' -- See 'Morhoop'

'Hulda' C, dr, 1845, Vibert; flowers dark velvety purple, medium, dbl.

'Hullabalou' Min, yb, 1990, Stoddard, Louis; bud pointed; flowers light orange on yellow with yellow reverse, aging to dull yellow, 20 petals; foliage small, medium green when new, aging to maroon, semi-glossy; prickles straight, sparse, small, red; bushy, low growth; ['Rise 'n' Shine' × unknown]

Hulthemia hardii (Cels) Rowley Sp, yb, Hardy; flowers yellow with the crimson eye of *hulthemia*, 2 in., 5 petals; foliage with 5-7 narrow leaflets; hips almost smooth, round; Simplicifoliae; [*R. clinophylla* × *Hulthemia persica*]; introduced by Hardy, about 1832; first described by Cels in 1836

Hulthemia persica (Michaux) Bornmueller Sp, yb; flowers buttercup-yellow with a scarlet-brown eye, 1 in., single; leaves simple, lacking stipules, bluish-green; hips prickly, round; Simplicifoliae, (14); brought from Iran to France in 1788; introduced to England in 1790 by Banks

'Hulthemosa'

'Humanity' -- See 'Harcross'

'Humboldt' HT, mp, 1922, E.G. Hill, Co.; flowers bright rose-pink, dbl., high-centered; foliage glossy, bronze; vigorous growth; ['Ophelia' × seedling]

'Humdinger' -- See 'Ocean Spray'

'Hume's Blush Tea-Scented China' ('Odorata', 'Tea Rose', 'Tea-Scented Rose', *R. thea*, *R. odorata*, *R. indica odoratissima*, *R. chinensis fragrans*) T, lp, 1809, Hume/Banks/Colville; flowers pale pearly pink, fading to creamy white at the edges, 9-10 cm., semi-dbl. to dbl., borne singly or in groups of 2-3, on weak stems, intense fragrance; foliage deep green, ovate, with 3-5 leaflets, quite shiny, purplish when young; prickles sparse, hooked; stems green to brown; hips found, depressed, reddish-scarlet; supposedly *R. chinensis* × *R. gigantea*

'Hummingbird' HT, ob, 1934, Scittine; bud pointed; flowers bronze-orange, 3 in., very dbl.; vigorous growth; [sport of 'Talisman']

'Humoreske' Min, lp, 1957, Spek; flowers white, tinged pink, small, dbl.; bushy, compact growth; ['Midget' × 'Pixie']

'Humpty-Dumpty' Min, lp, 1952, deVink; flowers soft carmine-pink, center deeper, very dbl., borne in clusters; growth to 6-8 in.; [((*R. multiflora nana* × Mrs Pierre S. duPont F2) × (*R. multiflora nana* × Mrs Pierre S. duPont F2)) × 'Tom Thumb']

'Hundred-Leaved Blush' C, lp, before 1759, from England

'Hungaria' F, mr

'Hunslet Moss' M, dp; bud heavily mossed; flowers large, deep pink cerise, full, intense fragrance; summer; growth to 3-5 ft.; said to have been grown for several generations by Humphrey Brook's ancestors; intr. 1984

'Hunter' ('The Hunter') HRg, mr, 1965, Mattock, R.H.; flowers bright crimson, 2½ in., 43 petals, borne in clusters, moderate sweet fragrance; recurrent bloom; foliage rugose, dark, glossy; vigorous (4-5 ft.) growth; [*R. rugosa rubra* × 'Independence']; originally registered as Shrub; intr. 1961

'Hunter Pink' HRg, mp; intr. 2001

'Hunter's Moon' HT, my, 1951, McGredy, Sam IV; flowers 30 petals; foliage glossy, dark; very vigorous growth; ['Condesa de Sástago' × 'Gorgeous']

'Huntingburg' F, lp, Peters; flowers soft pink, large, semi-dbl.; [sport of 'Festival Fanfare']; intr. 1997

'Huntington Brocade' B, rb, Robinson; flowers deep crimson-mauve with pink pinstripes and ribbons of light crimson, large, full, globular, moderate fragrance; [sport of 'Variegata di Bologna']; intr. 1973

'Huntington Rose' -- See 'Ausjive'

'Huntington's Hero' S, lp, Martin; flowers pale pink with yellow stamens, semi-dbl., slight fragrance; intr. 1995

'Huntsman' HT, rb, 1951, Robinson, H.; flowers spectrum-red, reverse yellow, 5½ in., 35-40 petals, moderate fragrance; foliage dark; PP1012; [('The Queen Alexandra Rose' × unknown) × 'Crimson Glory']

'Hurdal' -- See 'Hurdalsrosen'

'Hurdalsrosen' ('Hurdal', 'Moelvrosen') A, mp, 1860; May have originated in Germany, then carried on in Hurdal, Norway

'Hurdy Gurdy' -- See 'Macpluto'

'Huron' S, lp, 1932, Central Exp. Farm; flowers white flushed pink, semi-dbl., moderate fragrance; non-recurrent; foliage leathery; vigorous (2½ ft.), compact, bushy growth; a good hedge rose; very hardy; [(*R. spinosissima* × Pythagoras) × *R. cinnamomea*]

'Huron Sunset' -- See 'Renhuron'

Hurra® F, or, 1965, Tantau, Math.; bud pointed; flowers dbl., borne in clusters; foliage glossy, vigorous, bushy growth; intr. 1964

'Hurrikan' Pol, mr, VEG; flowers large, dbl.

'Hurst Charm' LCl, pb, 1936, Hicks; flowers pink, slightly tinted mauve, large

'Hurst Crimson' Pol, dr, 1933, Hicks; flowers deep crimson, borne in large trusses; [sport of 'Ideal']

'Hurst Delight' LCl, w, 1936, Hicks; flowers clear pale cream; vigorous growth

'Hurst Favourite' LCl, w, 1936, Hicks; flowers pure ivory-white, very large, semi-dbl., borne in clusters; very vigorous, climbing growth

'Hurst Gem' Pol, ob, 1931, Hicks; flowers brilliant orange-scarlet, small, semi-dbl.; [sport of 'Orléans Rose']

'Hurst Glory' HT, ob, 1936, Hicks; flowers pale salmon-cerise, flushed yellow, well-shaped, large, dbl.; vigorous growth

'Hurst Scarlet' HT, dr, 1933, Hicks; flowers deep scarlet, large, dbl.

'Husky' F, w, Dickson; intr. 2003

'Husmoderrose' HSpn, mp; flowers medium pink, fading to white, full, cupped, moderate fruity fragrance; large (7 × 6 ft.) growth

'Husnaa' S, pb, Ludwig; flowers cream white, petal edges turning salmon-pink, large, dbl., loose, borne singly or in clusters, intense fragrance; free-flowering; wide spreading, medium growth; intr. 1999

'Hutton Village' HT, my, 1974, Deamer; flowers bright yellow; [sport of 'Whisky Mac']; intr. 1973

'Hux1' ('Lily Freeman') S, mp, 1998, Huxley, Ian; flowers 5¼ in., single, flat, borne in small clusters, moderate fragrance; foliage small, medium green, dull; numerous prickles; bushy, medium tall growth; ['Schneezwerg' × 'Schneezwerg']

'Hviezdoslav' -- See 'Hwiezdoslav'

'Hvissinge-Rose' F, pb, 1943, Poulsen, S.; flowers pinkish with yellow, single, borne in clusters; vigorous growth; ['Orléans Rose' × seedling]

'Hwiezdoslav' ('Hviezdoslav') HT, rb, 1936, Böhm, J.; flowers copper-red to orange-copper-red, large, dbl., cupped; foliage glossy; vigorous, bushy growth

'Hybrida cum Bifera' -- See 'Petite Lisette'

'Hybride di Castello' -- See 'Ibrido di Castello'

'Hybride du Luxembourg' S, dp, before 1841, Hardy; flowers deep pink, shaded blush, medium, full, borne in clusters

'Hybride Stadtholder' ('Stadtholder') HCh, dp, before 1850; flowers deep pink, edged dark red

Hyde Hall™ -- See 'Ausbosky'

Hyde Park® ('Amber Abundance') F, ab, Harkness; flowers light rose-salmon, dbl., borne in large clusters, moderate fresh fragrance; intr. 1999

'Hylo' F, mp, 1961, Cant, B. R.; flowers salmon-pink, 2-2½ in., 28 petals, borne in clusters; bushy growth; [sport of 'Highlight']

'Hymenée' T, ly, about 1820, Hardy; possibly Laffay

'Hymenee' S, Delbard-Chabert; intr. 1969

'Hymne' F, mp, 1965, Verbeek; bud short, pointed; flowers Neyron rose, large, 38-52 petals, borne in large clusters; foliage dark, glossy; vigorous growth; ['Miracle' × seedling]; intr. 1963

'Hypacia' ('Hypathia', 'Hypatia') C, pb, before 1844, Hardy; flowers bright rose-pink spotted white, center whitish, large, dbl., cupped, moderate damask fragrance

'Hypathia' -- See 'Hypacia'

'Hypatia' -- See 'Hypacia'

'Hythe Cluster' Pol, dp, 1935, Archer; flowers glowing deep pink, semi-dbl., cupped, borne in large clusters; foliage small, glossy, light; vigorous growth

— I —

'I Have A Dream' -- See 'Albunda'

'I Love You' F, dp, 1981, Takatori, Yoshiho; flowers deep pink; [sport of 'Margaret Thatcher']; intr. 1983

'I Love You' -- See 'Geelove'

'I Promise' -- See 'Lyopri'

'I Zingari' HT, ob, 1925, Pemberton; flowers orange-scarlet, 3 in., semi-dbl., borne in cmall clusters, no fragrance; foliage dark; stems claret

'I. X. L.' ('Coolidge') HMult, dp, 1925, Coolidge; flowers magenta with white center, 3-4 cm., dbl., borne in small clusters; thornless; very vigorous growth; ['Tausendschön' × 'Veilchenblau']

'Ian Brinson' HT, dr, 1945, Bees; flowers crimson, compact, 4-5 in., 30 petals; foliage dark; ['Mrs J.J. Hedley-Willis' × 'J. C. Thornton']

'Ian Stuart' F, dr, 2005, Paul Chessum Roses; flowers full, borne in small clusters, slight fragrance; foliage medium size, medium green, semi-glossy; prickles medium, sharp, pink, moderate; growth compact, medium (2½ ft.); bedding, containers; [seedling × seedling]; intr. 2005

'Ian Thorpe' -- See 'Olijbrau'

Iberflora 95® -- See 'Febama'

'Ibica' -- See 'Ibiza'

'Ibis' F, ob, 1979, Godin, M.; bud ovoid; flowers orange, 14-16 petals; foliage dark; [Europeana® × Orangeade®]

'Ibisco' HRg, dp; flowers clear, deep pink, 5 petals, no fragrance; growth to 3-4 ft.

'Ibiza' ('Ibica') HT, w, 1938, Dot, Pedro; flowers well-formed; erect growth; ['Mme Butterfly' × 'Frau Karl Druschki']

'Ibrido di Castello' ('Hybride di Castello') HBank, ly, 1920, Ragionieri; flowers cream, fading to white, 4 cm., dbl., borne in small clusters, moderate tea and violets fragrance; [R. banksiae lutescens × 'Lamarque']

'Ibu Tien Suharto' HT, w; flowers white with apricot-pink blush in center, large, dbl., loose, intense fragrance; good repeat

'Ice Angel' -- See 'Jacber'

'Ice Breaker' -- See 'Briice'

'Ice Cascade' S, w, Williams, J. Benjamin; flowers very dbl., borne in sprays; intr. 1999

'Ice Cool' -- See 'Delgribla'

'Ice Cream' -- See 'Meisponge'

'Ice Cream' -- See 'Korzuri'

'Ice Crystal' -- See 'Cleice'

'Ice Fairy' -- See 'Sanmed'

'Ice Flower' HT, w, Teranishi; flowers green tint; intr. 2004

'Ice Follies' S, w, Williams, J. Benjamin; flowers white with delicate apricot tint in center, full, borne in large sprays, moderate unusual fragrance; foliage dark green; growth spreading, groundcover or can be trained as climber; intr. 1999

'Ice Girl' -- See 'Kormistiana'

'Ice-Girl' ('Ice Girl', 'Ice-Girl Panarosa') HT, w, Kordes; flowers snow white, medium, dbl., cupped, borne mostly singly, intense fragrance; free-flowering; foliage dark green, slightly glossy; stems wiry, almost thornless; tall growth

'Ice-Girl Panarosa' -- See 'Kormistiana'

'Ice Kordana Mini Brite' Min, w, Kordes; bud short, pointed ovoid, greenish white; flowers clear white, 1¾ in., 55-60 petals, borne singly and in clusters of 3 - 5, no fragrance; foliage small, abundant, glossy; prickles moderate, short, straight; vigorous, branching, upright (18 in.) growth; PP11147; PP11147; [seedling × seedling]; intr. 1998

'Ice Maiden' F, w, 1977, Garelja; bud pointed; flowers pure white, semi-formal, large, 15 petals, moderate fragrance; foliage narrow, glossy, light green; vigorous, upright growth; ['Iceberg' × 'Iceberg']

'Ice Meidiland® -- See 'Meivahyn'

Ice Meillandecor® (Ice Meidiland®) S, w, Meilland; bud conical, small; flowers white, open flat, 2½-3 in., 21-30 petals, flattened pompon, borne in clusters, no fragrance; free-flowering; foliage medium size, medium green, glossy; prickles medium; compact, mounding, ground cover growth; hips 1 cm., orange-red to red; PP11577; ['Katherina Zeimet' × ('Iceberg' × 'White Meidiland')]; intr. 1996

'Ice Princess' -- See 'Lavice'

'Ice Queen' -- See 'Korturek'

Ice Queen™ -- See 'Savanice'

'Ice White' (Vision Blanc®) F, w, 1966, McGredy, Sam IV; flowers 3 in., 25 petals, borne in clusters; foliage glossy; ['Mme Léon Cuny' × ('Orange Sweetheart' × 'Cinnabar')]

'Ice White, Climbing' ('Vision Blanc, Climbing') Cl F, w, McGredy, Sam IV; intr. after 1966

'Iceberg' Cl Pol, w, 1910, Paul, G.; flowers pure white

'Iceberg' ('Fée des Neiges', 'Schneewittchen') F, w, Kordes, R.; bud long, pointed; flowers pure white, 4 in., 20-25 petals, borne in clusters, moderate fragrance; good repeat; foliage large, light green, glossy, disease-resistant; few prickles; vigorous, upright, bushy growth; ['Robin Hood' × 'Virgo']; intr. 1958

'Iceberg, Climbing' ('Fée des Neiges, Climbing') Cl F, w, 1968, Cant, B. R.

Iceberg® ('Ice Queen', 'New Iceberg') HT, w, Kordes; flowers white, large; foliage glossy, dark green; stems 28; PP14900; intr. 2001

'Iced Ginger' F, ob, 1972, Dickson, A.; flowers inside of base strong orange to light orange, reverse deep pink with yellow base,, 4½ in., 45 petals, borne in trusses, moderate fragrance; free-flowering; foliage light green, red veined, medium; ['Anne Watkins' × unknown]

'Iced Parfait' F, lp, 1985, Xavier, Sister

M.; flowers pale pink, medium, 40 petals, urn-shaped, borne 6 per cluster, moderate fragrance; foliage light green; prickles straight, red; bushy, compact growth; ['Pink Parfait' × 'Iceberg']; intr. 1972

Iced Raspberry™ -- See 'Savaras'

'Iced Tea' -- See 'Morice'

'Iceland Queen' HSet, w, 1935, Horvath; flowers creamy white, 7-9 cm., dbl.; vigorous growth

'Icelantic Angel' Min, w, 2007, Bennett, John; flowers medium, 1½ in., full, borne mostly solitary; foliage dark green, semi-glossy; few prickles; growth upright, medium (18 in.); exhibition, garden decoration; ['Fairhope' × 'Peace']; intr. 2007

Ich hab Dich lieb™ -- See 'Poultry'

'Ichalkaranji 100' HT, m, Chiplunkar; flowers lavender pink, outer petal edges and reverse darker, large, full; intr. 1993

'Ichi Boh Fun' Pol, pb; from China

'Ichibanboshi' ('Evening Star') Min, ob, Keisei; intr. 1996

Ichiro™ -- See 'Moeichiro'

'ICI Golden Celebration' -- See 'Peaquant'

'Ico' F, m, 1987, Patil, B.K.; flowers light purple, 60-70 petals, globular, slight fragrance; foliage dark green, glossy; prickles brownish-green curving downward; vigorous, upright, bushy growth; [sport of 'Deep Purple']; intr. 1985

'Ico Ambassador' HT, my, Patil, B.K.; flowers light chrome yellow, dbl.; free-flowering; [sport of 'Ambassador']; intr. 1988

'Ico Beauty' HT, pb, 1987, Patil, B.K.; flowers rose pink, reverse flushed white, medium, 25-30 petals, high-centered, slight fragrance; foliage glossy; prickles pale green curving downward; upright, bushy growth; [sport of 'Red Planet']; intr. 1985

'Ico Delight' HT, w, Patil, B.K.; flowers pure white, large, full, high-centered; [sport of 'Eterna']; intr. 1989

'Ico Deluxe' HT, pb, Patil, B.K.; flowers broad petals, lasting; free-flowering; [sport of 'Mistraline']; intr. 1990

'Ico Pearl' F, pb, Patil, B.K.; flowers pink shaded apricot, full, borne in clusters; [sport of 'Dearest']; intr. 1990

'Ico Talk' F, pb, Patil, B.K.; flowers light pink stripes on both sides of petals, borne singly and in clusters; free-flowering; [sport of 'Double Talk']; intr. 1993

'Ico Trimurthi' HT, pb, Patil, B.K.; intr. 1989

'Icy Tiding' HT, w

'Ida' -- See 'Wisida'

'Ida' HMult, op, about 1890, Dawson; ['Dawson' × R. multiflora]

Ida Belle™ -- See 'Minayco'

'Ida Elizabeth' HT, mr, 1987, Welsh, Eric; flowers large, 30 petals, high-centered, borne singly, moderate fragrance; foliage matte; medium, bushy growth; ['Red Lion' × Mainauperle®]; intr. 1987

'Ida Eve Javior' HT, w, 2003, Cockerham, John E.; flowers blushed light pink when newly-opened, 3 in., full, borne mostly solitary; foliage medium size, medium green, semi-glossy; prickles 3/8 in., blade-shaped,; growth compact, vigorous, medium; garden decorative; ['Savoy Hotel' × unknown]; intr. 2004

'Ida Hoff' HT, mp; flowers large, dbl.

'Ida Klemm' HMult, w, 1907, Walter, L.; flowers snow-white, 3½ cm., semi-dbl., borne in large clusters; foliage large, dark green, glossy, long, strong stems; vigorous growth; [sport of 'Crimson Rambler']

'Ida McCracken' HT, op, 1952, Norman; flowers salmon and coral, well-formed, 4 in., 25-30 petals; foliage leathery, dark; free growth; ['Ethel Somerset' × 'Mrs Sam McGredy']

'Ida Red' -- See 'Ponred'

'Ida Scholten' HT, pb, 1933, Buisman, G. A. H.; flowers pink shaded carmine-red, very large, dbl.; foliage dark, leathery, glossy; bushy, dwarf, compact growth; ['Capt. F.S. Harvey-Cant' × 'Gen. MacArthur']

'Ida Sisley' B, dr; flowers violet-red, large, full

'Ideal' ('Becker's Ideal') HT, mp, 1904, Becker; flowers carnation pink, very large, full; [sport of 'La France']

'Ideal' Pol, mr, van Nes; flowers dark crimson scarlet; [sport of 'Miss Edith Cavell']; intr. 1921

'Ideal Home' ('Idylle') HT, pb, 1963, Laperrière; flowers carmine-pink, base white, well-formed, 5 in., 25-30 petals, moderate fragrance; vigorous, upright growth; ['Monte Carlo' × 'Tonnerre']

Idée Fixe® -- See 'Lendec'

'Idole' ('Ruimeys') HT, or

'Idun' F, mp, 1969, Lundstad; flowers Neyron rose, large, 41 petals, cupped, borne in clusters; foliage dark, glossy; bushy growth; ['Schneewittchen' × 'Fanal']

'Idylle' -- See 'Ideal Home'

'Iga 63' HT, pb, 1963, Moreira da Silva; flowers pink and red; ['Confidence' × seedling]

'Iga 83 Munchen' -- See 'Meibalbika'

'Iga Erfurt' F, op, GPG Bad Langensalza; flowers medium, semi-dbl.; intr. 1966

'Igloo' HT, w, 1969, Verbeek; bud ovoid; flowers medium, dbl.; foliage dark; [seedling × 'White Knight']

'Igna' HT, ob, Delbard; flowers orange-yellow with lighter reverse, medium, dbl., high-centered; cut flower trade

'Ignasi Iglesias' HT, mr, 1934, Dot, Pedro; flowers rose in early season, oriental red in summer, dbl., high-centered; foliage wrinkled; vigorous, bushy growth; ['Angel Guimera' × ('Souv. de Claudius Pernet' × 'Mme Butterfly')]

'Ignis' S, mr, 1934, Chotkové Rosarium; flowers fiery red, very large; non-recurrent; foliage leathery, dark; vigorous (3¼-6½ ft.) growth

'Igor' ; flowers carmine-white, medium, 36 petals; foliage dark; spreading growth

'Ikaruga' HT, yb, 1977, Ito; bud ovoid; flowers 6 in., 35 petals, high-centered, slight fragrance; vigorous, upright growth; ['McGredy's Ivory' × 'Garden Party']; intr. 1975

'Ilam' -- See 'Similam'

'Ilaria' F, dp, 1962, Borgatti, G.; flowers coral-red, well-formed, semi-dbl.; foliage dark; ['Cinnabar' × 'Fashion']

'Ildiko' F, mr, 1971, Institute of Ornamental Plant Growing; bud ovoid; flowers cherry-red, medium, semi-dbl., cupped; profuse, intermittent bloom; moderate, upright growth; ['Mardi Gras' × 'Paprika']

'Ile Bourbon' -- See 'Impératrice Eugénie'

'Ile de France' -- See 'Peksolred'

'Ile de France' -- See 'Adoration'

'Île de France' HWich, rb, 1922, Nonin; flowers bright scarlet, center white, 4-5 cm., semi-dbl., borne in medium to large clusters; foliage large, leathery, dark; numerous prickles; short, strong stems; very vigorous (15-20 ft.) growth; ['American Pillar' × unknown]

'Ilicifolia' -- See 'À Feuille de Chêne'

'Ilios' HT, dr; intr. 2002

'Illinois' Gr, or, 1969, Morey, Dr. Dennison; bud long, pointed; flowers large, 25 petals; foliage leathery; vigorous, bushy growth; ['Soprano' × 'Tropicana']

Illisca® -- See 'Lapem'

Illos® HT, m

'Illumination' F, dy, 1970, Dickson, Patrick; flowers deep sulfur-yellow, 3 in., 12 petals; foliage glossy, light; free growth; ['Clare Grammerstorf' × 'Happy Event']

'Illumination' F, ab, Pallek; intr. 1986

'Illusion' HT, my, 1961, Verbeek; flowers 50 petals; foliage glossy; vigorous growth; ['Peace' × seedling]

'Illusion' HKor, mr, Kordes, R.; flowers blood-red to cinnabar, 8-9 cm., dbl., borne in large clusters, moderate fragrance; foliage leathery, glossy, light green; vigorous growth; intr. 1961

'Illusion' HT, pb, Kordes; bud very large; flowers white with deep pink petal edges brushed downward on the petals, large, full, exhibition, borne mostly singly, no fragrance; no prickles on stems; stems long, slender; growth vigorous, medium; intr. 2002

'Illustre' ('Belle de Hesse', 'Surpasse Singleton', 'La Triomphante', 'La Prédestinée', 'La Glorieuse', 'Die Berühmte') HGal, pb, before 1820, Descemet; flowers lilac-pink, sometimes shaded light purple, medium, full

'Ilmenau' S, mr, Hetzel; intr. 1992

'Ilona' -- See 'Varlon'

Ilona™ -- See 'Marilo'

'Ilse' HT, pb, 2005, Edwards, Eddie & Phelps, Ethan; flowers full, borne mostly solitary, slight fragrance; foliage large, dark green, semi-glossy; few prickles; growth upright, tall (5-6 ft.); exhibition;

[seedling × seedling]; intr. 2006
'Ilse Haberland® F, mp, 1956, Kordes; flowers crimson-pink, very large, dbl., high-centered, moderate fragrance; foliage glossy; vigorous, upright, bushy growth
'Ilse Krohn' HKor, w, 1958, Kordes; flowers pure white, 12-13 cm., very dbl., high-centered, borne in small clusters; non-recurrent; foliage large, glossy; very vigorous growth; ['Golden Glow' × *R. × kordesii*]; intr. 1957
Ilse Krohn Superior® HKor, w, 1964, W. Kordes' Sohne; flowers pure white, buff at center, 12-13 cm., dbl., borne in small clusters, intense fragrance; remontant; foliage dark; vigorous (9 ft.) growth; [sport of 'Ilse Krohn']
Ilseta® -- See 'Tanatesil'
'Iluse' HT, ob, Urban, J.; flowers salmon-orange and yellow, large, dbl.; intr. 1968
'Image d'Epinal' LCl, mr, Croix; growth to 7-10 ft.; intr. 1997
Imagination™ -- See 'Pouldron'
'Imagination' -- See 'Wekmar'
'Imagine' -- See 'Renimag'
Imagine® HT, rb, Dorieux; intr. 1992
'Imagine' HT, w, Hiroshima; intr. 1999
'Imagine' S, ab, Clements, John; flowers soft apricot with brownish cast, 5 in., 36 petals, cup-and-saucer, moderate fragrance; recurrent; foliage dark green; vigorous, bushy (4 ft.) growth; intr. 2007
'Imagine' -- See 'Worcolourful'
'Imatra' F, pb, 1930, Poulsen, S.; flowers pink to white; ['Orléans Rose' × unknown]
'Imbricata' S, lp, 1869, Ducher; flowers delicate pink, large, full, cupped
'Imbroglio' -- See 'Benimbro'
'Imma' HT, lp; flowers high-centered, high-centered
'Immaculada Galan' F, w, 1970, LeGrice; flowers large, 60-70 petals, globular, borne in trusses; foliage small, blue-gray; very free growth; intr. 1968
Immensee® -- See 'Korimro'
'Immerblühender Crimson Rambler' -- See 'Flower of Fairfield'
'Immortal Juno' -- See 'Ausjuno'
'Imogen' F, Bidwell
'Imogen' HT, w, 1915, Paul; flowers creamy white aging to light yellow with orange-yellow, large, full, moderate fragrance
Imogene™ -- See 'Minyco'
'Imp' F, rb, 1971, Dawson, George; bud globular; flowers red, reverse silver-pink, small, dbl.; foliage large, dark, leathery; bushy growth; ['Daily Sketch' × 'Impeccable']; intr. 1970
'Impala' F, op, 1977, Herholdt, J.A.; bud ovoid, pointed; flowers coppery, reverse orange,, 2½-3 in., 30 petals, cupped; foliage bright green; bushy growth; [Zambra® × seedling]; intr. 1972
Impala® F, ob, Kordes; flowers orange, medium, dbl., high-centered, borne mostly singly; recurrent; stems moderate; intr. 2005
'Impala' -- See 'Rulimpa'
'Impatient' -- See 'Jacdew'
'Impeccable' HT, dr, 1955, Delbard-Chabert; flowers deep velvety red, well-shaped, dbl.; foliage dark
'Imperator' -- See 'Meiperator'
'Impératrice Charlotte' HP, dp, 1867, Verdier, E.
'Impératrice de Hollande' -- See 'Roi des Pays-Bas'
'Impératrice de Russie' HGal, dp, about 1825, Péan; flowers large, very full
'Impératrice Eugénie' B, m, Plantier; flowers purple-pink; intr. 1855
'Impératrice Eugénie' M, m, Guillot père; flowers lilac-pink, medium, dbl., moderate fragrance; some repeat; vigorous growth; intr. 1856
'Impératrice Eugénie' HP, w, Avoux & Crozy; flowers white, center light pink, aging white, medium, full, globular; intr. 1856
'Impératrice Eugénie' T, my, 1853, Pradel; flowers sulfur yellow, medium, very full
'Impératrice Eugénie' HP, w, Oger; bud spotted crimson; flowers delicately tinted at center with pink, aging to pure white, medium, full, globular; ['Mme Récamier' × unknown]; intr. 1856
'Impératrice Eugénie' ('Empress Eugénie', 'Marguerite Lartay', 'Ile Bourbon') B, mp, Béluze; flowers silvery rose pink, medium, full; foliage dark green, glossy; prickles very sharp, hooked, purple-red; intr. 1855
'Imperatrice Farah' ('Empress Farah', 'Kaiserin Farah', 'Strawberry Parfait') HT, w, Delbard; flowers white with deep pink edges, petals form points, large, full, high-centered, slight fragrance; vigorous, upright (3 ft.) growth; intr. 1992
'Impératrice Joséphine' ('Empress Joséphine') HGal, pb, before 1815, Descemet; flowers cerise pink, lighter at edges, dbl., borne singly and in small clusters; foliage elliptical, veined
'Impératrice Joséphine' B, lp, 1842, Verdier, V.; flowers flesh pink, edges whitish, medium, very full, globular
'Impératrice Joséphine' HP, lp, 1852, Lartay; flowers flesh pink, shaded white, large, full
'Impératrice Maria Alexandrina' HP, w, 1862, Damaizin
'Impératrice Maria Feodorowna' HP, mp, 1892, Lévêque; flowers delicate pink, large, globular; foliage glaucous green
'Impératrice Maria Féodorowna de Russie' ('Empress Marie of Russia') T, ly, 1883, Nabonnand; flowers canary yellow, fading to white, very large, imbricated, very full
'Impératrice Rouge' -- See 'Red Empress'
Imperial™ ('Imperial Palace') F, mr, Olesen, L. & M.; bud globular; flowers 8-10 cm., semi-dbl. to dbl., borne singly or in clusters of 3 - 4, slight wild rose fragrance; foliage medium size, medium to dark green, glossy; prickles moderate; growth bushy, 40-60 cm.; PP11151; ['Christian IV' × seedling]; intr. 1996
'Imperial' HT, rb, 1957, Moreira da Silva; flowers cardinal-red, reverse golden yellow, well-formed; ['Geranium' × 'Opera']
'Imperial Blaze' -- See 'Demokracie'
'Imperial Gold' ('Canadiana') HT, my, 1962, Swim, H.C.; bud ovoid; flowers lemon-yellow to Indian yellow,, 3½-4½ in., 30-35 petals, moderate fragrance; foliage leathery, dark, glossy; vigorous, upright growth; PP1894; ['Charlotte Armstrong' × 'Girona']; intr. 1962
'Imperial Palace' -- See 'Poulchris'
'Imperial Pink' HT, mp, 1942, Coddington; PP552; [sport of 'Royal Beauty']
'Imperial Potentate' HT, mp, 1921, Clarke Bros.; flowers large, 45 petals, high-centered; foliage dark, leathery; vigorous growth; ['Ophelia' × 'Hoosier Beauty']
'Imperial Queen' HT, mr, 1962, Lammerts, Dr. Walter; bud long, pointed; flowers cherry-red, 4½-5 in., 21 petals, cupped, moderate fragrance; foliage leathery, glossy; vigorous, compact growth; PP2121; [Queen Elizabeth® × 'Chrysler Imperial']; intr. 1961
'Imperial Rose' B, dp
'Impériale' -- See 'Regina Dicta'
Imposant® F, mp
'Impress' HT, rb, 1929, Dickson, A.; bud ovoid, cardinal-red, shaded orange; flowers salmon-cerise, tinted golden, very large, 40-45 petals; foliage dark, glossy; vigorous growth
'Improved Cécile Brünner' ('Rosy Morn') HG, op, 1948, Duehrsen; bud long, pointed; flowers salmon-pink, medium, 30 petals, high-centered, borne in clusters; foliage leathery, dull green; very vigorous, upright growth; PP851; ['Dainty Bess' × *R. gigantea*]
'Improved Lafayette' F, mr, 1935, H&S; flowers semi-dbl.; foliage soft; vigorous, bushy growth; ['E.G. Hill' × seedling]
'Improved Marquise Litta de Breteuil' -- See 'C. W. Cowan'
'Improved Orléans' Pol, mp, 1931, Green Norfolk Nurs.; [sport of 'Orléans']
'Improved Peace' HT, yb, 1959, Dean; bud ovoid; flowers yellow edged and flushed pink, large, dbl., high-centered; foliage leathery, wrinkled; very vigorous, bushy growth; [sport of 'Peace']
'Improved Premier Bal' HT, pb, Wheatcroft Bros.; flowers pale cream edged deep pink, large; foliage leathery; vigorous growth
'Improved Prince Philip' Gr, or, 1964, Leenders, J.; flowers well-formed; [Queen Elizabeth® × 'Prince Philip']
'Improved Princesse de Béarn' -- See 'Mme Jean Everaerts'
'Improved Rainbow' T, pb, about 1896, Burbank; flowers deep coral pink, striped and mottled with crimson, very large

'Improved Universal Favorite'   HWich, mp, 1901, Manda, W.A.; flowers brilliant pink

'Improved Verdun'   Pol, dp, 1946, Kluis; flowers vivid carmine-red, dbl., borne in clusters; foliage leathery; bushy growth

Impulse® -- See 'Barimp'

'Impulse'   Min, op, 1986, Jolly, Marie; flowers salmon-pink, light yellow reverse, small, 38 petals, cupped; foliage small, medium green, semi-glossy; prickles long, brownish; medium, upright growth; fruit not observed; ['Red Ace' × 'Chris Jolly']

Impulse®   HT, ob, Tantau; flowers brilliant orange, large , double, high-centered, borne mostly singly; recurrent; stems long; florist rose; intr. 2006

'In Appreciation'   HT, dp, Nieuwesteeg; flowers dbl., moderate fragrance; growth free branching

'In Dreams'   HT, pb, 2004, Edwards, Eddie & Phelps, Ethan; flowers medium pink with yellow base, 5 in., full, high-centered, borne mostly solitary, moderate fragrance; recurrent; foliage medium size, dark green, glossy; prickles small, hooked; growth upright, medium, 5-6 ft.,; [Veterans' Honor™ × 'Hot Princess']; intr. 2005

In the Mood™ -- See 'Wekfrancoly'

'In the Mood'   HT, m, Hiroshima; intr. 2005

'In the Mood' -- See 'Seamood'

'In the Pink'   F, mp, 1989, Ryan, C.; flowers medium, 60 petals, borne in sprays of 4 - 5, moderate musk fragrance; foliage greenish-red, glossy; prickles hooked, red; medium, bushy growth; ['Baby Faurax' × seedling]; intr. 1988

'In the Pink'   F, pb, Limes New Roses; intr. 1994

'Ina' -- See 'Talina'

Ina an' Mona®   S, ab, Jensen; intr. 1992

'Inano'   HT, dy, 1986, Teranishi, K.; flowers urn-shaped, medium, 40 petals, borne singly, moderate fruity fragrance; foliage medium size, light green; prickles small, brown; medium, bushy growth; ['Doreen' × 'Goldilocks']; intr. 1978

'Inata'   F, op, 1967, deRuiter; flowers pink shaded salmon, open, semi-dbl., borne in trusses; vigorous growth; [sport of 'Valeta']

Inca™   Min, ob, Poulsen Roser; intr. 2000

'Inca de Mallorca'   F, mr, 1958, Dot, Pedro; flowers strawberry-red, 20 petals; strong stems; compact growth; ['Soller' × 'Floradora']

'Incandescent'   HT, mr, Wagner, S.; bud globular and short; flowers velvety bright red vermillion-red, dbl., slight fragrance; foliage large, reddish dark green, glossy; ['Bond Street' × 'Dame de Coeur']; intr. 1991

'Incantation' -- See 'Ardspell74'

Incanto®   LCl, mp, Barni; flowers bright pink, golden stamens, single, flat, borne in clusters, slight fragrance; foliage dark green; vigorous (8-20 ft.) growth; intr. 2006

'Incarnata' -- See 'My Lady Kensington'

'Incarnata' -- See 'Double Carnée'

'Incarnata Major' -- See 'Great Maiden's Blush'

'Incarnata Maxima' -- See 'Belle Couronnée'

'Incarnate' -- See 'Vilmorin'

'Incense'   HT, dr, 1968, LeGrice; flowers deep red, pointed, dbl.; vigorous growth; [('Karl Herbst' × 'New Yorker') × Konrad Adenauer®]

Incense Indigo™ -- See 'Virmagenta'

'Inch'Allah'   HT, pb, 1944, Meilland, F.; bud long; flowers bright pink, reverse flesh, stamens yellow, very large, semi-dbl.; vigorous growth; ['Pres. Macia' × 'Editor McFarland']

'Inclination'   S, op, Williams, J. Benjamin; flowers salmon pink, dbl., moderate fragrance; recurrent; moderate (3 ft.) growth; intr. 2006

Incognito™ -- See 'Briincog'

'Incomparable'   HGal, dp, before 1813; flowers deep pink, nuanced purple; from Holland

'Incomparable'   HP, w, Giraud, A.; flowers rosy white, large; intr. 1923

'Incomparable d'Auteuil'   C, mp, before 1826, Laffay; flowers rose with carmine; non-remontant; growth to 5 ft.

'Incredible' ('That's Incredible')   S, yb, 1985, Buck, Dr. Griffith J.; bud ovoid, pointed; flowers yellow freckled and streaked with orange-red, large, 28 petals, urn-shaped, borne 1 - 10 per cluster, moderate fragrance; recurrent; foliage medium large, leathery, dark olive green, copper tinted when young; prickles awl-like, brown; vigorous, erect growth; hardy; ['Gingersnap' × 'Sevilliana']; intr. 1984

'Indéfectible'   Pol, mr, 1919, Turbat; flowers bright clear red, semi-dbl.; ['Annchen Muller' × unknown]

'Independance du Luxembourg'   HT, w, Lens, Louis; flowers creamy white with orange and pink tones, large, dbl., high-centered, intense fragrance; very disease-resistant; intr. 1990

'Independence' ('Geranium', 'Sondermeldung', 'Kordes' Sondermeldung', 'Reina Elisenda')   F, or, 1951, Kordes; bud urn-shaped; flowers pure scarlet, 4½ in., 35 petals, cupped, borne in clusters of up to 10, moderate fragrance; foliage glossy, dark; growth moderate; PP1036; [('Baby Chateau' × 'Crimson Glory') × ('Baby Chateau' × 'Crimson Glory')]

'Independence, Climbing' ('Kordes' Sondermeldung, Climbing')   Cl F, or, 1960, Balducci & Figli

'Independence 76'   F, mr, 1977, Byrum; bud short, pointed; flowers high-pointed, 3-4 in., 22 petals, moderate tea fragrance; vigorous, upright growth; PP3902; ['Cotillion' × 'Suspense']; intr. 1974

'Independence Day'   HT, ab, 1919, Bees; bud pointed; flowers sunflower-gold, stained flame-color and orange-apricot, large, dbl., high-centered, intense fragrance; foliage leathery, glossy, dark; vigorous growth; ['Mme Edouard Herriot' × 'Souv. de Gustave Prat']

'Independence Day, Climbing'   Cl HT, ab, 1930, Brown, W.&J.; flowers red, orange yellow center, medium, very full; [sport of 'Independence Day']

'Indian Baby'   S, my; flowers lemon yellow; free-flowering; graceful, trailing, groundcover growth

'Indian Chief'   HT, rb, 1967, Gregory; flowers currant-red shaded orange, pointed, dbl.; foliage dark; very free growth; ['Tropicana' × unknown]

'Indian Goddess'   Cl Min, pb, 1999, Sridharan, Dr. Lakshmi M.; flowers 2½ in., semi-dbl., borne singly and in small clusters; foliage dark green, semi-glossy, disease-resistant; few prickles; bushy, medium (4-5 ft.) growth; ['Crazy Dottie' × seedling]

'Indian Gold'   F, yb, 1961, Von Abrams; bud ovoid, flushed red; flowers yellow flushed soft pink, large, 30-45 petals, high-centered, borne in clusters, moderate fragrance; foliage glossy, light green; short stems; upright, compact growth; ['Goldilocks' × seedling]; intr. 1961

'Indian Love Call'   S, mp, 2008, Rupert, Kim L.; flowers medium, single, borne in small clusters; foliage medium, medium green, semi-glossy, turning purple on reverse in cooler weather; no prickles; stems red-mahogany; growth fountain shaped, tall (5-9 ft.); ['Ann Harkness' × 'Basye's Legacy']; intr. 2009

'Indian Maid'   HT, ob, Padilla; bud long, pointed; flowers salmon, reverse bronze-yellow, dbl., high-centered; foliage glossy; vigorous growth; [('Talisman' × unknown) × 'Souv. de Claudius Pernet']

'Indian Meillandina' -- See 'Carol-Jean'

'Indian Pink'   HT, pb, 1977, McDaniel, G. K.; flowers 5 in., 30-36 petals, globular; foliage leathery; very vigorous, upright, bushy growth; [seedling × 'Orange Tango']; intr. 1971

'Indian Princess' -- See 'Princess of India'

'Indian Princess' -- See 'Pixiprin'

'Indian Red'   HT, rb, 1948, Brownell; bud long, pointed; flowers red shaded deeper, large, dbl., high-centered, moderate fragrance; foliage small, glossy; vigorous, bushy, upright growth; hardy; ['Pink Princess' × 'Crimson Glory']

Indian Silk® -- See 'Lenlilo'

'Indian Song' ('Preziosa')   HT, pb, 1971, Meilland; flowers rose, reverse gold, 5 in., 40 petals, high-centered; foliage glossy, dark; vigorous, upright growth; [('Radar' × 'Karl Herbst') × 'Sabrina']

'Indian Summer' -- See 'Harwigwam'

'Indian Summer'   Cl HT, ob, 1938,

Duehrsen; bud pointed; flowers orange, streaked red, large, 25 petals, intense fragrance; foliage dark bronze, leathery, glossy; very vigorous (12-18 ft.) growth; PP448; ['Ednah Thomas' × 'Autumn']

'Indian Summer' ('Sweet Perfume') HT, ob, Pearce; flowers creamy orange, dbl., high-centered, intense fragrance; good rebloom; foliage dark green, healthy; bushy, compact (2½ ft.) growth; intr. 1991

'Indian Sunblaze' -- See 'Carol-Jean'

'Indian Sunset' HT, rb, Meilland; flowers vermilion-red, China yellow reverse, full, classic; cut flower rose; intr. 2004

'Indian Warrior' HT, dr

'Indiana' HGal, 1834, Vibert

'Indiana' M, mp, Vibert; flowers medium, very dbl., cupped; intr. 1845

'Indiana' HT, pb, E.G. Hill, Co.; flowers bright pink, faintly suffused orange, dbl.; bushy growth; ['Rosalind Orr English' × 'Frau Karl Druschki']; intr. 1907

'Indiana' HT, rb, Meilland, Marie Louise; bud large, ovoid, ruby red; sepals foliaceous; flowers rose-red, yellow at base, reverse lighter, white at base, 4¾-5¼ in., 34-38 petals, high-centered, borne mostly singly, but sometimes in small clusters, moderate tea fragrance; foliage medium size, medium green, leathery; prickles moderate, brown; growth bushy, branching; [('Happiness' × 'Independence') × ('Happiness' × 'Charles Mallerin')]; intr. 1965

'Indianapolis' HT, mp, 1971, Schloen, J.; flowers deep yellow-pink, medium, very dbl., cupped; foliage glossy, leathery; moderate, upright growth; ['Coloranja' × unknown]

Indiane® F, dy, Sauvageot; intr. 2007

'Indica Alba' ('White Daily Rose') Ch, lp, 1802; flowers very light blush; [sport of 'Old Blush']; discovered in an English garden

'Indica Major' -- See 'Fun Jwan Lo'

'Indica Purpurea' Ch, m, Chenault; flowers purple/pink, medium, single

'Indigo' P, m, before 1845, Laffay; flowers bluish violet, velvety, large, full, flat

'Indigoletta' ('Azubis') LCl, m, Van de Laak; flowers dbl.; intr. 1981

'Indira' HT, pb, 1975, Hetzel; bud ovoid; flowers pink, reverse lighter, medium, slight fragrance; foliage soft; vigorous, upright, bushy growth; [Baccará® × 'Prima Ballerina']; intr. 1973

'Indispensable' LCl, mp, 1947, Klyn; bud globular; flowers pink, medium, dbl., high-centered, borne in clusters; foliage glossy; moderate, upright, pillar growth; [sport of 'Roserie']

'Indra' HMult, dp, 1937, Tantau; bud pointed; flowers rose-pink, 6-8 cm., semi-dbl., open, borne in small clusters; foliage greyish-green, glossy; long stems; very vigorous, climbing growth; [('Ophelia' × R. multiflora) × 'Florex']

'Indraman' F, or, Chiplunkar; flowers bright fire-orange, non-fading, medium; intr. 1990

'Indraneel' HT, m, Mukherjee, K.P.; flowers lavender, large, moderate fragrance; intr. 1988

'Indu' HT, pb, Mandal, G.S.; flowers bright pink with gold reverse; free-flowering; [sport of 'Las Vegas']; intr. 2004

'Indu Singhal' Gr, pb, Singhal; flowers broad pink petals, marked and etched with white stripes; [sport of Queen Elizabeth®]; intr. 1995

'Indy 500' Gr, or, 1976, Williams, J. Benjamin; bud tapered; flowers brilliant orange-red, 4½-5 in., 32 petals, flat, intense fragrance; foliage large, glossy, dark, reddish; vigorous, upright growth; PP4361; [('Aztec' × (Queen Elizabeth® × unknown)) × ('Independence' × 'Scarlet Knight seedling')]

'Inermis' ('À Tiges sans Épines') HSpn, mr, before 1824, Nestler/DeCandolle; flowers varying shades of red, single, borne mostly solitary; foliage ovate, simply dentate, glabrous; nearly thornless

'Inermis Morletii' -- See 'Morletii'

'Inermis Sub Albo Violacea' -- See 'Bourbon'

'Ines' LCl, ob; flowers large, full; recurrent; intr. 2007

Infanta Pilar™ -- See 'Febima'

'Infantania' F, w, 1953, Heers; flowers snow-white, sometimes tinged green, small, dbl., borne in large clusters; ['Baby Alberic' × unknown]

'Infante Beatrice' HT, ob, 1930, Guillot, M.; flowers orange-yellow, tinted reddish-gold, base golden, dbl.; vigorous growth; ['Marie Adélaïde' × seedling]

'Infante Maria Cristina' HT, ob, 1930, Gaujard; bud pointed; flowers coppery, tinged carmine; foliage reddish bronze; vigorous growth

'Infante Marie-Thérèse' -- See 'Rosycola Panarosa'

'Inferno' -- See 'Arokunce'

'Infidélité de Lisette' -- See 'Mme Bureau'

'Infinity' -- See 'Resfini'

'Ingar Olsson' F, mr, 1931, Poulsen, S.; flowers brilliant cerise-red, semi-dbl., cupped, borne in clusters; foliage leathery; vigorous, rather compact growth; ['Else Poulsen' × 'Ophelia']

'Inge Horstmann' HT, rb, 1964, Tantau, Math.; bud long, red, reverse white tinged pink; flowers cherry-red, high-centered; long stems; vigorous, bushy growth

'Inge Pein' Pol, mr, 1939, Pein; flowers carmine-red, medium, semi-dbl.

Inge Schubert® -- See 'Maulave'

'Ingegnoli Prediletta' -- See 'Zéphirine Drouhin'

'Ingénieur Madèlé' HP, dp, 1874, Moreau-Robert; flowers currant pink, very large, full

'Ingénue' HGal, w, 1833, Vibert; flowers white, buff center, medium, dbl., cupped; foliage pale green; growth branching

'Ingenue' S, lp, Eve; flowers soft pink, undulating petals, 5 petals; recurrent; growth to 4-5 ft.; intr. 1972

'Ingrata' -- See 'Le Rire Niais'

'Ingrid' -- See 'Maning'

'Ingrid Bergman' -- See 'Poulman'

'Ingrid Mander-Fuchs' -- See 'Manfu'

'Ingrid Stenzig' ('Pink Triumph') Pol, dp, 1951, Hassefras Bros.; flowers rose-pink, small, buttercup form, borne in large clusters; [sport of 'Orange Triumph']

'Ingrid Weibull' -- See 'Tanweieke'

'Ingrid's Hawaiian Magic' -- See 'Manhawaii'

'Ingrid's Sister Elisabeth' -- See 'Mansis'

'Inigo Jones' HP, pb, 1886, Paul, W.; flowers pink tinted purple, large, full, globular

'Inisfree' ('Innisfree') F, yb, 1964, Dickson, Patrick; flowers yellow, orange and pink, 22 petals, borne in clusters; vigorous, tall growth; [('Karl Herbst' × 'Masquerade') × 'Circus']; intr. 1964

'Ink Spots' HT, dr, 1985, Weeks, O.L.; flowers medium, 35 petals, slight fragrance; foliage large, dark, semi-glossy; upright, bushy, spreading growth; PP5855; [seedling × seedling]

'Inka' HT, dy, Tantau; intr. 1993

Inka® -- See 'Tantreika'

'Inner Glow' -- See 'Pixinner'

'Inner Temple' -- See 'Horhoneylove'

'Inner Wheel' -- See 'Fryjasso'

'Innisfree' -- See 'Inisfree'

Innocence™ -- See 'Savinn'

'Innocence' HT, w, 1921, Chaplin Bros.; flowers stamens reddish, slightly waved, 5 in., 12 petals, borne in clusters, moderate fragrance; foliage dark; vigorous growth; supposedly R. × hibernica × a hybrid tea

'Innocence, Climbing' Cl HT, w, 1938, Armstrong, J.A.

'Innocence' HT, w, Croix

'Innocence 96' -- See 'Cocoray'

Innocencia® -- See 'Korstarnow'

Innocencia® -- See 'Korenbon'

'Innocent Blush' -- See 'Renblush'

'Innocente Pirola' T, w, 1878, Ducher, Vve.; flowers clouded white, medium, full

'Innovation' F, Combe, M.; intr. 1973

'Innovation Minijet' -- See 'Meijette'

'Innoxa Femille' -- See 'Harprincely'

'Inoa' F, mr, 1958, Arles; flowers bright velvety red; vigorous growth; ['Gruss an Teplitz' × 'Pioupiou']

Insel Mainau® F, dr, 1959, Kordes, R.; bud ovoid; flowers deep crimson, large, dbl., borne in clusters of up to 5; foliage leathery, dark; low, compact growth

'Insolite' -- See 'Morchari'

'Inspecteur Jagourt' F, m, 1932, Soupert & Notting; bud glowing red; flowers purplish pink to China-rose, large white stamens, large, 25-30 petals; foliage glossy; vigorous growth; ['Mrs Henry Winnett' × 'Eblouissant']

'Inspector Rose' HT, rb, 1969, Fryers Nursery, Ltd.; flowers maroon-red, reverse yellow, long, pointed, 35 petals; foliage coppery bronze-red; very free growth; [sport of 'Piccadilly']

'Inspektor Blohm' HMsk, w, 1942, Kordes; flowers medium, very dbl., borne in large corymbs, intense fragrance; recurrent bloom; foliage abundant, gray-green; vigorous, well-branched growth; ['Joanna Hill' × 'Eva']

'Inspiration' -- See 'Jaccoh'

'Inspiration' -- See 'Horkeepog'

'Inspiration' LCl, mp, 1946, Jacobus; flowers medium pink, fading to pale pink, 10-11 cm., semi-dbl., moderate fragrance; foliage large, dark green, glossy; moderate growth; ['New Dawn' × 'Crimson Glory']

'Inspiration' HT, rb, Perry; flowers medium red blend, moderate fragrance; intr. 1991

Inspiration® HT, pb, Noack; flowers pink blended with yellow, 4 in., dbl., borne in clusters; growth to 70-80 cm.; intr. 2004

'Inspiration 2000' HT, pb, Horner; flowers pearly pink and cream, dbl.; growth vigorous; intr. 2002

'Instigation' S, dr, Williams, J. Benjamin; flowers dbl., classic hybrid tea, moderate fragrance; recurrent; foliage medium green, semi-glossy; medium (4 ft.) growth; intr. 2006

Institut Lumière® S, op, Guillot-Massad; flowers pink tinted orange, dbl., slight fragrance; foliage dark green; growth to 1 m.; intr. 2004

'Instituteur Sirdey' HT, dy, 1905, Pernet-Ducher

'Institutrice Moulins' Ch, dp, 1893, Charreton

'Insulinde' HT, yb, Van Rossem; flowers clear yellow shaded golden yellow, dbl., slight fragrance; ['Mr Joh. M. Jolles' × 'Melody']; intr. 1923

'Insulinde' HT, op, Leenders, M.; flowers pink and salmon, dbl., moderate fragrance; ['Ophelia' × 'Jonkheer J.L. Mock']; intr. 1923

'Intasprint' HT, dy, Ilsink; intr. 1989

'Integrity' -- See 'Harvintage'

'Intel' Min, m, Spooner, Raymond A.; intr. 1996

Intense Cover™ -- See 'Poultw001'

'Intensity' HT, dr, 1908, Dingee & Conard; flowers very dark crimson scarlet, large, full, moderate fragrance; ['Gruss an Teplitz' × 'General MacArthur']

'Interabflo' F, ab, Ilsink; intr. 1999

'Interall' ('Rosy Hedge', Rosy Cushion®) S, pb, 1979, Ilsink; bud ovate; flowers pink with white toward center, small, 6 petals, flat, borne in large clusters, very slight fragrance; free-flowering; foliage dark green, glossy; prickles numerous, medium, straight; vigorous, sprawling (3 × 4 ft.) growth; [Yesterday® × seedling]

'Interama' -- See 'Intruma'

'Interamon' (White Diamond®) S, w; intr. 1994

'Interander' ('Oleander Rose') S, op, 1983, Interplant; flowers salmon-pink, small, 7 petals, borne in large clusters; repeat bloom; foliage medium size, medium green, semi-glossy; prickles very few, small; upright growth; ['Liverpool Echo' × seedling]

'Interbab' ('Yellow Dot') F, ly, Ilsink; intr. 1995

'Interbec' ('Espoir') HCh, w, 1983, Gailloux, Gilles; bud small; flowers small, single, slight fragrance; foliage very small, medium green, semi-glossy; upright, spreading growth; ['hybrid china seedling' × 'hybrid china seedling']

'Interbee' ('Beehive Gold') S, my, Interplant; intr. 1994

'Interbeegol' Min, dy

'Interbricor' ('Hot Fire') S, mr, Interplant; intr. 1995

'Interbronzi' (Suntan™) Min, r, 1992, Ilsink, G.P.; flowers bronze, little fading, 1½ in., 30 petals, urn-shaped, borne in sprays, slight fragrance; foliage small, dark green, glossy; upright, bushy, low (30 cm.) growth; [seedling × 'The Fairy']; intr. 1989

'Intercarp' ('Matador', Rosy Carpet®) S, dp, 1983, Interplant; flowers deep pink to red, 5 petals, shallow cup, borne in clusters, moderate fragrance; repeat blooming; foliage medium size, dark, glossy; prickles numerous, medium; spreading (to 4 ft.) growth; [Yesterday® × seedling]

'Intercell' (Red Blanket®) S, dp, 1979, Ilsink; flowers dull, deep pink, small, semi-dbl., borne in small clusters, slight fragrance; repeat bloom; foliage dark, glossy; prickles numerous, medium; vigorous (to 3-4 ft.) groundcover growth; [Yesterday® × seedling]

'Intercher' (Chimo®) S, mr, 1992, Ilsink, Peter; flowers red aging dark red, 1¼ in., 5 petals, cupped, borne singly; repeat bloom; foliage medium size, medium green, glossy; low (90 cm.), spreading growth; [seedling × Immensee®]; intr. 1988

'Interchimp' ('Pink Panoramic', Pink Chimo®) S, mp, 1992, Ilsink, Peter; flowers 1-1½ in., 5 petals, cupped, borne singly; repeat bloom; foliage medium size, medium green, semi-glossy; spreading, low (30 cm.) growth; [seedling × Immensee®]; intr. 1989

'Intercitira' ('Lime Glow') HT, my, Interplant

'Interclem' (New Face®) S, yb, 1982, Interplant; flowers yellow edged pink, small, 5 petals, borne in large clusters; repeat bloom; foliage medium size, medium green, semi-glossy; numerous prickles; upright growth

'Intercream' ('Ivora') F, w, 1986, Interplant; flowers near white, 35 petals, borne in clusters; foliage medium size, light green, matte; upright growth; ['AmRUda' × seedling]

'Interdain' ('Fellini') F, lp, Interplant; intr. 1996

'Interdays' ('Tropical Skies') HT, yb, Ilsink; intr. 1997

'Interdust' ('Stardust', 'Sun Runner') S, ly, 1998, Ilsink/Interplant; bud short, pointed ovoid; flowers light, bright yellow, 1½ in., 5-10 petals, shallow cup, borne in large clusters, self cleaning, slight fragrance; recurrent; foliage small, dark green, glossy; prickles moderate, short, red; spreading (3 ft.), mounding (18 in.), low, growth; PP10240; [seedling × seedling]; intr. 1992

'Interette' ('Flavia', Fleurette®) S, lp, 1982, Interplant; flowers 2 in., 5 petals, borne in clusters; repeat bloom; foliage medium green, glossy; prickles few, medium; vigorous (to 4 ft.) growth; groundcover; [Yesterday® × seedling]; intr. 1978

'Intereup' ('Peachy Creeper') S, ob, Interplant; intr. 1997

'Interfair' (Fair Play®) S, m, 1982, Interplant; flowers light violet, 18 petals, borne in large clusters; repeat bloom; foliage medium size, dark, matte; prickles dark green; groundcover; vigorous growth; [Yesterday® × seedling]; intr. 1978

'Interfire' ('Darthuizer Orange Fire', Orange Fire™) F, ob, 1992, Ilsink, Peter; flowers very bright orange, 3¼ in., 15-20 petals, urn-shaped, borne in sprays of 7 - 12, slight fragrance; foliage large, medium green, matte; upright growth; ['Orange Wave' × seedling]; intr. 1987

'Interflora' -- See 'Meiretni'

'Interflu' ('Fluffy', 'Patio Cloud') Min, w, 1984, Interplant; flowers white, shaded creamy pink, small, 15 petals, borne in clusters; foliage dark, glossy; prickles few, medium; groundcover; spreading growth; [seedling × 'Nozomi']

'Interflucco' ('Amber Flush') HT, ab, Ilsink; intr. 2003

'Interfour' (Petit Four®) Min, mp, 1982, Ilsink; flowers large, semi-dbl., borne in clusters, moderate fragrance; foliage small, medium green, glossy; prickles numerous, small; bushy growth; [('Marlena' × unknown) × seedling]; intr. 1986

'Interfrico' -- See 'Apricot Queen'

'Intergant' (Elegant Pearl®) Min, w, 1983, Interplant; flowers creamy white, patio, dbl., borne in large clusters; foliage small, medium green, glossy; prickles few, medium; bushy growth; [seedling × 'Nozomi']

'Intergeorge' (Carmela™, Georgeous™) Min, mp, 1992, Ilsink, Peter; flowers 1¼ in., 6-8 petals, cupped, borne in sprays of 3-8; foliage small, dark green, glossy; bushy, low (30-40 cm.) growth; [Candy Rose® × 'Eyeopener']; intr. 1990

'Interglo' ('Gloire des Anciens') S, pb, Interplant; intr. 1987

'Intergojod' HT, mp, Interplant

'Intergol' Min, dy, Ilsink; intr. 1990

'Intergri' (Silver Dream®) F, lp, 1993,

Ilsink, G.P.; flowers silver pink, medium, dbl., borne in sprays; foliage medium size, medium green, semi-glossy; few prickles; medium (60 cm.), upright growth; intr. 1992

'Interhappy' S, yb, Ilsink ; bud pointed, ovoid; intr. 1999

'Interhel' ('Stadt den Helder') F, mr, 1982, Interplant; flowers bright red, medium, 20 petals, cupped, borne in sprays, slight fragrance; recurrent; foliage large, dark green, matte; upright (3-5 ft.) growth; [Amsterdam® × (Olala® × Diablotin®)]; intr. 1979

'Interhenk' Min, w, Interplant; intr. 1989

'Interhyro' S, mr, Interplant; intr. 1987

'Interice' ('Coral Ice') HT, op, Interplant; intr. 1996

'Interictira' ('Glorius') HT, my, Interplant; intr. 2001

'Interim' S, mr, Ilsink; intr. 1991

'Interjada' F, dp, 1986, Interplant; flowers deep pink, 35 petals, borne in sprays; foliage medium size, dark, semi-glossy; upright growth; [seedling × seedling]

'Interjusti' HT, ab, Interplant

'Interlada' (Lady of the Dawn®) F, lp, 1984, Interplant; flowers large, ruffled, soft cream edged with pink, semi-dbl., borne in large clusters, moderate fruity fragrance; foliage large, medium green, matte, leathery; upright growth, arching, 4 ft.; PP6068; ['Interdress' × 'Stadt den Helder']

'Interlav' (Lavender Dream®) S, m, 1984, Interplant; bud long; flowers deep lilac pink, 1½ in., 11-15 petals, flat, borne in large clusters, no fragrance; repeat bloom; foliage medium size, light green, matte, narrow; prickles few, medium; bushy, arching, 5 ft., growth; PP5916; [Yesterday® × 'Nastarana']

'Interleer' ('Leersum 700') F, ob, 1985, Interplant; flowers light orange-yellow, medium, semi-dbl., borne in clusters, slight fragrance; foliage medium size, light green, matte; prickles numerous, small; upright growth; ['Lichtkonigin Lucia' × 'Marlena']; intr. 1979

'Interlien' ('Evelien') F, lp, 1986, Interplant; flowers 35 petals, borne in clusters, slight fragrance; foliage medium size, medium green, semi-glossy; PP7368; [seedling × 'Fresh Pink']; intr. 1985

'Interlight' (Day Light®) F, ab, 1992, Ilsink, G.P.; flowers apricot-yellow, apricot and light pink reverse, aging to champagne, 3¼ in., dbl.; foliage medium size, dark green, matte; upright, medium (36-48 cm.) growth; [seedling × New Year®]; intr. 1991

'Interlis' ('Lydia') F, lp, Ilsink; intr. 1995

'Intermezzo' HT, m, 1963, Dot, Pedro; bud ovoid; flowers deep lavender, large, 25 petals, moderate fragrance; foliage dark, glossy; moderately tall, compact growth; PP2430; ['Grey Pearl' × 'Lila Vidri']

'Interminer' ('Minerette') Min, lp, 1982, Interplant; flowers small, semi-dbl., borne in clusters; free-flowering; foliage small, medium green, glossy; prickles numerous, small; bushy growth; [('Marlena' × unknown) × seedling]

'Intermoto' (Joy®) F, dp, 1986, Interplant; flowers deep pink, 35 petals, borne in clusters, no fragrance; foliage medium size, medium green, semi-glossy; upright growth; ['Amruda' × seedling]; intr. 1985

'Intermug' ('Butterflies') S, my, Ilsink; intr. 1996

'Intermunder' ('Red Dot') S, mr, Interplant; intr. 1989

'International Gold' -- See 'Tomgold'

International Herald Tribune® -- See 'Harquantum'

'Interniki' (Nikita®) F, mr, 1993, Ilsink, G.P.; flowers small, dbl., borne in sprays; foliage medium size, medium green, glossy; some prickles; medium (45 cm.), bushy growth; intr. 1988

'Interonly' ('Only Love') HT, dr, 1986, Interplant; flowers large, 35 petals; foliage medium size, dark, semi-glossy; upright growth; PP6698; [seedling × 'Caramba']

'Interop' ('Erica', 'Eyeopener', 'Tapis Rouge') S, mr, 1986, Interplant; flowers small, semi-dbl., no fragrance; foliage medium size, medium green, glossy; spreading growth; [(seedling × Eyepaint®) × (seedling × Dortmund®)]

'Interorge' ('Georgette') F, w, 1985, Interplant; flowers large, 35 petals, slight fragrance; foliage large, medium green, semi-glossy; upright growth; [seedling × Bordure Rose®]; intr. 1983

'Interpeel' ('Ardennes', Eye Appeal®) S, dr, 1992, Ilsink, Peter; flowers 2 in., 8 petals, cupped, borne singly, no fragrance; repeat bloom; foliage medium size, medium green, glossy; spreading, medium (40-60 cm.) growth; ['Eyeopener' × unknown]; intr. 1992

'Interpin' ('Cottage Dream', 'Pink Fringe') F, mp, Ilsink; intr. 1995

'Interpink' (Pink Star®) S, mp, 1982, Interplant; flowers medium, semi-dbl., borne in clusters; foliage medium size, light green, semi-glossy; spreading growth; [Yesterday® × seedling]; intr. 1978

'Interpool' ('Verdi') HT, rb, 1960, Dorieux; bud ovoid; flowers brick-red, reverse veined darker, medium, dbl.; foliage dark, glossy; very vigorous, bushy growth; ['Cafougnette' × 'Independence']; intr. 1960

'Interprince' ('Princess®) F, w, 1993, Ilsink, G.P.; flowers medium, full, borne in large clusters; foliage medium size, dark green, glossy; some prickles; tall to medium (60 cm.), upright growth; ['Pink Delight' × seedling]; intr. 1989

'Interpur' (Purple Prince®) F, m, 1993, Ilsink, G.P.; flowers dark mauve to light purple, medium, full, borne in large clusters; foliage medium size, dark green, semi-glossy; some prickles; medium (55 cm.), upright growth; intr. 1991

'Interreflet' ('Glowing Cushion') S, mr, Ilsinksingle; intr. 1996

'Interrialow' S, my, Interplant; intr. 2006

'Interro' ('Red Jewel') Min, or, 1985, Interplant; flowers small, 20 petals, no fragrance; foliage small, medium green, semi-glossy; bushy growth; PP5769; ['Amanda' × seedling]; intr. 1984

'Interrob' ('Robin Red Breast', 'Robin Redbreast') MinFl, rb, 1983, Interplant; flowers dark red, white eye, reverse silver, small, single, borne in clusters, no fragrance; foliage small, medium green, glossy; prickles numerous, medium; bushy growth; [seedling × Eyepaint®]

'Intersina' HT, lp, 1985, Interplant; flowers large, 35 petals, no fragrance; foliage large, medium green, semi-glossy; upright growth; PP5836; [seedling × 'Red Success']; intr. 1984

'Intersiree' (Swing®) F, lp, 1993, Ilsink, G.P.; flowers cream pink, medium, dbl., borne in sprays; foliage medium size, dark green, glossy; few prickles; medium (60 cm.), upright growth; intr. 1990

'Intersmart' (Smarty®) S, lp, 1979, Ilsink; flowers pale pink with large white eye, 2 in., single, flat, borne in clusters, no fragrance; recurrent; foliage bright green, matte; prickles numerous, small; vigorous, bushy (3 ft. × 4 ft.) growth; groundcover; [Yesterday® × seedling]

'Intersnapni' HT, dpdbl.; intr. 2001

'Interstreep' ('Arabesque') S, pb, Interplant; intr. 1997

'Intersum' ('Summerrose') S, lp, 1982, Interplant; flowers 2 in., 6-8 petals, borne in large clusters, moderate fragrance; foliage medium size, medium green, matte; prickles numerous, long; groundcover; spreading growth; [Yesterday® × seedling]; intr. 1981

'Intertor' (Pink Torch®, Torche Rose®) S, mp, 1986, Interplant; flowers small, single, borne in large, pyramidal sprays; good repeat; foliage medium size, medium green, glossy; upright (to 4 ft.) growth; [('Mozart' × seedling) × (seedling × Eyepaint®)]; intr. 1987

'Intertra' (Chess®) F, m, 1993, Ilsink, G.P.; flowers deep purple, medium, full, borne in sprays, no fragrance; foliage medium size, dark green, glossy; few prickles; medium (55 cm.), upright growth; intr. 1991

'Intertropa' ('Temptation') HT, mr; intr. 1995

'Intertwik' (Twinkle™) Min, ly, 1992, Ilsink, Peter; flowers light yellow, do not fade, 2 in., 10 petals, urn-shaped, borne singly, slight fragrance; recurrent; foliage medium size, medium green, matte; upright, low (40 cm.) growth; ['McShane' × seedling]; intr. 1989

'Intertyn' (Sentyna®) F, op, 1993, Ilsink, G.P.; flowers light salmon pink, medium, dbl., borne in sprays; foliage medium size, medium green, glossy; few prickles; tall (80 cm.), upright growth; intr. 1990

'Interuept' S, mr, Interplant; intr. 2006

'Interval' ('Porcelain Bouquet', 'Porcelina') HT, w, 1985, Interplant; flowers cream with pink tint, 30 petals, borne singly or in small clusters, moderate fragrance; foliage large, dark, glossy; few prickles; upright growth; PP5648; [seedling × 'Golden Times']; intr. 1983

'Intervema' ('Orlando') HT, pb, Ilsink; bud pointed; intr. 1995

'Interview' ('Interflora') HT, dp, 1968, Meilland; flowers light madder-red, large, 40 petals, high-centered, slight fragrance; foliage leathery; vigorous, upright growth; PP2977; [((Baccará® × 'White Knight') × (Baccará® × 'Jolie Madame')) × (Baccará® × 'Paris-Match')]; intr. 1968

Intervilles® LCl, mr, 1970, Robichon; bud ovoid; flowers semi-dbl., cupped, borne in small clusters, moderate fragrance; foliage dark, glossy; vigorous, climbing growth; ['Etendard' × unknown]; intr. 1968

'Interway' ('Milky Way', 'Thornhem') HT, w, 1992, Ilsink, Peter; flowers white with hint of pink on reverse/edge, 4 in., 20 petals, urn-shaped, borne in sprays of up to 10, slight fragrance; foliage large, dark green, glossy; upright, medium (100-120 cm.) growth; ['Esmeralda' × 'True Love']; intr. 1991

'Interwell' ('Golden Nuggets') S, ly; intr. 1992

'Interyama' HT , lp, Interplant

'Interyassor' HT, dr, Ilsink, Peter; PP15538

'Interzabunel' HT, pb, Interplant

'Interzange' HT, dy, Interplant; intr. 2002

'Inti' HT, dy, deRuiter; intr. 2005

'Intimité' HT, ob, 1956, Delforge; bud long; flowers golden orange shaded yellow and chamois, open, large, dbl.; foliage glossy, dark; vigorous, bushy growth; ['Beauté' × seedling]

Intrepid™ -- See 'Perpid'

'Intrepid Red' HT, mp, 2001, Coiner, Jim; flowers medium pink, white reverse, 3 in., full, borne in small clusters, no fragrance; foliage medium size, light green, matte; growth compact, medium (36 in.); garden decorative; PP15824; [seedling × seedling]; intr. 2002

'Intrépide' LCl, or, Combe; flowers orange scarlet, large; intr. 1972

'Intrigue' -- See 'Korlech'

'Intrigue' -- See 'Jacum'

'Intropi' Min, mp, Interplant; intr. 2003

'Intruma' ('Interama', 'Onterama') F, dr, 1976, deRuiter; flowers 3 in., 18 petals; foliage large, glossy, dark; bushy growth; PP4018; ['Kohima' × (Europeana® × 'Kimona')]

'Invention' HT, dp, Patil, B.K.; flowers salmon and carmine; free-flowering; [sport of 'Ambossfunken']; intr. 1988

'Invertilis' HSpn, mr; flowers carmine-red, medium-large, single

'Invincible' HGal, mr, before 1819, Miellez; flowers fiery red

'Invincible' -- See 'Runatru'

'Invitation' HT, op, 1961, Swim & Weeks; bud long, pointed; flowers rich salmon-pink, base yellow, 4½ in., 30 petals, high-centered, intense spicy fragrance; foliage leathery, glossy; vigorous, compact, bushy growth; PP2018; ['Charlotte Armstrong' × 'Signora']; intr. 1961

'Involuta' (R. braunii, R. villosa, R. coronata, R. doniana, R. × involuta Smith, R. sabini) Misc OGR, lp, before 1800; flowers pale pink, single; growth moderate; [R. spinosissima × R. tomentosa]; from Scotland

'Involuta' (R. × involuta wilsonii Baker, R. wilsonii) Misc OGR, before 1862; vigorous, shrubby growth

'Iobelle' ('Iowa Belle') HT, pb, 1960, Buck, Dr. Griffith J.; bud ovoid; flowers ivory-white edged and overspread deep pink, large, high-centered, moderate fruity fragrance; foliage dark, glossy; vigorous, upright, compact growth; ['Dean Collins' × 'Peace']; intr. 1962

'Iode' F, dr, 1974, Schloen, J.; bud ovoid; flowers large, semi-dbl., cupped; foliage glossy; vigorous, upright growth; [Lichterloh® × 'Red Pinocchio']

'Iolanthe' HT, rb, 1940, Gaujard; flowers bright red, reverse yellow, large, semi-dbl.; vigorous growth

'Ion Phillips' HT, dy, 1934, Dickson, A.; flowers rich yellow, large, dbl.; vigorous growth

'Iona Herdman' HT, dy, 1914, McGredy; flowers brilliant yellow, dbl.

'Ione' Min, ly, 1990, Jerabek, Paul E.; bud ovoid; flowers white with pale yellow center, medium, 50 petals, high-centered, borne singly and in small clusters; foliage medium size, medium green, semi-glossy; prickles very few, very small, light green; bushy, medium growth; fruit not observed; [seedling × seedling]

'Ionian Rose' -- See 'Tanekily'

'Iowa Belle' -- See 'Iobelle'

'Ipitombi' -- See 'Jacorb'

'Ipsilanté' -- See 'Ypsilanti'

Iranja® -- See 'Lenira'

'Ireland Hampton' HT, pb, 1934, Hillock; flowers flame-pink suffused gold, base gold, large, dbl., cupped, moderate spicy fragrance; foliage glossy; vigorous, compact growth; PP194; ['Étoile de Feu' × seedling]

'Ireland Hampton, Climbing' Cl HT, pb, 1936, Hillock

'Irene' -- See 'Meiridol'

'Irene' -- See 'Worankle'

'Irene' -- See 'Richoilier'

'Irene' F, pb, Leenders, M.; flowers rose-white, reverse pure white, semi-dbl., moderate fragrance; [seedling × 'Permanent Wave']; intr. 1941

Irene® F, lp, Barni, Enrico; flowers clear, pearly pink, large, dbl., borne in clusters, slight fragrance; good repeat; foliage large, dark green; growth to 2 ft.; [seedling × Venere®]; intr. 2000

'Irène' HSpn, w, 1823, Vibert; flowers flesh white, 3-3½ in., dbl.

'Irene au Danmark' -- See 'Irene of Denmark'

'Irène Bonnet' Cl HT, mp, 1920, Nabonnand, C.; flowers hermosa pink, edges lighter, medium, dbl., moderate fragrance

'Irene Churruca' ('Golden Melody') HT, ly, 1934, La Florida; bud pointed, yellow; flowers light buff, fading cream, well-formed, large; ['Mme Butterfly' × ('Lady Hillingdon' × 'Souv. de Claudius Pernet')]

'Irene Curie' HT, mr, 1952, San Remo Exp. Sta.; bud very long, pointed; flowers scarlet, large, 20 petals; foliage glossy; very vigorous, bushy growth; [seedling × 'Lawrence Johnston (HT)']

'Irene Dean' -- See 'Horquestion'

'Irene Jane' HWich, m, Nobbs; intr. 1995

'Irene Marie' -- See 'Morlindsey'

'Irene of Denmark' ('Irene au Danmark', 'Irene von Danemark') F, w, 1948, Poulsen, S.; bud pointed; flowers 3 in., 40 petals, cupped, moderate fragrance; foliage dark; vigorous, upright, bushy growth; PP889; ['Orléans Rose' × ('Mme Plantier' × 'Edina')]; intr. 1950

'Irene of Denmark, Climbing' Cl F, w, Ruston, D.; [sport of 'Irene of Denmark']; intr. 1970

'Irene Smith' -- See 'Bosrexeye'

'Irene Thompson' HT, yb, 1921, McGredy; flowers deep ruddy gold shaded bronze or coppery, dbl.

'Irene Virag' -- See 'Zipvir'

'Irene von Danemark' -- See 'Irene of Denmark'

'Irène Watts' Ch, w, 1896, Guillot, P.; bud soft apricot-orange, long; flowers creamy white with tints of apricot, dbl.; foliage dark green, margined with purple; ['Mme Laurette Messimy' × unknown]

'Irene's Beauty' Min, yb, 1999, Jolly, Betty J.; flowers very colorful, yellow blend, reverse med. yellow, aging to orange-red, 1½ in., dbl., borne in small clusters; foliage medium size, dark green, semi-glossy; few prickles; compact, low (1 ft.) growth; ['Little Darling' × Kristin™]; intr. 1998

'Irene's Choice' HT, mp, 1977, Ellick; flowers azalea-pink, 4-5 in., 35-40 petals, slight fragrance; very free growth; ['Karl Herbst' × Blue Moon®]; intr. 1978

'Irene's Delight' HT, lp, 1982, Varney, E.; flowers large, dbl., high-centered; foliage medium size, dark, semi-glossy; upright growth; ['Admiral Rodney' × 'Red Lion']

'Irene's Delight' S, op, Lowe; flowers warm shades of orange to peach to apricot., single, borne in small clusters., moderate fragrance; once bloomer.; very cold hardy.; intr. 2001

'Irene's Surprise' -- See 'Kirbee'

'Irina' F, dr, 1969, Grabczewski; flowers dark crimson-red, large, semi-dbl.;

foliage soft, glossy; moderate, bushy growth
'Iris' -- See 'Ferecha'
'Iris' -- See 'Coczero'
'Iris' HSpn, w; flowers dbl.; foliage finely divided; dense, shrubby (3-4 ft.) growth; hips shining, black
'Iris Foster' HT, mp, 1998, Poole, Lionel; flowers medium pink, 6 in., very dbl., high-centered, borne mostly singly; foliage large, medium green, dull; some prickles; vigorous, upright, bushy, floriferous growth; ['Gavotte' × ('Solitaire' × 'Mischief')]
'Iris Gee' F, ab, Gee; flowers pale pink to apricot, fading to cream; growth tall; [sport of 'Liverpool Echo']; intr. 1987
'Iris Hilda' HT, mp, 2001, Hill, Ernest H.; flowers satin pink, lighter reverse, 4½-5 in., very full, borne mostly solitary, slight fragrance; foliage large, dark green, glossy; prickles moderate; growth upright, medium (3 ft.); exhibition; ['Silver Jubilee' × 'Red Devil']
'Iris May' -- See 'Worcherry'
'Iris Patricia Green' HT, mr, 1928, Pemberton; bud pointed; flowers cherry-red; foliage dark
'Iris Squire' F, mp, 1966, Bees; flowers soft rose, 4-5 in.; foliage dull; tall, vigorous growth; [seedling × Queen Elizabeth®]
'Iris Webb' -- See 'Chewell'
'Irischer Regen' -- See 'Irish Mist'
'Irish Afterglow' HT, ob, 1918, Dickson, A.; flowers very deep tangerine, passing to crushed strawberry; [sport of 'Irish Fireflame']
'Irish Beauty' -- See 'Macel'
'Irish Beauty' Cl HT, w, 1900, Dickson; flowers pure white with yellow stamens, single, moderate fragrance
'Irish Brightness' HT, mr, 1904, Dickson, A.; flowers velvety crimson shading pink at base of petals, medium, single
'Irish Charity' HT, rb, 1927, McGredy; bud intense fiery scarlet with golden sheen; flowers rosy scarlet, dbl.
'Irish Charm' HT, ab, 1927, McGredy; bud pointed; flowers base golden apricot passing to blush-pink, dbl., high-centered; foliage dark, leathery; vigorous growth
'Irish Courage' HT, op, 1927, McGredy; bud pointed; flowers soft shrimp-pink to salmon, dbl., high-centered; foliage rich green, leathery, glossy; vigorous growth
Irish Creme™ -- See 'Percreme'
'Irish Elegance' HT, ob, 1905, Dickson, A.; flowers bronze orange-scarlet, large, 5 petals, moderate fragrance; good repeat; vigorous growth
'Irish Engineer' HT, mr, 1904, Dickson, A.; flowers dazzling scarlet, large, single
Irish Eyes™ -- See 'Dicwitness'
'Irish Eyes' F, yb, 1975, Byrum; bud ovoid; flowers yellow edged red, 2½-3 in., 45 petals, high-centered, slight fragrance; vigorous growth; PP3631; [seedling ×

'Gemini']; intr. 1974
'Irish Fireflame' HT, ob, 1914, Dickson, A.; flowers orange to old-gold, veined crimson, anthers light fawn, 5 in., 5 petals, intense fragrance; foliage dark, glossy; compact, bushy growth
'Irish Fireflame, Climbing' Cl HT, ob, 1916, Dickson, A.; flowers orange-yrllow and peach, large, single; [sport of 'Irish Fireflame']
'Irish Glory' HT, pb, 1900, Dickson, A.; flowers silvery pink, reverse crimson, large, 10 petals; very vigorous growth
'Irish Gold, Climbing' Cl HT, Humphreys; intr. 1973
'Irish Gold' -- See 'Grandpa Dickson'
'Irish Harmony' HT, ly, 1904, Dickson, A.; flowers creamy white to saffron yellow
'Irish Heartbreaker' -- See Seaheart'
'Irish Hope' -- See 'Harexclaim'
'Irish Hope' HT, dr, 1927, McGredy; bud pointed; flowers rosy crimson shaded maroon, large, dbl., high-centered; foliage dark, leathery; vigorous growth
'Irish Lady' Min, pb, 1991, Schmidt, Richard; flowers small, full, slight fragrance; foliage small, dark green, glossy; bushy growth; [sport of 'Kathy Robinson']; intr. 1991
'Irish Luck' -- See 'Wekamanda'
'Irish Marbled' -- See 'Irish Rich Marbled'
'Irish Mist' ('Irischer Regen', Irish Summer®) F, op, 1966, McGredy, Sam IV; flowers orange-salmon, well-formed, 4½ in., borne in clusters; foliage dark; dense growth; PP3068; [Orangeade® × 'Mischief']
'Irish Modesty' HT, op, 1900, Dickson, A.; flowers light orange-pink, large, single
'Irish Morn' HT, pb, 1927, McGredy; flowers pink, center coral, dbl.
'Irish Pride' HT, rb, 1904, Dickson, A.; flowers red, coppery center, single
'Irish Rich Marbled' ('Burnet Irish Marbled', 'Irish Marbled') HSpn, rb; flowers rose to lilac-pink, flecked and marbled with lighter shading; hips shiny black
'Irish Rose of India' -- See 'Kencream'
'Irish Rover' HT, op, 1970, McGredy, Sam IV; flowers salmon-pink, 4 in., 36 petals; foliage coppery, dark; vigorous growth; ['Violet Carson' × 'Tropicana']
'Irish Simplicity' -- See 'Simplicity'
'Irish Squire' F, dp, Bees of Chester; flowers carmine-pink, large, dbl.; intr. 1966
'Irish Star' HT, mr, 1904, Dickson, A.; flowers rosy red, single
Irish Summer® -- See 'Irish Mist'
'Irish Sweetness' HT, rb, 1927, McGredy; bud pointed; flowers crimson suffused scarlet, large, dbl., high-centered; foliage dark, leathery; vigorous growth
'Irish Wonder' -- See 'Macev'
'Irma' Ch, w, 1824, Laffay; flowers flesh white
'Irma' T, pb, Vibert; flowers medium pink with apricot; intr. 1835
'Irma' S, lp, Carlsson-Nilsson; flowers full, cupped; bushy (6 ft.) growth; ['Friesia' × 'L83']; intr. 2001

'Irmela' F, w, Hetzel, K.; intr. 1983
'Iroquois' S, lp, 1932, Central Exp. Farm; flowers flowers pale amaranth-pink, semi-dbl., moderate fragrance; non-recurrent; foliage leathery; vigorous, bushy, compact growth; [(R. spinosissima × Pythagoras) × R. cinnamomea]
Irresistible™ -- See 'Tinresist'
'Irsnar' ('Australian Sunrise') S, rb, 2001, Spriggs, Ian Raymond; flowers cherry red, darker reverse, 10 cm., single, borne in small clusters, intense fragrance; foliage medium size, dark green, semi-glossy; prickles moderate; growth upright, tall (1¾ m.); garden decorative, cutting; [Altissimo® × ('Munchen' × 'Erfurt')]; intr. 2000
'Isa' HT, lp, 1931, Evans, F.&L.; flowers light pinkish cream, well-shaped, dbl.; vigorous growth; ['Abol' × unknown]
'Isa Carstens' -- See 'Morjoybon'
'Isa Murdock' HSpn, w, 1953, Skinner; flowers white, sometimes tinged with pink, dbl.; non-recurrent; foliage spinosissima type; numerous prickles; growth to 3 ft.; [R. spinosissima altaica × dbl. white spinosissima]
Isabel™ -- See 'Poulisab'
'Isabel' -- See 'First Gold'
'Isabel de Ortiz' ('Isabel Ortiz') HT, pb, 1962, Kordes, R.; flowers deep pink, reverse silvery, well-formed, 5 in., 38 petals, moderate fragrance; foliage dark, glossy; vigorous, upright growth; PP2449; ['Peace' × 'Kordes' Perfecta']; intr. 1962
Isabel Hit™ MinFl, dr, Poulsen; flowers dark red, 5-8 cm., dbl., no fragrance; foliage dark; growth bushy, 40-60 cm.; intr. 1999
'Isabel Llorach' HP, yb, 1929, Dot, Pedro; flowers nankeen yellow, tinted red, semi-dbl.; ['Frau Karl Druschki' × 'Benedicte Seguin']
'Isabel Ortiz' -- See 'Isabel de Ortiz'
'Isabel Renaissance' ('Isabella', 'Isabelle Renaissance', Isabel™) S, dr, Poulsen; flowers dark red, 4-6 in., dbl., moderate fragrance; foliage dark; bushy (3-5 ft.) growth; PP12825; intr. 1995
'Isabella' -- See 'Andenken an Alma de l'Aigle'
'Isabella' -- See 'Poulisab'
'Isabella' HT, ob, 1964, Leenders, J.; flowers orange, star-shaped; [Queen Elizabeth® × 'Pink Lustre']
'Isabella Cara' -- See 'Seaisa'
'Isabella Ducrot' T, pb, Branchi; intr. 2001
'Isabella Gray' N, dy, 1857, Gray, Andrew; flowers golden yellow, more fragrant, but otherwise similar to parent; ['Chromatella' × unknown]
'Isabella Rossellini' ('Wedding Celebration') HT, dr, Olesen; flowers intense dark red, medium, full, high-centered, borne singly and in clusters, very slight fragrance; recurrent; foliage dark green, glossy; strong, bushy growth; intr. 2006

'Isabella Skinner' S, mp, probably Skinner; flowers pink, well-formed, dbl., slight fragrance; blooms on new wood all summer; bushy growth; [(R. laxa × Tea) × floribunda seedling]; intr. before 1965

'Isabella Sprunt' ('Isabelle Sprungh') T, my, 1865, Sprunt/Buchanan; flowers sulfur-yellow, dbl.; recurrent; medium growth; [sport of 'Safrano']; intr. 1865

'Isabella Sprunt Single Seedling' HMsk, lp, Worl; flowers pale pink, 3 in., single, borne in large clusters, moderate fragrance; good rebloom if deadheaded; hips golden-orange; ['Isabella Sprunt' × unknown]; intr. 1980s

'Isabelle' -- See 'Héloïse'

'Isabelle' HGal, dr, Descemet; flowers velvety purple red marbled violet purple, small to medium, very full; growth erect; Jäger says this is the same as Héloïse; intr. before 1820

'Isabelle' HGal, mp, Vibert; intr. about 1830

'Isabelle' Ch, lp, about 1835, Laffay; flowers whitish flesh pink, full

Isabelle Autissier® HT, pb, Adam; flowers shades of pink, yellow in heart, dbl., intense fragrance; foliage glossy, beginning red; upright (4-5 ft.) growth; intr. 2000

'Isabelle de France' HT, or, 1958, Mallerin, C.; bud pointed; flowers vermilion, large, dbl., high-centered, slight fragrance; vigorous, upright growth; ['Peace' × ('Mme Joseph Perraud' × 'Opera')]; intr. 1957

'Isabelle d'Orléans' N, w, 1824, Vibert; flowers white, center straw yellow, large, full, semi-globular

Isabelle Mainoz® S, dp, Guillot-Massad; growth to 5 ft.

'Isabelle Milner' ('Mrs Isabel Milner') HT, ly, 1908, Paul, W.; flowers ivory white tinted pink, large, dbl., moderate fragrance

'Isabelle Nabonnand' T, pb, 1875, Nabonnand, G.; flowers fawn-pink, darker at center, large, dbl.

'Isabelle Renaissance' -- See 'Poulisab'

'Isabelle II' B, mp, 1853, Pradel; flowers vivid pink, large, full, borne in clusters, strong fragrance

'Isabelle Sprungh' -- See 'Isabella Sprunt'

'Isabel's Jewel' -- See 'Renjewel'

'Isidore Malton' -- See 'Mme Bravy'

Isarperle® F, ab, Noack; flowers cream to salmon, dbl.; free-flowering; growth to 70-80 cm.; intr. 2005

'Isella' Min, lp, 1980, Bartolomeo, Embriaco; flowers small, 22 petals, cupped, borne singly and several together, no fragrance; foliage small, green; prickles pale pink; vigorous, compact, upright growth; [(Baccará® × 'Generosa') × 'Miss Italia']; intr. 1973

'Iséran' LCl, or, Combe; flowers orange or light scarlet, medium to large, full, slight fragrance; intr. 1965

'Isidingo' LCl, op, Orard; bud green-yellow with pink edging; flowers coral, with deep gold in the heart, dbl., exhibition, borne mostly singly, slight fragrance; foliage glossy; tall (10 ft.) growth; intr. 1999

'Isidore' Ch, lp, from Angers; flowers flesh pink, medium, full

Isis™ -- See 'Poulari'

'Isis' N, w, 1853, Robert; flowers large, full, borne in small clusters; foliage dark green; prickles numerous, sturdy, hooked, flat

'Isis' F, w, Mattock; flowers ivory-white, 4-5 in., 40-45 petals, moderate fragrance; compact growth; ['Vera Dalton' × 'Shepherdess']; intr. 1973

'Iskara' -- See 'Meihati'

'Iskra' -- See 'Meihati'

'Iskra 82' LCl, mr

'Island Cloud' w; flowers small, single, borne in clusters, moderate fragrance; non-remontant; vigorous (20 × 8 ft.) growth; probably a HMult or HWich; intr. 2000

'Island Dancer' S, pb, Lim, Ping; flowers deep pink, reverse white, ruffled, 2 in., 18 petals, borne singly and in clusters; recurrent; low (2 ft.) growth; crown hardy to -30°F; intr. 2006

'Island of Dreams' F, dy, Spek; intr. 1995

'Island of Fire' -- See 'Kortemma'

'Island Pearl' lp; flowers pearly pink with slightly darker petal edges, single, borne in clusters, moderate fragrance; non-remontant; vigorous (15 × 12 ft.) growth; probably HMult or HWich; intr. 2000

'Island Wildfire' dp, Quin; flowers reddish pink, single, borne in clusters, moderate fragrance; non-remontant; 15 ft. × 12 ft. growth; intr. 2000

'Isle' HT, pb, Edwards, Eddie; intr. 2007

'Isle of Man' -- See 'Manx Queen'

'Isle of Roses' -- See 'Morisle'

'Ismène' N, lp, about 1835, Laffay; flowers light flesh pink, small, full

'Ismène' D, lp, Vibert; flowers delicate carnation pink, large, full; intr. 1845

'Ismène' M, lp, Robert; flowers flesh pink nuanced with lilac, 6 cm., full, rosette; intr. 1852

'Isn't She Lovely' HT, ly, Dickson; bud creamy gold with slight pink edges; flowers ivory with center showing tones of gold and pink, double, high-centered, borne mostly singly; recurrent; foliage medium, dark green, semi-glossy; upright, bushy growth; ['Poetry in Motion' × 'Glorious']; intr. 2008

'Isobel' HT, pb, 1916, McGredy; bud pointed; flowers light rose-pink, shaded apricot, large, 5 petals, cupped; foliage rich green, soft

'Isobel Champion' -- See 'Delgeot'

'Isobel Derby' -- See 'Horethel'

'Isobel Harkness' HT, dy, 1958, Norman; flowers bright yellow, 6 in., 32 petals, moderate fragrance; foliage dark, leathery, semi-glossy; vigorous, upright, bushy growth; PP1650; ['McGredy's Yellow' × 'Phyllis Gold']; intr. 1957

Isolde™ -- See 'Poulpah024(N)'

'Isolde' -- See 'Judsolde'

'Isolde Hit' (Isolde™) MinFl, rb, Poulsen; flowers red with white stripes, 5-8 cm., dbl., slight wild rose fragrance; foliage dark; growth bushy, 20-40 cm.; intr. 2004

'Isoline' -- See 'Paul Dupuy'

'Ispahan' ('Parfum d'Ispahan', 'Pompon des Princes') D, mp, before 1832; flowers bright pink, medium, petals larger at the edges, dbl., borne in small clusters, intense fragrance; blooms over long season; foliage small, bluish-green, with 5-7 leaflets; prickles few, strong

'Istropoliteana' S, Chorvath, F.; intr. 1990

'Ita Buttrose' HT, op, Armstrong; flowers peach to orange, with burned edges, dbl., moderate fragrance; small growth; intr. 1984

'Italia' HT, pb, 1905, Berti; flowers carmine-pink, with silvery aurora red, very large, full

'Italia' HFt, yb, Aicardi; flowers golden yellow, reverse carmine red; ['Julien Potin' × unknown]; intr. 1933

'Italia' HT, dr, Biga, Valentino; bud ovoid; flowers cardinal-red and cherry-red, to open, large, dbl., cupped, moderate fragrance; foliage leathery, dark; long, strong stems; bushy, upright growth; [Baccará® × 'Poinsettia']; intr. 1959

'Italian Four-Seasons Rose' -- See 'Quatre Saisons d'Italie'

'Italian Pink' S, mp, 1959, Leenders, J.; bud short, pointed; flowers begonia-pink, open, large, dbl., borne in clusters, moderate fragrance; foliage dark; vigorous, upright, well branched growth; ['Cocorico' × 'Yellow Holstein']

'Italie Impériale' HT, m, 1936, Capiago; flowers purplish garnet-red, large; vigorous growth

'Italienisches Doerfchen' F, or, 1967, Haenchen, E.; bud ovoid; flowers open, small, single, borne in clusters; foliage small, leathery; vigorous, bushy, low growth; ['Highlight' × unknown]

'It's A Winner' HT, yb, J & P; bud orange-yellow; flowers yellow with pink and apricot as it opens, large, dbl., high-centered, slight fragrance; foliage medium green, semi-glossy; tall (5-6 ft.) growth; intr. 2000

'It's Lovely Mary' -- See 'Liogift'

'It's Magic' -- See 'Mackalves'

'It's Magic' ('Clecupcake') S, mp, Clements, John; flowers violet pink, golden stamens, 4-5 in., 16 petals, shallow cup, very floriferous, moderate fruity fragrance; recurrent; foliage rich green; upright (4 ft.) growth; intr. 2002

It's Show Time™ -- See 'Morjoybon'

'ITV 50th Anniversary Coronation Street Rose' -- See 'Wekswetrup'

'Ivan Meneve' HT, dp, RvS-Melle; ['Ingrid Bergman' × 'Florex']; intr. 1996

'Ivan Misson' Pol, lp, 1922, Soupert & Notting; flowers small, dbl.; moderate (2 ft.) growth; ['Jeanny Soupert' × 'Katharina Zeimet']

'Ivanhoe' HT, rb, 1928, Easlea; bud pointed; flowers brilliant scarlet to rich crimson, large, dbl., high-centered; foliage glossy; vigorous growth

'Ivany' F, rb, 1985, Staikov, Prof. Dr. V.; flowers orange-yellow, shaded pink on petal edges, aging red, 50 petals, cupped, borne in clusters of 5-30; foliage dark, glossy; vigorous growth; ['Masquerade' × 'Rumba']; intr. 1975

'Ivemax' ('Delta Dawn') HT, my, 1999, Iverson, Halvor; flowers 5 in., full, borne mostly singly, intense fragrance; foliage medium size, medium green, semi-glossy; few prickles; upright, medium (5 ft.) growth; [sport of 'Out of Africa']

'Iver Cottage' HEg, lp, before 1846; flowers pale rose, single, cupped

Ivor™ Min, w, Olesen; intr. 2000

'Ivor Hunter' F, ab, Horner; intr. 2005

'Ivora' -- See 'Intercream'

'Ivor's Rose' -- See 'Beadonald'

'Ivory' ('White Golden Gate') T, w, 1901, Dingee & Conard; flowers ivory-white, large, dbl.; vigorous growth; [sport of 'Golden Gate']

'Ivory Ann' S, w, 1993, Jobson, Daniel J.; flowers creamy white, 3-3½ in., 5 petals, borne in small clusters; foliage large, medium green, glossy; medium, bushy, spreading growth; ['Ivory Fashion' × (('Valerie Jeanne' × Eyepaint®) × Twilight Trail™)]; intr. 1993

'Ivory Beauty' -- See 'Korivo'

'Ivory Buccaneer' HT, w

Ivory Carpet™ -- See 'Wilivory'

'Ivory Castle' -- See 'Guesoverlay'

'Ivory Charm' Cl F, w, 1968, Earing, Elsie A.; bud ovoid; flowers open, large, semi-dbl., intense fragrance; foliage glossy, leathery; vigorous, climbing growth; [sport of 'Ivory Fashion']

'Ivory Drift' S, w, Meilland; flowers cream, ending white , 1.5 in., 20-25 petals, cupped, borne in clusters of 5 - 8; recurrent; foliage small, dark green, semi-glossy; low, spreading growth; ['The Fairy' × seedling]; intr. 2006

'Ivory Fashion' F, w, 1959, Boerner; bud ovoid; flowers ivory-white, well-formed, 4-4½ in., 17 petals, borne in clusters, moderate fragrance; foliage leathery; vigorous, upright growth; PP1688; ['Sonata' × 'Fashion']; intr. 1958

'Ivory Fashion, Climbing' Cl F, w, 1964, Williams, J. Benjamin; bud slender; flowers white, with crimson stamens, 4½-5 in.; PP2409

Ivory Festival™ -- See 'Lavyip'

'Ivory Flush' F, pb, 1996, Bees of Chester; flowers orange centered with pink blended edges, fading to pale pink, large, very dbl.; foliage medium size, light green, dull; some prickles; bushy, medium (26 in.) growth; intr. 1995

'Ivory Grand' -- See 'Poulmount'

'Ivory Palace' -- See 'Morivory'

'Ivory Queen' HT, w, 1954, Fletcher; bud ovoid; flowers ivory-cream, 5-6 in., moderate fragrance; foliage dark, glossy; vigorous, bushy growth; ['Edina' × 'McGredy's Ivory']; intr. 1954

'Ivory Queen' Gr, w, Delforge; flowers ivory; [sport of Queen Elizabeth®]; intr. 1965

'Ivory Quill' MinFl, w, Williams, J.B.; flowers ivory white, quilled, dbl.; intr. 2003

'Ivory Silk' Min, w, Benardella, Frank; flowers pure white, large, dbl., hybrid tea; growth medium; intr. 2001

'Ivory Splendor' Min, w, 1991, Gruenbauer, Richard; bud rounded; flowers white, pale yellow center, white reverse, aging white, large, 35 petals, high-centered, slight fruity fragrance; foliage medium size, medium green, matte; upright, tall growth; ['Rise 'n' Shine' × seedling]; intr. 1993

'Ivory Tip Top' F, lp, 1977, Fryers Nursery, Ltd.; flowers ivory-pink, 2-2½ in., semi-dbl., slight fragrance; low, compact, bushy growth; [sport of 'Tip Top']; intr. 1976

'Ivory Tower' HT, w, 1977, Kordes, R.; bud very long, pointed; flowers ivory-white, shaded light pink and light yellow, 5½ in., 35 petals, high-centered, moderate fragrance; upright, bushy growth; PP4658; ['Colour Wonder' × King's Ransom®]; intr. 1978

'Ivory Triumph' F, w, 1963, Von Abrams; bud pointed; flowers ivory, 3-4 in., 12 petals, open, borne in clusters; foliage leathery, light green; upright, compact growth; ['Goldilocks' × seedling]; intr. 1961

'Ivory Warrior' -- See 'Ripwar'

'Ivresse' HT, rb, 1958, Combe; flowers clear red, reverse silvery, large; vigorous growth; ['Peace' × 'Spectacular']

'Ivy Alice' HWich, op, 1927, Letts; flowers soft pink to blush-salmon, splashed carmine when fading, dbl., cupped, borne in very large clusters; foliage glossy, light; very vigorous, climbing (6 ft.) growth; [sport of 'Excelsa']

'Ivy Evans' HT, mr, 1926, Evans; flowers light cerise; [('George C. Waud' × unknown) × 'Gen. MacArthur']

'Ivy May' HT, pb, 1925, Beckwith; bud pointed; flowers rose-pink, base and edges amber, dbl.; foliage dark; vigorous growth; [sport of 'Mme Butterfly']

'Iwara' (R. × iwara, R. yesoensis) HMult, w; flowers single, borne in clusters of 5-15; [R. multiflora × R. rugosa]; described by Siebold in 1832

'Izayoi' HT, pb, Tanaka; intr. 1963

'Izu no Odoriko' -- See 'Meidresia'

'Izumi' HT, m, 1999, Ohkawara, Kiyoshi; flowers lavender blended pale pink, 5-5½ in., 40 petals, high-centered; foliage bronze dark green; growth to 5 ft.; [('Intermezzo' × 'Soir d'Automne') × ('Intermesso' × 'Soir d'Automne')]; intr. 1997

'Izy' HT, pb, 1997, Ballin, Don & Paula; flowers large, white stripes frequently appear, 5-6 in., 26-50 petals, borne mostly singly; foliage long, narrow, medium size, medium green semi-glossy; some prickles; upright, medium to tall growth; [sport of 'Sheer Bliss']

— J —

'J. A. Escarpit' HP, m, 1883, Bernède; flowers velvety purple, edged with cherry reflections, large, very full

'J. A. Gomis' HT, rb, 1933, Camprubi, C.; flowers crimson-red and yellow, medium, dbl., cupped; foliage dark, glossy; upright growth; ['Sensation' × 'Souv. de Claudius Pernet']

'J. B. Clark' HP, dr, 1905, Dickson, H.; flowers deep scarlet, shaded blackish crimson, large, 25 petals, high-centered; very prickly; vigorous (8-10 ft.), bushy, almost climbing growth; ['Lord Bacon' × 'Gruss an Teplitz']

'J. B. Clark, Climbing' Cl HT, mr, 1939, Vogel, M.; flowers carmine-red, very large, dbl.

'J. B. M. Camm' B, lp, 1900, Paul, G.; flowers light salmon pink, large, very dbl., moderate fragrance; ['Mme Gabriel Luizet' × 'Mrs. Paul']

'J. B. Meilland' HT, ob, 1941, Meilland, F.; flowers orange, reverse golden yellow, large, very dbl.; very vigorous growth; ['Mme Joseph Perraud' × ('Charles P. Kilham' × 'Margaret McGredy')]

'J. B. Varonne' ('J. B. Waronne') T, dp, 1889, Guillot & fils; bud long; flowers deep pink, sometimes with a coppery yellow center, large, full

'J. B. Waronne' -- See 'J. B. Varonne'

'J. Bienfait' -- See 'Mr J. Bienfait'

'J. C. Hooper' -- See 'Hooray'

'J. C. Thornton' HT, mr, 1926, Bees; bud pointed; flowers glowing crimson-scarlet, dbl.; foliage light olive-green, glossy, leathery; vigorous, branching growth; ['Kitchener of Khartoum' × 'Red-Letter Day']

'J. F. Bailey' HT, Williams, A.; ['Frau Karl Druschki' × unknown]

'J. F. Barry' HT, my, 1912, Piper; flowers light daffodil-yellow; [sport of 'Arthur R. Goodwin']

'J. F. Müller' F, dr, 1929, Muller, J.F.; flowers large; foliage dark; bushy, dwarf growth; [sport of 'Rodhatte']

'J. F. Quadra' -- See 'Quadra'

'J. G. Glassford' HT, dr, 1921, Dickson, H.; bud pointed; flowers deep crimson, very large, high-centered; very vigorous, branching growth

'J. G. Mendel' S, or, Urban, J.

'J. G. Sandberg' -- See 'Jonkheer G. Sandberg'

'J. H. Bruce' HT, mr, 1937, Bees; flowers crimson-scarlet, over large, dbl., high-centered; foliage glossy; vigorous, bushy growth; ['H.V. Machin' × 'Marion Horton']

'J. H. Pemberton' HT, mr, 1931, Bentall;

flowers scarlet, moderate damask fragrance; vigorous growth

'J. H. Pierneef' ('Jacob H. Pierneef') F, or, Williams, J. Benjamin; flowers orange-red with white stripes and spots, semi-dbl., borne in clusters, no fragrance; upright, vigorous, tall growth; intr. 1994

'J. H. Van Heyst' HT, yb, 1936, Leenders, M.; bud pointed; flowers yellowish-flesh, reverse pink; vigorous growth; ['Comtesse Vandal' × 'Edith Nellie Perkins']

'J. J. Audubon' S, mr, 2005, Shoup, George Michael; flowers large, resembling a red Mutabilis, 3 in., single, borne mostly solitary, slight fragrance; remontant; foliage medium size, dark green, semi-glossy; prickles moderate; growth bushy, tall (6 ft.); hedging; [('Carefree Beauty' × 'Basye's Blueberry') × Altissimo®]; intr. 1998

'J. K. B. Roos' HT, m, 1933, Leenders, M.; bud pointed; flowers pale reddish-lilac, shaded salmon-flesh, large, dbl.; very vigorous growth

'J. K. Tyl' LCl, mp, 1936, Brada, Dr.; flowers bright pink, cactus form; very free bloom; vigorous growth

'J. M. López Picó, Climbing' Cl HT, dr, 1954, Camprubi, C.

'J. M. López Picó' HT, dr, 1947, Camprubi, C.; bud long, pointed; flowers crimson, large, dbl., high-centered; upright growth; ['Editor McFarland' × 'Comtesse Vandal']

J. Michael™ -- See 'Kinmike'

'J. Michel' HT, dy, 1930, Felberg-Leclerc; flowers dark golden yellow, large, dbl.; foliage leathery; vigorous growth; RULED EXTINCT 1/87; [seedling × 'The Queen Alexandra Rose']

'J. N. Hart' HT, dp, 1924, Chaplin Bros.; flowers rose-pink, dbl.; ['George Dickson' × 'Edith Cavell']

'J. Otto Thilow' HT, mp, 1927, Verschuren; bud pointed, well shaped; flowers rich glowing rose-pink, large, dbl., high-centered; very vigorous growth; ['Hadley' × 'Souv. de H.A. Verschuren']

'J. Otto Thilow, Climbing' Cl HT, mp, 1933, Howard Rose Co.

'J. P. Connell' S, my, 1987, Svedja, Felicitas; flowers pale, medium yellow at inner petals, yellow-white on upper petals, dbl., high-centered, borne 1-8 per cluster, intense tea fragrance; repeat bloom; foliage abundant, dark yellow-green, wide ovate, doubly serrated; no prickles; bushy, winter hardy growth; ['Arthur Bell' × 'Von Scharnhorst']; intr. 1986

'J. R. Byfield' Cl HT, dr, 1941, Clark, A.; flowers deep red flowers with petals edged purple, slight fragrance; stems strong and long; [sport of a 'Sensation' seedling]

'J. S. Baar' HT, dr, 1934, Mikes Böhm, J.; flowers pure dark carmine-red, dbl.; foliage leathery; long, strong stems; vigorous, bushy growth

'J. S. Fay' HP, rb, 1905, Walsh; flowers dark crimson tipped scarlet, dbl.; vigorous growth; ['Prince Camille de Rohan' × 'Souv. de Pierre Notting']

'J. W. Fargo' (variety of *R. arkansana*), mp; flowers wild-rose-pink, borne in clusters; non-recurrent; well branched (20 in.) growth

'Jacable' (Spice Twice™) HT, ob, 1998, Zary, Dr. Keith W.; bud long, pointed ovoid; flowers orange, 5-6 in., 30-35 petals, high-centered, borne mostly singly, moderate ginger fragrance; recurrent; foliage medium size, dark green, semi-glossy; prickles moderate, hooked downward; stems strong, medium; upright, tall (5 ft.) growth; PP8628; ['Spirit of Glasnost' × 'Kardinal']; intr. 1997

'Jacaby' HT, or, 1985, Warriner, William A.; flowers large, slight fragrance; foliage large, medium green; upright, bushy growth; PP4649; ['South Seas' × 'Tonight']; intr. 1979

'Jacacien' F, lp, Jackson & Perkins; intr. 2007

'Jacade' ('Home's Choice', 'Olympic Dream') HT, pb, 1984, J&P; flowers large, 35 petals; foliage large, dark, semi-glossy; upright growth; PP5842; [seedling × seedling]

'Jacadnof' (Radiant Perfume™) Gr, my, 2005, Zary, Keith W.; flowers , 25-30 petals, borne mostly solitary, intense lemony fragrance; foliage large, dark green, glossy; prickles 12 mm., hooked downward, greyed-orange, moderate; upright (5-6 ft.), branching, very vigorous growth; PP14915; [Henry Fonda™ × seedling]; intr. 2004

'Jacadyna' (High Society™) LCl, dp, 2005, Zary, Keith W.; flowers full, borne in large clusters, intense fragrance; foliage large, dark green, glossy; prickles 7-9 mm., hooked downward, greyed-orange, moderate; growth spreading, vigorous, tall (4 m.); climber; PP16187; [Dynamite™ × 'America']; intr. 2004

'Jacaebi' HT, dp, J&P; intr. 1993

'Jacaford' S

'Jacage' HT, yb, 1985, Warriner, William A.; flowers medium, 35 petals, slight fragrance; foliage medium size, dark, leathery; upright, bushy growth; PP4537; [seedling × 'Spellbinder']; intr. 1981

'Jacaim' ('Acclaim') HT, ob, 1982, Warriner, William A.; flowers orange, large, 34 petals; foliage medium green, semi-glossy; upright, bushy growth; PP5638; ['Sunfire' × 'Spellbinder']; intr. 1986

'Jacair' (Watermelon Ice™) S, dp, 1998, Zary, Dr. Keith W.; flowers dark lavender pink, lighter reverse, 1½ in., single, borne in large clusters, slight fragrance; repeats quickly; foliage small, dark green, semi-glossy; prickles moderate, straight; spreading, bushy, low (1½ ft.) growth; PP10229; ['The Fairy' × seedling]; intr. 1997

Jacakor® ('Jakaranda', Jacaranda®) HT, mp, 1985, Kordes, W.; bud long, pointed ovoid; flowers mauve-pink, lighter in center and reverse, darker on edges, large, 35 petals, high-centered , borne mostly singly, intense fragrance; recurrent; foliage large, medium green, glossy; prickles ordinary, hooked downward,; upright growth; PP6316; [('Mercedes' × 'Emily Post') × seedling]

'Jacal' HT, or, 1985, Warriner, William A.; flowers large, 35 petals, no fragrance; foliage medium size, dark, semi-glossy; upright growth; PP5341; ['Spellbinder' × 'Futura']; intr. 1983

'Jacale' ('Arc de Triomphe', 'Summer Fashion') F, yb, 1986, Warriner, William A.; bud pointed ovoid; flowers light yellow edged pink, pink spreading with age, 5 in., 20-30 petals, high-centered, borne singly and in flat clusters, moderate fragrance; recurrent; foliage large, medium green, semi-glossy; prickles numerous, long, hooked downward; stems short, strong; vigorous, upright (under 3 ft.) growth; PP5860; ['Precilla' × Bridal Pink™]; intr. 1985

'Jacalp' HT, or, 1985, Warriner, William A.; flowers brick red, large, 50 petals, slight fragrance; foliage large, dark, leathery; upright growth; PP4541; [seedling × Medallion®]; intr. 1980

'Jacameer' Warriner, W. A., Warriner, W. A.

'Jacamite' LCl, ob, Zary, Keith; bud pointed ovoid; intr. 2004

'Jacamque' (Amber Waves™) F, ab, 1999, Zary, Dr. Keith W.; bud copper/gold, pointed, ovoid; flowers amber yellow, reverse yellow/apricot, opens flat, 3½-4 in., full, cupped, borne singly and in small clusters, moderate fruity fragrance; foliage medium size, dark green, glossy; prickles moderate; upright, bushy, medium (3½ ft.) growth; PP11839; [seedling × Amber Queen®]; intr. 2001

'Jacams' ('Sweet Dreams') MinFl, lp; intr. 1995

'Jacanase' ('Michaela') Min, mp, J&P; intr. 2007

'Jacange' ('John-Paul II') HT, ob, 1985, J&P; bud blunt top; flowers dbl., 35-40 petals, borne mostly singly, no fragrance; recurrent; foliage medium size, dark, semi-glossy, resistant to powdery mildew; prickles numerous, hooked downward; upright growth; PP5639; ['Apricot Parfait' × 'Futura']; intr. 1984

'Jacangel' ('Spellcaster') Gr, m, 1991, Warriner, William A.; bud short, pointed ovoid; flowers lavender and deep mauve, heavy substance, 4 in., 25-30 petals, high-centered, borne mostly singly or in small clusters, moderate lemon fragrance; recurrent; foliage large, dark green, glossy; prickles some, medium, hooked downward; stems strong, 12 - 14 in.; tall (145-160 cm.), upright, spreading, very full, uniform growth; PP8568; [seedling × 'Angel Face']; intr. 1992

'Jacant' ('Topaz') F, r, 1985, Warriner, William A.; flowers tan, medium, 35 petals; foliage medium size, medium green, semi-glossy; upright growth; [seedling × 'Intrigue']; intr. 1986

'Jacanth' HT, mr, 1974, Warriner, William A.; bud ovoid, pointed

'Jacap' ('Apollo Tribute') F, ob, Christensen, Jack E.; intr. 1992

'Jacapri' ('Lucille Ball') HT, ab, 1991, Christensen, Jack E.; flowers apricot, amber blend, good petal substance, 2¾ in., full, borne mostly singly, moderate fragrance; foliage medium size, medium green, semi-glossy; some prickles; tall (145-160 cm.), upright, bushy growth; ['Hello Dolly' × seedling]; intr. 1993

'Jacapshr' S, ab; intr. 2003

'Jacara' ('Spirit of Glasnost') HT, pb, 1991, Warriner, William A.; flowers coral pink and ivory blend, large, full, borne mostly singly, moderate fragrance; foliage medium size, dark green, semi-glossy; upright, spreading growth; [seedling × seedling]; intr. 1991

Jacaranda® -- See 'Jacakor'

'Jacarber' F, my, J&P; intr. 2006

'Jacarch' ('Lace Cascade') LCl, w, 1992, Warriner, William A.; bud pointed, ovoid; flowers icy white, floriferous, 3-3½ in., full, borne in small and large clusters, moderate sweet fragrance; foliage large, medium green to dark green, semi-glossy; some prickles; growth tall (150-160 cm.), upright, spreading; PP8689; ['Iceberg' × 'Prairie Fire']

'Jacare' ('Class Act', 'First Class', 'White Magic') F, w, 1988, Warriner, William A.; bud long, pointed ovoid; flowers clear white, 3-4 in., 15-20 petals, high-centered, opening flat, borne in sprays of 3-6, slight fruity fragrance; recurrent; foliage medium size, dark green, semi-glossy; prickles moderate, long, narrow; stems strong, short; upright, bushy, medium growth; hips bright orange; PP6515; ['Sun Flare' × seedling]

'Jacared' HT, dr, 1978, Warriner, William A.; bud pointed, ovoid; intr. 1974

'Jacaret' ('Cabaret') Min, dr, 1983, Warriner, William A.; bud small; flowers small, 35 petals; foliage small, medium green, semi-glossy; upright, bushy growth; PP5576; [('Fire Princess' × 'Mary DeVor') × (seedling × 'Caliente')]

'Jacarina' ('Amorous') HT, lp, 1986, Warriner, William A.; flowers shell pink, 30 petals, high-centered, borne singly, slight fruity fragrance; foliage large, medium green, glossy; upright, tall growth; ['White Masterpiece' × Marina®]

'Jacarol' HT, yb, J & P; bud orange-yellow; intr. 2000

'Jacarque' ('Pam Golding', Honey Perfume™) F, ab, 2005, Zary, Keith W.; bud pointed, ovoid; flowers apricot-yellow, 10-12 cm., 30 petals, borne in large clusters, intense spicy fragrance; quick rebloom; foliage large, dark green, glossy; prickles 9-11 mm., straight, greyed-yellow, moderate; growth upright, branching, vigorous, compact, medium (110 cm.); ['AROfres' × Amber Queen®]; intr. 2004

'Jacary' ('Firstar', 'Golden Anniversary', 'Home's Pride', 'Olympic Spirit') HT, my, 1983; flowers large, semi-dbl., moderate fragrance; foliage medium size, medium green, glossy; bushy, spreading growth; ['New Day' × 'Oregold']; originally registered as Golden Anniversary

'Jacati' Min, or, Zary, Dr. Keith; intr. 1997

'Jacautel' ('Sara') HT, mp, 1997, J&P

'Jacav' F, w, Warriner, William A.; bud cream color; intr. 1991

'Jacavan' HT, mr, J&P

'Jacave' ('Blue Chip') F, m, 1983, Warriner, William A.; flowers medium, 20 petals; foliage medium size, medium green, semi-glossy; bushy, upright growth; PP5684; ['Heirloom' × 'Angel Face']

'Jacbassi' S, mr, J&P; intr. 2006

'Jacbeau' (Grand Prize™) F, ly, 2005, Zary, Keith W.; flowers yellow-white, reverse yellow-white, 4 in., dbl., borne in small clusters, moderate fragrance; foliage large, dark green, glossy; prickles 8-10 mm., hooked downward, greyed orange, moderate; upright, branching and vigorous, medium (100 cm.) growth; PP14754; ['Sunflare' × 'Impatient']; intr. 2003

'Jacbed' ('Red Rascal') S, mr, 1986, Warriner, William A.; bud short, pointed ovoid; flowers bright red, 2 in., 30 petals, cupped, borne in sprays of 2-5, self cleaning, slight fragrance; recurrent; foliage small, medium green, semi-glossy; prickles medium, red to brown, hooked downward; stems strong, short; tall (3-4 ft.), vigorous, bushy growth; PP6693; [seedling × seedling]

'Jacbelgo' ('100 Idées Jardin', 'Continued Friendship', Golden Zest™) S, my, 2005, Zary, Keith W.; flowers golden yellow, reverse golden yellow, 10 cm., very full, borne in small clusters, intense fragrance; foliage large, dark green, glossy; prickles 9-11 mm., hooked downward, greyed-orange, moderate; growth upright, branching, medium (120-130 cm.); PP16707; [Mirabella™ × 'Golden Celebration']

'Jacber' ('Ice Angel') Min, w, Zary, Dr. Keith W.; intr. 1997

'Jacbico' HT, pb, J&P; intr. 1998

'Jacbip' ('Wedding Pink') HT, lp, 1990, Nakashima, Tosh; bud ovoid; flowers light pink, reverse slightly paler pink, large, very dbl., high-centered, urn-shaped; foliage medium size, dark green, matte; prickles long, very narrow, reddish-brown; upright, tall growth; [sport of 'Bridal White']; intr. 1990

'Jacbitou' ('Millennium', 'Success Story', 'Weight Watcher Success') HT, yb, 1999, Zary, Dr. Keith W.; bud long, pointed ovoid; flowers light creamy yellow edged pink, 4½-5 in., 35 petals, high-centered, borne mostly singly, intense sweet and spicy fragrance; recurrent; foliage medium size, dark green, semi-glossy; prickles few, medium, hooked downward, tan; stems medium, strong; upright, spreading, tall (4-4½ ft.) growth; PP11838; [Henry Fonda™ × French Perfume™]; intr. 1999

'Jacblar' ('Evita Bezuidenhout') HT, m, J&P; intr. 1995

'Jacblem' HT, my, 1981, Warriner, William A.

'Jacblupo' HT, m, J&P; intr. 2005

'Jacboupu' (Lovestruck™) F, pb, 2007, Zary, Keith W.; flowers pink white handpaint, reverse light pink, 4 in., dbl., blooms borne in small clusters; foliage medium size, dark green, glossy; prickles 6-8 mm., hooked downward, greyed-orange, moderate; growth compact, medium (3½ ft.); [Sorbet Bouquet™ × 'Pure Poetry']; intr. 2008

'Jacbow' (Kaleidoscope™) S, m, 1998, Walden, John K.; flowers tan mauve blend, reverse yellow mauve blend, 3 in., full, borne in large clusters, slight fruity fragrance; foliage dark green, glossy; numerous prickles; spreading, bushy, 3½ ft. growth; hedging; PP11690; [Pink Pollyanna™ × Rainbow's End™]; intr. 1999

'Jacboy' ('Tango') HT, ob; intr. 1992

'Jacbrant' ('Sweet Valentine') Gr, mp, 2000, Zary, Keith; bud long, pointed ovoid; flowers warm pink, 5 in., 30-35 petals, high-cent., then flattens, borne singly and in large, open clusters, moderate spicy peach fragrance; recurrent; foliage large, dark green, glossy; prickles moderate, medium size, hooked slightly downward; stems strong, 12 - 16 in.; upright, medium (5 ft.) growth; PP12121; [Brandy™ × 'Tournament of Roses']; intr. 2001

'Jacbri' F, mp, 1967, Boerner; bud ovoid, pointed, long

'Jacbub' (Tiny Bubbles™) Min, w, 1990, Warriner, William A.; bud ovoid; flowers ivory, near white, fading to white, medium, dbl., cupped, borne usually singly, no fragrance; foliage medium size, medium green, semi-glossy; prickles straight, slightly angled downward, green-yellow; upright, spreading, medium growth; ['Zorina' × 'Funny Girl']; intr. 1990

'Jacbunch' (Raspberry Punch™) Min, dp, 1998, Zary, Dr. Keith W.; bud long, pointed ovoid; flowers full, 35 petals, high-centered, borne singly and in clusters of three to seven, slight fragrance; foliage medium size, dark green, semi-glossy; prickles moderate, straight; stems strong (6 - 8 in.); compact, upright, moderate (30 in.) growth; PP12050; ['Tournament of Roses' × seedling]; intr. 1999

'Jacbush' (Barbara Bush™) HT, pb, 1991, Warriner, William A.; flowers salmon pink where exposed to sun, lighter pink to ivory white where unexposed, 5 in., 25-30 petals, high-centered, borne mostly singly, moderate damask fragrance;

foliage medium size, medium green, glossy; tall, upright, spreading growth; PP7542; [Pristine® × 'Antigua']; intr. 1991

'Jacbute' ('Abracadabra') HT, pb, 1991, Warriner, William A.; bud pointed, ovoid, deep pink/yellow; flowers purple pink, tan and yellow, 4½-5 in., full, high-centered, borne mostly singly, intense fragrance; foliage large, dark green, semi-glossy; some prickles; medium (90-120 cm.), upright, bushy growth; PP8590; ['White Masterpiece' × 'Tribute']; intr. 1993

'Jaccart' ('Cartwheel') Min, rb, 1989, Warriner, William A.; bud ovoid; flowers red and white picotee, small, 20 petals, cupped, borne singly; foliage small, medium green, matte; prickles hooked, small, tan; low, bushy growth; PP7508; ['Libby' × seedling]; intr. 1990

'Jaccasp' ('Happy Trails') Min, pb, 1992, Warriner, William A. & Zary, Keith W.; flowers pink with cream center, medium, very dbl., borne in small clusters, no fragrance; foliage small, medium to dark green, glossy; some prickles; low (20-30 cm.), groundcover, spreading 60-90 cm.across. growth; PP8719; [Immensee® × 'Roller Coaster']; intr. 1993

'Jacchamp' HT, w, Zary, Keith; intr. 1999

'Jacchar' ('Little Diane') Min, lp, J&P; intr. 1994

'Jacchari' (Candy Mountain™) S, dp, 1998, Walden, John K.; flowers deep pink, 1½-2 in., single, borne in large clusters; foliage small, medium green, dull; prickles moderate; bushy, arching, low (2 ft.) growth; PP10616; ['Sweet Chariot' × seedling]; intr. 1997

'Jacchry' ('Breathless') HT, dp, 1993, Warriner, William A.; three sepals moderately bearded; flowers deep pink, 3-3½ in., dbl., borne mostly singly, moderate fragrance; foliage large, medium green, purple-red when young, semi-glossy; some prickles; tall (150 cm.), upright growth; PP8595; [seedling × 'Chrysler Imperial']; intr. 1993

'Jaccinqo' (Candelabra™) Gr, ob, 1998, Zary, Dr. Keith W.; bud long, pointed; flowers coral-orange, 4 in., 20-25 petals, borne in small clusters, slight tea fragrance; foliage medium size, dark green, glossy; prickles moderate; bushy, medium tall growth; PP11016; ['Tournament of Roses' × seedling]; intr. 1999

'Jacclam' LCl, op, Warriner, William A.; bud ovoid, pointed; intr. 1976

'Jacclip' ('Bunny Hop') Cl Min, mp, 1993, Zary, Dr. Keith W.; flowers medium, dbl., borne in large clusters, slight fragrance; foliage small, dark green, semi-glossy; some prickles; upright (180 cm.), spreading, climbing growth; [Pink Pollyanna™ × seedling]; intr. 1995

'Jacclist' Cl HT, pb, 1974, Reasoner; intr. 1976

'Jacclop' LCl, dr, 1974, Warriner, William A.; bud ovoid; intr. 1975

'Jacco' HT, w, Warriner, William A.; bud long; intr. 1976

'Jaccoeur' ('Gardens of the World') HT, pb, 1993, Christensen, Jack E.; bud small, ovoid; flowers magenta pink and cream blend, 3-3½ in., full, borne mostly singly, slight fragrance; foliage medium size, medium green, matte; few prickles; medium (120 cm.), upright growth; ['Dame de Coeur' × Sunbright®]; intr. 1991

'Jaccofl' (Brass Band™) F, ab, 1993, Christensen, Jack E.; flowers melon orange and yellow bicolor, 3-3½ in., 30-35 petals, borne in small clusters, slight fruity fragrance; foliage large, dark green, semi-glossy; some prickles; medium (100 cm.), upright, bushy growth; PP9171; [Gold Badge™ × seedling]; intr. 1994

'Jaccogel' ('Coral Sea', Orange Passion™) HT, ob, 1999, Zary, Dr. Keith W.; flowers coral-orange, reverse lighter, 4½-5 in., full, borne mostly singly; foliage large, dark green; prickles moderate; upright growth; PP9330; ['Anne Morrow Lindbergh' × 'Angelique']; intr. 1999

'Jaccoh' ('Inspiration') HT, op; apparently never introduced into commerce, per J&P

'Jaccol' ('Colette') HT, mp, 1991, Warriner, William A. & Zary, Keith W.; bud ovoid, pointed; flowers medium soft pink, aging slightly paler, large, 25-30 petals, urn-shaped, borne usually singly, slight damask fragrance; foliage large, dark green, semi-glossy; upright, bushy, tall growth; [Lorena® × seedling]; intr. 1990

'Jaccolap' (Catalina™) Gr, ab, 2007, Zary, Keith W.; flowers apricot-pink, 4½ in., full, blooms borne in small clusters; foliage medium size, dark green, glossy; prickles 8-10 mm., straight, greyed-orange; growth upright, tall (5 ft.); ['Color Magic' × seedling]; intr. 2008

'Jaccor' ('Glory Days') HT, mp, 1991, Warriner, William A.; flowers coral pink, large, full, moderate fragrance; foliage medium size, medium green, semi-glossy; growth tall, upright, bushy; PP7946; [seedling × 'Showstopper']; intr. 1991

'Jaccream' ('Angela') HT, yb, J&P

'Jacdal' ('Great Expectations') F, mp, 1993, J&P

'Jacdandy' (Caramel Kisses™) Min, m, 2007, Zary, Keith W.; flowers tan lavender blend, 1½-2 in., dbl., borne in small clusters; foliage small, dark green, glossy; prickles 4-6 mm., straight, greyed-orange, few; growth compact, medium (32-40 in.); ['Kaleidoscope' × 'Chipmunk']; intr. 2008

'Jacdash' ('Rose of Wagga Wagga', 'Sun Goddess') HT, dy, 1993, Warriner, William A.; bud long, pointed ovoid; three moderately bearded sepals; flowers bright yellow, 3 in., 20-25 petals, high-centered, flattens, borne mostly singly, moderate fragrance; recurrent; foliage medium size, dark green, matte; prickles some, medium, straight to hooked slightly downward; stems long; tall, upright, spreading growth; PP7659; [Sunbright® × seedling]; intr. 1993

'Jacdaz' ('Chorus Line') S, dr, 1992, Zary, Keith & Warriner, William; flowers red, cream base, 3-3½ in., 16-20 petals, borne in small clusters; foliage large, dark green, semi-glossy; some prickles; medium (120-135 cm.), upright, bushy, very vigorous growth; ['Razzle Dazzle' × seedling]

'Jacdebu' ('Paul Gauguin') HT, m, J&P; intr. 1992

'Jacdeep' ('Kiko') HT, lp, J&P; intr. 1994

'Jacdeli' ('Paul Cezanne') HT, yb, J&P; intr. 1992

'Jacder' HT, dr, 1974, Warriner, William A.; bud ovoid to globular

'Jacdesa' (Claude Monet®) HT, rb, J&P; intr. 1992

'Jacdew' ('Impatient') F, or, 1982, Warriner, William A.; flowers medium, orange-red, 4 in., 20-25 petals, borne in large clusters, slight fragrance; foliage medium size, light green, glossy; upright, bushy growth; PP5122; ['America' × seedling]; intr. 1984

'Jacdis' ('Fragrant Memory') HT, mp, 1974, Warriner, William A.

'Jacdor' ('Señorita') F, rb, 1991, Warriner, William A.; flowers orange-red to red on top of petal with a yellow petal base and yellow-tan reverse, medium, full, borne in large clusters, slight fragrance; foliage medium size, dark green, semi-glossy; numerous prickles; upright (75 cm.), bushy growth; [seedling × 'Matador']; intr. 1992

'Jacdouce' (Wildfire™) HT, ob, 2005, Zary, Keith W.; bud long, pointed ovoid; flowers strong orange, 9 cm., 35-40 petals, high-centered, quills, borne mostly solitary, very slight fragrance; recurrent; foliage dark green, glossy; prickles numerous, 5 mm., hooked slightly downward, brown; stems strong; upright, angular branching, vigorous (180 cm.) growth; PP16186; [seedling × Elina®]

'Jacdrama' HT, rb, Zary, Keith; intr. 2008

'Jacdreco' (Greetings™) S, m, 2005, Keith W. Zary; flowers red-purple with white reverse and yellow base, 2 in., semi-dbl., borne in large clusters; foliage small, dark green, glossy; prickles 6-7 mm., hooked downward, greyed orange, moderate; upright, branching, medium (4 ft.) growth; [Lavender Dream® × 'Roller Coaster']; intr. 1999

'Jacdrift' ('Blizzard') Min, w, 1991, Warriner, William A.; bud pointed; flowers medium, full, no fragrance; foliage small, dark green, glossy; low, spreading, compact growth; ['Petticoat' × 'Orange Honey']

'Jacdrive' ('Red Delicious') S, mr, J&P;

intr. 1998

'Jacdulav' HT, m, Zary; intr. 1999

'Jacduse' HT, my, Zary, Keith; intr. 2000

'Jacecond' (Timeless™) HT, dp, 1998, Zary, Dr. Keith W.; bud long, pointed ovoid; flowers red to deep pink, deep pink reverse, 4½ in., 25-30 petals, high-centered, borne singly and in small clusters, slight fragrance; recurrent; foliage medium size, dark green, semi-glossy, leathery; prickles numerous, medium length, hooked downward; stems medium; upright, bushy growth; PP11369; ['Spirit of Glasnost' × 'Kardinal']; intr. 1997

'Jaced' ('Home's Beauty', 'Olympic Glory') HT, dr, 1984, J&P; flowers medium, 35 petals; foliage large, medium green, glossy; upright growth; [seedling × seedling]

'Jaceibre' (Lavender Lace™) F, m, 2005, Zary, Keith W.; flowers light lavender, reverse light lavender, 7-9 cm., full, borne in small clusters, moderate fragrance; foliage large, dark green, glossy; prickles 9-10 mm., straight, greyed-red, few; growth upright, vigorous, medium (80 cm.); PP14760; [seedling × 'Herbie']; intr. 2004

'Jacel' ('Graceland') HT, my, 1988, Warriner, William A.; flowers medium yellow, aging lighter at margins, loose, medium, 30-35 petals, cupped, borne singly, no fragrance; foliage medium size, dark green, matte, smooth; prickles medium, reddish-green; upright growth; PP6069; ['New Day' × seedling]; intr. 1989

'Jaceleco' ('Touch of Coral', Sheer Magic™) HT, ob, 2007, Zary, Keith W.; flowers coral-red and cream blend, reverse coral-orange and cream blend, 4-4½ in., full, blooms borne mostly solitary; foliage medium size, dark green, glossy; prickles 8-10 mm., hooked downward, greyed-orange, moderate; growth upright, medium (5 ft.); PPAF; [Sheer Elegance™ × 'Color Magic']

'Jacelvet' HT, mr, J&Pdouble; intr. 2007

'Jacemu' ('Perfume Pleasure') HT, pb, J&P

'Jacenram' (Sweet Nothings™) Min, m, 2001, Zary, Keith; bud short, pointed, ovoid; flowers deep lavender, 1½-2 in., 20-25 petals, cupped, borne in large clusters, moderate antique rose fragrance; free-flowering; foliage small, light green, glossy; prickles moderate, medium size, hooked downward; stems strong; vigorous, compact (2½ ft.) growth; garden decorative; hips very few; PP12995; ['La Marne' × 'lavender miniature seedling']; intr. 2002

'Jacepirt' (Cabana™) HT, pb, 2001, Zary, Keith; buds long, pointed, ovoid; flowers rose pink with light yellow stripes., 4½ in., 25-30 petals, borne mostly solitary, slight spicy fragrance; foliage medium size, dark green, glossy; prickles moderate; growth upright, tall (5 ft.); garden decorative; PP13089; ['pink HT seedling'

× 'striped HT seedling']; intr. 2002

'Jacergma' ('Habitat for Humanity', Passionate™) HT, mr, 2001, Zary, Keith; bud pointed, ovoid; flowers bright red, ruffled, 5 in., 25-30 petals, high-centered, borne mostly solitary, slight light, sweet fragrance; recurrent; foliage medium size, dark green, glossy; prickles moderate; growth upright, tall (5 ft.); garden decorative; PP13332; ['Poulman' × 'hybrid tea seedling']; intr. 2002

'Jacern' ('Northern Gold', 'Radiant Gold') HT, my, 1984, J&P; flowers large, 35 petals; foliage large, dark, glossy; upright growth; ['Precilla' × 'Sunshine']

'Jacess' ('Moonstruck') F, w, J&P; intr. 1997

'Jacetima' (Stairway to Heaven™) Cl F, mr, 2002, Zary, Keith; bud pointed, ovoid; flowers ruffled, 3½-4 in., 25-35 petals, high-centered, borne in small clusters, slight light, sweet fragrance; recurrent; foliage medium size, dark green, glossy; prickles moderate; stems strong, medium; growth upright, spreading, tall (10-12 ft.); hips pear-shaped, yellow-green; PP14333; [Dynamite™ × Dream Weaver™]; intr. 2002

'Jacette' ('Regatta') HT, w, 1986, Warriner, William A.; flowers large, 48 petals, high-centered, borne singly; foliage medium size, medium green, matte; prickles medium red to brown, hooked downward; medium, upright growth; no fruit; PP5896; ['Bernadette' × 'Coquette']

'Jaceve' ('Venus') F, lp; intr. 1997

'Jacextra' F, lp, Zary; intr. 2001

'Jacezz' (Crimson Lace™) F, dr, 1998, Zary, Dr. Keith W.; flowers dark red, old-fashioned, 3-3½ in., dbl., borne in small clusters, slight fragrance; foliage medium size, dark green, glossy; prickles moderate; compact, medium growth; PP10284; ['Esprit' × 'Razzle Dazzle']; intr. 1997

'Jacfab' F, pb, 1969, Boerner; bud ovoid

'Jacfabco' ('Blanche de Castille', Pure Perfume™) S, w, 2005, Zary, Keith W.; bud pointed, ovoid; flowers 3-4 in., very full, cupped, borne in small clusters, intense grapefruit fragrance; foliage large, dark green, glossy; prickles 6-8 mm., straight, greyed-orange, moderate; upright, branching, medium (5 ft.) growth; PP16864; [Fabulous!™ × 'Perfume Perfection']; intr. 2005

'Jacfango' HT, w, Zary; buds green; intr. 1999

'Jacfare' ('Grannie's Bonnet') F, pb, J&P; intr. 1996

'Jacfed' HT, mp, 1993, Warriner, William A.; flowers 3-3½ in., very dbl., borne mostly singly; foliage large, medium green, semi-glossy; some prickles; tall (150-180 cm.), upright, spreading growth; ['Grand Masterpiece' × 'First Federal Renaissance']; intr. 1992

'Jacfehon' HT, ab, Zary, K.; intr. 1999

'Jacfiseg' ('Paper Doll') Min, ab, 1992,

Zary, Dr. Keith W.; flowers light apricot with a hint of pale pink fading to light amber, then white, large, dbl., borne in small clusters, no fragrance; foliage small, dark greeen, glossy; some prickles; low (45-60 cm.), upright growth; [Fiddler's Gold™ × Sequoia Gold™]

'Jacflapo' F, ob, J&P; intr. 2006

'Jacflare' ('Miss Daisy') Min, dy, 1991, Warriner, William A.; bud short, pointed ovoid; flowers full, 30-35 petals, high-centered, borne singly and several together; foliage small, dark green, glossy; prickles medium, hooked slightly downward; stems short, strong, vigorous, low, bushy growth; [seedling × 'Sun Flare']; intr. 1991

'Jacfog' ('Charm Bracelet') Min, dy, 1992, Christensen, Jack E.; flowers dark yellow, aging to pink, red blush on tips of outer petals, medium, very dbl., slight fragrance; foliage small, dark green, semi-glossy; some prickles; low (45 cm.), bushy, compact growth; ['Fool's Gold' × seedling]; intr. 1992

'Jacfon' (Heaven™) HT, w, 1993, Warriner, William A.; flowers ivory or cream with a light pink blend, 3-3½ in., full, borne mostly singly, intense fragrance; foliage large, dark green, matte; some prickles; tall (150-160 cm.), upright, bushy growth; PP7943; [Honor™ × 'First Prize']; intr. 1994

'Jacfrain' ('Vulcanic', Mardi Gras™) F, pb, 2007, Zary, Keith W.; flowers pink orange yellow blend, 4 in., dbl., blooms borne in small clusters; foliage medium size, dark green, semi-glossy; prickles 6-8 mm., hooked downward, greyed-orange, moderate; growth upright, medium (4 ft.); ['Arofres' × 'Singin' in the Rain']

'Jacfrens' (Fragrant Keepsake™) HT, yb, 2005, Zary, Keith W.; flowers yellow-pink blend, 12-13 cm., full, borne mostly solitary, intense fragrance; foliage large, dark green, glossy; prickles 8 mm., straight, greyed-green, few; growth upright, vigorous, medium (180 cm.); PP15773; [French Perfume™ × Sunbright®]; intr. 2004

'Jacfrepu' ('Bella Roma', 'Bella'roma') HT, pb, 2004, Zary, Keith W.; flowers yellow pink blend, reverse yellow pink blend, 4-4½ in., 30 -35 petals, borne mostly solitary, intense fragrance; foliage dark green, glossy; prickles 5 mm., hooked slightly downward,; growth upright, 4½ ft.; PP15075; [Sunbright® × 'Kelbian']; intr. 2003

'Jacfries' HT, dy, J&P; intr. 2001

'Jacfruit' ('Camille') HT, lp, 1993, Warriner, William A.; flowers light pink, near white, 3-3½ in., very dbl., borne mostly singly; foliage large, dark green, semi-glossy; some prickles; medium (120 cm.), upright, bushy growth; [Honor™ × 'Fragrant Memory']; intr. 1995

'Jacfun' ('Funny Girl') Min, lp, 1982, Warriner, William A.; flowers small, 20 petals, slight fragrance; foliage small, medium green, matte; upright, bushy growth; PP5249; [Bridal Pink™ × 'Fire Princess']; intr. 1983

'Jacgate' ('Brandenburg Gate', 'Red/White') HT, mr, 1991, Warriner, William A.; flowers red with light reverse, large, full, exhibition, moderate fragrance; foliage large, medium green, matte; tall, upright growth; [seedling × 'Madras']; intr. 1990

'Jacgbru' F, mr, J&P; intr. 2001

'Jacglow' HT, w, 1989, Warriner, William A.; bud ovoid, pointed; intr. 1990

'Jacgodde' (Tahitian Sunset™) HT, ab, 2007, Zary, Keith W.; bud pointed ovoid; flowers apricot yellow with pink blend, 5 in., 25-30 petals, blooms borne mostly solitary, intense licorice fragrance; recurrent; foliage medium size, dark green, semi-glossy; prickles few, 8-10 mm., hooked downward, greyed-orange; upright, tall (5 ft.) growth; [seedling × 'Sun Goddess']; intr. 2006

'Jacgold' ('Golden Emblem') HT, dy, 1982, Warriner, William A.; flowers large, 20 petals; foliage large, medium green, glossy; upright growth; PP5121; [(Bridal Pink™ × 'Dr. A.J. Verhage') × ('Golden Sun' × 'South Seas')]

'Jacgrant' (Fragrant Apricot™) F, ab, 1998, Zary, Dr. Keith W.; bud pointed, oval, apricot blend; flowers light apricot, copper tinted, light coral reverse, 4 in., full, borne in large clusters, slight musk fragrance; foliage large, dark green, glossy; prickles moderate; compact, medium (3 ft.) growth; PP11485; ['Impatient' × Amber Queen®]; intr. 1999

'Jacgray' (Billy Graham™) HT, lp, 1998, Zary, Dr. Keith W.; bud long, pointed; flowers light pink, 5 in., 25-30 petals, high-centered, borne singly, slight sweet fragrance; foliage large, dark green, glossy; prickles moderate; growth upright, tall (5 ft.); PP11049; [Honor™ × 'Color Magic']; intr. 1998

'Jacgrid' HT, dr, Zary; intr. 1997

'Jacgron' (Garden Blanket™) S, dp, 1998, Walden, John K.; flowers dark pink, white at base, lighter reverse, 1-1½ in., single, borne in large clusters, slight fragrance; foliage small. dark green, glossy; prickles moderate; spreading, bushy, tall (3½ ft.) growth; PP11563; ['Magic Carpet' × 'Happy Trails']; intr. 1998

'Jacgum' ('Gumdrop') Min, dr, 1982, Warriner, William A.; bud fat, pointed; flowers 25 petals, borne 3-12 per cluster; foliage small, semi-glossy; spreading growth; PP5152; [('San Fernando' × Bridal Pink™) × ('Fire Princess' × 'Mary DeVor')]; intr. 1981

'Jachal' (Sun Sprinkles™) Min, dy, 1999, Walden, John K.; bud pointed ovoid; flowers stable deep yellow, 2 in., 25-30 petals, high-centered, flattens, borne mostly singly and in small clusters, slight sweet, myrrh fragrance; recurrent; foliage medium size, dark green, glossy; prickles moderate; stems normal, short, hooked downward; compact, low (18-20 in.) growth; PP11883; ['Yellow Jacket' × ('Ferris Wheel' × seedling)]; intr. 2001

'Jachanpa' (Cherries 'n' Cream™) S, m, 2005, Zary, Keith W.; flowers cherry-maroon and white, handpainted, reverse white, 10-12 cm., 20 petals, borne in large clusters, intense fragrance; foliage large, dark green, glossy; prickles 10-12 mm., straight, greyed-orange, moderate; growth upright, very vigorous, tall (180 cm.); PP16705; ['Pure Poetry' × Fabulous!™]; intr. 2005

'Jachart' ('Starburst') F, ly; intr. 1997

'Jacheir' ('Fortune Teller') HT, m, 1993, Warriner, William A. & Zary, Keith W.; flowers deep mauve/purple, 3-3½ in., full, borne mostly singly, intense fragrance; foliage large, dark green, semi-glossy; some prickles; upright, spreading (150-160 cm.) growth; [seedling × 'Heirloom']; intr. 1993

'Jachenfo' -- See 'kykNet Ster'

'Jachill' (Suzy Q™) Min, mp, 1991, Warriner, William A. & Zary, Keith W.; bud ovoid; flowers medium shell pink, deeper color at petal margins, medium, 40-45 petals, cupped, no fragrance; foliage medium size, dark green, glossy; upright, bushy, medium growth; ['Rose Hills Red' × 'Baby Ophelia']; intr. 1991

'Jachoc' ('Suzette van der Merwe') HT, w; intr. 1994

'Jachon' ('Amazon Lady') HT, mp, J&P; intr. 1995

'Jachonew' (Aromatherapy™) HT, mp, 2005, Zary, Keith W.; flowers full, borne mostly solitary, intense fragrance; foliage large, dark green, glossy; prickles 7-9 mm., straight, greyed-yellow, moderate; growth upright, branching and vigorous, medium (150 cm.); [seedling × 'New Zealand']; intr. 2005

'Jachop' ('Haute Pink') HT, dp, 1987, Warriner, William A.; flowers rose pink fading little, loose, medium, 25-30 petals, cupped, borne singly; foliage medium size, medium green, matte; prickles long, narrow, red; upright, tall growth; no fruit; PP6653; [Bridal Pink™ × 'Grand Masterpiece']

'Jachotta' (Bedazzled™) Min, dp, 1999, Walden, John K.; flowers 2-2½ in., full, borne in small clusters, slight fragrance; foliage dark green, semi-glossy; prickles moderate; compact, medium (20-24 in.) growth; PP12352; [sport of 'Hot Tamale']; intr. 2000

'Jachy' ('Old Faithful') HT, dy, 1991, Warriner, William A.; flowers large, full, moderate fragrance; foliage large, dark green, semi-glossy; upright, bushy growth; PP6445; [Sunbright® × Medallion®]; intr. 1991

'Jachyp' ('Unforgettable') HT, mp, 1991, Warriner, William A.; bud long, pointed ovoid; flowers , 30-35 petals, high-centered, borne mostly singly, moderate fragrance; recurrent; foliage large, dark green, semi-glossy; prickles average, hooked downward; stems long, strong; tall (140 cm.), upright, spreading growth; PP6318; [Honor™ × 'American Dawn']; intr. 1992

'Jaciat' ('Patio Jewel', Little Sizzler™) Min, mr, 1989, Warriner, William A.; bud ovoid, pointed; flowers large, 38 petals, cupped, borne usually singly and in sprays of 16-20; foliage large, dark green, semi-glossy; prickles hooked downward, reddish-brown; bushy, medium growth; PP6091; [seedling × 'Funny Girl']; intr. 1989

'Jacibe' ('Caribe') Min, ab, 1982, Warriner, William A.; flowers apricot, semi-dbl.; foliage small, light green, semi-glossy; upright, bushy growth; PP5246; [Bridal Pink™ × 'Fire Princess']; intr. 1983

'Jacibras' ('Catherine McAuley') F, dy, Bear Creek Gardens; intr. 1993

'Jacice' ('Moonlight') HT, w, 1985, Warriner, William A.; flowers medium, 35 petals, no fragrance; foliage large, medium green, matte; upright growth; PP5743; ['Coquette' × seedling]; greenhouse rose; intr. 1984

'Jacideso' (Simply Marvelous!™) F, m, 2001, Zary, Keith; bud pointed, ovoid; flowers lavender with soft pink edges, 3-4 in., 30 petals, high-centered, borne in large clusters, moderate antique rose fragrance; good repeat; foliage medium size, dark green, glossy; prickles moderate; growth upright, medium (3½ ft.); garden decorative; PP13183; [Pink Pollyanna™ × 'Arosedi']; intr. 2002

'Jacient' ('Berkeley', 'Poesie', 'Tournament of Roses') Gr, pb, 1988, Warriner, William A.; bud pointed ovoid; flowers light coral pink, reverse deep pink, aging coral pink, 3-4 in., 25-30 petals, high-centered, borne singly and several together, very slight fragrance; recurrent; foliage large, dark green, semi-glossy, disease-resistant; prickles large; stems strong, medium length; upright, bushy, medium growth; PP6725; ['Impatient' × seedling]; intr. 1989

'Jacif' (Pacifica®) F, ab, 1983, Warriner, William A.; flowers medium, 35 petals; foliage medium size, light green, matte; upright, bushy growth; PP5261; ['Mercedes' × Marina®]

'Jacignat' (Moxie™) S, dp, 2001, Zary, Keith; flowers large, full, borne in large clusters, moderate fragrance; foliage medium size, dark green, glossy; prickles moderate; growth bushy, medium (4 ft.); garden decorative; PP13319; ['La Marne' × Matangi®]; intr. 2002

'Jacimgol' ('Forever Young', 'Queen Wilhelmina') F, dy, Zary, Keith; buds pointed, amber-copper; intr. 2000

'Jacimin' ('Small Miracle') Min, w, 1993, Warriner, William A.; bud plump, short, pointed ovoid; flowers clean white, 1½-2 in., 20-24 petals, classic hybrid tea, borne in clusters, slight fragrance; recurrent; foliage small, dark green, glossy, resistant to powdery mildew; prickles few, short, hooked downward; upright (20-24 in.), bushy growth; PP8850; ['Libby' × 'Sun Flare']; intr. 1993

'Jacimp' Warriner, W. A., Warriner, W. A.

'Jacina' (Wild Dancer™) S, dp, 1998, Walden, John K.; bud short, pointed ovoid; flowers bright magenta-pink, reverse lighter, 1½ in., single, cupped, flattens, borne in large clusters, slight spicy fragrance; recurrent; foliage small, medium green, matte, leathery; prickles moderate, short, hooked downward; stems short; compact, arching, low (2½ × 2.5 ft.) growth; PP10962; ['China Doll' × 'Sweet Chariot']; intr. 1998

'Jacinal' ('Debutante') F, mp, 1985, Warriner, William A.; flowers small, 20 petals; foliage medium size, medium green, matte; bushy growth; PP5729; [Bridal Pink™ × 'Zorina']

'Jacinber' ('Derrich Gardner, Flame of Fantasy', Lovers Lane™, Georges Dubœuf®) HT, mr, 2001, Zary, Keith; bud pointed, ovoid; flowers thick velvety petals, classic hybrid tea form; lighter, silvery reverse., 4½-5 in., 35 petals, borne mostly solitary, slight sweet fragrance; foliage large, dark green, semi-glossy; prickles moderate; stems tall, straight; growth upright, tall (5-6 ft.); garden decorative; PP13317; ['Jacpico' × 'Poulman']; intr. 2002

'Jacink' ('Pink Simplicity', Simplicity™) F, mp, 1979, Warriner, William A.; bud long, pointed; flowers phlox pink, 3-4 in., 14-20 petals, flat, borne several together, very slight fragrance; free-flowering; foliage large, leathery; prickles normal, hooked slightly downward; stems long, strong; bushy, upright growth; PP4089; ['Iceberg' × seedling]; intr. 1979

'Jaciraps' (Hugs 'n' Kisses™) Min, pb, 1999, Walden, John K.; flowers pink, white, reverse near white, 2½ in., dbl., borne in small to large clusters, moderate fragrance; foliage large, dark, grey-green, glossy; prickles moderate; compact, spreading, medium (16-18 in.) growth; PP12113; ['Small Miracle' × seedling]; intr. 1999

'Jacirst' ('Once Touched', Artistry™) HT, op, 1998, Zary, Dr. Keith W.; flowers coral-orange and creamy coral reverse, 4½ in., 30-35 petals, high-centered, borne singly, full, best form and color in heat, slight fragrance; foliage large, dark green, semi glossy; prickles moderate; upright, bushy, tall growth; PP10230; [seedling × seedling]; intr. 1997

'Jacis' ('Poesie') HT, lp, Warriner, William A.; bud ovoid, pointed; intr. 1976

'Jaciv' F, dr, 1973, Warriner, William A.; bud ovoid; intr. 1974

'Jacjel' HT, my, 1978, Warriner, William A.; bud long, pointed ovoid; intr. 1984

'Jacjem' ('Sun Flare', 'Sunflare') F, my, 1982, Warriner, William A.; bud pointed ovoid; flowers 4 in., 20-30 petals, flat, borne singly and 3-12 per cluster, very slight fragrance; recurrent; foliage small, glossy, disease-resistant; prickles numerous, long, pointing downwards, reddish; low, compact (3 ft.) growth; PP5001; ['Sunsprite' × seedling]; intr. 1983

'Jacjingl' (Party Lights™) Min, op, 2007, Zary, Keith W.; flowers coral-orange, reverse cream, 2 in., dbl., blooms borne in small clusters; foliage medium size, dark green, glossy; prickles 6-8 mm., hooked downward, greyed-orange, few; growth upright, medium (12-18 in.); [seedling × Jingle Bells™]; intr. 2006

'Jacjubel' (Mirabella™) F, my, 1994, Zary, Dr. Keith W.; intr. 1994

'Jack Collier' -- See 'Horjack'

'Jack Dayson' -- See 'Korwilma'

'Jack Folly' HT, w, 1978, H. Buss Nurseries; bud ovoid; flowers cream color, opening, 5½ in., 40 petals, cupped; foliage dull, leathery; spreading growth; intr. 1976

'Jack Frost' F, w, 1962, Jelly; bud pointed; flowers white to creamy, sweetheart, medium, 42 petals, high-centered, moderate fragrance; foliage dark; vigorous, upright growth; PP2447; ['Garnette' × seedling]; intr. 1962

'Jack Frost' HT, w, Howard, A. P.; bud medium, conical, high-centered; flowers pure white, large, 25-30 petals, high-centered, borne mostly singly; foliage medium size, medium green; growth upright, branching, tall (5-6 ft.); hips ovoid to pear-shaped, dark green; PP2522; ['Blanche Mallerin' × 'Joseph Hill']

'Jack Horner' Min, mp, 1955, Robinson, T.; flowers bright pink, 50 petals; no prickles; growth to 4-8 in.; ['Margo Koster' × 'Tom Thumb']

'Jack McCandless' HT, rb, 1935, McGredy; bud long, pointed, carmine and yellow; flowers amber-yellow, veined red, dbl., high-centered; foliage small, glossy, dark

'Jack of Hearts' F, 1968, Waterhouse Nursery; flowers cardinal red, trusses, semi-dbl., cupped; free bloom; foliage dark, glossy; low, bushy growth

'Jack O'Lantern' Gr, yb, 1960, Swim & Weeks; bud ovoid; flowers gold and yellow blend, 4½ in., 25 petals, high-centered, slight fragrance; foliage leathery; vigorous, tall, bushy growth; PP1985; ['Circus' × 'Golden Scepter']

'Jack Rose' -- See 'Général Jacqueminot'

'Jack Wood' ('Belle Danielle') F, dp, Fryer; flowers vibrant pink, dbl., slight fragrance; free-flowering; foliage dense, healthy, bright green; bushy, spreading, vigorous (2 ft.) growth; intr. 2000

'Jacka' ('Loving') HT, pb, J&P; intr. 1994

'Jackee' (Bees Knees™) Min, yb, 1998, Zary, Dr. Keith W.; flowers yellow/pink blend, 2½ in., full, borne in large clusters, slight fragrance; foliage medium size, dark green, dull; prickles moderate; growth bushy, tall (3 ft.); [seedling × 'Haute Pink']; intr. 1998

Jackie™ Min, ly, 1956, Moore, Ralph S.; flowers straw-yellow changing to white, 1½ in., 60 petals, high-centered, moderate fragrance; foliage glossy; vigorous, dwarf (12 in.), bushy, spreading growth; ['Golden Glow' × 'Zee']; intr. 1955

'Jackie, Climbing' Cl Min, ly, 1958, Moore, Ralph S.; flowers soft yellow to creamy white, 1-1½ in., 60 petals, moderate fragrance; foliage semi-glossy, leathery; growth to 10 ft.; ['Golden Glow' × 'Zee']; intr. 1957

'Jackie Clark' HT, dr, 1990, Wambach, Alex A.; bud pointed; flowers large, 35 petals, high-centered, borne singly; foliage medium size, dark green, matte, disease-resistant; prickles curved down, pink; vigorous, upright growth; ['White Masterpiece' × 'Red Planet']; intr. 1989

'Jackman's White' ('Brookdale Giant White') HT, w, Brookdale-Kingsway; flowers creamy white, very large, high-centered; vigorous growth; very hardy for this type; intr. 1940

'Jacko' F, or, 1974, Warriner, William A.; bud ovoid, blunt; intr. 1974

'Jackpot' -- See 'Driscobert'

'Jackpot' Min, mr, J&P

'Jackpot' -- See 'Morjack'

'Jackpot 99' -- See 'Driscobert'

'Jack's Fantasy' -- See 'Bilfan'

'Jack's Wish' HT, op, Kirkham; flowers salmon-orange, large, loose, borne singly and in small clusters; foliage starts dark copper, then dark green, glossy; medium growth; intr. 2001

'Jackson Square' -- See 'Taljac'

'Jacksonii' (R. × jacksonii Willmott) S, mr, before 1910; flowers bright crimson; very free bloomer; [R. rugosa × R. wichurana]

'Jacky's Favorite' S, pb, DVP Melle; foliage dark green, disease-resistant; ['Melglory' × 'Guirland d'Amour']; intr. 2000

'Jaclace' F, w, 1981, Warriner, William A.; bud pointed; intr. 1980

'Jacladin' (Burning Desire™) HT, mr, 2000, Zary, Keith; flowers velvety crimson red, 5 in., full, exhibition, borne mostly singly, no fragrance; foliage large, dark green, glossy; prickles moderate; upright growth to 5 ft.; PP12200; ['Macauck' × 'Poulman']; intr. 2001

'Jaclaf' (Moon Shadow™) HT, m, 1998, Warriner, William A.; bud long, pointed, oval; flowers medium lavendar, 4½-5 in., 35 petals, borne in small clusters, intense sweet pea fragrance; foliage medium size, dark green, semi glossy; few prickles; upright, tall, bushy (4½ ft.) growth; PP9538; intr. 1996

'Jaclam' ('Carmen') F, dr, 1987, Warriner, William A.; flowers deep red, very little fading, small, 30 petals, high-centered, borne usually singly, no fragrance;

foliage medium size, dark green, semi-glossy; upright, bushy growth; PP6070; [seedling × 'Samantha']; intr. 1986

'Jaclarud' Gr, mp, J&P; intr. 2000

'Jaclav' ('Heather', Silver Anniversary™) HT, m, 1991, Christensen, Jack E.; bud long, pointed ovoid; flowers medium lavender, spot of yellow at base, aging paler, 4½-5 in., 25-30 petals, high-centered, borne singly, intense damask fragrance; recurrent; foliage large, very dark green, semi-glossy to glossy; prickles ordinary, ¼ in. straight, red to brown; long, straight, sturdy stems; tall, upright, bushy growth; PP7658; [Crystalline™ × Shocking Blue®]; intr. 1990

'Jaclay' HT, my, Warriner, William A.; intr. 1991

'Jaclem' ('Sun Flare, Climbing') Cl F, my, 1983, Warriner, William A.; [sport of 'Sun Flare']; intr. 1987

'Jacles' HT, rb, 1984, Warriner, William A.; intr. 1985

'Jacleste' F, op; intr. 1999

'Jaclewt' (English Perfume™) Gr, m, 1999, Zary, Dr. Keith W.; flowers lavender blend, 5 in., 41 petals, intense fragrance; foliage medium size, dark green, semi-glossy; prickles moderate; upright growth; PP12220; [seedling × Carefree Wonder™]; intr. 1999

'Jacliang' ('Lilac Mystery', Plum Dandy™) Min, m, 1991, Warriner, William A.; bud ovoid, pointed, short; flowers medium lavender, lighter near petal base, fades to light lavender with age, 2-2½ in., 35 petals, cupped, borne several together in pyramidal clusters, moderate fruity fragrance; good repeat; foliage medium size, medium green, semi-glossy; prickles medium, medium size, hooked slightly downward; stems short, strong; bushy, spreading, medium growth; PP8402; [seedling × 'Angel Face']; intr. 1991

'Jaclib' ('Petite Michelle') Min, pb, J&P; intr. 1993

'Jaclin' ('Patriot') HT, dr, 1991, Warriner, William A.; flowers large, full, borne mostly singly, slight fragrance; foliage large, dark green, semi-glossy to dullish; upright (5 ft.), spreading growth; ['Showstopper' × Mister Lincoln®]

'Jaclinber' ('Derrich Gardner') HT, rb, J&P; intr. 2001

'Jacling' ('First Kiss') F, pb, 1991, Warriner, William A.; flowers light pink, light yellow blend at base, large, dbl., slight fragrance; foliage medium size, medium green, matte; bushy, compact growth; PP7951; ['Sun Flare' × 'Simplicity']; intr. 1991

'Jaclion' ('Monet', Grand Impression™) HT, ab, 1998, Warriner, William A.; flowers yellow/peach/pink blend, apricot yellow reverse, 6 in., very dbl., borne in small clusters, slight fragrance; foliage large, dark green, semi glossy; few prickles; growth upright, tall (5 ft.); PP10273; ['Spirit of Glasnost' × Medal-

lion®]; intr. 1999

'Jaclip' ('Le Pink') Min, lp, 1986, Warriner, William A.; flowers crowded, small, very dbl., cupped, borne in sprays of 3-20, slight damask fragrance; foliage small, light green, matte; prickles long, thin, numerous on pecuncle; very dense, bushy, upright, medium growth; PP6011; [seedling × 'Watercolor']

'Jaclite' ('Cloud Nine') Min, w, 1982, Warriner, William A.; flowers medium, semi-dbl.; foliage light green, matte; spreading growth; PP5557; ['Bon Bon' × 'Calgold']; intr. 1984

'Jacliy' ('Blondie') F, my, 1987, Warriner, William A.; flowers medium yellow, fading slightly, medium, 25 petals, high-centered, borne usually singly, slight fruity fragrance; foliage medium size, light green, semi-glossy; prickles straight, medium; upright, bushy, medium growth; no fruit; [[(Bridal Pink™ × 'Golden Wave') × 'Gold Rush']

'Jaclogo' ('Saturn') HT, ob, J&P; intr. 1997

'Jacloom' HT, m, 1971, Warriner, William A.; bud long, pointed; intr. 1972

'Jacloose' (Petal Pushers™) S, lp, 2007, Zary, Keith W.; bud pointed, ovoid; flowers soft pink with lighter pastel edges, 3 in., very full, pompon, blooms borne in small clusters; recurrent; foliage medium size, dark green, glossy; prickles few, 6-8 mm., hooked downward, greyed-orange; stems 12-14 in.; growth spreading, medium (3 ft.); groundcover; PPAF; [seedling × 'Footloose']; intr. 2006

'Jaclopi' ('Leading Lady') HT, mp, 1985, Warriner, William A.; flowers large, 35 petals; foliage large, light green, matte; upright growth; PP5859; [seedling × seedling]

'Jaclorna' ('Sugar Daddy') HT, dp; intr. 1992

'Jaclover' ('Tapis Magique') S, m, Zary, Keith & Warriner, William; intr. 1992

'Jaclow' Warriner, W. A., Warriner, W. A.; PP4650

'Jacmad' ('Winner's Choice') HT, pb; intr. 1992

'Jacmag' HT, pb, 1977, Warriner, William A.; bud long; intr. 1978

'Jacmalsp' HT, mp, J&P; intr. 2007

'Jacmantha' HT, mr, 1974, Warriner, William A.; bud ovoid, pointed

'Jacmar' ('Kaileen') F, ob, 1991, Nakashima, Tosh; flowers bright orange, yellow reverse, medium, full, borne in small clusters, slight fragrance; foliage medium size, dark green, glossy; some prickles, light green to yellow; upright (6 ft.) growth; [sport of 'Marina']; intr. 1992

'Jacmarne' (Demitasse™) Min, m, 2001, Zary, Keith; flowers magenta, 2½ in., full, borne in large clusters, moderate fragrance; foliage small, medium green, glossy; prickles moderate; growth compact, low (2½ ft.); garden decorative; PP12996; ['La Marne' × 'lavender

miniature seedling']; intr. 2002

'Jacmas' HT, w, 1969, Boerner; bud long, pointed

'Jacmat' ('Razzmatazz') Min, or, 1982, Warriner, William A.; bud pointed ovoid; flowers small, 27-30 petals, flat, borne in clusters, no fragrance; free-flowering; foliage semi-glossy; prickles numerous, long, hooked slightly downward, brown; vigorous, upright (2 ft.) growth; PP5118; ['Zorina' × 'Fire Princess']; intr. 1981

'Jacmearo' (Sweetness™) Gr, m, 2008, Zary, Keith W.; flowers lavender, 10-12 cm., full, borne in small clusters; foliage medium, dark green, glossy; prickles 5 mm., hooked slightly downward, greyed-orange, moderate; growth upright, medium, (5 ft.); [Melody Parfumée™ × (Lagerfeld™ × Shocking Blue®)]; intr. 2009

'Jacmebub' Min, mp, J&P; intr. 2000

'Jacmeen' ('Good Show') F, op, J&P; intr. 1998

'Jacmello' MinFl, dy, Walden; bud short, pointed ovoid; intr. 1998

'Jacmem' ('Mango') HT, yb, J&P; intr. 1994

'Jacment' ('Autumn Song', 'Pure Poetry') F, yb, 1998, Zary, Dr. Keith W.; flowers yellow-orange with pink petal edges, 4 in., 30-35 petals, high-centered, then flat, borne in small clusters, slight fragrance; recurrent; foliage medium size, dark green, glossy; prickles numerous, straight; compact (2½ ft.) growth; PP10282; [seedling × 'Tournament of Roses']; intr. 1997

'Jacmered' Min, dr, Walden; intr. 1999

'Jacmey' ('Sun Glory') HT, dy, 1987, Warriner, William A.; flowers medium, 30 petals, high-centered, borne singly, slight fruity fragrance; foliage medium size, medium green, matte; prickles long, red, pointed slightly downwards; upright growth; no fruit; PP6612; ['Golden Emblem' × seedling]

'Jacminno' ('Jitterbug') Min, ob, 1992, Warriner, William A.; flowers orange, slightly lighter on reverse, heavy petal substance, large, dbl., nicely formed, open, borne in small clusters; foliage medium size, dark green, glossy; some prickles; tall (60-75 cm.), upright, bushy growth; PP8766; ['Caribe' × 'Impatient']; intr. 1993

'Jacmint' ('Peppermint Stick') Min, pb, J&P

'Jacmirab' ('Habitat for Humanity Rose') S, ly, J&P; bud pointed, ovoid; intr. 2004

'Jacmirat' S, ab, J&P

'Jacmiryl' (Lemon Gems™) Min, my, 1999, Walden, John K.; flowers rich, deep yellow, 2½-2¾ in., full, cupped, borne mostly singly; recurrent; foliage medium size, dark green, glossy; prickles moderate; upright, spreading, low (18-20 in.) growth; PP12112; [seedling × 'Small Miracle']; intr. 1999

'Jacmiss' (Miss Perfect™) Min, lp, 1989,

Warriner, William A.; bud ovoid, pointed; flowers light pink to near white at edge, reverse lighter, medium, very dbl., cupped; foliage medium size, medium green, semi-glossy; prickles straight to slightly hooked downward, light yellow; spreading, low growth; PP7650; ['Over the Rainbow' × 'Lavender Lace']

'Jacmiy' (Sunsmile™) Min, my, 1989, Warriner, William A.; bud ovoid; flowers medium, 48 petals, high-centered, borne singly and in sprays of 2-3; foliage medium size, medium green, semi-glossy; prickles straight to slightly hooked downward, brown; bushy, spreading, compact, vigorous growth; ['Spanish Sun' × 'Calgold']; intr. 1989

'Jacmo' (Pride 'n' Joy™) Min, ob, 1991, Warriner, William A.; bud ovoid, pointed; appendages on all sepals; flowers bright, medium orange, reverse orange and cream, fades to salmon pink, 2 in., 30-35 petals, high-centered, borne singly and several together in pyramid shape, moderate fruity fragrance; recurrent; foliage medium size, dark green, semi-glossy; prickles medium, short, hooked slightly downward; bushy, spreading, medium growth; PP8578; [Chattem Centennial™ × Prominent®]; intr. 1992

'Jacmobli' (Barbie®) Min, mp, 1998, Walden, John K.; flowers medium pink, long lasting, 2 in., 41 petals, borne in small clusters, slight fragrance; foliage medium size, dark green, semi glossy; prickles moderate; upright, low, suitable for pots growth; PP11416; [(seedling × 'Watercolor') × Red Minimo™]; intr. 1999

'Jacmocl' (Orange Blossom Special™) Cl Min, ob, 1990, Warriner, William A.; bud ovoid, sepals serrated; flowers coral-orange, edges darker, reverse lighter coral pink, small, 55+ petals, high-centered, borne in sprays of 3 - 9; foliage small, dark green, semi-glossy; prickles straight to hooked down, reddish-green; upright, bushy, tall growth; ['Zorina' × 'Andrea']; intr. 1990

'Jacmonn' F, ab, Zary, Keith; bud pointed ovoid; intr. 2006

'Jacmorbl' F, pb, J&P

'Jacmorde' (Ruffled Cloud™) S, dp, 2007, Zary, Keith W.; flowers deep pink, reverse medium pink, 4 in., dbl., blooms borne in small clusters; foliage medium size, medium green, glossy; prickles 6-8 mm., straight, greyed-orange, few; growth bushy, medium (3½ ft.); landscape, bedding; ['Morden Blush' × seedling]; intr. 2007

'Jacmound' ('Pink & White Multirosa', Good 'n Plenty™) S, pb, 2007, Zary, Keith W.; flowers raspberry pink with white eye, reverse medium pink, 2½ in., single, borne in small clusters; foliage small, dark green, glossy; prickles 4-6 mm., hooked downward, greyed-orange, few; growth compact, short (2 ½ ft.); PPAF; [seedling × 'Footloose']; intr. 2007

'Jacmouse' ('Disneyland', Disneyland Rose®, 'Voodoo Charm') F, op, 2005, Walden, John K. & Zary, Keith W.; flowers orange pink blend, 7½ cm., 30-35 petals, borne in small clusters, slight fragrance; foliage medium size, dark green, glossy; prickles 5-7 mm., hooked downward, greyed-orange, moderate; growth upright, branching, compact, short (70-80 cm.); PP15114; [Sequoia gold™ × Hot Tamale™]

'Jacmpiad' ('Mother's Rose', Coral Hush™) HT, op, 2001, Zary, Keith; bud creamy coral, long, pointed, ovoid.; flowers deep coral and pink, 5 in., 30 petals, high-centered, borne mostly solitary, slight light and fresh fragrance; continuous; foliage medium size, dark green, semi-glossy; prickles moderate; growth upright, tall (6 ft.); garden decorative; PP13087; ['Olympiad' × 'hybrid tea seedling']; intr. 2002

'Jacmur' HT, w, 1985, Humenick, Muriel F.; intr. 1986

'Jacnel' ('Sundance') HT, dy, 1992, Warriner, William A.; flowers 3-3½ in., very dbl., borne mostly singly; foliage large, dark green, semi-glossy; some prickles; tall (180-120 cm.), upright growth; [seedling × Emblem™]; intr. 1991

'Jacnepal' ('St. John's College', Gemini™) HT, pb, 1999, Zary, Dr. Keith W.; bud pointed, ovoid; flowers cream, blushing coral pink, 4½-5 in., 25-30 petals, high-centered, borne usually singly, moderate sweet fragrance; foliage large, deep green, glossy; prickles moderate; long stems; upright, spreading, tall (5½ ft.) growth; PP11691; ['Anne Morrow Lindbergh' × New Year®]; intr. 2000

'Jacnereb' (Camisole™) F, ab, 2001, Zary, Keith; bud pointed, ovoid; flowers 4 in., full, borne in small clusters, moderate fragrance; foliage large, dark green, glossy; prickles moderate; growth upright, medium (3½ ft.); garden decorative; PP13210; ['Impatient' × Amber Queen®]; intr. 2002

'Jacnewpu' (Chelsea Morning™) S, ab, 2001, Zary; buds pointed, ovoid; flowers pink and apricot blend, aging to more intense pink, 4-5 cm., 40 petals, saucer-shaped, borne mostly solitary, moderate fruity fragrance; foliage medium size, dark green, glossy; prickles moderate; growth upright, medium (5 ft.); garden decorative; PP14755; [New Year® × French Perfume™]; intr. 2002

'Jacnewze' HT, lp, Zary, Keith; bud pointed; intr. 2007

'Jacnezen' F, w, J&P; intr. 2005

'Jacnon' HT, ob, 1985, Warriner, William A.; flowers medium, very dbl., slight fragrance; foliage large, medium green, matte; upright, bushy growth; PP5318; [Baccará® × seedling]

'Jacnor' (Signature®) HT, pb, 1998, Warriner, William A.; bud long, pointed, ovoid, deep pink; flowers deep pink and cream blend, light pink and cream reverse, 5-6 in., 30-35 petals, high-centered, borne singly, moderate fragrance; foliage large, dark green, semi glossy; numerous prickles; upright, bushy, tall (4-5 ft.) growth; PP9539; [Honor™ × 'First Federal Renaissance']; intr. 1996

'Jacnu' ('Nuance') HT, op, J&P; intr. 1993

'Jacnuel' ('Sterling '95') HT, m; intr. 1995

'Jacnuye' (Little Flame™) Min, ob, 1998, Walden, John K.; flowers brilliant orange, 2 in., dbl., borne in large clusters, no fragrance; foliage medium size, dark green, semi-glossy; prickles moderate, straight; growth compact, tall (3 ft.); borders; PP11632; [New Year® × seedling]; intr. 1998

'Jacob H. Pierneef' -- See 'J. H. Pierneef'

'Jacob van Ruysdael' ('Amber Star') F, op, Williams, J. Benjamin; flowers peach orange, semi-dbl.; upright, compact growth; intr. 1997

Jacob's Ladder™ -- See 'Weksacsodor'

Jacob's Robe™ -- See 'Wekausboy'

'Jacolber' (Opening Night™) HT, dr, 1998, Zary, Dr. Keith W.; bud ovoid, pointed; flowers bright, deep red, 4½ in., 25-30 petals, high-centered, borne singly, slight fruity fragrance; foliage medium size, dark green, semi glossy; prickles moderate, straight; upright, tall, slightly spreading growth; PP11265; ['Olympiad' × 'Ingrid Bergman']; intr. 1998

'Jacolfa' (English Sachet™) HT, lp, 1999, Zary, Dr. Keith W.; flowers cupped, ruffled, almost quartered, delicate petals, 4-4½ in., 40-50 petals, cupped, borne mostly singly, intense sweet fragrance; foliage medium size, medium green, matte; prickles moderate; upright, spreading, tall (5 ft.) growth; PP12118; ['Summer Fashion' × 'Silver Jubilee']; intr. 1999

'Jacolite' ('Honour', 'Silhouette', Michèle Torr®) HT, w, 1979, Warriner, William A.; bud ovoid, pointed; intr. 1980

'Jacolly' HT, yb, Zary

'Jacolman' ('Beloved', 'Grey Kollege', 'Merveille de Gien', 'Cesar E. Chavez') HT, dr, 2004, Zary, Keith W.; flowers 5 in., 30-35 petals, borne mostly solitary, slight fragrance; foliage large, dark green, glossy; prickles 5-7 mm., hooked slightly downward,; growth upright, tall (6 ft.), specimen, garden decoration; PP14104; ['Olympiad' × 'Ingrid Bergman']

'Jacolpur' (Purple Passion™) HT, m, 1999, Zary, Dr. Keith W.; bud pointed, ovoid; flowers rich purple/lavender, reverse lavender, 4½-5 in., 30-35 petals, high-centered, borne singly and in clusters of 3 - 7, intense lemony fragrance; recurrent; foliage large, dark green, glossy; prickles moderate; upright, spreading, tall (5 ft.) growth; PP11801; [seedling × seedling]; intr. 1999

'Jacomail' F, m, Zary

'Jacopper' ('City of Newcastle Bicentennary', Veterans' Honor™, 'Five-Roses Rose', 'Lady in Red') HT, dr, 1999, Zary, Dr. Keith W.; bud furled, pointed, 2 in.; flowers bright red, 5-5½ in., 25-30 petals, high-centered, borne mostly singly, slight raspberry fragrance; recurrent; foliage medium size, dark green, semi-glossy; prickles moderate; upright, spreading, tall (5 ft.) growth; ['Showstopper' × (seedling × 'Royalty')]; intr. 1995

'Jacoral' (Coral Sprite™) Min, mp, 1989, Warriner, William A.; bud ovoid, pointed; flowers medium, very dbl., urn-shaped, borne in sprays of 3-18, no fragrance; foliage medium size, dark green, matte; prickles straight to slightly angled downward, yellow-green; bushy, spreading, low growth; PP7717; ['Merci' × Party Girl™]; intr. 1989

'Jacorb' ('Ipitombi') HT, ob, J&P

'Jacorbet' ('Pastel Chameleon', Laura Bush™) F, or, 2007, Zary, Keith W.; flowers smoky orange, reverse orange, 4 in., dbl., blooms borne in large clusters; foliage medium size, dark green, glossy; prickles 8-10 mm., hooked downward, greyed-orange, numerous; growth upright, medium (3 ft.); PPAF; [Sorbet Bouquet™ × Outrageous™]; intr. 2008

'Jacorca' (Tropical Twist™) Min, op, 1998, Walden, John K.; bud pointed ovoid; flowers coral-orange and apricot with yellow-cream reverse, 1½-1¾ in., 30-35 petals, high-centered, borne mostly singly, floriferous, very slight fragrance; recurrent; foliage medium size, dark green, glossy; prickles moderate, short, angled downward,; compact, upright (22 - 24 in.) growth; hedging or border; PP10882; [('Funny Girl' × 'Galaxy') × 'Pink Polyanna']; intr. 1997

'Jacore' ('Encore') HT, dr, 1984, Warriner, William A.; flowers large, 20 petals; foliage medium size, dark, semi-glossy; upright growth; PP5658; [seedling × 'Samantha']

'Jacorflo' (Light My Fire™) F, or, 2008, Zary, Keith W.; flowers orange-red, 10 cm., dbl., borne in small clusters; foliage medium, dark green, glossy; prickles 5 mm., hooked slightly downward, greyed-orange, moderate; growth compact, short (2½ ft.); specimen, containers; [('Showbiz' × seedling) × seedling]; intr. 2009

'Jacorg' (Crackling Fire™) Min, ob, 1999, Walden, John K.; flowers copper orange, reverse deep red-orange, 2-2¼ in., 20-40 petals, borne in small clusters, no fragrance; foliage medium size, dark green, semi-glossy; prickles moderate; upright, compact, low (14-18 in.) growth; PP12322; [seedling × Rainbow's End™]; intr. 1999

'Jacormag' (Lady Bird™) HT, or, 2008, Zary, Keith W.; bud pointed, ovoid; flowers dark orange, 12-15 cm., full, borne mostly solitary, slight spicy fragrance; recurrent; foliage large, dark green, glossy; prickles 6-8 mm., hooked slightly download, greyed orange, moderate; growth upright, tall (5-6 ft.); ['Color Magic' × seedling]; intr. 2009

'Jacormin' ('Vixen') Min, or, 1989, Warriner, William A.; bud ovoid, pointed, green with reddish-brown; flowers red-orange with yellow base, aging red-orange to pink orange, 28 petals, cupped, no fragrance; foliage medium size, medium green, semi-glossy, small; prickles small, straight, reddish-brown; bushy, spreading, low growth; ['Petticoat' × Red Minimo™]; intr. 1990

'Jacosch' ('Opulence') HT, w, J&P; bud long, pointed ovoid; intr. 1997

'Jacosol' ('Moonlight Lady') HT, my, J&P; intr. 1995

'Jacotte' HWich, ab, 1920, Barbier; bud ovoid, orange and yellow; flowers deep coppery yellow, tinted coppery red, 3 in., semi-dbl., cupped, moderate fragrance; recurrent; foliage leathery, glossy, dark; long, strong stems; very vigorous, climbing growth; [R. wichurana × 'Arthur R. Goodwin']

'Jacouch' ('Soft Touch') Min, ab, 1982, Warriner, William A.; flowers medium, semi-dbl.; foliage medium size, medium green, semi-glossy; PP5578; [Bridal Pink™ × 'Fire Princess']; intr. 1984

'Jacout' ('Neon Lights') F, dp, 1991, Warriner, William A.; flowers hot magenta pink, large, dbl., borne in small clusters, moderate fragrance; foliage medium size, medium green, semi-glossy; medium, bushy growth; PP8692; ['Intrigue' × 'Impatient']; intr. 1992

'Jacoutra' (Cinnamon Twist™) F, ob, 2007, Zary, Keith W.; flowers orange turning coral-orange, 5 in., 25-30 petals, blooms borne mostly solitary; foliage medium size, dark green, glossy; prickles 6-8 mm., straight, greyed-orange, moderate; growth compact (3½ ft.); [seedling × Outrageous™]; intr. 2007

'Jacoyel' HT, op, 1981, Warriner, William A.; bud nearly globular; intr. 1982

'Jacpal' (Brigadoon™) HT, pb, 1991, Warriner, William A.; bud ovoid, pointed; flowers pink near center, coral pink at petal margin, rose pink and cream reverse, 5 in., 35-40 petals, high-centered, borne mostly singly, moderate spicy fragrance; foliage medium size, dark green, semi-glossy; upright, spreading, tall growth; PP8591; [seedling × Pristine®]; intr. 1992

'Jacpan' ('Meteor Shower') F, mp, J&P

'Jacpat' ('Jumpin' Jack') F, op, J&P

'Jacpehot' (Cinnamon Girl™) Min, ob, 2008, Zary, Keith W.; flowers dusty orange, reverse cream, 5 cm., full, borne in small clusters; foliage medium, dark green, glossy; prickles 5-7 mm., hooked downward, greyed-orange, moderate; growth upright, medium (30-40 cm.); [Petite Perfection™ × Hot Tamale™]; intr. 2010

'Jacperby' (Enchanted Evening™) F, m, 2008, Zary, Keith W.; flowers lavender, reverse silvery-lavender, 6-8 cm., dbl., borne in large clusters; foliage medium-size, dark green, glossy; prickles 6-8 mm., hooked slightly downward, greyed orange, moderate; growth upright, medium (3-4 ft.); ['Perfume Perfection' × 'Blue Bayou']; intr. 2009

'Jacpet' ('Petticoat') Min, w, 1982, Warriner, William A.; bud short; flowers white tinted pink, 55 petals; foliage dark, small, pointed; very compact, spreading growth; PP5039; ['Bon Bon' × 'Lemon Delight']; intr. 1981

'Jacpetex' -- See 'Flamenco'

'Jacpetor' F, my, J&P

'Jacpicl' (Dream Weaver™) Cl F, op, 1998, Zary, Dr. Keith W.; bud short, pointed; flowers coral pink, 3-3½ in., full, rosette, borne in large clusters, slight rose fragrance; foliage large, dark green, glossy; prickles moderate; growth tall, spreading, arching, climbing; PP9492; [seedling × Lady of the Dawn®]; intr. 1997

'Jacpico' (Pristine®) HT, w, 1977, Warriner, William A.; bud long, pointed ovoid; flowers near white, shaded light pink, imbricated, 5-6 in., 28-35 petals, high-centered, borne singly or several together, slight fragrance; good repeat; foliage very large, dark green, semi-glossy; prickles numerous, medium, hooked downward, brown; stems medium, strong; vigorous, upright growth; PP3997; ['White Masterpiece' × 'First Prize']; intr. 1978

'Jacpie' HT, mr, 1978, Warriner, William A.; bud ovoid, pointed

'Jacpif' ('Pleasure') F, mp, 1989, Warriner, William A.; bud ovoid, pointed; flowers coral pink, reverse lighter, large, 33 petals, cupped, borne in sprays of 3-7; foliage medium size, dark green, semi-glossy; prickles slightly hooked downward, reddish-brown; low, compact growth; globular fruit; PP7480; [('Merci' × 'Faberge') × 'Intrigue']; intr. 1990

'Jacpihi' (Grand Finale™) HT, w, 1998, Zary, Dr. Keith W.; bud long, ovoid; flowers ivory white, 4-4½ in., very dbl., high-centered, borne singly, slight honeysuckle fragrance; foliage large, medium green, semi-glossy; prickles moderate; upright, medium (4 ft.) growth; PP11007; [Honor™ × Pristine®]; intr. 1998

'Jacpik' ('African Sunset') HT, or, J&P; intr. 1994

'Jacpin' ('Dream Dolly') F, op, J&P; intr. 1993

'Jacpinap' (Apricot Passion™) HT, ab, 2000, Zary, Keith; flowers apricot-pink, reverse apricot yellow, medium, full, borne singly and in clusters, slight fragrance; foliage semi-glossy; growth medium, vigorous, upright; PP22202; ['yellow hybrid tea seedling' × Mirabella™]

'Jacpink' HT, op, J&P; intr. 2001

'Jacpluco' (Plum Frost™) S, m, 2007, Zary, Keith W.; flowers smoky purple, reverse lavender, 3½ in., semi-dbl., borne in small clusters; foliage medium size, dark green, glossy; prickles 8-10 mm., hooked downward, greyed-orange, moderate; growth upright, medium (4 ft.); hedge, in mixed perennial beds; PPAF; [seedling × 'Perfume Perfection (formerly Cotillion)']; intr. 2007

'Jacply' ('Somersault') HT, yb, 1993, Zary, Dr. Keith W.; flowers yellow and rose red/orange blend, medium, full, borne in clusters; foliage small, dark green, glossy; some prickles; low (45-50cm.), upright, bushy growth

'Jacpo' ('Goldpoint') Min, my, 1984, Warriner, William A.; flowers small, 20 petals, slight fragrance; foliage small, light green, matte; growth upright, bushy; PP5645; ['Rise 'n' Shine' × ('Faberge' × 'Precilla')]

'Jacpolpa' (Citrus Tease™) F, mp, 2000, Zary, Keith; flowers large, dbl., high-centered, borne in small clusters; foliage medium size, dark green, glossy; prickles moderate; upright, bushy growth (3½ ft.); PP12116; [Pink Pollyanna™ × 'Gnome World']; intr. 2001

'Jacpop' ('Prince of Peace') HT, yb, 1985, J&P; flowers yellow edged with pink, medium, 35 petals; foliage medium size, medium green, glossy; upright growth; PP5901; [Bridal Pink™ × unknown]

'Jacpoulp' (Kimberlina™) F, lp, 2008, Zary, Keith W.; flowers light pink, reverse medium pink, 8-10 cm., dbl., borne in large clusters; foliage medium, dark green, glossy; prickles 6-8 mm., hooked slightly downward, greyed-orange, moderate; growth upright, medium (4 ft.); [('Moon Shadow' × seedling) × seedling]; intr. 2009

'Jacpow' ('Fantasy') HT, w, J&P; intr. 1992

'Jacpoy' ('Sunbird', Hot Tamale™) Min, yb, 1993, Zary, Dr. Keith W.; flowers yellow-orange blend changing to yellow pink, finishing pink, large, full, high-centered, borne singly and in small clusters, slight fragrance; foliage small, dark green, semi-glossy; some prickles; low (36 cm.), bushy, compact growth; PP9015; intr. 1994

'Jacpri' ('Joyous Moment') Min, ab, J&P

'Jacpribe' (Spellbound™) HT, op, 2007, Zary, Keith W.; flowers coral pink, 4½ in., full, high-centered, blooms borne mostly solitary; foliage medium size, dark green, semi-glossy; prickles few, 8-10 mm., hooked downward, greyed-orange; growth upright, medium (5 ft.); ['Ingrid Bergman' × Pristine®]; intr. 2006

'Jacprize' (April in Paris™) HT, pb, 2007, Zary, Keith W.; flowers pink cream blend, 4½ in., full, blooms borne mostly solitary; foliage medium size, dark green, glossy;
prickles 8-10 mm., hooked downward, greyed-orange, few; growth upright, medium (5 ft.); [Pristine® × 'New Zealand']; intr. 2008

'Jacpurr' ('Purple Tiger') F, m, 1991, Christensen, Jack E.; bud pointed, ovoid; flowers very deep purple with stripes and flecks of white and mauve-pink, 3½-4 in., full, borne in small clusters, moderate damask fragrance; foliage medium size, medium green, glossy; nearly thornless; stems very glabrous (shiny); medium (70-90 cm.), bushy growth; ['Intrigue' × Pinstripe™]; intr. 1992

'Jacpursh' ('Neon Glory', 'Purple Simplicity') S, m, 1998, Zary, Dr. Keith W.; bud long, pointed ovoid; flowers raspberry purple, 3 in., semi-dbl., high-centered, then flat, borne in clusters of 5-9, slight fragrance; free-flowering; foliage medium size, medium green, semi-glossy; prickles few, straight, thin; growth tall, bushy; hedging; PP11251; [seedling × Love Potion™]

'Jacpuzle' S, rb, J&P; intr. 2007

'Jacquard' B, dp, 1842, Béluze; flowers carmine pink, medium, full

'Jacqueline' -- See 'Kororanki'

'Jacqueline' -- See 'Meger'

'Jacqueline' HT, mr, 1961, Byrum, Roy L.; bud short, pointed; flowers turkey-red, 4-4½ in., 30 petals, high-centered, moderate fragrance; foliage glossy; vigorous, well-branched growth; PP2183; ['Topper' × seedling]; intr. 1961

'Jacqueline' HEg, rb, 1923, Paul; flowers reddish-copper with yellow base, semi-dbl.; non-recurrent; growth moderate (3½ ft.); name released for re-use (MR 6); may be an older variety, reintroduced by Paul

Jacqueline du Pré® -- See 'Harwanna'

'Jacqueline Dufier' HT, dr, 1957, Kemp, M.L.; flowers crimson shaded black, high pointed, 4 in., 25 petals; foliage bronze; vigorous growth; ['Dicksons Red' × 'Ena Harkness']

'Jacqueline Humery' -- See 'LLX8851'

Jacqueline Nebout® ('City of Adelaide', 'Sanlam-Roos') F, mp, Meilland; flowers silvery pink, dbl.; intr. 1989

'Jacqueline Sternotte' HT, rb, 1976, Select Delforge; bud ovoid; flowers red and white, 4½ in., 51 petals, moderate fragrance; intr. 1974

'Jacquenetta' -- See 'Ausjac'

'Jacques Amyot' N, m, 1844, Varangot; flowers lilac pink, 4 in., very dbl.; good repeat bloom; foliage dark green, regularly dentate; almost thornless; tall growth; sometimes classed as Po

'Jacques Carroy' Pol, m, 1929, Turbat; flowers carmine, slightly tinted purple, center velvety, borne in clusters

'Jacques Carteau' HT, ly, 1957, Privat; bud long; flowers creamy yellow, medium; foliage glossy; moderate growth

'Jacques Cartier' Gr, or

'Jacques Cartier' P, lp, 1868, Moreau-Robert; flowers clear rose, center darker,
edges very pale, with a very small eye, 3½-4 in., 50 petals, quartered, borne singly and in small clusters, moderate fragrance; good repeat bloom; foliage medium green, matte; compact, low, branching growth

'Jacques Cartier, Climbing' Cl P, lp, Whartons; intr. 2002

'Jacques Cartier Blanc' P, w; flowers rosy-white; intr. about 1870

'Jacques Esterel' HT, m, Croix; flowers silvery red, large, very dbl., moderate fragrance; growth to 75-85 cm.; intr. 1973

'Jacques Hackenburg' HT, pb, 1919, Leenders, M.; flowers deep rose-pink and carmine, opening flesh-white, dbl.; ['Jonkheer J.L. Mock' × 'Marquise de Sinéty']

'Jacques Laffitte' HP, dp, 1846, Vibert; flowers carmine-pink, large, full

'Jacques Latouche' HT, pb, 1935, Mallerin, C.; flowers orange-pink in spring, red in summer, reverse yellow, very large, dbl., cupped; foliage glossy; vigorous growth; ['Souv. de Claudius Pernet' × 'Director Rubió']

'Jacques Pink' HT, mp, Meilland; intr. 2006

'Jacques Plantier' HP, pb, 1872, Damaizin; flowers pink, aging to flesh white, large, full

'Jacques Porcher' HT, w, 1914, Guillot, P.; flowers white with tints of carmine, saffron and deep yellow, small, dbl., moderate fragrance

Jacques Prévert® -- See 'Meimouslin'

'Jacques Proust' Pol, m, 1904, Robichon; flowers violet-red, small, semi-dbl.

'Jacques Vincent' HT, rb, 1908, Soupert & Notting; flowers coral-red, center golden; vigorous growth; ['Mme J.W. Budde' × 'Souv. de Catherine Guillot']

'Jacquie Williams' -- See 'Morwheels'

'Jacquinot' C, pb, before 1848; flowers deep rose, streaked with white, medium, dbl., flat; growth branching

'Jacquint' (Royal Wedding™) F, ab, 1998, Zary, Dr. Keith W.; bud globular; flowers pink-amber, 3½-4 in., 40-45 petals, cupped, borne mostly singly, with some small clusters, moderate fragrance; recurrent; foliage medium size, dark green, semi-glossy; prickles moderate, straight to hooked slightly downward; stems short; compact (3½ ft.), vigorous, old-fashioned growth; PP11170; ['Impatient' × Amber Queen®]; intr. 1998

'Jacquot' F, Dorieux, Francois; intr. 1973

'Jacrain' ('Kleine Renate') Min, pb, J&P; intr. 1993

'Jacraw' ('Peppermint Twist', 'Red and White Delight') F, rb, 1992, Christensen, Jack E.; sepals have glandular structures on back; flowers red/white/pink striped, large, very full, flat to slightly cupped, borne in small clusters; foliage large, medium green, semi-glossy; some prickles on peduncle; medium (90-110 cm.), upright, bushy growth; [Pinstripe™ × 'Maestro']; intr. 1992

'Jacraz' F, rb, 1976, Warriner, William A.; intr. 1977

'Jacrebin' F, ab, Zary, Keith; intr. 2008

'Jacredem' (Jingle Bells™) Min, dr, 1998, Zary, Dr. Keith W.; bud short, pointed ovoid; flowers dark red, light red reverse, 2 in., 30 petals, high-centered, borne in clusters, slight fragrance; recurrent; foliage medium size, dark green, semi-glossy; prickles moderate, short, straight; stems short, strong; bushy, medium (2 ft.) growth; border; PP9325; [seedling × seedling]; intr. 1997

'Jacredi' ('Colinda') HT, mr; intr. 1997

'Jacref' ('Limited Edition') HT, mr, 1984, J&P; flowers large, dbl., no fragrance; foliage medium size, medium green, semi-glossy; upright growth; PP5037; [seedling × seedling]

'Jacreflo' (Black Cherry™) F, dr, 2007, Zary, Keith W.; flowers 3-3½ in., 20-25 petals, blooms borne in large clusters; foliage medium size, medium green, glossy; prickles 8-10 mm., hooked downward, greyed-orange, moderate; growth bushy, medium (3½ ft.); [seedling × seedling]; intr. 2006

'Jacreg' ('Jubilation') F, lp, 1995, J&P

'Jacrenew' (Very Cherry™) Min, mr, 1999, Walden, John K.; bud short, pointed ovoid; flowers bright red, darken with age, 2-2½ in., dbl., cupped, borne singly and in small clusters, very slight fragrance; recurrent; foliage large, medium green, glossy; prickles moderate. short, angled slightly down, brown; upright, compact, globular, medium (20-26 in.) growth; hips light green; PP12618; [seedling × New Year®]; intr. 1999

'Jacrenim' (Feisty™) Min, mr, 2001, Zary; flowers medium, bold red, 2½ in., dbl., borne in small clusters, no fragrance; foliage small, dark green, glossy; prickles moderate; growth compact, low (2½ ft.); garden decorative; PP12994; [red miniature seedling × red miniature seedling]; intr. 2002

'Jacrepin' (Frankly Scarlet™) F, mr, 2007, Zary, Keith W.; flowers light red, 4 in., dbl., blooms borne in small clusters; foliage medium size, dark green, glossy; prickles 6-8 mm., hooked downward, greyed-orange, moderate; growth compact, medium (3 ft.); PPAF; [seedling × seedling]; intr. 2008

'Jacreraz' F, mr, J&P; intr. 2006

'Jacrette' ('Emperor') HT, mr, J&P; intr. 1997

'Jacrewai' F, dp, J&P; intr. 2004

'Jacrewhi' F, m, J&P; intr. 2004

'Jacrex' (Fabulous!™) F, w, 2000, Zary, Keith; bud pointed, ovoid buds; flowers pure white, 3-4 in., 25-30 petals, high-centered, borne in large clusters, slight sweet fragrance; recurrent; foliage dark green, glossy; prickles moderate; upright, bushy, vigorous (3-4 ft.) growth; PP12130; ['Iceberg' × 'Macrexy']; intr. 2001

'Jacrim' ('Target') F, rb, 1986, Warriner, William A.; flowers white with red petal edges, 25 petals, high-centered, borne usually singly; foliage medium size, medium green, semi-glossy; prickles straight, large and small; upright, bushy, medium growth; PP6255; [Prominent® × seedling]

'Jacrink' ('Day Glow') Min, dp, 1989, Warriner, William A.; bud ovoid, pointed; flowers deep pink, fading lighter, medium, 60 petals, high-centered, borne usually singly, slight fragrance; foliage medium size, dark green, matte; prickles straight, short; low growth; ['Petticoat' × 'Red Jewel']; intr. 1988

'Jacris' ('Contessa') S, dp, 1987, Warriner, William A.; flowers deep pink with yellow eye, reverse deep pink, fading slightly, 6-10 petals, flat, slight spicy fragrance; fast cycle; foliage medium size, medium green, semi-glossy; prickles straight, long, green-brown; upright, tall growth; PP6577; ['Sunsprite' × seedling]

'Jacrite' (Rio Samba™) HT, yb, 1991, Warriner, William A.; bud long, pointed, ovoid; flowers medium yellow fading to peach-pink, large, 25 petals, high-centered, borne singly and in small clusters, slight fragrance; foliage medium size, dark green, matte; prickles some, medium, hooked slightly downward; medium (110-120 cm.), upright, bushy growth; PP8361; [seedling × Sunbright®]; intr. 1993

'Jacro' ('Bravado') F, dr, 1986, Warriner, William A.; flowers 26 petals, high-centered, borne usually singly, slight fragrance; foliage medium size, dark, semi-glossy; prickles medium, red to brown, hooked downward; medium, upright growth; PP5978; [seedling × 'Gabriella']; intr. 1987

'Jacrogem' F, pb, Zary, Keith; bud long, pointed ovoid; intr. 1998

'Jacrolie' F, op, Zary

'Jacrom' ('Romance') HT, mp, 1983, Warriner, William A.; flowers medium salmon-pink, large, 35 petals; foliage large, medium green, semi-glossy; upright growth; PP5250; [seedling × Prominent®]

'Jacrose' ('Tribute') HT, dp, 1982, Warriner, William A.; bud long, pointed ovoid; flowers deep pink, loose form, 4½ in., 30 petals, high-centered, borne singly and several together, slight fragrance; recurrent; foliage large, dark green, leathery; prickles numerous, reddish, hooked downward; stems long, strong; upright growth; PP4850; [seedling × seedling]; intr. 1983

'Jacrove' ('Topsy, Perfectly Red™) HT, dr, 1999, Zary, Dr. Keith W.; bud pointed, ovoid; flowers velvety red, 4-4½ in., 25-30 petals, high-centered, borne mostly singly, slight sweet apple fragrance; recurrent; foliage medium size, dark green, semi-glossy; prickles moderate; upright (5 ft.) growth; PP11715; [seedling × 'Love']

'Jacroxa' F, mp, Zary; intr. 2000

'Jacrulav' (Wild Berry Breeze™) HRg, m, 1999, Zary, Dr. Keith W.; flowers lavender-pink, veined petals, large, single, borne in clusters, intense spicy clove fragrance; recurrent; foliage medium size, dark green, semi-glossy, deeply rugose; numerous prickles; upright, bushy, medium (3½ ft.) growth; hips round, large, orange; PP12055; ['Buffalo Gal' × seedling]; intr. 1999

'Jacruner' S, my, J&P; intr. 2007

'Jacruwhi' ('Wild Spice') HRg, w, 1999, Zary, Dr. Keith W.; flowers snowy white, delicate, ruffled, large, single, borne in small clusters, intense clove fragrance; foliage dark green, semi-glossy, deeply rugose; upright, bushy, medium (3½ ft.) growth; PP11575; ['Buffalo Gal' × seedling]; intr. 1999

'Jacrybi' (Petite Perfection™) Min, rb, 1999, Walden, John K.; bud long, ovoid; flowers bright red/yellow, reverse deep yellow, 2¼-2½ in., 25 petals, high-centered, borne singly and in small clusters, slight tea fragrance; foliage medium size, dark green, glossy; prickles moderate; upright, compact, medium (16-22 in.) growth; patio mini; PP12049; [seedling × seedling]; intr. 1999

'Jacrymin' HT, m, Zary, Keith; intr. 2008

'Jacsak' ('Riviera') HT, mr, J&P; intr. 1994

'Jacsal' ('Cherish') F, op, 1979, Warriner, William A.; bud short, flat; flowers coral-pink, 3 in., 28 petals, high-centered, slight fragrance; foliage large, dark; compact, spreading growth; PP4331; [Bridal Pink™ × 'Matador']; intr. 1980

'Jacsall' (Key Largo™) HT, op, 2001, Zary; bud pointed, ovoid; flowers clear coral, 4-5 cm., 30 petals, borne mostly solitary, slight citrus fragrance; foliage medium size, dark green, glossy; prickles moderate; growth upright, tall (5 ft.); garden decorative; PP13296; [Touch of Class™® × 'hybrid tea seedling']; intr. 2001

'Jacsalps' (Lemon Zest™) S, my, 2001, Zary, Keith; bud pointed, ovoid; flowers 3½-4 in., 40-50 petals, old-fashioned, borne in small clusters, moderate citrus fragrance; foliage medium size, dark green, glossy; prickles moderate; growth compact, medium (3½ ft.); garden decorative; PP13342; ['Jacyim' × 'yellow shrub seedling']; intr. 2002

'Jacsan' ('Pearl of Joy') Gr, ab, J&P; intr. 1994

'Jacsanet' F, mp, J&P

'Jacsash' ('Rose Sachet', Rose Rhapsody™) HT, dp, 1999, Zary, Dr. Keith W.; bud long, pointed ovoid; flowers deep, dusty pink, 5-6½ in., 41-50+ petals, high-centered, borne mostly singly, intense citrus fragrance; recurrent; foliage large, dark green, glossy; prickles moderate, medium size, hooked downward; stems medium, strong; upright, spreading, tall (4½-5 ft.) growth; PP11046; ['Fragrant Cloud' × 'Ingrid Bergman']; intr. 1999

'Jacsat' ('High Flyer', Dynamite™) LCl, dr, 1992, Warriner, William A.; flowers bright red, 4-4½ in., 30 petals, borne in small clusters, slight citrus fragrance; foliage large, dark green, glossy, resistant to powdery mildew; some prickles; tall (150-185 cm.), upright, spreading, arching growth; PP8741; [seedling × 'Simpathie']

'Jacsay' ('Avanti') HT, dr, 1990, Warriner, William A. & Zary, Keith W.; bud ovoid, pointed; flowers dark red, with hint of blue reverse, aging dark, dark red, large, 25-30 petals, high-centered, urn-shaped, slight fruity fragrance; foliage medium to large, dark green, matte to semi-glossy; upright, bushy, tall growth; ['Royalty' × 'Samantha']; intr. 1990

'Jacseboy' (Baby Bloomer™) Min, mp, 2007, Zary, Keith W.; flowers pure medium pink, 1-1½ in., semi-dbl., blooms borne in large clusters; foliage small, dark green, glossy; prickles 4-6 mm., straight, greyed-orange, few; growth spreading, medium (18 in.); [seedling × 'Boy Crazy']; intr. 2007

'Jacsedi' ('Purple Puff', Love Potion™) F, m, 1993, Christensen, Jack E.; flowers deep clear lavender, 3-3½ in., full, borne in small clusters, intense raspberry fragrance; foliage medium size, dark green, glossy; some prickles; medium (90-100 cm.), upright, spreading growth; PP9172; [seedling × 'Dilly Dilly']; intr. 1994

'Jacsee' ('New Horizons', Fragrant Lace™) HT, pb, 1998, Zary, Dr. Keith W.; flowers cream and lavender pink with cream and light yellow reverse, 5-5½ in., very dbl., borne mostly singly, intense fragrance; foliage large, dark green, glossy; prickles moderate; upright growth; PP11138; [seedling × 'Cherry Jubilee']; intr. 1998

'Jacsegra' (Pope John Paul II™) HT, w, 2007, Zary, Keith W.; flowers 5 in., full, blooms borne mostly solitary; foliage medium size, dark green, glossy; prickles 8-10 mm., hooked downward, greyed-orange, moderate; growth upright, tall (5 ft.); PPAF; [Secret™ × Fragrant Lace™]; intr. 2007

'Jacseoso' HT, lp, Zary; intr. 1999

'Jacseout' Gr, ly, J&P; bud pointed; intr. 2008

'Jacseraw' ('Orange Splash') F, ob, 1991, Christensen, Jack E.; flowers bright orange to orange-red with white and lighter orange stripes and flecks, 3-3½ in., dbl., borne in small clusters, moderate fragrance; foliage large, dark green, glossy; some prickles; medium (75-90 cm.), upright, bushy growth; [seedling × seedling]; intr. 1992

'Jacshaq' ('Diana, Princess of Wales', 'Diana') HT, pb, 1998, Zary, Keith W.; flowers pink cream blend, reverse pink cream blend, 5 in., full, borne mostly solitary, moderate fragrance; foliage large, medium green, glossy; prickles 6-8 mm., hooked upward; growth upright, well branched, tall (5-5½ ft.); specimen, garden; PP11482; ['Anne Morrow Lindbergh' × Sheer Elegance™]; intr. 1999

'Jacshe' ('Summer Dream') HT, ab, 1986, Warriner, William A.; bud pointed ovoid; flowers apricot-pink, 5½ in., 30-35 petals, high-centered, borne singly, slight fruity fragrance; recurrent; foliage medium size, medium green, matte; prickles numerous, long, straight, brown; stems long, strong; upright, tall (5 ft.) growth; PP5640; ['Sunshine' × seedling]; intr. 1987

'Jacshel' Warriner, W. A., Warriner, W. A.; PP4439

'Jacship' (Pink Pollyanna™) S, mp, 1990, Warriner, William A.; bud ovoid; flowers medium pink, reverse slightly darker, aging lighter, small, dbl., high-centered, moderate fruity fragrance; repeat bloom; foliage small, medium green, glossy; prickles small, straight, red to brown; growth upright, bushy, medium; ['Zorina' × 'Heidi']; intr. 1990

'Jacshlav' (Fragrant Lavender Simplicity™) S, m, 2007, Zary, Keith W.; flowers light lavender, 3½ in., full, borne in large clusters; foliage medium size, dark green, glossy; prickles 8-10 mm., hooked downward, greyed-orange, moderate; growth upright, tall (4-5 ft.); [seedling × seedling]; intr. 2006

'Jacsho' HT, dr, 1981, Warriner, William A.; bud pointed

'Jacshok' ('Perfume Perfection', Cotillion™, 'Serenissima') F, m, 1999, Zary, Dr. Keith W.; bud pointed, ovoid; flowers lavender, reverse pale lavender, 4 in., 41 petals, rosette, borne in large clusters, intense sweet fragrance; foliage medium size, dark green, glossy; prickles moderate; upright, spreading (3½ ft.) growth; PP11562; [seedling × Shocking Blue®]; intr. 1999

'Jacshume' HT, w, Zary, Keith; bud long, pointed; intr. 2006

'Jacshur' ('King Crimson') S, dr, 1991, Warriner, William A.; flowers large, semi-dbl., no fragrance; foliage large, dark green, semi-glossy; tall, upright, bushy growth; ['Razzle Dazzle' × seedling]; intr. 1991

'Jacsil' ('Eloquence', 'Little Silver') F, m, 1986, Warriner, William A.; flowers lavender, mini-flora, small, 20 petals, flat, borne singly and in clusters, slight spicy fragrance; foliage medium size, medium green, matte; upright, bushy growth; PP6010; [('Merci' × 'Faberge') × 'Angel Face']

'Jacsile' (Mirabella™) F, my, 1994, Zary, Dr. Keith W.; flowers very dbl., borne singly and in small clusters, intense fragrance; foliage medium size, dark green, glossy; some prickles; medium (80-100 cm.), upright,bushy growth; PP9657; ['Sunsprite' × 'Silver Jubilee']; intr. 1994

'Jacsilho' ('Rose Bayard', Pearl Essence™) HT, lp, 2000, Zary, Keith; bud long, pointed ovoid; flowers large, 30-35 petals, high-centered, borne mostly singly, moderate sweet fragrance; free-flowering; foliage medium size, dark green, glossy; prickles moderate, hooked downward; stems strong; vigorous, upright, medium (5 ft.) growth; PP12127; ['Sterling Silver' × Honor™]; intr. 2001

'Jacsim' ('Sweet Inspiration') F, mp, 1991, Warriner, William A.; bud short, pointed ovoid; flowers medium pink with some cream coloration at petal base, 4 in., full, high-centered, then flat, borne in large clusters, slight fragrance; fast repeat; foliage medium size, medium green, matte; prickles few, hooked slightly downward; stems short; upright (85-100 cm.), bushy growth; PP8581; ['Sun Flare' × 'Simplicity']; intr. 1993

'Jacsimpl' ('Red Simplicity') S, mr, 1991, Warriner, William A. & Zary, Keith W.; bud long, pointed ovoid; flowers bright red, a bit of blackening near petal edges, 3½-4 in., 20-25 petals, high-centered, then flat, borne singly and in small clusters, slight fragrance; foliage medium size, medium green, semi-glossy; prickles moderate, medium, hooked downward, red when young; medium, upright, spreading growth; PP8582; [seedling × 'Sun Flare']; intr. 1992

'Jacsling' (Legacy™) HT, mr, 1993, J&P

'Jacsmi' ('Smiles') Min, my, 1982, Warriner, William A.; flowers medium, 35 petals; foliage small, light green, semi-glossy; upright, bushy growth; PP5577; ['Spanish Sun' × 'Calgold']; intr. 1984

'Jacsnow' (White Simplicity®) V, w, Warriner ; bud pointed ovoid; intr. 1991

'Jacsod' ('Rhapsody') HT, mp, 1985, Warriner, William A.; flowers medium, 20 petals; foliage medium size, medium green, matte; [seedling × seedling]

'Jacsome' Min, dp, Walden, John; bud long, pointed, ovoid; intr. 1998

'Jacsos' ('Cherry Jubilee') S, mr, 1991, Warriner, William A.; flowers light to medium red, medium, dbl., no fragrance; foliage medium size, medium green, semi-glossy; upright, bushy growth; [seedling × 'Simplicity']; intr. 1991

'Jacsowe' ('Sowetan Peace') HT, dp; intr. 1994

'Jacspana' F, dp, J&Pdouble; intr. 2007

'Jacspec' F, pb, J&P

'Jacspif' ('Satin Doll') F, ly, 1986, Warriner, William A.; flowers cream to pale apricot; [sport of 'Pacifica']

'Jacspri' ('Eldorado') F, dy, Christensen, Jack E.; intr. 1992

'Jacstand' (Raspberry Swirl™) S, rb, 1999, Walden, John K.; flowers red, white, pink stripe, reverse same, 2 in., dbl., borne in large clusters, slight apple scent fragrance; foliage small, dark green, glossy; prickles moderate; upright, arching, medium (3-4 ft.) growth; PP11996; [seedling × Plum Dandy™]; intr. 1999

'Jacstine' ('Spirit of Peace') HT, yb, 1992, Warriner, William A.; flowers apricot yellow, opening with pink tinge where sun strikes the blooms, large, full, classic hybrid tea, borne mostly singly, slight spiced honey fragrance; recurrent; foliage medium size, dark green, semi-glossy; some prickles; tall (170-180 cm.), upright,spreading growth; [Pristine® × seedling]

'Jacsto' ('Future Award') HT, mr, J&P; intr. 1993

'Jacstop' ('Salsa') HT, dr, 1990, Warriner, William A.; bud ovoid, pointed; flowers large, 30-35 petals, high-centered, urn-shaped, borne singly, moderate damask fragrance; foliage medium size, dark green, semi-glossy; few prickles; upright, tall growth; PP6971; ['Showstopper' × seedling]

'Jscstrip' Min, rb, J&P; intr. 2000

'Jacsumio' (Welcome Home™) HT, ly, 2007, Zary, Keith W.; bud light yellow, pointed, ovoid; flowers peachy pink at center, aging to butter yellow, 4½ in., 30 petals, blooms borne mostly solitary, moderate licorice fragrance; foliage medium size, dark green, glossy; prickles 8-10 mm., straight, greyed-orange, moderate; growth upright, tall, 5½ ft.; PPAF; ['Sun Goddess' × O Sole Mio®]; intr. 2007

'Jacsumre' (Summer Samba™) F, op, 2000, Zary, Keith; bud long, pointed ovoid; flowers apricot orange, reverse apricot yellow, 4 in., 25-30 petals, high-centered, borne singly and in small clusters, moderate sweet damask fragrance; recurrent; foliage large, dark green, glossy; prickles moderate, medium, straight to hooked slighty downward; stems strong (14 - 18 in.); growth upright, medium (3½ ft.); landscape, containers; PP12114; [Sexy Rexy® × 'Summer Fashion']; intr. 2001

'Jacsun' ('Bojangles') Min, dy, 1982, Warriner, William A.; flowers deep yellow, small, 20 petals, no fragrance; foliage small, light green, semi-glossy; upright, bushy growth; PP4990; ['Spanish Sun' × 'Calgold']; intr. 1983

'Jacsunov' ('Super Nova') F, dp; intr. 1997

'Jacsur' (Bill Warriner™) F, op, 1998, Warriner, William A. & Zary, Keith W.; bud pointed, ovoid; flowers coral pink, ruffled edges, 3½-4 in., full, borne in large clusters, slight sweet fragrance; foliage medium size, dark green, semi-glossy; prickles moderate, straight; compact (3 ft.) growth; PP9494; ['Sun Flare' × 'Impatient']; intr. 1997

'Jacsuyel' (Golden Bounty™) S, my, 1999, Zary, Dr. Keith W.; flowers 2½ in., dbl., borne in large clusters, slight fragrance; foliage medium size, dark green, semi-glossy to glossy; few prickles; upright, arching, medium (3-4 ft.) growth; PP11849; ['Sun Flare' × seedling]; intr. 2001

'Jactafl' (Bridal Shower™) F, lp, 1998, Zary, Dr. Keith W.; flowers light pink, 4 in., very dbl., borne in small clusters, slight fragrance; foliage medium size, dark green, glossy; prickles moderate; upright, bushy, tall (4 ft.) growth; PP11220; [seedling × 'Sunflare']; intr. 1999

'Jactan' ('Butterscotch') LCl, r, 1986, Warriner, William A.; flowers tannish-orange, loose, 25 petals, cupped, borne in clusters of 3-5; foliage medium size, medium green, semi-glossy; no fruit; PP5895; [('Buccaneer' × 'Zorina') × 'Royal Sunset']

'Jactanic' (Moondance™) F, w, 2007, Zary, Keith W.; flowers full, blooms borne in large clusters; foliage medium size, dark green, glossy; prickles 8-10 mm., straight, greyed-orange, few; growth upright, tall (5 ft.); ['Hartanna' × 'Iceberg']; intr. 2007

'Jactanre' (Ronald Reagan™) HT, rb, 2005, Zary, Keith W.; bud long, pointed ovoid; flowers red, reverse white and red, 10-12 cm., 35 petals, high-centered, borne mostly solitary, slight fragrance; foliage medium size, dark green, glossy; prickles moderate, 6-10 mm., hooked downward, greyed orange; upright, branching, tall (150 cm.) growth; PP15061; [seedling × (seedling × 'Ingrid Bergman')]; intr. 2004

'Jactasy' F, w, Zary; bud long, pointed ovoid; intr. 1999

'Jacthain' (Tuscan Sun™) F, ab, 2005, Zary, Keith; bud pointed ovoid; flowers apricot-orange, 8-10 cm., 25 petals, high-centered, borne in small clusters of 3 - 7, slight spicy fragrance; recurrent; foliage large, dark green, glossy; prickles 8-10 mm., hooked slightly downward, greyed-orange, moderate; stems 10 - 12 in.; growth upright, branching, medium (100-120 cm.); PP17083; ['Singin' in the Rain' × (Pink Pollyanna™ × 'Impatient')]; intr. 2005

'Jactig' HT, ab, 1974, Warriner, William A.; bud ovoid

'Jactiger' ('Tiger Tail') F, ob, 1991, Christensen, Jack E.; flowers deep orange, white or cream colored stripes, cream colored reverse, medium, full, borne in small clusters, no fragrance; foliage medium size, medium green, glossy; medium, bushy growth; [Matangi® × Pinstripe™]; intr. 1992

'Jactoose' (Wild Thing™) S, dp, 2007, Zary, Keith W.; flowers hot pink, 3 in., semi-dbl., blooms borne in large clusters; foliage medium size, dark green, glossy; prickles 4-6 mm., hooked downward, greyed-orange, moderate; growth bushy, arching, medium (3½ ft.); landscape, bedding; PPAF; [seedling × 'Footloose']; intr. 2007

'Jactop' ('Legend', 'Top Star') HT, mr, 1992, Warriner, William A.; flowers 3-3½ in., very dbl., high-centered, borne mostly singly; foliage medium size, dark green, semi-glossy; prickles very small, on peduncle; tall (120-140 cm.), upright, bushy growth; PP6092; ['Grand Masterpiece' × seedling]

'Jactorob' HT, pb; bud pointed, ovoid; intr. 2007

'Jactorse' (Miss Behavin'™) F, pb, 2000, Zary, Keith; bud short, pointed ovoid; flowers deep pink, reverse cream pink, yellow at petal base, 4 in., 25-30 petals, high-centered, borne in small clusters, slight apple fragrance; foliage large, dark green, glossy; prickles moderate, hooked downward; upright, medium (3½ ft.) growth; PP12129; ['Tournament of Roses' × 'red floribunda seedling']; intr. 2001

'Jactosam' F, ob; intr. 2003

'Jactou' (Midas Touch™) HT, dy, 1992, Christensen, Jack E.; bud urn-shaped; flowers bright, non-fading yellow, 3½-4 in., dbl., high-centered, borne mostly singly, moderate musk fragrance; foliage large, medium green, matte; prickles small on peduncle; tall (150-160 cm.), upright, bushy growth; PP8706; [Brandy™ × 'Friesensohne']; intr. 1994

'Jactourn' ('Good Samaritan', Voluptuous!™) HT, dp, 2005, Zary, Keith W.; bud long, pointed ovoid; flowers fuchsia, reverse fuchsia, 4½-5 in., 35 petals, high-centered, borne mostly solitary, some small clusters, moderate spicy fragrance; recurrent; foliage large, dark green, glossy; prickles several, ½ in., slightly curved downward, brown; stems strong, medium; upright, medium (5 ft.) growth; PP16498; ['Tournament of Roses' × Trumpeter®]

'Jactred' ('American Spirit', 'Medal of Honor') HT, mr, 1986, Warriner, William A.; flowers large, 35 petals, high-centered, borne usually singly, no fragrance; foliage medium size, medium green, semi-glossy; upright, tall growth; PP6083; [seedling × 'American Pride']; intr. 1988

'Jactrig' (Fragrant Rhapsody™) HT, m, 1999, Zary, Dr. Keith W.; flowers light lavender blend, small, 20-40 petals, borne mostly singly, intense fragrance; foliage medium size, medium green, glossy; prickles moderate; upright, spreading, medium (4 ft.) growth; PP12072; ['Intrigue' × seedling]; intr. 1999

'Jactro' ('Sheer Bliss') HT, w, 1985, Warriner, William A.; flowers white with pink center, large, 35 petals, high-centered, borne singly, moderate spicy fragrance; foliage medium size, medium green, matte; prickles medium brown; medium, upright, bushy growth; PP6282; ['White Masterpiece' × 'Grand Masterpiece']; intr. 1987

'Jactu' ('Headliner') HT, pb, 1985, Warriner, William A.; flowers petals white, blending to deep pink at edges, large, 40 petals, high-centered, slight fragrance; foliage large, medium green, glossy; upright growth; PP5340; ['Love' × 'Color Magic']; intr. 1986

'Jacturpl' ('Turkish Delight', Tigress™) Gr, m, 2005, Zary, Keith; bud long; flowers striped with 2 slightly differing red-purples and white, reverse striping of red-purple and white, 9-11 cm., 25 petals, high-centered, borne singly and in small clusters, intense sweet gardenia fragrance; recurrent; foliage large, dark green, glossy; prickles few, 10mm., hooked downward, brown; stems strong, 18 in.; growth upright, branching, medium (1¼-1½ m.); PP13777; ['Purple Tiger' × seedling]

'Jactutti' ('Tutti-Frutti') Min, yb, 1991, Christensen, Jack E.; bud ovoid, pointed; flowers yellow with red-orange stripes, medium, 25-30 petals, cupped, slight fragrance; foliage medium size, dark green, semi-glossy; bushy, spreading, medium growth; ['Fool's Gold' × Pinstripe™]; intr. 1991

'Jactwin' ('Love') Gr, rb, 1979, Warriner, William A.; bud short, pointed; flowers bright scarlet red, reverse silvery white, large, 35 petals, high-centered, borne mostly singly, slight rose fragrance; foliage dark green, glossy, new growth is red; long stems; upright growth; PP4437; [unknown × 'Redgold']; intr. 1980

'Jactwist' ('Flirtatious™) F, yb, 2005, Zary, Keith W.; flowers full, borne in large clusters, moderate fragrance; foliage medium size, dark green, glossy; prickles 7-10 mm., hooked downward, greyed-orange, moderate; growth upright, medium (1¼ m.); PP15335; ['SunFlare (JACjem)' × 'JACraw']; intr. 2003

'Jacum' ('Intrigue') F, m, 1982, Warriner, William A.; flowers reddish-purple, large, 20 petals; foliage medium size, dark, semi-glossy; PP5002; ['White Masterpiece' × 'Heirloom']; intr. 1984

'Jscunkno' S, mp, J&P; intr. 2007

'Jacuntor' F, ab, J&P; intr. 2008

'Jacunu' F, w, J&P; intr. 2000

'Jacup' ('Upstart') Min, mr, 1982, Warriner, William A.; flowers small, semi-dbl.; foliage small, medium green, semi-glossy; upright growth; ['Merci' × 'Fire Princess']; intr. 1984

'Jacurnam' ('Nancy Reagan™) HT, ab, 2005, Zary, Keith W.; flowers full, 30 petals, borne mostly solitary, moderate fragrance; foliage large, dark green, glossy; prickles 5-6 mm., hooked downward, greyed-orange, moderate; growth upright, branching, medium (150 cm.) bush; PP15115; ['Jacient' × seedling]; intr. 2004

'Jacurp' ('Night Star') F, m, J&P; intr. 1997

'Jacute' ('Confection') Min, mp, 1989, Warriner, William A.; bud ovoid, pointed; flowers pink with small yellow to cream base, medium, very dbl., high-centered, then flattened, borne usually singly, slight fragrance; foliage medium size, dark green, matte; prickles straight to slightly hooked, light green; low, bushy growth; PP6518; [seedling × seedling]; intr. 1988

'Jacval' (Ultimate Pink™) HT, lp, 1998, Zary, Dr. Keith W.; bud pointed, ovoid; flowers clear medium pink, 4½-5 in., 25-30 petals, high-centered, borne mostly singly, slight sweet fragrance; recurrent; foliage large, medium green, dull, leathery; prickles numerous, short, straight to hooked downward; stems long (18 - 22 in.), strong; tall (4½ ft.), upright, vigorous growth; PP11048; [(Honor™ × 'Silver Jubilee') × 'Fragrant Memory']; intr. 1999

'Jacvelma' HT, dp, Zary, Keith; intr. 1999

'Jacven' F, w, 1973, Warriner, William A.; intr. 1974

'Jacvep' ('Corina', 'Peach Princess') HT, pb, 1992, Warriner, William A. & Zary, Keith W.; flowers salmon pink with darker edges and lighter, almost cream, reverse, medium, full, high-centered, moderate fragrance; foliage large, dark green, matte; few prickles; medium (150 cm.), upright growth; [Bridal Pink™ × 'Kardinal']; intr. 1993

'Jacveryp' ('Helen Suzman Rose', 'Our Lady of Guadalupe', Shining Hope™) F, pb, 2000, Zary, Keith; flowers light pink, reverse medium pink, 8-9 cm., 25 petals, borne in small clusters, moderate fragrance; foliage medium size, dark green, glossy; prickles moderate; growth upright, medium (80-90 cm.); ['Jacsedi' × 'Jacsim']; intr. 2001

'Jacvet' ('Velvet Treasure') HT, dr; intr. 1992

'Jacvetor' HT, mr, Zary; intr. 2002

'Jacvoo' ('First Affair') HT, w, J&P; intr. 1996

'Jacwade' ('Snow Shower') Min, w, 1992, Warriner, William A. & Zary, Keith W.; bud short, pointed ovoid; flowers snow white, 1-1½ in., 45-50 petals, high-centered to flat, borne singly and in small clusters, no fragrance; recurrent; foliage small, medium to dark green, glossy; prickles some, short, hooked downward; stems 5 - 6 in.; growth low (25-40 cm.), spreading (60-75 cm.) across; groundcover; PP9374; [Immensee® × 'Roller Coaster']; intr. 1993

'Jacweave' LCl, mp; bud pointed, ovoid; intr. 2004

'Jacwhim' ('Shy Girl') Min, w, 1989, Warriner, William A.; bud ovoid, pointed; flowers medium, 80 petals, high-centered, borne usually singly and in sprays of 2-4; foliage medium size, dark green, semi-glossy; prickles straight, short; upright, spreading, low growth; no fruit; PP6514; ['Petticoat' × Red Minimo™]; intr. 1988

'Jacwhink' S, w, J&P; intr. 2007

'Jacwhip' ('Snow Angel') S, w, 1993; flowers white with a light pink tone and a hint of yellow near petal base, medium, very dbl.; foliage small, dark green, semi-glossy; some prickles; medium (5 ft.), upright, bushy growth; [sport of Pink Pollyanna™]; intr. 1993

'Jacwhy' ('Tricia') F, w, 1972, Warriner, W. A.; buds medium, long pointed; intr. 1972

'Jacwig' (Wild Plum™) Min, m, 1998, Zary, Dr. Keith W.; flowers lavender blend, darker reverse, 1½-2 in., 25 petals, high-centered, borne in large clusters, slight fragrance; recurrent; foliage medium size, dark green, glossy; prickles few, straight; growth bushy, tall (3 ft.); hedging; PP9493; ['Winsome' × 'Elegance']; intr. 1995

'Jacwiht' ('Cathedral Peak') HT, w, J&P; intr. 1995

'Jacwipet' (Snowcone™) S, w, 2007, Zary, Keith W.; flowers pure white, yellow stamens, 1 in., single, shallow cup, blooms borne in large clusters, slight fragrance; foliage small, dark green, glossy; prickles few, 4-6 mm., hooked downward, greyed-orange; growth upright, short (2 ft.); mini shrub, mixed perennial beds; PPAF; [seedling × seedling]; intr. 2006

'Jacworro' ('Buttercream') HT, ly, 2004, Zary, Keith W.; flowers light yellow, reverse light yellow, 5 in., full, borne mostly solitary, moderate fragrance; foliage large, dark green, glossy; prickles 4-6 mm., hooked slightly downward; growth upright, tall (5 ft.); specimen, garden; PP13925; intr. 2003

'Jacwotte' (Vanilla Perfume™) HT, ab, 1999, Zary, Dr. Keith W.; bud plump, ovoid; flowers light cream, blushed apricot/pink, reverse light apricot, 4-4½ in., 35 petals, high-centered, borne mostly singly and in small clusters, intense sweet, spicy vanilla fragrance; recurrent; foliage medium size, dark green, semi-glossy to glossy; prickles moderate, medium, hooked downward, brown; stems strong; upright, tall (5 ft.) growth; PP12464; ['Anne Morrow Lindbergh' × (Honor™ × 'Silver Jubilee')]; intr. 1999

'Jacwypin' (Change of Heart™) HT, pb, 2007, Zary, Keith W.; flowers medium pink, reverse white, 4½ in., full, borne mostly solitary; foliage medium size, dark green, glossy; prickles 8-10 mm., hooked, greyed-orange, moderate; growth upright, tall (5 ft.); [seedling × seedling]; intr. 2007

'Jacyap' ('Anne Morrow Lindbergh', 'Melinda Gainsford') HT, pb, 1993, Warriner, William A.; flowers pink, white, yellow blend, 3-3½ in., full, borne mostly singly, moderate fragrance; foliage medium to large, medium green, semi-glossy; some prickles; tall (150-160 cm.), upright growth; [seedling × seedling]; intr. 1994

'Jacyarp' (Mai Tai™) Min, op, 2001, Zary, Keith; bud pointed, ovoid; flowers coral and yellow buds opening to a dusty orange, finishing in pink., 2 in., 20 petals, borne in small clusters, slight fresh fragrance; foliage medium size, dark green, glossy; prickles moderate; growth upright, compact, medium (2½ ft.); PP12993; [seedling × seedling]; intr. 2002

'Jacyef' (Shining Hour™) Gr, dy, 1990, Warriner, William A.; bud short, pointed ovoid; flowers deep, bright yellow, 4 in., 30-35 petals, high-centered, borne singly and in sprays, moderate fruity fragrance; recurrent; foliage large, dark green, semi-glossy; prickles fairly long, hooked downward, red to yellow; stems medium, strong; upright, bushy, medium growth; PP7949; [Sunbright® × 'Sun Flare']; intr. 1991

'Jacyeflo' F, my, J&P; intr. 2008

'Jacyelap' (Sultry™) HT, ab, 2000, Zary, Keith; flowers apricot yellow, 5½ in., full, high-centered, borne mostly singly, moderate fragrance; recurrent; foliage large, dark green, glossy; prickles moderate; upright, tall (6 ft.) growth; PP12126; [('Legend' × unknown) × ('Tansenfrie' × unknown)]; intr. 2001

'Jacyelgo' F, dy, Zary

'Jacyelsh' ('Lemon Bells', 'Yellow Simplicity') S, dy, 1998, Zary, Dr. Keith W.; bud long, pointed ovoid; flowers deep yellow, 3 in., 15-20 petals, cupped to globular, borne in small clusters, slight fragrance; free-flowering; foliage medium size, dark green, glossy, leathery; prickles moderate, long, hooked downward; stems medium, strong, vigorous, upright (4.5 ft.) growth; hedging; PP10283; [seedling × seedling]; intr. 1997

'Jacyem' ('Santa Fe') HT, my, 1993, Zary, Dr. Keith W.; bud long, pointed ovoid; flowers rich, medium yellow, 5-5½ in., 35-40 petals, high-centered, borne singly, moderate musk fragrance; good repeat; foliage large, dark green, matte; prickles few, medium to short, hooked downward; stems long, strong, straight; vigorous, upright (6-7 ft.) growth; PP9329; [Emblem™ × seedling]; greenhouse rose; intr. 1993

'Jacyepat' ('Gold Dust', 'Yellow Jacket') S, dy, 1992, Christensen, Jack E.; flowers rich yellow, loose, 2 in., full, cupped, borne mostly singly or small clusters, slight fragrance; free-flowering; foliage medium size, dark green, glossy, very disease-resistant; some prickles; vigorous, medium (2½-3 ft.), upright, bushy growth; [seedling × seedling]

'Jacyes' (Henry Fonda™) HT, dy, 1998, Christensen; bud pointed, ovoid; flowers deep yellow, pointed, 4½-5 in., 20-25 petals, high-centered, borne mostly singly; foliage medium size, dark green, glossy; tall growth; PP9390; intr. 1996

'Jacyesp' ('Golden Galaxy') F, my, J&P; intr. 1997

'Jacyim' (Sunsplash™) Min, dy, 1989, Warriner, William A.; bud short, ovoid, pointed; flowers deep yellow, aging pale yellow on petal edges, 1½ in., 40-45 petals, flat, borne in sprays of 18-21, very slight fragrance; free-flowering; foliage medium size, medium green, very glossy, attractive; prickles few, long, slightly hooked downward, red to green-tan; stems medium; bushy, upright (2 ft.), spreading growth; PP7127; ['Rise 'n' Shine' × 'Sun Flare']

'Jacyimp' (Honey Bouquet™) F, yb, 1999, Zary, Dr. Keith W.; bud pointed, ovoid; flowers light yellow, hint of pink, reverse light yellow, 4½-5 in., 35-40 petals, borne in small clusters, intense sweet fragrance; foliage medium size, dark green, semi-glossy; upright, spreading, medium (3½ ft.) growth; PP11882; [seedling × Amber Queen®]; intr. 1999

'Jacyo' (Dynasty™) HT, ob, 1990, Warriner, William A.; bud pointed; flowers bright orange with yellow blending at petal base, aging to coral, 30 petals, cupped, no fragrance; foliage medium size, medium green, semi-glossy; prickles hooked down slightly, red to yellow-green; upright, spreading, tall growth; PP6443; [seedling × seedling]; intr. 1991

'Jaczap' (Outrageous™) F, ob, 1999, Zary, Dr. Keith W.; bud pointed, ovoid; flowers soft orange tinged with yellow, 3½-4 in., 25-30 petals, high-centered, borne in small clusters, moderate lemon fragrance; foliage medium size, dark green, dull; prickles moderate; bushy, medium (3½ ft.) growth; PP12073; ['Summer Fashion' × seedling]; intr. 1999

'Jaczeeze' (Fragrant Wave™) F, w, 2005, Zary, Keith W.; flowers 8-9 cm., dbl., borne in small clusters, moderate fragrance; foliage large, dark green, glossy; prickles 8-10 mm., hooked downward, greyed-yellow, few; upright, branching, tall (4 ft.) growth; PP16664; [seedling × 'Vie en Rose']; intr. 2005

'Jaczeman' ('Stodels Beauty', Sundance™) HT, yb, 2005, Zary, Keith W.; bud long, pointed ovoid; flowers bright yellow, tipped orange, 9-11 cm., 25 petals, high-centered, borne singly and in small clusters of 3 - 5, moderate spicy fragrance; foliage large, dark green, glossy; prickles few, 8-10 mm., straight, greyed-yellow; stems medium, strong; upright, branching, medium (140-160 cm.) growth; PP16388; [seedling × 'AROgoru']

'Jaczeyel' (Solstice™) Gr, ly, 2007, Zary, Keith W.; flowers full, blooms borne in small clusters; foliage medium size, dark green, semi-glossy; prickles 8-10 mm., hooked downward, greyed-orange, moderate; growth upright, tall, 5-6 ft.; [seedling × seedling]; intr. 2005

'Jaczibwo' (Salsa™) F, dr, 2001, Zary, Keith; bud pointed, ovoid; flowers bright, velvety red, 3½-4 in., 20 petals, shallow cupped, borne in small clusters, slight light, fresh fragrance; repeats well; foliage medium size, dark green, glossy; prickles moderate; growth upright, medium (3 ft.); garden decorative; PP14245; ['Showbiz' × red floribunda seedling]; intr. 2002

'Jaczor' (Fame!™) Gr, dp, 1998, Zary, Dr. Keith W.; flowers deep shocking pink - almost light red, 5 in., 30-35 petals, high-centered, borne in small clusters; foliage large, dark green; shrubby, full bush, tall growth; PP11293; ['Tournament of Roses' × 'Zorina']; intr. 1998

'Jaczorba' ('Emile Debroise', Citrus Splash™, 'The Gardener') S, ob, 2007, Zary, Keith W.; flowers orange and yellow striped, 3½ in., dbl., blooms borne in small clusters; foliage medium size, dark green, glossy; prickles 6-8 mm., hooked downward, greyed-orange, moderate; growth upright, medium (4½ ft.); [seedling × seedling]

'Jaczotta' (Sorbet Bouquet™) F, pb, 1999, Zary, Dr. Keith W.; bud long, pointed ovoid; flowers rose pink, reverse light yellow, 4 in., 30 petals, high-centered, borne singly and several together, slight fragrance; recurrent; foliage medium size, dark green, glossy; prickles moderate, medium, hooked downward; stems strong; bushy, upright, medium (3½ ft.) growth; PP12128; ['Tournament of Roses' × 'floribunda seedling']; intr. 2000

Jade™ -- See 'Poulspan'

'Jade' HT, ob, Richardier; flowers yellow suffused with orange, very dbl., cupped; growth to 80-100 cm.; intr. 1999

'Jade' HT, w, Tantau; flowers creamy white with green tint on outer petals, medium, dbl., exhibition; cut flower rose; intr. 2000

'Jadis' ('Fragrant Memory') HT, mp, 1974, Warriner, William A.; flowers large, dbl., high-centered, intense fragrance; foliage large, light, leathery; vigorous, upright, bushy growth; PP3423; ['Chrysler Imperial' × 'Virgo']

'Jaen' HT, pb

'Jägerbataillon' (strain of R. canina), lp; almost thornless; growth once popular as an understock

'Jaguar' F, mr, Spek; PP4462; intr. 1977

'Jakaranda' -- See 'Jacakor'

'Jake McIlroy' HT, mp, Brundrett; intr. 1997

'Jakwen' ('Wenche') HT, w, 2006, Jaksland, Roger; flowers edged light red, 9 cm., full, borne mostly solitary; foliage medium size, medium green, semi-glossy; prickles 1 cm., sharp, red/brown, moderate; growth upright (80 × 80 cm.); bedding, borders, containers; ['Sekel' × Memoire®]; intr. 2003

'Jalact' ('Opening Act') Min, dr, 1993, Jalbert, Brad; flowers medium, single, borne in small clusters, no fragrance; foliage medium size, dark green, glossy;

some prickles; medium (30-35 cm.), upright growth; ['Anytime' × Black Jade™]; intr. 1994

'Jalanita' ('Anita Russell') Min, mp, 2004, Jalbert, Brad; flowers pink, petals having pointed tips, 1¼ in., dbl., borne in small clusters, slight fragrance; foliage medium green, semi-glossy; prickles medium, green, moderate; growth upright, medium (14-16 in.); ['Cherry Wine' × 'Glowing Amber']; intr. 2001

'Jalbelle' ('Vancouver Belle') S, lp, 2004, Jalbert, Brad; flowers pink, reverse lighter pink, 3-4 in., dbl., borne in small clusters, slight fragrance; recurrent; foliage medium size, medium green, glossy; prickles medium, green, moderate; growth bushy, medium (2-3 ft.); hedge, container, garden decoration; ['Thelma's Glory' × Sexy Rexy®]; intr. 1999

'Jalcoral' ('Super Cascade Coral') Min, op, 1996, Jalbert, Brad; flowers coral, petals very frilly, 1½ in., very dbl., borne in large clusters, slight fragrance; foliage medium size, dark green, glossy; few prickles; spreading, medium (12 in.), cascading growth; ['Orange Honey' × Sexy Rexy®]; intr. 1997

'Jalexhibit' ('Exhibitionist!') Min, m, 2004, Jalbert, Brad; flowers mauve, petal edges darker in cool weather, 1½ in., very full, borne mostly solitary, slight fragrance; foliage medium size, dark green, glossy; prickles small, hooked, green, moderate; bushy, medium growth; containers, garden decoration, exhibition; [seedling × Black Jade™]; intr. 2004

'Jalgalla' ('Len Gallagher') Min, rb, 2004, Jalbert, Brad; flowers mottled red with white stripes, reverse red with white stripes, 1½ in., full, borne in small clusters; foliage medium size, medium green, semi-glossy; prickles medium, green, moderate; growth upright, tall (16-18 in.); garden; [Sachet™ × Pinstripe™]; intr. 2002

'Jalgary' ('Gary Michael ') Min, my, 2004, Jalbert, Brad; flowers yellow, changing to buff or peach depending on weather, 1½ in., full, borne in small clusters, slight fragrance; foliage medium size, medium green, glossy; small, hooked, redish, no prickle; growth upright, medium (14 in.); containers, cutting; ['Sandalwood' × Sexy Rexy®]; intr. 2003

'Jalgerda' ('Gerda Hnatyshyn') HT, mp, 2004, Jalbert, Brad; flowers pure pink, 5 in., full, borne mostly solitary, intense fragrance; foliage medium size, dark green, very glossy, very thick; prickles large, dark, numerous; growth upright, medium (4 ft.); cut flower, garden rose; [Pristine® × 'New Zealand']

'Jalglory' ('Thelma's Glory') MinFl, dp, 2004, Jalbert, Brad; flowers self-cleaning, 2 in., semi-dbl., borne in large clusters, slight fragrance; foliage medium size, dark green, very glossy; prickles moderate, medium, hooked, green; growth bushy, medium (16-20 in.), very round; low hedge, containers, garden; very hardy; ['Anytime' × Flower Carpet™]; intr. 1999

'Jalgrad' ('Graduation Day') MinFl, ab, 2004, Jalbert, Brad; flowers apricot, petals frilled, 2 in., very dbl., old-fashioned, borne in large clusters; foliage medium size, dark green, very glossy, reddish when new; prickles medium, slight hook, reddish, few; bushy, medium (20 in.), mounding growth; ['Thelmas Glory' × Sexy Rexy®]; intr. 2000

'Jaljambor' ('John Jambor') Min, m, 2005, Jalbert, Brad; flowers full, borne mostly solitary, slight fragrance; foliage medium size, medium green, semi-glossy; prickles small, hooked, green, numerous; growth upright, medium (14 in.); [seedling × Rainbow's End™]; petals turn pink at the edges in cool weather; intr. 2005

'Jaljanet' ('Janet A. Wood') S, op, 2004, Jalbert, Brad; flowers orangey pink, reverse orange-pink, fading to pink, yellow eye, tiny, 1 in., single, borne in large clusters, slight fragrance; foliage small, medium green, semi-glossy; prickles small, hooked,; growth bushy, medium (3-4 ft.); hedge, garden decoration; ['Ana Ford' × 'Ballerina']; intr. 1998

'Jalmac' ('Rose MacKenzie') MinFl, dr, 2005, Jalbert, Brad; flowers very dark, velvety red, 2 in., full, borne in large clusters, slight fragrance; foliage medium size, dark green, glossy; prickles medium, pointed, dark, numerous; growth bushy, medium (2 ft.); ['Thelma's Glory' × 'Glad Tidings']; intr. 2005

'Jalmoon' ('Moondance Masquerade') MinFl, w, 2005, Jalbert, Brad; flowers white, sometimes with a cream-green hue, 1 in., full, borne mostly solitary, slight fragrance; foliage medium size, medium green, semi-glossy; prickles medium, pointed, green, moderate; growth upright, tall (2 ft.); ['Auntie Louise' × Marilyn Monroe™]; intr. 2006

'Jalnana' ('Nana's Rose') Min, m, 2004, Jalbert, Brad; flowers reddish-purple, striped white, reverse white-purple, ½ in., full, borne in small clusters, slight fragrance; foliage small, medium green, semi-glossy; prickles small, green, numerous; growth compact, bushy, dense, short (under 12 in.); containers, garden decoration; ['Fairy Moss' × 'Hurdy Gurdy']; intr. 2000

'Jalnicole' ('Reah Nicole') MinFl, pb, 2004, Jalbert, Brad; flowers pink and cream, 1½-2 in., full, borne in small clusters, slight fragrance; foliage medium size, medium green, semi-glossy; prickles moderate, medium size, green; growth upright, 18 in. and up; cutting, garden decoration; [Loving Touch™ × Kristin™]; intr. 2000

'Jalorangepat' ('Orange Patio Wonder') Min, ob, 2004, Jalbert, Brad; flowers orange, reverse light orange, 1½ in., very full, borne in large clusters, slight fragrance; foliage medium size, medium green, glossy; prickles moderate, small, green; upright, medium (14-16 in.) growth; ['Orange Honey' × Sexy Rexy®]; intr. 1999

'Jalouise' ('Auntie Louise') Min, ob, 2004, Jalbert, Brad; flowers orange tinged pink, reverse lighter orange, 1¼ in., full, borne in small clusters, slight fragrance; foliage medium size, medium green, semi-glossy; prickles medium, reddish brown, numerous; growth spreading, medium (14-16 in.); containers, garden decorative; ['Orange Honey' × Sexy Rexy®]; intr. 1999

'Jalpark' ('Sherry Parks Sunrise') MinFl, ab, 2005, Jalbert, Brad; flowers apricot, sometimes with slight salmon veining, 2½-3 in., very full, old-fashioned, borne in small clusters, slight fresh fragrance; foliage medium green, glossy; prickles medium, pointed, green, moderate; growth bushy, medium (20 in. or more); ['Graduation Day' × 'Fellowship']; intr. 2005

'Jalpink' ('Heaven Scent Pink') Min, lp, 1996, Jalbert, Brad; flowers wide, 2 in., full, flat, intense fragrance; foliage medium size, medium green, dull, reddish; few prickles; upright, tall (24 in.) growth; ['Rise 'n' Shine' × 'Rosemary Harkness']; intr. 1997

'Jalpinkpat' ('Pink Patio Wonder') Min, mp, 2004, Jalbert, Brad; flowers very full, borne in small clusters, slight fragrance; foliage very dark green, very glossy; prickles small, green, numerous; growth bushy, medium (14 in.); containers, garden decoration; ['seedling 68-91' × Sexy Rexy®]; intr. 1999

'Jalpurple' ('Color Purple', 'The Colour Purple') Min, m, 2004, Jalbert, Brad; flowers deep purple, 1¼ in., dbl., borne mostly solitary, moderate lemon fragrance; foliage medium size, dark green, very glossy, dark when new; prickles small, dark, moderate; growth upright, medium (14 in.); containers, garden decoration; [Loving Touch™ × 'Rubies']; intr. 2004

'Jalray' ('Reiko') Min, lp, 1995, Jalbert, Brad; flowers medium pink, lighter pink reverse, 1 in., dbl., borne in small clusters, moderate fragrance; foliage medium size, medium green, glossy; some prickles; medium (12 in.), compact, bushy growth; ['Winsome' × Springwood Gold™]; intr. 1995

'Jalreef' ('Coral Reef') Min, mp, 2004, Jalbert, Brad; buds heavily mossed, sticky, scented; flowers 1 in., full, borne mostly solitary, slight fragrance; foliage dark green, glossy; prickles small, green, numerous; growth compact, short, pot or garden; ['Dresdon Doll' × 'Silver Jubilee']; intr. 2000

'Jalshilo' ('Shiloh Hill Rose') F, rb, 2005, Jalbert, Brad; flowers red, reverse silver-white, 2-3 in., full, borne in large clusters, no fragrance; foliage medium size, dark green, glossy; prickles medium, pointed, reddish, moderate; growth bushy, medium (2½-3 ft.); ['Thelma's Glory' × 'Glad Tiding's']; intr. 2006

'Jalstar' ('Rising Star') Min, pb, 1995, Jalbert, Brad; flowers cream with strong pink blend edges, 1-2 in., full, borne mostly singly, slight fragrance; foliage medium size, medium green, semi-glossy; some prickles; tall (18 in.) upright, bushy growth; ['Sans Souci' × 'Pink Petticoat']; intr. 1995

'Jalsun' ('Sun Chariot') Min, my, 1995, Jalbert, Brad; flowers medium yellow with blush of salmon on edges, bright gold stamens, medium, dbl., borne in small clusters, moderate fragrance; foliage medium size, dark green, matte; numerous prickles; medium, upright, tall growth; ['Pink Petticoat' × Bright Smile®]; intr. 1996

'Jaltalat' ('Mrs Talat Rizvi') HT, ob, 2007, Jalbert, Brad; flowers orange, reverse apricot, 6 in., dbl., borne mostly solitary; foliage medium, dark green, glossy; prickles medium, slightly hooked, darkish purple, moderate; growth upright, medium (3-4 ft.); ['Rosemary Harkness' × 'New Zealand']; intr. 2008

'Jaltinskii Suvenir' F, ly, Klimenko, V. N.; flowers large, dbl.; intr. 1956

'Jalwater' ('Water Lily') MinFl, w, 2004, Jalbert, Brad; flowers cream white, 2 in., dbl., borne in very large clusters, slight fragrance; foliage medium size, medium green, semi-glossy; prickles moderate, medium, green; growth upright, tall (2 ft.); cut flower, garden rose; ['Pink Petticoat' × 'Alexander HT.']; intr. 1998

'Jalwed' ('Summer Wedding') Min, mp, 1995, Jalbert, Brad; flowers medium, full, borne in small clusters, slight fragrance; foliage medium size, medium green, semi-glossy; few prickles; compact, bushy, medium growth; [Maurine Neuberger™ × Sexy Rexy®]; intr. 1996

'Jalwhitepat' ('White Patio Wonder') Min, w, 2004, Jalbert, Brad; flowers white, edges turning pink in cool weather, 1½ in., very full, borne in small clusters, no fragrance; foliage medium size, dark green, glossy; prickles moderate, small, hooked, dark; spreading, wide, medium (14 in.) growth; ['Thelma's Glory' × Sexy Rexy®]; intr. 1999

'Jalwine' ('Cherry Wine') Min, mr, 1993, Jalbert, Brad; flowers medium, full, borne mostly singly, slight fragrance; foliage medium size, medium green, matte; some prickles; medium (30-35 cm.), spreading growth; [Dee Bennett™ × 'Winsome']; intr. 1994

'Jalwood' ('Sandalwood') Min, r, 1995, Jalbert, Brad; flowers russet with lighter edges, 1 in., dbl., borne in small clusters, no fragrance; foliage medium size, medium green, glossy; some prickles; medium (12 in.), compact, bushy growth; ['Blushing Blue' × Springwood Gold™]

'Jalyear' ('Year 2000') Min, yb, 2004, Jalbert, Brad; flowers yellow with scarlet petal edges, reverse yellow, 1¼ in., full, high-centered, borne in small clusters, no fragrance; recurrent; foliage medium size, very dark green, glossy, heavy; prickles moderate, medium, green-brown; growth bushy, medium (14-16 in.); garden and container; [Laura Ford® × 'Kristen']; intr. 2000

'Jam Session' -- See 'Zipjam'

'Jamaica' HT, mr, 1965, Lindquist; bud ovoid; flowers cherry-red, large, semi-dbl., cupped, moderate fragrance; foliage dark, glossy, leathery; vigorous, upright growth; PP2627; [('Charlotte Armstrong' × 'Floradora') × 'Nocturne']

'Jambo' HT, or, Kordes; flowers bright vermilion-orange, full, high-centered, borne singly and in clusters; cut flower rose; intr. 2002

'Jamboree' F, rb, 1964, Gregory; flowers cherry-red, reverse lighter, 1½-2 in., 26 petals, flat, borne in clusters; foliage glossy, light green; free growth; ['Masquerade' × unknown]

'James Appleby' F, ob, 1963, Wood; flowers orange-scarlet flecked deep crimson, medium, semi-dbl., borne in clusters; vigorous growth; [sport of 'Orangeade']

'James Biddle' -- See 'Wiljame'

'James Bond' -- See 'James Bond 007'

'James Bond 007' ('James Bond') HT, op, 1968, Tantau, Math.; flowers coral-pink, pointed; foliage glossy; bushy growth; [unknown × 'Fragrant Cloud']; intr. 1966

'James Bougault' -- See 'James Bourgault'

'James Bourgault' ('James Bougault') HP, w, 1887, Renaud-Guépet; flowers white, shaded rose; [sport of 'Auguste Mie']

'James Brownlow' HP, mp, 1890, Dickson, A.; flowers glossy pink, very large, full, moderate fragrance; ['Marquise de Castellane' × 'Paul Neyron']

'James Dickson' HP, pb, 1861, Verdier, E.; flowers carmine, shaded purple-violet, dbl.

'James Ferris' HT, w, 1927, Hall; flowers creamy white; vigorous growth

'James Galway' -- See 'Auscrystal'

'James Gibson' HT, mr, 1928, McGredy; bud pointed; flowers crimson-scarlet, large, dbl., high-centered; foliage dark, leathery; vigorous, bushy growth

'James Mason' HGal, mr, Beales, Peter; flowers bright crimson with golden anthers, large, semi-dbl., borne in clusters, profuse, moderate citrus fragrance; non-remontant; arching, spreading, vigorous (4 ft.) growth; intr. 1982

'James Mitchell' M, dp, 1861, Verdier, E.; flowers deep pink nuanced lilac, slaty, medium, dbl.; early bloom; very heavily mossed stems

James Pereire® HT, pb, Meilland; flowers bengal pink, clear rose reverse, 24-26 petals, moderate fragrance; foliage semi-glossy; intr. 1995

'James Power' -- See 'Kenniece'

'James Rea' HT, dp, 1930, McGredy; bud pointed; flowers rich carmine or rose-pink, very large, dbl., high-centered; foliage light, leathery; vigorous, bushy growth

'James Robert' -- See 'Rawlemal'

James Smile® HT, pb, 1987, Rogin, Josip; flowers China-pink, reverse pink-yellow blend, loose, medium, semi-dbl., cupped, borne in sprays of 3, moderate spicy fragrance; foliage medium size, medium green, semi-glossy; prickles rare, small, brown; upright, medium growth; hips rounded, medium size, pink-red; [sport of 'Sea Pearl']

'James Sprunt' Cl Ch, mr, 1858, Sprunt; flowers carmine-red, velvety, medium, dbl.; [sport of 'Cramoisi Supérieur']; possibly synonymous with 'Cramoisi Supérieur, Climbing']

'James Veitch' ('James Weltch') M, m, Verdier, E.; flowers violet-slate shaded fiery red, large, dbl., borne in clusters of 3-8; some repeat; moderately vigorous growth; intr. 1865

'James Veitch' HP, dp, 1852, Laffay; flowers flower deep pink to bright carmine, large, full; ['La Reine' × unknown]

'James Walley' HT, ab, 1923, Easlea; flowers apricot and fiery salmon, large, dbl.; foliage olive-green, leathery; vigorous growth; ['Ophelia' × seedling]

'James Weltch' -- See 'James Veitch'

'James Woodlock' -- See 'Horproper'

'Jamestown' -- See 'Wilcipks'

Jamie™ -- See 'Mogajam'

'Jamie Alexander' S, rb, Hannemann, F.; ['Ko's Yellow' × Eyepaint®]

'Jamie's Love' -- See 'Geljam'

'Jan Abbing' HT, rb, 1933, Tantau; bud pointed; flowers salmon-red shaded yellow, large, cupped; foliage leathery, dark; vigorous growth; ['Columbia' × 'Étoile de Hollande']

'Jan and Rick' -- See 'Moejanrick'

'Jan Böhm' HP, mr, 1934, Svoboda; flowers velvety fiery red, 40 petals, moderate fragrance; recurrent bloom; vigorous growth; ['Hugh Dickson' × 'King George V']

'Jan Guest' HT, pb, 1976, Guest; flowers carmine-pink with yellow reverse, 4 in., 43 petals; foliage glossy; vigorous, upright growth; ['Fragrant Cloud' × 'Irish Gold']

'Jan H. Meyer' HT, mr, 1954, Leenders, M.; flowers cinnabar-red, well-formed, large; vigorous growth; ['Tawny Gold' × 'Gaudia']

'Jan Hus' HT, lp, 1933, Böhm, J.; flowers large, dbl.

Jan Spek® F, dy, 1966, McGredy, Sam IV; flowers 3 in., 44 petals, flat, borne in clusters; foliage dark, glossy; ['Clare Grammerstorf' × 'Faust']

'Jan Steen' HT, mr, 1923, Spek; flowers brilliant scarlet-red, semi-dbl.; ['Mev. Dora van Tets' × 'Gruss an Dresden']

'Jan Steen' S, rb, Williams, J. Benjamin; bud high; flowers ivory and red striped, single; upright growth; intr. 1997

'Jan van Riebeeck' HT, m, 1952, Leenders, M.; flowers carmine, large, dbl.; vigorous growth

'Jan Vermeer' F, m, Williams, J. Benjamin; flowers purple/burgundy blend, borne in sprays, intense fragrance; intr. 1997

'Jan Wellum' ('Vancouver Centennial') Min, dr, 1986, Fischer, C.&H.; flowers large, 20 petals, borne singly and in sprays of 3-5, slight fruity fragrance; foliage medium size, medium green, matte; prickles small, straight, near-white; spreading growth; small, globular fruit; ['shrub seedling' × 'Dwarfking '78']

'Jana' -- See 'Yardley English Rose'

'Jana' HT, dy, Cocker; flowers large, dbl.; intr. 1976

'Jana' -- See 'Janna'

'Janal' HT, dp, 1982, Dawson, George; bud pointed; flowers deep pink, 55 petals, high-centered, intense fragrance; foliage bronze-red to dark green; prickles hooked red; vigorous growth; ['Charles Mallerin' × ('Duet' × 'Kordes' Perfecta')]; intr. 1978

'Jane' HSet, lp, about 1846, Pierce; flowers flesh to lilac-pink, medium, very dbl., borne in clusters of 25-30; foliage large, coarsely serrated

'Jane' HT, ob, Mee; flowers coppery orange suffused pink, well-formed, large, 24 petals, moderate fragrance; foliage dark; vigorous, upright growth; ['Signora' × 'Mrs Edward Laxton']; intr. 1956

'Jane Asher' -- See 'Peapet'

'Jane Bullock' S, my, ARE; flowers yellow, 2 in., semi-dbl., borne in abundance, moderate fragrance; recurrent; growth small (3 ft.), cascading bush; intr. 2004

'Jane Carrel' HT, yb, 1940, Gaujard; bud pointed; flowers yellow shaded orange, medium, dbl.; very vigorous, bushy growth

'Jane Eyre' -- See 'Mehpark'

'Jane Hardy' -- See 'Jean Hardy'

'Jane Isobella Linton' T, pb, L'Hay

'Jane Jackson' F, ob, 1977, Jackson, J.R.; flowers strawberry-orange, dbl.; low, vigorous, bushy growth; [sport of 'Tip Top']

'Jane Lathrop Stanford' HT, dr

'Jane Lazenby' F, mp, 1960, McGredy, Sam IV; flowers rose-pink, large, 25 petals, flat, moderate fragrance; foliage dark; very vigorous, bushy growth; ['Alain' × 'Mme Henri Guillot']; intr. 1959

'Jane Pauley' HT, ob, 1992, Weddle, Von C.; flowers orange, reverse orange, aging orange pink, 6½ in., 35 petals, high-centered, borne singly, moderate fragrance; foliage large, medium green, semi-glossy; upright, medium growth; ['Elizabeth Taylor' × 'Fortuna']; intr. 1993

'Jane Piekarski' HT, w, 1994, Hoshall, Howard; flowers 3-3½ in., very dbl., borne mostly singly; foliage medium size, medium green, matte; numerous prickles; medium (24 in.), upright growth; [Honor™ × 'John F. Kennedy']

'Jane Probyn' HT, dp, 1979, Anderson, K.; flowers deep pink; [sport of 'Red Devil']; intr. 1978

'Jane Rogers' HT, ab, 1991, Mander, George; flowers large, full, borne mostly singly, sometimes in small clusters, slight fragrance; foliage medium size, medium green, semi-glossy; medium, spreading growth; ['Fragrant Cloud' × 'Diamond Jubilee']

'Jane, Souvenir Du Barbicon' -- See 'Horlikorish'

'Jane Thornton' HT, rb, Bees; flowers velvety crimson shaded maroon

'Janet' -- See 'Auspishus'

'Janet' HT, ab, 1915, Dickson, A.; flowers golden fawn, shaded copper and rose, large, dbl., globular-cupped, moderate fragrance

'Janet A. Wood' -- See 'Jaljanet'

'Janet Bebb' -- See 'Mehgoldie'

'Janet Carnochan' HT, w, Pallek; flowers white blend with faint mauve in center, dbl., exhibition, intense fragrance; recurrent; intr. 1996

'Janet Frazer' F, op, 1967, McGredy; flowers shrimp-pink and yellow, large, semi-dbl., borne in clusters, slight fragrance; foliage light green; ['Mme Léon Cuny' × ('Orange Sweetheart' × 'Cinnabar')]

'Janet Greig' -- See 'Worapple'

'Janet Morrison' Cl HT, dp, 1936, Clark, A.; flowers deep pink, 3-3½ in., semi-dbl., borne in small clusters, moderate fragrance; long stems; vigorous growth; ['Black Boy' × unknown]

'Janet's Passion' -- See 'Worcollar'

'Janet's Pride' -- See 'Clémentine'

'Janette Murray' HT, op, 1985, Bell, Ronald J.; flowers orange pink, large, 35 petals, borne singly; foliage large, medium green, semi-glossy; vigorous growth; [('Daily Sketch' × unknown) × 'Montezuma']

'Janice' Min, mp, 1972, Moore, Ralph S.; bud ovoid; flowers small, dbl.; foliage small, glossy, leathery; vigorous, dwarf, upright, bushy growth; [(R. wichurana × Floradora) × 'Eleanor']; intr. 1971

'Janice Heyes' HT, lp, Dawson; intr. 1986

'Janice Kellog' -- See 'Janice Kellogg'

'Janice Kellogg' ('Janice Kellog') F, dr, Meilland; flowers dark burgundy, large, very full, cupped, slight fragrance; recurrent; foliage dark green, semi-glossy; medium, bushy growth; intr. 2006

'Janice Meredith' HCh, dp, 1903, Hill, E. G.; flowers carmine pink, large, full, moderate fragrance; ['Hermosa' × 'La France']

'Janice Tellian' Min, op, 1979, Moore, Ralph S.; bud pointed; flowers light coral-pink, 1 in., 40 petals, high-centered, slight fragrance; foliage small; dwarf, bushy, compact growth; PP4657; ['Fairy Moss' × 'Fire Princess']

'Janida' HT, rb, 1955, Robichon; bud long, pointed, blood-red veined maroon; flowers orange, dbl.; ['Crimson Glory' × 'Baby Chateau']

'Janie Harrison' -- See 'Horcharters'

Janina® -- See 'Tanija'

'Janine Astle' F, mp, 1971, Hunt; flowers clear pink, 3 in., 22 petals, high-centered; foliage bluish green; vigorous, upright growth; ['Charlotte Elizabeth' × 'Grand Slam']

'Janine Herholdt' HT, ab, Herholdt; bud pointed, golden; flowers golden apricot fading to caramel-cream, semi-dbl., slight fragrance; recurrent; foliage glossy, healthy; easy, willing (5-6 ft.) growth; [sport of 'Johannesburg Sun']; intr. 1989

'Janine Viaud-Bruant' HT, mr, 1910, Viaud-Bruant; flowers crimson-purple-ruby, large, dbl., moderate fragrance; ['Triomphe d'Orléans' × 'Princesse de Béarn']

'Janita Claassen' -- See 'Soleil Rouge'

'Janna' ('Jana') Min, pb, 1970, Moore, Ralph S.; bud pointed; flowers pink, reverse white, small, dbl.; foliage leathery; dwarf, bushy growth; PP3245; ['Little Darling' × ('Little Darling' × (R. wichuraiana × miniature seedling))]

'Janos' Pol, or, VEG; flowers medium, dbl.

'Jan's Wedding' -- See 'Adajan'

'Jan's Wedding Bouquet' -- See 'Adajan'

'Jantar' HT, dr, 1966, Grabczewski; bud elongated; flowers dark crimson, shaded darker, large; vigorous, upright growth

'Jantzen Girl' Gr, mr, 1961, Von Abrams; bud ovoid; flowers 4-5 in., dbl., high-centered, borne in clusters, slight fragrance; foliage glossy; upright growth; PP2242; ['Carrousel' × ('Chrysler Imperial' × seedling)]; intr. 1962

'Japonica' -- See 'Mousseux du Japon'

'Japonica Thornless' (strain of R. multiflora); prickle-free; growth popular as an understock

'Jaquenetta' ('Jacquenetta') S, ab, Austin, David; flowers apricot-peach, large, dbl., cupped, borne singly and in clusters, slight fragrance; strong, tall (6 ft.) growth; intr. 1983

'Jardin de Giverny' HT, ob, Gillet; intr. 1992

'Jardin de la Croix' HMacr, op, 1901, L'Hay

Jardinero Ortiz® HT, rb, Dot; flowers deep blackish crimson red, large, full; intr. 1969

Jardins d'Albertas® F, lp, Guillot-Massad; [(R. filipes × Sanguinea) × ('Artiste' × 'Anne Laure')]

Jardins de Bagatelle® -- See 'Meimafris'

Jardins de France™ -- See 'Meizebul'

Jardins de l'Essonne® S, lp, Delbard; flowers chamois-rose, lighter at edges, very dbl., rosette, moderate citron & herb fragrance; intr. 2000

'Jardins de Valloires' Pol, dp, Eve, A.; flowers full, rosette; good rebloom; foliage healthy, dark green; rounded (3 ft.) growth; intr. 1994

Jardins de Viels Maisons® S, mp, Guillot-Massad; intr. 1998

Jardins de Villandry® HT, mp, Delbard, Georges; flowers very large, very dbl., cupped, intense rose-fruit fragrance; intr. 1995

'Jardins et Loisirs' S, ab; intr. 2001

'Jaris Hudson' Min, mp

'Jarlina' -- See 'Poulena'

'Jarvis Brook' HT, rb, 1928, Low; flowers carmine, reverse orange, dbl.

'Jasdarter' ('Denny Arter') LCl, yb, 2003, Starnes, John A. Jr.; flowers buff yellow, reverse ivory-cream, 3 in., dbl., borne in small clusters, moderate fragrance; very remontant; foliage small, light green, semi-glossy; prickles small, straight, beige, moderate; stems very pliable; spreading (7 ft.) growth; shrub or pillar; ['Francis E. Lester' × Graham Thomas®]; intr. 2005

'Jasena' HT, dy, Urban, J.; flowers large, dbl.; intr. 1983

'Jasfair' ('Fairmount Memory') S, pb, 2004, Starnes, John A, Jr.; flowers deep pink, reverse silvery pink, 4 in., very full, borne mostly solitary, intense fragrance; very remontant; foliage medium size, medium green, semi-glossy; prickles medium, claw-shaped; growth bushy, medium (5 ft.); very hardy; intr. 2004

'Jasheels' ('Four Inch Heels') S, dr, 2003, Starnes, John A. Jr.; flowers burgundy, reverse magenta pink, 4 in., very full, borne mostly solitary, intense fragrance; early summer; foliage medium size, medium green, matte; prickles moderate, 1/3 in., cat-claw, green to brown, moderate; growth upright, short; ['Great Western' × 'Othello']; intr. 2003

'Jaslok' HT, m, 1999, Chiplunkar, C. R.; flowers light mauve with dark mauve stripes, reverse lighter, 4-5 in., 41 petals, borne mostly singly; foliage large, medium green, semi-glossy; prickles moderate; compact, medium (2½-3½ ft.) growth; [sport of 'Blue Ocean']; intr. 1992

'Jasmin-Rose' Misc OGR , w, Urban, Helga & Klaus; flowers pure white with yellow stamens, single, flat, borne in large clusters, moderate jasmine fragrance; non-remontant; foliage dark green, turning yellow-gold in autumn; large (5 - 8 meters) growth

Jasmina® -- See 'Korcentex'

'Jasmow' ('Brenda Mowery') A, lp, 2003, Starnes, John A. Jr.; flowers light pink, reverse light pink, 3½ in., very full, borne in small clusters, intense complex, spicy fragrance; foliage large, dark green, matte, disease-free; prickles moderate, ¼ in., curved, brown, moderate; growth upright, rampant vigor, tall (8-10 ft.); pillar; very hardy; ['Alba maxima' × 'Alfred Colomb']; intr. 2002

'Jasnaja Poljana' HT, pb, Shtanko, E.E.; flowers salmon-pink with light yellow, large, very dbl.; intr. 1958

'Jasoblush' ('Gold Blush') LCl, ab, 2003, Starnes, John A. Jr.; flowers apricot-gold, reverse apricot-gold, 4 in., dbl., borne in small clusters, strong cinammon fragrance; very remontant; foliage medium size, medium green, semi-glossy; prickles ¼ in., straight and flat, dark brown, few; growth upright, wide climber, tall (6-10 ft.); pillar; [R. moschata × Abraham Darby®]; intr. 2003

'Jason' -- See 'Sherice'

Jasper™ -- See 'Poulbella'

'Jasper Crane' HT, mr, Williams, J. B.; PP15680

'Jasru' ('Ruby Voodoo') S, dr, 2004, Starnes, John A. Jr.; flowers deep red, 3 in., very full, borne mostly solitary, intense rich, sweet fragrance; early summer; foliage medium size, medium green, matte; prickles small, cats claw; upright, short growth; short shrub or medium pillar; ['General Jacqueminot' × 'Stephen's Big Purple']; intr. 2004

'Jaswee' ('Sweet Passion') Tea, dp, 2003, Starnes, John A. Jr.; flowers magenta pink, reverse silvery pink, 4 in., very full, borne mostly solitary, intense citrus peel and old rose fragrance; very remontant; foliage medium size, medium green, semi-glossy; prickles few, tiny, straight bristles, beige; bushy, short (3 ft.) growth; specimen; ['Duchesse de Brabant' × 'Francis Dubreuil']; intr. 1999

'Jaunatella' HT, yb

'Jaunâtre' HSem, ly; flowers yellowish-white, moderate musk fragrance; probably a hybrid between R. sempervirens and a Noisette or Hybrid Musk

'Jaunâtre Pleine' Sp, my; flowers primrose yellow, dbl; [sport of R. banksiae lutea]

'Jaune Ancien' -- See 'Multiplex'

'Jaune Bicolor' S, yb, 1633; flowers yellow streaked red, medium, single; [sport of R. foetida bicolor]

'Jaune de William' -- See 'Williams' Double Yellow'

'Jaune Desprez' ('Desprez à Fleur Jaunes', 'Noisette Desprez') N, yb, about 1830, Desprez; flowers dull yellow to sulfur yellow, 6 cm., full, cupped, borne in small clusters, moderate fragrance; vigorous (to 20 ft.) growth; ['Blush Noisette' × 'Parks' Yellow Tea-scented China']

'Jaune d'Italie' HFt, ly, before 1846, from Italy; flowers pale straw yellow, darker center, dbl.

'Jaune d'Or' T, ob, Oger; flowers coppery yellow, large, dbl., globular

'Jaune Double' -- See 'Williams' Double Yellow'

'Jaune of Smith' -- See 'Smith's Yellow China'

'Jaune Serin' HBank, my; flowers canary yellow with gold, large, full; [sport of R. banksiae lutea]

'Jaune Soufré' -- See 'Sulphurea'

'Java' F, ob, 1958, Mallerin, C.; bud ovoid; flowers orange-red, medium, 40-45 petals, borne in clusters of 4-5, slight fragrance; foliage bronze; vigorous, upright, bushy growth; ['Francais' × seedling]; intr. 1955

'Jawahar' HT, w, 1981, Division of Vegetable Crops and Floriculture; flowers creamy white, 47 petals, high-centered, borne 2-6 per cluster, intense fragrance; foliage light green, glossy; prickles straight, brown; vigorous, bushy growth; ['Sweet Afton' × 'Delhi Princess']; intr. 1980

'Jawani' HT, or, Pal, Dr. B.P.; flowers large, full; strong growth; intr. 1985

'Jawarosa Mawa' HT, or; flowers large, dbl.

'Jay Jay' HT, w, 1971, Kern, J. J.; flowers white, edged pink, very large, very dbl., high-centered, slight fragrance; foliage large, dark, leathery; very vigorous, bushy growth; [sport of 'Peace']

'Jayanc' (Ancestry™) Min, mp, 1997, Jellyman, J.S.; flowers medium, 8-14 petals, borne in small clusters; foliage medium size, medium green, glossy; spreading, bushy, medium (30cm.) growth; [seedling × Party Girl™]

'Jayant' HT, pb, Gokhale, Anand; flowers pink and white stripes on deep vermilion; [sport of 'Maharshi']; intr. 1998

'Jayart' (Arthur Cox™) Min, pb, 1997, Jellyman, J.S.; flowers medium, dbl., borne in small clusters; foliage medium size, medium green, semi-glossy; compact, medium growth; ['Cotswold Gold' × 'Peaches 'n' Cream']

'Jayatsen' HT, pb, K&S; flowers deep pink with reverse pure white, large, full, exhibition; intr. 1998

'Jaybo' Min, rb, 1988, Bridges, Dennis A.; flowers very bright red, yellow at base, fading to pink, 22 petals, urn-shaped, slight fruity fragrance; foliage medium size, dark green, glossy; prickles long, pointed, pink; bushy, medium growth; ['Rise 'n' Shine' × seedling]

'Jaycai' (Caitlin May™) Min, ab, 2003, Jellyman, J.S.; flowers apricot-white, reverse white, 2 in., dbl., borne in small clusters, moderate fragrance; foliage medium size, medium green, semi-glossy; prickles 3 mm., curved, few; growth compact, medium (2½ ft.); garden decoration; ['Marylin Ross' × (Jean Kenneally™ × ('Sue Lawley' × 'Sue Lawley'))]

'Jayclar' (Clarice Wood™) Min, mr, 2001, Jellyman, J.S.; flowers 2 in., dbl., borne in small clusters, no fragrance; foliage small, dark green, glossy; prickles small, curved, few; growth upright, bushy, medium (18 in.); bedding, containers; [Jean Kenneally™ × 'Merrie']

'Jaycot' ('Cotswold Gold') Min, ob, 1992, Jellyman, J.S.; flowers orange, medium, 6-14 petals, borne in small clusters, slight fragrance; foliage small, medium green, semi-glossy; few prickles; low (20 cm.), bushy growth; ['Tony Jacklin' × 'Judy Fischer']; intr. 1993

'Jaydon' ('Beverley Stoop') F, mr, 1998, Jellyman, J. S.; flowers velvety red, reverse dame, medium, dbl, borne in small clusters, slight fragrance; foliage medium size, medium green, semi-glossy; growth upright, compact, medium (2½ ft.); [seedling × ('Tony Jacklin' × 'Andrea')]

'Jaydon' ('Donella') F, mr, Jellyman, J. S.; intr. 1997

'Jayemm' ('Emma Kate') F, mr, 1992, Jellyman, J.S.; flowers light red with lighter reverse, 35 petals, borne in clusters of 4-10, moderate fruity fragrance; foliage medium size, dark green, glossy; upright, bushy, medium growth; ['Tony Jacklin' × 'Cairngorm']

'Jayerel' ('Erin Elise') F, or, 2005, Jellyman, J.S.; flowers single, borne in small clusters, moderate fragrance; foliage medium size, medium green, semi-glossy; prickles moderate, 5/8 mm., curved; growth upright, compact, medium (2-2½ ft.); bedding, containers; ['Fragrant Cloud' × 'Baby Love']

'Jaygra' ('Granny Beryl') HT, my, 2007, Jellyman, J. S.; flowers medium, 4½ in., dbl., borne mostly solitary; foliage medium green, semi-glossy; prickles 6 mm., curved, few; growth upright, compact, medium (2½ ft.); bedding; [Behold™ × 'Baby Love']

'Jaygup' ('Diana H. Gupta') HT, op, 1999, Jellyman, J.S.; flowers orange-pink, reverse pale lemon yellow with faint white striping, 3 in., full, borne in small clusters, slight fragrance; foliage medium size, medium green, semi-glossy; few prickles; upright, bushy, medium (3 ft.) growth; ['Gavotte' × 'Bill Temple']

'Jayhac' (John Hackling™) Min, mr, 2001, Jellyman, J.S.; flowers variable red and white striping, 2 in., single, borne in small clusters; foliage small, dark green, glossy; prickles 6 mm., curved, few; growth compact, medium (10 in.); bedding, containers; ['Imbroglio' × 'Beverley Stoop']

'Jayhel' ('Helen Teresa') HT, mp, 2007, Jellyman, J. S.; flowers 9 cm., full, borne in small clusters; foliage medium, medium green, semi-glossy; prickles 1 cm., curved, few; growth upright, bushy, medium; ['Silver Jubilee' × 'Cotswold Sunset']

'Jayjow' ('John Owen') Min, yb, 2004, Jellyman, J.S.; flowers yellow-cream, reverse pink, medium, dbl, borne in small clusters; foliage medium size, medium green, semi-glossy; prickles 5-6 mm., curved,; growth upright, compact, medium (30-38 cm.); containers; patio; ['Cider Cup' × ('Ibroglio' × 'Beverley Stoop')]

'Jaykoo' (Kooshti-Bok™) F, or, 1997, Jellyman, J.S.; flowers medium, single, borne in small clusters; foliage medium size, dark green, semi-glossy; growth upright, spreading, medium to tall (3½-4ft.); [('Tony Jacklin' × seedling) × ('Tony Jacklin' × 'Andrea')]

'Jayllo' ('Susan Osborn Lloyd') HT, r, 2007, Jellyman, J. S.; flowers russet/brown, reverse yellow, medium, dbl., borne mostly solitary; foliage medium, dark green, glossy; prickles 7-10 mm., curved, moderate; growth upright, compact, medium (2½ ft.); bedding; [Remember Me® × 'Diana H. Gupta']

'Jaymar' ('Marilyn Ross') Min, my, 2000, Jellyman, J.S.; flowers medium, single, borne in small clusters, moderate fragrance; foliage medium size, dark green, semi-glossy; few prickles; growth bushy, medium (15 in.); patio, containers; ['Baby Love' × (Priscilla Burton® × ('Tony Jacklin' × 'Andrea'))]

'Jaymarj' (Marjorie Reid™) HT, pb, 1997, Jellyman, J.S.; flowers small, dbl.; foliage small, dark green, glossy; low (25 cm.) growth; [seedling × 'Wee Barbie']

'Jaymatt' (The Matthew™) HT, pb, 1997, Jellyman, J.S.; flowers medium, very dbl.; few prickles; ['Silver Jubilee' × 'Pres. Petts']

'Jaymer' ('Merrie') f, ab, 1994, Jellyman, J.S.; flowers apricot, pale pink, dbl., 30 petals, borne 6-20 per cluster; foliage medium size, dark green, semi-glossy; medium, upright, bushy growth; [Minnie Pearl™ × seedling]

'Jaymoll' (Molly Beckley™) F, pb, 1997, Jellyman, J.S.; flowers small, 8-14 petals, slight fragrance; foliage small, dark green, glossy; growth spreading, low (1½ ft.); [('Tony Jacklin' × 'Andrea') × 'Wee Barbie']

Jayne Austin™ -- See 'Ausbreak'

'Jaypru' ('Prunella Stack') HT, ab, 2000, Jellyman, J.S.; flowers apricot, reverse deep pink, 3 in., dbl., borne in small clusters, slight fragrance; foliage medium size, dark green, glossy; few prickles; growth upright, low (2 ft.); patio, containers; ['Cider Cup' × 'Don Charlton']

'Jayrea' ('Baby Ria') F, op, 2007, Jellyman, J. S.; flowers pink/peach, reverse pink, 8 cm., dbl., borne in small clusters; foliage medium, medium green, glossy; prickles 6 mm., curved, few; growth upright, bushy, medium; bedding; ['Kitty Hawk' × 'Baby Love']

'Jayrolo' ('Ron's Love') F, dr, 2007, Jellyman, J. S.; flowers dark, velvety red with almost-black edges, 2½ in., semi-dbl., borne in small clusters; foliage medium, dark green, glossy; prickles 6 mm., curved, few; growth upright, medium; bedding; [Hot Tamale™ × ((Priscilla Burton® × seedling) × ('Cider Cup' × seedling))]

'Jayrus' ('Joyce Ruston') HT, ob, 2007, Jellyman, J. S.; flowers orange, reverse yellow, 9 cm., full, borne mostly solitary; foliage medium, dark green, glossy; prickles 8-9 mm., curved, moderate; growth upright, compact, medium; bedding; ['Silver Jubilee' × ((Remember Me® × 'Baby Love') × Priscilla Burton®)]

'Jaysharr' ('Sharron with Two R's') HT, pb, 2008, Jellyman, J. S.; flowers pink and white, reverse pink, medium, dbl., borne mostly solitary; foliage medium, medium green, glossy; prickles 7-10 mm., curved, moderate; growth upright, compact, medium; garden decoration, exhibition; ['Silver Jubilee' × (Remember Me® × ('Baby Love' × seedling))]

'Jaysil' (Precious Gift™) F, dp, 1997, Jellyman, J.S.; flowers medium, dbl., borne in small clusters; foliage medium size, medium green, semi-glossy; few prickles; upright, bushy, medium (20cm.) growth; ['Silver Jubilee' × seedling]

'Jaysis' (Sister Hellie™) F, w, 2003, Jellyman, J.S.; flowers pearl pink to white, reverse white and pink, 2 in., single, borne in small clusters, moderate fragrance; foliage medium size, dark green, semi-glossy; prickles 8 mm., slightly curved, few; growth compact, medium (3 ft.); garden, bedding; ['Marylin Ross' × (Jean Kenneally™ × ('Sue Lawley' × 'Sue Lawley'))]

'Jaysow' ('Nesta Burnett Snowdon', 'Nesta Burnett Sowden') Min, my, 2004, Jellyman, J.S.; flowers semi-dbl., borne in small clusters, moderate fragrance; foliage medium green, glossy; prickles 9-10 mm., curved, few; growth bushy, medium (2½-3 ft.); garden; decorative; [Remember Me® × 'Marylin Robb']

'Jayspei' ('The Spiedel Rose') F, or, 2000, Jellyman, J.S.; flowers orange-red, reverse lighter, 3 in., semi-dbl., borne mostly singly, slight fragrance; recurrent; foliage large, medium green, glossy; few prickles; growth compact, tall (3 ft.); ['Wembley Stadium' × Alexander®]

'Jaysun' ('Cotswold Sunset') F, pb, 1992, Jellyman, J.S.; flowers gold, pink edge, pale pink, moderately full, 3-3½ in., dbl., high-centered, borne in small clusters; foliage medium size, dark green, glossy; some prickles; medium (80-90 cm.), upright, compact growth; [('Cairngorm' × unknown) × (Alexander® × 'Wembley')]; intr. 1993

'Jaysus' (Susan Munro™) HT, mp, 2001, Jellyman, J.S.; flowers medium pink with light pink reverse, 4½ in., dbl., borne mostly solitary; foliage medium size, dark green, semi-glossy; prickles few, small, curved; growth compact, bushy, medium (2½ ft.); bedding; [Jean Kenneally™ × (Starina® × 'Peachy White')]

'Jaytom' ('Joan F. Mills') HT, mr, 2000, Jellyman, J.S.; flowers medium red, reverse light red, 3 in., semi-dbl., borne in small clusters, slight fragrance; foliage medium size, dark green, glossy; few prickles; bushy, medium (2½ ft.) growth; [Minnie Pearl™ × seedling]

'Jazz' -- See 'That's Jazz'

'Jazz'   F, ob, 1960, deRuiter; flowers orange-yellow flushed crimson, 2 in., 26 petals, borne in clusters; foliage dark, glossy; vigorous growth; ['Masquerade' × seedling]; intr. 1960

'Jazz'   HT, ob, Tantau

'Jazz Band'   Min, pb, Benardella, Frank; flowers pale pink with carmine red and coffee stripes, hybrid tea; medium growth

'Jazz Club'   S, ab, Lowery/Robinson; flowers soft apricot shot with yellow and amber, semi-dbl., informal, slight fragrance; free-flowering; foliage bright green, glossy, disease-resistant; intr. 1995

'Jazz Dancer' -- See 'Seatwinkle'

'Jazz Fest'   F, mr, 1971, Armstrong, D.L.; bud long, pointed; flowers medium, semi-dbl., slight fragrance; foliage large, leathery; vigorous, upright, bushy growth; PP3323; ['Pink Parfait' × 'Garnette']

Jazz Time™ -- See 'Minacco'

'Jazzy Jewel' -- See 'Judjewel'

Je n'ai que 25 ans®   HT, op, Dorieux; flowers double , high-centered; recurrent; intr. 2007

'Jealous Joey' -- See 'Mattarb'

'Jean' -- See 'Cocupland'

'Jean Adrien Mercer'   F, Dorieux, Francois; intr. 1991

'Jean André'   T, yb, 1894, Pelletier; flowers orange-yellow with a darker center, medium, full, moderate fragrance; ['William Allen Richardson' × 'Ma Capucine']

'Jean Armour'   F, ab; intr. 2005

'Jean Bach Sisley'   Ch, pb, 1898, Dubreuil; flowers silvery rose, outer petals salmon-rose veined carmine, moderate fragrance; growth moderate

'Jean Baker'   HT, w, 1998, Edwards, Eddie; flowers white, full, exhibition, borne mostly singly, intense fragrance; foliage medium size, dark green, glossy; few prickles; upright, medium to tall (4-5 ft.) growth; [Crystalline™ × 'Classic Touch']; intr. 1998

'Jean-Baptiste'   HT, pb, Orard; intr. 2000

'Jean-Baptiste Casati' ('Duchesse d'Orléans')   HP, dp, 1886, Schwartz; flowers carmine-pink, large, very dbl.

'Jean-Baptiste Guillot'   HP, m, 1861, Verdier, E.; flowers violet, shaded with purple, very large, spherical

'Jean Bart'   P, m, before 1836, Trébucien; flowers dbl., moderate fragrance

'Jean Beeden' -- See 'Woraltitude'

'Jean Bodin'   M, lp, 1848, Vibert; flowers light rose-pink, 6 cm., quartered; foliage dark green; prickles short, straight, numerous; vigorous growth

'Jean Bostick' ('Yellow Condesa de Sastago')   HT, my, 1936, Bostick; flowers deep yellow, sometimes splotched red, large, 50 petals, globular; foliage leathery, glossy; very vigorous growth; [sport of 'Condesa de Sástago']

'Jean Brosse'   HP, mp, 1867, Ducher; flowers full, spherical

'Jean Brown'   HT, ly, 1930, Evans, F. David; flowers large, very dbl.

'Jean Burion'   HT, mp, RvS-Melle; ['Frederik Chopin' × 'Waanrode']; intr. 1995

'Jean C. N. Forestier'   HT, rb, 1919, Pernet-Ducher; flowers carmine, slightly tinted orange and yellow, very large, dbl.; foliage glossy, bronze; very vigorous growth; [seedling × 'Mme Edouard Herriot']

'Jean Campbell'   HT, pb, 1964, Sanday, John; flowers blush-pink suffused apricot, well-formed, 4½ in., 28 petals; foliage dark; upright growth; [('Ethel Sanday' × unknown) × 'Lady Sylvia']

'Jean Cherpin'   HP, m, 1865, Liabaud; flowers purple/pink, very large, very dbl.

'Jean Cote'   HT, yb, 1936, Gaujard; flowers old-gold, center deeper, very large, dbl.; foliage brilliant green; vigorous growth; PP321

'Jean Dalmais'   HP, dp, 1873, Ducher; flowers dark cherry pink, very large, full, spherical

'Jean de la Lune' ('Moon Magic', 'YelloGlo')   F, dy, 1969, Delbard-Chabert; flowers dbl., cupped, borne in clusters; foliage matte; low growth; PP2995; [('Orléans Rose' × 'Goldilocks') × ('Fashion' × ('Henri Mallerin' × unknown))]; also registered as Yelloglo in the same year; patent issued to Yelloglo

'Jean Desprez'   N, rb, about 1820, Desprez; flowers crimson-pink, shaded coppery, medium, full

'Jean Dorizy'   B, mp, 1850, Dorizy; flowers large, full

'Jean D'Ormesson'   HT, w, Gaujard; intr. 2004

'Jean du Tilleux'   HT, mp, 1981, Winchel, Joseph F.; bud long; flowers medium lavender pink, medium, 30 petals, high-centered, borne mostly singly, slight fragrance; recurrent; foliage deep green, waxy; prickles slightly hooked, red; medium, vigorous growth; ['King of Hearts' × 'Golden Masterpiece']; intr. 1980

'Jean Ducher' ('Comte de Sembui', 'Ruby Gold')   T, op, 1874, Ducher, Vve.; bud pale cream, occasionally streaked red; flowers salmon to peachy pink, 8-9 cm., semi-dbl. to dbl., globular, borne mostly solitary, moderate tea fragrance

'Jean Galbraith'   S, ab, Nieuwesteeg, J.; flowers buff apricot fading to soft buff, large, to 50 petals, cupped, borne in small clusters, moderate fruity fragrance; recurrent; foliage medium green, shiny; vigorous, bushy growth; [sport of 'Abraham Darby']; intr. 1999

Jean Gaujard®   HT, mr, 1978, Gaujard; flowers brilliant red, 40 petals; vigorous growth; ['Canasta' × Rose Gaujard®]; intr. 1977

Jean Giono™ -- See 'Meirokoi'

'Jean Girin'   HWich, pb, 1910, Girin; flowers bright rose-pink, base rosy white, yellow stamens, 3½-4 cm., dbl., no fragrance; profuse bloom, sometimes repeated in autumn; vigorous, climbing growth

'Jean Goujon'   HP, mr, 1862, Margottin; flowers deep rose red, very large, full, cupped; nearly thornless

'Jean Guichard'   HWich, pb, 1905, Barbier; bud bronzy crimson; flowers copper-pink, 7-8 cm., very dbl., flat, borne in small clusters; foliage dark green, glossy; stems flexible, coppery bronze to dark green; vigorous, climbing growth; [R. wichurana × 'Souv. de Catherine Guillot']

'Jean Hardy' ('Jane Hardy', 'Jeanne Hardy')   N, yb, 1859, Hardy; flowers golden yellow with flesh pink

'Jean Kathryn'   F, pb, 1973, Ellick; flowers Neyron rose, reverse white, 4 in., 45 petals; foliage light; very vigorous growth; ['Memoriam' × 'Gavotte']

Jean Kenneally™ -- See 'Tineally'

'Jean Lafitte'   HSet, mp, 1934, Horvath; bud pointed; flowers willowmere pink, darker at center, 7-8 cm., dbl., cupped, borne in tight clusters, moderate fragrance; foliage leathery; numerous prickles; growth very vigorous, climbing (8-10 ft.); very hardy; [(R. setigera × unknown) × 'Willowmere']

'Jean Lambert'   HP, mr, 1865, Verdier, E.; flowers fire-red, large, full

'Jean Lambert'   HT, rb, Laperrière; flowers red with yellow base; intr. 1903

'Jean Lapeyre'   S, my, 1960, Gaujard; flowers well-formed; recurrent bloom; foliage bronze; vigorous, bushy growth

'Jean Lelièvre'   HP, dr, 1879, Oger; flowers bright deep crimson, large, dbl., moderate fragrance

'Jean l'Hoste'   HWich, rb, 1926, Congy; flowers rosy carmine, base flesh-white, 7 cm., dbl., borne in clusters of 50-100; foliage large, glossy; ['Alexandre Girault' × 'Gerbe Rose']

'Jean Liabaud'   HP, dr, 1875, Liabaud; flowers crimson-maroon, shaded scarlet, large, 60 petals; some recurrent bloom; vigorous growth; ['Baron de Bonstetten' × unknown]

'Jean Lorthois'   HT, pb, 1879, Ducher, Vve.; flowers rose-pink, center darker, reverse silvery, well-formed, large; ['Gloire de Dijon' × unknown]

'Jean MacArthur'   HT, mr, 1942, Joseph H. Hill, Co.; bud long, pointed, begonia-red; flowers 3½-4 in., 30-40 petals, high-centered, slight fragrance; foliage leathery, wrinkled, dark; vigorous, upright growth; PP616; ['Joanna Hill' × 'California']

'Jean-Marc' -- See 'Jean Marc'

'Jean Marc' ('Jean-Marc')   F, or, Croix; intr. 1975

'Jean Marc Rosé'   F, Fineschi, G.; intr. 1995

'Jean Marmoz' -- See 'Jean Mermoz'

'Jean Maycock'   HT, mr, 1999, Rawlins, R.; flowers crimson pink, reverse lighter, 3 in., full, borne in small clusters, slight fragrance; foliage medium size, medium

The Official Registry and Checklist — Rosa   337

green, semi-glossy; prickles moderate; compact, medium (36 in.) growth; [Sexy Rexy® × 'Sharifa Asma']

'Jean McGregor Reid'   HT, w, 1962, Sunter; flowers cream, large; foliage dark, glossy; vigorous growth; [sport of 'Peace']

'Jean Mermoz' ('Jean Marmoz') Pol, mp, 1937, Chenault; flowers ruddy pink, imbricated, small, very dbl., borne in long clusters; foliage glossy, dark; vigorous growth; [R. wichurana × 'a hybrid tea']

'Jean Monford' -- See 'Jeanne de Montfort'

Jean Monnet® -- See 'Pekcram'

'Jean Morrison'   HT, or, Sutherland; intr. 1996

'Jean Muraour'   F, w, 1935, Vogel, M.; flowers pure white, center light yellow, large; [sport of 'Gruss an Aachen']

'Jean Noté'   HT, op, 1909, Pernet-Ducher; flowers light salmon-pink, large, dbl.

'Jean Pernet'   T, my, 1867, Pernet père; flowers medium to large, full; prickles large, straight; growth upright; ['Devoniensis' × unknown]

'Jean Piat'   HT, yb, Adam; flowers amber yellow, edged with orange-red, very large, dbl., high-centered; intr. 2003

Jean Pierre Coffe® -- See 'Weklezpat'

'Jean Pierre Ferland' -- See 'Wekosomit'

'Jean Rameau'   B, dp, 1918, Darclanne/Turbat; flowers iridescent rose, large, full; [sport of 'Mme Isaac Pereire']

'Jean Renton'   HT, my, 1940, Clark, A.; vigorous growth

'Jean Rex' -- See 'Rexjean'

'Jean Rose' -- See 'Tinjean'

'Jean Rosenkrantz'   HP, or, 1864, Portemer fils; flowers very bright coral-red, large, dbl., intense fragrance; ['Victor Verdier' × unknown]

'Jean Sisley'   HT, m, 1879, Bennett; flowers lilac-rose, large, no fragrance; moderate growth; ['Adam' × 'Emilie Hausburg']; rarely opens properly; prone to mildew

'Jean Soupert' ('Grand Mogul') HP, dr, 1875, Lacharme, F.; flowers crimson-maroon, large, dbl.; ['Charles Lefebvre' × 'Souv. du Baron de Sémur']

'Jean Stephenne'   HMsk, lp, Lens; bud light salmon-pink; flowers creamy pink, semi-double to double, flat, borne in large clusters, slight fragrance; recurrent; foliage dense, vigorous, upright (100 cm.) growth; intr. 2007

'Jean Thomson Harris'   F, op, 1976, Cocker; flowers salmon, shaded orange, 4 in., 30 petals; [('Fragrant Cloud' × 'Heidelberg') × ('Heidelberg' × 'Kingcup')]

'Jean Touvais'   HP, m, 1863, Touvais; flowers purple with carmine shades, large, full, spherical

'Jean Webb'   HT, rb, 1966, Marks; flowers cochineal, reverse light bronze, 4 in.; foliage dark; vigorous growth; [sport of 'Bettina']

Jeanette™ -- See 'Spojean'

'Jeanette Heller' -- See 'William R. Smith'

'Jeanette Talbot' -- See 'Webeyam'

'Jeanie'   HT, w, 1959, Eddie; flowers cream to pink, 4-4½ in., 66 petals, high-centered; foliage dark; vigorous, spreading growth; ['Condesa de Sástago' × 'Mme Edmond Labbe']; intr. 1958

'Jeanie Williams'   Min, rb, 1965, Moore, Ralph S.; flowers orange-red, reverse yellow, small, dbl.; foliage leathery; vigorous, bushy growth; ['Little Darling' × 'Magic Wand']

'Jeanine'   Gr, op

'Jeanine Defaucamberge'   Pol, pb, 1931, Turbat; flowers bright salmon-pink, passing to light pink, large, very dbl., peony-like; foliage slender; [sport of 'Merveille']

'Jeanine Weber'   HT, ob, 1954, Leenders, M.; flowers orange, large; vigorous growth; ['Soestdijk' × 'Mary Hart']

'Jeanne Buatois'   HT, w, 1902, Buatois; flowers pearly white, center light flesh pink, very large, moderate fragrance; ['Merveille de Lyon' × 'Mme Eugene Résal']

'Jeanne Cabanis'   HT, rb, 1922, Guillot, P.; bud coral-red; flowers bright rose-carmine, reverse silvery, center coppery rose, dbl.

'Jeanne Corboeuf'   HT, lp, 1902, Corboeuf; bud long; flowers satiny pink with carmine reflections on a yellow ground, very large, dbl., full, borne in cupped; ['Mme la Duchesse d'Auerstädt' × 'Mme Jules Grolez']

'Jeanne d'Arc' -- See 'Étendard de Jeanne d'Arc'

Jeanne d'Arc™ -- See 'Poulra023(N)'

'Jeanne d'Arc'   A, w, 1818, Vibert; flowers creamy flesh fading to ivory-white, medium to large, dbl., cupped, borne in clusters, intense fragrance; foliage dark grey-green; prickles strong; dense bush (to 5 ft.) growth; ['Elisa' × unknown]

'Jeanne d'Arc'   HP, w, Verdier, V.; flowers creamy white, dbl.; vigorous growth; intr. 1847

'Jeanne d'Arc'   M, w, Robert & Moreau; flowers lilac-white; intr. 1858

'Jeanne d'Arc'   T, my, Ducher; flowers full; intr. 1870

'Jeanne d'Arc'   Pol, w, Levavasseur; flowers pure milky white, moderate fragrance; ['Mme Norbert Levavasseur' × unknown]; intr. 1909

'Jeanne d'Arc Parade' (Jeanne d'Arc™) MinFl, w, Poulsen; flowers white, 5-8 cm., dbl., no fragrance; foliage dark; growth broad, bushy, 20-40 cm.; PP15191; intr. 2002

'Jeanne de Montfort' ('Jean Monford') M, mp, 1853, Robert; bud heavily mossed, dark carmine; flowers clear pink, edged silver, semi-dbl., flat, borne in large clusters, moderate fragrance; foliage emerald-green; tall, vigorous growth

'Jeanne Drivon'   Pol, w, 1883, Schwartz, J.; flowers white, faintly shaded pink, very dbl.

'Jeanne Excoffier'   HT, pb, 1921, Buatois; bud large, long, pointed; flowers daybreak-pink, inside buff, large, dbl.; ['Mme Philippe Rivoire' × 'Mme Edouard Herriot']

'Jeanne Gross'   HP, mp, 1871, Damaizin; flowers silky pink, large, full, cupped

'Jeanne Guillot'   HP, mp, 1869, Liabaud; flowers pink with purple shades, very large, full

'Jeanne Hachette'   HGal, dp, 1842, Vibert; flowers lilac rose, large, dbl., globular

'Jeanne Hachette'   M, mp, Coquerel; flowers medium pink, edges lighter, large, full; intr. 1851

'Jeanne Hachette'   M, m, Robert; flowers slaty violet; intr. 1851

'Jeanne Hachette'   HP, dp, Oger; flowers carmine-rose; intr. 1867

'Jeanne Halphen'   HP, mp, 1878, Margottin; flowers large, full

'Jeanne Hardy' -- See 'Jean Hardy'

'Jeanne Heloise'   w, Terre Noire; intr. 1991

'Jeanne Lajoie'   Cl Min, mp, 1976, Sima; bud long, pointed; flowers 1 in., 40 petals, high-centered, borne in small clusters and singly; foliage small, glossy, dark, embossed; upright, bushy growth; [('Casa Blanca' × 'Independence') × 'Midget']; intr. 1975

'Jeanne Lallemand'   LCl, pb, 1954, Buatois; flowers pink, reverse salmon-pink, large, 40-50 petals; very free, recurrent bloom; very vigorous growth; ['Mrs Pierre S. duPont' × 'George Dickson']

'Jeanne Lassalle'   LCl, mp, 1936, Lassalle; flowers borne in clusters of 50-60; free, recurrent boom; foliage broad, light; long, stiff stems; vigorous (5 ft.) growth

'Jeanne Masson'   HP, lp, 1891, Liabaud; flowers whitish pink, medium, dbl., moderate fragrance

'Jeanne Mermet'   Pol, w, 1909, Mermet; vigorous growth

Jeanne Moreau®   HT, w, Meilland; flowers pure white, full, high-centered, borne mostly singly, moderate fragrance; recurrent; moderate growth; intr. 2006

'Jeanne Nicod'   HT, w, 1929, Schwartz, A.; flowers white, center tinted cream, dbl.

'Jeanne Philippe' -- See 'Mlle Jeanne Philippe'

'Jeanne Richert'   HWich, w, 1929, Walter, L.; flowers cream, center red-brown, 4 cm., dbl., borne in large clusters, slight fragrance; foliage glossy; very vigorous, climbing growth; ['Leontine Gervais' × unknown]

'Jeanne Saultier'   HT, pb, 1927, Laperrière; flowers salmon-rose, reverse reddish-pink, base yellow, dbl.; ['Louise Catherine Breslau' × 'Mme Edouard Herriot']

'Jeanne Sury'   HP, dp, 1868, Faudon; flowers claret and crimson, very large, full, moderate fragrance

'Jeannette'   HGal, dp, before 1815, Descemet, M.; flowers bright light red,

fading light rose-pink, dbl.
'Jeannette' Min, pb, Spooner, Raymond A.; intr. 1997
'Jeannie Deans' HEg, dr, 1895, Penzance; flowers scarlet-crimson, medium to large, semi-dbl.; very free seasonal bloom; foliage fragrant; vigorous growth
'Jeannie Dickson' HP, pb, 1890, Dickson, A.; flowers rose-pink, edged silvery pink, large, 45 petals, high-centered; moderate bloom; vigorous growth
'Jeannine' Gr, op
'Jeannine' -- See 'Froneen'
'Jeannine Michelle' -- See 'Frojean'
'Jeanny Soupert' Pol, w, 1913, Soupert & Notting; flowers soft flesh-white, borne in large clusters; moderately vigorous growth; [('Mme Norbert Levavasseur' × 'Petite Léonie']
'Jean's Dream' HT, pb, 1970, Ellick; flowers orient pink to azalea-pink, 6 in., 30 petals, high-centered; foliage large; vigorous, upright, bushy growth; [('My Choice' × (seedling × 'Memoriam')]
'Jebsheim Mill' S, lp, Williams, J. B.; flowers blush pink with ruffled petals, borne in clusters, slight fragrance; growth to 4 ft.; intr. 2005
'Jeep' -- See 'Lucina'
'Jeeper's Creeper' -- See 'Korissel'
'Jeff Chait' -- See 'Zipjeff'
'Jeffrey' -- See 'Resjeff'
'Jehoca' -- See 'Tanjeka'
'Jelbar' ('Wee Barbie') Min, w, 1981, Jellyman, J.S.; bud globular; flowers cream-white, 43 petals, borne 10 - 20 per cluster, moderate fragrance; foliage dark; bushy growth; [seedling × seedling]; intr. 1980
'Jelcanodir' F, dy, 1976, Jelly; flowers aureolin-yellow, 2½-3 in., 30 petals; almost continuous bloom in glasshouse; vigorous, upright growth; [seedling × 'Golden Garnette']
'Jeldaniran' ('Mimi Rose', Mimi Pink™) F, lp, 1984, Jelly, Robert G.; flowers light pink, reverse darker, sweetheart, large, 35 petals, no fragrance; foliage medium size, dark, semi-glossy; upright growth; PP5636; [seedling × 'Misty Pink']; intr. 1980
'Jeleit' ('Virgin') F, w, 1972, E. G. Hill Co.; flowers dbl, 30-35 petals, globular, borne several together and in trusses; foliage large, leathery, dull; growth vigorous, upright; ['Seventeen' × 'Jack Frost']; intr. 1971
'Jelena de Belder' -- See 'Lenbracta'
'Jelfax' -- See 'Cancan'
'Jelico' HT, or, 1974, Jelly; flowers vermilion, reverse crimson, 5 in., 35 petals, cupped, slight fragrance; foliage large, dark; [Baccará® × ('Forever Yours' × seedling)]; intr. 1973
'Jelina' HRg, dp, 1894, Kaufmann; flowers dark velvety carmine, large, dbl., foliage elliptical, dark green, very stiff; [R. rugosa rubra × 'Perle de Lyon']
'Jello' F, my, 1971, Jelly; bud short, pointed

Jelly Bean™ Min, rb, 1982, Saville, F. Harmon; bud ovoid, pointed; flowers red-yellow blend, micro-mini, 20 petals, high-centered, borne 1 - 6 per cluster, moderate spicy fragrance; foliage small; no prickles; very compact, tiny growth; PP5093; [seedling × 'Poker Chip']; intr. 1982
'Jelona' HMult, pb; flowers pink with white eye, single, borne in large clusters; foliage medium green
'Jelpirofor' ('White Success') HT, w, 1986, Jelly; bud long ovoid; flowers clear white, 5 in., 55 petals, high-centered, borne singly, no fragrance; recurrent; foliage large, dark green, semi-glossy; prickles numerous, medium, straight, brown; stems strong; upright growth; PP5632; [Bridal Pink™ × seedling]; originally a greenhouse rose.; intr. 1985
'Jelrandoli' F, rb, 1976, Jelly; flowers vermilion-red, base cardinal-red, 3-3½ in., 35 petals; foliage large; vigorous, upright growth; ['San Francisco' × 'Little Leaguer']
'Jelroganor' ('Surprise Party') F, rb, 1977, Jelly, R. G.; bud ovoid
'Jelwhite' HT, w, 1971, Jelly; intr. 1969
'Jema' HT, ab, 1982, Perry, Astor; bud ovoid; flowers large, 45 petals, borne singly, moderate fragrance; foliage medium size, light green; prickles small, triangular, straw; tall, vigorous growth; ['Helen Traubel' × 'Lolita']; intr. 1982
'Jemma Giblin' -- See 'Horjemma'
'Jemne Losos Interflora' HT, op, Strnad
'Jen' -- See 'Prejen'
'Jenifer' HT, 1954, Fletcher; flowers pale flesh pink, 4-5 in.; foliage dull green; vigorous growth; RULED EXTINCT 1/85 ARM; [('Mrs Henry Bowles' × 'Phyllis Gold') × 'Edina']; intr. 1954
'Jenna Rose' S, w, 2005, Miladin, Suzanne; flowers white with pink stripes, 3½ in., very full, borne in small clusters, slight fragrance; foliage medium size, medium green, matte; prickles moderate, 1/8 in., tan; growth bushy, medium; [sport of 'Mary Rose']
Jennie Anne™ -- See 'Kinjen'
Jennie June™ -- See 'Tanjenju'
'Jennie Robinson' -- See 'Trobette'
'Jennie Sommer' -- See 'Gelsom'
Jennifer™ -- See 'Poulhi021(N)'
'Jennifer' F, dp, 1959, Fryers Nursery, Ltd.; RULED EXTINCT 1/85 ARM; ['Independence' × 'Fashion']
'Jennifer' HT, op, Select; flowers coral, 4 in., 40-45 petals; foliage dark green; intr. 2003
Jennifer™ -- See 'Benjen'
'Jennifer-Betty Kenward' -- See 'Lanbet'
'Jennifer Clark' -- See 'Rawfragjen'
'Jennifer Hart' HT, dr, 1982, Swim, H.C. & Christensen, J.E.; bud ovoid, pointed; flowers 45 petals, high-centered, borne singly, slight tea fragrance; foliage medium size, medium green, semi-glossy; medium, upright, bushy growth;

PP5219; ['Pink Parfait' × 'Yuletide']; intr. 1982
'Jennifer Hit' (Jennifer Patiohit™, Jennifer™) MinFl, dr, Olesen; bud pointed ovoid; flowers dark red, 5 cm., 43 petals, open cup, borne singly and in small clusters, very slight fragrance; free-flowering; foliage dark green, semi-glossy; prickles few, 3 mm., linear, greyed-orange; stems 14 cm; bushy (40-60 cm.) growth; PP15853; [sport of 'Valentina Hit']; intr. 2003
'Jennifer Jay' HT, pb, 1977, Thomas, Dr. A.S.; flowers light to medium pink; [sport of 'Christian Dior']
'Jennifer Joy' -- See 'Pouljenjoy'
Jennifer Patiohit™ -- See 'Poulhi021(N)'
'Jennifer's Rose' HT, mr, Dawson; intr. 1997
'Jennirene' HT, pb, 2005, Felts, Stephen D; flowers dark pink, reverse light yellow, 4¼ in., full, borne mostly solitary, no fragrance; foliage medium size, dark green, glossy; prickles small, slightly diagonally slanted; growth upright, tall (5 ft.); exhibition; [sport of 'Brooks Red']; intr. 2004
'Jenny' ('Rubra') HCh, dr, before 1836; flowers fiery purple-crimson; Lawrenciana
'Jenny' -- See 'Jenny Duval'
'Jenny Audio' P, mp, before 1836, Audio; flowers bright pink, large, full
'Jenny Brown' HT, or, 1976, Parkes, Mrs M.H.; bud long, pointed; flowers salmon-pink, center paler, open, 4 in., 5 petals, intense fragrance; foliage glossy; very vigorous growth; [('Pink Favorite' × 'Dorothy Peach') × 'Dainty Bess']; intr. 1974
'Jenny Butchart' HT, op, Hepworth, George; flowers deep orange pink fading to lighter pink, 30-35 petals, high-centered; foliage medium sized matte green; ['Miss Canada' × 'Fragrant Cloud']
'Jenny Charlton' -- See 'Simway'
'Jenny Duval' ('Jenny') HGal, mp, before 1842; flowers rosy blush, tinted magenta and mauve, aging lilac-grey, medium, semi-dbl. to dbl., quartered, borne singly or in clusters of 2-3; foliage medium green, large, elliptical; prickles moderate; sometimes classed as HCh; possibly from Duval; the rose currently in commerce does not match early descriptions
'Jenny Fair' HT, mp, 1967, Gregory; flowers pink, globular; foliage dark; slender, upright growth; ['Tropicana' × unknown]
'Jenny Gay' ('Mlle Jenny Gay') B, w, 1865, Guillot; flowers flesh white with light pink tints, medium, full
'Jenny Jones' T, 1890, Williams, A.
'Jenny Lind' M, mp, 1845, Laffay, M.; bud abundantly mossed; flowers medium, dbl.
'Jenny Lynn' HT, pb
'Jenny Reilly' -- See 'Horbondpeace'

'Jenny Wren' F, ab, 1957, Ratcliffe; bud salmon-red; flowers creamy apricot, reverse pale salmon, small, dbl., borne in large clusters, intense fragrance; foliage dark; ['Cécile Brunner' × 'Fashion']

'Jenny's Dream' HT, dp, 1980, Beckett, Ian; bud large; flowers deep pink, 102 petals, classic, borne 5 per cluster, no fragrance; free-flowering; foliage large, medium green, glossy; vigorous, tall, upright growth; [sport of 'Red Devil']; intr. 1979

'Jenny's Rose' -- See 'Cansit'

'Jens Munk' HRg, mp, 1977, Svedja, Felicitas; bud ovoid; flowers rose pink, yellow stamens, 3 in., 25 petals, intense fragrance; upright, bushy growth; ['Schneezwerg' × 'Frau Dagmar Hartopp']; intr. 1974

'Jeppe Gold' HT, yb, Kordes; intr. 2003

'Jeri Jennings' -- See 'Ardjeri'

'Jéricho' -- See 'Bourbon'

'Jericho' ('Dorbin') HT, Dorieux, Francois; intr. 1971

'Jerry' Gr, pb, 1987, Jerabek, Paul E.; flowers white, flushing carmine red, reverse carmine, grading to white, dbl., cupped, intense sweet fragrance; foliage medium size, medium green, semi-glossy; prickles medium, red-brown, hooked downward; bushy, tall growth; small, rarely sets fruit; [seedling × seedling]

'Jerry Desmonde' HT, mp, 1960, Norman; flowers rose-pink, reverse silvery, well-formed,, 5 in., 50 petals; foliage dark, glossy; vigorous, upright growth; ['Lord Rossmore' × 'Karl Herbst']; intr. 1959

Jerry Lynn™ -- See 'Tuckjerry'

Jerry-O™ -- See 'Savajerry'

'Jersey' -- See 'Jersey Beauty'

'Jersey Beauty' ('Jersey') HWich, ly, 1899, Horvath/Manda, W.A.; flowers pale yellow, fading white, 6 cm., single, borne in clusters of 3-5, intense fragrance; non-recurrent; foliage dark green, glossy, evergreen; vigorous, climbing growth; [R. wichurana × 'Perle des Jardins']

'Jersey Cream' S, ly, Sutherland; intr. 1996

'Jersey Gold' Min, dy, Benardella, Frank; flowers clear yellow, dbl., high-centered; tall growth; intr. 1999

'Jersey Queen' HT, ob, 1920, Le Cornu; flowers flame-orange, edged rose, reverse lemon, dbl.; ['Mme Mélanie Soupert' × 'Queen Mary']

'Jerusalem' -- See 'Holje'

'Jeslyn' -- See 'Brijes'

'Jesmond Dene' F, op, 1976, Wood; flowers pastel salmon-pink, large, dbl., intense fragrance; vigorous, upright growth; ['Arthur Bell' × 'Betty May Wood']

'Jessa Belle' ('Jezebel') HT, pb

'Jesse's Jewels' -- See 'Burjes'

'Jessica' -- See 'Rose Angle'

'Jessica' HWich, pb, 1910, Walsh; flowers cream-white, center light rose, 7-9 cm., semi-dbl., borne singly or in small clusters; foliage dark green, glossy; numerous prickles

'Jessica' S, mp, Clements, John; flowers soft pink becoming apricot-pink in the center, 4 in., 30 petals, deeply cupped., moderate fragrance; foliage deep green; growth bushy, compact (3½ ft. × 3 ft.); intr. 2003

'Jessica' -- See 'Tanjeka'

'Jessica Lauren' HRg, lp, Baskerville, Joanne; flowers blush pink, 4 in., single, moderate fragrance; blooms all summer; foliage crinkled, glossy; growth to 6 ft. tall and wide; hips large, orange-red; intr. 2000

'Jessica Rose' -- See 'Morbahny'

'Jessie' Pol, rb, 1909, Merryweather; flowers bright crimson, fading rose-pink, center white, 1½ in., semi-dbl.; foliage small, soft, glossy; bushy growth; [sport of 'Phyllis']

'Jessie Anderson' S, dp; flowers deep rose, well-formed, large, dbl.; blooms continuously on new wood; [('Old Crimson China' × R. canina) × 'Souv. d'Alphonse Lavallee']

'Jessie Brown' Min, mp, 1978, Dobbs; bud mossy; flowers loosely formed, 1½ in., 15 petals; foliage small; bushy growth; ['Fairy Moss' × 'Fairy Moss']

'Jessie Clark' LCl, mp, 1915, Clark, A.; flowers rosy pink, becoming lighter, 12 cm., single; non-recurrent; foliage dark, leathery; very vigorous growth; [R. gigantea × 'Mme Martignier']

'Jessie Mathews' -- See 'Beejes'

'Jessie Patricia' -- See 'Bosor'

'Jessie Segrave' HT, rb, 1937, Mee; flowers scarlet on deep chrome base, with pencil markings on inside, dbl.; vigorous growth

Jessika® -- See 'Tanjeka'

'Jet' HT, dr, 1948, Brownell; bud long, pointed; flowers red to very dark red, large, dbl., moderate fragrance; foliage glossy, dark; vigorous, bushy, compact growth; ['Pink Princess' × 'Crimson Glory']

'Jet Fire' F, or, 1965, Schloen, J.; bud ovoid; flowers large, dbl., cupped, moderate spicy fragrance; foliage dark, glossy; vigorous, upright, bushy growth; ['Sumatra' × 'Fashion']; intr. 1964

Jet Flame® -- See 'Lenpen'

Jet Flame Nirpaysage® -- See 'Lenpen'

'Jet Richards' HT, rb, 2000, Poole, Lionel; flowers medium red, reverse light red, 5½ in, full, exhibition, borne mostly singly, slight fragrance; free-flowering; foliage large, dark green, semi-glossy; prickles moderate; bushy, medium (2½ ft.) growth; [('Silver Jubilee' × 'Red Planet') × 'Gavotte']; intr. 2001

Jet Set® F, pb, Laperriere; flowers clear pink, reverse lighter, double, cupped to flat, borne in clusters; recurrent; foliage glossy; medium (60 - 80 cm.) growth; intr. 2008

Jet Spray® -- See 'Lencara'

'Jet Trail' Min, w, 1964, Moore, Ralph S.; bud pointed; flowers white, sometimes tinted pale green, small, 40 petals; bushy (12-14 in.) growth; PP2683; ['Little Darling' × 'Magic Wand']

'Jeune Fille' -- See 'Brocade'

'Jeune Fille' F, op, 1964, Gaujard; flowers bright salmon-pink, medium, dbl., borne in clusters; foliage leathery; very vigorous, bushy growth; [(Rose Gaujard® × unknown) × 'Vendome']

'Jeune France' -- See 'Young France'

'Jeune Henry' P, mr, before 1815, Descemet; flowers vivid rose/red, velvety, medium, full

'Jeunesse' HT, mp, 1959, Laperrière; flowers bright pink, dbl.; moderately bushy growth; [('Independence' × 'Tonnerre') × 'Michèle Meilland']

'Jeunesse Éternelle' -- See 'Eternal Youth'

'Jewel' HT, dr, 1938, Grillo; flowers velvety red, 5 in., 50 petals, moderate fragrance; PP367; [sport of 'Better Times']

'Jewel Box' -- See 'Morbox'

Jewel's Delight™ -- See 'Minbaco'

'Jezebel' -- See 'Jessa Belle'

'Jezebel' HT, mp, 1964, Leenders, J.; flowers dbl.; strong stems; [Queen Elizabeth® × 'Pink Lustre']

'JFK' -- See 'John F. Kennedy'

'Jian' Min, mr, 1965, Williams, Ernest D.; bud ovoid; flowers medium red, reverse lighter, very small, dbl.; foliage narrow, leathery; very vigorous, bushy, dwarf growth; ['Juliette' × 'Oakington Ruby']

'Jigs' -- See 'Geljig'

'Jihoceske Slunce' HT, w, 1937, Böhm, J.; flowers medium, dbl.

'Jill' F, mr, 1939, LeGrice; flowers cerise-scarlet, open, semi-dbl., borne in clusters; long stems; vigorous, bushy growth; [('Else Poulsen' × seedling) × (('single red seedling' × 'Étoile de Hollande') × 'Daily Mail Scented Rose')]

'Jill Carter' -- See 'Sherijill'

'Jill Dando' -- See 'Beajil'

'Jill Darling' HT, rb, 1937, Austin & McAslan; flowers rich cerise, reverse cinnamon-yellow; foliage glossy; vigorous growth

'Jillian Louise' Min, w, 1994, Fairweather, Mrs. P.H.; flowers white with light pink edge and center, large, full, borne in large clusters, slight fragrance; foliage medium size, medium green, semi-glossy; some prickles; medium to tall, upright growth; [sport of 'Magic Carrousel']

'Jillian McGredy' -- See 'Macarnhe'

'Jill's Rose' -- See 'Ganjil'

'Jilly Cooper' -- See 'Legcream'

'Jilly Jewel' -- See 'Benmfig'

'Jim Bowie' S, dp, Williams, J. Benjamin; flowers dark pink to light pink center, 4 in., semi-dbl., borne in sprays, intense fragrance; arching growth; hardy; intr. 1996

Jim Dandy™ -- See 'Benjim'

'Jim Delahanty' Pol, lp, 2008, Wilke, William; flowers 2 in., single, borne in large clusters; foliage medium, dark green, semi-glossy; prickles straight, red, moderate; growth bushy (2 ft.); containers, low hedges; [sport of 'Wee Butterflies']

'Jim Ingall' HT, mr, 1998, Thomas, D.; flowers medium red, 4 in., very dbl., borne singly; foliage medium size, dark green, semi-glossy; prickles moderate; bushy, upright, 120-150 cm. growth; ['Debbie Thomas' × 'Maria Theresa']

'Jim Larkin' -- See 'Bosaceball'

'Jim Lounsbery' S, or, 1995, Fleming, Joyce L.; flowers medium, 5-7 petals, borne in sprays of 5-25; foliage medium size, medium green, matte; upright (120-150 cm.), bushy growth; ['Liverpool Echo' × R. virginiana]; intr. 1994

'Jim Loves Peggy' MinFl, w, 2008, Smith, Joe and Landers-Smith, Brenda; flowers 2¾ in., dbl., high-centered, borne mostly solitary; foliage medium, medium green, semi-glossy; no prickles; growth upright, medium; [sport of 'Leading Lady']; intr. 2008

'Jim Pugh' -- See 'Hormemoriam'

'Jim Todd' HT, rb, 1940, Mallerin, C.; flowers nasturtium-red, reverse touched yellow, large, semi-dbl., cupped; very vigorous, bushy growth

'Jiminy Cricket' F, op, 1955, Boerner; bud ovoid; flowers coral-orange to pink-coral, 3-4 in., 28 petals, cupped, borne in clusters, moderate rose geranium fragrance; foliage glossy; vigorous, upright, bushy growth; PP1346; ['Goldilocks' × 'Geranium Red']; intr. 1954

'Jimmy' Min, ob, Chandrakant; flowers lustrous orange with white base, compact, full; free-flowering; [sport of 'Don Don']; intr. 1993

'Jimmy Greaves' HT, m, 1971, Gandy, Douglas L.; flowers red-purple, reverse silver, 5 in., 55 petals, high-centered, foliage large; erect, bushy growth; ['Dorothy Peach' × 'Prima Ballerina']

'Jimmy Savile' -- See 'Peapolly'

'Jindrich Hanus Böhm' HRg, mr, 1937, Böhm; flowers large, full

'Jinge Limm' HSem, w, Louette, Ivan; flowers pure white with yellow stamens, 3 cm., single, shallow cup, borne in clusters, slight fragrance; non-remontant; foliage dark green, glossy; vigorous (10 - 15 ft.), arching growth; intr. 2005

Jingle Bells™ -- See 'Jacredem'

'Jingles' F, mp, 1956, Boerner; bud ovoid; flowers pink overcast deep rose-pink, to open, 2½-3 in., 35-40 petals, cupped, moderate fragrance; foliage leathery, glossy; vigorous, upright, bushy growth; PP1570; ['Goldilocks' × 'Garnette']

'Jisraela Amira' HT, Nevo, Motke; intr. 1980

'Jitka' F, yb, Urban, J.

'Jitka' F, Strnad

'Jitrenka' HWich, lp, 1933, Mikes-Böhm, J.; flowers rich pink, fading to pale pink, white at base of petals, 4 cm., semi-dbl., borne in medium clusters

'Jitrenka' Pol, dy, Urban, J.; flowers medium, semi-dbl.; intr. 1978

'Jitterbug' -- See 'Jacminno'

Jive™ LCl, mr, Poulsen; bud pointed ovoid; flowers , 25 petals, open cup, borne in large clusters, slight floral fragrance; recurrent; foliage dark green, glossy; prickles few, 8 mm., hooked downward, greyed-orange; bushy (150-200 cm.) growth; PP15411; [seedling × 'Poulket']; intr. 2003

'Jkvr D. Baroness von Ittersum' -- See 'Baronesse von Ittersum'

Jo™ -- See 'Moejo'

'Jo-Jo' Min, dy, Interplant; intr. 1988

'Jo McMath' -- See 'Driscoaust'

'Joachim du Bellay' HP, mr, 1882, Moreau-Robert; flowers vermilion red, tinted flame, large, full; foliage dark green

'Joachim du Bellay' ('Hermitage') F, m, Sauvageot; bud globular; flowers deep lilac-pink center, pale lilac-pink to white edges, full, cupped; recurrent; moderate growth; intr. 2004

'Joan' HMsk, ob, 1919, Pemberton; bud peach; flowers copper, semi-dbl., borne in clusters; [Trier® × 'Perle des Jeannes']

'Joan Alder' HT, pb, 1950, Moss; bud long; flowers salmon-pink tinted mauve; foliage dark; very vigorous growth

'Joan Anderson' -- See 'Else Poulsen'

'Joan Austin' -- See 'Mordeb'

'Joan Ball' -- See 'Troball'

'Joan Beales' -- See 'Beaagile'

'Joan Bell' HT, dp, 1985, Bell, John C.; flowers light crimson, large, dbl.; [sport of 'Portland Trailblazer']; same as parent except for color

Joan Brickhill® -- See 'Hilgofan'

'Joan Cant' HT, pb, 1929, Cant, B. R.; bud pointed; flowers salmon-pink, reverse brighter, very large, dbl.; foliage light, leathery; vigorous, bushy growth

'Joan Davis' HT, ab, 1927, Allen; flowers salmon-apricot shaded cerise-pink, base yellow, dbl.; ['Ophelia' × unknown]

'Joan Elizabeth' HT, yb, 1949, Fletcher; bud long, pointed; flowers golden yellow, reverse flushed pink, well-formed, 5 in., 30 petals; foliage dark, glossy; vigorous growth

'Joan F. Mills' -- See 'Jaytom'

'Joan Fittall' HT, yb, 1946, Moss; bud long, pointed; flowers bronze and gold fading to pink, open, medium, semi-dbl.; foliage leathery; vigorous, bushy growth; ['Luis Brinas' × unknown]

Joan Fontaine™ -- See 'Clejon'

'Joan Frueh' HT, lp, 1924, Frueh; flowers shell-pink, dbl.; ['Ophelia' × 'General-Superior Arnold Janssen']

'Joan Howarth' HT, pb, 1924, Bees; flowers shell-pink shaded carmine, very large, dbl.; ['Lyon Rose' × 'Mme Abel Chatenay']

'Joan Knight' Cl HT, dr, 1928, Knight, J.; vigorous growth

'Joan Kruger' S, w, Kordes; bud globular, slightly pointed; flowers white with touches of ivory and pink in the center, very full, quartered, borne in clusters, basals produce candelabras, no fragrance; growth tall and vigorous; intr. 1997

Joan Longer™ -- See 'Wilktwo'

'Joan Margaret Derrick' Pol, dr, 1953, Derrick; flowers carmine-red, small, 15 petals; vigorous growth; [sport of 'Golden Salmon']

'Joan Ollis' HT, dp, 2000, Poole, Lionel; flowers 4½ in., full, exhibition, classic, borne mostly singly, slight fragrance; free-flowering; foliage medium size, dark red turning medium green, semi-glossy; prickles moderate; vigorous, bushy, medium (1 m.) growth; [('Selfridges' × 'Mischief') × 'Gavotte']; intr. 2001

'Joan Ross' HP, pb, 1933, Nicolas; bud pointed; flowers blush, reverse light pink, very large, dbl.; profuse, non-recurrent bloom; vigorous growth; ['Frau Karl Druschki' × 'Paul Neyron']

'Joanie' -- See 'Rawsharoo'

'Joanna Bridge' HT, yb, 1916, Hicks; flowers canary-yellow shaded strawberry, semi-dbl., borne on large trusses; vigorous growth

'Joanna Elise' -- See 'Rawcrazylady'

'Joanna Hill' HT, ly, 1928, J.H. Hill Co.; bud long, pointed; flowers creamy yellow, base flushed orange, large, 48 petals; foliage leathery; vigorous growth; ['Mme Butterfly' × 'Miss Amelia Gude']

'Joanna Hill, Climbing' Cl HT, ly, 1935, Howard Rose Co.

'Joanna Lumley' HT, ab, 1994, Poole, Lionel; flowers 3-3½ in., full, borne singly, slight fragrance; foliage medium size, dark green, glossy; some prickles; upright (100 cm.) growth; [Chicago Peace® × 'Joanne']; intr. 1995

'Joanna Troutman' HT, ob, 1929, Vestal; bud pointed; flowers orange-yellow, open, semi-dbl.; foliage bronze, glossy; ['Mme Alexandre Dreux' × unknown]

'Joanne' HT, op, 1985, Poole, Lionel; flowers medium shrimp pink, large, 43 petals, high-centered, borne singly; foliage large, dark, semi-glossy; prickles large, dark brown; medium, upright growth; hips large, globular, orange; [Courvoisier® × 'Princesse']

'Joanne' S, pb, Mekdeci; flowers two-toned blush pink, borne in floriferous; growth tall; intr. 2001

'Joannes Ginet' HT, pb, 1929, Gaujard; flowers white, tinted cream, edged oriental red; [sport of 'The Queen Alexandra Rose']

'Joanne's Wedding' -- See 'Denjo'

'Joan's Desire' -- See 'Twoadore'

'Joao Moreira da Silva' HT, my, 1959, Moreira da Silva; ['Mme Marie Curie' × 'Dr. Manuel Alves de Castro']

'Joao Pereira da Rosa' HT, rb, 1936, Moreira da Silva; flowers brilliant red shading orange and yellow, large, dbl., cupped; foliage light, soft; vigorous growth; ['Angèle Pernet' × 'Mme Méha

Sabatier']
'Joaquin Aldrufeu' HT, m, 1897, Aldrufeu; flowers garnet-purple, reverse violet to magenta, dbl.; foliage light green; moderate growth

'Joaquin Mir' HT, dy, 1940, Dot, Pedro; flowers golden yellow, large, dbl., cupped; foliage glossy, dark; upright growth; ['Mrs Pierre S. duPont' × 'Senora Gari']

'Joaquina Munoz' HT, Dot, Simon; intr. 1980

'Joasine Hanet' -- See 'Johasine Hanet'

'Jocelyn' F, r, 1970, LeGrice; flowers mahogany aging purplish-brown, 3 in., dbl.

'Jocelyne Pardo' -- See 'Jonise'

Jocelyne Salavert® S, ab, Guillot; intr. 2007

'Jockey' -- See 'Horrido'

'Jodrell Bank' HT, pb, 1967, Dale, F.; flowers light pink, reverse rose-pink; [sport of 'Charles F. Warren']

Joe Grey™ -- See 'Wiljoeg'

Joe-Joe™ -- See 'Kinjoe'

'Joe Longthorne' HT, op, 1995, Poole, Lionel; flowers orange pink, 3-3½ in., full, borne singly, intense fragrance; foliage medium size, dark green, matte; some prickles; medium (100 cm.), upright growth; ['Gavotte' × 'Pot of Gold']; intr. 1995

'Joe Roscoe' HT, mp, 1972, Wright & Son; flowers rose-red, 6 in., 62 petals, moderate fragrance; ['Karl Herbst' × 'Tzigane']

Joëlle® HT, w, 1986, Kriloff, Michel; flowers white, aging light pink, well-formed, dbl.; foliage glossy; [seedling × seedling]; intr. 1977

'Joëlle Marouani' S, dy, Guillot-Massad; flowers yellow with a whitish tinge on the petal tips, large, 60 petals, borne singly and in clusters, moderate fruity fragrance; foliage dark green; growth to 4 ft.; intr. 2001

'Joe's Little Red Creeper' ('Joe's Red Creeper') S, mr; flowers single; groundcover; spreading growth; PPAF; intr. 2001

'Joe's Red Creeper' -- See 'Joe's Little Red Creeper'

Joey's ™ -- See 'Pouljoey'

'Joey's Palace' (Joey's ™) S, ab, Poulsen; flowers apricot blend, 8-10 cm., full, slight wild rose fragrance; foliage dark; stems bushy, 40 - 60 cm; PP11598; intr. 1997

'Jofitali' F, rb, 1976, DeWitte; flowers rose-bengal, center cardinal-red; PP4083; [sport of 'Sonia']

'Jogan' HT, ab, Bansal, O.P.; flowers pale apricot, dbl., high-centered; intr. 1988

'Johan Ludwig Lumberg' HT, dr, 1905, Björn-Lindberg; flowers dark cherry red

Johann Strauss® -- See 'Meioffic'

'Johanna Ofman' HT, dp, 1962, Ofman; flowers carmine-pink, large, dbl.; [sport of 'Pink Sensation']

'Johanna Röpcke' -- See 'Johanna Röpke'

'Johanna Röpke' ('Johanna Röpcke') HWich, op, 1931, Tantau; bud pointed; flowers salmon-pink, resembling Ophelia but smaller, 7-9 cm., dbl., cupped, borne in small clusters, moderate fragrance; foliage dark, bronze-green; thornless; very vigorous, climbing growth; ['Dorothy Perkins' × 'Ophelia']

'Johanna Sebus' Cl HT, pb, 1894, Müller; flowers cherry pink with yellow at base, very large, full, strong heliotrope fragrance

'Johanna Tantau' Pol, w, 1928, Tantau; flowers white, center pinkish yellow, large, dbl., borne in clusters; foliage dark, leathery; bushy, dwarf growth; ['Dorothy Perkins' × 'Ophelia']

'Johanna Tantau, Climbing' Cl Pol, lp; flowers medium, semi-dbl.

Johanna Thuillard® S, lp, Huber; flowers dbl., cupped; intr. 2006

'Johannes Boettner' F, mr, 1943, Kordes; flowers light crimson, very large, dbl., high-centered, borne in clusters; vigorous, bushy, compact growth; [('Baby Chateau' × unknown) × 'Else Poulsen']

'Johannes Rau' S, yb, Noack; flowers dark yellow with soft pink on outer petals, 4 in., full; free-flowering; spreading (4 × 5 ft.) growth; intr. 2002

Johannes Schultheis® S, mp, Schultheis; flowers silvery rose, deeper in center, medium, dbl., cupped, borne in clusters, moderate fragrance; good repeat; foliage delicate, medium green, glossy; vigorous (5 × 5 ft.) growth; intr. 2000

'Johannes Wesselhöft' HT, my, 1899, Welter & Hinner; bud long; flowers sulphur yellow, aging to light yellow, large, full; ['Kaiserin Auguste Viktoria' × ('William Francis Bennett' × 'Comtesse de Frigneuse')]

'Johannes XXIII' HT, w

'Johannesburg Centennial' HT, dy

'Johannesburg Garden Club' -- See 'Poulfan'

'Johannesburg Sun' -- See 'Kordoubt'

'Johannisfeuer' HT, mr, 1910, Türke; flowers red, yellow center, large, dbl., cupped; [('Princesse de Béarn' × 'Deutschland') × R. foetida bicolor]

Johannisfeuer® S, mr, Tantau; flowers blood red, semi-dbl., borne in sprays; foliage large, dark green; bushy, upright, strong (4½ ft.) growth; intr. 1988

'Johannisröschen' HSpn, ly; flowers full; good repeat; growth to 5 ft.; very winter hardy

'Johanniszauber' HT, dr, 1926, Tantau; bud pointed; flowers dark velvety blood-red, very dbl.; vigorous growth; ['Château de Clos Vougeot' × seedling]

'Johasine Hanet' ('Glendora', 'Joasine Hanet', 'The Portland from Glendora', 'MacGregor's Damask', 'Portland from Glendora') P, m, 1846, Vibert; flowers deep rose tinged with violet, 5-6 cm., dbl., quartered, moderate fragrance; heavy bloomer; very hardy; roses sold as Amanda Patenaude in the U.S. in recent years are almost certainly Joasine Hanet

'Johillgold' ('Tropical Sunrise') Gr, dy, 1992, Hoy, Lowel L.; flowers deep yellow aging to medium yellow, 4 in., 21 petals, high-centered, borne singly and in small clusters; foliage medium size, medium green, semi-glossy; upright, medium growth; ['Golden Fantasie' × seedling]

'Johillgolf' ('Crimson Delight') S, mr, 1992, Hoy, Lowel L.; flowers 2½ in., dbl., borne in sprays of 3-4; foliage medium size, medium green, semi-glossy; upright, bushy, low growth; ['Volare' × seedling]

'Johillstar' ('Classical Velvet') HT, mr, 1992, Hoy, Lowel L.; flowers 5¼ in., 25 petals, borne in sprays of 4-5; foliage medium size, dark green, semi-glossy; upright, bushy, tall growth; ['Anniversary' × seedling]

'JOHilmar' ('After Glow') Gr, op

'John A. Allison' Gr, lp, 1974, Golik; bud ovoid; flowers large, very dbl., slight fragrance; very vigorous, upright growth; [Queen Elizabeth® × 'Montezuma']; intr. 1973

'John A. Macdonald' ('Sir John A. Macdonald') Gr, dr, Delbard; intr. 1974

'John A. Weall' LCl, dr; flowers velvet red, dbl., borne in clusters, slight fragrance; foliage medium green; growth vigorous; intr. 1994

'John Abrams' F, op, 1977, Sanday, John; flowers vermilion and salmon, 3 in., 15 petals; ['Vera Dalton' × Sarabande®]; intr. 1976

'John Allan' Sp, lp, 1944; flowers dbl.; recurrent bloom; growth to 18 in.; collected in S. Sask. by John Allan; may be same parentage as 'Woodrow'; a form of Rosa arkansana var. suffulta

'John Andrews' HT, dr, Williams, J. Benjamin; flowers large, moderate fragrance; foliage disease-resistant; growth to 5 ft.; intr. 1997

John Boy™ -- See 'Tuckjohnboy'

'John Bradshaw' -- See 'Harquisp'

'John Bright' HP, mr, 1878, Paul & Son; flowers bright crimson, medium, round, globular

'John Burton' HWich, mp, 1903, Hoopes & Thomas; flowers very full; [R. wichurana × 'Safrano']

'John C. M. Mensing' ('Pink Ophelia') HT, mp, 1924, Eveleens; flowers deep bright rose-pink, open, large, dbl.; vigorous growth; [sport of 'Ophelia']

'John Cabot' HKor, mr, 1978, Svedja, Felicitas; bud ovoid; flowers fuschia tinted red, opens flat, 2½ in., 40 petals, borne in clusters, moderate fragrance; foliage yellow-green; vigorous, upright, medium growth; [R. × kordesii × seedling]

'John Cant' S, dp, 1895, Cant, B. R.; flowers carmine-pink, small, semi-dbl.; sometimes classed as HEg

'John Church' F, or, 1964, McGredy, Sam IV; flowers orange-scarlet, well-formed, large, 30 petals, borne in clusters;

vigorous growth; ['Ma Perkins' × 'Red Favorite']
John Clare™ -- See 'Auscent'
'John Cook' HT, pb, 1917, Krüger; bud dark pink; flowers La France pink, reverse very dark, dbl., moderate fragrance; ['La France' × unknown]
'John Cramphorn' F, or, Kriloff; flowers large, dbl.; intr. 1980
'John Cranston' M, m, 1861, Verdier, E.; flowers crimson, shaded purple, expanded, medium, dbl.; some repeat; vigorous growth
'John Christopher' -- See 'Christopher Stone, Climbing'
'John Cronin' HT, dp, 1935, Clark, A.; flowers deep pink, large, dbl., globular; vigorous growth
'John Crou' -- See 'John Grow'
'John Cuff' HT, pb, 1909, Dickson, A.; flowers deep carmine pink with yellow at base of each petal, large, full
'John Davis' HKor, mp, 1986, Svedja, Felicitas; flowers medium pink, yellow at base, large, 40 petals, borne in clusters of up to 17, intense spicy fragrance; recurrent bloom; foliage glossy, leathery; prickles straight; trailing growth; [R. × kordesii × ('Red Dawn' × 'Suzanne')]
'John Davison' HT, dr, 1919, McGredy; flowers rich velvety crimson, dbl.
'John Dijkstra' ('Letkis') F, dr, 1965, Buisman, G. A. H.; bud ovoid; flowers medium, semi-dbl., borne in clusters; foliage dark; [Olala® × 'Paprika']
'John Donne' S, mp
'John Downie' HT, ob, 1921, Dobbie; flowers salmon; [sport of 'Lyon Rose']
'John E. Tovey' F, mp; intr. 2007
'John E. Sleath' HT, rb, 1937, Mee; flowers carmine-red, suffused vermilion-orange; vigorous growth
'John Edward Reed' HT, dy, 1950, Reed; bud long, pointed; flowers buttercup-yellow, 5½-6 in., 32 petals; vigorous, upright growth; [sport of 'Talisman']
'John F. Kennedy' ('JFK', 'President John F. Kennedy') HT, w, 1965, Boerner; bud ovoid, tinted greenish; flowers 5-5½ in., 48 petals, high-centered, moderate fragrance; foliage leathery; vigorous growth; PP2441; [seedling × 'White Queen']
'John Franklin' S, mr, 1980, Svedja, Felicitas; bud ovoid; flowers vibrant red, large, 25 petals, borne in clusters, floriferous; foliage rounded; prickles yellow-green with purple hues; upright, bushy growth (3-4 ft.); [Lilli Marleen® × seedling]
'John Fraser' M, rb, 1861, Lévêque; flowers bright red, shaded crimson and purple, 10-12 cm., dbl.; remontant; prickles reddish; shy growth
'John Gibb' F, ab, Cocker; flowers soft apricot-gold, dbl., cupped, slight fragrance; recurrent; foliage dark green, glossy; upright (2½-3 ft.) growth; intr. 2005
'John Gould Veitch' ('John Weitch') HP, mr, 1864, Lévêque; flowers brilliant red, large, full
'John Greenwood' F, mr, 1976, Lea; flowers bright red, 2½ in., 25 petals; foliage large, dark; vigorous, free growth; ['Marlena' × 'Fragrant Cloud']
'John Grier' HP, dp, 1865, Verdier, E.; flowers rose pink, reverse silver, large, full
'John Grooms' LCl, pb, Beales, Peter; flowers salmon pink, fading to medium pink, medium, dbl.; recurrent; relatively thornless; dense (10 ft.) growth; intr. 1993
'John Grow' ('John Crou') M, mp, 1859, Laffay, M.; flowers violet crimson red, shaded deep purple, large, full
'John H. Ellis' HT, dp, 1948, McGredy; flowers deep rose-pink, well-formed, large, 48 petals; free, bushy growth
John Hackling™ -- See 'Jayhac'
'John Harris' HT, pb, Dawson; intr. 1995
'John Hart' HT, mp, 1922, Hicks; flowers cherry-pink, dbl.
'John Henry' HT, mr, 1925, Beckwith; bud rosy scarlet; flowers rich pink
'John Hopper' HP, pb, 1862, Ward; flowers bright rose edged lilac, center carmine, large, 70 petals, semi-globular, intense fragrance; occasionally recurrent bloom; vigorous, upright, bushy growth; ['Jules Margottin' × 'Mme Vidot']
'John Hughes' -- See 'Sanphyllis'
'John Jambor' -- See 'Jaljambor'
John-John™ -- See 'Wekgibotex'
'John Keats' -- See 'Meiroupis'
'John Kemp' HWich, w
'John Keynes' HP, dr, 1864, Verdier, E.; flowers red shaded maroon, 48 petals, intense fragrance; vigorous growth
'John Kidman' HT, my, 1969, Fankhauser; bud ovoid; flowers lemon-yellow, very large, dbl., camellia-like; foliage leathery; vigorous, tall, compact growth; ['Radar' × Allgold®]
'John Laing' HP, dr, 1872, Verdier; flowers velvety crimson-maroon, small to medium, dbl.
'John Lawrence' F, my, 1991, Bracegirdle, Derek T.; bud pointed; flowers canary yellow, fading as it ages, medium, 18 petals, flat, borne in sprays of 5 - 7, moderate spicy fragrance; foliage medium size, glossy; medium, upright growth; [seedling × 'Sunsprite']; intr. 1990
John Leese™ -- See 'Poulrise'
'John Macmillan Pearson' -- See 'Worcauliflower'
'John McCarthy' HT, lp, 2003, McCarthy, John; flowers light pink, reverse medium pink, 6 cm., dbl., borne mostly solitary, no fragrance; foliage medium size, dark green, glossy, with ruffled edges; prickles 7 mm., triangular, numerous; growth upright, bushy, medium (20 in.); garden decorative; ['Savoy Hotel' × 'Polar Star']; intr. 1999
'John McDonald' F, op, Certified Roses; intr. 2007
'John McNabb' HRg, mp, 1932, Skinner; flowers dbl.; profuse midseason bloom, sometimes continuing later; [R. rugosa kamtchatica × R. beggeriana]
'John Moore' HT, yb, 1939, Gaujard; flowers buff shaded gold, well-shaped, very large, 47 petals, high-centered; foliage dark
'John Morley' HT, dp, 1945, Duehrsen; bud long, pointed; flowers glowing pink, very large, dbl., high-centered; foliage dark, leathery; vigorous, bushy growth; ['Joanna Hill' × 'J. C. Thornton']
'John Owen' -- See 'Jayjow'
'John-Paul II' -- See 'Jacange'
'John Phillip Sousa' S, rb
'John Raymond' LCl, ly; intr. 2007
'John Ruskin' -- See 'Ruskin'
'John Ruskin' HT, mp, 1903, Dickson, A.; flowers bright rosy carmine, very large, full, moderate fragrance
'John Russell' HT, dr, 1924, Dobbie; flowers glowing crimson flushed deeper, well-shaped, large, very dbl.; vigorous growth
'John Russell, Climbing' Cl HT, dr, 1930, Ketten Bros.
'John S. Armstrong' Gr, dr, 1961, Swim, H.C.; bud ovoid to urn-shaped; flowers 3½-4 in., 40 petals, high-centered, slight fragrance; foliage leathery, semi-glossy, dark; tall, bushy growth; PP2056; ['Charlotte Armstrong' × seedling]; intr. 1961
'John S. Bloomfield' HT, ab, 1964, Fankhauser; bud ovoid; flowers deep apricot flushed pink, open, large, dbl.; compact growth; ['Ma Perkins' × 'Burnaby']
'John Saul' HP, mr, 1878, Ducher; flowers red, reverse carmine, very full, spherical
'John Snowball' HT, w
'John Square' Cl HT, dy, 1937, Square; flowers sunflower-yellow, center deeper, very large, dbl., cupped; foliage glossy, dark; vigorous, climbing (6-8 ft in season) growth; PP259; [sport of 'Souv. de Claudius Pernet']
'John Stuart Mill' HP, mr, 1875, Turner; flowers rosy crimson, large, dbl.; ['Beauty of Waltham' × unknown]
'John Wallace' Pol, dr, 1941, Kluis; flowers deep red, open, large, dbl.; foliage large, leathery, glossy; bushy growth; [sport of 'Marianne Kluis Superior']
John Waterer® HT, dr, 1970, McGredy, Sam IV; flowers 4 in., 44 petals, high-centered, moderate fragrance; ['King of Hearts' × 'Hanne']
'John Weal' LCl, dr; intr. 2006
'John Weitch' -- See 'John Gould Veitch'
'John Willan' -- See 'Fryeager'
'JOHnago' HT, pb, 1962, Johnston
'Johnnie Walker' -- See 'Frygran'
'Johnny B Good' HT, mp, 2007, Bennett, John; flowers medium, 4-5 in., full, borne mostly solitary; foliage medium, dark green, matte; prickles moderate; growth upright, medium (3-4 ft.); garden decoration, exhibition; [Blueberry Hill™ × 'Elizabeth Taylor']; intr. 2007
'Johnny Becnel' F, ob, 2004, Edwards,

The Official Registry and Checklist — Rosa 343

Eddie; flowers coral and white, 5 in., full, high-centered, borne mostly solitary, intense fragrance; foliage medium size, dark green, glossy; growth upright, medium (5-6 ft.); exhibition; [Gemini™ × Crystalline™]; Registration changed to floribunda per request of hybridizer, July 2007.

'John's Rose' -- See 'Mejoria'

'Joia' F, yb, 1962, Moreira da Silva; flowers yellow shaded carmine; [seedling × 'Virgo']

'Joie' -- See 'Joie de Vivre'

'Joie de Vivre' ('Joie') HT, pb, 1949, Gaujard; flowers pink, base gold, well-shaped, very large, dbl.; foliage bronze green; moderately vigorous growth

'Joker' HT, ob, 1958, Lens; flowers orange-red, reverse lighter; foliage glossy; ['Peace' × 'Karl Herbst']

'Jolaft' ('Afternoon Delight') Min, mp, 1991, Jolly, Marie; flowers large, 21 petals, borne mostly singly and in small clusters, slight fragrance; foliage medium size, medium green, matte; few prickles; tall (45 cm.), upright, spreading, vigorous growth; [Party Girl™ × 'Fashion Flame']; intr. 1992

Jolanda™ -- See 'Poulhi012(N)'

'Jolanda' HT, dp, 1959, Malandrone; bud long, pointed; flowers rose, cupped; vigorous, upright, bushy growth

'Jolanda d'Aragon' -- See 'Yolande d'Aragon'

'Jolanda Hit' (Jolanda™) MinFl, w, Olesen; bud short, pointed ovoid; flowers white with green shading, 5 cm., 75-85 petals, borne mostly singly, no fragrance; recurrent; foliage dark green, semi-glossy; prickles numerous, 4 mm., linear; narrow, bushy (20-40 cm.) growth; PP14742; ['Patricia Kordana' × seedling]; container plant; intr. 2002

'Jolcher' ('Cherry Bomb') Min, ob, 1991, Jolly, Marie; flowers orange, medium, very dbl., borne mostly singly, no fragrance; foliage small, medium green, semi-glossy; few prickles; medium, upright growth; ['Fashion Flame' × 'Sheri Anne']; intr. 1991

'Jolcol' ('Color Guard') Min, mp, 1991, Jolly, Marie; flowers 2 in., 25 petals, borne mostly singly, no fragrance; foliage medium size, medium green, matte; few prickles; upright (20 cm.), bushy, very hardy growth; [Anita Charles™ × 'Poker Chip']; intr. 1993

'Jolene' Min, w, Buchanan; [sport of 'Pink Petticoat']

'Joli Coeur' F, dr, 1963, Gaujard; bud globular; flowers dark crimson, medium, dbl.; foliage dark; symmetrical growth; [Rose Gaujard® × (seedling × 'Josephine Bruce')]

'Joli Mome' HT, Ducher, Ch.; intr. 1969

'Joli Tambour' -- See 'Korassenet'

Jolie Comtoise® F, op, Sauvageot; flowers shrimp-pink and salmon, large, very dbl., borne in small clusters; intr. 1973

'Jolie Demoiselle' Pol, lp

'Jolie Madame' HT, or, 1959, Meilland, F.; bud ovoid; flowers vermilion-red, 4-4½ in., 65 petals, cupped, slight fragrance; foliage leathery, glossy; vigorous, upright, bushy growth; PP1700; [('Independence' × 'Happiness') × 'Better Times']; intr. 1958

Jolie Môme® -- See 'Fryxotic'

'Jolie Princesse' F, pb, 1955, Gaujard; flowers pink, shaded ochre, dbl., borne in large trusses, moderate fragrance; foliage leathery, bronze; very vigorous, bushy growth; ['Peace' × 'Independence']

'Jolie Rose' HT, Mondial Roses; intr. 1967

'Jolie Rose Pierret' -- See 'Agathe Incarnata'

Jolisquare® S, mp, Adam; intr. 1998

'Jollity Jane' Pol, m, 1993, Jobson, Daniel J.; flowers lilac-cream blend, medium, very dbl., borne in large clusters, slight fragrance; foliage small, medium green, glossy; few prickles; tall, upright, bushy growth; ['Valerie Jeanne' × Yesterday®]; intr. 1993

'Jollmea' ('Atlantic City') F, rb, 1995, Jolly, Marie; flowers ivory white with dark red blend, large, full, borne mostly singly; foliage medium size, dark green, semi-glossy; few prickles; medium (105 cm.), compact growth; ['Crimson Glory' × 'Orange Honey']; intr. 1996

'Jolly' Pol, m, 1934, Leenders, M.; flowers carmine-purple, center white, single, borne in clusters; foliage sparse, dark; dwarf growth; ['Miss Edith Cavell' × Tip-Top®]

'Jolly' HT, ab

'Jolly' -- See 'Lukor'

'Jolly Cupido' -- See 'Ruixandra'

'Jolly Dance' HKor, ob; [sport of 'Leverkusen']; possibly from Kordes

'Jolly Good' -- See 'LLX8559'

'Jolly Good' F, pb, 1975, Fuller; bud ovoid; flowers salmon-pink, large, 55 petals, moderate fragrance; foliage glossy, dark leathery; bushy, compact growth; ['Cupid's Charm' × 'Lucky Piece']; intr. 1973

'Jolly Good' HT, mp, Interplant; flowers soft pink, double, high-centered; recurrent; growth medium height

'Jolly Joker' F, w

'Jolly Roger' F, or, 1973, Armstrong, D.L.; bud ovoid, pointed; flowers bright reddish-orange, medium, semi-dbl., cupped, slight fragrance; foliage wrinkled; growth moderate, bushy; PP3457; ['Spartan' × 'Angelique']

'Jolsir' ('Sir') Min, ab, 1992, Jolly, Marie; flowers medium, semi-dbl., moderate fragrance; foliage medium size, dark green, semi-glossy; few prickles; medium growth; ['Olympic Gold' × 'Rise 'n' Shine']; intr. 1993

'Jolson' ('Sonata in Pink') Min, pb, 1991, Jolly, Marie; flowers medium pink fading to light pink, 1¼ in., 24 petals, borne mostly singly; foliage medium size, medium green, semi-glossy; few prickles; medium (44 cm.), upright growth; ['Chris Jolly' × Chattem Centennial™]; intr. 1992

'Joltip' Min, mp, 1988, Jolly, Marie; intr. 1988

'Joly Rose Primaplant' HT, mp, Vlaeminck; flowers medium to large, dbl.; intr. 1963

'Jonathan' ('Red Jonathan') F, mr, Asami; intr. 1988

'Jondad' ('For You Dad') Min, op, 1995, Jones, Steve; flowers coral, petals reflex to form star, medium, 5 petals, borne mostly singly; foliage medium size, dark green, semi-glossy; some prickles; upright, tall growth; ['Heartbreaker' × seedling]

'Jondorose' ('Dorothy Rose') Min, or, 1998, Jones, Steve; flowers white with orange, red-orange, and/or red stripes, 2 in., single, borne in small clusters; foliage medium size, medium green, semi glossy; growth upright, tall (4 ft.); [Sarabande® × 'Peggy T']; intr. 2005

'Jonetsu' HT, mr, 1978, Suzuki, Seizo; bud pointed; flowers dark scarlet, 4½-6 in., 30-35 petals, high-centered; foliage dark, leathery; vigorous growth; [('Kagayaki' × 'Prima Ballerina') × 'Kagayaki']

Jonise® ('Jocelyne Pardo') F, dy, Barni; flowers yellow-ocher, outer petals turning lighter, dbl., borne in clusters, moderate fragrance; foliage glossy; vigorous, bushy (3 ft.) growth

'Jonkheer G. Sandberg' ('J. G. Sandberg') HT, my, 1936, Buisman, G. A. H.; flowers clear yellow, dbl.; foliage dark, leathery; vigorous growth; ['Christine' × 'Mrs Wemyss Quin']; intr. 1941

'Jonkheer J. L. Mock, Climbing' Cl HT, pb, 1923, Timmermans; flowers whitish pink, large, full; [sport of 'Johkheer J. L. Mock']

'Jonkheer J. L. Mock' HT, pb, 1910, Leenders, M.; bud pointed; flowers silvery rose-white, reverse carmine-pink, bluing slightly, dbl., high-centered; foliage dark, leathery; vigorous growth; [(('Mme Caroline Testout' × 'Mme Abel Chatenay') × 'Farbenkonigin') × unknown]

'Jonkheer Mr G. Ruys de Beerenbrouck' ('Jonkheer Ruis de Beerenbrouck') HT, ob, 1919, Timmermans; flowers pure orange-yellow fading clear yellow, large, dbl.; vigorous growth; ['Mme Mélanie Soupert' × 'Joseph Hill']

'Jonkheer Ruis de Beerenbrouck' -- See 'Jonkheer Mr G. Ruys de Beerenbrouck'

'Jonone' Min, rb, Jones, Chris; intr. 2001

'Jonquille' -- See 'Deljonq'

'Jonwhite' ('White Sunshine') Min, w, 1998, Jones, Steve; flowers white, like My Sunshine, single; foliage medium size, medium green, semi-glossy; compact, bushy, medium, 2 ft. growth; [Sarabande® × 'Peggy T']

'Joost van der Westhuizen' ('Lime Glow') HT, my, Interplant; flowers soft yellow with green tints, double; growth medium height

'Jorianda' HT, m, Erica Intl.; flowers pinkish-mauve to crimson red, dbl., moderate fragrance; recurrent

'Jorja Julianna' -- See 'Webbrook'

'Joro' HT, ob, RvS-Melle; flowers pastel orange, dbl., high-centered, light fragrance; growth to 120-150 cm.; intr. 1979

'José Bonifacio' T, pb, 1910, Amaury Fonseca; flowers salmon with rose, medium, full

José Carreras™ -- See 'Poulnew'

José Carreras™ -- See 'Monsoon'

'Josef Angendohr' F, dp, 1985, Angendohr, Hans-Werner; flowers deep pink; [sport of 'Dame de Coeur']; intr. 1982

'Josef Peter' HT, m, 1929, Ketten Bros.; flowers pale blush, reverse mauve-rose, dbl.; ['Ruth' × 'Frank W. Dunlop']

'Josef Rothmund' -- See 'Joseph Rothmund'

'Josef Strnad' HT, rb, 1932, Böhm, J.; flowers dark red, with traces of yellow, orange and rose, very large, dbl., cupped; foliage leathery, glossy, dark, bronze; very vigorous, bushy, branching growth; ['Aspirant Marcel Rouyer' × 'Toison d'Or']; intr. 1934

'Josefa' HT, Laperriere, J.; intr. 1982

'Josefina de Salgado' ('Joséphine de Salgado') HT, dp, 1963, Dot, Simon; flowers bright pink, large, 30 petals; somewhat weak stems; very vigorous growth; [Queen Elizabeth® × 'Peace']

'Joseph Arles' Cl HT, rb, 1964, Arles; flowers vermilion-red, reverse silvery white; foliage leathery; vigorous, climbing growth; ['Aloha' × 'Gabychette']

'Joseph Baud' HT, yb, 1919, Gillot, F.; flowers golden yellow and orange-yellow, very large, dbl., intense fragrance; ['Rayon d'Or' × seedling]

'Joseph Bernacchi' N, w, 1878, Ducher; flowers cream white with yellow tints, slightly pink at center, full; very remontant

'Joseph Billard' HWich, mr, 1906, Barbier; flowers carmine-red, yellow at center, reverse lighter, 7-9 cm., single, borne in small clusters, moderate musk fragrance; foliage dark green, large, glossy; [R. wichurana × 'Mme Eugène Résal']

'Joseph Chappaz' -- See 'Mons Joseph Chappaz'

'Joseph Courbis' HT, pb, 1958, Arles; flowers carthamus-pink to orange-red, 48 petals; foliage dark, glossy; vigorous, upright growth; ['Margaret McGredy' × 'Emma Wright']

'Joseph Durand' HP, m, 1863, Ledéchaux; flowers slatey dark crimson, shaded velvety violet, large, full

'Joseph F. Lamb' S, dr, 1989, Buck, Dr. Griffith J.; bud ovoid, pointed; flowers dark red, reverse lighter, aging darker, loose, medium, 23 petals, cupped, moderate fruity fragrance; foliage medium size, medium green, semi-glossy; prickles awl-like, small, tan to reddish brown; upright, bushy, low, winter hardy growth; hips yellow-orange; [('Prairie Star' × ('(Dornroschen × Peace)' × 'Music Maker')) × ('Music Maker' × Topsi®)]

'Joseph Fiala' HP, rb, 1863, Verdier, E.; flowers large, full

'Joseph Gourdeau' -- See 'Joseph Gourdon'

'Joseph Gourdon' ('Joseph Gourdeau') B, pb, 1851, Robert; flowers dark flesh pink to incarnate red, 6-7 cm., full, globular; sometimes classed as HP

'Joseph Guy' Pol, mp, Westhus; flowers large, semi-dbl., slight fragrance; intr. 1950

'Joseph Guy, Climbing' Cl F, dp, 1928, Nonin; flowers dark scarlet-pink,; [sport of 'Lafayette']

'Joseph Guy' Pol, dp, Feldmann; flowers carmine-pink, medium, semi-dbl., slight fragrance; intr. 1930

'Joseph Guy' -- See 'Lafayette'

'Joseph Hill' ('Mons Joseph Hill') HT, pb, 1903, Pernet-Ducher; bud pointed; flowers pink shaded salmon, reverse coppery pink, dbl.; ['Mme Eugénie Boullet' × unknown]

'Joseph Klimes' HT, dr, Urban, J.; flowers large, very dbl.; intr. 1985

'Joseph Lamy' HWich, w, 1906, Barbier; flowers porcelain white, tinted pink, large, semi-dbl.; [R. wichurana × 'Mme Laurette Messimy']

'Joseph Liger' HWich, yb, 1909, Barbier; bud dark pink; flowers canary-yellow, edged and washed light pink, reverse cream-white, 7-10 cm., full, borne in small clusters; foliage glossy; vigorous, climbing growth; [R. wichurana × 'Irene Watts']

'Joseph Lowe' HT, op; flowers salmon-pink; [sport of 'Mrs W.J. Grant']

'Joseph Métral' T, rb, 1888, Bernaix; bud ovoid; sepals reddish; flowers magenta red, aging to cherry with purple tints, petals undulate and creped, very dbl., slightly flattened

'Joseph Paquet' T, pb, 1905, Ketten Bros.; bud very long; flowers rose pink, with light yellow petal base, large, full, moderate fragrance; ['G. Nabonnand' × 'Margherita di Simone']

'Joseph Pernet d'Annemasse' HT, op, 1934, Pernet-Ducher; bud pointed; flowers salmon, dbl.; foliage glossy, dark, bronze; very vigorous growth

'Joseph Rothmund' ('Josef Rothmund') HEg, ob, 1940, Kordes; bud small, ovoid, orange-red; flowers light red with pinkish yellow, very dbl., borne in clusters; profuse, non-recurrent bloom; foliage bronze, leathery; very vigorous growth; ['Joanna Hill' × 'Magnifica']

Joseph Sauvageot® HT, ob, Sauvageot; flowers luminous orange, full; intr. 1989

'Joséphina' HGal, lp, before 1813, possibly Savoureux; flowers spotted, medium, dbl.

'Joséphine' -- See 'Buffon'

'Joséphine' HGal, dp, before 1829, Boutigny; flowers semi-dbl.

'Joséphine' HGal, dp, Vibert; flowers dark pink, edges lighter, medium, very full; intr. about 1830

'Joséphine' M, dp; flowers deep rose pink, medium, dbl., globular; intr. before 1846

'Josephine' HT, lp, Paul, W.; flowers flesh pink with salmon-yellow at base, large, full; intr. 1914

'Josephine' Min, w, Moore, Ralph S.; flowers white or soft pink, micro-mini, small, dbl.; foliage small, glossy; dwarf, bushy growth; [(R. wichurana × Carolyn Dean) × 'Jet Trail']; intr. 1969

'Joséphine' A, lp

'Joséphine Baker' -- See 'Meimaur'

'Joséphine Baker, Climbing' Cl HT, dr, Orard; flowers rich crimson, 4 in., intense fragrance; intr. 1983

'Josephine Bruce' HT, dr, 1949, Bees; flowers crimson, 5-6 in., 24 petals, slight fragrance; foliage dark; vigorous, branching growth; PP1294; ['Crimson Glory' × 'Madge Whipp']; intr. 1953

'Josephine Bruce, Climbing' Cl HT, dr, Ross; flowers dark crimson, large; possibly introduced about 1952, certainly before 1968

'Josephine Carmody' S, lp, 1995, Collins, Frank E. Jr.; flowers light pink, medium sized, dbl., borne in small clusters; foliage small, dark green, glossy; numerous prickles; growth bushy, medium (36 in.); [sport of 'Sea Foam']

'Josephine Clermont' B, mp, 1857, Guillot

'Joséphine de Beauharnais' HP, lp, 1865, Guillot fils; flowers delicate pink, reverse silvery, very large, full

'Joséphine de Salgado' -- See 'Josefina de Salgado'

'Josephine Elizabeth' S, m, Peden, R.; intr. 1999

'Joséphine Guyet' ('Mlle Joséphine Guyet', 'Mlle Joséphine Guyot', 'Mme Joséphine Guyet') B, dr, 1873, Touvais; flowers deep red, medium, full, globular; recurrent bloom

'Josephine Lédéchaux' HP, ob, 1855, Lédéchaux

'Josephine Maille' HGal, mp, about 1825, Boutigny; flowers bright pink, large

'Josephine Malton' Ch, ab, about 1830, Guérin; flowers cream with apricot-orange, large, full

'Joséphine Maltot' -- See 'Mme Bravy'

'Joséphine Marot' HT, lp, 1894, Bonnaire; flowers white washed pink, large, full

'Joséphine Morel' Pol, dp, 1892, Alégatière; flowers carmine-pink, small, dbl.

'Joséphine Parmentier' HGal, mp, about 1840, Parmentier; flowers medium, full

'Josephine Ritter' HMult, mp, before

1900, Geschwind, R.; flowers rich pink, aging to silvery pink, 7 cm., dbl., quartered, quilled, moderate damask/musk fragrance; foliage dark green, large; numerous prickles

'Josephine Spiecker' HT, ob, 1939, Verschuren-Pechtold; flowers deep orange to yellow, very dbl., globular; foliage glossy, dark bronze; vigorous, bushy growth

'Josephine Thomas' HT, ob, 1924, H&S; flowers orange-salmon to cream-flesh, very dbl., high-centered; foliage leathery; vigorous, bushy growth

'Josephine Vestal' HT, lp, 1923, E.G. Hill, Co.; flowers soft pink, dbl., high-centered; very vigorous, bushy growth; ['Ophelia' × seedling]

'Josephine Wheatcroft' -- See 'Rosina'

Joseph's Coat® LCl, rb, 1964, Armstrong, D.L. & Swim, H. C.; flowers yellow and red, 3 in., 23-28 petals, borne in clusters; recurrent bloom; foliage dark, glossy; vigorous, pillar growth; PP2488; ['Buccaneer' × 'Circus']; patent issued as Cl F; intr. 1963

'Josh' -- See 'Tinjosh'

Josh Alonso™ -- See 'Alojosh'

Joshua™ -- See 'Mogajosh'

'Joshua Bradley' -- See 'Chrisgobro'

'Josi' S, ly, 2007, Pawlikowski, Martin & Elaine; flowers large, 4-5 in., very full, borne mostly solitary; foliage medium size, dark green, semi-glossy; prickles small, pointed, green, few; growth bushy, medium (4 × 4 ft.); landscape; [sport of English Garden®]; intr. 2007

'Josie Whitney' F, yb, Harkness; flowers yellow with red edges, dbl., borne in clusters, slight fragrance; growth to 3 ft.; intr. 2001

'Jospice' F, mr, 2004, Thomas William Yates; flowers red, reverse red, medium, single, borne in small clusters; foliage medium size, dark green, matte; prickles small; growth upright, tall; ['Birthday Girl' × 'Apricot Nectar']

'Jospink' ('Anne Marie Laing') F, lp, 1998, Shipway, John; flowers light pink, darker reverse, 4 in., very dbl., camellia-like, borne in large clusters; foliage medium size, dark green, dull; few prickles; upright, tall (110 cm.) growth; [('Iceberg' × 'Anytime') × Sexy Rexy®]; intr. 1998

'Josyane' S, m, Lens, Louis; flowers violet-red, small, dbl.; intr. 1980

'Josysigal' HT, mr, 1976, Delforge; flowers large, 60 petals, cupped, intense fragrance; intr. 1975

'Jour de Fête' HT, w, Lens; flowers pure white with touch of pink in heart, large, full, slight fragrance; growth to 3 ft.; intr. 1968

'Jour de Fête' F, op, Adam; flowers double, abundant flowering, intense fragrance; recurrent; robust (80 - 110 cm.) growth; intr. 2006

'Jour des Pères' -- See 'Vatertag'

'Jour d'Eté' HT, mr, 1964, Combe; bud very long; flowers bright red, open; vigorous growth; ['Coup de Foudre' × 'Berthe Mallerin']

'Journey's End' HT, ob, 1978, Gandy, Douglas L.; flowers Indian orange, pointed, 6 in., 37 petals; foliage large, glossy; vigorous, upright growth; ['Doreen' × 'Vienna Charm']

'Jouvencelle' HT, pb, 1978, Gaujard; flowers salmon-pink suffused red, 50 petals; foliage reddish; ['Prima Ballerina' × 'Helen Traubel']; intr. 1969

'Jove' F, or, 1968, Harkness; flowers scarlet, semi-dbl., borne in clusters; foliage glossy; low growth; ['Vera Dalton' × 'Paprika']

Jovita® F, or, 1986, Harkness; flowers borne in large clusters, slight fragrance; foliage bright green; medium, bushy growth; ['Jove' × 'Tip Top']; intr. 1975

'Jovita Pérez' HT, ob, 1929, Munné, B.; flowers coppery salmon, shaded coral, dbl., cupped; foliage soft, dark; long, strong stems; vigorous, compact growth; ['Mme Butterfly' × 'Souv. de Claudius Pernet']

'Joy' HT, pb, 1929, Beckwith; bud tangerine-red; flowers rose-pink suffused tangerine, base yellow, dbl., high-centered; foliage leathery; vigorous, branching growth

Joy™ Min, mp, Olesen; intr. 1997

Joy® -- See 'Intermoto'

Joy™ -- See 'Decjoy'

'Joy' -- See 'Yorokobi'

'Joy Bells' -- See 'Joybells'

'Joy Button' -- See 'Ludpinbu'

'Joy In The Morning' Min, ab, 2006, Hopper, Nancy; flowers single, borne mostly solitary; foliage medium size, medium green, matte; prickles ½ in., few; growth upright, medium (15 in.); [seedling × seedling]; intr. 2006

'Joy O'Brien' Gr, op, 1969, Verschuren; flowers pink shaded orange-salmon, large, dbl.; foliage dark; vigorous growth; [Queen Elizabeth® × seedling]

'Joy of Health' ('Applause') F, op, Harkness; flowers soft peachy salmon; modest growth; Australian nurseries call it a HT; intr. 1996

'Joy of Life' -- See 'Maxim'

'Joy Owens' -- See 'Macred'

'Joy Pagram' HT, lp, Dawson; intr. 1995

'Joy Parfait' F, lp, 1966, McIlroy; [sport of 'Pink Parfait']

'Joy Poynter' HT, Matthews; intr. 2002

'Joyance' HT, mr, 1939, Grillo; flowers velvety red, 4 in., 50 petals, camellia-like, moderate fragrance; foliage leathery, dark; very vigorous, upright growth; PP778; [sport of 'Regina Elena']

'Joybells' ('Joy Bells') F, mp, 1961, Robinson, H.; flowers rich pink, large, 30 petals, camellia-like, borne in clusters; [seedling × 'Fashion']

'Joybells' HT, ab, Kordes; flowers cream apricot with greenish guard petals, full, high-centered, no fragrance; free-flowering; healthy, vigorous, medium growth; intr. 1988

'Joyce' HT, dr, 1953, Cant, F.; flowers dark velvety crimson, pointed, medium, 24 petals; foliage leathery; vigorous growth; ['George Dickson' × 'Étoile de Hollande']

'Joyce' MinFl, lp, Williams, J.B.; flowers Ivory pink., single, borne in masses of blooms, moderate fragrance; intr. 2001

Joyce® HT, dy, J&P; intr. 2001

'Joyce Abounding' Min, op, 2008, Chapman, Dr.Bruce A.; flowers 6 cm., full, borne in small clusters; foliage large, medium green, semi-glossy; prickles small, straight, red, few; growth upright, medium (50 cm.); garden decoration; ['Rise 'n' Shine' × 'Pirouette']; intr. 2008

'Joyce Barden' -- See 'Ardour'

'Joyce Claire' F, dp, 1965, Tonkin; bud globular; flowers deep pink, open, small, dbl.; foliage glossy; very vigorous, upright growth; [Queen Elizabeth® × unknown]

'Joyce Edmonds' F, op, Nieuwesteeg, J.; flowers large, dbl., cupped, borne in small clusters, no fragrance; recurrent; intr. 1992

'Joyce Fairey' Cl HT, dp, 1929, Clark, A.; flowers soft red; pillar growth

'Joyce Hunt' ; ['Scented Bouquet' × 'Stella']

'Joyce Lomax' -- See 'Satan'

'Joyce Longley' HT, ob, 1970, Court; flowers in sunset shades; [sport of 'Opera']; intr. 1958

'Joyce Mary' HT, pb, 2003, Heath, William; flowers pink blush, outer petals creamy white, reverse cream, 4-5 in., full, borne mostly solitary; foliage medium size, medium green, semi-glossy; prickles medium, triangular, light, moderate; growth upright, medium; garden, exhibition; ['Silver Jubilee' × Pristine®]; intr. 2004

'Joyce Northfield' HT, ob, 1977, Northfield; flowers deep orange, high-pointed, 3-4 in., dbl.; foliage dark; vigorous, upright growth; ['Fred Gibson' × 'Vienna Charm']

'Joyce Riley' F, ob, 1979, Wood; bud well formed; flowers vermilion, yellow-salmon, 2½ in., 25 petals, slight fragrance; foliage dark, leathery; vigorous, upright growth; ['Paddy McGredy' × 'Arthur Bell']

'Joyce Robinson' HT, op, 1945, Selwood; flowers peach-pink, high-centered; foliage dark, leathery; vigorous, bushy growth; [sport of 'Rose Berkley']

'Joyce Ruston' -- See 'Jayrus'

'Joyce's Rose' HT, pb, Johnstone; intr. 2004

Joycie™ -- See 'Morjoyc'

'Joyena Pillar' LCl, m, 1969, Mason, P.G.; flowers spirea-red, reverse Tyrian purple, high-centered, borne in small clusters, moderate fragrance; foliage dark, bronze, leathery; vigorous growth; ['Blossomtime' × unknown]; intr. 1964

'Joyeux Anniversaire' HT, mr; intr. 2005

'Joyeux Noël' HT, or, 1960, Delbard-Chabert; bud long, pointed; flowers well-formed, medium, 30-35 petals; foliage bronze, leathery; vigorous, bushy growth; [('Floradora' × 'Independence') × ('La Vaudoise' × 'Léonce Colombier')]

'Joyful' HT, pb, 1931, Vestal; bud pointed; flowers pink, reverse streaked red, base red and orange; vigorous growth

'Joyful' -- See 'Weljoy 0505'

'Joyful Jubilee' S, dp; flowers strong pink, small, dbl., rosette, borne in clusters; free-flowering; foliage shiny, dark green; fast-growing, groundcover (24 × 36 in.) growth; intr. 2005

'Joyful Singer' S, mr, Clements, John; flowers scarlet red, 3 in., 30 petals, borne in clusters of 6 - 8 blooms; growth large shrub or low climber; intr. 2002

'Joyfulness' -- See 'Tansinnroh'

'Joyfulness' F, ab, 1965, Tantau, M.; flowers dbl, borne in clusters; foliage large, dark green, glossy; intr. 1963

'Joyfulness, Climbing' Cl HT, ob, Ruston, D.; flowers large, high-centered, moderate fragrance; recurrent; growth strong; [sport of 'Joyfulness']; intr. 1988

'Joyous' F, pb, 1939, deRuiter; flowers rose-pink, reverse slightly darker; vigorous, bushy growth; PP381; [sport of 'Else Poulsen']

'Joyous Cavalier' HT, mr, 1926, Archer; bud pointed; flowers brilliant red, open, large, 25-30 petals; foliage dark, glossy; very vigorous growth; ['Red-Letter Day' × 'Clarice Goodacre']

'Joyous Moment' -- See 'Jacpri'

'Joyride' -- See 'Renride'

'Juan Maragall' HT, mr, 1960, Dot, Simon; flowers bright strawberry-red, large, 35 petals; long, strong stems; vigorous, compact growth; ['Chrysler Imperial' × 'Buccaneer']

'Juan Pich' HT, m, 1921, Leenders, M.; flowers purplish wine-red, dbl.

'Juan Quevedo' HT, ly, 1921, Leenders, M.; flowers cream-yellow, dbl.; ['Entente Cordiale' × 'My Maryland']

'Juana de Darder' HT, yb, 1947, Munné, M.; flowers deep yellow shaded salmon, cupped; foliage bright green; strong stems; vigorous growth; ['Souv. de Claudius Pernet' × ('Sensation' × 'Souv. de Claudius Pernet')]

'Juane Adam' F, my, Adam, M.; intr. 1997

'Juanita' HGal, pb, 1836, Vibert; flowers pink edged paler, spotted with white, medium, dbl.; it appears that the Centifolia attributed to Robert, 1855, is the same as this cultivar; the descriptions given in Paul and the Robert catalog are nearly identical

'Juanita' HWich, Walsh; intr. 1907

Juanita® S, pb, Kordes; flowers strong pink with white eye, yellow stamens , 3 cm., single, shallow cup to flat, borne in clusters, slight fragrance; recurrent; foliage disease-resistant; bushy (80 cm. × 80 cm.) growth; intr. 2007

'Juanita du Plessis' HT, mr, J&P; flowers double , borne mostly singly; recurrent; foliage glossy; medium to tall growth; intr. 2007

'Jubilaire de Masaryk' -- See 'Masarykova Jubilejni'

'Jubilant' F, lp, 1967, Dickson, A.; flowers flesh pink, 2½ in., borne in clusters; foliage glossy; ['Dearest' × 'Circus']

'Jubilation' -- See 'Jacreg'

'Jubilation' F, or; intr. 2006

'Jubiläumsrose' HT, w, 1910, Schmidt, J. C.; flowers creamy white, large, semi-dbl.

'Jubiläumsrose' HFt, mp, Schmidt, J. C.; flowers large, dbl.; intr. 1929

Jubilé du Prince de Monaco® -- See 'Meisponge'

'Jubilé Loubert' HMult, mp, Loubert; flowers semi-dbl., borne in large clusters, slight fragrance; vigorous, tall (7-10 ft.) growth; intr. 1998

'Jubilee' HP, m, 1897, Walsh; flowers purple, shaded maroon, large, dbl., moderate fragrance; some recurrent bloom; moderate growth; ['Victor Hugo' × 'Prince Camille de Rohan']

'Jubilee' ('Allen's Jubilee') HT, w, Allen; bud pointed; flowers cream, tinged salmon-pink and Indian yellow, center coral-pink, dbl., high-centered, intense fragrance; vigorous growth; ['Paul's Lemon Pillar' × 'Aspirant Marcel Rouyer']; intr. 1930

Jubilee™ F, ab, Olesen; bud pointed ovoid; flowers apricot, 5 cm., 55-60 petals, cupped, borne in corymbs, slight fruity fragrance; recurrent; foliage dark green, glossy; prickles moderate, hooked downward; bushy, upright (5 ft.) growth; PP16552; ['Atlantis Palace' × seedling]; intr. 2004

'Jubilee' HRg, m; flowers deep purplish-red, 3 in., single, borne mostly singly; recurrent; foliage dark green, glossy, disease-resistant; vigorous (4-5 ft.) growth; hips large, round, red; imported from Russia

'Jubilee' -- See 'Masarykova Jubilejni'

'Jubilee 150' -- See 'Meicloux'

Jubilee Celebration™ -- See 'Aushunter'

'Jubilee Celebration' F, pb, 1977, Smith, E.; flowers pink shaded salmon, 4 in., 20 petals; foliage matte, green; growth moderate; [Elizabeth of Glamis® × 'Prima Ballerina']; intr. 1977

'Jubilee Sunset' -- See 'Taljub'

'Jubilejnaja' HT, pb, 1940, Kosteckij; flowers rose pink with dark yellow, medium, semi-dbl.

'Jubilejni' HT, m, Urban, J.

'Jubileum 110' HT, dp, Urban, J.

'Judann' ('Ann's Rose') Cl Min, op, 1996, Bell, Judy G.; flowers light orange pink, 1½ in., dbl., borne in small clusters; foliage medium size, light green, glossy; few prickles; tall (5 ft.), upright, pillar growth; intr. 1996

'Judbaby' ('Betty's Baby') MinFl, dp, 1994, Bell, Judy G.; flowers deep pink with white center, small, semi-dbl., borne in small clusters, no fragrance; foliage small, medium green, semi-glossy; few prickles; medium (12-14 in.), upright, bushy growth; [Twilight Trail™ × 'Charmglo']; intr. 1995

'Judbett's' ('Queen Bett's') Min, w, 2001, Bell, Judy G.; flowers white blushed pink, gold and red stamens, red stigma, 1½ in., full, borne mostly solitary, slight fragrance; foliage medium size, dark green, semi-glossy; prickles small, straight, moderate; upright, medium growth; garden decorative, exhibition, containers; [Party Girl™ × 'Giggles']; intr. 2002

'Judblush' ('Casey's Blush') Min, ab, 2001, Bell, Judy G.; flowers flesh-pink, medium, full, borne mostly solitary, no fragrance; foliage medium size, medium green, semi-glossy; prickles small, straight, few; growth upright, bushy; garden decorative, containers, exhibition; [Jean Kenneally™ × Rainbow's End™]; intr. 2001

'Judbright' ('Bright Sight') Min, ob, 1993, Bell, Judy G.; flowers light orange, medium, full, borne in large clusters, no fragrance; foliage small, medium green, matte; few prickles; upright (18 in.), bushy growth; ['Charmglo' × 'Poker Chip']; intr. 1994

'Juddance' ('Folk Dance') Min, m, 1993, Bell, Judy G.; flowers medium, full, borne mostly singly, slight fragrance; foliage small, dark green, glossy; few prickles; bushy (41 cm.) growth; [Dale's Sunrise® × 'Angel Face']; intr. 1994

'Juddoll' ('Diamond Doll') Min, ly, 1996, Bell, Judy G.; flowers light yellow, darker yellow center, petals quilled and reflexed, 1½ in., full, borne in small clusters, intense fragrance; foliage medium size, medium green, matte; few prickles; upright growth, 18 in.; medium (18 in winter hardy; ['Rise 'n' Shine' × 'Angel Face']; intr. 1997

'Jude the Obscure' -- See 'Ausjo'

'Judfest' (Bloomfest™) Min, ab, 1999, Bell, Judy G.; flowers 1 in., dbl., borne in small clusters; foliage medium size, medium green, dull; few prickles; compact, low (14 in.) growth; ['Rise 'n' Shine' × unknown]; intr. 1999

'Judfire' ('Firedance') Min, rb, 2003, Bell, Judy; flowers red/yellow, reverse yellow/white, 1 in., full, borne in small clusters; foliage medium size, dark green, semi-glossy; prickles small, hooked; growth upright, medium (18 in.); garden, containers, exhibition; ['Azure Sea' × 'Rise 'n' Shine']; intr. 2004

'Judgold' ('Golden Morning') Min, dy, 2001, Bell, Judy G.; flowers bright golden yellow with bright yellow stamens, 1½ in., single, borne mostly solitary, no fragrance; foliage light green, matte; prickles small, straight, few; growth upright, medium; garden decorative, containers, exhibition; [Loving Touch™

× Party Girl™]; intr. 2002

'Judi Dench' -- See 'Peathunder'

'Judian' ('Here's Ian') Min, mr, 1996, Bell, Judy G.; flowers 1½ in., semi-dbl., borne mostly singly, no fragrance; foliage small, medium green, semi-glossy, disease-resistant; few prickles; small, compact, rounded growth; low (12 in winter hardy; [Dale's Sunrise® × seedling]; intr. 1997

'Judie Darling' Cl Min, pb, 1979, Sudol, Julia; flowers marbled pink, reflexed, 1-1½ in., 45-50 petals; vigorous, climbing growth

'Judit' F, yb, Wagner, S.; flowers 35 petals, cupped, slight fragrance; foliage large, dark green, leathery, glossy; [(('Frankfurt am Main' × 'Maria Callas') × 'Dr Faust']; intr. 1997

'Judith' HT, rb, 1938, LeGrice; flowers glowing cerise, reverse golden yellow, dbl., globular, intense fruity fragrance; foliage glossy, bronze; vigorous, bushy growth

'Judith Ann' HT, dp, 1998, Schamel, Al; flowers deep pink with medium reverse and silvery sheen, 6-7 in., 41 petals, borne singly, candelabras in summer; foliage medium size, dark green, glossy; prickles moderate; growth upright, medium (4-5 ft.); [sport of 'Red Devil']; intr. 1998

'Judith Black' HT, dr, 1930, Clark, A.; bud pointed; flowers rich dark red flushed fiery red, dbl., globular; foliage soft; dwarf growth

'Judith I. B. Hall' HT, pb, 1953, Balcombe Nursery; flowers pink, base orange, 5 in., 32 petals; very vigorous growth; ['Crimson Glory' × 'Sterling']

'Judjewel' ('Jazzy Jewel') Min, dr, 2000, Bell, Judy; flowers dark red with bright yellow eye, reverse light red, 2½ in., single, borne mostly singly, no fragrance; foliage medium size, dark green, semi-glossy; few prickles; growth bushy, medium (16 in.); [Rainbow's End™ × unknown]; intr. 2000

'Judlee' ('Essie Lee') MinFl, ob, 1992, Bell, Judy G.; flowers white with orange picotee down ½ of petals, white to light orange reverse, small, full, globular, no fragrance; foliage small to medium size, dark green, semi-glossy; few prickles; upright (46 cm.), bushy growth; ['Tennessee' × 'Tennessee']; intr. 1994

'Judlov' ('Love in Bloom') Min, m, 1994, Bell, Judy G.; flowers mauve to tan with bright yellow stamens, medium, single, borne in small clusters, slight fragrance; foliage medium size, dark green, semi-glossy; few prickles; bushy, spreading (10-12 in.) growth; ['Angel Face' × unknown]; intr. 1995

'Judmarie' ('Ashley Marie') Min, m, 1995, Bell, Judy G.; flowers light lavender, 1-1½ in., dbl., borne mostly singly; foliage small, dark green, semi-glossy; few prickles; low (14 in.), bushy growth; [Dale's Sunrise® × 'Angel Face']; intr. 1996

'Judmon' ('Monday's Child') Min, m, 1995, Bell, Judy G.; flowers lavender and white, small, dbl., borne in small clusters, no fragrance; foliage medium size, medium green, glossy; few prickles; medium (16 in.), upright, bushy growth; [Dale's Sunrise® × 'Angel Face']; intr. 1996

'Judmorn' ('Misty Morning') MinFl, m, 1995, Bell, Judy G.; flowers lavender shaded yellow/tan, small, full, borne mostly singly, foliage medium size, medium green, matte; few prickles; tall (18 in.), upright, bushy growth; [Dale's Sunrise® × 'Angel Face']; intr. 1996

'Judnic' ('Baby Dominic') Min, op, 1992, Bell, Judy G.; fringed sepals; flowers light orange-coral pink, micro-mini, ½ in., dbl., high-centered, borne in small clusters; foliage small, light green, matte; few prickles; low, compact, bushy growth; ['Centergold' × 'Cuddles']

'Judpret' ('Pretty Little Thing') Min, dp, 2000, Bell, Judy; flowers dbl., high-centered, borne mostly singly, slight fragrance; foliage medium size, medium green, matte; prickles moderate; upright, compact, medium (16 in.) growth; [Jean Kenneally™ × 'Poker Chip']

'Judpride' ('P. J.'s Pride') Min, rb, 1996, Bell, Judy G.; bud medium, pointed; flowers white with bright pink to red edging shading down petals to white, 1 in., high-centered, borne in small clusters, no fragrance; foliage medium size, dark green, dull; some prickles; medium, upright growth; [American Rose Centennial™ × unknown]; intr. 1997

'Judriv' ('River City Jubilee') Min, ob, 1996, Bell, Judy G.; flowers orange, tight, full, high-centered, borne in small clusters, no fragrance; foliage medium size, dark green, semi-glossy, very disease-resistant; some prickles; medium (16 in.), upright growth; [Jean Kenneally™ × Rainbow's End™]; intr. 1996

'Judsar' ('Caesar's Rose') Min, dr, 1996, Bell, Judy G.; flowers dark red with yellow stamens, 1-1½ in., single, borne mostly singly, no fragrance; foliage small, dark green, matte; prickles numerous dark red, short; upright, medium (15-18 in.) growth; winter hardy; [Jean Kenneally™ × 'Angel Face']; intr. 1997

'Judsilk' ('Silk 'n' Satin') Min, ab, 1996, Bell, Judy G.; flowers apricot, with bright yellow stamens, 1½ in., 8-9 wide petals, borne in small clusters, no fragrance; foliage small, light green, matte; no prickles; low (10 in.), bushy, spreading growth; winter hardy; [seedling × unknown]; intr. 1997

'Judsolde' ('Isolde') MinFl, pb, 1994, Bell, Judy G.; flowers light pink in center shading darker toward edges, small, full, slight fragrance; foliage medium size, medium green, matte; few prickles; upright, bushy (14-16 in.) growth; [Dale's Sunrise® × 'Charmglo']; intr. 1995

'Judspunk' ('Spunky') Min, mr, 1993, Bell, Judy G.; flowers medium, dbl., borne in small clusters, no fragrance; foliage small, dark green, glossy; numerous prickles; medium (16 in.), bushy, upright growth; [Dale's Sunrise® × J. Michael™]; intr. 1994

'Judtrouble' ('Double Trouble') Min, ob, 2000, Bell, Judy; bud round; flowers light orange, 1 in., full, HT form, borne in large clusters, no fragrance; foliage medium size, medium green; few prickles; growth very full, bushy, upright (18 in.); [Party Girl™ × 'Gingersnap']; intr. 2001

'Judvee' ('Vee Marie') Min, dp, 1993, Bell, Judy G.; flowers bright deep pink, slight white on reverse, yellow stamens, medium, full, borne in small clusters, no fragrance; foliage small, dark green, glossy; few prickles; low (15 in.), bushy, spreading, compact growth; [Dale's Sunrise® × 'Angel Face']; intr. 1993

'Judvirg' ('Dorothy Virginia') Min, ly, 1999, Bell, Judy G.; flowers medium, dbl., borne mostly singly; foliage large, dark green, semi-glossy; few prickles; upright, medium growth; [Loving Touch™ × unknown]; intr. 1999

'Judy' -- See 'Tanydu'

'Judy' HT, mr, 1940, Grillo; flowers cerise-red, 4 in., 55 petals; [sport of 'Jewel']

'Judy Finnigan' HT, op, 1999, Poole, Lionel; flowers orange/peach, 4-4½ in., full, high-centered, borne in small clusters, moderate fragrance; foliage medium size, medium green, semi-glossy, very rain-resista; almost thornless; upright, tall (4 ft.) growth; ['Hazel Rose' × 'Joe Longthorne']; intr. 2000

'Judy Fischer' Min, mp, 1968, Moore, Ralph S.; bud pointed; flowers rose-pink, small, dbl.; foliage dark, bronze, leathery; vigorous, bushy, low growth; PP3137; ['Little Darling' × 'Magic Wand']

'Judy Garland' F, yb, 1977, Harkness; flowers yellow, petals edged orange-red, medium-large, 35 petals, borne singly and in small clusters; foliage semi-glossy; medium, bushy growth; [(('Tropicana' × 'Circus') × ('Sabine' × 'Circus')) × 'Pineapple Poll']; intr. 1978

'Judy Hart' HT, mp, 1959, Motose; bud ovoid; flowers 4-5 in., 30-40 petals, intense fragrance; foliage leathery; vigorous, bushy growth; PP1715; ['Pink Delight (HT)' × ('Senator' × 'Florex')]; intr. 1958

'Judy Robertson' Min, my, 1998, Warner, A.J.; flowers medium yellow, 2 in., 80 petals, high-centered, borne singly and in small clusters; foliage medium size, medium green, semi-glossy; no prickles; long, thin stems; growth upright, bushy (3 ft.); ['Little Darling' × 'Rise 'n' Shine']

'Judy Shaw' F, ab, 2000, Shaw, Dr. John A.; bud apricot; flowers deep apricot, reverse light apricot, 6½ cm., very full, cupped, borne in small clusters, slight fragrance; foliage medium size, medium green, semi-glossy, reddish when young; prickles moderate; upright, medium (100 cm.) growth; ['Etoile de Hollande' × 'Rise 'n' Shine']

'Judy's Song' HT, lp, 2007, Courage, Ray; flowers full, blooms borne mostly solitary; foliage medium size, dark green, semi-glossy; prickles medium, hooked, brown, few; growth bushy, medium (1¼ m.); garden decoration; ['Aotearoa' × 'Auckland Metro']; intr. 2007

'Jugoslavie' HT, w, 1936, Böhm, J.; flowers large, dbl.

Juillet® -- See 'Briletjui'

'Jujnoberejnaia' ('River's South Bank') F, dr, 1955, Klimenko, V. N.; flowers velvety red, well-shaped, medium; ['Independence' × 'Vaterland (?)']

JuJu™ -- See 'Bisred'

'Jules' LCl, dr, 1997, Jerabek, Paul E.; flowers dark to medium red, velvety, 2½ in., 41 petals, borne in small clusters, moderate fragrance; foliage medium size, light green turning medium green, sem-glossy; spreading, medium growth; [seedling × seedling]

'Jules Barigny' HP, mr, 1886, Verdier, E.; flowers carmine red with paler reverse, large, dbl., intense fragrance; foliage oval-rounded, irregularly toothed; prickles few, straight, large, pink; growth erect

'Jules Bire' HP, dp, 1887, Bire; flowers carmine, shaded lilac pink, very large, full; ['Général Jacqueminot' × 'Paul Neyron']

'Jules Bourgeois' HP, dr, 1867, Ledéchaux; flowers velvety dark red, dbl.

'Jules Bourquin' T, yb, 1893, Chauvry; flowers chrome yellow, reverse tinted lilac, edges whitish, very large, full; ['Gloire de Dijon' × unknown]

'Jules Calot' HP, pb, 1866, Verdier, E.; flowers carmine, white edges, large, full

'Jules Chrétien' HP, mp, 1869, Damaizin; flowers large, full

'Jules Chrétien' HP, mr, Schwartz; flowers poppy red, tinged with purple, reverse tinted violet, large, full; foliage very large, glossy; prickles whitish; growth upright; intr. 1878

'Jules Closen' HWich, dr, 1935, Opdebeeck; flowers darker and more, dbl.; [sport of 'Excelsa']

'Jules d'Asnières' Pol, w, 1900, d'Asnières

'Jules Finger' T, rb, 1879, Ducher, Vve.; flowers vivid red fading light red, shaded silvery, very large, dbl.; vigorous growth; ['Catherine Mermet' × 'Mme de Tartas']

'Jules Gaujard' HT, ob, 1928, Pernet-Ducher; flowers bright orange-red flushed carmine, very large, cupped; foliage bright green; very vigorous growth; ['Jean C.N. Forestier' × seedling]

'Jules Girodit' HT, op, 1900, Buatois; flowers light orange-pink, large, dbl.

'Jules Jamain' Ch, mp; flowers small to medium, full

'Jules Jürgensen' B, m, 1879, Schwartz; flowers purple-crimson, large, full, moderate fragrance

'Jules Lavay' HP, mp, 1864, Damaizin; flowers medium carmine pink, large, full

'Jules Lesourd' P, mr, 1863, Robert & Moreau; flowers light red, medium, full, globular

'Jules Levacher' HWich, lp, 1908, Barbier; bud globular; flowers creamy light rose pink, 3-4 cm., semi-dbl.; foliage small, dark green; [R. wichurana × 'Mme Laurette Messimy']

'Jules Margottin' HP, mp, 1853, Margottin; flowers carmine-rose, large, 90 petals, flat, slight fragrance; occasionally recurrent; numerous prickles; vigorous growth; very hardy; [probably a 'La Reine' seedling]

'Jules Margottin, Climbing' Cl HP, mr, 1874, Cranston; bud round; flowers red with purple tints, 10-11 cm., dbl., flat, borne singly or in small clusters, intense fragrance; numerous prickles; [sport of 'Jules Margottin']

'Jules Roussingihol' HP, mr, 1864, de Sansal; flowers bright carmine-red, large, full; ['Général Jacqueminot' × unknown]

'Jules Seurre' HP, mr, 1869, Liabaud, l.; flowers carmine red, tinted blue, large, full; ['Victor Verdier' × unknown]

'Jules Tabart' HT, pb, 1920, Barbier; flowers silvery salmon-pink, center coppery coral-pink, dbl.; [seedling × 'Mme Edouard Herriot']

'Jules Toussaint' HT, dr, 1900, Bonnaire; flowers dark brownish red, base of petals citron yellow, reverse silvery, very large, dbl., moderate fragrance

'Jules Verne' HT, yb, Adam; intr. 2000

'Juleschildren' ('Me Too') F, lp, 1998, Muha, Julius; flowers pink-purple, white eye, white reverse, ½-1½ in., 8-14 petals; foliage small, light green, dull; prickles moderate; upright, medium growth; ['Mackaukaup' × 'Nickelodeon']; intr. 1999

'Juleschke' -- See 'Tanjuka'

'Julesdear' ('Thanx Mom', 'Thanx Mum') HT, dp, 1998, Muha, Julius; flowers hot fuschia pink, 4-4½ in., full, decorative, borne in small clusters, intense raspberry fragrance; recurrent; foliage medium size, medium green, semi-glossy; prickles moderate; growth bushy, medium (3 ft.); ['Lancome' × 'Stephens' Big Purple']; intr. 1998

'Juleslove' ('Luv Ya') HT, lp, 1998, Muha, Julius; flowers soft apricot-pink, 4-4½ in., very dbl., borne mostly singly; foliage medium size, medium green, semi-glossy; prickles moderate; upright, 3-5 ft. growth; intr. 1998

Juli de Sala® -- See 'Femental'

Julia® -- See 'Pekcouliane'

Julia™ -- See 'Poulheart'

'Julia' -- See 'Pascal Sevran'

'Julia' Cl Min, ob; flowers orange with yellow base, 2 in., semi-dbl., borne singly and in clusters; foliage large; growth tall

'Julia Ann Bostick' Pol, pb, 1935, Bostick; flowers apple-blossom-pink, base white, small, single, cupped; dwarf growth; [sport of 'Ideal']

'Julia Bartet' HT, yb, 1920, Schwartz, A.; flowers dark canary-yellow, fading pale straw-yellow, dbl.; ['Lyon Rose' × 'Georges Schwartz']

Julia Child™ -- See 'Wekvossutono'

'Julia Clements' F, mr, 1958; flowers bright red, 3 in., single, borne in clusters; foliage dark, glossy; very vigorous growth; intr. 1957

'Julia Countess of Dartrey' HT, pb, 1927, Hall; flowers rose pink with golden yellow, very large, dbl.

'Julia Dymonier' ('Mlle Julie Dymonier') HP, lp, 1880, Gonod; flowers light pink, sometimes striped flesh pink, large, full

'Julia Faye' F, m, 2001, Certified Roses, Inc.; flowers lavender purple, mauve reverse, 2¾ in., dbl., borne in small clusters, moderate fragrance; foliage medium size, dark green, matte; prickles average, curved, moderate; growth compact, bushy; garden decorative; [seedling × seedling]; intr. 2001

'Julia Ferran' -- See 'Lady Trent'

'Julia Fontaine' B, lp, 1879, Fontaine; flowers bright flesh pink, medium, full

'Julia Mannering' HEg, lp, 1895, Penzance; flowers pearly pink, yellow stamens, semi-dbl., borne along the cane, moderate fragrance; summer bloom; vigorous growth

Julia Renaissance® (Julia™, Phillipa™) S, lp, Olesen; flowers light pink, 10-15 cm., full, moderate fragrance; foliage dark; growth bushy, 100-150 cm.; intr. 1996

'Julia Touvais' HP, lp, 1868, Touvais; flowers flesh pink, large, full

'Julia, Countess of Dartrey' HT, rb, 1927, Hall; bud pointed; flowers Tyrian rose, base yellow, very large, dbl., high-centered; foliage dark, leathery, glossy; very vigorous growth

'Juliana-Roos' Pol, op, 1920, den Ouden; flowers pale salmon; [sport of 'Orléans Rose']

Juliane® HT, r, McGredy; flowers light coffee-brown, dbl.; intr. 2000

'Julia's Kiss' HT, lp, 2001, Poole, Lionel; flowers cream/pink, 5-6 in., full, high-centered, borne mostly solitary, slight fragrance; foliage large, dark green, semi-glossy; prickles medium, long, narrow, few; stems very strong, vigorous; growth upright, bushy, medium (1 m.); exhibition, bedding, borders; [('Hazel Rose' × 'Cardiff Bay') × ('Hazel Rose' × 'Silver Jubilee')]; intr. 2003

Julia's Rose® HT, r, 1978, Wisbech Plant Co.; bud long, pointed; flowers parchment and copper shades, pointed, 2½ in., 22 petals, slight fragrance; foliage reddish; upright growth; [Blue Moon® × 'Dr. A. J. Verhage']; intr. 1980

'Julia's Rose, Climbing' Cl HT, r, St. Kilda's; [sport of 'Julia's Rose']; intr. 1994

'Julia's Secret' HT, r, Martin; flowers amber-fawn tinged lavender-pink, moderate fragrance; free-flowering; vigorous growth; intr. 2003

Julie™ -- See 'Poulra014(N)'

Julie® ('Kordes' Rose Julie') HT, dr, 1973, Kordes, R.; bud ovoid; flowers large, dbl., cupped, intense fragrance; foliage dark, soft; upright growth; [seedling × 'Red American Beauty']; intr. 1970

'Julie' Pol, dp, Clements, John; flowers dark reddish pink, small, borne in large clusters, candelabra style; intr. 2005

'Julie Andrews' -- See 'Fryvivacious'

Julie Ann™ -- See 'Savaweek'

'Julie Anne Ashmore' HT, yb, 1986, Owen, Fred; flowers deep yellow, suffused with pink throughout; [sport of 'Peace']; intr. 1985

'Julie Cussons' -- See 'Fryprincess'

'Julie de Fontenelle' B, dp, 1855, Portemer; flowers dark carmine pink, shaded violet, full

'Julie de Krüdner' -- See 'Julie Krüdner'

'Julie de Loynes' B, lp, 1835, Desprez; flowers flesh pink, full

'Julie de Mersan' ('Julie de Mersent') M, mp, 1854, Thomas; flowers rose shaded blush, striped white, full, borne in small clusters

'Julie de Mersent' -- See 'Julie de Mersan'

Julie Delbard® -- See 'Deljuli'

'Julie d'Étanges' HGal, m, 1834, Vibert; flowers rosy lilac, edged blush, large, dbl., cupped; erect, vigorous growth

'Julie Dupont' HP, mp, 1841, Dupont; flowers bright pink, center carmine, large, full

'Julie Evans' -- See 'Rawsetbo'

'Julie Krüdner' ('Julie de Krüdner') P, lp, 1847, Laffay; flowers pale flesh pink, medium, full

'Julie Link' -- See 'Morlink'

'Julie Lynne Zipper' -- See 'Zipjul'

'Julie Mansais' T, w, 1834, Mansais; flowers rich creamy white, large, full

Julie Newmar™ -- See 'Weklezpat'

'Julie Parade' (Julie™) MinFl, lp, Poulsen; flowers light pink, 5-8 cm., dbl., moderate fragrance; foliage dark; growth bushy, 20-40 cm.; PP14941; intr. 2001

'Julie Sharp' F, w, 1976, Sharp; flowers white, pink edge maturing to scarlet, large, 25-30 petals, cupped; foliage matte green; vigorous, upright growth; [sport of 'Evelyn Fison']

'Julie Sisley' B, pb; flowers bright pink, shaded lilac-violet, large, full

'Julie Strahl' HT, rb, 1928, Leenders Bros.; flowers nasturtium-red, passing to golden yellow, dbl.; ['Lady Greenall' × 'Gorgeous']

'Julie Y' ('Julie Youell') HT, or, Harkness; flowers bright, non-fading, dbl., high-centered, slight fragrance; growth to 3 ft.; intr. 1994

'Julie Youell' -- See 'Julie Y'

'Julien Potin' ('Golden Pernet') HT, ly, 1927, Pernet-Ducher; bud golden, pointed; flowers primrose-yellow, large, dbl., high-centered; foliage bright green; vigorous growth; ['Souv. de Claudius Pernet' × seedling]

'Julien Potin, Climbing' Cl HT, dy, 1935, Bostick; flowers yellow, with a blush; [sport of 'Julien Potin']

'Julien Renouard' -- See 'Dorjure'

'Julienne' HT, mp, 1940, Grillo; flowers silvery pink; [sport of 'Jewel']

'Julie's Choice' -- See 'Renjulie'

'Juliet' HP, pb, 1910, Paul, W.; bud globular, golden yellow; flowers rich rosy red to deep rose, reverse old-gold, large, dbl.; occasionally recurrent bloom; foliage curiously curled; vigorous growth; ['Captain Hayward' × 'Soleil d'Or']

'Juliet' S, ab, Austin, David; flowers soft creamy apricot, outer petals fade lighter, 90 petals, cupped, slight tea fragrance; recurrent; florist rose; intr. 2006

'Juliet Ann' -- See 'Harvissa'

'Juliet Staunton Clark' HT, w, 1933, Robichon; flowers white, center blush-white, turning white, large, very dbl.; [sport of 'Juliet']

'Juliet Williamson' Ayr, mp

'Julietta' HT, mp, Orard; intr. 2000

'Juliette' HGal, mr, before 1828, Miellez; flowers carmine-pink at the center, striped violet pink at the edges, medium, dbl., flat; growth upright

'Juliette' Min, mr; flowers brilliant crimson-scarlet, 30 petals; foliage bright red in fall; vigorous (10-12 in.) growth

'Juliette' -- See 'La Belle Sultane'

'Juliette E. van Beuningen' ('Mme Juliette') HT, dp, 1937, Buisman, G. A. H.; bud pointed; flowers bright pink, open, very large, semi-dbl.; foliage leathery, dark; ['Dame Edith Helen' × 'Mrs Sam McGredy']

Juliette Gréco® S, dy; flowers large, very dbl., quartered, intense herbal fragrance; recurrent; medium growth; intr. 1999

'Julio Iglesias' -- See 'Meisiastri'

Julischka® ('Juleschke') F, mr, 1974, Tantau, Math.; bud long, pointed; flowers bright red, medium, semi-dbl.; foliage glossy, bronze

'Julius Fabianics de Misefa' T, mr, 1902, Geschwind, R.; flowers crimson, full

'Julius Finger' HT, op, 1879, Lacharme; flowers salmon pink, large, full; ['Victor Verdier' × 'Mlle de Sombreuil']

'Julius Gofferje' HT, pb, 1930, Schmidt, J.C.; flowers peach-pink on yellow ground, dbl.; foliage bright green; vigorous growth

'Julklap' S, op, 1940, Krause; flowers light salmon-pink, large, semi-dbl.

'July Glory' HWich, dp, 1932, Chaplin Bros.; flowers rich rose-pink, 3 cm., dbl., borne in large clusters; foliage dark green, glossy; vigorous growth

'July Racecourse Rose' Min, my, Fryer; intr. 2008

'Jumpin' Jack' -- See 'Gnome World'

'Jumping Jack Flash' -- See 'Taljum'

'June' HT, pb, 1937, Archer; bud pointed; flowers shell-pink, center darker, well-shaped; vigorous growth

'June Aberdeen' F, ob, 1977, Cocker; flowers salmon, 2½ in., 20 petals; foliage dark; [Anne Cocker® × ('Sabine' × 'Circus')]

'June Anne' -- See 'Ripjune'

'June Boyd' HT, rb, 1924, McGredy; flowers salmon-carmine, base yellow, opening to bright peach-blossom, dbl.

'June Bride' Gr, w, 1957, Shepherd; bud pointed, greenish white tipped pink; flowers creamy white, 4 in., 30 petals, high-centered, borne in clusters of 3 - 7, moderate fragrance; foliage leathery, crinkled; vigorous, upright growth; PP1770; [('Mme Butterfly' × 'New Dawn') × 'Crimson Glory']; intr. 1957

'June Bug' -- See 'Pixjun'

'June Flame' HT, ob, 1949, Fletcher; bud small, tight; flowers bright orange-flame shaded copper; very early bloom

June Laver™ -- See 'Lavjune'

'June Moon' -- See 'June Morn'

'June Morn' ('June Moon') LCl, rb, 1939, Nicolas; bud ovoid; flowers carmine-red, reverse touched gold, 5 in., dbl., high-centered; some recurrent bloom; vigorous, climbing (8 ft.) growth; PP375; ['Mme Gregoire Staechelin' × 'Souv. de Claudius Pernet, Climbing']; sometimes classed as HMult

'June Opie' F, ab, 1959, Kordes; flowers apricot shaded salmon-pink, 3 in., semi-dbl., borne on trusses, slight fragrance; foliage leathery; very free, upright growth; ['Masquerade' × seedling]; intr. 1958

'June Park' HT, dp, 1959, Park; flowers rose-pink, 4½-5 in., 40 petals, intense fragrance; foliage dark; vigorous, spreading growth; ['Peace' × 'Crimson Glory']; intr. 1958

'June Patricia' HT, lp, 1966, Lees, H.; flowers silvery pink, 3 in., dbl., moderate fragrance; foliage dark, glossy; moderate growth; ['Peace' × 'Ena Harkness']

'June Time' Min, lp, 1963, Moore, Ralph S.; flowers light pink, reverse darker, small, 75 petals, borne in clusters; foliage glossy; bushy, compact (10-12 in. growth; PP2563; [(R. wichurana × Floradora) × (('Étoile Luisante' × unknown) × ('Red Ripples' × 'Zee'))]; intr. 1963

'June Way' HT, mp, 1976, Atkiss; flowers 4-5 in., 33 petals, cupped, slight fragrance; foliage glossy; spreading growth; ['Pink Favorite' × 'Chrysler Imperial']; intr. 1977

'June Wedding' HT, w, 1977, Graham; bud pointed; flowers white, tinted yellow,, 4 in., 27 petals, high-centered; foliage glossy, dark; upright growth; [sport of 'Bewitched']

'June Whitfield' -- See 'Harchutzpah'

'Juneen' HT, my, 1969, Mason, P.G.;

flowers, high-centered, slight fragrance; compact growth; ['Burnaby' × ('Burnaby' × unknown)]; intr. 1967

'June's Delight' F, w, 2000, Tucker, Dr. Kenneth; flowers full, high-centered, borne mostly singly, slight fragrance; foliage medium size, medium green, semi-glossy; few prickles; compact, medium growth; [sport of 'Sweet Inspiration']

'June's Joy' F, pb, Benardella, Frank; flowers ivory blushed pink, dbl., exhibition, borne in clusters and individual blooms, no fragrance; good repeat; stems short; compact, dense growth; intr. 2000

'Junior' HT, St Zila; intr. 1973

'Junior Bridesmaid' F, mp, 1962, Jelly; bud short, pointed; flowers sweetheart,, 2 in., 35 petals, slight fragrance; foliage leathery; vigorous, upright growth; PP2446; ['Stoplite' × 'Lovelight']; intr. 1962

'Junior Geisha' F, or, Keisei

'Junior Gilbert' HT, or, 1954, Mallerin, C.; flowers cupped, cupped; vigorous growth

'Junior Miss' -- See 'America's Junior Miss'

'Junior Miss' F, pb, 1943, Duehrsen; bud well formed; flowers pink and yellow, medium, semi-dbl., high-centered, borne in clusters; foliage glossy; vigorous, bushy growth; ['Joanna Hill' × 'Heidekind']

'Junior Prom' F, dr, 1962, Jelly; bud ovoid; flowers crimson, open, 1½-2 in., 30-45 petals; vigorous, upright growth; ['Orange Sweetheart' × 'Lovelight']; intr. 1962

'Junior Van Fleet' S, lp, 1923, Kemp, J.A.; flowers flesh-pink, dbl.; non-recurrent; ['Dr. W. Van Fleet' × 'Frau Karl Druschki']

'Juno' C, lp, before 1832; flowers blush pink, with a small center eye, large, very dbl., globular, quartered, strong fragrance; foliage bright green; arching growth; possibly synonymous with the HCh of this name from Laffay

'Juno' HCh, lp, Laffay, M.; flowers pale rose, very large, dbl., globular; intr. 1847

'Juno' HT, mp, Swim, H.C.; bud ovoid; flowers soft medium pink, large, 30 petals, high-centered, slight fragrance; foliage bright, leathery, wrinkled, glossy; moderate upright, bushy growth; PP895; ['Duquesa de Peñaranda' × 'Charlotte Armstrong']; intr. 1950

'Juno Rose' -- See 'Petite Junon de Hollande'

'Junon' -- See 'Surpasse Tout'

'Junon' ('Belle Junon', 'Junonis', 'Rouge Agréable') HGal, dp, before 1811, Dupont; flowers deep crimson pink, often plumed white, edges lighter, large, full, slight fragrance

Junon® -- See 'Gaucova'

'Junon Argentée' -- See 'Petite Junon de Hollande'

'Junonis' -- See 'Junon'

Jupiter® HT, dy, Tantau; flowers clear, unfading yellow, medium, double, high-centered, borne mostly singly; recurrent; stems medium to long; florist rose; intr. 2003

'Jupiter' S, pb, GPG Bad Langensalza; flowers ivory with pale to strong pink edges, large, dbl.; recurrent; upright, arching (4 ft.) growth; intr. 1987

'Jupiter' HT, pb

'Jupiter' HP, lp, Williams, A.; ['Prince Camille de Rohan' × unknown]; intr. 1900

'Jupiter' B, dr, 1845, Verdier, V.; flowers slatey dark red, medium, full

'Jupiter' HSpn, mp; flowers bright pink, dbl.; foliage finely divided; dense, shrubby (3-4 ft.) growth; hips shining, black; intr. before 1930

'Jupiter' -- See 'Brijup'

Jupon Rose® -- See 'Lenniro'

'Jura' -- See 'Berliner Luft'

'Jurassic Pink' HKor, mp

'Jurie Els' HT, yb, Orard; flowers yellow with pink edging as exposed to sun, dbl., high-centered, borne mostly singly, no fragrance; stems medium long; growth medium; intr. 2001

'Jusamanda' ('Amanda Kay') Min, w, 1991, Justice, Jerry G.; bud ovoid; flowers white to near white, some pink shading, small, dbl., high-centered, borne singly, intense spicy fragrance; foliage small, medium green, glossy; bushy, low growth; [seedling × seedling]; intr. 1991

'Jusclare' ('Nancy Clare') Min, w, 1995, Justice, Jerry G.; flowers nearly pure white with pink accent at outer edge, 1¾-2 in., 18-20 petals, borne mostly singly, moderate spicy fragrance; recurrent; foliage medium size, light green, semi-glossy; medium (32 in.), upright growth; ['Jennifer' × seedling]; intr. 1995

'Juselle' ('Giselle') Min, dp, 1991, Justice, Jerry G.; bud small, pointed with medium green sepals; flowers pink outer edges with very light pink throat, reverse rosy pink with white midline, 1¼ in., 18 petals, urn-shaped, loose, borne usually singly, no fragrance; foliage small, dark green, glossy, disease-resistant; bushy, low growth; ['Crazy Dottie' × seedling]; intr. 1992

'Jusfoggy' ('Foggy Day') Min, w, 2000, Justice, Jerry G.; flowers white, reverse ivory to white, medium size, dbl., high-centered, borne mostly singly, no fragrance; quick repeat; foliage small, medium green, semi-glossy; prickles moderate; compact, medium (14-18 in.) growth; ['Kiss 'n' Tell' × unknown]; intr. 2000

'Jushaze' ('Purple Haze') Min, m, 1996, Justice, Jerry G.; flowers soft mauve with light tan shading at the throat, 2¾ in., full, borne mostly singly, intense fragrance; foliage medium size, medium green, semi-glossy; some prickles; bushy, medium growth; PPAF; [Twilight Trail™ × seedling]; intr. 1996

'Jushoney' ('My Honey') Min, ob, 1991, Justice, Jerry G.; bud pointed; flowers orange with light yellow accent at base, acquiring a pinkish cast with age, medium, dbl., urn-shaped, loose, borne singly, no fragrance; foliage medium size, dark green, semi-glossy; spreading, medium growth; [sport of 'Orange Honey']; intr. 1991

'Jusknack' ('Knick Knack') Min, ob, 2000, Justice, Jerry G.; flowers peachy white, reverse pale orange, fading to white with gold edges, 1½ cm., semi-dbl., flat, borne mostly singly, slight fragrance; foliage medium size, medium green, semi-glossy; prickles moderate; growth upright, medium (18-22 in.); [Baby Diana™ × unknown]; intr. 2000

'Juslatte' ('Latte') Min, m, 1995, Justice, Jerry G.; flowers russet with lavender edge, 1½ in., 56 petals, borne singly, moderate spicy fragrance; foliage medium size, medium green, semi-glossy; medium, bushy growth; [Twilight Trail™ × seedling]; intr. 1995

'Juslemon' ('Lemon Meringue') Min, my, 1996, Justice, Jerry G.; flowers medium yellow, with white to ivory tips, reverse becomes lighter, petals highly reflexed, 1 in., full; foliage medium size, dark green, dull; nearly thornless; growth compact (16-20 in.); PPRR; ['Rise 'n' Shine' × seedling]; intr. 1997

'Jusmaiden' ('Snow Maiden') Min, w, 1995, Justice, Jerry G.; flowers pure white with ivory to bone white throat, reverse pure white, pink in cool temp, full, borne mostly singly, slight fragrance; foliage medium size, dark green, glossy; few prickles; upright, medium growth; [Snow Twinkle™ × seedling]; intr. 1996

'Jusmichael' ('Baby Michael') Min, dp, 1991, Justice, Jerry G.; bud pointed; flowers deep rose pink, reverse medium pink with a touch of silver at base, medium, 38-40 petals, high-centered, borne singly, slight spicy fragrance; foliage medium size, dark green, semi-glossy; upright, medium growth; [seedling × seedling]; intr. 1991

'Jusprop' ('Whirlygig') Min, pb, 1999, Justice, Jerry G.; flowers soft pink and white, reverse darker, 2 in., single, slight fragrance; foliage medium size, dark green, semi-glossy; upright, medium (20-22 in.) growth; [(seedling × Magic Carrousel®) × unknown]; intr. 1999

'Jusregal' ('Regal') Cl Min, dp, 1999, Justice, Jerry G.; flowers old rose pink, reverse same, 1¾ in., very dbl., borne mostly singly, no fragrance; foliage medium size, medium green, glossy; prickles moderate; upright, climbing, medium to tall (6 ft.) growth; ['Rosanna' × unknown]; intr. 1999

'Jussabra' ('Sabra') Min, mp, 1999, Justice, Jerry G.; flowers medium pink, reverse light pink, 1¾ in., single, borne mostly singly; foliage large, light green, dull; upright, medium (18-21 in.) growth; [('Fairy Moss' × unknown) × unknown]; intr. 1999

'Just Beautiful' HT, ab, Interplant; flowers large, double, cupped; recurrent; growth medium height

'Just Brilliant' ('Brilliant Sea-duction') F, pb, 2007, Ross, Andrew; flowers 8 cm., full, borne in small clusters; foliage medium size, dark green, matte; prickles medium, hooked, brown, few; growth compact, medium (1¼ m.); garden decoration; ['Seduction' × Manou Meilland®]; intr. 2007

Just Buddy™ -- See 'Kinbud'

'Just Dreamy' -- See 'Perjusdream'

'Just For Fun' -- See 'Strildew'

'Just For You' -- See 'Moryou'

'Just Happy' -- See 'Dictalent'

'Just Jennie' -- See 'Just Jenny'

'Just Jenny' ('Just Jennie') Min, ab; flowers soft peachy-apricot, dbl., moderate fragrance; intr. 1993

Just Joanna™ -- See 'Wiljoea'

'Just Joey' HT, ob, 1972, Cants of Colchester, Ltd.; flowers buff-orange, 5 in., 30 petals, classic, intense fragrance; foliage glossy, leathery; growth moderate; ['Fragrant Cloud' × 'Dr. A. J. Verhage']

'Just Judy' HT, lp, 1992, Poole, Lionel; flowers medium, full, borne mostly singly, slight fragrance; foliage medium size, dark green, semi-glossy; some prickles; upright growth; ['Mischief' × 'Simba']

'Just Lucky' HT, w, 1985, Bridges, Dennis A.; flowers well-formed, large, 35 petals, intense fragrance; foliage medium size, dark, glossy; bushy growth; ['Typhoo Tea' × Pascali®]; intr. 1985

'Just Magic' -- See 'Trobic'

'Just Married' F, op; flowers bright salmon-orange, double, cupped, borne in clusters; recurrent; strong, sturdy (36 in.) growth

'Just Peachy' -- See 'Gelpeach'

'Just Peachy' -- See 'Balets'

'Just Reward' -- See 'Guestall'

'Just Simon' -- See 'Burbrahmvidya'

'Just William' -- See 'Driscored'

'Justa Little Goofy' -- See 'Rengoofy'

'Justin' HT, mr, Kordes; flowers clear red, large, dbl., exhibition, borne mostly singly, no fragrance; foliage healthy, disease-resistant; growth medium; intr. 1997

'Justina' HT, mp

'Justine' ('Nouveauté de Provence') C, m, 1822, Vibert; flowers pale lilac-pink, medium, very dbl.

'Justine' T, Foulard; intr. 1827

'Justine' B, dp, Rousseau; flowers dark pink mixed with carmine, full; intr. 1845

'Justine' HT, ly, Joseph H. Hill, Co.; bud orange; flowers creamy yellow, base dark orange, reverse almost white, large, 30-35 petals; foliage dark, leathery; vigorous growth; PP154; ['Joanna Hill' × 'Sweet Adeline']; intr. 1935

'Justine' S, mp, Jerabek; intr. 2005

'Justine Mee Liff' Gr, mp, 2004, Jerabek, Paul; flowers light pink, reverse medium pink, 4½ in., very full, borne singly and in small clusters, moderate fragrance; foliage medium size, semi-glossy; prickles 3/16 in., straight; growth spreading, medium; [unknown × unknown]; intr. 2005

'Justine Ramet' C, m, 1845, Vibert; flowers purplish-rose, medium, dbl.

'Justine Silva' -- See 'Rita Sammons'

'Justino Henriques' HT, yb, 1926, deFreitas; flowers yellow tinted orange, stamens carmine, dbl.; [sport of 'Louise Catherine Breslau']

'Justizrat Dr Hessert' HT, pb, 1919, Lambert, P.; bud carmine-red; flowers salmon-pink shaded red and yellow, dbl.; ['Gen. MacArthur' × Tip-Top®]

Jutland™ (Chateau Montrose™, Nashira™) F, lp, Poulsen; flowers light pink, 8-10 cm., 25 petals; foliage dark, glossy; growth bushy, 100-150 cm.; intr. 1995

'Jutlandia' HWich, mp, 1913, Poulsen, D.T.; flowers dbl.; vigorous growth; ['Mme Norbert Levavasseur' × 'Dorothy Perkins']

'Jutta' Pol, mr, Scholle, E.; flowers medium, semi-dbl.; intr. 1970

'Jutta' Pol, lp, Rupprecht-Radke; flowers large, dbl.; intr. 1964

'Jutul' F, dp, 1983, Lundstad, Arne; flowers deep pink, small, 14 petals, cupped, borne in clusters of 7-9, slight fragrance; foliage dark, glossy; prickles curved, red-brown; vigorous growth; ['New Dawn' × Moulin Rouge®]

'Juwel' HT, ly, 1911, Hinner, W.; flowers lemon-white, large, dbl., moderate fragrance

'Juwena' ('Tanerou') F, ob, Tantau; intr. 1978

'Juwena' F, dy, Tantau; intr. 2003

'Jwala' F, or, K&S; free-flowering; strong, vigorous growth; intr. 2003

— K —

'K S G Centenary' HT, yb, K&S; intr. 1995

'K S R' HT, Keisei Rose Nurseries, Inc.; intr. 1987

'K. A. Viktoria' -- See 'Kaiserin Auguste Viktoria'

'K. of K.' -- See 'Kitchener of Khartoum'

'K. T.' -- See 'Talkev'

'K. T. Marshall' -- See 'Katherine T. Marshall'

'Kabjenn' ('Pretty Jennifer') S, w, 2000, Belcher, Kenneth A.; flowers cream, reverse lighter, medium, very full, borne in small clusters; foliage medium size, dark green, semi-glossy; few prickles; growth upright, tall (4-5 ft.); [sport of 'Ausjess']

'Kabuki, Climbing' Cl HT, my, Vidal; intr. after 1968

'Kabuki' -- See 'Meigold'

'Kadora' S, mr, Noack; flowers semidouble, borne in clusters; recurrent; low (60 - 80 cm.), spreading growth; intr. 2008

'Kagaribi' HT, yb, Oshima; flowers striped; intr. 1970

'Kagayaki' ('Brilliant Light', 'Glitter') F, rb, 1973, Suzuki, Seizo; flowers brilliant scarlet and yellow, large, dbl., high-centered, slight fragrance; foliage glossy, dark; vigorous, upright growth; [(('Aztec' × unknown) × ('Spectacular' × 'Aztec')) × ('Cover Girl' × unknown)]; intr. 1970

'Kagayaku Seishin' ('Lustrous Spirit') HT, my, Hiroshima; intr. 1997

'Kagerou' F, w, Hiroshima; flowers greengrey; intr. 2004

'Kagura' ('Festival Music') HT, rb, Hiroshima; intr. 1998

'Kagura'

'Kaguya-Fuji' HT, w, 2003, Matsumoto, Masayuki; flowers full, borne in large clusters; foliage medium size, dark green, glossy; few prickles; growth upright, medium (150 cm.); [seedling × seedling]

'Kaguyahime' HT, my, Keisei; intr. 1998

'Kaguyama' HT, w, Tanaka; intr. 1974

Kaikoura® -- See 'Macwalla'

'Kaileen' -- See 'Jacmar'

'Kaimai Sunset' -- See 'Somtabco'

'Kaina' HT, pb, G&L; intr. 1985

'Kaiser Friedrich' T, pb, 1890, Drögemüller; flowers silky China pink, center golden yellow, shaded cherry red, large, full, moderate fragrance; ['Gloire de Dijon' × 'Countess of Oxford']

'Kaiser Wilhelm der Siegreiche' T, pb, 1889, Drögemüller; flowers exterior petals yellowish-white, interior brilliant deep yellow with carmine pink, 10 cm., very dbl., borne singly or in small clusters, moderate fragrance; ['Mme Bérard' × 'Perle des Jardins']

'Kaiser Wilhelm I' HP, m, 1878, Ruschpler; flowers purple/pink, large, dbl., moderate fragrance; foliage dark green, grayish-green underneath; nearly thornless

'Kaiser Wilhelm II' ('Fürst Niclot') HT, mr, 1909, Welter; bud conical, long; flowers fiery red with poppy reflections, large, semi-dbl., moderate fragrance

'Kaiserin Auguste Viktoria' ('Grande Duchesse Olga', 'K. A. Viktoria', 'Reine Augusta Victoria') HT, w, 1891, Lambert, P.; bud long, pointed; flowers snowy white, center tinted lemon, well-formed, 100 petals, intense fragrance; foliage rich green, soft, very disease-resistant; growth moderate; ['Coquette de Lyon' × 'Lady Mary Fitzwilliam']; parentage also given as Perle des Jardins × Belle Lyonnaise

'Kaiserin Auguste Viktoria, Climbing' ('Mrs Robert Peary') Cl HT, w, 1897, Dickson, A. (also De Voecht & De Wilde, 1898); flowers cream-white, very large, dbl.; [sport of 'Kaiserin Auguste Viktoria']

'Kaiserin des Nordens' ('Himalayensis', 'Regeliana Flore Pleno', 'Regeliana Rubra', 'Zuccariniana') HRg, m, 1879;

flowers purple violet, large, dbl.; possibly synonymous with 'Taïcoun'
'Kaiserin Farah' -- See 'Delivour'
'Kaiserin Farah' HT, dr, W. Kordes Söhne; flowers very large, very dbl.; intr. 1965
'Kaiserin Friedrich' T, pb, 1890, Drögemüller; flowers golden yellow on pink, large, very dbl.; ['Gloire de Dijon' × 'Perle des Jardins']
'Kaiserin Goldifolia' HT, w, 1909, Conard & Jones; flowers identical to Kaiserin Auguste Viktoria; foliage bright golden yellow; [sport of 'Kaiserin Auguste Viktoria']
'Kaiserin Zita' HT, lp
'Kaiteri Gold' ClMin, dy, Warner; flowers soft golden-yellow, fading paler, dbl.; free-flowering; moderately vigorous (6 ft.) growth; intr. 2003
'Kaitlyn' S, dp, Williams, J.B.; flowers very deep reddish-pink, semi-dbl., globular; growth spreading; intr. 2003
'Kaitlyn Ainsley' HRg, m, Baskerville, Joanne; flowers mauve-pink, large, semi-dbl., intense fragrance; recurrent; foliage medium green, disease-resistant; tidy (4 ft.) growth; [Dagmar Hastrup® × 'Roseraie de l'Haÿ']; intr. 1998
Kaj Munk™ -- See 'Pouldunk(N)'
'Kakadu' S, w, Peden, R.; intr. 2000
'Kakayan' Pol (?), w; flowers single; intr. before 1867
'Kakwa' HSpn, w, Wallace, John A.; flowers creamy white, moderate fragrance; some repeat; arching, open growth, much suckering; open pollination of R. spinosissima hispida; intr. 1973
'Kala Agneta' -- See 'Agnes und Bertha'
'Kaladi' HT, op, K&S; flowers salmon with yellow base and reverse, aging to deeper tones of apricot-orange-red, dbl.; intr. 1998
'Kalahari' HT, op, 1971, McGredy, Sam IV; flowers salmon-pink, high-pointed, 4 in., 25 petals; foliage glossy, dark; ['Uncle Walter' × ('Hamburger Phoenix' × 'Danse de Feu')]
'Kalavalla' F, mp, 1935, Poulsen, S.; flowers dbl., borne in large clusters; vigorous growth; ['Else Poulsen' × seedling]
Kaleidoscope™ -- See 'Jacbow'
'Kaleidoscope' F, ob, 1970, Fryer, Gareth; flowers orange and yellow, 3 in., 28 petals, slight fragrance; foliage glossy; ['Circus' × 'Redgold']; intr. 1972
'Kalinka, Climbing' -- See 'Meihartforsar'
'Kalinka' -- See 'Pink Wonder'
Kalmar™ -- See 'Poulkalm'
'Kalmia' HWich, w, 1911, Walsh; flowers white, upper half of petals tinged pink, single, borne in clusters; foliage dark, glossy; vigorous, climbing growth
'Kalyana' HT, ob, Kasturi; flowers rich salmon with creamy yellow base and reverse, large; intr. 1995
'Kamakura' HT, my, 2004, Hironaka Ohtsuki; flowers medium yellow, reverse medium yellow, 14 cm., full, borne mostly solitary; foliage medium size, medium green, semi-glossy; no prickle; growth upright, 100-150 cm.; cutting exhibition; ['Kabuki' × 'Kewai']; intr. 2003
'Kamaladevi Chattopadhayay' HT, op, Pal, Dr. B.P.; intr. 1989
'Kamalakantha' HT, or, Deby's; flowers orange-red with clear, distinct white stripes; [sport of 'La Marseillaise']; intr. 2005
'Kambala' HT, my, Swane; intr. 1988
'Kamchin' ('Carlita') HT, mp, 1974, Kammeraad; flowers Neyron rose, outside rose, 4-5 in., 45 petals, cupped, slight fragrance; foliage dull, dark; vigorous growth; [sport of 'Carina']; intr. 1972
'Kameleon' HT, yb, de Groot; Henk C. A.; flowers yellow-cream at center, greenish-hued outer petals, 10-12 cm., 42 petals, no fragrance; prickles moderate; stems long; PP15796; intr. 2004
'Kamelia' HT, mr, Urban, J.; flowers large, dbl.; intr. 1969
'Kamikazari' ('Hair Ornament') Min, mp, Yoshida; intr. 1996
'Kamion' Min, or, 1988, Schoen-Jones, Helen; flowers bright orange-red, reverse matte finish, clear, golden stamens, 12 petals, high-centered; foliage large, dark green, glossy; prickles curved, small, reddish; upright, tall, sturdy growth; hips oval, large, light orange; [Starina® × seedling]; intr. 1988
'Kammersanger Karl Terkal' -- See 'Kammersanger Terkal'
'Kammersanger Terkal' ('Hartina', 'Kammersanger Karl Terkal') F, ob, 1974, Tantau, Math.; bud small, globular; flowers pure orange, medium, dbl., slight fragrance; foliage glossy; dwarf, bushy growth; intr. 1971
'Kammersingerin Perra' S
'Kamo' HT, w, Keihan; intr. 1978
'Kampai' -- See 'Kanpai'
'Kampaÿ' -- See 'Meipelmel'
'Kamtchatica' (R. × rugosa kamtchatica, R. kamtchatica) S, dr, about 1800; sepals entire; flowers velvety purple-carmine, medium, single; hips rounded, glabrous, reddish-brown; from Siberia, discovered by Ventenat; now thought to be a hybrid of R. davurica × R. rugosa
'Kana' HT, dr, 1985, Ota, Kaichiro; flowers large, 38 petals, high-centered, borne singly and in small clusters, no fragrance; foliage medium green; prickles small, slanted downward; tall, bushy growth; ['Ginger Rogers' × 'Chiyo']; intr. 1982
'Kanaal' F, op, RvS-Melle; intr. 1998
'Kanak' F, yb, Sunil Jolly; flowers pale yellow with petal edges blended pale pink; growth medium; [sport of 'Charisma']; intr. 1988
'Kanakangi' HT, ab, 1970, Pal, Dr. B.P.; bud globular; flowers gold and apricot, open, medium, semi-dbl., intense fragrance; foliage leathery; moderate, bushy, open growth; ['Mme Charles Sauvage' × unknown]; intr. 1968
'Kanarie' HT, dy, 1919, Verschuren; flowers clear dark yellow, dbl.; ['Golden Star' × 'Melody']
'Kanchani 2003' HT, my, K&S; bud pointed, ovoid; flowers non-fading yellow, well-formed, dbl.; intr. 2003
'Kanchi' HT, dp, Viraraghavan, M.S.; flowers hues of magenta, cerise, and purple, lighter reverse, dbl.; intr. 1976
'Kanegem' ('Caneghem', 'Carike Keuzenkamp') F, or, 1985, Rijksstation Voor Sierplantenteelt; flowers large, 42 petals, high-centered to cupped, borne 1-7 per cluster; foliage dark, glossy; upright growth; [Ludwigshafen am Rhein® × Satchmo®]; intr. 1982
'Kanon' HT, op, Keisei; intr. 2004
'Kanpai' ('Cheers', 'Kampai') HT, dr, 1985, Suzuki, Seizo; flowers deep red, 48 petals, high-centered, borne singly and in small clusters, moderate fragrance; foliage medium size, dark; upright growth; [('Yu-ai' × ('Happiness' × 'American Beauty')) × 'Pharoah']; intr. 1985
'Kansas City' HT, dp, 1903, Conard & Jones
'Kanten' HWich, m, 1910, Barbier; flowers lilac pink
'Kantha Selvon' -- See 'Evegaytime'
'Kanva' HT, op, Kasturi; flowers salmon pink, large, dbl., high-centered, moderate fragrance; intr. 1974
Kanyakumari™ -- See 'Virkanya'
Kapai® -- See 'Macgam'
'Kapiti' -- See 'Macglemil'
'Kara' ('Dear One') Min, mp, 1973, Moore, Ralph S.; bud long, mossy; flowers light to medium pink, micro-mini, mini-moss, small, single; foliage small, soft; vigorous, dwarf, bushy growth; ['Fairy Moss' × 'Fairy Moss']; intr. 1972
Karaoke™ -- See 'Pal-kar'
'Kardinal, Climbing' Cl HT, mr, Knight, J.; [sport of 'Kardinal']; intr. 1999
'Kardinal' HT, dr, 1934, Krause; flowers scarlet-red, sometimes tipped blackish, large, cupped; vigorous, compact, bushy growth; [('Château de Clos Vougeot' × unknown) × seedling]
Kardinal® -- See 'Korlingo'
'Kardinal 85' -- See 'Korlingo'
'Kardinal Kordana' Min, dr, Kordes; flowers full; container rose
'Kardinal Piffl' HT, ob, 1925, Leenders Bros.; flowers red-orange, reverse golden yellow, very large, dbl.; foliage good; [('Mme Edouard Herriot' × 'Rayon d'Or') × 'Mme Charles Lutaud']
'Kardinal Schulte' HT, mr, 1926, Leenders Bros.; flowers brilliant scarlet-red, dbl.; [('Jonkheer J.L. Mock' × 'Radiance') × 'Commandeur Jules Graveraux']
'Kardinal Schulte, Climbing' Cl HT, mr; flowers large, dbl.; [sport of 'Kardinal Schulte']
'Kardinal's Flame' HT, or
'Karel Hynek Mácha' HT, dr, 1936, Brada, Dr.; flowers velvety red, well-shaped
'Karel IV' HT, mr, 1935, Brada, Dr.; flowers large, dbl.
'Karen' F, my, 1961, Borgatti, G.; flowers straw-yellow shaded ochre-yellow, 3 in.,

30-35 petals; bushy growth; ['Goldilocks' × 'Fashion']
'Karen' S, w, Skinner; flowers creamy white flecked red, well-shaped, very dbl., moderate fragrance; non-recurrent; bushy, erect (5 ft.) growth; [R. primula × R. spinosissima cultivar]; intr. 1964
'Karen' HT, yb, Marciel; PP6582; intr. 1989
'Karen' ('Lovely') F, op, Keisei; intr. 1995
'Karen' -- See 'Nirpicered'
Karen Blixen™ -- See 'Poulari'
'Karen Julie' HT, or, Allender, Robert William; flowers flame orange, dbl., high-centered, slight fragrance; free-flowering; medium growth; [Alexander® × 'Weinerwold']; intr. 1979
'Karen Maria' HT, yb, 1972, Gates; flowers cream and yellow, flushed pink, 4 in., 40 petals, intense fragrance; foliage glossy, dark; free growth; [sport of 'Kordes' Perfecta']
'Karen Poulsen, Climbing' Cl F, mr, Roger; [sport of 'Karen Poulsen']
'Karen Poulsen' ('Bailey's Red') F, mr, 1932, Poulsen, S.; flowers scarlet, single, borne in huge trusses; vigorous growth; ['Kirsten Poulsen' × 'Vesuvius']; intr. 1933
'Karen Rudall' -- See 'Rawgolley'
'Karenina' Min, op; intr. 1999
'Karen's Cream' HT, Neil, J.; [sport of 'Shocking Blue']
'Karen's Pink Lace' F, mp, 1998, Prevatt, Clarence; flowers medium pink, creamy reverse at base, 41 petals, borne mostly singly; foliage medium size, medium green, dull; prickles moderate, medium size; bushy, medium (3-4 ft.) growth; [sport of 'French Lace']; intr. 1998
Karina™ -- See 'Poulpar029(N)'
'Karina Eloise' -- See 'Bedjust'
'Karina Parade' (Karina™) Min, mr, Olesen; bud pointed ovoid; flowers medium red, 3½ cm.-less than 5 cm., 30 petals, rosette, borne singly, slight floral fragrance; recurrent; foliage dark green, glossy; prickles moderate, straight; growth bushy, 20-40 cm.; PP16148; [Patricia Kordana Mini Brite™ × seedling]; intr. 2003
'Karine' Pol, mp, Knopf, Ruth; flowers bright pink with bright yellow stamens, single, slight fragrance; good repeat; seedling that appeared in Knopf's garden in South Carolina; intr. 1992
Karine Sauvageot® F, op, Sauvageot; flowers rose-peach and salmon, single, borne in small clusters, moderate fragrance; intr. 1989
'Karkulka' F, Urban, J.; intr. 1986
'Karkulka' HT, mr, Strnad
'Karl Diehl' S, dy, Schultheis; flowers gold-yellow, wavy petals, semi-dbl., borne in clusters; recurrent; foliage light green; strong (5-7 ft.) growth; intr. 1997
'Karl Fischer' S, or, Hetzel; intr. 1976
'Karl Förster' HSpn, w, 1931, Kordes; bud pointed; flowers snow-white, very large, semi-dbl. to dbl., high-centered; borne intermittently throughout the summer; foliage wrinkled, light; vigorous (7 ft.) growth; [R. spinosissima altaica × 'Frau Karl Druschki']
Karl Heinz Hanisch® -- See 'Meimafris'
'Karl Herbst' ('Red Peace') HT, mr, 1950, Kordes; flowers dull dark scarlet, well-shaped, large, 60 petals, intense fragrance; vigorous growth; ['Independence' × 'Peace']
'Karl Herbst, Climbing' Cl HT, mr; [sport of 'Karl Herbst']; intr. about 1980
'Karl Höchst' F, dp, Hetzel; flowers carmine-pink, large, dbl.; intr. 1983
'Karl Mayer' HT, Hetzel, K.; intr. 1970
'Karl Schneider' HMult, lp, 1934, Vogel, M.; flowers salmon pink, 9 cm., semi-dbl., flat, borne singly or in small clusters, moderate fragrance; [('Fragezeichen' × 'American Pillar') × 'Professor C. S. Sargent']
'Karl Weinhausen' F, dr, 1942, Tantau; flowers dark red tinted salmon, large, 20 petals, rosette, borne in clusters; vigorous, upright growth; ['Baby Chateau' × ('Heidekind' × 'Ingar Olsson')]
'Karla' -- See 'Frytrooper'
'Karlea' HT, pb, 1965, O'Brien; flowers pink and salmon, base yellow, dbl.; foliage glossy; vigorous, upright growth
'Karlian' HT, mr, 1991, Alde, Robert O.; flowers medium, full, borne mostly singly, intense fragrance; foliage medium size, medium green, semi-glossy; medium, upright, compact growth; [Pristine® × Burgund®]
'Karlsruhe' HKor, dp, 1958, Kordes; bud ovoid; flowers deep rose-pink, 12-14 cm., very dbl., cupped; repeat bloom; foliage dark green, glossy; vigorous, climbing growth; [R. × kordesii × seedling]; intr. 1957
'Karma' -- See 'Macnic'
'Karneol Rose' HT, op, Rupprecht-Radke; flowers dark salmon-pink, large, dbl.; intr. 1964
'Karolina' F, mr, Hempelmann; flowers carmine-red, medium, very dbl.; intr. 1994
'Karoline Reiber' Pol, mr, Hetzel; flowers carmine-red, small, dbl.; intr. 1991
'Karoline Svetla' Pol, lp, 1937, Brada, Dr.; flowers medium, semi-dbl.
'Karol's Rose' Min, mp
'Karolyn' -- See 'Coralin'
'Karoo' HT, lp, Elton Farm Nursery; flowers bright pink, large, high-centered; vigorous growth; RULED EXTINCT 2/88
'Karoo' -- See 'Poulkaro'
'Kasachstanskaia Jubilejnaja' HT, dr, Sushkov & Besschetnova; flowers large, very dbl.; intr. 1958
'Kasbah' HT, dp, 1977, Takatori, Yoshiho; bud pointed; flowers dark pink, reverse lighter, large, 80-110 petals, cupped, moderate fragrance; foliage leathery; upright growth; [seedling × 'Tropicana']
'Kasbek' HT, w, VEG; flowers medium to large, semi-dbl.
'Kashmir' Cl F, m, 1973, Thomson; bud ovoid; flowers clear mauve, medium, dbl.; foliage glossy, leathery; vigorous, climbing growth; ['Magenta' × 'Royal Tan']
'Kassel' HEg, or, 1958, Kordes, R.; bud ovoid; flowers orange-scarlet, large, semi-dbl., borne in clusters of up to 10, moderate fragrance; recurrent bloom; foliage dark, glossy; vigorous growth; not dependably hardy; ['Hamburg' × 'Scarlet Else']; intr. 1956
'Kasteel Van Ooidonk' F, lp, RvS-Melle; flowers 10 petals, flat; foliage matte; ['Melglory' × seedling]; intr. 1995
'Kasturi Rangan' HT, m, Agarwal; flowers dusky mauve with yellow base, dbl., high-centered, moderate fragrance; intr. 1983
'Kasumi' HT, op, Keisei; intr. 1998
'Kasuya no Sato' HT, pb, Hiroshima; intr. 2001
'Kätchen Meiner' Pol, op, 1914, Altmüller; flowers carmine pink with salmon, center darker, large
'Kätchen von Heilbronn' Pol, dr, 1922, Kiese; flowers very dark red, small, dbl.; ['Freudenfeuer' × seedling]
'Kate' HRg, Rieksta, Dr. Dz.
'Käte Beyer' Pol, op, 1947, Vogel, M.; flowers salmon-pink, medium, dbl.
'Kate Edwards' HT, m, 1965, Edwards; flowers magenta; [sport of 'Condessa de Mayalde']
'Kate Emily McCormack' -- See 'Kenmacho'
'Käte Felberg' HT, pb, 1930, Felberg-Leclerc; bud pointed; flowers creamy white, reverse violet-rose, large, dbl.; vigorous growth; [seedling × 'Mrs Wemyss Quin']
'Kate Hausburg' HP, lp, 1863, Granger; flowers very large, full
'Kate Moulton, Climbing' Cl HT, pb, 1928, Opdebeeck; [sport of 'Miss Kate Moulton']
'Kate Mull' HT, op, 1934, Easlea; flowers crushed strawberry and coppery rose, very dbl.
'Kate Rainbow' HT, pb, 1935, Beckwith; flowers blend of glowing pinks and gold, well-formed, very large, dbl.; foliage glossy, leathery; very vigorous growth
'Käte Schmid' HMult, dp, 1931, Vogel, R., Jr.; flowers deep rose-pink, very large, dbl., borne in clusters; foliage light; long stems; very vigorous, climbing growth; ['Fragezeichen' × 'Tausendschon']
'Kate Sheppard' F, mp, Sherwood; flowers clear, warm pink, dbl., high-centered, borne in clusters; free-flowering; medium growth; intr. 1994
'Kate Smith' HT, pb, 1954, Boerner; bud ovoid; flowers apricot overcast grenadine-pink, 4½-5 in., 35-40 petals, high-centered, intense fragrance; foliage glossy; vigorous growth; PP1317; [('Break o' Day' × 'Golden Rapture') × 'Ballet']
'Katelyn Ann' -- See 'Mickate'
'Katerina' HP, mr, Kosteckij; flowers large,

very dbl.; intr. 1955

'Katerina Lou' F, pb, 2005, Johnson, Kenneth E.; flowers pink blend with white stripes, pronounced stamens, 3 cm., dbl., borne in large clusters, slight fragrance; foliage medium size, medium green, semi-glossy; prickles 1¼ cm., acuminate; growth bushy, tall (3½ ft.); exhibition; [sport of 'Vera Daulton']

'Kateryna' -- See 'Clekate'

'Kate's Delight' Min, op, Benardella, Frank; flowers bright coral, fading to pink, dbl., high-centered; intr. 1999

'Kate's Rose' Pol, m, Cox, Mrs K.; ['Baby Faurax' × unknown]; intr. 1988

'Katharina Kündgen' S, mp, Michler, K. H.; flowers dbl.; intr. 1996

'Katharina Sophia' F, lp, Karwecki; intr. 1991

'Katharina von Bora'

'Katharina von Bora' LCl, pb, Schultheis; flowers deep pink in heart, soft pink on the outer petals, large , full, cupped, quartered, moderate fragrance; recurrent; foliage dark green; 3 - 5 meters growth; ['Pink Cloud' × 'Sämling']; intr. 2006

'Katharina Zeimet' ('Summer Snowflake', 'White Baby Rambler') Pol, w, 1901, Lambert, P.; flowers pure white, small, dbl., borne in clusters of 25 - 50, moderate fragrance; foliage small, rich green; short stems; dwarf, bushy growth; ['Étoile de Mai' × 'Marie Pavie']

'Katharine Pechtold' HT, ob, 1934, Verschuren-Pechtold; bud old-gold and bronzy orange; flowers coppery orange, flushed rose and gold, semidbl., moderate clove pink fragrance; foliage leathery; vigorous, bushy growth; ['Roselandia' × 'Charles P. Kilham']

'Katharine Worsley' F, mr, 1962; flowers bright oriental red, large, 28 petals, borne in large, well-spaced clusters; moderate, bushy growth; intr. 1962

'Käthchen' F, mr, Hetzel; flowers large, dbl.; intr. 1985

'Käthe Duvigneau' S, mr, 1942, Tantau; flowers glistening red tinted salmon, large, 15 petals, borne in clusters of 12 - 15, slight fragrance; foliage leathery, glossy, bright green; vigorous, upright growth; ['Baby Chateau' × *R. roxburghii*]

'Käthe von Saalfeld' HT, yb, 1914, Elbel; flowers orange yellow, large, very full, moderate fragrance

'Katherine Cook' HT, mr, 1927, Cook, J.W.; flowers cherry-red, dbl.; ['Crusader' × seedling]

'Katherine Harbour' HT, mp, 1974, Meyer, Harry; bud ovoid; flowers pink, tinted apricot, open, large, dbl., moderate fragrance; foliage glossy; vigorous, upright growth; [Queen Elizabeth® × 'Comtesse Vandal']; intr. 1973

'Katherine Helen' -- See 'Horoverture'

'Katherine Loker' F, my, 1978, Swim, H.C. & Christensen, J.E.; bud pointed; flowers medium golden yellow, imbricated, large, 28 petals, high-centered; upright, spreading growth; PP4666; ['Zorina' × 'Dr. A. J. Verhage']; intr. 1979

'Katherine Mansfield' -- See 'Meilanein'

'Katherine McCarty' Min, yb, 1991, Gruenbauer, Richard; bud ovoid; flowers yellow center, then white, with coral edges, coral spreads with age, medium, 60 petals, high-centered, moderate damask fragrance; foliage medium size, dark green, matte; bushy, medium growth; ['Poker Chip' × 'Rise 'n' Shine']; intr. 1993

'Katherine McGredy' HT, McGredy, Sam IV; intr. 1997

'Katherine Mock' HT, my, 1943, Mock; [sport of 'President Herbert Hoover']

'Katherine T. Marshall' ('K. T. Marshall') HT, mp, 1943, Boerner; flowers deep rose-pink, flushed yellow, 5 in., 22 petals, cupped, slight spicy fragrance; foliage leathery; vigorous, upright growth; PP607; [seedling × 'Chieftain']

'Kathleen' HT, op, 1895, Dickson, A.; flowers coral-pink, single

'Kathleen' HMult, pb, Paul, W.; flowers soft rose with white eye, small, single, borne in large clusters; ['Turner's Crimson Rambler' × 'Félicité et Perpétue']; intr. 1907

'Kathleen' HMsk, lp, Pemberton; flowers blush-pink, small, single, borne in large clusters; recurrent bloom; vigorous (6 ft.) growth; ['Daphne' × 'Perle des Jardins']; intr. 1922

'Kathleen' HT, op, Dickson, A.; bud very long; flowers light yellowish-salmon, medium to large, full, slight fragrance; vigorous, free branching growth; intr. 1934

'Kathleen Ferrier' F, op, 1952, Buisman, G. A. H.; flowers deep salmon-pink, 2½ in., 18 petals, borne in small clusters, moderate fragrance; foliage dark, glossy; vigorous, upright growth; ['Gartenstolz' × 'Shot Silk']

'Kathleen Ferrier, Climbing' Cl F, op; [sport of 'Kathleen Ferrier']

'Kathleen Harrop' B, lp, 1919, Dickson, A.; flowers soft shell-pink, semi-dbl., moderate fragrance; good repeat; foliage gray-green; prickles almost none; shrubby (10 × 6 ft.) growth; [sport of 'Zephirine Drouhin']

'Kathleen Jane' -- See 'Horcoed'

'Kathleen Jermyn' -- See 'Legneed'

'Kathleen Joyce' F, lp, 1970, McGredy, Sam IV; flowers soft pink, 4 in., 30 petals, high-centered, intense fragrance; ['Paddy McGredy' × 'Ice White']

'Kathleen Kaye' HT, mp, 1959, Kemp, M.L.; flowers rich rose-pink, 5 in., 60 petals; foliage dark; vigorous growth; ['Directeur Guerin' × 'Mirandy']

'Kathleen Kellehan' ('The Nanango Rose') S, rb, 1999, Laving, Peter; flowers 4 in., full, borne in large clusters, intense fragrance; foliage medium size, medium green, semi-glossy; prickles moderate; upright, medium (4 ft.) growth; [Lilian Austin® × 'Oklahoma']

'Kathleen Kennedy' HT, op, 1939, Dickson, A.; flowers light salmon-carmine, shaded orange, well-formed, large; strong stems; vigorous growth

'Kathleen King' HT, dp, 1930, Marriott; flowers carmine-pink, well-formed, large, high-centered; vigorous growth

'Kathleen Kirkham' -- See 'Kirkit'

'Kathleen Mills' HT, pb, 1934, LeGrice; bud long, pointed; flowers pale pink tinted silvery, reverse deep pink, large, semi-dbl.; foliage leathery; vigorous growth

'Kathleen Nash' HT, mr, 1944, Spera; bud urn shaped; flowers bright cerise, 4 in., 28 petals, globular, intense fragrance; foliage leathery, dark; vigorous growth; PP618; [sport of 'Pink Delight']

'Kathleen O'Rourke' HT, op, 1976, Dickson, Patrick; flowers soft orange-pink, 4 in., 38 petals, high-centered; foliage large, matte; ['Fragrant Cloud' × 'Red Planet']

'Kathleen Peden' HT, dr, 1959, Peden, G.H.; bud long pointed; flowers crimson, large, dbl., high-centered; foliage leathery, dark; very vigorous, upright growth; ['Crimson Glory' × 'Charles Mallerin']

'Kathleen Rumble' -- See 'Welrum'

'Kathleen Wiggin' Cl HP, w, 1932, Wiggin; bud long pointed, opening one at a time on each cluster; flowers white, sometimes tinged pink, large, very dbl., borne in clusters; foliage glossy, heavy; long stems; vigorous, climbing (12-15 ft.) growth; ['Frau Karl Druschki' × unknown]

'Kathleen's Rose' -- See 'Kirkit'

'Kathrinerl' ('Katrinerl') S, rb, Weihrauch, Jürgen; flowers mottled, hand painted, semi-dbl., flat, no fragrance; good spring flush, scattered later bloom; medium growth; ['Gruss an Teplitz' × 'Bonica Meidiland']; intr. 1992?

'Kathryn' S, ab, 1986, Eggeman, H.W.; bud copper; flowers apricot, aging to buff, copper stamens, 4-5 in., 25 petals, open, moderate fruity fragrance; foliage semi-glossy; vigorous growth; ['Wind Chimes' × 'yellow HT']

'Kathryn Bailey' F, w, 1992, Bailey, Dr. Edwin; flowers medium, full, slight fragrance; foliage light green, glossy; some prickles; medium tall, upright growth; [sport of 'Gene Boerner']; intr. 1993

'Kathryn Gram' F, ab, 1945, Moore, Ralph S.; bud urn shaped; flowers large, bushy, low growth; ['Talisman' × unknown]

'Kathryn McGredy' -- See 'Macauclad'

'Kathryn Morley' -- See 'Ausclub'

'Kathy' Min, mr, 1970, Moore, Ralph S.; bud pointed; flowers small, dbl., moderate fragrance; foliage small, leathery; moderate, dwarf, bushy growth; PP3246; ['Little Darling' × 'Magic Wand']

'Kathy Fiscus' F, mp, 1950, Duehrsen; bud ovoid; flowers deep flesh-pink, open, medium, 45 petals, borne in clusters, moderate fragrance; foliage leathery; very vigorous, upright, bushy growth; PP967; [seedling × 'Baby Chateau']

'Kathy Reid'   HRg, m, Sandbrook; intr. 1987

'Kathy Robinson'   Min, pb, 1975, Williams, Ernest D.; flowers pink, creamy reverse, 1 in., 26 petals, high-centered, slight fragrance; foliage small, glossy, dark, embossed; upright, bushy growth; PP3860; ['Little Darling' × 'Over the Rainbow']; intr. 1974

'Kathy Wade'   HT, mp; intr. 2007

'Katie'   LCl, mp, 1960, O'Neal; bud long, pointed; flowers reverse darker, large, 17 petals, cupped, intense fragrance; recurrent bloom; foliage glossy; vigorous growth; ['New Dawn' × 'Crimson Glory']; intr. 1959

'Katie Crocker' -- See 'Burbrindley'

'Katie Prior' -- See 'Worcard'

'Katiroy' -- See 'Eveglitter'

'Katja'   F, dp, J&P; flowers double, rosette, borne in clusters; recurrent; short, compact growth; intr. 2007

'Katkoff'   HP, mr, 1887, Moreau-Robert; flowers cerise red with carmine, tinted currant red, large, full; foliage glossy; ['Charles Lefebvre' × unknown]

'Katrin'   HT, op, GPG Bad Langensalza; flowers salmon-pink, large, dbl.; intr. 1972

Katrin Kron®   S, ab, Huber; flowers dbl., borne singly and in clusters, moderate tea rose fragrance; foliage dark green, glossy; growth to 3-5 ft.; intr. 2002

'Katrina'   HT, op, 1965, Samtmann, Charles; bud pointed; flowers orange-scarlet, medium, dbl., cupped, slight fragrance; foliage glossy, leathery; bushy, vigorous growth; PP2545; [sport of 'Baccará']; intr. 1964

'Katrinerl' -- See 'Kathrinerl'

Katy Girl™ -- See 'Pongirl'

'Katy Lampkin' -- See 'Talkat'

'Katy Mae'   F, w, Pagowski; flowers semi-dbl.; good bloomer; [sport of 'Regensberg']; intr. 2002

'Katy Road Pink' -- See 'Bucbi'

'Kauff' -- See 'Kauth'

'Kauth' ('Kauff') (strain of R. canina), lp; growth sometimes used as understock

'Kavita'   F, pb, 1972, IARI; buds small, pointed; flowers orient-pink with light yellow base, medium, dbl, open, borne in clusters; foliage medium size, soft; growth vigorous, compact, bushy (90 cm.); ['Margaret Spaull' × unknown]

'Kawamoblue' ('Purple Rain') HT, m, 1995, Kawamoto, Hiromoto; bud medium, pointed; flowers mauve, 4-5 in., 24-30 petals, high-centered, borne mostly singly, intense fragrance; good repeat; foliage medium size, dark green, semi-glossy; few prickles; growth upright, medium; PP9987; [seedling × Blue Moon®]; greenhouse rose; intr. 1994

'Kawkasskaja'   HGal, m; bud thick, spherical; flowers magenta to lilac-red, large, very full, dish-shaped, borne in clusters, moderate fragrance; medium strong (5 ft.) growth

'Kay'   F, or, 1971, Delforge; bud ovoid; flowers vermilion, large, dbl., cupped; foliage large, bronze; vigorous, upright growth; [Queen Elizabeth® × 'Numero Un']

'Kay Ann' -- See 'Wilkaya'

'Kay Barnard'   HT, lp, 1974, Dingle; bud long, pointed; flowers pale pink, high-centered; upright growth; ['South Seas' × Queen Elizabeth®]

'Kay Denise' -- See 'Tinkay'

'Kayla' -- See 'Morkay'

'Kaylee Rose'   MinFl, lp, 2001, Kuze, Hugo; flowers small, very full, borne in large clusters, no fragrance; foliage medium size, medium green, matte; prickles 5/8 in., straight, moderate; growth bushy, medium; garden decorative; [sport of 'Red Flush']

'Kayli Joy' -- See 'Brojoy'

'Kazaguruma' ('Pinwheel') F, mr, Keisei; intr. 2000

'Kazanlik'   D, dp, before 1700; flowers deep pink, aging to lighter pink, medium, 30 petals, loose, intense fragrance; foliage soft, light green; growth spindly, tall (2 m.); introduced from Bulgaria by Dr. Dieck about 1900; often assumed to be the same as Trigintipetala

'Kde Domov Muj'   HMult, dp, 1935, Böhm, J.; flowers carmine-pink, lighter at center, 4 cm., semi-dbl. to dbl., borne in clusters of 10-20, slight fragrance

'Kean' ('Shakespeare') HGal, m, before 1843; flowers velvety purple, scarlet crimson center, medium to large, full; growth branching, vigorous; possibly from Laffay or Godefroy; first reference in Verdier's 1843 catalog

'Kebu'   mr

'Keely'   Min, or, 1989, Bridges, Dennis A.; bud pointed; flowers bright, orange-red, reverse slightly darker, aging color fading, 20 petals, high-centered; foliage medium size, medium green, semi-glossy; prickles straight, pointed, medium, red; bushy, medium growth; [Party Girl™ × seedling]; intr. 1989

'Keep in Touch'   F, mr, Harkness; flowers bright red, semi-dbl., borne in clusters; recurrent; compact, low (2½ ft.) growth; intr. 1999

'Keep Smiling'   HT, dy, Fryer; flowers bright, unfading yellow, dbl., moderate fragrance; free-flowering; strong, vigorous (4 ft.) growth; intr. 2004

'Keepit'   HT, lp, Dawson; intr. 1988

'Keepsake'   HT, dr, 1941, Clark, A.; flowers deep red; RULED EXTINCT 7/81; ['Anne Leygues' × unknown]

'Keepsake' -- See 'Kormalda'

'Kees Knoppers'   Pol, w, 1930, Leenders, M.; flowers flesh-white, open, large, semi-dbl., borne in clusters; foliage rich green; vigorous, bushy growth; [sport of 'Mev. Nathalie Nypels']

'Keewatin'   HRg, w, 2002, Olsen, Paul G.; flowers large, semi-dbl., borne in small clusters, moderate fragrance; foliage medium size, gray-green, matte; prickles moderate; upright, tall (150 cm.) growth; ['Henry Hudson' × 'Henry Hudson']; intr. 2002

'Kegon'   HT, mr, 1979, Onodera, Toru F.; bud pointed; flowers deep red, 5 in., 30 petals, high-centered; foliage leathery; tall growth; ['Gruss an Berlin' × 'Christian Dior']; intr. 1976

'Kei'   Min, lp, 1980, Lyon, Lyndon; bud ovoid, pointed; flowers 33 petals, borne 1-3 per cluster; foliage tiny, dark; prickles straight; very compact, bushy growth; [seedling × seedling]; intr. 1979

'Keibelmi' (Shortcake™) Min, rb, 1991, Keisei Rose Nurseries, Inc.; bud ovoid, pointed, short; flowers red, white reverse, red color pales with age, blues slightly, 2 in., 30-35 petals, cupped, borne in flat clusters of 5 - 10, slight fragrance; recurrent; foliage large, dark green, glossy; prickles normal, medium, straight, red to brown; stems short (6 in.), strong; upright, bushy, tall (30 in.) growth; PP8602; [seedling × seedling]; intr. 1991

'Keibian' ('Mademoiselle's Bouquet', French Perfume™) HT, yb, 1993, Suzuki, Seizo; sepals very small, glandular, with soft prickles on reverse; flowers light yellow with rose pink picotee, 5-6½ in., 40-45 petals, borne mostly singly, intense fruity fragrance; foliage large, medium green, purple-red when new, semi-glossy; tall (110-150 cm.), upright, spreading growth; PP8476; [('Todoroki' × 'Montana') × seedling]; intr. 1993

'Keifupie' ('Hime', 'Princess') Min, dp, 1999, Hirabayashi, Hiroshi; flowers bright purplish pink, 1½-2 in., 20-25 petals, flat; foliage dark green, semi-glossy; growth to 10 in.; ['Ko's Yellow' × seedling]; intr. 1997

'Keifupira' ('Urara') F, dp, 1999, Hirabayashi, Hiroshi; flowers pale purplish pink, 3-4 in., 25-30 petals, cupped, no fragrance; foliage dark green, leathery; growth to 2-3 ft.; ['Mimi' × 'Minuette']; intr. 1995

'Keihatakao'   HT, mp, Keisei; intr. 2004

'Keihayanasa'   HT, ob, Keisei; intr. 2004

'Keihayokoki' ('Rose Yokohama') HT, dy, 2000, Hirabayashi, Hiroshi; flowers large, very full, borne mostly singly, moderate tea fragrance; foliage large, dark green, semi-glossy, leathery; numerous prickles; growth upright, medium; [seedling × seedling]

'Keimateo' -- See 'Alliance'

'Keimipia' ('Sayokyoku') Min, lp, 1999, Hirabayashi, Hiroshi; flowers soft pink, 2-2½ in., 45-50 petals, hybrid tea, slight fragrance; foliage dark green, leathery; growth to 1½-2 ft.; ['Sonia' × Petite Folie®]; intr. 1996

'Keimove'   HT, m, Keisei

'Keinoumi'   F, dr, Suzuki, Seizo; bud medium, conical; intr. 1992

'Keireb' (Mahalia™) HT, mr

'Keiren' ('Fairy-Tale') Pol, dp, Keiren; intr. 1995

'Keirofil' HT, w, Keisei; intr. 2004

'Keiromo' ('Silva') HT, op, Keisei

'Keishutoupi' S, lp, Takeuchi ; bud very long and slender; intr. 2008

'Keisola' F, ob, Keisei; intr. 2004

'Keisukita' F, my, Keisei; intr. 2005

'Keitaibu' (Laser™) Gr, dp, Keisei; bud medium, conical

'Keith Harder' HT, m, Harder, K.

'Keith Kirsten' -- See 'Tansirk'

'Keith Maughan' LCl, ab; flowers apricot to buff, fading to near white, yellow stamens, large, single, shallow cup to flat, borne in clusters; recurrent; broad growth; intr. 2008

'Keithie' F, rb

'Keith's Delight' -- See 'Morkeith'

'Keitoli' (FerdyTM®) S, dp, 1984, Suzuki, Seizo; flowers deep pink, small, 20 petals, no fragrance; foliage medium size, medium green, matte; spreading (to 5 ft.) growth; groundcover; ['climbing seedling' × (Petite Folie® × unknown)]

'Keizimba' HT, ob, Keisei; intr. 2004

'Keizoubo' HT, ob, Suzuki. Seizo; bud large, conical; intr. 1991

'Kejgard' ('Color-Guard') LCl, dp, 2002, Jones, Ken; flowers full, borne mostly solitary, moderate fragrance; foliage medium size, dark green, semi-glossy; prickles large, curved, numerous; growth spreading, very vigorous, tall (20-30 ft.); fences; [seedling × 'First Prize']

'Kejunvel' ('Unveiled') Min, pb, 2001, Jones, Ken; flowers light pink, medium yellow reverse, 1½ in., dbl., high-centered, borne mostly solitary, slight fragrance; foliage medium size, medium green, semi-glossy; prickles small, few; growth upright (24-36 in.); garden decorative, exhibition; [sport of 'Incognito']

'Keldaz' (Dazzler™) Min, yb, 1997, Kelly, Martin; flowers medium, light yellow, reverse lighter yellow with light red tips and edges, 1¾ in., dbl., borne mostly singly; foliage medium size, dark green, semi-glossy; upright, medium growth; PP10333; [Rainbow's End™ × Kristin™]; intr. 1998

'Kelleriis-Rose' -- See 'Poulsen's Supreme'

'Kelli Ann' Min, w, 1982, Dobbs, Annette E.; flowers small, 35 petals, slight fragrance; foliage small, medium green, matte; bushy growth; ['Patricia Scranton' × ('Patricia Scranton' × 'Fairy Moss')]; intr. 1981

'Kelly Country' LCl, pb, Sutherland; intr. 1997

'Kelly-Leigh' -- See 'Stekelly-Leigh'

'Kelly Reynolds' -- See 'Reykelly'

'Kempton Park' -- See 'Dorobla'

'Ken Davis' -- See 'Geldavis'

'Ken n Norma' -- See 'Horbabapapa'

'Ken Simmonds' HT, ab, Fryer's; flowers golden apricot, turning amber with age, large, double, high-centered, slow opening, borne singly and in clusters of several together, moderate fragrance; recurrent; strong, vigorous (3 ft.), branching growth; intr. 2007

'Kenbrog' ('Marian Finnucane') MinFl, dr, 2007, Kenny, David; flowers brownish-red, reverse red, small, 7.5 cm., dbl., borne in small clusters; foliage small, medium green, semi-glossy; prickles small, straight, brown, moderate; growth compact, bushy, short (60 cm.); bedding; [Shine On™ × 'Maestro']; very novel color; intr. 2006

'Kencream' ('Irish Rose of India') F, w, 2001, Kenny, David; flowers cream with soft yellow center, white reverse, medium, full, borne in small clusters, slight fragrance; foliage medium size, medium green, semi-glossy; prickles medium, hooked, few; growth bushy, medium; garden decorative; [('Mary Sumner' × 'Kiskadee') × 'Spek's Centennial']

'Kendad' ('May Graham') F, ab, 1996, Kenny, David; flowers coppery apricot, fading to pink, medium, 26 petals, borne in small clusters, slight fragrance; foliage medium size, medium green, glossy; numerous prickles; medium (3½ ft.), bushy growth; [Prominent® × 'Kiskadee']

'Kendanqu' ('Wiggy') F, or, 1993, Kenny, David; flowers orange-red with cerise, medium, full, borne in small clusters; foliage medium size, dark green, semi-glossy; some prickles; tall (90 cm.), upright, bushy growth; [(Prominent® × 'Kiskadee') × ('Mary Sumner' × 'Kiskadee')]; intr. 1993

'Kendixie' ('Róisín Ruddle') S, ob, 2004, Kenny, David; flowers orange, reverse orange/yellow, 2½ cm., dbl., borne in large clusters, no fragrance; continuous; foliage light green, matte; prickles small, pointed,; bushy, spreading, short growth; patio, groundcover; ['Mr.J.C.B.' × 'Pathfinder']

'Kenedel' ('Doris Read') S, ab, 2007, Kenny, David; flowers apricot-pink, reverse apricot, small, 4 cm., single, borne mostly solitary; prickles medium, straight, brown, moderate; growth to 120 cm.; beds, borders, hedges; ['DICyeti' × 'Jane Eyre']; intr. 2006

'Kenenchan' ('Nellie Deaser') F, ab, 2001, Kenny, David; flowers old-fashioned, apricot blend fading to cream, 3 in., very full, borne in large clusters; foliage medium size, dark green (red when young), matte; prickles large, hooked, moderate; growth upright, bushy, tall (4 ft.); garden decorative; [Sexy Rexy® × 'Wiggy']

'Kenesca' ('Treasured Memories') F, yb, 2001, Kenny, David; flowers red, petals edged with yellow, 3 in., dbl., borne in large clusters, moderate fragrance; foliage medium size, dark green, glossy; growth bushy, medium (3 ft.); garden decorative; ['Golden Wedding' × Bright Smile®]

'Kenetern' ('Mount Temple') F, my, 2001, Kenny, David; flowers bright lemon yellow, full, high-centered, borne in large clusters; foliage medium size, dark green (purple when young), semi-glossy; prickles large, pointed, moderate; growth upright, bushy, medium (3½ ft.); garden decorative; ['Golden Wedding' × Bright Smile®]

'Kenfine' ('Riverdance') Min, dp, 1997, Kenny, David; flowers medium, dbl., borne in small clusters, moderate fragrance; foliage small, medium green, glossy; bushy, medium (28 in.) growth; ['MEIdomonac' × Freegold®]

'Kengirl' ('Brendan Maguire') F, or, 2004, Kenny, David; flowers orange-red, reverse yellow, 7½ cm., dbl., borne in small clusters, slight fragrance; foliage large, dark green, glossy, disease-resistant; prickles medium, hooked; growth upright, tall (120 cm); garden decoration; [Laura Ford® × 'Fellowship']; intr. 2006

'Kenhandon' ('Ellie Johnson') MinFl, my, 2007, Kenny, David; flowers small, 5 cm., dbl., borne in small clusters; foliage dark green, glossy, disease-resistant; prickles small, straight, brown, moderate; growth compact, bushy, short (60 cm.); bedding, borders; ['Golden Handshake' × Shine On™]; intr. 2007

'Kenicma' ('Fiona Lynch') F, w, 2003, Kenny, David; bud soft yellow; flowers creamy yellow-white, reverse creamy yellow, fading to white, 3 in., dbl., borne in small clusters; foliage medium size, light green, semi-glossy; prickles small, hooked, brown, moderate; growth bushy, 75 × 75 cm.; [('Aunty Lil' × 'Rock'n Roll') × 'Kate Emily McCormack']; intr. 2004

'Kenlimon' ('Aaron Dean') F, ly, 2007, Kenny, David; flowers lemon yellow, 2½ in., single, borne mostly solitary; prickles medium, semi-hooked, light brown, moderate; growth to 120 cm.; ['Dicyeti' × 'The Arboretum Rose']; intr. 2007

'Kenly' ('Mary Cullen') S, dr, 2001, Kenny, David; flowers old-fashioned, 5 in., full, quartered, borne in small clusters, slight fragrance; foliage large, dark green, glossy; prickles large, slightly hooked, numerous; growth spreading, tall (5 ft.); garden decorative; [Laura Ford® × 'Phantom']

'Kenmacho' ('Kate Emily McCormack') F, rb, 1999, Kenny, David; flowers red, pink to white edges,handpainted with white eye, reverse silver, 3 in., 8-14 petals, borne in large clusters; foliage large, dark green, glossy; numerous prickles; spreading, bushy, tall (4 ft.) growth; [(('Mary Sumner' × 'Kiskadee') × Bassino®) × Little Artist®]

'Kenmado' ('Sister Joan') F, op, 1997, Kenny, David; flowers large, dbl., borne in small clusters; foliage large, dark green, semi-glossy; some prickles; upright, bushy, tall (3½ × 2½ ft.) growth; [('Mary Sumner' × 'Kiskadee') × 'Maestro']

'Kenmajes' ('Michael Flatley') F, ob, 2003, Kenny, David; flowers deep peach, reverse orange-salmon, 2½ in., dbl., borne in large clusters, moderate fragrance; foliage small, medium green, matte; prickles small, pointed, few; growth upright, medium (3 ft.); garden; ['Benita' × ('Mary Sumner' × 'Kiskadee')]; intr. 2002

'Kenmasnia' ('Aunty Lil') F, yb, 1995, Kenny, David; flowers yellow edged pink, fades to pink, medium, full, borne in large clusters, slight fragrance; foliage medium size, medium green, glossy; some prickles; medium, upright growth; [(('Friesia' × 'Kiskadee') × ('Mary Sumner' × Regensberg®)]; intr. 1994

'Kenmigqui' ('Margaret Lucas') F, w, 2001, Kenny, David; flowers white with pink edge, 3 in., semi-dbl., borne in large clusters, slight fragrance; foliage small, medium green, semi-glossy; prickles small, straight, moderate; growth upright, tall; garden decorative; ['Bonica' × 'Solitaire']

'Kenmoll' ('Tessa O'Keeffe') F, dy, 1999, Kenny, David; flowers 3 in., dbl., borne in small clusters; foliage medium size, dark green, glossy; few prickles; bushy, medium (30 in.) growth; ['Friesia' × 'Kiskadee']

'Kenmore' HT, dy, 1971, Macara; flowers deep yellow, 4½ in., 36 petals; foliage glossy; ['Jane Lazenby' × 'Golden Delight']

'Kennash' ('Patricia Eileen Adams') HT, mp, 2000, Kenny, David; flowers salmon pink, reverse lighter, 4 in., dbl., borne in small clusters, moderate fragrance; foliage medium size, dark green, glossy; prickles moderate; growth bushy, medium (2½ ft.); [('Avocet' × (Prominent® × 'Kiskadee')) × 'New Zealand']

'Kenneth Vincent Orpe Taylor' -- See 'Woramy'

'Kenniece' ('James Power') HT, ab, 2007, Kenny, David; flowers apricot, reverse apricot-pink, large, 5 in., dbl., borne in small clusters; foliage large, dark green, matte; prickles large, straight, red, moderate; growth upright, tall; ['Mount Temple' × 'Sr. Joan']; intr. 2008

'Kennorma' ('Ken n Norma') HT, mp, 2002, Horner, Colin P.; intr. 2003

'Kenny's Rose' -- See 'Gelken'

'Kenobsess' ('Audrey McCormack') F, ab, 1999, Kenny, David; flowers soft apricot yellow, 3 in., full, borne in large clusters, moderate fragrance; foliage large, medium green, glossy; numerous prickles; spreading, bushy, medium (3 ft.) growth; ['Golden Wedding' × Bright Smile®]

'Kenora Duet' F, ab, 1977, Tresise; bud long, pointed; flowers salmon-pink, open, medium, semi-dbl., slight fragrance; foliage glossy; vigorous, bushy growth; [sport of 'Duet']

'Kenpass' ('Castle Hyde') S, dr, 2001, Kenny, David; flowers dark velvety red, old fashioned, 4 in., full, borne in small clusters; foliage large, medium green (light green when young), semi-glossy; prickles large, hooked, numerous; growth spreading, bushy, tall (4 ft.); garden decorative; [(('Mary Sumner' × 'Kiskadee') × Bassino®) × 'Purple TIger']

'Kenposh' ('Garry Moore') S, mr, 2007, Kenny, David; flowers small, 5 cm., semi-dbl., borne in large clusters; foliage small, dark green, semi-glossy; prickles small, hooked, brown, moderate; growth bushy, spreading, medium (90 cm.); borders, hedges; ['Phantom' × Laura Ford®]; intr. 2006

'Kenrapp' MinFl, rb, 2007, Kenny, David; flowers red with yellow eye, reverse yellow, small, 1 in., semi-dbl., borne in large clusters; foliage small, dark green, semi-glossy, disease-resistant; prickles small, straight, brown, moderate; growth compact, bushy, short (20 in.); containers, bedding, borders; ['Horcoffitup' × 'Pathfinder']; intr. 2007

'Kenrhapso' ('Stardust Memory', 'Treasured Moments') F, ab, 2001, Kenny, David; flowers apricot with apricot/pink reverse, old-fashioned, 3 in., full, flat, borne in small clusters, moderate fragrance; foliage medium size, medium green, glossy; prickles moderate, medium, straight; growth bushy, medium; garden decorative; [Sexy Rexy® × ('Mary Sumner' × 'Kiskadee')]

'Kenseles' ('Le Masquerade en Villefranche') F, pb, 2006, Kenny, David; flowers pink to light apricot, reverse pink, 3 in., dbl., borne in small clusters; foliage medium size, light green, glossy; prickles small, pointed, brown, moderate; growth bushy, upright, medium (3 ft.); ['HORcoherent' × 'Rock'n Roll × Aunty Lil']; intr. 2007

'Kensheco' ('The Merrion Rose') MinFl, rb, 2003, Kenny, David; flowers pink/red with yellow eye, reverse yellow, 2 in., single, borne in large clusters, slight fragrance; continuous; foliage small, medium green, semi-glossy; prickles small, hooked downward, light brown; growth spreading, medium (2 ft. × 2 ft.); patio, containers; [New Year® × 'Eyeopener']; intr. 2004

'Kensingso' ('Mary Swindells') F, op, 1995, Kenny, David; flowers salmon pink, medium, full, borne in small clusters; foliage medium size, dark green, glossy; numerous prickles; tall, upright, bushy growth; [('Mary Sumner' × 'Kiskadee') × ('Mary Sumner' × Regensberg®)]; intr. 1990

Kensington™ F, dr, Olesen; bud pointed ovoid; flowers , 40-45 petals, open cup, borne in small clusters, slight fragrance; recurrent; foliage dark green, semi-glossy; prickles numerous, 6 mm., hooked downward, greyed-purple; vigorous, upright to bushy (60-100 cm.) growth; PP15288; [seedling × 'Redwood']; intr. 2002

'Kensoixnu' ('Dan Rafter') HT, mp, 2007, Kenny, David; flowers medium, 5 cm., dbl., borne singly and in small clusters; foliage medium green, semi-glossy; prickles medium, pointed, brown, moderate; growth upright, bushy, tall (120 cm.); bedding; ['DICzombie' × 'FRYromeo']; intr. 2006

'Kenspigi' ('Rose Atieno') S, or, 2007, Kenny, David; flowers deep orange red, reverse orange red, medium, 3 in., semi-dbl., borne in large clusters; foliage medium, dark green, glossy; prickles large, straight, brown, moderate; growth upright, tall (180 cm.); garden decoration; ['Phantom' × Laura Ford®]; intr. 2008

Kent™ ('Sparkler', Latina™, Pyrenees™, Sparkling White™, White Cover™) S, w, Olesen; bud ovate; flowers clear white, bright yellow stamens, 1½ in., 10-15 petals, flat, borne singly and in clusters, very slight fragrance; free-flowering; foliage medium green, semi-glossy; prickles some, 6 mm., hooked downward, brown; growth arching, compact, spreading, low (60-100 cm.); hips few, small ; PP10648; intr. 1991

'Kentfield' Pol, mp, 1922, Diener; flowers soft cameo-pink to deeper pink, small, dbl.; ['Cécile Brunner' × seedling]

'Kentrib' ('Timmy Williams') F, or, 2001, Kenny, David; flowers orange/salmon, orange reverse, 3 in., dbl., borne in small clusters; foliage medium size, medium green (red when young), semi-glossy; prickles medium, hooked, moderate; growth upright, bushy, medium (3 ft.); garden decorative; [('Mary Sumner' × 'Kiskadee') × 'Spek's Centennial']

'Kentucky' HT, w, Select; intr. about 1995

'Kentucky Derby' HT, dr, 1972, Armstrong, D.L.; flowers large, dbl., high-centered, slight fragrance; foliage large, glossy, leathery; vigorous, upright, bushy growth; PP3303; ['John S. Armstrong' × 'Grand Slam']

'Kenyacker' ('Valerie') HT, ly, 2007, Kenny, David; flowers lemon yellow, deeper yellow in the autumn, 6 in., dbl., borne mostly solitary; foliage large, medium green, semi-glossy; prickles large, hooked, reddish-brown, moderate; growth upright, bushy, tall (135cm.); ['Maria McGredy' × 'Simply Heaven']; intr. 2007

'Kerfany' F, dp; intr. 2005

'Kerry Anne' -- See 'Bosfordlish'

'Kerry Gold' F, yb, 1967, Dickson, A.; flowers canary-yellow, outer petals veined red, 3 in., globular, borne in clusters; foliage dark; ['Circus' × Allgold®]

'Kerry MacNeil' F, mr, 1967, Vincent; flowers bright vermilion; free growth; [Orangeade® × 'Anna Wheatcroft']

Kerryman® F, pb, 1971, McGredy, Sam IV; flowers salmon and pink, 4½ in., 24 petals, high-centered; ['Paddy McGredy' × ('Mme Léon Cuny' × 'Columbine')]

'Kersbergen' Pol, mr, 1927, Kersbergen; flowers bright currant-red, very small, full, borne in clusters; free-flowering; [sport of 'Miss Edith Cavell']

'Kesri' F, or, 1971, Singh; bud ovoid; flowers orient orange, small, dbl., open, slight fragrance; foliage leathery; vigorous growth; ['Orangeade, Climbing' × unknown]; intr. 1969

'Kessi' S, mp, Schultheis; flowers bright carmine rose, dbl., borne in clusters; free-flowering; spreading, low (2 ft.) growth; intr. 2000

Kessy® ('Tanyssek') HT, yb, Tantau; flowers peach-yellow with reddish hues, full, high-centered, borne singly and in clusters; good repeat; prickles moderate; stems upright, strong; intr. before 1993

'Ketje' HT, mr, 1938, Lens; bud pointed; flowers brilliant red mixed dark pink, well-formed, very dbl.; foliage bronze; very vigorous growth; ['Mrs Sam McGredy' × 'E.G. Hill']

'Kev' -- See 'Talkev'

'Kevin' HT, dp, Twomey, Jerry; intr. 1997

'Kew Beauty' HT, dr, 1918, Therkildsen; flowers crimson, dbl.

'Kew Rambler' HMult, mp, 1913, Royal Botanic Gardens, Kew; flowers pink, center paler, 4 cm., single, borne in large clusters, moderate fragrance; foliage gray-green; growth to 15 ft.; [*R. soulieana* × 'Hiawatha']

'Kewai' HT, yb, 1997, Ohtsuki, Hironaka; flowers yellow with orange-yellow center, 5 in., full; foliage medium size, medium green, semi-glossy; few prickles; upright, bushy, medium (6 ft.) growth; ['Izayoi' × 'Golden Emblem']; intr. 1997

Key Largo™ -- See 'Jacsall'

'Key Rock Rose' Misc OGR, yb

Key West™ (Cherry Cover®) S, dp, Poulsen; bud elongated, pointed-ovoid; flowers deep pink to light red, 3 in., 12-14 petals, shallow cup to flat , borne in clusters of 5 - 10, slight floral fragrance; recurrent; foliage dark green, glossy, leathery; prickles moderate, 3-5 cm., concave, brown; vigorous, compact (2 ft.) growth; PP13450; ['Mystic' × seedling]; intr. 2000

'Keystone' LCl, dy, 1904, Dingee & Conard; flowers deep lemon-yellow

'Ki Ki Paquel' F, or, 1960, Moreira da Silva; flowers bright brick color; ['SuperCongo' × 'Independence']

'Kia Ora' -- See 'Suncral'

'Kia Ora' F, or, 1962, Mason, P.G.; flowers orange-scarlet, large, 35 petals; foliage glossy, dark; vigorous, bushy, compact growth; ['Independence' × 'Independence']

'Kiboh' ('Gypsy Carnival', 'Hope', 'Lovita', 'Gypsy') F, rb, 1986, Suzuki, Seizo; flowers orange-red, reverse yellowish, large, 50 petals, high-centered, borne in clusters of 3; foliage dark, semi-glossy; prickles slanted downward; vigorous, upright growth; PP7139; ['Liberty Bell' × 'Kagayaki']

'Kibune' HT, rb, Keisei; flowers deep red with yellow base, large, exhibition

'Kickapoo' HT, rb, 1990, Stoddard, Louis; bud ovoid; flowers yellow, outer petals red, white reverse aging to light red blend, 20 petals; foliage medium size, medium green, dull; prickles straight, green aging to tan; bushy, medium, slightly spreading growth; hips round, green to light yellow; [('Daisy Mae' × 'First Prize') × seedling]

'Kickoff' HT, mr, Teranishi; intr. 2005

'Kiddy' Pol, mr, 1967, Delforge; bud pointed; flowers dark red, becoming brighter, medium, single, cupped; abundant, recurrent bloom; foliage glossy; vigorous, upright growth; ['Mme Dieudonne' × seedling]

'Kidwai' -- See 'Kidway'

'Kidway' ('Kidwai') HT, mp, 1933, Pernet-Ducher; bud long, pointed; flowers salmon-rose, lower half of petals golden yellow, large, semi-dbl.; foliage leathery, dark, bronze, glossy; very vigorous, bushy growth

'Kieran Ross Clark' -- See 'Horanyme'

'Kieran's Rose' -- See 'Agulily'

'Kiese' -- See 'Kiese's Unterlage'

'Kiese's Unterlage' ('Kiese') S, mr, 1910, Kiese; flowers bright red, medium, single to semi-dbl.; ['Général Jacqueminot' × *R. canina*]; hybrid canina

'Kiftsgate' Sp, w, 1954; flowers creamy white, 5 petals, borne in large clusters, moderate fragrance; very vigorous, sprawling growth; *R. filipes* form

'Kiftsgate Violett' S, m; flowers whitish-violet, small, single, shallow cup, borne in large clusters, moderate fragrance; non-remontant; strong (8-10 m.) growth

'Kiftsgate × Violet Hood' S, m, Lens; flowers violet, small, heavy spring bloom; once bloomer; tall (to 10 ft.)

'Kihachijou' HT, ob, Hiroshima; flowers striped; intr. 2005

'Kika' -- See 'Ortkee'

Kiki® F, ab, Select; flowers 9 cm., 30-35 petals, high-centered, borne mostly singly; stems 20 - 28 in; cut flower rose; intr. 2003

'Kiki' HT, Dorieux, Francois; intr. 1972

'Kiki Paquel' Gr, Moreira da Silva, A.; intr. 1960

Kiki Rose™ -- See 'Poulcat'

'Kiko' -- See 'Jacdeep'

'Kilbreda Centenary' HT, mr, 2007, Chapman, Bruce; flowers 9 cm., dbl., blooms borne singly and in small clusters; foliage large, dark green, semi-glossy; prickles medium, hooked, brown, few; growth compact, medium (1¼ m.); garden decoration; ['Kardinal' × 'Aotearoa']; intr. 2005

'Kilimanjaro' HT, w, 1977, Herholdt, J.A.; bud pointed; flowers pure white, 4½-5 in., 35-38 petals; foliage rich green; vigorous growth; [seedling × Pascali®]

'Kilkea Castle' S, pb, McCann, Sean; recurrent; intr. 2004

'Killarney' HT, mp, 1898, Dickson, A.; bud long, pointed; flowers bright medium pink, loose, large, dbl.; foliage bronze; ['Mrs W.J. Grant' × 'Charles J. Grahame']

'Killarney, Climbing' Cl HT, mp, 1908, Reinberg; [sport of 'Killarney']

'Killarney Brilliant' HT, dp, 1914, Dickson, A.; bud long, pointed; flowers brilliant pink to rosy carmine, open, dbl.; foliage rich green, soft; [sport of 'Killarney']

'Killarney Double Pink' HT, mp, 1935, Vestal; flowers sparkling shell-pink; [sport of 'Killarney Double White']

'Killarney Double White, Climbing' Cl HT, w, 1935, Howard Rose Co.

'Killarney Double White' ('Double White Killarney') HT, w, 1912, Budlong; flowers snowy white; [sport of 'Killarney']

'Killarney Queen' HT, dp, 1912, Budlong; flowers Tyrian rose, brighter than killarney; [sport of 'Killarney']

'Kilmore Rose' HRg, p, 2003, Collins, Leon; flowers dbl., borne in small clusters; foliage medium size, dark green, glossy; prickles small, hooked downwards,; growth bushy, medium (4 ft.); hedging, specimen; [*R. rugosa alba* × unknown]; intr. 2003

'Kilwinning' HSpn, w, Wright, Percy H.; foliage fern like; [*R. spinosissima altaica* × 'Hansen's Yellow']

'Kilworth Gold' HT, dy, 1977, Gandy, Douglas L.; flowers golden yellow, 28 petals, borne singly and several together, moderate fragrance; free-flowering; foliage large, dark green; bushy growth; [sport of 'Whisky Mac']

'Kilworth Pride' F, dr, 1955, deRuiter; flowers semi-dbl., borne in clusters; foliage bronze; dwarf, bushy growth; ['Better Times' × 'floribunda seedling']

'Kim' Pol, mp, 1956, Buyl Frères; flowers geranium-rose, small, borne in clusters; vigorous growth; ['Independence' × 'Salmon Perfection']

'Kim' F, my, Harkness; flowers 3 in., 28 petals; foliage small, light green, matte; dwarf growth; [(Orange Sensation® × Allgold®) × Elizabeth of Glamis®]; intr. 1971

'Kim Peters' -- See 'Worangry'

'Kim Rupert' -- See 'Moruncommon'

Kimberley™ ('Kimberley Hit') S, dp, Poulsen; flowers deep pink, 8-10 cm., dbl., slight fragrance; foliage dark; growth bushy, 20-40 cm.; PP15621; intr. 2002

'Kimberley Anne' HT, w, 1984, Evans, F. David; flowers large, 35 petals, intense fragrance; foliage medium size, medium green, matte; upright growth; ['Virgo' × 'Secret Love']

'Kimberley Hit' -- See 'Poulhi017(N)'

Kimberlina™ -- See 'Jacpoulp'

'Kimberly' -- See 'Mickim'

'Kimbo' F, Pineau; intr. 1977

'Kimmy' F, rb, Laperriere, L.; flowers brilliant red tinted red-orange, dbl.; growth to 60-70 cm.; intr. 1975

'Kimono, Climbing' Cl F, pb; [sport of 'Kimono']; intr. after 1962

Kimono® F, pb, 1962, deRuiter; flowers salmon-pink, 3 in., 30 petals, borne in broad clusters, moderate fragrance; vigorous, bushy growth; ['Cocorico' × 'Frau Anny Beaufays']

Kim's Cream™ -- See 'Rupkimcrm'

'Kinash' (Baby Ashley™) Min, yb, 1985, King, Gene; flowers light yellow, petals edged light pink, 24 petals, borne singly and in cluster of 3-5; foliage small, dark, matte; prickles straight, small, light brown; bushy growth

'Kinbarb' (Barbara Mandrell™) Min, ab, 1991, King, Gene; bud pointed; flowers dark apricot changing to apricot-pink at 3/4 open, yellow base, aging to white, medium, 28 petals, high-centered, borne singly or in sprays of 3 - 10, slight fragrance; foliage medium size, medium green, matte; prickles medium, dark brown; bushy, medium growth; [(seedling × Party Girl™) × Party Girl™]; intr. 1990

'Kinbay' (Tampa Bay™) Min, ob, 1989, King, Gene; bud pointed; flowers orange, edges aging darker, medium, 18 petals, high-centered, borne singly, slight fruity fragrance; foliage medium size, medium green, matte; prickles straight, red; growth upright, medium; hips ovoid, orange; [('Arthur Bell' × 'Orange Honey') × Baby Diana™]; intr. 1988

'Kinbee' (B. C.™) Min, dr, 1986, King, Gene; flowers dark red, reverse darker, 24 petals, high-centered; foliage small, medium green, matte; prickles long, hooked, brown; medium, upright, bushy growth; globular fruit; ['Evelyn Fison' × 'Magic Mist']

'Kinbelle' (Rosa Belle™) Min, dp, 1988, King, Gene; flowers deep pink to yellow-cream at base, medium, 21 petals, high-centered, borne usually singly; foliage medium size, medium green, matte; prickles straight with hook, few, dark brown; bushy, medium growth; no fruit; ['Vera Dalton' × Party Girl™]

'Kinbo' (Tobo™) Min, dy, 1989, King, Gene; bud pointed; flowers medium, 32 petals, high-centered, borne singly and in small clusters, slight fruity fragrance; recurrent; foliage medium size, light green, matte; prickles straight, slightly crooked, red to brown; upright, bushy, medium growth; hips ovoid, green; ['Arthur Bell' × 'Rise 'n' Shine']

'Kinbosco' (Boscobel™) Min, ob, 1991, King, Gene; flowers orange to burnt orange, small, dbl., borne mostly singly, no fragrance; foliage medium size, light green, matte; upright, medium growth; [('Cheers' × Rainbow's End™) × Breezy™]

'Kinbud' (Just Buddy™) Min, ly, 1985, King, Gene; flowers mini-flora, large, 45 petals, high-centered, borne singly; foliage medium size, light green, matte; prickles straight, light brown; medium upright, bushy growth; no hips; ['New Day' × 'Rise 'n' Shine']; intr. 1986

'Kinbuff' (Buffy™) Min, ab, 1987, King, Gene; flowers light apricot, reverse deeper, darker towards center, medium, 20 petals, high-centered, slight fragrance; foliage medium green, matte; prickles slightly hooked, light brown; mini-flora; bushy spreading growth; hips oval, green; ['Vera Dalton' × Party Girl™]; intr. 1987

'Kincap' (Captivation™) Min, or, 1991, King, Gene; flowers medium, full, borne mostly singly, slight fragrance; foliage medium size, light green, matte; some prickles; upright (60-70 cm.), bushy growth; [('Arthur Bell' × Little Jackie™) × Little Jackie™]; intr. 1992

'Kincha' (Charlie™) Min, mr, 1984, King, Gene; flowers small, 35 petals, high-centered; foliage small, dark, matte; upright, bushy growth; [seedling × 'Big John']

'Kinclaire' (Mollie Claire™) Min, w, 1989, King, Gene; bud pointed; flowers white, pink edge blushing toward center, reverse white tipped, 28 petals, high-centered; foliage small, medium green, matte; prickles crooked,very few, white to brown; bushy, low growth; no fruit; [('Evelyn Fison' × 'Magic Mist') × Baby Diana™]

'Kincoach' (Stagecoach™) Min, op, 1987, King, Gene; flowers medium salmon pink, medium, 18 petals, high-centered, borne usually singly or in sprays of 3-5; foliage medium size, light green, matte; prickles straight, white; upright, spreading growth; hips oval, green; ['Vera Dalton' × 'Orange Honey']; intr. 1987

'Kind Regards' F, mr, Pearce; intr. 1995

'Kind Regards' F, mr, 1956, Kordes; flowers crimson-red, very large, dbl., borne in clusters; free-flowering; vigorous, bushy growth

'Kindiddy' (Pink Diddy™) Min, mp, 1991, King, Gene; bud pointed; flowers medium, 28 petals, cupped, slight fruity fragrance; foliage small, medium green, semi-glossy; bushy, spreading, low growth; [(('B.C.' × Scamp) × Miss Dovey™) × Tudelum™]; intr. 1990

'Kindixie' (Dixie Dazzle™) Min, ob, 1991, King, Gene; bud ovoid; flowers orange-red to yellow, small, 16 petals, high-centered, no fragrance; foliage small, medium green, semi-glossy; upright, low growth; [(Rainbow's End™ × Miss Dovey™) × Jennie Anne™]; intr. 1990

'Kindness' HT, dp, Certified; flowers , high-centered, slight fragrance; intr. 1994

'Kindov' (Miss Dovey™) Min, ab, 1985, King, Gene; flowers deep apricot, 21 petals, high-centered, borne usually singly; foliage medium size, medium green, semi-glossy; prickles straight, reddish-brown; upright, bushy growth; sets hips; [Anne Harkness® × 'Rise 'n' Shine']

'Kinfancy' (Fancy Pants™) Min, rb, 1987, King, Gene; flowers deep pink to golden yellow base, edged red, fading deeper pink, 40 petals, high-centered, slight spicy fragrance; foliage medium size, medium green, matte; prickles medium, light red, slightly crooked on end; upright, bushy, medium growth; fruit not observed; [Baby Katie™ × 'Rose Window']; intr. 1987

'Kinfanta' (Fantasi™) MinFl, w, 1986, King, Gene; flowers cream, reverse cream shaded deep pink, large, 50 petals, high-centered, slight fragrance; foliage medium size, dark, matte; prickles medium, hooked, brown; tall, upright growth; no fruit; intr. 1985

'King Alexander I' -- See 'Roi Alexandre'

'King Arthur' -- See 'Harverag'

'King Arthur' F, op, 1967, Harkness; flowers salmon-pink, large, dbl., borne in clusters; foliage glossy; ['Pink Parfait' × 'Highlight']

King Arthur® HT, mp, Spek; flowers pastel pink, darker guard petals, 10-11 cm., 55-65 petals, cupped; recurrent; numerous prickles; stems medium to long; florist rose; intr. 2006

'King Boreas' F, my, 1941, Brownell; flowers pure yellow shading to nearly white, recurved, medium, 100 petals, moderate fragrance; vigorous growth; ['Golden Glow' × unknown]

'King Crimson' -- See 'Jacshur'

'King David' -- See 'Tanmarsa'

'King David' HP, 1910, California Rose Co.; [sport of 'Vick's Caprice']

'King Edward' HT, dr, Laver; flowers dbl., high-centered, no fragrance; good repeat; vigorous, medium (3 ft.) growth; intr. 2002

'King George IV' -- See 'Rivers' George IV'

'King George V' HP, dr, 1912, Dickson, H.; flowers crimson, large, 40 petals, high-centered; sparse, intermittent bloom; strong stems; very vigorous, open growth

'King George's Memorial' -- See 'Památnik Krále Jiriho'

'King Henry' -- See 'Genwine'

'King Hey' S, dr

'King J.' HRg, w, 1996, Fleming, Joyce L.; flowers yellow stamens, dbl., borne in small clusters, intense spicy fragrance; good repeat; foliage dark green, glossy, very healthy, disease/insect resistant; numerous prickles; growth bushy, medium; hardy to -10°F; [R. rugosa alba × 'Assiniboine']; intr. 1989

King Kong+ HT, ab, Voom, Lex; flowers apricot pink , double, high-centered, borne mostly singly; recurrent; stems medium to long; florist rose

'King Midas' LCl, my, 1942, Nicolas; bud long, pointed; flowers clear yellow, 4-5 in., 20 petals, cupped, borne in clusters of 4-6, slight fragrance; repeat bloom; foliage large, leathery, dark; vigorous, climbing or pillar (8-10 ft.) growth; PP586

'King o' Kings' HT, mr, 1973, Anderson's Rose Nurseries; flowers 6 in., 35-40 petals, high-centered; foliage dark; ['My Love' × 'Duftwolke']

'King of Hearts' HT, mr, 1968, McGredy, Sam IV; bud long, pointed; flowers medium, dbl., high-centered; foliage dark, leathery; vigorous, bushy growth; PP3091; ['Karl Herbst' × 'Ethel Sanday']

'King of Scotland' -- See 'King of Scots'

'King of Scots' ('King of Scotland', 'Large Double Two-Coloured', 'Roi d'Écosse') HSpn, dp, 1803, Brown, R.; flowers deep rosy purple-pink to red, pale reverse, medium, semi-dbl.; profuse, early bloom; foliage finely divided; dense, shrubby (3-4 ft.) growth; hips glossy, black

'King of Siam' HT, mr, 1912, Bräuer; flowers large, full; ['Mme Victor Verdier' × 'Safrano']

'King of Sweden' -- See 'Oscar II, Roi de Suéde'

'King of the Prairies' HSet, mr, 1843, Feast; flowers bright red

'King Richard' -- See 'Genruby'

'King Tut' Bailey, Dorothy J., Bailey, Dorothy J.; PP4396

'King Tut' -- See 'Lavtrek'

'King Tut' -- See 'Chewarvel'

'King William' -- See 'Genpink'

'Kingaroy' HT, dr, 1980, Perry, Astor; bud long, pointed; flowers 30 petals, urn-shaped, borne singly, slight fruity fragrance; foliage medium size, matte; prickles small; medium growth; [seedling × 'Red Lion']; intr. 1981

'Kingcup' HT, my, 1953, LeGrice; flowers buttercup-yellow, well-formed, 4 in., 40 petals, intense fruity fragrance; foliage dark, glossy; very free growth; ['Mrs Sam McGredy' × 'Ellinor LeGrice']

'Kingdon Ward No. 3505' Sp, dp; a form of R. pendulina oxyodon

'Kingdon Ward No. 6101' Sp, w; a form of R. pendulina oxyodon with cream-colored flowers and fern-like foliage

'Kingi' -- See 'Murki'

'Kingig' ('Giggles') Min, mp, 1987, King, Gene; flowers light pink, reverse light to dark pink, fading to creamy pink, 18 petals, high-centered; foliage medium size, medium green, matte; prickles slightly crooked, white; upright, tall growth; hips oval, green; ['Vera Dalton' × 'Rose Window']

'Kinglow' ('Glowry™') Min, ob, 1989, King, Gene; bud pointed; flowers bright orange-yellow bicolor, medium, 24 petals, high-centered, borne singly; foliage small, medium green, matte; prickles straight, red; bushy, low growth; no fruit; [('Arthur Bell' × 'Orange Honey') × Baby Diana™]

'King's Acre' HP, rb, 1864, Cranston; flowers dusty scarlet, reverse flesh pink, large, full

'King's Macc' HT, ab, Fryer; flowers yellow-apricot blend, beautifully formed, dbl., strong fragrance; repeats well; foliage dark green; upright (3 ft.) growth; intr. 2003

'King's Mountain' -- See 'Briking'

King's Ransom® HT, dy, 1961, Morey, Dr. Dennison; bud ovoid; flowers clear golden yellow, 5-6 in., 38 petals, high-centered, moderate fragrance; foliage leathery, glossy; vigorous, upright growth; PP2103; ['Golden Masterpiece' × 'Lydia']; intr. 1961

'King's Row' S, yb, 1965, Whisler; flowers yellow becoming rose-red, medium, dbl., borne in clusters, moderate fragrance; foliage bronze, leathery; vigorous (4 ft.), compact growth; PP2593; ['Easter Parade' × 'Herrenhausen']

'King's Treasure' F, my, Williams, J. Benjamin; intr. 1995

'Kingsmead Heritage' -- See 'Kordalsilk'

'Kingswood College' -- See 'Korloher'

'Kingun' (Top Gun™) Min, pb, 1990, King, Gene; bud pointed; flowers peony pink, yellow base, apricot yellow reverse, medium, 28 petals, high-centered, borne usually singly, no fragrance; foliage medium size, medium green, semi-glossy; tall, upright growth; [(Rainbow's End™ × 'Vera Dalton') × 'Vera Dalton']; intr. 1990

'Kinheart' (Heartlight™) MinFl, ob, 1985, King, Gene; flowers orange-yellow, reverse yellow, large, 16 petals, high-centered; foliage medium size, medium green, matte; prickles straight, light brown; upright, bushy, medium growth; ['Golden Slippers' × 'Rise 'n' Shine']

'Kinistino' S, dp, Erskine; flowers single; ['Aurora' × 'Leafland Glow']

'Kinjen' (Jennie Anne™) Min, rb, 1987, King, Gene; flowers red, reverse yellow, fading light yellow with red edge, medium, 16 petals, high-centered, no fragrance; foliage medium size, medium green, matte; prickles straight, small, white; bushy, medium growth; oval fruit; ['Gingersnap' × 'Charmglo']; intr. 1987

'Kinjoe' (Joe-Joe™) Min, ob, 1985, King, Gene; flowers orange-yellow, reverse yellow, 25 petals, cupped, borne singly; foliage medium size, dark, matte; prickles straight, light yellow to brown; bushy, spreading growth; [seedling × 'Rise 'n' Shine']

'Kinkaku' ('Golden Pavillion') HT, dy, 1986, Okamoto, K.; flowers golden yellow, large, 38 petals, high-centered, usually borne singly; foliage medium size, light green; prickles brown; medium, bushy growth; [seedling × 'Peace']; intr. 1975

'Kinliv' (Midwest Living®) Min, ob, 1991, King, Gene; bud globular; flowers orange, slight ruffle to petal edges, good substance, holding well, large, full, borne singly or in small clusters, slight fragrance; foliage medium size, medium green, semi-glossy; few prickles; bushy, spreading, medium (18 in.), healthy, vigorous growth; ['Evelyn Fison' × Party Girl™]; intr. 1992

'Kinlu' (Li'l Alleluia™) Min, rb, 1991, King, Gene; flowers wine to silver with yellow base, small, dbl., borne mostly singly, moderate fragrance; foliage medium size, medium green, matte; upright, tall growth; [(('B.C.' × Scamp™) × 'Tamango') × Magic Carrousel®]

'Kinlum' (Tudelum™) Min, dp, 1987, King, Gene; flowers deep pink to lighter shades, petal edges darken on opening, 30 petals, high-centered, no fragrance; foliage medium size, medium green, matte; prickles straight, medium, light pink; upright, bushy, medium, vigorous growth; no fruit; [Baby Katie™ × 'Watercolor']; intr. 1987

'Kinmac' (Merrimac™) Min, dr, 1989, King, Gene; bud pointed; flowers deeper at tips, medium, 18 petals, high-centered, borne usually singly and in sprays, slight fruity fragrance; foliage medium size, medium green, matte; prickles straight, small, red; upright, medium growth; hips ovoid, ornage; [('Alain' × Scamp™) × Lilli Marleen®]; intr. 1989

'Kinmike' (J. Michael™) Min, or, 1987, King, Gene; flowers orange-red, aging lighter, large, 18 petals, high-centered, borne usually singly, moderate fruity fragrance; foliage large, light green, matte; prickles straight, medium, white-green; mini-flora; upright, tall growth; ['Poker Chip' × 'Watercolor']

'Kinnight' (After Midnight™) Min, dr, 1991, King, Gene; bud ovoid; flowers dark red, tips show darker edge, outer petals darker, medium, 28 petals, high-centered, borne singly, no fragrance; foliage medium size, medium green, semi-glossy; medium, upright growth; [('B.C.' × Scamp™) × Black Jade™]; intr. 1990

'Kinnor' (New Orleans™) Min, mr, 1987, King, Gene; flowers medium to dark red toward base, non-fading, reverse medium red, medium, 32 petals, cupped, borne singly or in sprays of 3 - 5, slight spicy fragrance; foliage medium size, medium green, matte; prickles straight, small, red; bushy, spreading, medium growth; hips oval, small, green; ['Evelyn Fison' × 'Magic Mist']; intr. 1987

'Kinpai' -- See 'Poulgode'

'Kinpic' (Pink Picotee®) Min, pb, 1990, King, Gene; flowers white to cream with dark pink picotee edge, small, full, borne mostly singly, no fragrance; foliage medium size, light green, matte; upright, spreading, medium growth; [('Vera Dalton' × Fancy Pants™) × Magic Carrousel®]

'Kinpleas' (My Pleasure™) Min, pb, 1987, King, Gene; flowers lavender pink, reverse light pink, fading lighter pink, medium, 45 petals, high-centered, moderate fruity fragrance; foliage medium size, dark green, matte; prickles straight, white with brown tips; upright, medium growth; hips oval, medium green; ['Lavender Pinocchio' × seedling]; intr. 1987

'Kinrenpo' ('Golden Lotus Walk') F, my, Keisei; intr. 2008

'Kinsandy' (Pink Sandy™) Min, pb, 1991, King, Gene; flowers light pink to light apricot center, aging deep pink edges, small, full, borne mostly singly, slight fragrance; foliage small, medium green, matte; bushy, low growth; [('Vera Dalton' × Rainbow's End™) × Fancy Pants™]

'Kinschon' Min, rb, 1986, King, Gene

'Kinslam' (Little Slam®) Min, dr, 1990, King, Gene; flowers small, dbl., borne mostly singly, no fragrance; foliage small, medium green, semi-glossy; bushy, low growth; [(('B.C.' × Scamp™) × 'Red Ace') × Scamp™]; intr. 1990

'Kinsmen' HT, rb, Delbard; flowers white with red edges, dbl., moderate fragrance; recurrent; medium (4 ft.) growth

'Kinspeech' (Speechless™) Min, ob, 1987, King, Gene; flowers dark to light orange, fading darker, medium, 30 petals, high-centered, borne usually singly, no fragrance; foliage dark green, semi-glossy; prickles medium, hooked, red, with brown tips; upright, bushy growth; hips oval, medium, green; [seedling × 'Watercolor']; intr. 1987

'Kinsun' (Dale's Sunrise®) Min, yb, 1991, King, Gene; flowers yellow tipped medium pink, fading pink, small, dbl., borne mostly singly, slight fragrance; foliage small, medium green, semi-glossy; upright, bushy, medium growth; [(('B.C.' × Scamp™) × Rainbow's End™) × Tobo™]; intr. 1990

'Kintee' ('Peggy 'T') Min, mr, 1988, King, Gene; flowers medium red with white, circular base, reverse white, 5 petals; foliage medium size, medium green, matte; prickles straight with hook, white; bushy, medium growth; no fruit; ['Poker Chip' × 'Rise 'n' Shine']

'Kintenn' (Tennessee™) Min, op, 1988, King, Gene; flowers coral to white, reverse light coral to white, aging darker coral, medium, 18 petals, high-centered, borne singly or in small clusters; recurrent; foliage medium size, light green, matte; prickles straight, light green; upright, tall growth; hips oval, large, orange; ['Kiskadee' × 'Orange Honey']

'Kintoddy' (Hoddy Toddy™) Min, dr, 1990, King, Gene; bud pointed; flowers dark red, petals tipped darker, small, 28 petals, cupped, borne usually singly, no fragrance; foliage small, medium green, matte; prickles straight, very small, red; bushy, low growth; no fruit; [('Alain' × Scamp™) × Scamp™]; intr. 1989

'Kinugasa' ('Silk Parasol') HT, lp, 1986, Shibata, T.; flowers large, 45 petals, exhibition, borne usually singly, moderate fruity fragrance; foliage medium size, light green; prickles brown, hooked; medium, bushy growth; ['Michèle Meilland'

× ('Michèle Meilland' × 'Anne Letts')]; intr. 1984

'Kiora' F, mr, 1989, Cattermole, R.F.; bud pointed; flowers light vermillion shading to darker petal edges, small, dbl., flat, foliage dark green, shiny, veined; upright, bushy growth; ['Liverpool Echo' × 'John Church']

'Kir Royal' -- See 'Meinibur'

'Kirang' HT, pb, Tejganga; intr. 1995

'Kirari' ('Twinkle') F, yb, Keisei; intr. 2004

'Kirbee' ('Irene's Surprise') F, ab, 1993, Kirkham, Gordon Wilson; flowers medium, dbl., high-centered, borne in small clusters; foliage medium size, medium green, semi-glossy; medium (2½ ft.), upright growth; intr. 1993

'Kirbell' ('Berenice Neville') HT, dy, 1995, Kirkham, Gordon Wilson; flowers medium to large, dbl., borne in small clusters; foliage medium size, dark green, semi-glossy; numerous prickles; medium, upright growth; ['Tynwald' × Bright Smile®]; intr. 1996

'Kirbill' F, or, Kirkham, Gordon Wilson; intr. 1995

'Kirbronze' ('Elizabeth Ann') F, ob, 1993, Kirkham, Gordon Wilson; flowers bronze and gold, medium, dbl., borne in small clusters; foliage medium size, medium green, glossy; some prickles; medium, upright growth; ['Kathleen's Rose' × 'Eurorose']; intr. 1995

'Kirchief' HT, mr, Kirkham; intr. 2005

'Kircloud' ('Mary Hilda Law') HT, dp, 1995, Kirkham, Gordon Wilson; flowers deep pink, 3-3½ in., dbl.; foliage large, dark green, semi-glossy; medium, upright growth; ['Lady Helen' × 'Fragrant Cloud']; intr. 1997

'Kirdex' ('Roccana Diane') F, dp, 1985, Kirkham, Gordon Wilson; flowers deep pink, medium, 20 petals; foliage large, dark, glossy; upright growth; ['Pink Favorite' × 'Attraction']

'Kirfelix' Min, ob, Kirkam; intr. 1999

'Kirgale' F, mp, Kirkham; intr. 2001

'Kirhand' F, yb, Kirkham; bud lemon edged cherry pink; intr. 2002

'Kirhol' ('May Lawlor') HT, w, 1993, Kirkham, Gordon Wilson; flowers cream and pink, 2¾-3 in., dbl., borne mostly singly, intense fragrance; foliage large, dark green, semi-glossy; numerous prickles; tall, upright growth; ['Morgengruss' × 'Mary Sumner']

'Kirjack' ('Daphne Claire Jones') LCl, or, 1994, Kirkham, Gordon Wilson; flowers 3-3½ in., dbl.; foliage large, dark green, semi-glossy; numerous prickles; tall, upright growth; [Parkdirektor Riggers® × seedling]; intr. 1996

'Kirkcaldie' -- See 'Macclosup'

'Kirkit' ('Kathleen Kirkham', 'Kathleen's Rose') F, pb, 1985, Kirkham, Gordon Wilson; flowers variable - pink, apricot, peach and yellow, medium, semi-dbl., moderate fragrance; foliage medium size, medium green, semi-

glossy; upright growth; ['Manx Queen' × seedling]

'Kirlis' F, ob, Kirkham, S.; intr. 2001

'Kirlon' ('Woman O'th North', 'Women O'th North') F, lp, 1993, Kirkham, Gordon Wilson; flowers shell pink, medium, dbl., hybrid tea, borne in small clusters, moderate fragrance; foliage medium size, medium green, semi-glossy; few prickles; low (1½ × 1½ ft.), bushy growth; intr. 1994

'Kirlyl' ('Harlow Carr') F, mp, Kirkham, Gordon Wilson; intr. 1997

'Kirmac' ('Greenalls Glory') F, w, Kirkham, Gordon Wilson; intr. 1989

'Kirmelody' ('Bangor Cathedral') HT, dy, Kirkham, Gordon Wilson; intr. 1996

'Kirmyst ' F, ob, Kirkham; intr. 1999

'Kirora' LCl, ob, Kirkham; intr. 2008

'Kirpark' ('Ted Goves') HT, mr, 1985, Kirkham, Gordon Wilson; flowers medium, 20 petals, intense fragrance; foliage medium size, dark, matte; ['Prima Ballerina' × 'Teenager']; intr. 1983

'Kirpice' HT, mr, 1994, Kirkham, Gordon Wilson; intr. 1995

'Kirpink' ('Owen's Pride') F, mp, Kirkham, Gordon Wilson; intr. 1968

'Kirrad' ('Arejay') Min, ab, 1993, Kirkham, Gordon Wilson; flowers moderately small, dbl., borne in large clusters, slight fragrance; foliage small, medium green, glossy; few prickles; low, bushy growth; [seedling × seedling]; intr. 1995

'Kirrans' HT, my, Kirkham; intr. 2003

'Kirrans' Min, ab, Kirkham, Gordon; intr. 1999

'Kirsan' ('Chris') LCl, my, Kirkham, Gordon Wilson; intr. 1999

'Kirsandra' HT, op, Kirkham; intr. 2007

'Kirsch, Climbing' -- See 'Poullack'

Kirsch Cover™ -- See 'Petaluma'

'Kirscot' ('Graceland') MinFl, op, Kirkham, Gordon Wilson; intr. 1989

'Kirshru' S, w, Kirkham, Gordon Wilson; buds lemon yellow; intr. 1991

'Kirsi' HT, rb, 1967, Palmer, H.E.; flowers cream-white edged pink, becoming red over white, large, dbl.; very vigorous growth; PP2706; [sport of 'Rose Gaujard']

'Kirsil' HT, op, Kirkham; intr. 2001

'Kirsmile' ('Donald Thomas Heald') F, yb, 1994, Kirkham, Gordon Wilson; flowers small, semi-dbl., borne in small clusters, slight fragrance; foliage medium size, dark green, semi-glossy; numerous prickles; patio; low, compact growth; [seedling × Bright Smile®]; intr. 1996

'Kirstein' ('Sophie Deborah') HT, ob, 1999, Kirkham, Gordon Wilson; flowers 3 in., dbl., borne in small clusters; foliage medium size, dark green, semi-glossy; prickles moderate; upright, medium (2½ ft.) growth; ['Prunella' × 'Mary Sumner']

'Kirsten' -- See 'Poulkir'

'Kirsten Klein' HMsk, mp, Scarman; flowers single; intr. 1995

'Kirsten Poulsen' F, mr, 1924, Poulsen,

S.; flowers bright scarlet, single, borne in clusters; foliage leathery; vigorous growth; ['Orléans Rose' × 'Red Star']

'Kirsten Poulsen Improved' F, mr, 1938, Radmore; flowers scarlet, single, borne on trusses; free bloom; foliage dark; free growth

'Kirsty' -- See 'Loveaura'

'Kirsty Jane' -- See 'Simkayjay'

'Kirsun' S, dy

'Kirtyn' ('Heywood') S, ab, 1995, Kirkham, Gordon Wilson; flowers peach, medium, 6-14 petals, borne in large clusters; foliage medium size, medium green, matte; numerous prickles; tall, bushy growth; ['Tynwald' × Bright Smile®]

'Kirwim' ('Clara's Surprise') HT, mp, 1998, Kirkham, Gordon Wilson; flowers lilac pink, high centered, medium size, full, high-centered, borne in small clusters, moderate fragrance; foliage medium size, dark green, semi-glossy; few prickles; compact, low growth; ['Seaspray' × 'Admiral Rodney']

'Kirworjackie' ('Worjackie') HT, pb, 1993, Kirkham, Gordon Wilson; flowers pink blend, 2¾-3 in., full, borne mostly singly, moderate fragrance; foliage medium size, dark green, semi-glossy; numerous prickles; medium, upright growth; ['Solitaire' × 'Brandy Butter']; intr. 1994

Kiska® HT, pb, Meilland; flowers two-tone pink; intr. 2007

'Kiskadee' F, my, 1973, McGredy, Sam IV; flowers bright yellow, large, 25 petals, high-centered; foliage dark; ['Arthur Bell' × 'Cynthia Brooke']

'Kisme' F, pb, Raffel; flowers soft, warm pink, deepening with age, large, very full, borne in clusters, moderate fragrance; good repeat; intr. about 1960

Kismet™ -- See 'Tuckfate'

'Kismet' HT, my, 1930, Nicolas; flowers clear yellow, center deeper, large, dbl., cupped, intense fragrance; foliage light, glossy; PP153; [sport of 'Talisman']

'Kiss' Min, ob, 1980, Lyon, Lyndon; bud ovoid, pointed; flowers Indian orange, reverse lighter, 28 petals, high-centered, borne in clusters of 1-3, moderate fruity fragrance; foliage small, medium green; prickles straight; growth strong, upright; [seedling × seedling]; intr. 1979

Kiss™ F, op; flowers salmon-pink, small, dbl., high-centered, slight fragrance; growth vigorous, medium (18 in.); intr. 1988

'Kiss 'n' Tell' -- See 'Seakiss'

'Kiss Kordana' Min, dr, Kordes; flowers dbl.; container rose

'Kiss Kordana Mini Brite' Min, op, Kordes; PP11363

'Kiss Me' Gr, mp, Lim, Ping; flowers clear pink, 4 in., 20-25 petals, loose, borne in clusters, intense fragrance; recurrent; foliage disease-resistant; low (2-3 ft.) growth; intr. 2006

'Kiss Me Quick' -- See 'Seaquick'

'Kiss of Desire' -- See 'Korlupo'

'Kiss of Fire' F, rb, Gaujard; flowers pale yellow with red edges, dbl., borne in clusters, moderate fragrance; intr. 1960

'Kiss of Fire' HT, yb, Laveena Roses; intr. 1969

'Kiss the Bride' -- See 'Seawhi'

'Kissin' Cousin' S, op, 1978, Buck, Dr. Griffith J.; bud ovoid, pointed; flowers pink to coral-pink, 4-5 in., 28 petals, high-centered; foliage large, dark, leathery; vigorous, upright, spreading growth; [(('Ophelia' × 'Prairie Princess') × 'Tiki') × (('Corbeille Royale' × American Heritage®) × 'Hawkeye Belle')]

'Kit Delahanty' ('Mom-Mom') B, dp, 2008, Delahanty, James; flowers deep pink, reverse pink with white at the base, 3-5 in., very full, blooms borne mostly solitary; foliage medium, medium green, matte; prickles 3-4 mm., curved, grey, moderate; growth spreading, medium (3-5 ft.); specimen; ['Maggie' × unknown (possibly self)]; intr. 2009

'Kitana' HRg, m, 1927, Hansen, N.E.; flowers deep lavender-pink, large, semi-dbl., intense fragrance; non-recurrent; hips profuse, red; very hardy; ['Tetonkaha' × 'Rose Apples']

'Kitano' HT, w, Keihan; intr. 1985

'Kitayama' HT, w, Keihan; intr. 1994

'Kitchener of Khartoum' ('K. of K.') HT, mr, 1917, Dickson, A.; flowers dazzling velvety scarlet, 3 in., 10 petals; vigorous, branching growth

'Kitty' Pol, mr, 1925, Koster; flowers carmine-red, small, dbl.

'Kitty Bice' LCl, mp, 1932, Fitzhardinge; ['Ophelia, Climbing' × 'Lady Waterlow']

'Kitty Cleo' F, yb; intr. 2003

'Kitty Hawk' Min, pb, 1986, Bridges, Dennis A.; flowers deep pink, reverse lighter pink, 29 petals, high-centered, borne mostly singly; recurrent; foliage large, medium green, semi-glossy; prickles medium, long, red; medium, upright growth; ['Watercolor' × unknown]; intr. 1986

'Kitty Kingsbury' HT, mp, 1930, Evans; flowers shell-pink; vigorous growth; ['Abol' × unknown]

'Kitty Kininmonth' HG, dp, 1922, Clark, A.; flowers deep pink, lighter reverse, golden stamens, 12 cm., semi-dbl., cupped; some recurrent bloom; foliage dark, wrinkled; few prickles; vigorous, climbing growth; [seedling × R. gigantea]

'Kitty-Lew' -- See 'Houkitty'

'Kitty's Rose' -- See 'Beaarty'

'Kiwi' -- See 'Wekpaltlez'

'Kiwi' HT, w, 1989, Cattermole, R.F.; bud pointed; flowers creamy pink opening to creamy white, reflexed, pointed, medium, dbl.; foliage dark green, shiny; prickles needle-like, red to light brown; tall, upright growth; ['Judith Morton' × (Pascali® × Blue Moon®)]

'Kiwi Belle' F, pb, 1984, Cattermole, R.F.; flowers tan apricot to pink in cool weather, light pink in hot summer, large, 40 petals, globular, borne in clusters of 3 - 5, intense spicy fragrance; foliage bronze green when young, turning light green; prickles brown; upright, spreading growth; ['Silent Night' × 'Irish Mist']

'Kiwi Charm' HT, pb, 1972, Lindquist; bud ovoid; flowers creamy yellow, edged pink, large, semi-dbl., high-centered, moderate fragrance; foliage glossy, leathery; vigorous, bushy growth; ['Kordes' Perfecta' × 'Champagne']

'Kiwi Delight' HT, yb, 1984, Cattermole, R.F.; flowers golden yellow, petals edged deep pink, aging pink overall, large, 40 petals, globular, intense fragrance; foliage bronze green turning dark green, glossy; prickles gray-brown, very small and large; upright, bushy growth; ['Peace' × (Peer Gynt® × 'Irish Mist')]

'Kiwi Enterprise' HT, yb, 2000, Cattermole, R.F.; flowers full, high-centered, borne mostly singly, slight fragrance; foliage medium size, light green, glossy; nearly thornless; growth compact, medium (4 ft.); ['Royden' × 'Irish Gold']; intr. 2001

'Kiwi Gold' HT, yb, 1983, Cattermole, R.F.; bud pointed; flowers light yellow, reverse edges of petals flushed pink, 22 petals, high-centered, intense fragrance; foliage light green, glossy; prickles very few, light brown; upright growth; [('Pink Parfait' × 'Pink Parfait') × 'Waipounamu']; intr. 1984

'Kiwi Queen' HT, yb, 1984, Cattermole, R.F.; flowers yellow, shaded orange and pink, large, 44 petals, high-centered, slight fragrance; foliage medium green; prickles light brown; upright, spreading growth; [Peer Gynt® × 'Command Performance']

'Kiwi Reds' HT, mr, 2000, Cattermole, R.F.; flowers very large, borne in small clusters, moderate fragrance; foliage large, medium to dark green, glossy; prickles few, on basal shoots only; growth upright, tall (up to 6 ft.); ['Kiwi Gold' × 'Prima Ballerina']; intr. 2001

'Kiwi Sunrise' -- See 'Mactaumaruniu'

'Kiwiana' F, dp, 2002, Jones, Diana; flowers cerise pink, medium pink reverse, 7 cm., full, borne in large clusters, slight fragrance; foliage medium size, medium green, semi-glossy; prickles average, triangular, moderate; growth compact, short (80 cm.); garden decorative; [seedling × Dublin Bay®]

'Kiyosumi' HT, m, 1979, Onodera, Toru F.; bud slender; flowers clear light purplish blue,, 3 in., 25 petals, high-centered; foliage light green, leathery; upright growth; [seedling × 'Sterling Silver']

'Klassy Lady' Min, pb, 2006, Klassy, Diana; flowers deep pink, reverse white, 2 in., dbl., borne mostly solitary; foliage medium size, dark green, semi-glossy; prickles 3/16 in., hooked downward, deep pink, moderate; growth bushy, tall (20-24 in.); [sport of 'Miss Flippins']; intr. 2007

'Klaus Groth' -- See 'Claus Groth'
'Klaus Störtebeker' HT, mr, 1965, Kordes, R.; flowers well-formed, 5 in., 40 petals; foliage dark; low, bushy growth; intr. 1964
'Klein Tausendschön' HMult, mp, 1916, Kiese; ['Tausendschön' × unknown]
'Kleine Ballerina' Pol, Noack, Werner; intr. 1998
Kleine Dortmund® ('Kleine Dortmunderin') F, rb, Noack, Werner; flowers carmine-scarlet with white eye, small, borne in large clusters, no fragrance; good repeat; foliage glossy; bushy, spreading growth; intr. 1992
'Kleine Dortmunderin' -- See 'Kleine Dortmund'
'Kleine Echo' Pol, mp, 1925, Kiese; flowers small, semi-dbl.
'Kleine Eva' Pol, mp, Hetzel, Karl; recurrent; low (12 in.) growth; intr. 1995
'Kleine Leo' HT, mr, 1921, Timmermans; flowers brilliant red shaded dark red, dbl.; ['Farbenkonigin' × 'Gen. MacArthur']
Kleine Regina® -- See 'Helreg'
'Kleine Renate' -- See 'Jacrain'
'Kleine Rösel' HWich, m, 1929, Vogel, M.; flowers dark violet-pink, reverse lighter, 4 cm., single, borne in flat clusters, no fragrance; foliage glossy; numerous prickles
'Kleiner Alfred' Pol, or, 1904, Lambert, P.; bud garnet-red; flowers well-formed, medium; foliage glossy; dwarf growth; ['Anna-Maria de Montravel' × 'Shirley Hibberd']
'Kleiner Liebling' Pol, mp, 1895, Schmidt, J. C.; flowers carmine rose, medium, cupped, borne in very large clusters; ['Polyantha Grandiflora' × 'Fellemberg']
'Kleopatra' -- See 'Cleopatra'
Kleopatra® -- See 'Korverpea'
'Klerksdorp Horizon' -- See 'Kormöwe'
'Kletternde Ruby' Cl Pol, mr, 1946, Kordes; bud globular; flowers scarlet, small, dbl., borne in clusters; foliage dark, wrinkled; very vigorous, trailing growth; [sport of 'Ruby']
Klima™ -- See 'Savaklim'
'Klimentina' HT, mp, Klimenko, V. N.; flowers pink with silvery reverse, large, dbl.; intr. 1955
'Klondyke' HWich, my, 1911, Paul; flowers soft yellow, center deeper, passing to ivory-white, large, dbl.; very vigorous, climbing growth
'Klondyke' HT, my, LeGrice; flowers clear golden yellow; [sport of 'Lady Forteviot']; intr. 1934
'Klostertaler Power' S, ob, Schultheis; flowers bright orange, wavy petals, dbl., borne in clusters, slight fragrance; foliage dark green, glossy; dense, bushy (5 × 5 ft.) growth; intr. 2000
'Kluis Orange' -- See 'Klyn's Orange'
'Kluis Scarlet' F, mr, 1931, Kluis, R.; flowers brilliant red; very free growth; [sport of 'Lafayette']
'Klyn's Orange' ('Kluis Orange') Pol, or, Kluis; flowers orange-scarlet, small, dbl., borne in dense clusters; foliage light green; dwarf growth
'Klyn's Yellow' HT, my, 1948, Klyn; bud pointed; flowers clear yellow, open, large, dbl.; foliage glossy; very vigorous, compact growth; ['McGredy's Yellow' × unknown]
'Knezna Libuse' HT, op, Cerveny
'Knick Knack' -- See 'Jusknack'
Knirps® -- See 'Korverlandus'
Knock Out™ -- See 'Radrazz'
'Knockout' -- See 'Radrazz'
'Knocktopher Lady' -- See 'Seaknock'
'Ko-Choh' F, ob, 1986, Suzuki, Seizo; flowers orange, reverse yellow shaded orange, small, 45 petals, high-centered, borne 3-5 per cluster, moderate fragrance; foliage dark, semi-glossy; prickles small; low, compact growth; [('Rumba' × 'Olympic Torch') × Allgold®]; intr. 1983
'Koa' Min, op, 1979, Rovinski & Meredith; bud ovoid; flowers coral-pink, 1 in., 44 petals, high-centered, slight fragrance; tall, open, leggy growth; ['Persian Princess' × 'Gene Boerner']; intr. 1978
'Koai' HT, mr; intr. 1970
Koala® -- See 'Meitapov'
Koba® -- See 'Véronèse'
'Koba' -- See 'Meiroverna'
'Kobé' HG, lp, about 1900, Busby; flowers light flesh pink, large
'København' -- See 'Copenhagen'
'Kobold' F, op, McGredy, Sam IV; flowers large, semi-dbl.; intr. 1981
'Kocher Red' -- See 'Rhode Island Red'
'Kochiana' (R. × kochiana Koehne, R. oxyacanthos) S, dp, before 1869; flowers deep rose, 1½ in., borne solitary in clusters of 3; foliage small, with 9-11 leaflets; numerous prickles; probably R. spinosissima × R. carolina
'Koehneana' (R. × koehneana Rehder) S, m, before 1893; flowers purplish red, large; [R. carolina × R. rugosa]
'Kogane' ('Gold') F, my, Keisei; intr. 1993
'Koh-I-Noor' HT, pb, 1973, Ellick; flowers white, center deep pink, 5 in., 60 petals; foliage glossy, dark; vigorous growth; [('Memoriam' × 'Peace') × 'My Choice']
'Koha' HT, rb, 1984, Cattermole, R.F.; flowers medium red, reverse lighter, large, 32 petals, high-centered, slight fragrance; foliage light, glossy, veined; prickles brown; upright, branching growth; ['Silent Night' × ('Josephine Bruce' × 'Irish Mist')]
'Koharu-Biyori' F, lp, 1999, Yasuda, Yuji; flowers pale pink, 2 in., 5 petals; foliage medium green; growth to 2½ ft.; ['Hanagasumi' × seedling]; intr. 1994
'Kohima' F, rb, 1972, Ellick; flowers fire-red to orange, reverse cream, 4 in., 45-50 petals; vigorous growth; [Orange Sensation® × 'Mischief']
'Kohsai' -- See 'Mikado'
'Koigokoro' ('Loving Heart') HT, dp, Keisei; intr. 1992
'Koigoromo' HT, w, Hiroshima
'Koisan' HT, ob, Teranishi; intr. 1969
'Koise' ('Snow Diamond') HT, m, Teranishi; intr. 2005
'Kojack' -- See 'Miss Blanche'
'Kojo' -- See 'Sweet Dreams'
'Kojo no Tsuki' ('Moon Over the Castle Ruins') LCl, dy, 1977, Teranishi, K.; bud circular; flowers deep yellow, 4½-5 in., 35 petals, high-centered, slight fragrance; foliage light; vigorous, climbing growth; [('Souv. de Jacques Verschuren' × 'Thais') × 'Amarillo']; intr. 1975
'Koka' HT, ly, Keihan; intr. 1996
'Koki' ('Fragrant Treasure') HT, op, Keisei
'KoKo' Min, yb, 1983, Meredith, E.A. & Rovinski, M.E.; bud globular; flowers pale yellow, aging orange-red on petal edges, 55 petals, borne mostly singly, moderate fragrance; foliage medium size, medium green, matte; prickles thin, triangular, light brown; low, bushy growth
'Koksijde' F, pb, RvS-Melle; flowers 19 petals, flat; foliage matte; strong growth
'Kokulinsky's Unterlage' ('Kukolinsky') (strain of R. canina), lp; foliage susceptible to rust; growth once used as understock; used in Europe as an understock
'Kokyu' HT, w, Itami; flowers ivory with pink blush, shapely; growth medium; intr. 1990
'Kolbe's Diamond' HT, lp, Ludwig; [sport of 'Andrea Stelzer']; intr. 2003
'Koldinghus' F, dp, 1978, Poulsen, Niels D.; flowers deep rose, open,, 2-2½ in., 23 petals, slight fragrance; foliage dark, glossy; upright growth; [Pernille Poulsen™ × seedling]; intr. 1968
'Kolgian' S, lp, Kolster; Peter Rudolf; flowers single; PP16042
'Kolibre' F, mr, 1946, Leenders, M.; bud long, pointed; flowers 3 in., 20 petals, borne in small trusses; foliage bronze; moderately vigorous growth; ['Mev. Nathalie Nypels' × seedling]
'Kolkhoznitsa' HT, m, 1957, Sushkov & Besschetnova; flowers lilac-pink, large, 45 petals, moderate fragrance; recurrent; foliage dark; very vigorous, compact growth; ['Peace' × 'Mirandy']
'Köln am Rhein' ('Cologne') HKor, op, 1958, Kordes; flowers deep salmon-pink, 10-12 cm., semi-dbl., borne in large clusters, moderate fragrance; recurrent bloom; foliage dark, glossy; vigorous, climbing growth; [R. × kordesii × 'Golden Glow']; intr. 1956
'Kölner Karneval, Climbing' ('Blue Girl, Climbing') Cl HT, m, Kyle; flowers 12-15 cm.; PP4088; intr. 1977
'Kölner Karneval' -- See 'Cologne Carnival'
'Komala '89' HT, pb, K&S; bud ovoid; flowers rosy pink with almond, large, dbl.; intr. 1989
'Kombination' F, VEG; intr. 1982

'Komet' HT, mr, VEG; flowers vermilion red, medium to large, dbl.

'Komfort' F, mp, 1967, Tantau, Math.; flowers salmon-pink, large, semi-dbl., borne in clusters (to 20); foliage glossy; very vigorous, bushy growth

'Kommerzienrat W. Rautenstrauch' HFt, mp, 1909, Lambert, P.; flowers pure salmon-pink, center yellow, reverse lighter, 5-6 cm., semi-dbl., open, borne in small clusters, slight licorice fragrance; some repeat; nearly thornless; ['Léonie Lamesch' × *R. foetida bicolor*]

'Kommodore, Climbing' Cl F, mr; [sport of 'Kommodore']; intr. after 1959

'Kommodore' ('The Commodore') F, mr, 1959, Tantau, Math.; flowers blood-red, well-formed, large, dbl., borne in clusters; vigorous, low growth

'Kon-Tiki' F, mr, 1971, Institute of Ornamental Plant Growing; bud ovoid; flowers bright red, large, semi-dbl., cupped; foliage glossy, dark; vigorous, upright growth; ['Aztec' × 'Paprika']

Konfetti® -- See 'Tantau's Konfetti'

'Konfetti' ('Confetti') HT, pb, 1965, Tantau, Math.; bud globular; flowers claret-rose, reverse light cream, well-formed, 5 in., 40-45 petals; foliage dark, leathery; strong stems; bushy, upright growth

'Kong Frederik den IX' -- See 'Poulrise'

'König Friedrich II von Dänemark' HP, dr; flowers deep red, medium, dbl.

'König Friedrich II von Dänemark, Climbing' Cl HP, dr, 1840, Vogel; [sport of 'König Friedrich II von Dänemark']

'König Laurin' HT, w, 1910, Türke; flowers whitish pink, large, dbl., moderate fragrance; ['Mme Caroline Testout' × 'White Maman Cochet']

'König Ludwig-Rose' S, mp, Tantau; flowers large, dbl.; intr. 1994

'König von Sachsen' HGal, mp, 1878, Ruschpler; foliage light green, deeply serrated; numerous prickles; stems strong; growth vigorous

'Königen' HWich, mp; flowers small, dbl.

Königin Beatrix® -- See 'Hetkora'

'Königin Carola' -- See 'Königin Carola von Sachsen'

'Königin Carola von Sachsen' ('Königin Carola') HT, pb, 1904, Türke; bud pointed; flowers satiny rose-pink, reverse silvery white, very large, dbl.; foliage dark, leathery; vigorous growth; ['Mme Caroline Testout' × 'Viscountess Folkestone']

'Königin der Rosen' -- See 'Korbico'

'Königin Emma' HT, lp, 1903, Verschuren; flowers fleshy white with rosy center, large, dbl.; ['Kaiserin Auguste Viktoria' × seedling]

'Königin Juliana' F, 1948, Buisman, G. A. H.

Königin Kunigunde® F, mp, Tantau; flowers soft pink fading to white, dbl., rosette, borne in clusters; intr. 2002

'Königin Luise' HT, w, 1927, Weigand, C.; flowers very large, dbl., high-centered; foliage dark, leathery, glossy; vigorous, bushy growth; ['Frau Karl Druschki' × 'Sunburst']

Königin Margrethe™ -- See 'Poulskov'

'Königin Maria Therese' HT, dp, 1916, Lambert, P.; flowers carmine-pink, very large, very dbl.; ['Frau Karl Druschki' × 'Luise Lilia']

'Königin Viktoria von Schweden' HT, yb, 1919, Ries; flowers light saffron-yellow, aging to pale salmon-pink, dbl.; ['Mme Segond Weber' × 'Mrs Joseph Hill']

'Königin von Blatna' -- See 'Blatenskà Kràlovna'

'Königin von Dänemark' ('Dronningen af Danmark', 'Naissance de Vénus', 'New Maiden's Blush', 'Queen of Denmark', 'Reine du Dänemark') A, mp, 1816, Booth; flowers flesh-pink, center darker, petals recurved, with a very small center eye, medium, very dbl., quartered, flat, borne in clusters, intense fragrance; non-recurrent; foliage dark bluish-green, with 5-7 toothed, elliptical leaflets; prickles numerous, hooked; vigorous growth; [probably *R. alba* × Damask hybrid]

'Königin Wilhelmine' Pol, dp, 1925, Koster; flowers carmine-pink, medium, full; [sport of 'Orléans Rose']

'Koniginrosa' -- See 'Regina Dicta'

'Konigliche Hoheit' -- See 'Royal Highness'

'Königlicht Hoheit' -- See 'Royal Highness'

'Königsberg' HT, mr, 1940, Weigand, L.; flowers scarlet-red; ['Mrs Henry Winnett' × 'Marechal Petain']

'Koningin Astrid' ('Queen Astrid') HT, mr, 1935, Leenders, M.; bud long, pointed, nasturtium-red; flowers reddish-apricot and bronze, very large, dbl.; foliage dark, bronze; vigorous growth

'Koningin Juliana' F, mp, 1948, Buisman, G. A. H.; flowers salmon-pink becoming light yellow with salmon, large, dbl., borne in clusters; blooms late; foliage glossy; ['Poulsen's Pink' × 'Mrs Pierre S. duPont']

'Koningin Wilhelmina' HT, pb, 1904, Verschuren; flowers rose pink with coppery salmon, dahlia-like

'Konoe' HT, ob, Keihan; intr. 1989

Konrad Adenauer® ('Konrad Adenauer Rose') HT, dr, 1955, Tantau, Math.; bud globular; flowers blood-red, 4 in., 35 petals, cupped, intense fragrance; foliage light green, glossy; vigorous, upright growth; PP1452; ['Crimson Glory' × 'Hens Verschuren']; intr. 1955

'Konrad Adenauer Rose' -- See 'Konrad Adenauer'

'Konrad Glocker' F, dr, 1965, Kordes, R.; flowers 3 in., dbl.; foliage dark; vigorous, bushy, low growth; intr. 1964

Konrad Henkel® -- See 'Koriet'

'Konrad Thönges' HFt, op, 1929, Thönges; flowers salmon-orange/pink, large, semi-dbl.

'Kontiki' HT, rb

'Kontrast' HT, rb, Hchen; intr. 1981

'Kooiana Butterscotch' HT, my, Gibson, P.; [sport of 'Golden Times']; intr. 1995

'Kooiana Daybreak' HT, ab; flowers delicate cream-pink, fading with age, borne mostly singly; tall growth; intr. 1995

'Kooiana Moonlight' HT, ly, Gibson, P.; [sport of 'Gerdo']; intr. 1995

'Kooiana Watermelon' HT, Gibson, P.; [sport of 'Kooiana Daybreak']; intr. 1995

'Kookaburra' -- See 'Korlomet'

'Koopmanns Sport von Else Poulsen' Pol, mr, 1940, Koopmann; flowers medium, semi-dbl.

Kooshti-Bok™ -- See 'Jaykoo'

'Kootenay' ('Mary Greer') HT, lp, 1917, Dickson, A.; flowers primrose-color, tinged yellow, large, full, moderate fragrance

'Köpenicker Sommer' F, dy, Rupprecht-Radke; flowers medium-large, dbl.; intr. 1968

'Koppies' HT, lp, 1980, Perry, Astor; bud ovoid; flowers 35 petals, high-centered, borne usually singly, moderate fruity fragrance; foliage medium size, matte; prickles short, recurved; vigorous, tall growth; ['Tropicana' × 'Wendy Cussons']; intr. 1981

'Kor951721' F, mr, Kordessingle

'Korabemo' HT, my, Kordes; buds pointed; intr. 1999

'Korabmask' ('Harry Oppenheimer') HT, dy, Kordes; bud green-yellow, diamond shaped; intr. 1996

'Koraburg' ('Eliza Panarosa', Eliza®, 'Sweet Memory') HT, mp, 2006, Kordes; bud long, pointed ovoid; flowers silvery pink, 3.5 -4.5 in., 30 petals, high-centered , borne singly and in small clusters; recurrent; foliage dark green, glossy ; prickles moderate, medium, hooked downward ; stems medium to long; compact, upright, medium growth; PP9752; ['Saphir' × seedling]

'Koraby' ('Barby') HT, mp, Kordes; intr. 1995

'Koracona' ('Georgette') F, mp, Kordes; intr. 1995

'Korad' HT, yb, 1973, Kordes, R.; bud ovoid; intr. 1970

'Koradeigel' (Laguna®) LCl, dp, 2006, Kordes; bud round, magenta; flowers strong pink, 10 cm., very full, shallow cup , borne in clusters of 6-8, very strong, fruity fragrance; recurrent; foliage medium size, dark green, glossy, dense; bushy, erect, climbing (8 ft.) growth; intr. 2004

'Korades' ('Wild at Heart') S, dp, 1993, W. Kordes Söhne; flowers deep pink, 3-3½ in., dbl., borne in large clusters; foliage large, medium green, glossy; medium (120-130 cm.), bushy, spreading (180 cm.) growth; ['Bonanza' × seedling]; intr. 1994

'Korakaesci' HT, dy, Kordes; intr. 2005

'Koral' F, or, Kordes; bud ovoid; intr. 1969

'Koralanson' HT, or, Kordes; intr. 2001

'Koralbavan' Min, w, Kordesfull
'Koralbeid' S, pb, Kordes; intr. 2007
'Koralie' S, lp
'Koralle' F, mr, 1942, Koopman; flowers light red; [sport of 'Else Poulsen']
'Koralle' F, op, Harkness; intr. 1991
'Korallovyj Sjurpriz' F, op, Klimenko, V. N.; flowers luminous coral-red, large, dbl.; intr. 1966
'Koralogen' ('Apps Rose') F, ab, Kordes; intr. 1996
'Koralu' ('Perfecta') HT, pb, 1959, Kordes; bud urn-shaped; intr. 1957
'Koramasti' F, mr, Kordes; intr. 2005
'Koramator' ('Marjorie Chase') HT, ob, Kordes; intr. 1996
'Koramba' HT, ab, Kordes; intr. 1999
'Korambo' ('Professor Fred Ziady') HT, my, 1987, Kordes, R.; flowers clear medium yellow, 43 petals, high-centered, star-shaped, borne usually singly, moderate fragrance; foliage medium green; prickles straight, dark brown; growth medium, sturdy; ['Lusambo' × 'Deep Secret']; intr. 1985
'Korameget' ('Egoli') HT, dy, Kordes; intr. 1995
Koramgat® Min, ab, Kordes; bud pointed ovoid; intr. 2005
'Koramgis' ('Golden Spire') HT, dy, Kordes; intr. 1996
'Korami' ('Ami des Jardins') F, op, 1964, Kordes, R.
'Koramiro' Min, rb, Kordes; intr. 2005
'Korampa' ('Antique Silk', 'Champagne', Champagner®, 'Kordes' Rose Champagner') F, w, 1985, Kordes; flowers near white, flora-tea, large, 20 petals; foliage medium size, medium green, semi-glossy; upright, bushy growth; PP5411; [(Anabell® × unknown) × seedling]; intr. 1982
'Koramphi' HT, dr, Kordes; intr. 1996
'Koramvis' ('Lemon Dream') HT, ly, Kordes; intr. 1997
'Koranaorlo' HT, w, Kordes; intr. 1995
'Koranderer' ('Our Copper Queen', Kupferkönigin®) HT, dy, 2006; bud large, pointed; flowers copper-yellow, 11 cm., very full, high-centered, borne mostly solitary, slight fragrance; recurrent; foliage medium size, dark green, glossy; upright, medium (80 cm.) growth; intr. 1996
'Korandpunk' ('Madiba') HT, m, Kordes; bud deep maroon-pink; intr. 1996
'Korangeli' ('Kordes' Rose Angelique', Angelique®) HT, ob, 1985, Kordes; intr. 1980
'Korantel' (Tarantella®) HT, yb, 1986, Kordes, W.; flowers creamy yellow, petals edged and marked with pink, large, 54 petals, high-centered, borne singly; recurrent; foliage medium size, medium green, glossy; prickles light brown; upright growth; ['Colour Wonder' × Wiener Charme®]; intr. 1979
'Koranul' HT, ly, Kordes; intr. 1999
'Korapriber' F, mp, Kordes; bud salmon red; intr. 2007

'Koraroked' HT, mp, Kordes; intr. 2005
'Korascha' HT, mp, Kordes; intr. 2003
'Korassenet' ('Brothers Grimm Fairy Tales', 'Joli Tambour', Gebrüder Grimm®, 'Eternal Flame') F, ob, 2006; flowers dazzling orange and yellow, 7 cm., full, borne in small clusters; recurrent; foliage medium size, dark green, very glossy; vigorous, bushy, upright (70 cm.) growth; intr. 2002
'Korastor' -- See 'Koreklia'
'Koratomi' ('Fortuna Vigorosa', Fortuna®) F, lp, 2006, Kordes; flowers soft salmon pink with white center, 4 cm., single, borne in large clusters; foliage small, dark green, glossy, dense; growth bushy, upright (50 cm.); intr. 2002
'Koraubala' LCl, pb, Kordes; intr. 2002
'Koraucher' ('Deloitte & Touche') S, ab, Kordes; intr. 1996
'Koraureab' HT, mp, Kordes; bud pointed; intr. 2006
'Korav' ('New Ave Maria', Ave Maria®, 'Sunburnt Country') HT, op, 1986, Kordes, W.; flowers orange-salmon, large, 35 petals, high-centered, borne singly, moderate fragrance; foliage large, medium green, semi-glossy; prickles small; upright growth; [Uwe Seeler® × 'Sonia']; intr. 1981
'Korazerka' ('Ekstasse', 'Extase') HT, dr, Kordes; buds large, pointed; intr. 1994
'Korbacol' HT, my, Kordes; bud long, pointed ovoid; intr. 1993
'Korbad' ('Orange Fruitilia', Bad Füssing®) F, mr, 1980, Kordes, W.; bud large; flowers brilliant red, 23 petals, cupped, borne in clusters, moderate fragrance; foliage glossy, dark; few prickles; vigorous, upright, bushy growth; hips round; [Gruss an Bayern® × seedling]
'Korbalem' ('Little Lemmy') Min, my, Kordes; intr. 1988
'Korbalrom' Min, mp, Kordes
'Korbarkeit' S, w, Kordes; intr. 1998
'Korbasren' ('Simple Gifts', Pink Bassino®, 'St Tiggywinkles') F, mp, 2006; flowers apple blossom pink with white base and yellow stamens, 4 cm., single, cupped, borne in small clusters; foliage medium size, moss green, very glossy; growth bushy, medium (50 cm.); intr. 1995
'Korbasta' ('Tonsina') HT, my, Kordes; intr. 1992
'Korbaxand' ('Alexandra') HT, yb, Kordes; intr. 1973
'Korbe' ('Gruss an Heidelberg') HKor, mr, 1959, Kordes, R.; intr. 1958
'Korbeen' ('Goldy') HT, dy, 1982, Kordes, W.; flowers large, 35 petals, moderate fragrance; foliage medium size, medium green, semi-glossy; upright, bushy growth; ['Berolina' × seedling]; intr. 1981
'Korbefosa' Min, w, Kordes; intr. 2005
'Korbel Bicolor Pink' -- See 'Mrs Henry Morse'
'Korbelesp' Min, mp, Kordes
'Korbell' ('Annabelle', Anabell®, 'Kordes' Rose Anabel') F, ob, 1973, Kordes;

flowers orange and silvery blend, well-formed, 4 in., 30 petals, moderate fragrance; foliage small; ['Zorina' × 'Colour Wonder']; intr. 1972
'Korbelma' ('Goldsmith', Helmut Schmidt®, 'Simba') HT, my, 1980, Kordes, W.; bud large, long, pointed; flowers clear, even yellow, 4½-5 in., 30-40 petals, high-centered, borne 1-3 per cluster, moderate sweet tea fragrance; foliage dark green, matte; vigorous, upright, bushy growth; ['New Day' × seedling]; intr. 1979
'Korber' ('Fire Magic', Feuerzauber®, 'Magie de Feu') HT, or, 1974, Kordes, R.; flowers orange-red, reverse lighter, medium to large, dbl., high-centered, foliage dark, glossy; vigorous, upright growth; ['Fragrant Cloud' × seedling]
'Korberbeni' Gr, dy, Kordes; intr. 2001
'Korberis' (Felicitas®) S, dp, 2006; flowers carmine pink, 4 cm., single, borne in large clusters; foliage medium size, dark green, very glossy; bushy, spreading (3 × 5 ft.), arching growth; intr. 1998
'Korbersoma' Min, yb, Kordes
'Korberuhig' (Manita®) LCl, mp, 2006; flowers pink with white-yellow center, 9 cm., semi-dbl., borne in small clusters; foliage large; growth spreading, tall (250 cm.); intr. 1996
'Korbeteilich' (Crimson Bouquet™) Gr, dr, 1999, Kordes; flowers dark garnet red, reverse shiny dark red, good substance, 4-4½ in., 20-25 petals, high-centered, borne in large clusters, slight sweet fragrance; foliage large, dark green, glossy; prickles large; upright, medium (4½ ft.) growth; PP12001; [Bad Füssing® × 'Ingrid Bergman']; intr. 2000
'Korbever' Min, op, Kordes
'Korbi' ('Fièvre d'Or', Golden Giant®) HT, dy, 1965, Kordes, R.
'Korbico' ('Königin der Rosen', 'Queen of Roses', 'Reine des Roses') HT, ob, 1964, Kordes, R.; bud ovoid; intr. 1964
'Korbido' (Silver Star®) HT, m, 1966, Kordes, R.; intr. 1966
'Korbilant' ('Buxom Beauty', Parole®, 'XXL') HT, dp, 2006; bud large; flowers deep pink with a breath of purple, 14 cm., very full, high-centered, borne mostly solitary, intense fragrance; foliage large, green ,shiny; upright, medium (80 cm.) growth; intr. 2001
'Korbin' ('Fée des Neiges', 'Schneewittchen') F, w, Kordes, R.; bud long, pointed; intr. 1958
'Korbindu' (Elveshörn) S, mp, 1985, Kordes, W.; flowers medium, 35 petals; foliage medium size, dark, semi-glossy; bushy, spreading growth; ['The Fairy' × seedling]
'Korbirac' (Caribbean™) Gr, ab, 1992, Kordes, W.; flowers apricot orange/yellow blend with yellow reverse, 3-3½ in., 30-40 petals, high-centered, borne in small clusters, moderate fragrance; foliage large, dark green, semi-glossy, with red mid-vein and margins; numerous

prickles; medium (110-125 cm.), upright, bushy growth; PP8592; [‎'Mercedes'® × ('New Day' × seedling)]; intr. 1994

'Korbisch' ('Brillant', Kordes' Brillant®) S, ob, 1983, Kordes, W.; flowers orange, large, 35 petals; foliage medium size, medium green, glossy; upright, bushy growth; [(Sympathie® × unknown) × seedling]

'Korblekaf' HT, ob, Kordes; bud large, triangular; intr. 1999

'Korbltyp' ('Antigua') Min, pb, Kordes; bud ovoid; intr. 2002

'Korblue' F, m, 1975, Kordes; bud very large, pointed; intr. 1974

'Korboden' HT, op, Kordes; intr. 1997

'Korbolak' ('Melody') HT, lp, Kordes; bud long, pointed ovoid; intr. 1991

'Korbonnet' HT, mr, Kordes; bud pointed; intr. 1993

'Korbotaf' (Elveshörn®) S, mp, 1985, Kordes, W.

'Korbraufo' S, mr, Kordessingle; intr. 1992

'Korbravet' HT, or, Kordes; intr. 2002

'Korbreano' HT, rb, Kordes; intr. 2005

'Korbrespo' S, ab, Kordes; bud rounded, cream-apricot; intr. 2006

'Korbritta' Min, ab, Kordes

'Korbutte' F, mr, Kordessingle

'Korcalfer' HT, rb, Kordes; intr. 2002

'Korcapas' F, yb, Kordes, R.; bud globular; intr. 1964

'Korcapdra' HT, w, Kordes; intr. 2002

'Korcarill' Min, dp, Kordes; bud pointed ovoid

'Korcasirna' F, dr, Kordes; intr. 2007

'Korcelin' (Mandarin®) Min, ab, 2006; flowers salmon pink and mandarin orange-yellow with lighter center, 4 cm., full, borne in small clusters; foliage tiny, light green, glossy; growth compact, short (25 cm.); intr. 1987

'Korcentex' (Jasmina®) LCl, pb, 2006; flowers violet and pink, 6-7 cm., very full, cupped, borne in large clusters, moderate sweetish fragrance; foliage medium size, semi-glossy; bushy, well-branched (200 cm.) growth; intr. 2004

'Korcharm' HT, ab, Kordes; intr. 2005

'Korchumda' Min, lp, Kordes

'Korciate' ('Felicia Teichmann') HT, ob, Kordes; intr. 1991

'Korcigej' HT, rb, Kordes; intr. 2005

'Korcilmo' ('Escimo') F, w, Kordes; intr. 1991

'Korcleveth' S, pb, Kordes; intr. 2003

'Korcloco' S, ab, Kordes; intr. 2007

'Korcoeinf' Min, op, Kordes; intr. 2007

'Korcolla' HT, lp, Kordes; intr. 2005

'Korcoluma' ('My Valentine', 'Walter Sisulu') HT, mr, Kordes; bud pointed, red; intr. 2005

'Korconta' ('Country Song', 'Heideschnee', 'Moon River', 'Snow on the Heather') S, w, 1998, Kordes, W.; flowers white, 2 in., single, borne in large clusters, slight fragrance; foliage medium size, dark green, glossy; prickles moderate; medium tall groundcover (2½ ft.), spreading growth; PP10637; [Yesterday® × ('Sea Foam' × 'Red Max Graf')]; intr. 1996

'Korcoon' (Coon Carnival®) F, yb, 1985, Kordes, R.; bud ovoid; flowers yellow, changing to pink and red, large, 56 petals, borne singly or in clusters of up to 7, slight fragrance; foliage matte, green; prickles straight, brown; medium, bushy growth; [seedling × seedling]; intr. 1981

'Korcoptru' ('Triple Treat') S, w, Kordes; bud pointed, reddish; intr. 2004

'Korcountry' ('Bernalene') HT, ab, Kordes; intr. 1994

'Korcremkis' ('Madeo') F, w, Kordes; intr. 1991

'Korcremkis' F, w, Kordes; intr. 1991

'Korcrisett' ('Calibra') HT, or; intr. 1994

'Korcrozika' Min, lp, Kordes

'Kordaba' ('Lambada') HT, op, Kordes; bud long, pointed, ovoid; intr. 1992

'Kordadel' ('The Valois Rose') Min, yb, Kordes

'Kordaelf' ('Magma Freelander') HT, yb, Kordes; intr. 2005

'Kordaisy' ('Daisy Rose') F, pb, 1982, Kordes, W.; flowers pink with white eye, small, 5 petals, borne in large clusters; foliage medium size, medium green, semi-glossy; bushy growth; ['Robin Hood' × Topsi®]

'Kordakila' Min, ob, Kordes

'Kordalen' ('Antique 89', Antike 89®) LCl, w, 2006; flowers cream with carmine edging, 10 cm., full, borne in large clusters; foliage dark green, very glossy, leathery; growth vigorous, heavy canes, slow climber to 2½ m.; intr. 1988

'Kordalsilk' ('Kingsmead Heritage') F, w, Kordes; intr. 1996

'Kordalu' (Andalusien®) F, mr, 1977; bud long, pointed; flowers red, 3 in., 34 petals, cupped; vigorous, bushy growth; [seedling × 'Zorina']; intr. 1977

'Kordana Vanilla' Min, w, Kordes; flowers white with a greenish tint; intr. 2003

'Kordapt' ('Pheasant', Heidekönigin®, Palissade Rose®) HWich, lp, 1985, Kordes, W.; flowers medium to dark pink, touched coral, 5-6 cm., 35 petals; foliage small, medium green, glossy; groundcover; spreading growth; ['Zwerkönig '78' × (R. wichurana × unknown)]

'Kordatura' ('Sweet Vigorosa', Neon®) F, dp, 2006, W. Kordes' Söhne; bud small, rounded; flowers crimson pink, white at base of petals, yellow stamens, 5 cm., semi-dbl., shallow cupped, borne in small clusters; foliage medium size, reddish, turnin dark green, very glossy, disease-resistant; wide, bushy (60 cm.) growth; intr. 2001

'Kordauerpa' S, my, Kordes; intr. 2001

'Korday' ('Angelica', Angela®) F, dp, 1984, Kordes; flowers deep pink, 35 petals, cupped, borne singly and in clusters; foliage medium size, medium green, glossy; bushy growth; [Yesterday® × Peter Frankenfeld®]

'Kordehei' ('Malverns') F, m, Kordes

'Kordehn' ('Mireille Mathieu') F, or, 1973; bud ovoid; flowers large, 27 petals, high-centered; foliage soft; vigorous, upright, bushy growth; ['Fragrant Cloud' × Peer Gynt®]; intr. 1972

'Kordemas' ('Pink Button') Min, mp, Kordes; bud pointed; intr. 1990

Kordes' Brillant® -- See 'Korbisch'

'Kordes' Gärtnerfreude' -- See 'Gärtnerfreude'

'Kordes' Harmonie' -- See 'Harmonie'

'Kordes' Magenta' -- See 'Magenta'

'Kordes' Perfecta' ('Perfecta') HT, pb, 1959, Kordes; bud urn-shaped; flowers cream tipped and then flushed crimson, suffused yellow, 4½-5 in., 68 petals, high-centered, intense fragrance; foliage dark, leathery, glossy; vigorous, upright growth; PP1604; ['Golden Scepter' × 'Karl Herbst']; intr. 1957

'Kordes' Perfecta, Climbing' Cl HT, pb, 1962, Japan Rose Soc.; bud pointed; flowers creamy white, edged crimson, large, borne in small clusters, intense fragrance; [sport of 'Kordes' Perfecta']

'Kordes' Perfecta Superior' -- See 'Perfecta Superior'

'Kordes' Rose Aloha' -- See 'Kormarcus'

'Kordes' Rose Aloha' -- See 'Korwesrug'

'Kordes' Rose Anabel' -- See 'Korbell'

'Kordes' Rose Angelique' -- See 'Korangeli'

'Kordes' Rose Bella Rosa' -- See 'Korwonder'

'Kordes' Rose Champagner' -- See 'Korampa'

'Kordes' Rose Delicia' -- See 'Korgatum'

'Kordes' Rose Esmeralda' -- See 'Kormalda'

'Kordes' Rose Flamingo' -- See 'Korflüg'

Kordes' Rose Florentina® -- See 'Florentina'

'Kordes' Rose Gabriella' -- See 'Gabriella'

'Kordes' Rose Holstein' -- See 'Korholst'

Kordes' Rose Immensee® -- See 'Korimro'

'Kordes' Rose Julie' -- See 'Julie'

'Kordes Rose Kardinal' -- See 'Korlingo'

'Kordes' Rose Lady Rose' -- See 'Korlady'

'Kordes' Rose Park Wilhelmshöhe' -- See 'Korwilpa'

'Kordes' Rose Pasadena' -- See 'Korland'

Kordes' Rose Repandia® -- See 'Korsami'

Kordes' Rose Robusta® -- See 'Korgosa'

Kordes' Rose Sylt® -- See 'Korylt'

'Kordes' Rose Sylvia' -- See 'Korlift'

'Kordes' Rose Weisse Immensee' -- See 'Korweirim'

Kordes' Rose Westfalenpark® -- See 'Korplavi'

'Kordes' Silver Star' (Silver Star®) HT, m, 1966, Kordes, R.; flowers lavender, well-formed, 5 in., dbl., classic hybrid tea, borne singly, intense fragrance; free-flowering; foliage dark green; vigorous growth; ['Sterling Silver' × ('Magenta (F)' × unknown)]; intr. 1966

'Kordes' Sondermeldung' -- See 'Independence'

'Kordes' Sondermeldung, Climbing' -- See 'Independence, Climbing'

'Kordesii' (*R* × *kordesii* Wulff) HKor, dp, 1941, Kordes, W.; flowers bright red-pink, 2 in., semi-dbl., cupped; non-recurrent; foliage dark green, glossy; growth open, lax; hips elliptic-ovoid, vermilion; very hardy; ['Max Graf' × unknown]; intr. 1952

'Kordialo' ('Festival') MinFl, rb, Kordes; intr. 1994

'Kordiam' ('Heidi Kabel', Holsteinperle®, 'Testa Rossa') HT, op, 1987, Kordes, W.; flowers brilliant coral and salmon, open slowly, 4 in., dbl., high-centered, no fragrance; recurrent; foliage medium size, medium green, semi-glossy; bushy, vigorous, medium growth; [seedling × 'Flamingo']; intr. 1985

'Kordibor' (Rosendorf Sparrieshoop®) S, lp, Kordes; intr. 1988

'Kordibus' HT, rb, Kordes; intr. 2002

'Kordiena' ('Helen Naudé', 'New Pristine') HT, w, 1996, W. Kordes Söhne; flowers white flushed with pink, 4¾ in., very dbl.; foliage large, medium green, dull; prickles moderate; bushy, medium growth; intr. 1992

'Kordijau' HT, my, Kordes

'Kordisbad' HT, rb, Kordes; intr. 2003

'Kordisbad' Min, rb, Kordes

'Kordodo' (Larissa®) F, mr, 1987, Kordes, W.; flowers medium, full, no fragrance; foliage small, medium green, semi-glossy; spreading growth; [(seedling × Marina®) × 'Rumba']

'Kordomal' ('Global Rose') S, w, Kordes; intr. 1991

'Kordorsten' S, mr, Kordes; intr. 2000

'Kordoselbla' (Sunbeam®) HT, ab, 1987, Kordes, W.; flowers large, full; foliage large, dark green, semi-glossy; bushy growth; intr. 1986

'Kordoubt' ('Johannesburg Sun') HT, dy, 1988, W. Kordes Söhne; flowers deep golden yellow, large, 22 petals, borne singly, moderate fragrance; foliage glossy, deep green; prickles concave, brown; tall, upright growth; [seedling × seedling]; intr. 1988

'Kordrami' HT, op, Kordes; intr. 2002

'Kordreischi' HT, w, Kordes; bud creamy white; intr. 1997

'Kordrekes' ('Myrna's Dream') HT, ab, Kordes; intr. 1998

'Kordreweer' F , ly, Kordes; intr. 1998

'Kordrina' HT, op, Kordes; intr. 2005

'Kordroper' ('Lolly Pop') HT, op, Kordes; intr. 2001

'Kordruber' HT, rb, Kordes; intr. 2005

'Kordu' ('Duftzauber', 'Fragrant Charm') HT, mr, 1973, Kordes, R.; bud ovoid; flowers rose-red, large, dbl., high-centered, intense fragrance; foliage light, soft; moderate, upright growth; ['Prima Ballerina' × 'Kaiserin Farah']

'Korduran' HT, pb, Kordes; intr. 2006

'Kordurban' ('Durban July') F, rb, 1982, Kordes, W.; flowers yellow, orange to red, medium, semi-dbl.; foliage medium size, medium green, semi-glossy

'Korduvo' HT, w, Kordes; intr. 2002

'Kordwarul' ('Coffee Fruitilia') Min, dp, Kordes; intr. 2007

'Kordyrer' Min, mr, Kordesdbl.

'Kore' S, pb, Urban, J.; flowers yellowish-pink, with russet tints, large, dbl., intense fragrance; good repeat; vigorous (6 × 5 ft.) growth; intr. 1980

'Koreb' ('Diamond') F, or, Kordes, R.; bud ovoid; intr. 1962

'Korechtem' HT, w, Kordes; bud pointed-double; intr. 1994

'Koredan' ('Bluewunder', Blühwunder®, 'Ponderosa') F, mp, Kordes; intr. 1995

'Koregmobe' LCl, dr, Kordes; intr. 2002

'Koreibei' ('Bridget') F, dp, Kordesfull; intr. 1993

'Koreinek' HT, op, Kordes; intr. 2002

'Koreipark' (Rheinaupark®) S, mr, 1983, Kordes

'Koreistan' HT, op, Kordes ; bud slender, salmon-orange; intr. 2001

'Koreklia' ('Korastor', 'Valencia 89', Valencia®) HT, ab, 2006, Kordes; bud large, oval; flowers warm copper yellow, 12 cm., full, high-centered, borne mostly solitary, intense fragrance; recurrent; foliage fresh green, leathery; bushy, upright, medium growth; intr. 1989

'Korelasting' ('Summer Breeze', Linderhof®) S, mp, 2006; flowers brilliant pink with yellow stamens, 8 cm., single, borne in small clusters; foliage medium size, dark green, very glossy; vigorous (6 ft.) growth, canes arch over and down; intr. 1999

'Korelaval' Min, or, Kordesdbl.

'Koreledas' ('Big Fruitilia', 'Centenary', 'Heartache', 'National Radio', NDR 1 - Radio Niedersachsen®) F, dp, 2006; flowers 6 cm., semi-dbl., borne in small clusters; hips round to oval; intr. 1996

'Korelgas' ('Esme Euvrard') HT, lp, Kordes; intr. 1992

'Korelnobe' HT, mr, Kordes; intr. 2001

'Korelzoda' ('New Ballet') HT, dp, Kordes; bud round; intr. 1999

'Koremzila' HT, lp, Kordesfull; intr. 2004

'Korenbon' (Innocencia®) F, w, 1987, Kordes, W.; flowers medium, full, no fragrance; foliage medium size, medium green, matte; bushy growth; [sport of 'Lorena']; intr. 1986

'Korenlo' (Lorena®) F, mp, 1984, Kordes, W.; flowers medium salmon-pink, flora-tea, large, 35 petals, high-centered; foliage medium size, medium green, semi-glossy; upright growth; PP5679; ['Angelique' × seedling]; intr. 1983

'Korenon' F, op, Kordes; intr. 1993

'Korenpi' (Loretta®) F, mp, 1987, Kordes, W.; flowers medium, full, no fragrance; foliage medium size, medium green, matte; flora-tea, bushy growth; PP7479; [sport of 'Lorena']; intr. 1986

'Korescal' Min, dr, Kordes

'Koresswik' HT, mp, Kordes; intr. 2002

'Koretyal' HT, mp, Kordes; intr. 2005

'Koreubassa' HT, rb, Kordes; intr. 2005

'Korewala' Min, dy, Kordes

'Korfachrit' ('Andrea Stelzer') HT, lp, Kordes; intr. 1992

'Korfaduv' S, ab, Kordes; intr. 1999

'Korfalt' ('Goldmarie', Goldmarie Nirp®) F, dy, 1984, Kordes, W.; flowers deep yellow, red on reverse of outer petal, large, 35 petals, slight fragrance; foliage medium size, medium green, glossy; bushy growth; [(('Arthur Bell' × 'Zorina') × ('Honeymoon' × 'Dr. A.J. Verhage')) × (seedling × 'Sunsprite')]

'Korfan' ('Fantazia') HT, pb, 1974, Kordes; bud ovoid; intr. 1974

'Korfanto' ('Rosmarin 89', Rosmarin®) Min, dp, 2006; flowers full, borne in small clusters; foliage tiny, dark green, dense; compact, short (20 cm.) growth; intr. 1989

'Korfapal' HT, dp, Kordes; bud pointed intr. 2001

'Korfarim' ('Esther O'Farim') F, ob, Kordes, R.; bud ovoid; intr. 1972

'Korfativ' S, w, Kordes; intr. 2001

'Korfayfo' HT, ob, Kordes; buds pointed, urn-shaped, warm tangerine orange; intr. 2002

'Korfee' ('Dwarf Fairy') Min, or, 1979, Kordes, W.; bud globular

'Korfeimot' ('Countess Sonja', Gräfin Sonja®) HT, pb, 2006; bud long, pointed, cherry pink; flowers cherry pink with a lighter center, opening silvery pink, long lasting, 10 cm., full, high-centered, borne mostly solitary, slight, soft fragrance; foliage large, dark green, glossy; well-branched, upright (2½ ft.) growth; intr. 1994

'Korfeining' ('Caribbean Dawn', 'Dawn Sunsation', Maxi Vita®, 'Siena Vigorosa') F, op, 2006, W. Kordes' Söhne; flowers orange pink with yellow-orange petal base, 5 cm., semi-dbl., borne in large clusters, no fragrance; foliage medium size, fresh green, semi-glossy; compact, moderate, 60-70 cm. growth

'Korfeldwo' S, lp, Kordes; intr. 1997

'Korfenbak' Min, op, Kordes

'Korferse' ('Coco') LCl, or, Kordes; intr. 1989

'Korfi' ('Fiona') F, mr, 1976, Kordes; bud long, pointed; flowers 3 in., 24 petals, high-centered; foliage wrinkled; vigorous, upright growth; RULED EXTINCT 9/82 ARM; [seedling × Prominent®]

'Korfibi' ('Camilla Sunsation') S, dp, Kordes; intr. 1997

'Korfinger' (Marie-Luise Marjan®) HT, w, 2006; bud pointed, bright apricot; flowers cream white with a touch of pink and apricot, fading to clean white, 11 cm., dbl, high-centered, borne mostly solitary, moderate sweet/spicy fragrance; foliage first reddish, then dark green, leathery, glossy, upright, medium (120 cm.) growth; intr. 1999

'Korfirgo' ('Isabel', Satin Touch™) HT, dy, Kordes; buds elongated, sharply pointed

'Korfirona' ('Leigh Matthews Memorial Rose') HT, mp, Kordes; intr. 2002

'Korfischer' ('Hanza Park') S, m, Kordes; intr. 1994

'Korfisro' ('Sweet Sunsation') S, lp, Kordes

'Korfitase' HT, dp, Kordes; intr. 2001

'Korflamoni' HT, lp, Kordes; bud long, slender; intr. 2001

'Korflanka' HT, ob, Kordes; intr. 2003

'Korflapei' ('Pamela', Frisco®) F, my, 1987, Kordes, W.; flowers medium, full, slight fragrance; foliage medium size, dark green, semi-glossy; mini-flora bushy growth; PP6695; [(('New Day' × 'Minigold') × 'Banzai') × 'Antique Silk']; intr. 1986

'Korflata' ('Flame Dance') HEg, mr, 1955, Kordes' Söhne, W.

'Korfleur' ('Black Beauty®) F, rb, Kordes; intr. 1999

'Korflieder' Min, m, Kordes

'Korfloci' F, w, Kordes; intr. 2007

'Korfloci01' F, ly, Kordes; intr. 2008

'Korfloci02' F, ob, Kordesfull; intr. 2008

'Korfloci04' F, lp, Kordes; intr. 2008

'Korfloci05' ('Pom Pom Flower Circus') F, mp, Kordes; intr. 2008

'Korfloci08' F, ob, Kordes; intr. 2007

'Korfloci10' F, my, Kordes; intr. 2007

'Korfloci23' F, lp, Kordes; intr. 2008

'Korfloci24' F, dp, Kordes; intr. 2008

'Korflot' HT, dp, 1959, Kordes, R.

'Korflüg' ('Kordes' Rose Flamingo', 'Veronica', Flamingo®, 'Margaret Thatcher', 'Porcelain') HT, lp, 1979, Kordes, W.; bud large, long, pointed; flowers large, 24 petals, high-centered, borne singly, moderate fragrance; foliage matte, green; numerous prickles; vigorous, upright, bushy growth; PP5575; [seedling × 'Lady Like']; intr. 1978

'Korfobalt' (Cinderella®) S, lp, 2006, Kordes; flowers soft pink, 10 cm., very dbl., cupped, borne in clusters of 4-6, moderate fruity/apple fragrance; foliage medium size, dark green, very glossy, dense; growth very bushy, well branched, upright, 4-5 ft.; intr. 2003

'Korfolga' ('Splish Splash') S, w, Kordes

'Korfolklori' ('Herman Steyn') HT, rb, Kordes; intr. 1994

'Korfrauma' Min, op, Kordes

'Korfrilla' (Carnaval®) F, rb, 1987, Kordes, W.; flowers white with red edges, large, full, no fragrance; foliage medium size, dark green, matte; bushy growth; [seedling × ('Die Krone' × 'Simona')]; intr. 1986

'Korfriroy' Min, yb, Kordes

'Korfullwind' ('Baby Blanket', 'Summer Morning', 'Sommermorgen', 'Country Lass', 'Oxfordshire') S, lp, 1993, W. Kordes Söhne; flowers medium, dbl., borne in large clusters, slight fragrance; foliage small, dark green, glossy; few prickles; medium (60-75 cm.), bushy, spreading (120-150 cm.) growth; PP8872; [Weisse Immensee® × 'Goldmarie']; intr. 1993

'Korfungo' ('Country Prince') S, mr, Kordes

'Korgane' (Las Vegas®) HT, ob, 1980, Kordes, W.; bud large, pointed; flowers deep orange, reverse lighter, 26 petals, borne 1 - 3 per cluster, moderate fragrance; foliage green, slightly glossy; prickles brown; vigorous, upright, bushy growth; PP4798; [Ludwigshafen am Rhein® × 'Feuerzauber']; intr. 1981

'Korgater' HT, yb, Kordes

'Korgatine' ('Cream Sunsation') S, w, Kordes; buds deep cream, pointed, smallish; intr. 1996

'Korgatum' ('Delicia', 'Elegant Beauty', 'Kordes' Rose Delicia') HT, ly, 1982, Kordes, W.; flowers light yellow flushed pink, large, 20 petals; foliage large, dark, matte; upright, bushy growth; ['New Day' × seedling]

'Korgazell' ('Brilliant Vigorosa', Diamant®, 'Diamond', 'White Sunsation') S, w, 2006; bud small, pointed, oval; flowers pure white with large golden stamens, 6 cm., semi-dbl., flat, borne in small clusters, no fragrance; recurrent; foliage small, dark green, glossy, dense; groundcover; bushy (2 ft.) growth

'Korgenda' ('Shocking Sky') F, m, Kordes; bud pointed; intr. 1994

'Korgenoma' HT, w, Kordes; intr. 1998

'Korgera' ('Bagheera') F, or, 1976, Kordes, W.; bud ovoid; flowers 4 in., 35 petals, high-centered; foliage glossy, dark; vigorous, upright growth; ['Nordia' × seedling]

'Korgi' ('Blue Girl', 'Kölner Karneval') HT, m, 1965, Kordes, R.; intr. 1964

'Korgitte' ('Golden Queen') HT, ob, Kordes; intr. 1986

'Korglolev' Min, dp, Kordesfull

'Korglolev' Min, mp, Kordes; PP15717; ['Korengir' × 'Korfrauma']

'Korgo' ('Gold Topaz') F, my, 1963, Kordes, R.; bud ovoid

'Korgold' ('Goldy', 'Mabella', 'New Day') HT, my, 1973, Kordes, R.; bud ovoid, pointed; flowers mimosa-yellow, 4-5 in., 30 petals, cupped, intense fragrance; foliage large, light; upright growth; PP3228; ['Arlene Francis' × 'Roselandia']

'Korgolgat' LCl, dy, Kordes; intr. 2005

'Korgolki' HT, dy, Kordes; intr. 2003

'Korgorb' HT, ab, Kordes; intr. 1988

'Korgosa' (Kordes' Rose Robusta®, Robusta®) S, mr, 1979, Kordes, W.; bud long, pointed; flowers single, 5-8 petals, shallow cup, borne in clusters, slight fragrance; foliage large, dark green, glossy, leathery; numerous prickles; very vigorous, upright (6-7 ft.), bushy growth; [seedling × R. rugosa]

'Korgosumo' ('Yellow Angel', Gelber Engel®) F, ly, 2006; flowers light yellow with golden stamens, 6 cm., dbl., borne in small clusters; foliage very dense, dark green, very glossy, disease-resistant; low, erect and bushy (80 × 60 cm.) growth; intr. 2002

'Korgram' ('White Max Graf', Weisse Max Graf®) S, w, 1983, Kordes, W.; flowers white with yellow stamens, medium, semi-dbl., shallow cup, intense fragrance; foliage small, dark green, glossy; spreading (10 ft.) growth; groundcover; [seedling × (R. wichurana × unknown)]

'Korgrapet' ('Suncluster') F, my, Kordes

'Korgrasotra' ('Sister's Fairy Tale', Home & Garden®) F, lp, 2006; bud rounded, pink suffused greenish; flowers pure pink, aging softer, 8 cm., full, quartered, borne in large clusters, no fragrance; recurrent; foliage medium size, dark green, dense; bushy, upright (80 cm.) growth; intr. 2001

'Korgrayel' ('Saffex Rose') F, m, Kordes; intr. 1993

'Korgreeni' Min, w, Kordes

'Korgretaum' (Make-A-Wish Australia®, Petticoat®, Petticoat Fairy Tale™) F, w, 2006; flowers cream white with soft apricot coloured center, 6-7 cm., full, borne in small clusters; growth compact, medium (70 cm.); intr. 2004

'Korgreyel' ('The J. S. E. Rose') F, dy, Kordes

'Korgund' (Burgund®) HT, dr, 1977, Kordes, W.; bud long, pointed; flowers 4 in., 30 petals, high-centered; vigorous, bushy growth; [Henkell Royal® × seedling]

'Korgund '81' ('Burgund '81', 'Loving Memory', 'Red Cedar') HT, mr, 1983, Kordes, W.; flowers large, dbl., high-centered; foliage medium green, semi-glossy; upright, bushy growth; [seedling × ('Red Planet' × unknown)]; intr. 1981

'Korgust' ('Stadt Wurzburg', 'Sunsation', 'Veldfire', 'Wurzburg') HT, ab, 1988, W. Kordes Söhne; flowers orange, reverse chrome-yellow, medium, 38 petals, high-centered, borne singly, slight fragrance; recurrent; foliage glossy, medium green; prickles concave, yellow-brown; upright, well-branched, free-flowering growth; [seedling × seedling]; intr. 1988

'Korgutopf' S, w, Kordes ; buds long, pointed; intr. 1998

'Korgyzin' HT, lp, Kordes; intr. 2001

'Korhabib' HT, mr, Kordes; intr. 2007

'Korhagon' ('Pretoria') HT, dp, Kordes; bud long, pointed; intr. 1992

'Korhamp' ('Hampshire') S, mr, Kordes; intr. 1989

'Korhanbu' ('Belami', 'Woods of Windsor') HT, op, 1986, Kordes, W.; flowers orange pink, large, 35 petals, high-centered, moderate fragrance; foliage medium size, dark, glossy; upright, bushy growth; [(Prominent® × Carina®) × 'Emily Post']; intr. 1985

'Korharment' ('Francois Krige') S, dr, Kordes; intr. 1993

'Korhassi' ('Charles Notcutt', Hansaland®) HRg, dr, 2006; flowers bright, deep scarlet with yellow stamens, 7 cm., semi-dbl., cupped, borne singly and in small clusters; foliage reddish when young, turning light green, semi-glossy, rounded; bushy, upright (6 ft.) growth; intr. 1993

'Korhaugen' ('Cambridgeshire', 'Fun Sunsation') S, rb, Kordes

'Korhedani' Min, dr, Kordesdbl.

'Korheim' ('Morning Red', Morgenrot®) S, rb, 1986, Kordes, W.; flowers medium, 5 petals; foliage small, dark, matte; bushy growth; [('Marlena' × Europeana®) × (('Tropicana' × Carina®) × ('Clare Grammerstorf' × 'Fruhlingsmorgen'))]; intr. 1985

'Korherkul' S, m, Kordes; intr. 2007

'Korhitbel' F, pb, Kordes; intr. 2006

'Korhitom' ('Golden Fire', Sonnenkind®, 'Perestroika') Min, dy, 1987, Kordes, W.; flowers deep golden yellow, medium, dbl., high-centered, slight fragrance; recurrent; foliage small, dark green, semi-glossy; bushy, upright (14 in.) growth; [seedling × 'Goldmarie']; intr. 1986

'Korhocsel' HT, rb; intr. 2002

'Korhokhel' (La Vanoise Parc National®, Rosanna®) LCl, op, 2006, W. Kordes' Söhne; flowers salmon pink, 11 cm., full, borne in small clusters, slight fragrance; recurrent; foliage large, glossy; spreading, tall (200 cm.) growth; intr. 2002

'Korholesea' F, dy, Kordes; intr. 2004

'Korholst' ('City of Birmingham', 'Petit Marquis', 'Kordes' Rose Holstein', 'Holstein', Esprit®) S, dr, 1987, Kordes, W.; flowers deep red, aging darker, medium, 12 petals, flat, borne in sprays of 5-7, no fragrance; repeat bloom; foliage small, medium green, semi-glossy; prickles medium, tan, slightly down pointed; upright, bushy, tall growth; no fruit; PP6117; [seedling × Chorus®]; intr. 1989

'Korhomapo' Min, mr, Kordes; bud long, blunt topped; intr. 1998

'Korhood' ('Rooi Rose') HT, mr, Kordes; bud pointed; intr. 1993

'Korhoro' (Morgensonne 88®) LCl, ly, 2006, W. Kordes' Söhne; flowers rich yellow, fading quickly to cream, 10 cm., dbl., borne mostly solitary; foliage dark green, glossy; growth compact, tall (300 cm.); intr. 1988

'Korhota' ('Sarie Marals') HT, pb, Kordes

'Korhuba' ('Glendore') HT, ab, Kordes; intr. 1995

'Korhug' ('St Hughs') HT, my, 1987, Kordes, W.; flowers creamy yellow, large, full, moderate fragrance; foliage medium size, medium green, semi-glossy; upright, bushy growth; [seedling × seedling]; intr. 1986

'Korhurtlen' ('Copper Arch') LCl, ob, Kordes; buds golden, shapely; intr. 1991

'Korhuylou' S, lp, Kordes; intr. 2005

'Koriant' (Weisse Repandia®) S, w, 1983, Kordes, W.; flowers small, semi-dbl., foliage small, dark, glossy; spreading (7 ft.) growth; groundcover; ['The Fairy' × (R. wichurana × unknown)]

'Koribra' HT, op, Kordes; intr. 1995

'Koricesi' HT, pb, Kordes; intr. 2005

'Korichard' ('Plisiedame') F, ab, Kordes; intr. 1990

'Koricole' ('Nicole') F, w, 1985, Kordes, W.; flowers white with soft pink petal edges, large, 30-35 petals, high-centered to cupped, borne singly and in clusters, slight fragrance; recurrent; foliage large, dark, semi-glossy; moderate, upright growth; [seedling × Bordure Rose®]; intr. 1984

'Koriet' ('Avenue's Red', Konrad Henkel®) HT, mr, 1983, Kordes, W.; flowers large, 35 petals, high-centered, moderate fragrance; foliage large, medium green, semi-glossy; upright, bushy growth; [seedling × 'Red Planet']

'Koriganta' ('Antoinette') HT, ab, Kordes; intr. 1993

'Korignale' HT, w, Kordes; intr. 1995

'Korikon' ('Limelight', Golden Medaillon®) HT, ly, 1985, Kordes, W.; flowers large, 35 petals, high-centered, intense fragrance; foliage medium size, dark, semi-glossy; upright, bushy, spreading growth; ['Peach Melba' × seedling]

'Korildambu' Min, lp, Kordes

'Korilona' F, my, 1975, Kordes, R.; bud ovoid; intr. 1976

'Korimro' ('Grouse', Immensee®, Kordes' Rose Immensee®, Lac Rose®) S, lp, 1983, Kordes, W.; flowers light pink to near white, small, single; foliage small, dark, glossy; spreading (to 13 ft.) growth; groundcover; ['The Fairy' × (R. wichurana × unknown)]; intr. 1982

'Korinor' ('Mandy') HT, dr, Kordes; intr. 1987

'Korinter' ('Rosanna') LCl, op, 1985, Kordes, W.; flowers salmon pink, large, 35 petals, camellia, moderate fragrance; foliage medium size, medium green, glossy; upright, tall growth; [Coral Dawn® × seedling]; intr. 1982

'Korionluck' ('Trump') HT, ab, Kordes; intr. 2005

'Koriox' HT, dy, Kordes; intr. 2003

'Korislas' HT, mr, Kordes; intr. 2002

'Korisofus' F, ab, Kordes; bud slender, pointed, apricot colored

'Korissel' ('Jeeper's Creeper') S, w, 1993, W. Kordes Söhne; flowers medium, 6-14 petals, borne in large clusters; foliage medium size, dark green, semi-glossy; numerous prickles; low (40-50 cm.), spreading growth; PP8871; [Yesterday® × 'Edelweiss']; intr. 1994

'Koristava' Min, ab, Kordes

'Korita' ('Peach Melba') HT, ab, 1979, W. Kordes Söhne; bud long, pointed

'Korituscha' ('Triodene') F, op, Kordes

'Koriver' ('Esterel', 'Heidekind') S, dr, 1985, Kordes, W.; flowers medium, 20 petals; foliage small, medium green, glossy; upright, bushy growth; ['The Fairy' × seedling]

'Korivo' ('Ivory Beauty') F, w, Kordes; bud pointed, urn-shaped; intr. 1985

'Korizont' ('Summer Wine') LCl, op, 1985, Kordes, W.; bud conical; flowers salmon pink, red stamens, 3 in., single, flat, borne mostly in clusters, moderate fruity fragrance; recurrent; foliage large, medium green, semi-glossy; prickles large; upright (8 ft.), bushy growth

'Korjafir' HT, m, W. Kordes Söhne; bud urceolate; intr. 2002

'Korjan' HT, or, Kordes

'Korjepgo' HT, yb, Kordes; intr. 2003

'Korjoni' (Zitronenjette®) HT, my, 1987, Kordes, W.; flowers large, dbl.; foliage large, medium green, glossy; spreading growth; ['Sutter's Gold' × 'Sunblest']; intr. 1986

'Korjulon' ('Oranje Meisieskool') HT, ab, Kordes; intr. 2003

'Korkalba' Min, w; intr. 1994

'Korkandel' S, pb, Kordes; intr. 1991

'Korkat' HT, w, Kordes; bud white with green tinge; intr. 1995

'Korkeilich' ('Pepita') Min, dp, 1987, Kordes, W.; flowers deep pink, small, full, no fragrance; foliage small, medium green, semi-glossy; spreading growth; ['Lenpi' × ('Mercedes' × 'Garnette')]; intr. 1985

'Korkeindor' ('Nancy Gardiner') F, op, Kordes; intr. 1994

'Korkeltin' ('Tradition 95', Tradition®) LCl, mr, 2006; flowers luminous deep red, conspicuous yellow stamens, 8 cm., semi-dbl., cupped to flat, borne in large clusters, slight fragrance; recurrent; foliage medium size, dark green, very glossy; bushy, upright (10 ft.) growth; intr. 1995

'Korkengi' Min, mp, Kordesfull

'Korkilet' Min, mr, Kordes

'Korkilgwen' (Sunny Rose®) S, ly, 2006, Kordes; bud small, rounded; flowers pale yellow, 3 cm., dbl., cupped to flat, borne in small clusters, no fragrance; recurrent; foliage small, dark green, very glossy; bushy, short (40 cm.), growth; intr. 2001

'Korkilt' HT, lp, Kordes; intr. 1996

'Korkinteral' ('Reminiscence', Caramella®) S, my, 2006; flowers large, amber yellow, 10 cm., full, nearly quartered, borne in small clusters; foliage large, green, semi-glossy; vigorous, erect, upright growth to 120 cm.; intr. 2001

'Korkister' (Orange Juwel®) Min, op, 2006; flowers salmon orange, 3 cm., full, borne in small clusters; foliage medium size, dark green; bushy, short (30 cm.) growth; intr. 1987

'Korkisusa' HT, w, Kordes; bud pointed, urn shaped; intr. 2001

'Korkitoek' HT, lp, Kordes; intr. 2002

'Korkleiva' ('Vanilla Kordana Mini Brite') Min, ly, Kordes; intr. 2000

'Korklemol' (Moonlight®) LCl, yb, 2006, W. Kordes' Söhne; flowers copper yellow, fading lighter, 12 cm., semi-dbl., borne in clusters of 4-6; foliage large, dark green, very glossy; vigorous, tall (2 m.) growth; intr. 2004

'Korklieva' Min, w, Kordes; intr. 2003
'Korkojotie' HT, ab, Kordes; intr. 2008
'Korkompo' ('Anja') F, op, Kordes; bud sharply pointed; intr. 1993
'Korkönig' ('Dwarf King 78', Zwergkönig 78®) MinFl, mr, 2006; flowers vivid deep red, 5 cm., semi-dbl., borne in small clusters; foliage dark green, dense; growth compact, medium (50 cm.); intr. 1978
'Korkonopi' ('County of Cheshire') S, mp, Kordes; intr. 2001
'Korkopapp' F, dp, Kordes/Koopmann; intr. 2000
'Korkouw' F, ab, Kordes
'Korkragor' ('Coral Spire') HT, mp, Kordes; intr. 1994
'Korkufat' ('Babette Stutzer') HT, op, Kordes; intr. 1999
'Korkularis' HT, ly, Kordes; bud slender; intr. 1999
'Korkultop' ('Blue Bayou', 'Blue-Bijou') F, m, Kordes; intr. 1993
'Korkuma' ('Goldmarie, Climbing') Cl F, yb, Martens; intr. 1998
'Korkunde' ('Toscana') F, or, 1972, Warriner, William A.; bud long, pointed
'Korkunde' F, mr, Kordes; intr. 1991
'Korlabriax' (Amadeus®) LCl, dr, 2006; bud dark red; flowers dark red with little bluing, 8 cm., dbl., borne in clusters of 5-7; foliage large, dark green, very glossy; growth climbing, 8+ ft. tall; intr. 2003
'Korlady' ('Kordes' Rose Lady Rose', Lady Rose®) HT, op, 1978, W. Kordes Söhne; bud long, pointed; flowers salmon-orange, 5 in., 34 petals, high-centered, borne singly and in clusters, moderate fragrance; recurrent; foliage large, dense, glossy; vigorous, upright, bushy (3 ft.) growth; [seedling × 'Traumerei']
'Korlalla' LCl, dp, Kordes; intr. 1994
'Korlalon' S, my, Kordes; intr. 2000
'Korlamber' ('Pixie Hat') F, mr, Kordes; intr. 1993
'Korland' ('Kordes' Rose Pasadena', Pasadena®) HT, or, 1982, Kordes, W.; flowers large, lasting, 35 petals, high-centered, no fragrance; foliage large, medium green, matte; upright growth; ['Mercedes' × ('Sweet Promise' × ('Miss Ireland' × 'Zorina'))]; intr. 1981
'Korlanum' ('Gotenborgs Posten', 'Summer Breeze', 'Vent d'Été', 'Summerwind', 'Surrey', 'Sommerwind') S, lp, 1985, Kordes, W.; flowers soft pink, medium, semi-dbl., cupped, borne in clusters; recurrent; foliage small, medium green, semi-glossy; bushy (2-3 ft.), spreading growth; ['The Fairy' × seedling]
'Korlaper' F, lp, Kordes; intr. 1994
'Korlarkon' ('Delicate Beauty') HT, w, Kordes; buds pointed, light cream-yellow
'Korlasche' ('Magaliesburg Roos') HT, m, Kordes; intr. 1993
'Korlawe' S, ab, 1976, Kordes; bud ovoid; intr. 1969
'Korlech' ('Intrigue', 'Lava Flow', 'Lavaglow', Lavaglut®) F, dr, 1979, W. Kordes Söhne; flowers 2½ in., 24 petals, globular, borne in clusters; foliage glossy; vigorous, upright, bushy growth; [Gruss an Bayern® × seedling]

'Korlecobi' HT, op, Kordes; intr. 1999
'Korleen' ('Bavarian Girl', Schöne Münchnerin®) F, mr, 1985, Kordes, W.; flowers 22 petals, cupped, borne 2-3 per cluster; foliage medium size, medium green, semi-glossy; prickles medium, green; bushy growth; [Sympathie® × Tornado®]
'Korlehnig' LCl, op, Kordes; intr. 2004
'Korlette' ('Dorandi', 'Harlekin', Harlequin™) HT, m, 1998, Kordes, W.; flowers lavender pink, white reverse, 4 in., full, borne mostly singly, slight fragrance; foliage medium size, dark green, glossy; few prickles; bushy, low (3 ft.) growth; PP11271; ['Prima Ballerina' × 'Peace']; possibly synonymous with 'Korlupo'; intr. 1998
'Korleu' F, mr, Kordes; intr. 1978
'Korlexado' HT, yb, Kordes; intr. 2001
'Korlichtung' ('Ruth Pennington') F, my, Kordes; intr. 1993
'Korlidamo' HT, ab, Kordes; intr. 2002
'Korlift' ('Congratulations', 'Kordes' Rose Sylvia', 'Sylvia') HT, op, 1979, W. Kordes Söhne; bud long, pointed; flowers medium pink, 4½ in., 42 petals, high-centered, moderate fragrance; foliage semi-glossy; vigorous, upright, bushy growth; [Carina® × seedling]
'Korligel' HT, ly, Kordes; intr. 2001
'Korligora' S, w, Kordes; bud globular, slightly pointed; intr. 1997
'Korlillewa' Min, w, Kordes
'Korlilub' ('Lucia', 'Reine Lucia', 'Queen Lucia', Lichtkönigin Lucia®) S, my, 1985, Kordes, W.; flowers 18 petals, cupped, borne 3-5 per cluster, moderate fragrance; foliage medium size, dark, glossy; bushy, tall growth; ['Zitronenfalter' × 'Cläre Grammerstorf']; intr. 1966
'Korlima' ('Lili Marlene', Lilli Marleen®) F, mr, 1960, Kordes, R.; bud ovoid; intr. 1959
'Korlimit' ('Cora Marie', 'Dallas') HT, mr, 1987, Kordes, W.; flowers large, dbl., no fragrance; foliage large, dark green, semi-glossy; upright growth; ['Ankori' × seedling]; intr. 1986
'Korlinde' HT, ob, Kordes; intr. 1987
'Korlingo' ('Kardinal 85', 'Kordes Rose Kardinal', Kardinal®) HT, mr, 1986, Kordes, W.; flowers large, bright red, 4½-5 in., 30-35 petals, high-centered, borne singly, long vase life, slight fragrance; foliage medium size, dark, semi-glossy; upright growth, medium; PP5846; [seedling × 'Flamingo']; intr. 1985
'Korlinik' ('Sunny Kordana') Min, my, Kordes; intr. 1998
'Korlinsun' F, ob, Kordes; intr. 2005
'Korlirus' ('Cevennes', Heidesommer®) F, w, 1985, Kordes, W.; flowers medium, 20 petals; foliage small, dark, glossy; upright, bushy growth; ['The Fairy' × seedling]

'Korlitare' Min, w, Kordes; intr. 2005
'Korlitze' ('Lady Mavis Pilkington') HT, ob, Kordes; intr. 1992
'Korlo' ('Red Queen') HT, mr, 1968, Kordes; bud ovoid
'Korlobea' Min, pb, Kordes ; bud between urceolate and ovate
'Korlodera' ('Pink Spectacle') S, mp, Kordes; intr. 1995
'Korlodico' Min, mp, Kordes
'Korloher' ('Kingswood College') F, mr, Kordes; intr. 1990
'Korlomet' ('Kookaburra', 'Vogelpark Walsrode') S, lp, 2006; flowers light pink, shaded peach, darker at edges, 8 cm., semi-dbl., cupped, borne in airy clusters, slight fragrance; occasional repeat; foliage tiny, medium green, glossy; wide, bushy, medium growth; intr. 1988
'Korlore' HT, ob, 1976, Kordes; bud long, pointed; intr. 1975
'Korlortas' HT, pb, Kordes; bud very large; intr. 2002
'Korlougel' LCl, w, Kordes; intr. 2006
'Korlowi' ('Cathie Irwin') Gr, ob, Kordes
'Korludwig' ('Ludwigshafen') F, dp, 1976, Kordes; bud ovoid; intr. 1975
'Korlufter' HT, mr, Kordes; intr. 1997
'Korlumara' ('Circus 99') HT, yb, Kordes
'Korlungbre' F, pb, Kordes; intr. 1999
'Korlunta' (Daniela®) Min, lp, Kordesdbl.; intr. 1987
'Korlupo' ('Kiss of Desire', Harlekin®) LCl, pb, 2006; flowers cream white with clear red edging, 9 cm., full, borne in small clusters; foliage dark green, glossy; growth bushy, tall (250 cm.)
'Korluspo' HT, dr, Kordes; intr. 2005
'Korlyn' ('Lynette') HT, w, 1985, Kordes, R.; bud long, pointed; flowers cream blended with coral pink, well-formed, large, dbl., borne singly or in clusters of up to 5, no fragrance; foliage dark; prickles straight, brown; tall, upright growth; [Clivia® × 'MEltakilor']; intr. 1983
'Kormador' F, ab, Kordes; intr. 1988
'Kormagneto' Min, dp, Kordes
'Kormagoro' ('New Carousel') HT, pb, Kordes; intr. 2002
'Kormai' (Mainauperle®) HT, dr, 1973, Kordes, R.; bud ovoid; flowers large, dbl., high-centered, intense fragrance; foliage large, dark, leathery; vigorous, upright, bushy growth; [seedling × 'Americana']; intr. 1969
'Kormalda' ('Keepsake', Esmeralda®, 'Kordes' Rose Esmeralda') HT, pb, 1981, W. Kordes Söhne; bud ovoid; flowers deep pink blended with lighter pink shades, reflexed, large, 40 petals, exhibition, moderate fragrance; foliage dark; prickles large, stout; vigorous, bushy growth
'Kormamtiza' ('Afternoon Delight', 'Cervia', Floral Fairy Tale™, Sangerhäusen Jubiläumsrose®) F, ab, 2006, W. Kordes' Söhne; flowers soft apricot, fading to pink, 6-7 cm., full, old-fashioned, borne in trusses, moderate, sweetish

fragrance; foliage medium size, dark green, dense; bushy, medium (70 cm.) growth

'Kormantona' HT, r, Kordes; intr. 2002

'Kormapoki' S, m, Kordes; intr. 2004

'Kormarcus' ('Kordes' Rose Aloha') HT, yb, Kordes; intr. 1999

'Kormarec' ('Red Immensee', 'Summer Evening') S, dr, Kordes; intr. 1995

'Kormarie' ('Miss Pam Ayres', Bonanza®) S, yb, 1982, Kordes, W.; flowers yellow tipped red, large, 20 petals, slight fragrance; foliage medium size, dark, glossy; upright growth; [seedling × 'Arthur Bell']; intr. 1983

'Kormarter' ('Sunrise', Freisinger Morgenröte®) S, ob, 2006; flowers orange with yellow reverse and pink edges, 7 cm., semi-dbl., high-centered, borne in large clusters; foliage deep green, glossy; growth wide, tall, 150 cm; intr. 1988

'Kormasyl' ('Pink Pearl') HT, lp, Martens; intr. 1989

'Kormat' ('Mona Lisa') F, ab, 1981, Kordes; bud ovoid

'Kormate' ('Graaff-Reinet') HT, ab, 1988, W. Kordes Söhne; flowers apricot with orange on petal margin, large, 36 petals, borne in sprays, moderate fragrance; foliage dull, medium green; prickles concave, reddish-brown; compact, medium, well branched, free flowering growth; [seedling × seedling]; intr. 1988

'Kormatt' ('St Boniface') F, or, 1982, Kordes, W.; flowers bright vermilion red, medium, 35 petals, hybrid tea form, slight fragrance; foliage medium size, dark, semi-glossy; upright (2 ft.), bushy growth; [Diablotin® × 'Traumerei']

'Kormauret' ('Red Curtain') LCl, dr, Kordes; intr. 1994

'Kormax' ('Red Max Graf', Rote Max Graf®) HKor, mr, 1980, Kordes, W.; bud medium, ovoid; flowers deep red with white at petal base, 7 cm., 6 petals, borne in large clusters, moderate fragrance; recurrent; foliage small, leathery, matte; prickles dark brown; vigorous, trailing groundcover growth; [R. × kordesii × seedling]

'Kormazin' ('Country Gold') F, my, Kordes; intr. 1991

'Kormeeram' ('Royal Dream') HT, dp, Kordes; bud long, pointed ovoid, blunt tip; intr. 1997

'Kormeita' ('Agatha Christie') LCl, mp, W. Kordes' Sohne; intr. 1988

'Kormeneint' ('My Pretty Garden', Mein Schöner Garten®) S, mp, 2006, W. Kordes' Söhne; flowers soft pink with a breath of salmon, center lighter, 9 cm., dbl., borne in small clusters, slight fruity, fresh fragrance; foliage medium size, dark green, very glossy; growth compact, medium (120 cm.); intr. 1997

'Kormentoka' HT, m, Kordes; intr. 1999

'Kormerwind' S, lp; intr. 1993

'Kormetter' ('Anna Livia', 'Trier 2000', 'Sandton Smile') F, op, 1985, Kordes, W.; flowers orange pink, large, 20 petals; foliage medium size, medium green, semi-glossy; bushy growth; [(seedling × Tornado®) × seedling]

'Kormiach' ('City of Windsor', 'Crimson Spire', Liebeszauber®) HT, dr, 2006, W. Kordes' Söhne; bud large, oval, dark red; flowers brilliant deep red, 11 cm., very full, high-centered, borne mostly solitary; foliage reddish, turning dark green, leathery; large, spreading (4-6 ft.) growth

'Kormifari' ('Escimo') S, w, Kordes; intr. 2004

'Kormikflo' F, mp, Kordes; intr. 2006

'Kormiller' HT, pb; intr. 1997

'Korminuva' Min, dr, Kordesdbl.

'Kormiora' ('Rosi Mittermeier') F, or, 1976, Kordes; bud globular; intr. 1975

'Kormispag' Min, my, Kordesdbl.

'Kormisso' Min, dp, Kordes

'Kormistiana' ('Ice Girl', 'Ice-Girl Panarosa') HT, w, Kordes

'Kormixal' ('Suffolk', Bassino®) S, mr, 2006, W. Kordes' Söhne; flowers with ruffled petals and yellow stamens, 3 cm., single, cupped, borne in small, dense clusters; foliage small, glossy, dense; growth wide and bushy (25 cm.), canes at first upright, but later low

'Kormixsosia' ('Cinderella', 'Ruth Bell Graham Rose') HT, lp, Kordes; intr. 2003

'Kormobada' HT, ab, Kordes; intr. 2002

'Kormocent' S, op, Kordes; intr. 2001

'Kormocru' S, dr, Kordes; intr. 2005

'Kormodika' HT, op, Kordes; intr. 1998

'Kormoigol' HT, w, Kordes; intr. 2006

'Kormollis' ('Garden Party') F, mr, Kordes; intr. 1999

'Kormonajac' S, mr, Kordes; intr. 2002

'Kormonfri' Min, my, Kordesfull

'Kormorlet' (Salita®) LCl, or, 2006; bud large, ovoid; flowers orange scarlet, 9 cm., full, high-centered, borne in small clusters, no fragrance; foliage reddish when young, later dark green, glossy; upright, tall (250 cm.) growth; intr. 1987

'Kormöwe' ('Klerksdorp Horizon') HT, rb, 1988, W. Kordes Söhne; flowers tomato-red, reverse golden yellow, large, 32 petals, borne 1 - 3 per cluster, no fragrance; foliage medium green, large; prickles concave, reddish-brown; upright, medium, free-flowering growth; [seedling × seedling]; intr. 1988

'Kormun' ('Bavaria', Gruss an Bayern®) F, mr, 1973, Kordes, R.; flowers blood-red, medium, semi-dbl., globular, slight fragrance; foliage dark, leathery; vigorous, upright growth; ['Messestadt Hannover' × 'Hamburg']; intr. 1971

'Kormunde' ('Rosamunde') F, mp, Kordes; intr. 1975

'Kormuse' ('Beautiful Carpet', 'Elfrid') S, mp, Kordes; intr. 1993

'Kormutric' Min, ab, Kordes

'Kornacho' ('Gartenzauber '84', Gartenzauber®) F, mr, 1984, Kordes, W.; flowers large, 35 petals, high-centered; foliage medium size, dark, semi-glossy; upright growth; [(seedling × Tornado®) × Chorus®]

'Kornafiro' HT, mr, Kordes; intr. 1999

'Kornagent' ('Florence') F, lp, Kordes; intr. 1987

'Kornalist' HT, my, Kordes; bud large, pointed; intr. 1999

'Kornanze' (Golden Medaillon®) HT, dy, 2006; bud long, deep yellow with a breath of copper; flowers deep yellow, tinted copper, 11 cm., full, high-centered, borne in airy clusters; foliage dark green, shiny, tough; bushy, upright (3 ft.) growth; intr. 1991

'Kornauer' (Agnes Bernauer®) HT, lp, Kordes; bud globular; intr. 1989

'Korneamus' Min, dr, Kordes; intr. 2005

'Kornemark' HT, op, Kordes; intr. 1992

'Kornemuta' (Schneeküsschen®) Min, w, 2006; flowers white, suffused pink, 3 cm., dbl., borne in small clusters; foliage tiny, fresh green; growth compact, short (30 cm.); intr. 1993

'Kornends' ('Charlotte Searle') HT, mr, Kordes

'Körner' HMsk, yb, 1914, Lambert, P.; bud reddish; flowers orange-yellow tinted salmon, dbl., borne in clusters; [Trier® × 'Eugenie Lamesch']

'Kornicken' (Anjou®) S, op, Kordes

'Korniebon' LCl, lp, Kordes; bud small, deep pink; intr. 1998

'Kornieoch' HT, pb; intr. 1990

'Kornijfla' HT, rb, Kordes

'Kornilsca' Min, dp, Kordes; intr. 2005

'Kornita' F, or, 1955, Kordes

'Kornitzel' ('Boksburg Fantasia', 'Red Fantasy') HT, mr, 1988, W. Kordes Söhne; flowers large, 23 petals, borne in sprays of 1-3, moderate fragrance; foliage medium green; prickles needle point, brown; tall, well-branched growth; [seedling × seedling]; intr. 1988

'Kornokiva' HT, lp, Kordes; intr. 2000

'Kornolia' Min, lp, Kordes

'Kornuma' ('Red Pixie', Heinzelmännchen®) F, mr, 1983, Kordes, W.; flowers large, 35 petals; foliage medium size, medium green, glossy; bushy growth; [(Satchmo® × seedling) × ('Messestadt Hannover' × 'Hamburg')]

'Kornumiks' S, dy, Kordes; intr. 2003

'Koro' HT, mr, 1984, Cattermole, R.F.; flowers scarlet, large, 32 petals, high-centered, intense fruity fragrance; foliage medium green; prickles reddish; upright growth; [('Pink Parfait' × unknown) × 'Red Planet']

'Koroberfinz' ('Margaret Wasserfall') HT, w, Kordes; intr. 1994

'Korocken' HT, ob, Kordes; intr. 1997

'Korofaser' ('Peach Spire') HT, ob, Kordes; intr. 1994

'Korogesa' ('Helpmekaar Roos') HT, ab, Kordes; intr. 1993

'Koroketto' ('Futura') F, m, Kordes; intr. 1994

'Korokis' F, op; intr. 1988

'Korol' HT, yb, 1970, Kordes, R.; intr. 1968

'Korol' ('Coppertone', 'Old Time') HT, ob, 1969, Kordes, R.

'Korola' (Rheinaupark®) S, mr, 1983, Kordes; flowers large, 20 petals; foliage large, dark, glossy; upright, bushy growth; [(Gruss an Bayern® × seedling) × (*R. rugosa* × unknown)]

'Korolani' Min, rb, Kordes

'Korolesola' HT, pb, Kordes; bud large; intr. 2002

'Koromega' ('Pat's Choice') HT, or, Kordes; intr. 1996

'Korommerla' ('Peach Sunsation') S, ab, Kordes; intr. 1997

'Koromtar' ('Cream Dream') HT, w, Kordes; intr. 1997

'Korona' S, ab, Unmuth; flowers amber yellow, borne singly and in clusters; upright, branching (7 ft.) growth; intr. about 2000

Korona® F, or, 1955, Kordes; flowers orange-scarlet, 2½ in., 20 petals, borne in large trusses; vigorous, upright growth

'Korona, Climbing' Cl F, or, 1957, Kordes; [sport of 'Korona']

'Koronabaj' S, m, Kordes; intr. 2003

'Koronam' HT, w, Kordes; intr. 1994

'Koronet' HT, ob, 1941, Mallerin, C.; bud globular, lemon shaded orange; flowers orange, reverse deep primrose, 4½ in., 40-50 petals, high-centered; foliage dark, glossy, leathery; vigorous, upright, bushy, open growth; PP596; ['Julien Potin' × 'Bright Wings']

'Koronto' (Burghausen®) S, mr, 2006; flowers light red with ruffled petals, 8 cm., dbl., cupped, borne in small clusters and trusses with many flowers; foliage semi-glossy; bushy, upright, arching growth with heavy, well-branched canes; intr. 1991

'Koropas' (Sir Henry®) HRg, m, Kordes; intr. 1988

'Koropti' ('Champagnerperle') F, ab, W. Kordes Söhne; intr. 1983

'Kororagut' Min, ob, Kordes; intr. 2005

'Kororanki' ('Jacqueline') F, ob, Kordes; intr. 1994

'Kororbe' ('Summer Beauty', Aprikola®) F, ab, 2006; bud rounded, orange-yellow; flowers deep apricot yellow, change to apricot-pink, 6 cm., full, borne in small clusters, slight fruity, sourish fragrance; foliage medium size, dark green, very glossy, very disease-resistant; growth wide, medium, 70 cm.; intr. 2000

'Korosi' HT, w, Kordes; bud pointed; intr. 2008

'Koroskin' Min, ab, Kordes; intr. 2005

'Korovo' HT, op, 1931, Leenders, M.; bud pointed; flowers peach-blossom-pink and coppery old-rose, large, 30 petals, moderate fragrance; foliage thick; vigorous growth; ['Mrs T. Hillas' × 'Étoile de Hollande']

'Koroyness' ('Bride's Dream', 'Fairy Tale Queen', 'Märchenkönigin') HT, lp, 1985, Kordes, R.; bud long, pointed, ovoid; flowers very pale pink, 5 in., 25-30 petals, high-centered, borne singly, slight fragrance; foliage large, medium green, matte; prickles dark brown; tall, upright growth; ['Royal Highness' × seedling]; intr. 1984

'Korozon' (Mondiale®) HT, op, 2006; bud high-centered, darker on top; flowers salmon-pink, outer petals lighter, 10 cm., full, borne mostly solitary; foliage large, reddish, dense; well-branched, vigorous, upright (80 cm.) growth; intr. 1993

'Korp' (Prominent®) Gr, or, 1971, Kordes, R.; bud long, pointed; flowers large, 33 petals, cupped; free-flowering; foliage matte; upright growth; PP3380; ['Zorina' × 'Colour Wonder']; intr. 1970

'Korpagbel' Min, mp, Kordes; intr. 2005

'Korpagisa' Min, mr, Kordes

'Korpalmor' F, op, Kordes; intr. 1997

'Korpalud' ('Hamburg Girl', Hamburger Deern®) HT, op, 2006; flowers flower salmon, reverse creamy yellow, 11 cm., full, high-centered, borne mostly solitary, moderate spicy fragrance; recurrent; foliage large, dark green, very glossy; vigorous, upright, medium growth; intr. 1997

'Korpancom' ('Bad Birnbach', 'Nest Rose', 'Salmon Vigorosa', 'Electric Blanket', 'Busy Bee', 'Bonapart') F, op, 2006; flowers salmon to coral pink, 4 cm., full, borne in trusses; foliage medium size, glossy; growth compact, low (1½ × 2 ft.); groundcover

'Korpapie' S, op, Kordes; intr. 1989

'Korpapiro' ('Apricot Summer') F, ab, Kordes; intr. 1995

'Korpapis' HT, ab, Kordes; intr. 2005

'Korparau' ('Abundancia', 'Ronja') S, mp, Kordessemi-dbl.

'Korparesni' ('Halcyon Days', 'Rose Professor Sieber', Rosenprofessor Sieber®) F, mp, 2006; flowers pure pink, aging to porcelain pink, 5 cm., dbl., borne in small clusters; foliage medium size, dark green, glossy; compact, medium (70 cm.) growth

'Korparosa' HT, pb, Kordes; intr. 1999

'Korpastato' ('Amoretto', 'Fragrant Memories', Sebastian Kneipp®) HT, w, 2006; bud rounded, medium, green-white; flowers cream with a yellow-pink center, 11 cm., full, quartered, borne mostly solitary, strong, sweetish fragrance; foliage medium size, dark green, glossy; growth bushy, medium (120 cm.); intr. 1997

'Korpatetof' (Cubana®) S, ab, 2006, Kordes; flowers apricot fading to pink, 5 cm., dbl., borne in small clusters; foliage small, glossy; growth spreading, short (50 cm.); intr. 2001

'Korpatri' F, op, Kordes ; bud slim; intr. 1976

'Korpauvio' ('Perfume Passion') HT, pb, Kordes; intr. 2008

'Korpeahn' ('Carl Philip Kristian IV', 'Timeless Beauty', 'Carl Philip', 'Kristian IV', Mariandel®, 'The Times Rose') F, mr, 1987, Kordes, W.; bud pointed, dark red; flowers scarlet crimson-red, 7 cm., dbl., shallow cup, borne in clusters, slight fragrance; recurrent; foliage medium size, dark green, semi-glossy, disease-resistant; bushy (2 ft.) growth; [Tornado® × 'Redgold']; intr. 1985

'Korpeapro' F, ab, Kordes; intr. 2007

'Korpedia' Min, w, Kordes

'Korpek' ('Royal Red') HT, mr, 1985, Kordes, W.; flowers 20 petals; foliage dark, glossy; upright growth; [seedling × seedling]

'Korpeligo' (Charmant®) Min, pb, 2006; bud small, pointed; flowers pure pink with a yellow-white center, cream reverse, 4 cm., full, pompon, borne singly and in clusters, slight, sweetish fragrance; foliage small, dark green, very glossy; growth bushy, short (50 cm.); intr. 1999

'Korpemdrel' ('Hewlet-Packard 2000') HT, ab, Kordes; bud pointed, urn shaped

'Korperki' ('Trojan Victory') HT, dr, 1986, Kordes, R.; bud ovoid; flowers deep red, reverse lighter, 4½ in., 50-55 petals, high-centered, borne singly, slight damask fragrance; recurrent; foliage medium size, medium green, semi-glossy; prickles medium, hooked downward; stems long, strong; medium, spreading growth; PP5678; [seedling × Uwe Seeler®]

Korpersca® ('Rebell 03 Kordana') Min, dr, Kordesfull

'Korpesch' F, op, Kordes; intr. 1999

'Korpesh' Gr, ob, 1981, Kordes, R.; bud ovoid, pointed

'Korphorla' HT, mp, Kordes; intr. 2006

'Korpinka' ('Berkshire', Sommermärchen®, 'Xénia') F, dp, 2006; flowers non-fading, petals ruffled, 4 cm., semi-dbl., cupped, borne in large clusters, slight fragrance; recurrent; foliage dark green, glossy, robust; bushy, medium (50 cm.), wide growth; intr. 1992

'Korpinrob' ('Göteborg', Pink Robusta®, 'The Seckford Rose') S, mp, 1987, Kordes, W.; flowers large, semi-dbl.; foliage large, dark green, glossy; bushy, spreading growth; [('Zitronenfalter' × 'Grammerstorf, Climbing') × 'Robusta']; intr. 1986

'Korpitelo' HT, or, Kordes; intr. 1998

'Korplasina' ('Emely Kordana', 'Our Vanilla') F, w, Kordes; intr. 1994

'Korplavi' ('Chevreuse', Kordes' Rose Westfalenpark®, Westfalenpark®) S, ab, 1987, Kordes, W.; flowers large, full, cupped, moderate fragrance; recurrent; foliage large, dark green, glossy; bushy (5 ft.), spreading growth; [seedling × 'Las Vegas']

'Korpocus' F, rb, Kordes; intr. 2001

'Korpolber' S, my, Kordes; intr. 2008

'Korpompan' (Pomponella Fairy Tale™) F, dp, Kordes; bud small, rounded; intr. 2005

'Korpon' (Ponderosa®) F, or, 1973, Kordes, R.; bud globular; flowers red-orange, medium, dbl., cupped; foliage leathery; vigorous, dwarf, bushy growth;

[seedling × 'Marlena']; intr. 1970

'Korpoobea' S, ab, Kordes; intr. 2003

'Korpora' (Christel von der Post®) HT, dy, 2006; bud large, elongated; flowers medium size, lasting color, 10 cm., full, high-centered, borne mostly solitary, moderate fragrance; foliage fresh green, glossy; bushy, upright, vigorous growth to 3 ft.; intr. 1990

'Korport' ('Golden Summers', Funkuhr®, 'Laser Beam') HT, yb, 1984, Kordes, W.; flowers yellow, petals edged medium red, aging red, large, 35 petals; foliage medium size, medium green, glossy; upright growth; [seedling × seedling]

'Korpriblo' S, pb, Kordes; intr. 2003

'Korpriggos' F, w, Kordes; intr. 2007

'Korprill' ('Belami', 'Woods of Windsor') HT, op, 1986, Kordes, W.; intr. 1985

'Korpriwa' ('Berolina') HT, dy, 1984, Kordes, W.; bud large; intr. 1984

'Korproa' HT, yb, Kordes; bud triangular, deep yellow; intr. 1993

'Korprofko' F, op, Kordes

'Korproha' HT, dp, Kordes; intr. 2006

'Korprolit' ('Chica Kordana') Min, dp, Kordes; bud long, pointed ovoid; intr. 1998

'Korprovia' HT, ab, Kordes; intr. 1998

'Korquanni' S, dr, Kordes; intr. 2008

'Korquelda' ('Abbeyfield Gold', 'Elsie de Radt', 'Golden Fairy Tale', Sterntaler®) HT, yb, 2006; flowers flower medium yellow, partly edged red, 12 cm., full, cupped, borne singly and in small clusters, moderate fragrance; recurrent; foliage dark green, semi-glossy, very disease-resistant; upright, medium (90 cm.) growth; intr. 2004

'Korquemu' ('Queen Mum') F, lp, Kordes; intr. 1991

'Korquick' HT, ob, Kordes; bud egg-shaped; intr. 1988

'Korrabea' ('Roxy') HT, mr, Kordes; intr. 2001

'Korraffi' F, my, Kordes; intr. 1993

'Korrandiber' F, yb, Kordes; intr. 2001

'Korrantu' F, mr, 1970, Kordes; bud ovoid; intr. 1968

'Korravreli' ('Avril Elizabeth Home') F, ab, Kordes; intr. 2001

'Korred' ('Ace of Hearts', 'Toque Rouge', Asso di Cuori®) HT, dr, 1983, Kordes, W.; bud large, ovoid; flowers 30 petals, cupped, moderate fragrance; foliage large, dark; prickles dark green; bushy growth; intr. 1981

'Korrei' ('Dreaming', 'Reverie', Träumerei®) F, ob, 1974, Kordes; bud long, pointed; flowers salmon orange, 7 cm., dbl., cupped, borne singly or in clusters, intense fragrance; recurrent; foliage large, dark green, leathery; vigorous, upright, bushy growth; ['Colour Wonder' × seedling]; intr. 1974

'Korrein' HT, ly, Kordes; intr. before 2005

'Korresia' ('Friesia', 'Sunsprite') F, dy, 1973, Kordes, R.; bud ovoid, blunt top; flowers bright yellow, 3-3½ in., 25-30 petals, high-centered, borne singly and in flat clusters, intense fragrance; recurrent; foliage medium size, light green, semi-glossy; prickles moderate, long, hooked downward; stems medium; upright growth; PP3509; [seedling × 'Spanish Sun']

'Korresli' ('Love's Song', Rosenresli®) S, dp, 1987, Kordes, W.; flowers blend of orange pink to carmine red, 4 in., full, high-centereed, borne singly or in small clusters, intense tea rose fragrance; recurrent; foliage medium size, dark green, glossy; vigorous (5 ft.), bushy, arching, possibly climbing growth; [('New Dawn' × 'Prima Ballerina') × seedling]; intr. 1986

'Korretra' ('Mother's Value') HT, mr, Kordes; buds sharply pointed; intr. 1989

'Korrev' ('News Review') HT, rb, 1975; intr. 1962

'Korrigan' F, lp, 1978, Poulsen, Niels D.; bud globular; flowers dbl., 25 petals, slight fragrance; foliage glossy, dark, leathery; vigorous, bushy growth; [seedling × ('Orléans Rose' × Eden Rose®)]; intr. 1972

'Korrogilo' HT, dy, Kordes

'Korrohe' (Heckenfeuer®) F, mr, Kordes; intr. 1984

'Korromalu' ('Red Corsair', Roter Korsar®, 'Temptress') S, dr, 2006, W. Kordes' Söhne; flowers brilliant dark red, not bluing, 9 cm., semi-dbl., shallow cup, borne in clusters of 10-12, very slight fragrance; foliage medium size, dark green, slightly glossy; bushy, tall (4-5 ft.) growth

'Korrovino' Min, or, Kordes; intr. 1998

'Korruge' (Rugelda®) HRg, yb, 2006; flowers citron yellow edged reddish, 9 cm., dbl., cupped, borne in large clusters, moderate fragrance; recurrent; foliage dark green, glossy; numerous prickles; bushy, tall (200 cm.) growth; intr. 1989

'Korrundum' ('Heike') HT, my, Kordes; bud green-yellow; intr. 1993

'Korryme' F, dp, Kordes; intr. 2005

'Korsailer' Min, w, Kordes; bud short, pointed ovoid, greenish white; intr. 1998

'Korsaku' ('Playtime', Rosalina™, 'Roselina') S, dp, 1998, Kordes, W.; bud short, slender, pointed; flowers dark pink with traces of lavendar, dark pink reverse, 3 in., 5 petals, cupped to flat, borne in small clusters, slight fragrance; foliage medium size, medium green, dull, Rugosa-like; prickles numerous, narrow, sharp, hooked downward; stems short, strong; bushy, medium (3-4 ft.), sprawling growth; hedges; PP9011; ['The Fairy' × seedling]; intr. 1992

'Korsalfio' Min, or, Kordes; intr. 2006

'Korsalpro' F, op, Kordes; intr. 2005

'Korsalton' F, ab, Kordes; intr. 1998

'Korsami' (Kordes' Rose Repandia®, Repandia®) S, lp, 1983, Kordes, W.; flowers soft pink, small, semi-dbl., shallow cup, borne in clusters, moderate fragrance; foliage small, dark, glossy; low, spreading (to 5 ft.) growth; groundcover; ['The Fairy' × (R. wichurana × unknown)]; intr. 1982

'Korsanter' ('Paradisea') HT, pb, Kordes; buds egg shaped; intr. 1988

'Korsaphil' HT, ab, Kordes

'Korsata' HT, ab, Kordes; intr. 2006

'Korsavale' Min, or, Kordesdbl.

'Korschaprat' ('Charme de Vienne', 'Charming Vienna', Wiener Charme®) HT, ob, 1963, Kordes, R.; bud large, pointed; intr. 1963

'Korschloss' F, or, 1975, Kordes

'Korschnuppe' ('Olympic Gold', Goldener Olymp®) LCl, dy, 1984, Kordes' Sohne, W.; flowers large, with wavy petals, 4-5 in., 20 petals, borne singly or in small clusters, moderate fragrance; occasional repeat; foliage large, medium green, matte; upright, bushy (to 7 ft.) growth; [seedling × Goldstern®]

'Korschwama' ('Barry Fearn', 'Black Madonna', Schwarze Madonna®) HT, dr, 2006; bud velvety black; flowers velvety black-red, 11 cm., full, high-centered, borne mostly solitary, slight fragrance; recurrent; foliage reddish at first, then deep dark green, glossy; vigorous, upright (80 cm.) growth; intr. 1992

'Korsebue' ('Hanneli Rupert') HT, ob, Kordes; intr. 1995

'Korsee' ('Gitta Grummer', 'Orange Vilmoria', 'Orange Vilmorin', 'Rainer Maria Rilke', 'Reiner Maria Rilke', Uwe Seeler®) F, ob, 1973, Kordes, R.; bud ovoid; flowers salmon-orange, large, semi-dbl., high-centered, moderate fragrance; recurrent; foliage large, glossy, bronze, leathery; vigorous, upright, bushy growth; [Queen Elizabeth® × 'Colour Wonder']; intr. 1970

'Korselary' ('Bad Wörishofen 2005', 'Pink Emely') F, dp, Kordes; intr. 2006

'Korsered' HT, mr, Kordes; intr. 2001

'Korserump' F, op, Kordes; intr. 2001

'Korseubel' ('City of Pretoria') F, ab, Kordes

'Korshell' HT, op, Kordes, R.; bud short, pointed; intr. 1976

'Korsicht' (Blue River®) HT, m, 1984, Kordes, W.; bud large; flowers lilac, shaded deeper at petal edges, large, 35 petals, high-centered, intense fragrance; foliage medium size, medium green, semi-glossy; upright growth; [Blue Moon® × 'Zorina']; intr. 1984

'Korsiero' HT, pb, Kordes; bud long, pointed; intr. 1999

'Korsilan' ('Our Rosy Carpet', 'Palmengarten Frankfurt') S, dp, 2006; flowers rose pink, 4 cm., dbl., cupped/pompon, borne in small clusters; foliage fresh green, glossy; spreading, medium (70 cm.) growth; intr. 1988

'Korsincha' Min, dr, Kordesfull

'Korsineo' Min, m, Kordes; intr. 2007

'Korsion' Gr, my, Kordes; bud egg-shaped; intr. 1989

'Korsir' HT, rb, Kordes; intr. 1998
'Korsisten' ('Bienkie') F, op; intr. 1995
'Korsita' ('Pasita') HT, dr, 1985, Kordes, R.; flowers bright dark red, flora-tea, 25 petals, borne singly; foliage glossy; prickles straight, light brown; medium-high, densely branched growth; ['Mercedes' × seedling]; intr. 1982
'Korskadela' Min, mp, Kordesdbl.; intr. 2000
'Korskipei' ('Esther Geldenhuys') HT, op, 1988, W. Kordes Söhne; flowers light coral pink, petals clam-shaped, large, 32 petals, borne singly, moderate fragrance; foliage glossy, purple to medium green; prickles concave, yellow-brown; vigorous, very tall, well-branched growth; [seedling × seedling]; intr. 1988
'Korslyfo' S, mr, Kordes; intr. 2003
'Korsoalgu' ('Sonne des Allgäus') S, ab, Kordes; bud small, elongated, orange-yellow; intr. 2006
'Korsommer' (Roseromantic®) F, w, 1984, Kordes, W.; bud light pink; flowers light pink to white, medium, 5 petals, shallow cup, borne in large clusters, slight fragrance; foliage small, dark green, glossy; bushy, spreading (2 ft.) growth; [seedling × Tornado®]
'Korsonn' (Sonnenröschen®) F, dy, 1977, W. Kordes Söhne; bud ovoid; flowers deep yellow, 4 in., full, cupped; foliage glossy; vigorous, bushy growth; ['Arthur Bell' × 'yellow seedling']
'Korsorb' HT, ab, Kordes; intr. 1988
'Korsparko' ('Orange Sparkle') F, ob, 1985, Kordes, R.; flowers bright orange, yellow stamens, semi-dbl., borne in small clusters, moderate fragrance; foliage very glossy; prickles straight, brown; tall, bushy growth; [('Colour Wonder' × 'Zorina') × Uwe Seeler®]; intr. 1984
'Korspatax' ('Darling') HT, mp, Kordes; intr. 1994
'Korspunty' Min, my, Kordes; intr. 2005
'Korstacha' ('Nuage Blanc', 'White Cloud') S, w, Kordes; intr. 1993
'Korstarnow' ('Yorkshire', Innocencia®) F, w, 2006; flowers pure white, 5 cm., semi-dbl., flat, borne in clusters of 10-15; foliage dark green, very glossy; bushy, compact, upright (2 ft.) growth; intr. 2003
'Korstatis' (Rosenstadt Zweibrücken®) S, pb, 2006; flowers pink-red, center golden yellow, yellow stamens, 7 cm., semi-dbl., cupped, borne in large clusters; recurrent; foliage medium size, deep green, glossy; bushy, medium (3 ft.) growth; intr. 1989
'Korstesgli' ('Gardner's Pleasure', Gärtnerfreude®, 'Lancashire', 'Toscana', 'Toscana Vigorosa') S, dr, 2006, W. Kordes' Söhne; flowers flower raspberry red, 3 cm., dbl., borne in small clusters, no fragrance; recurrent; foliage small, dark green, very glossy; vigorous (4 ft × 2 ft.) growth
'Korstigma' Min, my, Kordes; bud long pointed, ovoid; intr. 1997
'Korstoffein' Min, lp, Kordes; intr. 2000
'Korstozau' F, pb, Kordes; intr. 1998
'Korstrunek' Min, mp, Kordes
'Korstutta' HT, pb, Kordes; intr. 2008
'Korsuflabe' F, ab; intr. 2003
'Korsulas' HT, ly, Kordes; intr. 1997
'Korsun' ('Sun City') HT, yb, 1985, Kordes, R.; flowers deep yellow with red petal edges, red spreading, 32 petals, high-centered, star-shaped, borne singly and in clusters of 2 or 3, slight fragrance; foliage deep green, red when young, leathery; prickles dark brown; upright, tall growth; [(('New Day' × 'Minigold') × seedling) × 'MEltakilor']
'Korsupigel' ('Smile') S, my, Kordes
'Korta' F, mr, 1965, Kordes, R.; intr. 1964
'Kortabo' ('Little Red Hedge') F, mr, Kordes; bud small, pointed
'Kortabris' -- See 'Korweiso'
'Kortag' (Clivia®) HT, ob, 1985, Kordes, W.; bud ovoid; flowers salmon orange-red blend, 30 petals, high-centered, borne singly; foliage medium size, medium green, matte; prickles brown; upright, bushy growth; ['Mercedes' × ('Sonia' × Uwe Seeler®)]; intr. 1979
'Kortaired' ('Red Taifun') F, mr, Kordes; intr. 2006
'Kortake' ('Germiston Gold') HT, dy, 1988, W. Kordes Söhne; flowers deep golden-yellow, large, petals slightly serrated and curly, 30-36 petals, borne singly and in clusters of 3, intense spicy fragrance; free-flowering; foliage medium green; prickles concave, brown; medium, well branched growth; [seedling × seedling]; intr. 1988
'Kortakmo' Min, lp, Kordes; intr. 2005
'Kortaly' (Lucinde®) S, dy, Kordes; intr. 1988
'Kortanken' ('Cathedral City', Domstadt Fulda®) F, or, 2006, W. Kordes' Söhne; flowers dazzling orange-red, 7 cm., dbl., borne mostly solitary; foliage dark green, glossy; growth vigorous, upright, 80 cm.; intr. 1994
'Kortara' ('Lagonda') F, dp, Kordes; intr. 1987
'Kortasto' ('Panthea') HT, pb, Kordes; intr. 1991
'Kortat' ('Rosenthal') HT, dr, 1973, Kordes, R.; bud long, pointed; intr. 1970
'Kortechna' ('Germania-Africana') HT, ob, Kordes; buds pointed; intr. 1992
'Kortelin' ('Spotted Gold') F, yb; intr. 1994
'Kortello' ('Red Barrier', Ulmer Münster®) S, dr, 1982, Kordes, W.; flowers clear dark red, 12 cm., 35 petals, cupped, borne in clusters, slight fragrance; recurrent; foliage large, dark green, glossy; bushy, upright (5 ft.) growth; [Sympathie® × seedling]
'Kortember' ('Harmony', Harmonie®) HT, op, 1980, Kordes, W.; bud long, pointed; flowers deep salmon, 20 petals, high-centered, intense fragrance; foliage slightly glossy; vigorous, upright, bushy growth; ['Fragrant Cloud' × Uwe Seeler®]; intr. 1981
'Kortemma' ('Chilterns', 'Fiery Sunsation', 'Island of Fire', 'Mainaufeuer', 'Red Ribbons') S, dr, 1998, Kordes, W.; bud short, pointed ovoid; flowers bright red, 3 in., 20 petals, cupped, borne in large clusters, slight fragrance; recurrent; foliage medium size, dark green, glossy; prickles moderate, short, hooked downward, red; stems short, strong; growth low (2 × 5 ft.), spreading; PP9115; [Weisse Max Graf® × 'Waltzertraum']; intr. 1990
'Kortenay' ('Bright Carpet', 'Lazy Susan', 'Sandefjord', 'Tommelise') S, dp, Kordes
'Kortensei' ('Fairy Castle', Dornröschenschloss Sababurg®, 'Fond Thoughts') S, mp, 2006; flowers pure pink, 10 cm., very full, high-centered, borne mostly solitary; foliage dark green, very glossy, leathery, ruffled; growth upright, robust, 4 ft.; intr. 1993
'Kortenses' ('Sergeant Pepper') Min, or, 1992, W. Kordes Söhne; flowers large, semi-dbl., borne in small clusters, no fragrance; free-flowering; foliage small, dark green, glossy; some prickles; low (45-60 cm.), upright, bushy, spreading growth; [seedling × LAVaglut®]; intr. 1992
'Korterschi' ('Belami', Bremer Stadtmusikanten®, 'Elegant', 'Elegant Fairy Tale', 'Pearl', 'Rose Pearl') S, pb, 2006, W. Kordes' Söhne; bud rounded, cream yellow, suffused reddish; flowers cream pink with darker center, 8 cm., full, camellia-like, borne mostly in large clusters, slight sweetish fragrance; foliage medium size, dark green, glossy; bushy, tall (120 cm.) growth; intr. 2000
'Kortersen' ('Seminole Wind', Rosarium Uetersen®, 'The Halcyon Days Rose', 'Uetersen') LCl, dp, 1977, Kordes, W.; bud ovoid, pointed; flowers deep pink, silvery reverse, ruffled petals, 10-12 cm., very dbl., borne in large clusters, moderate fragrance; recurrent; foliage large, medium green, glossy; vigorous, climbing (10 ft.) growth; ['Karlsruhe' × seedling]; intr. 1977
Kortexung® ('Europa', Fleurop®) F, mp, 1987, Kordes, W.; flowers medium, dbl.; foliage medium size, medium green, matte; bushy growth; PP6513; [(seedling × 'Banzai') × ('Mercedes' × 'Carol')]; intr. 1985
'Kortibli' Min, or, Kordes; intr. 1992
'Kortifhar' S, ab, Kordes; intr. 2003
'Kortiglo' F, ab, Kordes; intr. 2005
'Kortikel' ('Goldyla', 'Surprise') F, dy, Kordes; intr. 1989
'Kortime' ('Golden Times') F, my, 1985, Kordes, W.; flowers medium, dbl.; foliage medium size, dark, semi-glossy; bushy growth; ['New Day' × 'Minigold']
'Kortinava' Min, dp, Kordesdbl.
'Kortingle' ('Scarlet Patio') MinFl, mr,

Kordes; intr. 1993

'Kortionza' (Postillion®) S, my, 2006, Kordes; bud copper yellow; flowers shining yellow, 10 cm., dbl., shallow cupped, borne in small clusters; foliage medium size, dark green, glossy; vigorous, upright (5 ft.) growth; intr. 1998

'Kortisching' ('Yellow Sunsation') S, ly, Kordes

'Kortitper' Min, pb, Kordes

'Kortitut' S, mp, Kordes; intr. 1991

'Kortocrea' ('Marlena') HT, mr, Kordes; intr. 1998

'Kortonetec' ('Taifun') F, yb, Kordes; intr. 2002

'Kortor' (Tornado®) F, or, 1973, Kordes, R.; flowers bright scarlet, 6 cm., semi-dbl., cupped, borne in clusters; recurrent; foliage large, dark green, glossy, leathery; vigorous, bushy (2 ft.), open growth; [Europeana® × 'Marlena']; intr. 1973

'Kortossgo' ('Gold Topaz') F, my, 1963, Kordes, R.; bud ovoid

'Kortradkos' ('Parkwood Scarlet') F, mr, Kordes; intr. 1995

'Kortragfei' ('Red Mozart') S, or, Kordes; intr. 1989

'Kortraste' ('Grouse 2000', Medeo®) S, w, 2006; flowers white, blushed pink, 3 cm., single, flat, borne in large clusters; foliage small, dark green, glossy; moderate, low, spreading (60 × 80 cm.) growth; groundcover; intr. 2003

'Kortraupfi' ('New Duet') HT, pb, Kordes; intr. 2001

'Kortreu' (Fuggerstadt Augsburg®) F, or, 1985, Kordes, W.; flowers medium, semi-dbl.; foliage medium size, dark, glossy; upright, bushy growth; [Cordula® × Topsi®]

'Kortri' (Cordula®) F, or, 1973, Kordes, R.; bud globular; flowers red-orange, medium, dbl., slight fragrance; foliage dark, bronze, leathery; vigorous, dwarf, bushy growth; [Europeana® × 'Marlena']; intr. 1972

'Kortrilac' HT, pb, Kordes; intr. 1999

'Kortrolle' ('Bloemfontein') F, ob, Kordes; intr. 1988

'Kortron' ('Honey Kordana') Min, rb, Kordes, Wilhelm; bud long pointed, ovoid; intr. 1997

'Kortuel' ('White Bella Rosa') F, w, Kordes; intr. 1989

'Kortufee' (Pepita®) Min, dp, 2006; flowers full, borne in small clusters; foliage small, dark green, very glossy; growth bushy, medium (50 cm.); intr. 2004

'Kortumbon' HT, mr, Kordes; intr. 2005

'Kortuna' (Fortuna®) HT, op, 1986, Kordes, W.; flowers medium salmon-pink, large, 30 petals, high-centered, borne singly, moderate fragrance; foliage medium size, medium green, semi-glossy; medium, upright growth; ['Sonia' × seedling]; intr. 1977

'Korturek' ('Ice Queen', 'New Iceberg') HT, w, Kordes; intr. 2001

'Korturnus' ('Salmon Spire') HT, op, Kordes; bud long; intr. 1993

'Kortutu' S, mr, Kordes; bud pointed; intr. 2008

'Kortwente' ('Purple Kiss', Raspberry Vigorosa™) S, dp, Kordes

'Korub' S, yb, 1971, Kordes, R.; bud ovoid

'Korumelst' F, op, 1961, Kordes, R.; bud pointed

'Koruminno' HT, mp, Kordes; intr. 2002

'Korunalike' F, w, Kordes; intr. 2002

'Koruteli' F, w, Kordes; intr. 2005

'Korutilta' S, pb, Kordes; intr. 2003

'Korutzmo' Min, mr, Kordesdbl.

'Korvaky' HT, w, Kordes; intr. 2005

'Korvalue' ('Woman's Value') HT, op, 1985, Kordes, R.; bud pointed; flowers cream to soft coral, deepening to deep salmon, 42 petals, star-shaped, slight fragrance; free-flowering; foliage glossy, deep green; prickles straight, brown; medium, bushy, well-branched growth; [('Sonia' × ('(Dr. A.J. Verhage × Colour Wonder)' × 'Zorina')) × Asso di Cuori®]; intr. 1984

'Korvanaber' ('Champagne Moment', 'Lion's Fairy Tale', Lions-Rose®) F, w, 2006; flowers cream-white, opening tinted apricot and pink, center darker, 8 cm., full, borne in clusters of 3-5, slight fragrance; foliage medium size, green, shiny, dense; compact, medium (60 cm.) growth; intr. 2002

'Korvapoco' Min, ab, Kordes

'Korveco' HT, or, Kordes; intr. 1997

'Korvedsco' HT, or, Kordes; intr. 2002

'Korvegata' ('Australian Centenary of Federation', Rebell®) HT, mr, 2006; flowers flower brilliant red, 11 cm., full, high-centered, borne singly and in small clusters, moderate fragrance; foliage medium size, dark green, very glossy; growth upright, medium, 80 cm

'Korvejoh' F, ob, 1990, Kordes; buds pointed, salmon; intr. 1990

'Korvenlig' ('Sunbeam 2000') HT, ab, Kordes; intr. 1999

'Korvera' Gr, or, 1978, Kordes, R.; bud ovoid, pointed; intr. 1977

'Korveril' ('Cadillac') HT, op, Kordes; intr. 1990

'Korverlandus' ('Hampshire', Knirps®, 'Little Chap') F, dp, 2006; flowers full, rosette, borne in small clusters; foliage small, dark green, very glossy; growth spreading, short (30 cm.); intr. 1997

'Korverpea' ('Cleopatra', 'Peace of Vereeniging', 'New Kleopatra', Kleopatra®) HT, rb, 2006; bud large, round, pointed; flowers wine red with brass colored reverse, 11 cm., very full, high-centered, borne mostly solitary, moderate fragrance; foliage reddish at first, then large, dark green, shiny; erect, upright, vigorous, bushy growth with many canes, to 3 ft.; intr. 1994

'Korvestavi' HT, yb, Kordes; intr. 2000

'Korviga' Min, lp, Kordes; intr. 1988

'Korvignon' F, or, Kordes; intr. 1983

'Korvila' ('Vierländerin') F, mp, 1983, Kordes, W.; flowers medium salmon-pink, large, 35 petals; foliage medium size, medium green, matte; upright growth; [('Zorina' × 'Zorina') × 'Rosenelfe']; intr. 1982

'Korvillade' ('Red Finesse', Rotilia®, Ruby Vigorosa™) F, mr, 2006, W. Kordes' Söhne; bud small, pointed, dark red; flowers brilliant crimson, 5 cm., semi-dbl., cupped, borne in large clusters, moderate fragrance; recurrent; foliage medium size, deep dark green, very glossy; bushy, compact, medium (60 cm.) growth; intr. 2000

'Korvolomin' ('Saturday Star') HT, ab, Kordes; intr. 1994

'Korvondra' ('Flirt') F, mp, Kordes; intr. 1990

'Korwalbe' (Maidy®) Min, rb, 1984, Kordes, W.; flowers medium, 20 petals; foliage small, medium green, semi-glossy; bushy growth; [Regensberg® × seedling]

'Korwarpeel' ('Dame Elisabeth Murdoch', Speelwark®) HT, yb, 2006, Kordes; bud large, pointed, red with yellow stripes; flowers flower cream and golden yellow flushed with vermilion and pink, fading to reddish, 12 cm., full, high-centered, borne mostly solitary, intense fragrance; foliage medium size, reddish, then dark green, glossy; upright, medium (80 cm.) growth

'Korweirim' ('Kordes' Rose Weisse Immensee', 'Lac Blanc', 'Partridge', Weisse Immensee®) S, w, 1983, Kordes, W.; bud light pink; flowers small, 5 petals; foliage small, dark, glossy; spreading (10 ft.) growth; groundcover; ['The Fairy' × (R. wichurana × unknown)]; intr. 1982

'Korweiso' ('Hannah Gordon', 'Kortabris', 'Raspberry Ice', 'Tabris') F, pb, 1984, Kordes, W.; flowers white with deep pink to red petal edges, large, 20-25 petals, shallow cup to flat, borne singly and in clusters, slight fragrance; recurrent; foliage large, medium green, semi-glossy; strong, upright, tall, bushy growth; [seedling × Bordure Rose®]; intr. 1983

'Korwerk' ('Dwarf Queen '82', 'Zwergkönigin '82') Min, mp, 1985, Kordes, W.; bud deep pink; flowers lighten as they open, 4 cm., 35 petals, shallow cup, rosette, borne in clusters, slight fragrance; recurrent; foliage small, medium green, glossy; bushy (20 in.) growth; [Zwergkönig 78® × 'Sunday Times']

'Korwesrug' ('Aloha Hawaii', Aloha®, 'Kordes' Rose Aloha') LCl, ob, 2008, Kordes; bud red-orange, medium; flowers orange-apricot with pink and red shades, 4 in., full, borne in clusters of up to ten blooms, slight fruity fragrance; recurrent; numerous prickles; vigorous (8+ ft.), strong growth; intr. 2003

'Korwest' S, ab, 1976, Kordes; bud ovoid; intr. 1969

'Korwhit' HT, pb, Kordes; intr. 1994

'Korwibalk' ('White Balconia') S, w,

Kordes; intr. 2007

'Korwilma' ('Jack Dayson', Perfect Moment™) HT, rb, 1990, W. Kordes Söhne; bud pointed; flowers red on outer half of petals, yellow on inner, reverse yellow, 4-4½ in., 30-35 petals, high-centered, borne singly and in small clusters; foliage medium size, medium green, semi-glossy; prickles broad at base, narrowing, hooked down, red to brown; upright, bushy, medium growth; PP8007; ['New Day' × seedling]; intr. 1991

'Korwilpa' ('Kordes' Rose Park Wilhelmshöhe', 'Park Wilhelmshöhe') HGal, dp, 2006, Kordes; flowers carmine pink, 10 cm., full, borne in small clusters; nonrecurrent; foliage deep green, glossy; growth bushy, tall (180 cm.); intr. 1987

'Korwings' HT, ob, 1979, W. Kordes Söhne; bud ovoid

'Korwisco' S, w, Kordes; intr. 1997

'Korwitcil' ('Our Esther') HT, lp, Kordes; intr. 1999

'Korwitela' LCl, mp, Kordes; intr. 2003

'Korwiwi' HT, ly, Kordes; intr. 2003

'Korwonder' ('Kordes' Rose Bella Rosa', 'Toynbee Hall', Bella Rosa®) F, mp, 1982, Kordes, W.; flowers mini-flora, large, 34 petals, slight fragrance; foliage small, medium green, glossy; bushy growth; [seedling × 'Traümerei']

'Korworm' ('Romantic Hedgerose') F, mp, Kordes; intr. 1994

'Korxenna' ('Robina') HT, mr, Kordes; intr. 1988

'Korxomi' HT, pb, Kordes; intr. 2005

'Koryalasch' HT, dp, Kordes; intr. 2005

'Koryard' ('Jana') HT, mp, Kordesdouble; intr. 1990

'Koryell' (Yellow Taifun®) F, my, Kordesdouble; intr. 2006

'Korylt' ('Sylt', Kordes' Rose Sylt®) HKor, dr, 1982, Kordes, W.; flowers bright crimson, medium, semi-dbl., slight fragrance; foliage medium size, dark, glossy; spreading growth; hips long, orange-red; [R. × kordesii × seedling]; intr. 1981

'Korzaun' ('Duftzauber '84', 'Fragrant Charm 84', 'Royal William') HT, dr, 1984, Kordes, W.; flowers deep crimson red, large, 35 petals, high-centered, moderate spicy fragrance; free-flowering; foliage large, dark, semi-glossy; upright, bushy (3½ ft.) growth; ['Feuerzauber' × seedling]

'Korzeito' ('Silk Button') Min, w, Kordes; bud pointed; intr. 1991

'Korzentraf' F, op, Kordes; intr. 1999

'Korzimko' (Charmant®) Min, mr, 1987, Kordes, W.; flowers small, 40 petals; foliage small, medium green, semi-glossy; bushy growth; [((seedling × Tornado®) × 'Korkonig') × Trumpeter®]

'Korzinta' HT, pb, Kordes; intr. 1991

'Korzola' ('Zola Budd') F, rb, 1987, Kordes, R.; flowers white with ruby red painted over the petals, 5-7 petals, borne 1-3 per cluster, slight fragrance; recurrent; foliage deep green, leathery; prickles straight, light brown; vigorous, bushy, densely-branched growth; ['Mabella' × (('Dr. A. J. Verhage' × 'Colour Wonder') × 'Zorina')]; intr. 1985

'Korzuri' ('Ice Cream', Memoire®, Memory™) HT, w, 2006; flowers pure white shaded cream, 11 cm., full, high-centered, borne mostly solitary, moderate tea fragrance; foliage large, dark green, glossy; growth upright, medium (70 cm.); intr. 1992

'Ko's Yellow' -- See 'Mackosyel'

'Kosai' HT, or, Keisei; flowers bright red, reverse orange blend, full

KOSMOS® F, w, Kordes; flowers creamy white , 8 cm. , full, cupped, slight fragrance; recurrent; bushy (80 cm.), arching growth; intr. 2007

'Kosmos' F, dr, VEG; flowers medium, dbl.

'Koster Blanc' -- See 'Blanche Neige'

'Koster's Orléans' Pol, mr, 1920, Koster, M.; flowers brilliant scarlet-red; [sport of 'Orléans Rose']

'Koster's Triumph' Pol, or, 1920, Koster; flowers small, dbl.

'Kostior Arteka' ('Campfire Arteka') F, or, 1955, Klimenko, V. N.; flowers coral-red tinted orange, large; ['Independence' × unknown]

'Koto' ('Kyoto') HT, dy, 1973, Suzuki, Seizo; bud ovoid; flowers pure deep yellow, large, dbl., high-centered, moderate fragrance; foliage glossy, dark, leathery; vigorous, upright growth; [('Lydia' × unknown) × ('Peace' × unknown)]; intr. 1972

'Kotobuki' HT, yb, 1991, Ogura Rose Nurseries; bud pointed; flowers creamy to creamy yellow, creamy yellow reverse with light pink at fringe, large, 30-35 petals, high-centered, borne usually singly, slight fragrance; foliage dark green, glossy; medium growth; [sport of 'Souma']

'Kotobuki' ('Congratulations') HT, rb, Hiroshima; intr. 2000

'Kotohogi' Cl Min, dp, 2003, Tsuyoshi Ishii; flowers single, borne in small clusters; foliage small, medium green, semi-glossy; prickles sharp, numerous; growth spreading, short (100 cm.); groundcover; ['Azumino' × seedling]

'Kotone' F, ab, Keisei; intr. 2002

'Koukaku' LCl, my, Hiroshima; intr. 1998

'Kouzan' HT, dr, 2004, Matsumoto, Masayuki; flowers dark red, 12 cm., full, borne mostly solitary, moderate fragrance; foliage large, medium green, semi-glossy; prickles medium; growth upright, tall (200 cm.); exhibition; [seedling × seedling]

'Kovalam' HT, w, 1979, Viraraghavan, M.S. Viru; bud globular; flowers creamwhite, 4 in., 20-25 petals, cupped, intense fragrance; foliage wrinkled; moderate, bushy growth; [('Amberlight' × 'Traumland') × Western Sun™]; intr. 1976

'Kovsie Roos' S, m, Taschner, Ludwig; flowers lilac-crimson, dbl., cupped, intense fragrance; recurrent; stems long; vigorous, tall growth; intr. 2005

'Koyo' F, rb, 1989, Kikuchi, Rikichi; bud ovoid; flowers vermilion, reverse orange-yellow, small, 17-20 petals, cupped, borne in large sprays; foliage dark green, glossy; prickles ordinary; spreading growth; ['Masquerade' × 'Matador']; intr. 1990

'Koyuki' ('Snow Infant') Min, w, 1990, Yamasaki, Kazuko; bud ovoid; flowers light green, reverse white, aging white, small, full, borne in sprays, no fragrance; foliage small, light green, semi-glossy; prickles small, light green; upright, medium growth; hips ovoid, small, red; ['Katharina Zeimet' × seedling]

'Koza' HRg, dp, 1927, Hansen, N.E.; flowers deep pink, medium, semi-dbl.; vigorous (over 7 ft.) growth; extremely hardy; [(R. rugosa × La France) × 'La Mélusine']

'Krabentiger' (Bengal Tiger™) F, or, 2000, Kralovetz, Timm R.; flowers orange-red blend, 3-4½ in., semi-dbl., borne singly, slight fragrance; foliage small, dark green edged in dark red, glossy; prickles moderate; growth speading, medium (3-3½ ft.); PP14048; intr. 2002

'Krakow' HT, dr, Grabczewski; bud ovate; flowers very dbl.

'Kralj Alexander I' HT, dr, 1935, Böhm, J.; flowers velvety blood-red, reflexes fiery red, very large, dbl.; vigorous growth; ['Capt. Kilbee Stuart' × 'Jan Bohm']

'Kralj Petar II' HT, pb, 1936, Brada, Dr.; flowers salmon-pink, reverse carmine, with coppery sheen

'Kralj Tomislav' HT, mr, 1931, Leenders, M.; bud long, pointed; flowers solferino-red, open, very large, dbl., high-centered; vigorous growth; ['Dora Stober' × 'Étoile de Hollande']

'Kraljica Marija' HT, ly, 1935, Brada, Dr.; flowers creamy yellow to creamy white, large, dbl.; ['Frau Karl Druschki' × 'Golden Ophelia']

'Kranenburg' F, dp, 1965, Verschuren, A.; flowers very dark pink, 32 petals, borne in clusters; foliage glossy, dark; bushy growth; ['Pinocchio' × 'Ma Perkins']; intr. 1963

'Krasavitza Festivalia' ('Festival Beauty') HT, yb, 1955, Klimenko, V. N.; flowers yellow edged raspberry-red, medium, 28 petals; foliage glossy, light green; spreading growth; [('Peace' × 'Crimson Glory') × 'Poinsettia']

'Krasavitza Festivalia, Climbing' Cl HT, yb, Vidal; [sport of 'Krasavitza Festivalia']; intr. after 1955

'Krásná Azurea' -- See 'General Stefánik'

'Krásná Uslavanka' HT, ob, 1930, Böhm, J.; flowers orange-rose, reverse dark orange-yellow; very vigorous, bushy growth; ['Mrs Beckwith' × 'Arthur Cook']

'Krasnaia Moskva' ('Red Moscow') HT,

dr, 1955, Klimenko, V. N.; flowers dark velvety red, medium; ['Peace' × 'Crimson Glory']

'Krasni Mak-Sin' F, dr, Klimenko, V. N.; flowers dark, velvety red, medium, dbl.; intr. 1975

'Krasnokamenka' ('Red Stone') F, mr, 1955, Klimenko, V. N.; flowers crimson-red, medium, 12 petals; foliage dark, glossy; upright growth; ['Independence' × 'Kirsten Poulsen']

'Krasnyi Mak' ('Red Poppy') F, mr, 1955, Klimenko, V. N.; flowers scarlet, medium, 26 petals; foliage glossy, light green; short stems; upright growth; ['Independence' × 'Kirsten Poulsen']

'Krause Macrantha' S, pb, Krause; flowers medium pink outer half of petals with lighter center, semi-dbl.; foliage dark green; HMacrantha

'Krause's Rote Joseph Guy' -- See 'Feuerschein'

'Kretly' HGal, m, 1842, Bardou; flowers velvety lilac-violet, marbled purple-garnet, medium, full

'Kribasil' HT, w, 1986, Kriloff, Michel

'Kribatis' ('Comtesse d'Alcantara', 'Home & Country') HT, yb, 1982, Kriloff, Michel; flowers large, moderate fragrance; foliage medium green glossy; upright growth; [seedling × 'Peace']; intr. 1979

'Kribecy' HT, or, Kriloff; intr. 1973

'Kricarlo' ('D'Eleganta', 'Maréchal Le Clerc', Touch of Class™®) HT, op, 1985, Kriloff, Michel; bud pointed ovoid; flowers medium pink, shaded coral and cream, 4½-5½ in., 25-35 petals, high-centered, borne mostly singly, slight fragrance; recurrent; foliage large, dark green, semi-glossy; prickles several, medium, slightly hooked downward; stems strong, medium to long; upright, bushy growth; hips long, ovoid, conspicuous neck, very smooth ; PP5165; ['Micaela' × (Queen Elizabeth® × 'Romantica')]; intr. 1984

'Krilamy' ('Krilani') HT, op, Kriloff

'Krilani' -- See 'Harmonie'

'Krileville' ('St Quentin') HT, rb, 1986, Kriloff, Michel; flowers red, silver petal edges; foliage dark, glossy; [seedling × 'Tropicana']

'Krilexis' HT, dp, 1986, Kriloff, Michel; bud red

'Krimasar' ('Lucy Cramphorn, Climbing') Cl HT, or, Kriloff; intr. 1984

'Krimhilde' T, yb, 1893, Drögemüller; flowers chamois yellow, aging to carmine, center coppery golden yellow, medium to large, full, moderate fragrance; ['Mme Bérard' × 'Perle des Jardins']

'Krimisti' mp, Kriloff; intr. 1984

'Krimony' ('Hello') HT, ob, Kriloff; intr. 1994

'Krimrose' -- See 'Rote Krimrose'

'Krinico' ('Tresor') HT, ab, Kriloff

'Krinirosy' ('Helene de Savoie') HT, op, Kriloff; intr. 1995

'Krioga' F, lp, 1986, Kriloff, Michel; flowers 35 petals, borne in clusters; foliage dense; bushy growth; [seedling × 'Orange Garnet']

'Kripal' mp, Kriloff; intr. 1973

'Kripalli' -- See 'Annie Girardot'

'Kripordi' mr, Kriloff; intr. 1977

'Kriprile' F, yb, 1986, Kriloff, Michel

'Krira' HT, op, 1971, Kriloff, Michel; intr. 1967

Krishna's Peach™ -- See 'Virapricot'

Kristall® F, w, GPG Bad Langensalza; intr. 1979

'Kristi' HT, mp, 1976, Swim, H.C. & Ellis, A.E.; bud ovoid, pointed; flowers clear medium pink, 5 in., 45 petals, moderate spicy fragrance; foliage large; vigorous, upright growth; ['White Satin' × 'Bewitched']

'Kristian IV' -- See 'Korpeahn'

Kristin™ -- See 'Benmagic'

Kristin, Climbing™ -- See 'Benkricl'

'Kristina av Tunsberg' F, or, 1973, Lundstad; bud long, pointed; flowers large, very dbl., high-centered, slight fragrance; foliage glossy, dark; vigorous, bushy growth; ['Charleston' × 'Toni Lander']; intr. 1972

'Kristo Pienaar' -- See 'Herpot'

'Kritiban' HT, w, 1986, Kriloff, Michel; intr. 1977

'Kriwi' HT, ob, 1972, Kriloff, Michel; intr. 1968

Kronborg™ -- See 'Poultry'

'Kronborg Castle' -- See 'Poultry'

'Kronenbourg' ('Flaming Peace') HT, rb, 1965, McGredy, Sam IV; bud large, ovoid; flowers bright medium red, reverse straw-yellow veined red, large, dbl., high-centered, borne singly on long stems; foliage abundant, large, dark green, glossy, leathery; vigorous, full, rounded growth; PP2745; [sport of 'Peace']; intr. 1966

'Kronenbourg, Climbing' Cl HT, rb, Kasturi; flowers bicolor red and yellow; intr. 1973

'Kronjuwel' F, mr, Noack, Werner; flowers 6 cm., semi-dbl. to dbl., borne in clusters; good repeat; low to medium (2 ft.) growth; intr. 1997

Kronos® HT, dy, Tantau; flowers large, full, high-centered, borne mostly singly; stems long; greenhouse rose; intr. 2002

'Kronprincessin Victoria' -- See 'Kronprinzessin Viktoria von Preussen'

'Kronprinsesse Ingrid' -- See 'Kronprinzessin Ingrid'

Kronprinsesse Mary™ S, w, Olesen; bud urceolate; flowers white with yellow shading in center, 5 cm., 130 petals, cupped, borne in large clusters, moderate fragrance; recurrent; foliage dark green, glossy; prickles numerous, 10 mm., hooked downward, greyed-orange; upright to bushy (60-100 cm.) growth; PP16991; [seedling × 'Clair Renaissance']; intr. 2004

'Kronprinzessin Cecilie' HT, lp, 1907, Kiese; flowers large, very dbl.; ['Mme Caroline Testout' × 'Mrs W. J. Grant']

'Kronprinzessin Ingrid' ('Kronprinsesse Ingrid') F, mp, 1936, Poulsen, S.; bud long, pointed; flowers deep rose-pink, open, semi-dbl.; foliage dark; vigorous growth; ['Else Poulsen' × 'Dainty Bess']; intr. 1942

'Kronprinzessin Victoria' -- See 'Heltoria'

'Kronprinzessin Viktoria' -- See 'Kronprinzessin Viktoria von Preussen'

'Kronprinzessin Viktoria von Preussen' ('Kronprincessin Victoria', 'Kronprinzessin Viktoria') B, w, 1887, Volvert; flowers milk-white, center tinted yellow; free-flowering; growth compact; [sport of 'Souv. de la Malmaison']

'Krymchanka' F, m, Klimenko, V. N.; flowers dark purple-red, medium, dbl.; intr. 1955

'Krymskaja Notsch' HT, dr, Klimenko, V. N.; flowers large, dbl.; intr. 1955

'Kseelite' ('Bright Lights') Min, pb, 1996, Apple, Ken; flowers dark pink with bright yellow stripe on some petals, reverse, dbl.; foliage medium size, medium green, semi-glossy; numerous prickles; upright, medium (24 in.) growth; ['Red Delight' × 'Hurdy Gurdy']; intr. 1997

'Kühnhilda' S, mp, Weihrauch; flowers medium, single; intr. 1983

'Kukolinsky' -- See 'Kokulinsky's Unterlage'

'Kulu Belle' HT, dp, 1974, Pal, Dr. B. P.; buds medium, long pointed; flowers deep pink, medium to large, full, high-centered, borne singly; foliage medium size, leathery; growth vigorous, bushy (75 cm.); intr. 1972

'Kum Kum' HT, lp, Muckerjee, K.P.; flowers delicate pink, large, lasting, moderate fragrance; free-flowering; intr. 1994

'Kumaradhara' F, pb, K&S; flowers salmon with silvery white reverse; intr. 1988

'Kumari' F, mp, Kasturi; flowers , high-centered; ['White Junior Miss' × unknown]; intr. 1982

'Kumbaya' F, my, 1981, Sanday, John; bud pointed; flowers bright medium yellow, 22 petals, borne up to 15 per cluster; foliage deep green; prickles slightly hooked, red; low, bushy growth; ['Chatterbox' × Allgold®]

'Kumiko' HT, dp, Reuter; intr. 1997

'Kumkum' F, or, 1974, Pal, Dr. B. P.; buds small, pointed; flowers vivid orange-scarlet, medium, semi-dbl., open, borne in clusters; foliage medium size, glossy; growth vigorous, open, upright (115 cm.); intr. 1971

'Kunigunde' F, 1960, Horstmann; flowers pink, large, 35 petals, high-centered; vigorous growth

Kupferkönigin® -- See 'Koranderer'

'Kurama' HT, mr, Keihan; intr. 1977

'Kurenai' F, dp, Keisei; intr. 2004

'Kurenai Seishin' HT, ob, Hiroshima; intr. 2000

'Kurocho' ('Black Butterfly') F, dr, Keisei; intr. 2005

'Kuroshinju' ('Black Pearl') HT, dr, Suzuki, Seizo; intr. 1988

'Kurstadt Baden' HT, pb, Tantau, Math.; flowers pink and red, large, dbl.; intr. 1966

'Kurt Scholz' HT, mr, 1934, Kordes; bud pointed; flowers blood-red with some crimson, very large, dbl., high-centered; foliage leathery; vigorous, bushy growth; ['Cathrine Kordes' × 'W.E. Chaplin']

'Kushali' Gr, mp, Solanki-Tejganga; free-flowering; stems long; [sport of 'Prima Donna']; intr. 1996

'Kusum' F, lp, Padhye; flowers pale pink, long lasting, borne in clusters; [sport of 'Fusilier']; intr. 1978

'Kutno' Pol, m, 1965, Wituszynski, B.; flowers lavender-pink, dbl.; growth low; ['Margo Koster' × unknown]

'Kwinana' F, rb, 1962, Riethmuller; bud ovoid; flowers crimson overlaid carmine, single, open, borne in clusters; moderate fragrance; foliage leathery; strong stems; vigorous, tall growth; [Orange Triumph® × unknown]; intr. 1962

'kykNet Ster' ('Jachenfo') HT, my, J&P; flowers bright yellow, double; recurrent; stems long; tall growth

'Kynast' HT, mr, 1917, Krüger; flowers amaranth-red, large, full; ['Dr G. Krüger' × unknown]

'Kyo-Maiko' ('Maiko') F, op, 1973, Suzuki, Seizo; bud ovoid; flowers deep bright salmon-orange, small, dbl., cupped, slight fragrance; foliage small, glossy, light; moderate, dwarf, bushy growth; [(Sarabande® × unknown) × ('Ruby Lips' × unknown)]; intr. 1974

'Kyogoku' HT, pb; intr. 1989

'Kyoto' -- See 'Koto'

'Kyoto 1200' -- See 'Arashiyama'

'Kyria' -- See 'Pitica'

'Kyson' Cl HT, mr, 1940, Eacott; flowers bright red, open, very large, single, borne in clusters; recurrent bloom; foliage leathery, glossy, dark; short, strong stems; very vigorous, climbing (7 ft. or more) growth; ['New Dawn' × 'Allen Chandler']

— L —

'L. D. Braithwaite' -- See 'Auscrim'

'L. E. Longley' HT, mr, 1949, Longley, L.E.; flowers open, large to medium, semi-dbl.; foliage glossy, dark, bronze; very vigorous, bushy growth; ['Pink Princess' × 'Crimson Glory']

'L. G. Harris' HT, Gregory, C.; intr. 1972

'L. J. de Hoog' HT, mr, 1934, Leenders Bros.; flowers scarlet-red, well-formed, large, dbl.; vigorous, bushy growth; ['Hadley' × 'Hawlmark Scarlet']

'L. R. May' HT, dr, 1935, Chaplin Bros.; flowers scarlet-crimson, paling to silvery pink, base orange, well-formed; vigorous growth

'La Bamba' S, my, Dickson; flowers pale yellow, semi-dbl., open, borne in open clusters; low, spreading groundcover growth; intr. 2003

La Baraka® HT, or

'La Bella' HT, dr, 1975, Kordes; bud large, ovoid; flowers dbl., globular, slight fragrance; foliage glossy, dark; very vigorous, upright growth; ['Liebeszauber' × 'Herz As']; intr. 1976

La Belle® HT, pb, Kordes; flowers light pink, green tint on outer petals, medium, full, cupped, borne mostly singly; recurrent; thornless; stems medium to long; florist rose; intr. 2005

'La Belle Alsacienne' -- See 'Evelsac'

'La Belle Augusta' -- See 'Belle Auguste'

'La Belle Distinguée' ('Double Red', 'Double Scarlet Sweet Briar', 'La Petite Duchesse', 'Lee's Duchess', 'Scarlet Sweet Brier') HEg, mr, about 1820; flowers bright crimson, small, dbl.; non-recurrent; foliage dainty, fragrant; compact (3-4 ft.) growth

'La Belle Inconnue' S, mp

'La Belle Irisée' HT, ob, 1943, Gaujard; bud ovoid, coppery; flowers clear orange-yellow, medium, dbl., globular; foliage leathery; dwarf growth; ['Mme Joseph Perraud' × seedling]

'La Belle Marie' ('Belle Marie') T, dp, 1856, Raynaud; flowers pink, veined darker, reverse deep rose, center incurved; medium, moderate fruity fragrance; foliage smooth, pointed; vigorous, tall growth; ['Old Blush' × 'Mme Laurette Messimy']

'La Belle Mathilde' ('Belle Mathilde') HSpn, w, 1816, Descemet; flowers white, washed pink, 3-3½ in., semi-dbl., moderate fragrance; foliage very close-set, simply serrate

'La Belle Ninon' -- See 'Belle Ninon'

'La Belle Sultane' ('Aigle Rouge', 'Belle Sultane', 'Violacea', 'Rose du Sérail', 'Mahaeca', 'Gallica Maheca', 'Juliette') HGal, dr, before 1801; flowers velvety deep crimson-purple, becoming violet, base white, with prominent yellow stamens, medium, 10-12 petals, flat, borne solitary or in cluster of 2-3; early summer; foliage thick, medium green, round; prickles numerous, brown, slightly recurved, small; from Holland, distributed by Dupont; intr. ca. 1795

'La Belle Suzanne' T, lp; flowers light pink suffused white; foliage smooth, pointed; vigorous, tall growth; ['Old Blush' × 'Mme Laurette Messimy']

'La Belle Villageoise' -- See 'Panachée Pleine'

'La Biche' -- See 'Mlle de Sombreuil'

'La Biche' N, w, 1832, Trouillet; flowers white, center flesh, 7-9 cm., very dbl., cupped, borne in large clusters, strong damask/Tea fragrance; very remontant; foliage dark

'La Bien Aimé' -- See 'Bien-Aimée'

'La Bitta' S, dy; groundcover; intr. 2005

'La Blancheur' -- See 'Sodori-Himé'

'La Bonne Geneviève' -- See 'Bonne Geneviève'

'La Bonne Maison' HMsk, w, Masquelier, Odile; flowers white with pink blush, single, borne in large clusters, intense fragrance; recurrent; vigorous (6 ft.) growth; ['Francis E. Lester' × R. multiflora nana]; intr. 1997

'La Boule d'Or' T, dy, 1860, Margottin; flowers golden yellow, very large, full, globular

'La Brillante' -- See 'Général Jacqueminot'

'La Brillante' HP, mr, 1861, Verdier, V.; flowers bright crimson, well-formed, large, dbl.; numerous prickles; growth upright

'La Brunajeune' -- See 'La Brunoyenne'

'La Brunoyenne' ('La Brunajeune') HP, rb, 1908, Bourgeois; flowers velvety red with flame, center lighter madder red, large, very full, cupped

'La Caille' M, mp, 1857, Robert et Moreau; flowers bright rose-pink, nuanced violet, full, flat

'La Canada' Min, dp

'La Canadienne' HT, ob, 1967, Morey, Dr. Dennison; bud long, pointed; flowers orange to shrimp and cream, large, semi-dbl.; foliage dark, bronze, glossy; vigorous, bushy growth; ['Royal Sunset' × 'Sierra Sunset']

'La Centfeuilles Prolifère Foliacée' -- See 'Prolifera de Redouté'

'La Champagne' HT, ob, 1919, Barbier; bud long, pointed; flowers light coppery red, base yellow, edged light pink, large, 25 petals, globular; foliage rich green, leathery; vigorous growth

'La Chinoise' -- See 'Fortuniana'

'La Cicogne' HT, mp, 1903, Corboeuf

'La Cocarde' -- See 'Majestueuse'

'La Coquette' -- See 'Belle Couronnée'

'La Coquette de Lyon' -- See 'Coquette de Lyon'

'La Coquette de Marly-le-Roy' B, w, 1863, Cagneux; flowers white, shaded pink

'La Couronne Tendre' HGal, lp; flowers flesh-pink, small, dbl.

'La Croix d'Honneur' -- See 'Croix d'Honneur'

'La Dame Blanche' D, w, Miellez; bud red; flowers flesh white, large, dbl.; intr. about 1860

'La Dame Blanche' Ch, w, before 1830, Laffay; flowers pure white, medium, full

'La Delphinie' -- See 'Delphinie'

'La Désirée' HGal, about 1810, Descemet

'La Desirée' HCh, mp, before 1848; flowers very small, full; Lawrenciana

'La Detroite' HT, lp, 1904, Hopp & Lemke; flowers flesh-pink, shading to deep rose, large, dbl., intense fragrance; ['Mme Caroline Testout' × 'Bridesmaid']

'La Diaphane' M, lp, 1848, Laffay; flowers blush rose, large, very dbl., rosette

'La Digittaire' -- See 'Childling'

'La Divinité' -- See 'Damas Violacé'

'La Duchesse' HGal, mp, 1838

'La Duchesse de Morny' HP, mp, 1863, Verdier, E.; flowers tender rose-pink, reverse pale pink, nuanced silver, large,

dbl., globular, cupped; very remontant; foliage dark above, pale beneath, oval, pointed; prickles unequal
'La Esmeralda' -- See 'Esmeralda'
'La Favorita' ('Barpess') HT, or
'La Favorite' HGal, mr, about 1815, Descemet; flowers bright cherry red
'La Favorite' D, lp, Vibert; flowers flesh pink; sometimes classed as HGal; intr. about 1830
'La Favorite' HP, pb, Laffay; flowers flesh-white, shaded with carmine-garnet, medium, full; intr. 1847
'La Favorite' HP, dp, Guillot; flowers dark pink becoming light pink, large, full, globular, moderate fragrance; intr. 1872
'La Favorite' HT, mp, Schwartz; flowers blush white washed cream, large, dbl., cupped; ['Mme Caroline Testout' × 'Reine Emma des Pays-Bas']; intr. 1900
'La Félicité' ('Unique Panachée') D, pb, before 1810, Dupont; flowers light blush pink, speckled with white, large, semi-dbl.
'La Fiamma' HWich, ob, 1909, Walsh; flowers flame red, 3 cm., single, borne in very large clusters; foliage small, glossy; vigorous, climbing (15 ft.) growth
'La Fiancée d'Abydos' ('Bride of Abydos') T, w; flowers white, tinted with coppery carmine pink, full
'La Florida' HT, mp, 1932, La Florida; flowers salmon, well-formed; foliage glossy; strong stems; very vigorous growth
'La Florifère' B, dp, 1846, Bougère; flowers dark carmine pink, shaded silky pink, medium, full
'La Florifère' B, mp, Soupert; flowers glowing carmine; intr. 1865
'La Follette' ('Lafollette', 'Sénateur La Follette') HG, mp, about 1910, Busby; bud long, pointed; flowers pink and carmine, 13 cm., dbl., moderate fragrance; vigorous (to 20 ft half-hardy; [R. gigantea × unknown]
'La Fontaine' HP, mr, 1845, Vibert; flowers bright garnet, medium, full
'La Fontaine' M, lp, Robert; flowers delicate pink, shaded deep pink, 5-7 cm., full, flat; intr. 1852
'La Fontaine' HP, mp, Guinoisseau; flowers bright pink, large, full; intr. 1855
'La Fontaine' F, my, Meilland, Mrs. Marie-Louise; bud pointed, ovoid; flowers barium-yellow, 3½-4 in., 20-25 petals, high-centered to cupped, borne in clusters; foliage leathery, dark; vigorous, bushy growth; PP2040; ['Mme Charles Sauvage' × 'Fashion']; intr. 1961
'La Fraîcheur' ('Fraîcheur') HWich, mp, Turbat; flowers dark pink with lighter edges, 4 cm., dbl., borne in clusters of 15-20, slight fragrance; non-recurrent; foliage small, dark green; intr. 1921
'La Fraîcheur' Ch, lp, 1858, Robert & Moreau; flowers whitish pink, center dawn pink, small to medium, full, globular to cupped, borne in clusters, moderate fragrance
'La Fraîcheur' HT, lp, Pernet-Ducher; flowers whitish-pink, center carmine, very large, full, cupped; ['Victor Verdier' × 'Mme Falcot']; intr. 1891
'La France' HT, lp, 1867, Guillot et Fils; bud long, pointed; flowers silvery pink, reverse bright pink, large, petals slightly waved, 60 petals, intense fragrance; vigorous, short (2-3 ft.) growth; ['Mme Bravy' × 'Mme Victor Verdier']; considered to be one of the first Hybrid Teas introduced, and the prototype of the class; reported parentage is probably not correct
'La France, Climbing' Cl HT, lp, 1893, Henderson, P.; flowers rich peach pink, large, dbl.; [sport of 'La France']
'La France de '89' HT, rb, 1889, Moreau et Robert; bud long, pointed; flowers bright red, sometimes striped white, 3-3½ in., dbl., borne in small clusters; good repeat; very vigorous growth; ['Reine Marie Henriette' × 'La France']
'La France Striped' HT, pb, 1956, Hennessey; flowers deep pink to red, and white to blush; [sport of 'La France']
'La France Victorieuse' HT, dp, 1919, Gravereaux; flowers silvery carmine-pink, inside tinted yellow, very large, dbl., moderate fragrance
'La Garçonne' -- See 'Taneiglat'
'La Giralda' HT, mp, 1926, Dot, Pedro; ['Frau Karl Druschki' × 'Mme Edouard Herriot']
'La Globuleuse' HP, dp, 1862, Crousse; flowers silky dark pink
'La Gloire des Jardins' ('Gloire des Jardins') HGal, m, before 1815, Descemet; flowers carmine pink, tinted violet, large, dbl.
'La Gloire des Laurencias' HCh, dr, before 1829, Miellez; flowers dark crimson purple, small, full, flat; Lawrenciana
'La Glorieuse' -- See 'Illustre'
'La Gracieuse' -- See 'Célina'
'La Grand Obscurité' -- See 'Passe-Velours'
'La Grande Belgique' -- See 'Blush Belgiques'
'La Grande Junon' -- See 'Minerve'
'La Grande Parade' S, mr; flowers small, single, borne in clusters; free-flowering
'La Grande Violette' -- See 'Roxelane'
'La Grandeur' T, m, 1878, Nabonnand; flowers violet-pink, very large, full; very remontant
'La Grandeur' HT, my, Pernet-Ducher; flowers medium yellow, edges lighter and tinted pink, sometimes striped, very large, dbl.; ['Mme Honoré Defresne' × 'Lady Mary Fitzwilliam']; intr. 1894
'La Jago' S, yb, Delbard; intr. 2006
'La Joconde' -- See 'Deljacq'
'La Joconde' HT, my, 1920, Croibier; flowers pure golden yellow; RULED EXTINCT 2/88; [sport of 'Arthur R. Goodwin']
'La Jolie' HT, mr, 1956, Buyl Frères; bud long, pointed; flowers geranium-red, 30-35 petals; very vigorous growth; ['Independence' × 'Hens Verschuren']
'La Jolla' HT, pb, 1954, Swim, H.C.; bud long, pointed; flowers soft pink veined deeper, center cream and gold, 5 in., 65 petals, high-centered, moderate fragrance; foliage dark, glossy; upright growth; PP1103; ['Charlotte Armstrong' × 'Contrast']
'La Jonquille' T, my, 1871, Ducher; flowers medium, semi-dbl.; ['Lamarque' × unknown]
'La Julie' HGal, before 1815, Descemet
'La Laponne' HCh, mp, before 1829; flowers violety-pink, very small, flat; Lawrenciana
'La Liliputienne' HCh, dp, before 1829, Miellez; flowers deep violet pink, very small, full; Lawrenciana
'La Louise' -- See 'Louise'
'La Louise' ('Louise Simplex', 'Louise') C, m, before 1810, Dupont; flowers fleshy mauve-pink, semi-dbl.
'La Luna' HT, ly, Kordes; flowers lemon-yellow, dbl., high-centered, borne singly, occasionally two or three per stem; stems long, near thornless; intr. 1999
'La Lune' T, ly, 1878, Nabonnand; flowers creamy yellow, center darker, semi-dbl., globular
'La Maculée' ('Maculata', 'Pulmonaire') HGal, pb, before 1815, Dupont; flowers rose pink with carmine striping, medium, semi-dbl.
'La Madelon de Paris' F, lp, 1962, Robichon; flowers bright pink, well-formed, medium, dbl., borne in clusters of 6-8; vigorous growth; ['Cécile Brunner' × seedling]
'La Magie du Parfum' HT, mr; flowers intense red, double, high-centered, intense fragrance; recurrent; growth moderate height; intr. 2007
'La Magnifique' -- See 'Pourpre Charmant'
'La Maréchale Pétain' HT, mr, 1927, Sauvageot, H.; flowers carmine, dbl.; ['Col. Leclerc' × 'Château de Clos Vougeot']
'La Marne' Pol, pb, 1915, Barbier; flowers blush white, edged vivid pink, single, borne in large, loose clusters; vigorous growth; ['Mme Norbert Levavasseur' × 'Comtesse du Cayla']
La Marseillaise® -- See 'Delgeot'
'La Marylene' F, dr
'La Mascotte' Cl HT, dy, 1933, Schwartz, A.; flowers deep saffron-yellow, passing to straw-yellow, slightly tinted salmon, dbl.; foliage dark, glossy; ['Reine Marie Henriette' × 'Laurent Carle']
'La Mélusine' HRg, dp, 1906, Späth; flowers pinkish red, large, dbl., borne in large clusters, intense fragrance; very vigorous growth
'La Mère de St Louis' -- See 'Mère de St Louis'
'La Mère Gigogne' HGal, before 1815, Descemet
'La Mère Gigogne' Ch, dp, Vibert; flowers

dark pink, aging to purple, medium, very full; intr. about 1830

'La Mère Gigogne'   C, lp, Vibert; flowers light pink, medium, full; intr. about 1830

'La Merveille'   HGal, before 1820, Descemet

'La Mexique' -- See 'Le Mexique'

'La Mie au Roy'   HT, yb, 1927, Bernaix, P.; flowers yellow, salmon and copper large, dbl., globular, moderate fragrance; ['Duchess of Wellington' × 'Pax Labor']

'La Mienne' -- See 'Flon'

'La Minuette' -- See 'Minuette'

'La Moderne' ('À Fleur Double')   P, lp, before 1820; flowers blush, large, semi-dbl.; prickles feeble

'La Mortola'   Sp, w, 1970, Hanbury; flowers yellowish-white, 3 in., 5 petals, borne in trusses, intense fragrance; foliage downy gray-green; very vigorous, climbing growth; form of R. brunonii; intr. 1954

'La Motte Sanguine' -- See 'Lamotte Sanguin'

'La Mouche'   HCh, dp, before 1830, Miellez; flowers cerise, very small, full; Lawrenciana

'La Nankeen'   T, yb, 1871, Ducher; bud deep orange yellow at base, white at point; flowers coppery-yellow, outer petals lighter, large, full; foliage light green, smooth, oval-pointed; prickles reddish brown, upright, flattened; stems thin and reflexing, pale green

'La Nantaise'   HP, dr, 1885, Boisselot; flowers intense red darkened by deeper tints, large, full, cupped, borne singly and in small clusters; foliage dark green; prickles hooked, medium; growth erect; ['Général Jacqueminot' × unknown]

'La Napolitaine' -- See 'Charles X'

'La Napolitaine' -- See 'Ulysse'

'La Nationale' ('Nationale Tricolore')   HGal, pb, before 1836; flowers pink and red, striped and marbled with purplish crimson, medium, dbl.

'La Négresse' -- See 'Superbe en Brun'

'La Négresse'   D, dr, 1842, Vibert; flowers very deep crimson-purple, medium, full, flat; growth branching, small

'La Neige'   HGal, w, 1853, Robert; flowers white with green pip, full, flat rosette; foliage dark green; growth vigorous

'La Neige'   T, w, Perny; intr. 1885

'La Neige'   Ch, w, Reboul; flowers pure white, medium, full, borne in clusters; intr. 1893

'La Neige'   M, w, Moranville; flowers pure white, medium, dbl., flat to globular, borne in clusters of 3-5; foliage turns purple; vigorous growth; ['Blanche Moreau' × unknown]; intr. 1905

'La Nina'   HGal, about 1810, Descemet

'La Nina'   F, pb, Richardier; intr. 1998

'La Noble Fleur'   HGal, about 1810, Descemet

'La Noblesse'   C, lp, 1856, Pastoret; flowers soft pink with carmine center, somewhat silvery, large, dbl., borne singly or in clusters of 2-3, intense fragrance; later bloom than most centifolias; foliage light gray-green; bushy growth

'La Nuancée'   T, w, 1875, Guillot; flowers white, copper at base, edges tinted salmon, medium, full

'La Nubienne' ('Gloire des Héllènes', 'Nubienne')   HCh, m, 1825, Laffay; flowers deep velvety purple, medium, full, globular

'La Paloma' -- See 'Paloma'

La Paloma®   F, w, 1959, Tantau, Math.; flowers creamy white, well-formed, dbl., borne in clusters of up to 30; foliage dark, glossy; ['Yellow Rambler' × 'Goldene Johanna Tantau']

'La Paloma 85' -- See 'Tanamola'

'La Pâquerette' -- See 'Pâquerette'

'La Parfaite'   HT, op, 1956, Buyl Frères; bud pointed; flowers bright salmon-pink, large, 40-50 petals; vigorous, bushy growth; [R.M.S. Queen Mary × 'Lady Sylvia']

'La Parfumee'   HT, or

La Parisienne® -- See 'Sunpari'

'La Parisienne'   HT, or, 1937, Mallerin, C.; bud long, pointed, deep coral-red; flowers orange-coral, open, very large, semi-dbl.; foliage glossy, dark; very vigorous growth; ['Lucy Nicolas' × 'Charles P. Kilham']

'La Passionata' ('Betsy Ross')   HT, dr, 1970, Delbard; flowers deep red, large, dbl., high-centered, slight fragrance; vigorous, upright growth; [('Gloire de Rome' × 'La Vaudoise') × 'Divine']; intr. 1969

'La Passionata' ('Appassionata', 'Barapp')   HT, Barni, V.; intr. 1987

'La Passionata'   HT, rb, Delbard; flowers red and orange mixed, large, dbl.; good repeat; vigorous (50-100 cm.) growth; intr. 1997

'La Perie' -- See 'La Perle'

'La Perla'   F, lp, Kordes; intr. 1994

'La Perle' ('La Perie')   HWich, ly, 1905, Fauque; flowers pale yellow to white, 7 cm., full, borne in small clusters, moderate fragrance; foliage dark green, glossy; [R. wichurana × 'Mme Hoste']

'La Petite' -- See 'Umsapetite'

'La Petite Duchesse' -- See 'La Belle Distinguée'

'La Peyrouse' ('Admiral la Peyrouse')   HP, dr, 1854, Robert

'La Phocéenne'   HP, dp, 1862, Geoffre; flowers shining, velvety carmine, large, full

'La Pinta'   F, mr, Richardier; intr. 1998

'La Pivoine'   HP, mr, 1862, Moreau & Robert; flowers poppy red

'La Plus Belle des Ponctuées'   HGal, pb, before 1929; flowers deep rose, spotted pale rose, flat; probably much older than the stated date

'La Plus Élégante' -- See 'Cramoisie Triomphante'

'La Poilu' -- See 'Cumberland Belle'

'La Pologne'   HT, or, 1938, Chambard, C.; flowers orange-carmine, very large, cupped; foliage bronze; vigorous growth

'La Prédestinée' -- See 'Illustre'

'La Presumida' -- See 'Presumida'

'La Princesse Vera'   T, w, 1877, Nabonnand; flowers white with a coppery base, large, very full; few prickles

'La Promise'   HT, mr, 1956, Buyl Frères; bud long, pointed; flowers brick-red, semi-dbl.; tall growth; [seedling × 'Betty Uprichard']

'La Proserpine'   HMult, op, 1897, Ketten; flowers peach, yellow center, edge fading to white, medium, dbl., moderate fragrance; ['Georges Schwartz' × 'Duchesse Marie Salviati']

'La Provence' ('Archévêque')   HGal, dr, before 1819; flowers velvety crimson, 4 in.

'La Pucelle' -- See 'Pucelle de Lille'

'La Pucelle'   HGal, m, before 1811, Dubourg; bud pointed; flowers bright purple pink, small, dbl., pompon; foliage small, light green, finely dentate

'La Pudeur'   B, w, about 1835, Laffay; flowers flesh white, small, full; perhaps synonymous with La Pudeur from de Fauw

'La Pudeur'   B, w, de Fauw; flowers white with pink, large, full; possibly synonymous with 'La Pudeur' from Laffay; intr. 1853

'La Pyramidale' -- See 'Porcelaine'

'La Quintinie'   HCh, m, before 1848; flowers dark lilac pink, very large, cupped

'La Quintinie'   B, dp, Thomas; flowers dark carmine, aging to poppy red, full; sometimes classed as HP; intr. 1853

'La Ramée'   F, dr, 1949, Meilland, F.; flowers crimson, 13 petals, borne in clusters; foliage dark, bronze; vigorous growth; ['Holstein' × 'Alain']

'La Reine' ('Reine des Francais', 'Rose de la Reine')   HP, mp, 1842, Laffay, M.; flowers glossy rose-pink, large, 78 petals, cupped, moderate fragrance; vigorous growth; [possibly a seedling of 'William Jesse']

'La Reine d'Angleterre' -- See 'Reine d'Angleterre'

'La Reine de Hamburg'   P, mp

'La Reine de la Pape' -- See 'Reine de la Pape'

'La Reine de Provence' -- See 'Reine des Centfeuilles'

'La Reine Elizabeth' ('Reine Elizabeth')   Pol, mr, 1924, Oosthoek; flowers dark crimson, small, full, pompon, borne in clusters; compact, dwarf growth

'La Reine Victoria' -- See 'Reine Victoria'

'La Remarquable'   A, w, before 1833; flowers medium, full, cupped

'La Revenante' ('Revenante')   HGal, mp, 1825, Miellez; flowers cerise, dbl., loose

'La Roche aux Fees'   HT, yb, Adam, M.; intr. 1997

'La Rochefoucauld-Liancourt'   HGal, pb, 1825, Coquerel; flowers light pink, center brighter, shaded and marbled purple, very large, very full

'La Rose' -- See 'Meisocrat'

'La Rose Bordeaux'   S, mp, Guillot - Massad; flowers pale pink, deeper in center, full, borne in clusters, moderate fragrance; foliage medium size, medium green; vigorous (4 ft.) growth; intr. 2001

'La Rose de Mme Raymond Poincaré' -- See 'Mme Raymond Poincaré'

'La Rose de York' -- See 'White Rose of York'

'La Rose Évêque' -- See 'Le Rosier Évêque'

'La Rose Romantica' -- See 'Meisocrat'

'La Rose Tatouée' -- See 'The Rose Tatoo'

'La Rose Vert de Chine' -- See 'Green Rose'

'La Rosée' -- See 'Doctor F. Debat'

'La Rosée'   Pol, w, 1920, Turbat; flowers sulfur-white, passing to pure white, then to soft pink

'La Rosière, Climbing' -- See 'Prince Camille de Rohan'

'La Rosiere'   HP, 1861, Verdier, E.

'La Rosière'   HP, dr, 1875, Damaizin; bud long; flowers maroon crimson, shaded with black, medium, dbl., cupped

'La Rossa' -- See 'Barlar'

'La Roxelane'   HGal, m, 1828, Vibert

'La Royale' -- See 'Plena'

'La Royale' -- See 'Great Maiden's Blush'

'La Royale de Mulhouse'   F, ly, Sauvageot; flowers light yellow, darker towards center, petals ruffled, dbl.; intr. 2003

'La Rubanée' ('Belle Rubine', 'Panachée Double', 'Perle des Panachées', 'Village Maid') HGal, pb, before 1832, possibly Vibert; flowers rose pink, striped with white and violet, 8 cm., very dbl., early bloomer, moderate fragrance; foliage large, deep green; numerous prickles; open (6 ft.) growth

'La Sanguine' -- See 'Sanguinea'

'La Saumonée'   HCh, op, 1877, Margottin fils; flowers salmony pink, large, full, cupped; sometimes reblooming in autumn

'La Scala'   HT, rb, 1965, Lindquist; flowers reddish-orange, large, dbl., cupped, intense fragrance; foliage leathery; upright, open growth; [('Mme Henri Guillot' × 'Mirandy') × 'Peace']; intr. 1964

'La Séduisante' -- See 'Great Maiden's Blush'

'La Serenissima'   HT, (Italia)

'La Sevillana, Climbing' -- See 'Meigekanusar'

La Sevillana® ('Sevillana') F, or, 1978, Meilland, Mrs. Marie-Louise; bud conical; flowers vermilion, 8 cm., 10-15 petals, borne in clusters of 5 - 20, no fragrance; recurrent; foliage bronze, leathery; vigorous, bushy (3 ft.) growth; PP6384; [((('MEIbrim' × 'Jolie Madame') × (Zambra® × Zambra®)) × (('Tropicana' × 'Tropicana') × ('Poppy Flash' × 'Rusticana'))]; intr. 1982

'La Sirène' ('La Syrène') HP, m, 1867, Soupert & Notting; flowers dark reddish-purple

La Soleil® ('The Sunflower') F, or, 1961, Mallerin, C.; flowers bright vermilion, 3 in., 29 petals, borne in clusters; foliage clear green; dwarf, bushy growth

'La Somme'   HT, or, 1919, Barbier; bud large, ovoid; flowers deep coral-red tinted copper, turning salmon, large, semi-dbl., open, cupped, moderate fragrance; foliage medium size, leathery, dark green, glossy; ['Mme Caroline Testout' × 'Rayon d'Or']

'La Souveraine' ('Grand Edouard') HP, mp, 1874, Verdier, E.; flowers shining carmine pink, reverse silvery, very large, full, moderate melon fragrance

'La Stupenda'   HT, pb, 1966, Taylor, L.R.; bud long, pointed; flowers pink, reverse darker, large, very dbl.; foliage glossy; upright, bushy growth; ['Aztec' × 'First Love']

'La Superba'   Gr, Mansuino; intr. 1970

'La Surprise'   A, w, 1823, Poilpré; flowers medium, very dbl.; nearly thornless

'La Sylphide'   T, ly, 1838, Vibert

'La Sylphide'   T, m, Boyau; flowers flesh pink tinted lavender, deeper in fall, semi-dbl., globular; tall growth; sometimes classed as N; intr. 1842

'La Syrène' -- See 'La Sirène'

'La Syrène'   HP, mr, 1874, Touvais; flowers light cherry red, large, full

'La Temponaise'   HT, rb, Reuter; intr. 2000

'La Tendresse'   HGal, m, before 1820, Dupont; flowers pale violet pink

'La Tendresse'   HP, mp, Oger; flowers hydrangea pink, large, full; intr. 1864

'La Tosca'   HT, pb, 1901, Schwartz, Vve.; flowers shell-pink, center and reverse darker, 4 in., dbl., moderate fragrance; foliage rich green, leathery; vigorous, bushy growth; ['Josephine Marot' × 'Luciole']

'La Toulousaine'   HP, lp, 1877, Brassac; flowers flesh pink, aging to carmine, medium, full

La Tour d'Argent™ -- See 'Delricos'

'La Tour d'Auvergne'   HGal, rb, 1842, Vibert; flowers deep rosy crimson, flecked carmine, incurved, large, dbl.

'La Transparente' -- See 'Unique Carnée'

'La Très Haute' -- See 'Aigle Brun'

'La Triomphante' -- See 'Illustre'

'La Tulipe'   T, w, 1868, Ducher; flowers creamy white, tinted with pale carmine, large, semi-dbl.

'La Vaillante Bergère'   HP, dp, 1847, Cherpin; flowers medium, full

La Vanoise Parc National® -- See 'Korhokhel'

'La Variable' -- See 'Childling'

'La Vaudoise'   HT, mr, 1946, Heizmann, E.; bud oval; flowers blood-red touched brilliant scarlet, medium, dbl.; foliage leathery; vigorous, bushy growth

'La Vendômoise'   HT, pb, 1907, Moullière; flowers pink and red, large, dbl.; ['Mrs W. J. Grant' × 'Marie d'Orléans']

'La Vénissiane'   F, ly, Guillot - Massad; flowers yellow fading quickly to white with pink dots, large, slight fragrance; foliage dark green, glossy; solid (80 cm.) growth; intr. 2001

'La Vie'   HT, dr, 1931, Groshens; flowers crimson to scarlet, base orange to carmine, fading to red; PP3; [sport of 'Talisman']

'La Vie en Rose' -- See 'Vie en Rose'

'La Vierzionnaise'   HP, lp, 1893, André; sepals foliaceous; flowers light lilac pink, shaded darker pink, borne in small clusters; prickles red, hooked; growth upright

'La Villageoise' -- See 'Panachée Pleine'

'La Ville de Bruxelles' ('Ville de Bruxelles') D, mp, 1836, Vibert; sepals long, leafy; flowers pink tinted salmon, center incurved, with a small center eye, medium, very dbl., quartered, cupped, strong fragrance; non-remontant; foliage glossy, light green, elongated; tall (5 ft.) growth; R. centifolia may have been one parent

'La Ville de Londres'   HGal, dp, before 1844, Vibert; flowers deep rose pink, very large, full, cupped

'La Virginale' -- See 'Beauté Virginale'

'La Virginale' -- See 'Great Maiden's Blush'

'La Volumineuse'   P, lp, before 1835; flowers rosy flesh, large

'La Volupté' ('Laetitia', 'Volupté') HGal, dp, before 1828, Bizard; flowers bright glowing deep pink, large, full

'La Voulzie'   F, dr, 1953, Robichon; flowers garnet-red, very large, semi-dbl., borne in clusters; very vigorous growth; ['Brise Parfumee' × 'Alain']

'Labareda'   F, mr, Moreira da Silva; flowers bright red

'L'Abbandonata' -- See 'Lauré Davoust'

'L'Abondance'   HP, mr, 1864, Verdier, E.; flowers vivid red

'L'Abondance'   N, w, Moreau-Robert; bud slightly pink; flowers flesh-pink, opening to pure white, 5-6 cm., full, borne in large clusters; good repeat; foliage glossy; growth semi-climbing (8 ft.); intr. 1877

'Lac Blanc' -- See 'Korweirim'

'Lac La Nonne'   HRg, dp, 1950, Bugnet; bud pointed, deep red; flowers very deep pink, 2-3 in., semi-dbl., moderate fragrance; foliage light; growth vigorous (7-8 ft.); hardy; [R. rugosa plena × R. acicularis]

'Lac Majeau'   HRg, w, Bugnet; flowers large, semi-dbl.; recurrent; few prickles; upright, bushy (5 ft.) growth; intr. before 1984

Lac Rose® -- See 'Korimro'

'Lace'   HT, lp, Fryer; flowers soft pearl pink, full, high-centered, borne mostly singly, moderate fragrance; recurrent; medium height, bushy growth; intr. 2007

'Lace Cascade' -- See 'Jacarch'

'Lacépède'   HP, dp, 1865, Vibert; flowers

light red, aging to dark pink, large, full

'Lachs' Pol, or, 1943, Kordes; flowers glowing orange-red; [sport of 'Dick Koster']

'Lacination' S, mp, Twomey, Jerry; intr. 1997

'Lacre' F, mr, 1963, Moreira da Silva; flowers bright red, loose, semi-dbl.; ['Concerto' × seedling]

'Lacteola' -- See 'White Provence'

'Lada' HT, dp, Urban, J.

'Ladakh Rose' ('The Ladakh Rose') Ch, lp, before 1936; flowers light pink, aging to dark pink, large; from India

'Laddie' HT, or, 1926, McGredy; flowers deep carmine, flushed orange and scarlet, base orange; bushy growth

'Ladera' S, ob; intr. 2003

'Ladies Choice' HT, pb, 1969, Anderson's Rose Nurseries; flowers cerise, reverse silvery, high pointed, large, dbl.; foliage light green; free growth; ['Liberty Bell' × 'Prima Ballerina']

'Ladies' Choice, Climbing' Cl HT, pb, 1976, Anderson's Rose Nurseries; flowers cerise, reverse silvery, high-pointed, large, dbl., intense fragrance; foliage light green; [sport of 'Ladies' Choice']; intr. 1975

Ladies Home Journal® -- See 'Burwinladhom'

'Ladies In Waiting' S, ab; PP14334; intr. 2003

'Ladies' View' -- See 'Seaview'

'L'Admirable' -- See 'Admirable'

'L'Admiration' Ch, mp, 1856, Robert; flowers medium, single

Lady™ -- See 'Poulra021(N)'

'Lady' HT, mp, 1984, Weeks, O.L.; flowers medium, 35 petals, high-centered, slight fragrance; foliage large, medium green, matte to semi-glossy; upright, compact growth; ['Song of Paris' × 'Royal Highness']

'Lady Aberdeen' -- See 'Frybingo'

'Lady Alice Stanley' HT, pb, 1909, McGredy; bud pointed; flowers pale flesh-pink, reverse coral-rose, large, 75 petals, moderate fragrance; foliage rich green, leathery; branching growth

'Lady Anderson' HT, pb, 1920, Hall; flowers coral pink to flesh pink and yellow, dbl.

'Lady Angela' -- See 'Monangie'

'Lady Ann' Min, mp, 1961, Moore, Ralph S.; bud pointed; flowers rose-pink, 1¾ in., 42 petals, cupped; foliage leathery, glossy, dark; vigorous, bushy, low growth; [(R. wichurana × Floradora) × 'Little Buckaroo']; intr. 1961

'Lady Ann Kidwell' Pol, dp, 1948, Krebs; bud pointed; flowers deep pink, medium, dbl., star-shaped; foliage glossy, vigorous, upright growth; PP1226; ['Cécile Brunner' × unknown]

'Lady Arthur Hill' HP, lp, 1889, Dickson; flowers lilac-pink, large, full

'Lady Ashtown' HT, pb, 1904, Dickson, A.; bud pointed; flowers carmine-pink, base yellow, large, 43 petals, high-centered; foliage rich green, soft; vigorous, bushy growth; ['Mrs W.J. Grant' × unknown]

'Lady Ashtown, Climbing' Cl HT, pb, 1909, Bradley; [sport of 'Lady Ashtown']

'Lady Baillie' HSpn, ly, before 1848, Lee; flowers pale sulfur-yellow, semi-dbl.; profuse, early bloom; foliage finely divided; dense, shrubby (3-4 ft.) growth; hips glossy, black

'Lady Barbara' ('Chewba') LCl, ob, 1985, Warner, Chris; flowers tangerine, reverse yellow, medium, 20 petals, high-centered, moderate fragrance; foliage medium size, medium green, semi-glossy; upright growth; ['Red Planet' × (Elizabeth of Glamis® × (Galway Bay® × 'Sutter's Gold'))]; intr. 1987

'Lady Barbara Bossom' -- See 'Boshotearl'

'Lady Barham' HT, op, 1911, Dickson; flowers fleshy coral-pink, shaded orange pink, very large, full

'Lady Barnby' HT, pb, 1930, Dickson, A.; bud pointed; flowers glowing pink, shaded red, large, dbl., high-centered; foliage rich green, leathery; bushy, low growth

'Lady Barnett' HT, dr, 1958, Verschuren; flowers crimson, reverse darker, high-centered, moderate fragrance; vigorous, upright growth; intr. 1957

'Lady Battersea' ('Red Nipheros') HT, pb, 1901, Paul; flowers cherry-blossom, base orange, dbl.; ['Mme Abel Chatenay' × 'Liberty']

'Lady Be Good' -- See 'Seagood'

'Lady Beatty' HT, lp, 1918, Chaplin Bros.; flowers blush-pink, well-formed; vigorous growth

'Lady Beauty' HT, pb, 1985, Kono, Yoshito; bud ovoid; flowers light pink flushed yellow, reverse deeper, large, 33 petals, high-centered, slight fragrance; foliage medium size, medium green, glossy; prickles few, sickle-shaped; vigorous, upright growth; ['Lady' × 'Princess Takamatsu']; intr. 1984

'Lady Belper' HT, ob, 1948, Verschuren; flowers bronze-orange shaded light orange, semi-globular, 4 in., 38 petals, high-centered, borne mostly singly, moderate fragrance; foliage glossy, dark; vigorous growth; ['Mev. G.A. van Rossem' × seedling]

'Lady Betty' HT, ab, 1930, Bees; bud pointed; flowers apricot-pink, veined red, semi-dbl., high-centered; ['Sunburst' × 'Mrs Aaron Ward']

'Lady Beverley' F, lp, Owens; flowers clear pink; [sport of 'Independence']; intr. 1958

Lady Bird™ -- See 'Jacormag'

'Lady Bird' F, yb, 1966, Joseph H. Hill, Co.; flowers yellow shaded red at edge, small, dbl., borne in clusters; foliage leathery; vigorous, bushy growth; PP2626; [seedling × 'Rumba']

'Lady Bird Johnson' HT, or, 1970, Curtis, E.C.; bud long, pointed; flowers medium, dbl., moderate fragrance; vigorous, upright growth; PP3115; ['Montezuma' × 'Hawaii']; intr. 1971

'Lady Bissett' HT, ob, 1928, Lilley; flowers bright orange, reverse apricot

'Lady Blanche' LCl, w, 1913, Walsh; flowers snow-white, dbl., borne in large clusters; free bloom, sometimes repeated in fall; very vigorous, climbing growth

'Lady Bountiful' LCl, mr, 1938, Tait; flowers scarlet-rose, center white, open, large, single, borne in clusters; foliage leathery, dark; very vigorous, climbing or trailing growth; ['American Pillar' × unknown]

'Lady Braye' HT, dp, 1960, Verschuren; flowers deep rose-pink, long, pointed; foliage dark

'Lady Bren' Min, mp, 2004, Smith, Joe and Landers, Brenda; flowers med pink, reverse white, medium, dbl., borne mostly solitary; foliage medium size, dark green, glossy; prickles ¼ in.; growth upright, medium; [sport of Miss Flippins™]; intr. 2005

'Lady Brisbane' -- See 'Cramoisi Supérieur'

'Lady Brisbane, Climbing' -- See 'Cramoisi Supérieur, Climbing'

'Lady Cahn' HT, ab, 1937, Gaujard; bud long, pointed; flowers rich apricot-yellow, veined darker, large, 40-50 petals; long, strong stems; vigorous growth

'Lady Canada' HT, mp, 1927, Dale; flowers bright rose, dbl.; ['Mme Butterfly' × 'Premier']

'Lady Carolina' S, lp, 1990, Jeremias, Lephon L.; bud ovoid; flowers blush pink, same reverse, aging to white, decorative, small, 35-40 petals; repeat bloom; foliage average, dark, glossy; prickles small, hooked, reddish-brown; bushy, spreading, hedge-type, medium growth; hips round, very red, very small; [sport of 'Lady Gay']

'Lady Castlereagh' T, yb, 1888, Dickson, A.; flowers rosy yellow, well-formed; vigorous growth

'Lady Catherine' HT, or, 1976, Von Koss; bud urn shaped; flowers 3½-4 in., 32-45 petals, high-centered; foliage leathery; vigorous, upright, compact growth; ['Montezuma' × 'Rubaiyat']

'Lady Catherine Rose' HT, dp, 1912, Bide; ['Antoine Rivoire' × 'La Fraîcheur']

'Lady Cecily Gibson' -- See 'Evebright'

'Lady Charles Townshend' HT, ob, 1931, Daniels Bros.; flowers orange, overlaid salmon, large, dbl., globular; vigorous, bushy growth; ['The Queen Alexandra Rose' × 'Shot Silk']

'Lady Charmion' HT, mr, 1923, Bees; flowers bright cherry-carmine, dbl.; ['Lyon Rose' × 'Gen. MacArthur']

'Lady Clanmorris' HT, w, 1900, Dickson, A.; flowers creamy white with pale rose center, edged with deep rose, very large

'Lady Clonbrock' N, lp; flowers light pink, medium, dbl., borne in large clusters; introduced by Smith, 1903, but is pos-

The Official Registry and Checklist — Rosa

sibly an older variety

'Lady Coventry'   HT, m, 1913, Smith of Downley

'Lady Craig'   HT, ly, 1922, Dickson, H.; flowers cream-yellow, center apricot-yellow, well-formed, large, dbl.; vigorous, free branching growth

'Lady Cromwell'   HT, dr, 1956, Verschuren; flowers crimson, base gold, large, dbl.; foliage bronze; vigorous growth

'Lady Cunliffe Owen'   HT, pb, 1932, Ley; flowers salmon and cream, base yellow, flushed carmine-rose, outer petals reflexed, dbl., high-centered; foliage leathery; vigorous growth; [sport of 'Mrs A.R. Barraclough']

'Lady Curzon'   HRg, mp, 1901, Turner; flowers delicate pale pink, golden anthers, large, single, moderate fragrance; prickles very numerous; arching stems; vigorous growth; [R. macrantha × R. rugosa rubra]

'Lady Dallas Brooks'   HT, mp, 1955, Downes; [sport of 'Peace']

'Lady Dartmouth'   HT, pb, 1909, Bermaix fils

'Lady Dawson Bates'   HT, yb, 1939, McGredy; flowers golden yellow, flushed pink, opening, high-centered; vigorous growth

'Lady de Bathe'   HT, w, 1911, Cant, B.; flowers creamy white, center shaded peach-rose with yellow, large, full

Lady Di®   HT, lp, Huber; bud pointed; flowers soft pink, 25-29 petals, high-centered, slight fragrance; good repeat; upright, strong (80 cm.) growth; intr. 1982

'Lady Diana' -- See 'Dicxotic'

'Lady Diana'   HT, lp, 1986, Hoy, Lowel L.; flowers 37 petals, high-centered, borne in sprays of 3-4; foliage medium size, medium green, matte; prickles short, hooked; tall, upright growth; hips ovoid, orange; PP5360; ['Sonia' × 'Caress']; intr. 1983

'Lady Dixon'   HT, ab, 1919, Dickson, A.; flowers rich apricot, flushed salmon-pink, dbl.

'Lady Dixon-Hartland'   HT, pb, 1923, Cant, B. R.; flowers centers deep salmon, outer petals pale pink, high-centered; vigorous growth

'Lady Donaldson' -- See 'Canana'

'Lady Dorothea'   T, pb, 1898, Dunlop; flowers yellow over pink; [sport of 'Sunset']

'Lady Downe'   HT, my, 1911, Paul, W.; flowers medium to large, full, moderate fragrance

'Lady Dumas'   HT, pb, White, T.H.

'Lady Duncan'   HRg, pb, 1900, Dawson; flowers rich glowing pink, center and stamens yellow, 3 in., single, borne in small clusters; non-recurrent; foliage glossy; trailing (6 ft.) growth; [R. wichurana × R. rugosa]

'Lady Dunleath'   HT, w, 1913, Dickson, A.; flowers ivory-white edged yellow, small, dbl.

'Lady Dunmore'   HSpn, lp, before 1906, from England

'Lady Edgeworth David'   HT, mp, 1939, Fitzhardinge; bud long, pointed; flowers malmaison rose shaded soft pink, large, dbl., open, moderate fragrance; foliage glossy; vigorous growth; [seedling × 'Betty Uprichard']

'Lady Edine'   HSpn, w, before 1906, from Scotland

'Lady Eleanore'   Cl HT, yb, 1923, Dreer; flowers light yellow-cream splashed rose, center golden to copper; ['Gruss an Teplitz' × 'Barbara']

'Lady Elgin'   ('Thaïs') HT, yb, 1957, Meilland, F.; bud ovoid with conspicuous neck; flowers buff-yellow washed pink, large, 40 petals, cupped, borne singly, moderate fragrance; recurrent; foliage dark, leathery; stems medium; vigorous, upright, bushy growth; PP1469; ['Mme Kriloff' × ('Peace' × 'Geneve')]; intr. 1954

'Lady Elphinstone'   HT, yb, 1921, Dobbie; bud long, pointed; flowers Indian yellow to clear rose, very large, semi-dbl.; foliage dark green, glossy; [sport of 'Mme Edouard Herriot']

Lady Elsie May™ -- See 'Noaelsie'

'Lady Emily Peel'   N, w, 1862, Lacharme, F.; flowers white, tinged with blush, large, full; ['Mlle Blanche Lafitte' × 'Sapho']; sometimes classed as B

'Lady Emma Hamilton' -- See 'Ausbrother'

'Lady English'   HT, or, 1934, Cant, B. R.; flowers bright cerise, center orange, open, very large, dbl.; foliage glossy, bronze; long stems; vigorous growth

'Lady E'owyn' -- See 'Tuckladye'

'Lady Ethel'   S, ab, Sutherland, P; intr. 1998

'Lady Eve'   Min, op, 1979, Rovinski & Meredith; bud globular; flowers creamy white, edged coral-pink, 1½-2 in., 40 petals, high-centered, slight fragrance; vigorous, upright, tall, spreading growth; [Neue Revue® × 'Sheri Anne']; intr. 1978

'Lady Eve Price' -- See 'Caprice'

'Lady Eve Price, Climbing' -- See 'Caprice, Climbing'

'Lady Evelyn Guinness'   HT, mp, 1932, Evans; [sport of 'Ophelia']

'Lady Fairbairn'   HT, mp, 1929, Clark, A.; flowers bright pink, 40 petals; vigorous, upright growth; ['Mme Abel Chatenay' × seedling]

'Lady Faire'   HT, mp, 1907, Bentley; flowers salmon-pink; [sport of 'Mrs W.J. Grant']

'Lady Fairfax'   HT, ob, 1930, Cant, F.; flowers rose and orange-cerise, flushed orange to yellow, well-formed; foliage light green; long stems; vigorous growth

'Lady Florence Stronge'   HT, lp, 1925, McGredy; bud pointed; flowers pale flesh, base pink and gold, very large, dbl., high-centered; foliage leathery, glossy; vigorous, bushy growth

'Lady Fordwich'   HP, pb, 1838, Laffay; flowers bright carmine, shaded garnet-purple, fading to bluish pink, medium, full, cupped

'Lady Forteviot'   HT, yb, 1926, Cant, B. R.; flowers golden yellow to deep apricot, large, dbl., high-centered; foliage bronze, glossy; vigorous, bushy growth

'Lady Forteviot, Climbing'   Cl HT, yb, 1935, Howard Rose Co.; flowers golden-yellow to apricot, reverse darker; [sport of 'Lady Forteviot']

'Lady Fraser'   HT, mr, 1941, Clark, A.; flowers rich red; ['War Paint' × unknown]

'Lady Frost'   HT, dp, 1935, Bees; flowers deep rose, very large, dbl.; foliage leathery; vigorous, bushy growth; ['Lady Alice Stanley' × 'Dr. Herbert Hawkesworth']

'Lady Gay'   HWich, op, 1905, Walsh; flowers cherry pink fading to blush white, small, dbl., borne in clusters, no fragrance; foliage small, dark, glossy; vigorous, climbing (12-20 ft.) growth; [R. wichurana × 'Bardou Job']; virtually identical with Dorothy Perkins; some references say 1903

'Lady Gay'   HMult, mr, Geschwind; ['Crimson Rambler' × unknown]; intr. 1905

'Lady Genevieve'   HP, mr

'Lady Georgia'   HT, pb, 1974, Curtis, E.C.; flowers pink, base blending to ivory, medium, dbl., moderate fragrance; foliage dark, leathery, very vigorous, bushy growth; ['Miss Hillcrest' × 'Peace']; intr. 1973

'Lady Glencora' -- See 'Aroraju'

'Lady Godiva'   HWich, lp, 1908, Paul, G; flowers cameo-pink, small, dbl., borne in clusters, moderate fragrance; [sport of 'Dorothy Perkins']

'Lady Gowrie'   Cl HT, my, 1938, Fitzhardinge; bud long, pointed; flowers maize and champagne-yellow, large, very dbl.; intermittent bloom; foliage leathery, glossy, dark; long stems; very vigorous, climbing growth; ['Sunburst, Climbing' × 'Rev. F. Page-Roberts']

'Lady Grade'   ('Lady Kathleen Grade') HT, or, 1983, Gregory, C.; flowers vermilion, large, 35 petals, moderate fragrance; foliage large, medium green, semi-glossy; bushy growth; ['Tropicana' × seedling]; intr. 1982

'Lady Greenall'   HT, yb, 1911, Dickson, A.; flowers saffron-yellow, edges tinted shell-pink, dbl.

'Lady Greenall, Climbing'   Cl HT, yb, 1923, Lippiatt; [sport of 'Lady Greenall']

'Lady Guinevere' -- See 'Harbadge'

'Lady Gwendoline Colvin'   Cl HT, pb, 1918, Chaplin Bros.; flowers apricot-salmon, shaded chrome-yellow, outer petals stained carmine, dbl.; growth to 6-10 ft.

'Lady Hailsham'   HT, or, 1951, Knight's Nursery; bud pointed; flowers orange flushed red, 3 in., 30 petals; foliage glossy; vigorous growth; [sport of 'McGredy's Sunset']

'Lady Hamilton' HSpn, w; flowers creamy white, occasionally tinted rose, large, semi-dbl.; profuse, non-recurrent bloom; dwarf growth

'Lady Harriet' -- See 'Wilherb'

'Lady Heirloom' S, mp, Clements, John; flowers warm pink with touch of lilac, 4-5 inches, 100+ petals, globular, intense fragrance; recurrent; foliage medium green; moderate (3 ft.) growth; intr. 2005

'Lady Helen' HT, mp, 1971, McTeer, Gilbert; flowers soft clear pink, pointed, 5 in., 30 petals, intense fragrance; foliage glossy, dark; bushy growth; ['Margaret' × ('McGredy's Ivory' × 'Peace')]; intr. 1970

'Lady Helen Maglona' HT, dr, 1926, Dickson, A.; bud pointed; flowers bright crimson-red to scarlet-red, center deeper, very large, dbl., high-centered; foliage leathery; vigorous, bushy growth

'Lady Helen Stewart' HP, dr, 1887, Dickson, A.; flowers bright crimson shaded scarlet, dbl.; vigorous growth

'Lady Henry Grosvenor' HT, lp, 1892, Bennett; flowers flesh pink, large, full, globular

'Lady Hillingdon' T, yb, 1910, Lowe & Shawyer; bud long, pointed; flowers deep apricot-yellow, semi-dbl.; foliage bronze; bushy growth; sometimes as hardy as a Hybrid Tea; ['Papa Gontier' × 'Mme Hoste']

'Lady Hillingdon, Climbing' Cl T, yb, 1917, Hicks; bud long; flowers apricot-yellow, large, dbl., loose; foliage purplish; prickles moderate; growth rampant (20 ft.); [sport of 'Lady Hillingdon']

'Lady Hiroshima' HT, ob, Hiroshima; intr. 1996

'Lady Hudson' HT, ab, 1930, Chaplin Bros.; flowers deep apricot, large, dbl.; vigorous growth

'Lady Huntingfield' HT, my, 1937, Clark, A.; flowers rich golden yellow, reverse lighter, large, dbl., globular; long stems; vigorous, bushy growth; ['Busybody' × unknown]

'Lady Iliffe' HT, mr, 1976, Gandy, Douglas L.; flowers Tyrian rose, 5 in., 38 petals, intense fragrance; free-flowering; foliage large, olive-green; ['Saul' × 'Wendy Cussons']

'Lady in Red' -- See 'Jacopper'

'Lady in Red' -- See 'Sealady'

'Lady In Waiting' S, op, Harkness; flowers unusual copper salmon color, 4½ in., 80 petals, cupped, moderate sweet clove fragrance; recurrent; foliage medium green; growth bushy (3½ ft.); intr. 2003

'Lady Inchiquin' HT, or, 1922, Dickson, A.; flowers orange-vermilion, large, very dbl., high-centered; foliage leathery, rich glossy green; very vigorous, bushy growth

'Lady Jane' HT, dy, 1992, Poole, Lionel; flowers 3-3½ in., full, borne mostly singly; foliage medium size, medium green, semi-glossy; some prickles; medium (75 cm.), upright growth; [Dorothe® × 'Helmut Schimdt']; intr. 1993

'Lady Jane® HT, pb, Tantau; intr. 2004

'Lady Jane Grey' -- See 'Sue Hipkin'

'Lady Jennifer Green' -- See 'Woralps'

'Lady Joan' -- See 'Twogreen'

'Lady Johnstone' HG, dp, 1922, Nabonnand, P.; bud yellow; flowers reddish-pink, turning lilac-rose, stamens yellow, large, single, moderate fragrance; vigorous, climbing growth; [R. gigantea × 'Beauté Lyonnaise']; hybrid gigantea

'Lady Kathleen Grade' -- See 'Lady Grade'

'Lady Kathryn' Min, m, 1990, Jolly, Marie; bud pointed; flowers lavender, aging brown, medium, 22 petals, high-centered, urn-shaped, borne usually singly, moderate damask fragrance; foliage medium size, medium green, semi-glossy, disease-resistant; upright, medium, vigorous growth; hips round, green-brown; [Lavender Jade™ × 'Angel Face']; intr. 1991

'Lady Lauder' HT, yb, 1931, Morse; flowers deep canary-yellow, reverse flushed crimson, dbl., cupped; foliage thick, light; long stems; very vigorous growth

'Lady Lavender' HT, m, 1993, Weeks, O.L.; flowers 3-3½ in., full, borne mostly singly, moderate fragrance; foliage medium size, dark green, glossy; some prickles; bushy (40-48 in.) growth; [('Paradise' × seedling) × 'Swarthmore']; intr. 1993

'Lady Layton' HT, my, 1932, Layton; bud long, pointed; flowers light sunflower-yellow, deepening as it opens, large, moderate fragrance; vigorous growth; PP115; [sport of 'Joanna Hill']

'Lady Le-Ru' HT, mp, 1965, Lothrop; bud round; flowers deep pink, 3½-4 in., 50 petals, cupped, moderate fragrance; free,non-recurrent bloom; thornless; long stems; growth moderate, open (2½ ft.); hardy; PP2241; [R. rugosa hybrid × unknown hybrid tea]

'Lady Leconfield' HT, w, 1939, Burbage Nursery; bud long, pointed, cream, flushed pink; flowers cream-white, 25-30 petals, cupped; foliage leathery; vigorous, bushy growth

'Lady Leslie' HT, rb, 1929, McGredy; flowers rosy scarlet to scarlet-carmine suffused saffron-yellow, large, dbl., high-centered; foliage dark, leathery, glossy; vigorous growth

'Lady Liberty' HT, w, 1987, deVor, Tom; flowers clear white, yellow at base, large, 35 petals, high-centered, borne usually singly or in small clusters; foliage medium size, medium green, semi-glossy; prickles straight, medium, light yellow; extremely long stems; upright, profuse growth; hips globular, medium size, medium green; PP6142; [sport of 'Lady Diana']

'Lady Like' HT, ob, 1973, Tantau, Math.; bud globular; flowers dark orange, large, dbl.; vigorous, upright growth; [seedling × 'Tropicana']; intr. 1971

'Lady Like® ('Ionian Rose') HT, pb, Tantau; flowers deep pink, yellow base, large, 30 petals, low-centered, intense fragrance; free-flowering; foliage deep green, glossy; stems long; upright, medium (3 ft.) growth; intr. 1989

'Lady Lilford' HT, my, 1930, Gregory; flowers clear yellow, center deep golden yellow; foliage rich green, glossy; vigorous, bushy, branching, compact growth; [sport of 'Independence Day']

'Lady Loch' HT, 1885, Johnson; [sport of 'Aspasia']

'Lady Lou' HT, ob, 1948, Brownell; bud long, pointed; flowers coral-peach, large to medium, 50 petals, high-centered, moderate fragrance; foliage glossy, light; vigorous, dwarf growth; PP1059; ['Pink Princess' × 'Shades of Autumn']

'Lady Love' -- See 'Ribbon Rose'

'Lady Luck' HT, pb, 1957, Miller, A.J.; bud long, pointed; flowers blends of pale to rich pink, 4-4½ in., 38 petals, high-centered, intense damask fragrance; foliage dark, leathery; vigorous, upright, bushy growth; PP1579; ['Tom Breneman' × 'Show Girl']; intr. 1956

'Lady MacGregor' HT, 1911, Williams, A.; ['Boule de Neige' × 'a tea']

'Lady MacRobert' -- See 'Coclent'

'Lady Madeleine' -- See 'Eveleine'

'Lady Mandeville' HT, my, 1941, McGredy; flowers yellow, flushed amber, well-formed, 5 in., 35 petals, slight fruity fragrance; foliage dark, bronze; branching, moderate growth; PP461; [seedling × 'Mrs Sam McGredy']

'Lady Mann' HT, pb, 1940, Clark, A.; flowers rosy salmon, large, dbl., cupped, borne in small clusters, moderate tea fragrance; recurrent; foliage large, glossy; ['Lorraine Lee' × unknown]

'Lady Margaret Boscawen' HT, mp, 1911, Dickson, A.; flowers soft shell pink on fawn, large, dbl., intense fragrance

'Lady Margaret Stewart' HT, ob, 1926, Dickson, A.; bud long, pointed; flowers golden yellow shaded and streaked orange and red, very large, dbl., high-centered; foliage sage-green, leathery; vigorous, bushy growth

'Lady Marine' HT, or, 1981, DeLashmutt; flowers dark orange-red, 53 petals, high-centered, urn-shaped, borne 1-3 per cluster; foliage dark, leathery; prickles medium, reddish; medium growth; [seedling × 'Tropicana']

'Lady Mars' T, 1909, California Rose Co.; [sport of 'Gloire de Dijon']

'Lady Martha Bruce' HT, mp, 1925, Ferguson, W.; flowers pink, outer petals tinged peach-blossom-pink

'Lady Mary' HT, mr, 1999, Teranishi, K.; flowers crimson red, 40 petals, high-centered; foliage medium green; growth to 3 ft.; ['Princess Mikasa' × seedling]; intr. 1990

'Lady Mary Corry' T, dy, 1900, Dickson, A.; flowers deep golden yellow, large, moderate tea fragrance; growth vigorous, erect, branching

'Lady Mary Elizabeth' HT, dp, 1927, Dickson, A.; bud pointed; flowers brilliant carmine-pink, large, dbl., high-centered; vigorous, bushy growth

'Lady Mary Fitzwilliam' HT, lp, 1882, Bennett; flowers flesh-color, large, full, globular, intense fragrance; weak growth; ['Devoniensis' × 'Victor Verdier']

'Lady Mary Ward' HT, ob, 1913, McGredy; flowers orange, shaded deeper, dbl.

'Lady Maureen Stewart' HT, dr, 1920, Dickson, A.; flowers velvety blackish scarlet-cerise, reflex orange-maroon, dbl.

'Lady Mavis Pilkington' -- See 'Korlitze'

'Lady Maysie Robinson' HT, pb, 1957, Kordes; flowers deep pink, center white, large, 22 petals, cupped, moderate fragrance; foliage dark, glossy; vigorous, upright, bushy growth; [seedling × 'Peace']; intr. 1955

'Lady Medallist' HT, lp, 1912, Clark, A.; flowers pink with lighter reverse, large, high-centered; foliage dark green; growth vigorous, early summer climber

'Lady Meilland' -- See 'Meialzonite'

'Lady Meillandina' -- See 'Meilarco'

'Lady Miller' HT, dr, 1940, Clark, A.; flowers dark-red, well-formed

'Lady Mitchell' -- See 'Haryearn'

'Lady Mond' HT, w, 1920, Paul, W.; flowers deep cream, outer petals shaded rose

Lady Moss™ -- See 'Morgabriel'

'Lady Moyra Beauclerc' HT, mr, 1901, Dickson, A.; flowers carmine-red, large, dbl.

'Lady Moyra Cavendish' HT, mr, 1939, McGredy; bud long, pointed; flowers bright strawberry-red, flushed crimson, dbl., high-centered; foliage glossy, dark; bushy growth

'Lady Nutting' HT, mp, 1938, Wheatcroft Bros.; flowers soft salmon-pink, large, high-centered; foliage leathery, dark; vigorous growth

'Lady of Hertford' -- See 'Bosconpea'

'Lady of Megginch' -- See 'Ausvolume'

'Lady of Sky' HT, or, 1976, Gregory; flowers 35 petals, high-centered; foliage dark; vigorous, upright growth; [Queen Elizabeth® × unknown]; intr. 1974

'Lady of Stifford' F, or, 1982, Warley Rose Gardens; [sport of 'Matador']; intr. 1981

Lady of the Dawn® -- See 'Interlada'

'Lady of the Mist' S, ob, Harkness; flowers soft violet-pink at the edges, shading to cream and then coppery buff at center, 4-5 in., 100 petals, quartered; foliage rich green; growth upright, strong growing; large shrub or small climber; PPAF; intr. 2002

'Lady Overtoun' HP, op, 1907, Dickson; flowers salmon-flesh

'Lady Parade' (Lady™) MinFl, mp, Olesen; bud long, broad based; flowers 5 cm., 35-45 petals, cupped, to flat, borne mostly singly, no fragrance; recurrent; foliage matte; vigorous, bushy (20-40 cm.) growth; PP15506; [Isabel Hit™ × Patricia Kordana Mini Brite™]; container plant; intr. 2001

'Lady Penelope' -- See 'Chewdor'

'Lady Penzance' (R. × penzanceana) HEg, op, 1894, Penzance; flowers coppery salmon-pink with yellow center and yellow stamens, 1 in., single, slightly cupped; summer bloom; foliage dark; stems drooping; very vigorous growth; [R. rubiginosa × R. foetida bicolor]

'Lady Phelia' -- See 'Tomabra'

'Lady Pirrie' ('Mme Pirrie') HT, ab, 1910, Dickson, H.; bud pointed; flowers apricot-yellow, reverse coppery, large, dbl.; vigorous, bushy growth

'Lady Pirrie, Climbing' Cl HT, ab, 1938; [sport of 'Lady Pirrie']

'Lady Plymouth' T, w, 1914, Dickson, A.; bud long, pointed; flowers deep ivory-cream, very faintly flushed, large, dbl.; foliage rich green, leathery; vigorous, bushy growth, with numerous canes

'Lady Quartus Ewart' HT, w, 1904, Dickson, H.; flowers pure white, large, full

'Lady Rachel' -- See 'Candoodle'

'Lady Rachel Verney' HT, mp, 1935, Bees; flowers rose, base lemon, large, dbl., cupped; foliage glossy, bronze; vigorous, bushy growth; ['Annie Laurie' × 'Lord Charlemont']

'Lady Reading' Pol, mr, 1921, Van Kleef; flowers clear red, rosette, slight fragrance; good repeat; [sport of 'Ellen Poulsen']

'Lady Reay' HT, dp, 1911, Dickson or Cant; flowers dark pink, petals edged pearly white, moderate fragrance

'Lady Rhodes' HT, dp, 1934, Clark, A.

'Lady Roberts' T, ab, 1902, Cant, F.; flowers rich reddish-apricot, base coppery red, edges shaded orange, dbl., moderate fragrance; vigorous, tall growth; [sport of 'Anna Olivier']

'Lady Romsey' F, w, Beales, Peter; flowers creamy white, suffused pink and yellow, dbl., moderate sweet fragrance; free-flowering; foliage dark green, leathery; intr. 1985

'Lady Rose, Climbing' -- See 'Orakosar'

Lady Rose® -- See 'Korlady'

'Lady Rossmore' HT, mr, 1907, Campbell Hall; flowers reddish-crimson with claret shading, medium, dbl.

'Lady Roundway' HT, ab, 1923, Cant, B. R.; flowers bright apricot-orange, fading to creamy buff, open, semi-dbl.; vigorous, but stubby growth

'Lady Russon' -- See 'Orange Delbard'

'Lady Sackville' -- See 'Night'

'Lady Sackville' HT, w, 1933, Cant, B. R.; bud pointed; flowers pure white, very large, dbl., high-centered; foliage leathery, bronze; very vigorous growth

'Lady Seton' HT, lp, 1966, McGredy, Sam IV; flowers 4½ in., 35 petals; vigorous, tall growth; ['Ma Perkins' × 'Mischief']

'Lady Sheffield' HP, mp, 1881, Postans; flowers glowing cherry pink, aging to bluish pink, large, full, globular; ['François Michelon' × unknown]

'Lady Somers' HT, lp, 1930, Clark, A.; flowers fresh pink, tinted flesh, dbl.; foliage wrinkled, light; bushy growth; ['Comte G. de Rochemur' × 'Scorcher']

'Lady Sonia' S, my, 1961, Mattock; flowers golden yellow, 4-4½ in., 20 petals; foliage dark; vigorous, upright, branching growth; ['Grandmaster' × 'Doreen']

'Lady Stanley' B, dp, 1849, Dubos; flowers large, full

'Lady Stanley' T, m, Nabonnand; bud long; flowers lilac over a yellow base, edged darker purple, very large, dbl., globular, moderate fragrance; intr. 1886

'Lady Stuart' HCh, lp, 1851, Portemer fils; flowers flesh pink to blush, darker at center, large, very full, globular; foliage leaflets 5-7

Lady Sunblaze™ -- See 'Meilarco'

'Lady Sunshine' HT, my, 1965, Lens; bud ovoid; flowers large, very dbl.; foliage dark; ['Belle Étoile' × ('Michèle Meilland' × 'Tawny Gold')]

'Lady Susan Birch' HT, ab, 1934, Cant, B. R.; bud pointed; flowers large, dbl., high-centered; foliage glossy, dark; vigorous, bushy growth

'Lady Suzanne' HT, w, 1985, Bridges, Dennis A.; flowers creamy white, large, 32 petals, high-centered; foliage large, dark, glossy; bushy growth; ['Lady X' × 'Flaming Beauty']

'Lady Sydney Eardley-Wilmot' HT, mp, 1925, Chaplin Bros.; flowers coppery reddish-salmon, tinted fawn and apricot, semi-dbl.

'Lady Sylvia, Climbing' Cl HT, pb, 1933, Stevens, W.; flowers pink, cream and apricot, large, full, moderate fragrance; moderate (10 ft.) growth; [sport of 'Lady Sylvia']

'Lady Sylvia' HT, lp, 1926, Stevens, W.; flowers flesh-pink, deeper in center, dbl., moderate fragrance; moderate (3 ft.) growth; [sport of 'Ophelia']

'Lady Taylor' -- See 'Smitling'

'Lady Tervueren' Pol, mr, 1969, Buisman, G. A. H.; flowers medium to small, dbl.; foliage dark; [Allotria® × seedling]

'Lady Trent' ('Julia Ferran') HT, ob, 1940, Dot, Pedro; flowers coppery orange, large, 46 petals, high-centered; foliage dark, glossy; vigorous growth; ['Rosieriste Gaston Leveque' × 'Federico Casas']

'Lady Ursula' HT, pb, 1908, Dickson, A.; flowers pink fading lighter, reverse cameo-pink, base lemon, large, very dbl., high-centered; foliage dark, leathery, glossy; vigorous, bushy growth

'Lady Venables Vernon' HT, lp, 1922, Jersey Nursery; flowers soft flesh-color, overlaid blush; ['Mrs Amy Hammond' × 'Sir Alexander N. Rochfort']

'Lady Vera' HT, pb, 1975, Smith, R.W.; flowers silvery pink, reverse rose-pink, dbl.; vigorous growth; ['Royal Highness'

× 'Christian Dior']; intr. 1974

'Lady Verey' HT, mp, 1922, Hicks; flowers rose-pink, dbl.

'Lady Violet Astor' HT, dp, 1933, Cant, B. R.; flowers deep rose-pink, over large, dbl., high-centered; foliage leathery; vigorous growth

'Lady Wakefield' HT, ab, 1926, Cant, B. R.; bud pale orange; flowers bright apricot, fading to pink, moderate fragrance; foliage dark green; strong (80-100 cm.) growth

'Lady Warrender' -- See 'Clara Sylvain'

'Lady Waterlow' Cl HT, pb, 1903, Nabonnand, P.& C.; bud red; flowers salmon-pink edged carmine, 11 cm., dbl., moderate fragrance; vigorous (8-10 ft.) growth; ['La France de '89' × 'Mme Marie Lavalley']

'Lady Wenlock' HT, lp, 1904, Bernaix, P.; flowers China-pink tinted apricot, large, dbl.

'Lady White' D, w, 1901, Turner; flowers white, striped red, large, semi-dbl.; [R. macrantha × R. × damascena]

'Lady Willingdon' HT, lp, 1928, Dale; flowers very light pink, large, dbl.; foliage rich green, glossy; vigorous growth; ['Ophelia' × 'Premier']

'Lady Woodward' HT, lp, 1960, Riethmuller; bud long, pointed; flowers pink veined, large, dbl., high-centered, moderate fragrance; foliage dark, glossy; vigorous, upright, bushy growth; ['Heinrich Wendland' × 'Elli Knab']; intr. 1959

'Lady Worthington Evans' HT, dr, 1926, Dickson, A.; bud pointed; flowers deep crimson shaded blackish, semi-dbl., high-centered; foliage bronze, leathery; vigorous, bushy growth

'Lady X' HT, m, 1968, Meilland, Mrs. Marie-Louise; bud long, pointed; flowers large, dbl., high-centered; foliage leathery; vigorous, upright growth; PP2691; [seedling × 'Simone']; intr. 1966

'Lady X, Climbing' Cl HT, m, 1970, Ruston (also Takatori, 1976); [sport of 'Lady X']; intr. 1975

'Lady Yvonne' -- See 'Bosbigsouth'

'Lady Zia' HT, or, 1960, Park; flowers light orange-scarlet, well-formed, 5-6 in., 50 petals, moderate fragrance; foliage dark, glossy; vigorous growth; ['Peace' × 'Independence']; intr. 1959

'Lady Zoë Brougham' ('M. H. Graire') T, my, 1886, Nabonnand; bud elongated; flowers bright chamois yellow, darker at petal edges, large, imbricated, full; ['Isabelle Nabonnand' × unknown]

Ladybird® HT, my, Tantau; intr. 2003

Ladybug™ -- See 'Meicinelle'

'Ladybug' -- See 'Morbug'

'Ladylove' HT, mp, 1926, McGredy; flowers light rose-pink fading hydrangea-pink, flushed apricot, well-formed, dbl.; foliage dark; very vigorous growth; ['Ophelia' × seedling]

'Laelia' HP, mp, 1857, Avoux & Crozy; flowers very large; possibly synonymous with 'Louis Peyronny'

'Laetitia' -- See 'La Volupté'

'Laetitia Pujol' HT, pb, Tantau; intr. 2006

'Lafayette, Climbing' -- See 'Auguste Kordes'

'Lafayette' ('August Kordes', 'Joseph Guy') F, dp, 1924, Nonin; flowers bright cherry-crimson, large, semi-dbl., cupped, borne in clusters (up to 40); foliage rich green, glossy; vigorous, bushy growth; ['Rodhatte' × 'Richmond']

Lafayette™ ('Lafayette Hit', 'Lafayette Patio Hit') S, ab, Olesen; bud globular; flowers light apricot, 8 cm., 61 petals, open cup, borne mostly singly, slight fragrance; recurrent; foliage dark green, semi-glossy; thornless; stems 6 in.; growth vigorous, compact (20-40 cm.); PP16354; [sport of 'Tiffany Hit']; intr. 2003

'Lafayette Hit' -- See 'Poulhi020'

'Lafayette Patio Hit' -- See 'Poulhi020'

'Laffay' Ch, mr, about 1825, Laffay; flowers bright cerise red, full; probably extinct

'Lafollette' -- See 'La Follette'

'Laforcade' HP, mr, 1889, Lévêque; flowers carmine red, very large, cupped; foliage dark green; growth upright

'L'Africaine' LCl, dr, 1953, Mallerin, C.; flowers garnet shaded coppery, 4 in., dbl., borne mostly solitary; abundant early bloom, not recurrent; strong stems; very vigorous growth; ['Guinée' × 'Crimson Glory']

'Lafter' HT, yb, 1948, Brownell; bud pointed; flowers salmon-yellow, 4 in., 23 petals, moderate fragrance; vigorous, upright, branching growth; PP955; [('V for Victory' × ('Général Jacqueminot' × 'Dr. W. Van Fleet')) × 'Pink Princess']

Lagerfeld™ -- See 'Arolaqueli'

Lagerfeuer® ('Feu de Camp') F, mr, 1959, Tantau, Math.; bud pointed; flowers velvety scarlet, large, dbl., borne in clusters; foliage leathery, dark; vigorous, upright growth; ['Red Favorite' × 'Kathe Duvigneau']; intr. 1958

'Lago Maggiore' S, m, Kordes; intr. 2003

'Lagonda' -- See 'Schleswig 87'

'Lagoon' F, m, 1970, Harkness; flowers lilac, reverse darker, gold stamens,, 2½ in., 7 petals, moderate fragrance; foliage glossy; hips large, abundant, colorful; ['Lilac Charm' × 'Sterling Silver']

Laguna® -- See 'Koradeigel'

'Laguna' HT, or, 1975, Kordes; bud large, long, pointed; flowers dbl., cupped, moderate fragrance; foliage glossy; vigorous, upright growth; ['Hawaii' × 'Orange Delbard']; intr. 1974

'Laguna' ('Laguna Palace') S, ab, 1999, Poulsen; flowers apricot blend with tones of other hues, 8-10 cm., full, no fragrance; foliage dark, glossy; growth bushy, 40-60 cm.; PP11608; intr. 1998

'Laguna Palace' -- See 'Poulagun'

'Lahar' F, my, IARI; flowers mimosa yellow with tinge of pink; recurrent; intr. 1991

'Laila' F, ob, 1968, Abdullah; flowers bright orange, well-formed, dbl., borne on trusses; foliage glossy; vigorous growth; [Orangeade® × unknown]

'L'Aimable Beauté' ('Aimable Beauté') HGal

'L'Aimant' -- See 'Harzola'

'L'Aimont' -- See 'Harzola'

Lake™ -- See 'Poulcot006'

'Lake Como' F, m, 1968, Harkness; flowers lilac, semi-dbl., borne in turrses; ['Lilac Charm' × 'Sterling Silver']

'Lake Cottage' (Lake™) S, lp, Olesen; bud ovate, deep pink; flowers light pink, small, 6-7 petals, almost flat, borne in small clusters, no fragrance; recurrent; foliage dark green, glossy; prickles numerous, 10 mm., hooked; low (40-60 cm.), spreading growth; hips 15 × 13 mm., greyed-orange; PP16550; [Diamond Head™ × seedling]; intr. 2004

'Lake Kayoichou' F, m, Hiroshima; intr. 2002

'Lake Street' -- See 'Reine des Violettes'

'Lakeland' HT, lp, 1976, Fryer, Gareth; flowers soft shell-pink, 5-6 in., 36 petals; ['Fragrant Cloud' × Queen Elizabeth®]

'Lakeland Princess' -- See 'Poullack'

'Lakeland's Pride' -- See 'Double Feature'

'Lal' HT, pb, 1933, Easlea; bud long, pointed; flowers deep salmon pink, suffused yellow; foliage dark; vigorous growth; ['Commonwealth' × 'Florence L. Izzard']

'Lal, Climbing' Cl HT, mp, 1937, Vogel, M.; flowers very large, dbl.; [sport of 'Lal']

'L'Alcazar' -- See 'Tanelfe'

'Lalima' HT, mr, 1983, Pal, Dr. B.P.; flowers large, 50 petals, high-centered, borne singly, intense fragrance; foliage large; vigorous, upright growth; ['Picture' × 'Jour d'Ete']; intr. 1978

'Lallita' HT, mp, 1929, Mallerin, C.; flowers rose, very large, dbl.; foliage rich green, leathery; long, strong stems; ['Pres. Briand' × unknown]

'Lamarque' ('Général Lamarque', 'Thé Maréchal') N, w, 1830, Maréchal; flowers pure white, center lemon-yellow, 7-8 cm., dbl., flat, quartered, borne in small clusters, intense fragrance; prickles few, straight, thin; vigorous, climbing growth, with long, trailing shoots; ['Blush Noisette' × 'Parks' Yellow Tea-scented China']

'Lamarque Jaune' N, ly, 1869, Ducher; flowers light yellow, center golden yellow, medium, full

'Lamartine' B, mr, 1842, Guillot; flowers red, shaded light violet, medium, full

'Lamartine' HP, dp, Dubreuil; flowers velvety dark carmine, shaded violet over amaranth, medium, full, cupped; intr. 1890

'Lamartine' HT, op, Meilland, F.; flowers pearly pink shaded orange, dbl.; intr. 1943

'Lamb Chop' S, pb, Peden, R.; intr.

The Official Registry and Checklist — Rosa 387

1997

'Lambada' -- See 'Kordaba'

Lambert™ ('Lilac Castle') F, m, Poulsen; flowers lavender and purple, 4-6 in., full, slight fragrance; foliage dark green, glossy; growth bushy, 60-100 cm.; PP15643; intr. 2002

'Lambert Closse' S, mp, 1994, Ogilvie, Ian S.; flowers 3-3½ in., 53 petals, borne mostly singly, slight fragrance; foliage medium size, light green, glossy; some prickles; medium (85 cm.), upright growth; PP9978; ['Arthur Bell' × 'John Davis']; intr. 1994

'L'Ami E. Daumont' HP, mr, 1903, Vilin; bud conical, very large; flowers carmine-red, reverse silvery, large, very dbl.; foliage delicate green; few prickles

'L'Ami Maubray' HP, rb, 1890, Mercier; flowers light red, shaded delicate violet, borne mostly singly or in small clusters; ['Xavier Olibo' × unknown]

'L'Ami Noël' HP, mr, 1886, Chauvry; flowers bright velvety red

'Lamia' HT, or, 1918, Easlea; bud rich apricot; flowers intense reddish-orange, semi-dbl.; vigorous growth

'Laminuette' -- See 'Minuette'

'L'Amitié' D, lp, before 1813, Stegerhoek/Dupont; flowers flesh pink, sometimes spotted white, large, semi-dbl.

'LAMlam' HT, yb, 1965, Lammerts, Dr. Walter; bud long, pointed

'Lamoon' -- See 'Umslamoon'

'Lamotte Sanguin' ('La Motte Sanguine') HP, mr, 1869, Vigneron; sepals leaf-like; flowers bright carmine red, 4 in., full, widely cupped, borne singly and in small clusters; foliage thick, quite rugose, somber green; prickles numerous, reddish brown, straight, strong

'Lampion' F, or, 1959, Tantau, Math.; bud pointed; flowers blood-red shaded orange, large, 5 petals, open, borne in large clusters; foliage dark, leathery, glossy; dwarf, bushy growth; ['Fanal' × 'Kathe Duvigneau']; intr. 1957

'Lampion' HT, op, Tantau; intr. 2004

'Lamplighter' HT, yb, Joseph H. Hill, Co.; bud long, pointed; flowers mimosa-yellow, 4-4½ in., 55-60 petals, high-centered, moderate fragrance; foliage dark, semi-glossy, leathery; strong stems; vigorous, upright growth; PP1804; ['Peace' × 'Yellow Perfection']; intr. 1959

'Lamplighter' Cl HT, dy, 1948, Duehrsen; flowers blend similar to talisman and autumn, large, dbl., globular, intense fragrance; foliage leathery; very vigorous, climbing (10-15 ft.) growth; ['Talisman' × 'Gold Rush']

'Lamplighter' HT, pb, McGredy, Sam IV; flowers salmon-rose, reverse gold, very large, 37 petals, high-centered; foliage bronze; vigorous growth; ['Sam McGredy' × seedling]; intr. 1950

'Lampo' F, Cazzaniga, F. G.; intr. 1958

'Lamrhowitch' -- See 'Oyster Pearl'

'Lana Jane' -- See 'Worcrane'

'Lanbet' ('Jennifer-Betty Kenward') HT, or, 1986, Sealand Nurseries, Ltd.; flowers medium, 35 petals, slight fragrance; foliage medium size, medium green, glossy; spreading growth; ['Mildred Reynolds' × 'Whisky Mac']; intr. 1985

'Lancashire' -- See 'Korstesgli'

'Lancashire' HT, mr, 1950, Wright, R. & Sons; flowers fiery red; ['Christopher Stone' × seedling]

'Lancashire Lass' HT, mr, 1939, Archer; bud well shaped, crimson; flowers scarlet-cerise, semi-dbl.; foliage glossy, dark; vigorous growth

'Lancashire Life' -- See 'Ruilanca'

'Lancaster' Cl HT, mr, 1962, Hicks, S.J.; bud ovoid; flowers medium rose-red, 5 in., 35-40 petals, high-centered, intense fragrance; foliage leathery, dark; vigorous growth; PP1892; [sport of 'President Eisenhower']; intr. 1962

'Lancastrian' HT, mr, 1965, Gregory; flowers crimson-scarlet, 3½-4 in., 40 petals; foliage light green, glossy; vigorous, upright growth; ['Ena Harkness' × unknown]

'Lance Hird' HT, mp, 1973, Wood; flowers deep pink, reverse lighter, 4 in., 20-30 petals; free growth; [seedling × 'Greetings']

'Lancier' HT, dr, 1959, Mallerin, C.; flowers crimson-red; ['Karl Herbst' × seedling]

Lancôme® -- See 'Delboip'

'Lancoro' F, dp, Bees

Land Brandenburg™ -- See 'Pouloma'

'Land of the Long White Cloud' -- See 'Maclanoflon'

'Landen' ('Denman') HT, ly, 1989, Sealand Nurseries, Ltd.; flowers creamy yellow, large, 35 petals, urn-shaped, borne in sprays of 2-3, intense fragrance; foliage large, dark green, glossy; prickles medium, red; upright growth; ['Mildred Reynolds' × 'Arthur Bell']

'Lander Gold' -- See 'Micgold'

'Landia' ('Anne Diamond') HT, ab, 1989, Sealand Nurseries, Ltd.; bud pointed; flowers apricot, reverse pink, aging apricot, medium, 38 petals, urn-shaped, borne in sprays of 3 or 4; foliage medium size, dark green, semi-glossy; prickles slightly hooked, brown; upright, bushy growth; ['Mildred Reynolds' × 'Arthur Bell']; intr. 1988

'Landisney' ('Snow White') HT, w, Sealand Nurseries, Ltd.; intr. 1987

'Landmark' ('Landmark Rose') S, pb, 2005, Shoup, George Michael; flowers dbl., borne mostly solitary, moderate fragrance; remontant; foliage medium size, dark green, semi-glossy; prickles moderate; growth bushy, medium (3-4 ft.); hedging; ['Carefree Beauty' × 'Basye's Blueberry']; intr. 1995

'Landmark Rose' -- See 'Landmark'

'Landora, Climbing' -- See 'Clinora'

'Landora' -- See 'Sunblest'

'Landour' Cl HT, w, 1979, Takur; bud oval; flowers 6-6½ in., very dbl., high-centered, moderate fruity fragrance; intermittent bloom; foliage large, glossy, dark, leathery; upright growth; ['Peace, Climbing' × 'Peace, Climbing']; intr. 1978

'Landrover' HRg, mr; intr. 1995

'Landscape Splendor' -- See 'Cleland'

'Landwirtschaftsrat Hubert Schilling' Pol, or, Pieper; flowers medium, semi-dbl.; intr. 1964

'Lane' -- See 'Laneii'

'Lane' ('Latone') M, lp, 1860, Robert; flowers blush pink, lightly shaded with carmine, large, full

'Laneii' ('Lane', 'Lane's Moss') M, mr, 1846, Laffay, M.; bud large, globular, well-mossed; flowers rosy crimson, occasionally tinted purple, large, dbl., globular; foliage large, bright green, 5 leaflets; robust growth; ['a moss rose' × R. gallica]

'Lane's Moss' -- See 'Laneii'

'Lang Havey' -- See 'Ardwesternstar'

'Langdale Chase' -- See 'Fryrhapsody'

'Langenhoven' LCl, mp, Kordes; intr. 2003

'Langford' HSet, dp, about 1940, Preston; flowers dark pink to nearly red, dbl., borne in medium clusters; non-recurrent; late; foliage large, dark; needs protection in cold areas; [R. setigera × 'Aennchen Müller']

'Langford Light' -- See 'Lannie'

'Langley' HT, dy, 1942, Eacott; bud streaked red; flowers clear deep yellow, edges flushed old-gold, 4-5 in., 50 petals; foliage bronze, dark; ['Mrs Sam McGredy' × 'Phyllis Gold']

'Langley Gem' HMoy, dp, 1939, Eacott; flowers scarlet-cerise, single, open, borne in clusters; recurrent; foliage leathery, bronze; strong stems; vigorous growth; ['Karen Poulsen' × R. moyesii]

'Lanican' ('Great Expectations') HT, yb, 1988, Sealand Nurseries, Ltd.; flowers light pink, reverse light yellow, aging fading slightly, well-formed, 55 petals, high-centered; foliage medium size, medium green, semi-glossy, clean; prickles long, pointed, medium, red; upright growth; ['Rosenella' × 'Cassandra']

'Lanken' ('Felicity Kendal') HT, op, 1986, Sealand Nurseries, Ltd.; flowers salmon-orange, large, 35 petals; foliage large; bushy growth; ['Fragrant Cloud' × 'Mildred Reynolds']; intr. 1985

'Lannie' ('Langford Light') Min, w, 1985, Sealand Nurseries, Ltd.; flowers bright yellow stamens, small, semi-dbl.; foliage medium size, dark, matte; bushy growth; ['Ballerina' × 'Little Flirt']; intr. 1984

'Lanpipe' ('St Bruno') F, dy, 1986, Sealand Nurseries, Ltd.; flowers large, 35 petals, intense fragrance; foliage medium size, medium green, semi-glossy; bushy growth; ['Arthur Bell' × Zambra®]; intr. 1985

'Lansezeur' M, dp, before 1846, Panaget; flowers deep crimson, veined with lilac, medium, dbl., cupped; possibly synonymous with 'Panaget'

'Lantern' -- See 'Maclanter'

'Lantor' ('Torvill & Dean') HT, pb, 1985, Sealand Nurseries, Ltd.; flowers pink, yellow reverse, medium, 35 petals, high-centered, slight fragrance; recurrent; foliage medium size, dark, semi-glossy; upright growth; ['Irish Gold' × Alexander®]; intr. 1984

Lanvin™ -- See 'Arolemo'

'Lanwool' ('Chelsea Gold') F, ab, 1985, Sealand Nurseries, Ltd.; flowers medium, 20 petals; foliage medium size, medium green, semi-glossy; numerous prickles; bushy growth; ['Arthur Bell' × Elizabeth of Glamis®]

'Lap1288XT' ('Grimpant Pierre Bonnard') LCl, pb, Laperrière; intr. 2006

'Lapacil' HT, mr, Laperriére; intr. 1978

'Lapad' F, or, Laperrière; intr. 1971

'Lapadsar' Cl F, or, Laperrière; intr. 1976

'Lapam' (Golden Flame®) F, my, Laperrière

'Laparam' F, op, Laperriere, L.; intr. 1958

'Lapaso' HT, pb, Laperriere, R.very full; intr. 2005

'Lapav' ('Mme Louis Pradel') HT, ob, 1970, Laperrière; flowers clear orange, medium, dbl., high-centered; foliage bronze, glossy, leathery; vigorous, upright growth; ['Magicienne' × seedling]; intr. 1967

'Lapbal' (Horticolor®) HT, yb, Laperrière; intr. 1989

'Lapbau' HT, my, Laperrière; intr. 1991

'Lapbel' (Duchesse de Savoie®) HT, mr, Laperriere, L.; intr. 1988

'Lapbu' HT, op, Laperrière; intr. 1988

'Lapcal' (Fanette®) HT, rb, 1970, Laperrière; flowers red, reverse white, medium, 36 petals, high-centered, slight fragrance; foliage dark, glossy; vigorous, bushy growth; ['Jeunesse' × 'Souv. du President Plumecocq']; intr. 1966

'Lapci' F, mr, 1958, Laperrière

'Lapcli' ('Hillary First Lady') F, mr, Laperrière; intr. 1997

'Lapcol' F, yb, Laperriere, R.; intr. 2004

'Lapdade' HT, mr, Laperrière; intr. 1984

'Lapdal' (Roxane®) HT, yb, Laperrière; intr. 1990

'Lapdalsar' ('Grimpant Roxane') Cl HT, yb, Laperrière; intr. 2000

'Lapdef' HT, dy, Laperrière; intr. 1986

'Lapderle' HT, mr, Laperrière; intr. 1984

'Lapdev' (Plein Soleil®) F, or, Laperrière; intr. 1991

'Lapdi' (Renouveau de Provins®) HT, or, 1970, Laperrière; bud ovoid; flowers geranium color, open, very large, 36 petals; foliage glossy; vigorous, bushy growth; ['Magicienne' × 'Numero Un']; intr. 1967

'Lapdil' ('Blondie') HT, op, Laperrière; intr. 1988

'Lapdul' (Régence®) HT, pb, 1970, Laperrière; bud globular; flowers flesh color edged bright pink, open, dbl.; foliage glossy; vigorous, bushy growth; intr. 1967

'Lapdur' HT, op, Laperriere, L.; intr. 1989

'Laped' (Cabaret®) HT, rb, Laperrière; intr. 1992

'Lapej' HT, rb, Laperrière; intr. 1992

'Lapem' (Illisca®) HT, dp, Laperrière; intr. 1974

'Lapimade' ('Tarantelle') HT, op, 1965, Laperrière

'Lapjaminal' ('Magic Fire 83') F, ob, Laperrière; intr. 1983

'Laplam' (Mme Franck Augis®) HT, ob, 1969, Laperrière; bud ovoid; flowers clear orange, medium, dbl., high-centered; foliage glossy; vigorous, bushy growth; ['Magicienne' × seedling]

'Laplical' ('Mamy Laperrière') HT, rb, Laperrière; intr. 1991

'Lapman' (Ludmilla®) HT, m, 1970, Laperrière; bud ovoid; flowers medium, semi-dbl.; foliage glossy; vigorous, upright growth; [('Peace' × 'Independence') × 'Heure Mauve']; intr. 1968

'Lapmiravi' ('Carmosine') HT, mr, Laperriere, L.; intr. 1982

'Lapmis' F, ab, Laperrière; intr. 2005

'Lapmisal' (Mistraline®) HT, op, Laperrière; intr. 1986

'Lapnala' HT , dp, Laperrière; intr. 2006

'Lapnat' (Domila®) HT, op, Laperrière; intr. 1971

'Lapneuf' (Magic Fire®) F, or, 1970, Laperrière; bud pointed; flowers bright orange-red, small, semi-dbl., high-centered; foliage glossy; vigorous, bushy growth; intr. 1967

'Lapniro' F, ob, Laperrière

'Lapon' (Ursula®) HT, mr, 1970, Laperrière; bud ovoid; flowers clear red, open, medium, dbl.; foliage glossy; vigorous, upright growth; ['Jeunesse' × ('Peace' × 'Independence')]

'Laponda' HT, ob, Laperrièredbl.; intr. 1978

'Lapoval' F, pb, Laperriere; intr. 2006

'Lapovi' (Capitole®) F, mp, Laperrière; intr. 1986

Lapponia® -- See 'Tannipola'

'Lapra' F, pb, Laperriere; intr. 2008

'Lapran' S, Laperrière; intr. 1980

'Lapruni' (Banquise™) F, w, Laperrière; intr. 1974

'Lapstur' F, or, Laperriere, R.dbl.; intr. 2004

'Lapuli' F, rb, Laperriere, L.; intr. 1975

'Lapwon' F, ob, 1965, Laperrière

'Laque de Chine' HMsk, mr, Lens, Louis; once blooming' intr. 1991

'Lara' HT, op, 1971, Kriloff, Michel; flowers salmon-carmine, well-formed, large, 38 petals; foliage dark, glossy; vigorous, tall growth; PP3011; ['Tropicana' × 'Romantica'], intr. 1967

'Larado' -- See 'Spolar'

'L'Archévêque' -- See 'Pourpre Charmant'

'Large Double Two-Coloured' -- See 'King of Scots'

'Large Provence' -- See R. centifolia batavica

'L'Argentee' HT, rb

'Largo d'Haendel' ('Handel's Largo') HT, dp, 1947, Mallerin, C.; flowers reddish-apricot to salmon-carmine

'Larini' HT, rb, Olij; flowers medium red, reverse cream edged red, dbl., high-centered; cut flower rose; intr. 1998

'L'Arioste' N, lp, 1859, Moreau-Robert; flowers delicate pink

Larissa® -- See 'Kordodo'

'Lark' -- See 'Alouette'

'L'Arlésienne' -- See 'Fred Edmunds'

'Larry Burnett' HSpn, w, 1925, Skinner; flowers blush-white, center deeper, large, semi-dbl., cupped, intense fragrance; profuse bloom; foliage small, rich green, soft; short stems; dwarf, bushy, spreading growth; very hardy; [R. acicularis × R. spinosissima]

'Larry Daniels' HP, lp, Liggett, Thomas; flowers 2-3 in., very full; recurrent; intr. 2000

'Larry's Surprize' -- See 'Renlarry'

'Las Casas' -- See 'Las-Cases'

'Las-Cases' ('Las Casas') B, dp, 1828, Vibert; flowers purplish-pink, large, full, flat; non-remontant

Las Vegas® -- See 'Korgane'

'Las Vegas' HT, pb, 1956, Whisler, Milton; bud long, pointed; flowers salmon-pink, reverse darker, 5 in., 25-30 petals, high-centered; foliage leathery; vigorous, bushy growth; PP1486; RULED EXTINCE 6/80; ['Charlotte Armstrong' × 'Mission Bells']; intr. 1957

Laser™ -- See 'Keitaibu'

'Laser Beam' -- See 'Korport'

'Laska' F, lp, Dräger; flowers soft pink, medium, semi-dbl.; free-flowering; growth low (40-60 cm.); winter hardy; intr. 1990

'Lasker' HT, pb, 1980, Perry, Astor; bud very long; flowers very dbl., high-centered, borne singly, moderate fragrance; foliage glossy; prickles curved; tall growth; ['South Seas' × 'Oregold']; intr. 1981

'Lassie' HT, pb, 1946, Tuttle Bros. Nursery; bud long, pointed; flowers shell-pink, base canary-yellow, dbl., high-centered, moderate fragrance; foliage leathery; vigorous, compact growth; PP810; [sport of 'Picture']

'Last Tango' ('Garden Art Last Tango') S, mr, Ping Lim; flowers clear red with ruffled edges, 2½-3 in., 20-30 petals; excellent repeat; growth mounded habit with blooms distributed evenly over the plant, 1½-4 ft.; PP16505; intr. 2004

'Lasting Beauty' S, mp; flowers medium, semi-dbl., cupped, borne in clusters; once-bloomer; intr. 1998

'Lasting Impression' -- See 'Micimp'

'Lasting Love' ('Commandant Cousteau', 'Grand Huit', 'Grande Classe', 'Le Grand Huit') HT, dr, Adam, M.; flowers velvety red, dbl., moderate fragrance; PPAF; intr. 1993

'Lasting Peace'   Gr, ob, Meilland; bud conical; flowers brick red, 3½-4 in., 33 petals, cupped, borne 2-5 per stem; free-flowering; foliage medium size, medium green, glossy, dense; numerous prickles; growth semi-erect, compact (3 ft.); PP10544; [('Tropicana' × 'First Edition') × Catherine Deneuve®]; intr. 1997

'Latan'   HT, 1978, Williams, J. Benjamin; bud long; flowers light lavender-tan, 4½-5½ in., 43 petals, high-centered, intense fragrance; foliage leathery; upright, bushy growth; ['Lady X' × 'Bronze Masterpiece']

'Lathom Chapel'   F, w, 1973, Ellick; flowers buff-cream, blended to white, 4 in., 20-25 petals; vigorous growth; [Orange Sensation® × 'Sutter's Gold']

'Lathom Park'   F, dp, 1972, Ellick; flowers carmine, 4 in., very dbl.; foliage glossy, light; vigorous growth; [Orange Sensation® × 'Ballet']

'Lathom Sunrise'   F, ob, 1973, Ellick; flowers orange-flame, 4 in., 25-30 petals; vigorous growth; [(Orange Sensation® × 'Ballet') × 'Sutter's Gold']

'Lathom Sunset'   HT, ob, 1973, Ellick; flowers orange-yellow, pink and red, 4½ in., 20-25 petals; vigorous growth; ['Karl Herbst' × 'Mischief']

'Lathom Twilight'   HT, m, 1973, Ellick; flowers deep purple to Indian lake, 5 in., 28-30 petals; foliage dark; vigorous growth; ['Karl Herbst' × 'Mischief']

'Latin Gypsy Curiosa'   HT, yb

'Latina'™ -- See 'Poulcov'

'Latone' -- See 'Lane'

'Latte' -- See 'Juslatte'

'Laughing Cavalier' -- See 'Seacaval'

'Laughter Lines' -- See 'Dickerry'

'Laura' -- See 'Laure'

'Laura' -- See 'Gella'

'Laura' -- See 'Meidragelac'

'Laura'   S, pb, Clements, John; flowers creamy apricot and pink center shades to cream with a lipstick red picotee edge, 4 in., 70 petals; foliage light green, matte; moderate (3 × 3 ft.) growth; PPAF; intr. 2002

'Laura'   HT, op, 1968, Meilland, Mrs. Marie-Louise; flowers coral-pink, large, dbl., high-centered, moderate fragrance; foliage leathery; vigorous, upright, bushy growth; PP2986; [(('Happiness' × 'Independence') × 'Better Times') × (Baccará® × 'White Knight')]; intr. 1969

'Laura '81' -- See 'Meidragelac'

'Laura-Alexander'   S, yb, Matthews; flowers lemon tinged pink, golden stamens, large, semi-dbl., borne in clusters, moderate lemon scented fragrance; good repeat; foliage glossy, vigorous, upright, bushy (3 ft.) growth; intr. 2001

'Laura Anne' -- See 'Cocclarion'

'Laura Ashley' -- See 'Chewharla'

Laura Bush™ -- See 'Jacorbet'

'Laura Chantal' -- See 'Tomtal'

'Laura Clements' -- See 'Clespirit'

Laura Ford® -- See 'Chewarvel'

'Laura Jane'   HT, lp, Gandy; flowers soft pink, large, dbl.; foliage dark green, dense; sturdy, upright, medium growth; intr. 1990

'Laura Louisa' ('Laura Louise') HKor, dp, Riches; flowers deep cerise pink to salmon, dbl., loose, moderate fragrance; recurrent; growth vigorous (10-12 ft.); [sport of 'Leverkusen']; intr. 1996

'Laura Louise' -- See 'Laura Louisa'

'Laura Louise'   Cl Min, pb, Peden; intr. 1998

'Laura Rose Elliott'   HT, dp, 1995, Thomas, D.; flowers deep pink with light reverse, 4-4¾ in., very dbl., borne mostly singly; foliage medium size, medium green, dull; numerous prickles; medium (60-70 cm.), upright growth; ['Gavotte' × 'City of Gloucester']

'Laura Towill'   HT, yb, 1929, Towill; flowers copper-yellow, becoming copper-pink, semi-dbl.; ['Phantom' × 'Buttercup']

'Laura's Laughter' -- See 'Sealaura'

'Laura's Red Koster'   Pol, mr; intr. 1992

'Laure'   ('Laura') C, mp, before 1836; flowers hydrangea pink, large, full, cupped, borne in clusters of 10-12

'Laure Brémont'   T, m, 1884, Guillot; flowers light grenadine-purple, shaded darker, large, very full

'Laure Charton'   F, or, Guillot

'Lauré Davoust' ('L'Abbandonata') HMult, lp, 1846, Laffay, M.; flowers clear pink, fading to flesh, then white, small, dbl., cupped, quartered, borne in clusters; non-recurrent; foliage dark green; very susceptible to winter injury; [R. sempervirens × a Noisette]

'Laure de Broglie'   Ch, w, 1910, Dubreuil; bud very long; flowers blush ivory-white, full; growth shrubby, branching, robust; ['Baronne Piston de St.-Cyr' × 'G. Nabonnand']

'Laure de Fénelon'   T, mr, 1884, Nabonnand; flowers glowing silky red, large, dbl.

'Laure Dubourg'   B, mr, 1850, Pradel; flowers fire-red, large, full

'Laure Fontaine'   T, w, 1867, Fontaine; flowers cream white, center brighter, large, full

'Laure Gravereaux'   HRg, mp, 1901, L'Hay

'Lauré Soupert'   HMult, ly, 1927, Soupert & Notting; flowers yellowish-white to pure white, 3 cm., dbl., borne in clusters of 80, intense fragrance; recurrent bloom; foliage small, glossy; strong stems; vigorous, climbing or trailing growth; ['Tausendschön' × 'George Elger']

'Laure Wattinne'   HT, mp, 1902, Soupert & Notting; flowers bright pink, center more intense, large, dbl., moderate fragrance; ['Marie Baumann' × 'Mme Caroline Testout']

'Laureate'   F, m, 1990, Jobson, Daniel J.; bud pointed; flowers lavender with pink highlights, aging lighter, medium, dbl., high-centered, urn-shaped, slight fruity fragrance; foliage medium size, dark green, glossy, disease-resistant; prickles straight, medium, red; growth upright, bushy, medium; fruit not observed; winter-hardy; ['Baby Talk' × 'Angel Face']

'Laurel Louise'   MinFl, ab, Clements, John; flowers deep apricot, dbl., high-centered; foliage dark green, leathery; growth medium; intr. 1999

'Laurelle'   F, m, 1966, Harris, J.R.; flowers lavender-pink, base veined lemon, dbl., borne in clusters; foliage glossy; vigorous, bushy growth; ['Rumba' × 'Lavender Princess']

'Lauren'   Pol, m, Rupert, Kim; flowers small, borne in clusters, slight fragrance; recurrent; graceful (5 ft.) growth; [seedling × 'Baby Faurax']

'Lauren Amy'   HT, or, Dawson; intr. 1995

'Lauren Elizabeth' -- See 'Ortlae'

'Laurence Allen'   HP, mp, 1896, Cooling; flowers carnation pink, shaded lighter pink, large, full

'Laurence Olivier' -- See 'Wapiti'

Laurent™   ('Laurent Hit') S, yb, Poulsen; flowers yellow blend, 8-10 cm., dbl., slight wild rose fragrance; foliage dark; growth bushy, 40-60 cm.; intr. 2000

'Laurent Carle' ('Zeiber House Red') HT, mr, 1907, Pernet-Ducher; flowers brilliant velvety carmine, large, dbl., open, intense fragrance; foliage rich green, soft; bushy growth

'Laurent Carle, Climbing'   Cl HT, mr, 1923, Rosen, L.P. (also Mermet, 1924); flowers deep carmine, aging to blood-red, large, full; [sport of 'Laurent Carle']

'Laurent de Rillé'   HP, mr, 1885, Lévêque; flowers bright light cerise red, large, dbl., moderate fragrance; foliage glaucous green

'Laurent Descourt'   HP, m, 1862, Liabaud; flowers velvety purple, medium, full, cupped

'Laurent Heister'   P, mr, 1859, Robert et Moreau; flowers carmine red-purple, 7-9 cm.; very remontant

'Laurent Hit' -- See 'Poulrent'

'Laurentia'   my, Vire Aimery

'Laurette'   T, yb, 1853, Robert; flowers salmony flesh, 3 in., dbl.; few prickles

'Laurette'   HRg, lp, 1999, Hortico; flowers medium, dbl., moderate fragrance; recurrent; intr. 1999

'Laurie'   HT, lp, 1970, Scott, D.H.; flowers creamy pale pink, tipped salmon, 5 in., 28 petals; foliage matte green; vigorous growth; [sport of 'Princesse']

'Lauriston'   HT, rb; intr. 2001

'Lausitz'   S, mp, Berger, W.; flowers medium, semi-dbl.; intr. 1959

'Lava Flow' -- See 'Korlech'

'Lava Gold'   F, ob, Williams, J. Benjamin; flowers bright orange yellow, red overlay, deepens to copper orange, semi-dbl., borne in large clusters, intense fragrance; intr. 1999

'Lavaby'   Min, lp, Laver, Keith G.; bud tapered; intr. 1982

'Lavacek'   (Mountie™) Min, mr, 1984, Laver, Keith G.; bud medium, globular;

intr. 1985

'Lavaglow' -- See 'Korlech'

Lavaglut® -- See 'Korlech'

'Lavalette' ('Valette') D, dp, 1823, Vibert; flowers lilac-rose, medium, full; foliage wide, elliptical; prickles red, short, unequal, sparse, intermixed with red bristles

'Lavalette' HGal, m, Cartier/Prévost; flowers light lilac pink, medium, full; intr. about 1840

'Lavalier' Min, dp, 1989, Laver, Keith G.; bud pointed; flowers deep mauve-pink, reverse medium pink, small, 50 petals, cupped, borne singly; foliage small, medium green, matte, disease-resistant; prickles straight, small,light brown; upright, bushy, low, prolific growth; hips round, red; [Loving Touch™ × (Honest Abe™ × seedling)]

'Lavalot' (Potluck Pink™) Min, mp, 1992, Laver, Keith G.; flowers rose pink, 1½ in., full, borne mostly singly; foliage small, medium green, matte; few prickles; low (25-30 cm.), compact growth; [June Laver™ × Julie Ann™]

'Lavaluck' Min, dp, 1989, Laver, Keith G.; bud pointed; flowers vivid, deep cherry pink, aging fuchsia, small, 28 petals, urn-shaped; foliage small, medium green, matte, long sepals, disease resi; no prickles; bushy, low growth; hips ovoid, orange-red; [Blueblood™ × Julie Ann™]

'Lavalud' HT, pb, Laver; intr. 2003

'Lavamaze' Min, lp, 1989, Laver, Keith G.; bud ovoid; flowers light pink with deeper center, reverse light pink, small, 80 petals, high-centered; foliage small, medium green to red, disease-resistant; prickles straight, narrow, red; bushy, low growth; hips round, orange-red; [Loving Touch™ × 'Potluck']

'Lavande' ('Lavonda') F, m, Rennie, Bruce F.; flowers shades of lavender, small, dbl., borne mostly singly, moderate fragrance; good repeat; florist rose; intr. before 1994

Lavande Parfumée® F, m, Dorieux; flowers lavender, tinted silver, double, cupped, borne in small clusters, intense fragrance; recurrent; foliage medium green; vigorous growth; intr. 2007

'Lavaru' ('Springwood Ruby') Min, dr, 1993, Laver, Keith G.; flowers 1½ in., full, borne in small clusters, no fragrance; foliage medium size, medium green, matte; some prickles; low (20-25 cm.), compact growth; [(Breezy™ × June Laver™) × (June Laver™ × 'Ontario Celebration')]

'Lavaway' ('Snowbound') Min, w, 1989, Laver, Keith G.; bud ovoid; flowers ivory, reverse white, aging white, small, 55 petals, urn-shaped, borne usually singly; foliage small, dark green, matte, disease-resistant; prickles straight, narrow, greenish-brown; bushy, low, compact growth; hips round, yellow-orange; ['Tabris' × June Laver™]; intr. 1989

'Lavbert' (Springwood Red Victor®) Min, dr, 1995, Laver, Keith G.; flowers dark red, small, 40-60 petals, borne 3-10 per clusters; foliage medium size, medium green, semi-glossy; some prickles; medium (30-33 cm.), upright, compact growth; [seedling × seedling]; intr. 1995

'Lavblu' (Blueblood™) Min, mr, 1982, Laver, Keith G.; flowers velvety texture, small, 55 petals; foliage small, deep green, semi-glossy; spreading growth; PP5851; ['Dwarfking '78' × 'Hokey Pokey']

'Lavbound' Min, op, 1989, Laver, Keith G.; bud pointed; flowers coral to orange-pink, outer petals pink-apricot, reverse pink, 53 petals, high-centered; foliage medium size, medium green, semi-glossy, disease-resistant; upright, bushy, low, prolific growth; [June Laver™ × Black Jade™]

'Lavbric' ('Show Carpet') Min, lp, 1995, Laver, Keith G.; flowers pale pink with deeper tones, small, micro-mini, dbl., borne in large clusters, slight fragrance; foliage small, dark green, glossy; upright growth; [seedling × seedling]; intr. 1996

'Lavbrun' Min, ob, 1995, Laver, Keith G.; flowers orange, full, borne mostly singly, no fragrance; foliage medium size, medium green, semi-glossy; some prickles; bushy, medium growth; [seedling × 'Apricot Doll']; intr. 1995

'Lavcale' (Mountie™) Min, mr, 1984, Laver, Keith G.; bud medium, globular; flowers unusually stable red color, 1¼-1½ in., 35 petals, cupped, becoming flat, borne mostly singly, no fragrance; recurrent; foliage small, dark, semi-glossy; prickles medium, long, thin, straight, pointed; compact, upright (12-15 in.), bushy growth; hips none ; PP6054; [Party Girl™ × 'Dwarfking '78']; intr. 1985

'Lavcali' (Mountie™) Min, mr, 1984, Laver, Keith G.; bud medium, globular; intr. 1985

'Lavcap' (Peach Festival™) Min, op, 1997, Laver, Keith G.; flowers medium, very dbl., borne mostly singly, slight fragrance; foliage medium size, medium green, glossy; few prickles; upright, bushy, medium growth; [seedling × Painted Doll™]

'Lavchip' ('Blue Ice') Min, m, 1993, Laver, Keith G.; flowers lavender, petals reflex upon opening, large, full, borne mostly singly, moderate fragrance; foliage small, medium green, semi-glossy; some prickles; low (25-30 cm.), upright, bushy growth; [June Laver™ × 'Apricot Doll']; intr. 1993

'Lavchro' ('Gala Gold') Min, dy, 1993, Laver, Keith G.; flowers medium, full, borne mostly singly, no fragrance; foliage small, medium green, matte; some prickles; low (24-30 cm.), upright, bushy, compact growth; ['Golden Promise' × (June Laver™ × 'Tut's Treasure')]; intr. 1994

'Lavclass' (Springwood Classic™) Min, mp, 1999, Laver, Keith G.; flowers 2 in., full, borne in small clusters, no fragrance; foliage medium size, medium green, semi-glossy; few prickles; bushy, medium (10-12 in.) growth; [seedling × seedling]; intr. 1999

'Lavclo' ('Fiesta Clown') Min, rb, 1994, Laver, Keith G.; flowers scarlet with orange-yellow reverse, bicolor, pointed, recurved, large, full, intense fragrance; foliage medium size, dark green, semi-glossy; some prickles; medium (24-30 cm.), upright growth; [(June Laver™ × seedling) × (Painted Doll™ × June Laver™)]; intr. 1994

'Lavcoat' ('Colour Parade') F, yb, 1991, Laver, Keith G.; flowers yellow turning to red, small, full, borne in small clusters, slight fragrance; foliage medium size, medium green, glossy; some prickles; low (45 cm.), bushy growth; [Breezy™ × Julie Ann™]; intr. 1992

'Lavcom' (Silken Laumann®) Min, ob, 1993, Laver, Keith G.; flowers luminous orange, yellow reverse, large, full, high-centered, borne in large clusters, slight fragrance; foliage medium size, medium green, matte; few prickles; medium (18 in.), bushy growth; [June Laver™ × Potluck Red™]; intr. 1994

'Lavcream' (Potluck Cream™) Min, ly, 1988, Laver, Keith G.; flowers light yellow center, cream edges, reverse cream with yellow, 30 petals, high-centered, no fragrance; foliage medium size, medium green, matte; prickles slender, brown; bushy, low, very free-flowering growth; no fruit; [Cornsilk™ × seedling]; intr. 1988

'Lavcreme' ('Crème Glacée') Min, ly, 1989, Laver, Keith G.; bud pointed; flowers small, 23 petals, urn-shaped, borne singly, slight fragrance; foliage small, medium green, matte; prickles pointed and straight out, white-beige; bushy growth; hips globular, orange; [June Laver™ × 'Summer Butter']; intr. 1990

'Lavdance' ('Striped Pet') Min, pb, 1993, Laver, Keith G.; flowers variable pink stripes on white, large, dbl., borne singly; foliage medium size, dark green, matte; few prickles; low (25-30 cm.), upright,compact growth; [June Laver™ × (June Laver™ × 'Ontario Celebration')]; intr. 1993

'Lavdoll' ('Apricot Doll') Min, ab, 1991, Laver, Keith G.; bud ovoid; flowers apricot, yellow center, reverse lighter, aging light apricot, medium, 30-35 petals, urn-shaped, borne usually singly and in sprays of 1-4, moderate fragrance; foliage small, medium green, matte; spreading, low growth; [Painted Doll™ × Painted Doll™]; intr. 1990

'Lavdusk' (Springwood Pink™) Min, dp, 1992, Laver, Keith G.; flowers deep pink,

1½ in., dbl., borne in small clusters; foliage medium size, medium green, matte; some prickles; low (30-40 cm.), spreading growth; containers; [Maurine Neuberger™ × (June Laver™ × 'Ontario Celebration')]

'Laveena' HT, yb, 1969, Laveena Roses; bud long, pointed; flowers yellow tinged pinkish, large, dbl., high-centered; foliage glossy; vigorous, upright, compact growth; ['Kiss of Fire' × unknown]

'Lavelvet' ('Niagara Wildfire') Min, dr, 2001, Laver, Keith G.; flowers 1-1½ in., full, borne mostly solitary, no fragrance; foliage small, dark green, glossy; prickles 3/8 in., straight, reddish, moderate; growth bushy, medium (8-10 in.); garden decorative, containers; [seedling × seedling]; intr. 2001

'Lavendale' Min, m, 1990, Jolly, Marie; bud pointed; flowers deep lavender, medium, very dbl., high-centered, borne singly, intense fragrance; foliage medium size, medium green, semi-glossy; no prickles; growth upright, bushy, medium, vigorous; hips round, greenish-brown; [Lavender Jade™ × 'Angel Face']; intr. 1990

'Lavender' HT, m, Boerner; bud large, ovoid, purple-red; flowers Persian lilac, 4½-5 in., dbl., cupped, borne singly and in small clusters, strong centifolia fragrance; foliage medium-size, dark green; PP2421; ['Brownie' × 'Sterling Silver']; may be the same as Lavender Garnette; intr. about 1963

'Lavender Beauty' F, m, K & S; flowers lavender mauve, borne singly and small clusters, slight fragrance; intr. 1999

'Lavender Bird' HT, m, 1964, Herholdt, J.A.; bud long, spiral, pointed; flowers lavender-pink, well-formed, large, dbl., moderate lavender fragrance; vigorous growth

'Lavender Blue' -- See 'Leolavblu'

'Lavender Charm' HT, m, 1964, Boerner; flowers Persian lilac, 4½-5 in., 45-50 petals, cupped, intense fragrance; foliage dark, leathery; vigorous, bushy growth; PP2421; ['Brownie' × 'Sterling Silver']; intr. 1964

Lavender Cover™ -- See 'Poulrust'

'Lavender Crystal' ('Crystal Lavender') Min, m; flowers cool mauve, deeper in center, 2 in., very full, slight spicy fragrance; recurrent; growth to 16-20 in.; intr. 1985

'Lavender Delight' -- See 'Mororcheri'

Lavender Dream® -- See 'Interlav'

'Lavender Duet' HT, m, Zary; intr. 1999

'Lavender Floorshow' S, m, Harkness; flowers lavender, 2½-3½ in., 12 petals, intense expensive perfume fragrance; free-flowering; low, spreading (2 × 3 ft.) growth; intr. 2002

Lavender Folies® F, m, Meilland; bud globular, small; flowers violet-purple, 2½ in., 100 petals, dome-shaped, borne mostly singly or in small clusters; recurrent; foliage dark green, semi-glossy; prickles both short and long; growth bushy (70 cm.); PP14017; [Debut™ × (Dreamer™ × 'Lavender Meillandina ')]; florist rose; intr. 2004

'Lavender Friendship' S, m, Verschuren; flowers deep lavender to purple, white eye, small, semi-dbl., borne in trusses, slight fragrance; good repeat; spreading (2½ ft.) growth; intr. 1984

'Lavender Garnette' F, m, 1960, Boerner; bud globular; flowers lavender, open, medium, 35-45 petals, moderate fragrance; foliage leathery; vigorous, bushy growth; [('Grey Pearl' × unknown) × 'Garnette']; intr. 1959

'Lavender Girl' F, m, 1958, Meilland, F.; flowers rosy purple, reverse magenta, changing to lavender, large, 35-42 petals, cupped, moderate spicy fragrance; dwarf, bushy growth; PP1672; ['Fantastique' × ('Ampere' × ('Charles P. Kilham' × 'Capucine Chambard'))]; intr. 1957

Lavender Jade™ -- See 'Benalav'

'Lavender Jewel' Min, m, 1978, Moore, Ralph S.; bud pointed; flowers clear lavender-mauve, 1 in., 38 petals, high-centered; foliage dark; compact, bushy growth; PP4480; ['Little Chief' × 'Angel Face']

'Lavender Joy' S, m, Interplant

'Lavender Kordana' Min, m, Kordes; flowers lavender, full; container rose

Lavender Lace™ -- See 'Jaceibre'

'Lavender Lace, Climbing' Cl Min, m, 1971, Rumsey, R.H.

'Lavender Lace' Min, m, 1968, Moore, Ralph S.; flowers lavender, small, dbl., high-centered, moderate fragrance; foliage small, glossy; vigorous, bushy dwarf growth; PP2991; ['Ellen Poulsen' × 'Debbie']

'Lavender Lady' -- See 'Wiljoea'

'Lavender Lady' F, m, 1956, LeGrice; flowers pastel mauve, large, semi-dbl., borne in clusters; vigorous, upright growth; [seedling × 'Lavender Pinocchio']

'Lavender Lassie' HMsk, m, 1960, Kordes; flowers lilac-pink, 3 in., dbl., borne in large clusters, intense fragrance; very vigorous, tall growth; ['Hamburg' × 'Mme Norbert Levavasseur']; intr. 1960

'Lavender Love' F, m, 1964, Daugherty; flowers lavender, medium; low growth; ['Fashion' × 'Floradora']

'Lavender Mascara' HT, m, Meilland; bud conical, large; flowers light cyclamen pink to mauve, 4 in., 40 petals, high-centered, borne mostly singly; recurrent; foliage semi-glossy, dense; stems medium; growth narrow, bushy (5 ft.); PP14275; [('Sterling Silver' × 'Peace') × 'Meigormon']; florist rose; intr. 2003

'Lavender Meillandina' -- See 'Meiptima'

'Lavender Midinette' Min, m, Moore; flowers purple lavender, yellow stamens, pompon, borne in dense clusters, moderate fragrance; recurrent; willowy, arching (5 ft.) growth

'Lavender Mist' -- See 'Tinviolet'

'Lavender Mist' ('Mystic Mauve') LCl, m, 1981, Christensen, Jack E.; bud ovoid; flowers 35 petals, borne mostly 3 per cluster, slight tea fragrance; foliage large; prickles medium, hooked downward; vigorous growth; long arching canes; ['Angel Face' × 'Allspice']

'Lavender Pearl' HT, m, 1977, Shaw; flowers lavender, center shading to pearl, large, very dbl., moderate lemon fragrance; foliage small; moderate, bushy growth; [Blue Moon® × 'Grandpa Dickson']

'Lavender Pearl' F, m, Williams, J.B.; flowers lavender pink, small; intr. 2004

'Lavender Pinocchio' F, m, 1948, Boerner; bud ovoid, light chocolate-olive-brown; flowers pink-lavender, 3-3½ in., 28 petals, borne in clusters, moderate fragrance; vigorous, bushy, compact growth; PP947; ['Pinocchio' × 'Grey Pearl']

'Lavender Pixie' -- See 'Morlavpix'

'Lavender Princess' F, m, 1960, Boerner; bud ovoid; flowers lavender, lightly overcast purplish lilac, 3½-4 in., 25 petals, open, borne in large clusters, moderate fruity fragrance; foliage leathery; vigorous, upright growth; PP1905; [('World's Fair' × unknown) × ('Lavender Pinocchio' × unknown)]; intr. 1959

'Lavender Queen' HT, m, 1951, Raffel; bud pointed, touched red; flowers pinkish, lavender, 5-6 in., 20-35 petals, cupped; vigorous growth

Lavender Simplex™ -- See 'Mintco'

'Lavender Spoon' -- See 'Spolav'

Lavender Star™ -- See 'Minauco'

Lavender Sunblaze® ('Lavender Meillandina') Min, m, Meilland; bud conical; flowers lavender-mauve, 1-1½ in., 25-30 petals, cupped, borne singly and in small clusters; good repeat; foliage small, deep green, glossy; prickles few, small; bushy, compact, medium (18 in.) growth; PP11025; [('Prelude' × 'Blue Peter ') × 'Lavender Jewel']; intr. 1999

Lavender Sweetheart™ -- See 'Willash'

'Lavender Symphony' Min, m; intr. 2004

'Lavendula' F, m, 1965, Kordes, R.; flowers lavender, 4 in., borne in clusters, intense fragrance; foliage dark; ['Magenta' × 'Sterling Silver']

'L'Avenir' -- See 'Avenir'

'L'Avenir' -- See 'Avenir'

'Lavfal' (Fall Festival™) Min, rb, 1997, Laver, Keith G.; flowers tomato red with yellow stripes, medium, full, borne mostly singly, no fragrance; foliage medium size, dark green, semi-glossy; some prickles; upright, bushy, medium growth; PP11571; [seedling × Springwood Red Victor®]

'Lavfan' ('Fancy Potluck') Min, dr, 1998, Laver, Keith G.; flowers dark red, good substance, ½-1 in., very dbl., borne mostly singly; foliage small, dark green, matte; few prickles; low (15-20 cm.), compact growth; [seedling × 'Antique

Gold']; intr. 1998

'Lavfire' (Flame Bouquet™) Min, or, 1999, Laver, Keith G.; flowers brilliant orange-red, very long lasting, 2½-3 in., full, borne mostly singly, no fragrance; foliage medium size, medium green, semi-glossy; few prickles; upright, medium (12 in.) growth; intr. 1999

'Lavflame' ('Flaming Potluck') Min, or, 1995, Laver, Keith G.; flowers flaming orange-scarlet, deeper center, medium, full, borne mostly singly; foliage medium size, dark green, semi-glossy; some prickles; medium (30-40 cm.), upright, bushy growth; intr. 1994

'Lavflush' ('Double Date') Min, op, 1993, Laver, Keith G.; flowers orange pink, medium, very dbl., borne mostly singly, slight fragrance; foliage small, medium green, semi-glossy; some prickles; low, upright, bushy growth; [((Breezy™ × June Laver™) × (Breezy™ × June Laver™)) × seedling]

'Lavfuhr' ('Dainty Bouquet') Min, mp, 1994, Laver, Keith G.; flowers clear pink, medium, very dbl., borne mostly singly, slight fragrance; foliage medium size, medium green, semi-glossy; some prickles; medium (20 cm.), upright, spreading growth; [seedling × 'Pink Bouquet']; intr. 1994

'Lavfun' ('Blessed Event') Min, pb, 1993, Laver, Keith G.; flowers white suffused pink, large, full, borne singly and in small clusters, slight fragrance; foliage medium size, dark green, matte; some prickles; low (25-30 cm.), upright growth; ['Enjoy' × (June Laver™ × Party Girl™)]; intr. 1993

'Lavglo' ('Spicy Minijet', Potluck Yellow™, 'Yellow Mini-Wonder', 'Yellow Minijet') Min, my, 1984, Laver, Keith G.; flowers 20 petals, no fragrance; foliage small, medium green, semi-glossy; bushy growth; ['Rise 'n' Shine' × 'Lemon Delight']

'Lavgold' Min, dy, 1987, Laver, Keith; flowers deep, strong yellow, reverse slightly lighter, fading creamy, small, 20 petals, high-centered, borne singly; foliage small, medium green, matte; prickles light beige, finely pointed, set at right angles; growth upright, bushy, low, compact; fruit ovoid, orange-yellow; [Loving Touch™ × 'Gold Mine']; intr. 1986

'Lavgold' (Potluck Gold™) Min, my, 1991, Laver, Keith G.; flowers small, 20 petals, flat, borne in sprays of 3-5, no fragrance; foliage small, medium green, semi-glossy; bushy, low, very dwarf growth; [Dorola® × Julie Ann™]; intr. 1990

'Lavhomme' ('Bonhomme') Min, w, 1986, Laver, Keith G.; [sport of Blueblood™]

'Lavice' ('Ice Princess') Min, lp, 1983, Laver, Keith G.; flowers light pink, light yellow stamens, finishing white, medium, dbl.; foliage small, medium green, matte; ['pink seedling' × 'Lemon Delight']

'Lavictor' ('Royal Victoria') Min, op, 1991, Laver, Keith G.; flowers coral pink, white reverse, small, very full, cupped, borne mostly singly, moderate fragrance; recurrent; foliage small, medium green, semi-glossy; tall, upright, bushy growth; [(Painted Doll™ × June Laver™) × Mountie™]; intr. 1991

'Lavina' HT, dp, Strnad

'Lavina' HT, mp, 1962, Reynolds, W.H.; flowers buff-pink, large, 60 petals, high-centered; foliage dark, leathery; vigorous growth; [Queen Elizabeth® × 'Anne Letts']

'Lavinia' -- See 'Tanklewi'

'Lavinia Harrison' HT, mp, 1988, Harrison, G.; flowers shell pink with light undertones, large, 30-35 petals, borne in sprays of 1-3; foliage red to light green, aging dark green; prickles pyramidal, red-brown; vigorous growth; ['Duet' × seedling]

'Lavisle' (Springwood Mauvette®) Min, m, 1995, Laver, Keith G.; flowers deep mauve, medium, full, borne mostly singly, slight fragrance; foliage medium size, dark green, glossy; numerous prickles; spreading, bushy growth; ['Blue Ice' × seedling]; intr. 1996

'Lavjack' ('Orange Minijet', 'Orange Mini-Wonder', Potluck Orange™) Min, or, 1989, Laver, Keith G.; bud ovoid; flowers intense, dark orange, compact, small, 24 petals, borne in sprays; foliage small, medium green, matte; prickles straight, pointed, light brown; bushy, low, symmetrical growth; PP7326; [Julie Ann™ × 'Potluck']

'Lavjoy' ('Enjoy') Min, pb, 1989, Laver, Keith G.; bud pointed; flowers blush pink edged deeper pink, reverse white, small, 22 petals, high-centered, borne singly; foliage small, medium green, disease-resistant; prickles straight, very small, sparse, light brown; upright, low growth; hips ovoid, orange; [(Moulin Rouge® × seedling) × Party Girl™]; intr. 1989

'Lavjune' (June Laver™) Min, dy, 1988, Laver, Keith G.; flowers dark yellow, aging cream, large, 20-25 petals, high-centered, borne usually singly or in small sprays, no fragrance; foliage large, dark green, matte; prickles small, short, green; bushy, medium, compact growth; hips rounded, light orange-red; PP6859; [Helmut Schmidt® × 'Gold Mine']; intr. 1985

'Lavkin' ('Yellow Bouquet') Min, dy, 1993, Laver, Keith G.; flowers deep yellow, medium, dbl., borne in small clusters; foliage small, medium green, matte; few prickles; low (15-20 cm.), compact growth; [June Laver™ × Potluck Gold™]; intr. 1994

'Lavking' HT, dr, Laverdbl.; intr. 2002

'Lavlad' ('Rosy Forecast') Min, dp, 1993, Laver, Keith G.; flowers deep pink, medium, dbl., borne in small clusters, moderate fragrance; foliage small, dark green, matte; few prickles; low (15-18 cm.), compact growth; [(June Laver™ × 'Ontario Celebration') × Potluck Purple™]; intr. 1994

'Lavlemo' Min, my, 1989, Laver, Keith G.; bud ovoid; flowers lemon yellow, deeper in center, medium, 28 petals, high-centered, borne usually singly; foliage small, medium green, matte; prickles beige; upright, bushy, medium growth; hips ovoid, green; [Dorola® × 'Genevieve']

'Lavlight' ('Niagara Moonlight') Min, w, 2001, Laver, Keith G.; flowers 2 in., very full, borne in small clusters, slight fragrance; foliage medium size, medium green, semi-glossy; prickles 1/8 in., straight, light brown, few; growth bushy, medium (7-9 in.); garden decorative, containers; intr. 2001

'Lavlinc' ('Small Slam') Min, dr, 1984, Laver, Keith G.; flowers small, dbl.; foliage small, dark, semi-glossy; bushy growth; ['Nic Noc' × Party Girl™]

'Lavling' ('Living Bouquet', 'Yellow Festival') Min, ly, 1991, Laver, Keith G.; bud ovoid; intr. 1991

'Lavlinger' ('Living Bouquet', 'Yellow Festival') Min, ly, 1991, Laver, Keith G.; bud ovoid; flowers medium, 40-50 petals, flat, borne in sprays of 3 - 5, no fragrance; recurrent; foliage medium size, light green, semi-glossy; bushy, compact, semi-upright growth; PP9159; [Loving Touch™ × (Dorola® × 'Genevieve')]; intr. 1991

'Lavlow' Min, ob, 1991, Laver, Keith G.; flowers orange yellow, small, full, borne in small clusters, no fragrance; foliage small, medium green, semi-glossy; few prickles; low, compact growth; [(Painted Doll™ × June Laver™) × Potluck Yellow™]; intr. 1991

'Lavluv' ('Golden Promise') Min, dy, 1992, Laver, Keith G.; flowers medium, full, borne mostly singly, no fragrance; foliage small, dark green, glossy; few prickles; low (30 cm.), bushy growth; [June Laver™ × Potluck Gold™]; intr. 1993

'Lavmar' ('Margaret Laver') Min, w, 2001, Laver, Keith G.; flowers luminous cream, 1-1½ in., full, borne mostly solitary, moderate fragrance; foliage medium size, light green, matte; prickles ¼ in., straight, few; growth bushy, medium (10-12 in.); garden decorative, containers; [seedling × seedling]; intr. 1998

'Lavmilne' ('Alexander Milne') Min, lp, 1987, Laver, Keith G.; flowers light pink, reverse cream, small, 35 petals, high-centered, borne singly; foliage small, medium green, semi-glossy; prickles straight, light brown; bushy, low growth; hips rounded, orange; [Cornsilk™ × 'Ice Princess']

'Lavmin' (Potluck Red™) Min, dr, 1989, Laver, Keith G.; bud pointed; flowers deep red, compact, small, 35 petals, borne singly, no fragrance; foliage small, dark green, young edged in red, matte; no prickles; upright, low growth; hips globular, orange-red; [Breezy™ × June Laver™]; intr. 1989

'Lavming' (Striped Festival™) Min, rb, 1999, Laver, Keith G.; flowers velvety red with salmon stripes, 2½ in., dbl., high-centered, borne mostly singly, slight fragrance; foliage medium size, medium green, semi-glossy; prickles moderate; easy-growing, upright, medium (12-15 in.) growth; intr. 1999

'Lavmoth' ('Fair Genie') Min, pb, 1989, Laver, Keith G.; bud pointed; flowers light orange in center with pink outer petals, reverse pink, 33 petals, high-centered, moderate fragrance; foliage small, medium green, glossy; prickles slender, straight, almost white, translucent; upright, bushy, low, strong growth; hips ovoid, orange; [Breezy™ × June Laver™]; intr. 1990

'Lavmount' ('Ontario Celebration') Min, or, 1984, Laver, Keith G.; flowers small, 35 petals, moderate fragrance; foliage small, deep reddish green, semi-glossy; spreading, compact growth; ['Nic-Noc' × (Party Girl™ × 'Queen of the Dwarfs')]; intr. 1983

'Lavnew' (Springwood Beauty™) Min, op, 1995, Laver, Keith G.; flowers orange pink, reverse lighter, medium, full, borne mostly singly, no fragrance; foliage small, medium green, semi-glossy; few prickles; bushy, low growth; [seedling × 'Apricot Doll']; intr. 1995

'Lavnova' (Potluck Blue™) Min, m, 1995, Laver, Keith G.; flowers lavender, reverse white, dbl., semi-dbl., borne mostly singly; foliage medium size, medium green, semi-glossy; some prickles; upright, bushy, medium growth; ['Blue Ice' × seedling]; intr. 1995

'Lavonda' -- See 'Lavande'

'Lavont' ('Touché') Min, op, 1995, Laver, Keith G.; flowers orange-pink, medium, 40-60 petals, borne in small clusters; foliage medium size, medium green, semi-glossy; prickles mossed; bushy, medium growth; [seedling × seedling]; intr. 1996

'Lavoro' Min, dy, 1984, Laver, Keith G.; buds; intr. 1984

'Lavpaint' (Painted Doll™) Min, ob, 1984, Laver, Keith G.; flowers orange, reverse yellow, small, 35 petals; foliage small, light green, matte; bushy growth; [Party Girl™ × 'Dwarfking '78']

'Lavpert' ('Snow Princess') F, w, 1991, Laver, Keith G.; flowers medium, full, borne in large clusters, no fragrance; foliage large, dark green, glossy; some prickles; bushy, low (45 cm.), compact growth; [Regensberg® × June Laver™]; intr. 1992

'Lavpet' (Perfect Potluck™) Min, dy, 1992, Laver, Keith G.; flowers golden yellow, medium, dbl., borne in small clusters; foliage medium size, dark green, glossy; few prickles; low (30 cm.), compact growth; [Showbound™ × (Party Girl™ × June Laver™)]

'Lavplat' ('Platinum Lady') Min, m, 1989, Laver, Keith G.; bud pointed; flowers light lavender, reverse white, very slow to open, 21 petals, high-centered, borne singly, no fragrance; foliage small, dark green, young edged in red, semi-glossy; prickles slender; upright, bushy, medium growth; hips ovoid, orange; ['lavender seedling' × Lavender Jade™]; intr. 1989

'Lavplease' ('Pleasantly Pink') Min, mp, 1992, Laver, Keith G.; flowers clear pink, large, very dbl., borne in small clusters; foliage medium size, medium green, matte; some prickles; medium (30-35 cm.), bushy growth; [(June Laver™ × 'Rosamini Red') × ('Dwarfking' × Julie Ann™)]

'Lavpop' ('Party Popcorn') Min, w, 1993, Laver, Keith G.; flowers medium, full, borne mostly singly; foliage small, medium green, matte; few prickles; medium (20-25 cm.), bushy growth; [(June Laver™ × Painted Doll™) × 'Popcorn']; intr. 1993

'Lavpot' ('Potluck') Min, dr, 1984, Laver, Keith G.; flowers small, 20 petals; foliage small, medium green, glossy; compact, bushy, tiny growth; ['Dwarfking '78' × 'Little Liza']

'Lavpup' Min, dr, 1992, Laver, Keith G.

'Lavpurr' (Springwood Purple™) Min, dp, 1990, Laver, Keith G.; flowers fuchsia, medium to large, 25-30 petals, loose, borne in sprays of 3, no fragrance; foliage large, medium green, semi-glossy; bushy, spreading, medium, very compact growth; [June Laver™ × ('Small Slam' × Mountie™)]; intr. 1990

'Lavquest' ('Pink Bouquet', 'Pink Festival') Min, lp, 1991, Laver, Keith G.; bud pointed; flowers white to luminous blush pink, white reverse, aging white, medium, 50-60 petals, flat, borne in sprays of 1 - 3, no fragrance; foliage small, dark green, matte; bushy, spreading, low growth; [Loving Touch™ × 'Ontario Celebration']; intr. 1991

'Lavred' (Springwood Red™) Min, dr, 1988, Laver, Keith G.; flowers deep red, aging slightly lighter, small, full, urn-shaped, borne usually singly; foliage small, medium green, matte; prickles slightly recurved, light yellow-green; bushy, low growth; hips ovoid, orange; ['Small Slam' × Mountie™]

'Lavride' ('Red Rider') Min, dr, 1991, Laver, Keith G.; bud pointeddbl.; intr. 1990

'Lavrosy' ('Rosy Potluck') Min, mp, 1995, Laver, Keith G.; flowers medium, full, borne in small clusters, moderate fragrance; foliage small, dark green, semi-glossy; few prickles; low (20-30 cm.), compact growth; intr. 1995

'Lavsans' ('Heart 'n' Soul', 'Sans Souci') Min, dp, 1986, Laver, Keith G.; flowers deep fuchsia pink, fading slightly, medium, 40 petals, high-centered, borne usually singly, slight fragrance; foliage medium size, light green, matte; prickles numerous, very fine, light brown; bushy, medium growth; hips oblong, narrow, red; ['Rise 'n' Shine' × 'Ontario Celebration']; intr. 1986

'Lavsaph' ('Black Sapphire') Min, dr, 1995, Laver, Keith G.; flowers full, borne mostly singly; foliage medium size, medium green, glossy; few prickles; patio, upright, medium growth; ['Royal Victoria' × seedling]; intr. 1995

'Lavsask' ('Maverick') Min, rb, 1995, Laver, Keith G.; flowers red with white stripes and patches, large, dbl., high-centered, borne mostly singly; free-flowering; foliage medium size, medium green, dull; some prickles; upright, bushy, medium growth; ['Striped Pet' × 'Apricot Doll']; intr. 1995

'Lavsat' (Springwood Pink Satin®) Min, mp, 1997, Laver, Keith G.; flowers small, very dbl., borne in small clusters; foliage medium size, medium green, semi-glossy; few prickles; compact, bushy, low growth; ['Pleasantly Pink' × 'Springwood Ruby']

'Lavscent' (Springwood Coral™) Min, or, 1988, Laver, Keith G.; flowers coral-pink, turning slightly white at stem, loose, large, 23 petals, borne in sprays of 3-4, intense fragrance; foliage large, light green, matte; prickles curved, red; bushy, medium growth; hips round, light orange; ['Helmut Schimdt' × 'Potluck']; intr. 1986

'Lavser' ('Serene Bouquet') Min, pb, 1998, Laver, Keith G.; flowers pink with white reverse, 1½-2 in., very dbl., borne in sprays of 5; foliage medium size, medium green, matte; some prickles; upright, vigorous growth; [seedling × 'Antique Gold']; intr. 1998

'Lavsho' Min, lp, 1984, Laver, Keith G.; flowers small, 20 petals, borne in large clusters; foliage small, light green, glossy; spreading growth; ['Mighty Mouse' × 'Fairy Rose']

'Lavshrimp' ('Wilfred H. Perron') Min, mp, 1988, Laver, Keith G.; flowers clear shrimp-pink, aging paler, rosea, large, 70-80 petals, borne singly, no fragrance; foliage very small, medium green, matte; prickles straight out, very slender, greenish-red; bushy, low growth; hips round, very rare, green-red; [('Dwarfking '78' × Baby Katie™) × Painted Doll™]

'Lavsign' ('By Design') Min, ob, 1992, Laver, Keith G.; flowers orange, large, full, high-centered, borne in small clusters, slight fragrance; foliage medium size, medium green, semi-glossy; some prickles; medium (40-50 cm.), bushygrowth; [(Breezy™ × Julie Ann™) × (June Laver™ × Painted Doll™)]

'Lavsno' Min, w, 1985, Laver, Keith G.; flowers dbl., no fragrance; foliage small, medium green, matte; upright, bushy growth; ['Ice Princess' × 'Sue Lawley']

'Lavsnow' ('White Festival', Springwood White) Min, w, 1991, Laver, Keith G.;

flowers medium, very full, borne mostly singly, no fragrance; foliage small, medium green, matte; few prickles; low (22 cm.), bushy growth; [Loving Touch™ × June Laver™]; intr. 1991

'Lavson' (Potluck Crimson®) Min, dr, 1997, Laver, Keith G.; flowers medium, 41 petals, borne mostly singly and in small clusters; foliage medium size, medium green, semi-glossy; few prickles; compact, low growth; [June Laver™ × Springwood Red Victor®]

'Lavspring' ('Niagara Blossom') Min, pb, 2001, Laver, Keith G.; flowers 2 in., full, borne in small clusters, slight fragrance; foliage medium size, medium green, semi-glossy; growth upright, tall (9-11 in.); garden decorative, containers; [seedling × 'Lavlinger']; intr. 2001

'Lavstar' ('Sweet Butterfly') Min, m, 1989, Laver, Keith G.; bud rounded; flowers mauve pink, pointed, open, loose, medium, 12-15 petals, flat, star-like, borne singly, intense fragrance; foliage medium size, medium green, matte; prickles short, pointed, beige; bushy, low growth; hips globular, yellow; [('Dwarfking' × Baby Katie™) × ('Small Slam' × Mountie™)]

'Lavsum' (Summer Festival™) Min, rb, 1997, Laver, Keith G.; flowers medium, 41 petals, borne singly and in small clusters; foliage medium size, dark green, semi-glossy; some prickles; upright, compact, bushy, medium growth; [seedling × Painted Doll™]

'Lavsun' Min, lp, Laver, Keith G.; intr. 1984

'Lavtiki' (Lemon Bouquet™) Min, my, 1999, Laver, Keith G.; flowers medium yellow, reverse light yellow, 2-2½ in., full, high-centered, borne mostly singly, slight fragrance; foliage medium size, dark green, glossy; no prickles; growth upright, medium (12-15 in.); intr. 1999

'Lavtipaws' (Tiger Paws™) Min, ob, 1994, Laver, Keith G.; flowers orange with yellow reverse, large, full, borne mostly singly, no fragrance; foliage medium size, medium green, matte; medium (20 cm.), compact growth; [Painted Doll™ × seedling]; intr. 1994

'Lavtique' ('Antique Gold') Min, yb, 1995, Laver, Keith G.; flowers deep chrome yellow tipped with red, small, full, borne mostly singly; foliage medium size, light green, semi-glossy; some prickles; spreading, medium growth; [seedling × seedling]; intr. 1996

'Lavtrek' ('King Tut') Min, dy, 1989, Laver, Keith G.; bud pointed; flowers rich, deep yellow, reverse medium yellow, small, 45 petals, high-centered, borne singly; foliage small, dark green, disease-resistant; prickles curved down, light brown; upright, low, compact growth; hips ovoid, orange-red; [June Laver™ × 'Genevieve']

'Lavtrice' ('Orange Zest') Min, or, 1994, Laver, Keith G.; flowers medium, very dbl., borne mostly singly; foliage small, dark green, semi-glossy; few prickles; upright, bushy (25 cm.) growth; [seedling × Painted Doll™]; intr. 1994

'Lavtru' (True Gold™) Min, dy, 1997, Laver, Keith G.; bud egg-shaped, golden; flowers medium, very full, cupped, borne mostly singly, no fragrance; foliage medium size, medium green, dull; few prickles; upright, bushy, medium growth; ['Antique Gold' × 'Yellow Bouquet']

'Lavtuch' ('Painter's Touch') Min, ob, 1998, Laver, Keith G.; flowers luminous orange blend, 1½-3 in., very dbl., borne mostly singly; foliage large, medium green, matte; prickles moderate; bushy, medium tall growth; [seedling × 'Antique Gold']; intr. 1998

'Lavtynine' (Springwood Gold™) Min, my, 1989, Laver, Keith G.; bud pointed; flowers deep, buttery yellow, reverse lighter, medium, 20 petals, high-centered, borne usually singly; foliage small, medium green, semi-glossy; prickles very narrow, straight, green; upright, bushy, medium growth; hips globular, light orange; ['Rise 'n' Shine' × June Laver™]

'Lavwin' ('Niagara Winter') Min, w, 2001, Laver, Keith G.; flowers 2 in., very full, borne in small clusters, no fragrance; foliage medium size, dark green, glossy; growth upright, medium (8-10 in.); garden decorative, containers; [seedling × seedling]; intr. 2001

'Lavwyte' (Potluck White™) Min, w, 1985, Laver, Keith G.; flowers 35 petals; foliage small, light green, glossy; spreading growth; [Baby Katie™ × Mountie™]

'Lavyip' (Ivory Festival™) Min, w, 1997, Laver, Keith G.; flowers large, very dbl., borne singly and in small clusters; foliage medium size, dark green, glossy; compact, bushy, medium growth; [seedling × 'Living Bouquet']

Lawinia® -- See 'Tanklewi'

'Lawrence Johnston' ('Hidcote Yellow') LCl, my, 1923, Pernet-Ducher; flowers large, semi-dbl., borne in clusters, moderate fragrance; repeat bloom; very vigorous, climbing (to 30 ft.) growth; ['Mme Eugene Verdier' × R. foetida persiana]

'Lawrence Johnston' HT, yb, San Remo Exp. Sta.; bud pointed; flowers yellow edged red and salmon, large, semi-dbl., moderate fragrance; foliage light green; vigorous, upright, bushy growth; ['Souv. de Denier van der Gon' × 'Brazier']; intr. 1946

'Lawrence of Arabia' -- See 'Harverag'

'Lawrence of Arabia' HT, yb, 1938, Dickson, A.; flowers Indian yellow, flushed coppery rose, large, dbl.; vigorous, bushy growth

'Laxton's Monthly Rambler' -- See 'Monthly Rambler'

'Laxton's Pink Delight' -- See 'Pink Delight'

'Laxton's Standard' HT, mp, 1926, Laxton Bros.; flowers clear cerise-pink

'Lays' N, lp, about 1860, Guillot; flowers flesh pink, shaded white, medium, full, moderate fragrance

'Lays' T, my, Damaizin; flowers sulfur-yellow, medium; intr. 1863

Lazy Days™ ('Apricot Castle', Bavaria München™, Kalmar™) F, ab, Poulsen; flowers apricot blend, 8-10 cm., 25 petals, no fragrance; foliage dark; growth bushy, 60-100 cm.; intr. 1999

'Lazy Daze' -- See 'Tallaz'

'Lazy Susan' -- See 'Kortenay'

'Le Baron de Rothschild' -- See 'Baron de Rothschild'

'Le Bengale à Bouquets' -- See 'Slater's Crimson China'

'Le Bienheureaux de la Salle' -- See 'Mme Isaac Periere'

'Le Bourguignon' Pol, yb, 1901, Buatois; flowers light egg-yolk yellow, edged carmine, medium, full; ['Étoile de Mai' × 'Mme Chédane Guinoisseau or Lauretty Messimy']

'Le Camée' B, m, 1845, Béluze; flowers bluish pink, center darker, medium, full, cupped

'Le Chainon' -- See 'Wekhilpurnil'

'Le Chamois' F, mr, 1954, Combe, M.; flowers crimson, medium, semi-dbl., borne in small clusters

'Le Cid' HRg, mr, 1908, Vigneron; flowers dazzling crimson, large, semi-dbl., borne mostly solitary; vigorous growth; ['Conrad Ferdinand Meyer' × 'Belle Poitevine']

Le Cid® F, rb, Dorieux; flowers fire red with white reverse, semi-dbl., shallow cup, borne in clusters; recurrent; foliage glossy; vigorous (80-110 cm.) growth; intr. 1996

'Le Droit Humain' HMult, pb, 1907, Vilin; bud pale crimson; flowers pink with darker carmine-pink, 6-7 cm., very dbl., borne in small clusters, slight fragrance

'Le Flambeau' T, dr, 1907, Chédane-Guinoisseau & Pajotin; flowers dark red, center fiery, medium, dbl.; [sport of 'Mons Tillier']

'Le Florifère' M, dp, 1861, Robert & Moreau; flowers carmine pink

'Le Florifère' T, w, Ducher; flowers white with light salmon pink, medium, full; intr. 1872

'Le Florifère' HP, dp, Faudon; intr. 1873

'Le Géant' HP, dp, 1863, Bruant; flowers dark pink, shaded violet, large, full

'Le Grand Dauphin' -- See 'Enfant de France'

'Le Grand Huit' -- See 'Adharman'

'Le Grand Huit, Climbing' -- See 'Commandant Cousteau, Climbing'

'Le Grand Sultan' ('Grand Sultan', 'Grande Sultane') HGal, m, before 1815, Descemet; flowers purplish crimson, large, very dbl.; growth branching

'Le Grand Triomphe' -- See 'Nouvelle Pivoine'

'Le Grande Capitain' B, dr; bud fat, pink; flowers deep crimson, flushing purple, very dbl., quartered, slight fragrance; good repeat

'Le Gras St Germain' -- See 'Mme Legras de St Germain'

'Le Havre' HP, mr, 1870, Eude; flowers vermilion, imbricated, large; vigorous growth

'Le Jacobin' -- See 'Marcel Bourgouin'

'Le Jeune Roi Dauphin' -- See 'Enfant de France'

'Le Lobèrde' M, mp; flowers medium, very dbl.

'Le Loiret' Pol, mp, 1920, Turbat; flowers very brilliant pink to salmon-rose, borne in clusters of 10-15

'Le Majestueuse' -- See 'Majestueuse'

'Le Masquerade en Villefranche' -- See 'Kenseles'

'Le Météor' HP, dp; flowers carmine, shaded purple, very large, full, globular; intr. before 1880

'Le Météore' HCh, mr, before 1846, Thierry; flowers carmine, nuanced purple, very large, dbl., borne in large clusters

'Le Mexique' ('La Mexique') HWich, lp, 1912, Schwartz, A.; flowers pale silvery rose, reverse lighter, medium, semi-dbl., borne in clusters; some autumn repeat; foliage glossy; vigorous, climbing growth; ['Dorothy Perkins' × 'Marie Pavie']

'Le Mont Blanc' T, ly, 1870, Ducher; flowers light yellowish-white, full

'Le Nankin' T, yb, 1871, Ducher; flowers yellow shaded coppery, well-formed

'Le Pactole' ('Mme de Chalonges') T, ly, before 1841, Miellez; flowers pale yellow, large, dbl.; ['Lamarque' × 'a yellow tea']

'Le Pérou' ('Baron de Gossard', 'Pérou de Gossard') HGal, dr, before 1826, Gossard/Parmentier; flowers velvety cerise with very deep grenadine reflections, medium, full

'Le Petit Orange' Pol, ob, Adam

'Le Phoenix' HGal, mp, 1843, Vibert; flowers medium carmine-pink, large, very dbl.

'Le Pink' -- See 'Jaclip'

'Le Plessis Robinson' -- See 'Snow Cloud'

'Le Poilu' -- See 'Cumberland Belle'

'Le Poilu' HWich, mp, 1915, Barbier; flowers satiny rose, turning to lilac-rose, silvery reverse to medium, 5-6 cm., borne in clusters of 8-15; stems covered with numerous hairs or small thorns; ['Wichmoss' × 'Moussue de Japon']

'Le Ponceau' Pol, dr, 1912, Hémeray-Aubert; flowers deep garnet-red, small, semi-dbl.; ['Gruss an Teplitz' × 'Mme Norbert Levavasseur']

'Le Prince de Galles' P, dp, before 1826; flowers light red or deep pink, large, full; foliage large, dark green, sharply dentate; few prickles

'Le Progrès' HT, my, 1903, Pernet-Ducher; bud ovoid golden yellow; flowers nankeen yellow, aging lighter, very large, full, cupped; very vigorous growth

'Le Rêve' LCl, ly, 1923, Pernet-Ducher; bud pointed; flowers pale yellow, large, semi-dbl., moderate fragrance; foliage rich green, glossy; vigorous, climbing growth; ['Souv de Mme Eugene Verdier' × R. foetida persiana]

'Le Rhône' HP, mr, 1862, Guillot; flowers velvety vermilion, medium to large, full

'Le Rigide' HMult, mp, 1920, Turbat; flowers Neyron pink, semi-dbl., borne in clusters of 25-30; vigorous growth

'Le Rire Niais' ('À Odeur de Punaise', 'À Odeur Ingrate', 'Ingrata', 'Putidula') C, mp, before 1810, Dupont; flowers pink tinted lilac, medium, with a small center button, full, quartered, moderate unpleasant fragrance; foliage medium green, pointed; few prickles

'Le Roi de Siam' -- See 'Roi de Siam'

'Le Roitelet' B, mp, 1869, Soupert & Notting; flowers silky pink, small, dbl.

'Le Rosier Aurore Poniatowska' -- See 'Celestial'

'Le Rosier de Philippe Noisette' -- See R. × noisettiana

'Le Rosier du Jardin ou Cecile' S, op; flowers striped

'Le Rosier Évêque' ('La Rose Évêque', 'L'Évêque', 'Manteau d'Évêque', 'Pourpre Belle Violette', 'The Bishop') HGal, m, before 1790, from Holland; flowers violet, slightly striped, somtimes spotted white, medium, semi-dbl.

'Le Rosier Pompon Blanc' -- See 'Rose de Meaux White'

'Le Rouge et Le Noir' -- See 'Delcart'

'Le Royal-Époux' -- See 'Royal Époux'

'Le Soleil' T, my, 1891, Dubreuil; flowers silky glowing yellow, very large, very full, semi-globular

'Le Triomphe' -- See 'Aimable Rouge'

'Le Triomphe' -- See 'Majestueuse'

'Le Triomphe de Saintes' ('Triomphe de Saintes') HP, mr, 1885, Derouet; flowers scarlet, large, very full, round, slight fragrance; remontant; growth to 4 ft.

'Le Vésuve' ('Lemesle', 'Vésuve') Ch, pb, 1825, Laffay, M.; flowers carmine shading to pink, large, very dbl.; vigorous growth

'Le Vésuve, Climbing' Cl Ch, mp, 1904, Guillot; flowers variable, from pink to red, large, full; [sport of 'Le Vésuve']

'Le Vingt-Neuf Juillet' ('Coccinée Superbe') HCh, dr, before 1836; flowers crimson-purple, shaded with scarlet, large, full

'Léa' ('Lée', 'Rose Lée') HGal, dp, about 1825, Vétillart; flowers bright rose-pink, large, full, cupped; abundant early bloom

'Lea' F, dr, Urban, J.

'Lea Ann' Gr, w, 1976, Patterson; bud long, pointed; flowers clear white, 4 in., 25-30 petals, high-centered; foliage soft; vigorous growth; [Queen Elizabeth® × 'Ivory Fashion']

'Leader' HT, mr, 1924, E.G. Hill, Co.; [sport of 'Premier']

Leading Lady™ -- See 'Benuno'

'Leading Lady' -- See 'Jaclopi'

'Leading Lady' HT, lp, 1935, Dickson, A.; flowers flesh-pink, flushed peach-blossom, large, dbl., high-centered; foliage deep green, leathery; vigorous, bushy growth; RULED EXTINCT 1/85

'Leafy-Proliferous Cabbage Rose' -- See 'Prolifera de Redouté'

'League of Nations' HT, m, 1929, Leenders, M.; flowers reddish-lilac, shaded salmon-pink, semi-dbl.; ['Frau Felix Tonnar' × 'Solliden']

'Leah' Pol, mr, Holzman; intr. 1970

'Leah Alison' -- See 'Worcentigrade'

Leah June™ -- See 'Grelovie'

'Lealand Jewel' S, dp, 1963, Erskine; flowers deep pink, fading quickly, semi-dbl.; ['Athabasca' × unknown]

'Leana' -- See 'Roelanda'

Leander® -- See 'Auslea'

'Leandra' HT, ab, Tantau; flowers cream, white, and apricot tones, large, full, high-centered, borne mostly singly; good repeat; foliage medium green; prickles moderate; stems long; growth strong, vigorous; florist rose; intr. 2004

'Léandre' -- See 'Fleur de Pelletier'

'LeAnn Rimes' -- See 'Harzippee'

'LeAnn Rimes, Climbing' -- See 'Broclann'

'Leaping Salmon' -- See 'Peamight'

'Lebensfreude' HT, or, GPG Bad Langensalza; flowers large, dbl.; intr. 1979

'L'Eblouissante' Ch, mr, 1820, Vibert; flowers fiery cherry-red to light crimson, medium, very full

'L'Eblouissante' HP, mp, Touvais; flowers bright carmine, very large, full; intr. 1852

'L'Eblouissante' M, mr, Robert; flowers fiery red, becoming scarlet, medium, full; intr. 1853

'L'Eblouissante de La Queue' HGal, dr, about 1820, Noisette; flowers dark velvety crimson, large, very dbl.

'Lecbelpa' ('Belvedere Park') HT, dr, 1995, LeCroy, Jack; flowers dark red, edging to black, large, full, borne mostly singly; foliage medium size, dark green, glossy; few prickles; medium (4 ft.), spreading, bushy growth; ['Swarthmore' × 'First Prize']; intr. 1995

'Lecblu' ('Blushing June') F, or, 1996, LeCroy, Jack; flowers orange, vivid stamens, large, 6-14 petals, borne mostly singly, slight fragrance; foliage medium size, medium green, semi-glossy; some prickles; upright, medium growth; [Altissimo® × 'Frances Ashton']

'Lecocq-Dumesnil' HP, mr, 1882, Verdier, E.; flowers carmine-red, very large, very dbl., moderate fragrance; foliage dark green, deep irregular serration; prickles numerous, unequal, short, very pointed; stems reddish

'Léda' ('Leila', 'Painted Damask') D, w, 1826, Deschiens; bud long; flowers white to blush, edged crimson, medium, dbl., flat, with central rosette, moderate fragrance; sometimes recurrent bloom;

foliage dark green, large; compact (3 ft.) growth; hardy

'Leda' S, lp, 1960, Skinner; flowers pale pink, shallow, cupped, borne in clusters of 4-5; foliage dark; bushy (5 ft.) growth; hips large, apple-like, red

'Ledonneau-Leblanc' HGal, w, before 1834; flowers large, full

Ledreborg™ ('Ledreborg Castle', Rastede™, 'White Castle') F, w, Poulsen; flowers 5-8 cm., 25 petals, no fragrance; foliage dark; growth bushy, 60-100 cm.; PP15484; intr. 2001

'Ledreborg Castle' -- See 'Poulcs004(N)'

'Lée' -- See 'Léa'

'Leea Rubra' C, lp, before 1906; flowers pink, center darker, medium, dbl., moderate fragrance

'Leecal' ('Colleen Little') Min, my, 1992, Little, Lee W.; flowers medium, full, high-centered, borne usually singly or in sprays of 5-7, slight fragrance; foliage small, dark green, semi-glossy, disease-resistant; some prickles; medium (26-30 cm.), upright, bushygrowth; ['Luis Desamero' × 'Cheyenne']; intr. 1992

'Leeds Castle' -- See 'Tanrupeza'

'Leefir' ('Flashfire') LCl, rb, 1992, Little, Lee W.; flowers brilliant coppery red-orange with yellow eye, 3-3½ in., 5 petals, borne in small clusters; foliage large, dark green, glossy, disease-resistant; some prickles; tall (210 cm.), upright, spreading growth; [Altissimo® × Playboy®]; intr. 1992

'Leela' ('Mrs Leela Subhedar') HT, rb, Shastri, Dr. N. V.; flowers blend of red, white and yellow, large, full; strong growth; intr. 1999

'Leenders' Bergfeuer' F, mr, 1959, Leenders, J.; bud long; flowers scarlet, large, semi-dbl.; foliage dark, glossy; ['Independence' × 'Fashion']

'Leenders' Flamingo' F, ob, 1960, Leenders, J.; bud ovoid; flowers bright coral-peach, open, large, semi-dbl., borne in clusters, moderate fragrance; vigorous, bushy growth; ['Cocorico' × 'Ma Perkins']

'Leenders' Pink' F, mp, 1959, Leenders, J.; flowers bright pink, large, dbl., borne in heavy clusters; foliage dark, leathery, glossy; ['Goldilocks' × 'Mrs Inge Poulsen']

'Leepel' ('Royal Porcelain') Cl HT, mp, 1992, Little, Lee W.; flowers 3-3½ in., full, high-centered, borne in small clusters on strong upright laterals; foliage large, disease-resistant; some prickles; tall (260 cm.), upright, spreading growth; ['Pele' × Altissimo®]; intr. 1992

'Leerder's Harlequin' -- See 'The Jester'

'Leersum 700' -- See 'Interleer'

'Lee's Crimson Perpetual' -- See 'Comte Lelieur'

'Lee's Duchess' -- See 'La Belle Distinguée'

'Leesho' ('Rainbow Shower') LCl, pb, 1992, Little, Lee W.; flowers shrimp pink suffused with yellow and darker pink edge, aging, 3-3½ in., 5 petals; foliage medium size, medium green, glossy, disease-resistant; some prickles; tall (210 cm.), upright, spreading growth; [Altissimo® × Playboy®]; intr. 1992

Legacy™ -- See 'Jacsling'

'Legacy' HT, pb, 1963, Hamilton; flowers rose-pink streaked white, large, dbl.; foliage leathery; moderate growth; [sport of 'Mrs Bryce Allan']; intr. 1963

'Legacy Jubilee' HT, yb, 1974, Dawson, George; bud long, pointed; flowers yellow, edged red, large, dbl.; foliage large, glossy; vigorous, upright growth; ['Great Venture' × 'Fred Streeter']

'Legcream' ('Jilly Cooper') F, w, LeGrice; intr. 1998

'Legend' -- See 'Jactop'

'Legendary' HT, lp, 1962, Von Abrams; bud long, pointed; flowers soft pink, 5½ in., 55 petals, high-centered, moderate fragrance; foliage leathery; vigorous, upright growth; intr. 1962

Legends™ -- See 'Weksiamia'

'Legga' ('Midas', Dorothe®) HT, my, 1980, LeGrice, E.B.; bud pointed; flowers 48 petals, borne singly, slight fragrance; foliage glossy, medium green; prickles large, curved, light brown; vigorous, upright growth; ['Irish Gold' × 'Dr. A. J. Verhage']

'Leggab' ('Pearl Drift') S, w, 1980, LeGrice; flowers white flushed pink, 18 petals, borne in small clusters; foliage glossy, reddish to dark green; prickles small, light brown; vigorous, compact, spreading growth; ['Mermaid' × 'New Dawn']; intr. 1981

'Leggiero' HT, or, Teranishi; flowers single; intr. 2006

'Legglow' ('CanCan', 'Can-Can') HT, ob, 1985, LeGrice, E.B.; flowers orange, large, 24 petals, intense fragrance; foliage large, dark, semi-glossy; bushy growth; ['Just Joey' × ('Superior' × 'Mischief')]; intr. 1982

'Leggrey' ('Nimbus') F, m, 1990, LeGrice, E.B. Roses; bud pointed; flowers lilac-gray, medium, very dbl., cupped, borne in sprays; foliage medium size, medium green, semi-glossy; bushy, medium growth; ['Grey Dawn' × seedling]; intr. 1989

'Legion' ('American Legion') HT, dp, 1920, Towill; flowers deep cerise-red, dbl.; [('Milady' × unknown) × 'Hadley']

Légion d'Honneur® -- See 'Delsamar'

'Legneed' ('Kathleen Jermyn') HT, or, 1988, LeGrice, E.B.; flowers medium, dbl., urn-shaped, loose, borne usually singly, slight fragrance; foliage large, dark green, semi-glossy; growth bushy, medium; [Royal Dane™ × Alexander®]

'Legnews' F, m, 1968, LeGrice; intr. 1968

'Legram' ('Pink Fountain') LCl, dp, LeGrice; intr. 1990

'Legsweet' ('Deb's Delight') F, pb, 1983, LeGrice, E.B.; flowers silvery salmon-pink blend, patio, medium, 35 petals, moderate fragrance; foliage medium size, medium green, semi-glossy; low, bushy growth; ['Tip Top' × seedling]

'Leicester Abbey' -- See 'Nosab'

'Leigh Ann' Min, pb, 1987, Jolly, Marie; flowers pink, reverse cream, yellow center, fading to light pink, medium, 34 petals, high-centered; foliage medium size, medium green, semi-glossy; prickles bayonet-shaped, pinkish brown; upright, medium, vigorous growth; hips round, red-orange; ['Poker Chip' × 'Rise 'n' Shine']; intr. 1987

'Leigh-Lo' -- See 'Harpurl'

'Leigh Matthews Memorial Rose' -- See 'Cherry Girl'

'Leila' -- See 'Berlei'

'Leila' -- See 'Léda'

'Leila Francis' HT, pb, 1948, Francis; bud ovoid; flowers two-toned pink, large, dbl., high-centered; foliage leathery; vigorous, bushy growth; ['Earl Haig' × 'Crimson Glory']

'Leila Verde' F, m

'Leipzig' HMsk, or, 1939, Kordes; flowers orange-scarlet, open, semi-dbl., borne in clusters; recurrent bloom; foliage leathery, glossy, wrinkled; long, strong stems; vigorous, bushy growth; ['Eva' × 'Mermaid']

'Leitrim Glory' HT, dy, 1976, Hughes; flowers deep yellow, 5 in., 28-30 petals; foliage bronze, matte green; [sport of 'Whisky Mac']

'Lele' HT, dr, 1939, San Remo Exp. Sta.; bud pointed; flowers dark red, veined, very large, 30 petals; foliage bright green; strong stems; very vigorous growth; ['Marquise d'Andigne' × 'President Herbert Hoover']

'L'Élégante' -- See 'Élégante'

'L'Elégante' -- See 'Euphrosine'

'Lelia Laird' Min, ob, 1980, Bennett, Dee; bud long, pointed; flowers orange-red with yellow eye and reverse, 38 petals, high-centered, borne 1 - 4 per cluster, moderate tea fragrance; foliage medium green with red edging; prickles long, thin, red; upright growth; PP4922; ['Contempo' × 'Sheri Anne']; intr. 1979

'Lemania' HT, dr, 1937, Heizmann, E.; bud almost black; flowers velvety blackish red, well-formed, very large, dbl.; vigorous growth

'Lembut' Min, w, 1981, Lemrow, Dr. Maynard W.; bud globular

'Lemcar' ('Carl's Rose') Min, m, 1985, Lemrow, Dr. Maynard W.; flowers small, 35 petals, high-centered, borne in sprays; foliage small, medium green, semi-glossy; low, upright growth

'Lemesle' -- See 'Le Vésuve'

'Lemfall' (Snowfall™) Cl Min, w, 1988, Lemrow, Dr. Maynard W.; bud medium, ovoid, recessed center; flowers white, reverse greenish-white, 1½ in., 40-50 petals, flat, then pompon, borne usually singly or in sprays of 2-5, no fragrance; recurrent; foliage medium size, medium green, semi-glossy; prickles short, pointed, small, straight; spreading, tall, profuse, hardy growth; no fruit; PP6706; ['Jeanne Lajoie' × seedling]; intr. 1988

'Lemlil' Min, pb, 1984, Lemrow, Dr. Maynard W.

'Lemmar' Min, pb, 1981, Lemrow, Dr. Maynard W.

'Lemon' HSpn, w, from Scotland; flowers yellowish-white

'Lemon Beauty' HT, w, 1932, Cant, B. R.; flowers creamy white, quickly fading to paper-white, base lemon-yellow, moderate fruity fragrance; foliage light

'Lemon Bells' -- See 'Jacyelsh'

'Lemon Blush' -- See 'Sielemon'

Lemon Bouquet™ -- See 'Lavtiki'

'Lemon Chiffon' ('Yellow Rose of Texas') HT, my, 1955, Swim, H.C.; bud long, pointed; flowers lemon-yellow, to open, 3-4 in., very dbl., high-centered, intense spicy fragrance; compact, bushy growth; PP1241; RULED EXTINCT 9/86; ['Soeur Thérèse' × 'Golden Dawn']; intr. 1954

'Lemon Couture' S, ly; flowers bright yellow, slight fragrance; low (50 cm.) growth; intr. 2003

'Lemon Delight' Min, my, 1978, Moore, Ralph S.; bud mossy, long, pointed; flowers mini-moss, 1½ in., 10 petals; bushy, upright growth; PP4447; ['Fairy Moss' × 'Goldmoss']

'Lemon Diana' HT, ly, Tantau; flowers lemon yellow, dbl., moderate fragrance; foliage medium green; few prickles; growth strong, upright; intr. 2002

'Lemon Dream' -- See 'Koramvis'

'Lemon Drop' -- See 'Wekyegi'

'Lemon Drop' Min, ly, 1954, Moore, Ralph S.; flowers ¾ in., dbl.; foliage very small; very prickly; growth dwarf (6 in.); [(R. wichurana × 'Floradora') × 'Zee']

'Lemon Elegance' HT, my, 1965, Jones; bud long, pointed; flowers lemon-yellow, well-shaped, 4½-5 in., 38 petals, moderate fragrance; foliage leathery; vigorous, tall growth; intr. 1960

'Lemon Flower Circus' F, my, Kordes; flowers lemon yellow , 3.5 in., 20 petals, cupped, borne mostly in clusters, slight sweet fragrance; recurrent; low (25 - 30 in.), wide growth; intr. 2007

'Lemon Fluff' -- See 'Curlem'

Lemon Gems™ -- See 'Jacmiryl'

'Lemon Glow' HT, my, 1963, Schwartz, Ernest W.; bud long, pointed; flowers lemon-yellow, 6-7 in., 55 petals, high-centered, moderate fragrance; foliage soft; vigorous, upright growth; ['Sunlight' × 'Golden Masterpiece']; intr. 1963

'Lemon Honey' F, ly, Dickson, Patrick; flowers lemon yellow with paler margins; growth medium; intr. 1986

'Lemon Ice' HT, my, 1960, Kern, J. J.; bud pointed; flowers lemon-yellow, 4 in., 65 petals; foliage leathery, dark; vigorous, bushy, compact growth; [sport of 'Leonard Barron']

'Lemon Ice' Min, ly, Hannemann, F.; ['Oz Gold' × 'Lemon Delight']

'Lemon Light' LCl, ly

Lemon Meringue™ -- See 'Wekradler'

'Lemon Meringue' -- See 'Juslemon'

'Lemon Mist' Min, w, 1991, Gruenbauer, Richard; bud ovoid; flowers white with yellow center, aging white, medium, 50 petals, high-centered, slight fruity fragrance; foliage medium size, medium green, matte; upright growth; ['Rise 'n' Shine' × seedling]; intr. 1993

'Lemon Ophelia' HT, my, 1922, Leenders, M.; flowers lemon-yellow, dbl.; [sport of 'Ophelia']

'Lemon Parady' -- See 'Ausmas'

'Lemon Pearl' -- See 'Micpearl'

'Lemon Pearls' -- See 'Morpearls'

'Lemon Pillar' -- See 'Paul's Lemon Pillar'

'Lemon Queen' Cl HT, w, 1912, Hobbies; flowers creamy white, large, dbl.; ['Frau Karl Druschki' × 'Mme Ravary']

Lemon Romantic Folies® F, ly, Meilland; flowers light lemon, borne in sprays; intr. 2006

'Lemon Rosamini' Min, ly

'Lemon Sherbet' HT, ly, 1975, Kern, J. J.; bud ovoid; flowers white, center light yellow,, 4 in., 35 petals, high-centered; foliage large, leathery; upright growth; [sport of 'Florence']; intr. 1973

'Lemon Spice' HT, ly, 1966, Armstrong, D.L.; & Swim, H. C.; bud long, pointed; flowers 5½ in., 30-35 petals, high-centered to cupped, borne mostly singly, intense fragrance; recurrent; foliage dark, leathery; vigorous, spreading growth; PP2836; ['Helen Traubel' × seedling]

'Lemon Surprise' F, my, 1980, Slack; flowers lemon, 12 petals, moderate spicy fragrance; foliage glossy; low, upright growth; [Allgold® × Elizabeth of Glamis®]; intr. 1978

'Lemon Swirl' -- See 'Renswirl'

'Lemon Time' HT, my, Kasturi; flowers lemon yellow with green tinge, large, dbl.; intr. 1989

'Lemon Twist' -- See 'Foutwist'

'Lemon Up' Min, yb, 2006, Hopper, Nancy; flowers light yellow, edged pink, reverse light yellow, 2½ in., single, borne mostly solitary; foliage medium size, medium green, semi-glossy; prickles ½ in., brown, few; growth bushy, medium (14-15 in.); ['yellow seedling' × 'yellow seedling']; intr. 2006

'Lemon Yellow' F, my, 1977, Gandy, Douglas L.; flowers lemon-yellow, 2 in., 21 petals; foliage dark; bushy growth; [Orange Sensation® × King's Ransom®]

'Lemon Zen' N, ly, 2006, Starnes, John A., Jr.; flowers 3 in., single, borne in large clusters, intense cinnamon fragrance; foliage medium size, medium green, matte; prickles medium, claw-shaped, moderate; growth upright, tall (8 ft.), pillar; [R. moschata × Graham Thomas®]; intr. 2004

Lemon Zest™ -- See 'Jacsalps'

'Lemonade' F, w, 1976, Haynes Roses; flowers cream, 4½ in., 25 petals; foliage matte; [sport of 'Nancy West']; intr. 1974

'Lemonade' F, w, Kordes; flowers white, tinged green, medium, dbl., borne mostly singly; good repeat; florist rose; intr. 2002

'Lemsea' Min, mp, 1976, Lemrow, Dr. Maynard W.; bud short, pointed

'Lemsur' ('Surf's Up') Min, ob, 1984, Lemrow, Dr. Maynard W.; flowers orange, yellow reverse, small, 35 petals, high-centered, borne singly; foliage small, medium green, semi-glossy; upright growth; ['Avandel' × seedling]

'Lemswi' ('Swiss Lass') Min, rb, 1987, Lemrow, Dr. Maynard W.; flowers red, reverse almost all white, medium, very dbl.; foliage small, medium green, semi-glossy; upright growth; [seedling × seedling]

'Len 1' ('Bouquet Fait') S, pb, 1986, Lens, Louis; flowers medium pink with a white eye, 2 in., semi-dbl., borne singly and in small clusters, intense fragrance; non-recurrent; foliage grayish green, hairy; bushy (to 5 ft.) growth; [R. mollis × 'Complicata']; intr. 1985

'Len 2' ('Epoca Mondadori', 'Epoca') Gr, dr, 1986, Lens, Louis; flowers very dark red, large, 45 petals, high-centered, borne in sprays of 3-18, no fragrance; foliage very dark; prickles brown-green; upright, bushy growth; [seedling × seedling]; intr. 1966

'Len 3' ('Favori', 'Favorite') F, op, 1986, Lens, Louis; flowers light salmon-pink, 3 in., 23 petals, urn-shaped, borne in clusters of 8-24, intense fragrance; foliage dark; prickles hooked, brownish-green; large, bushy growth; [seedling × seedling]; intr. 1980

'Len 4' (Jet Spray®) S, m, 1986, Lens, Louis; flowers purple-pink, small, 21 petals, rosette; foliage very small, dark; no prickles; growth bushy, spreading, low (60 cm.); ['New Penny' × seedling]; intr. 1984

'Len Gallagher' -- See 'Jalgalla'

'Len Mace' HT, ly, 2003, Poole, Lionel; flowers cream tinged pink, 5 in., full, borne mostly solitary; foliage small, medium green, matte; prickles medium, triangular, moderate; growth upright, medium (36 in.); garden, exhibition; ['Tom Foster' × ('Joanna Lumley' × 'Pedrus Aquarius')]; intr. 2005

'Len Turner' -- See 'Dicjeep'

'Lena' T, ab, 1906, Dickson, A.; flowers apricot, edged yellow, borne in large clusters

'Lena' HT, or, deRuiter; intr. 1981

'Lena' HT, ab, Dickson; intr. 2004

'Lena' S, pb, Zuzek, Kathy; flowers frilly pink and white , single , borne in clusters; recurrent; foliage bright green, disease-resistant; intr. 2008

'Léna Turner' HP, rb, 1869, Verdier, E.; flowers deep carmine, brightened at center with flame, shaded with violet, large, full; foliage dark green; prickles reddish

'Lenabavi' (Fortissima®) Cl Pol, dp, 2000, Lens, Louis; flowers 1 in., single, borne in large clusters, slight fragrance; recurrent; foliage small, dark green, glossy, disease-resistant; few prickles; climbing, upright, spreading, tall (150-250 cm.) growth; [(R. adenocheata × 'Ballerina') × 'Violet Hood']; intr. 1994

'Lenadbi' (Frisson Frais®) HMsk, w, 2000, Lens, Louis; flowers light pink, reverse lighter, 1-1½ in., single to semi-dbl., borne in large clusters; recurrent; foliage medium green, semi-glossy, disease-resistant; prickles moderate; bushy, tall (120-150 cm.) growth; hedge; ['Ravel' × Rush®]; intr. 1991

'Lenadbial' (Matchball®) HMsk, w, 2000, Lens, Louis; flowers white, pink shade, reverse white, 1½ in., single, borne in large clusters, moderate fragrance; recurrent bloom; foliage medium size, medium green, semi-glossy, disease-resistant; prickles moderate; growth bushy, medium (80-100 cm.); hedge, border; [R. multiflora adenocheata × 'Kathleen']; intr. 1990

'Lenadeba' ('Claire Jolly') HMsk, mp, 2000, Lens, Louis; flowers medium pink, paler center, small, semi-dbl., borne in large clusters; recurrent; foliage small, medium green, glossy, disease-resistant; prickles moderate; upright, low (60 cm.) growth; hedge; [(R. multiflora adenocheata × 'Ballerina') × 'The Fairy']; intr. 1991

'Lenadne' ('Neige d'Eté') HMsk, w, 2000, Lens, Louis; flowers creamy white, 1-1½ in., semi-dbl., borne in large clusters; recurrent; foliage medium size, light green, semi-glossy, disease-resistant; few prickles; upright, medium (120-150 cm.) growth; hedge, border, cut flower; [R. multiflora adenocheata × 'Ballerina']; intr. 1991

'Lenalbi' ('Guirlande d'Amour') HMsk, w, 2000, Lens, Louis; flowers creamy white, nice stamens, 1 in., semi-dbl., borne in large clusters; recurrent bloom; foliage medium size, medium green, semi-glossy, disease-resistant; prickles moderate; upright, tall (180-200 cm.) growth; hedge, climber; ['Seagull' × (R. multiflora nana × 'Moonlight')]; intr. 1993

'Lenamo' ('Brigitte de Villenfagne') HMsk, lp, 2000, Lens, Louis; flowers pale pink, white center, reverse lighter, 1 in., single, borne in large clusters, moderate fragrance; recurrent; foliage medium size, medium green, semi-glossy, disease-resistant; prickles moderate; growth upright, tall (125-150 cm.); hedge, border; [R. multiflora adenocheata × (R. multiflora nana × 'Ballerina')]; intr. 1993

'Lenana' ('Flash') S, lp, 1986, Lens, Louis; flowers 1½ in., 22 petals, borne in clusters of 3-50; foliage small, dark; prickles hooked, green; bushy, spreading growth; [R. multiflora nana × seedling]; intr. 1984

'Lenarvere' ('Porcelaine de Chine') Ayr, lp, 2000, Lens, Louis; flowers pale pink to white, reverse lighter, 1½ in., semi-dbl., borne in large clusters; recurrent; foliage medium size, dark green, semi-glossy; thornless; upright, tall (4-5 ft.) growth; hedge, climber; [R. arvensis × R. chinensis minima]; intr. 1996

'Lenbaca' ('Magie d'Orient') HMsk, dp, 2000, Lens, Louis; flowers deep pink, white center, reverse paler, 1-1½ in., single, borne in large clusters; recurrent; foliage large, medium green, semi-glossy, disease-resistant; prickles moderate; spreading, medium (100-120 cm.) growth; [(R. multiflora adenocheata × 'Ballerina') × 'Puccini']; intr. 1991

'Lenbar' ('Sibelius') HMsk, m, 2000, Lens, Louis; flowers dark mauve, 1 in., semi-dbl., cupped, borne in large clusters; recurrent; foliage small, dark green, glossy; prickles moderate; upright, medium (80-120 cm.) growth; hedge; ['Mister Bluebird' × 'Violet Hood']; intr. 1984

'Lenbari' ('Vif Eclat') HMsk, mr, 2000, Lens, Louis; flowers bright red with white eye and yellow stamens, 2 cm., single, cupped, borne in large, pyramidal clusters; recurrent; foliage medium size, medium green, semi-glossy, disease-resistant; prickles moderate; upright, medium (60-80 cm.) growth; hedge, border; [(R. multiflora adenocheata × 'Ballerina') × 'Ravel']; intr. 1992

'Lenbaser' ('Robe de Neige') S, w, 2000, Lens, Louis; flowers white with pink shades, reverse white, small, single, borne in large clusters; recurrent; foliage medium size, medium green, semi-glossy; prickles moderate; growth spreading, medium (60 cm.); [Serpent Vert® × 'Ballerina']; intr. 1995

'Lenbefas' ('Easy to Cut') HMsk, lp, 2000, Lens, Louis; flowers light pink, reverse lighter, 2-2½ in., semi-dbl., borne in large clusters, moderate fragrance; recurrent; foliage medium size, medium green, semi-glossy; few prickles; upright, bushy, medium (3-4 ft.) growth; [(Trier' × 'Pinocchio') × ('Seagull' × 'Ballerina')]; intr. 1997

'Lenbit' ('Verdi') HMsk, m, 2000, Lens, Louis; flowers 2-3 cm., semi-dbl., borne in large clusters, slight fragrance; foliage medium size, dark green, glossy, disease-resistant; prickles moderate; upright, medium (100 cm.) growth; ['Mr Bluebird' × 'Violet Hood']; intr. 1984

'Lenblank' (White Dream®) Min, w, 1986, Lens, Louis; flowers small, 36 petals, high-centered, borne in clusters of 3 - 28; prickles hooked, greenish-brown; low, bushy growth; [seedling × seedling]; intr. 1982

'Lenbofa' (Bouquet Parfait®) HMsk, pb, 2000, Lens, Louis; flowers pale pink to cream, reverse lighter, 2 in., full, globular, borne in large clusters; recurrent; foliage medium size, dark green, glossy, disease-resistant; few prickles; upright, medium (4-5 ft.) growth; [(R. multiflora adenocheata × 'Ballerina') × White Dream®]; intr. 1989

'Lenborata' ('Ambiance') HMsk, pb, 2000, Lens, Louis; flowers deep pink, reverse lighter, 1 in., single, borne in large clusters; recurrent; foliage small, dark green, semi-glossy; few prickles; compact low (50-60 cm.) growth; [R. multiflora adenocheata × 'Vanity']; intr. 1994

'Lenbrac' ('Pink Surprise') HBc, lp, 2000, Lens, Louis; flowers light pink, nearly white, reverse white, red stamens, 10-11 cm., single, borne in small clusters, moderate fragrance; recurrent; foliage large, medium green, glossy, evergreen; numerous prickles; bushy, tall (1¾-2 m.) growth; [R. bracteata × 'La Rosee']; intr. 1987

'Lenbracta' ('Jelena de Belder') HBc, w, 2000, Lens, Louis; flowers single, borne in small clusters, moderate fragrance; recurrent; foliage yellow-green with bronze shadings, matte, evergreen; prickles moderate; growth bushy, medium (120-150 cm.); [R. bracteata × 'Schneezwerg']; intr. 1996

'Lenbrirus' ('Bukavu') HMsk, dp, 2000, Lens, Louis; flowers deep pink, reverse lighter, 4-5 cm., single, borne in large clusters; recurrent bloom; foliage medium size, dark green, glossy; prickles moderate; upright, medium (80-120 cm.) growth; ['Britannia' × Rush®]; intr. 1998

'Lenbru' ('Bruxelles', Bruocsella®) HT, dy, 1986, Lens, Louis; flowers golden yellow, large, 35 petals, high-centered, urn-shaped, borne singly or in small clusters, intense fragrance; prickles dark green; upright, bushy growth; ['Peace' × 'Golden Garnette']; intr. 1980

'Lencan' (Petit Canard®) Min, ly, 1986, Lens, Louis; flowers small, 20 petals, high-centered, borne in clusters of 12 - 22; foliage small; prickles few, green; bushy growth; ['Rosina' × ('Le Vesuve' × 'Belle Étoile')]; intr. 1984

'Lencara' (Jet Spray®) S, m, 1986, Lens, Louis; intr. 1984

'L'Enchantresse' ('Enchantress', 'Grande Henriette') HGal, mp, before 1824, François; flowers clear pink, fading with age, large, dbl.

'Lencil' -- See 'Cecile Lens'

'Lenclidon' ('White Crystal') HMsk, w, 2000, Lens, Louis; flowers white, shaded pink, reverse white, 3 cm., single, borne in large clusters, moderate fragrance; foliage medium size, dark green, glossy, disease-resistant; prickles moderate; upright, tall (150-200 cm.) growth; [(R. multiflora adenocheata × 'Ballerina') × 'Felicia']; intr. 1992

'Lenclima' ('Maaseik', Maaseik 750®) HMsk, pb, 2000, Lens, Louis; flowers light pink, reverse white, yellow stamens, 4-5 cm., single, borne in large clusters, moderate fragrance; foliage large, bronze-green, semi-glossy; prickles moderate; growth spreading, medium (1-1½ m.); [(*R. multiflora adenocheata* × 'Ballerina') × 'Kathleen']; intr. 1994

'Lenda' ('Anda') Pol, rb, 1986, Lens, Louis; flowers dark red, white eye, 2 in., 5 petals, borne in clusters of 18-24, moderate fruity fragrance; prickles purple; bushy growth; [('Britannia' × *R. moschata*) × ('Little Angel' × Europeana®)]; intr. 1980

'Lendadi' ('Violine') S, m, 1986, Lens, Louis; flowers lilac, pink, white blend, 2 in., 20 petals, borne in clusters of 5-28, moderate fruity fragrance; foliage light green; prickles few, small, brown; upright, bushy growth; [('Little Angel' × 'Picasso') × 'Skyrocket']; intr. 1985

'Lendec' (Idée Fixe®) F, or, 1986, Lens, Louis; flowers light orange-red, 2 in., 15 petals, borne in clusters of 3-18, slight fragrance; foliage small, dark; prickles hooked, light red; low, bushy growth; [seedling × (seedling × 'Floradora')]; intr. 1980

'Lendiro' ('Diamant Rose') HMsk, pb, 2000, Lens, Louis; flowers light pink, reverse lighter, 1 in., single, borne in large clusters; recurrent; foliage small, medium green, glossy, disease-resistant; few prickles; upright, bushy, low (2-3 ft.) growth; [(*R. multiflora adenocheata* × 'Ballerina') × seedling]; intr. 1995

'Lendori' ('Erna Doris') F, op, 1986, Lens, Louis; flowers medium salmon pink, 24 petals, high-centered, borne in clusters of 3-12, slight fragrance; foliage small, medium green; prickles small, hooked, brown-green; upright, bushy growth; ['Little Angel' × Elizabeth of Glamis®]; intr. 1985

'Leneli' ('Jolly Good') MinFl, op, 2000, Lens, Louis; flowers orange pink, reverse lighter, 3-4 cm., dbl., borne in small clusters, moderate fragrance; foliage medium size, medium green, matte; few prickles; growth bushy, medium (35 cm.); [('Little Angel' × Elizabeth of Glamis®) × Pernille Poulsen™]; intr. 1991

'L'Enfant de France' -- See 'Enfant de France'

'L'Enfant du Mont Carmel' HP, dp, 1851, Cherpin; flowers dark pink, shaded purple, large, full

'L'Enfant Trouvé' -- See 'Enfant Trouvé'

'Lenfeeli' (Feeling®) HMsk, yb, 2000, Lens, Louis; flowers light yellow to white, reverse lighter, 2-2¼ in., semi-dbl., borne in large clusters, moderate fragrance; recurrent; foliage medium size, medium green, dull; prickles moderate; bushy, medium (4-5 ft.) growth; [Trier® × 'Poesie']; intr. 1992

'Lenfil' (Fil d'Ariane®) S, w, 2000, Lens, Louis; flowers pink and creamy white, reverse white, yellow stamens, 2-3 cm., semi-dbl., flat, borne in large clusters, intense fragrance; recurrent; foliage small, medium green, glossy; prickles moderate; low, spreading (8 in. × 3 ft.) growth; groundcover; [Running Maid® × *R. multiflora nana*]; intr. 1988

'Lenfiltap' (Schoone Gezelle Blomme®) HMsk, w, 2000, Lens, Louis; flowers semi-dbl., open, borne in large clusters; foliage medium size, dark green, semi-glossy; prickles moderate; growth bushy, spreading, medium (80-120 cm.); [Fil d'Ariane® × Tapis Volant®]; intr. 1999

'Lenfiro' ('Dentelle de Malines', 'Lens Pink') S, lp, 2000, Lens, Louis; flowers pale pink to cream, reverse lighter, small, dbl., flat, borne in large clusters; foliage dark green, glossy; prickles moderate; bushy, tall (5-6 ft.) growth; [*R. filipes* × ('Robin Hood' × 'Baby Faurax')]; intr. 1986

'Lengodo' (Chamois Doré®) F, ab, 2000, Lens, Louis; flowers pale apricot, reverse lighter, 6 cm., dbl., borne in small clusters; recurrent; foliage medium size, medium green, semi-glossy; few prickles; bushy, low (60-70 cm.) growth; ['LLX7952' × 'Goldtopaz']; intr. 1990

'Lengra' ('Pleine de Grâce', 'The Songbird Rose') S, w, 1985, Lens, Louis; flowers creamy white, 4-5 cm., 5 petals, borne in clusters of 20-50, intense fragrance; non-recurrent; foliage yellowish-green; bushy, spreading growth; ['Ballerina' × *R. filipes*]; intr. 1983

'Lengrati' ('Alden Biesen') HMsk, lp, 2000, Lens, Louis; flowers medium pink, reverse lighter, 3-4 cm., single, borne in large clusters; recurrent; foliage medium size, dark green, semi-glossy; prickles moderate; upright, medium (4-5 ft.) growth; ['Pleine de Grace' × 'Pretty Pink']; intr. 1996

'Lengravi' (Gravin Michel d'Ursel®) HMsk, ab, 2000, Lens, Louis; flowers salmon-pink with a touch of lavender-brown, reverse lighter, 4-6 cm., single, borne in small clusters, moderate fragrance; recurrent; foliage large, dark green, semi-glossy; few prickles; upright, bushy, medium (4-5 ft.) growth; ['Lavender Pinocchio' × ('Ballerina' × 'Echo')]; intr. 1988

'Lenhele' ('Hélène de Gerlache') HT, w, 2000, Lens, Louis; flowers white, champagne center, reverse lighter, 3 in., full, borne in small clusters, intense fragrance; recurrent; foliage medium size, light green, glossy; prickles moderate; upright, medium (70 cm.) growth; [(Pascali® × 'Jour de Fete') × 'Vagabonde']; intr. 1982

'Lenhem' ('Hélène Maréchal') Cl Gr, w, 2000, Lens, Louis; flowers creamy white, 6 cm., dbl., borne in small clusters, moderate delicate fragrance; non-recurrent; foliage medium size, medium green, matte; prickles moderate; growth climbing, tall (6 m.); [*R. helenae* × 'Maréchal Niel']; intr. 1995

'Leni Neuss' HT, pb, 1933, Leenders, M.; bud pointed; flowers hydrangea-pink, reverse reddish old-rose, very large, dbl.; very vigorous, bushy growth; ['Lilly Jung' × 'Baronesse M. van Tuyll van Serooskerken']

'Lenidora' S, Lens, Louis; intr. 1990

'Lenip' (Blanche Pasca®) HT, w, 1963, Lens; intr. 1963

'Lenira' (Iranja®) F, or, 1986, Lens, Louis; flowers orange-red, 2 in., 35 petals, borne in clusters of 3-24, no fragrance; foliage small, brilliant green; prickles hooked, red-green; low, bushy growth; ['Little Angel' × ('Floradora' × 'Angelina Louro')]; intr. 1984

'Lenisur' ('Merle Blanc') S, lp, 1986, Lens, Louis; flowers blush pink, 2 in., 22 petals, borne in clusters of 3 - 22, intense fragrance; recurrent bloom; foliage dark; prickles hooked, brownish-green; tall, spreading growth; ['Ballerina' × 'Surf Rider']; intr. 1985

'Lenivill' ('Ville d'Ettelbruck') S, dr, 1986, Lens, Louis; flowers deep red, 2 in., 20 petals, borne in clusters of 5 - 18, moderate fruity fragrance; foliage dark, leathery; prickles hooked, green; upright, bushy growth; [Satchmo® × 'Skyrocket']; intr. 1983

'Lenjoma' ('Super Pink') LCl, mp, 2000, Lens, Louis; flowers pure, clear pink, 8-12 cm., full, cupped, borne in small clusters; recurrent; foliage large, dark green, glossy; prickles moderate; growth upright, tall (2-2½ m.); ['Jour de Fete' × Maria Teresa®]; intr. 1992

'Lenka' F, ly, Vecera, L.

'Lenkama' ('Pretty Pink') HMsk, pb, 2000, Lens, Louis; flowers single, borne in large clusters, moderate fragrance; recurrent; foliage large, medium green, semi-glossy; prickles moderate; bushy, medium (4-5 ft.) growth; [*R. multiflora adenocheata* × 'Ballerina']; intr. 1992

'Lenkivi' (Dentelle de Bruxelles®) S, mr, 2000, Lens, Louis; flowers dark carmine red, 1 in., semi-dbl., borne in large clusters; recurrent; foliage dark green-reddish, semi-glossy; prickles moderate; bushy, tall (5-6 ft.), arching growth; ['Kiftsgate' × 'Violet Hood']; intr. 1988

'Lenkliro' ('Art Deco') HMsk, mr, 2000, Lens, Louis; flowers medium red, 2 cm., single, borne in large clusters; recurrent; foliage medium size, medium green, semi-glossy; numerous prickles; upright, tall (7 ft.) growth, can be used as climber; ['Pleine de Grace' × 'Pretty Pink']; intr. 1993

'Lenlifra' (Cimarosa®) F, op, 2000, Lens, Louis; flowers orange-pink, 7-8 cm., very full, borne in small clusters, intense fragrance; recurrent bloom; foliage medium size, brown-green, glossy; prickles moderate; growth bushy, medium (2 ft.); ['Little Angel' × Fragrant Delight®]; intr. 1989

'Lenlilo' (Indian Silk®) MinFl, ab, 2000, Lens, Louis; flowers apricot, 3-4 cm., full, borne in small clusters, moderate fragrance; recurrent; foliage medium size, light green, glossy; few prickles; bushy, medium (14 in.) growth; patio, containers; ['Little Angel' × Love Letter®]; intr. 1991

'Lenlit' (Little Shrimp®) F, lp, 1986, Lens, Louis; flowers light shrimp-pink, rosette, 2 in., very dbl., borne in clusters of 3-24; foliage small; prickles hooked, brownish-red; bushy growth; ['Little Angel' × ('Little Angel' × 'Spartan')]; intr. 1984

'Lenlita' ('Petit Serpent') S, w, 2000, Lens, Louis; flowers white, shaded pink, reverse white, 2 cm., single, borne in large clusters, moderate fragrance; non-recurrent; foliage small, dark green, glossy; prickles moderate; spreading, low (10 × 80 cm.) growth; groundcover, containers; hips red; [Green Snake® × (R. multiflora × unknown)]; intr. 1994

'Lenlitlit' (Petite Fredaine®) MinFl, op, 2000, Lens, Louis; flowers orange pink, reverse lighter, 3-4 cm., dbl., borne in small clusters, moderate fragrance; foliage medium size, medium green, semi-glossy; few prickles; growth bushy, medium (35-40 cm.); [('Little Angel' × unknown) × 'Little Angel']; intr. 1991

'Lenlitpap' ('Rosy Ann') MinFl, op, 2000, Lens, Louis; flowers orange pink, 2-3 cm., full, borne in small clusters, slight fragrance; recurrent; foliage medium size, medium green, glossy; prickles moderate; growth bushy, low (25 cm.); ['Little Angel' × 'Papillon Rose']; intr. 1993

'Lenloro' (Belgian Lace®) S, lp, 2000, Lens, Louis; flowers light pink, reverse lighter, 3-4 cm., dbl., flat, borne in small clusters; once blooming; foliage small, medium green, semi-glossy; prickles moderate; spreading, medium (80-120 cm.) growth; ['Lovania' × ('Robin Hood' × seedling)]; intr. 1994

'Lenlosan' ('Waanrode') Gr, op, 2000, Lens, Louis; flowers salmon, 10 cm., full, borne in small clusters; recurrent; foliage medium size, dark green, semi-glossy, disease-resistant; numerous prickles; upright, medium (100 cm.) growth; [((R. wichurana × Floradora) × Coloranje) × 'Papillon Rose']; intr. 1990

'Lenmacra' ('Beautiful Bride', Maria Teresa®) S, lp, 1986, Lens, Louis; flowers 28 petals, cupped, borne in clusters of 32, intense fragrance; recurrent bloom; foliage light green; prickles hooked, brownish-green; bushy growth; [seedling × R. macrantha]; intr. 1984

'Lenmagi' ('White Magic') HMsk, w, 2000, Lens, Louis; flowers white with yellow stamens, 2-3 cm., single, flat, borne in large clusters, moderate fragrance; recurrent; foliage medium size, medium green, semi-glossy, disease-resistant; prickles moderate; bushy, medium (120 cm.), arching growth; ['Ravel' × Dupontii]; intr. 1989

'Lenmagika' ('Pink Magic') HMsk, pb, 2000, Lens, Louis; flowers single, borne in large clusters, slight fragrance; recurrent; foliage large, medium green, semi-glossy; prickles moderate; upright, arching, medium (4-5 ft.) growth; [(R. multiflora adenocheata × 'Ballerina') × 'Kathleen']; intr. 1990

'Lenmar' (Maria Mathilda®) F, w, 1986, Lens, Louis; flowers white, shaded pink, small, 24 petals, borne in clusters of 3 - 24, intense fragrance; foliage very dark, glossy; prickles hooked, brownish-red; growth upright, bushy (100 cm.); ['miniature seedling' × ('New Penny' × 'Jour de Fete')]; intr. 1980

'Lenmau' (Bluesette®) MinFl, m, 1986, Lens, Louis; flowers lilac, 2 in., 50 petals, flat, borne in clusters of 3-18, slight fragrance; prickles dark green; bushy growth; ['Little Angel' × ('Westmauve' × 'Blue Diamond')]; intr. 1984

'Lenmobar' ('Vivaldi') S, mr, 1986, Lens, Louis; flowers raspberry red, 1 in., 5 petals, shallow cup, borne in clusters of 7-50; free-flowering; foliage small; prickles very hooked,greenish-brown; bushy (2 ft.), spreading growth; [(R. multiflora × unknown) × (seedling × 'Robin Hood')]; intr. 1984

'Lenmobra' (Rush®) S, pb, 1986, Lens, Louis; flowers pink, white eye, 2 in., 5 petals, borne in clusters of 3 - 32, moderate fruity fragrance; recurrent; foliage light green; prickles hooked, brownish-green; upright, bushy growth; [('Ballerina' × 'Britannia') × R. multiflora]; intr. 1983

'Lenmol' (Si Bemol®) Min, m, 1986, Lens, Louis; flowers lilac blue and white, small, 30 petals, borne in clusters of 3-24; foliage dark; prickles few, green; bushy growth; [('Little Angel' × 'Le Vesuve') × 'Mr Bluebird']; intr. 1980

'Lenmor' (Schubert®) S, pb, 1986, Lens, Louis; flowers pink, white-eye, 1 in., 5 petals, borne in clusters of 7 - 60, slight fragrance; recurrent; foliage small; prickles very hooked, greenish-brown; bushy, spreading growth; ['Ballerina' × R. multiflora]; intr. 1984

'Lenmos' ('Puccini') HMsk, lp, 2000, Lens, Louis; flowers medium pink, white center, 2 cm., single, borne in large clusters, slight fragrance; foliage medium size, medium green, semi-glossy; prickles moderate; growth upright, medium (60-80 cm.); hips globular, red; [(R. luciae × unknown) × ('Ballerina' × 'Robin Hood')]; intr. 1984

'Lenmule' (Dentelle de Bruges®) S, w, 2000, Lens, Louis; flowers white, 2-3 cm., semi-dbl., borne in large clusters, moderate fragrance; non-recurrent; foliage medium size, medium green, semi-glossy; prickles moderate; bushy, tall (5-6 ft.) growth; ['Seagull' × 'Muhle Hamsdorf']; intr. 1990

'Lennedi' ('Heavenly Pink') HMsk, mp, 2000, Lens, Louis; flowers medium pink, reverse lighter, 3-4 cm., semi-dbl., borne in large clusters, slight fragrance; recurrent; foliage medium size, medium green, semi-glossy; prickles moderate; upright, medium (100 cm.) growth; ['Seagull' × seedling]; intr. 1997

'Lenniro' (Jupon Rose®) F, op, 1986, Lens, Louis; flowers light salmon pink, 28 petals, cupped, borne in clusters of 3-24, slight fragrance; foliage dark; prickles hooked, reddish-green; upright, bushy growth; ['Little Angel' × Pernille Poulsen™]; intr. 1982

'Lennop' (Little Pim®) Min, mr, 1986, Lens, Louis; flowers small, 24 petals, rosette, borne in clusters of 3 - 32, no fragrance; foliage dark; prickles hooked, greenish-brown; bushy growth; ['miniature seedling' × 'Ruth Leuwerick']; intr. 1984

'Lenobit' ('Poesie') HMsk, pb, 1986, Lens, Louis; flowers white shaded pink, 2 in., 20 petals, borne in clusters of 5 - 32, intense fragrance; foliage large, leathery, dark; prickles hooked, light brown; bushy, spreading growth; ['Ballerina' × 'Moonlight']; intr. 1982

'Lenomina' (Omi Oswald®) HMsk, ly, 2000, Lens, Louis; flowers light yellow to cream white, reverse white, 4-5 cm., single, borne in large clusters, slight fragrance; foliage medium size, medium green, semi-glossy; prickles moderate; growth upright, medium (120 cm.); ['Ravel' × Bright Smile®]; intr. 1988

'Lenor' ('Festivity') F, ob, 1986, Lens, Louis; flowers orange, 3 in., 24 petals, borne in clusters of 3-24, slight fragrance; foliage dark; prickles hooked, green; bushy growth; [seedling × seedling]; intr. 1980

'Lenoran' (Eurosong®) HT, lp, 1986, Lens, Louis; flowers 38 petals, high-centered, borne singly or in three's, slight fragrance; foliage dark reddish-green; prickles large, brownish-red; upright growth; [(Queen Elizabeth® × seedling) × Queen Elizabeth®]; intr. 1984

'Lenpac' ('Focus', 'Sweet Bouquet') HMsk, lp, 1986, Lens, Louis; flowers small, 20 petals, borne in large clusters, intense fragrance; recurrent bloom; foliage small, dark; prickles hooked, brownish-green; spreading growth; ['Marie Pavie' × seedling]; intr. 1984

'Lenpaga' ('Paganini', Harley®) HMsk, dr, 2000, Lens; flowers dark red, 3 cm., single, borne in large clusters, slight fragrance; recurrent; foliage medium size, dark green, glossy; prickles moderate; bushy, medium (80-100 cm.) growth; hips in autumn; [Running Maid® × R. multiflora nana]; intr. 1989

'Lenpas' (Pascaline®) Min, w, 1986, Lens, Louis; flowers long lasting, 35 petals, high-centered, borne singly or in clusters, no fragrance; foliage dark gray-green; prickles slightly hooked, brownish-red; upright, bushy growth; ['miniature seedling' × ('New Penny' × 'Jour de Fete')]; intr. 1984

'Lenpasti' ('Simplicity') F, op, 2000, Lens, Louis; flowers light salmon-pink, 6 cm., semi-dbl. to dbl., cupped to flat, borne in large clusters, moderate fragrance; foliage medium size, medium green, glossy; few prickles; growth bushy, medium (60-70 cm.); ['Little Angel' × Pascali®]; intr. 1990

'Lenpen' (Jet Flame Nirpaysage®, Jet Flame®) Min, m, 1986, Lens, Louis; flowers lavender-purple, small, 30 petals, rosette, borne in clusters, no fragrance; foliage very small, brilliant dark green; no prickles; bushy, spreading growth; ['New Penny' × 'Violet Hood']; intr. 1984

'Lenpenba' ('Robe Rose') S, mp, 2000, Lens, Louis; flowers medium pink, white center, 2 cm., single, borne in large clusters, moderate fragrance; foliage medium size, medium green, semi-glossy; prickles moderate; growth spreading, low (40-50 cm.); [Serpent Vert® × 'Ballerina']; intr. 1995

'Lenpetir' (Petit Rat de l'Opéra®) HMsk, pb, 2000, Lens, Louis; flowers deep pink, reverse lighter, 2 cm., single, borne in large clusters, slight fragrance; recurrent; foliage large, medium green, semi-glossy; few prickles; upright, medium (60-90 cm.) growth; [(R. multiflora adenocheata × 'Ballerina') × 'Ballerina']; intr. 1990

'Lenphide' (Reine Chabeau®) HMsk, w, 2000, Lens, Louis; flowers creamy white, 2-3 cm., semi-dbl., borne in large, long, pyramid-shaped clusters, moderate fragrance; foliage light green, semi-glossy; prickles moderate; compact, upright, arching, medium (80-120 cm.) growth; [('Seagull' × R. multiflora nana) × R. multiflora nana]; intr. 1994

'Lenpi' (Pink Delight®) Min, lp, 2000, Lens, Louis; flowers light pink, reverse lighter, 3-4 cm., full, borne in small clusters, moderate fragrance; recurrent; foliage medium size, medium green, matte; thornless; bushy, medium (35 cm.) growth; [('Le Vesuve' × 'Rouletii' × '(New Penny × Rosenelfe)') × 'Cecile Brunner']; intr. 1982

'Lenpic' (Tache de Beauté®) F, op, 1986, Lens, Louis; flowers 2 in., 22 petals, high-centered, borne in clusters of 3-24; foliage dark; prickles hooked, brown; upright, bushy growth; ['Little Angel' × 'Picasso']; intr. 1982

'Lenplat' (Tapis Volant®) S, pb, 1986, Lens, Louis; flowers white-pink blend, 2 in., semi-dbl., borne in clusters of 7 - 35, moderate fruity fragrance; recurrent bloom; foliage reddish green; prickles hooked, reddish-brown; groundcover; spreading growth; [(R. luciae × unknown) × (R. multiflora × 'Ballerina')]; intr. 1982

'Lenpli' ('White Spray') S, w, 2000, Lens, L.; flowers 2 cm., single, borne in large clusters, very slight fragrance; recurrent; foliage small, medium green, glossy, evergreen; prickles moderate; growth spreading, low (40-60 cm.); [R. wichurana yakachinensis × R. multiflora adenocheata]; intr. 1980

'Lenpoba' ('Robe de Soie') S, lp, 2000, Lens, Louis; flowers pink, center white, reverse lighter, 3 cm., single, borne in large clusters, slight fragrance; recurrent; foliage medium size, dark green, glossy; prickles moderate; growth spreading, low (40 cm.); groundcover; [Serpent Vert® × 'Ballerina']; intr. 1996

'Lenpon' (Asterix®) Min, or, 1986, Lens, Louis; flowers small, 65 petals, flat, borne in clusters of 12-22, no fragrance; prickles hooked, brown; bushy growth; [('Little Red' × ('Little Angel' × 'Robin Hood')) × Idée Fixe®]; intr. 1980

'Lenpucciba' ('Bel Esprit') HMsk, pb, 2000, Lens, Louis; flowers pale pink, center white, reverse lighter, 3-4 cm., single, borne in large, pyramidal clusters; recurrent; foliage medium green, dull, disease-resistant; prickles moderate; upright, medium (70-100 cm.) growth; [(R. multiflora adenocheata × 'Ballerina') × 'Puccini']; intr. 1992

'Lenraba' ('Francoise Drion') HMsk, mp, 2000, Lens, Louis; flowers deep pink reverse lighter, 3-4 cm., single, borne in large clusters; recurrent; foliage large, dark green, semi-glossy; few prickles; upright, tall (4-5 ft.) growth; ['Ravel' × 'Ballerina']; intr. 1995

'Lenrag' ('Ragtime') F, r, 1986, Lens, Louis; flowers brownish red, medium, 25 petals, hybrid tea, borne in clusters of 7-18, slight fragrance; foliage brownish-green; low, bushy growth; ['Little Angel' × Goldtopas®]; intr. 1980

'Lenramp' (Running Maid®) S, m, 1986, Lens, Louis; flowers lilac-red, white eye, 2 in., 5 petals, borne in clusters of 3 - 32, intense fragrance; recurrent bloom; foliage deep reddish-green, glossy; prickles hooked, brown; spreading growth; groundcover; [R. multiflora × (R. wichurana × Violet Hood)]; intr. 1985

'Lenrav' (Ravel®) HMsk, pb, 2000, Lens, Louis; flowers medium red, yellow stamens, 3 cm., single, borne in large clusters, moderate fragrance; recurrent; foliage medium size, medium green, semi-glossy; prickles moderate; growth bushy, medium (80-120 cm.); [R. multiflora adenocheata × 'Ballerina']; intr. 1988

'Lenreho' ('Red Robin') S, rb, 2000, Lens, Louis; flowers deep pink to crimson, reverse lighter, small, semi-dbl., borne in large clusters, moderate fragrance; non-recurrent; foliage medium green, matte; prickles moderate; stems red; growth bushy, tall (200 cm.); [R. helenae × 'Robin Hood']; intr. 1992

'Lenrohi' ('Pink Robin') S, mp, 2000, Lens, Louis; flowers dbl., borne in large clusters, moderate fragrance; non-recurrent; foliage small, yellow and red to medium green, matte; few prickles; stems red; growth bushy, tall (200 cm.); [R. helenae × 'Robin Hood']; intr. 1992

'Lenros' ('White Surprise') HBc, w, 2000, Lens, Louis; flowers white, green stamens, 10-12 cm., single, borne in small clusters, moderate fragrance; foliage large, medium green, glossy, evergreen; numerous prickles; bushy, tall (200 cm.) growth; [R. bracteata × R. rugosa rubra]; intr. 1987

'Lenruba' (Giant Pink®) S, pb, 2000, Lens, Louis; flowers deep pink, white center, reverse lighter, 2 in., single, borne in large clusters; recurrent; foliage medium green, glossy; prickles moderate; upright, medium (4-5 ft.) growth; [(R. multiflora adenocheata × 'Ballerina') × Rush®]; intr. 1990

'Lenruma' ('Sharon's Love') S, lp, 2000, Lens, Louis; flowers pale pink, reverse lighter, red stamens, petals wavy, 4 in., single, flat, borne in small clusters, slight fragrance; recurrent; foliage medium size, medium green, semi-glossy; prickles moderate; growth upright, medium (120-150 cm.); ['Rudolf Timm' × 'Maria-Mathilda']; intr. 1998

'Lens Pink' -- See 'LLX8603'

'Lensilve' (Silver Pink®) F, lp, 2000, Lens, Louis; flowers medium, full, cupped, borne in large clusters; recurrent; foliage medium size, dark green, glossy; prickles moderate; growth bushy, medium (60-80 cm.); [(R. multiflora adenocheata × 'Ballerina') × Running Maid®]; intr. 1990

'Lensim' (Eagle Wings®) F, m, 1986, Lens, Louis; flowers white, shaded lilac, 2 in., 5 petals, borne in clusters of 3-24, moderate spicy fragrance; foliage very dark; prickles hooked, brown; bushy growth; [seedling × 'Picasso']; intr. 1982

'Lensiver' (Silver River®) S, w, 2000, Lens, Louis; flowers white, shaded pink, reverse white, 3 cm., single, borne in large clusters; recurrent; foliage medium size, medium green, semi-glossy; prickles moderate; growth spreading, medium (40 cm.); groundcover; [(R. multiflora adenocheata × 'Ballerina') × Running Maid®]; intr. 1989

'Lensnaba' (Serpent Rose®) S, mp, 2000, Lens, Louis; flowers single, borne in small clusters, moderate fragrance; non-recurrent; foliage small, light green, glossy; prickles moderate; growth spreading, low; groundcover; [Serpent Vert® × 'Ballerina']; intr. 1994

'Lensouran' ('Sourire d'Antan') HMsk, dp, 2000, Lens, Louis; flowers rose fuchsia, small, dbl., cupped, borne in large clusters, moderate fragrance; recurrent; foliage medium size, medium green, semi-glossy; few prickles; bushy, medium (100 cm.) growth; [(R. multiflora × R. multiflora) × 'Violet Hood']; intr. 1988

'Lenspra' (Pink Spray®) S, dp, 2000, Lens, Louis; flowers deep pink, white center, reverse deep pink, 2 cm., single, borne in large clusters, slight fragrance; non-recurrent; foliage small, dark green, glossy, disease-resistant; prickles moderate; growth spreading (60 cm.); groundcover; [*R. wichurana yakachinensis* × seedling *R. multifora adenocheata*]; intr. 1980

'Lenstebrac' ('Pink Mystery') S, do, 2000, Lens, Louis; flowers deep pink to purple, reverse lighter, 7-8 cm., single, borne in small clusters; recurrent; foliage medium size, dark green, matte; numerous prickles; growth upright, medium (80-120 cm.); [*R. stellata mirifica* × (*R. bracteata* × *R. nutkana*)]; intr. 1997

'Lensun' ('Sunnyside '83') Min, yb, 1986, Lens, Louis; flowers yellow, spotted red, small, 20 petals, borne in clusters of 3-22, moderate fruity fragrance; foliage small; prickles small, hooked, green; bushy growth; [('Little Angel' × ('Rosina' × seedling)]; intr. 1983

'Lentapo' ('Jacqueline Humery') HMsk, lp, 2000, Lens, Louis; flowers white, pink shade, reverse white, 6 cm., semi-dbl., borne in large clusters, moderate fragrance; recurrent; foliage medium size, dark green, semi-glossy; prickles moderate; bushy (80-120 cm.) growth; [(Serpent Vert® × Tapis Volant®) × ('Robe Fleurie' × 'Poesie')]; intr. 1995

'Lentini' (Tineke van Heule®) F, lp, 1986, Lens, Louis; flowers , 7-12 petals, borne in clusters of 3-12; foliage large, leathery, greenish-brown; prickles few, reddish-brown; upright, bushy growth; [seedling × City of Belfast®]; intr. 1985

'Lentribal' ('Trianon') F, pb, 2000, Lens, Louis; flowers pink with apricot, 5 cm., semi-dbl., borne in small clusters, moderate fragrance; recurrent; foliage medium size, medium green, semi-glossy; prickles moderate; bushy, medium (80 cm.) growth; [(*R. multiflora adenocheata* × 'Ballerina') × 'Buff Beauty']; intr. 1990

'Lentrichin' (Apricot Bells®) HMsk, ab, 2000, Lens, Louis; buds apricot; flowers creamy apricot to pink and darker pink, 4 cm., semi-dbl., cupped, borne in large clusters, intense fragrance; recurrent; foliage large, brown to dark green, semi-glossy; prickles moderate; upright, tall (5 ft.) growth; [Trier® × 'Mutabilis']; intr. 1999

'Lentrifel' ('Twins') HMsk, m, 2000, Lens, Louis; flowers lilac pink, fading toward cream, reverse lighter, 3-4 cm., single, borne in very long, clusters, intense fragrance; recurrent; foliage large, brown to dark green, semi-glossy; prickles moderate; growth bushy, tall (125-150 cm.); [Trier® × 'Felicia']; intr. 1994

'Lentriga' ('Yellow Light') HMsk, ly, 2000, Lens, Louis; flowers light yellow to white, reverse white, 1½-2 cm., single, borne in large, pyramidal-shaped clusters; recurrent; foliage small, medium green, semi-glossy; prickles moderate; spreading, medium (60 cm.) growth; [Trier® × 'Seagull']; intr. 1994

'Lentrihel' ('Rosalita') HMsk, w, 2000, Lens, Louis; flowers white with yellow button center, 5-6 cm., single, borne in large clusters; foliage large, brown-green and dark green, glossy; few prickles; bushy, medium (120-150 cm.) growth; [(Trier® × 'Surf Rider') × *R. helenae*]; intr. 1997

'Lentrimera' ('Plaisanterie', 'Pleasant Valley') HMsk, pb, 2000, Lens, Louis; bud orange; flowers yellow, aging to pink and dark pink, reverse lighter, 4 cm., semi-dbl., borne in large clusters, slight fragrance; foliage dark green, semi-glossy; few prickles; upright (4-5 ft.) growth; [Trier® × 'Mutabilis']; intr. 1996

'Lentrita' ('Souv de Rose-Marie') HMsk, ly, 2000, Lens, Louis; flowers ochre, changing to light yellow, reverse light yellow, 5-6 cm., single, shallow cupped, borne in large clusters, moderate fragrance; recurrent; foliage medium size, medium green, semi-glossy; prickles moderate; growth upright, medium (80-100 cm.); hedges; [Trier® × 'Mutabilis']; intr. 1998

'Lentriter' ('Sourire Rose') HMsk, lp, 2000, Lens, Louis; flowers pale pink, reverse lighter, 6-7 cm., semi-dbl., shallow cup, borne in large clusters, slight fragrance; recurrent; foliage light green, glossy, disease-resistant; few prickles; upright, tall (6 ft.) growth; [Trier® × Maria Teresa®]; intr. 1996

'Lenverba' ('Robe Fleuri') S, mp, 2000, Lens, Louis; flowers medium pink, white center, 2 cm., single, borne in large clusters, moderate fragrance; recurrent; foliage medium size, dark green, semi-glossy; prickles moderate; growth spreading, low (40-50 cm.); groundcover; [Serpent Vert® × 'Ballerina']; intr. 1995

'Lenvie' (View®) Pol, dp, 1986, Lens, Louis; flowers deep pink, 2 in., 7-15 petals, borne in clusters of 3-32, no fragrance; foliage greenish-brown; prickles hooked, brown; low, bushy growth; ['Britannia' × *R. multiflora*]; intr. 1980

'Lenvir' (White Dream®) Min, w, 1986, Lens, Louis; intr. 1982

'Lenwal' ('Walferdange') HMsk, dp, 2000, Lens, Louis; flowers deep pink, reverse lighter, 4-5 cm., dbl., cupped, borne in large clusters, moderate fragrance; recurrent; foliage medium size, medium green, semi-glossy, disease-resistant; few prickles; bushy, medium (60-80 cm.) growth; [(*R. multiflora adenocheata* × 'Ballerina') × 'Felicia']; intr. 1990

'Lenway' (Waverland®) HT, yb, 1986, Lens, Louis; flowers deep yellow, edged orange-red, large, 30 petals, high-centered, borne singly, intense fragrance; recurrent; foliage dark, leathery; prickles brown; upright, bushy growth; [Peer Gynt® × 'Peace']; intr. 1982

'Lenwich' (Green Snake®, Serpent Vert®) S, w, 1986, Lens, Louis; flowers pure white, small, 5 petals, borne in clusters of 3 - 24; non-recurrent; foliage small, spoon-shaped; prickles hooked, light brownish-green; groundcover; spreading growth; [*R. arvensis* × *R. wichurana*]; intr. 1985

'Lenwil' ('Pirouette') S, dr, 2000, Lens, Louis; flowers dark red, white center, reverse dark red, 7 cm., single, borne in small clusters, slight fragrance; recurrent; foliage medium size, medium green, semi-glossy; prickles moderate; upright, medium (4-5 ft.) growth; ['Wilhelm' × 'Picasso']; intr. 1983

'Lenyak' ('Weepy') S, pb, 2000, Lens, Louis; flowers pink, white center, reverse lighter, 2-3 cm., single, borne in large clusters, slight fragrance; recurrent; foliage small, medium green, glossy, disease-resistant; prickles moderate; growth spreading, medium (60 cm.); [*R. wichurana yakachinensis* × *R. multiflora adenocheata*]; intr. 1996

'Lenzburger Duft' HT, mr, Schaiber; flowers cardinal red, shaded violet; intr. 1985

'Leo' ('The Lion') F, mp, Burston; flowers solid pink, dbl., cupped, borne in clusters; recurrent; foliage dark green, glossy; growth medium (80 cm.); intr. 2004

'Leo Ferre' HT, rb, Adam; intr. 2006

'Leobretak' ('Breathtaking') HT, dp, 1982, Leon, Charles F., Sr.; bud ovoid, long, pointed; flowers deep pink, 40 petals, high-centered, intense damask fragrance; foliage medium to large, medium green, semi-glossy; upright, bushy growth; [('Pink Silk' × unknown) × ('Pink Parfait' × 'Wendy Cussons')]; intr. 1981

'Leocok' ('Cockle Shells') Min, pb, 1985, Leon, Charles F., Sr.; flowers pale yellow tinged deep pink, medium, 35 petals; foliage medium; bushy, spreading growth; [('Kathy Robinson' × seedling) × ('Janna' × seedling)]

'Leocrel' ('Crimson Elegance') HT, dr, 1990, Leon, Charles F., Sr.; bud rounded; flowers crimson/scarlet, crimson reverse, aging darker red, 40 petals, high-centered, borne usually singly; foliage medium size, medium green, semi-glossy; upright, bushy, tall growth; ['Big Red' × 'Swarthmore']; intr. 1990

'Leoexbeau' ('Exotic Beauty') HT, op, 1990, Leon, Charles F., Sr.; bud rounded; flowers orange blend, reverse pink blend, large, dbl., high-centered, borne usually singly, slight fruity fragrance; foliage large, dark green, glossy; upright, bushy, medium growth; ['Silver Jubilee (surmised)' × seedling]; intr. 1990

'Leofire' ('Forest Fire') Min, or, 1985, Leon, Charles F., Sr.; flowers medium, dbl.; foliage medium size, medium to dark, semi-glossy; bushy growth; [((('Sheri Anne' × Starina®) × ('Persian Princess' × Starina®)) × (('Sheri Anne' × 'Persian

Princess') × Starina®)]

'Leoglo' ('Glorious') HT, ab, 1985, Leon, Charles F., Sr.; flowers medium pink tinted apricot, well-formed, large, 37 petals; foliage medium to large, medium green, semi-glossy; upright, bushy growth; [seedling × 'Mirato']

'Leolavblu' ('Lavender Blue') HT, m, 1982, Leon, Charles F., Sr.; flowers lavender, darker edges, large, dbl., high-centered; foliage medium size, dark, semi-glossy; upright, bushy growth; ['Silver Star' × 'Kolner Karneval']

'Leoloyros' ('Loyal Rosarian') HT, mr, 1990, Leon, Charles F., Sr.; bud ovoid; flowers medium red becoming darker red as it ages, large, 36-42 petals, high-centered, borne usually singly; foliage medium size, leathery, green; upright, bushy, tall growth; large fruit, germinates rapidly; ['Red Planet' × 'Red Devil (surmised)']; intr. 1990

'Léon Chenault' HT, pb, 1931, Pernet-Ducher; flowers carmine-rose shaded salmon, base deeper, very large, dbl.; foliage dark; very vigorous growth

'Léon de Bruyn' T, ly, 1895, Soupert & Notting; flowers light yellow with darker center, large, full, moderate fragrance

'Léon Delaville' HP, dr, 1885, Verdier, E.; flowers dark red strongly shaded carmine, tinted violet crimson, large, full; foliage dark green

'Léon Lecomte' D, dp, about 1854; flowers warm pink, fading paler, darker veins, large, full, moderate fragrance

'Léon Oursel' B, dp, 1847, Oger; flowers large, full

'Léon Renault' HP, mr, 1878, Lédéchaux; flowers cherry-red, reverse tinted carmine, very large, very dbl.

'Léon Robichon' HP, w, 1901, Robichon; flowers large, dbl.

'Léon Say' HT, rb, 1882, Lévêque; flowers bright red shaded brown, light pink, and lilac pink, very large, moderate centifolia fragrance; foliage large, thick, glaucous green

'Léon XIII' T, w, 1892, Soupert & Notting; flowers white, with shades of straw yellow, center ochre, large, full; foliage large; growth vigorous; ['Anna Olivier' × 'Earl of Eldon']

'Leona' F, mp, Noack; flowers 2 in., semi-dbl., borne in clusters; good repeat; growth to 2 ft.; intr. 2004

'Leonard Barron' HT, op, 1931, Nicolas; bud pointed; flowers salmon-copper and shell-pink, very large, dbl., moderate fragrance; foliage leathery; bushy growth; ['Schoener's Nutkana' × 'Souv. de Mme Boullet']

'Leonard Cheshire' HT, mr

'Leonard Dudley Braithwaite' -- See 'Auscrim'

Leonardo de Vinci® -- See 'Meideauri'

'Léonce Colombier' HT, mr, 1943, Meilland, F.; bud oval; flowers brilliant geranium-red, stamens yellow, medium, dbl., cupped; foliage leathery; very vigorous, bushy growth; ['Charles P. Kilham' × ('Charles P. Kilham' × 'Capucine Chambard')]

'Leonhart' ('Heart Throb') HT, mr, 1982, Leon, Charles F., Sr.; flowers 37 petals, high-centered, borne singly and several together, moderate damask fragrance; foliage medium to large, medium green, leathery; vigorous, bushy, tall growth; [Norita® × ((Norita® × seedling) × Papa Meilland®)]

'Leonidas' -- See 'Meicofum'

Leonie™ -- See 'Poulra019(N)'

'Leonie' ('Dazzler') F, mp, 1964, Leenders, J.; flowers dbl.; vigorous growth; [Queen Elizabeth® × 'Circus']

'Léonie Lambert' HP, lp, 1913, Lambert, P.; flowers silver-pink, shaded yellow and flesh, well-shaped, large, moderate fragrance; very vigorous growth; ['Frau Karl Druschki' × 'Prince de Bulgarie']

'Léonie Lamesch' ('Mme Léonie Lamesch') Pol, ob, 1899, Lambert, P.; flowers light coppery red, center yellow, edges flecked darker, semi-dbl.; foliage rich green, soft; vigorous, bushy growth; ['Aglaia' × 'Kleiner Alfred']

'Léonie Lartay' HP, mr, 1860, Lartay; flowers bright scarlet, large, full

'Léonie Osterrieth' T, w, 1892, Soupert & Notting; flowers porcelain white with very light yellow center, large, full, borne in large clusters, moderate fragrance; ['Sylphide' × 'Mme Bravy']

'Leonie Parade' (Leonie™) MinFl, mr, Olesen; bud pointed ovoid; flowers medium red, 2 in., 13-15 petals, cupped, borne mostly singly, slight fragrance; recurrent; foliage dark green, matte; prickles some, 3 mm., yellow-green, hooked downward; bushy, compact (20-40 cm.) growth; PP15573; [sport of 'Heidi Parade']; intr. 2001

'Léonor de March' HT, dr, 1958, Camprubi, C.; bud long, pointed; flowers deep blood-red, large, dbl., moderate fragrance; foliage glossy; upright growth; ['J.M. Lopez Pico' × 'Poinsettia']; intr. 1956

'Léonora' HT, mr, 1921, Paul, W.; flowers brilliant velvety red, center brighter, dbl.

'Leonorah' -- See 'Rawguapa'

Leonore Annenberg™ -- See 'Wilannb'

'Leonoro' ('Solid Gold') HT, my, 1982, Leon, Charles F., Sr.; flowers golden yellow, large, 36 petals, borne 3-6 per cluster; foliage dark, glossy; vigorous growth; [(('Royal Gold' × unknown) × Golden Giant®) × ('Bright Gold' × ('Phyllis Gold' × unknown))]

'Léontine Contenot' HT, yb, 1935, Ketten Bros.; bud pointed; flowers sunflower-yellow bordered pink and yellow, large, 45-50 petals, high-centered; foliage quaker green; vigorous growth; ['Joanna Hill' × 'Souv. de Claudius Pernet']

'Léontine Gervais' HWich, ab, 1903, Barbier; bud coppery red; flowers salmon-orange and yellow, 5 cm., semi-dbl., borne in clusters of 3-10, moderate fragrance; non-recurrent; foliage dark, glossy; very vigorous, climbing growth; [R. wichurana × 'Souv. de Catherine Guillot']

'Léopold Hausburg' HP, pb, 1863, Granger; flowers carmine, shaded purple to dark garnet, large, full

'Léopold Lambotte' HT, mr, 1944, Meilland, F.; bud long, pointed; flowers scarlet-red; very tall growth; ['Grenoble' × 'National Flower Guild']

'Léopold Premier' -- See 'Léopold I'

'Leopold Ritter' HMult, mr, about 1900, Geschwind, R.; flowers brilliant velvety red, aging to purplish crimson, medium, semi-dbl., borne in small clusters; somewhat recurrent; foliage large; numerous prickles

'Léopold I' ('Léopold I, Roi des Belges', 'Léopold Premier') HP, dr, 1863, Van Asche; flowers deep red, well-formed, large, dbl.; ['Général Jacqueminot' × unknown]

'Léopold I, Roi des Belges' -- See 'Léopold I'

'Leopold II' HP, lp, 1868, Margottin; flowers light pink, shaded salmon, very large, full, cupped

'Léopoldine' M, lp, Robert; flowers bright flesh pink, medium, full; intr. 1850

'Léopoldine' P, lp, 1826, Toutain; flowers flesh pink, tinted violet

'Léopoldine d'Orléans' HSem, w, 1828, Jacques; flowers white, shaded rose, medium, dbl.

'Leora Stewart' HT, op, Wilber; long continued bloom

'Leosilmu' ('Silvery Moon') HT, m, 1982, Leon, Charles F., Sr.; flowers lilac, large, 35 petals; foliage medium size, medium green, leathery, matte; upright growth; ['Silver Star' × Blue Moon®]; intr. 1981

'Leostra' ('Strawberry Sundae') Min, w, 1985, Leon, Charles F., Sr.; flowers ivory flushed pink, medium, 35 petals; foliage medium size, light to medium green, semi-glossy; bushy, spreading growth; [('Kathy Robinson' × seedling) × ('Kathy Robinson' × seedling)]

'Leotilde Minguez' HT, rb, 1961, Dot, Pedro; flowers carmine, shaded vermilion and yellow, large, 30 petals; upright growth; ['Pres. Herbert Hoover' × 'Vicky Marfá']

'Leotoelg' ('Touch of Elegance') Min, w, 1989, Leon, Charles F., Sr.; bud pointed; flowers white with creamy yellow center, large, dbl., high-centered, borne singly and in small clusters; foliage medium size, medium green, semi-glossy; upright, tall growth; [('Gavotte' × 'Buccaneer') × 'miniature seedling']; intr. 1987

'Leovelv' ('Touch of Velvet') HT, rb, 1989, Leon, Charles F., Sr.; bud pointed, long; flowers magenta red with lighter tones, 31 petals, high-centered, borne usually singly and in small clusters, moderate fragrance; foliage medium size, dark green, semi-glossy; upright, tall growth; [('First Prize' × 'Gypsy') × seedling]; intr. 1987

'Leprechaun' F, yb, 1972, Adams, M.R.; bud ovoid; flowers red, reverse yellow, small, dbl., globular, moderate fragrance; foliage glossy; growth moderate, upright; [('Easter Parade' × 'Masquerade') × 'Little Darling']

'L'Ermite' Ch, about 1826, from Angers

'Lerna' F, rb; intr. 2004

'Les Amis de Lille' HT, pb, 1928, Ketten Bros.; bud lincoln red on pale buff ground; flowers pale buff, edges and reverse suffused salmon-pink; ['Golden Emblem' × 'Pres. Bouche']

'Les Amis de Troyes' HT, mp, 1935, Vially; flowers China-pink, passing to carmine-pink, base ochre-yellow, well-formed, dbl.; vigorous growth; ['Feu Joseph Looymans' × seedling]

Les Amoureux de Peynet® ('Efekto 21', 'Simply Magic') F, dp, Meilland; flowers rose-carmine, medium, dbl., borne in large clusters; good repeat; foliage dark green, matte; growth to 50 cm.; intr. 1992

'Les Quatre Saisons' S, mp; flowers very dbl., pompon; intr. 2003

'Les Rosati' HFt, rb, 1906, Gravereaux; bud dark pink; flowers bright carmine, center yellow, medium, full

Les Sables d'Olonne® HT, ob, Dorieux; flowers nasturtium orange with touch of gold, petal edges darker, double, high-centered; recurrent; vigorous growth; intr. 2001

'Les Saisons d'Italie' HGal, mr; flowers carmine-red, medium, very dbl.

'Les Sjulin' Gr, pb, 1981, Buck, Dr. Griffith J.; flowers coral pink, reverse light red, 28 petals, urn-shaped to imbricated, moderate old rose fragrance; foliage medium size, dark olive green, leathery; prickles awl-like; erect, bushy growth; ['Country Dancer' × (('Dornroschen' × 'Peace') × Pink Peace®)]

'Les Sylphides' HT, op, 1960, Watkins Roses; flowers pink shading to yellow and orange, well-shaped; foliage reddish; long stems; very vigorous growth; [sport of 'Margaret']

'Les Trois Mages' ('Gentil') HGal, mp, 1823, Gentil; flowers medium, very full, borne in clusters of 3; sometimes classed as a D

Lesbos® LCl, op, Peden, R.

'Lesdain' HT, ob, RvS-Melle; [Roklea® × Candia™]; intr. 1989

'Lesja Jean' HT, lp, 1990, Weddle, Von C.; bud pointed; flowers large, 37 petals, high-centered, borne usually singly; foliage medium size, medium green, semi-glossy; prickles medium, light; upright, medium growth; [seedling × seedling]; intr. 1989

'Lesja Ukrajinka' HT, lp, Lempickij; flowers medium, dbl.; intr. 1964

'Lesley Anne' -- See 'Fryminiles'

'Lesley Dudley' ('Leslie Dudley') HT, op, 1932, McGredy; flowers warm carmine-pink shaded orange, well-shaped, large, dbl.; foliage dark; vigorous, bushy growth

'Lesley Johns' -- See 'Leslie Johns'

'Leslie' -- See 'Tinleslie'

'Leslie Dudley' -- See 'Lesley Dudley'

'Leslie Evans' HT, dr, 1927, Evans; flowers rich dark velvety crimson, semi-dbl.; vigorous growth; ['J.B. Clark' × 'Red-Letter Day']

'Leslie G. Harris' HT, mr, 1970, Gregory; flowers crimson-scarlet, pointed, 4 in., 27 petals; moderate growth

'Leslie Holland' HT, dr, 1911, Dickson, H.; flowers deep velvety crimson, large, dbl.

'Leslie Johns' ('Lesley Johns') HT, dp, 1973, Gregory; flowers Persian rose, 5-6 in., 32 petals, high-centered, moderate fragrance; foliage dark, glossy; ['Soraya' × unknown]; intr. 1972

'Leslie Pidgeon' HT, ob, 1922, Dickson, H.; flowers orange-buff, suffused terra-cotta, semi-dbl.

'Leslie Wheal' F, yb, 1978, Buss; bud ovoid; flowers cream-yellow, 1½ in., 25-35 petals, cupped; foliage light green; compact growth; [sport of 'Zorina']

'Leslie's Dream' -- See 'Dicjoon'

'L'Esperance' HP, pb, 1871, Lartay (or Fontaine); flowers light carmine, changing to rose with cherry red, large, dbl., flat

'Lessing' HMsk, rb, 1914, Lambert, P.; flowers reddish-rose streaked white, center citron-yellow, small, dbl.; foliage large, light; [Trier® × 'Entente Cordiale']

'Lest We Forget' F, mr, Matthews; flowers vibrant red, borne in clusters; repeats well; shrubby, compact (80 cm.) growth; intr. 2000

'Lestra Hibberd' HT, dy, 1935, Joseph H. Hill, Co.; bud dark yellow; flowers amber-yellow to orange-yellow, large, dbl., moderate fragrance; foliage leathery; strong stems; vigorous, compact growth; PP156; ['Joanna Hill' × 'Sweet Adeline']

'Lesueur' P, m, 1853, Robert; flowers violety red pink, 7-9 cm., full, cupped, borne in clusters; foliage dark green

Let Freedom Ring™ -- See 'Wekearman'

'Letchworth Centenary' S, mp, Harkness; flowers 2½ in., very dbl., borne in large, abundant clusters, moderate fragrance; continuous bloom; foliage glossy, light green; growth mounded, 2 × 2 ft.; bedding, borders; intr. 2004

Letchworth Garden City® -- See 'Harkover'

'L'Étincelante' HP, mr, 1891, Vigneron; flowers bright red, somewhat velvety within, large, full, cupped

'Letitia' HT, dr, 1949, Bees; bud long, pointed; flowers crimson, 5-6 in., 35 petals; foliage dark; very vigorous growth; ['Crimson Glory' × 'Southport']

'Letizia' -- See 'Baritzia'

'Letizia' Gr, Cazzaniga, F. G.; intr. 1962

'Letizia Bianca' HBanksiae, w, Mansuino; flowers pure white, 1½ in., dbl., high-centered, borne mostly solitary, slight fragrance; foliage small, medium green, semi-glossy; growth upright, small (24 in.); intr. 1963

'Letkis' -- See 'John Dijkstra'

'Letlyda' ('Lyda Rose') S, w, Lettunich, Kleine; intr. 1994

'L'Etna' Ch, mp, 1825, Laffay, M.; flowers pink, becoming brighter, medium, very dbl.

'Letrob' ('Aptos') HMsk, ab, Lettunich; intr. 1996

'Letsilk' ('Silk Butterflies') Ch, mp, Lettunich; intr. 1992

'Letty Coles' T, w, 1876, Coles/Keynes; flowers white, center pink; [sport of 'Mme Mélanie Willermoz']

'Leuchtfeuer' ('President Taft') HCh, mr, 1909, Türke; flowers bright red, large, full, moderate fragrance; ['Gruss an Teplitz' × 'Cramoisi Superieur']; sometimes classed as B

'Leuchtstern' HMult, pb, Kiese; flowers deep rose pink, center white, 3-4 cm., single, borne in clusters of 10-30; growth to 8-10 ft.; ['Daniel Lacombe' × 'Crimson Rambler']; intr. 1899

Leventina® HT, w, Huber; intr. 1984

'L'Évêque' -- See 'Le Rosier Évêque'

'Leverkusen' HKor, ly, 1956, Kordes; bud long, pointed; flowers clear lemon yellow, crinkly petals, dbl., borne in small clusters; recurrent bloom; foliage small, medium green, glossy; vigorous, creeper or pillar (to 8 ft.) growth; [R. kordesii × 'Golden Glow']

'Leverson-Gower' -- See 'Leweson-Gower'

'Leveson-Gower' -- See 'Leweson-Gower'

'Levfamagnes' ('Agnes My Oh!') F, ab, 2005, Michelle L. LeVan-Steklenski; flowers apricot blend, reverse light creamy apricot, 3½ in., dbl., borne mostly solitary; foliage medium size, medium green, semi-glossy; prickles small, straight and narrow, light green, moderate; growth compact, medium (3-4 ft.); hedge, garden decoration; [Fame™ × 'Anthony Meilland']; intr. 2007

'Levianthan' ; ['Great Venture' × 'Fritz Thiedemann']

'Levsplen' ('Splendid!') S, pb, 2008, LeVan-Steklenski, Michelle L.; flowers white with pink edges, reverse white, stamens form a bold red dot in the center of the bloom, 1½ in., semi-dbl, borne in small clusters; foliage small, medium green, semi-glossy; prickles 3-4 mm., narrow, tent-shaped, tan, moderate; growth compact, medium (3 × 3 ft.,); ['Small Miracle' × 'Simply Marvelous']; intr. 2008

'Leweson-Gower' ('Leverson-Gower', 'Leveson-Gower', 'Malmaison Rose', 'Souv de la Malmaison Rose') B, op, 1845, Béluze; flowers rose shaded

salmon, very large, dbl., cupped
'Lewiston' HT, my, 1982, Perry, Astor; flowers pointed, large, very dbl., high-centered, borne singly, intense fruity fragrance; foliage large, glossy; vigorous, tall growth; ['Red Lion' × King's Ransom®]
'Lexadama' HT, dr, Voom, Lex
'Lexaelat' HT, lp, Voom, Lex; intr. 2004
'Lexalleb' (Bella Vita+) HT, w, Voom, Lex; intr. 2005
'Lexani' HT, w, Voom, Lex; intr. 2004
'Lexannod' HT, ab, Voom, Lex; intr. 2004
'Lexativas' HT, my, Voom, Lex
'Lexatseif' HT, yb, Voom, Lex
'Lexecaf' HT, m, Voom, Lex
'Lexgnok' (King Kong+) HT, ab, Voom, Lex
'Lexhcaep' HT, ab, Van de Berg Roses; intr. 2007
'Lexie' Pol, Miers, A.
Lexington™ ('Kinpai', Golden Cover™, Sparkling Yellow™, Suffolk™, Yellow Cover™) S, my; flowers medium yellow, fading lighter, 5-8 cm., dbl., pompon, borne in clusters, slight wild rose fragrance; recurrent; foliage dark green, glossy; broad, bushy (60-100 cm.) growth; hips none
'Lexistym' HT, w, Tantau, M.; intr. 1998
'Lexjori' HT, w, Voom, Lex; intr. 2007
'Lexmei' HT, w, Voom, Lex
'Lexmied' HT, op, Voom, Lex
'Lexmuc' HT, op, Voom, Lex
'Lexode' HT, ab, Voom, Lex
'Lexohcam' HT, w, Voom, Lex
'Lexoris' HT, ob, Voom, Lex
'Lexplut' HT, ly, Voom, Lex
'Lexsara' F, dy, Voom, Lexdouble
'Lexteews' HT, lp, Voom, Lex; intr. 2006
'Lexus' Min, mp, Benardella, Frank; intr. 2004
'Lexy' S, mp, Clements, John; flowers old-fashioned, English style, 3 in., 70 petals, borne in clusters of 12 - 15, slight fragrance; foliage dark green, glossy; vigorous (5-6 ft.) growth; intr. 2000
'Ley's Perpetual' Cl HT, ly, 1936, Ley; bud apricot yellow; flowers pale yellow, fading to buff/cream, 4 in., dbl., cupped, moderate fragrance; vigorous, climbing (to 15 ft.) growth; intr. 1936
'Lheritieranea' -- See 'Boursault Rose'
'Li Burés' HT, rb, 1929, Dot, Pedro; flowers rose-red and yellow mixed (very variable), dbl., cupped; very vigorous, bushy growth; ['Château de Clos Vougeot' × 'Souv. de Claudius Pernet']
'Li Schluter' HT, Moreira da Silva, A.
'Li-Ying' HCh, w, Dening; bud creamy pink; flowers white with yellow stamens, small, semi-dbl., shallow cup, borne in sprays; modest (2 ft.) growth; [R. chinensis minima × unknown]; intr. 2007
'Lia' Min, or
'Lia' HT, pb, 1909, Ketten; flowers rosy scarlet, reverse crimson-pink, base of petals Indian yellow, medium to large, full; ['Farbenkönigin' × 'Mme Ravary']

'Liaison' -- See 'Wilpete'
Liane® LCl, ob, Cocker; flowers salmon pink, fading to pinkish-yellow, 5 in., high-centered, borne mostly solitary; foliage dark green, glossy; intr. 1989
'Liane des Champs' dp; flowers clear pink, semi-dbl. to dbl.; once bloomer; foliage glossy; vigorous (10 m.) growth; [sport of 'chance seedling']
'Lianne Reynolds' -- See 'Reylianne'
'Libby' Min, rb, 1979, Rovinski & Meredith; bud ovoid; flowers white, edged red, 1-1½ in., 20 petals, high-centered, then flat; foliage glossy; upright, compact growth; PP4597; ['Overture' × 'Perla de Alcañada']; intr. 1978
'Libby's Gold' HT, yb, 1977, Carpenter; bud long, slender; flowers 5 in., very dbl.; foliage dark; upright, compact growth; [sport of 'Apollo']
'Liberté' ('Crimson Masse') F, dr, 1946, Leenders, M.; flowers brilliant crimson-red, large, dbl.; ['Florentina' × seedling]
Liberty™ -- See 'Poulberty'
'Liberty' HT, dr, 1900, Dickson, A.; flowers brilliant velvety crimson, large, dbl., intense fragrance; foliage dark; vigorous growth; ['Mrs W.J. Grant' × 'Charles J. Grahame']
'Liberty, Climbing' Cl HT, dr, 1908, May; flowers velvety crimson; [sport of 'Liberty']
'Liberty Bell' -- See 'Benpete'
'Liberty Bell' ('Damas de Yuste', 'Freiheitsglocke') HT, rb, 1968, Kordes, R.; flowers claret-rose, reverse light cream, 5 in., 50 petals, globular, moderate fragrance; foliage leathery; vigorous growth; ['Detroiter' × 'Kordes' Perfecta']; intr. 1963
'Liberty Miss' -- See 'Ziplib'
'Liberty Parade' (Liberty™) MinFl, ob, Poulsen; flowers orange in heart with paler outer petals, 5-8 cm., dbl., slight wild rose fragrance; foliage dark; growth bushy, 20-40 cm.; PP13103; intr. 2000
'Libia' HT, w, 1934, Borgatti, G.; flowers milk-white, center creamy yellow, large, very dbl.; vigorous growth
'Libra' Min, dp, Burston; intr. 2004
'Librarian' F, m, Kaneko; intr. 2002
'Libre Ingenue' -- See 'Delciste'
'Libretto' LCl, w
'Libretto' HT, dp, 1967, Verschuren, A.; bud ovoid; flowers pink-red, medium, dbl., borne in clusters; foliage dark; ['Elli Knab' × seedling]; intr. 1966
'Lichfield Angel' -- See 'Ausrelate'
'Lichtblick' S, yb, VEG; flowers yellow and pink, large, dbl.; intr. 1972
Lichterloh® HMsk, mr, 1959, Tantau, Math.; bud ovoid; flowers velvety blood-red, semi-dbl., borne in clusters; foliage leathery, dark, glossy; vigorous, upright (3 ft.) growth; ['Red Favorite' × 'New Dawn']; intr. 1955
Lichtkönigin Lucia® -- See 'Korlilub'
'Licorice Twist' -- See 'Devlicor'
'Lída Baarová' ('Lida Paar') HT, mp, 1934, Böhm, J.; bud pointed; flowers

rosy salmon, large, dbl., cupped; foliage glossy; vigorous, bushy growth; ['Ophelia' × unknown]
'Lida O' -- See 'Bisyel'
'Lida Paar' -- See 'Lída Baarová'
'L'Idéal' N, mr, 1887, Nabonnand, G.; flowers geranium to turkey-red, base Indian yellow, semi-dbl.; vigorous, climbing growth
'Lidice' F, or, Wheatcroft; flowers large, dbl.; intr. 1961
'Lidka' HT, mr, Urban, J.
'Lidka Böhm' -- See 'Lidka Böhmova'
'Lidka Böhmova' ('Lidka Böhm') HT, mp, 1929, Böhm, J.; flowers salmon-pink, tips veined reddish, base golden yellow, large, dbl.; foliage soft, bronze; very vigorous, bushy growth; [sport of 'Una Wallace']
'Lido di Roma' -- See 'Delgap'
'Lie de Vin' HGal, dr, before 1815, Descemet; flowers wine red
'Liebesbote' HT, dr, 1935, Weigand, C.; bud pointed; flowers velvety dark red, very large, dbl., high-centered; foliage soft; very vigorous, bushy growth; ['Hadley' × 'Miss C.E. van Rossem']
'Liebeserklärung' HT, mr, Horstmann; flowers large, dbl.; intr. 1968
'Liebesglut' -- See 'Crimson King'
'Liebeslied' -- See 'Love Song'
Liebeslied® ('Sweet Sensation') F, lp, Noack, Werner; flowers soft pastel pink, 3 in., 30 petals, cupped to flat, borne in clusters, slight fragrance; recurrent; foliage glossy; growth medium; intr. 1990
'Liebestraum' ('Red Queen') HT, mr, 1968, Kordes; bud ovoid; flowers large, dbl.; foliage dark; vigorous, upright growth; ['Colour Wonder' × 'Liberty Bell']
Liebeszauber® -- See 'Kormiach'
'Liebeszauber' ('Charme d'Amour') HT, mr, 1959, Kordes; flowers velvety red, large, cupped; foliage dark; vigorous, upright growth; ['Detroiter' × 'Crimson King']
'Lied' -- See 'Bouquet'
'Lien Budde' -- See 'Caroline Budde'
Liesbeth Canneman® F, dy, Interplant; intr. 1997
'Liesbeth van Engelen' HT, w, 1960, Verschuren, A.; flowers creamy white edged lilac-pink, dbl.; foliage dark, glossy; upright growth; ['Briarcliff' × seedling]
'Liésis' -- See 'Céline Forestier'
'Lieutenant Chauré' HT, dr, 1909, Pernet-Ducher; flowers velvety crimson-red, shaded garnet, very large, dbl., cupped; foliage rich green, leathery; vigorous, bushy growth; ['Liberty' × Étoile de France']
'Lieutenant Colonel A. Fairrie' HT, my, 1930, Bees; bud pointed; flowers primrose, base deep yellow large, dbl., high-centered, moderate apple fragrance; ['Rev. F. Page-Roberts' × 'Mme Ravary']
'Lieutenant Colonel Desmaires' F, ob, 1967, Boerner; bud ovoid; flowers orange and yellow, dbl., borne in clusters;

foliage leathery; vigorous, low growth; ['Rondo' × ('Fashion' × unknown)]

'Lieve Louise' S, pb, Lens; bud slim; flowers pink on the outer half of the petals, with white in the center, single to semi-dbl., flat, borne in large clusters, slight fragrance; free-flowering; growth to 4 ft.; intr. 2002

'Lieven Gevaert' HT, mr, 1976, Delforge; bud ovoid; flowers dbl., 30 petals, moderate fragrance; foliage dark; intr. 1974

'Liewe Heksie' S, r, Ludwig; intr. 2003

'Liezl de Swardt' HT, ab; intr. 2003

'Life Begins at 40' -- See 'Horhohoho'

'Life Lines' -- See 'Sprolife'

'Lifeboat Jubilee' HT, mr, 1974, Sanday, John; flowers scarlet, shaded crimson, 4 in., 20 petals, high-centered; ['Karl Herbst' × ('Karl Herbst' × 'Crimson Glory')]

Lifestyle™ -- See 'Mordarain'

'Lifestyle' F, pb, Malanseuns; flowers strong pink with silvery pink reverse , cupped , borne in clusters; recurrent; stems short; tall growth

'Lifestyle' F, lp, Bell, Laurie; flowers dusky, soft pink, old-fashioned, moderate fragrance; medium growth

'Lifirane' HT, mp, 1976, Zwemstra; flowers Neyron rose, 3 in., 20-25 petals, high-centered; foliage dull; vigorous, upright growth; PP4034; [sport of 'Sweet Promise']

'Liga' HRg, lp, Rieksta; flowers soft pink in center, fading to white on outer petals, large, dbl., loose, moderate fragrance; recurrent; growth 3-5 ft. tall and wide

Light™ MinFl, my, Poulsen; flowers medium yellow, 5-8 cm., dbl., no fragrance; growth bushy, 20-40 cm.; PP13425; intr. 2000

'Light Editor McFarland' HT, lp, 1950, Thomasville Nursery; [sport of 'Editor McFarland']

'Light Fantastic' F, ly, Dickson; flowers light creamy lemon, full, cupped, borne in clusters, slight fragrance; recurrent; foliage dense, medium green, glossy; bushy, medium growth; intr. 2007

Light My Fire™ -- See 'Jacorflo'

Light of Day™ -- See 'Savibunda'

'Light Orlando' ('Orlando Sport') HT, pb; flowers light pink with light yellow reverse, pointed petals, large, dbl., high-centered; foliage glossy; stems long; [sport of 'Orlando']; intr. 2004

'Light Touch' S, pb, 1997, Weatherly, Lilia; flowers medium, dbl., borne in large clusters; foliage medium size, light green, very glossy; growth bushy, tall (2 m.); ['Cousin Essie' × unknown]

'Lighten Up' -- See 'Brilight'

Lights of Broadway™ -- See 'Savalights'

'Ligia' HT, Moreira da Silva, A.

'Ligne d'Arenberg' HT, w, 1903, Soupert & Notting; ['Souv du President Carnot' × 'Golden Gate']

'Lijiang Rose' HG, mp; flowers pink with shades of apricot and bronze, large, dbl., borne mostly singly, pendulous, moderate fragrance

'Lijnbaanroos' F, ly, 1961, Buisman, G. A. H.; bud yellow; flowers creamy yellow, semi-dbl., borne in clusters; foliage dark; vigorous, upright growth; ['Schneewittchen' × 'Koningin Juliana']

Li'l Alleluia™ -- See 'Kinlu'

'Lil' Rebel' -- See 'Sprorebel'

Li'l Rip™ -- See 'Mogarip'

Li'l Touch™ -- See 'Mogatouch'

'Lila' Pol, Miers, A.

'Lila Banks' -- See 'Riplila'

'Lila Queen of Bermuda' HT, m, Strnad, J.; flowers lilac-pink, large, dbl.; intr. 1970

'Lila Tan' HT, m, 1961, Dot, Pedro; flowers violet-cobalt, medium, 30 petals; vigorous, spreading growth; ['Grey Pearl' × 'Simone']

'Lila Vidri' HT, m, 1959, Dot, Simon; bud pointed; flowers lilac, 30 petals, exhibition, moderate fragrance; stems strong; upright, compact growth; [(seedling × 'Prelude') × 'Rosa de Friera']; intr. 1958

'Lila Zwerg' -- See 'Helzwerg'

'Lilac Airs' -- See 'Sanlilac'

'Lilac Belle' HT, m, Bell, Laurie; bud long, elegant; flowers soft lilac, dbl., well-formed, moderate fragrance; stems long; tall growth

'Lilac Castle' -- See 'Poulcs006(N)'

'Lilac Charm' F, m, 1962, LeGrice; bud pointed; flowers pastel mauve, anthers golden, filaments red, 4 in., 5-8 petals, flat, borne in clusters, moderate fragrance; foliage dark; upright, compact growth; PP2189; intr. 1961

'Lilac Chrysler Imperial' HT, m, Strnad

'Lilac Dawn' F, m, 1964, Swim, H. C.; bud pointed; flowers lavender-pink to lilac, 2½ in., 43 petals, borne in clusters, moderate lilac fragrance; foliage leathery, light green, vigorous, bushy growth; PP2225; ['Lavender Pinocchio' × 'Frolic']; intr. 1964

'Lilac Dream' F, m; intr. 2005

'Lilac Festival' MinFl, m, 2007, Read, Allan; flowers 6.3 cm., very full, borne in large clusters; foliage medium, medium green, semi-glossy; prickles medium, hooked, brown, few; growth upright, medium (70 cm.); ['Heartbreaker' × 'Sarah Anne']; intr. 2007

'Lilac Joseph Guy' Pol, m, Strnad

'Lilac Magic Carpet' S, m; groundcover

'Lilac Minimo' Min, m; flowers lilac mauve; growth 40 - 60 cm. height; intr. 1997

'Lilac Mystery' -- See 'Jacliang'

'Lilac Queen Elizabeth' Gr, m

Lilac Rose™ -- See 'Auslilac'

'Lilac Rose' HT, lp, 1964, Sanday, John; flowers soft silver pink with lilac shading, 5 in., 30 petals, moderate fragrance; foliage dark; vigorous, upright growth; ['Karl Herbst' × 'Chrysler Imperial']; intr. 1962

'Lilac Snow' HT, w, 1985, Williams, H.; flowers white, strong lilac tinge to inside petals; [sport of 'Admiral Rodney']

'Lilac Time' Min, m, 1955, Moore, Ralph S.; flowers lilac-pink to light red, becoming lilac tinted, small, dbl.; dwarf (10 in.) growth; ['Violette' × 'Zee']

'Lilac Time' HT, m, McGredy, Sam IV; flowers lilac, large, 33 petals, high-centered, moderate fragrance; foliage light green; growth moderate; ['Golden Dawn' × 'Luis Brinas']; intr. 1956

'Lilet Dot' F, Dot, Simon; intr. 1987

'Lilette Mallerin' HT, m, 1937, Mallerin, C.; bud pointed, yellow; flowers mauve-red to mauve pink, deepening in cooler weather, reverse yellow, dbl., cupped; foliage glossy; vigorous growth; ['Charles P. Kilham' × (R. foetida bicolor × unknown)]

'Lilette Mallerin Improved' HT, m, 1942, J&P; bud pointed; flowers mauve-red, reverse yellow, large, 25 petals, high-centered; foliage bronze, glossy; vigorous, upright, bushy growth; [sport of 'Lilette Mallerin']

'Lili Dieck' HRg, mr, 1899, Dieck; flowers rose-pink, tinted lilac, petals often striped with white, medium, semi-dbl., flat, borne in small clusters; medium (5 ft.) growth; intr. 1899

'Lili Marlene' -- See 'Korlima'

'Lilian' HT, dy, 1931, Cant, B. R.; flowers golden yellow, very large, dbl., cupped; foliage bronze, glossy; vigorous, bushy growth; RULED EXTINCT 12/85

Lilian Austin® S, pb, 1981, Austin, David; bud globular; flowers 33 petals, flat, borne 1-5 per cluster, moderate fragrance; foliage glossy, dark; prickles hooked, brown; spreading growth; ['Aloha' × 'The Yeoman']; intr. 1973

'Lilian Baylis' -- See 'Hardeluxe'

'Lilian Bootle' HT, dp, 1972, Bootle; flowers cerise, 4½-5 in., 35 petals, high-centered, moderate fragrance; foliage matte green; compact, bushy growth; ['Margaret' × 'seedling (red)']

'Lilian Doris' HT, mr, 2002, Poole, Lionel; flowers full, borne mostly solitary; foliage medium size, medium green, semi-glossy; prickles medium, hooked down, moderate; growth upright, bushy, medium (1 m.); garden, exhibition; ['Raewyn Henry' × 'Red Planet']; intr. 2004

'Lilian Harvey' HT, or, 2000, Poole, Lionel; flowers very bright orange-red, large, borne in small clusters, slight fragrance; foliage medium size, dark green, semi-glossy; prickles moderate; growth bushy, medium (3 ft.); ['Adrienne Berman' × Corso®]; intr. 2001

'Lilian Nordica' HT, w, 1898, Walsh; flowers large, dbl.; vigorous growth; ['Margaret Dickson' × 'Mme Hoste']

'Liliana' -- See 'Poulsyng'

'Liliana' HT, pb, 1956, Camprubi, C.; flowers soft pink, reverse carmine; RULED EXTINCT 12/85; ['Edith Krause' × 'Fashion']

'Liliana' Gr, w, 1986, Staikov, Prof. Dr. V.; flowers large, 50 petals; foliage light green, leathery; vigorous, tall, upright growth; [Queen Elizabeth® × seedling]; intr. 1977

'Liliana' LCl, dr; flowers strong red, borne in clusters; recurrent; foliage dark green, glossy; stems reddish; climbing (8 ft.) growth; intr. 2002

'Lilibet' ('Fairy Princess') F, lp, 1953, Lindquist; bud ovoid; flowers 2½-3½ in., 30 petals, borne in clusters, moderate spicy fragrance; foliage glossy; low, bushy growth; PP1209; ['Floradora' × 'Pinocchio']

Lill Lindfors™ -- See 'Poulrohill'

'Lillebror' Min, mr, 1978, Hubner; flowers dbl.; dwarf, bushy growth

Lilli Marleen® -- See 'Korlima'

'Lilli Marleen, Climbing' -- See 'Peklimasar'

'Lilli Marlene' ('Lili Marlene', Lilli Marleen®) F, mr, 1960, Kordes, R.; bud ovoid; flowers velvety crimson red, 3 in., 25 petals, cupped, moderate fragrance; foliage leathery; vigorous growth; PP1986; [('Our Princess' × 'Rudolph Timm') × 'Ama']; intr. 1959

'Lilli von Posern' HT, mp, 1910, Kiese; flowers large, dbl.; ['Mme Caroline Testout' × 'Oberbürgermeister Dr. Troendlin']

'Lillian' F, ob, Williams, J. Benjamin; flowers soft orange, borne in clusters; recurrent; ['Rose Parade' × 'Zorina']; intr. 1997

'Lillian' Min, pb, 1958, deVink; flowers rose pink, white center, small, semi-dbl.; very dwarf growth; ['Ellen Poulsen' × 'Tom Thumb']; intr. 1958

'Lillian French' HT, pb, 1985, French, Richard; flowers light to medium pink, reverse deep pink, large, 50-120 petals, quartered, borne in clusters of 1-5, moderate fragrance; foliage medium size, medium green, semi-glossy; prickles large, pointed downward; growth upright, bushy; ['Miss Hillcrest' × 'Bishop Darlington']

'Lillian Gibson' S, mp, 1938, Hansen, N.E.; flowers rose-pink, 3 in., very dbl., intense fragrance; non-recurrent; vigorous growth; very hardy; [R. blanda × 'Red Star']

'Lillian Gish' F, ly, 1985, French, Richard; flowers very pale yellow, large, 35 petals, borne singly and in small clusters; foliage medium size, medium green, semi-glossy; prickles few, straight; upright growth; [Queen Elizabeth® × Allgold®]

'Lillian Gomez-Mena' Cl HT, pb, 1927, Chambard, C.; flowers salmon-cream, reverse carmine, dbl.

'Lillian Moore' HT, yb, 1917, Dickson, H.; flowers white, shaded yellow over pink, medium, full, moderate fragrance

'Lillie Bell' HT, dp, 1979, Williams, J. Benjamin; bud ovoid to pointed; flowers deep pink to cerise-red, ruffled, 4½-5 in., 34 petals; foliage large; upright growth; [Pink Peace® × 'Miss All-American Beauty']

'Lillie Dawber' HT, dr, 1952, Kordes; flowers scarlet overlaid crimson, 5 in., 25 petals, cupped; foliage dark; free growth

'Lilliput' Cl Pol, mr, 1897, Paul, G.; flowers carmine-red, small, dbl.

'Lilly Jung' HT, dy, 1925, Leenders, M.; bud large, ovoid; flowers golden yellow, large, dbl., moderate fragrance

Lily Bertschinger® F, w, Hauser; intr. 1980

'Lily de Gerlache' HT, dp, 1971, Institute of Ornamental Plant Growing; bud long, pointed; flowers rose-red, large, dbl., cupped; foliage glossy, bronze, leathery; growth moderate, upright, bushy; ['Kordes' Perfecta' × 'Prima Ballerina']

'Lily Freeman' -- See 'Hux1'

'Lily Kemp' HT, dp, 1928, Morse; flowers deep cherry-cerise, dbl.; ['Mme Butterfly' × 'Capt. Ronald Clerk']

'Lily Mertscherskv' N, m, 1878, Nabonnand; flowers violet-red, fading to mauve-pink, 5 cm., very full, borne in clusters of up to 10, no fragrance

'Lily Pons' HT, ly, 1939, Brownell; flowers yellow center, shading to white outer petals, large, 50 petals, high-centered, moderate fragrance; foliage glossy; PP420; ['Glenn Dale' × 'Stargold']

'Lily the Pink' HT, lp, 1992, Scrivens, Len; flowers 3-3½ in., very dbl., borne mostly singly; foliage medium size, medium green, semi-glossy; some prickles; tall (100 cm.), upright growth; [seedling × seedling]

'Lily van Oost' HT, mp, 1938, Verschuren-Pechtold; flowers very large, dbl.

'Lily White' ('Starbright') HT, w, 1950, Hartgerink; bud ovoid; flowers 4½ in., very dbl., high-centered; foliage glossy; vigorous, upright growth; PP912; [sport of 'Starlite']

'Limberlost Plnk' -- See 'Super Jane'

'Limbo' HT, my, Kordes; bud large, pointed; flowers yellow with greenish tint, large, full, high-centered, borne mostly singly; free-flowering; stems long; growth vigorous; florist rose; intr. 1999

'Limburgia' HT, rb, 1921, Leenders, M.; flowers glowing deep carmine, reverse lilac-white, dbl.

'Lime Glow' -- See 'Intercitira'

'Lime Kiln' HWich, w; intr. 1970

Lime Sublime™ -- See 'Dicappeal'

'Limeburners Bay' Min, ob; flowers deep apricot with orange tonings, moderate fragrance; medium growth

'Limelight' -- See 'Wekamanda'

'Limelight' -- See 'Korikon'

'Limelight' F, r, 1960, Morse; flowers vermilion splashed golden, semi-dbl., borne in clusters; vigorous growth; RULED EXTINCT 5/85; [sport of 'Enterprise']; intr. 1959

'Limerick' -- See 'Ziplime'

'Limesglut' S, mr, Pearce; flowers bright blood-red, yellow stamens, small to medium, double, borne in clusters; recurrent; foliage small, dark green, glossy; compact (30 - 50 cm.) growth; intr. 2004

'Limesgold' S, dy, Pearce; bud small, rounded; flowers clean yellow, yellow stamens, medium, double, loose, borne in clusters of 5 - 10; recurrent; foliage small, dark green, glossy; strong, robust (50 - 70 cm.) growth; intr. 2004

'Limesjuwel' F, op, Pearce; flowers salmon-pink with yellow glow, medium, double, loose, borne in clusters, moderate fragrance; recurrent; foliage dark green, glossy; broad, low (40 - 60 cm.) growth; intr. 2004

'Limeszauber' F, pb, Pearce; bud pointed; flowers shades of pink, reverse creamy yellow, medium, semi-double, borne in clusters; recurrent; foliage dark green, glossy; broad, strong, low (40 cm.) growth; intr. 2004

'Limited Edition' -- See 'Jacref'

'Limo' HT, pb, Spek; flowers white with pink edges, 10-11 cm., 35-40 petals, high-centered, borne mostly singly; recurrent; prickles moderate; stems very long; intr. 2006

Limoges™ F, w, Poulsen; flowers 8-10 cm., 25 petals, no fragrance; foliage dark; growth bushy, 60-100 cm.; PP15549; intr. 2003

'Limona' HT, ly, Kordes; flowers cream yellow, large, dbl., high-centered, intense fragrance; stems long, PP11393; florist rose; intr. 1997

Lina™ -- See 'Poulen006(N)'

'Lina' Pol, lp, 1930, Vogel, M.; flowers creamy light pink, medium, dbl.

'Lina Renaissance' (Lina™) S, w, Poulsen; flowers white, 10-15 cm., dbl., moderate fragrance; foliage dark; growth bushy, 100-150 cm.; PP15695; intr. 2002

'Lina Schmidt-Michel' HT, yb, 1906, Lambert, P.; flowers yellowish-pink, large, semi-dbl.; ['Mme Abel Chatenay' × 'Kleiner Alfred']

'Lina Vogel' HFt, ob, 1936, Vogel, M.; flowers orange with golden and light yellow shades, medium, single

'Linburn Light' F, mp, Andersons; flowers dbl., high-centered, moderate fragrance; intr. 1986

'Lincelle' HGal, m, 1826, Dubourg; flowers violet, center darker, edges more red, medium, very full

'Lincoln Cathedral' -- See 'Glanlin'

'Lincolnshire Poacher' -- See 'Glareabit'

'Linda' -- See 'Lovclaire'

Linda™ -- See 'Poulra024(N)'

'Linda' HT, yb, 1997, Bracegirdle, A.J.; flowers medium, very dbl., borne in small clusters; foliage medium size, medium green, semi-glossy; upright, medium (3½ ft.) growth; ['Champion' × ('Pink Favourite' × 'Golden Autumn')]

'Linda Ann' Gr, mp, 1996, Dobbs, Annette E.; flowers medium pink, deeper pink than parents, more petals than parent, full; foliage medium size, medium green, semi-glossy; prickles moderate; upright, tall growth; [Queen Elizabeth® × 'Katherine T. Marshall']

'Linda Buford' -- See 'Tinbuford'

'Linda Campbell' -- See 'Morten'

'Linda Christine' F, pb, 1980, Taylor, W.J.; flowers cerise, silver reverse; [sport of 'Molly McGredy']

'Linda Guest' HT, ab, 1984, Guest, M.M.; flowers large, 20 petals, high-centered; foliage medium size, medium green, matte; bushy growth; [(('Golden Jewel' × 'Mischief') × 'Red Planet') × 'Valencia']

Linda Lou™ F, ob, 1987, Harvey, R.E.; flowers orange-yellow-red, medium, 30 petals, high-centered, borne in sprays of 1-8; foliage medium size, dark green; medium growth; ['Golden Slippers' × 'Roman Holiday']; intr. 1988

'Linda Mary' -- See 'Boseladnee'

'Linda Parade' (Linda™) MinFl, mp, Olesen; bud pointed ovoid; flowers medium pink, reverse slightly darker, 5 cm., 31 petals, cupped, borne singly or in pairs, slight fragrance; recurrent; foliage dark green, matte; prickles few, 4-5 mm., linear, greyed-yellow; compact, bushy (20-40 cm.) growth; PP15017; [sport of 'Heidi Parade']; intr. 2003

'Linda Porter' ('Miguel Aldrufeu') HT, op, 1957, Dot, Pedro; bud ovoid; flowers salmon-pink, 5-6 in., 55 petals, globular, intense fragrance; foliage leathery; vigorous, upright growth; PP1507; ['Senateur Potie' × 'Poinsettia']; intr. 1957

'Linda Radja' -- See 'Lindaraja'

'Linda Sue' -- See 'Gelsue'

'Linda Thomson' -- See 'Tomtwo'

'Linda Vista' F, de Ruiter, G.; intr. 1974

'Lindaraja' ('Linda Radja') HT, r; flowers nasturtium

'Linda's Choice' HT, m, Thomson

'Linda's Lipstick' -- See 'Sherilip'

'Lindbergh' Pol, mr, 1927, Croibier; flowers bright geranium-red; [sport of 'Orléans Rose']

'Lindee' Pol, w; flowers tiny, dbl., moderate fragrance; recurrent

'L'Indéfrisible' -- See 'Permanent Wave'

'Linden Heath' S, mp

Linderhof® -- See 'Korelasting'

'Lindliffe' ('Guyscliffe') F, op, 1985, Lindner, Richard; flowers orange-salmon, 12 petals, cupped, borne 3-5 per cluster, intense fragrance; foliage light green; prickles light brown; tall, densely branched growth; intr. 1984

'Lindsay's Rose' -- See 'Ardlinds'

'Lindsey' HT, op, 1973, Watkins Roses; flowers salmon-pink, shaded copper, pointed, 3-4 in., moderate fragrance; foliage large; free growth; [sport of 'Whisky Mac']

'Line Renaud' HT, mp, Meilland; flowers very full, cupped; recurrent; foliage dark green; medium to tall growth; intr. 2005

'Linette' Pol, dp, 1922, Turbat; bud reddish apricot; flowers shrimp-carmine-pink, passing to soft rose-pink, large

'L'Infante d'Espagne' -- See 'Cramoisie Éblouissante'

'L'Ingenue' C, w, 1848, Vibert; flowers pure white with a green center pip, 8-9 cm., full, rosette; [from 'Globe Hip']

'Linneanhall Beauty' Ayr, lp, before 1866; flowers light pink, fading to white, very full

'L'Innocence' HT, w, 1897, Pernet-Ducher; flowers large, full, globular; foliage bronze green; prickles small, few; [seedling × 'Mme Caroline Testout']

'Linrick' (Friendship™) HT, dp, 1978, Lindquist; bud ovoid; flowers deep pink, 5½-6 in., 28 petals, cupped, intense fragrance; foliage large, dark; vigorous, upright growth; PP4284; ['Fragrant Cloud' × 'Miss All-American Beauty']

'LINro' F, rb, 1966, Lindquist; bud ovoid

'Linville' Min, w, 1990, Bridges, Dennis A.; bud pointed; flowers light pink, aging white, large, 28 petals, high-centered, borne usually singly, slight fruity fragrance; foliage medium size, medium green, semi-glossy; prickles straight, medium, deep pink; upright, medium growth; PP7737; [seedling × seedling]; intr. 1990

'Lioang' ('Angela Davis') HT, pb, 2005, Poole, Lionel; flowers pink/apricot, reverse pink, 4-4½ in., dbl., borne singly and in small clusters, intense fragrance; foliage medium size, medium green, glossy; prickles moderate, medium, hooked down, light brown; bushy, medium (2½-3 ft.) growth; garden bedding, borders; ['Silver Jubilee' × 'Bernice Cooper']; intr. 2006

'Liobern' ('Bernice Cooper') HT, pb, 2005, Poole, Lionel; flowers ivory with pink edge, 5 in., very full, high-centered, borne mostly solitary, moderate fragrance; foliage medium size, dark green, semi-glossy; prickles medium, triangular, brown, moderate; growth bushy, medium (30 in.); garden decoration, exhibition; ['Pedrus Aquarius' × 'New Zealand']; intr. 2006

'Lioblanch' ('Susan Wilce') HT, w, 2006, Poole, Lionel; flowers full, high-centered, borne mostly solitary; foliage medium size, medium green, glossy; prickles medium, hooked, brown, moderate; growth upright, medium (3 ft.); exhibition; ['Silver Anniversary' × 'New Zealand']; intr. 2007

'Lioblush' ('Zena') HT, lp, 2006, Poole, Lionel; flowers light pink with apricot, 5 in., full, borne in small clusters; foliage medium size, medium green, glossy; prickles large, triangular, dark brown, moderate; growth bushy, tall (3 ft.); beds, borders, exhibition; [('Hazel Rose' × 'Cardiff Bay') × ('Solitaire' × 'Silver Jubilee')]; intr. 2007

'Liodoc' ('MontyJax') HT, dr, 2007, Poole, Lionel; flowers deep red/deeper edge, reverse deep red, large, 5 in., full, high-centered, borne mostly solitary; foliage medium, dark green, semi-glossy; prickles large, triangular, dark brown, moderate; growth bushy, medium (3 ft.); exhibition, bedding, borders; ['Veterans Honor' × 'Fiona Ivin']; intr. 2009

'Liodrag' ('Red Dragon') HT, mr, 2005, Poole, Lionel; flowers full, borne mostly solitary, slight fragrance; foliage medium size, dark green, semi-glossy; prickles moderate, medium size, slightly hooked, brown; upright, medium growth; garden decorative, exhibition; ['Raewyn Henry' × 'Unamed seedling (Hazel Rose × Cardiff Bay) × Red Planet']; intr. 2007

'Liogeorge' ('Anydale') HT, yb, 2005, Poole, Lionel; flowers yellow with pink edge, 4½ in., dbl., high, spiral center, borne mostly solitary, slight fragrance; foliage medium size, medium green, glossy; prickles medium, slightly hooked, brown, moderate; growth bushy, medium (1 m.); garden decoration; ['Joanna Lumley' × 'Healing Hands']; intr. 2006

'Liogift' ('It's Lovely Mary') HT, pb, 2007, Poole, Lionel; flowers medium pink/shaded deeper, reverse same, large, 5 in., full, high-centered, borne mostly solitary; foliage medium, medium green, semi-glossy; prickles medium, slightly hooked down, brown, moderate; growth upright, medium (3 ft.); bedding, exhibition; ['Gemini' × 'Bernice Cooper']; intr. 2008

'Lioglow' ('Eileen Bee') HT, lp, 2007, Poole, Lionel; flowers large, 5½ in., full, borne mostly solitary; foliage large, dark green, glossy; prickles small, narrow, pointed, dark brown, few; growth bushy, medium (2½ ft.); garden decorative, exhibition; ['Hazel Rose' × 'Duncan Reed Hill']; intr. 2008

'Liojoal' ('M.T. Ruby Sunday') HT, dr, 2005, Poole, Lionel; flowers deep red, 4 in., full, borne in small clusters, moderate fragrance; foliage medium size, dark green, semi-glossy; prickles moderate, medium, slightly hooked, dark brown; growth bushy, medium (30 in.); garden decoration, beds, borders; ['Raewyn Henry' × 'Red Planet']; intr. 2006

'Liokris' ('Miri') HT, pb, 2007, Poole, Lionel; flowers pale pink with cream center, reverse pale pink, medium, 5 in., full, borne mostly solitary; foliage medium, dark green, semi-glossy; prickles medium, hooked down, bronze, moderate; growth upright, medium (1 m.); garden decoration, exhibition; ['Gemini' × 'Pedrus Aquarius']; intr. 2009

'Liolà' HT, w, 1958, Giacomasso; flowers ivory edged crimson, dbl.; very vigorous growth; ['Peace' × ('Baiser' × 'Marguerite Chambard')]

Liolà® F, w, Barni; flowers creamy white with pink edges, aging ivory suffused lavender pink, single, borne in clusters; free-flowering; healthy (60-80 cm.) growth; intr. 2004

'Liolilac' ('Deborah Reilly') HT, m, 2007, Poole, Lionel; flowers lilac with deep pink edges, medium, 4 in., full, borne in small clusters; foliage medium green, matte; prickles medium, hooked down, brown, few; growth upright, medium

(30 in.); garden decoration, bedding, borders; ['Stephens' Big Purple' × 'Fiona Ivin']; intr. 2008

'Liolyn' ('Lynette Joseph') HT, mr, 2004, Poole, Lionel; flowers medium red, reverse medium red, 5 in., full, borne mostly solitary; foliage medium size, dark green, semi-glossy; prickles medium, triangular; growth bushy, vigorous, tall (45 in.); garden decoration, exhibition; ['Naomi Rebecca' × 'Adrienne Berman']; intr. 2005

'Liomich' ('The St Michael's Hospice Rose') HT, my, 2008, Poole, Lionel; flowers yellow, occassionally with fine carmine edge, reverse yellow, 4½ in., full, borne mostly solitary, strong almond fragrance; foliage dark green, glossy; prickles medium, hooked, brown, moderate; growth bushy, medium (3 ft.); garden decoration, exhibition; [('Hazel Rose' × 'Cardiff Bay') × 'Lydia']; intr. 2009

'Lion des Combats' HP, mr, 1850, Lartay; flowers reddish-violet, often shaded with scarlet, large, dbl.

'Lionel Barrymore' F, my, 1956, Silva; bud urn shaped; flowers yellow, center deeper, 3-3½ in., very dbl., cupped, intense fragrance; foliage dark; strong stems; bushy growth; PP1574; ['Duchess of Atholl' × 'Orange Everglow']

'Lionheart' -- See 'Minheart'

'Lionheart' HT, mr; flowers coral-red, intense fragrance; growth to 3 ft.; intr. 2004

'Lion's Fairy Tale' -- See 'Korvanaber'

'Lions International' ('Reta Elizabeth Lindsay') HT, dy, Fryer, Gareth; flowers golden yellow, dbl., high-centered, moderate spicy fragrance; good repeat; foliage dark green, glossy; vigorous, compact (3 ft.) growth; intr. 1998

Lions-Rose® -- See 'Korvanaber'

'Liopearl' ('Bill Heath') HT, w, 2007, Poole, Lionel; flowers upper ivory, tinged pink, reverse same, very large, 6 in., single, high-centered, borne mostly solitary; foliage dark green, glossy; prickles large, hooked down, dark brown, moderate; growth upright, medium (3 ft.); exhibition; ['Brad' × 'New Zealand']; intr. 2007

'Liosanz' ('April Moore') HT, w, 2007, Poole, Lionel; flowers white with pale pink, large, 5 in., full, borne mostly solitary; foliage medium size, dark green, glossy; prickles medium, slightly hooked down, brown, moderate; growth bushy, medium (3 ft.); garden decoration, borders; ['Silver Anniversary' × 'New Zealand']; intr. 2008

'Lioshell' ('Sweet Heart Shelley') HT, mr, 2005, Poole, Lionel; flowers 4½ in., full, borne mostly solitary, moderate fragrance; foliage medium size, medium green, semi-glossy; prickles medium, slightly hooked, brown, moderate; growth upright, medium (3 ft.); garden decoration, exhibition; ['Red Planet' × 'Raewyn Henry']; intr. 2006

'Liparfum' HT, m, RVS; flowers mauve blend; recurrent; intr. 1999

'Lippay János' Pol, dr, Márk, Gergely; flowers crimson-purple, 1¼ in., dbl., borne in clusters; foliage medium size, glossy, dark green; growth upright, short; intr. 2002

Lippe-Detmold® HT, mp, Noack, Werner; intr. 1985

'Lipsiana' Pol, 1952, Cazzaniga, F. G.

'Lipstick' HT, rb; intr. 2004

'Lipstick' F, rb, 1940, Verschuren; flowers deep cerise shaded salmon, 2 in., semi-dbl., cupped, borne in clusters; foliage glossy, dark; vigorous (3 ft.), bushy growth

'Lipstick 'n' Lace' -- See 'Clelips'

'Lisa' -- See 'Lisa Maree'

'Lisa' F, Zandri, R.; intr. 1988

'Lisa' HSpn, w, Sutherland, P; ['Single Cherry' × 'Primula']; intr. 1996

'Lisa' F, dy, Noack; flowers golden yellow, 2½ in., full, loose, borne in clusters; recurrent; growth to 70 cm.; intr. 2004

'Lisa' F, op, Kirkham; foliage large, dark green, semi-glossy; short to medium growth; intr. 2005

'Lisa Ann' -- See 'Rawlisan'

'Lisa Colfax' F, ob, 1976, Parkes, Mrs M.H.; bud ovoid; flowers vermilion, overlaid brown, medium, dbl., high-centered, intense fragrance; foliage leathery; very vigorous growth; ['Mignonne' × 'Sherry']; intr. 1975

'Lisa Kent' HT, dp, Dawson; correct name may be Lisa Kerr; intr. 1995

'Lisa Maree' ('Lisa') HT, dp, 1989, Cowper, Mrs. Maree; flowers deep pink, reverse lighter, exhibition; good repeat; growth vigorous; [sport of 'Esther Geldenhuys']; intr. 1989

'Lisa Michelle' HT, ab, 2006, Murray, Jean; flowers apricot, reverse mauve, medium, full, borne mostly solitary; foliage medium green, semi-glossy; prickles small, red, few; growth compact, medium; [seedling × seedling]; intr. 2006

'Lisbeth Prim' HT, or, 1934, Felberg-Leclerc; flowers coppery red, fading lighter, large, dbl.; vigorous growth; ['Hadley' × 'Lady Inchiquin']

'Lisbeth Stellmacher' Pol, or, 1919, Lambert, P.; bud coppery orange-red; flowers coppery red with golden yellow, striped pink, small, dbl.; ['Aglaia' × 'Marie van Houtte']

'Lisbeth von Kamecke' HMult, lp, 1910, Kiese; flowers light violet pink, 3 cm., semi-dbl., borne in large clusters; foliage small; ['Veilchenblau' × 'Katharina Zeimet']

'Lisboa' HT, dr, 1953, Moreira da Silva; flowers red shaded darker, large; very vigorous growth; ['Barcelona' × 'Crimson Glory']

'Lisboa de 1947' HT, mr, 1947, Moreira da Silva, A.; flowers bright red, dbl., moderate fragrance; recurrent; foliage medium green, matte; medium growth

'Lise Chiavassa' HT, mr, 1931, Buatois; flowers carmine, very large, dbl., cupped; foliage glossy; vigorous growth; ['Mme Philippe Rivoire' × 'Yves Druhen']

'Lise Palais' -- See 'Opal'

'Liselle' -- See 'Rulis'

'Liselotte Hollweg' F, mr; intr. 1962

'Lisette' HT, ly, Select Roses, B.V.

'Lisette de Béranger' HP, mp, 1867, Moreau, F.; flowers flesh pink, fading to almost white, medium, full, globular, borne in clusters; recurrent; vigorous (4 ft.) growth

'Lisima' -- See 'Gauzimi'

'Lissy Horstmann' HT, mr, 1943, Tantau; flowers brilliant scarlet-crimson, large, 28 petals, cupped; foliage leathery; vigorous growth; ['Hadley' × 'Heros']

'Litakor' HT, ab, Kordes, R.; intr. 1973

'Literary Giant' HT, pb; re-introduced by Heirloom Roses in 1991

'Litlin' ('Autumn Frost') Min, w, 1983, Rose, Euie; flowers medium, 35 petals, high-centered; foliage medium size, medium green, semi-glossy; bushy growth; [seedling × seedling]

'Little Alice' -- See 'Worcurrant'

'Little Amigo' -- See 'Tinamigo'

'Little Amy' -- See 'Batamy'

'Little Angel' F, mr, 1961, Verschuren; flowers salmon becoming scarlet, 30 petals, borne in large clusters; foliage dark, glossy; moderate growth; intr. 1961

'Little Angel' ('Petit Ange') Min, op, Lens; intr. 1974

Little Artist® -- See 'Macmanly'

'Little Awesome Beauty' Min, r, Taschner, Ludwig; flowers brownish, reverse greenish-yellow, dbl., cupped, moderate fragrance; recurrent; stems thin, wiry; vigorous, upright, tall growth; intr. 2005

'Little Baby Darling' Pol, lp, Tolmasoff; recurrent; growth 18 - 24 in. height; intr. 2005

'Little Ballerina' -- See 'Curbal'

'Little Beauty' ('Crown of Jewels') F, mp, 1935, Howard, F.H.; flowers bright cerise-pink, fading to pink, small, very dbl.; foliage leathery; vigorous, bushy growth; PP149; ['E.G. Hill seedling' × 'polyantha']

'Little Betty' S, lp, 1940, Wright, Percy H.; flowers soft pink, small; non-recurrent; growth to 3 ft.; ['Betty Bland' × R. nitida]

'Little Bit o' Sunshine' -- See 'Bit o' Sunshine'

Little Bo-Peep™ -- See 'Poullen'

'Little Boy' Pol

'Little Breeze' Min, ob, 1981, McCann, Sean; bud long, slender; flowers orange-red, fading to pink, loose, 17 petals, borne singly; foliage large, dark, glossy; prickles straight, gray; vigorous growth; ['Anytime' × Elizabeth of Glamis®]

'Little Bridesmaid' HT, lp, Archer; flowers shrimp-pink, well-shaped

'Little Brother' -- See 'Pixbro'

'Little Buckaroo' Min, mr, 1957, Moore, Ralph S.; flowers bright red, small, 23 petals, moderate fresh apple fragrance; foliage bronze, glossy, leathery; growth to 14-16 in.; PP1726; [(*R. wichurana* × 'Floradora') × ('Oakington Ruby' × 'Floradora')]; intr. 1956

'Little Butterfly' S, pb, Rupert; flowers light pink, darker pink reverse, small, single, borne in large clusters, moderate fragrance; intr. 2002

'Little Cameo' F, pb, 1982, Strahle, Robert; bud medium, pointed; flowers pink blend with cream outer petals, 26 petals, borne mostly singly; foliage medium green, leathery; prickles straight, short, red; vigorous, upright growth; PP5381; ['Lara' × seedling]; intr. 1981

'Little Carol' -- See 'Tincarol'

'Little Chameleon' Min, pb, 1977, Lyon; bud pointed; flowers rose-pink to red, 1½ in., 30 petals; upright growth; ['Little Amy' × unknown]

'Little Chap' -- See 'Korverlandus'

'Little Charm' -- See 'Lyolit'

'Little Cherub' Min, dr, Tantau; flowers deep red with yellow stamens, double, shallow cup, borne in large clusters, slight fragrance; recurrent; low (24 in.), bushy growth; intr. 2007

'Little Chief' Min, dp, 1972, Moore, Ralph S.; bud long, pointed; flowers small, semi-dbl.; foliage small, glossy, leathery; growth moderate, dwarf, bushy; ['Cotton Candy' × 'Magic Wand']

'Little Compton Creeper' HWich, dp, 1938, Brownell; flowers deep rose-pink, white at center, 6-7 cm., single, borne in small clusters; non-recurrent; foliage small, dark green, glossy; hips yellow-orange

'Little Crimson' -- See 'Savacrim'

'Little Curt' Min, dr, 1973, Moore, Ralph S.; bud long, pointed; flowers deep velvety red, medium, semi-dbl.; foliage dark, leathery; vigorous, upright, bushy growth; ['red Cl F seedling' × Westmont]; intr. 1971

'Little Darling' F, yb, 1957, Duehrsen; bud ovoid; flowers blend of yellow and soft salmon-pink, well-formed, 2½ in., 27 petals, moderate spicy fragrance; foliage dark, glossy, leathery; very vigorous, spreading growth; PP1581; ['Capt. Thomas' × ('Baby Chateau' × 'Fashion')]; intr. 1956

'Little Darling' F, w; intr. 2003

Little Deb™ -- See 'Willildeb'

'Little Devil, Climbing' -- See 'Delposar'

'Little Devil' -- See 'Delpo'

'Little Diamond' -- See 'Sundia'

'Little Diane' -- See 'Jacchar'

'Little Dickens' Min, ob, 1979, Schwartz, Ernest W.; bud ovoid; flowers orange-red and yellow, small, 25 petals, cupped; foliage small; compact growth; PP4693; [('Ma Perkins' × 'Sheri Anne') × 'Over the Rainbow']

'Little Dorrit' Pol, mp, 1930, Reeves; flowers glowing pink; growth to 2 ft.; [sport of 'Coral Cluster']

'Little Dorrit, Climbing' Cl Pol, mp, 1935, Letts

'Little Dot' Pol, lp, 1889, Bennett; flowers soft pink, flaked deeper on the outer petals, borne in clusters; very dwarf growth

'Little Dragon' Min, rb; intr. 2006

'Little Embers' F, rb, 1988, McFarland, John; flowers cerise to yellow, reverse yellow with cerise on tips, aging, 25 petals, high-centered; foliage medium size, medium green, matte; prickles long, narrow, small, light green; upright, low growth; no fruit; ['Rise 'n' Shine' × Prominent®]

'Little Emma' -- See 'Moremma'

'Little Eskimo' -- See 'Morwhit'

'Little Esperanza' F, mr, 2005, le Fevre, Ivan James; flowers bright red, reverse misty red, 2 in., semi-dbl., borne in large clusters, no fragrance; foliage medium size, dark green, matte; prickles small, straight; growth bushy, medium (4 ft.); specimen, hedging; [unknown × unknown]

'Little Fire' -- See 'Ogoniok'

'Little Fireball' Min, or, 1968, Moore, Ralph S.; bud ovoid; flowers bright coral-red, small, dbl.; foliage small, glossy; bushy, compact, low growth; [(*R. wichurana* × 'Floradora') × 'New Penny']

Little Flame™ -- See 'Jacnuye'

'Little Flirt' Min, rb, 1961, Moore, Ralph S.; bud pointed; flowers orange-red, reverse yellow, 1½ in., 42 petals, moderate fragrance; foliage light green; vigorous, bushy (12-14 in.) growth; PP2287; [(*R. wichurana* × 'Floradora') × ('Golden Glow' × 'Zee')]; intr. 1961

'Little Gem' -- See 'Sunsalm'

'Little Gem' ('Cramoisi de Meaux', 'Crimson Moss de Meaux') M, dp, 1880, Paul, W.; bud heavily mossed; flowers bright deep pink, small, dbl., borne in clusters, intense fragrance; dwarf, compact growth

'Little Gem' Pol, lp, Alderton; intr. about 1898

'Little Gigi' ('Citron-Fraise') S, pb, 1998, Delbard; bud yellow; flowers pink with pale yellow in heart, semi-dbl., borne in clusters; vigorous, shrubby (3 ft.) growth

'Little Girl' Cl Min, op, 1974, Moore, Ralph S.; bud long, pointed; flowers coral-salmon-pink, medium, dbl.; foliage glossy; bushy, climbing growth; ['Little Darling' × Westmont]; intr. 1973

'Little Green Snake' S, w, Lens, Louis; recurrent; spreading, low (12 in.) growth; intr. 1996

'Little Guy' Min, mr, 1986, Moore, Ralph S.; flowers medium red, reverse lighter, small, semi-dbl., borne in clusters of 3-7, no fragrance; foliage small, medium green, semi-glossy; low, bushy growth; no fruit; ['Magic Wand' × 'Violette']; intr. 1980

'Little Huzzy' -- See 'Tinhuzzy'

Little Jackie™ -- See 'Savor'

'Little Jewel' -- See 'Sunjew'

'Little Jewel' -- See 'Cocabel'

'Little Joe' HT, dr, 1921, Looymans; flowers crimson-red, single; ['Red-Letter Day' × 'H.V. Machin']

'Little John' Min, rb, 1959, Mason, F.; bud pointed; flowers scarlet, center white, medium, semi-dbl., high-centered, borne in clusters; foliage soft, vigorous, bushy (12-15 in.) growth; [sport of Baby Masquerade®]

'Little Joker' Min, pb, 1958, Spek; flowers rose-pink, center cream, well-shaped; bushy growth

'Little Juan' Min, mr, 1966, Williams, Ernest D.; flowers medium red, reverse lighter, small, dbl.; foliage small, leathery; vigorous, dwarf growth; ['Juliette' × seedling]

'Little Juliet' HT, yb, 1924, Looymans; flowers apricot and peach on yellow ground, dbl.; [('F.J. Looymans' × unknown) × unknown]

'Little Lady' Pol, w, 1967, Harkness; flowers blush to ice-white, small, 70 petals; dwarf growth; ['Schneewittchen (F)' × 'Baby Faurax']

'Little Leaguer' F, dr, 1962, Jelly; bud ovoid; flowers 2-2½ in., 28-40 petals, cupped; vigorous, upright growth; PP2623; [('Garnette' × unknown) × 'Yuletide']; intr. 1962

'Little Lemmy' -- See 'Korbalem'

'Little Len' MinFl, ab, Hatfield & Buckley; intr. 1987

'Little Lighthouse' -- See 'Clelight'

'Little Linda' Min, ly, 1977, Schwartz, Ernest W.; bud high-pointed; flowers micro-mini, 1 in., 17 petals, high-centered; compact growth; PP4264; [('Gold Coin' × unknown) × seedling]; intr. 1976

'Little Liza' Min, mp, 1976, Saville, F. Harmon; bud mossy; flowers rose-pink, ½-1 in., 15 petals; low, very compact growth; ['Fairy Moss' × 'Fairy Moss']

'Little Love' Min, mp, 1977, Lyon; bud pointed; flowers rose-pink, open, 1½ in., 25-30 petals; foliage tiny; very low, compact growth; ['Little Amy' × seedling]

'Little Lucy' -- See 'Houlucy'

'Little Lutea' LCl, my; intr. 1990

'Little Mabel' Min, mr, de Ruiter; intr. 1991

Little Magician™ -- See 'Wilmag'

'Little Marvel' -- See 'Ruigerdan'

'Little Meg' Pol, w, 1917, Easlea; flowers milk white, reverse shaded carmine, small, semi-dbl.; ['Shower of Gold' × 'Jersey Beauty']

'Little Meghan' -- See 'Spomeg'

'Little Melody' Min, pb, 1980, Strawn, Leslie E.; bud globular; flowers soft peach-yellow blend, 38 petals, high-centered, moderate fragrance; foliage medium green; prickles light brown, curved downward; compact, bushy growth; [Neue Revue® × 'Sheri Anne']; intr. 1979

'Little Mermaid' -- See 'Morwimer'

'Little Mike' Min, dr, 1967, Moore, Ralph S.; bud ovoid; flowers deep red, small, dbl., high-centered; foliage dark, glossy, leathery; vigorous, dwarf growth; PP2988; [((R. wichurana × 'Floradora') × seedling) × 'Little Buckaroo']

'Little Mischief' ('Little Mischief Garden Path') S, pb, Ping Lim; flowers deep pink with white eye, fading as they mature, 1 in., 19-24 petals, cupped; always in bloom; foliage medium green, semi-glossy; growth to 1½-2 ft.; PP17196; intr. 2004

'Little Mischief Garden Path' -- See 'Little Mischief'

'Little Miss Muffet' -- See 'Poulense'

'Little Miss Muffett' F, pb, 1940, LeGrice; bud pointed, cerise; flowers bright rose-pink, reverse deeper, open, large, semi-dbl., borne in clusters; strong stems; vigorous, bushy growth; ['Else Poulsen' × 'Étoile de Hollande']

'Little Miss Springtime' Min, rb, Williams, J.B.; flowers ivory white with deep pink edges, scarlet-purple when fully open, high-centered; growth to 6 in.; intr. 2001

'Little Muff' -- See 'Horluisbond'

'Little Nell' HT, yb, 1933, Archer; flowers deep cream, center apricot, reverse primrose, well-shaped; foliage glossy, dark; vigorous growth

'Little Nugget' Min, my, Schuurman, Frank B.; flowers golden yellow, 1½ in., dbl., slight fragrance; foliage small, medium green, semi-glossy; bushy growth; [Lorena® × 'Firefly']; intr. 1991

'Little One' -- See 'Sanone'

'Little Opal' -- See 'Sunpat'

Little Paradise™ -- See 'Weklips'

'Little Peaces' -- See 'Tinpeaces'

'Little Pearl' -- See 'Sunpearl'

'Little Pete' Min, or; intr. 2006

Little Pim® -- See 'Lennop'

'Little Pink' F, pb, 1965, Castleberry; flowers pink, center creamy pink, small, very dbl., high-centered; foliage glossy; vigorous, compact growth; ['Little Darling' × unknown]

'Little Pink Hedge' F, pb; flowers clear pink, semi-dbl. to dbl., borne in clusters, no fragrance; good rebloom; foliage glossy; medium (3 ft.) growth; intr. 1992

'Little Pinkie' -- See 'Morpinkie'

'Little Pioneer' -- See 'Curneer'

'Little Pooh' Min, or, 1980, Fong, William P.; bud slim, pointed; flowers , 5-6 petals, flat, borne 5-6 per cluster, moderate fragrance; foliage heavy, thick; prickles triangular; upright growth; ['Anytime' × seedling]

'Little Prancer' Cl HT, mr, 1996, Thurman, Robert R.; flowers red, lighter reverse, 3 in., dbl., borne mostly singly, moderate fragrance; foliage medium size, medium green striped with red, dull; prickles moderate; upright, tall (7-9 ft.) growth; ['Don Juan' × Joseph's Coat®]

'Little Prince' -- See 'Coccord'

'Little Princess' -- See 'Pixie'

'Little Princess' F, mp, Sodano, J.; flowers rose-pink, reverse lighter, 2 in., 50-75 petals, cupped, moderate fragrance; long stems; vigorous growth; PP1364; [sport of 'Garnette']; intr. 1955

'Little Princess' Pol, ob, 1937, Knight, G.; flowers pale salmon-coral, well-formed, dbl.; vigorous, bushy growth

'Little Purple' F, m

'Little Rambler' -- See 'Chewramb'

'Little Rascal' -- See 'Peaalamo'

'Little Rascal' Min, mr, 1981, Jolly, Betty J.; flowers medium red, shading to yellow at base, reverse lighter, 34 petals, high-centered; foliage tiny, light green; prickles slightly hooked; compact, bushy growth; ['Sheri Anne' × 'Rise 'n' Shine']

'Little Red' Min, or, 1979, Lens, Louis; bud ovoid; flowers red-orange, 1½ in., 18-22 petals, pompon; foliage glossy; compact growth; ['New Penny' × 'Coloranja']; intr. 1975

'Little Red' Min, mr, Tantau; flowers bright red, borne in clusters; free-flowering; growth to 12-16 in.; intr. 2004

'Little Red Devil' -- See 'Arovidil'

'Little Red Hedge' -- See 'Kortabo'

'Little Red Monkey' F, mr, 1954, Ratcliffe; flowers bright red, short stiff petals, very dbl., borne singly and in sprays; bushy growth; ['Donald Prior' × seedling]

'Little Ruby' MinFl, dr, Williams, J.B.; flowers deep crimson, with bright yellow stamens., single; intr. 2003

'Little Russel' -- See 'Trobric'

'Little Sapphire' -- See 'Sunsap'

'Little Scotch' Min, ly, 1959, Moore, Ralph S.; bud long; flowers straw-yellow to white, 1½ in., 55 petals, moderate fragrance; foliage leathery; vigorous, bushy (12 in.) growth; PP1952; ['Golden Glow' × 'Zee']; intr. 1958

'Little Showoff' Cl Min, yb, 1960, Moore, Ralph S.; bud pointed; flowers bright yellow, sometimes tinted red, 1-1½ in., 30 petals, high-centered, moderate fragrance; upright (to 4 ft.) growth; PP2176; ['Golden Glow' × 'Zee']; intr. 1960

Little Shrimp® -- See 'Lenlit'

'Little Silver' -- See 'Jacsil'

'Little Sir Echo' Min, mp, 1977, Schwartz, Ernest W.; bud long, pointed; flowers 1-1½ in., 48 petals, high-centered; foliage matte, green; compact, upright growth; ['Ma Perkins' × 'Baby Betsy McCall']

'Little Sir Echo, Climbing' Cl Min, mp, 1985, Watterberg, Leah; [sport of 'Little Sir Echo']

'Little Sister' -- See 'Pixsis'

'Little Sister' -- See 'Morsis'

Little Sizzler™ -- See 'Jaciat'

Little Slam® -- See 'Kinslam'

'Little Smiles' Min, yb, 1979, Lyon; bud ovoid; flowers chinese yellow vermilion, 1 in., 12 petals, moderate spicy fragrance; compact growth; ['Q17a' × 'Redgold']; intr. 1978

'Little Squirt' -- See 'Tinsquirt'

'Little Star' -- See 'Mini Wings'

'Little Star Rose' -- See 'Benstar'

Little Starburst™ Min, yb, 1991, Williams, J. Benjamin; flowers orange-red washing on golden yellow, small, full, borne mostly singly and in small clusters, slight fragrance; foliage small, medium green, semi-glossy; low, bushy growth; PP6821; [Prominent® × 'Rise 'n' Shine']

'Little Stephen' HT, mp, 1971, Sanday, John; flowers glowing pink, 3 in., very dbl., high-centered; foliage matte; upright growth; ['Gavotte' × seedling]

'Little Stripes' -- See 'Sherilowstri'

'Little Sunset' Min, yb, Kordes; flowers yellow with pink edges, 3 cm., double, high-centered, no fragrance; recurrent; upright (40 cm.) growth; intr. 2007

'Little Sunset' Min, pb, 1967, Kordes; flowers salmon-pink on yellow, star-shaped, borne in clusters; recurrent; foliage small, light green; [seedling × 'Tom Thumb']; intr. 1967

'Little Sunshine' Pol, my, 1915, Cumming/Pierson; flowers creamy yellow, varying to deep golden yellow, occasionally flecked crimson, 1½-2 in., dbl.; dwarf growth; [R. multiflora nana × 'Soleil d'Or']

'Little 't' -- See 'Trat'

'Little Tease' -- See 'Ziptease'

'Little Tiger' -- See 'Morshaki'

'Little Tiny' Min, mp; intr. after 1961

Little Tommy Tucker™ -- See 'Tucktommy'

'Little Tyke' -- See 'Renyke'

'Little Vegas' -- See 'Spovegas'

'Little Wallace' F, pb, 1952, Beall; bud very long; flowers light pink, center yellow, 25 petals, high-centered, borne in clusters; foliage leathery, dark; vigorous growth; PP1116; [sport of 'Elfe']

'Little Wendy' -- See 'Sarwen'

'Little White' Min, w, Tantau; flowers ivory white, double, cupped, borne in clusters; recurrent; compact (35 - 40 cm.) growth; intr. 2007

'Little White Lies' -- See 'Seafibs'

'Little White Pet, Climbing' -- See 'White Pet, Climbing'

'Little White Pet' -- See 'White Pet'

Little White Spray® Min, w, Lens, Louis; flowers small, 5 petals, borne in clusters; foliage small; growth dwarf; small gardens; intr. 1991

'Little White Star' Pol, w, 2007, Tolmasoff, Jan & William; flowers pearly white, 1 in., single, borne in large clusters; foliage medium size, medium green, semi-glossy; prickles medium, red, moderate; growth bushy, short (20-24 in.); borders, containers, low hedge; hips numerous; [seedling × seedling]; intr. 2004

Little Wings™ Min, ly, Smith; buds light yellow; flowers light yellow, fading quickly to white, yellow stamens, small, single, flat, no fragrance; recurrent; foliage dark green, matte; rounded, medium (2 ft.) growth; intr. about 1990

'Little Woman' -- See 'Diclittle'

'Little Wonder' F, or, 1979, Huber; bud pointed; flowers 3½-4 in., 22-28 petals, moderate spicy fragrance; foliage small; upright to spreading growth; ['Duftwolke' × 'Ena Harkness']; intr. 1975

'Little Wren' Min, mp, 2004, Smith, Redmond; flowers pink, medium, full, borne in small clusters, slight fragrance; foliage medium size, medium green, glossy; prickles 1/8 to ¼ in., recurved; growth upright, short (15 × 12 in.); patio rose; [sport of 'Little Buckaroo']; intr. 2003

'Littlest Angel' Min, my, 1976, Schwartz, Ernest W.; bud short, pointed; flowers medium to deep yellow, micro-mini, ½ in., 28 petals, high-centered; foliage small; low, compact, bushy growth; PP4168; [('Gold Coin' × unknown) × 'miniature seedling']; intr. 1975

'Littlest Spartan' -- See 'Grulit'

'Liv Tyler' -- See 'Meibacus'

Live Act® F, w, Spek; flowers pure white, 9-10 cm., 30-35 petals, high-centered, borne mostly singly; recurrent, very productive; prickles moderate; stems medium to long; florist rose; intr. 2006

Live Wire™ -- See 'Savawire'

'Lively' HT, dp, 1960, LeGrice; flowers rose pink, 4-6 in., 32 petals, intense fragrance; foliage dark, glossy; vigorous, compact, low growth; PP2061; ['Wellworth' × 'Ena Harkness']; intr. 1959

'Lively Lady' F, or, 1969, Cocker; flowers vermilion, large, dbl.; foliage dark, glossy; [Elizabeth of Glamis® × 'Tropicana']

Liverpool® -- See 'Liverpool Echo'

'Liverpool Daily Post' -- See 'Frytrooper'

'Liverpool Echo' (Liverpool®) F, op, 1971, McGredy, Sam IV; flowers salmon, 4 in., 23 petals, high-centered; foliage light; tall growth; [('Little Darling' × 'Goldilocks') × 'Munchen']

'Liverpool Remembers' -- See 'Frystar'

'Liverton Lady' Cl HT, mp, 1978, Warner; flowers 3-4 in., 16-20 petals; foliage small, glossy; tall, climbing growth; [Bantry Bay® × Sympathie®]

'Livia' -- See 'Meikola'

Livin' Easy™ -- See 'Harwelcome'

'Living' HT, rb, 1958, Lammerts, Dr. Walter; flowers reddish-orange, reverse copper streaked red, 5-6 in., 24 petals, high-centered, moderate spicy fragrance; foliage leathery, semi-glossy; vigorous growth; PP1463; ['Charlotte Armstrong' × 'Grande Duchesse Charlotte']; intr. 1956

'Living Bouquet' -- See 'Lavlinger'

'Living Coral' HT, op, 1975, Golik; bud ovoid; flowers soft coral-pink, 5 in., 28 petals, high-centered, moderate fruity fragrance; foliage glossy; moderate growth; ['Queen of Bermuda' × 'Tropicana']; intr. 1974

'Living Fire' ('Sunshine Girl') F, ob, 1973, Gregory; flowers orange, suffused orange-red, 2½ in., 33 petals, rosette, moderate fragrance; foliage dark; ['Tropicana' × seedling]

'Living Well' S, mp; intr. 1999

'Liz' -- See 'Meirebuc'

'Liz McGrath' -- See 'Dicqueue'

Liza® -- See 'Barliz'

'Lizabeth's Lullabye' -- See 'Wircurob'

'Lizfam' ('Lizzie's Fame') Gr, mp, 2007, Strong, Elizabeth; flowers medium, 5 in., full, borne in small clusters; foliage medium, dark green, semi-glossy; prickles ¼ in., normal, light green/brown, moderate; growth bushy, medium (5 ft.); [sport of Fame!™]

'Lizzie Ann' Min, lp, 2000, Stewart, Betty C.; flowers silvery light pink, 1½ in., full, high-centered, borne mostly singly, slight fragrance; foliage medium size, medium green, semi-glossy; few prickles; growth compact, medium (2 ft.); [sport of 'Winsome']

'Lizzie Molk' S, pb, 1984, Rusnock, Ann M.; flowers light pink, white center, 20 petals, borne in clusters, intense fragrance; does not repeat; foliage medium size, blue-green, glossy; spreading growth

'Lizzie's Fame' -- See 'Lizfam'

'L'jé' MinFl, mr, 2007, Espanol, Leslie; flowers 2½, dbl., high-centered, borne mostly solitary; foliage medium green, semi-glossy, disease-resistant; no prickles; growth upright, medium; beds, borders, containers, exhibition; [sport of 'Memphis Magic']; intr. 2007

Ljuba Rizzoli® ('Via Romana') HT, dr, 1981, Dot, Simon; bud pointed; flowers 25 petals, cupped, borne singly, intense fragrance; foliage large, dark, matte; prickles purple-green; upright, bushy growth; intr. 1978

'Lleida' HT, rb, 1936, Dot, Pedro; flowers bright red, reverse yellow; very vigorous growth; ['Edouard Renard' × 'Condesa de Sástago']

'Llorver' -- See 'Verdi'

'Lloyd Center Supreme' -- See 'Twoloy'

'Lloyds of London' -- See 'Canlloyd'

'Lloyds Supreme' HT, mp, Twomey, Jerry; ['Brion' × 'Silver Jubilee']

'Loads of Pink' -- See 'Fialopi'

'Loan Hulse' -- See 'Ardmizkernel'

'Lobo' HT, rb, 1988, Perry, Astor; flowers red-purple, reverse white, large, full, high-centered, intense fragrance; foliage large, dark green, matte; upright growth; ['Kordes' Perfecta' × 'Gavotte']; intr. 1989

'L'Obscurité' ('De Van Eeden', 'Purpurea Velutina Parva', 'Mons Van Eeden') HGal, m, before 1820, Van Eeden/Prévost; flowers purple aging to velvety brown, medium, dbl.

'L'Obscurité' M, dr, Lacharme, F.; flowers velvety, dark garnet-crimson, large, dbl.; intr. 1848

'L'Obscurité' B, dr, Robert; flowers velvety dark purple; intr. 1851

'Locarno' Pol, or, 1926, deRuiter; flowers large, borne in huge clusters; vigorous, bushy growth; [sport of 'Orléans Rose']

'Loch Lomond' HSpn, 1945, Wright, Percy; [R. spinossima altaica × 'Harison's Yellow']

'Lochinvar' -- See 'Ausbilda'

'Locomotion' HT, yb, 1965, Verschuren, H.A.M.; flowers salmon tinted peach, becoming citron-yellow; foliage dark, leathery; vigorous, bushy growth; [R.M.S. Queen Mary × 'Lady Sylvia']

'Lod. Lavki' HT, w, Lens; flowers white, apricot tones in center, dbl., cup and saucer, moderate fragrance; recurrent; foliage dark green; intr. 2005

'Lodestar' HT, pb, 1953, Boerner; bud ovoid to globular; flowers buff-pink, center peach, 4½-5 in., 35-40 petals, intense spicy fragrance; foliage leathery; bushy growth; PP1251; [('Diamond Jubilee' × unknown) × 'Serenade']

'Lodewijk Opdebeek' HT, dr, 1921, Leenders, M.; flowers oxblood-red, reverse rose, dbl.; ['Jonkheer J.L. Mock' × 'Mev. Dora van Tets']

'Lodovico' F, Cazzaniga, F. G.; intr. 1960

'Lœlia' -- See 'Louise Peyronny'

'Loeta Liggett' HT, pb, 1985, Liggett, Myron T.; flowers light pink, darker pink reverse, often with salmon center; [sport of 'Duet']; intr. 1984

'Lohengrin' HT, lp, 1903, Kiese; flowers silvery pink, large, dbl.; ['Mme Caroline Testout' × 'Mrs W. J. Grant']

'Lois' -- See 'Tinlois'

'Lois Crouse' HT, lp, 1937, Moore, Ralph S.; bud pointed; flowers light pink, suffused salmon, large, dbl., peony-like; foliage dark; vigorous, bushy growth; ['Mme Butterfly' × unknown]

'Lois Holin' HT, pb, 2002, McCall, Sharan; flowers white with fuchsia edging & veining, 6 in., very dbl., borne mostly solitary, intense fragrance; foliage medium size, medium green, semi-glossy; prickles ¼ in., slanting down, moderate; growth upright, medium (4½ ft.); garden decorative, exhibition; ['Elsie Melton' × 'Michèle Meilland']

'Lois Maney' LCl, op, 1953, Maney; flowers salmon-pink, 4-5 in., dbl.; abundant, non-recurrent bloom; foliage leathery; very vigorous (25 ft.) growth; [R. maximowicziana pilosa × 'Templar']

'Lois Wilson' HT, pb; flowers medium pink with yellow in heart, large, dbl.; good repeat; stems long; strong, upright growth; intr. 1998

'Lola' -- See 'Tanavilo'

'Lola de Porcioles' HT, Camprubi, C.

'Lola Montes' HT, mr, Dot; intr. 1969

'Lola Vendrell' HT, pb, 1958, Bofill; flowers soft pink streaked deeper, well-formed, large, full, moderate fragrance; foliage glossy; long stems; vigorous growth; ['Serafina Longa' × 'Mme Kriloff']; intr. 1957

'Lolette Dupain' Cl Pol, pb, 1918, Lottin; flowers yellowish-rose, reverse silvery rose, dbl., borne in clusters; sometimes recurrent bloom; vigorous growth; ['Casimir Moulle' × 'Mme Norbert Levavasseur']

'Loli Creus' HT, dp, 1953, Dot, Pedro; flowers carmine, well-formed, large; foliage glossy; strong stems; very vigorous growth; ['Cynthia' × 'Manuelita']

'Lolita' HT, w, 1937, Croibier; flowers white, center cream, overlarge, dbl., globular; foliage leathery; vigorous growth; ['Frau Karl Druschki' × 'hybrid tea seedling']

'Lolita, Climbing' Cl HT, ab; intr. after 1973

Lolita® HT, ab, Kordes, R.; flowers golden bronze, 5 in., 28 petals, moderate fragrance; ['Colour Wonder' × seedling]; intr. 1973

Lolita Lempicka® -- See 'Meizincaro'

'Lolita Lempicka, Climbing' -- See 'Peter Mayle, Climbing'

'Lollipop' Min, mr, 1960, Moore, Ralph S.; flowers bright red, 1-1½ in., 35 petals; foliage glossy; vigorous (14 in.), bushy growth; PP2080; [(R. wichurana × 'Floradora') × 'Little Buckaroo']; intr. 1959

'Lollo' HT, rb, 1949, San Remo Exp. Sta.; bud pointed; flowers purplish red, reverse crimson-carmine, well-formed, 32-36 petals; foliage dark; strong stems; vigorous, bushy growth; ['Lele' × 'Crimson Glory']

'Lolly Pop' -- See 'Lollypop'

'Lollypop' ('Lolly Pop') HT, op, Kordes; flowers salmon, large, dbl., high-centered, borne mostly singly; recurrent; florist rose; intr. 2001

'Lolo' -- See 'Cooplo'

'London Pride' HT, op, 1954, Ratcliffe; flowers deep salmon-pink shaded coral, high-centered; upright growth

'London Starlets' HT, ob, 1959, Maarse, G.; flowers orange to orange-red, well-shaped, large, 50 petals; long, strong stems; vigorous growth; ['Mission Bells' × ('Jiminy Cricket' × unknown)]

'London Town' HT, op, 1955, Letts; flowers salmon-pink, base buff, well-formed, medium, moderate fruity fragrance; vigorous growth; ['Peace' × 'Charles Gregory']

'Lone Star' HT, mr, 1925, Buller; flowers velvety cardinal-red, large, semi-dbl.; vigorous, upright growth; ['Étoile de France' × unknown]

'Lone Star State' HT, pb, 1943, Collins; flowers darker than parent, irregularly striped white; [sport of 'Texas Centennial']

'Lonesome Dove' -- See 'Tomkris'

'Lonette Chenault' Pol, lp, 1925, Chenault; flowers creamy rose pink, medium, dbl.

Long Island® -- See 'Caslon'

'Long John Silver' HSet, w, 1934, Horvath; bud pointed; flowers silvery white, 11 cm., dbl., cupped, borne in large clusters, moderate fragrance; occasional repeat; foliage large, leathery; growth vigorous, climbing; [(R. setigera × unknown) × 'Sunburst']

Long Tall Sally™ -- See 'Wekajazoul'

'Long White Cloud' -- See 'Maclanoflon'

'Longchamp' F, mr, 1962, Laperrière; flowers bright red cerise, medium, semi-dbl., borne in clusters; foliage glossy; vigorous, symmetrical growth; intr. 1960

'Longchamp 80' S, Laperrière; intr. 1980

'Longford' S, dp, before 1938, Preston; flowers carmine-pink to medium, 3½ cm., dbl., borne in clusters of 5-10, no fragrance; [R. helenae × a gallica]

'Longleat' -- See 'Macinca'

'Longueuil' -- See 'Wekplagneze'

'Longwood' LCl, mp, 1914, Wintzer; flowers semi-dbl.; ['American Pillar' × seedling]

'Longworth Rambler' LCl, mr, 1880, Liabaud; flowers light crimson, semi-dbl.; vigorous growth; possibly the same as 'Deschamps'

'Looking Good' -- See 'Welgood'

'Looks Like Fun' -- See 'Seafun'

Looping® -- See 'Meirovonex'

'Lord Allenby' HT, dr, 1923, Dickson, A.; flowers bright crimson, very large, dbl., high-centered; foliage rich green, leathery; dwarf, sturdy growth

'Lord Bacon' HP, dr, 1883, Paul & Son; flowers deep crimson shaded scarlet, large, dbl., globular; vigorous growth

'Lord Baden-Powell' HT, ob, 1937, Leenders, M.; bud orange striped red; flowers saffron-yellow, large, very dbl.; vigorous, bushy, compact growth

'Lord Beaconsfield' ('Earl of Beaconsfield') HP, dr, 1878, Christy; flowers blackish crimson, large, full, globular

'Lord Byron' -- See 'Meitosier'

'Lord Calvert' HT, dr, 1919, Cook, J.W.; flowers dark velvety red, dbl.; ['Radiance' × 'Hoosier Beauty']

'Lord Castlereagh' HT, dr, 1927, Dickson, A.; bud pointed; flowers dark blackish crimson, open, semi-dbl.; foliage dark, leathery; vigorous, bushy growth

'Lord Charlemont, Climbing' Cl HT, dr, 1932, Hurcombe; [sport of 'Lord Charlemont']

'Lord Charlemont' HT, dr, 1922, McGredy; bud long, pointed; flowers clear deep crimson, well-shaped, large, dbl., high-centered; foliage dark, leathery; bushy growth

'Lord Chelmsford' HT, mr, Williams, H.

'Lord Clyde' HP, dr, 1863, Paul & Son; flowers bright crimson, well-formed, large

'Lord Don' S, rb; flowers rich red, large, semi-dbl., cupped, slight fragrance; recurrent; robust, bushy growth; hips small, round, red; intr. 1993

'Lord Eldon' -- See 'Earl of Eldon'

'Lord Fairfax' HT, dp, 1925, Gray, W.R.; flowers cherry-rose-pink, moderate fragrance; foliage leathery; long stems

'Lord Frederick Cavendish' HP, mr, 1884, Frettingham; flowers bright scarlet

Lord Gold® -- See 'Delgold'

'Lord Herbert' HP, dp, 1864, Paul, W.

'Lord Hotspur'™ S, lp, Harkness; flowers blooms soft pink, 4 in., 35 petals, cupped, reflexed, slight fragrance; recurrent; vigorous, upright, tall growth; intr. 2007

'Lord Houghton of Sowerby' -- See 'Hartubond'

'Lord Kitchener' HT, dp, 1918, Chaplin Bros.; flowers bright carmine-rose, dbl.

'Lord Lambourne' HT, yb, 1925, McGredy; bud pointed; flowers buttercup-yellow, edged carmine-scarlet, very large, dbl., high-centered; foliage light, leathery, glossy; very vigorous, bushy growth

'Lord Lonsdale' HT, ab, 1933, Dickson, A.; bud pointed; flowers deepest orange-yellow, large, dbl., high-centered; foliage glossy, light; vigorous, bushy growth

'Lord Louie' -- See 'Harmantelle'

'Lord Louis' HT, dp, 1981, Gregory, C.; bud pointed; flowers light crimson, 30 petals, borne several together, moderate fragrance; foliage mid-green, glossy; vigorous growth; ['Pink Favorite' × seedling]; intr. 1982

'Lord Macaulay' HP, dr, 1863, Paul, W.; flowers crimson, large, full, nearly globular

'Lord Mountbatten' -- See 'Harmantelle'

'Lord Napier' HP, dp, 1874, Paul, W.

'Lord Palmerston' HP, mr, 1857, Margottin; flowers rose red, medium, full

'Lord Penzance' HEg, yb, 1894, Penzance; flowers soft rosy yellow, paler at base, yellow stamens, small, single, 1 in., borne in small clusters, moderate fragrance; summer bloom; foliage small, dark, fragrant; very vigorous growth; [R. rubiginosa × 'Harison's Yellow']

'Lord Raglan' HP, dr, 1854, Guillot Père; flowers bright velvety crimson, very large, very dbl.; ['Geant des Batailles' × unknown]

'Lord Robbie' HT, w; flowers ivory white with apricot buff shading; stems long

'Lord Rossmore' HT, w, 1930, Hall; flowers creamy white shaded rose toward edge, large, dbl., high-centered; foliage dark olive-green, leathery; vigorous growth

'Lord Scarman' HGal, pb, Scarman; intr. 1996

'Lord Stair' HT, dr, 1930, Smith, T.; bud pointed; flowers velvety crimson-scarlet, large, dbl., high-centered; foliage dark, leathery; very vigorous, bushy growth

'Lord Worthington' HT, mp, 1928, Dickson, A.; flowers medium, dbl.

'Lordly Oberon' -- See 'Ausron'

'L'Oréal Trophy' -- See 'Harlexis'

'Loredo' -- See 'Noalesa'

'Loree' F, w, 1969, Pal, Dr. B.P.; bud long, pointed; flowers white tinted pink, small, dbl., cupped; foliage leathery; vigorous, bushy, compact growth; ['Frolic' × unknown]

Lorelei™ S, mp, Poulsen; bud pointed ovoid; flowers 5 cm., 25 petals, reflexed open cup, borne in clusters, slight fragrance; recurrent; foliage dark green, semi-glossy; prickles numerous, 5 mm., hooked downward, greyed-red; bushy (80 cm.) growth; PP15748; [seedling × seedling]; intr. 2003

'Lorelei' S, ab, 1947, Fisher, R.C.; bud ovoid; flowers peach-pink, center yellow, 3-4 in., semi-dbl., intense fragrance; non-recurrent; foliage leathery, dark; vigorous, upright growth; ['Joanna Hill' × 'Harison's Yellow']

'Loreley' Pol, lp, 1913, Kiese; flowers creamy rose pink, medium, dbl.

Loreley 82® HT, dr, Noack, Werner; intr. 1982

Lorena® -- See 'Korenlo'

'Lorena Kordana' Min, dp, Kordes; flowers dbl., high-centered; pot rose

'Lorenz Schwamborn' Pol, mr, Schmid, P.; flowers medium, semi-dbl.; intr. 1960

'Lorenzo Pahissa' HT, op, 1941, Pahissa; flowers coral, 5-6 in., dbl., borne mostly solitary, moderate fragrance; good repeat; foliage abundant; very vigorous, upright growth; [seedling × 'Mari Dot']

'Loreto Gold' S, yb, 2007, Ross, Andrew; flowers medium yellow, reverse lighter, 8 cm., full, cupped, blooms borne mostly solitary; foliage medium size, dark green, glossy; prickles medium, hooked, brown, moderate; growth upright, tall (1¾ m.); garden decoration; [Gina Lollobrigida® × 'Friesia']; intr. 2007

Loretta® -- See 'Korenpi'

'Loretta' F, dp, Kordes; flowers rich pink, fading slightly as they open, full, cupped, borne mostly singly; recurrent; stems moderately long; florist rose; intr. 2005

'Loretto' LCl, pb, 1922, Clark, A.; flowers reddish, center white, semi-dbl., borne in clusters; few prickles; vigorous, climbing growth; ['Jersey Beauty' × seedling]

'Lori' LCl, or, 2007, Jerabek, Paul; flowers orange-red, reverse slighlty lighter, 3¼ in., 50 petals, borne in small clusters; foliage medium size, medium green, semi-glossy; prickles ¼ in., triangular red, moderate; growth upright, medium; garden decorative; [unknown × unknown]; intr. 2007

'Lori Ann' F, yb, 1991, Schneider, Peter; flowers bright amber yellow, flushed orange and pink, reverse yellow, large, 20 petals, cupped, loose, borne usually singly or in sprays of 3 - 5, moderate fruity fragrance; foliage medium size, medium green, semi-glossy, slightly elongated and narrow; slightly spreading, medium growth; ['Judy Garland' × 'Sutter's Gold']; intr. 1990

'Lori Nan' Min, dp, 1965, Moore, Ralph S.; bud globular; flowers rose-red, small, dbl.; foliage glossy, leathery; moderate growth; [(R. wichurana × 'Floradora') × (seedling × 'Zee')]

'L'Orientale' HGal, m, before 1829, Coquerel; flowers light purple, edges lighter, medium, very full

'L'Orléanaise' Bslt, lp, 1899, Vigneron; flowers very light pink, darker at center, 7-8 cm., very full, sometimes quartered, borne singly or in small clusters; foliage glaucous; thornless; ['Mme de Sancy de Parabère' × 'Blush Boursault']

'Lorna' -- See 'Cocringer'

'Lorna' HT, op, 1936, Cant, B. R.; bud pointed; flowers salmon, dbl., high-centered; foliage leathery, glossy, light; vigorous, bushy growth

'Lorna Anderson' HT, mr, 1940, Clark, A.; flowers well-formed

'Lorna Clare' -- See 'Rawgush'

'Lorna Doone' B, mr, 1894, Paul, W.; flowers magenta carmine, shaded with scarlet, large, full, globular

'Lorna Doone' F, mr, Harkness; flowers 4 in., 24 petals; foliage dark, glossy; ['Red Dandy' × Lilli Marleen®]; intr. 1970

'Lorna May' F, rb, 1959, deRuiter; flowers crimson-red, center white trusses, 2 in., single; foliage light green; vigorous growth; ['Poulsen's Pink' × 'Kathe Duvigneau']; intr. 1958

'Lorraine' HT, op, 1945, Meilland, F.; flowers salmon-carmine touched red, large, dbl.; vigorous growth; ['Peace' × 'Mme Mallerin']

'Lorraine' S, mp; intr. 1992

'Lorraine Lee' T, pb, 1924, Clark, A.; bud pointed; flowers rosy apricot-pink, dbl., cupped, moderate fragrance; foliage rich green, leathery, glossy; vigorous growth; ['Jessie Clark' × 'Capitaine Millet']

'Lorraine Lee, Climbing' Cl T, pb, 1932, McKay; bud pointed; flowers golden apricot-pink, darker reverse, semi-dbl.; [sport of 'Lorraine Lee']

'Lorraine Stebbings' Min, w, 1985, Morey, Dr. Dennison; flowers small, 23 petals, borne singly, slight honey fragrance; foliage small, glossy; upright, bushy growth; ['Cinderella' × 'Popcorn']

'Los Angeles, Climbing' Cl HT, pb, 1925, H&S; flowers light orange pink, yellow center, very large, full; [sport of 'Los Angeles']

'Los Angeles' HT, op, 1916, Howard, F.H.; bud pointed; flowers coral-pink, base gold, large, dbl.; foliage leathery; vigorous, spreading growth; ['Mme Segond Weber' × 'Lyon Rose']

'Los Angeles Beautiful' ('Waikiki') Gr, yb, 1967, Lammerts, Dr. Walter; flowers yellow blended with coral and scarlet, medium, dbl., high-centered; foliage dark, leathery; vigorous, upright, compact growth; PP2876; [Queen Elizabeth® × 'Rumba']

'Los Angeles Frost' HT, lp, Robinson; flowers soft ivory to ivory-pink, pale apricot at petal base, moderate fragrance; recurrent; foliage dark green; growth moderate to tall; intr. 1989

'Los Tejas' HT, mr, 1968, Patterson; bud globular; flowers large, dbl., high-centered, moderate fragrance; foliage leathery; vigorous, upright growth; PP3073; ['Chrysler Imperial' × 'Happiness']

'Lost in Paradise' Min, m, Spooner, Raymond A.; intr. 1997

'Lotte Günthart' HT, mr, 1964, Armstrong, D.L.; bud ovoid; flowers bright red, large, 90 petals, peony-like; foliage leathery; tall, upright, bushy growth; PP2585; [Queen Elizabeth® × 'Bravo']

'Lottie Forster' Pol, mr, Matthews, W.J.

'Lottum Abundance' -- See 'St Piers'

'Lou-Celina' S, dr, 1984, James, John; flowers large, 50 petals, moderate fragrance; repeat bloom; foliage medium size, dark red-green, semi-glossy; upright growth; [('Venture' × '(Cecilia × China Belle)' × 'Suzanne')) × ('Paula' × 'Soeur Kristin')]; intr. 1979

'L'Ouche' HCh, pb, 1901, Buatois; flowers rose shaded yellow, large, full, cupped, moderate peppery-tea fragrance; growth upright, large

'Louis Baldwin' -- See 'Louise Baldwin'

'Louis Barbier' ('Louise Barbier') HFt, ob, 1909, Barbier; flowers coppery orange with dark yellow striping, 7 cm., semi-dbl., borne in small clusters; ['Mme Bérard' × R. foetida bicolor]

'Louis Barlet' T, w, 1876, Ducher, Vve.; flowers flesh white with salmon

'Louis Béluze' B, mp, about 1840, Béluze; flowers bright pink, medium, full

'Louis Bernard' HT, or, Croix; intr. 1969

'Louis Bourgoin' HT, lp, 1921, Gillot, F.; flowers flesh-pink passing to silvery pink, dbl.; ['Jonkheer J.L. Mock' × 'Frau Karl Druschki']

'Louis Brassac' HP, mp, 1872, Brassac; flowers silky pink, reverse silver, large, full

'Louis Bruyère' Cl HT, dp, 1941, Buatois; flowers deep cerise pink, reverse and center lighter, 3-4 in., dbl., flat

'Louis Bulliat' HP, mp, 1867, Gonod; flowers carmine

'Louis Calla' HP, m, 1885, Verdier, E.; flowers purple/pink, large, dbl.

'Louis Cazas' D, lp, about 1850; flowers medium, very full, moderate fragrance

'Louis Chaix' B, mr, 1857, Lacharme; flowers bright red, shaded carmine, large, full; ['Géant des Batailles' × unknown]

'Louis Charlin' HP, pb, 1871, Damaizin; flowers bright pink, center red, very large, full

'Louis Clapot' HT, dp, 1906, Bidaud; flowers dark carmine with violet reflections, large, full, cupped

'Louis Corbie' HP, mr, 1871, Corbie; flowers bright crimson, large, full

Louis de Funes® -- See 'Meirestif'

'Louis Donadine' HP, dr, 1887, Gonod; flowers deep velvety maroon, nuanced flame, very large, full; very remontant; foliage dark green; growth upright; ['Duhamel-Dumonceau' × unknown]

'Louis d'Or' HT, Dorieux; intr. 1965

'Louis Doré' HP, mr, 1879, Fontaine; flowers shining cherry red, shaded purple, large to very large, full

'Louis' Double Rush' S, pb, Lens; bud red; flowers medium pink with white eye,

2-3 in., loose, borne in clusters, slight fragrance; foliage dark green, glossy; growth to 4 ft.; intr. 2001

'Louis Faurax' HT, ob, 1941, Gaujard; flowers coppery-salmon with dark yellow, large, dbl.

'Louis Faure' -- See 'Lucie Faure'

'Louis XIV' HGal, m, 1824, Hardy; flowers light lilac pink, large, full

'Louis XIV' HP, dr, Guillot et Fils; flowers dark crimson, medium, 25 petals, intense fragrance; foliage sparse; moderate growth; ['Général Jacqueminot' × unknown]; sometimes classed as Ch; intr. 1859

'Louis Gimard' M, mp, 1877, Pernet père; flowers bright pink, very large, dbl.; prickles very bristly, moss-like; long stems; vigorous growth

'Louis Gulino' HP, dr, 1859, Guillot; flowers purple-red, shaded pink, medium, full

Louis J. Appell, Jr.™ -- See 'Weklappell'

'Louis Joliet' -- See 'Louis Jolliet'

'Louis Jolliet' ('Louis Joliet') HKor, mp, 1991, Svejda, Felicitas & Ogilvie, Ian S.; flowers 6-7 cm., full, borne in large clusters, slight fragrance; foliage medium size, medium green, semi-glossy; spreading, low growth; PP9222; [(R. × kordesii × O.P. Max Graf) × (R. × kordesii × (Red Dawn × Suzanne × Champlain))]; intr. 1990

'Louis Kahle' HT, mr, 1922, Kiese; flowers bright cherry-red; ['Lieutenant Chauré' × 'Étoile de France']

'Louis Lévêque' -- See 'Erzherzog Franz Ferdinand'

'Louis Lille' HP, mr, 1887, Dubreuil; flowers bright red with light flame, very large, full, cupped; foliage dark green

'Louis Mon Ami' Ayr, pb, Louette; flowers magenta/lilac with white eye, dbl., pompon, borne in clusters, slight fragrance; non-remontant; foliage glossy; flexible, climbing growth; [R. arvensis plena × unknown]; intr. 2001

'Louis Noisette' HP, mp, 1865, Ducher; flowers carmine pink, large, full, borne in small clusters

'Louis Pajotin' HT, op, 1940, Mallerin, C.; flowers coral, stamens yellow, large, very dbl.; long, stiff stems; very vigorous growth; ['Souv. de Claudius Pernet' × 'Margaret McGredy']

'Louis Pajotin, Climbing' Cl HT, op, 1959, Pajotin-Chédane; [sport of 'Louis Pajotin']

'Louis-Philippe' ('Crown', 'Louis-Philippe d'Angers', 'Superbe du Bengale', 'Purple', 'Président d'Olbecque') Ch, rb, Guérin; flowers dark crimson with edges of center petals blush, aging crimson, dbl., globular; bushy growth; intr. 1834

'Louis-Philippe' ('Grandissima') HGal, m; flowers rosy crimson, sometimes purplish, aging to violet, very large, dbl., cupped, quartered; foliage medium green, rounded; prickles moderate; moderate, branching growth; possibly from Hardy, 1824; intr. before 1835

'Louis-Philippe' B, dr, Miellez; flowers purplish rose, center pinkish, large, very dbl., cupped; intr. 1835

'Louis-Philippe, Climbing' Cl Ch, rb, before 1955; flowers deep red; [sport of 'Louis-Philippe']

'Louis-Philippe' T, lp, about 1830, Cels; flowers vivid light pink, large, full

'Louis Philippe Albert d'Orléans' -- See 'Louis Philippe d'Orléans'

'Louis-Philippe d'Angers' -- See 'Louis-Philippe'

'Louis Philippe d'Orléans' ('Louis Philippe Albert d'Orléans') HP, mr, 1884, Verdier, E.; flowers cerise red, tinted purplish scarlet grenadine, large, full; foliage large, rounded, somber green; prickles unequal, short, hooked; growth upright

'Louis-Philippe I' P, dr, 1832, Duval, C.; flowers crimson shaded with purple and violet, very large, full, intense fragrance; probably extinct

'Louis Puyravaud' N, my, 1896, Puyravaud; flowers canary yellow, aging to light yellow, large, full; ['Rêve d'Or' × unknown]

'Louis' Rambler' HMult, w, Lens, Louis; bud yellow, pointed; flowers white, sometimes with yellow flush, large, single, flat, borne in panicles of 7-48, intense musk fragrance; non-remontant; prickles spines on pedicels; growth strong climber to 20 ft.; hips yellow-orange with black tip; [R. brunonii × R. multiflora adenocheata]; intr. 1997

'Louis Ricard' HP, m, 1902, Boutigny, P.; flowers velvety dark purple, shaded vermilion, very large, full

'Louis Richard' -- See 'Helvetia'

'Louis Riel' -- See 'Zublou'

'Louis Rödiger' LCl, ob, 1935, Kordes; bud pointed; flowers orange shaded yellow and red, open, very large, semi-dbl., moderate fruity fragrance; foliage leathery, wrinkled, dark; prickles numerous, large; very vigorous, climbing trailing growth; ['Daisy Hill' × ('Charles P. Kilham' × 'Mev. G.A. van Rossem')]

'Louis Rollet' HP, dr, 1886, Gonod; flowers purplish red, large, full; very remontant; foliage large; prickles large, red

'Louis Sauvage' HWich, m, 1914, Turbat; flowers purple/red, 3 cm., dbl., flat, borne in clusters of 5-15, no fragrance; foliage medium green; numerous prickles

'Louis van Houtte' HP, dp, 1863, Granger; flowers shining carmine pink, shaded velvety dark red, edges fire-red, reverse lighter, full

'Louis van Houtte' HP, dr, Lacharme, F.; flowers crimson-maroon, well-formed, large, 40 petals, intense fragrance; some recurrent bloom; ['Général Jacqueminot' × unknown]; intr. 1869

'Louis van Tyle' HGal, m, before 1846; flowers light crimson, shaded black or purple, small, semi-dbl.

'Louis Walter' HT, ab, 1938, Mallerin, C.; flowers golden orange-yellow, large, dbl.; foliage clear green, glossy; vigorous growth; [('Mrs Pierre S. duPont' × unknown) × 'Charles P. Kilham']

'Louis XII' HGal, m, before 1829, Coquerel; flowers lilac pink, becoming violet red, medium, full, cupped

'Louis XVI' -- See 'Achille'

'Louis XVIII' Ch, m, 1827, Mauget; flowers bright purple

'Louisa Jane' HT, pb, 1976, Ross, A., & Son; flowers center soft white, shading to deep pink, full, high-centered; growth medium; [sport of Baronne Edmond de Rothschild®]; intr. 1975

'Louisa Jane Morris' -- See 'Bosadson'

'Louisa Schultheis' HT, op, 1925, Schultheis, A.; flowers pink and salmon, center darker, 32-36 petals; ['Golden Ophelia' × 'Ruhm von Steinfurth']

Louisa Stone™ -- See 'Harbadge'

'Louise' -- See 'La Louise'

'Louise' S, dy, Zilligen, George D.; flowers golden yellow, blushing pink on petal ends, fading to bright yellow, small, semi-dbl., borne mostly solitary, moderate fragrance; foliage medium size, medium green, semi-glossy; spreading growth; bedding, borders; ['Golden Celebration' × unknown]; intr. 2004

'Louise' ('La Louise') HGal, dr, about 1840, Parmentier; flowers red, shaded purple, full

'Louise' HT, mp, Prince; bud pointed; flowers rose-pink shaded cerise, large, dbl., intense fragrance; foliage dark, leathery; vigorous growth; ['Isobel' × unknown]; intr. 1924

'Louise Abdy' F, mp, 1964, Abdy, S.; flowers pink, base yellow, 4 in., 6 petals, moderate fragrance; foliage dark; vigorous growth; ['Donald Prior' × 'McGredy's Yellow']

'Louise Aimé' P, 1845, Aimé

'Louise Baldwin' ('Louis Baldwin') HT, ob, 1919, McGredy; bud pointed; flowers rich orange, tinted soft apricot, dbl., high-centered; vigorous growth

'Louise Barbier' -- See 'Louis Barbier'

'Louise Béluze' B, dp, about 1840, Béluze; flowers dark carmine, medium, full

'Louise Bugnet' HRg, w, Bugnet, George; bud red; flowers white with hint of pink, dbl.; foliage tough; almost thornless; growth medium (4 ft.); intr. before 1960

'Louise Carique' -- See 'Mme Louise Carique'

'Louise Catherine Breslau' HT, op, 1912, Pernet-Ducher; flowers shrimp-pink shaded reddish coppery orange, reverse chrome-yellow, very large, dbl., moderate fragrance; foliage dark, bronze, leathery; bushy growth; [seedling × ('Soleil d'Or' × unknown)]

'Louise Catherine Breslau, Climbing' Cl HT, op, 1917, Kordes; flowers copper orange-red, large, very full, flat; [sport of 'Louise Catherine Breslau']

'Louise Clements' -- See 'Clelou'

'Louise Cretté' HP, w, 1915, Chambard, C.; flowers snow-white, center creamy white, well-formed, 6-7 in., 55 petals, high-centered, moderate fragrance; foliage dark; vigorous, bushy growth; ['Frau Karl Druschki' × 'Kaiserin Auguste Viktoria, Climbing']

'Louise Criner' HT, w, 1919, Chambard, C.; flowers snow-white, center creamy, dbl.; few prickles; ['Louise Cretté' × unknown]

'Louise Damaizin' HP, mp, 1864, Damaizin; flowers fresh pink, medium, full

'Louise d'Arzens' N, w, 1861, Lacharme, F.; flowers creamy white, small, full, cupped; [probably 'Mlle Blanche Laffitte' × 'Sappho' (Damask Perpetual)]; sometimes classed as B

'Louise d'Autriche' HP, m; flowers violet, large, full; [sport of 'La Reine']

'Louise de Savoie' T, ly, 1854, Ducher; flowers pale canary yellow, very large, full

'Louise de Vilmorin' HT, ab, 1944, Gaujard; bud ovoid; flowers orange-yellow, overlarge, very dbl.; foliage glossy, dark; dwarf growth

'Louise Emma' -- See 'Sarlet'

'Louise Estes' HT, pb, 1991, Winchel, Joseph F.; bud pointed; flowers pink blend, reverse white, aging medium pink, 4 in., 35 petals, high-centered, borne usually singly, moderate fruity fragrance; quick repeat; foliage medium size, medium green, matte, disease-resistant; upright, medium growth; [seedling × 'Miss Canada']; intr. 1992

'Louise Gardner' -- See 'Macerupt'

'Louise Gaujard' HT, op, 1941, Gaujard; flowers coppery pink shaded coral, open, very large, very dbl., cupped; foliage light green; vigorous, upright growth; ['Mme Joseph Perraud' × seedling]

Louise Hay™ -- See 'Wekwesytpla'

'Louise Hopkins' HMult, lp, 1923, Hopkins; flowers white, center shell-pink, 200-225 petals; non-recurrent; vigorous, climbing (20 ft. or more) growth; [sport of Trier®]

'Louise Joly' HT, or, 1922, Buatois; flowers coral-red, shaded shrimp-pink, large, dbl., cupped, borne mostly solitary, moderate fragrance; foliage glossy; few prickles; growth upright, bushy; ['Mme Edouard Herriot' × seedling]

'Louise Krause' HT, ob, 1930, Krause; flowers reddish-orange, passing to golden yellow, large, dbl.; foliage dark, glossy; vigorous, bushy growth; ['Mrs Beckwith' × 'Souv. de H.A. Verschuren']

'Louise L. Hay' -- See 'Worcentury'

'Louise le Cardonnel' HT, yb, 1939, Mallerin, C.; bud globular; flowers yellow tinted coral, very large, dbl.; stiff stems; very vigorous growth; [seedling × 'Mev. G.A. van Rossem']

'Louise Lilia' -- See 'Luise Lilia'

'Louise Mack' Min, dr, 1992, Jerabek, Paul E.; flowers 1¼ in., 30 petals, high-centered, borne usually singly; foliage medium size, dark green, semi-glossy; medium, spreading growth; [unknown × unknown]; intr. 1984

'Louise Magnan' HP, w, 1855, Fontaine; flowers pure white, medium, dbl.

'Louise Margottin' B, lp, 1862, Margottin; flowers silky light pink, medium, full

'Louise Méhul' HGal, pb, Parmentier; flowers light red, spotted white, large, flat

'Louise Odier' ('Mme de Stella') B, dp, 1851, Margottin; flowers bright rose-pink, well-formed, dbl., cupped; foliage medium green, matte; prickles very few; tall growth

Louise Park™ -- See 'Willork'

'Louise Pernot' HT, lp, 1903, Robichon; flowers delicate silvery pink, salmon at center, large, dbl.

'Louise Peyronny' ('Lœlia') HP, dp, 1844, Lacharme, F.; flowers deep pink shaded carmine, very large, dbl., moderate fragrance; moderate growth; [supposedly a seedling of 'La Reine']; possibly synonymous with 'Laelia'

'Louise Pigné' T, mp, 1905, Pigné; flowers China-pink, base buff-yellow, petals crinkled, very large, very dbl.; very vigorous growth; ['Mme Eugene Resal' × 'Mme Lombard']

'Louise Pommery' F, ab, Sauvageot; flowers apricot with carmine tints at edges, dbl.; intr. 2002

'Louise Simplex' -- See 'La Louise'

'Louise Verger' M, lp, 1860, Robert et Moreau; flowers bright pink, lighter at edges, 8-9 cm., dbl., cupped

'Louise Walter' Pol, pb, 1909, Walter, L.; flowers white and flesh-pink, open, dbl.; foliage small, rich green; very dwarf growth; ['Tausendschön' × 'Rosel Dach']

'Louise Weiss' F, ly, Pekmez; intr. 2006

'Louise Wood' HP, mp, 1869, Verdier, E.; flowers shining pink, large, dbl.

'Louisiana' HT, w, 1975, Weeks, O. L.; flowers creamy white, 3-4 in., 38 petals, high-centered; foliage dark, leathery; upright growth; PP3719; [seedling × seedling]; intr. 1974

'Louisiana, Climbing' Cl HT, w, Weeks; PP4797; [sport of 'Louisiana']; intr. 1985

'Louisiana' HT, op, Kordes; intr. 1992

Louisiana Lady™ -- See 'Tallou'

'Louisiana Purchase' HT, dp, 1955, Swim, H.C.; bud long, pointed; flowers rich cerise, 4-5 in., 20-25 petals, cupped, intense damask fragrance; foliage dark, leathery; very vigorous, upright growth; PP963; ['Charlotte Armstrong' × 'Piccaninny']; intr. 1954

'Louisville Lady' -- See 'Wellady'

'Louisville Lady' HT, pb, 1986, Weddle, Von C.; flowers bright pink, silver reverse, medium, 35 petals, high-centered; foliage medium size, dark, semi-glossy; bushy growth; ['Osiria' × seedling]

'Louita' F, rb

'Louksor' -- See 'Delcraf'

Loulou de Cacharel® ('Kempton Park') F, rb, Dorieux; flowers white with red to deep pink edges, semi-double, shallow cup, borne in clusters; recurrent; strong growth; intr. 1999

'Loumuskoka' ('Muskoka Moonlight') HT, w, 1999, Lougheed, Larry; flowers near white, medium, full; foliage medium size, medium green, glossy; some prickles; vigorous, spreading, tall growth; very hardy; [Pristine® × Lichtkönigin Lucia®]; intr. 1998

Louqsor® -- See 'Delcraf'

'Lourdes' HT, dy, 1960, Brownell, W. D.; bud ovoid; flowers golden yellow, 4-5 in., 35-50 petals, moderate fragrance; foliage leathery, glossy, dark; vigorous growth; hardy for the class; PP1491; ['V for Victory' × (sport of 'New Dawn' × sport of 'Copper Glow')]; intr. 1959

Lourdes Arroyo® -- See 'Feprogo'

'Louviola' ('Viola Lougheed') Gr, pb, 1997, Lougheed, Larry; flowers large, very dbl., borne in large clusters; foliage medium size, medium green, semi-glossy; numerous prickles; tall, spreading growth; [Pristine® × Peter Frankenfeld®]

Louvre® -- See 'Delfat'

'Lovable' HT, lp, 1979, Leon, Charles F., Sr.; bud long, pointed; flowers 4½-6 in., 30 petals, high-centered; vigorous, upright, bushy growth; [('Helen Traubel' × 'Michele Meilland') × (('Blanche Mallerin' × 'Peace') × ('Peace' × 'Virgo'))]

'Lovace' -- See 'Sheila Sorensen'

'Lovafred' F, mp, 2004, Paul Chessum Roses; intr. 2004

'Lovalady' ('Evelyn Tebbutt') F, ab, 2004, Paul Chessum Roses; flowers apricot-pink, reverse lighter, 6 cm., dbl., borne in small clusters, slight fragrance; foliage medium size, medium green, semi-glossy; prickles small, green, few; growth compact, bushy, medium (60 cm.); beds, borders, containers; intr. 2004

'Lovalish' HT, rb, 2004, Paul Chessum Roses; intr. 2004

'Lovandy' F, my, 2005, Paul Chessum Roses; intr. 2004

'Lovangle' ('Touching Lives') F, dy, 2004, Paul Chessum Roses; flowers full, borne in small clusters, moderate fragrance; recurrent; foliage large, medium green, semi-glossy; prickles moderate, medium, green; growth compact, bushy, medium (85 cm.); bedding, containers; intr. 2004

'Lovania' S, or, 1979, Lens, Louis; bud ovoid; flowers bright red-orange, 1½ in., 18-22 petals, pompon, moderate fruity fragrance; recurrent bloom; foliage dark; vigorous, upright, climbing growth; ['Robin Hood' × ('New Penny' × 'Coloranja')]; intr. 1978

'Lovanotion' F, dp, 2004, Paul Chessum Roses; intr. 2004

'Lovapure' F, w, 2004, Paul Chessum

The Official Registry and Checklist — Rosa 417

Roses; intr. 2004

'Lovasilk' F, ly, 2004, Paul Chessum Roses; intr. 2004

'Lovastripe' F, pb, 2004, Paul Chessum Roses; intr. 2004

'Lovatlas' ('The Papworth Hospital Rose') HT, dr, 2004, Paul Chessum Roses; flowers 7 cm., dbl., borne mostly solitary, slight fragrance; foliage medium size, medium green, semi-glossy; prickles moderate, medium, green; growth upright, medium (90cm.); bedding, borders, containers; intr. 2004

'Lovattitude' F, pb, 2005, Paul Chessum Roses; intr. 2004

'Lovauction' ('Daniel Greenway') HT, dy, 2004, Paul Chessum Roses; flowers 10 cm., dbl., borne mostly solitary, slight fragrance; foliage large, medium green, matte; prickles medium, green, moderate; growth upright, tall (110 cm.); bedding, borders, containers; [seedling × seedling]; intr. 2004

'Lovbang' ('Hazel Woodland') F, ab, 2005, Paul Chessum Roses; flowers apricot, 6 cm., semi-dbl., borne in small clusters, moderate fragrance; foliage medium size, dark green, glossy; spreading, medium growth; bedding, borders, containers; [seedling × seedling]; intr. 2005

'Lovbeadle' ('Nora Pugh') F, mp, 2005, Paul Chessum Roses; flowers dbl., borne mostly solitary, intense fragrance; foliage medium size, medium green, semi-glossy; prickles moderate, medium, green; growth compact, medium (18 in.); beds, borders and tubs; [seedling × seedling]; intr. 2004

'Lovbed' ('Sue Earley') F, w, 2005, Paul Chessum Roses; flowers white blend, 4 cm., semi-dbl., borne in large clusters, slight fragrance; foliage small, medium green, semi-glossy; growth compact, short; [seedling × seedling]; intr. 2005

'Lovblend' ('Angie') F, lp, 2005, Paul Chessum Roses; flowers dbl., borne in small clusters, slight fragrance; foliage small, medium green, glossy; prickles medium; bushy, short growth; bedding, borders, containers; [seedling × seedling]; intr. 2005

'Lovbloom' ('Nicole Morris') F, dp, 2005, Paul Chessum Roses; flowers pure deep pink, 6 cm., dbl., borne in small clusters, slight fragrance; foliage medium size, medium green, semi-glossy; prickles small; bushy, medium growth; bedding, borders, containers; [seedling × seedling]; intr. 2005

'Lovbonny' ('Dave McQueen') F, mr, 2005, Paul Chessum Roses; flowers light red, 6 cm., dbl., borne in small clusters, slight fragrance; foliage medium size, medium green, semi-glossy; prickles small; bushy, medium growth; bedding, borders, containers; [seedling × seedling]; intr. 2005

'Lovclaire' ('Linda') Min, mr, 2005, Paul Chessum Roses; flowers semi-dbl., borne in large clusters, slight fragrance; foliage medium size, dark green, glossy; prickles moderate, small, sharp, pink; growth bushy, medium (2 ft.); bedding, borders, containers; [seedling × seedling]; intr. 2005

'Love' -- See 'Jactwin'

'Love' Cl HT, or, 1935, Mallerin, Berthe; flowers scarlet, medium to large, semi-dbl., moderate fragrance; occasional repeat; foliage dark; long stems; vigorous, climbing (6½-10 ft.), bushy growth; declared extinct, ARA 1979; ['Hadley' × 'Ami Quinard']

'Love Affair' HT, dr, 1972, Jelly; bud short pointed; flowers brilliant red, large, very dbl., high-centered, moderate fragrance; foliage large, dark, leathery; vigorous, upright growth; PP3287; ['red seedling' × 'Forever Yours']; intr. 1970

'Love 'n' Kisses' -- See 'Seawalk'

Love and Peace™ -- See 'Baipeace'

'Love And Peace' -- See 'Morlove'

'Love Bug' Min, ob, 1987, Bridges, Dennis A.; flowers orange, white base, reverse orange, veining to white base, fades slightly, 14 petals, high-centered; foliage medium size, medium green, semi-glossy; prickles short, small, pink, hooked slightly downward; growth bushy, medium; [Heartland™ × seedling]

'Love Call' HT, pb, 1990, Bridges, Dennis A.; bud ovoid; flowers deep pink, lighter at base, reverse light pink, large, 50 petals, high-centered, borne singly, moderate damask fragrance; recurrent; foliage medium size, dark green, glossy; prickles pointed slightly downward, medium, light green; growth upright, tall; ['Lady X' × 'Wini Edmunds']; intr. 1990

'Love Dove' -- See 'Lyove'

'Love in Bloom' -- See 'Judlov'

'Love Knot' -- See 'Chewglorious'

Love Letter® F, w, 1979, Lens, Louis; flowers creamy white, 3-3½ in., 30-35 petals, cupped, intense fragrance; foliage glossy, dark; vigorous, bushy, upright growth; ['Pink Parfait' × 'Rosenelfe']; intr. 1977

'Love Me' -- See 'Wallove'

'Love Me Do' HT, w, Benny; flowers ivory white, opening with a peach center, dbl; foliage glossy

'Love Me Tender' HT, m; flowers light lavender, cream pink petal edges, moderate fragrance; intr. 2002

'Love Note' -- See 'Zipnote'

Love Potion™ -- See 'Jacsedi'

'Love Song' ('Liebeslied') HT, pb, 1956, Fisher, E. G.; bud ovoid; flowers Neyron rose, reverse yellow, 4½-5 in., 45 petals, cupped, intense fragrance; foliage dark, glossy; vigorous, upright growth; PP1360; ['Peace' × 'Orange Nassau']

Love Story® HT, ob, 1974, Tantau, Math.; bud ovoid; flowers orange, large, dbl., cupped; intr. 1972

'Love Surprise' -- See 'Ausroyal'

'Love Surprise' -- See 'Ausromeo'

'Love Token' F, mp, 1965, Gregory; flowers peach-pink, well-formed, 2 in., 28 petals; foliage dark, glossy; vigorous growth; intr. 1963

Love Torch™ -- See 'Minabeco'

'Love 'Ya Dad' -- See 'Tindad'

'Love You' -- See 'Nemlove'

'Loveaura' ('Kirsty') HT, dp, 2004, Paul Chessum Roses; flowers fuchsia pink, 8 cm., full, cupped, borne mostly solitary, moderate fragrance; recurrent; foliage medium size, medium green, semi-glossy; prickles medium size, medium green, moderate; growth compact, bushy, medium (80 cm.); beds, borders, containers; intr. 2004

'Lovebird' -- See 'Franmilro'

Loveglo™ -- See 'Minjco'

'Lovejoy' HT, w, 2008, Heath, William L.; flowers white edged deep pink, reverse white, large, 4 in., full, high-centered, borne mostly solitary; foliage medium, dark green, semi-glossy; prickles medium, hooked down, dark brown, few; growth upright, tall (5 ft.); exhibition, garden decoration; [sport of Signature®]; intr. 2008

'Loveliest' HT, lp, 1956, Leon, Charles F., Sr.; bud ovoid; flowers clear rose-pink, large, dbl., high-centered; foliage leathery, light green; vigorous, upright growth; ['Charlotte Armstrong' × 'Juno']

'Lovelight' F, mp, 1960, Jelly; bud short, pointed; flowers large, 33 petals, high-centered; vigorous, upright growth; PP1887; ['Garnette' × seedling]; originally registered as Pol; intr. 1959

'Loveliness' HWich, lp, 1933, Chaplin Bros.; flowers pale pink, white spot at base, round, large, dbl., borne in large clusters; foliage small, light green, glossy; vigorous, climbing growth

'Lovely' -- See 'Karen'

'Lovely' HT, dp, 1936, H&S; bud pointed; flowers carmine-pink, large, semi-dbl., high-centered, moderate violet fragrance; foliage soft; vigorous, compact growth

'Lovely Amazone' HT, ab, Pouw; bud ovate; flowers dbl., high-centered, star-shaped, borne mostly singly, slight fragrance; free-flowering; foliage glossy, abundant; prickles moderate; growth vigorous, narrow, upright (6 ft.); PP10914; [seedling × seedling]; greenhouse rose; intr. 1997

'Lovely Blue' Min, m, Keisei; intr. 1990

'Lovely Bride' -- See 'Meiratcan'

Lovely Child™ -- See 'Roschild'

'Lovely Cupido' Min

'Lovely Dream' -- See 'Hilraz'

'Lovely Fairy' -- See 'Spevu'

'Lovely Fairy' -- See 'Tornerose'

'Lovely Girl' HT, ob; flowers ochre and orange-yellow, dbl., high-centered; foliage matte; growth to 90-100 cm.; PP11731; [((seedling × 'Jelfax') × 'Meigerium') × seedling]; greenhouse rose; intr. 1984

'Lovely Green' F, w, Meilland; flowers creamy white with green tint, full, high-centered; florist rose; intr. 2002

'Lovely Jubilee' HT, m, Interplant; intr. 1992

'Lovely Lady' -- See 'Dicjubell'

'Lovely Lady' HT, mr, 1934, Asmus; bud long, pointed; flowers pure rose-red, large, very dbl., high-centered, intense fragrance; foliage leathery; long, strong stems; growth very vigorous, open; PP241; RULED EXTINCT 10/86; [sport of 'Better Times']

'Lovely Lady' HMsk, mp; intr. 2004

Lovely Lorrie™ Min, mp, Moore; flowers soft pink turning lighter as it opens, 1½ in., dbl., borne singly and in small clusters; recurrent; moderate (12-16 in.) growth; intr. 1998

'Lovely Louise' F, ab; intr. 1990

'Lovely Lynda' -- See 'Welbell'

'Lovely Meidiland' -- See 'Meiratcan'

'Lovely Meidiland' ('Lovely Bride', 'Lovely Meidiland') S, lp, Meilland; flowers clear rose pink, medium, dbl., borne in large clusters; growth to 60-80 cm.

'Lovely Red' HT, dr, Meilland; flowers deep, velvety red, dbl., high-centered, borne mostly singly; recurrent; florist rose; intr. 1998

'Lovely Rosamini' Min, lp

'Lovely Ruffles' F, pb; intr. 2002

'Lovely Symphonie' Min, mp, Meilland; flowers rose pink, dbl., borne in small clusters; growth to 40-45 cm.

'Loverly' F, ab, 1984, Stoddard, Louis; flowers medium, semi-dbl., moderate fragrance; foliage medium size, medium green, semi-glossy; bushy growth; ['Restless Native' × 'Apricot Nectar']; intr. 1986

Lovers Lane™ -- See 'Jacinber'

'Lovers' Meeting' HT, ob, 1980, Gandy, O.L.; bud pointed; flowers bright orange, 25 petals, high-centered, borne singly and in clusters, moderate fragrance; foliage bronze; prickles short; strong, upright growth; [seedling × 'Egyptian Treasure']

'Lovers Only' -- See 'Sealove'

'Love's Gift' -- See 'Tomgift'

'Love's Promise' -- See 'Meisoyris'

'Love's Song' -- See 'Korresli'

'Love's Spring' -- See 'Macivy'

'Lovesong' S, lp, Clements, John; flowers elegant shade of pink, 4 in., 28 petals, globular, borne in clusters of 5-8, intense grapefruit and tea fragrance; foliage dark green; growth upright (4-5 ft.); PPAF; intr. 2004

Lovestruck™ -- See 'Jacboupu'

'Loving' -- See 'Jacka'

'Loving Care' -- See 'Worcube'

'Loving Heart' -- See 'Koigokoro'

'Loving Memory' -- See 'Korgund '81'

'Loving Son' HT, w, 1994, Mengel, Russell R.; flowers 4-7 cm., very dbl., borne mostly singly, moderate fragrance; good rebloom; foliage medium size, medium green, semi-glossy; some prickles; medium, bushy growth; [Honor™ × 'Captain Harry Stebbings']; intr. 1994

Loving Touch™ Min, ab, 1983, Jolly, Nelson F.; flowers deep apricot, 25 petals, high-centered, borne usually singly, slight fragrance; foliage medium size, medium green, semi-glossy; bushy, spreading growth; globular fruit; PP5835; ['Rise 'n' Shine' × 'Angel Darling']; intr. 1982

'Loving Wishes' -- See 'Poulfiry'

'Lovita' -- See 'Kiboh'

'Lovita' F, ab; flowers brown apricot deepening as it opens, dbl., classic; intr. 1989

'Lovita' HT, mr, 1967, Meilland; bud ovoid; flowers bright red, large, dbl.; foliage dark; vigorous, upright growth; PP2598; [Baccará® × ('Independence' × 'Peace')]; intr. 1965

'Lowburn Rose' Misc OGR, dp

'Lowel Allen' S, op, Williams, J. Benjamin; flowers soft salmon-pink, single, slight fragrance; recurrent; medium (4 ft.) growth; intr. 2005

'Lowell Thomas' ('Botaniste Abrial') HT, dy, 1943, Mallerin, C.; bud long, pointed; flowers rich yellow, 4-4½ in., 38 petals, high-centered; foliage leathery; vigorous, upright, bushy, compact growth; PP595; ['Mme Mélanie Soupert' × 'Nonin']; intr. 1943

'Lowell Thomas, Climbing' Cl HT, dy, 1955, Armstrong, J.A.; PP1448; [sport of 'Lowell Thomas']; intr. 1954

'Lowe's Eglantine' HEg, dp, Lowe; flowers semi-dbl., flat, borne in huge spring flush, no fragrance; intermittent repeat; foliage not fragrant; growth to 20 ft.; groundcover or climber on low fence; intr. 2001

'Loyal Friend' MinFl, w, Gardner; intr. 2001

'Loyal Rosarian' -- See 'Leoloyros'

'Loyal Vassal' -- See 'Welvass'

'Loyalist' -- See 'Great Maiden's Blush'

'Loyalist Dream' Gr, w

Luana+ F, dy, Voom, Lex; flowers double, high-centered, borne mostly singly; recurrent; stems medium to long; florist rose

'Luarca' HT, Dot, Simon

'Lübeck' -- See 'Hansestadt Lübeck'

Lübecker Rotspon® -- See 'Tantide'

'Luberon' -- See 'Uhlwe'

'Lubov Chevtsova' HT, lp, 1956, Sushkov, K. L.; flowers light pink, base tinted orange, large (5 in) foliage glossy; strong stems; upright growth; ['Cathrine Kordes' × 'Peace']

'Lubra' HT, dr, 1938, Fitzhardinge; bud long, pointed; flowers dark crimson, dbl., high-centered; foliage leathery, dark; vigorous growth; [('Ophelia, Climbing' × unknown) × 'Black Boy']

'Luc Steeno' HT, mp, RvS-Melle; intr. 1997

'Luc Varenne' F, mr, 1959, Delforge; bud oval; flowers scarlet, open, medium, semi-dbl., borne in clusters; foliage dark, glossy; vigorous, bushy growth; ['Alain' × 'Montrouge']

'Lucdod' ('Rendez-vous') S, mp, 1986, Lucas, C.C.; flowers medium, semi-dbl., intense fragrance; foliage medium size, medium green, matte; bushy growth; [R. wichurana × 'Alain Blanchard']; intr. 1981

Luce di Todi™ -- See 'Willuce'

'Lucens Erecta' Misc OGR, lp, 1921, Paul, W.; flowers almost white, small to medium, semi-dbl.; non-recurrent; foliage dark green, glossy

Lucetta® -- See 'Ausemi'

'Lucette' HWich, pb, 1910, Guillot; flowers medium pink, base white, center yellow, medium, full

'Luchian' F, mr, Palocsay, R. and Wagner, S.; bud globular; flowers large, velvety vermillion red, 35 petals, slight fragrance; ['Paprika' × 'Coup de Foudre']; intr. 1972

'Lucia' -- See 'Korlilub'

Lucia Cotarelo® -- See 'Fetural'

'Lucia Zuloaga' HT, rb, 1932, Dot, Pedro; flowers velvety brownish scarlet with a golden undertone, open, very large, semi-dbl., moderate fruity fragrance; foliage glossy, dark; ['Duquesa de Peñaranda' × 'F. Cambo']; intr. 1934

'Lucie Duplessis' M, lp, 1854, Robert; flowers rosy white, 2½ in., full, rosette

'Lucie Faure' ('Louis Faure') T, w, 1898, Nabonnand; flowers ivory white, flesh/salmon centers, large, full, borne mostly solitary; ['Mme Léon Février' × 'Niphetos']

'Lucie Fernand-David' HT, w, 1924, Chambard, C.; flowers white, center slightly tinted cream, dbl.

'Lucie Hallouin' T, w, 1902, Corboeuf-Marsault; flowers white, center tinted garnet; ['Mme Charles' × 'Mme Hoste']

'Lucie Marie' HT, yb, 1930, Dickson, A.; bud pointed; flowers buttercup-yellow veined apricot-orange, and shaded salmon-cerise, dbl., high-centered; foliage dark, leathery, glossy; vigorous, compact, bushy growth

'Lucie Nicolas Meyer' HT, dp, 1922, Gillot, F.; flowers dark pink, edged lighter, dbl.; ['Jonkheer J.L. Mock' × seedling]

'Lucie Petzka' Pol, dr, 1953, Petzka; flowers medium, dbl.

'Lucien Chauré' HT, lp, 1913, Soupert & Notting; flowers flesh pink with light cream pink, very large, dbl.; ['Mme Abel Chatenay' × 'Pié X']

'Lucien de Lemos' HT, lp, 1905, Lambert, P.; flowers carnation pink, large, dbl., globular, moderate fragrance; ['Princesse Alice de Monaco' × 'Mme Caroline Testout']

'Lucien Duranthon' HP, mr, 1894, Bonnaire; flowers pure carmine red, large, dbl.; thornless; growth upright

'Lucie's Dream' -- See 'Meicitrem'

'Lucifer' Pol, or, 1931, Easlea; flowers small, dbl.

'Lucile' HWich, lp, 1911, Walsh; flowers flesh-pink, base tinged rosy salmon, dbl., borne in clusters; foliage large, rich green, glossy; vigorous, climbing growth

'Lucile Barker' HT, ab, 1922, Hicks; bud pointed; flowers apricot-yellow, semi-dbl., high-centered; foliage bronze; vigorous growth

'Lucile Dubourg' HGal, m, 1826, Dubourg; flowers velvety violet-purple

'Lucile Duplessis' ('Lucille') HGal, dp, 1836, Vibert; flowers deep pink, spotted with white, medium, full

'Lucile Hill' HT, dp, 1939, Joseph H. Hill, Co.; bud long, pointed, rose-red; flowers spinel-pink, very large, dbl.; foliage leathery; long stems; very vigorous, compact growth; PP305; [(('Senior' × 'De Luxe') × 'Sweet Adeline']

'Lucile Rand' HT, pb, 1930, Pernet-Ducher; bud pointed; flowers brilliant carmine, shaded yellow and orange, very large, dbl.; very vigorous, semi-climbing, bushy growth

'Lucile Supreme' HT, dp, 1941, Joseph H. Hill, Co.; flowers rose-red, 6 in., 25-35 petals; PP485; [sport of 'Lucile Hill']

'Lucilla' F, ab, 1992, Stainthorpe, Eric; flowers small, semi-dbl., borne in small clusters; foliage small, medium green, semi-glossy; some prickles; low (35 cm.), compact growth; [sport of 'Conservation']; intr. 1993

'Lucille' -- See 'Lucile Duplessis'

'Lucille Ball' -- See 'Jacapri'

'Lucille McWherter' -- See 'Wellsned'

'Lucille Ross' LCl, w, 1940, Ross; flowers white, center golden, open, semi-dbl.; vigorous, climbing (20-40 ft.) growth; [sport of 'Dr. W. Van Fleet']

'Lucina' ('Jeep') F, m; intr. 2005

'Lucinda' HT, dp, 1927, Heacock; [sport of 'Columbia']

Lucinde® -- See 'Kortaly'

'Luciole' T, pb, 1886, Guillot et Fils; bud long; flowers carmine-rose, base coppery yellow, large, intense fragrance; ['Safrano à Fleurs Rouges' × unknown]

'Luciole' HWich, rb, Nonin; flowers bright scarlet, center white, small, single, borne in large clusters; vigorous, climbing growth; ['Hiawatha' × unknown]; intr. 1923

'Lucious' -- See 'Resluc'

'Lucky'

'Lucky' F, dr, 1962, Leenders, J.; flowers deep velvety red, 3 in., 13 petals; ['Goldilocks' × 'Independence']

'Lucky' F, mp, Fryer; flowers lilac-pink , double, high-centered, borne in large clusters, moderate fragrance; recurrent; foliage disease-resistant; strong growth; intr. 2009

'Lucky Beauty' HT, pb, 1971, Fuller; bud ovoid; flowers pink, yellow reverse, large, 90 petals, high-centered, moderate fragrance; vigorous, upright, bushy growth; ['Kordes' Perfecta' × 'Lucky Piece']; intr. 1970

'Lucky Charm' -- See 'Morain'

'Lucky Charm' F, yb, 1961, Robinson, H.; flowers bright yellow tipped red, 3½-4 in., 18 petals, borne in clusters of 6-10; foliage glossy; vigorous growth

'Lucky Choice' HT, w, 1985, Ota, Kaichiro; flowers creamy white, flushed light pink in center, large, 35 petals, high-centered, borne 1-3 per stem; foliage large, medium green; prickles few, small, slender; upright growth; [American Heritage® × 'Sodori-Hime']

'Lucky Duck' Min, rb, Dickson; intr. 2001

'Lucky Four' F, dy, Hiroshima; flowers bluish-yellow; intr. 2002

'Lucky Kordana Mega Brite' Min, op, Kordes; intr. 2000

'Lucky Lady' Gr, lp, 1966, Armstrong, D.L. & Swim, H. C.; bud long, pointed; flowers light pink, reverse darker, large, 28 petals, high-centered; foliage dark, glossy; vigorous, upright growth; PP2829; ['Charlotte Armstrong' × 'Cherry Glow']

Lucky Lucy™ -- See 'Moelucky'

'Lucky Me' -- See 'Socluck'

'Lucky Piece' HT, pb, 1962, Gordon, Winifred; flowers copper, pink and gold blend, full, bowl-shaped, moderate fragrance; growth strong and stout; PP1948; [sport of 'Peace']; intr. 1962

'Lucky Star' HT, yb, 1936, Armacost; flowers golden yellow, suffused flame-scarlet; PP180; [sport of 'Souvenir']

'Lucky Star' F, mp, Zary; PPAF; intr. 2000

Lucpinkma Min, mp; intr. 2000

'Lucrèce' -- See 'Majestueuse'

'Lucrèce' HCh, lp, about 1830, Laffay; flowers bright light pink, medium, full

'Lucrèce' A, lp, Vibert; flowers pale rose, center deeper rose, 8-9 cm., dbl., globular; nearly thornless; intr. 1844

'Lucrèce' T, op, Oger; flowers salmon pink, aging to dark pink, large, full, cupped; intr. 1866

'Lucretia' F, mr

'Lucullus' ('Old Red Pet') Ch, dr, 1854, Guinoisseau-Flon; flowers velvety black purple, medium, very dbl.; probably extinct

'Lucy' -- See 'Barluc'

'Lucy' F, ob, Kirkham, S.; flowers bright orange with yellow reverse, dbl., borne in clusters, slight fragrance; good repeat; foliage bright, glossy; growth compact, upright; intr. 2001

'Lucy' Cl HT, dp, 1935, Williams, A. H.; flowers brilliant carmine, large; foliage glossy; growth very vigorous, climbing

'Lucy' Min, mp, Moore, Ralph S.; flowers bright pink, 1-1½ in., semi-dbl., flat; free-flowering; foliage medium green, semi-glossy; growth compact (8-12 in.); intr. 1997

'Lucy Ashton' HEg, w, 1894, Penzance; flowers pure white, edged pink, medium, single; mid-spring bloom, non-recurrent; foliage dark, fragrant; vigorous growth

'Lucy Bertram' HEg, rb, 1895, Penzance; flowers dark shining crimson, center white, single; mid-spring, non-recurrent; foliage dark, fragrant; very vigorous growth

'Lucy Caroline' -- See 'Horquinine'

'Lucy Constable' HT, pb, 1924, Lilley; flowers silver pink, reverse deep salmon pink

'Lucy Cramphorn, Climbing' -- See 'Maryse Kriloff, Climbing'

'Lucy Cramphorn' ('Maryse Kriloff') HT, or, 1960, Kriloff, Michel; flowers signal-red, well-formed, 5 in., very dbl.; foliage glossy; vigorous, upright growth; ['Peace' × Baccará®]; intr. 1960

'Lucy Locket' -- See 'Horoscope'

'Lucy Marguerite' HT, yb, 1977, Ellick; flowers buttercup-yellow, diffused red, 4 in., 35-40 petals, moderate fragrance; foliage small, glossy, dark; ['Val De Mosa' × 'Denise-Anne']; intr. 1978

'Lucy Nicolas' HT, r, 1935, Mallerin, C.; bud pointed; flowers coppery salmon, large, dbl., high-centered; foliage glossy, bronze; very vigorous growth; ['Odette Foussier' × 'Cécile Walter']

'Lucy Thomas' Cl HP, mp, 1924, Nabonnand, P.; flowers pink, center brighter, semi-dbl.; rarely recurrent bloom; ['Ulrich Brunner Fils' × 'Georg Arends']

'Lucyle' HT, mp, 1933, Vestal; flowers glowing pink, very large, dbl.; foliage leathery, dark; vigorous, bushy growth

'Ludbareza' HT, op, Taschner, Ludwig; bud pointed, coral pink; intr. 2005

'Ludbaurly' HT, pb, Taschner, Ludwig; bud pointed, urn-shaped; intr. 2004

'Ludbigcri' HT, mr, Taschner, Ludwig; intr. 2004

'Ludbrinco' Min, r, Taschner, Ludwig; intr. 2005

'Ludecoma' HT, mr, Taschner, Ludwig; intr. 2007

'Ludek Pik' HP, mr, 1933, Böhm, J.; flowers large, very dbl.

'Ludgeaberg' LCl, w, Taschner, Ludwig; intr. 2003

'Ludgeacent' S, m, Taschner, Ludwig; intr. 2005

'Ludgealytron' LCl, mr, Taschner, Ludwig; intr. 2005

'Ludgehex' S, r, Ludwig; intr. 2003

'Ludgret' Cl Min, w, Taschner, Ludwig; intr. 2003

'Ludhafelisa' F, op, Taschner, Ludwig; bud pointed; intr. 2004

'Ludheiblepo' HT, m, Ludwig, Heike; intr. 2004

'Ludlouest' HT, pb, Taschner, Ludwig; intr. 2004

'Ludlow Castle' -- See 'Ausrace'

Ludmilla® -- See 'Lapman'

'Ludmooirero' ('Roos Sonder Grense') F, or, Taschner, Ludwig; intr. 2004

'Ludosary' S, m, Delbard; bud pointed; intr. 2002

'Ludovic Létaud' HP, dp, 1849, Cherpin or Ducher; flowers medium, full

'Ludovicus' HGal, m, about 1845, Calvert; flowers violet-purple

'Ludpinbu' ('Joy Button') Min, ab, Taschner; intr. 1993

'Ludpribewi' HT, ab, Taschner, Ludwig; intr. 2007

'Ludredest' HT, mr, Taschner, Ludwig; intr. 1998

'Ludsehalo' Min, yb, Taschner, Ludwig; bud orange-red; intr. 2005

'Ludsponelle' -- See 'Anne Colle'

'Ludsporcoma' ('Flames 'n' Sparks') HT, rb, Taschner; intr. 1995

'Ludsporhekaar' S, dy, Taschner, Ludwig; intr. 2003

'Ludsporspense' HT, ab; intr. 2001

'Ludsportiana' ('Alberton Amor') HT, dp, Taschner; intr. 1995

'Ludstripea' Min, dp, Taschner, Ludwig; bud oval; intr. 2001

'Ludswenic' (Nicolette®) HT, ab, Taschner; intr. 1995

'Ludvic' S, my, Taschner, Ludwig; intr. 1997

'Ludvik Vecera' LCl, mr, Vecera, L.; flowers vermilion, 3 in., dbl., borne in large clusters, moderate fragrance; intr. 1981

'Ludwhibewi' HT, w, Taschner, Ludwig; intr. 2001

'Ludwig Möller' HP, ab, 1915, Kiese; flowers bright amber-yellow, fading white, large, full; ['Frau Karl Druschki' × ('Maréchal Niel' × unknown)]

'Ludwig Oppenheimer' HT, dr, 1932, Leenders Bros.; bud pointed; flowers crimson-scarlet, large, dbl.; foliage dark; vigorous growth; ['Villa Pia' × 'Capitaine Georges Dessirier']

'Ludwigshafen' -- See 'Korludwig'

Ludwigshafen am Rhein® ('Ludwigshafen') F, dp, 1976, Kordes; bud ovoid; flowers deep pink, flora-tea, 4 in., 45 petals, high-centered, moderate fragrance; foliage soft; vigorous, upright, bushy growth; [seedling × 'Pink Puff']; intr. 1975

'Lugdunum' HT, m, Orard; flowers soft lavender, full, cupped, intense fragrance; recurrent; medium height, robust growth; intr. 2008

'Luis Brinas' HT, ob, 1934, Dot, Pedro; bud long, pointed; flowers rose-orange, large, dbl., cupped, moderate fragrance; foliage soft; vigorous growth; PP102; ['Mme Butterfly' × 'Federico Casas']

'Luis Desamero' -- See 'Tinluis'

Luisa® HT, w, Tantau; flowers creamy white, pink blush on petals as they age, full; intr. 2004

'Luisa Fernanda da Silva' ('Luisa Fernanda de Silva') HT, rb, 1946, Dot, Pedro; flowers reddish, passing to purplish and then yellowish-red, base yellow; foliage dark, glossy; vigorous growth

'Luisa Fernanda de Silva' -- See 'Luisa Fernanda da Silva'

'Luise Kiese' -- See 'Frau Luise Kiese'

'Luise Kühnel' HT, dy, 1937, Kühnel; flowers medium, dbl.

'Luise Lilia' ('Louise Lilia') HT, dr, 1912, Lambert, P.; flowers deep crimson, large, full, intense fragrance; moderate growth; ['General MacArthur' × 'Frau Peter Lambert']

'Luisella Angelini' HT, Dot, Simon; intr. 1980

'Lukor' ('Jolly', 'Lustige') HT, rb, 1973, Kordes; bud ovoid; flowers copper-red, reverse yellow, large, dbl., cupped; foliage large, glossy, leathery; vigorous, upright growth; ['Peace' × 'Brandenburg']

'Lullaby' Pol, w, 1953, Shepherd; bud ovoid; flowers white, center flushed pink, 1½-2 in., 75 petals, cupped, borne in loose clusters; foliage dark, leathery; vigorous, bushy, compact growth; PP1495; [(R. soulieana × Mrs Joseph Hiess) × 'Mlle Cécile Brunner']

'Lullaby' HT, mp, Meilland; intr. 2006

'Lullaby' F, dp, Bishop; flowers rich rose-pink, 3 in., semi-dbl., flat, camellia-like, borne in clusters (to 28); vigorous growth; intr. 1957

'Lulu' HT, op, 1919, Easlea; bud very long, pointed, deep orange-red; flowers salmon-pink, large, 8 petals; foliage glossy; bushy, compact growth

'Lulu' ('Clubrose Lulu') F, ob, Kordes; flowers orange-pink, medium, dbl., high-centered; foliage glossy, dark, bronze; vigorous, upright, bushy growth; ['Zorina' × seedling]; intr. 1973

'Lulu' HT, rb, Kordes; flowers cream, pink and red, medium, full, high-centered, borne singly and in sprays; intr. 2002

'Luluette' Min, mp, 1986, Fischer, C.&H.; flowers small, single, borne singly and in small sprays; foliage small, medium green, semi-glossy; prickles small, straight, red; low, compact, tiny growth; ['Fairy Moss' × 'Fairy Moss']

Lumen® HT, ob; flowers coral, tinted red, with yellow at base of petals, large, 35-40 petals, high-centered, moderate fragrance; foliage matte; intr. 1973

'Lumen' HT, ab; flowers amber yellow, paler reverse, dbl.; recurrent; intr. 1990

'Lumière' HT, yb, 1944, Mallerin, C.; flowers golden yellow suffused capucine-red, large; foliage dark, leathery; vigorous growth

'Lumina' F, or, 1955, Tantau, Math.; flowers orange-scarlet, 2½ in., 25 petals, rosette, borne in large tursses; foliage dark; vigorous growth; ['Fanal' × 'Alpine Glow']

'Luminator' Pol, dr, 1938, Smith, J.; flowers scarlet-crimson; vigorous growth; [sport of 'Lady Reading']

Luminion® ('Rosi Mittermeier') F, or, 1976, Kordes; bud globular; flowers 3 in., 34 petals, cupped, moderate fragrance; foliage glossy, dark; vigorous, upright, bushy growth; [Hurra® × Peer Gynt®]; intr. 1975

'Luminosa' HT, or, 1964, Mondial Roses; bud long, pointed; flowers vermilion, large, 52 petals, high-centered; foliage dark, glossy; strong stems; vigorous, upright, bushy growth

'Luminosity' HT, my, Williams, J. Ben; flowers dbl., some fragrance; growth to 4 ft.; intr. 2005

'Luminous' Pol, or, 1932, deRuiter; flowers brilliant scarlet tinted orange, small, dbl., cupped; foliage small, light, wrinkled; dwarf growth; [sport of 'Gloria Mundi']

'Lum's Double White' HT, w, 1930, Lum; flowers pure white, overlarge, semi-dbl., high-centered; foliage dark, leathery; vigorous growth; [sport of 'Killarney Double White']

'Luna' HT, ly, 1918, Poulsen, S.; bud pointed; flowers pale yellow, large, dbl., high-centered; foliage dark; strong stems; very vigorous, bushy growth; ['Harry Kirk' × 'Sunburst']

'Luna Park' LCl, or, 1964, Croix, P.; flowers red shaded orange, large; recurrent bloom; vigorous, climbing growth; ['Gladiator' × seedling]

'Luna Rossa' HT, Delbard-Chabert

Lunar Mist™ -- See 'Meijacolet'

'Lunds Jubiläum' -- See 'Baby Blaze'

'Lunelle' ('George Sand') HT, lp, 1955, Meilland, F.; buds apricot; flowers pale pink, very large, 50 petals, high-centered, intense fragrance; vigorous growth; ['Young France' × 'Signora']

'Lupe's Buttons' HMsk, w, 2006, Hulse, Merrill; bud apricot; flowers ivory, blushed pink, 1¾ in., single, borne in very large panicles, very mild fragrance; foliage medium size, medium green, semi-glossy; prickles small, dilated, brown, few; growth bushy, bushy with tall basal breaks, tall (3 ft.); landscape, fences; intr. 2008

'Lupita' S, w, Hulse; intr. 2008

Lupo® ('Coffee Fruitilia') Min, dp, Kordes; flowers purplish to carmine red, overall appearance magenta , 3 cm., single, flat, borne in clusters, no fragrance; recurrent; broad, upright (40 cm.) growth; hips small, round; intr. 2007

'Lupo Kordana' Min, dp, Kordes; flowers full

'Luray' F, mr, 1962, Masek, R. J.; flowers rose-red, 2-3 in., 40-45 petals, moderate fragrance; foliage leathery, glossy; vigorous, bushy growth; PP2088; [sport of 'Patty's Pink']; patent issued as Pol; intr. 1958

'Lusambo' -- See 'Red Rock'

Lusambo® F, rb, Meilland; intr. 1998

'Luscious' HT, pb, Perry, Astor; flowers blend of magenta and amber, dbl., moderate fragrance; growth vigorous; intr. 2003

Luscious Lucy™ -- See 'Tucklucy'

'Lusiadas' -- See 'Céline Forestier'

'Lusitania' HG, 1905, Cayeux; ['Souv de Mme Léonie Viennot' × unknown]

'Lustige' -- See 'Lukor'

'Lustre' HT, mp, 1926, E.G. Hill, Co.; flowers rose-pink, large, semi-dbl.; ['Ophelia' × 'Hoosier Beauty']

'Lustre d'Église' ('Duchesse d'Orléans', 'Pivoine', 'Pourpre Double', 'Grandesse Royale', 'Grand St. Francis') HGal, mp, before 1790; flowers medium pink with lighter reverse, small, dbl., intense fragrance; from Holland

'Lustrous' -- See 'Celebrity'

'Lustrous Spirit' -- See 'Kagayaku Seishin'

'Lutea Flora'   T, my, 1874, Touvais; flowers brilliant yellow, fading to white, large, full

'Lutea Flore Pleno' -- See 'Multiplex'

'Lutea Plena' -- See 'Sulphurea'

'Luteola' ('Serin') HFt, ly, before 1821; bud round; flowers pale yellow, single; repeats in autumn; foliage ovate, pointed, ribbed, dark green; prickles numerous, unequal

'Lutescens Flavescens' -- See 'Parks' Yellow Tea-Scented China'

'Lutetia'   HT, yb, 1961, deRuiter; flowers coppery yellow, medium, 28 petals; vigorous, upright growth; ['The Optimist' × 'Tudor']

'Luther Russell'   F, op, 1956, Morse; flowers salmon, semi-dbl., borne several together; foliage olive-green; [sport of 'Korona']

'Lutin' -- See 'Rosey Gem'

'Lutin' ('Shady Lady') S, pb, Meilland; flowers bengal-rose, white eye, medium, semi-dbl., cupped, then flat, borne in clusters, moderate sharp fragrance; recurrent; foliage light green, glossy; upright (3-4 ft.) growth; intr. 1984

'Lutin'   Min, mp; [sport of Scarlet Gem®]

'Luv Ya' -- See 'Juleslove'

'Luvvie'   Min, pb, 1980, Bennett, Dee; bud ovoid; flowers soft to deep coral pink, micro-mini, very small, 38 petals, high-centered; foliage small, deep green with red peduncle and petiole; prickles straight, thin, red; low, bushy growth; PP4911; ['Little Darling' × 'Over the Rainbow']; intr. 1979

'Luxembourg' -- See 'Fanny Blankers-Koen'

'Luxembourg' -- See 'Ferrugineux du Luxembourg'

'Luxembourg' -- See 'Pourpre du Luxembourg'

'Luxembourg' -- See 'Marie Adélaïde'

'Luxembourg, Climbing'   Cl HT, op, 1932, Wight; flowers pinkish orange, base deep yellow; very vigorous, climbing growth; [sport of 'Marie Adélaide']

'Luxor', rb; flowers red with white reverse, 14 cm., 50 petals, high-centered, borne mostly singly, no fragrance; recurrent; prickles medium; stems long; florist rose; intr. 2004

'Luxor'   HT, mp

'Luxury'   HT, rb, 1968, Patterson; flowers light red, reverse white, large, dbl., high-centered; foliage soft; moderate growth; [seedling × 'Suspense']

'Lybelle'   LCl, mp, Noack, Werner; flowers large, dbl., borne in small clusters; intr. 1984

'Lybie' -- See 'Marlyb'

'Lycoris'   HGal, pb, 1835, Vibert; flowers light rosy red spotted white, large, dbl., flat; sometimes classes as M

'Lyda Rose' -- See 'Letlyda'

'Lydia' -- See 'Interlis'

'Lydia'   N, w, 1892, Geschwind; flowers white, center flesh pink, medium to large, dbl., cupped, borne in clusters, moderate fragrance; growth vigorous, climbing

'Lydia'   HT, op, Verschuren; bud pointed; flowers bright orange-rose, large, very dbl., moderate fragrance; foliage glossy; vigorous, bushy growth; ['Briarcliff' × 'Florex']

'Lydia'   HT, dy, Robinson, H.; bud long, pointed; flowers intense saffron-yellow, medium, very dbl., high-centered, moderate fragrance; foliage dark, leathery, glossy; vigorous, bushy growth; ['Phyllis Gold' × seedling]; intr. 1949

'Lydia' ('Clubrose Lydia') S, ob, Kordes; bud ovoid; flowers deep orange, reverse yellow, medium, semi-dbl., cupped, moderate fragrance; foliage glossy, dark, leathery; very vigorous, upright, climbing growth; [seedling × 'Circus']; intr. 1973

'Lydia'   HT, op, Croix

'Lydia Grimm'   HT, ly, 1907, Geduldig; flowers large, dbl.; [('Général Jacqueminot' × 'Mme Caroline Testout') × 'Kaiserin Auguste Viktoria']

'Lydia Kordana'   Min, mp, Kordes; flowers strong pink, dbl., high-centered; pot rose

'Lydia Morris'   S, m

'Lydie'   F, ob, Harkness; intr. 1993

'Lykkefund'   LCl, w, 1930, Olsen; bud small, pink; flowers cream color, small, semi-dbl., borne in clusters of 10-20, intense fragrance; foliage small, dark, glossy; nearly thornless; vigorous growth; [seedling from R. helenae, Barbier's form, possibly crossed with 'Zephirine Drouhin']

'Lyle Barbour'   HT, Watt, Mrs B.; intr. 1970

'Lyn Keppler'   S, lp, Taschner, Ludwig; intr. 2003

'Lynda'   HT, Mondial Roses; intr. 1970

'Lynda Hurst'   HT, mp, 1938, Clark, A.; flowers large, dbl.; vigorous growth; ['Mme Abel Chatenay' × seedling]

'Lyndarajha'   HT, Dorieux; intr. 1982

'Lynette' -- See 'Korlyn'

'Lynette Joseph' -- See 'Liolyn'

'Lynn Anderson' -- See 'Wekjoe'

'Lynn Anne'   Min, ob, 1980, Saville, F. Harmon; bud short, pointed; flowers orange-yellow blend, 38 petals, high-centered, borne singly and in large sprays, moderate fragrance; foliage medium; prickles long, thin; vigorous, upright, compact growth; PP4699; ['Rise 'n' Shine' × 'Sheri Anne']; intr. 1981

Lynne Elizabeth™ -- See 'Byrlynne'

Lynne Gold™ -- See 'Morlyn'

'Lynne's Gold' -- See 'Evegold'

'Lynnie'   S, mp, Rupert; flowers saturated dark pink fading to hot pink, semi-dbl., borne in clusters, slight fragrance; recurrent; prickles few to none; growth to 3 ft.; intr. 2002

'Lynn's Jubilee' -- See 'Majlynjub'

'Lynn's Saint' -- See 'Majlynt'

'Loyad' ('Added Touch') Min, or, 1984, Lyon; bud small; flowers orange-red, touch of yellow in the center and back of petals, 20 petals; foliage small, medium green, semi-glossy; upright, bushy growth; ['Dandy Lyon' × seedling]

'Lyoca' ('Care Deeply') Min, ab, 1983, Lyon, Lyndon; flowers medium, 35 petals, moderate fragrance; foliage medium size, medium green, semi-glossy; upright, bushy growth; ['Honey Hill' × seedling]; intr. 1982

'Lyoch' ('Cherokee Fire') Min, dr, 1982, Lyon, Lyndon; flowers deep red, medium, semi-dbl.; foliage medium green, semi-glossy; upright, bushy growth; [Merry Christmas × seedling]

'Lyocl' ('Classic Love') Min, mp, 1983, Lyon, Lyndon; flowers small, 20 petals, borne in clusters; foliage small, medium green, semi-glossy; upright, bushy growth; ['Baby Betsy McCall' × seedling]

'Lyoco' ('Coral Fantasy') Min, ab, 1982, Lyon, Lyndon; flowers medium, 34 petals; foliage medium green, semi-glossy; vigorous, upright, bushy growth; ['Dandy Lyon' × seedling]

'Lyodit' ('Ditto') Min, dr, 1986, Lyon, Lyndon; flowers very small, 14 petals, borne usually singly; foliage small, medium green, matte; no prickles; low, bushy growth; ['Baby Betsy McCall' × seedling]

'Lyodro' ('Sun Drops') Min, my, 1986, Lyon; flowers 35 petals, cupped, borne usually singly; foliage medium size, medium green, matte; prickles very small, reddish; low, bushy growth; [seedling × 'Redgold']

'Lyoet' ('Velvet Dreams') Min, dr, 1982, Lyon; flowers small, semi-dbl.; foliage small, medium green, semi-glossy; very miniature, upright, bushy growth; [seedling × seedling]

'Lyofi' ('Night Fire') Min, dr, 1982, Lyon, Lyndon; flowers deep red, petals often edged black, small, 20 petals; foliage medium size, dark, semi-glossy; upright, bushy growth; [seedling × seedling]

'Lyofin' ('Fine Touch') Min, ab, 1986, Lyon; flowers pale apricot, deeper in center, large, 37 petals, high-centered, borne singly, slight fragrance; foliage medium size, medium green, matte; prickles few, reddish; medium, upright growth; hips globular, medium, orange; ['Honey Hill' × unknown]

'Lyofor' ('Forevermore') Min, mr, 1986, Lyon; flowers large, 38 petals, high-centered, borne singly, intense spicy fragrance; foliage medium size, medium green, semi-glossy; prickles few, reddish, small; medium, upright growth; hips globular, medium, orange-red; [seedling × unknown]

'Lyogi' ('Giggles') Min, pb, 1982, Lyon, Lyndon; bud pointed; flowers medium pink, white center, small, semi-dbl.; foliage small, medium green, semi-glossy;

very small, upright, bushy growth; [seedling × seedling]

'Lyohi' ('High Style') Min, mr, 1983, Lyon; flowers cardinal red, 35 petals, borne in clusters; foliage medium size, medium green, semi-glossy; upright, bushy growth; [seedling × seedling]

'Lyolit' ('Little Charm') Min, mp, 1984, Lyon, Lyndon; flowers small, semi-dbl.; foliage small, medium green, semi-glossy; upright, bushy growth; [seedling × seedling]

'Lyolite' ('Peach Elite') Min, ab, 1986, Lyon; flowers peach, to loose form, large, 26 petals, high-centered, borne singly; foliage large, medium green, matte; prickles small; upright growth; hips globular, medium, orange-red; ['Dandy Lyon' × unknown]

'Lyoma' ('Magic Splendor') Min, dr, 1983, Lyon, Lyndon; flowers small, 35 petals, borne in clusters; foliage medium size, medium green, semi-glossy; upright, bushy growth; ['Baby Betsy McCall' × seedling]

'Lyon Rambler' HMult, dp, 1909, Dubreuil; flowers bright rose-pink, flushed carmine, medium, semi-dbl., borne in rounded clusters; foliage dark green, glossy; ['Crimson Rambler' × unknown]

'Lyon Rose, Climbing' Cl HT, op, 1924, Ketten Bros.; flowers copper pink, illumined by yellow-gold; [sport of 'Lyon Rose']

'Lyon Rose' HT, op, 1907, Pernet-Ducher; flowers shrimp-pink, center coral-red shaded yellow, large, 44 petals; ['Mme Mélanie Soupert' × ('Soleil d'Or' × unknown)]

'Lyonfarbige Druschki' HP, yb, 1928, Rosarium Sangerhausen; flowers yellowish-pink, large, dbl.; ['Frau Karl Druschki' × 'Lyon Rose']

'Lyonnais' HP, mp, 1872, Lacharme, F.; flowers large, dbl.; ['Victor Verdier' × unknown]

'Lyopin' ('Pink Charmer') Min, mp, 1984, Lyon, Lyndon; flowers medium, 20 petals; foliage small, medium green, semi-glossy; upright, bushy growth; ['Baby Betsy McCall' × seedling]

'Lyopr' ('Precious Moments') Min, my, 1982, Lyon; flowers medium, 35 petals, moderate fragrance; free-flowering; foliage medium size, medium green, semi-glossy; extremely short, upright, bushy growth; ['Dandy Lyon' × seedling]

'Lyopri' ('I Promise') Min, pb, 1986, Lyon; flowers pink, reverse pale yellow, medium, 28 petals, high-centered, borne usually singly, moderate spicy fragrance; foliage medium size, medium green, semi-glossy; prickles few, small; low, bushy growth; hips globular, very small, red-gold; [seedling × seedling]

'Lyopro' ('Promenade') Min, dr, 1985, Lyon; flowers very dark red, informal, ruffled, small, 35 petals, borne singly; foliage small, medium green, dark, matte; bushy growth; ['Red Can Can' × seedling]

'Lyora' ('Orange Sherbert') Min, ob, 1985, Lyon; flowers orange, small, 35 petals, cupped, borne singly; foliage medium size, medium green, matte; upright growth; ['Dandy Lyon' × unknown]

'Lyoren' ('Renegade') Min, mr, 1986, Lyon; flowers 52 petals, cupped, borne usually singly; foliage medium size, medium green, matte; prickles small, green; medium, upright growth; [seedling × seedling]

'Lyoshy' ('Shy Beauty') Min, mp, 1985, Lyon; flowers small, 55 petals, borne singly; foliage medium size, medium green, semi-glossy; bushy growth; [seedling × seedling]

'Lyoss' ('Endless Love') Min, mr, 1982, Lyon, Lyndon; flowers medium, 35 petals; foliage medium size, dark, semi-glossy; upright, bushy growth; ['Red Can Can' × seedling]

'Lyosun' ('Sun Sparkle') Min, yb, 1984, Lyon; flowers yellow blended red, small, 20 petals; foliage small, medium green, semi-glossy; upright, bushy growth; ['Dandy Lyon' × seedling]

'Lyoter' ('Cheery Chatter') Min, mr, 1984, Lyon, Lyndon; flowers medium, 20 petals; foliage small, medium green, semi-glossy; upright, bushy growth; ['Dandy Lyon' × seedling]

'Lyoto' ('Twinkle Toes') Min, mr, 1982, Lyon; flowers small, semi-dbl.; foliage small, medium green, semi-glossy; very compact growth; [Merry Christmas × seedling]

'Lyove' ('Love Dove') Min, w, 1982, Lyon, Lyndon; flowers near white, medium, 35 petals, high-centered; foliage medium size, medium green, semi-glossy; low growth; [seedling × seedling]

'Lyowe' ('Wild One') Min, mr, 1982, Lyon; flowers medium red, lighter center, medium, semi-dbl.; foliage medium size, dark, semi-glossy; bushy, upright growth; [Merry Christmas × seedling]

'Lyre de Flore' -- See 'Beauté Insurmontable'

'Lyric' S, mp, 1951, deRuiter; bud ovoid; flowers rose-pink, 28 petals, cupped, borne in large clusters, moderate fragrance; foliage leathery; vigorous (4 ft.), upright growth; good for hedge and border; PP1058; ['Sangerhausen' × seedling]

'Lyrical' F, pb, 1990, Jobson, Daniel J.; bud pointed; flowers salmon pink shading to cream at base, medium, 11 petals, flat, borne in sprays of 5-7, moderate spicy fragrance; foliage medium size, dark green, glossy, disease-resistant; prickles hooked downward, red; upright, bushy, low, winter-hardy growth; fruit not observed; ['Snow White' × Yesterday®]; intr. 1989

'Lys Assia' F, mr, 1959, Kordes, R.; flowers deep orange-scarlet, 4 in., 20 petals, high-centered, borne in small clusters; foliage glossy; vigorous, upright, bushy growth; ['Spartan' × 'Hens Verschuren']; intr. 1958

'Lysa' HT, lp, RvS-Melle; ['Windekind' × 'Melglory']; intr. 1989

'Lysbeth-Victoria' F, lp, 1977, Harkness; flowers light shell-pink, 4½ in., 11 petals; foliage matte; growth moderate; ['Pink Parfait' × 'Nevada']; intr. 1978

— M —

'M. A. Keessen' Pol, dp, 1923, Keessen; flowers darker; [sport of 'Ellen Poulsen']

'M. B.' HT, rb, 1941, Brownell; flowers red shading to pink, overlaid orange and yellow, open, large, 25 petals; long stems; vigorous, compact, upright growth; ['Dr. W. Van Fleet hybrid' × 'Frau Karl Druschki hybrid']

'M. Boncenne' -- See 'Mons Bonçenne'

'M. Bunel' -- See 'Mons Bunel'

'M. Geier' HT, dp, 1929, Felberg-Leclerc; flowers fiery dark carmine, shaded darker, dbl.; [Augustus Hartmann × 'Admiral Ward']

'M. H. Graire' -- See 'Lady Zoë Brougham'

'M. H. Walsh' HP, mr, 1905, Dickson, A.; flowers carmine-red, large, dbl.

'M. Kockel' Pol, lp, 1926, Kockel; flowers small, dbl.

'M. S. Hershey' HT, dr, 1941, Coddington; bud long, pointed; flowers velvety crimson, 4-4½ in., 33 petals, cupped; bushy growth; PP427; [seedling × 'E.G. Hill']

'M.T. Ruby Sunday' -- See 'Liojoal'

'Ma Capucine' T, yb, 1871, Levet; bud pointed, small; flowers bronzy yellow, shaded red, fading to white, medium, dbl.; ['Ophirie' × R. foetida]

'Ma Cherie' HT, op, Teranishi; intr. 2002

'Ma Fiancée' HT, dr, 1922, Van Rossem; flowers dark crimson, often nearly black, dbl.; [('Gen. MacArthur' × unknown) × 'Red-Letter Day']

'Ma Fille' HT, ob, 1962, Mallerin, C.; flowers orange, large, 45 petals; foliage glossy; vigorous, bushy, symmetrical growth; ['Berthe Mallerin' × seedling]; intr. 1960

'Ma Mie' HT, yb, 1955, Laperrière; flowers yellow, edge tinted pink, well-formed, very large, 50 petals; foliage bright green; very vigorous, upright growth; ['Peace' × seedling]

'Ma Pâquerette' -- See 'Pâquerette'

'Ma Perkins' F, pb, 1952, Boerner; bud ovoid; flowers sparkling salmon shell-pink, large, 25 petals, cupped, moderate fragrance; foliage rich green, glossy; vigorous, bushy growth; PP1143; ['Red Radiance' × 'Fashion']

'Ma Petite Andrée' ('Red Soupert') Pol, dr, 1898, Chauvry; flowers deep carmine red, large, dbl.

'Ma Pivoine du Roi' HGal, dp, 1810, Descemet; flowers bright pink, aging to red, shaded lighter, large, full

'Ma Ponctuée' ('Ponctuée') M, pb, 1857, Guillot père; flowers rose, spotted white, medium, dbl.; recurrent bloom; moderate growth

'Ma Ponctuée Semi-Double' M, rb, 1850, Moreau & Robert; flowers red, striped, semi-dbl.

'Ma Surprise' S, w, 1872, Guillot et Fils; flowers white tinged salmon, large, dbl.; [probably *R. roxburghii* × *R. odorata*]

'Ma Tulipe' HT, mr, 1899, Bonnaire; flowers carmine-red, large, semi-dbl.

Maaike™ HT, pb

'Maaseik' -- See 'Lenclima'

Maaseik 750® -- See 'Lenclima'

'Mab Grimwade' HT, yb, 1937, Clark, A.; flowers rich chrome, shaded yellow, center apricot, dbl.; ['Souv. de Gustave Prat' × unknown]

'Mabel Dot' Min, or, 1966, Dot; flowers rose-coral, small, dbl., borne in clusters; foliage small, bronze; ['Orient' × 'Perla de Alcañada']

'Mabel Drew' HT, w, 1911, Dickson, A.; flowers deep cream, center canary-yellow, dbl., borne in clusters

'Mabel Francis' HT, my, 1943, Bees; flowers rose-pink, 5 in., 35-40 petals, moderate fragrance; foliage light green; free growth; ['Leading Lady' × 'Southport']

'Mabel Jackson' HT, ab, 1924, Easlea; flowers apricot and pink, dbl.; ['Edith Part' × 'Queen Mary']

'Mabel Lynas' HT, dr, 1926, McGredy; bud pointed; flowers crimson-scarlet, base yellow, large, dbl.; foliage glossy; strong stems; very vigorous, bushy growth

'Mabel Morrison' HP, w, 1878, Broughton; flowers flesh-white, becoming pure white, sometimes tinged pink in autumn, 30 petals, cupped; seasonal bloom; stout, erect growth; [sport of 'Baronne Adolphe de Rothschild']

'Mabel Morse' HT, my, 1922, McGredy; bud pointed; flowers bright golden yellow, well-shaped, large, dbl.; foliage dark, bronze; bushy growth

'Mabel Morse, Climbing' Cl HT, my, 1931, Moulden (also Ley, 1932)

'Mabel Prentice' HT, mp, 1923, Lippiatt; flowers clear rose-pink

'Mabel Stewart' LCl, dr, 1942, Clark; bud almost black; flowers velvety crimson, semi-single

'Mabel Turner' HT, pb, 1923, Dickson, H.; bud pointed; flowers blush, center and reverse rosy carmine, very large, high-centered; foliage olive-green; vigorous growth

'Mabella' -- See 'Korgold'

'Mabella Kordana' Min, my, Kordes; flowers full, exhibition; recurrent

'Mabelle Stearns' ('Maybelle Stearns') S, mp, 1938, Horvath; flowers peach-pink with silvery reflex, 55 petals, blooms in clusters, intense fragrance; recurrent bloom; foliage small, glossy, dark; to 2 ft., spreading (6-8 ft.) growth; hardy; PP297; ['Mrs F.F. Prentiss' × 'Souv. de Georges Pernet']

'Mable Dot' Min, op, 1967, Dot; bud small, ovoid; flowers rose-coral, small, very dbl., open, borne several together and in clusters; foliage small, bright bronze green; no prickles; ['Orient' × 'Perle d'Alcanada']; intr. 1966

'Mable Ringling' F, mr, 2002, Mallory; flowers red, reverse yellow and red , medium, double, borne mostly singly, slight fragrance; recurrent; foliage medium, medium green, matte; prickles few, slightly hooked, 0.25 in.; bushy, medium growth

Macabo™ -- See 'Pouluf'

'Macaft' ('Margaret Trudeau') HT, op, 1977, McGredy, Sam IV; bud long, pointed; intr. 1978

'Macai' F, pb, 1961, McGredy, Sam IV; intr. 1961

'Macal' F, op, 1976, McGredy, Sam IV; intr. 1977

'Macamster' ('Matawhero Magic', Top Notch™, 'Simply the Best', Florida®) HT, ab, 1998, McGredy, Sam IV; flowers golden-apricot, 4 in., 30-40 petals, high-centered, borne mostly singly, intense fruit & anise fragrance; recurrent; foliage large, medium green, glossy; prickles moderate; bushy (120 cm.) growth; PPAF; ['Spek's Centennial' × New Year®]

'Macanat' ('Hi-de-hi') Min, mp, 1982, McGredy, Sam IV; flowers small, 20 petals, moderate fragrance; foliage small, dark, glossy; bushy growth; ['Anytime' × 'Gartendirektor Otto Linne']; intr. 1981

'Macangel' ('Snowball', Angelita®) Min, w, 1982, McGredy, Sam IV; bud small, ovoid, yellow; flowers pure white, 3 cm., 35 -40 petals, decorative, borne in sprays, slight fragrance; recurrent; foliage small, dark, glossy; prickles numerous, needle, declining, light brown; growth low (10 in.), spreading; hips few, globular, orange; PP5849; [Moana® × Snow Carpet®]; intr. 1982

'Macar' HT, rb, 1960, McGredy, Sam IV; intr. 1960

'Macarnhe' ('Jillian McGredy') F, lp, 1998, McGredy, Sam IV; flowers light pink, large, dbl., borne in small clusters, moderate fragrance; foliage medium size, medium green, semi-glossy; prickles moderate; bushy, 120 cm. growth; [Sexy Rexy® × Lagerfeld™]

'Macarom' ('Goldie') HT, ly, 1988, McGredy, Sam IV; flowers pale yellow, large, full, intense fragrance; foliage large, medium green, glossy; upright growth; [seedling × 'Golden Gate']

'Macauck' (Olympiad™) HT, mr, 1983, McGredy, Sam IV; flowers brilliant medium red, non-fading, 4½-5 in., 30-35 petals, high-centered, borne mostly singly; foliage large, medium green, matte; upright, bushy growth, vigorous; PP5519; ['Red Planet' × Pharaoh®]; intr. 1984

'Macauclad' ('Kathryn McGredy') HT, mp, 1998, McGredy, Sam IV; flowers 4½ in., dbl., borne mostly singly; foliage medium size, medium green, glossy; prickles slight; bushy, moderate (110 cm.) growth; ['City of Auckland' × Lady Rose®]; intr. 1996

'Macba' LCl, op, 1966, McGredy, Sam IV

'Macberli' HT, pb, McGredy; intr. 2003

'Macbern' ('Yellow Wonder', Young Quinn®) HT, my, 1976, McGredy, Sam IV; bud small, short, pointed ovoid; flowers bright yellow, fading with age, sometimes red blush on petal edges, 8-11 cm., 20-30 petals, high-centered, to cupped, borne singly and in small clusters, slight fragrance; recurrent; foliage heavily veined, medium green, semi-glossy; prickles several, medium, almost straight, brown; stems strong, short to medium; upright, tall, bushy growth; hips globular, yellow-green; PP4063; [Peer Gynt® × 'Kiskadee']; intr. 1975

'Macbeth' HT, dr, 1921, Bees; bud pointed; flowers deep crimson, shaded darker, large, dbl., high-centered; foliage dark, bronze; vigorous, bushy, compact growth; ['Richmond' × 'Admiral Ward']

'Macbigma' ('Redhot') F, pb, 1988, McGredy, Sam IV; flowers hand-painted, medium, dbl.; foliage small, medium green, semi-glossy; bushy growth; [Eyepaint® × 'Ko's Yellow']

'Macbipi' (Moana®) Min, mp, 1978, McGredy, Sam IV; flowers rose-pink, small, 35 petals; foliage glossy, dark; [seedling × 'New Penny']

'Macblackpo' F, yb, McGredy; intr. 2004

'Macbo' ('Flaming Peace') HT, rb, 1965, McGredy, Sam IV; bud large, ovoid; intr. 1966

'Macbotan' F, or, McGredy; intr. 2003

'Macbucpal' ('Auckland Metro', 'Métro', 'Precious Michelle') HT, w, 1988, McGredy, Sam IV; flowers large, creamy white, full, intense fragrance; foliage large, dark green, semi-glossy; bushy growth; [Sexy Rexy® × (seedling × 'Ferry Porsche')]; intr. 1988

'Macbunber' ('Hot Chile') S, or, 1998, McGredy, Sam IV; flowers orange-red, 2¾ in., semi-dbl., borne in small clusters; foliage small, dark green, glossy; prickles moderate; spreading, low (30 cm.), bushy growth; [Trumpeter® × 'Eyeopener']; intr. 1995

'Macca' ('Gerbe d'Or') LCl, ly, 1963, McGredy, Sam IV; intr. 1963

'Maccanter' -- See 'Scoop Jackson'

'Maccarib' ('Rexy's Baby') F, lp, 1992, McGredy, Sam IV; flowers medium, full, borne in clusters, slight fragrance; foliage small, medium green, glossy; bushy (90 cm.) growth; [Sexy Rexy® × ('Freude' × ('(Anytime × Eyepaint)' × 'Stars 'n' Stripes'))]; intr. 1992

'Maccarlto' ('Northland', 'Sweet Gesture') F, mp, 1991, McGredy, Sam IV; bud small, pointed; flowers clear pink, 3-3½ in., 55-60 petals, high-centered, then flat, borne in clusters of 6 - 12, slight sweet fragrance; recurrent; foliage large, medium green, semi-glossy; prickles numerous, short, slightly hooked; upright, bushy (100 cm.) growth; PP9275; [(Sexy Rexy® × New Year®) × West Coast®]; intr. 1992

'Maccarpe' ('Blanche Neige', 'Schneeteppich', Snow Carpet®) Min, w, 1979, McGredy, Sam IV; bud pointed, tapered; flowers pure white, open quickly, 1 in., 55 petals, high-centered, to loose, borne singly and in sprays, slight tea fragrance; foliage tiny, glossy, leathery; prickles few, long, recurved, red; low (8-10 in.), spreading (5 ft.) growth; hips oval, orange-red; PP4612; ['New Penny' × 'Temple Bells']; intr. 1980

'Maccatsan' ('Phantom') S, mr, 1992, McGredy, Sam IV; flowers scarlet red, large, semi-dbl., slight fragrance; foliage large, medium green, semi-glossy; spreading (80 cm.) growth; ['Pandemonium' × 'Eyeopener']

'Maccheup' Gr, ab, 1978, McGredy, Sam IV

'Macchome' ('Rita MacNeil', Big Daddy®) HT, or, 1994, McGredy, Sam IV; flowers scarlet-orange, 3 in., full; foliage large, medium green, semi-glossy; bushy (100 cm.) growth; PP896; ['Howard Morrison' × 'Mme Delbard']; intr. 1994

'Macchopsu' ('Painted Desert') Gr, or, 1998, McGredy, Sam IV; flowers orange-red, 4 in., dbl., borne in small clusters, slight fragrance; foliage large, medium green, bushy growth; prickles moderate; growth upright, bushy (110 cm.); PP10697; ['Louise Gardner' × 'Mme. Delbard']; intr. 1997

'Macci' F, or, 1968, McGredy, Sam IV

'Macclack' ('Paddy Stephens') HT, ob, 1991, McGredy, Sam IV; flowers large, dbl., slight fragrance; foliage large, dark green, red when young; bushy (100 cm.) growth; ['Solitaire' × (('Tombola' × '(Elizabeth of Glamis × (Circus × Golden Fleece))') × 'Mary Sumner')]; intr. 1991

'Macclosup' ('Carmel Sunset', 'Close Up', 'Kirkcaldie') HT, ab, 1998, McGredy, Sam IV; flowers apricot blend, 4½ in., dbl., borne mostly singly; foliage large, medium green, dull; prickles moderate; bushy, tall (120 cm.) growth; ['Freude' × 'Silver Jubilee']; intr. 1997

'Maccolumb' ('Carolyn') HT, mp, 1998, McGredy, Sam IV; flowers medium pink, 4 in., very dbl., borne mostly singly; foliage large, light green, dull; prickles moderate; bushy, medium (110 cm.) growth; [((Courvoisier® × 'Arthur Bell') × 'Traumerei') × (Tojo® × 'Vienna Woods')]; intr. 1995

'Maccompu' (Today™) Gr, ob, 1989, McGredy, Sam IV; bud ovoid; flowers light orange blending to yellow, medium, 33 petals, cupped, borne usually singly, slight fragrance; recurrent; foliage medium size, dark green, glossy; prickles recurved, medium, brown; bushy, medium growth; hips globular, medium, orange-red; PP7202; [(('Typhoo Tea' × '(Yellow Pages × Kabuki)') × (('Yellow Pages' × 'Kabuki') × ('MACjose' × 'Typhoon'))]; intr. 1988

'Maccourlod' ('Ragtime') Min, pb, 1985, McGredy, Sam IV; flowers small, dbl.; foliage small, dark, matte; bushy growth; ['Mary Sumner' × seedling]; intr. 1982

'Maccrackle' ('Howard Morrison') HT, dr, 1983, McGredy, Sam IV; flowers large, 35 petals; foliage medium size, medium green, semi-glossy; upright, bushy growth; [seedling × seedling]; intr. 1982

'Maccricke' ('Marriotta') Min, dp, 1990, McGredy, Sam IV; flowers deep pink, small, 20 petals, blooms with side buds and sprays; foliage small, medium green, semi-glossy, resistant to blackspot; bushy growth; PP9413; ['Seaspray' × Little Artist®]; intr. 1989

'Macdako' F, w, McGredy; intr. 1999

'Macdeepo' ('Guadalajara') HT, my, 1986, McGredy, Sam IV; flowers large, 24 petals, high-centered, borne singly, moderate fragrance; foliage large, medium green, semi-glossy; prickles large, deltoid, red to brown; medium, upright growth; fruit never observed; PP6263; ['New Day' × 'Yellow Bird']; intr. 1985

'Macdub' ('Grandhotel', Dublin Bay®) LCl, mr, 1976, McGredy, Sam IV; bud ovoid; flowers pure dark red, edges darker, 4½ in., 25 petals, moderate fragrance; foliage dark green, glossy; climbing growth; [Bantry Bay® × Altissimo®]; intr. 1975

'Macel' ('Elisabeth', 'Irish Beauty') F, op, 1964, McGredy, Sam IV; intr. 1964

'Macerupt' ('Louise Gardner', 'Orana Gold') HT, yb, 1988, McGredy, Sam IV; flowers large, dbl.; foliage medium size, medium green, matte; upright, bushy growth; ['Freude' × 'Sunblest' × unknown)]; intr. 1988

'Macesp' ('Old Master') F, rb, 1975, McGredy, Sam IV; flowers carmine, white eye and reverse, 4½ in., 15 petals; foliage semi-glossy, medium green; vigorous, bushy growth; [('Maxi' × 'Evelyn Fison') × ('Orange Sweetheart' × 'Fruhlingsmorgen')]; intr. 1973

'Macev' ('Irish Wonder') F, mr, 1962, McGredy, Sam IV; intr. 1962

'Maceye' ('Eye Paint', Eyepaint®, 'Tapis Persan') F, rb, 1976, McGredy, Sam IV; bud ovoid; flowers bright red, whitish eye, gold stamens, 2½ in., 5-6 petals, slight fragrance; foliage small, dark; tall, bushy growth; PP3985; [seedling × 'Picasso']; intr. 1975

'MacFarlane's Own' F, pb, Williams, J. Benjamin; flowers deep pink, ivory reverse, large, semi-dbl., flat, mass bloomer; intr. 1999

'Macfirinlin' ('Fiesta', 'War Dance') F, mr, 1998, McGredy, Sam IV; bud small; flowers medium red, handpainted in cool weather, 2½ in., 9-10 petals, borne in small clusters, slight fruity fragrance; foliage small, medium green, semi-glossy; prickles moderate, curved downward; compact, low (30 cm.) growth; hips globose, green with orange at top; PP10699; ['Howard Morrison' × 'Sue Lawley']; intr. 1997

'Macfirwal' ('Rock 'n' Roll', 'Stretch Johnson', 'Tango') S, rb, 1988, McGredy, Sam IV; bud small; flowers red with yellow eye, reverse pink with yellow tones, 4 in., semi-dbl., flat, borne in sprays of 5 - 25, slight sweet fragrance; recurrent; foliage large, medium green, semi-glossy; prickles few. thin, slightly curved downward; bushy, vigorous (2 m.) growth; hips globular, ½ in.; PP7472; [Sexy Rexy® × 'Maestro']; intr. 1988

'Macfrabro' ('Firefly') Min, ob, 1986, McGredy, Sam IV; flowers small, 20 petals; foliage small, dark, glossy; bushy growth; ['Mary Sumner' × 'Ko's Yellow']; intr. 1985

'Macfreego' ('Penelope Keith', Freegold®, Free Gold®) Min, dy, 1983, McGredy, Sam IV; flowers deep yellow, gold reverse, small, 20 petals, high-centered, moderate fragrance; foliage small, light green, semi-glossy; upright growth; PP5850; ['Seaspray' × Dorola®]

'Macfrothy' Min, w, McGredy, Sam IV; intr. 1992

'Macgam' (Kapai®) F, or, 1976, McGredy, Sam IV; flowers large, 30 petals, intense fragrance; foliage small; low, bushy growth; ['Madame Bollinger' × 'Tombola']; intr. 1977

'Macgem' ('Benson and Hedges', Benson and Hedges Gold®) HT, yb, 1979, McGredy, Sam IV; bud ovoid; flowers deep golden yellow flushed coppery red, medium, 33 petals; bushy growth; ['Yellow Pages' × ('Arthur Bell' × 'Cynthia Brooke')]

'Macgenev' ('Aotearoa-New Zealand', 'New Zealand') HT, lp, 1989, McGredy, Sam IV; flowers large, soft creamy pink, 4½-5 in., 34 petals, high-centered, borne singly, intense honeysuckle fragrance; foliage large, medium green, semi-glossy; upright, medium growth; PP8279; ['Harmonie' × 'Auckland Metro']; intr. 1990

'Macgeorgi' ('The PTA News Centenary') HT, yb, McGredy; intr. 1999

'Macghovie' ('Chateau Canon') S, dr, McGredy, Sam IV

'Macglemil' ('Kapiti') F, mp, 1991, McGredy, Sam IV; flowers medium, semi-dbl., slight fragrance; foliage medium size, medium green, semi-glossy; spreading growth (to 60 cm.); [Sexy Rexy® × 'Eyeopener']; intr. 1992

'Macgolold' ('Golden Oldie') F, ab, 1998, McGredy, Sam IV; flowers apricot blend, 2¾ in., dbl., borne in large clusters; foliage medium size, dark green, semi-glossy; prickles moderate; bushy, low (50 cm.) growth; ['Maiden Voyage' × 'Orange Honey']; intr. 1997

'Macgoofy' (Papageno®) HT, rb, 1990, McGredy, Sam IV; flowers deep rose red with cream stripes, large, dbl.; foliage large, light green, matte; upright growth; ['Freude' × (('Anytime' × Eyepaint®) × 'Stars 'n' Stripes')]; intr. 1989

'MacGregor's Damask' -- See 'Johasine Hanet'

'Macgremli' ('Deborah Beggs Moncrief') HT, rb, McGredy, Sam IV; bud medium, ovoid; intr. 1990

'Macgutsy' (Academy®) Min, pb, 1983, McGredy, Sam IV; flowers small, 20 petals, slight fragrance; foliage small, medium green, semi-glossy; bushy growth; ['Anytime' × Matangi®]; intr. 1982

'Macha' ('Händel', Haendel®) LCl, rb, 1965, McGredy, Sam IV

'Macha Méril' ('Copacabana') HT, rb, Adam; flowers red with white reverse, full, high-centered, intense fruity fragrance; intr. 2004

'Machaden' (Red Perfection™) HT, dr, 1987, McGredy, Sam IV; flowers dark red, reverse slightly lighter, fading purple-red, medium, 50-60 petals, high-centered, moderate old rose fragrance; foliage large, dark green, semi-glossy; prickles slightly recurved, average, green; tall growth; hips globular, large, dark red; PP5426; ['Karma' × 'Arturo Toscanini']; intr. 1986

'Machahei' ('Reba McEntire', 'Spirit of Hope') Gr, or, 1998, McGredy, Sam IV; bud medium, ovoid; flowers 4-4½ in., 30-35 petals, cupped to high-centered, borne in small clusters, slight spicy fragrance; free-flowering; foliage large, dark green, glossy; prickles moderate, large, hooked slightly downward; bushy, medium (110cm.) growth; hips none observed ; PP11489; [('Howard Morrison' × Red Perfection™) × 'Maiden Voyage']; intr. 1997

'Machana'   Min, my, McGredy, Sam IV; intr. 1983

'Machilver' ('Dame Cath') F, lp, 1998, McGredy, Sam IV; flowers light pink, 2¾ in., semi-dbl., borne in small clusters; foliage medium size, dark green, dull; prickles moderate; bushy, low (50 cm.) growth; ['Chaumant' × ('Seaspray' × Freegold®)]; intr. 1997

Macho+   HT, w, Voom, Lex; flowers creamy white , double, high-centered, borne mostly singly; recurrent; stems long; florist rose

'Macho Man' -- See 'Permach'

'Machomai' ('Grandee') Min, dr, 1985, McGredy, Sam IV; flowers gold stamens, medium, semi-dbl., moderate fragrance; foliage medium size, medium green, semi-glossy; upright growth; [Regensberg® × 'Ko's Yellow']; intr. 1984

'Machoro' ('Placido Domingo', 'Waikato', 'Velvet Ruby') HT, mr, 1990, McGredy, Sam IV; bud small, pointed ovoid; flowers medium to dark red, reverse lighter, 11-12 cm., full, imbricated, borne singly and in small clusters, slight fragrance; recurrent; foliage large, medium green, matte; prickles ordinary, medium, slightly curved downward, brown; upright, bushy growth; PP8953; [Candella® × 'Auckland Metro']

'Machorowhen' ('Sophileo') HT, or, 1993, McGredy, Sam IV; flowers medium, dbl.; foliage medium size, medium green, semi-glossy; medium, bushy growth

'Macinca' ('Longleat', Wanaka®, 'Young Cale') Min, or, 1978, McGredy, Sam IV; flowers bright scarlet, small, 40 petals, borne several together, slight fragrance; free-flowering; foliage light green; low, bushy growth; ['Anytime' × Trumpeter®]

'Macio' F, op, 1964, McGredy, Sam IV

'Macir' HT, or, 1961, McGredy, Sam IV; intr. 1961

'Macivy' ('Love's Spring', 'Singin' in the Rain', 'Spek's Centennial') F, ab, 1994, McGredy, Sam IV; flowers apricot/copper, medium, 25-30 petals, ruffled, borne in large clusters, moderate sweet musk fragrance; foliage medium size, dark green, glossy; some prickles; medium (3-4 ft.), upright, free-branching growth; PP8362; [Sexy Rexy® × 'Pot O'Gold']; intr. 1994

'Macjilli' ('Profile') Gr, op, 1988, McGredy, Sam IV; flowers orange blend, large, full; foliage large, medium green, semi-glossy; upright growth; ['Freude' × (('Arthur Bell' × unknown) × 'Sunsong')]; intr. 1988

'Macjocel' ('Dresselhuys', 'Petite Penny') F, w, 1988, McGredy, Sam IV; flowers small, semi-dbl., moderate fragrance; foliage small, medium green, semi-glossy; bushy growth; [(('Crepuscule' × seedling) × 'Royal Occasion']; intr. 1988

'Macjuliat' ('Old Spice', 'Siegfried Sassoon', 'Spiced Coffee', 'Vidal Sassoon') HT, r, 1991, McGredy, Sam IV; flowers pale lavender with brown overtones, large, dbl., cupped, borne mostly singly, intense fragrance; recurrent; foliage medium size, medium green, matte; upright, medium growth; ['Harmonie' × 'Big Purple']; intr. 1991

'Mackalves' ('Great Expectations', 'It's Magic', 'Magic') F, ab, McGredy; flowers apricot-pink, sometimes with green at center, 4 in., 50 petals, borne one to a stem or in clusters of 5-6, moderate sweet fragrance; recurrent; foliage starts bronze red and finishes rich, glossy green; growth to 3 ft.; intr. 2001

'Mackankaf' -- See 'Raspberry Red'

'Mackati' ('Old Port') F, m, 1990, McGredy, Sam IV; flowers medium, full, moderate fragrance; foliage medium size, medium green, matte; bushy growth; PP10698; [(('Anytime' × Eyepaint®) × 'Purple Splendour') × 'Big Purple']; intr. 1991

'Mackatwi' Gr, r, McGredy; intr. 2002

'Mackepa' ('Blushing Maid', Rocky™) LCl, ob, 1979, McGredy, Sam IV; bud ovoid; flowers coral-orange, reverse whitish, 2-3 in., 18-25 petals, loosely cupped, borne mostly in clusters of 5 or more, slight fragrance; foliage medium size, leathery, semi-glossy, dark yellow-green; prickles few, long, straight, yellow-brown; stems strong, medium to long; vigorous, tall, bushy growth; PP4669; ['Liverpool Echo' × ('Evelyn Fison' × ('Orange Sweetheart' × 'Fruhlingsmorgen'))]

'Mackinat' ('The Princess') S, ob, McGredy

'Mackinju' (Maestro®) HT, rb, 1981, McGredy, Sam IV; bud ovoid; flowers medium red, painted white, reverse lighter red and white, 28 petals; foliage olive green, matte; prickles narrow, red; upright, bushy growth; [('Picasso' × unknown) × seedling]; intr. 1980

'Mackosred' ('Paragon') Min, mr, 1983, McGredy, Sam IV; flowers 35 petals, moderate fragrance; foliage small, dark, glossy; bushy growth; ['Ko's Yellow' × Little Artist®]; intr. 1982

'Mackosyel' ('Ko's Yellow') Min, yb, 1978, McGredy, Sam IV; flowers yellow, edges marked red, fading to cream, classic form, medium, 39 petals; foliage dark, glossy; bushy growth; PP4385; [('New Penny' × 'Banbridge') × ('Border Flame' × 'Manx Queen')]

'Mackrasna' F, pb, McGredy; intr. 1999

'Mackung'   HT, my, McGredy, Sam IV; intr. 1980

'Maclanoflon' ('Full Sail', 'Land of the Long White Cloud', 'Long White Cloud') HT, w, 1998, McGredy, Sam IV; flowers white, 4½ in., full, high-centered, borne mostly singly, intense fragrance; foliage large, dark green, glossy; few prickles; bushy, medium (110 cm.) growth; [sport of 'New Zealand']; intr. 1998

'Maclanter' ('Lantern', Octoberfest™) Gr, ob, 1998, McGredy, Sam IV; bud long, pointed; flowers blended autmnal colors, cream through gold to red-orange, 5-5½ in., dbl., high-centered, borne in small clusters, slight fruity fragrance; foliage large, dark green, glossy; prickles moderate; reddish new growth, tall, upright (6 ft.) growth; ['Louise Gardner' × 'New Zealand']; intr. 1999

'Maclapaz' ('Beachcomber') F, r, 1987, McGredy, Sam IV; flowers medium, 6-14 petals, slight fragrance; foliage medium size, medium green, semi-glossy; bushy growth; [seedling × 'Colorbreak']

'Maclarayspo'   Min, ob, Jones, K.; intr. 2004

'Macleide' ('Wizard') F, or, 1998, McGredy, Sam IV; flowers orange-red with white eye, 2½ in., semi-dbl., borne in large clusters; foliage small, medium green, semi-glossy; prickles moderate; bushy, low (30 cm.) growth; [seedling × 'Genesis']; intr. 1996

'Maclocker' ('Chaumant', 'Maiden Voyage', 'Oriola') F, pb, 1992, McGredy, Sam IV; flowers medium, dbl., borne in small clusters; foliage medium size, medium green, glossy; medium (3½'), bushy growth; [Sexy Rexy® × New Year®]; intr. 1992

'Maclouisi' HT, op, McGredy; intr. 2001

'Macloupri' ('Too Hot To Handle') LCl, or, 1998, McGredy, Sam IV; flowers orange-red, 2¾ in., dbl., borne in small clusters, slight fragrance; foliage large, dark green, glossy; prickles moderate; upright, tall (150 cm.) growth; [Waiheke™ × 'Eyeopener']; intr. 1995

'Macman' (Matangi®) F, rb, 1975, McGredy, Sam IV; bud ovoid; flowers orange-red, silver eye and reverse, large, 30 petals; foliage small; bushy growth; [seedling × 'Picasso']; intr. 1974

'Macmanly' ('Top Gear', Little Artist®) Min, rb, 1983, McGredy, Sam IV; bud small, pointed; flowers open with hand-painted marks becoming solid medium red, off-white in base half, 1¼ in., semi-dbl., flat, borne mostly in clusters; recurrent; foliage small, medium green, semi-glossy; prickles profuse; upright, bushy (12-14 in.) growth; [Eyepaint® × 'Ko's Yellow']

'Macmatan' ('Ten Ten') HT, mr, McGredy; intr. 1987

'Macmelan' ('Melanie') Min, op, 1989, McGredy, Sam IV; bud ovoid; flowers light salmon-pink, reverse lighter, small, 23 petals, cupped, borne in sprays of 20-25; foliage small, medium green, semi-glossy; prickles straight, red-brown; bushy, low growth; ['Seaspray' × Wanaka®]; intr. 1989

'Macmi' HT, op, 1961, McGredy, Sam IV; intr. 1961

'Macmigmou' ('Mighty Mouse', 'Painted Star') F, ob, 1981, McGredy, Sam IV; bud small, short ovoid to globular; flowers bright orange, white eye, 2-2½ in., 10-14 petals, flat, then loosely cupped, borne 20 per cluster; free-flowering; foliage dark, very long, pointed; prickles slightly hooked, red; tall, spreading growth; hips orange-red; PP5036; ['Anytime' × Eyepaint®]; intr. 1980

'Macmillan Nurse' -- See 'Beamac'

'Macminmo' ('Minnie Mouse', 'Roller Coaster') Min, rb, 1988, McGredy, Sam IV; bud short, pointed ovoid; flowers red and white striped, 2-2½ in., 10-15 petals, flat, borne in clusters, slight fragrance; scattered repeat; foliage small, medium green, glossy; prickles numerous, medium, straight to hooked downward, brown; vigorous, upright (5 ft.), arching growth; hips bright orange; PP7319; [('Anytime' × Eyepaint®) × 'Stars 'n' Stripes']; intr. 1988

'Macmisech' (Taupo®) F, op, 1978, McGredy, Sam IV; flowers light rose-salmon, flora-tea, 5 in., full; tall growth; ['Liverpool Echo' × 'Irish Mist']

'Macmo' F, rb, 1969, McGredy, Sam IV

'Macmooblu' ('Moody Blues') F, m, 1998, McGredy, Sam IV; flowers mauve, 2¾ in., full, moderate fragrance; foliage large, medium green, semi-glossy; bushy, medium (100 cm.) growth; [Sexy Rexy® × Blue Nile®]; intr. 1991

'Macmoodre' ('Moody Dream') F, m, McGredy, Sam IV; intr. 1996

'Macmosco' ('Whistle Stop') Min, rb, 1989, McGredy, Sam IV; flowers red blend (striped), small, semi-dbl., slight fragrance; foliage small, medium green, semi-glossy; bushy growth; ['Mighty Mouse' × 'Hurdy Gurdy']; intr. 1989

'Macmota' ('Crimson Tide') HT, mr, 1983, McGredy, Sam IV; flowers crimson, large, 35 petals, high-centered, borne singly; foliage large, dark, leathery; upright growth; [seedling × seedling]

'Macmouhoo' ('Christine Horbiger', 'Foster's Melbourne Cup', 'Mount Hood', 'Mt Hood') HT, w, 1989, McGredy, Sam IV; bud medium, ovoid; intr. 1991

'Macmu' ('Muria') HT, op, 1979, McGredy, Sam IV; bud long, pointed; flowers salmon-orange, 4 in., 40 petals, high-centered; foliage light green; bushy growth; ['Miss Ireland' × 'Tropicana']; intr. 1966

'Macnauru' ('Penthouse', West Coast®) HT, mp, 1988, McGredy, Sam IV; flowers clear medium pink, large, dbl., urn-shaped, borne singly and in clusters, slight fragrance; recurrent; foliage large, light green, matte; medium to tall, bushy growth; [(('Yellow Pages' × 'Kabuki') × 'Golden Gate') × (seedling × 'Picasso')]; intr. 1986

'Macnecta' (Otago®) Min, or, 1978, McGredy, Sam IV; flowers medium, 35 petals, high-centered; bushy growth; ['Anytime' × 'Minuette']

'Macnewing' ('Sea Spray', 'Seaspray') Min, pb, 1983, McGredy, Sam IV; flowers pale pink flushed red, medium, semi-dbl., moderate fragrance; foliage medium size, medium green, matte; bushy growth; ['Anytime' × Moana®]; intr. 1982

'Macnewye' ('Arcadian', New Year®) Gr, ob, 1983, McGredy, Sam IV; flowers orange and gold blend, medium, 20 petals; foliage large, dark, glossy; upright growth; PP5428; ['Mary Sumner' × seedling]; intr. 1982

'Macnic' ('Karma', 'Pounder Star') HT, mr, 1978, McGredy, Sam IV; bud long, pointed; flowers currant red, non-fading, 4 in., 20-24 petals, high-centered, borne mostly singly, moderate old rose to spicy fragrance; recurrent; foliage large, dark green, glossy; prickles small, curved; growth upright, vigorous, medium (4½ ft.); hips small, long, ovoid, green with reddish tone; PP4694; [John Waterer® × 'Kalahari']; intr. 1982

'Macnickel' ('Nickelodeon') Min, rb, 1989, McGredy, Sam IV; flowers small, semi-dbl.; foliage small, dark green, semi-glossy; bushy growth; patio; ['Roller Coaster' × ('Freude' × ('(Anytime × Eyepaint)' × 'Stars 'n' Stripes'))]

'Macnijmeg' HT, mp, McGredy; intr. 1999

'Macnon' HT, mp, 1965, McGredy, Sam IV; bud ovoid, pointed

'Macoborn' ('Maggie Barry') HT, pb, 1995, McGredy, Sam IV; bud pointed; flowers salmon edged orange, 4 in., full, borne mostly singly; foliage large, light green, matte; prickles profuse, wing shaped, curved downward; bushy (100 cm.) growth; PP10938; ['Louise Gardner' × West Coast®]; intr. 1993

'Macoffer' ('City of Christchurch') HT, op, McGredy, Sam IV; intr. 1988

'Macon' HT, mr, 1963, McGredy, Sam IV

'Macoranlem' ('Oranges 'n' Lemons', 'Papagena') S, ob, 1994, McGredy, Sam IV; flowers striking orange and yellow striped, 3-3½ in., full, borne in small clusters, slight fruity fragrance; foliage medium to large, dark red when new, turning dark green; some prickles; tall, spreading, very vigorous growth; PP9191; [New Year® × ('Freude' × seedling)]; intr. 1995

'Macpa' F, mp, 1962, McGredy, Sam IV; bud ovoid; intr. 1962

'Macpandem' ('Claire Rayner', 'Pandemonium') F, yb, 1988, McGredy, Sam IV; flowers yellow and red stripes, full; foliage small, medium green, glossy; patio; bushy growth; [New Year® × (('Anytime' × Eyepaint®) × 'Stars 'n' Stripes')]

'Macparlez' ('Baby Sunrise', 'Gold Fever') Min, ab, 1984, McGredy, Sam IV; bud small; flowers copper apricot, small, semi-dbl.; foliage small, medium green, semi-glossy; bushy growth; PP7031; [Dorola® × Moana®]

'Macpaurmar' ('Kiwi Sunrise') Min, ob, 1993, McGredy, Sam IV; flowers florescent orange with yellow eye, light yellow to white accents, light yellow reverse, 2 in., dbl., borne in small clusters, moderate spicy fragrance; foliage medium size, dark green, glossy; few prickles; medium (24-30 in.), bushy growth; ['Orange Honey' × 'Pandemonium']; intr. 1994

'Macpennsyl' HT, dy, McGredy; intr. 2000

'Macpic' F, pb, 1971, McGredy, Sam IV

'Macpinderal' Min, mp, McGredy, Sam IV; intr. 1987

'Macpiopi' ('Graeme Douglas') HT, mp, 1995, McGredy, Sam IV; flowers 3 in., full; foliage large, medium green, semi-glossy; bushy (100 cm.) growth; ['Silver Jubilee' × ('Harmonie' × 'Auckland Metro')]; intr. 1994

'Macpluto' ('Hurdy Gurdy', 'Pluto') Min, rb, 1987, McGredy, Sam IV; flowers dark red with white stripes, small, full, slight fragrance; foliage small, medium green, semi-glossy; mini-flora; upright growth; [Matangi® × 'Stars 'n' Stripes']; intr. 1986

'Macponui' ('Pinky', 'Rebekah') HT, pb, 1988, McGredy, Sam IV; flowers large, full, high-centered, borne mostly singly, slight fragrance; recurrent; foliage large, dark green, glossy; upright growth; ['Freude' × 'Typhoo Tea']

'Macpow' (Chivalry®) HT, rb, 1978, McGredy, Sam IV; flowers red, yellowish reverse, large, 35 petals; foliage glossy, dark; PP4281; [Peer Gynt® × 'Brasilia']; intr. 1977

'Macraida' (Rainy Day®) HT, mp, 1982, McGredy, Sam IV; flowers large, 20 petals; foliage large, dark, semi-glossy; bushy growth; [Trumpeter® × 'Typhoon']

'Macramar' ('Tess') HT, lp, 1998, McGredy, Sam IV; flowers large, light pink to creamy apricot, 4½ in., very full, cupped, borne mostly singly, slight fragrance; recurrent; foliage large, medium green, semi-glossy; prickles moderate; growth bushy, tall (120 cm.); [((Sexy Rexy® × New Year®) × ('Freude' × '(Courvoisier × Arthur Bell)')) × 'Dreaming']; intr. 1997

'Macrantha Rubicunda' HGal, mr, before 1877; flowers light red, large, very dbl.

'Macrat' (Priscilla Burton®) F, rb, 1977, McGredy, Sam IV; flowers deep carmine pink and white blend (with variable combinations), 2½ in., 10 petals, borne in trusses, moderate fragrance; free-flowering; foliage glossy, dark green; free, hardy growth; ['Old Master' × seedling]

'Macred' ('Joy Owens') HT, mr, 1976, McGredy, Sam IV; bud ovoid; flowers 4 in., high-centered; foliage very dark; moderate, bushy growth; [Electron® × Pharaoh®]; intr. 1977

'Macredparap' ('Trinity') S, dr, 1994, McGredy, Sam IV; flowers deep scarlet, small, dbl., slight fragrance; recurrent; foliage small, dark green, semi-glossy; spreading (90 cm.) growth; [Sexy Rexy® × 'Eyeopener']; intr. 1994

'Macredsaus' (Red Magic Carpet™) S, mr, 1999, McGredy, Sam IV; flowers cerise-red, yellow stamens, 3 in., semi-dbl., borne in small clusters, moderate fragrance; foliage medium size, medium green, glossy; growth spreading, low (12 in.); groundcover; [Sexy Rexy® × 'Eyeopener']; intr. 1994

'Macrelea' ('Chardonnay', 'Release', Nobilo's Chardonnay®, 'Peachy') HT, my, 1985, McGredy, Sam IV; flowers orange yellow, large, 35 petals; foliage small, light green, glossy; bushy growth; ['Freude' × ('Wienerwald' × 'Benson & Hedges Gold')]; intr. 1984

'Macreno' ('Cardinal's Robe', 'Susan Devoy') HT, ob, 1994, McGredy, Sam IV; flowers orange blend, 3 in., full, slight fragrance; foliage large, medium green, matte; bushy (100 cm.) growth; PP10696; [Waiheke™ × 'Las Vegas']; intr. 1994

'Macrexy' ('Heckenzauber', Sexy Rexy®) F, mp, 1985, McGredy, Sam IV; bud pointed, ovoid to ovoid globular with conspicuous neck; flowers creamy medium to light pink, medium, 39-51 petals, cupped, borne in large clusters, slight fragrance; good repeat; foliage small, light green, glossy; prickles several, medium, hooked slightly downward, yellow-green; stems medium; compact, upright, bushy growth; hips globular, smooth, bright orange; PP6713; ['Seaspray' × 'Dreaming']; intr. 1984

'Macrophylla Scandens' -- See 'Scandens'

'Macroro' ('Bull's Red') HT, mr, 1976, McGredy, Sam IV; bud ovoid; flowers brilliant crimson, 4 in., 28 petals, high-centered; foliage dark; tall, upright growth; [Sympathie® × 'Irish Rover']; intr. 1977

'Macros' ('Rose Baby', 'Royal Salute') Min, mr, 1977, McGredy, Sam IV; flowers rose-red, 1½ in., 30 petals, rosette, borne in trusses; free-flowering; foliage small, dark green, matte; compact (2 ft.) growth; ['New Penny' × 'Marlena']; intr. 1976

'Macsalem' Min, mr, 1991, McGredy, Sam; intr. 1992

'Macsatur' ('Penthouse', 'Pink Charm') HT, mp, 1988, McGredy, Sam IV; flowers large, dbl., moderate fragrance; foliage large, medium green, matte; bushy growth; [seedling × 'Ferry Porsche']

'Macsausal' S, pb, McGredy, Sam IV; intr. 1994

'Macseatri' ('Happy Days') HT, pb, 1988, McGredy, Sam IV; flowers medium, dbl.; foliage medium size, medium green, matte; bushy growth; [(seedling × 'Picasso') × 'Paradise']; intr. 1988

'Macsee' F, dy, 1971, McGredy, Sam IV

'Macsev' ('Christina Atherton') HT, op, 1979, McGredy, Sam IV; flowers salmon-pink, 4 in., 33 petals, high-centered, slight fragrance; free growth; ['Tiki' × seedling]; intr. 1978

'Macshana' ('Benson & Hedges Special', Dorola®, 'Parkay') Min, dy, 1982, McGredy, Sam IV; flowers medium, 26 petals, moderate fragrance; foliage small, medium green, semi-glossy; bushy growth; PP5427; ['Minuetto' × 'Mabella']; intr. 1983

'Macsingal' ('Singalong') Min, op, 1988, McGredy, Sam IV; flowers salmon-orange and yellow, medium, full; foliage small, medium green, glossy; patio; bushy growth; [('Anytime' × Eyepaint®) × New Year®]

'Macsingap' ('Cup Final') HT, or, 1988, McGredy, Sam IV; flowers large, dbl., slight fragrance; foliage medium size, medium green, semi-glossy; upright growth; ['Benson & Hedges Gold' × ('Kalahari' × Papa Meilland®)]; intr. 1988

'Macsoda' ('Hot 'n' Spicy') F, or, 1991, McGredy, Sam IV; flowers medium, semi-dbl., borne in small clusters; foliage medium size, dark green, glossy; bushy growth; PP8066; ['Mary Sumner' × 'Precious Platinum']; intr. 1990

'Macspash' ('Sue Lawley') F, rb, 1980, McGredy, Sam IV; bud small, pointed; flowers medium red, petals edged light pink all around, ruffled, 4½ in., 19 petals, high-centered, then flat, borne in large sprays, slight fruity fragrance; free-flowering; foliage medium size, leathery, matte, red when young; prickles small, straight, pointed; bushy, compact (25-30 in.) growth; hips globular, small ; PP4993; [(('Little Darling' × 'Goldilocks') × ('Evelyn Fison' × '(Coryana × Tantau's Triumph)')) × ('Evelyn Fison' × ('Orange Sweetheart' × 'Fruhlingsmorgen'))]

'Macspeego' ('Eternally Yours', Candella®) HT, rb, 1990, McGredy, Sam IV; flowers large, dbl.; foliage large, dark green, glossy; bushy growth; PP9239; ['Howard Morrison' × 'Esmeralda']

'Macspice' Min, m, 1983, McGredy, Sam IV

'Macspike' Min, m, 1983, McGredy, Sam IV; flowers small, semi-dbl.; foliage small, medium green, semi-glossy; spreading growth; ['Anytime' × 'Gartendirektor Otto Linne']

'Macstewar' (Bradley Craig®) F, or, 1987, McGredy, Sam IV; flowers scarlet, medium, dbl., slight fragrance; foliage medium size, medium green, glossy; bushy growth; [Tojo® × 'Montana']; intr. 1986

'Macstra' ('Mary Sumner') F, or, 1976, McGredy, Sam IV; flowers semi-dbl., 15 petals; tall, upright growth; [seedling × seedling]

'Macsupbow' ('Cologne', 'Super Bowl') Gr, m, 1998, McGredy, Sam IV; flowers mauve, 4½ in., dbl., borne in small clusters, intense fragrance; foliage large, medium green, matte; prickles moderate; bushy, medium (110 cm.) growth; ['Harmonie' × Lagerfeld™]; intr. 1996

'Macsupcat' ('Miriam') HT, yb, 1989, McGredy, Sam IV; flowers golden yellow edged pink, medium, 20 petals; free-flowering; foliage medium size, dark green, semi-glossy; vigorous, bushy growth; [Sexy Rexy® × 'Yabadabadoo']; intr. 1990

'Macswanle' HT, ab, McGredy; intr. 2001

'Macsweetwa' ('Freshie', 'Sweetwaters') HT, op, 1988, McGredy, Sam IV; flowers medium salmon-pink, large, full, slight fragrance; foliage large, dark green, glossy; upright, tall, very big growth; [((Sympathie® × 'Red Lion') × Pharaoh®) × ('Tombola' × (Elizabeth of Glamis ® × '((Circus × Golden Fleece) × Ferry Porsche)'))]; intr. 1986

'Mactane' ('City of Auckland') HT, ob, 1982, McGredy, Sam IV; flowers large, deep gold and orange with a bit of pink, dbl., intense fragrance; foliage medium green, semi-glossy; growth bushy, medium; ['Benson & Hedges Gold' × 'Whisky Mac']; intr. 1981

'Mactaumaruniu' ('Kiwi Sunrise') Min, ob, 1993, McGredy, Sam IV; intr. 1994

'Mactaurang' ('Marvelle', Tropical Sunset™, 'Rainbow Niagara') HT, yb, 1998, McGredy, Sam IV; bud big, pointed, yellow with orange-red; flowers yellow, striped pink and orange, aging lighter, 4-4½ in., dbl., cupped, borne mostly singly, slight spice fragrance; recurrent; foliage large, light green, matte; prickles moderate; bushy, tall (4 ft.) growth; PP11484; ['Louise Gardner' × ('Auckland Metro' × '(Stars 'n' Stripes × unknown)')]; intr. 1995

'Mactel' (Hotel Royal®) LCl, mr, 1972, McGredy, Sam IV

'Mactemaik' ('Michelangelo', 'The Painter') F, rb, 1998, McGredy, Sam IV; flowers striped and splotched red, orange, cream and yellow, 4 in., dbl., spiral, borne in small clusters, slight fragrance; recurrent; foliage medium size, medium green, matte; prickles moderate; tall (120 cm.), bushy growth; ['Louise Gardner' × ('Auckland Metro' × '(Stars 'n' Stripes × unknown)')]; intr. 1995

'Mactenni' (Takapuna®) Min, op, 1978, McGredy, Sam IV; flowers light peach-pink, medium, 37 petals; tall, spreading growth; ['New Penny' × (('Cläre Grammerstorf' × 'Cavalcade') × Elizabeth of Glamis®)]

'Mactexa' HT, yb, McGredy; intr. 2001

'Mactitir' ('Hoagy Carmichael') HT, mr, 1990, McGredy, Sam IV; flowers large, full, moderate fragrance; foliage medium size, dark green, matte; upright, bushy growth; PP8001; [('Sir Harry Pilkington' × 'Elegy') × 'Pounder Star']; intr. 1990

'Mactrampol' ('Remuera') F, w, 1998, McGredy, Sam IV; flowers white, 2¾ in., 26-41 petals, borne in large clusters; foliage small, medium green, semi-glossy; prickles moderate; bushy, low (40 cm.) growth; ['Seaspray' × Sexy Rexy®]; intr. 1991

'Mactrum' (Trumpeter®) F, or, 1976, McGredy, Sam IV; bud ovoid; flowers bright orange-scarlet, 6-8 cm., 35-45 petals, cupped, borne usually in small clusters, slight fragrance; free-flowering; foliage medium green, glossy; prickles several, medium, slightly hooked downward, brown; bushy, compact growth; hips short, globular, reddish-orange; PP4297; [Satchmo® × seedling]; intr. 1977

'Mactual' ('Romeo') HT, dr, 1998, McGredy, Sam IV; flowers dark crimson-red, 4½ in., full, borne mostly singly, moderate fragrance; foliage large, dark green, semi-glossy; prickles moderate; bushy, tall (110 cm.) growth; ['Howard Morrison' × 'Harmonie']; intr. 1995

'Macturang' ('Maria McGredy') HT, pb, 1998, McGredy, Sam IV; flowers pink blend,, 4½ in., full, borne mostly singly, slight fragrance; foliage large, medium green, semi-glossy; prickles moderate; bushy, tall (120 cm.) growth; ['Freude' × Remember Me®]; intr. 1997

'Maculata' -- See 'La Maculée'

'Maculata' ('Double Marbrée', 'Marmorata') HSpn, w, before 1770; flowers blush white marbled with pink, small, semi-dbl.

'Macultra' ('Brown Velvet', 'Colorbreak') F, r, 1983, McGredy, Sam IV; flowers orange, tinged brownish, medium, 35 petals; foliage medium size, dark, glossy; upright, medium to tall growth; ['Mary Sumner' × Kapai®]; intr. 1982

'Macveni' HT, op, McGredy; intr. 2003

'Macvi' (Vision Blanc®) F, w, 1966, McGredy, Sam IV

'Macvisar' ('Vision Blanc, Climbing') Cl F, w, McGredy, Sam IV; intr. after 1966

'Macvolar' ('Volare') F, or, 1988, McGredy, Sam IV; flowers medium, dbl.; foliage large, medium green, glossy; upright growth; [Julischka® × Matangi®]; intr. 1988

'Macwaihe' ('Waikiki', Waiheke™) Gr, op, 1987, McGredy, Sam IV; bud long, pointed; flowers coral-pink with lighter reverse, fading lighter, 2 in., 30 petals, high-centered, borne in sprays of 5-9, slight spicy fragrance; recurrent; foliage medium size, dark green, glossy; prickles few, small, pointed, green; upright, bushy growth; hips ovoid, small, rare, tan-orange; PP5429; ['Tony Jacklin' × Young Quinn®]; intr. 1985

'Macwairar' ('Apéritif') HT, my, 1998, McGredy, Sam IV; flowers medium yellow, 4 in., dbl., borne mostly singly, slight fragrance; foliage large, light green, matte; prickles moderate; growth bushy, medium (110 cm.); ['Solitaire' × Sunbright®]

'Macwaiwer' ('Tara Allison', 'Tara') Min, or, 1987, McGredy, Sam IV; flowers small, semi-dbl.; foliage small, medium green, semi-glossy; bushy growth; [Wanaka® × Eyepaint®]; intr. 1986

'Macwalla' (Kaikoura®) Min, ob, 1978, McGredy, Sam IV; flowers orange, patio, medium, 27 petals; foliage glossy, dark; vigorous, bushy growth; ['Anytime' × Matangi®]

'Macweemat' ('Wee Matt', Waitemata®) Min, rb, 1978, McGredy, Sam IV; flowers medium, 42 petals; foliage light green, glossy; bushy growth; ['Wee Man' × Matangi®]; intr. 1980

'Macwhaka' ('Gwen Swane') S, mp, 1988, McGredy, Sam IV; flowers medium, dbl.; foliage small, medium green, matte; spreading growth; ['MACbroey' × Snow Carpet®]; intr. 1988

'Macwhenu' ('Derek Nimmo') HT, ob, 1981, McGredy, Sam IV; bud ovoid; flowers orange-red, silvery reverse, 30 petals, borne singly and in small clusters; foliage medium green; prickles red; vigorous growth; [seedling × seedling]

'Macwhitba' ('Massey University') HT, dp, McGredy; intr. 2003

'Macwhitout' ('Whiteout') Min, w, 1989, McGredy, Sam IV; flowers small, 20 petals, cupped, slight fragrance; foliage small, medium green, semi-glossy; bushy, medium growth; [Sexy Rexy® × 'Popcorn']; intr. 1989

'Macwoodma' ('Redwood') F, rb, 1988, McGredy, Sam IV; flowers hand-painted, medium, 14 petals; foliage large, dark green, glossy; bushy growth; ['Old Master' × 'Wienerwald']

'Macwooherm' ('Red Point') F, mr, 1998, McGredy, Sam IV; flowers 9 cm., dbl., borne in small clusters, slight fragrance; foliage large, medium green, glossy; prickles moderate; bushy, medium (110 cm.) growth; ['Maiden Voyage' × 'Eyeopener']; intr. 1993

'Macwynpin' ('Manapouri') F, mp, 1994, McGredy, Sam IV; flowers medium, dbl., slight fragrance; foliage medium size, medium green, semi-glossy; bushy (35 cm.) growth; ['Trinity' × 'Moody Blues']; intr. 1994

'Macwynscar' ('Hauraki') F, or, 1994, McGredy, Sam IV; flowers medium, dbl.; foliage small, medium green, semi-glossy; patio; bushy (30 cm.) growth; [Trumpeter® × 'Kapiti']; intr. 1994

'Macwyom' HT, ly, McGredy; intr. 1999

'Macyaba' (Yabadabadoo®) HT, dy, 1982, McGredy, Sam IV; flowers large, 20 petals, high-centered, slight fragrance; foliage medium size, medium green, semi-glossy; bushy growth; ['Yellow Pages' × Bonfire Night®]; intr. 1981

'Macyefre' ('Chartreuse', 'Solitaire') HT, yb, 1987, McGredy, Sam IV; flowers yellow tinted pink, reverse yellow, fading without blanching, large, 25 petals, cupped, borne in clusters of 2 or 3, slight fragrance; foliage medium size, dark green, semi-glossy; prickles slightly hooked, large, reddish-brown; bushy, strong growth; no fruit; ['Freude' × 'Benson & Hedges Gold']; intr. 1987

'Macyelkil' ('Gold Heart', 'Heart of Gold', 'Heavenly Gold') HT, dy, 1998, McGredy, Sam IV; flowers deep yellow, 4 in., dbl., borne in small clusters, moderate fragrance; foliage medium size, medium green, glossy; prickles moderate; upright, very tall, 160 cm. growth; PP10798; ['Solitaire' × Remember Me®]; intr. 1994

'Macyom' HT, my, McGredy; intr. 2001

'Macyoumis' ('Buffalo Bill', Regensberg®, 'Young Mistress') F, pb, 1978, McGredy, Sam IV; flowers pink, edged white, white eye, yellow stamens, 4½ in., 21 petals, cupped, moderate fragrance; low, bushy growth; ['Geoff Boycott' × 'Old Master']; intr. 1979

'Macy's Pride' ('Garden Art Macy's Pride') S, w, Lim; P. and Twomey; J.; bud lemon yellow, slim; flowers creamy white with a hint of pink as they age, 4-5 in., 22 petals, borne mostly in clusters of 3; recurrent; foliage red-trimmed, aging to semi-glossy, medium green.; prickles ½-¾ cm., grey-purple; upright, bushy (5 ft.) growth; PP15574; [Graham Thomas® × 'Carefree Beauty']; intr. 2003

'Mada' -- See 'Danse de Feu'

'Madam President' ('Madame President') F, pb, 1976, McGredy, Sam IV; bud long, pointed; flowers blend of pink shades, 4 in., 70 petals, hybrid tea, slight fragrance; bushy growth; [seedling × Handel®]; intr. 1975

'Madam Speaker' -- See 'Meizuzes'

'Mme A. Bouchayer' HT, op, 1927, Siret-Pernet; flowers shrimp-pink, base Indian yellow

'Mme A. Chatain' HT, 1940, Mallerin, C.

'Mme A. Étienne' T, dp, 1886, Bernaix; bud long; sepals long, pointed; flowers rosy pink with lighter center, large, full

'Mme A. Galland' HT, pb, 1928, Mallerin, C.; flowers rose-pink, shaded shrimp-pink, dbl.; ['Pharisaer' × ('Constance' × 'unnamed Hybrid Tea')]

'Mme A. Labbey' HP, pb, before 1885; flowers pink and lilac, medium or small, full

'Mme A. Lerche' HT, mp, 1928, Bernaix, P.; flowers China-rose shaded carmine, reverse silvery rose, dbl.; ['Mme L. Hot' × 'Mrs Henry Winnett']

'Mme A. Meilland' -- See 'Peace'

'Mme A. Meilland, Climbing' -- See 'Peace, Climbing'

'Mme A. Roure' HT, yb, 1932, Lens; flowers brilliant chrome-yellow shaded salmon, to amaranth-red, dbl.; ['Wilhelm Kordes' × 'Mev. G.A. van Rossem']

'Mme A. Schwaller' HT, mp, 1886, Bernaix; flowers large, full

'Mme Abel Chatenay' HT, pb, 1895, Pernet-Ducher; bud pointed; flowers pale pink, center deeper, reverse carmine-pink,, 3 in., dbl.; foliage bronze when young; ['Dr. Grill' × 'Victor Verdier']

'Mme Abel Chatenay, Climbing' Cl HT, pb, 1917, Page; flowers pale silvery pink, reverse dark salmon, 10-12 cm., full; [sport of 'Mme Abel Chatenay']

'Mme Achille Fould' T, yb, 1903, Lévêque; flowers yellow, shaded carmine rose and salmon, very large, dbl., globular

'Mme Achille Villey' HT, or, 1939, Colombier; flowers coral-red, tinted yellow, dbl.; foliage dark; very vigorous growth; ['Charles P. Kilham' × 'Mrs Aaron Ward']

'Mme Ada Carmody' T, w, 1898, Paul, W.; bud very long; flowers ivory white bordered with pink tints, center lightish yellow, large, full

'Mme Adélaïde Côte' HP, mr, 1882, Schmitt; flowers shining crimson with fire red, fading to dark brownish red, large, full, strong sweet fragrance; foliage dark green, glossy; growth compact, shrubby; ['Senateur Vaisse' × unknown]

'Mme Adélaïde Ristori' B, dp, 1861, Pradel; flowers cerise and fawn, full

'Mme Adolphe Dahair' -- See 'Mme Adolphe Dohair'

'Mme Adolphe Dohair' ('Mme Adolphe Dahair') T, ly, 1900, Puyravaud; flowers white and cream, satiny, large, dbl., cupped, moderate fragrance; ['Général Schablikine' × 'Mlle Lazarine Poizeau']

'Mme Adolphe Lafont' HT, ab, 1921, Croibier; flowers deep apricot-red tinted buff, semi-dbl.; [sport of 'Joseph Hill']

'Mme Adolphe Loiseau' HT, lp, 1897, Buatois; flowers rosy flesh pink, aging to creamy white, very large, very full; nearly thornless; ['Merveille de Lyon' × 'Kaiserin Auguste Viktoria']

'Mme Agathe Nabonnand' ('Agathe Nabonnand') T, lp, 1886, Nabonnand, G.; flowers rosy flesh tinted amber, petals shell-like, very large

'Mme Albert Barbier' HT, ob, 1925, Barbier; flowers salmon, tinted nankeen yellow, center darker, large, 50 petals, cupped; recurrent bloom; vigorous, bushy growth; ['Frau Karl Druschki' × unknown]

'Mme Albert Bernardin' T, w, 1904, Mari; flowers white, shaded with carmine, center yellow, medium, full; prickles small; ['Comtesse de Frigneuse' × 'Marie Van Houtte']

'Mme Albert Gilles' HT, op, 1934, Guillot, H.; flowers light coral-pink, very large, very dbl.; [seedling × 'Jean C.N. Forestier']

'Mme Alboni' M, lp, 1850, Verdier, V.; flowers flesh pink, medium, full

'Mme Alégatière' Pol, dp, 1888, Alégatière; flowers carmine-pink, medium, dbl.; ['Polyantha Alba Plena' × 'Jules Margottin']

'Mme Alexandre' HT, rb, 1926, Walter, L.; flowers crimson-vermilion-red, shaded velvety purple, dbl.

'Mme Alexandre Bernaix' HT, pb, 1877, Guillot; flowers shining dark pink with China pink, edged white, large, full, globular, moderate fragrance; ['La France' × unknown]

'Mme Alexandre Charvet' HT, or, 1943, Meilland, F.; bud long, pointed; flowers orange-red, edged lilac, medium, dbl., cupped; foliage leathery; moderate growth; ['Charles P. Kilham' × ('Charles P. Kilham' × 'Mme Joseph Perraud')]

'Mme Alexandre Dreux' HT, my, 1921, Soupert & Notting; bud pointed; flowers golden yellow, large, dbl.; ['Rayon d'Or' × 'Primerose']

'Mme Alexandre Jullien' HP, lp, 1882, Vigneron; bud elongated; flowers light, satiny pink, large, full; quite remontant; foliage light green; numerous prickles; growth upright; ['Elisabeth Vigneron' × unknown]

'Mme Alexandre Pommery' -- See 'Mme Veuve Alexandre Pommery'

'Mme Alfred Carrière' N, w, 1879, Schwartz, J.; bud pearly pink; flowers pale pinkish white, 10 cm., dbl., globular, borne in small clusters, intense fragrance; recurrent bloom; vigorous, climbing growth

'Mme Alfred de Rougemont' HP, lp, 1862, Lacharme, F.; flowers white tinted pink, medium, full, cupped, borne in small clusters, moderate fragrance; foliage light green; vigorous growth; ['Mlle Blanche Lafitte' × 'Sapho']; sometimes classed as B

'Mme Alfred Digeon' HT, my, 1911, Puyravaud; flowers lemon yellow tinted chamois, medium to large, slight fragrance; nearly thornless

'Mme Alfred Leveau' -- See 'Alfred Leveau'

'Mme Alfred Ponnier' HT, w, 1920, Bernaix, P.

'Mme Alfred Sabatier' HT, rb, 1904, Bernaix; flowers satiny peach-red, fading when open, large; foliage dark green

'Mme Alfred Schisselé' HT, m, 1930, Leenders, M.; flowers lilac-white, center coppery orange, large, dbl.; foliage bronze; ['Frau Felix Tonnar' × 'Angèle Pernet']

'Mme Alice Dureau' ('Alice Dureau') HP, lp, 1867, Vigneron; flowers lilac pink, large, full

'Mme Alice Garnier' ('Alice Garnier', 'Brownlow Hill Rambler') HWich, pb, 1906, Fauque; flowers bright rose, center yellow to light pink, 3-4 cm., full, borne in medium clusters, intense sweet fragrance; some autumn repeat; foliage dark, glossy; [R. wichurana × 'Mme Charles']

'Mme Alphonse Lavallée' -- See 'Marie Baumann'

'Mme Alphonse Seux' HP, mp, 1887, Liabaud; flowers delicate pink, very large, full; foliage glaucous green; growth upright; ['Victor Verdier' × unknown]

'Mme Alvarez del Campo' HRg, pb, 1903, Gravereaux; flowers rosy flesh, tinted salmon, large, semi-dbl.; prickles few for its type, straight

'Mme Amadieu' T, pb, 1880, Pernet; flowers shining carmine-pink, centers white shaded carmine, very large, dbl., strong fragrance

'Mme Amandinoli' T, lp, 1881, Brassac; flowers flesh pink

'Mme Ambroise Triollet' HP, op, 1869, Moreau & Robert; flowers pink over salmon, large, full

'Mme Ambroise Verschaffelt' HP, dp, 1865, Verdier, E.; flowers deep pink, large, full

'Mme Amélie Baltet' HP, lp, 1878, Verdier, E.; flowers satiny delicate pink, silvery, large, full, cupped; foliage light green, rounded, regularly dentate; prickles few, short, slightly recurved, yellowish

'Mme Anatole Leroy' HP, lp, 1892, Levet

'Mme Ancelot' HRg, lp, 1901, Gravereaux & Müller; flowers whitish pink, large, full, moderate fragrance; prickles numerous, small, straight, unequal

'Mme André Charmet' HT, mp, 1921, Croibier; flowers carnation-pink, dbl.; ['Mme Mélanie Soupert' × 'Mme Maurice de Luze']

'Mme André de Halloy' HT, ob, 1929, Ketten Bros.; flowers orange, reverse salmon-pink, very dbl.; ['Gloire de Hollande' × 'Benedicte Seguin']

'Mme André Dulin' HT, op, 1959, Gaujard; flowers bright coppery pink, large, dbl.; vigorous, bushy growth; ['Opera' × 'Ville de Gand']

'Mme André Duron' HT, mr, 1887, Bonnaire; flowers clear light red, very large; growth upright

'Mme André Gillier' HT, rb, 1934, Reymond; bud pointed; flowers coppery red, shaded yellow, semi-dbl., cupped; ['Padre' × seedling]

'Mme André Leroy' HP, mp, 1864, Trouillard; flowers salmon-rose, large, dbl.; vigorous growth

'Mme André Saint' HP, w, 1926, Barbier; flowers milk-white to pure white, center clear chamois, dbl.; prickles few thorns; stocky growth; ['Frau Karl Druschki' × 'Benedicte Seguin']

'Mme Angèle Dispott' HP, mr, 1879, Dauvesse; flowers fiery red, medium, full

'Mme Angèle Favre' HT, op, 1888, Perny; flowers pink and salmon

'Mme Angèle Jacquier' T, pb, 1879, Guillot; flowers bright pink, tinted coppery yellow, edged lighter, reverse dark pink, large, full; ['Mme Damaizin' × unknown]

'Mme Angèle Jacquier' T, pb, Veysset; flowers pink, striped; intr. 1890

'Mme Angélina' B, my, 1844, Chanet; flowers nankeen yellow, center creamy, tinted salmon, medium, very full

'Mme Angélique Veysset' ('Striped La France') HT, pb, 1890, Veysset; flowers pink, striped with bright red, large, dbl.; recurrent; [sport of 'La France']

'Mme Anna Bugnet' HP, lp, 1866, Gonod; flowers large, full

'Mme Anna de Besobrasoff' HP, w, 1877, Nabonnand; flowers flesh white, striped pink, edged white, center tinted carmine, large, full, moderate fragrance

'Mme Anna de Besobrasoff' HP, mr, Gonod; flowers bright cherry red, aging to purple, large, full; ['Charles Lefèbvre' × unknown]; intr. 1878

'Mme Anna Moreau' HP, lp, 1883, Moreau & Robert; flowers light pink, center lighter, edges and reverse white, very large, very full

'Mme Anne Béluze' ('Anne Béluze') B, mp, about 1840, Béluze; flowers bright pink aging to flesh pink, medium

'Mme Annette Aynard' HT, w, 1919, Leenders, M.; flowers milk-white edged pink, passing to amber-yellow, dbl.; ['Mme Caroline Testout' × 'Prince de Bulgarie']

'Mme Anth. Kluis' Pol, op, 1924, Kluis; flowers salmon-pink tinted orange, large, semi-dbl., borne in clusters

'Mme Antoine Mari' T, pb, 1901, Mari, A.; flowers rosy flesh, shaded lilac and rose, large, dbl.

'Mme Antoine Montagne' HT, lp, 1930, Richardier; flowers flesh-pink, with reflexes of old ivory

'Mme Antoine Rébé' T, rb, 1900, Laperrière; bud long; flowers bright red; ['Alphonse Karr' × 'Princesse de Sagan']

'Mme Antoine Rivoire' HP, lp, 1894, Liabaud; flowers delicate frosty pink with carmine reflections, very large, cupped; foliage light green; growth compact, erect

'Mme Antonin Charvet' HWich, lp, 1912, Girin; flowers silvery pink, edges lighter, large

'Mme Antony Choquens' T, pb, 1900, Bernais fils; flowers flesh pink, reverse apricot gold, large, full

'Mme Apolline Foulon' HP, pb, 1882, Vigneron; flowers light salmon, reverse touched with lilac, large, full; very remontant; few prickles; growth upright

'Mme Armand Souzy' HT, rb, 1945, Meilland, F.; flowers geranium-red and saffron-yellow, very large; ['Charles P. Kilham' × ('Charles P. Kilham' × 'Margaret McGredy')]

'Mme Arsène Bonneau' HP, mr, 1871, Bonnaire; flowers cherry red with white reflections

'Mme Arthaud' HT, ob, 1938, Mallerin, C.; flowers deep orange, large, very dbl.; vigorous growth; ['Charles P. Kilham' × ('Kitchener of Khartoum' × 'Mari Dot')]

'Mme Arthur Oger' Cl B, mp, 1899, Oger; flowers brilliant pink, very large, dbl.; very vigorous, climbing growth; ['Mme Isaac Pereire' × unknown]

'Mme Arthur Robichon' Pol, dp, 1912, Robichon; flowers carmine-pink, small, dbl.; ['Mme Norbert Levavasseur' × 'Mrs W. H. Cutbush']

'Mme Aude' B, m, 1839, Desprez; flowers lilac pink, large, full, globular

'Mme Audot' A, lp, 1844, Verdier, V.; flowers pale flesh, medium, full, cupped; growth branching

'Mme Auguste Chatain' HT, op, 1940, Mallerin, C.; bud very long; flowers coral-salmon, well-formed, large, dbl.; very vigorous growth

'Mme Auguste Choutet' LCl, ob, 1901, Godard; flowers orange-yellow, 7-9 cm., semi-dbl., borne in small clusters, intense tea fragrance; ['William Allen Richardson' × 'Kaiserin Auguste Viktoria']

'Mme Auguste Nonin' HWich, dp, 1914, Nonin; flowers deep shell-pink, center white, small, semi-dbl., cupped, borne in clusters of 20-30; foliage large, glossy; very vigorous, climbing (15-20 ft.), open growth; ['Dorothy Perkins' × 'Blush Rambler (?)']

'Mme Auguste Perrin' N, lp, 1878, Schwartz; flowers pearly pink, reverse whitish to medium, 7 cm., very full, moderate damask fragrance; foliage olive green

'Mme Auguste Rodrigues' B, mp, 1897, Chauvry; flowers frosty pink, reverse silvery, 9 cm., very full, globular, borne in small clusters, moderate fragrance; non-recurrent; ['Souv de Nemours' × 'Max Singer']; sometimes classed as HMult

'Mme Auguste Sommereau' HT, lp, 1892, Corboeuf-Marsault; flowers flesh pink, aging white, large, full, globular, moderate fragrance

'Mme Auguste van Geert' HP, pb, 1861, Robichon; flowers deep rosy-pink, striped white, medium, full

'Mme Augustine Hammond' HT, mp, 1897, Vigneron; flowers clear satin-rose, lighter at edges, very large, dbl., globular; foliage light green

'Mme Autrand' HT, ob, 1922, Leenders, M.; flowers coppery orange, dbl.; ['Mme Caroline Testout' × 'Prince de Bulgarie']

'Mme Azélie Imbert' T, yb, 1870, Levet, F.; flowers yellow, tinted with salmon, large, full; ['Mme Falcot' × unknown]

'Mme Badin' T, pb, 1897, Croibier; flowers bright carmine pink, shaded violet, center coppery yellow, medium, full

'Mme Ballu' HRg, m, 1904, Gravereaux; flowers violet-pink, medium, semi-dbl.; foliage not rugose; prickles large, nearly straight, reddish

'Mme Bardou Job' HT, ly, 1913, Dubreuil; flowers canary-yellow, center chrome-yellow, large, semi-dbl., cupped; ['Prince de Bulgarie' × unknown]

'Mme Barillet-Deschamps' T, w, 1853, Bernède; flowers white, shaded yellow, large, full

'Mme Barriot' HP, dp, 1867, Damaizin; flowers carmine pink, large, full

'Mme Barthélemy Levet' T, ly, 1879, Levet, F.; flowers canary-yellow, large, full; foliage brilliant green; growth vigorous; ['Gloire de Dijon' × unknown]

'Mme Baulot' HP, mp, 1885, Lévêque; flowers bright pink nuanced carmine, large, dbl.; foliage glaucous green

'Mme Bégault-Pigné' HP, dp, 1906, Bégault-Pigné; flowers very large, full, moderate fragrance

'Mme Bellenden Kerr' HP, w, 1866, Guillot père

'Mme Bellon' HP, mp, 1871, Pernet père; flowers cerise pink, very large, full

'Mme Bento Vidal' HT, mr, about 1910, Cotrim; flowers velvety crimson, large, full; [sport of 'Étincelante']

'Mme Bérard' Cl T, ob, 1870, Levet, F.; bud long; flowers salmon-yellow shaded salmon-rose, 10-11 cm., dbl., cupped, moderate fragrance; ['Mme Falcot' × 'Gloire de Dijon']

'Mme Berkeley' T, pb, 1898, Bernaix fils; flowers salmon-pink, cerise and gold, moderate fragrance; recurrent

'Mme Bernard' T, yb, 1875, Levet; flowers copppery yellow, aging to flesh pink, large, full; ['Mme Falcot' × unknown]

'Mme Bernède' T, pb, 1856, Bernède; flowers coppery pink, large, full

'Mme Bernutz' HP, mp, 1873, Jamain; flowers satiny pink, very large, full, cupped

'Mme Bertha Mackart' HP, mp, 1883, Verdier, E.; flowers bright carmine pink, reverse silvery, very large, full, cupped, globular; foliage oblong, dark green, regularly and deeply toothed; prickles long, straight, unequal, very sharp; growth upright

'Mme Berthe de Forge' HT, op, 1935, Chambard, C.; flowers orange-coral, tinted coppery salmon, very large, cupped; foliage bronze

'Mme Berthe Fontaine' HP, mp, 1898, Buatois; flowers bright pink, very large, very full, moderate fragrance; ['Luciole' × 'Cl. Jaquet']

'Mme Bessemer' HT, op, 1898, Conard & Jones; flowers peachy-pink, large, very full

'Mme Betty Hendlé' HP, dr, 1892, Boutigny, P.; flowers velvety red, shaded darker, large, full; ['Mme Victor Verdier' × 'Abel Carrière']

'Mme Bijou' HP, dr, 1886, Chauvry; flowers velvety red, shaded chestnut brown, reverse marbled violet, large, full

'Mme Blachet' T, mp, 1859, Boyau

'Mme Blondel' HT, mp, 1899, Veysset; flowers bright pink with silvery edge, very large, dbl., moderate fragrance; ['La France de '89' × unknown]

'Mme Blytha Pearkes' HT, ab, 1970, Blakeney; flowers light apricot flushed yellow and pink, medium, dbl.; bushy, compact growth; ['Karl Herbst' × 'Lady Hillingdon']

'Mme Boll' HP, dp, 1843, Boll, Daniel; flowers carmine-rose, large; recurrent bloom; foliage 5 leaflets per leaf; vigorous growth; two parentages given: HP × Belle Fabert, or Baronne Prévost × Portlandica; intr. 1859

'Mme Bollaert' HT, rb, 1938, Chambard, C.; bud long, coppery red; flowers carmine, shaded nasturtium-red, very large, dbl., cupped; strong stems; very vigorous, bushy growth; ['Ami F. Mayery' × seedling]

'Madame Bollinger' F, op, 1973, McGredy, Sam IV; flowers deep orange-salmon, 3 in., 25 petals, high-centered; free growth; [('Little Darling' × 'Goldilocks') × 'Bobbie Lucas']; intr. 1972

'Mme Bollinger' F, rb, McGredy, Sam IV; flowers coppery red with dark yellow, medium, semi-dbl.; intr. 1972

'Mme Bonnet-Aymard' T, w, 1874, Pernet; flowers pure white, center yellow, medium, full

'Mme Bonnet des Claustres' T, w, 1891, Reboul; flowers creme, center light yellow, very large, full

'Mme Bonnin' HP, op, 1877, Cochet; flowers bright silvery-salmon pink, large, very full; foliage dark green; few prickles

'Mme Bory d'Arnex' HT, op, 1907, Soupert & Notting; flowers coral-red, center flesh, large; ['Laure Wattine' × 'Antoine Rivoire']

'Mme Boutin' -- See 'Christina Nilsson'

'Mme Bovary' S, m, Delbard; flowers mauve pink with lighter reverse, large, dbl., rounded, intense floral and fruity fragrance; growth to 50-100 cm.; intr. 2002

'Mme Bravy ' ('Adèle Pradel', 'Mme de Sertot ', 'Joséphine Maltot', 'Isidore Malton', 'Danzille', 'Alba Rosea') T, w, 1846, Guillot Père; flowers creamy white shaded blush, dbl.

'Mme Bréon' Ch, dp, 1841, Verdier, V.; flowers carmine pink, shaded scarlet-salmon, large, full

'Mme Briançon' HP, rb, 1862, Fontaine; flowers carmine, shaded scarlet, large, full

'Mme Brosse' HP, mr, 1886, Brosse; flowers poppy red, large, full

'Mme Bruel' -- See 'Mme François Bruel'

'Mme Brunner' ('Aimée Vibert Jaune') N, ly, 1890, Brunner; flowers pale yellow; [sport of 'Aimée Vibert']

'Mme Bruno Coquatrix' Gr, or, Pineau; intr. 1978

'Mme Bruny' HP, m, 1858, Avoux & Crozy; flowers flesh-white, shaded lilac, large, full, globular

'Mme Bureau' ('Infidélité de Lisette', 'Mme de Rohan') HCh, w, before 1846; flowers white, centers straw yellow, large, very full, moderate fragrance

'Mme Butterfly' HT, lp, 1918, Hill, E.G.; flowers light creamy pink, tinted gold, well-formed, 30 petals; growth vigorous, well branched; [sport of 'Ophelia']

'Mme Butterfly, Climbing' Cl HT, lp, 1926, Smith, E.P.; flowers yellowish-pink, large, full; [sport of 'Mme Butterfly']

'Mme Byrne' N, w, 1840, Buist; flowers cream color, center rose, large, dbl.; ['Lamarque' × unknown]

'Mme C. Chambard' HT, lp, 1911, Chambard, C.; flowers rosy flesh-pink, shaded salmon, base yellow, very large, 72 petals, moderate fragrance; ['Frau Karl Druschki' × 'Prince de Bulgarie, or Lady Ashtown']

'Mme C. Liger' -- See 'Mme C. Ligier'

'Mme C. Ligier' ('Mme C. Liger') T, pb, 1900, Berland; bud round, very large; flowers pink with darker red, large, very dbl., intense fragrance

'Mme C. P. Strassheim' T, my, 1897, Soupert & Notting; flowers yellowish-white to sulphur-yellow, large, full, intense fragrance; foliage coppery-red, glossy; growth vigorous; ['Mlle Adèle Jougant' × 'Mme la Princesse de Bessaraba de Brancovan']

'Mme C. Richardier' HT, my, 1924, Richardier; flowers yellow, passing to clear yellow, dbl.

'Mme Cadeau-Ramey' HT, op, 1896, Pernet-Ducher; flowers deep flesh pink, center shaded yellow, edged carmine pink, large, full, moderate fragrance

'Mme Caillat' HP, mr, 1861, Verdier, E.; flowers shining cherry red, large, full

'Mme Calot' B, dp, 1850, Miellez

'Mme Camille' T, lp, 1871, Guillot et Fils; flowers aurora-pink, veined, with white reflections, well-formed, large, dbl.

'Mme Camille Laurens' HT, or, 1956, Dorieux; flowers crimson-red tinted orange, well-formed; foliage bright green; strong stems; ['Peace' × 'Happiness']

'Mme Campbell d'Islay' -- See 'Triomphe de Valenciennes'

'Mme Caradori-Allan' HMult, lp, 1843, Feast; flowers shining light pink, medium, dbl

'Mme Caristie Martel' HT, ly, 1916, Pernet-Ducher; flowers pure sulfur-yellow, center deeper, 5-6 in., full, globular

'Mme Carle' HT, mr, 1888, Bernaix; flowers bright cherry red, edged carmine pink, medium, full

'Mme Carnot' N, yb, 1889, Moreau et Robert; flowers golden yellow tinged orange, center darker, large, very dbl., globular; vigorous, climbing growth; ['William Allen Richardson' × unknown]

'Mme Caro' T, yb, 1880, Levet; flowers salmon-yellow, medium, very full; foliage dark green, purplish beneath; growth weak; ['Gloire de Dijon' × unknown]

'Mme Caroline Küster' ('Caroline Küster') N, yb, 1872, Pernet; flowers yellow and orange blend, medium, dbl.; ['Le Pactole' × unknown]

'Mme Caroline Schmitt' ('Caroline Schmitt') N, yb, 1878, Schmitt; flowers salmon-yellow, medium to large, dbl.; recurrent bloom; ['Solfaterre' × unknown]

'Mme Caroline Testout' ('Caroline Testout', 'City of Portland') HT, mp, 1890, Pernet-Ducher; bud pointed; flowers bright satiny rose, center darker, edged soft carmine-pink, very large, dbl., moderate fragrance; foliage rich green, soft; vigorous, bushy growth; ['Mme de Tartas' × 'Lady Mary Fitzwilliam']

'Mme Caroline Testout, Climbing' ('Caroline Testout, Climbing') Cl HT, mp, 1901, Chauvry; flowers satin pink with a deeper center, large, dbl., moderate fragrance; [sport of 'Mme Caroline Testout']

'Mme Carré' D, w, before 1885; flowers flesh white, medium, full

'Mme Casimir Moullé' -- See 'Casimir Moullé'

'Mme Catherine Fontaine' T, dp, 1892, Liabaud; flowers dark rose pink over cream, streaked darker pink, semi-dbl.; ['Marie van Houtte' × unknown]

'Mme Ceccaldi' HT, op, 1938, Chambard, C.; bud long; flowers salmon-carmine-pink, shaded vermilion, very large, dbl.; strong stems; very vigorous growth; ['Soeur Thérèse' × seedling]

'Mme Cécile Berthod' T, dy, 1871, Guillot; flowers sulfur-gold, reverse yellowish-white, medium to large, very full, slight fragrance

'Mme Cécile Brünner, Climbing' -- See 'Mlle Cécile Brünner, Climbing'

'Mme Cécile Brünner' -- See 'Mlle Cécile Brünner'

'Mme Cécile Morand' HP, dr, 1890, Corboeuf; flowers deep carmine red, reverse slightly silvery, large, very full

'Mme Cécile Piètre' HP, mr, 1909, Denis; flowers rose red, shaded vermilion, large, full

'Mme Céline Noirey' T, lp, 1868, Guillot et Fils; flowers soft pink, reverse purple, large, very dbl.

'Mme Céline Touvais' HP, mp, 1859, Touvais; flowers bright pink, dbl., peony-

shape
'Mme Céphalie Laurent' HP, mp, 1894, Boutigny, P.
'Mme César Brunier' HP, mp, 1887, Bernaix, A.; bud oval, long; flowers China pink, satiny, center petals muddled, very dbl., moderate centifolia fragrance; prickles numerous, unequal; growth upright
'Mme Chaban Delmas' HT, mr, 1957, Privat; flowers bright red, well-formed, large; foliage bright green
'Mme Chabanne' Cl T, yb, 1896, Liabaud; flowers canary yellow, outermost petals cream white, medium to large, full, cupped
'Mme Chamouton-Murgue' HT, op, 1925, Chambard, C.; flowers orange-carmine, shaded vermilion, very large, dbl., cupped; foliage dark; vigorous, erect, branching growth; [seedling × 'Mrs Edward Powell']
'Mme Charles' T, yb, 1864, Damaizin; flowers yellow, center salmon, large, full, semi-globular; ['Mme Damaizin' × unknown]
'Mme Charles Allizon' HT, w, 1928, Schwartz, A.; flowers rosy white, edges tinted yellow, dbl.; ['Mme Vittoria Gagniere' × 'Lady Pirrie']
'Mme Charles Baltet' B, lp, 1865, Verdier, E.; flowers delicate pink, large, very full, borne in clusters of 4-6; ['Louise Odier' × unknown]
'Mme Charles Boutmy' HT, lp, 1892, Vigneron; flowers light flesh pink, very large, full, cupped
'Mme Charles Chapelet' -- See 'Mme Charles Crapelet'
'Mme Charles Crapelet' ('Mme Charles Chapelet', 'Mme Hérivaux') HP, pb, 1859, Fontaine; flowers cerise, frosted and veined with lilac, large, full, moderate fragrance; foliage large, rugose; prickles numerous, small, unequal
'Mme Charles Damé' ('Belle Egarée') HP, lp, 1904, Damé; flowers fresh light pink, large, full
'Mme Charles de Lapisse' -- See 'Charles de Lapisse'
'Mme Charles de Luze' HT, w, 1903, Pernet-Ducher; flowers flesh white, center chamois-yellow, very large, full, globular, moderate fragrance
'Mme Charles Détreaux' B, mr, 1895, Vigneron; flowers bright carmine-red, large
'Mme Charles Druschki' -- See 'Frau Karl Druschki'
'Mme Charles Dubreuil' HT, pb, 1911, Guillot, P.; flowers salmon-rose, reverse shaded carmine, dbl.; [sport of 'Pharisaer']
'Mme Charles Frédéric Worth' ('C. F. Worth', 'Frédéric Worth') HRg, dp, 1889, Schwartz, Vve.; flowers rosy carmine, fading, large, semi-dbl., borne in large clusters, moderate fragrance; profuse early bloom, but sparse in summer and fall; foliage glossy, rugose; vigorous growth
'Mme Charles Guillaud' HT, op, 1943, Mallerin, C.; flowers orange-pink with fiery tints
'Mme Charles Guillot' HT, pb, 1943, Mallerin, C.; flowers carmine-pink and orange, large, dbl.
'Mme Charles Haas' HT, w, 1930, Ketten Bros.; flowers amber-white, tinted flesh-white, large, 60-70 petals, high-centered, moderate fragrance; foliage leathery; vigorous, free branching growth; ['Mme Abel Chatenay' × 'Golden Emblem']
'Mme Charles Joly' HT, op, 1942, Chambard, C.; flowers bright salmon shaded coppery yellow
'Mme Charles Lejeune' HWich, lp, 1924, Vandevelde; flowers soft pink, 7-8 cm., full, borne in small clusters, moderate fragrance; foliage glossy; ['Dr W. Van Fleet' × 'La Perle']
'Mme Charles Levet' T, op, 1870, Levet; flowers salmon pink
'Mme Charles Lutaud' HT, yb, 1912, Pernet-Ducher; flowers chrome-yellow, blending to rosy scarlet at edge, dbl.; [seedling × 'Marquise de Sinéty']
'Mme Charles Lutaud, Climbing' Cl HT, yb, 1922, Guillot, P.
'Mme Charles Magny' HT, rb, 1941, Gaujard; flowers coppery red and golden yellow, very large, very dbl., cupped; vigorous, bushy growth; ['Mme Joseph Perraud' × seedling]
'Mme Charles Mallerin' HT, ob, 1939, Mallerin, C.; flowers orange-salmon, large, dbl., cupped; foliage leathery, dark; vigorous growth; PP409; ['Lucy Nicolas' × 'Brazier']
'Mme Charles Meurice' HP, dr, 1878, Meurice; flowers velvety dark red, well-formed, large, dbl.; bushy growth
'Mme Charles Monnier' HT, op, 1901, Monnier/Pernet-Ducher; flowers flesh pink, center orange with golden salmon, very large, very full, globular
'Mme Charles Montigny' HP, mr, 1900, Corboeuf-Marsault; flowers blackish red, nuanced flame, large, full; ['Prince Camille de Rohan' × 'Éclair']
'Mme Charles Rouveure' HT, dy, 1946, Mallerin, C.; flowers 4-5 in., 36 petals, moderate fruity fragrance; foliage dark; free growth
'Mme Charles Roy' HP, mp, 1862; flowers rose pink, edges silky
'Mme Charles Salleron' M, mr, 1867, Fontaine; flowers carmine shaded fiery red, large, full; some repeat
'Mme Charles Sauvage' ('Mississippi') HT, yb, 1949, Mallerin, C.; flowers yellow tinted saffron, center orange-yellow, well-shaped, 5 in., 30 petals; bushy growth; ['Julien Potin' × 'Orange Nassau']
'Mme Charles Singer' T, dp, 1916, Nabonnand, C.; flowers garnet, becoming dark velvety purple-garnet, large, dbl.; vigorous growth
'Mme Charles Truffaut' HP, lp, 1878, Verdier, E.; flowers satiny rose, large; foliage light green, oblong, regularly dentate; prickles straight, pointed; growth vigorous, upright
'Mme Charles Verdier' HP, mp, 1863, Lacharme; flowers rosy pink, large, full, globular, moderate fragrance
'Mme Charles Wood' ('Dinsmore') HP, mr, 1861, Verdier, E.; flowers fiery scarlet, large, 45 petals; moderate growth
'Mme Charles Yojerot' HMult, mr, 1933, Thebault-Lebreton; flowers large, single
'Mme Charlet' T, yb, 1856, Corbie; flowers nankeen yellow, center salmon pink, large, semi-dbl.
'Mme Chaté' HP, rb, 1871, Fontaine; flowers cherry red, blended with white, large, full
'Mme Chatelaine de Lullier' HT, Meilland, L.; intr. 1987
'Mme Chauvel' HP, dp, 1855, Chauvel; flowers dark pink, aging to flesh pink, reverse light pink, large, full
'Mme Chauvry' N, yb, 1886, Bonnaire; flowers nankeen yellow, shaded copper-yellow, reverse China pink, 4½ in., full; foliage large, glossy, dark green; ['Mme Bérard' × 'William Allen Richardson']; sometimes classed as T
'Mme Chavaret' T, yb, 1872, Levet; flowers apricot with nankeen-yellow, shaded salmon and white, large, very full, globular, moderate fragrance; ['Mme Damaizin' × unknown]
'Mme Chédane-Guinoisseau' T, ly, 1880, Lévêque; bud pointed; flowers sulphur yellow, large, full; foliage glossy; [seedling or sport of 'Safrano']
'Mme Cheine Duguy' HT, pb, 1929, Schwartz, A.; flowers cerise-red, shaded scarlet, dbl.
'Mme Chevalier' B, mp, 1886, Pernet père; flowers bright pink, large, dbl.; growth upright
'Mme Chiang Kai-shek' ('Yellow Delight') HT, ly, 1942, Duehrsen; bud long, pointed; flowers lemon yellow, turning lighter, 5-5½ in., 27 petals, exhibition, moderate fragrance; foliage leathery, glossy, dark; vigorous, upright, compact growth; PP664; ['Joanna Hill' × 'Sir Henry Segrave']
'Mme Chirard' HP, mp, 1867, Pernet père; flowers rose, tinged with vermilion, large, full, globular, moderate fragrance
'Mme Claire Jaubert' T, ly, 1887, Nabonnand; flowers brick yellow, shaded to rose pink, imbricated, very large, semi-dbl.
'Mme Clara d'Arcis' ('Clara d'Arcis') HT, pb, 1931, Gaujard; flowers brilliant rose-pink, base yellow, large, dbl., moderate spicy fragrance; foliage dark, leathery; ['Julien Potin' × seedling]
'Mme Claude Olivier' HT, op, 1939, Mallerin, C.; bud long, pointed; flowers coral, tinted nasturtium-yellow, very large, dbl., high-centered; foliage leathery; strong

stems; very vigorous, bushy growth; ['Soeur Thérèse' × (R. foetida bicolor × unknown)]

'Mme Clémence Beauregard' ('Clémence Beaugrand') M, mp, 1851, Laffay; flowers crimson, shaded lilac, large, dbl.

'Mme Clémence Joigneaux' HP, pb, 1861, Liabaud; flowers pink and red, very large, dbl.; foliage large, dark green, regularly serrated; numerous prickles; growth upright

'Mme Clémence Marchix' T, rb, 1899, Bernaix, P.; bud deep cherry red, ovoid; flowers crimson and rose, cupped

'Mme Clément Massier' ('Mme G. Cossard') N, mp, 1884, Nabonnand; flowers bright pink, petal edges lighter, medium to large, very full

'Mme Clert' HP, op, 1868, Gonod; flowers salmon-rose, large, full

'Mme Clorinde Leblond' HP, dr, 1870, Dauvesse; flowers velvety garnet, medium, dbl.

'Mme Clothilde Perrault' B, dp, 1863, Vigneron; flowers dark pink, becoming light red, medium to large, full

'Mme Cochet-Cochet' HT, op, 1934, Mallerin, C.; bud very long; flowers coppery rose-pink, tinted coral, large, 30 petals, cupped, moderate fragrance; foliage glossy; vigorous growth; PP129; ['Mrs Pierre S. duPont' × 'Cécile Walter']

'Mme Colette Martinet' HT, yb, 1915, Pernet-Ducher; flowers old-gold shaded orange-yellow, dbl.

'Mme Collet' B, lp, 1864, Liabaud; flowers whitish pink, medium

'Mme Collet' HP, pb, Liabaud; flowers dark carmine-pink with salmon, large, full; intr. 1864

'Mme Comtesse' B, lp, 1857, Margottin; flowers bright flesh pink, medium, full

'Mme Constans' HWich, lp, 1902, Gravereaux; flowers medium pink, aging to light pink, 6 cm., very dbl., borne in small clusters, no fragrance; foliage light green

'Mme Constant David' HP, mr, 1909, Boutigny; bud long; flowers grenadine red with velvety vermilion, 5 in., full; foliage dark green; prickles long

'Mme Constant Soupert' T, yb, 1905, Soupert & Notting; bud long, pointed, upright, deep golden yellow; flowers yellow shaded peach, large, very full; foliage dark green, deeply serrated; ['Souv. de Pierre Notting' × 'Duchesse Marie Salviati']

'Mme Consuelo Brignone' HT, w, Croix, D.; flowers silky white with pink blush, slight fragrance; recurrent; foliage disease-resistant; robust growth; intr. 2006

'Mme Corboeuf' HT, mr, 1895, Corboeuf; flowers velvety scarlet, large, semi-dbl.; ['Reine Marie Henriette' × 'General Jacqueminot']

'Mme Cordier' HP, m, 1903, Leroy; flowers bright lilac-pink, large, dbl.

'Mme Cornélissen' B, lp, 1865, Corné-lissen; flowers white with blush-pink and yellow center, large, very dbl., moderate fragrance; [sport of 'Souv de la Malmaison']

'Mme Couibes' HT, ab, 1938, Meilland, F.; flowers salmon, center apricot, edged lighter, passing to golden coral, dbl.; foliage fresh green; long stems; vigorous, bushy growth; ['Charles P. Kilham' × 'Rochefort']

'Mme Cousin' B, dp, 1849, Margottin; flowers silky dark pink, large, full

'Mme Couturier-Mention' -- See 'Cramoisi Supérieur, Climbing'

'Mme Crespin' HP, m, 1862, Damaizin; flowers rose shaded violet

'Mme Creux' T, op, 1890, Godard; flowers light salmon-pink, 13-15 cm., dbl., moderate tea fragrance

'Mme Creyton' HP, rb, 1868, Gonod; flowers crimson, shaded rose pink, large, full

'Mme Croibier' -- See 'Mme J. B. Croibier'

'Mme Crombez' T, op, 1888, Nabonnand, G.; flowers rosy buff tinted bronze, well-formed, very large, dbl., moderate fragrance

'Mme Crosy' -- See 'Mme Crozy'

'Mme Crozy' ('Mme Crosy') HP, mp, 1881, Levet; flowers rose pink, large; foliage dark green; prickles very pointed

'Mme Cunisset Carnot' HT, op, 1900, Buatois; bud very long; flowers salmony carnation pink, medium, borne mostly solitary

'Mme Cusin' T, rb, 1881, Guillot et Fils; flowers crimson, center yellowish-white, well-formed, medium, dbl.; foliage light green, small

'Mme Dailleux' HT, pb, 1901, Buatois; flowers salmon pink with dark yellow, large, dbl.; ['Victor Verdier' × 'Dr. Grill']

'Mme Damaizin' T, w, 1858, Damaizin; flowers creamy white shaded salmon, poorly formed, very large, dbl.; [probably 'Caroline' × 'Safrano']

'Mme Damême' HP, pb, 1842, Cochet; flowers lilac pink, shaded bright pink, large, full

'Mme d'Arblay' ('Wells' White Climber') HMult, w, about 1835, Wells or Waldstein; flowers soft flesh changing to white, 2½-3 cm., semi-dbl., cupped, borne in large conical clusters, moderate musk fragrance; [R. moschata × R. multiflora]

'Mme Daurel' HP, rb, 1884, Bernède; flowers red, tinted violet, large, full, cupped

'Mme David' T, lp, 1895, Pernet Père; flowers pale flesh, center darker, medium, very dbl., flat, moderate fragrance

'Mme de Beauvoire' HT, lp, 1922, Schwartz, A.; flowers pinkish white, center pale pink, dbl.; ['Mme Vittoria Gagniere' × 'Lady Ashtown']

'Mme de Cambacérès' -- See 'Duchesse de Cambacérès'

'Mme de Canrobert' HP, m, 1862, Liabaud; flowers bluish-lilac, large, full

'Mme de Canrobert' HP, mr, Gonichon; flowers shining crimson, medium, very full; intr. 1868

'Mme de Carbuccia' HT, mr, 1941, Kriloff; bud long, pointed; flowers bright crimson-red, medium, dbl.; foliage leathery; very vigorous, upright growth; ['Admiral Ward' × 'Mme Méha Sabatier']

'Mme de Chalonges' -- See 'Le Pactole'

'Mme de Knorr' -- See 'Mme Knorr'

'Mme de la Boulaye' HP, op, 1877, Liabaud; flowers salmon pink, centers bright pink, large, full, cupped

'Mme de la Rôchelambert' M, m, 1851, Robert; flowers dark reddish-purple, 7-8 cm., dbl., globular; moderate growth

'Mme de Lamoricière' HP, pb, 1849, Portemer; flowers bright pink, reverse white, medium, full

'Mme de Loeben-Sels' HT, w, 1879, Soupert & Notting; flowers silvery white, nuanced salmon/dawn/gold, large, very full, flat

'Mme de Loisy' T, op, 1901, Buatois; flowers salmon pink, shaded carmine, large, full

'Mme de Plantamour' HRg, m; intr. before 1900

'Mme de Pompadour' HT, rb, 1945, Gaujard; flowers coppery red and bright yellow, medium, dbl., globular, borne on short stems; foliage dark, glossy; vigorous, bushy growth

'Mme de Ridder' HP, dr, 1871, Margottin; flowers dark shaded crimson, touched with violet, large, full, globular, moderate fragrance

'Mme de Rohan' -- See 'Mme Bureau'

'Mme de St Fulgent' HP, dr, 1872, Gautreau; flowers velvety slate-red, medium, full

'Mme de St Joseph' T, lp, 1846; flowers fawn shaded salmon, large, dbl., intense fragrance; moderate growth

'Mme de Sancy de Parabère' -- See 'Mme Sancy de Parabère'

'Mme de Sansal' P, mr, about 1850, de Sansal; flowers cherry red

'Mme de Selve' HP, mr, 1886, Bernède; flowers bright red with lilac reflections, very large; ['Monsieur Fillion' × unknown]

'Mme de Sertot ' -- See 'Mme Bravy'

'Mme de Serval' HP, rb, 1854, Desprez; flowers cherry red, shaded salmon, medium, full

'Mme de Sévigné' B, pb, 1874, Moreau et Robert; flowers bright rose in center, edges lighter, large, dbl., borne in small clusters; vigorous growth

'Mme de Sevigne' S, lp, Delbard; intr. 1998

'Mme de Sombreuil' -- See 'Mlle de Sombreuil'

'Mme de Soubeyran' -- See 'Mme Soubeyran'

'Mme de Staël' M, lp, 1857, Robert & Moreau; flowers flesh pink, 2-2½ in., full, cupped; some repeat

'Mme de Stella' -- See 'Louise Odier'

'Mme de Tartas' ('Mme de Thartas') T, lp, 1859, Bernède; flowers flush-pink, mixed with pale yellow, large, dbl., cupped; vigorous, sprawling growth

'Mme de Thartas' -- See 'Mme de Tartas'

'Mme de Tressan' ('Mme Tressan') HGal, mp, 1822, Sommesson; flowers flesh pink, large, full; sometimes classed as D

'Mme de Trotter' ('Mme Trotter') HP, pb, 1854, Granger; flowers pink and red, medium, dbl.

'Mme de Vatry' ('Mme de Vitry') T, dp, 1855, Guérin; flowers deep pink, center lighter, large, dbl.; recurrent bloom; vigorous growth

'Mme de Villars' M, mp, 1847, Béluze; flowers delicate pink, spotted; some repeat

'Mme de Ville-Mareuil' HP, w, 1853, Carré; flowers flesh white, large, full

'Mme de Vitry' -- See 'Mme de Vatry'

'Mme de Watteville' T, yb, 1883, Guillot et Fils; flowers lemon edged pink, large, dbl.

'Mme Delaunay' HT, Privat, J.; intr. 1963

Madame Delbard® -- See 'Deladel'

'Mme Dellevaux' HP, mp, 1883, Besson; flowers silky pink

'Mme Delville' HP, pb, 1890, Schwartz; flowers shining velvet-pink, edges lighter, reverse silvery, large, full

'Mme d'Enfert' B, lp, 1904, Vilin; flowers pale blushing flesh white, pinker towards center, full; growth upright; ['Mme Ernst Calvat' × 'Duchesse d'Auerstädt']

'Mme Denis' ('Mme Maurin') T, w, 1853, Guillot; flowers white shaded salmon, medium to large, very full

'Mme Denis' T, w, Gonod; flowers white, center sulfur-yellow, large, full; intr. 1872

'Mme Denise Cassegrain' -- See 'Denise Cassegrain'

'Mme Denise Gallois' HT, pb, 1941, Sauvageot, H.; flowers salmon shaded yellow, deeper reverse

'Mme Derepas-Matrat' ('Yellow Maman Cochet') T, dy, 1897, Buatois; bud large; flowers sulphur-yellow, center darker, dbl., borne mostly solitary; nearly thornless; growth vigorous; ['Mme Hoste' × 'Marie Van Houtte']

'Mme Derouet' HP, w, 1885, Derouet; flowers white, center rose, reverse lilac, large, full, globular

'Mme Derreult-Douville' HP, mp, 1863, Lévêque; flowers silky rose, becoming light red, edges silky white, large, full

'Mme Desbordes' T, pb, 1903, Corboeuf-Marsault; flowers pink with golden reflections, large, full, moderate fragrance; ['Cérès' × 'Louis Guillaud']

'Mme Désir Vincent' T, yb, 1898, Marqueton; flowers dark chrome yellow, salmon at base, reverse shaded pink-violet, large, full; ['Souv de Mme Levet' × unknown]

'Mme Desirée Bruneau' HT, mp, 1907, Moublot

'Mme Desirée Giraud' HP, pb, 1854, Van Houtte; flowers blush-white, striped rose; [sport of 'Baronne Prévost']

'Mme Deslongchamps' N, w, 1850, Lévêque; flowers white, shaded carmine-pink, medium, full

'Mme Desmars' HT, yb, 1929, Mallerin, C.; bud long; flowers golden yellow, tinted nasturtium-red, very large, dbl., high-centered; foliage glossy; vigorous, bushy growth; ['Ophelia' × 'Constance']; intr. 1932

'Mme Desmary' HT, yb, 1950, Moulin-Epinay; flowers ochre-yellow tinted orange, 30-35 petals; foliage bright green; vigorous growth; ['Aspirant Marcel Rouyer' × 'Emma Wright']

'Mme Desmazes' -- See 'Marie Desmazures'

'Mme Desprez' B, mp, 1831, Desprez; flowers rosy lilac, large, dbl., cupped, borne in large clusters; foliage dark green; ['Rose Edouard' × unknown]

'Mme Desprez' Ch, w, Desprez; flowers white tinged with lemon, large, very dbl., cupped, borne in small clusters, moderate fragrance; sometimes classed as N; intr. about 1835

'Mme Devacourt' -- See 'Mme Devoucoux'

'Mme Devacoux' -- See 'Mme Devoucoux'

'Mme Devert' HP, pb, 1876, Pernet; flowers flesh pink, center dark pink, very large, full, globular; ['Victor Verdier' × unknown]

'Mme Devoucoux' ('Mme Devacourt', 'Mme Devacoux') T, my, 1874, Ducher, Vve.; flowers bright yellow, well-formed, dbl.

'Mme d'Hébray' -- See 'Unique Panachée'

'Mme Didkowsky' HT, rb, 1943, Mallerin, C.; flowers fiery red, reverse golden yellow

'Mme Dieudonné, Climbing' Cl HT, rb, 1960, Anderson

'Mme Dieudonné' ('Mme L. Dieudonné') HT, rb, 1950, Meilland, F.; flowers rose-red, reverse gold, 4-5 in., 30 petals, slender, tulip-shaped, moderate fragrance; recurrent; foliage dark, glossy; vigorous growth; PP959; [('Mme Joseph Perraud' × 'Brazier') × ('Charles P. Kilham' × 'Capucine Chambard')]

Mme Dimitriu® -- See 'Delcrip'

'Mme Dr Jütté' T, yb, 1872, Levet; flowers salmon, orange and copper, intense fragrance; ['Ophirie' × unknown]

'Mme Domage' HP, mr, 1853, Margottin; flowers crimson

'Mme Doré' B, lp, 1863, Fontaine; flowers large, dbl., moderate fragrance; medium growth

'Mme Driout' Cl T, pb, 1902, Thirat, J.; flowers bright rose, striped carmine, large, dbl.; very vigorous, climbing growth; [sport of 'Reine Marie Henriette']

'Mme Dubarry' HGal, mp, before 1866; flowers bright shining carmine, medium, full

'Mme Dubois' HP, mr, 1866, Fontaine; flowers vermilion

'Mme Dubost' B, lp, 1890, Pernet Père; flowers flesh, center rose, medium, full, borne in small clusters; growth upright

'Mme Dubroca' T, pb, 1882, Nabonnand, G.; flowers salmon shaded carmine, large, dbl.

'Mme Dubuisson' HP, mp, 1861, Baudry; flowers carmine, large, full

'Mme Ducamp' HP, m, 1863, Fontaine; flowers bright garnet-purple, aging to currant, large, full

'Mme Ducher' HP, rb, Levet; flowers cherry red, petals edged dark purple, center petals whitish, very large, full; intr. 1880

'Mme Ducher' HP, mr, 1851, Cordier/Ducher; flowers cherry red

'Mme Ducher' T, ly, Ducher; flowers medium, full; ['Gloire de Dijon' × unknown]; intr. 1869

'Mme Dufesnois' HT, mp

'Mme Dufresnois' -- See 'Adelaïde Dufresnois'

'Mme Durand' T, w, Croibier; flowers white, center salmon pink, lrage, full, intr. 1903

'Mme Durand' T, dy, 1890, Moreau & Robert; flowers coppery dark yellow, large, full, globular

'Mme Dustour' HP, pb, 1869, Pernet; flowers carmine-pink, centers white, very large, full

'Mme E. A. Nolte' Pol, ly, 1892, Bernaix; flowers light nankeen yellow, passing to white

'Mme E. Rocque' HMult, m, 1918, Lottin; flowers violet, sometimes striped white, passing to amethyst, very dbl.; ['Veilchenblau' × 'Reine des Violettes']

'Mme E. Souffrain' N, yb, 1897, Chauvry; bud large, ovoid; flowers golden yellow tinged with salmon and pink, large, very full; foliage glossy; nearly thornless; ['Rêve d'Or' × 'Duarte de Oliveira']

'Mme E. Terracol' HT, yb, 1940, Meilland, F.; bud globular; flowers pure yellow, base orange, very large, dbl.; foliage leathery; very vigorous, upright growth; ['Julien Potin' × 'Soeur Thérèse']

'Mme Edmée Cocteau' ('Edmée Cocteau') Cl HT, lp, 1903, Margottin fils; flowers delicate pink, very large; ['Captain Christy' × unknown]

'Mme Edmée Metz' HT, pb, 1901, Soupert & Notting; flowers rosy carmine shaded salmon,, dbl.; ['Mme Caroline Testout' × 'Ferdinand Jamin']

'Mme Edmond Corpus' B, w, 1903, Boutigny, P.; flowers pure white, reverse fresh pink

'Mme Edmond Fabre' HP, mp, 1884, Verdier, E.; flowers large, dbl.

'Mme Edmond Gillet' HT, yb, 1921, Pernet-Ducher; flowers reddish nankeen

yellow, slightly shaded carmine at tips, dbl.; ['Mme Edmond Rostand' × 'Marquise de Sinéty']
'Mme Edmond Labbé' HT, rb, 1938, Mallerin, C.; bud pointed; flowers orange-red, reverse golden yellow, large, dbl.; long stems; very vigorous growth; ['Souv. de Claudius Pernet' × 'hybrid tea seedling']
'Mme Edmond LaPorte' B, pb, 1893, Boutigny; flowers silvery white within, fresh pink without, very large, semi-globular; foliage dark green, glossy
'Mme Edmond Raynal' HT, ly, 1927, Sauvageot, H.; flowers yellowish-cream, center salmon, dbl.
'Mme Edmond Rostand' HT, pb, 1912, Pernet-Ducher; flowers pale flesh, center shaded salmon and reddish orange-yellow, very large, dbl., moderate fragrance; [seedling × 'Prince de Bulgarie']
'Mme Edouard Estaunié' HT, yb, 1936, Buatois; bud long; flowers nankeen yellow, center reddish, edges and reverse flesh-pink, dbl.; long stems; very vigorous growth; ['Seabird' × 'Souv. de Claudius Pernet']
'Mme Edouard Helfenbein' T, yb, 1893, Guillot; flowers chamois yellow with carmine and China pink reflections, large, full
'Mme Édouard Herriot' ('Daily Mail Rose') HT, ob, 1913, Pernet-Ducher; bud pointed; flowers coral-red shaded yellow and bright rosy scarlet, passing to rose pink, large, semi-dbl., moderate fragrance; foliage bronze, glossy; vigorous, spreading, branching growth; ['Mme Caroline Testout' × 'a Pernetiana']
'Mme Édouard Herriot, Climbing' ('Daily Mail Rose, Climbing') Cl HT, ob, 1921, Ketten Bros.; flowers copper yellow red, large, semi-dbl., moderate fragrance; [sport of 'Mme Edouard Herriot']
'Mme Edouard Michel' HP, dp, 1886, Verdier, E.; flowers clear deep pink, very large, full; foliage delicate green, irregularly toothed; prickles unequal, straight; growth upright
'Mme Édouard Ory' M, dp, 1854, Robert; sepals foliaceous; flowers bright carmine-pink, 6-8 cm., dbl., globular, moderate fragrance; very remontant; foliage dark green, oval
'Mme Elie Dupraz' HT, mr, 1948, Gaujard; bud large; flowers brilliant red, medium, dbl., high-centered; foliage dark, glossy; very vigorous, bushy growth
'Mme Elie Lambert' T, w, 1890, Lambert, E.; flowers creamy white, faintly tinted with pale yellow, bordered with soft rose, very large, very full, cupped, globular; ['Anna Olivier' × 'Souv de Paul Neyron']
'Mme Elisa de Vilmorin' ('Mme Eliza de Vilmorin') HP, mr, 1864, Lévêque; flowers dark carmine, large, 30 petals; sparse bloom; upright, bushy growth; sometimes considered to be one of the earliest Hybrid Teas
'Mme Elisa Jaenisch' HP, rb, 1870, Soupert & Notting; flowers cherry red with bluish tints, shaded violet and flame-red, large, full
'Mme Elisa Tasson' HP, mr, 1879, Lévêque; flowers scarlet cerise, very large, full, globular; foliage glossy
'Mme Elise de Chénier' B, dp, 1857, Touvais; flowers deep pink, medium, full
'Mme Eliza de Vilmorin' -- See 'Mme Elisa de Vilmorin'
'Mme Emain' HP, m, 1862, Pernet; flowers purple, shaded slate, large, full
'Mme Emile Daloz' HT, pb, 1934, Sauvageot, H.; flowers satiny purplish pink, reverse bright rose-pink, very large, dbl., globular; foliage leathery, glossy; very vigorous, bushy growth; ['Frau Karl Druschki' × 'Souv. de Georges Pernet']
'Mme Emile Mayen' HT, ly, 1924, Chambard, C.; flowers sulfur-yellow passing to cream, dbl.
'Mme Emile Metz' HT, lp, 1893, Soupert & Notting; ['Mme de Loeben-Sels' × 'La Tulipe']
'Mme Emile Sénéclauze' HT, mp, Croix, P.; intr. 1966
'Mme Emile Thierrard' HT, yb, 1919, Turbat; flowers chamois-yellow and pink, stamens pure yellow, dbl.; ['Mrs Aaron Ward' × 'Joseph Hill']
'Mme Emilie Boyau' HP, lp, 1864, Boyau; flowers flesh pink, aging darker
'Mme Emilie Charrin' -- See 'Mme Emilie Charron'
'Mme Emilie Charron' ('Mme Emilie Charrin') T, mp, 1895, Perrier; flowers China-pink, large, cupped; very vigorous growth
'Mme Émilie Dupuy' -- See 'Émilie Dupuy'
'Mme Emilie Lafon' HT, mr, 1905, Moranville; flowers cerise red, large, dbl.; ['La France de 89' × unknown]
'Mme Emilie van der Goes' HT, op, 1925, Verschuren; bud pointed, orange-yellow and rosy shadings; flowers more pink than bud, large, semi-dbl.; foliage bronze, leathery; bushy growth; ['Columbia' × 'Irish Fireflame']
'Mme Emma Combey' HP, mp, 1872, Cordier/Gonod; flowers carmine
'Mme Emma Dampierre' HP, mp, 1842, Desprez; flowers bluish pink, shaded crimson, medium, full
'Mme Ernst Calvat' ('Mme Ernst Calvat', 'Pink Bourbon') B, mp, 1888, Schwartz, Vve.; flowers pink shaded darker, very large, semi-dbl.; [sport of 'Mme Isaac Pereire']
'Mme Ernest Charles' HT, or, 1933, Buatois; bud large, long; flowers coral-red, reverse shrimp-red, dbl., cupped; foliage leathery, glossy, bronze; vigorous, bushy growth; ['Mme Edmond Rostand' × 'Severine']
'Mme Ernest Dréolle' HP, m, 1861, Grujoire; flowers lilac pink
'Mme Ernest Levavasseur' HP, mr, 1900, Vigneron; flowers carmine-red, very large, very dbl.; ['Mme Isaac Pereire' × 'Ulrich Brunner']
'Mme Ernest Perrin' T, op, 1900, Schwartz; flowers light orange-pink, very large, dbl.
'Mme Ernest Piard' ('Mme Ernest Picard') HT, dp, 1888, Bonnaire; flowers carmine-pink, very large, dbl.
'Mme Ernest Picard' -- See 'Mme Ernest Piard'
'Mme Ernestine Verdier' T, pb, 1894, Perny/Aschery; flowers mauve-rose, shaded salmon, medium, very large, very full; numerous prickles; growth upright
'Mme Ernst Calvat' -- See 'Mme Ernest Calvat'
'Mme Errera' T, ob, 1899, Soupert & Notting; flowers salmon yellow, sometimes cerise, large, full, intense fragrance; ['Mme Lombard' × 'Luciole']
'Mme Etienne' T, mp, 1887, Bernaix, A.; flowers rose, well-formed; vigorous growth
'Mme Étienne Levet' HP, mr, 1878, Levet; flowers carmine-red, large, dbl., moderate fragrance; ['Antonine Verdier' × unknown]
'Mme Eugène Appert' HP, op, 1866, Trouillard; flowers salmon pink, large, full
'Mme Eugene Boullet' -- See 'Mme Eugénie Boullet'
'Mme Eugene Cavaignac' -- See 'Baron Heckeren de Wassenaer'
'Mme Eugène Chambeyran' HP, pb, 1878, Gonod; flowers deep pink, shaded aurora pink, large, full, globular; ['Victor Verdier' × unknown]
'Mme Eugène Mallet' N, yb, 1875, Nabonnand, G.; flowers pink and yellow, dbl.; moderate, climbing growth
'Mme Eugène Marlitt' -- See 'Eugène E. Marlitt'
'Mme Eugène Moreau' HT, my, 1925, Richardier; flowers dbl.; vigorous growth
'Mme Eugène Picard' HT, my, 1932, Gillot, F.; bud medium, oval, carmine-red; flowers medium, semi-dbl., high-centered, borne in small clusters, moderate fragrance; foliage medium size, dark green, leathery; [sport of 'Ariel']
'Mme Eugène Résal' Ch, pb, 1894, Guillot, P.; bud pointed; flowers bright pink shaded reddish-orange, base yellow, broad, dbl.; ['Mme Laurette Messimy' × unknown]
'Mme Eugène Sudreau' HP, dp, 1857, Bernède
'Mme Eugène Verdier' HP, mp, 1859, Guillot; flowers bright shining pink, very large, full, globular, moderate fragrance; ['Louise Peyrony' × unknown]
'Mme Eugène Verdier' HP, lp, Verdier, E.; flowers silvery pink, large, dbl., globular, moderate fragrance; vigorous growth; ['Gloire de Dijon' × possibly 'Mme Barthélemy Levet']; intr. 1875

'Mme Eugène Verdier' N, my, Levet; flowers varying from golden yellow to canary, to straw, large, moderate fragrance; foliage dark green; few prickles; ['Gloire de Dijon' × 'Mme Barthélemy Levet']; sometimes classified as a T; intr. 1878

'Mme Eugénie Boullet' ('Eugénie Boullet', 'Mme Eugene Boullet') HT, pb, 1897, Pernet-Ducher; flowers pink tinted yellow

'Mme Eugénie Bréon' B, my, 1847, Belet

'Mme Eugénie Frémy' HP, dp, 1885, Verdier, E.; flowers carmine-pink, large, very dbl.

'Mme Eugénie Savary' ('Mlle Eugénie Savary') HP, w, 1875, Gonod; flowers flesh white, reverse brighter pink, large, full

'Mme Falcot' T, my, 1858, Guillot et Fils; flowers nankeen yellow passing to clear yellow, darker at center, 7 cm., dbl., borne mostly solitary, moderate tea fragrance; ['Safrano' × unknown]

'Mme Fanny de Forest' N, lp, 1882, Schwartz; flowers pure white, very large, dbl.; foliage dark green; growth upright; sometimes classed as B

'Mme Fanny Pauwels' T, yb, 1885, Soupert, C.; flowers bright yellow, darker towards center, sometimes reddish-gold, medium, full

'Mme Farfouillon' HP, op, 1869, Liabaud; flowers silky pink with salmon and chamois

'Mme Faurax-Lille' HT, mr, 1933, Reymond; bud pointed; flowers bright vermilion-red passing to geranium-red, large, dbl.; ['Cuba' × 'Sir David Davis']

'Mme Fearnley Sander' HT, m, 1921, Ketten Bros.; flowers carmine, deepening to purple, base yellow, dbl.; ['Gen. MacArthur' × 'Rayon d'Or']

'Mme Félix Boulanger' N, 1910, Boulanger

'Mme Félix Faivre' HT, lp, 1901, Buatois; flowers silky light pink

'Mme Ferdinand Jamin' -- See 'American Beauty'

'Mme Fernand Gentin' HT, op, 1939, Mallerin, C.; bud long, pointed; flowers copper shaded coral, large, semi-dbl., cupped; vigorous growth; [seedling × 'Brazier']

'Mme Fernand Gregh' HT, yb, 1955, Robichon; flowers canary-yellow shaded coppery, large; foliage glossy; vigorous growth; ['Padre' × 'Madeleine Pacaud']

Mme Fernandel® ('Fernandel') F, dp, Meilland; flowers rose-purple, medium, dbl.; intr. 1989

'Mme Ferray' -- See 'Bernard'

'Mme Fey-Pranard' P, 1869, Cherpin

'Madame Figaro' (Figaro Panarosa™) S, lp, Delbard; flowers very dbl., cupped, moderate rose-citron fragrance; intr. 2000

'Mme Fillion' HP, op, 1865, Gonod; flowers salmon-pink, large, dbl.; ['Mme Domage' × unknown]

'Mme Florentin Laurent' HP, dp, 1870, Granger; flowers shining cherry pink, large, very full

'Mme Florentin Laurent' T, w, Bidaud; flowers white with cream reflections, large, full; intr. 1906

'Mme Fojo' HT, ob, 1937, Dot, Pedro; flowers orange, well-formed, large; strong stems; vigorous growth

'Mme Fontaine' -- See 'Prince Albert'

'Mme Forest' HT, mp, 1928, Walter, L.; ['Lieutenant Chauré' × 'Mrs George Shawyer']

'Mme Fortuné Besson' ('Fortunée Besson') HP, lp, 1881, Besson; flowers delicate flesh pink, very large, very full; ['Jules Margottin' × unknown]

'Mme Foureau' N, dy, 1913, Viaud-Bruant; flowers yellowish-salmon, medium, dbl.; ['Rêve d'Or' × unknown]

'Mme Fraculy' HT, dy, 1929, Siret-Pernet; flowers deep golden yellow, dbl.; foliage dark, glossy; long, strong stems; vigorous growth; ['Ophelia' × 'Constance']

'Mme Francis Buchner' HP, lp, 1884, Lévêque; flowers very light pink, darker towards center, large, full; foliage glossy

'Mme Francisque Favre' Pol, 1915, Dubreuil

Mme Franck Augis® -- See 'Laplam'

'Mme François Bolley' ('François Bollez') HT, op, 1934, Gillot, F.; bud shrimp-pink; flowers salmon, base orange, large, very dbl., moderate fragrance

'Mme François Bollez' HT, op, 1934, Gillot, F.; flowers coral-pink, center brighter, tinted orange, very large, dbl.; foliage dark, bronze; very vigorous growth

'Mme François Brassac' T, rb, 1883, Nabonnand; bud very large; flowers bright bronze-red, tinted with coppery yellow, large, very dbl.

'Mme François Bruel' ('Mme Bruel') HP, mp, 1882, Levet; flowers carmine-rose; very remontant; foliage light green; few prickles; ['Victor Verdier' × 'Comtesse d'Oxford']

'Mme François Graindorge' Pol, pb, 1922, Grandes Roseraies; flowers dark reddish-pink shaded magenta, base tinged lilac, large,; vigorous growth

'Mme François Hot' HT, pb, 1928, Schwartz, A.; flowers salmon shaded coppery rose, edged lighter, base salmon-yellow; ['Lady Pirrie' × 'Mme de Bauvoire']

'Mme François Janain' T, ob, 1872, Levet; flowers dark orange, becoming golden yellow, center coppery, medium, full, moderate fragrance

'Mme François Pittet' B, w, 1878, Lacharme, F.; flowers small to medium, very dbl., globular; ['Mlle Blanche Laffitte' × unknown]; sometimes classed as N

'Mme François Royet' HMult, mr, 1914, Royet; flowers bright red, 6-7 cm., cupped, borne in small clusters, moderate fragrance; foliage large, deeply dentate; numerous prickles; ['Crimson Rambler' × 'Général Jacqueminot']

'Mme Frank Augis' HT, Laperrière; intr. 1969

'Mme Frédéric Daupias' T, yb, 1899, Chauvry; flowers siena-yellow, center apricot, edges tinted violet-pink, large, full; ['Charles de Legrady' × unknown]

'Mme Frédéric Daupias' HT, pb, Soupert & Notting; flowers dark flesh pink, marbled silvery white, very large, full; ['Léonie Osterrieth' × 'Belle Siebrecht']; intr. 1899

'Mme Frédéric Weiss' Pol, rb, 1892, Bernaix; flowers carmine, shaded magenta, sometimes striped white

'Mme Freemann' HP, w, 1862, Guillot; flowers creme, medium, full; sometimes classified as N

'Mme Freemann' T, w, Nabonnand; flowers pure white, large, full; intr. 1874

'Mme Frémion' HP, mr, 1853, Margottin; flowers bright cherry, medium, full

'Mme Fresnoy' HP, mr, 1865, Pernet; flowers shining crimson, becoming carmine pink, large, full

'Mme Furtado' HP, dp, Verdier, V.; flowers shining carmine pink, very large, very full; intr. 1860

'Mme Furtado' B, dp, 1852, Bélot-Défougères; flowers dark pink, shaded poppy red, large, full

'Mme Furtado-Heine' HP, pb, 1887, Lévêque; flowers bright glowing pink, shaded carmine-lilac, large, full, globular

'Mme G. Cossard' -- See 'Mme Clément Massier'

'Mme G. Forest-Colcombet' ('G. Forest-Colcombet') HT, dp, 1928, Mallerin, C.; flowers deep carmine, strongly tinted scarlet; [sport of 'Hadley']

'Mme G. Hekkens' HT, dr, 1929, Faassen-Hekkens; flowers velvety dark red (nearly as dark as Chateau de Clos Vougeot), single; foliage glossy; ['Gloire de Holland' × 'Hawlmark Crimson']

'Mme Gabriel Hanra' HT, rb, 1929, Ketten Bros.; flowers strawberry-red, shaded carmine-purple, dbl.; ['The Adjutant' × 'Kitchener of Khartoum']

'Mme Gabriel Luizet' HP, lp, 1877, Liabaud; flowers light silvery pink, edged lighter, large, 34 petals, cupped, moderate fragrance; non-recurrent; vigorous growth; [sport of 'Jules Margottin']

'Mme Gadel' HP, m, 1872, Pernet; flowers lilac pink, large, full

'Mme Gaillard' B, mp, 1866, Pradel; flowers carmine-pink, medium

'Mme Gaillard' T, op, Ducher; flowers salmon yellow, large, full; intr. 1871

'Mme Galli-Marié' HCh, mp, 1876, Verdier, E; flowers medium, full, borne in small clusters

'Mme Gamon' T, ab, 1905, Gamon; bud long; flowers apricot on golden yellow, large, full; growth vigorous, bushy

'Mme Gaston Allard' T, w, 1893, Cailleau; flowers cream white, medium

'Mme Gaston Anouilh' N, w, 1899, Chauvry; bud tinged pink; flowers white tinted canary, medium to large, dbl., intense fragrance; nearly thornless

'Mme Gaston Doumergue' Pol, lp, 1934, Levavasseur; flowers soft salmon; [probably a sport of 'Gloria Mundi']

'Mme Gaston Mestreit' Pol, lp, 1922, Soupert & Notting; flowers very soft flesh-white, borne in clusters; ['Jeanny Soupert' × 'Katharina Zeimet']

'Mme Gaston Nocton' Pol, w, 1928, Soupert & Notting; flowers white, center flesh-pink, opening pure white, borne in clusters; dwarf growth; ['Amaury Fonseca' × 'Jeanny Soupert']

'Mme George Paul' HP, mr, 1886, Verdier, E.; flowers crimson, shaded dark pink, large, full

'Mme Georges Bénard' HT, dp, 1900, Corboeuf; flowers carmine-pink with silvery reverse, large, dbl.

'Mme Georges Brédif' HT, rb, 1955, Privat; flowers red mottled garnet, well-formed; strong stems

'Mme Georges Bruant' HRg, w, 1887, Bruant; bud pointed; flowers waxy white, large, semi-dbl., loose, borne in clusters, moderate fragrance; recurrent bloom; [R. rugosa alba × 'Mlle de Sombreuil']

'Mme Georges Clenet' HT, Godin, M.; intr. 1980

'Mme Georges Cozon' HT, pb, 1929, Laperrière; flowers shrimp-pink, reverse yellow; ['Mme Charles Lutaud' × 'hybrid tea seedling']

Mme Georges Delbard® -- See 'Deladel'

'Mme Georges Delbard' HT, or, 1959, Delbard-Chabert; flowers bright red suffused orange,, 5 in., 35-45 petals; foliage dull green; long, strong stems; very vigorous growth; RULED EXTINCT 4/85; ['Impeccable' × 'Mme Robert Joffet']

'Mme Georges Desse' HP, pb, 1897, Desse/Duprat

'Mme Georges Droin' HT, op, 1930, Gaujard, Jules; flowers orange-shrimp-pink; foliage bronze; very vigorous growth

'Mme Georges Halphen' T, op, 1899, Lévêque; flowers salmon pink, shaded yellow, large

'Mme Georges Landard' HT, lp, 1925, Walter, L.; flowers rose-red, large, full, borne mostly solitary, moderate fragrance; foliage glossy; ['Mme Abel Chatenay' × 'Lyon Rose']

'Mme Georges Paul' HP, mr, 1886, Verdier, E.; flowers crimson, shaded dark pink, large, full

'Mme Georges Petit' HT, mr, 1928, Ketten Bros.; bud pointed; flowers bright purple-red to velvety crimson-red, large, dbl., high-centered; very vigorous growth; ['Gen. MacArthur' × 'Mme Edouard Herriot']

'Mme Georges Renoard' -- See 'Delreno'

'Mme Georges Schwartz' HP, mp, 1871, Schwartz; flowers rose pink with soft lavender shading, fading to frosty pink, large, full

'Mme Georges Vibert' HP, mp, 1879, Moreau-Robert; flowers delicate pink, veined bright pink, center carmine, very large, full, borne in small clusters; foliage dark green

'Mme Ghys' HMult, m, 1912, Ghys; flowers lilac-rose, borne in clusters; growth to 6-10 ft.; ['Crimson Rambler' × unknown]

'Madame Gilberte Dubois' HT, op, RvS-Melle; flowers 30 petals, flat; foliage dense, luxurious; ['Silver Jubilee' × Mountbatten®]; intr. 1990

'Mme Gilberte Janaud' F, mp, 1957, Privat; flowers bright pink tinted salmon, very dbl.; dwarf growth

'Mme Gillen' -- See 'Mrs M. J. Gillon'

'Mme Gillet Lafond' HT, pb, 1930, Leenders, M.; flowers salmon-white, center old-rose, large, semi-dbl.; foliage light, leathery; vigorous growth; ['Frau Felix Tonnar' × 'Angèle Pernet']

'Mme Gina Demoustier' HT, mr, 1920, Laperrière; flowers pure garnet-red, dbl.; ['Étoile de France' × seedling]

'Mme Gonod' HP, mp, 1867, Moreau & Robert; flowers silky pink, large, full

'Mme Grandin-Monville' HP, rb, 1875, Verdier, E.; flowers crimson, edged bright pink, large, full, borne in small clusters

'Mme Grégoire Staechelin' ('Spanish Beauty') LCl, pb, 1927, Dot, Pedro; bud brushed deep maroon; flowers delicate pink, reverse stained crimson, ruffled, 5 in., semi-dbl., moderate fragrance; non-recurrent; foliage heavy, large, dark, glossy; vigorous (13-14 ft.) growth; hips pear-shaped, pinkish-orange, large; ['Frau Karl Druschki' × 'Château de Clos Vougeot']; intr. 1929

'Mme Grondier' HP, op, 1867, Gonod; flowers salmon pink, large, full, globular

'Mme Guimet' HT, dp, 1942, Laperrière; flowers large, dbl.

'Mme Gustave Bonnet' -- See 'Zéphirine Drouhin'

'Mme Gustave Fintelmann' HP, mp, 1853, Baumann; flowers large, full

'Mme Gustave Henry' T, op, 1899, Buatois; flowers bright coppery pink, very large

'Mme Gustave Metz' ('Frau Karl Smid') HT, lp, 1906, Lamesch; flowers creamy white, going to pink, very large, dbl.; [('Mme Caroline Testout' × 'Viscountess Folkestone') × unknown]

'Mme Gustave Soupert' HT, pb, 1928, Soupert & Notting; flowers purplish pink, center brighter, reverse silvery carmine, dbl.; [Augustus Hartmann × 'Souv. de Georges Pernet']

'Mme H. de Potworoska' T, dp, 1899, Bernaix; flowers amaranthe, shaded azalea pink with lighter reflections, medium, dbl.

'Mme H. Heinemann' -- See 'Meigalil'

'Mme Hardon' HP, mp, 1897, Cochet, P.; flowers bright pink and carmine

'Mme Hardy' -- See 'Félicité Hardy'

'Mme Hardy du Thé' -- See 'Clotilde Soupert'

'Mme Haussmann' -- See 'Baronne Haussmann'

'Mme Hébert' -- See 'Président de Sèze'

'Mme Hector Jacquin' HP, pb, 1853, Fontaine; flowers flower pink, shaded lilac, large, full

'Mme Hector Leuillot' HT, yb, 1903, Pernet-Ducher; bud pointed; flowers golden yellow on carmine ground, dbl.

'Mme Hélène Dapples' HT, mr, 1932, Heizmann, E.; flowers large, semi-dbl.

'Mme Hélène Duché' HT, pb, 1921, Buatois; flowers soft rose with silvery reflexes, edged carmine, dbl.; ['Mme Caroline Testout' × 'Reine Emma des Pays-Bas']

'Mme Hélène Parmentier' HT, or, 1935, Sauvageot, H.; bud long; flowers clear nasturtium-red, shaded orange, passing to pink, semi-dbl., cupped; foliage glossy, wrinkled, bronze; long stems; vigorous, bushy growth; [seedling × 'Angèle Pernet']

'Mme Helfenbein' B, m, 1852, Guillot; flowers lilac pink, large, full

'Mme Helmut Kohl' -- See 'Maslako'

'Mme Hélye' HP, mp, 1862; flowers carmine-lilac, large, full

'Mme Henri Berger' T, mp, 1901, Bonnaire; flowers China pink, very large, full, moderate fragrance

'Mme Henri Bonnet' HT, pb, 1948, Boerner; bud ovoid; flowers deep salmon-pink suffused golden orange, large, dbl., high-centered; foliage leathery; vigorous, upright, compact growth; ['Elite' × seedling]

'Mme Henri Fontaine' HT, lp, 1914, Guillot; flowers creamy pink with yellow base, large, dbl., moderate fragrance; ['Pharisäer' × unknown]

'Mme Henri Graire' T, pb, 1895, Lévêque; flowers pink, tinted bronze and chamois yellow, center deep peach, large, full; foliage dark green; growth vigorous

'Mme Henri Gravereaux' HRg, pb, 1904, Gravereaux; bud large, protrusive, reddish; flowers cream, with salmony pink center, large, dbl., cupped, borne mostly solitary; foliage not rugose; prickles sparse, small, upright; ['Marie Zahn' × 'Conrad Ferdinand Meyer']

'Mme Henri Gravereaux' HT, yb, Barbier; flowers coppery yellow tinted bronze-yellow, veined orange, dbl., moderate fragrance; ['Mrs Aaron Ward' × seedling]; intr. 1926

'Mme Henri Grimm' HT, lp, 1934, Buatois; bud long; flowers pinkish white tinged carmine, edged crimson, base yellow, dbl., high-centered; foliage leathery, dark; vigorous, bushy growth; ['Mme Charles Detreaux' × 'Mme Edouard Herriot']

'Mme Henri Guillot' HT, rb, 1938, Mallerin, C.; flowers orange-coral-red, large, 25 petals; foliage glossy; vigorous, bushy growth; PP337; ['Rochefort' × (R. foetida bicolor × unknown)]

'Mme Henri Guillot, Climbing' Cl HT, rb, 1942, Meilland, F. (also van Barneveld, 1947); flowers crimson-coral, 5-6 in., semi-dbl.; PP788

'Mme Henri Laforest' HT, my, 1942, Gaujard; bud pointed; flowers golden yellow, very large, semi-dbl.; foliage glossy; very vigorous, upright growth

'Mme Henri Lustre' HT, rb, 1924, Buatois; flowers purplish garnet tinted currant-red, very large, dbl., high-centered; foliage leathery; very vigorous, bushy growth; ['Mme Edouard Herriot' × 'Yves Druhen']

'Mme Henri Paté' HT, ly, 1929, Pernet-Ducher; bud pointed; flowers sulfur-yellow, very large, semi-dbl.; foliage bronze; very vigorous, bushy growth; ['Souv. de Claudius Pernet' × seedling]

'Mme Henri Pelley' HT, ly, 1928, Richardier; flowers transparent cream-yellow

'Mme Henri Pereire' HP, mr, 1887, Vilin; flowers crimson-red

'Mme Henri Perrin' HP, pb, 1892, Widow Schwartz; flowers bright carmine lilac pink, somtimes striped white, large; foliage bullate

'Mme Henri Queuille' HT, op, 1928, Pernet-Ducher; bud long, pointed; flowers bright shrimp-pink, center deeper, reverse coppery gold, large, semi-dbl., moderate fragrance; foliage bronze; very vigorous growth

'Mme Henri Thiebaut' HT, op, 1931, Chambard, C.; bud pointed; flowers salmon-coral base coral-orange, very large, dbl.; foliage bright green; strong stems; vigorous growth

'Mme Henriette' C, pb; flowers lilac pink, edged whitish pink, very large, full

'Mme Henriette Thomson' HT, op, 1909, Bruant; flowers orange-pink, edged carmine

'Mme Hérivaux' -- See 'Mme Charles Crapelet'

'Mme Hermann' N, op, 1861, Avoux / Crozy; flowers salmon pink with flesh white, medium, full

'Mme Hermann Haefliger' S, dr, 1951, Hauser; flowers velvety scarlet-crimson, yellow petal base, large, slight fragrance; some repeat; foliage dark; vigorous growth; [(R. foetida bicolor × unknown) × 'Charles P. Kilham']

'Mme Hermann Stenger' HP, mp, 1864, Gonod; flowers shining pink, medium

'Mme Herriot Panachée' HT, yb, 1921, Cassegrain; flowers coral and golden yellow; [sport of 'Mme Edouard Herriot']

'Mme Hersilie Ortgies' HP, lp, 1868, Soupert & Notting; flowers pink and pinkish lilac, medium, full

'Mme Hide' HT, pb, 1997, Ohta, Kaichiro; flowers blush edged pink, large, dbl.; foliage large, medium green, matte; some prickles; compact (1½ m.) growth

'Mme Hippolyte Dumas' HT, pb, 1924, Guillot, P.; flowers flesh tinted salmon-pink, base yellow, dbl.

'Mme Hippolyte Jamain' T, yb, 1869, Guillot; flowers yellowish-white, center coppery, large, full, globular

'Mme Hippolyte Jamain' HP, w, Garçon; flowers lightly blushing white, 4½ in., very full, cupped, borne singly or in small clusters; foliage light green, slightly glaucous, finely dentate; prickles numerous, slender, reddish; intr. 1871

'Mme Hoche' M, lp, 1859, Moreau & Robert; flowers whitish pink, medium, full

'Mme Honoré Defresne' Cl T, my, 1886, Levet, F.; flowers golden yellow, large, dbl.; vigorous growth; ['Mme Falcot' × unknown]

'Mme Hortense de Montefiori' B, op, 1900, Bernaix; flowers light salmon-flesh, brighter at edges, semi-dbl., moderate fragrance

'Mme Hoste' HP, w, 1865, Gonod

'Mme Hoste' T, w, 1887, Guillot et Fils; flowers yellowish-white, imbricated, large, globular; vigorous growth; ['Victor Pulliat' × unknown]

'Mme Huguette Despiney' -- See 'Huguette Despiney'

'Mme Hunnebel' HP, mp, 1873, Fontaine; flowers China pink, shaded darmine, very large, full

'Mme Isaac Periere' ('Le Bienheureaux de la Salle') B, dp, 1881, Garçon; flowers deep rose-pink shaded purple, large, dbl.; vigorous growth

'Mme J. B. Croibier' ('Mme Croibier', 'Mme Jean Croibier') HT, op, 1935, Gaujard; flowers bright salmon, open, very large, dbl.; foliage leathery; very vigorous growth; [seedling × 'Mme Nicolas Aussel']

'Mme J. Bonnaire-Pierre' -- See 'Mme Joseph Bonnaire'

'Mme J. Bonnaire Pierre' HP, 1892, Bonnaire

'Mme J. M. Fructus' HT, pb, 1935, Chambard, C.; flowers satiny carmine, shaded salmon, base yellow, well-formed, dbl., cupped; foliage dark; very vigorous growth

'Mme J. M. Gonod' ('Mme Julie Gonod') HP, dr, 1875, Gonod; flowers dark crimson, center flame red, very large, full

'Mme J. P. Soupert' HT, w, 1900, Soupert & Notting; flowers white with a yellow glow, very large, very dbl., moderate fragrance; ['Mme Caroline Testout' × 'Mlle Alice Furon']

'Mme J. Phillips' -- See 'Mlle Jeanne Philippe'

'Mme J. W. Büdde' HT, dp, 1906, Soupert & Notting; flowers bright carmine

'Mme Jacques Charreton' T, ab, 1897, Bonnaire; bud long, oval; flowers outer petals milky white, center coppery salmon, large, full; growth vigorous

'Mme Jacques Privat' HT, mr, 1959, Privat, J.; bud long; flowers red; foliage glossy; vigorous growth

'Mme Jacquier' HP, m, 1869, Guillot; flowers violet-pink, very large, full

'Mme James Gross' HP, mp, 1864, Baumann; flowers bright carmine-pink, large, full

'Mme Jard' B, mr, 1857, Guillot; flowers cherry red, medium

'Mme Jean Bonnet' T, pb, 1903, Godard; flowers very light pink, almost white, medium, full

'Mme Jean Croibier' -- See 'Mme J. B. Croibier'

'Mme Jean Demeshayne' HT, op, 1934, Nicolas; flowers yellowish salmon-pink, large, very dbl.

'Mme Jean Dupuy' T, yb, 1902, Lambert, P.; bud long, pointed; flowers golden yellow washed pink, large, dbl.; vigorous growth

'Mme Jean Everaerts' ('Improved Princesse de Béarn') HP, dr, 1907, Geduldig; flowers dark flame red, large, dbl., moderate fragrance; ['Eugene Furst' × ('Mme Eugene Verdier' × 'Johannes Wesselhoft')]

'Mme Jean Favre' HT, pb, 1900, Godard; bud long, deep carmine; flowers light carmine with bluish reflections, large; ['La France de 89' × 'Xavier Olibo']

'Mme Jean Gaujard' HT, yb, 1938, Gaujard; bud long, pointed; flowers creamy yellow, reverse shaded orange and carmine-pink, very large, dbl.; foliage leathery, light; very vigorous, bushy growth; PP338; ['Julien Potin' × seedling]

'Mme Jean Paquel' HT, ly, 1934, Walter, L.; bud long, pointed; flowers yellow, passing to cream; foliage glossy; ['Alice Stern' × 'Lilly Jung']

'Mme Jean Raty' HT, w, 1932, Ketten Bros.; bud pointed; flowers amber-white, edges tinted peach-blossom, well-formed, large, dbl.; ['Mme Abel Chatenay' × seedling]

'Mme Jean Sisley' Ch, w, 1885, Dubreuil; flowers matte white with pink reflections, medium, full, cupped, moderate fragrance; ['Ducher' × 'Sombreuil']

'Mme Jeanne Bouvet' HP, lp, 1887, Bernède; flowers silvery light pink, medium; ['Jules Margottin' × unknown]

'Mme Jeanne Philippe' -- See 'Mlle Jeanne Philippe'

'Mme Jeannine Joubert' B, dp, 1877, Margottin fils; flowers bright cerise-carmine, medium, full

'Mme Jenny' HMult, mp, 1925, Nonin; flowers satiny rose, fading to silvery pink, 4 cm., dbl., cupped, borne in clusters of 5-15, moderate fragrance; foliage dark green; vigorous, climbing growth; ['Dorothy Perkins' × unknown]

'Mme Jenny Gillemot' HT, ly, 1905, Pernet-Ducher; bud pointed; flowers light saffron-yellow, large, dbl., high-centered; ['Lady Mary Fitzwilliam' × 'Honourable Edith Gifford']

'Mme Joannes Beurrier' HT, op, 1942, Gaujard; bud pointed; flowers bright orange-pink, reddish reflections, very large, very dbl.; foliage glossy, bronze; very vigorous, bushy growth

'Mme John Twombley'   HP, dr, 1882, Schwartz; flowers bright currant red, large, full; ['Alfred Colomb' × unknown]

'Mme Jolibois'   HP, pb, 1879, Verdier, E.; flowers bright lilac-carmine-pink, edged silvery white, medium to large, full

'Mme Joly'   B, mp, 1859, Oger; flowers rose pink with carmine

'Mme Joseph Bonnaire'   ('Mme J. Bonnaire-Pierre') HT, pb, 1891, Bonnaire; bud very large; flowers China pink, reverse silvery, very large, very full; ['Adam' × 'Paul Neyron']

'Mme Joseph Bouvet'   HP, w, 1886, Bernède; flowers flesh white

'Mme Joseph Combet'   HT, pb, 1894, Bonnaire; flowers pink with yellow and white, large, very dbl.

'Mme Joseph Desbois'   HT, w, 1886, Guillot & fils; flowers flesh white, delicate salmon pink center, 6 in., full; ['Baronne Adolphe de Rothschild' × 'Mme Falcot']

'Mme Joseph Godier'   T, pb, 1887, Pernet-Ducher; flowers China pink, center carmine, shaded coppery yellow, large, very full, moderate fragrance; ['Souv de Marie Détry' × unknown]

'Mme Joseph Halphen'   T, pb, 1858, Margottin; flowers yellow-pink, medium, full

'Mme Joseph Jullien'   HT, pb, 1938, Chambard, C.; flowers coppery carmine, very large, dbl., cupped; foliage slightly bronze; ['Ami F. Mayery' × seedling]

'Mme Joseph Métral' -- See 'Souv de Mme Joseph Métral'

'Mme Joseph Perraud'   ('Sunburst') HT, yb, 1934, Gaujard; flowers yellow, center deeply tinted coppery, large, 33 petals, moderate fragrance; foliage glossy; ['Julien Potin' × seedling]

'Mme Joseph Perraud, Climbing'   Cl HT, yb, 1945, Marsh's Nursery

'Mme Joseph Schwartz'   ('White Duchesse de Brabant') T, w, 1880, Schwartz, J.; flowers white washed flesh-pink, medium, dbl.; vigorous growth; [probably a sport of 'Duchesse de Brabant']

'Mme Joséphine Guyet' -- See 'Joséphine Guyet'

'Mme Joséphine Mühle' -- See 'Safrano à Fleurs Rouges'

'Mme Jules Barandou'   HT, dp, 1900, Bonnaire; flowers dark China pink, very large

'Mme Jules Bouché'   ('Dr Jules Bouché') HT, w, 1911, Croibier; bud pointed; flowers white, center shaded primrose or pale blush, large, 34 petals, moderate fragrance; tall growth; ['Pharisaer' × seedling]

'Mme Jules Bouché, Climbing'   Cl HT, w, 1938, Bigot; flowers white, flesh center, 5 in., intense fragrance

'Mme Jules Cambon'   T, pb, 1888, Bernaix; flowers pint, edged carmine, with magenta shading, yellow at center

'Mme Jules Finger'   HT, lp, 1893, Guillot; flowers creamy white nuanced salmon pink at center, aging to pure white, very large, full, globular

'Mme Jules Fontaine-Lamarche'   HT, mr, 1936, Soupert & Notting; flowers velvety scarlet-red, large, dbl.; ['Sensation' × 'E.G. Hill']

'Mme Jules Francke'   N, w, 1887, Nabonnand; flowers white, fading to yellowish, medium, very full

'Mme Jules Gouchault'   Pol, op, 1913, Turbat; flowers bright pink, tinted coral and orange, dbl., cupped, borne in clusters; bushy growth; ['Maman Turbat' × 'George Elger']

'Mme Jules Graveraux'   Cl T, ab, 1901, Soupert & Notting; bud very long, pointed; flowers flesh, shaded peach or yellow, 10 cm., very dbl.; recurrent bloom; foliage large, dark, glossy; to 3-4 ft., bushy growth; ['Reve d'Or' × 'Viscountess Folkestone']

'Mme Jules Grévy'   HT, pb, 1881, Schwartz; flowers salmon-white within, bright carmine-pink outer, medim to large, full; ['Triomphe de l'Exposition' × 'Mme Falcot']

'Mme Jules Grolez'   HT, mp, 1896, Guillot, P.; bud long, pointed; flowers bright china-rose, dbl., high-centered; bushy growth; ['Triomphe de l'Exposition' × 'Mme Falcot']

'Mme Jules Grolez, Climbing'   ('Gamon's Climbing Grolez') Cl HT, mp, 1911, Gamon (also Dingee & Conard, 1920); flowers glowing China pink with coppery carmine reflections, large, dbl., moderate fragrance; [sport of 'Mme Jules Grolez']

'Mme Jules Guérin'   HT, ly, 1931, Gaujard; flowers deep cream, very large, dbl.; foliage bronze

'Mme Jules Margottin'   T, pb, 1871, Levet; flowers light pink, base yellow, center darker red, medium to large, full, moderate fragrance

'Mme Jules Siegfried'   T, w, 1894, Nabonnand; flowers creme white, shaded flesh, center darker, very large, dbl; ['Rêve d'Or' × 'Baronne Henriette de Loew']

'Mme Jules Thibaud'   Pol, op; flowers coral-pink, dbl., slight fragrance; good repeat; foliage bronzy; moderate (3 ft.) growth; [sport of 'Mlle Cécile Brunner']; according to some, color is peachy pink, definitely lighter than coral pink; sometimes classed as China

'Mme Jules Walthery'   HT, my, 1924, Allen; flowers outer petals becoming white

'Mme Julia Daran'   HP, dr, 1861, Touvais; flowers violet-crimson, very large, full, cupped

'Mme Julie Gonod' -- See 'Mme J. M. Gonod'

'Mme Julie Lasseu'   N, dp, 1881, Nabonnand; flowers large, very full, cupped

'Mme Julie Weidmann'   HT, op, 1881, Soupert & Notting; flowers silvery salmon pink with carmine and ocher, reverse silky violet, very large, full; ['Antoine Verdier' × unknown]

'Mme Julien Potin'   HRg, lp, 1913, Gravereaux; flowers pure flesh-pink, large, dbl., flat; recurrent bloom; foliage very leathery; vigorous growth; ['Germanica' × 'Gloire de Dijon']

'Mme Juliette' -- See 'Juliette E. van Beuningen'

'Mme Juliette Guillot'   F, dp, Guillot; flowers magenta-pink, dbl., cupped; free-flowering; vigorous (80 cm.) growth; intr. 1984

'Mme Just-Détrey'   B, dp, 1869, Just-Détrey; flowers velvety carmine, reverse lighter, large, full

'Mme Kahn'   HT, ly, 1939, Colombier; flowers canary-yellow, reverse slightly reddish; vigorous growth; ['Charles P. Kilham' × 'Ville de Paris']

'Mme Karen Shadish'   F, mp, 1999, Chaney, William; flowers 2-3 in., dbl., borne in small clusters; foliage small, medium green, semi-glossy; prickles moderate; upright, medium (2-3 ft.) growth; ('Pink Petticoat' × Mary Rose®)

'Mme Kastler'   HT, mr, 1934, Walter, L.; bud long, pointed; flowers large, dbl.; very vigorous growth; ['Mme Adele Gance' × 'Mme Caroline Testout']

'Mme Knorr'   ('Mme de Knorr') P, mp, 1855, Verdier, V.; flowers strong pink in center, outer petals fade, full, moderate fragrance

'Mme Kriloff'   HT, yb, 1944, Meilland, F.; flowers clear saffron-yellow, veined reddish-orange, large, dbl., globular; foliage leathery; vigorous, bushy growth; ['Peace' × 'Signora']

'Mme L. Cuny'   ('Mme Léon Cuny') HT, mr, 1955, Gaujard; bud long, pointed; flowers bright red, veined purple, very large, dbl., high-centered; foliage dark, bronze; upright growth; ['Peace' × seedling]

'Mme L. Dieudonné' -- See 'Mme Dieudonné'

'Mme L. Faucheron'   HT, w, 1911, Croibier; flowers cream white with light sulfur yellow reflections, large to very large, full, moderate fragrance

'Mme L. Hot'   HT, pb, 1926, Bernaix, P.; flowers reddish-salmon, shaded salmon-rose and chrome-yellow, dbl.; ['Gorgeous' × 'Rosomane Narcisse Thomas']

'Mme L. Ladoire'   F, op

'Mme L. Laperriere'   HT, 1951, Laperrière

'Mme la Baronne Berge'   ('Baronne Berge') T, pb, 1892, Pernet père; flowers cream and yellow, edged bright pink, medium to large, full, intense fragrance

'Mme la Baronne de Brezetz'   HT, dp, 1903, Chauvry; flowers dark porcelain pink, center cream, reverse carmine pink, very large, full

'Mme la Baronne de Rothschild' -- See 'Baroness Rothschild'

'Mme la Colonelle Desmaires'   F, dr, 1969, Delforge; flowers large, dbl.; foliage soft, bronze; moderate growth; ['Mercator' × 'Alain']

'Mme la Comtesse de Camondo' ('Comtesse de Camondo') HP, mr, 1880, Lévêque; flowers carmine red, tinged brown, very large, full

'Mme la Comtesse de Caserta' -- See 'Comtesse de Caserta'

'Mme la Comtesse de Jaucourt' ('Comtesse de Jaucourt') HP, mp, 1866, Desmazures père; flowers pink, shaded salmon at center, edges pale and silvery, very full; foliage light green; ['Triomphe de l'Exposition' × unknown]

'Mme la Duchesse d'Auerstädt' -- See 'Duchesse d'Auerstädt'

'Mme la Duchesse de Vallombrosa' -- See 'Duchesse de Vallombrosa'

'Mme la Générale Ardouin' HT, rb, 1927, Chambard, C.; flowers coppery carmine shaded chrome-yellow, dbl.

'Mme la Générale Decaen' HP, mp, 1869, Gautreau; flowers bright pink, center flesh pink, large, full

'Mme la Générale Paul de Benoist' Cl T, op, 1901, Berland; flowers salmon-pink, very large, very dbl.; ['Mme Chauvry' × unknown]; sometimes classed as N

'Mme la Princesse de Bessaraba de Brancovan' ('Princesse de Bassaraba de Brancovan') T, pb, 1900, Bernaix, A.; flowers flesh-pink, shaded copper, medium, dbl.

'Mme l'Abbey' C, mp, before 1846; flowers brilliant rose pink, large, full, cupped

'Mme Lacharme' HT, w, 1872, Lacharme; flowers white, very pale blush center, large, cupped; ['Jules Margottin' × 'Mlle de Sombreuil']

'Mme Lacoste' HP, dp, 1856, Bernède; flowers medium, full

'Mme Laffay' HP, mr, 1839, Laffay, M.; flowers bright crimson, dbl.; very vigorous growth; ['Général Allard' × unknown]

'Mme Lajotte' HT, pb, Gaujard; flowers bright salmon, reverse yellow, large, dbl.; very vigorous, bushy growth; ['Rome Glory' × 'Marie-Rose Toussaint']

'Mme Lambard' -- See 'Mme Lombard'

'Mme Lambert' D, mr, before 1848; flowers very large, full

'Mme Landeau' M, rb, 1873, Moreau et Robert; flowers light red with white striping and spotting, medium, dbl.; some repeat

'Mme Lanquetin' HT, ab, Ofman; flowers apricot

'Mme Lartay' T, lp, 1856, Lartay; flowers light pink, edged whitish pink, very large

'Mme Lauras' HT, mr, 1958, Gaujard; flowers bright red, medium, dbl.; foliage leathery; very vigorous growth; ['Rome Glory' × ('Mme Elie Dupraz' × unknown)]; intr. 1956

'Mme Laure Dupont' HCh, dp, 1906, Schwartz; flowers bright carmine, shaded silvery rose, reverse silvery pink; ['Hermosa' × 'Louis van Houtte']

'Mme Laurent' HP, dp, 1870, Granger; flowers shining cherry pink, large, very full

'Mme Laurent Simons' T, op, 1894, Lévêque; bud long; flowers coppery-pink, large, very dbl., moderate fragrance; foliage glossy; growth vigorous

'Mme Laurette Messimy' Ch, dp, 1887, Guillot et Fils; bud long; flowers rose-pink, base shaded yellow, large, dbl.; vigorous growth; [('Rival de Pæstum' × 'Mme Falcot') × 'Mme Falcot']

'Mme Lauriol de Barny' B, lp, 1868, Trouillard; flowers silvery pink, large, dbl., quartered, moderate fragrance; rarely repeats; growth to 5-6 ft.

'Mme le Guelinel' HT, mr, 1959, Gaujard, R.; flowers large; ['Mme Kriloff' × 'Marrakech']

'Mme Lecomte' HT, op, 1901, Buatois; flowers salmon pink, large, full

'Mme Lecomte-Bouquet' HP, dr, 1884, Singer; flowers garnet, shaded chestnut, large, full

'Mme Lefebvre' ('Mme Lefèvre') HP, mp, 1885, Moreau et Robert; flowers delicate satiny pink, center brighter, large, dbl., cupped, borne in small clusters; foliage glossy

'Mme Lefèvre' -- See 'Mme Lefebvre'

'Mme Lefrançois' ('Comtesse de Chabrillant Blanche') HP, op, 1870, Oger; flowers bright flesh-pink, large, full; ['Comtesse de Chabrillant' × unknown]

'Mme Legrand' M, pb, 1863, Fontaine; flowers pink and red, large, dbl.; some repeat

'Mme Legras de St Germain' ('Le Gras St Germain') A, w, before 1846; sepals long; flowers ivory-white, center rich cream, with a small central eye, large, very dbl., flat-cupped, borne in clusters, moderate fragrance; non-recurrent; foliage light gray-green; few prickles; vigorous (6-7 ft.) growth

'Mme Lelièvre de la Place' HP, mr, 1882, Verdier; flowers bright currant-red, shaded white along the edges, large, full, slight fragrance

'Mme Lemelles' -- See 'Mme Lemesle'

'Mme Lemerle' -- See 'Mme Lemesle'

'Mme Lemesle' ('Mme Lemelles', 'Mme Lemerle') HP, m, 1890, Moreau et Robert; flowers purple/violet, medium, dbl., globular; foliage dark green; prickles recurved

'Mme Léon Constantin' Cl T, pb, 1907, Bonnaire; bud long; flowers satiny pink with a light salmon interior, 10 cm., full, moderate fragrance

'Mme Léon Cuny' -- See 'Mme L. Cuny'

'Mme Léon de St Jean' T, m, 1875, Levet; flowers light lilac, center lilac tinted salmon, very large, full; ['Mme Falcot' × 'Mme Damaizin']

'Mme Léon Février' T, pb, 1884, Nabonnand, G.; flowers silvery rose shaded crimson, well-formed, dbl., intense fragrance; growth vigorous

'Mme Léon Guinotte' HT, pb, 1924, Verschuren; flowers glistening pink shaded yellow; ['Mme Edouard Herriot' × 'Old Gold']

'Mme Léon Halkin' HP, mr, 1886, Lévêque; flowers bright crimson red, nuanced purple, large, full, globular

'Mme Léon Pain' HT, pb, 1904, Guillot, P.; bud pointed; flowers silvery flesh-pink, center orange-yellow, reverse salmon-pink, large, 45 petals, moderate fragrance; vigorous, bushy growth; ['Mme Caroline Testout' × 'Souv. de Catherine Guillot']

'Mme Léon Pin' HT, ob, 1958, Gaujard; flowers soft orange, medium, dbl.; foliage dark, leathery; upright growth; ['Louise de Vilmorin' × ('Capucine' × unknown)]; intr. 1954

'Mme Léon Simon' HT, pb, 1909, Lambert, P.; flowers dark pink with cream, large, dbl.; ['Marie van Houtte' × 'Mme Caroline Testout']

'Mme Léon Troussier' HT, op, 1941, Mallerin, C.; flowers coral, base golden yellow

'Mme Léon Volterra' HT, mp, 1958, Leenders, M.; flowers salmon-pink, well-shaped, dbl.; vigorous growth; ['Ambassadeur Nemry' × 'Tawny Gold']

'Mme Léonce Colombier' HT, ly, 1926, Richardier; flowers center straw-yellow passing to white, reverse light rose, dbl.

'Mme Léonie Lamesch' -- See 'Léonie Lamesch'

'Mme Léopold Dupuy' HT, mp, 1912, Robichon; flowers carmine pink nuanced purple, large, dbl., intense fragrance; ['La France de '89' × 'Mme Ernst Calvat']

'Mme Léopold Moreau' HP, mr, 1882, Vigneron; flowers varnished red, large, dbl; ['Souv de Charles Montaut' × unknown]

'Mme Létuvée de Colnet' B, lp, 1887, Vigneron; flowers lilac pink, edges silvery, very large, full; foliage dark green; growth upright; ['Mme Dubost' × unknown]

'Mme Levet' Cl T, yb, 1870, Levet; flowers yellow, tinted violet, reverse salmon-yellow, shaded rose pink, large, very full, cupped; ['Gloire de Dijon' × unknown]

'Mme Liabaud' HP, w, 1858, Lacharme, F.; flowers white with flesh center, medium, dbl.; delicate growth habit

'Mme Lierval' HP, dp, 1868, Fontaine; flowers delicate pink mixed with bright crimson, large, full

'Mme Lilienthal' HP, dp, 1878, Liabaud; flowers rose red with salmon tints, large, full

'Mme Line Renaud' HT, mr, 1956, Mondial Roses; flowers velvety red; foliage bright green; ['Crimson Glory' × seedling]

'Mme Loeben de Sels' -- See 'Mme Loeben Sels'

'Mme Loeben Sels' ('Mme Loeben de Sels') HT, w, 1879, Soupert & Notting;

flowers silvery white shaded rose, large, dbl., flat; moderate growth
'Mme Loiseleur' -- See 'Adèle Pavié'
'Mme Lombard' ('Mme Lambard') T, op, 1878, Lacharme, F.; flowers rosy salmon, center darker, sometimes rosy flesh, large, very dbl.; vigorous growth; ['Mme de Tartas' × unknown]
'Mme Louis Armand' HT, pb, Croix; intr. 1974
'Mme Louis Blanchet' N, m, 1894, Godard; flowers lilac pink, marbled
'Mme Louis Donadine' HP, w, 1878, Gonod; flowers flesh white, center darker, large, full; [sport of 'Countess of Oxford']
'Mme Louis Gaillard' T, w, 1892, Liabaud; flowers white, shaded yellow, large, full; ['Mme Bérard' × unknown]
'Mme Louis Gravier' T, op, 1896, Gamon; flowers salmon with orange-yellow, edged pink, aging coppery apricot, large, full, moderate fragrance
'Mme Louis Henry' N, w, 1879, Ducher; flowers white, slightly yellowish in center, 7 cm., full, borne in small clusters; foliage light green; prickles numerous, short, reddish
'Mme Louis Ladoire' F, Arles, F.
'Mme Louis Laperrière' HT, mr, 1951, Laperrière; flowers rich scarlet, well-formed, medium, 48 petals, intense fragrance; foliage dark; upright, bushy growth; ['Crimson Glory' × seedling]
'Mme Louis Laurans' T, dr, 1894, Bonnaire; flowers dark red, shaded fiery magenta, very large, full, moderate fragrance
'Mme Louis Lens' HT, w, 1932, Lens, Louis; bud long, pointed; flowers large, unusually lasting, very dbl., high-centered, borne singly, moderate fragrance; continuous; foliage leathery; growth vigorous, upright; ['Kaiserin Auguste Viktoria' × 'Mrs Herbert Stevens']
'Mme Louis Lens, Climbing' Cl HT, w, 1935, Lens; [sport of 'White Briarcliff']
'Mme Louis Lévêque' ('Capt Christy Mossed') M, mp, Lévêque; flowers large, full, globular; some repeat in autumn; intr. 1903
'Mme Louis Lévêque' M, mp, Lévêque; flowers brilliant salmon-pink, large, full, globular, moderate fragrance; sometimes blooms in fall; upright, vigorous (4 ft.) growth; intr. 1898
'Mme Louis Lévêque' T, yb, Lévêque; flowers yellow washed pink, dbl.; moderate growth; intr. 1892
'Mme Louis Lévêque' HP, dp, 1864, Lévêque; flowers light rose, very large, dbl., globular, slight fragrance; moderate growth; ['Jules Margottin' × unknown]
'Mme Louis Poncet' T, pb, 1899, Guillot; flowers nasturtium-red, base coppery China pink, large, full, moderate fragrance
'Mme Louis Pradel' -- See 'Lapav'
'Mme Louis Puyravaud' T, mp, 1906, Puyravaud; flowers satiny China pink with darker reflections, large, dbl., moderate fragrance; ['Souv de Mme Détrey' × unknown]

'Mme Louis Ricard' B, lp, 1892, Duboc; flowers pale pink, brighter around center, petals reflexed, large, full, moderate fragrance; foliage oval; prickles few, straight; [possibly a seedling of 'Baron J. B. Gonella']
'Mme Louis Ricard' HP, mp, Boutigny, P.; intr. 1904
'Mme Louis Ricard, Climbing' Cl HP, mp, 1904, Boutigny; flowers bright pink, large, borne in small clusters; [sport of 'Mme Louis Ricard']
'Mme Louisa Cointreau' HT, mr, 1957, Robichon; flowers garnet-red, dbl.; vigorous growth; ['Crimson Glory' × 'Symbole']
'Mme Louise Carique' ('Louise Carique') HP, mp, 1859, Fontaine; flowers bright carmine, medium, full
'Mme Louise Collet' M, dp, 1840, Vibert; flowers bright, shining deep pink, large, full
'Mme Louise Guillot' F, Guillot, M.; intr. 1955
'Mme Louise Mulson' T, yb, 1897, Lévêque; flowers silvery white with sulfer yellow, shaded chrome over pink, large, full
'Mme Louise Piron' HP, lp, 1903, Piron-Medard; flowers large, full, moderate fragrance; remontant; upright (4 ft.) growth; ['La Reine' × 'Ulrich Brunner fils']
'Mme Louise Seydoux' HP, lp, 1856, Fontaine; flowers light silky pink, very large, full
'Mme Louise Trémeau' HT, op, 1931, Mallerin, C.; flowers pink, shaded nasturtium-red, center brighter, open, large, dbl., cupped; vigorous growth; [('Frau Karl Druschki' × 'Mme Edouard Herriot') × ('Mrs Edward Powell' × R. foetida bicolor)]
'Mme Louise Vigneron' HP, lp, 1882, Vigneron; bud elongated; flowers light pink, center darker, large, full; quite remontant; foliage light green; prickles fairly numerous, brown; growth upright; ['Elisabeth Vigneron' × unknown]
'Mme Lucien Baltet' HT, pb, 1911, Pernet'Ducher; flowers flesh pink, shaded coppery yellow, petals edged carmine, very large, full, globular
'Mme Lucien Chauré' HP, mr, 1884, Vigneron; flowers bright cerise red, 5 in., full, globular, borne mostly solitary; quite remontant; foliage dark green; prickles numerous, chestnut; growth upright
'Mme Lucien Duranthon' ('Blanche Duranthon') T, w, 1898, Bonnaire; flowers cream white, tinted coppery and salmon at center, large, cupped
'Mme Lucien Perrier' HT, rb, 1938, Gaujard; bud long; flowers coppery red, lighter on opening, open, very large, dbl.; foliage glossy, dark; vigorous growth
'Mme Lucien Picard' HT, w, 1910, Croibier; bud ovoid; flowers white with salmon tints, large, full; ['Mme Abel Chatenay' × unknown]

'Mme Lucien Villeminot' HRg, lp, 1901, Gravereaux & Müuller; flowers pale pink, large, dbl., globular, moderate fragrance; vigorous growth; ['Conrad Ferdinand Meyer' × 'Belle Poitevine']
'Mme Luizet' B, pb, 1867, Liabaud; flowers carmine, shaded salmon, large, full
'Mme Lureau-Escalaïs' HP, mp, 1886, Verdier, E.; flowers delicate pink, large, dbl.; ['Victor Verdier' × unknown]
'Mme Macker' HP, lp, 1863, Damaizin; flowers large, full
'Mme Madeleine Margat' T, w, 1900, Perny; flowers white, edged cherry red
'Mme Mallerin' HT, rb, 1924, Chambard, C.; flowers crimson-scarlet shaded vermilion; ['Mrs Edward Powell' × seedling]
'Mme Mantel' -- See 'Mme Montel'
'Mme Marcel Astic' F, Orard, Joseph; intr. 1978
'Mme Marcel Delauney' HT, pb, 1916, Leenders, M.; flowers pale pink or soft rose, shaded hydrangea-pink, large, dbl., moderate fragrance
'Mme Marcel Fauneau' HP, mr, 1886, Vigneron; flowers carmine-red, large, dbl.; ['Alexis Lepère' × unknown]
'Mme Marchal' B, w, 1858, de Fauw; flowers flesh white, edges lighter, medium, full
'Mme Margottin' T, yb, 1866, Guillot et Fils; flowers lemon-yellow, peach center, edges white, large, dbl., slightly globular; growth vigorous
'Mme Marguerite Lagières' HT, w, 1955, Privat; flowers cream, base golden yellow, very large, dbl.; foliage glossy; strong stems; vigorous growth
'Mme Marguerite Marsault' HP, m, 1894, Corboeuf; flowers reddish-violet, large, dbl.
'Mme Marie Accary' -- See 'Marie Accary'
'Mme Marie Berton' -- See 'Marie Berton'
'Mme Marie Bianchi' HP, m, 1881, Guillot; flowers lilac pink, centers brighter, reverse white, medium to large, full, globular; ['Victor Verdier' × 'Virginale']
'Mme Marie Brémond' T, m, 1866, Guillot; flowers light purple, shaded dark red, medium to large, full
'Mme Marie Cirodde' HP, dp, 1867, Verdier, E.; flowers deep pink, large, full
'Mme Marie Closon' -- See 'Mlle Marie Closon'
'Mme Marie Croibier' HT, dp, 1901, Croibier; bud long; flowers deep China pink, very large, dbl.; ['Mme Caroline Testout' × unknown]
'Mme Marie Curie' ('Québec') HT, dy, 1943, Gaujard; flowers clear yellow, 5 in., 25 petals, high-centered; foliage leathery, dark; vigorous, bushy, compact growth; PP727
'Mme Marie Dubourg' B, lp, 1851, Pradel; flowers light pink, medium, full
'Mme Marie Eberlin' HT, w, 1923, Walter,

A.; flowers cream, passing to white, base light yellow, dbl.; ['Comtesse Melanie de Pourtales' × 'Capt. Christy']

'Mme Marie Finger' -- See 'Mlle Eugénie Verdier'

'Mme Marie Finger' HP, op, 1872, Lacharme; flowers salmon pink

'Mme Marie Lavalley' ('Marie Lavalley') HT, pb, 1881, Nabonnand, G.; flowers bright rose tinted white, semi-dbl.; few prickles

'Mme Marie Legrange' HP, mr, 1882, Liabaud; flowers brilliant carmine, very large, full; ['Sénateur Vaïsse' × unknown]

'Mme Marie Moreau' -- See 'Mlle Marie Moreau'

'Mme Marie Rady' -- See 'Mlle Marie Rady'

'Mme Marie Röderer' HP, dp, 1881, Lévêque; flowers cherry pink; ['Jules Margottin' × unknown]

'Mme Marie Van Houtte' HP, lp, about 1870, van Houtte; flowers delicate, satiny pink, large, full

'Mme Marius Côte' HP, dp, 1872, Guillot; flowers fresh dark pink with light red, reverse lighter, very large, very full, cupped

'Mme Marius Dévigne' HT, pb, 1930, Reymond; bud long; flowers salmon-pink, reverse vivid carmine, large, globular

'Mme Martha Ancey' -- See 'Marthe Ancey'

'Mme Marthe d'Halloy' HP, mp, 1881, Lévêque; flowers carmine cerise pink, large, full; very remontant; foliage glaucous green

'Mme Marthe Dubourg' T, w, 1890, Bernaix; flowers white, washed violet-carmine with a blush border, aging to pale yellow washed blush, large, full

'Mme Martignier' Cl T, m, 1903, Dubreuil; flowers red tinted purplish, on yellow ground, medium, cupped; ['a Tea' × 'a Noisette']

'Mme Martin de Bessé' HP, w, 1866, Bernardin; flowers white, shaded light pink, large, full, cupped

'Mme Massicault' HP, lp, 1884, Schwartz; flowers fleshy pink-white with silvery highlights, medium to large, very dbl., borne mostly solitary; foliage large, dark green, glossy; prickles few, short, slightly hooked; growth straight, erect

'Mme Masson' ('Gloire de Châtillon') HP, dr, 1856, Masson; flowers pure crimson-rose, very large, very full, moderate fragrance; free bloom during long season; vigorous, compact growth

'Mme Massot' B, w, 1856, Lacharme, F.; flowers white, center flesh, medium, full; sometimes classified as N

'Mme Maurice Baudot' HT, ob, 1941, Gaujard; flowers bright orange, medium, semi-dbl., high-centered; foliage dark; very vigorous, bushy growth; ['Mme Joseph Perraud' × seedling]

'Mme Maurice Capron' HT, ab, 1914, Guillot, P.; flowers deep apricot-yellow tinted salmon

'Mme Maurice Cazin' HT, rb, 1931, Schwartz, A.; bud pointed; flowers dark scarlet, reverse clear reddish-crimson, large, dbl.; ['Gen. MacArthur' × 'Hadley']

'Mme Maurice de Luze' HT, pb, 1907, Pernet-Ducher; flowers rose-pink, center carmine, reverse paler, large, full, cupped, moderate sweet fragrance; ['Mme Abel Chatenay' × 'Eugene Fürst']

'Mme Maurice Fenaille' HT, lp, 1904, Boutigny, P.; flowers very light pink, nearly white, large, full

'Mme Maurice Genevoix' F, op, Hémeray-Aubert; intr. 1966

'Mme Maurice Kuppenheim' T, ab, 1877, Ducher, Vve.; flowers salmon-yellow tinged with pink, large, dbl.

'Mme Maurice Rafin' HT, mp, 1913, Bernaix fils; flowers clear pink, carmine center, large, full, moderate fragrance

'Mme Maurice Rivoire' HP, lp, 1876, Gonod; flowers deep flesh, exterior petals white, medium, full

'Mme Maurin' -- See 'Mme Denis'

'Mme Maxime Bonnet' B, mr, 1861, Pradel; flowers cherry-carmine

'Mme Maxime de la Rocheterie' HP, mp, 1880, Granger; flowers flesh pink, medium to large, full; [sport of 'Victor Verdier']

'Mme Méha Sabatier' HT, rb, 1916, Pernet-Ducher; flowers deep red, with white stripes in some petals, large, dbl.; [seedling × 'Château de Clos Vougeot']

'Mme Mélanie Soupert' HT, yb, 1905, Pernet-Ducher; bud pointed; flowers salmon yellow, suffused pink and carmine, large, semi-dbl., moderate fragrance; vigorous growth

'Mme Mélanie Soupert, Climbing' Cl HT, op, 1914, Burrell; flowers dawn pink, becoming salmon pink, very large, dbl.; [sport of 'Mme Mélanie Soupert']

'Mme Mélanie Vigneron' HP, m, 1882, Vigneron; flowers lilac pink, reverse silver, large, very full; ['Elisabeth Vigneron' × unknown]

'Mme Mélanie Willermoz' ('Mélanie Willermoz', 'Mme Willermoz') T, w, 1849, Lacharme, F.; flowers white tinted salmon pink at center, shaded cream, large, dbl, semi-globular, moderate fragrance; good repeat; growth compact

'Mme Melon du Thé' -- See 'Clotilde Soupert'

'Mme Mercier de Molin' HT, rb, 1921, Schwartz, A.; flowers fiery red, tinted crimson, edges slightly tinged rose-pink, dbl.; ['Comte G. de Rochemur' × 'Liberty']

'Mme Michel Dufay' HMoy, rb, 1932, Sauvageot, H.; flowers maroon, reverse purplish garnet, large, dbl., cupped; occaisionally recurrent; foliage dark; very vigorous, upright, bushy growth; ['George Dickson' × R. moyesii]

'Mme Millerand' HT, w, 1926, Walter, L.; flowers rosy white, shaded salmon, dbl.; ['Pharisaer' × 'Mme Henriette Schissele']

'Mme Miniver' HT, ob, 1947, Vilmorin-Andrieux; bud pointed; flowers orange-red tinted apricot, base yellow, large, dbl.; vigorous growth; ['Joanna Hill' × 'Charles P. Kilham']

'Mme Miolan Carvalho' N, dy, 1876, Chédane-Guinoisseau; flowers dark sulfur-yellow, large, full, moderate fragrance; ['Chromatella' × unknown]; sometimes attributed to Lévêque

'Mme Moisans' LCl, mp, 1955, Robichon; flowers hortensia-pink, dbl.; recurrent bloom; foliage glossy; ['Lady Sylvia' × seedling]

'Mme Montel' ('Mme Mantel', 'Mme Montet') HP, lp, 1880, Liabaud; flowers delicate rose pink, very large, dbl.; ['La Reine' × unknown]

'Mme Montet' -- See 'Mme Montel'

'Mme Morand Andrée' HT, dr, 1957, Privat; flowers blackish red, very large; foliage dark; vigorous growth

'Mme Moreau' T, yb, Moreau & Robert; flowers coppery yellow, center darker, reverse pink with apricot-yellow, very large, full; ['Mme Falcot' × 'Mme Bérard']; intr. 1889

'Mme Moreau' HP, mr, 1864, Moreau; flowers bright red, tinged violet, 4½-5½ in., very dbl., globular, borne mostly solitary; foliage dark green; ['Victor Verdier' × unknown]

'Mme Moreau' M, pb, Moreau & Robert; flowers vermilion, edged and striped white, large, dbl.; some repeat; upright, broad (5 × 5 ft.) growth; intr. 1872

'Mme Moser' HT, pb, 1889, Vigneron; flowers pink to rosy white, large, dbl.

'Mme Mouseur-Fontaine' HT, yb, 1931, Soupert & Notting; bud pointed; flowers sulfur-yellow, center saffron-yellow, large, dbl.; ['Sunburst' × 'Primerose']

'Mme Mulson' T, pb, 1895, Bernaix; flowers silky yellow, shaded salmon pink, center canary yellow with copper red, large, full

'Mme Myrja Sachs' HT, rb, Croix; flowers strong magenta red, overlaid silver, double; recurrent; foliage bright green, matte; growth 1 meter height; intr. 2007

'Mme Nabonnand' T, w, 1877, Nabonnand; flowers flesh white shaded pink; growth tall, not exceptionally vigorous

'Mme Nachury' HP, mp, 1873, Damaizin; flowers silky pink, very large, full, cupped; ['La Reine' × unknown]

'Mme Neige' -- See 'Youki San'

'Mme Nérard' B, pb, 1838, Nérard; flowers delicate blush pink, large, full, flat; ['Rose Edouard' × unknown]

'Mme Neumann' -- See 'Hermosa'

'Mme Nicolas Aussel' HT, ob, 1930, Pernet-Ducher; bud pointed; flowers salmon shaded carmine and ochre, large, dbl.; foliage dark; vigorous growth

'Mme Nicolas Boudler' HT, pb, 1934, Boudler; bud round; flowers rose, reverse shaded yellow, large, dbl.; ['Souv. de Georges Pernet' × 'Gloire de Dijon']

'Mme Nicolas Koechlin' C, mp, about 1860, Baumann

'Mme Nobécourt' B, lp, 1893, Moreau et Robert; bud very large and long; flowers light satiny pink very large, dbl., cupped, borne in small clusters, intense fragrance; foliage light green; ['Mme Isaac Pereire' × unknown]

'Mme Noël' HT, rb, 1939, Chambard, C.; flowers vermilion-red, reverse carmine-yellow, very large, dbl., cupped; foliage dark; vigorous growth

'Mme Noël le Mire' HT, rb, 1934, Sauvageot, H.; flowers brilliant crimson-red with yellow reflections, semi-dbl., cupped, borne in clusters; strong stems; dwarf growth; ['George Dawson' × 'Dance of Joy']

'Mme Noman' HP, w, 1867, Guillot père; flowers pure white, small, full, globular; foliage somewhat cimpled; prickles numerous, small; ['Mme Récamier' × unknown]

'Mme Norbert Levavasseur' ('Dwarf Crimson Rambler', 'Red Baby Rambler') Pol, mr, 1903, Levavasseur; flowers crimson-red, center lighter, bluing badly, small, semi-dbl., cupped, borne in large clusters; foliage glossy, dark; bushy, dwarf growth; ['Crimson Rambler' × 'Gloire des Polyantha']

'Mme Norman' HP, w, 1867, Guillot; flowers medium, dbl.

'Mme Ocker Ferencz' T, yb, 1892, Bernaix, A.; bud long, washed with violet pink; flowers canary and carmine, large, full

'Mme Ofman' HT, or, 1958, Ofman; bud long, pointed; flowers large, very dbl., high-centered, moderate fragrance; foliage dark, glossy; strong stems; vigorous, upright, bushy growth; intr. 1954

'Mme Olga' T, w, 1889, Lévêque; flowers white, finely and delicately shaded yellow, large, full; foliage dark green; growth vigorous

'Mme Olympe Téretschenko' B, w, 1882, Lévêque; flowers white with light blush, large, full, cupped; [sport of 'Louise Odier']

'Mme Orève' HT, ob, 1926, Chambard, M.; flowers rose-salmon, center coppery salmon

'Mme Oswald de Kerchove' HP, pb, 1879, Schwartz; bud oval; flowers white to coppery yellow at center, medium, very full, borne in clusters of 3-5; foliage medium green; prickles short, horizontal, unequal; ['Mme Falcot' × ('Mme Recamier' × unknown)]

'Mme P. Doithier' HT, pb, 1920, Chambard, M.; flowers glossy pink, shaded shrimp-pink

'Mme P. Euler' -- See 'Mme Pierre Euler'

'Mme P. Olivier' -- See 'Shining Star'

'Mme Paquel' HT, my, 1945, Mallerin, C.; flowers chrome-yellow, well-formed, dbl.; foliage wood and reddish

'Mme Paul Bouju' HT, ob, 1930, Chambard, C.; bud long, pointed; flowers carmine-orange, very large, cupped; foliage bronze

'Mme Paul Duringe' HT, mp, 1934, Chambard, C.; flowers deep coral, large; very vigorous growth

'Mme Paul Euler' -- See 'Mme Pierre Euler'

'Mme Paul Gravereaux' HRg, mr, 1901, L'Hay

'Mme Paul Lacoutière' HT, op, 1897, Buatois; flowers coppery-pink, large, semi-dbl.; ['Ma Capucine' × 'Baronne Adolphe de Rothschild']

'Mme Paul Marchandeau' HT, w, 1928, Barbaras; flowers white, base deep yellow, dbl.

'Mme Paul Marmy' T, yb, 1884, Marmy; bud large, globular, cream; flowers very light yellow at center, pale pink at edges, medium to large, full, borne mostly solitary; foliage thick, glossy; numerous prickles; ['Gloire de Dijon' × unknown]

'Mme Paul Olivier' HT, op, 1902, Pernet-Ducher; flowers salmon pink, shaded carmine, large, full, globular, moderate fragrance; ['Mme Eugene Boullet' × 'Mme Cadeau-Ramey']

'Mme Paul Ollivary' HT, op, 1924, Schwartz, A.; bud pointed; flowers coppery salmon, reverse shaded yellow, large, nearly single; ['Mme Mélanie Soupert' × 'Emma Wright']

'Mme Paul Parmentier' HT, ob, 1919, Gillot, F.; flowers salmon-yellow shaded flesh, copper and daybreak-pink, dbl.; ['Le Progres' × 'Lyon Rose']

'Mme Paul Rottier' F, rb, 1957, Buisman, G. A. H.; flowers red shaded orange, borne in large clusters; moderate growth

'Mme Paul Varin-Bernier' T, pb, 1906, Soupert & Notting; bud dark yellow; flowers various shades of melon, large, dbl.; foliage dark green; ['Mme C. P. Strassheim' × 'Mme Dr. Jütté']

'Mme Paula Guisez' -- See 'Heat Wave'

'Mme Paule Massad' -- See 'Maslupau'

'Mme Pauline Labonté' T, op, 1852, Pradel; flowers salmon-pink, large, dbl.; vigorous growth

'Mme Pauline Vilot' HP, mr, 1859, Marest

'Mme Pelisson' ('Mme Pellissier') T, ly, 1891, Brosse; flowers light citron, white reverse, medium, dbl.; growth vigorous, compact

'Mme Pellissier' -- See 'Mme Pelisson'

'Mme Pernet-Ducher' HT, dy, 1891, Pernet-Ducher; flowers canary yellow, outer petals washed carmine, fading to creamy white, large, very dbl., moderate fragrance; ['tea seedling' × 'Victor Verdier']

'Mme Petit' HP, dr, 1900, Corboeuf; flowers velvety carmine shaded purple, striped with one white line, borne in small clusters; ['Charles Lefebvre' × 'Pride of Reigate']

'Mme Ph. Tsirnana' -- See 'Mme Tsiranana'

'Mme Phélip' HP, lp, 1852, Lacharme; flowers light pink, edges brighter, large, full

'Mme Philbert Boutigny' HP, mp, 1913, Boutigny, P.; flowers bright, clear rose pink, full; ['Ulrich Brunner fils' × 'Paul Neyron']

'Mme Philémon Cochet' T, lp, 1887, Cochet, S.; bud large, truncated; flowers extremely light pink, often marked with blotches of light salmon pink, medium to large, very dbl., slightly cupped, borne mostly solitary, moderate fragrance; foliage bright green, purplish underneath; prickles triangular, few; growth upright; ['Sylphide' × unknown]

'Mme Philémon Plantamour' -- See 'Mme Philippe Plantamour'

'Mme Philippe Kuntz' T, pb, 1889, Bernaix; flowers cerise red fading to delicate blush pink toward center, large, full, cupped, moderate fragrance; foliage brilliant green

'Mme Philippe Plantamour' ('Mme Philémon Plantamour', 'Mme Plantamour') HRg, mr, about 1900; flowers flame red, large, semi-dbl.

'Mme Philippe Rivoire' HT, ab, 1908, Pernet-Ducher; flowers apricot-yellow, center nankeen yellow, reverse red, large, dbl., globular; vigorous growth

'Mme Pierre Cochet' N, yb, 1891, Cochet, S.; flowers saffron-yellow, shaded scarlet, center apricot, dbl.; vigorous, climbing growth; ['Reve d'Or' × unknown]

'Mme Pierre Euler' ('Mme P. Euler', 'Mme Paul Euler', 'Prima Donna') HT, rb, 1907, Guillot, P.; flowers silvery vermilion-pink, large, dbl., moderate fragrance; ['Antoine Rivoire' × 'Killarney']

'Mme Pierre Forestier' HT, ob, 1933, Chambard, C.; flowers orange, shaded shrimp-carmine to satiny China-pink, very large, cupped

'Mme Pierre Guillot' T, ob, 1888, Guillot & fils; flowers coppery orange yellow grading to a lighter shade at top, bordered with carmine, full, borne mostly solitary

'Mme Pierre Koechlin' HT, op, 1934, Sauvageot, H.; flowers salmon-pink, very large, dbl., high-centered; [seedling × 'The Queen Alexandra Rose']

'Mme Pierre Margery' HP, mp, 1881, Liabaud; flowers cerise pink, large, full; freely remontant; ['Jules Margottin' × unknown]

'Mme Pierre Oger' B, pb, 1878, Oger; flowers blush, reverse tinged rosy lilac, medium size, dbl., cupped, moderate sweet fragrance; good repeat; upright (5 ft.) growth; [sport of 'Reine Victoria']

'Mme Pierre Perny' T, ly, 1880, Nabonnand; bud elongated; flowers saffron yellow, large, semi-dbl.; nearly thornless

'Mme Pierre Place' HP, mp, 1854, Margot-

tin; flowers bright pink, medium, full
'Mme Pierre S. duPont, Climbing' -- See 'Mrs Pierre S. duPont, Climbing'
'Mme Pierre S. duPont' -- See 'Mrs Pierre S. duPont'
'Mme Pierson' HP, lp, 1860, Fontaine; flowers light pink, aging to light red with silvery tintes, large, full
'Mme Pirrie' -- See 'Lady Pirrie'
'Mme Pizay' HT, op, 1920, Chambard, C.; flowers light salmon; [seedling × 'Mme Mélanie Soupert']
'Mme Pizay, Climbing' Cl HT, op, 1920, Chambard, C.; flowers light salmon-pink, reverse darker, 4 in., dbl.
'Mme Plantamour' -- See 'Mme Philippe Plantamour'
'Mme Plantier' A, w, 1835, Plantier; sepals long; flowers creamy white changing to pure white, green pip, 6-7 cm., very dbl., flat, borne in clusters of 10-20, moderate fragrance; non-recurrent; foliage small, light gray-green; almost thornless; vigorous, spreading,bushy (about 5 ft.) growth; [thought to be R. × alba × R. moschata]; sometimes classed as hybrid N, HCh, or D
'Mme Platz' M, dp, 1864, Moreau et Robert; flowers carmine-pink, 7-9 cm., dbl., flat, intense fragrance; freely remontant
'Mme Plumecocq' HT, dy, 1931, Lens; flowers golden yellow, center brighter; ['Roselandia' × 'Ville de Paris']
'Mme Plumecocq' HT, pb, Gaujard; flowers bright pink, reverse silvery, very large, dbl., high-centered; foliage bronze; vigorous, upright growth; ['Peace' × seedling]; intr. 1954
'Mme Poincaré' -- See 'Mme Raymond Poincaré'
'Mme Portier Durel' HWich, w, 1910, Portier-Durel; flowers pure white, 3 cm., rosette, borne in medium clusters, slight fragrance
'Madame President' -- See 'Madam President'
'Mme Prévost' HP, w, 1900, Corboeuf; flowers white, tinted salmon pink
'Mme Prosper Laugier' HP, mr, 1875, Verdier, E.; flowers carmine-red, large, dbl., moderate fragrance; foliage dark green, irregularly dentate; prickles numerous, short, thick, brown; ['John Hopper' × unknown]
'Mme Prudhomme' HP, mr, 1872, Moreau & Robert; flowers bright cherry red, center flame red, large, full
'Mme Puissant' HP, mr, 1861, Moreau & Robert; flowers light cherry, edges shaded crimson, large, full
'Mme Pulliat' ('Alex Dickson') HP, pb, 1866, Ducher; flowers dark pink, shaded purple, medium to large, full, globular
'Mme Rambaux' HP, dp, 1881, Rambaux; bud conical; flowers carmine pink, paler on reverse, very large, very full, moderate fragrance; foliage dark green above, glaucescent beneath
'Mme Raoul Fauran' HT, m, 1934, Sauvageot, H.; flowers carmine shaded velvety purple, reverse light purple, very large, semi-dbl., cupped; foliage leathery, dark; vigorous, bushy growth
'Mme Rathswell' -- See 'Mme Therese Roswell'
'Mme Ravary' HT, ob, 1899, Pernet-Ducher; bud long, golden yellow, conical; flowers orange-yellow, large, dbl., cupped, moderate fragrance; foliage brownish-green; prickles strong; vigorous, bushy growth
'Mme Raymond Chevalier-Appert' HT, rb, 1917, Guillot, P.; flowers cerise-red, edged lighter, dbl., intense fragrance; robust (5 ft.) growth; ['Gen. MacArthur' × 'Richmond']
'Mme Raymond Chevalier-Appert, Climbing' Cl HT, rb, after 1917
'Mme Raymond Gaujard' -- See 'Olympiad'
'Mme Raymond Poincaré' ('La Rose de Mme Raymond Poincaré', 'Mme Poincaré') HT, pb, 1919, Graveraux; flowers pale pink and salmon, center yellow, large, dbl.; ['Antoine Rivoire' × 'Ophelia']
'Mme Récamier' HP, w, 1853, Lacharme; flowers flesh white, passing to pure white, medium, dbl., borne in small clusters
'Mme Remond' T, yb, 1882, Lambert, E.; flowers pale sulphur yellow, broadly margined with bright red, medium, full, moderate fragrance; nearly thornless; growth vigorous; ['Comtesse de Labarthe' × 'Anna Olivier']
'Mme Rémond' T, yb, Lambert, E.; flowers sulfur-yellow, edged red, very dbl.
'Mme Renahy' ('Mme Renshy') HP, dp, 1889, Guillot et Fils; flowers carmine, center brighter, reverse delicate pink, large, full, globular
'Mme Renard' HP, op, 1872, Moreau et Robert; flowers salmon-pink, very large, dbl.; ['Jules Margottin' × unknown]
'Mme René André' HT, lp, 1906; flowers large, dbl.
'Mme René Cassin' HT, pb, 1964, Delbard-Chabert; flowers cyclamen-pink, reverse silvery, 5 in., 24 petals, high-centered, moderate fragrance; foliage dark, glossy; vigorous, upright growth; ['Mme Armand Souzy' × 'Impeccable']
'Mme René Collette' HT, pb, 1909, Gamon; flowers yellowish-pink with red, large, dbl.; ['Mlle Anna Charron' × 'Kaiserin Auguste Viktoria']
'Mme René Coty' HT, rb, 1958, Meilland, F.; bud globular; flowers Persian red, reverse yellow, very large, dbl., moderate fragrance; foliage glossy, leathery; long, strong stems; vigorous, upright growth; ['Peace' × 'Brazil']; intr. 1955
'Mme René Gérard' T, yb, 1897, Guillot; flowers dark coppery yellow, shaded nasturtium red, large, full
'Mme René Graveraux' HRg, lp, 1902, Graveraux; flowers lilac pink with light violet, base tinted yellow, very large; ['Conrad Ferdinand Meyer' × 'Safrano']
'Mme René Lefèvre' HT, yb, 1938, Robichon; bud long, pointed, sulphur-yellow, edged cerise; flowers golden yellow, flushed carmine, open, large, semi-dbl.; foliage leathery, bronze; ['Elizabeth of York' × 'Mme Henri Pate']
'Mme René Truchot' HT, 1952, Orard, Joseph
'Mme Renée Baltet' B, dr, 1865, Verdier; flowers fiery carmine-purple, large, full
'Mme Renée Oberthür' HT, w, 1908, Vigneron; flowers procelain white, with occasional salmon tints at center, large, dbl., moderate fragrance; foliage dark green; ['Mme Caroline Testout' × unknown]
'Mme Renshy' -- See 'Mme Renahy'
'Mme Retornaz' T, yb, 1867, Guillot; flowers yellow with copper tings, large, full
'Mme Rival' -- See 'Auguste Mie'
'Mme Rival' HP, lp, 1866, Gonod; flowers light silky pink, large, full, slight fragrance
'Mme Rival Verne' HP, pb, 1874, Liabaud; flowers carmine pink over salmon pink, large, full
'Mme Rivers' HP, mp, 1850, Guillot; flowers flesh pink, medium, full, globular
'Mme Robert' HT, yb, 1917, Chambard, C.; flowers nankeen yellow with chamois reflexes, dbl.
'Mme Robert Fortin' HT, m, 1935, Buatois; flowers carmine-purple, large, dbl., cupped; very vigorous growth; ['Mme Caroline Testout' × 'Yves Druhen']
'Mme Robert Joffet' F, 1956, Delbard-Chabert; flowers salmon to geranium, reverse carmine-pink, well-formed, large, semi-dbl.
'Mme Robert Martin' HT, pb, 1943, Meilland, F.; bud long, pointed; flowers pink, center coral, very large, very dbl.; foliage leathery; vigorous, bushy growth; ['Charles P. Kilham' × 'Mme Joseph Perraud']
'Mme Robert Perrier' HT, ob, Orard, Joseph; flowers coppery, stamens saffron, large, semi-dbl.
'Mme Roberte Huet' HT, rb, 1960, Hémeray-Aubert; flowers velvety scarlet, reverse raspberry-red, base gold, dbl.; foliage glossy, slightly bronze; strong stems; vigorous growth
'Mme Rochefontaine' HP, pb; flowers rosy flesh to clear pink, large, dbl.
'Mme Rocher' HP, dr, 1878, Cochet, S.; flowers bright pink, with the inside of the petals darker, 5-5½ in., very full; numerous prickles; growth upright
'Mme Rodolphe Arnaud' HT, pb, 1911, Perdriolle; flowers dark pink, shaded yellow, with shrimp pink tints, moderate fragrance; ['Lyon Rose' × 'Mme Segond Weber']
'Mme Roger' HP, lp, 1877, Moreau-Robert; flowers delicate pink, nearly white, large, full
'Mme Roger Douine' HT, rb, 1926, Reymond; flowers crimson, shaded scarlet,

dbl.; ['Souv. de Claudius Denoyel' × 'Mme Edouard Herriot']

'Mme Roger Verlomme' HT, pb, 1951, Mallerin, C.; flowers ochre edged flesh-pink, very large, very dbl.; very vigorous growth

'Mme Roland' HP, pb, 1869, Roland; flowers flesh pink with salmon shades, large, full

'Mme Rolland' HGal, dp, before 1835, Girardon

'Mme Rolland' HP, dp, Moreau & Robert; flowers very large, full; ['Victor Verdier' × unknown]; intr. 1867

'Mme Rosa Monnet' ('Rosa Monnet') HP, dp, 1885, Monnet; flowers light crimson, large, cupped, moderate sweet fragrance; good repeat

'Mme Rose Caron' HP, mp, 1898, Lévêque; flowers monotone pink, nuanced carmine at center, large; foliage light green

'Mme Rose Chéri' M , mp, 1850, Laffay, M.; flowers delicate pink, medium, dbl.; foliage blackish green

'Mme Rose Romarin' T, rb, 1888, Nabonnand; bud tall, pointed; flowers light coppery red with salmon, large, full, moderate fragrance; ['Papillon' × 'Chromatella']

'Mme Roudillon' HP, mr, 1903, Vigneron; flowers bright carmine red, very large, very full, intense fragrance; foliage dark green; ['Mme Isaac Pereire' × 'Mme Ernest Levavasseur']

'Mme Roussel' ('Eugénie Jauvin') T, w, 1830, Desprez; flowers white, center flesh pink, large

'Mme Rousset' HP, lp, 1864, Guillot; flowers light silvery pink, large, full, cupped

'Mme Royet' LCl, m

'Mme Rozain-Boucharlat' T, yb, 1894, Liabaud; flowers chamois yellow, shaded pink, large, full, globular

'Mme Ruau' HFt, pb, 1909, Gravereaux; flowers orange/pink with dark yellow, large, dbl.; ['Pharisäer' × 'Les Rosati']

'Mme S. Croza' HT, ab, 1935, Laperrière; bud long; flowers flesh-pink, very large, dbl., high-centered; foliage leathery; long stems; vigorous growth; ['Sunburst' × unknown]

'Mme S. Mottet' N, my, 1899, Cochet-Cochet; bud pink; ['William Allen Richardson' × unknown]

'Mme Sachi' HT, w, Meilland; intr. 1984

'Mme Sancy de Parabère' ('Mme de Sancy de Parabère') Bslt, mp, 1874, Bonnet; flowers bright violet-pink, 5 in., semi-dbl. to dbl., peony-shaped, borne in clusters of 3-5, moderate clove fragrance; very early, non-recurrent bloom; thornless; growth to 7 ft.; very hardy; cross between a Boursault and a form of R. centifolia; intr. 1874

'Mme Saportas' HGal, dp; flowers bright rosy red, large, dbl.

'Mme Savary' HRg, dr, 1901, L'Hay; flowers red-violet

'Mme Schmitt' HP, mp, 1854, Schmitt; flowers rosy pink, shaded carmine, reverse silvery white, 12-15 cm., full; few prickles; growth upright

'Mme Schmitt' HT, ab, Schwartz, A.; flowers salmon-pink, shaded peach-blossom-pink, dbl.; intr. 1922

'Mme Schultz' N, yb, 1856, Béluze; flowers pale yellow, center darker, medium, dbl., intense fragrance; vigorous growth

'Mme Schwaller' HT, mp, 1886, Bernaix, A.; flowers large; vigorous growth

'Mme Scipion Cochet' HP, rb, 1872, Desmazures/Cochet; flowers shining cherry pink edged soft pink and white, center petals wrinkled, dbl., cupped; vigorous growth

Mme Scipion Cochet™ T, pb, Bernaix, A.; flowers pale pink to white, center yellow, large, dbl., cupped, moderate fragrance; vigorous growth; ['Anna Olivier' × 'Duchesse de Brabant']; intr. 1887

'Mme Segond Weber' HT, op, 1907, Soupert & Notting; bud ovoid, pointed; flowers clear salmon-pink, very large, dbl., cupped, moderate fragrance; long, strong stems; bushy growth; ['Antoine Rivoire' × 'Souv. de Victor Hugo']

'Mme Segond Weber, Climbing' Cl HT, op, 1911, Ardagh (also Reymond, 1929); flowers salmon pink, very large, full; [sport of 'Mme Segond Weber']

'Madame Seneclause' HT, lp

'Madame Shizuko' HT, mp, Hiroshima; intr. 1998

'Mme Simon Delaux' T, yb, 1891, Degressy; flowers yellow, shaded copper

'Mme Soetmans' -- See 'Mme Zoetmans'

'Mme Soledad de Ampuera de Leguizamon' HT, pb, 1928, Soupert & Notting; flowers hydrangea-pink, reverse carmine-rose, dbl.; ['General-Superior Arnold Janssen' × 'Mrs E.G. Hill']

'Mme Solvay' LCl, dp, Eve, A.; flowers crimson, flecked white at base, medium, semi-dbl., borne in large clusters, moderate fragrance; intr. 1992

'Mme Sophie Charlotte' A, lp, Weihrauch; intr. 1986

'Mme Sophie Froppot' ('Mme Sophie Tropot') HP, mp, 1876, Levet; flowers pale satin rose, large, dbl., cupped; foliage nearly thornless; ['Victor Verdier' × unknown]

'Mme Sophie Stern' HP, dp, 1887, Lévêque; flowers brilliant light bright rose, with metallic reflections, very large, dbl., globular

'Mme Sophie Tropot' -- See 'Mme Sophie Froppot'

'Mme Soubeyran' ('Mme de Soubeyran') HP, dp, 1872, Gonod; flowers bright rose, small, full

'Mme Souchet' B, pb, 1843, Souchet; flowers bluish rose pink, edges lighter, large, very full

'Mme Soupert' M, mr, 1851, Moreau & Robert; bud well mossed; flowers cerise red, medium, full, rosette, borne in small clusters

'Mme Soupert' HP, w, Portemer; flowers flesh white, medium, full; intr. 1863

'Mme Soupert' HP, w, Pernet; flowers pure white, medium, full; perhaps the same as Mme Soupert from Portemer, 1863; intr. 1864

'Mme Souveton' P, pb, 1874, Pernet père; flowers delicate pink, medium, full, cupped

'Mme Spotti' HT, m, 1955, Privat; flowers pink striped mauve, very dbl.; foliage glossy; very vigorous growth

'Mme Standish' ('Mrs Standish') HP, mp, 1860, Trouillard; flowers bright pink, medium, full

'Mme Steffen' HT, w, 1900, Buatois; flowers flesh white, large, full; ['Irene Watts' × 'Mavourneen']

'Mme Steinbach' HT, pb, 1934, Caron, B.; bud very long; flowers coppery pink tinted coral, very large, dbl.; ['Mrs Pierre S. duPont' × 'Cécile Walter']

'Mme Stolz' D, ly, before 1848; flowers pale straw yellow, medium to large, full, cupped, moderate fragrance; foliage light green

'Mme Suzanne Hervé' HP, dr, 1936, Hervé; bud very long, pointed; flowers velvety red, heavily streaked maroon; vigorous growth; ['Baron Girod de l'Ain' × unknown]

'Mme Taft' Pol, dp, 1909, Levavasseur; flowers ruby-pink medium, dbl., borne in clusters; vigorous, bushy growth; ['Crimson Rambler' × 'Mme Norbert Levavasseur']

'Mme Taha Hussein' HT, rb, 1939, Colombier; flowers Indian red, reverse darker, semi-dbl.; vigorous growth; ['Charles P. Kilham' × 'Betty Uprichard']

'Madame Takagi' HT, m, Teranishi; intr. 2007

'Mme Teresa Estaban' -- See 'Coral Fiesta'

'Mme Th. Cattier' T, my, 1900, Bénard; flowers canary yellow, medium, very full

'Mme Théobald Sernin' HP, mr, 1877, Brassac; flowers currant-red nuanced carmine, large, full

'Mme Théodore Cornet' HP, mr, 1899, Bénard; flowers currant red

'Mme Théodore Delacourt' HT, mp, 1913, Pernet-Ducher; bud long, rosy-scarlet; flowers reddish-salmon nuanced light yellow, large, very dbl., globular; foliage bronzy reddish green; prickles unequal, protrusive, few

'Mme Théodore Vernes' HP, mp, 1891, Lévêque; flowers bright pink with lighter edges, large, full; foliage dark green

'Mme Thérèse Deschamps' T, pb, 1888, Nabonnand; bud crimson; flowers very bright pink, striped on the upper surface with carmine, reverse whitish, large, semi-dbl., borne in small clusters; foliage thick, matte bronze-green; prickles few, small; growth erect

'Mme Thérèse Levet' -- See 'Mlle Thérèse Levet'

'Mme Therese Roswell' ('Mme Rathswell') T, dp, 1906, California Nursery Co.; bud carmine; flowers rose pink with deeper shadings, small; nearly thornless

'Mme Thévenot' HP, dr, 1878, Jamain, H.; flowers bright red, large, very dbl.

'Mme Thibaut' HP, lp, 1889, Lévêque; flowers delicate satiny pink nuanced carmine pink, dbl., camellia-like; foliage bright green

'Mme Thiers' B, pb, 1873, Pradel; flowers pink, center brighter, edged violet, medium, full

'Mme Tiret' HRg, mr, 1901, Gravereaux & Müller; flowers bright red, with silvery pink exterior, large, semi-dbl., cupped, borne mostly solitary; foliage large, light green, slightly dentate; prickles small, straight; stems reddish; [('Pierre Notting' × 'Cardinal Patrizzi') × 'Germanica']

'Mme Tixier' -- See 'Souv d'un Ami'

'Mme Tony Baboud' HT, my, 1895, Godard; flowers medium golden yellow, large, semi-dbl.

'Mme Tressan' -- See 'Mme de Tressan'

'Mme Trifle' N, yb, 1869, Levet; flowers deep yellow, center salmon yellow with copper, 9-10 cm., very dbl., cupped, moderate fragrance; good repeat; foliage large; tall, vigorous, climbing growth; ['Gloire de Dijon' × unknown]

'Mme Trotter' -- See 'Mme de Trotter'

'Mme Trottier' HT, yb, 1937, Leenders, M.; flowers yellowish-flesh, large, very dbl.; vigorous, bushy growth

'Mme Trudeaux' HP, dp, 1850, Boll; flowers shining dark pink, aging lighter pink, medium to large, full

'Mme Tsiranana' ('Mme Ph. Tsirnana') HT, mr, Croix; intr. 1971

'Mme V. Morrell' -- See 'V. Viviand-Morel'

'Mme Vachez' B, lp, 1864, Ducher; flowers whitish pink, very large

'Mme Valembourg' HP, m, 1863, Oger; flowers shining purple, shaded violet, large, full

'Mme Van de Voorde' HT, mr, 1928, Mallerin, C.; bud pointed; flowers brilliant scarlet, large, semi-dbl., cupped; very vigorous growth; ['Mme Méha Sabatier' × 'Kitchener of Khartoum']

'Mme van Houtte' HP, dp, 1857, Margottin; flowers dark pink, aging to flesh pink

'Mme Vannier' HT, or, Orard, Joseph; flowers coppery red, large, dbl., cupped

'Madame Verbelen' HT, dr, 1976, Delforge; flowers 4½ in., 65 petals, cupped, profuse bloom, intense fragrance; intr. 1973

'Mme Verdier' HP, w, 1840, Verdier, V.; sepals very long; flowers pale flesh; foliage gray-green

'Mme Verlot' HP, mp, 1876, Verdier, E.; flowers velvety pink, very large, very full, slightly cupped

'Mme Vermorel' T, yb, 1901, Mari/Jupeau; flowers dark coppery yellow with bronze center, medium, dbl.

'Mme Verrier-Cachet' HP, mr, 1895, Chédane-Guinoisseau; flowers carmine-red, very large, dbl.

'Mme Veuve Alexandre Pommery' ('Mme Alexandre Pommery', 'Mme Veuve Alexis Pommery') HP, lp, 1882, Lévêque; flowers delicate pink, nuanced bright pink within, petal edges very light pink, very large; foliage large, dark green

'Mme Veuve Alexis Pommery' -- See 'Mme Veuve Alexandre Pommery'

'Mme Veuve Ménier' HT, lp, 1891, Schwartz; flowers pale light rose, nuanced dawn gold and carmine, large, very full; foliage glaucous green; stems tinted purple; ['Camoëns' × unknown]

'Mme Vibert' HP, dp, about 1835, Vibert; flowers deep rose pink, edges carmine, medium, full

'Mme Victor Bozzola' HT, mp, 1935, Soupert, C.; bud pointed; flowers bright coral-pink, well-formed, large; ['Kardinal Piffl' × 'Mme Edouard Herriot']

'Mme Victor Caillet' T, pb, 1891, Bernaix; flowers peony pink with carmine and salmon, fading to white, large, dbl., cupped

'Mme Victor Lottin' HWich, rb, 1921, Lottin; flowers dark red, shaded crimson; vigorous, climbing growth

'Mme Victor Morlot' T, m, 1906, Chauvry; flowers violet-pink, base lighter, large, full; ['Marquise de Vivens' × 'Mme Caro']

'Mme Victor Rault' HT, w, 1920, Croibier; flowers white tinted salmon, center yellow,, dbl.; ['Mme Mélanie Soupert' × 'Lyon Rose']

'Mme Victor Verdier' HP, mr, 1863, Verdier, E.; flowers clear light crimson, large, 75 petals, flat, intense fragrance; seasonal bloom; vigorous growth; ['Senateur Vaisse' × unknown]

'Mme Victor Wibaut' HP, op, 1870, David; flowers salmon pink, medium, full

'Mme Vidot' HP, ab, 1854, Couturier; sepals long, acuminate; flowers flesh-white, large, full; foliage smooth, light green, oval-elliptical; prickles unequal, nearly straight, very sharp

'Mme Viger' HT, lp, 1901, Jupeau; flowers creamy pink, very large, dbl.; ['Heinrich Schultheis' × 'G. Nabonnand']

'Mme Vigneron' HP, op, 1858, Vigneron; flowers peach-pink, large, full

'Mme Villate' HT, ob, 1936, Walter, L.; flowers orange with yellow, dbl.; foliage glossy; ['Korovo' × seedling]

'Mme Ville' HGal, mp, before 1885; flowers carmine pink, medium, full

'Mme Vincent Auriol' HT, yb, 1951, Caron, B.; bud long; flowers golden coral, large, dbl., peony-like; foliage glossy; vigorous growth; ['Trylon' × seedling]

'Madame Violet' HT, m, 1986, Teranishi, K.; flowers lavender, 45 petals, high-centered, borne singly, no fragrance; foliage medium size, medium green, semi-glossy; prickles medium, reddish light-green; tall, upright growth; PP6315; intr. 1981

'Madame Violet, Climbing' Cl HT, m, 1999; flowers pale violet, 5½ in., 45 petals, high-centered, no fragrance; growth to 9-12 ft.; intr. 1992

'Mme Virgilio Pirola' HT, mr, 1939, Lens; bud long, pointed; flowers very bright red, dbl.; foliage dark; vigorous, bushy growth; ['Charles P. Kilham' × 'Étoile de Hollande']

'Mme Visseaux' HT, op, 1936, Mallerin, C.; bud long; flowers orange-pink, base yellow, 4-5 in., dbl.; ['Odette Foussier' × 'Elvira Aramayo']

'Mme Vittoria Gagnière' HT, w, 1909, Schwartz, Vve.; flowers white tinted pink; ['Anna Chartron' × 'Mrs W. J. Grant']

'Mme Viviand-Morel' Ayr, dp, 1882, Schwartz; flowers carmine pink tinted cerise, reverse violet-white, medium, full, borne in clusters; foliage reddish green; [R. arvensis × 'Cheshunt Hybrid']

'Mme Viviand-Morel' HP, mr, Bernaix; flowers carmine red with cherry-garnet shades, very large, dbl.; intr. 1887

'Mme Von Boch' -- See 'Frau Geheimrat Von Boch'

'Mme von Siemens' T, mp, 1895, Nabonnand; bud long; flowers flesh pink, very large, full

'Mme W. Baumann' HT, rb; flowers clear satin red-orange, large, dbl., high-centered; growth to 60-70 cm.; intr. 1973

'Mme W. C. Whitney' -- See 'Mrs W. C. Whitney'

'Mme Wagram, Comtesse de Turenne' T, pb, 1894, Bernaix, A.; flowers bright satiny rose suffused with darker rose, very large, full, moderate fragrance; vigorous growth; sometimes classed as HT

'Mme Walter Baumann' HT, rb, 1934, Reymond; bud long; flowers carmine, base yellow, open, dbl.; ['Mlle Franziska Kruger' × 'Gwynne Carr']

'Mme Welche' T, yb, 1878, Widow Ducher; bud pointed; flowers coppery orange-yellow within, outer petals pale yellow, large, full, globular, intense fragrance; growth vigorous

'Mme Willermoz' -- See 'Mme Mélanie Willermoz'

'Mme William' T, ly, 1856, Lartay; flowers straw yellow

'Mme William Paul' HP, m, 1862, Verdier, E.; flowers violet-purple, edged bright crimson, aging to flesh pink, medium to large, full

'Mme William Paul' ('Mrs William Paul') M, dp, Moreau & Robert; flowers bright rose, large, dbl., cupped; recurrent bloom; intr. 1869

'Mme William Wood' HP, pb, 1876, Verdier, E.; flowers carmine pink, centers bright red, edges lighter, large, very full

'Mme York' HP, dr, 1881, Moreau et Robert; flowers vermilion red shaded carmine and nuanced blackish purple, large, dbl., intense fragrance; foliage dark green

'Mme Yves Latieule' ('Nankin', 'Yves Latieule') HT, my, 1949, Meilland, F.; flowers primrose-yellow, 5 in., 70 petals; foliage glossy, dark; vigorous growth; PP1001; ['Mme Joseph Perraud' × 'Léonce Colombier']

'Mme Yvette Gayraud' HT, ob, Wisbech Plant Co.

'Mme Yvonne Chaverot' HT, op, Orard, Joseph; flowers rose-salmon, with yellow reverse, large, dbl; foliage glossy, disease-resistant; intr. 1976

'Mme Zélia Bourgeois' Pol, w, 1906, Vilin; flowers pure white, full, moderate fragrance; ['Bouquet de Neige' × 'miniature seedling']

'Mme Zoetmans' ('Mme Soetmans', 'Mme Zoutmann') D, w, 1830, Marest; flowers pale flesh, tinged with buff, medium, with a small green eye at center, very dbl., cupped, early bloomer, moderate fragrance; non-recurrent; foliage medium green, with 5-7 leaflets; few prickles; bushy, vigorous (5 ft.) growth

'Mme Zoutmann' -- See 'Mme Zoetmans'

'Madames de Villeparisis' M, pb, Morley, Dr B.; [sport of 'Henri Martin']

'Mmes Soeurs Chevandier' HP, dr, 1864, Pernet; flowers slatey-wine red, medium

'Madcap' F, mr, 1956, Kordes; bud urn-shaped; flowers scarlet-red, 4½ in., 20-25 petals, cupped, moderate fragrance; foliage leathery; bushy growth; PP1363; ['Independence' × 'Crimson King']; intr. 1954

'Madcap' HT, rb, 1955, Ratcliffe; bud dark red; flowers flame-scarlet striped yellow, or orange without stripe; [sport of 'Grand Duchesse Charlotte']

'Maddalena' HT, op, 1934, San Remo Exp. Sta.; bud pointed to ovoid; flowers salmon-pink, reverse begonia-rose, very large, 30-32 petals, cupped; foliage light green, glossy, leathery; long stems; very vigorous, upright, bushy growth; ['Julien Potin' × 'J. C. Thornton']

'Maddalena Scalarandis' Ch, dp, 1901, Scalarandis; flowers dark, rich rose with touches of scarlet and crimson, large; probably extinct

'Madeleine, Climbing' Cl HT, ly; intr. 2005

'Madeleine' MinFl, yb, 2005, Guillebeau, Ray; flowers yellow, edged pink or red depending on weather, reverse yellow, 1½ in., dbl., borne mostly solitary, no fragrance; foliage medium size, dark green, matte; prickles medium length, straight, slight downward angle, lt. green; bushy, medium (24-30 in.) growth; exhibition, garden decoration; ['Fairhope' × unknown]; intr. 2005

'Madeleine' HT, ly, Kordes; greenhouse rose; intr. before 2005

'Madeleine d'Aoust' T, lp, 1889, Bernaix; flowers light flesh pink, aging white, large, full

'Madeleine de Garnier des Garets' T, pb, 1900, Buatois; flowers dark coppery pink, very large, full

'Madeleine de Vauzelle' -- See 'Mlle Madeleine de Vauzelles'

'Madeleine Faivre' HT, lp, 1902, Buatois; flowers pinkish white, yellow center, large, very dbl.

'Madeleine Gaillard' HT, w, 1908, Bernaix; flowers white and cream, large, cupped

'Madeleine Guillaumez' T, w, 1892, Bonnaire; flowers white with salmony center, medium, globular; growth vigorous, upright; ['tea seedling' × 'Mlle de Sombreuil']

'Madeleine Lemaire' HWich, op, 1923, Nonin; bud medium, long-pointed; flowers bright salmon-pink, 5-6 cm., semi-dbl., cupped, slight fragrance; ['Mrs F.W. Flight' × unknown]

'Madeleine Lemoine' HG, w, before 1930, Franchetti; flowers cream-white, large, single to semi-dbl., moderate fragrance; [R. gigantea × R. moschata]

'Madeleine Monod' HT, op, 1939, Chambard, C.; bud long; flowers salmon-carmine, very large, dbl.; foliage bronze; vigorous growth

'Madeleine Nonin' -- See 'Mlle Madeleine Nonin'

'Madeleine Orosdy' Pol, mp, 1912, Gravereaux

'Madeleine Pacaud' HT, op, 1922, Chambard, C.; flowers silvery rose, tinted salmon

Madeleine Rivoire® HT, lp, Orard; intr. 1988

'Madeleine Seltzer' ('Madeleine Selzer', 'Mme Selzer', 'Yellow Tausendschön') HMult, ly, 1926, Walter, L.; flowers pale lemon, fading white, 5-6 cm., full, borne in large clusters; non-recurrent; foliage large; few prickles; vigorous growth; ['Tausendschön' × 'Mrs Aaron Ward']

'Madeleine Selzer' -- See 'Madeleine Seltzer'

'Madeleine Weidert' HMult, mp, 1928, Walter, L.; flowers rose-pink; ['Tausendschön' × 'Rosel Dach']

'Madeline' -- See 'Meijacolet'

'Madeline' ('Emmeline') HEg, w, Prévost; flowers creamy white edged pink, semi-dbl., borne in clusters, moderate fragrance; much confusion exists between this an a HCh of the same name; intr. about 1836

'Madeline Correy' HT, dp, 1971, Watson; bud globular; flowers cerise, medium, dbl., moderate lemon fragrance; foliage glossy, dark; moderate growth; ['Minnie Watson' × 'Sterling Silver']

'Madeline Spezzano' -- See 'Tinmad'

'Madeline's Choice' S, ab, Erskine; flowers pale yellow and pink, single, moderate fragrance; non-remontant, long blooming season

'Madelon' -- See 'Ruimeva'

'Madelon de Paris' F, Robichon, M.; intr. 1961

'Madelon Friquet' HGal, pb, 1842, Vibert; flowers rosy pink, spotted lighter, medium, very full; growth branching

'Madelyn Lang' Cl Min, dp, 1975, Williams, Ernest D.; bud slightly ovoid; flowers deep pink, 1 in., very dbl.; foliage small, glossy, dark, embossed; upright growth; ['Little Darling' × 'Little Chief']; intr. 1974

'Mademoiselle' -- See 'Meiplovon'

'Mademoiselle' F, dp, 1950, Boerner; bud ovoid; flowers rose-red, large, 50-60 petals; very vigorous, branching growth; PP1027; ['Goldilocks' × 'Marionette']

'Mlle Adèle Jougant' Cl T, my, 1862, Lédéchaux; flowers clear yellow, medium, dbl.; foliage small, light yellowish-green; ['Mlle de Sombreuil' × unknown]

'Mlle Adèle Launay' HP, dp, 1863, Boyau; flowers bright dark pink, large, full

'Mlle Adelina Viviand-Morel' N, ab, 1890, Bernaix; flowers apricot-yellow, shaded golden, with flesh pink reflections, medium to large, dbl., globular

'Mlle Alice Furon' HT, ly, 1896, Pernet-Ducher; flowers yellowish-white, large, full, globular; ['Lady Mary Fitzwilliam' × 'Mme Chedane-Guinoisseau']

'Mlle Alice Leroi' M, m, 1842, Vibert; flowers light violet-pink, medium, dbl.

'Mlle Alice Leroy' M, lp, 1856, Trouillard; flowers delicate pink, medium, full; some repeat

'Mlle Alice Marchand' B, lp, 1891, Vigneron; flowers delicate pink, shading to blush white, large, full

'Mlle Alice Morhange' HP, dp, 1879, Bernède; flowers velvety carmine, large, full, globular

'Mlle Alice Rousseau' Pol, lp, 1903, Vilin; flowers small, dbl.

'Mlle Amélie Halphen' HP, mp, 1864, Margottin; flowers bright carmine pink, very full

'Mlle Andrée Dourthe' N, mp, 1903, Chauvry; flowers silky procelain pink, becoming silvery pink, striped white, reverse lilac, large, full; ['Triomphe de la Duchère' × unknown]

'Mlle Andrée Worth' B, lp, 1890, Lévêque; flowers light pinkish white, sometimes washed with carmine, large, full; quite remontant; foliage glaucous green

'Mlle Angeline Seringe' HP, mp, 1852, Bernède; flowers bright pink, large, full

'Mlle Anna Charron' ('Mlle Anna Chartron') T, yb, 1896, Widow Schwartz; bud very long; flowers cream-yellow, washed lilac-rose, large, full, borne mostly solitary; foliage somber green edged purple; growth vigorous; ['Kaiserin Auguste Viktoria' × 'Luciole']

'Mlle Anna Chartron' -- See 'Mlle Anna Charron'

'Mlle Anna Vigier' T, yb, 1901, Puyravaud; flowers golden, shaded pink, with salmon tints, medium to large, full, moderate fragrance; ['General Schablikine' × 'Mlle Lazarine Poizeau']

'Mlle Annette Murat' T, my, 1884, Levet; flowers citron yellow, medium, full; ['Gloire de Dijon' × unknown]

'Mlle Annie Wood' ('Annie Wood') HP, mr, 1866, Verdier, E.; flowers clear red, 3½-4 in., dbl., moderate fragrance; recurrent bloom; foliage dark green; prickles strong, straight; stems reddish

'Mlle Antonia Decarly' T, dy, 1873, Levet; flowers dark canary yellow, full

'Mlle Antonine Veysset' T, yb, 1874, Veysset; flowers yellow, shaded red

'Mlle Argentine Cramon' ('Argentine Cramon') HT, w, 1915, Chambard; flowers white, center tinted salmon-rose, very large, full

'Mlle Aristide' N, ly, 1857, Robert; flowers straw yellow, centers reddish or shaded pink, large, full

'Mlle Aristide' ('Aristide') M, dp, Laffay; flowers velvety carmine with very dark crimson, medium, full, globular; intr. 1858

'Mlle Augustine Guinoisseau' -- See 'Augustine Guinoisseau'

'Mlle Bep van Rossem' HT, my, 1926, Van Rossem; flowers deep canary-yellow, dbl.; [seedling × 'Souv. de Claudius Pernet']

'Mlle Berger' B, lp, 1884, Pernet père; flowers delicate pink, orange, full; quite remontant; growth upright

'Mlle Bertha Ludi' Pol, w, 1891, Pernet-Ducher; flowers white with carmine pink, becoming flesh white, full; ['Mignonnette' × 'Jules Margottin']

'Mlle Berthe Chanu' HP, dp, 1867, Fontaine; flowers bright carmine, large, full

'Mlle Berthe Clavel' B, w, 1892, Chauvry; flowers white, center pink over yellow base, reverse tinted violet, large, full; [sport of 'Souv de la Malmaison']

'Mlle Berthe Lévêque' ('Berthe Lévêque') HP, lp, 1865, Céchet père; flowers flesh white, changing to pink, small; foliage large, rough; growth upright

'Mlle Berthe Levet' HP, mp, 1865, Cochet; flowers large, full

'Mlle Blanche Durrschmidt' T, lp, 1878, Guillot fils; flowers flesh pink, aging to white, medium, dbl., borne mostly singly and small clusters; foliage glossy; prickles hooked, few; ['Mme Falcot' × unknown]

'Mlle Blanche Lafitte' ('Blanche Lafitte') B, lp, 1851, Pradel; flowers whitish-rose, medium, dbl., borne in clusters, moderate fragrance; repeats in autumn; vigorous growth

'Mlle Blanche Martignat' T, yb, 1902, Gamon; flowers salmon, shaded with dawn-pink, creped, intense fragrance; [possibly a seedling of 'Marie Van Houtte']

'Mlle Blanche Rebatel' -- See 'Blanche Rebatel'

'Mlle Bonnaire' HP, w, 1859, Pernet père; flowers white, center sometimes pink, dbl.; growth moderate

'Mlle Brigitte Viollet' HT, m, 1878, Levet; flowers silvery-rose, tinged with violet, large, full, borne in small clusters; ['Antonine Verdier' × unknown]

'Mlle C. Riguet' -- See 'Caroline Riguet'

'Mlle Camille de Rochetaillée' Pol, w, 1886, Bernaix; flowers white, shaded carmine, medium, full, moderate fragrance

'Mlle Cécile Brünner' ('Cécile Brünner', 'Mme Cécile Brünner', 'Mignon', 'Sweetheart Rose') Pol, lp, 1880, Ducher, Vve.; bud long, pointed; flowers bright pink on yellow ground, small, dbl., borne in clusters, moderate fragrance; foliage sparse, soft, dark, 3-5 leaflets; prickles very few; growth like a tea, dwarf; ['a climbing polyantha' × 'Mme de Tartas']

'Mlle Cécile Brünner, Climbing' ('Cécile Brünner, Climbing', 'Mme Cécile Brünner, Climbing', 'Mignon, Climbing', 'Sweetheart Rose, Climbing') Cl Pol, lp, 1894, Hosp (also Ardagh, 1904); flowers soft, light pink, fading in sun, 2 in., borne in very large clusters, intense fragrance; good repeat; [sport of 'Mlle Cécile Brunner']

'Mlle Charlotte de la Trémoille' ('Princesse Charlotte de la Trémoille') HP, lp, 1877, Chédane-Guinoisseau; flowers very large, full, globular

'Mlle Christine de Noué' ('Christine de Noué') T, rb, 1890, Guillot; flowers deep rosy crimson, center shaded with salmon-rose, very large, full, moderate fragrance

'Mlle Claire Andruejol' HT, lp, 1920, Schwartz, A.; flowers pale pink tinted carmine, dbl.; ['Comte G. de Rochemur' × 'Mme Maurice de Luze']

'Mlle Claire Jacquier' -- See 'Claire Jacquier'

'Mlle Claire Truffaut' B, lp, 1887, Verdier, E.; flowers silvery pink medium, dbl.; prickles hooked, pinkish

'Mlle Clarisse Juranville' HT, lp, 1903, Corboeuf; [sport of 'Mme Caroline Testout']

'Mlle Claudine Perreau' -- See 'Mlle Claudine Perreault'

'Mlle Claudine Perreault' ('Mlle Claudine Perreau') T, mp, 1885, Lambert, E.; flowers rose flesh, center darker, very large, dbl.; free bloom; ['Souv d'Un Ami' × unknown]

'Mlle Danielle Dumur' HT, lp, 1910, Laroulandie; flowers delicate pink, fading to silvery pink, large, dbl., moderate fragrance; [sport of 'Mme Caroline Testout']

'Mlle de Dinant' F, w, 1979, Lens, Louis; bud globular; flowers creamy white, open, 3-3½ in., 22 petals, intense fruity fragrance; foliage light green; vigorous, spreading growth; ['Purpurine' × 'Lavender Pinocchio']; intr. 1966

'Mlle de la Vallette' HCh, rb, 1910, Schwartz; flowers coppery red over gold base, reverse ruby red, medium, very full, moderate fragrance; ['Mme Eugène Résal' × 'Aurore']

'Mlle de Labarthe' -- See 'Duchesse de Brabant'

'Mlle de Morlaincourt' HT, pb, 1934, Walter, L.; flowers pink and yellow; ['Cécile Walter' × 'Korovo']

'Mlle de Neux' HT, dp, 1901, Berland; flowers carmine-pink, medium, dbl.; ['Mme Caroline Testout' × unknown]

'Mlle de Sombreuil' ('La Biche', 'Mme de Sombreuil') T, w, 1850, Robert; flowers creamy white, often tinted pink, well-formed, large, dbl.; vigorous growth; [reputed to be a seedling of 'Parks' Yellow Tea-Scented China']; incorrectly called La Biche by some nurseries.

'Mlle Denise de Reverseau' -- See 'Cornelia Cook'

'Mlle Eglantine Guillot' ('Eglantine Guillot') F, op, Guillot; flowers orange pink, dbl., open, borne in clusters; growth to 2 ft.; intr. 1987

'Mlle Eléonore Grier' HP, dp, 1876, Verdier, E.; flowers large, full

'Mlle Elisabeth de la Rocheterie' HP, lp, 1881, Vigneron; flowers delicate flesh pink, reverse silvery, very large, full; quite remontant; foliage dark green; prickles numerous, chestnut brown; growth upright

'Mlle Elisabeth Marcel' N, yb, 1901, Berland; flowers coppery yellow, with metallic pink, reverse China pink, aging whitish pink; ['Ophirie' × unknown]

'Mlle Elise Chabrier' -- See 'Mlle Louise Chabrier'

'Mlle Emain' B, w, 1861, Pernet; flowers white with light pink center, large, full

'Mlle Emélie Verdier' HP, mp, 1875, Verdier, E.; flowers carmine pink, large, full, moderate fragrance

'Mlle Emélie Verdier, Climbing' Cl HP, lp, 1878, Paul, G.; [sport of 'Mlle Emélie Verdier']

'Mlle Emilienne Moreau' HT, yb, 1920, Verschuren; flowers dark yellow and creamy pink, medium, semi-dbl.

'Mlle Emma Hall' HP, op, 1876, Liabaud; flowers shining carmine and salmon pink, revers lighter, large, full, globular; ['Souv de la Reine d'Angleterre' × unknown]

'Mlle Emma Vercellone' T, rb, 1901, Schwartz; bud long; flowers bright coppery red, golden yellow at base, fading to coppery salmon pink, large, full; foliage purple red; ['Chamoïs' × 'Mme Laurette Messimy']

'Mlle Eugénie Savary' -- See 'Mme Eugénie Savary'

'Mlle Eugénie Verdier' M, mr, Schwartz; intr. 1872

'Mlle Eugénie Verdier ' HP, w, 1859, Verdier, E.; flowers white, edged pink

'Mlle Eugénie Verdier' ('Marie Finger', 'Mme Marie Finger') HP, mp, Guillot et Fils; flowers clear silvery pink, reverse silvery white, large, very dbl., moderate fragrance; vigorous, upright growth; ['Victor Verdier' × unknown]; intr. 1869

'Mlle Favart' B, lp, 1869, Lévêque; flowers light satiny pink, lightly edged white, medium, full

'Mlle Félicité Trouillot' B, mp, 1861,

Verdier, E.; flowers bright pink, medium, semi-dbl.

'Mlle Fernande de la Forest' HP, pb, 1872, Damaizin; flowers deep pink, reverse white, large, full

'Mlle Fernande Dupuy' Pol, dp, 1899, Vigneron; flowers carmine-pink, small, dbl.

'Mlle Franziska Krüger' ('Francisca Krüger', 'Frau Franziska Krüger', 'Grand Duc Héritier de Luxembourg') T, op, 1879, Nabonnand, G.; flowers coppery yellow and pink, center often green, large, very dbl., moderate fragrance; weak stems; hardy for this class; ['Catherine Mermet' × 'Gén. Schablikine']

'Mlle Gabrielle de Peyronny' HP, mr, 1863, Lacharme; flowers fiery red, nuanced violet towards center

'Mlle Gabrielle Touvais' HP, dp

'Mlle Geneviève Godard' T, yb, 1889, Godard; flowers yellow with pink and orange, medium, dbl.

'Mlle Germaine Caillot' HT, op, 1887, Pernet-Ducher; bud long; flowers salmon flesh pink, brighter at center, white at edge, very large, full, borne mostly solitary; foliage dark green; prickles few, nearly straight; growth upright; ['Baronne Adolphe de Rothschild' × 'Mme Falcot']

'Mlle Germaine Trochon' HT, pb, 1893, Pernet-Ducher; flowers salmon pink, aging to yellow-pink, center orange-nankeen, edges pink, large, full, globular, moderate fragrance; ['Victor Verdier' × 'Mme Eugene Verdier']

'Mlle Godard' HP, mp, 1857, Ducher

'Mlle Grévy' -- See 'Mlle Jules Grévy'

'Mlle Guiomar Cotrim' T, yb, about 1908, Fontes; flowers light yellow, edges carmine, large, full, moderate fragrance; ['Marie Budlow' × unknown]

'Mlle Hélène Croissandeau' HP, mp, 1882, Vigneron; bud very elongated; flowers velvety pink, center brighter, very large; quite remontant; foliage dark green; few prickles; growth upright; ['Victor Verdier' × unknown]

'Mlle Hélène Gambier' ('Helen Gambier') HT, op, 1895, Pernet-Ducher; flowers salmon-pink to coppery rose, large, dbl.

'Mlle Hélène Michel' HP, dr, 1883, Vigneron; flowers deep red, center brighter, outer petals velvety, large, full; foliage light green; prickles numerous, chestnut brown

'Mlle Henriette' HP, mp, 1857, Lartay; flowers bright pink

'Mlle Henriette de Beauveau' T, my, 1887, Lacharme

'Mlle Henriette Martin' HT, w, 1936, Reymond; flowers white, shaded ivory, edges lightly tinted pale pink

'Mlle Honorine Duboc' HP, dp, 1894, Duboc; flowers bright wine-pink, very large, dbl., borne mostly solitary; foliage brownish green

'Mlle Hortense Blanchette' B, w, 1860, Damaizin; flowers white touched with pink

'Mlle Irene Hennessy' HT, or, 1923, Guillot, P.; flowers bright vermilion-orange, dbl.; ['George C. Waud' × seedling]

'Mademoiselle Jacqueline' Pol, dp, Weihrauch; intr. 1985

'Mlle Jacquiline Bouvet' HP, dr, 1884, Bernède; flowers dark fiery red, medium to large; ['Aviateur Duvivier' × unknown]

'Mlle Jeanne Guillaumez' T, dp, 1889, Bonnaire; bud long, dark rose; flowers brick red with salmon, dark yellow at base, large, full; foliage evergreen

'Mlle Jeanne Lenail' Pol, mr, 1924, Schwartz, A.; flowers bright ruby-red shaded carmine, large, dbl.; ['Mrs W.H. Cutbush' × 'Mme Taft']

'Mlle Jeanne Marix' HP, m, 1866, Liabaud; flowers garnet purple, often marbled, large, full

'Mlle Jeanne Philippe' ('Jeanne Philippe', 'Mme J. Phillips', 'Mme Jeanne Philippe') T, yb, 1898, Godard; flowers nankeen yellow with chamois reflections, base ocher, edged carmine, very large, full

'Mlle Jenny Gay' -- See 'Jenny Gay'

'Mlle Joséphine Burland' Pol, w, 1886, Bernaix; flowers pure white, aging to light pink. large, very dbl., borne mostly solitary

'Mlle Joséphine Guyet' -- See 'Joséphine Guyet'

'Mlle Joséphine Guyot' -- See 'Joséphine Guyet'

'Mlle Jules Grévy' ('Mlle Grévy') HP, dr, 1879, Gautreau; flowers velvety dark red, large, full; quite remontant; ['Duhamel-Dumonceau' × unknown]

'Mlle Julie Dymonier' -- See 'Julia Dymonier'

'Mlle Julie Péréard' HP, mp, 1872, Pernet; flowers bright pink, very large, full; ['Jules Margottin' × unknown]

'Mlle Juliette Doucet' T, yb, 1881, Bernède; flowers cream yellow, washed with vermilion, large, full

'Mlle Juliette Halphen' HP, lp, 1869, Margottin; flowers light pink, aging flesh white, large, full, globular

'Mlle la Comtesse de Leusse' T, pb, 1878, Nabonnand; bud bright pink; flowers delicate pink with saffron at center

'Mlle Lazarine Poizeau' T, ob, 1876, Levet; flowers orange-yellow, medium, full; foliage glossy, reddish when young; few prickles

'Mlle Lenari la Granada' HT, Dot, Simon; intr. 1982

'Mlle Léonie Giessen' HP, lp, 1876, Lacharme; flowers pink washed white, large, full, centifolia-like; prickles long, recurved; growth bushy

'Mlle Léonie Persin' HP, lp, 1861, Fontaine; flowers frosty, silvery pink, large

'Mlle Loïde de Falloux' HP, w, 1864, Trouillard or Boyeau; flowers white with light pink shades

'Mlle Louise Boyer' HP, dp, 1881, Bernède; flowers silky dark pink, very large, full; ['Jules Margottin' × unknown]

'Mlle Louise Chabrier' ('Mlle Elise Chabrier') HP, lp, 1867, Gautreau/Cochet; flowers delicate pink, edged satiny blush white, large, dbl.

'Mlle Lucie Chauvin' T, op, 1893, Moreau & Robert; flowers salmon yellow, shaded apricot, very large, full, globular

'Mlle Madeleine de Vauzelles' ('Madeleine de Vauzelle') B, lp, 1881, Vigneron; flowers delicate pink, center brighter, large, full; quite remontant; foliage light green; few prickles; growth upright

'Mlle Madeleine Delaroche' T, lp, 1890, Corboeuf; flowers flesh pink, large, very full; ['Mlle Mathilde Lenaerts' × unknown]

'Mlle Madeleine Marot' N, w, 1902, Corboeuf-Marsault; flowers cream white, sometimes edged pink, large, full; ['Rêve d'Or' × 'Dr A. Carlès']

'Mlle Madeleine Nonin' ('Madeleine Nonin') HP, op, 1866, Ducher; flowers pink with some salmon, medium, full, globular

'Mlle Malvine Lartay' HP, mr, about 1855, Lartay; flowers flame red, center violet, medium, full

'Mlle Marcelle Gaugin' Pol, lp, 1910, Corboeuf; flowers creamy pink, small, dbl.

'Mlle Marguérite Appert' ('Marguérite Appert') HT, mr, 1896, Vigneron; flowers bright velvety red, very large, full, globular

'Mlle Marguerite Dombrain' -- See 'Marguerite d'Ombrain'

'Mlle Marie Achard' HP, lp, 1896, Liabaud; flowers delicate frosty pink, very large, cupped; foliage dark green; growth upright

'Mlle Marie Arnaud' T, my, 1872, Levet; flowers canary yellow, aging to white,large, full, moderate fragrance

'Mlle Marie Chauvet' HP, dp, 1881, Besson; flowers deep rose pink, center darker, fading lighter, very large, very full; ['Baronne Adolphe de Rothschild' × unknown]

'Mlle Marie Closon' ('Mme Marie Closon') HP, lp, 1882, Verdier, E.; flowers delicate pink, edged in white, medium to large, very full; foliage elongated, dark green; prickles very numerous, unequal, upright, brown; growth upright

'Mlle Marie Cointet' HP, mp, 1872, Guillot; flowers bright pink, silky, shaded whitish pink, large, full

'Mlle Marie Dauvesse' HP, mp, 1859, Vigneron; flowers bright light pink, medium, full

'Mlle Marie de la Villeboisnet' ('Mlle Marie Villeboisnet') HP, lp, 1864, Trouillard; flowers bright, delicate pink, large, full

'Mlle Marie Drivon' B, pb, 1887, Schwartz; flowers pink shaded with peach, sometimes marbled or spotted with carmine, medium, very dbl., borne in clusters; ['Apolline' × unknown]

'Mlle Marie Gaze' N, pb, 1892, Godard; flowers yellowish-pink with dark yellow,

7 cm., dbl., moderate tea fragrance; stems weak

'Mlle Marie Gonod' HP, lp, 1871, Gonod; flowers flesh white, aging pure white, large, full; ['Mme Laffay' × unknown]

'Mlle Marie Halphen' HP, mp; flowers shining carmine-pink, large, full

'Mlle Marie-Louise Bourgeoise' M, w, 1891, Corboeuf; flowers white, yellow center, large, full; some repeat

'Mlle Marie-Louise Oger' T, w, 1895, Lévêque; flowers milk white, very lightly shaded with yellow, very large; foliage dark green

'Mlle Marie Magat' HP, mr, 1889, Liabaud; flowers carmine-red, large, dbl.

'Mlle Marie Mascuraud' HT, w, 1909, Bernaix, P.; flowers white tinted flesh

'Mlle Marie Moreau' ('Mme Marie Moreau') T, w, 1879, Nabonnand, G.; flowers silver-white flushed crimson, well-formed

'Mlle Marie Page' N, lp, 1894, Corboeuf; flowers glossy light pink, large, full

'Mlle Marie Rady' ('Comtesse de Choiseul', 'Mme Marie Rady', 'Marie Rady') HP, mr, 1865, Fontaine; flowers vermilion-red shaded with crimson, large, very full, globular; foliage glossy; prickles numerous, red

'Mlle Marie Thérèse Coumer' B, mp, 1867, Liabaud; flowers bright, glowing pink, center lighter, large, full

'Mlle Marie Thérèse de la Devansaye' B, w, 1895, Chédane-Guinoisseau; flowers large, full

'Mlle Marie van Houtte' -- See 'Marie van Houtte'

'Mlle Marie Verdier' ('Marie Verdier') HP, mp, 1883, Verdier, E.; flowers bright silky pink, very large, full, moderate fragrance

'Mlle Marie Villeboisnet' -- See 'Mlle Marie de la Villeboisnet'

'Mlle Marthe Cahuzac' Pol, ly, 1901, Ketten Bros.; bud long, pointed; flowers yellowish-white, center silky yellow, passing to whitish pink, medium, full, flat; ['Mignonette' × 'Safrano']

'Mlle Marthe Carron' HWich, w, 1931, Mermet; flowers white, slightly tinted pink on opening, borne in clusters of 40 - 50; vigorous growth; [R. wichurana × R. wichurana]

'Mlle Marthe Moisset' HT, my, 1935, Ducroz; flowers chrome-yellow on ochre ground, very large, cupped; foliage glossy, dark; vigorous, erect, bushy growth; ['Mme Henri Queuille' × seedling]

'Mlle Mathilde Lenaerts' T, lp, 1880, Levet; flowers bright pink, silvered white, large, dbl., quartered, moderate fragrance; ['Gloire de Dijon' × unknown]

'Mlle Maurand' HP, lp; flowers pale flesh

'Mlle Pauline Bersez' HT, w, 1900, Pernet-Ducher; flowers white with cream-yellow center, large, full, globular

'Mlle Portier' HP, dp, 1864, Guillot; flowers bluish pink, medium

'Mlle Rachel' T, w, 1860, Damaizin; flowers greenish white, tinted with sulfur yellow, very large, full

'Mlle Renée Denis' HP, w, 1906, Chédane-Guinoisseau; flowers white with light pink wash, dbl.; ['Margaret Dickson' × 'Paul Neyron']

'Mlle Rosa Bonheur' -- See 'Rosa Bonheur'

'Mlle Simone Beaumez' HT, w, 1907, Pernet-Ducher; flowers flesh-white, center sometimes tinted saffron-yellow, dbl.

'Mlle Sontag' HGal, dp; flowers deep pink, reverse pale blush

'Mlle Sophie de la Villeboisnet' HP, mp, 1867, Touvais; flowers medium to large, full

'Mlle Stella Mallerin' HT, w, 1926, Chambard, C.; bud pointed; flowers white, center slightly shaded cream, very large, dbl., cupped

'Mlle Suzanne Bidard' Pol, op, 1913, Vigneron; bud very long, salmon; flowers light coppery salmon, bases lighter, stamens golden, medium, full, borne in clusters; ['Georges Pernet' × 'Perle d'Or']

'Mlle Suzanne Blanchet' T, mp, 1885, Nabonnand; flowers flesh pink, imbricated, large, very full, cupped, intense fragrance

'Mlle Suzanne-Marie Rodocanachi' -- See 'Suzanne-Marie Rodocanachi'

'Mlle Thérèse Appert' HP, lp, 1855, Trouillard; flowers light pink, shaded darker, large, full

'Mlle Thérèse Levet' ('Mme Thérèse Levet') HP, mp, 1864, Levet; flowers light carmine-rose, large, very dbl., moderate fragrance; ['Jules Margottin' × unknown]

'Mlle Victoire Hélye' HP, pb, 1878, Verdier, E.; flowers fresh pink, edges whitish, medium to large, full

'Mlle Yvette Bouquil' F, yb, 1955, Privat; flowers yellow edged orange; bushy growth

'Mlle Yvonne Gravier' T, yb, 1894, Bernaix; flowers cream yellow, shaded canary yellow, reverse pink, large, full, moderate fragrance

'Mademoiselle's Bouquet' -- See 'Keibian'

'Madeo' -- See 'Korcremkis'

'Madette' HT, op, 1922, Guillot, P.; bud medium, long, pointed, nasturtium-red; flowers coppery orange-pink, medium, full

'Madge Elliott' HT, lp, 1966, Darvall; flowers light pink, center shaded apricot, medium, dbl.; foliage dark, leathery; very vigorous, upright growth; [Queen Elizabeth® × unknown]; intr. 1964

'Madge Prior' F, pb, 1934, Prior; flowers brilliant claret, white eye, single, borne in large clusters; foliage dark; vigorous growth

'Madge Taylor' HT, dp, 1930, Clark, A.; flowers deep pink, large, dbl., globular; foliage light; vigorous growth; [('Rhea Reid' × unknown) × unknown]

'Madge Whipp' HT, or, 1936, Bees; flowers bright scarlet, dbl.; foliage leathery; vigorous, bushy growth; ['Lady Charmion' × 'J. C. Thornton']

'Madge Wildfire' HT, or, 1932, Dobbie; bud pointed; flowers Indian red, very large, very dbl., high-centered; foliage leathery; vigorous growth

'Madhatter' -- See 'Tinhat'

'Madhosh' HT, rb, 1976, IARI; bud globular; flowers deep magenta-red, streaked mauve and white, 4½ in., 45 petals; foliage leathery; vigorous, bushy, compact growth; [sport of 'Gulzar']; intr. 1975

'Madhumati' HT, mp, 1983, Pal, Dr. B.P.; flowers large, 55 petals, high-centered, borne singly, intense fragrance; foliage medium size, medium green, smooth; prickles brown; vigorous, upright, bushy growth; ['General MacArthur' × seedling]; intr. 1973

'Madhura' F, yb, 1980, Pal, Dr. B.P.; bud pointed; flowers 70 petals, high-centered, borne 3-6 per cluster, moderate fragrance; foliage glossy; vigorous, upright, bushy growth; ['Kiss of Fire' × 'Goudvlinder']; intr. 1979

'Mädi' Pol, or, GPG Bad Langensalza; flowers medium-large, semi-dbl.; intr. 1969

'Madiba' -- See 'Korandpunk'

'Madison' -- See 'Gelmad'

'Madison' T, w, 1912, Brant-Hentz; flowers pure white; ['Perle des Jaunes' × ('The Bride' × 'Meteor')]

Madison™ ('Devon', Bayernland™, Bayernland Cover™) S, mp, Poulsen; bud pointed, ovoid; flowers 5-8 cm., 20-25 petals, cupped, borne in large clusters, slight wild rose fragrance; recurrent; foliage dark; prickles moderate; growth broad, bushy, 60-100 cm.; PP12519; [seedling × 'Dorus Rijkers']; intr. 1996

'Madison' HT, mp, Tantau; intr. 2005

'Madlenka' F, mp, Vecera, L.

'Madness at Corsica' -- See 'Napoléon'

'Madoka' F, rb, 1977, Teranishi, K.; flowers 2-2½ in., 25 petals, high-centered; foliage glossy, dark; upright growth; [(Zambra® × 'Peace') × 'Cherry Brandy']; intr. 1975

'Madoka' HT, yb, Hiroshima; intr. 1996

'Madona' ('Madonna ') HT, pb, Meilland; bud long; flowers coral-peach, reverse amber blush, moderate fragrance; recurrent; intr. 1992

'Madonna ' -- See 'Meinopia'

'Madonna' HT, w, 1908, Cook, J.W.; ['Mlle Alice Furon' × 'Marie van Houtte']

Madonna™ ('Madonna Hit') MinFl, ab, Poulsen; flowers apricot blend, 5-8 cm., dbl., slight wild rose fragrance; foliage dark; growth bushy, 40-60 cm.; PP14971; intr. 2001

'Madonna Hit' -- See 'Poulhi009(N)'

'Madras' HT, pb, 1980, Warriner, William A.; bud ovoid; flowers rose with yellow and light pink reverse, 48 petals, borne singly, moderate fragrance; foliage large, leathery; prickles hooked downward; medium, spreading growth; PP4460; [seedling × seedling]; intr. 1981

'Madraz' -- See 'Radrazz'

'Madrigal'   HT, dp, 1950, Gaujard; bud long, pointed; flowers brilliant salmon-pink flushed coppery, very large, dbl., moderate spicy fragrance; vigorous growth; [(('Mme Joseph Perraud' × unknown) × seedling) × (('Mme Joseph Perraud' × unknown) × R. foetida bicolor)]

'Madrigal' ('Courageous', 'Fetzer Syrah Rose') S, dr; flowers deep, rich red, ruffled, 4 in., 50 petals, borne in clusters, intense rose/berry fragrance; recurrent; growth vigorous; intr. 1998

'Mady'   Cl HT, ly, 1925, Gemen & Bourg; flowers creamy white, with ruffled petals, 4 in., dbl., borne mostly solitary

'Mae Dean'   S, pb, ARE; flowers medium pink with lighter reverse, slight fragrance; growth tall (3-5 ft.); intr. 2004

'Maestro'   HT, dr, 1957, Delforge; bud oval; flowers deep velvety red, open, large, dbl.; foliage dark, glossy; vigorous, bushy growth; RULED EXTINCT 2/81; ['Crimson Glory' × 'Charles Mallerin']

Maestro® -- See 'Mackinju'

'Mafalda di Savoia' -- See 'Barsav'

'Magali' -- See 'Meigoufin'

'Magali'   HT, dp, 1952, Mallerin, C.; flowers carmine, open, medium, 35-40 petals; foliage abundant, leathery; very vigorous, upright, bushy growth; ['Charles P. Kilham' × 'Brazier']

'Magali Bonnefon'   HT, pb, 1916, Nabonnand; flowers pink, reverse bright salmon-pink, semi-dbl.; [sport of 'Mme Abel Chatenay']

'Magaliesburg Roos' -- See 'Mary Pope'

'Maganwilare'   HT, pb, Huber; flowers full, moderate spicy fragrance; foliage coppery colored; bushy, compact (50-60 cm.) growth; intr. 1995

'Magda'   HT, r; flowers tan apricot, large, very full, moderate fragrance; growth strong, bushy; intr. 2000

'Magda Wichmann'   HMult, pb, 1910, Kiese; flowers pink over cream-white, medium, very full; remontant

Magdalena®   HT, ob, Adam; flowers bright orange, reverse yellow, dbl., cupped, moderate fragrance; recurrent; compact (90-100 cm.) growth; intr. 2005

'Magdalena de Nubiola'   HT, op, 1932, Dot, Pedro; flowers salmon-rose, semi-dbl.; ['Li Bures' × 'Mari Dot']

'Magdeburg'   HT, VEG; intr. 1988

'Magdeleine Beauvillain'   T, ly, 1887, Beauvillain

'Magenta'   HT, mr, Leenders, M.; bud pointed; flowers crimson-carmine, large, dbl., intense fragrance; foliage glossy, dark; vigorous, bushy growth; intr. 1934

'Magenta' ('Kordes' Magenta) F, m, Kordes; bud ovoid; flowers rosy magenta to soft deep mauve, large, dbl., borne in large clusters, intense fragrance; foliage dark, leathery; vigorous, upright, bushy growth; ['Yellow Floribunda' × 'Lavender Pinocchio']; intr. 1954

'Magenta'   Pol, m, 1916, Barbier; flowers violet-red, semi-dbl.; dwarf growth

'Magenta Diadem' -- See 'Tandelbel'

'Magenta Floorshow' ('Purple Floorshow') S, m, Harkness; flowers deep reddish-purple, large, dbl., moderate fragrance; spreading (3½ × 4 ft.) growth

Magenta Mystique™ -- See 'Benlexa'

'Magenta Quartz'   F, m, Kakujitsu-en; intr. 2006

'Maggie'   HT, w, Nieuwesteeg; flowers white with soft lemon in center, very full, moderate fragrance; recurrent; growth to 4 ft.; intr. 2004

'Maggie Barry' -- See 'Macoborn'

'Maggie Tabberer' -- See 'Meichibon'

Magia Nera®   HT, dr; flowers very dark, velvety red, dbl., high-centered, no fragrance; recurrent; growth to 3 ft.

'Magic' -- See 'Mackalves'

Magic™ -- See 'Magic Hit'

'Magic'   HT, pb, 1954, Grillo; bud globular; flowers silver-pink, open, 5½ in., 75 petals; foliage leathery; very vigorous, upright growth; RULED EXTINCT 11/88; [sport of 'Thornless Beauty']

'Magic'   HT, mr, 1989, Strahle, Robert; bud pointed; flowers medium, 24 petals, high-centered, borne usually singly; foliage medium size, medium green, matte; prickles slender, straight, medium, light green; upright, tall growth; hips pear shaped, medium, orange; ['Volare' × 'Tonight']; intr. 1987

'Magic Baby' -- See 'Gelmagic'

'Magic Beauty' -- See 'Wilcans'

Magic Blanket™ -- See 'Tanigino'

'Magic Carpet'   LCl, yb, 1941, Brownell; flowers yellow, splashed orange, scarlet and rose, 9 cm., semi-dbl., borne in clusters, intense sweet fragrance; foliage small, dark green, glossy; strong stems; vigorous, climbing or trailing growth; ['Coral Creeper' × 'Stargold']

'Magic Carpet' ('Tapis Magique') S, m, Zary, Keith & Warriner, William; flowers lavender, 2 in., 12 petals, flat, borne in clusters, intense spicy fragrance; free-flowering; foliage medium size, dark green, glossy; prickles numerous, medium, hooked downward; growth spreading, low (18 in.); groundcover; PP9324; intr. 1992

Magic Carrousel®   Min, rb, 1973, Moore, Ralph S.; flowers white, edged red, small, dbl., high-centered; foliage small, glossy, leathery; vigorous, bushy growth; PP3601; ['Little Darling' × 'Westmont]; intr. 1972

'Magic Carrousel, Climbing'   Cl Min, rb; intr. after 1972

'Magic Charm'   HT, mp, 1966, Aufill; flowers medium, dbl., high-centered; vigorous growth; ['Mount Shasta' × 'Granada']

'Magic Day' -- See 'Horcointreau'

'Magic Dragon'   Cl Min, dr, 1973, Moore, Ralph S.; bud short, pointed; flowers small, dbl.; foliage leathery; very vigorous, upright growth; [((R. wichurana × 'Floradora') × seedling) × 'Little Buckaroo']; intr. 1969

'Magic East' -- See 'Virsplash'

'Magic Fire' -- See 'Meicurbos'

Magic Fire® ('Magic Fire 83') F, ob, Laperrière; flowers scarlet-orange, dbl.; intr. 1983

Magic Fire® -- See 'Lapneuf'

'Magic Fire 83' -- See 'Magic Fire'

'Magic Forez'   HT, Croix; intr. 1970

'Magic Hit' ('Magic'™) MinFl, rb, Poulsen; flowers red with yellow and orange reverse, 5 cm., full, hybrid tea, very slight fragrance; recurrent; foliage dark green, glossy; bushy (2 ft.) growth; intr. 2001

'Magic Lantern' -- See 'Starqueli'

'Magic Medley' ('Abhaya') HT, pb, 1997, Viraraghavan, M.S. Viru; flowers pink with dark red markings, white reverse, 6 in., full, borne mostly singly; foliage large, medium green, dull; bushy, medium (3 ft.) growth; [Pristine® × 'Priyatama']; intr. 1995

Magic Meidiland® -- See 'Meibonrib'

Magic Meillandecor® -- See 'Meibonrib'

'Magic Mikado'   F, mr, Tantau; flowers bright red, borne in clusters; florist rose

'Magic Mist'   Min, mr, 1981, Williams, Ernest D.; bud pointed; flowers medium red, veined darker, 47 petals, high-centered, borne usually singly, moderate fragrance; foliage small, medium to dark green, glossy; prickles thin, tan; bushy, spreading growth; ['Tom Brown' × 'Little Chief']; intr. 1980

'Magic Moment' -- See 'Makmaji'

'Magic Moment'   HT, mr, 1964, Buyl Frères; bud pointed; flowers scarlet to geranium-red, large, dbl., high-centered, moderate fragrance

'Magic Moments'   F, pb, 2007, Courage, Ray; flowers semi-dbl., blooms borne in small clusters; foliage medium size, dark green, semi-glossy; prickles small, hooked, brown, few; growth bushy, medium (1¼ m.); garden decoration; ['Friesia' × 'Michèle Meilland']; intr. 2007

'Magic Moon'   Gr, ob, 1970, Schwartz, Ernest W.; bud ovoid; flowers deep salmon, reverse silver, medium, very dbl.; foliage large, leathery; vigorous, upright growth; ['Little Darling' × 'Golden Scepter']

'Magic Mountain'   F, yb, 1971, Armstrong, D.L.; bud ovoid; flowers large, dbl., high-centered; foliage glossy, dark, leathery; vigorous, bushy growth; PP3315; ['Circus' × 'Texan']; intr. 1973

'Magic Red'   F, mr, 1942, Kordes; flowers large, 45 petals, globular, borne in clusters; foliage leathery, glossy; vigorous, bushy growth; ['Henri Panthier' × 'Dance of Joy']

'Magic Red® HT, dr, Tantau; flowers large, double, high-centered, borne mostly singly; recurrent; stems medium to long; florist rose; intr. 2007
'Magic Silver' HT, m, Kordes; intr. 1998
'Magic Splendor' -- See 'Lyoma'
'Magic Sunblaze' -- See 'SCHanbiran'
'Magic Sunset' F, ob, Tantau; flowers deep copper, dbl.; growth small; intr. 1995
'Magic Touch' HT, lp, 1975, Golik; bud ovoid; flowers soft pink, 5 in., 32 petals, high-centered, moderate fragrance; foliage glossy; moderate growth; ['Tropicana' × 'Queen of Bermuda']; intr. 1974
'Magic Wand' Cl Min, dp, 1958, Moore, Ralph S.; flowers light red, 1 in., 20 petals, borne in clusters; foliage small, dark; arching (to 4 ft.) growth; hips orange; ['Eblouissant' × 'Zee']; intr. 1957
Magician™ -- See 'Minimap'
'Magicienne' HT, or, 1957, Laperrière; flowers geranium-red, well-formed, 30 petals; foliage bronze; dwarf, bushy growth; ['Comtesse Vandal' × ('Peace' × 'Independence')]
Magicienne 78® HT, ob, Laperrière; flowers dbl.; intr. 1978
'Magie de Feu' -- See 'Korber'
'Magie des Jardins' -- See 'Gartenzauber'
'Magie d'Orient' -- See 'LLX8738'
Magitta® -- See 'Tanattigam'
'Magma' HT, or, Kordes; flowers bright orange-red with yellow at the petal base, dbl., high-centered, borne mostly singly; recurrent; stems medium; florist rose; intr. 1998
'Magma' ('Magma Freelander') HT, yb, Kordes; flowers yellow with red edges, large, 45 petals, high-centered, borne mostly singly; recurrent; few prickles; stems long; moderate (4 ft.) growth; intr. 2005
'Magma Freelander' -- See 'Magma'
'Magna Charta' ('Casper') HP, mp, 1876, Paul, W.; flowers bright pink, suffused carmine, very large, dbl., globular; some recurrent bloom; foliage thick, rich green; vigorous, compact growth
'Magnafrano' HT, mr, 1900, Van Fleet; flowers rich crimson-rose, large, dbl.; ['Magna Charta' × 'Safrano']
'Magneet' ('Feu d'Artifice', Feuerwerk®, 'Fireworks') S, ob, 1965, Tantau, Math.; flowers bright orange, semi-dbl., borne in clusters; foliage glossy; upright, bushy (to 5 ft.) growth; intr. 1964
'Magnet' F, mr, VEG; flowers luminous red, large, dbl.
'Magnifica' (R. rubiginosa magnifica) HEg, mr, Hesse; flowers light red, large, 10 petals; ['Lucy Ashton' × 'Lucy Ashton']; intr. 1916
'Magnifica' ('Rugosa Magnifica') HRg, dr, 1907, Van Fleet; bud carmine; flowers deep blood red, 4-5 in., full; [R. rugosa × 'Victor Hugo']
'Magnificence' HT, op, 1954, Gaujard; flowers salmon-pink tinted yellow, large, dbl., high-centered; foliage dark; vigorous, bushy growth; ['Peace' × unknown]
'Magnificent Mimosa' HT, dy, Delbard; flowers deep yellow, edges turning red in sunlight, 38 petals, cupped; foliage glossy; stems short; growth compact; intr. 2006
'Magnificent Perfume' S, lp, Clements, John; flowers soft pink shading to apricot at their center, 4-5 cm., 50 petals, heavy sweet and fresh fragrance; foliage rich, green; vigorous (4 × 3½ ft.) growth; PPAF; intr. 2003
'Magnifique' Pol, lp, 1928, deRuiter; flowers clear pink, open, large, semi-dbl., cupped, borne in clusters; foliage rich green, glossy; vigorous growth; [sport of 'Orléans Rose']
Magnolia Kordana® Min, lp, Kordes; flowers cream-pink, dbl.; recurrent; pot rose
'Magnolia Rose, Climbing' -- See 'Devoniensis, Climbing'
'Magnolia Rose' -- See 'Devoniensis'
Magnolia Springs™ -- See 'Talsprings'
'Magnolija' HP, w, 1940, Kosteckij; flowers creamy white, large, dbl.
'Magnum' HT, dr; bud conical, large; flowers 4 in., 30-35 petals, high-centered, borne mostly singly, no fragrance; good repeat; foliage medium green, semi-glossy; prickles numerous, medium; erect (5 ft.) growth; PP16493; [Mahalia™ × ('Challenger' × 'Meigormon')]; intr. 1998
'Magrana' F, or, 1954, Dot, Pedro; flowers well-formed, dbl.; vigorous growth; ['Méphisto' × 'Alain']
'Mahadev' F, or, 1976, Viraraghavan, M.S. Viru; bud long, pointed; flowers open, 1½ in., 20 petals; foliage glossy; vigorous, tall, bushy growth; [seedling × seedling]; intr. 1975
'Mahaeca' -- See 'La Belle Sultane'
'Mahaeca de Dupont' -- See 'Busard Triomphant'
'Mahagona' ('Mahogany') HT, pb, 1956, Kordes; bud pointed; flowers dull orange-scarlet, open, very large; foliage leathery, wrinkled; very vigorous, upright, bushy growth; ['Golden Rapture' × 'Hens Verschuren']
'Mahaja' HT, dp, 1936, Carbaugh; bud long, pointed; flowers deep rose-pink, center rose-red, base yellow, 4 in., dbl., high-centered, moderate fragrance; foliage glossy; long stems; vigorous growth; PP222; [sport of 'Rose Hill']
'Mahalaxmi' HT, yb, Patil, B.K.; intr. 1988
Mahalia™ -- See 'Keireb'
'Maharajah' HP, mr, 1904, Cant, B. R.; flowers velvety crimson, golden anthers, large, semi-dbl., borne in clusters, moderate fragrance; foliage dark, bronze, leathery
'Maharani' HT, pb; intr. 1996
'Maharishi' ('Orange Kardinal') HT, or, Tejganga; flowers vermilion orange, dbl., high-centered, recurrent; [sport of 'Kardinal']; intr. 1995
'Maheca' ('Bengale Hollandaise', 'Dutch Bengal', 'Hollandaise', 'Reversa Pourpre') Bslt, m, about 1815, Noisette; flowers purple crimson, nuanced light violet, medium, semi-dbl., borne in corymbs
'Maheca Nova' -- See 'Aigle Noir'
'Maheck à Fleurs Simples' -- See 'Holoserica'
'Maheka' -- See 'Purpurea'
'Mahina' HT, ab, 1952, Meilland, F.; flowers reddish-apricot, reverse golden yellow, large, 35 petals, moderate fragrance; foliage leathery; very vigorous, bushy growth; ['Peace' × 'Fred Edmunds']
'Mahogany' -- See 'Mahagona'
Mai Tai™ -- See 'Jacyarp'
'Maia' ('Baremp') HT, Barni, V.; intr. 1986
'Maid Marian' HT, pb, 1920, Therkildsen; flowers carmine-rose, reverse silvery pink, dbl.
'Maid Marion' -- See 'Red Imp'
'Maid Marion' HWich, w, 1909, Walsh; flowers white, tipped pink, center filled with yellow stamens, slightly incurved, single; foliage large, glossy; vigorous growth
'Maid Marion' HMsk, w, 1930, Pemberton; flowers white, opening blush, semi-dbl., borne in very large clusters; vigorous (3-4 ft.) growth
'Maid of Gold' Cl HT, my, 1936, Raffel; bud globular, reddish; flowers golden yellow, large, very dbl.; profuse, intermittent bloom; foliage glossy; vigorous, climbing (12 ft.), compact growth; PP246; ['Golden Emblem, Climbing' × unknown]
'Maid of Honour' HT, yb, Weddle, Von C.; flowers yellow, light pink center, large, dbl., borne singly and in small clusters, moderate fragrance; foliage large, dark, semi-glossy; tall, upright growth; [Folklore® × seedling]; intr. 1984
'Maid of Honour' T, mp, 1899, Hofmeister; flowers soft rose pink to flesh-pink, large, full; [sport of 'Catherine Mermet']
'Maid of Honour' ('Schleswig') F, op, Kordes; bud long, pointed; flowers salmon-pink, open, large, single, borne in trusses, moderate fragrance; foliage leathery, glossy, light green; vigorous, upright growth; RULED EXTINCT 1/86; ['Crimson Glory' × 'Holstein']; intr. 1951
'Maid of Kent' LCl, lp, Rumwood; delicate pink flowers, small, borne in clusters, slight fragrance; foliage dark, glossy; growth to 10 ft.; intr. 2000
'Maid of Kent' HT, op, 1929, Archer; flowers soft salmon-pink; ['Ophelia' × 'Mrs W. J. Grant']
'Maid of Orleans' F, ob, 1976, Ellick; flowers orange-flame blend, 4 in., very dbl.; foliage glossy, dark; very free growth; ['Val De Mosa' × 'Tropicana']; intr. 1977

'Maid of the Valley' -- See 'Unique Panachée'

'Maiden Voyage' -- See 'Maclocker'

'Maiden's Blush' -- See 'William R. Smith'

'Maiden's Blush' -- See 'Héloïse'

'Maiden's Blush' ('Belle Thérèse', 'Petite Anglaise', 'Cuisse de Nymphe à Ovaire Lisse', 'Cuisse de Nymphe Émue', 'Nymphe Naine Émue') A, w, 1802, Dumont de Courset; flowers whitish rose, medium, dbl., cupped, moderate fragrance; growth erect; probably a clone from the Royal Botanic Gardens, Kew

'Maiden's Blush' -- See 'Great Maiden's Blush'

'Maiden's Blush Sweet Briar' -- See 'Manning's Blush'

'Maidi' HT, pb

'Maids of Jubilee' -- See 'Talmaid'

'Maidstone' S, my, Kordes; groundcover; spreading growth; intr. 2001

Maidy® -- See 'Korwalbe'

'Maigold' S, dy, 1953, Kordes; flowers bronze-yellow, 4 in., 14 petals, cupped, borne singly or in small clusters, intense fragrance; non-recurrent; foliage glossy; numerous prickles; bushy (5 ft.), pillar or shrub growth; ['Poulsen's Pink' × 'Fruhlingstag']

'Maiko' -- See 'Kyo-Maiko'

'Mailoeur' ('Home Sweet Home') LCl, mr, Maillard

'Mainak' HT, dp, Ghosh; flowers deep rose pink, very large, dbl.; good repeat; intr. 2003

'Mainauduft' -- See 'Meizincaro'

'Mainaufeuer' -- See 'Kortemma'

Mainauperle® -- See 'Kormai'

'Mainz' HT, my, 1930, Leenders Bros.; flowers citron-yellow, very large, dbl., moderate fragrance; vigorous growth; [sport of 'Kardinal Piffl']

'Mainzer Fastnacht, Climbing' -- See 'Blue Moon, Climbing'

'Mainzer Fastnacht' -- See 'Tannacht'

'Mainzer Rad' -- See 'Mainzer Wappen'

'Mainzer Wappen' ('Mainzer Rad') S, or, 1963, Kordes, R.; bud pointed; flowers red, tinted orange, large, 25 petals, borne in clusters of up to 20, moderate fragrance; foliage dark; bushy, upright (5 ft.) growth

'Maiogi' ('Dancing Fan') HT, op, Keihan; intr. 1988

'Maisie' HT, op, 1926, Dickson, A.; flowers salmon-orange and pink, medium, semi-dbl.

'Maisie Gowie' HT, ?, 1968, Gowie; foliage dark, leathery; bushy growth

'Maison Pernet-Ducher' HT, my, 1934, Pernet-Ducher; bud pointed; flowers golden yellow, veined copper, large, dbl.; foliage glossy, dark; very vigorous, bushy growth

'Maisy Wakefield' -- See 'Worcrackle'

'Maitland White' T, w; flowers dbl., moderate fragrance; recurrent; growth medium; discovered in Bermuda.

'Maiwunder' S, ly, Kordes; intr. 1966

'Maizières' F, mr, RvS-Melle; flowers 29 petals, flat; foliage dense dark green; [seedling × 'Ernest H. Morse']; intr. 1993

'Maja' F, mr, 1960, deRuiter; flowers cinnabar-red, 30 petals, cupped, borne in broad clusters; vigorous, bushy growth; ['Independence' × 'Signal Red']

'Maja Mauser' -- See 'Cara Mia'

'Maja Mauser' F, or, 1978, Poulsen, Niels D.; flowers dark orange-red, 4 in., 20 petals; foliage glossy, dark; bushy, upright growth; ['Evelyn Fison' × seedling]; intr. 1970

'Maja Oetker' -- See 'Coronation Gold'

'Majestade' HT, w, 1957, Moreira da Silva; flowers cream-white, base deep yellow, well-formed; very vigorous growth; ['Mme Marie Curie' × 'Peace']

Majesté® -- See 'Dorma'

'Majestic' HT, or, 1955, Gaujard; bud long, purplish; flowers cinnabar-red, open, large, dbl.; vigorous growth; ['Peace' × seedling]

Majestic™ HT, lp, Poulsen; flowers light pink, 10-15 cm., 25 petals, borne one to a stem, no fragrance; foliage dark, glossy; growth bushy, 60-100 cm.; PP15600; intr. 2002

'Majestic' S, lp, Clements, John; flowers silvery pink, 6-7 in., 24 petals, moderate sweet, fresh fragrance; foliage large, bluish green; growth vigorous; large shrub or small climber.; PPAF; intr. 2004

'Majestic Kiwi' HT, rb, 2000, Cattermole, R.R.; flowers medium red, reverse yellow, 4½-5 in., full, borne singly or in small clusters, moderate fragrance; foliage medium size, light green, glossy; prickles moderate, aging light brown; growth upright, tall (5-6 ft.); ['Royden' × Chivalry®]; intr. 2001

'Majestic Sunrise' HT, my, Courage; flowers large, dbl., moderate fragrance; medium growth; charity rose for multiple schlerosis; intr. 2002

'Majestueuse' ('Boule Hortensia', 'Lucrèce', 'Maxima', 'Le Triomphe', 'Le Majestueuse', 'La Cocarde', 'De Hollande', 'Cocarde') HGal, lp, before 1790, from Holland; bud red; flowers pale rose, 3 in., full, moderate fragrance; Agathe group

'Majeure' -- See 'Tanya'

'Maji' -- See 'Makmaji'

'Majken' S, Thor; intr. 1974

'Majlaq' ('Amanda Justine') HT, rb, 2001, Hiltner, Martin J.; flowers medium red, white reverse, 4 in., full, high-centered, borne mostly solitary, or small clusters, no fragrance; foliage medium size, medium green, semi-glossy; prickles medium, hooked down, moderate; growth upright, medium (3-3½ ft.); garden decoration, exhibition; ['Lynn Anderson' × Amber Queen®]

'Majlara' ('Old Man Bailey') HT, pb, 2002, Hiltner, Martin; flowers deep pink, white eye, reverse light yellow, opening to lavender and white, 3½-4 in., semi-dbl., high-centered, borne mostly solitary; foliage medium size, medium green, semi-glossy; prickles straight, numerous; growth upright, medium (2½-5 ft.); garden, cut flower; ['Lynn Anderson' × Royal Amethyst™]; intr. 2003

'Majlybtwo' ('Tony's Two Tone') F, pb, 2002, Hiltner, Martin; flowers deep pink, reverse light yellow, 2-3 in., dbl., borne in small clusters; foliage medium size, light green, semi-glossy; prickles moderate, hooked down; growth spreading, low, short (2½ ft.); decorative, garden; ['Lynn Anderson' × (('Carefree Beauty' × 'Picasso') × unknown)]; intr. 2003

'Majlyniment' ('Heather Miranda') HT, rb, 2001, Hiltner, Martin J.; flowers dark red, blending to white, 2½-3 in., dbl., borne mostly solitary, slight fragrance; foliage medium size, medium green, semi-glossy; prickles 3/8 in., hooked downward; growth upright, bushy, medium (2½-3 ft.); garden decorative; ['Lynn Anderson' × Scentimental™]

'Majlynjub' ('Lynn's Jubilee') HT, pb, 2001, Hiltner, Martin J.; flowers light pink, aging to dark pink, 3½-4 in., dbl., high-centered, borne mostly solitary; foliage medium size, medium green, glossy; prickles 3/8-½ in., curved down, numerous; growth upright, medium (2½-3 ft.); garden decorative, exhibition; ['Lynn Anderson' × 'Silver Jubilee']

'Majlynlin' ('Uncle John') HT, mr, 2001, Hiltner, Martin; flowers medium red with lighter reverse, 3½-4 in., dbl., high-centered, borne mostly solitary, slight fragrance; recurrent; foliage medium size, medium green, semi-glossy; prickles moderate, ¼ in., hooked down; stems very red new growth; growth upright, medium (2½-3 ft.); garden decorative, exhibition; ['Lynn Anderson' × 'Dublin']

'Majlynlinto' ('Aunt Rosie') HT, pb, 2001, Hiltner, Martin J.; flowers 3-3½ in., dbl., borne mostly solitary; foliage medium size, medium green, semi-glossy; prickles ¼ in., curving down, moderate; growth upright, medium (2½-3 ft.); garden decorative, exhibition; ['Lynn Anderson' × 'Dublin']

'Majlynt' ('Lynn's Saint') HT, w, 2002, Hiltner, Martin; flowers large, fading to solid white, 3½-4½ in., full, borne mostly solitary; foliage medium size, medium green, semi-glossy; prickles hooked down, moderate; growth upright, medium (3-4 ft.); decorative, exhibition; ['Lynn Anderson' × St Patrick™]; intr. 2003

'Majmisem' ('Miss Emily') HT, dp, 2001, Hiltner, Martin J.; flowers 3-3½ in., very full, borne mostly solitary; foliage medium size, medium green, semi-glossy; prickles ¼ in., straight, numerous; growth upright, bushy, medium (3-3½ ft.); exhibition; ['Lynn Anderson' × seedling]

Majolika® -- See 'Tankeijoli'
'Major' -- See 'Alector Cramoisi'
'Major Frank Hayes' HT, dr, 1934, Bees; flowers crimson, center darker, very large, dbl., high-centered; foliage leathery, dark; vigorous growth; ['Joan Howarth' × 'J. C. Thornton']
'Major Multiplex' -- See 'Des Peintres'
'Major Shelley' HT, mr, 1939, Howard, F.H.; bud pointed; flowers rich crimson-scarlet, 5-6 in., 35 petals, high-centered; foliage leathery, dark; very vigorous, bushy growth; PP447; ['Mrs J.D. Eisele' × 'Crimson Glory']
'Majora' -- See 'Taneidol'
'Majorca' HT, op, Buyl Frères; bud short, thick; flowers rose-salmon, 52 petals; moderate growth; intr. 1958
'Majorca' ('Majorica') HT, mr, 1938, Dot, Pedro; flowers scarlet, large, dbl., cupped; foliage glossy, bronze; vigorous, bushy growth; ['Aribau' × 'Angels Mateu']; intr. 1941
'Majorette' Gr, lp, 1960, Carlton Rose Nurs.; bud medium, ovoid; flowers soft powder pink, medium, dbl., borne in clusters; foliage dark green, glossy, disease-resistant; growth very vigorous, upright; intr. 1958
Majorette® -- See 'Meipiess'
Majorette® -- See 'Meidad'
'Majorica' -- See 'Majorca'
'Majtelbel' ('Tell Belle') S, or, 2001, Hiltner, Martin J.; flowers small, full, borne in small clusters, intense fragrance; foliage medium size, medium green, semi-glossy; prickles moderate, ¼ - 3/8 in., straight; spreading, medium (2-2½ ft.) growth; ['Show 'n' Tell' × 'Hawkeye Belle']
'Majuna' -- See 'Makmajuna'
'Make A Wish' -- See 'Mehpat'
Make Believe™ -- See 'Mormake'
Make Mine Sherry™ Min, rb
'Make-Up' -- See 'Meixetal'
Make-A-Wish Australia® -- See 'Korgretaum'
'Makeddan' ('Eddan') S, rb, 2000, Makosch, Joachim; flowers dark red, reverse deep pink, medium size, full, borne mostly singly, intense fragrance; foliage medium size, light green, dull; few prickles; spreading, tall (4 ft.) growth; [sport of 'Auslo']; intr. 1987
'Making Memories' -- See 'Talmemo'
'Makmaji' ('Magic Moment', 'Maji') Min, pb, 2004, Jones, Mark W.; flowers pink, base yellow, reverse fringe pink, 2 in., full, borne mostly solitary, slight fragrance; foliage medium size, medium green, semi-glossy; prickles slightly hooked downward; growth upright, medium (18-24 in.); garden; exhibition; [sport of 'Marbutter']
'Makmajuna' ('Majuna') HT, yb, 2000, Makosch, Joachim; flowers light yellow, reverse light pink, medium, full, borne in large clusters, moderate fragrance; foliage large, dark green, semi-glossy; prickles moderate; growth upright, tall (4 ft.); [sport of 'Broadway']; intr. 1999
'Makybe Diva' HT, lp, Dickson; flowers pale pink with hint of apricot in center, large, double, high-centered, borne mostly singly; recurrent; stems long, firm; strong (4 ft.) growth; named for famous race horse; intr. 2007
'Mala Rubinstein' HT, mp, 1971, Dickson, A.; flowers 5½ in., 45 petals, high-centered, moderate fragrance; foliage large, matte; ['Sea Pearl' × 'Colour Wonder']
'Malaga' Cl HT, dp, 1971, McGredy, Sam IV; flowers reddish-pink, 4½ in., 36 petals, high-centered, borne in small clusters, intense fragrance; foliage glossy, dark; [('Hamburger Phoenix' × 'Danse de Feu') × 'Copenhagen']; originally registered as LCl
'Malaguena' S, mp, 1976, Buck, Dr. Griffith J.; bud ovoid, long, pointed; flowers 4½ in., 28 petals, cupped; foliage large, dark, leathery; erect, bushy growth; ['Tickled Pink' × 'Country Music']
'Malahat' -- See 'Betahat'
'Malak' HT, pb, Mahendrakumar C. Shah; flowers ivory and pale pink blend, large, full, high-centered; [sport of 'Admiral Rodney']; intr. 1988
'Malakarsiddha' HT, lp, Patil, B.K.; flowers porcelain pink, large, high-centered, slight fragrance; [sport of 'Century Two']; intr. 1987
'Mälar-Ros' HT, dr, 1932, Kordes; bud pointed; flowers glowing ruby-red indoors, dark blood-red with crimson outdoors, dbl., high-centered; very vigorous, bushy growth; ['Hadley' × 'Fragrance']
'Malcair' ('Grimpant Danse des Sylphes') LCl, or, 1959, Mallerin, C.
'Malcolm' HT, dp, 1977, Ellick; flowers carmine, 4-5 in., 35-40 petals; foliage large, glossy, dark; vigorous, free growth; ['Hector Deane' × 'Chopin']; intr. 1979
'Malcolm Sargent' -- See 'Harwharry'
'Malcolm Scott' -- See 'Bromal'
'Maleica' F, w, Tantau; flowers soft, creamy with apricot tints; growth compact, upright, medium; intr. 1988
'Maleica' HT, yb, Tantau; flowers gold and yellow, slight fragrance; intr. 2003
'Malek-Adel' ('Melik El Adel') HGal, lp; flowers soft pink, dotted white, large
'Malene' HT, Laperrière; intr. 1980
'Malesherbes' HGal, m, 1834, Vibert; flowers red, nuanced purple, spotted with white, very large, very full
'Malia' Min, mp, 1992, Mansuino, Dr. Domenico; flowers medium, very dbl., borne singly, no fragrance; highly recurrent bloom; foliage small, medium green, semi-glossy; some prickles; bushy (100-150 cm.) growth; ['seedling (Pink 1172)' × 'Rosa Maria']; intr. 1988
'Malibu' F, or, 1960, Morey, Dr. Dennison; bud pointed, ovoid; flowers coral-orange-red, becoming lighter, 4-4½ in., 35 petals, high-centered, intense fragrance; foliage leathery; vigorous, bushy, upright growth; PP1962; ['Charlotte Armstrong' × 'Independence']; intr. 1959
'Malibu Lake Shady Pink' HT, dp; intr. 1994
'Malicorne' -- See 'Delmator'
Malicorne® F, dr, Delbard; flowers dark, velvety red, 3 in., dbl., cupped, borne in clusters, slight fragrance; free-flowering; foliage bronzy green, glossy; medium (2-3 ft.) growth; intr. 2006
'Malin Jaune Delbard' S, dy, Delbard; intr. 2002
'Malin Rose Delbard' S, mp, Delbard; intr. 2002
'Malin Rouge Delbard' S, mr, Delbard; intr. 2002
'Malindall' F, mr, Noack, Werner; intr. 1996
'Malindi' F, mr, Noack, Werner; flowers medium, semi-dbl.; intr. 1974
'Malinovka' ('Raspberry Wine') F, dp, 1956, Sushkov, K. L.; flowers raspberry-red, medium; ['Staatsprasident Pats' × 'Independence']
'Maljoanna' ('Querida') HT, mp, 1994, Maltagliati, Mark G.; flowers 3-3½ in., full, borne mostly singly; foliage large, dark green, semi-glossy; few prickles; upright (5 ft.) growth; PP9769; ['Silver Anniversary' × unknown]; intr. 1995
'Malkarsiddha' HT, lp, 1989, Patil, B.K.; [sport of 'Century Two']; intr. 1987
'Mallif' F, pb, Malanseuns
'Mallory Marie' -- See 'Dwamallory'
'Malmaison Rose' -- See 'Leweson-Gower'
'Malmaison Rouge' ('Red Malmaison', 'Souv de la Malmaison Rouge') B, dr, 1882, Gonod; flowers velvety dark red, medium, full, cupped; [sport of 'Souv de la Malmaison']
'Malmesbury' HT, my, 1980, Sanday, John; bud pointed; flowers 23 petals, borne singly and several together; foliage medium green; prickles slightly hooked; compact, bushy growth; ['Vera Dalton' × 'Parasol']
'Malmiya' (Ayako™) Gr, ly, 1991, Maltagliati, Mark G.; flowers pale yellow cream, large, full, slight fragrance; foliage medium size, medium green, semi-glossy; medium, upright growth; [sport of 'Sonia']; intr. 1990
'Malnino' ('Saint Louis') Gr, w, 1989, Maltagliati, Mark G.; flowers white to ivory; PP6908; [sport of 'Lifirane']; intr. 1989
'Malred' F, dp, Malanseuns
'Malren' ('Nerene') HT, yb, Malanseuns; intr. 1993
'Malso' ('The Sunflower') F, or, 1961, Mallerin, C.
'Malton' ('Fulgens') HCh, mr, about 1830, Guérin; flowers bright crimson, paler reverse, 7-8 cm., full, borne in small clusters, intense tea fragrance; foliage dark, small
'Malva' F, m, 1935, Leenders, M.; flowers mauve, center white, open, large,

semi-dbl.; foliage large, glossy, light; very vigorous, bushy growth

'Malva Rambler' HMult, m, 1908, Puyravaud; flowers violet pink, fading lighter, 3 cm., semi-dbl.; non-recurrent

'Malvena' HT, lp, Dawson, George

'Malvern Hills' -- See 'Auscanary'

'Malverns' -- See 'Kordehei'

'Malvina' -- See 'Bourbon'

'Malvina' C, lp, 1841, Verdier, V.; flowers pale pink, edged lighter, well-formed, large, very dbl., borne in clusters; sometimes classed as M

'Malwa 94' HT, pb, Gokhale, J. & A.; flowers broad pink petals with white stripes, moderate fragrance; [sport of 'Eiffel Tower']; intr. 1994

'Malyi' (R. × malyi Kerner, R. pendulina malyi) S, dr, 1902; flowers deep, bright red, 1½ in., borne singly; foliage similar to spinosissima; growth to 6 ft.; hips scarlet, ovoid, ¾ in.; probably R. pendulina × R. spinosissima; first recorded in 1902 by Keller; from Austria

'Mama' HT, dr, Wänninger, Franz; flowers large, very dbl.; intr. 1991

'Mama' -- See 'Maman'

'Mama de Meyer' HT, w, 1931, Lens; flowers cream, center salmon, well-formed, large, dbl.; vigorous growth; ['Duchess of Wellington' × 'Aspirant Marcel Rouyer']

'Mama Lamesch' HT, op, 1922, Lambert, P.; flowers orange-rose, center deeper, reverse reddish-rose, dbl.; ['Frau Oberprasident von Grothe' × 'Mme Edouard Herriot']

'Mama Looymans' HT, dp, 1910, Leenders, M.; flowers carmine-pink, medium, semi-dbl.; ['Gruss an Teplitz' × 'Hortensia']

'Mama Mia' -- See 'Zipmia'

'Mama Pechtold' HT, 1938, Pechtold; bud long, pointed; flowers rosy salmon, dbl.; foliage bronze; long, strong stems; vigorous growth; ['Katherine Pechtold' × 'Briarcliff']

'Mama Teresa' F, pb, 2007, Auilar, Sergio; flowers orange-pink, reverse light yellow, 3½ in., semi-dbl, high-centered, borne mostly solitary; foliage small, matte, keeping a reddish shade until blooms finish; prickles medium, almost straight, moderate; growth upright, spreading, medium (4 ft.); garden decoration, cutting; ['Elizabeth Taylor' × Jean Kenneally™]; intr. 2008

'Mamaia' Pol, or, GPG Bad Langensalza; flowers semi-dbl.; intr. 1972

'Maman' ('Mama') HT, or, 1963, Delbard-Chabert; flowers orange-vermilion, well-formed,, 4-5 in., 30-40 petals; foliage bright green; bushy growth; [('Rome Glory' × 'La Vaudoise') × 'Impeccable']; intr. 1970

'Maman Chérie' -- See 'Delmanche'

'Maman Cochet' T, pb, 1893, Cochet, P.; bud pointed; flowers pale pink, center deeper, base lemon-yellow,, 4 in., dbl., high-centered, moderate fragrance; foliage dark, leathery; vigorous, bushy growth; ['Marie van Houtte' × 'Mme Lombard']

'Maman Cochet, Climbing' Cl T, pb, 1909, Upton (also Lee-Concord, 1909, H&S, 1915); flowers shades of pink and cream, darker at center, 10 cm., moderate fragrance; [sport of 'Maman Cochet']

'Maman Dental' HT, mp, 1921, Dental; flowers pure rose-pink; [sport of 'Mme Caroline Testout']

'Maman Geneviève' F, or, 1960, Hémeray-Aubert; flowers red tinted orange; bushy growth

'Maman Levavasseur' ('Baby Dorothy') Pol, dp, 1907, Levavasseur; flowers bright crimson-pink, dbl.; [sport of 'Mme Norbert Levavasseur']

'Maman Loiseau' T, yb, 1899, Buatois; flowers sulfur-yellow, center peach pink, edges cream yellow, large

'Maman Lyly' HT, lp, 1911, Soupert & Notting; bud long, oval; flowers pale coral pink, large, semi-dbl., cupped, moderate fragrance; recurrent; ['Mme Mélanie Soupert' × 'Mrs Peter Blair']

'Maman Pineau' -- See 'Godilofter'

'Maman Turbat' Pol, pb, 1911, Turbat; flowers China-rose shaded lilac, reverse almost white, large, semi-dbl., borne in clusters of 5-10; foliage dark, soft; bushy growth; ['Mme Norbert Levavasseur' × 'Katharina Zeimet']

'Mambo' Gr, mr, 1970, Swim, H. C.; bud ovoid; flowers currant-red to cardinal-red, medium, dbl., high-centered; foliage dark, leathery; vigorous, tall, bushy growth; ['Charlotte Armstrong' × seedling]; intr. 1968

'Mambo' F, op, Tantau, Math.; bud ovoid; flowers salmon-pink, medium, dbl.; dwarf, bushy growth; ['Tropicana' × 'Zorina']; intr. 1971

'Mambo' F, ob, Tantau; flowers orange, yellow and red on tips, small, dbl., borne in sprays; recurrent; greenhouse rose; intr. 1998

Mambo No. 5® F, yb, Tantau; flowers yellow with edges turning red, small, dbl., borne in sprays; recurrent; greenhouse rose; intr. 2002

'Mamie' HT, pb, 1902, Dickson, A.; flowers pink and red, large, dbl., moderate fragrance

'Mamie, Climbing' Cl HT, mr, 1938, Vogel; flowers rose red, large, full, moderate fragrance; [sport of 'Mamie']

'Mamie Serpa' F, w, 1955, Serpa; bud ovoid, creamy; flowers open, 2½ in., 50 petals; foliage dark, soft; vigorous, bushy, compact growth; ['Goldilocks' × 'Snowbird']

'Mamille' HT, my, 1976, Kordes; bud long, pointed; flowers 4½ in., 35 petals, high-centered; foliage soft; vigorous, upright growth; [Peer Gynt® × 'Valencia']

'Mamina' HWich, dp, Scheiber; flowers intense rose-pink, large, full, quartered; foliage matte green; strong, tall (10 ft.) growth

'Mamita' HT, mr, 1958, Robichon; flowers garnet-red, large; vigorous growth; ['Dickson's Red' × seedling]

'Mamma Mia' HT, op, Fryer; flowers coral , double, high-centered, borne mostly singly; recurrent; foliage bright green, glossy; vigorous, branching, medium growth; intr. 2006

'Mamouche' F, m, Lens; bud reddish-pink, globular; flowers lilac-pink with undertone of apricot, 6-7 cm., semi-double, cupped, borne in large clusters on overhanging stems, slight fruity fragrance; recurrent; foliage purplish brown when young, then dark green; 2 ft. growth,; intr. 2007

Mamy Blue® -- See 'Delblue'

'Mamy Laperrière' -- See 'Laplical'

'Mana' F, yb, 1989, Cattermole, R.F.; flowers creamy yellow, edges flushed pink, large, dbl., high-centered; foliage medium green, glossy, veined; prickles light brown; upright growth; ['Liverpool Echo' × 'Arthur Bell']

'Mana Böhm' -- See 'Mána Böhmová'

'Mána Böhmová' ('Mana Böhm') HMult, w, 1925, Böhm, J.; flowers greenish white, medium, full, globular, borne in clusters; foliage large, light green, soft; nearly thornless; [sport of 'Tausendschön']

'Manaia' -- See 'Sunmani'

'Manamsun' ('Amber Sunset') Min, ob, 1996, Mander, George; flowers orange with orange and dark yellow reverse, 1¾-2 in., full, high-centered, star-shaped, no fragrance; foliage medium size, dark green, glossy, disease-resistant; some prickles; very vigorous, medium (40-50 cm.), bushy growth; [June Laver™ × 'Rubies 'n' Pearls']; intr. 1996

'Manapouri' -- See 'Macwynpin'

'Manas' HT, ob, Londe & Gokhale; flowers salmon with stripes and blotches of white and red, dbl.; intr. 1997

'Manasi' F, lp, IARI; flowers light pink, deeper at the margins, small, dbl., borne in small and large clusters; ['Frolic' × unknown]; intr. 1991

'Manbella' (Bella Christina™) F, rb, 2006, Mander, George; flowers dark red, reverse cream, 4½ in., full, borne in large clusters; foliage large, dark green, very glossy, disease-resistant; prickles 3/8 in., needle-point, medium brown, moderate; growth upright, tall (4-5 ft.); garden decorative, exhibition; [Shades of Pink™ × 'Super Sun']; intr. 2007

'Manberyl' ('Golden Beryl') Min, yb, 1995, Mander, George; flowers deep yellow brushed orange inside of petals, 1¾-2 in., dbl., borne singly and in small clusters; foliage medium size, medium green, glossy; few prickles; medium (35-40 cm.), bushy growth; [June Laver™ × 'Rubies 'n' Pearls']; intr. 1995

'Mancarol' ('Alecia Carol') HT, mp, 2006, Mander, George; flowers luminous pink, reverse light pink, 5 in., full, borne in small clusters; foliage large, dark green, semi-glossy; prickles 3/8 in., needle point, medium brown, moderate; growth bushy, tall (4-5 ft.); garden, exhibition; ['Tiffany' × Pascali®]; intr. 2006

'Manclassic' ('Buffy Sainte-Marie', 'Valia Balkanska') HT, op, 1996, Mander, George; flowers blend of salmon, orange and pink with yellow center, 3¼-4¼ in., dbl.; foliage medium size, dark green, glossy, disease-resistant; very vigorous, medium (70-90 cm.), bushy growth; [June Laver™ × 'Rubies 'n' Pearls']; intr. 1996

'Mancoral' ('Coral 'n' Gold') Min, op, 1995, Mander, George; flowers coral/salmon/pink blend inside, yellow/cream reverse, some yellow stripes, full, borne in small clusters, no fragrance; foliage medium size, medium green, semi-glossy; few prickles; bushy, medium (40-45 cm.) growth; [June Laver™ × 'Rubies 'n' Pearls']; intr. 1995

Mandalay™ -- See 'Poulyv002'

'Mandalay' ('Helvétia') HT, my, 1942, Mallerin, C.; flowers clear yellow, open, 6 in., very dbl., moderate fragrance; foliage leathery; long stems; very vigorous, upright growth; PP775; ['Soeur Thérèse' × 'Feu Joseph Looymans']

'Mandalay Victory' (Mandalay™) S, my, Poulsen; flowers medium yellow,, 8-10 cm., 25 petals, moderate fragrance; foliage dark; growth bushy, 20-40 cm.; intr. 2002

Mandarin® -- See 'Korcelin'

'Mandarin' HT, my, 1946, Robichon; flowers golden yellow, intense fragrance; foliage glossy; vigorous growth; ['Betty Uprichard' × 'Ville de Paris']

'Mandarin' F, mr, Boerner; bud ovoid; flowers mandarin-red, 3-4 in., 18 petals, high-centered, borne in large clusters, moderate fragrance; foliage leathery, glossy; vigorous (3½-4 ft.), upright growth; PP1040; ['Lilette Mallerin' × 'red floribunda seedling']; intr. 1951

'Mandarin Delight' -- See 'Foumande'

'Mandarin Silk' -- See 'Denman'

Mandarin Sunblaze® -- See 'Meidarin'

'Mandarine' -- See 'Mandrina'

Mandarine Symphonie® -- See 'Meidarin'

'Manda's Pink Roamer' -- See 'Pink Roamer'

'Manda's Triumph' ('Double White Memorial Rose') HWich, w, 1899, Horvath; flowers pure white, 2 in., very dbl., borne in clusters of 10-12; some autumn repeat; very vigorous growth; [R. wichurana × 'Paquerette']

'Mander #1' -- See 'Mankana 1'

'Mander's Nutkana' -- See 'Mankana 1'

'Mander's Orange Dream' -- See 'Mandream'

'Mandiana' ('Bella Diana') F, pb, 2008, Mander, George; flowers light pink, reverse cream, petal edges more deeply colored in full sun, 2¾ in., full, high-centered, borne in small clusters; foliage large, dark green, glossy, disease-resistant; prickles 1 cm., needlepoint, medium brown, few; growth upright, medium (30-32 in.); garden decoration, exhibition; [(June Laver™ × 'Rubies 'n' Pearls') × 'Glowing Amber']; intr. 2008

'Mandream' ('Mander's Orange Dream') Min, ob, 2006, Mander, George; flowers dark burnt orange, reverse lighter orange, 2 in., full, high-centered, borne in small clusters; recurrent; foliage medium size, dark green, glossy; prickles moderate, 3/8 to ¼ in.es, needle point, light brown; growth compact, medium (20-24 in.); garden, containers, exhibition; [June Laver™ × 'Rubies 'n' Pearls']; intr. 2006

'Mandrina' ('Mandarine') F, or, 1964, deRuiter; flowers 2½-3 in., 30 petals, borne in clusters; foliage dark; vigorous, bushy growth; PP2557; [Moulin Rouge® × 'Frau Anny Beaufays']

'Mandryka' S, or, Mekdeci-Olsen; flowers medium red with orange, borne in clusters, moderate fragrance; intr. 1992

'Mandy' -- See 'Korinor'

'Mandy' F, ly, 1963, Robinson, H.; flowers creamy yellow to soft peach, large, dbl., foliage coppery; very free growth; ['Pinocchio' × 'Sweet Repose']

'Mandy Jo' HT, pb, 1970, Abrahams; flowers pale biscuit, flushed light pink, 4½ in., 22 petals; foliage very glossy, bright green; vigorous growth; [sport of 'Pink Favorite']

Mandy Kordana® Min, mr, Kordes; flowers dbl.; recurrent

'Mandy Singleton' HT, pb, Dawson; intr. 1995

'Maneca' HT, lp, 1929, Pernet-Ducher; flowers dbl., moderate fragrance

'Manette' HGal, rb, before 1820, Lecoffé; flowers violet, slatey edges, medium, very dbl., cupped; vigorous, upright growth; possibly synonymous with 'Nanette'; intr. 1820

'Manette' HGal, dp, Prévost; flowers dark pink, aging to red, edges lighter, medium, full; intr. about 1835

'Manettii' (R. chinensis manettii, R. noisettiana manettii, R. manettii) N, lp, 1835, Manetti, Dr.; flowers violet-rose, 2 in., single, borne in large clusters; foliage extremely susceptible to blackspot; stems red shoots; vigorous shrub growth; probably a cross of 'Blush Noisette' × 'Slater's Crimson China'; used as an understock by Thomas Rivers in 1850

'Manfu' ('Ingrid Mander-Fuchs') HT, pb, 2003, Mander, George; flowers pink/cream, 5 in., full, borne in small clusters; foliage large, dark green, glossy, disease-resistant; prickles 3/8 in., pointed,; growth upright, tall (4-5 ft.); garden, exhibition; [June Laver™ × 'Rubies 'n' Pearls']; intr. 2004

'Manglow' ('Glowing Amber') Min, rb, 1996, Mander, George; flowers scarlet red with deep yellow reverse and yellow center, 1½-2 in., full, borne mostly singly, slight fragrance; foliage medium size, dark green, glossy; some prickles; medium (40-50 cm.), bushy growth; [June Laver™ × 'Rubies 'n' Pearls']; intr. 1996

'Mango' -- See 'Jacmem'

Mango® HT, ob, Dorieux; flowers melon-orange with yellow center, large, dbl.; intr. 1988

'Mango Blush' S, ab; intr. 1999

'Mango Tango' -- See 'Geltan'

'Mangrace' ('Grace Sharington') MinFl, mp, 2007, Mander, George; flowers medium pink, reverse light pink, 3½ in., full, borne in small clusters; foliage medium size, dark green, semi-glossy, disease-resistant; prickles ¼ in., needle-point, light brown, moderate; growth bushy, medium (30-36 in.); garden, exhibition, containers; [Hot Tamale™ × 'Rubies 'n' Pearls']; intr. 2007

'Manhale' ('Haleakala') Min, m, 1996, Mander, George; flowers velvety dark ruby-purple inside with yellow center, 1¾-2 in., dbl.; foliage medium size, dark green, glossy; some prickles; medium (40-50 cm.), bushy growth; ['Rubies 'n' Pearls' × June Laver™]; intr. 1996

Manhattan™ -- See 'Poulharmu'

'Manhattan' ('Passion Rose') HT, or, 1936, Asmus; bud urn shaped; flowers jasper-red to coral-red, base yellow, very large, dbl., cupped, intense fragrance; very vigorous growth; PP179; [sport of 'Souvenir']

'Manhatten Blue' HT, m

'Manhawaii' ('Ingrid's Hawaiian Magic') MinFl, ob, 2008, Mander, George; flowers orange/yellow, reverse yellow, 3½ in., full, high-centered, borne in small clusters; foliage medium, dark green, glossy, disease-resistant; prickles ¼ in., needle point hooked, medium brown, few; growth bushy, medium (22-25 in.); garden decoration, exhibition, containers; [sport of 'Glowing Amber']; intr. 2008

'Manhazel' ('Hazel McCallion') MinFl, pb, 2008, Mander, George; flowers pink/cream, reverse cream, 3 in., full, high-centered, blooms borne mostly solitary; foliage disease-resistant; prickles ¼ in., needlepoint, medium brown, moderate; growth to 25-30 in.; garden decoration, exhibition, containers; [Hot Tamale™ × 'Rubies 'n' Pearls']; intr. 2008

'Manian' ('Shirynne Cowan') MinFl, op, 2007, Mander, George; flowers orange/pink, reverse cream, medium, 3 in., dbl., borne in small clusters; foliage medium, dark green, semi-glossy, disease-resistant; prickles 9 mm., needle point, light brown, moderate; growth vigorous, bushy, medium (24-28 in.); containers, garden, exhibition; [(June Laver™ × 'Rubies 'n' Pearls') × 'Glowing Amber']; intr. 2008

'Manifesto' HT, op, 1920, McGredy; flowers flesh-pink, tinged salmon, dbl.

'Manilla' HT, Kordes, R.
'Manille' HT, yb, 1951, Mallerin, C.; flowers golden yellow edged red, very large, 40-50 petals, globular; foliage leathery, bronze; vigorous, upright growth; ['Pierre' × 'Lumiere']
'Manille' HT, my, Kordes; flowers chrome yellow, aging to canary, large, dbl.; growth to 60-70 cm.
'Maning' ('Ingrid') MinFl, rb, 2005, Mander, George; flowers very dark velvety red, reverse yellow, 3½-4 in., 25-30 petals, high-centered, borne in small clusters, moderate fragrance; foliage large, dark green, glossy; prickles numerous, ¼ to 5/16 in.es, needle point, brown; growth upright, tall (28 to 32 in.); garden decoration, containers, exhibition.; [Hot Tamale™ × 'Rubies 'n' Pearls']; intr. 2006
Manipur Magic™ -- See 'Virdor'
'Manipuri' -- See 'Virmanipuri'
'Manit' -- See 'Umsdad'
Manita® -- See 'Korberuhig'
'Manitoba Centennial Rose' -- See 'Cuthbert Grant'
'Manitou' HT, rb, 1957, Swim, H.C.; flowers coppery red, reverse golden yellow, well-formed, very large, dbl.; upright, bushy growth
'Manja' -- See 'Six Flags'
'Manja Mourier' -- See 'Six Flags'
'Manjana' F, op, 1969, deRuiter; flowers salmon-pink-apricot, high-centered; free growth; [Orange Sensation® × ('Pink Parfait' × 'Lavender Pinocchio')]
'Mankana 1' ('Mander #1', 'Mander's Nutkana') S, dr, 2006, Mander, George; flowers red/crimson, reverse light red, 4-5 in., full, borne in small clusters; non-rem,ontant; foliage medium size, medium green, semi-glossy; prickles ¼ to 3/8 in., needle-point, light brown, few; growth bushy, tall (7-8 ft.); garden; hips brightly colored; [Shades of Pink™ × R. nutkana]; intr. 2000
'Manlissa' LCl, dp, 1991, Mander, George; flowers large, dbl., borne in small clusters, intense fragrance; foliage medium size, dark green, glossy; tall, upright, bushy growth; ['Morgengruss' × 'Whisky Mac']
'Manmariam' ('Mariam Ismailjee') MinFl, rb, 2006, Mander, George; flowers medium red, reverse cream, 2½ in., single, borne mostly solitary; prickles 5/16 in., needle point, dark brown, few; growth to 30-36 in.; garden decorative, exhibition, containers; [Hot Tamale™ × 'Rubies 'n' Pearls']; disease-resistant; intr. 2007
'Manmatha' F, m, Pal, Dr. B.P.; flowers smoky pink to silvery mauve, small, dbl.; a smaller version of Paradise; intr. 1989
'Manmichael' ('Dr Michael Noble') Min, ob, 2006, Mander, George; flowers orange, reverse dark yellow, 2½ in., full, borne in small clusters; foliage medium size, dark green, glossy, disease-resistant; prickles ¼ in., hooked, light brown, moderate; growth bushy, medium (20-24 in.); garden, containers, exhibition; [Hot Tamale™ × 'Rubies 'n' Pearls']; intr. 2007
'Manmike' ('Michael Mander') MinFl, pb, 2007, Mander, George; flowers medium pink, reverse medium yellow, small, long-lasting, 3-3½ in., single, borne mostly solitary; prickles 9 mm., needle point, medium brown, few; growth to 28-30 in.; exhibition, garden decoration, containers; [Hot Tamale™ × 'Rubies 'n' Pearls']; disease-resistant; intr. 2008
'Mannequin' F, mp, 1961, Lens; vigorous, upright growth; [('Peace' × 'Cinnabar') × 'Fashion']
Mannheim® S, dr, 1959, Kordes, R.; flowers crimson, large, dbl., borne in clusters; recurrent bloom; upright (3 ft.), bushy growth; ['Rudolph Timm' × 'Fanal']; intr. 1958
'Manning's Blush' ('Maiden's Blush Sweet Briar', 'Mossy Sweetbriar', 'Pubescens') HEg, w, before 1819, Manning; flowers white faintly flushed pink, very small, dbl.; foliage fragrant (apple); growth to 4-5 ft.
'Mannington Lavender' -- See 'Mannington Mauve Rambler'
'Mannington Mauve Rambler' ('Mannington Lavender') Misc OGR, m, 2007, Walpole, Lord; flowers small, dbl., borne in large clusters; foliage small, medium green, matte; numerous prickles; growth spreading, bushy, tall (5 m.), rambling; ['The Garland' × unknown]; discovered by Lord Walpole on grounds of Mannington Hall; intr. 2001
'Manola' -- See 'Fred Cramphorn'
'Manon' HT, ab, 1924, Bernaix, P.; flowers yellow mixed with apricot, semi-dbl.; ['Christine' × 'Mrs Farmer']
Manora® -- See 'Tanaronam'
'Manorsun' ('Orange Sunset') Min, ob, 1996, Mander, George; flowers salmon-orange inside, some yellow stripes, orange-yellow reverse, 1½-2 in., full; foliage medium size, dark green, glossy; some prickles; medium (40-50 cm.), bushy growth; [June Laver™ × 'Rubies 'n' Pearls']; intr. 1996
'Manosque' HT, mr, 1958, Buyl Frères; flowers well-formed, intense fragrance; moderately vigorous growth
'Manou' Gr, Meilland, L.; intr. 1979
'Manou Meilland, Climbing' -- See 'Meitulimonsar'
Manou Meilland® -- See 'Meitulimon'
'Manpaz' ('Pink Topaz') Min, pb, 2000, Mander, George; flowers dark pink with red tips, pink-cream blend reverse, 2½-3 in., full, high-centered, borne mostly solitary, no fragrance; foliage medium size, dark green, glossy; prickles 5/16 in., needlepoint, few; growth upright, tall (20-24 in.); garden, containers, exhibition; [Hot Tamale™ × 'Rubies 'n' Pearls']; intr. 2001
'Manpetals' ('Glowing Petals') Min, op, 1996, Mander, George; flowers blend of salmon orange and pink, dark yellow reverse, 2-2½ in., full, no fragrance; foliage large, dark green, glossy; some prickles; medium (45-60 cm.), bushy growth; [June Laver™ × 'Rubies 'n' Pearls']; intr. 1996
'Manpride' ('George's Pride') Min, ob, 2007, Mander, George; flowers orange blend, reverse dark yellow, 4-6 cm., full, high-centered, borne in small clusters; foliage medium size, dark green, glossy, disease-resistant; prickles ¼ in., needlepoint, light brown, moderate; growth bushy, medium (40-50 cm.); garden, exhibition, containers; [sport of 'Glowing Amber']; intr. 2007
'Manprincess' HT, lp, 1991, Mander, George; flowers large, very full, borne mostly singly, slight fragrance; foliage medium size, light green, semi-glossy; tall, upright growth; [('Tiffany' × Pascali®) × 'Super Sun']
'Manpurgold' ('Purple 'n' Gold') MinFl, m, 2004, Mander, George; flowers purple-red, reverse gold, 3-3½ in., full, high-centered, borne in small clusters, slight fragrance; foliage medium size, dark green, semi-glossy; prickles ¼ in., needlepoint; growth bushy, medium (2-2½ ft.); containers, garden, exhibition; [Hot Tamale™ × 'floribunda seedling']; intr. 2005
'Manpurpearl' ('Purple Gem', 'S.E.A. of Love') F, m, 1992, Mander, George; flowers purple/cream bicolor, mauve color intensifies with sun and aging, 3-3½ in., full, high-centered; recurrent; foliage medium size, dark green, semi-glossy; prickles very few; medium (3-4 ft.), bushy growth; ['Rise 'n' Shine' × 'MANpurple']
'Manpurple' HT, m, 1991, Mander, George; flowers purple/cream bicolor, large, dbl., borne mostly singly; foliage medium size, dark green, glossy; medium, bushy growth; ['Mount Shasta' × 'Super Sun']
'Manpursun' ('Purple Sunset') Min, m, 1992, Mander, George; flowers purple/cream bicolor, very attractive bicolor combination, medium, dbl., no fragrance; foliage small, dark green, glossy; few prickles; low (35-40 cm.), upright growth; ['Rise 'n' Shine' × 'MANpurple']
'Manrupearl' ('Rubies 'n' Pearls') Min, m, 1992, Mander, George; flowers purple/cream bicolor, 2 in., dbl., cupped, slight fragrance; recurrent; foliage small, medium green, semi-glossy; few prickles; stems long; low (40-50 cm.), upright, bushy growth; ['Rise 'n' Shine' × 'MANpurple']
'Mansais' T, pb, 1838, Mansais; flowers pink with yellow shades, verylarge, full
'Manscarlet' ('Scarlet Pearl') F, rb, 1993, Mander, George; flowers scarlet red with white eye and white reverse, medium, 5 petals, borne in large clusters, slight fragrance; foliage medium size, dark

green, glossy; prickles numerous on basals, few on laterals; medium (90-100 cm.), bushy, spreading, very vigorous growth; [Pink Meidiland® × seedling]; intr. 1993

'Mansis' ('Ingrid's Sister Elisabeth') MinFl, pb, 2006, Mander, George; flowers dark pink, reverse cream, 3 in., very full, borne in large clusters; foliage medium size, dark green, glossy, disease-resistant; prickles 5/16 in., needle point, medium brown, moderate; growth upright, tall (30-36 in.); garden, containers, exhibition; [Hot Tamale™ × 'Rubies 'n' Pearls']

'Mansopas' Cl F, op, 1991, Mander, George; flowers medium pink shaded coral and cream, medium, full, borne in small clusters, slight fragrance; foliage medium size, dark green, glossy; tall, upright, bushy growth; [Shades of Pink™ × Pascali®]

'Manstar' ('Amber Star', 'Brittany's Glowing Star') Min, ob, 1999, Mander, George & Pazdzierski, Jim; flowers amber/orange, reverse golden yellow, 1¾-2¼ in., full, borne in small clusters, slight fragrance; foliage medium size, dark green, glossy; prickles moderate; upright, tall (15-20 in.) growth; [sport of 'Glowing Amber']; intr. 1999

'Mansuino Rose' ('Generosa') HT, mr, 1964, Mansuino, Q.; flowers crimson to spirea-red, small to medium, 35 petals, cupped; foliage small, dark; thin stems; PP2577

'Mansun' ('Amber Sun', 'Callum's Glow') Min, ob, 2001, Shuttleworth, Sam; flowers dark amber orange, reverse golden yellow, 4-6 cm., full, borne in small clusters, slight fragrance; foliage medium size, dark green, semi-glossy; prickles small (¼ in.), needlepoint, moderate; growth upright, tall (40-50 cm.); containers, garden, exhibition; [sport of 'Glowing Amber']; blooms open extremely slowly; intr. 2002

'Manteau de Jeanne d'Arc' B, lp, about 1840, Béluze; flowers flesh pink, fading to white, medium, very full

'Manteau d'Évêque' -- See 'Le Rosier Évêque'

'Manteau d'Évêque' HP, m, 1853, Moulins; flowers purple, becoming amaranth-voilet, large, full; intr. 1853

'Manteau d'Évêque' HCh, dr, in Angers; flowers velvety dark red, large, full

'Manteau Pourpre' -- See 'Rouge Formidable'

'Manteau Pourpre' ('Manteau Rouge') HGal, m, before 1811; flowers bright carmine-purple, underside silvery, very large petals, semi-dbl.; foliage long, deeply toothed, bright green

'Manteau Rouge' -- See 'Manteau Pourpre'

'Manteau Rouge' -- See 'Rouge Formidable'

'Manteau Royal' HGal, dr, before 1820, Descemet; flowers fiery crimson to Roman purple, medium, very full

'Manteo' -- See 'Briman'

'Mantopas' ('Golden Topas') Min, dy, 1995, Mander, George; flowers 1¾-2 in., dbl., borne in small clusters; foliage medium size, medium green, semi-glossy; some prickles; medium (35 cm.), bushy growth; [June Laver™ × 'Rubies 'n' Pearls']

'Manu Mukerji' HT, my, 1972, Friends Rosery; [sport of 'Fragrant Cloud']

'Manuel Canovas' -- See 'Maspagui'

'Manuel P. Azevedo' HT, mr, 1911, Soupert & Notting; flowers carmine-red, large, dbl.; ['Étoile de France' × 'Ulrich Brunner fils']

'Manuel Pinto de Azevedo' HT, pb, 1958, Moreira da Silva; flowers deep rose-pink, reverse lighter, 4 in., 48 petals, moderate fragrance; foliage dark, glossy, leathery; vigorous, upright growth; [seedling × 'Peace']; intr. 1957

Manuela® HT, mp, 1970, Tantau, Math.; flowers large, 30 petals, high-centered, moderate fragrance; foliage glossy; vigorous, upright, bushy growth; intr. 1969

'Manuelita' HT, or, 1947, Dot, Pedro; flowers large; very vigorous growth; ['Cynthia' × 'Vive la France']

'Manureva' -- See 'Saudril'

'Manx Queen' ('Isle of Man') F, ob, 1963, Dickson, Patrick; flowers rich gold flushed bronze red, medium, 18 petals, borne in large clusters, moderate fragrance; foliage dark; bushy, compact growth; ['Shepherd's Delight' × 'Circus']; intr. 1963

'Many Happy Returns' -- See 'Harwanted'

'Many Moons' F, my, 1984, Stoddard, Louis; flowers deep yellow to light yellow, large, 35 petals, moderate fragrance; foliage medium size, medium green, matte; upright, bushy, tall, arching growth; [Chinatown® × 'Maigold']

'Many Summers' HT, ob, 1976, Fryer, Gareth; flowers orange-copper, 6 in., 30 petals, intense fragrance; vigorous growth; ['Arthur Bell' × 'Belle Blonde']; intr. 1975

'Many Thanks' Min, ab, Geytenbeek; [sport of 'Mary Marshall']; intr. 1976

'Manyo' ('Ten Thousand Leaves') F, ab, Keisei; intr. 1988

'Mao' HT, rb, Takatori

'Maori Doll' Min, yb, 1977, Bell Roses; bud pointed, somewhat ovoid; flowers straw yellow in heat, azalea pink overlaying yellow in cool weather, 50 petals, borne in clusters, moderate fragrance; free-flowering; foliage medium green, glossy; growth bushy, upright; [sport of 'Yellow Doll']; intr. 1977

'Maori Lullaby' F, pb, 1963, Mason, P.G.; flowers carmine-rose, base light yellow to white, 3-3½ in., 10-12 petals, borne in clusters; foliage bronze, leathery; bushy, low, compact growth; ['Traumland' × seedling]

'Maori Moon' F, pb, 1976, Clayworth; bud pointed; flowers pink, center cream, large, 10 petals, cupped; foliage light, aging darker; upright, compact, bushy growth; ['Bengali' × ('Pink Parfait' × 'King Boreas')]; intr. 1974

'Maorilander' HT, mr, 1956, Mason, P.; bud ovoid, pointed; flowers crimson, lighter reverse, large, dbl., high-centered; foliage bronze, leathery; bushy growth; ['Crimson Glory' × 'Peace']

'Maoz II' Pol, pb, Motke Nevo; flowers dbl., slight fragrance

'Marama' -- See 'Simaramam'

'Maranta' F, yb, 1974, Tantau, Math.; bud globular; flowers yellow, red, medium, semi-dbl.; foliage soft; upright, bushy growth

'Marathon' F, op, 1956, Mondial Roses; flowers salmon-rose, 4 in., semi-dbl., borne in clusters; moderate, compact growth; ['Fashion' × 'hybrid tea seedling']

'Marbel' ('Belle') HT, lp, 1999, Hiltner, Martin; flowers light pink, reverse medium pink, 4½ in., dbl., borne mostly singly; foliage small, dark green, semi-glossy; prickles moderate; upright, medium (2½ ft.) growth; ['First Prize' × Handel®]

'Marbled' -- See 'Marmorea'

'Marbled Gallica' HGal, m, Scarman; intr. 2000

'Marbol' (Bolivar™) F, pb, 2006, Martin, Robert B., Jr.; flowers hot fuchsia pink, reverse cream with yellow heart, 3 in., full, borne mostly solitary; foliage medium size, dark green, glossy, disease-resistant; prickles medium, slightly hooked, brown, few; growth upright, medium (36 in.); exhibition, garden decorative; ['Silver Jubilee' × 'Steppin' Out']; intr. 2006

'Marbrée' -- See 'Marmorea'

'Marbrée' P, rb, 1858, Moreau et Robert; flowers strawberry red marbled white, large, semi-dbl. to dbl., very slight fragrance

'Marbrée d'Enghien' HSpn, w, about 1830, Parmentier; flowers cream white marbled with med, medium, dbl.; foliage small, oval, closely-set; prickles numerous, unequal, narrow, straight

'Marbrée d'Enghien' M, m, Robert; flowers purple-violet, striped and marbled with pink; intr. about 1850

'Marbutter' (Butter Cream™) MinFl, my, 2003, Martin, Robert B., Jr.; flowers my, reverse my, 2 in., full, borne mostly solitary, no fragrance; foliage medium size, medium green, s`emi-glossy; prickles small, straight, black, few; growth upright, tall (30 in.); exhibition, cutting, borders; ['Anne Morrow Linbergh' × 'Fairhope']; intr. 2003

'Marc-Antoine Charpentier' S, yb, Guillot-Massad; flowers yellow, fading through vanilla to creamy white as they open, full, cupped, opening flat, borne in clusters, slight tea fragrance; recurrent; arching, dome-shaped (2 m.) growth

'Marc Guillot' F, dr, 1958, Mallerin, C.; bud ovoid; flowers dark scarlet-red, medium, 25-35 petals, cupped; foliage dull green, leathery; vigorous, upright growth; ['Happiness' × 'Demain']; intr. 1955

'Marcel Boivin' HT, op, 1954, Buatois; flowers coral-pink, base yellow, very large, 50-60 petals; vigorous growth; ['Souv. de Claudius Pernet' × 'Château de Clos Vougeot']

'Marcel Bourgouin' ('Le Jacobin') HGal, m, 1898, Corboeuf-Marsault; flowers velvety, rich scarlet-purple, mottled violet; intr. 1899

'Marcel Grammont' HP, dr, 1868, Vigneron; flowers dark brownish-red, large, full, globular

'Marcel Pagnol' -- See 'Meisoyris'

'Marcel Pajotin' F, Kriloff, Michel; intr. 1976

'Marcel Turbat' LCl, Moreira da Silva, A.

'Marcelin Roda' T, w, 1872, Ducher; flowers white with yellow base, large, very full

'Marceline' HT, rb, 1928, Buatois; flowers crimson, edge and reverse violet-rose, dbl., slight fragrance; recurrent; ['Frau Karl Druschki' × 'Yves Druhen']

'Marcella' HT, op, Paul, W.; bud yellow; flowers salmon flesh, large, full, borne mostly solitary; intr. 1913

'Marcella' HP, w, 1865, Liabaud

'Marcella Baldge' -- See 'Souv de Marcelle Balage'

'Marcelle Auclair' F, or, 1970, Robichon; flowers medium, semi-dbl., high-centered, borne in clusters of 5-8, intense fragrance; foliage glossy, leathery; vigorous, upright growth; ['Soleil de Lyon' × seedling]; intr. 1964

'Marcelle Gret' HT, my, 1947, Meilland, F.; bud long, pointed; flowers saffron-yellow,, 6 in., 28 petals; foliage dark; vigorous growth; ['Peace' × 'Prinses Beatrix']

'Marcelle Gret, Climbing' Cl HT, my, 1957, Frères, Brenier

Marcelle Marchand® HT, mp, Adam; intr. 2002

'Marcelle Petit' F, op, 1958, Arles; flowers glowing salmon-pink; foliage glossy; vigorous growth; ['Pinocchio' × 'Independence']

'Marcellin Champagnat' -- See 'Meipierar'

'Märchen' Pol, lp, 1927, Kiese; flowers light rose pink with white, small, single

'Marchen Hiroko' HT, lp, Kitagawa; [sport of 'Bride's Dream']; intr. 2002

'Märchenkönigin' -- See 'Koroyness'

'Märchenland' ('Exception') F, ob, 1951, Tantau; flowers bright rose tinted salmon, large, 18 petals, blooms in clusters of 40, moderate fragrance; foliage dark; vigorous, upright growth; ['Swantje' × 'Hamburg']

'Märchentag' HT, lp, 1929, von Württemberg, Herzogin Elsa; flowers creamy pink, large, dbl.

'Marchesa Boccella' -- See 'Marquise Boccella'

'Marchioness of Downshire' HP, pb, 1894, Dickson, A.; flowers glossy carnation pink, shaded light red, aging to ivory-white, large, full

'Marchioness of Dufferin' HP, mp, 1891, Dickson, A.; flowers very large, dbl.

'Marchioness of Exeter' HP, lp, 1877, Laxton; flowers pale pink, tinted with cherry pink, petals recurved, semi-globular, moderate fragrance; ['Jules Margottin' × unknown]

'Marchioness of Linlithgow' HT, dr, 1929, Dobbie; flowers deep blackish crimson, open, large, dbl.; foliage soft, bronze; vigorous growth

'Marchioness of Londonderry' HP, lp, 1893, Dickson, A.; flowers pale pink, very large, 50 petals, high-centered, moderate fragrance; very vigorous growth; [probably a seedling of 'Baronne Adolphe de Rothschild']

'Marchioness of Lorne' HP, pb, 1889, Paul, W.; flowers rich rosy pink shaded darker, large, dbl., cupped; vigorous growth

'Marchioness of Ormonde' HT, ly, 1918, Dickson, H.; flowers clear wheat-straw color, center deep honey-yellow, dbl.

'Marchioness of Salisbury' ('Marquise de Salisbury') HT, dr, 1890, Pernet père; flowers velvety intense red, medium, dbl.; foliage thick, dark green; prickles prominent, numerous; growth upright

'Marchioness of Waterford' HT, pb, 1910, Dickson, H.; flowers dark silvery pink, edges lighter, reverse glossy salmon pink, large, full, globular

'Marcia' HT, op, 1952, Raffel; flowers pink to coral, base yellow, well-shaped, large; foliage glossy; vigorous, upright growth; ['Étoile de Hollande' × 'Raffel's Yellow']

'Marcia Coolidge' HT, pb, 1927, Coolidge; flowers very light pink, reverse darker, stamens dark crimson, semi-dbl.; ['Gen. MacArthur' × unknown]

'Marcia Gandy' HT, rb, 1959, Verschuren; flowers crimson to rose-red, reverse rose-opal, intense fragrance; vigorous growth; intr. 1957

'Marcia Stanhope' HT, w, 1922, Lilley; flowers pure white, large, 25 petals, globular; foliage leathery; ['Frau Karl Druschki' × unknown]

'Marco' HWich, w, 1905, Guillot, P.; bud buff; flowers white, center coppery, aging to reddish orange-yellow, 6-7 cm., full, borne in clusters; foliage glossy, purplish; growth to 10 ft.; [R. wichurana × 'Souv. de Catherine Guillot']

'Marco Polo' HT, lp, 1971, Fankhauser; flowers soft dawn-pink, large, dbl., high-centered; foliage glossy; vigorous, upright growth; ['Memoriam' × 'Elizabeth Fankhauser']

'Marco Polo' -- See 'Meipaleo'

'Marcyana' (R. × marcyana Boullu, R. × mareyana, R. terebinthinacea) S, m; flowers pink to light purple, with notched petals, 2½-3 in., single; some repeat; stems long-stalked; low (2 ft., rarely 4 ft.) growth; hips almost round; first found near Marcy l'Étoile, France; presumed to be a natural hybrid between R. gallica and R. tomentosa

'Mardi Gras, Climbing' Cl HT, dr, 1956, Kordes

'Mardi Gras' HT, dr, 1953, Jordan, G.L.; bud ovoid; flowers deep velvety red, 5 in., 33 petals, high-centered, moderate fragrance; foliage leathery; vigorous, upright, bushy growth; PP1139; ['Crimson Glory' × 'Poinsettia']

Mardi Gras™ -- See 'Jacfrain'

'Mardonius' HP, m, 1845, Béluze; flowers bluish pink, medium, full

'Maréchal Bazaine' HP, dp, 1864, de Fauw; flowers dark carmine-pink, medium

'Maréchal Bugeaud' T, pb, 1843; flowers lilac pink, shaded chamois, large, full

'Marechal Carmona' HT, op, Moreira da Silva; flowers salmon-pink with reddish tones

'Maréchal Davoust' M, mp, 1853, Robert; flowers bright rose, large, full, cupped

'Maréchal de Canrobert' HP, pb, 1863, Pernet; flowers bright pink with red, shaded purple, very large, dbl

'Maréchal de Canrobert' HP, pb, Lévêque; flowers light cherry, shaded carmine-purple, large, full, globular; intr. 1885

'Maréchal de Villars' B, dp; flowers deep rose shaded violet,, cupped

'Maréchal du Palais' B, lp, 1846, Béluze; flowers rosy blush, large, full, cupped

'Maréchal Foch' ('Red Orléans Rose') Pol, dp, 1918, Levavasseur; flowers cherry-red to pink, semi-dbl., open, borne in compact clusters, moderate fragrance; vigorous, bushy growth; [sport of 'Orléans Rose']

'Maréchal Forey' HP, mr, 1862, Margottin; flowers bright crimson with velvety violet, large, cupped

'Maréchal Forey' HP, mp, Pradel; flowers large, full; intr. 1863

'Maréchal Le Clerc' -- See 'Kricarlo'

'Maréchal Lyautey' HT, dr, 1931, Croibier; flowers deep red, large, very dbl., high-centered; foliage thick, dark, bronze; very vigorous, bushy growth; ['Hadley' × 'Laurent Carle']

'Maréchal Mortier' -- See 'Deuil du Maréchal Mortier'

'Maréchal Niel' N, my, 1864, Pradel; bud long, pointed; flowers golden yellow, large, dbl., intense fragrance; foliage large, light green; weak stems; very vigorous, climbing growth; ['Chromatella' × unknown (possibly 'Isabella Gray')]

'Maréchal Niel a Feuilles Panachées' T, cy, 1895, Dienemann; foliage striped with yellow; [sport of 'Maréchal Niel']

'Maréchal Pétain' HT, yb, 1926, Reymond; flowers soft pink on yellow ground

'Maréchal Robert' T, yb, 1875, Widow Ducher; flowers yellow, blushing slightly along edges, very large, full, globular

'Maréchal Stalin' HT, mr, Mélichar; flowers carmine-red, large, dbl.; intr. 1965

'Maréchal Suchet' HP, mr, 1863, Guillot; flowers crimson, shaded chestnut, large, full; possibly synonymous with one of the same name from Damaizin, 1877

'Maréchal Vaillant' -- See 'Pourpre d'Orléans'

'Marella' HT, pb, 1961, Meilland, Mrs. Marie-Louise; bud globular; flowers pink-red, large, 35 petals; foliage glossy, leathery; vigorous growth; [('Happiness' × 'Independence') × 'Better Times']

'Marella 2002' HT, ob, Meilland; flowers orange center, outer petals lighter, dbl., high-centered; florist rose; intr. 2004

'Maren' -- See 'Wilgmar'

'Mareva' -- See 'Noamel'

'Marfa' HT, w, Shtanko, E.E.; flowers dbl.; intr. 1975

'Marfil' HT, w, 1962, Dot, Pedro; flowers ivory-white, large; strong stems; tall growth; ['White Knight' × 'Angelis']

'Marga' HRg, lp, Riekstra; flowers medium, semi-dbl.; intr. 1979

'Marga Weil' HT, or, 1938, Weil; flowers salmon-red, large, dbl.

'Margalit' HT, op, 2002, Poole, Lionel; flowers salmon pink, pale pink/cream reverse, 5 in., full, borne mostly solitary, moderate fragrance; foliage large, dark green, semi-glossy; prickles medium, hooked, moderate; growth upright, bushy, vigorous, medium (1 m.); garden decorative, cutting; ['Joanne' × 'Pot of Gold']

'Margaret' HT, lp, 1909, Paul, W.; flowers light carnation pink, large, full

'Margaret' HT, pb, Dickson, A.; flowers bright pink, reverse silvery pink, well-shaped, 70 petals, moderate fragrance; vigorous growth; [('May Wettern' × unknown) × 'Souv. de Denier van der Gon']; intr. 1954

'Margaret Amos' HT, dp, 1952, McGredy, Sam IV; flowers strawberry-red, large, 25 petals, high-centered; foliage dark reddish green; very free growth; ['McGredy's Scarlet' × unknown]

'Margaret Anderson' ('Broomfield Novelty') LCl, w, 1931, Thomas; flowers centers deep cream, outer petals cream-flesh, very large, dbl.; recurrent bloom; foliage thick, leathery; very vigorous, climbing growth

'Margaret Ann Silverstein' -- See 'Horjilly'

'Margaret Anne' HT, pb, Matthews, W.J.; intr. 1977

'Margaret Anne Baxter' HT, w, 1927, Smith, T.; bud pointed; flowers white, sometimes tinted flesh, large, 88 petals; foliage thick, leathery, glossy, bronze; vigorous, bushy growth; ['Harry Kirk' × unknown]

'Margaret Belle Houston' HT, dr, 1929, Vestal; flowers velvety crimson, very large, dbl.; foliage light, leathery

'Margaret Browning' S, lp; intr. 2001

'Margaret Bushby' S, pb, 2000, Weatherly, Lilia; flowers deep pink opening paler, fading to almost white, yellow base, 5-6 cm., full, borne in small clusters, slight fragrance; foliage medium size, dark green, semi-glossy; prickles moderate; growth spreading, medium (5 ft.); [R. macrantha × unknown]; intr. 1999

'Margaret Chase Smith' HT, dr, 1966, Brownell, H.C.; bud long, pointed; flowers large, dbl., moderate fragrance; vigorous, upright growth; PP2959; ['Red Duchess' × Queen Elizabeth®]

'Margaret Chessum' -- See 'Bossexpaint'

'Margaret Clara' HT, ab, 1999, Jones, L.J.; flowers 2 in., full, borne mostly singly, moderate fragrance; foliage medium size, dark green, glossy, impervious to rain; prickles moderate; upright, medium (3½ ft.) growth; ['Solitaire' × (Alexander® × Remember Me®)]

'Margaret Daintry' -- See 'Hormartim'

'Margaret Denton' -- See 'Denmar'

'Margaret Dickson' HP, w, 1891, Dickson, A.; flowers white, center pale flesh, well-formed, large, 65 petals, cupped; occasionally recurrent bloom; foliage dark; vigorous growth; ['Lady Mary Fitzwilliam' × 'Merveille de Lyon']

'Margaret Dickson Hamill' HT, yb, 1915, Dickson, A.; flowers straw-yellow, flushed salmon, petals shell-shaped, large, dbl.; foliage dark, leathery; bushy growth

'Margaret Egerton' HT, dp, 1931, Chaplin Bros.; flowers rosy cerise passing to carmine, base yellow, well-formed; vigorous growth

'Margaret Elbogen' Pol, w, 1936, Brada, Dr.; flowers pinkish white; very vigorous growth

'Margaret Fleming' HRg, mp, 1995, Fleming, Joyce L.; flowers very clear pink, no lavender tones, small, semi-dbl., borne up to 5 per cluster, no fragrance; foliage medium to large, medium green, semi-glossy, somewhat; bushy (to 120 cm.) growth; [R. rugosa alba × 'Masquerade']; intr. 1994

'Margaret H' -- See 'Moemargaret'

'Margaret Hall' -- See 'Horminstrel'

'Margaret Haywood' HP, lp, 1890, Haywood; flowers full; [sport of 'Mme Clémence Joigneaux']

'Margaret Herbert' HT, lp, 1956, Harrison

'Margaret Horton' HT, ab, 1921, Hicks; bud pointed; flowers apricot-yellow, open, large, dbl., high-centered; foliage leathery, glossy, light; vigorous growth

'Margaret Isabel' HT, w, 1984, Summerell, B.L.; flowers oyster white, cream center, delicately flushed pink petal edges, 45 petals, high-centered, intense fragrance; prickles red-brown; upright growth; ['Strawberry Ice' × 'Redgold']; intr. 1983

'Margaret Isobel Hayes' -- See 'Harquantum'

'Margaret Jean' -- See 'Ponjean'

'Margaret Jean' Min, dp, 1978, Dobbs, Annette E.; bud ovoid; flowers deep pink, very dbl., borne 4-8 per cluster; foliage small, dark; prickles very few; bushy, vigorous growth; ['Fairy Moss' × 'Fairy Moss']

'Margaret Laver' -- See 'Lavmar'

'Margaret Law' F, ob, 1981, McTeer, Gilbert; flowers luminous orange, pink on outer petals, 25 petals, high-centered, borne 3-23 per cluster; foliage dark, glossy; prickles hooked, red; vigorous growth; ['Princess Michiko' × 'Gold Gleam']

'Margaret Lucas' -- See 'Kenmigqui'

'Margaret M. Wylie' ('Mrs A. J. Wylie') HT, pb, 1921, Dickson, H.; flowers flesh, edges heavily flushed deep rosy pink, dbl.

'Margaret McDowell' -- See 'Seadow'

'Margaret McGredy, Climbing' Cl HT, or, 1936, Dixie Rose Nursery

'Margaret McGredy' HT, or, 1927, McGredy; flowers orange-scarlet, large, 35 petals, high-centered, moderate fragrance; foliage light, leathery, glossy; vigorous growth

'Margaret Mercer' HT, yb, 1977, Mercer; flowers pale yellow, edged light pink, 4½ in., 53-65 petals; foliage glossy, dark; vigorous growth; ['Pink Favorite' × 'Peace']

Margaret Merril® -- See 'Harkuly'

'Margaret Molyneux' HT, my, 1909, Dickson, A.; flowers canary-yellow

'Margaret Moore Jacobs' HT, mp, 1968, Fuller; bud ovoid; flowers large, dbl., cupped; foliage glossy; vigorous, bushy growth; ['Tiffany' × 'Pink Masterpiece']

'Margaret O' -- See 'Ortmar'

'Margaret Roberts' F, dp, 1976, Wood; flowers cerise, large, 20-25 petals; foliage small, dark; moderate, free growth; [Elizabeth of Glamis® × 'Wendy Cussons']

'Margaret Ruth' HT, w, 1969, Taylor, L.R.; flowers creamy white, center pale pink, large, dbl., high-centered; intermittent bloom; foliage glossy, leathery; vigorous, upright, bushy growth; ['Anne Letts' × 'Christian Dior']

'Margaret Sharpe' T, mp

'Margaret Spaull' HT, ob, 1928, Cant, B. R.; flowers variable orange and lilac, dbl.; ['Ophelia' × seedling]

'Margaret Telfer' -- See 'Seatel'

'Margaret Thatcher' -- See 'Korflüg'

'Margaret Thatcher' -- See 'Taksun'

'Margaret Trudeau' -- See 'Sweepstakes'

'Margaret Turnbull' Cl HT, yb, 1931, Clark, A.; flowers soft pink on amber ground, 4½ in., dbl., cupped; recurrent; foliage wrinkled, light; vigorous, pillar growth

'Margaret Turnbull' -- See 'Worcola'

'Margaret van Rossem' HT, op, 1946, Van Rossem; flowers coppery salmon, center old-gold; moderate growth

'Margaret von Hessen' HT, Hetzel, K.; intr. 1973

'Margaret Wasserfall' -- See 'Koroberfinz'

'Margaret Watson' HT, pb; flowers pink

and white, large, dbl., high-centered

'Margarete Fuchs' HT, m, Mander, George; flowers mauve pink, lighter reverse, 5½ in, 28-30 petals, high-centered, intense fragrance; recurrent; foliage mildew resistant; growth to 3 ft.; intr. 2006

'Margarete Gnau' HT, ob, 1930, Krause; flowers creamy white on orange ground, very large, dbl., high-centered; foliage leathery; very vigorous growth; ['Mrs Charles Lamplough' × 'Souv. de H.A. Verschuren']

'Margarete Herbst' Pol, dr, 1934, Herbst; flowers dark blood-red, dbl.; late bloom; recurrent; foliage ruby-red when young; vigorous, bushy growth

'Margarete Krüger' HT, or; flowers salmon-red, large, semi-dbl.

'Margaretha Adelheid' S, mr, Drummond; intr. 2000

'Margaretha Mühle' HT, pb, 1925, Mühle; flowers clear satiny pink with silvery reflex, dbl.; ['Mme Caroline Testout' × 'Mrs W. J. Grant']

'Margarethe van de Mandere' F, dp, 1952, Leenders, M.; flowers raspberry-red, large, single; very vigorous growth

'Margaret's Choice' Gr, or, 1999, Tough, Ian Murray; flowers orange-vermillion, reverse whitish, stiff petals, 4½ in., full, borne mostly singly, moderate fragrance; foliage medium size, dark green, semi-glossy; prickles moderate; upright, tall (3-5 ft.) growth

'Margaret's World' F, or, Kirkham, Gordon Wilson; intr. 1995

'Margarita' N, yb, 1868, Guillot; flowers shining yellow, edges white, shaded pink, medium, full

'Margarita Riera' HT, op, 1924, Dot, Pedro; flowers brilliant rose-salmon, base yellow, dbl.; ['Mme Ravary' × 'Mme Edouard Herriot']

'Margat Jeune' HCh, mr, before 1850; flowers crimson, center lighter garnet, large, full

'Marge' S, pb, 1999, Jerabek, Paul E.; flowers med. pink, creamy white at base, deep pink splotches on outer petals, 3 in., full, borne mostly singly, moderate fragrance; foliage medium size, medium green, dull; prickles moderate; spreading, medium to tall (5 ft.) growth

'Margherita Croze' HT, m, 1914, Ketten Bros.; flowers carmine-purple changing to purple-rose, base shaded deep rose, large, dbl., moderate fragrance; ['Étoile de France' × 'Earl of Warwick']

'Margherita di Simone' T, yb, 1898, Guillot, P.; bud elegant, carmine orange yellow; flowers bright pink to carmine, shaded with deep yellow, reverse orange-yellow, large, full

Margie™ -- See 'Marmie'

'Margie Burns' HT, mp, 1970; flowers rose-pink, reverse Tyrian rose, large, dbl., high-centered, moderate fragrance; foliage leathery; very vigorous, upright, bushy growth

'Margina' -- See 'White Fairy'

'Margined Hip' -- See 'Hebe's Lip'

'Margit' HT, op, Kordes; flowers peach salmon, large, dbl., high-centered, borne mostly singly; stems long; growth vigorous, tall; intr. 1999

'Margo Koster' ('Sunbeam') Pol, ob, 1931, Koster, D.A.; flowers coral, small, 25-30 petals, globular, cupped, borne in clusters, slight fragrance; recurrent; growth medium, mounded; [sport of 'Dick Koster']

'Margo Koster, Climbing' ('Sunbeam, Climbing') Cl Pol, ob, 1962, Golie; flowers coral-orange, semi-dbl. to dbl., borne in large clusters, no fragrance; PP2291; [sport of 'Margo Koster']; intr. 1962

'Margo Koster Superior' Pol, ob, 1956, Koster, D.A.; flowers deep salmon-pink; [sport of 'Dick Koster']

'Margo's Baby' Pol, yb, 1988, Partain, Joe L.; flowers creamy ivory, salmon edges, aging dark edge, small, 30 petals, cupped, no fragrance; foliage small, medium green, glossy; prickles few, medium, light green; upright, bushy, low, vigorous growth; winter hardy; [sport of 'Margo Koster']; intr. 1995

'Margo's Sister' Pol, lp, 1954, Ratcliffe; flowers shell pink; [sport of 'Margo Koster']

'Margot Amos' HT, op; bud high, pointed; flowers coral-pink flushed strawberry, large; foliage glossy, bronze

'Margot Anstiss' HT, lp, 1947, Norman; flowers glossy satin-pink, 6 in., 40-45 petals; vigorous, branching growth

'Margot Asquith' HT, mr, 1934, Prince; flowers shining cerise-red, well-formed; very vigorous growth; ['Betty Uprichard' × 'Kitchener of Khartoum']

'Margot Fonteyn' HT, op, 1964, McGredy, Sam IV; flowers salmon-orange, 4 in., very dbl.; very free growth; ['Independence' × 'Ma Perkins']

'Margraten' F, mr, 1949, Leenders, M.; flowers currant-red, 3-4 in., 16 petals, flat, borne in trusses; foliage light green; vigorous, bushy growth; ['Donald Prior' × 'World's Fair']

'Margrethe Möller' HT, dp, 1914, Poulsen, D.T.; flowers deep cerise-rose, well-formed, dbl.; stems weak necks; ['Lady Mary Fitzwilliam' × seedling]

'Margriet Hermans' HT, yb, RvS-Melle; ['Frederik Chopin' × seedling]; intr. 1993

'Marguerite' T, dp, 1869, Guillot; flowers deep pink, aging to light red, medium, full

'Marguerite Amidieu de Clos' HT, my, 1926, Ketten Bros.; flowers buttercup-yellow, dbl.; ['Souv. de Claudius Pernet' × 'Golden Emblem']

'Marguerite Anne' -- See 'Cocredward'

'Marguérite Appert' -- See 'Mlle Marguérite Appert'

'Marguerite Bonnet' B, w, 1864, Liabaud; flowers flesh white, medium

'Marguerite Bourgeoys' -- See 'Wekcryland'

'Marguerite Brassac' HP, dr, 1874, Brassac; flowers purplish crimson, large, full; perhaps the same as Mme F. Brassac

'Marguerite Carels' Cl HP, mp, 1922, Nabonnand; bud pointed, large; flowers Neyron pink, center darker, 5 in., dbl., moderate fruity fragrance; recurrent bloom; vigorous, climbing growth; ['Frau Karl Druschki' × 'General MacArthur']

'Marguerite Chambard' HT, or, 1928, Chambard, C.; bud pointed; flowers geranium-red to vermilion, very large, high-centered; foliage dark; very vigorous, bushy growth

'Marguérite d'Anjou' B, mp, Moreau-Robert; flowers silky, soft pink; intr. 1864

'Marguérite d'Anjou' HP, rb, Trouillard; flowers red over white, small; intr. 1862

'Marguérite d'Anjou' HP, m, Boyau; flowers silky lilac pink, medium to large, full; intr. 1847

'Marguérite d'Anjou' Ch, mp, 1827, Guérin; flowers small to medium

'Marguerite d'Autricho' -- See 'Dortiche'

'Marguérite de Fénelon' T, pb, 1884, Nabonnand; flowers pink, shaded sulfur-yellow, large, semi-dbl.

'Marguerite de Flandre' C, dr, before 1862; flowers slatey deep red, full

'Marguerite de Flandre' D, lp; flowers flesh pink, large, full; intr. before 1885

'Marguerite de Roman' HP, w, 1882, Schwartz; flowers flesh white with flesh pink center, very large, full, moderate fragrance; recurrent; foliage light green; growth upright, strong

'Marguerite de St Amand' HP, mp, 1864, De Sansal; ['Jules Margottin' × unknown]

'Marguerite Defforey' HT, Orard, Joseph; intr. 1973

'Marguerite Desrayaux' N, mp, 1906, Nabonnand; flowers peachy pink and white, 9-10 cm., semi-dbl., borne in small clusters; foliage large; nearly thornless; ['Mme Alfred Carrière' × 'Mme Marie Lavalley']

'Marguerite d'Ombrain' ('Mlle Marguerite Dombrain') HP, mp, 1865, Verdier, E.; flowers very large, very full

'Marguerite Dubourg' B, mp, 1854, Pradel; flowers bright pink, large, full

'Marguerite Gigandet' T, yb, 1902, Nabonnand; bud coppery yellow; flowers reddish-coppery yellow, aging to golden yellow, very large, very full; ['Mlle Franziska Kruger' × 'Reine Emma des Pays-Bas']

'Marguerite Guillard' HP, w, 1915, Chambard, C.; flowers white, with yellow stamens, 20 petals, flat; [sport of 'Frau Karl Druschki']

'Marguerite Guillot' HT, ly, 1902, Guillot; flowers cream colored, fading to pure white, very large, dbl., globular, moderate fragrance; ['Mme Caroline Testout' × unknown]

'Marguerite Heitzmann' HT, or, 1930,

Buatois; flowers salmon-pink, stamens golden yellow, very large, dbl., cupped; foliage leathery; very vigorous growth; ['Frau Karl Druschki' × 'Mme Edouard Herriot']

'Marguerite Hilling' ('Pink Nevada') HMoy, mp, 1965, Hilling; flowers large, single, moderate fragrance; recurrent; foliage grey-green; growth open, arching; [sport of 'Nevada']; intr. 1959

'Marguerite Jaffelin' T, pb, 1902, Buatois; flowers China pink, shaded yellow, petal edges bright carmine, large, dbl.

'Marguerite Jamain' HP, lp, 1873, Jamain, H.; flowers flesh pink, large, very dbl.

'Marguerite Ketten' T, yb, 1897, Ketten Bros.; bud elegant; flowers yellowish peach red, petal edges tinted pink, large, full, moderate fragrance; growth vigorous, medium; ['Mme Caro' × 'Georges Farber']

'Marguerite Lartay' -- See 'Impératrice Eugénie'

'Marguerite Lartay' B, m, 1873, Lartay; flowers purple-pink, aging to light red, large, full, globular

'Marguerite Lecureaux' HP, rb, 1853, Cherpin; flowers bright red, striped white, medium, full

'Marguerite Moulin' HT, pb, 1938, Moulin; flowers lilac-pink, center salmon, large, very dbl., cupped; vigorous, bushy growth; [('Mme Edouard Herriot' × 'Mrs Aaron Ward') × 'Mme Caroline Testout']

'Marguerite Rose' Pol, mp, 1905, Robichon; flowers medium, dbl., borne in clusters

Marguerite Rose® F, pb, Laperriere; flowers medium pink with white eye and reverse, petals notched like a daisy, single, shallow cup to flat, borne in clusters; low to medium (2 ft.) growth; intr. 2006

'Margy' Pol, mr, 1936, Sauvageot, H.; flowers brilliant red, open, semi-dbl., moderate spicy fragrance; foliage small, soft; bushy growth

'Mari Carolyn' HT, m, 1999, Sproul, James A.; flowers 4-5 in., dbl., borne mostly singly; foliage medium size, medium green, semi-glossy; few prickles; bushy, medium (5 ft.) growth; ['Heirloom' × 'Chrysler Imperial']; intr. 1999

'Mari Dot' HT, ab, 1927, Dot, Pedro; flowers bright salmon to salmon-pink, base yellow, borne in clusters; foliage glossy; long, strong stems; very vigorous growth; ['O. Junyent' × 'Jean C.N. Forestier']

Maria™ -- See 'Poulen010(N)'

'Maria' HT, rb, Staikov, Prof. Dr. V.; flowers red, yellow reverse, large, 60 petals, borne singly, moderate tea fragrance; foliage dark, glossy; vigorous growth; ['Rina Herholdt' × seedling]; intr. 1974

'Maria' F, or, 1963, Gregory; flowers orange-scarlet, 3 in., 10 petals, borne in clusters; foliage very large, dark, leathery; vigorous, upright growth; [seedling × 'Border Beauty']

'Maria Antonia Camprubi' HT, mp, 1956, Munné, M.; flowers soft carmine, well-formed, large; vigorous growth; ['Peace' × 'Rosa Munne']

'Maria Burnett' Min, yb, 1980, Dobbs, Annette; bud globular; flowers light yellow, edged pink, small, 70 petals, globular; foliage light green; low growth; ['Little Darling' × 'Patricia Scranton']

'Maria Callas' ('Miss All-American Beauty') HT, dp, 1965, Meilland, Mrs. Marie-Louise; bud ovoid, large; flowers large, 55 petals, cupped, borne usually singly, intense fragrance; recurrent; foliage leathery; vigorous, bushy growth; PP2625; ['Chrysler Imperial' × 'Karl Herbst']; intr. 1965

'Maria Callas, Climbing' -- See 'Meidaudsar'

'Maria Carta' HT, Zandri, R.; intr. 1976

'Maria Chavarri de Salazar' HT, lp, 1935, Dot, Pedro; flowers large, dbl.

'Maria Cinta' HT, op, 1970, Dot, Simon; bud long, pointed; flowers coral, large, 28 petals, moderate fragrance; foliage glossy, bronze; low, compact growth; ['Duet' × ('Soraya' × 'Chrysler Imperial')]; intr. 1967

'Maria Cristina' ('Reina Maria Christina') T, ob, 1895, Aldrufeu, Joaquin; flowers bright orange'yellow, tinted carmine, medium to large, full, globular

'Maria de Mello' HT, dr, 1935, Ketten Bros.; bud pointed; flowers bright velvety carmine-purple, large, 40-45 petals, cupped; foliage bronze Quaker green; vigorous, branching growth; ['Mme Gabriel Hanra' × 'Mrs John Bell']

'María de Rossi' mr, Requena; intr. 1976

'Maria Delforge' Pol, mp, 1959, Delforge; bud oval; flowers pink, rosette form, medium, dbl., borne in clusters; foliage glossy; vigorous, bushy, low growth; [Orange Triumph® × 'Ma Perkins']

'Maria Georgiana' F, mp, Horner; intr. 2005

'Maria Graebner' (R. × mariae-graebneriae) S, mp, about 1900; buds with leafy bracts; flowers bright rose pink, small, single, slight fragrance; a few borne all summer; foliage orange and red in fall; growth to 5 ft.; hips subglobose, red; [R. palustris × R. virginiana]

'Maria Guarro' HT, dp, 1935, Dot, Pedro; bud pointed; flowers pink in spring, blood-red in summer, large, very dbl., high-centered; foliage glossy, dark; very vigorous growth; ['Château de Clos Vougeot' × 'Li Bures']

'Maria Hofker' HT, my, Interplant; intr. 1993

'Maria Isabel' HT, mr, Camprubi, C.; flowers deep strawberry-red, base yellow, high-centered; foliage dark; vigorous growth

'Maria Iurato' Cl F, dp, 2002, Gareffa, N.; flowers full, borne in large clusters, moderate fragrance; foliage medium size, medium green, semi-glossy; prickles variable, sharp, numerous; growth climbing, tall (to 15 ft.); very hardy; [unknown × unknown]; intr. 1991

'Maria Kent' -- See 'Worcollege'

'Maria Leonida' ('Marie Leonida', R. × leonida) HBc, w, 1829, Lemoyne; flowers white, nuanced straw yellow, tinged rose at center, 6-8 cm., full, flat, quartered, intense tea fragrance; foliage small, dark green, glossy; prickles moderate; often confused with Alba Odorata; possibly R. bracteata × R. laevigata, or R. bracteata × Tea

'Maria Liesa' HMult, dp, 1925, Bruder Alfons; flowers carmine-pink, white center, prominent yellow stamens, 2½-3 cm., single, borne in very large clusters; foliage dark green; nearly thornless

'Maria Lisa' HWich, pb, 1936, Liabaud; flowers clear rose, center white, stamens yellow, open, small, single; profuse, non-recurrent bloom; foliage dark, leathery; very vigorous, climbing or trailing growth

'Maria Maass' HT, w, 1927, Maass; flowers very large, very dbl.

Maria Mathilda® -- See 'Lenmar'

'Maria McGredy' -- See 'Macturang'

'Maria Peral' HT, yb, 1941, Dot, Pedro; flowers yellow suffused red, large, dbl.; very vigorous growth

'Maria Reid' HT, dp, 1924, Ferguson, W.; flowers dark rose-pink tinted peach, base yellow, dbl.; ['Mme Caroline Testout' × 'George C. Waud']

'Maria Renaissance' (Maria™) S, dp, Olesen; bud broad based pointed ovoid; flowers deep pink to light red, white vertical line bisects reverse of petals, 8 cm., 50 petals, deep cup, borne in clusters of 5 - 9, moderate floral perfume fragrance; recurrent; foliage matte; upright to bushy (100-150 cm.) growth; PP15620; [seedling × 'Radox Bouquet']; intr. 2002

'Maria Serrat' HT, op, 1946, Munné, M.; flowers salmon-pink, base yellow, reverse deep yellow; ['Mrs Pierre S. duPont' × 'Baronesa de Ovilar']

'Maria Shriver' Gr, w, Dorieux; flowers large, pure white, 40 petals, borne in neat clusters, strong citrus fragrance; foliage polished, dark green; stems long; growth tall (4-5 ft.) and stately; PPAF; intr. 2005

'Maria Star' T, op, 1913, Pery-Gravereaux; flowers salmon-gold; ['Mme Gustave Henry' × 'Mme Jules Gravereaux']

'Maria Stern' HT, ob, 1969, Brownell, H.C.; bud pointed; flowers orange, large, 43 petals, globular, moderate fragrance; vigorous, upright growth; PP2960; ['Tip Toes' × Queen Elizabeth®]

Maria Teresa® -- See 'Lenmacra'

'Maria Teresa de Esteban' -- See 'Coral Fiesta'

'Maria Theresa' HP, lp, 1872, Ducher; flowers light pink, medium to large, very full, globular

'Maria-Theresa' HT, ab, Fryer, Gareth;

intr. 1994

'Mariaeburgensis' -- See 'De Marienbourg'

'Mariah Carey' -- See 'Hormarcar'

'Mariale'   HT, ab, 1956, de Boer; flowers orange-yellow, semi-dbl.; vigorous growth; [sport of 'Souv. de Jacques Verschuren']

'Mariam Ismailjee' -- See 'Manmariam'

'Marian Anderson'   HT, dp, 1964, Lammerts, Dr. Walter; flowers deep pink, large, semi-dbl., high-centered, moderate spicy fragrance; foliage glossy; vigorous, tall, compact growth; PP2526; [Queen Elizabeth® × 'Merry Widow']; intr. 1964

'Marian Colthorpe'   HT, op, 1946, Wheatcroft Bros.; flowers coral shaded lemon and pink

'Marian Finnucane' -- See 'Kenbrog'

'Mariana'   HT, ob, Kordes; flowers orange developing pink on the edges, medium to large, dbl., high-centered, borne mostly singly; stems long; greenhouse rose; intr. 2003

Mariandel® -- See 'Korpeahn'

'Mariandel 92'   F, rb, Hannemann, F.; ['Ko's Yellow' × Eyepaint®]

'Marianna Rolfs'   Cl HT, lp, 1926, Walter, L.; flowers silvery pink, semi-dbl.

'Marianne' -- See 'Meiklusy'

Marianne™ -- See 'Marianne Hit'

'Marianne' -- See 'Ardgoldeneyes'

'Marianne'   HT, yb, 1933, Krause; flowers mixture of copper-yellow, pink and red, large, high-centered; vigorous, bushy growth; ['Sybil' × 'Sunstar']

'Marianne Busse'   T, dr, 1901, Brauer; flowers medium

'Marianne Hit'   (Marianne™) MinFl, my, Poulsen; flowers medium yellow, 5-8 cm., semi-dbl., slight wild rose fragrance; foliage dark; growth bushy, 40-60 cm.; PP14990; intr. 2001

'Marianne Kluis'   Pol, mr, 1942, W. Kordes Söhne; flowers carmine-red, small, dbl.

'Marianne Kluis Superior'   Pol, mr, 1930, Kluis & Koning; flowers deep violet-red; [sport of 'Greta Kluis Superior']

'Marianne Pfitzer'   HT, lp, 1902, Jacobs; flowers flesh, with a deep pink and reddish sheen, very large, dbl.; ['Kaiserin Auguste Viktoria' × unknown]

'Marianne Powell'   HT, dr, 1987, Powell, G.; flowers large, 50 petals, moderate fragrance; foliage large, dark green, glossy; upright growth; [Kerryman® × 'Red Dandy']; intr. 1986

'Marianne Tudor'   ('Nuit d'Été') HT, mr, Fryer, Gareth; flowers bright red, large; growth strong, vigorous; intr. 1993

'Marianne Wolff'   S, mp, 2003, Wolff, Stefan; flowers 2½ in., full, borne mostly solitary, remontant; foliage medium size, medium green, semi-glossy, disease-resistant; few prickles; growth upright, medium (3-4 ft.); hardy to -30°F; ['Winnipeg Parks' × unknown]

'Mariano Vergara'   T, mr, 1896, Aldrufeu; flowers magenta-red with vermilion reflections, large, dbl.; vigorous growth

'Mariatheresia'   F, mp, Tantau; flowers full, quartered, borne in clusters, slight fragrance; recurrent; foliage dark green, glossy; growth strong, bushy; intr. 2004

'Maribel' -- See 'Cocdana'

'Maribell'   HT, rb, 1988, Gressard, J.; flowers carmine red, reverse silver white, large, 40-45 petals; upright, vigorous growth; [('Sea Pearl' × 'Zorina') × 'Lovita']; intr. 1988

'Marica'   HT, mp, 1964, Mondial Roses; flowers bright pink, large, dbl.; strong stems; vigorous, symmetrical growth

'Marica'   Cl Min, pb, Kono, Yoshito; flowers pink, reverse white; [sport of 'Ginza Komachi']; intr. 1989

'Marichu Zayas'   HT, lp, 1906, Soupert & Notting; bud long; flowers light strawberry, large, full; [('Mrs W. J. Grant' × unknown) × unknown]

'Marie' -- See 'Resmar'

'Marie Accary' ('Mme Marie Accary') N, pb, 1872, Guillot et Fils; flowers white tinted pink and yellow, fading to white, small, full, borne in small clusters

'Marie Adélaïde' ('Grande Duchesse de Luxembourg', 'Luxembourg') HT, yb, 1912, Soupert & Notting; bud pointed; flowers coppery yellow, center deeper, large, dbl., high-centered; foliage bronze, soft; vigorous, spreading growth; ['Mme J.W. Budde' × 'Lyon Rose']

'Marie-Antoinette'   HGal, m, 1829, Vibert; flowers lilac-rose, large, dbl.

'Marie Antoinette'   HT, mp, 1968, Armstrong, D.L.; bud long, pointed; flowers pink, reverse darker, large, dbl., cupped; foliage dark, glossy; very vigorous, upright growth; PP2928; [Queen Elizabeth® × 'Chrysler Imperial']

Marie Antoinette®   F, w, Tantau; flowers ivory, dbl., cupped, borne in clusters, intense spicy fragrance; recurrent; low (2 ft.) growth; intr. 2004

'Marie Antoinette Rety'   HT, Orard; intr. 1983

'Marie-Antoinette Rety'   HT, op

'Marie Baumann' ('Marie Beaumann', 'Mme Alphonse Lavallée') HP, mr, 1863, Baumann; flowers carmine-red, large, 55 petals, globular, moderate fragrance; foliage dark; vigorous growth; ['Alfred Colomb' × unknown]

'Marie Beaumann' -- See 'Marie Baumann'

'Marie Berton' ('Mme Marie Berton') T, ly, 1875, Levet; flowers straw yellow fading to cream, very large, full; ['Gloire de Dijon' × unknown]; sometimes classed as N

'Marie Boissée'   HP, w, 1864, Oger; flowers blush-white, aging to pure white, large, full, cupped

'Marie Boyer'   HP, dp, 1858, Lartay

'Marie Brissonet'   Pol, lp, 1913, Turbat; flowers flesh-rose, borne in pyramidal clusters of 75-100

'Marie Bugnet'   HRg, w, 1965, Bugnet; bud long, pointed; flowers snow white, 3 in., dbl., intense fragrance; recurrent bloom; foliage light green, rugose; vigorous (3 ft.), bushy, compact growth; [('Therese Bugnet' × seedling) × 'F.J. Grootendorst']; intr. 1959

'Marie Bülow'   N, pb, 1903, Welter; bud long, pointed; flowers China rose, changing to carmine and pure yellow, large, full; ['Maréchal Niel' × 'Luciole']

Marie-Caroline®   F, dp, Adam; flowers bright pink, large, full, cupped, then flat, borne in clusters; recurrent; squat, vigorous (2-3 ft.) growth; intr. 2006

'Marie Casant' -- See 'Marytje Cazant'

'Marie-Chantal'   F, mp, 1959, Gaujard; flowers bright pink, open, large, semi-dbl.; foliage glossy; vigorous, bushy growth; ['Peace' × 'Fernand Arles']

'Marie Chargé'   N, yb, 1853, Desponds; flowers golden yellow, shaded carmine pink, medium, full

'Marie Christina'   MinFl, lp; intr. 1988

'Marie Claire'   HT, or, 1938, Meilland, F.; bud deep orange-red; flowers golden coral-red, passing to orange-yellow, large, dbl.; foliage bronze, glossy; strong stems; very vigorous, cmpact growth; [('Charles P. Kilham' × 'Duquesa de Peñaranda') × ('Charles P. Kilham' × 'Margaret McGredy')]

'Marie Claire, Climbing' ('Grimpant Marie Claire') Cl HT, or, 1944, Meilland, F.

'Marie Curie' ('Romantic Dreams', 'Umilo') F, ob, Meilland; flowers orange with yellow base and pale pink edges, 30-35 petals, high-centered, borne in clusters, moderate clove fragrance; recurrent; foliage dark green; growth to 60-70 cm.; intr. 1996

'Marie Daly'   Pol, mp; bud long, pointed; flowers dbl., borne in small clusters, moderate sweet musk fragrance; good repeat; foliage large, rich green; few prickles; growth compact, bushy; [sport of 'Marie Pavie']; EarthKind; intr. 1999

'Marie de Blois'   M, mp, 1852, Moreau et Robert; flowers pink tinted lighter, 9-10 cm., full

'Marie de Bourgogne'   M, mp, Robert; flowers bright rose, 2½ in., dbl., globular/cupped, borne in clusters of 5-6; some repeat; intr. 1853

'Marie de Bourgogne'   A, pb, before 1844, Vibert; flowers rose, spotted white, medium, very dbl.

'Marie de Saint Jean'   P, w, 1869, Damaizin; flowers white, edged with carmine red, 6 cm., dbl., borne mostly solitary, intense fragrance; foliage glaucous green, rounded; prickles small, moderate; stems medium-sized, thin; growth vigorous, upright

'Marie Dermar'   N, ly, 1889, Geschwind, R.; flowers cream and flesh, 5 cm., dbl., borne in small clusters, moderate fragrance; numerous prickles; ['Louise d'Arzens' × unknown]

'Marie Desfossés'   B, mp, 1850, Desfos-

sés; flowers dark flesh pink, large, full
'Marie Desmazures' ('Mme Desmazes') HP, mp, 1868, Desmazures; flowers pink, shaded darker at center, medium, full
'Marie Dietrich' HWich, yb, 1928, Walter, L.; bud small, crimson; flowers yellowish-red, passing to white to medium, 4-5 cm., semi-dbl., borne in clusters of 10-20, moderate fragrance, foliage glossy; ['Leontine Gervais' × 'Eugenie Lamesch']
'Marie d'Orléans' Bslt, lp, 1825, Boutigny; flowers flesh pink, fading to white
'Marie d'Orléans' T, mp, Nabonnand, G.; flowers bright pink shaded darker, large, dbl., flat; vigorous growth; intr. 1884
'Marie Dougherty' F, dr, 1977, Linscott; bud long, slender; flowers large, 5 petals, slight tea fragrance; foliage glossy; moderate, bushy growth; [Sarabande® × Sarabande®]; intr. 1972
'Marie Ducher' T, lp, 1869, Ducher; flowers large, full, moderate fragrance
'Marie Duleau' B, w, about 1850, Desfossés; flowers flesh white, medium, full
'Marie Dutour' F, op, 1962, Arles; flowers reddish-salmon, well-formed, large; ['Aloha' × ('Gloire du Midi' × Edith de Martinelli®)]
'Marie Eads' Pol, mr, 1991, Eads, C.E.; bud rounded; flowers medium red with blue overtones, reverse light red, small, 25 petals, borne in sprays of 10 - 25, no fragrance; repeat bloom; foliage medium size, medium green, semi-glossy with fringed stipules; bushy, low growth; ['Baby Faurax' × 'Verdun']
'Marie Elizabeth' F, yb, 1965, McGredy, Sam IV; flowers yellow shaded rose-pink, 3 in., 28 petals, flat; foliage dark, heavily veined; vigorous growth; ['Clare Grammerstorf' × 'Cavalcade']
'Marie Faist' HT, op, 1925, Berger, V.; flowers shell-pink tinted salmon, center darker, with orange, dbl.; ['Mme Edmond Rostand' × 'Mrs T. Hillas']
'Marie Finger' -- See 'Mlle Eugénie Verdier'
'Marie-France' HT, my, 1957, Dorieux; bud apricot shaded orange; flowers pure yellow, large, semi-dbl.; very vigorous growth; ['Feu Pernet-Ducher' × 'Léonce Colombier']
'Marie-Francoise Saignes' HT, mr
'Marie Girard' HT, lp, 1898, Buatois; flowers flesh white nuanced yellowish-salmon, dbl., cupped, moderate fragrance; foliage large, dark green
'Marie Gouchault' HWich, mr, 1927, Turbat; flowers clear red passing to brilliant salmon-rose, reverse lighter, 4 cm., dbl., borne in clusters of 30-40, no fragrance; sometimes recurrent bloom; foliage medium green, glossy; nearly thornless; very vigorous growth
'Marie Greene' HT, mr, 1941, Clark, A.; flowers rich red
'Marie Guillot' T, w, 1874, Guillot et Fils; flowers white, tinged yellow, large, dbl.; strong stems; vigorous growth
'Marie Guillot, Climbing' Cl T, w, 1898, Dingee & Conard; flowers yellowish-white, extra large, full, moderate fragrance; [sport of 'Marie Guillot']
'Marie Henriette Gräfin Chotek' -- See 'Gräfin Marie Henriette Chotek'
'Marie Henry' HT, ly, 1900, Buatois; flowers white, lightly tinted canary yellow, large, dbl., moderate fragrance; ['Irene Watts' × 'Beauté Lyonnaise']
'Marie Isakoff' HT, yb, 1901, Dubreuil; flowers apricot yellow fading to pale canary, large, full; ['Mme Caroline Testout' × unknown]
'Marie-Jeanne' Pol, w, 1913, Turbat; flowers pale blush-cream, fading to white, 4 cm., dbl., round, borne in clusters of 20; remontant; no prickles; growth to 2-3 ft.
'Marie Jeannette' Min, yb, 2000, Fletcher, Ira R.; flowers light yellow to white, sometimes touch of light pink, medium, dbl., borne singly and in small clusters, slight fragrance; foliage medium size, medium green, matte; prickles moderate; growth upright, tall (to 120 cm.); [sport of 'Irresistible']; intr. 2001
'Marie Joly' B, lp, 1860, Oger; flowers light flesh pink, medium, full
Marie Laforêt® HT, w, Dorieux; flowers white to blush with thin pink edges, full, high-centered; intr. 1996
'Marie Lambert' ('Priscilla', 'Snowflake', 'White Hermosa') T, w, 1886, Lambert, E.; flowers pure white, semi-dbl. to dbl., loose; recurrent; growth low, compact; [sport of 'Mme Bravy']
'Marie Larpin' B, lp, 1867, Guillot; flowers light pink, tinted white, medium, full
'Marie Lavalley' -- See 'Mme Marie Lavalley'
'Marie Lavier' HT, yb, 1935, Buatois; bud brownish yellow; flowers reddish nankeen yellow to salmon-yellow, rather large, dbl.; vigorous, bushy growth; ['Souv. de Claudius Pernet' × 'Mme Edouard Herriot']
'Marie Lecomte' T, my, 1885, Singer; flowers butter yellow, tinted dark carmine, very large, full
'Marie Leczinska' HP, lp, 1847, Béluze; flowers flesh pink, center bright pink, medium, full
'Marie Leczinska' M, dp, Moreau-Robert; flowers 6-8 cm., full, globular; some repeat; intr. 1865
'Marie Leonida' -- See 'Maria Leonida'
'Marie-Louise' ('Agathe Couronnée', 'Belle Flamande', 'Tendresse Admirable', 'Caprice du Zéphyre', 'Agathe Rose', 'Orphée de Lille', 'Augustine Pourprée') D, dp, around 1811; flowers mauve-pink, very large, very dbl., quartered, intense fragrance; foliage medium green, elliptical; few prickles; bushy, shrubby (about 4 ft.) growth; cultivated at Malmaison; possibly from Prévost
'Marie Louise Marcenot' HT, op, 1900, Buatois; flowers salmon pink with copper and saffron tints, large, full; ['Victor Verdier' × 'Dr Grill']
'Marie-Louise Mathian' HT, ly, 1912, Fugier; flowers cream white, with a salmon tint at the center, large, dbl., intense fragrance
'Marie Louise Pernet' HP, dp, 1876, Pernet père; flowers deep rose, large, full, cupped
'Marie-Louise Poncet' HT, op, 1929, Gaujard; flowers coppery rose to pale coppery pink, reverse carmine-salmon
'Marie Louise Puyravaud' T, my, 1896, Puyravaud; flowers citron yellow, striped canary yellow, edged peach, reverse white, large, full; ['Mlle Lazarine Poizeau' × unknown]
'Marie-Louise Sondaz' HT, w, 1970, Gaujard; flowers cream shaded red, very large, dbl., moderate fragrance; foliage dark; very vigorous, upright growth; [Rose Gaujard® × 'Peace']; intr. 1967
'Marie-Louise Velge' F, lp, RvS-Melle; flowers light pink suffused white, 4 in., 20 petals, flat, borne in clusters, slight fragrance; recurrent; foliage dense dark green; intr. 1997
Marie-Luise Marjan® -- See 'Korfinger'
'Marie Lünnemann' HT, my, 1920, Timmermans; flowers clear pink, dbl.; ['Pharisaer' × 'Laurent Carle']
'Marie Maass' HT, w, 1928, Maass; flowers pure white to ivory-white, very large, dbl.; vigorous, bushy growth; ['Kaiserin Auguste Viktoria' × 'Marechal Niel']
'Marie Menudel' HP, op, 1927, Barbier; flowers rose-pink, tinted salmon, large, dbl.
'Marie Nordlinger' M, lp, Morley, Dr B.; ['Henri Martin' × unknown]; intr. 1988
'Marie Palit' HT, pb, Datt, Braham; flowers white with deep pink edges, dbl.; intr. 1988
'Marie Paré' B, lp, 1880, Paré/Jamain; flowers light flesh, center brighter, medium, full; ['Mistress Bosanquet' × unknown]
'Marie Paule Belle' mr, Requena; intr. 1984
'Marie Pavic' -- See 'Marie Pavié'
'Marie Pavié' ('Marie Pavic') Pol, w, 1888, Allégatière; flowers white, center flesh, 2 in., dbl., borne in clusters; foliage large, rich green; no prickles; vigorous, bushy growth
'Marie Pavié, Climbing' Cl Pol, lp, 1904, Bénard; flowers whitish pink, center darker, medium, full, rosette; [sport of 'Marie Pavié']
'Marie Perrachon' HP, m, 1864, Ducher; flowers violet-purple, medium
'Marie Pochin' -- See 'Mary Pochin'
'Marie Portemer' HP, m, 1857, Portemer; flowers purple, large, full
'Marie Rady' -- See 'Mlle Marie Rady'
'Marie Renfroe' Min, ab, 2007, Meyer, Lawrence E. & Doris J.; flowers light apricot to light yellow, pink at base, reverse cream to light yellow, 1 in., dbl., borne mostly solitary; foliage medium,

dark green, semi-glossy; prickles 5 cm., straight, clear to pale pink, few; growth open bush, medium (2 ft.); garden decoration, exhibition; [sport of 'Tiny Petals']; intr. 2007

'Marie Robert' P, m, 1850, Robert et Moreau; flowers lilac-pink, medium, dbl.

'Marie Robert' N, pb, Cochet; flowers bright rose marbled with salmon and apricot, large, full, no fragrance; ['Isabella Gray' × unknown]; intr. 1893

'Marie Roland' T, lp, 1870, Roland; flowers flesh pink, edges lighter, large, semi-dbl.

'Marie-Rose' Pol, mp, 1930, Truffaut, T.A.; flowers ruddy pink, large, dbl., carnation-like, borne in clusters of 30; foliage glossy; very vigorous growth; [sport of 'Marie-Jeanne']

'Marie-Rose, Climbing' Cl Pol, dp; flowers dbl.

'Marie-Rose Besson' HT, lp, 1939, Mallerin, C.; bud long, pointed, yellow, tinted coral; flowers light pink, tinted coral-orange, large, dbl.; foliage glossy; long stems; vigorous growth; ['Souv. de Claudius Pernet' × seedling]

'Marie-Rose Toussaint' HT, lp, 1946, Gaujard; flowers satiny pink, very large; foliage dark, leathery; strong stems; vigorous, bushy growth

'Marie Schmitt' HT, lp, 1910, Schmitt; flowers large, dbl.; [sport of 'Mme Caroline Testout']

'Marie Segond' T, pb, 1902, Nabonnand; bud elongated, coppery tinted carmine; flowers pink tinted flame, medium, full; ['Mme la Comtesse de Leusse' × 'Mlle Lazarine Poizeau']

Marie Shields™ -- See 'Mormari'

'Marie Sisley' T, yb, 1868, Guillot fils; flowers pale yellow, broadly margined with bright rose, large, full, globular

'Marie Soleau' T, mp, 1895, Nabonnand; flowers slivery pink, large, full; ['Mlle Suzanne Blanchet' × unknown]

'Marie Stuart' HGal, dp, 1820, Dubourg; flowers crimson pink, large, full

'Marie Teresa Bordas' HT, mp, 1958, Bordas; bud ovoid; flowers rose-pink, very large, very dbl., high-centered, moderate fragrance; foliage dark, glossy; very vigorous, upright, bushy growth; ['Sensation' × 'Peace']; intr. 1956

'Marie-Thérèse' HWich, dp, 1917, Turbat

'Marie Thérèse Dubourg' N, dy, 1888, Godard; flowers deep coppery golden yellow

'Marie Treusz' HMult, m, 1909, Walter

'Marie Tudor' HGal, dp, before 1835; flowers slaty violet-red

'Marie van Houtte' ('Mlle Marie van Houtte', 'The Gem') T, pb, 1871, Ducher; flowers deep cream, tinged pink, base buff-yellow, large, very dbl., high-centered; foliage rich green, leathery; vigorous, bushy, sprawling growth; ['Mme de Tartas' × 'Mme Falcot']

'Marie van Houtte, Climbing' Cl T, pb, 1936, Thomasville Nursery; flowers creamy, pink-tinged yellow; [sport of 'Marie Van Houtte']

'Marie Verbrugh' F, op, 1954, Leenders, M.; flowers yellow-salmon, reverse coral, well-formed, large, dbl.; bushy growth; ['Ambassadeur Nemry' × 'Souv. de Claudius Pernet']

'Marie Verdier' -- See 'Mlle Marie Verdier'

'Marie-Victoria Benoît' M, mp, 1905, Puyrvaud; flowers satiny pink, very large, cupped, moderate fragrance; foliage dark green; prickles small, short, reddish; ['Eugénie Guinoisseau' × unknown]

'Marie-Victorin' -- See 'AC Marie Victorin'

'Marie Victorin' S, op, L'Assomption; flowers 38 petals, flat

'Marie Young' HT, or; flowers brilliant orange-red, well-formed

'Marie Zahn' HT, lp, 1887, Müller, Dr. F.; bud long, pointed; flowers light pink, yellow at center, large, full, cupped; foliage light green; [('Reine des Ile-Bourbons' × 'Maréchal Niel') × ('Pierre Notting' × 'Safrano')]

'Mariechen' S, mp, Schultheis; flowers bright pink, dbl., loose, borne in clusters; recurrent; foliage dark green, glossy; growth upright, bushy (60-100 cm.); very winter hardy; does well in shady, windy conditions.; intr. 2000

'Mariee' S, ab, 2007, Iwata, Masaaki; flowers single, borne in large clusters; foliage medium size, light green, glossy; prickles 1 cm., few; growth spreading, shrub, medium (130 cm.); cutting, containers, garden decorat; [Graham Thomas® × 'Iceberg']; intr. 2008

'Marieken' F, ab, RvS-Melle; intr. 1987

'Marielle' F, mp, 1964, deRuiter; flowers deep rosy pink, 4 in., 25 petals, borne in large clusters, moderate fragrance; foliage dark; vigorous growth; ['Independence' × 'floribunda seedling']

Marietta® -- See 'Tanatiram'

'Marietta de Besobrasoff' T, pb, 1879, Nabonnand; flowers bright pink, shaded carmine, center darker, underlaid with copper, reverse lighter, medium, full, moderate fragrance

'Marietta Silva Tarouca' HMult, mp, 1925, Tarouca/Zeman; flowers bright rose, white center, large, semi-dbl., borne in small clusters, slight fragrance; foliage rich green; very vigorous, climbing growth; ['Colibri' × 'Crimson Rambler']

'Marigold' HT, op, 1955, Lens; bud long, pointed; flowers salmon-yellow lightly washed pink, 6 in., 52 petals, high-centered; foliage leathery, glossy, bright green; vigorous, upright growth; ['Peace' × 'Mme Joseph Perraud']

'Marijke Koopman' HT, mp, 1980, Fryer, Gareth; bud long, pointed; flowers 25 petals, borne singly and 3-5 per cluster, moderate fragrance; foliage dark, leathery; prickles red; vigorous, medium-tall,

upright growth; intr. 1979

'Mariko' -- See 'Devdorado'

'Marilena' HT, w; flowers white with pink tones in center, 9 cm., 30-35 petals, borne mostly singly; recurrent; stems 50 - 70 cm; florist rose; intr. 2004

'Marilo' (Ilona™) Min, ab, 1999, Martin, Robert B., Jr.; flowers orange/apricot striped, reverse lighter, 1 in., single, borne in small clusters; foliage small, dark green, near rugose, disease-resistant; prickles moderate; compact, low (18-24 in.) growth; [Altissimo® × 'Roller Coaster']

'Marilyn' Min, lp, Dot, M.; flowers light pink, base purplish, small, 60 petals, borne in clusters; very compact growth; ['Perla de Montserrat' × 'Bambino']; intr. 1955

'Marilyn' HT, ab, 1955, Fletcher; bud long, pointed; flowers apricot-pink veined red, intense fragrance; foliage dull, green; vigorous growth; ['May Wettern' × 'Phyllis Gold']; intr. 1954

'Marilyn Gowie' F, ?, 1968, Gowie; flowers borne in trusses; foliage bronze; bushy growth

Marilyn Monroe™ -- See 'Weksunspat'

'Marilyn O'Connor' S, mr, 2007, Fleming, Joyce L.; flowers 2-2½ in., semi-dbl, borne in large clusters; foliage medium, medium green, semi-glossy; prickles 7-10 mm., straight, moderate; growth bushy, medium (30 in.); low hedge, mass planting, specimen; ['Floranje' × 'breeding line 83']; intr. 2006

'Marilyn Ross' -- See 'Jaymar'

'Marilyn Wellan' -- See 'Moemarilyn'

'Marilyn Wellan' HT, mr, 2005, Edwards, Eddie & Phelps, Ethan; flowers medium to dark pink in hot weather; red in cool weather, 5 in., dbl., borne mostly solitary, moderate fragrance; foliage large, dark green, glossy; few prickles; upright, tall (5-6 ft.) growth; exhibition; [Veterans' Honor™ × 'Hot Princess']; intr. 2006

Marimba® F, mp, 1965, Dekkers; [sport of 'Garnette']

'Marime' -- See 'Mormarme'

Marina® F, ob, 1975, Kordes; bud long, pointed; flowers orange, base yellow, dbl., moderate fragrance; foliage glossy, dark, leathery; vigorous, upright growth; PP3789; ['Colour Wonder' × seedling]; intr. 1974

'Marina, Climbing' Cl F, ob, Teranishi; intr. 1997

'Marina Fontcuberta' HT, dp, 1924, Dot, Pedro; flowers brilliant carmine, center rose-carmine, dbl.; ['Entente Cordiale' × 'Laurent Carle']

Marina Marini® -- See 'Barmar'

'Marinette' -- See 'Auscam'

'Mario Clemente' HT, Moreira da Silva, A.

'Mario Lanza' -- See 'Horaardvark'

'Mariolina' S, Embriaco, B.; intr. 1989

'Marion' ('Salmon Sensation') F, op, 1956, deRuiter, G.; flowers pink tinted salmon, medium, dbl., high-centered, moderate fragrance; foliage first reddish, then light green; bushy (2 ft.) growth; ['Duchess of Rutland' × 'Fashion']

'Marion Brunell' T, 1917, Brunell; [sport of 'Reine Marie Henriette']

'Marion Cran' HT, or, 1927, McGredy; bud buttercup-yellow, flushed cerise; flowers scarlet veined orange and yellow, dbl., high-centered; foliage bronze, leathery, glossy; very vigorous, bushy growth

'Marion Dingee' HT, dr, 1889, Cook, J.W.; flowers crimson; [(('Comtesse de Caserta' × 'Général Jacqueminot') × 'Marechal Niel') × ('Pierre Notting' × 'Safrano')]

'Marion Foster' -- See 'Meicapula'

Marion Harkness® -- See 'Harkantabil'

'Marion Hess' HT, dr, Hetzel; intr. 1981

'Marion Horton' HT, my, 1929, Bees; flowers primrose-yellow; ['Gorgeous' × 'Sunstar']

'Marion Lawrie' HT, mp, 1976, Lawrie; flowers pink, base gold, 4 in., 75 petals; foliage dark, leathery; [sport of 'Kordes' Perfecta']

'Marion Manifold' -- See 'Miss Marion Manifold'

'Marion R. Hall' HT, dp, Balcombe Nursery; flowers bright cerise-red, well-formed, 5 in., 20 petals; vigorous growth; ['Crimson Glory' × 'Sterling']

'Marion Rich' HT, yb, 1997, Skinner, A.W.; flowers medium, dbl., borne mostly singly; foliage medium size, dark green, glossy; upright, medium (3-3½ ft.) growth; ['Solitaire' × Remember Me®]

'Marionette' F, w, 1944, deVor, Paul F.; bud cream-yellow; flowers 1½ in., 25-30 petals, borne in clusters, moderate fragrance; vigorous, bushy growth; PP569; [sport of 'Pinocchio']

'Mariposa' Pol, or, 1927, Allen; flowers deeper orange-red; [sport of 'Orange King']

'Mariposa Gem' -- See 'Mormagem'

'Mariquita' D, pb, 1860, Moreau & Robert; flowers flesh pink with lilac pink, large, full

Marisa™ -- See 'Ortisa'

'Mariska' -- See 'Valkita'

'Marista' HT, rb, 1985, Staikov, Prof. Dr. V.; flowers medium red, whitish reverse, large, 75 petals, borne singly, moderate tea fragrance; foliage dark, glossy; upright growth; ['Sarah Arnot' × 'Rina Herholdt']; intr. 1975

'Maristella' HT, 1952, Giacomasso

'Marita' F, ob, 1970, Mattock; flowers copper-orange, heavily veined yellow, medium, 30-40 petals, borne in trusses; foliage coppery; growth very free, straggly; ['Masquerade' × 'Serenade']; intr. 1961

'Marita Lindner' -- See 'Desmarita'

'Maritim' HT, m, Tantau; intr. 2001

'Maritime Bristol' -- See 'Santang'

'Maritime Heir' S, dp, 1987, James, John; flowers lavender pink, petals tight and frilled, carnation-like, large, 40 petals, intense fragrance; occasionally recurrent bloom; foliage small, light green, disease-resistant; prickles fine; upright, bushy, very hardy growth; ['Therese Bugnet' × R. nitida]; intr. 1986

'Marjan' HT, ob, Select Roses, B.V.

'Marjolaine' F, ab, Sauvageot; flowers ochre and vanilla-yellow, large, dbl., moderate fragrance; recurrent; intr. 2002

'Marjolin' HGal, dr, 1829, Hardy/Roeser; flowers dark crimson-purple, inclining to violet, 5 in., very full, cupped, borne in clusters of 2-3; foliage light green, semi-glossy

'Marjolin du Luxembourg' Ch, pb, about 1830, Desprez; flowers carmine-pink, shaded dark crimson, very large, very full

'Marjoline' HT, rb, 1949, Meilland, F.; flowers cardinal-red, reverse Indian yellow, 6 in., very dbl., cupped; vigorous, upright growth; ['Boudoir' × 'Léonce Colombier']

'Marjorie' HT, w, 1895, Dickson, A.; flowers white with pink, large, dbl.

'Marjorie Anderson' F, mp, 1973, Dickson, Patrick; flowers 5½ in., 26 petals; foliage very large, matte; ['Fragrant Cloud' × 'Sea Pearl']

'Marjorie Atherton' HT, my, 1977, Bell, Ronald J.; bud ovoid, large; flowers lemon yellow, large, dbl., high-centered, borne singly, moderate fragrance; good repeat; foliage light green, leathery; stems strong; vigorous, upright, bushy, tall growth; ['Mt. Shasta' × 'Peace']

'Marjorie Bulkeley' HT, yb, 1921, Dickson, H.; flowers buff, flushed rose-pink, passing to silvery pink, dbl.

'Marjorie Chase' -- See 'Koramator'

'Marjorie Conn' F, lp, 1981, Berry, Howard; bud ovoid; flowers 14 petals, borne in clusters of 5-7; foliage dark; prickles brown, hooked down; bushy growth; ['Bon Bon' × seedling]

'Marjorie Ellick' F, w, 1977, Ellick; flowers rowanberry, 4-6 in., 95 petals; foliage glossy, light; very vigorous, free growth; [('Spion-Kop' × 'Ena Harkness') × ('Sam Ferris' × 'Karl Herbst')]; intr. 1978

Marjorie Fair® ('Red Ballerina', 'Red Yesterday') S, rb, 1977, Harkness; flowers medium red, white eye, 1 in., 5 petals, borne in very large clusters; free-flowering; foliage small, light green, semi-glossy; dense, bushy growth; ['Ballerina' × 'Baby Faurax']; intr. 1978

'Marjorie Foster' HWich, dr, 1934, Burbage Nursery; flowers deep blood-red, small, dbl.; vigorous growth

'Marjorie LeGrice, Climbing' Cl HT, ob, 1959, Tantau, Math.; [sport of 'Marjorie Legrice']; intr. 1956

'Marjorie LeGrice' HT, ob, 1949, LeGrice; flowers orange and yellow, pointed, 5 in., 30 petals; foliage glossy; vigorous growth; ['Mrs Sam McGredy' × 'President Plumecocq']

'Marjorie Marshall' ('Celtic Pride') S, ab, Harkness; flowers apricot, dbl., borne in small clusters, slight fragrance; good repeat; shrubby, medium (3 ft.) growth; intr. 1996

'Marjorie May' -- See 'Horsunpegy'

'Marjorie Proops' HT, dr, 1969, Harkness; flowers crimson, dbl., high-centered; ['Red Dandy' × 'Ena Harkness']

Marjorie Reid™ -- See 'Jaymarj'

'Marjorie W. Lester' HMsk, lp; flowers soft pink with a lavender tinge; ['Kathleen' × unknown]

'Marjory Palmer' Pol, mp, 1936, Clark, A.; flowers rich pink, full, borne in clusters, intense fragrance; bushy, compact growth; ['Jersey Beauty' × unknown]

Mark One™ ('Apricot Sunblaze') Min, or, 1982, Saville, F. Harmon; flowers brilliant orange-red, 43 petals, cupped, borne singly and in clusters of up to 10, moderate spicy fragrance; foliage very glossy; prickles long, thin, soft on peduncles; compact, bushy growth; PP5044; ['Sheri Anne' × 'Glenfiddich']

'Mark Sullivan' ('Président Chaussé') HT, op, 1942, Mallerin, C.; flowers gold flushed and veined rose, 4-4½ in., 33 petals, high-centered, moderate fragrance; foliage dark, leathery, glossy; vigorous, upright. growth; PP599; ['Luis Brinas' × 'Brazier']

'Mark Sullivan, Climbing' Cl HT, ob

'Mark Twain' HT, dp, 1902, Hill, E. G.; bud pointed; flowers satiny rose-red, large, full, open

Mark Twain® Gr, lp, Huber; flowers silvery pink, full, borne singly and in clusters, moderate fragrance; recurrent; foliage matte green; growth strong, broad, 80-100 cm.; intr. 2001

'Markgräfin Wilhelmine' F, lp, Tantau; flowers large, dbl.; intr. 1995

'Markham Maiden' Gr, w; bud large, full, plump; flowers white with blush pink or buttery cream in the center, full, tea rose, borne in clusters, moderate fragrance; recurrent; intr. 2003

'Marlena' -- See 'Red Queen'

'Marlena' F, mr, 1965, Kordes, R.; flowers crimson scarlet, small, 18 petals, flat, borne in clusters; free-flowering; low, compact bushy growth; PP2700; ['Gertrud Westphal' × Lilli Marleen®]; intr. 1964

'Marlene' HT, lp, 2007, Bennett, John; flowers medium, 3-4 in., full, borne mostly solitary; foliage medium, dark green, matte; prickles moderate; growth upright, medium (3 ft.); garden decoration, exhibition; [Pristine® × 'The Lady']; intr. 2007

'Marlene Castronovo' -- See 'Webdance'

Marlène Jobert® Gr, pb, Guillot-Massad; bud small, pointed; flowers bright pink, reverse yellow, very full, borne in clusters; foliage matte; growth dwarf; intr. 2001

'Marlies' F, or

'Marliz' (Elizabeth Navarro™) Pol, lp, 2001, Martin, Robert B., jr.; bud elongated, pointed, brushed pink on reverse;

flowers 2 cm., dbl., borne in large clusters, no fragrance; foliage medium size, light green, matte; prickles medium, pointed, few; growth upright, medium (24-30 in.); borders; ['Nastarana' × 'Nastarana']

'Marlon's Day' -- See 'Wrimarlon'

'Marlyb' ('Lybie') HT, yb, 1999, Hiltner, Martin; flowers yellow blend, reverse medium yellow, 4 in., dbl., borne in small clusters; foliage medium size, dark green, semi-glossy; few prickles; upright, medium (3 ft.) growth; ['Lynn Anderson' × (('Carefree Beauty' × 'Picasso') × seedling)]

'Marlyn' -- See 'Tanliram'

Marlyse® -- See 'Pekomecli'

'Marmalade' HT, ob, 1976, Swim, H.C. & Ellis, A.E.; bud long, pointed; flowers bright orange, reverse deep yellow, 5 in., 30 petals, intense tea fragrance; foliage large, glossy, dark; upright growth; PP4243; ['Arlene Francis' × 'Bewitched']

Marmalade Mist™ HT, op, 1990, Lammerts, Dr. Walter; bud pointed; flowers medium salmon pink, with lighter salmon pink reverse, 25 petals, cupped, slight fruity fragrance; foliage large, dark green, semi-glossy; prickles deep plum and brown; upright, medium growth; PP7549; intr. 1990

Marmalade Skies™ -- See 'Meimonblan'

'Marmie' (Margie™) Cl Min, rb, 1999, Martin, Robert B., Jr.; flowers dark red with white eye, reverse lighter, 2 in., dbl., borne in small clusters, slight fragrance; foliage medium size, dark green, semi-glossy; prickles moderate; growth upright, climbing (5-7 ft.); shade tolerant; ['Roller Coaster' × 'Roller Coaster']

'Marmion' HT, pb, 1934, Dobbie; flowers pale rose flushed orange, reverse salmon-pink, dbl.; vigorous, branching growth

'Marmorata' -- See 'Maculata'

'Marmorea' ('À Fleurs Marbrée', 'Semi-Double Marbled Rose', 'Provins Marbré', 'Marbled', 'Marbrée') HGal, rb, before 1754; flowers pale red, tinted bluish, with lighter marbling, medium, semi-dbl.; sometimes considered to be a form of R. gallica officinalis

'Marnie Louise' -- See 'Tomwest'

Marondo® S, mp, Kordes; recurrent; growth to 5 ft.; intr. 1991

'Maroussia!' HT, w, Scheurs; intr. 2006

'Marovilla' F, or; intr. 1992

'Marpeach' (Peachy Cheeks™) F, ob, 2006, Martin, Robert B., Jr.; flowers cream with peach edges, 3 in., full, borne mostly solitary; foliage medium size, medium green, semi-glossy; prickles medium, slightly hooked, brown, few; growth upright, vigorous, medium (36 in.); exhibition, garden; ['Anne Morrow Lindbergh' × Bolivar™]; intr. 2006

'Marpeter' ('Peter Cottontail') MinFl, w, 2004, Martin, Robert B., Jr.; flowers dbl., high-centered, borne mostly solitary, slight fragrance; foliage medium size, medium green, semi-glossy, disease-resistant; prickles medium, pointed, on main canes only; bristles on rachis; bushy, tall (3 ft.,) growth; borders, small gardens, cutting; ['Anne Morrow Lindbergh' × 'Fairhope']; intr. 2004

'Marques de Narros' HT, ob, 1951, La Florida; flowers salmon-pink, pointed; thornless

'Marquesa de Aguilar' HT, mr, 1958, Bofill; bud ovoid; flowers cardinal-red to begonia pink, large, 60 petals, high-centered, moderate fragrance; foliage glossy; vigorous growth; ['Comtesse Vandal' × 'Caprice']; intr. 1954

'Marquesa de Bolarque' HT, my, 1945, Camprubi, C.; bud long, pointed; flowers lemon-yellow, large, dbl., high-centered; foliage dark, glossy; vigorous growth; ['Shot Silk' × 'Julien Potin']

'Marquesa de Casa Valdés' HT, or, 1958, Dot, Pedro; bud pointed; flowers scarlet-red slightly shaded orange, large, 35-40 petals, high-centered, moderate fragrance; foliage dark; very vigorous, compact growth; ['Peace' × 'Poinsettia']; intr. 1955

'Marquesa de Goicoerrotea' HT, ab, 1947, Dot, Pedro; flowers amber-yellow, well-formed; upright growth; ['Eclipse' × 'Joanna Hill']

'Marquesa de Urquijo, Climbing' -- See 'Pilar Landecho, Climbing'

'Marquesa de Urquijo' -- See 'Pilar Landecho'

'Marquesa del Vadillo' ('Spanish Main') HT, pb, 1945, Dot, Pedro; flowers Neyron pink, reverse silvery pink, open, 5 in.; foliage glossy, dark; upright growth; ['Girona' × 'Condesa de Sástago']

'Marquis d'Ailsa' -- See 'Dr Marx'

'Marquis d'Alex' HP, m, 1880, Brassac; flowers purple, center bright carmine, large, full

'Marquis de Bouillé' HT, dp, 1904, Schwartz; flowers light red tinted pale pink, very large, very full; foliage glaucous green

'Marquis of Salisbury' HP, mr, 1880, Paul, W.

'Marquise Adèle de Murinais' HP, mp, 1873, Schwartz; flowers silvery pink, aging to dark pink, large, full; ['Mme Laffay' × unknown]

'Marquise Boccella' ('Marchesa Boccella') HP, lp, 1842, Desprez; flowers delicate pink, edges almost blush, compact, large; petals smaller than other HP's, dbl., moderate fragrance; recurrent; stiff, erect stems; growth dwarf, robust habit

'Marquise d'Alex' T, w, 1880, Brassac; flowers white, center light yellow, large, very full

'Marquise d'Andigné' HT, dr, 1927, Leenders Bros.; flowers velvety scarlet-crimson, dbl.; [('Lieutenant Chauré' × 'George C. Waud') × 'Laurent Carle']

'Marquise de Balbiano' B, m, 1855, Lacharme, F.; flowers pink, tinged with lilac, medium, full, cupped

'Marquise de Barbentane' HT, ab, 1928, Fugier; flowers apricot-yellow, shaded orange and sunflower-yellow, dbl.; ['Mrs Farmer' × 'Severine']

'Marquise de Castellane' HP, dp, 1869, Pernet père; flowers dark rose-pink, well-formed, large, dbl., moderate fragrance; moderate growth; ['Jules Margottin' × unknown]

'Marquise de Chaponnay' T, yb, 1897, Bernaix; flowers butter yellow, edges tinted salmon, large, full

'Marquise de Chavaudon' HP, pb, 1853, Carré; flowers medium pink, center petals white-edged, large, full

'Marquise de Forton' T, yb, 1889, Charreton; flowers saffron yellow, center carmine pink, medium, cupped

'Marquise de Foucault' T, w, 1860, Margottin; flowers white, center cream, large, dbl.

'Marquise de Ganay' HT, mp, 1910, Guillot, P.; bud very large; flowers silvery rose, very large, dbl., cupped, moderate fragrance; foliage dark green; ['Liberty' × 'La France']

'Marquise de Gibot' HP, lp, 1868, De Sansal; flowers pale rose, large, full, globular; foliage dark green

Marquise de la Roche Jacquelein® S, ab, Guillot-Massad; flowers bright apricot, fading to white, 8 cm., full, cupped, slight fragrance; foliage glossy; growth to 1 m.; intr. 2006

'Marquise de Marat' HP, lp, 1855, Ducher; flowers large, full

'Marquise de Mortemart' HP, w, 1868, Liabaud; flowers blush-white, center pale flesh, large, full, cupped; ['Jules Margottin' × unknown]

'Marquise de Querhoënt' T, pb, 1901, Godard; flowers coppery pink with golden yellow at base of petals, medium, full; growth medium, bushy; ['G. Nabonnand' × 'Mme Laurette Messimy']

'Marquise de Salisbury' -- See 'Marchioness of Salisbury'

'Marquise de Salisbury' HP, lp, 1888, Lévêque

'Marquise de Sinéty' HT, yb, 1906, Pernet-Ducher; flowers golden yellow, shaded bronzy red, dbl.

'Marquise de Sinéty, Climbing' Cl HT, yb, 1912, Griffon

'Marquise de Verdun' HP, mp, 1868, Oger; flowers bright carmine pink, large, full, globular

'Marquise de Vivens' T, dp, 1886, Dubreuil; flowers carmine, base yellowish, large, dbl.

'Marquise d'Hautpoul' HT, pb, 1915, Hicks; flowers bright pink, shaded cream, moderate fragrance

'Marquise d'Ivry' HT, dp, before 1866; flowers dark pink with lilac tints, very large, full

'Marquise Jeanne de la Chataigneraye' HT, w, 1902, Soupert & Notting; flowers silky white with pink tints, center yel-

lowish, large, full, moderate fragrance; ['Souv de President Carnot' × 'Mme Jules Grolez']
'Marquise Litta de Bréteuil' HT, mr, 1893, Pernet-Ducher; flowers carmine pink, center vermilion red, 5 in., very full, cupped
'Marquise Spinola' ('Orsola Spinola') S, mp, Guillot-Massad; intr. 1996
Marquisette® Ch, op, 1872, Ducher; flowers pink with salmon
'Marr' Pol, op; flowers coral overcast orange, 1 in., cupped, borne in clusters; thornless; growth rangy (10-12 in.)
'Marraine' -- See 'Maslako'
'Marrakech' HT, dr, 1945, Meilland, F.; flowers oxblood-red shaded bright scarlet, well-formed, very large, dbl.; upright, vigorous growth; ['Rome Glory' × 'Tassin']
'Marriotta' -- See 'Maccricke'
Marry Me™ -- See 'Dicwonder'
'Mars' HT, op, 1927, Chaplin Bros.; flowers deep coral
Marselisborg™ -- See 'Poulreb'
Marsh™ -- See 'Marsh Cottage'
'Marsh Cottage' (Marsh™) S, dp, Olesen; bud ovate, red; flowers deep pink, small, single, almost flat, borne in clusters of 5 - 11, no fragrance; recurrent; foliage dark green, semi-glossy; prickles numerous, 8 mm., hooked downward; flat, bushy (40-60 cm.) growth; hips rounded to somewhat elliptical, greyed-orange; PP16941; [seedling × Diamond Head™]; intr. 2005
'Marshall P. Wilder' HP, dr, 1885, Ellwanger & Barry; flowers bright deep red, large, 45 petals, globular, intense fragrance; vigorous, tall growth; ['Général Jacqueminot' × unknown]
Marshmallow Fluff® -- See 'Bagmallow'
'Marstar' (Pasadena Star™) F, w, 2001, Martin, Robert B., Jr.; flowers ivory white with light pink edging and yellow at base, 4 in., full, high-centered, borne mostly solitary, no fragrance; foliage medium size, medium green, semi-glossy; prickles medium, downward pointed, brown; growth upright, medium (36 in.); exhibition; ['Anne Morrow Lindbergh' × 'Glowing Amber']; intr. 2001
'Marsyanka' HT, dp; flowers carmine-pink, medium, semi-dbl.; intr. 1958
'Marta' Min, or, 1983, Dobbs; flowers small, 20 petals; foliage small, light green, matte; upright growth; ['Persian Princess' × 'Anytime']
Marta Salvador® -- See 'Fedugia'
'Martha' Pol, pb, 1906, Lambert, P.; flowers coppery rose, dbl., borne in clusters of 7-20; dwarf growth; ['Thalia' × 'Mme Laurette Messimy']
'Martha' B, pb, Knudson/Zeiner; flowers pale coral, dbl., borne in clusters of 1-5, moderate fragrance; prickles few thorns; tall, climbing growth; [sport of 'Zéphirine Drouhin']; intr. 1912
'Martha Allen' Gr, ab, Williams, J. Benjamin; flowers apricot-pink with silvery overlay, dbl., moderate fragrance; recurrent; growth to 4 ft.; intr. 2005
'Martha Bugnet' HRg, mr, 1959, Bugnet; bud long, pointed; flowers purplish red, open, large, semi-dbl.; abundant, recurrent bloom; foliage dark rugosa type; weak stems; vigorous, bushy (5-6 ft.) tall and broad growth; very large fruit; [(R. rugosa kamtchatica × (R. amblyotis × R. rugosa plena)) × 'F.J. Grootendorst']
'Martha Drew' HT, w, 1919, McGredy; flowers creamy white, center rose, large, dbl., moderate fragrance
'Martha Ford' HMult, ab, Nobbs; intr. 1987
'Martha Keller' Pol, lp, 1912, Walter; flowers medium, very dbl.
'Martha Kordes' F, dp, 1941, Kordes; flowers light capucine-red, becoming pink, open, medium, semi-dbl., borne in clusters; vigorous, upright growth; ['Hedwig Fulda' × 'Holstein']
'Martha Lambert' Pol, rb, 1939, Lambert, P.; flowers brilliant scarlet with small yellow eye, small, single, borne in clusters, slight fragrance; recurrent bloom; foliage glossy; stems strong; vigorous, bushy growth; ['Frans Leddy' × 'Paul's Scarlet Climber']
'Martha Rice' F, dp, 1970, Raffel, Frank c.; buds pointed; flowers light red to rose-pink with some gold at base, medium, dbl, open, borne singly, several together and in clusters; foliage medium size, soft; growth vigorous, upright, bushy; ['Tropicana' × 'Sweet Vivien']
'Martha Washington' S, mp, before 1900; hybrid roxburghii
'Martha's Choice' HT, dp, 1977, Bailey; bud high-centered; flowers deep pink, 5 in., 37 petals; ['Gavotte' × 'Prima Ballerina']
Martha's Vineyard™ -- See 'Poulans'
'Marthe Ancey' ('Mme Martha Ancey') HT, w, 1932, Schwartz, A.; flowers cream, tinted salmon-pink, center with straw-yellow reflections, dbl.; vigorous growth; ['Souv. de Claudius Pernet' × 'Mme Mélanie Soupert']
'Marthe Cahuzac' Pol, ly, 1902, Ketten, Gebrüder; flowers medium, dbl.
'Martian Glow' F, mr, 1972, Gandy, Douglas L.; flowers red, reverse lighter, 1½ in., 10 petals, borne in clusters; foliage semi-glossy, medium green; vigorous, spreading growth; [Joseph's Coat® × 'Dorothy Wheatcroft']
'Martian Sunrise' S, or, 1980, Taylor, Thomas E.; bud ovoid; flowers 43 petals, high-centered, urn-shaped, borne singly or in small clusters; repeats well; foliage light to medium green, semi-glossy; prickles semi-hooked; upright, bushy growth; ['Paddy McGredy' × 'Heidelberg']
'Martin des Senteurs' ('Scented Whisper') F, ab, Adam; flowers soft chamois with salmon tints, medium, dbl., open, borne mostly in clusters, intense fragrance; foliage large, glossy; bushy (3-4 ft.) growth; intr. 2000
'Martin Faassen' HT, dp, 1965, Verbeek; bud ovoid; flowers pink-red, medium, dbl., borne in clusters; foliage dark; [Baccará® × seedling]
'Martin Frobisher' HRg, lp, 1970, Svedja, Felicitas; bud ovoid; flowers light pink, center darker, medium, dbl., intense fragrance; foliage light green; vigorous, tall growth; ['Schneezwerg' × unknown]; intr. 1968
'Martin Liebau' HP, mp, 1930, Kiese; flowers large, dbl.
'Martin Martin' -- See 'Seamar'
Martina™ -- See 'Poulanit'
Martina® HT, w, Noack, Werner; intr. 1989
Martina™ F, yb, Urban, J.
'Martina Hit' (Martina™) MinFl, dr, Poulsen; flowers dark red, 5-8 cm., semi-dbl., no fragrance; growth bushy, 40-60 cm.; PP11538; intr. 1998
'Martine Guillot' -- See 'Masmabay'
'Martine Hémeray' F, or, 1958, Gaujard, R.; flowers China-red, well-formed, dbl., foliage leathery; [(Orange Triumph® × 'Mme Edouard Herriot') × seedling]
Martinez® -- See 'Meinalpir'
'Martini' HT, Delforge; intr. 1967
Martinique™ -- See 'Poulpah027(N)'
'Martinique Hit' (Martinique™) MinFl, ab, Poulsen; flowers apricot blend, 5-8 cm., dbl., no fragrance; foliage reddish green; growth bushy, 20-40 cm.; intr. 2004
'Martone' Min, pb, 1990, Bridges, Dennis A.; bud pointed; flowers medium pink, lighter at base, reverse light pink, medium, 30 petals, high-centered, slight damask fragrance; foliage medium size, medium green, semi-glossy; prickles straight, medium, deep pink; upright, medium growth; ['Queen City' × seedling]; intr. 1990
'Marty' -- See 'Peasweet'
Marty's Triumph™ -- See 'Bismar'
'Marushka' HT, dy, 1985, Staikov, Prof. Dr. V.; flowers 35 petals, high-centered, borne 1-3 per stem; foliage dark, leathery, glossy; vigorous, bushy growth; ['Kabuki' × seedling]; intr. 1984
Marvel™ HT, dp, Zary, Keith; PPAF; intr. 1999
'Marvelle' -- See 'Mactaurang'
'Marvicka ' HT, w, Martin; intr. 2003
'Marvie' -- See 'Gelmar'
'Marvin Lassalle' S, my, Gilet; intr. 2005
'Marvlous' HT, mr, 1937, Cant, B. R.; flowers crimson, open, large, dbl.; foliage leathery; very vigorous growth
'Marx' HSpn, my, about 1825, Cartier; flowers sulfur yellow, small, full, moderate fragrance
'Mary' HT, ob, 1931, Bentall; flowers buff and orange, moderate fragrance; vigorous growth
'Mary' Pol, op, Qualm; flowers orange-cerise, borne in small clusters; vigorous growth; [sport of 'Orange Triumph']; intr. 1947
'Mary' -- See 'Pijama Party'

The Official Registry and Checklist — Rosa 469

'Mary Adair' Min, ab, 1966, Moore, Ralph S.; flowers buffy apricot, small, dbl., moderate fragrance; foliage light green, soft; vigorous, bushy, dwarf growth; PP2910; ['Golden Glow' × 'Zee']

Mary Adrienne™ -- See 'Wekswetrup'

'Mary 'n' John' -- See 'Seamary'

'Mary Ann' F, dp, 1959, Restani; bud ovoid; flowers rose-red, 2 in., 60-78 petals, high-centered; foliage dark; upright growth; PP1794; [sport of 'Garnette']

'Mary Ann' HT, m, Edwards, Eddie & Phelps, Ethan; flowers mauve with plum overtones in cool weather, 5-6 in., full, borne mostly solitary, intense fragrance; foliage large, dark green, glossy; few prickles; upright, tall (5-6 ft.) growth; exhibition; [seedling × 'Barbra Streisand']; intr. 2006

'Mary Barnard' F, op, 1978, Sanday, John; bud ovoid; flowers deep salmon-pink, large, 18 petals; foliage dark; low, vigorous growth; [('Karl Herbst' × Sarabande®) × 'Ernest H. Morse']

'Mary Beaufort' HT, lp, 1969, Sanday, John; flowers light peach-pink, well-shaped, small; compact, low growth; ['Gavotte' × ('Ethel Sanday' × 'Crimson Glory')]

'Mary Bell' Min, w, 1987, Bell, Charles E., Jr.; flowers small, full, moderate fragrance; foliage medium size, medium green, semi-glossy, disease-resistant; bushy, hardy growth; ['Cherish' × 'Rise 'n' Shine']; intr. 1987

'Mary Bennett' HP, dp, 1885, Bennett; flowers cherry pink, large, full; ['Baronne Adolphe de Rothschilde' × unknown]

'Mary Bostock' HT, lp, 1952, Clark, A.; flowers shell-pink tinted white, 60 petals; strong stems; vigorous growth

Mary Bradby™ -- See 'Byrbradby'

'Mary Bruni' Pol, lp, 1914, Gratama; flowers light creamy rose pink, small, dbl.

'Mary Burke' Min, op, Hannemann, F.

'Mary C' -- See 'Silbluebell'

'Mary Campbell' -- See 'Horlovequeen'

'Mary Carver' HT, lp, 1950, Chick; bud globular; flowers shell-pink, 5 in., 80 petals, cupped; foliage leathery, light green; vigorous, upright growth; [sport of 'Red Radiance']

'Mary Casant' -- See 'Marytje Cazant'

'Mary Cave' F, my, Harkness; flowers semi-dbl. to dbl.; intr. 1993

'Mary Clark' Min, lp, 1982, Hooper, John C.; flowers medium, 55 petals; foliage mid-green; prickles straight, light yellow; ['Janna' × 'Gene Boerner']; intr. 1981

'Mary Clay' HT, dr, 1951, Kordes; flowers blood-red, 6 in., 40-45 petals; foliage very heavy, dark; very free growth; ['Kardinal' × 'Crimson Glory']

'Mary Conn' S, mp, J. B. Williams; growth to 3 ft.; intr. 2005

'Mary Corelly' HP, op, 1901, Prince; flowers dark salmon-pink, medium, dbl.

'Mary Cullen' -- See 'Kenly'

'Mary Delahunty' HT, dr, 1991, Bell, Ronald J.; bud pointed; flowers large, 35-40 petals, borne usually singly, moderate damask fragrance; foliage dark green, glossy; bushy, tall growth; [('Daily Sketch' × 'Impeccable') × 'Red Planet']; intr. 1990

'Mary DeVor' ('Douchka') F, mr, 1970, Lammerts, Dr. Walter; flowers cardinal-red, sweetheart, medium, 35 petals, moderate fragrance; foliage leathery; vigorous, upright growth; PP2838; ['Christian Dior' × 'Rumba']; intr. 1967

'Mary Donaldson' -- See 'Canana'

'Mary Dutton' HT, op, 1949, Bees; bud long, pointed; flowers salmon-pink, 6 in., very dbl.; foliage glossy; very vigorous growth; ['Crimson Glory' × 'Mrs Sam McGredy']

'Mary E. Thomas' HT, dp, 2002, Thomas, D.; flowers medium, very full, borne mostly solitary, slight fragrance; foliage medium size, dark green, semi-glossy; prickles moderate; growth upright, medium; exhibition; ['Selfridges' × 'Red Devil']

'Mary Edith' -- See 'Talmar'

'Mary Egerton' F, rb, 1983, Lea, R.F.G.; flowers white, petals edged orange-red, spreading with age, reverse white, 35 petals; foliage large, dark, glossy; upright, bushy growth; ['Fragrant Cloud' × Prominent®]

'Mary Elizabeth' Min, lp, 1983, Dobbs; flowers small, 29 petals; foliage small, light green, matte; bushy growth; ['Fairy Moss' × 'Fairy Moss']

'Mary Fleming' F, mp, 1995, Fleming, Joyce L.; bud opening to very pale pink; flowers medium, 6-14 petals, borne 2-15 per cluster; foliage medium size, medium green, matte; bushy (90-100 cm.), spreading growth; ['Marchenland' × 'Golden Salmon Superieur']; intr. 1994

'Mary Gammon' -- See 'Mary Gamon'

'Mary Gamon' ('Mary Gammon') Min, op, Fryer, Gareth; flowers salmon orange, dbl., borne mostly in clusters; good repeat; neat, bushy (15 in.) growth; intr. 1993

'Mary Greer' -- See 'Kootenay'

'Mary Guthrie' Pol, mp, 1929, Clark, A.; flowers rich pink, small, single, borne in large clusters, moderate fragrance; foliage light; bushy (2½ ft.) growth; ['Jersey Beauty' × 'Scorcher']

'Mary Hankins' -- See 'Worcloud'

'Mary Hart' HT, mr, 1931, Hart, G.B.; PP8; [sport of 'Talisman']

'Mary Hart, Climbing' Cl HT, mr, 1937, Western Rose Co. (also Meilland, 1942)

'Mary Hayley Bell' ('Abundancia', 'Ronja') S, mp, Kordes; flowers semi-dbl.; growth to 3-4 ft.; winter hardy

'Mary Haywood' Min, mp, 1958, Moore, Ralph S.; flowers bright pink, base white, 1 in., 50 petals, moderate fragrance; foliage glossy; very compact (10 in.), bushy growth; PP1766; [(R. wichurana × 'Floradora') × 'Oakington Ruby']; intr. 1957

'Mary Helen Tanner' HT, dp, 1932, Tanner; flowers carmine, stems white or pinkish; PP151; [sport of 'Templar']

'Mary Hicks' HMult, dr, 1927, Hicks; flowers deep scarlet, 3-3½ cm., semi-dbl., moderate fragrance; foliage light; vigorous, climbing growth

'Mary Hilda Law' -- See 'Kircloud'

'Mary Hill' HT, w, 1916, E.G. Hill, Co.; flowers cream, center deep orange, dbl.; ['Ophelia' × 'Sunburst']

'Mary Hill' -- See Morhill'

'Mary Jean' -- See 'Haryen'

'Mary Jo' HT, my, 1959, Joseph H. Hill, Co.; bud short, pointed; flowers maize-yellow, large, 30-35 petals, high-centered; foliage leathery; strong stems; vigorous, upright, bushy growth; PP1504; [seedling × 'Orange Delight']; intr. 1958

'Mary Johnston' -- See 'Wammary'

'Mary Kate' Min, dp, 1977, Dobbs; bud mossy; flowers light red, 1 in., 29 petals, flat; foliage dark, soft; vigorous, upright growth; ['Fairy Moss' × 'Fairy Moss']

Mary Kay™ -- See 'Minoco'

'Mary Kittel' HT, dr, 1976, Harvey, R.E.; bud pointed; flowers 5 in., 35 petals, high-centered, intense fragrance; foliage large, glossy; vigorous growth; [('Chrysler Imperial' × 'Night 'n' Day') × 'Night 'n' Day']; intr. 1975

'Mary L. Evans' HRg, dp, 1936, Wright, Percy H.; flowers deep wild-rose-pink; non-recurrent; growth very similar to Tekonkaha but more spreading; ['Hansa' × R. macounii]

'Mary Lawrance's Shell Rose' Ch, mr, 1799; flowers dusky rose-crimson with small green pointel in center of bloom, full; stems light, slender

'Mary Lee Johnson Richards' HT, lp

'Mary Louise' -- See 'Taymar'

'Mary Louise' -- See 'Busmalou'

'Mary Lovett' HWich, w, 1915, Van Fleet; flowers snow-white, 7-8 cm., dbl., borne in clusters of 10-20, moderate fragrance; some repeat bloom; vigorous, climbing (to 10-12 ft.) growth; [R. wichurana × 'Kaiserin Auguste Viktoria']

'Mary Lynn' -- See 'Renlynn'

Mary Lyon™ -- See 'Wilmtho'

'Mary Magdalene' -- See 'Ausjolly'

'Mary Malva' HT, lp, 1979, Lens, Louis; bud long, pointed; flowers 3½-4½ in., 18-24 petals, high-centered, moderate spicy fragrance; foliage dark, leathery; upright growth; [(Pascali® × 'Charlotte Armstrong') × 'Lilac Charm']; intr. 1971

'Mary Mangano' Min, op, 1989, Papandrea, John T.; flowers deep coral pink; [sport of 'Petite Folie']

'Mary Manners' HRg, w, Leicester; flowers creamy white, sometimes with pink blush on petal edges, slight fragrance; recurrent; possibly a sport of 'Sarah van Fleet'; intr. 1970

'Mary Margaret' -- See 'Talmag'

'Mary Margaret McBride' HT, mp, 1942,

Nicolas; bud long, pointed; flowers salmon-pink, 4-5 in., 42 petals, high-centered, moderate fragrance; foliage dark, leathery, glossy; vigorous, upright, bushy growth; PP537; ['Sunkist' × 'Olympiad']

'Mary Marques' HT, or, 1958, Bofill; bud long, pointed; flowers orange-red tinted yellow, medium, very dbl., high-centered; upright growth; ['Mediterranea' × 'Suzanne Balitrand']; intr. 1955

'Mary Marshall' Min, ob, 1971, Moore, Ralph S.; bud long, pointed; flowers orange, base yellow, small, dbl., cupped, moderate fragrance; foliage small, leathery; vigorous, dwarf, bushy growth; PP3346; ['Little Darling' × 'Fairy Princess']; intr. 1970

'Mary Marshall, Climbing' -- See 'Minico'

'Mary Mathis' Min, lp, 2005, Singer, Judith A; flowers light pink with green eye, reverse medium pink, 1 in., full, borne mostly solitary, slight fragrance; foliage small, medium green; prickles small, moderate; bushy growth; ['Bonica' × seedling]

'Mary Maud' -- See 'Gelmaud'

'Mary May' -- See 'Sheriskep'

'Mary McHutchin' Cl Pol, mr, 1935, Cant, B. R.; flowers crimson, semi-dbl., cupped, borne in clusters; foliage large, leathery; vigorous, climbing (6-8 ft.) growth

'Mary McKillop' ('Mother Mary McKillop') HT, pb, Swane; flowers shell pink, edged rose pink, dbl., high-centered, borne singly or in clusters of 2 or 3, slight fragrance; free-flowering; foliage dense; growth medium; intr. 1989

'Mary Merryweather' HT, dy, 1925, Merryweather; bud pointed; flowers deep golden yellow, semi-dbl., cupped; foliage glossy; vigorous, bushy growth; ['Marquise de Sinéty' × 'Lady Hillingdon']

'Mary Mine' Gr, op, 1972, Harkness, R.; flowers salmon-pink to light rose, large, 27 petals, [Queen Elizabeth® × 'Buccaneer']; intr. 1971

'Mary Monro' HT, pb, 1921, Pemberton; flowers carmine-pink, flushed saffron-yellow, dbl.

'Mary Mulligan' HT, or, 1944, Mallerin, C.; bud long, pointed; flowers flame, dbl., cupped; vigorous growth

'Mary Murray' HT, ab, 1930, Prior; flowers deep apricot-yellow becoming lighter, 30 petals; foliage glossy, bronze; vigorous growth

'Mary Nish' ('White Radiance') HT, w, 1928, Pacific Rose Co.; flowers white, center tinted shell-pink, very large, dbl., moderate fragrance; foliage rich green, soft, glossy; vigorous, bushy growth; [sport of 'Radiance']

'Mary of Penola' -- See 'Tommop'

'Mary Pauline' HT, w, 1998, McCrury, Curtis; flowers palest pink, dbl., high-centered, borne mostly singly; foliage large, medium green, semi-glossy; some prickles; upright, tall growth; [Queen Elizabeth® × 'Chablis']

'Mary Pickford' HT, ab, 1923, H&S; bud pointed, orange-yellow; flowers pale yellow, center deeper, large, dbl.; foliage bronze; vigorous, bushy growth; [('Grange Colombe' × unknown) × 'Souv. de Claudius Pernet']

'Mary Pilkington' -- See 'Evepilk'

'Mary Pochin' ('Marie Pochin') HP, mr, 1881, Pochin; flowers bright red tinted velvety crimson, medium

'Mary Pope' F, yb, 1965, Sanday, John; flowers golden yellow suffused pink, edged darker, 3 in., 25 petals, borne in clusters; foliage glossy, dark; vigorous growth; [seedling × 'Independence']

'Mary Pope' ('Magaliesburg Roos') HT, m, Kordes; intr. 1993

'Mary Poppins' HT, mp, 1967, Morey, Dr. Dennison; [sport of 'Hallmark']

'Mary, Queen of Scots' HSpn, pb; flowers lavender-pink with a white eye, single

'Mary Rand' HT, w, 1965, Latham; flowers cream, edged rose-pink, well-formed, large; foliage glossy, light green; vigorous growth; ['Caprice' × 'Scandale']

'Mary Ratcliffe' HT, pb, 1958, Ratcliffe; flowers soft pink, reverse darker

'Mary Robertson' Pol, mr, 1969, Buisman, G. A. H.; bud ovoid; flowers medium, dbl.; foliage dark; ['Paprika' × seedling]

Mary Rose® -- See 'Ausmary'

'Mary Russell' HT, mr, 1940, Clark, A.; flowers well-formed, large

'Mary Sampere de Guanabara' F, Moreira da Silva, A.

'Mary Sheffield' -- See 'Debrah'

'Mary Summers' -- See 'Horanyfell'

'Mary Sumner' -- See 'Macstra'

'Mary Swindells' -- See 'Kensingso'

'Mary Taylor' HT, lp, Taylor, L.R.; intr. 1966

'Mary Thomson' S, pb, Thomson, G.A.

'Mary Toomey' -- See 'Seatoo'

'Mary Wallace' HWich, mp, 1924, Van Fleet; bud long, pointed; flowers warm rose pink, 8 cm., semi-dbl., cupped, moderate fragrance; seasonal bloom; foliage large, thick, glossy; vigorous, climbing (8-12 ft.) growth; [R. wichurana × a pink hybrid tea]

'Mary Warm' Cl Min, or; intr. 1997

'Mary Warren' Cl HT, mp, 1931, Clark, A.; flowers pink, open, large, semi-dbl.; recurrent bloom; foliage soft, large, dark; vigorous, pillar growth; ['Mrs Frank Guthrie' × 'Scorcher']

'Mary Washington' N, w; flowers white tinted pink, fading to white, medium, dbl., borne in clusters of 7-11, moderate fragrance; very vigorous growth; first evidenced in documents dated in 1891, but may be much older; sometimes classed as HSet

Mary Webb -- See 'Auswebb'

'Mary Wheatcroft' HT, ob, 1945, Robinson, H.; bud high-pointed; flowers deep copper; foliage bronze; ['Mrs Sam McGredy' × 'Princess Marina']

'Mary Wise' -- See 'Hermawi'

'Mary Woodcock' HMsk, mp, Stydd; intr. 1989

'Mary, Countess of Ilchester' ('Countess Mary of Ilchester', 'Countess of Ilchester') HT, mp, 1909, Dickson, A.; flowers deep rose-pink, open, large, dbl.; foliage rich green, leathery, glossy; very vigorous, bushy growth

Marybeth™ -- See 'Minibeth'

'Marycka Magdanová' Pol, dr, 1938, Böhm, J.; flowers small, semi-dbl.

'Maryellen' Min, pb, 1981, Lemrow, Dr. Maynard W.; flowers deep pink, yellow center, 5 petals, borne 3 or more per cluster; foliage small, deep green; prickles triangle-shaped; upright growth; ['Darling Flame' × seedling]

'Maryke-Marika' F, ob, 1975, Kordes; bud medium, ovoid; flowers orange, base yellow, dbl., globular; foliage glossy; vigorous, upright growth; ['Colour Wonder' × 'Zorina']; intr. 1973

'Marylea Johnson Richards' -- See 'Willea'

'Marylène' HT, mp, 1965, Gaujard; bud long, pointed; flowers pearl-pink, medium, dbl.; foliage dark, glossy; upright growth; ['Mignonne' × Queen Elizabeth®]

'Marylene' S, ob; flowers orange; free-flowering; moderate (3 ft.) growth

'Marylka' Min, Wituszynski, B.; intr. 1967

'Mary's Delight' HT, pb, Kordes; bud long, pointed; flowers deep pink blend, dbl., high-centered, intense fragrance; recurrent; growth vigorous; intr. 1999

'Mary's Favorite' F, dp, 1994, Hemphill, William J.; flowers deep pink, 3-3½ in., dbl., borne in small clusters; foliage large, medium green, semi-glossy, disease-resistant; few prickles; medium (48-54 in.), upright, compact growth; ['Pink Favorite' × unknown]

'Mary's Memory' F, pb, 2003, Roszko, Terry; flowers medium pink, reverse white, 2½-3 in., very full, borne in small clusters, moderate fragrance; foliage medium size, dark green, semi-glossy; prickles 3/8 in., typical, pink, few; growth bushy, medium; bedding, specimen; ['Gold Marie' × 'Morden Blush']; intr. 2005

'Mary's Pink' HT, mp, 1952, Spanbauer; bud long, pointed; flowers Neyron rose, 4-4½ in., 32 petals; foliage leathery; vigorous, compact, bushy growth; PP1237; [sport of 'Better Times']

'Mary's Pleasure - The Mary Woods Rose' -- See 'Woraugust'

'Mary's Pride' LCl, rb, 2005, Jerabek, Paul E.; flowers dark red, reverse red shaded silver, 3 in., dbl., borne in small clusters, slight fragrance; foliage medium size, medium green, semi-glossy; prickles moderate, 7/16 in., triangular; upright, short growth; [unknown × unknown]; intr. 2008

'Marysa' Pol, w, 1936, Brada, Dr.; flowers pure white, moderate lily-of-the-valley fragrance; vigorous growth

'Maryse Kriloff, Climbing' ('Lucy Cramphorn, Climbing') Cl HT, or, Kriloff; flowers large, dbl.; intr. 1984

'Maryse Kriloff' -- See 'Lucy Cramphorn'

'Marytje Cazant' ('Marie Casant', 'Mary Casant') Pol, ab, 1927, van Nes; bud globular; flowers coral-pink, borne in large clusters; dwarf growth; [sport of 'Jessie']

'Masako' -- See 'Ausmak'

'Masalber' F, lp, Guillot-Massad

'Masamcha' S, pb, Guillot-Massad; intr. 2005

'Masarykova Jubilejni' ('Jubilaire de Masaryk', 'Jubilee', 'Masaryk's Jubilee', 'Masaryk's Jubileums-Rose') HT, dr, 1931, Böhm, J.; flowers velvety red shaded black, very large, single; foliage dark, glossy; vigorous growth; [sport of 'Blanta']

'Masaryk's Jubilee' -- See 'Masarykova Jubilejni'

'Masaryk's Jubileums-Rose' -- See 'Masarykova Jubilejni'

'Masasch' S, pb, Guillot-Massadfull; intr. 2003

'Masayuki' HT, w, Keisei; intr. 1992

'Masbeles' S, rb, Guillot-Massad; intr. 2006

'Masbigui' S, dp, Guillot; intr. 2004

'Masbruper' S, mp, Guillot-Massad; intr. 1998

Mascara™ -- See 'Meidalnu'

'Mascarme' S, lp, Guillot-Massad; intr. 2000

'Mascatna' S, my, Guillot-Massad; intr. 1997

'Maschame' S, mp, Guillot-Massadvery dbl.; intr. 2000

'Maschaner' S, ab, Massad; intr. 2008

'Maschaumon' S, ab, Guillot-Massad; intr. 2007

'Mascombe' Gr, rb, Guillot-Massad; bud pointed; intr. 2005

'Mascorab' Gr, dy, Guillot-Massad; intr. 2004

'Mascotte' HT, mp, 1951, Meilland, F.; bud pointed; flowers hermosa pink, 4 in., dbl.; foliage dark; vigorous growth; ['Michèle Meilland' × 'Pres. Herbert Hoover']

Mascotte '77® -- See 'Meitiloly'

'Mascybel' S, m, Guillot-Massad; intr. 2000

'Masdecla' Gr, lp, Guillot-Massad; intr. 2002

'Masdeli' HT, op, Guillot-Massad; intr. 2004

'Masdhabi' S, mr, Guillot-Massad; intr. 2007

'Masdocha' HT, mp, Guillot-Massad; intr. 2005

'Masdogui' ('Sonia Rykiel') S, op, Guillot-Massad; intr. 1995

'Masdomo' ('Belle de Dom') S, pb, Guillot-Massad; intr. 1996

'Masedogui' HT, op, Guillot-Massad; intr. 2005

'Maselgi' ('Eliane Gillet') S, w, Guillot-Massad; bud white splashed with red; intr. 1998

'Maselgo' S, dp, Massadvery full; intr. 2008

'Maselma' S, dp, Guillot-Massad

'Maselstu' S, ab, Massad-Guillot; intr. 2004

'Masemgui' S, or, Guillot-Massad; intr. 2001

'Masfigel' S, ab, Guillot-Massad; intr. 2007

'Masflodel' ('Florence Delattre') S, m, Guillot-Massad; intr. 1997

'Masframb' S, mp, Guillot-Massad; intr. 1998

'Masfraro' F, dy, Guillot-Massad; intr. 2003

'Masgeden' F, yb, Guillot-Massad; intr. 2005

'Masgenti' S, dy, Guillot-Massad; intr. 2000

'Masgrma' ('Poncet') S, pb, Massad-Guillot; intr. 2000

'Mashahn' S, w, Guillot-Massad; intr. 2006

'Masinlum' S, op, Guillot-Massad; intr. 2004

'Masjanon' S, yb, Guillot - Massad; intr. 2007

'Masjorma' S, dy, Guillot-Massad; intr. 2001

'Masked Ball' HT, pb, 1968, Schwartz, Ernest W.; bud globular; flowers scarlet and gold, large, dbl., moderate fragrance; foliage dark, glossy; vigorous, bushy growth; ['Masquerade' × 'Peace']; intr. 1966

'Maslako' ('Marraine', 'Mme Helmut Kohl') S, dr, 1996, Guillot-Massad; intr. 1996

'Maslupau' ('Mme Paule Massad') S, ab, Guillot-Massad; intr. 1997

'Masmabay' ('Martine Guillot') S, w, Guillot-Massad; intr. 1996

'Masmacha' S, yb, Guillot-Massad

'Masmajo' Gr, pb, Guillot-Massad; bud small, pointed; intr. 2001

Masmaric® S, mp, Guillot-Massadvery dbl.; intr. 2000

'Masmaroch' S, ab, Guillot-Massad; intr. 2006

'Masmarti' ('Orsola Spinola') S, mp, Guillot-Massad; intr. 1996

'Masmijo' Min, yb, Guillot-Massad; intr. 2000

'Masmora' S, ab, Guillot; intr. 1997

'Masodmas' S, my, Guillot-Massad; intr. 2005

'Maspagui' ('Manuel Canovas') S, w, Guillot-Massad; intr. 1995

'Maspaujeu' ('Paul Bocuse') S, ab, Guillot-Massad; bud round, apricot; intr. 1997

'Maspeti' S, yb, Guillot-Massad; intr. 2001

'Masquerade' F, rb, 1949, Boerner; bud small, ovoid, yellow; flowers bright yellow turning salmon-pink and then dark red, 2½ in., 17 petals, borne in clusters of 10 - 25; foliage leathery, dark; vigorous, bushy, compact growth; PP975; ['Goldilocks' × 'Holiday']

'Masquerade, Climbing' Cl F, rb, 1958, Dillian

Masquerade® HT, pb, Kordes; flowers bright pink with white eye and reverse, dbl., high-centered, slight fragrance; growth to 3-4 ft.; intr. 2006

'Masrabla' S, pb, Guillot-Massad; intr. 2000

'Masrobo' S, mp, Guillot - Massad; intr. 2001

'Masrosch' S, ab, Guillot-Massad; intr. 2006

'Massabielle' HT, w, 1958, Guillot, M.; flowers well-formed, large; upright growth

'Massara' F, Sauvageot; intr. 1995

'Massey University' -- See 'Pride of Scotland'

'Master David' HT, pb, 1949, Cox; flowers pink, reverse carmine, pointed, 4 in., 25 petals; almost thornless; vigorous growth

'Master Hugh' S, dp, 1970, Mason, L.M.; flowers rich rose-pink, 2½-3 in., 5 petals, borne in clusters; [R. macrophylla × unknown]

'Master John' Cl HT, or, 1944, Duehrsen; flowers fiery orange-red, base gold, large, dbl., globular, intense fragrance; profuse spring bloom, then scattered until fall; foliage glossy, dark; very vigorous, climbing growth; ['Ednah Thomas' × 'Golden Rapture']

'Masterpiece' HP, mp, 1880, Paul, W.; flowers carmine pink, very large, full, globular; ['Beauty of Waltham' × unknown]

'Masverob' S, op, Guillot-Masad; intr. 2002

'Masversi' S, ob, Guillot-Massad; intr. 1998

'Masvive' F, ly, Guillot - Massad; intr. 2001

'Maswicri' S, mp, Guillot-Massad; intr. 2000

'Matador' -- See 'Intercarp'

'Matador' HT, dr, 1935, Van Rossem; bud long, pointed; flowers scarlet-crimson, shaded darker, large, very dbl., cupped, moderate fragrance; foliage leathery, dark; vigorous, bushy growth; PP170; [('Charles P. Kilham' × unknown) × 'Étoile de Hollande']

'Matador, Climbing' Cl HT, dr, 1938, Western Rose Co.

'Matador' ('Esther O'Farim') F, ob, Kordes, R.; bud ovoid; flowers light scarlet and orange, reverse gold, medium, dbl., high-centered; foliage large, dark, leathery; vigorous growth; PP3229; ['Konigin der Rosen' × 'Zorina']; intr. 1972

'Matangi, Climbing' Cl F, ob, Chiplunkar; intr. 1985

Matangi® -- See 'Macman'

'Matawhero Magic' -- See 'Macamster'

Matchball® -- See 'LLX8742'

'Matchless' HT, dp, 1926, Duckham-Pierson Co.; flowers cerise-pink, dbl.; upright, bushy growth; [sport of 'Premier']

'Matdoc' (The Physician™) LCl, lp, 2007, Mattock, Robert; flowers very full, usually quartered, borne in small clusters; foliage medium size, dark green, glossy; prickles medium, slightly hooked concave lower, moderate; growth climbing, tall (2½-3 m.); [sport of 'Penny Lane']; intr. 2007

'Matdove' ('Dove Dale') S, mp, 1998, Mather, Wendy; flowers medium pink, 3 in., 41 petals, borne in small clusters; foliage medium size, dark green, glossy; prickles moderate, medium, straight; spreading, low (3 × 6 ft.) growth; [seedling × seedling]

'Mateo's Silk Butterflies' ('Silk Butterflies') Ch, mp, Lettunich; flowers medium pink fading almost to white, single, slight fragrance; free-flowering; growth upright (4 ft.); intr. 1992

'Mater Casta' S, w; flowers semi-dbl.

'Mateus Rose' HT, pb, 1973, Winship; flowers peach, reverse pale pink, 4 in., 20 petals; ['Pink Parfait' × 'Mme Butterfly']

'Mathé Altéry' -- See 'Dresden'

'Matherin Regnier' HP, lp, 1855, Lévêque; flowers medium, full

'Mathilde' -- See 'Niphetos'

'Mathilde Bernard' HP, m, 1860, Bernède; flowers velvety purple, full

'Mathilde Jesse' P, dp, 1847, Laffay; flowers flame pink

'Mathilde Kärger' Pol, dp, 1929, Kärger; flowers carmine-pink, medium, dbl.

'Mati Bradová' HT, dp, 1934, Brada, Dr.; flowers dark rose-pink, sometimes almost carmine, very large, dbl., foliage glossy, dark; very vigorous, bushy growth; ['Gorgeous' × 'Gen. MacArthur']

Matilda™ -- See 'Meisoyris'

'Matilda, Climbing' -- See 'Nietar'

'Matilda' HT, my, Meilland; flowers dbl., high-centered, borne mostly singly; florist rose; intr. 2004

Matilda® -- See 'Meibeausai'

'Matilda Campbell' HT, dp, 1952, Campbell; bud ovoid; flowers bengal rose, 5-6½ in., very dbl., high-centered, intense fragrance; foliage glossy; vigorous, bushy growth; PP1274

'Matilda Jones' -- See 'Dawshadwell'

'Matka Vlast' HWich, pb, 1934, Böhm; flowers pink, striped red and white, small, full; [sport of 'Dorothy Perkins']

'Matson Modesty' HT, lp, 1946, Prosser; flowers pale pink, 4 in., 60 petals; vigorous growth; ['Mrs Sam McGredy' × 'Heinrich Wendland']

'Matsuo-Hime' HT, lp, 1999, Shimizu, Junji; flowers pale pink, 5½ in., 31-33 petals, high-centered; foliage medium green; growth to 4½ ft.; ['Hatakeyama' × 'Yonina']; intr. 1991

'Matsuri' ('Festival') LCl, rb, Keisei; flowers striped; intr. 1994

'Mattarb' ('Jealous Joey') F, ab, Matthews; intr. 1999

'Mattbay' LCl, mp, Matthews; intr. 2000

'Mattche' ('Chelsea Pensioner') Min, mr, 1983, Mattock, John, Ltd.; flowers scarlet, small, 20 petals, slight fragrance; foliage small, dark, semi-glossy; bushy growth; patio, containers; [('Gold Pin' × unknown) × seedling]; intr. 1982

'Mattdor' ('Northamptonshire') S, w, Mattock; intr. 1990

Matterhorn® HT, w, 1965, Armstrong, D.L. & Swim, H. C.; flowers medium to large, dbl., high-centered; foliage leathery; very tall, upright growth; PP2688; ['Buccaneer' × 'Cherry Glow']

'Mattgis' HT, dy, Matthews; intr. 2000

'Mattgrex' ('Spirit of SACS') F, w, Matthews; intr. 2000

'Mattgro' ('Pink Wave') F, mp, 1984, Mattock, John, Ltd.; flowers soft medium pink, medium, semi-dbl., moderate fragrance; foliage medium size, medium green, semi-glossy; groundcover; spreading growth; ['Moon Maiden' × Eyepaint®]; intr. 1983

'Matthew Duckett' HT, or, 1999, Jones, L.J.; flowers 2 in., dbl., borne mostly singly; foliage medium size, medium green, bronze when new, semi-glossy; few prickles; upright, tall growth; ['Solitaire' × (Alexander® × Remember Me®)]

'Matthew's Surprise' T, lp, 1889, Matthews, H.

Matthias Meilland® -- See 'Meifolio'

'Mattie Eloise' S, w, 2003, Nicholls, Deborah; flowers pale lavender, reverse light lavender, 4 in., full, borne mostly solitary, intense lavender fragrance; foliage medium size, medium green, semi-glossy; prickles ¼ in., needle, green/brown, moderate; growth compact, medium (3 ft.); ['Blue Girl' × Blue Moon®]; intr. 2002

'Mattinata' HT, Voightlander

'Mattjo' ('Snowman') HT, w, 1984, John Mattock, Ltd.; flowers large, dbl., moderate fragrance; foliage large, dark, semi-glossy; upright, bushy growth; [(Peer Gynt® × 'Isis') × 'Lady Seton']; intr. 1983

'Mattjop' HT, Matthews; intr. 2002

'Mattkiri' ('Kiri') HT, dp, Matthews; intr. 1994

'Mattlace' ('Anniversary') F, lp, Matthews; intr. 1998

'Mattmav' S, mp, Matthews; intr. 2001

'Mattmug' HT, pb, Matthews; intr. 2000

'Mattnot' ('Elizabeth Heather Grierson') LCl, lp, 1988, Mattock, John, Ltd.; bud coral pink; flowers soft pink, reverse darker, medium, dbl., borne in small clusters, moderate fragrance; foliage medium size, dark green, semi-glossy; upright growth; [Bonfire Night® × 'Dreaming Spires']; intr. 1986

'Mattspey' F, dr, Matthews

'Mattsun' ('Young Venturer') F, ab, 1979, Mattock; bud ovoid; flowers rich apricot, 4½ in., 30 petals; foliage dark, glossy, leathery; vigorous, upright growth; ['Arthur Bell' × 'Cynthia Brooke']

'Mattwai' HT, m, Matthews; intr. 2001

'Mattwyt' ('Tynwald') HT, ly, 1979, Mattock; bud ovoid; flowers cream, center yellow, 5 in., 60 petals, moderate fragrance; bushy, very upright growth; [Peer Gynt® × 'Isis']

'Matty' -- See 'Devhaute'

'Maturity' HT, mp, 1974, LeGrice; flowers rose-pink, pointed, 7 in., 50 petals; foliage large, dark; free growth; ['Duftwolke' × 'Lively']; intr. 1973

'Maud' HT, pb, 1921, Paul, W.; flowers salmon-pink

'Maud Alston' -- See 'Mrs Alston's Rose'

'Maud Betterton' HT, mp, 1965, Gregory; flowers rose-pink, medium, dbl.; vigorous growth; intr. 1958

'Maud Cole' F, m, 1968, Harkness; flowers mauve-purple, dbl.; foliage dark, glossy; ['Lilac Charm' × 'Africa Star']

'Maud Cuming' HT, op, 1923, Dickson, A.; bud pointed; flowers coral-pink, shaded peach and orange, very large, dbl., high-centered; foliage dark, glossy; vigorous, bushy growth

'Maud Dawson' ('Mrs Maud Dawson') HT, or, 1915, Dickson, A.; flowers orange-red, large, dbl., intense fragrance

'Maud E. Gladstone' Pol, pb, 1926, Bees; bud pointed; flowers malmaison pink, shaded coral and chrome-yellow, small, dbl., globular; foliage rich green, leathery, glossy; vigorous, bushy growth; ['Orléans Rose' × 'Edward VII']

'Maud Little' T, mp, 1891, Dingee & Conard; flowers full

'Maud Nash' HT, mr, 1942, Clark, A.; flowers rich red with fire; upright growth

'Maud Nunn' -- See 'Drisconun'

'Maude Elizabeth' S, mr, 2006, Beales, Amanda; flowers 8 cm., single, borne in large clusters; foliage medium size, dark green, semi-glossy; prickles average, straight, numerous; growth compact, spreading, bushy, short (60 cm.); landscape, containers; ['Robin Redbreast' × 'Cuthbert Grant']; intr. 2000

'Maude Sumner' F, ob; intr. 1994

'Mauget' M, dp, 1840, Prévost; flowers medium, full

'Maukeole' (Vent des Indes®) F, op

'Maulave' (Inge Schubert®) F, rb, (MAUI-ave)

'Mauna Loa' HT, mr, 1937, H&S; flowers bright red, large, dbl.; foliage heavy

'Maupertuis' M, mp, 1868, Moreau et Robert; bud very mossy; flowers rosy-pink, medium, full; some repeat

'Maure de Venise' -- See 'Othello Maure de Venise'

'Maureen Elizabeth' -- See 'Webrhapsody'

'Maureen Hendzel' HT, dp, 1974, Concord Floral Co.; buds medium, ovoid; flowers deep pink, large, very dbl., cupped, borne singly, strong spicy fragrance; foliage medium size, glossy; few prickles; growth vigorous, upright (4-6 ft.); [sport of 'Forever Yours']; intr. 1973

'Maureen Lipman' -- See 'Frantier'

'Maureen MacNeil' F, op, 1967, Vincent;

flowers salmon, borne in clusters; moderate growth; ['Anna Wheatcroft' × Orangeade®]

'Maureen Thompson' HT, dr, 1949, Cant, B. R.; bud pointed; flowers 3 in., 35 petals; foliage leathery; very vigorous growth

'Maurice' S, mr, J. B. Williams; intr. 2005

'Maurice' -- See 'McGredy's Triumph'

'Maurice Bernardin' ('Comte-Robert', 'Souv de l'Exposition de Brie', 'Exposition de Brie', 'Ferdinand de Lesseps') HP, mr, 1861, Granger; bud vermilion; flowers bright crimson, moderately large, dbl., borne in clusters, intense fragrance; vigorous growth; ['Général Jacqueminot' × unknown]; probably re-introduced by Verdier in 1869 as 'Ferdinand de Lesseps'

Maurice Chevalier® HT, mr, 1959, Delbard-Chabert; bud long; flowers rich red shaded garnet, large, 25 petals; foliage glossy; vigorous growth; ['Incendie' × (('Floradora' × unknown) × 'Independence')]

'Maurice Lepelletier' HP, dr, 1868, Moreau et Robert; flowers vermilion red

'Maurice Noyelle' HT, 1951, Buatois

'Maurice Perrault' HP, dr, 1869, Vigneron; flowers glowing dark cherry red, large, full

'Maurice Rouvier' T, pb, 1890, Nabonnand; bud long; flowers delicate pink, lightly veined red, pale on outer edge, very large, very full; foliage light green; prickles medium

'Maurice Utrillo' ('Artista Panarosa') F, rb, Delbard; flowers red with white stripes, dbl., moderate earthy fragrance; growth to 80 cm.; intr. 2003

'Maurice Vilmorin' HP, rb, 1868, Lédéchaux; flowers garnet-crimson to purple-maroon, dbl.; profuse bloom, sometimes repeated

'Mauricette Sistau' Pol, w, 1925, Turbat; flowers pure white to rosy white, large, dbl., borne in clusters of 25 - 50; thornless

Maurine™ -- See 'Poulrine'

Maurine Neuberger™ -- See 'Spomaur'

'Mauve' -- See 'Bourbon'

'Mauve' Pol, m, 1915, Turbat

'Mauve Mallerin' -- See 'Simone'

Mauve Melodee® HT, m, 1963, Raffell; bud long, pointed, purple; flowers rose-mauve, 4½-5 in., dbl., moderate fragrance; foliage dark, leathery, vigorous, upright growth; ['Sterling Silver' × seedling]

'Maverick' -- See 'Mavrik'

'Maverick' -- See 'Lavsask'

'Mavis Ballinger' -- See 'Horjurassic'

'Mavis Campbell' HT, dp, 1942, Clark, A.; bud long, deep pink; vigorous, tall growth

'Mavourneen' HT, lp, 1895, Dickson, A.; flowers pale silvery pink

'Mavourneen' S, rb, Buck, Dr. Griffith J.; bud medium-large, ovoid, pointed; flowers medium red, white reverse, large, 23 petals, borne in clusters of 1 - 10; repeat bloom; foliage large, leathery, semi-glossy, dark; prickles awl-like, tan; erect, bushy growth; [('Tickled Pink' × 'Prairie Princess') × 'El Catala']; intr. 1984

'Mavrik' ('Maverick') HT, pb, 2000, Edwards, Eddie; flowers pink, reverse white, 5-6 in., full, high-centered, borne mostly singly, slight fragrance; foliage large, dark green, glossy; few prickles; growth upright, tall (5-6 ft.); ['Louise Estes' × Signature®]

'Mawson' -- See 'Tomson'

'Max Colwell' Min, or, 1975, Moore, Ralph S.; bud long, pointed; flowers orange-red to red, 1½ in., 25 petals; foliage leathery; bushy, spreading growth; PP3963; ['red floribunda seedling' × ('Little Darling' × 'miniature seedling')]

'Max Graf' HRg, pb, 1919, Bowditch; flowers bright pink, petals somewhat crinkled, prominent golden stamens, 7-8 cm., single, borne in small clusters, slight musky fragrance; non-recurrent; foliage glossy, rugose, small; prickles numerous, reddish-brown; vigorous, bushy, trailing growth; groundcover; hardy; [R. rugosa × R. wichurana]

'Max Haufe' HEg, lp, 1939, Kordes; bud long, pointed, dark pink; flowers large, semi-dbl.; seasonal bloom; foliage large, leathery, light; somewhat arching, very vigorous (5-7 ft.), trailing growth; ['Joanna Hill' × R. rubiginosa]

'Max Hesdörffer' HT, dp, 1903, Jacobs; flowers deep rose, bordered with silvery rose, large, dbl., moderate fragrance; ['Kaiserin Auguste Viktoria' × unknown]

'Max Krause' HT, yb, 1930, Krause; flowers reddish-orange, opening golden yellow, very large, dbl.; foliage dark, glossy; vigorous growth; ['Mrs Beckwith' × 'Souv. de H.A. Verschuren']

'Max Krause, Climbing' Cl HT, yb, 1940, Moreira da Silva; flowers buff yellow, reverse apricot, large

'Max Krause Superior' HT, op, 1940, Heizmann, E.; flowers coppery pink, very large, very dbl.

'Max Schmeling' F, or, 1973, Tantau, Math.; bud ovoid; flowers large, dbl.; foliage large, glossy; upright, bushy growth; [unknown × unknown]

'Max Singer' -- See 'Rosiériste Max Singer'

'Max Vogel' HT, op, 1929, Leenders, M.; flowers coppery orange, large, very dbl.; foliage bronze; ['Fritz Maydt' × 'Lilly Jung']

'Maxi' F, rb, 1971, McGredy, Sam IV; flowers red, white eye, 3 in., 12 petals; free growth; [(('Evelyn Fison' × ('Tantau's Triumph' × 'Coryana')) × ('Hamburger Phoenix' × 'Danse de Feu')]

Maxi Vita® -- See 'Korfeining'

'Maxim' F, op, 1965, Tantau, Math.; bud ovoid; flowers salmon-pink, large, dbl., borne in broad clusters; foliage leathery; vigorous, bushy growth; intr. 1963

'Maxim' ('Joy of Life', 'Maxime') HT, rb, Tantau; flowers cream white flushed carmine, deepens with age, dbl., high-centered, moderate fragrance; growth strong, vigorous; intr. 1993

'Maxima' -- See 'Sultana'

'Maxima' -- See 'Majestueuse'

'Maxima' -- See 'Alba Maxima'

Maxima™ -- See 'Poulhi013(N)'

'Maxima' -- See 'Goliath'

'Maxima Hit' (Maxima™) MinFl, ob, Olesen; bud pointed ovoid; flowers orange and orange blend, 5 cm., 60-70 petals, hybrid tea, borne singly, very slight fragrance; recurrent; foliage dark green, matte; prickles some, 5 mm., linear; narrow, bushy (20-40 cm.) growth; PP15044; [Mandy Kordana® × Vanilla Kordana®]; intr. 2002

'Maxima Multiplex' -- See 'Des Peintres'

'Maxima Multiplex' A, w, before 1829, possibly Prévost; sepals foliaceous; flowers white, slightly yellow at center, large

'Maxime' -- See 'Maxim'

'Maxime Buatois' Pol, yb, 1900, Buatois; flowers fiery copper-yellow, aging to carmine pink, medium, full; ['Étoile de Mai' × 'Laurette Messimy']

'Maxime Corbon' HWich, rb, 1918, Barbier; flowers dark coppery red turning apricot-yellow, 6-7 cm., dbl., borne in small clusters, moderate fragrance; abundant seasonal bloom; foliage rich green, glossy, leathery; vigorous, climbing and trailing growth (8-18 ft.); [R. wichurana × 'Léonie Lamesch']

'Maxime de la Rocheterie' HP, dr, 1871, Vigneron; flowers velvety blackish purple red, large, full

'Maximin Chabuel' HT, op, 1943, Mallerin, C.

'Maxine' F, rb, 1957, Silva; bud globular, creamy pink; flowers camellia-red becoming maroon flecked pink and white, rosette, 37-40 petals, flat, moderate fragrance; foliage leathery, glossy; very vigorous, low, bushy growth; PP1879; ['Pinocchio' × 'Crimson Glory']

'Maxine' S, dp, Williams, J. Benjamin; bud cherry red; flowers single to semi-dbl.; growth prostrate; intr. 1999

'Maxine's Sister' S, dp, Williams, J.B.; bud cherry red; flowers dark red, single to semi-dbl.; growth prostrate; intr. 2000

'Maxistar' HT, or, 1979, Huber; bud round; flowers 5½-6 in., 70-80 petals; foliage dark, leathery, vigorous, upright growth; ['Duftwolke' × 'Pharaon']; intr. 1975

'May Alexandra Lippiat' HT, dp, 1909, Lippiat; flowers dark pink

'May Banks' T, ly, 1938, Banks; flowers lemon-yellow; [sport of 'Lady Hillingdon']

'May Graham' -- See 'Kendad'

'May Kenyon Slaney' HT, dp, 1911, Dickson, A.; flowers dark pink, lighter at base, large, full, moderate fragrance

'May Lawlor' -- See 'Kirhol'

'May Lyon' -- See 'Cocbay'

'May Martin' HT, ly, 1918, Martin & Forbes Co.; flowers pure canary-yellow, center darker, semi-dbl.; [sport of 'Ophelia']

'May Miller' HT, op, 1911, E.G. Hill, Co.; flowers coppery pink, large, dbl., moderate sweet fragrance; recurrent; [seedling × 'Paul Neyron']

'May Queen' HWich, lp, 1898, Van Fleet; bud light red; flowers lilac-pink, 7-8 cm., semi-dbl., flat, borne in small to medium clusters, intense fruity fragrance; occasional repeat; foliage glossy, rounded; vigorous, climbing or groundcover growth; [*R. wichurana* × 'Mrs DeGraw']

'May Quennell' HP, mr, 1878, Postans; flowers fiery crimson, petal edges shaded magenta and carmine, large, very full

'May Rivers' T, w, 1890, Rivers; flowers cream white, center citron yellow, large, full

'May Robinson' F, op; flowers bright salmon-pink

'May Taylor' HT, dp, 1966, Taylor, L.R.; flowers deep rose-pink, large, dbl., high-centered; foliage soft; vigorous, bushy growth; ['Tassin' × 'Ballet']

'May Turner' HP, op, 1874, Verdier, E.; flowers light salmon pink, reverse darker, very large, full, moderate fragrance

'May Wettern' HT, mp, 1928, Dickson, A.; bud pointed; flowers rosy pink, large, dbl., high-centered; foliage rich green, leathery; vigorous, bushy growth

'May Woolley' F, ab, 1976, Wood; flowers bronze-apricot to peach, 2½-3 in., 25-25 petals, cupped; foliage small, glossy; moderate, free growth; ['Fairlight' × 'Arthur Bell']

'Maya' F, or, 1986, Kriloff, Michel; flowers borne in clusters; foliage dense, bright; low growth; ['Zorina' × 'Lara']

Maya Kordana® Min, ab, Kordes; flowers copper-yellow, full; growth compact; [sport of 'Vanilla Kordana']; container rose; intr. 2005

'Maya Lee' HT, or, 1992, Jerabek, Paul E.; flowers 3-3½ in., 50 petals, borne mostly singly; foliage medium size, medium green, semi-glossy; numerous prickles; long stems; medium (100+ cm.), upright growth; [unknown × unknown]

'Maybe Baby' -- See 'Gelbe'

'Maybella' HT, my, Kordes; intr. 2006

'Maybelle Stearns' -- See 'Mabelle Stearns'

'Mayday' F, lp, 1959, Boerner; bud ovoid; flowers white overcast pink, 3 in., 25-30 petals, cupped, borne in clusters, moderate fragrance; foliage rich green, leathery; vigorous, bushy growth; PP1625; [(('Pinocchio' × unknown) × 'hybrid tea seedling') × 'Fashion']; intr. 1956

'Mayet' HT, mr, 1958, Dot, Pedro; flowers crimson-red passing to Neyron pink, base yellow, well-formed, 30 petals, intense fragrance; foliage olive-green; vigorous growth; ['Condesa de Sástago' × 'Mme Henri Guillot']; intr. 1951

'Mayfair' HT, dp, 1935, Bentall; flowers deep pink, well-formed, large; foliage bronze; very vigorous growth

'Mayflower' T, w, 1910, Hill, E. G.; flowers cream white, edges shaded pink, large

'Mayflower' HT, pb, Gregory; flowers light cerise, reverse silvery pink, 4 in., 30 petals, intense fragrance; foliage glossy; vigorous growth; [Eden Rose® × unknown]; intr. 1958

'Maylina' ('Mrs Charles E. F. Gersdorff') Cl HT, w, 1916, Gersdorff; flowers silvery white, reverse Killarney pink to shell-pink, very large, dbl., cupped, moderate spicy fragrance; abundant, intermittent bloom; foliage large, soft; growth vigorous, climbing (15 ft.); ['white climber' × 'Killarney']

'Mayor Baker' HT, or, 1928, Thomas; flowers terra-cotta to scarlet, base light orange, semi-dbl.; vigorous growth; ['Mons. Paul Lédé' × 'Hadley']

'Mayor Cermák' HT, dr, 1932, Böhm, J.; flowers very dark red, shaded purple, large; vigorous, branching growth; ['Mrs Henry Winnett' × 'Vaterland']; intr. 1934

'Mayor of Casterbridge' -- See 'Ausbrid'

'Maysa' HT

'Maytime' LCl, lp, 1953, Maney; bud red; flowers flesh-pink, reverse rose-pink, 5-6 in., single, borne in clusters of 5; profuse, non-recurrent bloom; foliage leathery; vigorous growth; [*R. maximowicziana pilosa* × 'Betty Uprichard']

'Maytime' S, pb, Buck, Dr. Griffith J.; bud ovoid, pointed; flowers carmine-rose, base yellow, shallowly-cupped, 3½-4 in., single, cupped, moderate fragrance; repeat bloom; foliage dark, leathery; upright, bushy growth; ['Elegance (HT)' × 'Prairie Princess']; intr. 1975

'Maywonder' Pol, or, Grootendorst; intr. 1968

'Maywood' HT, mr, 1924, Joseph H. Hill, Co.; flowers bright red, dbl.; ['Charles K. Douglas' × ('Killarney' × 'Ophelia')]

'Maywood Red' HT, mr, 1923, E.G. Hill, Co.; ['Premier' × seedling]

'Mazeppa' HGal, rb, before 1841; flowers red, edged and marbled with white, medium, dbl.

'Mazowsze' HT, dp, 1966, Grabczewski; bud oblong; flowers deep pink edged lighter, dbl.; foliage leathery; very vigorous growth; ['Marella' × unknown]

'Mazurka' -- See 'Meitune'

'Mazurka' F, mp, 1965, Verbeek; bud ovoid; flowers pink, medium, dbl., borne in clusters; foliage dark

'Mazzini' HT, w, 1925, Easlea; flowers blush-white suffused pink, dbl.; ['Mme Butterfly' × 'Gladys Holland']

'McCallun House' T, ly

'McCarthy Rose' -- See 'Worchurch'

'McCartney Rose' -- See 'Meizeli'

'McGredy's Coral' HT, op, 1936, McGredy; flowers coral-pink, overlaid salmon, shaded copper, large, high-centered; foliage dark cedar-green; very vigorous, branching growth

'McGredy's Gem' HT, lp, 1933, McGredy; bud pointed; flowers creamy pink, base yellow, deepening to rose-pink edges, full, cupped, slight fragrance; very vigorous growth

'McGredy's Ivory' ('Portadown Ivory') HT, w, 1930, McGredy; bud long, pointed; flowers creamy white, base yellow, large, 28 petals, high-centered, moderate damask fragrance; foliage dark, leathery, glossy; vigorous growth; ['Mrs Charles Lamplough' × 'Mabel Morse']

'McGredy's Ivory, Climbing' Cl HT, w, 1939, Raffel

'McGredy's Orange' ('Golden Thoughts', 'Morning Glory', 'Sunglow') HT, ob, 1936, McGredy; flowers deep Indian yellow, reverse orange, flushed salmon, dbl., high-centered; foliage dark, bronze; vigorous growth; [sport of 'Mrs Sam McGredy']

'McGredy's Peach' HT, op, 1933, McGredy; bud pointed; flowers creamy yellow, washed salmon, very large, cupped; foliage glossy, dark; vigorous growth

'McGredy's Perfection' HT, lp, 1936, McGredy; flowers large, dbl.

'McGredy's Pillar' HT, or, 1935, McGredy; flowers terra-cotta

'McGredy's Pink' HT, lp, 1936, McGredy; flowers bright rose, outer petals pearly cream and pink, base saffron, intense fragrance; foliage dark; vigorous, branching growth; PP341

'McGredy's Pride' HT, op, 1936, McGredy; bud long, pointed; flowers orange and salmon-pink, flushed saffron-yellow, reverse yellow, dbl., moderate fragrance; PP339; ['Angèle Pernet' × 'Mrs Charles Lamplough']

'McGredy's Salmon' HT, ab, 1940, McGredy; bud pointed; flowers apricot-salmon, dbl.; foliage dark, wrinkled; strong stems; vigorous, compact growth; PP410; ['Mrs Henry Morse' × seedling]

'McGredy's Scarlet' HT, mr, 1930, McGredy; flowers medium, 35 petals, high-centered; foliage leathery, glossy; vigorous growth

'McGredy's Sunset, Climbing' Cl HT, ob, 1957, Shamburger, P.; PP1633

'McGredy's Sunset' HT, ob, 1936, McGredy; bud long, pointed; flowers chrome-yellow shading to scarlet, reverse clear buttercup-yellow, 40 petals, globular, moderate fragrance; foliage glossy, bronze; vigorous growth; PP317; ['Margaret McGredy' × 'Mabel Morse']

'McGredy's Triumph, Climbing' Cl HT, dp, 1948, Simmonds Nursery

'McGredy's Triumph' ('Maurice') HT, dp, 1934, McGredy; flowers soft rose flushed orange, very large, dbl., high-centered, moderate fragrance; foliage dark reddish bronze, glossy; strong stems; vigorous, branching growth; PP190; ['Admiration' × seedling]

'McGredy's Wonder' HT, ob, 1934,

McGredy; flowers coppery orange, flushed orange-red, reverse orange-red, large, semi-dbl., cupped, moderate fruity fragrance; foliage glossy, olive-green; vigorous growth

'McGredy's Yellow' HT, my, 1933, McGredy; bud long, pointed; flowers bright buttercup-yellow, large, 30 petals, cupped; foliage glossy, bronze; vigorous growth; ['Mrs Charles Lamplough' × ('The Queen Alexandra Rose' × 'J.B. Clark')]

'McGredy's Yellow, Climbing' Cl HT, my, 1937, Western Rose Co.

'McLeod's Daughters' F, ab; flowers creamy apricot, reverse tinged copper, double, cupped, reflexed, moderate sweet lemon fragrance; recurrent; foliage light to medium green, glossy; 5 ft. growth

'McMillan's Pink' -- See 'Affirm'

'McMillan's Yellow' HT, my

'Me Darling' F, pb, 1971, Anderson's Rose Nurseries; flowers cream suffused pink, 3½-4 in., 37 petals, high-centered; foliage glossy, light; ['Evelyn Fison' × 'Dearest']

'Me-Gami' -- See 'Megami'

'Me Too' -- See 'Juleschildren'

Meadow™ -- See 'Meadow Cottage'

'Meadow Cottage' (Meadow™) S, my, Olesen; bud ovate; flowers medium yellow, small, semi-dbl., open cup to flat, borne usually in clusters of 7, slight fragrance; recurrent; foliage dark green, semi-glossy; prickles numerous, 9 mm., hooked downward, yellow-green; low (40 cm.), spreading growth; PP16303; [Diamond Head™ × seedling]; intr. 2004

'Meadow Dancer' Min, lp, 1991, Gruenbauer, Richard; bud ovoid; flowers medium, 45 petals, cupped, no fragrance; foliage medium size, medium green, semi-glossy; spreading, tall growth; [sport of 'Judy Fischer']; intr. 1990

'Meadow Fresh' Min, ab, Bell; flowers soft pink and buff apricot; free-flowering; growth medium

'Meadow Ruby' S, mr, 1982, James, John; flowers large, very dbl., high-centered, borne singly, moderate fragrance; repeat bloom; foliage leathery; prickles long, red; vigorous, upright growth; ['Prairie Princess' × (Queen Elizabeth® × 'Borealis')]; intr. 1978

'Meban' ('White Knight') HT, w, 1957, Meilland, F.; bud long, pointed; intr. 1955

'Mécène' HGal, pb, 1845, Vibert; flowers white, striped with rose and light pink, compact, medium, dbl.; prickles shoots very smooth; erect, moderate growth

'Mecertsar' -- See 'Concerto, Climbing'

'MeChabaku' F, mp, Poulsen; flowers dbl., cupped, borne in clusters; recurrent; stems short; growth tall (2 m.); intr. 2000

'Mechak' HT, dr, 1983, Pal, Dr. B.P.; flowers very large, 20 petals, high-centered, no fragrance; foliage medium size, dark, smooth; prickles brown; upright growth; ['Samourai' × seedling]; intr. 1979

'Mechliniae' S, lp; flowers very similar to *R. rubrifolia*; foliage touched with mauve

'Mechtilde von Neuerburg' HEg, mp, 1920, Boden-Kurtscheid; flowers pure pink, 1 in., semi-dbl., borne in corymbs; foliage typical sweetbriar; vigorous (10 × 10 ft.) growth; hips large, crimson; very hardy

Mecklenburg® LCl, lp, Lützow; intr. 1999

'Meda' HSet, op, 1942, Horvath; flowers shrimp-pink, open, imbricated, 3½-4 in., 40-60 petals, intense fragrance; foliage large, leathery; long stems; very vigorous, climbing (10-12 ft.) growth; PP518; [(*R. setigera* × Mme Butterfly) × 'Golden Dawn']

'Medal of Honor' -- See 'Jactred'

Medallion® HT, ab, 1972, Warriner, William A.; bud long, pointed; flowers light apricot, very large, dbl., moderate fragrance; foliage large, leathery; vigorous, upright growth; PP2997; ['South Seas' × King's Ransom®]; intr. 1973

'Medea' T, ly, 1890, Paul, W.; flowers lemon yellow with silk-yellow center, large, very full

Medeo® -- See 'Kortraste'

'Medeo' F, w, Kordes; flowers cream; growth vigorous, medium, healthy; [sport of 'Kiss']; intr. 1991

'Medialis' -- See 'Helmedia'

'Mediator' HT, op, 1949, Totty; flowers coral-pink shading to salmon base, medium, 45 petals, high-centered; foliage soft, dark green; vigorous, bushy growth

Medima™ -- See 'Poulvue'

'Medina' HT, w, 1918; [sport of 'Sunburst']; intr. 1923

'Mediterranea' HT, pb, 1943, Dot, Pedro; flowers carmine with yellow, passing to pink with white markings, 5 in., very dbl., high-centered; upright growth; [sport of 'Signora']

'Medley' HT, lp, 1962, Boerner; bud pointed; flowers bright salmon-pink, reverse flushed yellow, 5-5½ in., 35-40 petals, cupped, moderate fragrance; foliage leathery; vigorous, upright growth; PP2200; ['HT seedling' × 'Pageant']; intr. 1962

'Medley Pink' Min, mp, Noack; flowers 6 cm., dbl., borne in clusters; recurrent; growth to 10-14 in.; intr. 2003

'Medley Red' Min, mr, Noack; flowers 6 cm., dbl., cupped, borne in clusters; recurrent; growth to 10-14 in.; intr. 2003

'Medley Soft Pink' Min, lp, Noack; flowers 6 cm., dbl., borne in clusters; recurrent; growth to 10-14 in.

'Medusa' S, m, Noack, Werner; flowers lavender-pink, 2 in., dbl., borne in clusters; good repeat; bushy (80-100 cm.) growth; intr. 1996

'Méduse' (Simone Merieux®) HT, rb, 1982, Gaujard; flowers large, full; foliage large, dark green, semi-glossy; ['Chenonceaux' × 'Tropicana']; intr. 1981

Mee Maw™ -- See 'Sprolake'

Meera™ -- See 'Trsmeera'

'Meerzicht Glory' -- See 'Orange Delight'

'Meg' Cl HT, ab, 1954, Gosset; flowers salmon-apricot, stamens red, 5½ in., 10 petals, borne in large clusters, moderate fragrance; recurrent bloom; foliage dark, glossy; vigorous growth; [probably 'Paul's Lemon Pillar' × 'Mme Butterfly']

'Meg Merrilies' HEg, dp, 1894, Penzance; flowers rosy crimson, center white, small, single to semi-dbl., moderate fragrance; summer bloom; foliage very fragrant; very vigorous (10 ft.) growth; [*R. rubiginosa* × 'hybrid perpetual or bourbon']

'MEG X1-81' F, w, 1985, Gandy's Roses, Ltd.

'Megami' ('Me-Gami') HT, op, 1985, Suzuki, Seizo; flowers medium salmon-pink, large, 33 petals, high-centered, moderate fragrance; foliage dark, leathery; upright growth; [seedling × 'Fragrant Cloud']; intr. 1984

'Megan' HT, pb, 1981, Adams, Dr. Neil D.; bud pointed; flowers white with pink petal edges, high-centered, borne 3-5 per cluster; foliage medium green, glossy; prickles broad, slightly hooked; upright, strong growth; ['Daily Sketch' × seedling]

'Megan Dolan' -- See 'Devnovia'

'Megan Louise' HT, pb, 1981, Erich Welsh Roses; bud ovoid; flowers silvery pink, deep pink petal edges, large, 48 petals, high-centered, borne in clusters of 1 - 5, intense fragrance; foliage matte, green, tough; prickles red-brown; short, bushy growth; ['Red Lion' × 'Silver Lining']; intr. 1983

Megan's Melody™ -- See 'Harpmeg'

'Megastar' HT, or, 1981, Sohne, W. Kordes; bud globular; flowers very dbl., cupped, borne singly, intense fruity fragrance; foliage light green; prickles curved yellow-brown; intr. 1978

'Megastar '04' HT, mr; flowers cardinal red, slow opening, 12 cm., dbl., high-centered, moderate fragrance; recurrent; growth strong, medium (80-110 cm.); intr. 2005

Megenaris™ (Samsø™) F, rb, Olesen; flowers red with tones of yellow and orange, 8-10 cm., dbl., borne in small clusters, slight fragrance; foliage dark, glossy; growth bushy, medium (60-100 cm.); intr. 1998

'Meger' ('Baccarat', 'Jacqueline') HT, or, 1962, Meilland, F.; bud globular, medium; intr. 1954

'Megersar' Cl HT, or, 1965, Meilland

'Meggie' Min, lp

'Meghan's Arrival' -- See 'Bullmeg'

'Meghdoot' HT, w, 1974, Pal, Dr. B. P.; buds large, long pointed; flowers large, dbl., cupped, borne singly; foliage medium size, leathery; numerous prickles;

growth very vigorous, upright (170 cm.); intr. 1972

'Megiddo' F, or, 1971, Gandy, Douglas L.; flowers bright orange-red, 4½ in., 25 petals, borne in clusters, slight fragrance; recurrent; foliage large, olive-green, glossy; upright growth; ['Coup de Foudre' × 'S'Agaro']; intr. 1970

'Mehamber' ('Amber Nectar') F, ab, 1996, Mehring, Bernhard F.; flowers amber/apricot with amber yellow reverse, 2 in., full, borne in large clusters; foliage medium size, medium green, glossy; prickles moderate; upright, medium (60 cm.) growth; [Alexander® × 'Sweet Magic']; intr. 1997

'Mehblue' LCl, m, Mehring; intr. 2004

'Mehbronze' ('Free As Air') Min, r, 1996, Mehring, Bernhard F.; flowers orange-red/russet with light orange pink reverse, 1½ in., 8-14 petals, no fragrance; foliage medium size, dark green, glossy; few prickles; compact, medium (35 cm.) growth; PPPVRO 5448;; [Anna Ford® × 'Brown Velvet']; intr. 1996

'Mehbrown' ('Garry Brown') F, mr, 1997, Mehring, Bernhard F.; flowers medium, dbl., borne in small clusters; foliage large, dark green, glossy; some prickles; upright, medium (26in.) growth; ['Roger Lamberlin' × 'Arthur Bell']

'Meher' HT, mp, 1998, Pavri, Nadir J.; flowers medium pink, lighter reverse, 3-3½ in., full, high-centered, borne mostly singly, moderate fragrance; free-flowering; foliage medium size, medium green, semi-glossy; prickles numerous small and large; growth upright, tall (5 ft.); [American Heritage® × 'Paradise']

'Mehfever' F, or, Mehring; intr. 2006

'Mehgoldie' ('Janet Bebb') F, ly, 1997, Meahring, Bernhard F.; flowers medium, dbl., borne in small clusters; foliage large, medium green, glossy; compact, medium (100cm.) growth; [Golden Holstein® × 'Seafarer']

'Mehnan' ('Frechdachs') Min, yb, Mehring, Bernhard F.; intr. 1998

'Mehnina' ('Nina') S, dr, 2000, Mehring, B.F.; flowers semi-dbl., borne in large clusters, slight fragrance; foliage medium size, dark green, glossy; prickles moderate; bushy, medium (90-100 cm.) growth; [('Iceberg' × 'Anytime') × 'Eyeopener']

'Mehpark' ('Jane Eyre') LCl, mp, 1998, Mehring, Bernhard F.; flowers medium pink, 4½ in., dbl., borne in small clusters; foliage large, medium green, semi-glossy; prickles moderate; upright, climbing, medium (300cm.) growth; [Westfalenpark Dortmund × ((Anna Ford® × 'Frank Naylor') × (Westerland® × '(Casino × Mermaid) × (Vesper × Picasso))]; intr. 1998

'Mehpat' ('Make A Wish') Min, pb, 1996, Mehring, Bernhard F.; flowers salmon pink, light pink reverse, 2 in., very dbl., borne in large clusters, moderate fragrance; foliage medium size, dark green, glossy; prickles moderate; growth bushy, medium (35 cm.); ['Robin Redbreast' × Amber Queen®]; intr. 1996

'Mehpic' ('Golden Hope') F, yb, 1998, Mehring, Bernhard F.; flowers yellow, pink edge, reverse amber with pink edge, 2¾ in., dbl., borne in small clusters; foliage large, medium green, semi-glossy; no prickles; upright, medium, 80 cm. growth; ['Kronprinzessin Victoria von Schweden' × 'Goldene Holstein']; intr. 1998

'Mehrex' ('Sarah Jo') F, rb, 1993, Mehring, Bernhard F.; flowers red with white eye, salmon reverse, medium, dbl., borne in small clusters; foliage large, dark green, glossy; some prickles; medium (60 cm.), upright, bushy growth; ['Sheri Anne' × Dortmund®]; intr. 1994

'Mehsherry' ('The Holt') S, dp, Mehring, Bernhard F.

'Méhul' HGal, m, 1826, Cartier; flowers carmine-violet, large, very full

'Méhul' B, mp, Guillot; flowers carmine; intr. 1846

'Mei' S, lp, Komatsu

'Mei-li' HCh, pb, Dening; bud dark pink; flowers light pink, dbl., borne in sprays; growth to 2 × 2 ft.; [R. chinensis minima × unknown]; intr. 2007

'Mei975' HT, w, Meilland; intr. 2006

'Meiafone' ('Duftfestival', 'Sir Donald Bradman') HT, mr very dbl.; intr. 2002

'Meialate' (Mystic Meidiland®) S, yb, 1998, Selection Meilland; flowers coppery peach fading to butter cream yellow, 1-1½ in., semi-dbl., borne in small clusters, no fragrance; foliage medium size, dark green, semi-glossy; prickles moderate; compact, medium (3 ft.) growth; PP11044; intr. 1997

'Meialeric' F, ab

'Meialfi' F, ob, 1961, Meilland, Mrs. Marie-Louise; bud ovoid, pointed; intr. 1961

'Meialfisar' (Zambra, Climbing®) Cl F, ob, 1969, Meilland; [sport of 'Zambra']

'Meialoro' F, or, Meilland; intr. 2000

'Meialzonite' ('Lady Meilland') HT, op, Meilland; intr. 1986

'Meiarlo' HT, or, 1962, Meilland, Alain A.; intr. 1962

'Meiatjon' Min, mp, Meilland

'Meibacus' ('Liv Tyler', Comtesse de Provence™) HT, mp, 2001, Meilland, A.; bud conical; flowers medium coral-pink, 5 in., 80 petals, cupped, borne mostly solitary, intense fragrance; recurrent; foliage large, medium green, semi-glossy; prickles moderate, hooked downward; growth upright, medium (5½ ft.); hips smooth, rounded, yellow-green; PP13860; [(Centenaire de Lourdes® × 'Duc de Windsor ') × 'Regatta']; intr. 2001

'Meibaiprez' F, yb, Lim, Ping; bud pointed; intr. 2006

'Meibalani' ('Rétro') S, mp, Meilland; intr. 1980

'Meibalbika' ('Iga 83 Munchen', Meilland Rosiga 83®, 'Munchen 83', 'Rose Iga', 'The Wyevale rose') F, mr, 1985, Meilland, Mrs. Marie-Louise; bud oblong; flowers carmine-pink suffused with a scarlet blush on the edges, 3-3½ in., 17-20 petals, borne in clusters, no fragrance; recurrent; foliage medium size, dark green, semi-glossy; bushy (1 m.) growth; hips orange; PP6281; ['Coppélia 76' × ('Curiosa' × 'City of Leeds')]; intr. 1981

'Meibalneo' S, my, Meilland; intr. 2008

'Meibaltaz' ('Anthony Meilland') F, my, 1994, Meilland, Alain A.; bud egg-shaped; intr. 1990

'Meibarco' (Crimson Minuetto™) Min, dr, 2000, Meilland International; flowers very full, borne in small clusters, no fragrance; foliage medium size, dark green, matte; prickles moderate; growth compact, medium (8-12 in.); intr. 1999

'Meibarke' ('Douce Symphonie', 'Sweet Symphony', Debut™) Min, rb, 1988, Selection Meilland; flowers luminous scarlet blending to cream to yellow at base, aging, 1¾ in., 15-20 petals, cupped, borne singly and in clusters, no fragrance; recurrent; foliage medium size, dark green, semi-glossy; prickles slender, few, straw; bushy (16-20 in.) growth; hips ovoid, few, dull orange-red; PP6791; ['Coppelia' × Magic Carrousel®]; intr. 1989

'Meibarum' F, w; intr. 2000

'Meibderos' (Elle™) HT, pb, 2003, Meilland International; flowers light pink, reverse orange pink, large, 50-55 petals, borne mostly solitary, intense fragrance; foliage large, dark green, glossy; growth bushy, short (5 ft.); garden, cutting; PPAF; ['Purple Splendour' × (Chicago Peace® × 'Meikinosi')]; intr. 2000

'Meibeau' F, or, 1966, Meilland

'Meibeausai' ('Charles Aznavour', 'Seduction', 'Pearl of Bedfordview', Matilda®) F, pb, 1988, Meilland, Alain A.; bud oval, small; flowers light yellow, edged and suffused pink, 9-10 cm., 15-20 petals, flat, borne in clusters of 1 - 7, no fragrance; foliage medium size, dark green, semi-glossy; prickles moderate, large, tan; upright, low, compact, proliferous growth; PP7667; ['Coppelia 76' × 'Nirvana']

'Meibekarb' (Cherry Sunblaze®) Min, mr, 1993, Hutton, R.J.; flowers bright red, non-fading, 1-1½ in., 40-25 petals, borne in small clusters; foliage medium size, dark green, semi-glossy; some prickles; medium (35 cm.), bushy growth; PP8448; ['Coppelia' × Magic Carrousel®]; intr. 1993

'Meibeluxen' (Fiona®) S, dr, 1983, Meilland, Mrs. Marie-Louise; flowers small, bright red, 20 petals, borne in clusters; recurrent; foliage small, dark, semi-glossy; spreading growth; ['Sea Foam' × 'Picasso']; intr. 1982

'Meibicmarj' ('Elegance') HT, pb, Meilland; intr. 1996

'Meibigoud' ('Ambassador') HT, mr, Meilland; intr. 1995

'Meibil' HT, mp, 1959, Meilland, F.; bud medium, ovoid

'Meibilsar' (Pink Peace, Climbing®) Cl HT, mp, 1970, Meilland; [sport of 'Pink Peace']; intr. 1968

'Meibinosor' (Concertino®) F, or, 1979, Meilland, Mrs. Marie-Louise; flowers cherry-red, medium, 20 petals, cupped, slight fragrance; foliage matte, dark; vigorous, bushy growth; [(('Fidélio' × 'Fidélio') × (Zambra® × Zambra®)) × 'Marlena']; intr. 1976

'Meibionel' F, mr, Meilland International; bud ovoid; intr. 2004

'Meibiranda' (Candia™) HT, rb, 1985, Meilland, Mrs. Marie-Louise; flowers red and yellow blend, large, 38 petals, high-centered; foliage large, light green; PP4705; ['Matador' × ('Tropicana' × 'Flirt')]; intr. 1978

'Meibiru' HT, dr, Meilland; intr. 1998

'Meiblam' ('White Meillandina', 'Yorkshire Sunblaze') Min, w, 1984, Meilland, Mrs. Marie-Louise; flowers medium, semi-dbl., no fragrance; foliage small, light green, semi-glossy; bushy growth; ['Katharina Zeimet' × White Gem®]; intr. 1983

'Meiblanca' HT, w, Meilland; intr. 1998

'Meibleri' ('Alliance') HT, w, 1985, Meilland, Mrs. Marie-Louise; flowers glowing white, large, no fragrance; foliage medium size, dark, matte; upright growth; ['Rustica' × Youki San®]; intr. 1983

'Meiblonver' HT, w, Meilland

'Meibojat' HT, dy, Meilland; intr. 1987

'Meibolnay' ('Top Secret') HT, dr, Meilland

'Meibonrib' (Magic Meidiland®, Magic Meillandecor®) S, mp, 1994, Meilland, Alain A.; flowers red purple, lighter centers, medium, dbl., flat, borne in small clusters, no fragrance; foliage small, dark green, glossy; some prickles; medium to low, spreading, growth; groundcover; PP9469; [R. sempervirens × (Milrose® × 'Bonica')]; intr. 1992

'Meiborfil' ('Silver Anniversary') HT, m, Meilland

'Meibosnio' HT, yb; bud large, globular; intr. 2003

'Meiboulka' S, mr, Meilland; intr. 2007

'Meibrenec' (Peach Waterfall™) Min, lp, 2000, Meilland International; flowers light scarlet pink, reverse light carmine pink, 2½-3½ cm., very full, borne in small clusters, slight fragrance; foliage medium size, dark green, semi-glossy; prickles moderate; spreading, low (20-30 cm.) growth; PP10489; [('Meiplarzon' × 'Meitrisical') × 'Katharina Zeimet']

'Meibriacus' -- See 'Claude Brasseur'

'Meibrico' ('Bettina '78') HT, op, 1976, Paolino; flowers coral, 4 in., 30 petals; foliage dark, leathery; vigorous growth; PP3857; [('Jolie Madame' × 'Sunlight') × ('Lady Elgin' × 'Dr. A. J. Verhage')]; intr. 1976

'Meibrinpay' ('Romantic Seranade', Abbaye de Cluny™) HT, ab, 1996, Meilland International SA; flowers orange apricot, 4¼ in., full, borne mostly singly; foliage medium size, dark green, semi-glossy; prickles moderate; bushy, medium (90 cm.) growth; PP9609; ['Just Joey' × ('MEIrestif' × 'MEInarual')]; intr. 1993

'Meibuleux' HT, lp, Meillanddbl.; intr. 2004

'Meibulifa' HT, rb, Meilland; intr. 2004

'Meiburenac' (Swany®) S, w, 1977, Meilland, Mrs. Marie-Louise; bud ovoid; flowers pure white, large, 95 petals, cupped, slight fragrance; free-flowering; foliage glossy, bronze; very vigorous, spreading (2 × 6 ft.) growth; groundcover; [R. sempervirens × 'Mlle Marthe Carron']; intr. 1977

'Meiburgana' HT, mr, 1981, Meilland, Mrs. Marie-Louise; intr. 1982

'Meibyba' Min, or, 1965, Meilland, Alain A.

'Meibystar' ('Atoll') HT, or, 1972, Meilland; intr. 1971

'Meicairma' ('Courage', 'Paganini') F, mr, Meilland; intr. 1991

'Meicandy' F, rb, Meilland; intr. 2004

'Meicapinal' ('Aachener Dom', 'Panthere Rose', Pink Panther®) HT, pb, 1983, Meilland, Mrs. Marie-Louise; flowers silvery pink, edged deep pink, large, dbl., no fragrance; foliage medium size, semi-glossy; upright growth; ['MEIgurami' × 'MEInaregi']; intr. 1981

'Meicapula' ('Fiorella '82', 'Fiorella', 'Marion Foster') Gr, mp, 1985, Meilland, Mrs. Marie-Louise; flowers large, 35 petals; foliage medium size, dark, matte; upright growth; [(Queen Elizabeth® × 'Nirvana') × ('Tropicana' × 'MEInaregi')]; intr. 1981

'Meicarl' HT, dr, 1958, Meilland, F.; intr. 1957

'Meicarlsar' (Champs-Elysées, Climbing®) Cl HT, dr, 1969, Meilland; [sport of 'Champs-Elysees']

'Meicascal' S, pb, Meilland; intr. 2001

'Meicauf' ('Fiord', Amalia™) HT, dr, 1994, Meilland, Alain A.; flowers 3-3½ in., full, borne mostly singly, no fragrance; foliage medium size, dark green, semi-glossy; numerous prickles; medium (100-120 cm.), upright growth; PP7718; [(Queen Elizabeth® × 'Karl Herbst') × Papa Meilland®]; intr. 1986

'Meicauley' HT, w, Meillanddbl.; intr. 1998

'Meicellie' HT, dp, Richardier, M.dbl.; intr. 2005

'Meicelna' ('Your Garden') HT, mp, Meilland; intr. 1990

'Meiceppus' ('André le Nôtre') HT, pb, Meilland Intl.; intr. 2001

'Meicesar' HT, dr, 1963, Meilland, Alain A.; bud pointed

'Meicham' HT, pb, 1964, Meilland, Alain A.; bud long, pointed; intr. 1964

'Meichanso' ('Parador', 'Tchin-Tchin') F, or, 1978, Paolino; flowers large, 20 petals, cupped, borne in clusters of 3-17, slight fragrance; foliage matte; very vigorous growth; [((Sarabande® × 'MEIkim') × ('Alain' × Orange Triumph®)) × Diablotin®]

'Meichansosar' Cl F, ob, Meilland; intr. 1995

'Meichavrin' (Flora Romantica®) LCl, w, Meilland; intr. 1998

'Meichest' F, or, Meilland, Alain A.; bud long, pointed; intr. 1964

'Meichibon' ('Maggie Tabberer', Tchaikovski™) Gr, w, 2003, Meilland International; flowers white with apricot blush in center, 6-9 cm., very full, borne in small clusters; foliage medium size, dark green, semi-glossy; prickles moderate; growth bushy, tall (5-6 ft.); garden; [('Anthony Meilland' × 'Landora') × Centenaire de Lourdes®]

'Meichim' HT, mp, 1963, Meilland, Alain A.; intr. 1963

'Meichimsar' (Carina, Climbing®, Grimpant Carina®) Cl HT, mp, 1970, Meilland; [sport of 'Carina']; intr. 1968

'Meichoiju' ('City of Adelaide', 'Sanlam-Roos') F, mp, Meilland; intr. 1989

'Meichonar' ('Pearl Sevillana', 'Tutti Frutti', 'Tuff Stuff', Pearl La Sevillana™) S, w, 1996, Meilland International SA; bud conical; flowers white edged light pink, 6 cm., 18 petals, cupped, borne in clusters of 6 - 15, very slight fragrance; recurrent; foliage medium size, dark green, dull; prickles very few, small to medium, pinkish to brown; bushy, medium (4-5 ft.) growth; hips small, many, decorative, orange with black eye; PP9536; [('Bonica' × Pascali®) × 'Edelweiss']

'Meicijas' (Texas Girl™) HT, yb, 1991, Meilland, Alain A.; flowers creamy yellow, large, full, slight fragrance; foliage large, medium green; tall, upright growth; PP7784; [sport of 'Lovely Girl']; intr. 1991

'Meicinelle' (Ladybug™) F, rb, 2001, Meilland International; flowers red with white dots, 2½ in., semi-dbl., borne in small clusters, no fragrance; foliage medium size, dark green, semi-glossy; prickles moderate; growth bushy, low (3 ft.); PP13757; [('Meidanu' × 'Macev') × 'Tantide']; intr. 2001

'Meicitrem' ('Lucie's Dream') Min, my, 1995, Meilland, Alain A.; flowers large, very dbl., borne in small clusters, moderate lemony fragrance; foliage medium size, medium green, semi-glossy; some prickles; medium (25-30 cm.), bushy growth; [('Yellow Pages' × Gold Badge™) × 'Lemon Delight']; intr. 1994

'Meiclosal' ('Colossal') S, mr, Meilland; intr. 2000

'Meicloux' ('Chacok', 'Fakir', 'Jubilee 150', Pigalle®) F, ob, 1985, Meilland, Mrs. Marie-Louise; flowers yellow blended with orange and orange-red, large, 40 petals, no fragrance; foliage medium size, medium green, semi-glossy; bushy growth; ['Frenzy' × ((Zambra® × 'Suspense') × King's Ransom®)]; intr. 1983

'Meiclusif'   HT, mp, Meilland very full; intr. 2005

'Meicobuis' ('Terra Cotta') HT, r; bud conical; intr. 1999

'Meicofum' ('Leonidas') HT, rb, Meilland; bud conical, medium; intr. 1995

'Meicoublan' ('Blanc Meillandécor', 'Super Swany', 'White Midiland') S, w, 1987, Meilland, Mrs. Marie-Louise; bud oval; flowers white with slight pink edge, slight yellow cast at times, 8 cm., 60-70 petals, cupped, borne in clusters, no fragrance; recurrent; foliage medium size, dark green, glossy; large, spreading growth; PP6088; ['Temple Bells' × 'Coppélia 76']

'Meicrado' S, r, Meilland; intr. 2002

'Meicri' ('Cricri', 'Gavolda') Min, ob, 1959, Meilland, F.; intr. 1958

'Meicubasi' ('Scarlet Meillandina', Scarlet Sunblaze™) Min, dr, 1982, Meilland, Mrs. Marie-Louise; bud medium, conical; flowers currant red, 5½ cm., 20-30 petals, cupped, borne in clusters of 3 - 21, no fragrance; free-flowering; foliage medium size, dark green, matte; prickles average, small, slender, curved downward; bushy (20 in.) growth; PP4681; ['Tamango' × ('Baby Bettina' × 'Duchess of Windsor')]; intr. 1980

'Meicupag' (Golden Sunblaze™) Min, my, 1994, Selection Meilland; bud short, plump, ovoid; flowers bright golden yellow, like a zinnia, 1½ in., 40-45 petals, cupped, borne in small clusters; foliage medium size, dark green, glossy; few prickles; medium (15 in.), upright, bushy growth; PP8493; [('Rise 'n' Shine' × Mark One™) × 'Yellow Meillandina']; intr. 1993

'Meicurbos' ('Magic Fire') F, op, Meilland, Alain A.; intr. 1993

'Meidacinu' ('Baby Bettina') Min, or, 1981, Meilland, Mrs. Marie-Louise; bud ovoid; flowers vermilion, reverse carmine, deep, mini-flora, 15-20 petals, cupped, borne 3-11 per cluster, slight fragrance; foliage matte, dense; vigorous growth; [('Callisto' × 'Perla de Alcañada') × Starina®]; intr. 1977

'Meidad' (Majorette®, Minna Lerche Lerchenborg®) HT, op, 1970, Meilland; bud pointed; flowers coppery salmon, large, dbl., high-centered; foliage dark, leathery; vigorous, upright growth; [Zambra® × 'Fred Edmunds']; intr. 1967

'Meidali'   HT, pb, 1968, Meilland, Louisette

'Meidalnu' (Mascara™) HT, m, Meilland; bud conical, medium; intr. 1992

'Meidanclar' ('Romantique Meillandina', Candy Sunblaze™) Min, dp, 1991, Selection Meilland; bud ovoid, large; flowers deep pink, 6-7 cm., 85-95 petals, globular, then cupped, borne in clusters of 1-5, slight fragrance; recurrent; foliage medium size, dark green, glossy; prickles medium, light tan; tall, bushy, upright growth; PP7621; [sport of 'Lady Sunblaze']; intr. 1992

'Meidanego' ('Belle Sunblaze', Belle Meillandina®) Min, dr, 1984, Meilland, Mrs. Marie-Louise; PP5038; [sport of 'Meillandina']; intr. 1980

'Meidanover' ('Colibre 80', 'Star Trail') Min, ob, Meilland; intr. 1979

'Meidanu' F, dr, 1967, Meilland, Mrs. Marie-Louise

'Meidarin' (Mandarin Sunblaze®, Mandarine Symphonie®) Min, ab, 2003, Meilland International; bud elongated, medium; flowers apricot blend, reverse light yellow, 5-7 cm., 66 petals, cupped, borne in small clusters, no fragrance; free-flowering; foliage large, medium green, semi-glossy; prickles moderate; growth bushy, tall (2 ft.); garden decoration, containers; PP13291; [(Mark One™ × Teddy Bear™) × 'Leonidas']; intr. 2003

'Meidarwet' ('Relax Meidiland') S, pb, Meillandsemi-dbl.; intr. 1993

'Meidaud' ('Miss All-American Beauty') HT, dp, 1965, Meilland, Mrs. Marie-Louise; bud ovoid, large; intr. 1965

'Meidaudsar' ('Maria Callas, Climbing', 'Miss All-American Beauty, Climbing') Cl HT, dp, 1969, Meilland; [sport of 'Miss All-American Beauty']

'Meideauri' (Leonardo de Vinci®) F, lp, 1994, Meilland, Alain A.; bud globular, large; flowers bengal pink, 3½-4 in., 75-80 petals, borne in small clusters; free-flowering; foliage medium size, dark green, glossy; some prickles; bushy (70-110 cm.) growth; PP9980; ['Sommerwind' × (Milrose® × 'Rosamunde')]; intr. 1993

'Meidebenne' ('Black Baccara') HT, dr, 2004, Meilland International; flowers dark red, reverse dark red, 8 cm., full, borne mostly solitary, no fragrance; foliage dark green, glossy; growth upright, tall (up to 6 ft.); cutting; PP13152; ['Meifota' × 'Meilouzou']; intr. 2002

'Meideflash' HT, dp, Meilland; intr. 2004

'Meideinis' (Rosy Minuetto™) Min, lp, 2000, Meilland International; flowers 2-3 cm., very full, borne in small clusters, no fragrance; foliage medium size, medium green, semi-glossy; prickles moderate; compact, medium (8-12 in.) growth; PP17561; [sport of 'Fuchsia Minuetto']; intr. 1999

'Meidelweis' ('Bolero 2004', Bolero™) F, w, 2004, Meilland International; flowers large, very full, borne in small clusters, intense fragrance; foliage large, dark green, glossy; growth spreading, medium (3-4 ft.); garden; [(Kimono® × 'Ausreef') × 'Delge']; intr. 2004

'Meidési' Min, mp, 1963, Meilland, Alain; bud ovoid; intr. 1963

'Meideskri' F, my, Meilland; intr. 2004

'Meideuji' LCl, mr, Meilland; intr. 1989

'Meidia'   F, mp, 1960, Meilland, Mrs. Marie-Louise; bud ovoid; intr. 1960

'Meidiaphaz' HT, w, Meilland; intr. 2006

'Meidiland Alba' -- See 'Meiflopan'

'Meidinro' ('Altesse', 'Rodin') HT, rb, 1990, Meilland; intr. 1991

'Meidipser' ('Simply Sunblaze', Spot Meillandina®) Min, dp, 1994, Meilland, Alain A.; flowers rose bengal, small, 74 petals, borne in small clusters, no fragrance; foliage medium size, dark green, semi-glossy; few prickles; low (20-25 cm.), bushy growth; [(Orange Sunblaze™ × 'Pink Symphony') × Red Minimo™]; intr. 1992

'Meidirapo' HT, dr, 1976, Paolino; flowers red to purple, 3½-4 in., 25 petals, cupped; vigorous growth; [((Queen Elizabeth® × ('Peace' × 'Michele Meilland')) × (Baccará® × seedling)]

'Meido' ('Scarlet Pimpernel') Min, or, 1961, Meilland, Alain A.; bud ovoid; intr. 1961

'Meidomonac' ('Bonica Meidiland', 'Demon', Bonica '82®, BonicaTM ®) S, mp, 1985, Meilland, Mrs. Marie-Louise; bud ovoid, small; flowers medium pink center, lighter at edges, 6 cm., 53 petals, cupped, borne in clusters of up to 20, no fragrance; free-flowering; foliage small, dark green, semi-dull; prickles small, hooked down; bushy, low (80 cm.) growth; PP5105; [(R. sempervirens × Mlle Marthe Carron) × 'Picasso']; intr. 1981

'Meidona' ('Mme Neige') HT, w, 1965, Meilland

'Meidonfe' (Raspberry Sunblaze®) Min, dp, 1998, Meilland; buds egg-shaped; flowers raspberry red with lighter reverse, 2 in., 50 petals, cupped, borne in small clusters and singly, no fragrance; free-flowering; foliage medium size, medium green, semi-glossy; prickles moderate, small; bushy, medium, compact (15 in.) growth; PP10666; [(Orange Sunblaze™ × Prince Meillandina®) × Red Minimo™]

'Meidorsun'   HT, dy, Meilland, Alain A.; intr. 1992

'Meidragelac' ('Laura '81', 'Natilda', 'Laura') HT, or, 1985, Meilland, Mrs. Marie-Louise; flowers orange-red, lighter reverse, large, 30 petals; foliage small, dark, semi-glossy; medium growth; [(Pharaoh® × 'Colour Wonder') × (('Suspense' × 'Suspense') × King's Ransom®)]; intr. 1981

'Meidrason' ('Grimpant Eric Tabarly', 'Red Eden', 'Red Eden Rose', 'Red Pierre') LCl, dr, Meilland; bud medium, ovoid; intr. 2003

'Meidrepil' ('Symphonie No. 3', Sunny Waterfall™) Min, my, 2000, Meilland International; bud ovoid; flowers aureolin yellow, reverse straw yellow, 2½-3½ cm., 100 petals, flattened, borne in clusters of 6 - 15, slight fragrance; free-flowering; foliage medium size, dark green, semi-glossy; prickles moderate, small, pinkish; spreading, low (20-30 cm.) growth; hanging basket; PP10543; [('Meiplarzon' × 'Yellow Meillandina') × 'Katharina Zeimet']

'Meidresia' ('Dancing Girl', 'Izu no

Odoriko') F, my; intr. 2002

'Meidrifora' S, op; intr. 2006

'Meidrimy' ('Gp. Domaine de Courson') LCl, pb, Meilland; intr. 1995

'Meidrofal' Min, mr, Meilland

'Meidujaran' ('Pimlico '81', 'Pimlico') F, mr, 1984, Meilland, Mrs. Marie-Louise; flowers deep scarlet, gold stamens, large, 35 petals, no fragrance; foliage large, dark green, glossy; bushy growth; [('Tamango' × 'Fidélio') × ('Charleston' × Lilli Marleen®)]; intr. 1980

'Meidunkel' HT, dp, Meilland; intr. 2004

'Meidur' F, my, 1958, Meilland, F.

'Meielec' ('Scarlet Knight') Gr, mr, 1966, Meilland, Mrs. Marie-Louise; bud medium, ovoid with a conspicuous neck; intr. 1966

'Meielpa' LCl, mr, 1967, Meilland

'Meiestho' F, or, 1966, Meilland, Mrs. Marie-Louisesemi-dbl.

'Meifacul' HT, my, Meilland; bud medium yellow; intr. 2007

'Meifafio' S, mpvery dbl.; intr. 2003

'Meifaissel' (Queen Mary 2™) HT, w, 2004, Meilland International; flowers 8-10 cm., full, borne mostly solitary, intense fragrance; foliage dark green, glossy; growth upright, tall (5-6 ft.); garden decoration, cutting; PP16951; ['Meiban' × ('Poulari' × 'Lady Sylvia')]; intr. 2004

'Meifan' HT, rb, 1960, Meilland, F.; bud ovoid; intr. 1960

'Meifarent' (Solidor®) HT, my, Meilland; intr. 1986

'Meifazeda' HT, my; intr. 2004

'Meifebink' HT, dp, Meilland; intr. 2002

'Meifecham' HT, mp, Meilland; intr. 2004

'Meiferjac' ('Top Meillandina', Autumn Sunblaze™) Min, or, 1996, Selection Meilland; bud conical; flowers bright vermilion, reverse red, 4 cm., 40-45 petals, cupped, borne in clusters of 6 - 15, no fragrance; recurrent; foliage medium size, medium green, semi-glossy; prickles numerous, small, pinkish; medium (24 in.), bushy growth; heat tolerant; PP9652; [(Bonfire Night® × Orange Symphonie®) × 'Orange Jewel']; intr. 1995

'Meifersi' ('Trailblazer') HT, mr, Meilland; intr. 1987

'Meifiga' ('Pharaon') HT, or, 1970, Meilland, Mrs. Marie-Louise; bud ovoid; intr. 1967

'Meifigu' HT, m, 1968, Meilland, Mrs. Marie-Louise; bud long, pointed; intr. 1966

'Meifikalif' ('Allegeo '80') HT, or, 1985, Meilland, Mrs. Marie-Louise; flowers large, 35 petals, no fragrance; foliage medium size, medium green, semi-glossy; [('Diorette' × 'Tropicana') × (seedling × ('Diorette' × 'Tropicana'))]; intr. 1980

'Meifinaro' ('Air France Meillandina', 'American Independence', 'Air France', 'Rosy Meillandina') Min, yb, 1983, Meilland, Mrs. Marie-Louise; bud oval, small; flowers light yellow, pink petal edges, 1½ in., 50 petals, cupped, borne in small clusters, no fragrance; free-flowering; foliage small, dark green, matte; prickles small, numerous; bushy (18 in.) growth; PP5180; [Minijet® × ('Darling Flame' × 'Perle de Montserrat')]; intr. 1982

'Meiflamenc' HT, pb, Meilland; intr. 2002

'Meiflarol' F, ob, Meilland; intr. 1986

'Meiflizet' Min, rb, Meilland; intr. 2001

'Meifloccus' S, lp, Meilland; intr. 2003

'Meiflopan' ('Alba Meillandécor', 'Meidiland Alba', Alba Meidiland™) S, w, 1987, Meilland, Mrs. Marie-Louise; bud globular, small; flowers medium, very white, 3½-4 cm., 50-55 petals, cupped, borne in clusters of 8 - 15, no fragrance; free-flowering; foliage medium size, medium green, glossy; spreading growth, vigorous (4-5 ft.); PP6891; [R. sempervirens × 'Marthe Carron']; intr. 1985

'Meiflorem' F, or, 1971, Meilland; intr. 1970

'Meifluney' Min, dp, 1984, Meilland, Mrs. Marie-Louise; flowers deep pink, medium, dbl.; foliage medium size, medium green, matte; bushy growth; [('Alain' × 'Fashion') × ('Rumba' × (Zambra® × 'Cinderella'))]

'Meifolio' (Matthias Meilland®) F, mr, 1988, Meilland, Mrs. Marie-Louise; flowers large, dbl., no fragrance; foliage medium size, dark green, glossy, disease-resistant; upright, floriferous growth; [('Mme Charles Sauvage' × 'Fashion') × ('Poppy Flash' × 'Parador')]; intr. 1985

'Meifota' ('Celica') HT, mp, 1985, Meilland, Mrs. Marie-Louise; flowers large, 20 petals; foliage medium size, dark, semi-glossy; upright growth; PP5683; [seedling × (('Zambra × (Baccará × White Knight') × 'Golden Garnette') × seedling)]; intr. 1981

'Meifour' ('Anne Marie', Anne Marie Trechslin®) HT, dp, 1970, Meilland; bud long, pointed; flowers deep pink, large, dbl., high-centered, intense fragrance; foliage dark, leathery; vigorous, branching growth; ['Sutter's Gold' × ('Demain' × 'Peace')]; intr. 1969

'Meifovett' (Baby Paradise™) Min, m, 2003, Meilland International; flowers mauve, reverse mauve, 3-5 cm., very full, borne in small clusters, no fragrance; foliage medium size, medium green, semi-glossy; prickles moderate; growth bushy, medium (18-24 in.); garden decoration, containers; PPAF; ['Savarain' × ((Playboy® × 'Morrousel') × 'Meidanu']; intr. 2004

'Meifraboy' HT, pb, Meilland; intr. 1998

'Meifransa' F, my, Meilland; intr. 1998

'Meifrison' HT, op, 1970, Meilland; intr. 1968

'Meifructoz' ('Fruitee') F, ob, Meilland, L.; intr. 1984

'Meifruije' (Apricot Sunblaze™) Min, yb, 1994, Meilland, Alain A.; flowers yellow edged in bright orange, 1½ in., dbl, high-centered, borne mostly singly, no fragrance; foliage small, dark green, glossy; few prickles; medium, bushy growth, compact; PP9033; [(Mark One™ × 'Yellow Meillandina') × Gold Badge™]; intr. 1994

'Meifrypon' HT, ob, Meilland; intr. 2005

'Meifulcen' (Crimson Pillar™) LCl, rb, 2003, Meilland International; flowers medium red, reverse white, 4 in., dbl., borne in small clusters, no fragrance; foliage dark green, semi-glossy; numerous prickles; growth climbing, tall (to 10 ft.); hardy to 0°F; PPAF; intr. 2003

'Meigabi' Min, or, 1965, Meilland, Mrs. Marie-Louise; bud short, ovoid

'Meigadraz' S, dp, Meilland; intr. 2005

'Meigafor' (Confidence™) HT, w, 1995, Meilland; bud elongated, medium; flowers creamy white with pink petal tips, 5 in., 35 petals, borne mostly singly, slight fragrance; recurrent; foliage dark green, glossy; prickles few, small; growth upright (2-3 ft.); PP9223

'Meigalil' ('Hilda Heinemann', 'Mme H. Heinemann') HT, mr, 1971, Meilland

'Meigalpio' ('Nature Meillandecor') S, mr, Meilland; intr. 2006

'Meigancia' F, dp, Meilland; intr. 2004

'Meigand' HT, pb, 1961, Meilland, Mrs. Marie-Louise; bud globular

'Meigandor' ('Sabrina') HT, ab, 1985, Meilland, Mrs. Marie-Louise; flowers apricot-orange, large, 35 petals; upright growth; PP4520; [('Sweet Promise' × 'Golden Garnette') × ((Zambra® × 'Suspense') × (King's Ransom® × 'Whisky Mac'))]; intr. 1977

'Meigavesol' (Tequila®) F, ob, 1983, Meilland, Mrs. Marie-Louise; flowers light yellow, overlaid with orange, stained carmine on outer edges, 20 petals; foliage medium size, dark, matte; bushy growth; ['Poppy Flash' × ('Rumba' × ('MElkim' × 'Fire King'))]

'Meigekanu' ('Sevillana') F, or, 1978, Meilland, Mrs. Marie-Louise; bud conical; intr. 1982

'Meigekanusar' ('La Sevillana, Climbing') Cl F, or, Meilland; intr. 1997

'Meigelsi' F, op, Meilland; intr. 2005

'Meigene' Gr, mp, 1965, Meilland, Alain A.; bud ovoid, pointed; intr. 1965

'Meigenpf' Min, yb, Meilland; intr. 2005

'Meigenpi' Min, yb, Meilland; intr. 2006

'Meigerium' HT, or, 1976, Paolino; flowers light vermilion-red, 4-4½ in., 35 petals; foliage glossy; very vigorous growth; PP3803; [('Romantica' × 'Tropicana') × (('Show Girl' × Baccará®) × 'Romantica')]

'Meigeroka' ('Rosy La Sevillana', Pink La Sevillana®) F, mp, 1984, Meilland, Mrs. Marie-Louise; bud conical; flowers carmine pink, 8 cm., 10-15 petals, cupped, then flat, borne in clusters of 5 - 20, no fragrance; recurrent; foliage bronzed green, leathery; bushy, spreading (3 ft.)

growth; PP7117; [sport of 'La Sevillana']; intr. 1983

'Meigerokasar' Cl F, mp, Meilland; intr. 1993

'Meiggili' S, ab, Meilland; intr. 2006

'Meighivon' ('Snow Sunblaze') Min, w, Meilland; bud large, ovoid; intr. 1991

'Meigideon' F, lp, Meilland; intr. 2005

'Meiglassol' Min, my, Meilland; intr. 1995

'Meiglise' S, w, Meilland, Alain; bud small, ovoid; intr. 2004

'Meiglusor' (Concertino™) Min, dp, 1988, Meilland, Alain A.; flowers cardinal-pink, medium, full, no fragrance; foliage small, medium green, semi-glossy; bushy, compact growth; [('Anytime' × 'Julita') × 'Lavender Jewel']

'Meigold' ('Kabuki') HT, dy, 1970, Meilland, Mrs. Marie-Louise; buds medium, long pointed

'Meigosar' Cl F, ob, Meilland; intr. 1985

'Meigoudea' HT, op, Meilland; intr. 2007

'Meigoufin' ('Magali') F, mp, Meilland, Alain A.; intr. 1986

'Meigovin' ('Snow Sunblaze') Min, w, Meilland; bud large, ovoid; intr. 1991

'Meigrappo' LCl, mr, Meilland; intr. 2007

'Meigrelou' F, my, Meilland; bud conical; intr. 1989

'Meigriso' HT, rb, 1970, Meilland; intr. 1968

'Meigrisosar' ('Baronne de Rothschild, Climbing', Baronne Edmond de Rothschild, Climbing®, 'Grimpant Baronne de Rothschild') Cl HT, rb, 1979, Meilland, Mrs. Marie-Louise; flowers red with silver reverse, 14-16 cm., borne in small clusters, moderate fragrance; recurrent; foliage glossy; intr. 1974

'Meigrolet' Min, my, Meilland

'Meigronuri' ('Rimosa 79', Gold Badge™, Gold Bunny®) F, my, 1979, Paolino; bud conical, medium; flowers lemon-yellow, 3 in., 38 petals, cupped, borne in clusters, no fragrance; free-flowering; foliage dark green, semi-dull, leathery; prickles average, small; vigorous, bushy (70 cm.) growth; PP4625; ['Poppy Flash' × ('Charleston' × Allgold®)]

'Meigronurisar' ('Gold Bunny, Climbing', 'Rimosa, Climbing', 'Grimpant Rimosa') Cl F, my, Meilland; intr. 1991

'Meigrouge' HT, mr, Meilland; bud large, conical, elongated; intr. 1998

'Meigroupy' ('Classic Woman') HT, w, 2007, Meilland International; flowers 7-8 cm., very full, borne mostly solitary; foliage dark green, semi-glossy; prickles small, moderate; growth upright, tall (5½-6 ft.); cutting; [('Meilivar' × 'Sunbelt') × 'Meivildo']; intr. 2008

'Meigrume' HT, ob, Meilland; intr. 2004

'Meiguido' HT, ob, Meilland; intr. 2002

'Meiguimov' S, lp, Meilland; intr. 2007

'Meigurami' ('Coppélia 76') F, op, Meilland; intr. 1976

'Meigymnos' S, pb, Meilland; intr. 2005

'Meihaitoil' ('Romantic Sunrise') S, my, Meilland

'Meihand' F, or, 1958, Meilland, F.; intr. 1957

'Meihandica' Min, ob, Meilland; intr. 2008

'Meihandsar' Cl F, or, 1970, Meilland

'Meihartfor' ('Kalinka') F, lp, 1971, Meilland; intr. 1970

'Meihartforsar' ('Kalinka, Climbing', 'Pink Wonder, Climbing') Cl F, lp, 1979, Meilland, Mrs. Marie-Louise; [sport of 'Pink Wonder']; intr. 1976

'Meihati' ('Iskara', 'Iskra') Cl F, mr, 1971, Meilland; intr. 1970

'Meihauzrey' Min, dp, Meilland

'Meihecluz' F, my; intr. 2005

'Meihelvet' ('Sonia Meilland', 'Sonia') Gr, pb, 1971, Meilland; bud long, somewhat cylindrical

'Meihelvetsar' ('Sonia Meilland, Climbing', 'Sweet Promise, Climbing', Grimpant Sonia Meilland®) Cl Gr, pb, 1979, Meilland, Mrs. Marie-Louise; bud coral pink; intr. 1976

'Meihérode' Min, ob, 1970, Meilland

'Meihestries' Cl F, yb, Meilland; intr. 2002

'Meihigor' (Prince Igor®) F, rb, 1971, Meilland; intr. 1970

'Meihimper' ('Preziosa') HT, pb, 1971, Meilland

'Meihirvin' ('Thomas Barton') HT, mr, Meilland; intr. 1988

'Meihivano' F, mp, 1971, Meilland

'Meihouba' HT, my, Meilland; intr. 1991

'Meihourag' LCl, yb, Meilland; intr. 1991

'Meihud' ('Arioso') HT, or, 1976, Paolino; flowers light vermilion, 5 in., 25 petals, slight fruity fragrance; foliage glossy; dark; very vigorous, upright growth; [('Paris-Match' × Baccará®) × 'Marella']

'Meihuterb' ('Galaxy') F, yb, Meilland; intr. 1995

'Meihyago' HT, ob, Meilland; intr. 2007

'Meiirroy' Gr, rb, Meilland; intr. 2008

'Meijacolet' ('Madeline', Lunar Mist™, 'Yellow Colette', Yellow Romantica™) LCl, ly, 2007, Meilland International; flowers 5-6 cm., very full, borne in small clusters; foliage medium, dark green, semi-glossy; prickles small, moderate; growth spreading, medium (8-10 ft.); pillar; [sport of 'Colette']

'Meijade' LCl, pb; intr. 1989

'Meijason' HT, ob; intr. 1984

'Meijasper' HT, mr, Meilland; intr. 2002

'Meijelior' (Sonia Sunblaze®) Min, mp, 2003, Meilland International; bud conical, pointed; flowers full, cupped, borne in small clusters, no fragrance; recurrent; foliage medium size, medium green, matte; prickles moderate, hooked downward, pink to brown; growth upright, tall 2 ft.); garden, container; hips none ; PP14069; ['Apricot Sunblaze' × (Cumba Meillandina® × 'Meisancho')]; intr. 2003

'Meijenor' HT, or, 1958, Meilland, F.; bud pointed; intr. 1955

'Meijenorsar' (Grimpant Soraya®) Cl HT, or, 1960, Meilland; intr. 1960

'Meijette' ('French Liberty', 'Innovation Minijet') Min, my, 1987, Meilland, Mrs. Marie-Louise; flowers medium, dbl., slight fragrance; foliage small, light green, glossy; bushy growth; PP6177; [('Rumba' × 'Carol Jean') × (Zambra® × 'Darling Flame')]; intr. 1987

'Meijeunom' S, w, Meilland; intr. 2006

'Meijidiro' (Pink Meillandina®, Pink Sunblaze™) Min, mp, 1982, Meilland, Mrs. Marie-Louise; PP4961; [sport of 'Orange Sunblaze']; intr. 1980

'Meijikatar' ('Orange Meillandina', Orange Sunblaze™, 'Sunblaze') Min, or, 1982, Meilland, Mrs. Marie-Louise; flowers non-fading deep orange, 1½-2 in., 40 petals, cupped, borne 1-3 per cluster; foliage small, light green, matte; prickles straw-brown; upright, bushy (15 in.) growth; drops spent blooms; PP4682; ['Parador' × ('Baby Bettina' × 'Duchess of Windsor')]; intr. 1981

'Meijikatarsar' ('Orange Meillandina, Climbing', 'Orange Sunblaze, Climbing', Grimpant Orange Meillandina®) Cl Min, or, 1987, Meilland, Mrs. Marie-Louise; bud small, conical; flowers bright vermilion red, 2 in., 40 petals, cupped, then flat, borne singly or in clusters of 2 or 3, no fragrance; free-flowering; foliage small, medium green, matte; vigorous, upright (5 ft.) growth; PP6817; [sport of 'Orange Meillandina']; intr. 1986

'Meijocos' S, dp, Meilland; intr. 2006

'Meijulitasar' ('Chorus, Climbing') Cl F, or, Meilland; intr. 1986

'Meijulito' (Chorus®) F, or, 1976, Paolino; flowers vermilion-red, 4 in., 35 petals, borne several together, slight fruity fragrance; foliage glossy; vigorous growth; ['Tamango' × (Sarabande® × Zambra®)]; intr. 1975

'Meikans' F, or, 1959, Meilland; bud ovoid; intr. 1958

'Meikarouz' ('Alain Souchon', 'Caruso', Rouge Royale™, 'Royal Red') HT, rb, 2001, Meilland International; bud ovoid; flowers velvety red, reverse geranium red, 6-7 in., very full, cupped, borne mostly solitary, intense fragrance; recurrent; foliage large, medium green, glossy; prickles moderate, large, slightly concave undersurface; growth upright, medium (5-6 ft.); garden decorative, cutting; hips none ; PP14039; [Charlotte Rampling® × ('Ambassador' × 'Meicapula')]; intr. 2001

'Meikema' HT, r, Meilland; intr. 2005

'Meikentuk' (Colleen Mary™) HT, dr, 2003, Meilland International; flowers 8-10 cm., full, borne in small clusters; foliage medium green, Matte; prickles moderate; growth upright (5-6 ft.); garden, cutting; [('Duc de Windsor' × 'Chrysler Imperial') × 'Rouge Meilland']; intr. 2003

'Meikifunk' F, mp, Richardier; intr. 2006

'Meikiji' ('Destiny') F, w, Meilland; intr. 1989

'Meikinba' F, mr, Meilland; intr. 2002

The Official Registry and Checklist — Rosa 481

'Meikinba' S, mr, Meilland

'Meikinosi' ('Parador', 'Tchin-Tchin') HT, yb, 1978, Paolino; flowers chrome-yellow, 4½ in., 30 petals, cupped; vigorous growth; [((Zambra® × 'Suspense') × King's Ransom®) × ('Kabuki' × 'Dr. A. J. Verhage')]

'Meikister' F, dp, Meilland

'Meiklusy' ('Marianne') F, rb, Meilland; intr. 1993

'Meiklutz' (Fairy Meidiland™) S, mp, 2007, Meilland International; flowers fuchsia-pink, 2 cm., semi-dbl., borne in large clusters; foliage small, medium green, glossy; prickles small, moderate; growth spreading, medium (3 ft.): groundcover; [seedling × seedling]; intr. 2007

'Meikola' ('Livia') HT, mp, Meilland; bud ovoid, fairly short; intr. 1984

'Meikousie' LCl, or, Meilland; intr. 2001

'Meikrotal' ('Scarlet Meillandécor', Scarlet Meidiland™) S, mr, 1987, Meilland, Mrs. Marie-Louise; bud oval; flowers light cherry red, reverse dark carmine pink, 1½ in., 15-20 petals, borne in clusters of 10-15, no fragrance; recurrent; foliage medium size, dark green, glossy; spreading growth; PP6087; ['MEItiraca' × Clair Matin®]; intr. 1985

'Meikruza' HT, w, Meilland

'Meilabar' HT, dp, Meilland; intr. 2003

'Meilambra' HT, rb, Meilland; intr. 2004

'Meilanein' ('Katherine Mansfield', Charles de Gaulle®) HT, m, 1976, Meilland, Mrs. Marie-Louise; flowers lilac, 3½-4 in., 38 petals, cupped, intense fragrance; vigorous growth; [('Sissi' × 'Prelude') × ('Kordes' Sondermeldung' × 'Caprice')]; intr. 1974

'Meilano' F, or, 1951, Meilland, F.; bud pointed; intr. 1951

'Meilanodin' ('Paso Doble') F, or, 1976, Paolino; flowers geranium-red, 3 in., 9 petals; vigorous growth

'Meilarac' Min, ab, Meilland

'Meilarco' ('Lady Meillandina', Lady Sunblaze™, Peace Meillandina®, 'Peace Sunblaze') Min, lp, 1987, Meilland, Mrs. Marie-Louise; bud plump, pointed; flowers pale orient pink to light coral pink, 1½ in., 40 petals, high-centered, borne singly, no fragrance; foliage small, dark green, glossy; bushy growth; PP6170; [('Fashion' × Zambra®) × Belle Meillandina®]

'Meilasso' ('Birthday Girl', 'The Karnival') F, pb, Meilland

'Meilastel' HT, ly, Meilland; intr. 2004

'Meilaur' ('Florian') F, mr, 1971, Meilland

'Meilauron' Min, ob, Meilland; intr. 2004

'Meilaursar' ('Florian, Climbing', 'Tender Night, Climbing') Cl F, mr, 1979, Meilland, Mrs. Marie-Louise; intr. 1976

'Meilavio' ('Xaviere', Traviata™) HT, dr, 1998, Selection Meilland; bud large, globular; flowers dark currant red, 6.5-7 cm., very full, hollow cup, borne singly and in small clusters, very slight fragrance; recurrent; foliage large, dark green, glossy; prickles numerous, large, brown; stems 18 - 24 in.; upright, medium growth; PP10845; [('Porta Nigra' × 'Paolo') × William Shakespeare®]; intr. 1997

'Meileeuw' HT, ob, Meilland; intr. 2002

'Meiléna' ('Rusticana') F, or, 1972, Meilland

'Meilenangal' ('Mitzi 81') HT, my, Meilland-dbl.; intr. 1981

'Meilénasar' ('Rusticana, Climbing') Cl F, or, 1976, Paolino; intr. 1975

'Meileyet' (Emma de Meilland®) HT, lp, Meilland; intr. 1996

'Meilezpha' Min, mp; intr. 2004

'Meiliaxi' (Schuss®) S, lp, Meilland; intr. 1989

'Meilicafal' ('Cannes Festival') HT, yb, Meilland, Alain A.; intr. 1983

'Meilider' ('All In One', Grimpant Exploit®, Colonia®, 'Dorsland', Exploit®) LCl, dp, 1985, Meilland, Mrs. Marie-Louise; flowers deep pink, medium, 20 petals, borne in small clusters, no fragrance; foliage small, medium green, matte; very vigorous, spreading, climbing growth; [Fugue® × 'Sparkling Scarlet']; intr. 1983

'Meilie' HT, mr, 1959, Meilland, F.; bud ovoid, pointed; intr. 1958

'Meilimona' ('Banzai '76', Banzai™) HT, my, 1976, Paolino; flowers canary-yellow, 4 in., 35 petals, cupped; vigorous growth; PP4013; [Coed™ × ((seedling × seedling) × 'Verla')]

'Meilinday' Cl HT, mp, Meilland; intr. 2006

'Meilipo' Min, mp, Meilland

'Meilista' ('Princess Margaret of England', Princesse Margaret d'Angleterre®) HT, mp, 1970, Meilland, Mrs. Marie-Louise; flowers phlox-pink, large, dbl., high-centered, borne mostly singly, slight tea fragrance; free-flowering; foliage abundant, large, leathery; growth vigorous, upright; [Queen Elizabeth® × ('Peace' × 'Michele Meilland')]; intr. 1968

'Meilistasar' ('Princess Margaret of England, Climbing', 'Princesse Margaret d'Angleterre, Climbing') Cl HT, mp, 1970, Meilland; bud long; flowers medium pink, fading to silvery pink, borne mostly solitary; [sport of 'Princess Margaret of England']

'Meilivar' ('The Children's Rose', Gina Lollobrigida®) HT, dy, 1997, Meilland International SA; flowers large, 70-90 petals, borne mostly singly, moderate fragrance; foliage medium size, medium green, semi-glossy; some prickles; upright, medium (5ft.) growth; PP7541; ['Laura '81' × 'Tchin-Tchin']

'Meilland Decor Arlequin' -- See 'Meizourayor'

'Meilland Decor Rose' -- See 'Meituraphar'

Meilland Rosiga 83® -- See 'Meibalbika'

'Meillandina' -- See 'Meirov'

'Meilmera' ('Bridal Meillandina', Bridal Sunblaze®) Min, w, 1996, Meilland International SA; flowers 2 in., 30-40 petals, borne in small clusters; foliage large, dark green, dull; few prickles; compact, medium (18 in.) growth; PP10002; [('Meiringa' × 'Schneewitchen') × ('Meizogrel' × 'MEllarco')]; intr. 1996

'Meiloise' HT, op, Meilland; intr. 1985

'Meilomit' ('Romantic Dreams', 'Umilo') F, ob, Meilland; intr. 1996

'Meilontig' ('Repens Meidiland') S, w, 1987, Meilland, Mrs. Marie-Louise; bud conical; flowers single, 5 petals, flat to slightly cupped, borne in clusters of 5 - 10, no fragrance; moderate to low production; foliage medium size, light green, glossy; spreading, almost horizontal, strong growth; PP6598; [Swany® × 'New Dawn']; intr. 1985

'Meilotup' (Royal Velvet™) HT, dr, 1986, Meilland, Mrs. Marie-Louise; flowers large, 28 petals, high-centered, borne mostly singly; prickles large, straw-colored; medium, bushy growth; hips globular, small, medium green; [('Exciting' × 'Suspense') × 'Duke of Windsor']

'Meilouzou' ('Fuego Negro') F, dr, Meilland; intr. 1998

'Meilucca' ('Minuette', 'Minuetto') Min, or, 1971, Meilland

'Meilucre' ('Arturo Toscanini') HT, or, 1971, Meilland

'Meiludere' Gr, lp, Meilland; intr. 2007

'Meiluminac' (President L. Senghor®, Président Léopold Senghor®) HT, dr, 1979, Meilland, Mrs. Marie-Louise; bud conical; flowers velvety red, large, 25 petals, cupped, pointed; abundant; foliage glossy, dark; vigorous, bushy growth

'Meiluminacsar' Cl HT, dr, Meilland; intr. 1982

'Meilupin' HT, my, Meilland; bud spherical; intr. 1989

'Meilusam' ('Lusambo', 'Red Rocky') HT, mr, 1974, Meilland; intr. 1973

'Meilutida' (Muchacha®) F, or, 1979, Meilland, Mrs. Marie-Louise; bud conical; flowers brilliant vermilion, shallowly-cupped, medium, 12 petals, cupped; foliage dark; very vigorous, semi-shrub growth; [('Frenzy' × 'Frenzy') × ('Sangria' × 'Sangria')]; intr. 1977

'Meilyxir' F, or, Meilland; intr. 2008

'Meilyzro' HT, or, Meilland; intr. 1999

'Meimafris' ('Drottning Silvia', Jardins de Bagatelle®, Karl Heinz Hanisch®, 'Sarah') HT, w, 1987, Meilland, Mrs. Marie-Louise; flowers large, creamy white tinted pink, very dbl., borne mostly solitary, intense fragrance; foliage large, medium green, semi-glossy; upright growth; [(Queen Elizabeth® × 'Eleg') × 'MEldragelac']; intr. 1987

'Meimagarmic' ('Grace Kelly', 'Preference', 'Princess Grace', 'Princess of Monaco', Princesse de Monaco®) HT, w, 1982, Meilland, Mrs. Marie-Louise; bud large, oblong; flowers cream, edged pink, large, 35 petals, cupped, borne usually singly, slight fragrance; good repeat; foliage large, dark green, glossy; prickles moderate, large; growth upright, low, bushy; PP5067; [('Ambassador' × 'Peace']; intr. 1981

'Meimagul' ('Gypsy Minijet', Gypsy Sunblaze™) Min, rb, 1994, Meilland, Alain A.; flowers red/yellow bicolor, medium, dbl., borne mostly singly, no fragrance; foliage small, light green, matte; some prickles; growth medium, bushy; [(Bonfire Night® × Zambra®) × Tapis Jaune®]; intr. 1993

'Meimainger' ('Bushveld Dawn', Cary Grant™) HT, ob, 1987, Meilland, Mrs. Marie-Louise; flowers vivid orange blend, lighter at petal base, 5 in., 35-40 petals, high-centered, borne singly, opening slowly, intense spicy fragrance; foliage medium size, dark green, glossy; prickles slightly recurved, light green-straw; upright, medium growth; hips ovoid, green-red-orange; PP6792; [(Pharaoh® × Königin der Rosen') × ((Zambra® × 'Suspense') × King's Ransom®)]; intr. 1987

'Meimal' ('Colibre') Min, ob, Meilland, F.; bud ovoid; intr. 1958

'Meimaliss' F, w, Richardier; intr. 2005

'Meimalyna' ('New Rouge Meilland', 'Rouge Meilland') HT, mr, 1985, Meilland, Mrs. Marie-Louise; flowers large, very full, no fragrance; foliage large, dark green, semi-glossy; upright growth; [((Queen Elizabeth® × 'Karl Herbst') × 'Pharoah') × Antonia Ridge®]; intr. 1982

'Meimandinan' HT, ab, 1952, Meilland, F.

'Meimanesk' F, pb, Meilland; intr. 2004

'Meimanoir' ('Blossom Magic') LCl, mp, Meilland; intr. 1994

'Meimarène' HT, mr, Meilland

'Meimater' ('Sting') S, rb, Meilland; intr. 2000

'Meimaur' ('Joséphine Baker') HT, dr, 1974, Meilland; intr. 1972

'Meimelba' HT, my, Meilland; intr. 2004

'Meimex' HT, r, 1959, Meilland, F.; bud urn-shaped

'Meimexto' HT, lp, Meilland; intr. 2005

'Meimick' S, rb, 1958, Meilland, F.; bud pointed; intr. 1957

'Meimiros' Min, op, Meilland; bud ovoid; intr. 2004

'Meimit' HT, lp, 1958, Meilland, F.

'Meimodac' (Royal Bonica™) S, mp, 1994, Meilland, Alain A.; bud oval; flowers cardinal red, suffused with Neyron rose, medium, 53 petals, globular, then cupped, borne usually in small clusters, slight fragrance; recurrent; foliage medium size, medium green, semi-glossy; some prickles; bushy, medium (3 ft.), upright growth; PP8840; [sport of 'Bonica']; intr. 1993

'Meimonblan' (Marmalade Skies™, Tangerine Dream™) F, ob, 1999, Selection Meilland; bud conical, large; flowers dbl., flat, cupped, borne in large clusters, slight fragrance; foliage medium size, dark green, glossy; prickles moderate, large; bushy, medium (3-4 ft.) growth; hips round, 2 mm. orange-red; PP12579; [('Tamango' × 'Parador') × 'Patricia']; intr. 2001

'Meimont' ('Grimpant Clair Matin') LCl, mp, 1962, Meilland, Mrs. Marie-Louise; bud pointed; intr. 1960

'Meimoré' (Chorus®) F, or, 1976, Paolino; intr. 1975

'Meimouslin' (Cardinal Song™, Jacques Prévert®) Gr, mr, 1993, Selection Meilland; flowers 3-3½ in., very dbl., borne mostly singly; foliage large, dark green, glossy; some prickles; medium, semi-erect growth; PP8847; [('Olympiad' × (Michel Lis Le Jardinier® × Red Lady®)]; intr. 1992

'Meimucas' ('Arioso') HT, pb, Meilland; intr. 1995

'Meimuide' F, op, Meilland; intr. 1990

'Meimuide' ('Holstentor') F, op, Meilland; intr. 1990

'Meimurge' Gr, ob, Meilland; bud conical; intr. 1997

'Mein München' F, yb, Cocker; flowers yellow and red, large, dbl.; intr. 1987

'Mein Rubin' HT, dr, 1986, Teranishi, K.; flowers urn-shaped, well-formed, 35 petals, borne usually singly; foliage medium size, medium green, semi-glossy; prickles medium, lavender; medium, bushy growth; [('Helene Schoen' × 'Charles Mallerin') × ('Helene Schoen' × 'Charles Mallerin')]; intr. 1984

Mein Schöner Garten® -- See 'Korneneint'

'Meinabron' (Alba Meillandina®) Min, w, 1988, Meilland, Mrs. Marie-Louise; bud conical; flowers very dbl., 85-90 petals, flattened cup, borne singly and in small clusters, no fragrance; free-flowering; foliage small, medium green, semi-glossy; bushy (12 in.) growth; PP7347; ['MEIdonq' × ('Darling' × 'Jack Frost')]; intr. 1986

'Meinagre' ('Dazzler', 'Laurence Olivier', Dazzla®) F, rb, Meilland

'Meinalpir' ('Blue Bells', Bluebell®, Martinez®) HT, rb, Meilland; bud conical, large; intr. 1997

'Meinartemi' F, Meilland

'Meinarval' ('Sun King '74', 'Sun King') HT, my, 1976, Paolino; flowers yellow-ocher, large, 30 petals, high-centered, slight fragrance; free-flowering; foliage small, matte; vigorous, upright growth; [('Soroya' × 'Signora') × King's Ransom®]; intr. 1972

'Meinastur' ('Alpha') HT, or, 1976, Paolino; flowers bright vermilion, 4 in., 20 petals; foliage leathery; PP3926; [(('Show Girl' × Baccará®) × 'Romantica') × ('Romantica' × 'Tropicana')]

'Meinatac' ('Susan Hampshire') HT, lp, 1976, Paolino; flowers light fuchsia-pink, 5½ in., 40 petals, globular, intense fragrance; free-flowering; foliage medium green, matte; vigorous, upright growth; [('Monique' × 'Symphonie') × 'Miss All-American Beauty']; intr. 1972

'Meindeert Hobbema' S, rb, Williams, J. Benjamin; flowers red, striped ivory and pink, semi-dbl.; landscape shrub; intr. 1997

Meine Oma™ -- See 'Pouloma'

'Meineble' ('Rouge Meidiland', Rouge Meillandécor®, Red Meidiland™) S, rb, 1989, Meilland, Alain A.; bud conical; flowers red with white eye, medium, 5 petals, cupped, borne in sprays of 7-15; repeat bloom; foliage medium size, dark green, glossy, disease-resistant; prickles gray-brown; spreading, medium, very winter hardy growth; hips globular, small, red; PP7116; ['Sea Foam' × ('Picasso' × Eyepaint®)]; intr. 1989

'Meinececa' ('Tempo') F, mr, Meilland; intr. 1977

'Meinelvis' HT, dy, Meilland; intr. 2004

'Meinereau' (Centennial Star™) HT, yb, 1996, Meilland International SA; bud conical; flowers yellow with pink edge, 4¾ in., 50 petals, borne usually singly, slight fragrance; free-flowering; foliage large, dark green, semi-glossy; numerous prickles; bushy, medium (3 ft.) growth; PP10668; [('Peace' × 'Landora') × King's Ransom®]; intr. 1996

'Meineyta' ('Fiery Sunblaze', Cumba Meillandina®) Min, ob, 1994, Meilland, Alain A.; flowers large, very dbl., borne in small clusters; foliage large, medium green, semi-glossy; some prickles; medium, bushy growth; ['Orange Honey' × ('Darling Flame' × Tapis Jaune®)]; intr. 1992

'Meiniacin' ('Fragrant Lady', Perfume Beauty™) HT, mp, 1991, Meilland, Alain A.; bud conical; flowers rose bengal, medium, very dbl., cupped, borne singly, moderate fragrance; foliage large, dark green; upright, tall growth; PP7819; ['Princess Margaret of England' × (Carina® × 'Silvia')]; intr. 1990

'Meinibur' ('Kir Royal') LCl, pb, Meilland; intr. 1995

'Meinical' ('Edith Piaf') HT, dr, Meilland; bud conical and elongated; intr. 1999

'Meinieves' HT, w, Meilland; intr. 2004

'Meinimo' ('21 Again!', 'Penny Coelen', 'Prestige de Lyon', Regatta™) HT, lp, 1994, Meilland, Alain A.; bud medium, ovoid; flowers soft dawn pink, large, 32-35 petals, high-centered, borne mostly singly, moderate spicy fragrance; free-flowering; foliage large, dark green, matte; prickles numerous, large, greenish tan; medium (3 ft.), bushy growth; PP8390; ['Coppélia 76' × ('Meinaregi' × 'Laura 81')]; intr. 1992

'Meininrut' (Orange Symphonie®) Min, or, 1994, Meilland, Alain A.; flowers orange vermilion, large, full, borne mostly singly or in small clusters, no fragrance; foliage medium size, dark green, semi-glossy; some prickles; low (35-45 cm.), bushy growth; [('Baby Bettina' × 'Anytime') × 'Meteor']; intr. 1993

'Meinirlo' ('Festival Meidiland') S, mr,

Meillanddbl.; intr. 1992

'Meinissime' F, lp, Meilland; intr. 2004

'Meinitper' (Caramella®) HT, ab, Meilland; intr. 1986

'Meinivoz' ('Moondance', 'Summer's Kiss', 'Spirit of Peace', 'Paul Richard', 'Paul Ricard') HT, yb, 1994, Meilland, Alain A.; bud ovoid, large; flowers amber yellow, 4 in., 40-44 petals, cupped, borne usually singly, intense anise fragrance; free-flowering; foliage large, medium green, matte; prickles numerous, medium, light tan; tall (110-120 cm.), upright growth; PP9001; [(Hidalgo® × 'Mischief') × 'Ambassador']; intr. 1990

'Meinixode' HT, dy, Meilland; intr. 2004

'Meinochot' Min, dr, Meilland

'Meinofrai' (Red Mini-Wonder™) Min, dr, 1990, Selection Meilland; bud rounded; flowers currant red, cardinal red reverse, aging to dark red, small, 40-43 petals, cupped; foliage small, medium green, very dense, semi-glossy; prickles small, green to tan; bushy, low growth; PP7384; [('Anytime' × 'Parador') × 'Mogral']; intr. 1987

'Meinoiral' (Play Rose®) S, mp, Meillanddbl.; intr. 1990

'Meinomad' ('Desert Peace') HT, yb, 1992, Meilland, Alain A.; bud conical, large; flowers yellow edged with red, 14 cm., 22 petals, cupped, borne mostly singly, some small clusters, slight fragrance; good repeat; foliage large, dark green, glossy; prickles numerous, large; tall (120-130 cm.), upright growth; PP8248; [('Sonia' × 'Rumba') × (Piccadilly® × Chicago Peace®)]; intr. 1991

'Meinopia' ('Madonna ') HT, pb, Meilland; bud long; intr. 1992

'Meinorep' HT, pb, Meilland; intr. 1995

'Meinronsse' ('Christoph Colombus', 'Flamboyance', 'Christophe Colomb', 'Christopher Columbus', 'Cristobal Colon', 'Cristoforo Colombo') HT, ob, 1992, Selection Meilland; bud oval, large; flowers orange blend/copper, 4-5 in., 25-27 petals, cupped, borne mostly singly, slight fragrance; good repeat; foliage large, dark green, semi-glossy; prickles numerous, large; medium (120-140 cm.), upright growth; PP8496; ['Coppélia 76' × ('Ambassador' × 'MEInaregi')]

'Meinusian' ('Rabelais', Francois Rabelais™) F, mr, 1998, Selection Meilland; flowers bright red, 2-2½ in., 41 petals, borne in small clusters, slight fragrance; foliage medium size, dark green, glossy; prickles moderate; bushy, medium (3 ft.) growth; [('Tchin-Tchin' × Matthias Meilland®) × 'Lilli Marlene']; intr. 1996

'Meinustrel' F, Meilland

'Meinuzeten' (Ambassador®) HT, ob, 1977, Meilland; bud conical, large; flowers orange-red, reverse blended with golden yellow (orange-apricot), 4 in., 30-35 petals, cupped, borne mostly singly, slight fragrance; recurrent; foliage dark green, semi-glossy; prickles large, average number; bushy (4½ ft.) growth; PP4224; [(('Meialfi' × 'Meifan 00186F') × King's Ransom®) × 'Whisky Mac']; intr. 1979

'Meioffic' ('Forever Friends', Johann Strauss®, 'Sweet Sonata') F, pb, 1994, Meilland, Alain A.; flowers orient pink slightly suffused with aureolin yellow, 3-5 in., 100 petals, cupped, borne in clusters of 3 - 7, slight sweet fragrance; foliage medium size, dark green, semi-glossy; few prickles; low (50-60 cm.), bushy, compact growth; PP9998; [('Flamingo' × ('Pink Wonder' × 'Tip Top')]; intr. 1993

'Meionagre' ('Michaelhouse Centenary') HT, mr, Meilland; intr. 1995

'Meiouscki' (Crimson Meidiland®) S, dr; intr. 1996

'Meipadan' S, w; bud ovoid; intr. 2003

'Meipaede' Min, mr, Meillanddbl.; intr. 2002

'Meipaga' F, yb; intr. 2000

'Meipaleo' ('Marco Polo') HT, my, 1994, Meilland, Alain A.; bud conical, large; flowers lemon yellow, lighter at the edges, 3-3½ in., 35 petals, cupped, borne mostly singly or in small clusters, moderate fragrance; good repeat; foliage medium green, semi-glossy; prickles numerous, medium, pink; tall, upright growth; PP9042; ['Ambassador' × (Sunbright® × 'Oregold')]; intr. 1992

'Meipaonia' HT, yb, Meilland; intr. 2004

'Meiparadon' (Antonia Ridge®) HT, mr, 1976, Paolino; flowers cardinal-red, 4-4½ in., 30 petals, high-centered; vigorous growth; [('Chrysler Imperial' × 'Karl Herbst') × seedling]

'Meiparnin' ('Romantic Days', Honore de Balzac™) HT, pb, 1998, Selection Meilland; bud globular, large; flowers light creamy yellow suffused with carmine, 4½-5½ in., 58 petals, borne 1-3 per stem, moderate peach-like fragrance; good repeat; foliage medium size, medium green, semi-glossy; prickles numerous, medium, reddish; upright, bushy, medium (3 ft.) growth; PP10477; [('Marion Foster' × 'KORav') × 'Lancome']; intr. 1996

'Meiparos' ('Perfumella') HT, mp, Meilland, bud medium, conical; intr. 1999

'Meipazdia' ('Poker') HT, w, Meilland; intr. 1998

'Meipelmel' ('Kampaÿ', Pretty Sunrise®) S, op, Meilland; intr. 2007

'Meipelta' ('Cyclamen Meillandecor', Fuchsia Meidiland™, Fuchsia Meillandecor®) S, dp, 1994, Meilland, Alain A.; bud ovoid, small; flowers Bengal rose, medium, 15 petals, flat cup, borne in large clusters, slight fragrance; free-flowering; foliage medium size, light green, glossy; few prickles; low, spreading growth; PP8839; [Borderella® × Clair Matin®]; intr. 1993

'Meipeluj' LCl, lp, Meilland; intr. 1993

'Meiperator' ('Imperator') F, mr, 1972, Meilland

'Meipicoty' F, yb, Meilland; intr. 2007

'Meipierar' ('Cameo Cream', 'Caroline de Monaco', 'Marcellin Champagnat', 'Sacred Heart') HT, w, 1993, Meilland, Alain A.; bud conical, large; flowers cream white, 3-4½ in., 40-45 petals, borne mostly singly, no fragrance; good repeat; foliage large, dark green, semi-glossy; prickles large; medium, bushy growth; PP7622; [Chicago Peace® × 'Tchin-Tchin']; intr. 1993

'Meipiess' (Majorette®) MinFl, mr, 1987, Meilland, Mrs. Marie-Louise; flowers medium cardinal-red, medium, dbl., no fragrance; foliage small, medium green, semi-glossy; growth bushy; [Magic Carrousel® × ('Grumpy' × Scarletta®)]; intr. 1985

'Meipikon' HT, pb, Meilland; intr. 1999

'Meipinjid' ('Duc Meillandina', 'Duke Meillandina', 'Duke Sunblaze', Classic Sunblaze®) Min, mp, 1985, Meilland, Mrs. Marie-Louise; bud conical, small; flowers rich pink, 1½-2 in., 40 petals, borne mostly singly; foliage medium size, dark green, matte; prickles medium, fairly numerous; growth short (15 in.), bushy; PP5958; [sport of 'Pink Sunblaze']

'Meipitac' (Carefree Wonder™, Dynastie®) S, pb, 1990; bud pointed, ovoid; flowers medium pink with light pink reverse, aging to medium pink, 4-4½ in., 26-30 petals, cupped, borne in sprays of 1-4, slight fragrance; free-flowering; foliage medium size, medium green, semi-glossy; prickles narrow, reddish; bushy, medium growth; suitable for hedges; hips oval, reddish-brown; hardy; PP7783; [('Prairie Princess' × 'Nirvana') × (Eyepaint® × 'Rustica')]; intr. 1978

'Meiplatin' (Pearl Meidiland™, Perle Meillandécor®) S, lp, 1989, Meilland, Alain A.; bud ovoid; flowers light ochre pink, aging white, 2½ in., 28-32 petals, flat cup, borne in sprays of 3-15, no fragrance; good repeat bloom; foliage medium size, dark green, glossy; prickles small, reddish-brown; spreading, low growth; hips globular, small dish, reddish; PP6807; [('Sea Foam' × 'MElsecaso') × 'Sea Foam']; intr. 1989

'Meiplovon' ('Mademoiselle') HT, mp, Meilland

'Meipobil' ('Châtelaine de Lullier') HT, dp, Meilland; intr. 1987

'Meipojona' F, my, Meilland; intr. 2008

'Meipomolo' F, ab; bud conical; intr. 2004

'Meiponal' ('Sunblaze', Sunny Meillandina®, 'Sunny Sunblaze') Min, ob, 1986, Meilland, Mrs. Marie-Louise; bud slightly globular; flowers light orange-yellow, pale yellow reverse, 2 in., 35 petals, cupped, borne 1 - 5 per stem, no fragrance; free-flowering; foliage small, dark green, matte; bushy (12 in.) growth; PP6810; [(Sarabande® × Moulin Rouge®) × (Zambra® × 'Meikim')]; intr. 1985

'Meipoppie' HT, dr, Meillandfull; intr. 2006

'Meipopul' ('Amstelveen', Coral Meidiland™, Douceur Normande®, 'Goose Fair', 'Sandton City', 'Stadt Hildesheim') S, mp, 1994, Meilland, Alain A.; bud conical, small; flowers scarlet pink, medium, 5 petals, cupped, borne in small clusters, no fragrance; free-flowering; foliage small, medium green, semi-glossy; prickles numerous, small to medium; medium (70-90 cm.), bushy growth; PP9777; [(Immensee® × Green Snake®) × ('Temple Bells' × 'Red Cascade')]

'Meipoque' ('Rose Meillandécor', Pink Meidiland®, 'Schloss Heidegg') S, pb, 1985, Meilland, Mrs. Marie-Louise; bud conical; flowers deep pink with white eye, reverse whitish suffused red, 3 in., 5 petals, flat, borne in large clusters, no fragrance; good repeat; foliage small, medium green, semi-glossy; bushy, arching (5 ft.) growth; PP5956; ['Anne de Bretagne' × 'Nirvana']; intr. 1983

'Meipotal' ('Carefree Beauty', 'Evermore', 'Carefree Delight', Bingo Meillandecor®, Bingo Meidiland®) S, pb, 1994, Meilland; bud short, ovoid; flowers dark pink fading to light pink at center, slight eye effect, reverse lighter, 2-2½ in., 5-10 petals, flat cup, borne mostly in clusters, slight fragrance; free-flowering; foliage small, dark green, glossy; numerous prickles; arching, medium (2½ ft.) growth; PP8841; [(Eyepaint® × 'Nirvana') × Smarty®]; intr. 1991

'Meipraserpi' (Catherine Deneuve®) HT, op, Meilland; intr. 1981

'Meipreston' (Ruby Meidiland®) S, mr, 2001, Meilland International; bud globose, small to medium; flowers show shades of red, 1½ in., 15 petals, cupped, borne in large clusters, no fragrance; free-flowering; foliage small, dark green, glossy; prickles moderate; growth bushy, low (3 ft.); landscape; PP13500; [(Red Meidiland™ × Scarlet Meidiland™) × 'The Fairy']; intr. 2000

'Meiprille' F, dp, Meilland; intr. 1992

'Meipsidue' S, mr, Meilland; bud conical, small; intr. 1999

'Meipsilon' (Yakimour®) HT, rb, Meilland; intr. 1986

'Meiptima' ('Lavender Meillandina') Min, m, Meilland; bud conical; intr. 1999

'Meiptipier' ('Eden Folies', 'Mini Eden') Min, pb, Meilland; intr. 2002

'Meipuma' (Scherzo®) F, rb, 1976, Paolino; bud pointed; flowers bright scarlet, reverse white and crimson, large, 40 petals, spiraled, borne in clusters, moderate fragrance; foliage dark; vigorous, bushy growth; ['Tamango' × 'Frenzy']

'Meiqualis' HT, mr, Meilland; bud conical, medium; intr. 1995

'Meirabande' F, or, 1958, Meilland, F.; intr. 1957

'Meiradia' ('Lutin') Min, mp, 1972, Meilland

'Meirameca' ('Alpha Meidiland', 'Anadia', Carefree Marvel™) S, dp, 2003, Meilland International; bud globular, small; flowers 2 in., 24-28 petals, flattened, borne in large clusters, no fragrance; free-flowering; foliage medium green, glossy; prickles moderate; growth spreading, medium (2-3 ft.); groundcover, landscape, containers; PP16030; [Flower Carpet™ × (Magic Meidiland® × Immensee®)]; intr. 2003

'Meirandival' ('Miriana') HT, yb, 1983, Meilland, Mrs. Marie-Louise; PP5046; [sport of 'Meibiranda']

'Meiranoga' ('Brilliant Meillandina') Min, or, 1985, Meilland, Mrs. Marie-Louise; flowers 15 petals, cupped, borne in clusters of 3-20, no fragrance; foliage dark, semi-glossy; ['Parador' × ('Baby Bettina' × 'Duchess of Windsor')]; intr. 1975

'Meiranovi' (Candy Rose®) S, rb, 1982, Meilland, Mrs. Marie-Louise; bud conical; flowers deep pink, reverse medium red, 2 in., 15-20 petals, borne in clusters, no fragrance; foliage small, medium green, semi-glossy; arching, spreading growth; PP6385; [(R. sempervirens × Mlle Marthe Carron) × ((Lilli Marleen® × 'Evelyn Fison') × ('Orange Sweetheart' × 'Fruhlingsmorgen'))]; intr. 1980

'Meirasimac' ('Royal Show') S, mr, Meilland; bud tinted crimson; intr. 1983

'Meiratcan' ('Lovely Bride', 'Lovely Meidiland') S, lp, Meilland

'Meirebuc' ('Liz') F, w, Meilland; intr. 1995

'Meirecrom' ('Puy du Fou') HT, ob, Meilland; bud conical, large; intr. 1999

'Meired' ('Visa') HT, mr, 1972, Meilland; flowers turkey-red, 5 in., 38 petals, high-centered; foliage large, leathery; vigorous, upright growth; PP3452; [(Baccará® × Queen Elizabeth®) × 'Lovita']

'Meireibat' F, pb, Meilland; intr. 1995

'Meirestif' ('Charleston 88', Louis de Funes®) HT, ob, 1987, Meilland, Mrs. Marie-Louise; flowers orange capucine reverse cadmium yellow, large, dbl.; foliage medium size, dark green, glossy; upright, strong growth; [('Ambassador' × 'Whisky Mac') × ('Arthur Bell' × 'Kabuki')]; intr. 1983

'Meiretni' ('Interflora') HT, dp, 1968, Meilland; intr. 1976

'Meirevolt' ('Golden Conquest', Toulouse Lautrec®) HT, my, 1994, Meilland, Alain A.; bud globular; flowers clear lemon yellow, 3-4 in., 87-90 petals, cupped, borne mostly singly, very slight fragrance; good repeat; foliage medium size, medium green, glossy; prickles numerous, medium, greenish; medium (70-80 cm.), bushy growth; PP9582; ['Ambassador' × (King's Ransom® × 'Sunblest')]; intr. 1992

'Meirgano' HT, dr, Meilland; intr. 1992

'Meirianopur' ('Orange Bunny®) F, or, 1981, Meilland, Mrs. Marie-Louise; bud pointed; flowers orange-red, reverse darker, 13 petals, cupped, borne singly and in clusters of up to 25; foliage bronze, matte, very dense; bushy growth; [Scherzo® × (Sarabande® × 'Frenzy')]; intr. 1979

'Meiridge' F, yb, 1965, Meilland, Alain A.; bud pointed

'Meiridgesar' Cl F, yb, 1966, Rumsey, R.H. (also Keisei, 1978); intr. 1966

'Meiridol' ('Irene') F, dp, Meilland; intr. 1983

'Meiridorio' ('Gilbert Bécaud') HT, yb, 1985, Meilland, Mme. Marie-Louise; flowers orange and yellow blend, large, 45 petals; foliage bronze, matte; upright growth; [('Peace' × 'Mrs John Laing') × Bettina®]; intr. 1979

'Meiriental' ('Gavroche', 'Paprika') LCl, or, Meilland International SA; bud oblong; flowers vermilion, reverse lighter, 3 in., single, flat cup, borne in small clusters, no fragrance; free-flowering; foliage large, dark green, semi-glossy; prickles numerous, medium to large; growth spreading, tall (8+ ft.); PP9537; [(Centenaire de Lourdes® × 'Picasso') × 'Sparkling Scarlet']; intr. 1992

'Meirigalu' ('Colourama', 'Dr R. Maag') HT, rb, 1968, Meilland, Mrs. Marie-Louise; bud ovoid

'Meirillo' ClMin, dy, Meilland; intr. 2002

'Meirilocra' ('Capella', 'Zambra '80') HT, ab, 1985, Meilland, Mrs. Marie-Louise; flowers large, 35 petals; foliage medium size, dark, matte; PP4868; [seedling × 'Banzai']; intr. 1979

'Meiringa' (Carte Blanche™) HT, w, 1976, Paolino; flowers flora-tea, 4 in., 38 petals; foliage matte; vigorous growth; PP3804; [(Carina® × 'White Knight') × 'Jack Frost']

'Meirinlor' HT, my, 1976, Paolino; flowers 4 in., 15-18 petals; foliage dark; ['Golden Garnette' × (('Golden Garnette' × Bettina®) × 'Dr. A.J. Verhage')]

'Meirisouru' ('Gunnels Ros', Nirvana®) F, lp, 1979, Meilland, Mrs. Marie-Louise; bud ovoid; flowers large, 20 petals, cupped; foliage glossy; bushy growth; [('Pink Wonder' × 'Kalinka') × Centenaire de Lourdes®]; intr. 1977

'Meirivoui' ('Carefree Days') Min, mp, Meilland; intr. 1997

'Meirobidor' ('Carte d'Or', Supra™) HT, dy, 1984, Meilland, Mrs. Marie-Louise; flowers flora-tea, large, 20 petals, no fragrance; foliage medium size, dark, semi-glossy; upright growth; PP5042; [((Zambra® × ('Baccará × White Knight')) × 'Golden Garnette') × seedling]; intr. 1980

'Meirodium' ('Red Success') HT, rb, 1976, Paolino; bud oval; flowers blood-red, base cardinal-red, 4-4½ in., 40-45 petals, high-centered, borne mostly singly, slight fragrance; good repeat; foliage large, dark green, semi-glossy; prickles medium; stems long; vigorous, upright (5 ft.) growth; PP4037; [('Tropicana' × 'Meialto') × (('Meibrem' × Zambra®) × 'Tropicana')]; greenhouse rose

'Meirokad' ('Red Meilove') F, dr, Meilland; intr. 1994

'Meirokoi' ('Outback Angel', Jean Giono™, 'Romantic Moments') HT, yb, 1998, Selection Meilland; bud globular, large; flowers sunny yellow, veined and edged in orange/apricot, 3-4 in., 110-120 petals, borne singly and in small clusters, slight fragrance; good repeat; foliage medium size, medium green, glossy; prickles numerous, large; upright, bushy, medium (90 cm.) growth; PP9979; [(Yakimour® × 'Landora') × Graham Thomas®]

'Meirolange' HT, pb, Meilland; intr. 1999

'Meirolour' ('Concerto 94', 'Starstruck') S, ab, Meilland; intr. 1994

'Meirolyz' HT, or, Meilland; intr. 1999

'Meiromar' ('Gin Fizz') HT, w, Meilland; intr. 1995

'Meironssesar' ('Christophe Colomb, Gpt.') Cl HT, or, Meilland

'Meirosfon' (Fuchsia Minuetto™) Min, mp, 2000, Meilland International; flowers fuchsia pink, 2-3 cm., very full, borne in small clusters, no fragrance; foliage medium size, medium green, semi-glossy; prickles moderate; compact, medium (8-12 in.) growth; PP11571; intr. 1999

'Meirotego' ('Mini Jet', Minijet®) Min, mp, 1977, Paolino, Mrs M. L.; intr. 1977

'Meiroupis' ('Genevieve', Colette™, 'John Keats') LCl, mp, 1996, Meilland International SA; bud conical, small; flowers ruffled, 3-3½ in., 135 petals, borne in small clusters, intense fragrance; good repeat; foliage small, dark green, glossy; prickles numerous, small to medium; spreading, medium (2 m.) growth; PP9994; [('Fiona' × 'Friesia') × 'Prairie Princess']; intr. 1995

'Meirouve' ('Alphonse Daudet') HT, ab, Meilland; intr. 1997

'Meiroux' F, rb, Meilland; intr. 2004

'Meirov' ('Meillandina') Min, mr, 1976, Paolino; bud globular, medium; flowers currant-red, then imbricated, 1½-1¾ in., 30-35 petals, cupped, then flat, borne in clusters, no fragrance; foliage yellow-green, matte; vigorous, bushy (16-20 in.) growth; ['Rumba' × ('Dany Robin' × 'Fire King')]

'Meiroverna' ('Koba') HT, or, 1979, Meilland, Mrs. Marie-Louise; flowers scarlet, medium, 40 petals, cupped; foliage dark; very vigorous, upright growth; [((seedling × 'Rouge Meilland') × 'Independence') × Queen Elizabeth®]

'Meirovonex' (Looping®) LCl, ob, 1979, Meilland, Mrs. Marie-Louise; bud conical; flowers orange-coral, medium, 40 petals, cupped; spring bloom; foliage dark; vigorous, climbing growth; [((Zambra® × Danse des Sylphes®) × Cocktail®) × 'Royal Gold']; intr. 1977

'Meirozrug' ('Turbo Rugostar', 'Turbo', Turbo Meidiland®) HRg, mp, 1994, Meilland, Alain A.; bud oblong, medium; flowers fuchsia pink, 3½-5 in., 21-23 petals, flat cup, borne singly and in small clusters, no fragrance; good repeat; foliage medium size, light green, semi-glossy; prickles numerous, medium to large, greenish; tall (130-140 cm.), bushy growth; PP9468; [('Frau Dagmar Hastrup' × Manou Meilland®) × 'Pink Grootendorst']; intr. 1993

'Meirulex' ('Fuchsia Sunblaze') MinFl, op, Meilland; intr. 2004

'Meirumour' ('Cherry Meidiland', 'Cherry Meillandecor', 'Pride Meidiland') S, rb, 1995, Meilland; bud oval, medium; flowers red with a white eye, reverse lighter, 2 in., 5 petals, flat cup, borne in small clusters, no fragrance; good repeat; foliage medium size, dark green, semi-glossy; prickles numerous, medium; upright, bushy growth (5½-6 ft.); PP9251; [Pink Meidiland® × (Regensberg® × Fair Play®)]

'Meirutral' ('Prince Sunblaze', Prince Meillandina®, Red Sunblaze®) Min, dr, 1988, Meilland, Alain A.; bud oval, small; flowers dark currant-red, 1½-2 in., 20-22 petals, cupped, borne singly and in clusters, no fragrance; free-flowering; foliage medium size, dark green, semi-glossy; bushy, branching (15 in.) growth; PP7021; ['Parador' × 'Mogral']

'Meirypoux' ('Rotary Rose') HT, dr, 1990, Meilland, Alain A.; bud pointed; flowers 27 petals, high-centered, borne usually singly; foliage medium green; prickles large, red; vigorous, upright growth; PP7408; [(Mister Lincoln® × 'Pres. Leopold Senghor') × 'Karl Herbst']; intr. 1989

'Meisadina' ('Golestan') HT, or, 1979, Meilland, Mrs. Marie-Louise; bud tapering; flowers vermilion, small, 25 petals, high-centered; foliage glossy, dark; vigorous, upright growth; [('Tropicana' × 'Tropicana') × ((seedling × 'Rouge Meilland') × 'Independence')]; intr. 1975

'Meisar' HT, dr, 1963, Meilland, Alain A.; bud pointed

'Meisardan' ('Romantic Occasion') S, yb, Meilland; intr. 1993

'Meisarsar' (Grimpant Papa Meilland®) Cl HT, dr, 1971, Stratford (also Meilland, 1976)

'Meisashen' F, w, Meilland; intr. 2004

'Meisazy' ('Gala Charles Aznavour') F, lp, Meilland; intr. 1997

'Meisecaso' ('Shady Lady') S, pb, Meilland; intr. 1984

'Meiselgra' (Pink Mini-Wonder™) Min, mp, 1990, Selection Meilland; bud rounded; flowers light rose bengal, reverse pale rose bengal, aging pale rose, 39-42 petals, cupped; foliage medium green, semi-glossy; prickles small, very few, green, aging tan; bushy, medium growth; PP7361; [('Anytime' × 'Parador') × 'Mogral']; intr. 1987

'Meiselgra' Min, mp, Meilland

'Meisha' ('Sunlight') HT, my, 1958, Meilland, F.; bud ovoid with conspicuous neck; intr. 1956

'Meishasar' ('Grisbi, Climbing') Cl HT, my, 1963, Meilland, Mrs. Marie-Louise

'Meishasen' HT, w, Meilland; intr. 2004

'Meishulo' (Salmon Sunblaze™) Min, op, 1996, Meilland International SA; bud egg-shaped, medium; flowers salmon pink, 1½-2 in., 35-40 petals, cupped, borne in small clusters; free-flowering; foliage small, dark green, semi-glossy; prickles numerous, small, pinkish; compact, upright, low (12-16 in.) growth; PP10015; ['Parador' × (Lady Sunblaze™ × 'Dwarf Queen '82')]; intr. 1997

'Meisiastri' ('Julio Iglesias') F, w, 2007, Meilland International; flowers pink and white, 7-8 cm., dbl., borne in small clusters; foliage large, dark green, semi-glossy; prickles small, few; growth upright, medium (3½-4 ft.); ['(Shocking Blue × Lancome') × Scentimental™]; intr. 2008

'Meisinplox' ('Sorbet') HT, my, Meilland; buds large, conical, lemon yellow; intr. 1996

'Meisionver' ('Best Friend', 'Caprice') HT, mp, Meilland; intr. 1998

'Meiskaille' ('Gold Symphonie 2002', Yellow Sunblaze™, 'Yellow Sunblaze 2004') Min, my, 2004, Meilland International; bud ovoid, medium; flowers bright lemon yellow, 4-6 cm., 44-46 petals, cupped, borne in small clusters, no fragrance; free-flowering; foliage medium size, medium to dark green, semi-glossy; prickles 5 mm, straight, yellow-green; growth compact, short (18-24 in.); garden decoration, containers; PP14274; [((Cumba Meillandina® × seedling) × Good Morning America™]; intr. 2002

'Meiskimov' ('Nicole Carol Miller') Gr, m, 2004, Meilland International; flowers light lavender, 10-12 cm., dbl., borne in small clusters, intense fragrance; foliage medium green, semi-glossy; growth upright, medium (to 6 ft); garden; PPAF; [Charles de Gaulle® × (Shocking Blue® × 'Sterling Silver')]; intr. 2004

'Meisocrat' ('La Rose Romantica', Guy de Maupassant™, 'La Rose', 'Romantic Fragrance') F, mp, 1996, Meilland International SA; bud globular, large; flowers carmine pink, 3-3½ in., 90-100 petals, cupped, borne in clusters, intense green apple fragrance; good repeat; foliage large, dark green, glossy; prickles moderate; bushy, tall (70-90 cm.) growth; PP9613; [('Anne de Bretagne' × 'Mrs John Laing') × Egeskov™]; intr. 1995

'Meisogrel' -- See 'White MiniJet'

'Meisolroz' ('Comtesse Jeanne de Flandre', 'Sandra Kim', 'Heidepark', 'Sandra') S, mp, Meilland; intr. 1990

'Meisoyris' ('Love's Promise', 'Marcel Pagnol', Matilda™, 'Red Cross', 'Velveteen', Graf Lennart®) HT, mr, 1994, Meilland; buds pointed, large; flowers dark ruby-red, 5-5½ in., full, cupped, borne singly and in small clusters, moderate fragrance; good repeat; foliage dark green, glossy; prickles numerous, medium; growth strong, well-branched, upright (2½ ft.); PP9253; ['Fragrant

Cloud' × ('Oklahoma' × 'Royal William')]; registered as Gr; intr. 1993

'Meispola' ('Preview') HT, w, Meilland

'Meisponge' ('Diamond Rose', Prince de Monaco™, Jubilé du Prince de Monaco®, Cherry Parfait™, 'Ice Cream') Gr, rb, 2001, Meilland International; bud conical; flowers white with red edges, 5 in., 30-35 petals, high-centered, borne in small clusters, no fragrance; foliage medium size, dark green, semi-glossy; prickles medium, moderate; growth bushy, medium (4-5 ft.); specimen, landscape; PP12802; ['Meichoiju' × ('Meidanu' × 'Macman')]; intr. 2000

'Meispreyo' ('Golden Folies', 'Mimi Golden') F, my, Meilland; intr. 1998

'Meissner' HT, dp, Meilland; intr. 2004

'Meistadi' F, m, Meilland; bud globular, small; intr. 2004

'Meistefy' F, ob, Meilland; intr. 1998

'Meistefyel' F, my, Meilland

'Meisterstück' F, mr, 1940, Kordes; bud ovoid; flowers velvety crimson, large, dbl., cupped, borne in clusters; foliage dark, glossy; upright, bushy growth; ['Holstein' × 'Kardinal']

'Meistocko' ('Flash Meidiland') S, dp, Meilland; intr. 1993

'Meistrelia' HT, pb, Meilland; intr. 2002

'Meisunaj' ('Fernandel') F, dp, Meilland; intr. 1989

'Meisylpho' F, mp, Meilland

'Meitakilor' HT, my, Meilland, Mrs. Marie-Louise; bud elongated; intr. 1977

'Meitalbaz' ('Anthony Meilland') F, my, 1994, Meilland, Alain A.; bud egg-shaped; flowers 3-3½ in., 27-30 petals, cupped, borne in small clusters, no fragrance; good repeat; foliage large, medium green, semi-glossy; prickles large; medium (3 ft.), bushy growth; PP8449; [('Sunblest' × 'Mitzi 81 ') × 'Spek's Yellow']; intr. 1990

'Meitam' LCl, dr, 1959, Meilland, Mrs. Marie-Louise; bud globular; intr. 1958

'Meitandar' LCl, mp, Meilland; intr. 2004

'Meitanet' F, ly, Meilland; bud conical; intr. 1995

'Meitapov' (Koala®) LCl, w, Meilland; intr. 1993

'Meitaras' HT, pb, 1964, Meilland, Alain A.; bud pointed ovoid, with conspicuous neck; intr. 1964

'Meitasma' HT, or, Meilland; intr. 2006

'Meitchico' Min, r, Meilland; intr. 2004

'Meitebros' ('The Children's Rose', Frederic Mistral™) HT, lp, 1998, Selection Meilland; bud conical; flowers Venetian pink, reverse suffused rose, 4½ in., 40-45 petals, cupped, borne mostly singly, intense fragrance; good repeat; foliage large, dark green, semi-glossy; prickles moderate; upright, tall, 6 ft. growth; PP10004; [('Perfume Delight' × 'Prima Ballerina') × The McCartney Rose™]; intr. 1995

'Meitelov' ('Gracious Queen') HT, my, Meilland; intr. 1997

'Meithion' F, mr, 1959, Meilland, Mrs. Marie-Louise; bud oval

'Meitifran' ('Baron Sunblaze', Baron Meillandina®) Min, rb, 1987, Meilland, Mrs. Marie-Louise; flowers white with red edges, medium, dbl., umbrella-shaped; foliage small, medium green, glossy; bushy growth; PP6818; [Magic Carrousel® × (('Alain' × 'Mutabilis') × ('Medar' × 'Caprice'))]; intr. 1986

'Meitiloly' (Mascotte '77®) HT, yb, 1977, Paolino; flowers yellow, edged cardinal-red, 4½ in., 40 petals; foliage glossy; vigorous growth; [('MEIrendal' × ('Rim' × 'Peace')) × 'Peace']

'Meitinirol' (Galia®) HT, or, 1981, Meilland, Mrs. Marie-Louise; flowers 38 petals, cupped, borne singly, no fragrance; foliage matte, dense; vigorous growth; ['Interview' × 'Elegy']; intr. 1977

'Meitinor' ('Cindy') F, pb, Meilland; intr. 1997

'Meitiraca' F, pb

'Meitiver' F, w, Meilland; intr. 2002

'Meitixia' ('Hans Rosenthal') HT, mr, Meilland; intr. 1989

'Meitizado' HT, pb; bud conical; intr. 2002

'Meitobla' ('Efekto 21', 'Simply Magic') F, dp, Meilland; intr. 1992

'Meitoflapo' ('Caremo') F, mp, 1985, Meilland, Mrs. Marie-Louise; flowers large, 29 petals, no fragrance; foliage small, dark, semi-glossy; PP4912; [(('Jack Frost' × (Zambra® × ('Baccará × White Knight')) × ((Zambra® × '(Baccará × White Knight)') × seedling)]; intr. 1980

'Meitoifar' ('Auguste Renoir') HT, mp, 1994, Meilland, Alain A.; bud ovoid; flowers Bengal pink, 3-4 in., 50-65 petals, cupped with flat center, borne mostly singly, moderate fragrance; repeats in flushes; foliage medium size, medium green, semi-glossy; numerous prickles; medium, bushy growth; PP9564; [('Versailles' × Pierre de Ronsard®) × Kimono®]; intr. 1992

'Meitoleil' ('Golden Symphony', Gold Symphonie®) Min, my, 1994, Meilland, Alain A.; flowers large, very dbl., borne mostly singly or in small clusters; foliage medium size, dark green, semi-glossy; some prickles; medium (40-50 cm.), bushy growth; [('Rise 'n' Shine' × 'Yellow Meillandina') × Gold Badge™]; intr. 1993

'Meitomkin' ('Symphonie Lumiere') Min, yb, Meilland

'Meitongas' S, my, Meilland; intr. 2006

'Meitonje' ('Pink Symphony', 'Pretty Polly', Sweet Sunblaze®) Min, lp, 1987, Meilland, Mrs. Marie-Louise; bud oval, small; flowers light cardinal pink, unfading, 1½-2 in., 26 petals, flat, borne singly and in small clusters; good repeat; foliage medium size, dark green, glossy, disease-resistant; prickles small; vigorous, bushy (18 in.) growth; PP7277; ['Darling Flame' × 'Air France']

'Meitosier' ('Lord Byron', Polka™, 'Polka 91', 'Scented Dawn', 'Twilight Glow') LCl, ab, 1996, Meilland International SA; bud ovoid, large; flowers ivory yellow, 3½-4 in., 90-100 petals, quartered, borne singly and in small clusters, moderate fragrance; good repeat; foliage large, medium green, semi-glossy; few prickles on young stems, numerous on adult wood; upright, climbing, tall (12 ft.) growth; PP9233; [('MEIpalsar' × Golden Showers®) × 'Lichtkonigin Lucia']; intr. 1991

'Meitozaure' (Raspberry Rugostar™) HRg, dp, 2003, Meilland International; flowers mauve, reverse deep pink, 6-8 cm., 5 petals, flattened cup, borne in clusters, moderate spicy, sweet clove fragrance; recurrent; foliage large, light green, matte; prickles moderate; growth spreading, short (2-3 ft.); groundcover; hips sub-globose, 14 × 18 cm., orange-red; PP15937; ['Schneekoppe' × 'Frau Dagmar Hastrup']; intr. 2003

'Meitrainaz' F, mr; intr. 2002

'Meitravia' HT, dp, Meilland; bud globular, intr. 2006

'Meitrido' Min, mr, Meilland

'Meitrisical' ('Yellow Meillandina', 'Yellow Sunblaze') Min, yb, 1982, Meilland, Mrs. Marie-Louise; flowers yellow, petals edged pink, 20 petals; foliage medium size, dark, semi-glossy; bushy growth; [('Poppy Flash' × ('Charleston' × Allgold®)) × 'Gold Coin']; intr. 1980

'Meitrogana' ('Vabene') HT, my, 1979, Meilland, Mrs. Marie-Louise; bud conical; flowers medium, 30 petals, high-centered; very vigorous, upright growth; ['Arthur Bell' × ('MEIgold' × 'Kabuki')]; intr. 1977

'Meitrosra' LCl, mr

'Meitulandi' ('Michel Hidalgo', Hidalgo®) HT, mr, 1979, Meilland, Mrs. Marie-Louise; bud conical; flowers currant-red, very large, 30 petals, cupped; foliage matte, bronze; vigorous, upright growth; [((Queen Elizabeth® × 'Karl Herbst') × ('Lady X' × 'Pharaon')) × ('MEIcesar' × Papa Meilland®)]

'Meitulimon' (Manou Meilland®) HT, dp, 1979, Meilland, Mrs. Marie-Louise; bud conical; flowers mauve-pink, medium, 50 petals, cupped; foliage glossy, dark; vigorous, bushy growth; [(Baronne Edmond de Rothschild® × Baronne Edmond de Rothschild®) × 'Ma Fille' × 'Love Song')]

'Meitulimonsar' ('Manou Meilland, Climbing') Cl HT, dp, Meilland; intr. 1997

'Meitune' ('Mazurka') F, mp, Meillanddbl.; intr. 1995

'Meituraphar' ('Decor Rose', 'Meilland Decor Rose', Anne de Bretagne®) S, dp, 1979, Meilland, Mrs. Marie-Louise; bud conical; flowers 20 petals, shallow cupped; foliage semi-glossy; vigorous, upright growth; [(('Malcair' × Danse des Sylphes®) × (Zambra® × Zambra®)) × 'Centenair']; intr. 1976

'Meiturbo' HT, lp, Meilland; intr. 2007

'Meiturusa' Min, w, 1976, Meilland; bud long
'Meitylpic' HT, dy, Meillanddbl.; intr. 1999
'Meiunipare' HT, ab, Meilland; intr. 2006
'Meivahyn' (Ice Meidiland®) S, w, Meilland; bud conical, small; intr. 1996
'Meivaleir' ('Michka', Garden Sun™) LCI, ab, 2001, Meilland International; flowers 5 in., full, slight fragrance; foliage large, dark green, glossy; prickles moderate; growth climbing, tall (to 10 ft.); ['Meipalsar' × (Westerland® × 'Circus')]; intr. 1998
'Meivamo' (Paris de Yves St Laurent™) HT, dp, 1995, Meilland; bud conical, large; flowers deep pink, 5 in., 32-35 petals, high-centered, borne mostly singly, slight fragrance; good repeat; foliage large, dark green, glossy; prickles moderate; upright (5 ft.) growth; PP8619; [sport of 'Silva']; intr. 1992
'Meivanama' ('Ondella') HT, or, 1979, Meilland, Mrs. Marie-Louise; bud conical; flowers vermilion, large, 33 petals; foliage dark; vigorous, upright growth; [('Elegy' × 'Arturo Toscanini') × ('Peace' × 'Demain')]
'Meivanery' (Cyrano de Bergerac®, Full Moon Rising™) LCI, ly, 2007, Meilland International; flowers 10 cm., very full, borne in small clusters; foliage large, medium green, semi-glossy; prickles large, numerous; growth climbing, tall (5 ft. or more); pillar; [sport of 'Meitosier (Polka)']; intr. 2007
'Meivanthou' HT, dr; bud conical, large; intr. 1998
'Meivarfal' (Saffron Minuetto™) Min, dy, 2000, Meilland International; flowers deep yellow, reverse medium yellow, 2-3 cm., very full, no fragrance; foliage medium size, dark green, glossy; prickles moderate; compact, medium (8-12 in.) growth; containers, forcing; PPAF; intr. 1999
'Meivestal' ('Dreams Come True', Senator Burda®, 'Spirit of Youth', Victor Hugo®) HT, dr, 1988, Meilland, Mrs. Marie-Louise; flowers brilliant currant-red, large, full, high-centered, intense fragrance; recurrent; foliage large, medium green, semi-glossy; upright, strong, floriferous growth; [('Karl Herbst' × ('Royal Velvet' × 'Suspense')) × Erotika®]
'Meivibroum' ('Pinky Rugostar') HRg, lp, Meillandsingle; intr. 1996
'Meivilanic' ('Stadt Basel', Rustica®, 'Ville de Bâle') F, yb, 1981, Meilland, Mrs. Marie-Louise; bud very long; flowers yellow-peach blend, reverse buff yellow-orange, 35 petals, cupped, borne in clusters, slight fragrance; good repeat; foliage dark green, semi-matte, dense; half-upright growth; [(Queen Elizabeth® × seedling) × 'Sweet Promise']; intr. 1979
'Meivildo' ('Queen Adelaide', Yves Piaget®, 'The Royal Brompton Rose') HT, mp, 1985, Meilland, Mrs. Marie-Louise;

bud globular, fairly large; flowers Neyron pink, 5 in., 80 petals, globular, then cupped, borne mostly singly, intense fragrance; good repeat; foliage medium size, dark green, semi-glossy; upright (3 ft.) growth; PP6895; [((Pharaoh® × 'Peace') × ('Chrysler Imperial' × 'Charles Mallerin')) × 'Tamango']; intr. 1983
'Meivilibor' HT, mr, Meilland; intr. 1981
'Meiviolin' ('Eden Rose 85', Pierre de Ronsard®, 'Eden', Eden Climber™, Grimpant Pierre de Ronsard®) LCI, pb, Meilland, Marie-Louise; bud globular; flowers cream white suffused with carmine pink, 4½-5 in., 40-55 petals, hollow cup, borne in clusters, slight fragrance; recurrent; foliage medium size, deep green, semi-glossy, spreading, climbing growth; [(Danse des Sylphes® × Handel®) × 'Pink Wonder, Climbing']; intr. 1985
'Meiviowit' ('Blanc Pierre de Ronsard', 'Palais Royal', White Eden™) LCI, w, 2004, Meilland International; bud medium, globular; flowers creamy white, 12-13 cm., very full, cupped, borne in small clusters, slight fragrance; recurrent; foliage large, dark green, glossy; prickles very few, short, straight, brown; growth spreading, tall (to 12 ft.); garden; hips round, yellow-green; PP16739; [sport of 'Pierre de Ronsard']
'Meivirgi' Gr, my, 1960, Meilland; bud pointed; intr. 1959
'Meivostro' ('Carinita') Min, pb, Meilland; intr. 1995
'Meivraivou' Min, dr, Meilland; intr. 1994
'Meivrita' ('Seduction') HT, op, Meilland; intr. 1999
'Meivrofix' (Zurella™) F, mp, Meilland
'Meiwaton' ('Hagenbecks Tierpark') LCI, dp, Meilland; intr. 1994
'Meiwhiflo' (September Mourn™) F, w, 2003, Meilland International; bud narrow, ovoid; flowers large, very similar to Iceberg, but with better form, 3½ in., 36 petals, cupped, borne in small clusters; recurrent; foliage large, medium green, semi-glossy; few prickles; bushy, medium (3-4 ft.) growth; specimen, hedge, landscape; [('Iceberg' × 'Sunsprite') × 'Sun Flare']; intr. 2003
'Meiwiling' HT, m, Meilland; bud conical, large; intr. 2003
'Meiwimova' HT, w, Meilland; intr. 2006
'Meiwonder' Pol, mr, 1965, Grootendorst, F.J.; bud globular; flowers small, dbl., borne in clusters; [sport of 'Marianne Kluis Superior']
'Meixerul' ('Peach Meillandina', 'Peach Sunblaze') Min, ab, Meilland; bud conical, small; intr. 1991
'Meixetal' ('Caprice', 'Make-Up') S, lp, Meilland; intr. 1988
'Meiyacom' ('Claudia') HT, mp, Meilland; bud ovoid, large; intr. 1997
'Meiyaki' F, dp, Meilland; intr. 2004
'Meiyolki' ('Golden Starlite') HT, dy, Meillanddbl.; intr. 2002
'Meizabo' S, pb, Meilland; intr. 2000

'Meizalitaf' ('Banzai 83') LCI, yb, Meilland; intr. 1983
'Meizebul' (Jardins de France™, Passionate Kisses™) F, mp, 2001, Meilland International; flowers bright salmon-pink, 3 in., semi-dbl., borne in large clusters, slight fragrance; foliage medium size, medium green, semi-glossy; prickles small, few; growth bushy, tall (4-5 ft.); hedges, landscape; PPAF; ['Celine Delbard' × 'Laura']
'Meizeli' ('McCartney Rose', 'Paul McCartney', 'Sweet Lady', The McCartney Rose™) HT, mp, 1995, Meilland, Alain; bud oval, medium; flowers medium pink, reverse lighter, 4½-5 in., 20-22 petals, cupped, borne mostly singly and in small clusters, intense fragrance; good repeat; foliage large, medium green, semi-glossy; prickles numerous, medium, brownish; bushy, medium growth; PP8391; [('Nirvana' × Papa Meilland®) × 'First Prize']
'Meizepline' HT, dr, Meillanddbl.; intr. 2004
'Meizerbil' (Crimson Meidiland™) S, mr, 2007, Meilland International; flowers small, semi-dbl., borne in large clusters; foliage small, dark green, glossy; prickles small, moderate; growth spreading, short (3 ft.); groundcover; [seedling × seedling]; intr. 2008
'Meiziba' F, pb; intr. 2007
'Meizincaro' ('First Blush', Peter Mayle™, Lolita Lempicka®, 'Mainauduft') HT, dp, 2003, Meilland International; bud conical; flowers rose magenta, 4-5 in., 55 petals, cupped, borne mostly solitary, intense fruity and acidulous fragrance; good repeat; foliage dark green, glossy; bushy (4 ft.) growth; PP11660; [('Miss All-American Beauty' × Papa Meilland®) × 'Susan Hampshire']; intr. 2002
'Meizincarosar' ('Lolita Lempicka, Climbing') Cl HT, dp; intr. 2005
'Meizmea' ('Red Carefree Delight') S, rb, Meilland; intr. 2006
'Meizoele' ('Philippe Noiret', Glowing Peace™) Gr, yb, 1999, Selection Meilland; flowers yellow and orange blend, medium, 35-40 petals, borne in small clusters, slight fragrance; foliage medium size, dark green, glossy; prickles moderate; upright, bushy, medium growth; ['Sun King' × Roxane®]; intr. 2001
'Meizogrel' ('Spot Minijet', White MiniWonder™) Min, w, 1988, Meilland, Alain A.; bud conical, small; flowers clear white, thin petals, 1½ in., 40 petals, flat cup, borne in small clusters, no fragrance; free-flowering; foliage small, medium green, matte; prickles few, very small; short (12 in.), bushy growth; PP7276; [White Gem® × 'Cinderella']
'Meizourayor' ('Decor Arlequin', 'Meilland Decor Arlequin') S, rb, 1979, Meilland, Mrs. Marie-Louise; flowers strawberry-red and yellow, medium, 18 petals, cupped; foliage dark; very vigorous,

upright growth; [((Zambra® × Zambra®) × ('Suspense' × 'Suspense')) × 'Arthur Bell']; intr. 1977

'Meizules' HT, rb, Meilland; intr. 2001

'Meizuzes' ('Madam Speaker') HT, rb; intr. 1996

'Mejakka' ('Rosy Wings') S, rb, 1997, Mekdeci, John; flowers large, 8-15 petals, borne in large clusters; foliage large, medium green, glossy; spreading, tall (6 ft.) growth; ['Dornroschen' × 'Golden Wings']

'Mejoria' ('John's Rose') S, ob, 1995, Mekdeci, John; flowers brilliant orange to fluorescent pink, 3-3½ in., dbl., borne in small clusters, no fragrance; free-flowering; foliage large, dark green, glossy; some prickles; tall, upright growth; [(('Tropicana' × 'Queen of the Lakes') × seedling) × 'Golden Wings']; intr. 1995

'Mekkada' ('Butterflies') S, ob, 1997, Mekdeci, Dr. Anthony Casimir; flowers medium, single, borne in large clusters; foliage medium size, medium green, semi-glossy; bushy (5ft.) growth; ['Dornroschen' × 'Golden Wings']; intr. 1989

'Mel Hulse' -- See 'Ardkernel'

'Mel Lippincott' Gr, rb, Williams, J. B.; flowers burgundy red with ivory-pink striping, borne in clusters; intr. 1998

'Mel Rince' Min; intr. 2000

'Melanie' S, dr, 1946, Wright, Percy H.; flowers deep red, semi-dbl.; non-recurrent; foliage reddish; hardy (to about -15); [R. rubrifolia × 'Gruss an Teplitz']

'Melanie' HT, dp, Combe; bud long; flowers carmine-pink, dbl.; vigorous growth; ['Sterling' × 'Mme Auguste Chatain']; intr. 1958

'Melanie' -- See 'Macmelan'

'Mélanie Cornu' HP, m, 1841, Cornu; flowers bright reddish-violet, large, full

'Mélanie de Montjoie' HSem, w, before 1829, Jacques; flowers pure white, large, full, flat, borne in corymbs; foliage widely-set, small, lanceolate, glossy; prickles few, equal, straight, thin; stems smooth, tinted reddish; vigorous growth

'Mélanie Lemarié' -- See 'Hermosa'

'Mélanie Soupert' T, w, 1881, Nabonnand, G.; flowers pure white, large, very full; ['Gloire de Dijon' × unknown]

'Mélanie Waldor' HGal, w, 1836, Vibert; flowers chalk white, medium, full

'Mélanie Waldor' M, m, 1865, Moreau et Robert; flowers lilac pink, white center, medium, flat; some repeat; intr. 1865

'Mélanie Willermoz' -- See 'Mme Mélanie Willermoz'

'Melany' -- See 'Poulen008(N)'

'Melba' -- See 'Times Past'

'Melba' F, yb, 1963, Sanday, John; flowers soft cream and peach, well-formed, small, dbl., borne in clusters; foliage light green; spreading growth; ['Masquerade' × ('Independence' × unknown)]

'Melba Jean' -- See 'Geljean'

'Melchior Salet' -- See 'Salet'

'Meleagris' -- See 'Pintade'

'Meletta' -- See 'Geletta'

'Melflor' F, lp, RvS-Melle; intr. 1988

'Melglory' F, mr, 1985, Rijksstation Voor Sierplantenteelt; flowers large, 23 petals, borne in clusters of 4-16, no fragrance; foliage dark, matte; upright growth; [Lilli Marleen® × 'Patricia']; intr. 1982

'Melgold' HT, dy, 1985, Rijksstation Voor Sierplantenteelt; flowers large, 62 petals, cupped, borne singly and in small clusters, no fragrance; foliage dark, matte; prickles reddish-green; upright growth; ['Sunblest' × 'Souv. de Jacques Verschuren']; intr. 1980

Meli-Melo® HT, rb, Orard; flowers clear red, white reverse, striped yellow, slight fragrance; growth medium, vigorous; intr. 1998

'Melica' HT, op, Hicl

'Melik El Adel' -- See 'Malek-Adel'

Melina® -- See 'Tanema'

'Melinda' -- See 'Rulimpa'

Melinda Alonso™ -- See 'Alolinda'

'Melinda Claire' -- See 'Taymel'

'Melinda Gainsford' -- See 'Jacyap'

'Melinda Marie' F, lp, 1977, Linscott; bud ovoid; flowers clear light pink, 3 in., 20-25 petals, flat; foliage dark, leathery; bushy growth; [Sarabande® × Sarabande®]; intr. 1972

'Mélisande' HT, lp, 1964, Mondial Roses; bud long; flowers soft pink, reverse darker, well-formed, large, dbl.; foliage dark; long, strong stems; vigorous, symmetrical growth

'Mélissa' HT, dy, Sauvageot; flowers chrome yellow, tinted at center with salmon, dbl.; intr. 2003

'Melissa' HT, mp, 1977, McDaniel, Earl; flowers 4 in., 27-32 petals, globular; foliage leathery; very vigorous, upright, bushy growth; PP4082; [seedling × seedling]; intr. 1975

'Melissa' Min, rb, Martin, J.; intr. 1985

'Melissa' F, lp, Noack, Werner; intr. 1996

'Melissa Joyce' -- See 'Renhom'

'Melissa McCartney' F, dp, 1991, Troyer, Ray & Pat; bud ovoid; flowers hold color well, do not fade, 5 in., 36 petals, high-centered, borne usually singly; foliage medium size, dark green, glossy, slight red tinge to new growth; growth bushy, low (70 cm.); [sport of 'Cherish']

'Melita' HWich, mp, 1934, Easlea; flowers carnation-pink, 5-6 cm., dbl., borne in small to medium clusters; non-recurrent; foliage glossy, light; vigorous, climbing growth; [sport of 'Thelma']

'Melle Fischer' Pol, mp, 1914, Pfitzer; flowers small, dbl.

'Mellow' HT, ab, Dawson; intr. 1995

'Mellow Glow' HT, pb, 1990, Bridges, Dennis A.; bud ovoid; flowers medium pink, reverse creamy yellow, medium, 52 petals, high-centered, borne usually singly, intense damask fragrance; foliage medium size, medium green, semi-glossy; prickles pointed slightly downward, large, yellow; bushy growth; ['Thriller' × 'Wild Cherry']; intr. 1990

'Mellow Yellow' -- See 'Wekosomit'

'Mellow Yellow' -- See 'Cocyearn'

'Mellow Yellow' HT, my, 1968, Waterhouse Nursery; flowers sunflower-yellow, edged pink, urn-shaped; free growth; [sport of 'Piccadilly']

'Melmore Terrace' HSem, w

'Melo-melo-day' Cl F, mp, 1955, Motose; bud ovoid; flowers cameo-pink, 2-2½ in., very dbl., cupped, moderate fragrance; climbing (10-15 ft.) growth; PP1428; [sport of 'Demure']

Melodie® F, mr, Noack, Werner; intr. 1980

'Mélodie' HT, ly, Dickson; flowers creamy pale lemon with white, well-formed, dbl.; good repeat; growth to 90-100 cm.; intr. 1999

'Melodie Parfumée' -- See 'Dorient'

'Melodie Parfumée, Climbing' ('Violette Parfumee, Climbing', Grimpant Violette Parfumée®) Cl HT, m, Dorieux; flowers purple with silver tones, large, intense fragrance; [sport of 'Melodie Parfumee']; intr. 2004

'Melody' -- See 'Korbolak'

Melody™ -- See 'Melody Hit'

'Melody' HT, yb, 1911, Scott; flowers intense saffron yellow bordered spring yellow, medium to large, very dbl.; foliage dark violet green

'Melody' HT, pb, Lammerts, Dr. Walter; bud urn-shaped; flowers deep pink, edged lighter, large, 35 petals, moderate fragrance; low, bushy growth; ['Joanna Hill' × 'Miss C.E. van Rossem']; intr. 1946

'Melody Hit' (Melody™) MinFl, dp, Poulsen; flowers deep pink, 5-8 cm., dbl., no fragrance; growth narrow, bushy, 40-60 cm.; PP11514; intr. 1998

'Melody Lane' -- See 'Miclane'

'Melody Maker' F, or, 1990, Dickson, Patrick; flowers light vermillion with silver reverse, large, full, high-centered, borne in clusters; foliage medium size, dark green, semi-glossy; bushy growth; ['Anisley Dickson' × 'Wishing']; intr. 1991

'Melody Marshall' -- See 'Mormelma'

Melody Parfumée™ -- See 'Dorient'

'Melody Queen' HT, pb, Ghosh, Mr. and Mrs. S.; bud conical; flowers white with pink glow, large; intr. 1998

'Melonda' HT, ob, J&P; flowers yellowish salmon-orange, very large, dbl.; intr. 1974

'Melpink' F, lp, RvS-Melle; ['Centurion' × 'Patricia']; intr. 1983

'Melrose' HT, rb, 1963, Dickson, A.; flowers creamy white flushed cherry-red, large, 35 petals, moderate fragrance; foliage dark, leathery; vigorous, bushy growth; ['Silver Lining' × 'E.G. Hill']

'Melrose' F, dp, RvS-Melle; flowers 3 in., 24 petals, borne in large clusters, intense fragrance; growth to 2 ft.; ['Melflor' × 'Melglory']; intr. 1992

'Melvena' HT, op, 1972, Dawson, George; bud ovoid; flowers salmon-pink, medium, dbl., moderate fragrance; foliage leathery; vigorous, upright growth; ['Daily Sketch' × 'Impeccable']

'Melvin' F, rb, 1981, Jerabek, Paul E.; bud pointed; flowers ivory, flushed red, aging darker red, 30 petals, high-centered, borne in clusters of up to 11; foliage medium green; prickles triangular, hooked; medium, dense growth; [seedling × seedling]

'Memaj' ('Thaïs') HT, yb, 1957, Meilland, F.; bud ovoid with conspicuous neck; intr. 1954

'Mémé Buy' HT, or, 1935, Chambard, C.; flowers coppery coral-red, lightly streaked golden yellow, large, very dbl., cupped; foliage bronze; very vigorous growth

'Mémée Arles' HT, dr, 1955, Arles; flowers deep red tinted vermilion; foliage glaucous green; ['Peace' × 'Emma Wright']

'Mémée Azy' HT, pb, 1921, Gillot, F.; flowers pink shaded carmine, bordered whitish, stamens orange-yellow, dbl.; ['Étoile de France' × 'Le Progres']

'Mémée Chanteur' F, dr, 1961, Arles; bud ovoid; flowers deep crimson, large, dbl., cupped, borne in clusters; foliage dark, leathery; vigorous, upright growth; ['Karl Herbst' × 'Pioupiou']; intr. 1959

Memento® -- See 'Dicbar'

Memoire® -- See 'Korzuri'

Memorial Day™ -- See 'Wekblunez'

'Memoriam' HT, lp, 1961, Von Abrams; bud long, pointed; flowers pastel pink to nearly white, 6 in., 55 petals, high-centered, moderate fragrance; foliage dark, leathery; moderately tall growth; PP2280; [('Blanche Mallerin' × 'Peace') × ('Peace' × 'Frau Karl Druschki')]; intr. 1961

'Memories' -- See 'Hamera'

'Memories' HT, dy, 1979, Byrum; bud short, pointed, ovoid; flowers empire-yellow, 2½-3 in., 25-30 petals, high-centered, intense tea fragrance; continuous bloom in greenhouse; foliage large, glossy; vigorous, upright, bushy growth; PP4407; ['Spanish Sun' × 'Hoosier Gold']; intr. 1977

'Memories' S, mp, Clements, John K.; flowers warm pink, large, very full, moderate fragrance; free-flowering; foliage rich green; slightly spreading (4 × 3 ft.) growth; intr. 1996

Memory™ -- See 'Pouldata'

Memory™ -- See 'Korzuri'

'Memory' HT, pb, 1932, Cant, B. R.; bud pointed; flowers light pink to deeper pink, base yellow, very large, dbl., high-centered; foliage rich green, leathery; vigorous, compact growth

'Memory' HT, dp, Kordes; flowers bright magenta pink, medium, dbl., high-centered, borne mostly singly; intr. 2001

'Memory Bells' -- See 'Poulma'

'Memory Hit' (Memory ™) MinFl, ob, Poulsen; flowers orange and orange blend, 5-8 cm., dbl., slight wild rose fragrance; foliage dark; growth bushy, 20-40 cm.; intr. 2000

Memory Lane™ -- See 'Poulbella'

'Memory Lane' -- See 'Peavoodoo'

'Memory Lane' Min, lp, 1974, Moore, Ralph S.; bud ovoid; flowers rose-pink, small, very dbl.; foliage leathery; vigorous, dwarf, bushy growth; [('Pinocchio' × 'William Lobb') × 'Little Chief']; intr. 1973

'Memory of D. M. Roy' HT, w, Ghosh

Memphis™ (Intense Cover™) S, mr, Poulsen; flowers bright red, fading as they mature, small, semi-dbl., slight wild rose fragrance; foliage dark, glossy; broad, bushy (60-100 cm.) growth; PP15111; intr. 2002

'Memphis' HT, dp, Select Roses, B.V.

'Memphis Bell' -- See 'Welhis 0464'

'Memphis Blues' -- See 'Welblue'

'Memphis Cajun' -- See 'Welcajun'

'Memphis Heritage' Gr, pb, 1969, Patterson; bud long, pointed; flowers pink blended with gold, large, dbl., high-centered, moderate fragrance; very vigorous, compact growth; PP3113; [Queen Elizabeth® × 'Happiness']

'Memphis King' -- See 'Welking'

'Memphis Magic' -- See 'Welmagic'

'Memphis Music' -- See 'Welmusic'

'Memphis Queen' -- See 'Welqueen'

'Ménage' A, w, 1847, Vibert; flowers flesh, 6 cm., dbl., cupped

'Ménage' M, mp, Robert & Moreau; flowers bright carmine pink, 7-9 cm., full, flat; intr. 1858

'Menaka Durga Roy' -- See 'Driscoroy'

'Ménap' HT, my, 1955, Meilland, F.

'Mendel' F, mr, 1946, Leenders, M.; bud pointed; flowers cherry-red, 4 in., 15 petals, borne in trusses; foliage reddish green; vigorous, bushy growth; ['Florentina' × seedling]

'Mendocino Delight' HWich, w, Demits; once-bloomer; growth to 20 ft.; intr. 1988

'Mendocino Gothic' HMsk, w, Demits, Joyce; flowers borne in flushes; recurrent; chance seedling; possibly 'The Gift' × 'Lamarque'; intr. 1993

Mengia® S, dp, Huber; flowers rose pink , 5-6 in., full, borne singly and in clusters, moderate fruity fragrance; recurrent; foliage large, dark green; strong (150 - 200 cm.) growth; intr. 2006

'Menine' HT, mr, Laperrière; flowers carmine red, moderate fragrance; intr. 1977

'Menja' HMsk, mp, Petersen; flowers medium pink when opening, fading quickly to pale pink, small, single, cupped, borne in medium clusters, slight fragrance; foliage light green; growth to 4-5 ft.; intr. 1960

'Mennie d'Agnin' F, mr, 1962, Orard, Joseph; flowers vermilion-red, large; ['Independence' × 'Fashion']

'Menoux' B, lp, 1845, Lacharme; flowers light carmine pink, large, full

'Menoux' HMult, dp, Jobert; flowers pink, with a bluing edge, medium, full, borne in large clusters; ['Laure Davoust' × unknown]; intr. 1848

'Mentor' S, mp, 1960, Wyant; bud globular; flowers light pink, reverse darker, medium, dbl., intense fragrance; recurrent bloom; foliage dark, glossy; very vigorous (6 ft.), bushy, upright growth; ['Tallyho' × 'New Dawn']; intr. 1959

'Menuett' HT, ob, Hill, S. H.; flowers orange and yellow, large, dbl.; intr. 1961

'Menuett' HT, yb, GPG Bad Langensalza; flowers dark yellow with carmine pink, large, dbl.; intr. 1988

'Menut' Min, dp, 1958, Dot, Simon; flowers carmine, small, 20 petals; abundant, intermittent bloom; dwarf, bushy, compact growth; ['Rouletii' × 'Perla de Alcañada']; intr. 1956

'Mepal' HT, op, 1953, Meilland, F.

'Mepalsar' (Grimpant Bettina®) Cl HT, op, 1959, Meilland, F.; intr. 1958

'Méphisto' F, or, 1951, Mallerin, C.; flowers geranium-red, medium, semi-dbl., borne in clusters; foliage leathery; vigorous, upright, bushy growth; ['Francais' × seedling]

'Mephisto' Pol, or, GPG Bad Langensalza; flowers large, semi-dbl.; intr. 1985

'Mercantour' F, my, Dickson; intr. 2008

'Mercator' HT, dr, 1962, Delforge; flowers deep red, large, dbl.; foliage dark; ['Chrysler Imperial' × 'Tango']

'Mercedes' HGal, lp, 1847, Vibert; flowers white and lilac, changing to pale pink, large, dbl., moderate fragrance; spring flowering; growth to 3-5 ft.; sometimes classed as M

'Mercedes, Climbing' Cl F, or, Ruston, D.; [sport of 'Mercedes']; intr. 1982

Mercedes® F, or, Kordes, R.; bud ovoid; flowers bright scarlet, medium, 33 petals, high-centered; foliage large, leathery; PP3724; [Anabell® × seedling]; greenhouse rose; intr. 1974

'Mercedes' HMult, lp, Geschwind; flowers pale lilac pink, medium; sometimes classified as HSet; intr. 1886

'Mercédès' HRg, lp, Guillot, P.; flowers delicate carnation pink on a white ground, outer petals white, large, full; very hardy; intr. 1900

'Mercedes Gallart' Cl HT, dp, 1932, Munné, B.; flowers deep pink, base yellow, very large, dbl.; recurrent bloom; foliage glossy; very vigorous, climbing growth; ['Souv. de Claudius Denoyel' × 'Souv. de Claudius Pernet']

'Mercedes Juncadella' HT, op, 1933, Munné, B.; flowers salmon-orange; ['Frau Karl Druschki' × 'Angèle Pernet']

Mercedes Kordana® Min, or, Kordes; flowers dbl., high-centered; recurrent; pot rose

'Mercedes Mendoza' HT, or, 1962, Dot, Simon; flowers large, 30 petals; foliage glossy; vigorous growth; ['Asturias' × 'Grand'mère Jenny']

'Mercedia' HT, or, Kordes; greenhouse

rose; intr. 2002
'Merci' F, mr, 1972, Warriner, William A.; bud ovoid, long, pointed; flowers medium, dbl.; foliage dark, leathery; vigorous growth; PP3144; intr. 1971

Merci® F, mr, Kordes; flowers velvety red, small to medium, full, high-centered, flat top, borne mostly singly; free-flowering; stems moderate; florist rose; intr. 2005

'Mercurius' LCl, op, 1940, Horvath; flowers light coral-pink, large, semi-dbl., cupped, borne in clusters; profuse seasonal bloom; foliage glossy; vigorous, climbing growth; PP385; [('Doubloons' × 'damask') × 'Clio']

'Mercury' HT, mr, Kordes; flowers bright red, large, full, high-centered; foliage dark green, glossy; intr. 2005

'Mercury' F, or, 1967, Sanday, John; flowers orange-scarlet edged mahogany, borne in clusters; foliage dark; low, bushy growth; ['Independence' × 'Paprika']

'Mercy' -- See 'Simmer'

'Mère de la Patrie' -- See 'Mother's Country'

'Mère de St Louis' ('La Mère de St Louis') HP, w, 1851, Lacharme; flowers waxy flesh-white aging to delicate pink, medium, dbl.

'Mère Gigogne' -- See 'Prolifera de Redouté'

Meredith™ -- See 'Wekmeredoc'

'Meredith' LCl, lp, 1983, Thomson, Richard; flowers light pink to almost white, large, 20 petals, high-centered, moderate fragrance; repeat blooming; foliage large, dark, semi-glossy; long stems; upright (to 12 ft.) growth; [('Charlotte Armstrong' × 'New Dawn') × 'Araby']; intr. 1984

'Meredith Anne' -- See 'Tinmere'

'Meredith Bohls' -- See 'Ponmer'

'Meredith Hughes' Min, op, 1984, Dobbs, Annette E.; flowers medium coral pink, medium, dbl., high-centered; foliage medium size, medium green, glossy; bushy growth; ['Anne Scranton' × 'Patricia Scranton']

Merengue™ -- See 'Poulra026'

'Merengue' -- See 'Poulcy012'

'Merengue Parade' (Merengue™) Min, yb, Poulsen; flowers yellow blend, medium, dbl., no fragrance; growth bushy, 20-40 cm.; intr. 2003

'Merete Stenbock' HCh, w; flowers creamy white, suffused with rose-brown, dbl.; borne in small clusters; foliage dark green; vigorous (80 cm.) growth; intr. 1996

'Mériame de Rothschild' T, dp, 1897, Cochet; flowers carmine pink, edged silver, center darker, reverse shaded dark red, dbl.

'Meridian' HT, mr, VEG; flowers luminous red, very large, dbl.

Meridiana® -- See 'Barmeri'

'Meriggio' S, op, 1998, Barni, V.; flowers coral, edges darker, 15-20 petals, high-centered; growth to 130-150 cm.

'Merindah' HMult, mp, Sutherland; intr. 1994

'Merindah Red' HMult, mr, Sutherland; intr. 1995

'Meringue Kisses' -- See 'Talming'

'Merit' F, mp, 1952, Domilla; bud short, pointed; flowers brilliant rose, reverse lighter, base white, 1½-2 in., 50-90 petals, flat, borne in clusters, intense fragrance; foliage leathery, dark; very vigorous, bushy growth; PP1061; [sport of 'Garnette']

'Merit' -- See 'Spomerit'

'Merko' F, or, Kordes, R.; bud ovoid; intr. 1974

'Merkor' F, or, Kordes, R.; bud ovoid; intr. 1974

'Merle Blanc' -- See 'Lenisur'

'Merlin' F, pb, 1967, Harkness; flowers yellow, pink and red, 2½ in., dbl., borne in clusters; foliage glossy; ['Pink Parfait' × 'Circus']

'Merlin' S, lp, Poulsen; intr. 1991

'Merlot' -- See 'Benfebu'

Mermaid™ -- See 'Mermaid Palace'

'Mermaid' HBc, ly, 1918, Paul, W.; flowers creamy yellow, amber stamens,, 5-6 in., 5 petals; dependably recurrent; foliage dark, glossy; vigorous, climbing, pillar or trailer (6-9 ft.) growth; tender incold regions; [R. bracteata × double yellow tea]

'Mermaid Palace' (Mermaid™) Min, or, Poulsen; flowers orange-red, 5 cm., dbl., no fragrance; foliage dark; growth bushy, 40-60 cm.; PP15570; intr. 2003

'Mernieuw' -- See 'Romeo'

'Merrie' -- See 'Jaymer'

'Merrie England' HP, pb, 1897, Harkness; flowers crimson pink, striped silvery; [sport of 'Heinrich Schultheis']

'Merrie Miss' HT, mp, 1975, Fuller; bud long, ovoid; flowers soft rose-pink, 4 in., 60 petals, high-centered, intense fragrance; foliage dark, matte; upright, bushy growth; ['Pink Favorite' × 'Margaret']

Merrimac™ -- See 'Kinmac'

'Merriment' Min, yb, 1986, Bridges, Dennis A.; flowers bright yellow tipped red, reverse yellow edged red, 8 petals; foliage large, medium green, semi-glossy; prickles medium, long, pink; tall, upright growth; ['Rise 'n' Shine' × unknown]

'Merry Christmas' Min, mr, 1977, Lyon; bud pointed; flowers currant-red, open, 2 in., 5 petals; foliage dark; upright, compact, branching growth; ['Red Can Can' × unknown]

'Merry England' HP, mr, 1897, Harkness; flowers satiny light red, shaded carmine, 50 petals, intense fragrance; vigorous growth

'Merry-Go-Round' HT, op, 1950, Fisher, G.; bud pointed, becoming urn shaped, orange; flowers orange and pink blend, 5 in., 25 petals; foliage dark, leathery; tall, compact growth; PP1081; ['Talisman' × R.M.S. Queen Mary]

'Merry Go Round' F, rb; flowers greenwhite with thick petal edging of deep carmine, full, rosette, borne mostly in clusters; recurrent; healthy, vigorous, medium growth

'Merry Go Round' F, w; intr. 2006

'Merry Heart' Gr, rb, 1960, Swim, H.C.; bud ovoid; flowers Orient red, 3½-4 in., 30 petals, high-centered, borne in small clusters; foliage glossy, dark; vigorous, upright growth; PP1846; ['El Capitan' × seedling]; intr. 1960

'Merry Widow' Gr, dr, 1958, Lammerts, Dr. Walter; bud long, pointed; flowers velvety crimson, 6 in., 23 petals, cupped, intense spicy fragrance; foliage dark, glossy; vigorous growth; PP1711; ['Mirandy' × 'Grande Duchesse Charlotte']; intr. 1957

Merryglo™ -- See 'Minimerr'

'Merryweather's Crimson' HT, mr, 1958, Merryweather; flowers bright crimson, well-formed; strong stems; vigorous, bushy growth

'Mers du Sud' -- See 'South Seas'

'Merveille' -- See 'Tausendschön'

'Merveille d'Anjou' HP, m, 1867, Touvais; flowers bright garnet-purple, very large, full

'Merveille de Gien' -- See 'Jacolman'

'Merveille de la Brie' HWich, mr; flowers scarlet red, white eye, 3-4 cm., semi-dbl., borne in medium clusters; once-blooming

'Merveille de l'Univers' HGal, rb, before 1827, from Belgium; flowers carmine, edged lilac, large, very full

'Merveille de Lyon' HP, w, 1882, Pernet Père; flowers pure white, tinted satiny rose, 4 in., dbl., cupped, borne mostly solitary; some recurrent bloom; foliage light green; prickles numerous, upright; vigorous growth; ['Baronne Adolphe de Rothschild' × 'Safrano']

'Merveille des Blanches' HP, w, 1894, Pernet; flowers medium-large, dbl.

'Merveille des Jaunes' Pol, yb, 1920, Turbat; flowers bright coppery golden yellow, dbl., borne in clusters; dwarf growth

'Merveille des Polyanthas' Pol, w, 1909, Mermet; flowers white, aging to lilac pink; foliage light green

'Merveille des Rouges' Pol, rb, 1911, Dubreuil; flowers deep velvety crimson, center whitish, semi-dbl., cupped, borne in large clusters; dwarf growth

'Merveille du Monde' -- See 'Roi des Pays-Bas'

'Merveilleuse' HT, Dot, Simon

'Mervelle' HT, McGredy, Sam IV; intr. 1995

'Meryl Jane Gaskin' HT, pb, 1948, Mee; flowers shell-pink edged deeper pink, well-formed, 5-6 in., 48 petals; free, branching growth; [sport of 'Rose Berkeley']

'Message' ('White Knight') HT, w, 1957, Meilland, F.; bud long, pointed; flowers clear white, 4 in., 28-35 petals, high-centered, opens cupped, borne singly,

no fragrance; recurrent; foliage leathery, light green; prickles several, medium, straight, pointed downward; vigorous, upright growth; hips none ; PP1359; [('Virgo' × 'Peace') × 'Virgo']; intr. 1955
'Message, Climbing' ('White Knight, Climbing') Cl HT, w, 1967, Meilland (also Komatsu, 1959)
'Message 91' HT, my, Meilland; flowers clear Naples yellow, full, high-centered; cut flower variety; intr. 1991
'Messagere' -- See 'Betty Herholdt'
'Messara' F, ab; flowers creamy vanilla with touches of rose, deepens with age, very dbl., hybrid tea, borne in clusters; growth compact; intr. 1997
'Messestadt Hannover' ('Hannover') F, mr, 1965, Kordes, R.; flowers large, dbl., borne in clusters; foliage light green, glossy; moderate growth; intr. 1964
'Messidor' HT, dy
'Messire' LCl, mr, 1963, Laperrière; flowers bright scarlet red, 3 in., 10-15 petals, borne singly or in small clusters; profuse, repeated bloom; foliage bronze; moderately vigorous growth; [seedling × 'Spectacular']
Messire Delbard® -- See 'Delsire'
'Mrs Gillen' -- See 'Mrs M. J. Gillon'
'Meta' T, rb, 1898, Dickson, A.; flowers strawberry red touched with saffron yellow
'Metallina' HT, r, Kordes; flowers metallic silver, opening to pale mauve; greenhouse rose; intr. 1999
Metanoia® LCl, ob; flowers semi-dbl.; growth to 10 ft.
'Meteor' N, dp, 1887, Geschwind, R.; flowers deep rose tinted carmine-purple, 7 cm., dbl., moderate fragrance; good repeat; vigorous growth
'Meteor, Climbing' Cl HT, mr, 1901, Dingee & Conard
Meteor® F, or, 1959, Kordes, R.; flowers orange-scarlet, 3 in., 40 petals, cupped, borne in clusters (up to 10); foliage light green; vigorous, bushy, low growth; patio; ['Feurio' × 'Gertrud Westphal']
'Meteor' -- See 'The Meteor'
'Meteor Shower' -- See 'Jacpan'
'Meteor Sparks' Min, ob; intr. 2004
'Metis' ('Simonet') S, mp, 1975, Harp; bud ovoid; flowers soft rose, 2½-3 in., 35 petals, flat; spring bloom; foliage small, glossy; [R. nitida × 'Therese Bugnet']; intr. 1967
'Métro' -- See 'Macbucpal'
'Metropole' HT, mp, 1961, deRuiter; flowers 4-6 in., 45 petals, globular; foliage matte, green; vigorous growth; ['Sidney Peabody' × 'Peace']
'Metset' -- See 'Christian'
'Metset' ('Cristian') F, m, (METset)
Mette™ -- See 'Poulpar032(N)'
'Mette Parade' (Mette™) MinFl, w, Poulsen; flowers white, 5-8 cm., full, no fragrance; recurrent; bushy (20-40 cm.) growth; intr. 2004
'Mevrouw A. del Court van Krimpen' HT, lp, 1917, Leenders, M.; flowers flesh-white and pale pink, tinted copper, large, dbl., moderate fragrance; [seedling × 'Prince de Bulgarie']
'Mevrouw A. H. de Beaufort' HT, pb, 1934, Van Rossem; flowers clear salmon-pink, large, dbl.; foliage bronze, glossy; vigorous growth; ['Morgenglans' × 'Gooiland Beauty']
'Mevrouw Amélie Müller' HT, yb, 1927, Verschuren; flowers old-gold, shaded orange, dbl., moderate fragrance; growth to 3 ft.; ['Golden Ophelia' × 'Golden Emblem']
'Mevrouw Boreel van Hogelander' HT, w, 1918, Leenders, M.; flowers flesh-white shaded carmine and pink, medium, dbl., intense fragrance; ['Mme Leon Pain' × 'Mme Antoine Mari']
'Mevrouw C. van Marwijk Kooy' HT, w, 1921, Leenders, M.; flowers white, center Indian yellow, sometimes coppery orange, large, dbl., moderate fragrance; ['Mme Caroline Testout' × 'Mrs Aaron Ward']
'Mevrouw D. A. Koster' Pol, mr, 1934, Koster, D.A.; flowers bright red; [sport of 'Dick Koster']
'Mevrouw Daendels' -- See 'Mrs Henri Daendels'
'Mevrouw Dr L. Crobach' HT, pb, 1928, Leenders, M.; flowers carmine, base salmon, dbl.; ['Pink Pearl' × 'Red Star']
'Mevrouw Dora van Tets' HT, mr, 1913, Leenders, M.; flowers velvety deep crimson, medium, dbl., moderate fragrance; ['Farbenkonigin' × 'Gen. MacArthur']
'Mevrouw G. A. van Rossem' ('Mrs G. A. van Rossem') HT, ob, 1929, Van Rossem; flowers orange and apricot on golden yellow, veined red, reverse often dark bronze, large, dbl., intense fragrance; foliage very large, dark, bronze, leathery; vigorous, upright growth; ['Souv. de Claudius Pernet' × 'Gorgeous']
'Mevrouw G. A. van Rossem, Climbing' ('Mrs G. A. van Rossem, Climbing') Cl HT, ob, 1937, Gaujard; flowers dark orange yellow, large, full; [sport of 'Mevrouw G. A. van Rossem']
'Mevrouw G. de Jonge van Zwynsbergen' HT, pb, 1923, Leenders, M.; flowers pale flesh, center flesh-pink and salmon, dbl.; ['Mme Mélanie Soupert' × 'George C. Waud']
'Mevrouw H. Cremer' HT, mr, 1932, Buisman, G. A. H.; flowers large, dbl.
'Mevrouw Henri Daendels' HT, op, 1931, Buisman, G. A. H.; flowers light salmon, large, very dbl.
'Mevrouw L. C. van Gendt' HT, ab, 1925, Van Rossem; flowers salmon-apricot on yellow ground, dbl.; [seedling × 'Golden Emblem']
'Mevrouw Lala Philips' HT, or, 1931, Leenders Bros.; flowers brilliant orange-toned shrimp-red, well-formed, large, dbl.; foliage dark; vigorous growth; [sport of 'Elvira Aramayo']
'Mevrouw M. J. Gillon' -- See 'Mrs M. J. Gillon'
'Mevrouw Nathalie Nypels' ('Nathalie Nypels') Pol, mp, 1919, Leenders, M.; flowers rose-pink, medium, semi-dbl.; dwarf, spreading growth; ['Orléans Rose' × ('Comtesse du Cayla' × 'Jaune Bicolore')]
'Mevrouw S. van den Bergh, Jr.' -- See 'Mrs Vandenbergh'
'Mevrouw Smits Gompertz' HT, op, 1917, Leenders, M.; flowers yellowish-salmon and coppery orange shaded lilac, medium, dbl., intense fragrance; ['Lady Wenlock' × ('Mme J.W. Budde' × 'Souv. de Catherine Guillot')]
'Mevrouw van Straaten van Nes' -- See 'Permanent Wave'
'Mevrouw Welmoet van Heexk' HT, dp, 1933, Buisman, G. A. H.; flowers carmine-red, well-formed; foliage dark; vigorous, bushy growth
'Mexica Aurantia' -- See 'Tricolore'
'Mexicali Rose' F, yb, 1957, Whisler; bud short, pointed, yellow suffused red; flowers deep yellow turning deep rose-pink, then cerise-red, open, 3 in., 65-70 petals, slight spicy fragrance; foliage dark; vigorous, upright growth; PP1496; [(('Herrenhausen' × unknown) × 'Golden Rapture') × 'Easter Parade']; intr. 1956
'Mexican Festival' S, dp, Dickson, Patrick; flowers single; intr. 1996
Mexican Girl® HT, rb, Tantau; flowers red, reverse yellow and red, medium , double, high-centered , borne mostly singly; recurrent; stems medium; florist rose; intr. 2007
'Mexicana' HT, rb, 1966, Boerner; bud ovoid; flowers red, reverse silvery, large, 33 petals, high-centered, moderate fragrance; foliage dark, glossy, leathery; vigorous, upright growth; PP2636; ['Kordes' Perfecta' × seedling]
'Mexico' HP, m, 1863, Bruant; flowers velvety purple, shaded black, large, full
'Mexico' F, or, Krause; bud globular, deep carmine; flowers deep scarlet, suffused orange, 4 in., 18 petals, cupped, borne in clusters; foliage leathery; strong stems; vigorous, bushy growth; ['Baby Chateau' × 'Helgoland']; intr. 1944
'Mexico' Min, rb
'Meyerbeer' HP, dr, 1867, Verdier; flowers purple red, tinted flame, petals wavy, very large, full
'Meypink' ('Stéphanie de Monaco') HT, pb, 1971, Meyer, C.; bud ovoid
'Mhairi's Wedding' HT, w, 1983, MacLeod, Major C.A.; flowers 35 petals, flat; foliage large, dark, matte; upright growth; ['Dalvey' × 'Virgo']
'Mi Amor' Ht, mp, Schreurs; flowers medium pink, outer petals tinted green, large , double, high-centered, borne mostly singly; recurrent; intr. 2006
'Mia' HT, lp, Urban, J.
'Mia-Lucy Rose' -- See 'Horluvlush'
'Mia Maid' HT, mp, 1953, Swim, H.C.; bud ovoid; flowers phlox-pink, open, 3½-4

in., 40-50 petals; foliage leathery, glossy; upright, compact growth; ['Charlotte Armstrong' × 'Signora']

'Mia Snock' HT, ly, 1925, Leenders, M.; flowers lemon-yellow, dbl.; ['Mrs T. Hillas' × 'Mrs Wemyss Quin']

'Miami' HT, yb, 1953, Meilland, F.; flowers orange, veined, reverse yellow, long, pointed, 5 in., 25 petals; foliage dark; very vigorous, branching growth; PP977; ['Mme Joseph Perraud' × 'Fred Edmunds']

'Miami Holiday' Min, rb, 1977, Williams, Ernest D.; bud pointed; flowers red, reverse yellow, 1-1½ in., 60 petals, moderate fragrance; foliage small, glossy; upright, bushy growth; [seedling × 'Over the Rainbow']; intr. 1976

Miami Moon™ -- See 'Wekvosuimp'

'Miami Playa' HT, rb, Dot; flowers red, reverse white, dbl., high-centered

'Mic Mac' -- See 'Miomac'

'Micada' ('Orlando Sunshine') Min, pb, 1992, Williams, Michael C.; flowers pink and yellow blend, large, dbl., borne mostly singly; foliage large, medium green, semi-glossy; some prickles; medium (18-24 in.), bushy growth; ['miniature seedling' × 'miniature seedling']

'Micaela' M, lp, 1864, Moreau et Robert; flowers blush, compact, medium, very dbl.; erect growth

'Micaëla' ('Trudor') HT, or, 1986, Kriloff, Michel; flowers orange-red, fading to dark carmine red, borne in clusters; vigorous growth; ['Manola' × seedling]

'Micalex' (Alexandria's Rose™) Min, mp, 2004, Williams, Michael C./Houston, John P; flowers medium pink, reverse outer part of petals have a whitening effect, 1½ in., dbl., borne singly and in small clusters, moderate fragrance; foliage medium size, dark green, semi-glossy; prickles slant down, moderate; growth upright, angular, medium to tall (18-24 in.); garden, exhibition; [seedling × seedling]

'Micam' ('Carolina Morning') Min, rb, 1990, Williams, Michael C.; bud pointed; flowers red with yellow center, aging red, small, 20 petals, high-centered, borne singly and in small clusters, no fragrance; foliage small, medium green, semi-glossy; prickles straight, small, red; bushy, medium growth; hips round, orange; ['Rise 'n' Shine' × Rainbow's End™]; intr. 1990

'Micandie' MinFl, or, 2003, Williams, Michael C.; intr. 2004

'Micangel' ('Angel's Blush') Min, ab, 1996, William, Michael C.; flowers apricot, darkest color on the very edge of the petals, large, dbl.; foliage small, medium green, semi-glossy; few prickles; medium (50 cm.), upright growth; [seedling × unknown]; intr. 1997

'Micarol' ('Carolina Lady') Min, mr, 2000, Williams, Michael C.; flowers medium to dark red, reverse medium red, white at base, 2 in., full, exhibition, borne mostly singly, no fragrance; foliage medium size, dark green, semi-glossy; few prickles; upright, medium (18-24 in.) growth; [seedling × unknown]; intr. 2000

'Micaroline' ('Sweet Caroline') Min, rb, 1998, Williams, Michael C.; flowers white with light to medium red on outer petals, 1½ in., dbl., high-centered, borne mostly singly, no fragrance; recurrent; foliage medium size, dark green, semi-glossy; prickles moderate, small; tall (28-36 in.), slightly spreading growth; [seedling × unknown]; intr. 1999

'Micautumn' ('Autumn Splendor', 'Cotlands Rose') MinFl, yb, 1999, Williams, Michael C.; flowers yellow tinted orange and red, 2 in., full, high-centered, borne mostly singly, slight fragrance; foliage large, medium green, semi-glossy; upright, tall (30-40 in.) growth; intr. 1999

'Miccountry' ('Old Country Charm') Min, pb, 1996, Williams, Michael C.; flowers medium to dark pink with salmon, full, borne mostly singly, no fragrance; foliage medium size, dark green, dull; upright, medium growth; [seedling × unknown]; intr. 1996

'Micdeb' (Debidue™) Min, dp, 1991, Williams, Michael C.; flowers magenta, medium, full, borne mostly singly; foliage medium size, dark green, semi-glossy; some prickles; medium (12 cm.), upright growth; PP8690; ['Jazz Fest' × Party Girl™]; intr. 1992

'Micedi' ('Edisto') MinFl, rb, 2007, Williams, Michael C.; flowers medium red, reverse medium red/yellow, medium, full, borne mostly solitary; foliage medium size, dark green, matte; prickles ¼ in., slightly curved down, reddish brown, moderate; growth upright, medium (30-36 in.); garden decoration, exhibition; ['Chelsea Belle' × unknown]; intr. 2007

'Miceven' ('Evening Shadows') Min, pb, 1990, Williams, Michael C.; bud pointed; flowers medium, 20 petals, high-centered, borne usually singly, slight fruity fragrance; foliage large, medium green, semi-glossy; prickles slight downward curve, small, red; growth bushy, medium; hips globular, light orange; ['Tiki' × Party Girl™]; intr. 1990

'Micexplore' ('Explorer's Dream') Min, op, 1992, Williams, Michael C.; flowers deep orange pink, just a touch of yellow at base of each petal, medium, dbl., no fragrance; foliage medium size, dark green, semi-glossy; some prickles; medium (50 cm.), upright growth; [miniature seedling × 'Homecoming']

'Micfinest' ('Finest Hour') Min, ob, 1996, Williams, Michael C.; flowers very bright orange with yellow at base, creamy orange yellow reverse, medium, very full, borne mostly singly, no fragrance; foliage medium size, medium green, semi-glossy; some prickles; upright, medium growth; [Glowry™ × unknown]; intr. 1996

'Micgold' ('Lander Gold') Min, my, 1986, Williams, Michael C.; flowers 36 petals, high-centered, borne usually singly, moderate fruity fragrance; foliage medium size, medium green, semi-glossy; prickles very few, small, straight; medium, bushy growth; no fruit; ['Rise 'n' Shine' × Little Jackie™]

'Michael' ('Mickael', 'Mikäel') F, or,

'Michael Bates' Moss' -- See 'Princesse Adélaïde'

Michael Crawford™ -- See 'Poulvue'

'Michael Fish' F, mp, Kirkham; flowers mid-pink with yellow stamens, semi-dbl. to dbl., borne up to 12 per stem, moderate sweet fragrance; foliage medium green, glossy; growth to 30 in.; intr. 2001

'Michael Flatley' -- See 'Kenmajes'

'Michael Jon Halvorson' HT, lp, 1999, Adams, Dr. Neil D.; flowers 3 in., dbl., borne in small clusters; foliage medium size, medium green, semi-glossy; prickles moderate; spreading, tall (6 ft.) growth

'Michael Jones' ('Grimpant Michael Jones') LCl, mr, Tantau; flowers bright red , semi-double to double, high-centered early, then open , borne in clusters; recurrent; intr. 2007

'Michael Leek' F, or, 1995, Fleming, Joyce L.; flowers bright orange-red, medium, 5-8 petals; borne 2 - 8 per cluster; foliage medium size, dark green, glossy; bushy (75-90 cm.) growth; ['Liverpool Echo' × 'Traumerei']; intr. 1994

'Michael Mander' -- See 'Manmike'

'Michael Saunders' HT, pb, 1879, Bennett; flowers deep pink and coppery red, well-formed, medium, very dbl., moderate fragrance; moderate growth; ['Adam' × 'Mme Victor Verdier']

'Michaela' -- See 'Angel Wings'

'Michaelhouse Centenary' -- See 'Meionagre'

'Michal' F, rb, Neeman; flowers dbl., slight fragrance

'Michal Kowal' -- See 'Rawmolazy'

'Michel-Ange' HP, dp, 1863, Oger; flowers bright grenadine, large, full

'Michel Bonnet' -- See 'Catherine Guillot'

'Michel Bras' S, mp, Delbard; flowers semi-dbl., cupped, borne in clusters of up to 40 - 50, intense fragrance; medium growth; intr. 2002

'Michel Cholet' -- See 'Foumich'

'Michel Hidalgo' -- See 'Meitulandi'

Michel Joye® Min, yb, Guillot-Massad; intr. 2000

Michel Lis le Jardinier® ('Trailblazer') HT, mr, Meilland; flowers luminous red, large, 45-50 petals, high-centered; intr. 1987

Michel Serrault® F, yb, Meilland; flowers yellow ocher, veined, spotted and splashed with pink , double, high-centered , borne in clusters; recurrent; medium (3 ft.) growth; intr. 2007

'Michel Strogoff' HP, dr, 1882, Barault; flowers slatey violet red, shaded crimson, medium, full; few prickles; growth upright

'Michel Trudeau Rose' HRg, dp, 2008, Dening, Betsy; bud long, pointed, reddish-pink; flowers deep pink, center splashed white, reverse silvery-pink, large, 12½ cm., single, borne in small clusters; foliage medium, medium green, matte, plum-red in autumn; prickles to 7 mm., slightly curved down, pale reddish-brown, numerous; growth upright, medium (120 cm); shrub, hedge, mass plantings; [unknown × unknown]; intr. 2008

'Michelangelo' -- See 'Mactemaik'

'Michelangelo' ('Gracious Queen') HT, my, Meilland; flowers mimosa-yellow, medium, 42-45 petals, cupped, slight fragrance; free-flowering; foliage semi-glossy; growth to 110-130 cm.; intr. 1997

'Michèle' F, op, 1970, deRuiter; flowers deep salmon-pink, large, 25 petals; foliage light green; bushy growth; [seedling × Orange Sensation®]; intr. 1968

Michele Bross' F, Dorieux; intr. 1975

Michele Laroque® HT, yb, Panozzo?; flowers striped; intr. 2007

'Michele Lemming' -- See 'Horsolbond'

'Michèle Meilland' HT, lp, 1945, Meilland, F.; flowers light pink shaded lilac, center salmon, large, dbl., high-centered, moderate fragrance; vigorous, upright (3 ft.) growth; ['Joanna Hill' × 'Peace']

'Michèle Meilland, Climbing' ('Grimpant Michèle Meilland') Cl HT, lp, 1951, Meilland, F.; bud pearly pink; flowers dbl., intense fragrance

Michèle Torr® -- See 'Jacolite'

'Micheline' HT, dp, 1953, de Basso, Mata; flowers deep salmon-pink, base darker, 30-35 petals; foliage dark; ['Edouard Renard' × 'Luis Brinas']

'Micheline' HT, dp, Guillot; free-flowering; foliage green, healthy; growth to 4 ft.; intr. 1985

'Michelle' F, rb; intr. 1998

'Michelle Chetcuti' HT, mr, Kirkham; flowers bright red, aging to soft scarlet, medium, dbl., high-centered; recurrent; foliage large, plum when young, mature green, matte; medium growth; intr. 2005

'Michelle Claire' -- See 'Horseekfell'

'Michelle d'Hoop' F, w, DVP Melle; ['Melglory' × 'Porcelaine de Chine']; intr. 1998

'Michelle Joy' -- See 'Aroshrel'

'Michelle Rosa' -- See 'Horcassiopeia'

'Michelle Wright' -- See 'Pensioners Voice'

'Michigan' HT, pb, 1948, Mallerin, C.; flowers salmon-carmine, reverse Indian yellow, very large, dbl.; bushy growth; ['Mme Joseph Perraud' × 'Vive la France']

'Michigan Perpetual' -- See 'Perpetual Michigan'

'Michka' -- See 'Meivaleir'

'Michome' ('Home-Coming') Min, mp, 1989, Williams, Michael C.; bud pointed; flowers medium pink with slightly darker petal edges, medium, 35 petals, high-centered; foliage medium size, medium green, semi-glossy; prickles straight, green; upright, tall growth; no fruit; PP7454; ['Tiki' × Party Girl™]

'Micimp' ('Lasting Impression') Min, pb, 1998, Williams, Michael C.; flowers medium pink with darker pink edges, 1½ in., dbl., borne mostly singly; foliage medium size, dark green, semi-glossy; thornless; growth compact, medium (20 in.); [seedling × unknown]; intr. 1998

'Mick Micheyl' Gr

'Mickael' -- See 'Michael'

'Mickate' ('Katelyn Ann') F, mp, 1992, Williams, Michael C.; bud small, ovoid; flowers deep pink, reverse pale pink with hint of yellow, aging paler, 2½ in., 60 petals, cupped, borne singly and in small clusters, intense fruity fragrance; foliage medium size, dark green, glossy; prickles moderate, grayish-green; medium, upright (3-3½ ft.) growth; PP8968; [unknown × unknown]; intr. 1992

'Micki' HT, or, 1982, James, John; flowers light tangerine, 36 petals, high-centered; foliage dark, glossy, leathery; prickles small, brown; vigorous, upright growth; ['Fragrant Cloud' × 'Tropicana']; intr. 1979

'Mickim' ('Kimberly') Min, ab, 1986, Williams, Michael C.; flowers 24 petals, high-centered, urn-shaped, borne usually singly, moderate fruity fragrance; foliage medium size, medium green, semi-glossy; no prickles; upright, medium growth; hips globular, small, orange; [Party Girl™ × 'Sheri Anne']

'Micky' HT, op, 1951, Houghton, D.; bud long, pointed; flowers coral-pink, 9 petals; foliage leathery; prickles few thorns; very vigorous, upright, bushy growth; ['Lulu' × 'Vesuvius']

'Micky' Cl Min, mr, Warner, Chris; intr. 1995

'Miclane' ('Melody Lane') Min, m, 1991, Williams, Michael C.; flowers small, full, borne in small clusters, no fragrance; foliage small, medium green, semi-glossy; low (6 cm.) growth; ['Lavender Jewel' × Party Girl™]; intr. 1992

'Miclee' Min, yb, 1991, Williams, Michael C.; bud pointed; intr. 1991

'Miclee' ('Virginia Lee') Min, yb, 1989, Williams, Michael C.; bud ovoid; flowers creamy yellow with pink border, reverse creamy yellow, aging pink, medium, 30 petals, cupped, borne usually singly, no fragrance; recurrent; foliage medium size, dark green, glossy; prickles straight, green; slightly spreading, medium growth; hips globular, green to orange-yellow; ['Rise 'n' Shine' × Baby Katie™]

'Micmac' S, w, Central Exp. Farm; flowers borne in clusters; non-recurrent; foliage deep purplish red; open habit (4 ft.) growth; hardy; [R. rubrifolia × R. rugosa]

'Micmag' ('Mini Magic') Min, rb, 1988, Williams, Michael C.; flowers white with red edges, reverse more red color, small, 35 petals, cupped; foliage small, medium green, semi-glossy; prickles straight, light green; slightly spreading, low growth; [Baby Katie™ × 'Watercolor']

'Micmissc' (Miss Charleston™) Min, m, 2003, Williams, Michael C.; flowers medium mauve, reverse darker, 2½ in., dbl., borne mostly solitary, no fragrance; foliage medium size, light green, semi-glossy; prickles ¼ in., slightly curved down, moderate; growth upright, tall (25-30 in.), garden, exhibition; [seedling × unknown]; intr. 2003

'Micodessa' ('Odessa') Min, m, 1998, Williams, Michael C.; flowers 1½ in., full, high-centered, borne mostly singly, no fragrance; foliage medium size, dark green, matte; prickles few, small; upright, tall (30 in.) growth; [Jean Kenneally™ × unknown]; intr. 1998

'Micone' ('Bill Cone') Min, mr, 1989, Williams, Michael C.; bud ovoid; flowers medium, 35 petals, cupped, borne usually singly; foliage medium size, medium green, semi-glossy; prickles light green, globular; upright, tall growth; hips round, green to orange-yellow; [Heartland™ × Anita Charles™]

'Micpal' ('Palmetto Sunrise') Min, ob, 1992, Williams, Michael C.; flowers orange with a yellow base, yellow reverse, opening orange, large, 20-25 petals, high-centered, borne mostly singly, no fragrance; foliage medium size, medium green, semi-glossy; prickles ¼ in., straight; growth vigorous, upright (50 cm.); hips round, ½ in.; PP9252; ['Orange Honey' × 'miniature seedling']; intr. 1993

'Micpat' ('Patriot's Dream') MinFl, rb, 2000, Williams, Michael C.; flowers medium red, reverse white, medium, full, high-centered, borne mostly singly, slight fragrance; foliage medium size, dark green, semi-glossy; few prickles; upright, tall growth; [seedling × unknown]

'Micpearl' ('Lemon Pearl') Min, ly, 1998, Williams, Michael C.; flowers light yellow, 1-1½ in., 41 petals, borne mostly singly; foliage medium size, light green, matte; prickles few, small, straight; compact, medium (22 in.) growth; [seedling × unknown]; intr. 1998

'Micpie' ('Pierrine') Min, op, 1988, Williams, Michael C.; flowers medium pink, reverse slightly lighter, medium, 40 petals, high-centered, borne singly, slight damask fragrance; foliage medium size, medium green, semi-glossy serrated edges; prickles curved down slightly, light green; upright, medium growth; hips round, green-orange-yellow; ['Tiki' × Party Girl™]

'Micpride' ('Founder's Pride') Min, pb, 1991, Williams, Michael C.; bud pointed; flowers deep pink, white center, mostly white reverse, aging deep pink to strawberry red, large, 24 petals, high-centered, borne mostly singly, slight spicy fragrance; foliage large, dark green, semi-glossy; upright growth; [seedling × Party Girl™]; intr. 1990

'Micro White' -- See 'Weemicrowhite'

'Micrugosa' (*R.* × *micrugosa* Henkel, *R. roxosa*, *R. vilmorinii*, *R. wilsonii*) S, lp, before 1905; flowers 3 in., single to semi-dbl.; some repeat; hips orange-red, depressed-globose, about 1 3/4 in. diameter; [*R. roxburghii* × *R. rugosa*]; spontaneous hybrid, originating in the Botanical Garden at Strasbourg

'Micrugosa Alba' (*R.* × *micrugosa alba*) S, w, about 1910, Hurst, C. C.; flowers white, otherwise similar to micrugosa, single; blooms for many months; foliage compound; arching, colonizing growth; ['Microgosa' × unknown]; possibly *R. roxburghii* × *R. rugosa*

'Micsaluda' ('Saluda') Min, ob, 2006, Williams, Michael C.; flowers light, creamy orange, small, dbl., high-centered, borne in small clusters; recurrent; foliage small, dark green, matte; prickles few, less than 1/4 in., straight, dark reddish brown; growth upright, medium (18-22 in.); garden decoration, borders, containers; ['Finest Hour' × Party Girl™]; intr. 2007

'Micshade' ('Shady Charmer') Min, yb, 1990, Williams, Michael C.; bud ovoid; flowers light yellow base with light pink edges, aging cream, medium, 43 petals, high-centered, slight spicy fragrance; foliage medium size, dark green, semi-glossy; prickles straight, very few, small,lightgreen; bushy, medium growth; no fruit; [Party Girl™ × Anita Charles™]; intr. 1990

'Micsox' ('Sox') Min, rb, 1986, Williams, Michael C.; flowers medium red with a white eye, 1 in., 7 petals, borne singly; foliage medium size, dark; prickles small, straight; medium, upright growth; hips small, globular, orange; [Baby Katie™ × 'Angel Darling']

'Micsteal' ('Stolen Dream') Min, mp, 1995, Williams, Michael C.; flowers medium pink, touch of yellow at base of petals, large, dbl., no fragrance; foliage small, dark green, semi-glossy; upright (55 cm.) growth; intr. 1995

'Micsurf' ('Surfside') Min, pb, 1988, Williams, Michael C.; flowers medium pink to creamy yellow to creamy white, 24 petals, high-centered, borne usually singly; foliage large, light green, semi-glossy; prickles curved down, very few, red-green; upright, medium growth; hips round, medium, green orange-yellow; ['Tiki' × Party Girl™]

'Mictooga' ('Chattooga') Min, dp, 2004, Michael C Williams; flowers 2 in., dbl., borne mostly solitary, no fragrance; foliage large, dark green, matte; prickles 1/8 in., curved down; growth upright, tall (24-36 in.); garden decoration, cutting, exhibition; ['Pierrine' × unknown]; intr. 2005

'Mictwist' ('Tangerine Twist') Min, ob, 1996, Williams, Michael C.; flowers medium orange with yellow, light yellow reverse edged orange, medium, dbl., high-centered, borne singly and in small clusters, no fragrance; recurrent; foliage medium size, medium green, semi-glossy; few prickles; upright, medium growth; ['Pierrine' × unknown]; intr. 1996

'Micurin' LCl, mr, 1936, Böhm, J.; flowers bright red, very large, semi-dbl., globular, borne in large clusters; abundant seasonal bloom; foliage dark, soft; vigorous, climbing growth

'Micvoyage' ('Voyager') Min, yb, 1996, Williams, Michael C.; flowers yellow blend, at times touch of pink, large, full, borne mostly singly, no fragrance; recurrent; foliage medium size, dark green, semi-glossy; medium (50 cm.), upright growth; [seedling × unknown]; intr. 1997

'Midas' -- See 'Legga'

Midas Touch™ -- See 'Jactou'

'Middleborough Football Club' -- See 'Horflame'

'Middlesbrough Pride' -- See 'Nosmid'

'Middlesex County' -- See 'Bosanne'

'Middo' F, Laperrière; intr. 1971

'Midget' Min, mr, 1941, deVink; bud pink; flowers carmine-red, micro-mini, 1/2 in., 20 petals; foliage fern-like; dwarf growth; PP466; ['Ellen Poulsen' × 'Tom Thumb']

Midget Gem® S, ly, Dickson, Patrick; flowers yellow, fading white, 2 in., 5-8 petals, flat, borne in conical clusters, slight fragrance; growth to 50 cm.; intr. 1994

Midi® HT, op

'Midinette' HT, mp, 1962, Delforge; flowers cyclamen-pink, well-formed, dbl.; vigorous growth; ['Pink Spiral' × seedling]

'Midjet' Min, 1941, deVink, J.

'Midnapur Delight' HT, w, Pushpanjali; flowers white with red edge, dbl.; compact growth; intr. 1997

'Midnight' HT, dr, 1957, Swim, H.C.; bud urn shaped; flowers currant-red to cardinal-red, 3½-4½ in., 23-30 petals, high-centered, intense fragrance; foliage dark, glossy; long, strong stems; vigorous, compact growth; PP1542; ['Gay Lady' × 'Texas Centennial']; intr. 1956

Midnight Blue™ -- See 'Wekfabpur'

Midnight Magic™ -- See 'Wilmnmg'

'Midnight Rambler' -- See 'Talmid'

'Midnight Rendezvous' Min, dr, 1985, Hardgrove, Donald L.; flowers small, 27 petals; foliage small, dark, semi-glossy; bushy growth; ['Scarlet King' × 'Big John']

'Midnight Sun' HT, dr, 1921, Grant; flowers deep crimson flushed velvety black, semi-dbl.; ['Star of Queensland' × 'Red-Letter Day']; intr. 1921

'Midnite Sun' HT, yb, 1955, Brownell; flowers buttercup-yellow edged red, becoming lighter, 5 in., very dbl., moderate fragrance; bushy growth; PP1510; ['Sutter's Gold' × (*R. wichurana* × unknown)]

'Midsummer' HT, mp, 1947, Prosser; flowers 4-5 in., 20 petals, high-centered, moderate fruity fragrance; foliage leathery, dark; ['Heinrich Wendland' × 'Lady Sylvia']

'Midsummer Night's Dream' -- See 'Pat James'

'Midsummer Night's Dream' -- See 'Rawroyal'

Midwest Living® -- See 'Kinliv'

'Mie' Min, mr, 1980, Lyon; bud long, pointed; flowers 18 petals, cupped, borne several together; foliage very tiny, medium green; prickles tiny, curved; very compact growth; ['Red Can Can' × seedling]; intr. 1979

'Miellez' Ch, w; flowers cream, fading to pure white, medium, full

'Mien de Jonge' F, mr, 1969, Verschuren, A.; bud ovoid; flowers scarlet, large, semi-dbl., cupped; vigorous, bushy growth; ['Sumatra' × seedling]

'Mier y Teran' S, pb, 2005, Shoup, George Michael; flowers very full, borne mostly solitary, moderate fragrance; remontant; foliage large, medium green, glossy; few prickles; growth bushy, tall (6-8 ft.); hedging; [seedling from China × unknown]; intr. 1998

'Mies Bouwman' F, op, 1978, Buisman, G. A. H.; bud round; flowers salmon-reverse yellow; foliage glossy, dark; vigorous, bushy growth; ['Lijnbaanroos' × seedling]; intr. 1973

'Mieszko' Pol, lp, 1966, Grabczewski; flowers pale pink, small; foliage small, light green; low growth

'Mieze' Pol, ob, 1909, Lambert, P.; flowers orange-yellow, borne in small clusters; vigorous growth; very hardy; ['Petite Léonie' × *R. foetida bicolor*]

'Mieze Schwalbe' Pol, mr, 1927, Lohse & Schubert; flowers rose-red; [sport of 'Frau Rudolf Schmidt']

'Mighty Moe' -- See 'Moemighty'

'Mighty Mouse' -- See 'Macmigmou'

'Mignard' HP, mp, 1858, Baltet; flowers silky pink

'Mignardise' Pol, mr, 1971, Delforge; bud ovoid; flowers open, large, single; foliage large, leathery; vigorous, upright growth; ['Luc Varenne' × seedling]

'Mignon, Climbing' -- See 'Mlle Cécile Brünner, Climbing'

'Mignon' -- See 'Mlle Cécile Brünner'

'Mignon' Pol, ly, 1904, Mille-Toussaint; flowers flesh yellow fading to white; ['Mme Laurette Messimy' × 'Marie Pavie']

'Mignonette' Pol, lp, 1881, Guillot et Fils; flowers rose, sometimes blush white bordered with wine-red spots, 1 in., dbl., borne in short, full panicles of 50, resembling the Chinas; foliage dark green above, reddish beneath, glossy, 5-7 leaflets; prickles hooked, red; stems branches dark red; very dwarf, bushy growth; ['double-flowered multiflora' × probably China or Tea]

'Mignonne' HT, 1962, Gaujard; bud long, pointed; flowers bright salmon-pink, large, 80 petals, moderate fragrance; foliage leathery; very vigorous growth; PP2456; ['Mme Butterfly' × 'Fernand Arles']; intr. 1966

'Miguel Aldrufeu' -- See 'Linda Porter'

'Mijayima' F, dy, Tagashira, Kazuso; flowers large, dbl.; intr. 1992

'Mikado' Ch, dy, Dobbie; flowers deep golden yellow; vigorous growth; RULED EXTINCT 2/87; intr. 1929

'Mikado' F, mp, Tantau; flowers bright pink, borne in clusters; florist rose

'Mikado' F, dy, Guillot; flowers old yellow gold, semi-dbl., moderate fragrance; foliage healthy, beginning red; growth to 80 cm.; intr. 1972

'Mikado' HRg, dr, 1888, Morlet; flowers deep red, large, full

Mikado™ ('Kohsai') HT, rb, Suzuki, Seizo; flowers brilliant luminous light scarlet, suffused with yellow at base, fading darker, medium, 30-35 petals, high-centered, borne usually singly; foliage medium size, medium green, glossy; prickles slightly recurved, medium green, tinged purple; upright, tall growth; hips rounded, dull orange-red; PP6470; ['Fragrant Cloud' × 'Kagayaki']; intr. 1987

'Mikado' Cl HT, mr, Kiese; flowers large, semi-dbl.; intr. 1913

'Mikäel' -- See 'Michael'

'Mikagura' HT, dp, 1999, Hayashi, Shunzo; flowers bright velvet red, 30 petals, high-centered; foliage medium green; growth to 4½ ft.; ['Christian Dior' × seedling]; intr. 1992

'Mikayla Paige' F, w; flowers creamy white, dbl., high-centered, moderate fragrance; medium growth; intr. 2005

'Mike Peterson' -- See 'Moemike'

'Mike Sheppard' HT, mr, 2001, Poole, Lionel; flowers 6 in., full, high-centered, borne mostly solitary, slight fragrance; foliage large, dark green, semi-glossy; prickles medium, wide, angular, moderate; growth upright, bushy, vigorous (1 m.); exhibition, beds, borders; [('Royal William' × 'Gabi') × ('Hazel Rose' × 'Silver Jubilee')]; intr. 2003

'Mike Thompson' -- See 'Sheriired'

'Mike's Old-Fashioned Pink' ('Bon Chance') S, lp, 1999, Lowe, Malcolm; flowers 2½ in., full, borne in small clusters; foliage large, dark green, semi-glossy; prickles moderate; bushy, medium (4 ft.) growth; [Heritage® × 'William Baffin']; intr. 2001

'Mikheil' F, m; flowers light mauve blending to darker edges, medium, dbl., borne singly or in clusters, moderate fragrance; intr. 1998

'Mikulás Ales' HT, lp, 1936, Bojan; flowers rosy salmon-white; very vigorous growth

'Miky Tea' -- See 'Sherimiky'

'Mil Lamp' HT, w, 1991, Colclasure, C.E.; flowers white with pink border, medium, dbl., intense fragrance; foliage medium size, medium green, semi-glossy; bushy growth; [sport of 'Admiral Rodney']

'Milady' HT, dp, 1914, Towill; flowers deep pink, large, dbl., high-centered, moderate fragrance; foliage small, soft; dwarf, sparse bloom. growth; ['J. B. Clark' × 'Richmond']

'Milagros de Fontcuberta' HT, m, 1968, Dot, Simon; bud pointed; flowers violet-mauve, medium, 50 petals; upright, compact growth; [('Sterling Silver' × 'Intermezzo') × ('Sterling Silver' × 'Simone')]

'Milan' F, rb, 1986, Jerabek, Paul E.; flowers red, silver or yellow reverse, medium, 28 petals; foliage medium size, medium green, semi-glossy; upright, bushy growth; [seedling × seedling]

'Milano' HWich, op, 1923, Ingegnoli; bud very long, pointed; flowers nasturtium-pink on Indian yellow ground, dbl., borne in large clusters; foliage glossy; vigorous, climbing (10 ft.) growth

'Milaya' mp, Kriloff; intr. 1984

'Milben' ('Dr B. Benacerraf') Min, pb, 1988, Miller, F.; flowers white to light pink, dark pink borders, opening to light pink, 15-20 petals; foliage ovoid, medium green, matte, disease-resistant; vigorous, compact growth; [(Double Delight™ ® × 'Simplex') × Magic Carrousel®]

'Mildewfree Else Poulsen' F, pb, 1937, Poulsen, S.; flowers pink slightly tinged yellow, medium, single; ['Else Poulsen' × 'Dainty Bess']

'Mildred Cant' HT, mr, 1935, Cant, B. R.; bud pointed; flowers bright crimson, very large, dbl., high-centered; foliage leathery; vigorous, open growth

'Mildred Grant' HT, w, 1901, Dickson, A.; flowers silvery white, tinted pink at edge, dbl., high-centered; very large, vigorous growth; ['Niphetos' × 'Mme Mélanie Willermoz']

'Mildred Reynolds' F, mr, 1966, Dorieux; flowers cardinal-red, 3 in., cupped, borne in large, compact clusters; foliage glossy; ['Peace' × seedling]

'Mildred Scheel' -- See 'Deep Secret'

'Milena' HT, mp, Vecera, L.; intr. 1971

'Milestone' HT, rb, 1984, Warriner, William A.; flowers medium red, silvery red reverse, opening to coral-pink, dbl., cupped; foliage large, medium green, semi-glossy; upright growth; PP5000; ['Sunfire' × 'Spellbinder']; intr. 1985

'Milevsko' S, mp, Vecera, L.; flowers medium pink, yellow stamens, medium, semi-dbl. to dbl., cupped; heavy spring flush, scattered repeat bloom; bushy, branching (5 ft.) growth; intr. 1980

'Mili de Vega' HT, Moreira da Silva, A.

'Milkana' HT, rb, 1985, Staikov, Prof. Dr. V.; flowers brick-red, outer petals shaded pink, large, 50 petals; foliage dark, glossy; vigorous, upright, tall growth; ['Tallyho' × 'Spartan']; intr. 1974

'Milkmaid' N, w, 1925, Clark, A.; flowers white tinted fawn, 5 cm., semi-dbl., borne in medium clusters, moderate fragrance; foliage dark green; stems slender; very vigorous, climbing growth; ['Crépuscule' × unknown]

'Milky Way' -- See 'Amanogawa'

'Milky Way' HWich, w, 1900, Walsh; flowers pure white, tips lightly tinged pink, stamens yellow, very large, semi-dbl.; seasonal bloom; foliage glossy; vigorous, climbing growth; RULED EXTINCT 9/86

'Milky Way' Min, w, Keihan; intr. 2005

'Milky Way' -- See 'Interway'

'Milkyway' Gr, w, 1987, Ohlson, John; flowers yellow stamens, loose, medium, 21 petals, cupped, borne singly, slight fruity fragrance; foliage small, medium green, semi-glossy; prickles straight, small, greenish-yellow; spreading, medium growth; [seedling × seedling]; intr. 1982

'Mill Beauty' -- See 'Miller's Climber'

'Mille' -- See 'Rose Mille'

Mille et Une Nuits® HT, ob, Dorieux; flowers orange in center, outer petals fading as it opens, dbl.; intr. 2000

'Milledgeville' (natural variation of R. setigera), mp, 1842; flowers carmine

'Millefleurs' Min, ob; flowers bright orange, dbl., cupped, borne in clusters

'Millenium' LCl, lp, Schultheis; bud spherical; flowers mother of pearl pink, full, cupped, moderate fragrance; recurrent; foliage dark green, glossy; growth rapid, tall (10-13 ft.); intr. 2000

Millennium™ -- See 'Permill'

Millennium® -- See 'Graelove'

'Millennium' -- See 'Jacbitou'

'Millennium Memories' F, lp; intr. 2001

'Miller-Hayes' ('Millier-Hayes') HP, mr, 1873, Verdier, E.; flowers crimson red with brighter center, nuanced poppy, dbl., moderate fragrance; ['Charles Lefebvre' × unknown]

'Miller's Climber' ('Mill Beauty', 'Mill's Beauty') Ayr, dp, before 1838; flowers purple pink, large, semi-dbl.; foliage large; sometimes listed as a HSet, or a setigera × arvensis cross; some say origin is England, but the U.S. is more likely

'Millgrove' HMult, lp; intr. 1998

'Millicent' HMult, dp, 1914, Paul, W.

'Millicent' S, mp, Central Exp. Farm; flowers light coral-red fading to flesh-pink, reverse yellowish; non-recurrent; foliage dark green veined red-brown; medium-tall growth; hips flattened, globe shape, light red; hardy; intr. before 1952

Millie™ -- See 'Poulren013'

'Millie' Pol, rb, 1937, Russ; flowers light cherry-red, base yellow, borne in clusters; foliage dark; strong stems

'Millie Perkins' HT, mr, 1960, Maarse, G.; flowers velvety red, well-formed, large, dbl.; long, strong stems; vigorous growth; ['Ena Harkness' × 'Chrysler

Imperial']
Millie Walters™ -- See 'Mormilli'
'Millier-Hayes' -- See 'Miller-Hayes'
'Millionaire' -- See 'Peazara'
'Mills and Boon' F, mr, Gandy; flowers bright red, borne in clusters; foliage deep green; bushy, compact growth; intr. 2002
'Mill's Beauty' -- See 'Miller's Climber'
'Milord' F, dr, Gaujard; flowers large, dbl., borne in clusters; foliage dark; vigorous growth; ['Opera' × 'Ville de Gand']; intr. 1961
'Milord' HT, mr, 1962, McGredy, Sam IV; flowers crimson-scarlet, well-formed, 5-6 in., 35 petals, intense fragrance; foliage dark; upright growth; ['Rubaiyat' × 'Karl Herbst']; intr. 1962
'Milou' F, dr, 1964, Mondial Roses; flowers dark vermilion-red, medium, semi-dbl.; vigorous, low growth
Milrose® -- See 'Delbir'
'Milsweet' ('Elsie Warren') F, ab, 1990, Milner, William; flowers apricot with lemon yellow eye, medium, dbl., moderate fragrance; foliage large, medium green, semi-glossy; upright growth; ['Arthur Bell' × 'Arthur Bell']; intr. 1990
Milva® F, m, 1985, Tantau, Math.; intr. 1983
Milva® HT, ob, Tantau; flowers orange-apricot, edges copper-colored, large, long lasting, dbl., high-centered, borne mostly singly; recurrent; foliage full and green; stems medium to long; florist rose; intr. 1999
Milva Gold® HT, dy, Tantau; flowers golden yellow, large, double, high-centered, borne mostly singly; recurrent; stems medium to long; florist rose; intr. 2007
'Mimi' Min, mp, 1963, Meilland, Alain; bud ovoid; flowers 1-1½ in., 33 petals, cupped, borne in clusters; foliage leathery; vigorous, bushy (14 in.) growth; [Moulin Rouge® × ('Fashion' × 'Perla de Montserrat')]; intr. 1963
'Mimi Coertse' Gr, mp, 1963, Herholdt, J.A.; bud pointed; flowers bright rose-pink, 4 in., dbl., high-centered; foliage glossy; upright growth; [Queen Elizabeth® × 'Constantia']
'Mimi Eden' ('Eden Folies', 'Mini Eden') Min, pb, Meilland; flowers pink with white reverse, full, urn-shaped, borne in clusters; PP14194; cut flower rose; intr. 2002
Mimi Fariña™ -- See 'Harhefty'
'Mimi Golden' -- See 'Meispreyo'
'Mimi Mathy' ('Mimie Mathy') F, ab, Dorieux; bud rosy white; flowers apricot brushed with pink, semi-dbl., intense violets fragrance; solid (2 ft.) growth; intr. 1999
Mimi Pearl™ F, w
Mimi Pink™ -- See 'Jeldaniran'
'Mimi Pinson' Pol, dp, 1919, Barbier; flowers clear crimson, passing to purplish rose and then to Neyron purple
'Mimi Rose' -- See 'Jeldaniran'

'Mimie Mathy' -- See 'Mimi Mathy'
'Mimollet' F, lp, 1977, Ota, Kaichiro; bud pointed; flowers bright light pink, 3-4 in., very dbl., high-centered; foliage glossy; upright growth; [(Queen Elizabeth® × 'Ethel Sanday') × Zambra®]; intr. 1975
'Mimosa Cocktail' -- See 'Talmimosa'
'Min Jurgensen' HT, w, 1974, Bauer; flowers center buff, aging to pink edges, medium, dbl.; foliage dark, soft; very vigorous, upright growth; [sport of 'Pascali']; intr. 1973
'Minaaco' (Cindy™) Min, dp, 1985, Williams, Ernest D.; flowers deep pink, well-formed, small, dbl.; foliage small, dark, glossy; ['Tom Brown' × 'Over the Rainbow']
'Minabbco' (Redglo™) Min, mr, 1991, Williams, Ernest D.; flowers very color fast, velvety nap, outstanding substance, small, full, high-centered, borne mostly singly, slight fragrance; recurrent; foliage small, dark green, semi-glossy; some prickles; low (36 cm.), bushy growth; ['Starburst' × 'Over the Rainbow']; intr. 1992
'Minabcco' (Space Walk™) Min, m, 1991, Williams, Ernest D.; flowers mauve-tan/yellow, russet reverse, small, full, borne mostly singly, intense fragrance; foliage small, dark green, semi-glossy; few prickles; low (30 cm.), bushy growth; [seedling × Twilight Trail™]; intr. 1992
'Minabco' (Touch o' Midas™) Cl Min, yb, 1985, Williams, Ernest D.; flowers deep yellow, petals edged deep pink, small, 35 petals, borne singly; foliage small, dark, semi-glossy; upright (to 5 ft.) growth; ['Little Darling' × 'Over the Rainbow']
'Minabdco' ('Pretty Woman') Min, pb, 1991, Williams, Ernest D.; flowers pink with yellow and orange, deeper at edges, aging darker, good substance, small, full, high-centered, borne mostly singly, moderate fragrance; foliage small, medium green, glossy; few prickles; low (30 cm.), bushy growth; ['Tom Brown' × 'Over the Rainbow']; intr. 1992
'Minabeco' (Love Torch™) Min, rb, 1992, Williams, Ernest D.; bud long, pointed; flowers red, orange and yellow blend, holds color well, heavy substance, medium, full; foliage small, dark green, glossy; some prickles; low (30 cm.), upright, bushy growth; hardy; ['Starburst' × 'Over the Rainbow']
'Minacco' (Jazz Time™) Cl Min, dp, 1985, Williams, Ernest D.; flowers deep pink, small, 35 petals, borne in clusters; foliage small, dark, semi-glossy; upright, bushy (4-5 ft.) growth; ['Little Darling' × 'Little Chief']; intr. 1986
'Minaco' (Angelglo™) Min, m, 1983, Williams, Ernest D.; flowers lavender, micro-mini, small, dbl., slight fragrance; foliage small, dark, semi-glossy; bushy growth; PP5356; ['Angel Face' × ('Angel Face' × 'Over the Rainbow')]; intr. 1982

'Minacon' ('Space Probe') Min, rb, 1995, Williams, Ernest D.; flowers red edges on white petals, medium, dbl., moderate fragrance; foliage small, medium green, semi-glossy; some prickles; medium, upright, bushy growth; ['Little Darling' × 'Over the Rainbow']; intr. 1995
'Minadco' (Royalglo™) Min, m, 1987, Williams, Ernest D.; flowers non-fading, small, 40 petals, high-centered, borne usually singly, intense damask, sweet fragrance; foliage small, dark green, semi-glossy; prickles few, long, light tan; bushy, medium growth; no fruit; PP6673; ['Angel Face' × Anita Charles™]
'Minaeco' (Apricot Charm™) Min, ab, 1987, Williams, Ernest D.; flowers apricot, reverse slightly deeper, blending to yellow at base, 42 petals, high-centered, borne usually singly, slight fragrance; foliage small, dark green, glossy; prickles few, thin, light tan; bushy, spreading, medium growth; no fruit; ['Gingersnap' × Anita Charles™]; intr. 1986
'Minafco' (Orange Love™) Min, pb, 1987, Williams, Ernest D.; flowers orange, reverse deeper orange to dark red, fading lighter, 45 petals, high-centered, foliage small, dark green, semi-glossy; prickles very few, short, light tan; upright, bushy, medium growth; no fruit; PP6546; ['Tom Brown' × 'Over the Rainbow']; intr. 1986
'Minagco' (Honey 'n' Spice™) Min, r, 1987, Williams, Ernest D.; flowers tan with red highlights, reverse deeper tan with more red, small, 45-49 petals, borne usually singly, moderate fresh honey fragrance; foliage small, medium green, semi-glossy; prickles few, short, thin, light tan; bushy, medium growth; no fruit; ['Tom Brown' × 'Over the Rainbow']; intr. 1986
'Minahco' (Summer Beauty™) Min, dy, 1987, Williams, Ernest D.; flowers small, dbl., high-centered, borne usually singly or in sprays of 3-5, moderate fragrance; foliage small, dark green, semi-glossy; prickles very few, thin, short, light; upright, bushy, medium growth; no fruit; [seedling × seedling]; intr. 1986
'Minaico' (Red Delight™) Cl Min, mr, 1987, Williams, Ernest D.; bud pointed; flowers deep medium red, yellow at base, small, 33 petals, high-centered, borne singly and in sprays, intense spicy fragrance; foliage small, dark green, semi-glossy; prickles few, small, tan, slanted downwards; tall, bushy, upright growth; hips round, red; PP6547; ['Golden Song' × 'Magic Mist']; intr. 1986
'Minajco' (Purple Majesty™) Min, m, 1987, Williams, Ernest D.; bud short, pointed; flowers mauve, edged red, reverse reddish-mauve, 1½ in., 40 petals, high-centered, borne usually singly, slight fragrance; recurrent; foliage small, medium green, semi-glossy; prickles few, tan, needle-like, dilated at base; stems slender, wiry; growth

bushy, medium; PP6894; ['Tom Brown' × Black Jack™]

'Minakco' (Pink Kiss™) Min, lp, 1987, Williams, Ernest D.; flowers light pink, non-fading, small, 40-45 petals, high-centered, borne singly or in sprays; foliage small, medium green, semi-glossy; prickles tan-red, dilated at base; bushy, medium growth; ['Tom Brown' × Anita Charles™]

'Minalco' (Orange Star™) Min, ob, 1987, Williams, Ernest D.; bud short, pointed; flowers orange, reverse orange with yellow at base, non-fading, 1½ in., 35 petals, high-centered, borne usually singly, intense damask fragrance; foliage small, medium green, semi-glossy; prickles few, tan, dilated at base, hooked slightly downward; stems thin, wiry; bushy, upright, medium growth; PP6893; ['Tom Brown' × 'miniature seedling']

'Minamco' (Ethel Orr™) Min, mr, 1987, Williams, Ernest D.; flowers small, 35 petals, high-centered, borne usually singly or in sprays of 3 - 5, slight fragrance; foliage small, medium green, glossy; prickles few, small, tan; upright, bushy, medium, profuse growth; no fruit; ['miniature seedling' × 'Big John']

'Minanco' (Oriental Simplex™) Min, or, 1987, Williams, Ernest D.; flowers bright orange-red, reverse creamy yellow, aging deeper, non-fading, small, 5 petals, flat, borne usually singly, no fragrance; foliage small, medium green, glossy; prickles tan, declining, dilated at base; upright, bushy, medium growth; hips none observed; [('Starburst' × 'Over the Rainbow') × 'Little Chief']

'Minapco' (Amberglo™) Min, r, 1989, Williams, Ernest D.; flowers small, 34 petals, intense fragrance; foliage small, dark green, semi-glossy; bushy, sturdy growth; ['Tom Brown' × Twilight Trail™]; intr. 1988

'Minaqco' (White Charm™) Min, w, 1989, Williams, Ernest D.; bud long; flowers near white to soft yellow, sweetheart, 33 petals, high-centered, intense fragrance; foliage small, medium green, glossy; bushy, medium to tall growth; ['Tom Brown' × 'Over the Rainbow']; intr. 1988

'Minarco' (Evelyn Rogers™) Min, mp, 1989, Williams, Ernest D.; flowers small, 34 petals, slight fragrance; foliage small, medium green, glossy; upright, bushy growth; ['Tom Brown' × 'Over the Rainbow']; intr. 1988

'Minasco' (The Garden Editor®) Min, dy, 1989, Williams, Ernest D.; flowers small, 33 petals, moderate fragrance; foliage small, medium green, glossy; upright, bushy growth; [Gold Badge™ × 'Yellow Jewel']; intr. 1988

'Minatco' ('Ta Ta') Min, mp, 1989, Williams, Ernest D.; flowers small, 33 petals, no fragrance; foliage small, medium green, semi-glossy, dense; bushy growth; ['Tom Brown' × 'Over the Rainbow']; intr. 1988

'Minauco' (Lavender Star™) Min, m, 1989, Williams, Ernest D.; flowers mauve blended lavender-tan, small, 5 petals, intense fragrance; foliage small, dark green, semi-glossy; upright, bushy, dense growth; [seedling × Lavender Simplex™]

'Minavco' (Sue Jo™) Min, r, 1990, Williams, Ernest D.; flowers russet, outside petals tan-lavender, inside petals golden-amber, 1½ in., 33 petals, high-centered, borne mostly singly, intense fragrance; recurrent; foliage small, medium green, glossy; prickles few, slender, inclined downward, tan; stems slender, wiry; upright, bushy growth; PP7606; ['Tom Brown' × Twilight Trail™]; intr. 1989

'Minawco' (Suntan Beauty™) Min, r, 1990, Williams, Ernest D.; bud short, pointed; flowers tan to russet with rosy highlights, 1½ in., 33-45 petals, high-centered, borne usually singly, moderate fragrance; recurrent; foliage small, dark green, glossy, disease-resistant; prickles few, slender, short, hooked downward, light tan; stems slender, wiry; bushy, upright growth; hips few ; PP7596; [('Angel Face' × 'Golden Angel') × 'Yellow Jewel']; intr. 1989

'Minaxco' (Smoke Signals™) Min, m, 1990, Williams, Ernest D.; bud short, pointed; flowers smoky, lavender-gray, adding pinkish tone with aging, 1½ in., 30-40 petals, high-centered, borne usually singly, intense fragrance; recurrent; foliage small, medium green, glossy; prickles few, slender, hooked slightly downward, tan; stems slender, wiry; upright (12-14 in.), bushy growth; PP7604; [('Tom Brown' × ('Rise 'n' Shine' × 'Watercolor')) × Twilight Trail™]; intr. 1989

'Minayco' (Ida Belle™) Min, m, 1990, Williams, Ernest D.; flowers lavender with blends of amber, very long-lasting, small, 33 petals, high-centered, intense fragrance; foliage small, medium green, glossy; bushy growth; PP7605; [('Tom Brown' × ('Rise 'n' Shine' × 'Watercolor')) × Twilight Trail™]; intr. 1989

'Minazco' (Sands of Time™) Min, r, 1990, Williams, Ernest D.; bud short. pointed; flowers soft russet, 1½ in., 32 petals, high-centered, borne usually singly, moderate fragrance; recurrent; foliage small, medium green, semi-glossy; prickles few, slender, long, almost straight, tan; stems slender, wiry; upright, bushy growth; hips few ; PP7607; ['Tom Brown' × Twilight Trail™]; intr. 1989

'Minbaco' (Jewel's Delight™) Min, mp, 1990, Williams, Ernest D.; flowers small, 33 petals, moderate fragrance; foliage small, medium green, glossy; bushy growth; ['Tom Brown' × Twilight Trail™]; intr. 1989

'Minbco' ('Great Day') Min, dy, 1983, Williams, Ernest D.; bud long, pointed; flowers well-formed, small, 35 petals, moderate fragrance; foliage small, light green, glossy; bushy growth; PP5358; [('Little Darling' × 'Gold Coin') × ('Little Darling' × 'Gold Coin')]; intr. 1982

'Mincco' ('Peggy's Delight') Min, pb, 1983, Williams, Ernest D.; bud medium to long, slender; flowers deep pink, white base and reverse, 1½ in., 45 -50 petals, high-centered, borne usually singly, slight fragrance; good repeat; foliage small, dark, semi-glossy; prickles few, slender, hooked downward, tan; stems slender, wiry; dwarf, bushy, upright growth; hips none ; PP5357; ['Little Darling' × 'Over the Rainbow']; intr. 1982

'Mindco' ('Orange Charm') Min, or, 1983, Williams, Ernest D.; flowers well-formed, small, dbl.; foliage small, medium green, glossy; bushy growth; ['Starburst' × 'Over the Rainbow']; intr. 1982

'Minden' -- See 'Sunday Press'

'Mindor' F, yb, 1976, Station Exp. de Roses; flowers deep yellow, slightly flushed orange, 3 in., 30-60 petals, urn-shaped; foliage dark; vigorous, low growth; ['Dr. Faust' × 'Mme Lucky']

'Mindream' ('Twilight Dream') Min, m, 1992, Williams, Ernest D.; flowers medium, have good color stability, heavy substance, very dbl., high-centered, borne mostly singly, intense fragrance; good repeat; foliage small, dark green, glossy; few prickles; low (30 cm.), bushy growth; hardy; ['Tom Brown' × 'Twilight Beauty']

'Mineco' ('Spring Beauty') Min, pb, 1983, Williams, Ernest D.; flowers pastel pink and yellow blend, small, 35 petals; foliage small, medium green, glossy; upright growth; ['Little Darling' × 'Over the Rainbow']; intr. 1982

'Minerette' -- See 'Interminer'

'Miners Cottage' Misc OGR, dp

'Minerve' HP, mr, Gonod; flowers crimson, shaded velvety fire-red, large, full; intr. 1868

'Minerve' HP, dp, Jamain; flowers medium, full; intr. 1869

'Minerve' HT, yb, Meilland, F.; flowers chrome-yellow shaded red, high pointed, 36 petals, moderate fragrance; foliage thick, dark; vigorous, branching growth; ['Peace' × 'Prinses Beatrix']; intr. 1947

'Minerve' ('La Grande Junon') HGal, dp, before 1811, Miellez; flowers very deep pink

'Minette' C, lp, 1819, Vibert; flowers pink edged blush white, small, full; foliage elliptical, light green; sometimes classed as A

'Minfco' ('Break o' Dawn') Cl Min, pb, 1983, Williams, Ernest D.; flowers white with deep pink edges, white reverse, small, 35 petals, slight fragrance; foliage small, dark, glossy; upright, bushy, climbing growth; ['Little Darling' × 'Over the Rainbow']; intr. 1982

'Minfire' ('Watchfire') Min, or, 1998, Williams, Ernest D.; flowers bright coral-red with deep yellow base, 1¼-1½ in., 35 petals, high-centered, borne mostly singly; foliage medium size, medium green, semi-glossy; prickles moderate; upright, compact, bushy, medium (18 in.) growth; [Sue Jo™ × Twilight Trail™]; intr. 1997

'Minfriv' ('Frivolous') Min, mr, 1998, Williams, Ernest D.; flowers cherry red, with 8-10 broad petals, good substance, 1½ in., 8 petals, borne mostly singly, no fragrance; foliage medium size, semi-glossy; almost thornless; upright, medium (18 in.) growth; [Twilight Trail™ × seedling]; intr. 1997

'Ming Toy' F, dp, 1947, Krebs; bud globular; flowers deep rose-pink, loose trusses, 2 in., 50 petals, moderate fragrance; foliage leathery, dark; vigorous, upright, bushy growth; PP900

'Mingco' (Fiesta Time™) Min, rb, 1983, Williams, Ernest D.; flowers yellow to orange to red, reverse yellow, small, dbl.; foliage small, dark, glossy; bushy growth; ['Starburst' × 'Over the Rainbow']

'Minha Mulher' HT, Moreira da Silva, A.; intr. 1969

'Minhco' ('DeGrazia's Pink') Min, mp, 1983, Williams, Ernest D.; flowers small, of heavy substance, dbl., slight fragrance; foliage small, dark, glossy; bushy growth; [(seedling × 'Over the Rainbow') × (seedling × 'Over the Rainbow')]

'Minheart' ('Lionheart') Min, r, 1998, Williams, Ernest D.; flowers russet with coral edge, deep yellow reverse, 1¼ in., 25 petals, borne mostly singly; foliage medium size, dark green, semi-glossy; prickles moderate; upright, bushy, medium growth; [seedling × Twilight Trail™]; intr. 1997

'Mini Champagne' Min, ab; flowers buff yellow to apricot, double; foliage bronze when new; small growth; intr. 2006

'Mini Eden' -- See 'Meiptipier'

'Mini Jet' -- See 'Meirotego'

'Mini Love' -- See 'Chewcreepy'

'Mini Magic' Min, yb, Walsh; intr. 1998

'Mini Magic' -- See 'Micmag'

'Mini Mercedes' Min, mr

'Mini Metro' -- See 'Rufin'

'Mini Nicole' Min, pb; flowers white with carmine edges, high-centered; free-flowering; rugged, medium to tall growth; holds half open stage for a long time

'Mini Pink Folies' F, mp, Meilland; flowers borne in sprays; intr. 2007

'Mini Pink Melodies' Min, mp, 1991, Spooner, Raymond A.; flowers small, dbl.; foliage small, medium green, semi-glossy; bushy growth; [seedling × seedling]

Mini-Poul® Min, pb, 1985, Poulsen, Niels D.; flowers yellow and deep pink blend, small, 25 petals, no fragrance; foliage small, dark, glossy; compact growth; ['Darling Flame' × seedling]; intr. 1978

'Mini Tango' Min, pb, 2001, Williams, Michael C.; flowers deep pink, with halo at base of petals, medium, dbl., borne mostly solitary, no fragrance; foliage medium size, dark green, semi-glossy; prickles few, ¼ in., straight; growth upright, tall (23 in.); garden decorative, exhibition, containers; [seedling × unknown]; intr. 2002

'Mini White Folies' F, w, Meilland; flowers borne in sprays; intr. 2006

'Mini Wings' ('Ayanishiki', 'Little Star') Min, rb, Asami, Hitoshi; flowers white base with bright red petal edges, yellow stamens, semi-double, shallow cup to flat; intr. about 1985

'Miniature' Pol, lp, 1884, Alégatière; flowers pink, becoming yellowish-white, very small, very dbl.; moderate growth

'Miniature, Climbing' ('Rankende Miniature') Cl Pol, lp, 1908, Lambert; flowers whitish pink, very small, very full

'Miniature Moss' M, lp, before 1838, Rivers; flowers light crimson, small, semi-dbl.; ['Rivers' Single Crimson Moss' × unknown]

'Minibeth' ('Marybeth™) Min, m, 1994, Williams, Ernest D.; flowers pastel mauve, very dbl., high-centered, borne mostly singly, moderate fragrance; foliage small, medium green, semi-glossy; few prickles; medium (18-20 in.), upright growth; [seedling × Twilight Trail™]; intr. 1994

'Minibid' (Forbidden™) Min, m, 1994, Williams, Ernest D.; flowers medium lavender with dark lavender on edges, medium, full, moderate fragrance; foliage small, dark green, semi-glossy; few prickles; low (14-16 in.), bushy growth; [seedling × Twilight Trail™]; intr. 1994

'Minicin' (Cinnamon Delight™) Min, r, 1993, Williams, Ernest D.; flowers russet with deep yellow base, medium, full, borne mostly singly, intense fragrance; foliage small, dark green, semi-glossy; few prickles; medium (40 cm.), upright growth; [seedling × Twilight Trail™]; intr. 1993

'Minico' ('Mary Marshall, Climbing') Cl Min, ob, 1983, Williams, Ernest D.; intr. 1982

'Minidor' ('Fall Splendor') Min, yb, 1996, Williams, Ernest D.; flowers rich yellow with orange blush on edges, 1¼-1½ in., full, blooms borne mostly singly, moderate fragrance; foliage medium size, dark green, semi-glossy; some prickles; medium (16 in.), compact, bushy growth; ['Rise 'n' Shine' × Twilight Trail™]; intr. 1996

'Minifire' ('Rigadoon', Dragon's Fire™) Min, rb, 1993, Williams, Ernest D.; flowers bright red with deep yellow at base of petals, yellow reverse, medium, full, moderate fragrance; foliage small, medium green, semi-glossy; few prickles; medium (35 cm.), upright, compact growth; ['Starburst' × Twilight Trail™]; intr. 1993

'Minigold' F, my, 1970, Tantau, Math.; flowers pointed, 2½ in., 35 petals, moderate fragrance; foliage glossy, dark; PP3103; ['Whisky Mac' × 'Zorina']

Minijet® -- See 'Meirotego'

'Minilights' -- See 'Dicmoppet'

'Minimag' (Magician™) Min, m, 1993, Williams, Ernest D.; flowers mauve with deeper petal edges, large, very dbl., borne mostly singly, intense fragrance; foliage small, medium green, semi-glossy; few prickles; medium (45 cm.), upright, bushy growth; [seedling × Twilight Trail™]; intr. 1993

'Minimerr' (Merryglo™) Min, m, 1995, Williams, Ernest D.; flowers medium lavender, 1¼ in., full, borne mostly singly, intense fragrance; foliage medium size, medium green, semi-glossy; some prickles; medium (18 in.), bushy growth; [seedling × Twilight Trail™]; intr. 1995

'Minimoon' (Red Moon™) Min, mr, 1995, Williams, Ernest D.; flowers 1-1½ in., full, borne in small clusters, no fragrance; foliage medium size, medium green, semi-glossy; some prickles; upright, bushy, climbing (5 ft.) growth; ['Red Delight' × Twilight Trail™]; intr. 1995

'Minimys' (Mysterious™) Min, m, 1995, Williams, Ernest; flowers full, borne mostly singly, moderate fragrance; foliage medium size, medium green, semi-glossy; some prickles; upright (16-18 in.), bushy growth; [seedling × Twilight Trail™]; intr. 1995

'Minirasp' (Raspberry Beauty™) Min, mr, 1994, Williams, Ernest D.; flowers non-fading raspberry red, medium, full, high-centered, borne mostly singly; foliage small, medium green, semi-glossy; few prickles; medium (16-20 in.), bushy growth; ['Angel Face' × Anita Charles™]; intr. 1994

'Minirosa' Min, pb, VEG; flowers bright pink with white eye, small, semi-dbl., flat, borne in clusters, slight fragrance; free-flowering; bushy, compact (40 cm.) growth; intr. 1976

'Minirot' Min, m, VEG; flowers purple/pink with cream reverse, small, semi-dbl.

'Miniryl' (Royal Lady™) Min, m, 1993, Williams, Ernest D.; flowers lavender pink, petals ruffled, medium, full, borne mostly singly, intense fragrance; foliage small, medium green, semi-glossy; few prickles; medium (40 cm.), bushy growth; ['Angel Face' × 'Twilight Beauty']; intr. 1993

'Minisa' HRg, mr, 1927, Hansen, N.E.; flowers deep crimson, medium, 17 petals, intense fragrance; bloom repeats; very hardy; [R. rugosa × 'Prince Camille de Rohan']

'Minishow' ('Showdown') Min, dr, 1996, Williams, Ernest D.; flowers 1¼ in., full, borne mostly singly, no fragrance; foliage dark green, semi-glossy; some prickles; medium (16-18 in.), upright, bushy growth; ['Rise 'n' Shine' × Twilight Trail™]; intr. 1996

'Minisong' ('Morning Song') Min, ob, 1996, Williams, Ernest D.; flowers orange with yellow base, 1¼ in., full, borne mostly singly; foliage medium size, medium green, semi-glossy; some prickles; medium (16-18 in.), upright, bushy growth; [Sue Jo™ × Twilight Trail™]; intr. 1996

'Minister Afritsch' F, or, 1973, Tantau, Math.; flowers large, dbl.; vigorous, bushy growth; [seedling × Signalfeuer®]; intr. 1964

'Minister Luns' F, dp, 1968, Wijnhoven; bud ovoid; flowers pink-red, medium, semi-dbl.; foliage dark; ['Marchenland' × 'Florence Mary Morse']

'Minister Rasín' -- See 'Ministre des Finances Rasín'

'Ministorm' (Stormy Weather™) Min, m, 1994, Williams, Ernest D.; flowers medium lavender, medium, full, high-centered, borne mostly singly, moderate fragrance; foliage small, medium green, semi-glossy; few prickles; tall (24-30 in.), upright growth; [seedling × Twilight Trail™]; intr. 1994

'Ministre des Finances Rasín' ('Minister Rasín') HT, dp, 1930, Böhm, J.; bud long; flowers carmine-rose, large, dbl.; vigorous growth; ['Mme Maurice de Luze' × 'Hadley']

'Minitoc' ('Touch o' Cloves') Min, r, 1995, Williams, Ernest; flowers 1-1¼ in., dbl., borne mostly singly; foliage medium size, dark green, semi-glossy; few prickles; upright (18 in.), bushy growth; [seedling × Twilight Trail™]; intr. 1995

'Minitok' (Golden Token™) Min, dy, 1993, Williams, Ernest D.; flowers deep golden yellow, small, very full, borne in small clusters; foliage small, medium green, glossy; few prickles; medium (40 cm.), upright, bushy growth; [unknown × unknown]; intr. 1993

'Miniumber' (Umberglo™) Min, r, 1996, Williams, Ernest D.; flowers russet with red blush on edges, 1-1¼ in., full, borne mostly singly, moderate fragrance; foliage medium size, dark green, semi-glossy; few prickles; low (12-14 in.), compact, bushy growth; [seedling × Twilight Trail™]; intr. 1996

'Minivig' (Vigilance™) Min, w, Williams, Ernest; flowers 1½-1¾ in., full, borne in small clusters, no fragrance; foliage medium size, medium green, glossy; numerous prickles; spreading (6 ft.), climbing growth; [sport of 'Jeanne Lajoie']; intr. 1995

'Minivision' ('Heavenly Vision') Min, mp, 1996, Williams, Ernest D.; flowers clear, medium pink, 1½ in., dbl., borne mostly singly; foliage medium green, semi-glossy; few prickles; medium (16-18 in.), upright, bushy growth; ['Angel Face' × 'Tom Brown']; intr. 1996

'Miniwack' (Paddywack™) Min, pb, 1993, Williams, Ernest D.; flowers medium, full, borne mostly singly; foliage small, medium green, semi-glossy; few prickles; medium (50 cm.), upright, compact growth; ['Tom Brown' × 'Over the Rainbow']; intr. 1993

'Miniwin' (Winter Wheat™) Min, ly, 1995, Williams, Ernest; flowers 1¼ in., full, borne mostly singly; foliage medium size, medium green, semi-glossy; some prickles; upright (16-18 in.), bushy growth; [seedling × Twilight Trail™]

'Miniwon' (Wonderglo™) Min, r, 1994, Williams, Ernest D.; flowers unusual russet with red highlights, medium, very dbl., borne mostly singly, moderate fragrance; foliage small, medium green, semi-glossy; few prickles; medium (18 in.), bushy growth; [seedling × Twilight Trail™]; intr. 1994

'Minjco' (Loveglo™) Min, op, 1983, Williams, Ernest D.; flowers light coral pink and cream, small, dbl., high-centered; foliage small, dark, glossy; bushy growth; PP5677; ['Little Darling' × 'Over the Rainbow']

'Mink' -- See 'Minx'

'Minkco' (Black Jack™) Min, dr, 1983, Williams, Ernest D.; flowers deep red, golden stamens, small, 40 petals, high-centered; foliage small, dark, semi-glossy; bushy growth; PP5671; ['Tom Brown' × 'Over the Rainbow']

'Minlco' (Arctic Snow™) Min, w, 1983, Williams, Ernest D.; flowers small, dbl., high-centered; foliage small, dark, glossy; upright, bushy growth; ['miniature seedling' × 'Over the Rainbow']

'Minmco' (Spring Melody™) Min, ob, 1983, Williams, Ernest D.; flowers orange, small, 35 petals, slight fragrance; foliage small, bronze green, semi-glossy; bushy (12 in.) growth; ['Little Darling' × 'Over the Rainbow']

'Minna' HEg, w, 1895, Penzance; flowers white, tinted blush-lilac, large, semi-dbl.; very vigorous growth

'Minna' F, mp, 1930, Kordes; flowers rosy pink, large, dbl., borne in clusters; foliage rich green, leathery; bushy, dwarf growth; [sport of 'Gruss an Aachen']

'Minna Kordes' -- See 'World's Fair'

Minna Lerche Lerchenborg® -- See 'Meidad'

'Minnco' (Pink Carpet™) Min, mp, 1983, Williams, Ernest D.; flowers small, dbl., borne in large clusters, no fragrance; foliage small, light to medium green, glossy; low, spreading (to 6 ft.) growth; hanging baskets; PP5606; ['Red Cascade' × 'Red Cascade']

'Minnehaha' HWich, lp, 1905, Walsh; flowers pink fading white, small, dbl., borne in large clusters; non-recurrent; foliage small, glossy, dark; climbing (15-20 ft.) growth; [R. wichurana × 'Paul Neyron']

'Minnelli' ('Minnelli Patiohit') MinFl, ab, Olesen; bud ovate; flowers apricot, outer petals fading lighter, 2½ in., 40-50 petals, cupped, borne usually singly, slight wild rose fragrance; recurrent; foliage dark green, semi-glossy; prickles few, 4 mm., linear; growth compact, upright, bushy (8-16 in.); [seedling × Patricia Kordana Mini Brite™]; intr. 2003

'Minnelli Patiohit' -- See 'Poulpah022'

'Minnie' Min, rb, 1978, Williams, Ernest D.; bud long, pointed; flowers red and yellow blend,, 1 in., very dbl., high-centered, moderate fragrance; foliage small, glossy; upright growth; ['Starburst' × 'Over the Rainbow']; intr. 1977

'Minnie Dawson' HMult, w, 1896, Dawson; flowers pure white, borne in very large clusters; ['Dawson' × R. multiflora]

'Minnie Francis' T, dp, 1905, Griffing Nursery; flowers deep pink, open; vigorous growth

'Minnie Marcus' HT, pb, 1983, Rodgers, Shafner R.; flowers large, 35 petals; foliage large, dark, glossy; upright growth; [Queen Elizabeth® × 'Windsounds']; intr. 1984

'Minnie Mouse' -- See 'Macminmo'

Minnie Pearl™ -- See 'Savahowdy'

'Minnie Pearl White' Min, w, Lee; [sport of 'Minnie Pearl']; intr. 1993

'Minnie Saunders' HT, mr, 1921, Hicks; flowers bright red, single; vigorous growth

'Minnie Watson' HT, op, 1965, Watson; bud globular; flowers semi-dbl.; foliage glossy; compact, bushy growth; ['Dickson's Flame' × 'Dickson's Flame']

'Minoco' (Mary Kay™) Min, lp, 1984, Williams, Ernest D.; flowers small, 35 petals; foliage small, dark, glossy; upright, bushy growth; PP5631; ['Tom Brown' × 'Over the Rainbow']

'Minor' -- See 'Pompone Jaune'

'Minor' -- See 'Petite de Hollande'

'Minor Details' -- See 'Savaminor'

'Minor Prolific' -- See 'Gracilis'

'Minori' HT, ob, Hiroshima; intr. 2002

'Minou' F, Moreira da Silva, A.

'Minouchette' LCl, lp, Croix; flowers medium, dbl., borne in small clusters, slight fragrance; free-flowering; foliage clear green, disease-resistant; vigorous growth; intr. 1971

'Minpco' (Partyglo™) Min, yb, 1985, Williams, Ernest D.; bud long, pointed; flowers yellow with pink petal edges, yellow reverse, 1½ in., 35 petals, high-centered, borne usually singly; recurrent; foliage small, dark green, semi-glossy; prickles average, slender, hooked downward, tan; stems slender, wiry; growth bushy, upright to slightly spreading; few hips; PP5880; ['Little Darling' × 'Over the Rainbow']; intr. 1984

'Minpeep' (Peep-Eye™) Cl Min, mr, 1992, Williams, Ernest D.; flowers very distinct shade of medium red, medium, 25 petals, borne in large clusters; foliage small, dark green, glossy; some prickles; tall (4 ft.), upright, bushy growth; hardy (both heat & cold); ['Red Delight' × seedling]

'Minprop' ('Prophecy') Min, mr, 1998, Williams, Ernest D.; flowers rose red, heat stable, 1-1¼ in., very dbl., high-centered, borne mostly singly; foliage medium size, medium green, semi-glossy; prickles moderate; upright, bushy, medium (18 in.) growth; ['Red Delight' × Twilight Trail™]; intr. 1997

'Minpum' (Pumpkin Frost™) Min, r, 1995, Williams, Ernest; flowers russet, 1-1¼ in., dbl., borne in small clusters; foliage medium size, dark green, semi-glossy; some prickles; low (12 in.), compact growth; [seedling × Twilight Trail™]; intr. 1995

'Minqco' (Red Love™) Min, mr, 1985, Williams, Ernest D.; flowers spiral form, small, 35 petals; foliage small, dark, semi-glossy to glossy; upright, bushy growth; ['Tom Brown' × 'Over the Rainbow']; intr. 1984

'Minrco' (Cheryl's Delight™) Min, pb, 1985, Williams, Ernest D.; flowers medium pink, reverse white, small, 35 petals, slight fragrance; foliage small, dark, semi-glossy; bushy growth; PP5910; ['Little Darling' × 'Over the Rainbow']; intr. 1984

'Minrid' ('Dreamrider') Min, yb, 1998, Williams, Ernest D.; flowers med. yellow, pink edge, reverse yellow, 1¾ in., very dbl., borne mostly singly; foliage medium size, medium green, semi-glossy; few prickles; upright, bushy, medium (18 in.) growth; [Sue Jo™ × Twilight Trail™]; intr. 1997

'Minsco' (Pink Bounty™) Min, mp, 1985, Williams, Ernest D.; flowers small, 35 petals, high-centered; foliage small, medium green, semi-glossy; very dense, bushy growth; ['Tom Brown' × 'Over the Rainbow']; intr. 1984

'Minsounds' ('Heartsounds') Min, mp, 1998, Williams, Ernest D.; flowers clear medium pink, cream reverse, 1-1¼ in., 30-35 petals, borne mostly singly; foliage medium size, medium green, semi-glossy; few prickles; long stems; upright, bushy, medium (18 in.) growth; ['Rise 'n' Shine' × Twilight Trail™]; intr. 1997

'Minstrel' F, mr, 1967, Sanday, John; flowers scarlet, 2½ in., single to semi-dbl., borne in clusters; foliage dark, glossy; very free growth; ['Independence' × 'Paprika']

'Mint Julep' -- See 'Arogresh'

'Mintco' (Lavender Simplex™) Min, m, 1985, Williams, Ernest D.; flowers lavender, purple stamens, small, single, borne usually singly, moderate fragrance; recurrent; foliage small, dark, semi-glossy; growth upright, bushy; ['Angel Face' × 'Yellow Jewel']; intr. 1984

'Minuco' (Royal Carpet™) Min, mr, 1985, Williams, Ernest D.; flowers small, dbl., borne in clusters, no fragrance; foliage small, dark, semi-glossy; groundcover; spreading growth; PP5909; ['Red Cascade' × 'Red Cascade']; intr. 1984

'Minuet' HT, my, 1930, Thompson's, J.H., Sons; flowers open,large, semi-dbl.; foliage leathery; vigorous growth; [sport of 'Joanna Hill']

'Minuette' -- See 'Meilucca'

'Minuette, Climbing' Cl F, w, Kato; flowers white, edged crimson; intr. 1974

'Minuette' ('La Minuette', 'Laminuette') F, rb, 1969, Lammerts, Dr. Walter; bud ovoid, pointed; flowers with heart-shaped, ivory-white petals, tipped red, medium, dbl.; foliage glossy, dark green; bushy, branching, strong (2 ft.) growth; PP3162; ['Peace' × 'Rumba (F)']

'Minuetto' -- See 'Meilucca'

'Minvco' (Red Pendant™) Min, dr, 1985, Williams, Ernest D.; flowers small, 35 petals, no fragrance; foliage small, medium green, very glossy; low, spreading growth; ['Red Cascade' × 'Red Cascade']; intr. 1984

'Minwco' (Beautyglo™) Min, lp, 1985, Williams, Ernest D.; flowers small, 35 petals, high-centered; foliage small, dark, semi-glossy; bushy growth; PP6199; ['Tom Brown' × Black Jack™]

'Minx' ('Mink') F, ob, 1959, Boerner; bud globular; flowers orange-pink, 2½ in., 75-80 petals, flat, borne in pyramidal clusters, moderate fragrance; strong stems; vigorous, upright growth; PP1513; [('Pinocchio' × unknown) × 'Garnette']; intr. 1955

'Minxco' (Twilight Trail™) Min, m, 1985, Williams, Ernest D.; bud long, pointed; flowers lavender-tan, 3 cm., 30-35 petals, high-centered, borne singly and several together, intense fragrance; recurrent; foliage small, dark green, semi-glossy; prickles average, slender; stems slender, wiry; upright, bushy growth; PP6198; ['Angel Face' × Anita Charles™]

'Minyco' (Imogene™) Min, yb, 1985, Williams, Ernest D.; flowers yellow, marked red, well-formed, small, 45 petals; foliage small, dark, glossy; upright, bushy growth; ['Little Darling' × 'Over the Rainbow']

'Minzco' (Fiddler's Gold™) Min, dy, 1985, Williams, Ernest D.; flowers small, dbl.; foliage small, dark, glossy; bushy growth; ['Tom Brown' × 'Golden Angel']

'Mio Mac' -- See 'Miomac'

'Miomac' ('Mic Mac', 'Mio Mac') F, dy, 1976, Tantau, Math.; bud ovoid; flowers coppery yellow, medium, dbl.; foliage glossy; growth moderate, upright, bushy; intr. 1973

Mirabella™ -- See 'Jacsile'

'Mirabile' -- See 'Mirabilis'

'Mirabilia' F, Cazzaniga, F. G.; intr. 1960

'Mirabilis' -- See 'Admirable'

'Mirabilis' ('Mirabile') T, ab, about 1845, Boyau; flowers apricot yellow, shaded aurora pink, medium, full

'Miracle' HT, ob, Pouw; bud medium, ovate; sepals short; flowers orange-yellow, again to salmon-orange to orange, 3-4 in., 33 petals, high-centered, star-shaped, borne singly, slight fragrance; good repeat; foliage medium size, matte; prickles few, concave; growth vigorous, narrow, bushy (5 ft.); PP10907; [seedling × seedling]; greenhouse rose; intr. 1997

'Miracle' F, op, 1961, Verbeek; flowers soft coral, 3 in., 16-35 petals, high-centered, borne in large trusses; foliage glossy; vigorous growth; PP1863; [seedling × 'Fashion']; intr. 1961

'Miragaia' HT, pb, 1958, Moreira da Silva; flowers lilac-pink; ['Peace' × 'Coimbra']

'Mirage' Gr, op, 1966, Gaujard; bud ovoid; flowers bright salmon shaded red, medium, dbl.; foliage dark; very vigorous, bushy growth; ['Peace' × 'Circus']

'Mirai' ('Elegant Lady') HT, lp, Teranishi; intr. 2005

'Mirakel' F, yb, VEG; flowers dark yellow with orange and red, medium, dbl.

'Miralba' -- See 'Miralda'

'Miralda' ('Chévrier', 'Miralba') HCh, m, about 1825, Laffay; flowers dark crimson-purple, nearly black, striped carmine, small, very dbl.; prickles very small; vigorous, branching growth; perhaps Vibert, rather than Laffay

'Miramar' -- See 'Almirante Américo Tomás'

'Miramar' F, or, 1956, Gaujard; bud globular; flowers cinnabar shaded coppery, large; foliage dark; very vigorous growth; [('Opera' × unknown) × seedling]

'Miramare' HT, yb, Keisei; intr. 2002

'Miranda' -- See 'Dicrobot'

'Miranda' P, mp, 1869, de Sansal; flowers satiny pink, with a small center button, large, 8 cm., semi-dbl., moderate fragrance; recurrent; growth upright, medium

'Miranda' S, pb, Austin, David; flowers deep rose pink in center, outer petals paler and some streaked with green, large, full, cupped, slight fruity fragrance; recurrent; used for bouquets; intr. 2007

'Miranda Jane' F, op, 1973, Cocker; flowers salmon, 4 in., 20 petals, high-centered, moderate fragrance; [Orange Sensation® × 'Red Dandy']; intr. 1972

Mirandolina® Min, w, Interplant; flowers pure white, 4-5 cm., dbl.; recurrent; foliage dark green; compact (10 in.) growth; intr. 1989

'Mirandy, Climbing' Cl HT, dr, 1961, Moore

'Mirandy' HT, dr, 1945, Lammerts, Dr. Walter; flowers garnet-red, aging darker, 5-6 in., 45 petals, globular, intense damask fragrance; foliage leathery; vigorous, upright, bushy growth; PP632; ['Night' × 'Charlotte Armstrong']

'Mirato' -- See 'Tanotax'

'Mirato' HT, mp, 1974, Tantau, Math.; bud ovoid; flowers pink to salmon, dbl., intense fragrance; foliage large, glossy; upright, bushy growth; [unknown × unknown]

'Mireille' HT, mr, 1952, Gaujard; flowers coppery crimson-red, 4 in., 26 petals, moderate fragrance; foliage rich green; vigorous growth; ['Opera' × seedling]

'Mireille Mathieu' F, or, Kordes; flowers brilliant orange-red, full, slight fragrance; intr. 1983

'Mireille Mathieu' -- See 'Kordehn'

'Mirela'   F, pb, Wagner, S.; flowers intense pink with yellow, medium to large, 50 petals, borne in clusters, slight fragrance; foliage medium size, dark green, glossy; ['Castanet' × 'Carillon']; intr. 2003

Mirella® -- See 'Barnec'

'Miri' -- See 'Liokris'

'Miriam'   HT, my, 1919, Pemberton; flowers nasturtium-yellow, dbl., globular

'Miriam' -- See 'Macsupcat'

'Miriam's Climber'   LCl, op, 1950, Rosen, H.R.; bud ovoid, apricot-pink; flowers peach-pink, lighter at tip, large, dbl., borne in clusters; foliage dark, soft; very vigorous, climbing (25 ft.) growth; [seedling × 'Edith Nellie Perkins']

'Miriam's White (found)' -- See 'Sleigh Bells, Climbing'

'Miriana'   HT, mr, 1981, Meilland, Mrs. Marie-Louise; flowers large, dbl.; foliage medium size, dark, semi-glossy; upright growth; intr. 1982

'Miriana'   dp, Richardier; intr. 1997

'Miriana' -- See 'Meirandival'

'Miroir de Perfection'   B, mp, 1846, Armand, Étienne; flowers rose pink, shaded violet, medium, full

'Mirza'   F, ob, 1976, Kordes; bud ovoid; flowers 4 in., 35 petals, cupped, moderate fragrance; foliage glossy; vigorous, upright, bushy growth; ['Zorina' × 'Samba']; intr. 1974

'Mischief'   HT, op, 1961, McGredy, Sam IV; flowers salmon-pink, 4 in., 28 petals, moderate fragrance; foliage light green; vigorous, upright growth; ['Peace' × 'Spartan']; intr. 1961

'Miss Aalsmeer'   F, Spek, J.; PP3051

'Miss Ada'   F, lp, 1998, Pawlikowski, Martin & Elaine; flowers light pink, darker edges, reverse darker pink, 2-4 in., single, borne singly and in small clusters; foliage medium size, medium green, semi-glossy; prickles few, brown; upright, bushy, medium growth; [sport of 'Playgirl']; intr. 1998

'Miss Agnes C. Sherman'   T, rb, 1901, Nabonnand; flowers rose, salmon and red; ['Paul Nabonnand' × 'Catherine Mermet']

'Miss Alice' -- See 'Moealice'

'Miss Alice' -- See 'Ausjake'

'Miss Alice de Rothschild'   T, ly, 1910, Dickson, A.; flowers light canary-yellow, center deeper, dbl.

'Miss All-American Beauty' -- See 'Maria Callas'

'Miss All-American Beauty, Climbing' -- See 'Meidaudsar'

Miss All-American Dream™ -- See 'Wildrem'

'Miss All Australian Beauty'   HT, dp, 1969, Armbrust; bud ovoid; flowers light red, reverse darker, medium, dbl.; upright growth; ['Aztec' × 'Impeccable']

'Miss Amber'   HT, or, 2001, Coiner, Jim; flowers yellow/orange blend, 6 in., dbl., high-centered, borne mostly solitary, no fragrance; foliage medium green, matte; prickles 1/8-¼ in., wide, curved; growth bushy, medium (48 in.); garden decorative; PP16157; [seedling × seedling]

'Miss Amelia Gude'   HT, dy, 1921, Lemon; flowers deep yellow center shading to cream, 35-40 petals; foliage dark; vigorous growth; ['Columbia' × 'Sunburst']

'Miss America'   HT, pb, 1938, Nicolas; flowers light pink, flushed salmon and gold,, 6 in., 65 petals, moderate fragrance; foliage dark, leathery; vigorous growth; PP264; ['Joanna Hill' × 'S.M. Gustave V']

'Miss Annamarie Bally'   HT, or, 1926, Easlea; flowers reddish-copper, reverse suffused whitish fawn; ['Aspirant Marcel Rouyer' × 'Lamia']

'Miss Annie Crawford' -- See 'Annie Crawford'

'Miss Ashley'   HT, w, 2001, Coiner, Jim; flowers 6 in., dbl., borne mostly solitary; foliage medium size, light green, matte; prickles small, few; growth bushy, medium (48 in.); garden decorative; [seedling × seedling]

'Miss Australia'   HT, mp, 1933, Knight, G.; flowers pink, center salmon, very large, 50 petals, globular; foliage thick; very vigorous, bushy growth; ['Dame Edith Helen' × 'Mme Segond Weber']

'Miss B. Wright'   HT, mp, 2007, Edwards, Eddie and Phelps, Ethan; flowers 5 in., full, high-centered, borne mostly solitary; foliage medium, dark green, semi-glossy; prickles few, concaved; growth upright, medium (5 ft.); ['Mavrik' × Moonstone™]; intr. 2008

Miss Behavin'™ -- See 'Jactorse'

'Miss Blanche' ('Kojack') HT, w, 1981, Warriner, William A.; bud long; flowers 38 petals, urn-shaped to high-centered, borne usually singly, very slight fragrance; foliage large, dark, leathery; prickles straight, reddish; upright growth; PP4899; ['Evening Star' × 'Coquette']; intr. 1980

'Miss Bloomsalot' -- See 'Ponalot'

'Miss Brenda'   HT, m, 2006, Popwell, Larry G., Sr.; flowers mauve, reverse lighter, large, single, borne mostly solitary; foliage medium size, dark green, glossy; prickles medium, straight, light tan, moderate; growth upright, 4-5 ft.; [Queen Elizabeth® × 'Love']; intr. 2006

'Miss Brisbane'   HT, lp, 1955, Ulrick, L.W.; flowers shell-pink, medium, dbl., cupped, moderate fragrance; foliage light green; vigorous growth; [unknown × 'The Doctor']

'Miss C. E. Bernays' ('Mrs C. E. Bernays') HT, 1905, Williams, A.; ['Mme Lombard' × unknown]

'Miss C. E. van Rossem'   HT, mr, 1919, Verschuren; bud long, pointed; flowers crimson-scarlet shaded carmine and black, open, medium to small, semi-dbl., cupped; foliage leathery, bronze, dark; vigorous, bushy growth; ['Leuchtfeuer (HCh)' × 'Red-Letter Day']

'Miss California'   HT, dp, 1933, Smith, J.; flowers deep glowing pink; [sport of 'Dame Edith Helen']

'Miss Canada' ('Pacific Beauty') HT, pb, 1963, Blakeney, F.; bud ovoid; flowers rose-madder, reverse silver, large, dbl., high-centered; foliage glossy, leathery; vigorous, upright, spreading growth; ['Peace' × 'Karl Herbst']; intr. 1962

'Miss Caroline'   T, pb, 1997, Knopf, Ruth; flowers medium, 50-60 petals, borne in small clusters; foliage medium size, medium green, semi-glossy; bushy, medium (4-5ft.) growth; [sport of 'Duchesse de Brabant']; intr. 2000

Miss Charleston™ -- See 'Micmissc'

'Miss Clipper'   HT, pb, 1942, Lammerts, Dr. Walter; bud long, pointed to ovoid; flowers pale salmon-pink shaded yellow, 3½-4 in., 25-30 petals, high-centered, moderate spicy fragrance; foliage glossy, light; strong stems; vigorous, upright, bushy growth; PP522; ['Angèle Pernet' × 'Pres. Herbert Hoover']

'Miss Conner'   HT, ly, 1920, Dickson, A.; flowers canary-yellow on lemon-yellow, dbl.

'Miss Cynthia Forde' ('Cynthia Forde', 'Mrs Cynthia Forde') HT, dp, 1909, Dickson, A.; flowers deep brilliant rose-pink, reverse lighter, large, dbl., moderate fragrance; long stems; vigorous, bushy growth

'Miss Daisy' -- See 'Jacflare'

'Miss Delightful'   F, my, 1966, Sanday, John; flowers bright yellow, 3 in., 30 petals, rosette, borne in heavy clusters; foliage glossy; vigorous, upright growth; [('Masquerade' × seedling) × 'Golden Scepter']

'Miss Dior' -- See 'Harencens'

Miss Dovey™ -- See 'Kindov'

'Miss Edith Cavell' ('Edith Cavell', 'Nurse Cavell') Pol, dr, 1917, deRuiter; flowers scarlet-crimson overlaid velvety crimson, small, semi-dbl., flat, borne in large clusters; low (2 ft.), bushy growth; [sport of 'Orléans Rose']

'Miss Edith Gifford' -- See 'Hon. Edith Gifford'

'Miss Elvis' ('Elvis') HT, ob, 2000, Edwards, Eddie; flowers full, high-centered, borne mostly singly, slight fragrance; foliage medium size, medium green, semi-glossy; few prickles; growth upright, medium (4½ ft.); [seedling × seedling]; intr. 2002

'Miss Emily' -- See 'Majmisem'

'Miss England'   HT, w, 1936, Cant, B. R.; flowers creamy, very large, dbl.; foliage leathery, dark; vigorous, compact growth

'Miss Ethel Brownlow' -- See 'Ethel Brownlow'

'Miss Ethel Richardson'   HP, w, 1897, Dickson, A.; flowers white tinged pink, very large, dbl.

'Miss Evelyn Davey'   T, 1905, Williams, A.; ['Souv de S.A. Prince' × 'Niphetos']

'Miss Finland'   F, ob

Miss Flippins™ -- See 'Tuckflip'

'Miss Flora Mitten' ('Flora Mitten') LCl, lp, 1913, Lawrenson; flowers soft pink, stamens yellow, 3 in., single, borne in small clusters, moderate fragrance; vigorous growth; [*R. wichurana* × *R. canina*]

'Miss France' ('Pretty Girl') Gr, or, 1955, Gaujard; flowers bright scarlet, large, dbl., globular; foliage bronze; vigorous growth; ['Peace' × 'Independence']

'Miss Frotter' HSpn, lp, before 1906, from Scotland

'Miss G. Mesman' ('Baby Rambler, Climbing') Cl Pol, mr, 1910, Mesman; flowers purplish red, borne in small clusters; sport of 'Mme Norbert Levavasseur']

'Miss G. Radcliffe' HT, 1900, Williams, A.; ['Pharisaer' × unknown]

'Miss Georgie' HT, ab, 1981, Warriner, William A.; flowers 35 petals, borne usually singly, moderate fragrance; foliage large, semi-glossy; prickles long; upright, compact growth; ['South Seas' × seedling]; intr. 1976

'Miss Glegg' N, w, 1835, Vibert; flowers white, center salmon, small, full

'Miss Gunnell' HSet, lp, about 1846, Pierce; flowers pale pink, with a tinge of buff, medium, dbl., cupped, borne in clusters of 25-30; foliage large, undulated, partially rugose

'Miss Harp' ('Anneliesse Rothenberger', 'Silhouette', 'Oregold') HT, dy, 1970, Tantau, Math.; flowers dbl., high-centered, borne mostly singly; foliage large, glossy, dark; vigorous, upright, bushy growth; PP3415; [Piccadilly® × 'Colour Wonder']; intr. 1970

'Miss Hassard' HP, lp, 1874, Turner; flowers delicate flesh pink, large, full, loose, moderate fragrance; prickles numerous, large; ['Marguerite de St Amand' × unknown]

'Miss Havisham' -- See 'Sabfairbanks'

'Miss Hawaii' HT, w, 1976, Payne; flowers creamy white, 5½-6 in., 30-35 petals, high-centered; foliage leathery; very vigorous growth; [sport of 'Hawaii']

'Miss Helyett' ('Miss Heylett') HWich, pb, 1909, Fauque; bud coral, rounded; flowers bright carmine-pink, center yellowish salmon-pink, 8-9 cm., dbl., open, borne singly or in small clusters; foliage large, dark green, glossy; vigorous, climbing (10-12 ft.) growth; [*R. wichurana* × 'Ernest Metz']

'Miss Henriette Tersteeg' HT, pb, 1922, Van Rossem; flowers flesh and salmon-pink, dbl.; [('Mme Abel Chatenay' × unknown) × 'Mrs Joseph Hill']

'Miss Heylett' -- See 'Miss Helyett'

'Miss Hillcrest' -- See 'Poulsalfai'

'Miss Hillcrest' HT, or, 1969, Curtis, E.C.; flowers large, dbl., high-centered, intense fruity fragrance; foliage glossy; vigorous, tall growth; PP3027; ['Peace' × 'Hawaii']

'Miss Hiroshima' HT, lp, Hiroshima; intr. 1983

'Miss House' HP, w, 1838, House; flowers satin white

'Miss Huntington' HT, ob, 1972, Patterson; bud ovoid; flowers bright orange, large, dbl., high-centered, moderate fragrance; foliage leathery; vigorous, upright growth; ['Ma Perkins' × 'San Francisco']; intr. 1971

'Miss Ingram' HP, w, 1867, Ingram; flowers white, shaded light flesh pink, center darker pink, large, full, globular

'Miss Ireland' HT, or, 1961, McGredy, Sam IV; flowers orange-red, yellow reverse, 5 in., 37 petals; foliage dark; vigorous, bushy growth; ['Tzigane' × 'Independence']; intr. 1961

'Miss Italia' S, Mansuino; intr. 1963

'Miss Jekyll' Ayr, lp, before 1934, from England; flowers light rose pink, medium, dbl.

'Miss Joan' Cl HT, op, 1943, Duehrsen; flowers copper-bronze and salmon-pink, large, dbl., globular; foliage dark, glossy; very vigorous, climbing growth; ['Ednah Thomas' × 'Golden Dawn']

'Miss Kate Moulton' HT, pb, 1906, Monson; flowers rosy pink shaded rosy salmon, large, dbl.; ['Mme Caroline Testout' × ('La France' × 'Mrs W.J. Grant')]

'Miss Kate Sessions' Cl HT, pb, 1953, Hieatt; flowers deep rose-pink on white base, reverse shell-pink, open, large, dbl., moderate fragrance; profuse, intermittent bloom; foliage light green, leathery; moderate, climbing growth; ['Heart of Gold' × 'Ednah Thomas']

'Miss Katherine G. Warren' T, mr, 1895, Bernaix; flowers carmine, shaded garnet, aging China pink, medium, full

'Miss Kitty' -- See 'Bezkit'

'Miss Koganei' Cl Min, rb, 1986, Asano, S.; flowers medium red, white eye, yellow stamens, 7-10 petals, cupped; foliage small; few prickles; vigorous (to 3 ft.) growth; ['Nozomi' × unknown]; intr. 1985

'Miss Lakeland' Min, dp, 2004, Barnes, Fred; flowers deep pink, reverse medium pink, 1½ in., dbl., borne in large clusters, slight fragrance; foliage small, medium green, glossy, healthy; prickles ¼ in., slight hooked; growth vigorous, bushy, medium (15 in.), exhibition, garden; [Minnie Pearl™ × unknown]; intr. 2004

'Miss Leslie' HT, w, 1998, Garrett, Troy O.; flowers white with light pink edges, very dbl., high-centered, borne mostly singly; foliage medium size, medium green, semi-glossy; prickles moderate; upright, tall growth; [sport of 'Rina Hugo']

'Miss Liberté' -- See 'Arovule'

'Miss Liberty' LCl, mp, 1959, Boerner; bud ovoid; flowers Tyrian rose, 9-10 cm., 15-20 petals, cupped, borne singly or in small clusters, moderate fragrance; repeat bloom; foliage dark, leathery; numerous prickles; strong stems; vigorous, climbing (10-12 ft.) growth; PP1529; ['New Dawn' × 'Minna Kordes']; intr. 1956

'Miss Liberty' -- See 'Arovule'

'Miss Lillian' S, pb, 2005, Shoup, George Michael; flowers semi-dbl., borne in small clusters, moderate fragrance; remontant; foliage large, dark green, semi-glossy; few prickles; growth spreading, tall (6-8 ft.); hedging; [('Buff Beauty' × Heritage®) × Heritage®]; intr. 2004

'Miss Lolita Armour' HT, or, 1919, Howard, F.H.; flowers deep coral-red suffused coppery red, base yellow, very large, dbl., cupped

'Miss Lolita Armour, Climbing' Cl HT, or, H&S

'Miss Lorraine' -- See 'Evelora'

'Miss Lowe' -- See 'Miss Lowe's Variety'

'Miss Lowe's Variety' ('Miss Lowe') Ch, mr, 1887, Lowe; flowers bright red, single; recurrent bloom; dwarf growth; possibly a sport of 'Slater's Crimson China'

'Miss Luann' Min, ob, 2000, Close, Clarence; flowers dark orange, 1½ in., dbl., borne in small clusters; growth medium (20-24 in.); [sport of 'Pink Meidiland']; intr. 2001

'Miss M. J. F. Gostling' Pol, Williams, A.; ['Miss Pollock' × unknown]

'Miss M. J. Spencer' HT, my, 1920, Dickson, H.; flowers clear bright golden yellow,, dbl.

'Miss M. Robertson' Pol, 1902, Williams, A.; ['Mlle Cécile Brünner' × unknown]

'Miss Maine 1999' S, dp, 1999, Law, Stephen; flowers deep pink, reverse medium pink, 2 in., full, borne in small clusters, slight fragrance; foliage small, medium green, semi-glossy; numerous prickles; bushy, medium (4 ft.) growth; hardy to -30°F; [sport of 'Henry Kelsey']

'Miss Maine 2000' S, lp, 2001, Law, Stephen; flowers light pink with white center, 3 in., single, borne in small clusters, slight fragrance; continuous bloom; foliage medium size, dark green, semi-glossy; prickles average, numerous; growth spreading, medium (3-4 ft.); garden decoration, hedge; very hardy; ['Henry Kelsey' × unknown]

'Miss Marion Manifold' ('Marion Manifold') Cl HT, mr, 1913, Adamson; flowers velvety scarlet, shaded crimson, large, dbl., globular, moderate fragrance; foliage large, leathery; vigorous, climbing (12 ft.) growth

'Miss Marston' T, pb, 1889, Pries/Ketten Bros.; flowers yellowish-white, bordered very deep pink, center yellow/peach/red, large, full, moderate violet fragrance; growth bushy

'Miss Mary' -- See 'Gelmiss'

'Miss May Marriott' HT, ab, 1917, Robinson, T.; flowers glowing apricot to orange-red, large, semi-dbl.; [sport of 'Mme Edouard Herriot']

'Miss May Paul' T, m, 1880, Levet; flowers lilac white, reverse red, large, full, globular to cupped, moderate fragrance; ['Mme Thérèse Genevay' × unknown]

'Miss May Thurlowe' T, Williams, A.

'Miss Mayne' HT, Williams, A.; ['Marie van

Houtte' × 'General Jacqueminot']
Miss Megan™ Min, mp, 2004, Rickard, Vernon; intr. 2004
'Miss Melanie' -- See 'Denmel'
'Miss Middleton' F, op, 1965, Hill, A.; flowers coral-pink, 2½-3 in., 20 petals, cupped, borne in small clusters; foliage light green; low, bushy growth; ['Independence' × 'Masquerade']
'Miss M'liss' F, mp, 1960, Jelly; bud short pointed; flowers phlox-pink, 2½-3 in., 25-30 petals, high-centered; very vigorous, upright growth; PP1888; ['Garnette' × ('Garnette' × unknown)]; intr. 1958
'Miss Modesto' HT, my, 1934, Brooks, L.L.; flowers pure yellow, very large, dbl., high-centered; [sport of 'Rev. F. Page-Roberts']
'Miss Muffett' Min, mp, 1955, Robinson, T.; bud rather mossy; flowers apple-blossom-pink, compact growth, 4-6 in., 80 petals; ['Baby Bunting' × 'Tom Thumb']
'Miss Muriel Jamison' -- See 'Muriel Jamison'
'Miss Murine' F, dp, 1937, Fitzgerald; flowers deep pink, base yellow, small, dbl.; upright, bushy growth; PP469; [seedling × 'Cécile Brunner']
'Miss N. Robertson' Pol, Williams, A.; ['Mlle Cécile Brünner' × unknown]
'Miss Newell' -- See 'Rawreport'
'Miss P. Williams' Pol, Williams, A.; ['Perle d'Or' × unknown]
'Miss Pam Ayres' -- See 'Kormarie'
'Miss Paris' mp, Cant; flowers clear rose pink; intr. 1987
'Miss Paula' Min, pb, 2004, Carman, Howard; flowers medium pink blend, reverse white, 2 in., dbl., borne mostly solitary, no fragrance; foliage medium size, dark green, glossy; growth upright, medium; exhibition, garden, cutting; [sport of 'Miss Flippins']; intr. 2006
Miss Pearl™ -- See 'Hoopearl'
Miss Perfect™ -- See 'Jacmiss'
'Miss Personality' F, pb, 1973, Sherwood; bud ovoid; flowers cerise-pink, white eye, open, medium, semi-dbl.; foliage small, dark, leathery; vigorous, bushy growth; ['Pink Parfait' × ('Ophelia' × Parkdirektor Riggers®)]; intr. 1972
'Miss Pollock' P, 1906, Williams, A.
'Miss Poole' HP, mp, 1875, Turner; flowers bright silvery pink, large, full; ['Victor Verdier' × unknown]
'Miss Pretty' HT, ob, Keisei; PP13438; intr. 2004
'Miss Prissy' HT, w, Wells; flowers white with pink tint on petal edges; intr. 1995
'Miss Rainbow' HT, rb; intr. 2004
'Miss Reus' HT, op, Dot; flowers salmon orange to vermilion
'Miss Rita' F, lp, Robertson; intr. about 1986
'Miss Rose' Gr, Dorieux
'Miss Rose Hill' HT, 1913, Williams, A.
'Miss Rowena Thom' HT, pb, 1927, H&S; flowers fiery rose and rosy mauve, center washed gold, 6 in., 50 petals, intense fragrance; vigorous growth; ['Radiance' × 'Los Angeles']
'Miss Rowena Thom, Climbing' Cl HT, pb, 1937, van Barneveld
'Miss Ruth' N, mp, Lowery, Gregg; flowers rose pink, fading lighter, small, 15-20 petals, cupped, borne in clusters, intense fragrance; recurrent; thornless; upright (6 ft.), arching growth; found as a seedling, possibly from R. moschata and/or The Garland.; intr. 2005
'Miss Salsa' -- See 'Twopaul'
'Miss Schweiz' -- See 'Tanziewsim'
'Miss Smithson' HSpn, m, 1827, Dagonnet; flowers violet-purple
'Miss Stewart Clark' HT, dy, 1916, Dickson, A.; flowers golden yellow, shaded citron and chrome yellow, medium, full, globular, moderate fragrance
'Miss Talmadge' HT, dy, 1927, Pacific Rose Co.; flowers dbl.; [sport of 'Constance']
'Miss Universe' HT, rb, 1956, Gaujard; bud long, pointed; flowers orange-red, reverse tinted copper, large; foliage dark; vigorous growth; [('Peace' × seedling) × seedling]
'Miss Universe, Climbing' Cl HT, rb; intr. after 1956
'Miss Wenn' T, mp, 1890, Guillot & fils; flowers large, full
'Miss Willmott' T, rb, 1899, Paul, G.; flowers coppery red; ['L'Ideal' × unknown]
'Miss Willmott' HT, ly, McGredy; bud large; flowers soft sulfur-cream, edges flushed pale pink, large, dbl., cupped, moderate fragrance; vigorous growth; intr. 1917
'Miss Windsor' HT, mr, 1967, Heron; flowers medium, dbl., high-centered; foliage light green, leathery; very vigorous, upright growth; [sport of 'Tropicana']
'Miss Winifred Denham' T, Williams, A.; ['Marie van Houtte' × unknown]
'Missing You' -- See 'Horcakebread'
'Mission Bells' HT, pb, 1949, Morris; bud long, pointed; flowers vermilion-pink, 5 in., 43 petals, high-centered, moderate fragrance; foliage dark, soft; vigorous, bushy growth; PP923; ['Mrs Sam McGredy' × 'Malar-Ros']
'Mission Supreme' HT, ab, 1981, Sanday, John; bud pointed; flowers pale peach pink to apricot, 30 petals, borne singly; foliage deep green; prickles straight, red-brown; vigorous, bushy, medium growth; ['City of Glouchester' × seedling]
'Mississippi' -- See 'Mme Charles Sauvage'
'Mississippi' HT, dr, 1976, Williams, J. Benjamin; bud pointed; flowers deep red, 4½-5 in., 38 petals, moderate damask fragrance; foliage dark; upright growth; ['Charlotte Armstrong' × Mister Lincoln®]; intr. 1976
'Mississippi Rainbow' HT, yb, 1977, Graham; flowers full, 4 in., 41 petals; foliage thick, glossy; upright growth
'Missy' Min, mr, 1979, Lyon; bud pointed; flowers cardinal-red, 1½ in., 22 petals; foliage small; compact, bushy growth; [seedling × seedling]; intr. 1978
'Missy Eleanor' S, pb, 1999, Watson, Thomas L, & Glenda; flowers light pink, yellow eye, reverse medium pink, 2½ in., single, borne in large clusters; foliage medium size, light green, glossy; prickles moderate; bushy, medium (4-6 ft.) growth; [Anna Ford® × 'Ballerina']
'Mistee' Min, ly, 1979, Moore, Ralph S.; bud long, pointed; flowers white, tinted yellow, 1½ in., 28 petals, flat, moderate fragrance; foliage small; bushy, upright growth; PP4618; ['Little Darling' × 'Peachy White']
'Mister America' LCl, dr, 1971, Zombory; flowers blood-red, very large, dbl., high-centered, moderate fragrance; abundant bloom; foliage leathery; very vigorous, climbing growth; [('Paul's Scarlet Climber' × 'Golden Climber') × 'Pinocchio']; intr. 1974
'Mr Bluebird' Min, m, 1960, Moore, Ralph S.; bud ovoid; flowers lavender-blue, 1¼ in., 15 petals; foliage dark; compact, bushy (10-14 in.) growth; ['Old Blush' × 'Old Blush']; intr. 1960
'Mr Chips' HT, yb, 1970, Dickson, A.; flowers yellow and orange, large, dbl., high-centered; foliage glossy; ['Irish Gold' × 'Miss Ireland']
'Mr E. E. Greenwell' -- See 'Harjoobily'
'Mr Ernest Holmes' ('Big Pink') HT, dp, 2000, Lindquist, Jr., Robert; flowers full, 25-31 petals, high-centered, borne mostly singly; large, medium green, semi-glossy foliage; spreading, pillar, tall (4-8 ft.) growth; introduced originally prior to 1940
'Mr Faithful' F, mp, 1968, Harkness; flowers dbl., borne in trusses; ['Pink Parfait' × 'Pink Parfait']
'Mr Feast's No. 1' -- See 'Queen of the Prairies'
'Mr Gladstone' HP, mp, 1866, Paul, G.; flowers medium, full
'Mr J. Bienfait' ('J. Bienfait') HT, mr, 1923, Van Rossem; flowers brick-red; ['Mme Leon Pain' × 'Red-Letter Day']
'Mr J. C. B.' ('Mr Joseph Cyril Bamford') S, dy, Dickson, Patrick; flowers small, single to semi-dbl., flat, open, borne in small clusters; foliage small, medium green, semi-glossy; growth spreading (groundcover), small; intr. 1993
'Mr Joh. M. Jolles' HT, ly, 1920, Van Rossem; flowers clear creamy yellow, shaded apricot and golden yellow,, dbl.; ['Frau Karl Druschki' × 'Mrs Joseph Hill']
'Mr John Laing' HP, mp, 1887, Bennett; flowers silky pink
'Mr Leigh' F, mp
'Mr Lenard' -- See 'Welscot'
Mister Lincoln® HT, dr, 1965, Swim & Weeks; bud urn-shaped; flowers 4½-6 in., 35 petals, high-centered to cupped, intense fragrance; foliage leathery, dark green, matte; vigorous, tall growth; PP2370; ['Chrysler Imperial' × 'Charles

Mallerin']; intr. 1965

'Mister Lincoln, Climbing' Cl HT, dr, 1976, Ram; intr. 1974

'Mr McCawber' -- See 'Whicaw'

'Mister Otis' -- See 'Curmist'

'Mr Pat' HT, dr, 1966, Patterson; bud globular; flowers large, dbl., high-centered, intense spicy fragrance; foliage leathery; compact growth; PP2881; ['Red Jacket' × 'Mirandy']

'Mister Sam' Min, yb, 2003, Guillebeau, Ray; flowers light yellow with pink, varying to dark pink with light yellow, reverse light yellow, 2 in., very full, borne mostly solitary, no fragrance; foliage medium size, medium green, semi-glossy; prickles average, curving down, brown, moderate; growth bushy, medium; garden decoration, exhibition; ['Dora Delle' × unknown]; intr. 2005

'Mister Softee' HT, w, 1964, Morton's Rose Nursery; flowers creamy white edged pink, open, 4½ in., very dbl.; foliage glossy, dark; very free growth

'Mr Standfast' HT, w, 1968, Harkness; flowers cream, large, dbl.; foliage glossy; ['Dr. A.J. Verhage' × 'Kordes' Perfecta']

'Mr Tall' HT, op, 1958, Wyant; bud long, pointed; flowers salmon-pink, open, 4 in., 7 petals, intense cinnamon fragrance; foliage dark, leathery; vigorous, upright growth; ['Vogue' × 'Grande Duchesse Charlotte']; intr. 1957

'Misterre' HT, pb

'Mistica' HT, m, 1967, Dot; bud ovoid; flowers lilac, very large, dbl., cupped, intense fragrance; foliage dark; vigorous growth; ['Sterling Silver' × 'Intermezzo']; intr. 1966

'Mistigri' -- See 'Molde'

'Mistigri' Min, dp, Dickson; flowers fuchsia, dbl., slight fragrance; growth to 50-60 cm.; intr. 2001

Mistral ™ -- See 'Mistral Parade'

'Mistral' S, ab, Barni; flowers deep apricot, outer petals fade, full, high-centered; growth to 4-5 ft.; intr. 2004

'Mistral Parade' (Mistral ™) MinFl, dy, Poulsen; flowers deep yellow, 5-8 cm., full, moderate fragrance; foliage dark, glossy; bushy (20-40 cm.) growth; intr. 2000

Mistraline® -- See 'Lapmisal'

'Mrs A. Glen Kidston' -- See 'Mrs Glen Kidston'

'Mrs A. Gordon' Cl T, 1916, Fell, J.B.

'Mrs A. Hudig' -- See 'Flaming June'

'Mrs A. J. Allen' HT, pb, 1930, Allen; flowers rich pink, base lemon-yellow, tipped almost white, large, dbl.; ['Richmond' × 'Souv. de Mme Boullet']

'Mrs A. J. Wylie' -- See 'Margaret M. Wylie'

'Mrs A. Kingsmill' S (HLaev), lp, 1911, Paul, G.; flowers pale pink, reverse soft rose, single; growth dwarf; ['Anemone' × unknown]

'Mrs A. M. Kirker' HP, mr, 1906, Dickson, H.; flowers glossy cherry red, very large, full, moderate fragrance

'Mrs A. R. Barraclough' HT, mp, 1926, McGredy; bud long, pointed; flowers bright carmine pink, large, dbl., high-centered; vigorous growth

'Mrs A. R. Barraclough, Climbing' Cl HT, mp, 1935, Fryers Nursery, Ltd.

'Mrs A. W. Atkinson' HT, w, 1918, Chaplin Bros.; flowers ivory-white, dbl.

'Mrs Aaron Ward' HT, yb, 1907, Pernet-Ducher; bud long, pointed; flowers yellow, occasionally washed salmon (quite variable), dbl., high-centered; dwarf, compact growth

'Mrs Aaron Ward, Climbing' Cl HT, yb, 1922, Dickson; flowers Indian yellow, nuanced salmon, very large, full, moderate fragrance; [sport of 'Mrs Aaron Ward']

'Mrs Albert Nash' HT, dr, 1929, Clark, A.; buds small; flowers deep black red, medium, dbl., loose, moderate fragrance; recurrent; growth to 1 m.

'Mrs Alfred Tate' HT, rb, 1909, McGredy; flowers coppery red shaded fawn, base shaded ochre

'Mrs Alfred West' HT, op, 1922, Cant, F.; flowers salmon-pink, dbl.

'Mrs Alice Broomhall' T, yb, 1910, Schwartz, A.; bud long; flowers salmon apricot, tinted coppery orange yellow, fading to pale pink, large, dbl.; ['Dr. Grill' × 'G. Nabonnand']

'Mrs Allen Chandler' B, w, 1903, Chandler; ['Mrs Paul' × unknown]

'Mrs Alston's Rose' ('Maud Alston', 'Mrs Maud Alston') Pol, dp, about 1940, Clark; flowers reddish-pink with lighter eye, semi-dbl., borne in large trusses

'Mrs Ambrose Ricardo' HT, yb, 1914, McGredy; flowers deep honey-yellow, overlaid brighter yellow, very large, dbl., moderate fragrance

'Mrs Amy Hammond' HT, pb, 1911, McGredy; flowers cream and amber, sometimes flushed pink, base apricot, large, dbl., moderate fragrance; ['Mme Abel Chatenay' × unknown]

'Mrs Andrew Carnegie' HT, w, 1913, Cocker; flowers white, center lightly tinted lemon-yellow, very large, dbl.; recurrent; ['Niphetos' × 'Frau Karl Druschki']

'Mrs Anne Dakin' LCl, pb, 1973, Holmes, R.; flowers salmon-pink, reverse cream, large, dbl.; foliage glossy; moderate, climbing growth; intr. 1972

'Mrs Annie Beaufays' -- See 'Frau Anny Beaufays'

'Mrs Anthony Spalding' HT, or, 1934, McGredy; flowers strawberry-red flushed orange, reverse shaded orange, dbl.; vigorous growth

'Mrs Anthony Waterer' HRg, dr, 1898, Waterer; flowers deep crimson-carmine, large, semi-dbl., intense fragrance; free-flowering; growth vigorous, spreading, 3-4 ft.; hardy; [R. rugosa × 'Général Jacqueminot']

'Mrs Archie Gray' HT, ly, 1914, Dickson, H.; flowers deep creamy yellow, opening light canary-yellow, large

'Mrs Arnold Burr' HT, w, 1945, Burr, A.; flowers pure white, large, very dbl., high-centered; foliage glossy; vigorous, upright growth; ['Peace' × unknown]

'Mrs Arthur Bide' HT, 1914, Bide

'Mrs Arthur Curtiss James' ('Golden Climber') LCl, my, 1933, Brownell; bud long, pointed; flowers golden yellow, 10-12 cm., 18 petals, borne mostly solitary, moderate fragrance; non-recurrent; foliage dark green, glossy; prickles large; vigorous, climbing growth; PP28; ['Mary Wallace' × unknown]

'Mrs Arthur E. Coxhead' HT, dr, 1911, McGredy; flowers claret-red, shaded brighter red, dbl.

'Mrs Arthur Johnson' HT, yb, 1920, McGredy; flowers rich orange-yellow to chrome-yellow

'Mrs Arthur Moore' HT, 1911, Moore, A.K.; ['Victor Hugo' × 'C.J. Graham']

'Mrs Arthur Munt' HT, yb, 1910, Dickson, A.; flowers dark creamy yellow with peach reflections, large, full

'Mrs Arthur Robert Waddell' HT, op, 1909, Pernet-Ducher; bud long, pointed; flowers reddish-salmon, reverse garnet-red, large, semi-dbl., open, slight apricot fragrance; vigorous growth

'Mrs Atlee' HT, op, 1926, Chaplin Bros.; flowers silvery pink, shaded soft salmon

'Mrs B. L. Rose' T, yb, 1902, Bernais fils; flowers coppery aurora yellow, shaded flesh, edges silvery rose-amaranth, medium, full, moderate fragrance

'Mrs B. R. Cant' ('Mrs Benjamin R. Cant') T, mp, 1901, Cant, B. R.; flowers silvery rose, base suffused buff, reverse deep rose, dbl., cupped, moderate fragrance; vigorous growth

'Mrs B. R. Cant, Climbing' Cl T, mp, 1960, Hjort; flowers rose-red to silvery pink; growth to 10-12 ft.; [sport of 'Mrs B. R. Cant']

'Mrs B. Story' T, pb, 1905, Williams, A.; ['Mme Lombard' × unknown]

'Mrs B. T. Galloway' HT, 1918, Byrnes

'Mrs Baker' HP, mr, 1876, Turner; flowers bright carmine shaded crimson, very large, full, globular, slight fragrance; stems bushy, shrubby (3 ft.) growth; ['Victor Verdier' × unknown]

'Mrs Bayard Thayer' HT, pb, 1915, Waban Conservatories; flowers clear silvery pink, reverse deep rose; [sport of 'Mrs Charles E. Russell']

'Mrs Beatty' HT, my, 1926, Cant, B. R.; flowers Marechal Niel yellow, moderate fragrance; foliage bronze; vigorous growth

'Mrs Beckwith' HT, my, 1922, Pernet-Ducher; bud long, pointed; flowers buttercup-yellow, edged lighter, open, semi-dbl.; vigorous growth

'Mrs Belmont Tiffany' HT, yb, 1918, Budlong; flowers golden yellow, base apricot-orange; [sport of 'Sunburst']

'Mrs Benjamin R. Cant' -- See 'Mrs B. R. Cant'

The Official Registry and Checklist — Rosa 505

'Mrs Bertram J. Walker'   HT, dp, 1915, Dickson, H.; flowers bright cerise-pink, large, dbl.

'Mrs Billy Crick'   LCl, mp, Scarman; intr. 1995

'Mrs Blamire Young'   HT, op, 1932, Young; flowers salmon pink, slightly more petals than parent; [sport of 'Una Wallace']

'Mrs Bosanquet' -- See 'Mistress Bosanquet'

'Mistress Bosanquet' ('Mrs Bosanquet', 'Pauline Bonaparte', 'Thé Sapho') B, lp, 1832, Laffay, M.; flowers rosy flesh. large, very dbl., cupped; vigorous growth

'Mrs Breedlove'   HT, pb, 1947, Breedlove; bud ovoid; flowers pink, base yellow, very large, very dbl.; foliage leathery, glossy, dark; vigorous, bushy growth; [sport of 'Golden Dawn']

'Mrs Brook E. Lee'   HT, 1918, Byrnes

'Mrs Brownell'   HT, rb, 1942, Brownell; flowers red to pink and coppery orange, medium, semi-dbl., moderate spicy fragrance

'Mrs Bryce Allan'   HT, dp, 1916, Dickson, A.; flowers rose-pink, very dbl.

'Mrs Bullen'   HT, rb, 1917, Pernet-Ducher; flowers crimson, shaded yellow, passing to carmine, large, dbl.

'Mrs C. E. Bernays' -- See 'Miss C. E. Bernays'

'Mrs C. E. Prell'   HT, rb, 1938, Fitzhardinge; bud long, pointed; flowers dark cerise, reverse pink, stamens golden, very large, dbl.; long stems; very vigorous growth; ['Gustav Grunerwald' × 'Betty Uprichard']

'Mrs C. E. Salmon'   HT, mp, 1917, Cant, F.; flowers single

'Mrs C. J. Bell' -- See 'Mrs Charles J. Bell'

'Mrs C. L. Fitzgerald'   F, pb, 1937, Fitzgerald; bud pointed; flowers deep pink, base apricot-yellow, small, dbl.; foliage glossy; upright growth; PP468; [seedling × 'Cécile Brunner']

'Mrs C. V. Haworth'   HT, ab, 1919, Dickson, A.; flowers cinnamon-apricot, passing to buff, large, semi-dbl., intense fragrance; ['Mrs Wemyss Quin' × 'Hugh Dickson']

'Mrs C. V. Haworth, Climbing'   Cl HT, ab, 1932, Cant, F.; flowers dark apricot with pink, large, semi-dbl.; [sport of 'Mrs C. V. Haworth']

'Mrs C. W. Dunbar-Buller'   HT, dp, 1919, Dickson, A.; flowers deep rosy carmine, large, dbl.

'Mrs C. W. Edwards'   HT, rb, 1924, McGredy; bud pointed; flowers crimson-carmine, base yellow, reverse veined yellow, over large, dbl., high-centered; foliage dark, glossy; long stems; very vigorous growth

'Mrs C. W. Thompson'   HMult, dp, 1920, U.S. Dept. of Agric.; flowers deep pink, quilled, small, dbl., borne in clusters; good seasonal bloom; vigorous, climbing growth

'Mrs Calvin Coolidge'   HT, yb, 1924, U.S. Cut Flower Co.; bud long, pointed; flowers golden yellow, deepening to rich orange, semi-dbl.; [sport of 'Ophelia']

'Mrs Campbell Hall'   T, ab, 1914, Hall/Dickson; flowers soft creamy buff, edged or suffused rose, center warm salmon, high-centered, intense fragrance; foliage leathery, dark; vigorous growth

'Mrs Caroline Swailes'   HP, lp, 1884, Swailes; flowers light flesh pink to flesh white, large, full; ['Eugénie Verdier' × unknown]

'Mrs Cecily McMullen' -- See 'Bosemwine'

'Mrs Chaplin'   HT, pb, 1918, Chaplin Bros.; flowers creamy pink, base shaded yellow

'Mrs Charles Bell' -- See 'Mrs Charles J. Bell'

'Mrs Charles Custis Harrison'   HT, m, 1910, Dickson, A.; flowers purple/pink, large, dbl.

'Mrs Charles E. Allan'   HT, ly, 1911, Dickson, H.; bud large, globular; flowers ocher yellow, aging to light yellow, medium to large, very full

'Mrs Charles E. F. Gersdorff' -- See 'Maylina'

'Mrs Charles E. Pearson'   HT, ob, 1913, McGredy; bud pointed; flowers orange-apricot, flushed fawn and yellow, large, globular to flat, slight fragrance

'Mrs Charles E. Russell' ('Pink American Beauty') HT, dp, 1914, Montgomery, A.; bud long, pointed; flowers rosy carmine, large, dbl., globular; foliage leathery; long stems; vigorous growth; ['Mme Caroline Testout' × ('Mme Abel Chatenay' × 'Marquise Litta de Breteuil')]

'Mrs Charles E. Shea'   HT, rb, 1917, McGredy; flowers shrimp pink, shaded scarlet, petals edges shaded dark red

'Mrs Charles H. Rigg'   HT, my, 1946, McGredy; bud long, pointed; flowers lemon-yellow, large, dbl.; vigorous growth

'Mrs Charles Hunter'   HT, dp, 1912, Paul, W.; flowers carmine-pink, large, dbl.

'Mrs Charles J. Bell' ('Mrs C. J. Bell', 'Shell-Pink Radiance', 'Salmon Radiance', 'Mrs Charles Bell') HT, op, 1915, Bell, Mrs. C.J.; flowers shell-pink, shaded soft salmon, large, dbl.; [sport of 'Radiance']

'Mrs Charles J. Bell, Climbing'   Cl HT, op, 1929, Thomasville Nursery

'Mrs Charles Lamplough'   HT, ly, 1920, McGredy; flowers pale lemon-yellow, very large, dbl.; vigorous growth; ['Frau Karl Druschki' × unknown]

'Mrs Charles Reed'   HT, w, 1914, Hicks; flowers pale cream, tinted deep peach, base soft golden yellow, dbl.

'Mrs Charles Steward'   HT, mp, 1960, Verschuren; flowers bright pink, large, dbl., intense fragrance; foliage dark; vigorous growth; intr. 1959

'Mrs Charles Tennant'   HT, yb, 1936, Cant, F.; flowers clear primrose, shaded rich canary-yellow; foliage bronze; vigorous growth

'Mrs Charlotte Guilfoyle'   HT, 1885, Johnson; ['M. Berard' × unknown]

'Mrs Claude Aveling'   HT, rb, 1929, Bees; flowers scarlet-cerise, tinted orange, base buttercup-yellow, anther, semi-dbl., moderate fruity fragrance; ['The Queen Alexandra Rose' × 'Gorgeous']

'Mrs Clement Yatman'   HT, dr, 1927, Hicks; flowers deep crimson, dbl.

'Mrs Cleveland' -- See 'Général Jacqueminot'

'Mrs Cocker'   HP, mp, 1899, Cocker; flowers carnation pink, becoming bluish red, large, full, globular, intense fragrance; ['Mrs John Laing' × 'Mabel Morrison']

'Mrs Colville'   HSpn, m; flowers bright crimson-purple, white eye, single; foliage dark; arching, vigorous (4 ft.) growth; [probably R. spinosissima × R. pendulina]

'Mrs Conway Jones'   HT, w, 1904, Dickson, A.; flowers velvety cream white, center tinted salmon pink, very large, very full, moderate fragrance

'Mrs Cornwallis-West'   HT, w, 1911, Dickson, A.; flowers white, center blush, very large, imbricated, globular; vigorous growth

'Mrs Courtney Page'   HT, ob, 1922, McGredy; bud long, pointed; flowers orange-cerise, shaded carmine, very large, dbl., high-centered; strong stems

'Mrs Cripps'   HP, mp, before 1845, Laffay; flowers delicate rose pink, with a deeper center, large, dbl.

'Mrs Curnock Sawday'   HT, mp, 1920, Hicks; flowers satiny pink, dbl.

'Mrs Cynthia Forde' -- See 'Miss Cynthia Forde'

'Mrs D. A. Koster'   Pol, 1934, Koster, D.A.

'Mrs Dan Prosser'   HT, rb, 1946, Prosser; flowers red shaded gold,, 5½ in., 60 petals, high-centered; foliage glossy, dark red when young; ['Mrs Sam McGredy' × 'Heinrich Wendland']

'Mrs David Baillie'   HT, dp, 1912, Dickson, H.; flowers carmine, penciled deeper, dbl.

'Mrs David Jardine'   HT, mp, 1908, Dickson, A.; flowers bright rosy pink, shading in the outer petals to salmon pink, very large, full

'Mrs David McKee'   HT, ly, 1904, Dickson, A.; flowers creamy yellow, well-formed, large, full, moderate fragrance; dwarf, compact growth; ['Frau Karl Druschki' × 'Kaiserin Auguste Viktoria']

'Mrs de Graw' -- See 'Champion of the World'

'Mrs DeGraw'   B, op, 1885, Burgess; flowers bright coral pink, borne in small clusters

'Mrs d'Ombrain'   HP, dr, 1862, Trouillard; flowers red, shaded black

'Mrs Doreen Pike' -- See 'Ausdor'

'Mrs Douglas Copeland'   HT, mp, 1945,

Clark, A.; flowers dbl.; vigorous growth

'Mrs Dudley Cross' ('Dudley Cross') T, yb, 1908, Paul, W.; flowers pale yellow, tinted in autumn with crimson, dbl.; vigorous growth

'Mrs Dudley Fulton' Pol, w, 1931, Thomas; flowers silver-white, large, single, borne in large clusters; dwarf growth; PP122; ['Dorothy Howarth' × 'Perle d'Or']

'Mrs Dunlop Best' -- See 'Cleveland II'

'Mrs Dunlop-Best, Climbing' Cl HT, ab, 1933, Rosen, L.P.

'Mrs Dunlop-Best' HT, ab, 1916, Hicks; bud long, pointed; flowers reddish-apricot, base coppery yellow, large, 28 petals, moderate fragrance; foliage leathery, bronze, glossy; vigorous growth

'Mrs E. Alford' HT, lp, 1913, Lowe; flowers silvery pink, large, dbl., high-centered

'Mrs E. Claxton' HT, pb, 1928, Cant, F.; flowers light pink, shaded salmon and carmine

'Mrs E. G. Hill' HT, w, 1906, Soupert & Notting; flowers alabaster-white, reverse rose-coral, well-shaped, large, dbl.; vigorous growth; ['Mme Caroline Testout' × 'Liberty']

'Mrs E. Gallagher' HT, dr, 1924, McGredy; flowers dark crimson

'Mrs E. J. Hudson' HT, mp, 1923, Lilley; flowers bright pink, dbl., globular; ['Mrs W.J. Grant' × unknown]

'Mrs E. J. Manners' HT, dr, 1938, Burbage Nursery; flowers deep velvety crimson, becoming darker, well-shaped; long, strong stems; vigorous, branching growth

'Mrs E. M. Gibson' HT, dr, 1940, Clark, A.; ['Countess of Stradbrooke' × unknown]

'Mrs E. M. Gilmer' HT, mr, 1927, Cook, J.W.; [seedling × 'Crusader']

'Mrs E. T. Stotesbury' HT, pb, 1918, Towill; flowers light cream-pink, reverse dark pink, very dbl.; [('Joseph Hill' × 'My Maryland') × 'Milady']

'Mrs E. Townsend' -- See 'Mrs Edward Townsend'

'Mrs E. W. Sterling' HT, mp, 1916, Cook, J.W.; flowers rose-pink; ['Antoine Rivoire' × 'pink seedling']

'Mrs E. Willis' HT, lp, Weightman; flowers semi-dbl.; growth moderate; ['Mme Segond Weber' × unknown]

'Mrs E. Willis' HT, op, 1923, Poulsen; flowers light salmon-pink, large, dbl., moderate fragrance

'Mrs E. Willis, Climbing' Cl HT, lp, 1948, Wilson

'Mrs E. Wood' HT, yb, 1934, Dickson, A.; bud very long; flowers light buff-yellow, tinted yellowish-salmon, becoming cream-yellow; vigorous growth

'Mrs Edith Stanley' HT, w, 1919, Easlea; flowers creamy white, shaded Indian yellow

'Mrs Edward J. Holland' HT, op, 1909, McGredy; flowers salmon-rose, large; moderately vigorous growth

'Mrs Edward Laxton' HT, ob, 1935, Laxton Bros.; flowers flaming orange and old-rose, large, very dbl., high-centered; foliage leathery, dark; very vigorous growth; ['Mrs Henry Bowles' × 'Shot Silk']

'Mrs Edward Mawley' T, pb, 1899, Dickson, A.; flowers bright rich pink, shading to rose or flesh, very large, full, moderate fragrance

'Mrs Edward Powell' HT, dr, 1911, Bernaix, P.; flowers velvety crimson, large, dbl., globular, moderate fragrance

'Mrs Edward Townsend' ('Mrs E. Townsend') HT, pb, 1911, Guillot; flowers soft rosy fawn, orange carmine reverse, large, full; ['Mme Laurette Messimy' × 'Mme Léon Pain']

'Mrs Elisha Hicks' HT, w, 1919, Hicks; flowers flesh, nearly white, dbl.; ['Frau Karl Druschki' × 'Mme Gabriel Luizet']

'Mistress Elliot' HP, m, 1841, Laffay; flowers purplish pink, silky, large, full, cupped, borne in clusters of 3-4; prickles short, pointed, reddish

'Mrs Erskine Pembroke Thom' HT, my, 1926, Howard, F.H.; bud long, pointed; flowers clear yellow, well-formed, large, 40 petals, moderate fragrance; vigorous growth; ['Grange Colombe' × 'Souv. de Claudius Pernet']

'Mrs Erskine Pembroke Thom, Climbing' Cl HT, my, 1933, Dixie Rose Nursery

'Mrs Eveline Gandy' HT, dr, 1965, Verschuren; flowers dark velvety crimson-scarlet, well-formed, large, 50 petals, high-centered, intense fragrance; bushy, healthy growth; intr. 1959

'Mrs F. F. Prentiss' HSet, lp, 1925, Horvath; flowers pale pink, 7-9 cm., dbl., borne in clusters of 5-10, moderate musky fragrance; vigorous, climbing growth; extremely hardy; [(R. setigera × R. wichurana) × 'Lady Alice Stanley']

'Mrs F. J. Jackson' HT, mr, 1933, LeGrice; bud pointed; flowers cerise, dbl.; foliage leathery, bronze; vigorous growth

'Mrs F. J. Knight' HT, mr, 1928, Knight, J.; flowers velvety scarlet; [sport of 'Lord Charlemont']

'Mrs F. Millar' HT, lp, 1904, Williams, A.

'Mrs F. R. Pierson' HT, dr, 1926, Pierson, F.R.; bud pointed; flowers crimson, shaded scarlet, very large, dbl.; [sport of 'Premier']

'Mrs F. W. Flight' HMult, dp, 1905, Flight/Cutbush; flowers rose-pink, fading to light pink, 4 cm., semi-dbl., open, borne in large clusters; non-recurrent; foliage large, rich green, soft; pillar (6-8ft.) growth; ['Crimson Rambler' × 'The Garland']

'Mrs F. W. Sanford' ('Pride of the Valley') HP, lp, 1898, Curtis; flowers pink tinged white, moderate fragrance; good repeat; [sport of 'Mrs John Laing']

'Mrs F. W. Woodroffe' T, lp, 1904, Williams, A.

'Mrs Farmer' HT, yb, 1918, Pernet-Ducher; bud pointed; flowers yellow, reverse reddish-apricot, dbl.

'Mrs Foley-Hobbs' T, pb, 1910, Dickson, A.; flowers soft ivory-white, edges tinged clear pink, dbl., moderate fragrance; vigorous, upright growth

'Mrs Forde' HT, pb, 1913, Dickson, A.; flowers carmine-rose on soft rose-pink, base chrome-yellow, large, dbl., moderate fragrance

'Mrs Francis King' HT, ly, 1934, Nicolas; flowers cream-white shaded straw-yellow, large, 80 petals, high-centered; foliage leathery; vigorous, bushy growth; PP253; ['Lady Lilford' × 'Leonard Barron']

'Mrs Frank Bray' HT, yb, 1912, Dickson, A.; flowers dark coppery yellow, aging to pink, large, full, moderate fragrance

'Mrs Frank Cant' HP, mp, 1898, Cant, F.; flowers carnation pink, base darker, reverse silvery white, large, very full; ['Mme Gabriel Luizet' × 'Baronne Nathalie de Rothschild']

'Mrs Frank Guthrie' HT, lp, 1923, Clark, A.; flowers deep flesh in autumn, pale in summer, semi-dbl.; foliage dark, leathery; [(R. gigantea × unknown) × unknown]

'Mrs Frank J. Usher' HT, yb, 1920, Dobbie; flowers rich yellow, edged rosy carmine, very dbl.; stems weak; ['Queen Mary' × seedling]

'Mrs Frank Schramm' HT, pb, 1934, Schramm; flowers bright glowing rose-pink, reverse slightly lighter, dbl., moderate fragrance; foliage leathery, dark; very large, long stems; very vigorous growth; PP72; [sport of 'Briarcliff']

'Mrs Frank Serpa' Pol, dp, 1954, Serpa; flowers deep pink, borne in clusters; dwarf (18 in.) growth; ['Rouletii' × 'China Doll']

'Mrs Frank Verdon' HT, my, 1935, Bees; flowers creamy yellow, very large, dbl.; foliage leathery, dark; vigorous growth; ['Joan Horton' × 'Marion Horton']

'Mrs Frank Workman' HT, dp, 1911, Dickson, H.; flowers bright rose-pink

'Mrs Franklin D. Roosevelt' HT, dy, 1933, Traendly & Schenck; bud long, pointed; flowers golden yellow, large, dbl., globular, moderate fragrance; foliage glossy; very vigorous growth; PP80; [sport of 'Talisman']

'Mrs Franklin Dennison' HT, w, 1915, McGredy; bud long, pointed; flowers porcelain-white, veiled primrose-yellow, base ochre, very large, dbl., high-centered

'Mrs Fred Cook' HT, ob, 1920, Easlea; flowers light terra-cotta, edged silvery white, dbl.

'Mrs Fred Danks' HT, m, 1951, Clark, A.; bud long, pointed; flowers pink tinted lilac, large, 15 petals; foliage leathery; very vigorous, upright, pillar growth

'Mrs Fred H. Howard' HT, ob, 1926, Dobbie; flowers orange-apricot edged straw-yellow, dbl.

'Mrs Fred L. Lainson' HT, pb, 1934, Scittine; bud long, pointed; flowers deep pink, almost red, base yellow and bronze, reverse orange, dbl.; foliage leathery, glossy, bronze; vigorous growth; [sport of 'Talisman']

'Mrs Fred Poulsom'   HT, mp, 1920, Therkildsen; flowers vivid pink; prickles thorny; vigorous growth; ['Edith Part' × seedling]

'Mrs Fred Searl'   HT, pb, 1917, Dickson, A.; flowers fawny shell-pink, reflex silvery carmine-rose, deeper at edges, large, full, globular, moderate fragrance

'Mrs Fred Straker'   HT, yb, 1910, Dickson, A.; flowers light orange-yellow, medium, dbl.

'Mrs Frederick Lee'   S, pb, J. B. Williams; flowers cherry pink with ivory center, 5 petals, borne usually in clusters, slight fragrance; growth to 5 ft.; intr. 2005

'Mrs Frederick W. Vanderbilt'   HT, or, 1912, McGredy; flowers deep orange-red, shaded apricot, large, dbl., pointed, moderate musky, tea fragrance

'Mrs G. A. van Rossem' -- See 'Mevrouw G. A. van Rossem'

'Mrs G. A. van Rossem, Climbing' -- See 'Mevrouw G. A. van Rossem, Climbing'

'Mrs G. A. Wheatcroft'   HT, pb, 1926, Wheatcroft Bros.; flowers coppery pink to silver-rose at tips, reverse soft salmon-pink, dbl.; [sport of 'Lady Pirrie']

'Mrs G. M. Smith'   HT, dr, 1935, Bees; bud long, pointed; flowers deep crimson, dbl., cupped; vigorous growth; ['Red-Letter Day' × 'Mrs J.J. Hedley-Willis']

'Mrs G. Payne'   T, lp, 1911, Williams, A.

'Mrs G. W. Kershaw'   HT, mp, 1906, Dickson, A.; flowers shining carnation pink, very large, full

'Mrs George B. Easlea'   HT, dp, 1939, Easlea; flowers sparkling carmine-pink, well-formed, very large, high-centered; strong stems

'Mrs George C. Thomas'   HMsk, op, 1925, Thomas; flowers salmon-pink, center orange, 2-2½ in., semi-dbl.; repeat bloom; climbing growth to 10ft.; ['Mme Caroline Testout, Climbing' × 'Moonlight']

'Mrs George Dickson'   HP, mp, 1884, Bennett; flowers brilliant satiny pink, large, dbl.; ['Mme Clémence Joigneaux' × unknown]

'Mrs George Geary'   HT, ob, 1929, Burbage Nursery; bud pointed; flowers orange-cerise, shaded cardinal, very large, 35-40 petals, high-centered; vigorous growth; ['Red-Letter Day' × 'Mrs Wemyss Quin']

'Mrs George Gordon'   HT, mr, 1915, Dickson; flowers glossy rose red, edged silvery pink, base yellowish-pink, large, full

'Mrs George Marriott'   HT, w, 1918, McGredy; bud long, pointed; flowers deep cream and pearl, suffused rose, very large, dbl., high-centered

'Mrs George Preston'   HT, lp, 1910, Dickson, A.; flowers silvery pink, very large, full, globular

'Mrs George Shawyer'   HT, pb, 1911, Lowe & Shawyer; flowers rosy pink, reverse pale pink, very large, dbl.; ['Mme Hoste' × 'Joseph Lowe']

'Mrs George Shawyer, Climbing'   Cl HT, pb, 1918, Lindquist, E.J.

'Mrs Georgia Chobe'   HT, lp, 1937, H&S; bud long; flowers large, dbl., high-centered; foliage leathery, light; vigorous growth; ['Miss Rowena Thom' × 'Renault']

'Mrs Glen Kidston' ('Mrs A. Glen Kidston')   HT, dp, 1916, Dickson; flowers carmine-pink, large, full, moderate fragrance

'Mrs Gordon Sloan'   HT, op, 1912, Dickson, A.; flowers bright coppery salmon pink, center flesh white, edged cream white, large, full

'Mrs Graham Hart'   Cl T, lp, 1900, Williams, A.

'Mrs H. Cobden Turner'   HT, rb, 1948, Mee; flowers cherry-cerise flushed orange, base yellow, 3-4 in., 26 petals; foliage glossy; moderately vigorous growth; ['Ophelia' × seedling]

'Mrs H. D. Greene'   HT, rb, 1918, Easlea; flowers reddish-bronze, becoming flame and coppery pink; [sport of 'Joseph Hill']

'Mrs H. G. Johnstone'   HT, mp, 1930, Bees; bud long; flowers rose-pink, base and edges rose, very large, dbl., high-centered; vigorous growth; ['Mme Caroline Testout' × 'Mrs George Shawyer']

'Mrs H. J. Hedley-Willis'   HT, dr, 1930, Bees of Chester; flowers medium, semi-dbl.

'Mrs H. L. Wettern'   HT, mp, 1922, McGredy; flowers vivid pink, dbl.

'Mrs H. M. Eddie'   HT, w, 1932, Eddie; flowers creamy white, passing to purest white, 5-6 in., 40-45 petals, high-centered; foliage dark, leathery, glossy; vigorous, bushy growth; PP753; ['Mrs Charles Lamplough' × 'Mev. G.A. van Rossem']

'Mrs H. M. Eddie, Climbing'   Cl HT, w, 1944, Eddie

'Mrs H. P. Abbot'   T, lp, 1901, Williams, A.; ['Mme Lombard' × unknown]

'Mrs H. R. Darlington'   HT, ly, 1919, McGredy; bud long, pointed; flowers clear creamy yellow, well-formed, balling in wet weather; long stems; vigorous growth

'Mrs Harkness' -- See 'Paul's Early Blush'

'Mrs Harkness'   HP, pb, 1894, Harkness; flowers white striped pink; [sport of 'Heinrich Schultheis']

'Mrs Harold Alston'   Cl HT, mp, 1940, Clark, A.; flowers dbl.; good repeat; ['Sunny South' × unknown]

'Mrs Harold Bibby'   HT, pb, 1936, Bees; flowers soft pink veined red, outer petals silvery pink; foliage dark

'Mrs Harold Brocklebank'   HT, w, 1907, Dickson, A.; flowers creamy white, center buff, base soft yellow, dbl.

'Mrs Harold Brookes'   HT, mr, 1931, Clark, A.; flowers very bright red, large, dbl., cupped, moderate fragrance; foliage light; vigorous, bushy growth; ['Frau Oberhofgartner Singer' × 'Firebrand']

'Mrs Harry Turner'   HP, mr, 1880, Turner; flowers shining scarlet-crimson, shaded chestnut, large, full, globular; ['Charles Lefèbvre' × 'Alfred de Rougemont']

'Mrs Harvey Thomas'   HT, pb, 1905, Bernaix fils; flowers carmine with coppery red reflections, large, full, cupped, moderate fragrance

'Mrs Henri Daendels, Climbing'   Cl HT, ab, 1950, Buisman, G. A. H.

'Mrs Henri Daendels' ('Mevrouw Daendels')   HT, ab, 1931, Buisman, G. A. H.; flowers apricot shaded orange, reverse violet-pink, large, very dbl.; foliage bronze; strong stems; very vigorous growth; ['Mrs Henry Bowles' × 'Rev. F. Page-Roberts']

'Mrs Henry Balfour'   HT, pb, 1918, McGredy; flowers ivory-white, base primrose, edge penciled rose, like a picotee

'Mrs Henry Bowles'   HT, mp, 1921, Chaplin Bros.; flowers rosy-pink, flushed salmon, well-formed, large, 50 petals, high-centered; foliage dark, glossy; vigorous growth; ['Lady Pirrie' × 'Gorgeous']

'Mrs Henry Bowles, Climbing'   Cl HT, mp, 1929, Dobbie; flowers pink, peach at base, very large

'Mrs Henry Morse' ('Korbel Bicolor Pink')   HT, pb, 1919, McGredy; bud long, pointed; flowers cream, tinted rose, marked and veined red, large, dbl., high-centered; dwarf growth; ['Mme Abel Chatenay' × 'Lady Pirrie']

'Mrs Henry Morse, Climbing'   Cl HT, pb, 1929, Chaplin Bros.; flowers yellowish-pink, very large, full; [sport of 'Mrs Henry Morse']

'Mrs Henry Winnett'   HT, dr, 1917, Dunlop; bud long, pointed; flowers deep rich red, large, dbl., high-centered; foliage leathery; vigorous growth; ['Mrs Charles E. Russell' × 'Mrs George Shawyer']

'Mrs Henry Winnett, Climbing'   Cl HT, dr, 1930, Bernaix, P.; flowers large, full, moderate fragrance; [sport of 'Mrs Henry Winnett']

'Mrs Herbert Carter'   HT, ab, 1934, Cant, F.; flowers apricot-yellow, center deeper, veined bronze, dbl., moderate fragrance; vigorous growth

'Mrs Herbert Dowsett'   HT, pb, 1928, Easlea; flowers several shades deeper, otherwise similar to parent; [sport of 'Los Angeles']

'Mrs Herbert Hawksworth'   T, r, 1912, Dickson, A.; flowers ecru on milk-white, dbl.

'Mrs Herbert Hoover'   HT, mr, 1928, Coddington; bud long, pointed; flowers rich velvety red, dbl.; foliage dark, leathery; vigorous growth; ['Ophelia' × 'Hoosier Beauty']

'Mrs Herbert Nash'   HT, dr, 1925, Chaplin Bros.; flowers scarlet-crimson shaded deep crimson, overlarge; long, strong stems; vigorous growth

'Mrs Herbert Stevens' HT, w, 1910, McGredy; bud long, pointed; flowers white tinged with soft pink, dbl., high-centered, moderate fragrance; foliage light; vigorous, bushy growth; ['Frau Karl Druschki' × 'Niphetos']

'Mrs Herbert Stevens, Climbing' ('Grimpant Mrs Herbert Stevens', 'Stevens,Climbing') Cl HT, w, 1922, Pernet-Ducher; bud large, pure white; flowers semi-dbl., intense fragrance; foliage large; growth to 12 ft.; [sport of 'Mrs Herbert Stevens']

'Mrs Hilton Brooks' HT, yb, 1929, Cant, F.; flowers saffron-yellow, base deeper, suffused pink and carmine, dbl., moderate fragrance

'Mrs Hornby Lewis' HT, ob, 1921, Hicks; flowers orange-yellow, very dbl.; ['Gorgeous' × 'Mme Mélanie Soupert']

'Mrs Hovey' HSet, w, 1850, Pierce; flowers blush to almost white, large, full; foliage dark green; [R. setigera × unknown]

'Mrs Hubert Taylor' T, pb, 1910, Dickson, A.; flowers shell pink, edges with ivory white; susceptible to mildew

'Mrs Hugh Dettmann' Cl HT, ab, 1930, Clark, A.; flowers bright apricot-yellow, dbl.; non-recurrent; climbing growth; pillars

'Mrs Hugh Dickson' HT, yb, 1915, Dickson, H.; flowers deep cream, heavily suffused orange and apricot, large, 44 petals

'Mrs Inge Poulsen' ('Fru Inge Poulsen') F, pb, 1949, Poulsen, S.; flowers pink with a yellow center, open, medium, semi-dbl.; foliage light, matte; vigorous, compact (80 cm.) growth; PP1050; ['Poulsen's Pink' × seedling]; intr. 1949

'Mrs Iris Clow' -- See 'Harbrite'

'Mrs Isabel Milner' -- See 'Isabelle Milner'

'Mrs J. Berners' HP, dp, 1866, Ward; flowers magenta pink, small

'Mrs J. C. Ainsworth' HT, mp, 1918, Clarke Bros.; flowers rose-pink, very dbl.; [sport of 'Mrs Charles E. Russell']

'Mrs J. C. Manifold' HP, lp, 1915, Adamson; ['Prince Camille de Rohan' × unknown]

'Mrs J. D. Eisele' HT, pb, 1933, Howard, F.H.; bud long, pointed; flowers brilliant cherry-pink, center shaded scarlet, very large, dbl., intense fragrance; vigorous growth; PP67; ['Premier Supreme' × 'McGredy's Scarlet']

'Mrs J. D. Russell' HT, dr, 1930, Bees; flowers deep crimson, center maroon, almost black in certain lights, dbl., cupped; ['Prince Camille de Rohan' × 'Mrs Aaron Ward']

'Mrs J. F. Redly' HT, lp; flowers pale flesh-pink, center tinted salmon, large, very dbl.; lightly repeats in late summer.; vigorous growth

'Mrs J. Heath' HT, yb, 1924, McGredy; flowers maize-yellow, tinted peach-red, center yellow, dbl.

'Mrs J. J. Hedley-Willis' HT, dr, 1929, Bees; bud pointed; flowers dark crimson, center almost plum-black, dbl., high-centered; ['Admiral Ward' × 'Richmond']

'Mrs J. Pierpont Morgan' T, dp, 1895, May; flowers bright cerise or rose pink, large, very dbl.; [sport of 'Mme Cusin']

'Mrs J. T. McIntosh' HT, ab, 1935, McIntosh; flowers creamy apricot, center deeper apricot, base golden yellow, dbl.; vigorous growth

'Mrs J. Wylie' HT, lp, 1923, Dickson, H.; flowers silvery blush-pink

'Mrs James Craig' HT, op, 1909, Dickson, H.; flowers salmon pink, petal edges peach, large, full

'Mrs James Garner' HT, ab, 1931, Cant, F.; flowers buff, base orange

'Mrs James Lynas' HT, pb, 1914, Dickson, H.; flowers pearly pink, reverse and edges flushed rosy peach, dbl.

'Mrs James Shearer' HT, w, 1923, Ferguson, W.; flowers pure white, base yellow, large, dbl., high-centered; [seedling × 'Mme Colette Martinet']

'Mrs James White' HT, w, 1911, Dickson, H.; flowers muddy whitish-pink, medium, full

'Mrs James Williamson' HT, mp, 1922, Dickson, H.; flowers clear pink, dbl.

'Mrs James Wilson' T, yb, 1889, Dickson, A.; flowers deep lemon yellow, edged pink, very large, full, moderate fragrance; growth upright, vigorous

'Mrs Jeannette G. Leeds' HT, rb, 1942, Joseph H. Hill, Co.; bud globular, jasper-red and apricot-buff; flowers venetian pink, 5-6 in., 50-60 petals; foliage dark, leathery; very vigorous, upright growth; PP515; ['Joanna Hill' × R.M.S. Queen Mary]

'Mrs Jennie Deverman' HT, pb, 1933, Deverman; flowers cerise edged silvery, base tinted gold; [sport of 'Pres. Herbert Hoover']

'Mrs Jessie Fremont' T, w, 1891, Dingee & Conard; flowers white, aging to deep flesh pink, sometimes shaded with coppery red, medium; ['Duchesse de Brabant' × unknown]

'Mrs Joan Lewis' S, m, 2000, Lewis, Victor; flowers mauve-pink, reverse light pink, 11-12 cm., very full, borne mostly singly; foliage large, light green, matte; numerous prickles; growth spreading, tall (2 m.)

'Mrs John Bateman' HT, dp, 1905, Dickson, A.; flowers dark China pink, base tinted yellow, very full

'Mrs John Bell' HT, dr, 1928, Bell, Judy G.; bud long; flowers carmine, large, dbl., cupped

'Mrs John Cook' HT, w, 1920, Cook, J.W.; bud long, pointed; flowers white, suffused soft pink, deepening in cool weather, large, dbl., cupped; ['Ophelia' × seedling]

'Mrs John Foster' HT, dr, 1915, Hicks; flowers rich vermilion, large, dbl., moderate fragrance

'Mrs John Inglis' HT, dr, 1920, McGredy; flowers rich crimson, dbl.

'Mrs John K. Allan' HT, lp, 1920, Dickson, H.; flowers soft rosy pink, reverse darker, dbl.

'Mrs John Laing' HP, mp, 1887, Bennett; bud pointed; flowers soft pink, large, 45 petals, moderate fragrance; recurrent bloom; foliage light; vigorous, rather dwarf growth; ['Francois Michelon' × unknown]

'Mrs John McLaren' HP, dp, 1905, California Nursery Co.; flowers deep silvery pink

'Mrs John McNabb' S, w, 1941, Skinner; bud with very long sepals; flowers very dbl.; non-recurrent; foliage large, dark, slightly rugose, prickly underneath; few prickles; growth to 5 ft.; [R. beggeriana × R. rugosa]

'Mrs John Taylor' T, mp, 1887, Bennett; flowers silky pink

'Mrs Jones' -- See 'Centenaire de Lourdes'

'Mrs Joseph H. Welch' HT, mp, 1911, McGredy; flowers brilliant rose-pink, large, dbl.; vigorous growth

'Mrs Joseph H. Welch, Climbing' Cl HT, mp, 1922, Perkins, H.S.

'Mrs Joseph Hiess' Pol, lp, 1943, Shepherd; flowers Mary Wallace pink, base white, 40 petals, cupped, borne in clusters of 3-16; foliage leathery; strong stems; growth vigorous, upright, bushy, compact; ['Roserie' × unknown]

'Mrs Jowitt' HP, rb, 1880, Cranston; flowers glossy crimson, shaded salmon red, very large, full, globular

'Mrs K. B. Sharma' HT, w, Pal, Dr. B.P.; buds long; flowers flower petals very large, slight fragrance; intr. 1989

'Mrs L. B. Coddington' HT, mp, 1931, Coddington; bud long, pointed; flowers large, dbl.; foliage leathery; vigorous growth; ['Templar' × 'Souv. de Claudius Pernet']

'Mrs L. B. Copeland' F, pb, 1934, Fitzgerald; flowers salmon-pink, veined, base yellow, small, dbl., globular, intense fragrance; foliage dark, glossy; vigorous growth; PP467; [seedling × 'Cécile Brunner']

'Mrs Laing' HP, mp, 1872, Verdier, E.; flowers bright carmine pink, medium, full

'Mrs Laing' HP, mp, Cranston; flowers carmine pink; intr. 1882

'Mrs Laxton' HP, mp, 1875, Laxton; flowers bright crimson-pink, very large, very full, moderate fragrance

'Mrs Leela Subhedar' -- See 'Leela'

'Mrs Leonard Petrie' HT, yb, 1911, Dickson, A.; flowers sulfur-yellow, reverse petal edges with wine red reflections, large, full, moderate fragrance

'Mrs Leslie Moss' Cl HT, dp, 1944, Moss; flowers carmine-pink, medium, semi-dbl.; foliage leathery; vigorous, climbing growth

'Mrs Lincoln' HT, dr, Williams, J. Benjamin; flowers large, dark red with velvet texture, slight fragrance; growth strong, upright plant; intr. 1997

'Mrs Littleton Dewhurst' HWich, w, 1912, Pearson; flowers small, semi-dbl., borne in large, loose trusses; [sport of 'Lady Gay']

'Mrs Lovell Swisher' HT, pb, 1926, Howard, F.H.; bud pointed; flowers salmon-pink, edged flesh, well-formed, dbl., moderate fragrance; foliage bronze; very vigorous growth; [seedling × 'Souv. de Claudius Pernet']

'Mrs Lovell Swisher, Climbing' Cl HT, pb, 1930, H&S

'Mrs Luther Burbank' HT, mp, 1954, Swim, H.C.; bud long, pointed; flowers rose-pink, 4-4½ in., 34 petals, cupped, intense spicy fragrance; foliage leathery; vigorous growth; PP952; ['Christopher Stone' × 'Charlotte Armstrong']; intr. 1954

'Mrs M. H. Horvath' HT, ly, 1940, Horvath; bud long, pointed; flowers pale yellow, open, large, 40 petals; foliage glossy; long stems; very vigorous, upright growth; [('Mme Butterfly' × unknown) × 'Souv. de Claudius Pernet']

'Mrs M. H. Walsh' HWich, w, 1913, Walsh; flowers pure snow-white, small, dbl., borne in clusters; foliage large, glossy, very vigorous, trailing growth

'Mrs M. J. Gillon' ('Mevrouw M. J. Gillon', 'Mme Gillen', 'Mrs Gillen') HT, dr, 1976, Rijksstation Voor Sierplantenteelt; bud ovoid; flowers red-purple, 4 in., 37 petals, globular, moderate fragrance; foliage glossy, dark; upright growth; ['Super Star' × 'Prima Ballerina']; intr. 1974

'Mrs Mabel V. Socha' HT, my, 1935, H&S; bud pointed; flowers pure lemon-yellow, dbl.; long, strong stems; [seedling × 'Souv. de Claudius Pernet']

'Mrs MacDonald's Rose' HRg, dp, Reid; non-recurrent; apparently R. rugosa plena × R. acicularis

'Mrs MacKellar' HT, my, 1915, Dickson, A.; flowers deep citron or pure canary, passing to primrose, large, dbl., high-centered, moderate fragrance

'Mrs Mary D. Ward' HT, pb, 1927, Ward, F.B.; flowers shell-pink and gold, reverse ivory-white; ['Double Ophelia' × 'Souv. de Claudius Pernet']

'Mrs Mary Thomson' -- See 'Tomone'

'Mrs Matso's Moss' M, dr

'Mrs Matthews' HT, dp, 1923, Matthews, W.J.

'Mrs Maud Alston' -- See 'Mrs Alston's Rose'

'Mrs Maud Dawson' -- See 'Maud Dawson'

'Mrs Mavis Watson' -- See 'Woranchor'

'Mrs Maynard Sinton' HT, pb, 1909, McGredy; flowers silvery white suffused pink, very large; moderately vigorous growth

'Mrs Mina Lindell' Sp, lp, 1927; flowers, 10-12 petals; non-recurrent; growth to 4 ft.; hardy; a form of R. macounii, found in S. Dakota

'Mrs Miniver' ('Souv de Louis Simon') HT, mr, 1944, Chambard, C.; flowers scarlet-crimson, reverse slightly darker, 5½-6 in., 20 petals, cupped, moderate fragrance; foliage soft; vigorous, upright, bushy, compact growth; PP725

'Mrs Mona Hunting' HT, yb, 1916, Dickson, H.; bud long, pointed, deep chamois yellow; flowers pure fawn, medium, dbl.

'Mrs Moorfield Storey' HT, lp, 1915, Waban Conservatories; flowers shell-pink, center deeper, large, dbl.; [('Gen. MacArthur' × unknown) × 'Joseph Hill']

'Mrs Moyna' HT, 1913, Dickson

'Mrs Muir MacKean' HT, dr, 1912, McGredy; flowers carmine-crimson, large, high-centered; vigorous growth

'Mrs Murray Allison' HT, pb, 1925, Prior; flowers rose-pink, base carmine, dbl.

'Mrs Myles Kennedy' T, pb, 1906, Dickson, A.; flowers silvery white tinted buff, center and reverse pink, large, dbl.; vigorous growth

'Mrs Nancy Cannon' HMsk, m, 2004, Clyde W. Cannon; flowers mauve, reverse light mauve, 1 in., single, borne in clusters of 15-20, no fragrance; continuous; foliage medium size, medium green, matte; prickles 3/16 in., slightly curve, few; growth bushy, short; border, containers; [sport of 'Ballerina']; intr. 2003

'Mrs Nieminen' HT, rb, 1954, Buyl Frères; flowers blood-red shaded scarlet, well-formed, large, very dbl.; bushy, compact growth; ['Hens Verschuren' × 'Poinsettia']

'Mrs Norman Watson' Cl HT, dp, 1930, Clark, A.; flowers deep cherry-pink, lighter at edges, 5 in., borne mostly solitary; growth very vigorous, pillar; ['Radiance' × 'Gwen Hash']

'Mrs Norris M. Agnew' HT, ob, 1934, Bees; bud pointed; flowers orange-cerise, large, dbl.; foliage leathery, light; very vigorous growth; ['J.C. Thornton' × 'Florence L. Izzard']

'Mrs O. G. Orpen' HGal, dp, 1906, Orpen; flowers glowing carnation pink, center lighter, large

'Mrs Oakley Fisher' HT, dy, 1921, Cant, B. R.; flowers deep orange-yellow, very large, single, borne in clusters, moderate fragrance; foliage dark, bronze, glossy; vigorous growth

'Mrs Octavia Hill' -- See 'Harzeal'

'Mrs Olive Sackett' F, mr, 1931, Wirtz & Eicke; flowers bright red, well-formed, 2-2½ in., semi-dbl.; foliage bronze in autumn; vigorous growth; [sport of 'Else Poulsen']

'Mrs Oliver Ames' T, pb, 1898, Montgomery, R.; flowers delicate pink, edged deep pink, nearly white at base, ruffled, full; growth compact, bushy; [sport of 'Mme Cusin']

'Mrs Oliver Ames' T, dp, May; flowers deep pink with darker edges; intr. 1902

'Mrs Oliver Ames' HT, my, Verschuren; bud long, pointed; flowers lemon-yellow, 3½-4 in., 63 petals, globular, intense fragrance; foliage leathery; long stems; vigorous growth; PP497; ['Max Krause' × 'Julien Potin']; intr. 1941

'Mrs Oliver Mee' HT, rb, 1948, Mee; flowers scarlet shaded gold, 5-6 in., 35 petals, high-centered; foliage glossy, bronze; very vigorous growth; ['Mrs Charles Lamplough' × 'Edith Mary Mee']

'Mrs Opie' T, op, 1877, Bell; flowers glowing salmon pink, medium to large, full

'Mrs Oswald Lewis' HT, yb, 1936, Cant, F.; flowers soft canary-yellow, outer petals edged flame, well-formed, dbl.; long stems; vigorous growth

'Mrs Oswald Smeaton' HT, pb, 1932, Easlea; flowers ivory-cream, center and petal tips pink, very large, 50-60 petals; long stems; vigorous growth

'Mrs P. H. Coats' HT, w, 1909, Dickson, H.; flowers cream white, large, full

'Mrs Pat' Pol, lp, 1928, Lilley; flowers Chatenay pink, small, dbl., moderate fragrance

'Mrs Paul' B, lp, 1891, Paul & Son; flowers blush-white shaded rosy peach, large, moderate Damask fragrance; recurrent; stout, upright, modest growth; ['Mme Isaac Pereire' × unknown]

'Mrs Paul Goudie' ('Shining Sun') HT, yb, 1932, McGredy; flowers deep buttercup-yellow, edged carmine-scarlet, very large, dbl., moderate fruity fragrance

'Mrs Paul Hvid' B, w

'Mrs Paul J. Howard' Cl HT, rb, 1938, Howard, F.H.; bud long, pointed; flowers brilliant crimson, reverse flame-red, 5 in., 30 petals, moderate spicy fragrance; foliage large, bronze,leathery; long stems; very vigorous, climbing (12-15 ft.) growth; PP450; ['Miss Rowena Thom' × 'Paul's Lemon Pillar']

'Mrs Paul M. Pierson' HT, pb, 1930, Pierson, P.M.; bud long, pointed; flowers soft pink, reverse brighter, very large, dbl., high-centered; [sport of 'Premier']

'Mrs Paul R. Bosley' HT, my, 1941, Bosley Nursery; flowers apricot-yellow; PP441; [sport of 'Mme Joseph Perraud']

'Mrs Percy V. Pennybacker' HT, pb, 1929, Vestal; flowers peach-pink shaded silver, dbl., cupped; ['Mme Butterfly' × unknown]

'Mrs Peter Blair' HT, yb, 1906, Dickson, A.; flowers lemon-chrome, center golden yellow, well-formed, large

'Mrs Philip Russell' HT, dr, 1927, Clark, A.; bud long, pointed; flowers dark red, shaded black, semi-dbl.; foliage glaucous green; vigorous, semi-climbing growth; pillar or large bush; ['Hadley' × 'Red Letter Day']

'Mrs Pierce' HSet, mp, 1850, Pierce; flowers rose pink, well-formed

'Mrs Pierre S. duPont' ('Mme Pierre S. duPont') HT, my, 1929, Mallerin, C.;

bud long, pointed, reddish gold; flowers golden yellow, becoming lighter, 40 petals, moderate fruity fragrance; foliage rich green; moderate growth; [('Ophelia' × 'Rayon d'Or') × (('Ophelia' × 'Constance') × 'Souv. de Claudius Pernet')]

'Mrs Pierre S. duPont, Climbing' ('Mme Pierre S. duPont, Climbing') Cl HT, my, 1933, Hillock; flowers yellow on an ochre ground, large, full, moderate fragrance; [sport of 'Mrs Pierre S. Dupont']

'Mrs Potter Palmer' HT, op, 1909, Breitmeyer; flowers salmon red, edged silvery pink, reverse darker, medium to large, full

'Mrs Prentiss Nichols' HT, dp, 1923, Scott, R.; flowers brilliant deep pink, dbl.; ['Ophelia' × seedling]

'Mistress Quickly' -- See 'Ausky'

'Mrs R. B. McLennan' HT, pb, 1924, Easlea; flowers satiny rose suffused yellow, very dbl.; ['George C. Waud' × 'Mme Caristie Martel']

'Mrs R. B. Moloney' HT, mr, 1925, McGredy; flowers brilliant carmine-red, dbl.

'Mrs R. C. Bell' HT, mr, 1920, Clark, A.; flowers bright red; ['Gen. MacArthur' × 'Château de Clos Vougeot']

'Mrs R. D. McClure' HT, op, 1913, Dickson, H.; flowers salmon-pink, very large, dbl.

'Mrs R. G. Sharman-Crawford' HP, pb, 1894, Dickson, A.; flowers rosy pink, outer petals tinted flesh, large, 75 petals, cupped, moderate fragrance; good repeat; vigorous growth; general appearance and recurrent bloom suggest that it is a descendent of Victor Verdier

'Mrs R. M. Finch' Pol, mp, 1923, Finch; flowers rosy pink, becoming lighter, medium, dbl., borne in large clusters; bushy growth; ['Orléans Rose' × unknown]

'Mrs R. M. Finch, Climbing' Cl Pol, mp

'Mrs R. M. King' HT, ab, 1927, Harrison, A.; ['Mme Abel Chatenay' × 'W.R. Smith']

'Mrs Ramon de Escofet' HT, dr, 1919, Easlea; flowers flame-crimson, large, dbl.

'Mrs Redford' HT, ab, 1919, McGredy; flowers bright apricot-orange, medium, semi-dbl., intense fragrance; foliage dark green, glossy, holly-like

'Mrs Reynolds Hole' T, pb, 1900, Nabonnand, P.&C.; flowers carmine shaded purple rose, reverse carmine, large, dbl.; ['Archiduc Joseph' × 'André Schwartz']

'Mrs Richard Draper' HT, mp, 1912, Dickson, H.; flowers glossy carmine pink, center lighter silvery flesh pink, very large, full

'Mrs Richard Turnbull' LCl, w, 1945, Clark, A.; bud yellow; flowers cream, handsome stamens, 14 cm., single; hybrid gigantea

'Mrs Richards' F, pb, 1968, Harkness; flowers pink tinged apricot, single, borne in trusses; foliage dark, glossy; ['Ann Elizabeth' × 'Circus']

'Mrs Robert Bacon' HT, ab, 1934, Bertanzel; flowers golden apricot shading to coral, base yellow, large, very dbl., cupped; [sport of 'Talisman']

'Mrs Robert Garrett' HT, mp, 1900, Cook, J.W.; flowers shell pink, center deeper, medium, dbl.; ['Comtesse de Caserta' × 'Mme Eugene Verdier']

'Mrs Robert Mitchell' HT, pb, 1926, Jersey Nursery; flowers salmon-rose, overlaid coppery pink, very large, full; foliage glossy; ['St. Helena' × 'Mrs Redford']

'Mrs Robert Peary' -- See 'Kaiserin Auguste Viktoria, Climbing'

Mrs Robinson™ F, pb, 2005, Orent, Clifford; flowers white center with pink outers, 2-3 in., single, borne in small clusters, moderate fragrance; foliage small, dark green, glossy, bushy, short (18-24 in.) growth; [seedling × seedling]; intr. 2006

'Mrs Rosalie Wrinch' LCl, lp, 1915, Brown, W.&J.; flowers shell-pink, large, semi-dbl.; vigorous, pillar (5-8 ft.) growth; ['Frau Karl Druschki' × 'Hugh Dickson']

'Mrs Roy Green' HT, dr, 1940, Clark, A.; flowers very large; long stems

'Mrs Rumsey' HP, mp, 1899, Rumsey; flowers rosey pink; [sport of 'Mrs George Dickson']

'Mrs Russell Grimwade' T, mp, 1938, Grimwade; flowers fuchsia-pink; [sport of 'Lorraine Lee']

'Mrs S. K. Rindge' HT, yb, 1919, H&S; bud long, pointed; flowers deep golden yellow, suffused soft pink with age, over large, semi-dbl., cupped; long stems; ['Rayon d'Or' × 'Frau Karl Druschki']

'Mrs S. Paton' HT, ob, 1928, McGredy; bud long, pointed; flowers orange-carmine, base orange, large, dbl.

'Mrs S. Peters' HT, dp; flowers rich pink, dbl., high-centered, moderate fragrance

'Mrs S. T. Wright' T, ob, 1914, Dickson, A.; flowers old gold, center suffused rose-pink on orange, dbl.; [sport of 'Harry Kirk']

'Mrs S. W. Burgess' HT, ab, 1925, Burgess, S.W.; flowers apricot-yellow, base deeper, dbl.; ['Mme Mélanie Soupert' × 'Joseph Hill']

'Mrs Sam McGredy' HT, op, 1929, McGredy; bud pointed; flowers scarlet-copper-orange, reverse heavily flushed red, large, 40 petals, high-centered, moderate fragrance; foliage glossy, reddish bronze; vigorous growth; [('Donald Macdonald' × 'Golden Emblem') × (seedling × 'The Queen Alexandra Rose')]

'Mrs Sam McGredy, Climbing' ('Geneviève Genest') Cl HT, op, 1937, Buisman, G. A. H.; flowers copper orange-red, large, full, moderate fragrance; PP394; [sport of 'Mrs Sam McGredy']

'Mrs Sam Ross' HT, ly, 1912, Dickson, H.; flowers pale straw to light chamois-yellow, buff reverse, very large, full, cupped; foliage dark green

'Mrs Spencer Browne' HT, mp, 1928, Harrison, A.

'Mrs Standish' -- See 'Mme Standish'

'Mrs Standish' ('Froissard') HP, mp, Liabaud; flowers bright pink, large, full; intr. 1865

'Mrs Standish' HP, mr, 1853, Cherpin; flowers scarlet, striped

'Mrs Stewart Clark' HT, mp, 1906, Dickson, A.; flowers bright cerise pink to brilliant rose, large, dbl., moderate fragrance; foliage glossy; ['Rubens' × 'Tom Wood']

'Mrs T. B. Doxford' HT, rb, 1932, Dickson, A.; bud pointed; flowers salmon-carmine to peach-blossom-pink, reverse old-rose, large, dbl., high-centered

'Mrs T. Hillas' HT, my, 1913, Pernet-Ducher; flowers pure chrome-yellow, dbl.

'Mrs T. J. English' HT, ab, 1922, English; flowers apricot and amber, tinted salmon-flesh, heavily veined

'Mrs Talbot O'Farrell' HT, rb, 1926, McGredy; bud small to medium, long, pointed; flowers cerise flushed bronze, reverse old-gold, medium, dbl., moderate fragrance; foliage small, dark bronzy green, leathery, glossy; few prickles; growth upright, bushy

'Mrs Theodore Roosevelt' HT, lp, 1903, E.G. Hill, Co.; flowers cream white with a pink center, very large, dbl., moderate fragrance; vigorous, bushy growth; ['La France' × unknown]

'Mrs Theodore Salvesen' HT, op, 1922, Dobbie; flowers salmon-pink

'Mrs Theonville van Berkel' HT, pb, 1935, Buisman, G. A. H.; bud long, pointed; flowers pink, reverse flushed yellow, large, dbl., high-centered; foliage leathery, dark; vigorous growth; ['Briarcliff' × 'Mrs Sam McGredy']

'Mrs Tom Henderson' Pol, dp

'Mrs Tom Paul' HT, yb, 1920, Dickson, H.; flowers saffron-yellow, suffused pink, dbl.

'Mrs Tom Smith' HT, mr, 1924, Smith, T.; flowers glowing cerise, dbl.

'Mrs Tom Whitehead' HT, ab, 1938, Whitehead; flowers cream, center apricot-orange, outer petals veined, very large, dbl., high-centered; very vigorous growth; ['Mrs Charles Lamplough' × seedling]

'Mrs Treseder' T, ly, 1889, Paul, G.; flowers citron pink

'Mrs Tresham Gilbey' HT, op, 1923, Chaplin Bros.; bud pointed; flowers coral-rose shaded salmon, very large, dbl.; ['Waltham Flame' × 'Edith Cavell (HT)']

'Mrs Tresham Gilbey, Climbing' Cl HT, op, 1938, Vogel, M.; flowers light salmon-pink, very large, dbl., moderate fragrance

'Mrs U. M. Rose' HT, dp, 1931, Vestal; bud long, pointed; flowers cerise-pink, semi-dbl., cupped

'Mrs V.A.Treloar' -- See 'Bridget Mary'

'Mrs van Beresteyn-Frowein'   HT, op, 1935, Buisman, G. A. H.; flowers salmon, large, very dbl.; foliage leathery, light; vigorous growth; ['Souv. de Claudius Pernet' × 'Mrs Henry Bowles']

'Mrs Van Nes' -- See 'Permanent Wave'

'Mrs Vandenbergh' ('Mevrouw S. van den Bergh, Jr.') HT, mr, 1938, Buisman, G. A. H.; flowers bright red, semi-dbl., high-centered; foliage dark; strong stems; vigorous growth; ['E.G. Hill' × 'Étoile de Hollande']

'Mrs Veitch'   HP, mp, 1872, Verdier, E.; flowers carmine pink, medium, full, slight fragrance

'Mrs Verschuren' -- See *R. M. S. Queen Mary*

'Mrs W. A. Lindsay'   HT, pb, 1920, Dickson, H.; flowers peach-pink, center golden yellow, dbl.

'Mrs W. A. Taylor'   HT, 1918, Byrnes

'Mrs W. C. Whitney' ('Mme W. C. Whitney') HT, lp, 1894, May; buds long; flowers flesh-pink, large, intense fragrance; ['Mme Ferdinand Jamin' × 'Souv d'Un Ami']

'Mrs W. E. Nickerson'   HT, pb, 1927, McGredy; bud pointed; flowers silvery pink deeply shaded old-gold and salmon, large, dbl.

'Mrs W. Ewart'   T, pb, 1909, Williams, A.; ['Souv de Catherine Guillot' × unknown]

'Mrs W. H. Cutbush'   Pol, mp, 1907, Levavasseur; flowers rich pink, variable, with light and dark pink blooms in one cluster, dbl., rosette; [sport of 'Mme Norbert Levavasseur']

'Mrs W. H. Cutbush, Climbing'   Cl Pol, mp, 1911, Paling; flowers rich pink, variable, with light and dark pink blooms in one cluster; foliage light green; growth strong, upright (6 ft.); [sport of 'Mrs W. H. Cutbush']

'Mrs W. J. Grant' ('Belle Siebrecht') HT, lp, 1895, Dickson, A.; bud long, pointed; flowers light pink fading purplish, dbl.; ['La France' × 'Lady Mary Fitzwilliam']

'Mrs W. J. Grant, Climbing' ('Belle Siebrecht, Climbing') Cl HT, lp, 1899, E.G. Hill, Co.; flowers large, full; [sport of 'Mrs W. J. Grant']

'Mrs W. R. Groves'   HT, dr, 1941, Clark, A.; flowers deep red; foliage good

'Mrs Wakefield Christie-Miller'   HT, pb, 1909, McGredy; flowers blush, shaded salmon, reverse vermilion-rose, very large, dbl.; foliage light, leathery; dwarf growth

'Mrs Wallace H. Rowe'   HT, m, 1912, McGredy; flowers bright sweet-pea mauve, large, full, high-centered; vigorous growth

'Mrs Walter Brace'   HT, dp, 1939, Beckwith; flowers vivid cerise-rose-pink, slightly larger; [sport of 'Picture']

'Mrs Walter Burns'   F, mp, 1978, Harkness; bud ovoid; flowers patio size, 2½ in., very dbl., flat; foliage fragrant (musky), medium size, matte, dark; compact, bushy growth; [(((Queen Elizabeth® × Escapade®) × ('Orangeade × Lilac Charm') × ('Sterling Silver × Africa Star')')) × ('Cläre Grammerstorf' × 'Fruhlingsmorgen')]

'Mrs Walter Easlea'   HT, dr, 1910, Dickson, A.; flowers glowing crimson-carmine, deepening to intense crimson-orange, large, dbl., moderate fragrance

'Mrs Walter Jones'   HT, rb, 1930, Cant, B. R.; flowers brilliant coral-red, shaded orange, dbl.

'Mrs Walter T. Sumner'   HT, dp, 1920, Clarke Bros.; flowers carmine to deep rose-pink, large, 12-18 petals; ['Ophelia' × 'Hadley']

'Mrs Walter T. Sumner, Climbing'   Cl HT, dp, 1932, Hazlewood Bros.

'Mrs Ward'   HP, mp, 1866, Ward; flowers bright pink, center crimson, large, full

'Mrs Warren E. Lenon'   HT, dr, 1924, E.G. Hill, Co.; bud long, pointed; flowers crimson, large, dbl., globular; vigorous growth; ['Hoosier Beauty' × 'Premier']

'Mrs Warren G. Harding'   HT, dp, 1923, Pierson, A.N.; [sport of 'Columbia']

'Mrs Wemyss Quin'   HT, dy, 1914, Dickson, A.; flowers intense lemon-chrome, washed with maddery orange, medium, dbl., moderate fragrance; foliage dark, glossy; bushy, branching growth; ['Harry Kirk' × unknown]

'Mrs Whitman Cross'   Cl HT, ob, 1943, Cross, C.W.; bud long, pointed; flowers orange-apricot, overlaid pinkish, reverse sometimes striped, semi-dbl.; foliage glossy, soft; growth to 8-9 ft. as climber or pillar, upright; ['Nanjemoy' × 'Marion Cran']

'Mrs Wilfred Lloyd'   HT, dp, 1911, Dickson, A.; flowers fiery pink, large, full, globular

'Mrs William C. Egan'   HT, lp, 1922, H&S; bud long, pointed; flowers soft pink, 35 petals, moderate fragrance

'Mrs William C. Egan, Climbing'   Cl HT, lp, 1933, Howard Rose Co.

'Mrs William Fife'   HT, pb, 1926, Dobbie; flowers soft rose-pink, flushed blush-pink, dbl.

'Mrs William G. Koning'   Pol, w, 1917, Kluis & Koning; flowers pure white, open, dbl., borne in clusters; vigorous, bushy growth; [sport of 'Louise Walter']

'Mrs William Paul' -- See 'Mme William Paul'

'Mrs William R. Hearst'   HT, dp, 1915, Pierson, A.N.; flowers clear dark pink; [sport of 'My Maryland']

'Mrs William Sargent'   HT, ab, 1923, Dickson, H.; flowers apricot and peach, edges flushed rose-pink, dbl.

'Mrs William Sprott'   HT, my, 1938, McGredy; bud long, pointed; flowers large, dbl.; foliage glossy, bronze; vigorous, compact growth; ['Portadown Glory' × 'Mrs Sam McGredy']

'Mrs William Watson'   HP, m, 1890, Dickson, A.; flowers purple-pink, large, full, globular; ['Mme Vidot' × 'Merveille de Lyon']

'Mrs Yamada'   B, dr, Beales, Peter; flowers purple red, double, cupped, moderate fragrance; 5 - 6 ft. growth; [sport of 'Variegata di Bologna']; discovered by Peter Beales at Barakura Gardens in Japan; intr. 2006

'Misty'   HT, w, 1975, Armstrong, D.L.; bud ovoid, pointed; flowers creamy white, 4 in., 35 petals, cupped to formal, moderate tea fragrance; foliage large, leathery; vigorous, upright growth; PP3983; ['Mount Shasta' × Matterhorn®]; intr. 1976

'Misty'   HT, lp, Zary; PPAF; intr. 1999

Misty™ ('Diamond Wishes', 'Misty Hit') Min, mp, Olesen; bud pointed ovoid; flowers medium pink, outer petals fading lighter, medium, 30 petals, shallow cup, borne in large clusters, no fragrance; recurrent; foliage semi-glossy; prickles moderate, 8 mm., hooked downward; bushy (40-60 cm.), vigorous growth; PP15252; [sport of 'Pink Hit']

'Misty'   HT, m, Kordes; flowers small, moderate fragrance; stems short; cut flower trade; intr. 2003

'Misty Blue'   HT, m, Zary, Keith; flowers steely lilac, double, urn-shaped, heavy bloomer, intense fragrance; recurrent; intr. 2008

'Misty Dawn'   Min, w, 1979, Schwartz, Ernest W.; bud ovoid, pointed; flowers pure white, 1 in., 33 petals, cupped; foliage small, dark; vigorous, compact, spreading growth; PP4630; ['Charlie McCarthy' × seedling]

'Misty Delight'   HT, mp, 1990, Christensen, Jack E.; flowers full, borne mostly singly; foliage large, dark green, glossy; upright growth; ['Blue Wonder' × seedling]; intr. 1991

'Misty Eyed' -- See 'Seamit'

'Misty Gold'   F, my, 1954, Boerner; bud ovoid, pointed; flowers empire-yellow, 3½-4 in., 45-50 petals, cupped, moderate fragrance; foliage glossy; vigorous growth; PP1380; ['floribunda seedling' × 'floribunda seedling']; intr. 1954

'Misty Hit' -- See 'Poulhi011(N)'

Misty Moonlight™ -- See 'Segmisty'

'Misty Morn'   HT, ly, 1949, McGredy; flowers pale lemon-yellow, pointed, large, 45 petals; foliage dark; [seedling × 'Mrs Charles Lamplough']

'Misty Morning' -- See 'Judmorn'

'Misty Pink'   F, mp, 1973, Swim & Weeks; PP2945; intr. 1971

'Misty Twilight' -- See 'Balrihus'

'Misty Veil'   S, mp, Williams, J. Benjamin; flowers delicate pink, large, single, cupped to flat; free-flowering; intr. 1999

'Mitcheltonii' (*R.* × *mitcheltonii*) S, mp, 1967, Armbrust; flowers pink, small, single; profuse spring bloom; foliage small, leathery; thornless; very vigorous, climbing growth; [*R. multiflora* × 'I.X.L.']

'Mitchie's Gold' -- See 'Moegold'

Mitsouko® -- See 'Delnat'

'Mitzi' HT, yb, 1956, Meilland, F.; flowers pearly tints flushed mauve-rose, well-formed, 35 petals; foliage dark; strong stems; upright, bushy growth; [('Peace' × 'Mme Joseph Perraud') × ('Mrs Pierre S. duPont' × 'Mrs John Laing')]

'Mitzi' ('Mitzi 81') HT, my, Meilland; flowers dbl.; intr. 1981

'Mitzi 81' -- See 'Mitzi'

'Miwaku' ('Fascination') HT, w, Suzuki, Seizo; intr. 1988

'Mix 'n' Match' -- See 'Chewily'

'Mixed Emotions' Min, rb, Jalbert; flowers striped; intr. 2003

'Mixed Marriage' F, pb, Ruston, D.; [sport of 'Bridal Pink']; intr. 1987

'Miyabi' HT, w, 1977, Teranishi, K.; bud ovoid; flowers near white, 4-4½ in., 30 petals, high-centered; upright growth; [('Amatsu-Otome' × 'Samba') × ('Kordes' Perfecta' × American Heritage®)]; intr. 1976

'Miyagino' Cl Min, pb, 1979, Onodera, Toru F.; bud rounded; flowers light pink, small, 5 petals, flat; scattered rebloom; foliage tiny; ['Nozomi' × seedling]; intr. 1978

'Miyako Oji' ('Highway to the Capital') HT, pb, Keihan; intr. 1988

'Miyoshino' Min, mp; intr. 2001

'Ms Amanda Coombes' -- See 'Newmand'

'Ms Linda' HT, rb, 2006, Premeaux John W.; flowers red, sometimes with darker edges, reverse pink, 4½ in., full, borne mostly solitary; foliage medium size, medium green, semi-glossy; prickles average, straight, red, moderate; growth upright, medium; ['Elizabeth Taylor' × 'Hot Princess']; intr. 2006

'Ms Mary' -- See 'Tinmary'

'Ms Wendy Poulier' -- See 'Newwend'

'Mizar' -- See 'Barmiz'

'Mizuho' HT, yb

'Mlada' F, yb, Urban, J.; flowers yellow and red, medium, dbl.; intr. 1983

'Mme Baptiste Desportes' -- See 'Baptiste Desportes'

'Mme Figaro' HT, dp, Lens, Louis; intr. 1954

'Mme Myrja Sachs'

'Mme Myrja Sachs' HT, rb, Croix, Paul

'Mme Pocquet' LCl, ob; flowers orange , semi-double; recurrent

'Mme Selzer' -- See 'Madeleine Seltzer'

'Mme Thérèse Meyer' S, mr, Huber; flowers cherry red, 6 in., single, flat, intense fragrance; vigorous (5-6 ft.) growth; intr. 2005

'Mo Mama' -- See 'Houmom'

Moana® -- See 'Macbipi'

'Mobile Jubilee' -- See 'Talmobile'

'Möckel Rose ' HT, dr, Huber; flowers flower dark wine red; intr. 2005

'Mockin' Bird' S, rb; flowers Striped.; intr. 2001

'Mock's Rosa Druschki' Cl HP, mp, before 1935, Mock; flowers rose pink, fading lighter, 3½-4 in., dbl.; foliage glossy

'Model of Perfection' F, ob, 1977, Dickson, A.; bud globular; flowers yellow, pink and orange, large, 28 petals; free-flowering; small growth; ['Zorina' × 'Arthur Bell']

'Modèle de Perfection' B, mp, 1859, Guillot; flowers bright silky pink, medium, full; ['Louise Odier' × unknown]

Modern Art™ -- See 'Poulart'

'Modern Crusader' S, dr, Kordes; flowers burgundy red, large, dbl., open cup; recurrent; vigorous, tall growth; intr. 2005

Modern Magic™ -- See 'Chrisgood'

'Modern Miss' F, pb, Benny; flowers medium pink with amber glow in center, dbl., high-centered, spiral; medium growth; intr. 2005

'Modern Times' HT, rb, 1956, Verbeek; flowers red, striped pink; [sport of 'Better Times']

'Modesty' HT, pb, 1916, McGredy; bud pointed; flowers white to pearly-cream, center rose-pink, edges vermilon-pink, large, dbl., high-centered, intense fragrance

'Moealetha' ('Aletha June') Min, lp, 2000, Moe, Mitchie; flowers full, high-centered, borne mostly singly, slight fragrance; foliage medium size, medium green, semi-glossy; few prickles; growth upright, medium (15-18 in.); ['Grace Seward' × 'Blue Peter']

'Moealexa' ('Alexa') MinFl, dp, 2001, Moe, Mitchie; flowers deep pink, reverse light pink, 1½-2 in., dbl., high-centered, borne mostly singly, slight fragrance; foliage medium size, dark green, semi-glossy; prickles medium, straight, light green, few; growth spreading, tall (24-30 in.); garden decoration, exhibition; ['Grace Seward' × 'Blue Peter']; intr. 2001

'Moealice' ('Miss Alice') Min, m, 2000, Moe, Mitchie; flowers full, high-centered, borne mostly singly, moderate fragrance; foliage medium size, dark green, glossy; few prickles; growth upright, medium (15-18 in.); [Vista™ × unknown]

'Moealpha' ('Alpha Moe') Min, ob, 1998, Moe, Mitchie; flowers cream white with orange edges, 1½ in., 6-11 petals, borne mostly singly, slight fragrance; foliage medium size, medium green, semi-glossy; few prickles; upright, medium (18 in.) growth; ['Pink Petticoat' × seedling]; intr. 1999

'Moeanna' ('Anna Milam') F, mp, 2000, Moe, Mitchie; flowers medium, petals ruffled, 3-4 in., full, high-centered, borne in large clusters; foliage medium size, medium green, semi-glossy; prickles moderate; growth vigorous, upright, tall (3-4 ft.); [Pristine® × City of London®]

'Moeanne' ('Anne Hering') Min, r, 1999, Moe, Mitchie; flowers pale russet, reverse lighter, yellow base, 1-2 in., dbl., high-centered; foliage medium size, medium green, semi-glossy; few prickles; upright, medium (15 in.) growth; ['Fairhope' × 'Wistful']; intr. 1999

'Moebaldo' (Baldo™) Min, yb, 2003, Moe, Mitchie; flowers full, high-centered, borne mostly solitary, moderate fragrance; foliage medium size, medium green, semi-glossy; prickles small, straight, light tan, few; growth upright, medium; exhibition, garden decoration; [Hot Tamale™ × 'Elegant Beauty']; intr. 2003

'Moebecky' ('Becky Adams') Min, m, 2001, Moe, Mitchie; flowers mauve, developing red petal tips in intense sun, 1½-2 in., full, high-centered, borne mostly singly, moderate fragrance; foliage medium size, dark green, Semi-glossy; prickles medium, hooked, red, moderate; growth spreading, medium (18-24 in.); exhibition, garden decorative; ['Fairhope' × 'Wistful']; intr. 2001

'Moecougar' ('Cougar') MinFl, rb, 2000, Moe, Mitchie; flowers medium red, reverse light pink, 1-1½ in., full, high-centered, borne mostly singly; foliage large, medium green, semi-glossy; few prickles; growth vigorous, upright, tall (24-30 in.); [Klima™ × unknown]; intr. 2000

'Moecrescent' (Crescent Moon™) Cl Min, my, 2001, Moe, Mitchie; flowers 1-1½ in., dbl., borne in small clusters, slight fragrance; foliage small, medium green, semi-glossy; growth vigorous, upright, spreading, tall (30-36 in.); garden decoration; [Klima™ × 'Blue Peter']; intr. 2002

'Moeder des Vaderlands' -- See 'Mother's Country'

'Moedotcom' ('Dot Com') Min, dr, 2000, Moe, Mitchie; flowers very small, ½ in., semi-dbl., high-centered, borne mostly singly; foliage small, dark green, semi-glossy; few prickles; growth upright, medium (12 in.); [Vista™ × unknown]; intr. 2000

'Moegold' ('Mitchie's Gold') Min, dy, 2000, Moe, Mitchie; flowers dbl., high-centered, borne mostly singly, slight fragrance; foliage medium size, medium green, semi-glossy; few prickles; growth upright, medium (15-18 in.); [Vista™ × unknown]; intr. 2001

'Moehi' ('Hi') Min, yb, 2000, Moe, Mitchie; flowers yellow edged with pink, ½-¾ in., semi-dbl., high-centered, borne mostly solitary, slight fragrance; foliage small, dark green, semi-glossy; prickles very small, straight, few; growth compact, medium (12-14 in.); garden decorative, exhibition; [Klima™ × 'Stretch Johnson']; intr. 2001

'Moehot' (Hot To Trot™) MinFl, or, 2006, Moe, Mitchie; flowers extremely vivid orange-red, reverse orange-red blend, 2½-2¾ in., dbl., high-centered, borne mostly solitary; foliage medium size, medium green, semi-glossy; prickles medium, straight, light tan, few; growth upright, tall (24-30 in.); [Klima™ × 'Freisinger Morgenrote']; intr. 2007

'Moeichiro' (Ichiro™) Min, mr, 2002, Moe, Mitchie; flowers dbl., high-centered, borne mostly solitary, slight fragrance; foliage medium size, dark green, glossy; prickles small, straight, light tan, moderate; growth upright, medium (20-24 in.); garden decorative, exhibition; ['Anne Hering' × Miss Flippins™]; intr. 2002

'Moejanrick' ('Jan and Rick') Gr, w, 2000, Moe, Mitchie; flowers white with pale pink tint, 3-4 in., full, exhibition, borne in large clusters, intense fragrance; foliage medium size, dark green, semi-glossy; prickles moderate; upright, vigorous, tall (5-6 ft.) growth; [Pristine® × City of London®]; intr. 2000

'Moejo' (Jo™) Min, op, 2001, Moe, Mitchie; flowers light russet, reverse orange pink, 1-1½ in., dbl., borne mostly singly, slight fragrance; foliage medium size, dark green, glossy; prickles small, hooked down, light tan, moderate; growth spreading, medium (18-24 in.), exhibition, garden; ['Violet Mist' × 'mixed yellow pollen']; repeats quickly, lots of blooms; intr. 2002

'Moejo-netsu' Min, dp, 1998, Moe, Mitchie; flowers magenta pink, 1-1½ in., dbl., high-centered, borne mostly singly, slight fragrance; foliage medium size, dark green, semi-glossy; no prickles; upright, tall (18 in.) growth; [Klima™ × 'seedling (mauve)']; intr. 1999

'Moelucky' (Lucky Lucy™) Min, m, 2004, Moe, Mitchie; flowers mauve, reverse mauve, ½ in, full, high-centered, borne mostly solitary, moderate fragrance; free-flowering; foliage small, medium green, semi-glossy; prickles small, straight; growth compact, medium (18-20 in.); exhibition, garden decoration; [Vista™ × 'Elegant Beauty']; intr. 2005

'Moelvrosen' -- See 'Hurdalsrosen'

'Moemargaret' ('Margaret H') S, my, 2001, Moe, Mitchie; flowers medium yellow, light yellow reverse, 2½-3 in., single, borne in small clusters, moderate fragrance; fast repeat; foliage medium size, medium green, semi-glossy; prickles medium, slightly hooked, few; growth upright, tall (5-6 ft.), vigorous; garden decorative; [Pristine® × City of London®]; intr. 2001

'Moemarilyn' ('Marilyn Wellan') Min, lp, 1999, Moe, Mitchie; flowers apricot-pink, reverse lighter, 1-2 in., dbl., high-centered; foliage medium size, dark green, semi-glossy; few prickles; upright, tall (18 in.) growth; ['Sheri Anne' × 'Wistful']; intr. 1999

'Moemighty' ('Mighty Moe') Min, ob, 1999, Moe, Mitchie; flowers orange, reverse lighter, micro-mini, ½ in., semi-dbl., high-centered, slight fragrance; foliage small, medium green, dull; few prickles; compact, medium (12 in.) growth; ['Luis Desamero' × seedling]; intr. 1999

'Moemike' ('Mike Peterson') MinFl, ly, 2000, Moe, Mitchie; flowers dbl., high-centered, borne mostly singly, slight fragrance; foliage medium size, medium green, semi-glossy; few prickles; growth upright, tall (20-24 in.); ['Tracey Wickham' × unknown]

'Moemoondream' (Moonlight Dreamer™) Min, m, 2002, Moe, Mitchie; flowers petals quill to star-shaped, obvious stamens, 1½-2 in., single, borne mostly solitary, slight fragrance; foliage medium size, dark green, semi-glossy; prickles small, straight, light tan, few; growth upright, medium (18-20 in.); garden decorative, exhibition; ['Anne Hering' × Miss Flippins™]; intr. 2002

'Moepatty' (Patty Cakes™) Min, dy, 2005, Moe, Mitchie; flowers dbl., high-centered, borne mostly solitary, moderate fragrance; foliage small, medium green, matte; prickles few, small, straight, light brown; growth upright, short (15-18 in.), micro-mini; exhibition, garden; ['Snow Bunny' × 'Mighty Moe']; intr. 2006

'Moepiggy' (This Little Piggy™) Min, mp, 2005, Moe, Mitchie; flowers dbl., high-centered, borne mostly solitary, slight fragrance; foliage small, dark green, matte; prickles few, small, straight, light brown; growth compact, short (12-14 in.); exhibition, garden decoration; [Miss Flippins™ × 'Anne Hering']; intr. 2005

'Moeralph' ('Ralph T') Min, my, 2001, Moe, Mitchie; flowers single, borne mostly singly, slight fragrance; foliage small, medium green, semi-glossy; prickles few, very small, straight, white; growth upright, tall (24-30 in.); garden decoration, exhibition; [Klima™ × 'Blue Peter']; intr. 2001

'Moesassy' ('Sassy Girl') Min, op, 2000, Moe, Mitchie; flowers orange-pink, 2½ in., full, high-centered, borne mostly singly, slight fragrance; foliage medium size, medium green, semi-glossy, disease-resistant; few prickles; growth upright, vigorous, medium (15-18 in.); ['Violet Mist' × unknown]

'Moescott' ('Scott') Cl Min, mr, 2000, Moe, Mitchie; flowers bright red, 1-1½ in., dbl., borne in small clusters, slight fragrance; foliage medium size, dark green, semi-glossy; few prickles; growth vigorous, climbing, upright (30-36 in.); [Klima™ × unknown]; intr. 2000

'Moeseattle' (Seattle Sunrise™) MinFl, ab, 2005, Moe, Mitchie; flowers dbl., high-centered, borne mostly solitary, slight fragrance; foliage medium size, dark green, semi-glossy; prickles few, medium, hooked down, light tan; growth upright, medium (18-24 in.); exhibition, garden; [(Pristine® × 'Selfridges') × 'Finest Hour']; intr. 2006

'Moesmoke' (Smoking Gun™) Min, m, 2003, Moe, Mitchie; flowers light mauve, 1½ in., dbl., high-centered, borne mostly solitary, slight fragrance; foliage small, light green, semi-glossy; prickles small, straight, light tan, few; growth upright, medium (18-20 in.); exhibition, garden decorative; [Vista™ × 'Anne Hering']; intr. 2003

'Moesnow' ('Snow Bunny') Min, w, 2000, Moe, Mitchie; flowers dbl., high-centered, borne mostly singly, slight fragrance; foliage small, medium green, semi-glossy; few prickles; growth upright, medium (10-12 in.); micro-mini; ['Grace Seward' × 'Blue Peter']

'Moeterri' ('Terri King') HT, yb, 2001, Moe, Mitchie; flowers 3-4 in., dbl., high-centered, borne mostly solitary, moderate fragrance; foliage medium size, medium green, semi-glossy; prickles few, medium, hooked, light brown; growth upright, tall (3-4 ft.); garden decorative, exhibition, greenhouse; [Pristine® × 'Selfridges']; intr. 2001

'Moewhoop' (Whoop De Doo™) Min, rb, 2004, Moe, Mitchie; flowers red with yellow on lower portion of petals and somewhat on reverse, 1½-1¾ in., dbl., high-centered, borne mostly solitary, slight fragrance; recurrent; foliage medium size, medium green, semi-glossy; prickles medium, straight; growth upright, medium (18-20 in.); exhibition, garden; ['Olympic Gold' × 'Finest Hour']; intr. 2005

'Mogador' ('Crimson Superb', 'Roi des Pourpres') P, dp, after 1810, Descemet; flowers carmine, shaded purple, medium, full; [sport of 'Rose du Roi']

'Mogajam' (Jamie™) Min, lp, 1992, Moglia, Thomas; flowers outer petals horizontal at exhibition stage, large, very dbl., high-centered, borne in small clusters; foliage medium size, medium green, semi-glossy; some prickles; medium (45-50 cm.), spreading growth; [Party Girl™ × 'Fairlane']; intr. 1993

'Mogajosh' (Joshua™) Min, pb, 1990, Moglia, Thomas; bud pointed; flowers clear, deep pink with yellow at base, reverse lighter to white, 20 petals, high-centered, slight fragrance; foliage medium size, medium green, semi-glossy; prickles hooked, small, red; long stems; upright, medium growth; fruit not observed; [Loving Touch™ × Rainbow's End™]; intr. 1989

'Mogaline' (Party Line™) Min, op, 1992, Moglia, Thomas; flowers coral, medium, dbl., borne in clusters of 6 or more on basal canes; foliage small, medium green, matte; few prickles; medium (45-50cm.), compact growth; [Party Girl™ × 'Fairlane']; intr. 1993

'Mogarip' (Li'l Rip™) Min, w, 1992, Moglia, Thomas; flowers white with yellow center, medium, full, borne in small clusters; foliage small, medium green, matte; few prickles; medium (35-45 cm.), narrow, upright growth; [Loving Touch™ × Cupcake™]; intr. 1993

'Mogatouch' (Li'l Touch™) Min, ab, 1992, Moglia, Thomas; flowers apricot, yellow stamens showing, moderately open, medium, dbl.; foliage medium size, medium green, matte; some prickles; medium (40-50 cm.), upright growth; [Loving Touch™ × 'Prima Donna']; intr. 1993

'Mohak' HT, ob, Chiplunkar; intr. 1993

'Mohana'® HT, my, Tantau; flowers clear yellow, very large, double, high-centered, borne mostly singly; recurrent; stems long; florist rose; intr. 2006

'Mohawk' S, m, Central Exp. Farm; flowers brighter than aster-purple, center white, single; profuse, non-recurrent bloom; foliage dull green; rounded, dwarf growth; hardy; [R. rubrifolia × R. rugosa]

'Mohican' HT, mr, 1937, J.H. Thompson's Sons; bud long, pointed; flowers cherry-red, large, dbl.; foliage leathery, glossy, dark; long stems; very vigorous growth; PP289; [seedling × 'Briarcliff']

'Mohican' F, mr, Thompson's, J.H., Sons; flowers dark rose-red; PP2123; [sport of 'Garnette']; intr. 1961

'Mohini' F, ob, 1970, Division of Vegetable Crops and Floriculture; bud long, pointed; flowers chocolate-brown, base tinged yellow, medium, full; foliage glossy, dark; moderate, bushy growth; ['Sea Pearl' × 'Shola']

'Mohykan' HT, dr, Strnad

'Moiret' T, yb, 1843, Moiret; flowers whitish yellow, shaded pink and chamois, large, full

'Moïse' ('Moyse') HGal, m, 1828, Parmentier; flowers rosy-carmine, shaded purplish slate, expanded, large, dbl.; moderate upright growth

'Moja Mesta' S, mp, Lempickji; growth to 10 ft.; intr. 1956

'Mojave' HT, ob, 1954, Swim, H.C.; bud long; flowers apricot-orange tinted red, prominently veined, 4-4½ in., 25 petals, high-centered, moderate fragrance; foliage glossy; vigorous, upright growth; PP1176; ['Charlotte Armstrong' × 'Signora']

'Mojave, Climbing' Cl HT, ob, 1964, Trimper, K.; [sport of 'Mojave']

Moje Hammarberg® HRg, m, 1931, Hammarberg; flowers reddish-violet, large, dbl., intense fragrance; recurrent bloom; short, weak stems; vigorous growth; hips large, red; hardy

'Moksha' HT, op; flowers large

Molde® ('Mistigri') F, or, 1964, Tantau, Math.; flowers dbl., borne in clusters; foliage dark, glossy; bushy, low, compact. growth

'Molhip' ('High Point') Min, w, 1986, Molder, W.A.; [sport of 'Helen Boehm']

Molineux™ -- See 'Ausmol'

Molitor® -- See 'Gautira'

Mollie Claire™ -- See 'Kinclaire'

'Molly' -- See 'Brimolly'

'Molly Abdy' HT, rb, 1956, Abdy; bud pointed; flowers deep scarlet to lighter red, medium, dbl., moderate fragrance; vigorous growth; ['Southport' × unknown]

Molly Beckley™ -- See 'Jaymoll'

'Molly Bishop' HT, op, 1951, Robinson, H.; bud long, pointed; flowers large, dbl., high-centered; foliage leathery, rich green; vigorous growth

'Molly Bligh' HT, pb, 1917, Dickson, A.; flowers deep pink, base deep orange, large, full, moderate fragrance

'Molly Darragh' HT, pb, 1930, McGredy; bud pointed; flowers bright old-rose, base orange-yellow, very large, dbl., high-centered, moderate fragrance

'Molly de Balkany' -- See 'Worcrab'

'Molly Doyle' F, pb, 1965, Barter; flowers old-rose-pink, base silvery white, 5 in., 6 petals, intense fragrance; foliage light green; low, bushy growth; ['Étoile de Hollande' × Queen Elizabeth®]

'Molly Kirby' F, or, 1984, Wilson, George D.; flowers vermilion; [sport of 'Matangi']; intr. 1980

'Molly Lloyd Lee' -- See 'Rawmollbee'

'Molly McGredy' F, rb, 1969, McGredy, Sam IV; flowers medium red, reverse silver, well-formed, large, 35 petals, borne in trusses; foliage dark, glossy; PP3111; ['Paddy McGredy' × ('Mme Léon Cuny' × 'Columbine')]

'Molly Sharman-Crawford' T, w, 1908, Dickson, A.; bud long, pointed; flowers greenish white, becoming whiter, very dbl., high-centered, moderate fragrance; foliage sparse, rich green; bushy growth

'Mollycita' -- See 'Houmoll'

'Molodost' ('Youth') HT, lp, 1956, Sushkov, K. L.; flowers 5 in., 37 petals; foliage dark; strong stems; vigorous, upright growth; ['Staatsprasident Pats' × 'Cathrine Kordes']

'Molodost Mira' ('Early Peace') HT, mr, 1955, Klimenko, V. N.; flowers coral-red, well-formed, large, 50 petals; foliage dark; vigorous, well branched growth; ['Peace' × ('Crimson Glory' × 'Poinsettia')]

'Molsunlem' ('Sunday Lemonade') HT, lp, 1986, Molder, W.A.; flowers pale pink, 30 petals, high-centered to cupped, borne usually singly, intense fruity fragrance; recurrent; foliage medium size, dark, matte; prickles medium, amber, hooked downward; upright, medium-tall growth; [sport of 'Lemon Spice']

'Mom-Mom' -- See 'Kit Delahanty'

'Moments' S, op, J. B. Williams; flowers single; recurrent; growth to 4 ft.; intr. 2005

'Momo' HT, dp, 1988, Ota, Kaichiro; flowers deep pink, large, 35-40 petals, borne usually singly; foliage medium size, dark green; prickles pointed, straight; hips medium, copper; [('Picnic' × 'Kordes' Perfecta') × 'Christian Dior']

'Momo' LCl, dr, Noack, Werner; flowers cherry crimson, 1½ in., very dbl., borne in very large clusters; foliage small, dark green, glossy; growth to 8 ft.; intr. 1995

'Momoka' ('Peach Fragrance') HT, ob, Keisei; intr. 2004

'Momoyama' ('Peach Mountain') HT, op, Keihan; intr. 1981

'Momozono' ('Peach Garden') F, mp, Hiroshima; intr. 1990

'Mom's Fancy' -- See 'Renmom'

'Mom's Rose' -- See 'Winmom'

'Momy' F, dp

'Mon Aimée' mp, Kriloff; intr. 1973

'Mon Ami' Min, mr, Justice; intr. 2001

'Mon Amour' Cl HT, pb, 1967, Coggiatti, Stelvio; bud ovoid; flowers phlox-pink, reverse silver-rose, large, dbl., cupped, moderate fragrance; profuse, intermittent bloom; foliage dark, leathery; very vigorous growth; ['Peace, Climbing' × 'Caprice']

Mon Cheri™ -- See 'Arocher'

Mon Cherie® F, mp, Spek; flowers medium pink, outer petals fading lighter, 6 cm., 60-65 petals, cupped, borne in clusters; recurrent; prickles moderate; stems medium; intr. 2005

'Mon Jardin et Ma Maison' (Flora Romantica®) LCl, w, Meilland; flowers large, slight fragrance; free-flowering; foliage glossy; strong (7 ft.) growth; intr. 1998

'Mon Pays' ('Rigobec') Gr, w, 1983, Gailloux, Gilles; flowers large, dbl.; foliage medium to large, medium green, glossy; upright growth; ['Iceberg' × 'Peace']

'Mon Petit' Min, dp, 1947, Dot, Pedro; flowers light red, 80 petals; foliage pointed; dwarf, compact growth; ['Merveille des Rouges' × 'Pompon de Paris']

'Mon Tresor' -- See 'Red Imp'

'Mon Trésor' HGal, m, about 1845, Calvert; flowers light purple, medium, full

'Mona' F, mr, 1958, Kordes, R.; flowers light crimson, center lighter, 2 in., dbl., high-centered, borne in large clusters; foliage light green; vigorous, upright, bushy growth; ['Rudolph Timm' × 'Fanal']; intr. 1957

'Mona Lisa' -- See 'Kormat'

Mona Lisa® F, or, Meilland; intr. 2008

'Mona Lisa' LCl, pb, 1956, Malandrone; bud ovoid; flowers warm pink overcast cameo-pink, 4-4½ in., 35-40 petals, cupped, borne singly or in small clusters, intense fragrance; free, recurrent boom; foliage dark, leathery; vigorous growth; bushy pillar or climbing (8-10 ft.); PP1459; ['Mrs Sam McGredy' × ('Mrs Sam McGredy' × (seedling × 'Capt. Thomas'))]

Mona Lisa® HT, lp, Kordes; flowers porcelain pink, 35-40 petals, high-centered, borne singly; recurrent; stems long; [sport of 'Eliza']; florist rose; intr. 2005

'Mona Rosette' F, pb, 1963, Manski; bud ovoid; flowers pink and white striped, medium, dbl., cupped, borne in clusters; foliage dark, leathery; bushy, low growth; [sport of 'Pink Rosette']; intr. 1963

'Mona Ruth' Min, mp, 1960, Moore, Ralph S.; flowers 1-1½ in., 30 petals; foliage leathery; vigorous (12-14 in.), bushy growth; PP2081; [(('Soeur Thérèse' × 'Skyrocket') × (seedling × 'Red Ripples')) × 'Zee']; intr. 1959

'Monangie' ('Lady Angela') S, mp, 2003, Monteith, Joan; flowers medium, full, borne in large clusters, intense fragrance; foliage medium green, matte; growth upright, tall; [Heritage® × Wes-

terland®]
'Monarch'   HT, mp, 1926, Dobbie; bud pointed; flowers silvery pink, very large, dbl., high-centered, moderate fragrance
'Mönch'   F, mp, 1959, Tantau; flowers pink, large, dbl., borne in large corymbs; foliage dark, leathery; vigorous, upright growth; ['Karl Weinhausen' × unknown]; intr. 1952
'Moncton'   HRg, lp, 1978, Svejda, Felicitas; bud ovoid; flowers dbl., 20 petals, intense fragrance; foliage gray-green; upright, bushy growth; ['Schneezwerg' × R. chinensis]; intr. 1977
'Monday's Child' -- See 'Judmon'
'Mondial Pink'   HT, pb, 1967, Hendrickx; flowers pink, base yellow, medium, high-centered; foliage glossy; intr. 1965
Mondiale® -- See 'Korozon'
'Mondorf-les-Bains'   HT, r, Lens; flowers bright yellow, turning cream as it fades to white, 7 cm., semi-dbl., shallow cup to flat, borne in clusters, slight fragrance; recurrent; foliage dark green; growth to 40-45 cm.; intr. 2006
'Mondovision'   HT, dp, 1969, Delbard, G.; flowers cyclamen-pink, 4-5 in., 35-45 petals, moderate fragrance; ['Dr. Albert Schweitzer' × ('Bayadere' × 'Mme Rene Cassin')]; intr. 1969
'Monet' -- See 'Jaclion'
'Monet'   HT, m, Great Western; flowers smoky-mauve, large, quartered, flat, moderate tea-damask fragrance; intr. 1996
'Moneta'   F, pb, 1969, Freytag; bud ovoid; flowers pinkish red, small, very dbl.; foliage dark; [sport of 'Garnette']
'Monette'   HWich, w, 1921, Hémeray-Aubert; flowers small, very dbl., borne in clusters, intense fragrance; vigorous, climbing growth; [(R. wichurana × unknown) × 'Yvonne Rabier']
'Monette'   Pol, rb, Turbat; flowers fiery red, passing to rose, with many white streaks, small, full, borne in clusters of 60-100; ['Phyllis' × seedling]; intr. 1922
'Money For Nothing' -- See 'Talmoney'
'Mongioia'   Gr, Mansuino; intr. 1966
Monica™ -- See 'Poulra001(N)'
'Monica'   A, lp, before 1838; flowers delicate pink, medium, full; possibly synonymous with 'Monique'
'Monica Astmann'   F, or; flowers light orange, large, dbl.
'Monica Mary' -- See 'Rawqueenb'
'Monica Mitchell' -- See 'Rawqueenb'
Monika® -- See 'Tanakinom'
'Monique'   A, lp, 1828, Prévost; flowers medium, 60-80 petals, globular; foliage ovoid, acuminate, simply serrate; few prickles
'Monique'   HT, op, Paolino; flowers medium salmon-pink, well-shaped, large, 25 petals, intense fragrance; vigorous, upright growth; ['Lady Sylvia' × seedling]; intr. 1949
Monique Laperrière®   HT, dp, Laperrière; flowers fuchsia, double, cupped; vigorous (90 - 110 cm.) growth; intr. 2006
'Monique van Honsebrouck'   Gr, Delforge, H.
Monna Lisa®   HT, w; flowers ivory white, large
Monna Lisa, Climbing®   Cl HT, w; flowers ivory white, large
'Monplaisir'   HGal, m, about 1845, Calvert; flowers purple
'Monroe St. Yellow Tea' -- See 'Étoile de Lyon'
Monrose+ ('Geneve')   F, ab, Perfecta Plant; flowers soft apricot, double, high-centered, borne mostly singly; recurrent; stems medium to long; [sport of Amsterdam+]; florist rose
'Monseigneur Fournier' ('Mons Fournier')   HP, mr, 1876, Lalande; flowers brilliant light red, very large, full
'Monseigneur Touchet'   T, w, 1895, Corboeuf-Marsault; flowers cream white, large, full; ['Niphetos' × 'Mme Chédane-Guinoisseau']
'Mons A. Maille'   B, pb, 1889, Moreau & Robert; flowers shining carmine, shaded dark red, very large, full, borne in small clusters; foliage dark green; prickles recurved
'Mons Aimé Colcombet'   T, mp, 1891, Bernaix; flowers bright carmine, center rose pink with flesh pink, medium
'Mons Albert Dureau' -- See 'Albert Dureau'
'Mons Alexandre Pelletier'   B, mp, 1879, Duval, H.; flowers velvety pink, medium, full
'Mons Alfred Daney'   M, dp, 1886, Bernède; flowers dark pink with silvery reflections, very large, full
'Mons Alfred Leveau' -- See 'Alfred Leveau'
'Mons Barillet-Deschamps' ('Barillet')   HP, mp, 1867, Vigneron; flowers bright carmine, medium to large, full, globular; ['Comte Bobrinsky' × unknown]
'Mons Barthélemy Levet'   HP, mp, 1878, Levet; flowers bright pink, large, full; ['Victor Verdier' × unknown]
'Mons Bonçenne' ('M Boncenne')   HP, dr, 1864, Liabaud; flowers deep crimson, medium, full, moderate fragrance; moderate growth; ['Général Jacqueminot' × 'Géant des Batailles']
'Mons Bunel' ('M. Bunel')   HT, pb, 1899, Pernet-Ducher; flowers rosy peach, shaded with yellow, edged with bright rose, very large, full, somewhat flat
'Mons Chaix d'Est-Ange'   HP, mr, 1866, Lévêque; flowers bright scarlet-vermilion, large, full
'Mons Charles de Lapisse' -- See 'Charles de Lapisse'
'Mons Charles de Thézillat'   T, yb, 1888, Nabonnand; flowers creamy yellow, centers chamois, very large, full, globular
'Mons Chédane-Guinoisseau' ('Chédane-Guinoisseau')   HRg, lp, 1895, Chédane-Guinoisseau; flowers very large, dbl.
'Mons Cordeau'   B, dp, 1892, Moreau et Robert; flowers deep red with violet, very dbl., globular, intense fragrance; prickles very thorny
'Mons Cordier'   HP, mr, 1871, Gonod; flowers scarlet, very large, full, flat; ['Géant des Batailles' × unknown]
'Mons de Montigny'   HP, dp, 1855, Paillet; flowers carmine-pink, large, dbl.
'Mons de Morand'   HP, rb, 1891, Schwartz, J.; flowers bright crimson cerise nuanced bluish lilac purple, large, full; [sport of 'Général Jacqueminot']
'Mons de Pontbriand'   HP, dr, 1864, Damaizin; flowers brownish-crimson, shaded dark carmine, medium to large
'Mons Désir'   N, dr, 1888, Pernet père; flowers crimson red, darkened with violet, 8 cm., full; ['Gloire de Dijon' × unknown (possibly 'Général Jacqueminot')]
'Mons Dorier'   T, dp, 1897, Croibier; flowers bright pink, aging to crimson, large, full
'Mons Dubost'   B, op, 1864, Vigneron; flowers very light salmon
'Mons E. Y. Teas' -- See 'E. Y. Teas'
'Mons Edg. Blanchard' -- See 'Edgar Blanchard'
'Mons Edouard Detaille'   HP, m, 1893, Gouchault; flowers purple/pink, large, dbl.
'Mons Edouard Littaye'   T, pb, 1891, Bernaix; bud large, long; flowers rosey carmine, tinted light pink, often shaded with violet pink, full
'Mons Édouard Ory'   HP, mr, 1864, Moreau & Robert; flowers vermilion, large, full
'Mons Émile Lelong'   HP, mp, 1887, Bire; flowers rose pink, shaded lilac, globular; ['Général Jacqueminot' × unknown]
'Mons Ernest Dupré'   HP, mr, 1904, Boutigny; bud long; flowers bright carmine red, nuanced deep carmine, velvety, large, dbl., camellia-like
'Mons Étienne Dupuis' -- See 'Mons Étienne Dupuy'
'Mons Étienne Dupuy' ('Mons Étienne Dupuis')   HP, lp, 1873, Levet; flowers pale satin and rosy pink, reverse silvery, large, full; ['Victor Verdier' × 'Anna de Diesbach']
'Mons Eugène Delaire'   HP, mr, 1879, Vigneron; flowers velvety red illuminated with bright flame, large, full, borne singly or in small clusters; prickles chestnut brown; growth upright
'Mons Fillion'   HP, mp, 1876, Gonod/Lévêque; flowers carmine-rose, center brighter, large, full
'Mons Fontaine'   HT, w, 1932, Soupert & Notting; flowers pure white, large, full, slight fragrance
'Mons Fournier' -- See 'Monseigneur Fournier'
'Mons Fraissenon'   HT, dp, 1911, Gamon; bud long; flowers deep frosty pink, large, dbl., moderate fragrance; ['Lady Ashtown' × unknown]
'Mons Francisque Rive'   HP, mr, 1883, Schwartz, J.; flowers cerise red nu-

anced carmine, petals concave, reverse glaucescent, large, full; very remontant

'Mons Frédéric Daupias' T, w, 1898, Chauvry; flowers silvery cream white, shaded carmine pink, center darker, very large, very full, moderate fragrance

'Mons Furtado' T, ly, 1867, Laffay; flowers light sulfur-yellow, large, very full; may be synonymous with Duchesse de Bragance (T, 1997, Dubreuil)

'Mons Georges Cain' -- See 'Georges Cain'

'Mons Georges de Cadoudal' -- See 'Georges de Cadonel'

'Mons Guillaume Popie' HP, mr, 1894, Corboeuf; flowers bright red, large, full

'Mons Gustave Bienvêtu' ('Bienvêtu') HRg, pb, 1906, Gravereaux; flowers bright salmony pink with darker reflections, large, dbl., borne mostly solitary; prickles relatively few, straight or slightly hooked; [('Pierre Notting' × 'Safrano') × 'Conrad Ferdinand Meyer']

'Mons Hélye' HRg, lp, 1900, Morlet; flowers creamy pink, medium, semi-dbl.

'Mons Hippolyte Marchand' HP, rb, 1881, Vigneron; flowers light red, edges carmine-lilac, very large, full

'Mons Hoste' HP, mr, 1884, Liabaud; flowers velvety crimson red, large, dbl.; foliage thick, dark green

'Mons Jacobs' HP, mp; flowers carmine pink, large, full, globular

'Mons Jard' B, m, before 1866; flowers dark garnet-purple, large, full

'Mons Jean France' HP, m, 1866, Levet; flowers dark purple

'Mons Joseph Chappaz' ('Joseph Chappaz') HP, m, 1882, Schmitt; flowers violet-pink, large, dbl., globular; [sport of 'Jules Margottin']

'Mons Joseph Hill' -- See 'Joseph Hill'

'Mons Journaix' ('Mons Journaux') HP, mr, 1868, Marest; flowers scarlet, nuanced darker, large, full; very remontant

'Mons Journaux' -- See 'Mons Journaix'

'Mons Jules Deroudilhe' HP, m, 1886, Liabaud; flowers purple/pink, medium, dbl.

'Mons Jules Lemaître' HP, dp, 1890, Vigneron; flowers carmine-pink with lighter reverse, very large, dbl.; ['Mme Isaac Pereire' × unknown]

'Mons Jules Maquinant' HP, mr, 1882, Vigneron; flowers light red, center brighter, large, dbl.; ['Jules Margottin' × unknown]

'Mons Jules Monges' HP, mp, 1881, Guillot fils; flowers carmine pink, very large, full, cupped; foliage light green; growth upright; ['Souv de la Reine d'Angleterre' × unknown]

'Mons Just-Détrey' HP, mp, 1883, Just-Détrey; flowers shining carmine, medium to large, full

'Mons Lauriol de Barney' HP, dr, 1866, Trouillard; flowers currant red, shaded purple, large, full

'Mons le Capitaine Louis Frère' HP, dr, 1883, Vigneron; flowers velvety crimson, large; freely remontant; prickles small, chestnut brown, numerous; growth upright

'Mons le Chevalier Angelo Ferrario' -- See 'Chevalier Angelo Ferrario'

'Mons le Préfet Limbourg' -- See 'Préfet Limbourg'

'Mons Claude Levet' -- See 'Claude Levet'

'Mons Louis Ligier' HP, dr, 1899, Berland; flowers dark red aging to bring carmine, reverse silvery, very large, full, globular

'Mons Louis Ricard' HP, mr, 1899, Boutigny, P.; flowers currant red, large, full; ['Simon St. Jean' × 'Abel Carrière']

'Mons Mathieu Baron' HP, dr, 1886, Schwartz; flowers dark violet-red, large, dbl.

'Mons. Moreau' HP, m, 1864, Guillot; flowers purple, medium, full

'Mons. Moreau' HP, mp, Vigneron; flowers shining pink, petals edges silvery, large, full, globular; intr. 1885

'Mons Morlet' HRg, dp, 1900, Morlet; flowers deep carmine

'Mons Nomann' HP, lp, 1866, Laffay or Guillot; flowers light pink, edged white, large, full; ['Jules Margottin' × unknown]

'Mons Paul Lédé' ('Paul Lédé') HT, pb, 1902, Pernet-Ducher; flowers carmine-pink, shaded yellow, large, dbl., cupped

'Mons Paul Lédé, Climbing' ('Paul Lédé, Climbing') Cl HT, pb, 1913, Low; flowers carmine pink and dawn yellow, large, full; [sport of 'Mons Paul Lédé']

'Mons Pélisson' -- See 'Pélisson'

'Mons Pierre Migron' T, yb, 1898, Chauvry; flowers chamois yellow, petals edged dark pink, streaked China pink, large, full

'Mons Pierson' HP, mr, 1864, Fontaine; flowers amaranth and crimson, large, full

'Mons Plaisançon' HP, dp, 1866, Ducher; flowers dark carmine, large, full

'Mons Rosier' T, pb, 1887, Nabonnand; flowers rose and yellow, 9-10 cm., full, cupped; ['Mlle Mathilde Lenaerts' × unknown]

'Mons Seringe' HP, m, 1856, Guillot; flowers purple, aging brown, medium; ['Géant des Batailles' × unknown]

'Mons Thiers' HP, mr, 1866, Trouillard; flowers shining red, large, full

'Mons Tillier' T, op, 1891, Bernaix, A.; flowers rosy flesh, shaded salmon-rose and purple-rose, fairly large, dbl., cupped; recurrent; vigorous growth

'Mons Van Eeden' -- See 'L'Obscurité'

'Monsieur Victor Verdier' -- See 'Victor Verdier'

'Mons Woolfield' HP, mp, 1868, Guillot; flowers bright pink, large, full, globular

Monsoon™ (José Carreras™) HT, w, Poulsen; flowers 10-15 cm., 25 petals, borne in clusters of 2 or 3, no fragrance; foliage dark, glossy; growth bushy, 60-100 cm.; PP13300; intr. 2001

'Monstrueuse' -- See 'Bullata'

'Monstrueux' D, lp, before 1830; flowers pale pink, large, full, globular

'Mont-à-camp' HT, yb, 1928, Delobel; flowers pure yellow, reverse shaded orange, very large, dbl.; vigorous, upright growth

'Mont Blanc' ('Montblanc') HRg, w, Baum; flowers semi-dbl. to dbl., moderate fragrance; recurrent; growth to 3 ft.; hips numerous, plump, orange-red; very hardy; intr. 1986

'Mont d'Or' T, w, 1863, Ducher; flowers white, shaded light carmine-purple, aging to tan, large, full

'Mont Hamel' LCl, mp, 1937, Constantin; flowers semi-dbl., globular, borne in clusters; foliage glossy; very vigorous, climbing growth

'Mont Rosa' ('Montrosa') T, yb, 1872, Ducher; flowers dawn gold with flesh pink, medium, full

'Montagny' -- See 'Flaminaire'

'Montagut' HT, Dot, Simon; intr. 1991

'Montalembert' HGal, m, 1852, Moreau-Robert; flowers dark violet, plumed and often spotted with white and crimson, large, full, globular

'Montana' -- See 'Savamont'

Montana® -- See 'Royal Occasion'

'Montauban' HT, dr, Croix; flowers large, 50 petals, moderate fragrance; free-flowering; foliage large, disease-resistant

Montauban de Bretagne® -- See 'Adamonbu'

'Montblanc' -- See 'Mont Blanc'

'Monte Carlo' HT, ob, 1949, Meilland, F.; flowers Indian yellow suffused russet-orange, well-shaped, 5 in., 45 petals; foliage glossy; vigorous growth; ['Peace' × seedling]

Monte Carlo Country Club® HT, rb, Adam; flowers bright red, reverse pale yellow suffused red, dbl., high-centered; medium growth; intr. 2006

'Monte Cassino' HRg, dr, Baum; flowers medium, semi-dbl., borne in clusters, moderate fragrance; recurrent; growth to 3 ft.; hips plump, orange-red; intr. 1987

'Monte Cristo' -- See 'Evemas'

'Monte Cristo' HP, dr, 1861, Fontaine; flowers large, 50 petals, globular; low growth

'Monte Igueldo' HT, dr, 1944, La Florida; flowers velvety dark red, well-formed, open; upright, open habit growth; ['Étoile de Hollande' × 'Majorca']

'Monte Nevoso' HT, 1929, Cazzaniga, F. G.

'Monte Rosa' HRg, mp, Baum; flowers large, semi-dbl., moderate fragrance; growth to 3 ft.; numerous hips; intr. 1984

'Monte Toro' HT, pb, 1962, Dot, Simon; flowers strawberry-pink shaded red, large, dbl.; ['Berthe Mallerin' × 'Grand'mère Jenny']

'Monteariosa' HG, about 1920, Franchetti; [*R. gigantea* × *R. moschata*]

'Montebello' HP, mr, 1859, Fontaine; flowers medium, full

'Montecito' HG, w, 1930, Franchetti; flowers white to blush, 6 in., 5 petals; foliage medium green, disease-resistant; vigorous, climbing (to 50 ft.) growth; [*R. gigantea* × *R. moschata*]

'Monterey' HT, rb, 1933, Lester Rose Gardens; flowers light gold flushed rose, veined and edged crimson, reverse lighter, dbl., moderate fruity fragrance; [sport of 'The Queen Alexandra Rose']

'Monterosa' HT, pb, 1958, Giacomasso; flowers deep rose, edged lighter, full, peony-like; very vigorous growth; ['Elettra' × 'Superba']; intr. 1952

'Montesquieu' HT, pb, 1959, Dot, Simon; flowers deep rose shaded crimson, 45 petals, high-centered; strong stems; very vigorous growth; ['Loli Creus' × 'Tahiti']

'Montesuma Rosice' HT, Strnad

'Montézuma' HGal, m, before 1830, Coquerel; flowers lilac pink, edges paler, large, full, semi-globular; nearly thornless

'Montezuma' Gr, op, 1956, Swim, H.C.; bud urn-shaped; flowers 3½-4 in., 36 petals, high-centered; foliage leathery, semi-glossy; very vigorous, compact growth; PP1383; ['Fandango' × 'Floradora']; intr. 1955

'Montezuma, Climbing' Cl HT, op, Langbecker; [sport of 'Montezuma']; intr. 1970

'Monthly Rambler' ('Laxton's Monthly Rambler') HWich, dr, 1926, Laxton Bros.; flowers brilliant crimson-red, 5-6 cm., semi-dbl., borne in large clusters, moderate fragrance; some autumn repeat; [*R. wichurana* × 'Old Crimson China']

'Monthly Rose' -- See 'Parsons' Pink China'

'Monthyon' -- See 'Crignon de Montigny'

Monticello™ (Sweet Cover™) S, mp, Olesen; bud short, pointed ovoid; flowers medium pink, reverse lighter, ruffled, 5 cm., 10-15 petals, shallow cup, borne in clusters of 2 - 7, slight fruity fragrance; free-flowering; foliage dark; prickles moderate, 8 mm., concave; broad, bushy (60-100 cm.) growth; PP12125; [seedling × seedling]; intr. 1999

'Montigny' -- See 'Crignon de Montigny'

'Montigny-le-Tilleul' S, pr, RvS-Melle; flowers 60 petals, flat; foliage medium dark green; ['Frederik Chopin' × 'Florex']; intr. 1990

'Montijo' F, dr, 1954, Dot, Pedro; bud ovoid; flowers crimson-red, medium, very dbl.; very vigorous growth; ['Méphisto' × 'Magrana']

'Montmartre' F, m, 1955, Gaujard; bud ovoid; flowers bright purplish red, large, dbl.; foliage dark, bronze; very vigorous growth; ['Peace' × seedling]

'Montparnasse, Climbing' Cl HT, ab, 1986, Kodoya, Y.; flowers large, 34 petals, high-centered; foliage coppery green, leathery, semi-glossy; bushy, vigorous growth; [sport of 'Montparnasse']; intr. 1980

'Montrea' F, mr, 1970, Mosselman & Terreehorst; buds ovoid; flowers light red, small, very dbl., borne in clusters; foliage dark green; ['Coronet' × unknown]

Montreal® HT, pb, 1981, Gaujard, Jean; bud long; flowers cream and pink blend, large, 45 petals, high-centered, moderate fragrance; foliage large, dark; prickles green; ['Americana' × 'Dora']; intr. 1979

'Montresor' -- See 'Red Imp'

'Montrosa' -- See 'Mont Rosa'

'Montrose' -- See 'Talmontrose'

'Montrose' HT, dp, 1916, Cook, J.W.; flowers deep pink; ['red seedling' × 'Laurent Carle']

'Montrouge' F, rb, 1958, Gaujard; flowers clear red, center tinted copper, medium, semi-dbl.; foliage glossy; vigorous, bushy growth; ['Peace' × ('Alain' × unknown)]; intr. 1956

'Montseny' HT, op, 1944, Dot, Pedro; flowers salmon-pink, well-formed, very dbl., high-centered; foliage glossy; upright growth; ['Mme Butterfly' × 'Jean C.N. Forestier']

'Montserrat' HT, op, 1958, Camprubi, C.; flowers orange-salmon-pink, large, dbl., cupped, moderate fragrance; foliage dark, glossy; very vigorous, upright growth; ['Comtesse Vandal' × 'Angels Mateu']; intr. 1954

'Montuna' HP, 1928, Luke, E.R.; ['Prince Camille de Rohan' × unknown]

'MontyJax' -- See 'Liodoc'

'Monty's White' -- See 'White Ensign'

'Monument' HT, mr, Urban, J.; flowers large, dbl.; intr. 1969

'Monumental' HT, dr, Weeks, O.L.; intr. 2005

'Monviso' HT, pb, 1958, Giacomasso; bud pointed; flowers white streaked pink, large, dbl.; strong stems; ['Julien Potin' × 'Monterosa']; intr. 1955

'Monymusk' HMsk, my, 1954, Ratcliffe; flowers clear yellow, large, semi-dbl.; recurrent bloom; vigorous (3-4 ft.) growth; ['Pax' × 'Phyllis Gold']

'Monyna' HT, ob, Delbard; buds elongated, apricot with green overlay; flowers cream with coral-orange edges, flowing toward the center, large, high-centered, spiral, borne mostly singly; stems strong, upright; growth vigorous; intr. 2003

'Monza' HT, Leenders; intr. 1965

'Mood Music' Min, op, 1977, Moore, Ralph S.; bud mossy; flowers orange to orange-pink, mini-moss, 1 in., 45 petals, flat to rounded; foliage small; upright, bushy growth; PP4254; ['Fairy Moss' × 'Goldmoss']

'Moody Blues' -- See 'Macmooblu'

'Moody Dream' -- See 'Macmoodre'

'Moon Adventure' HT, my, Kordes; buds pointed; flowers clear yellow, dbl., high-centered; free-flowering; stems long; growth tall, strong, vigorous; intr. 1999

'Moon Glow' LCl, pb, 1937, Brownell; flowers creamy primrose, center soft yellow, 3 in., 60-75 petals, moderate fragrance; strong stems; vigorous growth; ['Glenn Dale' × 'Mrs Arthur Curtiss James']

'Moon Magic' -- See 'Delbut'

'Moon Maiden' F, ly, 1970, Mattock; flowers creamy yellow, 3½-4 in., 55 petals; foliage dark; ['Fred Streeter' × Allgold®]

Moon Mist™ -- See 'Piximis'

'Moon Over Miami' HT, w, 2007, Edwards, Eddie and Phelps, Ethan; flowers 5-6 in., full, high-centered, borne mostly solitary; foliage small, dark green; few prickles; growth upright, to 5 ft.; [seedling × Crystalline™]; intr. 2007

'Moon Over the Castle Ruins' -- See 'Kojo no Tsuki'

'Moon River' -- See 'Korconta'

'Moon River' -- See 'Benlavscent'

Moon Shadow™ -- See 'Jaclaf'

'Moon Shadow' Min, m, Benardella, Frank; flowers lavender and silvery blue, moderate fragrance; free-flowering; medium growth

'Moon Star' HT, or, 2003, Atherton, Kyle B.; flowers scarlet orange, reverse silvery, 4 in., full, borne mostly solitary, moderate fragrance; foliage medium size, dark green, semi-glossy; prickles small to medium, curved down, moderate; growth upright, medium (3 ft.); ornamental; [sport of 'Killarney']; intr. 2003

'Moonbeam' -- See 'Ausbeam'

'Moonbeam' -- See 'Bribeam'

'Moonbeam' HT, dy, 1950, Robinson, H.; flowers deep golden yellow, large, high-centered; foliage dark, glossy; RULED EXTINCT 4/92; [seedling × 'McGredy's Yellow']

'Moonbeam, Climbing' Cl HT, dy, 1955, Kordes

'MoonBerry' HT, dp, Dorieux; flowers deep pink, 4-6 in., 40-45 petals, intense sweet fragrance; foliage dark green, glossy; growth tall (3-5 ft.); PPAF; intr. 2005

'Moondance' -- See 'Meinivoz'

Moondance™ -- See 'Jactanic'

'Moondance Masquerade' -- See 'Jalmoon'

'Moondrops' HT, op, 1965, Delforge; bud ovoid; flowers rose-amaranth shaded salmon, open, single, intense spicy fragrance; vigorous growth; ['Sunny Boy' × seedling]

'Moondrops 85' HT, m, Delforge; flowers violet mauve with pink shadings, classical, moderate fragrance; intr. 1985

'Moonglow' -- See 'Gueslaylow'

Moonja® HT, op, Tantau; flowers shades of coral orange, medium, double, high-centered, wide, borne mostly singly; recurrent; stems medium; intr. 2005

'Moonlight' -- See 'Tsukiakari'

'Moonlight' -- See 'Gekko'

Moonlight® -- See 'Korklemol'
'Moonlight' -- See 'Jacice'
Moonlight™ MinFl, ly, Olesen; flowers dbl., 25-30 petals, borne mostly solitary, moderate wild rose fragrance; foliage medium green, semi-glossy; growth narrow, bushy, low (40-60 cm.); PP13658
'Moonlight' HT, ly, Kordes; flowers clear yellow, large, double, high-centered, borne mostly singly; recurrent; stems long; Florist rose; intr. 2001
'Moonlight' HMsk, ly, 1913, Pemberton; flowers lemon-white, prominent yellow stamens, single, borne in small clusters, moderate fragrance; repeat bloom; foliage dark, glossy; vigorous (4-5 ft.) bushy growth; [Trier® × 'Sulphurea']
'Moonlight and Roses' -- See 'Brirose'
'Moonlight Bay' -- See 'Renmobay'
Moonlight Dreamer™ -- See 'Moemoondream'
'Moonlight Fragrance' LCl, ly
'Moonlight Lady' -- See 'Jacosol'
'Moonlight Lady' -- See 'Socalp'
'Moonlight Magic' HT, m, 1991, Burks, Larry; flowers lavender, medium, dbl., borne mostly singly, slight fragrance; foliage medium size, medium green, matte; medium, bushy growth; [seedling × seedling]; intr. 1991
'Moonlight Mist' HT, w, 1965, Armbrust; bud pointed; flowers ivory-white, very large, dbl.; very vigorous growth; ['Buccaneer' × 'Golden Harvest']
Moonlight Niagara® HT, or, 1987, Rogin, Josip; flowers orange, reverse pale orange, loose, medium, 60 petals, high-centered, star-shaped, borne singly, moderate spicy fragrance; foliage large, dark green, matte; prickles semi-thick, medium, brown-red; growth upright, tall; hips rounded, medium, orange-red; [sport of 'Red Queen']
'Moonlight Panarosa' S, yb, Kordes; flowers light yellow with pink and apricot tones, outer petals fade, large, full, borne in large clusters, slight fragrance; arching growth; intr. 2004
'Moonlight Scentsation' -- See 'Savamoon'
'Moonlight Serenade' -- See 'Tanalzergo'
'Moonlight Serenade' HT, yb, 1994, Ohata, Hatsuo; flowers yellow with red fringe, 3-3½ in., full, moderate fragrance; foliage large, medium green, semi-glossy; numerous prickles; medium (120 cm.), spreading growth; ['Garden Party' × 'Jana']
'Moonlight Smooth Touch' -- See 'Hadmoo'
'Moonlight Sonata' -- See 'Grebetoven'
'Moonlight Sonata' HT, ab, 1966, Boerner; bud ovoid; flowers large, dbl., cupped, moderate fragrance; foliage dark, glossy; vigorous, upright, bushy growth; PP2652; [('Diamond Jubilee' × unknown) × ('Goldilocks' × 'Orange Nassau')]
'Moonlit' MinFl, w, 2007, Read, Allan; flowers 6 cm., very full, borne in small clusters; foliage small, medium green, semi-glossy; prickles small, hooked, brown, few; growth upright, medium (60 cm.); [Bluesette® × 'Rise 'n' Shine']; intr. 2007

'Moonlit Spire' HT, yb, Kordes; intr. 2008

Moonraker® F, ly, 1968, Harkness; flowers pale yellow to white, large, dbl., borne in clusters; foliage light green; ['Pink Parfait' × 'Highlight']

'Moonrise' HT, ly, 1997, McMillan, Thomas G.; flowers medium, full, cupped, borne mostly singly, no fragrance; foliage medium size, medium green, semi-glossy; upright, low (2 ft.) growth; [('Lady X' × 'Antigua') × Midas Touch™]

'Moonshine' Cl HT, w, before 1920; flowers single; foliage blue-green, glossy

'Moonsprite' F, ly, 1956, Swim, H.C.; bud ovoid; flowers creamy white, center pale gold, 2-2½ in., 80 petals, cupped, blooms in clusters, intense fragrance; foliage leathery, semi-glossy; dwarf, bushy growth; PP1450; ['Sutter's Gold' × 'Ondine']; intr. 1956

Moonstone™ -- See 'Wekcryland'

'Moonstruck' -- See 'Jacess'

'Moonwalker' S, ob, 2005, Valentic, Dzejna; flowers coral-orange, reverse coral, 4 in., full, borne mostly solitary, moderate fragrance; intermittent bloom; foliage medium size, medium green, semi-glossy; prickles small, moderate; growth upright, medium (5-7 ft.); hedging, specimen; ['Kon 35-02' × ('Camelot' × 'Kon 13')]; intr. 2006

'Moorcap' Cl Min, dr, 1976, Moore, Ralph S.; bud pointed

'Moorcar' Min, rb, 1973, Moore, Ralph S.; intr. 1972

'Moore's Classic Perpetual' -- See 'Morclassic'

'Moore's Odorata' w, Moore, Ralph S.; flowers white with pale pink centers, small, dbl.; a form of Odorata 22449

'Moore's Pink Perpetual' -- See 'Morpinkper'

'Moore's Striped Rugosa' -- See 'Morbeauty'

'Moore's Yellow' -- See 'Golden Angel'

'Moose Range' HRg, mr, 1944, Wright, Percy H.; ['Hansa' × 'Mary L. Evans']

'Morabito' S, ab, Guillot; intr. 1997

'Morag Ross' -- See 'Horseekship'

'Morain' ('Lucky Charm') Min, yb, 1990, Moore, Ralph S.; bud ovoid; flowers yellow, reverse tinting red, aging to pink to red, lightly striped, small, 50-60 petals, high-centered, borne in sprays of 3 - 5, no fragrance; foliage small, medium green, matte; prickles straight, small, brown; bushy, spreading, low growth; no fruit; ['Rumba' × Pinstripe™]; intr. 1989

'Moralbuque' ('Albuquerque Enchantment') Min, rb, 1997, Moore, Ralph S.; flowers medium, dbl., borne in small clusters; foliage medium size, medium green, semi-glossy; medium (30-45 cm.) bushy, spreading growth; ['Poker Chip' × Cherry Magic™]

'Moralert' ('Red Alert') Min, mr, 1991, Moore, Ralph S.; bud pointed, long; flowers medium red, slightly lighter reverse, aging similar, 4 cm., 35-40 petals, high-centered, borne usually singly or in sprays of 3-4, slight fragrance; foliage medium size, medium green, semi-glossy; prickles several, thin, straight; stems slender, wiry; upright, bushy, medium growth; hips none ; PP8193; [Orangeade® × Rainbow's End™]; intr. 1991

'Moramber' ('Amber Gem') HBc, ob, 2003, Moore, Ralph S.; flowers orange/ pink, reverse lt pink - white, 1½ in., full, borne in small clusters, slight fragrance; foliage small, medium green; prickles small, hooked, light green, few; growth compact, short (15 in.); pots, garden, borders; [Joycie™ × 'Out of Yesteryear']; intr. 2003

'Moranium' ('Autumn Fire') Min, or, 1983, Moore, Ralph S.; flowers medium, semi-dbl.; foliage small, medium green, semi-glossy; bushy, very spreading growth; ['Little Chief' × 'Anytime']; intr. 1982

'Moranyblac' ('Red Cameo') Min, dr, 1993, Moore, Ralph S.; flowers dark red, do not burn, large, 6-14 petals, borne mostly singly; foliage medium size, medium green, semi-glossy; few prickles; medium (34-38 cm.), upright, bushy growth; ['Anytime' × Black Jade™]; intr. 1994

'Moranyface' ('Halo Star') Min, ob, 1992, Moore, Ralph S.; flowers reddish on outside, orange to pink on inside, reddish-lavender at base, medium, single, no fragrance; foliage small, medium green, matte; medium (35-40 cm.), upright, bushy growth; [('Anytime' × 'Angel Face') × ('Anytime' × 'Angel Face')]; intr. 1993

'Morart' ('Work of Art') Min, ob, 1989, Moore, Ralph S.; bud short; flowers orange blended with yellow, reverse slightly more yellow, 4-5 cm., 35 petals, high-centered, borne in loose sprays of 3 - 7, slight fruity fragrance; recurrent; foliage medium size, bronze aging to medium green, semi-glossy; prickles few, slender, nearly straight, average, brown; stems slender, wirey; upright, spreading, tall growth; hips globular, medium, orange; PP7617; [('Little Darling' × 'Yellow Magic') × Gold Badge™]

'Morava' HT, Strnad; intr. 1970

'Morbaby' (Baby Austin™) Min, ab, 2002, Moore, Ralph S.; flowers peach/pink, peach/apricot reverse, micro-mini, 1 in., full, cupped/quartered, borne in small clusters, slight fragrance; foliage small, medium green, semi-glossy; prickles small, straight, few, green; growth bushy, short (10-12 in.); [Joycie™ × seedling]; intr. 2001

'Morbahny' ('Jessica Rose') Min, pb, 2003, Moore, Ralph S.; flowers light to medium pink, reverse medium to dark pink, 1¼ in., full, borne in large clusters; foliage medium size, medium green,

Semi-glossy; prickles small, straight, brown, few; growth bushy, medium, (12 in.); containers, garden, borders; [seedling × 'Red Fairy']; intr. 2003

'Morballet'   Gr, pb, Moore, Ralph; intr. 2007

'Morbeauty' ('Moore's Striped Rugosa') HRg, rb, 2004, Ralph S. Moore; flowers red/white stripes, reverse red, 4 in., full, borne in small clusters, moderate fragrance; recurrent; foliage medium size, dark green, matte; prickles medium, straight; growth bushy, medium (4 ft.); hedge, specimen; [(('Golden Angel' × '44st') × 'Rugosa Magnifica']; intr. 2005

'Morben' ('Doris Bennett') Min, pb, 2002, Moore, Ralph S.; flowers dark pink, reverse medium pink, 1-1½ in., very full, borne in small clusters; foliage medium size, medium green, Semi-glossy; prickles small, straight, green, few; growth spreading, short (12-15 in.); containers, garden, borders; intr. 2002

'Morberg' ('Ann Moore') Min, or, 1981, Moore, Ralph S.; bud long, pointed; flowers 30 petals, high-centered, borne usually singly, moderate fragrance; foliage leathery, semi-glossy; prickles long; vigorous, bushy, upright growth; ['Little Darling' × 'Fire Princess']

'Morberk' (Berkeley Beauty™) Min, m, 1988, Moore, Ralph S.; flowers picotee white, edged lavender to pink (striped), small, dbl., high-centered; foliage medium size, medium green, semi-glossy, abundant; prickles varying green to brown; bushy, medium, neat growth; ['Pink Petticoat' × Make Believe™]; intr. 1987

'Morbigleave'   HRg, pb, Moore, Ralph; intr. 2008

'Morblack' ('Don Marshall') Min, dr, 1982, Moore, Ralph S.; flowers medium red, reverse blackish-red, small, 35 petals, high-centered, slight fragrance; foliage small, dark, matte; bushy, spreading growth; [Baccará® × 'Little Chief']

'Morbouquet' ('Grandma's Pink') S, mp, 1991, Moore, Ralph S.; flowers medium, very full, borne in small clusters, no fragrance; foliage medium size, medium green, matte; medium, upright, bushy growth; ['Shakespeare Festival' × 'Marchioness of Londonderry']; intr. 1991

'Morbox' ('Jewel Box') Min, pb, 1984, Moore, Ralph S.; flowers light to deep pink blend, reverse lighter, small, 20 petals; foliage small, medium green, semi-glossy; bushy growth; PP5722; ['Avandel' × 'Old Master']; intr. 1983

'Morboy' ('Billy Boy') Min, mr, 1990, Moore, Ralph S.; bud pointed, short; flowers small, 15-18 petals, cupped, borne usually singly; foliage small, medium green, matte, dense; prickles slender, straight, small, brownish; bushy, low to medium, compact growth; ['Anytime' × 'Happy Hour']

'Morbrights' ('Spotlight') Min, ob, 1999, Moore, Ralph S.; flowers bright orange, blended rose, with white star-shaped eye, reverse white, 1½ in., 5 petals, borne mostly singly, no fragrance; recurrent; foliage medium size, medium green, semi-glossy; bushy, compact (12-18 in.) growth; [Orangeade® × Little Artist®]; intr. 1999

'Morbrown' ('Apricot Twist') Min, ab, 1993, Moore, Ralph S.; flowers medium, dbl., borne in small clusters; foliage small, medium green, semi-glossy; few prickles; low (30-32 cm.), bushy, compact growth; PP9656; ['Golden Angel' × Sequoia Gold™]; intr. 1994

'Morbug' ('Ladybug') Min, mr, 1992, Moore, Ralph S.; flowers medium, semi-dbl., borne in small clusters; fast repeat; foliage small, medium green, semi-glossy; few prickles; low (30-40 cm.), bushy, compact growth; ['Sheri Anne' × Cherry Magic™]; intr. 1993

'Morcade' ('Pink Cascade') Cl Min, mp, 1982, Moore, Ralph S.; flowers small, 35 petals; foliage small, medium green, matte to semi-glossy; spreading (5-7 ft; similar to Red Cascade) growth; [(R. wichurana × 'Floradora') × 'Magic Dragon']; intr. 1981

'Morcake' ('Wedding Cake') F, w, 2007, Moore, Ralph S.; flowers pink changing to green/white, reverse pale pink to white, medium, 3 in., very full, borne in small clusters; foliage medium green, semi-glossy; prickles small, straight, brown, moderate; growth upright, 3-4 ft.; specimen, large containers; ['Sheri Anne' × unknown]; intr. 2006

'Morcalyn' ('Coral Cameo') Min, dp, 1986, Moore, Ralph S.; flowers deep pink, dbl., high-centered, borne singly and in small sprays; foliage small, medium green, semi-glossy; prickles very few; medium, upright, bushy growth; hips small, globular, orange; ['Little Darling' × 'Anytime']; intr. 1982

'Morcara' (Antique Rose™) Min, mp, 1981, Moore, Ralph S.; bud pointed; flowers rose pink, mini-flora, medium, 38 petals, high-centered, borne usually singly, slight fragrance; foliage dark, semi-glossy; prickles straight, brown; vigorous, upright growth; [Baccará® × 'Little Chief']

'Morcarlet' (Scarlet Moss™) Min, mr, 1988, Moore, Ralph S.; bud long, pointed, mossy; very mossy sepals; flowers intense scarlet-red, 2 in., 12-15 petals, high-centered, then flat, borne singly and in loose sprays of 3-10, no fragrance; free-flowering; foliage medium size, medium green, glossy, leathery; prickles slender, various, green to brown; stems slender, wiry; upright, bushy, tall growth; hips round, elongated, orange; PP7128; [(Dortmund® × 'miniature seedling') × (Dortmund® × 'miniature striped seedling')]

'Morcas' ('White Rain') Min, w, 1991, Moore, Ralph S.; flowers small, dbl., borne in large clusters, moderate fragrance; foliage small, light green, semi-glossy; some prickles; low (22 cm.), spreading, groundcover growth; ['Papoose' × 'Renae']; intr. 1992

'Morcat' ('Copy Cat') Min, mp, 1986, Moore, Ralph S.; [sport of 'Beauty Secret']; intr. 1985

'Morcd' ('Cee Dee Moss') S, pb, 1991, Moore, Ralph S.; bud pointed; intr. 1990

'Morcebru' ('Baby Cécile Brunner') Min, lp, 1982, Moore, Ralph S.; flowers soft pink, 1 in., dbl., slight fragrance; recurrent; foliage small, medium green, matte; upright, bushy (12 in.) growth; ['Cécile Brunner, Climbing' × 'Fairy Princess']; intr. 1982

'Morceedee' ('Cee Dee Moss') S, pb, 1991, Moore, Ralph S.; bud pointed; flowers pink with occasional white stripe, lighter reverse, ages lighter, 2½-3¼ in., dbl., cupped, loose, borne in sprays of 3-5; foliage medium size, light green, glossy; bushy, spreading, medium growth; ['Carolyn Dean' × seedling]; intr. 1990

'Morcelebrate' ('Celebrate Life') Min, ob, 2005, Moore, Ralph S.; flowers orange, reverse orange/pink, 1½ in., semi-dbl., borne in small clusters, slight fragrance; foliage medium size, medium green, semi-glossy; no prickles; bushy, medium (15 in.) growth; containers, borders; ['Golden Gardens' × 'Sequoia Ruby']; intr. 2005

'Morchari' ('Insolite', Sweet Chariot™) Min, m, 1985, Moore, Ralph S.; bud small, ovoid to pointed; flowers lavender to purple blend, 1½ in., 55-60 petals, cupped, then rounded, borne in clusters of 5-20, intense fragrance; recurrent; foliage small, medium green, matte; prickles several, short, curved to straight, brown; stems slender, wiry; low (12 in.), spreading growth; hips few to none; PP5975; ['Little Chief' × 'Violette']; intr. 1984

'Morcharlie' ('Charlie Brown') Min, rb, 1996, Moore, Ralph S.; flowers red and white stripe, 1-1¼ in., 8-14 petals, borne singly or in small clusters; foliage small, medium green, semi-glossy; few prickles; compact, bushy, low (12-15 in.) growth; [seedling × Pinstripe™]; intr. 1997

'Morcheer' (Cheerleader™) Min, dr, 1986, Moore, Ralph S.; flowers small, very dbl., borne in sprays of 5-10; foliage small, medium green, semi-glossy; bushy, spreading growth; no fruit; PP5977; ['Fairy Moss' × 'Orange Honey']; intr. 1985

'Morchermag' (Cherry Magic™) Min, dr, 1988, Moore, Ralph S.; flowers deep red, reverse lighter red with silver sheen, aging lighter, 25 petals, high-centered; foliage small, medium green, matte; prickles short, small, brown; bushy, spreading, low growth; hips round, small, orange-red; PP7061; ['Anytime'

× 'Lavender Jewel']

'Morchick' ('Chick-a-dee') Min, mp, 1990, Moore, Ralph S.; bud pointed; flowers medium pink with occasional white stripes, reverse similar, 40-50 petals, high-centered, slight fragrance; foliage small, medium green, matte to semi-glossy; prickles small, hooked downward, brownish; bushy, low, compact, rounded growth; ['Cécile Brunner' × (Dortmund® × ('Fairy Moss' × 'Little Darling × Ferdinand Pichard'))]

'Morcingold' ('Cinderella Gold') Min, my, 1995, Moore, Ralph S.; flowers small, dbl., borne mostly singly and in small clusters; foliage small, light green, semi-glossy; no prickles; low (15 cm.) bushy growth; ['Cal Poly' × 'Cal Poly']; intr. 1996

'Morclassic' ('Moore's Classic Perpetual') S, dp, 1999, Moore, Ralph S.; flowers 3 in., 41 petals, borne in small clusters, moderate fragrance; foliage medium size, medium green, semi-glossy; few prickles; growth bushy, compact (16-24 in.); ['Anytime' × 'Paul Neyron']; a dwarf hybrid perpetual; intr. 1998

'Morclchick' ('Chick-A-Dee, Climbing') Cl Min, mp, 2000, Moore, Ralph S.; flowers medium pink, 4-7 cm., full, borne in large clusters; foliage medium size, dark green, glossy; few prickles; growth upright, spreading to 6 ft tall; [sport of 'Chick-A-Dee']

'Morclilav' ('Orchid Jubilee') Cl Min, m, 1992, Moore, Ralph S.; flowers mauve blend, holds color well in heat, large, dbl., borne in small clusters, no fragrance; profuse repeat bloom; foliage medium size, medium green, matte; few prickles; tall (2 m.), upright, climbing growth; [('Little Darling' × 'Yellow Magic') × Make Believe™]; intr. 1993

'Morclim' ('High Stepper') Cl Min, yb, 1983, Moore, Ralph S.; flowers yellow overlaid pink, reverse yellow, small, dbl.; foliage medium size, dark, semi-glossy; growth bushy, spreading (to 5 ft; needs support); [('Little Darling' × 'Yellow Magic') × 'Magic Wand']

'Morclip' ('Playgirl, Climbing') Cl F, mp, 1993, Moore, Ralph S.; flowers 3-3½ in., 5-7 petals, borne in small clusters; foliage medium size, medium green, semi-glossy; tall (2-3 m.), upright, spreading, climbing growth; [sport of 'Playgirl']; intr. 1995

'Morclpoly' Cl Min, my, Moore, Ralph; intr. 2000

'Morcoat' ('Tag-a-long') Min, rb, 1992, Moore, Ralph S.; flowers contrast of reddish-lavender against white, large, semi-dbl., borne in small clusters, no fragrance; recurrent; foliage medium size, medium green, new bronze, matte; few prickles; medium (30-40 cm.), upright, bushy growth; [('Little Darling' × 'Yellow Magic') × Make Believe™]; intr. 1993

'Morcofair' ('Coral Fairy') HWich, pb, 1995, Moore, Ralph S.; flowers 1½ in., single, borne in large clusters; foliage small, dark green, semi-glossy; few prickles; tall (3-4 m.), upright, bushy, spreading growth; [(R. wichurana × 'Floradora') × 'Hallelujah']; intr. 1995

'Morcojo' ('Country Joy') Min, pb, 1984, Moore, Ralph S.; flowers light pink, yellow reverse, small, dbl.; foliage small, medium green, matte; compact growth; ['Pinocchio' × 'Yellow Jewel']

'Morcrest' F, dp, Moore; sepals long, fern-like, fluffy, much like those of Chapeau de Napoleonsemi-dbl.; intr. 2005

'Mordal' ('The Dahlia Rose') F, pb, 2004, Moore, Ralph S.; flowers medium pink to white, hand-painted, reverse white, 3 in., very full, borne in small clusters, slight fragrance; foliage medium size, medium green, semi-glossy; prickles small, straight, light green, few; growth spreading, medium (28-36 in.); containers, landscape, cutting; ['Fairy Moss' × 'Old Master']; intr. 2004

'Mordan' ('Red Wagon') Min, mr, 1981, Moore, Ralph S.; flowers 23 petals, borne 1-3 or more per cluster; foliage glossy; prickles brown; vigorous, bushy, rounded growth; ['Little Darling' × 'Little Chief']; intr. 1980

'Mordarain' ('Lifestyle™') Min, pb, 1992, Moore, Ralph S.; flowers large, color holds well, dbl., borne mostly singly; foliage medium size, medium green, semi-glossy; few prickles; medium (35-45 cm.), upright, bushy, rounded growth; ['Little Darling' × Rainbow's End™]; intr. 1993

'Mordarcrest' ('Elegant Design') F, pb, 1994, Moore, Ralph S.; sepals crested; flowers medium, dbl., borne in small clusters; foliage medium size, medium green, matte; few prickles; medium to tall (45-60cm.), upright, bushy growth; ['Little Darling' × 'Crested Jewel']; intr. 1995

'Mordashin' ('Southern Delight') Min, yb, 1991, Moore, Ralph S.; bud pointed; flowers yellow edged with red, aging to pink and yellow, 1¾ in., 40 petals, high-centered to rounded, borne singly and in small clusters, slight fragrance; recurrent; foliage medium size, medium green, semi-glossy; prickles few, slightly inclining downwards; medium (14-16 in.), upright, bushy growth; PP8815; ['Little Darling' × 'Rise 'n' Shine']; intr. 1992

'Morday' ('Sunday Brunch') Min, yb, 1984, Moore, Ralph S.; flowers soft creamy yellow, petal tips becoming red, which spreads, 20 petals, variable, moderate fragrance; foliage small to medium size, medium green, semi-glossy; vigorous, upright, bushy growth; ['Rumba' × 'Peachy White']; intr. 1983

'Mordazz' Min, ob, Moore, Ralph; intr. 2001

'Mordeb' ('Joan Austin') Min, pb, 1981, Moore, Ralph S.; bud pointed; flowers light to medium pink, white stripes, 38 petals, high-centered, borne singly, sometimes 3 or more per cluster, intense fragrance; foliage small, medium green, semi-glossy to matte; very bushy, compact growth; PP5117; ['Avandel' × seedling]

'Mordelahanty' ('Baby Jane Clare') Min, mp, 2007, Moore, Ralph S.; flowers ½ in., dbl., borne mostly solitary; foliage small, medium green, semi-glossy; no prickles; growth compact, short (6 in.); containers; discovered as a root sport of a seedling of Sequoia Ruby

'Morden Amorette' S, dp, 1977, Marshall, H.H.; bud pointed; flowers carmine, 3 in., 28 petals; foliage dark; compact growth; [('Independence' × ('Donald Prior' × R. arkansana)) × ('Fire King' × 'J.W. Fargo' × 'Assiniboine'))]; hybrid suffulta

'Morden Belle' S, mp, Ag. Canada; flowers dusky pink, full; free-flowering; foliage medium size, dark green, glossy; bushy (3 × 3 ft.) growth; very hardy to -40°F; Parkland series; intr. 2005

'Morden Blush' S, lp, 1988, Collicutt, L.M. & Marshall, H.H.; flowers light pink, fading to ivory, small, flat, 51 petals, flat, borne in sprays of 1-5; repeat bloom; foliage medium size, medium green, matte; prickles straight; bushy, low (3-4 ft.) growth; hardy; PP8054; [('Prairie Princess' × 'Morden Amorette') × ('Prairie Princess' × ('White Bouquet' × (R. arkansana × 'Assiniboine')))]

'Morden Cardinette' S, mr, 1980, Marshall, H.H.; bud ovoid; flowers cardinal red, 25 petals, cupped, borne singly or in clusters of up to 15; foliage 7 leaflets, globulous, dark; bushy, low growth; hardy

'Morden Centennial' S, mp, 1980, Marshall, H.H.; bud ovoid; flowers medium-pink, shapely, 40 petals, borne 1-15 per cluster; repeat bloom; foliage 7 leaflets, dark, slightly glossy; prickles slightly recurved; typical shrub growth, 3-4 ft.; ['Prairie Princess' × ('White Bouquet' × ('J.W. Fargo' × 'Assiniboine'))]

'Morden Fireglow' S, or, 1990, Collicutt, L.M. & Marshall, H.H.; bud pointed; flowers brilliant red-orange, reverse red, loose, 3 in., 28 petals, cupped, borne in sprays; repeat bloom; foliage medium size, medium green, matte; prickles slight downward curve, tan; growth bushy, low (4 ft.); globular, reflexed calyx fruit; PP8060; [seedling × 'Morden Cardinette']; intr. 1990

'Morden Magic' F, rb; intr. 2006

'Morden Ruby' S, pb, 1977, Marshall, H.H.; bud ovoid; flowers 2½-3½ in., very dbl.; heavy bloom; vigorous, irregular growth; ['Fire King' × ('J. W. Fargo' × 'Assiniboine')]; hybrid suffulta

'Morden 6910' HWich, mr; flowers bright red, single, borne in clusters of 5 - 10, slight fragrance; spring bloom; vigorous (20+ ft.) growth

'Morden Snow Beauty' -- See 'Morden Snowbeauty'

'Morden Snowbeauty' ('Morden Snow Beauty', 'Snow Beauty') S, w, 1998, Davidson, C.G. & Colicutt, L.M.; flowers semi-dbl., 8-14 petals, borne in small clusters, slight fragrance; foliage medium size, medium green, semi-glossy; prickles small; compact, low growth; PP11730; [('Prairie Princess' × 'Morden Amorette') × ('Mount Shasta' ('Adelaide Hoodless' × *R. arkansana*))]; intr. 1997

'Morden Sunrise' S, yb, Davidson, C.G.; bud orange-yellow, pointed; flowers dark orange with yellow base, opening to light orange with bright yellow, 3 in., 12 petals, borne in clusters, moderate fragrance; foliage dark green, glossy; upright (70 cm.), open growth; PP13969; intr. 1999

'Mordora' ('Sequoia Ruby') Cl Min, mr, 1995, Moore, Ralph S.; flowers cherry red, yellow stamens, 2 in., dbl., cupped, borne in small clusters, no fragrance; recurrent; foliage medium size, dark green, matte; some prickles; tall (5 ft.), arching shrub, upright, bushy spreading growth; [('Little Darling' × 'Yellow Magic') × 'Floradora']; intr. 1996

'Mordoris' ('Pink Twist') Min, pb, 2007, Moore, Ralph S.; flowers dark pink, petals quilled, revealing white reverse, medium, 1½ in., dbl., borne in large clusters; foliage medium size, medium green, semi-glossy; prickles small, straight, brown, few; growth upright, tall (24 in.); hedging, containers; ['Doris Bennett' × 'Doris Bennett']; intr. 2007

'Mordort' ('Sincerely Yours') Min, mr, 1991, Moore, Ralph S.; flowers rich red, yellow stamens, medium, semi-dbl., borne in small clusters, no fragrance; foliage medium size, medium green, semi-glossy; some prickles; medium (20-24 cm.), bushy growth; ['Sheri Anne' × Dortmund®]; intr. 1992

'Mordream' Min, mp, Moore, Ralph; intr. 2001

'More Vale Pride' Gr, mp, 1957, Ulrick, L.W.; ['Ma Perkins' × 'Overloon']

'Moreau' T, w, 1825, Foulard; flowers greenish white, center flesh pink shaded red, large, very full

'Morecli' ('Baby Eclipse™) Min, ly, 1984, Moore, Ralph S.; bud small; flowers small, semi-dbl.; foliage small, medium green, matte; bushy, spreading growth; [(*R. wichurana* × 'Floradora') × 'Yellow Jewel']

'Mored' ('Edna Marie') Min, lp, 1988, Moore, Ralph S.; flowers very soft pink, soft yellow base, aging becomes near white,, 20 petals, high-centered, slight fruity fragrance; foliage small, light green, semi-glossy; prickles small, brown; upright, bushy, medium growth; ['Pinocchio' × 'Peachy White']

'Moredfar' ('Red Fairy') Pol, mr, 1995, Moore, Ralph S.; bud short, rounded; flowers cherry red, often with red line down center of petals, 1¼ in., 24-30 petals, rounded, borne in conical sprays, somewhat pendulous, slight fragrance; free-flowering; foliage long, bright medium green, semi-glossy; prickles some, hooked downward, brown; wiry, sturdy stems; bushy, medium, semi-cascading growth; hips small; PP10150; ['Simon Robinson' × 'Simon Robinson']; intr. 1996

'Morelfire' ('Pink Elf') Min, pb, 1983, Moore, Ralph S.; flowers medium pink, blended with yellow, small, semi-dbl., no fragrance; foliage small, medium green, matte to semi-glossy; upright, bushy growth; ['Ellen Poulsen' × 'Fire Princess']

'Moremma' ('Little Emma') Min, my, 2004, Moore, Ralph S.; flowers dbl., borne in small clusters, slight fragrance; foliage small, medium green, semi-glossy; prickles small, hooked,; growth compact, short (12-15 in.); pot, low hedge, border planting; [('Little Darling' × 'Yellow Jewel') × 'Clytemnestra']; intr. 2005

Morena® Min, op, Cocker; intr. 1983

'Morena' Min, mp, 2000, Cattermole, R.F.; flowers very full, borne in small clusters, no fragrance; foliage medium size, very dark blue-green, glossy; growth upright, bushy, tall (3 ft.); intr. 2001

'Moreny' ('Renny', 'Renny's Dream') Min, mp, 1989, Moore, Ralph S.; bud pointed; flowers medium rose pink, reverse lighter, old fashioned, medium, 25 petals, borne in sprays of 3-7, moderate fragrance; foliage medium size, medium green, matte; no prickles; upright, bushy, low growth; no fruit; ['Anytime' × 'Renae']

'Moreyes' ('Halo Karol') Min, pb, 1998, Moore, Ralph S.; flowers dark pink, lavendar base creates halo effect, 1-1½ in., 10 petals, borne singly, no fragrance; foliage medium size, medium green, semi-glossy; few prickles; bushy, compact growth; [('Anytime' × 'Angel Face') × ('Anytime' × 'Angel Face')]; intr. 1998

'Morey's Pink' S, mp, Morey; flowers medium pink, aging lighter, full, borne in clusters; intr. 1994

'Morey's Salmon' HT, pb, 1953, Morey, Dr. Dennison; growth to 3 ft.

'Morfair' ('Pink Cherub') Min, lp, 1981, Moore, Ralph S.; bud ovoid; flowers medium to light pink, often lighter at tips, 43 petals; foliage small, medium green, matte; prickles straight, small; compact, very bushy growth; ['Fairy Moss' × 'Fairy Moss']; intr. 1980

'Morfairpol' ('Fair Molly') Pol, w, 1999, Moore, Ralph S.; flowers white blend, 1-1½ in., semi-dbl., borne in small clusters; foliage small, medium green, semi-glossy; few prickles; bushy, spreading, medium (16-24 in.); landscape shrub growth; [(*R. polyantha nana* × unknown) × 'Fairy Moss']; intr. 1999

'Morfakir' ('Fakir's Delight') S, w, 2006, Moore, Ralph S.; bud mossy; flowers creamy white, reverse white, 2½-3 in., very full, borne in small clusters; recurrent; foliage medium size, medium green, glossy, new growth reddish; prickles medium, straight, green, numerous; growth upright, tall (6-8 ft.) spreading; shrub/climber; [('Little Darling' × 'Lemon Delight') × (seedling × 'Out of Yesteryear')]; intr. 2006

'Morfeat' ('White Feather') Min, w, 1986, Moore, Ralph S.; flowers pure white, small, 15 petals, loose, borne in clusters of 3 - 5, slight fragrance; foliage small, light green, semi-glossy; prickles very few; medium, bushy growth; no fruit; [(*R. wichurana* × 'Floradora') × 'Peachy White']; intr. 1980

'Morfed' ('Patriot Song') Min, dr, 2003, Moore, Ralph S.; flowers semi-dbl., borne mostly solitary, slight fragrance; foliage medium size, medium green,; prickles small, straight, light green, few; growth upright, tall (18 in.); garden, landscape, hedge; [('Sheri Anne' × Dortmund®) × Orangeade®]; intr. 2003

'Morfenn' ('Nurse Donna') Min, pb, 2003, Moore, Ralph S.; flowers dark pink, reverse white/lt pink, 1½ in., dbl., borne in small clusters, slight fragrance; foliage medium size, medium green,; prickles small, straight, green, few; growth spreading, medium (15 in.); containers, garden, borders; ['Pink Petticoat' × Rainbow's End™]; intr. 2003

'Morfever' ('Gold Fever') Min, my, 1990, Moore, Ralph S.; bud pointed; flowers medium yellow, aging lighter, 40-50 petals, high-centered, borne usually singly or in sprays of 3-5, moderate spicy fragrance; foliage medium size, medium green, semi-glossy; prickles slender, straight, medium to long, brownish; upright, bushy, medium growth; hips round, small, orange; ['Sheri Anne' × Gold Badge™]

'Morfing' ('Fingerpaint') Min, ob, 1990, Moore, Ralph S.; bud short, pointed; flowers orange blend, yellow base, with light yellow reverse, 12-14 petals, flat, no fragrance; foliage medium size, medium green, semi-glossy; prickles small, brownish,straight; bushy, spreading, low-medium growth; [Orangeade® × Little Artist®]

'Morfire' (Ring of Fire™) Min, yb, 1987, Moore, Ralph S.; bud ovoid to pointed; flowers yellow blended orange, reverse yellow, fading lighter, imbricated, 1½ in., 60 petals, high-centered, borne usually singly, but some small clusters, slight fragrance; foliage medium size, medium green, semi-glossy; prickles slender, sharp pointed, medium, green to brown; stems sturdy, wiry; upright, bushy, vigorous growth; no fruit; ['Pink Petticoat' × Gold Badge™]; intr. 1986

'Morflame' ('Persian Flame') S, rb, 2007, Moore, Ralph S.; buds appear yellow; flowers Chinese red with a deep red eye, reverse yellow, large, 2½ in., single, borne in small clusters; foliage medium size, light green, matte; prickles medium, hooked, brown, moderate; growth spreading, medium (3-5 ft.); specimens hedge; ['Tigris' × Playboy®]; *Hulthemia* hybrid; intr. 2007

'Morflash' (Blastoff™) F, ob, 1993, Moore, Ralph S.; flowers scarlet orange, white reverse, petals ruffled, 1½-2 in., 35-40 petals, quartered, borne in large clusters, slight slight spice fragrance; foliage medium size, dark green, semi-glossy; numerous prickles; medium (100-120 cm.), upright growth; PP9405; [Orangeade® × Little Artist®]; intr. 1995

'Morforest' ('Rainforest') F, pb, 2004, Moore, Ralph S.; flowers pink, aging to light green with pink highlights, reverse white, 3 in., semi-dbl., borne in small clusters, slight fragrance; foliage medium size, medium green, semi-glossy; prickles small, straight, brown, few; upright, tall (3-4 ft. growth); pillar, specimen, cutting; ['Sheri Ann' × 'Scarlet Moss']; intr. 2004

'Morfree' ('Softee') Min, w, 1983, Moore, Ralph S.; flowers creamy white, small, 35 petals, slight fragrance; foliage small to medium size, medium green, matte; no prickles; bushy (2 ft.), spreading growth; [seedling × seedling]; intr. 1982

'Morfrenzy' ('Orange Frenzy') Min, ob, 2002, Moore, Ralph S.; flowers dbl., borne mostly solitary, slight fragrance; foliage medium size, medium green, glossy; prickles small, straight, green; growth upright, tall (18-24 in.); containers, garden decorative, cutting; ['Avandel' × 'Golden Salmon']; intr. 2002

'Morfriend' ('Best Friend', My Best Friend™) Min, pb, 2002, Moore, Ralph S.; bud mauve to red; flowers light pink, mauve/pink reverse, 1-1½ in., semi-dbl., borne in small clusters, slight fragrance; foliage medium size, dark green; prickles small, straight, green; growth spreading, medium (15-18 in.); containers, garden decorative; ['Sugar Plum' × 'striped seedling']; intr. 2002

'Morfuzzy' M, mr, Moore, Ralph ; bud bright red, mossy buds; intr. 2004

'Morga' HRg, mp; flowers dbl., borne in clusters

'Morgabriel' (Lady Moss™) F, ab, 2004, Moore, Ralph S.; flowers apricot, reverse white, 3 in., semi-dbl., borne in small clusters, moderate fragrance; recurrent; foliage medium size, medium green, semi-glossy; prickles small, straight; growth upright, tall (4 ft.); specimen, cutting; ['Fairy Moss' × 'Gabriel Noyelle']; intr. 2005

'Morgal' (Galaxy™) Min, dr, 1980, Moore, Ralph S.; bud long, pointed; flowers deep velvety red, 23 petals, high-centered, borne 3, sometimes 5-10 per cluster; foliage small to medium; prickles slightly curved; vigorous, bushy, upright growth; PP4680; ['Fairy Moss' × 'Fairy Princess']

'Morgan Gilet' S, mp, Gilet; intr. 2005

'Morgel' ('Angel Pink', 'Pink Angel') Cl Min, op, 1987, Moore, Ralph S.; flowers pink to soft coral pink, holds color, dbl., high-centered, borne in sprays of 3-7, slight fragrance; foliage medium size, light green, semi-glossy; prickles medium, brown, slightly hooked downwards; upright, tall, climbing (5-7 ft.) growth; no fruit; ['Little Darling' × 'Eleanor']

'Morgenglans' HT, op, 1916, Van Rossem; bud coppery orange; flowers salmon-flesh, medium, semi-dbl.

'Morgengruss' ('Morning Greeting', 'Morning-Red') HKor, op, 1962, Kordes, R.; bud ovoid; flowers light pink tinted orange-yellow, 8-9 cm., dbl., borne in small clusters, intense fragrance; foliage glossy, light green; very vigorous (13-14 ft.), bushy growth

'Morgenluft' F, pb, 1965, Verschuren, A.; flowers dark pink, reverse lighter, 55-60 petals, borne in clusters; foliage dark buff-green; upright, bushy growth; ['La France' × seedling]; intr. 1963

Morgenrot® -- See 'Korheim'

'Morgenrot' ('Morning Red') Cl HT, dr, 1903, Lambert; flowers dark carmine red, white eye, large, single

'Morgenröte' HT, mp, 1951, Burkhard; RULED EXTINCT 12/85

'Morgensen' -- See 'Morgensonne'

'Morgensonne' ('Morgensen', 'Morning Sun') F, my, 1954, Kordes; bud ovoid; flowers golden yellow, very large, moderate fragrance; foliage glossy, light green; very vigorous, upright, bushy growth

Morgensonne 88® -- See 'Korhoro'

'Morgenster' HT, ob, 1916, Nyvelt; flowers coppery orange, large, semi-dbl.

Morgenstern® S, ly, Liebig; intr. 1989

'Morgentau' HT, w, 1908, Hinner; flowers very large, full, moderate fragrance

'Morgina' (Gina's Rose™) S, rb, 2006, Moore, Ralph S.; flowers medium red, reverse light red, 2-2½ in., single, borne in small clusters; rapid repeat bloom; foliage medium size, medium green, semi-glossy; no prickles; growth spreading, medium (3-5 ft.); specimen, border, arching shrub; [Playboy® × 'Basey's Legacy']; intr. 2006

'Morglo' ('Gypsy Fire') Min, or, 1982, Moore, Ralph S.; flowers small, semi-dbl., borne in clusters, no fragrance; foliage small, medium green, semi-glossy to glossy; upright, bushy growth; [(*R. wichurana* × 'Carolyn Dean') × 'Fire Princess']; intr. 1981

'Morglory' ('Halo Glory') Min, pb, 2004, Moore, Ralph S.; flowers light pink with darker pink to lavender base, reverse light pink to white, 1½-2 in., single, borne in small clusters, no fragrance; foliage medium size, medium green, semi-glossy; prickles small, straight, light green, few; growth compact, medium (1 ft.); containers, specimen, border; [(Gold Badge™ × ('Anytime' × 'Angel Face')) × unknown]; intr. 2004

'Morgogard' ('Golden Gardens', 'Summer Sun') Min, my, 1989, Moore, Ralph S.; bud ovoid; flowers bright, clear medium yellow, reverse slightly lighter, 28 petals, cupped, informal, no fragrance; foliage medium size, medium green, semi-glossy; prickles slender, inclined downward, small, brownish; upright, medium growth; no fruit; [('Little Darling' × 'Yellow Magic') × Gold Badge™]

'Morgoldart' ('Splish Splash') Min, pb, 1993, Moore, Ralph S.; flowers deep pink, yellow heart and reverse, large, full, cupped to rosette, borne in small clusters, slight fragrance; recurrent; foliage medium size, medium green, semi-glossy; few prickles; medium (30 cm.), bushy, spreading growth; [Sequoia Gold™ × Little Artist®]; intr. 1994

'Morgoldpoly' ('Polly Sunshine') Pol, my, 1999, Moore, Ralph S.; flowers 2-3 in., full, borne in small clusters; foliage medium size, medium green, glossy; few prickles; bushy (16-24 in.) growth; ['Golden Angel' × seedling]; intr. 1999

'Morgrapes' ('Vineyard Song') S, m, 1999, Moore, Ralph S.; flowers 1-1½ in., dbl., borne in large clusters, moderate fragrance; foliage dark green, glossy; some prickles; medium (12-16 in.) growth; [seedling × 'self']; intr. 1999

'Morhalfire' (Halo Fire®) Min, rb, 1995, Moore, Ralph S.; flowers bright orange-red with darker red halo, 1½-2½ in., 8-10 petals, borne in small clusters; foliage small, medium green, matte; medium (35-45 cm.), upright, bushy growth; [Orangeade® × seedling]; intr. 1996

'Morharmony' ('Condoleezza') F, pb, 2006, Moore, Ralph S.; bud lightly mossed; flowers pink, reverse yellow, with wavy petals, 2 in., semi-dbl., borne in small clusters; foliage medium size, medium green, semi-glossy; prickles small, straight, green, moderate; growth compact, medium (2-4 ft.); specimen, border, cut flower; ['Lemon Delight' × 'Angel Face']; intr. 2006

'Morheaven' ('Closer to Heaven') LCl, dr, 2004, Moore, Ralph S.; sepals frilly; flowers deep ruby red, reverse medium red, 3½ in., semi-dbl., borne in large clusters, slight fragrance; early summer bloom; foliage medium size, dark green, semi-glossy; prickles hooked; growth upright, climbing, cascading, medium (7-10 ft.); pillar; [(*R. wichurana* × 'Floradora') × (Queen Elizabeth® × 'Crested Moss')]; intr. 2005

'Morhill' ('Mary Hill') Min, pb, 1990, Moore, Ralph S.; bud pointed; flowers medium pink, yellow reverse, aging lighter, medium, 30-35 petals, high-centered, moderate fruity fragrance; foliage medium size, medium green, semi-glossy; prickles slender, straight, small, brownish; upright, bushy, medium growth; PP7994; ['Little Darling' × 'Golden Angel']

'Morhoney' ('Sun Honey') Min, my, 1984, Moore, Ralph S.; [sport of 'Orange Honey']; intr. 1983

'Morhoop' ('Hula Hoop') F, pb, 1991, Moore, Ralph S.; bud pointed; flowers white with pink to red edge, aging less intense, 2½-3 in., 15 petals, flat, borne in sprays of 5-15, no fragrance; foliage medium size, medium green, matte; upright, medium growth; PP8201; [(Dortmund® × seedling) × 'self']; intr. 1991

'Morhoot' ('Hoot Owl') Min, rb, 1990, Moore, Ralph S.; bud pointed; flowers red with white eye, small, 5 petals, borne usually singly or in sprays of 3 - 5, no fragrance; foliage small, medium green, semi-glossy; bushy, low growth; [Orangeade® × Little Artist®]; intr. 1991

'Morhopjo' ('Hope And Joy') Min, ob, 2007, Moore, Ralph S.; bud pale yellow; flowers orange-red, reverse light yellow, medium, 1½-2 in., dbl., borne in small clusters; foliage medium size, medium green, semi-glossy; prickles small, straight, reddish, few; growth bushy, medium (15 in.); containers, borders, garden decoration; ['Show 'n' Tell' × unknown]; intr. 2007

'Morhorizon' ('Golden Horizon') Min, my, 2006, Moore, Ralph S.; flowers 1½-2 in., full, borne in small clusters; foliage medium size, medium green, semi-glossy; prickles small, straight, green, few; growth compact, medium (15-18 in.); containers, borders, garden; ['Cal Poly' × 'Strawberry Ice']; intr. 2006

'Moriah' -- See 'Ganhol'

'Morice' ('Iced Tea') Min, r, 2002, Moore, Ralph S.; flowers tan/russet, russet/peach reverse, 1-1½ in., single, borne mostly solitary, slight fragrance; foliage medium size, medium green, matte; growth upright, tall (18-24 in.); ['Sequoia Ruby' × 'Sequoia Ruby']; intr. 2001

'Morinaye' F, yb; flowers yellow with red stripes, semi-double to double, borne in clusters; recurrent; compact (40 - 50 cm.) growth

'Morink' Min, op, Moore, Ralph; intr. 2001

'Morisle' ('Isle of Roses') Min, yb, 1993, Moore, Ralph S.; flowers large, full, borne in small clusters, no fragrance; foliage medium size, medium green, semi-glossy; few prickles; medium to tall (18-24 in.), upright,bushy growth; ['Pink Petticoat' × Gold Badge™]; intr. 1994

'Morivory' ('Ivory Palace') Min, w, 1991, Moore, Ralph S.; bud ovoid; flowers ivory white, white reverse, medium, very dbl., high-centered, borne in sprays of 3-8, slight fragrance; foliage medium size, medium green, semi-glossy; bushy, medium growth; ['Sheri Anne' × 'Pinocchio']; intr. 1991

'Morjack' ('Jackpot') Min, dy, 1985, Moore, Ralph S.; flowers small, dbl., moderate fragrance; foliage small, medium green, matte; vigorous, bushy, spreading growth; ['Little Darling' × Sunspray™]; intr. 1985

'Morjoybon' ('Isa Carstens', It's Show Time™) HT, ab, 1996, Moore, Ralph S.; flowers apricot blend, reverse slightly lighter, 4-4½ in., dbl., borne mostly singly; foliage medium size, dark green, semi-glossy; upright, medium (3-5 ft.) growth; PP10324; [Joycie™ × 'Bon Siléne']; intr. 1997

'Morjoyc' (Joycie™) Min, ob, 1988, Moore, Ralph S.; flowers orange-apricot, reverse lighter, small, dbl., high-centered, borne singly or in small clusters, moderate fruity fragrance; foliage small, medium green, semi-glossy; prickles slender, small, brown; bushy, medium growth; hips globular, orange; PP7055; [('Little Darling' × 'Yellow Magic') × Gold Badge™]

'Morkay' ('Kayla') Min, pb, 1994, Moore, Ralph S.; flowers 2-3½ in., dbl., borne mostly singly, but some in small clusters; foliage large, medium green, semi-glossy; few prickles; tall (45-55 cm.), upright, bushy growth; ['Sheri Ann' × 'Violette']; intr. 1995

'Morkeith' ('Keith's Delight') HRg, yb, 2004, Moore, Ralph S.; flowers pale yellow to white, reverse pale yellow, 3 in., full, borne in small clusters; recurrent; foliage medium size, medium green, glossy; prickles small, hooked; growth upright, tall (5-6 ft.); low climber, free standing shrub; hips orange; [('Little Darling' × 'Yellow Jewel') × Rugelda®]; intr. 2005

'Morkinshine' ('Rise 'n' Shine, Climbing') Cl Min, my, 1990, King, Gene; bud pointed; flowers medium yellow, aging lighter, small, 35 petals, high-centered, borne usually singly or in small clusters; foliage medium size, medium green, semi-glossy; prickles straight, inclined slightly downward, brown; upright, spreading, tall, climbing. growth; hips round, orange; [sport of 'Rise 'n' Shine']; intr. 1990

'Morkita' (Chiquita™) Min, dr, 1988, Moore, Ralph S.; flowers rich, dark red with fluorescent glow, 20 petals, flat, borne singly, slight fragrance; foliage small, medium green, matte; prickles hooked, short, brown; upright, bushy, medium growth; few to no hips; ['Anytime' × 'Happy Hour']

'Morlavmag' ('Surprise Surprise') Min, m, 1994, Moore, Ralph S.; flowers mauve-lavender with occasional petals being striped red, medium, semi-dbl., shallow cup to flat, borne in clusters, no fragrance; recurrent; foliage small, dark green, semi-glossy; few prickles; low (12-16 in.), bushy, compact growth; [sport of 'Cherry Magic']; intr. 1994

'Morlavpix' ('Lavender Pixie') Min, m, 2007, Moore, Ralph S.; flowers 1 in., semi-dbl., borne mostly solitary; foliage small, medium green, semi-glossy; prickles small, straight, tan, few; growth compact, short (10 in.); containers, small borders; [sport of 'Lavender Jewel']; intr. 1984

'Morlaw' Min, mp, Moore; intr. 1998

'Morlem' ('Sungold') Min, ob, 1983, Moore, Ralph S.; flowers yellow overlaid with orange on outer half of petals, reverse light yellow, 20 petals, cupped, then flat, no fragrance; foliage small, medium green, matte to semi-glossy; upright, bushy growth; ['Rumba' × 'Lemon Delight']; intr. 1982

'Morletii' ('Inermis Morletii', *R. inermis morletii*) Bslt, lp, 1883; flowers blush pink, 4-5 cm., semi-dbl., borne in small clusters; prickles branches plum-colored, without thorns; growth to 5 ft.; very hardy; rediscovered and put in commerce by Morlet; often confused with Mme Sancy de Parabère

'Morliday' ('Holiday Cheer') Min, dr, 1983, Moore, Ralph S.; flowers small, 35 petals, borne in clusters, no fragrance; foliage small, dark, matte; upright, bushy growth; ['Red Pinocchio' × 'Little Chief']; intr. 1982

'Morlight' ('Twilight Skies') Min, m, 2003, Moore, Ralph S.; flowers semi-dbl., borne in small clusters, slight fragrance; foliage medium size, medium green, semi-glossy; prickles small, straight, light green; growth bushy, medium (15 in.); containers, borders,; ['Vi's Violet' × 'Anytime']; intr. 2003

'Morlindsey' ('Irene Marie') Cl Min, yb, 2006, Moore, Ralph S.; flowers yellow/orange, reverse yellow, 1½-2 in., single, borne in small clusters; recurrent; foliage medium size, medium green, semi-glossy; thornless; growth upright, tall (4-6 ft.); climber, free standing arching shrub; ['(Little Darling × Yellow Magic)' × Playboy®]; intr. 2006

'Morlink' ('Julie Link') Min, op, 2004, Moore, Ralph S.; flowers peachy pink, reverse pink, 2 in., full, borne mostly solitary, moderate fragrance; foliage medium size, medium green, semi-glossy; prickles small, straight; growth upright, bushy, tall (24-30 in.); specimen, pot, hedge, cutting; [('Halo' × unknown) × (Queen Elizabeth® × 'striped seedling')]; intr. 2005

'Morliyel' ('Sierra Sunrise') Min, yb, 1980, Moore, Ralph S.; bud medium, pointed; flowers soft yellow, petals tipped pink, 1½ in., 35-45 petals, cupped, open, borne singly or 3 - 5 per cluster, slight fragrance; foliage medium size, medium green; prickles long, straight; vigorous, bushy, upright growth; PP4662; ['Little Darling' × 'Yellow Magic']

'Morliz' ('Spanish Dancer') Min, or, 1986, Moore, Ralph S.; flowers small, 18 petals, open, borne in sprays of 5 - 7; foliage medium size, medium green, semi-glossy; prickles small, brown; medium, bushy, spreading growth; no fruit; [Sarabande® × 'Little Chief']; intr. 1980

'Morlogen' ('Namib Sunrise') Min, yb,

1985, Moore, Ralph S.; flowers yellow blended with coral pink, 64 petals, borne in clusters of 15; foliage light; prickles straight, light brown; dense growth; ['Rumba' × 'Yellow Jewel']; intr. 1984

'Morlove' ('Love And Peace') Min, rb, 2007, Moore, Ralph S.; bud mossy; flowers red and lavender striped, reverse red, medium, 1½ in., dbl., borne in small clusters; foliage medium size, medium green, semi-glossy; prickles small, straight, green, numerous; growth bushy, medium (15 in.); containers, border, specimens; [seedling × 'striped seedling']; intr. 2007

'Morlu' ('Vintage Visalia') F, mp, 1992, Moore, Ralph S.; flowers pink, reverse of outer petals deeper pink than inside surface, large, very dbl., borne mostly singly, slight fragrance; foliage large, medium green, semi-glossy; few prickles; medium (50-60 cm.), upright, bushy growth; ['Pink Petticoat' × 'Lulu']; intr. 1993

'Morlucy' Min, mp, Moore, Ralph S.; intr. 1997

'Morlyn' (Lynne Gold™) Min, my, 1983, Moore, Ralph S.; flowers micro-mini, small, 20 petals; foliage small, medium green, semi-glossy; bushy, spreading growth; PP5742; ['Ellen Poulsen' × 'Yellow Jewel']

'Mormagem' ('Mariposa Gem') S, rb, 1995, Moore, Ralph S.; flowers red with yellow reverse and white eye, 2½ in., semi-dbl., flat, borne in clusters of 5-20; foliage medium size, medium green, semi-glossy; few prickles; growth upright, bushy, spreading (3-5 ft.), with arching canes; ['Little Darling' × 'Magic Wand']; intr. 1995

'Mormake' (Make Believe™) Min, m, 1986, Moore, Ralph S.; flowers mauve and white blend, reverse red-purple, 10 petals, borne in sprays, no fragrance; foliage medium size, dark, semi-glossy; prickles very few, hooked, dark brown; upright, bushy growth; hips small, globular, orange; ['Anytime' × 'Angel Face']; intr. 1980

'Mormari' (Marie Shields™) Min, mp, 1988, Moore, Ralph S.; flowers medium pink, reverse pink veined white, small, very dbl., high-centered, borne usually in sprays or clusters; foliage small, medium green, semi-glossy; prickles slightly hooked, small, brown; bushy, medium growth; ['Avandel' × ('Rumba' × 'unnamed Floribunda mossed seedling')]

'Mormarme' ('Marime') Min, mr, 1992, Moore, Ralph S.; flowers excellent medium red, good form, large, semi-dbl., borne mostly singly, no fragrance; foliage medium size, medium green, semi-glossy; few prickles; medium (35-45 cm.), upright, bushy growth; ['Anytime' × 'Happy Hour']

'Mormelma' ('Melody Marshall') Min, ly, 1993, Moore, Ralph S.; flowers large, dbl., borne mostly singly; foliage medium size, medium green, semi-glossy; no prickles; medium (25-35 cm.), upright, bushy growth; [sport of 'Mary Marshall']; intr. 1989

'Mormilli' (Millie Walters™) Min, op, 1984, Moore, Ralph S.; bud small, long, pointed; flowers deep coral pink, 1½ in., 45 petals, high-centered, borne singly and in clusters of 3-5; good repeat; foliage small, medium green, matte; prickles medium to long, straight; stems slender, wiry; growth upright, bushy (14-18 in.); PP5741; ['Little Darling' × 'Galaxy']; intr. 1984

'Mormint' ('Hall of Flowers') Min, my, 1991, Moore, Ralph S.; bud pointed; flowers lemon yellow, aging slightly lighter, medium, dbl., high-centered, borne singly, slight fragrance; foliage medium size, medium green, semi-glossy; upright, bushy, medium growth; ['Avandel' × Gold Badge™]; intr. 1991

'Mormitchell' ('Annie R. Mitchell') Min, ly, 1996, Moore, Ralph S.; flowers light yellow to white, 1½-2 in., full, borne in small clusters, moderate fragrance; foliage medium size, medium green, semi-glossy; few prickles; spreading, bushy, medium (15-18 in.) growth; [sport of 'Mary Hill']; intr. 1996

'Mormum' ('Strange Music', 'Striped Meillandina') Min, rb, 1986, Moore, Ralph S.; bud mossy; flowers red, striped white, reverse near white, medium, 50 petals, high-centered, borne in clusters of 5-7, no fragrance; recurrent; foliage medium size, medium green, matte; prickles small to medium, straight, brown; bushy, spreading growth; ['Little Darling' × ('Fairy Moss' × ('Little Darling' × 'Ferdinand Pichard'))]; intr. 1982

'Mormuri' ('Muriel') HBc, lp, 1990, Moore, Ralph S.; bud ovoid; flowers light to medium pink, aging slightly lighter, large, 15 petals, flat, borne singly and in sprays of 3 - 5; foliage large, medium green, semi-glossy; prickles sharp, pointed, average, brown; spreading, tall growth; hips short, oval, large, prickly, orange; [R. bracteata × 'Guinee']

'Mormyval' Min, dr, 1975, Moore, Ralph S.

'Mornet' ('Annette Dobbs') Min, op, 1991, Moore, Ralph S.; bud pointed; flowers coral-red, lighter reverse, ages slightly lighter, medium, 15 petals, flat, edges turned up, borne in sprays of 3-5, no fragrance; foliage medium size, medium green, semi-glossy; bushy, medium growth; ['Anytime' × Playgirl™]; intr. 1990

'Mornick' ('Muriel Humenick') S, ly, 2002, Moore, Ralph S.; flowers dbl., borne mostly solitary; foliage medium size, light green, matte; prickles small, straight, green, few; bushy, tall (5-6 ft.) growth; ['Golden Angel' × 'Honorine de Brabant']; intr. 2002

'Mornight' S, w, 2006, Moore, Ralph S.; flowers full, borne in small clusters; foliage medium size, medium green, semi-glossy; prickles small, hooked, brown, moderate; growth compact (2-2½ ft.); containers, borders; ['Yellow Jewel' × 'Out of Yesteryear']; intr. 2006

'Mornine' (Roses Are Red™) S, rb, 2005, Moore, Ralph; flowers red with darker red eye, 2½ in., semi-dbl., cupped, borne in clusters of 3-5; scattered repeat; foliage large, dark green; numerous prickles; arching (6 ft.) growth; ['Tigris' × Playboy®]; hybrid Hulthemia; intr. 2005

'Morning Blush' -- See 'Duquesa de Peñaranda'

'Morning Blush' A, ly, Sievers; flowers pure white edged strawberry red, 3-4 in., full; profuse spring bloom with occasional repeat; few prickles; growth center upright (4-5 ft.), outer canes spreading; intr. 1988

'Morning Call' Min, w, 2007, Yasuda, Yuji; flowers small, single, borne in small clusters; foliage small, medium green, matte; prickles medium, straight, moderate; growth compact, short (30 cm.); containers; [seedling × Pride 'n' Joy™]; intr. 2008

'Morning Cloud' -- See 'Asagumo'

'Morning Dawn' LCl, lp, 1955, Boerner; flowers silvery rose flushed salmon, 5 in., 63 petals, high-centered, borne singly or in small clusters, moderate spicy fragrance; foliage dark, glossy, leathery; vigorous, pillar (6-8 ft.) growth; PP1447; [('New Dawn' × unknown) × R.M.S. Queen Mary]; intr. 1955

'Morning Dew' -- See 'Asatsuyu'

'Morning Fog' HT, pb

'Morning Glory' -- See 'McGredy's Orange'

'Morning Glory' Cl HT, rb, 1937, Beckwith; flowers carmine, reverse sulfur-yellow stained carmine, well-formed, dbl.; very vigorous, compact growth; [sport of 'Portadown Sally']

'Morning Glow' T, op, 1902, Paul, W.; flowers bright crimson pink tinted orange and maroon, large, full

'Morning Glow' Min, ly, Jolly, Betty J.; flowers light yellow, slight blushing on top surface in cool weather, 1¼ in., dbl., high-centered, borne mostly singly, no fragrance; foliage large, medium green, semi-glossy; few prickles; upright, tall (24 in.) growth; ['Tidewater' × Kristin™]; intr. 1998

'Morning Greeting' -- See 'Morgengruss'

'Morning Has Broken' -- See 'Clewedding'

'Morning in Moscow' -- See 'Utro Moskvy'

'Morning in Nemuro' -- See 'Nemuro no Asa'

Morning Jewel® LCl, mp, 1968, Cocker; flowers rich pink, lighter reverse, white towards petal bases, 8-9 cm., semi-dbl., flat, borne in small clusters, moderate fragrance; recurrent bloom; foliage glossy; ['New Dawn' × 'Red Dandy']

'Morning Joy'   HT, ab, 1968, Williamson; flowers creamy amber, reverse flushed coppery pink, well-formed, dbl.; foliage light green; vigorous, upright growth; [sport of 'Mischief']

'Morning Light' -- See 'Harlecho'

Morning Magic™ -- See 'Radmor'

'Morning Mist' -- See 'Ausfire'

'Morning Mist'   HT, m, 1950, Fisher, G.; flowers lavender tinted gray, large, 15-20 petals, high-centered, moderate fragrance; moderately vigorous, upright growth; PP999

'Morning Mist 96' -- See 'Ausfire'

'Morning Red' -- See 'Morgenrot'

'Morning-Red' -- See 'Morgengruss'

'Morning Red' -- See 'Korheim'

'Morning Skies' -- See 'Gelskies'

'Morning Song' -- See 'Minisong'

'Morning Star'   S, yb; intr. 1998

'Morning Stars'   S, w, 1949, Jacobus; bud ovoid; flowers dbl., cupped, borne in clusters, moderate fragrance; free, recurrent boom; foliage glossy; upright, bushy, compact growth; [('New Dawn' × 'Autumn Bouquet') × ('New Dawn' × 'Inspiration')]

'Morning Sun' -- See 'Arosumo'

'Morning Sun' -- See 'Morgensonne'

'Morning Sun' -- See 'Asahi'

'Mornita' (Anita Charles™) Min, op, 1981, Moore, Ralph S.; bud pointed; flowers bright pink, reverse lighter pink-yellow blend, 43 petals, high-centered, borne singly, sometimes 2-3 per cluster, moderate tea fragrance; foliage small, leathery, matte; prickles straight; vigorous, upright, spreading growth; ['Golden Glow (Brownell)' × 'Over the Rainbow']

'Mornothorns' ('My Stars') S, pb, 2004, Moore, Ralph S.; flowers pink, reverse white, 3 in., single, borne in small clusters, slight fragrance; recurrent; foliage medium size, medium green, glossy; thornless; stems turn reddish bronze in autumn; growth bushy, medium (3 ft.); specimen, containers, garden decoration; [Playboy® × 'Basye's Legacy']; intr. 2005

'Morocco'   HT, mr, 1961, Von Abrams; bud pointed; flowers velvety red, 5 in., 30 petals, high-centered; foliage glossy; vigorous, upright growth; ['Carrousel' × 'Charles Mallerin']; intr. 1961

'Morolé' ('Café Olé') Min, r, 1990, Moore, Ralph S.; bud pointed; flowers medium to large, 40-50+ petals, cupped, borne singly or in sprays of 3-5, moderate spicy fragrance; foliage medium to large, medium green, dull to semi-glossy; prickles slender, hooked downward, brown; upright, bushy, tall, vigorous growth; hips round, orangish; [sport of 'Winter Magic']

'Morongo' S, dr, Peden, G.H.

'Mororcheri' ('Lavender Delight') Min, m, 1993, Moore, Ralph S.; flowers medium, semi-dbl., borne in small clusters; foliage medium size, medium green, semi-glossy; few prickles; medium, upright, bushy growth; [Orangeade® × Cherry Magic™]; intr. 1994

'Morose' (Rose Gilardi™) Min, rb, 1987, Moore, Ralph S.; bud slender, mossy; flowers red and pink striped, aging well, small, 12-15 petals, informal, borne in small clusters, slight fragrance; recurrent; foliage small, medium green, semi-glossy; prickles slender, straight, small to medium, brownish; bushy, spreading, medium growth; hips oblong, covered with prickles, orange; [Dortmund® × (('Fairy Moss' × '(Little Darling × Ferdinand Pichard)') × seedling)]; intr. 1986

'Morpale' ('Painter's Palette') Min, rb, 1985, Moore, Ralph S.; bud mossy; flowers creamy white, striped deep pink to deep red, 72 petals, borne 3 - 5 per cluster; foliage deep green; prickles needle straight, brown; shrubby growth; intr. 1984

'Morpapplay' ('Chunga', 'Ralph's Creeper', 'Highveld Sun', 'Creepy', 'Glowing Carpet') S, rb, 1988, Moore, Ralph S.; bud small, long, pointed; flowers dark orange-red, bright yellow eye, reverse bright yellow to white, medium, 15-18 petals, loose, borne in sprays of 10-15, moderate apple-blossom fragrance; repeat bloom; foliage small, dark green, matte; prickles brownish, straight, inclined downward; spreading, low, groundcover growth; hips round, orange-red; PP6548; ['Papoose' × Playboy®]; intr. 1988

'Morpeaches' ('Persian Peach') S, yb, 2007, Moore, Ralph S.; flowers peachy-yellow with red eye, reverse yellow, medium, 2½ in., semi-dbl., blooms borne mostly solitary; foliage medium size, matte; prickles medium, straight, tan to brown, numerous; growth upright, 3-5 ft.; ['Cal Poly' × '*Hulthemia* seedling']; intr. 2007

'Morpearls' ('Lemon Pearls') HBc, my, 2003, Moore, Ralph S.; flowers yellow, reverse light yellow, 2 in., full, borne mostly solitary, moderate fragrance; foliage medium size, medium green, glossy; prickles small, hooked, brown, few; growth spreading, medium (24 in.); landscape, pots, specimen; [seedling × 'Out of Yesteryear']; intr. 2003

'Morpepper' ('Peppermint Parfait') Min, rb, 2007, Moore, Ralph S.; bud yellow; flowers red/yellow striped, reverse yellow, 2 cm., single, borne mostly solitary; foliage small, medium green, matte, slightly serrated; prickles small, straight, tan to brown, numerous; growth to 18 in.; borders, containers specimens; [Sequoia Gold™ × 'striped seedling']; intr. 2007

'Morpetti' ('Hoot 'n' Holler) Min, rb, 1993, Moore, Ralph S.; flowers pleasing blend of red changing to lavender, large, semi-dbl., borne in small clusters, no fragrance; foliage medium size, medium green, matte; few prickles; upright, bushy growth; ['Pink Petticoat' × Make Believe™]; intr. 1993

'Morpho' F, Leenders

'Morpico' ('Circus Clown') Min, rb, 1991, Moore, Ralph S.; flowers medium, semi-dbl., borne mostly singly or in small clusters, slight fragrance; foliage small, medium green, semi-glossy; few prickles; low (18-22 cm.), bushy, compact growth; ['Pink Petticoat' × Make Believe™]; intr. 1992

'Morpinkie' ('Little Pinkie') Min, mp, 2000, Moore, Ralph S.; flowers dbl., borne in small clusters, no fragrance; foliage small, medium green, semi-glossy; thornless; growth small, bushy, compact (8-12 in.); micro-mini; ['Anytime' × 'Renae']

'Morpinkper' ('Moore's Pink Perpetual') S, pb, 1999, Moore, Ralph S.; flowers pink blend, 3-3½ in., very dbl., borne in small clusters, moderate fragrance; foliage medium size, medium green, semi-glossy; numerous prickles; dwarf hybrid perpetual, bushy, compact (16-24 in.) growth; [seedling × 'Paul Neyron']; intr. 1998

'Morpints' (Pinstripe™) Min, rb, 1985, Moore, Ralph S.; flowers red with white stripes, well-formed, small, 35 petals; foliage small, medium green, semi-glossy; low, mounded growth; ['Pinocchio' × seedling]; intr. 1986

'Morplag' (Playgirl™) F, mp, 1986, Moore, Ralph S.; bud long pointed, slender; flowers pink with yellow stamens, wavy petal edges, 3½ in., 5-7 petals, flat to slightly cupped, borne singly and in sprays; recurrent; foliage medium size, medium green, semi-glossy; prickles few, straight, brown; growth upright, bushy; PP6468; [Playboy® × 'Angel Face']

'Morplati' (Playtime™) F, or, 1990, Moore, Ralph S.; bud pointed; flowers vibrant orange-red, aging slightly darker, medium, 5 petals, flat, borne singly and in sprays of 3 - 5; foliage medium size, dark green, semi-glossy; prickles straight, slightly hooked, medium, light brown; upright, bushy, medium growth; hips round, medium, orange-red; [Playboy® × 'Old Master']; intr. 1990

'Morplaygold' ('Playgold') Min, ob, 1997, Moore, Ralph S.; flowers small, semi-dbl., borne in small clusters; foliage small, medium size, green, glossy; low (12-18 in.) growth; ['Playgold' × Sequoia Gold™]

'Morplum' ('Sugar Plum') Min, m, 1994, Moore, Ralph S.; flowers lavender purple, opening to expose a silver shading on inside of petals, 1½-2½ in., semi-dbl., borne mostly singly or in small clusters, no fragrance; foliage medium size, medium green, semi-glossy; medium (12-16 in.), bushy, spreading growth; ['Anytime' × 'Angel Face']; intr. 1995

'Morpoly' ('Cal Poly') Min, my, 1991, Moore, Ralph S.; flowers non-fading, large, dbl., borne in small clusters;

foliage medium size, medium green, semi-glossy; few prickles; medium (24 cm.), upright, bushy growth; PP8453; [('Little Darling' × 'Yellow Magic') × Gold Badge™]; intr. 1992

'Morpoodle' ('Pink Poodle') Min, pb, 1991, Moore, Ralph S.; flowers pink changing to lighter pink to white, medium, very full, borne in small clusters, moderate fragrance; foliage small, medium green, matte; few prickles; low (26-30 cm.), upright growth; [('Little Darling' × 'Yellow Magic') × 'Old Blush']; typical china characteristics; intr. 1992

'Morporc' ('English Porcelain') Min, lp, 1994, Moore, Ralph S.; flowers medium, dbl., borne mostly singly, slight fragrance; foliage medium size, medium green, matte; no prickles; low to medium (28-34 cm.), bushy, spreading, compact growth; ['Anytime' × 'Angel Face']; intr. 1995

'Morposa' S, rb, Moore; intr. 1997

'Morprepen' ('Pretty Penny') Min, ob, 1994, Moore, Ralph S.; flowers large, semi-dbl., borne mostly singly or in small clusters, no fragrance; foliage medium size, medium green, matte; no prickles; medium (28-34 cm.), bushy, spreading, compact growth; [seedling × seedling]; intr. 1995

'Morprom' ('Prom Date') Min, dp, 1989, Moore, Ralph S.; bud short, pointed; flowers deep pink, aging lighter, medium, 38 petals, globular, borne singly, no fragrance; profuse; foliage medium size, medium green, matte; prickles straight, pointed, medium, gray to brown; upright, bushy, medium growth; hips globular, orange; ['Sheri Anne' × (seedling × 'Fairy Moss')]

'Morpuff' ('Pink Powderpuff') HBc, lp, 1991, Moore, Ralph S.; bud pointed; flowers light pink, aging slightly lighter, old garden rose type, large, 100 petals, high-centered, loose, borne heavily in the spring, intense damask fragrance; repeat bloom; foliage large, medium green, semi-glossy; tall, spreading, climbing growth; ['Lulu' × 'Muriel']; intr. 1990

'Morquake' (Earthquake™) Min, rb, 1984, Moore, Ralph S.; flowers striped red and yellow, reverse yellow, small, dbl., no fragrance; foliage small, medium green, semi-glossy; upright, bushy growth; PP5791; ['Golden Angel' × seedling]; intr. 1984

'Morrainbow' (Halo Rainbow®) Min, pb, 1994, Moore, Ralph S.; flowers pink edging with center of each petal creamy white, and base pink, a picotee halo, large, 5 petals, borne in small clusters; foliage medium size, medium green, semi-glossy; no prickles; medium (28-35 cm.), bushy, spreading growth; [seedling × Make Believe™]; intr. 1995

'Morredrug' HRg, mr, Moore; intr. 2004

'Morris' F, or, J. B. Williams; intr. 2005

'Morrobi' ('Robi') Min, or, 2000, Moore, Ralph S.; flowers orange-red, medium, very full, cupped, borne in small clusters, no fragrance; prolific; foliage medium size, medium green, semi-glossy; few prickles; growth bushy, spreading, medium (15-18 in.); ['Pink Petticoat' × 'Sincerely Yours']

'Morrousel' Min, rb, 1973, Moore, Ralph S.; intr. 1972

'Morrubi' ('Ruby Magic') Min, mr, 1986, Moore, Ralph S.; flowers cherry red, small to medium, 20 petals, borne singly and in sprays of 3-5, slight fragrance; foliage small to medium size, medium green, semi-glossy; prickles brown; medium, upright, bushy growth; usually no fruit; [Orangeade® × Pinstripe™]

'Morsally' S, my, Moore, Ralph; bud clear yellow; intr. 2000

'Morsalvatore' (Thanks To Sue™) MinFl, ab, 2004, Moore, Ralph S.; bud peach-apricot; flowers peachy-pink, 2 in., semi-dbl., borne mostly solitary, moderate fragrance; fast repeat; foliage medium size, medium green, semi-glossy; prickles small, straight; growth upright, spreading, tall (30 in.); specimen, containers, exhibition; [Joycie™ × Playboy®]; intr. 2005

'Morsdag' -- See 'Mothersday'

'Morsdag Alba' ('White Mothersday') Pol, w; low (40 cm) growth

'Morsdag Red' Pol, mr

'Morsea' ('Chelsea') Min, mp, 1986, Moore, Ralph S.; lacy sepals; flowers small, 25 petals, cupped, borne in clusters of 5 or more, slight fragrance; foliage small to medium size, medium green, semi-glossy; upright, bushy growth; hips few, globular, medium size, orange; [('Little Darling' × 'Yellow Magic') × 'Crested Jewel']

'Morsegold' (Sequoia Gold™) Min, my, 1987, Moore, Ralph S.; flowers medium yellow, fading lighter, medium, 30 petals, high-centered, borne usually singly, moderate fruity fragrance; foliage medium size, medium green, glossy; prickles slender, medium, pale green-brown; bushy, spreading growth; hips round, orange; PP6617; [('Little Darling' × 'Lemon Delight') × Gold Badge™]; intr. 1986

'Morsemuri' ('Star Magic') S, pb, 1995, Moore, Ralph S.; flowers pink blend, small, 5 petals, borne in small clusters; foliage small, dark green, glossy; some prickles; groundcover; medium (3 × 8 ft.), spreading, compact growth; [Sequoia Gold™ × 'MORmuri']; intr. 1996

'Morsetwist' ('Sequoia Twist') Min, yb, 2004, Moore, Ralph S.; flowers yellow/orange, varying in pattern, reverse yellow, 1½-2 in., semi-dbl., borne in small clusters, moderate fragrance; foliage medium size, medium green, semi-glossy; prickles small, straight; growth spreading, medium (15-18 in.); containers, specimen, borders; [sport of 'Sequoia Gold']; intr. 2005

'Morsewel' ('Sequoia Jewel') Min, mr, 1990, Moore, Ralph S.; bud rounded; flowers medium, 33 petals, cupped, borne in sprays of 3 - 7; foliage medium size, medium green, matte; prickles straight, short, brown; upright, bushy, medium growth; hips round, medium, orange-red; ['Sheri Anne' × 'Paul Neyron']; intr. 1990

'Morshack' ('Exotic Treat', Phyllis Shackelford™) Min, ob, 1987, Moore, Ralph S.; flowers orange, fading pink, small, 20 petals, high-centered, borne usually singly, moderate fruity fragrance; foliage small, medium green, semi-glossy; prickles few, medium, brownish, slightly hooked downwards; upright, bushy, medium growth; hips rounded, medium, orange; ['Anytime' × Gold Badge™]

'Morshaki' ('Little Tiger') Min, rb, 1989, Moore, Ralph S.; bud short, pointed; flowers red, yellow and white stripes of varying patterns, reverse with more yellow, very dbl., high-centered, no fragrance; foliage small, medium green, matte; prickles average, slender, inclined downward, brown; bushy, low, rounded growth; ['Golden Angel' × Pinstripe™]

'Morshakrug' ('Yesterday's Garden') S, pb, 1992, Moore, Ralph S.; flowers medium, very dbl., borne in small clusters, no fragrance; foliage medium size, medium green, semi-glossy; tall to medium (over 50 cm.), upright, bushy, spreading growth; ['Shakespeare Festival' × 'Belle Poitevine']; intr. 1993

'Morsharon' ('Sharon's Delight') S, w, 1996, Moore, Ralph S.; flowers pure white, yellow stamens, 3½ in., single, shallow cup, borne in small clusters; free-flowering; foliage medium size, medium green, semi-glossy; few prickles; bushy, medium (2-3 ft.) growth; ['Golden Angel' × 'Safrano']; intr. 1996

'Morshefran' ('New Adventure') Min, w, 1989, Moore, Ralph S.; bud pointed; flowers creamy white, medium, 25 petals, flat, borne singly and in sprays of 3 - 5, no fragrance; foliage small, medium green, matte; prickles short, pointed, brownish-gray; upright, bushy, medium growth; hips globular, orange; ['Sheri Anne' × 'Safrano']

'Morsheri' Min, or, 1975, Moore, Ralph S.; bud long, pointed; intr. 1973

'Morshodot' ('Cherry Hi') Min, dr, 1996, Moore, Ralph S.; flowers dark red, reverse slightly lighter, 1½ in., very dbl., borne in small clusters, no fragrance; few prickles; PP11099; ['Show 'n' Tell' × 'Sincerely Yours']; intr. 1997

'Morshook' ('Earthquake, Climbing') Cl Min, rb, 1991, Moore, Ralph S.; bud rounded; flowers red/yellow stripes, yellow reverse, aging similar, medium, 40 petals, urn-shaped, borne usually singly or in sprays of 3 - 5, no fragrance; foliage small, medium green, semi-glossy; upright, tall growth; [sport of 'Earthquake']; intr. 1991

'Morsis' ('Little Sister') Min, lp, 2004, Moore, Ralph S.; flowers 1 in., semi-dbl., borne in small clusters; abundant bloom; foliage small, medium green; no prickles; growth compact (8-12 in.); containers, borders, cutting; [sport of 'Little Pinkie']; intr. 2004

'Morsixty' ('Diamond Anniversary') Min, m, 1996, Moore, Ralph S.; flowers mauve, reverse mauve or slightly lighter, 1½ in., 40 petals, borne in small clusters; few prickles; PP11063; [Joycie™ × Cherry Magic™]; intr. 1997

'Morsno' (Snow Twinkle™) Min, w, 1987, Moore, Ralph S.; bud long, pointed; flowers ivory to white, opening to a star shape, 1½ in., 35-45 petals, high-centered, borne singly and in small, loose sprays, slight fragrance; free-flowering; foliage small, medium green, semi-glossy to matte; prickles small, slender, slightly curved downward, brown; stems slender, wiry; bushy, medium growth; hips round, orange; PP6822; [('Little Darling' × 'Yellow Magic') × Magic Carrousel®]

'Morsnop' ('Buttermint') Min, my, 1993, Moore, Ralph S.; flowers large, dbl., borne mostly singly, slight fragrance; foliage medium size, medium green, semi-glossy; few prickles; medium to tall (36-40 cm.), upright, bushy growth; ['Pink Petticoat' × Gold Badge™]; intr. 1994

'Morstar' ('Star Delight', 'Starry Eyed') HRg, mp, 1990, Moore, Ralph S.; bud pointed; flowers rose pink, white base, silvery pink reverse, medium, 5 petals, flat, borne usually singly and in sprays of 3-5; repeat bloom; foliage medium size, olive to bluish-green, semi-glossy; upright, bushy, tall growth; ['Yellow Jewel' × 'Rugosa Magnifica']; intr. 1990

'Morstardust' ('Star Dust') HBc, w, 2002, Moore, Ralph S.; flowers white/yellow, reverse white, 1-1½ in., dbl., borne in small clusters; foliage medium size, medium green, semi-glossy; prickles small, pointed, green, few; growth bushy, medium (18-24 in.); containers, specimen; [seedling × 'Out of Yesteryear']; intr. 2002

'Morstock' ('Woodstock') Min, yb, 1999, Moore, Ralph S.; flowers bright yellow, aging red, 1-1½ in., full, borne mostly singly, slight fragrance; recurrent; foliage small, medium green, semi-glossy; few prickles; low (8-12 in.), bushy, compact growth; [seedling × 'Clytemnestra']; intr. 1999

'Morstrort' (Shadow Dancer™) LCl, pb, 1999, Moore, Ralph S.; bud very pointed to somewhat ovoid; flowers striped, swirled two-tone pink, 3½-4 in., 14-18 petals, cupped, borne usually in large clusters, sometimes singly, slight fruity fragrance; recurrent; foliage medium size, dark green, holly-like; prickles moderate, straight, angled downward; stems medium to long; climbing, tall (8-10 ft.) growth; hips globular; PP11089; [(Dortmund® × unknown) × Dortmund®]; intr. 1998

'Morsun' ('Sweet Sunshine') Min, my, 1982, Moore, Ralph S.; flowers small, 20 petals, intense fragrance; foliage small, medium green, semi-glossy; upright, bushy growth; ['Rumba' × 'Yellow Jewel']; intr. 1981

'Morsunrise' Min, yb, Moore, Ralph; intr. 1997

'Morsunset' ('Halo Sunset') Min, ob, 2000, Moore, Ralph S.; flowers orange blend with reddish-pink center, large, 8-10 petals, borne in small clusters; foliage medium size, medium green, semi-glossy; few prickles; upright, bushy, medium (15-18 in.) growth; [seedling × 'Show 'n' Tell']; intr. 2000

'Morsweet' ('Crested Sweetheart') LCl, mp, 1988, Moore, Ralph S.; flowers medium rose pink, large, very dbl., cupped, borne in sprays of 3-5, intense damask fragrance; foliage large, medium green, matte, rugose; prickles small, gray to brown; upright, tall growth; ['Little Darling' × 'Crested Moss']; intr. 1988

'Morsweetie' ('Halo Sweetie') Min, pb, 2002, Moore, Ralph S.; flowers single, borne in small clusters, no fragrance; foliage small, light green, matte; growth compact, medium (12-15 in.); containers, garden decorative, exhibition; [seedling × Halo Rainbow®]; intr. 2002

'Morswiss' ('Two-Timer') Min, ob, 1991, Moore, Ralph S.; bud ovoid; flowers orange-red with lighter shades of orange and white stripes, lighter reverse, medium, very dbl., high-centered, borne usually singly or in sprays of 3-5, no fragrance; foliage medium size, medium green, semi-glossy; bushy, spreading, low growth; [Orangeade® × Pinstripe™]; intr. 1991

'Morsycheek' S, op, Moore; intr. 1984

'Mort de Virginie' HGal, m, 1824, in Brussels; flowers dark violet, large

'Mortange' ('Tangerine Jewel') HBc, ob, 2002, Moore, Ralph S.; flowers orange, reverse orange/pink, 2-2½ in., single, borne in small clusters, moderate fragrance; foliage medium size, medium green, semi-glossy; prickles few, small, pointed, light green; growth bushy, medium (24-36 in.); garden shrub, containers, specimen; [Joycie™ × 'Out of Yesteryear']; intr. 2002

'Morten' ('Linda Campbell', 'Tall Poppy') HRg, mr, 1991, Moore, Ralph S.; bud pointed; flowers medium red, slightly lighter reverse, aging medium red, medium, 25 petals, cupped, borne in sprays of 5-25; fast repeat; foliage large, dark green, semi-glossy; growth upright, bushy, medium; PP8199; ['Anytime' × 'Rugosa Magnifica']; intr. 1991

'Morthirthree' ('Persian Autumn') S, ab, 2004, Moore, Ralph S.; flowers orange/apricot with red eye, reverse orange/apricot streaked with red, 2½ in., single, borne in small clusters, slight fragrance; recurrent; foliage medium size, medium green, semi-glossy; prickles medium, hooked; growth spreading, vigorous, arching canes, tall (4-5 ft.); specimen; ['Tigris' × ('Anytime' × Gold Badge™)]; hybrid Hulthemia; intr. 2005

'Morthirtythreebee' ('Persian Sunset') S, ob, 2006, Moore, Ralph S.; bud yellow; flowers pink/orange/red with a distinct red blotch at center, reverse yellow, 2-2½ in., semi-dbl., borne in small clusters; foliage medium size, medium green, matte; prickles small, straight, green, moderate; growth spreading, medium (3-5 ft.); ['Tigris' × seedling]; Hulthemia hybrid; intr. 2006

'Morthree' ('Persian Light') S, yb, 2006, Moore, Ralph S.; flowers medium yellow with a distinct red splotch at center, reverse light yellow, 2½ in., semi-dbl., borne in small clusters; some repeat; foliage small, medium green, matte; prickles small, straight, brown, many prick; growth spreading, medium (3-5 ft.); arching shrub, specimen; ['Tigris' × 'unnamed yellow mini']; Hulthemia hybrid; intr. 2006

'Mortime' ('Precious Dream') HBc, pb, 2002, Moore, Ralph S.; flowers pink/apricot, reverse pink/yellow, 2-2½ in., full, borne in small clusters; foliage medium size, medium green, semi-glossy; prickles small, pointed, green, few; bushy, medium (2-3 ft.) growth; containers, specimen; intr. 2002

Mortimer Sackler™ -- See 'Ausorts'

'Mortoday' (Halo Today®) Min, op, 1994, Moore, Ralph S.; flowers have distinct pink/lavender area at base of each petal, large, 5-8 petals, no fragrance; foliage medium size, medium green, semi-glossy; no prickles; low (16-18 in.), upright, bushy growth; [('Anytime' × Gold Badge™) × ('Anytime' × 'Lavender Jewel')]; intr. 1994

'Mortopaz' ('Peach Candy') Min, ab, 1995, Moore, Ralph S.; flowers soft peach, small, dbl., borne in small clusters, slight fragrance; foliage small, light green, matte; few prickles; medium (24-30 cm.), upright, bushy growth; ['Sheri Anne' × Topaz Jewel™]; intr. 1996

'Mortorch' (Torch of Liberty™) Min, or, 1986, Moore, Ralph S.; bud long, pointed; flowers orange-red, silver reverse, 1½ in., 20-30 petals, high-centered, borne singly and several together, slight fragrance; recurrent; foliage small, medium green, semi-glossy; few prickles; upright, bushy growth; hips ball-shaped, orange; PP6254; [Orangeade® × 'Golden Angel']; intr. 1985

'Mortreat' ('Double Treat') Min, yb, 1986, Moore, Ralph S.; bud mossy; flowers bright red and orange-yellow, striped, mini-moss, dbl., cupped, borne usually singly; foliage small to medium size, medium green, semi-glossy; prickles slender, brown; medium, upright, bushy growth; hips small, globular with numerous spines, orange; ['Arizona' × (('Fairy Moss' × 'Fairy Moss') × ('Little Darling' × 'Ferdinand Pichard'))]; intr. 1985

'Mortrip' ('Crazy Quilt') Min, rb, 1980, Moore, Ralph S.; bud pointed; flowers red and white striped, dbl., flat, borne singly or in clusters of 3 or more; foliage medium green; prickles small, straight; compact, bushy growth; PP4867; ['Little Darling' × seedling]

'Mortuit' HRg, pb, Moore, Ralph; intr. 2000

'Mortwist' ('Orange Twist') Min, ob, 1986, Moore, Ralph S.; flowers tannish-orange; [sport of 'Sungold']; same as parent except for color; intr. 1985

'Mortwister' ('Twister') Cl Min, rb, 1997, Moore, Ralph S.; flowers striped red and white, 1½ in., full, rosette, borne in small clusters, slight fragrance; recurrent; foliage medium size, medium green, dull; few prickles; upright, climbing, tall (5-6 ft.) growth; ['Little Darling' × 'Little Magic']

'Moruby' ('Ruby Princess') Min, rb, 2002, Moore, Ralph S.; flowers ruby red, reverse red, 1 in., dbl., borne mostly solitary; foliage small, medium green, semi-glossy; prickles small, pointed, green, few; growth compact, short (12 in.); potted plant, specimen; [Joycie™ × Cherry Magic™]; intr. 2002

'Moruncommon' ('Kim Rupert') Min, rb, 2003, Moore, Ralph S.; bud moderate, balsam scented mossing; flowers red/light yellow stripes, reverse red and yellow, 2 in., dbl., borne in small clusters; foliage medium size, medium green, semi-glossy; prickles straight; growth upright, tall (16-24 in.); containers, raised beds, borders; ['Golden Angel' × (Dortmund® × 'striped moss seedling')]; intr. 2003

'Morunusual' ('Most Unusual Day') F, pb, 1999, Moore, Ralph S.; flowers 1½-2½ in., dbl., borne in small clusters, no fragrance; foliage medium size, medium green, semi-glossy; few prickles; medium (16-24 in.), upright, bushy growth; ['Show 'n' Tell' × Blastoff™]; intr. 1999

'Morvandel' Min, yb, 1977, Moore, Ralph S.; bud long, pointed

'Morvi' ('Vi's Violet') Min, m, 1991, Moore, Ralph S.; bud lavender pink; flowers soft lavender, small, full, slight fragrance; free-flowering; foliage small, medium green, matte; upright, bushy, compact growth; [seedling × 'Angel Face']

'Morwategye' ('Halo Dolly') Min, pb, 1992, Moore, Ralph S.; flowers bicolor, reddish outside, pink inside with reddish-lavender, medium, semi-dbl., no fragrance; foliage medium size, medium green, semi-glossy; few prickles; medium (30-45 cm.), upright, bushy, rounded growth; ['Anytime' × ('Anytime' × 'Angel Face')]; intr. 1993

'Morwheels' ('Jacquie Williams') Min, rb, 1997, Moore, Ralph S.; flowers medium, full, borne mostly singly, but some clusters; foliage medium size, medium green, semi-glossy,; low to medium (30-45 cm.) growth; [('Yellow Jewel' × 'Tamango') × 'Strawberry Ice']; intr. 1998

'Morwhit' ('Little Eskimo') Min, w, 1981, Moore, Ralph S.; bud long, pointed; flowers near white, 55 petals, borne 3 - 7 per cluster, sometimes singly; foliage small, semi-glossy, leathery; prickles long, slender; vigorous, bushy, upright growth; [(R. wichurana × 'Floradora') × 'Jet Trail']

'Morwhy' ('Why Not') Min, rb, 1984, Moore, Ralph S.; bud long, pointed; flowers medium red, yellow eye, reverse yellow, 3 cm., 7 petals, shallow cup, borne singly and in clusters, very slight fragrance; recurrent; foliage small, medium green, matte to semi-glossy; prickles moderate, slender, curved slightly downward, brown; upright, bushy growth; hips small, globe-shaped ; PP5676; ['Golden Angel' × seedling]; intr. 1983

'Morwimer' ('Little Mermaid') Cl Min, ly, 1995, Moore, Ralph S.; flowers medium, 5 petals, borne in small clusters, no fragrance; foliage small, medium green, semi-glossy; some prickles; growth bushy, spreading; [sport of 'Mermaid']; intr. 1995

'Morwings' ('Yellow Butterfly') S, ly, 1989, Moore, Ralph S.; bud pointed; flowers light yellow, aging to near white, medium, 5 petals, informal, borne in sprays of 3-7, no fragrance; foliage medium size, light green, semi-glossy; prickles slender, inclined downward, small, brownish; bushy, spreading, medium, clean growth; hips ovoid, small, yellowish-orange; ['Ellen Poulsen' × 'Yellow Jewel']; intr. 1989

'Morwinst' ('Secret Recipe') Min, rb, 1994, Moore, Ralph S.; bud pointed, mossy; flowers combination of burgundy, red and white stripes, yellow stamens, 1¾ in., semi-dbl., flat, borne mostly singly, slight fragrance; foliage medium size, medium green, semi-glossy; some prickles; upright, bushy (12-18 in.) growth; ['Little Darling' × seedling]; intr. 1995

'Morwood' ('Redwood Empire') Min, or, 1984, Moore, Ralph S.; flowers small, 20 petals; foliage small, medium green, semi-glossy; upright, bushy growth; ['Rumba' × 'Sheri Anne']; intr. 1983

'Moryears' ('Out of Yesteryear') S, w, 1999, Moore, Ralph S.; flowers white blend, 3 in., very dbl., borne in large clusters, moderate fragrance; foliage medium size, dark green, glossy; numerous prickles; upright, spreading (4-6 ft.) growth; ['Golden Angel' × 'Muriel']; intr. 1999

'Moryelrug' ('Frau Dagmar Hastrup Geel', 'Rustica 91', 'Yellow Dagmar Hastrup', 'Yellow Fru Dagmar Hartopp', 'Gelbe Dagmar Hastrup', 'Gull Dagmar') HRg, my, 1987, Moore, Ralph S.; bud large, pointed; intr. 1987

'Moryelyol' Min, my, Moore, Ralph; intr. 2001

'Moryettem' (Saint Mary™) Min, m, 1986, Moore, Ralph S.; flowers deep red-purple, small, dbl., cupped, slight fragrance; foliage small, medium green, semi-glossy; prickles small, brown; medium, upright, bushy growth; no fruit; ['Little Chief' × 'Angel Face']

'Moryou' ('Just For You') Min, dp, 1991, Moore, Ralph S.; bud pointed; flowers dark pink to light red, lighter reverse, aging lighter, medium, 35 petals, high-centered, borne singly or in sprays of 3 - 5, slight fragrance; foliage medium size, medium green, semi-glossy; bushy, medium growth; [Orangeade® × Rainbow's End™]; intr. 1991

'Mosaik' F, rb, VEG; flowers red with dark yellow, medium, dbl.; intr. 1978

'Mosaïque' F, yb, 1960, Lens; flowers light yellowish-pink, becoming red, open, semi-dbl.; foliage light green; low, bushy growth; [('Alain' × 'Cinnabar') × 'Circus']

'Mosaïque' S, op, Croix; flowers soft orange and salmon tones; flowers generously; foliage disease-resistant; intr. 2002

'Moschata Grandiflora' (R. moschata grandiflora, R. multiflora grandiflora, R. polyantha grandiflora) HMult, w, 1866, Bernaix, A.; flowers prominent golden stamens, large, single, intense fragrance; very vigorous growth; [R. moschata × R. multiflora]

'Moschata Himalayica' -- See 'Paul's Himalayan Musk Rambler'

Moscow+ F, dp, Perfecta Plant; flowers double , high-centered, borne mostly singly; recurrent; stems medium to long; florist rose

'Moscow Morn' -- See 'Utro Moskvy'

'Mosel' HMult, m, 1920, Lambert, P.; flowers bluish violet, center reddish-violet, medium, dbl.; sometimes recurrent bloom; ['Mme Norbert Levavasseur' × Trier®]

'Moselblümchen' HCh, dp, 1889, Lambert

'Mosella, Climbing' Cl Pol, yb, 1909, Conard & Jones; flowers golden yellow and cream, borne in small clusters; [sport of 'Mosella']

'Mosella' Pol, w, 1895, Lambert & Reitner; flowers cream white, medium, borne in large clusters; ['Mignonette' × ('Mme Falcot' × 'Shirley Hibberd')]

'Mosellied' HMsk, m, 1932, Lambert, P.; flowers purplish red, center white, stamens golden yellow, medium, single, intense fragrance; non-recurrent; foliage dark; vigorous (about 6½ ft.), broad growth; [('Geheimrat Dr. Mittweg' × Tip-Top®) × ('Chamisso' × 'Parkzierde')]

'Moss Magic' Min, mp, 1977, Sudol, Julia; bud cupped, mossy; flowers medium to dark pink, circular, 1 in., 48 petals, flat; profuse bloom, repeating well; foliage

dark; spreading growth; ['Fairy Moss' × unknown]
'Moss Provence Rose' -- See 'Centifolia Muscosa'
'Moss Rose' -- See 'Centifolia Muscosa'
'Mossman' S, mp, 1954, Skinner; flowers heavily mossed, pale dusty pink, 2½ in., very dbl.; vigorous (4 ft.) growth; [(R. acicularis × R. rugosa) × a moss rose]
'Mossy de Meaux' -- See 'Mossy Rose de Meaux'
'Mossy Gem' Min, mp, 1984, Kelly, Martin; bud small, mossy; flowers medium pink, outer petals fading, small, dbl.; foliage medium size, dark, semi-glossy; bushy growth; ['Heidi' × 'Violette']
'Mossy Rose de Meaux' ('Mossy de Meaux', 'Pompon Moss', 'Pompon Mousseux', 'Pomponia Muscosa') M, mp, about 1813, from England; flowers blush, peach center, small, full, cupped, borne in clusters of 2-3; foliage ovate, pointed, small; prickles red, straight, small, very numerous and dense; growth dwarf (1 ft.); hybridizer possibly Sweet; sport of 'Rose de Meaux' or 'Pompon de Mai'
'Mossy Sweetbriar' -- See 'Manning's Blush'
'Most Unusual Day' -- See 'Morunusual'
'Moth' ('The Moth') S, m, Austin, David; flowers pale grey-pink fading to nearly white, yellow stamens, large, semi-dbl., flat, intense myrrh fragrance; recurrent; low (1 ft.), spreading (1½ ft.) growth; hips rounded; intr. 1983
'Mother' HT, pb, 1939, Cant, B. R.; flowers white edged bright pink; [sport of 'Memory']
Mother and Baby® -- See 'Sanbaby'
Mother Lode™ -- See 'Savalode'
'Mother Marie' Pol, w, 1954, Podesta; flowers white, center green, 1½-2 in., very dbl., flat, borne in clusters; foliage light green; PP1243; [sport of 'Garnette']
'Mother Mary McKillop' -- See 'Mary McKillop'
Mother of Pearl™ Gr, lp, Meilland; flowers soft pink, medium , 22-25 petals, high-centered, wide, slight fragrance; recurrent; foliage medium green; tall, bushy growth; PPAF; intr. 2007
'Mother of Pearl' HT, lp, Tantau; flowers very pale pink , double, high-centered; recurrent; intr. 2006
'Mother Theresa' HT, w, IARI; flowers white with pink tones, lasting, high-centered; stems long; intr. 1994
'Mother's Country' ('Mère de la Patrie', 'Moeder des Vaderlands') F, mr, 1958, Leenders, M.; flowers bright vermilion-red; strong stems; vigorous growth; ['Ambassadeur Nemry' × 'Cinnabar']; intr. 1957
'Mothers Day' -- See 'Mothersday'
'Mother's Day' HT, w, 1937, Knight, G.; flowers white, at times shaded pink, very large; very vigorous growth
'Mother's Day Orange Sport' Pol, ob, 1958, Klyn; flowers orange-yellow; [sport of 'Mothersday']
'Mother's Heart' S, m, Thomson; flowers lavender , double, moderate fragrance; recurrent; intr. 2002
'Mothers Joy' S, mp; flowers soft pink, dbl., high-centered, borne usually in clusters, intense fragrance; foliage medium green, glossy; growth to 3 ft.
'Mother's Love' -- See 'Tinlove'
'Mother's Love' HT, pb, Meilland; flowers soft white with a shell pink center, large, very full, borne singly and in clusters, intense sweet fragrance; good repeat; foliage dark green; stems long, strong; vigorous, upright (5 ft.) growth; intr. 1999
'Mother's Love' HT, mr; intr. 2004
'Mother's Rose' -- See 'Jacmpiad'
'Mother's Value' -- See 'Korretra'
'Mothersday' ('Fête des Mères', 'Morsdag', 'Mothers Day', 'Muttertag', 'Paree Red', 'Red Mothersday') Pol, dr, 1949, Grootendorst, F.J.; flowers medium, dbl., globular, borne in clusters of up to 20; foliage glossy, small; dwarf growth; containers, forcing; [sport of 'Dick Koster']
'Mothersday, Climbing' ('Fête des Mère, Climbing', 'Muttertag, Climbing') Cl Pol, dr, 1956, Kordes
'Motiv' HT, mp, VEG; flowers large, dbl.; intr. 1983
'Motrea' F, mr, 1968, Mosselman & Terreehorst; bud ovoid; flowers light red, small, very dbl.; foliage dark; [sport of 'Coronet']
'Mottled Moss' -- See 'Prolifère'
'Motylek' ('Butterfly Papilio') HT, w, 1954, Shtanko, I.; flowers cream, base yellow, medium, 40-45 petals, high-centered; moderate growth with thin, strong shoots; ['Freiburg II' × 'Golden Dawn']
Moulin Rouge® ('Sans souci') F, mr, 1952, Meilland, F.; flowers 2 in., 20-25 petals, cupped, borne in clusters; foliage glossy; upright, very bushy growth; PP1298; ['Alain' × Orange Triumph®]
'Moulin Rouge, Climbing' Cl F, mr, 1958, Hendrick; intr. 1957
Mouna® ('Pekcouflash') HT, mr
'Mount Eden' LCl, mp, 2007, Janon, Jocelyn; flowers 8 cm., single, borne mostly solitary; red, hairy new shoots on lime green foliage; prickles 5 mm., straight, red, few; growth to 5 m.; hedge/climber; ['Polyantha Grandiflora' × seedling]; intr. 2007
Mt Everest® HT, w, Tantau; flowers clear white, very large, double, high-centered, borne mostly singly; recurrent; stems long; intr. 2005
'Mount Everest' S, mp; flowers crimson with a white eye and soft yellow stamens, large, slight fragrance; heavy spring bloom and scattered repeat; hips bottle-shaped; hybrid of R. pendulina
'Mount Hobben' HT, mr, 1985, Ota, Kaichiro; flowers bright scarlet, large, 30 petals, high-centered, borne 1-3 per stem, no fragrance; foliage medium green; prickles numerous, small; tall, upright growth; ['Fragrant Charm' × 'Christian Dior']
'Mount Homan' HT, ab, 1985, Ota, Kaichiro; bud ovoid; flowers large, petals quilled, dbl., high-centered, borne 1-3 per stem; foliage dark, semi-glossy; prickles large; tall, upright, bushy growth; ['Ginger Rogers' × 'Sunblest']; intr. 1984
'Mount Hood' -- See 'Macmouhoo'
'Mt Hood' -- See 'Macmouhoo'
'Mount Nelson' F, w, J&P; flowers white with pink edges, semi-dbl., borne in clusters; free-flowering; vigorous, short growth; intr. 1998
'Mt Rai' HT, w, 1988, Ota, Kaichiro; flowers white, pale cream at center, aging pale pink at edges,, 42 petals, high-centered, urn-shaped; foliage dark green, semi-glossy; prickles medium, downward-shaped, slightly dented, green; bushy, medium growth; hips medium, yellow-green; [('Golden Scepter' × 'Narcissus') × 'Ginger Rogers']
'Mt St Helens' Gr, dp, 1982, Northwest Rose Growers; bud long, pointed; flowers deep pink, 35 petals, urn-shaped, borne singly and in small clusters, slight spicy fragrance; foliage dark, leathery; prickles bronze; growth to 4-5 ft.; [seedling × Queen Elizabeth®]; intr. 1981
'Mount Shasta' Gr, w, 1962, Swim & Weeks; bud long, pointed; flowers 4½-5 in., dbl., cupped, moderate fragrance; foliage leathery, gray-green; vigorous, upright growth; PP2132; [Queen Elizabeth® × 'Blanche Mallerin']; intr. 1963
'Mount Shasta, Climbing' Cl Gr, w, Knight, G.; flowers white, tinted yellow at center, 5-6 in., cupped; [sport of 'Mount Shasta']; intr. 1968
'Mt Tara' HT, or, 1988, Ota, Kaichiro; flowers large, 35 petals, high-centered, borne usually singly; foliage dark green, semi-glossy; prickles medium, downward-shaped, slightly dented, green; bushy, medium growth; hips medium, yellow-green; ['Ginger Rogers' × 'Fragrant Charm']
'Mount Temple' -- See 'Kenetern'
'Mountain Haze' F, m, 1967, Morey, Dr. Dennison; flowers lavender, reverse silver, medium, 55-60 petals, high-centered; foliage dark, leathery; vigorous, low, spreading growth; ['Amy Vanderbilt' × 'Lilac Time']
Mountain High® S, w, Warner; intr. 2007
'Mountain Mist' S, m, 1990, Jobson, Daniel J.; bud pointed; flowers purple-lavender shading to white at base, small, 5 petals, flat, borne in sprays of 10-35, intense multiflora, vanilla fragrance; foliage small, light green, semi-glossy; prickles very few, red; spreading, medium (4 × 6 ft.), prolific growth; hips globular, red; [Yesterday® × Yesterday®]
'Mountain Music' S, pb, 1985, Buck, Dr.

Griffith J.; flowers pink and yellow blend, medium, 23 petals, cupped, borne 5 - 15 per cluster, moderate fragrance; repeat bloom; foliage leathery, semi-glossy; prickles awl-like, tan; vigorous, erect, bushy growth; hardy; ['Sevilla' × 'Tom Brown']; intr. 1984

'Mountain Side' S

'Mountain Snow' -- See 'Aussnow'

'Mountaineer' HT, op, 1963, Wyant; bud long, pointed, orange-red; flowers orange-pink, reverse creamy yellow, 5 in., 35 petals, high-centered; foliage glossy; vigorous growth; ['Mrs Sam McGredy' × 'Crimson Glory']

Mountbatten® -- See 'Harmantelle'

Mountie™ -- See 'Lavcali'

'Mountjoy' (natural variation of *R. setigera*), lp; flowers blush, center darker

'Mourne Gold' HT, yb, 1981, Kane Brothers; flowers deep yellow, pink flush; [sport of 'Whisky Mac']; intr. 1980

'Mouse' -- See 'Seamou'

'Mousha' HT, lp, 1976, Kordes; bud long, pointed; flowers 4 in., 24 petals, high-centered; foliage glossy, dark; vigorous, upright growth; ['Königin der Rosen' × King's Ransom®]; intr. 1974

'Mousha' S, yb; flowers striped; intr. 2002

'Mousseau Ancien' -- See 'Centifolia Muscosa'

'Mousseline' -- See 'Alfred de Dalmas'

'Mousseline' M, w, 1881, Moreau-Robert; flowers blush white, medium to large, full, moderate fragrance; recurrent; prickles numerous, very fine; growth upright

'Mousseuse Blanche' -- See 'Shailer's White Moss'

'Mousseuse Blanche Nouvelle' -- See 'White Bath'

'Mousseux Anémone' -- See 'Anémone'

'Mousseux du Japon' ('Japonica', 'Moussu du Japon', 'Muscosa Japonica') M, m, before 1906; bud and stems heavily mossed; flowers purplish rose, quickly fading to lavender, many stamens, semi-dbl.; growth moderate; in actuality, a mutation of the rugosa group, not from the Centifolias

'Moussu du Japon' -- See 'Mousseux du Japon'

'Moussue des Quatre Saison Blanc' -- See 'Quatre Saisons Blanc Mousseux'

'Moussue Partout' -- See 'Zoé'

'Moustique' Min, w, Dickson; intr. 2003

'Movement' LCl, ob, Williams, J. Benjamin; flowers clear orange, yellow eye and stamens, single, shallow cup, moderate fragrance; recurrent; growth to 6 ft.; intr. 2006

'Movie Star' -- See 'Taneivom'

Moxie™ -- See 'Jacignat'

'Moyse' -- See 'Moïse'

'Mozart' HMsk, pb, 1937, Lambert, P.; flowers deep pink with large white eye, small, single, borne in clusters, moderate fragrance; repeat bloom; vigorous, trailing or bushy growth; ['Robin Hood' × 'Rote Pharisaer']

'Mr Gavin' Min, dr, Wells, Whit; flowers medium , double, slight fragrance; recurrent; foliage medium, dark green, semi-glossy; medium to tall growth; [Seedling × Seedling]; intr. 2005

'Mr Joseph Cyril Bamford' -- See 'Mr J. C. B.'

'Mridula' HT, w, 1976, IARI; bud long, pointed; flowers white, center soft pink, large, 35 petals, high-centered, moderate fragrance; foliage large, light, soft; very vigorous, upright, compact growth; [Queen Elizabeth® × ('Sir Henry Segrave' × unknown)]; intr. 1975

'Mrigasira' HT, w, Kasturi & Sriram; flowers cream with pale pink at petal edges, dbl., well formed; free-flowering; intr. 2004

'Mrinalini' HT, mp, 1972, IARI; bud long, pointed; flowers phlox pink, very large, dbl., high-centered, borne singly, moderate fragrance; foliage medium size, medium green, soft; vigorous, bushy growth; ['Pink Parfait' × 'Christian Dior']; intr. 1975

'Mrs Talat Rizvi' -- See 'Jaltalat'

'Mu Lan' F, m

'Mu Lan' ('MuLan') HT, ob, 2003, Edwards, Eddie; flowers coral, 5½ in., full, borne mostly solitary, slight fragrance; foliage medium size, dark green, semi-glossy; growth upright, medium (5½ ft.); high-centered, exhibition; ['Gemini' × 'Fantasy']; intr. 2003

'Mucaba' HT, pb, 1962, Moreira da Silva; flowers pink stained carmine; ['Marechal Carmona' × 'Suzon Lotthe']

Muchacha® -- See 'Meilutida'

'Mudgee Red' HT, mr, Dot

'Muff's Pet' Min, pb; flowers deep pink, reverse white shaded pink, double, high-centered; intr. 2007

'Muffy' LCl, op, Bell, Laurie; flowers bright coral pink with yellow stamens, borne in large clusters; free-flowering; intr. 2001

'Mühle Hermsdorf' HWich, w, 1928, Dechant; flowers pure white, 5 cm., dbl., borne in large clusters; nearly thornless; [*R. wichurana* × 'Gruss an Zabern']

'Muhme Löffler' HT, dr, 1940, Krause; flowers large, dbl.

'MuLan' -- See 'Mu Lan'

'Mulbarton' LCl, mr, 1965, Hooney; flowers 4½ in., dbl.; foliage coppery; vigorous growth; ['Paul's Lemon Pillar' × ('Ena Harkness' × 'Richmond')]

'Mulbry Rose' -- See 'Tanolgnil'

'Mullard Jubilee' ('Elektron', Electron®) HT, dp, 1971, McGredy, Sam IV; flowers shocking pink, 5 in., 32-40 petals, high-centered, borne mostly singly, intense fragrance; foliage large, dark green, glossy; stems fully branched; upright, medium, bushy growth; PP3226; ['Paddy McGredy' × 'Prima Ballerina']; intr. 1970

'Mullem' HT, rb, RvS-Melle; flowers 4 in., 29 petals, cupped, intense fragrance; foliage dense dark green; ['Mme A. Meilland' × 'Melglory']; intr. 1996

'Multiflora' -- See 'Red Damask'

'Multiflora' -- See 'Royale'

'Multiflora' -- See 'Œillet'

'Multiflora Nana Perpétuelle' Pol, lp, 1893, Lille; flowers small, single

'Multiflore de Vaumarcus' N, lp, 1875, Menet; flowers soft pink, medium, very dbl., borne in large clusters; good repeat

'Multiflore Tricolore' -- See 'Tricolore'

'Multiplex' -- See 'Admirable'

'Multiplex' ('Double Jaune', 'Sulphurea', 'Lutea Flore Pleno', 'Jaune Ancien') Misc OGR, my, before 1629; bud large, round; flowers sulphur yellow, very large, very dbl., globular, no fragrance; foliage oval, dentate, pale green, small; prickles numerous, strong, hooked

'Multnomah' HT, rb, 1948, Swim, H.C.; bud long, pointed; flowers carmine, base gold, open, 4-5 in., 18-22 petals; foliage glossy, dark; vigorous, upright, compact growth; hardy in Pacific Northwest; PP883; ['Contrast' × 'Charlotte Armstrong']

'Mum in a Million' -- See 'Poulren013'

'Mum Mum' Min, w, 1986, McDaniel, Earl; flowers pure white, small, 55 petals, cupped, borne in clusters of 3-25; foliage light green, semi-glossy; prickles short, curved, light green; low, upright, bushy, spreading growth; [seedling × seedling]

'Mum's Blessing' -- See 'Guesimage'

'München' HMsk, dr, 1940, Kordes; bud long, pointed; flowers scarlet-crimson, large, semi-dbl., borne in clusters; repeat bloom; foliage dark, glossy; very vigorous, trailing growth; ['Eva' × 'Reveil Dijonnais']

'Munchen 83' -- See 'Meibalbika'

München Kindl® -- See 'Dickimono'

'Münchener Fasching' S, mr, 1963, Kordes, R.; bud ovoid; flowers bright red, 30 petals, borne in large clusters (up to 40); foliage dark, glossy; vigorous, bushy (6-6½ ft.) growth

'Münchener Herz' -- See 'Münchner Herz'

'Munchkin' Min, pb, 1987, Bridges, Dennis A.; flowers pink edging, white center, reverse slight pink edged on white, 22 petals, high-centered; foliage medium size, medium green, semi-glossy; prickles short, pointed, small, tan; bushy, low growth; ['Watercolor' × seedling]

Münchner Herz® ('Münchener Herz') F, ab, Cocker; flowers apricot with pink tones on ourter petals, large, full, hybrid tea, light fragrance; recurrent; foliage medium green, glossy; upright (2 ft.), bushy growth; intr. 1990

'Münchner Kindl' -- See 'Dickimono'

Munot® Gr, or, Huber, Richard; bud pointed, oblong; flowers dbl., high-centered, borne singly and in clusters, moderate spicy fragrance; new foliage reddish, turning to green; upright (70 cm.) growth; intr. 1983

'Munro's Improved Premier' HT, dp, 1927, Munro

'Munstead Wood' -- See 'Ausbernard'

'Munster' S, pb, 1959, Kordes; flowers soft pink shaded deeper, large, 28 petals, high-centered, borne in trusses; foliage light green; intr. 1958

Münsterland® S, pb, Noack, Werner; flowers light pink, deeper in center, 4 in., dbl., borne in clusters; free-flowering; growth to 6 ft.; intr. 1986

'Mur-Ray' HT, pb, 1936, Murray; flowers darker pink, tinged salmon; PP181; [sport of 'Briarcliff']

'Murasaki no Sono' F, m, 1985, Kobayashi, Moriji; flowers silver lilac, 13 petals, flat, borne singly and in small clusters; foliage light green; prickles slanted downward; vigorous, tall growth; ['Tasogare' × seedling]

'Murasakisuisho' Min, m; intr. 1984

'Muraskino' ('Purple Meadow') HT, m, Keihan; intr. 1992

'Murca' ('Plum Cake') HT, dr, 1987, Murray, Nola; flowers deep plum red, pointed, 27 petals, borne in sprays of 3-7; almost everblooming; foliage medium size, dark green, glossy; prickles pointed, brown; bushy growth; [('Chanelle' × 'Sabine') × 'Pompadour']; intr. 1986

'Murdina Lowe' -- See 'Battmurdina'

'Murfri' ('Frilly Dilly') F, dp, 1987, Murray, Nola; flowers light magenta red, pointed, small, 25 petals, borne in sprays of 5-7, slight fragrance; foliage large, medium green, flat; prickles pointed, brown; upright growth; ['Red Lion' × 'Magenta']; intr. 1986

'Murgo' ('Hipango') F, yb, 1983, Murray, Nola; flowers deep yellow, petals edged orange, reverse yellow, shapely, large, 21 petals; foliage medium size, medium to light green; vigorous growth; ['Smiley' × 'Una Hawken']

'Murha' ('Aroha') HT, mp, 1987, Murray, Nola; flowers medium, soft pink, elongated, 43 petals, borne in sprays of 3-5, slight fragrance; foliage medium size, light green; prickles pointed, brown; tall growth; ['Rifleman' × Pascali®]; intr. 1986

'Muria' -- See 'Macmu'

'Muriel' -- See 'Mormuri'

'Muriel' -- See 'Harvool'

'Muriel' HT, dr, 1929, Archer; bud long, pointed; flowers brilliant velvety scarlet, semi-dbl.; strong stems

'Muriel Armitage' HT, dp, 1972, Ellick; flowers deep rose-pink, 5 in., 60-70 petals; foliage large, glossy, dark; vigorous, upright growth; [(Orange Sensation® × 'Ballet') × 'Mischief']

'Muriel Dickson' HT, ob, 1915, Dickson, H.; flowers reddish-copper

'Muriel Grahame' ('Yellow Mermet') T, yb, 1898, Dickson, A.; flowers light canary yellow, tipped with rosy pink, very large, full; [sport of 'Catherine Mermet']

'Muriel Humenick' -- See 'Mornick'

'Muriel Jamison' ('Miss Muriel Jamison') T, ob, 1910, Dickson, H.; flowers dark orange, becoming cadmium yellow, large

'Muriel Moore' HT, w, 1916, Moore, F.M.; [sport of 'My Maryland']

'Muriel O'Leary' HT, pb, 1980, Murray, Nola; bud long; flowers light and deep pink, well-formed, 3 in., 27 petals; foliage large, glossy; vigorous, upright growth; ['Honey Favorite' × Rose Gaujard®]

'Muriel Pasquill' HT, pb, 1927, Pasquill; flowers strawberry-pink, reverse golden yellow, semi-dbl.; [sport of 'Padre']

Muriel Robin® ('First Great Western') HT, m, Orard; flowers magenta, dbl., cupped, intense fruity fragrance; medium growth; intr. 2006

'Muriel Wilson' T, ly, 1923, Hall; flowers rich lemon-cream, dbl.

'Murillo' HP, m, 1862, Fontaine; flowers velvety violet-purple, reverse amaranth, medium to large, dbl

'Murki' ('Kingi') F, pb, 1983, Murray, Nola; flowers yellow flushed rose pink, large, 35 petals; foliage dense, dark; prickles large, red; bushy growth; ['Liverpool Echo' × 'Una Hawken']

'Murmure' LCl, dr, Croix; flowers scarlet, medium, dbl., borne in small clusters; ['Luna Park' × Moulin Rouge®]; intr. 1971

'Murphy's Law' -- See 'Seamurp'

'Murray Hill' HT, my, 1939, Coddington; PP405; [sport of 'Joanna Hill']

'Murse' ('Sedgebrook') HT, lp, 1987, Murray, Nola; flowers very pale pink, almost white, 47 petals, high-centered; foliage large, medium green, flat; prickles pointed, brown; low growth; [('Chanelle' × 'Prima Ballerina') × 'Deep Secret']; intr. 1986

'Murta' ('Tasman') Min, dp, 1983, Murray, Nola; flowers deep pink, small, 17 petals, flat; foliage medium size, dark, leathery; compact growth; ['Smiley' × (('Pink Parfait' × 'Una Hawken') × 'Anytime')]

'Musashino' HT, op, 1989, Takahashi, Takeshi; bud ovoid; flowers orange-pink, changing to pink, large, 35 petals, high-centered, urn-shaped, borne usually singly; foliage medium green, oblong, semi-glossy; few prickles; upright, medium growth; ['Garden Party' × 'Daimonji']

'Muscade Rouge' -- See 'Evratina'

'Muscosa Japonica' -- See 'Mousseux du Japon'

'Muscosa Rubra' -- See 'Old Red Moss'

'Muscosa Simplex' (R. centifolia andrewsii, R. muscosa simplex) M, mp, 1807; flowers single; native to the Caucasus Mountains and in France; discovered by Shailer

'Musette' F, dr, 1936, Tantau; flowers glowing light crimson, open, large, single, borne in clusters; foliage leathery, wrinkled, dark; strong stems; bushy growth; ['Ingar Olsson' × 'Johanniszauber']

'Music' F, rb, Asami, Hitoshi; flowers 7 cm.; intr. 1986

'Music, Climbing' Cl F, rb; [sport of 'Music']; intr. after 1986

'Music Maker' S, lp, 1972, Buck, Dr. Griffith J.; flowers medium, dbl., high-centered, moderate fragrance; foliage glossy, light, leathery; vigorous, dwarf, upright, bushy growth; intr. 1973

'Music Man' -- See 'Broman'

'Musicale' Gr, rb, 1964, Buck, Dr. Griffith J.; bud long, pointed; flowers straw-yellow changing to cherry red, small, dbl.; foliage glossy, bronze; moderate, bushy growth; [(('Bravo' × 'Nellie E. Hillock') × 'lobelle']

'Musician' S, rb, 1953, Wright, Percy H.; flowers bicolor, nearer red than yellow, with gray tones, 20 petals, borne in small clusters; non-recurrent; foliage modified rugose; hardy to -50F; ['Hansa' × 'Hazeldean']

'Musikantenland' F, mp, Hetzel; intr. 1993

Musimara® LCl, mr

'Musketeer' -- See 'Wilfolk'

'Musketeer' HMsk, w, Lester Rose Gardens; flowers stamens bright yellow, semi-dbl.; spring bloom; vigorous (20-25 ft.) growth

'Muskoka Moonlight' -- See 'Loumuskoka'

'Muso' HT, op, Keisei; intr. 1999

'Musquée Sans Soucis' S, w, Louette; flowers white, single, borne in large clusters; recurrent; growth to over 2 m.; hips small, borne in large clusters, orange; intr. 2003

'Mustang' ('Coloranja') HT, or, 1965, Lens; bud ovoid; flowers large to medium, dbl., high-centered; foliage dark, leathery; vigorous, bushy growth; PP2657; ['Fandango' × ('Independence' × 'Papillon Rose')]; intr. 1964

'Mutabilis' -- See 'White Provence'

'Mutabilis' -- See 'Cocarde'

'Mutabilis' (R. chinensis mutabilis, R. mutabilis, 'Tipo Ideale') Ch, yb, before 1894; flowers sulfur-yellow, changing to orange, red and finally crimson, 7 cm., single, borne in small clusters; foliage bronze-green; prickles large; possibly a sport of R. chinensis spontanea

'Mutabilis Variegata' -- See 'Unique Panachée'

'Mutace Caramba' HT

'Mutter Brada' HT, ab, 1934, Brada, Dr.; flowers apricot-yellow and red, varying; vigorous growth; ['Lady Craig' × 'Freifrau Ida von Schubert']

'Mutter Brada II' HT, dp, 1934, Brada, Dr.; flowers large, dbl., intense fragrance; upright (80 cm.) growth

'Mutter Brada III' HT, lp, 1934, Brada, Dr.; flowers large, dbl.

Muttergruss® F, dr

'Muttertag, Climbing' -- See 'Mothersday, Climbing'

'Muttertag' -- See 'Mothersday'

'My Amore' -- See 'Twojoan'

'My Angel' F, dp, 1987, Pencil, Paul S.;

flowers deep pink, medium, dbl., borne singly or in sprays of 6-10; foliage medium size, medium green, matte; upright, hardy growth; ['Pink Parfait' × 'Roman Holiday']; intr. 1988

'My Baby'   Min, dp, 1967, Quackenbush; bud ovoid; flowers deep pink, small, very dbl., cupped; foliage small, glossy, dark; moderate, dwarf growth; ['Cinderella' × 'Rouletti']

'My Beautiful English Rose' -- See 'Rawblaf'

'My Beauty'   HT, lp; intr. 1999

My Best Friend™ -- See 'Morfriend'

'My Blue Heaven' -- See 'Blue Heaven'

'My Choice'   HT, pb, 1959, LeGrice; flowers pink, reverse pale yellow, 4½-5 in., 33 petals, intense damask fragrance; foliage leathery; vigorous, upright growth; PP1769; ['Wellworth' × 'Ena Harkness']; intr. 1958

'My Dad' -- See 'Boselftay'

'My Delight' -- See 'Tinmyde'

'My Dream'   HT, dp, 1969, Winchel, Joseph F.; bud long, pointed; flowers deep pink, medium, dbl., high-centered; foliage glossy; upright growth; ['Pink Favorite' × 'Karl Herbst']; intr. 1970

'My Estelle'   F, pb, Kordes; flowers deep salmon with cream-golden reverse, semi-dbl. to dbl., borne in clusters, slight fragrance; good repeat; growth medium; intr. 1998

'My Everything' -- See 'Coccastle'

'My Fair Lady'   F, pb, 1959, Wheatcroft Bros.; flowers rose-pink, reverse darker, large, semi-dbl., borne in large clusters; foliage glossy; tall growth

'My Fancy'   F, or, 1971, Meilland; flowers Dutch vermilion, imbricated, 3 in., 25-30 petals; foliage dull, dark; vigorous, upright, bushy growth; [('Dany Robin' × 'Fire King') × 'Rumba']; intr. 1970

'My Fifi'   ('Vierge Folle', 'White Beauty') S, w, Delbard; flowers single; intr. 1998

'My Friend'   F, lp, 1956, Motose; bud ovoid; flowers apple-blossom-pink, 2½ in., 30 petals, flat; dwarf, bushy growth; PP1460; [('Garnette' × unknown) × 'sport of Summer Snow']

'My Gail' -- See 'Rawprimy'

'My Gal Gale'   F, lp, 1958, Marsh; flowers soft pink, very dbl., borne in clusters; dwarf growth; ['Pinocchio' × 'Morning Star']

'My George'   HT, mr, 2002, McCall, Sharan; flowers large, petals reflexing, 6 in., full, high-centered, borne mostly solitary, moderate fragrance; foliage medium size, dark green, semi-glossy; prickles ¼ to ½ in., hooked downwards, moderate; growth upright, tall (5 ft.); garden decorative, exhibition; ['Dorothy Anne' × 'Dara']

'My Gina'   S, mp, 1972, Shortland; [sport of 'Dorothy Wheatcroft']

'My Girl'   ('Curiosa') F, op, 1964, deRuiter; flowers deep salmon, large, 30 petals, cupped to open, borne in clusters; foliage dark; vigorous growth; ['Dacapo' × 'floribunda seedling']

'My Girl'   HT, mp, McGredy; flowers satin pink with hint of lavender, dbl.; low to medium growth; intr. 1999

'My Girl'   S, dp, Lim, Ping; bud round, deep pink; flowers flower ruffled, double, cupped to open, borne in clusters of 5 to 30; recurrent; intr. 2008

'My Grandad' -- See 'Bosseedgard'

'My Grandma' -- See 'Boskathrex'

My Granny™ -- See 'Pouloma'

'My Guy'   F, or, 1987, Milner, William; flowers bright orange-red, fading darker, medium, 13 petals, cupped, borne in sprays of 7-20, moderate fragrance; foliage medium size, medium green, semi-glossy; prickles medium, light brown, slightly hooked; bushy, medium growth; hips round, medium, light green; ['Rosalynn Carter' × 'Dorothy Wheatcroft']; intr. 1979

My Hero™   S, mr, Bailey; bud red; flowers red, fading to deep pink as they mature, 3½ in., 23 petals; produced continuously; foliage satiny, light green; mounded (3 ft.) growth; PP15400; intr. 2003

'My Hometown' -- See 'Welmy 0525'

'My Honey' -- See 'Jushoney'

'My Inspiration' -- See 'Welinspir'

'My Inspiration'   F, w, 2004, Sawyer, Rosemary; flowers white with pink edges, reverse white, 4 in., full, borne mostly solitary, with some clusters in warm weather, moderate fragrance; foliage medium size, medium green, matte; growth compact, medium; exhibition, garden decoration; [sport of 'Sweet Inspiration']

'My Jeannie' -- See 'Horperfect'

'My Joy'   HT, mp, 1976, Wood; flowers fuchsia pink, dbl., high-centered, moderate fragrance; [sport of 'Red Devil']

'My Kim'   F, dr, 2000, Horres, Marietta; flowers dark blue-red, white center, reverse dark red, 2¾ in., very full, borne in large clusters, slight fragrance; foliage medium size, mahogany red, turning dark green, glossy; prickles moderate; growth spreading, bushy, medium (3-3½ ft.); [sport of 'Europeana']

'My Lady'   HT, ab, 1957, Robinson, H.; bud pointed; flowers apricot flushed gold, 5 in., 46 petals, high-centered, moderate fragrance; foliage dark, leathery; very vigorous, bushy growth; [seedling × 'Peace']; intr. 1956

'My Lady Kensington' ('Anna', 'Constance des Hollandaises', 'Incarnata') C, lp, before 1819; bud round; flowers flesh pink, exterior petals washed white, 4½ in.; foliage large

'My Little Boy'   Min, my, Burrows, Steven; intr. 1982

'My Love' -- See 'Cogamo'

'My Love'   HT, dr, 1960, Anderson, P & J; flowers deep red, large, 45 petals, high-centered, intense fragrance; foliage dark; vigorous growth; ['Bayadere' × 'Ena Harkness']

'My Love, Climbing'   Cl HT, dr

'My Lucky Starr'   HT, mr, 1987, Evans, F. David; flowers large, full, no fragrance; foliage large, dark green, semi-glossy, leathery; spreading growth; ['Secret Love' × 'Karl Herbst']

'My Maryland'   HT, pb, 1908, Cook, J.W.; flowers bright salmon-pink, edged paler, large, dbl., vigorous growth; ['Madonna' × 'Enchanter']

'My Maryland, Climbing'   Cl HT, op, 1915, Dingee & Conard; [sport of 'My Maryland']

'My Mum' -- See 'Webmorrow'

'My Ouma' -- See 'Pouloma'

'My Own' -- See 'Coosyl'

'My Pink' -- See 'Brypink'

My Pleasure™ -- See 'Kinpleas'

'My Prayer'   HT, op, 1953, H&S; bud long, pointed; flowers peach-pink, 5 in., 25-30 petals, high-centered; foliage leathery; vigorous, upright growth; [seedling × 'The Doctor']

'My Pretty Garden' -- See 'Kormeneint'

'My Sister' -- See 'Socsis'

'My Stars' -- See 'Mornothorns'

'My Sunshine' -- See 'Tinshine'

'My Sweet Girl' -- See 'Bosrexsplender'

'My Sweetie' -- See 'Bendiez'

'My Valentine' -- See 'Grande Amore'

My Valentine™   Min, dr, 1975, Moore, Ralph S.; flowers deep red, 1 in., 65 petals, high-centered; foliage small, glossy, tinted bronze; vigorous, bushy growth; PP3935; ['Little Chief' × 'Little Curt']

'My Way'   HT, w, Simpson; intr. 1988

'My Wife Kathryn' -- See 'Welwife'

'My Wild Irish Rose' -- See 'Seairish'

'Myfanwy Welbourne'   HT, pb, 1999, Poole, Lionel; flowers 4½ in., full, borne mostly singly, intense fragrance; foliage medium size, dark green, semi-glossy; prickles moderate; upright, bushy, medium (3 ft.) growth; [('Hazel Rose' × 'Cardiff Bay') × 'Darling Jenny']; intr. 2000

'Myra' -- See 'Battoo'

'Myra'   LCl, w, 1926, Wilber; flowers creamy white, very large, dbl., borne in clusters of 2-3; foliage dark, bronze; vigorous, climbing growth; RULED EXTINCT 1/92; ['Dr. W. Van Fleet' × 'Lady Roberts']

'Myra Stegmann'   Gr, op, Ludwig's Roses; flowers salmon-apricot, softening on the petal edges, dbl., high-centered; free-flowering; stately, medium to tall growth; intr. 1991

'Myriam' -- See 'Cocgrand'

'Myrianthes Renoncule'   HSem, pb; flowers pale peach, large, dbl.; free bloom; not dependably hardy

'Myrna Courage'   HT, dr, 2007, Courage, Ray; flowers 9 cm., full, blooms borne mostly solitary; foliage medium size, dark green, glossy; prickles medium, hooked, brown, few; growth upright, medium (1¼ m.); garden decoration; [('Charles Mallerin' × 'Chrysler Imperial') × ('Chrysler Imperial' × Mister Lincoln®)]; intr. 2007

'Myrna's Dream' -- See 'Kordrekes'
'Myrniong'   HT, pb, Bell, Ronald J.; intr. 1994
'Myrrh-Scented Rose' -- See 'Splendens'
Myrthe®   HT, rb, Spek; flowers dark red, reverse white tinted red, 10 cm., 26-32 petals, high-centered, borne mostly singly; recurrent; prickles moderate; stems medium to long; florist rose; intr. 2006
'Mystelle'   HT, dy, deRuiter; flowers yellow shaded green; intr. 2001
'Mystère'   T, pb, 1877, Nabonnand; flowers pink, veined and marbled darker, very large, full, cupped; sometimes classed as N
'Mystère'   HT, dp, 1978, Gaujard; bud long; flowers scarlet pink, 45 petals; RULED EXTINCT 10/86; ['Premiere Ballerine' × ('Femina' × unknown)]; intr. 1969
Mysterious™ -- See 'Minimys'
'Mysterium'   F, yb, 1966, Kordes, R.; bud long, pointed; flowers golden yellow striped scarlet, 3 in., 25 petals, borne in clusters (up to 20); foliage glossy; bushy, spreading, low growth; ['Masquerade' × 'Kordes' Perfecta']; intr. 1963
'Mystery' -- See 'Hermesy'
Mystery™   Min, lp, Poulsen; flowers light pink, medium, dbl., no fragrance; foliage dark; growth bushy, 20-40 cm.; intr. 1996
'Mystery Girl'   HT, ly, Dickson; flowers lemon yellow, fading lighter, large, full, high-centered, borne in clusters and singly, moderate fragrance; recurrent; foliage large, dark green, glossy; upright growth; intr. 2008
Mystic™ -- See 'Poulor'
'Mystic'   HT, w, Tantau, M.; flowers creamy white, large, 30-35 petals; healthy, vigorous growth; intr. 1998
'Mystic'   HT, m, Dot; flowers deep lavender, well-formed; free-flowering
'Mystic Beauty' -- See 'Rosbeauty'
'Mystic Fairy' ('Garden Path Mystic Fairy')   S, mr, Bailey; flowers rich red with pink tones, 3 in., 27 petals, borne in large clusters; blooms continuously; foliage glossy red giving way to dark green.; growth compact (3 ft.), vigorous; hardy to -30°F; PP16131; intr. 2004
'Mystic Gem'   HT, dp, 1960, Armbrust; bud long, pointed; flowers reddish-pink, large to medium, dbl., high-centered; foliage leathery; vigorous, upright growth; ['Rod Stillman' × 'Bravo']; intr. 1959
'Mystic Mauve' -- See 'Lavender Mist'
Mystic Meidiland® -- See 'Meialate'
Mystique™ -- See 'Devstica'
'Mystique'   F, ob, Kirkham; flowers rustic orange, aging reddish-pink, yellow stamens, dbl., borne usually in clusters of 7-12, occasionally singly; good repeat; foliage young shoots plum red, maturing medium green, glossy; growth to 3-3½ ft.; intr. 1999
'Mystique'   HT, mp, Kordes; flowers dusty pink with soft mauve tints, moderate fragrance; stems short to medium; greenhouse rose; intr. 2001
'Mystique'   HT, mp, Neil, J.; [sport of 'Mysty']
'Mysty' ('Mysty Blue') HT, Neil, J.; [sport of 'Shocking Blue']
'Mysty Blue' -- See 'Mysty'
Mythos®   HT, w, Tantau; flowers creamy white with greenish tones, full, high-centered; intr. 2004

— N —

'N. L. Chrestensen'   Pol, or, GPG Bad Langensalza; flowers medium, semi-dbl.; intr. 1968
'Naarden Red'   HT, rb, 1932, Van Rossem; bud pointed; flowers crimson-red shaded orange, large, dbl., high-centered; ['Étoile de Hollande' × 'Charles P. Kilham']
'Naas Botha' -- See 'Tanrosilb'
'Nabab'   F, Delbard; intr. 1959
'Nacha Pobeda' ('Our Victory') HT, dr, Costetske; flowers dark velvety red
'Nachsommer'   LCl, mp, Wänninger, Franz; flowers coral pink, large, dbl., borne in clusters; foliage glossy; intr. 1990
'Nachtfalter'   HT, dr, Baum, Oswald; flowers large, dbl.; intr. 1971
Nadia™ -- See 'Poulen007(N)'
'Nadia'   HT, dr, 1956, Delforge; foliage light green; ['Mme G. Forest-Colcombet' × seedling]
Nadia Meillandecor®   S, my, Meilland; flowers fading lighter, large, 95-98 petals, pompon, borne in clusters, slight fragrance; recurrent; foliage clear green, glossy; low (50 - 60 cm.), spreading growth; intr. 2008
'Nadia Renaissance' (Nadia™) S, dr, Olesen; bud broad based, ovoid; flowers dark red, 8-10 cm., 40-60 petals, cupped rosette, borne in clusters, moderate floral perfume fragrance; recurrent; foliage dark green, semi-glossy; prickles few, 5 mm., hooked downward; upright to bushy (100-150 cm.) growth; PP15197; [seedling × Queen Margrethe™]; intr. 2002
'Nadine'   F, dr, 1962, Schwartz, Ernest W.; bud long, pointed; flowers maroon-red, 3 in., 38 petals, cupped; foliage bronze, soft; vigorous, bushy growth; ['Red Pinocchio' × seedling]; intr. 1962
'Nadine'   HT, ob, Croix; flowers delicate orange, 40 petals
'Nadine de Karadec'   Ch, w, 1852, Dorisy; flowers white, shaded light flesh pink, medium, full
'Nadine Faye'   HCh, mp, 1847, Bélot-Défougères; flowers bright carmine, medium, very full
'Nadja'   HT, mr, Rupprecht-Radke; flowers large, dbl.; intr. 1964
Naga Belle™ -- See 'Vircarefree'
'Naheglut' -- See 'That's Jazz'
'Nahéma'   LCl, lp, Delbard; flowers very dbl., cupped, moderate fruit and citrus fragrance; growth to 100 cm.; intr. 1998
'Naia'   F, Gaujard
'Nain' -- See 'De Chartres'
'Nain' -- See 'Rosier d'Amour'
'Naina'   HT, op, Kordes; flowers light salmon with almost brown center, medium; free-flowering; foliage full green, healthy; few prickles; intr. 1998
'Nair'   HFt, or, 1936, Chambard; flowers vermilion red, reverse yellow, semi-dbl.; recurrent; growth to 6 ft.; [R. foetida bicolor × (R. wichurana × unknown)]
'Naïr'   HFt, yb, 1936, Chambard, C.; bud long, yellow and carmine; flowers vermilion-red, reverse yellow, stamens yellow, large, semi-dbl.; recurrent bloom; vigorous, bushy growth; [R. foetida bicolor × (R. wichurana × unknown)]
'Naissance de Vénus' -- See 'Königin von Dänemark'
'Nakbet' ('Golden Phoenix') HT, my, 1986, Nakashima, Tosh; [sport of 'Bettina']; intr. 1985
'Nambour'   F, w, 1953, Ulrick, L.W.; flowers white flushed pink, medium, very dbl., borne in clusters; foliage bronze; very vigorous growth; ['Yvonne Rabier' × 'Mrs Tom Henderson']
'Nämenlose Schöne'   T, w, 1886, Deegen; flowers white tinted blush, well-formed, large
'Namib Sunrise' -- See 'Morlogen'
N-Amour®   HT, dp, Spek; flowers 4 in., 45-55 petals, high-centered, borne mostly singly; recurrent; numerous prickles; stems medium; florist rose; intr. 2006
'Nan Anderson'   F, op, 1970, Anderson's Rose Nurseries; flowers deep pink, coral sheen, 2½-3 in., 30 petals; foliage glossy, dark; low, bushy growth
'Nan Mac'   HT, m, Ludwig, Heike; flowers blend of brown, mauve and lilac, high-centered, moderate fragrance; quick repeat; growth medium; intr. 2004
'Nan Poole'   Min, pb, 1983, Meredith, E.A. & Rovinski, M.E.; bud globular; flowers yellow and pink blend, giving an overall coral-pink effect,, 25 petals, high-centered; foliage small, dark, semi-glossy; prickles thin; low, spreading growth; [seedling × 'Libby']
'Nana Mouskouri'   F, w, 1976, Dickson, A.; flowers well-formed, 2½ in., 30 petals, borne usually in clusters, moderate fragrance; growth shrubby; ['Redgold' × 'Iced Ginger']; intr. 1975
'Nanako Rose'   Pol, pb; flowers can be pink or white; intr. before 1867
'Nana's Rose' -- See 'Jalnana'
'Nance Christy'   HT, op, 1906, Cant, B. R.; flowers salmon pink, large, semi-dbl.
Nancy™ -- See 'Poulninga'
'Nancy'   HT, dr, 1929, Ferguson, W.; flowers bright scarlet-crimson, semi-dbl.
'Nancy'   HWich, lp, Williams; flowers semi-dbl., moderate fragrance; intr. 1932
'Nancy'   HT, my, Mallerin, C.; flowers chamois-yellow, semi-dbl., cupped; ['Mrs T. Hillas' × 'Souv. de Claudius Pernet']; intr. 1934

'Nancy' F, or, Croix, Paul; flowers intense orange-red; free-flowering; foliage glossy, healthy; dedicated to the town of Nancy, France; intr. 1982

'Nancy' F, mr; flowers bright red, very small, single; foliage very glossy

'Nancy Bennett' -- See 'Bospardon'

'Nancy Bergh' F, pb, 1968, Fankhauser; bud ovoid; flowers pink, reverse silver-pink, open, large, semi-dbl.; foliage dark, glossy, leathery; vigorous, open growth; ['Independence' × 'Impeccable']

'Nancy Clare' -- See 'Jusclare'

'Nancy Elizabeth' HT, w, 1947, Mason, F.; bud pointed; flowers cream, large, dbl., high-centered; foliage glossy, vigorous, upright growth; ['Korovo' × 'Florinda Norman Thompson']

'Nancy Gardiner' -- See 'Korkeindor'

'Nancy Hall' Min, pb, 1973, Moore, Ralph S.; buds small, long pointed; flowers pink with some yellow or apricot undertones, small, dbl., high-centered, borne singly and several together, moderate fragrance; continuous; foliage small, soft, light green; bushy, dwarf (10 in.) growth; [sport of 'Mary Adair']; intr. 1972

'Nancy Hayward' LCl, mr, 1937, Clark, A.; flowers rich bright cerise, large, single; very vigorous, climbing growth; ['Jessie Clark' × unknown]; hybrid gigantea

Nancy Jean™ -- See 'Ricnancy'

'Nancy Lee' HT, dp, 1879, Bennett; flowers deep pink, small, intense fragrance; dwarf, slender, weak growth; ['Mme Bravy' × 'Edward Morren']; susceptible to mildew

'Nancy Pretty' HWich, pb, 1917, MacLellan; flowers pink, reverse lighter, small, dbl., borne in clusters; ['Dorothy Perkins' × 'Ellen Poulsen']

Nancy Reagan™ -- See 'Jacurnam'

'Nancy Reagan' HT, or, 1967, Morey, Dr. Dennison; flowers orange-scarlet, 5-5½ in., 28 petals, high-centered; foliage dark, bronze, glossy, leathery; vigorous, tall growth; ['Orange Delight' × 'Hawaii']

'Nancy Renaissance' (Nancy™) S, rb, Poulsen; flowers red, striped and painted yellow, 10-15 cm., semi-dbl., moderate fragrance; foliage dark; growth bushy, 100-150 cm.; PP12267; intr. 1998

'Nancy Shaw' -- See 'Wiwancy'

'Nancy Steen' F, pb, 1976, Sherwood; flowers blush pink, center pale cream, 3½ in., 30 petals, flat, moderate fragrance; foliage glossy, dark, bronze, leathery; ['Pink Parfait' × ('Ophelia' × Parkdirektor Riggers®)]

'Nancy West' F, yb, 1970, Haynes; flowers medium yellow, suffused peach; [sport of 'Elizabeth of Glamis']

'Nancy Wilson' HT, mp, 1940, Clark, A.

'Nancy Wilson, Climbing' Cl HT, mp, 1959, Campton

'Nancy's Keepsake' HT, lp, 1995, Grierson, Mrs. Nancy; flowers pale pink, medium, full, borne mostly singly; foliage medium size, medium green, glossy; some prickles; medium (2½ ft.), upright growth; [sport of 'Keepsake']; intr. 1995

'Nanda' HT, mp, 1959, Sartore; bud ovoid to urn shaped, claret-red; flowers light rose, large; vigorous growth; ['Dame Edith Helen' × 'Eternal Youth']

'Nandini' HT, pb, 1984, Pal, Dr. B.P.; bud long, pointed; flowers pink with creamy white reverse, 46 petals, high-centered, borne singly, intense fragrance; foliage large, medium green, leathery; prickles brown-gray, hooked; compact growth; ['Kiss of Fire' × unknown]; intr. 1983

'Nanette' HGal, pb, before 1848; flowers rosy crimson, marbled with purple, medium, very dbl., cupped; growth erect; possibly synonymous with 'Manette' from Écoffay

'Nanette' HWich, w, Hicks; flowers creamy white to medium, 5-6 cm., semi-dbl. to dbl., flat, borne in large clusters, strong musky fragrance; foliage small, glossy; intr. 1926

'Nanjemoy' Cl HT, mp, 1937, Cross, C.W.; bud long, pointed; flowers pink, open, large, semi-dbl.; free, intermittent bloom; foliage dark; strong stems; vigorous, climbing growth; ['Mme Gregoire Staechelin' × 'Bloomfield Comet']

'Nankin' -- See 'Mme Yves Latieule'

'Nankin' HSpn, w, before 1818, Descemet; flowers flesh-colored, percepibly yellowish, pink at center, medium, single; prickles numerous, uneven, bristly; hips globular or flattened, nearly black

'Nankin Double' HSpn, pb, 1827, Vibert; flowers flesh pink, tinted yellowish, dbl.

'Nano Nagle' HT, dr, 1997, Xavier, Sister M.; flowers medium, very dbl., borne mostly singly; foliage medium size, medium green, semi-glossy; medium (114 cm.) upright growth; [Papa Meilland® × 'Northern Lights']

'Nantucket' HT, ab, 1973, Kern, J. J.; flowers peach apricot, large, dbl., high-centered; foliage leathery; vigorous, upright growth; [sport of 'Chantré']; intr. 1972

'Naomi' HT, ob, 1926, Pemberton; flowers coppery buff, dbl., moderate fragrance; RULED EXTINCT 1/88

'Naomi' HT, dr, 1988, Poole, Lionel; flowers dark red, shaded very dark in center, fading to red-purple,, 32 petals, high-centered; foliage large, dark green, semi-glossy; prickles flat, medium, medium green; tall, spreading, upright growth; ['Red Lion' × seedling]

'Naomi' HT, pb; intr. 1998

'Naomi' F, mp, Takatori

'Naomi Rebecca' HT, pb, 1996, Poole, Lionel; flowers deep pink, reverse pale pink, large, full, borne mostly singly; foliage large, dark green, dull; some prickles; upright, bushy, tall growth; ['Solitaire' × 'Gavotte']

'Napa Valley' -- See 'Poulnino'

'Napoléon' HGal, m, Hardy; flowers bright rose, shaded purple, very large, dbl.; erect, vigorous growth; intr. 1846

'Napoléon' ('Madness at Corsica') Ch, pb, Laffay; flowers pale blush pink, tinted with crimson, large, dbl., cupped; intr. about 1835

'Napoléon' HGal, pb, 1814; flowers pink, shaded with purple, lightly spotted, small center eye, medium, very double, cupped, quartered, usually solitary, but also in clusters of 2-4, slight fragrance; foliage dark green; possibly from Holland, or by Dupont

'Napoléon III' B, mp, 1852, Bacot; flowers carmine

'Napoléon III' HP, rb, 1864, Verdier, E.; flowers very bright scarlet and deep slatey violet, large, full; intr. 1864

Naranga™ HT, ob, Tantau; flowers deep orange, lighter reverse, large, dbl., high-centered, borne mostly singly, moderate fragrance; stems length 60 - 80 cm.; greenhouse rose; intr. 1998

'Narcisse' ('Enfant de Lyon', 'Sweet Anise Rose') T, my, 1859, Avoux & Crozy; flowers large, dbl.

'Narcisse de Salvandy' HGal, mp, 1843, Parmentier/Van Houtte; flowers deep rose-pink, prominent yellow stamens, large, flat, borne in clusters; large, spreading growth

'Narcisse Gravereaux' HRg, mr, 1901, L'Hay; flowers blood red

'Nardy' N, dy, 1888, Nabonnand; flowers coppery yellow, occasionally tinted pink, very large, very full, globular; foliage bronzy green; ['Gloire de Dijon' × unknown]

'Nardy Frères' HP, m, 1865, Ducher; flowers violet-pink, tinted slate, very large, full, globular; ['Mme Boll' × unknown]

'Narita Korinkaku' HT, dy, 1979, Kikuchi, Rikichi; bud pointed; flowers light orange, 5-6 in., 35-40 petals, high-centered, intense fragrance; foliage glossy, dark; upright growth; ['Burnaby' × 'Montparnasse']

'Narmada' F, pb, Kasturi; flowers pink with darker edges

'Narmada Lahari' HT, pb, 1980, Hardikar, Dr. M.N.; bud ovoid; flowers 90 petals, borne singly, moderate fragrance; foliage small, green; prickles beak-shaped; bushy, dwarf growth; [sport of 'Shree Dayananda']; intr. 1979

'Narragansett' S, mp, Schneider; intr. 2005

'Narre Fragrance' HT, ob, 1942, Brundrett; flowers golden orange; [sport of 'Portadown Fragrance']

'Narre Peace' HT, yb, 1960, Brundrett; [sport of 'Peace']

'Narrow Water' N, lp, 1883, Daisy Hill Nursery; flowers very pale pink, almost white, 1½-2 in., single to semi-dbl., borne in cluster of 6-12, slight fragrance; repeats reliably

'Nartaki' Pol, m, Kasturi; flowers deep lavender with yellow stamens; intr. 1977

'Narvik' HT, op, 1960, Robichon; bud

long, pointed; flowers salmon-pink to coppery, large, dbl.; foliage leathery; long, strong stems; vigorous growth; [seedling × 'Praline']

'Narzisse' HT, my, 1942, Krause; bud long, pointed; flowers apricot to maize-yellow, large, 23 petals, high-centered, moderate fragrance; foliage dark, leathery; vigorous, upright growth; ['Golden Rapture' × 'Golden Glory']

'Nascapee' S, w, 1946, Preston; flowers open, 5 petals; free, recurrent boom; tall, vigorous growth; hardy; [('Ross Rambler' × (*R. rugosa* × *R. eglanteria*)) × unknown]

'Nase Národni' HP, m, 1935, Böhm, J.; flowers purple/pink with white, medium, dbl.

'Naseby Rose' HGal, m

Nashira™ -- See 'Poulkini'

Nashville™ (Candy Cover™, Christopher Columbus™) S, rb, Poulsen; flowers red with modest stripes, 5-8 cm., dbl., very slight fragrance; foliage dark, glossy; bushy, medium (60-100 cm.) growth; hips none; PP12491; intr. 1996

'Nastarana' ('Persian Musk Rose', *R. pissardii*, *R. moschata pissardii*, 'Pissardii', *R. moschata nastarana*) N, w, 1879, Paul; flowers white tinged pink, 2 in., semi-dbl., blooms in clusters on new wood; recurrent bloom; very vigorous growth; [probably an early *R. chinensis* × *R. moschata* hybrid]

'Natacha' -- See 'Cara Mia'

'Natacha' dr, Pekmez; intr. 1989

'Natal Briar' ; understock for greenhouse roses

Natali® -- See 'Tanrotreili'

'Natali' F, dr, 1973, Tantau, Math.; bud ovoid; flowers small, semi-dbl.; foliage glossy; dwarf, upright growth; RULED EXTINCT 4/85; [unknown × unknown]

'Natalie' Pol, ob, GPG Bad Langensalza; flowers orange to orange-red, with dark yellow, medium, semi-dbl.; intr. 1972

'Natalie Ann' -- See 'Rawsumose'

'Natalie Böttner' HT, my, 1909, Boettner; flowers sulfur-yellow, passing to cream-yellow, tinted flesh, large, dbl.; ['Frau Karl Druschki' × 'Goldelse']

'Natalie Ward' F, mp, 1976, Thomas, R.; bud ht type; flowers pink, base yellow, 2-2½ in., 20 petals; bloom repeats quickly; foliage light; bushy growth; ['Pink Parfait' × unknown]; intr. 1975

'Natalka' HT, lp, Costetske

'Natascha' -- See 'Harwharry'

'Natasha' F, my, 1985, Staikov, Prof. Dr. V.; flowers lemon yellow, fading white, large, 135 petals, borne in clusters of 7-13; foliage dark, glossy; bushy growth; ['Highlight' × 'Masquerade']; intr. 1974

'Natasha Maria' LCl, or, 1995, Fleming, Joyce L.; flowers bright, intense, vibrant orange-red, yellow base, medium, semi-dbl., borne 2 - 5 per cluster, moderate fragrance; foliage medium size, dark green, glossy; growth to 60-80 cm.; ['Wilfrid H. Perron' × 'Golden Olymp']; intr. 1994

'Natasha Monet' HT, m, 1993, Pawlikowski, Martin & Elaine; flowers very light lavender, large, full, borne mostly singly; foliage medium size, medium green, semi-glossy; some prickles; tall, upright, bushy growth; [sport of 'Crystalline']

Natasja ™ -- See 'Natasja Hit'

'Natasja Hit' (Natasja ™) MinFl, lp, Poulsen; flowers light pink, 5-8 cm., semi-dbl., no fragrance; foliage dark; growth bushy, 40-60 cm.; intr. 2005

Natchez™ -- See 'Poullen'

'Nathalie' Ch, mr, about 1835, Laffay; flowers cherry pink, aging to light lilac, small to medium, full

'Nathalie' M, dp, Vibert; flowers dark pink, medium, full; intr. 1849

'Nathalie Daniel' B, pb, 1845, Verdier, V.; flowers light peach pink, medium, very full, cupped

'Nathalie Nypels' -- See 'Mevrouw Nathalie Nypels'

'Natilda' -- See 'Meidragelac'

National Beauty™ HT, mr, 1983, Burks, Joe J.; [sport of 'The Alamo']

'National Emblem' HT, dr, 1915, McGredy; flowers velvety dark crimson, edged vermilion, dbl., high-centered

'National Flower Guild' HT, mr, 1927, Mallerin, C.; flowers pure scarlet-red, large, dbl.; long stems; very vigorous growth; [('Capt. F. Bald' × 'Kitchener of Khartoum') × 'Mme Van de Voorde']; intr. 1930

'National Radio' -- See 'Koreledas'

'National Trust' ('Bad Nauheim', 'Bad Naukeim', 'Nationalstolz') HT, dr, 1970, McGredy, Sam IV; flowers bright red, 4 in., 53 petals, classic; ['Evelyn Fison' × 'King of Hearts']

National Velvet™ -- See 'Buralp'

'Nationale Tricolore' -- See 'La Nationale'

'Nationalstolz' -- See 'National Trust'

'Native Wedding' S, lp, 1980, Stoddard, Louis; bud short, pointed; flowers 14 petals, cupped, borne singly; repeat bloom; foliage broad, waved, medium green, semi-glossy, 5-7 leaflet; prickles straight; upright, medium growth; ['Restless Native' × ('Mount Shasta' × *R. suffulta*)]

'Nativity' S, ab, Williams, J. Benjamin; flowers very soft apricot and pink, fading to almost white, single, flat, slight fragrance; recurrent; growth to 3 ft.; intr. 2006

'Natural Beauty' -- See 'Rogscriv'

'Nature Meillandecor' -- See 'Meigalpio'

'Nature's Wonder' -- See 'Welnat'

'Naughty But Nice' -- See 'Tinnaughty'

'Naughty Nancy' F, pb, 1970, Cants of Colchester, Ltd.; flowers cream to red, 2 in., 12 petals; foliage dull, matte green; moderate growth

'Naughty Patricia' -- See 'Bilpat'

'Nautilus' F, op, 1960, deRuiter; flowers coral-salmon, open, 30 petals, borne in clusters; vigorous growth; ['Signal Red' × 'Fashion']

'Nav-Sadabahar' F, pb, 1981, Division of Vegetable Crops and Floriculture; bud pointed; flowers deep pink striped white, 20 petals, borne in clusters of 15, no fragrance; foliage medium size, green; prickles straight, pink to brown; medium, spreading, bushy growth; [sport of 'Sadabahar']; intr. 1980

'Navaho' (Fire Fox™) HT, ob

'Navajo' HT, dp, 1959, Malandrone; bud long, pointed; flowers dark red to rose-red, 4½-5 in., 35-40 petals, high-centered, intense fragrance; foliage leathery; vigorous, upright growth; ['Hortulanus Budde' × 'E.G. Hill']

'Navarro Rambler' LCl, pb

'Navarro Ridge' N, lp

'Navid' F, or, 1985, Payne, A.J.; flowers patio, medium, semi-dbl.; foliage medium size, medium green, semi-glossy; bushy growth; ['Roydon Hall' × Trumpeter®]

'Navigator' LCl, mp, 1925, Verhalen; bud globular; flowers radiance pink, large, 25 petals, cupped; foliage soft; long stems; very vigorous, climbing growth; [*R. soulieana* × 'Radiance']; intr. 1943

'Navneet' F, w, 1973, IARI; buds medium, pointed; flowers cream-white, large, semi-dbl., open, borne singly and several together; foliage large, green, soft; growth vigorous, bushy; ['Prelude' × 'Africa Star']; intr. 1971

'Nayika' HT, pb, 1976, Pal, Dr. B.P.; bud pointed; flowers delft-rose, reverse and base darker, 4 in., 45 petals, high-centered, slight tea fragrance; foliage leathery; moderate, upright, bushy growth; intr. 1975

'Nazneen' HT, lp, 1970, Pal, Dr. B.P.; bud ovoid; flowers very soft pink, large, very dbl., high-centered, moderate fragrance; foliage light green, glossy; vigorous, upright growth; [Queen Elizabeth® × unknown]; intr. 1969

'Nazr-e-Nazar' HT, mp, 1970, Singh, Raja Surendra; bud pointed; flowers light pink edges flushed darker, large, dbl., high-centered; foliage leathery; vigorous, upright, compact growth; ['Clovelly' × unknown]

N-Courage® HT, mr, Spek; flowers 4 in., 55-60 petals, high-centered, borne mostly singly; recurrent; numerous prickles; stems medium; florist rose; intr. 2006

NDR 1 - Radio Niedersachsen® -- See 'Koreledas'

'Ne Plus Ultra' N, w; flowers creamy white

'Néala' HGal, dp, 1822, Vibert; flowers deep rose edged lighter, medium, dbl.

'Near You' -- See 'Seanear'

'Nearly Black' HT, dr; may be Dame de Coeur

'Nearly Wild' F, pb, 1941, Brownell; bud small, long, pointed; flowers rose-pink, white eye, 5 petals, moderate sweet fragrance; bushy (2-3 ft.) growth; ['Dr.

W. Van Fleet' × 'Leuchtstern']

'Nearly Wild, Climbing' Cl F, mp, 1962, Burks; intr. 1962

'Nearly Wild Gallica' HGal, dp

Nébuleuse® F, dr, 1978, Gaujard; flowers deep crimson, medium, dbl.; vigorous growth; ['Ritz (F)' × Lilli Marleen®]; intr. 1971

'Nec Plus Ultra' HGal, mp, about 1810, Descemet; flowers large, full

Nectarine® F, yb, Spek; flowers golden yellow, outer petals with green tints, 8-9 cm., 50-55 petals, high-centered, borne mostly singly; recurrent; thornless ; stems medium to long; florist rose; intr. 2006

'Nedbank Rose' -- See 'Delverjaune'

'Nederland' HT, dr, 1919, Verschuren; flowers deep glowing red, very large, 60 petals; ['General-Superior Arnold Janssen' × 'George C. Waud']

'Neela' HT, m, K&S; flowers pale lavender with a tinge of pink, petal edges deeper lavender; [sport of 'Paradise']; intr. 1989

'Neelakanti' F, m, Chiplunkar; flowers deep purple mauve, deepening with age, rosette, borne singly and in small clusters; intr. 1993

'Neelambari' F, dr, 1976, IARI; flowers deep red, large, 35 petals; foliage dark, glossy; vigorous, compact, bushy growth; [Blue Moon® × 'Africa Star']; intr. 1975

'Neena' HT, lp, Bulsara; [sport of 'Queen Elizabeth']; intr. 1990

'Neervelt' Cl HT, mr, 1910, Verschuren; flowers carmine-red, lighter reverse, aging to purple, 9 cm., dbl., borne mostly solitary, moderate fragrance; reliable repeat; ['Gloire de Dijon' × 'Princesse de Béarn']

'Nefertiti' -- See 'Viramber'

'Négretienne' -- See 'Subnigra'

'Negrette' -- See 'Subnigra'

'Negridte' F, dr, Urban, J.; flowers medium, dbl.; intr. 1972

'Nehru Centenary' HT, dr, 1990, IARI; bud pointed; flowers dark red, reverse deeper, large, 60 petals, high-centered, borne singly; foliage very large, dark green, dense; prickles hooked, brown; tall, upright growth; ['Christian Dior' × 'Avon']; intr. 1989

'Neige' -- See 'White Provence'

'Neige' Ch, w, about 1840, Miellez

'Neige d'Avril' HMult, w, 1908, Robichon; flowers pure white, stamens yellow, 4-5 cm., semi-dbl., borne in large pyramidal clusters; early, non-recurrent; foliage light green; thornless; very vigorous, climbing (to 8 ft.) growth; R. wichurana is one parent

'Neige de Printemps' HMsk, w, Lens, Louis; intr. 1991

'Neige d'Été' -- See 'LLX8743'

'Neige d'Été' -- See 'Tanigino'

'Neige Parfum' HT, w, 1942, Mallerin, C.; flowers white, sometimes tinted cream, large, dbl., intense fragrance; foliage leathery; vigorous growth; ['Joanna Hill' × ('White Ophelia' × seedling)]

'Neige Rose' LCl, pb, 1955, Delbard-Chabert; flowers center deep pink, becoming lighter at petal edges, large, borne in small clusters; very vigorous growth

'Neiges d'Été' -- See 'Rigobec 2'

'Neisse' S, pb, Berger, W.; flowers yellowish-pink, medium, dbl.; intr. 1959

'Nejenka' ('Tender One') F, m, 1955, Klimenko, V. N.; flowers purplish pink, large, 57 petals; foliage dark, glossy; upright growth

'Nelie Niel' ('Nellie Niel') HT, w, 1975, Dawson, G.

'Nelkenrose' -- See 'F. J. Grootendorst'

'Nell Gwyn' HT, or, 1968, Cobley; flowers orange-copper, globular; upright growth; [sport of 'Tzigane']

Nella Martinetti® HT, op, Meilland; flowers salmon pink with lighter reverse, dbl., high-centered, intense fragrance; upright (80 cm.) growth; intr. 1990

'Nellie Charlton' HT, mp, 1923, Lilley; flowers silvery pink, reverse salmon-pink, dbl.; ['Mme Abel Chatenay' × unknown]

'Nellie Deaser' -- See 'Kenenchan'

'Nellie E. Hillock' HT, mp, 1934, Hillock; flowers silvery pink, base deep gold, reverse old-rose, 60 petals, cupped, peony, moderate fragrance; foliage leathery, dark; low, spreading growth; PP185; ['Golden Dawn' × seedling]

'Nellie E. Hillock, Climbing' Cl HT, mp, 1948, Buck, Dr. Griffith J.

'Nellie Maud Powell' HT, yb, 1977, Powell; flowers yellow edged red, 4-5 in., 75-80 petals; foliage glossy; vigorous growth; ['Columbine' × 'Kordes' Perfecta']

'Nellie Niel' -- See 'Nelie Niel'

'Nellie Parker' HT, w, 1916, Dickson, H.; flowers creamy white, center darker, well-shaped, large, dbl.; vigorous, upright growth

'Nelly Custis' HSet, w, 1934, Conard-Pyle; flowers small, dbl., borne in clusters of 7-9, moderate fragrance; vigorous, upright growth

'Nelly Johnstone' T, mp, 1906, Paul, G.; bud long; flowers pure rose pink often shot with light pale violet on the outside, large, full, moderate fragrance; ['Mme Berkeley' × unknown]

'Nelly Verschuren' HT, my, 1918, Verschuren; flowers clear yellow, large, intense fragrance; [seedling × 'Duchess of Wellington']

'Nelson Girls' HT, ab, Warner; flowers apricot, classic hybrid tea; free-flowering; 125th Ann. of Nelson College for Girls; intr. 2006

'Nelson's Pride' -- See 'Beacake'

Nemesis™ -- See 'Tucknemesis'

'Némésis' Ch, dr, 1836, Bizard; flowers purplish crimson, dbl., pompon; dwarf growth

'Nemlove' ('Love You') S, mp, 1999, Nemko, Martin; flowers ¾-1 in., borne in large clusters; foliage medium size, medium green, glossy; prickles moderate; bushy, low (2 ft.) growth; intr. 1999

Nemo® S, w, Noack; flowers clear white with yellow stamens, 4 cm., single, cupped, borne in clusters; low, bushy (80-100 cm.) growth; intr. 2002

'Nemuro no Asa' ('Morning in Nemuro') HT , lp, Suzuki; intr. 1957

'Nénette Leydier' Pol, mr, 1924, Richardier; flowers crimson-scarlet, base lighter

'Nenikujaku' F, pb, 1986, Kikuchi, Rikichi; flowers pink, blended with yellow and red, 15 petals, cupped, borne in clusters, moderate fragrance; vigorous growth; ['Masquerade' × 'Matador']; intr. 1984

'Nenita' F, w, 1962, Moreira da Silva, A.; flowers large, 22 petals, moderate fragrance; foliage light green; vigorous, low growth; [seedling × 'Virgo']

Neon® -- See 'Kordatura'

'Neon' HT, mr, 1936, Nicolas; flowers crimson-scarlet, large, very dbl., moderate fragrance; vigorous, branching growth

'Neon' F, ob, Waterhouse Nursery; flowers intense orange, 2 in., 26 petals; compact growth; intr. 1970

'Neon' F, op, Kordes; flowers deep salmon pink, 4 in., 30-35 petals, high-centered, borne in clusters; good repeat; stems strong; growth short, well-branched; PP11273; originally a greenhouse rose; intr. 1993

'Neon Cowboy' -- See 'Wekemilcho'

'Neon Glory' -- See 'Jacpursh'

'Neon Lights' -- See 'Jacout'

'Néphis' HSpn, dp, 1825, Dagonnet

Neptune™ -- See 'Wekhilpurnil'

'Neptune' HSpn, dr, before 1848; flowers deep crimson, medium, full

'Neptunia' HT, pb, 1998, Poole, Lionel; flowers pink blending to white, classic, 6 in., very dbl., high-centered, borne mostly singly; foliage large, dark green, semi-glossy; some prickles; upright, medium growth; [('Precious Platinum' × 'Silver Jubilee') × seedling]

'Nerene' -- See 'Malren'

'Nerissa' HT, ly, 1912, Paul, W.; bud short, sharply pointed; flowers cream-yellow, shaded white, very large, dbl., high-centered

'Nero' -- See 'Néron'

'Néron' ('Nero') HGal, rb, 1841, Laffay, M.; flowers crimson, blotched and marbled violet; growth to 4 ft.

'Nerone' HT, Cazzaniga, F. G.

'Nerrière' HBc, w, before 1847, Vibert; flowers cream with a darker center, large, full, cupped

'Nervi' HT, Mansuino

'Nescapee' LCl; derivative of Ross Rambler

'Nessie' LCl, lp, Rupert, Kim; bud apricot and gold; flowers blush pink, 2 in., dbl., borne in clusters, intense spicy, sweet fragrance; spring flowering; stems long; growth to 20 ft.; [sport of 'Montecito'];

intr. 2001

'Nest Rose' -- See 'Korpancom'

'Nesta Burnett Snowdon' -- See 'Jaysow'

'Nesta Burnett Sowden' -- See 'Jaysow'

'Nestor' HGal, mr, 1834, Vibert; flowers crimson, edges tinted lilac, medium, dbl., quartered, borne in clusters of 2-3; foliage light green, oval; numerous prickles; very vigorous growth

'Nestor Bolderdijk' HT, pb, 1938, Leenders, M.; bud long, pointed; flowers pale ecru, reverse yellowish-salmon, base golden, very large, dbl.; foliage glossy; vigorous growth; ['Comtesse Vandal' × 'Pres. Macia']

'Netravathy' F, mp, Kasturi; flowers pink, deepening with age, borne in compact trusses; intr. 1975

'Netsujo' ('Passion') HT, dr, Keisei; intr. 1993

'Netujoh' ('Passion') HT, dr, 1999, Hirabayashi, Hiroshi; flowers deep red, 4-5 in., 30-35 petals, high-centered; foliage dark green, semi-glossy; upright (3-4 ft.) growth

Neue Revue® ('News Review') HT, rb, 1975; flowers yellow-white, touched dark red, well-formed, 4½ in., 30 petals, intense fragrance; foliage leathery; prickles many large; upright growth; ['Colour Wonder' × unknown]; intr. 1962

'Neues Europa' -- See 'Nouvelle Europe'

'Neuheit' ('Fragrant Alizée') HT, pb, Adam; intr. 2003

Neus® -- See 'Fesaru'

'Neutron' (form of R. rugosa), m, 1985, Lundstad, Arne; flowers purple, shallow-cupped, 3 in., 10 petals, cupped, borne singly or in small clusters, intense fragrance; repeat bloom; foliage thick, rugose, shining, dark; prickles straight, gray; upright, dense growth; [grown from neutron-irradiated seed of R. rugosa × unknown]; intr. 1984

'Nevada' HMoy, w, 1927, Dot, Pedro; bud ovoid, pink or apricot; flowers white, reverse sometimes splashed carmine, on strong stems, 4 in., single; may repeat; vigorous (7 ft.), shrubby growth; ['La Giralda' × R. moyesii]

'Never Forgotten' -- See 'Gregart'

'Nevertheless' -- See 'Hennev'

'Neville Chamberlain' HT, ob, 1940, Lens; bud ovoid; flowers salmon, center orange, 4 in., 26 petals, high-centered; foliage bronze; vigorous, tall growth; PP428; ['Charles P. Kilham' × 'Mrs Sam McGredy']

'Neville Gibson' -- See 'Harportly'

'Nevis Moss' M, mp

'New Adventure' -- See 'Morshefran'

'New Age' -- See 'Wekbipuhit'

'New Antique' -- See 'Bronew'

'New Arrival' MinFl, or, Chessum; flowers coral-red, yellow stamens, slight fragrance; foliage neat, medium green; bushy (18 in.) growth; intr. 1998

'New Ave Maria' -- See 'Korav'

'New Ballerina' HT, lp, Kordes; flowers full, high-centered; intr. 2004

'New Ballet' -- See 'Korelzoda'

New Beginning™ -- See 'Savabeg'

'New Beginnings' F, op, Kordes; flowers peach pink, double, cupped, borne in clusters, slight fragrance; recurrent; foliage medium green, glossy; compact (80 cm.) growth

'New Blaze' -- See 'Demokracie'

New Blush™ -- See 'Virblush'

'New Blush Hip' -- See 'Blush Hip'

'New Carousel' -- See 'Carousel'

'New Castle' Min, rb, 1983, Bridges, Dennis A.; flowers red, white reverse, small, 20 petals, no fragrance; foliage medium size, dark, semi-glossy; upright growth; ['Watercolor' × seedling]; intr. 1984

'New Century' ('The New Century') HRg, pb, 1900, Van Fleet; flowers flesh-pink, center light red, edges creamy, 3-4 in., dbl., moderate fragrance; intermittent rebloom; foliage wrinkled, light, tough; vigorous (4-5 ft.), bushy growth; [R. rugosa alba × 'Clotilde Soupert']

'New Columbia' HT, mp, 1924, E.G. Hill, Co.; flowers true pink, deepening to glowing pink; [sport of 'Columbia']

'New Cork' LCl, ob

'New Daily Mail' (Pussta®) F, dr, 1972, Tantau, Math.; bud globular; flowers large, semi-dbl.; vigorous, upright, bushy growth; ['Letkis' × 'Walzertraum']

'New Daily Mail, Climbing' ('Pussta, Climbing') Cl F, dr, 1989, Patil, B.K.; [sport of 'New Daily Mail']; intr. 1987

'New Dawn' ('Everblooming Dr W. Van Fleet', 'The New Dawn') LCl, lp, 1930, Dreer/Somerset Rose Nursery; flowers same as parent, 35-40 petals, borne singly and in clusters, moderate sweet fragrance; recurrent; foliage medium size, dark green; climbing to 20 ft. growth; PP1; [sport of 'Dr. W. Van Fleet']; intr. 1930

'New Dawn Rouge' -- See 'Étendard'

'New Dawn White' LCl, w, Schultheis; flowers dbl., looser than New Dawn; foliage dark green, glossy; bushy, vigorous (3-5 m.) growth; intr. 2000

'New Dawning' ('Grand Parcours') LCl, lp, Horner; flowers medium, shallow cup; free-flowering; foliage deep green, glossy, healthy; long, strong growth; intr. 2001

'New Day' -- See 'Korgold'

'New Debbie' F, ob; good repeat; growth to 3 ft.; intr. 2001

'New Design' HT, yb, Tantau; flowers medium yellow with outer petals fading and showing pink wash, large, dbl., high-centered, borne mostly singly; good production; stems 70 - 90 cm; growth upright; greenhouse rose; intr. 2001

'New Duet' -- See 'Kortraupfi'

'New Emely' HT, lp; intr. 2001

'New Era' -- See 'Wekwinwin'

'New Europe' -- See 'Nouvelle Europe'

New Face® -- See 'Interclem'

New Fashion™ -- See 'Patio Princess'

'New Fashion' HT, rb; flowers bright yellow heart and reverse with bright red petal edges on face; intr. 2002

'New Gold' Min, dy, 1977, Lyon; bud long, pointed; flowers buttercup-yellow, open, 2-2½ in., 20 petals; foliage small, very dark; vigorous, upright growth; ['Yellow Jewel' × Allgold®]

'New Hampshire' Min, yb, Benardella, Frank; flowers golden yellow, flushed apricot to red, dbl., cupped; medium growth; intr. 2002

'New Haven Queen' HT, ob, 1939, Grillo; bud pointed; flowers tangerine, large, 40 petals; foliage leathery; vigorous growth; [sport of 'Token']

'New Hope' Min, w, 1989, Bridges, Dennis A.; bud pointed; flowers creamy white, slight pink edge, medium, high-centered, borne usually singly; foliage medium size, dark green, semi-glossy; prickles straight, pointed, medium, medium red; bushy, medium growth; [Party Girl™ × seedling]; intr. 1989

'New Horizon' -- See 'Dicplay'

'New Horizons' -- See 'Jacsee'

'New Iceberg' -- See 'Korturek'

New Imagine® HT, rb, Dorieux; flowers white striped with carmine red; intr. 2004

'New Kleopatra' -- See 'Korverpea'

'New Life' F, ab, Cocker; flowers peach-pink blend with reverse light apricot, double, hybrid tea, borne in clusters, slight fragrance; recurrent; foliage medium green, very glossy; very full (60 - 75 cm.) growth; [(Anne Cocker® × 'Arthur Bell') × 'Sunsprite']; intr. 2008

'New Look' F, rb, 1963, Gaujard; flowers maroon, reverse silver, 3 in., 50 petals, borne in clusters, moderate fragrance; foliage glossy, coppery; vigorous, bushy growth; [('Charles Gregory' × unknown) × (Orange Triumph® × unknown)]; intr. 1962

'New Look' F, ob; intr. 2003

'New Love' HT, rb, 1970, Morey, Dennison; flowers cardinal-red, reverse golden yellow, large, dbl., high-centered; foliage glossy, bronze; vigorous, bushy growth; ['South Seas' × 'Coronado']; intr. 1968

'New Maiden's Blush' -- See 'Königin von Dänemark'

'New Mexico' HT, mr, 1967, Aufill; flowers medium, dbl., high-centered; foliage bronze, leathery; very vigorous growth; ['Mount Shasta' × 'Granada']

'New Moonlight' HT, my, 1935, Elmer's Nursery; flowers very large, dbl.; foliage glossy; long stems; very vigorous growth; ['Sun Gold' × 'Joseph Hill']

'New Orange' Min, ob

New Orleans™ -- See 'Kinnor'

'New Orleans' HT, yb, 1966, Tate; bud ovoid; flowers yellow, veined light red, large, dbl., globular, moderate fragrance; foliage glossy; vigorous, upright growth; PP2787; RULED EXTINCT 2/87; [sport of 'Peace']

New Orleans™ S, dp, John Clements; flowers hot raspberry-pink, shaded plum-purple, 5 in., 40 petals, quartered, borne one to a stem and in clusters of three to five, intense fragrance; growth vigorous, upright, well foliated, 4 × 3½ ft.; PPAF; intr. 2005

'New Orleans Lady' -- See 'Talnola'

'New Orleans Lady' HT, mp, 2004, Edwards, Eddie & Phelps, Ethan; flowers full, borne mostly solitary, slight fragrance; foliage large, dark green, glossy; prickles hooked; growth upright, tall (5-6 ft.); exhibition; [unknown × unknown]; intr. 2005

New Peace™ -- See 'Aronewp'

'New Penny' Min, or, 1962, Moore, Ralph S.; bud short, pointed; flowers orange-red to coral-pink, 1½ in., 20 petals; foliage leathery, glossy; bushy, dwarf (10 in.) growth; [(R. wichurana × Floradora) × seedling]; intr. 1962

'New Planet' HT, MP, 1930, Cleveland Cut-Flower Co.; flowers bright rose-pink, center light pink, dbl.; [sport of 'Premier']

'New Polyantha' Pol, lp, Scarman?; intr. 2001

'New Pristine' -- See 'Kordiena'

'New Red Pet' -- See 'Red Pet'

'New Rouge Meilland' -- See 'Meimalyna'

'New Scotland Yard' -- See 'Bedsinker'

'New Star' HT, my, Keisei Rose Nurseries, Inc.; intr. 1987

'New Style' HT, mr, 1965, Meilland, Alain A.; bud oval; flowers crimson flushed brighter, large, 25 petals; foliage leathery, glossy; long stems; very vigorous, bushy growth; [('Happiness' × 'Independence') × 'Peace']

'New Wave' HT, m, Teranishi; intr. 2000

'New White Moss' -- See 'White Bath'

'New William Shakespeare' -- See 'Ausromeo'

'New World' F, rb, 1945, Jacobus; flowers velvety red and crimson, reverse lighter, dbl.; foliage soft, glossy; bushy growth; ['Crimson Glory' × 'Château de Clos Vougeot']

'New Year, Climbing' -- See 'Buryear'

New Year® -- See 'Macnewye'

'New Yorker' HT, mr, 1947, Boerner; flowers velvety bright scarlet, 4-4½ in., 35 petals, high-centered, moderate fruity fragrance; vigorous, bushy growth; PP823; ['Flambeau' × seedling]

'New Yorker, Climbing' Cl HT, mr, 1951, Boerner; PP1056

'New Zealand' -- See 'Macgenev'

'New Zealand, Climbing' Cl HT, lp; intr. 2000

'Newbury Angel' -- See 'Bardorg'

'Newcomer' ('Novitchkova') HT, ob, Novitchkov; flowers orange-yellow, medium; foliage dark, leathery; low growth

'Newgreg' ('Cup of Joy') HT, mp, 2006, Newman, Laurie; flowers soft pink, 4 in., full, borne mostly solitary; foliage medium green, semi-glossy; prickles small, moderate; growth upright, medium; ['China Sunrise' × 'Vol de Nuit']; intr. 2007

'Newly Wed' -- See 'Dicwhynot'

'Newmand' ('Ms Amanda Coombes') S, or, 2006, Laurie Newman; flowers deep scarlet, reverse red, 2½ in., single, borne in small clusters; foliage large, dark green, glossy; prickles medium, red/brown, moderate; growth bushy, tall, pillar; very healthy and vigorous; ['China Sunrise' × 'Vesper']; intr. 2007

'Newport' -- See 'Poulma'

'Newport Fairy' ('Newport Rambler') HWich, pb, 1908, Gardner; flowers very deep rosy pink, white eye, golden stamens, 3 cm., single, borne in clusters of 15-20; foliage medium green, glossy; [R. wichurana × 'Crimson Rambler']

'Newport Rambler' -- See 'Newport Fairy'

'Newry pink' -- See 'Paulii Rosea'

News® F, m, 1968, LeGrice; flowers red-purple, semi-dbl., borne in trusses, moderate fragrance; foliage olive-green, glossy; ['Lilac Charm' × 'Tuscany Superb']; intr. 1968

'News Review' -- See 'Neue Revue'

'Newsace' HT, ab, 1963, Wyant; bud ovoid; flowers light apricot, center darker, 4 in., 70 petals, moderate fragrance; foliage glossy; strong stems; vigorous, upright growth; ['Horace McFarland' × 'Good News']; intr. 1961

'Newsgate' HT, op, 1964, Verbeek; flowers rose and persimmon-orange, base yellow, reverse darker, 4 in., 50-58 petals; foliage dark, glossy; vigorous growth; ['Paulien Verbeek' × ('Jolie Madame' × Baccará®)]

'Newton' -- See 'Horoldnewt'

'Newwend' ('Ms Wendy Poulier') S, pb, 2006, Newman, Laurie; flowers pink, reverse salmon, 3 in., single, borne in large clusters, no fragrance; foliage large, dark green, semi-glossy; prickles medium, brown, few; growth upright, tall (6 ft.), pillar; ['Parador' × unknown]; intr. 2006

'Newxu' ('Sweet Osmanthus', 'Xu Gui Hua') Gr, ab, 2006, Newman, Laurie; flowers dbl., borne in small clusters; foliage medium size, dark green, glossy; prickles medium, regular, maroon, moderate; growth upright, medium (1½ m.); garden decoration; ['Parador' × 'Buff Beauty']; intr. 2008

'Ngarla' P, lp, 1955, Riethmuller

'NH NH #1' -- See 'Ezzy'

'Nhrosy' ('Rosy Vision') S, mp, 2005, Arnold, Dr. Neville, and Arnold, Catherine; flowers pink, reverse pink with yellow base, large, full, borne in large clusters, no fragrance; foliage medium size, medium green, semi-glossy, disease-resistant; prickles ½ in., hooked slightly downward, reddish brown, numerous; growth bushy, medium (5 ft.); ['L 83' × 'Dornroshen']; intr. 2006

'Niagara' HT, mr, 1952, Davis; bud long, pointed; flowers bright red, dbl., high-centered, intense fruity fragrance; ['Crimson Glory' × seedling]

Niagara™ (Avon™, Fairy Lights™, Pomona™, Snow Cover™, Sunnyside ™) S, w, Poulsen; bud blush pink; flowers pearl white, small, full, flat, borne usually in clusters, slight wild rose fragrance; foliage dark green, glossy; compact, spreading (1 × 2½ ft.) growth; intr. 1996

'Niagara Blossom' -- See 'Lavspring'

'Niagara Mist' HT, pb, 1968, Davis; bud ovoid; flowers light pink, base yellow, large, dbl., high-centered; foliage glossy; vigorous, upright growth; ['Tiffany' × 'Mrs A.R. Barraclough']

'Niagara Moonlight' -- See 'Lavlight'

'Niagara Pride' -- See 'Deldal'

'Niagara Sunrise' -- See 'Aalrise'

'Niagara Sunshine' HT, dy, 1969, Davis; flowers chrome-yellow, large, dbl., globular; foliage glossy, light green; vigorous, upright growth

'Niagara Wildfire' -- See 'Lavelvet'

'Niagara Winter' -- See 'Lavwin'

'Nic-Noc' Min, mr, 1985, Poulsen, Niels D.; flowers medium red, lighter reverse, 20 petals, cupped, borne in clusters; foliage small, dark, semi-glossy; spreading growth; ['Anytime' × Gruss an Bayern®]; intr. 1978

Niccolo Paganini® ('Courage', 'Paganini') F, mr, Meilland; flowers small, compact, velvety red, dbl., high-centered, borne in large clusters, slight fragrance; growth to 70-90 cm.; intr. 1991

'Nice 'n' Easy' -- See 'Horcoherent'

'Nice Day' -- See 'Chewsea'

'Nicholas Sweetbriar' (strain of R. eglanteria), lp, Nicholas; foliage fragrant; prickles very thorny; growth to 6-8 ft.; hips abundant, red; intr. 1959

'Nickelodeon' -- See 'Macnickel'

'Nicky' F, or, 1970, Institute of Ornamental Plant Growing; bud medium, pointed; flowers large, semi-dbl., cupped, borne in clusters, no fragrance; foliage medium size, light green, sparse, leathery; vigorous, upright, bushy growth; ['Cyclamen' × 'Fire King']

Nicola™ -- See 'Poulpar033(N)'

'Nicola' F, dp, 1981, Gandy, Douglas L.; flowers deep rose pink, 8 petals, borne 6 - 10 per cluster; prickles green; bushy growth; [seedling × seedling]; intr. 1980

'Nicola Parade' (Nicola™) MinFl, pb, Poulsen; flowers medium pink striped and painted with white, 5-8 cm., dbl., no fragrance; foliage dark; growth bushy, 20-40 cm.; intr. 2004

'Nicolas' S, mr, L'Assomption; flowers bright red, 3 in., 18 petals, flat, no fragrance; good repeat; foliage disease-resistant; compact growth; hardy; intr. 1996

'Nicolas Hulot' HT, my; flowers primrose yellow, dbl., high-centered; free-flowering; growth to 90-100 cm.; intr. 2004

'Nicolas Koechlin' HGal, m, about 1860,

Baumann; flowers dark purple

'Nicolas Rolland' B, mp, 1846, Dorisy; flowers bright carmine, medium, full

'Nicole' -- See 'Koricole'

'Nicole' HT, yb, 1931, Gaujard; bud long, pointed; flowers yellow, center coppery, shaded carmine; very vigorous growth; RULED EXTINCT 11/80

'Nicole' HT, rb, Kordes; flowers deep red with cream white reverse, large, dbl., high-centered, borne mostly singly; florist rose; intr. 1998

'Nicole, Climbing' Cl HT, yb, 1933, Kordes

'Nicole Carol Miller' -- See 'Meiskimov'

'Nicole Debrosse' HT, dr, 1962, Croix, P.; flowers dark red, shaded scarlet; vigorous growth; [seedling × Baccará®]

'Nicole Kordana' Min, rb, Kordes; flowers red, cream reverse, dbl., globular; pot rose

'Nicole Marie' MinFl, ly, 2002, LeBlanc, Albert; flowers light yellow to white, reverse white, 1¾-2¼ in., full, borne in small clusters, no fragrance; foliage medium size, medium green, semi-glossy; prickles 3/8 in., hooked, red to tan, moderate; growth spreading, tall (24-30 in.); garden, exhibition; ['Little Darling' × 'Linville']; petals have pink edges in warm weather; intr. 2002

'Nicole Mioulane' S, ab, Guillot-Massad; bud globular; flowers apricot/amber/yellow, medium, full, cupped, borne mostly singly, slight fragrance; growth to 4 ft.; intr. 2005

'Nicole Morris' -- See 'Lovbloom'

'Nicoletta' HT, mp, 1969, deRuiter; bud ovoid; flowers pink, medium, dbl.; foliage dark; [sport of 'Carla']

Nicolette® -- See 'Ludswenic'

'Nicolina' -- See 'Zipnic'

Nicoline™ -- See 'Nicoline Parade'

'Nicoline Parade' (Nicoline™) MinFl, or, Poulsen; flowers orange-red, 5-8 cm., dbl., no fragrance; foliage dark; growth bushy, 20-40 cm.; PP13108; intr. 2000

'Nida Senff' Pol, mp, 1946, Kersbergen; flowers soft rosy pink, borne in large clusters

'Nietar' ('Matilda, Climbing', 'Seduction, Climbing') Cl F, pb, 2001, Nieuwesteeg, John; flowers white, edged pink, large, semi-dbl. to dbl., borne in small clusters, slight fragrance; foliage medium to large, dark green, semi-glossy; prickles large, hooked, moderate; growth climbing; [sport of 'Matilda']

'Nigel Hawthorne' -- See 'Harquibbler'

'Nigel Quiney' -- See 'Sherinigel'

'Nigger Boy' HT, dr, 1933, Knight, G.; bud long, pointed; flowers very dark velvety blackish maroon, 56 petals, high-centered; foliage thick, glossy, bronze; low, compact growth; ['Hadley' × 'Yves Druhen']

'Night' ('Lady Sackville') HT, dr, 1930, McGredy; bud long, pointed; flowers deepest blackish crimson, shaded maroon, dbl., high-centered, intense fragrance; foliage dark, glossy; bushy growth

'Night, Climbing' Cl HT, dr, 1936, Armstrong, J.A.; PP439

'Night 'n' Day' HT, dr, 1968, Swim & Weeks; bud pointed; flowers large, dbl., moderate fragrance; foliage dark, leathery; vigorous, tall, bushy growth; PP2655; [('World's Fair' × 'Chrysler Imperial') × 'Happiness']

'Night Fire' -- See 'Lyofi'

'Night Flight' -- See 'Delrio'

'Night Lady' Min, rb, 1983, Meredith, E.A. & Rovinski, M.E.; flowers red, white reverse, medium, 36 petals, high-centered, borne singly; foliage medium size, dark, semi-glossy; upright growth; [seedling × 'Libby']

'Night Life' -- See 'Brolife'

Night Light™ -- See 'Poullight'

'Night Music' -- See 'Zipmusic'

'Night of the Midnight Sun' -- See 'Hakuya'

'Night Out' -- See 'Brinight'

Night Owl™ -- See 'Wekpurosot'

'Night Sky' F, rb, Dickson; flowers carmine red, striped, and with an ivory/pale yellow center, 6 petals, shallow cup, borne in clusters of 5 - 19, moderate fragrance; free-flowering; foliage large, dark green with hint of bronze, glossy; upright to bushy, slightly taller than average growth; intr. 2004

'Night Song' S, dr, 1985, Buck, Dr. Griffith J.; flowers large, 33 petals, borne singly and in clusters of up to 10, moderate fragrance; repeat bloom; foliage medium-large, dark bronze green, semi-glossy; prickles awl-like, tan; compact, erect, bushy growth; hardy; [('Rosali' × 'Music Maker') × 'Meisterstuck']; intr. 1984

'Night Star' -- See 'Jacurp'

'Night Time' HT, dr, 1976, Weeks; bud long, pointed; flowers dark black-red, 39 petals, high-centered, intense fragrance; foliage dark, leathery; vigorous growth; PP3924; ['Forty-niner' × 'Oklahoma']; intr. 1975

Nighthawk™ -- See 'Dohhawk'

'Nightingale' HT, pb, 1970, Herholdt, J.A.; flowers rich rose-red, blended lighter, large, 25 petals, high-centered; moderate growth; ['Rina Herholdt' × 'Tiffany']

'Nightmoss' -- See 'Ardarkness'

'Nightmoss #1' -- See 'Ardfara'

'Night's Musk' LCl, w; possibly Demits, 1986; HFilipes

'Nigra' HCh, m, before 1835; flowers very dark purple, reverse nearly black, very small, full; Lawrenciana

'Nigrette' -- See 'Subnigra'

'Nigrette' HT, dr, 1934, Krause; flowers blackish maroon or plum color, varying with season and weather, medium, dbl., open; bushy growth; PP87; ['Château de Clos Vougeot' × 'Lord Castlereagh']

'Nigritella' F, dr, 1953, Cazzaniga, F. G.; flowers red shaded darker, dbl.; dwarf, bushy growth

'Nigritiana' -- See 'Superbe en Brun'

'Nigrorum' HGal, m, about 1845, Calvert; flowers velvety dark purple-violet, small, full

Nikita® -- See 'Interniki'

'Nikitskaja Rosowaja' HP, mp, 1937, Kosteckij; flowers medium, very dbl.

'Nikki' F, ob, 1982, Bracegirdle, A.J.; flowers vermilion, white eye and reverse, medium, semi-dbl., no fragrance; foliage medium size, medium green, semi-glossy; bushy growth; ['Dusky Maiden' × Eyepaint®]; intr. 1981

'Nil Bleu' -- See 'Delnible'

'Nil Desperandum' HT, ob, 1977, Ellick; flowers Indian orange, 4 in., 25-30 petals; foliage large, light matte green; very vigorous growth; ['Gavotte' × 'Montezuma']; intr. 1979

'Niles Cochet' ('Red Maman Cochet') T, rb, 1906, California Nursery Co.; flowers cherry-red on outer petals, lighter within; [sport of 'Maman Cochet']

'Nilima' HT, m, Ghosh, Mr and Mrs S.; flowers silvery mauve, large, high-centered; intr. 2001

'Nilsson Guy' F, dp, 1930, Leenders, M.; flowers deep rose-pink, open, large, semi-dbl., borne in clusters; [sport of 'Lafayette']

'Nimble' S, pb, 1995, Jobson, Daniel J.; flowers handpainted birght pink, stippling to white center, white reverse, 4 in., 6-14 petals, borne in small and large clusters; foliage medium size, medium green, dull; some prickles; medium (5 × 5 ft.), upright, bushy growth; [('Valerie Jeanne' × Eyepaint®) × Twilight Trail™]

'Nimbus' -- See 'Leggrey'

'Nimes' F, rb, 1978, Gaujard; flowers vermilion, reverse gold, dbl.; ['Pampa' × Piccadilly®]; intr. 1970

'Nina' -- See 'Mehnina'

'Nina' T, lp, 1825, Vibert; flowers light lilac pink, large, full, globular

'Nina Marshall' HT, dp, 1967, Golik; flowers cerise, base gold, semi-dbl., cupped; foliage glossy; moderate growth; ['Serenade' × 'Queen o' the Lakes']; intr. 1966

'Nina Nadine' HT, yb, Kirkham; bud lemon edged cherry pink; flowers cream with pink blush on petal edges, full; foliage dark green, glossy; vigorous (4 ft.) growth; intr. 2002

'Nina Poulsen' F, mr, 1940, Poulsen, S.; flowers clear red, semi-dbl.; ['Grethe Poulsen' × 'red hybrid tea seedling']

Nina Renaissance™ S, w, Poulsen; flowers ivory to white , 10 -15 cm., very full, cupped, slight fragrance; recurrent; foliage matte; bushy, tall (100 - 150 cm.) growth; intr. 2006

'Nina Rosa' HT, op, 1946, Robichon; flowers coppery pink shaded yellow, very large, dbl.; ['Frank Reader' × 'Condesa de Sástago']

'Nina Weibull, Climbing' Cl F, dr

Nina Weibull™, ® F, dr, 1965, Poulsen, S.; flowers dbl., 25 petals, no fragrance; foliage dark; compact, bushy (100-150 cm.) growth; ['Fanal' × 'Masquerade']; intr. 1961

'Nine-Eleven' -- See 'Welzero'

1997 Traditional Home™ -- See 'Wamhome'

Ninetta® -- See 'Tanattenin'

Ninetta® ('Honeybun') Min, ab, Tantau; flowers dark orange , full, shallow cup, borne in clusters, slight fragrance; recurrent; foliage olive green, glossy; vigorous (24 in.) growth; intr. 2006

'Ninette' M, mr, 1857, Robert & Moreau; flowers bright cherry red, 4-5 cm., full

'Ninety-Niner' -- See 'Wekwinwin'

'Ninfea' HT, Borgatti, G.; intr. 1957

'Nini' T, mp, 1825, Barrier

'Ninie Vandevelde' Pol, mp, 1924, Vandevelde; flowers salmon

'Ninon Vallin' HT, ab, 1936, Gaujard; flowers apricot, reverse fresh yellow, large, dbl.; foliage bright green; very vigorous growth

'Niobe' F, w, 1942, J&P; flowers white, center sometimes flushed light pink; [sport of 'Rosenelfe']

'Nioumiya' Min, w, 1999, Yamazaki, Kazuko; flowers ivory white, 1½ in., 35 petals, high-centered, borne 2-5 per cluster; foliage medium size, dark green; vigorous, bushy, compact (10 in.) growth; [seedling × 'Hatuzakura']; intr. 1995

'Niphetos' ('Mathilde') T, w, 1841 or before, Bougère; bud pointed; flowers large, globular, intense fragrance

'Niphetos, Climbing' ('Paul Krüger') Cl T, w, 1889, Keynes, Williams & Co.; bud pale pink; flowers pure whiter than bush form, 9-10 cm., globular, intense fragrance; [sport of 'Niphetos']

'Nipper' -- See 'Hareco'

'Nippy' HT, yb, 1932, Cant, B. R.; flowers canary-yellow, reverse splashed red, moderate fruity fragrance; foliage dark

'Niramol' -- See 'Umsnira'

'Nirpaybla' F, w, NIRP; intr. 2005

'Nirpette Pink & White' Min, pb; intr. 1997

'Nirpfraga' HT, dy, Interplant; intr. 2006

'Nirpicered' ('Karen') HT, rb, NIRP; flowers cerise, reverse lighter, medium, full, high-centered, borne mostly solitary, slight fragrance; intr. 1999

'Nirpnufdeu' ('Ambiance') HT, yb; intr. 1995

'Nirporsa' HT, rb, NIRP; intr. 2007

'Nirpventyel' HT, op; bud pointed, green tinted; intr. 1996

'Nirpyelasif' HT, dy, NIRP; intr. 2003

'Nirpylos' HT, pb, Nirp; intr. 2003

Nirvana® -- See 'Meirisouru'

Nirvana® HT, lp, Meilland; flowers dbl., high-centered, borne mostly singly; intr. 2004

'Nisette' F, dp, 1967, van't Kruis; flowers pink-red, globular, borne in trusses; foliage small, dark; moderate growth; [sport of 'Garnette']

'Nishiki' F, yb, Keisei; intr. 2000

'Nishiki-E' F, ob, 1986, Suzuki, Seizo; flowers orange-yellow, 38 petals, high-centered, borne 2-5 per stem; foliage dark, semi-glossy; prickles small slanted downward; upright growth; [(Sarabande® × 'Amanogawa') × 'Kagayaki']; intr. 1981

'Nisida' C, lp, 1822, Vibert

'Nisida' HGal, mr, Noisette; intr. 1827

'Nisida' T, pb, Goubault; flowers pink, shaded fawn, medium, full, very fragrance; intr. 1840

Niso Fumagalli® F, w, Barni; flowers pure white, large, full, cupped, borne in clusters, slight fragrance; recurrent; medium (60-80 cm.) growth; intr. 2006

'Nita' Min, ab, 1986, McDaniel, Earl; flowers apricot, lighter apricot reverse, 55 petals, high-centered, borne singly; foliage medium size, dark, semi-glossy; prickles few, light green; medium, upright, bushy growth; [seedling × 'unknown miniature']; intr. 1987

'Nita Weldon' T, w, 1908, Dickson, A.; flowers ivory-white edged light pink

Nitouche® F, pb, 1978, Poulsen, Niels D.; flowers silvery, deep salmon pink reverse, 4 in., 25 petals, borne 3 - 5 per cluster; recurrent; foliage glossy, dark; bushy, upright growth; [seedling × 'Whisky Mac']; intr. 1974

'Nivalda' HT, ab, Kordes; flowers soft apricot, firm petaled , star-shaped; stems long, slender; tall growth; intr. 1997

'Nivea' -- See 'White Provence'

'Nivea' -- See 'Aimée Vibert'

'Nivea' HT, w, 1949, Dot, Pedro; bud long, pointed; flowers medium, dbl., high-centered; foliage sparse; dwarf growth; ['Nuria de Recolons' × 'Blanche Mallerin']

'Nivescens' HT, lp; flowers medium, semi-dbl.

N-Joy® HT, pb, Spek; flowers white with deep pink edges, lighter pink spreading down petals, 4 in., 55-60 petals, high-centered, borne mostly singly; recurrent; numerous prickles; stems medium; intr. 2005

No Worries™ Min, yb, White, W. R.; bud pointed, yellow with orange tips; flowers orange and yellow with gold stamens, 1½ in., semi-dbl., borne in small, open clusters; growth micro-mini (12-15 in.); PPRR; intr. 2005

'Noa151498A' S, dr, Noack; intr. 2006

'Noa167897' Min, lp, Noack

'Noa168098' S, mp, Noack; intr. 2007

'Noa250092' S, mp, Noack; intr. 2003

'Noa75800' F, ob, Noack; intr. 2006

'Noa83100B' ('Scarlet Flower Carpet') S, mr, Noack; intr. 2006

'Noa84497D' F, or, Noack; intr. 2005

'Noa97400A' ('Sedana Flower Carpet') S, ob, Noack; intr. 2006

'Noabell' F, mp, Noack, Werner; intr. 1997

Noack's Überraschung® HT, yb, Noack, Werner; flowers caramel colored, 12 cm., dbl., high-centered; good repeat; intr. 1985

'Noacres' -- See 'Crescendo'

'Noadort' F, mp, Noack, Werner; intr. 1991

'Noaelsie' (Lady Elsie May™) S, op, 2001, Noack, Reinhard; intr. 2002

'Noafeuer' ('Flower Carpet Red') F, dr, Noack, Werner; intr. 1995

'Noagut' ('Showtime') Gr, op, Noack, Werner; bud rounded, orange-red; intr. 1997

'Noah' HT, ob, 1985, Nevo, Motke; flowers orange; [sport of 'Dr. A.J. Verhage']; intr. 1976

'Noahan' ('Hannover's Weisse') S, w, Noack, Wernersingle; intr. 1997

'Noala' ('Coral Flower Carpet') S, op, Noack; intr. 2002

'Noalesa' ('Flower Carpet Gold', 'Loredo', 'Suneva') S, dy, Noack; intr. 2003

'Noaley' Min, mp, Noack; intr. 2003

'Noamel' ('Apple Blossom Flower Carpet ', 'Mareva', 'Sommermelodie') S, mp, Noack, Werner; intr. 1997

'Noamet' ('Rose Minarett') F, mp, Noack, Werner; intr. 1997

'Noanes' F, op, Noack; intr. 2002

'Noapu' Min, mr, Noack; intr. 2003

'Noarda' ('Danica') S, w, Noack, Wernersingle; intr. 1997

'Noare' ('Alcantara', 'Vesuvia') S, mr, Noack, Werner; buds pointed; intr. 2001

'Noaroca' ('Red Facade') LCl, mr, Noack, Werner; intr. 1997

'Noasa' S, m, Noack, Werner; intr. 1996

'Noaschnee' ('Flower Carpet Blanc', 'Snowflake', Opalia® , Schneeflocke®) F, w, Noack, Werner; intr. 1991

'Noastrauss' S, pb, Noack, Werner; intr. 1989

'Noasun' ('Sunshine Flower Carpet', 'Yellow Flower Carpet') S, dy, Noack, Werner; bud pointed; intr. 1997

'Noatraum' ('Blooming Carpet', Emera®, 'Emera Pavement', Heidetraum™, 'Pink Flower Carpet') S, dp, 1989, Noack, Werner; bud globular; intr. 1990

'Noatwi' S, dp, Noack, Werner; intr. 1997

'Noawild' -- See 'Wildfang'

'Noazauber' F, w, Noack; bud light rose; intr. 2001

'Nobal' ('Thornfree Wonder') HMult, w, 1986, Nobbs, Kenneth J.; flowers peach pink, fading to white, 14 petals, cupped, blooms in clusters of up to 14; summer bloom; no prickles; long canes; spreading growth; intr. 1985

'Nobam' ('Daughter Margaret') S, w, 1986, Nobbs, Kenneth J.; flowers peach, fading to white, 48 petals, borne in clusters of 2-6, slight fragrance; repeat bloom; foliage typical China; prickles broad, pink; compact growth; ['Mutabilis' × 'Cornelia']; intr. 1985

'Nobilia' S, mp, Roman, G., and Wagner, S.; flowers medium to large, 40 petals, high-centered, borne in clusters, slight fragrance; foliage medium to large, medium green, glossy; ['Rosabunda' × 'Dr Faust']; intr. 1998

'Nobility' ('Elle') HT, lp, 1961, Boerner; bud ovoid; flowers ivory lightly overcast pink, center deeper, 5-5½ in., 35-40 petals, high-centered, moderate fragrance; foliage leathery; vigorous, upright growth; PP2093; [('Peace' × unknown) × 'Peace']; intr. 1961

Nobilo's Chardonnay® -- See 'Macrelea'

Noble™ -- See 'Noble Hit'

'Noble Antony' -- See 'Ausway'

'Noble Hit' (Noble™) MinFl, mr, Poulsen; flowers medium red, 5-8 cm., dbl., no fragrance; growth bushy, 40-60 cm.; PP10728; intr. 1998

'Noblesse' HT, pb, 1917, McGredy; flowers apricot primrose-yellow, outer edges flushed deep pearl pink, medium, dbl.; name released, MR 8

'Noblesse' HT, or, 1969, Spek or Lens; flowers very large, 28 petals; foliage glossy; moderate growth; PP3227; ['Coloranja' × 'Coloranja']

'Noblesse' HT, op, Tantau; greenhouse rose; intr. 1989

'Noces d'Or' -- See 'Golden Wedding'

'Nocturne' HT, dr, 1947, Swim, H.C.; bud long, pointed; flowers 4½ in., 24 petals, cupped, moderate spicy fragrance; foliage leathery, dark; vigorous, upright, bushy growth; PP713; ['Charlotte Armstrong' × 'Night']

'Nocturne, Climbing' Cl HT, dr, 1956, Armstrong, J.A.; PP1088

'Nocturne' F, dr, Archer; flowers dbl.; moderate growth; intr. before 1958

'Noëlla Nabonnand' Cl T, dr, 1901, Nabonnand, G.; bud tall; flowers velvety crimson-red, much lighter reverse, 15-16 cm., semi-dbl., loose, moderate fragrance; ['Reine Marie Henriette' × 'Bardou Job']

'Noella Virebent' Cl T, lp, 1922, Nabonnand, P.; flowers flesh-pink, center brighter, semi-dbl., moderate fragrance; foliage dark, glossy; prickles few thorns; very vigorous growth; [R. gigantea × 'Archiduc Joseph']

'Noelle Marie' Min, ab, Eagle, Barry; flowers soft apricot with peach tonings; tall growth; ['Pink Petticoat' × unknown]; intr. 1990

'Noémie' HCh, m, about 1820, Hardy; flowers violet pink, large, very full

'Noémie' D, dp, Vibert; flowers deep rose, slightly spotted, large, full; intr. 1845

'Noémie' HP, lp, Aubert; flowers bright flesh pink, full, cupped; intr. 1845

'Noémie' HT, mr, Foulard; flowers red, marble light pink, large, full; intr. 1850

'Nogawa' HT, w, 1989, Takahashi, Takeshi; bud ovoid; flowers cream, fringed with pink, large, 30 petals, high-centered, borne usually singly; foliage medium size, dark green, semi-glossy; prickles almost right-angled to stem; bushy, tall growth; ['Garden Party' × 'Kordes' Perfecta']

'Noire' -- See 'Hector'

'Noire Couronnée' ('Gaillarde Marbrée') HGal, dr, before 1810, Dupont; sepals short, pointed; flowers velvety, purple-violet marbled crimson, medium to large, very dbl.; foliage narrow, wavy

'Noire de Holland' -- See 'Subnigra'

'Noire Pourpre Panachée' -- See 'Ombre Panachée'

'Noisette Ayez' -- See 'Spectabilis'

'Noisette de l'Inde' -- See R. × noisettiana

'Noisette Desprez' -- See 'Jaune Desprez'

'Noisette Jaune' -- See 'Smith's Yellow China'

'Noisette Moschata' N, w, 1873, Schwartz; flowers blush white

'Noisette Rose' ('Belle Noisette', 'Rosier de Philippe Noisette', 'Noisette de l'Inde', 'Bengale Noisette', 'Le Rosier de Philippe Noisette', R × noisettiana Thory) N, w, 1814, Noisette; flowers blush white

'Nokomis' HWich, dp, 1918, Walsh; flowers dark rose-pink, larger than lady gay or dorothy perkins, dbl., borne in clusters of 5-30, intense fragrance; foliage light, glossy; vigorous, climbing growth; [R. wichurana × 'Comte Raimbaud']

'Nola Emily' HT, mp, Allender, Robert William; [sport of 'Peter Benjamin']

'Noldanyu' ('Sunny Sam') F, my, 1997, Nolan, Gordon D.; flowers medium, 41 petals, borne in small clusters; foliage medium size, medium green, semi-glossy; upright, compact, low (2½-3ft.) growth; [(Gold Bunny® × Gold Bunny®) × seedling]

'Nolhelen' F, w, 2004, Nolan, Gordon, D.; flowers very full, borne in small clusters, moderate fragrance; foliage medium size, dark green, semi-glossy; prickles small, straight; growth bushy, medium (100 cm.); garden display; cutting; ['Bonica' × 'Angel Face']

'Nolpeg' ('The Little Mermaid') MinFl, m, 2004, Nolan, Gordon D.; flowers full, borne in small clusters, no fragrance; foliage medium size, medium green, semi-glossy; prickles small, straight; growth upright, medium (90 cm.); garden display; [Jean Kenneally™ × 'Angel Face']

'Nolsue' MinFl, pb, 2004, Nolan, Gordon D.; flowers light pink, reverse medium pink, 5 cm., dbl., borne in small clusters, slight fragrance; foliage medium size, dark green, matte; prickles small, straight; growth bushy, medium (75 cm.); garden display; [Jean Kenneally™ × 'Angel Face']

'Non Plus Ultra' ('Weigand's Crimson Rambler') HMult, dr, 1904, Weigand, C.; flowers semi-dbl., borne in large clusters; none; vigorous growth; ['Crimson Rambler' × 'Mlle Blanche Rebatel']

'Nona' HT, op, 1924, Easlea; bud long, tapering, flame and orange; flowers flame and pink, medium, semi-dbl., moderate fragrance; foliage medium size, leathery; ['Mme Edouard Herriot' × 'Constance']

'Nonin' HT, yb, 1938, Mallerin, C.; flowers golden yellow, tinted coral-orange, very large, dbl.; foliage glossy; vigorous growth; ['Souv. de Claudius Pernet' × seedling]

'Nonino' F, mr; intr. 1997

'Noon Sunshine' Min, ly, 2006, Hopper, Nancy; flowers semi-dbl., borne mostly solitary; foliage medium size, medium green, matte; prickles 1/8 in., tan, moderate; growth bushy, medium (13 in.); [sport of 'Tobo']; intr. 2006

'Nora' -- See 'Bernora'

'Nora Cunningham' Cl HT, lp, 1920, Clark, A.; flowers flesh-pink, center paler, large, semi-dbl., cupped; free bloom, sometimes recurrent; foliage wrinkled, light; vigorous growth, long stems; climbing; ['Gustav Grunerwald' × unknown]

'Nora Henslow' HT, dp, 1925, Evans; flowers crimson-cerise, single; ['Mme Mélanie Soupert' × 'Gen. MacArthur']

'Nora Hooker' F, mr, 1971, Hooker, W. J.; flowers 4 in., 22 petals; free growth; [sport of Queen Elizabeth®]; intr. 1970

'Nora Johnson' HMoy, dp, 1957; flowers cerise, small; hips small, bright; [believed to be R. willmottiae × R. moyesii]

'Nora Power' Cl HT, ab, Dearing

'Nora Pugh' -- See 'Lovbeadle'

'Norah Cruickshank' HT, op

'Norah Gabbatass' -- See 'Driscorob'

'Norah Longley' Pol, ob, 1948, Longley; flowers flame-orange, borne in trusses; foliage bright green; vigorous, branching growth; [sport of 'Cameo']

Nordfeuer® F, mr, Noack, Werner; intr. 1986

'Nordhausen' S, dp, 1940, Krause; flowers carmine-pink, large, semi-dbl.

'Nordia' F, or, 1967, Poulsen, N. D.; flowers medium, dbl.; PP2850

'Nordic Chant' HT, mp, 1976, Golik; bud long, pointed; flowers salmon-pink, 4½ in., 40 petals, high-centered, moderate spicy fragrance; foliage glossy, light; vigorous growth; ['Tropicana' × 'Queen of Bermuda']; intr. 1974

Nordina™ -- See 'Poulskab'

'Nordlandrose' -- See 'Geschwind's Nordlandrose'

'Nordlicht' HT, or, 1910, Kiese; flowers coppery red, large, semi-dbl.; ['Mme Caroline Testout' × 'Luciole']

'Nordlicht' -- See 'Northlight'

'Nordstern' F, Kordes, R.; intr. 1964

'Noreen Mackey' -- See 'Evesilvergold'

'Norfolk' -- See 'Poulfolk'

'Norfolk Harmony' HT, dp, 1940, LeGrice; bud long, pointed; flowers rosy cerise, large, dbl., high-centered; foliage glossy, dark; very vigorous, tall growth; ['Comtesse Vandal' × 'Mrs Sam McGredy']

'Norida' F, dp, Poulsen; flowers light crimson-scarlet, medium, dbl.; [('Pinocchio' × 'Pinocchio') × 'Elsinore']; greenhouse rose; intr. 1967

Norita® (Schwarze Rose®) HT, dr, 1973, Combe; flowers very deep red, large, dbl., high-centered, moderate fragrance; foliage dark, leathery; vigorous, bushy growth; ['Charles Mallerin' × seedling]; intr. 1971

'Norma' HT, lp, 1904, Dingee & Conard; flowers glossy light pink, very large, very full, moderate fragrance

'Norma' HT, mr, Gaujard; flowers brilliant red, large, 50 petals; ['Clio' × 'Credo']; intr. 1976

'Norma Bennett' F, dr, 1958, Bennett, H.; flowers crimson; ['Florence Mary Morse' × 'Border Queen']

'Norma Major' HT, mp; flowers dbl., high-centered, moderate sweet fragrance; tall growth; intr. about 1998

'Norma Margaret' -- See 'Fronorm'

'Norman' HT, mr, 1934, Dickson, A.; flowers well-formed, borne in bright scarlet-red; vigorous growth

'Norman Hartnell' HT, mr, 1964, Kordes, R.; flowers crimson-red, well-formed, large, 21 petals; foliage dark; very vigorous growth; ['Ballet' × 'Detroiter']

'Norman Lambert' HT, ob, 1926, McGredy; bud long, pointed; flowers deep salmon-orange, suffused bronze and yellow, base lighter, large, dbl., high-centered

'Norman Rogers' HT, dp, 1933, Chaplin Bros.; flowers deep rose-pink, base yellow, large

'Normandica' -- See 'Petite de Hollande'

'Normandie' HWich, mp, 1929, Nonin; flowers salmon-pink, aging lighter, 4 cm., dbl., borne in medium clusters, no fragrance; vigorous growth

'Normandie' -- See 'Chewarvel'

Norris Pratt® HT, my, 1964, Buisman, G. A. H.; flowers bright yellow, large; foliage leathery; growth moderate; ['Mrs Pierre S. duPont' × 'Marcelle Gret']

'Norrköping' HT, mr, 1961, Poulsen, S.; bud pointed; flowers scarlet, reverse darker; long stems; very vigorous growth; ['Karl Herbst' × (Baccará® × 'Golden Sun')]

'Norseman' F, mp, 1963, Von Abrams; flowers pink, medium, dbl.; foliage soft; vigorous, upright growth; [seedling × 'Pinocchio']

'North Star' HT, lp, 1964, Golik; bud ovoid; flowers light silvery pink, 6 in., 60 petals; foliage glossy; vigorous, medium growth; ['Marcia Stanhope' × 'Peace']

'Northamptonshire' -- See 'Mattdor'

'Northern Dancer' HT, ob, 1965, Schloen; bud ovoid; flowers orange-yellow, edges flushed pink, large, dbl.; foliage dark, glossy, leathery; vigorous, tall, compact growth; [sport of 'Tzigane']

'Northern Encore' ('Polar Joy') S, lp, Lim, Ping; flowers light pink, 2 in., single, shallow cup, borne in clusters, slight fragrance; repeats well; foliage light green; stems reddish tone; growth upright (5-8 ft.) tall and wide; very winter hardy; intr. 2004

'Northern Gold' HT, my; flowers non-fading golden yellow, large; possibly from Delbard, about 1999

'Northern Gold' -- See 'Jacern'

'Northern Light' HWich, lp, 1898, van Fleet; flowers whitish pink, large, single

'Northern Lights' S, mp, Noack, Werner; intr. 1997

Northern Lights® HT, yb, 1969, Cocker; flowers lemon-cream, tinted pink, 5 in., 50 petals; ['Fragrant Cloud' × 'Kingcup']

Northern Lights™ -- See 'Poultika'

'Northern Sensation' S, dp, Lim, Ping; flowers 2.5 in., 16 petals, borne in clusters; recurrent; 3 - 5 ft. growth ; PPAF; intr. 2006

'Northern States' HSpn, w, 1952, Shepherd; bud long, pointed; flowers white tinged pink and yellow, open, large, 5 petals; profuse, non-recurrent bloom; foliage leathery; bushy, compact (2½ ft.) growth; makes a good hedge; hardy; [R. spinosissima × 'Irish Charm']

Northern Sunburst™ S, dy, Lim, Ping; flowers 2 in., 35-40 petals; non-remontant; upright (4 ft.) growth; intr. 2007

'Northern Yellow' HGal, yb, Sievers; intr. 1977

'Northland' -- See 'Maccarlto'

'Northland Rose' -- See 'Geschwind's Nordlandrose'

'Northlander' S, mp, 1985, James, John; flowers 4 in., 5 petals, borne singly and in clusters of 3; repeat bloom; foliage medium size, dark, matte; vigorous, upright (to 8 ft.) growth; ['Baronne Prevost' × (('Magnifica' × 'Joanna Hill') × ('Blanche Mallerin' × R. laxa))]

'Northlight' ('Nordlicht') F, or, 1958, Kordes, R.; flowers deep cinnabar-red, large, dbl., high-centered, borne in small clusters; foliage leathery; very vigorous, low, bushy growth; ['Bergfeuer' × 'Gertrud Westphal']; intr. 1957

'Northumberland W. I.' HT, ab, 1988, Thompson, Robert; flowers deep apricot, reverse lighter, medium, full; foliage large, dark green, glossy; bushy growth; ['Silver Jubilee' × Doris Tysterman®]; intr. 1988

'Norwich Castle' F, ob, 1980, Beales, Peter; flowers copper orange, 30 petals, borne 3 - 5 per cluster, slight fruity fragrance; foliage medium green, shiny, smooth; prickles wedged; vigorous, upright growth; [('Whisky Mac' × 'Arthur Bell') × seedling]; intr. 1976

'Norwich Cathedral' -- See 'Beacath'

'Norwich Cerise' HT, mr, 1962, Morse; flowers cerise, 4-5 in., 25-30 petals; vigorous growth; [sport of 'Bettina']

'Norwich Gold' S, ob, 1965, Kordes; bud well-formed; flowers yellow shaded orange, large, 55 petals, moderate fragrance; vigorous, upright growth; intr. 1962

'Norwich Pink' HKor, dp, 1965, Kordes; flowers bright cerise, 4 in., 16 petals, moderate fragrance; foliage dark green, glossy; vigorous, pillar, well-branched growth; intr. 1962

'Norwich Salmon' HKor, op, 1965, Kordes; flowers salmon-pink, 6-7 in., 30 petals, borne in medium clusters, moderate fragrance; foliage dark green, thick, glossy; vigorous, pillar, well-branched growth; intr. 1962

Norwich Sweetheart™ -- See 'Bernor'

'Norwich Union' F, my, 1976, Beales, Peter; flowers bright yellow, changing to lemon as they age, 3 in., cupped, intense fragrance; foliage glossy, leathery; compact growth; ['Arthur Bell' × (seedling × Allgold®)]; intr. 1975

'Nosab' ('Leicester Abbey') HT, mr, 1987, Greensitt, J.A.; flowers large, very dbl., moderate fragrance; foliage large, dark green, glossy; bushy growth; [('Gavotte' × ('E.H. Morse' × unknown)) × Erotika®]; intr. 1981

'Noschal' ('Challis Gold') HT, dy, 1987, Greensitt, J.A.; flowers medium, 15-20 petals, high-centered; foliage medium size, medium green, glossy; spreading growth; [sport of 'Gold Dot']; intr. 1983

'Noscook' ('Catherine Cookson') HT, lp, 1987, Greensitt, J.A.; flowers large, full, moderate fragrance; foliage large, dark green, glossy; bushy growth; ['Gavotte' × King's Ransom®]; intr. 1985

'Nosman' ('City of Manchester') HT, pb, 1987, Greensitt, J.A.; flowers large, dbl., moderate fragrance; foliage large, dark green, semi-glossy; bushy growth; ['Gavotte' × 'Red Lion']; intr. 1982

'Nosmid' ('Middlesbrough Pride') HT, pb, 1987, Greensitt, J.A.; flowers medium, full, moderate fragrance; foliage medium size, medium green, semi-glossy; bushy growth; ['Prima Ballerina' × 'E.H. Morse']; intr. 1984

'Nossa Senhora de Fátima' HT, rb, Moreira da Silva; flowers deep red, reverse golden yellow

'Nosshef' ('City of Sheffield') HT, yb, 1987, Greensitt, J.A.; flowers medium, dbl., intense fragrance; foliage medium size, medium green, matte; spreading growth; [sport of 'Diorama']; intr. 1978

'Nossun' ('Sunderland Supreme') HT, lp, 1987, Greensitt, J.A.; flowers medium, full; foliage medium size, medium green, semi-glossy; upright growth; ['Paul Neyron' × 'Royal Highness']; intr. 1980

Nostalgia™ -- See 'Savarita'

'Nostalgica' S, m, Roman, G., and Wagner, S.; flowers mauve-pink, medium, 35 petals, globular, borne in clusters, very strong sweet fragrance; semi-recurrent; foliage large, dark green, glossy, very healthy; ['Vigorosa' × 'Angela']; intr. 1998

'Nostalgie' HRg, dp, Delbard, Georges; intr. 2003

'Nostalgie' ('Antique Nostalgia', 'La Garçonne') HT, rb, Tantau; flowers cream white with cherry red edges, dbl.; foliage leathery, glossy, reddish; intr. 1995

'Nostarn' ('Arnold Greensitt') HT, yb, 1987, Greensitt, J.A.; flowers medium, full, intense fragrance; foliage large, light green, matte; bushy growth; ['E.H. Morse' × 'Summer Sunshine']; intr. 1982

'Nostpri' ('Priory Pride') HT, mp, 1987, Greensitt, J.A.; flowers medium, full, moderate fragrance; foliage medium size, medium green, semi-glossy; bushy growth; [Pink Peace® × Chicago Peace®]; intr. 1981

'Nostrad' ('Radiant Superglaze') HT, w, 1987, Greensitt, J.A.; flowers near white, large, very dbl., moderate fragrance; foliage large, dark green, glossy; ['Gavotte' × Erotika®]; intr. 1982

'Nostros' ('Priory Rose') HT, mp, 1987, Greensitt, J.A.; flowers medium, full, intense fragrance; foliage medium size, medium green, semi-glossy; upright growth; [seedling × seedling]; intr. 1976

'Noswan' ('Pride of Wansbeck') HT, dp, 1987, Greensitt, J.A.; flowers light red, medium, 26-49 petals, moderate fragrance; foliage medium size, medium green, semi-glossy; bushy growth; ['Christian Dior' × seedling]; intr. 1979

'Notaire Bonnefond' HP, m, 1868, Liabaud; flowers velvety purple, very large, full

'Notre Dame' LCl, dp, Peden, R.; intr. 1997

'Notre Dame de Fourvière' HP, lp, 1861, Ducher

'Notre Pere' F, mr, Croix, Paul; flowers bright red, borne mostly in clusters; foliage disease-resistant; compact growth; intr. 1982

'Nottingham' HT, yb, 1938, Robinson, H.; flowers clear yellow, center tinted orange; vigorous growth

'Nottingham' F, dy, Gandy; flowers golden yellow, large, borne in trusses, slight fragrance; foliage olive green, disease-resistant; strong, bushy growth; intr. 2002

'Nottingham Forest' F, mr, 1971, deRuiter; flowers large, 28 petals; foliage dark; moderate, bushy growth; ['Metropole' × 'Diamant']

'Nottingham's Pride' S, my; intr. 2000

Notturno® HT, dr, 1983; flowers dark purplish red, 35 petals, intense fragrance; foliage large, dark; prickles reddish, hooked; upright, bushy growth; [Papa Meilland® × seedling]; intr. 1981

'Nouveau Intelligible' HGal, m, before 1811; bud round, inflated; flowers deep violet, 3 in., very dbl.; foliage small, oval, very bullate

'Nouveau Monde' ('Grande Brune') HGal, m, before 1811; bud large, round; flowers purple violet, dark and velvety, petals thick, very dbl.; foliage oval, dark green, largely dentate; nearly thornless

'Nouveau Petite Serment' C, m, before 1811; flowers deep purple, lightening from center to edge, small, very dbl., moderate fragrance; foliage oval, deeply and finely dentate; prickles numerous, hooked, red

'Nouveau Rouge' HGal, dr, before 1811; bud round, nearly glabrous; flowers sparkling purple red, very dbl., moderate fragrance; foliage nearly round, finely dentate, medium green

'Nouveau Triomphe' -- See 'Duc de Chartres'

'Nouveau Vulcain' HGal, m, before 1843; flowers dark purple, medium, very dbl.

'Nouveauté de Provence' -- See 'Justine'

'Nouvelle Duchesse d'Orléans' HGal, w; flowers flesh white, center touched violet, large, full

'Nouvelle Etoile' HT, yb, 1966, Delbard-Chabert; flowers creamy yellow, edged carmine-red, well-shaped, 40-48 petals; free growth; ['Chic Parisien' × 'Provence']

'Nouvelle Europe' ('Neues Europa', 'New Europe') F, or, 1964, Gaujard; flowers bright cinnabar orange, 3 in., dbl., high-centered, borne in small clusters, slight fragrance; free-flowering; foliage dark green; vigorous, bushy growth; hardy; ['Miss France' × 'Vendome']

'Nouvelle Europe, Climbing' Cl F, or; tall (2-4 m.), vigorous growth; intr. after 1964

'Nouvelle Gagnée' HGal, mp, before 1813, Miellez

'Nouvelle Héloïse' -- See 'Héloïse'

'Nouvelle Pivoine' ('Le Grand Triomphe', 'Pivoine de Lille') HGal, m, before 1818, Lille; flowers violet tinted, center vivid red, large

'Nouvelle Transparente' HGal, dp, 1835, Miellez; flowers rosy crimson, large, dbl.

'Nova' F, or, 1969, Harkness, R.; flowers semi-dbl., borne in clusters; foliage dark, glossy; ['Ann Elizabeth' × 'Paprika']; intr. 1967

Nova™ ('Nova Hit') Min, lp, Poulsen; flowers light pink, medium, dbl., no fragrance; foliage dark; growth bushy, 40-60 cm.; PP10082; intr. 1996

'Nova Coelestis' -- See 'Celestial'

'Nova Hit' -- See 'Nova'

'Nova Incarnata' -- See 'Elisa'

'Nova Lux' HT, yb, 1955, Aicardi, D.; flowers chrome-yellow with red reflections; foliage glossy; very vigorous growth; ['Julien Potin' × 'Sensation']

'Nova Red' Min, mr, 1964, Moore, Ralph S.; bud pointed; flowers crimson, small, 10 petals, borne in clusters; low (12 in.) growth; [seedling × 'Little Buckaroo']

'Nova Zembla' HRg, w, 1907, Ruys/Mees; flowers light pink to white, large, dbl., moderate fragrance; good repeat; vigorous, erect (6 ft.) growth; [sport of 'Conrad Ferdinand Meyer']

'Novaia' ('Carousel Panarosa') F, rb, Orard; flowers flushed bright red, heart yellow, reverse silver, dbl., borne in clusters, slight fragrance; free-flowering; growth to 90-100 cm.

Novelty™ -- See 'Weznov'

'November Rain' HT, m, Urban, J.

'Novitchkova' -- See 'Newcomer'

'Noweta' F, mr, 1960, Boerner; bud ovoid; flowers rose-red, medium, dbl., borne in clusters; foliage leathery; vigorous, upright, bushy growth; ['Spice' × ('Garnette' × unknown)]; intr. 1960

'Nozomi' ('Heideröslein Nozomi') Cl Min, lp, 1968, Onodera, Toru F.; flowers pearl-pink, single, flat, borne in trusses; foliage small, glossy; trailing growth; ['Fairy Princess' × 'Sweet Fairy']

N-Tertain® HT, pb, Spek; flowers white with pink stripes, 4 in., 55-60 petals, high-centered, borne mostly singly; recurrent; numerous prickles; stems medium; florist rose; intr. 2006

'Nu Gold' Min, my; flowers bright yellow

'Nuage Blanc' -- See 'Weisse Wolke'

'Nuage Parfumé' -- See 'Tanellis'

'Nuage Parfumé, Climbing' -- See 'Colfragrasar'

'Nuance' Min, or, 1992, White, Al; flowers medium, full, borne mostly singly; foliage small, medium green, matte; few prickles; medium, upright growth; [sport of 'Pierrine']; intr. 1991

'Nuance' -- See 'Jacnu'

'Nuancée de Bleu' -- See 'Celestial'

'Nubia' -- See 'Wekpaltlez'

'Nubian' LCl, dr, 1937, B&A; flowers dark velvety red, 4 in., dbl., high-centered; sometimes recurrent bloom; foliage large, leathery; vigorous (6-8 ft.) growth

'Nubienne' -- See 'La Nubienne'

Nubya® F, ob; flowers dark orange to brownish orange; intr. 2006

'Nucarina' HT, mr

'Nugget' F, my, 1974, Warriner, William A.; bud ovoid; flowers small, very dbl., high-centered; foliage large, glossy, dark; vigorous growth; PP3650; ['Yellow Pinocchio' × seedling]; intr. 1973

'Nuggets' HT, dy, 1941, Joseph H. Hill, Co.; bud short, pointed, buff-yellow; flowers pale orange-yellow, open, 2-3 in., 15-20 petals; foliage small, dark, leathery; PP517; ['Joanna Hill' × seedling

'Nuit de Chine' S, m, Tantau; intr. 2005

'Nuit d'Été' -- See 'Marianne Tudor'

'Nuit d'Orient' -- See 'Stebigpu'

'Nuits de Velours' F, rb; intr. 2002

'Nuits de Young' ('Black Moss', 'Old Black') M, dr, 1845, Laffay, M.; bud well mossed; flowers reddish-purple shading to dusky violet-maroon, medium, very dbl., moderate fragrance; non-recurrent; upright, medium (3 ft.) growth

'Numa Fay' HT, op, 1938, Richard; flowers salmon-pink, edged pale pink, well-formed, large, dbl.; vigorous growth

'No. 15/2000' S, mp, Adam; intr. 2002

'Numéro Un' HT, or, 1963, Mallerin, C.; flowers scarlet-red passing to vermilion-red, 5 in., 35-40 petals, globular; foliage bronze, glossy; growth vigorous, bushy, symmetrical

'Nuntius Pacelli' HT, w, 1929, Leenders Bros.; flowers white, center cream, large, dbl.; ['Mrs David McKee' × 'British Queen']

'Nuntius Schioppa' HT, my, 1931, Leenders Bros.; flowers golden yellow, sometimes washed peach-blossom-pink; [sport of 'Los Angeles']

'Nur Mahal' HMsk, mr, 1923, Pemberton; flowers bright crimson, medium, semi-dbl., borne in clusters, moderate musk fragrance; recurrent bloom; foliage small; strong stems; vigorous bush or pillar growth; ['Château de Clos Vougeot' × 'hybrid musk seedling']

'Nuria de Recolona' -- See 'Nuria de Recolons'

'Nuria de Recolons' ('Nuria de Recolona') HP, w, 1933, Dot, Pedro; flowers well-formed, on a very short peduncle, very dbl.; foliage dense; ['Canigo' × 'Frau Karl Druschki']

'Nurjehan' HT, dp, 1981, Division of Vegetable Crops and Floriculture; bud long, pointed; flowers deep pink, 50 petals, high-centered, borne singly, intense fragrance; foliage medium size, dark green, coppery when young; prickles straight; medium, spreading growth; ['Sweet Afton' × 'Crimson Glory']; intr. 1980

'Nurse Cavell' -- See 'Miss Edith Cavell'

'Nurse Donna' -- See 'Morfenn'

'Nurse Masako' HT, lp, Kadoya

'Nurse Tracey Davies' F, dy, Fryer; flowers golden yellow, dbl., cupped, borne in clusters; recurrent; foliage dark green, disease-resistant; compact, low (50 cm.) growth; intr. 2006

'Nursing Centenary' -- See 'Arobipy'

'Nutkhut' F, or, 1970, Pal, Dr. B.P.; bud long, pointed; flowers coral-red, small, very dbl., globular; foliage leathery; very vigorous, bushy, open growth; ['Rumba' × 'Cocorico']; intr. 1969

'Nutneyron' S, mp, Schoener; flowers semi-dbl.; occasionally repeats sparingly; growth to 4 ft.; ['Paul Neyron' × R. nutkana]

'Nutzwedel' F, mr, 1937, Schmidt, K.; flowers light crimson; [sport of 'Else Poulsen']

'Nymph' F, op, 1953, Dickson, A.; flowers coral-salmon, 3 in., 30 petals, borne in trusses; foliage dark, glossy; very free growth; ['Fashion' × seedling]

'Nymphaea Alba' ('Weisse Seerose') HT, w, 1889, Drögemüller; flowers glossy satin-white, medium, dbl.; ['Mlle Eugene Verdier' × 'Gloire de Dijon']

'Nymphe' LCl, w, 1910, Türke; flowers white, center pale yellow, 6 cm., full, borne in small clusters, moderate fragrance; ['Mignonette' × 'Maréchal Niel']

'Nymphe Egeria' HMult, mp, 1892, Geschwind, R.; flowers deep pink, aging to pure pink, 4-5 cm., dbl., globular, borne in small clusters; supposedly a hybrid multiflora, but bearing more resemblance to R. canina (perhaps crossed with a Bourbon)

'Nymphe Naine Émue' -- See 'Maiden's Blush'

'Nymphe Tepla' HMult, dp, 1886, Geschwind, R.; flowers carmine pink, fading lighter, 6-7 cm., very dbl., cupped, opening loosely, borne in medium clusters; numerous prickles; ['De la Grifferaie' × unknown]; sometimes classified as HSet

'Nymphenburg' HMsk, op, 1954, Kordes; flowers salmon-pink shaded orange, very large, semi-dbl., flat, borne in clusters, moderate fragrance; recurrent bloom; foliage large, glossy; upright growth; ['Sangerhausen' × 'Sunmist']

'Nypels Perfection' Pol, pb, 1930, Leenders, M.; flowers hydrangea-pink, shaded deep pink, large, semi-dbl., borne in clusters; vigorous, bushy growth; [sport of 'Mevrouw Nathalie Nypels']

'Nyveldt's White' HRg, w, 1965, Nyveldt; flowers snow-white, large, single; hips orange-red; [(R. rugosa rubra × R. cinnamomea) × R. nitida]; intr. 1958

— O —

'O. Junyent' ('Olegario Junyent') HT, mr, 1924, Dot, Pedro; bud large, ovoid; flowers coral-red, base yellow, large, semi-dbl., borne in small clusters; foliage large, dark green, glossy; numerous prickles; ['Frau Karl Druschki' × 'Mme Edouard Herriot']

'O. L. Weeks' HT, dr, Weeks, O.; flowers deep red, 40 petals; stems strong; intr. 2006

O Sole Mio® -- See 'Delosol'

'Oakington Ruby' Min, mr, 1933, Bloom; bud deep crimson; flowers ruby-crimson, white-eye, 1-1½ in., dbl.; dwarf (1 ft or less) growth; [sport of 'Rouletii']

'Oakley' HT, pb, 1937, Fairhead; flowers bright rose, base deep red, tipped flesh-pink, large; vigorous growth

'Oakmont' HP, pb, 1893, May; flowers deep pink, reverse lighter, borne in clusters; recurrent bloom

'Oamaston Pride' HT, yb, 1954, C.W.S. Ltd. Hort. Dept.; flowers buttercup-yellow suffused deep carnation-pink, large, dbl.; foliage dark, glossy; very vigorous growth; [sport of 'Haisha']; intr. 1954

'Oasis' Min, mp, Kamiyama; intr. 2000

'Oasis' -- See 'Rose Bengal'

'Oasis Sunset' -- See 'Sunmani'

'Obbo' HT; [sport of 'Alfred Colomb']

Obélisque® -- See 'Delmont'

'Oberbürgermeister Boock' Pol, dr, GPG Bad Langensalza; flowers medium, dbl.; good repeat; upright (50 cm.), branching growth; intr. 1964

'Oberbürgermeister Dr Külb' HT, op, 1931, Nauheimer; flowers flame-colored, passing to salmon; [sport of 'Roselandia']

'Oberbürgermeister Dr Troendlin' ('Dr Troendlin') HT, lp, 1904, Kaiser; flowers delicate flesh pink, large, very dbl.; [sport of 'Mme Caroline Testout']

'Oberbürgermeister Heimerich' HP, mp, 1929, Weigand, C.; flowers fresh rose, some petals with reverse lighter, dbl.; ['Frau Karl Druschki' × 'Souv. de Claudius Pernet']

'Obergärtner Burgner' HT, mr, 1934, Burgner; flowers medium, semi-dbl.

'Obergärtner Wiebicke' F, mr, 1950, Kordes; bud long, pointed; flowers light red, open, very large, semi-dbl., borne in clusters; foliage glossy, light green; vigorous, bushy growth; ['Johannes Boetnner' × 'Magnifica']

'Oberhofgärtner A. Singer' HP, mr, 1904, Lambert, H.; flowers carmine, center darker, 40 petals; dwarf, compact growth; ['Mme Caroline Testout' × 'Marie Baumann']

'Oberhofgärtner Terks' HT, pb, 1902, Welter; flowers flesh pink, muddled with carmine, tinted salmon-nankeen-yellow, very large, very full, moderate fragrance; ['Belle Siebrecht' × 'La France']

'Oberlehrer L. Burkhardt' HT, dp, 1939, Burkhardt; flowers carmine-pink, large, dbl.

'Oberleutnant Immelmann' HT, lp, 1916, Henniger; flowers soft yellowish-pink, center deeper, petals incurved, globular

'Oberon' F, ab, 1955, Dickson, A.; flowers salmon-apricot, 2-2½ in., 38 petals, borne in trusses; bushy growth; ['Nymph' × seedling]

'Obsession' -- See 'Devtinta'

'Ocarina' -- See 'Ocaru'

'Ocaru' ('Ocarina', Angela Rippon®) Min, op, 1976, deRuiter; flowers salmon-pink, patio, small, moderate fragrance; dwarf, compact growth; ['Rosy Jewel' × 'Zorina']; intr. 1977

Occhi di Fata® F, pb, Barni; flowers open white, then turn deep pink in sun, semi-dbl., borne in very large clusters, slight fragrance; compact, upright (2 ft.) growth; intr. 2005

'Ocean Song' HT, w, Tantau; greenhouse rose; intr. 2004

'Ocean Spray' ('Humdinger') Min, op, 1976, Schwartz, E. w.; buds pointed; flowers coral pink, medium, full, high-centered, borne singly and several together; foliage dark green, glossy, serrated; growth upright, bushy, branched; PP4294; intr. 1975

'Oceana' -- See 'Osiana'

'Océane' S, rb, Guillot-Massad; intr. 2000

'Ocho' HT, ab, Suzuki, Seizo; flowers full, high-centered; intr. 1983

'Ocooch Mountain Rose' S, mp, 1980, Hall, William W.; bud small, pointed; flowers 5 petals, borne 3-4 per cluster, intense spicy fragrance; foliage 9 leaflet, small, slightly rugose, medium green; prickles straight, fine; arching growth; intr. 1981

'Octandre' T, pb

'Octavia Hill' -- See 'Harzeal'

'Octavie' HGal, dp, about 1810, Descemet; flowers dark pink, edges lighter; possibly re-introduced by Vibert about 1835

'Octavie' HGal, lp, Coquerel; flowers

light pink, edged blush, open, medium, dbl.; vigorous, branching growth; intr. before 1829

'Octavie' HGal, dp, Vibert; flowers dark pink, edges whitish, small to medium, very full, moderate fragrance; this is possibly the 'Octavie' from Descemet, re-introduced by Vibert; intr. 1835

'Octavie' N, m, Vibert; flowers bright velvety purple-pink, medium, full, moderate fragrance; intr. 1845

'Octavie Fontaine' B, w, 1858, Fontaine; flowers white, shaded light flesh pink, medium, full

'Octet' S, m, 1979, Rowley; bud narrow, pointed; flowers pale purple, 3 in., 5 petals; prolific bloom in summer only; foliage gray-green; extrememly vigorous growth; [*R. rudiuscula* × *R. subglauca*]; intr. 1977

'October' HT, ob, 1980, Weeks, O.L.; bud long, pointed; flowers rich salmon orange, 30 petals, high-centered, borne singly and 2 - 3 per cluster, moderate fragrance; foliage leathery, dark; prickles long, hooked; tall, upright growth; PP4708; [seedling × seedling]

'October Moon' -- See 'Ardshine'

Octoberfest™ -- See 'Maclanter'

'Oddball' -- See 'Horodd'

Odense By-Rose™ -- See 'Poulspan'

'Odense City' -- See 'Poulspan'

'Odeon' -- See 'Gaufrarner'

'Oderic Vital' ('Orderic Vital') HP, lp, 1858, Oger; flowers delicate silvery-rose pink, large, full; [sport of 'Baronne Prévost']

'Odessa' -- See 'Micodessa'

'Odette' F, mp, GPG Bad Langensalza; flowers medium, dbl.; intr. 1972

'Odette Chêne' HT, mp, 1940, Colombier; flowers pink, base coral; vigorous growth; ['Richmond, Climbing' × 'Charles P. Kilham']

'Odette Foussier' HT, mp, 1924, Chambard, C.; flowers salmon-pink, inside chrome on yellow ground, dbl.

'Odette Foussier, Climbing' Cl HT, mp, 1929, Chambard, C.

'Odette Joyeux' LCl, op, 1959, Robichon; bud globular, coral-orange; flowers pink to lilac-pink, large, dbl., cupped; abundant, recurrent bloom; foliage leathery, glossy; very vigorous growth; ['Lady Sylvia' × unknown]

Odile Masquelier® S, my, Guillot-Massad; flowers light yellow at edges, darker golden at center, very full; intr. 2005

'Odine' -- See 'Ondine'

'Odorata' HT, pb, 1928, Van Rossem; flowers carmine-pink, reverse white edged pink, base golden yellow, dbl.; ['Sunburst' × 'Ma Fiancee']

'Odorata' -- See 'Hume's Blush Tea-Scented China'

'Odorata 22449' -- See 'Fun Jwan Lo'

'Odyssée' F, or, 1981, Gaujard, Jean; flowers well-formed, 25 petals, borne 3-5 per cluster, moderate fragrance; foliage dark; prickles small, brown; ['Pampa' × seedling]; intr. 1979

'Odyssey' -- See 'Franski'

'Œillet' ('Caryophyllata', 'Dianthaeflora', 'Guenille', 'Multiflora', 'Onguiculata Cariophillata', 'Unguiculata') C, lp, 1789, Poilpré; flowers bright pink, sometimes variegated, small, petals small and lacinated, dbl., borne in clusters of 3-6, moderate fragrance; foliage ovate, toothed; prickles numerous, unequal, reddish, slightly recurved; vigorous growth

'Œillet de Saint-Arquey' -- See 'Serratipetala'

'Œillet Double' HGal, m, about 1835, Prévost; flowers lilac pink, striped

'Œillet Flamand' HGal, pb, 1845, Parmentier or Vibert; flowers pale pink striped white and brighter pink, medium, very dbl., flat, intense fragrance; foliage medium green, oval; very vigorous growth

'Œillet Panachée' ('Striped Moss') M, pb, 1888, Verdier, C.; flowers pale pink striped deep pink, petals quilled, small, full, flat, moderate fragrance

'Œillet Parfait' HGal, pb, 1841, Foulard; flowers blush, striped lilac and dark red, medium, dbl., flat; dwarf growth; sometimes classed as Damask; possibly a Gallica × Damask hybrid

'Oekonomierat Echtermeyer' HT, dp, 1913, Lambert, P.; flowers deep carmine, shaded lighter, very large, dbl., moderate fragrance; ['Rose Benary' × unknown]

'Offrandé' HT, Gaujard; intr. 1982

'Offranville' F, dp, Eve, A.; intr. 1993

'Ognewaja' HT, mr, 1937, Kosteckij; flowers medium, dbl.

'Ogni Jalty' F, mr, Klimenko, V. N.; flowers medium, dbl.; intr. 1955

'Ogoniok' ('Little Fire') F, ob, 1955, Sushkov, K. L.; flowers fiery orange edged darker, medium

'Oh-Choh' HT, yb, 1986, Suzuki, Seizo; flowers yellow tinted rose, aging red, large, 38 petals, high-centered, moderate fragrance; foliage dark, semi-glossy; prickles small, slanted downward; upright growth; [('Rumba' × 'Olympic Torch') × 'Wisbech Gold']; intr. 1983

'Oh Darlin' -- See 'Rendar'

'Oh La La' -- See 'Olala'

'Oh My God' -- See 'Wekjoe'

'Oh My Stars' Min, ly, 1996, Bough, Melvin; flowers medium, full, high-centered, borne mostly singly; foliage medium size, medium green, dull; prickles moderate; upright, tall (2-2½ ft.) growth; [sport of 'Giggles']

'Oharame' HT, w; intr. 1974

'Ohio' S, mr, 1949, Shepherd; flowers bright red, semi-dbl.; recurrent bloom; growth to 4 ft.; hardy; [*R. soulieana* × ('Gruss an Teplitz' × unknown)]

'Ohio Belle' LCl, lp, 1975, Jerabek, Paul E.; bud globular; flowers dbl., 53 petals; repeat bloom; foliage glossy, dark; tall (15-20 ft.) growth; ['New Dawn' × unknown]; intr. 1974

'Ohl' HGal, m, before 1839; flowers violet-purple, center bright red, large, dbl.; vigorous growth

'Ohlala' -- See 'Olala'

'Ohshima Rose' -- See 'Cochuster'

'Oil Painting' -- See 'Aburae'

'Oirase' HT, mr, 1977, Ito; bud ovoid; flowers 5½ in., 24 petals, high-centered, moderate fragrance; below-average bloom continuity; foliage glossy, dark; vigorous, upright growth; ['Red Lion' × 'Christian Dior']; intr. 1973

'Oiseau Bleu' HT, m, 1978, Poulsen, Niels D.; flowers mauve-rose, 4-4½ in., 30 petals, intense fragrance; foliage large, glossy, dark; vigorous growth; intr. 1970

'Oiseau de Feu' ('Fire Bird') F, mr, 1956, Mallerin, C.; flowers scarlet-red, 2 in., 35 petals, cupped, borne in clusters; bushy growth; ['Chant Indou' × 'Peace']

'Ojibway' LCl, w, 1946, Preston; bud pointed; flowers 3 in., 12-15 petals, borne in clusters; free, non-recurrent bloom; foliage dark; vigorous, spreading growth; hardy; ['Ross Rambler' × ((*R. rugosa* × *R. eglanteria*) × unknown)]

'Okaga' HRg, dp, 1927, Hansen, N.E.; flowers deep pink, semi-dbl.; non-recurrent; low, bushy growth; very hardy; ['Alika' × 'Tetonkaha']

'Okaku' LCl, my, Hiroshima

'Oklahoma' HT, dr, 1964, Swim & Weeks; bud ovoid, long, pointed; flowers very dark red, 4-5½ in., 48 petals, high-centered, intense fragrance; foliage leathery, dark, matte; vigorous, bushy growth; PP2326; ['Chrysler Imperial' × 'Charles Mallerin']

'Oklahoma, Climbing' Cl HT, dr, 1968, Swim & Weeks (also Ross, 1972); PP2649; patent issued to Swim & Weeks

'Okresni Heitman Cubr' HT, mp, 1933, Böhm, J.; flowers large, dbl.

'Oksana' -- See 'Wisoks'

'Okuyoshino' Min, w; intr. 2001

Olala® ('Oh La La', 'Ohlala') F, mr, 1959, Tantau, Math.; bud pointed; flowers blood-red, center lighter, large, semi-dbl., borne in clusters of up to 25; foliage leathery, dark, glossy; vigorous, bushy, upright growth; ['Fanal' × 'Crimson Glory']; intr. 1956

'Olave Baden-Powell' HT, mr, 1974, Cobley, A.; flowers scarlet, 5 in., dbl., borne singly; free-flowering; foliage dark, leathery; very free growth; hardy; intr. 1972

'Olavus' M, lp, 1932, Nielsen; flowers salmon-pink, medium, semi-dbl.; ['Cristata or Blanche Moreau' × 'Mme Edouard Herriot']

'Olbrich's Merry Red' -- See 'Radbrich'

'Old Baylor' S, w, 2005, Shoup, George Michael; flowers semi-dbl., borne in small clusters, slight fragrance; remontant; foliage medium size, dark green, semi-glossy; numerous prickles; growth bushy, medium (3-4 ft.); hedging; [('Carefree Beauty' × 'Basye's Blueberry') × Heritage®]; intr. 1996

'Old Black' -- See 'Nuits de Young'
'Old Blush' ('Blush Monthly', 'Monthly Rose', 'Pallida', 'Common Monthly', 'Common China', 'Common Blush China') Ch, mp, 1751, Parsons; flowers two-tone pink, semi-dbl., borne in loose sprays; dependably recurrent; vigorous, upright growth
'Old Blush, Climbing' ('Parsons' Pink China, Climbing') Cl Ch, mp; flowers bright to medium pink, medium, semi-dbl. to dbl., moderate tea fragrance; [sport of 'Parsons' Pink']
'Old Blush Single' Ch, pb
Old Charleston™ -- See 'Poulterp'
'Old Country Charm' -- See 'Miccountry'
'Old Crimson' -- See 'Slater's Crimson China'
'Old Crimson China' -- See 'Slater's Crimson China'
'Old Danish' LCl, mp
Old Dutch® F, pb, Spek; flowers soft pink with green on outer petals , 7 -8 cm., 30-35 petals, high-centered, borne singly and in sprays; recurrent; few prickles; stems medium to long; florist rose; intr. 2006
'Old Faithful' -- See 'Jachy'
'Old Fashion Red' HT, mr, 1947, Brownell; flowers spectrum-red fading blush, large, very dbl., high-centered, moderate fragrance; foliage glossy; vigorous, bushy growth; ['Pink Princess' × 'Crimson Glory']
'Old Fashioned Girl' -- See 'Tinold'
'Old Fashioned Lady' S, w
Old Fashioned Romance™ -- See 'Byroldfashion'
'Old Flame' -- See 'Dickitty'
'Old Glory' HT, mp, 1940, Hausermann; flowers clear brilliant pink, large, dbl.; RULED EXTINCT 2/88; [sport of 'Briarcliff']
'Old Glory' HT, mr, Devor; intr. 1995
Old Glory™ -- See 'Benday'
'Old Glory' -- See 'Gloire de Dijon'
'Old Gold' HT, or, 1913, McGredy; flowers vivid reddish-orange, shaded coppery red and apricot, medium, 10 petals, borne mostly solitry, moderate fragrance; foliage dark coppery green; short stems
Old John™ -- See 'Dicwillynilly'
'Old Lavender' Ayr, m
'Old Lilac' -- See 'Auslilac'
'Old Man Bailey' -- See 'Majlara'
'Old Master' -- See 'Macesp'
'Old of Days' HT, mp
'Old Pink Daily' ('Blush Monthly', 'Monthly Rose', 'Pallida', 'Common Monthly', 'Common China', 'Common Blush China') Ch, mp, 1751, Parsons; flowers two-tone pink, semi-dbl., borne in loose sprays; dependably recurrent; vigorous, upright growth
'Old Pink Monthly' ('Blush Monthly', 'Monthly Rose', 'Pallida', 'Common Monthly', 'Common China', 'Common Blush China') Ch, mp, 1751, Parsons; flowers two-tone pink, semi-dbl., borne in loose sprays; dependably recurrent; vigorous, upright growth
'Old Pink Moss' -- See 'Centifolia Muscosa'
'Old Port' -- See 'Mackati'
'Old Red' HCh, mr
'Old Red Boursault' Bslt, mr; flowers pale red, boursault type, poorly formed, semi-dbl., borne in large clusters; hips nearly round; probably the original, typical form of R. lheritieranea
'Old Red Moss' ('Muscosa Rubra') M, mr; flowers carmine-red, medium, very dbl., moderate fragrance; heavy bloom; non-recurrent; vigorous (5 ft.) growth
'Old Red Pet' -- See 'Lucullus'
'Old Smokey' F, Murley, J.J.; intr. 1976
'Old Smoothie' HT, mr, 1970, Weeks; flowers large, very dbl., high-centered; foliage large, glossy, leathery; largely thornless; vigorous, upright growth; PP3098; ['Night 'n' Day' × (('First Love' × unknown) × (Queen Elizabeth® × 'Chrysler Imperial'))]
'Old Spanish Rose' -- See 'Russelliana'
'Old Spice' -- See 'Macjuliat'
'Old Stone School' Misc OGR, mp
'Old Time' -- See 'Oldtimer'
'Old Time, Climbing' -- See 'Oldtimer, Climbing'
'Old Time Fragrance' Gr, dp; flowers deep pinkish red, very strong, thick petals, large, dbl., intense fragrance; growth to 3-4 ft.; intr. 2003
'Old Tuscan' -- See 'Tuscany'
'Old Velvet Moss' -- See 'William Lobb'
'Old Velvet Rose' -- See 'Tuscany'
'Old White Moss' -- See 'Shailer's White Moss'
'Old Yella' Min, dy, Benardella, Frank; bud golden yellow; flowers buttercup yellow with splashings of red on petal edges; tall growth; [sport of 'Old Glory']; intr. 1999
'Old Yellow' ('Old Yellow St. Albans') HSpn, ly; bud yellow, rounded; flowers quickly turn white, full, cupped, borne in clusters along the canes; vigorous (1½ m.) growth; hardy
'Old Yellow Scotch' HSpn, dy; flowers golden yellow, small, dbl., moderate fragrance; foliage small, fern-like; prickles numerous, needle-like; compact (4 ft.) growth
'Old Yellow St. Albans' -- See 'Old Yellow'
'Old Yellow Tea' -- See 'Parks' Yellow Tea-Scented China'
'Oldcastle' HT, mp, 1985, LeMire, Walter; flowers large, 55 petals, high-centered, borne singly; foliage large, dark, glossy; medium, upright growth; [Queen Elizabeth® × 'Charlotte Armstrong']
'Olde English' F, dp, 1976, Orard, Joseph; flowers light red, 3-4 in., 30-35 petals; foliage glossy, bronze; free growth; [('Floradora' × 'Independence') × 'Siren']; intr. 1974
'Olde Fragrance' -- See 'Tanschaubud'
'Olde Lace' -- See 'Hadlace'
Olde Romance™ HT, mp, 1996, Davidson, Harvey; flowers peach pink, lighter reverse, 9 cm., very full, old-fashioned, quartered, flat, borne mostly singly, moderate fragrance; foliage medium size, medium green, glossy; prickles moderate; growth bushy, medium (1 m.); ['Shining Ruby' × ('Smooth Sailing' × 'Futura')]; intr. 1996
Olde Romance™ -- See 'Hadfling'
'Olde Romeo' -- See 'Hadromeo'
Olde Sweetheart™ -- See 'Hadswee'
Olde Tango™ -- See 'Hadango'
'Olden Days' Pol, mr, 1989, Vash, Ernest J.; flowers small, 10 petals, borne in sprays of 36; foliage small, light green, elliptical, slightly serrated, ma; prickles brown; bushy, compact growth; [sport of 'Paul Carpel']; intr. 1987
'Oldtimer' ('Coppertone', 'Old Time') HT, ob, 1969, Kordes, R.; flowers bronze, long, pointed, dbl., high-centered; good repeat; vigorous (4-5 ft.) growth; PP2999
'Oldtimer, Climbing' ('Old Time, Climbing') Cl HT, ab, Itami; intr. 2007
'Olé' Gr, or, 1964, Armstrong, D.L.; bud well-shaped; flowers medium, 50 petals, high-centered to cupped, moderate fragrance; foliage glossy; vigorous growth; PP2474; ['Roundelay' × 'El Capitan']; intr. 1964
'Ole' S, lp, Zuzek, Kathy; flowers blush pink to white, 2 inches, semi-double, shallow cup, borne in clusters of 5 - 15, slight fragrance; recurrent; upright (2 ft.) growth; winter hardy; intr. 2008
Olé, Climbing™ -- See 'Arohaiclo'
'Oleander Rose' -- See 'Interander'
'Olegario Junyent' -- See 'O. Junyent'
'Oleifolia' HGal, dp, 1900, Dieck; flowers large, very full; growth tall
'Olga' HT, Delforge; intr. 1988
'Olga' HT, Mansuino
'Olga Marix' B, lp, 1873, Schwartz; flowers flesh, changing to pure white, medium, full
'Olga Rippon' -- See 'Hortyard'
'Olga Tschechowa' HT, ly, Cocker; flowers creamy yellow, very large, very dbl.; intr. 1978
'Olijbrau' ('Ian Thorpe', Estelle de Meilland®) HT, r, Olij, Huibert W; intr. 1997
'Olijcrem' F, w, Olij; bud conical, elongated; intr. 1997
'Olijdum' ('Tamango Folies') F, dr, Olijfull; intr. 1998
'Olijfaon' F, pb, Olij, Huibert; intr. 1995
'Olijglu' HT, lp, Olij ; bud large, ovoid; intr. 1999
'Olijkroet' ('Faria') HT, yb, Olij, Huibert; intr. 1996
'Olijnol' HT, rb, Olij; intr. 1998
'Olijplam' ('Red Berlin') HT, mr, Olijdbl.; intr. 1999
'Olijprin' -- See 'Rendez-vous'
'Olijsab' ('Orange Flame') HT, ob; intr. 1999
'Olijzouc' ('Daytona') HT, dp, Olij; intr. 1997

'Olitel' ('Olytel') F, pb, Olij, Huibert W. ; bud small, conical; intr. 1994
'Olive' -- See 'Harpillar'
'Olive Cook' HT, w, 1934, Cant, F.; flowers white, base faintly tinged lemon-yellow, large, high-centered; foliage glossy; vigorous growth
'Olive Elsie' F, mr, Bossom, W.E.; flowers medium red, lighter reverse, 3 in., very full, borne in small clusters; foliage medium size, light green, semi-glossy; prickles moderate; medium (2½ ft.) growth; [Sexy Rexy® × 'Wonder of Woolies']; intr. 1999
'Olive Elsie' -- See 'Bossexwonder'
'Olive McKenzie' HT, yb, 1971, Dawson, George; bud long, pointed; flowers orange-yellow, marked red, large, dbl., moderate fragrance; foliage large, dark; vigorous, upright, bushy growth; ['Daily Sketch' × 'Manitou']
'Olive Moore' HT, lp, 1927, Allen; flowers pale rose-pink, reflexed silver-pink
'Olive Percival' HT, rb, 1948, Howard, P.J.; bud long, pointed; flowers intense cherry-red, base gold, 3½-4 in., 14-20 petals, cupped, intense fragrance; foliage leathery, bronze; very vigorous, upright, free branching growth; PP944; ['California' × 'Eternal Youth']
'Olive Taylor' -- See 'Peap'
'Olive Whittaker' HT, op, 1920, Easlea; flowers rich coppery rose to cerise and salmon
'Oliver Delhomme' HP, mr, 1861, Verdier, V.; flowers carmine-red, medium, full
'Oliver Mee' HT, mp, 1927, Dickson, S.; flowers deep salmon tinted fawn, becoming deep salmon-pink, large, dbl., high-centered
'Oliver Orange' -- See 'Gelora'
'Oliver Twist' -- See 'Sabbyron'
'Olivers' HT, m, 1965, Oliver, H.; flowers purple to pink, medium, semi-dbl., moderate fragrance; ['Pres. Herbert Hoover' × unknown]
'Olivet' HMult, mr, 1892, Vigneron; flowers light red, center slightly darker, 10-11 cm., full, flat; foliage dark green; growth tall (4 m.); ['De la Grifferaie' × 'Mme Baron Veillard']
Olivia® ('Lola') HT, mr, Tantau
Olivia® HT, rb, Tantau; flowers white with wide red borders, very large , double, high-centered, borne mostly singly; recurrent; stems medium; florist rose; intr. 2003
'Olivier Belhomme' HP, mr, 1861, Verdier, V. & C.; flowers fiery purplish red, medium, full
'Olivier Métra' HP, mr, 1885, Verdier, E.; flowers bright cerise red, large, very full; foliage dark green, irregularly dentate; prickles numerous, very long, recurved; growth upright
'Olivier Roellinger' S, pb, Delbard; flowers yellow heart with pink flush on petals, semi-dbl., cupped, open, borne usually in clusters, moderate fruity fragrance; free-flowering; vigorous (5 ft.) growth; intr. 2003

'Ollie' HT, mr, 1982, James, John; bud globular, pointed; flowers 45 petals, borne singly; foliage large, leathery, rounded; prickles red brown; vigorous, tall growth; [('Pink Garnette' × 'Pink Hat') × (('Frau Karl Druschki' × 'McGredy's Yellow') × ('Baronne Prevost' × 'Gruss an Teplitz'))]; intr. 1974
'Olwyn' HT, mp, 1946, Bird; bud long, pointed; flowers pink, medium, high-centered; foliage leathery; vigorous, bushy growth
'Olympe' HT, Gaujard; intr. 1974
'Olympe' D, dr, 1843, Vibert; flowers crimson purple, medium, full
'Olympe Frécinay' T, w, 1861, Damaizin; flowers white, becoming yellow
'Olympia' HT, mr, 1935, Tantau; flowers bright red, large, dbl., moderate fragrance; long, strong stems; vigorous growth; ['Johanniszauber' × 'Hadley']
'Olympia' HT, my, Delforge; bud bright yellow, well formed; bushy, semi-upright growth; ['Eclipse' × seedling]; intr. 1955
'Olympiad' ('Mme Raymond Gaujard') HT, rb, 1931, Pernet-Ducher; bud long, pointed; flowers blood-red, shaded copper and yellow, large, dbl., intense fragrance; RULED EXTINCT 11/82
'Olympiad, Climbing' Cl HT, rb, 1938, Raffel
Olympiad™ -- See 'Macauck'
Olympic™ -- See 'Poulymp'
'Olympic Champion' HT, yb, 1995, Pugh, D. J.; flowers yellow/pink blend, medium, very dbl.; foliage medium size, dark green, semi-glossy; some prickles; medium (70 cm.), bushy growth; [sport of 'Champion']
'Olympic Charm' HT, lp, 1965, Barter; flowers silvery, reverse bright pink, well-formed, large, 65 petals, intense fragrance; foliage dark, glossy; ['Grand'mere Jenny' × 'Claude']
'Olympic Dream' -- See 'Jacade'
'Olympic Fire' -- See 'Olympisches Feuer 92'
'Olympic Flame' F, or, 1962, Brett; bud pointed; flowers orange-vermilion, 3 in., 8 petals, borne in clusters; foliage glossy, bright green; vigorous, upright, bushy growth
'Olympic Glory' -- See 'Jaced'
'Olympic Gold' MinFl, ly, 1983, Jolly, Nelson F.; flowers large, 31 petals, high-centered; foliage medium size, medium green, semi-glossy; upright, bushy growth; ['Rise 'n' Shine' × 'Bonny']
'Olympic Gold' -- See 'Korschnuppe'
'Olympic Palace' (Olympic™) F, ob, Olesen; bud pointed; flowers orange to golden bronze, 3 in., 25-30 petals, cupped, borne mostly singly, slight spice fragrance; free-flowering; foliage dark green, glossy; prickles few, 5-6 mm., yellow-green; narrow, bushy (40-60 cm.) growth; PP16744; [seedling × seedling]; intr. 2001

'Olympic Spirit' -- See 'Jacary'
'Olympic Spirit' -- See 'Peaprince'
'Olympic Star' HT, mp, 1959, Trebbin; flowers cerise-pink; vigorous growth; [sport of 'Picture']
'Olympic Torch' ('Sacred Fire', 'Sei-Ka', 'Seika') HT, rb, 1968, Suzuki, Seizo; bud long, pointed; flowers white and red, becoming all red, medium, dbl., high-centered; foliage glossy, bronze, leathery; vigorous growth; PP2968; [Rose Gaujard® × 'Crimson Glory']; intr. 1966
'Olympic Torch, Climbing' -- See 'Seika, Climbing'
'Olympic Triumph' F, rb, 1973, Dickson, Patrick; flowers red and yellow, 4½ in., dbl., globular, foliage sage green; upright growth; ['Shiralee' × 'Apricot Nectar']
Olympisches Feuer® -- See 'Tanolfeu'
'Olympisches Feuer 92' ('Olympic Fire') F, or, Tantau; flowers bright, full, borne in clusters; recurrent; intr. 1992
'Olympus' -- See 'Baroly'
'Olysko' -- See 'Yellow River'
'Olytel' -- See 'Super Disco'
'Omar Khayyám' D, lp, 1894, Simpson/ Kew; flowers clear pink, center incurved, small, with a small center eye, very full, quartered, moderate fragrance; foliage small, downy; numerous prickles; dense, prickly growth (to 3 ft.)
'Omar Pacha' ('Omer-Pacha') B, mr, 1863, Pradel; flowers bright cherry, large, full; recurrent bloom; growth vigorous, upright
Omara® HT, lp, Tantau; flowers fresh soft pink; intr. 2004
'Ombre Panachée' ('Noire Pourpre Panachée') HGal, m, before 1811; bud round; flowers dark velvety purple, petals folding back, 4 in., dbl.; foliage long, regularly dentate
'Ombre Superbe' ('Pourpre Noir', 'Sanguineo-Purpurea Atra') HGal, m, before 1811; flowers dark black-purple, large, dbl., flat; foliage dark green, nearly ovoid, pointed; prickles moderate; from Holland
'Ombrée Parfaite' HGal, m, 1823, Vibert; flowers variable, light pink to deep purple, often in the same flower, dbl.
'Ombretta' S, Embriaco, B.; intr. 1991
'Omega' -- See 'Emily Post'
'Omer-Pacha' -- See 'Omar Pacha'
Omi Oswald® -- See 'Lenomina'
'Omni' S, yb, Lens, Louis; intr. 1988
'Omokage' HT, r, Hiroshima; flowers grayish-brown; intr. 2007
'Omphale' HGal, lp, Vibert; supposedly different from the Omphale of 1839, but no references prior to 1846; intr. 1820
'Omphale' HGal, mp, 1839, Vibert or Robert; flowers rosy pink, sometimes spotted with white, large, very dbl., cupped; growth erect; this first appears in Vibert's 1839 catalog, but the description is revised in the catalog of 1845
'Omul' S, dy, GPG Bad Langensalza;

flowers dark golden yellow, large, dbl.; intr. 1974
'On Fire' S, pb, Peden, R.; intr. 1999
'Once Touched' -- See 'Jacirst'
Onda Rose® S, mp
'Ondella' ('Red Meilove') F, dr, Meilland; flowers medium, borne in clusters; free-flowering; groundcover; spreading growth; intr. 1994
'Ondella' -- See 'Meivanama'
'Ondina' F, m, 2005, Kobayashi, Moriji; flowers semi-dbl., borne in small clusters, intense fragrance; foliage medium size, light green, matte; prickles medium; growth compact, medium (140 cm.); cutting, garden; [seedling × seedling]
'Ondine' ('Odine') HT, w, 1936, Ketten Bros.; bud pointed; flowers creamy white, slightly tinted pink, high pointed, large, 20-25 petals; foliage dark gray-green; long, strong stems; very vigorous growth; ['Louise Criner' × 'Souv. de Claudius Pernet']
'100 Idées Jardin' -- See 'Jacbelgo'
'O'Neal's Bequest' S, yb, 1986, O'Neal, Conrad; flowers yellow with pink petal edges, medium, semi-dbl.; foliage large, medium green, glossy; upright growth
'O'Neal's White' LCl, w, 1961, O'Neal; flowers large; vigorous growth; ['Blossomtime' × 'New Dawn']
'Onex' HGal, dr; flowers crimson violet, yellow stamens, small, semi-dbl., slight fragrance; foliage emerald green, tinted bronze; many, fine, needle-like prickles
'Onguiculata Cariophillata' -- See 'Œillet'
'Onkaparinga' -- See 'Tomring'
'Onkel Svend' F, rb, 1985, Poulsen, Niels D.; flowers medium red and silvery red blend, 23 petals, borne in sprays, moderate spicy fragrance; foliage medium size, dark, matte; low, bushy, spreading growth; ['Sonia' × 'Ernest H. Morse']; intr. 1978
'Only Love' -- See 'Interonly'
'Only You' HT, dp, 1971, Vahldiek-Bissingen; flowers rose-carmine, 4½-5 in., dbl., high-centered, borne singly, slight fragrance; good repeat; foliage medium size, leathery; very vigorous, dense growth; [sport of Carina®]; intr. 1970
'Ontario Celebration' -- See 'Lavmount'
'Onterama' -- See 'Intruma'
'Onyx Flamboyant' HT, lp, 1967, Delbard-Chabert; flowers peach to shell-pink, 4 in., high-centered; foliage serrated; vigorous, bushy growth; ['Sultane' × Queen Elizabeth®]; intr. 1965
'Oodnadatta' Pol, pb, Sutherland; intr. 2000
'Oonagh' -- See 'Seaoona'
'Ooo! Baby!' -- See 'Tinbaby'
'Oor Wullie' Min, mp, 1978, Anderson's Rose Nurseries; flowers salmon-pink, medium, 24 petals; foliage glossy, leathery; free growth; [sport of 'New Penny']
'Opa Pötschke' -- See 'Precious Platinum'
'Opal' ('Lise Palais') HT, mp, 1934, Gaujard; flowers salmon to opal, 5½ in., 45 petals, high-centered; vigorous growth; ['Julien Potin' × (R. foetida bicolor × unknown)]; intr. 1941
'Opal Brünner' Cl F, lp, about 1948, Marshall, O.C.; bud very small; flowers blush-pink to pale rose, dbl., borne in large clusters, slight musk fragrance; tall (10 ft.), pillar growth
'Opal Gold' HT, ab, 1936, Bate; flowers apricot, changing to pink; PP245; [sport of 'Joanna Hill']
'Opal Jewel' Min, mp, 1962, Morey, Dr. Dennison; bud ovoid; flowers pink, center darker, 1 in., 45 petals; foliage leathery; vigorous, compact (8-10 in.) growth; PP2292; ['Mothersday' × 'Rosy Jewel']; intr. 1962
'Opal of Arz' HT, ob, 1938, Brownell; flowers variable orange shades, dbl., moderate fragrance; [sport of Mary Wallace × unknown]
Opalia® -- See 'White Flower Carpet'
'Opaline' HT, pb, 1922, Lippiatt; flowers pale pink, shaded carmine and old-gold; ['Louise Catherine Breslau' × 'Frau Karl Druschki']
'Opaline' Cl HT, pb, Clause; flowers apricot-pink, lighter at edges, moderate fragrance; foliage large, dark green; intr. 1982
'Open Arms' -- See 'Chewpixcel'
Open d'Australie® -- See 'Dorsafr'
'Open Field' -- See 'Ausblush'
'Open Secret' -- See 'Weepaint'
'Opening Act' -- See 'Jalact'
Opening Night™ -- See 'Jacolber'
'Opéra' HT, rb, 1950, Gaujard; bud long, pointed; flowers light scarlet-red, base yellow, 6 in., dbl., moderate fragrance; foliage leathery, light green; vigorous, erect growth; PP1017; ['La Belle Irisee' × seedling]
'Opera, Climbing' ('Grimpant Opera') Cl HT, rb, 1956, Armbrust
'Operetta' Bailey, Dorothy J., Bailey, Dorothy J.; PP4429
Operettenrose® HT, lp
'Ophelia' HT, lp, 1912, Paul, W.; bud long, pointed; flowers salmon-flesh, center tinted light yellow, 28 petals, moderate fragrance; foliage leathery; vigorous growth; seed parent probably 'Antoine Rivoire'; pollen parent either Mme Caroline Testout, Pharisäer, or Prince de Bulgarie; intr. 1914
'Ophelia, Climbing' Cl HT, lp, 1920, Dickson, A.; flowers soft salmon pink, large, dbl., flat; [sport of 'Ophelia']
'Ophelia Queen, Climbing' Cl HT, lp, 1923, Westbury Rose Co.; [sport of 'Ophelia']
'Ophelia Supreme' HT, lp, 1917, Dailledouze Bros.; flowers light rose-pink, center darker; [sport of 'Ophelia']
'Ophie O' HT, lp, 2001, Adlong, Paula; flowers medium, full, borne mostly singly, slight fragrance; ['Crystilline' × 'Elizabeth Taylor']; intr. 2001
'Ophir' HMsk, my, about 1835, Laffay; flowers nankeen yellow, small, full
'Ophirie' N, op, 1841, Goubault; flowers reddish-copper, reverse rosy and fawn, very dbl., cupped; vigorous growth
'Opium!' HT, dr, Schreurs; intr. 2002
'Oporto' HT, dr, 1930, Allen; flowers port-wine-red, petals very leathery, dbl.; ['Château de Clos Vougeot' × 'Betty Uprichard']
'Optima Orange' Min, or, Pouw, A.; flowers very dbl., 40-50 petals, no fragrance; growth low (8-12 in.); containers; PP10820; [seedling × seedling]; intr. 1997
'Opulence' -- See 'Jacosch'
'Opus' Pol, or, VEG; flowers medium to large, semi-dbl.
'Or Hatabor' HT, dy, Fischel; intr. 1989
'Ora Kelly' Min, op, Moore, Ralph; flowers peach pink with a light halo, 1½-2 in., 5-10 petals, borne singly and in small clusters; recurrent; vigorous, healthy (18 in.) growth; intr. 2001
'Ora Kingsley' -- See 'Clehonor'
'Orablan' HT, w, Orard; intr. 1992
'Oracham' HT, rb, Orard; intr. 2002
'Oracharpam' ('First Great Western') HT, m, Orard; intr. 2006
'Oracle' HT, or, Select; intr. 2003
'Oracleon' HT, ab, Orard, Pierre dt Joseph; intr. 2005
'Oracreps' ('Hope') F, pb, Orard, P.; intr. 2000
'Oradal' ('Hacienda', 'Red 'n' Fragrant', Firefighter™) HT, dr, 2004, Orard, Pierre; flowers velvety dark red, reverse medium red, 4½ in., 40-45 petals, borne mostly solitary, intense fragrance; foliage small, semi-glossy; prickles smallish, straight, brown, few; growth upright, tall (60 in.); cutting, exhibition, garden decoration; ['Adharmon' × 'Meitulandi']; intr. 2000
'Oradit' (Edith de Martinelli, Climbing®) Cl F, op, 1983, Orard, Joseph; growth climbing (to 3 m.)
'Oradiwu' S, w, Orardsingle; intr. 1996
'Oradon' ('Tanned Beauty') HT, ab, Orard
'Oradour' F, dr, 1955, Mallerin, C.; flowers dbl.; ['Happiness' × 'Demain']
'Orafarcom' HT, m, Orard; intr. 2008
'Orafe' HT, pb; intr. 1997
'Orafuna' (Cyclamen®) F, pb, Orard; intr. 1992
'Oragofe' ('Carousel Panarosa') F, rb, Orard
'Oraju' ('Tassili') HT, ly, Orard; intr. 1993
'Orakah' HT, m, Orard, Joseph; intr. 1994
'Orakosar' ('Lady Rose, Climbing') Cl HT, or, Orard; intr. 1993
'Oralamar' ('Ville de Moulins') HT, mr, Orard
'Oraland' HT, my, Orard; intr. 2000
'Oramaucoq' HT, ob, Orard; intr. 2002
'Oramont' (Orangina®) F, or, 1983, Orard, Joseph; [sport of 'Royal Occasion']
'Orana Gold' -- See 'Macerupt'
'Oranat' HT, dr, Orard; intr. 1997

'Orange Ace'   HT, or, Roman, G., and Wagner, S.; flowers deep orange-red, medium to large, 25 petals, slight fragrance; foliage medium size, glossy, healthy; ['Rosabunda' × 'Galia']; intr. 1999

Orange Adam®   F, ob, Adam, M.; intr. 1993

'Orange Appeal' -- See 'Renapp'

'Orange Baby' -- See 'Tanegnaro'

'Orange Babyflor' -- See 'Tanegnaro'

'Orange Beauty'   Min, ob

'Orange Beauty'   Cl F, op, 1961, Raffel; flowers orange to salmon, medium, dbl., high-centered, borne in clusters; foliage glossy; vigorous (6-8 ft.) growth; ['Little Darling' × 'Gertrude Raffel']; intr. 1961

'Orange Blossom'   S, w, McLeod, J.; [R. brunonii × unknown]; intr. 1990

Orange Blossom Special™ -- See 'Jacmocl'

'Orange Bouquet'   F, ob, 1972, Northfield; flowers coppery orange, turning pink, 2½ in., 25 petals, rosette; foliage dark; upright, free growth; ['Masquerade' × 'Paris-Match']

Orange Bunny® -- See 'Meirianopur'

'Orange Butterfly'   S, or, Williams, J. Benjamin; flowers orange-red with prominent yellow stamens and eye, single, mass blooming; intr. 1997

'Orange Cascade'   Cl Min, ob, 1979, Moore, Ralph S.; bud pointed; flowers yellow-orange, 1 in., 20 petals, moderate fragrance; foliage small, fern-like; slender, willowy growth; PP4596; ['yellow seedling' × 'Magic Wand']

'Orange Chalice'   S, ob, Williams, J.B.; flowers delicate light orange, single; foliage dark green and glossy; growth shrub that can be trained as a climber; intr. 2003

'Orange Charm' -- See 'Mindco'

'Orange Chateau' -- See 'Hatuzakura'

'Orange Cheer'   Pol, ob, 1937, Letts; flowers clear orange, almost, dbl.; vigorous growth

'Orange-Cherry Up'   Min, or, 2006, Hopper, Nancy; flowers full, borne mostly solitary; foliage medium size, medium green, semi-glossy; prickles 1/8 in., brown, few; growth bushy, short (10-12 in.); ['orange seedling' × 'Ralph Moore']; intr. 2006

'Orange Chiffon'   F, ob, 1966, Mease; flowers orange-salmon, reverse silvery orange, medium, dbl., cupped; foliage dark, leathery; vigorous, bushy growth; ['Little Darling' × 'Goldmarie']

'Orange Class'   Min, ob

'Orange Classic'   Min, ob, Spooner; flowers clear orange, dbl., high-centered, moderate fruity fragrance; recurrent; medium growth; intr. 2006

'Orange Cluster'   S, or, Williams, J. Benjamin; flowers orange-red with ivory reverse, medium, dbl., open cup, borne in large clusters, slight fragrance; recurrent; foliage small, medium green; growth to 3 ft.; intr. 2006

'Orange Combe'   HT, ob, 1956, Combe; flowers orange, very dbl., globular; vigorous, upright growth; ['Charlotte Armstrong' × seedling]

'Orange Cup'   F, or, 1969, Pal, Dr. B.P.; bud pointed; flowers orange-scarlet, open, medium, single, borne in clusters, intense fragrance; foliage dark, glossy; vigorous, compact growth; ['Cocorico' × unknown]; intr. 1965

'Orange Darling'   Cl Min, ob, 1979, Sudol, Julia; flowers orange, 1½ in., 32 petals; foliage dark, leathery; climbing or pillar growth

'Orange Dawn'   F, ob, 1973, Ellick; flowers orange, tinted vermilion, 4 in., 30-35 petals; foliage glossy; dark; vigorous growth; [Orange Sensation® × 'Sutter's Gold']

'Orange Delbard' ('Lady Russon') HT, or, 1959, Delbard-Chabert; flowers bright orange, well-formed, large, dbl.; strong stems; vigorous growth; ['Impeccable' × 'Mme Robert Joffet']

'Orange Delight' ('Meerzicht Glory', 'Queen Juliana') HT, ob, 1950, Verschuren-Pechtold; bud urn shaped; flowers orange, reverse veined red, 5½-6 in., 30 petals, cupped, intense fragrance; foliage glossy, dark; vigorous, tall growth; PP874

'Orange Delight, Climbing'   Cl HT, ob, 1957, Verschuren-Pechtold

'Orange d'Éte' -- See 'Dornice'

'Orange Dot'   HT, ob, 1963, Dot, Pedro; bud long; flowers carthamus-red, large, 50 petals; bushy growth; ['Chrysler Imperial' × 'Soraya']

'Orange Drop'   Min, ob, 1988, Bridges, Dennis A.; flowers soft orange, white at base, reverse soft orange edging veining, 20 petals, high-centered; foliage medium size, medium green, semi-glossy; prickles long, very pointed, medium, light green; bushy, medium, vigorous growth; [Heartland™ × seedling]

'Orange Elf'   Cl Min, ob, 1960, Moore, Ralph S.; bud pointed; flowers orange, fading lighter, small, 25 petals; vigorous, climbing growth; trailer or groundcover; ['Golden Glow' × 'Zee']; intr. 1959

'Orange Elizabeth of Glamis'   F, ob, 1976, Thames Valley Rose Growers; flowers orange-flame, 3 in., 30 petals, intense fragrance; foliage glossy; compact, bushy growth; [sport of Elizabeth of Glamis®]; intr. 1974

'Orange Everglow'   LCl, ob, 1942, Brownell; flowers orange slightly shaded red and yellow, semi-dbl.; PP505; [sport of 'Copper Glow']

'Orange Festival'   HT, op, 1961, Leenders, J.; flowers pink to coral-orange, small; ['Souv. de Jacques Verschuren' × 'Serenade']

'Orange Fire'   Min, op, 1975, Moore, Ralph S.; bud short, pointed; flowers orange, pink, carmine, rose, 1 in., 40 petals; foliage very glossy, leathery; upright growth; PP3876; [(R. wichurana × 'Floradora') × 'Fire Princess']

Orange Fire™ -- See 'Interfire'

'Orange Flame'   HT, or, 1963, Meilland, Mrs. Marie-Louise; bud ovoid, pointed; flowers 4½-5 in., 33 petals, high-centered, moderate fragrance; foliage leathery, glossy; vigorous growth; PP2141; ['Monte Carlo' × 'Radar']; intr. 1962

'Orange Flame'   Min, or; flowers flame orange; free-flowering

'Orange Flame'   F, ob, Williams, J. Benjamin; flowers brilliant orange and yellow blend; growth to 3 ft.; border/container; intr. 1983

'Orange Flame' -- See 'Olijsab'

'Orange Flare'   F, ob

'Orange Floorshow'   S, or, Harkness; flowers orange with yellow stamens, semi-dbl., flat, borne in clusters, moderate fragrance; low, spreading (60 × 80 cm.) growth; intr. 1999

'Orange Flower Circus'   F, ob, Kordes; flowers full , cupped, borne in clusters; recurrent; medium growth; intr. 2008

'Orange Frenzy' -- See 'Morfrenzy'

'Orange Fruitilia' -- See 'Korbad'

'Orange Garnet'   F, or, 1965, Swim & Weeks; bud ovoid; flowers small, dbl.; foliage dark, leathery; vigorous, upright, bushy growth; PP2710; [('Garnette' × 'Circus') × 'Spartan']

'Orange Glory'   HT, ob, 1936, Leenders, M.; flowers orange, open, large, semi-dbl.; foliage leathery, light; vigorous growth; [seedling × 'Charles P. Kilham']

'Orange Glow'   Pol, ob, 1936, Verschuren; flowers bright golden orange, borne in large trusses

'Orange Goliath'   HT, op, 1978, Gandy, Douglas L.; bud long, pointed; flowers copper-orange, 8 in., 26 petals, moderate fragrance; foliage matte, green; vigorous growth; ['Beauté' × 'Serenade']; intr. 1975

'Orange Honey'   Min, ob, 1979, Moore, Ralph S.; bud pointed; flowers orange-yellow, 1½ in., 23 petals, high-centered to cupped, moderate fruity fragrance; foliage matte, green; bushy, spreading growth; PP4496; ['Rumba' × 'Over the Rainbow']

'Orange Ice'   F, or, 1963, Thomson, R.; bud ovoid; flowers light orange-red, 3 in., 25 petals, cupped, borne in clusters; foliage leathery, dark; vigorous, upright, bushy growth; ['Fashion' × 'Sumatra']; intr. 1963

'Orange Ice'   F, ob, Williams, J. Benjamin; flowers orange with ivory streaks, semi-dbl.; intr. 1999

Orange Ilseta® -- See 'Tanilvoba'

'Orange Impressionist' ('Garden Art Orange Impressionist') S, ob, Lim, P, & Twomey, J.; flowers orange, 3½ in., 25 petals; free-flowering; foliage medium green; upright, compact (3 ft.) growth; hardy; PP15738; intr. 2004

'Orange Jade'   Min, or, 1991, Cole, Catherine W.; flowers medium, full, borne mostly singly, slight fragrance; foliage medium size, dark green, semi-glossy; upright, medium growth; [sport of Black Jade™]; intr. 1990

'Orange Juice' -- See 'Aroraju'

Orange Juwel® -- See 'Korkister'

'Orange Kardinal' -- See 'Maharishi'

Orange Keops® Cl Min, ob; flowers orange to red, white eye, yellow stamens, large , semi-double, borne in clusters; recurrent; flexible canes; 2.5 meter growth; intr. 2008

'Orange Killarney' -- See 'Duchess of Wellington'

'Orange King' Pol, ob, 1922, Cutbush; flowers light coral-red, fading greenish, ¾ in., dbl., open, borne in clusters; foliage glossy, dark; bushy, dwarf growth; [sport of 'Orléans Rose']

'Orange Kordana' Min, or, Kordes; growth containers; intr. 1992

'Orange Kordana' Min, ob, Kordes; flowers bright orange, 35+ petals; recurrent; growth compact; containers; intr. 2005

'Orange Korona' F, or, 1961, Morse; flowers orange-scarlet, well-formed, 4 in., 20 petals, borne in clusters; foliage olive-green; vigorous, upright growth; ['Bergfeuer' × 'Independence']; intr. 1959

'Orange Koster' Pol, or

Orange Love™ -- See 'Minafco'

'Orange Marmalade' Min, ob, 1991, Williams, J. Benjamin; flowers bronze with yellow blend, small, full, borne mostly singly and in small clusters, moderate fragrance; foliage medium size, light green, matte; low, upright, bushy growth; PP6820; ['Gingersnap' × 'Orange Honey']

'Orange Marvel' Pol, op, 1928, Van der Vis; flowers salmon-orange; [sport of 'Miss Edith Cavell']

'Orange Masterpiece' F, or, 1970, deRuiter; flowers small, dbl., borne in trusses; foliage dark; bushy growth; [seedling × Orange Sensation®]

'Orange Meillandina' -- See 'Meijikatar'

'Orange Meillandina, Climbing' -- See 'Meijikatarsar'

'Orange Mikado' F, ob, Tantau

'Orange Mini-Wonder' -- See 'Lavjack'

Orange Minijet® Min, ob, Meilland

'Orange Minijet' -- See 'Lavjack'

'Orange Miss Edith Cavell' Pol, ob; flowers medium, full; free-flowering; bushy (50 cm.) growth; intr. 1998

'Orange Mist' F, ob, 1959, Boerner; flowers orange-salmon to yellow-orange, 4 in., dbl., moderate fragrance; dwarf, bushy growth; PP1757; ['Ma Perkins' × seedling]; intr. 1955

'Orange Morsdag, Climbing' Cl Pol, ob; growth height 250 cm.; intr. after 1956

'Orange Morsdag' ('Orange Mothersday', 'Orange Muttertag') Pol, ob, 1958, Grootendorst, F.J.; flowers deep orange, dbl., cupped, borne in clusters, slight fragrance; good repeat; upright, low growth; hardy; [sport of 'Muttertag']; intr. 1956

'Orange Mothersday' -- See 'Orange Morsdag'

'Orange Muttertag' -- See 'Orange Morsdag'

'Orange Nassau' HT, ob, 1941, Verschuren; bud long, pointed; flowers two-toned coppery orange, reverse yellow, dbl., cupped, moderate fragrance; foliage leathery; PP350; ['Mev. G.A. van Rossem' × seedling]

'Orange Nymph' F, or, 1960, Tulp; flowers medium, dbl., borne in small clusters; [sport of 'Nymph']

Orange Paillette™ -- See 'Poulrouge'

'Orange Parfait' HT, ob, 1982, Weeks, O.L.; bud ovoid, pointed; flowers orange, yellow reverse, large, 45 petals, high-centered, borne singly, slight tea fragrance; foliage medium to large, bronze green, leathery; prickles long, narrow, hooked downward, reddish at base; vigorous growth; PP5098

'Orange Parfait' Min, ob, Moore; flowers flower clean, soft orange, 1-1½ in., 18-24 petals, high-centered, no fragrance; recurrent; medium (12-18 in.) growth; intr. 1998

'Orange Passion' F, ob, Dorieux; flowers bright, deep orange, dbl., high-centered, borne in clusters, slight fragrance; good repeat; foliage bronze green; vigorous (80-100 cm.) growth; intr. 2005

Orange Passion™ -- See 'Jaccogel'

Orange Pastel™ -- See 'Wilorpat'

'Orange Patio Wonder' -- See 'Jalorangepat'

'Orange Pekoe' F, ob, Hiroshima; intr. 2006

'Orange Perfection' Pol, or, 1927, Spek; [sport of 'Ideal']

'Orange P'ins' -- See 'Wekcatlart'

'Orange Pixie' Min, or, 1978, Moore, Ralph S.; bud ovoid, pointed; flowers bright orange-red, 1 in., 48 petals, high-centered; foliage small, glossy, leathery; bushy, compact, upright growth; PP4484; ['Little Chief' × 'Fire Princess']

'Orange Queen' Pol, op, 1923, van Nes; flowers salmon-orange; [sport of 'Orléans Rose']

'Orange Queen Elizabeth' Gr, ob

'Orange Rapture' HT, op, 1935, Schmidt, K.; bud long, pointed; flowers orange with pink, large, dbl., high-centered; [sport of 'Rapture']

'Orange Red Supreme' F, or, 1959, Boerner; bud ovoid; flowers open, 2½-3 in., 18-24 petals, borne in clusters, moderate fragrance; foliage glossy, wrinkled; bushy growth; ['Spice' × ('Garnette' × unknown)]; intr. 1958

Orange Rosamini® -- See 'Ruiseto'

'Orange Rosette' Pol, or, 1941, deRuiter; flowers scarlet-orange, 1-1¼ in., 30 petals, borne in clusters; vigorous, compact growth; PP745; [sport of 'Gloire du Midi']

'Orange Ruffels' HT, ob, 1952, Brownell; bud long, pointed; flowers orange to saffron-yellow, petals frilled, 4-5 in., 40 petals, high-centered, moderate fragrance; foliage dark, glossy; vigorous, compact growth; PP1124; [('Dr. W. Van Fleet' × 'Général Jacqueminot') × 'Lafter']

'Orange Rumba' F, ob, 1962, Zieger; flowers orange; PP2111; [sport of 'Rumba']

'Orange Sauvageot' F, ob, Sauvageot; flowers shining orange, dbl.; foliage matte; intr. 1987

'Orange Scepter' HT, yb, 1953, Verschuren-Pechtold; flowers orange-yellow with dark golden yellow, large, dbl.; PP1164

'Orange Schoon' HT, ob, 1938, Lens; flowers pure orange; [sport of 'Katharine Pechtold']

'Orange Seabreeze' MinFl, op, Williams, J. Benjamin; intr. 1996

Orange Sensation® F, or, 1961, deRuiter; flowers 3 in., 24 petals, borne in clusters; foliage dark; vigorous, bushy growth; intr. 1961

'Orange Sensation, Climbing' Cl F, or; [sport of Orange Sensation®]

'Orange Sherbert' -- See 'Lyora'

'Orange Silk' F, or, 1968, McGredy, Sam IV; flowers orange-vermilion, large, dbl., shallow-cupped, borne in large clusters; good repeat; foliage dark, glossy; vigorous, compact growth; [Orangeade® × ('Ma Perkins' × 'Independence')]

'Orange Silk' -- See 'Apricot Silk'

'Orange Slippers' -- See 'Golden Slippers'

'Orange Smoke' F, ob, 1964, Hennessey; flowers orange, with blue haze in cool weather, 3-4 in.; very vigorous growth; ['Orange Ruffels' × ('Eva' × 'Guinee')]

'Orange Sovereign' Pol, ob

Orange Sparkle' -- See 'Korsparko'

'Orange Sparks' HT, or, 1969, Vasishth; flowers orange-vermilion blend, striped gold, medium, dbl.; foliage glossy, bronze; vigorous, bushy growth; [sport of 'Cherry Brandy']

'Orange Special' F, or, 1958, deRuiter; flowers orange-scarlet, 1½ in., 30-35 petals, cupped, borne in large trusses; dwarf, bushy growth; [sport of 'Salmon Perfection']; intr. 1957

'Orange Spice' Min, ob, 1980, Lyon; bud ovoid, pointed; flowers orange, deeper on petal edges, 23 petals, cupped, borne singly or several together, moderate fragrance; foliage small, medium green; prickles recurved; bushy, upright growth; [seedling × seedling]

'Orange Spice' -- See 'Socotra'

'Orange Splash' -- See 'Jacseraw'

'Orange Splendor' F, ob, Select Roses, B.V.; intr. 1998

Orange Star™ -- See 'Minalco'

'Orange Starina' Min, ob, 1982, Graff, Roy; bud pointed; flowers light orange, 30 petals, high-centered, borne mostly singly, moderate fragrance; foliage small; abundant growth; [sport of Starina®]; intr. 1981

'Orange Sunblaze, Climbing' -- See 'Meijikatarsar'

Orange Sunblaze™ -- See 'Meijikatar'

'Orange Sunset' -- See 'Manorsun'

'Orange Sunshine' Min, ob, 1968, Moore, Ralph S.; flowers orange; [sport of 'Bit o' Sunshine']

'Orange Supreme' HT, ob

'Orange Surprise' F, ob; intr. 1998

'Orange Sweetheart' F, op, 1952, Boerner; bud ovoid; flowers 3-3½ in., 20-25 petals, cupped, slight fruity fragrance; foliage dark; upright, bushy growth; PP1155; [('Pinocchio' × unknown) × 'Fashion']

Orange Symphonie® -- See 'Meininrut'

'Orange Tango' HT, or, 1973, McDaniel, G. K.; flowers large, very dbl., high-centered; foliage bronze; vigorous growth; PP3407; intr. 1972

'Orange Thérèse' HT, ob, 1943, Howard Rose Co.; flowers orange-yellow; [sport of 'Soeur Thérèse']

'Orange Thor' S, ob, Pedersen, Thor; flowers orange with touch of yellow, 5-10 petals, slight fragrance; free-flowering; growth to 2-3 ft.; intr. 1976

'Orange Time' Min, ob, Bell, Laurie; flowers bright orange, borne in large clusters; good repeat; short growth

'Orange Treasure' HT, ob; intr. 2001

'Orange Triumph, Climbing' Cl Pol, mr, 1945, Leenders, M.; flowers salmon orange-red, 2 in., semi-dbl., borne in medium to large clusters, no fragrance; [sport of Orange Triumph®]; intr. 1948

Orange Triumph® Pol, mr, 1937, Kordes; flowers small, semi-dbl., cupped, borne in clusters; foliage glossy; compact, bushy growth; ['Eva (HMsk)' × 'Solarium']

'Orange Triumph Improved' Pol, or, 1960, Cant, F.; flowers orange, dbl., borne in large clusters; [sport of Orange Triumph®]

'Orange Triumph Superba' Pol, ob, 1953, Maarse, J.D.; flowers clear orange; [sport of Orange Triumph®]

'Orange Twist' -- See 'Mortwist'

'Orange Unique' HT, ob, Pouw ; bud medium, ovate; flowers medium orange with yellow at base, reverse rose pink, 3-4 in., 24 petals, star-shaped, borne mostly singly, slight fragrance; good repeat; foliage small to medium size, semi-glossy; few prickles; long stems; growth vigorous, narrow, tall (6 ft.); PP10674; [seedling × seedling]; intr. 1996

'Orange Van Gogh' F, ob, Williams, J.B.; flowers orange with white stripes and splashes, semi-dbl., cupped, borne in clusters; intr. 2002

'Orange Velvet' LCl, or, 1987, Williams, J. Benjamin; flowers bright orange-red with dark velvet overlay, reverse orange-red to orange pink, fading to orange-pink, with dark velvet overlay on inside petals, large, 37 petals, high-centered, borne singly and in sprays of 3-5, moderate damask fragrance; foliage large, dark green, glossy, dark-waxed; upright, tall, vigorous growth; hips medium, rounded, medium bright orange; PP6596; ['Tropicana, Climbing' × 'Swarthmore']; intr. 1977

'Orange Vilmoria' -- See 'Korsee'

'Orange Vilmorin' -- See 'Korsee'

'Orange Wave' F, ob; intr. 2001

Orange Waves™ S, ob, Clements, John; flowers velvety true orange painted with scarlet toward the petal edges, 3½-4 in., 12-18 petals, slight clove fragrance; growth 3½ ft. tall and wide; PPAF; intr. 2005

'Orange You Happy' Min, ob, 2006, Hopper, Nancy; flowers orange, reverse white, 2½ in., dbl., borne mostly solitary; foliage medium size, medium green, semi-glossy; prickles ¼ in., yellow, few; growth bushy, medium (13-14 in.); ['orange seedling' × 'orange seedling']; intr. 2006

'Orange Zest' -- See 'Lavtrice'

Orangeade® F, or, 1960, McGredy, Sam IV; flowers bright scarlet orange, wide, semi-dbl., borne in clusters; foliage dark; very vigorous, bushy growth; hips large, ribbed, orange; ['Orange Sweetheart' × 'Independence']; intr. 1959

'Orangeade, Climbing' Cl F, or, 1964, Waterhouse Nursery

'Oranges 'n' Lemons' -- See 'Macoranlem'

'Orangextra' F, ob; intr. 2001

Orangina® -- See 'Oramont'

'Oraniën' F, or, 1962, Verschuren, A.; flowers orange-red, sometimes lined yellow, base light yellow, large, 42 petals; foliage dark; upright, compact, symmetrical growth; ['Highlight' × seedling]

'Oranje Meisieskool' -- See 'Valencia'

'Oranzova Garnette' F, or, Strnad

'Orapaymel' (Heart 'n' Soul™) S, rb, 2001, Orard, Pierre; flowers white with red border, reverse same, 7-9 cm., dbl., borne in small clusters, slight fragrance; foliage medium size, dark green, glossy; prickles average, pointed, brown, moderate; stems new growth dark red; growth upright to spreading, medium (110-130 cm.); garden decorative; PP14500; ['Tamango' × 'Iceberg']; intr. 2001

'Orapent' -- See 'Côte Jardins'

'Oraperf' HT, dp, Orard; intr. 2000

'Orared' (Romy Schneider®) F, mr, Orard; intr. 1991

'Orareg' F, lp, Orard; intr. 1997

'Orarojou' HT, yb, Orard; intr. 2001

'Oraroro' HT, ly, Orard; intr. 1990

'Orasarpal' LCl, op, Orard; bud green-yellow with pink edging; intr. 1999

'Orasil' HT, mp, Orard; intr. 2000

'Orasim' HT, pb, Orard; intr. 2000

'Orasoglo' HT, my, Orard; intr. 2001

'Orastrip' HT, rb, Orard; intr. 1998

'Oratam' D, pb, 1939, Jacobus; bud globular; flowers pink edged copper-pink, base and reverse yellow, large, dbl., intense damask fragrance; non-recurrent; foliage leathery, dark, matte, yellow-green; bushy, tall (5-6 ft.) growth; PP257; [R. damascena × 'Souv. de Claudius Pernet']

'Oratia Maid' F, lp, Garelja, Anita; intr. 1986

'Oratorio' -- See 'Wardido'

'Oratrinov' F, rb, Orard; intr. 2006

'Oraval' HT, my, Orard; intr. 1996

'Orawest' ('President Wilson') S, yb, Orard; intr. 1999

'Orawichkay' S, w, Orard; bud pointed, conspicuous neck; intr. 2002

'Orchard's Pride' HT, pb, 2006, Coiner, Jim; flowers dbl., borne mostly solitary; foliage medium size, light green, matte; prickles ½ in., triangle, light green, moderate; growth upright, medium (4½ ft.); garden; [seedling × seedling]; intr. 2006

'Orchid Jubilee' -- See 'Morclilav'

'Orchid Lace' -- See 'Benorchid'

'Orchid Masterpiece' HT, m, 1961, Boerner; bud ovoid, deep orchid; flowers lavender-orchid, large, 68 petals, moderate fruity fragrance; foliage leathery, dark; vigorous growth; PP2039; ['Golden Masterpiece' × ('Grey Pearl' × unknown)]; intr. 1960

'Orchid Masterpiece, Climbing' Cl HT, m, Buckner, G.; PP3566; [sport of 'Orchid Masterpiece']

'Orchid Melody' HT, m, Benardella, Frank; flowers dark lilac, paling to light lilac as they open, dbl.; foliage glossy; intr. 2003

'Orchid Splendour' -- See 'Tanmaritan'

'Orderic Vital' -- See 'Oderic Vital'

'Oregold' -- See 'Miss Harp'

'Oregon Centennial' HT, mr, 1959, Von Abrams; bud pointed; flowers rose-red, 4-5 in., 30-35 petals, high-centered to cupped, moderate fruity fragrance; foliage dark; long, strong stems; vigorous, upright, bushy growth; PP1914; ['Charles Mallerin' × ('Charles Mallerin' × 'Chrysler Imperial')]; intr. 1959

'Oregon Ophelia' HT, mp, 1921, Clarke Bros.; flowers salmon, edged pink, base yellow, dbl.; [sport of 'Ophelia']

'Oregon Rainbow' -- See 'Clerain'

'Oregon Trail' S, op, Clements, John; flowers deep pink, amber and bronze blended together, 5 in., 40+ petals, old fashioned; foliage deep green with a bluish tone; vigorous (4½ × 3½ ft.) growth; PPAF; intr. 2004

'Oreseed' -- See 'Valerie Howard'

'Oreste Sgaravatti' HT, Sgaravatti, A.

'Orfeo' LCl, dr, Leenders, J.; flowers bright crimson, fading to cerise, 4 in., full, borne in clusters, moderate fragrance; ['Curly Pink' × 'Guinée']; intr. 1963

'Orfuna' (Cyclamen®, Cyclamen La Sevillana) F, pb, Orard; intr. 1992

'Organdi' HT, dr

'Orgeuil de Lyon' HP, mr, 1886, Besson; flowers velvety poppy crimson, highlighted vermilion, medium, dbl.; nearly thornless

'Oriana' HT, rb, 1970, Tantau, Math.; flowers cherry-red, reverse white, 5 in., 38 petals; foliage glossy, dark

'Oribe' HT, r, Hiroshima; intr. 1995

'Orient' HT, dr, 1959, Dot, Simon; bud pointed; flowers crimson becoming vermilion, reverse vermilion with yellow base, 22 petals; ['Queen of Bermuda' × 'Henri Mallerin']

'Orient Express' HT, or, 1978, Wheatcroft; flowers deep orange-red, reverse lighter, 4-5 in., 40 petals, intense fragrance; foliage bronze; vigorous growth; ['Sunblest' × seedling]

'Orient Express' -- See 'Baipeace'

'Orient Silk' -- See 'Ahimsa'

'Orient Spice' ('Rajni') HT, m, 1996, Viraraghavan, M.S.; flowers pinkish lilac, 5 in., full, borne mostly singly, intense fragrance; foliage large, medium green, semi-glossy; prickles moderate; bushy, medium growth; ['Violaine' × 'Margaret Merrill']; intr. 1984

Oriental™ ('Oriental Palace') S, op, Poulsen; flowers 8-10 cm., semi-dbl., no fragrance; foliage dark; growth bushy, 40-60 cm.; PP11622; intr. 1999

'Oriental Charm' HT, or, 1961, Duehrsen; bud globular; flowers 3-4 in., 11 petals; foliage leathery, glossy, dark; vigorous, upright, bushy growth; PP2106; [('Charlotte Armstrong' × 'Gruss an Teplitz') × ('Mme Butterfly' × 'Floradora')]; intr. 1960

'Oriental Dawn' -- See 'Asagumo'

'Oriental Emperor' Cl Min, or, deRuiter (?); flowers lacquer orange-red; free flowering; 7 - 8 ft. growth; [sport of 'Minimo']; intr. 1999

'Oriental Glamour' F, mr, 1972, Gandy, Douglas L.; flowers orient red, 4-5 in., 15 petals, high-centered; foliage bronze; free growth; ['Coup de Foudre' × 'Tropicana']

'Oriental Palace' -- See 'Oriental'

'Oriental Queen' Ch, or, 1926, McGredy; flowers brilliant orange-scarlet, base yellow, fading to vivid carmine, 26 petals; foliage dark; prickles few thorns

Oriental Simplex™ -- See 'Minanco'

'Oriental Staer' HT, op, 2006, Yasuda, Yuji; flowers full, borne mostly solitary; foliage medium size, medium green, matte; prickles medium, numerous; growth upright, medium (1 m.); garden decorative, cutting; [seedling × 'Laura']; intr. 2006

'Orientale' Cl HT, op, 1946, Robichon; flowers coral, becoming old-rose, 5 in., dbl., borne mostly solitary, moderate fragrance; free, recurrent boom; foliage glossy; very vigorous growth; not dependably hardy; ['George Dickson' × 'Mrs Pierre S. duPont']

'Oriflamme' D, rb, 1819, Bozérian; flowers red, marbled

'Oriflamme' HMult, pb, Paul, G.; flowers deep rose-pink, suffused coppery gold, 2½ in., semi-dbl. to dbl., borne in small clusters, moderate fragrance; foliage dark green, glossy; vigorous, climbing growth; intr. 1914

'Oriflamme de St Louis' HP, dp, 1858, Baudry & Hamel; flowers brilliant rose-crimson, very large, full; ['Général Jacqueminot' × unknown]

Origami™ -- See 'Arocharm'

'Orihime' HT, pb, 1986, Itami Rose Nursery; flowers light pink flushed rose pink, reverse pearly light pink; [sport of 'Confidence']; intr. 1983

'O'Rilla' -- See 'Resilla'

'Orimanda' HT, dr, 1976, Kordes; bud long, pointed; flowers large, 27 petals, high-centered; foliage glossy, dark; vigorous, upright, bushy growth; ['Duftwolke' × seedling]; intr. 1975

'Orinda' HSpn, ly, 1922, Central Exp. Farm; flowers deep cream to amber, medium, dbl.; profuse, non-recurrent bloom; foliage soft, dark; vigorous (5 ft.), bushy growth; ['Harison's Yellow' × unknown]

'Oriola' -- See 'Maclocker'

'Oriole' HMult, ly, 1912, Lambert, P.; bud yellowish-pink; flowers creamy yellowish-white, small, dbl., rounded, borne in large tight clusters, moderate fragrance; foliage dark green, glossy; vigorous, climbing growth; ['Aglaia' × unknown]

'Orion' F, mr, 1968, Harkness; flowers scarlet, medium, dbl.; foliage glossy; ['Pink Parfait' × 'Red Dandy']

'Orion' Gr, ob, J. B. Williams; flowers orange-yellow, borne in large clusters, moderate fragrance; growth to 5 ft.; intr. 2004

Orione® ('Barnerio') HT, ob

'Orlando' -- See 'Intervema'

'Orlando Sport' -- See 'Light Orlando'

'Orlando Sunshine' -- See 'Micada'

'Orléans Improved' Pol, mp, 1931, Norfolk Nursery; flowers vivid rose-pink; [sport of 'Orléans Rose']

'Orléans Rose, Climbing' Cl Pol, rb, 1913, Levavasseur

'Orléans Rose' Pol, rb, 1909, Levavasseur; flowers vivid rosy crimson, center white, semi-dbl.; repeat bloom; foliage glossy; vigorous, bushy growth; ['Mme Norbert Levavasseur' × unknown]

'Orléans Simmgen' Pol, dr, 1925, Simmgen

'Ormiston Roy' S, dy, 1953, Doorenbos; flowers large, single; non-recurrent; bushy (3 ft.) growth; [R. spinosissima × R. xanthina]

Ornella Muti® ('Barmut') HT, pb

'Ornement de Carafe' -- See 'Ornement de Parade'

'Ornement de la Nature' ('Anémone Ancienne') HGal, m, before 1813; flowers deep lilac-rose, large, full, slight fragrance; from Holland

'Ornement de Parade' ('Ornement de Carafe') HGal, dp, before 1811, from Holland; flowers varying from deep pink to violet-purple, 3 in., semi-dbl., moderate fragrance; foliage oval, deeply toothed; nearly thornless

'Ornement des Bosquets' HSem, dp, 1860, Jamain, H.; flowers dark pink, aging to lilac pink, 5 cm., dbl., borne in clusters of 10-15; foliage small, glaucous; sometimes classed as Bslt

'Ornement du Luxembourg' HP, m, 1840, Hardy; flowers violet/red, small, dbl.

'Orphée de Lille' -- See 'Marie-Louise'

'Orpheline de Juillet' HGal, m, before 1836, Parmentier or Vibert; flowers crimson-purple, base of petals fiery red with occasional striping, very dbl.; erect, moderate growth

'Orphèse' -- See 'Orphise'

'Orpheus' HT, op, 1965, Verschuren, A.; flowers salmon-orange, medium, 35-40 petals; foliage glossy, dark; long stems; vigorous growth; ['Montezuma' × seedling]; intr. 1963

'Orphise' ('Admirable de Lille', 'Orphèse', 'Rouge Admirable') HGal, m, before 1826, Vibert; flowers purple crimson, large, full

'Orpington Gem' HT, or, 1953, Buckwell; bud long, pointed; flowers coppery orange shaded gold,, 3 in., 32 petals; foliage dark, leathery; vigorous growth; ['Princess Marina' × 'Alamein']

'Orpington Jewel' HT, op, 1953, Buckwell; bud very long; flowers coral-pink shaded coppery, base orange, 3 in., 30 petals; foliage dark, leathery; vigorous growth; ['Princess Marina' × 'Picture']

'Orsola Spinola' -- See 'Marquise Spinola'

'Ortana' ('Anna Katherine') HT, w, 1994, Ortega, Carlos; flowers white blend, medium, dbl., borne mostly singly; foliage large, medium green, matte; some prickles; tall, upright growth; ['Osiana' × seedling]; intr. 1994

'Ortcal' ('California Glory') HT, rb, 1995, Ortega, Carlos; flowers 3-3½ in., very dbl., borne mostly singly; foliage medium size, dark green, matte; numerous prickles; tall (150 cm.), upright growth; ['Osiana' × 'Kardinal']

'Ortisa' (Marisa™) HT, mp, 1996, Ortega, Carlos; flowers medium pink, lighter pink reverse, 5 in., dbl., high-centered, urn-shaped; foliage medium size, dark green, semi-glossy; prickles moderate; upright, tall (5 ft.) growth; [sport of 'Paris d'Yves St. Laurent']; intr. 1996

'Ortkee' ('Kika') HT, ly, 1993, Ortega, Carlos; flowers 3-3½ in., dbl., borne mostly singly; foliage medium size, dark green, semi-glossy; no prickles; medium (150 cm.), upright growth; ['JACice' × seedling]; intr. 1993

'Ortlae' ('Lauren Elizabeth') HT, m, 1991, Ortega, Carlos; flowers mauve blend, large, full, borne mostly singly, intense fragrance; foliage large, dark green, matte; tall, upright growth; ['Moonlight' × seedling]

'Ortmar' ('Margaret O') HT, w, 1995, Ortega, Carlos; flowers medium, very dbl., borne mostly singly; foliage medium size, dark green, matte; some prickles; tall (180 cm.), upright growth; [Pristine® × 'Lauren Elizabeth']; intr. 1995

'Ortsar' (Sterling Star™) HT, m, 1997, Ortega, Carlos; flowers large, 41 petals, borne mostly singly; foliage medium size, medium green, dull; upright, tall (8-10ft.) growth; ['Lauren Elizabeth' × 'Sterling Silver']

'Ortsea' (Chelsea™) HT, pb, 1997, Ortega, Carlos; flowers medium, dbl., borne mostly singly; foliage small, dark green, semi-glossy; upright, medium (4-5 ft.)growth; ['Lauren Elizabeth' × 'Paul's Pink']

'Ortvic' (Victoria's Song™) HT, w, 1997, Ortega, Carlos; flowers large, dbl., borne mostly singly; foliage medium size, medium green,semi-glossy; upright, tall (6½-7ft.) growth; ['Moonlight' × seedling]

'Osahachi' Min, w; intr. 1997

'Oscar' S, pb, Hauser; intr. 1994

'Oscar Chauvry' N, mp, 1900, Chauvry; flowers deep China pink on golden ground, purple reverse, 8-10 cm., dbl., borne in small, tight, clusters, moderate fragrance; numerous prickles; ['Elise Heymann' × unknown]

'Oscar II, Roi de Suéde' ('King of Sweden') HP, mr, 1889, Soupert & Notting; bud long; flowers carmine-vermilion with silvery reflections, large, very dbl., moderate fragrance

'Oscar Leclerc' M, dr, 1853, Robert; flowers red, tinged with violet, spotted with white, 2-2½ in., full; some repeat; foliage dark green; growth upright

'Oshun' -- See 'Ardorisha'

'Osiana' ('Oceana') HT, ab, Tantau; bud large, pointed ovoid; flowers pastel cream, slightly darker in the center, 5-6 in., 30 -35 petals, high-centered, borne mostly singly, moderate fragrance; good repeat; foliage large, long, dark green, leathery; prickles few, medium (¼ in.), hooked downward; stems long, strong; vigorous, upright, branching growth; PP7660; [seedling × seedling]; intr. 1988

'Osiria' HT, rb, 1979, Kordes, W.; bud long, pointed; flowers dark red, white reverse, 4½ in., 50 petals, high-centered, intense fragrance; short stems; vigorous, upright, bushy growth; ['Snowfire' × seedling]; intr. 1978

'Osjen' HT, dp; flowers carmine-pink, medium, dbl.

'Oskar Cordel' -- See 'Oskar Kordel'

'Oskar Kordel' ('Oskar Cordel') HP, mp, 1897, Lambert, P.; flowers carmine, large, 40 petals, cupped, moderate fragrance; vigorous, compact growth; ['Merveille de Lyon' × 'Andre Schwartz']

'Oskar Scheerer' S, dr, 1961, Kordes, R.; flowers velvety dark red, large, dbl., borne in large clusters; vigorous (6 ft.), well-branched growth

'Osmunda' Pol, dr, 1923, Holland (?); flowers dark carmine; [sport of 'Jessie']

'Oso Easy' -- See 'Scented Carpet'

'Ostara' F, mr, 1964, deRuiter; flowers bright red, medium, dbl., borne in clusters; foliage dark; ['Highlight' × 'Valeta']

'Ostrava' S, mr, Vecera, L.

'Oswald Sieper' HT, w, 1933, Krause; bud long, pointed; flowers creamy white, very large, dbl., high-centered, foliage glossy; vigorous growth; ['Mrs Charles Lamplough' × 'Ville de Paris']

Otago® -- See 'Macnecta'

'Othello' HT, dr, Paul; flowers dark maroon red, large, full; ['unrecorded' × 'Gustav Grünerwald']; intr. 1911

'Othello' F, or, Leenders, J.; flowers light orange-red, 2½ in., 22 petals, cupped; ['Ma Perkins' × 'Cocorico']; intr. 1961

'Othello' HGal, dr, before 1829, Trébucien; flowers vivid purple, center crimson, medium, very full, moderate fragrance

'Othello' HT, mr, Verschuren, A.; flowers velvety bright red, large, 48-60 petals, moderate fragrance; foliage dark; vigorous, upright, bushy growth; ['New Yorker' × seedling]; intr. 1963

Othello® -- See 'Auslo'

'Othello Maure de Venise' ('Maure de Venise') HCh, m, before 1828, from Angers; flowers dark violet with garnet purple, medium, full

'Otohime' ('Fancy Princess') HT, or, 1977, Keisei Rose Nurseries, Inc.; bud pointed; flowers 6-6½ in., 58 petals, high-centered, moderate fragrance; foliage large, glossy, dark; vigorous growth; [('Hawaii' × 'Tropicana') × ('Tropicana' × 'Peace')]

'Otome Pink' HT, pb, 1967, Rumsey, R.H.; flowers salmon-pink, reverse buff-yellow; [sport of 'Amatsu Otome']

'Otto Krause' HT, dy, 1931, Weigand, C.; flowers coppery yellow, large, dbl., high-centered; foliage soft, glossy, bronze,dark; vigorous growth; ['Mme Caroline Testout' × 'Souv. de Claudius Pernet']

'Otto Miller' HT, mr, 1968, Morey, Dr. Dennison; bud long, pointed; flowers deep red, 6 in., dbl., high-centered, foliage glossy, leathery; vigorous, upright growth; [('Chrysler Imperial' × 'Independence') × ('Mrs Charles Russell' × 'Happiness')]

'Otto von Bismarck' HT, mp, 1908, Kiese; flowers large, dbl.; ['Mme Caroline Testout' × 'La France']

'Oudtshoorn Joy' HT, ob, Kordes; bud egg-shaped; flowers vermilion, large, long-lasting, dbl., high-centered, borne singly and in clusters, slight fragrance; free-flowering; vigorous, medium to tall growth; intr. 1988

'Oui' -- See 'Ardyes'

'Ouma Smuts' F, ly, 1950, Leenders, M.; flowers straw-yellow shaded rosy flesh; ['Egalite' × 'Vanessa']

'Our Allies' Pol, lp, 1915, Matthews, W.J.

'Our Annie' HT, op, 1937, Letts; flowers vivid orange-cerise, large, dbl., globular; foliage glossy; very vigorous growth

'Our Anniversary' -- See 'Twoyel'

'Our Baby' -- See 'Boslovebell'

'Our Beth' -- See 'Beacarol'

'Our Bob' HT, mr, 1928, Dawes; flowers velvety red, center golden

'Our Copper Queen' -- See 'Koranderer'

'Our Coral Pearl' -- See 'Dospearl'

'Our Daughter' -- See 'Bossufrex'

Our Diana™ -- See 'Twoex'

'Our Dream' Min, ly; flowers lemon yellow, slight fragrance; 18 inch growth; intr. 2007

'Our Esther' -- See 'Korwitcil'

'Our Freedom' HT, rb, Diby; flowers red with white stripes and splashes; [sport of Mon Cheri™]; intr. 2005

'Our George' Min, ab, Kirkham, Gordon; flowers apricot-orange, golden yellow in summer heat, dbl., cupped; recurrent; foliage dense; stems long; medium (18-24 in.), speading growth; intr. 1999

'Our Hilda' F, dp, Bees

'Our Indira' HT, w, Viraraghavan, M.S.; bud long, pointed; flowers ivory, edged lilac, moderate fragrance; intr. 1998

'Our Jane' -- See 'Horengland'

'Our Joy' -- See 'Horjoy'

'Our Jubilee' -- See 'Coccages'

'Our Julie' -- See 'Rawsetbo'

'Our Lady' F, mr, 1956, Leenders, M.; flowers carmine; vigorous growth; [seedling × 'Soestdijk']

'Our Lady of Guadalupe' -- See 'Jacveryp'

'Our Little Secret' -- See 'Umsasecret'

'Our Love' -- See 'Andour'

'Our Molly' -- See 'Dicreason'

'Our Pearl' LCl, pb, 1993, Jerabek, Paul E.; flowers white with pink edges, medium, 13-18 petals, semi-dbl. to double, borne in small clusters; foliage medium size, medium green, matte; some prickles; medium (7 ft.), bushy, spreading growth

'Our Princess' ('Crimson Glow') F, dr, 1949, Robinson, H.; flowers deep velvety crimson, semi-dbl., borne in large trusses; foliage glossy, dark; vigorous growth; ['Donald Prior' × Orange Triumph®]

'Our Rodeo' F, rb, Kordes; intr. 1997

'Our Rosamond' HT, pb, 1982, Bell, Ronald J.; flowers silver and pink blend, large, 35 petals, high-centered, borne singly; foliage medium size, medium green, glossy; upright growth; [('Daily Sketch' × unknown) × 'Red Planet']; intr. 1983

'Our Rosy Carpet' -- See 'Korsilan'

'Our Sacha' -- See 'Spekes'

'Our Shirley' HT, w, 1989, Wilson, George D.; bud pointed; flowers medium, 28 petals, borne singly; foliage small, medium size, dark green; prickles long, slender, red; medium, upright growth; ['Judith Morton' × 'Sylvia']

'Our Son' -- See 'Bosrexfolk'

'Our Sweet Ann' F, op, 1976, Horsfield;

flowers warm pink, with orange glow, 3½-4 in., 28 petals, intense fragrance; foliage dark, leathery; vigorous, upright growth; [Queen Elizabeth® × Elizabeth of Glamis®]
'Our Terry' -- See 'Webcrimson'
'Our Town' -- See 'Ziptown'
'Our Vanilla' -- See 'Vanilla'
'Our Victory' -- See 'Nacha Pobeda'
'Out of Africa' HT, ob, Kordes; flowers bronze, apricot and orange, 4 in., dbl., high-centered, moderate nutty, tea fragrance; free-flowering; growth to 3½ ft.; intr. 1997
'Out of Canada' HT, pb, Williams, J. Benjamin; flowers peach and ivory blend, yellow stamens, dbl., intense fragrance; foliage dark green; intr. 1998
Out of India™ -- See 'Virred'
'Out of the Night' S, w, 2006, Moore, Ralph S.; intr. 2006
'Out of Yesteryear' -- See 'Moryears'
'Outback Angel' -- See 'Meirokoi'
Outrageous™ -- See 'Jaczap'
'Outsider' F, mr, 1959, Tantau, Math.; bud ovoid; flowers bright blood-red, open, medium, semi-dbl., borne in clusters; foliage glossy; vigorous, upright growth; ['Fanal' × 'Red Favorite']; intr. 1956
'Outta the Blue' -- See 'Wekstephitsu'
'Ovation' HT, or, 1978, Weeks; bud ovoid; flowers 4-4½ in., 25 petals, high-centered; foliage dark, leathery; vigorous, upright growth; PP4558; ['First Prize' × seedling]; intr. 1977
'Over the Rainbow' Min, rb, 1972, Moore, Ralph S.; flowers red, yellow reverse, small, dbl., high-centered; foliage leathery; vigorous, bushy growth; PP3472; ['Little Darling' × Westmont]
'Over the Rainbow, Climbing' Cl Min, rb, 1975, Rumsey, R.H.; [sport of 'Over the Rainbow']; intr. 1974
'Overloon' F, dp, 1949, Leenders, M.; flowers rosy pink, medium, dbl.; vigorous growth; ['Irene' × 'Hebe (F)']
'Overnight Scentsation' -- See 'Savanight'
'Overton on Dee' HT, pb, 1976, Ellick; flowers pink, reverse cream, 4½ in., 40 petals; [('Ballet' × 'Gavotte') × Orange Sensation®]
'Overture' F, m, 1960, LeGrice; flowers lilac-lavender, well-formed, 3-3½ in., 18 petals; foliage dark; vigorous, low growth; [(seedling × 'Lavender Pinocchio') × 'Prelude']
'Ovid' HSet, mp, 1890, Geschwind, R.; flowers flesh and velvety pink, large, full, flat, borne in clusters of 3-5; non-recurrent
'Owen's Pride' -- See 'Kirpink'
'Ownwid' ('The Widow of the South') S, dp, 2008, Owen, Anne; flowers self-cleaning, 3½-4 in., very full, borne in small clusters; foliage small, dark green, semi-glossy; prickles small, slightly hooked, brown, few; growth compact, medium (30-36 in.); hedging; ['Madame Isaac Pereire' × 'Knockout']; intr. 2008

'Oxbow' -- See 'Berbow'
'Oxfam' HT, pb, 1976, Cobley; flowers deep pink, shaded lilac, 5 in., 40 petals, intense fragrance; foliage dark; upright growth; ['Fragrant Cloud' × Blue Moon®]; intr. 1973
'Oxford' HT, yb, 1930, Prince; flowers deep warm peach, tipped orange-gold, well-shaped, large
'Oxford' -- See 'Harzola'
'Oxfordshire' -- See 'Korfullwind'
'Oyster Pearl' ('Lamrhowitch') HT, lp; flowers pale cream-pink with hint of deeper pink in center, dbl., high-centered, borne singly, intense fragrance; vigorous, tall growth; [sport of 'Bewitched']
'Oz Baby' Min, yb, Hannemann, F.; ['Poker Chip' × 'Oz Gold']
'Oz Gold' Min, yb, McGredy, Sam IV; flowers deep yellow with orange reverse, dbl.; intr. 1981

— P —

P. G. Wodehouse™ (Paul Red Star™, The Jubilee Rose™, True Love™) HT, dr, Poulsen; flowers dark red, 8-10 cm., full, cupped, slight fragrance; foliage dark green, glossy; bushy, tall (100-150 cm.) growth; hips none; intr. 2000
'P. H. Kulkarni' HT, pb, 2005, Shastri, N.V.; flowers full, borne mostly solitary, slight fragrance; foliage medium size, medium green, matte; prickles medium, straight; growth upright, medium (38 in.); rose bed, exhibition; ['Headliner' × 'Ariana']; intr. 2001
'P. J.'s Pride' -- See 'Judpride'
'P. L. Baudet' HT, lp, 1915, Lourens; flowers large, dbl.; ['Veluwezoom' × 'Le Progrès']
'P. M. Leenders' -- See 'President Macia'
'Pablo Diez' HT, Moreira da Silva, A.
'Pace Setter' ('Pacesetter') Min, w, 1979, Schwartz, Ernest W.; bud long, pointed; flowers pure white, 1½ in., 46 petals, high-centered, borne singly and in small clusters, moderate fragrance; foliage dark, matte; few prickles; vigorous, compact growth; PP4513; ['Ma Perkins' × Magic Carrousel®]
'Pacemaker' -- See 'Harnoble'
'Pacesetter' -- See 'Savapace'
'Pachinko' -- See 'Sunpach'
'Pacific' HT, lp, 1927, Pacific Rose Co.; flowers soft pink, semi-dbl.; [sport of 'Los Angeles']
'Pacific' HT, lp, Heers, C W; ['Catherine Kordes' × 'Rose Marie']; intr. 1948
'Pacific' F, mr, Gaujard; flowers bright red, semi-dbl.; foliage bright green; ['Alain' × 'Chanteclerc']; intr. 1958
'Pacific Beauty' -- See 'Miss Canada'
'Pacific Belle' HT, mp, 1989, Cattermole, R.F.; bud pointed; flowers light pink, reverse deeper pink, reflexed, pointed, medium, 31 petals; foliage light green, veined, glossy; prickles pointed, light brown; bushy, branching, upright growth; [(Peer Gynt® × unknown) × 'Josephine Bruce']

'Pacific Blue' HT, m; flowers lavender, large, full, high-centered, borne mostly singly; PP14410; greenhouse rose; intr. 2002
'Pacific Darling' Min, pb, 1991, Sudol, Julia; flowers large, semi-dbl., borne in large clusters, slight fragrance; foliage large, dark green, glossy; low, upright, bushy, compact growth; ['Winifred Coulter' × seedling]
'Pacific Dream' -- See 'Pejamblu'
'Pacific Pearls' HRg, lp, 2007, Olsen, Paul G.; flowers very light pink, fading quickly to white, 7½ cm., semi-dbl., borne in small clusters; foliage medium, medium green, semi-glossy; prickles moderate; growth bushy, medium (1.2 m.); landscape; ['Hansa' × 'Charles Albanel']; intr. 2007
'Pacific Princess' HT, mp, 1989, Cattermole, R.F.; bud tapering; flowers medium, 56 petals, globular, borne usually singly and in sprays of 3-4; foliage dark green, semi-glossy, veined; upright, branching growth; ['Pink Parfait' × 'Red Planet']; intr. 1988
Pacific Serenade™ -- See 'Savanade'
'Pacific Sunset' HT, pb, 1978, Fong; bud deep pointed; flowers pink to orange-scarlet, 5 in., semi-dbl., high-centered; foliage dark; upright growth; ['Mme Henri Guillot' × 'California']; intr. 1977
'Pacific Triumph' Pol, mp, 1949, Heers; flowers salmon-pink, intense fragrance; growth like parent; [sport of Orange Triumph®]
Pacifica® -- See 'Jacif'
'Paco Rabanne' F, dy, Adam; intr. 2003
'Pacoima' HT, lp, 1927, Pacific Rose Co.; flowers flesh tinted yellow, dbl.; [sport of 'William F. Dreer']
'Pacsix' Min, mp, Jauchen; Dan; PP15657
'Paddy McGredy' F, mp, 1962, McGredy, Sam IV; bud ovoid; flowers deep rose-pink, 4 in., 33 petals, cupped, borne in clusters, moderate fragrance; foliage leathery; vigorous, bushy growth; PP2327; ['Spartan' × 'Tzigane']; intr. 1962
'Paddy 'n' Elizabeth' -- See 'Seaeliz'
'Paddy Stephens' -- See 'Macclack'
Paddywack™ -- See 'Miniwack'
'Paderborn' -- See 'Bischofsstadt Paderborn'
'Padmavathi '95' HT, pb, Kasturi & Sriram; flowers creamy white with pink petal edges, large; [sport of 'Uncle Joe']; intr. 1995
'Padre' HT, rb, 1921, Cant, B. R.; flowers bright coppery scarlet, flushed yellow, large, semi-dbl., cupped, moderate fruity fragrance; foliage small, sparse, dark green; vigorous growth
'Padre Américo' HT, mr, 1956, Moreira da Silva; flowers carmine-red; ['Crimson Glory' × 'Peace']
'Padre Cruz' HT, w, 1956, Moreira da Silva; flowers rosy white edged ruby; ['Branca' × 'Peace']

'Padre Mañanet'   HT, dr, 1958, Dot, Pedro; flowers bright purple-garnet, reverse crimson-red, large, 30 petals, high-centered, moderate fragrance; strong stems; upright growth; ['Charles Mallerin' × ('Satan' × 'Mirandy')]; intr. 1957

'Paeonia'   HT, m, Strnad

'Pæonia'   HP, dp, Geduldig; flowers large, full; ['Frau Karl Druschki' × ('Ulrich Brunner fils' × 'Mrs John Laing')]; intr. 1914

'Pæonia' ('Plonia')   HP, dr, 1855, Lacharme, F.; flowers crimson, large, dbl., intense fragrance

'Paeonienrose'   HGal, mp; flowers peony pink, full, quartered, slight fragrance; 4 × 4 ft. growth

'Pagan Beauty'   F, pb, 1965, Verschuren; flowers bright vermilion, reverse salmon-pink, 4-5 in., 42 petals, globular; foliage dark, leathery; vigorous growth; ['Montezuma' × seedling]

'Paganini'   HT, pb, Meilland; flowers light pink, reverse darker, full, high-centered, borne mostly singly; cut flower trade; intr. 1999

'Paganini' -- See 'Lenpaga'

'Paganini' -- See 'Niccolo Paganini'

'Pageant'   HT, rb, 1953, Boerner; bud ovoid; flowers red, reverse yellow, 4½-5 in., 35-40 petals, high-centered, moderate fragrance; foliage leathery; vigorous, upright growth; PP1252; [hybrid tea seedling × ('Orange Nassau' × unknown)]

'Pagliacci'   Gr, yb, 1969, Von Abrams; bud pointed; flowers yellow, becoming cerise, medium, semi-dbl.; foliage glossy, bronze; vigorous, upright growth

'Pagoda'   S, dr, 1995, Jobson, Daniel J.; flowers dark velvet red with showy gold stamens, small, 5 petals, borne in large clusters; foliage medium size, medium green, semi-glossy; no prickles; low (3 × 6 ft.), spreading, bushy growth; ['Anytime' × 'Mountain Mist']

'Pahadi Dhun'   HT, m, Pal, Dr. B.P.; intr. 1981

'Paharan'   F, lp, 1974, Pal, Dr. B. P.; buds medium, pointed; flowers shell-pink, medium, semi-dbl., open, borne singly and several together; foliage small, bronzy, glossy; stems reddish; growth moderate, bushy, open (45 cm.); ['Anna Wheatcroft' × unknown]; intr. 1971

Pailine™   HT, ob, Melle; flowers yellow with pink edges; [Lorena® × 'Kardinal']; intr. 1989

'Paint Box'   F, yb, 1963, Dickson, Patrick; bud ovoid; flowers red and golden yellow, becoming deep red, 3 in., semi-dbl., flat, borne in clusters; foliage dark; vigorous, upright growth; [seedling × 'St Pauli']

'Paint-Pot' -- See 'Trobglow'

'Paint the Town'   S, mr, Lim, Ping; flowers bright red, 3½ in., 20 petals, cupped, borne in clusters; free-flowering; foliage dark green, glossy, disease-resistant; mounding (2-3 ft.), spreading growth; intr. 2005

'Paintbrush'   Min, ly, 1975, Moore, Ralph S.; bud mossy; flowers soft yellow to white, mini-moss, 1½ in., 8-10 petals; foliage small, glossy, leathery; vigorous, upright, bushy growth; ['Fairy Moss' × 'Goldmoss']

'Painted Damask' -- See 'Léda'

'Painted Desert'   HT, op, 1965, Lone Star Rose Nursery; bud long, pointed; flowers pink and copper, open, dbl.; foliage leathery; vigorous, upright growth; [sport of 'Talisman']

'Painted Desert' -- See 'Macchopsu'

Painted Doll™ -- See 'Lavpaint'

'Painted Lady'   HT, mp, 1931, Ward, F.B.; bud long, pointed; flowers bright cerise, base old-gold, large, 42 petals; [('Crusader' × 'Premier') × 'Julien Potin']

'Painted Lady'   HT, yb, Herholdt, J.A.; bud pointed; flowers cream and gold, red tipped, 4 in., dbl.; foliage glossy, bronze; bushy growth; intr. 1980

'Painted Melody'   HT, yb, Kasturi & Sriran; intr. 1993

'Painted Moon' -- See 'Dicpaint'

'Painted Spain'   Min, ob, 1995, Jobson, Daniel J.; flowers handpainted orange stippled with white, white reverse, medium, dbl., borne in small clusters; foliage medium size, medium green, semi-glossy; numerous prickles; tall (3 ft.), almost climbing, upright growth; ['Rise 'n' Shine' × (Queen Elizabeth® × Eyepaint®)]

'Painted Star' -- See 'Macmigmou'

'Painter's Palette' -- See 'Morpale'

'Painter's Touch' -- See 'Lavtuch'

'Paisley Anniversary' -- See 'Andpai'

'Pakeha'   HT, ly, Dawson; intr. 1980

'Pal'   HT, ob

'Palacky'   HT, ob, 1936, Böhm, J.; flowers orange-yellow, open, large, single; foliage glossy; vigorous growth; ['Mme Mélanie Soupert' × 'Sunburst']

'Paladin'   F, or, 1960, deRuiter; flowers open, 2½ in., semi-dbl., borne in clusters; moderate growth; ['Signal Red' × 'Fashion']

'Palais de Laeken' -- See 'Grand Palais de Laeken'

Palais des Papes®   HT, dr, Dorieux; flowers intense, unfading deep crimson, medium, dbl., high-centered, moderate fragrance; recurrent; foliage dark green, glossy, disease-resistant; moderate growth; intr. 2005

'Palais Royal' -- See 'Meiviowit'

'Palatino'   Min, rb, Dickson; intr. 2004

'Palatino'   F, mr, 1956, Buyl Frères; flowers dbl.; very vigorous growth

'Pale-Flowered' -- See 'Vilmorin'

'Pale Hands'   HT, ab, 1969, Pal, Dr. B.P.; bud pointed; flowers ivory-white to buff and peach, very large, dbl., moderate fragrance; foliage leathery; vigorous, upright growth; ['McGredy's Ivory' × unknown]; intr. 1965

'Pale Moon'   HT, my, 1967, Patterson; flowers large, dbl., high-centered, moderate fragrance; foliage glossy; vigorous, compact growth; PP2984; ['Ma Perkins' × 'Peace']

'Pale Pink Folies'   F, lp, Meilland; flowers pale pink, borne in sprays; recurrent; intr. 2006

'Pale Rouge Panaché' -- See 'Belle Aimable'

'Pâle Rouge Superbe' -- See 'Bouquet Charmant'

'Paleface'   Gr, w, 1960, Lindquist; bud ovoid; flowers nearly white, base naples yellow, 3-5 in., dbl., high-centered; foliage leathery, semi-glossy; vigorous, upright growth; PP1971; ['Joanna Hill' × seedling]; intr. 1959

'Palestro'   HP, rb, 1859, Boyau; flowers lilac red

'Palette'   F, yb, 1960, Leenders, J.; bud ovoid; flowers yellow to salmon-pink and then red, dbl., borne in clusters; foliage glossy; compact growth; ['Masquerade' × 'High Noon']

'Palhel' ('Helena Johanna')   HT, mp, 2001, Palmer, Bobby J.; flowers medium pink with lighter pink reverse, 5 in., full, borne mostly solitary, slight fragrance; foliage medium size, dark green, glossy; prickles moderate; growth compact, medium (5 ft.); garden decorative, exhibition; ['Kardinal' × 'Gene Boerner']

Palisades™ (Honey Border™)   S, mp, Olesen; bud ovate; flowers soft medium pink, 5 cm., 14 petals, open cup, borne in clusters of 3-6, no fragrance; recurrent; foliage dark green, glossy; prickles numerous, pointed, brown; upright to bushy (60-100 cm.) growth; PP16466; [seedling × seedling]; intr. 2004

Palissade Rose® -- See 'Kordapt'

Paljas®   HT, pb

'Pal-kar' (Karaoke™)   Min, pb, 2008, Palmer, Bobby J.; flowers medium pink, reverse lighter, 1-1½ in., dbl., borne mostly solitary; foliage medium, dark green, glossy; prickles medium, hooked downward, light brown, moderate; growth upright, tall (18-30 in.); exhibition, cutting, garden decoration; [Miss Flippins™ × 'Little Darling']

'Pallas' ('Reine des Pourpres')   HGal, m, before 1811, Miellez; bud round; flowers purple, large, full, moderate fragrance; foliage long, dark green; prickles numerous, flexible, brown

'Pallas'   HT, dr, Murray & Hawken; flowers garnet-red, reverse paler, 40 petals, high-centered, intense spicy fragrance; foliage large, dull, dark; tall growth; ['Chrysler Imperial' × Shannon®]; intr. 1975

'Pallas' -- See 'Harvestal'

'Pallida'   HFt, ly, 1824, Souchet; flowers light sulphur yellow, medium, single; numerous prickles; [R. foetida bicolor × unknown]

'Pallida'   HSet, lp, Feast; flowers very pale blush, almost white, dbl.; intr. 1843

'Pallida' -- See 'Parsons' Pink China'

'Pallidior' -- See 'Agathe Incarnata'

'Palm Springs'   F, rb, 1965, Duehrsen; bud ovoid; flowers oriental red to light bronze, center yellowish-pink, 50 petals, intense fragrance; foliage bronze; vigorous, upright growth; PP2466; ['Oriental Charm' × 'Circus']

'Palm Springs' -- See 'Ripspring'

'Palmengarten Frankfurt' -- See 'Korsilan'

'Palmetto Sunrise' -- See 'Micpal'

'Palmira Bastos'   HT, Moreira da Silva, A.

'Palmira Feijas'   HG, pb, 1905, Cayeux

'Palmyre'   P, lp, 1817, Vibert; flowers pale pink, shaded lilac, medium, full; often repeats; probably extinct

'Palmyre'   C, lp, Vibert; flowers flesh pink, center dark pink, medium, full; intr. about 1825

'Palmyre'   B, lp, Lartay; intr. 1852

'Palo Alto'   T, ab, 1898, Conard & Jones; flowers chamois rose, tinged at center with golden-yellow and creamy white, large, full

'Palocsay Rudolf'   HT, ob, Palocsay, R.; bud long; flowers well-shaped suitable for glasshouse as cut flower, 30 petals, high-centered, moderate fragrance; leaves medium size, medium green, glossy; growth semi-vigorous upright; [('Charles P Kilham' × R. harisonii) × 'Ville de Paris']; intr. 1955

'Palok'   F, pb, Long, P.; intr. 1993

'Paloma' ('La Paloma') HT, w, 1973, Swim & Weeks; buds medium, long-pointed to urn-shaped; flowers large, dbl, high-centered, borne mostly singly; foliage dark green, leathery; growth vigorous, upright (4½-5 ft.); PP2853; ['Mount Shasta' × 'White Knight']; intr. 1968

Paloma®   HT, w; flowers full, 30-40 petals, high-centered, borne mostly singly; stems long; cut flower trade; intr. 2002

'Paloma Blanca'   S, w, 1985, Buck, Dr. Griffith J.; flowers ivory-white, medium, 35 petals, cupped, borne in clusters of 3 - 10, moderate fragrance; repeat bloom; foliage leathery, dark olive green; prickles awl-like, tan; erect, spreading, bushy, compact growth; hardy; ['Vera Dalton' × (('Pink Princess' × 'Lillian Gibson') × ('Florence Mary Morse' × ('Josef Rothmund' × R. laxa)))]; intr. 1984

'Paloma Falcó'   HT, op, 1930, Dot, Pedro; flowers coral-salmon, dbl.; ['Li Bures' × 'Château de Clos Vougeot']

'Palpink' ('Pretty 'n' Pink') HT, mp, 2000, Palmer, Bobby J.; flowers medium pink, reverse light pink, 5½ in., very full, borne mostly singly; foliage large, dark green, glossy; prickles moderate; upright, tall (5-7 ft.) growth; ['Miss All-American Beauty' × 'Rebekah']; intr. 2001

'Palpitation'   F, mr, Kunieda; intr. 1995

'PALS Niagara'   S, mr, 2004, Fleming, Joyce L.; flowers medium red, reverse slightly lighter, 3 in., full, borne in large clusters, no fragrance; foliage medium size, dark green, semi-glossy, disease-resistant; prickles 4 mm., D-shaped; stems sturdy; upright, tall (5 ft.) growth; back of border; hedging; hardy to -30°F; ['Red Hot' × 'breeding line 83, issued by Ag Canada']; intr. 2004

'Pam'   F, yb, 1965, Annabel; bud ovoid; flowers yellow edged red, becoming deep red, small, semi-dbl., cupped; moderate, bushy growth; ['Masquerade' × unknown]; intr. 1962

'Pam Golding' -- See 'Jacarque'

'Pam Tillis' -- See 'Savapam'

'Památník Komenského'   LCl, mp, 1936, Bojan; flowers salmon-pink, medium, moderate fragrance; free early bloom; vigorous, climbing growth

'Památník Krále Jiřího' ('King George's Memorial') HT, dr, 1936, Böhm, J.; bud pointed; flowers deep crimson, marked velvety purple, large, dbl.; foliage glossy, dark; vigorous growth; ['Gorgeous' × 'Gen. MacArthur']

'Pamela'   HT, yb, 1924, Therkildsen; flowers canary-yellow and bright blush-pink shaded deep carmine, dbl.

Pamela®   HT, ob, Tantau; flowers copper-orange, outer petals fading and developing red-orange edges, full; intr. 2003

Pamela™   Min, pb, Olesen; flowers dbl., 25-30 petals, slight fragrance; foliage dark green, glossy; growth bushy, low (40-60 cm.)

'Pamela' -- See 'Korflapei'

'Pamela' -- See 'Worcreek'

'Pamela Ann'   HT, mr, Tudor; intr. 1998

'Pamela Jane Taylor' -- See 'Webyoung'

'Pamela Joy'   S, yb, Hannemann, F.; ['Oz Gold' × 'Eye Paint']; intr. 1999

'Pamela Louise Webb'   F, ly, 2004, Paul Chessum Roses; flowers semi-dbl., borne in large clusters, slight fragrance; foliage small, light green, semi-glossy; prickles small; growth compact, short (50 cm.); bedding, borders, containers; [seedling × seedling]; intr. 2004

'Pamela Travers'   HT, mp, 1966, Morey, Dr. Dennison; flowers large, dbl.; foliage leathery; vigorous, upright growth; ['Pink Favorite' × Queen Elizabeth®]; intr. 1966

'Pamela's Choice'   HT, my, 1966, Bardill Nursery; flowers golden yellow, 4½ in.; foliage bronze; [sport of Piccadilly®]

Pamina®   HT, dp, Liebig; intr. 1991

'Pampa'   F, mr, 1978, Gaujard; bud pointed; flowers brilliant vermilion-red, dbl.; foliage dark; ['Colisee' × Atlantic®]; intr. 1971

'Pampa'   HT, dy, K&S; flowers large, full; intr. 1988

'Pam's Passion' -- See 'Gelpam'

'Pan America'   HT, ob, 1941, Boerner; flowers deep orange suffused tawny yellow, becoming light gold, open, 5½ in., 30-40 petals, moderate fragrance; foliage glossy, bronze; long stems; vigorous, upright, bushy, open, growth; PP437; ['Heinrich Wendland' × 'Max Krause']

'Panaché'   Gr, mp, 1959, Lens; flowers light salmon-pink, well-formed, large; vigorous growth; ['Rubin (HT)' × 'Cinnabar']

'Panache' -- See 'Socpan'

Panache™ -- See 'Poultop'

'Panachée' ('Semi-Double Striped Moss', 'Striped Moss', 'Variegata') M, w, around 1818, Shailer; bud with moss arranged in longitudinal bands; flowers pure white plumed light pink, medium, semi-dbl.; thornless; [sport of 'Old White Moss' or 'White Bath']

'Panachée' ('Variegated Damask') D, pb, Godefroy (possibly Girardon); flowers white variegated with pink, medium, dbl.; intr. about 1820

'Panachée'   C, from Chartres; intr. about 1825

'Panachée'   HGal, m, Vibert; flowers violet, striped white, medium, full; intr. 1830

'Panachée a Fleurs Pleine' -- See 'Panachée Pleine'

'Panachée d'Angers' -- See 'Commandant Beaurepaire'

'Panachée de Bordeaux' -- See 'Coquette Bordelaise'

'Panachée de Lyon' ('Rose du Roi Panachée', 'Striped Crimson Perpetual') P, pb, 1895, Dubreuil; flowers pink, variegated crimson, medium, dbl., intense fragrance; recurrent; upright, medium growth; [sport of 'Rose du Roi']

'Panachée d'Orléans'   HP, pb, 1854, Dauvesse; flowers blush-white striped deep rose, full, borne in clusters of 5-7; [sport of 'Duchesse d'Orléans']

'Panachée Double' -- See 'Panachée Pleine'

'Panachée Double' -- See 'La Rubanée'

'Panachée Langroise'   HP, rb, 1873, Rimancourt; flowers bright cherry red, plumed deep carmine, large, full; [sport of 'Jules Margottin']

'Panachée Pleine' ('Belle Villageoise', 'La Belle Villageoise', 'Panachée Double', 'Panachée a Fleurs Pleine', 'La Villageoise') HGal, pb, 1839, Vibert; flowers violet-purple, strongly striped with white, small, petals recurved, green center, dbl., cupped, slight fragrance; foliage light green, elliptical

'Panachée Pleine' -- See 'Panachée Pleine a Petales Etroites'

'Panachée Pleine a Petales Etroites' ('Double White Striped Moss', 'Panachée Pleine', 'Striped Moss') M, w, before 1844, possibly Robert; flowers white or flesh, sometimes plumed pink, medium, full, cupped; [possibly a sport of 'White Bath']

'Panachée Superbe'   HGal, dr, before 1811, from Holland; flowers velvety purple red, lighter reverse, some petals folding back to give the striped, full, moderate fragrance

'Panachée Superbe' -- See 'Beauté Insurmontable'

'Panaget'   M, rb, before 1844; flowers purple striped and spotted with red, medium, semi-dbl.; possibly synonymous with 'Lansezeur'

'Panama' HT, lp, 1913, Cook, J.W.; flowers flesh edged lighter, dbl.; ['Frau Karl Druschki' × 'pink seedling']

'Panamaril' HT, dydbl.

'Paname' LCl, mp, 1959, Delbard-Chabert; flowers bright pink, reverse apricot tinted salmon, large, dbl., borne mostly solitary; free, recurrent boom; long, strong stems; well branched growth; ['Spectacular' × unknown]

'Pancha Ganga' ('Panchaganga') HT, pb, Patil, B.K.; flowers dbl., high-centered; intr. 1993

'Panchaganga' -- See 'Pancha Ganga'

'Panchu' F, mr, 1970, Pal, Dr. B.P.; bud globular; flowers ruby-red, open, medium, semi-dbl.; foliage leathery; very vigorous, upright, compact growth; intr. 1966

'Pand565' HT, pb, de Groot; Henk C. A.; PP15533

'Panda Meidiland' S, w; bud ovoid; flowers bright white, 6-7 cm., 5-7 petals, flat saucer, borne usually in clusters of 3-5, slight fragrance; free-flowering; foliage dark green, glossy, disease-resistant; prickles 1 cm.; growth low (40-60 cm.), spreading (70-120 cm.); no hips; PP15487; ['Fiona' × 'The Fairy']; intr. 2003

'Pandemonium' -- See 'Macpandem'

'Pandora' HT, my, 1947, Barké; bud ovoid; flowers cream to deep yellow, 5 in., 35-55 petals, high-centered, moderate fragrance; foliage dark, semi-glossy; very vigorous, tall growth; PP918; ['Golden Rapture' × R.M.S. Queen Mary]

'Pandora' -- See 'Harwinner'

'Paneera' HT, w, 1984, Fumagalli, Niso; flowers large, 35 petals, moderate fragrance; foliage medium size, dark, glossy; upright growth; [seedling × seedling]; intr. 1983

'Panhay' S, mp, Panozzo, Bernard; intr. 2006

'Pania' HT, lp, 1968, McGredy, Sam IV; flowers pure pink, well-formed; foliage leathery; strong, bushy growth; ['Paddy McGredy' × ('Kordes' Perfecta' × 'Montezuma')]

'Paniculé' -- See 'Reversa'

'Panlexpaimt' HT, yb, Panozzo?; intr. 2007

'Pannaran' HT, ob, deRuiter

'Panochre' -- See 'Peach Calypso'

'Panorama' HT, mp, 1943, McGredy; flowers rose-pink, reverse silvery pink, 5 in., 30 petals, cupped, moderate fragrance; foliage glossy; vigorous, upright, compact growth; PP614; ['Mrs A.R. Barraclough' × seedling]

'Panorama' -- See 'Panorama Holiday'

'Panorama Holiday' ('Panorama') F, mp, 1973, Gregory; flowers rose, pointed, large, 34 petals; foliage glossy, dark; [Queen Elizabeth® × seedling]

'Panpast' HT, ab, Pouw; bud ovate; intr. 1997

'Panroug' HT, dr

'Pansomro' HT, rb

'Panthea' -- See 'Women's Institute'

'Pantheon' -- See 'Dicjoon'

'Panthere Rose' -- See 'Meicapinal'

'Pantomime' F, dp, 1965, McGredy, Sam IV; flowers deep pink, 4 in., 30 petals, high-centered, borne in clusters, moderate fruity fragrance; ['Ma Perkins' × 'Karl Herbst']

'Paola' -- See 'Tanaloap'

Papa Falcon™ -- See 'Fevrusa'

'Papa Gontier' T, pb, 1883, Nabonnand, G.; bud long, pointed; flowers bright pink, reverse carmine-red, large, semi-dbl.; intermittent bloom; foliage rich green; vigorous, bushy growth; ['Duchess of Edinburgh' × unknown]

'Papa Gontier, Climbing' Cl T, pb, 1898, Hosp (also Vigneron/Chevrier, 1904, and Chase & Co; flowers intense pink, shaded yellow towards center, reverse purplish-red, dbl.; [sport of 'Papa Gontier']

'Papa Gouchault' HMult, dr, 1922, Turbat; bud long, pointed; flowers pure crimson-red, 3 cm., dbl., open, borne in clusters of 10-20; foliage large, glossy; few prickles; long stems; very vigorous, climbing growth; ['Rubin' × unknown]

'Papa Hémeray' Ch, rb, 1912, Hémeray-Aubert; flowers red, center white, single, borne in clusters; very vigorous growth; ['Hiawatha' × 'Parsons' Pink China']

'Papa Hendrickx' HT, or, 1964, Mondial Roses; bud long, pointed; flowers vermilion-orange, large, 45-50 petals, high-centered; foliage bronze; very vigorous, upright growth; [('Jolie Madame' × R. rugosa rubra) × seedling]

'Papa Joao XXIII' HT, lp, 1963, Moreira da Silva; flowers pearl-pink; ['Plaisir de France' × 'La Jolla']

'Papa Klein' HT, or, 1934, Ketten Bros.; flowers reddish coppery orange, passing to salmon-pink, imbricated,, dbl.; foliage cedar-green; very vigorous growth; ['Margaret Spaull' × 'Norman Lambert']

'Papa Lambert' HT, mp, 1899, Lambert, P.; flowers vivid pink, darker outside, large, dbl., cupped, borne mostly solitary, intense fragrance; [('White Lady' × 'Marie Baumann') × 'Oskar Cordel']

'Papa Leo' F, dy, Vidal

Papa Meilland® HT, dr, 1963, Meilland, Alain A.; bud pointed; flowers dark velvety crimson, large, 35 petals, high-centered, intense fragrance; foliage leathery, dark, glossy, olive-green; vigorous, upright growth; ['Chrysler Imperial' × 'Charles Mallerin']

Papa Meilland, Climbing® (Grimpant Papa Meilland®) Cl HT, dr, 1971, Stratford (also Meilland, 1976); flowers velvety red, 4-5 in., borne mostly solitary, intense fragrance

'Papa Pirosha' HT, my, Bulsara; flowers greenish yellow; stems long; [sport of Yankee Doodle®]; intr. 1990

'Papa Reiter' HT, lp, 1900, Hinner; flowers cream tinted pink; [sport of 'Mme Caroline Testout']

'Papa Rouillard' HWich, mr, 1923, Turbat; flowers bright carmine, reverse lighter, 3-4 cm., dbl., borne in long clusters of 15-25; abundant seasonal bloom; foliage rich green, glossy, thornless; long stems; very vigorous, climbing growth; ['Leontine Grevais' × seedling]

'Papa Schneider' HT, dr, 1961, Kriloff, Michel; flowers dark red-purple, large, dbl.; foliage glossy; vigorous, upright growth; ['Crimson Glory' × seedling]

'Papa Vibert' P, pb; flowers deep rose-red in cool weather, rich pink in heat, spotted, full, globular, then reflexing to convex, moderate fragrance; recurrent; vigorous, stiff (3 ft.), tidy growth

'Papagayo' HT, rb, Kordes; flowers medium red, striped yellow, medium, full, high-centered, borne mostly singly; recurrent; stems long (70 cm); greenhouse rose; intr. 2003

'Papagena' -- See 'Macoranlem'

Papageno® -- See 'Macgoofy'

'Papaverina Major' -- See 'Grosse Mohnkopfs Rose'

'Paper Anniversary' Min, w; flowers creamy white, dbl., cupped, borne mostly in clusters, slight fragrance; foliage glossy; growth to 24 in.; intr. 2003

'Paper Doll' -- See 'Jacfiseg'

'Paper Moon' F, w, Teranishi; intr. 2000

'Papi Delbard' -- See 'Delaby'

'Papilio' HT, Aicardi, D.; intr. 1955

'Papillon' Ch, mr, about 1826, Dubourg

'Papillon' T, op, Nabonnand; flowers coppery salmon rose, 6 cm., semi-dbl., borne in medium clusters, slight fragrance; intr. 1881

'Papillon' -- See 'Tanollipa'

'Papillon Rose' F, mp, 1956, Lens; flowers pink tinted salmon, dbl., high-centered, borne in clusters, intense fragrance; vigorous, bushy growth; ['White Briarcliff' × ('Lady Sylvia' × 'Fashion')]

'Papoose' Cl Min, w, 1956, Moore, Ralph S.; bud pointed; flowers 1 in., single, borne in clusters; foliage small, fern-like, semi-glossy; vigorous, spreading (to 3-4 ft.) growth; trailer or groundcover; [R. wichurana × 'Zee']; intr. 1955

Paprika® F, or, 1959, Tantau, Math.; bud long, pointed; flowers brick red, semi-dbl., borne in large clusters; foliage leathery, glossy, olive-green; vigorous, upright growth; ['Marchenland' × 'Red Favorite']; intr. 1958

Paprika™ HT, or, Meilland; intr. 2006

'Paprika' S, ob, Warner, Chris; flowers reddish-orange with yellow eye, single, flat, borne in clusters; recurrent; foliage glossy; low (1 -2 ft.), mounded growth; PPAF; claimed to be blackspot free; intr. 2006

'Paprika' -- See 'Meiriental'

'Papst Johannes XXIII' HT, w, Brauner; flowers large, dbl.; intr. 1963

'Papworth Hospital Rose' F, dr; flowers semi-dbl., flat cup, borne in clusters, slight fragrance; good repeat; growth to

90 cm.; intr. 2005

'Pâquerette' Pol, w, Guillot et Fils; flowers white, tinged with clear pink, very dbl., globular, borne in pyramidal clusters, moderate fragrance; good repeat; Beales form

'Pâquerette' ('La Pâquerette', 'Ma Pâquerette') Pol, w, 1875, Guillot et Fils; flowers pure white, with imbricated petals, 1 in., very dbl., cupped, borne in broad clusters of up to 40; foliage glossy, with 5-7 leaflets; prickles very few; stems bright green; dwarf (12-15 in.), bushy growth; seedling of a seedling of R. multiflora 'Polyantha', blooms much like a Noisette, claimed to be the first polyantha

'Paquita' HGal, m, before 1841; flowers violet, medium to large, full

'Para Ti' ('For You', 'Pour Toi', 'Wendy') Min, w, 1949, Dot, Pedro; flowers white, base tinted yellow, semi-dbl.; foliage glossy; very bushy (6-8 in.) growth; ['Eduardo Toda' × 'Pompon de Paris']; intr. 1946

'Parade' LCl, dp, 1953, Boerner; bud ovoid; flowers deep rose-pink, lighter reverse, medium to large, 33 petals, cupped, moderate fragrance; foliage dark green, glossy; vigorous growth; PP1253; [('New Dawn' × unknown) × 'World's Fair, Climbing']

'Parade Marshal' F, mr, 1975, Byrum; flowers full, 2-2½ in., 25-30 petals, high-centered; vigorous growth; PP3639; ['Little Leaguer' × 'Gemini']; intr. 1974

'Paradis' HT, mr, 1944, Gaujard; bud pointed; flowers clear red, medium, dbl., cupped; foliage glossy; vigorous growth

'Paradise' HWich, pb, 1907, Walsh; flowers rose-pink, center white, tips of petals notched, 6-7 cm., single, borne in large clusters; non-recurrent; foliage glossy; vigorous, climbing (10-15 ft.) growth; RULED EXTINCT 1/79

'Paradise, Climbing' Cl HT, m, Weeks; PP4796; [sport of 'Paradise']; like its parent except for climbing habit and blooming on laterals from climbing canes; intr. 1985

'Paradise' Min, ob; flowers orange with a yellow heart, semi-dbl., shallow cup; free-flowering; vigorous, tall (3 ft.) growth; intr. 2005

Paradise™ -- See 'Wezeip'

'Paradisea' -- See 'Korsanter'

'Parador' -- See 'Meichanso'

'Parador' -- See 'Meikinosi'

'Paraglider' S, ob, 1985, Buck, Dr. Griffith J.; bud ovoid, pointed; flowers light pink, reverse orange-red, medium-large, 28 petals, cupped, borne in clusters of 1-10; recurrent; foliage medium size, dark green tinted copper, leathery; prickles awl-like, tan; vigorous, bushy, spreading growth; hardy; [('Country Dancer' × 'Carefree Beauty') × Alexander®]; intr. 1984

'Paragon' HT, mp, 1964, Macres, T.; bud large, long, pointed; flowers brilliant cerise, 5½ in, 36-50 petals, high-centered, borne mostly singly; foliage dark green, leathery; few prickles; growth very vigorous, erect tall; [sport of 'Better Times']; intr. 1963

'Paragon' -- See 'Patricia Neal'

'Paragon' -- See 'Mackosred'

'Parallel Dreams' HT, w, Drummond; intr. 1994

'Paramount' HT, ab, 1950, Swim, H.C.; bud long, pointed; flowers orange-salmon-buff, becoming,, 4-5 in., 30 petals, high-centered; foliage glossy; very vigorous, upright, bushy growth; PP984; ['Charlotte Armstrong' × 'Glowing Sunset']

'Parapluie de Neige' LCl, w

'Parasol' HT, dy, 1964, Sanday, John; flowers rich yellow, 5 in., 28 petals; foliage dark; compact growth; ['Peace' × ('Ethel Sanday' × unknown)]

'Paray' F, mr

Parc des Princes® -- See 'Dorpurp'

'Pardinas Bonet' HT, yb, 1931, Dot, Pedro; bud large, oval; flowers deep yellow, reverse red, large, dbl., globular, intense fragrance; foliage medium glossy; few prickles; ['La Giralda' × 'Souv. de Claudius Pernet']

'Paree Pink' Pol, mp

'Paree Red' -- See 'Mothersday'

'Paree Salmon' -- See 'Vatertag'

'Paree White' -- See 'Sneprinsesse'

'Parel van Aalsmeer' -- See 'Perle von Aalsmeer'

Pareo® F, ob, Meilland; flowers exotic orange-mandarine and citron-yellow, dbl.; intr. 1986

Pareo™ HT, ob, Suzuki. Seizo; bud large, conical; flowers light tangerine orange, reverse Chinese yellow, edges suffused tangerine orange, 4 in., 30-38 petals, high-centered, borne usually singly, no fragrance; good repeat; foliage dark green, semi-glossy; few prickles; upright (4-5 ft.) growth; PP8024; [('Elmera' × 'Capella') × 'Keivlanox']; cut flower trade; intr. 1991

'Parfait' F, rb, 1976, Knight, C.; bud small, pointed, ovoid; flowers white with yellow base and red edges, spreading down the petals as they open, 3-3½ in., 30-48 petals, globular, borne singly and in clusters of 2 - 4, slight mild cinnamon fragrance; good repeat; foliage large, leathery, glossy; prickles grayed-orange, 10-13 mm.; compact, upright (4-6 ft.), branching, vigorous growth; hips fertile, round, orange-red; PP4046; [sport of 'Minuette']; intr. 1975

'Parfait Delight' F, pb; flowers watermelon pink with ivory reverse; free-flowering; medium growth

Parfum d'Armor® -- See 'Adanuamn'

'Parfum de Franche Comté' HT, op, Sauvageot; flowers rose and coral, large, dbl.; intr. 1989

Parfum de Grasse® HT, op, Adam; flowers strong orange-pink with yellow reverse, full, high-centered, intense fragrance; recurrent; modest (70 - 90 cm.) growth; intr. 2008

'Parfum de la Neige' HT, w, 1939, Mallerin, C.; flowers large, dbl.

'Parfum de l'Hay' -- See 'Rose à Parfum de l'Hay'

'Parfum de Liberté' -- See 'Wekblunez'

'Parfum d'Ispahan' -- See 'Ispahan'

Parfum d'Orleans® S, yb, Sauvegeot; flowers yellow, center apricot-orange , full , cupped, intense fragrance; growth 70 cm. height; intr. 2007

'Parfum Liffreen' F, m, Adam; intr. 1995

'Parfum Rose' HT, dp, Orard; intr. 2000

'Paris' Pol, mr, 1929, deRuiter; flowers bright red; vigorous growth

Paris de Yves St Laurent™ -- See 'Meivamo'

'Paris-Match' HT, dp, 1958, Meilland, F.; flowers carmine to rose, center darker, dbl.; foliage leathery; vigorous growth; ['Independence' × 'Grand'mère Jenny']; intr. 1957

'Paris Match' ('Farouche') HT, mr, Richardier; flowers rose red, large, full, high-centered, heavy rebloom in autumn, intense fragrance; vigorous, moderate (80-100 cm.) growth; intr. 2004

'Paris Pink' -- See 'Arodousna'

'Paris Red' -- See 'Rouge de Paris'

'Paris Superior' Pol, mr, deRuiter; flowers have more lasting color than parent; [sport of 'Paris']

'Paris 2000' S, mp, Delbard; flowers pink/soft lavender, yellow stamens and white eye when fully open, semi-dbl., shallow cup, borne in clusters, moderate fragrance; free-flowering; vigorous, short to medium growth; intr. 2001

Paris 2000® -- See 'Delsamo'

Pariser Charme® HT, mp, 1965, Tantau, Math.; bud ovoid; flowers pink, well-formed, 5 in., 28 petals, borne in clusters of up to 10, intense fragrance; foliage dark, glossy; vigorous, upright growth

'Parish Life' Gr, or, 1999, Wilson, George D.; flowers orange, red edged, reverse orange, fades to light pink, 4 in., full, borne mostly singly, slight fragrance; foliage medium size, medium green, semi-glossy; few prickles; upright, tall (5 ft.) growth; [Piccadilly® × 'Marijke Koopman']; intr. 2000

'Park Avenue' HT, dr, 1962, Jelly; bud ovoid; flowers cardinal-red, 3-4 in., 38-48 petals, open, moderate fragrance; foliage leathery, dark; vigorous, upright growth; ['Yuletide' × 'San Fernando']; greenhouse rose

'Park Jewel' -- See 'Parkjuwel'

'Park Place' HT, m, 2004, Edwards, Eddie; flowers mauve & white, reverse lighter, 5 in., full, high-centered, borne mostly solitary, moderate fragrance; foliage large, dark green, glossy; upright, medium (5-6 ft.) growth; exhibition; [Crystalline™ × 'Barbra Streisand']; intr. 2004

'Park Place' -- See 'Arocruby'

'Park Royal' F, ob, 1967, Eddie, J.H.; bud ovoid; flowers coral-pink, center white, reverse silver, medium, dbl., open; foliage light green; vigorous, upright growth; ['Tropicana' × 'Shepherd's Delight']

'Park Wilhelmshöhe' -- See 'Korwilpa'

'Parkay' -- See 'Macshana'

Parkdirektor Riggers® HKor, dr, 1958, Kordes, R.; bud long, pointed; flowers velvety crimson, occasionally flecked white, 5-6 cm., semi-dbl., borne in very large clusters; recurrent bloom; foliage dark, glossy, leathery; very vigorous, climbing growth; [R. × kordesii × 'Our Princess']; intr. 1957

'Parkfeuer' HFt, or, 1906, Lambert, P.; flowers bright scarlet, medium, single to semi-dbl., borne in small clusters; non-recurrent; thornless; vigorous (6-8 ft.) growth; [R. foetida bicolor × unknown]

'Parkjewel' -- See 'Parkjuwel'

'Parkjuwel' ('Park Jewell', 'Parkjewel') S, mr, 1956, Kordes; bud ovoid; flowers very large, very dbl., cupped, intense fragrance; non-recurrent; foliage leathery, wrinkled, light green; vigorous (4 ft.), bushy growth; ['Independence' × 'Red Moss']; intr. 1950

'Parklane' HT, my, 1961, Jelly; bud ovoid; flowers canary-yellow, 4½-5 in., 25-35 petals, high-centered; foliage glossy; vigorous, upright growth; ['Peace' × 'Dawn']; intr. 1961

'Parkprinzessin' HT, mp

'Parkrose' S, dr, Elvinge, H.; flowers large, dbl.

'Parks' Yellow Tea-Scented China' ('Amber Rose', R. odorata ochroleuca, 'Flavescens', 'Lutescens Flavescens', 'Old Yellow Tea', R. indica ochroleuca) T, my, 1824, Parks; flowers bright yellow, dbl.; the rose in commerce today under this name is, most likely, not correct; int. into England in 1824

'Parkside Rose' S, dp; flowers deep pink, single; vigorous (6 ft.) growth

'Parkstone Pride' S, Delforge

'Parkstown's Pride' -- See 'Tandirpkrap'

'Parkstrauchrose' S, rb, Scholle, E.; flowers dark red with golden yellow, small to medium, semi-dbl.; intr. 1975

'Parkwood Scarlet' -- See 'Kortradkos'

'Parkzauber' M, dr, 1958, Kordes; bud long, pointed; flowers dark crimson, large, dbl., moderate fragrance; non-recurrent; foliage dark, leathery; very vigorous (4 ft.), upright, bushy growth; ['Independence' × 'Nuits de Young']; intr. 1956

'Parkzierde' B, dr, 1909, Geschwind; flowers scarlet crimson, petals shell-shaped, dbl., moderate fragrance; non-recurrent; foliage dark green; long stems; very vigorous (2 m.) growth

'Parly 2' HT, lp; flowers large, dbl.

'Parme' -- See 'Simone'

'Parmelia' HT, mr, 1957, Lennard; bud long, pointed; flowers flamingo-red,, 5-5½ in., 24-30 petals, high-centered; foliage dark, glossy, leathery; very vigorous, upright, compact growth; [sport of 'Mme Chiang Kai-shek']

'Parmentier' HP, dp, Guillot et Fils; flowers medium to deep pink with silvery whitish reverse; growth to 5 ft.; intr. 1860

'Parmentier' M, mp, 1847, Robert/Vibert; flowers dbl., cupped

'Parnassine' HRg, m, 1825, Noisette, E.; flowers light violet, dbl., borne in clusters of 3-5; foliage elongate; prickles straight, unequal; growth erect

Parole® -- See 'Korbilant'

'Parsifal' F, op, 1968, deRuiter; flowers coral-salmon, well-shaped, 34 petals; vigorous, bushy growth; ['Dacapo' × 'Ballade']

'Pársla' HRg, w, Rieksta, Dr. Dz; flowers clean white, medium, semi-dbl., cupped, slight fragrance; recurrent; bushy (4 ft.), broad growth; hardy; originated in Latvia; intr. 1980

'Parsons' Pink China' ('Blush Monthly', 'Monthly Rose', 'Pallida', 'Common Monthly', 'Common China', 'Common Blush China') Ch, mp, 1751, Parsons; flowers two-tone pink, semi-dbl., borne in loose sprays; dependably recurrent; vigorous, upright growth

'Parsons' Pink China, Climbing' -- See 'Old Blush, Climbing'

Parthenon® -- See 'Delbro'

'Partridge' -- See 'Korweirim'

'Party Doll' F, ab, 1960, Boerner; bud ovoid; flowers pink, 2½ in., 40 petals, cupped, moderate fragrance; foliage leathery, glossy; vigorous, bushy growth; [('Goldilocks' × unknown) × 'Fashion']; intr. 1959

'Party Dress' HT, ab, 1961, Robinson, H.; flowers deep apricot shaded buff-peach, 5 in., 25 petals, high-centered; foliage glossy; vigorous, bushy, compact growth; ['Gay Crusader' × seedling]

Party Girl™ Min, yb, 1979, Saville, F. Harmon; bud long, pointed; flowers soft apricot-yellow, 1-1½ in., 23 petals, high-centered, borne mostly singly, moderate spicy fragrance; compact, bushy growth; PP4598; ['Rise 'n' Shine' × 'Sheri Anne']

'Party Girl's Daughter' -- See 'Welparty'

Party Lights™ -- See 'Jacjingl'

Party Line™ -- See 'Mogaline'

'Party Pink' F, mp, 1958, Raffel; flowers bright pink, 1-1½ in., 30-50 petals, borne in clusters, moderate fragrance; moderate growth; [seedling × ('Pinocchio' × unknown)]; intr. 1957

'Party Popcorn' -- See 'Lavpop'

'Party Time' HT, yb, 1987, Weeks, O.L.; flowers lemon yellow with pink overlay, reverse lemon yellow, large, 45 petals, cupped, borne singly, moderate fruity fragrance; foliage medium size, medium green, semi-glossy; prickles medium, reddish, hooked downwards; upright, medium growth; PP6457; ['Perfume Delight' × 'Half Time']; intr. 1986

Party Trick™ -- See 'Dicparty'

Partyglo™ -- See 'Minpco'

'Parure' HT, dp, 1967, Delbard-Chabert; flowers carmine-rose, 5 in., cupped; foliage serrated; tall to medium growth; ['Michèle Meilland' × 'Chic Parisien']; intr. 1965

'Parure des Vierges' D, w, before 1810; flowers medium, dbl.; foliage rounded, light green

Parure d'Or® -- See 'Delmir'

'Parviflora' -- See 'Pompon de Bourgogne'

'Parvifolia' -- See 'Pompon de Bourgogne'

'Parvula Nobis' HMult, m, 1866, Cochet; flowers light lilac pink, aging white, very small, full

'Parwana' F, yb, 1975, Pal, Dr. B.P.; bud pointed; flowers golden yellow, edged plum-red, open, 3 in., 37 petals, cupped; foliage glossy, dark; vigorous growth; [unknown × unknown]; intr. 1974

Pas de Deux™ LCl, my, Poulsen; flowers medium yellow, fading to white, 8-10 cm., 18-20 petals, borne in clusters, slight wild rose fragrance; recurrent; foliage dark green, glossy; bushy (150-200 cm.) growth; intr. 2000

'Pasadena' HT, yb, 1927, Coolidge; flowers golden yellow, edged flame, dbl.; RULED EXTINCT 1/82; [sport of 'The Queen Alexandra Rose']

Pasadena® -- See 'Korland'

Pasadena Star™ -- See 'Marstar'

'Pasadena Tournament' ('Red Cécile Brünner') F, mr, 1942, Krebs; bud long, pointed; flowers velvety red, small, 36 petals, cupped, moderate fragrance; foliage bronze; long stems; very vigorous, bushy growth; PP578; ['Cécile Brunner' × seedling]

'Pasadena Tournament, Climbing' ('Red Cécile Brünner, Climbing') Cl F, mr, 1945, Marsh's Nursery; PP797; [sport of 'Pasadena Tournament']

'Pascal Sevran' ('Julia') HT, rb, Adam; flowers white with red edges that spread down the petals as it opens, full, high-centered, borne mostly singly, moderate fragrance; foliage dark green, glossy, disease-resistant; moderate (3 ft.) growth; intr. 2002

Pascali® (Blanche Pasca®) HT, w, 1963, Lens; flowers creamy white, medium, 30 petals, high-centered, borne singly and in small clusters, slight fragrance; good repeat; foliage large, dark green; vigorous, upright, bushy growth; PP2592; [Queen Elizabeth® × 'White Butterfly']; intr. 1963

'Pascali, Climbing' Cl HT, w, 1978, Anderson's Rose Nurseries; [sport of Pascali®]

Pascaline® -- See 'Lenpas'

'Pascha' HT, mr, Kordes; flowers bright red, medium, full, borne mostly singly; greenhouse rose; intr. 2001

'Pashmina' HT, mp, Kordes; flowers soft pink, medium, full, high-centered, borne mostly singly; good repeat; greenhouse

rose; intr. 2003
'Pasita' -- See 'Korsita'
'Paso Doble' -- See 'Meilanodin'
'Passaya' HT, w; flowers blush to white, double, high-centered, intense fragrance; recurrent; moderate (70 - 90 cm.) growth
'Passe-Princesse' HGal, mp, before 1813, Prévost; flowers light lilac-rose, very large, full
'Passe-Velours' ('La Grand Obscurité') HGal, m, before 1820, Descemet; flowers dark violet-purple, medium, dbl.
'Passion' HT, dr, Preesman; flowers double, high-centered; recurrent
'Passion' HT, mr, 1955, Gaujard; bud long, pointed; flowers scarlet-cerise, 4 in., 36 petals, moderate fragrance; foliage dark; very vigorous, bushy growth; ['Peace' × 'Alain']
'Passion' -- See 'Showy Pavement'
'Passion' -- See 'Netujoh'
'Passion' -- See 'Netsujo'
'Passion' -- See 'Wezeip'
Passion de J. Renoard® HT, m
'Passion Rose' -- See 'Manhattan'
Passionate™ -- See 'Jacergma'
Passionate Kisses™ -- See 'Meizebul'
'Passion's Flame' -- See 'Renpaflame'
Passoa® HT, ob, Select; flowers flowes soft orange, 4 in., 30-40 petals, high-centered, borne mostly singly; recurrent; foliage dark green; stems long; florist rose; intr. 2005
'Passport' Cl HT, dr, 1940, Clark, A.; flowers well-formed; vigorous growth
'Pastel' HT, ab, 1961, Von Abrams; bud long, pointed; flowers creamy yellow and soft pink, 5 in., 25 petals, high-centered; foliage glossy, wrinkled; strong stems; vigorous, upright growth; [('Sutter's Gold' × seedling) × 'Fred Edmunds']; intr. 1961
'Pastel Chameleon' -- See 'Jacorbet'
'Pastel Delight' HT, lp, Kasturi; flowers delicate pastel pink, dbl., high-centered; intr. 1984
'Pastel Princess' HT, pb
'Pastel Tower' HT, Ruston, D.; [sport of 'Eiffel Tower']; intr. 1968
'Pastelina' -- See 'Sunpaste'
Pastella® F, pb, Tantau; flowers medium pink in center, outer petals creamy white, 8 cm., full, cupped, borne mostly in clusters, moderate fragrance; recurrent; compact (60-80 cm.), bushy growth; intr. 2005
'Pasteur' HT, pb, 1978, Gaujard; bud long; flowers brilliant pink, flushed red, dbl.; upright growth; ['Firmament' × 'Femina']; intr. 1973
Pastorale® -- See 'Pourale'
'Pastorella' HT, 1953, Meilland, F.
'Pastourelle' HT, op, 1952, Robichon; flowers salmon-pink, very large; very free bloom; RULED EXTINCT 12/85; ['Comtesse Vandal' × 'Étoile d'Or']
'Pastourelle' -- See 'Pourale'
Pat Austin™ -- See 'Ausmum'
'Pat James' ('Midsummer Night's Dream')

F, ob, Harkness; flowers soft rosy copper, dbl., high-centered, borne singly and in clusters; intr. 1991
'Pat Nixon' F, dr, 1973, Meilland, Marie Louise; bud ovoid; flowers large, dbl., moderate fragrance; foliage large, glossy, dark; vigorous, upright, bushy growth; PP3546; ['Tamango' × ('Fire King' × 'Banzai')]; intr. 1972
'Pat Phoenix' HT, yb, 1964, Latham; flowers cream to yellow, flushed pink, base yellow, 4½-5 in., 40 petals; foliage dark, leathery; very vigorous growth; [('Wellworth' × 'Clarice Goodacre') × 'Peace']
'Pat Stewart' HT, dp, 1977, Stewart, G.; flowers cerise to deep rose-pink, 5-5½ in., 26 petals; foliage dark; vigorous, upright growth; ['Red Devil' × 'Honey Favorite']
'Patchwork' HT, rb, Bailey, Dorothy J.; PP4012
'Patchwork, Climbing' Cl HT, rb, Conklin, H. A.; PP4441; intr. 1980
'Patchwork Quilt' Min, ob, 1991, Jolly, Marie; bud ovoid; flowers orange-yellow-pink blend, aging light orange, medium, 60 petals, urn-shaped, borne usually singly, slight fragrance; foliage small, medium green, matte; upright, bushy, medium growth; ['Rise 'n' Shine' × 'Dandy Lyon']; intr. 1991
'Pathfinder' -- See 'Chewpobey'
'Patience' HT, ob, 1927, McGredy; bud pointed; flowers scarlet-carmine shaded orange and orange-scarlet, large, dbl., high-centered
'Patience, Climbing' Cl HT, ob, 1935, Shamburger, C.S.
'Patience Strong' HT, mr, 1969, Trew, C.; flowers crimson-scarlet, pointed, large, dbl.; foliage dull, gray-green; free growth; ['Basildon Belle' × 'Red Dandy']
'Patina' HT, w, Tantau; flowers creamy white with pink and green tones, dbl., borne mostly singly; florist rose; intr. 1997
'Patio Charm' -- See 'Chewapri'
'Patio Cloud' -- See 'Interflu'
Patio Dance™ -- See 'Wilpada'
'Patio Delight' F, op, Dot
'Patio Flame' -- See 'Poulcot'
'Patio Gem' -- See 'Sunsalm'
Patio Gold™ -- See 'Wilpago'
'Patio Honey' Cl Min, ly, Warner, Chris; intr. 1995
'Patio Jewel' MinFl, m, 1976, Williams, J. Benjamin; bud pointed; flowers purple to clear amethyst, open, 2½ in., 5-7 petals; foliage leathery; very vigorous growth; [Europeana® × 'Angel Face']; intr. 1975
'Patio Jewel' -- See 'Jaciat'
'Patio Orange' MinFl, or, Harkness
'Patio Patty' MinFl, yb, 1976, Williams, J. Benjamin; bud pointed; flowers yellow, washed peach and orange, 2 in., 16 petals, globular, intense fragrance; foliage small, reddish-green; PP4360;

[('Circus' × 'The Optimist') × ('Little Darling' × Starina®)]
'Patio Pearl' MinFl, pb, 1976, Williams, J. Benjamin; flowers light pearl-pink, base deeper, 1-1½ in., 18-20 petals, high-centered; foliage small, glossy, dark; vigorous growth; ['Fairy Queen' × 'The Optimist']; intr. 1975
'Patio Pearl' MinFl, lp, Olesen; flowers soft creamy pink, large, open; low, compact growth; intr. 1990
'Patio Pearl, Climbing' Cl MinFl, lp; bud pointed; flowers soft pink, open quickly, cupped, slight fragrance; growth to 2 m.; intr. after 1990
'Patio Prince' -- See 'Poulcrim'
Patio Princess™ (Hørsholm By-Rose™, New Fashion™, Surrey™) S, op, Olesen; flowers blend of orange, pink and apricot, 8-10 cm., dbl., little to none fragrance; foliage reddish green; broad, bushy (100-150 cm.) growth; intr. 1990
'Patio Queen' -- See 'Chewsea'
'Patio Ribbon' MinFl, dr, 1976, Williams, J. Benjamin; bud ovoid; flowers velvety bright dark scarlet, 2½-3 in., 16 petals, cupped, moderate fragrance; foliage dark; strong growth; [Europeana® × 'Red Favorite']; intr. 1975
Patio Snow™ -- See 'Wilpasn'
'Patissier' HT, dr, Hiroshima; intr. 2007
'Patrice' HT, w, 1985, Bartolomeo, Embriaco; flowers large, 25 petals, high-centered; foliage medium size, dark, semi-glossy; upright, bushy growth; [(Baccará® × 'Generosa') × Zecchino d'Oro']
'Patricia' F, ab, Fermor, E. R.; flowers apricot, base shaded gold; [sport of Elizabeth of Glamis®]; intr. 1972
'Patricia' F, op, Kordes ; bud slim; flowers salmon pink; intr. 1976
'Patricia' HT, mr, 1932, Chaplin Bros.; flowers carmine flecked pink, base orange-yellow, moderate fragrance; foliage glossy, dark; vigorous growth
'Patricia Anne' HT, dp, 1965, Buzza; flowers deep pink, reverse silvery pink, 4-5 in., moderate fragrance; foliage dark, glossy; vigorous growth; [sport of 'Kordes' Perfecta']
'Patricia Beucher' HMsk, m, Lens; flowers dark purplish pink, fading toward cream, 2 in., single, borne in large, pyramidal trusses of up to 50 or more; foliage red brown when young, changing to dark green; vigorous (150-200 cm.), arching growth; hips none; [Trier® × 'Mutabilis']; intr. 2001
'Patricia C. Oppmann' F, w, 1981, Jerabek, Paul E.; bud pointed; flowers very light yellow, 43 petals, cupped, borne singly and in clusters of up to 7; foliage medium green, glossy; prickles slightly hooked; vigorous, upright, dense growth; [seedling × seedling]
'Patricia Dawn' HT, or, 1998, Austin, M.L.; flowers orange-red, lighter reverse, 4 in., very dbl., high-centered, borne singly, moderate fragrance; foliage medium

size, medium green, dull; prickles moderate; upright, medium growth

'Patricia Eileen Adams' -- See 'Kennash'

'Patricia Harknett' HT, dp, 1961, Harkness, A. & P.; flowers deep pink, 4 in., 23 petals, moderate fragrance; foliage bronze-red; vigorous growth; [sport of 'Lady Sylvia']

'Patricia Hyde' F, mp, 1969, Harkness; flowers medium, semi-dbl.; ['Ann Elizabeth' × 'Red Dandy']

'Patricia Kent' S, ly, Harkness; flowers yellow with outer petals fading white, full, cupped, moderate fragrance; growth to 4 ft.; intr. 2004

Patricia Kordana Mini Brite™ Min, lp, Kordes; PP11242; intr. 2000

'Patricia Lewis' HT, dp, Kordes; bud pointed; flowers strong, deep pink to red, full, high-centered, borne usually singly; good repeat; foliage dark green, glossy; stems long, strong; vigorous, tall growth; intr. 2001

'Patricia Macoun' LCl, w, 1945, Preston; flowers small, dbl., loose, borne in clusters of 15-25, moderate fragrance; non-recurrent; foliage dark, glossy; hardy; [R. helenae × unknown]

'Patricia Mary' -- See 'Worcradle'

'Patricia Miller' HT, w, 1977, Miller, J.; bud ovoid; flowers pure white, open, large, semi-dbl.; foliage leathery; vigorous, bushy growth; [Queen Elizabeth® × 'sport of Queen Elizabeth']; intr. 1978

'Patricia Neal' ('Paragon') HT, mr, 1970, Macres; flowers bright cerise, large, dbl., high-centered; foliage dark, leathery; vigorous, tall growth; [sport of 'Better Times']; intr. 1968

'Patricia Piesse' HT, lp, 1971, Fankhauser; flowers luminous light pink, medium, 50-60 petals, high-centered; foliage glossy; vigorous, upright growth; ['Elizabeth Fankhauser' × 'Memoriam']

'Patricia Scranton' Cl Min, yb, 1977, Dobbs; bud pointed; flowers light yellow, streaked red, 1½ in., 17 petals; foliage glossy, dark, soft; ['Fairy Moss' × 'Fairy Moss']

'Patricia Watkins' F, lp, 1947, Watkins Roses; flowers bright pink, medium, 5 petals, borne in trusses; foliage dark; vigorous growth; [sport of 'Karen Poulsen']

'Patricia Weston' -- See 'Reypat'

'Patricia Willats' S, op, 1973, Bottle, A. W.; flowers peach pink, 3 in., full, borne singly and in trusses; foliage small, light green, matte; growth upright 5-6 ft.; [Golden Showers® × 'Hamburger Phoenix']

'Patrician' HT, mr, 1976, Warriner, William A.; bud ovoid, pointed; flowers cardinal red, 4-5 in., 28 petals, high-centered, intense fragrance; foliage large, dark; very upright growth; PP4043; ['Fragrant Cloud' × 'Proud Land']; intr. 1977

'Patrick Anderson' HT, dp, 1938, McGredy; bud long, pointed; flowers deep rose-pink, large, dbl., high-centered, intense fragrance; foliage leathery; vigorous growth; PP411; ['John Henry' × 'Portadown Fragrance']

'Patrick Rudden's Rose' -- See 'Rawfegum'

'Patrick Vincent' HT, dr, 1967, Vincent; flowers crimson; foliage dark; free growth; ['Mirandy' × 'F.W. Alesworth']

'Patriot' HT, pb, 1973, Meilland; buds large, long pointed; flowers pale pink to cream with petal margins shaded through pin to red, large, dbl, high-centered, borne mostly singly; foliage medium size, dark green, leathery, disease-resistant; growth vigorous, upright, bushy; intr. 1975

'Patriot' -- See 'Jaclin'

'Patriot Flame' -- See 'Clescrub'

'Patriot Kordana' Min, rb, Kordes; flowers red and white striped, small, dbl., cupped, borne in clusters; recurrent; compact growth; pot rose; intr. 2005

'Patriot Song' -- See 'Morfed'

'Patriot's Dream' -- See 'Micpat'

'Pat's Choice' -- See 'Koromega'

'Pat's Delight' -- See 'Wilrss'

'Patsy' HT, w, 1930, Dickson, H.; bud pointed; flowers pure white, open, very large, dbl., cupped

Patsy Cline™ -- See 'Arocomu'

Patte de Velours® ('Sting') S, rb, Meilland; flowers red with white at base, medium, dbl., borne in small clusters; growth to 60-120 cm.; intr. 2000

'Patti Quarles' HT, pb, 2005, Edwards, Eddie & Phelps, Ethan; flowers 4-5 in., full, borne mostly solitary, slight fragrance; foliage dark green, semi-glossy; prickles moderate; growth upright, medium (4-5 ft.); garden, exhibition; [seedling × 'Barbra Streisand']; intr. 2006

Patty Cakes™ -- See 'Moepatty'

'Patty Lou' ('Petite') Min, pb, 1955, Moore, Ralph S.; bud ovoid; flowers rose pink, reverse silvery pink, 1 in., 55 petals, moderate fragrance; foliage small; dwarf (10-12 in.), bushy growth; PP1335; ['Oakington Ruby' × 'Oakington Ruby']; intr. 1953

'Patty Sue' -- See 'Tinpat'

'Patty's Pink' F, lp, 1960, Spanbauer; bud long, pointed; flowers rose-opal, reverse camellia-rose, 2½ in., 40-45 petals, high-centered; foliage leathery, glossy; very vigorous, upright, compact growth; PP1860; [('Cécile Brunner' × 'Mrs R.M. Finch') × ('Cécile Brunner' × 'Mrs R.M. Finch')]

'Patty's Red' F, mr, 1968, Paulen Park Nursery; flowers cherry-red; [sport of 'Patty's Pink']

'Paul Bigot' HWich, dp, 1924, Turbat; flowers bright rose, shaded vermilion, borne in clusters of 5-10; vigorous, climbing growth

'Paul Bocuse' -- See 'Maspaujeu'

'Paul Bouclainville' HT, yb, 1930, Buatois; flowers carmine on yellow ground, reverse pinkish white tinted yellow, semi-dbl., cupped; very vigorous growth; ['Mme Charles Detreaux' × 'Mme Edouard Herriot']

'Paul Buatois' Cl HT, dr, 1931, Buatois; flowers velvety red, base yellow passing to purplish carmine, very large, dbl., cupped; foliage leathery; very vigorous, climbing growth; ['Marie Baumann' × 'Mme Edouard Herriot']

'Paul Bunyan' Gr, dr, 1961, Von Abrams; bud long, pointed; flowers deep red, 5 in., 55 petals, high-centered; foliage leathery; very vigorous, upright growth; ['Charles Mallerin' × 'Carrousel']; intr. 1961

'Paul Cezanne' -- See 'Jacdeli'

'Paul Cottingham' -- See 'Woraardvark'

'Paul Crampel' ('Paul Krampel') Pol, or, 1930, Kersbergen; flowers deep orange-scarlet, brighter and larger than Gloria Mundi, but not as double, borne in large clusters

'Paul Crampel, Climbing' Cl Pol, or, 1934, Vially (also Appleton, 1934; Tantau, 1937); [sport of 'Paul Crampel']

'Paul Dauvesse' HMult, my, 1933, Barbier; bud long, golden yellow; flowers bright canary-yellow, large, dbl., borne in clusters of 4 - 8; vigorous, climbing growth

'Paul de Fontainne' -- See 'Deuil de Paul Fontaine'

'Paul de la Meilleraye' HP, mr, 1863, Guillot; flowers carmine-red with lighter reverse, very large, dbl.

'Paul de Zutter' HT, ab, Van Gampelaere, J.; ['Kanegem' × Graham Thomas®]; intr. 2008

'Paul Délépine' Pol, mp, 1933, Délépine; flowers brilliant rose-pink, dbl., globular, borne in clusters; foliage leathery, glossy; vigorous growth; ['Yvonne Rabier' × 'Dorothy Perkins']

'Paul Dupuy' ('Isoline') HP, mr, 1852, Dupuy-Jamain; flowers crimson-scarlet, shaded velvety dark violet, large, full

'Paul Duvivier' HT, mr, 1932, Laperrière; flowers carmine, base yellow, dbl.; ['Constance' × 'Pax Labor']

Paul Ecke, Jr.™ -- See 'Wekpascisou'

'Paul et Virginie' B, m, 1847, Oger; flowers light lilac, mixed with flesh pink, large, full

'Paul Fontaine' HP, m, 1852, Fontaine; flowers lilac pink, medium, full

'Paul Fromont' -- See 'Boudoir'

'Paul Gauguin' -- See 'Jacdebu'

'Paul Gold' HT, my, Poulsen; flowers buttercup yellow, large, dbl., high-centered; intr. 1998

'Paul Harris' HT, dy, 1993, Weeks, O.L.; flowers 3-3½ in., full, borne mostly singly; foliage medium size, medium green, matte; some prickles; medium (40-48 in.), bushy growth; [('Summer Sunshine' × 'Georgia') × seedling]; intr. 1993

'Paul Holtge' -- See 'Grace Moore'

'Paul Jamain' HP, dr, 1878, Jamain; flowers bright dark red, large, full

'Paul Jamain' -- See 'Charles Lefèbvre'

'Paul Jerabek' LCl, pb, 2007, Jerabek,

Paul; flowers cream shading to pink, reverse white, 3 in., dbl., borne in large clusters; foliage large, dark green, semi-glossy; prickles moderate, medium to large, awl-like, green to brown; growth upright, tall (5-7 ft.); pillars, arbors, trellises; hardy; [unknown × unknown]; intr. 2006

'Paul Kadolozigue' ('Paul Kadolozigue') HMult, mp, 1912, Lambert, P.; flowers crimson, fading to lilac pink, 3½-4 cm., dbl., cupped to rosette, borne in clusters of 10-20, moderate damask and musk fragrance; foliage light green; few prickles

'Paul Kadolozique' -- See 'Paul Kadolozigue'

'Paul Krampel' -- See 'Paul Crampel'

'Paul Krüger' -- See 'Niphetos, Climbing'

'Paul Lafont' HT, ly, 1920, Guillot, P.; flowers golden yellow to white tinted yellow, dbl.; low to medium growth; ['Mme Maurice Capron' × seedling]

'Paul Lédé' -- See 'Mons Paul Lédé'

'Paul Lédé, Climbing' -- See 'Mons Paul Lédé, Climbing'

'Paul Lucchini' HT, dr, 1931, Buatois; flowers purplish garnet, shaded velvety red, dbl., cupped; foliage bronze, leathery; vigorous growth; ['Rhea Reid' × 'Yves Druhen']

'Paul Marot' HT, mp, 1893, Bonnaire; bud ovoid; flowers China pink, large, full; ['Baronne Adolphe de Rothschild' × 'Souv de Victor Hugo']

'Paul McCartney' -- See 'Meizeli'

'Paul Meunier' ('Paul Monnier') HT, yb, 1902, Buatois; bud elongated; flowers light yellow shaded salmon, very large, full; foliage bronzy green

'Paul Monnier' -- See 'Paul Meunier'

'Paul Nabonnand' T, mp, 1877, Nabonnand, G.; flowers satiny rose, large, dbl., cupped; vigorous growth

'Paul Neyron' HP, mp, 1869, Levet, A.; flowers clear pink to rose-pink, tinted lilac, 6 in., 50 petals, cupped, good repeat, moderate fragrance; occasionally recurrent bloom; foliage large, rich green; vigorous growth; ['Victor Verdier' × 'Anna de Diesbach']

'Paul Neyron Panachée' -- See 'Coquette Bordelaise'

'Paul Noël' HWich, pb, 1913, Tanne; bud salmon-orange-pink, with yellow base; flowers old rose and pale yellow, fading to medium pink, 2-3 in., very full, borne in clusters of 4-6, moderate fragrance; intermittent repeat; foliage small, dark green; vigorous, climbing growth; [R. wichurana × 'Mons. Tillier']

'Paul Perras' ('Crepe Rose', 'The Crepe Rose') HP, lp, 1870, Levet; flowers pale rose, compact, large, very dbl.; sets many hips; sometimes classed as B

'Paul Ploton' HWich, mr, 1910, Barbier; flowers bright crimson red, reverse lighter, 3 cm., dbl., rosette, borne in clusters of 10-12; foliage dark; [R. wichurana × 'Mme Norbert Levavasseur']

'Paul Potter' ('Connie's Choice') S, rb, Williams, J. Benjamin; flowers bright red with ivory stripes, ruffled, dbl., borne in sprays, moderate fragrance; recurrent; compact, upright growth; intr. 1997

Paul Red Star™ -- See 'P. G. Wodehouse'

'Paul Revere' HT, mr, 1940, Roland; flowers carmine, opening scarlet-crimson, 4-5 in., 24-30 petals, cupped, moderate fragrance; vigorous, upright growth; PP480; [sport of 'Talisman']

'Paul Ricard' -- See 'Meinivoz'

'Paul Ricault' C, mp, 1845, Portemer fils; flowers rose-pink, large, dbl., quartered, intense fragrance; growth to 5 ft.; sometimes classed as B

'Paul Richard' -- See 'Meinivoz'

'Paul Shirville' -- See 'Harqueterwife'

'Paul Transon' HWich, op, 1900, Barbier; bud dark pink; flowers pale salmon, darker at center, aging to lighter pink, 6 cm., dbl., borne in clusters of 3-5; foliage dark green, glossy; short, strong stems; growth to 10 ft.; ['L'Idéal' × R. wichurana]

'Paul Verdier' HP, dp, 1866, Verdier, C.; flowers bright rose, cupped, borne on laterals from longer canes, moderate fragrance; good repeat

'Paul Vogel' HT, mp, 1932, Vogel, M.; flowers medium, dbl.

'Paula' T, ly, 1908, Paul, G.; flowers straw yellow, center ocher yellow, very large, semi-dbl.; ['Marechal Niel' × 'Gilbert Nabonnand']

'Paula' Gr, or, James, John; flowers dusty salmon; [radiation-induced sport of Queen Elizabeth]; intr. 1980

'Paula Anne Creasey' F, rb, 1999, Dobbs, Annette E.; flowers 2/3 medium red, lower 1/3 white, reverse light pink, 2½ in., 26 petals, borne in small clusters; foliage medium size, medium green, dull; prickles moderate; compact, low (2½ ft.) growth; ['Tamango' × 'Anne Scranton']; intr. 1998

'Paula Clegg' HT, mr, 1912, Kiese; flowers bright scarlet; ['Kaiserin Auguste Viktoria' × R. foetida bicolor]

'Paula Louise' F, yb, 2000; flowers light yellow, reverse medium yellow, medium, dbl., slight fragrance; foliage medium size, dark green, semi-glossy; prickles moderate; growth bushy, medium (60 cm.); [Matangi® × 'Mood Music']; intr. 2001

'Paula Mayer' HT, pb, 1929, Leenders Bros.; flowers silvery carmine-pink, reverse yellowish-pink, semi-dbl.; ['Mme Edmee Metz' × 'Betty Uprichard']

'Paula Meidinger' HT, lp, 1923, Meidinger; flowers large, dbl.

'Paula Nunn' -- See 'Horpaula'

'Paula Scholle' S, mp, Scholle, E.; flowers medium, semi-dbl.; intr. 1975

'Paula Scholle II' F, op, Scholle, E.; flowers large, dbl.; intr. 1980

'Paula Vapelle' HSpn, w, Louette; flowers 8 cm., dbl., rosette, moderate fragrance; free-flowering; foliage bluish green; vigorous (5 ft.) growth; hardy; ['Stanwell Perpetual' × unknown]; intr. about 1990

'Paule Delavey' Pol, ly, 1957, Privat; flowers creamy yellow; vigorous, bushy growth

'Paulette' F, ly, 1934, Buatois; flowers saffron-yellow to yellowish-white, very dbl., cupped, borne in clusters, intense fragrance; foliage leathery, glossy; vigorous growth; ['Leontine Gervais' × 'Paul Monnier']

'Paulette' HT, dp, Meilland, F.; flowers bright rosy scarlet, center tinted salmon, well-formed, large, very dbl.; foliage rich green; tall growth; ['Peace' × 'Signora']; intr. 1946

'Paulette Bentall' HMult, m, 1916, Bentall; flowers purple/pink, small, semi-dbl., borne in very large clusters

'Paulette Buffet' HT, lp, 1921, Gillot, F.; flowers pale flesh-pink, reverse silvery pink, dbl.; ['Jonkheer J.L. Mock' × seedling]

'Paulette Coquelet' HT, mr, 1947, Mallerin, C.; bud long; flowers salmon-red tinted bright coral, large, dbl.; very vigorous growth; [seedling × 'Daniel']

'Paulien Verbeek' HT, ob, 1959, Verbeek; flowers orange-yellow, large, 55 petals; very vigorous growth; intr. 1958

'Paulii' -- See 'Repens Alba'

'Paulii Rosea' ('Newry pink', R. × paulii rosea, R. × paulii, 'Repens Rosea', R. × rugosa repens rosea) HRg, pb, 1904, Smith; flowers medium pink, white eye, yellow stamens, single; [sport of 'Paulii']

'Pauline' -- See 'Tinpauline'

'Pauline Bonaparte' -- See 'Mistress Bosanquet'

'Pauline Dawson' HWich, dp, 1916, Dawson; flowers deep pink, large, single; vigorous, climbing growth

'Pauline Lancezeur' ('Pauline Lansezeur') HP, dr, 1854, Lancezeur; flowers crimson shaded violet, large, dbl.; recurrent bloom

'Pauline Lansezeur' -- See 'Pauline Lancezeur'

'Pauline Plantier' T, w, 1841, Plantier; flowers medium, full

'Pauliska' HP, lp, 1856, Avoux & Crozy; flowers flesh white, large, full, moderate fragrance

'Paul's Carmine Pillar' ('Carmine Pillar') HMult, mr, 1895, Paul; bud long, pointed; flowers carmine-red, open, 8-10 cm., single, borne in clusters of 5-20; very early bloom; foliage rich green; vigorous growth; ['Gloire de Margottin' × unknown]; sometimes classed as HCh or HGal

'Paul's Double Musk' S, w

'Paul's Early Blush' ('Mrs Harkness') HP, lp, 1893, Paul; flowers blush, large, dbl., recurrent, intense fragrance; upright, low (2 ft.) growth; [sport of 'Heinrich Schultheis']; blooms earlier than other

HPs

'Paul's Himalayan Musk Rambler' ('Brunonii Himalayica', 'Moschata Himalayica') HMsk, lp, 1899, Earle/Paul; flowers blush-lilac-pink, fading to white, yellow stamens, 3 cm., dbl., borne in clusters, strong musk fragrance; thread-like stems; growth to 30 ft.; [*R. brunonii* × unknown]

'Paul's Himalayica Alba Magna' Sp, w, 1899, Paul; flowers semi-dbl., borne in huge, rhododendron-like clusters; form of *R. brunonii*

'Paul's Himalayica Double Pink' Sp, lp, 1899, Paul, G.; flowers semi-dbl., borne in large clusters; form of *R. brunonii*

'Paul's Lemon Pillar' ('Lemon Pillar') Cl HT, ly, 1915, Paul; bud pale lemon-yellow; flowers pale sulfur-yellow to almost white, 12-13 cm., dbl., high-centered, intense fragrance; non-recurrent; foliage large; long, strong stems; vigorous growth; not dependably hardy; ['Frau Karl Druschki' × 'Maréchal Niel']

'Paul's Perpetual White' -- See 'Paul's Single White'

'Paul's Pink' HT, lp, 1979, deVor, Paul F.; flowers soft pink, small, 28 petals, intense fragrance; vigorous growth; PP4613; ['Snowsong Supreme' × 'Pink Puff']; intr. 1978

'Paul's Scarlet Climber' LCl, mr, 1916, Paul, W.; flowers vivid scarlet, shaded bright crimson, 6-7 cm., semi-dbl., borne in large clusters; sometimes slightly recurrent; vigorous, climbing or pillar growth; very hardy; ['Paul's Carmine Pillar' × 'Reve d'Or']

'Paul's Single White' ('Paul's Perpetual White', 'Paul's Single White Perpetual') N, w, 1883, Paul; flowers pure white, single, borne singly or in small clusters; foliage light green; vigorous growth; sometimes classed as Cl HP

'Paul's Single White Perpetual' -- See 'Paul's Single White'

'Paul's Tree Climber' HMsk, w, 1916, Paul, G.; flowers blush white, small, dbl.; hybrid of *R. brunonii* or *R. himalayica*

'Paulspride' LCl, yb, 1996, Jerabek, Paul E.; flowers yellow with pink edge changing to mostly pink, reverse medium yellow, 3½ in., full, borne in small clusters, moderate fragrance; foliage medium size, medium green, semi-glossy; few prickles; growth spreading, medium (8 ft.)

'Pavane' HT, Herholdt, J.A.; intr. 1969

'Pavarotti' HT, pb, deRuiter; bud medium, ovate; flowers medium pink, reverse somewhat lighter, 6 in., 25 petals, high-centered, borne mostly singly; good repeat; foliage medium size, medium green, semi-glossy; prickles medium, hooked downward, tan; vigorous, narrow, bushy (6 ft.) growth; hips funnel-shaped ; PP8631; [sport of 'Vivaldi']; greenhouse rose; intr. 1993

'Pavarotti' -- See 'Dicjoon'

'Pavilion Pride' F, my, J&P; flowers medium yellow, outer petals fading lighter, double, cupped to rosette, borne in clusters, moderate fragrance; recurrent; medium growth

'Pavillon de Prégny' N, m, 1863, Guillot père; bud small; flowers light violet-pink, 10-11 cm., full, globular, moderate fragrance; foliage small

'Pavot' -- See 'Grosse Mohnkopfs Rose'

'Paw Maw' Gr, m, 1994, Jerabek, Paul E.; flowers mauve turning red at edges of petals, large, 25-30 petals, borne singly or in clusters of up to 5, moderate fragrance; foliage large, medium green, semi-glossy; some prickles; tall, upright growth; [unknown × unknown]

'Paws' -- See 'Beapaw'

'Pax' HMsk, w, 1918, Pemberton; flowers pure white, prominent golden anthers, 3-4 in., semi-dbl., borne in clusters, intense fragrance; recurrent bloom; foliage large, leathery, dark green; long, strong stems; vigorous (4 ft.), bushy growth; [Trier® × 'Sunburst']

'Pax' F, w, 1946, Leenders, M.; flowers white tinted greenish, large, semi-dbl.; ['Irene' × 'Mme Alexandre Dreux']

'Pax Amanda' S, lp, 1937, Hansen, N.E.; flowers light pink, turning to white, 17 petals, borne in clusters; free, non-recurrent bloom; thornless; vigorous (7 ft.), growth; very hardy; ['Frau Georg von Simson' × *R. blanda*]

'Pax Apollo' S, dp, 1938, Hansen, N.E.; flowers deep pink, 14 petals, borne in large clusters; non-recurrent; thornless; vigorous (7 ft.), growth; very hardy; [*R. sempervirens* × *R. blanda*]

'Pax lola' S, lp, 1938, Hansen, N.E.; flowers clear shell-pink, passing to nearly white, large, 25 petals, borne in large clusters; non-recurrent bloom; prickles thorness; vigorous, pillar, growth; very hardy; ['Anci Bohmova' × *R. blanda*]

'Pax Labor' HT, yb, 1918, Chambard, C.; flowers pale golden yellow, slightly shaded coppery carmine, large, dbl., globular; foliage dark bronzy green; vigorous growth; [sport of 'Beauté de Lyon']

'Pax Labor, Climbing' Cl HT, yb, 1929, Gaujard

'Paxton' -- See 'Sir Joseph Paxton'

'Payable' ('Anusheh') F, rb, 1992, Payne, A.J.; flowers red with yellow reverse, medium, full, borne in large clusters, slight fragrance; foliage medium size, dark green, glossy; numerous prickles; medium, upright growth; ['Len Turner' × seedling]

'Pays d'Iroise' F, mr, Adam, Michel; flowers large, 20-30 petals, cupped to flat, borne in small clusters, slight fragrance; recurrent; foliage medium size, glossy, dark green; bushy (3 ft.), spreading growth; intr. 2005

'Paysagiste Faure-Laurent' HT, ob, 1947, Gaujard; flowers orange, reverse orange-yellow, large, dbl.; foliage glossy, dark; vigorous growth

'Paz Vila' HT, mr, 1931, Munné, B.; flowers large, dbl.; foliage glossy; vigorous growth; ['Jovita Perez' × 'Jean C.N. Forestier']

'Pazstar' ('Chloe', Chloe's Star™) Min, my, 2002, Pazdzierski, Jim; flowers dbl., high-centered, borne in small clusters, slight fragrance; foliage medium size, dark green, glossy; prickles ¼ in., needle-point, moderate; growth upright (20-24 in.); garden decorative, exhibition, containers; [sport of 'Brittany's Glowing Star']; intr. 2002

'Peaadante' LCl, mr, Pearce; intr. 2005

'Peaalamo' ('Little Rascal') F, dp, Pearce; intr. 1998

'Peacap' ('Ragtime') F, ab, 1980, Pearce, C.A.; flowers apricot-pink, 65 petals, borne 10-15 per cluster; foliage small, mid-green, glossy; prickles large, straight, red; bushy growth; ['Vesper' × 'Aloha']; intr. 1981

Peace™ ('Peace Palace') S, dy, Poulsen; flowers deep yellow, 8-10 cm., semi-dbl., no fragrance; foliage dark; growth bushy, 40-60 cm.; PP12885; intr. 2000

'Peace, Climbing' ('Gioia, Climbing', 'Gloria Dei, Climbing', 'Mme A. Meilland, Climbing') Cl HT, yb, 1950, Brandy (also Kordes, 1951); flowers 6 in.; PP932; [sport of 'Peace']

'Peace' ('Gioia', 'Mme A. Meilland', 'Gloria Dei') HT, yb, 1945, Meilland, F.; flowers golden yellow edged rose-pink, 6 in., 43 petals, high-centered to cupped, slight fragrance; foliage large, very dark, leathery, glossy; very vigorous, tall, bushy growth; PP591; [(('George Dickson' × 'Souv. de Claudius Pernet') × ('Joanna Hill' × 'Charles P. Kilham')) × 'Margaret McGredy']; intr. 1945

'Peace' T, ly, 1902, Piper

'Peace Maker' F, ob, Tagashira, Kazuso; flowers borne in clusters; intr. 1990

Peace Meillandina® -- See 'Meilarco'

'Peace of Vereeniging' -- See 'Korverpea'

'Peace Palace' -- See 'Poulpeacy'

'Peace Sunblaze' -- See 'Meilarco'

'Peaceful' HT, pb, 1956, Boerner; bud globular; flowers deep coral rose pink, reverse lighter, 5½-6 in., 50 petals, cupped, moderate fragrance; foliage leathery; vigorous, upright growth; PP1599; [seedling × 'Peace']; intr. 1956

'Peaceful Habitations' -- See 'Pontions'

'Peacekeeper' -- See 'Harbella'

'Peaceport' HT, op, 1960, Rokos; flowers deep orange-pink with yellow base and thin white outer edge, moderate fragrance; PP1282; [sport of 'Peace']; similar to it parent, Peace, in all respects but color and fragrance; intr. 1960

'Peaceport, Climbing' Cl HT, op

Peach™ Min, ab, Poulsen; intr. 1998

Peach™ -- See 'Poulache'

Peach Avalanche+ HT, ab, Van de Berg Roses; flowers soft peach , double, high-centered, borne mostly singly;

recurrent; stems medium to long; [sport of Avalanche+]; florist rose; intr. 2007

'Peach Beauty' HT, pb, 1970, Boerner; bud ovoid; flowers peach-pink, large, dbl.; foliage large, leathery; vigorous, bushy growth; ['Ma Perkins' × 'Polynesian Sunset']

'Peach Belle' HT, ob, Lim, Ping; flowers 4 in., 25 petals, borne mostly singly, slight rosy fragrance; recurrent; upright (4 - 5 ft.) growth; [Seedling × 'Acadia Sunrise']; intr. 2006

'Peach Blossom' Pol, op, Nyveldt; flowers peach pink, medium, semi-dbl., borne in clusters of 50-100; intr. 1914

'Peach Blossom' F, dp, Chaplin Bros.; bud orange-red; flowers soft carmine-rose, medium, semi-dbl., borne in clusters of 6-12; vigorous growth; intr. 1931

'Peach Blossom' T, op, 1890, Dingee & Conard; flowers golden rose or peach blossom

'Peach Blossom' -- See 'Egeria'

'Peach Blossom' -- See 'Ausblossom'

'Peach Brandy' Min, ab, 1979, Schwartz, Ernest W.; bud pointed; flowers small, 23 petals, high-centered, moderate fragrance; compact, bushy growth; intr. 1978

'Peach Calypso' ('Panochre') HT, dy, de Ruiter

'Peach Candy' -- See 'Mortopaz'

'Peach Castle' -- See 'Pouldron'

'Peach Clementine' ('Sweetie') Min, ab, Tantau; flowers creamy peach, large, full, cupped; free-flowering; growth to 40 cm.; intr. 2002

'Peach Delight' -- See 'Savapeach'

'Peach Dream' F, op, 1996, Bees of Chester; bud opening to peach orange center with pink edging; flowers 2½ in., dbl., high-centered, borne in small clusters; foliage medium size, dark green, glossy; few prickles; upright, medium (26 in.) growth; patio; intr. 1995

Peach Drift® S, ab, Meilland; flowers peach apricot, 1.5 in., 15-20 petals, cupped, borne in clusters of 5 - 8; recurrent; foliage small, dark green, semi-glossy; low, bushy, rounded growth; PPAF; intr. 2006

'Peach Elite' -- See 'Lyolite'

Peach Festival™ -- See 'Lavcap'

'Peach Fragrance' -- See 'Momoka'

Peach Fuzz™ -- See 'Wekhelen'

'Peach Garden' -- See 'Momozono'

'Peach Glow' F, pb, 1960, Boerner; bud ovoid; flowers golden coral, base pink, 3 in., 30 petals, cupped, moderate spicy fragrance; foliage leathery; vigorous, upright, compact growth; PP1999; ['Goldilocks' × 'Fashion']; intr. 1960

'Peach Kordana' Min, ab, Kordes; bud pointed ovoid; flowers apricot, yellow, peach and pink, 5 cm., 20-24 petals, high-centered, borne mostly singly, slight fragrance; recurrent; foliage dark green, glossy; prickles few, thin, small, green-white; upright (16 in.), bushy growth; PP15612; ['Amber Kordana' ×

'Golden Gate']; pot rose; intr. 2005

'Peach Meillandina' -- See 'Meixerul'

'Peach Melba' HT, yb, 1960, Dicksons of Hawlmark; flowers yellow marked flame and pink; vigorous growth; ['Golden Scepter' × 'Hazel Alexander']

'Peach Melba' -- See 'Gitte'

'Peach Mikado' F, ab, Tantau; flowers peachy apricot, borne in clusters; florist rose

'Peach Mountain' -- See 'Momoyama'

'Peach Nature' S, ab; flowers yellow-apricot in center, pink on edges, medium, single; free-flowering; intr. 1999

'Peach Parade' (Peach™) MinFl, ab, Poulsen; flowers apricot blend, 5-8 cm., dbl., no fragrance; foliage dark growth bushy, 20-40 cm.; intr. 2000

Peach Parfait™ -- See 'Carfait'

'Peach Pastel' MinFl, ab, Williams, J.B.; intr. 2003

'Peach Petticoat' F, ab, J&P; flowers soft peachy-apricot, double, borne in clusters; recurrent; growth medium height; intr. 2008

'Peach Princess' -- See 'Jacvep'

'Peach Schnapps' S, ab; flowers amber-peach, semi-dbl., flat, borne mostly singly; foliage glossy, disease-resistant; compact, upright growth; hardy; intr. 2000

'Peach Sherbet' F, pb, 1999, Teranishi, K.; flowers salmon pink, 4 in., 30 petals, high-centered, slight fragrance; ['Sonia' × seedling]; intr. 1996

Peach Silk™ LCl, op, Clements, John; flowers soft peach pink, 4-5 in., 24+ petals, slight fragrance; abundant; growth vigorous to 8-10 ft.; PPAF; intr. 2004

'Peach Silks' -- See 'Clepeach'

'Peach Spire' -- See 'Korofaser'

'Peach Sunblaze ' -- See 'Meixerul'

'Peach Sunsation' -- See 'Korommerla'

Peach Surprise™ -- See 'Poulrise'

'Peach Treat' HT, pb, 1968, Fuller; bud ovoid; flowers peach-pink, large, very dbl.; foliage leathery; vigorous, bushy growth; ['Beauté' × 'Kordes' Perfecta']

Peach Waterfall™ -- See 'Meibrenec'

'Peachblow' HT, lp, 1942, Coddington; bud long, pointed; flowers large, dbl.; foliage glossy; vigorous growth; ['Mme Butterfly' × 'yellow seedling']

'Peaches' -- See 'Bouquet Vanille'

'Peaches and Cream' HT, ob, 1936, H&S; flowers salmon shaded gold and rose-pink, very dbl.; bushy growth; RULED EXTINCT 4/77; [seedling × 'Miss Rowena Thom']

'Peaches 'n' Cream' Min, pb, 1977, Woolcock; bud tapering; flowers light peach-pink blend, 1 in., 52 petals, high-centered, slight fragrance; foliage dark; upright, spreading growth; PP4278; ['Little Darling' × 'Magic Wand']; intr. 1976

'Peaches 'n' Cream' HT, pb, J&P; intr. 1998

'Peachy' Min, pb, 1964, Moore, Ralph S.; flowers pink tinted yellow, small, 50 petals; foliage light green, soft; vigorous, bushy (12 in.) growth; ['Golden Glow' × 'Zee']

'Peachy' -- See 'Macrelea'

Peachy Cheeks™ -- See 'Marpeach'

'Peachy Cream' -- See 'Horcoherent'

'Peachy Creeper' -- See 'Intereup'

'Peachy Keen' Min, ab, 1979, Bennett, Dee; bud long, pointed; flowers soft apricot-pink,, 1 in., 18-20 petals, bushy, spreading growth; PP4769; ['Little Darling' × 'Sheri Anne']

'Peachy Pink' -- See 'Welpink'

Peachy Pink Magic Carpet™ -- See 'Poulor'

'Peachy Queen' -- See 'Denpea'

'Peachy White' Min, w, 1976, Moore, Ralph S.; bud long, pointed; flowers near white, often tinted pink, 1½ in., 18 petals, moderate fragrance; foliage leathery; upright, bushy growth; ['Little Darling' × 'Red Germain']

'Peacock' HT, op, 1985, LeMire, Walter; bud ovoid, pointed; flowers orange-coral, reverse cream, 5½ in., dbl., high-centered, borne usually singly, moderate spicy fragrance; foliage large, dark, semi-glossy; vigorous, upright, bushy growth; hips large, globular, orange-red; ['Red Queen' × 'Red Queen']

'Peafanfare' HT, w, Pearce; intr. 2006

'Peafever' ('Fever') F, dp, 1983, Pearce, C.A.; flowers deep pink, large, dbl., intense fragrance; foliage large, dark; upright growth; intr. 1982

'Peafirst' ('Dr McAlpine', 'Pink Toddler') F, dp, 1981, Pearce, C.A.; flowers deep rose-pink, large, 30 petals, high-centered, borne singly and in clusters of up to 10, intense fragrance; foliage dark; prickles straight, red; low, bushy growth; patio, containers; intr. 1983

'Peahaze' ('Geraldine') F, ob, 1983, Pearce, C.A.; flowers orange, medium, 20 petals, slight fragrance; foliage medium size, light green, semi-glossy; upright growth; [seedling × seedling]; intr. 1983

'Peahigh' ('Daily Telegraph', 'Gilda') F, lp, 1987, Pearce, C.A.; flowers pale shell pink, medium, dbl., intense fragrance; foliage medium size, medium green, matte; upright, spreading growth; [seedling × seedling]

'Peak Performance' HT, dr, 1991, Burks, Larry; flowers large, full, borne mostly singly; foliage medium size, dark green, matte; tall, bushy, spreading growth; [seedling × seedling]; intr. 1991

'Peallure' Min, lp, Pearce; intr. 2000

'Peamax' ('Dame Vera Lynn') F, or, 1986, Pearce, C.A.; flowers brick red, large, 20 petals; foliage medium size, dark, semi-glossy; upright growth; [seedling × seedling]

'Peamight' ('Emmanuelle', 'Leaping Salmon') LCl, op, 1984, Pearce, C.A.; flowers salmon pink, 5 in., 20 petals, moderate fragrance; foliage large, medium green, semi-glossy; upright (to 8-10 ft.) growth;

PP7196; [(('Vesper' × 'Aloha') × ('Paddy McGredy' × 'Maigold')) × 'Prima Ballerina']; intr. 1986

'Peanob' ('Bush Baby') Min, pb, 1984, Pearce, C.A.; flowers small, 35 petals, slight fragrance; foliage small, medium green, matte; bushy growth; intr. 1985

'Peanut' ('Pot Black') Min, dr, 1984, Pearce, C.A.; flowers small, dbl., no fragrance; foliage small, medium green, matte; bushy growth; [seedling × seedling]; intr. 1985

'Peanut Butter & Jelly' -- See 'Pixichip'

'Peap' ('Olive Taylor') Min, rb, 1989, Pearce, C.A.; flowers vermillion red with yellow eye, small, 20 petals; foliage medium size, dark green, glossy; bushy growth; [seedling × seedling]; intr. 1988

'Peapatio' ('Royal Flush') MinFl, pb, Pearce; intr. 1992

'Peaperfume' ('Sweet Perfume') HT, ob, Pearce; intr. 1991

'Peapet' ('Jane Asher') Min, mr, 1988, Pearce, C.A.; flowers scarlet, aging slightly paler, rounded, small, very dbl., borne in sprays, no fragrance; foliage small, medium green, semi-glossy; prickles straight, average, red; patio; bushy, low growth; [seedling × seedling]

'Peapolly' ('Jimmy Savile') F, ob, 1988, Pearce, C.A.; flowers coppery-orange, aging lighter, medium, 25-30 petals, cupped, loose, borne usually singly, moderate fruity fragrance; foliage medium size, medium green, matte; bushy, low growth; [seedling × seedling]; intr. 1988

'Peapost' ('Carol Ann') F, mr, 1990, Pearce, C.A.; bud rounded; flowers scarlet, loose, medium, 42 petals, borne in sprays of 3-15; foliage large, medium green, semi-glossy; prickles straight, large, red; spreading, medium growth; ['Geraldine' × seedling]; intr. 1990

'Peaprince' ('Olympic Spirit') F, ob, 1988, Pearce, C.A.; flowers orange, reverse yellow, aging orange-brown, medium, semi-dbl., cupped, borne in sprays of 4 - 5, slight fruity fragrance; foliage small, dark green, glossy; prickles pointed, medium, red; bushy, low growth; [seedling × seedling]; intr. 1988

'Peaproof' ('Freddy') F, op, 1990, Pearce, C.A.; bud ovoid; flowers deep coral pink, aging paler, medium, 25 petals, urn-shaped, borne in sprays of 3-21, slight fragrance; foliage medium size, medium green, matte; prickles hooked, medium,red; bushy, even growth; rare fruit; [seedling × seedling]; intr. 1989

'Peaquant' ('ICI Golden Celebration') Gr, dy, 1988, Pearce, C.A.; flowers golden yellow, large, full, moderate fragrance; foliage medium size, medium green, glossy, mildew resistant; bushy, healthy growth; [seedling × seedling]

'Pearich' ('Alistair Sheridan') HT, ob, 1992, Pearce, C.A.; flowers orange, reverse orange, aging pinky orange, 4¾ in., dbl., urn-shaped, borne usually singly; foliage large, medium green, glossy; upright growth; ['floribunda seedling' × 'hybrid tea seedling']; intr. 1991

'Pearl'   HT, w, Bentall; flowers white, shaded pink, moderate fragrance; intr. 1933

'Pearl'   P, Matthews, D.W.

'Pearl'   HMult, w, Turner; flowers whitish pink, 2 in., single, borne in large clusters; intr. 1915

'Pearl'   HT, lp, 1879, Bennett; flowers flesh pink, shaded carmine, medium, very dbl., moderate Bourbon fragrance; slender, weak growth; ['Adam' × 'Comtesse de Serenye']

Pearl™ (Pearl Palace™) Min, w, Olesen; flowers dbl., 25-30 petals, borne mostly solitary, slight fragrance; foliage dark green, glossy; growth bushy, low (40-60 cm.); PP11641

'Pearl' -- See 'Benmfig'

'Pearl' -- See 'Wekpearl'

'Pearl' -- See 'Korterschi'

'Pearl Abundance' -- See 'The Soham Rose'

'Pearl Anniversary'   MinFl, lp, Chessum, Paul; flowers delicate pearl pink, full, cupped, borne in clusters of 3-5, no fragrance; good repeat; foliage medium green, matte; compact (18 in.), bushy growth; intr. 1995

'Pearl Bright' HT, w; flowers single; foliage dark green, glossy; small to medium, compact growth; intr. 2006

'Pearl Chatsworth' -- See 'Tanrostax'

'Pearl Costin' HT, yb, 1959, Reithmuller; bud long, pointed; flowers light yellow, center pink, large, semi-dbl., cupped; foliage leathery, wrinkled; vigorous, upright, bushy growth; ['Elli Knab' × 'Amy Johnson']

'Pearl Dawn' Min, mp, 1976, Saville, F. Harmon; bud short, pointed; flowers micro-mini, 1 in., 38 petals; very compact, bushy growth; [('Cécile Brunner' × 'Perla de Montserrat') × 'Perla de Montserrat']; intr. 1975

'Pearl Drift, Climbing' -- See 'E. B. LeGrice'

'Pearl Drift' -- See 'Leggab'

Pearl Essence™ -- See 'Jacsilho'

'Pearl Harbor'   HT, pb, 1943, Howard, F.H.; bud long, pointed; flowers light pink, reverse China-rose, 3-3½ in., 45 petals, high-centered, intense fragrance; foliage leathery, dark; very vigorous, upright growth; PP637; [seedling × 'Miss Rowena Thom']

'Pearl Kordana'   Min, w, Kordes; flowers cream white, dbl., high-centered; pot rose

Pearl La Sevillana™ -- See 'Meichonar'

Pearl Meidiland™ -- See 'Meiplatin'

Pearl Mirato® ('Pearl Chatsworth') S, lp, Tantau; bud pointed ovoid; flowers light pink, fading white, 2 in., 25-28 petals, high-centered, to pompon, borne in clusters of 7 - 15; starts late, then free flowering; foliage medium green, leathery, disease-resistant; prickles 4 mm., hooked downward, dark brown; low (50-60 cm.), spreading growth; groundcover; hips none ; PP12851; [sport of 'Footloose']; intr. 2002

'Pearl Nature' S, lp; intr. 2001

'Pearl of Baltimore'   HT, lp, 1925, Cook, J.W.; flowers shell-pink, center deeper, very dbl.; ['Ophelia' × 'Glorified La France']

'Pearl of Bedfordview' -- See 'Meibeausai'

'Pearl of Canada' -- See 'Perla de Alcañada'

'Pearl of Joy' -- See 'Jacsan'

Pearl Palace™ -- See 'Poulpear'

'Pearl Queen'   HWich, w, 1901, Van Fleet; flowers pearly white, finely tinted withdeep rose, large, very dbl.

'Pearl Rivers' T, w, 1890, Dingee & Conard; bud peachy-red; flowers ivory-white, tinted and bordered light pink, intense fragrance; ['Devoniensis' × 'Mme de Watteville']

'Pearl S. Buck' HT, yb, 1940, Kordes; bud long, pointed, deep orange; flowers golden yellow suffused apricot, 4½ in., 45 petals, moderate fragrance; foliage leathery, dark; long stems; vigorous, bushy growth; PP423; ['Joanna Hill' × 'Étoile d'Or']

Pearl Sanford™ -- See 'Spropearl'

'Pearl Sevillana' -- See 'Meichonar'

'Pearl Wilson Kissel' HT, dp, 1954, Kissel and Motose; flowers bright red, 4½ in., 30-40 petals; foliage leathery; vigorous, bushy growth; ['Red Columbia' × 'Chrysler Imperial']

'Pearl Wishes' -- See 'Snow Hit'

'Pearlie Mae'   Gr, ab, 1981, Buck, Dr. Griffith J.; bud ovoid, pointed; flowers yellow blended with pink, reverse pink, 35 petals, cupped, borne singly and in clusters of up to 8, moderate fragrance; foliage leathery, semi-glossy, dark olive green, tinted copper; prickles awl-shaped; erect, bushy growth; ['Music Maker' × (Queen Elizabeth® × 'Country Music')]

'Pearls' -- See 'Rawlii'

Pearly Gates™ -- See 'Wekmeyer'

'Pearly King' S, w, Genesis

'Pearly Peace' HT, lp, 1959, Fryers Nursery, Ltd.; flowers soft pearl-pink; [sport of 'Peace']

'Pearly Queen'   F, lp, 1963; flowers well-formed, 4 in., 22 petals, moderate fragrance; vigorous growth; [sport of Queen Elizabeth®]; intr. 1963

'Pearly Shell' HT, pb, 1972, Sherwood; flowers shell pink, center cream, large, 30 petals, high-centered; foliage glossy; vigorous, upright growth; ['Pink Parfait' × 'Michèle Meilland']

'Pearly Shores' -- See 'Eughien'

'Pearly White'   LCl, w, 1942, Brownell; bud long, pointed; flowers white tinted pearl, open quickly, 21 petals; long, strong stems; vigorous, climbing (to 20 ft.), upright growth; [('Glenn Dale' × 'Mrs Arthur Curtiss James') × ('Glenn Dale' × 'Mrs Arthur Curtiss James')]

'Pearly Wonder' HRg, lp, Williams, J.B.; flowers very soft pink, dbl., globular, borne in clusters; intr. 2004

'Pearobin' ('Gary Lineker') F, ob, 1991, Pearce, C.A.; flowers luminous orange, yellow reverse, medium, single to semi-dbl., borne in small clusters, slight fragrance; foliage medium size, medium green, glossy; numerous prickles; medium (50-90 cm.), upright growth; [seedling × seedling]; intr. 1991

'Pearoyal' ('William David') F, dy, 1990, Pearce, C.A.; intr. 1990

'Peashine' ('Anthea Fortescue') F, pb, 1992, Pearce, C.A.; flowers pink, yellow center, buff reverse, 2½ in., dbl., urn-shaped, borne in sprays of 3-9, slight fragrance; foliage small, medium green, glossy, immune to powdery milde; low, spreading growth; ['floribunda seedling' × 'floribunda seedling']; intr. 1991

'Peaspecial' ('Audrey Gardner') Min, lp, 1990, Pearce, C.A.; bud rounded; flowers shell pink, reverse slightly darker, aging same, large, 45 petals, cupped, borne in sprays of 25-30, no fragrance; foliage small, medium green, semi-glossy; prickles pointed, red; bushy, medium growth; no fruit; [seedling × seedling]; intr. 1990

'Peastack' HT, dp, Pearce; intr. 2005

'Peasweet' ('Marty') F, mr, 1991, Pearce, C.A.; flowers dusty red, medium, very full, hybrid tea form, borne in small clusters; foliage small, medium green, semi-glossy; few prickles; low (40-60 cm.), bushy growth; [seedling × 'Sweetheart']; intr. 1991

'Peat Fire Flame' HT, op, 1985, MacLeod, Major C.A.; flowers pale orange, reverse salmon-pink, medium, 20 petals; foliage medium size, medium green, glossy; upright growth; ['Red Planet' × 'Bonnie Anne']

'Peathunder' ('Judi Dench', 'Red Velvet ') F, dr, 1995, Pearce, C.A.; flowers deep red with a hint of brown, medium, full, borne in large clusters, slight fragrance; foliage medium size, dark green, semi-glossy; low (50 cm.), bushy, spreading growth; intr. 1996

'Peatiger' F, mr, Pearce; intr. 1995

'Peatrophy' ('Charisma') F, ly, Pearce

'Peaudouce' -- See 'Dicjana'

'Peavandyke' F, m, Pearce; intr. 1995

'Peavenus' Min, m, Pearce; bud slender; intr. 1995

'Peavenus' ('St Katherine's') S, m, Pearce

'Peaverity' F, pb, Limes New Roses; intr. 1994

'Peavesta' ('Ginger Toddler') F, ob, Pearce; intr. 1996

'Peavoodoo' ('Memory Lane') F, ab, 1994, Pearce, C.A.; flowers apricot-pink, 3-3½ in., full, borne in small clusters; foliage large, dark green, semi-glossy; some prickles; upright (60 cm.) growth; ['Carol Ann' × seedling]; intr. 1995

'Peawinner' ('Ruby Celebration') F, dr, Pearce; bud near black; intr. 1995

'Peaxanadu' ('Pink Midinette') S, mp, Pearce; intr. 1996

'Peaxanthous' ('Bronze Baby') MinFl, yb, Pearce

'Peaxi' Cl HT, dr, 1977, Pearce

'Peaxi' -- See 'Bright Fire'

'Peayellow' HT, my, Pearce; intr. 2000

'Peayetti' ('Dream Lover') MinFl, mp, Pearce; intr. 1998

'Peazara' ('Millionaire') F, dp, Pearce; intr. 1998

'Peazephyr' Min, w, Pearce; intr. 2003

'Peazoe' Min, mr, Pearce; intr. 2001

Pebble Beach™ -- See 'Pouleas'

'Pebble Mill' F, rb, 1973, Gregory; flowers magenta, reverse spirea-red, large, 28 petals, flat; foliage dark; ['Paddy McGredy' × seedling]

'Peccato di Giola' -- See 'Tansinnroh'

Pêche Meillandina® ('Peach Meillandina', 'Peach Sunblaze ') Min, ab, Meilland; bud conical, small; flowers azalea pink tinted orange-buff, 2 in., 30-34 petals, cupped, borne mostly singly or in pairs, slight fragrance; recurrent; foliage medium green, semi-dull; few prickles; growth short, bushy; PP8000; [Pink Meillandina® × ('Frenzy' × 'Ann Moore')]; intr. 1991

'Pechtold's Flame' -- See 'Tudor'

'Pechtold's Triumph' F, dr, 1961, Verschuren-Pechtold; flowers oxblood-red, medium, semi-dbl., borne in large clusters; ['Red Favorite' × 'Frensham']

'Pedrálbes' HT, my, 1931, Camprubi, C.; flowers butter yellow, shaded gold, 5 in., 30 petals; foliage dark, glossy; very vigorous growth; ['Frau Karl Druschki' × 'Souv. de Mme Boullet']

'Pedro Costa' HT, yb, 1889, da Costa; flowers yellow, with red and orange

'Pedro Veyrat' HT, ab, 1933, Dot, Pedro; bud long, pointed; flowers large, dbl., cupped; ['Li Bures' × 'Benedicte Seguin']

'Pedrus Aquarius' HT, w, 1999, Poole, Lionel; flowers white/ivory, 6 in., full, borne mostly singly, slight fragrance; foliage medium size, dark green, glossy; prickles moderate; upright, bushy, medium (3 ft.) growth; ['Solitaire' × 'Joe Longthorne']; intr. 1999

'Peek a Boo' -- See 'Dicgrow'

Peep-Eye™ -- See 'Minpeep'

'Peep o' Day' F, op, 1972, Harkness; flowers salmon, shaded orange, large, 28 petals; foliage dark; [('Pink Parfait' × 'Highlight') × 'Orion']; intr. 1973

'Peeping Tom' S, dp, 1968, MacLeod; flowers deep pink, pointed, large, dbl.; recurrent bloom; foliage medium size, medium green, matte; vigorous, tall growth; ['Kordes' Perfecta' × 'Parade']

Peer Gynt® HT, yb, 1970, Kordes, R.; flowers yellow, outer petals edged red, large, 50 petals, slight fragrance; vigorous, bushy growth; ['Colour Wonder' × Golden Giant®]; intr. 1968

'Peerless' HT, mr, 1935, Joseph H. Hill, Co.; bud long, pointed; flowers bright velvety scarlet-carmine, large, 38-40 petals; PP157; [sport of 'Better Times']

'Pegasus' -- See 'Ausmoon'

'Peggy' HT, my, 1905, Dickson, A.; flowers safron yellow, becoming primrose, semi-dbl.

'Peggy' HT, dp, Bees; bud long, pointed; flowers deep rose, dbl., high-centered, intense fragrance; foliage glossy, light; vigorous growth; ['Ophelia' × 'Red-Letter Day']; intr. 1934

'Peggy A. Smith' HT, pb, 1936, Smith, A.; flowers pink with yellow tints, medium, dbl.

'Peggy Ann Landon' LCl, ob, 1938, Brownell; flowers yellow-orange, becoming lighter, 3½-5 in., dbl., high-centered, moderate fragrance; foliage large, leathery, glossy, dark; long, strong stems; very vigorous, climbing (15-25 ft.) growth; ['Glenn Dale' × ((seedling × seedling) × 'Mary Wallace')]

'Peggy Astbury' HT, ab, 1920, Easlea; flowers soft amber to light yellow

'Peggy Bell' HT, ab, 1929, Clark, A.; flowers peach-buff pink, copper reverse, large, full, moderate tea myrrh fragrance; good repeat; vigorous, very tall (10-12 ft.) growth

'Peggy England' HT, ab, 1923, Lilley; flowers cream-apricot, sometimes tinted carmine

'Peggy Gordon' Gr, r, McGredy; flowers shades of apricot brown, reverse russet, dbl., high-centered, borne in large candelabras of up to 25; good repeat; foliage deep bronze, very glossy; stems medium; neat, medium high growth, many basals; intr. 2002

'Peggy Grant' Min, lp, 1954, Moore, Ralph S.; flowers shell-pink, small, 25 petals; foliage light green; dwarf (5-6 in.), bushy growth; [('Robinette' × 'Mons. Tillier') × 'Zee']

Peggy Jane™ -- See 'Savapeg'

'Peggy Joan Reynolds' -- See 'Reypeg'

'Peggy Lee' HT, lp, 1983, Feigel, John R.; flowers pale pink; PP5467; [sport of 'Century Two']; same description as Century Two, except for color; intr. 1982

'Peggy M' S, pb, 1996, Jerabek, Paul E.; flowers pink gradually turning white on outer petals, reverse yellow, 2½-3 in., 75 petals; foliage medium size, light green, glossy; numerous prickles; upright, medium (5 ft.) growth

'Peggy Netherthorpe' HT, mp, 1976, Delbard; flowers 5 in., 35 petals; foliage light; [('Voeux de Bonheur' × 'Chic Parisien') × ('Michèle Meilland' × 'Mme Joseph Perraud')]; intr. 1974

'Peggy Newton' F, my, 1959, Boerner; flowers primrose-yellow, 2½-3 in., 40-50 petals, globular, borne in clusters; foliage small, leathery, glossy; dwarf, spreading growth; PP1682; ['Golden Glow' × 'Goldilocks']; intr. 1957

Peggy Rockefeller™ -- See 'Wilace'

'Peggy 'T'' -- See 'Kintee'

'Peggy's Delight' -- See 'Mincco'

'Peintre Renoir' HT, mp, 1925, Roseraie de St. Jean; flowers large, dbl.

'Pejamblu' ('Blue For You', 'Pacific Dream') F, m, 2006, James, Peter J.; flowers lilac, reverse lighter, 3-4 in., semi-dbl., borne in large clusters; foliage medium size, medium green, semi-glossy; prickles straight, few; growth bushy, medium (3 ft.); garden decorative; ['Rogscriv' × 'dark purple floribunda seedling']; intr. 2007

'Pejpur' ('Diana Holman') F, m, 2006, James, Peter J.; flowers purple, reverse lighter, 3-4 in., full, borne in large clusters, intense fragrance; foliage medium size, dark green, semi-glossy; prickles straight, moderate; growth vigorous, bushy, tall (4 ft.); garden decoration; ['Natural Beauty' × 'Rhapsody in Blue']; intr. 2007

'Pekaledon' ('Femnet') HT, dp, Pekmez, Paul; intr. 1993

'Pekali' HT, ob, 1985, Pekmez, Paul; flowers orange, large, 35 petals, no fragrance; foliage large, glossy; upright growth; [seedling × Marina®]

'Pekamecel' F, or, 1985, Pekmez, Paul; flowers 20 petals; foliage dark; upright growth; [seedling × seedling]; intr. 1984

'Pekatan' ('Clo-Clo') HT, pb, 1985, Pekmez, Paul; flowers 20 petals; foliage dark; upright growth; ['Emily Post' × 'Bellona']; intr. 1984

'Pekbord' S, mp; intr. 1992

'Pekcoubo' HT, op, Pekmez, Paul; intr. 1997

'Pekcoucan' HT, or, Pekmez, Paul; intr. 1992

'Pekcouflash' -- See 'Mouna'

'Pekcougel' (Anna®) HT, lp, Pekmez, Paul; bud cream white; intr. 1998

'Pekcougraine' dr, Pekmez; intr. 1989

'Pekcoujalapp' F, ly, Pekmez; intr. 2006

'Pekcoujenny' (First Red®) HT, dr, Pekmez, Paul; bud long, pointed; intr. 1988

'Pekcouliane' (Julia®) HT, ob, Pekmez

'Pekcoulieu' or, Pekmez; intr. 1988

'Pekcourofondu' HT, pb, Pekmez, Paul; intr. 1997

'Pekcram' (Jean Monnet®) F, mp, Pekmez, Paul; intr. 1988

'Pekgold' HT, dy, 1985, Pekmez, Paul; flowers medium, moderate fragrance; foliage dark, glossy; upright growth; [seedling × seedling]; intr. 1984

'Pekinois' ('Tapis Afghan') Pol, dr, 1979, Pekmez, Paul; bud round; flowers 1-2 in., 15 petals, cupped; dwarf growth; ['Marlena' × 'Lampion']; intr. 1975

'Peklican' HT, dy, 1985, Pekmez, Paul; flowers large, 35 petals, moderate fragrance; foliage medium size, light green, matte; bushy growth; [seedling × 'Bellona']; intr. 1984

'Peklimasar' ('Lilli Marleen, Climbing', Grimpant Lilli Marleen®) Cl F, mr, 1983, Pekmez, Paul

'Peklipink' ('Claridge') F, mp, 1985, Pekmez, Paul; flowers large, 35 petals, moderate fragrance; foliage medium size, light green, semi-glossy; upright growth; [seedling × seedling]; intr. 1984

'Pekminou' -- See 'Etoile Rouge'

'Pekmiwhite' S, lp, Pekmez, Paul; intr. 1991

'Pekomecli' (Marlyse®) HT, pb; intr. 1985

'Pekomegir' ('President Souzy') F, mp, 1985, Pekmez, Paul; flowers 20 petals, moderate fragrance; upright growth; ['Emily Post' × seedling]; intr. 1984

'Pekouzelia' my, Pekmez; intr. 1989

'Pekpus' HT, mp, Pekmez; intr. 2002

'Peksolred' ('Ile de France') S, mr, Pekmez, Paul; intr. 1992

'Pektarampe' ('Alsace') S, dr, Pekmez, Paul; intr. 1992

'Pekwhina' ('Virginia') HT, w, Pekmez, Paul; intr. 1994

'Pelé' LCl, w, 1980, Benardella, Frank A.; bud ovoid; flowers pale pink, fading to pearly pink, 6 in., 35 petals, borne mostly solitary, slight soft, fruity fragrance; repeat bloom; foliage medium green; prickles triangular, hooked; upright growth with long canes; [seedling × seedling]

'Pélisson' ('Mons Pélisson') M, dr, 1849, Vibert; flowers velvety red, turning purple, 6 cm., full, rosette

'Pelletier' HGal, lp, about 1825, Pelletier; flowers pale pink, medium, full

'Pelletier' -- See 'Fleur de Pelletier'

'Pellion' HT, w, Keisei; greenhouse rose; intr. 2004

'Pellonia' T, w, 1874, Touvais; flowers creme, center white with light pink, large, very full, globular

'Pelton Lonnen' HT, my, 1977, Wood; flowers pure yellow, 28-30 petals, cupped, moderate fragrance; foliage light; bushy, compact growth; [sport of 'Whisky Mac']; intr. 1975

'Pemberton's White Rambler' HMult, w, 1914, Pemberton; flowers dbl., rosette, borne in large clusters, strong musky fragrance; non-recurrent; foliage glossy; prickles large

'Pembridge' HT, ob, 1934, Stevens, E.; flowers richer, deeper orange-yellow; [sport of 'Roselandia']

'Pénélope' D, dp, 1818, Vibert; flowers deep grenadine-rose, large, very dbl., globular; foliage edges tinged with red

'Pénélope' B, lp, Robert; flowers light lilac pink, medium, full; intr. 1851

'Penelope' T, rb, Williams, J.; flowers dark red, center creamy white, medium, full, high pointed, moderate fragrance; recurrent; growth to 4 ft.; intr. 1906

'Penelope' HMsk, lp, Pemberton; flowers shell-pink fading to white, center lemon, semi-dbl., borne in clusters, moderate fragrance; recurrent bloom; foliage dark green; shrubby growth; ['Ophelia' × 'William Allen Richardson']; intr. 1924

'Penelope, Climbing' Cl T, rb, 1932, Rosen, L.P.

Pénélope® -- See 'Gaubiroc'

'Penelope Keith' -- See 'Macfreego'

'Penelope Mayo' -- See 'Duchesse de Caylus'

'Penelope Plummer' F, dp, 1970, Beales, Peter; bud orange; flowers vivid flamingo-pink,, 4 in., 16 petals, flat; foliage dark green; moderate growth; ['Anna Wheatcroft' × 'Dearest']; intr. 1970

'Penguin' HT, w, Kordes; bud pointed; flowers white tinted green, double, high-centered, borne mostly singly, moderate fragrance; recurrent; foliage glossy, disease-resistant ; stems long, slender; strong, tall (2 m.) growth; intr. 2008

'Penkala Slavoljub' -- See 'Rogslav'

'Pennant' LCl, mp, 1941, Clark, A.; flowers begonia-pink, dbl., moderate fragrance; profuse, non-recurrent bloom; ['Flying Colours' × 'Lorraine Lee']; hybrid gigantea

Pennies from Heaven™ -- See 'Wekwapunk'

'Pennsylvania' HT, pb, 1934, Neuner; bud long, pointed; flowers salmon-pink, center apricot, outer petals striped dark pink, semi-dbl., high-centered; [sport of 'Joanna Hill']

'Pennsylvanian' HT, ob, 1953, Ohlhus; bud pointed; flowers apricot-orange, 4-5 in., 25-30 petals, moderate fragrance; upright, bushy growth; PP936; ['Luna' × ('Mrs Pierre S. duPont' × 'Mrs Sam McGredy')]

'Penny' F, rb, 1973, Sanday, John; flowers strawberry-red, base orange, rosette form, 2 in., 17 petals; dwarf growth; [Sarabande® × 'Circus']

'Penny Annie' -- See 'Bisfra'

'Penny Ante' Min, yb, 2003, Cochran, L.C.; flowers yellow, reverse orange-tinted, 1½ in., full, borne in small clusters, no fragrance; foliage large, medium green, matte; prickles straight; upright, medium (24-30 in.) growth; ['Poker Chip' × unknown]; intr. 2003

Penny Candy™ Min, ob, 1982, Saville, F. Harmon; bud small, ovate, long pointed; flowers orange with yellow heart, yellow reverse, 1 in., 25-30 petals, cupped, borne singly or several together, slight fragrance; foliage small, glossy; prickles few, small, long, thin; tiny, compact growth; PP5031; ['Rise 'n' Shine' × 'Sheri Anne']; intr. 1981

'Penny Coelen' -- See 'Meinimo'

'Penny Girl' MinFl, ab, 2007, Read, Allan; flowers 6.5 cm., very full, borne in large clusters; foliage medium, medium green, semi-glossy; prickles small, straight, brown, few; growth upright, short (66 cm.); ['Rise 'n' Shine' × 'Fireglow (Ablaze)']; intr. 2007

'Penny Heyns' -- See 'Tanpen'

'Penny Lane' -- See 'Hardwell'
'Penny Lane' -- See 'Talpen'
'Pensioners Voice' ('Michelle Wright') F, ab, Fryer, Gareth; flowers orange apricot with shades of pink, large, dbl., high-centered, borne in clusters, moderate fragrance; free-flowering; vigorous, upright (3 ft.) growth; intr. 1989
'Penthouse' -- See 'Macnauru'
'Penthouse' -- See 'Macsatur'
'Peon' -- See 'Tom Thumb'
'Peony Blanc' HRg, w, Johnson, M.; flowers large, mound of petaloids in the center, very full, rosette, intense sweet fragrance; good repeat; numerous prickles; vigorous, tall (6 ft.) growth; hips insignificant; [unknown × unknown]; intr. 2002
'Peony of Fragrance' HP, mp, 1933, Pahissa; flowers pink, peony-like, large; recurrent bloom
'People' ('The People') F, dr, 1957, Tantau, Math.; flowers crimson shaded pink, large, 26 petals, flat, borne in large trusses; foliage light green; vigorous, bushy growth; ['Cinnabar' × ('Kathe Duvigneau' × 'Cinnabar')]; intr. 1956
'People's Princess' -- See 'Suntick'
'Pepe' HT, rb, 1961, deRuiter; flowers flame, base and reverse gold, 4 in., dbl.; foliage dark, glossy; vigorous growth; ['Amor' × 'Sutter's Gold']; intr. 1961
Pepino® -- See 'Tanipep'
'Pépita' HGal, pb, about 1850, Moreau; flowers soft rosy pink striped white
Pepita® F, pb, Kordes; flowers rich pink, lighter reverse, outer petals take on green tint, small, full, cupped, borne in sprays; good repeat; florist rose; intr. 2006
Pepita® -- See 'Kortufee'
'Pepita' -- See 'Korkeilich'
'Pepita Kordana' Min, w, Kordes; flowers cream white, double, cupped, then flat
'Pepita Kordana' Min, w, Kordes; flowers white with pink blush on reverse, dbl., urn-shaped; compact growth; container rose; intr. 2005
'Pépite' -- See 'Souv de J. Chabert'
'Pepper Pot' F, pb, 1973, Fryers Nursery, Ltd.; flowers rose-pink to red, splashed yellow, 3 in., 24 petals, high-centered; foliage light; free growth; ['Circus' × seedling]
'Peppermint' F, rb, 1965, Boerner; bud ovoid; flowers red, reverse cream, medium, dbl., cupped; foliage leathery; vigorous, bushy growth; PP2549; ['Jingles' × 'Jingles']; intr. 1964
'Peppermint' HT, r, Kordes; flowers russet with green tint on outer petals; greenhouse rose; intr. 2002
'Peppermint' LCl, rb; flowers striped
'Peppermint Candy' Min, w, 1991, Williams, J. Benjamin; flowers ivory with red blend, medium, full, borne mostly singly, intense fragrance; foliage small, dark green, glossy; medium (12-18 in.), upright, bushy growth; PP6819; ['Rose Parade' × 'Easter Morning']

'Peppermint Delight' LCl, rb
'Peppermint Ice' -- See 'Bosgreen'
Peppermint Kordana® Min, w, Kordes; flowers cream with a greenish tint, full, high-centered; pot rose
'Peppermint Parfait' -- See 'Morpepper'
'Peppermint Patty' Min, rb, 1990, Gruenbauer, Richard; bud pointed; flowers white with red edging, same reverse, aging darker red, 33 petals, urn-shaped, slight fruity fragrance; foliage medium size, medium green, semi-glossy; prickles straight, very few, tan; very hardy, upright growth; hips oblong, orange; ['Libby' × 'Libby']
'Peppermint Stick' -- See 'Jacmint'
'Peppermint Stripe' Min, rb, 1991, Spooner, Raymond A.; flowers small, dbl., intense fragrance; foliage small, medium green, semi-glossy; bushy growth; ['Roller Coaster' × seedling]
Peppermint Swirl™ -- See 'Devmenta'
'Peppermint Twist' -- See 'Jacraw'
Pepperoni® S, or, Poulsen; intr. 1994
'Per Chance' -- See 'Floper'
Perce Neige® S, lp, Pekmez, Paul; intr. 1991
'Perception' -- See 'Harzippee'
'Perchè Si?' HT, rb, 1958, Giacomasso; flowers carmine-red, reverse silvery white, well-formed; foliage dark, glossy; very vigorous growth; ['Peace' × 'Crimson Glory']; intr. 1956
'Percohn' ('Dr Edwin J. Cohn') HT, my, 2001, Perry, Astor; flowers 4 in., dbl., borne mostly solitary, slight fragrance; foliage medium size, dark green, semi-glossy; prickles average, recurved, moderate; growth upright, medium; garden decorative; [seedling × seedling]; intr. 2002
'Percreme' (Irish Creme™) HT, w, 1999, Perry, Astor; flowers light beige, reverse same, 4 in., full, borne mostly singly, moderate fragrance; foliage medium size, medium green, dull; prickles moderate; upright, medium (5 ft.) growth; ['Butterscotch' × 'Mandelon']; intr. 2000
'Percussion' -- See 'Zipcuss'
'Percy Izzard' HT, yb, 1936, Robinson, H.; flowers maize-yellow, reverse buff flushed warm rose, large, dbl., high-centered; foliage leathery; vigorous growth; ['May Wettern' × 'Barbara Richards']
'Percy Pilcher' F, op, 1961, Verschuren; flowers salmon-orange, large, dbl., borne in large clusters
'Percy Thrower' HT, mp, 1964, Lens; flowers rose-pink, well-formed, 4-5 in., 28 petals, moderate fragrance; foliage glossy; vigorous, tall growth; ['La Jolla' × 'Karl Herbst']; intr. 1964
'Percy Thrower, Climbing' Cl HT, mp, Stoneham; [sport of 'Percy Thrower']; intr. 1978
'Perdita' F, lp, Bidwell
Perdita® -- See 'Ausperd'
'Perennial Blue' LCl, m, Mehring; flowers deep magenta with lilac tones, base of petals white, small, semi-dbl., cupped, borne in large clusters, moderate sweet fragrance; recurrent; foliage medium green, semi-glossy; growth to 8-10 ft.; intr. 2004
'Perennial Blush' LCl, lp; flowers blush pink, fading quickly to white, small, semi-dbl., shallow cup, borne in large clusters; vigorous growth; intr. 2007
'Perestroika' -- See 'Korhitom'
Perfect™ -- See 'Perfect Hit'
'Perfect Day' -- See 'Poulcrem'
'Perfect Hit' (Perfect Paillette™, Perfect™) MinFl, op, Poulsen; bud short, pointed ovoid; flowers salmon pink, 2 in., 30-35 petals, high-centered, then flat, borne singly or in small clusters, no fragrance; foliage small, glossy; prickles moderate, short, straight; stems short and strong; bushy, low (40-60 cm.) growth; PP10083; [seedling × 'Ruiforto']; intr. 1996
Perfect Moment™ -- See 'Korwilma'
Perfect Paillette™ -- See 'Perfect Hit'
'Perfect Peace' -- See 'Dorothy Goodwin'
Perfect Potluck™ -- See 'Lavpet'
'Perfecta' Pol, dr, 1920, Spek; flowers scarlet-crimson under glass, dark crimson in the open, large, dbl.; vigorous growth; ['Ellen Poulsen' × 'Merveille des Rouges']
'Perfecta' -- See 'Koralu'
'Perfecta Superior' ('Kordes' Perfecta Superior') HT, mp, 1965, Kordes; flowers bright pink; [sport of 'Kordes' Perfecta']; intr. 1964
'Perfection' HP, dp, Lartay; flowers vivid dark pink, shaded with crimson, medium, full; intr. 1853
'Perfection' B, mp, Laurentius; flowers shining pink, reverse dull, large, full; intr. 1858
'Perfection' HP, mp, Touvais; flowers silky pink, medium to large, full; intr. 1866
'Perfection' HT, mp, Stielow Bros.; [sport of 'Columbia']; intr. 1925
'Perfection' Pol, op, Prior; flowers softer coral-pink; [sport of 'Marytje Cazant']; intr. 1932
'Perfection' F, pb, Ulrick, L.W.; flowers pink turning red, reverse white; ['Masquerade' × 'Masquerade']; intr. 1957
'Perfection' Min, dp, Benardella, Frank; flowers dusky, deep cerise pink, large, dbl., high-centered, moderate fruity fragrance; medium growth; intr. 1999
'Perfection' HP, mp, 1851, Miellez; flowers vivid carmine-pink, large, full
'Perfection de Lyon' HP, pb, 1868, Ducher; flowers pink, reverse lilac, very large, full
'Perfection de Montplaisir' T, 1871, Levet, A.; flowers clear lemon, medium, full, moderate fragrance; ['Canari' × unknown]
'Perfection des Blanches' N, w, 1873, Schwartz, J.; flowers medium, dbl., borne in corymbs; vigorous growth
'Perfection Orange' -- See 'South Orange Perfection'

Perfectly Red™ -- See 'Jacrove'

'Perfeita' F, or, Moreira da Silva; flowers orange and carmine; ['Cocorico' × 'Vogue']

'Perflight' ('First Flight') HT, mr, 2001, Perry, Astor; flowers 4 in., 35 petals, borne mostly solitary, slight fragrance; foliage medium size, dark green, semi-glossy; prickles average, curved, moderate; growth upright (5 ft.); garden decorative; [seedling × seedling]; intr. 2003

'Perfume' HT, dr, 1929, Marriott; bud long, pointed; flowers velvety, fiery deep crimson, 15 petals; vigorous growth

'Perfume' HT, lp, Spek; intr. 1995

Perfume Beauty™ -- See 'Meiniacin'

'Perfume of Multiflore' HT, m, 1935, Pahissa; flowers purple/pink, large, dbl.

'Perfume Delight' HT, mp, 1973, Swim & Weeks; bud long, pointed; flowers large, 26-35 petals, high-centered, borne mostly singly, intense fragrance; free-flowering; foliage large, leathery, glossy; prickles short to medium, hooked downward, brown; stems long, strong; vigorous, upright, bushy growth; PP3282; ['Peace' × (('Happiness' × 'Chrysler Imperial') × 'El Capitan')]

'Perfume Passion' -- See 'Korpauvio'

'Perfume Perfection' -- See 'Jacshok'

'Perfume Pleasure' -- See 'Touch of Spring'

'Perfume Simplex' Min, yb

Perfume Tiger™ -- See 'Winptig'

'Perfumed Bride' HT, pb, Bell; intr. 1994

'Perfumella' -- See 'Meiparos'

'Pergolèse' P, m, 1860, Robert et Moreau; flowers bright purplish crimson, shading to lilac, medium, very dbl., moderate fragrance; occasionally recurrent bloom; often classed as HP

'Perhope' ('Rose of Hope') HT, my, 2004, Astor Perry; flowers medium, full, borne mostly solitary, slight fragrance; foliage medium size, medium green, semi-glossy; prickles few, average, curved; bushy, medium (50 in.) growth; garden decoration; ['Grandpa Dickson' × seedling]; intr. 2004

'Péricles' D, dp, before 1826, Vibert; flowers purple-pink, marbled, medium, dbl.

'Péricles' HCh, lp, Laffay; intr. about 1835

'Perigord' -- See 'Chewharla'

'Perjusdream' ('Just Dreamy') HT, yb, 1999, Perry, Astor; flowers yellow-gold, reverse apricot gold, 3½-4 in., dbl., borne mostly singly, slight fragrance; foliage medium size, medium green, semi-glossy; few prickles; upright, bushy, medium growth; [Folklore® × 'Golden Gate']; intr. 2000

'Perky' Min, dp, 1959, Moore, Ralph S.; bud pointed; flowers 1 in., dbl., intense fragrance; foliage glossy; very bushy (12 in.), compact growth; [(R. wichurana × Floradora) × 'Oakington Ruby']; intr. 1958

Perl-Ilseta® -- See 'Tanilsepo'

'Perla de Alcañada' ('Baby Crimson', 'Wheatcroft's Baby Crimson', 'Perle de Alcañada', 'Pearl of Canada') Min, dp, 1944, Dot, Pedro; bud small, ovoid; flowers carmine, 18 petals; foliage dark, glossy; dwarf, very compact (6-10 in.) growth; ['Perle des Rouges' × 'Rouletti']

'Perla de Alcañada, Climbing' Cl Min, dp, Dot, Pedro

'Perla de Montserrat' Min, pb, 1945, Dot, Pedro; bud small; flowers hermosa pink edged pearl, 18 petals, borne in clusters; dwarf, very compact growth; ['Cécile Brunner' × 'Rouletti']

'Perla d'Oriolo' S, Embriaco, B.; intr. 1992

'Perla Rosa' Min, mp, 1946, Dot, Pedro; bud well-formed; flowers bright pink, very full; very compact (6-8 in.) growth; ['Perle des Rouges' × 'Rouletti']

'Perla Rosa, Climbing' Cl Min, mp, 1947, Dot, Pedro

'Perla Transilvaniei' F, pb, Roman, G., and Wagner, S.; flowers mauvish-pink, small, 30 petals, borne in clusters, slight fragrance; foliage small to medium, dark green, glossy, healthy; ['Rusticana' × Lavender Dream®]; intr. 2004

'Perle' Pol, pb, 1913, Kiese; flowers delicate pink, base yellow, small to medium, borne in clusters of 20-30

'Perle, Climbing' Cl Pol, pb, about 1913; [sport of 'Perle']

'Perle' Pol, w, Easlea; intr. 1920

'Perle Angevine' Pol, lp, 1920, Délépine; flowers pale rose, small, dbl., borne in clusters; prickles few thorns; ['Jeanne d'Arc' × 'Mrs W. H. Cutbush']

'Perle Blanche' -- See 'Delanche'

'Perle d'Amour' B, lp, Weihrauch

'Perle d'Angers' B, lp, 1879, Moreau et Robert; flowers delicate frosty flesh-pink, nearly white, large, very full, borne in small clusters

'Perle d'Anjou' Min, mp

'Perle de Alcañada' -- See 'Perla de Alcañada'

'Perle de Feu' T, yb, 1893, Dubreuil; flowers yellow with copper-red and purplish tints, medium, dbl.; ['Mme Falcot' × 'Claire Carnot']

'Perle de France' A, w, 1824, Dematra; flowers medium, full

'Perle de l'Orient' HGal, rb, before 1811, Schwarzkopf; bud round; flowers purple red with edges nuanced violet

'Perle de Lyon' T, dy, 1872, Ducher; flowers apricot yellow, large, dbl.

'Perle de Weissenstein' -- See 'Perle von Weissenstein'

'Perle des Blanches' N, w, 1872, Lacharme, F.; bud hard, round, slightly pinkish; flowers creamy-white, aging to pure white, 5-7 cm., full, globular, borne in large clusters; growth tall; ['Mlle Blanche Laffitte' × 'Sappho (Damask Perpetual)']

'Perle des Jardins' T, ly, 1874, Levet, F.; flowers straw-yellow, large, dbl., globular, intense fragrance; foliage dark green; slender growth; [sport of a 'Mme Falcot' seedling]

'Perle des Jardins, Climbing' Cl T, ly, 1890, Henderson, J.; flowers golden-yellow, fading to very light yellow, very large, very full, cupped, intense fragrance; foliage dark green; [sport of 'Perle des Jardins']

'Perle des Jaunes' T, dy, 1903, Reymond; flowers golden yellow tinted salmon, large, dbl., moderate fragrance

'Perle des Neiges' HMult, w, 1902, Dubreuil; flowers medium, semi-dbl., borne in corymbs of 25-30

'Perle des Panachées' ('Cottage Maid') HGal, m, 1845, Vibert; flowers white striped with lilac and violet or rose, small, dbl., borne in clusters of 3-8, moderate fragrance; foliage medium green, pointed, usually with 3 leaflets; possibly also has a synonym of 'Panachée Double'

'Perle des Panachées' -- See 'La Rubanée'

'Perle des Rouges' Pol, dr, 1896, Dubreuil; flowers velvety crimson

'Perle d'Or' ('Yellow Cécile Brünner') Pol, yb, 1875, Rambaux; flowers golden pink, very dbl., borne in clusters, intense fragrance; foliage rich green, soft; growth to 3 ft.; ['Polyantha alba plena' × 'Mme Falcot']

'Perle d'Or, Climbing' ('Yellow Cécile Brünner, Climbing') Cl Pol, yb; flowers deep yellow, opening lemon-yellow; [sport of 'Perle d'Or']

'Perle d'Or Yellow' -- See 'Ravensworth'

'Perle du Lac' -- See 'Dorouvi'

'Perle du Lac Annecy' -- See 'Dorouvi'

Perle Meillandécor® -- See 'Meiplatin'

Perle Noire® -- See 'Delurt'

'Perle Orléanaise' Pol, dp, 1913, Duveau; flowers carmine-pink, medium, dbl.; ['Mme Norbert Levavasseur' × 'Frau Cecilie Walter']

'Perle vom Wienerwald' HMult, pb, 1913, Praskac; flowers carmine-rose, reverse soft rose-pink, 2 in., semi-dbl., borne in medium to large clusters; foliage medium green; nearly thornless; vigorous, climbing growth; ['Helene' × 'Crimson Rambler']

'Perle von Aalsmeer' ('Parel van Aalsmeer') HT, dr, 1941, Verschuren; flowers deep red; [sport of 'Better Times']

'Perle von Britz' HMult, lp, 1910, Kiese; flowers pearly pink, fading to white, 3 cm., semi-dbl., borne in clusters of 30-50; ['Tausendschön' × unknown]

'Perle von Godesburg' HT, ly, 1902, Schneider; flowers cream, shaded lemon, large, full, moderate fragrance; [sport of 'Kaiserin Auguste Viktoria']

'Perle von Heidelberg' HT, lp, 1905, Scheurer; flowers silvery pink, reverse lilac pink, very large, full, intense fragrance; vigorous growth; [sport of 'La France']

'Perle von Heidelberg, Climbing' Cl HT, lp; intr. 1906

'Perle von Hohenstein' Pol, lp, 1923,

Kiese; flowers carmine-red, small, semi-dbl., borne in clusters; ['Freudenfeuer' × seedling]

'Perle von Remagen' HT, lp, 1959, Burkhard; bud pointed; flowers soft pink, reverse tinted creamy white, large, dbl., high-centered, moderate fragrance; foliage glossy, leathery; long stems; vigorous, upright growth; [R.M.S. Queen Mary × 'Peace']; intr. 1957

'Perle von Weissenstein' ('Perle de Weissenstein') HGal, m, 1773, Schwartzkopf; flowers brownish, center purple, medium, dbl.; foliage dark green, finely dentate; prickles very small, straight, brown

'Perlmutt-Prinzessin' S, lp, Wänninger, Franz; flowers small, very dbl.; intr. 1990

'Permach' ('Macho Man') HT, m, 1999, Perry, Astor; flowers lavender, medium, dbl., borne mostly singly, moderate fragrance; foliage medium size, medium green, dull; few prickles; bushy growth; intr. 2000

'Permanent Wave' ('Duchess of Windsor', 'Van Nes', 'Mrs Van Nes', 'Mevrouw van Straaten van Nes', 'L'Indéfrisible') F, mr, 1932, Leenders, M.; flowers bright carmine, petals wavy, large, semi-dbl., borne in clusters; foliage glossy, dark green; vigorous, bushy growth; PP107; [sport of 'Else Poulsen']; intr. 1935

'Permax' ('Anna Caroline Maxwell') HT, dr, 2000, Perry, Astor; flowers rich dark red, 4½ in., full, borne mostly singly, slight fragrance; foliage medium size, dark green, matte; few prickles; growth upright, tall; ['Karl Herbst' × 'Burgundy']

'Permeate Peace' HT, pb, Dawson; intr. 1990

'Permill' (Millennium™) HT, mr, 1997, Perry, Astor; flowers large, full, borne mostly singly; foliage medium size, medium green, semi-glossy; upright, medium (5ft. 6 in.) growth; ['Fire Magic' × 'Precious Platinum']

'Permoser' HT, yb, Institut für Obstbau Dresden Pillnitz; flowers light yellow with carmine edges, large, dbl.

'Pernetiana'

Pernille™ -- See 'Poulnil'

'Pernille Hit' (Pernille™) MinFl, pb, Olesen; bud pointed ovoid; flowers soft pink, overlaid with pale greenish-yellow, reverse slightly darker, 5-7½ cm., 16-19 petals, classic hybrid tea, borne mostly singly, slight wild rose fragrance; recurrent; foliage dark green, glossy; prickles few, 4-5 mm., linear, greyed-yellow; vigorous, bushy (40-60 cm.) growth; PP13301; [seedling × seedling]; intr. 1998

Pernille Poulsen™ F, mp, 1965, Poulsen, Niels D.; flowers large, 18 petals, borne in clusters, moderate fragrance; foliage pointed, light green; ['Ma Perkins' × 'Columbine']; intr. 1965

'Pernille Poulsen, Climbing' Cl F, mp, 1985, Poulsen, Niels D.; [sport of Pernille Poulsen™]; intr. 1980

'Pero d'Alenquer' F, dr, Moreira da Silva; flowers dark velvety red, center lighter; [seedling × 'Alain']

'Pérou de Gossard' -- See 'Le Pérou'

'Perpetual Michigan' ('Michigan Perpetual', 'Perpetual Pink') HSet, m, 1843, Feast; flowers rosy pink, changing to purple, large, full, globular, borne in large clusters; not remontant, but having a long bloom period

'Perpetual Pink' -- See 'Perpetual Michigan'

'Perpetual Red' S, mr, 1955, Gaujard; flowers bright red, open, medium, semi-dbl.; recurrent bloom; foliage abundant; very vigorous growth; ['Gruss an Teplitz' × seedling]

'Perpetual Red Moss' -- See 'Perpétuelle Mauget'

'Perpetual Scotch' ('Scotch Perpetual') HSpn, lp, 1819, from Scotland; flowers pale flesh pink, medium to large, dbl., flat, moderate fragrance; quite remontant

'Perpetual Thalia' -- See 'Thalia Remontant'

'Perpetual White Moss' -- See 'Quatre Saisons Blanc Mousseux'

'Perpetually Yours' ('Canterbury') LCl, my, Harkness; flowers creamy lemon yellow, large, 70 petals, slight fragrance; recurrent; foliage glossy, light green; growth shrubby climber to 8 ft., medium vigor; intr. 1999

'Perpétuelle' P, 1827, Vibert

'Perpétuelle d'Anjou' D, lp, before 1845; flowers whitish pink, petals edged lighter

'Perpétuelle de Neuilly' HP, mp, 1834, Verdier, V.; flowers lilac-pink, medium, full, cupped, globular; growth erect; ['Athalin' × unknown]

'Perpétuelle de St Ouen' -- See 'De Tous Mois'

'Perpétuelle Mauget' ('Perpetual Red Moss') M, mp, 1844, Mauget; flowers rose pink, 8-10 cm., full, cupped; very remontant; foliage light green, medium

'Perpétuelle Sapho' -- See 'Sapho'

'Perpid' (Intrepid™) HT, dr, 1998, Perry, Astor; flowers dark velvety red, 4-4½ in., very dbl., high-centered, borne singly, moderate fragrance; foliage medium size, dark green, dull; prickles moderate; medium (5 ft.), upright growth; ['Karl Herbst' × 'Burgundy']; intr. 1999

'Perroquet' LCl, dy, 1957, Robichon; flowers large; foliage glossy; vigorous growth

'Perroquet' F, rb, Lens; flowers red, reverse yellow, becoming dark red, well-formed; foliage bronze; vigorous growth; ['Peace' × ('Cinnabar' × 'Circus')]; intr. 1960

'Persane' HT, Dorieux; intr. 1984

'Persepolis' ('Truper') HT, dy, 1986, Kriloff, Michel; flowers 25 petals, intense tea fragrance; foliage clear green, glossy; [seedling × seedling]

'Persian Autumn' -- See 'Morthirthree'

'Persian Carpet' -- See 'Persian Delight'

'Persian Delight' ('Persian Carpet') F, rb, 1995, Fleming, Joyce L.; flowers rich crimson with yellow base of petal and reverse, medium, 10 petals, slight fragrance; foliage medium size, dark green, glossy; upright (up to 70 cm.) growth; ['Masquerade' × 'Traumerei']; intr. 1994

'Persian Flame' -- See 'Morflame'

'Persian Light' -- See 'Morthree'

'Persian Musk Rose' -- See 'Nastarana'

'Persian Peach' -- See 'Morpeaches'

'Persian Princess' Min, or, 1970, Moore, Ralph S.; bud small, pointed; flowers coral-red, small, 25 petals, high-centered to cupped, borne singly and in sprays of 4-6, slight fragrance; free-flowering; foliage medium small, semi-glossy, leathery; prickles medium, slender, hooked slightly downward; vigorous, bushy, dwarf (12-14 in.) growth; PP3161; [Baccará® × 'Eleanor']

'Persian Sunset' -- See 'Morthirtythreebee'

'Persicifolia' -- See 'À Feuilles de Pêcher'

'Persistence' -- See 'Broper'

'Personality' HT, yb, 1960, Morey, Dr. Dennison; bud large, ovoid; flowers golden yellow splashed red, 4½ in., 35-40 petals, open, borne singly, intense very sweet fragrance; recurrent; foliage large, leathery, glossy; prickles ordinary, medium length, hooked downward; vigorous, upright growth; hips none ; PP2097; ['Peace' × 'Sutter's Gold']; intr. 1960

'Persuader' HT, mp, 1960, Eacott; flowers bright pink, large, 30 petals, high-centered; vigorous growth; ['Golden Scepter' × 'Southport']

'Persuasion' F, lp, 1972, Sanday, John; flowers pale blush-pink, base orange, large, 30 petals, high-centered; foliage glossy; ['Vera Dalton' × 'Tropicana']

'Persue de Gossart' C, dp; flowers velvety cerise, with garnet reflexes, dbl.

'Persus' (Colossus™) HT, dy, 1998, Perry, Astor; flowers golden yellow, medium sized, full, borne in small clusters, moderate fragrance; foliage medium size, medium green, glossy; growth upright, medium (5 ft.); [Folklore® × 'Golden Gate']; intr. 1999

'Pertwentyfirst' ('21st Century', 'Twenty First Century') HT, dy, 1999, Perry, Astor; flowers large, full, borne mostly singly, slight fragrance; foliage medium size, dark green, semi-glossy; few prickles; upright, tall (5 ft.) growth; ['Butterscotch' × 'Mandelon']; intr. 2000

Petal Pushers™ -- See 'Jacloose'

Petaluma™ (Kirsch Cover™) S, rb, Poulsen; flowers medium red, fading as they open to medium pink on upper side, 5-8 cm., semi-dbl., flat, very slight fragrance; recurrent; foliage dark green, glossy; broad, bushy (60-100 cm.)

growth; intr. 2004
'Pete Musser' -- See 'Wilpete'
'Pete Paul' -- See 'Warpel'
'Peter Beales' S, mr, Clements, John; flowers crimson-red with pronounced golden eye, 3 in., 5-8 petals, moderate sweet, honey fragrance; free-flowering; foliage dark green; rounded and densely foliaged (4 × 3½ ft.) growth; PPAF; intr. 2000
'Peter Benjamin' HT, ab, 1981, Allender, Robert William; bud long; flowers light apricot-pink, 40 petals, rounded, borne 2 - 3 per cluster, moderate fragrance; free-flowering; foliage small to medium size, light green; prickles red; medium-tall growth; ['Benjamin Franklin' × Peter Frankenfeld®]; intr. 1978
'Peter Cottontail' -- See 'Marpeter'
'Peter Cottrell' -- See 'Sunny Abundance'
Peter Frankenfeld® HT, dp, 1966, Kordes, R.; flowers rose-pink, well-shaped, large, dbl., high-centered; good repeat; foliage medium green, leathery, disease-resistant; rugged (4-5 ft.), spreading growth; flower size diminished noticeably in warmer climates
'Peter Frankenfeld, Climbing' Cl HT, dp, 1976, Welsh, E.; [sport of Peter Frankenfeld®]; intr. 1975
'Peter Goldman' -- See 'Dicname'
'Peter Hood' -- See 'Worcarbon'
'Peter John' HMsk, op, 2000, Jerabek, Paul E.; flowers light pink, yellow at base, 4 in., full, borne in small clusters, moderate fragrance; foliage medium size, light green turning dark green, semi-glossy; prickles moderate; spreading, medium (5-6 ft.) growth
'Peter Lambert' HWich, dp, 1936, Vogel, M.; flowers carmine-pink, 6 cm., dbl., globular, borne in small to medium clusters, no fragrance; foliage very glossy; prickles numerous, long
'Peter Lawson' HP, dr, 1862, Thomas; flowers deep scarlet shaded purple
'Peter Long' HT, or
'Peter Mac Gold Jewel' -- See 'Tanledolg'
'Peter Mayle, Climbing' ('Lolita Lempicka, Climbing') Cl HT, dp; [sport of Peter Mayle™]; intr. 2005
Peter Mayle™ -- See 'Meizincaro'
'Peter Nay' HT, mr, 1959, Verschuren; flowers scarlet, large, dbl., intense fragrance; foliage leathery; long stems; very vigorous growth; ['The Doctor' × 'New Yorker']; intr. 1958
'Peter Pan' HT, dr, 1935, Knight, G.; flowers dark crimson, large; vigorous growth
'Peter Pan' -- See 'Chewpan'
'Peter Pan' -- See 'Sunpete'
'Peter Pan' -- See 'Presumida'
'Peter Piper' HT, or, 1969, Waterhouse Nursery; flowers Chinese orange, large, semi-dbl., urn-shaped; bushy growth; [sport of Piccadilly®]
'Peter Rosegger' HMult, op, 1914, Lambert, P.; bud coral; flowers coral-pink, fading to white, 5-6 cm., dbl., rosette, borne in clusters of 5-15, strong musk fragrance; repeat bloom; foliage dark green; vigorous, climbing growth; ['Geheimrat Dr. Mittweg' × Tip-Top®]
'Peter Turvey' HT, rb, 2003, Poole, Lionel; flowers red, reverse red/peach blend, 4½ in., full, borne mostly solitary, slight fragrance; foliage large, dark green, semi-glossy; prickles large, triangular; upright, bushy, medium (36 in.) growth; garden, exhibition; ['Mike Thompson' × 'Royal William']; intr. 2004
'Peter Wessel' -- See 'Tantide'
'Peter's Briarcliff' HT, mp, 1940, J&P; flowers true unshaded rose-pink, long pointed, well-formed; foliage dark; vigorous, free growth
'Pétillante' -- See 'Roter Champagner'
'Petit Ange' -- See 'Little Angel'
'Petit Bonheur' LCl, mp, Adam; intr. 2001
Petit Canard® -- See 'Lencan'
'Petit Constant' Pol, mr, 1899, Soupert & Notting; flowers nasturtium-red, small, dbl.; vigorous growth; ['Mignonette' × 'Luciole']
Petit Four® -- See 'Interfour'
'Petit François' F, or, 1957, Dorieux; flowers semi-dbl.; foliage glossy; very dwarf growth; ['Alain' × ('Brazier' × 'Léonce Colombier')]
'Petit Jean' HT, ob, 1926, Vestal; flowers deep orange-buff, shaded to yellow, edged peach-pink, large, dbl., moderate fragrance; ['White Killarney' × 'Sunburst']
'Petit Louis' HWich, op, 1912, Nonin; flowers shrimp-pink, 3½ cm., very dbl., borne in medium clusters; foliage small; vigorous, climbing growth; ['Dorothy Perkins' × unknown]
'Petit Marquis' -- See 'Korholst'
'Petit Poucet' F, mr, 1955, Combe; flowers bright red, center tinted yellow, petals wavy, single; dwarf growth; ['Cocorico' × seedling]
'Petit Prince' Pol, mr, 1956, Laperrière; flowers geranium-red, borne in clusters of 8-10; very dwarf growth
'Petit Quatre Saisons' D, dp, Noël; flowers deep pink, small, dbl.; growth dwarf
Petit Rat de l'Opéra® -- See 'LLX8744'
'Petit René' HWich, mr, 1925, Nonin; bud small, globular; flowers brilliant red, 3½ cm., very dbl., borne in small to medium clusters, intense fragrance; non-recurrent; vigorous, climbing growth
'Petit St François' ('De Reims') C, m, about 1850, Robert; flowers bluish-pink with purple-violet, full, globular; dwarf Centifolia
'Petit St. François' -- See 'Pompon de Saint-François'
Petit Sam® F, dp, Adam
'Petit Serpent' -- See 'Lenlita'
'Petit Trianon' F, lp, Meilland; flowers clear Neyron pink, 34-37 petals, cupped, borne in clusters, slight fragrance; recurrent; foliage dark green; growth to 60-70 cm.; intr. 2005
'Petit Vermilion' HGal, mr, about 1823, from Angers
'Petite' -- See 'Patty Lou'
'Petite Agathe' -- See 'Sommesson'
'Petite Aimée' HGal, before 1814, Descemet
'Petite Anglaise' -- See 'Maiden's Blush'
'Petite Carrousel' Min, w, 1985, Michelis, Dorothy; flowers ivory, coral pink petal edges, small, borne singly and in clusters, slight fragrance; foliage small, dark, semi-glossy; upright, tiny growth; ['thought to be Magic Carrousel' × unknown]
'Petite Chalons' -- See 'Pompon de Bourgogne'
'Petite de Hollande' ('Bordeaux des Dames', 'Minor', 'Rosier Petit à Cent Feuilles', 'Rosier des Dames', 'Rosier de Bourgogne à Grandes Fleurs', R. × centifolia minor, 'Pompon des Dames', 'Normandica', 'Gros Pompon', 'De Bordeaux', 'Centfeuilles de Bordeaux', 'Burgundiaca',) C, mp, before 1791; flowers rose pink, small, dbl., borne in small clusters, moderate fragrance; foliage ovoid, pointed, serrated; prickles small, sharp, slightly hooked; short (18 in.) growth; from Holland
'Petite de Terre Franche' HMsk, pb, Louette; flowers light rosy pink dotted with carmine, fading to white, 3-4 cm., semi-dbl., pompon, borne in large clusters, slight fragrance; free-flowering; canes up to 2½ m. long, spreading growth; intr. 1996
'Petite Écossaise' HSpn, lp, before 1826, Vibert or Prévost; flowers flesh, small, semi-dbl.; non-recurrent; moderate growth
'Petite Ernestre' -- See 'Petite Junon de Hollande'
'Petite Évêque' HGal, before 1815, Descemet
Petite Folie® Min, ob, 1970, Meilland; flowers vermilion, reverse carmine, small, dbl., globular, borne in trusses, slight fruity fragrance; foliage leathery; vigorous growth; [('Dany Robin' × 'Fire King') × ('Cricri' × 'Perla de Montserrat')]
'Petite Francoise' Pol, lp, 1915, Gravereaux
Petite Fredaine® -- See 'Lenlitlit'
'Petite Frolic' Min, yb, Taschner, Ludwig; bud orange-red; flowers yellow base with varying orange and red markings over the petals, single, shallow cup to flat; free-flowering; compact growth; intr. 2005
'Petite Hessoise' ('À Fleurs Doubles') HEg, mp, about 1810, Redouté/Lahaye; bud pointed; flowers bright rose, small, semi-dbl.; foliage large, light green, round; prickles protrusive, strong
'Petite Hollande' -- See 'Petite de Hollande'
'Petite Jeanne' HWich, mr, 1912, Nonin; flowers currant-red; ['Dorothy Perkins'

× unknown]
'Petite Junon de Hollande' ('Juno Rose', 'Roi de Perse', 'Petite Ernestre', 'Junon Argentée') C, lp, before 1820, from Holland; flowers small, full; Petite Ernestre may be a separate cultivar (D) from Descemet

'Petite Léonie' Pol, w, 1893, Soupert & Notting; flowers pinkish white, small; ['Mignonette' × 'Duke of Connaught']

'Petite Lisette' ('Hybrida cum Bifera') A, dp, 1817, Vibert; flowers rich rose, with a small center eye to medium, 1 in., full, pompon, borne in small clusters, slight fragrance; non-remontant; foliage matte, pointed, grayish-green, toothed, small; few prickles; growth to 3-4 ft.; sometimes classified as C or D, but listed by Vibert as A; probably a hybrid of an Alba and a Damask Perpetual

'Petite Louise' LCl, op; flowers salmon-pink

'Petite Louise' -- See 'Belle Mignonne'

'Petite Marcelle' Pol, w, 1910, Dubreuil; flowers snow white, small, borne in clusters of 5-10; foliage dark green

'Petite Michelle' -- See 'Jaclib'

'Petite Odette' HWich, lp, 1923, Nonin; flowers very dbl., borne in clusters; vigorous, climbing growth; ['Lady Godiva' × seedling]

'Petite Orléanaise' HGal, mp, before 1843; flowers strong pink, with a small central eye, small, dbl., flat, rosette at center, borne in clusters of 2-6, slight fragrance; vigorous, almost climbing. growth; sometimes classed as C; documented in Vibert's catalog of 1843

'Petite Penny' -- See 'Macjocel'

Petite Perfection™ -- See 'Jacrybi'

'Petite Perle d'Or' -- See 'Ripdor'

'Petite Provins' -- See 'Rosier d'Amour'

'Petite Red Scotch' -- See 'Double Dark Marbled'

'Petite Reine' -- See 'Queenie'

'Petite Renoncule Violette' -- See 'Félicie'

'Petite Rosamund' -- See 'Fabros'

'Petite Violette' HGal, m, before 1815, Descemet; flowers violet, small

'Petito' F, yb, Agel

'Petra' F, mr, 1975, Kordes; bud medium, globular; flowers blood-red, dbl.; foliage dark, leathery; moderate, bushy growth; [seedling × Taora®]; intr. 1974

'Petra' F, mp, Roman, G., and Wagner, S.; flowers pure pink, small, 40 petals, rosette, borne in clusters, slight fragrance; foliage medium size, medium green, glossy; practically thornless; [Bonica '82® × 'Rosabunda']; intr. 2004

'Petrine' HT, ob, 1921, Therkildsen; flowers coral-red, shaded chrome-yellow, dbl.; ['Old Gold' × 'Mme Edouard Herriot']

'Petro' F, w

'Petrol' HT, r, Spek; flowers deep brownish red, 4 in., 55-60 petals, high-centered, borne mostly singly; recurrent; numerous prickles; stems moderately long; intr. 2005

'Petronella' HT, rb, 1980, MacLeod, Major C.A.; flowers pointed, 49 petals, borne singly; foliage dark, glossy; prickles straight, red; compact growth; ['Gail Borden' × ('Dalvey' × 'Fragrant Cloud')]

'Pétronille' -- See 'Beauté Superbe Agathée'

Petticoat® -- See 'Korgretaum'

'Petticoat' -- See 'Jacpet'

Petticoat Fairy Tale™ -- See 'Korgretaum'

'Petticoat Lane' -- See 'Socamp'

'Petula Clark' HT, mr, 1963, Lens; flowers clear red, well-formed, dbl., high-centered; foliage bronze; vigorous, bushy growth; ['Purpurine' × 'Lavender Pinocchio']

'Petula Clark, Climbing' Cl HT, mr, 1979, Lens; intr. 1967

'Pfaffstädt' HP, ly, 1929, von Württemberg, Herzogin Elsa; flowers yellowish-white, large, dbl., moderate fragrance

Pfälzer Gold® -- See 'Tanalzergo'

'Pfander's Canina' (strain of R. canina), lp

'Pfuss Pfree' F, mp, 1989, Stoddard, Louis; bud ovoid, pointed; flowers light pink, reverse medium pink, small, 25 petals, cupped, borne in sprays of 4-6; foliage medium size, medium green, very glossy, blackspot resistant; prickles straight, tan-brown; spreading growth; hips round, deep orange; ['Sea Foam' × (('Restless Native' × unknown) × Europeana®)]

'Phab Gold' -- See 'Frybountiful'

'Phaenomen' ('Phenomenon') HT, op, 1934, Chotkové Rosarium; flowers slightly rosy salmon, reverse light rosy red, very large, dbl.; foliage dark; very vigorous growth

'Phaloé' HGal, mp, about 1845, Calvert; flowers bright pink, shaded lilac, medium to large, very full

'Phaloé' N, yb, Vibert; flowers light yellow, shaded dawn pink, large, full; intr. 1846

'Phantasy' HT, lp, 1927, Dunlop; flowers medium light pink, base yellow, dbl.; ['Lady Alice Stanley' × 'Royal (or Priscilla)']

'Phantom' HT, ob, 1920, Towill; flowers coppery yellow, center lighter, semi-dbl.; RULED EXTINCT 4/92; [('Joseph Hill' × ('My Maryland' × unknown)) × 'Lady Hillingdon']

'Phantom' -- See 'Maccatsan'

Pharaoh® ('Pharaon') HT, or, 1970, Meilland, Mrs. Marie-Louise; bud ovoid; flowers bright orange-red, 5 in., dbl., high-centered, moderate fragrance; foliage dark, glossy, leathery; vigorous, upright growth; PP2859; [('Happiness' × 'Independence') × 'Suspense']; intr. 1967

'Pharaon' B, mr, before 1889, Bernède; flowers velvety red

'Pharaon' -- See 'Meifiga'

Phare® LCl, or, 1961, Delbard-Chabert; flowers bright orange-red, 3 in., 33 petals, borne in small clusters; foliage glossy, dark green; vigorous (to 10 ft.) growth; ['Spectacular' × ('Floradora' × seedling)]

'Pharericus' HGal, dp, about 1829, Calvert; flowers dark pink to light red, large, full

'Pharisäer' HT, op, 1903, Hinner, W.; bud long, pointed; flowers rosy white, shaded salmon, dbl., high-centered, moderate fragrance; foliage bronze; long, weak stems; vigorous growth; ['Mrs W.J. Grant' × unknown]

'Pheasant' -- See 'Kordapt'

'Pheidippides' F, mr, 1977, Ellick; flowers currant-red, 4 in., 35 petals; foliage light green; moderately vigorous, low growth; ['Sam Ferris' × 'Chopin']; intr. 1979

'Phelan's Flag' HCh, rb, 1952, Phelan; bud ovoid, greenish white flushed purplish red; flowers red when newly opened, changing to pink, then white with a red eye, 2½-3 in., 75-100 petals, quartered, intense fragrance; semi-recurrent bloom; foliage dark; vigorous (6 ft. or more) growth, with tendency to climb; PP1152

'Phénice' HGal, dp, 1843, Vibert; flowers reddish-rose, spotted, medium, dbl.

'Phenomène' LCl, w, Delbard; flowers cream, fading qhite, medium, semi-dbl., borne in small clusters, moderate apple fragrance; intr. 1989

'Phenomenon' -- See 'Phaenomen'

'Philadelphia' -- See 'Tommac'

'Philadelphia' -- See 'Philadelphia Rambler'

'Philadelphia Rambler' ('Philadelphia') HMult, dr, 1904, Van Fleet; flowers scarlet-crimson, center lighter, 4 cm., dbl., borne in large clusters, no fragrance; midseason bloom; numerous prickles; vigorous, climbing growth; ['Crimson Rambler' × 'Victor Hugo']

'Philadelphica' HBank, w; flowers cream white, single; [sport of R. banksiae lutea]

'Philatelie' HT, rb, McGredy; flowers red and white striped, dbl., high-centered, borne singly and in clusters; foliage dark green; compact (70-80 cm.) growth; intr. 2000

'Philémon' Ch, m, 1821, Cochet or Vibert; flowers dark purple, becoming lilac pink, medium, dbl.

'Philémon' N, m, Laffay; flowers lilac, striped purple, small, full; intr. about 1835

'Philémon' -- See 'Philémon Cochet'

'Philémon Cochet' ('Philémon') B, dp, 1895, Cochet, Sc.; flowers deep bright pink, very large, very full, somewhat globular, borne mostly solitary; foliage dark green; prickles slightly recurved, reddish; growth semi-climbing

'Philibert Boutigny' HP, mp; flowers silvery rose, very large; vigorous growth

'Philip Harvey' F, ob, 1972, Harkness; flowers salmon-red, shaded orange,

5 in., 25 petals, moderate fragrance; foliage glossy, dark; ['Fragrant Cloud' × 'Circus']

'Philipp Melanchthon' F, dr, Hetzel; intr. 1994

'Philipp Paulig' HP, dr, 1908, Lambert; flowers large, full, moderate fragrance; ['Captain Hayward' × 'Baronne Adolphe de Rothschild']

'Philippe' ('Bel Ami') F, op, 1959, Delforge; bud oval; flowers peach-salmon, open, medium, 15 petals, borne in clusters; foliage glossy; moderate growth; ['Cognac' × 'Fashion']

'Philippe Bardet' HP, mr, 1874, Moreau-Robert; flowers red nuanced carmine, very large, full, borne in small clusters

'Philippe Noiret' -- See 'Meizoele'

'Philippe Pétain' HT, dp, 1940, Nabonnand, C.; flowers velvety carmine with coppery reflections, not turning blue,, cupped; foliage bright chive-green

'Philippe Rivoire' HT, op, 1941, Gaujard; flowers large, dbl.

'Philippine Lambert' HMult, op, 1903, Lambert; flowers bright salmon and peach, darker center, borne in clusters; [('Euphrosyne' × 'Safrano') × 'Dr. Grill']; sometimes classed as Pol

Phillipa™ -- See 'Poulheart'

'Phillipp Paulig' HP, dr, 1908, Lambert, P.; flowers large, dbl.

'Philomèle' N, lp, 1844, Vibert; flowers flesh pink

'Philomene' C, m, Hardy; growth to 4 ft.

'Philomène Crozy' HP, m, 1857, Avoux; flowers lilac pink

'Philomène Pollaert' HT, or, 1925, Pollaert; flowers crimson tinted orange, dbl.; [('Gen. MacArthur' × unknown) × 'Old Gold']

Phloxy® F, rb

'Phoebe' HT, w, 1922, Cant, B. R.; flowers cream-white, sometime pure white, dbl.; ['Ophelia' × 'Verna Mackay']

'Phoebe' -- See 'Harvander'

Phoebe's Choice™ -- See 'Bilice'

'Phoebe's Frilled Pink' -- See 'Fimbriata'

'Phoebus' HP, mp; flowers bright pink, shading lighter, large, dbl., moderate fragrance; bushy growth; intr. 1837

'Phoebus' D, m; flowers lilac blush, centers rosy crimson, large, full; growth erect; intr. before 1848

'Phoebus' HGal, mp, 1818

'Phoenix' HT, dp, 1973, Armstrong, D.L.; flowers light cerise, large, dbl., high-centered, moderate fragrance; foliage large, glossy, leathery; vigorous, upright growth; PP3438; ['Manitou' × 'Grand Slam']

'Phoenix' -- See 'Beauté Insurmontable'

'Phoenix' -- See 'Harvee'

'Phoenix First' F, dr, 1959, Kernovske, V.R.; bud ovoid; flowers dark red shaded black, small, very dbl., borne in clusters; foliage leathery; bushy growth; ['Our Princess' × 'Pompon Beauty']; intr. 1959

'Phoenix Rising' Min, ob, 2007, Smith, Joe and Landers-Smith, Brenda; flowers variegated, dramatically colored, reverse yellow, medium, dbl., borne mostly solitary; foliage dark green, glossy; prickles red, moderate; growth upright, tall (36 in.); exhibiton; [sport of Bees Knees™]; intr. 2008

'Photogenic' S, w, 1999, Jerabek, Paul E.; flowers white with pink edge, reverse white with narrow pink edge, 2½-3 in., 10 petals, borne in small clusters, moderate fragrance; foliage large, medium green, semi-glossy; upright, tall (10 ft.) growth; intr. 1998

'Phyllis' Pol, mr, 1908, Merryweather; flowers bright red, small, dbl., borne in large clusters; recurrent bloom; ['Mme Norbert Levavasseur' × unknown]

'Phyllis Bide' Cl Pol, yb, 1923, Bide; flowers pale gold, shaded pink, 3 cm., semi-dbl., borne in large clusters, slight fragrance; dependably recurrent; growth to 6-10 ft.; ['Perle d'Or' × 'Gloire de Dijon']

'Phyllis Burden' HT, op, 1935, Cant, B. R.; bud long, pointed; flowers shrimp-pink and orange, large, dbl.; foliage glossy, light; very vigorous growth

'Phyllis Diller' -- See 'Wekjojojap'

'Phyllis Gold' HT, my, 1935, Robinson, H.; flowers butter-yellow, edged lighter, dbl., high-centered; foliage rich olive-green; very vigorous, branching growth; ['Lady Florence Stronge' × 'Julien Potin']

'Phyllis Gold, Climbing' Cl HT, my, 1949, Fryers Nursery, Ltd.

'Phyllis Lucas' HT, ob, 1961, Wheatcroft Bros.; flowers orange shaded bronze, well-shaped; [sport of Bettina®]

'Phyllis McDonald' ('The Ionian Rose') HT, dp; intr. 1998

'Phyllis Poyser' HT, op, 1969, Fankhauser; bud long, pointed; flowers orange-pink, large, 50 petals, high-centered, intense spicy fragrance; foliage light green, soft, elongated; vigorous, compact, bushy growth; ['Golden Sun' × 'Spartan']

Phyllis Shackelford™ -- See 'Morshack'

'Phynelia' HT, mr, 1928, Reeves; flowers crimson-cerise, borne in clusters

'Pia Berghout' Pol, mp, 1967, Buisman, G. A. H.; flowers pink, medium, dbl., borne in clusters; foliage dark; ['Saskia' × seedling]

'Pia-Nissimo' HT, w, Keisei; flowers dbl., high-centered, slight fragrance; intr. 1996

Piacenza™ -- See 'Albella'

'Piano' HT, mr, Tantau; intr. 1998

'Piarsco' ('Revue de Dauville') F, dy, Pineau; intr. 1982

'Pic-Nic' -- See 'Picnic'

'Picador' F, mr, 1964, Verschuren, A.; flowers cherry-red, dbl., borne in clusters; foliage glossy, dark; upright, compact growth; [sport of 'Oranien']

'Picaninni' -- See 'Wripic'

'Picante' HT, ob, Weeks; flowers iridescent orange; foliage dark green; medium to tall growth; PPAF; intr. 2005

'Picardy' HT, dp, 1967, Trew, C.; flowers rose-bengal, globular; foliage dark, glossy; free growth; [Rose Gaujard® × 'Bayadere']

'Picasso' F, pb, 1971, McGredy, Sam IV; flowers deep pink, petal edges lighter, white eye and reverse, 3 in., 18 petals; foliage small; PP3351; ['Marlena' × ('Evelyn Fison' × ('Frulingsmorgen' × 'Orange Sweetheart'))]

'Picayune' Ch, lp, before 1843; flowers light pink to white, small, dbl., borne in clusters

Piccadilly® HT, rb, 1960, McGredy, Sam IV; flowers scarlet, base and reverse gold, 4½-5 in., 28 petals, high-centered; foliage dark, glossy; vigorous, upright, branching growth; ['McGredy's Yellow' × 'Karl Herbst']; intr. 1960

'Piccadilly, Climbing' Cl HT, rb, 1973, Minzen, 1963; Sutton, 1973; flowers scarlet at base, reverse gold, 1½-3 in., 25-30 petals; [sport of Piccadilly®]; 1963 version was never introduced into commerce

'Piccadilly Sunset' HT, ob, 1971, Goodwin; flowers orange flushed apricot, reverse gold, high pointed, 4-5 in., 34 petals, foliage glossy, dark; moderate, upright growth; [sport of Piccadilly®]; intr. 1970

'Piccaninny' HT, dr, 1941, Lammerts, Dr. Walter; bud long, pointed; flowers stamens yellow, large, 5-6 petals; foliage dark, glossy; vigorous growth; ['Night' × 'Sanguinaire']

'Picciola Ina' Pol, op, 1937, Giacomasso; flowers pure salmon, borne in clusters of 10-50; vigorous, bushy growth

'Piccola Es' S, lp, 1984, Fumagalli, Niso; flowers medium, 20 petals, foliage medium size, medium green, semi-glossy; bushy growth; [seedling × seedling]; intr. 1983

'Piccolo' F, dr, 1959, Tantau, Math.; bud ovoid; flowers velvety dark red, open, dbl., borne in clusters; foliage dark, leathery, glossy; moderate, bushy growth; RULED EXTINCT 4/85; ['Red Favorite' × 'Kathe Duvigneau']; intr. 1957

Piccolo® -- See 'Tanolokip'

'Piccolo Pete' S, mr, 1985, Buck, Dr. Griffith J.; flowers 4 in., 7-10 petals, flat, borne 1-10 per cluster, moderate fragrance; repeat bloom; foliage large, leathery, dark olive green; prickles slightly hooked, tan; upright, bushy growth; hardy; ['Carefree Beauty' × (('Peace' × 'Dornroschen') × 'Country Music')]; intr. 1984

'Pick Me Up' HT, mr, 1941, Clark, A.; flowers well-shaped

'Pickering Red HP (found)' -- See 'Star of Waltham'

'Pickwick' -- See 'Sabclive'

'Picnic' ('Pic-Nic') F, or, 1975, Warriner, William A.; bud short, pointed; flowers shrimp-red, petal base yellow, 3-3½ in., 70 petals, high-centered, borne singly and in flat clusters, slight fragrance; foliage medium size, leathery; prickles medium, long, straight, brown; vigorous, upright, branching growth; PP3829; ['South Seas' × seedling]; intr. 1976

'Pico' HT, rb, 1962, Buyl Frères; bud pointed; flowers salmon-red and canary-yellow, dbl.; foliage glossy; bushy growth

'Picobello' F, or; intr. 1998

'Picotee' F, rb, 1960, Raffel; flowers white, edged red, 2½-3½ in., 24 petals, cupped to flat, borne in clusters, slight fragrance; foliage dark green, glossy; vigorous, upright, bushy growth; PP1987; ['Little Darling' × 'Gertrude Raffel']; intr. 1961

'Picotee' -- See 'Benpico'

'Picpa' HT, Dorieux; intr. 1974

'Picture, Climbing' Cl HT, lp, 1942, Swim, H.C.; flowers pale pink, darker at center, reverse creamy, high-centered; PP524; [sport of 'Picture']

'Picture' HT, lp, 1932, McGredy; flowers 34 petals, high-centered, slight fragrance; foliage glossy, dark green; vigorous growth

'Picture Book' -- See 'Sabcook'

'Picture of Health' S, ab, Harkness; flowers blush white with pale apricot center, large, very full, borne in compact trusses; vigorous growth; intr. 1999

'Picture Page' HT, lp, 1953, Jordan, B.L.; flowers peach-pink shading to flesh-pink, base yellow, well-formed, 4 in., 23-25 reflexed petals; foliage dark; very free growth; ['Picture' × 'Mme Butterfly']

'Picture Perfect' -- See 'Elsie Melton'

'Picture Perfect' -- See 'Weltrue'

'Picturesque' HT, lp, 1950, Eddie; bud long; flowers pale pink with pronounced red veining, large, 30-35 petals, high-centered; foliage leathery; vigorous, upright, bushy growth; ['Mrs H.M. Eddie' × 'Mrs Sam McGredy']

'Pie IX' -- See 'Pius IX'

'Pie X' HT, w, 1905, Hildebrand; flowers cream white aging to delicate pink, center darker, large, very full, cupped, moderate fragrance; ['Kaiserin Auguste Viktoria' × 'Mrs W. J. Grant']

'Piece d'Or' S, dy

'Pied Piper' F, mr, 1969, Lindquist; flowers small, dbl., globular; foliage leathery; moderate, low growth; PP3069; ['Garnette' × Moulin Rouge®]

'Piera Rose' S, ob, Harkness; flowers soft orange, full, cupped, moderate fragrance; growth to 100 cm.; intr. 2005

'Pierette' ('Pierette Pavement', 'Yankee Lady') HRg, dp, Uhl, J.; flowers semi-dbl. to dbl., moderate fragrance; recurrent; low (30 in.), spreading growth; hardy; intr. 1987

'Pierette Pavement' -- See 'Pierette'

'Pierre' HT, yb, 1945, Mallerin, C.; bud large, ovoid; flowers deep golden yellow edged red, very dbl.; foliage glossy; vigorous, upright, bushy growth; ['Soeur Thérèse' × 'Lumiere']

'Pierre' HT, ab

'Pierre Aguetant' HT, my, 1938, Gaujard; bud long, pointed; flowers chamois-yellow, open, very large, dbl.; foliage leathery; vigorous growth

'Pierre B' HT, ab, Bell, Ronald J.; flowers soft apricot, long lasting when cut; medium growth; [sport of 'Dr A.J. Verhage']; intr. 1982

'Pierre Bonnard' ('Grimpant Pierre Bonnard') LCl, pb, Laperrière; flowers cream with magenta pink edges, full, cupped, quartered; strong (3 - 3.5 m) growth; intr. 2006

'Pierre Bredy' HT, rb, 1958, Arles; flowers currant-red, reverse silvery; foliage dark; low growth; ['Peace' × 'Scheherazade']

'Pierre Caro' HP, dr, 1879, Levet; flowers dard red, fading lighter, medium to large, dbl., intense fragrance; foliage dark green; growth upright

'Pierre Cormier' Pol, or, 1926, Turbat; flowers brilliant scarlet-red, center lighter, borne in clusters; dwarf growth

'Pierre Cuillerat' HT, w, 1900, Buatois; flowers flesh white, very large, full

Pierre de Ronsard® -- See 'Meiviolin'

'Pierre de St Cyr' B, lp, 1838, Plantier; flowers glossy pale pink, large, very dbl., cupped; vigorous growth

'Pierre Dupont' HP, dr, 1861, Clément; flowers glowing dark red, medium

'Pierre Durand' HP, mp, 1881, Pernet; flowers bright pink, large, dbl.

Pierre Gagnaire® S, ab, Delbard; bud small, orange; flowers cream, with tones of orange and pink fading to white, single, borne in large clusters, moderate floral, fruity fragrance; good repeat; foliage olive green, glossy; vigorous (5 ft.) growth; intr. 2003

'Pierre Gaujard' HT, rb, 1944, Gaujard; bud pointed; flowers fiery shades, very large, dbl.; foliage glossy; vigorous growth

'Pierre Guillot' HT, rb, 1879, Guillot; flowers red with white, large, dbl., moderate fragrance; ['Mme Falcot' × 'hybrid perpetual seedling']

'Pierre Larousse' HT, mr, Meilland

'Pierre Notting' HP, dr, 1863, Portemer fils; flowers large, 42 petals, globular, moderate fragrance; not often recurrent; upright growth; ['Alfred Colomb' × unknown]

'Pierre Seletzky' HP, dr, 1872, Levet; flowers fiery dark purple with slatey tints, large, full

Pierre Troisgros® HT, pb, Dorieux; flowers soft pink in center, fading toward white with brighter pink edges on opening, large, dbl., high-centered, borne mostly singly, moderate fragrance; good repeat; stems short; growth medium (3 ft.); intr. 1991

'Pierre Wattinne' HT, dp, 1901, Soupert & Notting; flowers cherry pink nuanced salmon yellow, large, dbl., moderate fragrance; ['Papa Gontier' × seedling]

'Pierrette' HT, rb, 1931, Tantau; flowers blackish red streaked white, passing to steel-blue, small, very dbl., cupped; foliage small; short stems; dwarf growth; [sport of 'Felix Laporte']

'Pierrette' HT, or, Tantau; flowers bright copper red, flecked brighter, large, 25 petals, intense fragrance; upright, bushy growth; [sport of 'Texas Centennial']; intr. 1945

'Pierrine' -- See 'Micpie'

'Pierrot' F, rb, 1979, Lens, Louis; bud ovoid; flowers white marked red, becoming red, 2½ in., 30 petals, cupped, moderate spicy fragrance; foliage leathery; vigorous, compact growth; ['Poupee' × 'Fillette']; intr. 1971

'Pierson's Pink' HT, dp, 1950, Pierson, A.N.; bud long, pointed; flowers rose-pink, 5 in., 32 petals, high-centered; very vigorous, upright growth; PP915; [sport of 'Better Times']

'Piet Retief' F, dr, 1950, Leenders, M.; flowers dark morocco-red; ['Irene' × 'Donald Prior']

'Piet Saverys' F, ob, 1955, Buyl Frères; flowers orange, semi-dbl.; bushy growth; ['Independence' × 'Border King']

'Pietermaritzburg Rose' S, lp; flowers translucent pink with yellow stamens, single, shallow cup, moderate fragrance; foliage dark green, disease-resistant; stately, tall growth; intr. 1993

'Pietro Tione' ('Tione Pietro') HT, rb, 1907, Fugier-Bonnaire; flowers brick red, shaded orange-yellow, large, full

'Pigalle, Climbing' Cl HT, m

'Pigalle' HT, ob, Keisei; flowers tangerine orange, full, high-centered, borne mostly singly; florist rose; intr. 2004

'Pigalle' HT, m, 1955, Meilland, F.; flowers reddish-violet, 4 in., dbl.; foliage bronze; bushy growth; ['Fantastique' × 'Boudoir']; intr. 1951

Pigalle® -- See 'Meicloux'

'Pigmy Gold' F, dy, 1953, Boerner; bud ovoid; flowers golden yellow, small, dbl., moderate fragrance; foliage dark, glossy; dwarf growth; PP1114

'Pigmy Lavender' F, m, 1961, Boerner; bud ovoid; flowers lavender tinted pink, 2 in., 30-35 petals, cupped, moderate fragrance; foliage leathery, dark; short, strong stems; vigorous, dwarf growth; PP2195; [('Lavender Pinocchio' × unknown) × 'hybrid tea seedling']; intr. 1961

'Pigmy Red' F, dr, 1953, Boerner; bud ovoid; flowers deep red, white eye, small, dbl., borne in clusters, moderate fragrance; foliage glossy; dwarf growth; PP1319; ['Chatter' × 'Red Pinocchio']

'Pihca' -- See 'Pitica'

Pijama Party® ('Mary') HT, or, Tantau; flowers orange red, cream yellow reverse edged red, large, double, high-centered, borne mostly singly; recurrent; stems medium to long; florist rose; intr. 2003

'Pike's Peak' S, pb, 1940, Gunter; bud long, pointed; flowers light bright red, center yellow, fading white, large, 13 petals, borne in clusters of up to 17; non-recurrent; foliage light, wrinkled; very vigorous (6 ft.), bushy growth; [*R. acicularis* × 'Hollywood']; HAcicularis

'Pilar de Arburua'   HT, op, Camprubi, C.; flowers salmon, large, dbl., high-centered; foliage dark reddish green; free growth; ['Comtesse Vandal' × 'Fashion']

'Pilar Dot'   Min, op, 1964, Dot, Pedro; flowers coral, well-formed, small; vigorous, well-branched growth; ['Orient' × 'Perla de Alcañada']

'Pilar Landecho' ('Marquesa de Urquijo') HT, ob, 1940, Camprubi, C.; bud long, pointed; flowers yellow, reverse dark coral-orange, large, dbl., high-centered; foliage dark, leathery; vigorous growth; [('Sensation' × 'Julien Potin') × 'Feu Joseph Looymans']

'Pilar Landecho, Climbing' ('Marquesa de Urquijo, Climbing') Cl HT, ob, 1954, Folgado, Comes; bud marked with red; [sport of 'Pilar Landecho']

'Pilarín Vilella'   HT, or, 1936, Dot, Pedro; flowers lacquer-red, large, dbl., cupped; foliage dark; vigorous growth; ['Mrs Pierre S. duPont' × 'Lucia Zuloaga']

'Pilgrim'   HT, dr, Armstrong, D.L.; bud ovoid; flowers large, dbl., cupped, moderate fragrance; foliage dark, leathery; vigorous, upright, bushy growth; PP3132; [seedling × 'Chrysler Imperial']; intr. 1970

'Pilgrim'   HT, pb, 1920, Montgomery Co.; bud long, pointed; flowers silvery pink reverse clear rose-pink, large, dbl., high-centered, moderate fragrance; foliage leathery, rich green; vigorous, bushy growth

'Pilina Mata'   HT, ob, 1934, Munné, B.; flowers orange-yellow; ['Souv. de Claudius Pernet' × 'Los Angeles']

'Pillar Box' -- See 'Chewaze'

'Pillar of Fire'   Cl F, or, 1963, Shamburger, P.; bud short, ovoid; flowers coral-red, 2-2½ in., 33 petals, cupped, borne in clusters; foliage leathery, matte; vigorous growth; PP2329; [sport of 'Floradora, Climbing']; originally registered as LCl; intr. 1963

'Pillar of Gold' -- See 'E. Veyrat Hermanos'

'Pillar Stratford'   Cl HT, lp, 1946, Watkins, A.F.; flowers silvery pink, base deeper, large, very dbl., intense fragrance; vigorous, upright (8 ft.) growth; PP784; [sport of 'Stratford']

'Pillnitzer Marcellina'   Pol, dr, Institut für Obstbau Dresden Pillnitz; flowers semi-dbl.

Pillow Fight™ -- See 'Wekpipogop'

'Pillow Talk'   F, m, 1980, Weeks, O.L.; bud short, ovoid; flowers reddish-lavender, 28 petals, high-centered, borne singly or several together, moderate tea fragrance; foliage medium size, thin, leathery, dark; prickles long, hooked downward; low to medium, rounded growth; PP4714; ['Plain Talk' × 'Angel Face']

'Pilona'   pb, 1965, Hendrickx; bud ovoid; flowers pink with white, medium, very dbl., borne in clusters; foliage dark green

'Pilurett'   F, or, Schmadlak, Dr.; flowers medium, semi-dbl.; intr. 1966

'Pimbonson'   LCl, mp, 1953, Muraour; flowers cerise pink, semi-dbl.

'Pimlico' -- See 'Meidujaran'

'Pimlico '81' -- See 'Meidujaran'

'Pimpant'   F, or, 1963, Laperrière; flowers bright orange-red, 25-30 petals, borne in clusters of 7-8; moderate, bushy growth; [seedling × 'Soleil']

'Pimpernel'   F, or, 1954, LeGrice; flowers turkey-red, open, semi-dbl., borne in clusters; foliage dark; [seedling × ('Poulsen's Pink' × 'Golden Dawn')]

'Pimprenelle' ('Berendina') S, dy, Delbard; flowers sunny yellow, fading lighter, single to semi-dbl., cupped to flat, borne in clusters; free-flowering; vigorous (2-3 ft.) growth; intr. 1997

'Pin-up'   F, dp, 1959, Fletcher; flowers deep China-rose, medium, 16-18 wavy petals, borne in clusters; foliage light green; low, bushy growth; ['Else Poulsen' × unknown]

'Piña Colada' -- See 'Alopiña'

'Pinafore'   Pol, ly, 1960, Swim, H.C.; flowers pale yellow to white, tinged pink, 1½-2 in., single, flat, borne in large, rounded clsuters; foliage glossy; low, bushy, compact growth; PP1810; ['China Doll' × 'Mrs Dudley Fulton']; intr. 1959

'Pinal'   Pol, mr, Institut für Obstbau Dresden Pillnitz; flowers medium, single

'Piñata'   F, yb, Bailey, Dorothy; bud Chinese yellow, very pointed, small; flowers Chinese yellow with orange, 3½-4 in., 22-24 petals, high-centered, becoming flat, borne singly and in small clusters, slight fragrance; foliage medium-size, ovoid, leathery; few prickles; hips globular, medium; PP4854; intr. about 1980

'Piñata' -- See 'Fure-Daiko'

'Pinault' ('Revue de Dauville') F, dy, Pineau; intr. 1982

'Pinchu Quiye'   HT, w; flowers pure white; free-flowering; almost thornless; vigorous growth

'Pincushion'   S, mp, Kordes; flowers strong pink, fading lighter, small, full, rosette, borne in large clusters, slight fragrance; free-flowering; low (12 in.), spreading growth; intr. 1992

'Pineapple Poll'   F, ob, 1970, Cocker; flowers orange-yellow, flushed red, 2½ in., 30 petals; foliage glossy; [Orange Sensation® × 'Circus']

'Pinehurst'   Min, pb, 1988, Bridges, Dennis A.; flowers light pink, fading lighter at base, reverse light pink to cream, 60 petals, moderate fruity fragrance; foliage medium size, dark green, semi-glossy; prickles straight, medium, pink; bushy, medium, vigorous, neat growth; ['Rise 'n' Shine' × seedling]

'Pingan'   F, w, 1980, Fong, William P.; bud ovoid, pointed; flowers white with pink petal edges, 13 petals, borne 4-6 per cluster; foliage large, leathery; prickles long; upright growth; [seedling × ('Ivory Fashion' × 'Little Darling')]

'Pink-A-Boo'   F, mp, 1961, Boerner; bud ovoid; flowers 3-3½ in., 33 petals, borne in large clusters, moderate fragrance; foliage leathery; vigorous, upright growth; PP2149; ['Spartan' × 'Pink Garnette']; intr. 1961

'Pink-a-ling' -- See 'Zippink'

Pink Above All™ -- See 'Chewpearl'

'Pink Abundance'   F, op; flowers deep coral-salmon pink. long lasting, 4 in., 60 petals, slight sweet pear and mint fragrance; foliage glossy, dense; bushy, compact (3½ ft.) growth; PPAF; intr. 1999

'Pink Agatha' -- See 'Agathe Incarnata'

'Pink Alain'   F, mp; intr. 2001

'Pink Alicia'   HT, mp, 1968, Dale, F.; flowers pink, pointed; spreading growth; ['Duftwolke' × 'Gavotte']

'Pink American Beauty' -- See 'Queen of Edgely'

'Pink American Beauty' -- See 'Mrs Charles E. Russell'

Pink 'n' White®   Min, pb

'Pink & White Multirosa' -- See 'Jacmound'

'Pink Angel'   HT, mp, Parkes, Mrs M.H.; intr. 1977

'Pink Angel'   Min, mp, 1982, Hunton, Claude B.; [sport of Starina®]

'Pink Angel' -- See 'Morgel'

'Pink Anne'   F, mp, 1951, Cant, B. R.; flowers borne in trusses; [sport of 'Anne Poulsen']

'Pink Arctic' -- See 'Show Garden'

'Pink Avalanche' -- See 'Wilpavl'

'Pink Babyflor' -- See 'Tanybab'

'Pink Banksia Rose' -- See 'Tausendschön'

Pink Bassino® -- See 'Korbasren'

'Pink Beauty'   HT, mp, 1919, Cook, J.W.; flowers clear pink, large, semi-dbl., cupped; ['Ophelia' × 'My Maryland']

'Pink Bedder'   HT, mp, 1920, Paul, W.; flowers rose-pink, center yellow, borne in clusters

'Pink Belle'   HT, dp, 1975, Harkness; flowers deep rose pink, large, 28 petals, moderate fragrance; foliage dark; RULED EXTINCT 11/83; ['Fragrant Cloud' × Elizabeth of Glamis®]; intr. 1973

Pink Bells™ -- See 'Poulbells'

'Pink Bianca'   S, pb; intr. 2006

'Pink Blush'   HT, lp, 1975, Warriner, William A.; bud long, pointed; flowers 4-5 in., 30 petals, cupped; foliage large, leathery; very free growth; PP3729; [Bridal Pink™ × seedling]; intr. 1974

'Pink Bountiful'   F, mp, 1945, Joseph H. Hill, Co.; bud short, pointed; flowers 3 in., 55 petals, borne in clusters, moderate fragrance; foliage dark, leathery; vigorous, upright, much-branched growth; PP601; ['Juanita' × 'Mrs R.M. Finch']

Pink Bounty™ -- See 'Minsco'
'Pink Bouquet' F, mp, 1954, Brownell; flowers China-rose pink, slightly tinted yellow, to ovoid, 3-4 in., 60-75 petals, high-centered, moderate fragrance; foliage leathery; upright, open, compact growth; PP1371; RULED EXTINCT 11/90; ['Curly Pink' × 'Free Gold']
'Pink Bouquet' HWich, pb, Treasure
'Pink Bouquet' -- See 'Lavquest'
'Pink Bourbon' -- See 'Mme Ernest Calvat'
'Pink Bowie' ('Windstar') S, pb, Williams, J.B.; flowers pink and ivory, single, borne in clusters, slight fragrance; free-flowering; upright (4 ft.) growth; intr. 2003
'Pink Brocade' F, lp, 1977, Bees; flowers very full, 3 in., 70 petals; foliage glossy; small, compact growth; ['Spartan' × 'Lilli Marlene']
'Pink Bunting' -- See 'Talpin'
'Pink Butterfly' S, pb, Williams, J.B.; flowers pink and ivory, single, borne in large clusters; free-flowering; foliage dark green; intr. 2003
'Pink Butterfly' HT, dp, 1926, Brown, A.C.; flowers bright cerise, base light buff; [sport of 'Mme Butterfly']
'Pink Button' -- See 'Kordemas'
Pink Calypso® HT, lp; florist rose
'Pink Cameo' ('Cameo, Climbing') Cl Min, mp, 1954, Moore, Ralph S.; flowers rose-pink, center darker, 1¼ in., 23 petals, borne in clusters of up to 20; foliage small, glossy, rich green; growth to 3-5 ft.; PP1451; [('Soeur Thérèse' × 'Skyrocket') × 'Zee']
'Pink Candy' HT, pb, Thomas; [sport of 'Candy Stripe']; intr. 1992
'Pink Cardinal Hume' S, mp, Rupert, Kim L.; flowers small, dbl., loose, borne in clusters, slight fragrance; recurrent; small (under 3 ft.), tidy growth; intr. 1998
Pink Carpet™ -- See 'Minnco'
'Pink Carrousel' Min, mp; flowers clear, strong pink; [sport of Magic Carrousel®]; grows like its parent, Magic Carrousel®; intr. 2000
'Pink Cascade' Pol, lp, 1945, Lammerts, Dr. Walter; flowers la france pink, small, very dbl., borne in clusters; foliage glossy; vigorous, bushy growth; RULED EXTINCT 12/81; ['Mrs Dudley Fulton' × 'Tom Thumb']
'Pink Cascade' -- See 'Morcade'
'Pink Cavalcade' F, pb, 1959, Shamburger, C.S.; flowers deep pink, reverse light yellow to white, 2½-3 in., 28-32 petals, cupped, borne in pyramidal clusters, moderate fragrance; foliage leathery, glossy, bronze; vigorous, bushy growth; PP1456; [sport of 'Cavalcade']; intr. 1955
'Pink Cavalier' S, mp, Courage, R.; flowers full, pompon, moderate fragrance; long flowering season; Australian patent 54257/01; intr. 2001
'Pink Cécile Brunner' Pol, dp, 1918, Western Rose Co.; flowers rose-pink; [sport of 'Mlle Cécile Brunner']
'Pink Chalice' S, pb, Williams, J.B.; flowers light pink blend, single to semi-dbl., borne in clusters on upright canes, slight fragrance; vigorous, spreading growth, can be trained as a climber.; intr. 2000
'Pink Chameleon' Pol, pb, 1945, Lammerts, Dr. Walter; bud rose-red; flowers venetian pink, darkening to purple, open, small, single, borne in clusters; abundant, recurrent bloom; foliage dark, glossy; very vigorous, bushy growth; ['Mrs Dudley Fulton' × 'Mutabilis']
'Pink Champagne' HT, mp, 1956, Jelly; bud long, pointed; flowers 5-6 in., 32-48 petals, high-centered, moderate fragrance; foliage leathery; vigorous, bushy growth; PP1375; [seedling × 'Pink Bountiful']
'Pink Champagne' Min, pb; flowers shades of pink, slight fragrance; growth to 50 cm.; hanging basket; intr. 2003
'Pink Champagne' -- See 'Clecham'
'Pink Charles Austin' S, pb, Austin, David; intr. 1992
'Pink Charm' F, dp, 1938, Kordes; flowers deep clear pink, very dbl.; foliage leathery; short stems; bushy growth
'Pink Charm' -- See 'Macsatur'
'Pink Charmer' -- See 'Lyopin'
'Pink Charming' HT, lp, 1953, Leenders, M.; flowers pale pink, loosely formed, 5½ in., 36 petals; vigorous growth
'Pink Chateau' HT, w, 1999, Teranishi, K.; flowers white, center soft pink, 5 in., 35 petals, high-centered; growth to 4½ ft.; [('Sheer Bliss' × seedling) × seedling]; intr. 1997
'Pink Cherokee' -- See 'Anemone'
'Pink Cherub' -- See 'Morfair'
'Pink Chiffon' F, lp, 1958, Boerner; bud ovoid; flowers 3½-4 in., 53 petals, cupped to flat, intense fragrance; foliage glossy; vigorous, bushy growth; PP1564; ['Fashion' × 'Fantasia']; intr. 1956
'Pink Chiffon, Climbing' Cl F, lp; intr. after 1956
Pink Chimo® -- See 'Interchimp'
'Pink Christian Dior' HT, dp, 1966, Chang, Chi-Shiang; bud ovoid; flowers light red and deep pink, large, dbl., high-centered; foliage glossy; very vigorous, upright growth; [sport of 'Christian Dior']
'Pink Cloud' LCl, mp, 1952, Boerner; bud ovoid; flowers rich pink, large, 28 petals, cupped, borne in clusters of 5-20, moderate fragrance; recurrent bloom; foliage glossy; vigorous, climbing (6-8 ft.) growth; PP1140; ['New Dawn' × ('New Dawn' × unknown)]
'Pink Clouds' Cl Min, dp, 1956, Moore, Ralph S.; flowers deep rose pink, small to medium, single, borne in clusters; foliage dark, glossy; vigorous (5-8 ft.) growth; ['Oakington Ruby' × R. multiflora]
'Pink Cluster' F, op, 1938, Morse; flowers salmon-pink, shaded gold, borne in clusters
'Pink Coctail' HT, pb, 1965, Barter; flowers light pink, reverse darker, 5 in., 38 petals; foliage dark, glossy; very free growth; [Queen Elizabeth® × 'Claude']
'Pink Confection' -- See 'Ripcon'
'Pink Cottage' -- See 'Chewily'
Pink Cover™ -- See 'Poulnoz'
'Pink Crinoline' HT, pb, Kordes; flowers deep pink on inside, silvery pink on reverse, large, full, globular, borne singly and in candelabras, slight fragrance; recurrent; foliage deep green; stems firm, wiry; vigorous, medium high growth; intr. 1999
'Pink Crumble Bar' HT, mp, Thomson, G.A.; [sport of 'Crumble Bar']
'Pink Crystal' -- See 'Wekslats'
'Pink Curtain' LCl, dp, Kordes; flowers deep, clear pink, borne on cane tips and side stems, intense sweet fragrance; recurrent; vigorous, arching growth; intr. 1994
'Pink Cushion' Pol, mp
Pink Danyland® S, dp
'Pink Dawn' HT, mp, 1935, H&S; bud long, pointed; flowers large, 60 petals, high-centered, intense fragrance; foliage soft; vigorous growth; ['Joanna Hill' × seedling]
'Pink Dawn, Climbing' Cl HT, mp, 1941, H&S
'Pink Delight' ('Laxton's Pink Delight') Pol, dp, 1922, Laxton Bros.; flowers rose-pink, single, moderate fragrance
'Pink Delight' ('Vierlanden') HT, op, Kordes; bud long, pointed; flowers deep salmon-pink, large, dbl., high-centered, intense fragrance; foliage leathery, light green; vigorous growth; ['Senator' × 'Florex']; intr. 1936
Pink Delight® -- See 'Lenpi'
'Pink Devil' HT, mp
Pink Diadem® -- See 'Tanspolett'
'Pink Diamond' HT, lp, 1942, Howard, F.H.; bud long pointed; flowers shell-pink, base yellow, 3½-4 in., 38 petals, cupped; foliage leathery; vigorous, upright growth; PP516
'Pink Diane' F, dp, 1959, Sodano, A.; bud ovoid; flowers deep rose-pink, 3½-4 in., 50-55 petals, cupped, intense fruity fragrance; foliage leathery, glossy, dark; vigorous, upright growth; PP2022; [sport of 'Rosenelfe']
Pink Diddy™ -- See 'Kindiddy'
'Pink Diëlma' HT, mp, 1969, Tas; bud ovoid; flowers pink, medium, very dbl.; foliage dark; [sport of 'Furore']
'Pink Don Juan' LCl, mp, 1996, Nelson, Brian; flowers medium, semi-dbl., borne in small clusters, slight fragrance; foliage medium size, medium green, semi-glossy; some prickles; tall, upright, spreading, climbing growth; [sport of 'Don Juan']; intr. 1997
Pink Double Knock Out™ -- See 'Radtkopink'
'Pink Dream' Min, mp, Moore, Ralph; flowers cherry pink., 1-1½ in., dbl., borne

in small clusters; free-flowering; foliage healthy and attractive; short (12 in.), compact and neat growth; intr. 2001

'Pink Dream' HT, pb, 1951, McGredy, Sam IV; flowers pink, inside rosy white, 6-7 in., 45 petals, high-centered; foliage dark; vigorous growth; ['Mrs Sam McGredy' × R.M.S. Queen Mary]

Pink Drift® S, dp, Meilland; flowers 1.5 inches, 7-8 petals, borne in large clusters; recurrent; foliage small, dark green, semi-glussy; low, spreading growth; intr. 2006

Pink Drift™ -- See 'Poulcat'

'Pink Druschki' HT, mp, 1949, Longley; flowers bright pink, well-formed, 5 in., 27 petals; very vigorous growth

'Pink Duchess' HT, dp, 1960, Boerner; bud ovoid; flowers rose-red, 5-6 in., 38 petals, cupped, moderate fragrance; foliage glossy; vigorous, upright, bushy growth; PP1834; [('Peace' × unknown) × seedling]; intr. 1959

'Pink Elegance' HT, lp, 1960, Hoefer, P.; bud long, pointed; flowers bright pink, medium, dbl., high-centered; foliage glossy; very vigorous growth; ['White Butterfly' × Baccará®]; intr. 1960

'Pink Elf' -- See 'Morelfire'

'Pink Elizabeth Arden' (Geisha®) F, mp, 1965, Tantau, Math.; bud long; flowers 2½-3 in., semi-dbl., borne in clusters of 1-3; foliage dark; growth bushy, medium; intr. 1964

'Pink Emely' -- See 'Emely Vigorosa'

'Pink Emperor' HT, mp, 1965, Jones; flowers clear pink, 4-5 in., 50-60 petals; foliage glossy; vigorous, bushy growth; ['Peace' × 'Crimson Glory']; intr. 1958

'Pink Empress' -- See 'Hadempress'

'Pink Euphoria' S, mp; flowers single, borne in sprays; recurrent; intr. 1999

'Pink Eutin' F, mp, 1962, Lindquist; bud pointed, globular; flowers fuchsine pink, 1½-2 in., 25-35 petals, cupped, borne in clusters; recurrent; foliage large, semi-glossy; prickles few, medium, sepia brown; growth vigorous, bushy, somewhat spreading; PP2269; [sport of 'Eutin']; intr. 1962

'Pink Fairy' Pol, mp; flowers , 10-20 petals; bushy (2-3 ft.) growth; [sport of 'The Fairy']; grows much like The Fairy

'Pink Fantasy' HT, mp, K&S; flowers glowing pink, non-fading; free-flowering; [sport of 'Mme Denise Gallois']; intr. 1995

'Pink Fantasy' S, dp; flowers open deep pink, fade to medium pink, 3 in., full, pompon, borne in clusters; free-flowering; foliage disease-resistant; low (2-3 ft.), spreading (5 ft.) groundcover growth

'Pink Favorite' ('Pink Favourite') HT, mp, 1956, Von Abrams; bud pointed; flowers Neyron rose, 3-4 in., 25 petals, loosely cupped, slight fragrance; foliage very glossy, bright green; vigorous, upright, bushy growth; PP1523; ['Juno' × ('Georg Arends' × 'New Dawn')]

'Pink Favourite' -- See 'Pink Favorite'

'Pink Festival' -- See 'Lavquest'

Pink Fire® ('Cottage Dream', 'Pink Fringe') F, mp, Ilsink; intr. 1995

Pink Fizz™ (Bournonville™) LCl, lp, Poulsen; bud medium pink; flowers light pink with yellow stamens, 8-10 cm., dbl., cupped, borne in clusters, no fragrance; recurrent; foliage reddish green; bushy, tall (150-200 cm.) growth; hips none; intr. 2000

'Pink Flair' F, mp, 1966, Swim & Weeks; bud urn shaped; flowers small, dbl.; foliage leathery; vigorous, bushy growth; PP2724; ['Verona' x 'Escort']

'Pink Flamingo' HT, pb, 1958, Kern, J. J.; flowers rose-pink tinted lighter, 2½-3½ in., 50 petals, intense fragrance; foliage dark, leathery; dwarf, bushy growth; [sport of 'Golden Dawn']; intr. 1957

'Pink Floradora' F, op, 1951, Shamburger, P.; bud ovoid; flowers shrimp-pink, 3 in., 35-40 petals, cupped; foliage glossy, light green; bushy growth; PP1121; [sport of 'Floradora']

'Pink Flower Carpet' -- See 'Noatraum'

'Pink Flower Circus' F, lp, Kordes; flowers light to medium pink , double, cupped, borne in clusters; recurrent; short growth; intr. 2008

'Pink Flurries' F, lp; intr. 1999

'Pink Formal' S, pb, 1978, Williams, J. Benjamin; bud pointed; flowers bright coral-pink, loosely-ruffled, 3½-4 in., 23 petals; foliage leathery; vigorous, upright growth; [(Queen Elizabeth® × 'Gladiator') × ('Aztec' × 'Little Darling')]

'Pink Fountain' -- See 'Legram'

'Pink Fragrance' HT, mp, 1957, deRuiter; bud long, pointed; flowers rose-pink, open, 4½-5 in., 78-85 petals, borne in pyramidal clusters, moderate spicy fragrance; foliage glossy, leathery; very vigorous, bushy, upright growth; PP1493; [(Orange Triumph® × 'Golden Rapture') × 'Peace']; intr. 1956

'Pink Frau Karl Druschki' HP, mp, 1910, California Rose Co.; [sport of 'Frau Karl Druschki']

'Pink French Lace' F, lp, 2000, Roses Unlimited (also Takefuji, 2005); flowers 4½ in., full, high-centered, borne in small clusters, slight fragrance; foliage medium size, dark green, semi-glossy; few prickles; growth bushy, medium; [sport of 'French Lace']; intr. 2001

'Pink Friendship' S, mp, Verschuren; intr. 1986

'Pink Frills' F, lp, 1954, Carlton Rose Nursery; [sport of 'Garnette']

'Pink Fringe' -- See 'Pink Fire'

'Pink Frost' HT, mp, 1954, Swim, H.C.; bud ovoid; flowers rose, 4-5 in., 38-45 petals, high-centered, intense fragrance; foliage glossy, leathery; vigorous, bushy growth; PP1269; ['Charlotte Armstrong' × 'Texas Centennial']; intr. 1954

'Pink Frostfire' Min, lp, 1968, Moore, Ralph S.; [sport of 'Frostfire']

'Pink Frosting' -- See 'Renfrost'

'Pink Garland' S, mp, 1935, Skinner; flowers clear pink, open,, 3-3½ in., semi-dbl.; non-recurrent; upright (3 ft.) growth; [R. blanda × R. spinosissima cultivar]

'Pink Garnette' F, dp, 1950, Schneeberg (also Boerner, 1951); flowers Tyrian rose; PP913; [sport of 'Garnette']

'Pink Garnette Supreme' F, mp, 1959, Perkins, C.H.; flowers rose-pink, 2½ in., 35-40 petals, cupped, borne in clusters, moderate fragrance; foliage glossy, leathery; vigorous, upright growth; PP1642; [sport of 'Garnette Supreme']; intr. 1957

'Pink Gem' HT, lp, 1949, Fletcher; bud long, pointed; flowers pearl-pink, 4-5 in., 30 petals, flat, intense fragrance; foliage bluish green; vigorous, tall growth

'Pink Gem' Min, lp, Meilland; bud ovoid; flowers rose-pink, medium, dbl.; foliage soft; moderate, upright, bushy growth; [sport of Scarlet Gem®]; intr. 1974

'Pink Gemini' F, pb, Zary, Keith; bud long, pointed ovoid; flowers 35 petals, high-centered, borne in clusters of 5-7; good repeat; foliage medium size, leathery, glossy; prickles medium, hooked downward; stems medium, strong; vigorous, upright (4½ ft.), branching growth; PP11140; [('Jacpray' × Party Girl™) × 'Jacanne']; greenhouse rose; intr. 1998

'Pink Ghislaine de Féligonde' HMult, mp, Ducher and David; flowers medium pink, fading quickly through light pink to white, double, cupped to rosette, borne in clusters, slight musk fragrance; recurrent; growth 2 - 2.5 m. height; ['Ghislaine de Feligonde' × Unknown]; intr. 2007

'Pink Gift' Pol, lp; recurrent; growth to 3-4 ft.; intr. 1999

'Pink Gin' HT, mp; flowers medium, dbl.

'Pink Glory' HT, mp, 1960, Boerner; bud long, pointed; flowers clear pink, 5 in., 25 petals, high-centered, intense fragrance; foliage leathery; vigorous, upright growth; PP1998; [('Ernie Pyle' × unknown) × 'Peace']; intr. 1960

'Pink Glow' HT, lp, 1951, Boerner; bud globular; flowers rose-pink, 5-5½ in., 40 petals, cupped, moderate fragrance; foliage leathery, glossy; vigorous, upright growth; PP1018; [(('Schoener's Nutkana' × seedling) × 'Mrs Pierre S. duPont') × 'Home Sweet Home']

'Pink Gnome' ('Garden Path Pink Gnome') S, pb; bud pink; flowers light pink with white centers, ¾ in., 5 petals, cupped; free-flowering; foliage medium green, disease-resistant; growth compact (12 in.), with tight, round habit; PP16602; intr. 2004

'Pink Golden Dawn' HT, mp, 1938, Bostick; flowers large, dbl.; [sport of 'Golden Dawn']

'Pink Gown' HT, lp, 1971, Sanday, John; flowers light clear pink, 4 in., 20 petals; foliage matte green; tall, very free growth; ['Vera Dalton' × 'Tropicana']

'Pink Grootendorst' ('Grootendorst Pink') HRg, mp, 1923, Grootendorst, F.J.;

flowers clear pink, carnation style petal edges, very dbl., borne in small clusters, slight fragrance; free-flowering; foliage medium size, dark green, rugose; tall growth; [sport of 'F.J. Grootendorst']

'Pink Gruss an Aachen' F, op, 1929, Kluis & Koning; flowers light salmon pink, very full; [sport of 'Gruss an Aachen']

'Pink Hadley' HT, mp, 1928, Knight, G.; flowers clear rose pink; [sport of 'Hadley']

'Pink Hat' F, pb, 1980, James, John; bud pointed; flowers light pink, center deep pink, 24 petals, high-centered, borne singly of 3-7 per cluster; foliage red turning dark green, glossy; prickles red; vigorous, upright, bushy growth

'Pink Haze' F, pb, 1973, Khanna, K. R., & Lata, P.; buds medium, long pointed; flowers pink with yellow centers, large, semi-dbl., open, borne several together and in clusters; foliage medium size, green, soft; few prickles; growth very vigorous, bushy; ['Pink Parfait' × 'Edward Mawley']

'Pink Haze' S, mp, Tantau; groundcover; spreading growth; intr. 1999

'Pink Heather' Min, lp, 1960, Moore, Ralph S.; flowers lavender-pink to white, very small, 45 petals, borne in clusters; foliage very small, glossy; vigorous (10-12 in.), bushy growth; PP2082; [(*R. wichurana* × 'Floradora') × ('Violette' × 'Zee')]; intr. 1959

'Pink Hedge' HRg, mp, Nyveldt; flowers bright pink, medium, single to semi-dbl., flat, borne in clusters; good repeat; foliage small, bronze; low, spreading growth; hips red; [(*R. rugosa rubra* × *R. cinnamomea*) × *R. nitida*]; intr. 1956

'Pink Hedge' F, dp, Interplant; intr. 1996

'Pink Heidelberg' HKor, mp

'Pink Hit' ('Silver Wishes') Min, mp, Poulsen; flowers medium pink, 2 in., dbl., cupped, borne in clusters, no fragrance; recurrent; foliage dark green, glossy; bushy (40-60 cm.) growth; intr. 1996

'Pink Hit' -- See 'Poulink'

'Pink Honey' Min, mp, 1988, Bridges, Dennis A.; flowers medium honey-pink, yellow at base, reverse light yellow at base, 20 petals, high-centered, slight fruity fragrance; foliage large, medium green, semi-glossy; prickles long, pointed, medium, pink; bushy, tall growth; ['Summer Spice' × seedling]

'Pink Ice' F, pb; flowers striped; intr. 2006

'Pink Ice' -- See 'Andpin'

Pink Iceberg™ ('Blushing Pink Iceberg') F, pb, Weatherly, Lilia; flowers light to medium pink blend, darkens in cool weather, 3 in., 35 petals, borne singly and in sprays of 3-4, slight fragrance; recurrent; foliage large, light green, glossy; prickles few, thin, curved downward, tan; growth upright, rounded, medium; PP9600; [sport of 'Iceberg']; intr. 1995

'Pink Ilseta' Gr, Tantau; intr. 1986

'Pink Intuition' HT, pb, Delbard; flowers medium pink with deep pink to red stripes, double, high-centered; intr. 2006

'Pink Jacqueline' HT

'Pink Jenny' HT, mp, 1961, Ruston, D.; flowers rose-pink; [sport of 'Grand'mere Jenny']

'Pink Jewel' F, mp, 1940, Kordes; flowers arbutus-pink, center camellia-pink, semi-dbl., cupped; foliage leathery; vigorous growth; ['Crimson Glory' × 'Holstein']

'Pink Jewel' HT, mp, de Ruiter

'Pink Jonathan' F, mp, Asami; intr. 1997

'Pink Joy' Min, dp, 1958, Moore, Ralph S.; flowers deep pink, well-shaped, 1 in., 30 petals, moderate sweet violet fragrance; dwarf (12in.), bushy growth; PP1378; ['Oakington Ruby' × 'Oakington Ruby']; intr. 1953

'Pink Kardinal' HT, dp, Stratford; [sport of 'Kardinal']

'Pink Karen Poulsen' F, mp, 1936, Poulsen, S.; [sport of 'Karen Poulsen']

'Pink Keops' Cl Min, mp; flowers silvery pink , double, borne in clusters; recurrent; flexible canes; growth 2.5 meters height; intr. 2008

'Pink Key' HT, mp, 1920, Pierson, F.R.; [sport of 'Francis Scott Key']

Pink Kiss™ -- See 'Minakco'

'Pink Knock Out' S, mp, Radler, W. ; bud cherry red.; flowers medium pink., single; foliage blackspot resistant; growth to 3 × 3 ft.; PP15070; [sport of Knock Out™]; intr. 2004

'Pink Koster' Pol, mp, Koster, D.A.; flowers dbl., cupped, slight fragrance; growth under 3 ft.; [sport of 'Margo Koster']; intr. after 1931

Pink La Sevillana® -- See 'Meigeroka'

'Pink Lace' F, pb, 1961, Watkins Roses; flowers light pink, becoming darker and then red, medium (2-2 1/2"), 20 petals, flat; foliage dark; vigorous growth; ['The Optimist' × 'Korona']

'Pink Lady' HT, mp, 1947, Wiltgen; bud urn-shaped; flowers soft pink, reverse darker, large, semi-dbl.; medium, vigorous growth; PP740; [sport of 'Pink Delight']

'Pink Lafayette' F, mp, 1925, Griffin; flowers clear rose-pink; [sport of 'Lafayette']

'Pink Lamesch' Pol, lp, Hiroshima; [sport of 'Léonie Lamesch']; intr. 2001

'Pink LD' S, dp, 2003, Jennings, George; flowers very full, borne mostly solitary; foliage medium size, medium green, matte; prickles small, straight, reddish-brown, moderate; growth upright, medium (4½ - 5½ ft.); garden, decorative; [sport of 'Leonard Dudley Braithwaite']; intr. 2002

'Pink Léda' D, mp, before 1827; flowers flesh pink to carmine lilac, fading to pale pink; [sport of 'Leda', or vice-versa]

'Pink Lemonade' -- See 'Arofrichee'

'Pink Licorice' -- See 'Resink'

'Pink Lorraine' HT, w, 1973, Williams, J. Benjamin; flowers pink, paling to white, base cream, 4½ in., 40 petals; foliage matte green; vigorous, upright growth; ['Milord' × 'Farah']

'Pink Love' HT, mp; flowers double , high-centered, borne mostly singly; recurrent; stems long; growth medium height; intr. 1998

'Pink Lovejoy' HT, lp, 2007, Heath, William L.; flowers silvery pink, reverse lighter, 3½ in., full, borne mostly solitary; foliage medium, medium green, semi-glossy; prickles medium, hooked down, brown, few; growth upright, tall (5 ft.); exhibition, garden decoration; [sport of 'Lovejoy']; intr. 2008

'Pink Lustre' HT, lp, 1958, Verschuren; bud ovoid; flowers 5 in., 48 petals, high-centered, intense fragrance; foliage dark, glossy, leathery; vigorous, upright growth; PP1641; ['Peace' × 'Dame Edith Helen']; intr. 1957

'Pink Macartney Rose' HBc, lp

'Pink Mme Plantier' -- See 'Garden's Glory'

'Pink Magic' HT, dp, 1952, Joseph H. Hill, Co.; bud long, pointed, spinel-red; flowers phlox-pink, 4-6 in., 40-45 petals, intense fragrance; foliage leathery; vigorous, upright growth; PP1118; ['Better Times (white)' × 'Snow White']

'Pink Magic' -- See 'Randilla Rose'

'Pink Magic' -- See 'Lenmagika'

Pink Magic Carpet™ S, pb, McGredy, Sam IV; flowers open pink, then fade to white, semi-dbl., borne in clusters at tips and on laterals; recurrent; spreading, arching growth; intr. 1994

'Pink Maiden' F, mp, 1965, Boerner; bud ovoid; flowers large, dbl., borne in clusters, slight fragrance; foliage dark; [('Spartan' × unknown) × Queen Elizabeth®]

'Pink Majesty' F, mp, 2003, McMillan, Thomas; flowers large, with scalloped petal edges, 4½ in., dbl., pointed center, borne in small clusters, no fragrance; foliage medium green, semi-glossy; prickles small, needle-shaped, moderate; growth compact, medium (2 ft.); garden decorative; [Lagerfeld™ × Love Potion™]; intr. 2004

'Pink Maman Cochet, Climbing' Cl T, mp, 1915, Conard & Jones

'Pink Mandy' Min, mp, 1975, Moore, Ralph S.; bud globular, small; flowers medium pink blending into white near base, 1 in., 40-50 petals, borne usually in clusters of 3-5; recurrent; foliage small, medium green, very glossy, leathery; prickles numerous, medium, curved downward, brown; growth low, bushy, spreading; PP3869; ['Ellen Poulsen' × 'Little Chief']; intr. 1974

'Pink Margaret Thatcher' F, pb, Takatori; flowers striped

Pink Marina® Min, dp, Kordes; flowers strong pink, dbl., high-centered; part of Kordana series

'Pink Marvel' F, dp, 1960, deRuiter;

The Official Registry and Checklist — Rosa 579

flowers spirea-red, 2½ in., 45-55 petals, flat, borne in clusters; foliage leathery; bushy, compact growth; PP1763; ['Rosemary Rose' × ('Cécile Brunner' × 'Floribunda seedling')]; intr. 1960

'Pink Masquerade' S, op, Simonet; flowers 5 petals; ['Suzanne' × 'Red Dawn']

'Pink Masterpiece' HT, pb, 1962, Boerner; bud ovoid, pointed; flowers La France pink, tinted shrimp-pink, 6 in., 38 petals, high-centered, borne mostly singly, moderate fragrance; foliage leathery; vigorous, upright growth; PP2294; [('Serenade' × unknown) × 'Kate Smith']; intr. 1962

Pink Meidiland® -- See 'Meipoque'

Pink Meillandina® -- See 'Meijidiro'

'Pink Meilove' F, mp, Richardier; intr. 2006

'Pink Melody' HT, op, K&S; flowers pale salmon-pink; good repeat; [sport of 'Pasadena']; intr. 1993

'Pink Meringue' S, lp, 1999, Bennett, Frank David; flowers large, 41 petals, borne in small clusters; foliage medium size, medium green, semi-glossy; numerous prickles; upright, tall (6 ft.) growth; [sport of Mary Rose®]

'Pink Mermaid' LCl, mp, 1940; flowers soft pink, large, single, very heavy first bloom flush, moderate fragrance; good repeat; growth tall (15-20 ft.), climbing; intr. about 1960

'Pink Meteor' F, mp, 1964, Timmerman's Roses; [sport of 'Meteor']

'Pink Midinette' -- See 'Peaxanadu'

'Pink Millie' -- See 'Watmill'

Pink Mini-Wonder™ -- See 'Meiselgra'

'Pink Minijet' Min, mp, Meilland

'Pink Minimo' Min, mp

'Pink Mist' HT, mp, 1959, Joseph H. Hill, Co.; bud pointed, ovoid; flowers phlox-pink, becoming darker, 4-5 in., 25-35 petals, high-centered, intense fragrance; foliage dark, leathery; vigorous, bushy growth; PP1774; [sport of 'Red Better Times']

'Pink Mist' S, op

'Pink Montezuma' Gr, lp, 1964, Williams, J. Benjamin; flowers light pink, reverse blush-pink, large, dbl., high-centered; foliage dark, leathery; vigorous, bushy growth; [sport of 'Montezuma']

'Pink Mothersday' Pol, mp

Pink Multirosa® S, mp, J&P; flowers borne in clusters; recurrent; foliage glossy, disease resistant; mounding growth; intr. 2007

'Pink Mystery' -- See 'Lenstebrac'

'Pink-n-Pretty' -- See 'Welpretty'

'Pink Nature' S, mp; intr. 1999

'Pink Nevada' -- See 'Sancharm'

'Pink Nevada' -- See 'Marguerite Hilling'

'Pink Nymph' Ch, mp, before 1958; flowers dbl.; [sport of R. chinensis minima]

'Pink Nymph' F, mp, Koster, D.A.; flowers clear pink; [sport of 'Nymph']; intr. 1959

Pink Ocean® -- See 'Havink'

'Pink Oklahoma' HT, dp; intr. 1999

'Pink Olympiad' HT, mp, Humenick, Muriel F.; intr. 1995

'Pink Ophelia' ('Rose-Pink Ophelia') HT, mp, 1916, Breitmeyer; flowers rose-pink; [sport of 'Ophelia']

'Pink Ophelia' -- See 'John C. M. Mensing'

'Pink Osiana' -- See 'Tanpinaiso'

Pink Pagode™ Min, lp, Poulsen; flowers light pink, medium, dbl., no fragrance; foliage dark; cascading growth, hanging basket type; PP13452; intr. 2000

'Pink Paillette' Min, mp, Poulsen; flowers small, borne in sprays; intr. 1998

'Pink Panoramic' -- See 'Interchimp'

Pink Panther® -- See 'Meicapinal'

'Pink Parade' (Rosy Paillette™) Min, pb, Poulsen; flowers pink blend, medium, dbl., slight wild rose fragrance; foliage dark; growth narrow, bushy, 20-40 cm.; intr. 1996

'Pink Parasol' HT, mp, 1950, Fisher, G.; bud long, pointed; flowers clear pink, 6 in., 25-30 petals; foliage leathery, dark; very vigorous growth; PP998; ['Rapture' × 'Rome Glory']

'Pink Parfait' Gr, pb, 1960, Swim, H.C.; bud ovoid to urn-shaped; flowers outer petals medium pink, center blended pale orange, 3½-4 in., 23 petals, high-centered to cupped, slight fragrance; foliage leathery, semi-glossy; vigorous, upright, bushy growth; PP1904; ['First Love' × 'Pinocchio']; intr. 1960

'Pink Passion' S, mp; intr. 2004

'Pink Passion' Min, mp, 1979, Schwartz, Ernest W.; bud pointed; flowers shell-pink and ivory, 1½ in., 26 petals, high-centered, moderate fragrance; upright, bushy growth; ['Sweet and Low' × unknown]; intr. 1978

'Pink Patio' -- See 'Ribbon Rose'

'Pink Patio Wonder' -- See 'Jalpinkpat'

'Pink Pavement' HRg, op, Baum; flowers salmon pink, semi-dbl., moderate fragrance; recurrent; foliage dark green, disease-resistant; compact, spreading (2½ ft.) growth; intr. 1991

Pink Peace® HT, mp, 1959, Meilland, F.; bud medium, ovoid; flowers dusty pink, 4½-6 in., 58 petals, cupped, borne mostly singly, intense tea fragrance; free-flowering; foliage leathery; stems long, strong; vigorous, tall, bushy growth; PP1759; [('Peace' × 'Monique') × ('Peace' × 'Mrs John Laing')]

Pink Peace, Climbing® -- See 'Meibilsar'

'Pink Pearl' HWich, op, 1901, Manda; bud crimson; flowers salmony pink, often darker at center, 6-7 cm., dbl., borne in small clusters; [R. wichurana × 'Meteor']

'Pink Pearl' Cl HT, op, Hobbies; flowers pink shaded salmon, single; ['Irish Elegance' × 'Una']; intr. 1913

'Pink Pearl' HT, mp, Leenders, M.; flowers Neyron pink, base salmon, dbl., intense fragrance; long stems; vigorous growth; ['Ophelia' × ('Gen. MacArthur' × 'Marie van Houtte')]; intr. 1924

'Pink Pearl, Climbing' Cl HT, mp, 1933, Dixie Rose Nursery

'Pink Pearl' -- See 'Kormasyl'

'Pink Pearls' S, dp, Lim, Pink; flowers frilly, 1.5 in., 20 petals; recurrent; foliage medium green, disease resistant; sturdy, compact, low growth; intr. 2007

'Pink Perfection' HT, mp, 1927, Ward, F.B.; flowers clear rose-pink, 45 petals; ['Premier' × 'Baroness Rothschild']

'Pink Perfection' HT, mp; intr. 1998

'Pink Perfekta' HT, pb, 1962, Ross, A.; flowers deep pink, often edged red; [sport of 'Kordes' Perfecta']; intr. 1962

'Pink Perfume' HT, op, Robinson, H.; intr. 1955

'Pink Perpétué' LCl, mp, 1965, Gregory; flowers bright rose-pink, medium, 32 petals, globular, borne in clusters, moderate fragrance; recurrent bloom; foliage glossy, light green; vigorous growth; ['Spectacular' × 'New Dawn']

'Pink Pet, Climbing' ('Caldwell Pink Cl.') Cl Ch, mp; flowers bright pink, fading lighter, medium, dbl., pompon, borne in large clusters; recurrent; growth to 5-10 ft.; [sport of 'Pink Pet']

'Pink Pet' ('Caldwell Pink') Ch, mp, 1928, Lilley; flowers bright pink, fading lighter, dbl., pompon, borne in clusters, slight fragrance; recurrent; moderate (3 ft.) growth

'Pink Petticoat' Min, pb, 1979, Strawn; bud pointed; flowers creamy white, edged coral-pink, 1½-2 in., 33 petals, high-centered, rounded, borne singly, slight sweet fragrance; recurrent; foliage glossy, dark; prickles very few, needle shape, declining, light tan; stems upright, slender; tall, vigorous, upright growth; hips globular, form readily ; PP4636; [Neue Revue® × 'Sheri Anne']

Pink Picotee® -- See 'Kinpic'

'Pink Pillar' LCl, mp, 1940, Brownell; flowers clear medium pink, small, dbl., slight fragrance; good repeat; hardy

Pink Pin's® Min, mp, Interplant; intr. 2003

'Pink Pirouette' -- See 'Harboul'

'Pink Pixie' -- See 'Pixie Rose'

Pink Pollyanna™ -- See 'Jacship'

'Pink Poodle' -- See 'Morpoodle'

Pink Popcorn™ -- See 'Wilpop'

'Pink Porcelain' -- See 'Tinporce'

'Pink Posy' Ch, dp; flowers deep pink, fading to lighter lavender pink, single, flat, borne in clusters; good repeat; growth to 3-4 ft.; forms hip readily; [R. chinensis minima × unknown]; intr. 2003

'Pink Posy' -- See 'Cocanelia'

'Pink Powder Puff' F, mp, 1970, Pal, Dr. B.P.; bud ovoid; flowers soft pink, open, medium, dbl.; foliage leathery; vigorous, upright, compact growth; intr. 1965

'Pink Powderpuff' -- See 'Morpuff'

Pink Prelude™ -- See 'Vireterna'

'Pink Pride' HT, lp, 1959, Fletcher; flowers silvery pink, 5-6 in., 30-35 petals, high-centered; foliage light green; free growth; ['May Wettern' × 'Peace']

'Pink Princess' HT, pb, 1939, Brownell; flowers deep rose pink to yellowish, large, dbl., high-centered, intense fragrance; foliage dark, leathery, glossy; vigorous, bushy growth; PP459; [('Dr. W. Van Fleet' × 'Général Jacqueminot') × 'Break o' Day']

'Pink Princess' Min, mp

'Pink Profusion' HSet, pb, 1938, Horvath; flowers pale flesh-pink, reverse deep coral-rose, small, 80 petals, globular, borne in clusters; non-recurrent; foliage large, glossy; long, strong stems; very vigorous growth; PP298; ['Mrs F.F. Prentiss' × 'Lady Alice Stanley']

'Pink Profusion' F, op, Kordes; flowers clear, intense coral pink, medium, 20 petals, cupped, borne in clusters, slight sweet fragrance; free-flowering; foliage glossy; stems short; bushy (2-3 ft.), vigorous growth; intr. 2001

'Pink Promise' HT, pb, 2007, Coiner, Jim; flowers smooth, veined, reverse veined, medium, 4¼ in., 34 petals, borne mostly solitary; foliage large, dark green, semi-glossy; prickles ½ in. wide at base, moderate; growth to 42 in.; [seedling × seedling]; intr. 2008

'Pink Promises' -- See 'Silpinke'

Pink Prophyta™ HT, mp, de Ruiter; PP10532; florist rose

'Pink Prosperity' HMsk, lp, 1931, Bentall; flowers medium, dbl., borne in large trusses, moderate musk fragrance; very vigorous growth

'Pink Puff' F, lp, 1965, Boerner; bud medium, ovoid; flowers soft pink, 3½-4 in., 25-30 petals, cupped, borne singly and several together, moderate fruity (russet apple) fragrance; free-flowering; foliage medium size, dark green, leathery; prickles medium, short, hooked downward; stems long, strong; growth vigorous, upright; no hips; PP2634; [('Pinocchio' × unknown) × ('Red Pinocchio' × 'Garnette')]

'Pink Queen' F, dp

'Pink Quill' -- See 'Weequill'

'Pink Radiance, Climbing' -- See 'Radiance, Climbing'

'Pink Radiance' -- See 'Radiance'

'Pink Rambler' -- See 'Euphrosyne'

Pink Reflection® Min, pb

'Pink Revelation' F, lp, 1980, Schramm, D.; flowers small, cupped, borne in clusters of 3 - 12, slight fragrance; recurrent; foliage light green; prickles very few; growth bushy; [sport of 'Summer Snow']

'Pink Rhapsody' LCl, op, 1973, Ellick; flowers deep vermilion-pink, 4 in., 35-40 petals; very vigorous growth; [('Heidelberg' × 'Bonn') × 'Pink Parfait']

'Pink Rhythm' Min, op, 1991, Jolly, Marie; bud pointed; flowers coral pink, white center, medium pink reverse, aging light pink, 18 petals, high-centered, loose, borne usually singly, moderate fruity fragrance; foliage medium size, medium green, matte; upright, spreading, medium growth; [Party Girl™ × 'Fashion Flame']; intr. 1991

'Pink Ribbon' Min, lp, 1966, Moore, Ralph S.; flowers soft pink, small, dbl.; foliage glossy, light green; vigorous, bushy, dwarf growth; [(R. wichurana × 'Floradora') × 'Magic Wand']

'Pink Ribbon' -- See 'Clos Fleuri Rose No. 2'

'Pink Ribbon' -- See 'Delpomp'

'Pink Ripples' F, lp, 1956, Sanders, H.T.; flowers pink, open, 2½-3 in., 15-20 wavy petals, borne in clusters; very vigorous, upright, compact growth; PP1659; [sport of 'Red Ripples']

'Pink River' -- See 'Ausmary'

'Pink Roadrunner' HRg, mp, Uhl; flowers 2 in., semi-dbl. to dbl., cupped, intense rugosa fragrance; recurrent; foliage dark green, leathery, disease-resistant; vigorous, bushy (18-24 in.), spreading growth; intr. 2003

'Pink Roamer' ('Manda's Pink Roamer') HWich, pb, 1897, Horvath; flowers pink, center white, fading to pale mauve pink, 3 cm., single, borne in medium clusters, moderate fragrance; foliage small; vigorous growth; [R. wichurana × 'Cramoisi Supérieur']

'Pink Robin' -- See 'Resink'

'Pink Robin' -- See 'LLX8548'

Pink Robusta® -- See 'Korpinrob'

'Pink Rocket' S, pb, 1949, Longley, L.E.; bud ovoid; flowers deep pink suffused copper, open, large, single to semi-dbl.; profuse, non-recurrent bloom; foliage glossy, bronze, dark; very vigorous, upright growth; hardy; ['Skyrocket' × unknown]

'Pink Rosette' F, lp, 1948, Krebs; bud small, ovoid; flowers soft pink, 2 in., 50 petals, cupped, rosette, borne in clusters, slight fragrance; foliage leathery, dark; growth vigorous, dwarf, bushy; PP902

'Pink Roundelay' HT, mp, Taylor, L.R.; [sport of 'Roundelay']; intr. 1968

'Pink Rover' Cl HT, lp, 1891, Paul, W.; bud long; flowers pale pink, deeper in center, borne mostly solitary, moderate fragrance

'Pink Royal' HT, mp, 1928, Vestal; flowers glowing pink, dbl.; ['Columbia' × 'Mme Butterfly']

'Pink Ruby' HT, mp, 1966, Anstiss; flowers high pointed, 4-4½ in.; foliage light green; vigorous growth; [sport of 'Rubaiyat']

'Pink Ruffles' F, mp, 1976, Ellis; bud pointed; flowers rose-pink, ruffled, 3 in., 5-7 petals, slight tea fragrance; foliage very glossy, dark; very bushy growth; [('Frolic' × 'Frolic') × 'Pinafore']; intr. 1977

'Pink Ruffles' HT, dp, Williams, J. Benjamin; flowers strong pink, ruffled, 4 in., full, moderate fragrance; intr. 1996

'Pink Sachet' HT, dp, Shinoda, D. S. & Umeda, G. Y.; PP3959

Pink Sandy™ -- See 'Kinsandy'

'Pink Sarabande' F, mp, Keihan; intr. 1981

'Pink Satin' F, mp, 1945, Cross, Mrs. C.W.; bud large; flowers clean rose-pink, showy stamens, open, semi-dbl., cupped, moderate fragrance; foliage soft,light green; very vigorous, bushy, compact growth; ['Indiana' × 'William F. Dreer']

'Pink Satin' F, lp, Warriner, William A.; bud ovoid; flowers 4-5 in., 30-35 petals, high-centered; foliage large; vigorous, very free growth; PP3825; [seedling × Bridal Pink™]; intr. 1974

'Pink Scotch' HSpn, mp

'Pink Secret' -- See 'Trobina'

'Pink Seduction' HT, dp, Meilland; intr. 2003

'Pink Semi' (form of R. laxa), lp; flowers resemble R. blanda

'Pink Sensation' HT, mp, Bos, Henry; bud urn-shaped; flowers deeper pink in center, lighter on outer petals, 3½-4 in., 30 petals, high-centered, cupped, borne singly, intense fragrance; free-flowering; foliage large, dark green, glossy; stems long, strong; vigorous (5-6 ft.) growth; PP1584; [sport of 'Pink Delight']; intr. 1958

'Pink Shadow' Min, dp, 1978, Williams, Ernest D.; bud plump, pointed; flowers dusty pink, reverse darker, 1 in., 52 petals, moderate fragrance; foliage glossy; growth bushy, spreading; ['Over the Rainbow' × 'Over the Rainbow']; intr. 1977

'Pink Sheri' -- See 'Reneri'

'Pink Showers' Pol, mp, Ramson; intr. 1968

'Pink Showers' Cl HT, lp, 1978, Verschuren, Ted; flowers satin pink, large, dbl., loose, borne in small clusters; good repeat; vigorous, tall, climbing growth; PP3612; ['Carla' × Golden Showers®]; intr. 1974

'Pink Silk' ('Heart of England') HT, mp, 1972, Gregory; flowers carmine-rose, 4 in., 42 petals, high-centered, borne singly and sometimes in small clusters, moderate fragrance; medium growth; ['Pink Parfait' × seedling]

'Pink Simplicity' -- See 'Jacink'

'Pink Skyliner' LCl, mp, Cowlishaw; flowers soft pink, small, semi-dbl. to dbl., cupped, borne in clusters; recurrent; vigorous (8 ft.) growth; intr. 2003

'Pink Snow' ('Pink Summer Snow, Climbing') Cl F, pb, 1981, Reed, Harry, Jr. (also Hanneman, 1987); flowers light pink shading to white in center, deeper on edges of petals; [sport of 'Summer Snow, Climbing']

'Pink Soupert' Pol, mp, 1896, Dingee & Conard; flowers glossy rose red, shaded violet, small to medium, full, cupped, borne in clusters; vigorous growth; ['Clotilde Soupert' × 'Lucullus']

'Pink Spectacle' -- See 'Korlodera'

'Pink Spice' HT, lp, 1962, Von Abrams;

bud long, pointed; flowers light pink flushed yellow, 5 in., 30 petals, high-centered; foliage leathery, light green; vigorous, upright growth; intr. 1962

'Pink Spiral' HT, dp, 1953, McGredy, Sam IV; flowers deep China-rose-pink, 4 in., dbl., high-centered; foliage cedar-green; growth very vigorous

'Pink Spire' HT, mp

'Pink Splendour' HT, mp, 1951, McGredy, Sam IV; flowers rose-pink, 6-7 in., 48 petals; foliage dark; very free growth; ['Sam McGredy' × 'Crimson Glory']

Pink Spray® -- See 'Lenspra'

Pink Star® -- See 'Interpink'

'Pink Starina' Min, pb, Asami; intr. 1975

'Pink Starina, Climbing' Cl Min, pb; intr. after 1975

'Pink Stream' LCl, mp, Teranishi; intr. 2003

'Pink Strike' Min, lp, Laver, Keith G.; intr. 1998

'Pink Sublime' HMsk, pb

'Pink Summer Snow' F, lp; [sport of 'Summer Snow']; similar to 'Summer Snow' except for flower color.

'Pink Summer Snow, Climbing' -- See 'Pink Snow'

Pink Sunblaze™ -- See 'Meijidiro'

'Pink Super Bouquet' -- See 'Sanjith'

'Pink Supreme' HT, lp, 1964, deRuiter; flowers 4-5 in., 23 petals; foliage light green; vigorous, upright, well-branched growth; ['Amor' × 'Peace']

'Pink Supreme Flower Carpet' S, mp, Noack; flowers bright, iridescent pink, double, cupped to flat, borne in clusters of 5 - 9; recurrent; foliage medium, dark green, glossy; dense, compact, low (30 - 38 in.) growth ; PPAF; intr. 2007

'Pink Surprise' S, dp, Ottawa; intr. 1975

'Pink Surprise' Min, mp, 1980, Lyon; bud ovoid, pointed; flowers 48 petals, borne singly or several together; foliage tiny, medium green; prickles curved; compact, bushy growth; [seedling × seedling]; intr. 1979

'Pink Surprise' -- See 'LLX8654'

'Pink Swany' S, mp, Meilland; flowers strong pink, small, full, rosette, borne in clusters; recurrent; growth mounding (50 cm.); intr. 2004

Pink Sweetheart™ -- See 'Wilpksh'

'Pink Sweetie' Pol, lp, 2007, Tolmasoff, Jan & William; flowers semi-dbl., borne in large clusters, intense sweet fragrance; foliage medium size, medium green, semi-glossy, disease-free; prickles medium, greenish red, moderate; growth bushy, short (20-24 in.); borders, containers, low hedge; [unknown × unknown]; intr. 2004

'Pink Symphony' -- See 'Meitonje'

'Pink Talisman' HT, op, 1943, Howard Rose Co.; flowers orange to pink with pink predominating, large; upright growth; [sport of 'Talisman']

'Pink Tapestry' F, dp, Williams, J. Benjamin; flowers fluorescent pink; free-flowering; compact growth; intr. 1997

'Pink The Fairy' Pol, dp; flowers very deep pink; [sport of 'The Fairy']; intr. 1985

'Pink Tiara' Min, mp; flowers bright pink, yellow stamens, semi-dbl., shallow cup; foliage dark green; growth to 20 × 20 in.; intr. 2003

'Pink Tingle' Min, mp, 1979, Lyon; bud ovoid; flowers dawn-pink, to recurved, 1 in., 20 petals, cupped; foliage tiny; compact growth; intr. 1978

'Pink Toddler' -- See 'Peafirst'

'Pink Topaz' -- See 'Manpaz'

Pink Torch® -- See 'Intertor'

'Pink Traumland' ('Sogno Rosa') F, mp, Tantau; flowers luminous pink, medium-large, dbl.; intr. 1996

'Pink Traviata' HT, dp, Meilland; bud globular; flowers hot pink, 3 in., very full, shallow cup, borne in clusters of 2-5, very slight fragrance; recurrent; foliage dark green, semi-glossy; prickles very numerous, large; growth tall (4 ft.), upright; PP16890; [sport of 'Traviata']; intr. 2006

'Pink Treasure' S, mp, Williams, J.B.; flowers 3 in., dbl.; intr. 2004

'Pink Treasure' -- See 'Hadpleasure'

'Pink Triumph' Min, mp, 1983, Jolly, Nelson F.; flowers small, 48 petals, borne usually singly; foliage small, medium green, semi-glossy; upright, bushy growth; ['Operetta' × 'Bonny']

'Pink Triumph' -- See 'Ingrid Stenzig'

'Pink Twist' -- See 'Mordoris'

'Pink Twister' S, mp

'Pink Vogue' F, mp, 1962, Kelleher, Mrs J.; bud pointed; flowers pink, medium, semi-dbl., borne in clusters, moderate fragrance; moderate, upright growth; [sport of 'Vogue']; intr. 1960

'Pink Wave' -- See 'Mattgro'

'Pink Wedding' LCl, lp; [sport of 'Wedding Day']; intr. 2000

'Pink Wings' HT, lp

'Pink Winks' -- See 'Flowin'

'Pink Wonder' ('Kalinka') F, lp, 1971, Meilland; flowers imbricated, 3 in., 28 petals, intense fragrance; foliage large, glossy, leathery; vigorous, upright growth; [Zambra® × (Sarabande® × ('Goldilocks' × 'Fashion'))]; intr. 1970

'Pink Wonder, Climbing' -- See 'Meihartforsar'

'Pinkces' LCl, yb, 1962, Schmalz & Limpert; bud pointed; flowers light yellow to pink, open, 3½-4 in., 30 petals, moderate fragrance; abundant, non-recurrent bloom; foliage leathery; vigorous, tall, compact growth; PP2268; [sport of 'Doubloons']

'Pinkeis' LCl, pb, Schultheis; intr. 2006

'Pinkerton' HT, mp, 1949, Eacott; bud long, pointed; flowers pink shaded deeper, 4 in., 30 petals; foliage light green; vigorous growth

'Pinkie, Climbing' Cl Pol, mp, 1952, Dering; flowers rose-pink, fading to pale pink, 1¾-2½ in., semi-dbl., cupped, borne in large clusters; foliage glossy; thornless; PP1076; [sport of 'Pinkie']

'Pinkie' Pol, mp, 1947, Swim, H.C.; flowers Neyron rose, 1¾-2½ in., 16 petals, cupped, borne in large trusses, intense fragrance; soft, glossy, mostly 7 leaflet leaves; dwarf, bushy growth; PP712; [sport of 'China Doll']

'Pinky' -- See 'Macponui'

'Pinky Rugostar' -- See 'Meivibroum'

'Pinnacle' -- See 'Beniowa'

'Pinnatifide' S, mp, before 1828; wild form found in the French Pyrenees

'Pinocchio' ('Rosenmärchen') F, op, 1940, Kordes; flowers pink suffused salmon, edged deeper, 2 in., 30 petals, cupped, borne in long sprays, moderate fruity fragrance; foliage leathery; vigorous, bushy growth; PP484; ['Eva' × 'Golden Rapture']; intr. 1942

'Pinocchio, Climbing' ('Rosenmärchen, Climbing') Cl F, pb, 1951, Parmentier, J.; good rebloom; PP1142; [sport of 'Pinocchio']

'Pinocchio' -- See 'Sunpino'

'Pinocchio' -- See 'Delki'

'Pinson' LCl, my, 1909, Barbier; flowers chamois-yellow, tinted rosy white, very large, semi-dbl., borne in clusters; early; vigorous, climbing growth; [R. wichurana × 'Souv. de Catherine Guillot']

Pinstripe™ -- See 'Morpints'

'Pinta' HT, w, 1976, Beales, Peter; flowers creamy white, large, 23 petals, moderate sweetbriar fragrance; foliage dark, matte; ['Ena Harkness' × Pascali®]; intr. 1973

'Pintade' ('Meleagris') HGal, mp, before 1817, Loiseleur-Deslongchamps; flowers pink, spotted white

'Pinturnia' Gr, or, Pineau; intr. 1978

'Pinwheel' Min, pb, 1977, Moore, Ralph S.; flowers pink and yellow blend; [sport of 'Jeanie Williams']; intr. 1979

'Pinwheel' -- See 'Kazaguruma'

'Pione' F, m, Hiroshima; intr. 2000

'Pioneer' HT, mr, 1971, LeGrice; flowers very full, 4 in., 50 petals, intense fragrance; foliage small, dark; very free growth; intr. 1970

'Pioneer Spirit' LCl, mp, 2005, Shoup, George Michael; flowers very full, borne in small clusters, moderate fragrance; foliage large, dark green, semi-glossy; numerous prickles; growth mannerly climber, tall (8 ft.); climber/pillar; [(('Seafoam' × 'Himilayan Musk') × 'Carefree Beauty') × 'Crimson Glory']; intr. 1996

'Pionerka' ('Woman Pioneer') F, ob, 1955, Sushkov, K. L.; flowers reddish-orange, medium; vigorous growth

'Pioupiou' F, mr, 1958, Arles; flowers cerise-red, large; very vigorous, bushy, low growth; ['Alain' × ('Alain' × seedling)]

'Pip' Min, mr, 1978, Lyon; bud pointed; flowers small, 12-15 petals, cupped; foliage tiny; very compact, bushy growth; RULED EXTINCT 7/90; ['N74' × seedling]

'Pip' HT, w, 1991, Stoddard, Louis; bud ovoid; flowers white rimmed pink, white reverse, aging same, medium, 30 petals, high-centered, borne singly, slight fragrance; foliage medium size, light to medium green, matte; bushy, medium growth; [('Poker Chip' × Helmut Schmidt®) × ('Rise 'n' Shine × Granada' × Handel®)]

'Pipe Dreams' S, mp, 1985, Buck, Dr. Griffith J.; flowers medium pink, reverse darker, 5 in., 28 petals, cupped, borne 5 - 10 per cluster, intense clove fragrance; repeat bloom; foliage leathery, medium olive green; prickles awl-shaped, red-brown; bushy, compact, upright growth; hardy; ['Countryman' × (('Meisterstuck' × 'Prairie Princess') × ('Tickled Pink' × 'Prairie Princess'))]; intr. 1984

'Pipi' Min, dp, Hiroshima; intr. 1998

'Pippa's Song' S, mp, 1985, Buck, Dr. Griffith J.; flowers imbricated, 3 in., borne 3-10 per cluster; repeat bloom; foliage medium size, leathery, dark olive green; prickles awl-shaped, tan; shrubby, erect, bushy growth; hardy; ['Prairie Princess' × (Queen Elizabeth® × ('Morning Stars' × 'Suzanne'))]; intr. 1984

Pippy® MinFl, pb, Barni, V.; flowers medium pink with darker pink to red edges, dbl., high-centered, moderate fragrance; growth to 40 - 45 cm.; intr. 1995

'Pipsqueak' Min, m, 1986, Dobbs; flowers pinkish mauve, quilled, small, 40 petals, flat, borne in sprays of 5-20; foliage small, light green, matte; prickles very small, brown, hooked downward; bushy, spreading growth; no fruit; ['Blue Mist' × 'Snow Magic']

'Pirate Gold' F, dy, 1973, deRuiter; flowers dbl., globular; foliage glossy, leathery; vigorous, upright growth; PP3377; ['Golden Wave' × seedling]; intr. 1972

'Pirbright' F, mp, 1948, Norman; flowers semi-dbl., borne in trusses; foliage dark; vigorous growth

'Piridance' F, Pineau; intr. 1980

'PiRo 3' ('Pirosa') S, lp, Stritzke; flowers deep rose pink, single, borne in clusters; once-blooming; foliage glossy; few prickles; growth to 6 ft.; hips oblong, 3 in. long, very high in vitamin C ; hardy; [R. dumalis × R. pendulina salaevensis]; bred to produce hips that contain very high levels of vitamin C; selection from Institute for Horticulture, Dresden-Pillnitz; intr. 1995

'Piroja' HT, m, 1999, Chiplunkar, C. R.; flowers deep mauve, medium, full, high-centered, borne in small clusters, moderate fragrance; foliage medium size, medium green, semi-glossy; few prickles; upright, medium (3-3½ ft.) growth; [Blue Moon® × 'Heirloom']; intr. 1992

'Pirol' HT, dy, Tantau; florist rose; intr. 2002

'Pirol' -- See 'Tanlorip'

'Piron-Médard' HP, mp, 1906, Piron-Médard; bud long; flowers satin pink, large, dbl.; foliage nearly thornless; growth upright

'Pironia' ('Centenaire du Vesinet') Gr, op, 1979, Pineau; bud pointed; flowers salmon-orange, 3 in., 32 petals, slight fragrance; vigorous, upright growth; ['Sonia' × Prominent®]; intr. 1977

'Pironti Arabian' HT, Pironti, N.

'Pironti Blithe' F, Pironti, N.; intr. 1970

'Pironti Critow' Cl HT, Pironti, N.

'Pironti Konrad' Gr, Pironti; intr. 1971

'Pironti Tornedos' F, Pironti; intr. 1971

'Pirontina' LCl, mp, Pironti; flowers small, dbl., cupped, slight fragrance; recurrent; vigorous (10-12 ft.) growth; hips none; hardy; intr. 1975

'Pirosa' -- See 'PiRo 3'

Piroschka® -- See 'Tanpika'

'Pirosel' or, Pineau; intr. 1981

Pirouette™ LCl, pb, Poulsen; flowers pink blend with touch of apricot in center, small, full, shallow cup, slight wild rose fragrance; recurrent; broad, bushy (150-200 cm.) growth; hips none ; PP15106; intr. 2002

'Pirouette' F, pb, 1968, Fankhauser; flowers pink tinged orange-red, open, medium, dbl.; ['Ma Perkins' × 'Radar']

'Pirouette' -- See 'Lenwil'

'Pirouette' -- See 'Benmagic'

'Pisadora' w, Pineau; intr. 1981

'Pisces' Fl, mp, Burston; flowers soft pink, large, dbl., cupped; foliage glossy; upright (30 in.) growth; intr. 2004

'Pisen' HT, op, Brabec

'Pismi' HT, rb, 1972, Pecollo; bud ovoid; flowers solferino-purple to spirea-red, large, dbl., cupped; foliage large, dark, leathery; vigorous, upright bushy growth; ['Dame Edith Helen' × 'Rote Rapture']

'Pissardii' -- See 'Nastarana'

'Pitica' ('Kyria', 'Pihca') F, lp, 1976, Royon; flowers full, 4 in., 25-30 petals, high-centered; PP4017; [sport of 'Sweet Promise']

'Pitord' HP, rb, 1867, Lacharme; flowers fiery red, center velvety violet, large, full

'Pitstop' HT, dr, Select; flowers velvety dark red, 4 in., 30-35 petals, high-centered, borne mostly singly; recurrent; foliage dark green; stems long

'Pittsburgh' HP, lp, 1929, Schoener; flowers flesh-pink, base yellow, very large, 25 petals, globular; foliage leathery; long stems; very vigorous growth; [((R. gigantea × unknown) × Frau Karl Druschki) × 'Mrs John Laing']

'Pius IX' ('Pie IX', 'Pope Pius IX', 'Pius the Ninth') HP, mp, 1849, Vibert; flowers violet-rose, large, very dbl., flat, intense fragrance; vigorous growth

'Pius the Ninth' -- See 'Pius IX'

'Pius XI' ('Pope Pius XI') HT, w, 1925, Leenders, M.; bud long, pointed; flowers cream-white, center cream-yellow, very large, dbl.; ['Ophelia' × seedling]

'Pivoine' -- See 'Lustre d'Église'

'Pivoine' -- See 'Bourbon'

'Pivoine de Lille' -- See 'Nouvelle Pivoine'

'Pivoine des Hollandais' -- See 'Great Royal'

'Pixanah' ('Savannah Miss') Min, ab, 1990, Chaffin, Lauren M.; bud pointed; flowers dark apricot, edges lighter, medium apricot reverse, fading to soft pink, medium, 40-50 petals, high-centered, borne singly, moderate fragrance; foliage medium size, medium green, semi-glossy; prickles needle-shaped, light tan; bushy, tall growth; hips globular, medium green; ['Pounder Star' × 'Ann Moore']

'Pixanne' ('Rebecca Anne') Min, mp, 1993, Chaffin, Lauren M.; flowers large, very dbl., borne mostly singly; foliage medium size, medium green, semi-glossy; some prickles; medium (40-45 cm.), upright, bushy, vigorous growth; ['Gene Boerner' × 'Pink Petticoat']; intr. 1993

'Pixarla' ('Starla') Min, w, 1990, Chaffin, Lauren M.; bud pointed; flowers medium, 20-25 petals, high-centered, borne singly, slight fruity fragrance; recurrent; foliage medium size, medium green, semi-glossy; prickles needle-shaped, tan; bushy, medium (18-24 in.) growth; [Honor™ × Rainbow's End™]; intr. 1991

'Pixbeth' ('Bethany Grace') Min, mp, 2003, Chaffin, Lauren M.; flowers finish pink as they age, 2 in., very full, borne mostly solitary, slight fragrance; foliage medium size, dark green, semi-glossy; prickles slightly curved; growth upright, bushy, tall (18-24 in.); garden, containers; [unknown × unknown]; intr. 2003

'Pixbro' ('Little Brother') Min, mr, 1998, Chaffin, Lauren M.; flowers medium red, 2 in., full, borne mostly singly, slight fragrance; foliage medium size, medium green, semi-glossy; compact, medium growth; ['Pink Petticoat' × 'Happy Hour']; intr. 1998

'Pixchek' ('Checkers') Min, mr, 1990, Chaffin, Lauren M.; bud pointed; flowers medium red, aging darker, 20 petals, high-centered, borne singly, slight spicy fragrance; foliage small, medium green, semi-glossy; prickles needle-shaped, tan; bushy, low growth; rarely forms fruit; ['Deep Purple' × 'Happy Hour']

'Pixcook' ('Sugar Cookie™) Min, mp, 2003, Chaffin, Lauren; flowers medium pink, white at base, reverse white, 2 in., dbl., borne mostly solitary, slight fragrance; foliage medium size, medium green, semi-glossy; prickles medium, straight, moderate; growth bushy, medium (14-16 in.); garden, containers; [Matangi® × Little Artist®]; intr. 2003

'Pixhar' ('Summer Harvest') Min, ob, 1998, Chaffin, Lauren M.; flowers very bright orange blend, gold stamens, 2 in., 5 petals, borne in small clusters; foliage large, dark green, glossy; prickles moderate, medium, straight; bushy, tall (24 in.) growth; ['Ann Moore' × Sequoia Gold™]; intr. 1998

'Pixhoney' ('Honey Butter') Min, ly, 1998, Chaffin, Lauren M.; flowers creamy yellow center, near white outer edges, 2-2½ in., very dbl., borne mostly singly;

foliage medium size, medium size, semi-glossy; prickles few, small, straight; bushy, medium growth; ['Deep Purple' × Rainbow's End™]; intr. 1998

'Pixichar' ('Real Charmer') Min, lp, 1992, Chaffin, Lauren M.; flowers 3-3½ in., full, borne in small clusters, moderate fragrance; foliage large, medium green, semi-glossy; tall (45 cm.), upright growth; ['Gene Boerner' × 'Crissy']

'Pixichip' ('Chipmonk', 'Chipmunk', 'Peanut Butter & Jelly') Min, r, 1991, Chaffin, Lauren M.; flowers tannish brown blending with mauve when full blown, large, full, borne mostly singly, moderate fragrance; foliage medium size, medium green, semi-glossy; few prickles; medium (30 cm.), bushy, neat, compact growth; ['Deep Purple' × Rainbow's End™]; intr. 1992

'Pixie' ('Little Princess', 'Princesita') Min, w, 1940, deVink; flowers white, center light pink, small, 55 petals; foliage very small, soft; short stems; dwarf, compact growth; PP408; ['Ellen Poulsen' × 'Tom Thumb']

'Pixie, Climbing' Cl Min, w, 1964, Ruston, D.

Pixie Delight™ -- See 'Wilbentur'

'Pixie Dust' -- See 'Denpix'

'Pixie Gold' Min, my, 1961, Dot, Pedro; flowers mimosa-yellow, 1-1½ in., 11 petals; foliage very small, thin, dark; bushy growth; PP2091; ['Perla de Montserrat' × ('Rosina' × 'Eduardo Toda')]; intr. 1961

'Pixie Hat' -- See 'Korlamber'

'Pixie Hedge' -- See 'Baby Jayne'

'Pixie Pearl' ('Estralia', 'Estralita') Min, w, about 1910; flowers pearly white, small, very dbl., borne in clusters; vigorous, compact growth

'Pixie Rose' ('Pink Pixie') Min, dp, 1961, Dot, Pedro; flowers , 43 petals, high-centered to cupped, borne in irregular clusters; foliage very small, dark; dwarf, much-branched growth; PP2095; ['Perla de Montserrat' × 'Coralín']; intr. 1961

'Pixifull' ('Fullerton Centennial') Min, or, 1987, Chaffin, Lauren M.; flowers orange-red with white base, bright, fading darker, medium, 20-25 petals, high-centered, borne singly or in sprays of 3-5, slight fragrance; foliage small, medium green, semi-glossy, disease-resistant; prickles needle-declining, sparse, light tan; upright, bushy, medium, neat, symmetrical growth; sometimes forms globular, medium-green hips; ['Orange Honey' × 'Rise 'n' Shine']; intr. 1987

'Pixihon' ('Honey Bear') Min, ab, 1987, Chaffin, Lauren M.; flowers deep apricot, yellow base, reverse light apricot, aging cream, 50-55 petals, cupped; foliage small, medium green, semi-glossy, disease-resistant; prickles needle-like, straight, light tan; bushy, low compact growth; PP6844; ['Rise 'n' Shine' × Holy Toledo™]

'Piximis' (Moon Mist™) Min, w, 1985, Strawn, Leslie E.; flowers ivory tinged pale pink, well-formed, small, 20 petals, moderate fragrance; foliage small, medium green, semi-glossy; bushy growth; ['The Optimist' × 'Darling Flame']

'Pixink' ('Tickle Me Pink') Min, mp, 1989, Chaffin, Lauren M.; bud pointed; flowers medium pink to soft cream at base, reverse cream blush, aging, dbl., moderate spicy fragrance; foliage small, medium green, semi-glossy; prickles needle-like, light tan; bushy, low growth; hips globular, rare, medium green; ['Osiria' × Magic Carrousel®]

'Pixinner' ('Inner Glow') Min, rb, 1990, Chaffin, Lauren M.; bud ovoid; flowers red with golden yellow base, yellow reverse, red veining towards outer edges, 40 petals, high-centered; foliage medium size, medium green, semi-glossy; prickles hooked, tan; bushy, medium growth; hips round, medium green; ['Ann Moore' × Rainbow's End™]; intr. 1991

'Pixiprin' ('Indian Princess') Min, r, 1982, Strawn, Leslie E.; flowers tan flushed orange, reverse burnt umber, shaded garnet-brown, 20 petals; foliage small, dark, semi-glossy; upright growth; ['Yellow Jewel' × 'Golden Cougar']

'Pixiree' ('Free Spirit') Min, ab, 1985, Strawn, Leslie E.; flowers small, 20 petals; foliage small, medium green, semi-glossy; upright growth; PP6188; [Prominent® × 'Gold Pin']; intr. 1984

'Pixislip' ('Silver Slippers') Min, m, 1991, Chaffin, Lauren M.; bud slender; flowers unique silvery lavender, medium, full, borne mostly singly, moderate fragrance; foliage medium size, medium green, semi-glossy; medium (30 cm.), bushy growth; ['Deep Purple' × 'Jennifer']; intr. 1992

'Pixisun' ('Sunshine Girl') Min, my, 1985, Woolcock, Edward P.; flowers small, 35 petals, multi-star shaped, slight fragrance; foliage small, medium green, semi-glossy; upright growth; ['Sunsilk' × 'Rise 'n' Shine']

'Pixiter' ('Tiger Butter') Min, dy, 1982, Strawn, Leslie E.; flowers small, 20 petals; foliage small, dark, semi-glossy; upright, bushy growth; ['Sunblest' × 'Over the Rainbow']

'Pixiwow' ('Wow!') Min, ob, 1985, Strawn, Leslie E.; bud pointed; flowers bright orange, reverse more red tones, small, 25-35 petals, cupped, borne singly, slight fragrance; recurrent; foliage small, dark green, glossy; prickles few, needle, declining slightly; stems upright, slender; bushy, rounded growth; PP6469; ['Ann Cocker' × ('Puerto Rico' × 'Darling Flame')]

'Pixjun' ('June Bug') Min, ob, 1994, Chaffin, Lauren M.; flowers bright medium orange, slightly lighter reverse, yellow base, 1½ in., full, borne mostly singly, slight fragrance; foliage medium size, dark green, semi-glossy; some prickles; medium (12 in.), bushy, compact growth; [(Prominent® × 'Orange Honey') × 'Ann Moore']; intr. 1994

'Pixkick' ('Side Kick') Min, or, 1995, Chaffin, Lauren M.; flowers orange-red, medium, 40-60 petals, borne mostly singly; foliage medium size, medium green, semi-glossy; few prickles; medium (30 cm.), bushy growth; ['Dandenong' × 'Ann Moore']; intr. 1996

'Pixkiss' ('Sun Kissed') MinFl, yb, 2003, Chaffin, Lauren M.; flowers yellow w/ blush pink edges, reverse medium yellow, 2½ in., full, borne mostly solitary, slight fragrance; foliage medium size, medium green, semi-glossy; prickles straight; growth upright, bushy, medium (2-3 ft.); garden, containers; [Honor™ × 'Rise 'n' Shine']; intr. 2004

'Pixric' ('Ric Rac') F, rb, 1996, Chaffin, Lauren M.; flowers white edged red, non-fading color, long lasting, 2½-3 in., full; fast repeat; foliage small, medium green, semi-glossy; prickles moderate; upright, low (18-20 in.) growth; ['Hannah Gordon' × 'Pink Petticoat']; intr. 1996

'Pixsar' ('Sarah Elizabeth') F, ab, 1998, Chaffin, Lauren M.; flowers apricot blend, 2½-3 in., 41 petals, old-fashioned, rosette, borne in small clusters, slight fragrance; foliage medium size, dark green, glossy; prickles few, medium, straight; upright, medium growth; ['City of Auckland' × seedling]; intr. 1998

'Pixsis' ('Little Sister') Min, mp, 1995, Chaffin, Lauren M.; flowers large, 40-60 petals, borne mostly singly, occasional side buds, slight fragrance; foliage medium size, medium green, semi-glossy; few prickles; growth medium (30 cm.), bushy; ['Gene Boerner' × 'Crissy']; intr. 1996

'Pixsno' ('Sno Cone') F, rb, 1996, Chaffin, Lauren M.; flowers white edged red, 2½-3 in., dbl., borne in small clusters; foliage small, medium green, semi-glossy, disease-resistant; prickles moderate; bushy, low (18 in.) growth; ['Hannah Gordon' × 'Pink Petticoat']; intr. 1996

'Pixsta' ('Christa') Min, w, 1993, Chaffin, Lauren M.; flowers large, full, high-centered, borne mostly singly, slight fragrance; foliage medium size, medium green, semi-glossy, disease-resistant; some prickles; long stems; tall (45 cm.), upright, vigorous growth; [Honor™ × 'Rise 'n' Shine']; intr. 1993

'Pixsummer' (Summer Splash™) MinFl, my, 2003, Chaffin, Lauren; flowers dbl., borne mostly solitary, slight fragrance; foliage medium size, medium green, semi-glossy; prickles straight, moderate; growth upright, medium (18-24 in.); garden, containers; ['Rise 'n' Shine' × Dorola®]; intr. 2003

'Pixsun' ('Sunny Side Up') F, ob, 1994, Chaffin, Lauren M.; flowers blended soft yellow to tangerine, 3-3½ in., 6-14 petals, borne in small clusters; foliage medium size, dark green, glossy; some prickles; medium (2-3 ft.), bushy growth; ['City of Auckland' × Rainbow's End™];

intr. 1994

'Pixzig' ('Zig-Zag') Min, rb, 1993, Chaffin, Lauren M.; flowers white with dark red picotee edge, large, very dbl., high-centered, borne mostly singly; foliage similar to Peaches 'n' Cream, medium size, medium green; some prickles; low (30 cm.), upright, bushy, compact growth; ['Osiria' × 'Pink Petticoat']; intr. 1993

'Pizzazz' Min, rb, 1991, Jolly, Marie; bud ovoid; flowers various yellows, pink hues, aging to orange-red, 1½ in., 50 petals, borne usually singly or in sprays of 2-3, slight fragrance; foliage medium size, medium green, semi-glossy; upright, spreading, medium growth; ['Orange Honey' × Loving Touch™]; intr. 1992

Pizzazz™ -- See 'Savapizzazz'

'Pizzicato' S, lp, 1964, Buck, Dr. Griffith J.; bud ovoid, long, pointed; flowers light salmon-rose, 3-4 in., 40 petals, cupped, moderate fragrance; foliage leathery, bronze; vigorous, upright (3-4 ft.), bushy. growth; ['Florence Mary Morse' × ('Josef Rothmund' × *R. laxa*)]; intr. 1962

'Placet' S, w, 1981, Bevan, Mrs. Ruth M.; bud small, ovoid; flowers 5 petals, borne 40 or more per cluster; all summer bloom; foliage soft green, 7 leaflet; bushy growth

'Placida' HT, mr, 1959, Cayzer; bud ovoid; flowers crimson, large, dbl.; foliage glossy, dark; vigorous, bushy, compact growth; ['Crimson Glory' × 'Una Wallace']

'Placidie' A, mp, 1820, Prévost/Vibert; flowers bright pink, medium, semi-dbl.; foliage small, narrow, deep green; nearly thornless; stems slender; growth vertical; [sport of 'Great Maiden's Blush']

'Placido Domingo' -- See 'Machoro'

'Plain Talk' F, mr, 1965, Swim & Weeks; bud long-pointed; flowers bright, clear red, 2½-2¾ in., 25-30 petals, borne in flat to rounded clusters of 3 or more, slight fragrance; free-flowering; foliage large, dark green, leathery; prickles few, straight, grayish-brown; growth vigorous, bushy, low; PP2538; ['Spartan' × 'Garnette']

'Plaisante' F, mp, 1957, Riethmuller; flowers bright pink, base and reverse lighter, semi-dbl.; low growth; ['Borderer' × seedling]

'Plaisanterie' -- See 'LLX8886'

'Plaisir de France' HT, dp, 1952, Gaujard; flowers bright deep coppery pink, 6 in., 35 petals; foliage glossy, dark; vigorous growth; ['Peace' × seedling]

'Plameny' HT, mr, Urban, J.; flowers large, dbl.; intr. 1970

'Plamya Vostoka' ('Flame of the East') F, or, Klimenko, V. N.; flowers fiery red tinted darker, medium, 30 petals; medium growth; ['Independence' × 'Kirsten Poulsen']; intr. 1955

'Planten un Blomen' -- See 'Cheerio'

'Plate Bonde Seedling' Pol, mp; recurrent; growth to 2-3 ft.

'Platinum Lady' -- See 'Lavplat'

'Plato' HSpn, mr, about 1850, Vibert; flowers clear red, dbl.; non-recurrent; foliage finely divided; dense, shrubby (3-4 ft.) growth; hips glossy, black

'Platyphylla' -- See 'Seven Sisters'

'Play Girl' F, or; intr. 2002

Play Rose® -- See 'Meinoiral'

Playboy® ('Cheerio') F, rb, 1976, Cocker; flowers scarlet, gold eye, large, single, flat to slightly cupped, borne singly and in clusters, slight apple fragrance; recurrent; foliage glossy, dark green; growth moderate (3-4 ft.); ['City of Leeds' × ('Chanelle' × Piccadilly®)]

'Player' -- See 'Sunplay'

'Playfair' -- See 'Wiwait'

'Playful' HT, ab, 1970, Watson; flowers light apricot, edged pink; [sport of 'Mischief']

'Playful' F, mp, Wilke, William; flowers pink, reverse deeper pink, golden stamens, 3 in., single, borne in large clusters, slight fragrance; foliage medium size, dark green, glossy; prickles ¼ in., straight out, no hook, brown; upright, medium growth; containers, bedding; [sport of Playgirl™]; intr. 2003

'Playfulness' F, mp, Williams, J.B.; recurrent; intr. 2004

Playgirl™ -- See 'Morplag'

'Playgirl, Climbing' -- See 'Morclip'

'Playgold' -- See 'Morplaygold'

Playgroup Rose® -- See 'Horsun'

'Playmate' S, ab, Williams, J.B.; recurrent; low (2 ft.), spreading (3 ft.) growth; intr. 2003

'Playmate' -- See 'Horcohabit'

'Playmate' -- See 'Weokay'

Playpretty™ S, op, 2000, Cockerham, John E.; flowers orange pink, reverse deep pink, large, semi-dbl., borne mostly singly, slight fragrance; foliage medium size, medium green, matte; few prickles; upright, low (2-3 ft.) growth

'Playrose' ('American Shakira') HT, dp, Ferrer; florist rose; intr. 2004

'Playtime' -- See 'Korsaku'

Playtime -- See 'Morplati'

'Pleasant Valley' -- See 'LLX8886'

'Pleasantly Pink' -- See 'Lavplease'

Pleasure!® HT, w, Schreurs; intr. 2002

'Pleasure' -- See 'Jacpif'

'Plein Ciel' HT, mp, 1967, Hendrickx, Adolf; bud pointed; flowers large, dbl., high-centered, moderate fragrance; foliage dark, glossy; vigorous, well branched growth; [seedling × 'Golden Rapture']; intr. 1965

Plein Soleil® -- See 'Lapdev'

'Pleine de Grâce' -- See 'Lengra'

'Pleins Feux 92' Pol, rb, Dorieux; flowers bright red, reverse lighter, semi-dbl., flat, borne in clusters; intr. 1992

'Plena' ('À Fleurs Doubles', 'Rose de l'Hymen', 'Blanc Ordinaire', 'Double', 'Flore Pleno', 'La Royale') A, w; bud slightly pink; flowers washed nankeen in center,, single to semi-dbl., borne in large clusters; foliage ovoid, pointed, dentate, dark green; prickles reddish, shield-shaped; intr. before 1770

'Plena' ('Blanc à Fleurs Pleines', 'Double White Noisette', *R. sempervirens major*, 'Sempervirens Major', 'Sempervirens Pleno') HSem, lp, Laffay, M.; flowers flesh-tinted, dbl.; intr. before 1830

'Plenissima' -- See 'Double Hugonis'

'Plentiful' F, dp, 1961, LeGrice; bud globular; flowers 3-4 in., 75 petals, flat, quartered, borne in large clusters, slight fragrance; good repeat; foliage light green; vigorous, bushy growth; intr. 1961

'Plisiedame' -- See 'Polisiedame'

'Plnokvety Super Star' HT, or, Strnad

'Plomin' F, pb, 1951, Tantau; flowers golden peach, fading thru peach/blush pink to white, large, semi-dbl., borne in large clusters, intense fragrance; foliage leathery; bushy, dwarf growth; [('Johanna Tantau' × 'Karen Poulsen') × 'Stammler']

'Plonia' -- See 'Pæonia'

'Pluie de Feu' LCl, or, 1964, Mondial Roses; flowers bright scarlet, semi-dbl., borne in clusters; vigorous growth

'Plukovnik Svec' ('Colonel Svec') HT, dr, 1935, Böhm, J.; bud long (over 3 in.), pointed; flowers blood-red, large, semi-dbl.; foliage small; vigorous, bushy growth; ['Pres. Jac. Smits' × 'Kitchener of Khartoum']

'Plum Brandy' Min, m; flowers plum/purple/pink, small, full, rosette, slight fragrance; growth low (10-14 in.)

'Plum Cake' -- See 'Murca'

'Plum Crazy' -- See 'Arograju'

Plum Dandy™ -- See 'Jacliang'

'Plum Duffy' Min, m, 1978, Bennett, Dee; bud ovoid; flowers deep plum, 1½ in., 25 petals, high-centered, slight fragrance; foliage dark; growth compact; [Magic Carrousel® × Magic Carrousel®]

Plum Frost™ -- See 'Jacpluco'

Plum Pudding™ -- See 'Wilplpd'

'Plume d'Ange' F, w, Richardier; flowers white, shaded salmon pink, with ruffled petals, full, rounded; intr. 2005

'Plums 'n' Cream' -- See 'Weeplumsncream'

'Pluto' C, dr, before 1799; flowers very dark red

'Pluto' -- See 'Macpluto'

'Pluton' ('Rose Pluton') HGal, m, 1843, Vibert; flowers very deep blackish purple, medium, full

'Plzen' ('City of Pilsen', 'Stadt Pilsen') HT, dr, 1930, Böhm, J.; bud very long; flowers dark blood-red, very large, semi-dbl.; very vigorous growth; ['Étoile de Hollande' × 'Macbeth']

'Pobjeditel' HT, dp, 1940, Kosteckij; flowers large, dbl.

'Poblet' HT, ob, Dot; flowers bright vermilion, long lasting

'Pocahontas' -- See 'Wilkaya'

'Poco' Min, pb, 1987, Bridges, Dennis A.; flowers pink, white center, fades slightly, medium, 29 petals, urn-shaped, borne usually singly; foliage medium size, medium green, semi-glossy; prickles medium, light green, pointed downwards; growth bushy, medium; [Heartland™ × seedling]

'Podruga' ('Girl Friend') HT, mp, 1939, Costetske; flowers bright pink, base dark red, oval, irregular shape; low, rather weak growth; ['Vaterland' × 'Mme Edouard Herriot']

'Poëma' Cl Pol, mp, 1933, Brada, Dr.; flowers bright pink, passing to La France pink, 4-5 cm., semi-dbl., borne in clusters of 10-20; recurrent bloom; foliage bright, dark; vigorous (5-10 ft.) growth; ['Tausendschön' × 'Farbenkonigin']

'Poema' HT, dr; intr. 2004

'Poeme!' HT, lp, Schreurs; intr. 2002

'Poente' F, ob, Moreira da Silva; flowers orange and carmine; ['Pinocchio' × 'Goldilocks']

'Poesie' S, w; groundcover; intr. 1997

'Poesie' -- See 'Promise'

'Poesie' -- See 'Jacient'

'Poesie' -- See 'Lenobit'

'Poète Jean du Clos' HT, op, 1919, Gillot, F.; flowers pink, shaded salmon, dbl.; ['Le Progres' × 'Lyon Rose']

Poetry® HT, lp, Kordes; flowers delicate pink, large, very full, high-centered, borne mostly singly, intense fragrance; good repeat; foliage fresh green; stems long, strong; intr. 2002

'Poetry' -- See 'Zipoet'

'Poetry in Motion' -- See 'Harelan'

Poetry Kordana® Min, lp, Kordes; flowers silvery pink, full, high-centered; pot rose; intr. 2005

'Pohadka Maje' HT, mr, Certek

'Poiana' HT, dy, GPG Bad Langensalza; flowers large, dbl.; intr. 1972

'Poinsettia' HT, mr, 1938, H&S; bud long, pointed; flowers bright scarlet, large, 28 petals, moderate spicy fragrance; recurrent; foliage glossy; growth vigorous, compact; [('Mrs J.D. Eisele' × 'Vaterland') × 'J. C. Thornton']

'Poinsettia, Climbing' Cl HT, mr, 1950, Thompson, D.L.

'Point Clear' -- See 'Talpoi'

'Point de Avignon' F, or

Point du Jour® -- See 'Candide'

'Pointsfield' HT, ab, 1977, McKenzie Clan; flowers 5 in., 35 petals; foliage glossy, reddish-green; vigorous growth; ['Bonsoir' × 'Percy Thrower']

'Pointsfield' HT, ab, 1977, Simpson, J. W.; buds high pointed; flowers dbl, high-centered, borne singly and in small clusters; foliage glossy, reddish green; growth vigorous, medium tall; ['Bonsoir' × 'Percy Thrower']; intr. 1977

'Poise' S, lp, Williams, J. Benjamin; flowers soft, creamy pink, darker center, semi-dbl., cupped, moderate fragrance; recurrent; foliage dark green, semi-glossy; low (2 ft.), spreading growth; intr. 2006

Poison!® HT, dp, Schreurs; intr. 2002

'Poiteau' HP, dp, 1855, Robert; flowers large, full

'Poker' -- See 'Meipazdia'

Poker® -- See 'Havaps'

'Poker Chip' Min, rb, 1979, Saville, F. Harmon; bud pointed; flowers red with yellow reverse, medium, 28 petals, high-centered, intense fragrance; foliage glossy, dark; vigorous, compact growth; large fruit; PP4582; ['Sheri Anne' × ('Yellow Jewel' × ('Tamango' × unknown))]

'Pokornyana' (R. × pokornyana, R. scopulosa) S, lp, before 1916; sepals appendaged; flowers 1¾ in.; foliage leaflets doubly serrate; [R. canina × R. glauca]; from Hungary

'Pol Robson' F, dr, Klimenko, V. N.; flowers medium, very dbl.; intr. 1955

'Polar Bear' HP, w, 1934, Nicolas; flowers white tinted blush, becoming pure white, large, very dbl., globular, intense fragrance; recurrent bloom; foliage large, leathery, wrinkled; vigorous, bushy growth; PP132; ['Schoener's Nutkana' × 'New Century']

'Polar Cap' -- See 'Brocap'

'Polar Joy' -- See 'Northern Encore'

'Polar Spire' -- See 'Tanlarpost'

Polar Star® HT, w, Tantau; flowers very large, double, high-centered, borne mostly singly; recurrent; stems medium to long; vigorous growth; florist rose; intr. 2006

'Polar Star' -- See 'Tanlarpost'

'Polar Sun' -- See 'Polarsonne'

'Polareis' -- See 'Ritausma'

'Polaris' HSet, w, 1939, Horvath; flowers pure snow-white, open, dbl., borne in clusters, intense fragrance; profuse, non-recurrent bloom; foliage glossy, light; very vigorous, climbing (12-15 ft.) growth; PP386; [(R. setigera × R. wichurana) × R. foetida bicolor]

Polaris™ Min, mp, Olesen; intr. 2000

'Polarsonne' ('Polar Sun') HRg, mp, Strobel; flowers medium, dbl., slight fragrance; growth to 2 ft.; intr. 1991

Polarstern® -- See 'Tanlarpost'

'Pôle Nord' HT, w, 1944, Mallerin, C.; bud long, pointed; flowers pure white, base tinted greenish; vigorous growth

'Pole Position' HT, mr, Select; flowers 4½ in., 35-40 petals, high-centered, borne mostly singly; good repeat; stems long, straight; florist rose; intr. 2003

'Polestar' -- See 'Polstjärnan'

'Poliarchus' S, w, Central Exp. Farm; flowers cream flushed salmon, fading rapidly; non-recurrent; spreading shrub (4 ft.) growth; hardy; [seedling × 'Harison's Yellow']

'Polichinelle' Min, yb, Delbard; flowers yellow with red stripes, small, semi-dbl.; free-flowering; stems vigorous (2 ft.) growth; intr. 2000

'Polina' HT, dp, 1985, Staikov, Prof. Dr. V.; flowers deep pink, large, 38 petals; foliage dark, leathery; bushy growth; ['Mistica' × 'Chenon']; intr. 1984

'Polisiedame' ('Plisiedame') F, ab, Kordes; intr. 1990

'Polka' F, mp, 1960, Meilland, Mrs. Marie-Louise; bud ovoid; flowers 3-3½ in., 42 petals, high-centered, borne in clusters, moderate fragrance; foliage leathery; vigorous, bushy growth; PP1939; [Moulin Rouge® × 'Fashion']; intr. 1960

Polka™ -- See 'Meitosier'

'Polka 91' -- See 'Meitosier'

'Polka Dot' Min, w, 1956, Moore, Ralph S.; flowers ivory white, small, dbl.; foliage dark, leathery; vigorous, dwarf (10 in.), bushy growth; ['Golden Glow' × 'Zee']

'Polka Time' S, op, 1985, Buck, Dr. Griffith J.; bud ovoid, pointed; flowers salmon tinted yellow, veined pink, petals imbricated, 5 in., 38 petals, cupped, borne in clusters of 1-10, moderate fragrance; repeat bloom; foliage dark, leathery; prickles awl-like, tan; growth low, bushy, compact; hardy; [Bonfire Night® × 'Countryman']; intr. 1984

'Pollentia' HT, dp, 1942, Dot, Pedro; bud large, long pointed; flowers satiny strawberry-red, 40 petals, high-centered; foliage dark, glossy; upright, compact growth

'Polleriana' -- See 'Pollmeriana'

'Polliniana' (R. × polliniana) Misc OGR, w, 1820; flowers white to pale pink, occasionally tinted rose, large, borne singly or in pairs; long stems; [R. arvensis × R. gallica]

'Pollmeriana' ('Polleriana') (strain of R. canina), lp; almost thornless; very vigorous growth; ['De la Grifferaie' × R. canina]; used for understock

Polluce® (Pollux®) S, mr, Barni, V.; intr. 1987

Pollux® -- See 'Polluce'

'Polly' HT, w, 1927, Beckwith; bud long, pointed; flowers cream, center tinted pink or light orange, fading white, large, 38 petals, high-centered, intense fragrance; [('Ophelia' × unknown) × 'Mme Colette Martinet']

'Polly Flinders' Min, w, 1954, Robinson, T.; flowers cream tinted copper-orange, 1 in., 30 petals; foliage veined red; ['Little Princess (Pol)' × 'Fashion']

'Polly Perkins' HT, op, 1969, Gregory; flowers orange-cerise, pointed, moderate fragrance; foliage dark; very free growth; intr. 1967

'Polly Sunshine' -- See 'Morgoldpoly'

'Polo' -- See 'Tanolop'

Polo Club™ -- See 'Arotigy'

Polo Queen™ -- See 'Haybarb'

'Polonaise' HT, mr, 1961, Von Abrams; flowers bright red, ruffled petals, 6 in., 40-50 petals, high-centered, moderate fragrance; foliage glossy; growth vigorous, upright, compact; ['Carrousel' × ('Chrysler Imperial' × seedling)]; intr. 1962

'Polonaise' S, dp, Buck, Dr. Griffith J.; bud ovoid, pointed; flowers deep pink, imbricated, 3 in., 43 petals, borne 5 - 10 per cluster; repeat bloom; foliage leathery, dark green with reddish veination; prickles awl-like, red-brown; dwarf, upright, bushy growth; hardy; ['San Francisco' × 'Prairie Princess']; intr. 1984

'Polstjärnan' ('Polestar', 'The Polar Star', 'White Star of Finland', 'White Rose of Finland', 'Wasastiernan', 'The Wasa Star') LCl, w, 1937, Wasastjerna; flowers pure white, very small, borne in clusters; non-recurrent; very vigorous (to 18 ft.) growth; very hardy

Polvere di Stelle® LCl, w, Barni; flowers pure white, 25 petals, borne in large clusters, no fragrance; foliage medium size, dark green; 250 - 400 cm. growth; intr. 2006

'Poly Peace' F, yb, 1960, Leenders, J.; flowers golden yellow edged rose-pink, large, semi-dbl., high-centered; foliage dark, glossy; strong stems; very vigorous, tall, bushy growth; ['Masquerade' × 'Peace']; intr. 1959

'Poly Prim' F, dy, 1953, Eddie; flowers well-shaped, 3 in., 70 petals, borne in clusters; foliage dark, glossy; very vigorous, bushy growth; ['Goldilocks' × 'Golden Rapture']

'Polyana' S, dp, 1925, Skinner; [R. rugosa × 'Mme Norbert Levavasseur']

'Polyantha Grandiflora' ('Gentiliana') HMult, w, 1886, Bernaix; flowers pure white, medium, single to semi-dbl., flat, borne in large clusters; not recurrent; foliage large, light to medium green, glossy; probably R. multiflora hybrid × R. moschata hybrid; intr. 1886

'Polybag Joshi' HT, lp, 1999, Chiplunkar, C. R.; flowers light pale pink, reverse deeper, 4-5 in., very dbl., borne mostly singly, moderate fragrance; foliage large, medium green, dull, leathery; numerous prickles; spreading, medium (3-4 ft.) growth; ['First Prize' × ('First Prize' × 'Perfume Delight')]; intr. 1995

Polygold® -- See 'Tanlypolo'

'Polynesian Pearl' Gr, lp, 1977, Takatori, Yoshiho; bud ovoid; flowers shell-pink, 2 in., 35-59 petals, high-centered, moderate fruity fragrance; foliage leathery; upright growth; ['Floribunda' × 'Tropicana']

'Polynesian Sunset' HT, op, 1965, Boerner; bud long; flowers coral-orange, 6 in., dbl., high-centered, moderate fruity fragrance; foliage leathery; vigorous, bushy growth; PP2530; [('Diamond Jubilee' × unknown) × 'Hawaii']

'Pom-Pom' HWich, 1910, USDA; ['Crimson Rambler' × R. wichurana]

'Pom Pom Flower Circus' -- See 'PomPon Flower Circus'

'Pommifère à Fleur Double' -- See 'Duplex'

'Pomona' F, ob, Fryer, Gareth; flowers dusky peach, dbl., high-centered, borne in well-spaced clusters, slight fragrance; good repeat; neat, even, medium (2 ft.) growth; intr. 1994

Pomona™ -- See 'Niagara'

'Pompadour' HT, dp, 1978, Murray, Nola; bud pointed; flowers deep pink, 5½ in., 43 petals, high-centered, intense fruity fragrance; foliage dark, glossy; bushy, compact growth; ['Molly McGredy' × 'Prima Ballerina']; intr. 1979

'Pompadour Red' F, dp, 1951, deRuiter; bud globular; flowers rose-red, large, 30-35 petals, cupped, moderate fruity fragrance; vigorous growth; PP1045; [Orange Triumph® × 'Anne Poulsen']

'Pompeii' HT, rb, Bailey, Dorothy J.; bud large, ovoid; flowers velvety red with yellow reverse, 4½-5½ in., 30-32 petals, high-centered, borne usually singly, moderate damask fragrance; free-flowering; foliage large, leathery; prickles very few, flat, medium; growth vigorous, upright (4 ft.); hips globular; PP4430; ['Grand Gala' × 'Peace']; intr. 1980

'Pompon' HGal, dr, 1835, Joly; flowers brilliant crimson

'Pompon' -- See 'Pompon Panachée'

'Pompon Bazard' A, lp, before 1835, Bazard; flowers flesh pink, edges lighter, full

'Pompon Beauty' F, or, 1949, deRuiter; flowers scarlet, very dbl., borne in large trusses; vigorous growth; ['polyantha seedling' × 'hybrid tea seedling']

'Pompon Blanc' C, w; bud round; flowers small, very dbl., moderate fragrance; foliage oval, doubly dentate; nearly thornless; probably synonymous with 'De Meaux White'; intr. before 1811

'Pompon Blanc' ('Alba Flore Multiplici', 'Albo Pleno', 'Blanc à Fleurs Doubles', 'Double Blanche') HSpn, w, before 1817, Descemet; flowers very large, full, borne mostly solitary; foliage round, or rounded-ovate, deeply dentate, bright green; prickles uneven, straight; hips globose, bright red maturing to black

'Pompon Blanc' C, w, Mauget; intr. 1827

'Pompon Blanc Parfait' ('Blanc Parfait') A, lp, 1876, Verdier, E.; flowers blush-white, small, dbl., pompon, borne in clusters, intense fragrance; occasional rebloom in fall; prickles very few; compact, upright (4 ft.) growth; intr. 1876

'Pompon Commun' -- See R. × centifolia pomponia

'Pompon de Bourgogne' ('Burgundian Rose', R. burgundiaca, R. parvifolia, R. remensis, R. pomponia, R. gallica remensis, R. ehrrhartiana, R. × centifolia parvifolia, 'Petite Chalons', 'Parvifolia', 'Parviflora', 'Cramoisi', R. provincialis minor, 'Burgundy Rose',) HGal, pb, before 1650; flowers deep pink suffused purple, center paler, 1 in., dbl., rosette; foliage dark gray-green; few prickles; compact (18 in.) growth

'Pompon de Bourgogne à Fleurs Blanches' HGal, w, 1827, Mauget; flowers pure white, flesh at center, very small, very dbl., cupped

'Pompon de Bretagne' S, dp, Adam; growth low; groundcover; intr. 1997

'Pompon de Kingston' C, lp, before 1817; flowers flesh pink, very small, full

'Pompon de Lyon' Pol, mp, 1912, Dubreuil; flowers bright carmine pink, small, cupped

'Pompon de Meaux' -- See R. × centifolia pomponia

'Pompon de Panachée' -- See 'Pompon Panachée'

'Pompon de Paris' Ch, mp, 1839; bud very pointed; flowers bright pink, very small, dbl.

'Pompon de Paris, Climbing' ('Rouletti, Climbing') Cl Ch, mp, about 1839; flowers bright pink, button-like, 3-4 cm., dbl., borne in small clusters, slight fragrance; scattered rebloom; foliage small, greyish-green; tall and arching, wiry canes, twiggy growth; [sport of 'Pompon de Paris']

'Pompon de St. Francis' -- See 'Pompon de Saint-François'

'Pompon de Saint-François' ('Petit St. François', 'St. Francis', 'Pompon de St. Francis') C, dp, about 1850, Robert; flowers deep violet-pink, small, dbl., globular; low, bushy growth

'Pompon des Dames' -- See 'Petite de Hollande'

'Pompon des Princes' -- See 'Ispahan'

Pompon Diadem® F, mp, Tantau; intr. 1984

'PomPon Flower Circus'

'PomPon Flower Circus' ('Pom Pom Flower Circus') F, mp, Kordes; flowers medium pink in center, fading to white on outer petals, full, deeply cupped, borne in clusters; recurrent; short growth; intr. 2008

'Pompon Moss' -- See 'Mossy Rose de Meaux'

'Pompon Mousseux' -- See 'Mossy Rose de Meaux'

'Pompon Panachée' ('Pompon de Panachée', 'Pompon', 'Pompon Robert') HGal, w, 1857, Robert et Moreau; flowers cream to white, striped light pink, well-formed, dbl., flat; foliage very small; wiry, erect growth

'Pompon Perpetual' -- See 'Bernard'

'Pompon Perpétuel' M, lp, 1849, Vibert; flowers delicate pink, 4-5 cm., full, rosette; sometimes repeats; sometimes classed as C or P

'Pompon Robert' -- See 'Pompon Panachée'

'Pompon Rose' -- See R. × centifolia pomponia

'Pompon Rouge' F, mr, 1971, Delforge; bud ovoid; flowers brilliant red, medium, very dbl.; foliage soft; dwarf, bushy growth; ['Reverence' × 'Miracle']

'Pompon Spong' -- See 'Spong'

'Pompon Varin' ('Centfeuilles Nain', 'Sara') C, mp, before 1819; flowers pink, darker in center, small, semi-dbl.; foliage oval-rounded

'Pompone Jaune' ('Minor', R. sulphurea nana, 'Sulphurea Nana', 'Yellow Pompon') Misc OGR, my, before 1806; flowers sulphur yellow, small, very dbl., globular; foliage small, close-set; nearly thornless; growth dwarf (2 ft.); [sport of *R. hemisphaerica*]; from France

Pomponella™ (Pomponella Fairy Tale™) F, dp, Kordes; bud small, rounded; flowers 4 cm., dbl., globular, borne in clusters of 5 - 7, slight fragrance; recurrent; foliage dark green, dense, semi-glossy; vigorous, upright (80 cm.) growth; intr. 2005

Pomponella Fairy Tale™ -- See 'Pomponella'

'Pomponia Muscosa' -- See 'Mossy Rose de Meaux'

'Ponalot' ('Miss Bloomsalot') S, op, 2006, Ponton, Ray; flowers 2 in., single, borne in small clusters; recurrent; foliage medium size, dark green, glossy, disease-resistant; prickles medium, straight, moderate; growth upright, medium (4 ft.); [('Paloma Blanca' × 'Hippolyte') × 'Baby Love']; intr. 2006

'Ponanita' ('Sarah Juanita') S, my, 2003, Ponton, Ray; flowers 3-4 in., dbl., borne in small clusters, moderate fragrance; recurrent; foliage medium size, dark green, glossy, disease-resistant; prickles medium, curved, few; growth compact, short (1-2 ft.); bedding, hedge, container; decorative hips; ['Lillian Austin' × 'Baby Love']; intr. 2003

'Ponanna' ('Deanna') S, pb, 2004, Ponton, Ray; flowers pink stripe, 3-4 in., single, borne mostly solitary, intense fragrance; foliage medium size, medium green, semi-glossy; prickles large, hooked, moderate; growth upright, medium (4 ft.); ['Carefree Beauty' × Fourth of July™]

'Ponark' ('After Dark') S, dr, 2004, Ponton, Ray; flowers dark red, 3-4 in., semi-dbl., borne mostly solitary, slight fragrance; foliage medium size, medium green, semi-glossy; prickles medium, curved; stems wine-colored; upright, medium (4 ft.) growth; ['Lillian Austin' × 'San Gabriel']

'Ponbohls' (Cameron Bohls™) S, dr, 2000, Ponton, Ray; flowers single, borne in small clusters; quick repeat; foliage medium size, dark green, glossy; prickles moderate; upright, medium growth; orange hips; ['Carefree Beauty' × Lichterloh®]

'Ponbriel' (San Gabriel™) S, yb, 2002, Ponton, Ray; flowers yellow-red, 2-3 cm., single, borne in small clusters, moderate fragrance; foliage medium green, semi-glossy; prickles medium, hooked, moderate; growth upright, medium (3-4 ft.); landscape; ['Katy Road Pink' × 'Reveil Dijonnaise']; intr. 2002

'Poncal' ('Callie Liane') MinFl, lp, 2007, Ponton, Ray; flowers blush pink, 2 in., full, borne in small clusters; foliage medium, dark green, semi-glossy; prickles medium, straight, moderate; growth compact, medium (2 ft.); [('Paloma Blanca' × 'Hippolyte') × Fourth of July™]; intr. 2008

'Poncet' -- See 'Masgrma'

'Poncheau-Capiaumont' ('Rosa Poncheaux', 'Rose Ponceau', 'Rose Poncheaux') HCh, dr; flowers borne in clusters of 3; foliage curiously stiff, thick, deeply veined

'Ponctué' HP, pb, before 1845, Laffay; flowers rose pink, spotted with lilac and white, medium, dbl., flat

'Ponctuée' M, pb, 1829, Hébert

'Ponctuée' M, pb, Laffay; flowers rose, spotted with white, large, very dbl.; intr. 1846

'Ponctuée' -- See 'Belle Herminie'

'Ponctuée' -- See 'Ma Ponctuée'

Ponderosa® HT, ab, Kordes; flowers creamy apricot, outer petals adding pink tone, medium, full, high-centered, borne mostly singly; good repeat; [sport of 'Sioux']; florist rose; intr. 2002

'Ponderosa' -- See 'Koredan'

Ponderosa® -- See 'Korpon'

'Pondora' ('Splendora') S, dp, 2004, Ponton, Ray; flowers uniform deep pink, medium, full, borne mostly solitary, slight fragrance; foliage medium size, light green, semi-glossy; prickles large and small, hooked; spreading, medium (4-5 ft.) growth; ['Lillian Austin' × 'San Gabriel']

'Pondream' ('Rustler's Dream') S, lp, 2006, Ponton, Ray; flowers very full, borne in small clusters; recurrent; foliage medium green, semi-glossy, disease-resistant; prickles medium, straight, moderate; growth compact, medium (4 ft.); ['(Paloma Blanca × Hippolyte)' × 'Baby Love']; intr. 2006

'Ponfest' ('Schulenfest') S, ly, 2006, Ponton, Ray; flowers full, borne mostly solitary; foliage dark green, semi-glossy; prickles medium, straight, moderate; growth compact, short (2 ft.); [Lilian Austin® × 'Schulenberg Apricot']; intr. 2006

'Pongirl' (Katy Girl™) S, lp, 2000, Ponton, Ray; flowers semi-dbl., borne mostly singly, slight fragrance; quick repeat; foliage medium size, medium green, disease-resistant; few prickles; bushy, tall (6 ft.) growth; landscape, short climber; ['Carefree Beauty' × unknown]; intr. 2000

'Pongold' ('Atocha Gold') S, my, 2006, Ray Ponton; flowers semi-dbl., borne mostly solitary; recurrent; foliage medium green, semi-glossy, disease-resistant; prickles medium, hooked, moderate; growth upright, spreading, medium; hips fragrant; ['Lillian Austin' × ('Carefree Beauty' × 'Reveil Dijonnaise')]; intr. 2006

'Poniatowska' -- See 'Belle Aurore'

'Poniatowsky' ('Elvire') HEg, lp, 1821, Cartier; flowers flesh pink, medium, semi-dbl.

'Ponjean' ('Margaret Jean') S, pb, 2006, Ponton, Ray; flowers deep pink, reverse light pink, 2-3 in., dbl., borne mostly solitary; foliage medium green, semi-glossy; prickles medium, straight, moderate; growth upright, short (2 ft.); ['Carefree Beauty' × Scentimental™]; intr. 2006

'Ponmer' ('Meredith Bohls') S, mp, 2003, Ponton, Ray; flowers medium, full, borne in small clusters, slight fragrance; foliage medium size, medium green, semi-glossy; prickles medium, straight, moderate; spreading, medium (3-4 ft.) growth; [Brass Band™ × Lichterloh®]; intr. 2003

'Ponnell' ('Annie Nell') S, mp, 2003, Ponton, Ray; flowers medium, full, borne in small clusters; foliage medium size, dark green, semi-glossy, disease-resistant; prickles medium, curved, moderate; growth upright, medium (4 ft.); specimen, hedge; ['Lillian Austin' × ('Carefree Beauty' × 'Reveil Dijonnaise')]

'Ponred' ('Ida Red') S, mr, 2006, Ponton, Ray; flowers full, borne mostly solitary and in small clusters; foliage medium size, medium green, semi-glossy; prickles medium, straight, moderate; growth upright, short (3 ft.); [Brass Band™ × Cameron Bohls™]; intr. 2006

'Ponreno' (Chireno™) S, dp, 2002, Ponton, Ray; flowers 3-4 in., single, borne mostly solitary; foliage medium size, medium green, semi-glossy; prickles medium, straight, few; growth upright, spreading, medium (4 ft.); landscape; ['Carefree Beauty' × 'Mutabilis']; intr. 2002

'Ponshen' ('Elizabeth of Goshen') S, m, 2007, Ponton, Ray; flowers 3 in., full, borne in small clusters; foliage medium, medium green, semi-glossy; prickles medium, straight, moderate; growth upright, medium (4 ft.); [('Paloma Blanca' × 'Hippolyte') × ("San Filipe Noisette" × Cameron Bohls™)]; intr. 2008

'Pont d'Avignon' F, or, Dot; flowers vermilion, non-fading, reflexed petals

'Pontbriant' HT, mp, 1948, Gaujard; flowers bright pink, very large, dbl.; foliage leathery; vigorous growth; ['Mme Joseph Perraud' × 'Kidwai']

'Pontcarral' HT, dp, 1943, Meilland, F.; bud long, pointed; flowers strawberry-red, reverse dull yellow, medium, semi-dbl., cupped; foliage leathery; moderate, bushy growth; ['Charles P. Kilham' × ('Charles P. Kilham' × 'Margaret McGredy')]

'Ponte d'Arrabida' HT, op, 1963, Moreira da Silva; flowers salmon-pink veined deep pink; ['Grand'mere Jenny' × seedling]

'Ponte Rosa' LCl, mr

'Ponte Salazar' F, Moreira da Silva, A.

'Pontejas' ('Tejas') LCl, pb, 2002, Ponton, Ray; flowers white to pink, 2 in., single, borne in small clusters; recurrent bloom; foliage medium size, medium green, semi-glossy; prickles medium, straight, moderate; growth upright, tall (10-12 ft.); pillar, fence; hips numerous; ['Katy Road Pink (Carefree Beauty)' × 'Reveil Dijonnais']; intr. 2003

'Pontevedra' HT, Moreira da Silva, A.; intr. 1969

'Pontiana' ('Aldégonde', 'Manteau Rouge', 'Manteau Pourpre', 'Violet Brillant', 'Pourpre Cramoisi', 'Du Pont', 'Belle Bourbon', 'André Du Pont', 'Grand Condé', 'Porcia') HGal, mr, before 1811

'Pontions' ('Peaceful Habitations') S, mp, 2001, Ponton, Ray; flowers show some striping with age, medium, semi-dbl., borne mostly solitary, moderate fragrance; foliage medium size, medium green, matte; prickles medium, straight, moderate; growth upright, medium; garden decorative; ['Folksinger' × Lichterloh®]; intr. 2000

'Pontrop' ('Baron de Bastrop') S, dr, 2004, Ponton, Ray; flowers single, borne in small clusters, slight fragrance; foliage medium size, light green, semi-glossy; prickles medium; spreading, medium (4 ft.) growth; ["San Felipe Noisette" × Cameron Bohls™]

'Pony' HGal, dr, before 1828, Deschiens; flowers cark crimson

'Pooh Bear' S, ab, Kordes; flowers deep apricot, outer petals fading to near white, medium, full, cupped, borne in small clusters, slight fragrance; free-flowering; foliage dark green, glossy; neat, compact, short growth; intr. 2003

Poopsie™ -- See 'Grefairlynn'

'Poornima' HT, ly, 1983, Pal, Dr. B.P.; bud long, pointed; flowers large, 46 petals, high-centered, borne singly, moderate fragrance; foliage medium size, medium green, smooth; bushy, tall growth; ['Fernand Arles' × seedling]; intr. 1971

'Pop Warner' HT, pb, 2000, Edwards, Eddie; flowers pink and white, 4-5 in., full, high-centered, borne mostly singly, slight fragrance; foliage medium green, semi-glossy; few prickles; growth upright, medium (4-5 ft.); [Crystalline™ × 'Fantasy']; intr. 2001

'Popcorn' Min, w, 1976, Morey, Dr. Dennison; bud ovoid; flowers pure white, 1 in., 13 petals, moderate honey fragrance; foliage glossy; upright growth; ['Katharina Zeimet' × 'Diamond Jewel']; intr. 1975

'Pope' D, dr, before 1844, Laffay; flowers crimson and purple, centers sometimes fiery, very large, full; growth branching

Pope John Paul II™ -- See 'Jacsegra'

'Pope Pius IX' -- See 'Pius IX'

'Pope Pius XI' -- See 'Pius XI'

'Poppet' F, mp, 1978, Bees; flowers large, 60 petals, cupped; foliage light green, matte; upright growth; ['Spartan' × 'Arthur Bell']; intr. 1979

'Poppi John' S, ab, 2005, Paul Chessum Roses; flowers dbl., borne in small clusters, slight fragrance; foliage medium size, dark green, semi-glossy; prickles large, red, numerous; growth upright, medium (4 ft.); bedding, containers; [seedling × seedling]; intr. 2005

'Popping White' Min, w, 1977, Lyon; bud ovoid; flowers 1 in., 12 petals; vigorous, compact growth

'Poppius' HSpn, mp, Steinberg; flowers deep pink, fading to lilac pink, semi-dbl., cupped, slight fragrance; few prickles; growth medium (3-4 ft.); hardy

'Poppy' HT, op, 1939, Archer; flowers coral-pink, passing to shell-pink, petals serrated, dbl., moderate fragrance; vigorous growth

'Poppy' F, or, Soenderhousen; flowers scarlet, 2-2½ in., semi-dbl., open, borne in clusters; very vigorous growth; ['Cocorico' × 'Geranium Red']; intr. 1960

'Poppy Flash' ('Rusticana') F, or, 1972, Meilland; flowers vermilion, 3 in., 20 petals, slight fruity fragrance; vigorous, bushy growth; [('Dany Robin' × 'Fire King') × ('Alain' × 'Mutabilis')]

'Poppy Flash, Climbing' ('Rusticana, Climbing') Cl F, or, 1976, Paolino; [sport of 'Poppy Flash']; intr. 1975

'Poppy Rose' -- See 'Grosse Mohnkopfs Rose'

'Pops' -- See 'Tinpops'

'Popsy' S, op, Peden, G.H.

Popular™ -- See 'Poulpal024(N)'

'Popular Palace' (Popular™) Min, ob, Poulsen; flowers orange and orange blend, 5 cm., dbl., no fragrance; foliage dark; growth broad, bushy, 40-60 cm.; intr. 2005

'Porcelain' F, lp, 1984, Gobbee, W.D.; flowers shell pink over cream, medium, semi-dbl.; foliage small, dark, semi-glossy; upright, bushy growth; ['Dainty Maid' × (('Tropicana' × 'Anna Wheatcroft') × ('Tropicana' × 'Anna Wheatcroft'))]

'Porcelain' -- See 'Korflüg'

'Porcelain Bouquet' -- See 'Interval'

'Porcelain Bride' HT, lp, Interplant; flowers soft pink, full, cupped; tall growth

Porcelain Panarosa™ S, lp, Kordes; flowers pale pink, center darker, full, high-centered; recurrent; very tall growth; intr. 2005

'Porcelain Pink' -- See 'Tinporce'

'Porcelain Princess' Min, pb, 1990, Gruenbauer, Richard; bud rounded; flowers cream with pale pink edging, aging light pink, medium, 35 petals, high-centered, borne in sprays of 2-3; foliage medium size, dark green, semi-glossy; prickles straight, tan; bushy, medium growth; hips oblong, orange-red; ['Libby' × seedling]

'Porcelaine' ('La Pyramidale', 'Pyramidale') HGal, lp, before 1815, Descemet; flowers light pink, aging white, large, semi-dbl.

'Porcelaine de Bayeux' S, lp, Adam; groundcover; spreading growth; intr. 2006

'Porcelaine de Chine' -- See 'Lenarvere'

'Porcelaine Royale' HGal, m, about 1840, Miellez; flowers lilac, marbled, small, full

'Porcelina' -- See 'Interval'

'Porcia' -- See 'Rouge Formidable'

Porsalino™ -- See 'Poulander'

'Port St John' HT, Herholdt; intr. 1974

'Port Sunlight' -- See 'Auslofty'

'Porta Nigra' HT, dr, Meilland; flowers large, dbl., moderate fragrance; intr. 1992

Porta Westfalica® F, dr

'Portadown' HT, dr, 1928, McGredy; bud long, pointed; flowers velvety deep crimson, large, dbl., high-centered; vigorous, bushy growth

'Portadown Bedder' HT, op, 1929, McGredy; bud long, pointed; flowers scarlet-cerise on orange ground, reverse orange-yellow flush, dbl., high-centered; foliage glossy, dark; vigorous, bushy growth

'Portadown Crimson' HT, dr, 1928, McGredy; flowers dark crimson, globular, moderate fragrance

'Portadown Fragrance' HT, op, 1931, McGredy; bud long, pointed; flowers brilliant orange-salmon-pink, flushed orange-scarlet, dbl., high-centered, intense fragrance; foliage thick, bronze; low, sprawling growth

'Portadown Glory' HT, my, 1932, McGredy; flowers clear canary-yellow, well-formed, large, dbl.; foliage glossy, bright; vigorous growth

'Portadown Glow' -- See 'Portadown Yellow'

'Portadown Ivory' -- See 'McGredy's Ivory'

'Portadown Sally' HT, mr, 1931, McGredy; bud long, pointed; flowers crimson-carmine, base yellow, reverse sulfur-yellow, semi-dbl., high-centered; foliage thick, glossy; vigorous growth

'Portadown Scarlet' HT, mr, 1927, McGredy; flowers scarlet

'Portadown Yellow' ('Portadown Glow') HT, my, 1927, McGredy; flowers chrome yellow, shaded golden yellow, medium, very dbl., moderate fragrance

'Portail Rouge' LCl, mr, Combe, C.; flowers crimson, 4 in., moderate fragrance; intr. 1973

'Portchester Pink' HT, dp, 1979, Poole, K. E.; flowers deep rose-pink, intense fragrance; [sport of 'Red Devil']

'Porthos, Climbing' Cl F, or, Laperrière; [sport of Porthos®]; intr. 1976

Porthos® F, or, Laperrière; intr. 1971

'Portia' HT, lp, 1910, Paul, W.; flowers pale rose, center yellow, large, full

'Portia' HT, mr, Bees; flowers nasturtium-red, paling to pink, dbl., moderate fragrance; ['Bridesmaid' × 'Sunburst']; intr. 1921

'Portland' HT, dp, 1958, Lowe; flowers rose-madder, large, dbl.; foliage dark, glossy; vigorous, symmetrical growth; intr. 1958

'Portland Blanc' P, w, 1836, Vibert; flowers medium, full, flat

'Portland Crimson Monthly Rose' -- See 'Duchess of Portland'

'Portland Dawn' -- See 'Seatip'

'Portland from Glendora' -- See 'Johasine Hanet'

'Portland Pink'   F, dp, 1957, Murrel, E.; flowers glowing deep pink; [sport of 'Pinocchio']

'Portland Pourpre'   P, dp, about 1830, Prévost; flowers deep bright crimson, medium, semi-dbl.

'Portland Rose' -- See 'Duchess of Portland'

'Portland Rose Festival' -- See 'Dorjure'

'Portland Trailblazer' -- See 'Big Chief'

'Portlandia'   LCl, pb, Clements, John; flowers golden apricot center shading to pink and cream, 3½-4 in., 80 petals, borne in good size clusters, moderate fruity fragrance; foliage dark green, leathery; stems long; growth climbing (8-10 ft.); PPAF; intr. 2002

'Portmeirion' -- See 'Ausguard'

'Porto'   HT, dr, 1934, Mallerin, C.; flowers deep garnet tinted bright scarlet, large, dbl.; foliage leathery; vigorous growth; ['Capt. F. Bald' × 'Mrs Edward Powell']

'Portofino'   F, rb, 1964, Delforge; flowers red, reverse deep yellow; low growth; ['Miramar' × seedling]

'Portofino'   Min, w, Adam; flowers white with thin, bright fuchsia pink edges, full; free-flowering; growth to 10-12 in.; intr. 2006

'Portrait' ('Stéphanie de Monaco') HT, pb, 1971, Meyer, C.; bud ovoid; flowers medium pink and light pink blend, medium, dbl., high-centered, moderate fragrance; good repeat; foliage glossy, dark; growth upright, bushy; PP3097; ['Pink Parfait' × Pink Peace®]

'Portrait of Jenny'   F, dr, 1951, Hope; flowers crimson, 2 in., 30 petals, borne in trusses; foliage dark; vigorous, bushy growth; ['Donald Prior' × unknown]

'Portuense'   HP, m, 1890, da Costa; flowers purple

'Portugal Pink'   HT, dp, 1959, Mondial Roses; bud globular; flowers deep pink, large, dbl., cupped; foliage leathery; vigorous, upright growth; ['Independence' × seedling]

'Post Office'   F, rb, J&P; intr. 1997

Postillion® -- See 'Kortionza'

'Postillon'   HT, ab, 1962, Verbeek; flowers coppery yellow, large, dbl.; foliage glossy; moderate growth; ['Peace' × seedling]

'Posy'   F, pb, 1951, LeGrice; flowers clear pink, reverse deeper, 3 in., 30 petals, borne in large clusters; foliage dark; dwarf growth; ['Rosenelfe' × 'Dusky Maiden']

'Pot Black' -- See 'Peanut'

'Pot o' Gold' -- See 'Dicdivine'

'Potager du Dauphin'   HRg, mp, 1899, Gravereaux

'Potch Pearl' -- See 'Hertroci'

'Potifar' ('Wieteke van Dordt') HT, ab, 1985, Poulsen, Niels D.; flowers pale peachy orange, large, 25 petals, urn-shaped, borne usually singly, slight fragrance; foliage large, leathery, dark green, matte; bushy growth; [Royal Dane™ × 'Pjerrot']; intr. 1979

'Potluck' -- See 'Lavpot'

Potluck Blue™ -- See 'Lavnova'

Potluck Cream™ -- See 'Lavcream'

Potluck Crimson® -- See 'Lavson'

Potluck Frosty® Min, w

Potluck Gold™ -- See 'Lavgold'

Potluck Orange™ -- See 'Lavjack'

Potluck Pink™ -- See 'Lavalot'

Potluck Purple™   Min, dr, 1992, Laver, Keith G.; flowers fuchsia, 1½ in., dbl., borne in small clusters, no fragrance; foliage small, medium green, matte; few prickles; micro-mini; low (25-30 cm.), compact growth; [(June Laver™ × Painted Doll™) × Springwood Purple™]

Potluck Red™ -- See 'Lavmin'

Potluck White™ -- See 'Lavwyte'

Potluck Yellow™ -- See 'Lavglo'

'Potter & Moore' -- See 'Auspot'

'Potton Heritage' -- See 'Harsprice'

'Poubicarbe' ('Chipie') F, ab, 1978, Poulsen, Niels D.; flowers rose-begonia to apricot, open, 4 in., 24 petals; foliage light green; bushy growth; [(Elizabeth of Glamis® × ('Heidelberg' × '8366-2')) × (Pernille Poulsen™ × ('Danish Gold' × 'Mischief'))]; intr. 1974

'Poudola'   F, pb, 1978, Poulsen, Niels D.; intr. 1974

'Poudunclub'   S, dp, Poulsensingle; intr. 1998

'Pouganda' (Springs 75™) F, dp, 1978, Poulsen, Niels D.; intr. 1975

'Poulac002'   MinFl, yb, Poulsen; bud short, globular; intr. 2000

'Poulac003(N)' ('Dream Palace') S, my, Poulsen; intr. 2000

'Poulac004(N)' (Anjou™, Sweet Chariot™) S, mr, Poulsen; intr. 2002

'Poulac005(N)' ('Roman Palace') S, op, Poulsen; intr. 2001

'Poulac006'   S, or, Poulsen; intr. 2001

'Poulac007' (Aladdin™) MinFl, ab, Poulsen; intr. 2002

'Poulac008(N)' (Duke of Edinburgh™) F, dy, Olesen; intr. 2003

'Poulac009(N)' (Capitoule™) MinFl, dr, Poulsen; intr. 2002

'Poulac010' (Spring™) MinFl, mp, Olesen; bud pointed ovoid; intr. 2003

'Poulac011(N)' (Flirting™) MinFl, mr, Olesen; bud pointed-ovoid with broadened base; intr. 2003

'Poulac012(N)' (Mermaid™) Min, or, Poulsen; intr. 2003

'Poulac013(N)' (Spectacular™) MinFl, ab, Poulsen; intr. 2003

'Poulac014(N)' (Amazing™) MinFl, ab, Poulsen; bud pointed ovoid; intr. 2004

'Poulac015(N)' (Regina™) MinFl, mp, Olesen; bud globular; intr. 2002

'Poulac016(N)' (Bordeaux™) MinFl, mr, Poulsen; intr. 2004

'Poulac017(N)' (Rialto™) MinFl, w, Poulsen; intr. 2002

'Poulac018(N)' (Gloria™) MinFl, lp, Olesen; bud broad based ovoid; intr. 2003

'Poulache' (Peach™) MinFl, ab, Poulsen; intr. 2000

'Poulagun' ('Laguna Palace') S, ab, 1999, Poulsen; intr. 1998

'Poulaksel' (Sunburst Border™) S, dy, Poulsen; intr. 2000

'Poulalo' (Coral Border™, Coral Gables™) S, op, Poulsen; bud pointed, ovoid to globular; intr. 1998

'Poulals'   Min, rb, Olesen; intr. 1996

'Poulamb' -- See 'Apricot Hit'

'Poulander' ('Hans Christian Andersen', America's Choice™, H. C. Andersen™, Porsalino™, Touraine™) F, dr, 1987, Olesen, Pernille & Mogens N.; flowers large, semi-dbl., cupped, borne in sprays of 1-25, slight fragrance; foliage medium size, dark green, glossy; bushy, tall growth; PP6265; ['Royal Occasion' × seedling]; intr. 1979

'Poulanit' (Martina™) MinFl, dr, Poulsen; intr. 1998

'Poulanlis'   S, mr, Poulsen; intr. 1998

'Poulann' (Queen™) Min, dp, Poulsen; intr. 1996

'Poulans' (Gaby Cover™, Martha's Vineyard™) S, dp, 1995, Olesen, Pernille & Mogens N.; flowers hot pink, blending to white at center, 2-4 in., dbl., borne in small clusters; foliage small, light green, semi-glossy; few prickles; spreading (36 in.) growth, tall, vigorous; PP9664; intr. 1995

'Poulaps' ('White Knights', Château Angelus™, Armorique™, White Nights™) S, ly, 1985, Olesen, Pernille & Mogens N.; bud long, pointed; flowers light, creamy yellow to white, 10-15 cm., full, high-centered, urn-shaped, borne singly and in clusters of up to 5, moderate fragrance; recurrent; foliage large, leathery, dark, glossy; tall, upright, bushy growth; [seedling × 'Kalahari']; intr. 1985

'Poularbso' (Soraya™) MinFl, mp, Poulsen; intr. 2000

'Poulari' ('Susan Blixen', Isis™, Karen Blixen™, Roy Black™, Silver Anniversary™) HT, w, 1994, Poulsen Roser APS; flowers 3-3½ in., very dbl., borne in small clusters; foliage large, medium green, glossy; some prickles; medium (60-80 cm.), upright growth; PP9274; intr. 1994

'Poulart' ('Prince de Monaco', Modern Art™) HT, rb, 1985, Olesen, Pernille & Mogens N.; bud medium, pointed; flowers scarlet, reverse silvery with red wash, 3½-4 in., 25 petals, high-centered, borne singly and several together in large sprays; foliage medium size, dark, matte; upright, bushy (4 ft.) growth; hips small ; PP5646; [seedling × seedling]; intr. 1983

'Poulasor' (Drottningholm™) F, lp, Poulsen; intr. 2000

'Poulattra' (Baton Rouge™) S, dr, Poulsen; intr. 2000

'Poulave' ('Apricot Cottage Rose') S, ab, Poulsen; intr. 1991

'Poulavon' ('Nova Hit') Min, lp, Poulsen; intr. 1996

'Poulbambe' (Taos™) S, ab, Olesen; bud

ovate; intr. 2001

'Poulbao' ('Bravo Parade') Min, mr, Poulsen; intr. 1998

'Poulbella' ('Berleburg Castle', Bewitched™, Memory Lane™, Jasper™, Herrenchiemsee™, Cuyahoga™, 'Fuchsia Pink Castle') F, dp, Poulsen; intr. 1996

'Poulbells' (Pink Bells™) Min, dp, 1984, Poulsen Roser APS; flowers deep pink, small, 35 petals; foliage small, medium green, semi-glossy; groundcover; spreading growth; [Mini-Poul® × 'Temple Bells']; intr. 1983

'Poulberin' (Bering™, Eleanor™) S, m, Poulsen; intr. 1997

'Poulbero' (Solitude™) Gr, ob, 1991, Olesen, Pernille & Mogens N.; bud large, elongated; flowers orange-yellow with red on petal edges, 4½-5 in., 20-23 petals, cupped, borne singly and in clusters of 3 - 10, slight spicy fragrance; recurrent; foliage medium size, medium green, semi-glossy; prickles few to moderate, medium size, tan; medium (4 ft.), bushy growth; PP8230; ['Selfridges' × seedling]; intr. 1992

'Poulberty' (Liberty™) MinFl, ob, Poulsen; intr. 2000

'Poulbian' Min, w, Olesen; intr. 1996

'Poulbico' (Candy Cover™, Christopher Columbus™) S, rb, Poulsen; intr. 1996

'Poulbon' (Bonbon™) MinFl, yb, Poulsen; intr. 1992

'Poulbota' LCl, w, Olesen; intr. 1999

'Poulbrez' (Breeze™) Min, ab, Poulsen

'Poulbrido(N)' (Paul Red Star™, The Jubilee Rose™, True Love™) HT, dr, Poulsen; intr. 2000

'Poulbright' F, or, Poulsen; intr. 1985

'Poulbufi' ('Bushfire') S, ob, Poulsen

'Poulbut' (Butterflies Cover™, Telluride™) S, pb, Poulsen; intr. 1998

'Poulcape' (Summer™) S, w, Olesen; bud pointed; intr. 1998

'Poulcar' (Pink™, Rosy Paillette™) Min, pb, Poulsen; intr. 1996

'Poulcas018(N)' S, w, Olesen; bud urceolate; intr. 2004

'Poulcas022(N)' S, or, Poulsen; intr. 2005

'Poulcas023(N)' S, ab, Poulsen; intr. 2005

'Poulcas024(N)' S, pb, Olesen; bud urceolate with pointed apex; intr. 2005

'Poulcas025(N)' F, my, Poulsen; intr. 2005

'Poulcas026(N)' (Ronda ™) MinFl, mr, Poulsen; intr. 2005

'Poulcat' (Caterpillar™, Charming Bells™, Kiki Rose™, Pink Drift™) S, lp, 1985, Olesen, Pernille & Mogens N.; flowers small, dbl., borne in large trusses, no fragrance; foliage small, dark, glossy; growth broad, bushy, tall (100-150 cm.); ['Temple Bells' × seedling]; intr. 1984

'Poulchris' ('Imperial Palace') F, mr, Olesen, L. & M.; bud globular; intr. 1996

'Poulclaus' ('Santa Claus') Min, dr, 1991, Olesen, Pernille & Mogens N.; bud long, well-formed; sepals sepal insides tinted red; flowers velvety dark red, medium, dbl., high-centered, borne mostly singly, slight fragrance; foliage medium size, dark green, glossy; few prickles; medium (50-60 cm.), upright, bushy growth; PP9063; ['floribunda seedling' × 'miniature seedling']; intr. 1995

'Poulclimb' (Berries 'n' Cream™, Calypso™, Concert™) LCl, pb, 1999, Olesen; flowers pink striped white, reverse same, 4-5 in., full, borne in large clusters, moderate apple fragrance; foliage large, medium green, glossy; few prickles; climbing, tall (10-12 ft.) growth; PP10639; ['Evita' × seedling]

'Poulcolop' Min, yb, Poulsen Roser; intr. 2000

'Poulcot' ('Apricot Medinette', 'Apricot Midinette', 'Patio Flame') Min, ab, 1985, Olesen, Pernille & Mogens N.; flowers apricot-orange, well-formed, small, 20 petals, borne in clusters; foliage leathery, glossy; prickles brown; spreading growth; [Mini-Poul® × 'Mary Sumner']; intr. 1984

'Poulcot001' (Meadow™) S, my, Olesen; bud ovate; intr. 2004

'Poulcot003' (Bay ™) S, dp, Poulsen; intr. 2004

'Poulcot005' (Marsh™) S, dp, Olesen; bud ovate, red; intr. 2005

'Poulcot006' (Lake™) S, lp, Olesen; bud ovate, deep pink; intr. 2004

'Poulcot007' (Heather™) S, mr, Poulsen; intr. 2005

'Poulcot008' (Hill ™) S, w, Poulsen; intr. 2004

'Poulcov' ('Sparkler', Latina™, Pyrenees™, Sparkling White™, White Cover™) S, w, Olesen; bud ovate; intr. 1991

'Poulcrack' ('Crackerjack') F, ob, Olesen; intr. 1989

'Poulcrem' ('Perfect Day') F, w, Poulsen; intr. 2001

'Poulcrim' ('Crimson Medinette', 'Patio Prince') Min, dr, 1985, Olesen, Pernille & Mogens; flowers small, 33 petals, borne in clusters of 3-5, no fragrance; foliage small, leathery; prickles straight brown; dense growth; [seedling × Pygmae®]; intr. 1984

'Poulcs001' ('Abendglut™) F, dr, Olesen; intr. 2000

'Poulcs002' F, w, Poulsen; intr. 2000

'Poulcs003(N)' (Acadia™) F, ab, Olesen; bud long; intr. 2001

'Poulcs004(N)' ('Ledreborg Castle', Rastede™, 'White Castle') F, w, Poulsen; intr. 2001

'Poulcs005(N)' F, dr, Olesen; bud pointed ovoid; intr. 2002

'Poulcs006(N)' ('Lilac Castle') F, m, Poulsen; intr. 2002

Poulcs007N F, mp, Olesen; bud broad based ovoid; intr. 2003

'Poulcs008(N)' (Colchester™) F, yb, Olesen; bud long, pointed ovoid; intr. 2002

'Poulcs009(N)' F, op, Olesen; bud broad based ovoid; intr. 2003

'Poulcs010(N)' F, or, Olesen; bud pointed ovoid; intr. 2003

'Poulcs011(N)' F, ab, Olesen; bud short, pointed, broad-based; intr. 2003

'Poulcs012(N)' F, my, Poulsen

'Poulcs014(N)' F, w, Poulsen; intr. 2003

'Poulcs015(N)' S, lp, Poulsen; intr. 2003

'Poulcs016(N)' S, mp, Poulsen; bud pointed ovoid; intr. 2003

Poulcs017N S, w, Olesen; bud pointed ovoid; intr. 2003

'Poulcub' (Tiger Cub™) Min, yb, Olesen; intr. 1998

'Poulyc010' LCl, lp, Poulsen; intr. 2004

'Poulcy011' LCl, mp, Poulsen; intr. 2004

'Poulcy012' ('Merengue') LCl, mr, Olesen; bud pointed ovoid, broad base; intr. 2004

'Pouldacen' ('Sundance') MinFl, dy, Olesen ; bud blunt to ovoid; intr. 1999

'Pouldahle' F, pb, Poulsen; intr. 2001

'Pouldani' Min, pb, Olesen; intr. 1998

'Pouldata' (Memory ™) MinFl, ob, Poulsen; intr. 2000

'Pouldava' ('Augusta') S, ab, 1995, Olesen, Pernille & Mogens N.; flowers peach, 2-3 in., dbl.; foliage small, medium green, dull; some prickles; low (24 in.), spreading growth; intr. 1995

'Pouldel' (Pure™) MinFl, w, Poulsen; bud short; intr. 1996

'Pouldiram' (Diamond Border™) S, w, Poulsen; intr. 1997

'Pouldol' (Springs 75™) F, dp, 1978, Poulsen, Niels D.; intr. 1975

'Pouldom' (Gold Reef™) F, dy, Poulsen; intr. 1998

'Pouldotage' ('Addo Heritage') HT, pb, Poulsen

'Pouldra' ('Princesse Alexandra', Alexandra™, 'The Ridge School') S, dp, Olesen, P. & M.; intr. 1997

'Pouldrik' (Bryce Canyon™, Frederiksborg™) F, op, Poulsen; intr. 1998

'Pouldron' ('Peach Castle', Coral Palace™, 'Viking Princess', Schackenborg™, Rosenburg Riederburg™, Imagination™, Countess Celeste™, Gute Besserung™) S, op, 1999, Poulsen Roser APS; flowers coral pink, old-fashioned form, 2½-3 in., very dbl., borne in small clusters, moderate fragrance; foliage medium size, dark green, glossy; prickles moderate; compact, rounded low (20-24 in.) growth; PP10923; [Queen Margrethe™ × seedling]

'Poulduce' ('Chateau Pavie', Tivoli 150™, 'Tivoli Gardens', 'Tivoli') HT, my, 1994, Olesen, Pernille & Mogens N.; flowers soft yellow, 4-5 in., 50-65 petals, cupped, borne in small clusters, slight fragrance; recurrent; foliage large, dark green, semi-glossy; some prickles; tall (100-150 cm.), spreading growth; intr. 1995

'Poulduf' ('Roy Castle Rose') HT, dr, Poulsen; intr. 1998

'Pouldunk(N)' (Kaj Munk™) HT, my, Poulsen

'Pouldyb' (Fantasy™) MinFl, dr, Poulsen; intr. 1993

'Pouleas' (Easy Cover™, Pebble Beach™, Sparkling Pink™) S, mp, Poulsen; intr. 1996

'Pouledel' (Edelweiss™) F, w, 1971, Poulsen, Niels D.; intr. 1970

'Pouleden' Min, mp, Olesen; intr. 1996

'Poulege' (Shenandoah™, Søren Kanne™) F, op, 1999, Poulsen; intr. 1996

'Poulelap' (Queen's™) S, mp, Poulsen; bud pointed to ovoid; intr. 1997

'Poulemb' ('Cliffs of Dover', Cliffs of Dover Cover™) S, w, 1995, Olesen, Pernille & Mogens N.; flowers white, bright yellow stamens, 1-1½ in., 5 petals, borne in small clusters, no fragrance; foliage small, dark green, glossy; few prickles; low (36 in.), arching, spreading growth; PP9650; [seedling × seedling]; intr. 1995

'Poulen001' ('Susan Renaissance', Gettysburg™) S, w, Poulsen; intr. 2000

'Poulen002' ('Solo Mio', Rita Barbera™, Sophia™) S, dy, Olesen; bud long, pointed; intr. 1999

'Poulen003(N)' (Chloe™, Hjemmerosen™) S, lp, Poulsen; intr. 2001

'Poulen005(N)' (Sandra™) S, m, Poulsen; bud pointed ovoid; intr. 2002

'Poulen006(N)' (Lina™) S, w, Poulsen; intr. 2002

'Poulen007(N)' (Nadia™) S, dr, Olesen; bud broad based, ovoid; intr. 2002

'Poulen008(N)' ('Melany', Amie™) S, lp, Poulsen; bud ovoid; intr. 2002

'Poulen009(N)' (Bonita™, The St. Edmund's Rose™) S, pb, Olesen; bud pointed ovoid; intr. 2001

'Poulen010(N)' (Maria™) S, dp, Olesen; bud broad based pointed ovoid; intr. 2002

'Poulen011(N)' (Amelia™) S, ab, Poulsen; intr. 2002

'Poulen012(N)' (Sissel™) S, lp, Poulsen; bud pointed ovoid; intr. 2003

'Poulena' ('Jarlina') HT, yb, 1978, Poulsen, Niels D.; intr. 1976

'Poulense' ('Little Miss Muffet') Cl Min, ly, Olesen; intr. 1995

'Poulerry' (Cherry Cover®) S, dp, Poulsen; bud elongated, pointed-ovoid; intr. 2000

'Poulesta' (Fiesta™) Min, dp, Poulsen; bud pointed ovoid; intr. 1999

'Pouletta' ('Henrietta') HT, ab, 1986, Olesen, Pernille & Mogens N.; flowers large, 25 petals, urn-shaped, borne singly, slight fruity fragrance; foliage large, dark, glossy; vigorous, upright, bushy growth; [seedling × ('Pink Nordia' × 'Sonny Boy')]; intr. 1984

'Poulezy' (Frosty Paillette™, Frosty ™) Min, w, Poulsen; intr. 1998

'Poulfair' ('Gelbe The Fairy', Yellow Fairy™) S, my, 1989, Olesen, Pernille & Mogens N.; flowers medium yellow, outer petals fading lighter, 5-8 cm., double, cupped, borne in clusters, very slight fragrance; recurrent; foliage small, light green, semi-glossy; bushy (60-100 cm.) growth; no hips; ['Texas' × 'The Fairy']; intr. 1988

'Poulfame' MinFl, mp, Olesen; intr. 1999

'Poulfan' ('Cape Cod', 'Johannesburg Garden Club', 'Rosenreigen') S, lp, 1995, Olesen, Pernille & Mogens N.; flowers soft pink, 2-3 in., 5 petals, borne in large clusters; foliage small, medium green, semi-glossy; few prickles; medium (36-42 in.), spreading growth; PP9641; intr. 1995

'Poulfancy' (Fancy™) MinFl, or, Poulsen; intr. 1994

'Poulfect' (Perfect Paillette™, Perfect™) MinFl, op, Poulsen; bud short, pointed ovoid; intr. 1996

'Poulfeld' (Gråsten™) F, w, Poulsen; intr. 1996

'Poulfi' (Alfi™, Elfin®) Min, dp, 1986, Olesen, Pernille & Mogens N.; flowers soft lavendar to pink, small, 40-45 petals, borne in large clusters and candelabras, no fragrance; foliage small, light green, glossy; compact growth, free flowering; PP5058; [Mini-Poul® × 'Harriet Poulsen']; intr. 1981

'Poulfio' (Fiona Old™) Min, rb, Poulsen; intr. 1998

'Poulfiry' ('Loving Wishes', Fiery™) MinFl, ob, Poulsen

'Poulfl001(N)' F, dr, Olesen; bud pointed ovoid, broad base; intr. 2003

'Poulfl002(N)' F, pb, Poulsen; intr. 2003

'Poulfl003(N)' F, ab, Olesen; bud pointed ovoid; intr. 2004

'Poulflag' MinFl, ob, Olesen; intr. 2001

'Poulflash' ('Flashdance') HT, my, 1985, Olesen, Pernille & Mogens N.; flowers urn-shaped, large, dbl., borne singly, slight fragrance; foliage large, medium green, semi-glossy; upright growth; ['Berolina' × seedling]; intr. 1984

'Poulfolk' ('Norfolk') S, my, Poulsendbl.; intr. 1990

'Poulfre' ('Fresh Hit') Min, dp, Poulsen; intr. 1990

'Poulfuna' Min, dp, Poulsen Roser; intr. 1995

'Poulfyl' LCl, mp, Poulsen; intr. 2001

'Poulgan' ('City Lights') MinFl, dy, Poulsen; intr. 1992

'Poulgav' (Buck's Fizz™, Candide™, Gavnø™) F, ob, 1989, Olesen, Pernille & Mogens N.; flowers orange, medium, 20 petals, no fragrance; foliage medium size, dark green, glossy; bushy growth; [seedling × 'Mary Sumner']; intr. 1988

'Poulgelb' (Sunset™) Min, dy, Poulsen; intr. 1996

'Poulgewfa' ('Gwen Fagan') S, lp, Poulsen; intr. 1992

'Poulgildo' MinFl, my, Poulsen; intr. 2000

'Poulglow' -- See 'Everglow'

'Poulgo001' MinFl, w, Poulsen; intr. 2000

'Poulgo002' Min, lp, Poulsen; intr. 2000

'Poulgo003' MinFl, pb, Poulsen; intr. 2000

'Poulgo004' MinFl, mr, Poulsen; intr. 2000

'Poulgo005' MinFl, my, Poulsen; intr. 2000

'Poulgo006' MinFl, mp, Poulsen; intr. 2002

'Poulgode' ('Kinpai', Golden Cover™, Sparkling Yellow™, Suffolk™, Yellow Cover™) S, my

'Poulgold' (Golden™) MinFl, dy, Poulsen; intr. 1996

'Poulgrad' ('Grand Palace') S, dr, Poulsen; intr. 1998

'Poulgrandel' S, dp, Poulsen; intr. 2004

'Poulgren' F, w, Poulsen; intr. 1982

'Poulgrena' (Dr Ingrid™, Grenadine™, Dronning Ingrid™) HT, ob, Poulsen; intr. 2001

'Poulgret' (Hampton Palace®) MinFl, w, Poulsen; intr. 1996

'Poulhappy' (Charming™) Min, or, Poulsen

'Poulharmu' (Manhattan™, Schwarzwaldfeuer™) S, mr, Olesen; bud pointed-ovoid; intr. 2000

'Poulheart' (Julia™, Phillipa™) S, lp, Olesen; intr. 1996

'Poulhi001' Min, my, Poulsen; intr. 2000

'Poulhi002' Min, pb, Olesen

'Poulhi003' Min, dy, Olesen

'Poulhi004(N)' (Magic™) MinFl, rb, Poulsen; intr. 2001

'Poulhi005(N)' (Valentina™) Min, mr, Poulsen; intr. 2001

'Poulhi006(N)' (Marianne™) MinFl, my, Poulsen; intr. 2001

'Poulhi008(N)' ('Tiffany Hit') S, mp, Poulsen; intr. 2001

'Poulhi009(N)' ('Madonna Hit') MinFl, ab, Poulsen; intr. 2001

'Poulhi011(N)' ('Diamond Wishes', 'Misty Hit') Min, mp, Olesen; bud pointed ovoid

'Poulhi012(N)' (Jolanda™) MinFl, w, Olesen; bud short, pointed ovoid; intr. 2002

'Poulhi013(N)' (Maxima™) MinFl, ob, Olesen; bud pointed ovoid; intr. 2002

'Poulhi014(N)' ('Elegance Hit') Min, or, Olesen; bud short, pointed ovoid; intr. 2003

'Poulhi015(N)' ('Feminine Hit') Min, pb, Olesen; bud pointed ovoid; intr. 2003

'Poulhi016(N)' (Amor™) Min, dr, Olesen; bud globular; intr. 2003

'Poulhi017(N)' ('Kimberley Hit') S, dp, Poulsen; intr. 2002

'Poulhi018(N)' ('Toledo Hit') S, yb, Poulsen; intr. 2003

'Poulhi019(N)' ('Cornelia Patiohit', Cornelia™) MinFl, my, Poulsen; intr. 2003

'Poulhi020' ('Lafayette Hit', 'Lafayette Patio Hit') S, ab, Olesen; bud globular; intr. 2003

'Poulhi021(N)' (Jennifer Patiohit™, Jennifer™) MinFl, dr, Olesen; bud pointed

ovoid; intr. 2003
'Poulhilda' ('Annette Hit') MinFl, mp, Olesen; intr. 1998
'Poulhit' ('Red Hit') Min, dr, 1985, Olesen, Pernille & Mogens N.; flowers small, 20 petals, no fragrance; foliage small, dark, matte; low, bushy, compact growth; [Mini-Poul® × seedling]; intr. 1984
'Poulholm' (Hørsholm By-Rose™, New Fashion™, Surrey™) S, op, Olesen; intr. 1990
'Poulht001(N)' (Remember™) HT, lp, Olesen; bud pointed ovoid
'Poulht002(N)' ('Bitten Clausen') HT, ab, Poulsen; intr. 2003
'Poulht003(N)' HT, ab, Poulsen; bud long, pointed ovoid; intr. 2003
'Poulht006' ('Wedding Celebration') HT, dr, Olesen; intr. 2006
'Poulhult' LCl, my, Poulsen; intr. 2000
'Poulhyr' (Cherry™) Min, dp, Poulsen; intr. 1999
'Poulidor' S, yb, Adam; intr. 2003
'Poulina' Min, lp; intr. 1996
'Poulink' ('Pink Hit') Min, mp, 1988, Olesen, Pernille & Mogens N.; flowers small, 6-14 petals; foliage small, medium green, semi-glossy; bushy, compact, even, abundant growth; [seedling × seedling]; intr. 1986
'Poulion' ('Fashion Parade') Min, mp, Poulsen; intr. 1996
'Poulisab' ('Isabella', 'Isabelle Renaissance', Isabel™) S, dr, Poulsen; intr. 1995
'Poulit' ('Angel Eve', Baby Grand™) Min, mp, 1994, Poulsen Roser APS; flowers clear pink, medium, full, quartered, borne in small clusters, slight fragrance; foliage small, medium green, matte, very disease-resistant; some prickles; low (25-30 cm.), bushy, compact, rounded growth; [Egeskov™ × seedling]; intr. 1995
'Pouljenjoy' ('Jennifer Joy') Min, lp, 1985, Olesen, Pernille & Mogens N.; flowers 75 petals, borne in clusters, no fragrance; foliage light green; compact, low, bushy growth; [Mini-Poul® × seedling]; intr. 1983
'Pouljill' ('Belle Renaissance', Child of Achievement™, Bella™) S, my; intr. 1995
'Pouljoey' ('Joey's ™) S, ab, Poulsen; intr. 1997
'Pouljol' Min, my, Olesen
'Pouljose' (José Carreras™) HT, w, Poulsen; intr. 2001
'Pouljub' ('Poulsen's Jubilaeumsrose') Min, yb, 1985, Poulsen, Niels D.; flowers deep pink and yellow blend, 28 petals, borne in clusters; foliage dark, glossy; upright growth; ['Darling Flame' × seedling]; intr. 1978
'Poulkalm' ('Apricot Castle', Bavaria München™, Kalmar™) F, ab, Poulsen; intr. 1999
'Poulkardi' MinFl, dr, Olesen
'Poulkaro' ('Karoo') F, or, 1988, Poulsen Roser APS; flowers orange-red, aging watermelon-pink, medium, 32 petals, borne in sprays, no fragrance; good repeat; foliage medium size, medium green, very hardy; prickles concave, yellow-brown; neat, medium, densely branched growth; [seedling × seedling]; intr. 1988
'Poulkini' ('Chateau Montrose™, Nashira™) F, lp, Poulsen; intr. 1995
'Poulkir' ('Kirsten') HT, lp, Poulsen; intr. 1985
'Poulkrid' LCl, w, Poulsen; intr. 2000
'Poulkrue' Min, ob, Olesen; intr. 2000
'Poullack' ('Kirsch, Climbing', 'Lakeland Princess', 'Vintage Wine') Cl HT, rb, 1983, Poulsen, Niels D.; flowers burgundy red, straw-yellow reverse, large, 40 petals, high-centered, slight old rose fragrance; foliage large, moss green; prickles red when new, then tan; pillar (8-10 ft.) growth; [Royal Dane™ × 'Arthur Bell']; intr. 1983
'Poullak' (Wonder™) Min, pb, Poulsen; intr. 1996
'Poulland' (Wagtail Cover™, Wagtail™) S, w; intr. 1994
'Poullen' (Gentle Cover™, Little Bo-Peep™, Natchez™, White Carpet™) Min, mp, 1994, Olesen, Pernille & Mogens N.; flowers small, full, borne in small clusters; foliage small, dark green; few prickles; low (65 cm.), compact growth; patio; PP9273; intr. 1994
'Poullight' (Night Light™) LCl, dy, 1985, Poulsen, Niels D.; flowers deep yellow with red on some petal edges, aging to crimson, 8-10 cm., 27 petals, borne in medium clusters, moderate fragrance; foliage large, dark, reddish green, glossy; prickles large, dark red; bushy growth, 150-200 cm.; [Westerland® × Pastorale®]; intr. 1980
'Poullitam' ('Carmelita Castle', Fredericia™) F, my, Poulsen; intr. 1998
'Poullow' ('Yellow Hit') Min, dy, 1988, Olesen, Pernille & Mogens N.; flowers small, dbl.; foliage small, dark green, semi-glossy; bushy, compact, even growth; PP6860; [seedling × seedling]
'Poullug' (Gripsholm™) F, dy, Poulsen; intr. 2000
'Poullute' MinFl, mp, Olesen; intr. 1996
'Poully' F, Poulsen; intr. 1991
'Poulma' ('Memory Bells', 'Newport', 'Waxwing') S, mp, 1994, Olesen; bud small, round to slightly ovoid; flowers pink, old fashioned, 3 in., very full, pompon, borne usually in large clusters, slight fragrance; foliage medium size, medium green, glossy; some prickles; compact, bushy growth; PP9261; intr. 1994
'Poulman' ('Ingrid Bergman') HT, dr, 1984, Olesen; flowers large, clear bright red, 5 in., 35-40 petals, high-centered, borne singly, slight spice fragrance; foliage medium size, dark, semi-glossy; upright growth, vigorous, compact; PP6264; [seedling × seedling]; intr. 1983
'Poulmanti' ('Romantic Palace') S, mp, 1999, Poulsen; bud ovoid to globular; intr. 1998
'Poulmar' ('Rosy Hit') Min, op, Poulsen; intr. 1994
'Poulmax' ('Shrimp Pink Castle', Solliden™, Fascination™, Fredensborg™, Schloss Herrenchiemsee™) F, op, Poulsen; intr. 1996
'Poulming' ('Harmony Parade') Min, lp, Olesen; intr. 1996
'Poulmiro' Min, dr, Poulsen; intr. 2000
'Poulmist' (Mistral™) MinFl, dy, Poulsen; intr. 2000
'Poulmo' (Ruby Wishes™, Scarlet™) MinFl, dr, Olesen, L & M; bud pointed ovoid to globular; intr. 1996
'Poulmona' (Ramona™) MinFl, dp, Poulsen; intr. 2000
'Poulmoon' MinFl, ly, Olesen
'Poulmount' ('Ivory Grand') Gr, w, Poulsen; intr. 1996
'Poulmulti' (Avon™, Fairy Lights™, Pomona™, Snow Cover™, Sunnyside ™) S, w, Poulsen; bud blush pink; intr. 1996
'Poulmundo' Min, mp, Poulsen; intr. 2000
'Poulna' ('Helena Renaissance', Helena™) S, lp, 1997, Olesen; flowers light pink, 10-15 cm., dbl., intense fragrance; foliage dark; growth bushy, 100-150 cm.; intr. 1997
'Poulnana' (Swift™) S, w, Poulsen; intr. 1992
'Poulnaris' (Samsø™) F, rb, Olesen; intr. 1998
'Poulneto' Min, ab, Poulsen; intr. 1998
'Poulnew' (José Carreras™) HT, w, Olesen, Pernille & Mogens N.; intr. 1998
'Poulnil' (Pernille ™) MinFl, pb, Olesen; bud pointed ovoid; intr. 1998
'Poulninga' (Nancy™) S, rb, Poulsen; intr. 1998
'Poulnino' ('Napa Valley', 'Red Wing') S, mr, 1995, Olesen, Pernille & Mogens N.; flowers bright red, 2 in., semi-dbl., borne in clusters; foliage small, dark green, glossy; low (36 in.), spreading growth; PP9554; intr. 1995
'Poulnish' (Sunbird™) Min, my, 1988, Poulsen Roser APS; flowers medium yellow opening to light yellow, fading to light pastel, 25-30 petals, high-centered; foliage medium size, dark green, matte, convex; bushy, medium growth; hips ovoid, few, pale orange-red; [Mini-Poul® × seedling]; intr. 1988
'Poulnoev' ('Salmo Hit', Coral Midinette™) S, op, Olesen
'Poulnoish' (Pink™) Min, mp, Poulsen; intr. 1998
'Poulnorm' ('Jazz', 'Naheglut') LCl, dr, Olesen; bud pointed ovoid; intr. 1997
'Poulnou' ('Snow Parade') Min, w, Poulsen; intr. 1998
'Poulnoz' (Aquitaine™, Essex™, Pink Cover™) S, mp, Poulsen; intr. 1991
'Poulnye' (Royal™) Min, mp, Poulsen; intr. 1996
'Poulnys' Min, my, Poulsen; intr. 2000
'Poulobe' (Noble™) MinFl, mr, Poulsen;

intr. 1998

'Poulody' (Melody™) MinFl, dp, Poulsen; intr. 1998

'Pouloesy' (Rosy Border™, Santa Barbara™) S, mp, Olesen, P & M; bud long, pointed ovoid; intr. 2000

'Pouloma' ('My Ouma', Land Brandenburg™, The Faun™, Meine Oma™, Granny™, My Granny™) F, mp, Olesen; intr. 1996

'Pouloni' (Benoni '75™, Vision®) HT, op, 1977, Poulsen, Niels D.; flowers medium salmon red, well-formed, large, 22 petals, borne 1-3 per stem; foliage dark, glossy; vigorous, spreading growth; PP6939; intr. 1978

'Poulor' (Mystic™, Peachy Pink Magic Carpet™, Supreme Cover™) S, dp, Olesen; intr. 1996

'Pouloral' (Dreaming™) Min, op, Poulsen; intr. 1996

'Poulorin' ('Oriental Palace') S, op, Poulsen; intr. 1999

'Poulover' (Rosenholm™) LCl, lp, Poulsen; intr. 1994

'Poulpah022' ('Minnelli Patiohit') MinFl, ab, Olesen; bud ovate; intr. 2003

'Poulpah024(N)' (Isolde™) MinFl, rb, Poulsen; intr. 2004

'Poulpah025(N)' (Andromeda™) MinFl, w, Poulsen; intr. 2004

'Poulpah026(N)' (Donnaway™) MinFl, ab, Poulsen; intr. 2004

'Poulpah027(N)' (Martinique™) MinFl, ab, Poulsen; intr. 2004

'Poulpah028(N)' (Estepona™) MinFl, ob, Poulsen; intr. 2004

'Poulpah029(N)' ('Cartier Hit') S, pb, Poulsen; intr. 2004

'Poulpah030(N)' (Emerald™) MinFl, w, Poulsen; intr. 2004

'Poulpah031(N)' ('Armani Hit') S, mp, Poulsen; intr. 2005

'Poulpah032(N)' ('Havana Hit', 'Sweet Wishes') Min, dr, Poulsen; intr. 2005

'Poulpah033(N)' MinFl, dp, Poulsen; intr. 2004

'Poulpah034(N)' (Natasja™) MinFl, lp, Poulsen; intr. 2005

'Poulpah035' ('Fashion Hit') S, dr, Poulsen; intr. 2005

'Poulpah036(N)' (Sullivan™) MinFl, my, Poulsen; intr. 2005

'Poulpah037(N)' MinFl, mr, Poulsen; intr. 2005

'Poulpai001' S, yb, Poulsen; intr. 2005

'Poulpal019(N)' ('Bangalore Palace') S, mp, Poulsen; intr. 2004

'Poulpal021(N)' (Adventure™) Min, dr, Poulsen; intr. 2005

'Poulpal022(N)' ('Stromboli Palace') S, rb, Poulsen; intr. 2004

'Poulpal024(N)' (Popular™) Min, ob, Poulsen; intr. 2005

'Poulpal026(N)' (Sunglow™) MinFl, my, Poulsen; intr. 2005

'Poulpal028(N)' ('Catalina Palace') S, lp, Poulsen; intr. 2005

'Poulpar' ('Alto') MinFl, ab, Poulsen; intr. 2004

'Poulpar029(N)' (Karina™) Min, mr, Olesen; bud pointed ovoid; intr. 2003

'Poulpar031(N)' (Etna™) Min, or, Poulsen; intr. 2004

'Poulpar032(N)' (Mette™) MinFl, w, Poulsen; intr. 2004

'Poulpar033(N)' (Nicola™) MinFl, pb, Poulsen; intr. 2004

'Poulpar034(N)' (Andrea™) MinFl, m, Poulsen; intr. 2004

'Poulpar036(N)' (Clara™) MinFl, w, Poulsen; intr. 2004

'Poulpar038(N)' (Hot™) MinFl, dp, Poulsen; intr. 2005

'Poulpar039(N)' (Breeze™) Min, ab, Poulsen

'Poulpar040(N)' (Flair™) Min, mp, Poulsen; intr. 2005

'Poulpar042' (Belle™) MinFl, lp, Poulsen; intr. 2005

'Poulpeacy' ('Peace Palace') S, dy, Poulsen; intr. 2000

'Poulpear' (Pearl Palace™) Min, w, Olesen

'Poulpearl' MinFl, lp, Olesen; intr. 1990

'Poulper' F, mp, 1965, Poulsen, Niels D.; intr. 1965

'Poulpm001(N)' HT, lp, Poulsen; intr. 2002

'Poulpm002(N)' HT, mp, Poulsen; bud pointed ovoid, broad base; intr. 2003

'Poulpm003(N)' HT, my, Poulsen; intr. 2003

'Poulpm004(N)' HT, m, Olesen; bud globular; intr. 2003

'Poulpol' ('Sweet Paillette') HT, ob, Poulsen; intr. 1997

'Poulpollo' (Apollo™) Min, ab, Poulsen; intr. 1998

'Poulprima' ('Purple') Min, m, Poulsen; intr. 1996

'Poulpunt 005' HT, my, Poulsen; intr. 2005

'Poulpyg' ('Central Park') S, ab, 1995, Olesen, Pernille & Mogens N.; flowers peach, bright yellow stamens, fading white, 2 in., dbl., borne in small clusters; foliage small, medium green, glossy; few prickles; low (2 ft.), spreading growth; PP9665; intr. 1995

'Poulra001(N)' (Columbine™, Monica™) MinFl, lp, Poulsen; intr. 2000

'Poulra002' (Heidi™) MinFl, op, Poulsen; bud short, pointed ovoid; intr. 2000

'Poulra003' ('Flair Parade') Min, op, Olesen; intr. 2000

'Poulra004(N)' (Claudia™) MinFl, lp, Poulsen; intr. 2000

'Poulra005(N)' (Nicoline™) MinFl, or, Poulsen; intr. 2000

'Poulra007(N)' (Real™) MinFl, dr, Poulsen; intr. 2002

'Poulra008' ('Ecco Parade') Min, dy, Olesen; intr. 2000

'Poulra009' Min, mp, Olesen; intr. 2000

'Poulra010' Min, mp, Olesen; intr. 2000

'Poulra011' Min, mp, Olesen

'Poulra012(N)' (Carmen™, Sensuous™) Min, mr, Poulsen; intr. 2000

'Poulra013' Min, w, Olesen; intr. 2000

'Poulra014(N)' (Julie™) MinFl, lp, Poulsen; intr. 2001

'Poulra015(N)' (Denise™) MinFl, w, Olesen; bud pointed ovoid; intr. 2001

'Poulra016(N)' (Sterling™) MinFl, mr, Poulsen; intr. 2001

'Poulra017(N)' (Blanca™) MInFl, w, Poulsen; intr. 2001

'Poulra018(N)' (Chic™) MinFl, lp, Poulsen; intr. 2001

'Poulra019(N)' (Leonie™) MinFl, mr, Olesen; bud pointed ovoid; intr. 2001

'Poulra021(N)' (Lady™) MinFl, mp, Olesen; bud long, broad based; intr. 2001

'Poulra022(N)' (Camilla™) MinFl, w, Poulsen; intr. 2002

'Poulra023(N)' (Jeanne d'Arc™) MinFl, w, Poulsen; intr. 2002

'Poulra024(N)' (Linda™) MinFl, mp, Olesen; bud pointed ovoid; intr. 2003

'Poulra026' (Merengue™) Min, yb, Poulsen; intr. 2003

'Poulra028(N)' (Sonja™) MinFl, yb, Poulsen; bud pointed ovoid to globular; intr. 2003

'Poulracos' (Scarlet™) Min, dr, Poulsen; intr. 2000

'Poulrael' Min, mp, Olesen; intr. 1998

'Poulrang' (First™) Min, or, Poulsen; intr. 1995

'Poulrato' ('Spring Parade') Min, dy, Poulsen; intr. 2000

'Poulreb' (Eurostar™, Marselisborg™, Schloss Neuschwanstein™, Summer Gold™) F, my, Olesen; bud short, globular; intr. 1996

'Poulred' (Red Bells™) Min, mr, 1984, Poulsen Roser APS; flowers bright red, small, 35 petals, cupped, borne in clusters; foliage small, medium green, semi-glossy; groundcover; spreading (2 × 4 ft.) growth; [Mini-Poul® × 'Temple Bells']; intr. 1983

'Poulrek' ('Cristel Palace', 'Crystal Palace') F, lp, Poulsen Roser APS; intr. 1996

'Poulren013' ('Mum in a Million', Millie™, Ghita™) S, mp, Olesen; bud urceolate

'Poulren018' S, w, Poulsen; intr. 2006

'Poulrent' ('Laurent Hit') S, yb, Poulsen; intr. 2000

'Poulria' (Red Fairy™, Velvet Cover™) S, dr, Olesen; bud short, globular; intr. 1995

'Poulriber' (Riberhus™) F, op, Poulsen; bud pointed ovoid; intr. 1998

'Poulrijk' ('Devon', Bayernland™, Bayernland Cover™) S, mp, Poulsen; bud pointed, ovoid; intr. 1996

'Poulrim' (Flora Danica™, Garden News™, Spellbound™) HT, ob, Poulsen Roser APS; intr. 1996

PoulrineN (Bangsbo™, Prince Albert™, Maurine™) F, mp, Poulsen; flowers medium pink, 8-10 cm., 25 petals, no fragrance; foliage dark, glossy; growth bushy; intr. 1996

'Poulrise' ('Kong Frederik den IX', John Leese™, Peach Surprise™) HT, yb, 1994, Poulsen Roser APS; flowers peach and cream, large, full, borne mostly singly, moderate fragrance; foliage large, dark green, glossy; numerous prickles; spreading (80-100 cm.) growth; [sport of 'Freude']; intr. 1995

'Poulrohill' (Enduring Spirit™, Lill Lindfors™, Rosehill™) F, mp, 1985, Olesen, Pernille & Mogens N.; bud long, pointed ovoid; intr. 1982

'Poulrolyt' ('Colour Hit', Colour™, 'Colour Patiohit') MinFl, or, Poulsen; bud long, pointed, ovoid; intr. 1998

'Poulrosit' (Rosita™) MinFl, yb, Poulsen; intr. 2000

'Poulrouge' (Absolute™, Orange Paillette™) MinFl, or, Poulsen; intr. 1996

'Poulruk' (Emotion™) Min, dp, Poulsen; intr. 1997

'Poulrusset' ('Russet Beauty') Min, or, 1985, Olesen, Pernille & Mogens N.; flowers small, 46 petals, borne in clusters of 3-15; foliage matte; prickles straight, brown; compact, bushy growth; [Mini-Poul® × seedling]; intr. 1983

'Poulrust' (Lavender Cover™) S, m, Poulsen; bud short, ovoid; intr. 1997

'Poulsabel' MinFl, dr, Poulsen; intr. 1999

'Poulsail' (Versailles™) F, or, Olesen; bud pointed ovoid; intr. 1999

'Poulsak' F, mp, Poulsen; intr. 2000

'Poulsalfai' ('Miss Hillcrest') S, op, 1993, Poulsen

'Poulscho' Min, m, Poulsen; intr. 2000

'Poulscots(N)' HT, m, Olesen; bud pointed ovoid; intr. 2001

'Poulsendo' (Yellow™) MinFl, my, Poulsen; intr. 1998

'Poulsen's Bedder' ('Poulsen's Grupperose') F, lp, 1948, Poulsen, S.; flowers clear pink, 3 in., semi-dbl., borne in trusses; foliage bronze; vigorous, upright growth; ['Orléans Rose' × 'Talisman']; intr. 1948

'Poulsen's Copper' F, op, 1940, Poulsen, S.; flowers rose-pink to orange, base yellow, 3-3½ in., 25-35 petals, cupped, borne in clusters, slight spicy fragrance; foliage small, light green; vigorous growth; PP446; ['Grethe Poulsen' × 'Souv. de Claudius Pernet']; intr. 1940

'Poulsen's Crimson' F, dr, 1985, Poulsen, S.; flowers 6 petals, borne in clusters; foliage medium size, dark, matte; vigorous, bushy growth; [Orange Triumph® × ('Betty Uprichard' × 'Johanniszauber')]; intr. 1950

'Poulsen's Delight' ('Fru Julie Poulsen') F, lp, 1948, Poulsen, S.; flowers appleblossom-pink, 5-7 petals, borne in trusses; foliage dark, glossy; vigorous, upright growth; ['Else Poulsen' × seedling]

'Poulsen's Fairy' ('Rodovrerosen') F, lp, 1940, Poulsen, S.; flowers light pink with amber-pink stamens, single, borne in large clusters; free-flowering; very vigorous, tall growth; ['Orléans Rose' × 'Dainty Bess']

'Poulsen's Grupperose' -- See 'Poulsen's Bedder'

'Poulsen's Jubilaeumsrose' -- See 'Pouljub'

'Poulsen's Park Rose' S, lp, 1953, Poulsen; flowers silvery pink, well-shaped, 4-5 in., dbl., borne in trusses; vigorous (6 × 6 ft.) growth; ['Great Western' × 'Karen Poulsen']

'Poulsen's Peach' F, ab, 1985, Poulsen, S.; flowers peach, large, semi-dbl., cupped, borne in clusters; foliage medium size, medium green, semi-glossy; growth medium, bushy; intr. 1948

'Poulsen's Pearl' F, lp, 1949, Poulsen, S.; flowers pearly pink, 5 petals, borne in trusses; foliage light green; vigorous growth; ['Else Poulsen' × seedling]; intr. 1948

'Poulsen's Pink' F, lp, 1939; flowers soft pink with yellow base, semi-dbl., cupped, borne in clusters, slight fragrance; foliage glossy, light green; vigorous growth; ['Golden Salmon' × 'yellow HT']; intr. 1942

'Poulsen's Scarlet' F, dp, 1941, Poulsen, S.; flowers bright rose, 2½ in., 30 petals, borne in clusters; bushy growth; ['D.T. Poulsen' × 'Red HT']

'Poulsen's Supreme' ('Kelleriis-Rose') F, mp, 1945, Poulsen, S.; flowers 3 in., semi-dbl., borne in trusses; foliage light green; very free growth; ['Poulsen's Pink' × seedling]; intr. 1953

'Poulsen's Yellow' F, my, 1938, Poulsen, S.; bud ovoid; flowers semi-dbl., borne in clusters, intense fragrance; foliage glossy; ['Mrs W.H. Cutbush' × 'Gottfried Keller']; intr. 1939

'Poulset' ('Sweet Party') Min, mp, Poulsen; intr. 1999

'Poulsha' ('Flammenmeer') F, or, 1978, Poulsen, Niels D.; bud globular; intr. 1973

'Poulshine' (Aberdeen™, Rutland Cover™, Shiner™) S, lp, Poulsen; intr. 1988

'Poulshrimp' ('Birthday Wishes', Shrimp™) MinFl, or, Poulsen; bud broad ovate; intr. 2001

'Poulsiana' (Atlantis™) F, dy, Poulsen; intr. 1998

'Poulsint' (Red™) Min, mr, Poulsen; intr. 1998

'Poulsiv' ('Silvia Hit') S, dy, Poulsen; intr. 2000

'Poulskab' (Nordina™) LCl, pb, Poulsen; intr. 2000

'Poulske' ('Arlette') F, rb, Poulsen; intr. 1996

'Poulskov' ('Drottning Margretha', Dronning Margrethe™, Queen Margrethe™, Königin Margrethe™, Dr Margrethe™, Enchantment™) S, lp, 1994, Olesen; bud short, pointed to ovoid; flowers pastel pink, old-fashioned form, medium, very full, quartered, borne in small clusters, moderate apple fragrance; free-flowering; foliage small, medium green, glossy, clean; few prickles; stems strong, short to medium; low to medium (2 ft.), bushy, compact, rounded growth; PP9062; [seedling × Egeskov™]; intr. 1995

'Poulslas' ('Salsa') LCl, w, Poulsen; intr. 2002

'Poulsnows' ('Pearl Wishes', Snow™) MinFl, w, Poulsen; intr. 2000

'Poulspan' ('Odense City', Devon™, Jade™, Odense By-Rose™, Borussia™) S, my, Poulsen; intr. 1990

'Poulstar' (Starlight™) Min, w; bud short, pointed ovoid; intr. 1991

'Poulstigh' ('Delight Hit') MinFl, ab, Olesen

'Poulstri' LCl, pb, Poulsen; intr. 2000

'Poulsum' ('Dawn Weller') F, op, Poulsen; intr. 1995

'Poulsun' ('Golden Wishes', Sun™) MinFl, my, Olesen; bud long, pointed ovoid; intr. 1996

'Poulsyng' ('Clair', 'Liliana') S, lp, Olesen; intr. 1995

'Poultal' (Eva Gabor™, Sentimental™) HT, dp, 1983, Olesen, Pernille & Mogens N.; flowers deep pink, large, 40 petals, moderate fragrance; foliage large, medium green, glossy; vigorous, upright, bushy growth; PP4940; [seedling × seedling]; intr. 1983

'Poultc004' (Kirsch Cover™) S, rb, Poulsen; intr. 2004

'Poultc005' (Honey Border™) S, mp, Olesen; bud ovate; intr. 2004

'Poultc006' (Ruby Border™) S, mr, Olesen; bud urceolate

'Poultc007' (Silk Cover™) S, my, Poulsen; intr. 2005

'Poultc010' (Soft Cover™) S, dp, Poulsen; intr. 2005

'Poultc011' S, mr, Poulsen; intr. 2005

'Poultc012' (Explosion Border™) S, mp, Poulsen; intr. 2005

'Poultc014' (Golden Eye Cover™) S, my; intr. 2005

PoulteenyN ('Felicity II', Teeny WeenyN) Min, dp, 1981, Poulsen Roser APS; bud small; intr. 1980

'Poulterp' (Brilliant Cover™, Old Charleston™) S, w, Poulsen; intr. 1998

'Poultex' (Golden Piccolo™, Texas™) Min, my, 1985, Olesen; bud long, pointed ovoid; flowers buttercup yellow, 2 in., 20 petals, high-centered, borne singly and several together, slight apple-rose fragrance; recurrent; foliage small, medium green, semi-matte; prickles some, short, slightly curved, green; upright (40-50 cm.), bushy growth; hips globular, 15 mm., yellow-orange; PP6261; [Mini-Poul® × seedling]; intr. 1984

'Poulthe' (Topkapi™) S, dp, Olesen; bud ovoid; intr. 1996

'Poultieme' LCl, dp, Poulsen; intr. 2000

'Poultika' (Northern Lights™) LCl, mp, Poulsen; intr. 1998

'Poultimes' F, my, Poulsen; intr. 1993

'Poultin' (Violet Paillette™, Violet™) MinFl, m; intr. 1995

'Poultipe' ('Silver Wishes', Pink™) Min, mp, Poulsen; intr. 1996

'Poultn003' (Bright Cover™) S, w, Poulsen; intr. 2003

'Poultop' ('Special Wishes', Carrot Top™, Panache™, Top Hit™, Brilliant Hit™) Min, ob, 1991, Olesen, Pernille & Mogens N.; bud ovoid, slightly pointed; flowers orange to orange-red, clear lasting color, medium, 18-22 petals, high-centered to cupped, borne singly or in small clusters, slight fragrance; prolific bloom; foliage medium size, medium green, matte; prickles few, long, straight, angled downward, brown; low (40-50 cm.), bushy, compact growth; hips short, globular, orange; PP9048; [floribunda seedling × miniature seedling]; intr. 1994

'Poultory' (Fame™) Min, dr, Poulsen; intr. 1996

'Poultrav' (Amber™) MinFl, ab, Poulsen; intr. 2000

'Poultre' Min, mp, Olesen; intr. 1997

'Poultress' (Cherry Velvet®) HT, dp, 1989, Olesen, Pernille & Mogens N.; flowers deep pink, large, 20 petals, moderate fragrance; foliage large, medium green, glossy; upright, vigorous growth; ['Vision' × seedling]; intr. 1987

'Poultroi' (Adele Duttweiler™, Troika™) HT, ob, 1973, Poulsen, D. T.; intr. 1971

'Poultry' ('Kronborg Castle', Ich hab Dich lieb™, Kronborg™, Schloss Linderhof™, Tryfosa™) F, dr, Poulsen; intr. 1996

'Poultumb' (Tumbling Waters™) S, w, Olesen; bud short, pointed ovoid; intr. 1998

'Poultver' Min, lp, Poulsen; intr. 1996

'Poultw001' (Intense Cover™) S, mr, Poulsen; intr. 2002

'Poultw002' (Special Border™) S, mr, Poulsen; intr. 2002

'Poulty001' Min, ob, Poulsen Roser; intr. 2000

'Poulty002' ('Vital Parade') Min, my, Olesen; bud long, pointed ovoid; intr. 2000

'Poulty004(N)' Min, ob, Poulsen; intr. 2002

'Poulty007(N)' MinFl, w, Poulsen; intr. 2005

'Pouluf' ('Dream Sequence', Charentes™, Egon Schiele™, Macabo™) S, lp, Poulsen; bud medium pink; intr. 1991

'Poululla' Min, mr, Olesen; intr. 1996

'Poululv' ('Good Wishes', Favourite™) MinFl, ab, Poulsen; bud broad based, pointed ovoid; intr. 2002

'Poulurt' (Chitina™, Gold Magic Carpet™, Golden Plover™, Gwent™, Sun Cover™) S, my, 1996, Olesen, Pernille & Mogens N.; intr. 1995

'Poulusa' ('Dame de Köbenhavn', Princess Marianna™) S, w, 1999, Poulsen Roser APS; flowers ivory white, old-fashioned form, 2½-3 in., very dbl., borne in small clusters, moderate fragrance; foliage medium size, dark green, glossy; prickles moderate; compact, bushy, rounded, low (20-24 in.) growth; PP10638; [seedling × Queen Margrethe™]; intr. 1998

'Poulvam' LCl, mp, Poulsen; intr. 2000

'Poulvam' LCl, dp, Poulsen; intr. 2000

'Poulvang' HT, dr, 1988, Olesen, Pernille & Mogens N.; intr. 1987

'Poulviaks' Min, my, Olesen; intr. 1999

'Poulvic' ('Victory Parade') Min, mr; intr. 1996

'Poulviol' (Belle™) MinFl, lp, Poulsen; intr. 2005

'Poulvita' ('Evita') Min, w, 1985, Olesen, Pernille & Mogens N.; flowers white with touch of pale pink, small, 20 petals, borne in clusters, slight fragrance; foliage small, dark, glossy; bushy growth; [Mini-Poul® × seedling]; intr. 1984

'Poulvok' Min, or, Poulsen; intr. 1996

'Poulvue' (Medima™, Victor Borge™, Michael Crawford™) HT, ob, Olesen; bud medium, pointed ovoid; intr. 1991

'Poulwarb' ('Fairy Moon') S, my, Olesen

'Poulwee' (Rainbow Yellow Parade™, Yellow Parade™) Min, dy, 1990, Olesen, Pernille & Mogens N.; bud cupped, globular; flowers bright yellow, aging slightly, small, 28-30 petals, cupped, borne singly, slight damask fragrance; foliage small, dark green, semi-glossy; no prickles; upright, low, compact growth; [seedling × 'Texas']; intr. 1985

'Poulweeto' (Sweet Cover™) S, mp, Olesen; bud short, pointed ovoid; intr. 1999

'Poulwei' F, dr, 1965, Poulsen, S.; intr. 1961

'Poulweno' Min, ob, Olesen

'Poulwest' HT, dy, 1965, Poulsen, Niels D.

'Poulwhite' (White Bells™) Min, w, 1984, Poulsen Roser APS; bud bright yellow; flowers pale yellow to white, 35 petals, rosette, borne in clusters, slight fragrance; scattered repeat; foliage small, medium green, semi-glossy; groundcover; spreading growth; [Mini-Poul® × 'Temple Bells']; intr. 1983

'Poulxas' (Gingerbread Man™) Min, ab, 1994, Poulsen Roser APS; flowers deep, long-lasting apricot amber, medium, full, quartered, borne in small clusters; foliage small, dark green, semi-glossy; some prickles; medium (40-45 cm.), upright, bushy, vigorous growth; PP9420; [seedling × 'Texas']; intr. 1995

'Poulyc001' (Bournonville™) LCl, lp, Poulsen; bud medium pink; intr. 2000

'Poulyc002' LCl, dr, Poulsen; intr. 2002

'Poulyc003' LCl, pb, Poulsen; intr. 2002

'Poulyc004' LCl, dy, Poulsen; intr. 2002

'Poulyc005' LCl, lp, Poulsen; intr. 2002

'Poulyc006' LCl, mp, Poulsen; intr. 2002

'Poulyc007' LCl, lp, Olesen; bud broad based; intr. 2002

'Poulyc008' LCl, yb, Olesen; bud broad-based, pointed-ovoid; intr. 2003

'Poulyc009' LCl, mr, Poulsen; bud pointed ovoid; intr. 2003

'Poulymp' (Olympic™) F, ob, Olesen; bud pointed; intr. 2001

'Poulyn' (Fashion™) Min, mp, Poulsen; intr. 1998

'Poulypso' ('Arrow Hit', 'Arrow Patiohit', Arrow™) MinFl, dr, Poulsen; intr. 1998

'Poulyv001' (Diamond™) S, w, Poulsen; intr. 2000

'Poulyv002' (Mandalay™) S, my, Poulsen; intr. 2002

'Poulzazz' (Pzazz™) MinFl, rb, Poulsen; intr. 1996

'Poulzin' ('Prince Palace') S, rb, Poulsen; bud ovoid to globular; intr. 1998

'Pounder Star' -- See 'Macnic'

'Poupée' F, lp, 1979, Lens; flowers flesh-pink, 3-3½ in., 25-30 petals, cupped; foliage glossy; vigorous, upright growth; intr. 1965

'Pour Toi' -- See 'Para Ti'

'Pour Vous Madame' F, dp, 1961, Gaujard; flowers rose-red, reverse lighter, open, 4 in., 25 petals; foliage dark; vigorous growth; intr. 1961

'Pourale' ('Pastourelle', Pastorale®) S, pb, 1986, Poulsen, Niels D.; flowers deep pink, yellow reverse, large, 25 petals, urn-shaped, borne in sprays; foliage large, leathery, dark, glossy; prickles dark green; very vigorous, upright, bushy growth; [seedling × Royal Dane™]; intr. 1970

'Pourpre' -- See 'Rubra'

'Pourpre' ('Bengale Pourpre') Ch, m, 1827, Vibert; flowers deep purple-red, small, 5-8 petals, borne in clusters; growth to 2 ft.

'Pourpre Ancien' ('Purpurea Plena') Misc OGR, m, about 1829; flowers purple, sometimes striped with white, large, very full; foliage small, glossy

'Pourpre Ardoisée' -- See 'Busard Triomphant'

'Pourpre Belle Violette' -- See 'Le Rosier Évêque'

'Pourpre Brillant' HGal, m, before 1815, Descemet; flowers glossy purple

'Pourpre Brun' HCh, dr, before 1844; flowers purplish crimson, very small, full; Lawrenciana

'Pourpre Charmant' ('Grande Pompadour', 'Rouge Admirable', 'La Magnifique', 'L'Archévêque') HGal, m, before 1811; flowers deep velvety purple-pink, 3-4 in., very dbl., moderate sweet fragrance

'Pourpre Cramoisi' -- See 'Rouge Formidable'

'Pourpre d'Orléans' ('Maréchal Vaillant') HP, m, 1861, Dauvesse; flowers bright garnet purple, large, full; sometimes attributed to Viennot or Lecomte/Jamain

'Pourpre Double' -- See 'Lustre d'Église'

'Pourpre du Luxembourg' ('Luxembourg') M, m, 1848, Hardy; flowers deep crimson, shaded with purple, medium, dbl., moderate fragrance; scattered rebloom; growth to 5 ft.

'Pourpre d'Yèbles' Ch, m, 1830, Desprez; flowers dark purple

'Pourpre Favorite' -- See 'Belle de Stors'

'Pourpre Foncé' ('Bengale Noire') HGal, m, before 1815, Descemet; flowers dark purple, small

'Pourpre Marbrée' ('Arlequin', 'Bizarre Changeant') HGal, m, before 1821; flowers violet purple, marbled, small, very full

'Pourpre Noir' -- See 'Ombre Superbe'

'Pourpre Rouge' -- See 'Temple d'Apollon'

'Pourpre Violet' M, m, before 1862; flowers violet purple, medium, full

'Poustinia' F, ab, Orye; flowers yellow-apricot in center and cream white on outer petals, large, dbl., pompon, intense fragrance; growth to 80 cm.; intr. 1994

'Powder Puff' F, lp, 1962, Mason, A.L.; flowers creamy light pink, becoming darker, open, medium, dbl., slight fragrance; foliage glossy; bushy growth; ['Masquerade' × ('Masquerade' × unknown)]; intr. 1959

Power Point™ -- See 'Bennovecientos'

'Pozdrav Prohunice' S, mp, Schmidt; intr. 1915

'Poznan' HT, dr, 1966, Grabczewski; bud ovoid; flowers vivid dark crimson, well-formed, large, dbl.; vigorous growth

'PP20385Mos' F, dp, Perfecta Plant-double

'PP2088Ams' F, op, Perfecta Plant

'PP30880Gen' ('Geneve') F, ab, Perfecta Plant

'Praecox' (form of R. sericea), w

'Praeddy' HT, lp, Pratt, Florence; bud pink; intr. 1994

'Prague' HSpn, pb; flowers single

Prairie® HT, dy, Kordes; flowers soft yellow, medium, full, high-centered, borne mostly singly; good repeat; ['Sioux' × unknown]; florist rose; intr. 2003

'Prairie Belle' -- See 'Queen of the Prairies'

'Prairie Breeze' S, m, 1979, Buck, Dr. Griffith J.; bud ovoid, pointed; flowers Tyrian purple, 4½ in. 25 petals, cupped, moderate spicy fragrance; repeat bloom; foliage olive-green, leathery; upright, bushy, spreading growth; ['Dornroschen' × ('Josef Rothmund' × R. laxa)]; intr. 1978

'Prairie Celebration' S, dp, Ag Canada; flowers single, slight fragrance; vigorous (4 ft.) growth; winter hardy; one of the Parkland series; intr. 2003

'Prairie Charm' S, op, 1959, Morden Exp. Farm; flowers bright salmon-coral, semi-dbl.; free, non-recurrent bloom; foliage light green; growth to 4 ft., arching; hardy on prairies; ['Prairie Youth' × 'Prairie Wren']

'Prairie Clogger' S, mr, 1985, Buck, Dr. Griffith J.; bud medium-small, ovoid, pointed; flowers 2½ in., 8-10 petals, shallow-cupped to flat, borne 1-10 per cluster, moderate fragrance; repeat bloom; foliage leathery, dark olive green; prickles awl-like, tan; vigorous, erect, bushy growth; ['Carefree Beauty' × ('Marlena' × 'Pippa's Song')]; intr. 1984

'Prairie Dawn' S, mp, 1959, Morden Exp. Farm; flowers glowing pink, 2-2½ in., dbl.; repeat bloom on current season's wood; foliage dark, glossy; upright (5 ft.) growth; hardy on prairies; ['Prairie Youth' × ('Ross Rambler' × ('Dr. W. Van Fleet' × R. spinosissima altaica))]

'Prairie Fire' S, mr, 1962, Phillips, R. A.; bud pointed; flowers bright red, base white, 2½-3 in., 9 petals, borne in clusters of 35-50, moderate fragrance; recurrent; foliage glossy, dark; long stems; very vigorous, tall growth; ['Red Rocket' × R. arkansana]; intr. 1960

'Prairie Flower' S, rb, 1975, Buck, Dr. Griffith J.; bud ovoid, pointed; flowers cardinal-red, center white, 2-3 in., 7 petals, flat, slight old rose fragrance; repeat bloom; foliage dark, leathery; erect, bushy growth; ['Rose of Tralee' × (Queen Elizabeth® × ('Morning Stars' × 'Suzanne'))]; intr. 1975

'Prairie Harvest' S, ly, 1985, Buck, Dr. Griffith J.; flowers medium yellow, petals imbricated, 4-5 in., 43 petals, borne singly and in clusters of up to 15, moderate fragrance; repeat bloom; foliage leathery, glossy, medium size, dark; prickles awl-like, tan; growth upright, bushy; hardy; ['Carefree Beauty' × 'Sunsprite']; intr. 1984

'Prairie Heritage' S, op, 1978, Buck, Dr. Griffith J.; bud ovoid, pointed; flowers peach to coral-pink, 4-5 in., 50 petals, cupped; repeat bloom; foliage dark, leathery; vigorous, upright, spreading, bushy growth; [('Vera Dalton' × 'Prairie Princess') × ('Apricot Nectar' × 'Prairie Princess')]

'Prairie Joy' S, mp, 1990, Marshall, H. H.; flowers medium pink, aging to light pink, medium, 30-40 petals, cupped, borne singly or in sprays of 2-6, slight fragrance; sparse repeat bloom; foliage medium size, medium green, matte, very disease-resistant; growth tall, bushy; ['Prairie Princess' × 'Morden Cardinette']; intr. 1990

'Prairie Lass' S, pb, 1978, Buck, Dr. Griffith J.; bud ovoid, pointed; flowers claret-rose to rose-red, large, 28 petals, moderate spicy fragrance; repeat bloom; foliage dark, leathery; vigorous, upright, spreading, bushy growth; [('Hawkeye Belle' × 'Vera Dalton') × ('Dornroschen' × ('World's Fair' × 'World's Fair'))]; intr. 1978

'Prairie Maid' S, w, 1959, Morden Exp. Farm; flowers cream, 25 petals; intermittent bloom; compact (4 ft.) growth; hardy on prairies; [('Ophelia' × 'Turkes Rugosa Samling') × R. spinosissima altaica]

'Prairie Moon' LCl, ly, 1953, Maney; bud ovoid, deep yellow; flowers creamy yellow, large, 30-35 petals, borne in clusters of 4-5; abundant, non-recurrent bloom; foliage glossy, dark, leathery; vigorous, climbing (15 ft.) growth; [R. maximowicziana pilosa × 'Autumn']

'Prairie Peace ' HSpn, yb, Erskine; flowers yellow and pink, sometimes peach, semi-dbl. to dbl., cupped, moderate fragrance; recurrent, two crops of blooms per year; ['Beauty of Leafland' × 'Hazeldean']

'Prairie Pinkie' S, op, 1958, Skinner; flowers deep coral-pink, dbl., intense fragrance; midsummer bloom; foliage like R. spinossissima; growth upright (2½ ft.), bushy

'Prairie Princess' S, op, 1971, Buck, Dr. Griffith J.; bud ovoid, long, pointed; flowers light coral-pink, large, semi-dbl.; repeat bloom; foliage large, dark, leathery; vigorous, upright growth; ['Carrousel' × ('Morning Stars' × 'Suzanne')]; intr. 1972

'Prairie Red' Min, rb, 1981, Lyon; flowers red-yellow blend, 18 petals, borne singly or several together, moderate fragrance; foliage tiny, medium green; prickles brownish, curved downward; growth bushy, upright; [seedling × seedling]; intr. 1980

'Prairie Sailor' HSpn, yb, 1946, Morden Exp. Farm; flowers golden yellow deeply edged bright red, single; profuse, non-recurrent bloom; vigorous (6 ft.) growth; hardy on prairies

Prairie Schooner™ Min, rb, 1986, King, Gene; flowers red, reverse yellow edged red, 22 petals, high-centered, borne singly and in sprays; foliage small, dark, matte; prickles straight, brown; upright growth; no fruit; PP6748; ['Vera Dalton' × 'Sheri Anne']

'Prairie Squire' S, mp, 1985, Buck, Dr. Griffith J.; flowers 4-5 in., 20 petals, cupped, borne singly and in clusters of up to 10, slight fragrance; repeat bloom; foliage leathery, dark green, tinted copper; prickles awl-like, tan; vigorous, erect, bushy, spreading growth; hardy; ['Countryman' × 'Carefree Beauty']; intr. 1984

'Prairie Star' S, w, 1975, Buck, Dr. Griffith J.; bud ovoid, pointed; flowers pale chrome-yellow, tinted pink, 3½-4 in., 54 petals, cupped, moderate green apple fragrance; repeat bloom; foliage dark, leathery; vigorous, erect, bushy growth; ['Tickled Pink' × 'Prairie Princess']; intr. 1975

'Prairie Sunrise' S, ab, 1997, Buck, Dr. Griffith J.; flowers golden apricot yellow, 4 in., 50+ petals, borne in small clusters, intense fragrance; foliage large, medium green, glossy; glossy, compact, bushy, medium growth; ['Friesia' × 'Freckle Face']

'Prairie Sunset' S, pb, 1985, Buck, Dr. Griffith J.; flowers deep pink, reverse yellow, 4 in., 38 petals, urn-shaped, borne 5 - 10 per cluster, moderate fragrance; repeat bloom; foliage moderately large, leathery, dark; prickles tan; erect, bushy, slightly spreading growth; hardy; [Bonfire Night® × ('Music Maker' × 'Athlone')]; intr. 1984

'Prairie Valor' S, mr, 1985, Buck, Dr. Griffith J.; flowers 4-5 in., 38 petals, cupped, borne 3-5 per cluster, moderate damask fragrance; repeat bloom; foliage leathery, dark; prickles awl-like, brown; upright, bushy growth; hardy; [(('Dornroschen' × ('Josef Rothmund' × *R. laxa*)) × 'Rose du Roi a Fleurs Pourpres') × ('Music Maker' × Topsi®)]; intr. 1984

'Prairie Wren'   S, mp, 1946, Morden Exp. Farm; flowers rich pink, large, semi-dbl.; heavy, non-recurrent bloom; very hardy

'Prairie Youth'   S, op, 1948, Morden Exp. Farm; flowers pure salmon-pink, semi-dbl., borne in clusters, slight fragrance; repeat bloom; vigorous (6 ft.) growth; completely hardy on prairies; [(('Ross Rambler' × 'Dr. W. Van Fleet') × *R. suffulta*) × (('Dr. W. Van Fleet' × 'Turkes Rugosa Samling') × *R. spinosissima altaica*)]

'Praise of Jiro'   F, or, 1959, Kordes, R.; bud ovoid; flowers large, 30 petals, borne in clusters; foliage leathery; vigorous, upright, bushy growth; ['Korona' × 'Spartan']

'Praline'   HT, dr, 1955, Robichon; flowers carmine-purple to crimson; foliage glossy; ['Camelia' × seedling]

'Pranabandajee'   HT, dr, Pushpanjali; flowers deep crimson, large, full; vigorous growth; intr. 1999

'Präsent' ('Present')   F, ab, 1969, Haenchen, E.; flowers yellow-orange, reverse yellow, large, 27 petals, high-centered; foliage dark, glossy, leathery; vigorous, upright, bushy growth; ['Highlight' × Allgold®]

'Präsident Dr H. C. Schröder' -- See 'President H. C. Schroder'

'Präsident Hindenburg'   Pol, mr, 1927, Bom; flowers carmine to deep red, base white, dbl.; ['Greta Kluis' × unknown]

Praterstern®   HT, yb

'Prato Rosso'   Min, Motta; intr. 1984

'Prattigosa'   HRg, mp, 1953, Kordes; bud long, pointed, red; flowers pink, overlarge, single; foliage leathery, light green; vigorous (3½ ft.), upright, bushy growth; [*R. prattii* × *R. rugosa alba*]

'Pray'   Gr, Delforge; intr. 1987

'Précieuse' -- See 'Prolifère'

'Precilla'   HT, dy, 1973, Kordes; bud ovoid; flowers deep golden yellow, medium, dbl., cupped, moderate fragrance; foliage dark, leathery; vigorous, upright growth; PP3726; [Peer Gynt® × seedling]

'Preciosa'   HT, pb, Meilland; flowers pink and yellow, large, dbl.; intr. 1972

'Precious'   HT, pb, 1985, Dawson, Charles P.; flowers blend of light, medium and deep pink, reverse medium pink, l, 35 petals, high-centered, moderate fragrance; foliage medium size, medium green, semi-glossy; prickles very few; upright, bushy growth; [('Briarcliff' × ('Carla' × unknown)) × 'Pink Parfait']; intr. 1987

'Precious Anya' -- See 'Horeducate'
'Precious Child' -- See 'Geaaura'

'Precious Dream' -- See 'Mortime'
Precious Gift™ -- See 'Jaysil'
'Precious Lady' -- See 'Rawprelad'
'Precious Memories'   F, op, World of Roses; foliage glossy; 75 cm. growth
'Precious Michelle' -- See 'Macbucpal'
'Precious Moments' -- See 'Lyopr'
'Precious Moments'   F, ob, World of Roses; flowers yellow-orange, edges turning full, full, high-centered, moderate fragrance; growth to 3 ft.

'Precious Pet'   S, mp, Matthews; intr. 2001

'Precious Platinum' ('Opa Pötschke', 'Red Star')   HT, mr, 1976, Dicksons of Hawlmark; flowers cardinal-red, medium to large, 35 petals, high-centered, borne mostly singly, slight fragrance; good repeat; foliage dark green, glossy, leathery; stems long, strong; vigorous, upright (4 ft.) growth; ['Red Planet' × 'Franklin Englemann']; intr. 1974

'Precision'   S, dr, Williams, J. Ben; flowers semi-dbl., slight fragrance; recurrent; growth to 4 ft.; intr. 2005

'Précoce'   M, dp, 1843, Vibert; flowers rosy red, sometimes spotted at the edge, medium, dbl.; very early bloom

'Prediction'   HT, mp, 1975, Golik; flowers luminous pink, 4 in., 35 petals, high-centered; foliage leathery; moderate growth; ['Queen of Bermuda' × Golden Giant®]; intr. 1974

'Preference' -- See 'Meimagarmic'

'Préférence'   HT, mr, Meilland; bud large, conical, elongated; flowers strawberry red, reverse cardinal red, 4 in., 40-45 petals, high-centered, cupped, borne mostly singly; good repeat; foliage dark green, matte; prickles numerous, tan; growth erect (4-5 ft.); PP7383; ['Visa' × 'Royalty']; florist rose; intr. 1998

'Preference'   F, mr, Meilland International; bud ovoid; flowers deep scarlet red, 3 in., 20-25 petals, borne singly and in clusters of up to 6, very slight fragrance; free-flowering; foliage dense, dark green, semi-glossy; numerous prickles; growth compact (3-4 ft.), bushy; PP15878; [('Tamango' × 'Korona') × 'Pharaon']; intr. 2004

'Préfet Limbourg' ('Mons le Préfet Limbourg')   HP, dr, 1878, Margottin fils; flowers velvety crimson, tinged with violet, large, dbl.; ['Pierre Notting' × unknown]

'Préfet Monteil'   T, my, 1901, Bernaix fils; flowers canary yellow, shaded sulfur yellow, aging to coppery carmine, large, full

'Prejen' ('Jen')   HT, yb, 2001, Premeaux, John; flowers yellow and pink, ruffled edges on petals, 4 in., dbl., borne mostly solitary, slight fragrance; foliage medium size, medium green, semi-glossy; prickles moderate; growth spreading, tall; garden decorative, exhibition; [sport of 'Sorbet']; intr. 2001

'Prekrasnaja Rossijanka'   HT, mr, Klimenko, V. N.; flowers large, dbl.; intr. 1966

'Prelud'   F, mr, Urban, J.

'Prélude'   HT, m, 1958, Meilland, F.; bud medium, stubby; flowers lilac-mauve, well-formed, medium, 25 petals, borne singly or several together, moderate fragrance; free-flowering; foliage dense, soft; strong stems; vigorous, bushy growth; ['Fantastique' × ('Ampere' × ('Charles P. Kilham' × 'Capucine Chambard'))]; intr. 1954

'Prélude'   HT, m, Keisei; flowers lavender pink, dbl., high-centered, borne mostly singly; good repeat; florist rose

'Preludium'   F, ab, Hannemann, F.; ['Poker Chip' × unknown]

'Prema'   F, pb, 1970, Division of Vegetable Crops and Floriculture; flowers soft pink, petals edged deep pink, medium, dbl., high-centered; foliage leathery; vigorous, upright growth; ['Sea Pearl' × 'Shola']

'Prémice des Charpennes'   B, m, 1845, Cherpin; flowers lilac pink, edges white, medium, full, globular

'Premier' ('Hiltig')   Jelly, R. G.; PP4408

'Premier, Climbing'   Cl HT, mr, 1927, Vestal

'Premier'   HT, mr, 1918, E.G. Hill, Co.; bud long, pointed; flowers dark velvety rose-rev, veined darker, reverse lighter, open, dbl.; foliage rich green, leathery; vigorous growth; [('Ophelia' × 'Mrs Charles E. Russell') × unknown]

'Premier Amour' -- See 'First Love'

'Premier Bal'   HT, w, 1950, Meilland, F.; flowers ivory edged carmine, 30-40 petals, cupped, intense fragrance; name released for re-use (MR 6); ['Fantastique' × 'Caprice']

'Premier Bal'   HT, w, 1955, Meilland, F.; flowers ivory edged cyclamen-rose, picotee effect, large, 45 petals, intense fragrance; recurrent; vigorous, bushy growth; [('Fantastique' × 'Caprice') × 'Peace']

'Premier Bal'   HT, pb, Richardier; flowers deep pink with silvery pink reverse, dbl., high-centered; good repeat; growth to 80-100 cm.; intr. 1999

'Premier Essai'   S, w, 1866, Geschwind; flowers flesh white, center carminy, medium, full; [*R. roxburghii* × 'Reine de la Lombardie']

'Premier Supreme'   HT, dp, 1927, Zieger; bud long, pointed; flowers deep rose-pink, almost scarlet, very large, dbl., high-centered; foliage dark, leathery; long stems; very vigorous growth; [sport of 'Premier']

'Première Ballerine' -- See 'Prima Ballerina'

'Présence' -- See 'Delprat'
'Present' -- See 'Präsent'
'Présent Filial'   HT, pb, 1956, Delbard-Chabert; bud long; flowers old rose tinted coppery yellow, center salmon-pink, reverse, 85 petals; foliage dense; ['Verschuren's Pink' × seedling]

'Preservation' -- See 'Bosiljurika'

'Preservation' S, lp
'President' -- See 'Adam'
'President' HSet, dp, about 1846, Pierce; flowers reddish-pink, small, very dbl., borne in clusters of 15-20; foliage medium size, rugose, deeply serrated; prickles puplish red
President Armand Zinsch® HT, dy, Delbard; flowers bright, large, dbl., high-centered, intense rose, lemon and raspberry fragrance; free-flowering; growth vigorous, medium; intr. 1998
'Président Blondeau' N, w, 1909, Denis; flowers pure white
'President Boone' HT, dr, 1936, Howard, F.H.; bud long, pointed; flowers scarlet-crimson, large, dbl., globular, intense fragrance; foliage leathery; stems sometimes weak; vigorous growth; PP314; [seedling × 'Miss Rowena Thom']
'Président Bouché' HT, or, 1917, Pernet-Ducher; flowers coral-red, shaded carmine, large to medium, full; vigorous growth; [seedling × 'Lyon Rose']
'President Bray' HT, op, 1954, Privat; flowers salmon-pink veined pink; strong stems; vigorous growth
'Président Briand' HP, op, 1929, Mallerin, C.; flowers pink suffused salmon, overlarge, dbl., globular, moderate fragrance; recurrent; foliage wrinkled; strong stems; vigorous, compact growth; [(('Frau Karl Druschki' × unknown) × 'Lyon Rose') × ('Frau Karl Druschki' × 'Willowmere')]
'Président Carnot' HP, mr, 1891, Degressy; flowers bright reddish-pink, nuanced carmine, large, full; foliage dark green, bullate; nearly thornless
'Président Charles Hain' -- See 'Amelia Earhart'
'Président Chaussé' -- See 'Mark Sullivan'
'Président Chérioux' HT, rb, 1923, Pernet-Ducher; flowers red and salmon-pink, shaded yellow, dbl.
'President Cleveland' -- See 'Frances E. Willard'
'Président Cochet-Cochet' HT, dr, 1937, Mallerin, C.; flowers deep garnet-red, tinted scarlet, very large, dbl.; foliage leathery; very vigorous growth; ['Grenoble' × seedling]
'President Coolidge' HSet, dr, 1925, Horvath; flowers glowing crimson, dbl.; very hardy; [(R. setigera × R. wichurana) × 'Château de Clos Vougeot']
'President Cosnier' HT, mp, Orard; intr. 1994
'Président de la Rochterie' B, m, 1891, Vigneron; flowers dark purple/red, very large, dbl.; [sport of 'Baron J. B. Gonella']
'Président de Sèze' ('Mme Hébert') HGal, m, 1828, Hébert, Mme.; flowers magenta center, paler at edges, small eye at center, very dbl., cupped, then convex, borne in clusters of 2-3, moderate to strong fragrance; non-remontant; foliage medium size, rounded; prickles moderate, hooked

'Président Deville' HT, mr, 1929, Leenders, M.; flowers dbl.; ['Fritz Maydt' × 'Mme J.W. Budde']
'Président d'Olbecque' -- See 'Louis-Philippe'
'Président Duhem' Pol, mr, 1930, Reymond; flowers bright red, dbl.; foliage dark; vigorous growth
'Président Dutailly' ('Charlemagne') HGal, m, 1888, Dubreuil; bud globular; flowers reddish-purple, dbl., cupped, borne in small clusters, intense fragrance; foliage matte; prickles numerous, small; stems strong, erect
'President Eisenhower' HT, mr, 1953, Joseph H. Hill, Co.; bud ovoid; flowers rose-red, 4-5 in., 35-40 petals, high-centered to open, intense fragrance; foliage dark, leathery; vigorous, bushy growth; PP1217; [sport of a seedling ('Captivator' × 'Red Delicious')]
'President F. A. des Tombe' HT, ab, 1925, Van Rossem; flowers apricot on golden yellow ground, reverse peach, dbl.; ['Mr Joh. M. Jolles' × 'Golden Emblem']
'Président Férier' HT, op, 1938, Gaujard; flowers reddish coppery pink, base tinted yellow, very dbl.; foliage bright green; very vigorous growth
'Président Franklin D. Roosevelt' HT, or, 1933, Traendly & Schenck; flowers velvety scarlet, large, 35-40 petals; [sport of 'Templar']
'President Gaupin' HT, dr
'Président Gausen' B, mr, 1862, Pradel; flowers bright carmine red, large, full
'Président Georges Feuillet' LCl, yb, 1954, Vially; flowers sulfur-yellow edged vermilion, reverse saffron, semi-dbl.
'President H. C. Schroder' ('Präsident Dr H. C. Schröder') HT, mr, 1970, Kordes, R.; flowers velvety deep red, large, dbl.; strong stems; ['New Yorker' × seedling]
'President Heidar Aliyev' -- See 'Cocosimber'
'Président Henri Queuille' HT, mr, 1952, Gaujard; flowers carmine-red, very large, dbl.; very vigorous, upright growth; ['Rome Glory' × seedling]
'President Herbert Hoover' HT, pb, 1930, Coddington; bud long, pointed; flowers orange, rose and gold, reverse lighter, large, 25 petals, moderate spicy fragrance; recurrent; foliage leathery; vigorous, tall growth; ['Sensation' × 'Souv. de Claudius Pernet']
'President Herbert Hoover, Climbing' ('President Hoover, Climbing') Cl HT, pb, 1931, Dixie Rose Nursery (also Cant, B. R., 1937); flowers pink, tinted cream and apricot, large; [sport of 'Herbert Hoover']
'President Hoover, Climbing' -- See 'President Herbert Hoover, Climbing'
'Président J. B. Croibier' HT, ob, 1940, Colombier; bud well shaped, pure orange; flowers dark orange, reverse yellow; foliage light green; very vigorous growth; ['Mrs Pierre S. duPont' ×

'Talisman']
'President Jac. Smits' ('President Jacob Smith') HT, dr, 1928, Verschuren; bud long, pointed; flowers brilliant dark red, large, semi-dbl.; foliage bronze, leathery; very vigorous growth; ['Étoile de Hollande' × 'Kitchener of Khartoum']
'President Jacob Smith' -- See 'President Jac. Smits'
'President John F. Kennedy' -- See 'John F. Kennedy'
'President Kekkonen' ('Emotion') F, or, de Ruiter, G.; flowers medium, single; free-flowering; hardy; intr. 1983
President L. Senghor® -- See 'Meiluminac'
'Président Léon de St Jean' HP, mr, 1875, Lacharme; flowers crimson, shaded velvety flame red, large, full; ['Charles Lefèbvre' × unknown]
Président Léopold Senghor® -- See 'Meiluminac'
'President Leopold Senghor, Climbing' Cl HT, dr, Meilland; flowers deep velvety crimson, 5-6 in., borne mostly solitary; intr. 1982
'Président Lincoln' HP, dr, 1862, Granger; flowers dark red shaded crimson, large, dbl., slight fragrance; recurrent; growth to 5 ft.
'President Macia' ('P. M. Leenders') HT, lp, 1933, Leenders, M.; flowers light pink, darker veining, 6 in., 25 petals; foliage dark; vigorous, bushy growth; [('Ophelia' × 'Gloire de Hollande') × ('Ophelia' × 'Sensation')]
'President MacKinley' HP, mp, 1900, Charltons; flowers carnation pink
'Président Magnaud' Ch, dr, 1916, Nabonnand, C.; flowers small, semi-dbl.
'Président Menoux' HP, lp, 1854, Guillot; flowers silky light pink, reverse lighter, large, full
'Président Morel Journel' HT, rb, 1934, Chambard, C.; flowers scarlet, reverse yellow, large, cupped; foliage bronze; vigorous growth; ['Mrs Edward Powell' × R. foetida bicolor hybrid]
'Président Nomblot' -- See 'Horace McFarland'
'Président Pacaud' HT, yb, 1946, Sauvageot, H.; flowers ochre-yellow shaded dark carmine-red and copper, well-formed, dbl.; foliage glossy; ['Mme Joseph Perraud' × seedling]
'Président Parmentier' HT, ab, 1926, Sauvageot, H.; flowers apricot-pink, dbl.; ['Col. Leclerc' × 'Le Progres']
'Président Pats' -- See 'Staatspräsident Päts'
'Président Paul Martin' HT, my, 1942, Moulin-Epinay; flowers purplish carmine-red, large, semi-dbl.; vigorous growth; ['Charles K. Douglas' × 'Souv. de Georges Pernet']
'Président Paulmier' Pol, dr, 1932, Turbat; flowers pure blood-red, passing to garnet, well-formed, very dbl., borne in clusters; dwarf growth
'Président Plumecocq' ('Director Plume-

cock') HT, yb, 1931, Gaujard; flowers coppery buff and deep salmon, large, 34 petals, cupped, moderate fruity fragrance

'Président Poincaré' HT, 1920, Grandes Roseraies; flowers reddish-magenta, center crimson, shaded yellow, reverse brighter, dbl.

'Président Rodolphe Burghes' HP, mr, 1886, Bire; flowers bright rose red, shaded lilac, medium, full; ['Jules Margottin' × 'Jean Bart']

'Président Schlachter' HP, m, 1877, Verdier, E.; flowers purple/violet, large, dbl.

'Président Seize' F, dp, 1958, Delbard-Chabert; bud long; flowers light red becoming darker, 4 in., 10-15 petals; foliage dark; strong stems; upright growth

'Président Sénélar' HP, dr, 1883, Schwartz; flowers dark cerise ved, velvety, fading to purple, large, full

'President Smith' -- See 'William R. Smith'

'President Sono' HT, ly, 1978, Kikuchi, Rikichi; bud pointed; flowers cream-yellow, 45-50 petals, high-centered, intense fragrance; foliage dark; very large (5-6 in.) upright growth; ['Burnaby' × 'Montparnasse']; intr. 1972

'President Souzy' -- See 'Pekomegir'

'President Taft' -- See 'Leuchtfeuer'

'Président Thiers' HP, mr, 1871, Lacharme; flowers fiery red, very large, full, globular; ['Victor Verdier' × unknown]

'Président Van Oost' HT, my, 1934, Lens; flowers golden yellow, edged deeper, large, dbl.; foliage glossy; long, strong stems; vigorous growth; ['Souv. de Claudius Pernet' × 'Ville de Paris']

'President Viard' HT, mr

'Président Vignet' HT, dr, 1911, Pernet-Ducher; flowers deep carmine-red, large, full, slight fragrance; strong, bushy (3-5 ft.) growth

'Président Vignet, Climbing' Cl HT, dr, 1942, Vogel, M.; flowers large, full, slight fragrance; recurrent; strong, upright (8 ft.) growth; [sport of 'Président Vignet']

'President W. H. Taft' HT, op, 1908, McCullough; bud long, pointed; flowers salmon-pink, large, dbl., high-centered; foliage glossy; long, strong stems; vigorous growth

'Président Willermoz' HP, mp, 1867, Ducher; flowers birght rose, full, globular

'President Wilson' -- See 'Orawest'

'President Wilson' HT, op, 1918, Easlea; flowers shrimp-pink, large, dbl.

'President Wm. R. Smith' -- See 'William R. Smith'

'Presidente' HT, or, Croix; flowers large, 60 petals; free-flowering; vigorous growth

'Presidente Carmona' HT, dr, 1937, Moreira da Silva; flowers blackish crimson, shaded salmon, large, dbl., cupped; foliage soft; vigorous, bushy growth; ['Hortulanus Budde' × 'Château de Clos Vougeot']

'Presidente Craveiro Lopes' HT, rb, 1958, Moreira da Silva; flowers cherry, reverse yellow, medium, 33 petals, moderate fragrance; foliage dark; strong stems; very vigorous, upright growth; ['Sirena' × 'Peace']; intr. 1955

'Presidential' Gr, lp, 1960, Lammerts, Dr. Walter; bud long, pointed; flowers light crimson, reverse China-rose, 5½ in., dbl., cupped; foliage leathery, glossy; vigorous, tall growth; ['Charlotte Armstrong' × ('Charlotte Armstrong' × 'Floradora')]; intr. 1960

'Presque Bleu' HGal, dr, about 1815, Descemet

'Presque Partout' M, dp, before 1850; flowers rose, medium, dbl., cupped; vigorous growth

'Press and Journal' -- See 'Coclion'

'Pressin' HT, Dorieux; intr. 1975

'Prestance' HT, Dorieux; intr. 1985

'Prestatyn Rover' HT, op, 1929, Lavender; flowers salmon-pink, reverse darker, dbl.; ['Alfred Colomb' × 'Mrs Wemyss Quin']

'Prestige' HEg, mr, 1958, Kordes, R.; flowers light crimson, large, semi-dbl., open, borne in clusters, slight fragrance; recurrent bloom; foliage dense, dark green, glossy; vigorous, bushy growth; hardy, tips freeze; ['Rudolph Timm' × 'Fanal']; intr. 1957

Prestige® HT, mr, Tantau; flowers large , double, high-centered, borne mostly singly; recurrent; stems medium to long; vigorous growth; florist rose; intr. 2004

Prestige de Bellegarde® F, mr, Eve, A.; flowers pure red, 8 cm., semi-dbl., borne in clusters; good repeat; foliage dense, disease-resistant; growth to 2-3 ft.; intr. 1974

'Prestige de Lyon' -- See 'Meinimo'

Prestige de Seine-et-Marne® F, yb, Eve, A.; flowers soft yellow and chamois, fading as it opens, 3 in., semi-dbl., borne in large, broad clusters; good repeat; foliage dense, glossy; growth to 70-100 cm.; intr. 1992

'Presumida' ('Baby Talisman', 'La Presumida', 'Peter Pan') Min, yb, 1948, Dot, Pedro; flowers pumpkin-yellow to white, center yellowish, small, dbl.; dwarf growth; ['Eduardo Toda' × 'Pompon de Paris']

'Pretoria' -- See 'Korhagon'

'Pretoria' HT, or, 1953, Moro; bud long; flowers copper-red to orange, large; very vigorous growth

'Pretoria Boys Centenary' HT, mr, Kordes; flowers bright red, medium, dbl., high-centered, borne mostly singly; free-flowering; vigorous, medium growth; intr. 2001

Pretty™ Min, or, Poulsen; flowers orange-red, medium, dbl., no fragrance; foliage dark; growth bushy, 20-40 cm.; intr. 1996

'Pretty 'n' Pink' -- See 'Palpink'

'Pretty 'n' Single' -- See 'Umspretty'

'Pretty Baby' Min, pb, 1982, Jolly, Betty J.; flowers light pink, reverse creamy yellow, medium, 35 petals, high-centered; foliage small, medium green, semi-glossy; bushy, spreading growth; [Baby Katie™ × 'miniature seedling']

Pretty Belinda® HT, ab, Tantau; flowers apricot with orange shading, large , double, high-centered, borne mostly singly; recurrent; stems medium to long; florist rose; intr. 2003

'Pretty Bride' HT, mp, Keisei; flowers soft pink, dbl., high-centered, borne mostly singly; good repeat; florist rose; intr. 2004

'Pretty Celine' -- See 'Rencel'

'Pretty Cupido' Min, mp, de Ruiter; bud ovate; flowers bright pink, 1-1½ in., 25 petals, rosette, borne in small clusters; good repeat; prickles sparse, 5 mm.; PP10819; [seedling × seedling]

'Pretty Fairy' S, dp, Spek; flowers bright pink , pompon , borne n large clusters, moderate fruity fragrance; recurrent; foliage small, glossy; groundcover; spreading growth; intr. 1990

'Pretty Girl' HT, w, Meilland; flowers ivory white, dbl., high-centered, borne mostly singly; good repeat; florist rose; intr. 1998

'Pretty Girl' -- See 'Miss France'

Pretty in Pink™ -- See 'Dicumpteen'

'Pretty Jennifer' -- See 'Kabjenn'

'Pretty Jessica' -- See 'Ausjess'

'Pretty Lady' -- See 'Scrivo'

'Pretty Little Thing' -- See 'Judpret'

'Pretty Penny' -- See 'Morprepen'

'Pretty Pink' -- See 'LLX8749'

'Pretty Pink' -- See 'Barprett'

'Pretty Pink' LCl, dp, 1968, Patterson; flowers deep pink, open, medium, dbl.; recurrent bloom; foliage glossy; very vigorous, climbing growth; ['New Dawn' × 'Spartan']

'Pretty Please' Min, lp, 1986, Epperson, Richard G.; flowers small, 25 petals, urn-shaped, borne usually singly, no fragrance; foliage medium size, light green, semi-glossy; prickles very thin, long, straight, light red; medium, bushy growth; ['Bride's White' × 'miniature seedling']; intr. 1985

'Pretty Polly' -- See 'Meitonje'

'Pretty Poly' Pol, mr, 1954, Bishop; flowers cherry-red, flat, camellia-like, borne in clusters; vigorous, upright growth; ['Mme Butterfly' × 'Our Princess']; intr. 1954

'Pretty Princess' HT, dp, Meilland; flowers fuchsia pink, dbl., high-centered, borne mostly singly; good repeat; florist rose; intr. 2002

Pretty Sunrise® -- See 'Meipelmel'

'Pretty Tiny' -- See 'Renpiny'

'Pretty Woman' -- See 'Minabdco'

Pretty Woman® HT, lp, Ferrer; flowers soft pink, small to medium, dbl., high-centered; florist rose; intr. 1999

'Preussen' HT, dr, 1920, Löbner; flowers

glowing dark blood-red, dbl.; ['Farbenkonigin' × 'Richmond']
'Préval' P, lp, about 1821, Prévost; flowers blush pink, large, full, moderate fragrance
'Prevalent' F, Verbeek
'Preview' -- See 'Meispola'
'Prevue' S, w, 1984, James, John; flowers medium, semi-dbl., no fragrance; foliage medium size, medium green, semi-glossy; bushy growth; [('Tausendschon' × ('Perle d'Or' × 'Old China')) × 'Safrano']; originally registered as Pol; intr. 1978
'Preyasi' HT, dp, IARI; bud pointed; flowers flower fuchsia pink, large, intense fragrance; abundant bloomer; stems long; intr. 1991
'Preziosa' -- See 'Meihimper'
Priceless® HT, pb, Tantau; flowers light pink with medium pink edges, very large, double, high-centered, borne mostly singly; recurrent; stems medium to long; florist rose; intr. 2004
'Priceless Pearl' HT, ab, Taschner, Ludwig; flowers ivory with apricot and pale pink tones, double, high-centered, borne mostly singly, moderate fragrance; recurrent; stems long; tall, stately growth; [sport of 'Bewitched']; intr. 2007
Pride® HT, dr; flowers full, 30-35 petals, high-centered, borne usually singly; good repeat; florist rose; intr. 2004
Pride 'n' Joy™ -- See 'Jacmo'
'Pride Meidiland' -- See 'Meirumour'
'Pride of Canada' HT, dp, 1981, Collins; bud long, ovoid; flowers deep pink, 34 petals, high-centered, borne in pairs; foliage dark; prickles small, brown; tall growth; ['Ena Harkness' × 'Charlotte Armstrong']
'Pride of Daylesford' Hmult, dp, Huxley, Ian; intr. 1994
'Pride of England' -- See 'Harencore'
'Pride of Hurst' Pol, op, 1926, Hicks; flowers coral-pink, small, very dbl., borne in clusters; [sport of 'Coral Cluster']
'Pride of Ichalkaranji' HT, yb, Patil, B.K.; intr. 1989
'Pride of Leicester' HT, pb, 1960, Verschuren; flowers rose-pink, base yellow, large, dbl., high-centered; foliage light green; vigorous growth; [R.M.S. Queen Mary × seedling]; intr. 1960
'Pride of Lille' -- See 'Triomphe de Lille'
'Pride of Maldon' -- See 'Harwonder'
'Pride of Midnapur' HT, rb, Mandal, G.S.; flowers blackish red with distinctive pink stripes and streaks; free-flowering; vigorous growth; [sport of 'Carmousine']; intr. 2004
'Pride of Mountbarker' -- See 'Tommount'
'Pride of Nagpur' HT, dr, Datt, Braham; flowers dark, dusky red, large, moderate sweet fragrance; intr. 1983
'Pride of New Castle' HT, dr, 1930, E.G. Hill, Co.; flowers deep velvety crimson, large, dbl.; vigorous, bushy growth; ['Hoosier' × ('Beauty' × unknown)]
'Pride of Newark' F, lp, 1968, Morey, Dr. Dennison; flowers shell-pink, 4 in., dbl., cupped, intense fragrance; foliage glossy, bronze, leathery; very vigorous, upright, compact growth; ['Joanna Hill' × 'The Fairy']; intr. 1966
'Pride of Oakland' F, mp, 1977, Lindquist; bud pointed; flowers 2½ in., 26 petals, rosette, moderate spicy fragrance; upright, spreading growth; ['Pinocchio' × 'China Doll']; intr. 1976
'Pride of Pacific' F, op, 1957, Silva; flowers salmon-pink, dbl., borne in clusters of 4-7; symmetrical growth; ['Pinocchio' × 'Maxine']
'Pride of Park' F, ob
'Pride of Reigate' HP, rb, 1884, Brown, J.; flowers carmine, striped and mottled white and soft pink, dbl.; recurrent; upright (4 ft.), bushy growth; [sport of 'Comtesse d'Oxford']
'Pride of Reigate, Climbing' Cl HP, rb, 1941, Vogel, M.; flowers red with pink or white striping, 10-12 cm., dbl., moderate fragrance; occasional repeat; [sport of 'Pride of Reigate']
'Pride of Runcorn' HT, Williams, A.
'Pride of Scotland' ('Massey University') HT, dp, McGredy; flowers deep pink, changing to salmon pink as they age, dbl., slight fragrance; good repeat; foliage large, medium green, matte; upright (3½-4 ft.), bushy growth; intr. 2003
'Pride of Sunnybank' Gr, mp, 1957, Ulrick, L.W.; ['Ma Perkins' × 'Charlotte Armstrong']
'Pride of the Valley' -- See 'Mrs F. W. Sanford'
'Pride of Tryon' S, ab, Lowe, Malcolm; flowers with apricot, peach and pink tones, dbl., borne in small clusters, slight fragrance; repeat flowering; growth low, prostrate, groundcover; intr. 2002
'Pride of Waltham' HP, mp, 1881, Paul, W.; flowers silvery rose, large, dbl.; vigorous growth; [sport of 'Comtesse d'Oxford']
'Pride of Wansbeck' -- See 'Noswan'
'Pride of Washington' HSet, m, 1849, Pierce; flowers rosy violet, medium, very dbl., cupped, borne in clusters of 10-20; foliage medium size, slightly serrated
'Pridwin' HT, m, Kordes; flowers mauve maroon, large, dbl., high-centered to globular, borne mostly singly, intense fragrance; recurrent; stems strong, sturdy; medium to tall growth; intr. 1999
'Prima' -- See 'Harwanted'
Prima™ Min, mp, Olesen
'Prima Ballerina' -- See 'Solistka Baleta'
Prima Ballerina® ('Première Ballerine', Primaballerina®) HT, dp, 1959, Tantau, Math.; bud long, pointed; flowers cherry-pink, medium to large, 20 petals, high-centered, intense fragrance; recurrent; foliage leathery, light green; upright (3 ft.) growth; [unknown × 'Peace']; intr. 1957
'Prima Donna' HT, op, 1944, Dickson, A.; bud pointed; flowers rich deep salmon-pink tinted buff, 5 in., 45 petals, high-centered; foliage glossy; vigorous, upright, open growth; PP639; ruled extinct 01/1985; ['Heinrich Wendland' × seedling]
Prima Donna™ ('Toboné') Gr, dp, 1985, Shirakawa, Takeshi; bud pointed; flowers deep fuchsia pink, large, 27 petals, high-centered, slight fragrance; foliage large, medium green, semi-glossy; prickles greyed-orange, hooked slightly downward; vigorous (6 ft.), bushy, spreading growth; [(seedling × 'Happiness') × Prominent®]; intr. 1983
Prima Donna® HT, pb, J&P; flowers creamy yellow with pink edges, gradually covering the petals, dbl., high-centered, intense fragrance; free-flowering; upright (3 ft.) growth; intr. 2000
'Prima Donna' -- See 'Mme Pierre Euler'
Prima Donna+ HT, ab, Voom, Lex; flowers peach, double, high-centered, borne mostly singly; recurrent; stems medium to long; florist rose; intr. 2004
Primaballerina® -- See 'Prima Ballerina'
Primaballerina® HT, pb, Tantau; flowers soft pink, outer petals greenish white, medium, double, high-centered, borne mostly singly; recurrent; stems medium to long; florist rose; intr. 2005
'Primarosa' HT, dp, 1950, Giacomasso; bud long; flowers carmine, base yellow, streaked orange, very large; strong stems
'Primavera' HT, op, 1936, Aicardi, D.; flowers salmon-pink, well-formed, dbl., moderate musk fragrance; vigorous growth; ['Julien Potin' × 'Sensation']
'Prime Time' Min, my, 1985, Hardgrove, Donald & Mary; flowers medium, 35 petals, high-centered; foliage small, medium green, semi-glossy; upright, bushy growth; ['Picnic' × 'Rise 'n' Shine']; intr. 1984
'Primerose' HT, my, 1913, Soupert & Notting; flowers melon-yellow, deeper in autumn, shaded apricot, dbl.; ['Mme Mélanie Soupert' × 'Mrs Peter Blair']
'Primrose Sistau' ('Primrose Sistau') Pol, pb, 1925, Turbat; flowers carmine, shaded yellow, medium, double, cupped to pompon, borne in clusters of 5-6; recurrent; prickles few thorns; half-dwarf growth
'Primevère' ('Primrose') HWich, yb, 1929, Barbier; flowers primrose-yellow to canary-yellow, 7 cm., dbl., borne in small clusters; non-recurrent; foliage dark green, glossy; long stems; very vigorous, climbing and trailer growth; [R. wichurana × 'Constance']; intr. 1930
Primo Passo® S, ly, Barni, V.; flowers creamy yellow, golden stamens, medium, semi-dbl., cupped to flat, borne in large clusters, slight fragrance; good repeat; rapid, arching (70-90 cm.) growth; intr. 1995
'Primo Premio' HT, pb, 1964, Giacomasso; flowers rose suffused yellow, well-formed, medium

Primo Sole® -- See 'Barpris'
'Primrose' -- See 'Primevère'
'Primrose' T, ly, 1908, Dingee & Conard
'Primrose Bedder' F, my, 1957, Kordes; flowers primrose-yellow, dbl., borne in large trusses; foliage light green; intr. 1956
'Primrose Pet' Pol, 1913, Williams, A.
'Primrose Pirrie' HT, my, 1920, Dobbie; [sport of 'Lady Pirrie']
'Primrose Queen' Ch, ly, before 1918, Lippiat; flowers medium, full; [sport of 'Arethusa']
'Primrose Queen' HT, my
'Primrose Sistau' -- See 'Primrose Sistau'
'Primula' Pol, pb, 1900, Soupert & Notting; flowers carmine pink with white eye, small, dbl.; ['Mignonette' × unknown]
'Primula' HT, Aicardi; intr. 1956
Prince™ ('Prince Palace') S, rb, Poulsen; bud ovoid to globular; flowers 8-10 cm., 60+ petals, borne singly and in small clusters, no fragrance; foliage dark, glossy; prickles moderate, ¼ in., straight, greyed-orange; vigorous, compact, bushy (2 ft.) growth; hips none observed ; PP11626; [Dalli Dalli® × seedling]; intr. 1998
'Prince A. de Wagram' HP, m, 1891, Cochet; bud globular; flowers bright purple, aging carmine, large, very full
'Prince Abricot' -- See 'Gingersnap'
Prince Albert™ -- See 'Poulrine'
'Prince Albert' -- See 'Souv de la Reine des Belges'
'Prince Albert' HP, rb, 1837, Laffay, M.; flowers carmine-rose changing to dark, velvety crimson, large, globular; ['Gloire des Rosomanes' × 'a damask perpetual']; sometimes classes as B
'Prince Albert' ('Mme Fontaine') B, mr, Fontaine/Paul; flowers brilliant crimson-scarlet, medium, full, borne in small clusters; nearly thornless; ['Comice de Seine-et-Marne' × unknown]; intr. 1852
'Prince Antoine d'Arenberg' HGal, about 1830, Parmentier
'Prince Arthur' ('Triomphe de Caen') HP, mr, 1875, Cant, B. R.; flowers deep crimson, medium, 55 petals, intense fragrance; vigorous growth; ['Général Jacqueminot' × unknown]
'Prince Bernhard' HT, mr, 1937, Van Rossem; bud pointed; flowers shining red, shaded strawberry-red, well-formed, large, dbl.; foliage dark; vigorous growth; [(sport of 'Matador' × unknown)]; intr. 1941
'Prince Camille de Rohan' ('La Rosière, Climbing') HP, dr, 1861, Verdier, E.; flowers very deep velvety crimson-maroon, well-formed, large, 100 petals, cupped, intense fragrance; rarely repeats; rather weak stems; vigorous, upright growth; [possibly 'Général Jacqueminot' × 'Geant des Batailles']
'Prince Charles' B, dp, 1842, Hardy; flowers deep red-purple, fading to lavender, veined magenta, base of petals near white, semi-dbl., loose, intense fragrance; non-recurrent; foliage large, dark; prickles very few; growth vigorous (to 5 ft.); sometimes classed as Ch
'Prince Charles' Gr, dr; flowers deep, royal red, dbl., high-centered; vigorous, tall growth; intr. 1992
'Prince Charles d'Arenberg' HP, mp, 1888, Soupert & Notting; flowers silky carmine pink, silvery reflections, center bright pink, very large, full, cupped; ['Dupuy Jamain' × 'Mme Sévigné']
'Prince Charles du Luxembourg' Ch, dp; flowers bright carmine, cupped
'Prince Charlie' HT, op, 1932, Dobbie; bud long, pointed; flowers coral-pink, overlaid salmon, base orange, large, dbl., cupped; foliage leathery, bronze tinted; vigorous, bushy growth
'Prince Charming' S, lp, Skinner; flowers pale blush-pink, dbl., intense fragrance; prolonged bloom; upright (2½ ft.), bushy growth; intr. 1958
'Prince Charming' HT, rb, 1916, Dickson, H.; flowers reddish-copper, base bright gold, medium, full
'Prince Charming' Min, mr, deVink; flowers bright crimson, 1 in., dbl.; foliage tinted red; dwarf (8-12 in.) growth; ['Ellen Poulsen' × 'Tom Thumb']; intr. 1953
'Prince Damask' HT, dr, 1954, LeGrice; flowers maroon, medium, 30 petals; foliage small, dark; ['Guineé' × unknown]
'Prince d'Arenberg' -- See 'Duc d'Arenberg'
'Prince de Beïra' HP, mr, 1888, Verdier, E.; flowers vermilion-red, shaded lighter, glossy red, large, full
'Prince de Bulgarie' HT, lp, 1900, Pernet-Ducher; bud long, pointed; flowers silvery flesh, center deeper, shaded salmon and saffron-yellow, dbl., cupped, moderate fragrance; foliage bright green; vigorous growth
'Prince de Galles' P, rb, before 1826, Blinière; flowers red, aging violet pink, large, full
'Prince de Joinville' HP, mr, 1867, Paul, W.; flowers bright carmine-crimson, medium, dbl.
Prince de Monaco™ -- See 'Meisponge'
'Prince de Monaco' -- See 'Poulart'
'Prince de Porcia' HP, dr, 1865, Verdier, E.; flowers deep scarlet-vermilion, 10 cm., dbl.
'Prince de Vaudémont' -- See 'Princesse de Vaudémont'
'Prince Englebert Charles d'Arenberg' HT, or, 1909, Soupert & Notting; flowers scarlet shaded purple, very large, dbl., moderate fragrance; ['Étoile de France' × 'Richmond']
'Prince Eugène' -- See 'Eugène de Beauharnais'
'Prince Eugène de Beauharnais' ('Eugène de Luxembourg') HP, dr, 1864, Moreau et Robert
'Prince Félix de Luxembourg' HT, mr, 1930, Ketten Bros.; flowers carmine-red, shaded purplish, large, 30-35 petals, moderate fragrance; foliage dark; very vigorous, bushy growth; ['Gen. MacArthur' × 'George C. Waud']
'Prince Frédéric' -- See 'Prince Frederick'
'Prince Frederick' ('Prince Frédéric') HGal, mr, about 1840, Parmentier; flowers bright red, large, very dbl.
'Prince Henri' F, mr, 1954, Reuter, A.; flowers large, dbl.
'Prince Henri des Pays-Bas' HP, mp, 1862, Soupert; flowers bright carmine, reverse lilac, medium, full
'Prince Henri d'Orléans' HP, dp, 1886, Verdier, E.; flowers light carmine cerise red, large, dbl., cupped; foliage dark green, deeply serrated; prickles numerous, unequal, thing and sharp, slightly hooked; growth erect
'Prince Henry' F, mp, 1926, Easlea; bud long, pointed; flowers bright pink, passing to blush-pink, borne in clusters of 18-20; ['St. Helena' × seedling]
Prince Igor® -- See 'Meihigor'
'Prince Igor, Climbing' Cl F, ob, Meilland; intr. 1985
'Prince Jean de Luxembourg' Pol, w, 1926, Soupert & Notting; flowers pure white, very small, dbl., borne in immense clusters of 100-150; moderately dwarf growth; ['Jeanny Soupert' × 'miniature seedling']
'Prince Klaus' -- See 'RUprins'
'Prince Klaus' F, ob; flowers salmon-red, large, dbl.; intr. 1986
Prince Meillandina® -- See 'Meirutral'
'Prince Napoléon' B, pb, 1864, Pernet; flowers bright rose, very large, very full, moderate fragrance; recurrent; upright (4-5 ft.) growth
'Prince Noir' HP, m, 1854, Boyau; flowers dark velvety crimson-purple, full, cupped, intense sweet fragrance; free-flowering; moderate (4-5 ft.) growth
'Prince of Denmark' HT, mp, 1964, McGredy, Sam IV; flowers rose-pink, 4 in., dbl.; free growth; [Queen Elizabeth® × 'Independence']
'Prince of Orange' HT, ob, Williams, J. B.; flowers dusky orange-salmon, high-centered; intr. 1998
'Prince of Peace' -- See 'Jacpop'
'Prince of Peace' HT, pb, 2005, Murray, Jean; flowers medium, semi-dbl., borne mostly solitary; recurrent; foliage medium size, dark green; prickles moderate; upright, tall growth; ['Peace' × 'Love']
'Prince of Wales' HT, mr, 1921, Easlea; bud long, pointed; flowers brilliant cherry-scarlet, semi-dbl.
'Prince Orange' F, op
'Prince Palace' -- See 'Poulzin'
'Prince Philip' -- See 'Tudor Prince'
'Prince Prosper d'Arenberg' T, op, 1880, Soupert & Notting; flowers reddish-salmon with flesh pink, reverse carmine, medium, full; ['Mme Bérard' × unknown]
'Prince Regent' -- See 'Genpen'

'Prince Stirbey' HP, dp, 1871, Schwartz; flowers flesh pink, 3½-4 in., full, flat

'Prince Sunblaze' -- See 'Meirutral'

Prince Tango® -- See 'Delgus'

'Prince Theodore Bonney' HT, 1898, Dingee & Conard; ['Bon Silène' × 'W. F. Bennett']

'Prince Waldemar' HP, rb, 1885, Verdier, E.; flowers bright carmine cerise, bordered whitish, large, full, cupped; foliage large, delicate green

'Prince Wasiltchikoff' -- See 'Duchess of Edinburgh'

'Prince Yugala' HT, dr, 1923, Cant, F.; bud long, pointed; flowers deep velvety maroon, dbl.

'Princeps' LCl, mr, 1942, Clark, A.; flowers deep crimson, reverse lighter, medium to large, dbl., cupped, slight fragrance; may repeat in hot climates; pillar (10 ft.) growth

'Prince's Trust' -- See 'The Prince's Trust'

'Princes van Oranje' ('Princess van Oranje', 'Princesse d'Orange') Cl Pol, or, 1933, Sliedrecht; flowers blazing red and orange, borne in large clusters; PP106; [sport of 'Gloria Mundi']

'Princesa Carmen de Borbon' F, Dot, Simon; intr. 1979

'Princesa Sofia' HT, Dot, Simon; intr. 1972

'Princesita' -- See 'Pixie'

'Princess' -- See 'Keifupie'

Princess® -- See 'Interprince'

'Princess Aiko' F, mp, Keisei; intr. 2002

'Princess Alexandra' F, yb, 1970, Cobley; flowers creamy yellow suffused carmine-pink, medium, 30-35 petals, borne in trusses, moderate fragrance; foliage dark, glossy; very vigorous growth; ['Masquerade' × seedling]; intr. 1962

Princess Alexandra™ ('Princesse Alexandra', Alexandra™, 'The Ridge School') S, dp, Olesen, P. & M.; flowers 4 in., 20-30 petals, shallow cup, borne 1-4 per stem, intense spicy fragrance; free-flowering; foliage medium size, dark green, glossy; prickles moderate, ¼ in., hooked downward, yellow-green; growth moderate (3-4 ft.), upright to bushy; PP12999; [Margaret Merril® × seedling]; intr. 1997

'Princess Alexandra of Kent' -- See 'Ausmerchant'

'Princess Alice' -- See 'Hartanna'

'Princess Alice' M, m, 1853, Paul, A.; bud globular; flowers violet-rose, not very mossy, small, full, borne in small clusters; non-recurrent; stems long, covered with moss with citrus scent; ['Pourpre du Luxembourg' × unknown]

'Princess Angela' HT, lp, 1991, Alde, Robert O.; flowers large, very full, borne mostly singly, slight fragrance; foliage medium size, dark green, semi-glossy; tall, upright, bushy growth; [Pristine® × 'Granada']

'Princess Angeline' HT, mp, 1945, Swim, H.C.; flowers pink, becoming open, 4½-5½ in., 35-50 petals, cupped, intense damask fragrance; foliage leathery; vigorous, tall growth; ['Charlotte Armstrong' × 'Times Square']

'Princess Aurora' -- See 'Aurora-Hime'

'Princess Beatrix' T, yb, 1887, Bennett; flowers dark golden yellow, reverse lighter, edged pink, large, full, moderate fragrance

'Princess Bonnie' T, dr, 1896, Dingee & Conard; bud long; flowers vivid crimson, large, semi-dbl., intense fragrance; ['Bon Silène' × 'William Francis Bennett']

'Princess Charming' -- See 'Fryeager'

'Princess Chichibu' F, pb, 1971, Harkness; flowers two-toned pink, 2½-3 in., 30 petals, borne several together, slight fragrance; free-flowering; foliage glossy, dark green; hardy; [('Vera Dalton' × 'Highlight') × 'Merlin']

'Princess des Roses' -- See 'Principessa delle Rose'

'Princess Diana' HT, op, Noack; flowers coral, salmon and pink blend, dbl., high-centered; recurrent; intr. 1981

'Princess Elizabeth' HT, ob, 1927, Wheatcroft Bros.; flowers orange-gold, striped with dark cherry red, large, full, some fragrance; [sport of 'The Queen Alexandra Rose']

'Princess Elizabeth of Greece' HT, my, 1926, Chaplin Bros.; flowers golden yellow shaded terra-cotta, well-shaped, high-centered

'Princess Ena' Pol, mp, 1906, May, H. B.

'Princess Fair' HT, ab, 1965, Morey, D.; flowers light apricot, large, dbl., cupped, moderate fragrance; foliage glossy; vigorous, upright growth; [Queen Elizabeth® × ('Crimson Glory, Climbing' × 'Happiness')]; intr. 1964

'Princess Fukuyma' HT, ly, Hiroshima; intr. 1991

'Princess Grace' -- See 'Meimagarmic'

'Princess Louise' HP, w, 1869, Laxton/Paul; flowers blush, medium, globular; vigorous growth; ['Mme Vidot' × 'Virginal']

'Princess Margaret' -- See 'Prinsesse Margrethe'

'Princess Margaret of England, Climbing' -- See 'Meilistasar'

'Princess Margaret of England' -- See 'Meilista'

'Princess Margaret Rose' HT, pb, 1933, Cant, B. R.; bud long, pointed; flowers glowing pink suffused orange, large, dbl., cupped; foliage leathery; vigorous growth; [('Los Angeles' × unknown) × seedling]

Princess Marianna™ -- See 'Poulusa'

'Princess Marina' HT, ab, 1938, Robinson, H.; flowers apricot, shaded salmon and copper, well-shaped, dbl.; stiff stems; vigorous growth

'Princess Mary of Cambridge' HP, lp, 1867, Paul, G.; flowers flesh pink, large, full; ['Duchess of Sutherland' × 'Jules Margottin']

'Princess May' HT, lp, 1893, Paul, W.; flowers very light pink, slightly darker reverse, 10 cm., dbl., globular, borne singly or in small clusters, moderate fragrance; remontant; ['Gloire de Dijon' × unknown]

Princess Michael of Kent® -- See 'Harlightly'

'Princess Michiko' F, ob, 1966, Dickson, A.; flowers coppery orange, yellow eye, 3 in., 15 petals, cupped, borne in clusters; foliage glossy; bushy growth; ['Circus' × 'Spartan']

'Princess Michiko, Climbing' Cl F, ob, Keisei; [sport of 'Princess Michiko']; intr. 1977

'Princess Mikasa' HT, dp, 1986, Teranishi, K.; flowers deep pink, 45 petals, urn-shaped, borne singly, no fragrance; foliage large, medium green, semi-glossy; prickles small, light green; tall, bushy growth; [('Red Lion' × 'Samantha') × ('Red Lion' × 'Samantha')]; intr. 1983

'Princess Nagako' HT, rb, 1922, Pemberton; flowers fiery red, shaded yellow, small, semi-dbl.

'Princess Nobuko' -- See 'Coclistine'

'Princess of Holland' ('Princess of Orange') HT, op, Williams, J. B.; flowers dusky orange-salmon, reverse lighter, dbl., high-centered, moderate fragrance; recurrent; intr. 1998

'Princess of India' ('Indian Princess') HT, rb, 1983, Pal, Dr. B.P.; flowers outer petals deep red, inner petals carmine, large, 35 petals, high-centered, intense fragrance; foliage medium to large, dark, smooth; prickles brown to gray; upright, bushy growth; ['Tropicana' × 'Granada']; intr. 1980

'Princess of Monaco' -- See 'Meimagarmic'

'Princess of Nassau' -- See 'Princesse de Nassau'

'Princess of Orange' -- See 'Princess of Holland'

'Princess of Wales' HP, lp, 1871, Laxton; flowers light pink center with outer petals fading to white, full, cupped, borne in clusters, intense fragrance; frequent flowering; growth medium (4-5 ft.)

'Princess of Wales' HP, mr, Paul, W.; flowers vivid crimson; intr. 1874

'Princess of Wales' T, yb, Bennett; bud long, pointed; flowers exterior petals pink yellow, center deep waxy yellow, medium, dbl., cupped; ['Adam' × 'Elise Sauvage']; intr. 1882

'Princess of Wales' ('Princesse de Galles', 'The Princess of Wales') F, w, Harkness; flowers clear white, yellow stamens, medium, 25-30 petals, open, borne in clusters, slight fragrance; good repeat; foliage dark green, glossy; stems upright, medium (2-2½ ft.); intr. 1997

'Princess Pearl' F, w, 1960, Beldam Bridge Nursery; flowers white center blush, 3 in., 40 petals, borne in clusters; foliage leathery, dark; moderate growth; [sport of 'Carol Amling']

'Princess Rose Blossom' S, pb, Kordes; flowers combination of cream, white and shades of coral, large, deeply cupped to globular, borne singly and in clusters, slight fragrance; growth to 4 ft.; intr. 2003

'Princess Royal' -- See 'Dicroyal'

'Princess Royal' HT, mp, 1935, Dickson, A.; flowers rose-pink to hydrangea-pink, petals shell-shaped, very large; foliage dark, glossy; vigorous growth; RULED EXTINCT 4/92

'Princess Takamatsu' HT, pb, 1977, Kono, Yoshito; bud globular; flowers 6 in., 50 petals, high-centered; vigorous, upright growth; ['Bonsoir' × 'Christian Dior']; intr. 1974

'Princess van Orange' -- See 'Princes van Oranje'

'Princess Victoria' HT, or, 1920, McGredy; flowers glowing scarlet-crimson shaded orange, passing to carmine, b, dbl.

'Princess White' F, w, 1957, Boerner; bud pointed; flowers medium, dbl., flat, moderate fragrance; foliage leathery; strong stems; vigorous, upright, bushy growth; PP1540; ['orange seedling' × 'Demure']; intr. 1956

'Princesse' HGal, dp, 1824, Hardy

'Princesse' HT, or, 1965, Laperrière; flowers geranium-red, 4-5 in., 45 petals, globular; vigorous, upright growth; [('Peace' × 'Magicienne') × ('Independence' × 'Radar')]

'Princesse Adélaïde' ('Michael Bates' Moss') M, lp, 1845, Laffay, M.; flowers pale carmine pink, medium to large, dbl., moderate fragrance; non-recurrent; foliage dark, often variegated; vigorous growth

'Princesse Adélaïde d'Orléans' -- See 'Adélaïde d'Orléans'

'Princesse Alexandra' -- See 'Pouldra'

'Princesse Alice de Monaco' T, yb, 1893, Weber; flowers cream-yellow edged pink

'Princesse Alix de Ligne' HT, mp, RvS-Melle; ['Korland' × seedling]; intr. 1993

'Princesse Amédée de Broglie' HT, or, Mallerin, C.; bud very long, fiery red; flowers nasturtium-red, deeper in autumn, well-formed, large; foliage dark, glossy; vigorous growth; [('Charles P. Kilham' × unknown) × 'Colette Clément']; intr. 1935

'Princesse Amédée de Broglie' HP, lp, 1885, Lévêque; flowers light pink, silvery towards center, reverse blush, large, full, globular; very remontant; foliage large, dark green

'Princesse Amélie' M, m, 1851, Robert; flowers lilac-carmine, large, dbl.

'Princesse Amélie d'Orléans' HP, lp, 1884, Lévêque; flowers silky flesh pink, very large, full, globular

'Princesse Bacchiochi' M, mp, 1866, Moreau et Robert; flowers raspberry pink, buttoned eye, medium, dbl., cupped, loose, moderate fragrance; non-remontant

'Princesse Béatrice' -- See 'Prinses Béatrix'

'Princesse Blanche d'Orléans' HP, dp, 1877, Verdier, E.; flowers dark carmine pink, shaded purple-violet, medium, full

'Princesse Charles d'Arenberg' HP, pb, 1877, Soupert; flowers silvery lilac rose, center darker carmine, large, full; ['Dupuy Jamain' × 'Mme de Sévigné']

'Princesse Charlotte de la Trémoille' -- See 'Mlle Charlotte de la Trémoille'

'Princesse Christine von Salm' -- See 'Baron Girod de l'Ain'

'Princesse de Bassaraba de Brancovan' -- See 'Mme la Princesse de Bessaraba de Brancovan'

'Princesse de Béarn' HP, mr, 1885, Lévêque; flowers velvety poppy-red, large, dbl., globular; vigorous growth; ['Duc de Cazes' × unknown]

'Princesse de Galles' -- See 'Princess of Wales'

'Princesse de Joinville' B, mp, 1840, Poncet; flowers bright pink, medium; sometimes classed as HP

'Princesse de Lamballe' ('Princesse Lamballe') A, w, before 1830, Miellez; sepals long; flowers milky white, sometimes tinted flesh, medium, very dbl., borne in clusters of 6-10, moderate fragrance; foliage gray-green; growth vigorous, compact, branching

'Princesse de Metternich' HP, mp, 1871, de Sansal; flowers bright, shining pink, large, full

Princesse de Monaco® -- See 'Meimagarmic'

'Princesse de Monaco, Climbing' Cl HT, w; [sport of Princesse de Monaco®]; intr. 1985

'Princesse de Naples' HP, lp, 1897, Gaëtano, Bonfiglioli & Figlio; flowers silvery pink on ground of cream, reverse lilac, very large, full; foliage light green

'Princesse de Nassau' HGal, dp, about 1840, Miellez

'Princesse de Nassau' ('Princess of Nassau') N, ly, 1835, Laffay, M.; bud yellowish, tinted pink; flowers creamy yellow, fading to cream, 5-7 cm., very dbl., cupped, borne in large clusters, moderate musk fragrance; growth with crossing branches; sometimes classed as HMsk

'Princesse de Parme' M, mp, Morley, Dr B.; ['William Lobb' × unknown]; intr. 1988

'Princesse de Portugal' HGal, mp, before 1828, Pelletier; flowers bright cerise pink, very large, full; sometimes classes as D

'Princesse de Sagan' Ch, dr, 1887, Dubreuil; flowers crimson shaded with purple, medium, dbl., cupped; vigorous growth

'Princesse de Vaudémont' M, lp, about 1825, Vibert; bud globular, large; flowers medium, dbl., peony-like, moderate fragrance

'Princesse de Vaudémont' ('Prince de Vaudémont') M, lp, Robert; flowers 2¼ in., full, globular; intr. 1854

'Princesse de Venosa' T, w, 1895, Dubreuil; bud long, ovoid; flowers white tinted blush and yellow

'Princesse d'Orange' -- See 'Princes van Oranje'

'Princesse d'Orient' HT, Poulsen

'Princesse Éléonore' HGal, mr, before 1826, Miellez; flowers crimson red, large, dbl.; nearly thornless

'Princesse Étienne de Croy' T, m, 1898, Ketten Bros.; flowers violet rose, dbl.; ['Comtesse de Labarthe' × 'Mme Eugène Verdier']

'Princesse Ghika' T, mr, 1922, Nabonnand, P.; flowers brilliant red with dark reflexes, large, dbl.; ['Gén. Schablikine' × 'Papa Gontier']

'Princesse Hélène' HP, dp, 1837, Laffay; flowers rosy purple, medium, very dbl., globular; growth erect

'Princesse Hélène d'Orléans' HP, mp, 1886, Verdier, E.; flowers fresh, brilliant pink, large, full, cupped; foliage dark green, irregularly dentate; prickles numerous, strong, fairly straight; growth erect

'Princesse Henri des Pays-Bas' HP, w, 1868, Soupert; flowers white, tinted silvery pink and flesh, large, full

'Princesse Hohenzollern' ('S. A. R. Mme La Princesse de Hohenzollern, Infante de Portugal') T, rb, 1886, Nabonnand; flowers peach-red to crimson, well-formed, very large, dbl.

'Princesse Ita' HT, yb, 1943, Meilland, F.; bud oval; flowers Indian yellow edged red, open, medium, semi-dbl.; foliage leathery; vigorous, bushy growth; ['Julien Potin' × 'Charles P. Kilham']

'Princesse Jaune' HT, my, 1945, Fessel; flowers citron-yellow, large, dbl.

'Princesse Joséphine-Charlotte' Pol, op, 1945, Lens; flowers bright pink suffused apricot-salmon, small, semi-dbl., cupped, slight fragrance; very vigorous, bushy growth; [sport of Orange Triumph®]

'Princesse Joséphine de Flandres' Pol, pb, 1888, Soupert & Notting; flowers blush pink on a ground of salmon; growth to 80 cm.; ['Mignonette' × 'Marquise de Vivens']

'Princesse Josephine de Hohenzollern' D, mp, 1840, Baumann; flowers medium, full

'Princesse Julie d'Arenberg' T, yb, 1885, Soupert & Notting; flowers yellow, shaded dark yellow, center canary, large, very full, cupped

'Princesse Lamballe' -- See 'Princesse de Lamballe'

'Princesse Liliane' HT, mr, 1954, Buyl Frères; flowers blood-red, 5 in., 25-30 petals; foliage dark; vigorous, upright growth; ['Happiness' × 'Hens Verschuren']

'Princesse Lise Troubezkoi' HP, lp, 1878,

Lévêque; flowers delicate pink, bordered white, medium, full

'Princesse Louise' HSem, w, 1829, Jacques; bud crimson; flowers creamy white, back petals shaded with rose, 2-2½ in., dbl., cupped, borne in clusters of 3-20; foliage dark green, smooth, sharply and regularly toothed; prickles numerous, strong, straight; [R. sempervirens × 'Parson's Pink']

'Princesse Louise' Cl HT, m, 1924, Nabonnand, P.; bud long, pointed; flowers rich purple, center tinted brilliant garnet, large, semi-dbl.; vigorous, climbing growth; ['La France de '89' × 'Victor Hugo']

'Princesse Louise d'Orléans' HP, mp, 1886, Verdier, E.; flowers glowing, silky pink, silvery edges, large, full

'Princesse Louise-Victoria' HP, op, 1872, Knight; flowers dark carmine-pink, shaded peach, medium to large

'Princesse Margaret d'Angleterre, Climbing' -- See 'Meilistasar'

Princesse Margaret d'Angleterre® -- See 'Meilista'

'Princesse Margaretha' Pol, lp, 1985, Poulsen, S.; flowers pale pink, dbl., borne in clusters, no fragrance; foliage medium size, medium green, semi-glossy; medium, bushy growth; intr. 1932

'Princesse Marguerite d'Orléans' HP, dp, 1888, Verdier, E.; flowers deep pink, shaded darker pink, large to very large, full

'Princesse Marguerite d'Orléans' T, lp, Nabonnand; flowers light pink, center carmine, reverse silvery, very large, full; ['Papa Gontier' × 'Isabelle Nabonnand']; intr. 1890

'Princesse Marie' ('Belvedere') HSem, mp, 1829, Jacques; flowers bright pink, fading to pale pink, medium, full, flat, quartered, borne in clusters of 3-12; non-remontant; foliage oval, pointed, sharply dentate; prickles moderate

'Princesse Marie Adelaide de Luxembourg' Pol, w, 1895, Soupert & Notting; flowers white with pink tones, full, borne in clusters; foliage dark green, glossy; growth to 2 ft.; ['Mignonette' × unknown]

'Princesse Marie-Astrid' HT, mp, 1964, Mondial Roses; bud globular; flowers deep rose to camellia-pink, large, dbl.; moderate, bushy growth; [('Mme Edouard Herriot' × R. rugosa rubra) × 'La Jolie']

'Princesse Marie-Christine' HT, dr, 1955, Buyl Frères; bud ovoid to long; flowers blood-red, 25-30 petals; vigorous, bushy growth; ['Poinsettia' × 'Ena Harkness']

'Princesse Marie Clotilde Napoléon' Pol, w, 1924, Opdebeeck; flowers white shaded pink, base pale yellow, large, dbl.; vigorous growth

'Princesse Marie Dagmar' -- See 'Socrate'

'Princesse Marie Dagmar' T, 1919, Lévêque

'Princesse Marie Dolgorouky' HP, lp, 1878, Gonod; flowers light pink, often striped with white, very large, dbl.; ['Anna de Diesbach' × unknown]

'Princesse Marie d'Orléans' HP, mp, 1885, Verdier; flowers bright cerise pink shaded silvery, large, full; foliage light green, glossy; growth upright

'Princesse Marie José' Pol, w, 1924, Opdebeeck; flowers white shaded rose, base yellow, large, dbl.; vigorous growth

'Princesse Marie José' HT, or, Klettenberg-Londes; bud long, pointed; flowers orange-scarlet, dbl., moderate fruity fragrance; intr. 1925

'Princesse Olympie' ('Grossherzogin Mathilde') HP, w, 1858, Béluze; flowers greenish white

'Princesse Paola' HT, mp, 1967, Hendrickx; bud cerise-pink; flowers bright pink, 5 in., dbl., high-centered, intense fragrance; foliage glossy; vigorous growth

'Princesse Queen' Pol, pb

'Princesse Radziwill' HP, mp, 1883, Lévêque; flowers carmine pink shaded bright crimson, large, full; foliage light green

'Princesse Royale' M, mp, 1846, Portemer; bud well mossed; flowers rosy flesh, 5-6 cm., dbl., globular, borne in clusters; foliage dark green, oval, pointed, much serrated; prickles short, saffron; ['Ponctuée' × 'Tuscany']

'Princesse Sophie de Bavière' F, lp, RvS-Melle; ['Melglory' × seedling]; intr. 1996

'Princesse Stéphanie' -- See 'Fiançailles de la Princesse Stéphanie et de l'Archiduc Rodolphe'

'Princesse Stéphanie' T, op, 1880, Levet, A.; flowers salmon-yellow, large, dbl.; very vigorous growth; ['Gloire de Dijon' × unknown]

'Princesse Stéphanie de Belgique' HT, dp, 1929, Soupert & Notting; bud long, pointed; flowers carmine, center deeper, dbl.; ['Gen. MacArthur' × seedling]

'Princesse Vera Orbelioni' HT, op, 1909, Schwartz; flowers light salmon-pink, large, dbl.; ['Kaiserin Auguste Viktoria' × 'Sénateur Saint-Romme']

'Princesse Verona' S, mp, 1985, Buck, Dr. Griffith J.; flowers Neyron rose, 4 in., 30 petals, cupped, high-centered, borne singly and in clusters of up to 15, slight honey clove fragrance; repeat bloom; foliage leathery, dark olive green; prickles awl-like, tan; upright (4 ft.), bushy, compact growth; hardy; ['Verona' × 'Prairie Princess']; intr. 1984

'Princesse Wilhelmine des Pays-Bas' Pol, w, 1886, Soupert & Notting; flowers bright white, greenish at center, small to medium, full, moderate fragrance; ['Mignonette' × 'Mme Damaizin']

'Princesse Yvonne Ghika' HT, w, 1927, Mühle; flowers white, center salmon, dbl.; ['Stadtrat Glaser' × unknown]

'Principal A. H. Pirie' HT, mp, 1910, Bernaix fils; flowers silvery pink, medium, very full, moderate fragrance

'Principe da Beïra' HP, m, 1890, da Costa; flowers purple

'Principe de Napoli' HT, my, 1937, Aicardi Bros.; bud long; flowers large, dbl.; foliage clear green; vigorous growth

'Principe de Piemonte' HT, dr, 1929, Giacomasso; flowers crimson-red, large; ['Mrs Edward Powell' × 'Gen. MacArthur']

'Principessa delle Rose' ('Princess des Roses') HT, mr, 1953, Aicardi, D.; bud long, pointed; flowers lilac-rose, large, 30-40 petals, cupped, moderate fragrance; very vigorous, upright growth; PP1355; ['Julien Potin' × 'Sensation']

'Principessa di Napoli' T, lp, 1898, Brauer/Ketten Bros.; bud long; flowers pale rose, base of petals cream, large, full, borne mostly solitary, moderate like Maréchal Niel fragrance; ['Duc de Magenta' × 'Safrano']

'Prins Claus' ('Prince Klaus', 'Rosalynn Carter') Gr, or, 1973, deRuiter; flowers coral-red with orange tones, 3½-4 in., 30 petals, high-centered, moderate spicy fragrance; tall, vigorous, bushy, upright growth; ['Mischief' × (Queen Elizabeth® × 'Scania')]; originally registered as HT; re-registered as Rosalynn Carter, ARA 1979; intr. 1978

'Prins Hamlet' HT, lp, 1927, Mohr; bud long, pointed; flowers light pink, base yellow, open, large, semi-dbl., high-centered; foliage light, leathery; vigorous, bushy growth; [sport of 'Ophelia']

'Prins Willem-Alexander' F, ob, 1973, Verschuren; flowers coral-vermilion, 2-3 in., single, borne in trusses, slight fragrance; free-flowering; foliage dark green, red when young; growth bushy, large; ['Tropicana' × Europeana®]; intr. 1972

'Prinses Astrid' HT, yb, DVP Melle; [Australian Gold® × 'Princesse Alix de Ligne']; intr. 2000

'Prinses Béatrix' ('Princesse Béatrice') HT, ob, 1940, Busiman; bud long, pointed; flowers terra-cotta, shaded light apricot, large, dbl., cupped, intense fruity fragrance; foliage leathery, bronze; vigorous, bushy growth; ['Heinrich Wendland' × 'Max Krause']

'Prinses Christina' F, mr, 1945, Buisman, G. A. H.; bud large; flowers clear carmine-red, dbl., borne in clusters; very vigorous growth; ['Lafayette' × 'Donald Prior']

'Prinses Juliana' HT, dr, 1918, Leenders, M.; bud long, pointed; flowers deep crimson-red, shaded darker, dbl.; foliage dark; vigorous growth; ['Gen. MacArthur' × 'Marie van Houtte']

'Prinses Mathilde' F, r, DVP Melle; flowers large, dbl, moderate soft fragrance; ['Melglory' × 'Marchenland']; intr. 2004

'Prinses van Oranje, Climbing' -- See 'Gloria Mundi, Climbing'

'Prinsesse Astrid af Norge' F, ob, 1958,

Poulsen, S.; flowers bright orange, semi-dbl.; vigorous, upright growth; ['Pinocchio' × 'Pinocchio']

Prinsesse Benedikte™ S, yb, Poulsen; flowers yellow blend, 10-15 cm., 25 petals, slight fragrance; foliage dark; growth narrow, bushy (20-40 cm); intr. 2005

'Prinsesse Margrethe' ('Princess Margaret') HT, op, Poulsen, S.; flowers dark salmon-orange, dbl., slight fragrance; free-flowering; strong stems; growth vigorous, upright; [Queen Elizabeth® × ('Independence' × 'Golden Scepter')]; intr. 1963

'Printemps' HT, pb, 1948, Mallerin, C.; bud long; flowers old-rose tinted light red, reverse yellow, 4 in., dbl.; foliage glossy, dark; very vigorous growth; ['Trylon' × 'Brazier']

'Printemps Fleuri' HMult, m, 1922, Turbat; flowers bright purple passing to carmine-pink, stamens yellow, 3 cm., semi-dbl., borne in clusters of 5-15; ['Étoile Luisante' × unknown]

'Prinz Hamlet' HT, lp, 1927, Mohr; flowers large, dbl.

'Prinz Hirzeprinzchen' HMult, m, 1912, Geschwind, R.; flowers purple-red, striped white, lighter reverse, 5-6 cm., semi-dbl., borne in clusters of up to 20, moderate fragrance

'Prinz Max zu Schaumburg-Lippe' HT, op, 1934, von Würtemberg, Herzogin Elsa; flowers salmon-pink, large, dbl., intense fragrance; vigorous growth; ['Frau Karl Druschki' × 'Lyon Rose']

'Prinzessin Bathildis zu Schaumburg-Lippe' ('Prinzessin Elsa zu Schaumburg-Lippe') HT, ly, 1929, von Württemberg, Herzogin Elsa; flowers yellowish-white, very large, dbl.; sometimes classed as HP

'Prinzessin Elsa zu Schaumburg-Lippe' -- See 'Prinzessin Bathildis zu Schaumburg-Lippe'

'Prinzessin Hildegard' -- See 'Prinzessin Hildegard von Bayern'

'Prinzessin Hildegard von Bayern' ('Prinzessin Hildegard') HT, my, 1917, Lambert, P.; flowers bright yellow, fading to cream-yellow, large, dbl., moderate fragrance; ['Frau Karl Druschki' × 'Friedrich Harms']

'Prinzessin Irrlieb' F, mr, 1963, Kordes, R.; flowers velvety bright red, dbl., borne in large clusters; moderate, symmetrical growth

'Prinzessin Leontine Fürstenberg' T, my, 1908, Chalupecky; flowers large, full; [sport of 'Mme Lombard']

'Prinzessin Ludwig von Bayern' HMult, mp, 1911, Brög; flowers bright pink, lighter reverse, 3½ cm., dbl., borne in medium clusters, no fragrance; ['Turner's Crimson Rambler' × unknown]

'Prinzessin M. von Arenberg' HT, w, 1928, Leenders, M.; flowers rosy white, shaded pale rose-pink, dbl., cupped, intense fragrance; ['Ophelia' × 'Los Angeles']

'Prinzessin Maria Teresa' F, lp, Lens, Louis; flowers medium, dbl.; intr. 1982

'Prinzessin Marie' HT, lp, 1907, Lindemann; flowers large, full; ['Mme Caroline Testout' × 'Mme Mélanie Willermoz']

'Prinzessin Tatiana Wasiltchikoff' HT, lp, 1941, Spath; flowers flesh-pink, dbl., long stems; upright growth

'Prinzessin von Battenberg' T, w, 1912, Brauer; flowers white, aging to flesh pink

'Prior M. Oberthau' HMult, dp, 1923, Bruder Alfons; flowers rose red, white center, 3½ cm., dbl., flat, borne in medium clusters, slight fragrance; non-recurrent; few prickles

'Priory Pride' -- See 'Nostpri'

'Priory Rose' -- See 'Nostros'

'Priscilla' HT, mp, 1922, Montgomery Co.; bud long, pointed; flowers pink, outer petals rose-pink, very large, dbl., cupped; foliage leathery, glossy; vigorous growth; [seedling × 'Ophelia']

'Priscilla' -- See 'Marie Lambert'

Priscilla Burton® -- See 'Macrat'

'Prissy Missy' Min, mp, 1965, Williams, Ernest D.; flowers medium pink, reverse lighter, small, very dbl., moderate spicy fragrance; vigorous, bushy, dwarf growth; ['Spring Song' × seedling]

Pristine® -- See 'Jacpico'

'Pristine, Climbing' Cl HT, w; intr. after 1978

'Pristine Pavement' ('Schneeberg', 'White Perfection') HRg, w, Baum; flowers pure white, semi-dbl., moderate fragrance; foliage glossy; compact, mounding (3 ft.) growth; intr. 1990

'Prithi Rani' HT, pb, Ghosh, Mr. & Mrs. S.; flowers porcelain pink with deep center, reverse pinkish white, dbl.; strong growth; intr. 2001

'Priti' Pol, lp, Kasturi; flowers pink to white, globular; prolific; [sport of 'Margo Koster']; intr. 1971

'Priub' -- See 'Umspriub'

Prive™ Gr, mp

'Privet iz Alma-Aty' ('Greetings from Alma-Aty') HT, op, 1958, Sushkov & Besschetnova; flowers pink tinted orange, large, 60 petals; foliage dark, glossy; very vigorous growth; ['Independence' × 'Peace']

'Priyadarshini' HT, pb, IARI; flowers rhodamine pink with darker edges; free-flowering; dedicated to late Mrs. Indira Gandhi; intr. 1988

'Priyatama' ('The Beloved') HT, pb, 1984, Viraraghavan, M.S. Viru; bud ovoid; flowers deep pink, paler edges and reverse, medium, 35 petals, high-centered, borne singly; foliage glossy, slightly wrinkled; prickles red; growth bushy; [Inge Horstmann × 'Picasso']; intr. 1981

'Proberg' ('Blushing Pink Iceberg') F, pb, Weatherly, Lilia; intr. 1995

'Probril' ('Bright Pink Iceberg', Brilliant Pink Iceberg™) F, pb, 1999, Weatherly, Lilia; flowers deep pink, reverse white, 3½-4 in., dbl., borne in large clusters, moderate fragrance; foliage large, light green, glossy; few prickles; upright, rounded, medium (30-36 in.) growth; PP12645; [sport of Pink Iceberg™]; intr. 1999

'Probuzeni' ('Awakening') LCl, lp, 1992, Böhm, J.; flowers medium, full, quartered, moderate fragrance; [sport of 'New Dawn']; brought from Czechoslovia to England by R. Balfour and re-introduced; intr. 1935

'Prodaná Nevesta' S, w, 1934, Brada, Dr.; flowers snow-white, center tinted yellow, borne in large clusters; non-recurrent; foliage light, glossy; vigorous growth

'Prodigieuse' HT, ob, Croix; flowers orange with silver reverse, large, 65 petals; good repeat; foliage dark green, disease-resistant; intr. 1969

'Professeur Bérard' HT, dp, 1930, Laperrière; flowers bright purple-carmine, base yellow, petals laciniated, dbl.; foliage leathery, dark; very vigorous growth; ['Hadley' × 'The Queen Alexandra Rose']

'Professeur Christian Cabrol' HMsk, pb, Lefebvre; flowers carmine with white center, small, single, borne in clusters of 8-10; free-flowering; growth compact (3 ft.), vigorous; named for professor of cardiac surgery.; intr. 1993

'Professeur Déaux' HT, ly, 1935, Pernet-Ducher; flowers light yellow streaked chamois, dbl.; foliage glossy, dark, bronze; long stems; very vigorous growth

'Prof Émile Perrot' D, mp, 1931; flowers light pink, medium, dbl.; brought from Persia by Prof. Perrot; may be synonymous with Ispahan, Kazanlik, or Trigintipetala

'Professeur Ganiviat' T, pb, 1890, Perrier; flowers salmon carmine, shaded carmine purple, large, very dbl., high-centered; growth to 1 m.

Professeur Jean Bernard® -- See 'Deljaber'

'Professeur Jolibois' HP, dr, 1888, Verdier, E.; flowers dark red, magenta, carmine and flame, large, full, globular

'Professeur Jules Courtois' HP, mr, 1886, Bire; flowers glowing red, shaded lilac, medium, dbl.; ['Général Jacqueminot' × unknown]

'Professeur Maxime Cornu' HP, mr, 1885, Lévêque; flowers cerise red, very large, full, some fragrance; recurrent; foliage lanceolate, glaucous green

'Prof Alfred Dufour' F, mr, 1970, Cazzaniga, F. G.; flowers bright red, medium, semi-dbl.; foliage light green; compact growth; ['Paprika' × 'Coup de Foudre']; intr. 1961

'Professor Baranov' HT, yb, 1947, Vogel, M.; flowers large, dbl.

'Prof Bento Carqueja' HT, op, 1936, Moreira da Silva; bud long, pointed; flowers pink and salmon, shaded coral-red, large, dbl., high-centered; foliage soft; vigorous growth; ['Ophelia' × 'Mme Edouard Herriot']

'Professor Boesman' F, mp, RvS-Melle; flowers dbl.; ['Melflor' × 'Melglory']; intr. 1992

'Professor Borza' HT, or, 1940, Ambrosi; flowers medium, dbl.

'Prof C. S. Sargent' HWich, my, 1903, Farrell; flowers yellow, center deeper, fading to cream, 2½ in., dbl., borne in small clusters, moderate fragrance; early bloom; foliage small, ornamental; vigorous growth; [*R. wichurana* × 'Souv. d'Auguste Metral']

'Prof Chris Barnard' HT, mr, 1972, Fisher, P.; flowers blood-red, pointed, 4 in., 40 petals; foliage glossy; upright growth; ['Ena Harkness' × 'Karl Herbst']; intr. 1970

'Prof Costa Leite' HT, my, 1955, Moreira da Silva; very vigorous growth; ['Peace' × 'Julien Potin']

'Professor Dr Hans Molisch' Cl HT, mp, 1923, Mühle; flowers silvery pink, medium to large, very dbl., borne in small clusters; numerous prickles

'Professor Dr Kurth' HT, mr, Schmid, P.; flowers large, dbl.; intr. 1960

'Prof Dr von Beck' HT, pb, 1927, Ries; flowers bright rose-pink, reverse carmine-red, dbl.; ['Mme Abel Chatenay' × 'Farbenkonigin']

'Professor Erich Maurer' Cl HT, mp, 1939, Tepelmann; flowers dark pink, lighter at center, 5-6 in., semi-dbl. to dbl.

'Professor Fred Ziady' -- See 'Korambo'

'Professor Gnau' HT, w, 1928, Tantau; bud long, pointed; flowers creamy white; ['Oskar Cordel' × seedling]

'Professor Ibrahim' LCl, mp, 1937, Krause; flowers rose-pink, base yellow, large, borne in clusters of 4-5; very vigorous, climbng (over 13 ft.) growth; ['Daisy Hill' × 'Talisman']

'Professor Knöll' HT, mr, Berger, W.; flowers very large, very dbl.; intr. 1964

'Prof Leite Pinto' HT, mr, 1960, Moreira da Silva; flowers cherry-red, center ochre; ['Buccaneer' × 'La Jolla']

'Prof M. C. Nath' ('Prof Madhab Chandra Nath') HT, dp, 2005, Shastri, N.V.; flowers deep mauve pink, 11 cm., dbl., borne mostly solitary, moderate fragrance; free-flowering; foliage medium size, medium green, matte; prickles medium, elongated, gray, moderate; compact, medium (35 in.) growth; ['Jadis' × 'Swarthmore']; intr. 1998

'Prof Madhab Chandra Nath' -- See 'Prof M. C. Nath'

'Prof N. E. Hansen' HRg, dr, 1892, Budd; flowers rich velvety red

'Prof O. L. Kunz' S, mp, Hetzel; intr. 1980

'Professor Panalla' HT, Dot, Simon; intr. 1988

'Prof Reynaldo Santos' HT, Moreira da Silva, A.

'Professor Schmeil' HFt, yb, 1925, Kröger; flowers light orange-yellow, large, semi-dbl.

'Profil' HT, op, VEG; flowers coral pink, large, dbl.; intr. 1985

'Profile' -- See 'Macjilli'

Profondo Rosso® F, dr, Kordes; flowers very dark red, semi-dbl.; upright (60-70 cm.), compact, strong growth

'Profumo Romano' HT, Zandri, R.

'Profusion' HT, dp, 1939, Dickson, A.; bud long, pointed; flowers carmine, base orange-yellow, dbl., moderate fragrance; vigorous growth

'Profusion' HT, op, Meilland, F.; bud very long; flowers orange-salmon and carmine; foliage glossy; ['Mme Henri Guillot' × 'Signora']; intr. 1944

'Progress' -- See 'Fortschritt'

'Progress' HT, pb, 1890, Drögemüller; flowers shining carmine, shaded yellow, large, dbl., moderate fragrance; ['Mme Bérard' × 'Marie van Houtte']

'Prohadka Maje' HT

'Prolet' S, pb, 1985, Staikov, Prof. Dr. V.; flowers brick, shaded deep pink, medium, 85 petals; non-recurrent; foliage light green; vigorous, upright, branching growth; ['General Stefanik' × 'Bonn']; intr. 1975

'Prolifera' -- See 'Childling'

'Prolifera de Redouté' ('La Centfeuilles Prolifère Foliacée', 'Steeple Rose', 'Leafy-Proliferous Cabbage Rose', 'Mère Gigogne', *R. centifolia prolifera foliacea*, 'Rose Prolifère') C, mp, before 1824; sepals long, fringed; flowers rose pink, large, full, rosette, intense fragrance; non-remontant; growth to 6 ft.; new buds often protrude from the center of bloom; probably synonymous with 'King of Holland'

'Prolifère' -- See 'Childling'

'Prolifère' ('Précieuse') HGal, lp, before 1804, Dupont (?); flowers medium size, delicate pink, petals shell-shaped, very dbl.; prickles light brown; Agathe group; very subject to proliferation

'Prolifère' ('Mottled Moss') M, dp, Philippe; flowers deep-rose, too full to open well at times, large, cupped; vigorous growth; intr. before 1826

'Prom Date' -- See 'Morprom'

'Prom Night' -- See 'Zippro'

'Promenade' -- See 'Lyopro'

'Promethean' S, rb, 1985, James, John; flowers medium red, reverse darker, white eye, medium, 12 petals; repeat bloom; foliage medium size, light green, smooth, matte; bushy growth; [('Blanche Mallerin' × 'Pink Hat') × *R. multibracteata*]

'Prométhée' D, m, about 1835, Vibert

'Prométhée' HT, my, Croix; flowers bright yellow, non-fading, large, 35-40 petals, moderate fruity fragrance; recurrent; vigorous growth; intr. 2005

Prominent® -- See 'Korp'

'Promise' ('Chin Chin') HMult, op, 1929, Cant, F.; flowers salmon-pink, stamens bright yellow, single, borne in large clusters, moderate fragrance; non-recurrent; foliage almost evergreen; vigorous, climbing growth; [sport of 'Mme Eugène Résal']

'Promise' ('Poesie') HT, lp, Warriner, William A.; bud ovoid, pointed; flowers camellia pink, 4½-5 in., 40-45 petals, high-centered, borne usually singly; good repeat; foliage large, glossy; prickles medium, hooked downward; stems long, strong, vigorous growth; PP3492; ['South Seas' × 'Peace']; intr. 1976

'Promise Me' HT, w, 1971, Jelly; flowers 4 in., 45 petals, high-centered, slight sweetbriar fragrance; foliage matte, dark, leathery; vigorous, upright growth; PP3167; ['Snowsong Supreme' × seedling]; intr. 1969

'Promotion' F, mp, 1966, Verbeek; bud ovoid; flowers pink, medium, dbl., borne in clusters; foliage dark; [seedling × 'Miracle']

'Prophecy' -- See 'Minprop'

Prophyta™ HT, ab, de Ruiter, G.

'Prose' -- See 'Burgundy Iceberg'

'Proserpine' HGal, m, 1835, Prévost; flowers velvety black-purple, shaded bronze, medium, full

'Proserpine' B, m, Mondeville/Verdier, V.; bud round; flowers crimson to purplish crimson, variable, medium, full, borne in clusters of 3-4; foliage dark green; prickles hooked, red; the cultivar sold in the U.S. as Meteor may be the same as this; intr. 1841

'Prosper Laugier' HP, mr, 1883, Verdier, E.; flowers scarlet-red, large, 30 petals, cupped, moderate fragrance; recurrent bloom; growth tall (5 ft.)

'Prosperity' HMsk, w, 1919, Pemberton; bud creamy white flushed pale pink; flowers ivory white, small to medium, semi-dbl., rosette, borne in very large clusters, moderate fragrance; recurrent bloom; foliage glossy; vigorous, pillar (6-8 ft.) growth; ['Marie-Jeanne' × 'Perle des Jardins']

Prospero® -- See 'Auspero'

'Proteiformis' (*R.* × *heterophylla*, *R.* × *proteiformis*) HRg, w, 1894; flowers semi-dbl., borne in clusters; foliage variable; [*R. rugosa alba* × unknown]

Proud Bride® S, ab, Austin, David; intr. 1992

'Proud Heritage' Min, dr, 1986, Jolly, Nelson F.; flowers patio, large, 28 petals, high-centered, borne in sprays of 2-3; foliage medium size, medium green, matte; prickles light green to brown, hooked downward; upright, bushy growth; hips globular, orange; PP6561; ['Red Beauty' × 'Big John']

'Proud Land' HT, dr, 1969, Morey, Dennison; bud urn-shaped, large; flowers deep red, large, very full, cupped, borne singly and several together, moderate tea fragrance; free-flowering; foliage large, dark green, leathery; prickles medium; stems long, strong; growth vigorous, upright; PP2737; ['Chrysler Imperial' × seedling]

'Proud Mary' -- See 'Twohave'
'Proud Titania' -- See 'Austania'
'Provence' -- See 'Dorlina'
'Provence' HT, ob, 1945, Paolino; flowers orange, tinted copper and pink, well-formed
'Provence Bergsoe' C, mp
'Provence Blanc' HT, w; intr. 2007
'Provence Moss' -- See 'Unique Moss'
'Provence Pink' C, mp, 1759
Providence™ -- See 'Tucprov'
'Province d'Anjou' F, mr, Croix; flowers luminous red; intr. 1967
'Provincialis Hybrida' -- See 'Spong'
'Provins Ancien' HGal, lp, before 1906, Cochet, P.
'Provins Blanc' -- See 'Fausse Unique'
'Provins Marbré' -- See 'Marmorea'
'Provins Panaché' ('Gros Provins Panaché') B, pb, about 1860, Fontaine; flowers light pink, striped deep pink, dbl., cupped, borne in clusters, intense fragrance; recurrent; foliage bluish-green; upright (6 ft.), narrow growth; sometimes classed as P
'Provins Renoncule' ('Anémone', 'Renoncule', 'Provins Renonculée') HGal, mp, before 1810, Cartier/Dupont; flowers clear purple-pink, lighter at edges, green pip center, very dbl., moderate fragrance; foliage oval, edged pink, finely dentate; prickles small, straight, numerous, brown
'Provins Renonculée' -- See 'Provins Renoncule'
'Prudence' Cl HT, op, 1938, Fitzhardinge; flowers salmon-pink, large, semi-dbl., cupped; recurrent bloom; very vigorous, climbing (10 ft.) growth; ['Warrawee' × 'Souv. de Claudius Pernet']
'Prudence Besson' HP, mp, 1865, Lacharme; flowers cerise pink to carmine red, very large, dbl., flat
'Prudence Elizabeth' HT, w, 2007, Jacobs, Mrs. Margaret; flowers 12 cm., dbl., borne mostly solitary; foliage large, medium green, semi-glossy; prickles medium, regular, maroon, moderate; growth upright, tall (1½ m.); garden decoration; ['Mount Shasta' × ('Elizabeth Arden' × 'Crimson Glory')]; intr. 2008
'Prudhoe Peach' HT, ab, 1971, Wood; flowers apricot-peach, 25 petals; foliage glossy, dark, leathery; free growth; [sport of Piccadilly®]; intr. 1970
'Pruhonice' S, mp, Vecera, L.; flowers light coral-pink, golden stamens, large, semi-dbl., flat, slight fragrance; recurrent; foliage pewter-green, matte; flowers can be double in fall; intr. 1973
'Prunella Stack' -- See 'Jaypru'
'Psyche' HMult, mp, 1899, Paul, W.; flowers medium pink, paler reverse to medium, 5 cm., dbl., borne in clusters of 15-25; tall (4-5 m.) growth; ['Turner's Crimson Rambler' × 'Golden Fairy']
'Pteragonis' (R. × pteragonis, R. omeiensis pteragonis) S, ly, 1937, Krause; flowers creamy yellow, medium, single, moderate fragrance; prickles pinkish-red

'P'tit Pacha' F, rb, 1965, Combe; bud pointed; flowers geranium-red edged dark red, large, semi-dbl.; moderate growth; [seedling × 'Coup de Foudre']
'PTMR' HT, Kurowski, L.; intr. 1975
'Pu Tâo Hóng' Ch, mr
'Puanani' F, lp, 1997, Belendez, Kitty; flowers medium, single, borne in small clusters; foliage medium size, medium green, semi-glossy; bushy, medium (3 ft.) growth; [sport of Playgirl™]
'Pubescens' -- See 'Manning's Blush'
'Puccini' -- See 'LLX8267'
'Puccini' HT, rb, 1968, Ellick; flowers red, veined yellow, 4-6 in., 26-33 petals; foliage large, light; very vigorous growth; ['Opera' × 'Teenager']
'Puccini's Daughter' F, ob, 1972, Ellick; flowers orange-flame, reverse streaked yellow, 4 in., 20-25 petals; foliage glossy, dark; very vigorous, upright growth; [('Puccini' × 'Peace') × Orange Sensation®]
'Pucelle de Lille' ('La Pucelle', 'Théagène') HGal, pb, before 1828, Miellez; flowers deep purple-red, fading quickly to pink, medium to large, full, borne in clusters
'Puck' F, or, Leenders, J.; bud globular; flowers cinnabar-red, large, dbl., cupped; foliage leathery; moderate growth; ['Pour Toi' × 'Margaret McGredy']; intr. 1960
'Puck' HT, mr, 1921, Bees; bud long, pointed; flowers cherry-crimson, dbl., moderate fragrance; ['Lyon Rose' × 'Gen. MacArthur']
'Puck Pulling' Cl Min, lp, 1997, Pulling-Smith, Mrs. Pam; flowers small, single, borne in large clusters; foliage medium size, medium green, semi-glossy; spreading, tall (8 ft.) growth; [seedling × seedling]
'Pucker Up' -- See 'Tinpuck'
'Pudsey Bear' -- See 'Bedchild'
Puerta del Sol® -- See 'Delglap'
'Puerto del Sol' -- See 'Delorvi'
'Puerto Rico' -- See 'Delsob'
'Puerto Rico Shell Pink Noisette' N, lp
'Pullman Orient Express' -- See 'Baipeace'
'Pulmonaire' -- See 'La Maculée'
Pulsar® HT, mr; flowers bright red, dbl., high-centered, no fragrance; growth to 3 ft.
'Pumila' -- See 'Rosier d'Amour'
'Pumila' Ch, w, about 1806, Colville; flowers star-like, small to medium
'Pumila' Min, dp; bud long, pointed; flowers bright pink to red, dbl.; good repeat; almost thornless; dwarf (8-10 in.) growth
'Pumila Alba' N, w, 1847, Hardy; flowers pure white, very small, cupped; foliage dark green
Pumpkin Frost™ -- See 'Minpum'
'Punch' F, dp, 1960, Delforge; flowers raspberry-red, open, medium, semi-dbl., borne in clusters; foliage glossy; moderate, bushy growth; ['Luc Varenne' × 'Lafayette']
'Punctata' -- See 'Belle Herminie'

'Punkin' -- See 'Tinkin'
'Puppy Love' Min, ob, 1978, Schwartz, Ernest W.; bud pointed; flowers pink, coral, orange blend, 1½ in., 23 petals, high-centered, borne mostly singly, slight fragrance; good repeat; foliage matte; prickles very few, soft. thin, pointed; upright, compact growth; PP4292; ['Zorina' × seedling]
'Pur Caprice' ('Chameleon') S, w, Delbard; few prickles; intr. 1997
'Pur Sang' -- See 'Wiener Walzer'
Pure™ -- See 'Pouldel'
'Pure Abundace' -- See 'Hareasy'
'Pure and Simple' -- See 'Horcogwheel'
Pure Bliss™ -- See 'Dictator'
'Pure Gold' ('Créme Caramel', 'The Sir Steven Redgrave Rose', 'Steve Redgrave') S, my; flowers amber to creamy yellow, large, dbl., borne in clusters of three, moderate fragrance; repeats quickly and freely; foliage dark green; growth upright, vigorous (4 × 3 ft.); intr. 2002
'Pure Hit' MinFl, w, Poulsen; bud short; flowers ivory, 2-3 in., 30 petals, high-centered, borne singly and in clusters, moderate fragrance; good repeat; foliage dark green, glossy; prickles medium, short, straight; growth bushy, upright (40-60 cm.); PP9996; ['Pink Delight' × seedling]; intr. 1996
Pure Love™ -- See 'Burlov'
'Pure Magic' ('Spirit of SACS') F, w, Matthews; intr. 2000
'Pure Magic' Min, ob; [sport of 'Sweet Magic']; intr. 1999
'Pure Orange Typhoon Sport' HT, ob; [sport of 'Typhoon']
Pure Perfume™ -- See 'Jacfabco'
'Pure Poetry' -- See 'Jacment'
'Puregold' ('Fanion') HT, dy, 1961, Robichon; bud long, pointed; flowers rich yellow, 3-3½ in., 30 petals, high-centered, intense fragrance; foliage leathery, dark, glossy; vigorous, upright growth; PP1859; ['Helen Fox' × ('Mrs Pierre S. duPont' × 'Joanna Hill')]; intr. 1961
'Purezza' ('The Pearl') LCl, w, 1961, Mansuino, Q.; flowers dbl., pompon, borne in clusters of 39-50, moderate fragrance; may repeat; foliage small, glossy, leathery; thornless; growth very vigorous, climbing; ['Tom Thumb' × R. banksiae lutescens]
'Puritas' HT, Borgatti, G.; intr. 1969
'Purity' B, w, 1899, Cooling; flowers pure white with light rosy center, medium; growth semi-climbing; ['said to be Devoniensis' × 'Madame Bravy']
'Purity' LCl, w, 1917, Farrell; flowers pure unshaded white, 4 in., semi-dbl., globular, borne in small clusters; some autumn repeat; foliage bronze-green, glossy; prickles heavy; vigorous, climbing growth; [(R. wichurana × Marion Dingee) × 'Mme Caroline Testout']
Purple™ -- See 'Poulprima'
'Purple' -- See 'Louis-Philippe'

'Purple 'n' Gold' -- See 'Manpurgold'
'Purple Angel' S, m; groundcover; spreading growth; intr. 2001
'Purple Beauty' HT, m, 1979, Gandy, Douglas L.; flowers red-purple, 5 in., 30 petals, high-centered, moderate damask fragrance; foliage leathery; growth vigorous, upright; ['Éminence' × 'Tyrius']
'Purple Bengal' ('Violet Bengal') Ch, dr, 1827, Vibert; flowers maroon shaded darker
Purple Buttons™ S, m, Rupert, Kim L.; flowers deep red-purple, 2 in., full, rosette, borne in clusters, moderate fragrance; recurrent; growth small (under 3 ft.); [Cardinal Hume® × unknown]; intr. 1993
'Purple Carpet' S, m, Clements, John K.; intr. 1999
'Purple Chateau' HT, m, Teranishi; intr. 1996
'Purple Cloud' HT, m, Keisei Rose Nurseries, Inc.; flowers purple magenta, large, 40-50 petals, high-centered, intense fragrance; good repeat; short stems; growth to 4 ft.; intr. 1993
'Purple Dawn' -- See 'Bridawn'
'Purple East' HMult, dp, 1900, Paul, W.; flowers light crimson, fading to deep pink to medium, 4 cm., semi-dbl., borne in tight clusters; early, non-recurrent; numerous prickles; ['Turner's Crimson Rambler' × 'Beauté Inconstante']
'Purple Elf' Min, m, 1964, Moore, Ralph S.; flowers fuchsia-purple, small, 43 petals; foliage glossy; dwarf, bushy (10 in.) growth; ['Violette' × 'Zee']; intr. 1963
'Purple Fantasy' Min, m, 1983, Dobbs, Annette E.; flowers deep purple, small, dbl., no fragrance; foliage small, medium green, matte; bushy growth; ['Blue Mist' × 'Snow Magic']; intr. 1982
'Purple Floorshow' -- See 'Magenta Floorshow'
'Purple Floorshow' S, m; flowers deep magenta purple with large, deep golden centers., 2-3 in., 10-12 petals, moderate fragrance; low (2 ft.), spreading (3 ft.) growth; intr. 2002
'Purple Fragrance' -- See 'Shiko'
'Purple Gem' -- See 'Manpurpearl'
'Purple Haze' -- See 'Tanrupeza'
'Purple Haze' -- See 'Jushaze'
Purple Heart™ -- See 'Wekbipuhit'
'Purple Heart' HT, m, 1946, Moore, Ralph S.; bud long, pointed; flowers dahlia-purple to blackish red-purple, large, semi-dbl., cupped; upright, bushy growth; ['Crimson Queen' × 'Crimson Queen']
'Purple Iceberg' -- See 'Burgundy Iceberg'
'Purple Imp' Min, m, 1967, Wiliams, E.D.; bud ovoid; flowers magenta to purple, small, dbl.; foliage small, narrow, glossy; vigorous, very compact growth; ['Baby Faurax' × 'Red Imp']
'Purple Keops' Cl Min, m; flowers fuchsia, double, double, borne in clusters; recurrent; flexible canes; growth 2.5 meters height; intr. 2008
'Purple Kiss' -- See 'Roseberry Blanket'
Purple Majesty™ -- See 'Minajco'
'Purple Mary' F, m, Takatori
'Purple Meadow' -- See 'Muraskino'
'Purple Mikado' F, m, Tantau; flowers small, borne in clusters; florist rose
'Purple Noisette' -- See 'Purpurea'
'Purple Parade' (Purple™) Min, m, Poulsen; flowers mauve, medium, no fragrance; foliage dark; growth bushy, 20-40 cm.; intr. 1996
Purple Passion™ -- See 'Jacolpur'
'Purple Pavement' ('Rotes Meer', 'Rotesmeer') HRg, m, Baum; flowers purplered with yellow stamens, large, semi-dbl., cupped, borne in small trusses, moderate fragrance; recurrent; foliage rugose, glossy; mounding (3 ft.) growth; hips plump, red
'Purple Pleasure' -- See 'Brypurple'
Purple Popcorn™ -- See 'Wilpurp'
Purple Prince® -- See 'Interpur'
'Purple Puff' -- See 'Jacsedi'
'Purple Rain' -- See 'Kawamoblue'
'Purple Reign' -- See 'Wekpluroco'
'Purple Roadrunner' HRg, m, Uhl; flowers purple-violet, 5 cm., double, cupped, intense fragrance; recurrent; bushy (70 × 70 cm.) growth; intr. 2007
'Purple Simplicity' -- See 'Jacpursh'
'Purple Skyliner' LCl, m, Cowlishaw; flowers purple, fading to mauve, small, borne in clusters, intense fragrance; growth large shrub or small climber; intr. 2002
'Purple Spires' F, m, Hortico; intr. 1997
'Purple Splendour' F, m, 1976, LeGrice; flowers glowing purple, 4 in., 26 petals, slight fragrance; foliage dark; upright growth; [News® × 'Overture']
'Purple Springs' HRg, m, 2006, Olsen, Paul G; flowers semi-dbl., borne in small clusters, moderate fragrance; foliage medium size, medium green, semi-glossy; prickles small, straight, brown, moderate; growth bushy, medium (1½ m.); landscape, hedging; hardy to -40°F; ['Hansa' × R. foliolosa]; intr. 2006
'Purple Sunset' -- See 'Manpursun'
'Purple Temptation' HT, m, Preesman; flowers double, high-centered, borne mostly singly; recurrent
'Purple Tiger' -- See 'Jacpurr'
'Purple Times' F, m, Tantau; flowers borne in large clusters; intr. 1999
'Purple Torch' HT, m; flowers purple, large, dbl.; growth to 3 ft.; intr. 2005
'Purple Velvet' S, m, Clements, John; flowers velvet purple. magenta-crimson in heat of summer, 4-5 in., 85 petals, old-fashioned, moderate wine fragrance; foliage serrated, matte green; growth vigorous, somewhat spreading (4 × 3 ft.); PPAF; intr. 2000
'Purpurea' -- See 'Purpurine de France'
'Purpurea' ('Maheka', 'Purpuria', 'Violacée'), m, Buist; no prickles on sepals or receptacle; flowers purple-crimson or purplish-rose; [R. roxburghii × unknown]
'Purpurea' ('Purple Noisette') N, dr, 1822, Laffay, M.; flowers purple-crimson, poorly formed, semi-dbl.; possibly a Boursault × Noisette hybrid
'Purpurea' Ch, m, Chenault; growth small; intr. 1930
'Purpurea di Bologna' B, m, Ruston, D.; flowers purple, striped maroon, medium, dbl., cupped, borne in large clusters, intense fragrance; recurrent; growth to 6 ft.; [sport of 'Variegata di Bologna']; intr. 1980
'Purpurea Plena' -- See 'Pourpre Ancien'
'Purpurea Rubra' M, m, before 1870; flowers violet-purple, well mossed, large, dbl., intense fragrance
'Purpurea Velutina Parva' -- See 'L'Obscurité'
'Purpuria' -- See 'Purpurea'
'Purpurine' F, m, Lens; bud long; flowers fuchsia-purple to rhodamine-purple, dbl.; foliage dark; vigorous, bushy growth; [('Peace' × seedling) × 'Fashion']
'Purpurine de France' ('Purpurea') HGal, m, before 1770; flowers brilliant purple-red, semi-dbl., moderate fragrance; foliage oval; nearly thornless; growth upright; possibly synonymous with R. gallica officinalis
'Purpurtraum' HWich, dr, 1923, Kayser & Seibert; flowers deep purple red with a white eye, 3 cm., semi-dbl., borne in medium to large clusters, no fragrance; foliage small, glossy; strong, bushy (12 ft.) growth; ['Excelsa' × unknown]
'Purpurtraum 2000' S, m, Schultheis; flowers magenta-violet with golden stamens, semi-dbl., shallow cup, borne in clusters; low (2 ft.), bushy growth; intr. 2000
'Pusa Christina' HT, mp, 1976, IARI; bud globular; flowers 3 in., 50 petals, high-centered, foliage soft; vigorous, upright growth
'Pusa Pitambar' F, yb, IARI; flowers golden yellow with shadings of pink, high-centered, borne in large clusters, intense fragrance; intr. 2000
'Pusa Priya' HT, lp, IARI; buds long; flowers pale pink, long lasting; stems sturdy; intr. 2000
'Pusa Sonia' HT, dy, 1968, IARI; bud long, pointed; flowers golden yellow, large, 24 petals; foliage leathery; vigorous, upright growth; ['McGredy's Yellow' × unknown]
'Pusa Sonora' HT, pb, 1984, Division of Floriculture and Landscaping; flowers rose pink, deeper reverse, medium, 5 petals; foliage medium green; bushy, upright growth; [Queen Elizabeth® × 'First Prize']
'Pushkala' Min, w, Kasturi; flowers clear white, tiny, borne in large clusters; free-flowering; intr. 1973
'Pushkarini' F, w, Chiplunkar; intr. 1990
'Pussta, Climbing' -- See 'New Daily Mail, Climbing'
Pussta® -- See 'New Daily Mail'

'Putidula' -- See 'Le Rire Niais'
'Puy du Fou' -- See 'Meirecrom'
'Pye Colour' F, mr, 1973, Dickson, A.; flowers turkey-red, ovate, 2 in., 30 petals; foliage leathery; free growth; ['Marlena' × Elizabeth of Glamis®]; intr. 1972
Pygmae® ('Pygmy') Min, or, 1978, Poulsen, Niels D.; bud globular; flowers bright orange-red, yellow center, 1 in., 13 petals, borne in clusters; foliage small, glossy, dark; low, compact, spreading, bushy growth; ['Anytime' × 'Minuette']; intr. 1977
'Pygmee' Min, yb, Delbard; flowers yellow shaded with apricot and flame; intr. 1978
'Pygmy' -- See 'Pygmae'
'Pyramidale' -- See 'Porcelaine'
Pyrenees™ -- See 'Poulcov'
'Pythagoras' HSpn, pb, probably Vibert; flowers light pink, flecked deep pink, semi-dbl.; early bloom; foliage finely divided; dense, shrubby (3-4 ft.) growth; hips glossy, black
Pzazz™ -- See 'Pzazz Hit'
'Pzazz Hit' (Pzazz™) MinFl, rb, Poulsen; flowers red blend, 5-8 cm., dbl., no fragrance; foliage dark; growth bushy, 40-60 cm.; intr. 1996

— Q —

'QE2' HT, rb, Ruston, D.; [sport of Queen Elizabeth®]
'Quadra' ('J. F. Quadra') HKor, dr, Svejda, F.J. & Ogilvie, Ian S.; bud ovoid; flowers dark red, reverse slightly lighter, 60 petals, flat, somewhat quartered, borne singly or in clusters of up to 4, slight fragrance; recurrent; foliage dark green with red tinge, glossy; very low, trailing growth or may be trained as climber to 8 ft.; very hardy; PP9995; [seedling from B08 line × seedling from U11 line]; intr. 1994
'Quadroon' S, dr, Wright, Percy H.; flowers rich dark red, small, single; non-recurrent; growth rather poor; ['supposedly Hansa' × ('Hansa' × R. nitida')]
'Quaker Beauty' HT, ab, 1936, Brookins; bud long, pointed; flowers glowing apricot, large, high-centered; PP272; [sport of 'Joanna Hill']
'Quaker Maid' F, or, 1960, Byrum, Roy L.; bud ovoid; flowers nasturtium-red, 1½-2 in., 18-20 petals, flat, borne in clusters, moderate spicy fragrance; foliage leathery; vigorous, upright, bushy growth; PP1789; ['Orange Sweetheart' × 'Pinocchio']; originally registered as Pol; intr. 1959
'Quaker Star' -- See 'Dicperhaps'
'Quantock Star' HT, or, 1968, Heard; flowers vermilion shaded pink, small, dbl.; foliage variegated; free growth; [sport of 'Tropicana']
'Quatre Saisons' -- See 'Quatre Saisons Continue'
'Quatre Saisons Blanc Mousseux' ('Moussue des Quatre Saison Blanc', 'Perpetual White Moss', 'Quatre Saisons Blanche', 'Rosier de Thionville') M, w, 1835, Laffay, M.; bud very mossy; flowers medium, dbl., borne in large clusters; repeats sparingly in fall; growth medium (4 ft.); [sport of 'Autumn Damask']
'Quatre Saisons Blanche' -- See 'Quatre Saisons Blanc Mousseux'
'Quatre Saisons Continue' ('Autumn Damask', R. × damascena bifera, R. × damascena semperflorens, 'Rosier des Quatre Saisons', 'Damask Monthly', 'Quatre Saisons', R. bifera) D, mp, before 1849; flowers pink, lighter at edges, less full than R. × damascena, dbl., borne singly or in small clusters, moderate fragrance; foliage light gray-green, oval, with 5-7 leaflets; known to be very ancient, but the first botanical description was made by Loiseleur-Deslongchamps at the beginning of the 19th century; recent research (Japan) indicates parentage is (R. moschata × R. gallica) × R. fedtschenkoana
'Quatre Saisons d'Italie' ('Henriette Boulogne', 'Italian Four-Seasons Rose', R. damascena italica, 'Rosier de la Malmaison') P, dp, before 1815, Dupont, Andre; flowers vermilion, sometimes striped, medium, semi-dbl., borne in clusters of 3, moderate fragrance; foliage large, ovate, simply serrate; prickles very numerous, small, short, straight; brought from Florence to Luxembourg in 1795 by Dupont; re-introduced by Verdier in 1865; sometimes classed as D
'Quatre Saisons Rose' D, mp, 1580; flowers deep rose; possibly brought to France from Italy by Montaigne
'Québec' -- See 'Mme Marie Curie'
'Queen' B, mp, 1900, Paul, W.; flowers pink, shaded darker, large, full
'Queen Adelaide' -- See 'Meivildo'
'Queen Aishwarya' -- See 'Aishwarya'
'Queen Alexandra' -- See 'The Queen Alexandra Rose'
'Queen Alexandra' HMult, mp, 1901, Veitch; flowers rosy white, medium, semi-dbl., borne in large corymbs
'Queen Alexandra' HMsk, ly, Pemberton; flowers light yellow, flushed with pink, stamens prominent, 2-3 cm., single, borne in large clusters, slight fragrance; sometimes classed as HT; intr. before 1916
'Queen Ann' HT, dr, 1949, Spandikow; bud long, pointed; flowers crimson, medium, dbl., high-centered; strong stems; vigorous growth; PP964; [sport of 'Better Times']
'Queen Astrid' -- See 'Koningin Astrid'
'Queen Bagatelle' HT, ob, Teranishi; intr. 2006
'Queen Beatrice' HT, lp, 1909, Kramer; flowers bright silvery pink, large to medium, very dbl.; vigorous growth; ['Mme Abel Chatenay' × 'Liberty']
'Queen Beatrix' -- See 'Hetkora'
'Queen Bee' S, dr, 1985, Buck, Dr. Griffith J.; flowers 4-5 in., 35 petals, high-centered to cupped, borne 5-8 per cluster, moderate old rose fragrance; repeat bloom; foliage large, leathery, dark olive green; prickles awl-like, brown; erect, bushy, branching growth; hardy; [('Rosali' × 'Music Maker') × ('Square Dancer' × Tatjana®)]; intr. 1984
'Queen Bett's' -- See 'Judbett's'
'Queen Charlotte' -- See 'Harubondee'
'Queen City' Min, ob, 1987, Bridges, Dennis A.; flowers orange, yellow base, fading lighter, medium, 20 petals, high-centered, borne usually singly, slight fragrance; foliage medium size, medium green, semi-glossy; prickles long, straight, medium, light colored; bushy, medium growth; ['Rise 'n' Shine' × seedling]
'Queen Dina' Gr, dr, 1964, Soenderhousen; flowers deep scarlet, large, dbl.; foliage leathery; very vigorous, upright, bushy growth; ['Cocorico' × 'Geranium Red']
'Queen Dorothy Bell' HT, dr, 1940, Stell; flowers velvety scarlet, very dbl., globular; foliage light, leathery; vigorous growth; [sport of 'Oswald Sieper']
'Queen Elizabeth, Climbing' ('Grimpant Queen Elizabeth', 'The Queen Elizabeth Rose, Climbing') Cl Gr, mp, 1957, Whisler; PP1615; [sport of Queen Elizabeth®]; intr. 1957
Queen Elizabeth® ('Queen of England', 'The Queen Elizabeth Rose') Gr, mp, 1954, Lammerts, Dr. Walter; bud pointed; flowers 3½-4 in., 38 petals, high-centered to cupped, borne singly and in clusters, moderate fragrance; good repeat; foliage dark, glossy, leathery; very vigorous, upright, bushy growth; PP1259; ['Charlotte Armstrong' × 'Floradora']; intr. 1954
'Queen Elizabeth Abricot' -- See 'Apricot Queen Elizabeth'
'Queen Elizabeth Blush' -- See 'Blushing Queen'
'Queen Elizabeth Jaune' -- See 'Yellow Queen Elizabeth'
'Queen Elizabeth Rouge' -- See 'Scarlet Queen Elizabeth'
'Queen Esther' HT, w, 1985, Poole, Lionel; flowers cream, pale pink petal edges, spiraled, large, 35 petals; foliage medium size, medium green, matte; numerous prickles; ['Golden Masterpiece' × Peer Gynt®]; intr. 1984
'Queen Fabiola' ('Fabiola') Gr, op, 1965, Hazenberg, G.; bud ovoid; flowers salmon-pink, medium, dbl., borne several together; foliage dark green; numerous prickles; [sport of 'Montezuma']; intr. 1962
'Queen Frances Connally' HT, mr, 1939, Stell; flowers spectrum-red, base lemon-chrome, reverse yellow edged red; [sport of 'Katharine Pechtold']
'Queen Gertrude Anne Windsor' HT, dp, 1936, Dixie Rose Nursery; flowers darker; [sport of 'Francis Scott Key']
'Queen Juliana' -- See 'Orange Delight'

'Queen Louise Boren'   HT, op, 1935, Nicolas; flowers pink suffused salmon, large, dbl.; very vigorous growth; [('Emile Charles' × 'La France') × 'Marechal Niel']

'Queen Lucia'   F, op, 1954, Maarse, G.; flowers salmon-pink, pompon form, dbl., borne in large trusses; vigorous growth; ['Pinocchio' × 'Tapis Rose']

'Queen Lucia' -- See 'Korlilub'

'Queen Mab'   Ch, ab, 1896, Paul, W.; flowers soft rosy apricot, center shaded orange, reverse tinted rose, dbl.; free-flowering; bushy, compact (2-3 ft.) growth

'Queen Margaret Hunt'   HT, dr, 1936, Nicolas; bud long, pointed, spiral; flowers dark velvety crimson-maroon, stamens golden yellow, large, cupped; foliage leathery; very vigorous growth; ['Templar' × 'Ami Quinard']

Queen Margrethe™ -- See 'Poulskov'

'Queen Marie'   HT, pb, 1925, Chervenka; flowers rose-pink, reverse deeper pink, base bronze yellow, dbl.; ['Mme Butterfly' × 'Lamia']

'Queen Marie of Jugoslavia'   HT, my, 1935, Hicks; flowers bright yellow, slightly flushed pink; [sport of 'Mme Butterfly']

'Queen Mary'   HT, yb, Dickson, A.; flowers bright canary yellow, shaded red, medium, semi-dbl., moderate fragrance; intr. 1913

'Queen Mary'   HT, lp, 1911, Williams, A.; ['Frau Karl Druschki' × unknown]

Queen Mary 2™ -- See 'Meifaissel'

'Queen Mother' ('Queen Mum')   F, lp, Kordes; flowers small, semi-dbl., flat; low, spreading growth; intr. 1991

'Queen Mum' -- See 'Queen Mother'

Queen Nefertiti® -- See 'Ausap'

'Queen of Bath'   HT, dy, 1931, Bees; bud long, pointed; flowers deep buttercup-yellow, outer edged chrome-yellow, dbl., high-centered; foliage thick, glossy, bronze; vigorous growth; ['Souv. de Claudius Pernet' × 'Cleveland']

'Queen of Beauty and Fragrance' -- See 'Souv de la Malmaison'

'Queen of Bedders'   B, dp, 1876, Noble; flowers deep carmine, well-shaped, medium to large, full; dwarf, compact growth; ['Sir Joseph Paxton' × unknown]

'Queen of Bermuda'   Gr, or, 1961, Bowie; bud ovoid; flowers orange-vermilion, 4 in., 35 petals, high-centered, borne in small clusters, moderate fruity fragrance; foliage glossy, bronze; vigorous, bushy growth; [('Independence' × Orange Triumph®) × Bettina®]; intr. 1960

'Queen of Bourbons' -- See 'Reine des Iles-Bourbons'

'Queen of Bourbons'   B, w, 1930, Burch; flowers pure white, moderate fragrance

'Queen of Colors' -- See 'Farbenkönigin'

'Queen of Denmark'   D, lp, 1846, Vibert; flowers light flesh pink

'Queen of Denmark' -- See 'Königin von Dänemark'

'Queen of Diamonds' -- See 'Scarlet Queen Elizabeth'

'Queen of Diamonds'   Gr, mr, 1966, Dickson; bud ovoid; flowers light red, medium, dbl, borne several together; foliage dark green; [('Korona' × unknown) × Queen Elizabeth®]; intr. 1965

'Queen of Edgely' ('Pink American Beauty')   HP, mp, 1901, Florist's Exchange; flowers bright pink, large, deeply cupped; [sport of 'American Beauty']

'Queen of England' -- See 'Queen Elizabeth'

'Queen of Fragrance'   HT, lp, 1915, Paul, W.; flowers shell-pink, tipped silver, well-shaped, large, dbl.; foliage soft; dwarf growth

Queen of Hearts™ -- See 'Harfond'

'Queen of Hearts' -- See 'Dame de Coeur'

'Queen of Hearts'   Cl HT, mp, 1920, Clark, A.; bud globular; flowers rich pink, aging lighter, 4½ in., semi-dbl. to dbl., cupped, moderate fragrance; foliage dark green, glossy; numerous prickles; very vigorous, climbing growth; ['Gustave Grunerwald' × 'Rosy Morn']

'Queen of Hearts'   HT, rb, Kordes; flowers cherry red and apricot, large, full, cupped, borne mostly singly, slight fragrance; foliage glossy; strong (5 ft.) growth; intr. 2005

'Queen of Hearts' -- See 'Taser Bibi'

'Queen of Pearl'   HWich, lp, 1898, Van Fleet; non-remontant

'Queen of Queens' ('Reine des Reines')   HP, pb, 1882, Paul, W.; flowers pink, with blush edges, large, full, globular; ['Victor Verdier' × ('La Reine' × 'Maiden's Blush')]

'Queen of Queens, Climbing'   Cl HP, mp, 1892, Paul, W.; flowers very large; [sport of 'Queen of Queens']

'Queen of Roses' -- See 'Korbico'

'Queen of Scarlet' -- See 'Cramoisi Supérieur'

'Queen of Spain'   HT, lp, 1907, Bide; flowers flesh pink, center darker, large, very full; ['Antoine Rivoire' × unknown]

'Queen of Sweden' -- See 'Austiger'

'Queen of the Belgians' -- See 'Reine des Belges'

'Queen of the Belgians'   HT, op, 1916, Hicks; bud long, pointed; flowers salmon-pink, semi-dbl.

'Queen of the Dwarfs' ('Dwarf Queen', 'Zwergkönigin')   Min, dp, 1955, Kordes; flowers deep pink, dbl.; foliage rather coarse; growth to 10-12 in.

'Queen o' the Lakes'   HT, dr, 1949, Brownell; bud ovoid, long, pointed; flowers large, dbl., high-centered, moderate fragrance; foliage glossy; vigorous, bushy growth; PP1003; ['Pink Princess' × 'Crimson Glory']

'Queen o' the Lakes, Climbing'   Cl HT, dr, 1965; intr. 1965

'Queen of the Musks'   HMsk, pb, 1913, Paul, W.; bud coppery red; flowers deep blush and white, centers darker, small, semi-dbl., borne in large clusters, intense fragrance; recurrent bloom; foliage dark ivy-green; prickles numerous, small, bristly; bushy (3 ft.) growth

'Queen of the Night'   HT, Sgaravatti, A.

'Queen of the Prairies' ('Beauty of the Prairies', 'Prairie Belle', 'Mr Feast's No. 1')   HSet, pb, 1843, Feast; flowers bright rose pink, frequently striped white, large, dbl., globular, borne in clusters of 10-15, moderate fragrance; foliage large, dark green; vigorous, climbing growth; hardy; [R. setigera × a Gallica]

'Queen of the Violets' -- See 'Reine des Violettes'

'Queen Olga of Greece' -- See 'Reine Olga de Wurtemberg'

'Queen Olga of Wurtemburg' -- See 'Reine Olga de Wurtemberg'

'Queen Parade'   Min, dp, Poulsen; flowers deep pink, medium, no fragrance; foliage dark; growth bushy, 20-40 cm.; intr. 1996

'Queen Thornless, Climbing'   Cl HT, dp, Kittle; bud pointed; flowers deep pink, 3-4 in., 20-40 petals, high-centered, moderate fragrance; intermittent bloom; foliage leathery, dull green; thornless; strong stems; vigorous, arching growth; PP2275

'Queen Victoria' -- See 'Brennus'

'Queen Victoria' -- See 'Souv d'un Ami'

'Queen Victoria'   HP, lp, 1850, Fontaine; flowers blush-pink, large, dbl.; ['La Reine' × unknown]

'Queen Wilhelmina' -- See 'Jacimgol'

'Queen Wilhelmina'   HT, ob, 1942, Deverman; flowers brilliant orange, base light orange-yellow; [sport of 'Hinrich Gaede']

'Queenie' ('Petite Reine')   F, lp, 1962, Boerner; bud ovoid; flowers 4 in., 33 petals, cupped, borne in clusters, moderate fragrance; foliage leathery; vigorous, upright, bushy growth; PP2238; [('Pinocchio' × unknown) × 'Spartan']; intr. 1962

'Queenie Robinson'   HT, op, 1924, Easlea; bud long, pointed; flowers orange-cerise to flame-pink, semi-dbl.

'Queenie's Love'   HT, dp, 1970, Verschuren, A.; bud globular; flowers begonia-rose, medium, dbl., moderate fragrance; foliage leathery; vigorous growth; ['Libretto' × 'Mme Butterfly']; intr. 1968

'Queen's Knight'   S, mp, 1980, Stoddard, Louis; bud short, conical; flowers , 6-10 petals, cupped, borne 3 per cluster; profuse for 6 weeks; non-recurrent; foliage semi-glossy, deep green, 7 leaflets; prickles hooked; erect, arching, self-supporting growth; ['Don Juan' × R. laxa]

'Queen's Palace'   S, mp, Poulsen; bud pointed to ovoid; flowers medium pink, 3 in., 20-25 petals, flattened, borne in large clusters; quick repeat; foliage medium size, dark green, semi-glossy; prickles moderate, ¼ in., straight, red; growth vigorous, compact (2 ft.),bushy; PP10821; [Sexy Rexy® × seedling]; intr. 1997

'Queen's Scarlet' ('Red Hermosa', 'Rote Hermosa') Ch, mr, 1880, Hallock & Thorpe; flowers rich velvety scarlet, small, dbl.; foliage small; bushy, compact growth

'Queen's Visit' HT, dr, 1955, Viney; bud long, pointed; flowers dark velvety red veined darker, medium, dbl., high-centered; foliage leathery; vigorous growth; ['Crimson Glory' × 'Crimson Glory']; intr. 1955

'Queensday' HT, ab, Tantau; flowers apricot-orange, large, full, high-centered, borne mostly singly; good repeat; greenhouse rose; intr. 1997

'Queensland Beauty' HT, pb, 1934, Alderton & Williams; flowers coppery pink; [sport of 'Golden Dawn']

'Queenstown' HT, dr, 1991, Cattermole, R.F.; bud pointed; flowers deep crimson to ruby red, 5 in., 32 petals, cupped, borne up to 6 per cluster, slight fragrance; foliage leathery, mid-green, semi-glossy; upright, spreading growth; ['Silent Night' × 'Josephine Bruce']; intr. 1991

'Quercifolia' -- See 'À Feuille de Chêne'

'Querida' -- See 'Maljoanna'

'Querido Padre' HT, ly, 2007, Auilar, Sergio; flowers light yellow, with light apricot center which darkens in cool weather, 5 in., full, borne mostly solitary; foliage medium, medium green, matte; prickles medium, slightly hooked, moderate; growth upright, medium (3-4 ft.); garden decoration, cutting; [Pristine® × St Patrick™]; intr. 2008

'Quicksilver' -- See 'Arostal'

Quickstep™ LCl, mp, Poulsen; flowers dusty rose, lightens with age, 8-10 cm., dbl., cupped, no fragrance; foliage dark green, glossy; bushy (10 ft.) growth; intr. 2001

'Quiet Reflections' T, dy, Hay

'Quiet Time' -- See 'Tinquiet'

'Quietness' S, lp, 2003, Buck, Dr. Griffith J.; flowers soft pink, 4 in., very full, borne in small clusters, intense spicy fragrance; foliage medium size, medium green, semi-glossy, disease-resistant; prickles medium, awl, light brown, moderate; growth spreading, tall (4-5 ft.); landscape, mixed plantings; [seedling × seedling]; tolerant of partial shade; intr. 2003

'Quinella' HT, ob

'Quintet' -- See 'Victoria Park'

'Quiproquo' HT, my, Richardier; intr. 1999

'Quite Unforgettable' -- See 'Worantelope'

'Quito' HT, yb; intr. 1999

'Quo Vadis?' HT, pb, 1961, Giacomasso; bud oval; flowers silvery pink becoming red, large, 50-60 petals; very vigorous growth; ['Peace' × ('Baiser' × unknown)]

— R —

'R. B. Cater' HP, dp, 1899, Cooling; flowers glossy carmine-magenta

'R. B. Stewart' -- See 'Freestew'

'R. K. Witherspoon' HT, w, 2005, Pike, David V.B.; buds long, pointed; flowers white with pink-blushed petals, colors stronger in cool weather, 4-5 in., dbl., high-centered, borne mostly solitary, intense fragrance; foliage medium size, dark green, semi-glossy; prickles moderate; upright, medium growth; [sport of 'Tiffany']; intr. 2006

'R. M. S. Queen Mary' ('Mrs Verschuren') HT, mp, 1937, Verschuren; flowers salmon-pink suffused orange, very large, dbl., cupped; foliage leathery; vigorous growth; PP249; ['Briarcliff' × 'Mrs Sam McGredy']

'R. S. Hudson' HT, yb, 1939, Wheatcroft Bros.; flowers yellow tinged red, large, well-formed; vigorous, upright growth

'R. W. Proctor' F, dp, 1947, Proctor; flowers deep rose-pink, 4 in., 10-12 petals, borne in trusses; foliage glossy; vigorous growth; [sport of 'Anne Poulsen']

'Raalte's Golden Harvest' S, dy, Interplant; intr. 1992

'Raat-ki-Rani' HT, mr, 1975, IARI; bud pointed; flowers velvety crimson-red, 4½ in., 30 petals; foliage glossy; vigorous, upright growth; [seedling × ('Samourai' × unknown)]; intr. 1975

'Rabbie Burns' HT, mr, 1960, Arnot; bud long, pointed; flowers bright light red, semi-dbl., intense fragrance; foliage dark; vigorous, upright growth; ['Ena Harkness' × 'Sutter's Gold']; intr. 1959

'Rabble Rouser' -- See 'Horcoffitup'

'Rabelais' -- See 'Meinusian'

'Rachael Fox' -- See 'Rawfox'

'Rachael's Smile' LCl, or, 2007, Tolmasoff, Jan; flowers orange-red with yellow at very base, 3½ in., dbl., borne mostly solitary; very early blooming; foliage medium size, medium green, semi-glossy; prickles medium to large, tan, moderate; growth climbing, tall (12-14 ft.); trellises/fences; [unknown × unknown]; intr. 2001

Rachel™ -- See 'Ricrachel'

'Rachel' -- See 'Tangust'

'Rachel' -- See 'Booyol'

'Rachel'   HT, ob, 1929, Pemberton; flowers orange-buff, flushed carmine, large, dbl., high-centered; foliage dark; very vigorous growth; RULED EXTINCT 5/84

'Rachel Bowes Lyon' -- See 'Harlacal'

'Rachel Buchanan' Min, ly, 2000, Buchanan, Hedley; flowers cream-lemon, large, very full, borne mostly singly, slight fragrance; foliage medium size, dark green; few prickles; growth upright, tall; [sport of 'Pink Petticoat']

'Rachel Crawshay' HT, op, 1978, Harkness; flowers pink to orange-salmon, 5 in., 30 petals; foliage olive-green; ['Fragrant Cloud' × 'Mary Mine']; intr. 1977

'Rachel Esta' HT, w, 2002, Poole, Lionel; flowers white with pink edge, 5 in., full, high-centered, borne mostly solitary, intense fragrance; foliage medium size, medium green, semi-glossy; prickles medium, triangular, moderate; growth upright, bushy, vigorous, medium (3 ft.); exhibition; bedding; [('Hazel Rose' × 'Cardiff Bay') × 'New Zealand']; intr. 2003

'Rachel Farrant' -- See 'Horsimkor'

'Rachel Jayne' HT, op, 2001, Poole, Lionel; flowers coral/amber, 4 in., full, borne mostly solitary, intense fragrance; free-flowering; foliage medium size, dark green, glossy; prickles medium, long, angular; upright, bushy, medium growth; borders, beds; ['Augustus Stone' × 'Joanna Lumley']; intr. 2002

'Rachel Kathleen' F, mr; flowers bright red, dbl., cupped; intr. 2006

'Rachel Louise Moran' HT, rb, Zary, Keith; flowers striped and spotted red, pink and white, large , double, borne singly and in small clusters, moderate rich, fruity fragrance; recurrent; robust, medium growth; intr. 2008

'Rachel Townsend' HT, yb, 1963, Townsend; flowers golden yellow tipped carmine, 4-4½ in., 30 petals; foliage dark, glossy; free growth; [sport of 'Sultane']

'Rachelle' F, mp, 1976, Warriner, William A.; bud long; flowers French rose, 2-3 in., 30 petals, nearly flat; upright growth; ['Antigua' × unknown]

Racy Lady™ -- See 'Dicwaffle'

'Rada' HT, dr, 1985, Staikov, Prof. Dr. V.; flowers large, 75 petals; foliage medium green, glossy; [Baccará® × seedling]; intr. 1975

'Radames' HT, dr, 1984, Fumagalli, Niso; flowers large, 35 petals, intense fragrance; foliage large, medium green, glossy; upright growth; [seedling × seedling]; intr. 1983

'Radar' HT, or, 1953, Meilland, F.; bud long; flowers light geranium-red, well-formed, large, 45 petals; vigorous growth; ['Charles Mallerin' × 'Independence']

'Radar, Climbing' Cl HT, or, 1959, Meilland, Mrs. Marie-Louise

'Radar Italiana' HT, or, 1944, San Remo Exp. Sta.; bud pointed; flowers nasturtium-red edged rose, large, 32-34 petals; foliage bright green; vigorous, bushy growth; ['Souv. de Denier van der Gon' × 'Brazier']

'Radbrich' ('Hallelujah!', 'Olbrich's Merry Red') S, mr, 2000, Radler, William J.; flowers large, semi-dbl., borne in small clusters, slight fragrance; foliage medium size, medium green, matte, blackspot-resistant; prickles moderate; growth upright, tall; hedge; very hardy; ['Carefree Beauty' × (('(('(Fairy Moss ×

First Prize) × unknown)' × '(Lucky Lady × Eddie's Crimson)') × 'G48')]

'Radbrite' LCl, pb, Radler; intr. 2006

'Radcliffe Flame' HT, mr, 1987, Thomson, Colin; flowers medium, full, no fragrance; foliage medium size, dark green, matte; upright growth; [Alec's Red® × 'Grandpa Dickson']

'Radcon' S, mp, Radler, W. ; bud cherry red.; intr. 2004

'Radcor' S, pb, Radler; bud slender; intr. 2007

'Radhe' -- See 'Horradhe'

'Radiance, Climbing' ('Pink Radiance, Climbing') Cl HT, lp, 1926, Griffing, W.D. (also Catt, 1928); flowers salmon pink with yellow, large, full; [sport of 'Radiance']

'Radiance' ('Pink Radiance') HT, lp, 1904, Cook, J.W.; bud globular; flowers rose-pink, reverse lighter, large, 23 petals, cupped, intense damask fragrance; foliage leathery; vigorous growth; ['Enchanter' × 'Cardinal']; intr. 1908

Radiant™ -- See 'Benrad'

'Radiant' HT, or, 1962, Fletcher; bud spiral; flowers orange-flame, reverse shaded red, 4-5 in., 30 petals; foliage glossy; very free growth; RULED EXTINCT 9/87; ['Mrs Sam McGredy' × 'Fantasia']; intr. 1962

'Radiant Beauty' HT, mr, 1934, Cleveland Cut-Flower Co.; flowers deeper crimson than parent, not turning blue, dbl., moderate fragrance; PP97; [sport of 'Francis Scott Key']

'Radiant Glow' F, or, 1953, Quinn; bud pointed; flowers bright orange-salmon tinted peach, medium, dbl., cupped, borne singly and in clusters; foliage leathery, light green; vigorous, upright growth; ['Pinocchio' × unknown]

'Radiant Gold' -- See 'Jacern'

Radiant Perfume™ -- See 'Jacadnof'

'Radiant Superglaze' -- See 'Nostrad'

'Radiation' F, mr, 1960, deRuiter; flowers open, 3-3½ in., semi-dbl., borne in clusters; foliage glossy; vigorous growth; ['Poulsen's Pink' × 'Pompadour Red']

'Radieuse' HT, mr, 1955, Laperrière; bud long; flowers clear red, well-formed, large, 30-35 petals; vigorous, bushy growth

'Radiman' F, ly, 1985, Staikov, Prof. Dr. V.; flowers 50 petals, cupped, borne in clusters of 5-35, moderate tea fragrance; foliage dark, glossy; vigorous growth; ['Highlight' × 'Masquerade']; intr. 1975

'Radio' HT, yb, 1937, Dot, Pedro; flowers yellow slightly tinted pink, striped and marked rose, large, 50 petals, cupped, moderate spicy fragrance; foliage wrinkled, light green; vigorous growth; PP197; [sport of 'Condesa de Sástago']

'Radio Lancashire' F, or, 1987, Bracegirdle, A.J.; flowers orange-red, reverse slightly lighter, rosette, medium, 38 petals, borne in sprays of 10-15, slight fruity fragrance; foliage medium size, dark green, glossy; prickles triangle-shaped, brown; upright, medium growth; hips round, orange; ['Dusky Maiden' × Matangi®]; intr. 1987

'Radio Times' -- See 'Aussal'

'Radiosa' HT, Aicardi; intr. 1956

'Radium' Pol, lp, 1913, Houry; flowers delicate pink, pearly gold at center, borne in clusters of 15-20

'Radium' HT, rb, Lippiatt; flowers carmine, shaded coppery red; ['Beauté Lyonnaise' × 'Capt. Hayward']; intr. 1922

'Radka' HT, dy, Vecera, L.; flowers large, dbl.; intr. 1975

'Radmor' (Morning Magic™) LCl, lp, 2007, Radler, William; flowers soft shell pink, large, 4 in., single, borne in small clusters; foliage large, dark green, semi-glossy; prickles moderate; growth upright, tall (8-10 ft.,); ['Radsbs' × 'Radspot']; intr. 2008

'Radome' F, lp, 1966, Nicol; flowers pale rose; [sport of Queen Elizabeth®]

'Radox Bouquet' -- See 'Harmusky'

'Radral' S, op, Radler; intr. 2008

'Radramblin' ('Ramblin' Red') LCl, mr, 2001, Radler, William; bud slender, small to medium; flowers cardinal red, 3 in., 35 petals, borne in large clusters, slight spicy fragrance; recurrent; foliage deep green, satiny; prickles moderate; upright, vigorous (6-9 ft.) growth; PP14270; ['Razzle' × 'Henry Kelsey']

'Radrazz' ('Knockout', Knock Out™, 'Madraz') S, rb, 1999, Radler, William; flowers medium, light red to deep pink, 2½ in., single, borne in small clusters, slight tea fragrance; foliage large, medium green, semi-glossy, very resistant to blackspot; prickles moderate; bushy, rounded, medium (3 ft.) growth; PP11836; [(('Carefree Beauty' × '((Tampico × Applejack) × Playboy)') × 'self') × ('Razzle Dazzle' × ('Deep Purple' × ('Faberge × Eddie's Crimson)'))]; intr. 2000

'Radsun' ('Carefree Sunshine') S, ly, 2001, Radler, William J.; flowers 3 in., single, borne in small clusters, no fragrance; foliage medium size, light green, matte; prickles moderate; growth upright (3½-4 ft.); landscape; very resistant to blackspot; PP13063; [seedling × seedling]; intr. 2001

'Radsunny' (Sunny Knock Out™) S, ly, 2007, Radler, William; flowers medium, 3 in., single, borne in small clusters; foliage large, dark green, semi-glossy; prickles moderate; growth upright, medium (4½ ft.); hedging; ['Radbrite' × 'Radsweet']; intr. 2008

'Radsweet' S, lp, Radler, William; intr. 2008

'Radtko' (Double Knock Out™) S, mr, 2004, Radler, William; flowers red, reverse red, 4 cm., full, borne in small clusters, no fragrance; foliage small, medium green, semi-glossy; growth bushy, medium (3-4 ft.); garden decoration; PP16202; [('Carefree Beauty' × unknown) × ('Razzle Dazzle' × unknown)]; intr. 2004

'Radtkopink' (Pink Double Knock Out™) S, mp, 2007, Radler, William; flowers medium, 3 in., dbl., borne in small clusters; foliage small, light green, matte; few prickles; growth upright, short; hedging, landscape; [sport of Double Knock Out™]

'Radway Charm' HT, dp, 1960; flowers deep pink, base deep yellow, 20 petals, moderate fragrance; vigorous growth; ['Christopher Stone' × 'sport of McGredy's Wonder']; intr. 1959

'Radway Glow' F, op, 1960; flowers coral-pink, 14 petals, borne in large, open clusters; foliage dull green; vigorous growth; intr. 1960

'Radway Jewel' F, dr, 1960; flowers yellow, becoming orange and deep red, medium, 40 petals, borne in large clusters; foliage light green; intr. 1960

'Radway Pink' F, mp, 1965; flowers rose-pink, large, 42 petals, borne in clusters; foliage dull green; very free growth; ['Margaret' × 'Korona']; intr. 1965

'Radway Scarlet' F, mr, 1963, Waterhouse Nursery; low growth; ['Karl Weinhausen' × seedling]

'Radway Sunrise' S, ob, 1962; flowers yellow, shading through orange to red, 3½-4 in., 7 petals, borne in clusters, slight fragrance; free-flowering; foliage dark, glossy; very vigorous growth; ['Masquerade' × unknown]; intr. 1962

'Radwin' (Winner's Circle™) LCl, dr, 2007, Radler, William; flowers large, 3½-4 in., single, borne in large clusters; foliage large, dark green, semi-glossy; numerous prickles; growth upright, tall; ['Radliv' × 'Radkoswe']; intr. 2008

'Radyod' ('Blush Knock Out', 'Blushing Knockout') S, lp, Bell, John; intr. 2004

'Rae Dungan' HT, yb, 1972, Dawson, George; bud long, pointed; flowers creamy yellow, edged deep pink, large, dbl., borne singly, moderate fragrance; moderate, intermittent repeat; foliage dark green; stems long; vigorous, upright growth; ['Daily Sketch' × 'Fred Streeter']

'Raewyn Henry' HT, mr, 2001, Poole, Lionel; flowers medium red, lighter reverse, 5½ in., full, high-centered, borne mostly solitary, slight fragrance; free-flowering; foliage medium size, dark green, matte; prickles medium, hooked down, moderate; growth upright, bushy, vigorous, medium (1 m.); exhibition, bedding; ['Naomi Rebecca' × 'Adrienne Berman']; intr. 2002

'Raf' -- See 'Rafaël Braeckman'

'Rafaël Braeckman' ('Raf') F, ob, RvS-Melle; ['Mullard Jubilee' × Satchmo®]; intr. 1985

'Rafaela G. de Peña' Pol, ob, 1938, Dot, Pedro; flowers pure orange, dbl.; foliage bright green, leathery; vigorous, bushy growth

'Raffel's Pride' HT, mr, 1937, Raffel; bud

small; flowers oriental red, reverse gold-splashed, open, dbl.; vigorous growth; ['Talisman' × unknown]

'Raffel's Yellow' HT, my, 1942, Raffel; flowers pure yellow, well-shaped, large, 25-35 petals; foliage bronze turning very dark; vigorous growth; [probably 'Mrs Beatty' × 'Maid of Gold']

'Raffles Bruce' HT, ab, 1943, Bees; flowers apricot and gold, well-shaped, 3-4 in.; foliage dark; compact growth; ['Mrs Sam McGredy' × 'Aureate']

'Rafzerfeld' HGal, mp, Hauenstein Rafz; flowers clear pink; modest (60 - 80 cm.) growth

'Ragamuffin' Min, yb

'Ragazzina' F

'Ragged Robin' -- See 'Gloire des Rosomanes'

'Raggedy Ann' F, mr, 1956, Joseph H. Hill, Co.; bud short, pointed; flowers 13 petals, borne in clusters; foliage dark, leathery; vigorous, upright growth; PP1403; ['Garnette' × 'Sister Kenny']

'Ragini' F, mp, 1974, Pal, Dr. B. P.; buds medium, pointed; flowers large, semi-dbl., open, borne singly and several together; foliage medium size, dark green, glossy; growth very vigorous, upright (140 cm.); intr. 1972

'Ragtime' -- See 'Peacap'

Ragtime™ LCl, dp, Poulsen; flowers deep pink, reverse lighter, 8-10 cm., dbl., no fragrance; recurrent bloom; foliage dark green, glossy; bushy (7-10 ft.) growth; intr. 2000

'Ragtime' -- See 'Maccourlod'

'Ragtime' -- See 'Lenrag'

'Rahima' Pol, mp, 2004, Valentic, Dzejna; flowers pink with golden center and white edged petals, reverse blush pink with white, semi-dbl., borne mostly solitary, no fragrance; foliage small, medium green, glossy; upright, medium (12-18 in.) growth; garden, decorative, containers; [seedling × seedling]

'Rainbow' T, pb, 1889, Sievers; flowers pink, striped carmine and blush, semi-dbl., moderate fragrance; recurrent; [sport of 'Papa Gontier']

'Rainbow' S, op, Mattock; flowers peachy-salmon, shaded orange and lemon, large, dbl.; recurrent; growth tall; can serve as small climber or shrub; intr. 1974

'Rainbow 02' LCl, rb, Hiroshima; flowers striped; intr. 2002

Rainbow Bliss™ -- See 'Devdicha'

Rainbow Cerise™ -- See 'Devclavel'

Rainbow Crimson™ -- See 'Devmesi'

'Rainbow Delight' Min, mr; intr. 1998

Rainbow Eclipse™ -- See 'Deveclipsar'

Rainbow Gold™ -- See 'Devoro'

Rainbow Hot Pink™ -- See 'Deviente'

'Rainbow Knock Out' S, pb, Radler; bud slender; flowers light coral pink with yellow eye, 2 in., single, shallow cup to flat, borne in small clusters, slight spice fragrance; recurrent; foliage medium green, satiny finish; prickles 1-1½ cm., brown; vigorous, round, bushy (3 ft.) growth; hips greyed-orange; PP17346; ['Radtee' × 'Radral']; intr. 2007

Rainbow Magic™ -- See 'Dicxplosion'

'Rainbow Nation' -- See 'Camille Pissarro'

Rainbow Niagara -- See 'Mactaurang'

Rainbow Pink™ -- See 'Devrosado'

Rainbow Red™ -- See 'Devrojo'

'Rainbow Robe' HT, m, Kordes; flowers mauve, edges of outer petals turning red with exposure to sun, large, dbl., high-centered, intense fragrance; intr. 1991

'Rainbow Shower' -- See 'Leesho'

Rainbow Sorbet™ F, yb, Lim, Ping; bud pointed; flowers bright yellow, red and orange petal edges, 3½ in., 15-18 petals, cupped, no fragrance; recurrent; foliage dark green, glossy; upright (to 5 ft.) growth; intr. 2006

Rainbow Stanford™ -- See 'Devrico'

Rainbow Sunblaze™ Min, yb, Meilland; flowers yellow with red petal edges, small, 30-40 petals, cupped, borne in clusters, no fragrance; recurrent; foliage medium green, semi-glossy; medium, bushy growth; PPAF; intr. 2005

Rainbow Sunrise™ -- See 'Devaurora'

Rainbow Surprise™ -- See 'Devpresa'

'Rainbow Warrior' -- See 'Chrisgood'

Rainbow Yellow™ -- See 'Devamarillo'

Rainbow Yellow Parade™ -- See 'Poulwee'

Rainbow's End, Climbing™ -- See 'Savaclend'

Rainbow's End™ -- See 'Savalife'

'Rainbows Heaven Scent' -- See 'Webmoment'

Raindrops™ -- See 'Savarain'

'Raindrops' S, pb, Williams, J. Benjamin; flowers medium pink, ivory reverse, semi-dbl.; compact growth; intr. 1997

'Rainer Maria Rilke' -- See 'Korsee'

'Rainforest' -- See 'Morforest'

'Rainy' -- See 'Scrivjam'

Rainy Day® -- See 'Macraida'

Raissa® HT, mp, Cocker; intr. 1990

'Raita' HRg, Rieksta, Dr. Dz.

'Raja of Nalagarh' ('Raja Surendra Singh of Nalagarh') HT, or, 1979, Pal, Dr. B.P.; bud pointed; flowers bright orange-red with salmon tints, 4 in., 32 petals, high-centered, borne singly, slight fragrance; recurrent; foliage dark, leathery; vigorous, upright growth; ['Samourai' × 'Montezuma']; intr. 1977

'Raja Surendra Singh of Nalagarh' -- See 'Raja of Nalagarh'

'Rajbala' F, pb, 1976, Pal, Dr. B.P.; bud pointed; flowers open, 4 in., 10 petals; foliage large, glossy, light; very vigorous, upright, compact growth; ['Delhi Princess' × seedling]; intr. 1975

'Rajkumari' HT, dp, 1976, IARI; bud pointed; flowers deep fuchsine-pink, 4 in., 70 petals; foliage glossy, light; vigorous, compact growth; [('Charles Mallerin' × 'Delhi Princess') × seedling]; intr. 1975

'Rajni' -- See 'Orient Spice'

'Raketa' ('Rocket') HT, op, 1952, Shtanko, E.E.; flowers golden orange-pink, 5 in., 50 petals; foliage reddish bronze; vigorous, upright, compact growth; ['Narzisse' × 'Comtesse Vandal']

'Rakete' HT, mr, GPG Bad Langensalza; flowers large, dbl.; intr. 1972

'Raktagandha' HT, or, 1976, IARI; bud long, pointed; flowers vermilion, 3 in., 35 petals, high-centered; foliage glossy; vigorous, upright growth; ['Christian Dior' × ('Carrousel' × unknown)]; intr. 1975

'Rakthima' HT, mr, IARI; flowers bright red, dbl., high-centered; recurrent; stems strong, straight; intr. 1991

'Rakuen' HT, ob, Keisei; intr. 1996

'Rakuhoku' HT, pb, Keihan; intr. 1990

'Rakuyô' HT, rb; intr. 1995

'Rallye' Pol, r, 1966, Delforge; bud ovoid; flowers cognac color with pink, large, dbl., borne in clusters; foliage dark, glossy; vigorous, upright growth; ['Cognac' × 'Fashion']

Ralph® HT, ab, deVor; intr. 1993

'Ralph Leighty' F, w, 1972, Leighty; bud ovoid; flowers near white, medium, dbl., high-centered; foliage light, soft; moderate, upright growth; PP3545; [sport of 'Gene Boerner']; intr. 1971

'Ralph Moore' -- See 'Savaralph'

'Ralph T' -- See 'Moeralph'

'Ralph Tizard' F, op, 1979, Sanday, John; flowers pure salmon, pointed, 4 in., 28 petals, borne singly and several together, moderate fragrance; free-flowering; foliage medium size, dark green; prickles straight; growth average, vigorous; ['Vera Dalton' × 'Tropicana']

'Ralph's Creeper' -- See 'Morpapplay'

'Ramapo' -- See 'Zipram'

'Ramat-Gan' F, dy, 1975, Holtzman; bud urn-shaped; flowers deep lemon-yellow, 1 in., 25 petals, cupped to urn-shaped, moderate fragrance; foliage light; moderate growth; ['Golden Masterpiece' × 'Zorina']; intr. 1974

'Ramble and Tumble' LCl, op, Kordes; flowers intense salmon pink, full, cupped, borne in clusters; late bloomer, rapid repeat; vigorous, spreading, tumbling growth; intr. 2004

'Rambler-Königin' HWich, mp, 1907, Kohler & Rudel; flowers small, full; somewhat remontant

'Rambling Rector' HMult, w, 1910, from England; flowers pink-white, 4 cm., semi-dbl., borne in large clusters, moderate fragrance; vigorous growth; hips small, oval; very probably an older rose, renamed

'Ramblin' Red' -- See 'Radramblin'

'Rambling Rosie' -- See 'Horjasper'

Ramira® ('Agatha Christie') LCl, mp, W. Kordes' Sohne; flowers large, borne singly or in small clusters, slight fragrance; good repeat; foliage dark green, glossy; intr. 1988

'Ramón Bach' HT, ob, 1938, Dot, Pedro; flowers bright orange, edged lighter, reverse reddish-gold, stamens bright yellow, 80 petals, globular, intense fruity fragrance; foliage glossy, dark; vigorous growth; PP366; ['Luis Brinas' × 'Condesa de Sástago']

Ramona™ -- See 'Poulmona'

'Ramona' ('Red Cherokee') S, mr, 1913, Dietrich & Turner; flowers carmine-crimson, fading to rose pink with age, large, single; some repeat; [sport of 'Anemone']; most characteristics like Anemone, but bloom deeper color

'Ramona Hit' (Ramona™) MinFl, dp, Poulsen; flowers deep pink, 5-8 cm., dbl., no fragrance; foliage dark; growth bushy, 40-60 cm.; intr. 2000

'Rampa Pal' HT, pb, 1976, Pal, Dr. B.P.; bud ovoid; flowers fuchsia-pink, reverse lighter, 4½ in., 60 petals, high-centered; foliage glossy; moderate, upright, bushy growth; intr. 1975

'Rampant' HSem, w, 1830, Jacques; profuse bloom, sometimes in autumn

'Ran' S, mp, 1973, Lundstad; bud globular; flowers pink, open, small, semi-dbl.; foliage small, light, soft; vigorous, upright growth; [R. cinnamomea × R. helenae hybrid]; intr. 1972

'Rancho Mirage' -- See 'Ripmir'

'Randall' HGal, mp; flowers dbl.; not as hardy as Alika; an old variety taken by early pioneers to western Canada

Randers™ (Colchester™) F, yb, Olesen; bud long, pointed ovoid; flowers yellow-apricot-orange blend, 2½-4 in., 28-33 petals, open cup, borne in large clusters, very slight fragrance; free-flowering; foliage dark green, glossy; prickles linear to slightly concave; bushy, upright (3 ft.) growth; PP15609; [seedling × Aspen™]; intr. 2002

'Randfontein Gold' Gr, my, Kordes; bud egg-shaped; flowers clear golden-yellow, dbl., cupped, borne in large clusters; vigorous, medium growth; intr. 1989

'Randilla Geel' -- See 'Randilla Jaune'

Randilla Jaune® ('Randilla Geel', 'Yellow Magic', 'Yellow Profusion') Min, my; flowers bright yellow, large, full, cupped, to flat, borne in clusters; recurrent; foliage medium green; compact (12 - 16 in.) growth

Randilla Rose® ('Pink Magic') Min, mp; flowers bright pink, shallow cup, borne in clusters; recurrent; compact (12 - 16 in.) growth

Randilla Rouge® ('Red Magic', 'Red Profusion') Min, mr; flowers bright red, 5 -6 cm., borne in clusters; recurrent; compact growth

'Randy Scott' -- See 'Siljonscott'

'Rangatarang' HT, pb, Chiplunkar; intr. 1993

'Range View Cream Tea' -- See 'Devoniensis'

'Ranger' -- See 'Barger'

'Rangila' HT, rb, Tejganga; intr. 1995

'Rangitoto' -- See 'Suntoto'

'Rangoli' F, op, 1979, Thakur; bud tapered; flowers coral-pink, 3-3½ in., 25 petals, high-centered, slight fruity fragrance; foliage glossy; dwarf, bushy growth; [sport of 'Golden Slippers']

'Rangoli' HT, w, Chakraborty, Dr. K.; flowers creamy white with strong pink flush, large, dbl.; intr. 1999

'Rangshala' HT, ab, 1971, IARI; bud pointed; flowers apricot, shaded peach and amber yellow, open, medium, dbl.; foliage glossy; moderate growth; ['Margaret Spaull' × unknown]; intr. 1969

'Ranjana' HT, or, 1976, Pal, Dr. B.P.; bud pointed; flowers rose-opal, 4½ in., 38 petals, intense fragrance; foliage dark, leathery; very vigorous, upright, bushy growth; ['Samourai' × unknown]; intr. 1975

'Rankende Johanna Tantau' Cl Pol, 1942, Tantau, Math.

'Rankende Miniature' -- See 'Miniature, Climbing'

'Ranuncula' HT, rb, Kordes; flowers red with soft yellow stripes and splashes, medium, dbl., cupped, borne mostly singly; recurrent; stems long; florist rose; intr. 2005

'Ranunculiflora' HSet, lp, about 1846, Pierce; flowers pale flesh, darker center, small to medium, borne in clusters of 20-30, moderate fragrance; foliage rugose; prickles purplish

'Ranunculus Musk Cluster' HMsk, w; flowers pure white, very dbl.; very vigorous growth

'Ranunkel Mikado' F, dy, Tantau; greenhouse rose

'Ranzan' ('Stormy Mountain') HT, dr, Keihan; intr. 1990

'Raoul Chauvry' T, yb, 1896, Chauvry; flowers capucine yellow, shaded coppery, center apricot, large, dbl., moderate fragrance; ['Mme Lombard' × unknown]

'Raoul Follereau' HT, dp, Delbard; flowers rose-magenta, large, very dbl., moderate fruit and spice fragrance; intr. 2005

'Raphael' M, w, 1856, Robert; flowers well mossed, pinkish white, full, borne in clusters of 12-20; slightly recurrent bloom

'Raphaela' HT, ob, Tantau; bud long pointed, ovoid; flowers orange to orange-red, with thick petals, 5 in., 20 petals, high-centered, borne singly, slight fragrance; recurrent; foliage large, leathery, glossy; prickles moderate, hooked slightly downward, red; stems long (24-28 in.); vigorous, upright (6 ft. in greenhouse) growth; PP9064; [seedling × 'TANettelur']; originally a florist rose; intr. 1994

Rapperswil® HT, or, 1979, Huber; bud globular; flowers 4 in., 30 petals, cupped, intense fragrance; foliage dark, leathery; ['Fragrant Cloud' × 'Ena Harkness']; intr. 1975

Rapsodia® ('Barasd') F, ob

'Rapture' HT, pb, 1926, Traendly & Schenck; flowers deeper pink, flushed gold at base; [sport of 'Mme Butterfly']; growth much like parent

'Rapture, Climbing' Cl HT, pb, 1933, Dixie Rose Nursery

'Raquel Meller' HT, lp, 1958, Camprubi, C.; flowers soft pink, large, dbl., cupped, intense fragrance; foliage glossy; ['Edith Krause' × 'Fashion']; intr. 1957

'Rare Edition' F, rb, Kasturi; flowers scarlet, striped and splashed white; [sport of 'Kusum']; intr. 1982

'Raschamp' Min, r, Rasmussen; intr. 2002

'Rashmi' Pol, dr, Kasturi; flowers blackish crimson, globular; intr. 1977

Raspberry Beauty™ -- See 'Minirasp'

'Raspberry Bouquet' -- See 'Brorasp'

'Raspberry Delight' HT, rb, 1980, Taylor, Thomas E.; flowers medium red on outer petals shading to creamy coral on inner, 30 petals, high-centered, moderate raspberry fragrance; foliage medium green, semi-glossy; prickles hooked; upright, bushy growth; ['Carrousel' × 'First Prize']

'Raspberry Ice' -- See 'Zipberry'

'Raspberry Ice' -- See 'Korweiso'

'Raspberry Meillandina' Min, dp, Meilland

Raspberry Punch™ -- See 'Jacbunch'

'Raspberry Red' ('Mackankaf') F, mr, McGredy; intr. 1995

'Raspberry Ripple' F, rb, Delbard; flowers red with white stripes, semi-dbl. to dbl., cupped to flat, borne in clusters; recurrent; vigorous (24-30 in.) growth; intr. 1998

'Raspberry Ripple' HSet, pb

'Raspberry Ripple Folies' F, dp, J&P; intr. 2004

'Raspberry Rose' F, mr

'Raspberry Royale' S, dp; flowers raspberry red, dbl., cupped; foliage glossy; growth to 20 × 20 in.; intr. 2003

'Raspberry Ruffles' -- See 'Talras'

Raspberry Ruffles™ S, pb, Harkness Roses; flowers ruffled, raspberry with brushed white edges, 2½ in., 12 petals, slight fragrance; compact, upright (3½ ft.) growth with many canes; PPAF; intr. 2005

Raspberry Rugostar™ -- See 'Meitozaure'

'Raspberry Star' Min, dp; intr. 2000

Raspberry Sunblaze® -- See 'Meidonfe'

Raspberry Swirl™ -- See 'Jacstand'

'Raspberry Swirls' HT, pb, 2000, Edwards, Eddie; flowers raspberry, reverse white, 4-5 in., dbl., high-centered, borne mostly singly, slight fragrance; foliage large, medium green, semi-glossy; few prickles; growth upright, medium (4 ft.); [Crystalline™ × 'Suffolk']

'Raspberry Trail' S, mr, Bell, Laurie; flowers rich raspberry red, very full; growth vigorous, low, spreading; groundcover; [seedling × 'Red Cascade']

Raspberry Vigorosa™ -- See 'Roseberry Blanket'

'Raspberry Wine' -- See 'Malinovka'

'Rassvet' ('Daybreak') HT, pb, 1955,

Klimenko, V. N.; flowers soft pink, base creamy yellow, medium, 48 petals; foliage dark; spreading growth; ['Peace' × unknown]

Rastede™ -- See 'Poulcs004(N)'

'Ratan' HT, my, Bulsara, S.P.; flowers lemon yellow; intr. 1990

'Ratgeber Rose' HWich, mr, 1930, Verlag Praktischer Ratgeber; flowers light red, 4-5 cm., dbl., borne in small clusters

'Rathernice' HT, ob, 1957, Bishop; flowers coppery orange; foliage coppery; moderate growth

'Ratnaar' HT, mp, Pal, Dr. B.P.; flowers coral pink, large, dbl., high-centered; intr. 1985

'Raubritter' S, lp, 1936, Kordes; flowers medium, dbl., globular, borne in clusters, moderate fragrance; foliage leathery, wrinkled; vigorous, climbing growth; ['Daisy Hill' × 'Solarium']

Ravel® -- See 'LLX8684'

'Ravel' -- See 'Ruisteenka'

'Ravellae' ('Cavallii') HSpn, w, Christ; flowers creamy white

Raven™ -- See 'Frytrooper'

'Ravenna' S, dp, Noack; flowers dark pink with lighter tones in center, 4 cm., single, shallow cup, borne in clusters, slight fragrance; free-flowering; upright (80 cm.), then spreading growth; crown frost hardy; intr. 2001

Ravensberg® S, mr, Noack, Werner; flowers blood red with a darker overlay on the petal edges, small, dbl., borne in clusters, slight fragrance; recurrent; ['Alpengruss' × (('Ruth Leuwerik' × 'Paprika (Tantau, 1958)') × ('Lili Marlene' × Molde®))]; intr. 1986

'Ravenswood' Min, yb, 1992, Catt, Graeme Charles; flowers gold, outer petals flushed pink, ½ in., 18-20 petals, borne 3-4 per cluster; foliage healthy; upright, bushy growth; ['Rise 'n' Shine' × unknown]; intr. 1989

'Ravenswood Village' HT, ly, 1996, Poole, Lionel; flowers light yellow, deeper in autumn, very large, full, high-centered, borne mostly singly; foliage medium size, medium green, glossy; some prickles; upright, medium growth; ['Golden Splendour' × 'Queen Esther']; intr. 1997

'Ravensworth' ('Perle d'Or Yellow', 'Yellow Perle d'Or') Pol, my; flowers soft yellow; [sport of 'Perle d'Or']; identical to Perle d'Or in all respects except bloom color; intr. 1998

'Ravikanchan' HT, lp, 2003, Bhate, N.B.; flowers large, full, borne mostly solitary, slight fragrance; foliage medium size, medium green, semi-glossy; prickles slightly pointed; bushy, medium growth; [sport of 'Garden Party']; intr. 2002

'Raving Beauty' HT, mp, 1948, Joseph H. Hill, Co.; bud ovoid, rose-red; flowers Tyrian rose, 3-4 in., 35-40 petals, globular, intense fragrance; foliage leathery, dark; vigorous, upright growth; PP809

'Rawana' ('Golden Wonders 99') HT, dy, 1999, Rawlins, R.; flowers large, dbl., borne in small clusters; foliage medium size, medium green, semi-glossy; prickles moderate; bushy (2½ ft.) growth; [(Gold Bunny® × ('Baby Love' × seedling)) × 'Golden Celebration']

'Rawanitra' ('Anitra Louisa') F, rb, 2006, Rawlins, Ronnie; flowers red/pink striped, reverse red, medium, full, borne in small clusters, moderate fragrance; foliage medium size, medium green, semi-glossy; prickles ½ in., triangular, moderate; growth compact, medium (30 in.); garden decoration; ['Kanagem' × 'Candle in the Wind']

'Rawbamb' ('Ann Elizabeth Vear') HT, ab, 2003, Rawlins, R.; flowers apricot, reverse apricot yellow, medium, dbl., borne in small clusters; foliage medium size, medium green, matte; prickles 1 cm., triangular, few; growth compact, medium (30 in.); garden decoration; [('Baby Love × Amber Queen' × Amber Queen®) × Amber Queen®]

'Rawblaf' ('My Beautiful English Rose') F, ly, 2007, Rawlins, Ronnie; flowers pale yellow, 5 in., very full, borne in small clusters; foliage medium, dark green, semi-glossy; prickles 1 cm., triangular, moderate; growth compact, medium (36 in.); garden decoration; [('Baby Love' × Amber Queen®) × 'Golden Future']; intr. 2007

'Rawblight' ('Atholl Grant') HT, yb, 2000, Rawlins, R.; flowers yellow suffused red, reverse yellow, medium, very full, borne in small clusters, slight fragrance; foliage medium green, semi-glossy; prickles moderate; growth upright, medium (30 in.); [Chinatown® × Remember Me®]; intr. 2000

'Rawblister' ('Sheena F. Gordon') HT, dy, 2000, Rawlins, R.; flowers 3 in., full, borne in small clusters, slight fragrance; foliage medium size, medium green, glossy; prickles 1 cm., triangular, moderate; growth upright, medium (3 ft.); garden decorative; ['Golden Quill' × 'Lichtkonigin Lucia']

'Rawblob' ('Andy Gray') HT, pb, 2000, Rawlins, R.; flowers pink-apricot, reverse pink, medium, very full, borne in small clusters; foliage medium size, dark green, semi-glossy; prickles moderate; growth upright, tall (48 in.); ['Solitaire' × Abraham Darby®]

'Rawbus' ('Strawberry Fields') S, m, 2001, Rawlins, R.; flowers purple with pink flecks, reverse purple, 1 in., dbl., borne in small clusters, slight fragrance; foliage small, medium green, semi-glossy; prickles small, few; growth spreading, low (18 in.); garden decorative; ['Intrigue' × 'Christopher Columbus']; intr. 2001

'Rawchinme' ('Clara Eileen') F, ob, 2006, Rawlins, Ronnie; flowers orange/yellow, reverse yellow, 2½ in., full, borne in small clusters; foliage medium size, medium green, glossy; prickles ½ in., triangular, moderate; growth upright, medium (36 in.); garden decoration; [Chinatown® × Remember Me®]

'Rawcleet' ('Vera Brown') F, ab, 2000, Rawlins, R.; flowers apricot, reverse pink, 5 in., full, borne in small clusters, moderate fragrance; foliage medium size, medium green, semi-glossy; prickles moderate; upright, medium (36 in.) growth; ['Golden Future' × 'Sharifa Asma']

'Rawcrack' ('Claude's Cracker') HT, dr, 2006, Rawlins, Ronnie; flowers crimson, 3 in., full, borne mostly solitary; foliage large, dark green, glossy; prickles ½ in., triangular, few; growth upright, medium (36 in.): garden decoration; [seedling × 'Ingrid Bergman']

'Rawcrazylady' ('Joanna Elise') F, w, 2005, Rawlins, R.; flowers semi-dbl., borne in large clusters, slight fragrance; foliage medium size, dark green, glossy; upright, tall (120 cm.) growth; garden; ['Pretty Lady' × 'Crazy For You']

'Rawdan' ('Danielle Turner') F, ab, 2008, Rawlins, R.; flowers 4 in., very full, borne in small clusters; foliage medium, light green, matte; prickles ½ in., hooked, pink, moderate; growth bushy, medium (3 ft.); [('Baby Love' × Amber Queen®) × ('Solitaire' × ('Baby Love' × Amber Queen®))]

'Rawdawn' ('G'Mundi's Rose') HT, mr, 2000, Rawlins, R.; flowers scarlet, reverse slightly darker, medium, full, borne in small clusters, no fragrance; foliage medium size, dark green, semi-glossy; prickles moderate; upright, low (30 in.) growth; ['Kanagem' × 'Florange']; intr. 1999

'Rawdenqueen' ('Rose For Elaine') HT, ob, 2003, Rawlins, R.; flowers orange brown, medium, dbl., borne in small clusters, moderate fragrance; foliage medium size, medium green, semi-glossy; prickles 2 cm., scimitar-shaped, moderate; upright, medium (36 in.) growth; garden; ['Edith Holden' × ('Baby Love' × Amber Queen®)]; intr. 2003

'Rawdred' ('Vince Butterworth') F, rb, 2006, Rawlins, Ronnie; flowers red, reverse gold, 2½ in., full, borne in small clusters; foliage medium size, dark green, glossy; prickles ½ in., triangle, moderate; growth upright, tall (48 in.); garden decoration; [Chinatown® × 'Ingrid Bergman']; intr. 2006

'Rawfegum' ('Patrick Rudden's Rose') HT, r, 2000, Rawlins, R.; flowers russet, 4 in., very full, borne mostly singly, no fragrance; foliage medium size, dark green, semi-glossy; prickles moderate; upright, medium (27 in.) growth; ['Kanagem' × 'Fellowship']

'Rawfling' ('Bobo's Rose') F, dr, 2005, Rawlins, R.; flowers dr, reverse dr, 10 cm., full, borne in small clusters; foliage medium size, medium green, semi-glossy; growth upright, medium; garden decorative; ['Florange' × 'Ingrid Bergman']

'Rawfox' ('Rachael Fox') F, mr, 2006, Rawlins, Ronnie; flowers 2½ in., dbl., borne in small clusters, moderate fragrance; foliage medium size, medium green, semi-glossy; prickles ½ in., triangle, few; growth compact (24 in.); garden decoration; [('Summer Wine' × International Herald Tribune®) × 'Ingrid Bergman']

'Rawfragjen' ('Jennifer Clark') HT, ob, 2003, Rawlins, R.; flowers orange apricot, medium, full, borne in small clusters; foliage medium size, dark green, semi-glossy; prickles 2 cm., triangular, moderate; growth upright, tall (38 in.); garden; ['L'Oreal Trophy' × ('Fragrant Cloud' × *R. bella*)]; intr. 2003

'Rawgecko' ('Alie Dool') HT, m, 2003, Rawlins, R.; flowers lavender pink, medium, dbl., borne in small clusters; foliage medium size, medium green, semi-glossy; prickles 1 cm., triangular, few; growth compact, short (28 in.); garden decoration; [Samara® × ('Seaspray' × (Queen Elizabeth® × *R. laxa*))]

'Rawgeel' ('Alan Butterworth') HT, ob, 2000, Rawlins, R.; flowers, 3¾ in., full, borne mostly solitary, slight fragrance; foliage dark green, glossy; prickles ½ in., triangular, moderate; growth upright, tall (5 ft.); garden decorative; [seedling × seedling]

'Rawgoldrog' ('The Constance Pink') F, yb, 2003, Rawlins, R.; flowers yellow with pink edge, small, dbl., borne in small clusters; foliage medium size, dark green, glossy; prickles 1 cm., triangular, moderate; growth upright, medium (1 m.); garden; ['Golden Future' × ('Silver Jubilee' × 'Pretty Lady')]

'Rawgolface' ('Terry Ann') F, yb, 2003, Rawlins, R.; flowers primrose with pink edge, reverse primrose, medium, dbl., borne in small clusters, intense fragrance; foliage medium size, dark green, glossy; prickles moderate, 1½ cm., hooked; growth upright, tall (48 in.); garden; ['Golden Future' × 'Baby Face']; intr. 2003

'Rawgoljub' ('Gillian Levy') F, yb, 2005, Rawlins, Ronnie; flowers yellow blend, reverse yellow and pink, 10 cm., full, borne in small clusters; foliage medium size, dark green, glossy; growth upright, medium (1 m.); garden; ['Golden Future' × ('Baby Love' × 'Silver Jubilee')]

'Rawgolley' ('Karen Rudall') F, bp, 2000, Rawlins, R.; flowers light pink with orange center, reverse light yellow, 3 in., full, borne in large clusters, moderate fragrance; foliage medium size, medium green, semi-glossy; prickles 1 cm., triangular, moderate; growth upright, medium (3 ft.); garden decorative; [Laura Ford® × 'Golden Celebration']

'Rawguapa' ('Leonorah') F, ob, 2003, Rawlins, R.; flowers medium, semi-dbl., borne in small clusters; foliage medium size, medium green, semi-glossy; prickles triangular; growth compact, medium (30 in.); garden decoration; [Laura Ford® × Heritage®]

'Rawgush' ('Lorna Clare') F, ab, 2000, Rawlins, R.; flowers apricot-orange, 3 in., full, borne in small clusters, moderate fragrance; foliage medium size, light green, matte; prickles 1 cm., triangular, moderate; growth compact, low (24 in.); garden decoration; [(Laura Ford® × 'Goldbusch') × ('Baby Love' × Amber Queen®)]

'Rawjen' ('Beatrice Jennings') F, op, 2006, Rawlins, Ronnie; flowers vermilion/pink stripe, reverse vermilion, 2 in., semi-dbl., borne in small clusters, no fragrance; foliage medium size, dark green, glossy; prickles ½ in., triangle, moderate; growth upright, tall (42 in.); garden decoration; ['Florange' × 'Candle in the Wind']

'Rawlavlan' ('Amy Donelan') F, m, 2006, Rawlins, R.; flowers lavender, 5 in., full, borne in small clusters; foliage medium size, medium green, glossy; prickles ½ in., triangular, few; growth medium (3½ ft.); garden decoration; [('Summerwine' × ('Montezuma' × ('Violacea × Montezuma'))) × 'Golden Future']; intr. 2006

'Rawlemal' ('James Robert') HT, m, 2001, Rawlins, R.; flowers mauve/pink, 2¼ in., full, borne mostly solitary, no fragrance; foliage medium size, dark green, semi-glossy; prickles 9 mm., triangular, moderate; growth compact, tall (42 in.); garden decorative; ['Oranges 'n' Lemons' × (Blue Moon® × 'Jenny Duval')]

'Rawlil' ('Pearls') F, w, 2001, Rawlins, R.; flowers small, semi-dbl., borne in small clusters, moderate fragrance; foliage small, medium green, semi-glossy; prickles small, moderate; growth upright, low (60 cm.); garden decorative; [Laura Ford® × 'Margaret Merrill']; intr. 2001

'Rawlisan' ('Lisa Ann') HT, dr, 2003, Rawlins, R.; flowers dark red, reverse gold, medium, very full, borne mostly solitary; foliage medium size, dark green, glossy; prickles triangular; growth compact, medium (39 in.); garden decoration; ['Solitaire' × 'Ingrid Bergman']

'Rawmolax' ('Andrea Jones') F, pb, 2003, Rawlins, R.; flowers medium, dbl., borne in small clusters; foliage medium size, dark green, glossy; prickles hooked; growth upright, tall (5½ ft.); garden; ['Golden Future' × ('Florange' × 'Sealax']; intr. 2003

'Rawmolazy' ('Michal Kowal') F, pb, 2003, Rawlins, R.; flowers pink with white stripe, medium, single, borne in small clusters, no fragrance; foliage medium size, medium green, semi-glossy; prickles 1½ cm., scimitar-shaped, numerous; growth compact, medium (32 in.); garden decoration; ['Golden Future' × 'Crazy For You']

'Rawmollbee' ('Molly Lloyd Lee') F, ab, 2003, Rawlins, R.; flowers full, borne in small clusters, slight fragrance; foliage medium size, medium green, semi-glossy; prickles triangular; growth upright, medium (40 in.), garden; ['Golden Future' × ('Baby Love' × Amber Queen®)]

'Rawodes' ('Helen Rhodes') F, pb, 2000, Rawlins, R.; flowers pale pink with fawn center, reverse primrose, large, very dbl., borne in small clusters, moderate fragrance; foliage medium size, dark green, semi-glossy; prickles 1 cm., triangular, few; growth upright, medium (3 ft.); [Sexy Rexy® × 'Golden Celebration']

'Rawood' ('Dorothy Hilda Wood') HT, rb, 2006, Rawlins, Ronnie; flowers dark red, reverse gold, 2½ in., very full, borne mostly solitary; foliage medium size, dark green, glossy; prickles ½ in., triangular, few; growth upright, tall (43 in.); garden decoration; [Chinatown® × 'Ingrid Bergman']; intr. 2006

'Rawperp' ('Samantha-Jane') F, m, 2008, Rawlins, R.; flowers small, 3 in., single, borne mostly solitary; foliage medium-size, dark green, semi-glossy; prickles 1 cm., triangular, crimson, moderate; growth upright (36 in.); garden decoration; ['English Courtyard' × 'Cohort']

'Rawprelad' ('Precious Lady') HT, w, 2003, Rawlins, R.; flowers medium, very full, borne mostly solitary, slight fragrance; foliage medium size, dark green, semi-glossy; prickles 2 cm., triangular, few; upright, medium (39 in.) growth; garden; ['Solitaire' × 'Silver Anniversary']

'Rawprimy' ('My Gail') F, ly, 2006, Rawlins, Ronnie; flowers primrose, reverse primrose, 2½ in., full, borne in small clusters, moderate fragrance; foliage medium size, dark green, semi-glossy; prickles ½ in., triangular, few; growth upright (33 in.); garden decoration; [(Laura Ford® × 'Goldbusch') × 'Crazy For You']

'Rawqueenb' ('Monica Mary', 'Monica Mitchell') HT, dy, 2003, Rawlins, R.; flowers lemon yellow, medium, full, borne in small clusters, moderate fragrance; foliage medium size, medium green, semi-glossy; prickles 1 cm., triangular, moderate; growth upright, medium (33 in.); garden; [(Laura Ford® × 'Goldbusch') × ('Baby Love' × Amber Queen®)]

'Rawreport' ('Miss Newell') F, m, 2006, Rawlins, Ronnie; flowers mauve, 2½ in., full, borne mostly solitary; foliage medium size, dark green, semi-glossy; prickles ½ in., triangular, few; growth upright, medium (30 in.); garden decoration; ['Len Turner' × 'Old Port']; intr. 2006

'Rawril' ('Babyface') MinFl, w, 2001, Rawlins, R.; flowers 2 in., borne in large clusters, intense fragrance; foliage medium size, dark green, glossy; prickles moderate; growth bushy, medium (2 ft.); garden decorative; [Laura Ford® × 'Margaret Merrill']; intr. 2001

'Rawroyal' ('A Midsummer Nights Dream', 'Midsummer Night's Dream') Gr, dr, 2003, Rawlins, R.; flowers red, reverse lighter, small, single, borne in large clusters; foliage medium green, semi-glossy; prickles medium, sharp, moderate; growth upright, 30 in., garden, decorative; [seedling × seedling]

'Rawsaddle' ('Saddleworth Male Voice Choir') F, rb, 2003, Rawlins, R.; flowers crimson with white stripe, reverse magenta, large, single, borne in small clusters, no fragrance; foliage medium size, medium green, semi-glossy; prickles ½ in., hooked; growth bushy, medium (42 in.); garden; ['Golden Future' × 'Crazy For You']

'Rawsetbo' ('Julie Evans', 'Our Julie') F, dp, 2003, R Rawlins; flowers light primrose red, reverse primrose, medium, single, borne in small clusters, slight fragrance; foliage light green, semi-glossy; prickles 1½ cm., hooked; growth compact, short (24 in.); garden; ['Sunset Boulevard' × ('LF' × 'BQ/S')]; intr. 2004

'Rawsexan' ('Rosemeade') HT, or, 2003, Rawlins, R.; flowers vermilion, medium, full, borne in small clusters, slight fragrance; foliage medium size, medium green, semi-glossy; prickles moderate, 1 cm., triangular; upright, medium (33 in.) growth; garden; [Sexy Rexy® × 'Kanagem']

'Rawsharoo' ('Joanie') F, ab, 2003, Rawlins, R.; flowers full, borne in small clusters; foliage medium size, medium green, semi-glossy; prickles triangular; growth upright, medium (36 in.); garden; ['World Peace 2000' × (Laura Ford® × 'Sharifa Asma')]

'Rawshermo' ('Saddleworth') HT, w, 2000, Rawlins, R.; flowers semi-dbl., slight fragrance; foliage medium size, medium green, semi-glossy; prickles moderate; growth upright, medium; ['Golden Future' × ('Sheri Ann' × (Queen Elizabeth® × R. laxa (Retzius)))]

'Rawslam' ('Alastair McEwan') F, ly, 2005, Rawlins, R.; flowers full, borne in small clusters, slight fragrance; foliage dark green, semi-glossy; upright, medium (1 m.) growth; garden; ['Solitaire' × ('Baby Love' × Amber Queen®)]

'Rawsob' ('Desert Orchid') S, ly, 2001, Rawlins, R.; flowers 3 in., full, borne in large clusters, moderate fragrance; foliage medium size, medium green, semi-glossy; prickles pointed, moderate; growth upright, medium (3 ft.); garden decorative; ['Solitaire' × (Mountbatten® × ('Angelina' × ('Flamenco' × R. bella)))]; intr. 2001

'Rawsolann' ('Snow Crystal') HT, w, 2003, Rawlins, R.; flowers medium, full, borne mostly solitary; foliage medium size, dark green, glossy; prickles 2 cm., triangular,; growth upright, tall (45 in.); garden, exhibition; ['Solitaire' × 'Silver Anniversary']; intr. 2003

'Rawsolbab' ('Daddy Anstey') HT, dy, 2005, Rawlins, R.; flowers deep yellow, reverse blend of yellow and orange pink, 11 cm., full, borne mostly solitary, slight fragrance; foliage medium size, dark green, glossy; upright, tall (110 cm.) growth; ['Solitaire' × ('Baby Love' × 'Tequila Sunrise')]

'Rawsolly' ('English Courtyard') HT, m, 2003, Rawlins, R.; flowers medium, full, borne in small clusters, slight fragrance; foliage medium size, dark green, semi-glossy; prickles ½ in., triangular, moderate; growth bushy, tall (42 in.); garden decoration; ['Solitaire' × ('Kanagem' × Abraham Darby®)]

'Rawsoltan' ('Eric Green') HT, yb, 2003, Rawlins, R.; flowers yellow picotee, medium, dbl., borne in small clusters; foliage medium size, medium green, semi-glossy; prickles 1 cm., triangular, moderate; growth upright, short (30 in.); garden; ['Solitaire' × ('Tango' × 'Tequila Sunrise')]

'Rawsplits' ('Banana Splits') HT, my, 2000, Rawlins, R.; flowers straw yellow, 4 in., full, borne in small clusters, slight fragrance; foliage medium size, light green, matte; prickles 1 cm., triangular, moderate; growth bushy, medium (39 in.); garden decorative; ['Solitaire' × ('Baby Love' × Amber Queen®)]

'Rawstone' ('Alex Brackstone') F, dy, 2006, Rawlins, Ronnie; flowers yellow, reverse yellow, 2½ in., full, borne in large clusters; foliage medium size, dark green, glossy; prickles ½ in., triangular, few; growth upright, medium (33 in.); garden decoration; [('Baby Love' × Amber Queen®) × (Laura Ford® × 'Goldbusch')]

'Rawsumose' ('Natalie Ann') F, m, 2003, Rawlins, R.; flowers palest lavender, medium, semi-dbl., borne in small clusters, slight fragrance; foliage medium size, dark green, glossy; prickles 2 cm., triangular,; growth upright, medium (36 in.); garden; ['Odyssey' × ('Golden Future' × Mary Rose®)]; intr. 2003

'Rawvad' HT, ab, 2002, Rawlins, R.; intr. 2007

'Rawville' ('Alma June Seville') HT, mp, 2006, Rawlins, Ronnie; flowers pink, reverse pink, 3 in., full, borne mostly solitary; foliage medium size, dark green, glossy; prickles triangular, moderate; growth upright, medium (36 in.); garden decorative; ['Ingrid Bergman' × 'Silver Anniversary']

'Ray Adeline' HT, my, 1990, Bevard, Harry D.; bud pointed; flowers medium, 40 petals, high-centered, borne usually singly and in sprays of 2-4, moderate fragrance; foliage medium size, dark green, semi-glossy; prickles straight, hooked down, light green; upright growth; hips small, light green; ['First Prize' × King's Ransom®]

'Ray Bunge' Cl HP, dp, 1959, Bunge; flowers dark rose, reverse lighter, 4-5 in., 30-40 petals, borne singly or clusters of 7-8; prolific early spring bloom, repeating later in season; foliage dark; very long stems; very vigorous (15½ ft.) growth; quite hardy; PP1637; [sport of 'Paul Neyron']; intr. 1959

'Ray of Hope' -- See 'Cocnilly'
'Ray of Sunshine' -- See 'Cocclare'
'Ray Still' -- See 'Houstill'

'Ray Torey' F, mr, 2003, Gill, Mathew; flowers medium, semi-dbl., borne in large clusters, slight fragrance; foliage medium size, medium green, semi-glossy; prickles small, hooked; compact, medium (50 cm.) growth; intr. 2003

'Raymond' HT, pb, 1917, Pernet-Ducher; bud long, pointed; flowers peach-blossom-pink, center salmon-carmine, dbl.; ['Rayon d'Or' × unknown]

'Raymond Blanc' S, mp; flowers bright cerise pink, full, old fashioned, moderate almond fragrance; recurrent; bushy growth; intr. 2006

'Raymond Carver' -- See 'Horraycar'

'Raymond Chenault' HKor, mr, 1963, Kordes, R.; flowers bright red, 4 in., 16 petals, borne in medium clusters, moderate fragrance; foliage dark, glossy; vigorous (9-12 ft.) growth; [R. × kordesii × 'Montezuma']; intr. 1960

'Raymond Chevalier-Appert, Climbing' Cl HT, mr; flowers pale red, semi-dbl.

'Raymond Kopa' -- See 'Wekjuvoo'

'Raymond Nazereau' F, dp, Adam; intr. 2000

'Raymond Privat' Pol, m, 1935, Privat; flowers violet, dbl., borne in clusters; vigorous growth

'Raymond's Pearl' F, yb, 1997, Rawlins, R.; flowers medium, 41 petals, borne in small clusters; foliage medium size, medium green, semi-glossy; some prickles; upright, medium (75 cm.) growth; [Amber Queen® × 'Brown Velvet']

'Rayon Butterflies' S, pb, Rupert; flowers single; intr. during the 1980s

'Rayon d'Or' HT, my, 1910, Pernet-Ducher; flowers golden yellow, sometimes streaked crimson on the outer petals, large, dbl., globular; foliage large, glossy; ['Mme Mélanie Soupert' × ('Soleil d'Or' × unknown)]

'Rayon d'Or' HT, my, Combe; flowers well-formed; intr. 1962

'Ray's Joy' F, ob, 2000, Jerabek, Paul E.; flowers orange-brownish, velvety, reverse orange, 3 in., full, borne singly or in small clusters, slight fragrance; foliage medium medium green, semi-glossy,new growth bronze; prickles moderate; growth upright, medium (3 ft.)

'Raywen Henry' HT, mr, Poole; intr. 2004

'Razzle Dazzle' -- See 'Frybright'

'Razzle Dazzle' F, rb, 1976, Warriner, William A.; flowers red, reverse white, 2½ in., 25 petals, slight fragrance; foliage dark, leathery; bushy growth; PP3995; intr. 1977

'Razzmatazz' -- See 'Jacmat'

'Rdsarrow' (Straight Arrow™) HT, pb, 2003, Streeper, Richard; flowers medium pink to medium red, 4½ in., dbl., borne mostly solitary, slight fragrance; recurrent; foliage large, dark green, glossy, mildew-free; prickles hooked; very long, straight stems; growth upright, tall (5-7 ft.); garden, exhibition; [seedling × 'First Prize']; intr. 2004

'Rea Silvia' HT, or, 1959, Giacomasso; flowers fiery red; ['Baiser' × ('Peace' × seedling)]; intr. 1958

'Reach for Recovery' HT, mp, Delbard; bud globular; flowers large, full, borne mostly singly, intense fragrance; good repeat; tall growth; intr. 2001

'Reaclibal' ('Ballerina, Climbing') HMsk, pb, 1997, Rearsby; flowers white in center, deepening to pink outer edge, reverse white, medium, semi-dbl., borne in large clusters, moderate fragrance; foliage medium size, light green, semi-glossy; some prickles; upright (15 ft.) growth; [sport of 'Ballerina']

Ready™ -- See 'Tuckready'

'Reah Nicole' -- See 'Jalnicole'

'Real Charmer' -- See 'Pixichar'

'Real Hit' MinFl, dr, Poulsen; flowers dark red, 5-8 cm., dbl., no fragrance; foliage dark; growth bushy, 20-40 cm.; PP13170; intr. 2002

'Reality' -- See 'Broreal'

'Rea's Rose' HT, pb, Kordes; flowers coral pink with cream reverse, full, high-centered, borne mostly singly; recurrent; stems sturdy, medium long; medium to tall growth; intr. 1997

Reba K. Rowland™ -- See 'Wekamarsodo'

'Reba McEntire' -- See 'Machahei'

Rebecca® -- See 'Tanrekta'

'Rebecca' HT, pb, 1930, Pemberton; bud large, long, pointed; flowers silvery pink, reverse salmon-pink, dbl.; foliage dark, leathery; vigorous growth

'Rebecca' Min, dp, Style; flowers deep raspberry pink, dbl., cupped, borne in clusters; free-flowering; foliage medium green, glossy; growth to 2 ft.; [sport of 'Sweet Dream']; intr. 2004

'Rebecca Anne' -- See 'Pixanne'

'Rebecca Claire' HT, op, 1981, Law, M.J.; flowers coppery orange edged light coral, 28 petals, borne singly and in small clusters; foliage medium green, semi-glossy; prickles medium brown; vigorous, bushy growth; [Blessings® × 'Redgold']

'Rebecca Gue' B, mp, 1983, Gue, Derek J.; flowers distinction from parent not described; [sport of 'Mme Ernst Calvat']

'Rebecca Kathleen' F, mr; intr. 2002

'Rebecca Louise' S, mp, Clements, John; flowers soft candy pink, golden stamens., 3 in., 25 petals, borne consistently in clusters of 6; foliage bronzy early, turning dark green, glossy; upright (5 × 5 ft.) growth; PPAF; intr. 2000

'Rebecca Paul' -- See 'Horcockalorum'

'Rebecca Susan' HT, op, Athy, M.; flowers orange pink with shades of tan and brown, dbl., moderate fragrance; recurrent; intr. 2006

'Rebecca's Delight' F, mp, 1975, Harkness; flowers soft salmon pink, shaded darker, large, 24 petals; foliage light green; vigorous, upright growth; [('Pink Parfait' × 'Highlight') × 'Circus']; intr. 1973

'Rebekah' -- See 'Macponui'

Rebell® -- See 'Korvegata'

'Rebell' -- See 'Feybell'

'Rebell 03 Kordana' -- See 'Rebell Kordana'

'Rebell Kordana' ('Rebell 03 Kordana') Min, dr, Kordes; flowers full, cupped; pot rose

'Rebellastar' HT, Hetzel; intr. 1970

'Recompense' HT, dp, 1957, Ratcliffe; flowers deep pink, well-shaped, medium; moderate growth; ['Charles P. Kilham' × 'Polly']

'Reconciliation' -- See 'Hartillery'

'Record' -- See 'Décor'

'Recuerdo de Angel Peluffo' HT, rb, 1928, Soupert & Notting; flowers cardinal-red, center garnet-red, large, dbl., moderate fragrance; ['Mme Edouard Herriot' × 'Duchess of Wellington']

'Recuerdo de Antonio Peluffo' T, yb, 1910, Soupert & Notting; flowers light yellow, edged pink, dbl.; ['Mme Mélanie Soupert' × 'Mme Constant Soupert']

'Recuerdo de Blas Munné' Cl HT, rb, 1948, Munné, M.; flowers carmine-red shaded cerise red; foliage dark; long, strong stems; very vigorous growth; ['Maria Serrat' × 'Recuerdo del Doctor Ferran']

'Recuerdo de Felio Camprubi' HT, rb, 1931, Camprubi, C.; flowers crimson suffused pink, reverse yellow suffused red, large, dbl.; vigorous growth; ['Hugh Dickson' × 'Souv. de Claudius Pernet']

'Recuerdo del Doctor Ferrari' HT, rb, 1935, Munné, B.; bud long, pointed; flowers scarlet-crimson, shaded fiery red, open, large, very dbl.; foliage dark; vigorous growth; ['Sensation' × 'Kitchener of Khartoum']

'Red Abundance' ('Songs of Praise', 'Velvet Abundance') F, dr, Harkness; flowers blood red, 2½ in., full, cupped, borne in large clusters, slight fragrance; good repeat; foliage dark green, glossy; upright (2½ ft.), bushy growth; intr. 2005

'Red Ace' -- See 'Amruda'

'Red Ace' Min, mr, 1981, Saville, F. Harmon; flowers 23 petals, high-centered, borne usually singly; prickles long, thin, straight; low, compact, bushy growth; PP4840; ['Rise 'n' Shine' × 'Sheri Anne']; intr. 1980

'Red Admiral' F, mr, 1940, Archer; flowers scarlet, borne in clusters

'Red Admiral' HT, mr, 1913, Paul, W.; flowers cerise, large, semi-dbl., borne in small clusters, slight fragrance

'Red Alert' -- See 'Moralert'

Red Alpha® HT, dr, Meilland; flowers full, high-centered, borne mostly singly; recurrent; intr. 2006

'Red American Beauty' HT, mr, 1960, Morey, Dr. Dennison; bud ovoid; flowers scarlet overcast rose-red, 4½-5 in., 30-35 petals, high-centered, intense fragrance; foliage leathery, dark; long stems; vigorous, upright, bushy growth; PP1982; ['Happiness' × 'San Fernando']; intr. 1959

'Red 'n' Fragrant' -- See 'Oradal'

'Red and White Delight' -- See 'Jacraw'

'Red Arrow' Min, mr, 1962, Moore, Ralph S.; flowers 1¼ in., 40 petals, high-centered, borne in clusters; foliage leathery; vigorous (12-18 in.) growth; [(R. wichurana × 'Floradora') × seedling]; intr. 1962

'Red Azteca' -- See 'Selazteca'

'Red Baby' S, Embriaco, B.; intr. 1992

'Red Baby Rambler' -- See 'Mme Norbert Levavasseur'

'Red Ballerina' S, mr, 1976, Fryer, Gareth; flowers bright crimson, small, 10 petals; foliage glossy; ['Ballerina' × 'Evelyn Fison']

'Red Ballerina' -- See 'Marjorie Fair'

'Red Baron' HT, or; flowers bright red orange, 30-35 petals, high-centered, borne mostly singly, slight fragrance; recurrent; stems long; intr. 2007

'Red Barrier' -- See 'Kortello'

'Red Beauty' HT, mr, 1929, Dunlop; [sport of 'Matchless']

'Red Beauty' Min, dr, Williams, Ernest D.; flowers dark red, yellow hinge, small to medium, 35 petals, high-centered; foliage small, dark, glossy; bushy growth; ['Starburst' × 'Over the Rainbow']; intr. 1981

'Red Belgic' mr; flowers full; in England before 1759

Red Bells™ -- See 'Poulred'

'Red Berlin' -- See 'Olijplam'

'Red Better Times' HT, mr, 1937, Asmus; flowers bright clear red; PP323; [sport of 'Better Times']

'Red Bird' -- See 'Gelbird'

'Red Bird' HT, mr, 1959, Manda, Jr., E.A.; flowers bright red; PP1687; [sport of 'Better Times']; intr. 1958

Red Blanket® -- See 'Intercell'

'Red Blush' A, mr, Sievers; flowers rose-red with darker edges, small, dbl., moderate fragrance; non-remontant; foliage soft green, glossy; arching growth; intr. 1988

'Red Bonica' S, mr; growth to 4 ft.; [sport of 'Bonica']; intr. after 1986

'Red Boy' HT, or, 1939, Hansen, N.J.; bud long, pointed; flowers fiery orange-red, fading to dominant pink, open, single to semi-dbl.; foliage dark, glossy; vigorous, bushy growth; ['Charles K. Douglas' × 'Pres. Herbert Hoover']

'Red Brigand' -- See 'Santor'

'Red Built' HT, dr; florist rose; intr. 2005

'Red Button' Min, dr, 1979, Moore, Ralph S.; bud short, pointed; flowers deep red, small, full; foliage very small, glossy; bushy, compact, spreading growth; [(R. wichurana × 'Floradora') × 'Magic Dragon']; intr. 1978

'Red Calypso' HT, dr; flowers large, full, high-centered, borne mostly singly; foliage glossy; stems very long

'Red Camellia' F, or, 1943, Krause; bud small; flowers orange-scarlet, 20-30 petals; foliage dark, leathery; vigorous, upright, bushy growth; ['Baby Chateau' × 'Folkestone']

'Red Camellia' HT, mr

'Red Cameo' -- See 'Moranyblac'

'Red Can Can' Min, mr, 1977, Lyon; bud pointed; flowers cardinal-red, 2 in., 28 petals, moderate fruity fragrance; foliage dark; vigorous, upright growth; [seedling × unknown]

'Red Candy' F, mr, Wagner, S.; bud short; flowers simple light red with white eye, 8 petals, flat, borne in clusters, slight fragrance; foliage medium large, dark green, glossy; [sport of 'Candy Rose' seedling]; intr. 1995

'Red Carefree Delight' -- See 'Meizmea'

'Red Carpet' Cl F, dr, 1971, Williams, J. Benjamin; bud ovoid; flowers dark scarlet, overlaid darker, medium, dbl., globular; foliage large, dark, leathery; very vigorous, climbing growth; ['Don Juan' × 'Red Favorite']; originally registered as LCl

'Red Carrousel' Min, dp, 1984, Rumsey, R.H.; flowers small, full, slight fragrance; foliage glossy, leathery; bushy growth; [sport of Magic Carrousel®]

'Red Cascade' Cl Min, dr, 1976, Moore, Ralph S.; bud pointed; flowers deep red, 1 in., 40 petals, cupped, borne singly or in small clusters, very slight fragrance; free-flowering; foliage small, leathery, semi-glossy; prickles moderate, straight; prostrate, bushy growth; hips none ; PP3962; [(R. wichurana × 'Floradora') × 'Magic Dragon']

'Red Cavalier' S, mr, Courage; flowers rich red, ruffled, dbl., borne in small clusters; recurrent; intr. 2002

Red Caviar™ F, dr, Olesen; bud pointed ovoid, broad base; flowers dark red, 8 cm., 30 petals, pompon, borne in large clusters, very slight fragrance; recurrent; foliage dark olive-green, glossy; prickles few, 5 mm., hooked downward, brown; upright to bushy (60-100 cm.) growth; PP16033; [Dalli Dalli® × seedling]; intr. 2003

'Red Cécile Brünner, Climbing' -- See 'Pasadena Tournament, Climbing'

'Red Cécile Brünner' -- See 'Pasadena Tournament'

'Red Cedar' -- See 'Korgund '81'

'Red Centre' LCl, or, Peden

Red Champ® F, mr, Select; flowers bright red, 9 cm., 40-45 petals, high-centered, borne mostly singly; recurrent; stems 50 - 70 cm; florist rose; intr. 2001

'Red Chateau' HT, mr, 1999, Teranishi, K.; flowers crimson red, 35 petals, high-centered; growth to 3½ ft.; [('Samantha' × seedling) × seedling]; intr. 1997

'Red Chatenay' HT, mr, before 1910

'Red Cheer' Min, mr, 1978, Lyon; flowers cherry-red, 1 in., 45 petals; foliage very small, dark; compact, bushy growth; [seedling × seedling]; intr. 1975

'Red Cheerful' HT, dr, 1951, Blixen; bud pointed; flowers deep red, 4½ in., 30-40 petals, high-centered, moderate fragrance; foliage glossy, leathery, veined red; vigorous, upright growth; PP1556; [sport of 'Better Times']; intr. 1951

'Red Cherokee' -- See 'Ramona'

'Red Chief' HT, mr, 1967, Armstrong, D.L.; bud large, ovoid; flowers , 35-40 petals, high-centered, borne usually singly, but sometimes 2 or 3 per stem, intense fragrance; good repeat; foliage medium to large, leathery, semi-glossy; prickles several, medium, hooked slightly downward, brown; vigorous, upright, bushy growth; hips short, globular, smooth, chrysolite green; PP2927; [seedling × 'Chrysler Imperial']

'Red Coat' -- See 'Redcoat'

'Red Columbia' HT, mr, 1920, Joseph H. Hill, Co.; flowers rich velvety scarlet, large, dbl.; foliage leathery; very vigorous growth; [sport of 'Columbia']

'Red Corsair' -- See 'Korromalu'

'Red Corvette' -- See 'Vital'

'Red Cottage' ('Dictech ??') S, rb, Dickson, Patrick; flowers red with pink stripes and yellow eye , single, shallow cup , borne in clusters, no fragrance; 4 - 5 ft. growth; intr. 1998

'Red Cross' -- See 'Meisoyris'

'Red Cross' HT, mr, 1969, Gregory; flowers crimson scarlet, pointed, borne several together; foliage medium size, medium green; intr. 1967

'Red Cross' HT, ob, 1916, Dickson, A.; flowers orange-crimson-scarlet, dbl., moderate fragrance; Ruled extinct 1969 ARA

Red Cupido® Min, mr; bud ovoid, rounded; flowers 3-4 cm., 35-45 petals, rosette, borne in clusters of up to 9, no fragrance; recurrent; foliage smooth, leathery; compact (12 in.), rounded, dense growth; hips rarely observed ; PP9634; [seedling × seedling]; containers

'Red Curtain' -- See 'Kormauret'

'Red Cushion' F, dr, 1966, Armstrong, D.L.; bud pointed; flowers small, semi-dbl., borne in clusters; foliage dark, glossy, leathery; vigorous, bushy growth; PP2845; ['Circus' × 'Ruby Lips']; intr. 1966

'Red Dagmar' -- See 'Speruge'

'Red Damask' ('À Fleurs Rouges Doubles', 'Multiflora', 'Rouge', 'Rubro-Purpurea', 'Bouquet Tout Fait', 'Corimbosa') D, mr, before 1789; flowers rose red, medium, dbl., intense fragrance

'Red Dandy' F, mr, 1960, Norman; flowers cherry-red, velvety, 3 in., 40 petals, high-centered, moderate fragrance; free-flowering; foliage dark green; vigorous, upright growth; ['Ena Harkness' × 'Karl Herbst']; intr. 1959

'Red Dawn' S, mr, 1957, Simonet; flowers deep rose-red, well-formed; recurrent bloom; hardy; ['New Dawn' × unknown]

'Red Deer' -- See 'Waskasoo'

'Red Delicious' -- See 'Jacdrive'

'Red Delicious' HT, mr, 1942, Joseph H. Hill, Co.; bud carmine, shaded oxblood-red; flowers brilliant rose-red, 4-6 in., 30-35 petals, intense fragrance; foliage leathery, dark; stems weak necks; vigorous, upright growth; PP620; ['Rome Glory' × 'Chieftain']

Red Delight™ -- See 'Minaico'

'Red Delight' HT, mr, Avansino; flowers bright red; RULED EXTINCT 11/86; [sport of 'Pink Delight']; intr. 1935

'Red Det' Min, mr, 1986, Harkness; flowers dbl., flat, borne in clusters; foliage small, deep green, glossy; vigorous, bushy growth; [('Marlena' × 'Kim') × 'Little Buckaroo']; intr. 1978

'Red Det 80' Min, dr, Cocker; flowers dark scarlet-red, very dbl.; bushy, compact growth; intr. 1980

'Red Devil' ('Coeur d'Amour') HT, mr, 1967, Dickson, A.; bud ovoid; flowers medium red, reverse lighter, large, 72 petals, high-centered, borne singly, moderate fragrance; foliage large, glossy; stems long; vigorous growth; PP3037; ['Silver Lining' × 'Prima Ballerina']; intr. 1970

Red Diadem® -- See 'Tanetorde'

'Red Dorothy Perkins' -- See 'Excelsa'

'Red Dot' -- See 'Dart's Red Dot'

'Red Dragon' -- See 'Liodrag'

'Red Dragon' HP, dr, 1878, Paul, W.; flowers vivid crimson, large, very dbl., cupped; foliage grey-green; ['Charles Lefèbvre' × unknown]

'Red Dragon' F, mr, Cants of Colchester, Ltd.; flowers 3½-4 in., 5 petals; vigorous growth; ['Anna Wheatcroft' × seedling]; intr. 1970

Red Drift® ('Nature Meillandecor') S, mr, Meilland; flowers scarlet red, 3/4 in., 15 petals, cupped, borne in large clusters; recurrent; foliage small, dark green, semi-glossy; low (18 in.), spreading growth; intr. 2006

'Red Druschki' -- See 'Ruhm von Steinfurth'

'Red Duchess' HT, mr, 1942, Brownell; bud long, pointed; flowers 3½-5 in., 35-45 petals, high-centered, moderate fragrance; foliage glossy, bronze; long, strong stems; vigorous, upright, bushy growth; PP846; ['Pink Princess' × 'Crimson Glory']

'Red Duchess, Climbing' Cl HT, mr, 1955, Brownell; PP1370

'Red Echo' Pol, or, 1932, Kluis & Koning; flowers vermilion tinted crimson, dbl., cupped; foliage dark, wrinkled; dwarf growth; ['Echo' × 'hybrid tea seedling']

'Red Eden' -- See 'Meidrason'

'Red Eden Rose' -- See 'Meidrason'

Red Elegance™ HT, dr, Twomey, Jerry; flowers 4-4.5 in., 35 -40 petals, high-centered; recurrent; 4 - 5 ft. growth;

intr. 1996

'Red Elf' Min, dr, 1949, deVink; bud ovoid; flowers dark crimson, ¾-1 in., 23 petals; foliage soft, tiny; vigorous, bushy, dwarf growth; PP973; ['Eblouissant' × 'Tom Thumb']

'Red Ellen Poulsen' ('Dunkelrote Ellen Poulsen') Pol, mr, 1918, Poulsen, S.; [sport of 'Ellen Poulsen']

'Red Ember' HT, or, 1953, Cant, F.; flowers flame, well-formed, 4-5 in., 30 petals; foliage glossy, dark; free growth

'Red Emblem' F, dr, 1959, Boerner; bud ovoid; flowers deep red, open, 2½ in., 30-35 petals, moderate fragrance; foliage leathery; upright, bushy growth; [('Garnette' × unknown) × 'Pageant']; intr. 1959

'Red Emperor' -- See 'Broemp'

'Red Empress' ('Impératrice Rouge', 'Robur') LCl, mr, 1957, Mallerin, C.; bud ovoid; flowers cardinal-red, 3½ in., 33 petals, high-centered to cupped, borne usually singly, sometimes in small clusters, intense tea fragrance; recurrent; foliage medium size, leathery; prickles several, medium, hooked downward, oval base; vigorous, climbing growth; PP1573; [('Holstein' × 'Decor') × ('Holstein' × 'Decor')]

'Red Ensign' HT, mr, 1947, Norman; flowers crimson,, 4-5 in., 40-45 petals, high-centered, intense damask fragrance; foliage dark; very vigorous growth; ['Crimson Glory' × 'Southport']

'Red Euphoria' S, mr, Interplant; flowers bright red, semi-dbl., borne in small clusters; intr. 1999

'Red Explorer' Cl Pol, dr, 1928, Penny; flowers deep brilliant crimson, small, dbl., borne in medium clusters; recurrent bloom; vigorous, climbing growth; [sport of 'Miss Edith Cavell']

'Red Facade' -- See 'Rotfassade'

'Red Fairy' -- See 'Moredfar'

Red Fairy™ -- See 'Poulria'

'Red Fan' HT, or, Keisei; intr. 1991

'Red Fantasy' -- See 'Kornitzel'

'Red Fantasy' S, mr; flowers 3 in., full, pompon, borne in clusters; free-flowering; foliage disease-resistant; low (2-3 ft.), spreading (5 ft.), groundcover growth

'Red Favorite, Climbing'

'Red Favorite' ('Holländerin', 'Schweizer Gruss', 'Salut à la Suisse', 'Red Favourite') F, dr, 1954, Tantau, Math.; bud ovoid; flowers velvety oxblood-red, 2½ in., 13 petals, borne in trusses; good repeat; foliage dark, leathery, glossy; vigorous, bushy growth; PP1189; ['Karl Weinhausen' × 'Cinnabar']; intr. 1951

'Red Favourite' -- See 'Red Favorite'

'Red Fawn' -- See 'Beni-Kanoko'

'Red Festival' -- See 'Delfesrou'

'Red Figurine' Min, dr, Saville; flowers bright crimson red, dbl., borne mostly singly; recurrent; slender, 8 in. stems; medium to tall growth; intr. 2001

'Red Finch' Pol, mp, 1937, Stielow, F.C.; flowers cerise, more cupped, more open, more dbl. than parent, borne in clusters; PP292; [sport of 'Mrs R.M. Finch']

'Red Finesse' -- See 'Korvillade'

'Red Flame' -- See 'Commandant Cousteau, Climbing'

'Red Flare' LCl, dr, 1954, Mansuino, Dr. Ada; bud globular; flowers carmine overcast spectrum-red, 4-4½ in., 40 petals, cupped, borne singly and in small clusters, moderate fragrance; profuse bloom repeated sparingly; foliage dark, glossy; growth to 7-8 ft.; PP1366; ['Reine Marie Henriette' × 'Paul's Scarlet Climber']; intr. 1954

'Red Fleurette' S, mr

'Red Flower Carpet' ('Alcantara', 'Vesuvia') S, mr, Noack, Werner; buds pointed; flowers pure velvet red with bright yellow stamens, 2 in., 25 petals, cupped to flat, borne in large trusses, no fragrance; recurrent; foliage dark green, glossy; prickles medium; growth spreading (2½ × 3 ft.); PP11308; [('Evelyn Fison' × 'Paprika') × Flower Carpet™]; intr. 2001

'Red Flush' Min, mr, 1978, Schwartz, Ernest W.; bud ovoid; flowers rose red, satiny, 1½ in., 30-35 petals, cupped, borne usually in sprays of 3 - 7, no fragrance; fast repeat; foliage medium size, green, matte; prickles few, thin, pointed; very compact (15 in.) growth, breaks readily from soil; hips none observed ; PP4369; ['Zorina' × seedling]

'Red Fountain' LCl, dr, 1974, Williams, J. Benjamin; bud ovoid, pointed; flowers scarlet, medium, 20-25 petals, cupped, borne in clusters, intense old rose fragrance; recurrent; foliage large, dark, leathery; prickles moderate, flat base, hooked downward, red; very vigorous, climbing growth; hips globular, smooth, persimmon orange; PP3615; ['Don Juan' × 'Blaze']; intr. 1975

'Red France' -- See 'Fazcanne'

'Red Friendship' S, mr, Verschuren; flowers bright red, small, dbl., borne in clusters; low (30 in.), sprawling growth; intr. 1986

'Red Frost' HT, rb, 1993, Lienau, David W.; flowers medium red, suffused white, shaded light yellow at base, 3-3½ in., full, high-centered; foliage medium size, dark green, glossy; some prickles; medium (90-120 cm.), bushy growth; ['First Prize' × seedling]; intr. 1993

'Red Fruitilia' F, mr, Kordes; flowers single; recurrent; growth 80 cm. height ; hips round

'Red Garnette' -- See 'Garnette'

'Red Garter' -- See 'Brogar'

'Red Germain' Min, rb, 1976, Moore, Ralph S.; bud long, pointed; flowers red, reverse lighter, 1 in., 25 petals, flat; foliage small, leathery; vigorous, bushy growth; [(R. wichurana × 'Floradora') × ('Oakington Ruby' × 'Floradora')]; intr. 1975

'Red Giant' HT, mr, Kordes; flowers clear red, large, full, high-centered, borne mostly singly; good repeat; stems long, upright, firm; florist rose; intr. 2002

'Red Globe' F, mr, 1971, Delforge; bud ovoid; flowers full,large, dbl.; foliage soft; moderate, bushy growth

'Red Glory' F, mr, 1963, Swim, H.C.; bud ovoid, pointed; flowers cherry to rose-red, 2½-3½ in., 11 petals, cupped to flat, borne in rounded clusters, slight fragrance; foliage leathery, semi-glossy; very vigorous, tall, bushy growth; good as fence or hedge; PP1885; ['Gay Lady' × ('Pinocchio' × 'Floradora')]; intr. 1958

'Red Gold' -- See 'Redgold'

'Red Gruss an Coburg' -- See 'Clotaria'

'Red Guard' HT, rb, 1935, Verschuren; flowers dark blood-red, well-formed, very dbl.; very vigorous growth

'Red Halo' F, mr, 1968, Oliver, W.G.; flowers crimson, flat, borne in trusses; foliage glossy; vigorous, bushy growth; ['Tabarin' × 'Karl Herbst']

'Red Haze' -- See 'Tanzahde'

'Red Head' HT, mr, Dickson; intr. 1985

'Red Hedge' HRg, mr, 1958, Nyveldt; flowers single; hips small, red; [(R. rugosa rubra × R. cinnamomea) × R. nitida]

'Red Hedges' S, mr, Williams, J.B.; flowers bright red with yellow stamens, ruffled petals, semi-dbl., borne in masses of bloom; intr. 2000

'Red Hermosa' -- See 'Queen's Scarlet'

'Red Hill' HT, mr, 1941, Clark, A.; flowers well-formed, large; ['E.G. Hill' × unknown]

'Red Hiroshima' HT, mr, Hiroshima; intr. 1990

'Red Hit' -- See 'Poulhit'

'Red Hoover' HT, rb, 1937, Lens; flowers brilliant red, center salmon-red; [sport of 'President Herbert Hoover']

'Red Hot' S, mr, Carruth, Tom; flowers bright red, small, single, shallow cup to flat, borne in clusters; free-flowering; foliage small, medium green, glossy; vigorous, low (15-18 in.) growth; intr. 2006

'Red Hot Friendship' F, rb, Fleming; intr. 2006

'Red Immensee' -- See 'Sommerabend'

'Red Imp' ('Maid Marion', 'Mon Tresor', 'Montresor') Min, dr, 1951, deVink; bud ovoid; flowers deep crimson, micro-mini, ¾-1 in., 54 petals, flat, slight fragrance; upright, bushy, dwarf (9 in.) growth; PP1032; ['Ellen Poulsen' × 'Tom Thumb']

'Red Intuition' HT, rb, Delbard; flowers mix of bright red and dark red in stripes and splotches, medium , dbl., high-centered, borne mostly singly; recurrent; stems long; vigorous, tall growth; originally a greenhouse rose; intr. 2004

'Red Jacket' HT, mr, 1950, Swim, H.C.; bud ovoid, pointed; flowers 3¾ in., 21 petals, urn-shaped, then flat, slight fragrance; foliage leathery; upright, bushy growth; PP968; ['World's Fair'

× 'Mirandy']

'Red Jewel' -- See 'Interro'

'Red Jewel' HT, mr, Verbeek; bud medium, oval, violet-red; flowers currant red, reverse lighter, petals scalloped, 3-4 in., 44-62 petals, full, opening flat, borne several to a stem; foliage large, dark green, glossy; prickles moderate, 9 mm., reddish; growth bushy; hips pear-shaped, smooth, thin-walled; PP2546; ['Poinsettia' × ('Baccara' × seedling)]

'Red Jewel' HT, dr, deRuiter

'Red Jonathan' -- See 'Jonathan'

'Red Joy' HT, mr; intr. 1997

'Red Kelly' LCl, rb, Sutherland, P; intr. 1999

'Red Knight' LCl, dr, 1965, Booy, P.J.; flowers maroon, medium, very vigorous growth, semi-dbl., globular; recurrent bloom; [sport of 'Dr. Huey']

'Red La France' -- See 'Duchess of Albany'

Red Lady® HT, mr, Laperriére; flowers velvety red, dbl.; intr. 1978

'Red Leonardo da Vinci' F, dr, Meilland; flowers rich, dark red, lightening in strong sun, dbl., rosette; free-flowering; robust, low growth; intr. 2004

'Red-Letter Day' HT, dp, 1914, Dickson, A.; flowers velvety rose-red, white streak in center of inner petals, stamens cinnamon, 3½ in., semi-dbl.; foliage glaucous sage-green; short stems; vigorous growth

'Red Lion' HT, mr, 1964, McGredy, Sam IV; flowers red becoming rose-red, 5 in., 38 petals, high-centered; ['Kordes' Perfecta' × 'Detroiter']

Red Love™ -- See 'Minqco'

'Red Magic' -- See 'Randilla Rouge'

'Red Magic' Min, mr, 1977, Lyon; bud pointed; flowers deep cherry-red, open, medium, 10-15 petals; vigorous, upright growth; ['Red Can Can' × unknown]

Red Magic Carpet™ -- See 'Macredsaus'

'Red Maid' F, or, 1976, Sanday, John; flowers coral-red, 3 in., 18 petals; ['Vera Dalton' × 'Stephen Langdon']; intr. 1975

'Red Malmaison' -- See 'Malmaison Rouge'

'Red Maman Cochet' -- See 'Niles Cochet'

'Red Manikin' F, rb, Orard; flowers bright red with white eye, single, borne in clusters; recurrent; compact growth; intr. 2006

'Red Maréchal Niel' -- See 'Grossherzog Ernst Ludwig von Hesse'

'Red Margo Koster' Pol, mr

'Red Martini' HT, dr, 1967, Delforge; bud ovoid; flowers large, dbl.; foliage bronze; vigorous, bushy growth; ['Chrysler Imperial' × seedling]

'Red Masquerade' F, mr, 1965, Hill, A.; bud pointed; flowers red becoming darker, 2½-3 in., 10 petals, borne in clusters; vigorous growth; ['Masquerade' × 'Independence']

'Red Masterpiece' HT, dr, 1974, Warriner, William A.; bud ovoid to globular; flowers cardinal red, 4½-5 in., 45-50 petals, high-centered, borne usually singly, intense fragrance; foliage large, dark green, leathery; prickles moderate, long, hooked downward; vigorous, upright growth; PP3508; [('Siren' × 'Chrysler Imperial') × ('Carrousel' × 'Chrysler Imperial')]

'Red Masterpiece, Climbing' Cl HT, dr, Kasturi & Sriram; flowers very large; free-flowering; [sport of 'Red Masterpiece']; intr. 2004

'Red Max Graf' -- See 'Kormax'

Red Meidiland™ -- See 'Meineble'

Red Meillandina® Min, mr, Meilland; intr. 1982

'Red Meilove' -- See 'Meirokad'

'Red Mercedes' F, mr

'Red Midinette' Cl Min, mr, Orard; flowers bright red, yellow stamens, semi-dbl. to dbl., borne in clusters; recurrent; tall (8 ft.), vigorous growth; intr. 2004

'Red Mikado' F, mr, Tantau; florist rose

Red Mini-Wonder™ -- See 'Meinofrai'

Red Minimo™ -- See 'Ruimired'

'Red Minimo, Climbing' Cl Min, dr, Takefuji (Muto?); intr. 1998

'Red Minuetto' Min, mr; PPAF; intr. 2004

'Red Mirato' -- See 'Tanoronez'

'Red Monarch' HT, dr, Meilland; flowers dbl., high-centered, borne mostly singly; good repeat; florist rose; intr. 2004

'Red Moon' M, m, Teranishi; intr. 2003

Red Moon™ -- See 'Minimoon'

'Red Moscow' -- See 'Krasnaia Moskva'

'Red Moss, Climbing' Cl M, mr, Foote

'Red Moss' -- See 'Henri Martin'

'Red Moss Rambler' HWich, mr, Moore; bud mossy; flowers deep, bright crimson, semi-dbl., moderate fragrance; recurrent; numerous prickles; intr. 1988

'Red Mothersday' -- See 'Mothersday'

'Red Mountain Peak' HT, mr, Taschner, Ludwig; flowers large, full, high-centered, borne usually singly; recurrent; tall growth; intr. 2004

'Red Mozart' -- See 'Rote Mozart'

'Red Multirosa' S, rb, J&P; flowers medium red with white reverse, red blues as it matures; [seedling × seedling]; intr. 2007

'Red-n-White Glory' -- See 'Candystick'

'Red Nearly Wild' F, mr, 1960, Brownell, H.C.; bud globular; flowers rose-red, small, single, cupped, borne in clusters; foliage soft; vigorous, bushy growth; ['Nearly Wild' × seedling]; intr. 1960

'Red Nella' HT, dp, Allender, Robert William; intr. 1991

'Red Nelly' -- See 'Single Red'

'Red New Dawn' -- See 'Étendard'

'Red Niphetos' -- See 'Lady Battersea'

'Red Nostalgie' -- See 'Tantumleh'

'Red One' HT, dr; bud large, cylindrical; flowers, 11-12 cm., 22 petals, cupped, borne singly, no fragrance; recurrent; prickles numerous, strong, 1 cm., curved downward, green; upright (6 ft.), vigorous growth; hips pitcher shaped, 1 cm ; PP14468; [seedling × 'Tina']; intr. 2001

'Red Opal' F, mr, 1968, Northfield; bud pointed; flowers red, reverse cerise, flat, borne in small clusters; foliage small, dark; free growth; ['Karl Herbst' × 'Korona']

'Red Orléans Rose' -- See 'Maréchal Foch'

Red Pagode™ MinFl, mr, Poulsen; flowers medium red, 5-8 cm., dbl., no fragrance; foliage dark; cascading growth, hanging basket type; PP13592; intr. 2000

Red Paillette™ Min, mr, Poulsen; flowers medium red, medium, no fragrance; foliage dark; growth narrow, bushy, 40-60 cm.; intr. 1998

'Red Parade' F, mr, 1972, Patterson; bud ovoid; flowers carmine-red, medium, dbl., high-centered; foliage glossy, bronze; vigorous, bushy growth; [('Frolic' × 'Peace') × 'Texan']

Red Parfum® Cl F, mr, Eve, A.; flowers soft red, 9 cm., dbl., borne in clusters, intense fragrance; foliage glossy; vigorous (10-13 ft.) growth; intr. 1972

'Red Passion' S, mr; intr. 2004

'Red Pastel' -- See 'Wilrib'

'Red Pat' S, mr; groundcover; spreading growth; intr. 2003

'Red Patio Wonder' MinFl, mr, Jalbert; flowers crimson red, large, full, slight fragrance; recurrent; compact (14 in.), tidy growth; intr. 1999

'Red Peace' -- See 'Dame de Coeur'

'Red Peace' -- See 'Karl Herbst'

'Red Pearl' HT, mr, 1970, Watkins Roses; flowers bright red, pointed, 5 in., 40 petals; foliage large, dark; very vigorous growth; ['Josephine Bruce' × 'Kordes' Perfecta']

Red Pendant™ -- See 'Minvco'

Red Perfection™ -- See 'Machaden'

'Red Pet' ('New Red Pet') Ch, dr, 1888, Parker/G. Paul; flowers deep rich red, round, small, very dbl.; growth low, bushy; probably extinct

'Red Petticoat' F, mr, 1967, Watkins Roses; flowers blood-red, short petaled, dbl., flat, borne in trusses; foliage dark, glossy; very vigorous growth; ['Buisman's Triumph' × 'Lilli Marlene']

'Red Pierre' -- See 'Meidrason'

'Red Pinocchio' F, dr, 1947, Boerner; flowers velvety carmine-red, 3 in., 28 petals, cupped, borne in clusters, moderate fragrance; vigorous, bushy growth; PP812; [('Pinocchio' × unknown) × 'Donald Prior']

'Red Pistols' Min, dy, 1982, Ballmer, Gordon W.; flowers deep golden yellow, small, 15-20 petals; foliage medium green, matte; prickles brown, needle-like; upright, bushy growth; ['Rise 'n' Shine' × seedling]

'Red Pixie' -- See 'Kornuma'

'Red Planet' HT, dr, 1970, Dickson, Patrick; flowers crimson, 5½-6 in., 30-35 petals, high-centered, intense fragrance; foliage glossy; ['Red Devil' × seedling]

'Red Plume' F, or, 1966, Sanday, John; flowers bright scarlet, 3 in., 35 petals, rosette, borne in clusters; foliage glossy; vigorous, bushy growth; ['Masquerade' × ('Independence' × unknown)]

'Red Point' -- See 'Macwooherm'

'Red Popcorn' S, dp, Williams, J. Benjamin; flowers reddish-pink, small, dbl., pompon, borne in large sprays, slight fragrance; recurrent; foliage small, bluish-green; groundcover, small climber; spreading (2 ft.) growth; intr. 2005

'Red Poppy' -- See 'Krasnyi Mak'

'Red Premier' HT, dp, 1924, Scott, R.; bud long, pointed; flowers bright carmine, large, dbl.; foliage leathery; vigorous growth; [sport of 'Premier']

'Red Pride' F, mr, 1968, Verbeek; bud ovoid; flowers small, dbl.

Red Prince® -- See 'Fountain'

'Red Princess' -- See 'Benihime'

'Red Profusion' -- See 'Randilla Rouge'

'Red Prolific' -- See 'Delific'

'Red Provence' -- See 'Rubra'

'Red Queen' -- See 'Korlo'

'Red Queen, Climbing' Cl HT, mr; intr. after 1968

'Red Queen' ('Marlena') HT, mr, Kordes; flowers velvety red, large, dbl.; free-flowering; florist rose; intr. 1998

'Red Radiance' HT, dp, 1916, Gude Bros.; flowers brilliant cerise-red, large, 23 petals, cupped, intense damask fragrance; free-flowering; foliage leathery; vigorous growth; [sport of 'Radiance']

'Red Radiance, Climbing' Cl HT, dp, 1927, Pacific Rose Co. (also Catt, 1929); bud very large, long-pointed; flowers very large, dbl., moderate fragrance; foliage large, dark green, glossy; [sport of 'Red Radiance']

'Red Rascal' -- See 'Jacbed'

'Red Recker' HT, dr, Kasturi; flowers deep crimson, dbl., high-centered; intr. 1986

'Red Reflection' HT, mr, 1975, Warriner, William A.; bud ovoid, pointed; flowers velvet red with faint blue tint on reverse, 4-5 in., high-centered, slight fragrance; recurrent; foliage large, leathery; upright growth; PP3664; ['Tropicana' × 'Living']; intr. 1964

'Red Rhapsody' -- See 'Weksanpoly'

Red Ribbon™ -- See 'Wilrib'

'Red Ribbon' F, mr, McGredy, Sam IV; intr. 1973

Red Ribbon® HT, mr, Kordes; flowers brilliant red, large, dbl., high-centered, borne mostly singly; recurrent; stems moderately long; intr. 2005

'Red Ribbons' -- See 'Kortemma'

'Red Riddle' -- See 'Wilrib'

'Red Rider' -- See 'Red Rover'

'Red Rider' Cl F, rb, 1970, Guest; flowers red, base yellow, 2-3 in., 50 petals; foliage large, glossy; vigorous growth; ['Circus' × 'Danse de Feu']

'Red Riding Hood' -- See 'Rödhätte'

'Red Riding Hood' Min, dr, 1955, Robinson, T.; flowers brilliant dark red; [sport of 'Red Imp']

'Red Ripples' ('Willi Maass') F, dr, 1942, Krause; bud globular; flowers deep red, petals wavy, small, semi-dbl., borne in large clusters; foliage leathery, glossy, wrinkled; upright, bushy growth; ['Hamburg' × 'Anne Poulsen']

'Red River' F, Kordes

'Red Robin' -- See 'Lenreho'

'Red Robin' HT, rb, 1940, Brownell; flowers red, tending toward scarlet; vigorous growth

'Red Robin' -- See 'Gloire des Rosomanes'

'Red Rock' ('Lusambo', 'Red Rocky') HT, mr, 1974, Meilland; flowers cherry-red, open, petals imbricated, 5 in., 35 petals; very vigorous growth; [('Royal Velvet' × 'Chrysler Imperial') × Pharaoh®]; intr. 1973

'Red Rocket' S, mr, 1949, Longley, L.E.; bud ovoid; flowers crimson, large, semi-dbl., borne in clusters; non-recurrent; foliage large, dark, glossy, bronze; vigorous, upright growth; ['Skyrocket' × unknown]

'Red Rocky' -- See 'Red Rock'

'Red Roma' HT, mr; flowers large, dbl.

'Red Romance' S, dr; flowers deep red, small, semi-dbl. to dbl., cupped; growth to 20 × 20 in.; intr. 2003

Red Rosamini® -- See 'Ruiredro'

'Red Rose Marie' HT, rb, 1938, Mordigan Evergreen Nursery; bud ovoid; flowers cerise-red, large, dbl., high-centered; foliage dark, leathery; vigorous, bushy growth; [sport of 'Rose Marie']

'Red Rose of Denman' S, dr; intr. 1958

'Red Rose Wave' HT, mr, Preesman

'Red Roulette' Min, mr

'Red Rover' HP, mr, 1864, Paul, W.; flowers fire-red, large, full

'Red Rover' ('Red Rider') Min, dr, 1991, Laver, Keith G.; bud pointed; flowers dbl., exhibition, loose, borne usually singly, no fragrance; foliage small to medium size, dark green, semi-glossy to glossy; bushy, low growth; [sport of Mountie™]; intr. 1990

'Red Ruffles' F, dr, 1960, Von Abrams; bud pointed; flowers dull dark red, petals ruffled, 2½-3 in., 45 petals, cupped to flat, borne in large clusters, slight fragrance; foliage dark, glossy; vigorous, bushy, compact growth; PP2110; ['Improved Lafayette' × 'Carrousel']; intr. 1960

'Red Rugostar' HRg, mr, Meilland; flowers carmine-red, medium-large, semi-dbl.; intr. 1995

'Red Rum' F, mr, 1976, Bees; flowers red, shaded scarlet, 2½ in., 24 petals; foliage dark; vigorous growth; [Handel® × 'Arthur Bell']

'Red Safrano' -- See 'Safrano à Fleurs Rouges'

'Red Sarong' HT, dr, 1975, Golik; bud ovoid; flowers deep red, 5 in., 36 petals, high-centered, moderate fragrance; foliage dark, leathery; tall growth; [Baccará® × Golden Showers®]; intr. 1974

'Red Satin' -- See 'Devpajaro'

Red Scentsation™ -- See 'Savared'

Red Sea® -- See 'Barred'

'Red Sea' -- See 'Casred'

'Red Seafoam' S, dp; flowers fuchsia pink, semi-dbl., borne in clusters, slight fragrance; low, spreading growth; intr. 2000

Red Shadows™ -- See 'Savmore'

'Red Simplicity' -- See 'Jacsimpl'

'Red Skelton' HT, or, 1968, Whisler, D.; bud long, pointed; flowers vermilion, 5-6 in., 20-30 petals, high-centered to cupped, borne mostly singly, moderate fragrance; recurrent; foliage bronze-green when young, dark green when mature, leathery; prickles few, bronze; vigorous, upright growth; hips none observed; PP3020; ['Rose Queen' × 'Charlotte Armstrong']

'Red Smith's Parish' T, rb, 1997, Manners, Dr. Malcolm; flowers small, color variable, dbl., borne in small clusters, slight fragrance; recurrent; foliage medium size, light green, semi-glossy; bushy, medium (4-6 ft.) growth; [sport of 'Smith's Parish']

'Red Soldier' -- See 'Fusilier'

'Red Soupert' -- See 'Ma Petite Andrée'

'Red Spark' HT, mr, Meilland; intr. 2006

'Red Sparkler' HT, rb, 1975, Buck, Dr. Griffith J.; flowers red, striped pink and white, 4-4½ in., 55 petals, cupped, intense damask fragrance; foliage dark, leathery, upright growth; PP3489; ['Scarlet Royal' × 'Rouge Mallerin']; intr. 1974

'Red Spectacle' S, dr, Poulsen; flowers crimson red, large, full, cupped; free-flowering; vigorous, tall (6-7 ft.) growth; intr. 1993

'Red Spice' F, dr, 1959, Boerner; bud short, flat topped; flowers 2-2½ in., 80-85 petals, cupped, moderate fragrance; foliage dark, leathery; vigorous, bushy growth; PP1784; ['Spice' × 'Garnette']; intr. 1958

'Red Spire' HT, or; flowers large, full, high-centered, borne mostly singly; stems strong; very tall, stiffly upright growth; intr. 2000

Red Spirit™ HT, mr, Zary; intr. 2000

'Red Spirit' HT, mr, J&P; florist rose

'Red Splendor' HT, mr, 1954, Grillo; flowers bright red, 6 in., 55 petals; foliage leathery; vigorous, upright growth; [sport of 'Joyance']

'Red Splendour' -- See 'Davona'

Red Spot® F, mr, Barni; bud globular; flowers velvet red, double, borne in clusters of 5 - 7, no fragrance; recurrent; compact (40 - 60 cm) growth; suitable for hedges; intr. 2007

'Red Sprite' F, mr, 1976, LeGrice; flowers glowing red, 2-2½ in., 35 petals; foliage small, glossy, dark; low growth; intr. 1974

'Red Star' -- See 'Precious Platinum'

'Red Star' HT, mr, 1918, Verschuren; flowers scarlet-red, very large, semi-dbl., moderate fragrance

'Red Stone' -- See 'Krasnokamenka'

'Red Storm' Min, dr

'Red Success' -- See 'Meirodium'

'Red Summer' F, or, Noack, Werner; intr. 1996

'Red Summerwind' ('Röd Summerwind') S, mr

'Red Summit' Min, dr, 1981, Lyon; bud ovoid, pointed; flowers 33 petals, borne usually singly; prickles long, thin, straight; low, compact, bushy growth; [seedling × seedling]; intr. 1980

Red Sunblaze® -- See 'Meirutral'

'Red Sweetheart' Pol, rb, 1944, Krebs; bud pointed; flowers crimson-carmine, 1-1½ in., 25 petals, high-centered, moderate spicy fragrance; foliage small, glossy; strong stems; vigorous, bushy growth; PP577; intercrossing of Cécile Brunner seedlings

'Red Tag' Min, rb, 1979, Williams, Ernest D.; bud ovoid, pointed; flowers medium red, white reverse, 1 in., 48 petals, high-centered, moderate fragrance; foliage small, glossy, dark; upright, spreading growth; [seedling × 'Over the Rainbow']; intr. 1978

'Red Taifun' -- See 'Red Typhoon'

'Red Talisman' HT, rb, 1931, Amling Bros.; flowers deep cerise, base yellow, intense fruity fragrance; recurrent; PP59; [sport of 'Talisman']

'Red Talisman, Climbing' Cl HT, rb

'Red Tausendschön' HMult, rb, 1931, Walter, L.; flowers vivid red with white eye, but varies considerably; [sport of 'Tausendschön']

'Red Tornado' HT, mr, 1999, McCall, Sharan; flowers medium red, reverse light red, 5-5½ in., full, borne mostly singly, slight fragrance; foliage medium size, dark green, glossy; prickles moderate; upright, medium (4 ft.) growth; ['Dorothy Anne' × 'Classic Touch']

'Red Trail' S, mr, Ilsink; flowers bright red with golden stamens, 3½ in., single; recurrent; low, spreading, groundcover growth; roots easily wherever it touches the ground; intr. 1991

'Red Treasure' HT, dr; intr. 2001

'Red Triumph' Pol, or, 1956, Morse; [sport of Orange Triumph®]

'Red Trooper' F, dr

'Red Tropicana' HT, or; intr. 2006

'Red Typhoon' ('Red Taifun') F, mr, Kordes; intr. 2006

'Red Unique' HT, mr; intr. 2000

'Red Velvet' -- See 'Tanorelav'

'Red Velvet ' -- See 'Peathunder'

'Red Velvet' F, mr, 1940, Kordes; bud ovoid; flowers vivid crimson, semi-dbl., cupped, slight fragrance; vigorous, compact growth

'Red Velvet' -- See 'Velvet Flower Carpet'

'Red Wagon' -- See 'Mordan'

'Red Wall' LCl, dr, Teranishi

'Red Walls' HT, mr; intr. 2007

'Red Wand' Cl Min, mr, 1964, Moore, Ralph S.; bud small, ovoid-pointed; flowers light crimson-red, golden stamens, small, 18-25 petals, cupped, borne in clusters, slight green tea fragrance; recurrent; foliage small, semi-glossy, leathery; prickles moderate, slender, hooked slightly downward, brown; vigorous, climbing (3½-4 ft.) growth; PP2717; [((R. wichurana × 'Floradora') × Orange Triumph®) × 'unknown miniature']

'Red Wand' S, mr, Kordes; flowers bright blood-red, semi-dbl., borne in clusters; tall, strong growth; intr. 1994

'Red Wave' F, mr, 1964, Moore, Ralph S.; flowers tulip shaped, small; low growth; containers; ['Carolyn Dean' × 'floribunda seedling']

'Red Wine' HT, mr, 1970, Sanday, John; flowers large, 22 petals, high-centered, borne in clusters; foliage medium green, matte; upright growth; ['Lilac Rose' × seedling]

'Red Wing' -- See 'Poulnino'

'Red Wing' S, ly, about 1950, possibly Doorenbos; flowers pale yellow, 3 cm., single, borne in clusters; prickles large, winged, translucent red; growth to 6 ft.; hardy; [probably R. sericea pteracantha × R. hugonis]

'Red Wings' F, dr, 1959, Boerner; bud ovoid; flowers rich dark red, large, 20 petals, cupped, moderate fragrance; foliage dark, leathery; vigorous, upright, bushy growth; PP1788; [('Improved Lafayette' × 'Herrenhausen') × 'Lavender Pinocchio']; intr. 1959

'Red Wonder' F, dr, 1954, deRuiter; bud globular; flowers crimson-carmine, 3-3½ in., 24-28 petals, cupped, borne in large clusters, moderate fragrance; foliage medium size, leathery, semi-glossy; prickles several, straight, pointed downward; vigorous, bushy growth; hips none ; PP1341; ['Better Times' × 'polyantha seedling']; intr. 1954

'Red Yesterday' -- See 'Marjorie Fair'

'Red Zinnia' Min, dr; flowers frilly, long lasting; free-flowering; low growth

'Red/White' -- See 'Jacgate'

'Redcap' F, mr, 1954, Swim, H.C.; bud ovoid; flowers semi-dbl., 18 petals, high-centered, borne in clusters; foliage leathery, semi-glossy, vigorous, upright, bushy growth; PP1292; ['World's Fair' × 'Pinocchio']

'Redcliffe' F, mr, 1976, Sanday, John; flowers bright crimson, large, 15 petals; [seedling × Sarabande®]; intr. 1975

'Redcoat' ('Red Coat') F, mr, 1981, Austin, David; bud pointed; flowers 10 petals, borne 1-5 per cluster, slight fragrance; free-flowering; foliage dark; prickles hooked, brown; bushy growth; [seedling × Golden Showers®]; intr. 1973

'Redcraze' HT, ob, 1959, Doley; bud long, pointed; flowers orange-scarlet, medium, dbl., high-centered; foliage glossy, dark; vigorous, bushy growth; ['Independence' × 'Independence']

'Reddy Teddy' -- See 'Sunhino'

'Redemption' HT, dp, 2005, Edwards, Eddie & Phelps, Ethan; flowers deep pink, reverse deep pink, 5-6 in., full, borne mostly solitary; foliage large, dark green, glossy; few prickles; growth upright, tall (5-6 ft.); exhibition; [Veterans' Honor™ × 'Hot Princess']; intr. 2006

Redglo™ -- See 'Minabbco'

'Redgold, Climbing' -- See 'Dicorsar'

'Redgold' ('Red Gold', 'Rouge et Or') F, yb, 1967, Dickson, A.; bud ovoid, pointed; flowers gold edged deep pink, 4½ in., 25 petals, high-centered, borne usually in clusters, slight fragrance; free-flowering; foliage medium size, dark green, leathery; prickles numerous, broad base, slightly hooked downward; vigorous, upright (2½ ft.) growth; PP3006; [(('Karl Herbst' × 'Masquerade') × 'Faust') × Piccadilly®]; intr. 1971

'Redgold, Climbing' Cl F, yb, 1972, Stratford (also Lynch, 1974); buds medium, ovoid; flowers gold with deep pink edging, medium, dbl, borne singly and several together; foliage medium size, medium green; [sport of 'Redgold']; intr. 1970

'Redhead' Cl Min, dr, 1956, Moore, Ralph S.; flowers blood-red; growth to 2½ ft.; [(('Soeur Thérèse' × 'Skyrocket') × (seedling × 'Red Ripples')) × 'Zee']

'Redhot' -- See 'Macbigma'

'Redhots' Min, dr, 1983, Meredith, E.A. & Rovinski, M.E.; flowers 22 petals, high-centered, borne singly; foliage small, long, medium green, finely serrated; very small, tiny growth; [seedling × 'Darling Flame']

'Rediffusion Gold' -- See 'Harquorgold'

'Redipuglia' HT, w, 1933, Ingegnoli; bud long, pointed; flowers pinkish white, reverse golden rose, base chrome-yellow, large, dbl.; vigorous growth

'Redland Court' F, ab, 1982, Sanday, John; flowers soft apricot, small, 20 petals, slight fragrance; foliage small, medium green, glossy; bushy growth; ['Red Maid' × Sarabande®]

Redlands Century™ -- See 'Burcen'

'Redneck Girl' -- See 'Gelred'

'Redonda' HT, mr, 1968, Patterson; bud globular; flowers large, dbl.; foliage leathery, wrinkled; vigorous, upright growth; [Queen Elizabeth® × 'Happiness']

'Redouté' -- See 'De Marienbourg'

Redouté™ S, lp, Austin, David; bud short, slightly pointed ovoid; flowers 3 in., 97 petals, cupped, quartered, borne in clusters of 1 - 6, moderate sweet, heavy fragrance; recurrent; vigorous (4 ft.) growth; PP8789; [sport of Mary Rose®]; intr. 1992

'Redutea Glauca' -- See 'De Marienbourg'

'Redway' HT, mr, 1954, Waterhouse Nursery; flowers crimson-carmine, high-centered, moderate fragrance; foliage leathery; moderate, upright growth; ['Ena Harkness' × seedling]

'Redwood' -- See 'Macwoodma'

Redwood™ ('Kronborg Castle', Ich hab Dich lieb™, Kronborg™, Schloss Linderhof™, Tryfosa™) F, dr, Poulsen; flowers dark red, 8-10 cm., full, cupped, then rounded, no fragrance; bushy (60-100 cm.) growth; hips none; intr. 1996

'Redwood Empire' -- See 'Morwood'

'Referenz' F, mp, VEG; flowers dbl.; intr. 1983

'Reflection' HT, yb, 1952, Ratcliffe, R. & E.; bud long, pointed; flowers amber, reverse streaked scarlet, moderate fragrance; vigorous growth; [sport of 'Mme Henri Guillot']

'Reflection' HT, dr, Brady, M.; intr. 1995

'Reflections' F, mp, Simpson; flowers warm shell pink, dbl., borne in clusters; free-flowering; medium growth; intr. 2000

'Reflections' HT, pb, Tantau; flowers cream with bright pink edges, large, full, high-centered, moderate fragrance; recurrent; foliage medium green, glossy; growth medium height; intr. 2007

'Reflets' F, or, 1964, Croix, P.; flowers large, single; free-flowering; upright growth; ['Gertrud Westphal' × Sarabande®]

Reflets de Nacre® S, lp, Dorieux; flowers pearly pale pink with a touch of apricot, large, dahlia shaped; foliage dark green, glossy, elongated; 80 cm growth; intr. 2007

'Reflets de Saint Malo' ('Fragrant Alizée') HT, pb, Adam; flowers pink with light yellow reverse, full, low-centered, intense fragrance; recurrent; foliage dark green, glossy; moderate growth; intr. 2003

'Refresher' HWich, w, 1929, Clark, A.; flowers pure white, 4 cm., single, borne in medium to large clusters; early; vigorous, climbing growth

'Refulgence' HEg, mr, 1909, Paul, W.; flowers scarlet, aging to crimson, large, semi-dbl.; foliage very fragrant; vigorous growth; very hardy

'Reg Willis' HT, dp, 1966, McGredy, Sam IV; flowers deep rose-pink, base yellow, well-formed, 4½ in.; ['Golden Masterpiece' × 'Karl Herbst']

'Regal' -- See 'Jusregal'

'Regal Gold' HT, dy, 1958, Dale; bud pointed; flowers clear golden yellow, open, 5 in., 40-45 petals; foliage glossy, leathery; vigorous, upright, bushy growth; [sport of 'Golden Rapture']; intr. 1957

'Regal Lady' Min, pb, 1990, Jolly, Nelson F.; bud pointed; flowers white, edged pink, 27 petals, high-centered, borne usually singly or in sprays of 3 - 5, slight fragrance; foliage medium size, medium green, semi-glossy; no prickles; upright, spreading, tall growth; round fruit; ['Sassy Lassie' × 'First Prize']; intr. 1990

'Regal Pink' HT, mp, 1980, Thomas, Dr. A.S.; [sport of 'Red Queen']

'Regal Red' -- See 'Cocfoster'

'Regalia' HT, rb, 1964, Robinson, H.; flowers cherry-red, reverse silver, well-formed, 5½ in., 60 petals; foliage bronze; [Rose Gaujard® × seedling]

'Regalis' -- See 'Great Royal'

'Regalis' -- See 'Royale'

'Regatta' -- See 'Jacette'

Regatta™ -- See 'Meinimo'

'Regeliana Flore Pleno' -- See 'Kaiserin des Nordens'

'Regeliana Rubra' -- See 'Kaiserin des Nordens'

Régence® -- See 'Lapdul'

Regensberg® -- See 'Macyoumis'

'Regensberg, Climbing' Cl F, pb; intr. 2002

'Regente Agricola' HT, Moreira da Silva, A.

'Reggae' HT, ob, Tantau; flowers soft orange, reverse lighter, medium, dbl., high-centered, borne mostly singly; good repeat; stems 18 in. length; greenhouse rose; intr. 1997

'Regia' -- See 'Beauté Tendre'

'Regia Purpurea' HGal, m, before 1835, Coquerel; flowers dark purple, center carmine, medium, full

'Regierungsrat Rottenberger' HMult, mp, 1926, Praskac; flowers rich pink, lighter towards edges, reverse darker, 4-5 cm., dbl., flat, circular, borne in large clusters, strong musky fragrance; ['Fragezeichen' × 'Tausendschön']

'Regierungsrat Stockert' HP, lp, 1888, Soupert & Notting; flowers silky, silvery pink, reverse edged light carmine, large, full, moderate fragrance; ['Dupuy-Jamain' × 'Mme de Sévigné']

'Regina' -- See 'Sultana'

Regina™ -- See 'Poulac015(N)'

'Regina' HWich, w, 1916, Walsh; flowers creamy white tipped pink large panicles, single; foliage large, glossy, vigorous, climbing growth

'Regina' HT, or, Kordes; flowers orange-red, reverse yellow, dbl., high-centered, moderate fragrance; growth to 70-90 cm.; intr. before 1976

'Regina' HT, pb, Twomey; intr. about 1997

'Régina Badet' HRg, dp, 1908, Gravereaux & Müller; flowers deep violet pink, large, very dbl., flat, often quartered, intense fragrance; repeat bloom; foliage dark; bushy growth; [('Général Jacqueminot' × 'Empereur du Maroc') × R. rugosa]

'Regina Centifolia' HRg, mp; recurrent; 3-5 ft. growth; intr. 2001

'Régina de Alvéar' HT, w, 1922, Sauvageot, H.; flowers white, center slightly shaded pink, dbl.; ['Mme Mélanie Soupert' × 'Mme Segond Weber']

'Regina della Neve' -- See 'Tanigino'

'Regina Dicta' ('De la Reine', 'Koniginrosa', 'Impériale') HGal, m, before 1791; flowers light violet, edged white, often mottled, medium, full; often shows proliferation

'Regina Elena' HT, mp, 1938, Grillo; bud long, pointed; flowers darker rose-pink than briarcliff, 5 in., 50 petals, moderate fragrance; foliage dark; PP417; [sport of 'Briarcliff']

'Regina Lee' -- See 'Welreg'

'Regina Lee's Sister' -- See 'Welinspir'

'Regina Louise' -- See 'Cleconcert'

'Regina Pacis' HT, w, 1945, Dot, Pedro; buds long; flowers 5 in., high-centered, intense fragrance; foliage soft; branching growth; ['Nuria de Recolons' × 'Ibiza']

Regina Palace™ MinFl, mp, Olesen; bud globular; flowers bright pink, fading slightly as they open, 5 cm., 65 petals, high-centered, borne usually singly, very slight fragrance; recurrent; foliage dark green, glossy; bushy (40-60 cm.) growth; PP15171; [Patricia Kordana Mini Brite™ × seedling]; intr. 2002

'Reginald Fernyhough' HT, op, 1949, Bees; flowers pink lightly suffused orange, long, pointed, 5 in., 35 petals; foliage olive-green; very vigorous growth; ['Southport' × seedling]

Regine™ -- See 'Hefqueen'

'Regine Crespin' -- See 'Delcreme'

'Reginella' -- See 'Sweet Home'

'Regulus' ('Comtesse de Woronzoff') T, pb, 1860, Robert & Moreau; flowers bright coppery pink, medium, dbl., flat, intense fragrance

'Reichsgraf E. von Kesselstatt' T, rb, 1898, Lambert; flowers brilliant carmine, aging to rose-pink, edged with crimson, very large, very dbl.; growth erect; ['Princesse Alice de Monaco' × 'Duchesse Marie Salviati']

'Reichspräsident von Hindenberg' HP, pb, 1933, Lambert, P.; flowers dark pink to carmine, veined lighter, reverse darker, button center, 6 in., very dbl., moderate fragrance; floriferous; foliage broad; very vigorous, bushy growth; ['Frau Karl Druschki' × 'Graf Silva Tarouca']

'Reigen' F, ob, GPG Bad Langensalza; flowers medium, dbl.; intr. 1984

'Reiko' -- See 'Jalray'

'Reiko' HT, op, 1963, Teranishi, K.; bud long, pointed; flowers bright coral-peach, 3½-4 in., 25 petals, high-centered; foliage dark, leathery; vigorous, upright growth; ['Spartan' × 'Fred Streeter']

'Reikor' ('Dreaming', 'Reverie', Träumerei®) F, ob, 1974, Kordes; bud long, pointed; intr. 1974

'Reims' HT, yb, 1924, Barbier; bud long, pointed; flowers bright nankeen yellow shaded fiery red, orange-apricot and copper-pink, large

'Reina Elisenda' -- See 'Independence'

'Reina Maria Christina' -- See 'Maria Cristina'

'Reinaerdiana' F, or, Delforge; intr. 1974

'Reine Amelia' HGal, mp

'Reine André' HWich, 1900, Barbier; ['L'Idéal' × R. wichurana]

'Reine Astrid' HT, rb, 1937, Gaujard;

The Official Registry and Checklist — Rosa 625

bud long, pointed; flowers bright deep coppery red, reverse golden yellow, dbl., cupped; foliage glossy; vigorous growth

'Reine Augusta Victoria' -- See 'Kaiserin Auguste Viktoria'

'Reine Blanche'   HP, w, 1868, Damaizin; flowers white, shaded light pink, large, full, globular; ['La Reine' × unknown]

'Reine-Blanche'   M, w, 1857, Moreau et Robert; flowers pure white, large, dbl., flat

'Reine Blanche' -- See 'Hebe's Lip'

'Reine Carola de Saxe' ('Helen Mills') HT, pb, 1902, Gamon; flowers silvery pink on a deep salmony pink ground, large, full, moderate fragrance

Reine Chabeau® -- See 'LLX8838'

'Reine d'Angleterre' ('La Reine d'Angleterre') T, dp; flowers carmine, shaded purple, medium, very full

'Reine de Castille'   HP, dr, 1852, Lartay; flowers deep carmine red, large, full, globular

'Reine de Castille'   B, mp, Pernet; bud rose-white; flowers bright rose, well-formed; vigorous growth; intr. 1863

'Reine de Danemark'   HP, lp, 1857, Granger; flowers flesh-lilac, large, full; foliage small, pointed, very serrate; nearly thornless

'Reine de Fontenay'   HP, mp; flowers medium, full

'Reine de la Lombardie'   Ch, dr, before 1835; flowers deep cerise passing to crimson purple, medium, dbl., globular

'Reine de la Pape' ('La Reine de la Pape') HP, m, 1863, Guillot; flowers violet pink, large, full

'Reine de Perse'   HGal, lp, before 1825; flowers light cream-pink, small to medium, very dbl., intense fragrance

'Reine de Portugal'   T, yb, Guillot et Fils; flowers coppery yellow shaded pink, large, very dbl.

'Reine de Prusse' -- See 'Duchesse d'Angoulême'

'Reine de Prusse'   HGal, mr, 1824, possibly Asselin; flowers bright red, aging to lilac pink, medium, full

'Reine de Saxe'   C, mp, before 1820; flowers medium, dbl., moderate fragrance

'Reine de Vibert'   HGal, m, about 1835, Vibert; flowers purple

'Reine des Amateurs'   HGal, m, before 1829, Hébert, Mme.; flowers clear lilac, edged pale pink, well-shaped, very large

'Reine des Ayrshire' -- See 'Ayrshire Queen'

'Reine des Beautés'   HP, lp, 1870, Gonod; flowers light flesh pink with white, medium to large, full

'Reine des Belges'   B, lp, 1831, Jacques; flowers lilac-pink, large, full, globular to cupped

'Reine des Belges' ('Queen of the Belgians') Ayr, w, Jacques; flowers creamy white, lightly touched with pink, 4-5 cm., very dbl., slight musk fragrance; non-recurrent; foliage evergreen; stems long, slender, reddish; mixed parentage of R. sempervirens, R. arvensis, and a China; intr. 1832

'Reine des Belges'   HP, lp, Vibert; flowers flesh pink; intr. about 1836

'Reine des Belges'   HCh, w, Sc. Cochet; flowers creamy white, medium, full, globular; sparse bloom; vigorous growth; ['Globe Hip' × R. chinensis]; sometimes classed as T; intr. 1867

'Reine des Belges'   HP, dp, Cochet; flowers velvety light red to pink, large, full; intr. 1867

'Reine des Blanches'   HP, w, Crozy; flowers white, shaded light pink, large, full; ['Victor Verdier' × unknown]; intr. 1870

'Reine des Blanches'   HP, w, 1868, Avoux or Pernet; flowers white shaded pink, large, full; ['La Reine' × unknown]

'Reine des Bordures' -- See 'Border Queen'

'Reine des Centfeuilles' ('La Reine de Provence') C, mp, 1824, from Belgium; flowers clear pink, reflexed, central rosette, very large, dbl., cupped/globular, moderate fragrance; foliage somber green; very vigorous growth

'Reine des Couleurs' -- See 'Farbenkönigin'

'Reine des Fées' -- See 'Rosalie'

'Reine des Fleurs' ('De la Reine') HP, mr, 1846, Portemer; flowers crimson, edged with lilac-pink, large, full, globular

'Reine des Francais' -- See 'La Reine'

'Reine des Iles-Bourbons' ('Bourbon Queen', 'Queen of Bourbons', 'Souv de la Princesse de Lamballe') B, pb, 1834, Mauget; flowers fawn and rose, small to medium, dbl., cupped, intense fragrance

'Reine des Mousseuses'   M, lp, about 1860, Moreau et Robert; flowers flesh pink, medium, full; possibly synonymous with 'Gloire des Mousseux'

'Reine des Nègres' -- See 'Superbe en Brun'

'Reine des Neiges' -- See 'Frau Karl Druschki'

'Reine des Neiges, Climbing' -- See 'Frau Karl Druschki, Climbing'

'Reine des Pays-Bas'   HGal, dp, 1824, in Brussels; flowers velvety carmine, medium

'Reine des Pays-Bas'   T, lp, Fontaine; intr. 1858

'Reine des Poètes' -- See 'Des Poètes'

'Reine des Pourpres' -- See 'Pallas'

'Reine des Reines' -- See 'Queen of Queens'

'Reine des Roses' -- See 'Korbico'

'Reine des Vierges'   B, lp, 1844, Béluze; flowers pale pink, flesh towards center, medium, semi-dbl.

'Reine des Violettes' ('Lake Street', 'Queen of the Violets') HP, m, 1860, Mille-Malet; flowers violet-red, large, 75 petals, intense fragrance; recurrent bloom; foliage sparse; ['Pie IX' × unknown]

'Reine d'Espagne'   HP, mr, 1861, Fontaine; flowers brilliant red, medium, full; foliage light; bushy growth; sometimes classed as HGal

'Reine d'Italie'   Ch, dr, 1886, Perny; flowers dark red with carmine

'Reine du Congrès'   B, lp, 1842, Béluze; flowers flesh pink, shaded bright pink, medium, full

'Reine du Dänemark' -- See 'Königin von Dänemark'

'Reine du Forez'   HT, rb, Croix; flowers red with silver reverse, nuanced with orange, 45 petals, globular; foliage dark green, resistant; upright growth; intr. 1969

'Reine du Matin'   HP, m, 1845, Béluze; flowers bluish lilac, medium, full

'Reine du Midi'   HP, mp, 1867, Roland; flowers lilac pink, very large, full, flat, moderate fragrance; ['La Reine' × unknown]

'Reine Elisabeth'   HT, mr, 1955, Buyl Frères; flowers velvety blood-red; ['Princesse Liliane' × 'Ena Harkness']

'Reine Elizabeth' -- See 'La Reine Elizabeth'

'Reine Elizabeth'   HT, rb, 1925, Opdebeeck; bud long, pointed; flowers coral-red, changing to prawn-red, tinted yellow, dbl., intense fragrance

'Reine Emma des Pays-Bas'   T, my, 1879, Nabonnand, G.; flowers coppery yellow, reverse almost flame-colored, large, semi-dbl.

'Reine France'   HT, op, Delbard-Chabert; flowers large, dbl.

'Reine Lucia' -- See 'Korlilub'

'Reine Marguerite' -- See 'Tricolore'

'Reine Marguerite d'Italie'   HT, mr, 1904, Soupert & Notting; flowers carmine red, vermilion toward center, very large, very full; foliage dark green; ['Baron Nathaniel de Rothschild' × 'Mme la Princesse de Bessaraba de Brancovan']

'Reine Maria de Roumanie'   HT, w, 1927, Mühle; bud long, pointed; flowers marble-white, center yellow, dbl.; ['Stadtrat Glaser' × unknown]

'Reine Maria Pia'   T, dp, 1880, Schwartz, J.; flowers deep pink, center crimson, lighter reverse, 9-10 cm., full, globular, borne singly or in small clusters, moderate fragrance; very vigorous growth; ['Gloire de Dijon' × unknown]

'Reine Marie Henriette' ('Gloire de Dijon à Fleur Rouges') Cl T, mr, 1878, Levet, F.; bud large, plump, pointed; flowers pure cherry-red, fading to magenta, reverse lighter, 10-11 cm., dbl., moderate fragrance; foliage dark green; vigorous, climbing growth; ['Mme Berard' × 'Général Jacqueminot']; sometimes classed as a Cl HT or a N

'Reine Mère d'Italie'   HT, dy, 1910, Bernaix; flowers apricot-ochre yellow, medium, dbl.

'Reine Nathalie de Serbie'   T, lp, 1885, Soupert & Notting; flowers flesh pink and creme, shaded light yellow, large to very large, full, flat to globular; ['Mme Lombard' × 'Sulfureux']

'Reine Olga de Wurtemberg' ('Queen Olga of Greece', 'Queen Olga of Wurtemburg') N, mr, 1881, Nabonnand, G.; flowers bright red, 9 cm., dbl., moderate fragrance; reliable repeat; growth very vigorous; pillar

'Reine Sammut' S, pb, Guillot-Massad ?; intr. 1999

'Reine Victoria' ('La Reine Victoria') B, mp, 1872, Labruyère/Schwartz; flowers rich pink, well-formed, large, dbl., cupped, intense damask fragrance; repeat bloom; foliage soft green; slender, upright (to 6 ft.) growth

'Reiner Maria Rilke' -- See 'Korsee'

'Reinhard Bädecker' HP, my, 1918, Kordes; flowers clear golden yellow, red shadings on edge and reverse, very large, dbl.; ['Frau Karl Druschki' × 'Rayon d'Or']

'Reinhard Pusch' HT, yb, Tagashira, Kazuso; flowers large, dbl.; intr. 1992

'Reinhardt Voigt' HT, mr, Taschner, Ludwig; flowers crimson, large, double, high-centered, borne mostly singly; recurrent; stems long; tall growth; intr. 2007

'Rejoice' Gr, pb, 1985, McMillan, Thomas G.; flowers salmon-pink blended with yellow, large, 40 petals, high-centered, borne in clusters of 1-6, moderate fragrance; foliage large, medium green, glossy; tall, upright, bushy growth; ['Little Darling' × 'Color Magic']

'Rejouissence' HT, Croix; intr. 1977

'Rekordblüher' F, mp, 1965, Tantau, Math.; flowers rose-pink, 2-3 in., semi-dbl., borne in large trusses; foliage dark, glossy; bushy growth

'Rektor Foerster' HT, pb, 1936, Weigand, C.; flowers solferino-pink, flushed yellow, large, dbl., high-centered; foliage leathery; vigorous growth; ['Golden Ophelia' × 'Mme Caroline Testout']

'Relax' S, or; flowers orange-red with yellow center, lighter reverse, yellow stamens, single, borne in small clusters; non-remontant; intr. 1979

'Relax Meidiland' -- See 'Relax Meillandecor'

'Relax Meillandecor' ('Relax Meidiland') S, pb, Meilland; flowers semi-dbl.; free-flowering; growth to 50 cm.; intr. 1993

'Release' -- See 'Macrelea'

'Reliance' HT, lp, 1909, Hill, E. G.; flowers light pink, edged creamy white, large, full; ['Etoile de France' × 'Chateau de Clos Vougeot']

'Relief' HT, w, 1919, Verschuren; flowers ivory-white, center yellowish-pink; ['Kaiserin Auguste Viktoria' × 'Sunburst']

'Remarkable' -- See 'Brimark'

'Rembrandt' P, m, 1883, Moreau-Robert; flowers vermilion, sometimes striped with white, large, full; remontant; stems long, strong; growth vigorous

'Rembrandt' HT, ob, Van Rossem; flowers salmon, tinted orange-red, well-formed, large, 40 petals; foliage leathery; vigorous growth; ['Frau Karl Druschki' × 'Lyon Rose']; sometimes classed as HP; intr. 1914

'Rembrandt' F, mr, McGredy, Sam IV; flowers bright scarlet, large, 15 petals, borne in clusters; foliage light green; ['Tivoli' × 'Independence']; intr. 1964

'Rembrandt van Ryn' S, rb, Williams, J. Benjamin; flowers burgandy red with lighter striping and spotting, dbl., cupped, borne in clusters; upright growth; intr. 1997

Remember™ -- See 'Royal Copenhagen'

Remember Me® -- See 'Cocdestin'

Remembering Dee™ -- See 'Savaremember'

'Remembering Michael' HT, m, 2005, Halvorson, Donald A.; flowers mauve, reverse mauve, 4 in., full, borne mostly solitary, intense fragrance; foliage medium size, medium green, semi-glossy; prickles medium; growth bushy, medium (4-5 ft.); garden, exhibition; ['Royal Highness' × Charles de Gaulle®]; intr. 2005

'Remembrance' -- See 'Harxampton'

'Remembrance' HT, yb, 1953, Howard, A.P.; bud ovoid; flowers soft yellow edged dawn-pink, 4-5 in., 50 petals, high-centered, moderate fragrance; profuse bloom; foliage leathery, glossy, coppery green; vigorous, upright growth; PP1145; RULED EXTINCT 4/92; ['Fred Howard' × seedling]

'Reminiscence' -- See 'Korkinteral'

'Remuera' -- See 'Mactrampol'

'Remy Martin' -- See 'Starqueli'

'Renack' ('Wee Ack') Min, lp, 1995, Rennie, Bruce F.; flowers 1 in., dbl., borne mostly singly; foliage small, light green, semi-glossy; few prickles; medium (15-18 in.), upright growth; [seedling × 'Pink Sheri']; intr. 1994

'Renae' Cl F, mp, 1954, Moore, Ralph S.; bud pointed; flowers warm pink, 2½ in., 43 petals, cupped, borne in clusters, intense fragrance; recurrent bloom; foliage small, glossy; prickles few to none; vigorous, climbing growth; PP893; ['Étoile Luisante' × 'Sierra Snowstorm']

'Renaissance' ('Born Again', 'Cameo Perfume') HT, lp; flowers pale blush pink, dbl., high-centered, intense fruity, Damask fragrance; recurrent; bushy (2½ ft.) growth; intr. 1994

'Renaissance' HT, ab; greenhouse rose; intr. 2002

Renaissance® HT, ob, 1987, Gaujard, Jean; flowers brilliant orange, dbl., high-centered, moderate fragrance; foliage large; prickles small; rounded fruit; [seedling × 'Pampa']; intr. 1980

Renaissance® HT, rb, 1945, Gaujard; bud pointed; flowers red and gold, medium, dbl.; foliage glossy; low growth; ruled extinct 10/86

'Renaissance de Flecheres' HT, my, Ducher; flowers yellow, petal edges turn white, full, cupped, moderate fragrance; free-flowering; growth to 3-4 ft.; intr. 2004

'Renal' ('Grandpa Alex') Min, w, 1995, Rennie, Bruce F.; flowers 1½ in., full, borne in small clusters, moderate fragrance; foliage medium size, dark green, semi-glossy; few prickles; medium (15-18 in.), bushy growth; ['Hap Renshaw' × 'Summer Scent']; intr. 1993

'Renangel' ('Blue Angel') F, m, 1992, Rennie, Bruce F.; flowers medium, dbl., borne mostly singly; foliage medium size, dark green, semi-glossy; few prickles; medium, bushy growth; ['Lavonde' × Shocking Blue®]

'Renapp' ('Orange Appeal') Min, or, 1995, Rennie, Bruce F.; flowers 2¾ in., very dbl., borne mostly singly; foliage large, medium green, semi-glossy; some prickles; tall (24 in.), spreading, bushy growth; ['Justa Little Goofy' × seedling]; intr. 1992

'Renata' HT, op, Williams, J. Benjamin; flowers orange and peach blend with hint of green, dbl., cupped, moderate fragrance; recurrent; growth to 4 ft.; intr. 2005

'Renata Tebaldi' -- See 'Delredi'

'Renate' HT, w, 1925, Berger, V.; flowers cream-white, dbl.; ['Kaiserin Auguste Viktoria' × unknown]

'Renate' HT, ab, Preesman; flowers champagne colored

'Renbaby' ('Dream Baby') Min, lp, 1993, Rennie, Bruce F.; flowers medium, dbl., borne mostly singly, slight fragrance; foliage small, medium green, semi-glossy; few prickles; medium, bushy growth; [Party Girl™ × 'Silver Phantom']; intr. 1993

'Renblonde' ('California Blonde') Min, yb, 1993, Rennie, Bruce F.; flowers medium, dbl., slight fragrance; foliage medium size, medium green, semi-glossy; few prickles; medium, upright growth; [Party Girl™ × 'Tooth of Time']; intr. 1995

'Renblue' ('Blushing Blue') Min, m, 1988, Rennie, Bruce F.; flowers lavender with magenta edge, yellow-tan at base, medium, 30-35 petals, high-centered, borne usually singly; repeat bloom; foliage medium size, medium green, semi-glossy; prickles straight, medium, transparent yellow-green; upright, bushy growth; hips rounded, medium size, orange; [Shocking Blue® × Twilight Trail™]; intr. 1989

'Renblush' ('Innocent Blush') Min, lp, 1990, Rennie, Bruce F.; bud ovoid; flowers pale blush pink, reverse white, aging white, medium, 40 petals, high-centered, borne usually singly and in sprays of 5-7, no fragrance; foliage medium size, medium green, matte; prickles straight, medium, yellow; upright, medium growth; fruit not observed; ['Paul Shirville' × Party Girl™]; intr. 1990

'Renboy' ('Augie Boy') Min, rb, 1995, Rennie, Bruce F.; flowers 1-1½ in., dbl., borne mostly singly; foliage medium size, medium green, glossy; few prickles; low (12-15 in.), compact growth; [Party Girl™ × 'California Dreaming']; intr. 1994

'Renbun' ('Easter Bunny') Min, m, 1995, Rennie, Bruce F.; flowers 2 in., 5 petals, borne mostly singly; foliage large, medium green, semi-glossy; few prickles; tall (2 ft.), upright growth; ['Lavonde' × seedling]; intr. 1992

'Rencel' ('Pretty Celine') Min, pb, 1995, Rennie, Bruce F.; flowers 1¼ in., dbl., borne mostly singly; foliage medium size, medium green, semi-glossy; some prickles; medium (15 in.), upright, bushy growth; ['Strawberry Delight' × 'Strawberry Delight']; intr. 1994

'Rendan' ('Duet') F, rb, Keisei; intr. 1987

'Rendar' ('Oh Darlin') Min, ab, 1995, Rennie, Bruce F.; flowers 1¼ in., 6-14 petals, borne mostly singly; foliage small, dark green, glossy; few prickles; low (10-12 in.), compact growth; ['Pink Sheri' × 'Hap Renshaw']; intr. 1992

'Rendez-vous' -- See 'Day of Triumph'

'Rendez-vous' -- See 'Lucdod'

'Rendez-Vous' ('Châtelaine de Lullier') HT, dp, Meilland; flowers rose-mauve, large, dbl., intense fragrance; intr. 1987

'Rendez-Vous' HT, dp, J&P; cut flower rose; intr. 1993

'Rendez-vous' ('Olijprin') HT, dr

'Rendez Vous 81' HT, Meilland, L.; intr. 1981

'Rendude' ('Cool Dude') Min, m, 1995, Rennie, Bruce F.; flowers 1 in., dbl., borne mostly singly; foliage small, medium green, semi-glossy; no prickles; low (10-12 in.), compact growth; [seedling × 'Blushing Blue']; intr. 1995

'Rene' F, Byrum; PP4016

'René André' HWich, ab, 1901, Barbier; bud coppery; flowers saffron-yellow, becoming pale pink and carmine, 2-2½ in., semi-dbl., borne in clusters, moderate fragrance; very vigorous growth; [R. wichurana × 'L'Ideal']

'René Boulanger' B, lp, 1913, Boulanger; flowers flesh pink with salmon, large, full

'René Buatois' LCl, mp, 1936, Buatois; flowers ruddy pink; [sport of 'Leontine Gervais']

'René Daniel' HP, dp, 1868, Damaizin; flowers cherry-pink, aging to crimson, large, full

'René d'Anjou' M, dp, 1853, Robert; flowers deep pink, veined, small, dbl., globular; some repeat

'René Denis' ('Eugène Bourgeois') N, ly, 1897, Denis; [sport of 'Mme Bérard']

'René Gosciny' HT, ob, Meilland; flowers warm orange suffused with vermillion, 80-90 petals, cupped, moderate fruity fragrance; vigorous (60-80 cm.) growth; intr. 2005

'René Javey' HT, ab, 1934, Gillot, F.; flowers clear apricot, reverse salmon-pink shaded yellow, passing to, dbl.; foliage clear bronze green

'Renée Brightman' HT, rb, 1936, Hurran; flowers brilliant scarlet, shaded orange, reverse striped yellow, dbl.; vigorous growth; ['Emma Wright' × unknown]

'Renee Columb' -- See 'Gauvila'

'Renée Danielle' HWich, my, 1913, Guillot, P.; flowers jonquil-yellow to golden yellow, passing to white, 5 cm., dbl., cupped, borne in small clusters; sometimes blooms again in autumn; foliage glossy, purplish; nearly thornless; vigorous, climbing growth

'Renée Wilmart-Urban' HT, pb, 1908, Pernet-Ducher; bud long, pointed; flowers salmon-flesh, edged carmine, large, dbl.

'Reneen' ('Caribbean Queen') Min, r, 1986, Rennie, Bruce F.; flowers apricot-copper, reverse yellow, 33 petals, high-centered, borne singly, slight fragrance; foliage small to medium size, medium green, semi-glossy; prickles medium, orange-red; vigorous, bushy growth; hips ovoid, yellow; ['Sunday Brunch' × 'Gold Mine']; intr. 1987

'Renegade' -- See 'Lyoren'

'Renegade' MinFl, lp, Spooner, Raymond A.; intr. 1995

'Reneri' ('Pink Sheri') Min, lp, 1985, Rennie, Bruce F.; [sport of 'Sheri Anne']

'Renerry' ('Strawberry Delight') Min, pb, 1989, Rennie, Bruce F.; bud pointed; flowers white with medium pink freckles, reverse white with pink edg, 28 petals, high-centered; foliage medium size, dark green, semi-glossy; prickles straight, medium, brown; spreading, medium growth; fruit not observed; ['Little Darling' × 'California Dreaming']; intr. 1990

'Rene's Rose' HT, pb, Dawson; intr. 1995

'Renfer' ('Surfer Girl') Min, or, 1988, Rennie, Bruce F.; flowers light orange-red, salmon, reverse lighter, medium, 25-30 petals, high-centered, borne usually singly, moderate spicy fragrance; foliage medium size, medium green, matte; prickles hooked, medium, transparent yellow-brown; bushy, medium growth; hips round, small, yellow-orange; ['Pink Sheri' × 'Paul Shirville']

'Renfire' ('Touch of Fire') Min, ob, 1989, Rennie, Bruce F.; bud ovoid; flowers orange-yellow, reverse light orange, aging apricot-orange, 25 petals, urn-shaped, moderate spicy fragrance; foliage small, medium green, semi-glossy; prickles straight, small, orange-red; bushy growth; no fruit; ['Tangerine Mist' × 'California Girl']; intr. 1989

'Renfragobses' ('Fragrant Obsession') Min, m, 1995, Rennie, Bruce F.; flowers 1½ in., dbl., borne mostly singly; foliage medium size, medium green, semi-glossy; few prickles; medium (18 in.), upright growth; ['Lavonde' × 'Blushing Blue']; intr. 1995

'Renfrost' ('Pink Frosting') HT, mp, 1992, Rennie, Bruce F.; flowers 3-3½ in., full, borne mostly singly, intense fragrance; foliage large, medium green, matte; some prickles; tall, upright growth; [seedling × 'Prima Ballerina']

'Rengoofy' ('Justa Little Goofy') F, or, 1992, Rennie, Bruce F.; flowers medium, full, borne mostly singly, moderate fragrance; foliage medium size, medium green, semi-glossy; some prickles; medium, bushy growth; [seedling × seedling]

'Renhap' ('Hap Renshaw') Min, ab, 1991, Rennie, Bruce F.; flowers small, dbl., borne mostly singly, slight fragrance; foliage small, dark green, semi-glossy; upright growth; [Party Girl™ × 'Lavonde']; intr. 1991

'Renheart' ('Young Hearts') Min, dr

'Renhom' ('Melissa Joyce', 'Silver Phantom') Min, m, 1988, Rennie, Bruce F.; bud pointed; flowers silver-lavender, large, 33 petals, high-centered, borne usually singly, slight licorice fragrance; foliage medium size, dark green, semi-glossy; prickles hooked, medium, light tan-red to dark; upright, bushy, tall growth; hips globular, medium, yellow-orange; [Shocking Blue® × Angelglo™]; intr. 1989

'Renhuron' ('Huron Sunset') Min, ly, 1990, Rennie, Bruce F.; flowers small, full, borne in small clusters, no fragrance; foliage small, medium green, semi-glossy; bushy growth; [Party Girl™ × 'Golden Rule']; intr. 1991

'Renica' -- See 'Tanrekta'

'Renimag' ('Imagine') Min, pb, 1995, Rennie, Bruce F.; flowers 1 in., full, borne in clusters; foliage small, medium green, semi-glossy; few prickles; low (12-15 in.), compact growth; ['Forever Mine' × 'Pink Sheri']; intr. 1995

'Renirl' ('California Girl') Min, ab, 1986, Rennie, Bruce F.; flowers apricot, reverse yellow blend, 28 petals, high-centered, borne singly, moderate fruity fragrance; foliage medium to large, medium green, semi-glossy; prickles small; bushy, spreading growth; hips orange-red; [Julie Ann™ × Red Love™]; intr. 1987

'Renist' ('Tangerine Mist') Min, ob, 1988, Rennie, Bruce F.; flowers orange, medium, 15 petals, high-centered, borne singly, moderate fruity fragrance; foliage medium size, light green, glossy; prickles straight, medium, red-brown; upright growth; hips round, small, orange; [('Avandel' × seedling) × 'Gold Mine']; intr. 1988

'Renity' ('Royal City') Min, dr, 1989, Rennie, Bruce F.; bud ovoid; flowers medium, 23 petals, high-centered, urn-shaped, borne singly; foliage medium size, medium green, semi-glossy; prickles hooked, medium, yellow; upright, tall growth; hips globular, medium, ornage-red; ['Goldmarie' × 'Pink Sheri']; intr. 1990

'Renjewel' ('Isabel's Jewel') Min, ob, 1995, Rennie, Bruce F.; flowers 1¼ in., 6-14 petals, borne mostly singly; foliage medium size, medium green, glossy; some prickles; medium (15-18 in.), spreading, bushy growth; ['Forever Mine' × 'Fragrant Morning']; intr. 1993

'Renjulie' ('Julie's Choice') Min, ly, 1991, Rennie, Bruce F.; flowers small, full, borne in small clusters, slight fragrance; foliage small, medium green, glossy; bushy growth; [seedling × seedling]; originally registered as pink blend; intr. 1991

'Renlarry' ('Larry's Surprize') Min, dy, 1991, Rennie, Bruce F.; flowers small, semi-dbl., borne mostly singly; foliage small, light green, matte; bushy (15 in.) growth; ['Golden Rule' × 'Rise 'n' Shine']; intr. 1991

'Renlover' ('Dream Lover') Min, lp, 1995, Rennie, Bruce F.; flowers 1-1½ in., full, borne mostly singly, moderate raspberry fragrance; foliage medium size, medium green, glossy; some prickles; medium (18 in.), upright growth; ['Pink Sheri' × 'Innocent Blush']; intr. 1995

'Renlynn' ('Mary Lynn') HT, dr, 1988, Rennie, Bruce F.; flowers maroon red, reverse lighter, aging darker, medium, 15 petals, high-centered, borne usually singly, intense damask fragrance; foliage medium size, medium green, semi-glossy; prickles hooked, medium, red-brown; upright, tall growth; hips oblong, medium, yellow; [(Electron® × 'Watercolor') × 'Lavonde']; intr. 1988

'Renmer' ('Endless Summer') Min, op, 1989, Rennie, Bruce F.; bud pointed; flowers shrimp-pink, reverse light pink, small, 33 petals, high-centered, borne singly, slight spicy fragrance; foliage small, dark green, semi-glossy; prickles straight, small, transparent to brown; low, bushy growth; no fruit; ['Paul Shirville' × 'California Dreaming']; intr. 1990

'Renmercy' ('Tender Mercy') Min, mr, 1995, Rennie, Bruce F.; flowers 1-1½ in., dbl., borne mostly singly; foliage small, medium green, glossy; few prickles; low (12-15 in.), compact growth; ['California Dreaming' × seedling]; intr. 1992

'Renmine' ('Forever Mine') Min, ob, 1993, Rennie, Bruce F.; flowers medium, full, slight fragrance; foliage small, medium green, matte; some prickles; medium, bushy growth; ['Hap Renshaw' × Party Girl™]; intr. 1994

'Renmobay' ('Moonlight Bay') F, w, 1995, Rennie, Bruce F.; flowers 3¼ in., very dbl., borne mostly singly; foliage small, light green, glossy; some prickles; medium (3 ft.), upright growth; [('Paul Shirville' × 'Lavonde') × Party Girl™]; intr. 1991

'Renmom' ('Mom's Fancy') Min, lp, 1995, Rennie, Bruce F.; flowers slight moss on buds, 1¼ in., dbl., borne in large clusters; foliage small, medium green, semi-glossy; some prickles; low (12-15 in.), compact growth; ['Pink Sheri' × 'Hap Renshaw']; intr. 1994

'Renmorning' ('Fragrant Morning') Min, my, 1991, Rennie, Bruce F.; flowers small, full, borne mostly singly, intense fragrance; foliage small, light green, semi-glossy; upright (18 in.) growth; ['Sunsprite' × miniature seedling]; intr. 1991

'Rennie's Pink' Min, pb, Rennie; flowers deep salmon pink inner petals blending to soft pink and white outer petals., hybrid tea, slight fragrance; recurrent; intr. 2000

'Renny' -- See 'Moreny'

'Renny's Dream' -- See 'Moreny'

'Reno' Gr, op, 1957, Silva; bud long, pointed, ovoid; flowers coral-salmon, wavy petals, 3-3½ in., 16-20 petals, globular, cupped, borne singly and in clusters; free-flowering; foliage bronze; prickles reddish-brown; vigorous (4 ft.), branching growth; hips round, yellow; PP1690; ['Mrs Sam McGredy' × 'Mme Henri Guillot']; intr. 1957

'Renoir' Gr, pb, 1980, Hall, William W.; bud plump, pointed; flowers flesh pink with peach tones toward base, 18 petals, borne 1-4 per cluster, moderate tea fragrance; repeat bloom; foliage 7-9 leaflet, dark, smooth; prickles curved; vigorous, upright to arching growth; intr. 1982

'Renoncule' -- See 'Provins Renoncule'

'Renoncule' Pol, dp, 1913, Barbier; flowers deep pink tinted lighter, buttercup-like

'Renoncule Noirâtre' -- See 'Roi des Pourpres'

'Renoncule Ponctuée' HGal, mr, 1833, Vibert; flowers crimson, spotted and marbled with rose, medium, dbl.

Renouveau de Provins® -- See 'Lapdi'

'Renove' ('California Dreaming') Min, mr, 1986, Rennie, Bruce F.; flowers medium red, reverse lighter, 28 petals, high-centered, borne usually singly, moderate fruity fragrance; foliage medium size, dark, semi-glossy; prickles tiny, maroon; medium, bushy growth; hips globular, yellow-orange; [Julie Ann™ × Black Jack™]; intr. 1987

'Renown' HT, or, 1927, Burbage Nursery; flowers glowing orange-cerise, shaded cardinal, dbl.; ['Red-Letter Day' × 'Mrs Wemyss Quin']

'Renown's Desert Glo' -- See 'Harblend'

'Renown's Rosario' -- See 'Tanoras'

'Renown's Samaritan' -- See 'Harverag'

'Renown's Summer Lady' -- See 'Summer Lady'

'Renpaflame' ('Passion's Flame') Min, dp, 1995, Rennie, Bruce F.; flowers deep pink, 1½ in., 6-14 petals, borne in small clusters; foliage medium size, medium green, semi-glossy; some prickles; tall (18-24 in.), spreading growth; intr. 1993

'Renpie' ('Cutie Pie') Min, ly, 1989, Rennie, Bruce F.; bud ovoid; flowers light to medium yellow, small, 23 petals, high-centered, borne usually singly and in small clusters, moderate fruity fragrance; foliage small, dark green, glossy; prickles straight, small, yellow-red; bushy, low growth; hips globular, very small, yellow-orange; ['Tangerine Mist' × 'California Girl']; intr. 1989

'Renpiny' ('Pretty Tiny') Min, w, 1995, Rennie, Bruce F.; flowers 1 in., dbl., borne in small clusters; foliage small, medium green, semi-glossy; few prickles; low (8-10 in.), compact growth; intr. 1995

'Renride' ('Joyride') Min, mp, 1995, Rennie, Bruce F.; flowers 2¾ in., very dbl., borne mostly singly; foliage large, medium green, semi-glossy; few prickles; tall (24 in.), upright growth; [seedling × 'Innocent Blush']; intr. 1994

'Renruby' ('Ruby Tuesday') Min, dr, 1988, Rennie, Bruce F.; flowers dark, velvety red, reverse lighter, aging darker, small, 25-30 petals, cupped pompom, no fragrance; foliage small, dark green, semi-glossy; prickles slightly hooked, small, brownish; bushy, low growth; hips round, small, red-orange; ['Pink Sheri' × Black Jack™]; intr. 1989

'Rensand' ('Coral Sand') F, op, 1991, Rennie, Bruce F.; flowers coral, large, full, borne mostly singly, intense fragrance; foliage medium size, medium green, semi-glossy; bushy growth; ['Paul Shirville' × Shocking Blue®]; intr. 1991

'Renscent' F, pb, 1988, Rennie, Bruce F.; bud ovoid; intr. 1990

'Rensecobses' ('Secret Obsession') Min, lp, 1995, Rennie, Bruce F.; flowers 3 in., full, borne mostly singly; foliage large, medium green, semi-glossy; few prickles; tall (24-30 in.), upright growth; [seedling × 'Innocent Blush']; intr. 1994

'Rensilen' ('Golden Silence') Min, yb, 1995, Rennie, Bruce F.; flowers 1½ in., dbl., borne mostly singly; foliage medium size, dark green, semi-glossy; some prickles; medium (15-18 in.), upright growth; intr. 1995

'Rensum' ('Summer Scent') Min, lp, 1990, Rennie, Bruce F.; bud ovoid; flowers medium pink with white center, reverse lighter, medium, 30 petals, high-centered, borne singly, moderate spicy fragrance; foliage medium size, dark green, glossy; prickles straight, small, few, brown; bushy, low growth; fruit not observed; ['Paul Shirville' × seedling]; intr. 1990

'Rensun' ('California Sun') Min, ab, 1988, Rennie, Bruce F.; flowers golden apricot, opening to golden center, reverse lighter, 30-35 petals, high-centered, no fragrance; foliage large, medium green, matte; prickles straight, medium, pinkish; upright, tall growth; patio, containers; hips rounded, medium, yellow-orange; [Shocking Blue® × 'Rise 'n' Shine']; intr. 1989

'Rensweet' ('Sweet Scent') Min, mp, 1993, Rennie, Bruce F.; flowers medium, full, moderate fragrance; foliage small, medium green, semi-glossy; few prickles;

medium, upright growth; [Party Girl™ × 'Silver Phantom']; intr. 1994

'Renswirl' ('Lemon Swirl') Min, ly, 1992, Rennie, Bruce F.; flowers large, dbl., borne in small clusters; foliage medium size, light green, glossy; few prickles; growth tall, upright; [seedling × 'Sunsprite']

'Rentdel' ('Timeless Delight') Min, m, 1995, Rennie, Bruce F.; flowers 2¼ in., dbl., borne mostly singly; foliage large, medium green, dull; some prickles; tall (24-36 in.), upright growth; ['Silver Phantom' × 'Innocent Blush']; intr. 1996

'Rentime' ('Tooth of Time') Min, w, 1990, Rennie, Bruce F.; bud pointed; flowers white with cream, small, 25 petals, urn-shaped, borne usually singly and in sprays of 3-5, slight spicy fragrance; foliage small, dark green, semi-glossy; prickles hooked downward, medium, light yellow; growth bushy, medium; [Party Girl™ × 'Paul Shirville']; intr. 1990

'Renuggle' ('Snuggles') Min, mp, 1995, Rennie, Bruce F.; flowers 1½ in., dbl., borne in small clusters; foliage medium size, medium green, semi-glossy; some prickles; medium (15-18 in.), bushy growth; intr. 1993

'Renurf' ('California Surf') Min, w, 1988, Rennie, Bruce F.; flowers creamy white with peachy-pink edging, small, 20 petals, urn-shaped, borne usually singly, slight fragrance; foliage small, medium green, semi-glossy; prickles straight, small, reddish-brown; upright growth; hips round, small, yellow-orange; [seedling × seedling]; intr. 1988

'Renwinnie' ('Winnie Renshaw') Min, lp, 1991, Rennie, Bruce F.; flowers small, dbl., borne in small clusters, moderate fragrance; foliage small, medium green, semi-glossy; medium growth; ['Lavonde' × Party Girl™]; intr. 1991

'Renyke' ('Little Tyke') Min, pb, 1986, Rennie, Bruce F.; flowers medium pink, white reverse, loose, 25 petals, borne singly; foliage small, medium green, matte; prickles small, reddish; small, bushy, very compact growth; small fruit; [Julie Ann™ × Red Love™]

'Renyoung' ('Young 'n' Innocent') Min, w, 1993, Rennie, Bruce F.; flowers small, white, very dbl., borne in small clusters, moderate fragrance; foliage small, medium green, semi-glossy; some prickles; low, spreading growth; ['Hap Renshaw' × 'Tooth of Time']; intr. 1994

'Renyours' ('Tenderly Yours') Min, w, 1993, Rennie, Bruce F.; flowers small, white, full; foliage small, medium green, semi-glossy; some prickles; low, spreading growth; [Party Girl™ × 'Tooth of Time']; intr. 1993

'Renzie Park' Min, ob, Consigliero; intr. 2005

'Renzig' ('Ziggy Stardust') Min, r, 1995, Rennie, Bruce F.; flowers 1¼ in., dbl., borne mostly singly; foliage medium size, medium green, semi-glossy; few prickles; medium (15 in.), upright growth; ['Silver Phantom' × Party Girl™]

Repandia® -- See 'Korsami'

'Repartee' HSpn, w

'Repelsteeltje' -- See 'Rumpelstilzchen'

'Repens' -- See 'Aimée Vibert'

'Repens' -- See 'Splendens'

'Repens Alba' ('Paulii', R. × paulii, R. × rugosa repens alba) HRg, w, 1903, Paul, G.; flowers pure white with bright yellow stamens, 2½ in., single, borne in small clusters; prostrate shrub growth; [R. rugosa alba × R. wichurana]

'Repens Meidiland' -- See 'Meilontig'

'Repens Rosea' -- See 'Paulii Rosea'

'Rephidy' HT, pb; flowers pink with darker pink edges, medium, full, high-centered; tall growth

'Republic of Texas' S, ly, 2005, Shoup, George Michael; buds bright yellow; flowers light yellow with pink tints, 1-1½ in., dbl., borne in small clusters, moderate fragrance; remontant; foliage small, dark green, semi-glossy; numerous prickles; spreading, medium (3-4 ft.) growth; container/border or in mass; [('The Fairy' × R. wichurana) × 'Baby Love']; intr. 2000

République de Genève® HT, rb, Laperrière; flowers yellow heart and reverse, outer half of petals turning red, dbl., high-centered; free-flowering; intr. 1992

'Resage' ('Golden Age') HT, yb, 2004, Sheldon, John; flowers yellow, changing quickly to white, 3½-4½ in., full, borne mostly solitary, moderate fragrance; foliage medium size, medium green, matte; prickles medium, pointed, green, moderate; growth bushy, medium (3-5 ft.); ['Spirit of Glasnost' × Lanvin™]; intr. 2002

'Resand' ('Gene Sandberg') HT, lp, 1996, Sheldon, John, Jennifer & Robyn; flowers light pink with a dark pink line around outer edge of each p, 4-6 in., full; foliage medium size, dark green, dull; prickles moderate; upright, medium (2-3 ft.) growth; ['Touch of Elegance' × 'First Prize']

'Resbobie' ('Bobbie Vesely') HT, pb, 1996, Sheldon, John, Jennifer & Robyn; flowers medium pink blend, reverse medium pink with yellowish tinge, full; foliage medium size, medium green, dull; prickles moderate; upright, medium growth; [Pristine® × Gold Medal®]; intr. 1995

'Rescard' ('Christmas Card') HT, ly, 1995, Sheldon, John & Robin; flowers light yellow, fading to white on outer petals, large, full, borne mostly singly, moderate fragrance; foliage medium size, medium green, matte; upright, medium growth; ['Spirit of Glasnost' × Lanvin™]

'Resclara' ('Clara') HT, ab, 1995, Sheldon, John & Robin; flowers unusual apricot, medium, full, borne mostly singly; foliage medium size, medium green, matte; upright, medium growth; ['Nantucket' × 'Lovely Lady']

'Resfini' ('Infinity') HT, mp, 1995, Sheldon, John & Robin; flowers medium, full, borne mostly singly, slight fragramce fragrance; foliage medium size, medium green, matte; upright, tall growth; ['Kordes' Perfecta' × 'Prima Donna']

'Resgold' ('Doris Reese') HT, my, 1996, Sheldon, John, Jennifer & Robyn; bud urn-shaped with tips of petals folding downward; flowers medium yellow, center of rose darker than outer petals, 4 in., full, high-centered, moderate fragrance; foliage medium size, dark green, semi-glossy; prickles moderate; upright, medium (3 ft.) growth; [seedling × Lanvin™]

'Reshollywood' ('Hollywood Star') HT, ab, 2001, Sheldon, John; flowers medium, full, borne mostly solitary, slight fragrance; foliage medium size, medium green, semi-glossy; prickles average, recurved, few; growth upright, medium (5 ft.); garden decorative; ['Summer Dream' × Lanvin™]; intr. 2002

'Reshonor' ('Sheldon's Honor') HT, w, 1995, Sheldon, John & Robin; flowers full, borne in small clusters, slight fragrance; foliage medium size, medium green, matte; upright, medium growth; ['Sheer Bliss' × 'Anastasia']

'Reshope' ('Hopeful') HT, lp, 1995, Sheldon, John & Robin; flowers medium, full, borne mostly singly; foliage medium size, medium green, matte; upright, medium growth; ['Sheer Bliss' × 'Elizabeth Taylor']

'Reshopie' ('Hopie Girl') HT, ly, 2003, Sheldon, John; flowers dbl., high-centered, borne mostly solitary; foliage medium size, medium green, matte; prickles medium, pointed; growth upright, medium, shrub; PPAF; [Polarstern® × Lanvin™]; intr. 2004

'Resilla' ('O'Rilla', 'Rilla') HT, r, 1996, Sheldon, John, Jennifer & Robyn; flowers 5-7 in., full, high-centered, borne mostly singly, slight fragrance; foliage medium size, dark green, semi-glossy; prickles moderate; upright, medium (3-4 ft.) growth; [Lanvin™ × 'First Prize']

'Resine' ('White Wine') HT, w, 1995, Sheldon, John & Robin; flowers white with pink tinge, medium, full, borne mostly singly; foliage medium size, medium green, matte; upright, medium growth; [Pristine® × ('Spirit of Glasnost' × Lanvin™)]

'Resink' ('Pink Licorice', 'Pink Robin') HT, pb, 1995, Sheldon, John & Robin; flowers pink blend, medium, full, borne mostly singly, slight licorice fragrance; foliage medium size, medium green, matte; upright, medium growth; ['Osiria' × 'Elegant Beauty']

'Resjeff' ('Jeffrey') HT, my, 1995, Sheldon, John & Robin; flowers medium, full, borne in small clusters; foliage medium size, light green, matte; upright, medium growth; [Polarstern® × ('Spirit of Glasnost' × Lanvin™)]

'Resland' ('Dreamland') HT, ob, 1995, Sheldon, John & Robin; flowers orange blend tipped with darker orange, dbl., borne mostly singly; foliage medium size, medium green, matte; upright, medium growth

'Resline' ('White House') HT, w, 1995, Sheldon, John & Robin; flowers white with pink tinge, medium, full, borne mostly singly; foliage medium size, medium green, matte; upright, medium growth; [Pristine® × ('Spirit of Glasnost' × Lanvin™)]

'Resluc' ('Lucious') HT, mr, 1995, Sheldon, John & Robin; flowers intense medium red, dbl., borne mostly singly; foliage medium size, dark green, semi-glossy; upright growth

'Resmar' ('Marie') HT, w, 1995, Sheldon, John & Robin; flowers medium, full, borne mostly singly; foliage medium size, medium green, matte; upright, medium growth

'Resolut' F, or, 1962, Tantau, Math.; bud oval; flowers 4-5 in., 30 petals, borne in large sprays; foliage glossy; upright, bushy growth

'Resonanz' F, mr, Noack; flowers bright red, bright yellow stamens, colorfast, 2½ in., semi-dbl., cupped, borne in clusters, slight fragrance; recurrent; foliage dark green, glossy; growth to 90-100 cm.; intr. 2006

'Resone' ('Violet Dawson') HT, m, 1991, Sheldon, John & Jennifer; flowers mauve blend, medium, full, borne in small clusters, moderate fragrance; foliage medium size, dark green, disease-resistant; medium, bushy growth; winter hardy; ['Paradise' × seedling]

'Resox' ('Roxie') HT, mr, 1995, Sheldon, John & Robin; flowers medium, full, borne mostly singly, slight fragrance; foliage medium size, medium green, matte; upright, medium growth; ['Sheer Bliss' × 'Headliner']

'Respad' ('Grandpa Dan') HT, pb, 1995, Sheldon, John & Robin; flowers pink blend, medium, full, borne mostly singly; foliage medium size, medium green, matte; upright, extremely vigorous, medium growth; [Pristine® × Touch of Class™®]

'Respar' ('Grandpa Ray') HT, pb, 1995, Sheldon, John & Robin; flowers light pink blend, medium, full, borne mostly singly; foliage medium size, medium green, matte; upright, medium growth; [Pristine® × Touch of Class™®]

'Respat' ('Grandpa Toni') HT, pb, 1995, Sheldon, John & Robin; flowers light pink blend, medium, full, borne mostly singly; foliage medium size, medium green, matte; upright, medium growth; [Pristine® × Touch of Class™®]

'Respect' HT, mr, Spek; flowers bright red, full, high-centered, borne mostly singly; intr. 2002

'Resplenda' HT, w, 1975, Golik; bud ovoid; flowers 4 in., 30 petals, moderate fruity fragrance; foliage glossy; moderate growth; ['Queen of Bermuda' × Golden Giant®]; intr. 1974

'Resplendent' HP, lp, 1896, Williams, A.

'Respond' HT, pb, 1995, Sheldon, John & Robin; flowers dark pink blend, large, full, borne mostly singly, slight fragrance; foliage medium size, medium green, matte; upright, medium growth; [Sheer Elegance™ × seedling]

'Responso' F, yb, GPG Bad Langensalza; flowers medium, dbl.; intr. 1981

'Resrob' ('Robin') HT, m

'Resruth' ('Ruthe') HT, yb

'Ressins Etienne Gautier' -- See 'Dorster'

'Resstraw' ('Strawberry Romance') HT, pb, 2003, Sheldon, John; flowers red, pink & cream, aging to almost white, 5-6 in., full, high-centered, borne mostly solitary; recurrent; foliage medium size, medium green, matte; prickles medium, pointed; bushy, medium growth; PPAF; [Pristine® × Gold Medal®]; intr. 2004

'Rest in Peace' MinFl, w, Chessum, Paul; flowers creamy white, large, full; foliage medium green, glossy; growth to 3 ft.; intr. 1997

'Restful' HT, my, 1995, Sheldon, John & Robin; flowers large, full, borne mostly singly, slight fragrance; foliage medium size, medium green, matte; upright, tall growth; ['Miyabi' × Lanvin™]

'Restless' HT, dr, 1938, Clark; flowers dark red, semi-dbl.; almost thornless

'Restless Native' S, or, 1973, Stoddard, Louis; bud ovoid; flowers orange-scarlet, base white, 2½ in., 8-12 petals, cupped; foliage large, dark, leathery; vigorous, compact, bushy growth; [Orangeade® × R. carolina]

'Resto' ('Thoughtful') HT, pb, 1995, Sheldon, John & Robin; flowers dark pink blend, large, full, borne mostly singly; foliage medium size, dark green, matte; upright, medium growth; [Pristine® × 'Nightingale']

'Results' HT, pb, 1995, Sheldon, John & Robin; flowers red, white, pink, purple hues, depending on temperature, large, dbl., borne mostly singly; foliage medium size, dark green, matte; upright, tall growth; [Pristine® × seedling]

'Resunc' ('Uncle Steve') HT, mr, 1995, Sheldon, John & Robin; flowers large, full, borne mostly singly, slight fragrance; foliage medium size, dark green, matte; upright, medium growth; [Pristine® × Touch of Class™®]

Resurrection® HT, dp, 1986, Kriloff, Michel; bud red; flowers bright pink, large, moderate sweet fragrance; foliage dark; [seedling × seedling]

'Reta Elizabeth Lindsay' -- See 'Frycharm'

'Retina' Min, mr, 1981, Williams, Ernest D.; flowers medium red, reverse lighter, base gold, 43 petals, borne singly, slight fruity fragrance; foliage green, matte; prickles straight, long, tan; bushy, spreading growth; [seedling × 'Over the Rainbow']; intr. 1980

'Retour du Printemps' HCh, dp, before 1835; flowers medium, semi-dbl.; Lawrenciana

'Rétro' -- See 'Meibalani'

'Rétro Blanc' S, w

'Reubis' F, dp, Reuter; intr. 2003

'Reuham' F, rb, Reuter; intr. 2006

'Reuhug' HT, dr, Reuterdouble; intr. 2008

'Reunion' HT, dp, Weeks, O.L.; flowers rich light red to deep pink, 35 petals, high-centered; recurrent; intr. 2005

'Reus' HT, m, 1949, Dot, Pedro; bud long, pointed; flowers magenta, large, dbl., high-centered; ['Cynthia' × 'Manuelita']

'Rêve de Capri' HT, op, 1953, Buyl Frères; flowers salmon-orange and yellow; foliage bronze; compact, low growth; ['Pres. Herbert Hoover' × seedling]

'Rêve de Deauville' ('Revue de Dauville') F, dy, Pineau; intr. 1982

'Rêve de Mome' HT, yb, Dorieux; flowers bright yellow, edged with salmon red, large, full, high-centered; intr. 2005

'Rêve de Môme' HT, yb, Dorieux; flowers yellow with broad red edges, dbl., high-centered; foliage dark green, glossy; intr. 2006

Rêve de Paris® HT, op, Meilland; flowers rose-scarlet, large, dbl.; intr. 1985

Rêve de Valse® F, mr, Tantau; flowers velvety blood red, dbl.

'Rêve d'Hélène' HT, mp, 1959, Orard, Joseph; flowers bright pink edged silvery, large; foliage clear green; free growth; ['Michèle Meilland' × seedling]

'Rêve d'Or' ('Condesa da Foz', 'Golden Chain') N, my, 1869, Ducher, Vve.; flowers buff-yellow tinted lighter at edges, fading to pale buff, medium to large, dbl., loose, borne in small clusters, moderate fragrance; foliage dark green, glossy, tinted red when young; vigorous, climbing growth; ['Mme Schultz' × unknown]

'Rêve d'un Soir' HT, m, Croix; flowers large, well-formed, intense fragrance; free-flowering; intr. 1997

'Rêve Rose' F, mp, 1950, Mallerin, C.; flowers 60 petals, borne in large clusters

'Réveil' HT, yb, Van Rossem; flowers golden yellow, reverse striped red, dbl., moderate fragrance; ['Mr Joh. M. Jolles' × 'Mrs Wemyss Quinn']; intr. 1924

'Réveil' HP, mp, 1849, Lacharme; flowers pink, spotted lighter pink, large, full

'Réveil' B, rb, Guillot père; flowers cherry red, tinted and shaded violet, large, full; growth to 80 cm.; intr. 1854

'Réveil de l'Empire' HP, mp, 1852, Bernède; flowers silky pink, large, full

'Réveil Dijonnais' Cl HT, rb, 1931, Buatois; flowers cerise, golden yellow center, reverse yellow streaked carmine, 5 in., 13 petals, cupped, borne in small clusters, moderate fragrance; intermittent repeat; foliage thick, glossy, bronze; short stems; vigorous, climbing growth;

['Eugene Furst' × 'Constance']
'Réveil du Printemps' HP, w, 1883, Oger; flowers delicate flesh white, large, very full
'Reveille' HT, pb, 1941, Nicolas; flowers light salmon-buff-pink, center deeper pink, open, large, 40-50 petals, cupped; foliage dark, leathery; vigorous, upright, bushy, compact growth; ['Kidwai' × 'Golden Main']
'Revelation' HT, pb, 1938, Witter; bud long; flowers thulite-pink to rose-red, 4½-5 in., 35 petals, high-centered, moderate fragrance; foliage dark; very vigorous growth; PP373; [sport of 'Briarcliff']
Revelry™ -- See 'Swishrev'
'Revelry' F, dp, 1959, Boerner, E. S.; bud large, blood-red, ovoid; flowers open rose-red, aging to rose-pink, very large, semi-dbl., open; continuous; foliage leathery, dark green, disease-resistant; growth vigorous, upright, bushy; PP1850; [Enchantment × seedling]; intr. 1959
'Revenante' -- See 'La Revenante'
'Révérence' F, mr, 1962, Delforge; flowers geranium-red, 2 in., 26 petals, carnation-like, borne in large clusters; foliage dark, glossy; vigorous, upright growth; [Orange Triumph® × seedling]
'Reverend Alan Cheales' HP, mr, 1897, Paul, G.; flowers pale pink, reverse darker, very large, dbl., peony-like
'Rev. David R. Williamson' ('David R. Williamson', 'Rev Williamson') HT, mr, 1921, Pernet-Ducher; bud long, pointed, deep coral-red; flowers coral-red, tinted orange, large, very full, globular, moderate fragrance
'Rev F. Page-Roberts' HT, yb, 1921, Cant, B. R.; bud long, pointed; flowers yellow shaded red, large, dbl., high-centered, intense fragrance; free-flowering; growth to 4 ft.; ['Queen Mary' × seedling]
'Rev. F. Page-Roberts, Climbing' Cl HT, yb, 1931, Beverley
'Rev. Floris Ferwerda' -- See 'Ben Stad'
'Rev. H. d'Ombrain' B, mr, 1863, Margottin; flowers brilliant red, large, full, cupped; recurrent bloom; vigorous growth
'Rev James Sprunt' Cl HCh, mr, 1858, Sprunt; flowers crimson-red, larger than parent; [sport of 'Cramoisi Supérieur']; intr. 1858
'Rev. Peter Lewis' -- See 'Sarpet'
'Reverend Seidel' HMsk, w, Robinson; flowers white with yellow stamens, small, single, flat, borne in large clusters, moderate fragrance; free-flowering; growth compact, Noisette-like; intr. 2005
'Rev T. C. Cole' Cl T, dy, 1880, Cole, Rev T.C.; ['Chromatella' × 'Marechal Neil']
'Rev Williamson' -- See 'Rev. David R. Williamson'
'Rev. Williamson' HT, or, 1921, Pernet-Ducher; bud long, pointed; flowers coral-red, shaded carmine,, dbl.

'Reverie' -- See 'Reikor'
'Rêverie' HT, ab, 1925, Ketten Bros.; flowers apricot, reverse shrimp-pink veined rose, dbl.; ['Mme Mélanie Soupert' × 'Jean C.N. Forestier']
'Reversa' (R. × reversa Waldstein & Kitaibel, R. × rubella) Misc OGR, mr, 1820; foliage very dark green; growth upright, to 5 ft.; hips scarlet, 3/4 in., obovoid, pendulous; [R. pendulina × R. spinosissima]; found in the Alps and southern Europe
'Reversa' ('Bengale Violet', 'Violet Bengal', 'Common Purple Boursault', 'Paniculé') Bslt, m, about 1810, Vilmorin; flowers violet purple, medium, semi-dbl., borne in small clusters; foliage lanceolate, glabrous, simply dentate at the tips; nearly thornless; stems glaucous, usually purple; hips ovoid, red
'Reversa Pourpre' -- See 'Maheca'
'Review' HT, mp, 1951, Fletcher; flowers bright rose, reverse flesh, 6-7 in., 50 petals; foliage dull, green; medium, dwarf growth; ['Mrs Henry Bowles' × 'Trigo']
'Revival' HT, ab, 1981, Rose Barni-Pistoia; flowers honey amber, fading to creamy yellow, dbl., high-centered, slight fragrance; recurrent; stems strong; growth to 4 ft.; [sport of Folklore®]; intr. 1979
Revival® HT, mp, Tantau; flowers large, double, high-centered, borne mostly singly; recurrent; stems medium to long; florist rose; intr. 2007
'Revolution' Pol, or, GPG Bad Langensalza; flowers medium, semi-dbl., loose, borne in clusters; bushy (2 ft.) growth; intr. 1972
Révolution Française® ('Hans Rosenthal') HT, mr, Meilland; intr. 1989
Revue® HT, pb, Kordes; bud large; flowers white with pink edges, strong contrast, medium size, 40-45 petals, high-centered, borne usually singly, no fragrance; good repeat; foliage dark green, glossy; prickles few, bending downward; stems 60 cm.; vigorous, upright, bushy growth; PP14440; [seedling × seedling]; greenhouse rose; intr. 2002
'Revue de Dauville' -- See 'Pinault'
'Reward' HT, yb, 1934, Dickson, A.; bud long, pointed; flowers clear yellow shaded peach, medium; foliage dark, glossy; vigorous, bushy growth
'Rex' HT, mr, 1960, Spanbauer; bud long, pointed; flowers velvety cardinal-red, large, semi-dbl., cupped; foliage leathery, glossy; vigorous, upright growth; ['Senior' × 'Better Times']; intr. 1959
'Rex Anderson' HT, w, 1938, McGredy; flowers ivory-white, very well-formed, large, dbl., high-centered, moderate fruity fragrance; shy bloom; foliage gray-green; vigorous growth; PP335; ['Florence L. Izzard' × 'Mrs Charles Lamplough']
'Rexjean' ('Jean Rex') S, dr, 1999, Rex, Dr. Robert W.; flowers dark red

(3 shades), center vein darkest, 4-4½ in., very dbl., borne in small clusters, intense fragrance; foliage medium size, dark green, matte; numerous prickles; bushy, very vigorous, strong, medium (4 ft.) growth; [sport of Prospero®]; intr. 1995
'Rexy's Baby' -- See 'Maccarib'
'Reycantpri' ('Canterbury Pride') Min, r, 1992, Reynolds, Ted; flowers 1½ in., very dbl.; foliage small, medium green, semi-glossy; low (28 cm.), upright growth; ['Hot Chocolate' × 'miniature seedling']
'Reycidun' ('City of Dunedin') Min, yb, 1995, Reynolds, Ted; flowers old gold changing to yellow then white with red edge, small, full, borne in small clusters; foliage medium size, medium green, glossy; few prickles; upright, medium growth; [('Rise 'n' Shine' × seedling) × Rainbow's End™]; intr. 1995
'Reyfaye' ('Faye Reynolds') Cl F, dp, 1992, Reynolds, Ted; flowers deep pink, 3-3½ in., full, borne in small clusters, moderate fragrance; foliage sage green, semi-glossy; some prickles; growth medium (6½ ft.); [Westerland® × 'Gingersnap']
'Reyinver' ('City of Invercargill') HT, dp, 1996, Reynolds, Ted; bud very dark red; flowers deep pink, large, very dbl., borne mostly singly; foliage medium size, medium green, glossy, disease-free; few prickles; upright, medium growth; [Westerland® × 'Perfume Delight']; intr. 1996
'Reykelly' ('Kelly Reynolds') HT, pb, 1999, Reynolds, Ted; flowers apricot peach pink blend, large, full, high-centered, borne mostly singly, slight fragrance; foliage large, medium green, glossy; few prickles; upright, medium growth; ['Perfume Delight' × seedling]; intr. 1999
'Reylianne' ('Lianne Reynolds') F, lp, 1996, Reynolds, Ted; flowers light pink, china-porcelain appearance, full, borne in small clusters, no fragrance; foliage small, medium green, glossy; some prickles; compact, medium growth; ['Gloire de Dijon' × 'Hot Pewter']; intr. 1997
'Reynolda House' -- See 'Wilangil'
'Reynolds Hole' B, mp, 1862, Trouillard; flowers medium, very dbl.
'Reynolds Hole' HP, rb, Paul, G.; flowers chestnut-brown-red, shaded scarlet-purple or amaranthe, large, full, globular; ['Duke of Edinburgh' × unknown]; intr. 1874
'Reynold's Rugosa' -- See 'Reyrug'
'Reypat' ('Patricia Weston') LCl, lp, 1992, Reynolds, Ted; flowers 3-3½ in., full, borne in small clusters, moderate fragrance; foliage large, dark green, glossy; some prickles; medium (2 m.), upright growth; [Westerland® × 'Perfume Delight']
'Reypeg' ('Peggy Joan Reynolds') S, mp, 1992, Reynolds, Ted; flowers 1½ in., 5 petals, borne in small clusters; very

remontant, almost perpetual; foliage medium size, light green, semi-glossy, disease-resistant; few prickles; upright (150 cm.) growth; very hardy; possibly HCh × *R. gigantea*

'Reyred' ('Ted's Red') HT, mr, 1992, Reynolds, Ted; flowers 3-3½ in., full, borne mostly singly; foliage medium size, medium size, semi-glossy; few prickles; medium, upright growth; [Alec's Red® × seedling]

'Reyrug' ('Reynold's Rugosa') HRg, mr, 2000, Reynolds, Ted; flowers 100 petals, borne mostly singly; foliage large, dark green, glossy; numerous prickles; bushy, medium growth; intr. 2002

'Reysel' ('Selina') HMsk, dp, 1992, Reynolds, Ted; flowers deep pink, medium, single, borne in small clusters; foliage small, medium green, semi-glossy; few prickles; medium, spreading growth; ['Cornelia' × Trier®]; intr. 1992

'Reyshelley' ('Shelley Higgins') HT, ab, 1998, Reynolds, Ted; flowers apricot-peach blend, dbl., high-centered, borne mostly singly, intense spicy fragrance; foliage medium size, medium green, semi-glossy; some prickles; upright, medium growth; [Westerland® × seedling]; intr. 1998

'Rhapsody' -- See 'Jacsod'

'Rhapsody' HT, ob, 1951, Houghton, D.; bud long, pointed; flowers orange, reverse terra-cotta, medium, 20 petals, high-centered; foliage leathery; vigorous, bushy growth; RULED EXTINCT 1/85; ['Lulu' × 'Cecil']

'Rhapsody in Blue' -- See 'Frantasia'

'Rhea Reid' HT, mr, 1908, E.G. Hill, Co.; bud long, pointed; flowers crimson-red, large, dbl., high-centered, moderate fragrance; foliage soft; ['American Beauty' × 'red seedling']

'Rhea Reid, Climbing' Cl HT, mr, 1914, California Nursery Co.

'Rheda-Wiedenbruck' F, mp

'Rhein' HT, r, Hiroshima; intr. 2006

Rheinaupark® -- See 'Korola'

'Rheingold' HT, my, Leenders, M.; flowers golden yellow, large, very dbl., intense fragrance; foliage leathery, light; dwarf, bushy, compact growth; PP138; ['Mrs T. Hillas' × 'Mabel Morse']; intr. 1934

'Rheingold' T, my, 1889, Lambert

'Rhode Island Red' ('Field of Woods', 'Fields of the Wood', 'Kocher Red') LCl, dr, 1958, Brownell; flowers carmine red, large, delicate substance, 4-5 in., 33 petals, cupped to globular, moderate fragrance; remontant; foliage dark green, glossy; moderate growth; ['Everblooming Pillar No. 73' × seedling]; intr. 1957

'Rhodes Rose' HMult, w

'Rhodologue Jules Gravereaux' T, yb, 1908, Fontes; flowers yellowish-pink, medium, very full, slight fragrance; ['Marie Van Houtte' × 'Mme Abel Chatenay']

'Rhodophile Gravereaux' HFt, yb, 1900, Pernet-Ducher; flowers dark yellow with pink, large, semi-dbl.; ['Antoine Ducher' × *R. foetida persiana*]

'Rhona' HT, mp, 1984, Gobbee, W.D.; flowers large, 20 petals; foliage medium size, medium green, semi-glossy; bushy growth; ['Anne Letts' × ('Dainty Maid' × 'Pink Favorite')]

'Rhona Beck' HT, lp, Kordes; bud long, slender; flowers porcelain-pink, dbl., high-centered, borne mostly singly, intense fragrance; free-flowering; vigorous, tall growth; intr. 2001

'Rhona Catherine' MinFl, dr, 2001, Bailey, John; flowers scarlet, crimson reverse, 3 in., dbl., borne in small clusters, moderate fragrance; foliage medium size, dark green, glossy; prickles small, slightly hooked, few; bushy, medium (42 in.) growth; garden decorative; [('Whisky Mac' × 'Adrian Bailey') × ('Adrian Bailey' × Peer Gynt®)]; intr. 2002

'Rhonda' LCl, mp, 1967, Lissemore; bud globular; flowers carmine-rose, 7-8 cm., dbl., borne in medium to large clusters; foliage dark, glossy; vigorous, climbing growth; PP2854; ['New Dawn' × 'Spartan']; intr. 1968

'Rhosyn Margaret Williams' HT, ob, Fryer; flowers two-tone brick and terracotta, dbl., spiral, moderate fragrance; recurrent; moderate growth; intr. 2005

'Rhotare' Pol, mr; flowers medium, semi-dbl.

'Rhumba' -- See 'Rumba'

'Rhythm 'n' Blues' LCl, dp, Poulsen; flowers warm pink with almost purple overtones, 10-15 cm., dbl., cupped, borne in clusters, no fragrance; free-flowering; foliage medium green, matte; bushy, strong (8-10 ft.) growth; intr. 2000

'Ria Wenning' HT, dp, 1932, Leenders, M.; bud long, pointed; flowers carmine, semi-dbl.; vigorous growth; ['Mme Maurice de Luze' × 'Red Star']

Rialto™ -- See 'Rialto Palace'

'Rialto Palace' (Rialto™) MinFl, w, Poulsen; flowers white, 5-8 cm., semi-dbl., no fragrance; growth bushy, 20-40 cm.; PP15000; intr. 2002

'Ribambelle' F, op, Croix; flowers luminous salmon-pink, borne in clusters of 25 - 30; free-flowering; foliage glossy; intr. 1972

'Ribatejo' F, w, 1962, Moreira da Silva; flowers white, center deep yellow; ['Virgo' × seedling]

'Ribbon Parade' Cl Min, rb; flowers apricot yellow and cherry red, well-formed, moderate fragrance

'Ribbon Rose' ('Lady Love', 'Pink Patio', 'The Ribbon Rose') Min, lp; flowers shell pink, very full, cupped; recurrent; foliage light green, glossy; growth to 18-24 in.; sold to support Breast Cancer Care, a charity; intr. 1997

Riberhus™ -- See 'Poulriber'

'Ric Rac' -- See 'Pixric'

'Ricanna' (Anna Marie™) Min, ly, 2004, Rickard, Vernon; flowers light yellow, blushed medium pink in cool weather, 1¾ in., dbl., borne mostly solitary, no fragrance; foliage medium size, dark green, semi-glossy; prickles straight, red, numerous; growth spreading, tall (36 in.); exhibition, garden decoration; ['Fairhope' × 'Sweet Caroline']; intr. 2004

Ricarda® F, op, Noack, Werner; intr. 1989

'Ricbetty' (Betty Lou™) Min, dp, 2004, Rickard, Vernon; flowers dark pink, blending to yellow at center when fully open, 1¾ in., dbl., borne mostly solitary, no fragrance; foliage medium size, dark green, glossy; prickles curved down, tan, numerous; growth spreading, tall (36 in.); ['Fairhope' × 'Ruby Baby']; intr. 2004

'Riccordo di Fernando Scarlatti' HP, dr, about 1925; flowers large, dbl., intense fragrance

'Riccordo di Geo Chavez' HT, dp, 1911, Bonfiglio, A.; flowers large, dbl.

'Riccordo di Giosue Carducci' HT, lp, 1909, Bonfiglio, A.; flowers very large, very dbl.

'Riccordo di Giovanni Spotti' HT, mr; flowers large, dbl.

'Ricfra' MinFl, my, Rickard, Vernon; intr. 2005

'Rich and Rare' -- See 'Searich'

'Richafic' F, rb, Meilland; intr. 1998

'Richague' F, pb, Richardier; intr. 1998

'Richaly' F, mr, Richardier; intr. 1998

'Richanize' ('Richdame', Koba®) HT, mp, Richardierfull; intr. 2004

'Richard' HT, dr, 1978, Ellick; bud long, pointed; flowers spinel-red, 4-5 in., 25-30 petals, intense fragrance; foliage light green; bushy, upright growth; ['Gavotte' × 'Memoriam']; intr. 1979

'Richard Buckley' -- See 'Smitshort'

'Richard E. West' HT, my, 1924, Dickson, A.; bud long, pointed; flowers large, dbl., moderate lemon fragrance; recurrent; foliage leathery; vigorous growth

'Richard Hayes' S, mp, 1974, Holmes, R.A.; flowers 4 in., moderate fragrance; foliage light; vigorous, tall, upright growth; [sport of 'Fred Loads']; intr. 1965

'Richard Smith' -- See 'Général Jacqueminot'

Richard Strauss® S, pb, Noack, Werner; flowers rose-pink and white, 3 cm., single, shallow cup, borne in large clusters of up to 30; recurrent; upright (3-4 ft.) growth; intr. 1989

Richard Tauber® HT, rb, Pouw; intr. 1986

'Richard's Rose' S, mp, 2008, Zipper, Herbert; flowers pink, reverse white to pink, large, 3 in., very full, borne mostly solitary; foliage medium, dark green, matte; prickles medium, downward, light brown, moderate; growth upright, tall (6 ft.); garden decoration, containers; ['Tamango' × unknown]; intr. 2008

'Richardson Wright' HT, pb, 1931, C-P;

flowers pearl with carmine dashes and lemon reflexes, large, globular; foliage dark, leathery; vigorous growth; ['Radiance' × 'Ville de Paris']

'Richdame' -- See 'Véronèse'

'Richelieu' Ch, m, 1845, Verdier, V.; flowers violet-pink, large, very dbl., cupped; growth compact, branching

'Richerne' HT, ob, Richardier; intr. 1999

'Richicket' F, my, Richardier; intr. 1999

'Richipio' dp, Richardier; intr. 1997

'Richmond' ('Everblooming Jack Rose') HT, mr, 1905, E.G. Hill, Co.; bud long, pointed; flowers bright scarlet, varying greatly at times, large, dbl., moderate damask fragrance; vigorous growth; ['Lady Battersea' × 'Liberty']

'Richmond, Climbing' Cl HT, mr, 1912, Dickson, A.; flowers red-scarlet, medium, full, moderate fragrance; [sport of 'Richmond']

'Richodda' HT, my, Richardier; intr. 1999

'Richofle' HT, pb, Richardier; intr. 1999

'Richoilier' ('Irene') HT, w, Richardier; intr. 1999

'Richotale' ('Farouche') HT, mr, Richardier; intr. 2004

'Richulon' HT, mr, Richardier; intr. 1999

'Richulri' F, or, Richardier; intr. 1998

'Richupare' HT, ab, Richardier; intr. 1999

'Richvicia' HT, dp, Richardier; intr. 1999

'Richzone' ('Femme Actuelle') HT, mr, Richardier; intr. 1999

'Rick Stein' -- See 'Rikita'

Rickie-Tickie™ -- See 'Grerickie'

Ricky® -- See 'Hauric'

'Ricky Hendrick' -- See 'Briricky'

'Ricmegan' Min, mp, 2004, Rickard, Vernon; flowers dbl., borne mostly solitary, slight fragrance; foliage medium size, dark green, glossy; prickles angled down, red, moderate; growth spreading, tall (36 in.); exhibition; garden; ['Fairhope' × 'Ruby']; intr. 2004

'Ricnancy' (Nancy Jean™) Min, ab, 2004, Rickard, Vernon; flowers apricot, reverse apricot blend, 1¾ in., dbl., borne mostly solitary, no fragrance; foliage large, dark green, glossy; prickles angled down, red, moderate; growth upright, tall (36 in.); exhibition; ['Fairhope' × 'Michel Cholet']; intr. 2004

'Ricordo di Geo Chavez' HT, mr, 1911, Gaetano, Bonfiglioli; flowers large, full

'Ricordo di Giosue Carducci' ('Souv de Giosue Carducci') HT, lp, 1909, Gaetano, Bonfiglioli; flowers whitish pink, very large, very full

'Ricordo di Leone Sgaravatti' HT, Sgaravatti, A.

'Ricpink' (Elegant Pink™) Min, pb, 2005, Rickard, Vernon; flowers light pink, reverse medium pink, 1½ in., dbl., borne mostly solitary, no fragrance; foliage medium size, dark green, semi-glossy; prickles ¼ in., straight, brown, few; growth upright, medium (24 in.); exhibition-garden; ['Fairhope' × 'mixed pollen']; intr. 2005

'Ricrachel' (Rachel™) MinFl, dp, 2005, Rickard, Vernon; flowers deep pink, reverse medium pink, 1½ in., full, borne mostly solitary, moderate fragrance; foliage medium size, dark green, semi-glossy; prickles small 3 mm., straight, red, few; growth upright, vigorous, tall, 30 in; exhibition, garden decoration; ['Fairhope' × 'Signature®]; intr. 2006

'Rictammy' (Tammy Darlene™) Min, pb, 2004, Rickard, Vernon; flowers light pink, reverse white, 2 in., dbl., borne singly and in small clusters, no fragrance; foliage medium size, medium green, semi-glossy; prickles moderate, angled down, red; growth bushy, tall (36 in.); exhibition, garden decoration; ['Fairhope' × 'Sweet Caroline']; intr. 2004

'Riczach' (Zach™) F, or, 2005, Rickard, Vernon; flowers orange, 3 in., dbl., borne mostly solitary, no fragrance; foliage medium size, dark green, glossy, disease-resistant; prickles moderate, ½ in., straight, brown; growth bushy, medium (48 in.); hedges, garden decoration; [Playboy® × Orangeade®]; intr. 2005

'Ridgeway' HT, pb, 1953, Ratcliffe; flowers salmon-pink shaded apricot, well-shaped, dbl.; foliage rather sparse; strong stems; very vigorous growth; ['Princess Marina' × 'Vanessa']

'Rieder's Solin' Cl HT, mr, 1930, Rieder; flowers large, dbl.

'Riégo' HCh, mp, 1831, Vibert; flowers bright carmine pink, large, full, globular, intense raspberry fragrance; foliage dark green, thick; growth branching, robust

'Rifleman' HT, or, 1980, Murray, Nola; bud ovoid; flowers light vermilion, large, 35-43 petals, high-centered; tall, very vigorous, bushy growth; ['Tropicana' × Orange Sensation®]

'Rigadoon' -- See 'Minifire'

'Rigaudon' F, dr, 1957, Combe; flowers dark red tinted geranium, dbl.; very dwarf, dense growth; [('Independence' × seedling) × seedling]

'Right Bright' -- See 'Gelrite'

'Right Royal' HT, mp, 1980, Hawken, Una; flowers silvery pink, 4 in., 30 petals; foliage dark; moderate growth; ['Scented Air' × 'Anne Letts']

'Rigobec' -- See 'Mon Pays'

'Rigobec 2' ('Neiges d'Été', 'Summer Snows') Min, w, 1984, Gailloux, Gilles; flowers small, 37 petals; foliage medium size, medium green, glossy; upright growth; [Baby Masquerade® × (Baby Masquerade® × unknown)]; intr. 1985

'Rigobec 3' ('Danse Azteque') Min, yb, 1984, Gailloux, Gilles; flowers yellow-pink blend, medium, semi-dbl., flat, slight fragrance; foliage medium size, medium green, semi-glossy; vigorous, upright growth; [Baby Masquerade® × unknown]; intr. 1985

'Rigoletto' F, ab, 1954, Leenders, M.; flowers apricot-yellow tinted copper, well-formed, large, semi-dbl.; vigorous growth; ['floribunda seedling' × 'Souv. de Claudius Pernet']

Rigoletto® HT, pb, Kordes; flowers cream with pink edges, spreading down the petals, large, full, high-centered, borne usually singly; recurrent; stems long; intr. 2005

'Rijswijk' F, ob, 1964, Buisman, G. A. H.; bud deep yellow; flowers orange-yellow, semi-dbl., borne in clusters; foliage dark, glossy; vigorous growth; ['Goldmarie' × 'Fata Morgana']

Rikita® ('Rick Stein') HT, ab, Tantau; flowers soft apricot with touch of pink, full, cupped, moderate sweet fragrance; recurrent; foliage glossy; intr. 2005

'Riksbyggerosen' F, or, 1978, Poulsen, Niels D.; flowers open, 3 in., 23 petals; foliage glossy, light green; low, compact growth; ['Irish Wonder' × seedling]; intr. 1969

'Rilla' -- See 'Resilla'

'Rim' -- See 'Happiness'

'Rima' HT, lp, 1964, Samuels; flowers light silvery pink; PP2570; [sport of 'Prima Ballerina']

'Rimosa, Climbing' -- See 'Meigronurisar'

'Rimosa' F, my, 1958, Meilland, F.; flowers Indian yellow to citron-yellow, well-formed, medium, 18-25 petals, borne in clusters; foliage leathery; upright, symmetrical, compact growth; ['Goldilocks' × 'Perla de Montserrat']

'Rimosa 79' -- See 'Meigronuri'

'Rimrose' F, my, 1959, Meilland, F.; buds small, pointed, dark yellow; flowers Indian-yellow, aging to lemon yellow, medium, semi-dbl., borne in small clusters; continuous; foliage leathery, disease-resistant; few prickles; growth vigorous, compact, bushy; ['Goldilocks' × 'Perla de Montserrat']; intr. 1958

'Rin' F, pb, Keisei; intr. 2008

'Rina' HT, w, 1999, Yonzda, Kazuo; flowers cream white blended pink, 5 in., 32 petals, high-centered; foliage medium size, medium green, semi-glossy; tall (6 ft.) growth; ['Royal Highness' × 'Shizunomai']; intr. 1997

'Rina Herholdt' HT, pb, 1960, Herholdt, J.A.; bud long, pointed; flowers milky white, flushed deep pink at edges, darkening with age, 3½-4 in., 60 petals, semi-cupped, borne singly, moderate sharp, sweet fragrance; recurrent; foliage medium green, leathery, glossy; prickles moderate, broad base, slightly recurved; vigorous, upright, bushy growth; hips spherical; PP1970; ['Peace' × seedling]; intr. 1962

'Rina Herholdt, Climbing' Cl HT, pb, 1974, Arora, Bal Raj; bud large, long pointed; flowers ivory white, edged bright pink, large, full, high-centered, borne singly, slight fragrance; intermittent, moderate; foliage large, dark green, glossy; few prickles; stems medium; vigorous growth; [sport of 'Rina Herholdt']; intr. 1973

'Rina Hugo' -- See 'Dorvizo'

'Rinakor' F, ob, 1975, Kordes; bud long, pointed; intr. 1974

Rinascimento® -- See 'Barinas'

'Ring-A-Ling' HT, mp, Ringrose, Dr. V.P.; intr. 1995

Ring of Fire™ -- See 'Morfire'

'Ringfield' HT, or, 1977, Plumpton, E.; flowers deep vermilion, 5 in., 30 petals; vigorous growth; ['Ernest H. Morse' × 'Fragrant Cloud']

'Ringlet' LCl, pb, 1922, Clark, A.; flowers white, tipped pink and lilac to medium, 2½ in., single, borne in clusters; good repeat; few prickles; vigorous, climbing growth; ['Ernest Morel' × 'Betty Berkeley']

'Rio Grande' HT, dr, 1973, Tantau, Math.; bud ovoid; flowers velvety dark red, medium, dbl.; foliage soft; moderate, upright, bushy growth; [unknown × unknown]

'Rio Rita' HT, w, 1931, Joseph H. Hill, Co.; bud long, pointed; flowers white tinged pink, large, dbl., intense fragrance; foliage glossy; vigorous growth; PP117; ['Mme Butterfly' × 'Premier']

'Rio Rita, Climbing' Cl HT, w, 1935, Elmer's Nursery; flowers velvety scarlet-crimson, very large, dbl., cupped, intense fragrance; foliage glossy; very vigorous growth; [sport of 'E.G. Hill']

'Rio Rita' -- See 'Worattack'

Rio Samba™ -- See 'Jacrite'

'Ripaud' ('Audrey's Rose') F, m, 2003, Rippetoe, Robert Neil; flowers deep mauve, reverse white, 2¼ in., dbl., borne mostly solitary, intense fragrance; foliage medium size, medium green, semi-glossy, disease-resistant; prickles small, slightly hooked, brown, few; growth bushy, short (2 ft.); bedding, hedges; ['Lilac Charm' × unknown]; intr. 2002

'Ripbon' ('Bonnie Rosalie') F, w, 2006, Rippetoe, Robert Neil; flowers white-pink edge, reverse white, red stamens, 2-2½ in., single, borne mostly solitary, moderate clove fragrance; foliage medium size, medium green, matte; prickles medium, slightly hooked, red brown, moderate; growth bushy, medium (3 × 3 ft.); landscape, bedding; ['Sweet Vivien' × unknown]; intr. 2006

'Ripbutter' ('Buttercream') Ch, ab, 2003, Rippetoe, Robert Neil; flowers light yellow, often deep yellow in cool weather, fading to creamy white, 2¼ in., dbl., borne mostly solitary, no fragrance; foliage medium size, medium green, semi-glossy; prickles medium, slightly curved, brown, few; growth compact, medium (3 ft.); hedge, specimen, standards; ['Mutabilis' × unknown (probably selfed)]

'Ripcal' ('Callista') S, w, 2005, Rippetoe, Robert Neil; flowers white, becoming pink and apricot in cool weather, 3-5 in., full, borne mostly solitary, intense fragrance; foliage medium size, medium green, semi-glossy; prickles medium, straight, tan, moderate; growth bushy, tall (4-6 ft.); ['Sweet Afton' × Abraham Darby®]; intr. 2005

'Ripchase' ('Steve Chase') F, ob, 2006, Rippetoe, Robert Neil; flowers creamy, blushing orange, aging to mostly orange, 3-4 in., full, borne mostly solitary; good repeat; foliage medium size, dark green, glossy; prickles large, slightly curved, tan, moderate; growth bushy, medium (2½ ft.); bedding, exhibition, hedging; hips few; ['Little Darling' × unknown]; intr. 2006

'Ripcher' ('Cherry Drop') Ch, rb, 2003, Rippetoe, Robert Neil; flowers light red, 2 in., very full, borne in small clusters, moderate cherry-candy fragrance; foliage medium size, dark green, semi-glossy; prickles medium, hooked, brown, moderate; growth spreading, angular, medium (3-4 ft.); hedge, specimen, bedding; [sport of 'Serratipetala']; intr. 2002

'Ripcon' ('Pink Confection') B, mp, 2007, Rippetoe, Robert Neil; flowers 2 in., very full, borne mostly solitary; foliage medium green, matte; prickles small, sickle, tan, moderate; growth compact, short (18 in.); containers, short hedges; ['Louise Odier' × unknown]; intr. 2006

'Ripdor' ('Petite Perle d'Or') Min, ab, 2007, Rippetoe, Robert Neil; flowers ¾ in., dbl., borne in small clusters; foliage small, medium green, semi-glossy; no prickle; growth bushy, dense, twiggy, short (12 in.); border hedge, containers; ['Perle d'Or' × 'Cinderella']; intr. 2006

'Ripelise' ('Fur Elise') S, pb, 2006, Rippetoe, Robert Neil; flowers semi-dbl., borne mostly solitary, strong old rose fragrance; foliage medium size, matte; prickles medium, slightly curved, tan, few; stems very short; growth spreading, medium (3 ft.); no hips; ['Reveille Dijonnais' × unknown]; intr. 2006

'Ripjune' ('June Anne') Noisette, mp, 2004, Robert Neil Rippetoe; flowers medium pink, fading to light pink, 1 in., very full, borne in small clusters, intense fragrance; foliage medium size, medium green,; prickles ¼ in., sickle-shaped; growth spreading, tall (8-10 ft.); pillar, climber; ['Champney's Pink Cluster' × 'Katherine Zeimet']; intr. 2004

'Riplady' ('Sophisticated Lady') HT, ab, 2006, Rippetoe, Robert, Neil; flowers single, borne mostly solitary, strong fruity fragrance; foliage large, dark green, semi-glossy; prickles medium, straight, tan, moderate; growth bushy, 2½ ft.; garden decorative, cutting, exhibit; ['Just Joey' × unknown]; intr. 2006

'Riplila' ('Lila Banks') S, m, 2003, Rippetoe, Robert Neil; flowers light mauve, reverse deeper mauve, 2 in., single, borne mostly solitary; good repeat; foliage medium size, medium green, semi-glossy, puckered, banksia-like; prickles small, straight, brown, few; growth compact, short (2 ft.); specimen, hedge, bedding; ['Lilac Charm' × (R. banksiae alba-plena × Old Blush)]

'Ripmir' ('Rancho Mirage') F, mr, 2005, Rippetoe, Robert Neil; flowers small, single, borne in large clusters, no fragrance; foliage medium size, dark green, glossy; prickles moderate, medium, hooked, light tan; growth compact, short (2 ft.); bedding; [Dortmund® × unknown]; intr. 2005

'Ripples' F, m, 1971, LeGrice; flowers lilac-lavender, wavy petals, large, 18 petals, cupped, slight fragrance; foliage small, green, matte; [('Tantau's Surprise' × 'Marjorie LeGrice') × (seedling × 'Africa Star')]

'Ripriver' ('Riverbanks') S, mp, 2005, Rippetoe, Robert Neil; flowers semi-dbl., borne in small clusters, moderate fragrance; foliage medium size, medium green, semi-glossy; prickles moderate, medium size, straight, tan; growth upright, medium (4 ft.); ['Antoine Rivoire' × 'Lila Banks']

'Ripspring' ('Palm Springs') S, mr, 2006, Rippetoe, Robert, Neil; flowers heat-resistant, long-lasting, 2-2½ in., single, borne mostly solitary; foliage medium size, dark green, glossy; prickles medium -large, slightly curved, tan, moderate p; growth bushy, 3 ft.; hedge, shrub, bedding; [Dortmund® × unknown]; intr. 2006

'Ripwar' ('Ivory Warrior') S, w, 2006, Rippetoe, Robert Neil; flowers single, borne mostly solitary, moderate musky fragrance; foliage medium size, semi-glossy; prickles small to medium, slightly curved, tan, moderate; growth upright, 3 × 4 ft.; ['Country Dancer' × unknown]; intr. 2006

'Rise 'n' Shine' ('Golden Meillandina', 'Golden Sunblaze') Min, my, 1977, Moore, Ralph S.; bud long, pointed; flowers rich medium yellow, 1½ in., 35 petals, high-centered, borne singly and in small clusters, moderate sweet tea rose fragrance; recurrent; foliage small, leathery, semi-glossy to matte; prickles moderate, slender, hooked downward, brown; bushy, upright growth; PP4231; ['Little Darling' × 'Yellow Magic']

'Rise 'n' Shine, Climbing -- See 'Morkinshine'

'Rising Star' -- See 'Hareast'

'Rising Star' -- See 'Jalstar'

'Rising Sun' HT, rb, 1924, Hicks; bud long, pointed; flowers rich copper, base old-gold, cactus dahlia form, large

'Risqué' Gr, rb, 1985, Weeks, O.L.; bud short, pointed; flowers medium red, light yellow reverse, 4 in., 20-28 petals, high-centered, borne singly and several together, no fragrance; recurrent; foliage medium size, dark green, semi-glossy; prickles very few, flat, pointed down, reddish-brown; upright (4-4½ ft.), slightly spreading growth; PP5828; ['Bob Hope' × seedling]

'Rita' F, mp, 1960, Fryers Nursery, Ltd.; flowers rich pink, dbl., borne in large clusters; foliage glossy; vigorous growth; ['Karl Herbst' × 'Pinocchio']

'Rita' F, rb, Vidal

'Rita Applegate' -- See 'Tinrita'

Rita Barbera™ -- See 'Sophia Renaissance'

'Rita Bugnet' HRg, w, Bugnet; intr. 1958

'Rita Jackson' HT, rb, 1973, Jackson, F.; flowers striped carmine and yellow, large, dbl., high-centered, borne mostly singly, slight fragrance; stems long; upright, bushy growth; [sport of 'Tzigane']; intr. 1964

Rita Levi Montalcini® -- See 'Barlev'

'Rita MacNeil' -- See 'Macchome'

'Rita Perfumella® HT, lp, Meilland; flowers light buff-colored pink, dbl., high-centered, borne usually singly; recurrent; florist rose; intr. 2005

'Rita Sammons' ('Justine Silva') Pol, pb, 1925, Clarke, B.; flowers deep rose-pink, opening pink, edged lighter; [sport of 'Cécile Brunner']

'Ritausma' ('Polareis') HRg, lp, Rieksta; bud slim; flowers soft blush and light pink, deeper in the center, medium, dbl., high-centered, moderate fragrance; foliage glossy; vigorous, arching (1 × 1 m.) growth; winter hardy; [R. rugosa plena × 'Abelzieds']; registered incorrectly as Polareis; intr. 1963

'Rite Brite' -- See 'Gelrite'

Rittenhouse™ -- See 'Wilhkpk'

'Ritter Taler' HT, rb

'Ritter von Barmstede' HKor, dp, 1959, Kordes; flowers very dark pink, lighter reverse white eye, 2 in., 20 petals, borne in clusters of 30-40; foliage light green, glossy; vigorous (10-15 ft.) growth; [R. × kordesii × a polyantha]

'Ritz' LCl, mr, 1955, Horvath; flowers velvety red, 3 in., 11 petals, borne in clusters; recurrent bloom; vigorous (8-9 ft.) growth; [R. setigera × unknown]; intr. 1955

'Ritz' F, mr, Gaujard; flowers bright scarlet, large, 16 petals; foliage dark, glossy, vigorous, well branched growth; intr. 1961

'Riva Ligure' HT, dp, 1947, San Remo Exp. Sta.; bud pointed; flowers velvety carmine, 24-35 petals; foliage dark; vigorous, bushy growth; [seedling × 'Crimson Glory']

'Rival' HT, mr, 1954, Fletcher; flowers cherry-scarlet, loosely formed, 4-5 in., flat; foliage bronze; free growth; ['Southport' × 'The Rev. W.S. Crawford']; intr. 1954

'Rival de Paestum' T, w, 1841, Béluze; bud tinged pink; flowers white, base blush and ivory, dbl.; foliage dark; moderate growth; often classed as a China

'River City Jubilee' -- See 'Judriv'

'Riverbanks' -- See 'Ripriver'

'Riverdance' -- See 'Kenfine'

'Riverdance' Min, pb, Laver, Keith G.; bud pointed; flowers white with pink stripes, dbl., high-centered; foliage dark green, semi-glossy; growth to 12-15 in.; intr. 1998

'Riverina Sunset' T, mp, Hay

'Rivers' HP, mr, 1832, Laffay, M.; flowers bright crimson, large, dbl., borne in corymbs; recurrent bloom; vigorous growth

'Rivers' George IV' ('George IV', 'King George IV') HCh, dr, 1830, Rivers; flowers vivid crimson, shaded with dark purple, dbl., loosely cupped; non-recurrent; stems branching shoots tinged with purple; vigorous growth; ['thought to be Damask' × R. chinensis]

'Rivers' Musk Cluster' HMsk, mp, before 1846, Rivers; flowers rosy buff, small, dbl., intense fragrance

'Rivers' Single Crimson Moss' ('Single Crimson Moss Rose') M, dr, before 1838, Rivers; flowers brilliant crimson, changing to purplish crimson, large, single to semi-dbl.; foliage dark green

'River's South Bank' -- See 'Jujnoberejnaia'

'Rivers' Super Tuscan' -- See 'Tuscany Superb'

'Riverview' -- See 'Riverview Centennial'

'Riverview Centennial' ('Riverview') HT, dr; flowers very dark red, large, dbl.; strong, tall growth; intr. 1980

'Riviera' -- See 'Jacsak'

'Riviera' LCl, mr

'Riviera' HT, or, 1939, Dot, Pedro; bud globular, yellow; flowers orange-scarlet, reverse lighter, base yellow, open, large, dbl., cupped; foliage glossy, wrinkled, dark; very vigorous, bushy growth; PP378; ['Luis Brinas' × 'Catalonia']; intr. 1940

'Riviere de Diamant' -- See 'Brisiness'

'Rivierenhof' F, pb, DVP Melle; flowers pink and red, large, borne in clusters; growth strong, branching; ['Melglory' × 'Guirlande d'Amour']; intr. 1998

'Road to Freedom' -- See 'Franlac'

'Roadman' HT, w, 1977, Ota, Kaichiro; bud pointed; flowers near white, 6 in., 40-50 petals, high-centered; foliage leathery; upright growth; ['Hawaii' × 'Kordes' Perfecta']; intr. 1974

'Roaming' HT, dp, 1970, Sanday, John; flowers reddish-pink shades, pointed, large, 24 petals; foliage green, matte; ['Vera Dalton' × 'Tropicana']

'Roar!' -- See 'Garlion'

Rob Roy® F, dr, 1970, Cocker; flowers scarlet-crimson, 4½ in., 30 petals, hybrid tea, borne several together; free-flowering; foliage glossy; vigorous growth; ['Evelyn Fison' × 'Wendy Cussons']

'Robbie Burns' -- See 'Ausburn'

'Robe de Neige' -- See 'LLX8819'

'Robe de Soie' -- See 'LLX8818'

'Robe d'Eté' F, or, 1979, Lens; flowers salmon-orange, 3-3½ in., 22-24 petals, high-centered; foliage bronze; bushy, upright growth; [('Chatelaine' × 'Mannequin') × ('Montezuma' × 'Floradora')]; intr. 1966

'Robe Fleuri' -- See 'Lenverba'

'Robe Rose' -- See 'LLX8817'

'Robert' P, pb, 1856, Robert; flowers carmine, marbled white

'Robert Aliano' -- See 'Wilalno'

'Robert Betten' HT, mr, 1920, Schmidt, J.C.; flowers clear dark carmine-red, not turning blue, dbl.; ['Frau Karl Druschki' × 'Corallina']

'Robert Bland' S, dp, 1960, Wright, Percy H.; flowers open, small, dbl.; non-recurrent; foliage richgreen; thornless; vigorous, bushy growth; quite hardy; [(('Hansa' × R. macounii × 'Betty Bland') × (R. blanda × Betty Bland)]

'Robert Burns' HT, mr; flowers scarlet, dbl., rounded, moderate fragrance; strong (3 ft.), healthy growth; intr. 2005

'Robert Clements' S, ob, Clements, John; bud long and pointed; flowers deep apricot-blush overlayed with orange-red, 4 in., 20 petals, high-centered, moderate sweet old rose fragrance; foliage bright green, glossy; well foliaged (3½ ft. × 3 ft.) growth; PPAF; intr. 2003

'Robert Cotton' HT, w, 1968, Golik; bud ovoid; flowers white, edges flushed pink, large, dbl.; foliage glossy, serrated, leathery; moderate growth; ['Marcia Stanhope' × 'Karl Herbst']

'Robert Craig' HWich, my, 1903, Hoopes & Thomas; bud yellow-apricot; flowers yellow, center darker; [R. wichurana × 'Beauté Inconstante']

'Robert de Brie' HP, m, 1860, Granger; flowers violet-pink with white stripes, large, dbl.

'Robert Dubol' HT, mr, 1946, Sauvageot, H.; flowers warm orient red, stamens golden, very dbl., high-centered

'Robert Duncan' HP, pb, 1897, Dickson, A.; flowers purplish pink, sometimes flamed brilliant red, well-formed, large, 70 petals, moderate Damask fragrance; repeat bloom; vigorous growth

'Robert F. Kennedy' HT, mr, 1968, Takatori, Yoshiho; flowers scarlet, high-centered, borne singly, intense fragrance; foliage dark green, semi-glossy; very vigorous, upright growth; ['Chrysler Imperial' × 'Ena Harkness']

'Robert Fortune' M, m, 1853, Robert; flowers striped lilac and pale violet, 2½ in., dbl., globular

'Robert Huey' HT, dp, 1911, Dickson, A.; bud long, pointed; flowers carmine edged lighter, bluing slightly, dbl.; moderate growth

'Robert le Diable' HGal, m, before 1885; flowers scarlet-pink aging to deep purple, center often green, full, moderate fragrance; low (3 ft.), lax growth; sometimes classed as C; perhaps as early as 1831 (see Beales, and Prince)

'Robert Léopold' M, pb, 1941, Buatois; flowers salmon-flesh-pink edged light carmine, large, dbl., loose, moderate fragrance; remontant; upright (4 ft.) growth

'Robert Perpétuel' P, m, 1856, Robert; flowers violet-pink, medium, dbl., rosette when open; growth medium

'Robert Pineau' F, ob, Pineau; intr. 2000

'Robert Scott' HT, mp, 1901, Scott; flowers medium pink, edges flesh pink, very large, dbl.; ['Merveille de Lyon' × 'Belle Siebrecht']

'Robert Snowden' -- See 'Worcarrot'

'Robert Stolz' F, dr, deRuiter; flowers medium, semi-dbl.; intr. 1974

'Roberta' -- See 'Albgiovi'

'Roberta' -- See 'Ausblush'

'Roberta Bondar' LCl, my, 1993, Fleming, Joyce L.; flowers medium, full, borne 1-8 per truss, moderate fragrance; foliage large, dark green, semi-glossy; climbing (6-8 ft.) growth; [King's Ransom® × 'Buff Beauty']; named for first Canadian woman in space; intr. 1993

Roberto Capucci® HT, lp, Barni; flowers light pink deepening toward the center, 10-12 cm., full, old fashioned, cupped, moderate fragrance; foliage very large, glossy, light green; growth to 4 ft.; hips globular, orange, medium; [Antico Amore® × 'Letizia']; intr. 2001

'Robertson Garden' F, op, Kordes; flowers roses salmon-pink, dbl., borne in clusters, slight sweet fragrance; recurrent; foliage leathery, disease-resistant; low to medium growth; intr. 2005

'Robespierre' Pol, pb, 1976, Delforge, S.; bud full; flowers very dbl., 88 petals, cupped, moderate fragrance; foliage bronze; intr. 1975

'Robi' -- See 'Morrobi'

'Robin' -- See 'Resrob'

'Robin' Min, mr, 1957, Dot, Pedro; bud urn-shaped; flowers rich red, 1¼ in., 65 petals, flat, borne in clusters of 15; foliage leathery, green, matte; vigorous, dwarf (12 in.), bushy growth; PP1663; ['Perla de Montserrat' × 'Perla de Alcañada']; intr. 1957

Robin Alonso™ -- See 'Alorobin'

'Robin Beard's Rugosa' HRg, dp, Beard; flowers dark magenta pink with small white flash at center, creamy yellow stamens, 5 in., semi-dbl., cupped to flat, intense fragrance; recurrent; growth to 4-5 ft.; ['Roseraie de l'Hay' × unknown]; intr. 2003

'Robin des Bois' -- See 'Robin Hood'

'Robin Hood' HP, mr, before 1850; flowers bright cherry red, large, full, globular

'Robin Hood' HT, mr, E.G. Hill, Co.; flowers soft bright rosy scarlet, changing to bright scarlet-crimson, dbl., intense fragrance; intr. 1912

'Robin Hood' ('Robin des Bois') HMsk, mr, Pemberton; flowers cherry-red, single, borne in large clusters; recurrent bloom; vigorous (4-5 ft.), dense, compact growth; [seedling × 'Miss Edith Cavell']; intr. 1927

'Robin Red Breast' -- See 'Interrob'

'Robin Redbreast' -- See 'Interrob'

'Robina' -- See 'Korxenna'

'Robinette' HMult, rb, 1943, Moore, Ralph S.; flowers amaranth-red, white eye, open, small, single, borne in large clusters, intense fragrance; foliage glossy; growth to 10-12 ft.; ['Hiawatha' × 'Hiawatha']

'Robur' -- See 'Red Empress'

'Robusta' B, mr, 1877, Soupert & Notting; flowers velvety red, aging to purple, large, full, borne in small clusters

'Robusta' Cl T, mp

Robusta® -- See 'Korgosa'

'Roby' HMult, rb, 1912, Guillot, P.; bud deep pink; flowers rose red, yellow center, 6-7 cm., single, borne in medium to large clusters, moderate fragrance; ['Léonie Lamesch' × 'Leuchtstern']

'Roccana Diane' -- See 'Kirdex'

'Roche Centenary' -- See 'Dicvintage'

'Roche du Theil' -- See 'Cocgold'

'Rochefort' HT, ab, 1936, Mallerin, C.; flowers large, dbl., intense fruity fragrance; foliage leathery; vigorous growth; PP191; ['Mrs Pierre S. duPont' × 'Charles P. Kilham']

'Rochelle Hudson' HT, rb, 1937, Moore, Ralph S.; bud long, pointed; flowers carmine, base yellow, orange undertone deepening with age, semi-dbl., slight fruity fragrance; foliage dark; vigorous growth; ['Isobel' × 'Mme Edouard Herriot']

'Rochemenier Village' -- See 'Britannia'

'Rochester' F, ab, 1934, Nicolas; flowers buff, reverse orange-carmine, medium, dbl., moderate fragrance; foliage leathery; vigorous, bushy growth; PP131; ['Echo' × 'Rev. F. Page-Roberts']

'Rochester Cathedral' -- See 'Harroffen'

Rocio Elias® -- See 'Fetrone'

'Rock 'n' Roll' -- See 'Macfirwal'

Rock & Roll™ -- See 'Wekgobnez'

'Rock Creek' -- See 'Gardorty'

'Rockabye Baby' Min, dy, Dickson; flowers non-fading yellow, full, cupped, then pompon; free-flowering; foliage dark green, glossy; bushy, compact (20 in.) growth; intr. 2006

'Rocket' HT, mr, 1935, Nicolas; flowers brilliant scarlet, reverse crimson, large, dbl., high-centered, intense fragrance; foliage leathery, dark, bronze; very vigorous growth; PP171; ['Dame Edith Helen' × 'Scorcher']

'Rocket' -- See 'Raketa'

'Rocketeer' -- See 'Chewallop'

Rockin' Robin™ -- See 'Wekboroco'

'Rockwall Sesquicentennial' S, lp, 2005, Shoup, George Michael; flowers very full, borne mostly solitary, moderate fragrance; remontant; foliage medium size, medium green, semi-glossy; numerous prickles; growth compact, medium (3-4 ft.); containers; [('Carefree Beauty' × 'Granny Grimmetts') × 'City of York']; intr. 1999

Rocky™ -- See 'Mackepa'

'Rocky Top' -- See 'Weltop'

'Rococo' F, mr, 1964, McGredy, Sam IV; flowers scarlet, 3 in., 15 petals, borne in clusters; free growth; [Moulin Rouge® × 'Fire Opal']

'Rod Stillman' HT, lp, 1948, Hamilton; flowers light pink, base flushed orange, large, 35 petals, intense melons and peaches fragrance; foliage dark green; vigorous, tall growth; ['Ophelia' × 'Editor McFarland']

'Röd Summerwind' -- See 'Red Summerwind'

Roddy MacMillan' -- See 'Cocared'

'Rodeo' F, or, 1960, Kordes, R.; flowers bright scarlet, 3 in., dbl., borne in clusters of up to 10; foliage light green; bushy, low growth; ['Obergärtner Wiebicke' × 'Spartan']; intr. 1960

Rodeo Drive™ -- See 'Arocore'

Rodeo Kordana® Min, or, Kordes; flowers dbl., high-centered, borne singly and in small clusters; pot rose

'Rödhätte' ('Red Riding Hood') F, mr, 1912, Poulsen, D.T.; flowers clear cherry-red, large, semi-dbl., borne in large clusters; foliage rich green; bushy, compact growth; ['Mme Norbert Levavasseur' × 'Richmond or Liberty']

'Rödhätte, Climbing' Cl F, mr, 1925, Grootendorst, F.J.

'Rodheo' HT, rb

'Rodin' S, dp, Meilland; flowers clear, deep pink, aging lighter, semi-dbl., shallow cup, borne in clusters; free-flowering; foliage very disease-resistant; growth to 60-70 cm.; descended in a direct line from Knock Out; intr. 2005

'Rodin' -- See 'Meidinro'

'Rödinghausen' S, mr, Noack, Werner; flowers brilliant orange-red, lavender petal bases, slight fragrance; recurrent; hips brilliant orange; intr. 1987

'Rodovrerosen' -- See 'Poulsen's Fairy'

'Rody' ('Viking') S, mr, Tantau; flowers raspberry red, 2 in., dbl., borne in clusters, intense fragrance; free-flowering; foliage dark green, glossy; low (2 ft.), spreading growth; intr. 1995

'Roedean' -- See 'Bencamelia'

'Roelanda' ('Leana') HT, w; intr. 1993

'Roelof Buisman' HT, mr, 1966, Kordes, R.; bud ovoid; flowers bright pure red, well-formed, large; vigorous, upright, bushy growth; intr. 1964

'Roemer's Hip Happy' S, mp, 2005, Shoup, George Michael; flowers small, single, shallow cup, borne in small clusters, moderate fragrance; foliage medium size, dark green, semi-glossy; few prickles; bushy, medium (4 ft.) growth; containers, landscape; hips very numerous; [('Carefree Beauty' × Heritage®) × 'Iceberg']; intr. 2000

'Roger Boudou' Pol, mr, 1957, Privat; flowers very bright red; ['Lafayette' × unknown]

'Roger Lambelin' HP, rb, 1890, Schwartz, Vve.; flowers bright crimson fading maroon, petals margined white, very distinct, 30 petals, petals fringed; recurrent bloom; vigorous growth; [sport of 'Fisher Holmes']

'Roger Lambelin Striped' HP, rb, 1953, Hennessey; flowers deep maroon to pink stripes on white ground; recurrent

The Official Registry and Checklist — Rosa 637

bloom; [sport of 'Roger Lambelin']
'Roger Secretrain'   LCl, Moreira da Silva, A.
'Rogscriv' ('Natural Beauty') HT, pb, 1999, Scrivens, Len; flowers pink/apricot blend, reverse pink blend, 3 in., full, rosette, borne in small clusters, intense fragrance; foliage medium size, medium green, semi-glossy; few prickles; compact, medium (3 ft.) growth; ['Pretty Lady' × 'Silver Jubilee']; intr. 1998
'Rogslav' ('Penkala Slavoljub') HT, ab, 1995, Rogin, Josip; flowers apricot-orange striped, medium, full, borne mostly singly; foliage medium size, dark green, semi-glossy; few prickles; medium (100 cm.), bushy growth; [sport of 'Ambassador']; intr. 1995
'Rogzag' ('Zagreb') HT, pb, 1995, Rogin, Josip; flowers pink striped, medium, full, borne mostly singly, intense fragrance; foliage large, medium green, matte; few prickles; tall (150 cm.), upright growth; [sport of 'Eiffel Tower']
'Roi Albert'   HT, pb, 1925, Klettenberg-Londes; bud long, pointed; flowers bright carmine-rose, center tinted scarlet; [('Laurent Carle' × unknown) × 'Mme Abel Chatenay']
'Roi Alexandre' ('King Alexander I', 'S. M. Alexander I') HT, ob, 1937, Gaujard; flowers coppery orange, tinted salmon, over large, dbl.; foliage leathery, glossy, bronze; very vigorous growth
'Roi d'Angleterre' -- See 'Duc de Berry'
'Roi de Nains'   Min, mr
'Roi de Perse' -- See 'Petite Junon de Hollande'
'Roi de Rome' -- See 'Enfant de France'
'Roi de Siam' ('Le Roi de Siam') Cl T, lp, 1825, Laffay, M.; flowers pale pink and cream, large, semi-dbl., moderate tea fragrance; cultivar now in commerce is probably not correct
'Roi d'Écosse' -- See 'King of Scots'
'Roi des Aunes' ('Erlkönig') S, dp, 1885, Geschwind, R.; flowers carmine tinted red, fading to medium pink, 5-6 cm., full, globular, borne in medium to large clusters; non-recurrent; very vigorous growth; ['De la Grifferaie' × unknown]
'Roi des Bengales'   F, rb, 1958, Arles; flowers grenadine-red; vigorous, low growth; [('Hermosa' × 'Gruss an Teplitz') × 'Independence']
'Roi des Bordures' -- See 'Border King'
'Roi des Cramoisis'   Ch, mr; flowers bright red, cupped
'Roi des Pays-Bas' ('Impératrice de Hollande', 'Merveille du Monde') D, dp, before 1826; flowers deep pink, large, dbl., cupped; foliage very large; from Holland
'Roi des Pourpres' ('Renoncule Noirâtre') HGal, dr, before 1817, Descemet; bud round, small; flowers dark crimson-purple, small, very dbl., pompon
'Roi des Pourpres' -- See 'Mogador'
'Roi des Rois'   F, Delbard-Chabert; intr. 1955

'Roi d'Italie'   T, w; flowers flesh white, medium, full
'Roi Maximilian de Bavière' HP, m, 1857, Touvais; flowers velvety purple, shaded darker, medium, full
'Roi Soleil'   HT, my, 1962, Dorieux; bud long, pointed; flowers citron-yellow; very vigorous growth; ['Peace' × ('Independence' × unknown)]
'Róisín Ruddle' -- See 'Kendixie'
Roklea®   HT, ob, 1985, Tantau, Math.; flowers bright orange, large, 20 petals, high-centered, moderate fragrance; foliage large, dark, semi-glossy; upright growth; greenhouse rose; intr. 1975
'Rokoko' -- See 'Showy Pavement'
Rokoko® -- See 'Tanokor'
'Roland'   F, ob, 1961, Leenders, J.; flowers salmon-orange-red; low growth; ['Karl Weinhausen' × 'Independence']
Roland Garros® -- See 'Brigarold'
'Roletta'   F, op, GPG Bad Langensalza; flowers salmon-orange/pink, large, dbl.; intr. 1983
'Roller Coaster' -- See 'Macminmo'
'Roma'   Min, mr, NIRP Intl.; flowers full, cupped, borne in clusters, slight fragrance; recurrent; foliage dark green; bushy (12 - 24 in.) growth; intr. 2007
'Roma'   HT, op, Spronk; [sport of 'Duet']; intr. 1970
'Roma di Notte'   HT, Zandri, R.; intr. 1980
'Romaine Desprez'   B, mr, before 1835, Desprez; flowers crimson, aging to light red, medium
'Román'   HT, mp, 1961, Dot, Simon; flowers nilsson pink, becoming hermosa pink, large, 35 petals; ['Asturias' × 'Rosa de Friera']
Roman™ ('Roman Palace') S, op, Poulsen; flowers orange pink and orange blend, 8-10 cm., full, high-centered, no fragrance; foliage dark green, glossy; bushy, low (40-60 cm.) growth; intr. 2001
'Roman'   HT, rb, Keisei; intr. 2007
'Roman Festival'   F, pb, 1968, Williams, J. Benjamin; bud ovoid; flowers coral, base yellow, medium, high-centered, borne in clusters; foliage dark, glossy; vigorous, low, compact growth; [Queen Elizabeth® × 'Sumatra']
'Roman Herzog'   F, or, Noack; flowers shiny red, non-fading, 8 cm., dbl., high-centered, borne in clusters, slight fragrance; recurrent; growth to 70-90 cm.; intr. 1999
'Roman Holiday'   F, rb, 1966, Lindquist; bud ovoid; flowers orange turning blood-red, base yellow, medium, 28 petals, high-centered, borne in clusters, moderate fragrance; foliage dark, leathery; vigorous, bushy, low growth; PP2725; [('Pinkie' × 'Independence') × 'Circus']
'Roman Palace' -- See 'Poulac005(N)'
'Roman Triumph'   F, mr, 1978, Harkness; flowers large, 13 petals; foliage glossy; upright, bushy growth; ['Jove' × 'City of Leeds']; intr. 1977

'Romana'   HT, or, Roman, G., and Wagner, S.; flowers deep orange-red, 60-80 petals, high-centered; continuous bloom; foliage large, medium green, semi-glossy; ['Rosabunda' × 'Landora']; intr. 2003
'Romana'   HT, rb, Vecera, L.
'Romana'   HT, rb, 1938, Ringdahl; bud long, pointed; flowers rose-red to light purple, open, large, dbl.; foliage leathery, glossy, dark; very vigorous growth; PP295; [sport of 'Better Times']
'Romance, Climbing'   Cl HT, lp, 1933, Beckwith; flowers shell-pink, fading to pale blush, large, semi-dbl to dbl., intense sweet fragrance; vigorous, climbing growth; [sport of 'Isa']
Romance®   HT, op, Tantau; flowers soft orange and pink, very large, double, high-centered, borne mostly singly; recurrent; stems medium to long; florist rose; intr. 2007
'Romance'   HT, my, 1931, Towill; bud long, pointed; flowers golden yellow, shading toward lemon, open, large, dbl.; foliage thick; very vigorous growth; RULED EXTINCT 11/82; ['Souv. de Claudius Pernet' × ('Buttercup' × unknown)]
'Romance' -- See 'Jacrom'
'Romance' -- See 'Tanezamor'
'Romance Mikado'   F, pb, Tantau; flowers pink and cream blend, borne in clusters; florist rose
'Romane Estenou'   S, op, Gilet; intr. 2005
'Romanina'   F, Zandri, R.; intr. 1974
Romantic™ ('Romantic Palace') S, mp, 1999, Poulsen; bud ovoid to globular; flowers medium pink, 3 in., 40-50 petals, borne 1 - 4 per stem, slight fragrance; free-flowering; foliage dark green, glossy; prickles moderate, straight to curved downward; bushy, upright (2 - 2½ ft.) growth; PP11540; [sport of Queen Margrethe™]; intr. 1998
'Romantic Angel'   HT, lp, Imai; intr. 2004
'Romantic Curiosa'   HT, yb; florist rose
'Romantic Days' -- See 'Meiparnin'
'Romantic Dreams' -- See 'Marie Curie'
'Romantic Fragrance' -- See 'Meisocrat'
'Romantic Hedgerose' -- See 'Korworm'
'Romantic Moments' -- See 'Meirokoi'
'Romantic Occasion' -- See 'Meisardan'
'Romantic Palace' -- See 'Poulmanti'
'Romantic Panarosa'   S, ab, Kordes; bud pointed; flowers creamy apricot with touch of pink, large, full, rosette; vigorous, tall growth; intr. 2004
Romantic Roadrunner®   HRg, dp, Uhl; flowers strong pink, large, dbl., rosette, intense fragrance; recurrent; foliage dark green, leathery; upright (70 cm.), but bushy, spreading growth; intr. 2004
'Romantic Ruffles'   F, mr; intr. 2002
'Romantic Seranade' -- See 'Meibrinpay'
Romantic Spire™   HT, w, Kordes; flowers ivory white with touch of pink, large , full; recurrent; strong, tall growth; intr. 2006
'Romantic Sunrise' -- See 'Meihaitoil'
'Romantica'   HT, mp, 1962, Meilland, Mrs.

Marie-Louise; bud oval; flowers phlox-pink, large, 40 petals, high-centered, slight fragrance; foliage leathery, glossy; very vigorous, upright growth; [Baccará® × 'White Knight']; forcing variety

Romantica 76® HT, op

'Romantique Meillandina' -- See 'Meidanclar'

'Romany' F, op, 1965, McGredy, Sam IV; flowers salmon, well-formed, large, borne in clusters; free growth; [Orangeade® × 'Mischief']

'Romanze' -- See 'Tanezamor'

'Rome Glory' ('Gloire de Rome', 'Gloria di Roma', 'Glory of Rome') HT, mr, 1937, Aicardi, D.; bud ovoid; flowers scarlet, reverse cerise, 4-5 in., 55 petals, globular, moderate fragrance; recurrent; vigorous, bushy growth; PP304; ['Dame Edith Helen' × 'Sensation']

'Rome Glory, Climbing' Cl HT, mr

'Romeo' -- See 'Mactual'

'Romeo' HT, yb, 1918, Therkildsen; flowers Indian yellow, suffused coppery pink; [('Edith Part' × unknown) × 'Ophelia']

'Romeo' HWich, dr, Easlea; flowers deep red, small, dbl., high-centered, borne in small clusters; vigorous, climbing growth; intr. 1919

'Romeo' ('Mernieuw') F , or, Nieuwkoop, Jacob; flowers salmon-orange-red; PP4626; [sport of 'Mercedes']; intr. 1979

Romeo® F, or, Barni, Enrico; flowers bright geranium-red, 4-5 cm., 20-25 petals, high-centered, slight fragrance; foliage medium size, light green, matte; growth to 2-3 ft.; ['Feeling' × 'Mathias Meilland']; intr. 2000

'Romina' -- See 'Tananim'

'Romstar' HT, dr, Wagner, S.; bud long; flowers medium red, velvety, high centered, 34 petals, moderate fragrance; foliage medium size, medium-green, semi-glossy; ['Baccara' × 'Coronado']; intr. 1991

'Romy' HT, w, Select Roses, B.V.

Romy Schneider® -- See 'Orared'

'Ron West' HT, pb, 1985, West, Ronald; flowers white with deep pink petal edges; [sport of Admiral Rodney]

'Ronald George Kent' -- See 'Brandypink'

'Ronald Healy' HT, pb, 1932, Dobbie; bud long, pointed; flowers old-rose, shaded salmon and yellow, dbl., high-centered; foliage glossy; bushy growth

'Ronald McDonald' -- See 'Tommac'

Ronald Reagan™ -- See 'Jactanre'

'Ronald Tooke' HT, dr, 1927, Morse; flowers deep blackish crimson; [sport of 'Col. Oswald Fitzgerald']

'Ronald William Pearce' F, ab, Fryer; flowers light peach and warm apricot blend , double, high-centered, borne singly and several together, moderate fragrance; recurrent; foliage glossy, disease-resistant; neat (85 cm.) growth; intr. 2007

'Roncalli' S, rb, Noack, Werner; intr. 1997

Ronda ™ -- See 'Ronda Palace'

'Ronda Palace' (Ronda ™) MinFl, mr, Poulsen; flowers medium red, 5-8 cm., semi-dbl., no fragrance; foliage dark; growth bushy, 60-100 cm.; intr. 2005

'Ronde Endiablée' F, or, 1963, Combe; flowers geranium-red, edged darker, large, semi-dbl.; foliage dark, glossy; moderate growth

'Rondo' HT, or, 1955, Tantau, Math.; bud ovoid; flowers 3½-4 in., 15-20 petals, high-centered, moderate fruity fragrance; foliage dark, leathery; vigorous, upright, compact growth; PP1454; ['Danzig' × ('Crimson Glory' × ('Baby Chateau' × R. roxburghii))]; intr. 1955

'Rongotai Rose' S, dr, Ball; intr. 1995

'Ronja' -- See 'Mary Hayley Bell'

'Ronny Temmer' F, mp, 1976, Delforge, S.; bud ovoid; flowers large, 44 petals, moderate fragrance; intr. 1974

'Ron's Love' -- See 'Jayrolo'

'Ronsard' HFt, rb, 1932, Gaujard; bud long, pointed, yellowish edged red; flowers brilliant red, reverse yellow and cream, semi-dbl., cupped; sometimes recurrent; foliage leathery, dark; bushy, compact growth; PP284; ['Conrad Ferdinand Meyer' × R. foetida bicolor]

'Rooi Rose' -- See 'Korhood'

'Rooibus Rose' S, dr, Delbard; flowers unfading crimson red , classic hybrid tea; recurrent

'Rookie' Min, w, Fischer; [sport of 'Giggles']; similar to Giggles except for bloom color; intr. 2000

'Roos Sonder Grense' -- See 'RSG Roos'

'Roosendaal' F, mr, 1965, Buisman, G. A. H.; flowers medium, dbl.; foliage dark; ['Gartendirektor Glocker' × 'Alpine Glow']

'Roquebrune' HT, ob, 1959, Delforge; bud oval; flowers ochre-yellow edged orange, medium, dbl.; foliage dark, glossy; strong stems; moderate, bushy growth

'Roro' HT, 1954, San Remo Exp. Sta.

'Rory Carlton' HT, dp, 1996, Macredie, W.R.; flowers deep pink, full, borne mostly singly; foliage medium size, dark green, semi-glossy; few prickles; medium (100-120 cm.), upright growth; ['Sylvia' × 'Royal Highness']

'Ros Gardner' HT, pb, 2003, Poole, Lionel; flowers pink/cream, 4 in., full, borne mostly solitary; foliage medium size, medium green, glossy; prickles medium, triangular,; growth upright, bushy, medium (30 in.); garden; ['Silver Jubilee' × 'New Zealand']; intr. 2004

R. acicularis × R. rugosa HRg, mr; flowers magenta-crimson, single; occasional autumn repeat; hips pear-shaped; natural hybrid from Japan

R. × alba -- See 'White Rose of York'

R. alba anglica minor -- See 'Alba Maxima'

R. alba staxon cymbaefolia -- See 'Cymbaefolia'

R. × alba var. florepleno -- See 'Alba Maxima'

R. × alba incarnata -- See 'Great Maiden's Blush'

R. × alba maxima -- See 'Alba Maxima'

R. × alba nivea -- See 'Alba Semi-plena'

R. × alba regalis -- See 'Great Maiden's Blush'

R. × alba var. rubicunda -- See 'Great Maiden's Blush'

R. × alba semi-plena -- See 'Alba Semi-plena'

R. × alba suaveolens -- See 'Alba Semi-plena'

R. × andersonii -- See 'Andersonii'

R. × anemonoides -- See 'Anemone'

R. × arnoldiana -- See 'Arnold Rose'

R. arvensis ayreshirea -- See 'Ayrshire Rose'

R. arvensis splendens -- See 'Splendens'

R. × aschersoniana -- See 'Aschersoniana'

R. balsamea -- See 'Tackholmii'

R. banksiae rosea -- See 'Tausendschön'

R. batavica -- See 'Cabbage Rose'

R. belgica -- See 'Summer Damask'

Rosa Belle™ -- See 'Kinbelle'

R. bengalensis -- See 'Slater's Crimson China'

R. bifera -- See 'Quatre Saisons Continue'

R. bifera alba -- See 'White Four Seasons Rose'

'Rosa Blossom' F, lp; flowers blush pink, heavy bloom; low growth

'Rosa Bonheur' ('Mlle Rosa Bonheur') M, mp, Laffay, M.; flowers pink or bright rose, large, dbl.; moderate growth

R. borboniana -- See 'Bourbon Rose'

R. boursaulti -- See 'Boursault Rose'

R. boursaultiana -- See 'Boursault Rose'

R. boursaultii -- See 'Boursault Rose'

R. × bracteata alba odorata -- See 'Alba Odorata'

R. braunii – See 'Involuta'

R. burgundensis -- See 'Pompon de Bourgogne'

R. burgundiaca -- See 'Pompon de Bourgogne'

R. calendarum -- See 'Summer Damask'

R. × calocarpa -- See 'Calocarpa'

R. campanulata – See 'Francofurtana'

R. canina andersonii -- See 'Andersonii'

R. canina burboniana -- See 'Bourbon Rose'

R. cannabifolia -- See 'Cymbaefolia'

R. × cantabrigiensis -- See 'Cantabrigiensis'

R. carnea -- See 'Great Maiden's Blush'

R. cathayensis platyphylla -- See 'Seven Sisters'

R. centifolia -- See 'Cabbage Rose'

R. × centifolia albomuscosa -- See 'Shailer's White Moss'

R. centifolia andrewsii -- See 'Muscosa Simplex'

R. centifolia anglica rubra -- See 'Rubra'

R. × centifolia bullata -- See 'Bullata'
R. centifolia cristata -- See 'Crested Moss'
R. × centifolia maxima -- See 'Des Peintres'
R. × centifolia minima -- See 'Rouletii'
R. × centifolia minor -- See 'Petite de Hollande'
R. × centifolia muscosa -- See 'Centifolia Muscosa'
R. centifolia muscosa cristata -- See 'Crested Moss'
R. centifolia mutabilis -- See 'White Provence'
R. centifolia nivea -- See 'White Provence'
R. × centifolia parvifolia -- See 'Pompon de Bourgogne'
R. centifolia prolifera foliacea -- See 'Prolifera de Redouté'
R. centifolia sancta -- See 'St John's Rose'
R. centifolia variegata -- See 'Variegata'
R. chinensis fragrans – See 'Hume's Blush Tea-Scented China'
R. chinensis manettii -- See 'Manettii'
R. chinensis mutabilis -- See 'Mutabilis'
R. chinensis pseudindica -- See 'Fortune's Double Yellow'
R. chinensis semperflorens -- See 'Slater's Crimson China'
R. chinensis serratipetala -- See 'Serratipetala'
R. chinensis viridiflora -- See 'Green Rose'
R. × collina -- See 'White Rose of York'
R. × cooperi -- See 'Cooper's Burmese'
R. coronata – See 'Involuta'
R. × coryana -- See 'Coryana'
R. cretica sabina -- See 'Clémence Isaure'
R. cymbifolia -- See 'Cymbaefolia'
'Rosa d'Abril' HT, dp, 1948, Dot, Pedro; flowers carmine, large, very dbl., globular; very vigorous growth
R. × damascena -- See 'Summer Damask'
R. damascena aurora -- See 'Celestial'
R. × damascena bifera -- See 'Quatre Saisons Continue'
R. damascena italica -- See 'Quatre Saisons d'Italie'
R. damascena rubra -- See 'Hebe's Lip'
R. damascena rubrotincta -- See 'Hebe's Lip'
R. × damascena semperflorens -- See 'Quatre Saisons Continue'
R. × damascena trigintipetala -- See 'Trigintipetala'
R. damascena variegata -- See R. × damascena versicolor
R. davidii syvdal -- See 'Syvdal'
R. dawsoniana -- See 'Dawson'
'Rosa de Ferra' HT, pb, 1958, Dot, Pedro; flowers violet-pink with carmine reflections, large, 35 petals, intense fragrance; strong stems; vigorous growth; ['Rosa Gallart' × 'Paulette']; intr. 1956
'Rosa de los Andes' Gr, op, 1975, Gutierrez; bud ovoid; flowers pink-salmon-peach, 4-4½ in., 44-46 petals; vigorous growth; [sport of 'Duet']
R. diversifolia -- See 'Slater's Crimson China'
R. doncasterii -- See 'Doncasterii'
R. doniana – See 'Involuta'
R. × dupontii -- See 'Dupontii'
R. earldomensis -- See 'Earldomensis'
R. eglanteria eos -- See 'Eos'
R. ehrrhartiana -- See 'Pompon de Bourgogne'
R. fimbriata -- See 'Fimbriata'
R. foetida harisonii -- See 'Harison's Yellow'
R. foliolosa × R. rugosa HRg, mp; flowers rose-pink, single; growth compact (3 ft.)
R. fortuneana -- See 'Fortune's Double Yellow'
R. fortuneana -- See 'Fortuniana'
R. fortuniana -- See 'Fortune's Double Yellow'
R. × fortuniana -- See 'Fortuniana'
R. × francofurtana Muenchhausen -- See 'Francofurtana'
R. fraseri -- See 'Fraser's Pink Musk'
R. fraxinifolia -- See 'Turneps'
R. freundiana -- See 'Dupontii'
'R. G. Casson' HT, pb, 1923, Cant, B. R.; flowers rose and copper
'Rosa Gallart' HT, mp, 1935, Dot, Pedro; bud long, pointed; flowers rose-pink, large, dbl., cupped; foliage glossy; vigorous growth; [seedling × ('Li Bures' × 'Rose Marie')]
R. gallica agatha -- See 'Francfort Agathé'
R. gallica agatha delphiniana -- See 'Enfant de France'
R. gallica agatha incarnate -- See 'Agathe Incarnata'
R. gallica centifolia -- See 'Cabbage Rose'
R. gallica complicata -- See 'Complicata'
R. gallica conditorum -- See 'Conditorum'
R. gallica damascena -- See 'Summer Damask'
R. gallica grandiflora -- See 'Alika'
R. gallica macrantha -- See 'Gallica Macrantha'
R. gallica remensis -- See 'Pompon de Bourgogne'
R. gallica splendens – See 'Francofurtana'
R. germanica – See 'Francofurtana'
R. glabrata – See R. × spinulifolia
Rosa glauca Nova -- See 'Glauca Nova'
'Rosa Gruss an Aachen' F, pb, 1930, Spek; flowers satiny yellowish-pink, large, full; [sport of 'Gruss an Aachen']
R. × harisonii -- See 'Harison's Yellow'
R. × harisonii vobergii -- See 'Vobergii'
R. headleyensis -- See 'Headleyensis'
R. × heterophylla -- See 'Proteiformis'
R. × hibernica -- See 'Tackholmii'
R. × hibernica -- See 'Hibernica'
R. × highdownensis -- See 'Highdownensis'
R. × hillieri -- See 'Hillier Rose'
R. hugonis flora pleno -- See 'Double Hugonis'
R. incarnata -- See 'Alba Semi-plena'
R. incarnata -- See 'Great Maiden's Blush'
R. indica creunta -- See 'Sanguinea'
R. indica ochroleuca -- See 'Parks' Yellow Tea-Scented China'
R. indica odoratissima -- See 'Hume's Blush Tea-Scented China'
R. indica semperflorens -- See 'Slater's Crimson China'
R. indica sertulata -- See 'Slater's Crimson China'
R. inermis – See 'Francofurtana'
R. inermis morletii -- See 'Morletii'
R. × involuta Smith – See 'Involuta'
R. × involuta wilsonii (Borrer) Baker -- See 'Involuta'
R. × iwara -- See 'Iwara'
R. × jacksonii Willmott -- See 'Jacksonii'
'Rosa Kaiserin' HT, mp; flowers large, dbl.
R. kamtchatica -- See 'Kamtchatica'
R. × kochiana Koehne -- See 'Kochiana'
R. × koehneana Rehder -- See 'Koehneana'
R. × kordesii Wulff -- See 'Kordesii'
R. × leonida -- See 'Maria Leonida'
R. × lheritierana -- See 'Boursault Rose'
R. lutea hoggii -- See 'Harison's Yellow'
R. macrantha -- See 'Gallica Macrantha'
R. macrophylla coryana -- See 'Coryana'
R. macrophylla doncasterii -- See 'Doncasterii'
R. × malyi Kerner -- See 'Malyi'
'Rosa Mamie' HT, mr, 1956, Asseretto, V.; bud ovoid; flowers bright rose, large, 35 petals, moderate fragrance; long stems; vigorous growth; PP1356; [sport of 'Rome Glory']
R. manettii -- See 'Manettii'
R. × marcyana Boullu -- See 'Marcyana'
R. × mareyana -- See 'Marcyana'
R. × mariae-graebneriae -- See 'Maria Graebner'
R. × microphylla alba odorata -- See 'Alba Odorata'
R. × micrugosa Henkel -- See 'Micrugosa'
R. × micrugosa alba -- See 'Micrugosa Alba'
R. × mitcheltonii -- See 'Mitcheltonii'
'Rosa Monnet' -- See 'Mme Rosa Monnet'
R. monstrosa -- See 'Green Rose'
R. moschata grandiflora -- See 'Moschata Grandiflora'
R. moschata nastarana -- See 'Nastarana'
R. moschata nivea -- See 'Dupontii'
R. moschata pissardii -- See 'Nastarana'
R. × moyesii hillieri -- See 'Hillier Rose'
R. multiflora grandiflora -- See 'Moschata Grandiflora'
R. multiflora nana hort. Pol, w, after 1875; flowers white to pink, very small, single to semi-dbl., borne in clusters; recurrent bloom; bushy, dwarf (1-2 ft.) growth
R. multiflora platyphylla -- See 'Seven

Sisters'

'Rosa Mundi' T, dr, 1898, Conard & Jones; flowers deep crimson, large, cupped

'Rosa Munné' HT, rb, 1952, Munné, M.; flowers red to saffron-pink, large, dbl.; foliage clear green; very vigorous growth; ['Maria Serrat' × 'Paz Vila']

R. muscosa -- See 'Centifolia Muscosa'

R. muscosa alba -- See 'Shailer's White Moss'

R. muscosa anemonflora -- See 'De La Flèche'

R. muscosa multiplex -- See 'Centifolia Muscosa'

R. muscosa simplex -- See 'Muscosa Simplex'

R. mutabilis -- See 'Mutabilis'

R. × noisettiana Thory -- See 'Noisette Rose'

R. noisettiana manettii -- See 'Manettii'

R. odorata -- See 'Hume's Blush Tea-Scented China'

R. odorata ochroleuca -- See 'Parks' Yellow Tea-Scented China'

R. odorata pseudindica -- See 'Fortune's Double Yellow'

R. omeiensis pteragonis -- See 'Pteragonis'

'Rosa Orange Triumph' Pol, mp, 1943, Verschuren; flowers small, semi-dbl.

R. oxyacanthos -- See R. × kochiana

R. paestana -- See 'Comte Lelieur'

R. parviflora provincialis -- See 'Blandford Rose'

R. parvifolia -- See 'Pompon de Bourgogne'

R. parvula -- See 'Très-Petite Fleur'

R. × paulii -- See 'Paulii Rosea'

R. × paulii -- See 'Repens Alba'

R. × paulii rosea -- See 'Paulii Rosea'

R. pendulina malyi -- See R. × malyi

R. × penzanceana -- See 'Lady Penzance'

R. pissardii -- See 'Nastarana'

R. platyphylla -- See 'Seven Sisters'

R. × pokornyana -- See 'Pokornyana'

R. × polliniana -- See 'Polliniana'

R. polyantha -- See 'Summer Damask'

R. polyantha grandiflora -- See 'Moschata Grandiflora'

R. pomifera duplex -- See 'Duplex'

R. pomponia -- See 'Pompon de Bourgogne'

'Rosa Poncheaux' -- See 'Poncheau-Capiaumont'

R. portlandica -- See 'Duchess of Portland'

'Rosa Prattigora' S, mr, 1956, Kordes, W.; bud long, pointed; flowers light red, very large, open, borne in small clusters, slight fragrance; continuous; foliage light green, leathery; stems light brown; growth vigorous, upright, bushy (to 6 ft.); [R. prattii × R. rugosa alba]

R. procera -- See 'White Rose of York'

'Rosa Prominent' Gr, mp, Sieber; flowers large, dbl; [sport of Prominent®]; intr. 1982

R. × proteiformis -- See 'Proteiformis'

R. provincialis -- See 'Cabbage Rose'

R. provincialis alba -- See 'White Provence'

R. provincialis minor -- See 'Pompon de Bourgogne'

R. × pruhoniciana -- See 'Hillier Rose'

R. pseudindica -- See 'Fortune's Double Yellow'

R. × pteragonis -- See 'Pteragonis'

R. × rapa -- See 'Turneps'

R. rapa -- See 'Rose d'Amour'

R. reclinata -- See 'Boursault Rose'

R. remensis -- See 'Pompon de Bourgogne'

R. × reversa -- See 'Reversa'

R. richardii -- See 'St John's Rose'

R. rouletii -- See 'Rouletii'

R. roxosa -- See R. × microrugosa

R. rubella -- See R. × reversa

R. rubicans -- See 'Great Maiden's Blush'

R. rubiginosa magnifica -- See 'Magnifica'

R. rubra plena spinosissima pedunculo muscosa -- See 'Centifolia Muscosa'

R. rubrosa -- See 'Carmenetta'

R. × rubrosa Preston S, mp, before 1903; flowers large; [R. glauca × R. rugosa]

R. × ruga -- See 'Ruga'

R. × rugosa atropurpurea -- See 'Atropurpurea'

R. × rugosa calocarpa -- See 'Calocarpa'

R. × rugosa kamtchatica -- See 'Kamtchatica'

R. × rugosa repens alba -- See 'Repens Alba'

R. × rugosa repens rosea -- See 'Paulii Rosea'

R. rugosa scabrosa -- See 'Scabrosa'

R. × rugotida -- See 'Rugotida'

R. russeliana Loudon HSem; [R. sempervirens × R. chinensis]

R. sabini -- See 'Involuta'

R. salaevensis perrieri (Songeon ex Déséglise) Rouy – See 'Salaevensis'

R. sancta -- See 'St John's Rose'

R. × scharnkeana -- See 'Scharnkeana'

R. scopulosa -- See 'Pokornyana'

R. semperflorens -- See 'Slater's Crimson China'

R. sempervirens major -- See 'Plena'

'Rosa Sinfonie' F, mp, VEG; flowers medium, semi-dbl.

R. × spaethiana -- See 'Spaethiana'

R. spinosissima lutea plena -- See 'Williams' Double Yellow'

R. spinulifolia dematriana -- See R. × spinulifolia

'Rosa Stern' -- See 'Bel Ange'

Rosa Sternenflor® S, mp, Schultheis; flowers bright pink, fading to white, yellow stamens, small, single, flat, borne in large clusters, moderate fragrance; recurrent; low (2 ft.), spreading growth; ['Sternenflor' × unknown]; intr. 1995

R. sublaevis -- See 'Sublaevis'

R. sulphurea nana -- See 'Pompone Jaune'

R. × tackholmii -- See 'Tackholmii'

R. terebinthinacea -- See R. marcyana

R. thea -- See 'Hume's Blush Tea-Scented China'

R. thoryi -- See 'Seven Sisters'

'Rosa Traum' F, mp, 1976, Kordes; bud pointed; flowers 2½ in., 32 petals, high-centered; foliage glossy; vigorous, upright, bushy growth; ['Duftwolke' × seedling]; intr. 1974

R. trigintipetala -- See 'Trigintipetala'

R. turbinata – See 'Francofurtana'

'Rosa Union' HT, Dot

R. usitatissima -- See 'White Rose of York'

'Rosa Verschuren' HT, lp, 1904, Verschuren; flowers large, full, loose

R. villosa – See 'Involuta'

R. vilmorinii -- See R. × microrugosa

R. virginiana plena -- See 'Rose d'Amour'

R. viridiflora -- See 'Green Rose'

'Rosa Vollendung' F, pb, 1943, Kordes; bud long, pointed; flowers salmon-pink, reverse capucine-red, large, dbl., borne in clusters; foliage leathery, wrinkled; vigorous, bushy growth; ['Crimson Glory' × 'Else Poulsen']

R. vobergii -- See 'Vobergii'

R. × wadeii Hurran – See 'Wadeii'

R. × waitziana -- See 'Waitziana'

R. × waitziana macrantha -- See 'Gallica Macrantha'

R. × warleyensis -- See 'Warleyensis'

R. wichurana grandiflora – See 'Wichurana Grandiflora'

R. wilsonii – See Involuta

R. wilsonii -- See R. × microrugosa

R. × wintoniensis -- See 'Wintoniensis'

R. xanthina slingerii -- See 'Allard'

R. xanthina spontanea Rehder -- See 'Canary Bird'

R. yesoensis -- See 'Iwara'

'Rosa Zwerg' ('Admiration', 'Dwarf Pavement', 'Rosazwerg', 'Zwerg') HRg, mp, Baum; flowers medium, semi-dbl., flat, moderate fragrance; recurrent; spreading, low (2 ft.) growth; hips orange-red; very winter hardy; intr. 1984

'Rosabel Walker' HT, mr, 1922, Cant, F.; bud long, pointed; flowers brilliant velvety crimson, large, dbl.; very vigorous, bushy, spreading growth

'Rosabell' -- See 'Cocceleste'

'Rosabella' HT, mr, 1941, Giacomasso; flowers red with cerise reflections, very large; foliage abundant; long stems; ['Mrs J.D. Russell' × 'Julien Potin']

'Rosabella' F, op, Maarse, G.; flowers salmon-pink shaded orange, well-shaped, very dbl., borne in very large clusters; vigorous growth; ['Pinocchio' × unknown]; intr. 1955

'Rosabelle' Cl T, op, 1900, Bruant; bud long; flowers light pink with salmon reflections, pink reverse, large, borne in small clusters; remontant; foliage glossy, bronze, purplish when young; numerous prickles; ['Fortune's Double Yellow' × 'Mme de Tartas']

'Rosabelle Barnett' F, op, 1970, Gregory; flowers coral, 2½ in., 32 petals, globular; foliage dark; very free growth; ['Tropicana' × unknown]

'Rosabunda' F, dp, Wagner, S.; bud cylindrical and short; 30 petals, cupped, borne in flowers in clusters of 3-9 florets, moderate fragrance; foliage dark green, medium large, glossy; ['Frankfurt am Main' × 'Maria Callas']; intr. 1978

'Rosada' ('Rosata') Min, op, 1950, Dot, Pedro; flowers peach edged pink, 25 petals, cupped; foliage small, glossy; compact (7-8 in.) growth; ['Perla de Alcanada' × 'Rouletii']

'Rosadoll' F, pb, Roman, G., and Wagner, S.; flowers intense mauvish-pink, small to medium, semi-dbl., flat, borne in clusters, slight fragrance; foliage medium size, dark green, glossy, healthy; ['Rusticana' × Lavender Dream®]; intr. 2005

'Rosadora' F, lp, Wagner, S.; flowers 25 petals, rosette, slight fragrance; leaves small, medium green, glossy; growth spreading; [Candy Rose® × Yesterday®]; intr. 1996

'Rosagold' F, dy, Wagner, S.; bud medium long; flowers yellow-apricot, 35 petals, cupped, borne in clusters, intense very fragrance; foliage medium large, light green, glossy; vigorous upright tall growth; ['Vigorosa' × Allgold®]; intr. 1996

'Rosalba' HT, pb, 1934, Borgatti, G.; bud long, pointed, streaked carmine; flowers lilac-pink, center shaded salmon-pink, large, dbl.; vigorous growth; ['Souv. de Claudius Pernet' × 'Willowmere']

'Rosaleda' HT, yb, 1958, Moreira da Silva; flowers yellow and white, well-formed, large, dbl.; foliage dark; strong stems; upright, bushy growth; ['Monte Carlo' × 'Michèle Meilland']

'Rosaleen' HMsk, dr, 1932, Bentall; flowers crimson, small, dbl., borne in large clusters, slight fragrance; recurrent bloom

'Rosaleen Dunn' HT, mr, 1942, McGredy; flowers crimson-red, 5½ in., 22 petals, cupped, intense fragrance; foliage dark; vigorous growth; PP483

'Rosaletta' -- See 'Frystassi'

'Rosali' F, mp, 1973, Tantau, Math.; bud long, pointed; flowers large, dbl., moderate fragrance; vigorous, upright growth; RULED EXTINCT 4/85; [seedling × 'Junior Miss']; intr. 1971

Rosali® -- See 'Tanilasor'

Rosali 83® -- See 'Tanilasor'

'Rosalia' HT, dp, 1954; bud long, pointed, light cerise; long stems

'Rosalie' -- See 'Unique Carnée'

'Rosalie' ('Fairy Queen', 'Reine des Fées') T, mp, 1884, Ellwanger & Barry; flowers clear pink, medium, very full, moderate fragrance; ['Marie Van Houtte' × unknown]

Rosalie® HT, lp, Tantau; flowers medium, full, high-centered, borne mostly singly; recurrent; stems medium to long; florist rose; intr. 2005

'Rosalie' -- See 'Rosella Sweet'

'Rosalie Coral' -- See 'Chewallop'

'Rosalie Richardson' HT, lp, 1932, Evans; flowers soft pink

Rosalina™ -- See 'Korsaku'

'Rosalind' S, lp, Austin, David; bud small; flowers blush pink, full, cupped, moderate fruity fragrance; recurrent; intr. 2006

'Rosalind' HT, op, 1918, Pierson, F.R.; bud bright coral; flowers apricot-pink becoming shell-pink, dbl.; [sport of 'Ophelia']

'Rosalind' HT, pb, Bell; intr. 1993

'Rosalind Orr English' HT, op, 1905, E.G. Hill, Co.; flowers salmon-pink, large, dbl.; ['Mme Abel Chatenay' × 'Papa Gontier']

'Rosalind Russell' HT, mp, 1950, Grillo; bud long, well formed; flowers bright pink, 5 in., 45-50 petals, high-centered, moderate fragrance; foliage dark, leathery; very vigorous, upright growth; PP1049; ['Briarcliff' × 'Regina Elena']

'Rosalinda' HT, dp, 1945, Camprubi, C.; flowers carmine, well-formed, large, very dbl.; very vigorous growth; ['Editor McFarland' × 'Comtesse Vandal']

'Rosalinda' F, mp, Wagner, S.; flowers medium pink, 39 petals, cupped, borne in clusters, slight fragrance; foliage medium green, semi-glossy; growth vigorous; [('Frankfurt am Main' × 'Maria Callas') × Foc de Tabara™]; intr. 1994

'Rosalinde' F, mp, 1944, Krause; bud round, fat; flowers clear, soft pink, dbl., cupped, borne in large clusters, moderate apples fragrance; recurrent; foliage dark; stout, upright growth

'Rosalita' -- See 'LLX8898'

'Rosalpina' HT, pb, 1958, Giacomasso; flowers coppery pink, very large, 50 petals; foliage glossy; strong stems; very vigorous growth; ['Signora' × seedling]; intr. 1953

'Rosalynn Carter' -- See 'RUprins'

'Rosamaria' S, Mansuino; intr. 1974

'Rosamond' HT, op, 1927, Burbage Nursery; flowers orange-salmon, stamens golden, single; ['Red-Letter Day' × *R. foetida bicolor*]

'Rosamunde' -- See 'Kormunde'

'Rosamunde' F, pb, 1941, Leenders, M.; flowers salmon-carmine, reverse hydrangea-pink, large, dbl.; [seedling × 'Permanent Wave']

Rosanna® -- See 'Korhokhel'

'Rosanna' HT, mp, 1959, Biga, Valentino; bud urn shaped; flowers spinel-rose, open, medium to large; foliage leathery; vigorous, upright, compact growth; RULED EXTINCT 4/77; [Baccará® × 'Gruss an Coburg']

'Rosanna' -- See 'Korinter'

'Rosaperle' S, mp; groundcover; intr. 2002

'Rosarama' HT, op, Martin; intr. 1988

Rosario® ('Renown's Rosario') S, mp, Tantau; flowers bright pink, dbl., cupped, borne in loose clusters, moderate fragrance; foliage dark green, glossy; vigorous, arching growth; intr. 1993

'Rosario Algorta' -- See 'Seaurug'

'Rosarito' HT, Moreira da Silva, A.

'Rosarium den Blakken' F, lp, RvS-Melle; intr. 1998

'Rosarium Dortmund' (Deutsches Rosarium Dortmund®) LCl, pb, Noack, Werner; flowers bright pink, 4 cm., dbl., rosette, borne in large clusters; recurrent; growth to over 8 ft.; intr. 1995

'Rosarium Glücksburg' -- See 'Glücksburg'

Rosarium Uetersen® -- See 'Kortersen'

'Rosary' -- See 'Roserie'

'Rosata' -- See 'Rosada'

'Rosatherapy' HT, dp, 2000, Chiplunkar, C.R.; flowers dark pink, reverse light pink, medium, very full, high-centered, borne mostly singly, slight fragrance; foliage medium size, medium green, semi-glossy; prickles moderate; compact, medium (2½-3 ft.) growth; [sport of 'Ace of Hearts']; intr. 1996

'Rosatop' F, mr, Roman, G., and Wagner, S.; flowers carmine-red with a white eye, small to medium, semi-dbl., flat, slight fragrance; foliage small to medium, dark green, semi-glossy; intr. 2004

'Rosazwerg' -- See 'Rosa Zwerg'

'Rosbeauty' ('Mystic Beauty') B, lp, 2003, Patterson, William; flowers large, full, borne in small clusters, intense fragrance; foliage medium size, medium green, matte; prickles curved; growth compact, medium (3½ ft.); specimen; [sport of 'Kronprincessin Viktoria']; intr. 2002

'Röschen Albrecht' F, or, Tantau; flowers medium, semi-dbl.; intr. 1981

'Roschild' (Lovely Child™) S, ab, 2006; flowers apricot to yellow, outer petals fading near white, medium, full, cupped, borne mostly solitary, moderate fragrance; recurrent; foliage small, medium green; no prickles; growth upright, short; [sport of 'Tamora']; intr. 2006

'Rose 2,000' -- See 'Cocquetrum'

'Rose à Bois Jaspé' S, mr, 1876, Brassac; flowers bright carminy cherry red, large, full; hybrid canina

'Rose à Cent Feuilles' -- See 'Cabbage Rose'

'Rose à Feuilles de Laitue' -- See 'Bullata'

'Rose à Feuilles Luisantes' M, lp, 1843, Vibert; flowers soft pink edged blush, medium, dbl., globular, borne in clusters; foliage glossy; branching growth

'Rose à Parfum de Bulgarie' D, mp; flowers medium, dbl., intense fragrance; possibly the same as 'Kazanlik'

'Rose à Parfum de Grasse' D, mp, before 1867; flowers medium, dbl., intense fragrance

'Rose à Parfum de l'Hay' ('Parfum de l'Hay') HRg, mr, 1901, Gravereaux; flowers cherry-carmine-red, turning blue in heat, large, dbl., globular, intense fragrance; recurrent bloom; foliage not typically rugose; vigorous (5 ft.)

growth; [('Summer Damask' × 'Général Jacqueminot') × *R. rugosa*]

'Rose Aimée' HT, m, 1955, Gaujard; flowers gold, flushed and splashed crimson, well-formed, dbl.; very vigorous, bushy growth; ['Peace' × seedling]

'Rose Angle' ('Angle', 'Jessica', 'Rose Angle Blush') Ayr, mp, before 1838, Martin; flowers bright lilac rose, semi-dbl., cupped; foliage very fragrant; very vigorous growth

'Rose Angle Blush' -- See 'Rose Angle'

'Rose Anil' -- See 'Viranil'

'Rose Anne' Cl HT, ob, 1938, Thomas; flowers orange-apricot, base deeper yellow, semi-dbl., cupped; recurrent bloom; foliage large, glossy; very vigorous, climbing (15 ft.) growth; RULED EXTINCT 4/77; ['Francesca' × 'Margaret McGredy']

'Rose Apples' HRg, dp, 1895, Paul; flowers carmine-rose, large, semi-dbl., moderate fragrance; vigorous growth

'Rose Atieno' -- See 'Kenspigi'

'Rose Ayez' -- See 'Spectabilis'

'Rose Baby' -- See 'Macros'

'Rose Ball' -- See 'Roseball'

'Rose Bampton' HT, dp, 1940, Van Rossem; bud carmine; flowers bright China-red, 5½ in., 50 petals, camellia-like, moderate fragrance; foliage dark; vigorous growth; PP425; ['Charles P. Kilham' × 'Margaret McGredy']

'Rose Bansal' HT, yb, 1972, Friends Rosery; flowers yellow, petal edges sometimes crimson; [sport of 'Ambossfunken']

'Rose Bayard' -- See 'Jacsilho'

'Rose Benary' HT, mp, 1908, Lambert, P.; flowers pink, yellow center, large, dbl., moderate fragrance; ['Ferdinand Batel' × 'Liberty']

'Rose Bengal' ('Oasis') HT, rb, Ghosh, Mr & Mrs S.; flowers dark, velvety crimson, creamy white reverse, dbl., high-centered, moderate sweet fragrance; intr. 2001

'Rose Berkley' ('Souv de Rose Berkley') HT, op, 1928, McGredy; bud long, pointed; flowers deep rosy salmon-pink suffused orange, base orange, large, high-centered; foliage rich green, glossy; very vigorous growth

'Rose Bicolore' HT, ob, Croix

'Rose Blanche' HT, w, Croix

'Rose Bleu' -- See 'Busard Triomphant'

'Rose Bleu' HGal, m, about 1810, Descemet; flowers purple with bluish marbling

'Rose Bleue' HT, m

'Rose Bordée de Blanc' -- See 'Comtesse de Chamoïs'

'Rose Bowl' HT, mr, 1961, Morey, Dr. Dennison; bud urn shaped; flowers bright red, large, 35 petals, high-centered, intense fragrance; foliage leathery; long, strong stems; vigorous, upright, bushy growth; PP2188; ['Mardi Gras' × 'Chrysler Imperial']; intr. 1961

'Rose Bradwardine' ('Bradwardine') HEg, mp, 1894, Penzance; flowers clear rose-pink, center white, single, borne in graceful clusters; seasonal bloom; foliage very fragrant; vigorous growth

'Rose Bretagne' S, mp

'Rose Brillante' -- See 'Brillante'

'Rose Bruford' HT, ab, 1961, Wheatcroft Bros.; flowers creamy peach, shaded rosy bronze; [sport of 'Soraya']

'Rose Buffon' -- See 'Buffon'

'Rose Cascade' -- See 'Delcouro'

Rose Céleste® -- See 'Delroceles'

'Rose Charm' HT, mp, 1934, Scittine; flowers sanguineous pink; [sport of 'Talisman']

'Rose Cheal' HT, mp, 1970, Herincx; flowers rose-pink, spiral form, 4-5 in., 42 petals; foliage glossy, dark; free growth; ['New Style' × Scarlet Queen Elizabeth®]

'Rose Cherry Pastel' Min, mr

'Rose Chou de Hollande' -- See 'Cabbage Rose'

'Rose City of Nashik' ('Gulab Angree Nashik') HT, dp, Bulsara; [sport of 'Christian Dior']; intr. 1990

'Rose Cornet' -- See 'Cornet'

'Rose Country' -- See 'Sprose'

'Rose Csárdás' F, mr, Berger, W.; flowers medium, dbl.; intr. 1965

'Rose d'Amour' ('Duplex', 'The St Mark's Rose', *R. rapa*, *R. virginiana plena*, 'St Mark's Rose') Misc OGR, dp; bud deep pink with long sepals; flowers rose pink, outer petals fading to pale pink receptacle wide, semi-dbl., moderate fragrance; summer bloom; foliage leaflets 5-7, rich green, marked with red on leaf stalks & stipules; prickles mixed sizes, scattered; lax growth to 10 ft.; cultivated in Europe since 1768

'Rose d'Amour' HT, ob, Reynaud; flowers brown-red, reverse yellow, open, large, dbl.; foliage glossy, dark; vigorous growth; intr. 1935

'Rose d'Amour' -- See 'Cocdestin'

'Rose d'Anjou' T, dp, before 1836, Vibert; flowers dark pink, center lighter, large, dbl, slight fragrance

Rose d'Annecy® S, mp, Adam; flowers clear, bright pink, medium, dbl., borne in clusters, slight fragrance; recurrent; bushy (80 × 60 cm.) growth; intr. 1995

'Rose Dawn' HT, pb, 1924, Towill; bud long, pointed; flowers soft shell-pink, base yellow, large, dbl., high-centered; foliage light; vigorous growth; [('Joseph Hill' × ('Mrs George Shawyer' × unknown)) × 'Ophelia']

'Rose de Batavie' -- See 'Cabbage Rose'

Rose de Bayonne® F, mp, Horner; flowers deeper pink in center, full, cupped to almost flat, borne in clusters; recurrent; growth 70 - 80 cm. height; intr. 2008

Rose de Beaune® S, lp, Tantau; flowers clear pink , cupped , borne in clusters; recurrent; foliage dark green, glossy; vigorous, mounding growth; intr. 2006

'Rose de Bengale' -- See 'Sanguinea'

'Rose de Cahors' F, rb, Reuter; flowers dark red with silver reverse, dbl., borne in clusters, slight fragrance; recurrent; vigorous (70-80 cm.) growth; intr. 2006

'Rose de Cornouaille' F, mp, Harkness; flowers pastel pink, large, full, shallow cup, abundant, moderate fragrance; recurrent; foliage dark green; growth to 3 ft.; intr. 2003

'Rose de Dijon' -- See *R. × centifolia pomponia*

'Rose de France' HP, mp, 1893, Verdier, E.; flowers carmine pink, reverse silvery, medium to large, full

'Rose de France' HT, op, Gaujard; bud ovoid; flowers brilliant salmon tinted orange, very large, dbl.; foliage glossy; dwarf growth; intr. 1942

'Rose de la Floride' -- See 'Calypso'

'Rose de La Maître-Ecole' ('De la Maître-Ecole', 'Du Maître d'École', 'Rose du Maître d'École') HGal, m, 1831, Coquereau; flowers soft pink to lilac, center petals not opening, very large, dbl., cupped, borne in clusters of 2-3, intense fragrance; foliage dark green, oval, medium to large; some prickles, intermixed with fine bristles

'Rose de la Petite Chabote' F, pb, Lens; flowers pink changing to white, small, dbl., cupped, borne in large clusters, slight fragrance; recurrent; foliage dark green; growth to 80 cm.; intr. 2005

'Rose de la Reine' -- See 'La Reine'

'Rose de l'Hymen' -- See 'Plena'

'Rose de Limoux' ('Dukat') HT, my, Tantau; flowers yellow ocher, dbl., cupped, borne singly and in clusters, slight fragrance; recurrent; robust, medium growth; intr. 2005

'Rose de l'Inde' Ch, dp

'Rose de Lyon' HT, ob, 1945, Gaujard; bud pointed; flowers orange-yellow, medium, dbl.; foliage glossy

'Rose de Meaux' -- See *R. × centifolia pomponia*

'Rose de Meaux White' ('De Meaux White', 'White Rose de Meaux', 'White de Meaux', 'Le Rosier Pompon Blanc') C, w, before 1824; flowers white with pink centers

Rose de Monplaisir® HMult, dp, Ducher/David; flowers deep pink with mauve reflections , very full, pompon, borne in clusters, slight musk fragrance; recurrent; flexible, vigorous (5 - 10 ft.) growth; ['Ghislaine de Feligonde' × 'Veilchenblau']; intr. 2007

'Rose de Montfort' F, dp, Adam; intr. 1993

'Rose de Pelletier' -- See 'Fleur de Pelletier'

'Rose de Puebla' -- See 'François Fontaine'

Rose de Rennes® HT, lp, Adam, M.; flowers large , double , high-centered, borne mostly singly, intense fragrance; recurrent; vigorous (3 - 4 ft.) growth; intr. 1995

'Rose de Rescht' P, dp, about 1880, from Iran; flowers bright fuchsia-red, fading with lilac tints, very dbl., rosette, borne mostly singly, intense damask fragrance; recurrent; foliage dense; vigorous, compact growth; originally introduced into England about 1880, but was then forgotten about and re-introduced in the 1940's.

'Rose de Schelfhout' HGal, lp, 1840, Parmentier; flowers delicate pink, full, quartered, moderate fragrance; non-remontant

'Rose de Tavel' F, dp, Reuter; flowers intense deep pink, dbl., high-centered, borne in clusters, slight fruity fragrance; recurrent; growth to 70-80 cm.; intr. 2003

'Rose de Trianon' P, mp, about 1830, Vibert; flowers medium, dbl., cupped, borne in large clusters; growth small, vigorous; probably extinct

'Rose de Trianon Double' -- See 'Adèle Mauzé'

'Rose de Van Huysum' -- See 'Belle Couronnée'

'Rose des 4 Vents' S, dr, Delbard; intr. 2007

'Rose des Blés' LCl, rb, Eve; flowers bright shades of red, dbl., cupped, slight fragrance; recurrent; vigorous (180-250 cm.) growth; intr. 2006

'Rose des Cisterciens' -- See 'Delarle'

'Rose des Maures' ('Sissinghurst Castle') HGal, dr; flowers deep plum-crimson, yellow stamens, 2½ in., semi-dbl. to dbl., rosette, borne singly or in clusters of 2-7, slight fragrance; non-remontant; foliage medium green, oval, with 3 leaflets; prickles numerous, hooked; vigorous, upright (4 ft.) growth; a very old variety, believed lost, but rediscovered by Sackville-West in 1947 at Sissinghurst

'Rose des Parfumeurs' -- See 'Rose du Puteaux'

'Rose des Peintres' -- See 'Des Peintres'

'Rose d'Espérance' HT, dr, 1918, Verschuren; flowers dark red to deep black, medium, dbl.

'Rose d'Evian' T, pb, 1895, Bernaix, A.; bud long, magenta; flowers pink, center carmine, very large, very dbl., cupped; foliage glossy

'Rose d'Herbeys' -- See 'Souv de J. B. Guillot'

'Rose d'Hivers' D, w; flowers whitish, center shell-pink, well-shaped

'Rose d'Or' HT, dy, 1941, Gaujard; bud long, pointed; flowers intense yellow, 4½-5 in., 35 petals; foliage dark, bronze, glossy; very vigorous growth; PP482; ['Julien Potin' × seedling]

'Rose d'Or de Montreux' -- See 'Adatonysil'

'Rose d'Orsay' -- See 'D'Orsay Rose'

'Rose Dot' HT, rb, 1962, Dot, Simon; flowers red, reverse white, large, 35 petals, intense fragrance; foliage dark; vigorous, upright growth; [Baccará® × 'Peace']

'Rose du Barri' HT, pb, 1940, Archer; flowers salmon-pink, reverse carmine, large, single; vigorous growth

Rose du Ciel® -- See 'Delfror'

'Rose du Maître d'École' -- See 'Rose de La Maître-Ecole'

'Rose du Prince' HT, mr, 1962, Dorieux; bud long, pointed; flowers strawberry-rose, large, dbl.; foliage leathery, light green; vigorous, upright growth; ['Blanche Mallerin' × 'Profusion']; intr. 1959

'Rose du Puteaux' ('Rose des Parfumeurs') D, mp, before 1826; flowers rose pink to rose red, moderate fragrance; recurrent; a form of Quatre Saisons, cultivated at Puteaux, near Paris, for the perfume industry; sometimes credited to Cochet

'Rose du Roi' -- See 'Comte Lelieur'

'Rose du Roi à Fleurs Blanches' -- See 'Célina Dubos'

'Rose du Roi à Fleurs Pourpres' P, dr, 1844, Varangot; flowers crimson, shaded with purple, large, medium, full, cupped; repeats sparingly; growth branching, moderate (4 ft.); breeder and date based on Revue Horticole, 1846; usually considered to be a sport of Rose du Roi, but is not, according to Joyaux

'Rose du Roi Panachée' -- See 'Panachée de Lyon'

'Rose du Roi Strié' -- See 'Capitaine Rénard'

'Rose du Sérail' -- See 'La Belle Sultane'

'Rose Dubreuil' -- See 'Rose Edouard'

'Rose d'York' -- See 'Duc d'York'

'Rose Edouard' ('Rose Dubreuil', 'Rose Neumann') B, mp, 1818, Perichon/Neumann; bud pointed; flowers bright pink, small, dbl., cupped, often muddled, moderate sweet with hint of pepper fragrance; recurrent; foliage gray-green, waxy; broad, tall (5-6 ft.) growth; ['Tous-les-Mois (DP)' × 'Parsons' Pink']

'Rose Edward' -- See 'Bourbon Rose'

'Rose Elf' -- See 'Rosenelfe'

'Rose Ellen' S, lp, Lykke; intr. 1995

'Rose Eutin' F, mp, 1958, Hennessey; flowers rose-pink; [sport of 'Eutin']

'Rose Festival' S, mr, Sutherland, P; ['Black Beauty' × 'Candy Cane']; intr. 1996

'Rose Foncé' -- See 'Rubra'

'Rose For Elaine' -- See 'Rawdenqueen'

'Rose Foucheaux' -- See 'Foucheaux'

'Rose Fukuoka' HT, pb, 1985, Ota, Kaichiro; flowers blend of light, medium and deep pink, (deeper at petal edges, 27 petals, high-centered; foliage small, dark, glossy; compact growth; [('Utage' × 'Kordes' Perfecta') × 'Miss Ireland']; intr. 1983

'Rose Fukuyama' HT, dp, Hiroshima; intr. 1985

'Rose Garnette' Pol, mp

'Rose Gaujard, Climbing' (Grimpant Rose Gaujard®) Cl HT, rb, 1964, Nakashima, Tosh; [sport of Rose Gaujard®]

Rose Gaujard® HT, rb, 1958, Gaujard; bud small to medium, ovoid to globular; flowers cherry-red, reverse pale pink and silvery white, 3-4 in., 80 petals, high-centered to cupped, borne usually singly, slight fragrance; free-flowering; foliage leathery, glossy; prickles several, medium, hooked downward, brown; stems medium; vigorous, bushy growth; PP1829; ['Peace' × ('Capucine Bicolore' × 'Opera')]; intr. 1964

'Rose Gaujard × Leverkusen' S, rb, Scholle, E.; flowers white with red edges, large, single to semi-dbl.; recurrent; tall (200 cm.), arching growth

Rose Gilardi™ -- See 'Morose'

'Rose Gold' -- See 'Garrose'

'Rose Hannes' ('Hannes') HT, w, 1982, Wheatcroft, Christopher; flowers large, dbl.; foliage medium size, medium green, glossy; upright growth; [Pascali® × seedling]

'Rose Hill' HT, dp, 1928, Joseph H. Hill, Co.; bud long, pointed; flowers darker than briarcliff, very large, dbl., high-centered; [sport of 'Columbia']

'Rose Hills Red' Min, dr, 1977, Moore, Ralph S.; bud pointed; flowers deep red, 1½ in., 30 petals; foliage glossy, leathery; vigorous, upright growth; [(R. wichurana × 'Floradora') × Westmont]; intr. 1978

'Rose Iga' -- See 'Meibalbika'

'Rose Impériale' HT, ob, 1942, Gaujard; flowers flame and gold, over large, very dbl., globular; foliage dark, glossy; vigorous growth

'Rose Jacques' -- See 'Rosier de Bourgon'

'Rose Jay' -- See 'Clémentine'

'Rose Lée' -- See 'Léa'

'Rose Lelieur' -- See 'Comte Lelieur'

'Rose Love' HT, or, Delbard; flowers tender orange, dbl.; intr. 1978

'Rose MacKenzie' -- See 'Jalmac'

'Rose Magic' -- See 'Gellando'

'Rose Marguerite' -- See 'Tricolore'

'Rose-Marie' -- See 'Ausome'

'Rose Marie' HT, mp, 1918, Dorner; flowers clear rose-pink, very large, dbl., cupped, moderate fragrance; recurrent; foliage glossy, dark; vigorous growth; ['Hoosier Beauty' × 'Sunburst']

'Rose Marie, Climbing' Cl HT, mp, 1927, Pacific Rose Co.; bud very large, long-pointed; flowers very large, dbl.; [sport of 'Rose Marie']

'Rose Marie' F, m

'Rose Marie Gorst' -- See 'Worcart'

'Rose Marie Reid' HT, mp, 1956, Whisler; bud globular; flowers Neyron rose, 5-6 in., 48 petals, cupped, moderate fragrance; foliage dark, leathery; vigorous growth; PP1487; ['Charlotte Armstrong' × 'Katherine T. Marshall']; intr. 1956

'Rose-Marie Viaud' ('Rosemary Viaud') HMult, m, 1924, Igoult; flowers same as parent except bluer and more double, 3 cm., dbl., rosette, borne in large clusters, no fragrance; thornless; ['Veilchenblau' × unknown]

'Rose Mary' HT, mp

'Rose Mauve' -- See 'Bourbon'
'Rose Meillandécor' -- See 'Meipoque'
'Rose Merk'   HT, or, 1931, Cant, F.; flowers bright geranium-red; vigorous growth
'Rose Mille' ('Mille') A, w, 1826, Cartier; flowers pure white, medium, full
'Rose Minarett' -- See 'Noamet'
Rose mit Herz®   S, dr, Huber; intr. 2003
'Rose Moet'   HT, my, 1962, Dorieux; flowers golden yellow, large, dbl.; foliage leathery; long, strong stems
'Rose Mousseuse Ordinaire' -- See 'Centifolia Muscosa'
'Rose Music'   F, dp, Kakujitsu-en; intr. 1988
'Rose Myra Grimbley' -- See 'Webfascin'
'Rose Nabonnand'   T, pb, 1883, Nabonnand, G.; flowers salmon-pink tinted yellow, large, full, intense fragrance; few prickles
'Rose Neumann' -- See 'Rose Edouard'
'Rose Noble'   HT, lp, 1927, Mühle; bud long, pointed; flowers silvery pink, semi-dbl.; ['Mme Caroline Testout' × unknown]
'Rose Nuggets'   Min, lp, 1991, Michelis, Dorothy; bud pointed; flowers light pink, aging lighter, self-cleaning, many petaloids, small, 30 petals, high-centered, borne singly, no fragrance; foliage small, dark green, glossy, frequently 7 leaflets; very full, bushy, low growth; [sport of 'Red Ace']; intr. 1992
'Rose O'Bree'   F, O'Bree, Nancy
'Rose Odyssey 2000' -- See 'Balparty'
'Rose Œillet de Saint-Arquey (Vilfroy)' -- See 'Serratipetala'
'Rose of Castile' -- See 'Summer Damask'
'Rose of Clifton'   F, yb, 1978, Sanday, John; bud pointed; flowers gold edged peach-pink, large, 27 petals; foliage dark, matte; vigorous, upright growth; ['Vera Dalton' × 'Parasol']
'Rose of Freedom'   HT, mr, 1948, Swim, H.C.; bud ovoid; flowers clear rose red, 3½-4½ in., 50 petals, intense tea and spice fragrance; foliage leathery, dark; vigorous, upright, bushy growth; PP791; ['Charlotte Armstrong' × 'Night']
'Rose of Hope' -- See 'Perhope'
'Rose of Lidice'   HT, yb, 1961, Wheatcroft Bros.; flowers lemon-yellow shaded poppy red; [sport of 'Tzigane']
'Rose of Narromine' -- See 'Wekdykstra'
'Rose of Paestum' -- See 'Summer Damask'
'Rose of Picardy' -- See 'Ausfudge'
'Rose of Provence' -- See 'Cabbage Rose'
'Rose of Rhone' -- See 'Cabbage Rose'
'Rose of Rove' -- See 'Cabbage Rose'
'Rose of the Tombs' -- See 'St John's Rose'
'Rose of Torridge'   HT, dp, 1961, Allen, E.M.; flowers deep pink, 6 in., 36 petals; foliage glossy; vigorous growth; ['Karl Herbst' × 'Pink Charming']
'Rose of Tralee'   S, op, 1964, McGredy, Sam IV; flowers deep pink shaded salmon, 4 in., 35 petals, borne in small clusters, slight fragrance; foliage dark; very vigorous, bushy growth; ['Leverkusen' × 'Korona']
'Rose of Wagga Wagga' -- See 'Jacdash'
'Rose 1'   F, w, Teranishi; intr. 1999
'Rose Opal'   HT, dp, 1961, LeGrice; flowers pink-opal, well-formed, 4-5 in., 25-30 petals, moderate fragrance; foliage dark (reddish when young); vigorous, upright, bushy growth; PP2190; ['Wellworth' × 'Independence']
'Rose Optimiste'   HT, pb, Gaujard
'Rose Osaka'   HT, dr, 2003, Teranishi, Kikuo; flowers 15 cm., very full, borne mostly solitary, slight fragrance; foliage large, medium green, semi-glossy; prickles large; growth upright, tall (150 cm.); garden, exhibition; [('Helene Schoen' × seedling) × seedling]; intr. 2003
'Rose Parade'   F, pb, 1974, Williams, J. Benjamin; bud ovoid; flowers coral-peach to pink, large, dbl., cupped, moderate fragrance; foliage large, glossy; vigorous, bushy, compact growth; PP3065; ['Sumatra' × Queen Elizabeth®]
'Rose Pavot' -- See 'Grosse Mohnkopfs Rose'
'Rose Pearl' -- See 'Korterschi'
'Rose-Pink Ophelia' -- See 'Pink Ophelia'
'Rose Pluton' -- See 'Pluton'
'Rose Ponceau' -- See 'Poncheau-Capiaumont'
'Rose Poncheaux' -- See 'Poncheau-Capiaumont'
'Rose Professor Sieber' -- See 'Korparesni'
'Rose Prolifère' -- See 'Prolifera de Redouté'
'Rose Queen'   HT, mp, 1911, Hill, E. G.; bud long, pointed
'Rose Queen'   HT, or, Whisler; bud globular; flowers 4-5 in., 38 petals, high-centered, moderate fragrance; foliage leathery, dark; vigorous, upright, bushy growth; PP2203; ['Chrysler Imperial' × seedling]; intr. 1962
Rose Rhapsody™ -- See 'Jacsash'
'Rose Sachet' -- See 'Jacsash'
'Rose Sachet'   HT, dp, J&P; intr. 1998
'Rose Schelfhout' -- See 'De Schelfhout'
'Rose Sherbet'   F, dp, 1970, Pal, Dr. B.P.; bud globular; flowers deep rose-pink, medium, dbl., intense fragrance; foliage glossy; vigorous, upright, open growth; ['Gruss an Teplitz' × unknown]; intr. 1962
'Rose Tulipe'   HFt, yb, before 1817, Dupont/Noisette; flowers yellow with poppy bands
'Rose Two Thousand' -- See 'Cocquetrum'
'Rose Unique' -- See 'White Provence'
'Rose Valmae'   S, mr, 1981, Watts, Mrs. M.A.; flowers decorative, 40 petals, borne in clusters of 3; foliage light green, 7 leaflet; upright, medium growth
'Rose van Sian' -- See 'Cardinal de Richelieu'
'Rose Verreux' ('Verhaux') D, dp, before 1848; flowers red, tinged lilac, paler at edges, medium, full, globular
'Rose Verte' ('Croix Verte') HT, w, Croix; flowers creamy white with green tinges and touch of apricot in center; intr. 1989
'Rose Window'   Min, ob, 1979, Williams, Ernest D.; bud ovoid, pointed; flowers orange, yellow, and red blend, 1 in., 15-20 petals, hybrid tea, borne singly, slight fragrance; recurrent; foliage small, dark green, rounded leaflets; prickles small, thin; spreading, bushy growth; [seedling × 'Over the Rainbow']; intr. 1978
'Rose Yokohama' -- See 'Keihayokoki'
'Rosea' -- See 'Gallica Alba'
'Rosea'   Bslt, lp, 1824, Boursault; [R. banksiae alba-plena × unknown]
'Rosea'   F, Delforge; intr. 1974
'Rosea Centfeuilles'   HP, dp, Touvais
'Roseanna'   Cl Min, dp, 1977, Williams, Ernest D.; bud pointed; flowers deep pink with slightly darker reverse, 1-1½ in., 50+ petals, high-centered, borne singly and in clusters; recurrent in cycles; foliage glossy, firm, medium green; tall, semi-climbing growth; ['Little Darling' × seedling]; intr. 1976
'Roseanne'   HT, dr; intr. 2000
'Roseate'   Cl HT, mr, 1931, Clark, A.; flowers large, semi-dbl., cupped; foliage wrinkled; vigorous, climbing growth; good as a pillar
'Roseball' ('Rose Ball') S, lp, 2006, Beales, Amanda; flowers light powder pink, 15 cm., dbl., globular, borne in large clusters; foliage medium size, dark green, semi-glossy; prickles moderate; growth bushy, medium (1 m.); hedging; ['Bonica' × 'English Miss']; intr. 2002
'Roseberry Blanket' ('Purple Kiss', Raspberry Vigorosa™) S, dp, Kordes; flowers fuchsia-toned, 2½ in., 15-20 petals, borne in clusters, slight spicy fragrance; groundcover; spreading growth; PPAF
'Rosebud'   S, pb, Demits; flowers single; hybrid filipes; intr. 1997
'Rosecarpe'   HT, yb, 1993, Poole, Lionel; flowers cream shaded pink, 3-3½ in., full, borne mostly singly; foliage large, dark green, semi-glossy; some prickles; medium (100 cm.), upright growth; ['Selfridges' × 'Mischief']; intr. 1994
'Rosée du Matin' -- See 'Elisa'
'Rosee O'Bree'   F, mp, 1998, O'Bree, Nancy; flowers medium pink, lighter reverse, multi-clored, ¾-2½ in., dbl., borne in large clusters; foliage medium green, semi-glossy; prickles moderate; spreading, rambling, medium growth
'Roseford'   LCl, lp, 1982, Jerabek, Paul E.; bud ovoid; flowers light pink, slightly darker reverse, 28 petals, cupped, borne 6 per cluster, slight fragrance; repeats well; foliage dark, semi-glossy; prickles straight, red; bushy growth; [seedling × seedling]
'Roseglen Bouquet'   F, pb, 1953, Quinn;

flowers ivory-white edged deep pink, small, very dbl., high-centered; foliage dark, glossy, leathery; vigorous, upright growth; ['Pinocchio' × unknown]

Rosehill™ -- See 'Poulrohill'

'Roseketeer' -- See 'Tinketeer'

'Rösel Dach' Pol, mr, 1906, Walter; flowers cherry red, edges lighter, very full

'Rosel Vogel' S, m, 1938, Vogel, M.; flowers small, dbl.

'Roseland Rosette' F, dp, 1952, Houghton, T.B.; bud globular; flowers deep rose-pink, small, dbl.; vigorous, bushy growth; [sport of 'Crimson Rosette']

'Roselandia' HT, my, 1924, Stevens, W.; flowers darker and larger; [sport of 'Golden Ophelia']

'Roselandia, Climbing' Cl HT, my, 1933, Lens

'Roselette' F, mp, 1957, Lens; flowers soft salmon-pink; foliage bright green; very vigorous growth; [Orange Triumph® × 'Alain']

'Roselina' -- See 'Korsaku'

'Roseline de Kersaint' HT, dp, Adam; flowers fuchsia, double, high-centered, borne mostly singly, intense citronné fragrance; recurrent; compact, vigorous (90 - 110 cm.) growth; intr. 1997

Rosella™ -- See 'Fetosa'

'Rosella' -- See 'Bobby Dazzler'

'Rosella' Cl HT, pb, Dot, Pedro; bud long, pointed; flowers velvety carmine, base yellow, orange undertone, 2¾ in., single, borne in clusters; foliage large, glossy; vigorous (8 ft.) growth; [('Mme Edouard Herriot' × 'Roger Lambelin') × unknown]; intr. 1931

'Rosella' HGal, lp, about 1830, Racine; flowers light pink, medium to large, full, borne in clusters

'Rosella' F, pb, Prior; flowers salmon-rose-pink, ruffled, semi-dbl., borne in large trusses; vigorous growth; [sport of 'Else Poulsen']; intr. 1930

'Rosella Grace Cremer' F, dp, 1957, Cremer; bud conical to ovoid; flowers dark Tyrian rose, reverse lighter, rosette center, medium, 35-40 petals, moderate fragrance; very vigorous, bushy growth; PP1607; [sport of 'Garnette']

'Rosella Sweet' ('Rosalie') HT, op, 1930, Pernet-Ducher; flowers nasturtium-yellow suffused salmon-pink, large

Rosellana® -- See 'Barros'

'Rosemarie Hinner' HT, mp, 1949, Hinner, P.; bud long, pointed; flowers large, high-centered, foliage leathery, light green; very vigorous, upright, bushy growth; ['Frau Karl Druschki' × ('Ellen' × 'Una Wallace')]

Rosemarin® ('Rosmarin') Min, pb, 1965, Kordes, R.; flowers light pink, reverse light red, small, globular, borne several together, slight fragrance; recurrent; foliage glossy, light green; dwarf, bushy growth; ['Tom Thumb' × 'Dacapo']

'Rosemary' HGal, m, 1842, Vibert; flowers lilac-pink, spotted white, large, full, rosette; foliage large, marbled with yellowish splotches; ['Boule de Neige' × unknown]

'Rosemary' HT, lp, Hill, E. G.; flowers translucent, silky pink, very large, very full; intr. 1907

'Rosemary, Climbing' Cl HT, lp, 1920, Dingee & Conard; flowers very large, dbl.; [sport of 'Rosemary']

'Rosemary' HT, lp, Cant, F.; bud long, pointed; flowers carmine-pink shaded old-gold, medium, very dbl., high-centered, borne several together on long stems, moderate fragrance; free, recurrent boom; foliage large, leathery; few prickles; growth vigorous, climbing; very hardy; intr. 1925

'Rosemary' Min, mp, Letts; flowers apple-blossom-pink; intr. 1955

'Rosemary' F, dp, Schenkel; bud ovoid; flowers rose-pink, 2½ in., 55-60 petals, flat, borne in clusters, moderate fragrance; foliage leathery; vigorous, bushy growth; PP1398; [sport of 'Garnette']; intr. 1955

'Rosemary Clooney' F, ab, 1985, French, Richard; flowers creamy apricot, 20 petals, borne in clusters of 3-6; foliage small, medium green, matte; prickles small, red; upright, bushy growth; ['Vera Dalton' × Elizabeth of Glamis®]

'Rosemary Duncan' F, my, 1964, Duncan; flowers yellow, edged lighter, medium, 40 petals; foliage glossy; vigorous, bushy growth; [sport of 'Pinocchio']

'Rosemary Eddie' F, mp, 1956, Eddie; flowers bright pink, well-formed; ['New Dawn' × 'Fashion']

'Rosemary Foster' LCl, lp, 2000, Foster, Maurice; flowers medium pink, fading to white, slightly darker at edges, orange stamens, 3 cm., single, borne in very large clusters, slight fragrance; foliage large, medium green, semi-glossy; prickles moderate; growth climbing, vigorous, tall (35 ft.); ['Kiftsgate' × unknown]; intr. 1996

'Rosemary Gandy' ('Flash') F, yb, 1959, Gaujard; flowers yellow and coppery, medium, semi-dbl., cupped, moderate fragrance; foliage glossy, bronze; bushy, strong, upright growth; [('Tabarin' × unknown) × ('Jolie Princesse' × unknown)]; intr. 1958

'Rosemary Harkness' -- See 'Harrowbond'

'Rosemary Ladlau' S, m, Delbard; bud pointed; flowers deep mauve-violet, full, high-centered, then quartered, intense sweet fragrance; recurrent; foliage dark green, glossy ; stems medium long; vigorous, well-branched, medium growth; intr. 2002

'Rosemary McCoy' -- See 'Burcoy'

'Rosemary Murray' F, my, Harkness; flowers yellow, fading toward white on outer petals, full, rosette, moderate fragrance; recurrent; growth to 80 cm.; intr. 2005

'Rosemary Roache's Burnett' HSpn, pb, Roache, Rosemary; flowers lilac-pink centers with cream edges, medium, semi-dbl., shallow cup, borne in small clusters, intense fragrance; recurrent; foliage fine, ferny; growth to 3 × 3 ft.; hips elongated, black; ['Irish Rich Marble' × unknown]; this may be Irish Rich Marble and not a seedling of it

'Rosemary Rose' F, dp, 1957, deRuiter; flowers medium, dbl., camellia-shaped, borne in large trusses, moderate fragrance; foliage coppery; vigorous, bushy growth; ['Gruss an Teplitz' × 'floribunda seedling']; intr. 1954

'Rosemary Stone' HT, mp, 1970, Stone; flowers pink, very dbl., high-centered; foliage leathery; moderate, upright growth; [sport of 'Waltzing Matilda']

'Rosemary Viaud' -- See 'Rose-Marie Viaud'

'Rosemary's Dream' Min, lp, 2000, Sawyer, Rosemary; bud ovoid; flowers light pink, aging to almost white, reverse white, medium, full, high-centered, borne mostly singly, slight fragrance; foliage medium size, medium green, semi-glossy; prickles moderate; upright, bushy, medium (24 in.) growth; [sport of 'Chelsea Belle']

'Rosemeade' -- See 'Rawsexan'

'Rosemere Cancer Foundation' HT, mr, 2004, Poole, Lionel; flowers 5 in., full, spiral-shaped, borne mostly solitary, slight fragrance; free-flowering; foliage medium size, dark green, semi-glossy; prickles medium, triangular; growth upright, bushy, medium (3 ft.); garden, bedding, exhibition; ['Raewyn Henry' × 'Red Planet']; intr. 2005

'Rosemonde' D, pb, 1825, Toutain; flowers pink, plumed white; probably the same as R. gallica versicolor

Rosemoor™ -- See 'Austough'

'Rosen-Lambert' LCl, dr, 1937, Vogel, M.; flowers oxblood-red, very large, dbl.; foliage large, bronze, leathery; vigorous, climbing (9 ft.) growth; ['Fragezeichen' × 'American Pillar']

'Rosen-Müller' S, mr, 1940, Vogel, M.; flowers medium, single

'Rosenau' F, dr, Eggert; flowers glowing dark red, large, dbl., borne in clusters, slight fragrance; recurrent; even, low (50 cm.) growth; winter hardy; intr. 1961

Rosenborg™ (Drottningholm™) F, lp, Poulsen; flowers light pink, deeper in center, 10-15 cm., full, cupped, borne in clusters, no fragrance; recurrent; foliage dark green, glossy; bushy, medium (60-100 cm.) growth; intr. 2000

Rosenburg Riederburg™ -- See 'Pouldron'

Rosendal™ F, pb, Poulsen; flowers pink blend, 8-10 cm., dbl., cupped, borne in clusters, no fragrance; recurrent; foliage dark green, glossy; bushy, tall (100-150 cm.) growth; PP13451; intr. 2001

'Rosendel' F, m

'Rosendorf Schmitshausen' LCl, dr, Cocker; flowers dark scarlet-crimson, large, dbl., borne usually singly, slight fragrance; good repeat; foliage dark green; intr. 1977

Rosendorf Sparrieshoop® -- See 'Kordibor'

'Rosendorf Steinfurth' S, mp, Schultheis; flowers medium pink, fading to white, small, semi-dbl., cupped, borne in clusters, slight fragrance; fast repeat; foliage medium green; growth to 8-10 ft.; intr. 1993

'Rosendorf Ufhoven' HEg, dr, 1949, W. Kordes Söhne; flowers magenta-crimson, very large, very dbl., globular, borne in small clusters; non-recurrent; foliage leathery, glossy, dark; weak stems; vigorous, upright, bushy growth; ['Gen. MacArthur' × 'Magnifica']

'Rosenelfe' ('Rose Elf') F, mp, 1939, Kordes; bud long, pointed; flowers 2½ in., dbl., high-centered, borne in clusters, moderate fragrance; foliage leathery, glossy, light; vigorous, bushy growth; ['Else Poulsen' × 'Sir Basil McFarland']

'Rosenella' HT, mp, 1964, Mondial Roses; flowers clear pink, reverse brighter

Rosenfee® F, lp, Boerner; intr. 1967

Rosenfee® F, mp, Kordes; bud salmon red; flowers pure pink, 7-8 cm., very full, cupped, borne in clusters, slight fresh fragrance; recurrent; arching (70 cm.) growth; intr. 2007

'Rosenfest' LCl, op, GPG Roter Oktober; flowers pale crimson/cherry, large, semi-dbl., borne in clusters, moderate fragrance; foliage large, glossy, rounded; strong (8-12 ft.) growth; [(Dortmund® × unknown) × seedling]; intr. 1981

Rosenholm™ -- See 'Poulover'

'Rosenkavalier' F, or, Huber; intr. 1995

'Rosenkavalier' F, dp, 1965, Verschuren, A.; flowers deep rose, 45 petals, borne in clusters, intense fragrance; foliage dark; vigorous, upright, bushy growth; intr. 1963

'Rosenkreis Neunkirchen' F, mr, Michler, K. H.; flowers luminous red, semi-dbl.; intr. 1995

'Rosenmärchen' F, mp, (Kordes per CRL); flowers strong pink; intr. 1992

'Rosenmärchen, Climbing' -- See 'Pinocchio, Climbing'

'Rosenmärchen' -- See 'Pinocchio'

'Rosenpfarrer Meyer' HT, or, 1930, Soupert & Notting; flowers coral-red passing to prawn-red, semi-dbl.; very vigorous growth; ['Mme Edouard Herriot' × 'Louise Catherine Breslau']

'Rosenprinz' S, dp, Wänninger, Franz; flowers small, dbl.; very low, almost dwarf growth; intr. 1990

'Rosenprinzessin' -- See 'Helprinzess'

'Rosenprinzessin' (Rosenprinzessin Evi®) HT, mp, 1976, Hetzel; bud ovoid; flowers 3½-5 in., dbl., moderate fragrance; foliage glossy; upright growth; ['Nordia' × 'Sans Souci']; intr. 1975

'Rosenprinzessin Andrea' HT, mr, Hetzel; intr. 1993

Rosenprinzessin Evi® -- See 'Rosenprinzessin'

Rosenprofessor Sieber® -- See 'Korparesni'

'Rosenreigen' -- See 'Poulfan'

Rosenresli® -- See 'Korresli'

Rosenrot® HT, mr, Tantau; flowers velvety deep crimson, moderate fragrance; intr. 1978

Rosenstadt Freising® ('Triple Treat') S, w, Kordes; bud pointed, reddish; flowers white with red edges, aging to white with red splashes and pink tones, 7 cm., dbl., cupped, borne in clusters, slight fragrance; recurrent; foliage dark green, glossy; upright (4 ft.), bushy growth; intr. 2004

Rosenstadt Zweibrücken® -- See 'Korstatis'

'Rosentanz' -- See 'Frydarkeye'

'Rosenthal' -- See 'Tatjana'

Rosenwalzer® S, pb, Dickson, Patrick; intr. 1993

'Rosenwunder' HEg, dp, 1934, Kordes; bud long, pointed; flowers rose pink to rose red, 3 in., semi-dbl., globular to cupped, borne in small clusters; non-recurrent; foliage large, leathery, glossy, wrinkled; very vigorous, bushy growth; hips squat, turban-shaped, fleshy, bright orange; ['W.E. Chaplin' × R. rubiginosa]

'Rosenwunder von Schloss Hexenagger' Pol, dp, Hetzel, Karl; flowers strong pink, 0.75 in., semi-double, shallow cup, borne in clusters, slight fragrance; recurrent; foliage medium, medium green, glossy; short (40 - 50 cm.), bushy growth; intr. 2001

'Rosenzauber' -- See 'White Fleurette'

'Rosenzauber' F, lp, Wänninger, Franz; flowers medium, semi-dbl.; intr. 1991

'Roseraie de Blois' -- See 'Dorfuri'

'Roseraie de l'Hay' HRg, dr, 1901, Cochet-Cochet; flowers crimson-red changing to rosy magenta, 4 in., dbl., intense fragrance; recurrent bloom; foliage medium green, rugose; vigorous (4-5 ft.) growth; [R. rugosa rubra × unknown]

'Roseraie du Châtelet' F, pb, Sauvageot; flowers rose-carmine and bengal-rose, dbl., rosette; intr. 1999

'Roserie' ('Rosary') HMult, mp, 1917, Witterstaetter; flowers Tyrian pink, base white, darkening with age, 3¾ in., semi-dbl., open, borne in clusters; foliage large, rich green, leathery, glossy; thornless; very vigorous, climbing growth; [sport of 'Tausendschön']

Roseromantic® -- See 'Korsommer'

Roses Are Red™ -- See 'Mornine'

'Rosetime' -- See 'Bentem'

Roseto Carla Fineschi® ('Barfine') F, ab, Barni; bud elongated; flowers chamois and pale pink, 25 petals, tea rose, borne in clusters of 5 - 7, moderate fragrance; recurrent; foliage very dark green; upright (60 - 80 cm.) growth; intr. 2007

'Rosetone' Min, mp, 1977, Moore, Ralph S.; bud ovoid, pointed; flowers 1 in., 60 petals, high-centered; foliage small, dark, leathery; very bushy growth; ['Dream Dust' × 'Little Chief']

'Rosetta' -- See 'Sporose'

'Rosette' Pol, mr, 1926, Grandes Roseraies de la Loire; flowers fuchsia-red, medium, dbl.; semi-dwarf growth

'Rosette' HT, or, Dickson, A.; flowers rose red, shaded orange, base yellow, well-formed, large, dbl., moderate fragrance; vigorous, bushy growth; intr. 1934

'Rosette' F, op, Archer; flowers peach-pink, dbl., borne in clusters; vigorous growth; intr. before 1958

'Rosette de la Légion d'Honneur' HT, op, 1896, Bonnaire; flowers salmon-pink, medium, semi-dbl.

'Rosette Delizy' T, yb, 1922, Nabonnand, P.; flowers yellow, apricot reflexes, outer petals dark carmine, well-formed, dbl., slight fragrance; free-flowering; vigorous (3-5 ft.) growth; ['Général Galliéni' × 'Comtesse Bardi']

'Rosetti Stone' -- See 'Rossetti Rose'

'Roseville College' -- See 'The Roseville College Rose'

'Rosewood' HT, dp, 1998, Prescott, Cheryl; flowers neon pink, dbl., 4-4½ in., dbl., borne in small clusters; foliage medium size, medium green, semi-glossy; prickles medium; upright, compact, medium growth; [sport of 'Kardinal']

'Roseworld' -- See 'Similam'

'Rosey Garland' HMult, mp, Robinson; flowers rose pink, borne in clusters, moderate fragrance; non-remontant; vigorous growth; [sport of 'The Garland']; intr. 2002

'Rosey Gem' ('Lutin') Min, mp, 1972, Meilland; flowers Neyron rose, small, 50-60 petals, cupped, then flat, borne in compact trusses; recurrent; foliage small, semi-glossy, dark green; medium, bushy, vigorous growth; [sport of Scarlet Gem®]

'Rosey Lou' Min, pb, McCann, Sean; flowers medium, dbl., slight fragrance; foliage medium; intr. 2005

'Rosey Meidiland' S, dp, Meilland; low, spreading growth; intr. 2006

'Rosi Mittermeier' -- See 'Kormiora'

Rosie™ -- See 'Benros'

'Rosie Jane' F, mp, 2005, Paul Chessum Roses; flowers single, borne mostly solitary, no fragrance; foliage medium size, medium green, semi-glossy; prickles small, short, red, few; growth bushy, medium (24 in.); bedding, containers; [seedling × seedling]; intr. 2005

'Rosie Larkin' -- See 'Fryyippee'

'Rosie O'Donnell' -- See 'Wekwinwin'

'Rosier d'Amour' ('Austriaca', 'Rosier d'Autriche', 'Pumila', 'Petite Provins', 'Dwarf Austrian Rose', 'Nain') HGal, m, before 1806, possibly Crantz; sepals lanceolate; flowers whitish outside light purple within, large, 5 petals, borne in small clusters, moderate fragrance; foliage ovate, doubly dentate; prickles straight or slightly curved; growth branching; hips somewhat bristly, reddish or orange, persistent

'Rosier d'Autriche' -- See 'Rosier d'Amour'

'Rosier de Bourgogne à Grandes Fleurs' -- See 'Petite de Hollande'

'Rosier de Bourgon' ('Bourbon Jacques', 'Rose Jacques') B, dp, 1821, Breon/Jacques; flowers deep pink with lilac, medium, semi-dbl., cupped; somewhat remontant; ['Rose Edouard' × unknown]

'Rosier de Damas' D, mp, about 1840, from France; flowers medium, dbl., moderate fragrance

'Rosier de la Malmaison' -- See 'Quatre Saisons d'Italie'

'Rosier de Normandie' -- See 'Vivid'

'Rosier de Philippe Noisette' -- See R. × noisettiana

'Rosier de Portland' -- See 'Duchess of Portland'

'Rosier de Thionville' -- See 'Quatre Saisons Blanc Mousseux'

'Rosier des Dames' -- See 'Petite de Hollande'

'Rosier des Quatre Saisons' -- See 'Quatre Saisons Continue'

'Rosier d'Or' Pol, ob, 1969, Delbard; flowers orange-yellow, shaded apricot-yellow, 2½-3½ in., 20-28 petals; [Zambra® × ('Orléans Rose' × 'Goldilocks')]

'Rosier du Bengale' -- See 'Slater's Crimson China'

'Rosier Gloriette' Min, op; flowers orange-salmon, rosette form

'Rosier Mousseux' -- See 'Centifolia Muscosa'

'Rosier Panaché d'Angleterre' -- See R. × damascena versicolor

'Rosier Petit à Cent Feuilles' -- See 'Petite de Hollande'

'Rosier Tenuifolia' HRg, w, 1904, Bénard; foliage finely lacinate and curled; [R. rugosa alba × R. pimpinellifolia]

'Rosière d'Enghien' B, lp, 1875, Dallemagne; flowers whitish pink, small

'Rosiériste Chauvry' HP, mr, 1885, Gonod; flowers shining fiery red, large, full, globular; ['Victor Verdier' × unknown]

'Rosiériste Gaston Lévêque' HT, dp, 1932, Dot, Pedro; bud long, pointed; flowers brilliant carmine, large, dbl., cupped; foliage dark; very vigorous growth; ['Mme Butterfly' × 'Jean C.N. Forestier']

'Rosiériste Harms' HP, mr, 1879, Verdier, E.; flowers velvety scarlet, large, full; foliage delicate green, deeply serrated; prickles numerous, very fine and pointed; growth upright

'Rosiériste Jacobs' ('Duke of Wellington') HP, mr, 1880, Ducher; flowers velvety bright red, shaded darker, large, full, globular; repeats well

'Rosiériste Max Singer' ('Max Singer') HMult, dr, 1885, Lacharme, F.; flowers ruby-red, aging lighter, 7-8 cm., dbl., cupped, borne singly or in small clsuters, moderate tea fragrance; good repeat; foliage large; few prickles; growth vigorous (2½ m.); ['Polyantha Alba Plena Sarmentosa' × 'Général Jacqueminot']

'Rosiériste Pajotin-Chédane' Pol, dr, 1934, Délépine; flowers deep red, with white, thread-like markings, semi-dbl., cupped, borne in clusters on strong stems; foliage leathery; strong stems; vigorous, bushy growth

'Rosiériste Philbert Boutigny' HT, mp, 1904, Boutigny, P.; flowers carmine, globular; ['Reine Marie Henriette' × 'Victor Hugo']

'Rosika' -- See 'Harmusky'

'Rosilia' -- See 'Chewallop'

'Rosina' ('Josephine Wheatcroft', 'Yellow Sweetheart') Min, my, 1951, Dot, Pedro; flowers sunflower-yellow, small, 16 petals, borne in clusters, slight fragrance; foliage glossy, light; dwarf, compact growth; ['Eduardo Toda' × 'Rouletii']; intr. 1935

'Rosine' HT, pb, 1935, Lens; bud citron-yellow with red; flowers flesh-pink, base clear salmon, very dbl.; foliage bronze

'Rosine Dupont' HCh, w, Jacques; flowers flesh white, center violet, medium, very full

'Rosine Margottin' HP, lp, 1849, Margottin; flowers very pale flesh pink, medium, full

Rosita™ -- See 'Rosita Parade'

'Rosita' HT, lp, 1956, Delforge; bud long; flowers soft pink, large, dbl.; foliage glossy; vigorous growth; ['The Doctor' × seedling]

'Rosita Mauri' HT, dp, 1914, Ketten Bros.; flowers deep rose-pink, large, full, borne mostly solitary; ['Mme Abel Chatenay' × 'Étoile de France']

'Rosita Missoni' -- See 'Barmiss'

'Rosita Parade' (Rosita™) MinFl, yb, Poulsen; flowers yellow with red edges, 5-8 cm., semi-dbl., slight wild rose fragrance; foliage dark; growth bushy, 20-40 cm.; PP13111; intr. 2000

'Rosita Vendela' HT, dp, Tantau; greenhouse rose; intr. 2004

'Roslaw' ('D. H. Lawrence') HT, yb, 1985, McCarthy, Mrs. Rosemary; [sport of Gay Gordons®]

'Roslyn' HT, dy, 1929, Towill; bud long, pointed, deep orange; flowers golden yellow, reverse darker orange, large, semi-dbl.; vigorous, compact growth; ['Souv. de Claudius Pernet' × 'Buttercup']

'Roslyn, Climbing' Cl HT, dy, 1937, Vestal

'Roslyne' -- See 'Strawberry Ice'

'Rosmari' HT, pb, 1962, Dot, Simon; bud pointed; flowers pink, reverse purplish, 30 petals; strong stems; vigorous, upright growth; ['Vigoro' × 'First Love']

Rosmarin® -- See 'Korfanto'

'Rosmarin' -- See 'Rosemarin'

'Rosmarin 89' -- See 'Korfanto'

'Rosnella' Gr, Moro, L.; intr. 1958

'Rosoft' (Soft Morning™) F, ab, 2006; flowers medium, full, borne mostly solitary, no fragrance; foliage medium size, medium green,; spreading, medium growth; [sport of 'Rose Parade']; intr. 2006

'Rosomane Alix Huguier' HT, w, 1895, Bonnaire; flowers white with flesh pink reflections, center tinted salmon, very large, full

'Rosomane E. P. Roussel' HT, mr, 1907, Guillot; flowers glossy light crimson, reverse bright carmine, very large, full, moderate fragrance

'Rosomane Gravereaux' HT, w, 1899, Soupert & Notting; bud large, long; flowers silvery white, exterior tinted very lightly with flesh pink, very large, very full

'Rosomane Hubert' T, dy, 1883, Bernède; ['Gloiire de Dijon' × unknown]

Rosomane Janon® S, yb, Guillot - Massad; flowers yellow, adding red tints as it opens and ages , full, globular, moderate fruity fragrance; recurrent; 1 meter growth; intr. 2007

'Rosomane Narcisse Thomas' T, rb, 1908, Bernaix fils; flowers crimson suffused apricot-yellow, small

'Rosorum' F, or, 1959, Buisman, G. A. H.; flowers orange-scarlet, semi-dbl., borne in large clusters; foliage dark, glossy; vigorous, upright growth; ['Buisman's Triumph' × 'Alpine Glow']

'Ross Gowie' HT, dr, 1968, Gowie; flowers conical, large; vigorous, tall growth

'Ross Rambler' LCl, w, 1938; flowers small, single; blooms all summer; growth to 9 ft.; very hardy; discovered at the Dominion Forestry Station, Indian Head, Saskatchewan; probably a hybrid of R. beggeriana

'Rossana' HT, dr, 1958, Buyl Frères; flowers blood-red, well-shaped, large, dbl.; vigorous, spreading growth; ['Orange Delight' × 'Tudor']

'Rossetti Rose' ('Rosetti Stone') F, mp, Harkness; flowers large, delicate mid pink, very dbl., borne in large clusters, slight herbal fragrance; repeats freely; foliage dark green; bushy (3 × 3 ft.) growth; intr. 2004

Rossi® HT, my, Select; flowers 5 in., 25-35 petals, high-centered, borne singly; recurrent; stems 70-90 cm; florist rose; intr. 2003

'Rossini' HT, pb, deRuiter; florist rose

'Rosslyn' HP, mp, 1900, Dickson, A.; flowers rosy flesh, large, full

'Rosso Giacomasso' HT, Giacomasso; intr. 1967

'Rostock' HMsk, lp, 1937, Kordes; bud long, pointed; flowers very large, dbl., cupped, borne in clusters, slight fragrance; recurrent; foliage leathery, glossy, dark; very vigorous, bushy (4 ft.) growth; ['Eva' × 'Louise Catherine Breslau']

'Rostwo' HT, yb, Ross; intr. 2006

'Roswytha' F, mp, 1968, van der Meyden; bud ovoid; flowers pink, small, very dbl., borne in clusters; foliage dark; [sport of 'Carol']

'Rosy' Min, mp, Chandrakant; flowers non-fading pink, very full, rosette; free-flowering; [sport of 'Don Don']; intr. 1993

'Rosy Ann' -- See 'Lenlitpap'

Rosy Border™ -- See 'Pouloesy'

Rosy Carpet® -- See 'Intercarp'

'Rosy Cheeks' HT, rb, 1976, Anderson's Rose Nurseries; flowers red, reverse yellow, 7 in., 35 petals, intense fragrance; foliage dark, glossy; [unknown × 'Irish Gold']; intr. 1975

'Rosy Cheeks' S, op, Moore; flowers coral pink, small, semi-dbl., borne in clusters; recurrent; foliage small, glossy; vigorous, spreading (3 × 6 ft.) growth; intr. 1984

'Rosy Cheeks, Climbing' -- See 'Andros'

'Rosy Creeper' -- See 'Suma'

Rosy Cushion® -- See 'Interall'

'Rosy Dawn' Min, yb, 1982, Bennett, Dee; bud ovoid; flowers yellow, edged deep pink, medium, 25-30 petals, cupped, borne singly, slight tea fragrance; recurrent; foliage small, medium green, glossy; prickles small, slender, reddish; vigorous, erect (24 in.) growth; PP5274; [Magic Carrousel® × Magic Carrousel®]

'Rosy Floorshow' S, pb; flowers rosy pink with white eye, 3½ in., 75 petals, cupped; foliage mid-green; growth compact, bushy plant (3 × 2 ft.); intr. 1999

'Rosy Forecast' -- See 'Lavlad'

'Rosy Future' -- See 'Harwaderox'

'Rosy Glow' HT, mp, 1947, Joseph H. Hill, Co.; bud long, pointed; flowers hermosa pink, 4-5 in., 25-35 petals, high-centered, intense fragrance; foliage leathery; vigorous, bushy growth; PP694; [sport of 'Better Times']

'Rosy Glow' F, mp, Hensen

'Rosy Hedge' -- See 'Interall'

'Rosy Hit' -- See 'Poulmar'

'Rosy Jewel' Min, pb, 1959, Morey, Dr. Dennison; bud ovoid; flowers rose-red, reverse lighter, center white, 1 in., 25 petals, moderate fragrance; low (6-8 in.), compact growth; PP1899; ['Dick Koster' × 'Tom Thumb']; intr. 1959

'Rosy Koster' Pol, mp

'Rosy La Sevillana, Climbing' Cl F, mp, Meilland; [sport of 'Rosy La Sevillana']; intr. 1993

'Rosy La Sevillana' -- See 'Meigeroka'

'Rosy Life' ('Vie en Rose') HT, mp, 1971, Delbard; flowers sparkling pink, 3-4 in., 25 petals; foliage glossy; vigorous growth; ['Walko' × 'Souv. de J. Chabert']

'Rosy Mantle' LCl, mp, 1968, Cocker; flowers pale coral pink, 12-14 cm., dbl., borne in small clusters, moderate fragrance; recurrent; foliage dark, glossy; growth to 8-10 ft.; ['New Dawn' × 'Prima Ballerina']

'Rosy Meillandina' -- See 'Meifinaro'

'Rosy Minimo' ('Ruinanny') Min, mp

Rosy Minuetto™ -- See 'Meideinis'

'Rosy Morn' HP, op, 1878, Paul, W.; flowers soft peach shaded salmon-pink, well-formed, very large; very vigorous growth; ['Victor Verdier' × unknown]

'Rosy Morn' LCl, mp, Clark, A.; flowers large; ['Frau Karl Druschki' × unknown]; intr. 1922

'Rosy Morn' Pol, mp, Burbage Nursery; flowers rose-pink, large, borne in large clusters, moderate fragrance; vigorous growth; intr. 1930

'Rosy Morn' -- See 'Improved Cécile Brünner'

'Rosy Outlook' -- See 'Wektorroc'

Rosy Pagode™ MinFl, mp, Poulsen; flowers medium pink, 5-8 cm., dbl., slight wild rose fragrance; foliage dark; growth broad, bushy, 40-60 cm.; PP14942; intr. 2002

Rosy Paillette™ -- See 'Pink Parade'

Rosy Pillow® S, dp, Kontor; intr. 1998

'Rosy Potluck' -- See 'Lavrosy'

'Rosy Purple' HMsk, m, Lens, Louis; flowers reddish-purple, yellow stamens, small, single, flat, borne in clusters, slight fragrance; recurrent; foliage disease-resistant; tall (5+ ft.) growth; intr. 1995

'Rosy Star' HT, dp; flowers bright, strong pink, dbl., high-centered

'Rosy Vision' -- See 'Nhrosy'

'Rosy Wings' -- See 'Mejakka'

'Rosy Wings' HT, dp, 1962, Delforge; flowers pink shaded light red, 2-2½ in., 35 petals, globular; foliage dark, glossy; vigorous growth; ['Pink Spiral' × seedling]

'Rosycola Panarosa' ('Infante Marie-Thérèse') F, r, Delbard; flowers deep scarlet orange, maturing to orange brown, petals curly, semi-dbl., open, borne in clusters; recurrent; vigorous growth; intr. 2001

Rotana® F, dy, Spek; flowers golden yellow, 4 in., 40-45 petals, urn-shaped, borne mostly singly; recurrent; few prickles; stems medium; florist rose; intr. 2006

'Rotaria' Min, or

'Rotarian' HT, mr, 1921, Lemon; bud long, pointed; flowers bright cherry-crimson, 35-40 petals; ['Ophelia' × unknown]

'Rotary Centennial Rose' S, dy, Taschner, Ludwig; intr. 2003

'Rotary Jubilee' HT, yb, 1973, Lindquist; bud ovoid; flowers yellow blend, creamy yellow, large, dbl., high-centered, moderate fragrance; foliage large, glossy, dark, leathery; vigorous, bushy growth; [Queen Elizabeth® × 'Peace']; intr. 1971

'Rotary-Lyon' HT, yb, 1936, Chambard, C.; bud long, pointed, well formed, golden pink; flowers old-gold shaded carmine, reverse yellow, stamens deep yellow, dbl., cupped; foliage dark; very vigorous growth

'Rotary President' F, or, 1976, Wood; flowers deep vermilion, 4 in., dbl., intense fragrance; foliage small, plum color, turning dark green; dwarf, bushy growth; ['Fairlight' × Summer Holiday®]

'Rotary Rose' -- See 'Meirypoux'

'Rotary Sunrise' ('The Rotarian', 'Voeux de Bonheur') HT, yb, Fryer; flowers golden orange, bright orange at petal edges, dbl., high-centered, borne mostly singly, moderate fragrance; recurrent; medium growth; intr. 2004

'Rote Apart' -- See 'Scarlet Pavement'

'Rote Better Times' HT, mr, 1940, Noack, Werner; flowers large, dbl.

'Röte Centifolie' C, dr, 1938, Krause; flowers deep red, medium, very dbl., intense fragrance

'Rote Else Poulsen' F, dp, 1934, Koopmann; [sport of 'Else Poulsen']

Rote Flamme® HKor, dr, Kordes; flowers dark blood-red, 8-9 cm., dbl., borne in small clusters, no fragrance; some repeat; foliage large, dark green, glossy; bushy, upright (13 ft.) growth; intr. 1967

'Rote Fox' -- See 'Scarlet Pavement'

'Rote Gabrielle Privat' ('Gabrielle Privat Rouge') Pol, mr, 1940, Koopmann; flowers raspberry red; 40 - 50 cm. growth; [sport of 'Gabrielle Privat']; intr. 1940

'Rote Hannover' S, mr; intr. 1998

'Rote Hermosa' Ch, mr, 1899, Geissler; flowers carmine-red, medium, dbl., moderate fragrance

'Rote Hermosa' -- See 'Queen's Scarlet'

'Rote Hiroshima' HT, mr, Tagashira, Kazuso; flowers carmine-red, large, dbl.; intr. 1990

'Rote Krimrose' ('Krimrose') HGal, dp; flowers bright pink to purple-pink, yellow stamens, large, full, intense fragrance; bushy, upright (5 ft.) growth; the Oilrose of Crimea

Rote Max Graf® -- See 'Kormax'

'Rote Mevrouw G. A. van Rossem' HT, or, 1934, Kordes; flowers nasturtium-red, reverse lightly tinted yellow, large, dbl., open, intense fragrance; foliage glossy, dark; vigorous growth; [sport of 'Mev. G.A. van Rossem']

Rote Mozart® ('Red Mozart') S, or, Kordes; intr. 1989

'Rote Perle' F, dr, 1962, Tantau, Math.; flowers deep red, 1½ in., 25 petals; foliage dark; vigorous, bushy growth

'Rote Pharisäer' HT, mr, 1927, Hinner, W.; bud very long, pointed; flowers well-shaped, large, dbl.; foliage reddish green,leathery; very vigorous growth; ['Pharisaer' × 'George C. Waud']

'Rote Rapture' HT, mr, 1934, Weber, J.; flowers bright cherry-red; [sport of 'Rapture']

'Rote Tausendschön' HMult, mr, 1918, Isenhut, Frau; flowers ruby red; ['Tausendschön' × 'Bordeaux']

'Rote Teschendorffs Jubiläumsrose' Pol, dp, 1930, Grunewald; flowers dark crimson-pink to light red, large, dbl., borne in large clusters; vigorous growth

Rote Woge® ('Festival Meidiland') S, mr, Meilland; flowers dbl., cupped, borne in clusters; spreading (80-100 cm.) growth;

intr. 1992

'Rotelfe' HT, dr, 1922, Tantau; flowers very dark red, medium, semi-dbl.; RULED EXTINCT 4/85; ['Château de Clos Vougeot' × 'Ulrich Brunner Fils']

Rotelfe® -- See 'Tanrecktor'

'Roter Champagner' ('Pétillante') HT, dp, 1963, Tantau, Math.; bud pointed; flowers red champagne color, large, dbl.; foliage bright green; long, strong stems; vigorous, upright growth

Roter Kobold® F, dr, Interplant; intr. 1994

Roter Korsar® -- See 'Korromalu'

'Roter Schmetterling' HFt, mr, 1935, Vogel, M.; flowers medium, semi-dbl.

'Roter Stern' ('Exciting') HT, mr, Meilland; flowers geranium red, dbl., cupped, borne mostly singly, very slight fragrance; recurrent; medium growth; intr. 1958

'Rotes Meer' -- See 'Purple Pavement'

'Rotes Meer' Pol, or, 1960, Verschuren, A.; flowers dbl., borne in large clusters; foliage glossy, dark; upright, bushy, symmetrical growth; [Orange Triumph® × seedling]

'Rotes Phænomen' HRg, m, Baum; flowers dark magenta purple, intense fragrance; foliage rough; numerous prickles; dense growth; hips round; intr. 2002

'Rotesmeer' -- See 'Purple Pavement'

Rotfassade® ('Red Facade') LCl, mr, Noack, Werner; flowers red with white base and yellow stamens, 6 cm., semi-dbl., cupped to flat, borne in clusters; recurrent; foliage medium to dark green, glossy; growth to 10 ft.; intr. 1997

'Rothsay' -- See 'Brosay'

Rotilia® -- See 'Korvillade'

'Rotkäppchen' Pol, mr, 1887, Geschwind, R.; flowers magenta-red, 6 cm., 30 petals, rosette, borne in small clusters; good repeat; bushy (50 cm.) growth; winter hardy

Rotkäppchen® F, dr, Kordes; flowers 7 cm., very full, rosette, borne in clusters, slight fragrance; recurrent; bushy, upright (70 cm.) growth; intr. 2007

'Rotorua' F, or, 1963, McGredy, Sam IV; bud ovoid; flowers orange-scarlet, large, 27 petals, high-centered, borne in clusters; foliage leathery, dark; short, strong stems; very vigorous, bushy growth; ['Independence' × 'Spartan']; intr. 1962

'Rotraut' Pol, dr, 1931, Grunewald; flowers dbl., borne in clusters; vigorous growth; [sport of 'Miss Edith Cavell']

'Rotrou' ('Routrou') M, m, 1849, Vibert; flowers reddish-violet, medium, dbl.

'Rouge' -- See 'Red Damask'

'Rouge' -- See 'Rubra'

'Rouge' -- See 'Rubra'

'Rouge' ('Double Red', 'Rubra Plena') HSpn, mp, about 1808, Descemet; bud nearly round; flowers delicate flesh pink, medium, dbl., borne mostly singly on the secondary branches; foliage round or elliptical, simply dentate; prickles unequal, short, almost straight; hips cherry-sized, red at first, blackening at maturity

'Rouge' T, mr, Nicolle; flowers crimson, medium to large, full, moderate fragrance; intr. about 1825

'Rouge' T, mr, Touvais; flowers vivid red, medium, full; intr. 1875

'Rouge' Pol, mr, Verschuren; flowers brilliant scarlet-crimson, open, semi-dbl.; foliage leathery; strong stems; dwarf growth; intr. 1934

Rouge Adam® ('Velvet Alibi®) HT, dr, Adam, M.; flowers velvety dark red, full to very full, high-centered, borne singly, slight fragrance; recurrent; foliage medium size, dark green, glossy; bushy, medium growth; intr. 1996

'Rouge Admirable' -- See 'Orphise'

'Rouge Admirable' -- See 'Pourpre Charmant'

'Rouge Admirable Strié' HGal, m, before 1836, Vibert; flowers striped purple

'Rouge Agréable' -- See 'Junon'

'Rouge Angevine' HP, mr, 1907, Chedane-Pajotin; flowers large, dbl.

'Rouge Ardoisé' HGal, dr, about 1845, Calvert; flowers slatey red

Rouge Baiser™ HT, mr, Delbard; flowers red to reddish-orange, high-centered; greenhouse variety

'Rouge Brillant' HGal, dr, about 1830, Vibert; flowers vivid light purple-red, medium, very full

'Rouge Captain Christy' HT, dp, 1898, Perrier; [sport of 'Captain Christy']

'Rouge Champion' HT, mr, 1956, Buyl Frères; flowers bright red, 40-50 petals; very vigorous growth; ['Happiness' × 'Princesse Liliane']

'Rouge de Belgique' ('Belgica Rubra', 'Vitex Spinosa') HGal, mr, before 1791; flowers large, dbl.; foliage dark green, often marbled yellow, wavy edges; Agathe group

'Rouge de Paris' ('Paris Red') F, mr, 1958, Delbard-Chabert; flowers light red, 3 in., 35-45 petals; foliage purplish; vigorous, bushy growth; [('Floradora' × unknown) × (Orange Triumph® × unknown)]; intr. 1964

'Rouge de Parme' HT, pb, 1963, Dorieux; flowers mauve-pink, large, dbl., high-centered; foliage dark, dull; [('Peace' × 'Fred Edmunds') × 'Buccaneer']

Rouge Dorieux® -- See 'Dormal'

'Rouge Dot' HT, mr, 1962, Dot, Simon; flowers currant-red, 20 petals; vigorous growth; [Baccará® × 'Lydia']

'Rouge Éblouissant' -- See 'Assemblage de Beauté(s)'

'Rouge et Or' -- See 'Redgold'

'Rouge et Or, Climbing' -- See 'Dicorsar'

'Rouge Formidable' ('Aldégonde', 'Manteau Rouge', 'Manteau Pourpre', 'Violet Brillant', 'Pourpre Cramoisi', 'Du Pont', 'Belle Bourbon', 'André Du Pont', 'Grand Condé', 'Porcia') HGal, mr, before 1811; flowers crimson-violet-purple, medium, very dbl.

Rouge Keops® Cl Min, mr; flowers bright red, yellow stamens when open, double, high-centered, borne in clusters; recurrent; flexible canes; growth 2.5 meter height; intr. 2008

'Rouge Koster' Pol, mr

'Rouge Mallerin' ('Henri Mallerin') HT, mr, 1934, Mallerin, C.; bud long, pointed; flowers brilliant red, large, dbl., high-centered, intense damask fragrance; compact growth; ['Mme Van de Voorde' × 'Lady Maureen Stewart']

'Rouge Marbrée' B, rb; flowers red and violet

'Rouge Meidiland' -- See 'Meineble'

'Rouge Meiland' -- See 'Meimalyna'

'Rouge Meilland' -- See 'Happiness'

'Rouge Meilland, Climbing -- See 'Happiness, Climbing'

Rouge Meillandécor® -- See 'Meineble'

'Rouge Meilove' F, dr, Meilland; flowers Bordeaux red, double, slight fragrance; recurrent; foliage disease-resistant; bushy (40 - 60 cm.) growth; intr. 2003

Rouge Panaramic® S, mr, Interplant; intr. 2006

'Rouge Pineau' F, Pineau; intr. 1980

'Rouge Plein' C, mr, 1826, Laffay; flowers full

Rouge Prolific® -- See 'Delific'

'Rouge Rayé' -- See 'Beauté Tendre'

Rouge Royale™ -- See 'Meikarouz'

'Rouge Saint-Victor' Pol, mr, Croix, Paul; flowers floriferous; recurrent; foliage glossy

'Rouge Striée' -- See 'Striata'

'Rouge Superbe Actif' HGal, dr, before 1811; bud round; flowers velvety crimson, small, very dbl., moderate fragrance

'Rouge Vif' -- See 'Capricornus'

'Rougeau Virginale' -- See 'Héloïse'

'Rougemoss' F, or, 1973, Moore, Ralph S.; bud ovoid, pointed; sepals covered densely with bristles mimicking moss; flowers scarlet, 2½ in., 30-40 petals, cupped, borne singly and in small clusters, moderate fragrance; recurrent; foliage medium to dark green, leathery, glossy; prickles numerous, medium, slender, straight, sharp, brown; vigorous, bushy (2½-3 ft.) growth; hips none ; PP3563; ['Rumba' × 'moss hybrid']; intr. 1972

'Rougextra' F, mr; flowers luminous scarlet; always in bloom

'Rouletii' ('Centifolia Minima', R. × centifolia minima, R. rouletii) Ch, mp, 1815, rediscovered in 1922 by Major Roulet; flowers rose-pink, ½ in., dbl.; recurrent bloom; dwarf growth; sometimes considered (Jäger) to be a dwarf form of R. semperflorens or R. bengalensis; probably synonymous with R. semperflorens minima (Lawrence)

'Rouletii, Climbing' Cl Ch, mp; possibly synonymous with 'Pompon de Paris, Cl.'

Roulette® HT, rb, Tantau; flowers medium red with white reverse, very large

, double, high-centered, borne mostly singly; recurrent; stems long; [sport of 'Vino Rosso']; florist rose; intr. 2004

'Rouletti, Climbing' -- See 'Pompon de Paris, Climbing'

'Round Robin' Min, mr, Hannemann, F.; ['Avandel' × 'Oz Gold']; intr. 1990

'Roundabout' -- See 'Zipround'

'Roundelay, Climbing' Cl Gr, dr; flowers deep crimson red; recurrent; vigorous (10 ft.) growth; [sport of 'Roundelay']; discovered in Australia; intr. 1970

'Roundelay' Gr, dr, 1954, Swim, H.C.; bud ovoid; flowers medium-large, 3-4 in., 35-40 petals, high-centered, then flat, borne mostly in clusters of 3-4, some singly, moderate tea fragrance; free-flowering; foliage dark green, glossy, leathery; prickles numerous, medium, hooked slightly downward, tawny; stems strong, long; very vigorous growth; hips globular, smooth, green; PP1280; ['Charlotte Armstrong' × 'Floradora']

'Rountuit' HRg, pb, Moore, Ralph; flowers rose pink, 2½ in., very dbl.; borne all season; growth somewhat spreading, to 5 ft.; intr. 2000

Roussillon® F, mr

Route 66™ -- See 'Wekmorfis'

'Routrou' -- See 'Rotrou'

'Roville' -- See 'Evero'

'Rowdy Roy' -- See 'Tinroy'

'Rowena' HWich, dp, 1912, Paul, W.; flowers carmine, changing to mauve-pink, small, dbl., borne in clusters; vigorous, climbing growth

'Roxana' HT, yb, 1933, Dickson, A.; bud large, long, pointed; flowers orange-yellow and copper, open, semi-dbl.; foliage glossy, light; vigorous, bushy growth

'Roxana' HT, or, Urban, J.

Roxane® -- See 'Lapdal'

'Roxane, Climbing' ('Grimpant Roxane') Cl HT, yb, Laperrière; flowers yellow with carmine red edges, slight fruity fragrance; growth to 3-5 m.; [sport of Roxane®]; intr. 2000

'Roxanne' F, Laperrière; intr. 1990

'Roxburghe Rose' -- See 'Cocember'

'Roxburghiana' -- See 'Grevilii'

'Roxelana' -- See 'Roxelane'

'Roxelane' ('Grande, Violette, et Belle', 'La Grande Violette') HGal, dp, 1811; flowers light purple, semi-dbl.

'Roxelane' ('Roxelana') HCh, mp, Prévost; flowers medium pink, inner petals often marked with white, small, dbl., cupped; sometimes classed as HGal; intr. about 1825

'Roxette' F, op, Select; flowers salmon pink, 9 cm., 30-40 petals, high-centered, borne mostly singly; recurrent; florist rose; intr. 2003

'Roxie' -- See 'Resox'

Roxie™ -- See 'Tuckgrinnel'

Roxie Baby™ -- See 'Tuckrox'

Roxy® Min, m, Kordes; flowers violet, 4 cm., very full, flat, almost quartered, no fragrance; recurrent; foliage disease-resistant; bushy, upright (40 cm.) growth; intr. 2007

'Roxy' -- See 'Roxy 2001'

'Roxy 2001' ('Roxy') HT, mr, Kordes; flowers large, dbl., high-centered, borne mostly singly; good repeat; stems long (80 cm) in greenhouse; florist rose; intr. 2001

'Roxy Kordana Mini Brite' Min, mr, Kordes; bud long, blunt topped; flowers medium red, reverse slightly darker, occasional white streak, 2-2¼ in., 35-40 petals, high-centered, then flat, borne singly and in small clusters, no fragrance; free-flowering; foliage leathery, glossy; prickles moderate, short, straight; stems 8-10 in.; vigorous, upright (3 ft.) growth; PP11148; [seedling × seedling]; intr. 1998

Roy Black™ -- See 'Poulari'

'Roy Castle Rose' -- See 'Poulduf'

Royal™ -- See 'Royal Parade'

Royal™ Min, mp, Poulsen; intr. 2000

'Royal Air Force' HT, m, 1969, Laperrière; flowers light lavender-blue, 6 in., 35 petals, high-centered, slight tea and lavender fragrance; foliage dark, matte

'Royal Albert Hall' HT, rb, 1972, Cocker; flowers wine-red, reverse gold,, 5 in., 32 petals, intense tea fragrance; foliage dark; compact growth; ['Fragrant Cloud' × 'Postillon']

'Royal Amber' S, ab, Clements, John; flowers rich apricot-amber, very ruffled, 4 in., 33 petals, pompon, moderate old rose fragrance; recurrent; bronzy red leaves become medium green, matte; compact (4 × 3½ ft.) growth; PPAF; intr. 2000

'Royal America' LCl, w, 1994, Cooper, Curt; flowers ivory, medium, semi-dbl., borne in small clusters, slight fragrance; foliage medium size, light green, matte; tall, bushy, spreading growth; [sport of 'America']; intr. 1995

Royal Amethyst™ -- See 'Devmorada'

'Royal Anniversary' -- See 'Harbonny'

Royal Ascot® -- See 'Delsab'

'Royal Baby' -- See 'Debrad'

Royal Baccara® HT, mr, Meilland; flowers velvety red, dbl., high-centered, bonre mostly singly; good repeat; florist rose; intr. 2002

'Royal Ballgown' -- See 'Harwicklow'

'Royal Bassino' ('Country Prince') S, mr, Kordes; flowers bright red to scarlet with yellow stamens, medium, semi-dbl., shallow cup to flat, borne in clusters, slight fragrance; continuous blooms; medium (2-3 ft.), spreading, ground-cover growth

'Royal Bath & West' Gr, lp, 1977, Sanday, John; flowers pastel pink, 4 in., 20 petals; foliage green, matte; [seedling × 'Prima Ballerina']

'Royal Beauty' HT, dr, 1940, Coddington; flowers dark velvety red, 5 in., 25 petals, high-centered, moderate spicy fragrance; foliage bronze; PP452; [sport of 'Better Times']

'Royal Blush' -- See 'Sieroyal'

Royal Bonica™ -- See 'Meimodac'

'Royal Bouquet' -- See 'Tanmeda'

'Royal Bright' HT, my, 1977, Kono, Yoshito; bud ovoid; flowers 6 in., very dbl., high-centered, vigorous, upright growth; ['Garden Party' × ('Bronze Masterpiece' × 'Memoriam')]; intr. 1976

'Royal Canadian' HT, mr, 1967, Boerner, E. S.; bud ovoid; flowers deep, clear red, very large, dbl., open, borne singly and several together; foliage large, leathery; vigorous, upright growth; [seedling × seedling]

'Royal Canadian' HT, mr, 1968, Morey, Dennison H., Jr.; buds large, ovoid to urn-shaped; flowers scarlet, 5-5½ in., 25-30 petals, cupped, borne mostly singly; free-flowering; foliage leathery, glossy; prickles moderate, medium, hooked downward; stems medium, strong; growth upright, vigorous; no hips; PP2736

Royal Carpet™ -- See 'Minuco'

'Royal Celebration' F, m, Carruth, Tom; flowers velvet purple, dbl., cupped, borne in clusters, intense clove fragrance; recurrent; foliage semi-glossy; slender, fairly short growth; intr. 2004

'Royal Chinook' HT, mr, 1939, Chase; flowers brilliant rose-red; PP383; [sport of 'Rapture']

Royal Circus® HT, rb, Kordes; flowers bright red, reverse yellow suffused with red from the outer edge, medium, full, high-centered, borne mostly singly; recurrent; stems medium; [sport of 'Circus']; florist rose; intr. 2005

'Royal City' -- See 'Renity'

'Royal Class' HT, dr; flowers deep classic red; intr. 2004

'Royal Cluster' HMult, lp, 1899, Dawson; flowers blush white, 4 cm., single, borne in clusters of up to 100; ['Hermosa' × 'Dawson']; intr. 1899

Royal Copenhagen™ (Remember™) HT, lp, Olesen; bud pointed ovoid; flowers light blush pink, 3½-4 in., 25-30 petals, hybrid tea, borne one to a stem, moderate old rose with lemon and grapefruit fragrance; recurrent; foliage very glossy; prickles medium, deeply concave; upright, bushy (100-150 cm.) growth; PP15195; [seedling × 'Tivoli Gardens']

Royal Dane™ (Adele Duttweiler™, Troika™) HT, ob, 1973, Poulsen, D. T.; flowers orange, outer petals red, 4-6 in., full, high-centered, borne mostly singly, intense sweet fragrance; recurrent; foliage large, dark, glossy, leathery; vigorous, upright, bushy growth; [('Tropicana' × (Baccará® × 'Princesse Astrid')) × 'Hanne']; intr. 1971

'Royal Dawn' LCl, mp, 1964, Morey, Dr. Dennison; flowers coral-pink, large, 35 petals, moderate fragrance; foliage dark, glossy; vigorous, climbing growth; ['Royal Sunset' × 'Aloha']; intr. 1962

'Royal Delight' -- See 'Aroreroy'

'Royal Dot' HT, pb, Dot, P.; flowers well-formed; intr. 1980

'Royal Dream' -- See 'Kormeeram'

'Royal Edward' S, mp, 1994, Ogilvie, Ian S.; bud ovoid; flowers medium pink, fading to pale pink, 2 in., 18 petals, flat, borne mostly in large clusters, slight fragrance; heavy spring bloom, lesser repeat; foliage small, medium green, glossy; few prickles; low (45 cm.), bushy, spreading growth; winter hardy ; PP9972; [R. × kordesii × ((R. × kordesii × (Red Dawn × Suzanne)) × Zeus)]; intr. 1994

'Royal Emblem' HT, w, 2003, Ishii, Tsuyoshi; flowers semi-dbl., borne in small clusters, slight fragrance; foliage small, dark green, glossy; prickles medium, sharp, moderate; growth spreading, medium (5 ft.); ground cover, weeping standard; [R. yakushimensis × unknown]

'Royal Époux' ('Le Royal-Époux') HP, mp, 1859, Damaizin; flowers bright glossy pink, large, full

'Royal Flare' HT, rb, 1988, Wambach, Alex A.; flowers red and white blend, large, high-centered, borne singly; foliage medium size, dark green, disease-resistant; prickles down-turned, dark green; upright, medium growth; [Pristine® × 'Standout']

'Royal Flush' -- See 'Peapatio'

'Royal Flush' LCl, pb, 1970, Fuller; bud ovoid; flowers cream, edges blending pink, medium, semi-dbl., cupped; repeat bloom; foliage dark, leathery; vigorous, upright, climbing growth; ['Little Darling' × 'Suspense']

'Royal Garnet' Min, mr; flowers rich, moderate fragrance; moderate growth

'Royal Gem' F, lp, Brooks, M.L.; intr. 1959

'Royal Gold' LCl, my, 1958, Morey, Dr. Dennison; bud medium, ovoid; flowers golden yellow, 4-5 in., 35-45 petals, cupped, borne singly and in clusters of 3-7, moderate fruity fragrance; recurrent; foliage large, dark green, glossy; prickles numerous, medium, straight; stems medium, strong; vigorous, pillar (5-7 ft.) growth; hips none ; PP1849; ['Goldilocks, Climbing' × 'Lydia']; intr. 1957

'Royal Highness' ('Konigliche Hoheit', 'Königlicht Hoheit') HT, lp, 1962, Swim & Weeks; bud long, pointed; flowers soft light pink, 5-5½ in., 40-45 petals, high-centered, borne mostly singly, intense tea fragrance; recurrent; foliage large, dark, glossy, leathery; prickles several, long, straight, brown; stems long, strong; tender, upright, bushy growth; hips globular, smooth ; PP2032; ['Virgo' × 'Peace']; intr. 1962

Royal Lady™ -- See 'Miniryl'

'Royal Lavender' LCl, m, 1961, Morey, Dr. Dennison; bud medium, ovoid; flowers lavender tinted gray and pink, 3 in., 35-40 petals, cupped, borne in clusters, intense old rose (centifolia) fragrance; intermittent; foliage large, dark green, leathery; prickles moderate, medium, hooked downward; stems medium, strong; vigorous (6-9 ft.) growth; hips none ; PP2194; ['Lavender Queen' × 'Amy Vanderbilt']; intr. 1961

'Royal Lustre' HT, op, McGredy; flowers orange-buff overlaid salmon, 6-7 in., 45 petals; foliage coppery; very free growth; ['Mrs Sam McGredy' × 'Crimson Glory']

'Royal Mail' -- See 'Androi'

'Royal Marbré' HGal, m, before 1837, Moreau & Robert; flowers lilac and purple, marbled (striped) pink, medium, very dbl.; upright, bushy (5 ft.) growth

'Royal Meillandina' -- See 'Schobitet'

'Royal Midinette' S, rb, Moore; flowers gold-cream and deep royal red, borne in clusters; foliage dark green; medium, vigorous, arching growth; intr. 1997

'Royal Occasion' (Montana®) F, or, 1976, Tantau, Math.; bud long, pointed; flowers luminous orange-scarlet, 3 in., 20 petals, cupped, borne in small clusters, slight fragrance; recurrent; foliage glossy, large, leathery; prickles numerous, narrow base, brown; stems long; upright, compact, strong (3 ft.) growth; hips round, smooth, orange-scarlet; PP3824; ['Walzertraum' × Europeana®]; intr. 1974

'Royal Pageant' -- See 'Harblend'

Royal Palace™ MinFl, yb, Poulsen; bud short, globular; flowers yellow-orange, 2 in., 20-28 petals, flat, borne in clusters, slight fruity fragrance; recurrent; foliage medium size, dark, glossy; prickles few, 3-4 mm., concave; bushy (40-60 cm.) growth; PP13277; [Flora Danica™ × Easter™]; intr. 2000

'Royal Parade' (Royal™) Min, mp, Poulsen; flowers medium pink, medium, dbl., no fragrance; growth bushy, 20-40 cm.; intr. 1996

'Royal Parks' HT, ab, Harkness; flowers copper shading blending with apricot and caramel, 4½ in., 35 petals, high-centered, borne mostly singly, moderate sweet & spicy fragrance; recurrent; foliage leathery; strong (4 ft.) growth; intr. 2005

Royal Pashmina® HT, dp, Kordes; flowers rich pink, medium, dbl., cupped, borne mostly singly; recurrent; stems medium; [sport of 'Pascha']; florist rose; intr. 2005

'Royal Perfection' ('Royale Perfection') HT, or, 1964, Delbard; flowers orange-coral, 4½ in., 20 petals; vigorous growth; ['Rome Glory' × 'Bayadere']; intr. 1964

'Royal Philharmonic' HT, w, Harkness; flowers white with a hint of pink, full, high-centered, borne mostly singly, slight fragrance; recurrent; medium to tall growth; intr. 1997

'Royal Porcelain' -- See 'Leepel'

'Royal Princess' Min, pb, 1982, Lyon; bud ovoid; flowers pink and yellow blend, 65 petals, borne singly and in small clusters, moderate fruity fragrance; foliage dark, leathery; prickles hooked, bronze; upright, bushy growth; [seedling × seedling]; intr. 1981

'Royal Princess' S, Meilland; intr. 1997

'Royal Prophyta' HT, mp, deRuiter; flowers cerise, full, cupped, borne mostly singly; recurrent; [sport of Prophyta™]; florist rose; intr. 2001

'Royal Queen' ('Royal Queen Elizabeth') Gr, w, 1965, Verschuren; bud ovoid; flowers greenish white, medium, dbl., borne several together; foliage dark green; [sport of Queen Elizabeth®]

'Royal Queen, Cl.' ('Royal Queen Elizabeth, Cl.') Cl Gr, w, after 1965, Verschuren

'Royal Queen Elizabeth' -- See 'Royal Queen'

'Royal Queen Elizabeth, Cl.' -- See 'Royal Queen, Cl.'

'Royal Red' -- See 'Meikarouz'

'Royal Red' HT, mr, 1924, E.G. Hill, Co.; bud pointed; flowers intense crimson-scarlet, shaded black, very large, very full, cupped, moderate fragrance; foliage leathery; vigorous growth

'Royal Red' HT, dr, Lowe; flowers deep scarlet, well-formed; moderate growth; [sport of 'Happiness']; intr. 1956

'Royal Red' HT, mr, Preesman; flowers full , high-centered

'Royal Red' -- See 'Korpek'

'Royal Renate' HT, m, Preesman; flowers lilac pink

'Royal Robe' S, mr, 1946, Wright, Percy H.; flowers crimson, almost purple, rather large, semi-dbl.; non-recurrent; vigorous growth; [(R. rugosa × a Hybrid Perpetual) × (R. multiflora × R. blanda)]

'Royal Romance' HT, my, 1975, Fryer, Gareth; flowers bright lemon-yellow, 5 in., 30 petals, moderate fragrance; foliage leathery; very free growth; ['Pink Parfait' × seedling]; intr. 1974

'Royal Romance' -- See 'Rulis'

'Royal Rose' HT, mp, 1999, Teranishi, K.; flowers rose pink, 80 petals, high-centered; growth to 4½ ft.; ['Happiness' × Peter Frankenfeld®]; intr. 1987

'Royal Ruby' Min, mr, 1974, Morey, Dr. Dennison; bud small, globular; flowers red, base white, small, full, globular, borne singly and in small clusters, slight sweet fragrance; free-flowering; foliage small, dark green, leathery. glossy; stems long; vigorous, upright (12-18 in.) growth; ['Garnette' × ('Tom Thumb' × 'Ruby Jewel')]; intr. 1972

'Royal Salute' -- See 'Macros'

'Royal Scarlet' HP, mr, 1899, Paul, G.; flowers bright scarlet-red; recurrent; ['Mme Rady' × 'Cheshunt Scarlet']

'Royal Scarlet' HT, mr, Kraus; bud ovoid; flowers scarlet-red, large, dbl., high-centered, moderate fragrance; foliage glossy; vigorous, bushy growth; ['McGredy's Scarlet' × 'Christian Dior'];

intr. 1966

'Royal Scarlet Hybrid' HWich, mr, 1926, Chaplin Bros.; flowers bright crimson red, 6-7 cm., semi-dbl., borne in small clusters, slight fragrance; foliage small, glossy

'Royal Scot' HT, yb, 1928, Dobbie; flowers golden yellow, edged crimson, open, semi-dbl.; foliage dark; vigorous growth

'Royal Show' -- See 'Meirasimac'

'Royal Show' HT, mr, 1973, Gregory; flowers light red to deeper red, pointed, 4 in., 27 petals, borne singly, slight fragrance; recurrent; foliage medium green, glossy; vigorous (3 ft.) growth; [Queen Elizabeth® × unknown]

'Royal Smile' HT, w, Beales, Peter; flowers creamy white with soft pink shadings, dbl., cupped, intense fragrance; free-flowering; short to medium growth; intr. 1980

'Royal Star & Garter' LCl, mp, Fryer; flowers candy pink, large, dbl., cupped, borne in clusters of several together., moderate fragrance; constant bloom.; stems long, supple; growth to 8-9 ft.; intr. 2001

Royal Success™ -- See 'Aroreroy'

Royal Sunblaze® -- See 'Schobitet'

'Royal Sunset' LCl, ab, 1960, Morey, Dr. Dennison; bud large, ovoid; flowers 4½-5 in., 20 petals, cupped, borne singly and several together, moderate fruity fragrance; recurrent; foliage large, leathery; prickles numerous, medium, straight; stems medium, strong; vigorous, upright (6 ft.) growth; hips none ; PP2072; ['Sungold' × 'Sutter's Gold']; intr. 1960

'Royal Tan' HT, m, 1956, McGredy, Sam IV; flowers pale purple feathered violet and chocolate, high-pointed, 5 in.; foliage dark; vigorous growth; ['Charles P. Kilham' × 'Mrs Sam McGredy']

'Royal Touch' -- See 'Androy'

'Royal Velvet' HT, dr, 1960, Meilland, F.; flowers rich, velvety cardinal-red, 4-5 in., 55-65 petals; vigorous, tall growth; PP1911; RULED EXTINCT 3/86 ARM.; [('Happiness' × 'Independence') × ('Happiness' × 'Floradora')]; intr. 1959

Royal Velvet™ -- See 'Meilotup'

'Royal Victoria' -- See 'Lavictor'

'Royal Victoria Hospital' F, pb; intr. 2002

'Royal Virgin Rose' -- See 'Aimable Rouge'

'Royal Visit' HT, op, 1939, Eddie; flowers deep tangerine-orange, reverse coral passing to apricot, dbl.; foliage leathery, glossy, dark; bushy growth; ['Picture' × 'Mrs Pierre S. duPont']

'Royal Volunteer' -- See 'Cocdandy'

Royal Wedding™ -- See 'Jacquint'

'Royal Welcome' HT, rb, 1955, Homan; flowers velvety dark red, reverse deep rosy pink, well-formed; foliage glossy; vigorous growth; ['Crimson Glory' × 'Peace']; intr. 1955

'Royal Welsh Show' HT, w, 2000, Poole, Lionel; flowers full, high-centered, borne in small clusters, slight fragrance; foliage medium size, medium green, semi-glossy; few prickles; bushy, vigorous, medium (36 in.) growth; ['Solitaire' × 'Hazel Rose']; intr. 2004

'Royal William, Climbing' Cl HT, dr, 1995, Newman, F. S.; flowers other growth similar to parent; [sport of 'Royal William']

'Royal William' -- See 'Korzaun'

Royal Worcester® -- See 'Trobroy'

'Royale' -- See 'Belle Époque'

'Royale' ('Agathe Royale', 'Regalis', 'Multiflora', 'Bouquet Parfait') HGal, lp, before 1811, Godefroy; flowers light pink or cerise, edges lighter, mottled with red, medium, dbl., borne in small clusters; foliage stiff, bidentate; prickles numerous, slender, unequal; Agathe group

'Royale Aurore' -- See 'Celestial'

Royale de Mulhouse® F, w, Sauvegeot; intr. 2005

'Royale Perfection' HT, or, Delbard-Chabert; flowers large, dbl.; intr. 1964

'Royale Perfection' -- See 'Royal Perfection'

'Royale Veloutée' -- See 'Holoserica Regalis'

'Royalet' HT, mr, 1977, Herholdt, J.A.; flowers crimson-red, 4½-5½ in., 35-40 petals; foliage dark; upright, bushy growth; [seedling × 'Chrysler Imperial']; intr. 1968

Royalglo™ -- See 'Minadco'

'Royalist' HT, mp, 1954, McGredy, Sam IV; flowers deep rose-pink, large, 28 petals, high-centered; foliage dull green; very free growth; [('Billy Boy' × 'Blossom') × 'Mrs Redford']

'Royalty' HT, dr, 1976, Jelly; bud globular, pointed; flowers deep cardinal red, 4-4½ in., 20-22 petals, high-centered to cupped, borne mostly in small clusters; free-flowering; foliage leathery; prickles few, medium, hooked downward; stems long, strong; vigorous growth; hips medium, globular body with conspicuous neck, smooth; PP4057; ['Forever Yours' × 'Love Affair']; originally a greenhouse rose; intr. 1976

'Royalty' Bailey, Dorothy J., Bailey, Dorothy J.; PP4397

'Royat Mondain' HP, mr, 1901, Veysset; flowers crimson red, large, petals pointed, some edges thinly bordered white, full

'Royden' F, my, 1989, Cattermole, R.F.; flowers bright gold, fading quickly to white, 40 petals, cupped, borne in sprays; foliage light green, glossy; tall, upright growth; ['Liverpool Echo' × 'Arthur Bell']

'Roydon Hall' F, mr, 1985, Scrivens, Len; flowers large, 35 petals, no fragrance; foliage medium size, medium green, semi-glossy; bushy growth; ['City of Leeds' × ('Paprika' × Rose Gaujard®)]; intr. 1983

'Roze Koningin' HT, mr, 1938, Lens; bud long, pointed; flowers medium red, passing to pink, well-formed large, dbl.; vigorous growth; [('Lady Sylvia' × unknown) × 'Étoile de Hollande']

'Rozenamateur A. Bok' F, mr, 1961, Buisman, G. A. H.; flowers bright red, single, borne in large clusters; foliage dark; vigorous, upright growth; ['Prinses Christina' × 'Kathe Duvigneau']

'Rozenmini' Min, pb; flowers medium pink with white streaks, small, single, shallow cup to flat, borne in clusters; recurrent; growth to 12 in.

Rozorina -- See 'Zorina'

'Roztomila' F, w, Urban, J.

'RSG Roos' ('Roos Sonder Grense') F, or, Taschner, Ludwig; flowers bright vermilion orange, intensifying to red, yellow base, medium, dbl., high-centered, borne in small clusters; free-flowering; foliage large, medium green; stems straight; tall, upright growth; intr. 2004

'Ruatara' LCl, dp, Nobbs; intr. 1995

'Rubaiyat' HT, dp, 1946, McGredy; bud long, pointed; flowers rose-red, reverse lighter, 4½-5 in., 25 petals, high-centered, intense Damask & spice fragrance; foliage dark, leathery; vigorous, upright growth; PP758; [(('McGredy's Scarlet' × 'Mrs Sam McGredy') × (seedling × 'Sir Basil McFarland')]

'Ruban Doré' -- See 'Tricolore'

'Ruban Rouge' F, dr, 1957, Lens; bud globular; flowers deep velvety red, borne in clusters; foliage dark, leathery; vigorous growth; ['Alain' × 'Cinnabar']

'Rubella' F, dr, 1973, deRuiter; flowers deep red, 2½-3 in., 24 petals, open, borne in trusses; free-flowering; bushy growth; hardy; [Kimono® × Lilli Marleen®]; intr. 1972

'Rubens' HP, yb, Verdier; intr. 1864

'Rubens' HT, mr, Gaujard; bud pointed; flowers vermilion red, large, dbl.; vigorous growth; [Rose Gaujard® × 'Miss France']; intr. 1972

'Rubens' T, w, Moreau & Robert; flowers white, shaded with rose, center bronzy yellow, large, wavy petals, dbl., cupped, moderate fragrance; free-flowering; dense (3-5 ft.), spreading growth; intr. 1859

'Rubens' HP, mr, 1852, Laffay; flowers amaranth-red, loose

'Rübezahl' HT, mr, 1917, Krüger; flowers large, dbl.; ['Julius Fabianics de Misefa' × 'Mrs W. J. Grant']

Rubiela® F, w, NIRP; intr. 2005

'Rubies 'n' Pearls' -- See 'Manrupearl'

'Rubiginosa' -- See 'Rubra'

'Rubiginosa' -- See 'Hebe's Lip'

'Rubin' HMult, mr, 1899, Kiese; flowers crimson to spinel-red, 4-5 cm., semi-dbl., borne in clusters of 10-30, moderate fragrance; growth to 10-12 ft.; ['Daniel Lacombe' × 'Fellemberg']; sometimes attributed to Schmidt; intr. 1899

'Rubin' HT, or, Lens; flowers orange-red, base yellow, large, semi-dbl.; vigorous growth; ['Mme Henri Guillot' × 'Grande Duchesse Charlotte']; intr. 1956

'Rubin' F, dr, Kordes; bud long, pointed; flowers deep red, dbl., borne in broad clusters; foliage dark; bushy, compact, low growth; intr. 1962

Rubina® F, dr, Dickson, Patrick; intr. 1989

'Rubinette' F, dr, 1971, deRuiter; flowers deep red, large, 28 petals; foliage dark; vigorous, upright growth; PP3383; [('Mandrina' × Baccará®) × ('Mandrina' × 'Baccara')]

'Rubino' S, Mansuino; intr. 1966

'Rubis' Ch, lp, before 1835, Laffay; flowers light pink to red, center brighter, small to medium, semi-dbl. to dbl.

'Rubis' Pol, rb, Nonin; flowers bright ruby-red, center white, medium, dbl., borne in clusters; dwarf growth; ['Merveille des Rouges' × 'Jessie']; intr. 1926

'Rubis' Cl HT, mr, Mallerin, C.; flowers blood-red, 4 in., dbl., intense fragrance; foliage bronze; vigorous growth; ['Mme G. Forest-Colcombet' × unknown]; intr. 1948

'Rubnispa' Min, rb

'Rubor' HT, mp, 1947, Dot, Pedro; flowers Neyron pink, dbl.; foliage dark; very vigorous growth; ['Cynthia' × 'Director Rubió']

'Rubra' -- See 'Jenny'

'Rubra' -- See R. barbierana

'Rubra' ('Centfeuilles Anglais', 'Rubiginosa', 'Unique Rouge', 'Unique Anglais', 'Rouge', R. centifolia anglica rubra, 'Red Provence', 'Cumberland', 'Cramoisi', 'Centifolia Unica', 'Unique Rose') C, mr, before 1629; flowers crimson red, 3 in., dbl., slight fragrance; foliage large

'Rubra' ('Des Peintres', 'Rouge', 'Rose Foncé', 'Pourpre') M, mr, from England; flowers deep pink to medium red, medium, dbl.; intr. before 1777

'Rubra Plena' -- See 'Rouge'

'Rubra Variegata' -- See 'Striata'

'Rubro-Purpurea' -- See 'Red Damask'

'Rubrosa' -- See 'Carmenetta'

'Rubrotincta' -- See 'Hebe's Lip'

'Ruby' -- See 'Benmjul'

'Ruby' Pol, mr, 1932, deRuiter; flowers glowing scarlet

'Ruby Anniversary' -- See 'Harbonny'

'Ruby Baby' Min, rb, 2000, Christopher, Lonnie H.; flowers red-orange, reverse yellow, 1½ in., dbl., high-centered, borne mostly singly, slight fragrance; foliage medium size, medium green, semi-glossy; prickles moderate; upright, medium (12-18 in.) growth; [sport of Hot Tamale™]

'Ruby Bay' HMsk, mr; flowers ruby red, small, semi-dbl., borne in clusters; shrubby (5 ft.), semi-climbing growth; ['Ballerina' × unknown]; intr. 1994

'Ruby Belle' Min, dr, Bell, Laurie; flowers deep velvety red, moderate fragrance; free-flowering; medium growth

Ruby Border™ -- See 'Sausalito'

'Ruby Celebration' -- See 'Peawinner'

'Ruby Celebration, Climbing' ClF, dr; intr. after 1995

'Ruby Dee' Gr, mr, 1968, Patterson; bud ovoid; flowers large, dbl., high-centered, borne in clusters, moderate fragrance; foliage dark, glossy; vigorous, upright growth; PP3074; [Queen Elizabeth® × 'Happiness']

'Ruby Garland' LCl, mr, Pearce; flowers ruby red, medium, dbl., high-centered; recurrent; supple canes, tall growth; intr. 2005

'Ruby Gem' HT, mr, 1962, Leenders, J.; flowers bright red, large, 28 petals; [seedling × 'Red Favorite']

'Ruby Glow' LCl, mr, 1955, Jacobus, Martin; bud short, oval; flowers spectrum-red, open, 3 in., 13-15 petals, borne in clusters, moderate fragrance; foliage glossy; moderate pillar (7 ft.) growth; PP1234; ['Dream Girl' × 'New World']; intr. 1955

'Ruby Gold' -- See 'Jean Ducher'

'Ruby Jewel' Min, mr, 1959, Morey, Dr. Dennison; bud ovoid; flowers ruby-red, reverse lighter, open, ½ in., 35-40 petals, moderate fragrance; foliage glossy; low (6-8 in.), compact growth; PP1907; ['Dick Koster' × 'Tom Thumb']; intr. 1959

'Ruby Lips' F, mr, 1959, Swim, H.C.; bud short, ovoid, pointed; flowers bright cardinal-red, 3 in., 18-20 petals, loose, borne in clusters, slight fragrance; recurrent; foliage medium size, leathery, semi-glossy; prickles several, medium, almost straight, brown; stems short to medium; vigorous, semi-spreading, bushy growth; hips globular, smooth, orange; PP1775; ['World's Fair' × 'Pinocchio']; intr. 1958

'Ruby Lips' Min, mr, J&P; flowers ruby red, small , double, high-centered; recurrent; compact growth

'Ruby Magic' -- See 'Morrubi'

'Ruby Manwaring' HT, dp, 1932, Longley; flowers rich rosy cerise; [sport of 'Betty Uprichard']

Ruby Meidiland® -- See 'Meipreston'

'Ruby Pearl' F, dp, Malanseuns; flowers deep pink to burgundy, white eye, silver reverse , semi-double, flat, borne in clusters; recurrent; stems short; medium to tall growth

'Ruby Pendant' Min, m, 1980, Strawn, Leslie E.; bud pointed; flowers red-purple, 25-30 petals, high-centered, borne singly, slight fragrance; recurrent; foliage reddish-green; prickles needle-shaped; vigorous growth; [('Lotte Gunthart' × 'Salvo') × 'Baby Betsy McCall']; intr. 1979

'Ruby Princess' -- See 'Moruby'

'Ruby Princess' HT, mr, 1949, Grillo; flowers velvety red, 5 in., 50 petals, moderate fragrance; PP1043; [sport of 'Jewel']

'Ruby Queen' HWich, dp, 1899, Van Fleet; flowers deep rose-pink, reverse lighter, 4-5 cm., dbl., loose, borne in clusters of 5-7; non-recurrent; foliage small, medium green, glossy; numerous prickles; stems stiff; growth to 10 ft.; [R. wichurana × 'Cramoisi Supérieur']

'Ruby Rain' Cl Min, mr

'Ruby Ring' HWich, w, 1926, Clark, A.; flowers white with ruby edge, 4-5 cm., dbl., borne in clusters of 5-15; foliage glossy

Ruby Ruby™ -- See 'Weksactrumi'

'Ruby Star' -- See 'Umstar'

'Ruby Superior' Pol, mr, deRuiter; flowers have more lasting color; [sport of 'Ruby']

'Ruby Talisman' HT, mr, 1935, Eddie; flowers rich ruby-red, more shapely than parent, with reflexed petals; [sport of 'Talisman']

'Ruby Treasure' Min, dr, Hannemann, F.; ['Oz Gold' × 'Lemon Delight']

'Ruby Tuesday' -- See 'Renruby'

'Ruby Ulrick' F, dp, 1953, Ulrick, L.W.; flowers deep pink, base white, dbl., borne in clusters; foliage leathery; very vigorous growth; ['Mrs Tom Henderson' × 'Gloria Mundi']

'Ruby Velvet' -- See 'Hinruby'

Ruby Vigorosa™ -- See 'Korvillade'

'Ruby Voodoo' -- See 'Jasru'

'Ruby Wedding, Climbing' Cl HT, dr; vigorous (12 ft.) growth; [sport of 'Ruby Wedding']; intr. after 1979

'Ruby Wedding' HT, dr, 1980, Gregory; bud flat, pointed; flowers deep, velvety red, medium, 44 petals, borne 3 - 4 per cluster, moderate fragrance; good repeat; foliage medium green; prickles slightly hooked; vigorous (3 ft.), somewhat spreading growth; ['Mayflower' × seedling]; intr. 1979

'Ruby Wedding Anniversary' F, mr; flowers brilliant red, slight fragrance; medium growth; intr. 2005

'Ruby Wedding Celebration' F, w; intr. 2005

Ruby Wishes™ -- See 'Scarlet Hit'

'Rudelsburg' HMult, dp, 1919, Kiese; flowers shining carmine-rose, fading to slatey pink, 3-4 cm., semi-dbl., flat, borne in large clusters; non-recurrent; no prickles; vigorous, climbing growth

'Rudi Korte' Pol, or, 1929, Kersbergen; flowers medium, semi-dbl.

'Rudi Neitz' HT, yb, Dorieux; bud long, pointed; flowers golden-yellow with touch of pink on petal edges, cupped; foliage deep green, glossy; prickles very few; stems long, straight; vigorous, medium growth; intr. 2004

'Rudola' F, mr, 1974, deRuiter; bud ovoid; flowers light geranium-red, open, large, semi-dbl.; foliage leathery; very vigorous, bushy growth; ['Dacapo' × Kimono®]; intr. 1972

'Rudolf Alexander Schröder' HT, w, 1930, Kordes; bud long, pointed; flowers white, center tinted lemon, large, dbl., high-centered; foliage leathery, light; vigorous growth; ['Mrs Herbert Stevens' × 'Pius XI']

'Rudolf Schmidt's Jubiläumsrose' F, my, 1958, Kordes; flowers golden yellow, large, semi-dbl., high-centered, borne in clusters, moderate fragrance; foliage light green, glossy; very vigorous, upright, bushy growth; intr. 1955

'Rudolf Schock' HT, mr, 1970, Verschuren, A.; flowers bright currant-red, large, dbl., moderate fragrance; foliage dark, leathery; vigorous growth; ['Josephine Bruce' × seedling]; intr. 1968

'Rudolf von Bennigsen' LCl, mp, 1932, Lambert, P.; bud pointed; flowers rosy-pink, edges fading, large, semi-dbl., borne in clusters of 5-20, slight fragrance; recurrent bloom; foliage broad, dark, glossy; vigorous, bushy, semi-climbing growth; [('Geheimrat Dr. Mittweg' × 'Souv. de Paul Neyron') × 'Joanna Hill']

'Rudolph Kluis' Pol, mr, 1922, Kluis & Koning; bud globular; flowers pure vermilion-red, dbl., foliage rich green, glossy; bushy growth; [sport of 'Ellen Poulsen']

'Rudolph Kluis Superior' Pol, mr, 1928, Kluis; flowers glowing scarlet; more compact growth than Rudolph Kluis; [sport of 'Ellen Poulsen']

'Rudolph Timm' F, rb, 1951, Kordes; flowers white, reverse red, open, 2 in., 15-20 petals, borne in trusses to 40; foliage glossy, light green; very free growth; [('Johannes Boettner' × 'Magnifica') × ('Baby Chateau' × 'Else Poulsen')]

'Rudolph Valentino' HT, op, 1929, Pernet-Ducher; flowers lively shrimp-pink or coral-red, suffused golden coppery, dbl.; vigorous growth

'Rudy Rambler' ClMin, mr; intr. 2005

Ruffian™ -- See 'Decruf'

Ruffled Cloud™ -- See 'Jacmorde'

'Ruffles' HT, mp, 1994, Perry, Astor; flowers magenta pink, ruffled petals, medium, full, high-centered, borne mostly singly, slight fragrance; recurrent; foliage large, medium green; some prickles; tall, upright growth; [seedling × Alec's Red®]; intr. 1997

Ruffles & Flourishes™ -- See 'Wekquahofa'

'Ruffle's Dream' S, yb

'Ruffles 'n' Flourishes' -- See 'Cleruff'

'Ruffle's Passion' S, m

'Rufin' ('Finstar', 'Mini Metro', Finnstar®) Min, op, 1982, deRuiter, George; flowers orange-salmon, small, 20 petals; foliage small, medium green, semi-glossy; bushy growth; ['Minuette' × seedling]; intr. 1979

'Rufus' Pol, mr, 1925, Allen; flowers intense scarlet, dbl., borne in clusters; compact growth; [sport of 'Orléans Rose']

'Ruga' (R. × ruga, 'Tea-Scented Ayrshire') Ayr, w, before 1820; flowers creamy flesh pink, fading lighter, 5-6 cm., semi-dbl., cupped, borne in small clusters, moderate tea fragrance; non-recurrent; numerous prickles; stems long, slender; trailing (up to 30 ft.) growth; ['thought to be R. arvensis' × R. odorata]; brought to England from Italy by John Lindley

Rugelda® -- See 'Korruge'

'Ruggolda' ('Golden Days') HT, dy, 1982, deRuiter, George; flowers large, 35 petals; foliage large, medium green, semi-glossy; bushy growth; [Peer Gynt® × seedling]; intr. 1980

'Rugosa Copper' S, ob, 1958, Gaujard; flowers coppery orange, large; recurrent bloom; vigorous growth; ['Conrad Ferdinand Meyer' × seedling]; intr. 1955

'Rugosa Magnifica' -- See 'Magnifica'

'Rugosa Ottawa' HRg, m, L'Assomption; flowers 5 petals, flat

'Rugosa Superba' -- See 'Scabrosa'

'Rugotida' (R. × rugotida) HRg, mp, 1950, Darthuis

'Rugspin' HRg, dr, Petersen; flowers deep scarlet crimson, large, single, flat, moderate fragrance; recurrent; foliage dark green, glossy; healthy (4 ft.) growth; hips rounded; intr. 1966

'Rugul' ('Gulletta', Tapis Jaune®) Min, my, 1976, deRuiter; flowers dbl., 20 petals; foliage small, glossy, dark; low, compact growth; ['Rosy Jewel' × Allgold®]; intr. 1973

'Rühkor' ('Athena') HT, w, 1985, Kordes, W.; flowers clear white, large, 35 petals, moderate fragrance; foliage large, medium green, matte; upright, bushy growth; [seedling × Helmut Schmidt®]; greenhouse rose; intr. 1981

'Ruhm der Gartenwelt' HP, dr, 1904, Jacobs; flowers fiery red, large, dbl.; ['American Beauty' × 'Francis Dubreuil']

'Ruhm von Steinfurth' ('Red Druschki') HP, mr, 1920, Weigand, C.; bud long, pointed; flowers bright carmin, large, 34 petals, cupped, intense fragrance; recurrent; foliage dark, leathery; vigorous growth; ['Frau Karl Druschki' × 'Ulrich Brunner Fils']

'Ruhm von Thalwitz' ('Gloire de Thalwitz') HP, mr, 1866, Peters; flowers poppy red with salmon pink reflections, medium to large, full

'Ruia07922' F, ob, de Ruiter; intr. 2007

'Ruia0806' F, op, de Ruiter; intr. 2007

'Ruiabri' Min, op, Pouw; bud ovoid; intr. 2004

'Ruibel' F, dr, 1973, deRuiter; intr. 1972

'Ruibengal' HT, rb

'Ruibleu' Min, m, deRuiter; intr. 2003

'Ruiblun' ('Azulabria', 'Blue Peter', 'Bluenette') Min, m, 1983, deRuiter, George; flowers lilac-purple, patio, small, semi-dbl.; foliage small, light green, semi-glossy; bushy growth; ['Little Flirt' × seedling]

'Ruibuyel' HT, pb, deRuiter; intr. 2001

'Ruicany' Min, yp, de Ruiter; intr. 2002

'Ruicharo' ('Charming Rosamini') Min, ob, deRuiter

'Ruico' F, ob, 1968, deRuiter

'Ruiconti' HT, dy, de Ruiter ; bud medium, ovate; intr. 1997

'Ruicrevi' ('White Timeless') HT, w, Pouw; bud ovate; intr. 1995

'Ruidriko' HT, lp; bud medium, pointed, ovate; intr. 1988

'Ruidusty' HT, ob, deRuiter

'Ruifarol' ('Favourite Rosamini') Min, mp, deRuiter; intr. 1989

'Ruiflami' ('Flaming Rosamini') Min, mr, deRuiter; intr. 1987

'Ruigerdan' ('Little Marvel') Min, or, 1988, deRuiter, George; flowers bright orange-scarlet, small, 6-14 petals; foliage small, medium green, semi-glossy; bushy growth; PP7572; [seedling × seedling]

'Ruihoudris' HT, mp, deRuiter; intr. 2001

'Ruijamu' HT, ab, de Ruiter

'Ruijoho' HT, dy, van der Hoorn; bud medium, ovate

'Ruikalla' Min, mr; bud ovoid, rounded

'Ruiklij' HT, lp

'Ruikoovi' HT, pb, deRuiter

'Ruikuik' HT, w, de Ruiter

'Ruikuiros' HT, mp, de Ruiter

'Ruilanca' ('Lancashire Life') F, or, 1984, deRuiter, George; flowers scarlet, semi-dbl., borne in clusters; foliage medium size, medium green, semi-glossy; bushy growth; ['Robert Stolz' × Diablotin®]

'Ruilav' HT, m, Pouw; intr. 1997

'Ruiliro' HT, mp, deRuiter

'ruimarso' -- See 'Sweet Rosamini'

'Ruimats' Min, or, Pouw, A.; intr. 1997

'Ruimeva' ('Madelon') HT, or, 1983, deRuiter, George; flowers medium, 20 petals; foliage medium size, medium green, semi-glossy; upright growth; PP5820; ['Varlon' × 'MEIgenon']; intr. 1981

'Ruimeys' -- See 'Idole'

'Ruimired' (Red Minimo™) Min, dr, 1991, deRuiter, George; bud pointed ovoid; flowers Orient red, small, 22-25 petals, flat, borne in small clusters, no fragrance; free-flowering; foliage small, dark green, semi-glossy; prickles long, hooked slightly downward; stems short, strong; low, bushy growth; PP5770; [seedling × seedling]; intr. 1986

'Ruimz15' HT, w, de Groot; Henk

'Ruinanny' -- See 'Rosy Minimo'

'Ruiodnine' HT, dr, deRuiter

'Ruioldoros' HT, op, de Ruiter

'Ruioran' HT, ob, Pouw ; bud medium, ovate; intr. 1996

'Ruiortro' F, ob; intr. 2001

'Ruipiko' Min, mp

'Ruipinvi' HT, mp, de Ruiter

'Ruiquin' F, or, de Ruiter; intr. 1977

'Ruiredro' (Red Rosamini®) Min, dr, 1988, deRuiter, George; flowers clear crimson, white at base, 1-1½ in., 30-40 petals, cupped, borne in small clusters; free-flowering; foliage medium size, medium green, matte; few prickles; bushy, medium (15 in.) growth; PP5976; [seedling × seedling]; intr. 1988

'Ruiroone' HT, rb, deRuiter

'Ruirorap' HT, dr; bud large, cylindrical; intr. 2001

'Ruiroskee' HT, pb, deRuiter; bud large, soft pink
'Ruirosora' Min, ob, Pouw; bud pear-shaped; intr. 2001
'Ruiroug' HT, mr; intr. 2000
'Ruirupo' ('Scarlet Rosamini') Min, mr, deRuiter; intr. 1989
'Ruisalro' Min, op, deRuiter; intr. 1984
'Ruiseto' (Orange Rosamini®) Min, or, 1988, deRuiter, George; flowers semi-dbl.; medium growth; PP6236; [seedling × Red Rosamini®]
'Ruisnowy' F, w; intr. 2001
'Ruisteenka' ('Ravel') HT, dp; bud medium, ovate; sepals shorter than bud, generally simple to slightly foliated; intr. 1994
'Ruitapaf' Min, mr
'Ruitenor' HT, ob, Pouw; bud medium, ovate; sepals short; intr. 1997
'Ruitulvi' HT, pb, deRuiter; bud medium, ovate; intr. 1993
'Ruitween' Min, dp, deRuiter; intr. 2004
'Ruivonk' HT, lp, deRuiter; intr. 2001
'Ruiwita' Min, w
'Ruiwitun' HT, w, Pouw; A. A.; bud ovate; sepals long, foliated; intr. 1998
'Ruix001' Min, w, deRuiter; intr. 2004
'Ruix69010' HT, lp, deRuiter; intr. 2001
'Ruixandra' ('Jolly Cupido') Min, rb, deRuiter; intr. 1992
'Ruiy0016' F, dp, de Ruiter; intr. 2007
'Ruiy5451' HT, or, de Groot; H. C. A.; PP15993
'Ruiyel' HT, yb, Ammerlaan; bud ovate; intr. 1999
'Ruiz0561' F, mr, de Ruiterdbl.; intr. 2007
'Ruiz18915' F, pb, de Ruiter; intr. 2007
'Ruiz19751' F, my, de Ruiterdbl; intr. 2007
'Ruiz2516' F, dr, de Ruiterdbl; intr. 2007
'Ruiz99925' HT, yb, de Groot; Henk C. A.; intr. 2004
'Ruizesac' ('Astra') HT, pb, deRuiter; intr. 1989
'Ruizon' HT, dr, deRuiter
'Rukhsaar' HT, w, 1971, Singh; flowers cream, center shell-pink, medium, dbl., high-centered; foliage glossy; moderate growth; ['Virgo' × unknown]; intr. 1969
'Rulimpa' ('Impala', 'Melinda') HT, rb, 1983, deRuiter, George; flowers scarlet, gold reverse, large, 35 petals, moderate fragrance; foliage medium size, dark, glossy; upright growth; ['Whisky Mac' × 'Criterion']; intr. 1980
'Rulis' ('Liselle', 'Royal Romance') HT, ob, 1982, deRuiter, George; flowers orange-peach, well-formed, large, 35 petals; foliage large, dark, semi-glossy; bushy growth; ['Whisky Mac' × 'Matador']; intr. 1980
'Rum Butter' -- See 'Talrum'
'Rum Candy' -- See 'Umsrum'
'Rumba' HT, op, 1956; bud long, pointed; flowers salmon-orange, intense fragrance; long stems; ['Talisman' × unknown]
Rumba® ('Rhumba') F, rb, Poulsen, S.; bud ovoid; flowers poppy-red, center yellow, 2-2½ in., 30-35 petals, cupped, borne in clusters, slight spicy fragrance; recurrent; foliage dark, glossy, leathery; vigorous, bushy growth; PP1919; ['Masquerade' × ('Poulsen's Bedder' × 'Floradora')]; intr. 1958
'Rumba, Climbing' Cl F, rb, 1972, Bansal, O.P.; flowers medium, dbl, cupped; [sport of 'Rumba']
'Rumpelstilzchen' ('Repelsteeltje') S, dr, 1956, deRuiter; flowers deep red, small, single; dwarf growth
'Runatru' ('Fennica', 'Invincible') F, dr, 1983, deRuiter; bud large; flowers large, 20 petals; foliage large, medium green, glossy; upright growth; ['Rubella' × 'National Trust']; intr. 1982
Running Maid® -- See 'Lenramp'
'Rupali' F, dp, 1973, IARI; buds medium, pointed; flowers deep rose-pink, medium, dbl, open, borne singly and several together; foliage medium size, green; growth very vigorous, upright; ['Sweet Afton' × 'Delhi Princess']; intr. 1971
'Rupert Brooke' HT, pb, 1928, Easlea; flowers fawn-pink to cream, dbl.; ['Miss Cynthia Forde' × 'Mrs Wemyss Quin']
'Rupfespin' (Festival Pink™) S, mp, 1991, Rupert, Kim L.; bud pointed; flowers clear medium pink, white petal base, golden stamens, medium, 5-7 cm. petals, borne in small and large clusters, slight fragrance; foliage medium size, bright green,glossy; numerous prickles; tall (4-5 ft.), bushy,spreading growth; [sport of 'Festival Fanfare']
'Rupgoljul' (Golden Julia™) HT, my, 1992, Rupert, Kim L.; bud long, pointed; flowers medium golden mustard, opening medium golden yellow, fading, 3-4 in., 18-22 petals, flat, slight fragrance; foliage medium size, medium green, matte; prickles few, yellow; stems green wood; growth medium (75-90 cm.), upright, bushy; [sport of Julia's Rose®]
'Rupkimcrm' (Kim's Cream™) F, w, 1991, Rupert, Kim L.; bud ovoid, pointed; flowers cream with coffee and gold tints, opening cream, tint remains in cool weather, 3-3½ in., full, flat, borne in small clusters, intense spicy fragrance; foliage leathery, medium size, medium green, semi-glossy; some prickles; low (45-50 cm.), bushy, compact, vigorous growth; ['Lavender Pinocchio' × 'Lavender Pinocchio']
'RUprins' ('Prince Klaus', 'Rosalynn Carter') Gr, or, 1973, deRuiter; intr. 1978
'Rural England' LCl, mp, Beales; flowers soft pink, medium , double, cupped, then rosette, borne in large clusters; recurrent; foliage medium green ; few prickles; vigorous (10 ft.) growth; intr. 2007
'Rural Rhythm' S, lp, 1985, Buck, Dr. Griffith J.; flowers 4 in., 30 petals, shallow cupped, borne 1-5 per cluster, moderate myrrh fragrance; repeat bloom; foliage dark, leathery; prickles awl-like, tan; erect, bushy, spreading growth; hardy; ['Carefree Beauty' × 'The Yeoman']; intr. 1984
'Ruritania' HT, or, 1971, Curtis, E.C.; bud ovoid; flowers medium, very dbl., intense fragrance; foliage dark, leathery; vigorous, upright growth; ['Miss Hillcrest' × 'Hawaii']; intr. 1972
'Ruru' F, pb, Keisei; intr. 2007
'Rusalka' LCl, dp, 1934, Brada, Dr.; flowers carmine to sunset-rose, base yellow, very large, semi-dbl., high-centered; profuse, repeated bloom; foliage glossy, light; climbing growth; ['Tausendschön' × 'Farbenkonigin']
Rush® -- See 'Lenmobra'
'Rushing Stream' -- See 'Austream'
'Rushton-Radclyffe' HP, mr, 1864, Verdier, E.; flowers bright cherry red, large, full
'Ruskin' ('John Ruskin') HRg, dr, 1928, Van Fleet; bud ovoid; flowers deep crimson, large, petals twisted, 50 petals, cupped, intense fragrance; sparingly recurrent; foliage large, rich green, leathery; vigorous, bushy (4-5 ft.) growth; hips rare; ['Souv. de Pierre Leperdrieux' × 'Victor Hugo']
'Russell Supreme' HT, lp, 1927, Pacific Rose Co.; [sport of 'Mrs Charles E. Russell']
'Russelliana' ('Old Spanish Rose', 'Russell's Cottage ', 'Scarlet Grevillea', 'Souv de la Bataille de Marengo') HMult, m, before 1826, Cormack & Sinclair; flowers magenta-crimson fading to mauve, 5-7 cm., dbl., flat, borne in clusters, moderate fragrance; foliage coarse; growth to 20 ft.
'Russell's Cottage ' -- See 'Russelliana'
'Russet Beauty' -- See 'Poulrusset'
'Rust Spot' Min, or, 2003, Barnes, Karen W.; flowers full, borne mostly solitary, no fragrance; foliage medium size, medium green, semi-glossy; prickles small, curved, red/brown, few; compact, short (18 in.) growth; containers; [seedling × seedling]; intr. 2003
'Rustica' HSpn, yb, 1929, Barbier; flowers straw-yellow and gold, center apricot, reverse citron-yellow, semi-dbl., moderate fragrance; non-recurrent bloom; growth to 6 ft.; ['Mme Edouard Herriot' × 'Harison's Yellow']
Rustica® -- See 'Meivilanic'
'Rustica 91' -- See 'Moryelrug'
'Rusticana' F, lp, Wagner, S.; bud short; flowers pale pink, 15 petals, flat, borne in clusters, slight fragrance; foliage medium large, dark green, glossy; groundcover; spreading growth; [Candy Rose® × Yesterday®]; intr. 1995
'Rusticana, Climbing' -- See 'Poppy Flash, Climbing'
'Rusticana' -- See 'Poppy Flash'
'Rustington Rose' -- See 'Worchina'
'Rustler's Dream' -- See 'Pondream'
'Ruston's Blush' HG, w, Morley, Dr B.; [sport of R. gigantea hybrid]
'Rusty' F, r; flowers burnt orange to rus-

set, striped, semi-dbl., borne in trusses, slight fragrance; recurrent; strong growth; intr. 2004

'Ruth' HT, ob, 1921, Pemberton; flowers orange flushed carmine, large, dbl., high-centered, moderate fragrance; vigorous, bushy growth

'Ruth, Climbing' Cl HT, ob, 1928, Prior; flowers light orange shaded to red at edges, very large, very dbl., intense fragrance; recurrent bloom; foliage very large, glossy, olive-green; vigorous, climbing growth; not hardy; [sport of 'Ruth']

'Ruth' HGal, mr, Wright, Percy H.; flowers less bright than Alika, more double than Alika, dbl.; non-recurrent; upright growth (to 7 ft.); ['Mary L. Evans' × 'Alika']; intr. 1947

'Ruth Alexander' LCl, ob, 1937, Wilber; bud long, pointed; flowers orange, base yellow, large, semi-dbl., high-centered, moderate fragrance; foliage leathery, glossy, bronze; vigorous, climbing growth; PP178; ['Myra' × 'Constance Casson']

'Ruth Bell Graham Rose' -- See 'Cinderella Freelander'

'Ruth Christine' -- See 'Hormonet'

'Ruth Clements' S, op, Clements, John; flowers blend of coral-pink and soft pink, 4 in., 69 petals, moderate green apple fragrance; free-flowering; foliage matte green.; very bushy (4½ × 3½ ft.) growth; PPAF; intr. 2000

'Ruth Harker' -- See 'Harpooh'

'Ruth Hewitt' F, w, 1963, Norman; flowers 4 in., 36 petals, cupped, borne in open clusters; foliage dark; vigorous, compact growth; [seedling × Queen Elizabeth®]; intr. 1962

'Ruth Knopf' LCl, mp

'Ruth Leuwerik' F, mr, 1961, deRuiter; flowers bright red, 3 in., 30 petals, borne in clusters, moderate fragrance; foliage bronze; vigorous, bushy growth; ['Kathe Duvigneau' × 'Rosemary Rose']

'Ruth Leuwerik, Climbing' Cl F, mr

'Ruth Pennington' -- See 'Korlichtung'

'Ruth Shamburger' F, lp, 1934, Shamburger, C.S.; [sport of 'Kirsten Poulsen']

'Ruth Staley' -- See 'Tinstaley'

'Ruth Turner' Pol, dp, 1941, Moore, Ralph S.; flowers rose-pink, small, dbl., high-centered, borne in clusters of 5-10; foliage glossy, pointed; vigorous, bushy growth; ['Étoile Luisante' × 'Sierra Snowstorm']

'Ruth Vestal' ('Bride, Climbing') Cl T, w, 1908, Vestal; flowers snow-white, well-formed, very large; recurrent bloom; vigorous growth; [sport of 'The Bride climbing']

'Ruth Warner' F, m, 1984, Warner, A.J.; flowers deep lavender, medium, 48 petals, high-centered, borne singly and in clusters up to 5, intense fragrance; foliage dark, smooth; prickles very few; upright growth; ['Little Darling' × 'Angel Face']; intr. 1978

'Ruth Woodward' -- See 'Dicpleasant'

'Ruthchen' Pol, mr, 1937, Vogel, M.; flowers carmine-red, medium, dbl.

'Ruthe' -- See 'Resruth'

'Ruthie' -- See 'Tinruth'

'Rutilant' HT, mr, 1962, Arles, F.; bud ovoid; flowers carthamus-red, open, medium, semi-dbl.; foliage glossy; vigorous, bushy growth; ['Gloire de Cibeins' × 'Independence']; intr. 1960

Rutland Cover™ -- See 'Poulshine'

'Rutrulo' ('True Love', 'Yorkshire Bank') HT, w, 1981, de Ruiter, George; flowers ivory with shades of pink that fade as they open, 36 petals, borne 3-5 per cluster, moderate fragrance; recurrent; foliage bright green; prickles pointed, brown; stems long; vigorous, medium, bushy growth; [Pascali® × Peer Gynt®]; intr. 1979

'Ruyton' ('Ruyton Girl's School') HT, mp, Bell, Ronald J.; flowers strong pink in center, petals fading quickly to blush pink as they open, dbl., high-centered, very slight fragrance; recurrent; medium growth; intr. 1989

'Ruyton Girl's School' -- See 'Ruyton'

'Ruzova Lavina' F, dp, Strnad

'Ruzyne' HT, rb, 1936, Mikes Böhm, J.; flowers carmine-red marked rose, large

'Ryk Neethling' HT, dy, Harkness; intr. 2008

'Ryokkoh' ('Chidori', 'Green Light') F, ly, 1999, Suzuki, Seizo; flowers light yellow green turning to green, 1-2 in., 15-20 petals, no fragrance; foliage dark green, leathery; growth to 3-4 ft.; [Bridal Pink™ × (seedling × 'Tasogare')]; intr. 1991

'Ryokukou' F, ly

Rythm 'n Blues™ LCl, mp, Poulsen; flowers medium pink, 10-15 cm., semi-dbl., no fragrance; foliage matte; growth bushy, 200-300 cm.; intr. 2000

— S —

'S. A. Prince Youssof Kamal' HP, rb, 1922, Nabonnand, P.; bud long, pointed; flowers crimson, streaked brilliant scarlet, large, semi-dbl.; ['Souv. de Mme Chedane-Guinoisseau' × 'Ulrich Brunner Fils']

'S. A. R. Ferdinand Ier' HRg, mp, 1901, Gravereaux

'S. & M. Perrier' HT, pb, 1936, Mallerin, C.; flowers very pale rose-pink, with orange glow, large, 60 petals, high-centered; foliage glossy; vigorous growth; ['Magdalena de Nubiola' × 'Pres. Cherioux']

'S. Antonio di Padova' HT, Sgaravatti, A.; intr. 1960

'S.E.A. of Love' -- See 'Manpurpearl'

'S. M. Alexander I' -- See 'Roi Alexandre'

'S. M. Gustave V' -- See 'Sa Majesté Gustave V'

'S. M. I. Abdul-Hamid' ('Abdul-Hamid') HRg, mr, 1901, Gravereaux; flowers purple red

'S. S. Pennock' HT, pb, 1922, Kordes; flowers light rose-pink, with sulfur-yellow sheen, dbl., moderate fragrance; ['Lieutenant Chaure' × 'Mrs George Shawyer']

'S. S. Pennock, Climbing' Cl HT, pb, 1932, Lens; [sport of 'S. S. Pennock']

'S. W. A. L. K.' -- See 'Seawalk'

'Sa Majesté Gustave V' ('S. M. Gustave V') HP, dr, 1922, Nabonnand, P.; bud long, pointed, brilliant crimson; flowers carmine, reverse crimson, well-formed, very large, 30 petals, cupped, moderate fragrance; vigorous growth; ['Frau Karl Druschki' × 'Avoca']

'Saarbrücken' S, mr, 1959, Kordes; flowers scarlet-red, 3 in., semi-dbl., borne in clusters of up to 20; foliage dark; vigorous, bushy (5 ft.) growth

'Saarlandwelle' HT, or, Hetzel; intr. 1976

'Sabaudia' HT, pb, 1934, Cazzaniga, F. G.; flowers pink with gold reflections, base light chrome-yellow, large, dbl., cupped; foliage leathery, glossy, dark; vigorous, bushy growth; [R. foetida hybrid × 'Harison's Yellow']

'Sabbelief' ('Artful Dodger') Min, rb, 1996, Burrows, Steven; flowers cherry red, cream reverse, 1 in., dbl., borne in large clusters; foliage medium size, dark green, glossy; some prickles; tall (45 cm.), upright, spreading, bushy growth; ['Sheri Anne' × 'Richard Buckley']; intr. 1997

'Sabbyron' ('Oliver Twist') Min, w, 1996, Burrows, Steven; flowers creamy white, 1 in., dbl., borne in large clusters; foliage medium size, dark green, glossy; some prickles; tall (45-60 cm.), upright, spreading, bushy growth; ['Sheri Anne' × 'Richard Buckley']; intr. 1996

'SABchurchill' ('Sweet Bouquet') HT, lp, Burrows, Steven; intr. 1996

'Sabclive' ('Pickwick') Min, w, 1998, Burrows, Steven; flowers cream and white, medium, dbl., borne in small clusters; foliage medium size, medium green, semi-glossy; prickles moderate; compact, bushy, medium growth; ['Buttons' × 'Richard Buckley']; intr. 1998

'Sabcook' ('Picture Book') F, ob, 2002, Burrows, Steven; flowers bright orange, reverse soft orange with medium yellow, medium, full, borne in small clusters, moderate fragrance; foliage medium size, medium green, semi-glossy; prickles small to medium, moderate; growth bushy, medium (3½ ft.); garden decorative; [Buck's Fizz™ × Bright Smile®]; intr. 2002

'Sabfairbanks' ('Miss Havisham') Min, pb, 2003, Burrows, Steven; flowers lavender pink, reverse warm cream, medium, dbl., borne in small clusters, slight fragrance; foliage medium size, dark green, glossy; prickles small, few; growth bushy, medium (18 in.); containers, patio; ['Lavender Jewel' × ('Sheri Anne' × 'Richard Buckley')]; intr. 2003

'Sabine' HT, ob, 1958, Buyl Frères; flowers salmon, well-formed, 40 petals; vigorous growth; ['Dame Edith Helen' × seedling]

'Sabine' ('Sabine Sinjen') HT, dp, Tantau, Math.; bud pointed; flowers cherry-red, medium, 30 petals, urn-shaped, intense fragrance; foliage dark, glossy; upright, bushy growth; intr. 1962

'Sabine' HT, pb, RvS-Melle; flowers fresh pink with yellow heart, dbl., high-centered; moderate growth

'Sabine Plattner' F, op, Taschner, Ludwig; bud pointed; flowers deep salmon, dbl., cupped, borne singly and in clusters; recurrent; vigorous (6 ft.) growth; intr. 2004

'Sabine Rancy' HT, Croix; intr. 1972

'Sabine Ruf' -- See 'Helsabine'

'Sabine Sinjen' -- See 'Sabine'

'Sabinia' HT, pb, 1940, Aicardi, D.; bud ovoid; flowers dark eglantine-pink passing to reddish-yellow, large, dbl., high-centered; foliage dark, leathery; very vigorous, upright growth; ['Julien Potin' × 'Sensation']

'Sable Chaud' -- See 'Delsob'

'Sabra' -- See 'Jussabra'

'Sabre Dance' F, rb, 1976, Bees; flowers scarlet, reverse gold, 4 in., 40 petals, high-centered, slight fragrance; foliage dark; vigorous growth; ['Mildred Reynolds' × 'Arthur Bell']; intr. 1975

'Sabrina' HT, rb, 1960, Meilland, Mrs. Marie-Louise; flowers crimson, reverse amber-yellow marked crimson, 5 in., 35 petals, high-centered, intense fragrance; foliage dark, leathery; vigorous, bushy growth; ruled extinct ARA 1985; ['Grand Gala' × 'Premier Bal']; intr. 1960

'Sabrina' -- See 'Meigandor'

'Sacajawea' F, mr, 1983, Elliott, Charles P.; bud small, short, flat top; flowers have ruffled petals, 1¾ in., 20 petals, cupped, borne singly and in flat clusters, very slight fragrance; recurrent; foliage medium size, medium green, smooth; prickles medium, hooked downward; stems short; vigorous, upright (3 ft.) growth; PP4892; [(Baccará® × 'Garnet') × unknown]; intr. 1982

'Sacha' -- See 'Spekes'

'Sachalin' HRg, pb; flowers medium pink in center, blending to blush pink on outer petals, dbl., cupped, moderate spicy, clove fragrance; recurrent; foliage wrinkled; vigorous, medium growth; intr. 1988

Sachet™ -- See 'Savasach'

'Sachiko' HT, rb, Takatori

'Sächs. Lichtenstein' S, lp, Noack, Werner; flowers medium-large, semi-dbl.; intr. 1996

'Sachsengruss' ('Tendresse') HP, lp, 1912, Neubert; flowers soft flesh, well-formed, very large, full, moderate sweet fragrance; recurrent; thornless; stems short; vigorous, tall growth; ['Frau Karl Druschki' × 'Mme Jules Gravereaux']

'Sachsenrose' Pol, dp; flowers carmine-pink, small, semi-dbl.

'Saclay' F, pb, 1970, Inst. National Agronomique; flowers opal, 2-3 in., 20-22 petals, cupped; foliage dull, sage-green; bushy growth; [sport of 'Miss France']

'Sacramento' HT, dr, GPG Bad Langensalza; flowers dark velvety red, medium, dbl.; intr. 1981

'Sacred Fire' -- See 'Olympic Torch'

Sacred Heart™ -- See 'Wezsacheart'

'Sacred Heart' -- See 'Meipierar'

'Sadabahar' F, mp, 1970, IARI; bud pointed; flowers pink, open, medium, semi-dbl.; foliage glossy, dark; very vigorous, bushy growth; ['Frolic' × unknown]

'Sadabahar, Climbing' Cl F, mp, IARI; flowers borne in large clusters; [sport of 'Sadabahar']; intr. 1991

'Sadaranga' HT, mp, 1978, Hardikar, Dr. M.N.; bud ovoid; flowers 4½ in., 60 petals, globular; foliage glossy; vigorous, upright, compact growth; ['Kronenbourg' × 'Peace']; intr. 1977

'Saddler's Gold' -- See 'Horsaddler'

'Saddleworth' -- See 'Rawshermo'

'Saddleworth Male Voice Choir' -- See 'Rawsaddle'

'Sadie' -- See 'Desmother'

'Sadie Hawkins' -- See 'Spohawk'

'Sadler' -- See 'Biscof'

'Sadler's Wells' S, pb, Beales, Peter; flowers silvery-pink, laced with cherry red at the edges, semi-dbl., shallow cup, borne in large clusters, slight fragrance; free-flowering; foliage dark green, glossy; vigorous (4 ft.) growth; intr. 1983

'Safari' S, op, Clements, John; flowers soft coppery-bronze shading to rich coral toward the outer edge of the petals, 3-4 in., 35 petals, deeply cupped., moderate sweet fragrance; free-flowering; growth compact, bushy plant (3½ × 3 ft.); PPAF; intr. 2004

'Safari' F, my, 1970, Tantau, Math.; flowers large, 22 petals, cupped, borne in trusses; vigorous, compact growth; intr. 1966

'Safari' F, ab, Kordes; intr. 1998

'Safe Haven' F, mr, J&P; flowers medium, dbl., cupped, borne in large clusters, slight fragrance; free-flowering; foliage medium green, glossy; bushy, strong (3 ft.) growth; intr. 2006

'Saffex Rose' -- See 'Korgrayel'

'Saffo' HT, 1934, Aicardi, D.

'Saffran' HT, ly; intr. 2006

Saffron Minuetto™ -- See 'Meivarfal'

'Safrano' ('Aimé Plantier') T, ab, 1839, Beauregard; bud pointed; flowers saffron and apricot-yellow, large, semi-dbl., moderate fragrance; good repeat; vigorous growth

'Safrano à Fleurs Rouges' ('Mme Joséphine Mühle', 'Red Safrano') T, yb, 1867, Oger; flowers saffron yellow, shaded with coppery red, medium, semi-dbl.; [sport of 'Safrano']

'Saga' S, w, 1974, Harkness; flowers cream-white, 2½ in., 12 petals, borne in clusters; free-flowering; foliage medium green; ['Rudolph Timm' × ('Chanelle' × Piccadilly®)]

'Saga Holiday' -- See 'Harzest'

'Sagano' HT, op, Keihan; intr. 1982

'S'Agaró' HT, mr, 1959, Dot, Simon; bud long, pointed; flowers geranium-red, large, 30 petals, high-centered; foliage dark, glossy; compact growth; ['Angels Mateu' × ('Radar' × 'Grand'mere Jenny')]

'Sagittarius' F, mp, Chessum, Paul; flowers strong pink, dbl., borne in clusters; foliage glossy; bushy (75 cm.) growth; intr. 2004

'Sahara' HT, w, 1956, Stevenson; bud golden yellow; flowers creamy buff, well-shaped; rather late bloom; very vigorous, upright growth; ['Mrs Wemyss Quinn' × 'Mev. G.A. van Rossem']

'Sahara' S, yb, Tantau; flowers golden yellow with bronze red shades, large , dbl.; free-flowering; foliage medium green, glossy; tall (5 ft.) growth; intr. 1996

'Sahara' F, w, Olij; bud conical, elongated; flowers cream with light yellow and orange tints, 3½-4 in., 35 petals, high-centered, borne 1-3 per stem; good repeat; foliage medium green; prickles numerous, medium, greenish to yellow-brown; erect (4-5 ft.) growth; PP10281; [Prophyta™ × 'Olytel']; greenhouse rose; intr. 1997

'Sahasradhara' HT, pb, Thakur, Arpi; flowers deep pink with white streaks; [sport of 'Century Two']; intr. 1981

'Sai-Un' HT, ob, 1986, Suzuki, Seizo; flowers yellow-orange shaded deep orange-red, large, 50 petals, high-centered, moderate fragrance; foliage dark, glossy; prickles slanted downward; upright growth; [('Miss All-American Beauty' × 'Kagayaki') × seedling]; intr. 1980

'Sai Zan Tsuin' HCh, ab

'Sai Zhao Jun' HCh, ab; flowers blush pink, sometimes with honey tints, 2-2½ in., dbl., flat, moderate old rose fragrance; recurrent; growth to 5 ft.

'Saïd' F, rb, 1964, Arles; bud ovoid; flowers cinnabar-red, reverse dark red, medium, 28 petals, cupped, borne in clusters; short stems; ['Aloha' × 'Pioupiou']

'Saigon' HT, yb, 1943, Gaujard; flowers dark yellow with coppery pink tints, large, dbl.

'Saiki' HT, ly, Hiroshima; intr. 1999

'Sailoz Mookherjea' F, or, 1974, Pal, Dr. B.P.; flowers cadmium-orange to orange-vermilion, 3 in., 20 petals, high-centered; very vigorous growth; [unknown × unknown]

'St Alban' -- See 'Auschesnut'

'Saint Alban' F, mr, 1977, Harkness; flowers 3 in., 15 petals; foliage glossy; dwarf growth; ['Marlena' × unknown]

'St Alban's Gem' S, m

'St. Andrews' -- See 'Dicogle'

'St Boniface' -- See 'Kormatt'
'St. Brennus' -- See 'Brennus'
'St. Brigid's Rose'   HT, pb; intr. 1999
'St Bruno' -- See 'Lanpipe'
'St Catherine'   LCl, pb
'St Cecilia' -- See 'Ausmit'
'St Christopher' -- See 'Harcogent'
'St Clair's Rose'   HT, w
'St Clare' -- See 'Horoffside'
'St Dunstan's Rose'   S, w, Kirkham, Gordon Wilson; buds lemon yellow; flowers white, sometimes yellow streaked, full, rosette, intense fragrance; foliage pale green, glossy; growth to 3-4 ft.; commemorating the War Blind Association; intr. 1991
Saint-Émilion®   HT, mr, Briant; intr. 2001
'St Ethelburga' -- See 'Beabimbo'
'Saint-Exupéry'   S, mp; flowers Indian-rose, large, dbl., cupped, intense rose fragrance; growth to 80 cm.; intr. 2003
Saint-Exupéry®   ('Waltz Time') HT, m, 1960, Delbard-Chabert; flowers mauve tinted silvery, fading quickly, 5 in., dbl., high-centered, borne mostly solitary, slight fragrance; vigorous, bushy growth; [('Christopher Stone' × 'Marcelle Gret') × ('Holstein' × 'Bayadere')]
'Saint Fiacre'   Pol, or, 1965, Delforge; bud ovoid; flowers geranium-red, single, cupped, borne in clusters; vigorous, upright growth; ['Reverence' × 'Sumatra']
'Saint Fiacre d'Orléans'   Pol, op, Eve, A.; flowers salmon-pink, 6 cm., full, turbinate, borne in large clusters; recurrent; compact (2 ft.) growth; intr. 1997
'St. Francis' -- See 'Pompon de Saint-François'
'St Francis Xavier' -- See 'Tomxav'
'Saint Galmier'   S, w, Eve, André; flowers 3 cm.; foliage glossy; lax, groundcover or climbing growth; hips small, red; intr. 2005
'St Helena'   HT, ly, 1912, Cant, B. R.; flowers creamy yellow, center pinkish, large, full; RULED EXTINCT 6/83
'St Helena' -- See 'Canlish'
'St Hilaire'   (R. blanda form), mp; no prickles
'St Hildas'   HT, ab; flowers bright bronze-yellow, borne in clusters, moderate fragrance; stems moderately long; medium growth; intr. 1996
'St Hughs' -- See 'Korhug'
'St Ignatius'   HT, dy, Courage; flowers clear yellow, semi-dbl. to dbl., star-like, intense fragrance; recurrent; intr. 2001
'St Ingebert'   HP, w, 1926, Lambert, P.; bud long, pointed; flowers white, center yellowish and reddish, large, 62 petals; vigorous growth; ['Frau Karl Druschki' × 'Mme Mélanie Soupert']
'St John' -- See 'Harbilbo'
'St. John'   HT, mr; flowers mid-red, large, double, slight fragrance; recurrent; compact, medium growth; intr. 2005
'St. John Nonacentenary'   F, w, Poulsen; flowers white with soft apricot-cream in the center, dbl., low-centered, borne in dense clusters; recurrent; growth medium; intr. 2000
'St John Ogilvie' -- See 'Blestogil'
'St. John's College' -- See 'Jacnepal'
'St John's Rose'   ('Abyssinian Rose', R. centifolia sancta, R. richardii, R. sancta, 'Rose of the Tombs', 'Sancta') S, lp, before 1867; flowers rose to salmon-pink, 2-2½ in., single, borne in small corymbs; foliage somewhat rugose; prickles robust, hooked; growth low, trailing; [R. gallica × R. phoenicia]; introduced in Europe by Dammann around 1895; described by Rehder in 1902; known from Ethiopian & Egyptian tombs between 100-400 AD
'St Katherine's' -- See 'Peavenus'
'Saint Louis' -- See 'Malnino'
St Lucia®   HT, mp, 1975, Tantau, Math.; bud ovoid; flowers pink, medium, dbl., moderate fragrance; foliage glossy; moderate, upright, bushy growth; [unknown × unknown]
'St Margaret's'   HT, ob, Bell, Ronald J.; intr. 1998
'St Mark's Rose' -- See 'Rose d'Amour'
Saint Mary™ -- See 'Moryettem'
'St Nicholas'   D, dp, Hilling; flowers rich pink, yellow stamens, medium, semi-dbl., moderate apple fragrance; vigorous, erect (3 ft.) growth; [sport of 'Hebe's Lip']; probably a very old variety; found in England and re-introduced in 1950
'Saint Patrick' -- See 'Wekamanda'
St Patrick™ -- See 'Wekamanda'
'St Paul'   ('St. Pauli') F, yb, 1959, Kordes, R.; bud long, pointed; flowers golden yellow edged red to pink, becoming fused, open, 3 in., 15 petals, borne in clusters, moderate fragrance; foliage large, dark green, glossy; very vigorous, upright, bushy growth; ['Masquerade' × 'Spek's Yellow']; intr. 1958
'St. Pauli' -- See 'St Paul'
'St Piers'   ('Lottum Abundance', 'Salmon Abundance') F, mp; flowers rose pink, medium, full, cupped, borne in clusters, slight to moderate fragrance; good repeat; foliage dark green, glossy; modest (2-3 ft.) growth; intr. 1998
'St Priest de Breuze'   ('St Prist de Breuze') Ch, rb, 1838, Desprez; flowers rich deep crimson with rose center, medium, dbl., globular; upright (3-4 ft.) growth
'St Prist de Breuze' -- See 'St Priest de Breuze'
'St Quentin' -- See 'Krileville'
'St. Richard of Chichester'   ('Sherlock Holmes') S, ab, Harkness; flowers golden-amber, full, cupped, slight fragrance; moderate (100 cm.) growth; intr. 2006
'St Swithun' -- See 'Auswith'
'St Theresa'   HT, op, Williams, J.B.; flowers warm coral pink, dbl., cupped, borne in clusters; recurrent; intr. 2002
'St Tiggywinkles' -- See 'Korbasren'
'Saint Trop'   dp, INRA; intr. 1978
'Saint-Victor'   HT, mr, Croix; flowers large; free-flowering; foliage resistant; intr. 1979
Saint-Vincent® -- See 'Deltrap'
'St Wilfrid's Hospice'   F, mr, 1994, Sawday, Mrs. D.R.; flowers medium, semi-dbl., borne in small clusters, slight fragrance; foliage small, medium green, semi-glossy; some prickles; medium, bushy growth; [sport of 'Len Turner']; intr. 1995
'Sainte-Genevieve'   S, w, Guimont, G.; non-remontant; intr. 1987
'Saison Bluete'   HT, dy
'Sakaura-Hime'   Min, lp; flowers light to medium pink, large, dbl., pompon, borne in clusters; recurrent; intr. before 1979
'Sakura-Gasumi, Climbing'   Cl F, lp, Washimi; [sport of 'Sakura-Gasumi']; intr. 2001
'Sakura-Gasumi'   ('Cherry Blossom Haze', 'Sakuragasumi') F, lp, 1999, Suzuki, Seizo; flowers pale pink, turning deeper, 1½-2 in., 20-25 petals; foliage dark green, semi-glossy; dwarf, compact (1 ft.) growth; [seedling × seedling]; intr. 1990
'Sakuragai'   ('Cherry Blossom Clam') F, lp, Keisei; intr. 1996
'Sakuragasumi' -- See 'Sakura-Gasumi'
'Salaevensis'   (R. × salaevensis perrieri (Songeon ex Déséglise) Rouy) S; flowers rose-purple, borne 1-3 together; [R. dumalis × R. pendulina]
'Salam Aleik'   HT, mr; flowers pure red, very large, dbl.
Salamanca™   S, ab, Poulsen; flowers apricot blend, 5-8 cm., 25 petals, no fragrance; foliage dark; growth bushy, 60-100 cm.; intr. 2005
'Salamander'   HP, mr, 1891, Paul, W.; flowers bright scarlet-crimson, large, dbl., cupped; non-recurrent; upright growth
'Salambo'   HT, mr, 1959, Kordes, R.; flowers carthamus-red
Salammbô®   LCl, dr, Delbard; flowers dark, velvety crimson, medium, very full, borne in small clusters, slight fragrance; growth to 7-8 ft.; ['Grimpant Delbard' × Perle Noire®]; intr. 1994
'Salazar'   HT, rb, Moreira da Silva; flowers bright velvety red with salmon reflections, petals waved
'Salden Monarch'   HT, mp, 1970; flowers large, dbl.; foliage glossy; vigorous growth; ['Ballet' × unknown]; intr. 1968
'Salet'   ('Melchior Salet') M, mp, 1854, Lacharme, F.; bud well mossed; flowers rosy pink, lighter at edges, very large, full, cupped to flat, moderate fragrance; some recurrence; vigorous growth; apparently part Damask
Salita® -- See 'Kormorlet'
Salita Kordana®   Min, or, Kordes; compact growth; pot rose; intr. 2006
'Sallie'   HT, w, 1915, Cant, B. R.; flowers cream white, center darker with yellow reflections, large, full
'Sallie Lewis'   HT, ab, 1924, Morse; bud long, pointed; flowers creamy apricot, center deeper, dbl., intense fragrance;

['Mme Charles Lutaud' × 'Gladys Holland']; similar to Souv. de Mme. Boullet

'Sallijane' ('Sally Jane') HT, pb, 2001, Adlong, Paula; flowers medium, full, borne mostly singly, slight fragrance; [Crystalline™ × 'Elizabeth Taylor']; intr. 2001

'Sally' HT, mp, 1938, Spandikow; bud long, pointed; flowers pink, dbl., high-centered; foliage leathery; long stems; vigorous growth; PP187; RULED EXTINCT 3/81; ['Mrs Charles Russell' × 'Mme Butterfly']

'Sally' F, ab, 1981, Walker, B.; flowers pale apricot, fading to ivory, with pink veins; [sport of Elizabeth of Glamis®]

'Sally Alder' HT, mp, 1944, Moss; bud long, pointed; flowers pink, medium, semi-dbl., high-centered; foliage dark; moderate, bushy growth; ['Portadown' × seedling]

'Sally Forth' S, yb, Peden, R.

Sally Holmes® S, w, 1976, Holmes, R.; bud pointed, apricot; flowers creamy white, 3½-4 in., single, borne in large clusters; recurrent; foliage dark, glossy; few prickles; straight, long stems; vigorous, bushy growth; ['Ivory Fashion' × 'Ballerina']; intr. 1976

'Sally Jane' -- See 'Sallijane'

'Sally Jean' -- See 'Tomsal'

'Sally Kane' HT, w, Fryer; flowers creamy white with green tints on outer petals and champagne in the center, large, full, high-centered, borne usually singly, moderate fragrance; recurrent; foliage dark green, dense; medium growth; intr. 2006

'Sally Krisman' HT, w, 2002, Poole, Lionel; flowers cream to pale pink, 4½ in., full, borne mostly solitary, slight fragrance; foliage medium size, medium green, glossy; prickles medium, hooked down, moderate; growth upright, bushy, medium (3 ft.); garden decorative, exhibition; ['Joanna Lumley' × 'New Zealand']

'Sally Mac' F, ab, 1981, McCann, Sean; flowers apricot-pink blend, yellow at base, 40 petals, borne in clusters of 4; foliage medium size, dark, glossy; prickles hooked, red-brown; vigorous, upright growth; [('Joyfulness' × 'Paddy McGredy') × ('Circus' × 'Joyfulness')]

'Sally Pigtail' HT, pb, 1959, Mee; flowers cream flushed rose-pink, high pointed, large, 32 petals; free growth; ['Wilfred Pickles' × 'Karl Herbst']

'Sally Tite' HT, dr, 1930, Dickson, S.; flowers glowing crimson, over large, dbl., high-centered

'Sally's Rose' -- See 'Canrem'

Salmo™ ('Salmo Hit', Coral Midinette™) S, op, Olesen; flowers salmon-pink to orange, 5-8 cm., dbl., high-centered, borne in clusters, slight fragrance; free-flowering; foliage dark green, glossy; bushy, low (40-60 cm.) growth

'Salmo Hit' -- See 'Salmo'

'Salmon Abundance' -- See 'St Piers'

'Salmon Ange' HT, op

'Salmon Arctic' ('Everblooming Pillar No. 83') LCl, lp, 1954, Brownell; flowers dawn-pink, 3½-4½ in., 90-100 petals; growth like a hybrid tea, followed by 4-5 ft. canes; PP1297; [seedling × 'Break o' Day, Climbing']

'Salmon Beauty' Pol, op, 1929, Wezelenburg; flowers peach-pink, passing to soft salmon, medium, very dbl., borne in clusters; dwarf growth; [sport of 'Orange King']

'Salmon Button' Min, ob

'Salmon Charm' -- See 'Ginger Rogers'

'Salmon Cupido' Min, op, Pouw; bud ovoid; flowers salmon, 1½ in., 78 petals, rosette, borne singly and in large sprays, very slight fragrance; free-flowering; foliage dark green, glossy; prickles moderate, 4 mm., straight, brown; upright (15 in.), spreading growth; PP12642; [seedling × seedling]; containers; intr. 2004

'Salmon Dream' MinFl, op; intr. 1999

'Salmon Drops' Gr, op, Williams, J. Benjamin; flowers salmon-pink, dbl., high-centered, intense fragrance; foliage glossy; intr. 1999

'Salmon Gaujard' HT, op, Gaujard; flowers salmon-pink, large, full, high-centered; vigorous, sturdy growth; intr. 1985

'Salmon Glory' Pol, op, 1937, deRuiter; flowers pinkish salmon; [sport of 'Gloria Mundi']

'Salmon Glow' F, op, 1970, Sanday, John; flowers salmon, 3 in., 25 petals; foliage matte green; compact, bushy growth; ['Vera Dalton' × seedling]

'Salmon Impressionist' S, op, Lim, P, & Twomey, J.; bud medium, rounded; flowers coral, maturing to mauve-pink, 3½ in., 30 petals, tea rose form, borne in cluster of about 8, moderate fragrance; recurrent; foliage medium to dark green, satiny, disease-resistant; compact, upright (3 ft.), bushy growth; PP15739; [seedling × 'Lillian Gibson']; intr. 2004

'Salmon Keops' Cl Min, op; flowers salmon pink touched with orange , double, borne in clusters; recurrent; flexible canes; 2.5 meter growth; intr. 2008

'Salmon-King' F, rb, 1972, Ellick; flowers red, inside orange-red, high pointed, 5 in., 28-30 petals, intense fragrance; foliage glossy; vigorous, bushy growth; ['Show Girl' × Orange Sensation®]

'Salmon LD' S, op, Rogue Valley Roses; flowers salmon; [sport of 'Leonard Dudley Braithwaite']; like its parent except in flower color; intr. 2007

'Salmon Marvel' F, op, 1959, deRuiter; flowers orange-salmon, 2½-3 in., 44 petals, rosette, borne in trusses; foliage dark, glossy, crinkled; bushy, upright growth; ['Red Pinocchio' × 'Signal Red']; intr. 1958

'Salmon Midinette' Cl Min, op, Moore; flowers deep salmon-pink, borne singly and in clusters; recurrent; vigorous, tall (4 m.), willowy growth; intr. 1996

Salmon Panarosa™ S, op, Kordes; flowers deep salmon, medium, dbl., high-centered; upright, tall growth; intr. 2004

'Salmon Perfection' F, rb, 1952, deRuiter; flowers scarlet-red shaded orange, medium, 25 petals, cupped, borne in trusses; foliage dark, leathery; vigorous growth

'Salmon Pink Garnette' Pol, op

'Salmon Queen' Pol, op, 1923, Den Ouden; flowers deep salmon; [sport of 'Juliana Rose']

'Salmon Radiance' -- See 'Mrs Charles J. Bell'

'Salmon Rosamini' Min, op, deRuiter; flowers orange salmon, pompon; free-flowering; vigorous, tall, densely branched growth; intr. 1984

'Salmon Sensation' -- See 'Marion'

'Salmon Sorbet' F, pb

'Salmon Spire' -- See 'Korturnus'

'Salmon Splash' F, ob, K&S; flowers salmon with white stripes and splashes, borne in large sprays; free-flowering; compact growth; [sport of 'Orange Splash']; intr. 1997

'Salmon Spray' F, pb, 1923, Grant; flowers light salmon-pink, reverse shaded carmine, semi-dbl., cupped, borne in clusters, moderate fragrance; recurrent; foliage rich green, leathery; very vigorous, bushy growth; ['Orléans Rose, Climbing' × 'Midnight Sun']

'Salmon Sprite' F, op, 1964, LeGrice; flowers salmon suffused strawberry, 3 in., 40 petals, borne in clusters of up to 15; upright growth; [seedling × 'Jiminy Cricket']

Salmon Sunblaze™ -- See 'Meishulo'

'Salmon Sunsation' S, op, Kordes; flowers deep salmon, dbl., cupped, borne in clusters; low, groundcover growth; intr. 1989

'Salmon Symphony' HT, op

'Salmon Vigorosa' -- See 'Korpancom'

'Salmona' HT, op, Ghosh, Mr. & Mrs. S.; bud long; flowers salmon, veined deeper salmon, dbl., high-centered; intr. 2001

'Salmone' Gr, lp, 1968, Faassen-Gouba; bud ovoid; flowers medium, borne in clusters; foliage dark; [sport of Queen Elizabeth®]

'Salmonea' Pol, op, 1927, Cutbush; flowers salmon-pink

'Salomé' HT, op, 1945, Gaujard; bud ovoid; flowers salmon-flesh-pink, medium, dbl., moderate fragrance; foliage glossy; very vigorous, upright growth

'Salomé' F, pb, Buyl Frères; flowers rose-orange, dbl.; vigorous growth; intr. 1958

'Salome' HT, yb; florist rose; intr. 2002

'Salomi' S, mr, William, J. Benjamin; flowers cherry red , single, slight fragrance; 4 ft. growth; intr. 2004

'Salomon' HGal, pb, about 1825, Cartier; flowers dark pink, striped white, large, full

'Salou' F, pb, 1971, Delforge; bud long, pointed; flowers deep pink to flesh-pink, open, large, dbl.; foliage dark, leathery; very vigorous, upright growth; ['Astoria' × 'Tiffany']

'Salsa'™ -- See 'Jaczibwo'

'Salsa' -- See 'Poulslas'

'Salsa' -- See 'Jacstop'

Salt Lake™ (Silk Cover™) S, my, Poulsen; flowers medium yellow, 5-8 cm., semi-dbl., cupped to flat, borne in clusters, very slight fragrance; recurrent; foliage dark green, glossy; broad, bushy (60-100 cm.) growth; intr. 2005

'Saltaire' HT, dr, 1925, Dickson, A.; bud long, pointed; flowers deep velvety crimson, dbl.

'Saltatina' F, or, 1979, Lens, Louis; bud ovoid; flowers orange-copper to red, open, 2½-3 in., 18-22 petals, moderate spicy fragrance; foliage dark; bushy, spreading growth; ['Zorina' × 'Fillette']; intr. 1974

'Saltwell Park' F, mr, 1976, Wood; flowers very deep scarlet, 3 in., 20 petals; foliage dark; moderate, upright growth; ['Paddy McGredy' × 'Arabian Nights']

'Saluda' -- See 'Micsaluda'

'Salut' HT, op, VEG; flowers salmon-orange, large, dbl.; intr. 1987

'Salut à la Suisse' -- See 'Red Favorite'

'Salut d'Aix la Chapelle' -- See 'Gruss an Aachen'

'Salutation' LCl, op, 1972, Oliver, W.G.; flowers salmon, 2½ in., 38 petals; foliage glossy, dark; very vigorous growth; ['Salute' × 'Mme Isaac Pereire']

'Salute' -- See 'Savasalute'

'Salute' F, rb, 1959, McGredy, Sam IV; flowers cherry and ochre bicolor, 1½ in., 20 petals, borne in trusses; foliage dark, leathery; free growth; ['Masquerade' × 'Lady Sylvia']; intr. 1958

'Salvation' -- See 'Tomsave'

'Salvation' F, ab, Harkness; flowers amber infused with apricot, full, pompon, borne in clusters of 3 - 7, moderate fruity fragrance; recurrent; compact, sturdy, bushy growth; intr. 2005

'Salvator Adamo' or, Pineau; intr. 1981

'Salvo' HT, mr, 1959, Herholdt, J.A.; flowers velvety crimson, 5 in., 45 petals; vigorous, bushy growth; ['Happiness' × 'Grand Gala']

'Salza' S, dp, Berger, W.; flowers carmine-pink, medium, dbl.; intr. 1956

'Salzagold' HT, dy

'Salzajubiläum' F, or, GPG Bad Langensalza; flowers salmon-red, large, semi-dbl.; intr. 1982

'Salzaperle' HT, mp, GPG Bad Langensalza; flowers large, dbl.; intr. 1977

'Salzaquelle' HT, m, GPG Bad Langensalza; flowers light lilac, large, dbl.; intr. 1977

'Salzburg' S, op, W. Kordes Söhne; flowers medium, dbl.; intr. 1967

'Sam' -- See 'Stesam'

'Sam Buff' -- See 'Afterglow'

'Sam Ferris' F, ob, 1967, Ellick; flowers orange-scarlet, dbl., borne in trusses; vigorous growth; [sport of 'Heidleberg']

'Sam Houston' -- See 'Sam Houston Rose'

'Sam Houston Rose' ('Sam Houston') S, pb, Antique Rose Emporium; bud long, pointed; flowers medium pink fading into yellow eye, outer petals fade to pale pink, 3 in., semi-dbl., loose, flat, borne in small clusters, no fragrance; recurrent; growth to 3-4 ft.; ['Carefree Beauty' × 'Mrs. Oakley Fisher']; intr. 1996

'Sam McGredy' HT, yb, 1937, McGredy; flowers dark cream, base sunflower-yellow, large, high-centered, slight fragrance; foliage dark, leathery; vigorous growth; ['Delightful' × 'Mrs Charles Lamplough']

'Sam Trivitt' -- See 'Sprotri'

'Samandi' F, w, 1997, Rawlins, R.; flowers dbl., borne in small clusters; foliage medium; medium (1 m.) growth; [Sexy Rexy® × 'Brownie']

Samantha® HT, dr, Noack, Werner; intr. 1984

'Samantha, Climbing' Cl HT, mr; [sport of 'Samantha']

Samantha® HT, mr, 1974, Warriner, William A.; bud ovoid, pointed; flowers currant red, 4 in., 45-50 petals, high-centered, borne singly and several together, slight fragrance; recurrent; foliage medium size, leathery; prickles moderate, long, straight; stems long, strong; vigorous, upright growth; PP3727; [Bridal Pink™ × seedling]; flora-tea

'Samantha' -- See 'Worcall'

'Samantha Barker' -- See 'Webfree'

'Samantha-Jane' -- See 'Rawperp'

'Samantha Jose Home' -- See 'Worcable'

'Samantha Ruth' -- See 'Welsam'

Samara® HT, dy, Noack, Werner; flowers golden yellow, 4 in., dbl., high-centered; free-flowering; moderate growth; intr. 1989

'Samaritan' -- See 'Harverag'

'Samba' F, yb, 1963, Poulsen, N.; flowers cream yellow rimmed vermilion, 2½ in., 15 petals, high-centered, borne in clusters; foliage dark green; intr. 1962

Samba® F, yb, Kordes, R.; bud globular; flowers golden yellow touched red, becoming fiery red, 6 cm., dbl., borne in clusters, no fragrance; recurrent; foliage dark green, glossy; upright (2 ft.), bushy growth; intr. 1964

Samba® F, ob, Kordes; flowers copper-orange, sweetheart size, full, high-centered, borne mostly singly; recurrent; stems moderate; florist rose; intr. 2005

Samba Kordana® Min, yb, Kordes; flowers deep yellow, edged red, full, cupped; pot rose

Sambina® HT, pb; florist rose; intr. 2002

'Sammetglut' F, dr, 1943, Kordes; bud long, pointed; flowers crimson, open, very large, semi-dbl., borne in clusters; foliage dark, leathery; very vigorous, upright, bushy growth; ['Holstein' × 'Kardinal']

Sammi Minijet® Min, op, Meilland; flowers salmon, dbl., rosette, borne in clusters; containers

'Sammy' F, ab, Athy, Mike; bud pinky red; flowers apricot, ruffled, full, rosette, intense musk fragrance; recurrent; low to medium growth; intr. 2004

'Sammy' HMsk, dr, 1921, Pemberton; bud small; flowers carmine, single, borne in erect clusters; recurrent bloom; foliage glossy, bronze; very vigorous, bushy growth; [(Trier® × 'Gruss an Teplitz') × unknown]

'Samoa' -- See 'Fred Cramphorn'

Samoa® HT, ob, Tantau; flowers bright orange, medium, double, high-centered, borne mostly singly; recurrent; foliage glossy ; stems medium to long; florist rose; intr. 2001

'Samoa Sunset' HT, ob, 1965, Lone Star Rose Nursery; flowers chrome-yellow and copper-orange, open, large, dbl.; foliage glossy, bronze; vigorous, bushy, compact growth; [sport of 'McGredy's Sunset']

'Samouraï' ('Scarlet Knight') Gr, mr, 1966, Meilland, Mrs. Marie-Louise; bud medium, ovoid with a conspicuous neck; flowers crimson-scarlet, 4-5 in., 25-30 petals, cupped, borne singly and in small clusters, slight tea fragrance; recurrent; foliage large, leathery; prickles several, brownish; vigorous, upright, bushy growth; hips medium, globular, smooth, green, shaded red; PP2692; [('Happiness' × 'Independence') × 'Sutter's Gold']; intr. 1966

'Samourai, Climbing' ('Scarlet Knight, Climbing') Cl Gr, mr, 1974, Jack; [sport of 'Scarlet Knight']; intr. 1972

'Samptosa' F, dr, Institut für Obstbau Dresden Pillnitz; flowers large, dbl.; intr. 1969

Samsø™ -- See 'Poulnaris'

Samson™ -- See 'Savasam'

'Samuel Holland' -- See 'Captain Samuel Holland'

'Samuel Marsden' Ch, mp, 1989, Nobbs, Kenneth J.; [sport of 'Slater's Crimson China']; intr. 1987

'Samuel Pepys' HT, w, 1934, Cant, B. R.; flowers white, center slightly shaded cream, very large, dbl., globular; foliage leathery; bushy growth

'San Antonio' ('Armoton') Gr, or, 1967, Armstrong, D.L.; bud medium, medium; flowers cardinal red, 3½-5 in., 35-45 petals, high-centered to cupped, borne singly and in small clusters, slight fragrance; free-flowering; foliage dark, glossy, leathery; prickles several, short, almost straight; stems strong, medium to long; very vigorous, upright, bushy growth; hips globular, rough, apricot-orange to hazel; PP2844; ['Roundelay' × 'El Capitan']

'San Diego' HT, ob, 1937, Hieatt, Forrest L.; bud medium to large, ovoid; flowers deep orange-yellow, shading to apricot, fading to soft buff, large, dbl., strong fruity fragrance; good repeat bloom; foliage glossy; growth vigorous upright, bushy (3 ft.)

'San Diego' HT, my, Armstrong, D.L.; bud ovoid; flowers light yellow, large, 50 petals, high-centered, moderate fragrance; foliage leathery; vigorous, upright, bushy, compact growth; PP2900; ['Helen Traubel' × 'Tiffany']; intr. 1968

'San Diego' HT, pb, deVor; intr. 1993

'San Fernando' HT, mr, 1948, Morris; bud fat; flowers scarlet, large, 30 petals, high-centered, intense fruit/tea fragrance; recurrent; vigorous, upright growth; PP785; ['Heart's Desire' × ('Crimson Glory' × 'Poinsettia')]

'San Fernando, Climbing' Cl HT, mr, 1951, Whisler; PP1123; [sport of 'San Fernando']

'San Francisco' HT, mr, 1962, Lammerts, Dr. Walter; bud ovoid; flowers signal-red, 4-5 in., 40 petals, high-centered, moderate fragrance; foliage dark, glossy, leathery; vigorous, compact, branching growth; PP2045; ['Dean Collins' × 'Independence']; intr. 1962

'San Francisco Sunset' -- See 'Seaset'

San Gabriel™ -- See 'Ponbriel'

'San Gabriel' HT, op, 1947, Morris; bud long, pointed; flowers deep salmon-pink, 5½ in., 45 petals, high-centered, moderate fragrance; foliage dark, leathery; vigorous, bushy growth; PP860; ['Poinsettia' × seedling]

'San Joaquin' HT, ob, 1939, Moore, Ralph S.; flowers glowing orange; [sport of 'Talisman']

'San Jordi' HT, Camprubi, C.

'San José' HT, ob, 1933, Denoyel, Vve.; bud ovoid; flowers orange-salmon suffused gold, very large, dbl.; foliage glossy; very vigorous growth

'San Jose Sunshine' -- See 'Fousun'

'San Luis Rey' HT, dy, 1947, Morris; bud ovoid; flowers deep saffron-yellow, 4½ in., 40 petals, cupped, intense orange-clove tea fragrance; foliage dark, glossy; bushy growth; PP861; ['Lady Forteviot' × 'Pedralbes']

'San Rafael Rose' -- See 'Fortune's Double Yellow'

'San Valentino' Pol, Dot, Simon; intr. 1971

'Sanaran' HT, w, Sandbrook; intr. 1995

'Sanbaby' (Mother and Baby®) HT, dr, 1988, Sanday, John; flowers dark red with a velvet sheen, some black marking, reverse deep red-matte, medium, 48 petals, quartered, flat, borne usually singly, sometimes in sprays; foliage medium size, medium green, semi-glossy; prickles barbed, light brown; low growth; ['Bristol' × ('Lilac Rose' × ('Magenta' × 'Crimson Glory'))]

'Sanbi' HT, pb, Suzuki; intr. 1991

'Sancharm' ('Pink Nevada') HMoy, lp, 1985, Sanday, John; flowers pale lilac pink; [sport of 'Nevada']

'Sanchette' HGal, dp, 1837, Vibert; flowers crimson pink to rose, medium to large, full, cupped; growth erect

'Sancol' ('Edward Colston') F, dr, 1990, Sanday, John; bud rounded; flowers dark red with medium red reverse, aging dark red, 40-45 petals, cupped, borne in sprays of 3-5, slight fruity fragrance; foliage medium size, medium green, matte; prickles barbed, red; upright, medium growth; no fruit; ['Vera Dalton' × 'Stephen Langdon']; intr. 1982

'Sancta' -- See 'St John's Rose'

'Sanctus' HKor, w, 1982, James, John; flowers pure white, large, 36 petals, high-centered, borne singly, moderate fragrance; repeat bloom; foliage large, dark, leathery; prickles large, straight, rust-brown; vigorous, upright, tall growth; ['Borealis' × 'Borealis']; intr. 1978

'Sandalwood' -- See 'Jalwood'

'Sandar' HT, rb, 1946, Laperrière; flowers carmine, center yellow, large, 25 petals; foliage dark; very vigorous growth; ['Charles P. Kilham' × 'Lleida']

'Sandaya' ('Enhance') S, ly, 1992, Sanday, John; flowers soft apricot yellow, 1½ in., dbl., borne in large clusters, moderate fragrance; foliage medium size, medium green, glossy; some prickles; low (25 cm.), spreading growth; ['Malmesbury' × 'The Fairy']

'Sandberg' HT, pb

'Sandefjord' -- See 'Kortenay'

'Sander's White Rambler' HWich, w, Sander; flowers golden stamens, 3 cm., dbl., rosette, borne in large clusters, moderate fragrance; some autumn repeat; foliage bright green, glossy; vigorous growth; intr. 1912

'Sandhya Bela' F, ob, 1974, Pal, Dr. B. P.; buds small, ovoid; flowers orange with lighter reverse, medium, semi-dbl., open, borne singly and several together; foliage medium size, glossy; growth vigorous, bushy, open (60 cm.); [Zambra® × unknown]; intr. 1971

'Sandkor' (Sandra®) HT, op, 1982, Kordes, W.; bud long; flowers salmon, large, 35 petals, high-centered, slight fragrance; foliage medium size, medium green, matte; upright, medium growth; ['Mercedes' × seedling]; intr. 1981

'Sandokan' ('Sanmez') F, rb, 1979, Sande; flowers , 27-32 petals

'Sandolina de Major' HT, dp, 1978, W. Kordes Söhne; bud ovoid; flowers deep pink, 4 in., 57 petals, cupped, moderate fragrance; vigorous, upright growth; ['Dr. A.J. Verhage' × 'Königin der Rosen']; intr. 1977

'Sandra' -- See 'Meisolroz'

Sandra™ -- See 'Poulen005(N)'

'Sandra' HT, op, Kordes; flowers ivory with coral-pink edges spreading down the petals, dbl., high-centered, borne mostly singly; recurrent; stems long, strong; vigorous, upright growth; intr. 2002

Sandra® -- See 'Sandkor'

'Sandra Kim' -- See 'Meisolroz'

'Sandra Kordana' Min, op, Kordes

'Sandra May Williamson' HT, mp, Williamson; flowers single; intr. 1988

'Sandra Renaissance' (Sandra™) S, m, Poulsen; bud pointed ovoid; flowers lavender and purple, 4-6 in., 30 petals, deep cup, borne singly and in small clusters, moderate floral fragrance; recurrent; foliage dark, glossy; prickles some, deeply concave; upright (3-5 ft.), bushy growth; PP15730; [seedling × 'Evening Star']; intr. 2002

'Sandrina' S, Embriaco, B.; intr. 1996

'Sandrina' HT, yb, Kordes; intr. 1997

'Sandrine' F, lp, Eve, A.; flowers pale pink, 4 in., dbl., high-centered; recurrent; growth to 3-4 ft.; intr. 1975

'Sandringham' F, my, 1955, Kordes; flowers 2½ in., 30 petals, borne in large clusters; foliage light green, glossy; vigorous, tall growth

'Sandringham Centenary' ('Sandringham Century') HT, op, 1980, Wisbech Plant Co.; bud pointed; flowers deep salmon-pink, 22 petals, borne singly; foliage dark, glossy; vigorous, upright growth; [Queen Elizabeth® × Baccará®]

'Sandringham Century' -- See 'Sandringham Centenary'

Sands of Time™ -- See 'Minazco'

'Sandton City' -- See 'Meipopul'

'Sandton Smile' -- See 'Kormetter'

'Sandy' HT, op, Wisbech Plant Co.; flowers coppery-pink, large, dbl.; intr. 1981

Sandy ® F, ly, Spek; flowers pale yellow to apricot, 9 cm., 30-35 petals, high-centered, borne mostly singly; recurrent; prickles moderate; stems medium length; florist rose; intr. 2002

'Sandy Lundberg' -- See 'Gelberg'

'Sang' -- See 'Hector'

'Sang de Boeuf' -- See 'Sanguineo-Purpurea Simplex'

'Sang de Venus' P, mr, 1823, Bizard

'Sangerhausen' HMsk, dp, 1938, Kordes; bud long, pointed; flowers large, semi-dbl., cupped, borne in large clusters, slight fragrance; recurrent; foliage large, leathery, wrinkled; vigorous (4-5 ft.), bushy growth; ['Ingar Olsson' × 'Eva']

Sangerhäusen Jubiläumsrose® -- See 'Kormamtiza'

'Sangerhausen Roi de Siam' Cl T, dp; flowers deep cherry pink, loosely formed, semi-dbl.

'Sanglant' Ch, mp, 1873, Cherpin/Liabaud; flowers varying from light to dark pink

Sangria® F, or, 1966, Meilland, Mrs. Marie-Louise; flowers semi-dbl., borne in large trusses; vigorous growth; ['Fire King' × ('Happiness' × 'Independence')]

'Sangria' F, dp, Meilland; flowers fuchsia pink tinted carmine, 60-80 petals, rosette, borne in small clusters; growth compact (80-90 cm.); intr. 1992

'Sanguinaire' HRg, or, 1933, Gillot; bud long, pointed; flowers brilliant oxblood-red with orange, stamens yellow, open, 4 in., 18 petals; repeats sparingly; foliage glossy; short stems; growth shrub or pillar (6½ ft.); ['Bergers Erfolg' × 'Capt. Ronald Clerk']

'Sanguine d'Angleterre' -- See 'Hector'

'Sanguinea' -- See 'De La Flèche'

'Sanguinea' ('Bengal Cramoisi Double', 'Bengal Crimson', 'Rose de Bengale', *R. indica creunta*, 'Blood-red China Rose', 'La Sanguine') Ch, dr, before 1818; flowers velvety, vivid purple crimson, petals concave with white base, very dbl., globular; branches, leaves, and flowered stalks very purple; weak, spreading growth

'Sanguineo-Purpurea Atra' -- See 'Ombre Superbe'

'Sanguineo-Purpurea Simplex' ('Blutpurpurne Rose', 'Sang de Boeuf') HGal, dr, before 1820; flowers oxblood red, medium, single; foliage oval, singly dentate, light green upper, dull green reverse; prickles moderate

'Sanjith' ('Pink Super Bouquet') F, pb, K&S; flowers bright pink with broad white eye, single, shallow cup, borne in clusters; recurrent; compact growth; intr. 2001

'Sanka' ('Enchantment') HT, ob, Keisei Rose Nurseries, Inc.; flowers dbl., high-centered; intr. 1986

'Sankt Anton' Pol, mr, 1971, Delforge; bud long, pointed; flowers brilliant red, open, small, single; profuse, continuous bloom; foliage leathery; vigorous, upright growth; ['Alain' × seedling]

'Sanktflorian' F, mr, Meilland; flowers medium to large, dbl.; intr. 1971

'Sanlam-Roos' -- See 'Meichoiju'

'Sanlilac' ('Lilac Airs') HT, lp, 1988, Sanday, John; flowers soft lilac pink, yellow at base, reverse silver at base, large, 36 petals, exhibition, intense damask fragrance; foliage large, medium green, semi-glossy; prickles long, fairly straight, medium brown, matt; bushy, tall, strong growth; ['Fred Gibson' × 'Whisky Mac']; intr. 1988

'Sanmar' ('Bright Eyes') F, or, 1983, Sanday, John; flowers yellow stamens, medium, dbl.; foliage medium size, dark, matte; bushy growth; [seedling × 'Circus']

'Sanmed' ('Ice Fairy') Pol, w, 1984, Sanday, John; bud small; flowers ice white, small, full, borne in large clusters, slight fragrance; recurrent; foliage small, light green, semi-glossy; spreading growth; [sport of 'The Fairy']

'Sanmez' -- See 'Sandokan'

'Sanolence' ('Benevolence') HT, or, 1986, Sanday, John; flowers rich vermilion, large, 35 petals, high-centered, moderate fragrance; foliage large, dark, semi-glossy; prickles long, narrow; bushy growth; ['Vera Dalton' × seedling]; intr. 1986

'Sanone' ('Little One') S, rb, 1988, Sanday, John; flowers red with white eye, 5 petals, borne in sprays of 12-20; repeat bloom; foliage medium size, medium green, glossy; prickles average, light brown; bushy, low growth; [(Sarabande® × seedling) × 'Circus']

'Sanphyllis' ('John Hughes') F, ab, 1987, Sanday, John; flowers soft apricot, medium, 6-14 petals, slight fragrance; foliage medium size, dark green, glossy; bushy growth; ['City of Gloucester' × 'Bristol Post']; intr. 1986

'Sanremo' HT, mr, 1962, Mansuino, Q.; bud ovoid, pointed; flowers cardinal-red, 5½-6 in., 20-30 petals, high-centered, moderate fragrance; foliage glossy; strong stems; vigorous, upright, bushy growth; PP2134; [('Pink Delight' × 'Rome Glory') × Baccará®]

'Sanroc' ('Corsair') F, or, 1985, Sanday, John; flowers medium, 20 petals; foliage medium size, dark, glossy; bushy growth; [('Vera Dalton' × 'Stephen Langdon') × 'Fiesta Flame']

'Sanrozo' ('Esperanto Jubileo') HT, pb, 1987, Sanday, John; flowers cream, edged deep rose pink, yellow suffused at base, large, dbl., slight fragrance; foliage medium size, medium green, matte; bushy growth; ['Gavotte' × Piccadilly®]

'Sans Pareille Pourpre' HGal, dr, before 1811; bud oval; flowers velvety crimson-violet, full, moderate fragrance; foliage long, pointed, regularly dentate; prickles stright, red, pointed, unequal

'Sans Pareille Rose' HGal, dp, before 1811; bud oval; flowers delicate rose pink, lighter at edges, large, very dbl., moderate fragrance; foliage long, pointed, regularly dentate; prickles straight, red, pointed, few

'Sans Sépales' M, lp, 1839; flowers silvery flesh-pink, medium, dbl.

'Sans Souci' -- See 'Barsan'

'Sans Souci' Pol, or, Schmid, P.; flowers small, dbl.; intr. 1960

'Sans Souci' -- See 'Lavsans'

'Sans souci' -- See 'Moulin Rouge'

Sansibar® HT, ob, Tantau; flowers soft orange, large , doble, classic hybrid tea, borne mostly singly; recurrent; stems medium; florist rose; intr. 2005

'Sanspic' ('Apricot Spice') HT, ab, 1985, Sanday, John; flowers orange-apricot, medium, 35 petals; foliage medium size, medium green, matte; bushy growth; ['City of Gloucester' × seedling]

'Santa Anita' HT, mp, 1932, Howard, F.H.; bud pointed; flowers warm, clear pink, 3½-4 in., 22 petals, high-centered, moderate fragrance; foliage light; vigorous, bushy growth; PP539; [('Mrs J.D. Eisele' × seedling) × 'E.G. Hill']

'Santa Anita, Climbing' Cl HT, mp, 1946, Howard, F.H.; PP834; [sport of 'Santa Anita']

Santa Barbara™ -- See 'Pouloesy'

'Santa Catalina' Cl F, lp, 1970, McGredy, Sam IV; bud dark pink; flowers pale pink, reverse darker, 3½ in., 18 petals, borne in small clusters; foliage dark green, glossy; vigorous, tall (15 ft.) growth; ['Paddy McGredy' × 'Gruss an Heidelberg']; originally registered as LCl

'Santa Claus' HT, rb, Ghosh, Mr. & Mrs. S.; flowers carmine red with white reverse, large, full, high-centered; free-flowering; intr. 1998

'Santa Claus' -- See 'Poulclaus'

'Santa Fe' HT, op, 1967, McGredy, Sam IV; flowers deep salmon-pink, reverse lighter, large, dbl.; ['Mischief' × 'Tropicana']

'Santa Fe' -- See 'Jacyem'

'Santa Maria' F, mr, 1969, McGredy, Sam IV; flowers scarlet, borne in trusses; foliage small; ['Evelyn Fison' × ('Ma Perkins' × Moulin Rouge®)]

'Santa Rita' HT, op, 1961, Lens; flowers salmon-pink, well-formed, large; vigorous growth; ['Independence' × 'Papillon Rose']

'Santa Rosa' Ch, mp, 1899, Burbank; flowers bright rose-pink shading lighter, large, dbl., moderate fragrance; recurrent; moderate growth; ['Hermosa' × 'Bon Silene (or a seedling thereof)']

Santa Rosa™ (Special Border™) S, mr, Poulsen; flowers medium red, 5-8 cm., slight wild rose fragrance; foliage dark; growth broad, bushy, 100-150 cm.; PP15230; intr. 2002

'Santa Rosa' F, op, Silva; bud ovoid; flowers salmon-pink tipped brick, small, dbl., globular, intense fragrance; foliage glossy, soft, bronze; vigorous, bushy growth; ['Golden Salmon' × 'Pinocchio']; intr. 1954

'Santa Tereza d'Avila' HT, op, 1959, Moreira da Silva; flowers salmon-pink and orange, reverse gold, well-formed; foliage glossy; vigorous growth; ['Monte Carlo' × 'Michèle Meilland']

Santana® -- See 'Tanklesant'

'Santang' ('Maritime Bristol') HT, ob, 1983, Sanday, John; flowers tangerine, large, 35 petals; foliage medium size, dark, semi-glossy; upright, bushy growth; ['City of Gloucester' × seedling]

Santiago® -- See 'Adamona'

'Santor' ('Red Brigand') F, or, 1984, Sanday, John; flowers medium, 20 petals; foliage large, dark, semi-glossy; prickles short, slightly hooked; bushy growth; ['Vera Dalton' × 'Stephen Langdon']

'Sanwife' ('Wiltshire Pride') HT, rb, 1988, Sanday, John; flowers scarlet with yellow at base, reverse yellow with red edging, 28 petals, high-centered; foliage large, dark green, semi-glossy; prickles slightly hooked, dark brown; upright, tall growth; ['Bristol' × Piccadilly®]; intr. 1989

'Saohime' HT, lp, 1999, Hayashi, Shunzo; flowers clean, light pink, 38 petals, high-centered; foliage medium green, half-leathery; growth to 3½ ft.; ['Gavotte' × 'Bridal Robe']; intr. 1990

'Saonara' HT, mr, 1962, Borgatti, G.; flowers geranium-red, dbl.; foliage dark; strong stems; vigorous growth; [Baccará® × 'Peace']

'Saphir' -- See 'Tanrikas'

'Saphir' -- See 'Song of Paris'

'Sapho' HT, ob, Gaujard; flowers salmon, tinted coppery, very large, dbl.; foliage leathery, glossy, dark; very vigorous growth; intr. 1933

'Sapho' ('Beauté Rare') HGal, pb, 1818, Vibert; flowers purple center, edges a mixture of deep pink and delicate pink, medium, very dbl., flat; Agathe group

'Sapho' ('Perpétuelle Sapho') P, w, Vibert; flowers white, shaded flesh pink, small, full, borne in large clusters; sometimes classed as HP; intr. 1847

'Sappho' T, pb, 1889, Paul & Son; flowers fawn shaded pink, center yellow, large, full, moderate like Gloire de Dijon fragrance; vigorous growth

'Sappho' A, w; may not really exist

'Sara' -- See 'Jacautel'

'Sara' -- See 'Albella'

'Sara' -- See 'Pompon Varin'

'Sara' F, dr; intr. 2000

'Sara May Price' LCl, mp, 2005, Cunningham, Sam; flowers medium pink, reverse light pink, 4+ in., very full, borne mostly solitary, intense fragrance; foliage large, dark green, semi-glossy; prickles few, ¼ in., triangular, brown; growth upright, open, tall (11 ft.); lattice, fence; ['Maman Cochet, Cl.' × 'New Dawn (?)']; intr. 1988

Sarabande® F, or, 1958, Meilland, F.; flowers light orange-red, stamens yellow, 2½ in., 13 petals, cupped to flat, borne in large trusses, slight fragrance; recurrent; foliage semi-glossy; low, bushy growth; PP1761; ['Cocorico' × Moulin Rouge®]; intr. 1957

Sarabande, Climbing® Cl F, or, 1970, Meilland; [sport of Sarabande®]

'Saragat' HT, rb, 1968, Malandrone; flowers deep strawberry to cream, large, dbl., globular; foliage leathery; very vigorous growth; [seedling × seedling]

'Sarah' ('Varin') C, mp, 1822, Calvert; flowers medium pink, center brighter

'Sarah' S, op, Clements, John; flowers soft pink, peach and coral, 3½ in., 30 petals, intense fruity fragrance; foliage rich green; vigorous, bushy (3-4 ft.) growth; PPAF; intr. 2001

'Sarah' Min, ab, Hannemann, F.; ['Poker Chip' × Holy Toledo™]

'Sarah' -- See 'Meimafris'

'Sarah Ann Morgan' Min, w, 2003, Hover, Flora C.; flowers full, borne in small clusters, slight fragrance; foliage medium size, medium green, semi-glossy; prickles 1/8 in., straight, moderate; growth bushy, tall (4 ft.); garden decorative, exhibition; [sport of 'Giggles']; intr. 2002

'Sarah Anne' MinFl, mp, 2002, Read, Allan; flowers medium, colour varying from white with pink splashes to solid pink, 2½ in., full, borne in large clusters, no fragrance; foliage medium size, medium green, semi-glossy; prickles 3/16 in. pointed, few; growth compact, medium (3 ft.); garden decorative, exhibition; [Bluesette® × unknown]; intr. 2003

'Sarah Arnot' HT, mp, 1958, Arnot, David; flowers warm rose-pink, 4½ in., 25 petals, moderate fragrance; foliage leathery; vigorous, upright growth; ['Ena Harkness' × 'Peace']; intr. 1957

'Sarah Bacherach' F, mp, 1965, Buisman, G. A. H.; flowers pink, medium, dbl.; foliage dark; ['Harmonie' × 'Buisman's Triumph']

'Sarah Bernhardt' Cl HT, dr, 1906, Dubreuil; flowers scarlet-crimson, very large, semi-dbl.

'Sarah Coventry' F, dr, 1959, Boerner; bud ovoid; flowers cardinal-red, open, medium, 40-45 petals, cupped, borne in irregular clusters, moderate fragrance; foliage bright green; vigorous, compact, bushy growth; PP1611; ['Red Pinocchio' × 'Garnette']; intr. 1956

'Sarah Darley' HT, dy, 1938, Wheatcroft Bros.; flowers clear deep golden yellow, well-shaped; foliage dark; vigorous growth

'Sarah, Duchess of York' -- See 'Dicracer'

'Sarah Elizabeth' -- See 'Pixsar'

'Sarah Eluned' F, pb, 2004, Paul Chessum Roses; flowers small, semi-dbl., borne in small clusters, slight fragrance; foliage medium size, medium green, matte; growth compact, short (50 cm.); bedding, borders, containers; [seedling × seedling]; intr. 2004

'Sarah Hartas' -- See 'Worcastle'

'Sarah Hill' F, mp, 1956, Joseph H. Hill, Co.; bud short, pointed; flowers phlox-pink, open, 2½-3 in., 25-30 petals, slight spicy fragrance; foliage dark, leathery; vigorous, upright, bushy growth; PP1397; ['Garnette' × 'Pink Bountiful']

'Sarah Jane' HT, pb, 1970, Heath, W.L.; flowers rose-pink, edged deeper, reverse white, 4½-5 in., 35 petals; foliage glossy; very vigorous, tall growth; [sport of Rose Gaujard®]

'Sarah Jayne' -- See 'Socbob'

'Sarah Jo' -- See 'Mehrex'

'Sarah Juanita' -- See 'Ponanita'

'Sarah Lynn' HT, mp, 1991, Ohlson, John; flowers medium, full, borne mostly singly, slight fragrance; foliage large, dark green, semi-glossy; strong stems; vigorous, medium, compact growth; [seedling × 'Prima Ballerina']

'Sarah Maud' HT, dy, 1934, Mallerin, C.; bud long; flowers golden yellow, large; foliage bright, dark; very vigorous growth

'Sarah Nesbitt' T, yb, 1910, Dorrance; flowers light carnation-yellow, center darker; [sport of 'Mme Cusin']

'Sarah Penrose' -- See 'Websun'

'Sarah Philp' Min, ab

'Sarah Robinson' -- See 'Trobinette'

'Sarah Van Fleet' HRg, mp, 1926, Van Fleet; flowers wild-rose-pink, large, semi-dbl., cupped, intense fragrance; recurrent bloom; foliage leathery, rugose; compact (6-8 ft.) growth; [R. rugosa × 'My Maryland']

'Sarah Wright' HT, dp, 1927, Morse; bud long, pointed; flowers rose-pink, dbl.; ['Ophelia' × 'Emma Wright']

'Sarah's Rose' HT, op; intr. 2003

'Sarajean' Min, pb, 1980, Williams, Ernest D.; bud pointed; flowers peach-pink, 1 in., 50 petals, globular, moderate fragrance; foliage small, bronze-green, glossy; upright, bushy growth; PP4755; [seedling × 'Over the Rainbow']; intr. 1979

'Saramouche' Min, rb, Delbard; flowers striped; intr. 2002

'Sarannla' ('Annie Laurie') HT, pb, 2003, Renfroe, Samuel; flowers full, borne mostly solitary; foliage medium size, medium green, semi-glossy; growth upright, tall (4-6 ft.); garden, exhibition; [sport of 'Virginia']

'Sarasota Spice' N, w, 2006, Starnes, John A., Jr.; flowers dbl., borne in large clusters, intense cinnamon-clove fragrance; foliage medium size, medium green, matte; prickles small, cats claw, tan, moderate; growth upright, climbing, medium (6 ft.); pillar/climber; ['The Gift' × 'Blush Noisette']; at times produces massive panicles of dozens of blooms; intr. 2005

'Saratoga' F, w, 1963, Boerner; bud ovoid; flowers , 33 petals, gardenia-like, borne in irregular clusters, intense fragrance; foliage glossy, leathery; vigorous, upright, bushy growth; PP2299; ['White Bouquet' × 'Princess White']

'Sardane' F, rb, 1962, Laperrière; bud long; flowers coral-red tinted silvery, 3 in., 35-40 petals; foliage bright green; very bushy, compact growth

'Saremo' S, mp, Noack; flowers soft, medium pink, 3-4 in., full, borne in clusters, slight fragrance; recurrent; spreading (4 × 4 ft.) growth; hips decorative; intr. 2001

'Sargent' HWich, pb, 1912, Dawson; flowers apple-blossom-rose to pale pink, base amber-yellow, 3 in., semi-dbl., borne in large clusters, moderate fragrance; growth to 10-12 ft.; [(R. wichurana × Turner's Crimson Rambler) × 'Baronne Adolphe de Rothschild']

'Sari Hou' S, lp, 2003, Law, Stephen; flowers 2-3 in., dbl., borne in small clusters, slight fragrance; foliage small, medium green, matte; prickles small; growth to 2-3 ft.; decorative; ['Morden Centennial' × unknown]

'Sarie' HT, mp, 1976, Herholdt, J.A.; flowers 4½-5 in., 35 petals; foliage glossy, bright green; vigorous growth; ['Pink Favorite' × 'Nightingale']; intr. 1977

'Sarie Marais' -- See 'Korhota'

'Sarie Mareis' F, mr, 1950, Leenders, M.; flowers glowing scarlet; ['Irene' × 'Donald Prior']

'Saris Sepals' M, mp, 1839

'Sarlet' ('Louise Emma') MinFl, op, 2007, Pullen, Sarah Mary; flowers pink, reverse orange/pink, medium, 2.5 in., very full, borne mostly solitary; foliage small, dark green, semi-glossy; prickles small, downward pointing, brown, few; growth bushy, medium (18-24 in.); bedding, containers; [June Laver ™ × 'Ruby Pendant']; intr. 2007

'Sarmemory' ('Alison Pitt') MinFl, w, 2008, Pullen, Sarah Mary; flowers 1½ in., full, borne in small clusters; foliage small, medium green, glossy; prickles small, straight, light brown, moderate; growth bushy, medium; bedding; [Irresistible™ × seedling]; intr. 2008

'Saroda' ('Sharada') Gr, lp, 1985, Gupta, Dr. M.N., Datta, Dr. S.K. & Nath, P.; [sport of Queen Elizabeth®]; intr. 1983

'Saroja' F, pb, Pal, Dr. B.P.; intr. 1984

'Sarong' -- See 'Glanlin'

'Saroor' F, or, 1971, Singh; bud ovoid; flowers orange-scarlet, open, large, dbl.; foliage large, leathery; upright growth; ['Gertrud Westphal' × unknown]; intr. 1969

'Sarpet' ('Rev. Peter Lewis') F, rb, 2006, Pullen, Sarah Mary; flowers red striped, reverse red, 2-3 in., semi-dbl., borne in large clusters; foliage medium size, medium green, semi-glossy; prickles small, straight, light brown, moderate; growth upright, medium (30 in.); ['Pirouette' × seedling]; intr. 2006

'Sarvesh' HT, or, K&S; bud pointed, long; flowers intense, deep orange-red, large, dbl., high-centered; free-flowering; sturdy growth; intr. 2004

'Sarwen' ('Little Wendy') Min, w, 2004, Pullen, Sarah Mary; flowers white, reverse white, 1½-2 in., single, borne in small clusters, intense fragrance; foliage small, dark green, semi-glossy; prickles few, small, downward, green; growth bushy, short (12-15 in.); [June Laver™ × Winter Magic™]; intr. 2004

'Sasa' -- See 'Delrima'

'Saskabec' -- See 'Tant Mieux'

'Saskia' F, mp, 1961, Buisman, G. A. H.; flowers single, borne in large clusters; foliage dark; bushy growth; ['Pinocchio' × 'Gartenstolz']

Sassy™ -- See 'Hiltaco'

'Sassy Cindy' -- See 'Bricindy'

'Sassy Girl' -- See 'Moesassy'

'Sassy Lassy' Min, yb, 1976, Williams, Ernest D.; bud pointed; flowers yellow and pink blend, 1 in., 28 petals, cupped to high-centered, borne singly or several together, slight fragrance; foliage small, bronze, glossy, leathery; upright, spreading growth; PP4036; [seedling × 'Over the Rainbow']; intr. 1975

'Satan' ('Joyce Lomax', 'Satanas') HT, dr, 1939, Pahissa; flowers very dark red, reverse lighter, large, semi-dbl. to dbl., high-centered, moderate fragrance; foliage leathery; bushy growth; PP379; [('Mme Edouard Herriot' × 'Angèle Pernet') × 'Mari Dot']

'Satanas' -- See 'Satan'

Satchmo® F, or, 1970, McGredy, Sam IV; flowers bright scarlet, 3 in., 25 petals, hybrid tea, borne in large clusters, slight fragrance; foliage reddish early, then dark green; bushy, compact growth; ['Evelyn Fison' × 'Diamant']

'Satellite' -- See 'Delsatel'

Satellite® HT, dr, 1959, Priestly; bud pointed; flowers deep crimson, 4½ in., 30 petals, high-centered, intense fragrance; foliage dark, glossy; vigorous, upright, compact growth; ['Editor McFarland' × 'William Harvey']; intr. 1958

'Satin' HT, dp; flowers deep satiny pink, dbl., high-centered, borne mostly singly; recurrent; growth to 3½ ft.; intr. 1996

'Satin' HT, ab, Tantau; thornless; greenhouse rose; intr. 2002

'Satin Beauty' HT, op, Kordes; flowers clear salmon, softening to cream salmon in the sun, dbl., high-centered, borne mostly singly; recurrent; few prickles; stems long, strong, upright; medium growth; intr. 2002

'Satin Doll' -- See 'Jacspif'

'Satin Ribbon' HT, yb, Delbard; bud creamy yellow; flowers deep yellow with light apricot tones; moderate growth; intr. 2001

'Satin Tears' F, mp, Williams, J.B.; flowers pink with yellow stamens, semi-dbl.; recurrent; intr. 2004

Satin Touch™ -- See 'First Gold'

'Satina' -- See 'Snow Cloud'

Satina® ('Harewood') S, mp, Tantau; flowers medium, semi-dbl., rosette, borne in large clusters, slight fragrance; free-flowering; foliage deep green, glossy; compact, bushy growth; intr. 1992

'Satinette' Pol, w, 1971, Delforge; bud ovoid; flowers large, dbl., cupped; foliage large, light, leathery; vigorous, upright growth; ['Maria Delforge' × 'Irene of Denmark']

'Satinglo' F, mp, 1954, Boerner; bud globular; flowers glowing coral, 2½ in., 45-50 petals, cupped, borne in clusters, moderate fragrance; foliage leathery, glossy; vigorous growth; PP1285; [('Pinocchio' × unknown) × 'Vogue']

'Satisfaction' HT, dp, 1960, Verbeek; flowers carmine-pink, large, dbl., intense fragrance; ['Parfum' × seedling]; intr. 1958

'Satmir' HT, dr, 1956, Dot, Pedro; flowers carmine-red, dbl.; long, strong stems; very vigorous growth; ['Satan' × 'Mirandy']

Saturday® HT, pb, McGredy, Sam IV; flowers rose pink with yellow tones in center, large, dbl., borne singly and several together, slight fragrance; recurrent; foliage dark green; stems strong, strong, upright (100 cm.) growth; intr. 1990

'Saturday Star' -- See 'Korvolomin'

'Saturn' -- See 'Jaclogo'

'Saturnia' HT, rb, 1936, Aicardi, D.; bud long, pointed; flowers bright scarlet with gold, large, 20 petals, cupped, moderate fruity fragrance; foliage dark, glossy; vigorous growth; PP349; ['Julien Potin' × 'Sensation']

'Satvika' HT, rb, K&S; flowers hand-painted scarlet-crimson with prominent white base, silvery white reverse, dbl.; free-flowering; intr. 2001

'Saubaflor' ('Heriflor') F, lp, Sauvageot-dbl.; intr. 1990

'Sauban' F, pb, Sauvageot; intr. 1999

'Saubera' HT, ob, Sauvageot; intr. 1989

'Saubima' F, op, Sauvageot; intr. 1994

'Saublim' ('Atida') HT, mr, Sauvageot; intr. 1991

'Saubord' (Gustave Courbet®) HT, dp, Sauvageot; intr. 1992

'Saucabou' ('Hermitage') F, m, Sauvageot; bud globular; intr. 2004

'Saucobol' HT, pb, Sauvageot; intr. 2006

'Saucy Sue' F, mp, 1975, Lowe; flowers large, 20-25 petals, moderate fragrance; free growth; ['Pink Parfait' × Europeana®]; intr. 1973

'Saudade d'Anibal de Morais' HT, dr, 1935, Moreira da Silva; bud velvety crimson; flowers salmony crimson-red, dbl.; vigorous growth; ['Sir David Davis' × 'Pres. Jac. Smits']

'Saudero' ('Dance of Joy 95') F, mr, Sauvageot, H.; intr. 1995

'Saudime' F, rb, Sauvageot; intr. 1999

'Saudive' F, ab; intr. 1997

'Saudora' ('Eclipse') F, pb, Sauvageot; intr. 1997

'Saudril' ('Manureva') F, lp, Sauvageot; intr. 1997

'Saugamu' F, yb, Sauvageot; intr. 2000

'Saukaro' F, op, Sauvageot; intr. 1989

'Saul' HT, dp, 1970, Gandy, Douglas L.; flowers light rose-madder, 4 in., 28 petals; foliage large, dark; upright growth; ['Tropicana' × 'Sterling Silver']

'Saulina' F, ly, Sauvageot; intr. 2003

'Saulina' F, w, Sauvegeot; intr. 2005

'Saumonia' HT, op; intr. 1998

'Saunalid' S, yb, Sauvegeot; intr. 2007

'Saunel' HT, dy, Sauvageot; intr. 2003

'Sauniber' F, ab, Sauvageot; intr. 2002

'Sauraline' F, dy, Sauvageot; intr. 2007

'Sauredupt' F, ab, Sauvageot; intr. 2002

Sausalito™ (Ruby Border™) S, mr, Olesen; bud urceolate; flowers medium red, reverse lighter, 5 cm., 30-35 petals, open cup, flowers borne in large panicles, slight floral fragrance; recurrent; foliage dark green, glossy; prickles numerous, 7 mm., concave, brown; broad, bushy (60-100 cm.) growth; PP16583; [Charming Cover™ × seedling]

'Sauvachild' S, dp, Sauvageto; intr. 2004

'Sauvami' F, mp, Sauvageot; intr. 2004

'Sauvrima' HT, pb, Sauvageot; intr. 2007

'Savabe' ('Glory Be') Min, dy, 1994, Saville, F. Harmon; flowers small, dbl., borne singly or in small clusters, no fragrance; foliage small, dark green, semi-glossy; growth medium (16-20 in.), upright, bushy; PP9506; [Party Girl™ × Sonnenkind®]; intr. 1995

'Savabean' Min, rb, 1982, Saville, F. Har-

The Official Registry and Checklist — Rosa 665

mon; bud ovoid, pointed; intr. 1982

'Savabear' (Teddy Bear™) Min, r, 1990, Saville, F. Harmon; bud small, ovate; flowers terra-cotta, reverse lighter, aging to mauve-pink, ¾ in., 28 petals, high-centered, then flat, borne singly or in clusters of 5 - 20, slight fragrance; recurrent; foliage medium size, dark green, semi-glossy; prickles slight downward curve, medium, purple; upright, bushy, medium, vigorous growth; hips ovoid to globular, brownish-orange; PP7424; [Sachet™ × Rainbow's End™]; intr. 1990

'Savabeg' (New Beginning™) Min, ob, 1988, Saville, F. Harmon; flowers bright orange-yellow bicolor, decorative, medium, 40-50 petals, borne usually singly, no fragrance; foliage medium size, medium green, semi-glossy; prickles very few; bushy, compact (16-20 in.) growth; no fruit; PP6707; ['Zorina' × seedling]; intr. 1989

'Savabet' (Single's Better™) Min, mr, 1985, Saville, F. Harmon; bud mossy; flowers medium red, yellow hinge, minimoss, small, 5 petals; foliage medium size, medium green, semi-glossy; bushy growth; [('Yellow Jewel' × 'Tamango') × (('Little Chief' × Sarabande®) × 'Lemon Delight')]

'Savabino' ('Bambino') Min, or, 1997, Saville, F. Harmon; flowers small, micro mini, vibrant orange, full, borne in small clusters, no fragrance; foliage small, medium green, semi-glossy changing to matte; compact, bushy, low (to 14in.) growth; PP10980; [Sequoia Gold™ × Sparks™]; intr. 1998

'Savabrez' (Breezy™) Min, ob, 1984, Saville, F. Harmon; bud small; flowers bright orange-red, yellow reverse, small, 20 petals, high-centered, borne in sprays; foliage small, medium green, semi-glossy; upright growth; ['Sheri Anne' × seedling]

'Savabusy' ('Busy Bee') Min, ab, 2001, Saville, F. Harmon; flowers coral-orange, soft yellow reverse, 1¼ in., full, borne in small clusters, slight fragrance; continuous; foliage medium size, dark green, matte; prickles ¼ in., thin, straight, numerous; growth compact, bushy, medium (14-20 in.); garden decorative, containers; [Sequoia Gold™ × Sparks™]; intr. 2001

'Savacall' (Total Recall™) Min, or, 1985, Saville, F. Harmon; flowers medium, dbl., no fragrance; foliage small, medium green, semi-glossy; bushy growth; ['Zorina' × Baby Katie™]; intr. 1984

'Savacamp' (Scamp™) Min, mr, 1985, Saville, F. Harmon; flowers micro-mini, small, 35 petals, high-centered, slight fragrance; foliage small, medium green, semi-glossy; compact, bushy growth; [Baby Katie™ × ('Yellow Jewel' × 'Tamango')]; intr. 1984

'Savacent' ('Atkins Beauty', 'Australian Centre Gold') Min, dy, 1981, Saville, F. Harmon; bud pointed

'Savachase' (Chasin' Rainbows™) Min, rb, 1989, Saville, F. Harmon; bud ovoid; flowers very brilliant yellow, edged red with scarlet becoming more red with age, 21 petals, high-centered, slight spicy fragrance; foliage small, dark green, semi-glossy; prickles long, thin, angled, light brown; bushy, low growth; no hips; PP7058; ['Zorina' × Rainbow's End™]; intr. 1988

'Savachild' (Child's Play™) Min, pb, 1991, Saville, F. Harmon; flowers porcelain white with pink edges, 1½ in., 20 petals, high-centered, borne singly or in small clusters, moderate sweet fragrance; foliage medium size, dark green, matte; upright, medium growth; PP8175; [('Yellow Jewel' × 'Tamango') × Party Girl™]

'Savacin' (Cinnamon Toast™) Min, r, 1986, Saville, F. Harmon; flowers russet brown, small, 28 petals, high-centered; foliage small, medium green, semi-glossy; prickles small, red; low, upright, bushy growth; ['Zorina' × ('Sheri Anne' × 'Glenfiddich')]

'Savaclend' (Rainbow's End, Climbing™) Cl Min, yb, 1998, O'Brien, Susan; flowers yellow suffused with red at edges, 1½ in., 30-35 petals, high-centered, borne singly and in small clusters; foliage small, medium green, semi-glossy; prickles moderate, thin, angling downward; short, thick stems; climbing to 10 ft. growth; PP11257; [sport of Rainbow's End™]

'Savacloud' Min, w, 1988, Saville, F. Harmon

'Savacon' ('Constellation') Min, w, 2000, Saville, F. Harmon; flowers near white, medium, 35-40 petals, high-centered, borne mostly singly; foliage medium size, dark green, semi-glossy to glossy; no prickles until plant matures, then few; upright, spreading, well-branched, medium (24-28 in.) growth; PP12652; [Sachet™ × 'New Zealand']; intr. 1999

'Savacook' ('Fortune Cookie') Min, ab, 1995, Saville, F. Harmon; flowers apricot blend, small, dbl., borne singly and in small clusters, no fragrance; foliage small, medium green, semi-glossy; no prickles; medium (16-18 in.), upright, compact growth; [Baby Katie™ × 'Mazurka']; intr. 1996

'Savacop' (Copper Sunset™) Min, ob, 1988, Saville, F. Harmon; bud pointed; flowers coppery-orange, flushed orange-red, reverse medium red, 21 petals, high-centered; foliage medium size, dark green, semi-glossy; prickles long, thin, slanted, gray-red; upright, medium, angular growth; hips ovoid, orange; PP7032; [Acey Deucy™ × Rainbow's End™]

'Savacrim' ('Little Crimson') Min, dr, 1994, Saville, F. Harmon; flowers small, dbl., borne mostly singly, no fragrance; foliage small, dark green, semi-glossy; few prickles; medium (16-20 in.), upright, bushy growth; [Teddy Bear™ × ('Zorina' × Baby Katie™)]; intr. 1995

'Savaday' (Heavenly Days™) Min, op, 1988, Saville, F. Harmon; flowers glowing Indian-orange, reverse lemon yellow, flushed fire-red, 28-32 petals, cupped, no fragrance; foliage medium size, medium green, glossy, underside matte; bushy, medium, compact growth; PP6808; ['climbing yellow miniature' × ('Sheri Anne' × 'Glenfiddich')]

'Savadee' (Dee Bennett™) Min, ob, 1989, Saville, F. Harmon; flowers yellow and orange becoming orange-yellow, medium, 25 petals, high-centered, borne usually singly, slight fruity fragrance; foliage medium size, dark green, semi-glossy; prickles long, thin, curved, gray-orange; bushy, medium growth; no fruit; PP6951; ['Zorina' × ('Sheri Anne' × ('Yellow Jewel' × 'Tamango'))]; intr. 1989

'Savaden' (Denver's Dream™) Min, ob, 1995, Saville, F. Harmon; flowers copper orange with red reverse, small, full, cupped, borne mostly singly, no fragrance; foliage medium size, dark green, semi-glossy; medium (16-20 in.), upright growth; PP9435; ['Gingersnap' × Klima™]; intr. 1994

'Savadi' (Baby Diana™) Min, or, 1986, Saville, F. Harmon; flowers orange-red, yellow reverse, small, 20 petals, high-centered, borne usually singly; foliage small, medium green, semi-glossy; prickles long, thin, hooked, brown; bushy growth; PP5957; ['Zorina' × ('Sheri Anne' × 'Glenfiddich')]

'Savadiana' ('Sweet Diana') Min, dy, 2001, Saville, F. Harmon; bud ovate; flowers deep yellow, medium yellow reverse, 1⅞ in., 20 petals, high-centered, then flat, borne in small clusters, very slight fragrance; recurrent; foliage medium size, dark green, matte, disease-resistant; prickles few, 5/16 in., angled slightly down; growth bushy, medium (14-18 in.); borders, containers, exhibition, cutting; hips apple-shaped ; PP16797; ['Cal Poly' × June Laver™]; intr. 2002

'Savadoll' Min, ob, 1979, Saville, F. Harmon; bud ovoid, pointed

'Savadouble' (Double Gold™) MinFl, yb, 2002, White, Wendy R.; flowers light yellow, reverse golden yellow, 2½-3¼ in., full, borne mostly solitary, intense fragrance; foliage medium size, dark green, glossy; prickles straight or slightly angled down, moderate; growth upright, spreading, medium (18-30 in.), exhibition, cut flower; PP16056; [(('Zorina' × Baby Katie™) × June Laver™) × 'Old Glory']; intr. 2003

'Savadream' (Dreamer™) Min, mp, 1991, Saville, F. Harmon; bud ovoid, pointed; flowers dusty pink, medium, 20 petals, cupped, borne singly or in sprays of 3-5, no fragrance; foliage medium size, dark green, semi-glossy; upright, bushy, medium growth; PP7757; [Baby Katie™

× Shocking Blue®]; intr. 1991

'Savaface' (Happy Face™) Min, dp, 1991, Saville, F. Harmon; bud ovoid; flowers clear rosy pink, medium, 35-40 petals, cupped, borne usually singly or in sprays of 3 - 5, no fragrance; foliage medium size, dark green, glossy; bushy, medium, compact growth; [('Sheri Anne' × 'Rise 'n' Shine') × Mountie™]; intr. 1991

'Savafire' (Fireworks™) Min, rb, 1991, Saville, F. Harmon; flowers brilliant orange-yellow bicolor, 1½ in., 35 petals, high-centered, borne singly or in small clusters, slight fragrance; profuse; foliage medium size, dark green, semi-glossy; bushy, medium growth; PP8182; [('Rise 'n' Shine' × 'Sheri Anne') × Rainbow's End™]; intr. 1992

'Savafish' (Gone Fishin'™) Min, ob, 1992, Saville, F. Harmon; flowers bright orange, 1¼ in., 28-35 petals, cupped, borne singly and in sprays of 4-10; foliage medium size, dark green, glossy, very disease-resistant; bushy, medium growth; ['Fairlane' × 'Zorina']; intr. 1993

'Savafront' ('Front 'n' Center') Min, mr, 2002, Saville, John M.; flowers dbl., borne in small clusters; foliage medium size, medium green, matte; prickles 3/16 in., thin, angled down, few; growth upright, compact, medium (14-18 in.); garden, border, containers; [(('Zorina' × Baby Katie™) × (Little Jackie™ × Rainbow's End™)) × Lavender Jade™]; drought resistant; intr. 2002

'Savagala' ('Gala') Min, dp, 1999, Saville, F. Harmon; flowers 1½ in., dbl., borne mostly singly and in small clusters, loose sprays, no fragrance; foliage medium size, dark green, semi-glossy; prickles moderate; upright, spreading, medium (15-16 in.) growth; [High Jinks™ × seedling]; intr. 2000

'Savagen' (Genevieve™) Min, yb, 1983, Saville, F. Harmon; flowers yellow, streaked scarlet, scarlet increasing with age, small, 35 petals, moderate spicy fragrance; foliage medium size, medium green, semi-glossy; upright, bushy growth; PP5145; [climbing miniature seedling × miniature seedling]; intr. 1983

'Savagood' (Good Morning America™) Min, my, 1991, Saville, F. Harmon; bud ovoid, urn-shaped; flowers sunshine yellow, 1½ in., 55-60 petals, urn-shaped, borne mostly singly, moderate fruity fragrance; foliage medium size, dark green, semi-glossy; long stems; upright, bushy, tall growth; PP7761; ['Fantasia' × Rainbow's End™]; intr. 1991

'Savagrand' (Happy Thoughts™) Min, ob, 2006, White, Wendy R.; intr. 2007

'Savahalo' (Golden Halo™) Min, my, 1991, Saville, F. Harmon; bud ovoid, pointed; flowers bright yellow, medium, 24-26 petals, cupped, borne mostly singly, slight fragrance; foliage medium size, medium green, semi-glossy; upright, bushy growth; PP7770; ['Arthur Bell' × Rainbow's End™]; intr. 1991

'Savahold' (Behold™) Min, my, 1996, Saville, F. Harmon; bud medium; flowers clear, bright medium yellow, reverse lighter, holds color, dbl., borne mostly singly, no fragrance; foliage medium size, medium green, semi-glossy; few prickles; upright, compact, medium (22-26 in.) growth; PP10249; [('Rise 'n' Shine' × 'Sheri Ann') × ('Heideroslein' × 'Nozomi')]; intr. 1997

'Savahowdy' (Minnie Pearl™) Min, pb, 1983, Saville, F. Harmon; flowers light pink, reverse darker, yellow base, 25 petals, high-centered, borne mostly singly; foliage small, medium green, semi-glossy; few prickles; thin, wiry stems; upright growth; PP5097; [('Little Darling' × 'Tiki') × Party Girl™]; intr. 1982

'Savajerry' (Jerry-O™) Min, mr, 1998, Saville, F. Harmon; flowers light ot medium red, 1½ in., 25 petals, high-centered, borne singly, intense fragrance; PP10630

'Savajinks' (High Jinks™) Min, pb, 1992, Saville, F. Harmon; flowers 1½ in., 25-32 petals, high-centered, borne singly and in sprays of 4-30; foliage medium size, dark green, semi-glossy; upright, bushy, medium to tall growth; ['Rise 'n' Shine' × 'Sheri Anne']; intr. 1993

'Savaklim' (Klima™) Cl Min, dy, 1993, Saville, F. Harmon; flowers medium, semi-dbl., no fragrance; foliage small, medium green, semi-glossy; few prickles; tall (4-5 ft.), upright, climbing growth; PP8411; ['Ferris Wheel' × 'Golden Jubilee']; intr. 1993

'Savalav' (Vista™) Min, m, 1994, Saville, F. Harmon; bud short, pointed; flowers soft lavender, 1¾-2 in., 22-25 petals, high-centered, becoming flat, borne mostly singly, some small clusters, very slight fragrance; recurrent; foliage medium size, medium green, semi-glossy; prickles some, thin, straight; medium (16 in.), compact growth; hips globular, orange; PP9031; [Sachet™ × Copper Sunset™]; intr. 1994

'Savalife' (Rainbow's End™) Min, yb, 1984, Saville, F. Harmon; bud long pointed; flowers deep yellow, red petal edges, aging red all over, 1¼-1¾ in., 30-35 petals, high-centered, borne singly and in small clusters, no fragrance; free-flowering; foliage small, dark green, glossy; prickles moderate, thin, pointed, angled slightly downward; upright (18 in.), bushy growth; hips globular, orange-red; PP5482; ['Rise 'n' Shine' × 'Watercolor']

'Savalights' (Lights of Broadway™) Min, rb, 1993, Saville, F. Harmon; flowers yellow with broad red edge, yellow reverse, medium, very dbl., borne mostly singly, no fragrance; foliage medium size, medium green, semi-glossy; some prickles; medium (16-20 in.), upright, bushy growth; PP8918; [('Tamango' × 'Yellow Jewel') × Party Girl™]; intr. 1994

'Savalode' (Mother Lode™) Min, yb, 2006, White, Wendy R.; flowers golden yellow, reverse light orange or orange/yellow blend, 1¾-2 in., dbl. to full, borne in small clusters; foliage small, medium green, matte; prickles few, 3/32 - 3/16 in., straight; attenuate, crimson; growth bushy, mounded, short, (10-14 × 16-22 in.); containers, garden; [Light of Day™ × Sachet™]; intr. 2007

'Savalot' (Cheers™) Min, ob, 1984, Saville, F. Harmon; flowers orange-red, cream reverse, 20 petals; foliage small, medium green, semi-glossy; compact, bushy growth; ['Poker Chip' × 'Zinger']

'Savaluck' (Happy Go Lucky™) Min, ob, 1987, Saville, F. Harmon; flowers brilliant orange-yellow blend, small, 17-24 petals, high-centered, borne usually singly, slight sweet fragrance; foliage small, dark green, semi-glossy; prickles long, thin pointed; bushy, medium growth; no fruit; PP6506; ['Cheers' × ('Sheri Anne' × ('Yellow Jewel' × 'Tamango'))]

'Savalute' (Absolutely™) Min, yb, 1998, Saville, F. Harmon; bud medium, ovate; flowers pale to medium yellow, dusted apricot-pink, lighter reverse, 22 -40 petals, high-centered , borne singly and in small clusters, floriferous, slight fragrance; free flowering; foliage medium size, medium green, semi-glossy; few prickles; upright, compact, spreading, bushy, vigorous growth; PP11132; [seedling × 'Rise 'n' Shine']; intr. 1998

'Savamae' (Ellamae™) Min, ab, 1986, Saville, F. Harmon; flowers 35 petals, high-centered, borne singly and in sprays of 3-5, moderate fragrance; foliage medium size, dark, glossy; prickles long, thin; medium, upright, bushy growth; PP6053; ['Zorina' × ('Sheri Anne' × 'Glenfiddich')]

'Savamark' ('Apricot Sunblaze') Min, or, 1982, Saville, F. Harmon; flowers brilliant orange-red, 43 petals, cupped, borne singly and in clusters of up to 10, moderate spicy fragrance; foliage very glossy; prickles long, thin, soft on peduncles; compact, bushy growth; PP5044; ['Sheri Anne' × 'Glenfiddich']

'Savaminor' ('Minor Details') Min, pb, 2002, White, Wendy R.; flowers white edged deep pink, reverse magenta, 1⅛-1¼ in., dbl., borne in small clusters; foliage small, dark green, semi-glossy; growth upright, compact, short (12-16 in.); containers, border, garden; [Vista™ × 'Cal Poly']; drought resistant; intr. 2002

'Savamist' (Apricot Mist™) Min, ab, 1987, Saville, F. Harmon; flowers apricot with tones of pink and yellow, medium, 40-45 petals, high-centered, borne singly; foliage small, dark green, glossy; prickles long, thin, straight, brown; bushy, low, profuse, compact, symmetrical growth; no fruit; PP6507; ['Fantasia' × Baby Katie™]

'Savamont' ('Montana') Min, dr, 2001,

The Official Registry and Checklist — Rosa 667

Saville, F. Harmon; flowers dark red, medium red reverse, 1½ in., dbl., borne mostly solitary, slight fragrance; foliage medium size, dark green, disease-resistant; prickles 3/16 in., thin, tapered, slightly curved, moderate; growth upright, compact, medium (18-22 in.); garden decorative, containers; [Lavender Jade™ × Red Minimo™]; intr. 2001

'Savamoon' ('Moonlight Scentsation') MinFl, w, 2004, White, Wendy R.; flowers very pale lavender, near white, 2½-2-¾ in., very full, borne mostly solitary, intense fragrance; foliage small, medium green, matte; prickles ¼ in. long, acute triangular; growth upright, medium (3-3½ ft.); garden decoration, cutting; ['Admirable' × Pacific Serenade™]; intr. 2005

'Savamor' (Scentsational™) Min, m, 1995, Saville, F. Harmon; bud ovoid; flowers light mauve with pink tones, 2 in., 24 -30 petals, high-centered, borne mostly singly, but some clusters of up to 7, intense lilac fragrance; recurrent; foliage medium green, semi-glossy; prickles on main canes few, on laterals numerous, angled downward; stems long; vigorous, upright (24-30 in.), branching growth; hips globular ; PP9798; [Lavender Jade™ × 'Silverado']; intr. 1996

'Savanade' (Pacific Serenade™) Min, dy, 1997, Saville, F. Harmon; flowers bright yellow, medium, dbl., cupped, borne mostly singly, moderate fragrance; foliage medium size, medium green, semi-glossy; no prickles; upright, compact, spreading, bushy, vigorous growth; PP11810; ['Cal Poly' × 'New Zealand']

'Savanhour' (Happy Hour™) Min, mr, 1984, Saville, F. Harmon; flowers bright medium red, yellow eye, small, 20 petals, moderate fragrance; foliage small, dark, glossy; bushy, spreading growth; PP5449; [('Tamango' × 'Yellow Jewel') × 'Zinger']; intr. 1983

'Savanice' (Ice Queen™) Min, w, 1991, Saville, F. Harmon; bud ovoid, pointed; flowers medium, 60 petals, high-centered, borne mostly singly or in sprays of 5 - 8, no fragrance; foliage medium size, dark green, semi-glossy; bushy, medium growth; PP7771; [sport of Cupcake™]; intr. 1991

'Savanight' ('Overnight Scentsation') MinFl, mp, 1997, Saville, F. Harmon; flowers large, very dbl., borne mostly singly, intense fragrance; foliage medium size, medium to dark green, semi-glossy; upright, medium (2 ft.) growth; PP11303; ['Taxi' × Lavender Jade™]

'Savanin' Min, rb, 1987, Saville, F. Harmon; flowers medium red with yellow center, small, dbl.; foliage small, medium green, semi-glossy; bushy growth; ['Rise 'n' Shine' × 'Zinger']; intr. 1986

'Savannah' HT, ab, 1980, Weeks, O.L.; bud ovoid, pointed; flowers soft apricot, 4-4½ in., 32 petals, cupped, borne singly or 2-3 per cluster, slight spicy fragrance; recurrent; foliage moderately leathery; prickles long, hooked down; vigorous, upright growth; PP4735; [seedling × 'Arizona']

'Savannah Miss' -- See 'Pixanah'

'Savanne' HT, dy, Noack, Werner; intr. 1985

'Savapace' ('Pacesetter') Min, w, 1979, Schwartz, Ernest W.; bud long, pointed

'Savapaint' (Flying Colors™) Min, rb, 1983, Saville, F. Harmon; flowers red and yellow blend, aging to pink and white, micro-mini, semi-dbl., slight fragrance; foliage medium green, semi-glossy; upright, bushy growth; PP5094; [('Yellow Jewel' × 'Tamango') × 'Sheri Anne']; intr. 1983

'Savapam' ('Pam Tillis') MinFl, ab, 2004, Saville, F. Harmon; flowers pastel pink and yellow blend, reverse lighter yellow and pink blend, 2½-3 in., very full, old-fashioned, borne mostly solitary, slight fragrance; foliage small, medium green, semi-glossy, very disease-resistant; prickles ¼ in., sharply acuminate,; growth upright, as wide as tall (26-32 in.); garden decorative; ['Cal Poly' × 'New Zealand']; intr. 2004

'Savapeach' ('Peach Delight') MinFl, ab, 2001, Saville, F. Harmon; bud pale apricot; flowers deep peach, 2⅜ in., very full, borne mostly solitary, intense fragrance; foliage medium size, dark green, semi-glossy; prickles ¼ in., hooked down, numerous; growth upright, spreading, bushy, medium (20-26 in.); garden decorative; [Sequoia Gold™ × 'Harmony']; intr. 2001

'Savapeg' (Peggy Jane™) Min, lp, 1986, Utz, Peggy L.; flowers light pink, with lighter petal edges and base; PP5999; [sport of Starina®]

'Savapie' (Something Else™) Min, rb, 1991, Saville, F. Harmon; flowers white with very contrasting red edge, medium, dbl., cupped, borne usually singly, slight fragrance; foliage small, medium green, semi-glossy; upright, bushy, medium growth; PP7769; [('Yellow Jewel' × 'Tamango') × 'Party Girl™]; intr. 1985

'Savapiece' (Centerpiece™) Min, mr, 1985, Saville, F. Harmon; flowers deep medium red, small, 35 petals, high-centered; foliage small, dark, semi-glossy; bushy growth; PP5692; [('Sheri Anne' × 'Tamango') × ('Sheri Anne' × ('Yellow Jewel' × 'Tamango'))]; intr. 1985

'Savapizzazz' (Pizzazz™) Min, rb, 2003, White, Wendy R.; flowers medium red, reverse medium yellow, 2-2½ in., dbl., borne mostly solitary, moderate fragrance; recurrent; foliage large, dark green, glossy, disease-resistant; prickles straight, flat, triangular, few; growth upright, compact, medium (16-24 in.); container, decorative; PP15870; [Sachet™ × 'Pierrine']; intr. 2003

'Savapple' ('Applause') Min, ab, 1999, Saville, F. Harmon; flowers medium coral, reverse lighter, 1¼ in., dbl., slight fragrance; foliage small, medium green, semi-glossy; prickles moderate; upright, compact, low growth; PP13055; [Sequoia Gold™ × Sparks™]; intr. 2000

'Savapup' Min, ob, 1978, Schwartz, Ernest W.; bud pointed

'Savarain' (Raindrops™) Min, m, 1990, Saville, F. Harmon; bud ovoid; flowers light mauve-purple, light yellow at base, reverse lighter, 1½ in., 24 petals, high-centered, borne in sprays of 5 - 20, slight fragrance; foliage small, dark green, semi-glossy; prickles straight, slanted downward, small, gray-red; upright, medium growth; fruit not observed; PP7448; [Sachet™ × Rainbow's End™]; intr. 1990

'Savaralph' ('Ralph Moore') Min, mr, 1999, Saville, F. Harmon; bud small, ovate; flowers dark cherry red, lighter reverse, medium, 20 -24 petals, high-centered, borne mostly singly, with some sprays, slight fragrance; free-flowering; foliage medium size, dark green, semi-glossy; prickles few, straight; upright, compact, well-branched, medium (16 in.) growth; hips near globular, deep orange; PP13056; [Sachet™ × seedling]; intr. 2000

'Savaras' (Iced Raspberry™) Min, rb, 2005, White, Wendy R; flowers dark and medium red, reverse white and red, 1¾ in., very full, borne mostly solitary, slight fragrance; foliage medium size, dark green, matte, disease-resistant; prickles moderate, ¼ in., fine point, angled down slightly; growth upright, compact, medium (15-20 in.); cutting, garden decoration; ['Jilly Jewel' × ('Zorina' × Baby Katie™)]; intr. 2006

'Savared' (Red Scentsation™) Min, mr, 2002, White, Wendy R.; bud ovate with an acuminate tip; flowers medium red, reverse streaked with burgundy, 2 in., 24 petals, high-centered, borne mostly solitary, with some small clusters, intense fragrance; recurrent; foliage medium size, dark green, matte; prickles thin, tapered, angled down; stems long; growth upright, bushy, medium (18-24 in.); cut flower, decorative, container; PP16040; ['Taxi' × ((Party Girl™ × Sparks™) × 'New Zealand')]; intr. 2003

'Savaremember' (Remembering Dee™) MinFl, w, 2007, Sparks, Richard & Carol; flowers pure white, 6 cm., 40-50 petals, borne singly and in small clusters; foliage medium size, medium green, semi-glossy; prickles moderate, 6-7 mm., slightly hooked; growth upright, well-branched, medium (40-60 cm.); garden, cutting, containers; [sport of 'Madeline Spezzano']; intr. 2007

'Savarend' (Adam's Smile™) Min, dp, 1988, Saville, F. Harmon; flowers deep pink, medium, 23-27 petals, high-centered, borne usually singly and in sprays of 3-5, no fragrance; foliage medium size, medium green, semi-glossy; prickles long, thin, pointed slightly downward, gray-red; upright, bushy, medium growth; no fruit; PP6570; [('Rise 'n' Shine' × 'Sheri Anne') × Rainbow's End™]

'Savaria' Pol, Mark; intr. 1972

'Savarist' (Aristocrat™) Min, dp, 2002, White, Wendy R.; flowers deep pink/ near red, reverse medium to dark pink, 2 in., full, borne mostly solitary; foliage medium size, dark green, semi-glossy; prickles 5/16 in., tapered and angled down, moderate; growth upright, compact, medium (14-18 in.); cutting, exhibition, garden; [June Laver™ × 'New Zealand']; intr. 2002

'Savarita' (Nostalgia™) Min, mp, 1990, Saville, F. Harmon; bud ovoid; flowers medium pink, reverse lighter, aging lighter, medium, 38 petals, cupped, quartered, borne usually singly and in sprays of 3 - 5, no fragrance; foliage medium size, medium green, semi-glossy; prickles thin, straight, medium, gray-purple to brown; spreading, low growth; fruit not observed; PP7418; ['Rita' × ('Rise 'n' Shine' × 'Sheri Anne')]; intr. 1990

'Savars' ('A. R. S. Centennial', American Rose Centennial™) Min, pb, 1991, Saville, F. Harmon; bud ovoid; flowers creamy white, edged soft pink, 1½ in., 50-55 petals, high-centered, borne singly or in sprays of 3-5, slight fragrance; foliage medium size, dark green, semi-glossy; bushy, medium growth; PP8181; [High Spirits™ × Rainbow's End™]; intr. 1992

'Savasach' (Sachet™) Min, m, 1986, Saville, F. Harmon; bud small, ovate, pointed; flowers lavender, yellow stamens, 1½-2 in., 30 petals, urn-shaped, then flat, borne singly and in small sprays, intense damask fragrance; foliage small, dark, semi-glossy; prickles few, medium, thin, angled slightly downward; medium upright, bushy growth; PP5967; [yellow miniature seedling × Shocking Blue®]

'Savasalute' ('Salute') Min, dr, 2003, White, Wendy R.; flowers 1½-1¾ in., dbl., borne mostly solitary; foliage medium size, dark green, matte, good disease resistance; prickles ¼ in., angled slightly downward; upright (15-22 in.), compact, bushy growth; cut flower, exhibition,; PP15899; [(Vista™ × Party Girl™) × (Party Girl™ × Teddy Bear™)]; intr. 2004

'Savasam' (Samson™) Min, mr, 1986, Saville, F. Harmon; flowers brilliant scarlet red, 28 petals, urn-shaped, borne in sprays of 20-60; foliage large, dark, semi-glossy; prickles long, thin; tall, upright growth; ['Sheri Anne' × ('Yellow Jewel' × 'Tamango')]

'Savascent' (Scentsational™) Min, m, 1995, Saville, F. Harmon; bud ovoid; intr. 1996

'Savaschool' ('School Days') Min, dy, 1993, Saville, F. Harmon; flowers medium, full, borne mostly singly, no fragrance; foliage medium size, medium green, semi-glossy; few prickles; medium (14-18 in.), bushy, compact growth; [Klima™ × Sonnenkind®]; intr. 1994

'Savaseat' (Seattle Scentsation™) Min, pb, 1996, Saville, F. Harmon; bud small, ovate, pointed; flowers yellow, apricot base and mauve-pink, large, 18-20 petals, flat, borne singly and in small clusters, intense classic rose fragrance; recurrent; foliage small, dark green, semi-glossy; prickles very few, short, thin, straight; stems variable; medium (26-30 in.), upright, bushy, vigorous growth; hips pear-shaped ; PP9821; [Lavender Jade™ × 'New Zealand']; intr. 1996

'Savashel' (Shelly Renee™) Min, pb, 1989, Saville, F. Harmon; bud medium, ovate; flowers shrimp pink, reverse peach, aging light pink to white, 1 in., 35 -38 petals, cupped, to flat, borne in clusters, slight fragrance; recurrent; foliage small, dark green, semi-glossy; prickles average, long, thin, slanted slightly downwards, olive green; vigorous, compact (12-14 in.) growth; PP6952; [sport of Spice Drop™]; intr. 1989

'Savasilk' (Cornsilk™) Min, ly, 1983, Saville, F. Harmon; flowers light pastel yellow, small, 40 petals, high-centered, borne mostly singly, moderate fragrance; foliage medium size, medium green, semi-glossy; vigorous, bushy growth; PP5164; ['Rise 'n' Shine' × 'Sheri Anne']

'Savasleep' ('Sleeping Beauty') MinFl, pb, 2005, White, Wendy R.; flowers salmon, reverse light pearl salmon, 1?-2? in., very full, borne in large clusters, intense fragrance; foliage medium size, medium green, semi-glossy, disease-resistant; prickles 5/16, tapered, hooked, slight angle, dark, mahogany brown,; growth compact, bushy, medium (18-22 in.); garden perennial, borders; [seedling × 'New Zealand']; intr. 2005

'Savasorc' (Sorcerer™) Min, mr, 1994, Saville, F. Harmon; bud small, pointed, ovate; flowers bright, medium red, 1¾ in., 22-26 petals, high-centered, borne mostly singly, no fragrance; free-flowering; foliage small, medium green, semi-glossy; prickles some, thin, straight, angled downward; medium (16-20 in.), upright, bushy growth; PP9507; ['Ginger Snap' × Rainbow's End™]; intr. 1995

'Savaspark' (Sparks™) Min, mr, 1995, Saville, F. Harmon; bud oval, pointed; flowers bright scarlet, 1½ in., 18-24 petals, high-centered, borne mostly in clusters, no fragrance; recurrent; foliage small, medium green, semi-glossy; few prickles; compact, upright (14-16 in.) growth; hips globular to bowl-shaped ; PP9799; [('Zorina' × Baby Katie™) × Red Minimo™]; intr. 1996

'Savaspir' (High Spirits™) Min, mr, 1984, Saville, F. Harmon; flowers small, 35 petals, high-centered, borne in sprays, slight fragrance; foliage small, dark, semi-glossy; upright growth; PP5450; ['Sheri Anne' × 'Tamango']

'Savasun' (Sunny Day™) Min, dy, 1987, Saville, F. Harmon; bud long, pointed; flowers bright yellow, fading lighter, slight red blush on edges, 1½ in., 30 petals, high-centered, then flat, borne singly and in small clusters, slight spicy fragrance; recurrent; foliage small, dark green, semi-glossy; prickles long, thin, angled slightly downwards; upright, bushy, low (14-16 in.) growth; no fruit; PP6213; ['Golden Slippers' × 'Rise 'n' Shine']; intr. 1987

'Savasweet' (Spice Drop™) Min, op, 1982, Saville, F. Harmon; bud small, ovoid

'Savathoughts' (Happy Thoughts™) Min, ob, 2006, White, Wendy R.; flowers dark yellow w/orange edges, reverse medium yellow, 2 in., semi-dbl., borne mostly solitary, slight fragrance; foliage medium size, dark green, matte, disease-resistant; prickles angled and curved downward, tan-brown, few; growth compact, short (10-12 in.); decorative garden perennial; [('Zorina' × Baby Katie™) × (June Laver™ × 'New Zealand')]; intr. 2007

'Savathree' (Acey Deucy™) Min, mr, 1983, Saville, F. Harmon; flowers small, 20 petals, high-centered, moderate fragrance; foliage small, medium green, semi-glossy; bushy growth; [('Yellow Jewel' × 'Tamango') × 'Sheri Anne']; intr. 1982

'Savaval' Min, dp, 1981, Saville, F. Harmon; bud globular

'Savavel' ('Velvet Touch') Min, mr, 1993, Saville, F. Harmon; bud medium, pointed; flowers medium red, reverse darker, 1¼ in., 27 -32 petals, high-centered, then flat, borne mostly singly, very slight fragrance; recurrent; foliage medium size, medium green, semi-glossy; prickles some, short, slightly curved, reddish brown; medium, bushy, compact growth; hips globular, orange; PP8919; [Rainbow's End™ × Acey Deucy™]; intr. 1994

'Savawed' (Wedded Bliss™) Min, mp, 1985, Saville, F. Harmon; flowers semi-dbl., borne in clusters, slight fragrance; foliage small, medium green, glossy; groundcover; very spreading growth; [('Yellow Jewel' × 'Tamango') × 'Nozomi']

'Savaweek' (Julie Ann™) Min, or, 1984, Saville, F. Harmon; flowers brilliant vermillion orange, 1-1½ in., 20 petals, high-centered, borne mostly singly; foliage small, medium green, semi-glossy; prickles moderate; upright, bushy growth; PP5415; ['Zorina' × 'Poker Chip']

'Savawhoop' (Whoopi™) Min, rb, 1991, Saville, F. Harmon; flowers white with red edges, suffused more with red as blooms age, medium, 28-32 petals, high-centered, borne mostly singly or in small clusters, slight spicy fragrance; foliage medium size, dark green, semi-glossy; bushy, medium growth; PP8176; [('Yellow Jewel' × 'Tamango') × Party Girl™]; intr. 1992

'Savawin' (Winsome™) Min, m, 1985, Saville, F. Harmon; flowers lilac-lavender with red tinge, 1¾-2 in., 30 -35 petals, high-centered, borne singly and in sprays, no fragrance; recurrent; foliage medium size, dark green, semi-glossy; prickles some, medium, straight, purplish; upright, bushy growth; PP5691; [Party Girl™ × Shocking Blue®]; intr. 1985

'Savawire' (Live Wire™) Min, dp, 1988, Saville, F. Harmon; flowers deep cardinal red-pink, reverse darker, aging lighter, loose, 27-30 petals, cupped, no fragrance; foliage small, medium green, semi-glossy; prickles thin, straight, dark gray-purple; micro-mini; bushy, low, compact growth; no fruit; PP6811; [('Rise 'n' Shine' × 'Sheri Anne') × Rainbow's End™]

'Savawist' ('Wistful') Min, m, 1994, Saville, F. Harmon; bud pointed, ovate; flowers lilac lavender, 1½ in., 20 -24 petals, high-centered, becoming flat, borne singly and in small clusters, slight fragrance; recurrent; foliage small, dark green, semi-glossy; prickles some, short, straight, angled slightly downward; medium (16-22 in.), upright, bushy growth; PP9562; [Sachet™ × Rainbow's End™]; intr. 1995

'Savaworry' Min, yb, White, W. R.; bud pointed, yellow with orange tips; intr. 2005

'Save the Children' -- See 'Hartred'

'Savember' ('Ember') Min, or, 1994, Saville, F. Harmon; flowers small, dbl., borne mostly singly, no fragrance; foliage small, medium green, semi-glossy; few prickles; medium (16-22 in.), upright, bushy, compact growth; [Copper Sunset™ × ('Zorina' × Baby Katie™)]; intr. 1995

'Saverne' HT, rb, 1937, Heizmann, E.; flowers nasturtium tinted brownish red, reverse tinted yellow, large, dbl.; foliage bright, bronze

'Savgine' Min, dr, Saville; intr. 2001

'Savibunda' (Light of Day™) F, my, 2006, Nor'East Miniature Roses; flowers 2-3¼ in., full, borne in singly and in clusters; foliage large, medium green, matte, disease-resistant; prickles deltoid with concave upper and, dark reddish-brown; growth upright, full and rounded, medium (32-38 in.); garden decoration; very hardy; PPAF; ['Cal Poly' × 'Sunsprite']

'Savinn' (Innocence™) Min, w, 1997, Saville, F. Harmon; flowers medium, pure ivory white, 26-41 petals, borne mostly singly; foliage medium size, dark green, glossy; few prickles; upright, spreading, bushy, medium (30 in.) growth; PP10352; ['SAVajinks' × 'SAValite']

Savita+ HT, my, Voom, Lex; flowers creamy yellow , double, high-centered, borne mostly singly; recurrent; stems medium to long; florist rose

'Savkar' HT, mr, Patil, B.K.; intr. 1988

'Savmore' (Red Shadows™) Min, dr, 1984, Saville, F. Harmon; flowers show dark shadings on petal edges, small, dbl., high-centered, no fragrance; foliage small, medium green, semi-glossy; bushy, slightly spreading growth; ['Tamango' × 'Sheri Anne']

'Savoia' HT, m, 1937, Aicardi, D.; bud pointed, rosy lilac; foliage glossy; vigorous growth; ['Julien Potin' × 'Sensation']

'Savor' (Little Jackie™) Min, ob, 1982, Saville, F. Harmon; flowers light orange-red, yellow reverse, small, 20 petals, intense fragrance; foliage medium size, medium green, semi-glossy; vigorous growth; PP5090; [(Prominent® × 'Sheri Anne') × 'Glenfiddich']

'Savorockies' (Gem o' the Rockies™) MinFl, pb, 2008, White, Wendy R.; flowers russet-pink, reverse lighter, 3 in., full, borne mostly solitary; foliage medium-siz, dark green, glossy; prickles 5-7 mm., angled down, dark crimson, few; growth compact, upright, well-branched, medium; garden decoration containers, exhibition, cutting; [(Lavender Jade™ × unknown) × 'Pam Tillis']; rose of the 2008 National Rose Convention in Denver, Colorado; intr. 2008

'Savoy Hotel' -- See 'Harvintage'

'Savplenti' Min, ob, 1982, Saville, F. Harmon; bud small, ovate, long pointed; intr. 1981

'Savrojet' Min, dp, 1987, Saville, F. Harmon; flowers deep pink, moderately small, dbl., no fragrance; foliage small, medium green, semi-glossy; bushy growth; [('Tamango' × 'Yellow Jewel') × 'Watercolor']; intr. 1985

'Savsay' Min, op, 1982, Saville, F. Harmon; bud short, pointed

'Savswat' ('Windjammer') Min, dp, 1982, Saville, F. Harmon; flowers deep pink, reddened by sun, small, 35 petals; foliage medium size, medium green, semi-glossy; PP5091; ['Sheri Anne' × 'Watercolor']

'Savswet' (Spice Drop™) Min, op, 1982, Saville, F. Harmon; bud small, ovoid; flowers light salmon-pink, 1 in., 25-35 petals, hybrid tea, borne singly and in sprays, slight fragrance; recurrent; foliage small, medium green, glossy; prickles few, short, straight, thin, slanting slightly downward; compact (8 in.), bushy, micro-mini growth; PP5089; [('Sheri Anne' × 'Glenfiddich') × ('moss seedling' × (Sarabande® × 'Little Chief'))]

'Savyk' ('Y2K') Min, dy, 1999, Saville, F. Harmon; flowers deep yellow with coating of coral, reverse medium yellow, 1½-2 in., dbl., borne mostly singly, slight fragrance; recurrent; foliage medium size, dark green, glossy; few prickles; bushy, low (12-15 in.) growth; ['Cal Poly' × 'New Zealand']; intr. 2000

'Saxo' -- See 'Harqueterwife'

'Saxy Bob' F, op, Liggett; bud pointed; flowers blend of peach, apricot and pink , double, high-centered, borne in sprays, slight fragrance; recurrent; medium (3 - 5 ft.) growth; [sport of Marina®]; intr. 2000

'Saya' Min, ob

'Sayokyoku' -- See 'Keimipia'

'Sayonara' HT, yb, 1959, Grillo; bud long, pointed; flowers yellow blend tinted pink, 5 in., 50 petals; foliage leathery; vigorous, upright growth; [sport of 'Sunnymount']

'Sazanami' Min, lp, 1986, Suzuki, Seizo; flowers soft pink, small, 60 petals, flat, borne 2 - 5 per cluster, moderate fragrance; foliage dark green, semi-glossy; prickles slanted downward; bushy growth; [('Yorokobi' × unknown) × 'Yellow Doll']; intr. 1984

'Sázava' S, mr, Pajer, J.; flowers medium, semi-dbl.; intr. 1964

'Scabrata' S, m; flowers rich pinkish purple, large, single; foliage downy; [R. corymbifera (?) × R. gallica]

'Scabriusculus' HBc, w, before 1822, Noisette; flowers single; foliage small; prickles needle-like, straight, intermixed with numerous bristles; stems thin

'Scabrosa' (R. rugosa scabrosa, 'Rugosa Superba') HRg, m, 1950; flowers mauve-pink, stamens light sulfur, 5 in., 5 petals, borne in clusters of 5 or more, moderate carnation fragrance; recurrent bloom; foliage light, glossy, soft; very bushy (5 ft.) growth; hips large, bright red

'Scala' -- See 'Clubrose Scala'

'Scala' HT, dp, Gaujard

'Scaldia' HT, Delforge; intr. 1987

Scamp™ -- See 'Savacamp'

'Scandale' HT, pb, 1959, Gaujard; bud pink; flowers crimson shaded coppery, 4 in., 25 petals, moderate fragrance; foliage glossy, dark; long stems; vigorous, upright growth; ['Peace' × 'Opera']

'Scandens' ('Alice Gray', 'Macrophylla Scandens') Ayr, w, before 1804, from Italy; flowers salmony cream white, darker edges, darker reverse, 5 cm., semi-dbl., borne in clusters of up to 15, strong musky fragrance; moderately vigorous growth; possibly R. arvensis × R. gallica

'Scandia' HT, m, Cooper; flowers pale mauve blend, dbl., slight fragrance; [sport of 'Paradise']; intr. 1996

'Scandia' Pol, op, 1951, van de Water; flowers salmon-orange; [sport of 'Margo Koster']

'Scandica' -- See 'Scania'

'Scania' ('Scandica') F, dr, 1965, deRuiter; flowers deep red, well-formed, 3½ in., borne in clusters, slight fragrance;

foliage matte; vigorous (80-100 cm.) growth; ['Cocorico' × seedling]

'Scar P97'   Misc OGR, lp, Scarman; intr. 1997

'Scaramouche'   F, mr, 1969, Fankhauser; bud long, pointed; flowers coral-red, large, 30-35 petals, high-centered; foliage leathery; vigorous, compact, tall growth; ['Ma Perkins' × 'Duet']

Scarborough Fair™ -- See 'Ausoran'

'Scarlano' ('Faust') HSet, mr, 1938, Horvath; flowers cerise-red, open, semi-dbl., borne in clusters; sometimes recurrent bloom; foliage leathery, dark; short, strong stems; bushy (2½ ft.) growth; PP288; [(*R. setigera* × Papoose) × 'Paul's Scarlet Climber']

Scarlet™ -- See 'Scarlet Hit'

Scarlet™ -- See 'Scarlet Parade'

'Scarlet Abundance' -- See 'Harxampton'

'Scarlet Adventurer'   HT, dr, 1958, Lowe; flowers scarlet, medium, dbl.; foliage dark; intr. 1957

'Scarlet Beauty'   HT, dr, 1934, Vestal; flowers crimson-scarlet, very large, dbl.; vigorous growth; ['Mme Butterfly' × 'Premier Supreme']

'Scarlet Bedder'   HT, ob, 1927, Henderson, W.H.; flowers rich orange-scarlet; dwarf growth; ['Mme Edouard Herriot' × 'Gen. MacArthur']

'Scarlet Betty Uprichard'   HT, dr, 1930, Allen; bud long, pointed, shaded black; flowers intense scarlet, semi-dbl., cupped; foliage thick, light; vigorous growth; ['Betty Uprichard' × unknown]

'Scarlet Button'   Pol, dr, 1932, Dreer; flowers brilliant scarlet; [sport of 'Locarno']

'Scarlet Crampel'   Pol, dr; flowers scarlet; [sport of 'Paul Crampel']

'Scarlet Else'   F, dr, Kordes; flowers scarlet, 3-4 in., 10-12 petals, borne in trusses; foliage leathery; very free growth; ['Else Poulsen' × red hybrid tea seedling]

'Scarlet Emperor'   HT, mr, 1961, LeGrice; flowers scarlet-red, large, dbl., high-centered; vigorous, upright growth; ['Karl Herbst' × 'Fandango']

'Scarlet Fire' -- See 'Scharlachglut'

'Scarlet Flame'   HT, mr, 1934, Burbank; flowers brilliant red, petals recurved and fringed, large, dbl.; very vigorous growth

'Scarlet Flower Carpet' -- See 'Sorrento'

'Scarlet Garnette'   F, mr, 1971, Newberry; flowers scarlet, small, 45 petals, globular; foliage dark; vigorous growth; [sport of 'Garnette']

Scarlet Gem® ('Scarlet Pimpernel') Min, or, 1961, Meilland, Alain A.; bud ovoid; flowers orange-scarlet, 1 in., 58 petals, cupped, borne singly and in irregular clusters, slight fragrance; recurrent; foliage dark, glossy, leathery; prickles several, brown; stems short; bushy, dwarf (12-15 in.) growth; PP2155; [(Moulin Rouge® × 'Fashion') × ('Perla de Montserrat' × 'Perla de Alcanada')]; intr. 1961

'Scarlet Glory'   HT, ob, 1925, Dickson, A.; bud long, pointed; flowers orange-scarlet, dbl., high-centered; foliage leathery, rich green

'Scarlet Glow'   HT, dr, 1945, Sodano, A.; flowers brilliant velvety scarlet; PP688; [sport of 'Briarcliff']

'Scarlet Glow' -- See 'Scharlachglut'

'Scarlet Grevillea' -- See 'Russelliana'

'Scarlet Hit' (Ruby Wishes™, Scarlet™) MinFl, dr, Olesen, L & M; bud pointed ovoid to globular; flowers open quickly, 2 in., 18-22 petals, flat, borne in sprays of 8-10, very slight fragrance; free-flowering; foliage dark green, semi-glossy; prickles numerous, slight downward curve; growth vigorous, compact (50 cm.), upright to bushy; PP12490; [H. C. Andersen™ × Red Minimo™]; intr. 1996

'Scarlet Kardinal'   HT, or, Tapanchev; [sport of 'Kardinal']; intr. 2001

'Scarlet Knight, Climbing' -- See 'Samouraï, Climbing'

'Scarlet Knight' -- See 'Samouraï'

'Scarlet Lady'   Min, mr, 1991, Jolly, Nelson F.; bud ovoid; flowers medium red, aging light pink, large, 30 petals, cupped, borne singly, no fragrance; foliage medium size, dark green, semi-glossy; upright, medium growth; [Anita Charles™ × 'Chris Jolly']; intr. 1991

'Scarlet Leader'   Pol, ob, 1927, Wezelenburg; flowers brilliant orange-scarlet, large, dbl., borne in clusters

'Scarlet Maria Leonida'   HBc, mr, before 1846, Rivers; flowers crimson red, large, full, cupped

'Scarlet Mariner'   F, mr, 1972, Patterson; flowers bright scarlet-red, medium, dbl., high-centered; foliage leathery; vigorous, bushy growth; [seedling × 'Showboat']

'Scarlet Marvel'   F, mr, 1960, deRuiter; flowers orange-scarlet, 2½ in., 45-50 petals, flat, borne in clusters; foliage leathery; vigorous, compact growth; PP1771; ['Alain' × floribunda seedling]; intr. 1959

Scarlet Meidiland™ -- See 'Meikrotal'

'Scarlet Meillandécor' -- See 'Meikrotal'

'Scarlet Meillandina' -- See 'Meicubasi'

'Scarlet Midinette'   Min, mr, Horner; flowers scarlet-red, small, dbl., high-centered; free-flowering; vigorous (5-7 ft.) growth; intr. 2003

Scarlet Mimi™   F, dr, Suzuki, Seizo; bud medium, conical; flowers bright red, 2½ in., 21 petals, cupped, borne singly and in clusters of up to 9, no fragrance; good repeat; foliage dark green, semi-glossy; prickles very few, small, greenish; vigorous, upright (3-4 ft.) growth; PP8484; [seedling × Sassy™]; greenhouse rose; intr. 1992

'Scarlet Moss' -- See 'De La Flèche'

Scarlet Moss™ -- See 'Morcarlet'

'Scarlet Ovation'   Min, mr, deRuiter; intr. 2000

'Scarlet Panarosa'   HRg, mr, Moore; flowers scarlet, large, semi-dbl., loose, borne in clusters; recurrent; foliage dark green, rugose; robust growth; intr. 2004

'Scarlet Parade' (Scarlet™) Min, dr, Poulsen; flowers dark red, medium, dbl., slight wild rose fragrance; foliage dark; growth bushy, 20-40 cm.; PP11543; intr. 2000

'Scarlet Patio' -- See 'Kortingle'

'Scarlet Pavement' ('Hanuhi', 'Rote Apart', 'Rote Fox') S, mr, Uhl, J.; bud pink; flowers light fuchsia red, semi-dbl., borne in clusters, moderate fragrance; recurrent; spreading (2½ × 3 ft.) growth; hips numerous, dark red; intr. 1991

'Scarlet Pearl' -- See 'Manscarlet'

'Scarlet Pimpernel' -- See 'Meido'

'Scarlet Provence'   C, mr, before 1867; flowers faint carmine

'Scarlet Queen'   F, dr, 1939, Kordes; bud long, pointed; flowers pure scarlet, open, large, dbl., borne in clusters; foliage glossy, leathery, bronze; long stems; vigorous, bushy growth; ['Dance of Joy' × 'Crimson Glory']

Scarlet Queen Elizabeth® ('Queen Elizabeth Rouge', 'Queen of Diamonds') F, or, 1965, Dickson, Patrick; flowers flame-scarlet, medium, dbl., globular, borne in clusters, slight fragrance; foliage dark; vigorous, tall growth; [('Korona' × seedling) × Queen Elizabeth®]; intr. 1962

'Scarlet Ribbon'   Cl Min, dr, 1961, Moore, Ralph S.; bud ovoid; flowers red, sometimes almost maroon, 1¼ in., 50 petals, high-centered; vigorous (3 ft.) growth; [(('Soeur Thérèse' × 'Wilhelm') × (seedling × 'Red Ripples')) × 'Zee']; intr. 1961

'Scarlet Ripple'   S, rb, Williams, J.B.; flowers ruffled petals of pink, dark red and white stripes, yellow stamens, cupped, borne in clusters; recurrent; foliage medium green; bushy growth; intr. 2004

'Scarlet Rosamini' -- See 'Ruirupo'

'Scarlet Royal'   HT, mr, 1963, Park; flowers scarlet, base yellow, well-formed; vigorous growth; ['Karl Herbst' × 'Independence']

'Scarlet Ruffles'   Min, or, 1990, Gruenbauer, Richard; bud pointed; flowers orange-red with yellow eye, aging to light red, loose, large, 8 petals, intense spicy fragrance; foliage medium size, dark green, glossy; prickles straight, slightly hooked downwards, tan; spreading, medium growth; hips oblong, gold and orange; ['Poker Chip' × 'Zinger']; intr. 1984

'Scarlet Sensation' ('Brownell's Everblooming Pillar No. 73', 'Everblooming Pillar No. 73') LCl, dr, 1954, Brownell; bud high pointed, crimson; flowers rose-madder, 3½-4½ in., 35 petals, borne in clusters, moderate fragrance; free bloom; growth like a hybrid tea, followed by 4-5 foot canes; PP1261; [seedling × 'Queen o' the Lakes']

'Scarlet Showers'   LCl, mr; flowers bright

red; recurrent; [Golden Showers® × 'Chrysler Imperial']

Scarlet Spreader™ -- See 'Wilscarlet'

'Scarlet Star' -- See 'Wilstar'

Scarlet Sunblaze™ -- See 'Meicubasi'

'Scarlet Sunset' F, or, 1970, deRuiter; flowers small, 12 petals, borne on trusses; foliage dark, leathery; moderate bushy growth; [Orange Sensation® × seedling]

'Scarlet Sweet Brier' -- See 'La Belle Distinguée'

'Scarlet Swimmer' Min, rb; flowers red with yellow center; [sport of 'Tracey Wickham']; intr. 2001

'Scarlet Triumph' F, rb, 1951, Poulter; bud ovoid; flowers deep scarlet, base yellow, small, semi-dbl., cupped, borne in clusters; foliage glossy, light green; vigorous, bushy growth; [sport of Orange Triumph®]

Scarlet Velvet™ S, mr, Clements, John; flowers velvety scarlet, 4 in., very full, cupped, quartered, borne singly and in clusters, slight to moderate fruity tea fragrance; recurrent; compact (3 ft.) growth; intr. 2006

'Scarlet Waves' F, mr, 1961, Bennett, H.; flowers bright scarlet, ruffled petals; tall growth; [('Florence Mary Morse' × 'Border Queen') × 'Mrs Inge Poulsen']

'Scarlet Wonder' F, or, 1959, deRuiter; flowers bright orange-scarlet, 3 in., semi-dbl., flat, borne in clusters; foliage dark, glossy; vigorous growth; ['Signal Red' × 'Fashion']; intr. 1958

'Scarletina' Min, or, 1985, Hardgrove, Donald L.; flowers spiraled, dbl., borne mostly singly; foliage small, medium green, semi-glossy; upright, bushy growth; ['Futura' × 'Poker Chip']

'Scarlett O'Hara' Pol, rb, 1947, Klyn; bud ovoid; flowers brilliant red, overcast orange, open, large, dbl., borne in clusters; foliage leathery; vigorous, bushy growth; RULED EXTINCT 2/88; [sport of 'Gloria Mundi']

Scarlett O'Hara™ -- See 'Aroresas'

'Scarletta, Climbing' Cl Min, mr; [sport of Scarletta®]; intr. after 1972

Scarletta® Min, mr, deRuiter; flowers scarlet red, small, dbl.; recurrent; growth to 2 ft.; intr. 1972

'Scarman's Crimson China' Ch, mr, Scarman; flowers medium red, fading quickly, dbl., borne in clusters; growth to 80 cm.; intr. 1995

Scent From Above™ -- See 'Chewgoldtop'

'Scent-Sation' -- See 'Fryromeo'

'Scent to Remember' -- See 'Somspice'

'Scentasia' -- See 'Sunscent'

'Scented Abundance' -- See 'Harzola'

'Scented Air' F, op, 1965, Dickson, Patrick; flowers salmon-pink, well-formed, 5 in., dbl., borne in clusters; foliage very large; vigorous growth; [('Spartan' × unknown) × Queen Elizabeth®]

'Scented Bouquet' ; ['My Choice' × 'Great Venture']

'Scented Bowl' HT, dr, 1970, Pal, Dr. B.P.; bud ovoid; flowers bright red, medium, dbl., intense fragrance; foliage glossy; open, upright growth; ['Gen. MacArthur' × unknown]; intr. 1965

'Scented Carpet' ('Fragrant Spreader', 'Oso Easy') S, m, Warner, Chris; bud lanceolate; flowers red-purple, 2 in., single, borne is small terminal clusters, moderate sweet fragrance; foliage dark green, glossy; prickles dense, triangular, sharp; vigorous, low (16 in.), spreading (5 ft.), freely branching growth; hips ovoid, fleshy, smooth ; PP15981; ['Grouse' × Yesterday®]; intr. 2002

'Scented Dawn' -- See 'Meitosier'

Scented Memory™ ('Bitten Clausen') HT, ab, Poulsen; flowers apricot blend with pink flush, 10-15 cm., full, cupped, borne one to a stem, moderate fragrance; foliage large, dark green, glossy; narrow, upright (3-5 ft.), bushy growth; intr. 2003

'Scented Star' HT, lp, 1974, Lowe; flowers coral-pink, 5-5½ in., 30-35 petals, high-centered, intense fragrance; foliage dark; moderate growth; ['Fragrant Cloud' × 'Spek's Yellow']; intr. 1973

'Scented Whisper' -- See 'Martin des Senteurs'

'Scentillating Blues' -- See 'Socblue'

Scentimental™ -- See 'Wekplapep'

Scentsational™ -- See 'Savascent'

'Scepter'd Isle' -- See 'Ausland'

'Sceptre' HT, ob, 1923, McGredy; flowers bright flame, base shaded orange, reverse dull yellow; low growth

Schackenborg -- See 'Pouldron'

'Schaffners Erfolg' F, mr, 1958, Tantau; flowers bright scarlet, 2 in., 30 petals, borne in well-spaced clusters; foliage medium green; vigorous, bushy growth; ['Red Favorite' × 'Fanal']; intr. 1955

'SCHanbiran' ('Magic Sunblaze') Min, rb, Schwartz; intr. 1984

'Scharlachglut' ('Scarlet Fire', 'Scarlet Glow') HGal, dr, 1952, Kordes; flowers scarlet-crimson, golden stamens, 5 in., single, borne in clusters; foliage dull green; vigorous (8-10 ft.), dense, arching, spreading growth; hips large, urn-shaped, sealing-wax red; ['Alika' × 'Poinsettia']; originally registered as S

'Scharnkeana' (R. × scharnkeana) S, m, before 1900; flowers rose-purple, borne in small clusters; growth to 3 ft.; a natural hybrid of R. californica × R. nitida

'Schéhérazade' HT, mr, 1942, Mallerin, C.; bud large, oval; flowers fiery red, dbl., cupped, slight fragrance; foliage dark, glossy; vigorous, bushy growth

Scherzo® -- See 'Meipuma'

'Schiehallion' HT, mr, 1982, MacLeod, Major C.A.; flowers 4½ in., 50 petals, foliage medium size, medium green, glossy; upright growth; ['Red Planet' × 'Bonnie Anne']

'Schiller' HMult, mp, 1913, Lambert, P.; flowers clear pink, medium, borne in clusters; [Trier® × 'Lady Mary Fitzwilliam']

'Schirus' HT, w, Schreurs; Petrus Nicolaas Johannes; PP15725

'Schleswig' -- See 'Maid of Honour'

Schleswig 87® ('Lagonda') F, dp, Kordes; intr. 1987

'Schleswig-Holstein' HT, rb, 1921, Engelbrecht; flowers reddish-yellow, large, semi-dbl., cupped, borne singly or in small clusters; foliage glossy; [sport of 'Mme Edouard Herriot']

Schloss Balthasar® F, op, Kordes; intr. 1997

'Schloss Dryburg' Cl HT, dy, GPG Bad Langensalza; flowers luminous golden yellow, 4 in., dbl., borne in small clusters; foliage small; prickles numerous, large; ['Lydia' × 'Le Rêve']; intr. 1969

Schloss Eutin® S, ab, Kordes; bud rounded, cream-apricot; flowers soft apricot with darker center, 8 cm., full, imbricated, camellia-like, borne mostly in large clusters, slight sweet fragrance; recurrent; foliage medium size, dark green, glossy; vigorous, upright (4 ft.), arching growth; [sport of Bremer Stadtmusikanten®]; intr. 2006

'Schloss Friedenstein' HMult, m, 1915, Schmidt, J. C.; flowers reddish-violet, 3-4 cm., dbl., moderate fragrance; ['Veilchenblau' × 'Mme Norbert Levavasseur']

'Schloss Glücksburg' -- See 'Ausbuff'

'Schloss Heidegg' -- See 'Meipoque'

Schloss Herrenchiemsee™ -- See 'Poulmax'

Schloss Linderhof™ -- See 'Poultry'

'Schloss Luegg' ('Château Luegg) HMult, mp, 1886, Geschwind; flowers shining carmine pink, full; ['de la Grifferaie' × unknown]

'Schloss Lützow' S, ly, Jensen; flowers light lemon yellow, 7-9 cm., full, shallow cup, borne singly and several together, moderate fragrance; recurrent; foliage medium, dark green; strong, upright (4 - 5 ft.), bushy growth; [sport of 'Evelyn']; intr. 1999

Schloss Mannheim® F, or, 1975, Kordes; flowers red-orange, medium, dbl., globular, borne in clusters, slight fragrance; free-flowering; foliage dark green, medium size, leathery; vigorous, upright, bushy growth; ['Marlena' × Europeana®]

'Schloss Moritzburg' F, dr, 1967, Haenchen, E.; flowers medium, semi-dbl., cupped; foliage dark, leathery; vigorous growth; ['Donald Prior' × unknown]

Schloss Neuschwanstein™ -- See 'Poulreb'

'Schloss Seusslitz' HSpn, ly, 1933, Dechant; flowers creamy yellow, fading to white, 2½-3 in., semi-dbl., flat, borne in small clusters; once-blooming, very early; moderate growth; ['Frau Karl Druschki' × 'Harison's Yellow']

'Schlössers Brilliant, Climbing' -- See 'Detroiter, Climbing'

'Schlosser's Brilliant' -- See 'Detroiter'
'Schlossgarten' S, mp, GPG Bad Langensalza; flowers large, dbl., high-centered, borne singly and in clusters; upright growth; intr. 1989
'Schmetterling' HFt, yb, 1905, Müller, Dr. F.; flowers yellow and red, medium, semi-dbl.
'Schmid's Ideal' Sp, lp; prickles thorny; growth used as an understock; strain of R. canina
'Schmid's Rekord' S, lp, 1930, Schmid, R.; flowers soft pink, golden stamens, 5 petals, moderate fragrance; spring-flowering; moderate (3-5 ft.) growth; hybrid canina
'Schnee-Eule' -- See 'White Pavement'
'Schneeball' HWich, w, 1905, Weigand, C.; flowers semi-dbl., borne in clusters, moderate fragrance
'Schneeberg' -- See 'Pristine Pavement'
Schneeflocke® -- See 'White Flower Carpet'
'Schneekönigen' -- See 'Frau Karl Druschki'
'Schneekönigin' -- See 'Tanigino'
'Schneekopf' Pol, w, 1903, Lambert, P.; flowers snow-white or light pink, regular form; recurrent bloom; vigorous growth; ['Mignonette' × 'Souv. de Mme Sablayrolles']; sometimes classified as HP
'Schneekoppe' ('Snow Pavement') HRg, w, Baum; bud light lavender-pink; flowers white with lavender tint, semi-dbl., cupped, borne in clusters, moderate fragrance; foliage light green; groundcover; spreading (2½ ft.) growth; hips red; very hardy; intr. 1986
Schneeküsschen® -- See 'Snow Kiss'
Schneeküsschen® -- See 'Kornemuta'
'Schneelicht' HRg, w, 1894, Geschwind, R.; flowers pure white, large, single, borne in clusters; very vigorous, climbing growth; makes an impenetrable, prickly hedge; very hardy; [R. rugosa × R. phoenicia]
'Schneeprinzessin' HT, w, 1946, Meilland, F.; bud long; flowers large; vigorous growth
'Schneeschirm' F, w, 1946, Tantau; flowers white, center tinted rose-yellow, large, single, shallow cup, borne in clusters; foliage dark; low, bushy, spreading growth; ['Johanna Tantau' × ('Karen Poulsen' × 'Stammler')]
Schneesturm® ('Blenheim') S, w, Tantau
'Schneeteppich' -- See 'Maccarpe'
'Schneewalzer 87' ('Snow Waltz', 'Valse des Neiges') LCl, w, Tantau; flowers very pale lemon-white, 5-6 in., dbl., high-centered, borne singly or in small clusters; foliage large, dark green, glossy; tall, bushy growth; intr. 1987
'Schneewalzer' -- See 'Tanschneewa'
Schneeweissschen® -- See 'Tanensch'
'Schneewittchen' Pol, ly, 1901, Lambert, P.; flowers yellow fading to white, dbl., rosette, borne in clusters; foliage glossy; low (16 in.) growth; ['Aglaia' × ('Paquerette' × 'Souv. de Mme Levet')]
'Schneewittchen' HMsk, w, Kordes, W.; bud large, long-pointed; flowers pure white, large, long-lasting, semi-dbl., open, borne in clusters, strong fragrance; foliage large, light green, glossy, resistant; few prickles; stems long, strong; growth vigorous, upright, bushy; ['Robin Hood' × 'Virgo']; intr. 1958
'Schneewittchen' -- See 'Iceberg'
'Schneewolke' S, w, Noack, Werner; intr. 1996
'Schneezwerg' ('Snow Dwarf', 'Snowdwarf') HRg, w, 1912, Lambert, P.; flowers snow-white, stamens golden yellow, small, semi-dbl., flat, borne in clusters of 3 - 10; recurrent bloom; foliage dark, glossy, rugose; prickles spiny; vigorous (3-4 ft.) growth; hips abundant, small, red; [possibly R. rugosa × polyantha hybrid]
'Schobitet' ('Royal Meillandina', Royal Sunblaze®) Min, my, 1987, Schwartz, Ernest W.; bud ovoid; flowers lemon yellow, quilled petals, 4-5 cm., very dbl., rosette, borne in small clusters, slight fragrance; free-flowering; foliage medium size, medium green, semi-glossy; prickles red; compact, bushy (15 in.) growth; PP5690; [seedling × seedling]; intr. 1984
'Schoener's Musk' HMsk, w, Schoener; flowers milk-white, medium enormous trusses; vigorous, pillar growth
'Schoener's Nutkana' S, mp, 1930, Schoener; flowers clear rose-pink, 4 in., single, blooms on arching canes, moderate fragrance; non-recurrent; foliage grey-green; few prickles; stems red-brown; vigorous, shrub (4-6 ft.) growth; [R. nutkana × 'Paul Neyron']
'Scholle's Golden Moss' M, dy, Scholle, E.; flowers amber-yellow, medium, dbl.; intr. 1985
'Schön Ingeborg' HP, lp, 1921, Kiese; flowers light pink with darker center, large, dbl., shallow cup; recurrent; upright (5 ft.) growth; ['Frau Karl Druschki' × 'Natalie Böttner']
'Schöne aus Kaiserslautern' ('Schöne von Kaiserslautern') F, op, 1958, Kordes; bud long, pointed; flowers orange tinted salmon-red, 4 in., 30 petals, high-centered, intense fragrance; free, intermittent bloom; foliage dark, leathery; strong stems; very vigorous, upright, bushy growth; [R.M.S. Queen Mary × 'Obergärtner Wiebicke']; intr. 1957
Schöne Berlinerin® HT, mp, Tantau; flowers warm, bright rose pink, 8-10 cm., dbl., high-centered, slight fragrance; recurrent; strong (80-100 cm.) growth; intr. 1986
Schöne Dortmunderin® F, mp, Noack, Werner; flowers intense pure pink, 2 in., dbl., cupped, borne in clusters; recurrent; upright (60-70 cm.) growth; intr. 1991
Schöne Münchnerin® -- See 'Korleen'
'Schöne von Holstein' Pol, mp, 1919, Tantau; flowers pure hermosa pink, yellow stamens, dbl., cupped, borne in large clusters, no fragrance; recurrent; foliage apple green; ['Orléans Rose' × unknown]
'Schöne von Kaiserslautern' -- See 'Schöne aus Kaiserslautern'
'Schöne von Marquardt' HWich, rb, 1928, Clauberg; flowers bright dark red, variegated with white; vigorous, climbing growth; [sport of 'Sodenia']
'Schonerts Meisterklasse' HT, or, 1952, Leenders, M.; flowers salmon and coral-red, well-formed, very large, dbl.; vigorous growth
'School Days' -- See 'Savaschool'
'School Girl' ('Schoolgirl') LCl, ab, 1964, McGredy, Sam IV; flowers orange-apricot, 4 in., dbl., loose, flat, borne mostly solitary, moderate fragrance; recurrent bloom; foliage dark green, glossy, sparse; prickles numerous, large; fairly vigorous (10 ft.) growth; [Coral Dawn® × 'Belle Blonde']
'Schoolgirl' -- See 'School Girl'
Schoone Gezelle Blomme® -- See 'Lenfiltap'
'Schrenat' HT, dp, Schreurs, Petrus Nicolaas Johannes; PP16075
Schubert® -- See 'Lenmor'
'Schulenfest' -- See 'Ponfest'
'Schuprak' ('Susan Elizabeth') HT, pb, 1990, Schlueter, Barry; bud ovoid; flowers cream tipped with very deep purple-pink, reverse cream to pale yellow at base, edging broadening with age, full, high-centered, slight fruity fragrance; foliage medium size, medium green, semi-glossy; prickles slightly recurved, sparse, red; upright, medium growth; fruit not observed; [Pristine® × 'Akebono']; intr. 1989
Schuss® -- See 'Meiliaxi'
'Schwabenland' HRg, mp, 1928, Berger, V.; flowers amaranth-pink, open, large, dbl.; profuse, repeated bloom; foliage large, rich green, leathery; vigorous (3 ft.) growth; [(R. rugosa × unknown) × 'Elizabeth Cullen']
'Schwabenmädel' F, dr; flowers velvety dark red, dbl., cupped, borne in clusters; bushy, well-branched growth
'Schwäbische Heimat' HT, dr, 1934, Pfitzer; flowers deep amaranth-red, dbl.; [sport of 'Jonkheer J.L. Mock']
Schwanensee® -- See 'Swan Lake'
'Schwarzaldmädel' F, Hetzel, K.; intr. 1977
Schwarze Madonna® -- See 'Korschwama'
Schwarze Rose® -- See 'Norita'
'Schwarzer Samt' ('Black Velvet') HKor, dr, Hänchen; buds medium, long pointed; flowers dark velvety blackish red, 7-9 cm., semi-dbl., open, borne several together and in clusters, slight fragrance; continuous; foliage medium size, dark green, glossy, leathery; ['Alain' × 'Oskar Scheerer']; intr. 1969
Schwarzwaldfeuer™ -- See 'Poulharmu'

Schwarzwaldmädel® F, ob, Hetzel; flowers orange with red tones, moderate fragrance; recurrent; intr. 1977

'Schweizer Garten' F, ly, Huber; flowers white with yellow centers, 9 cm., 25-30 petals, cupped, borne in clusters of 10 - 12, slight fragrance; recurrent; foliage copper-colored when new, then dark green, glossy; bushy (80-120 cm.) growth; intr. 2001

'Schweizer Gold' ('Swiss Gold') HT, ly, 1975, Kordes; bud ovoid; flowers dbl., high-centered; foliage large, light; vigorous growth; [Peer Gynt® × King's Ransom®]

'Schweizer Gold' HT, dy, Urban, J.

'Schweizer Gruss' -- See 'Red Favorite'

'Schweizer Gruss, Climbing'

Schweizer Woche® HT, w, Huber; bud roundish; flowers creamy white, some with yellow or apricot tints, dbl., borne mostly singly, intense tea rose fragrance; foliage dark green, leathery; stems strong; upright, medium growth; intr. 1989

'Schwerin' HMsk, dp, 1937, Kordes; bud long, pointed; flowers light crimson, open, cupped, borne in large clusters, moderate musk fragrance; profuse, intermittent bloom; foliage large, leathery, glossy, bronze; long, strong stems; very vigorous, bushy growth; ['Eva' × 'D.T. Poulsen']

'Scintillation' S, lp, 1967, Austin, David; flowers blush pink, small, semi-dbl., shallow cup to flat, borne in large clusters, intense fragrance; non-remontant; foliage dark, matte; vigorous, wide growth; [*R. macrantha* × 'Vanity']; intr. 1968

'Scipion' HP, pb, 1852, Avoux & Crozy; flowers shining carmine pink with white, large, full

'Scipion Cochet' B, dp, 1850, Cochet, P.; flowers bright pink to grenadine, medium, dbl.; sometimes classed as T

'Scipion Cochet' HP, dr, Verdier, E.; flowers glowing velvety chestnut purple, shaded fiery carmine-scarlet, large, full; intr. 1887

'Scoop' F, or, Richardier; flowers vivid orange, dbl.; growth to 80-90 cm.; intr. 1998

'Scoop Jackson' ('Canterbury', 'Fidelity', 'Maccanter') Gr, dr, 1980, McGredy, Sam IV; flowers large, 20 petals; foliage glossy; upright growth; PP5142; ['Kalahari' × John Waterer®]; intr. 1981

'Scorcher' HWich, dr, 1922, Clark, A.; flowers brilliant scarlet-crimson, 8-9 cm., semi-dbl., flat, borne singly or in small clusters; some repeat; foliage small, dark green, glossy, vigorous, climbing or pillar (to 10 ft.) growth; ['Mme Abel Chatenay' × seedling]

'Scorpio' ('The Scorpion') HT, mr; flowers bright crimson, dbl., high-centered; recurrent; foliage glossy; stems stiff, upright; moderate growth; intr. 2004

'Scotch Blend' HT, pb, 1976, J&B Roses; bud long, pointed; flowers 5-6 in., 35 petals, high-centered; foliage dark, leathery; upright growth; [Queen Elizabeth® × 'Peace']; intr. 1975

'Scotch Double White' -- See 'Double White Burnet'

'Scotch Heather' HSpn, yb, Sutherland; flowers single; intr. 1996

'Scotch Perpetual' -- See 'Perpetual Scotch'

'Scotch Yellow' HT, my, Mercer; intr. 1991

'Scotland Wink' F, dp, Adam; intr. 2001

'Scotland Yard' HT, ab

'Scotland's Trust' -- See 'Coclands'

'Scott' -- See 'Moescott'

'Scott Chait' -- See 'Zipcha'

'Scott Williams' F, yb, Hannemann, F.; ['Oz Gold' × Gold Bunny®]; intr. 1992

'Scottish Celebration' F, pb; intr. 2004

Scottish Highlands™ S, ob, Cocker; flowers bronzy-copper, 7 in., very full, moderate fragrance; recurrent; strong (4-5 ft.) growth; intr. 1991

'Scottish Soldier' S, yb, Williams, J. Benjamin; flowers yellow with red tints on some petal edges, semi-dbl., cupped to flat; intr. 1996

'Scottish Special' -- See 'Cocdapple'

'Scottish Tartans' F, yb; flowers begin yellow, red starts on petal edges as it opens, spreading down the petals, semi-dbl. to dbl., borne in clusters; recurrent

'Scott's Columbia' HT, dp, 1928, Scott, R.; flowers clear bright pink; [sport of 'Columbia']

'Scout' -- See 'Boy Scout'

'Scouts Honor' ('Venerie') F, w; intr. 2006

'Scrabo' F, op, 1970, Dickson, A.; flowers light salmon-pink, large, dbl., high-centered, moderate fragrance; free growth; ['Celebration' × Elizabeth of Glamis®]

'Scrivjam' ('Rainy') F, mr, 2006, Scrivens, Len; flowers crimson, 4 in., very full, borne in large clusters; foliage medium size, dark green, matte; prickles straight, few; growth bushy, tall (4 ft.); garden decoration; [(seedling × 'Cuthbert Grant') × 'Big Purple']; intr. 2007

'Scrivleo' ('Albert Weedall') HT, ly, 1997, Scrivens, Len; flowers large, dbl., borne in large clusters; foliage medium size, medium green, semi-glossy; some prickles; upright, tall (5ft.) growth; [seedling × seedling]

'Scrivluv' Min, dy, 1992, Scrivens, Len; bud small, pointed; intr. 1992

'Scrivo' ('Pretty Lady') F, lp, 1997, Scrivens, Len; flowers semi-dbl., 8-14 petals; foliage medium size, dark green, semi-glossy; numerous prickles; medium (4ft.) growth; [(seedling × (*R. davidii elongata* × seedling)) × ((Troika™ × Alpine Sunset®) × 'Freedom')]

'Scudbuster' -- See 'Clescrub'

'Scugog Sunrise' Min, pb, Jalbert, Brad; flowers blend of pink, orange and yellow, hybrid tea; 14 - 16 in. growth; intr. 2006

'Sea Foam' HBc, w, 1919, Paul, W.; flowers white, shaded slightly with cream, small, dbl.; foliage dark green, glossy; ['Mermaid' × a polyantha]

Sea Foam® S, w, Schwartz, Ernest W.; bud short, pointed, globular with conspicuous neck; flowers white to cream, 2-2½ in., 60-70 petals, high-centered to cupped, borne in clusters, slight spicy fragrance; recurrent; foliage small, glossy, leathery; prickles numerous, pointed downward, brown; vigorous, climbing trailer, semi-prostrate growth; hips globular, smooth, green; PP2463; [((White Dawn® × 'Pinocchio') × (White Dawn® × 'Pinocchio')) × ('WhiteDawn' × 'Pinocchio')]; intr. 1964

'Sea Foam Rosa' S, Zandri, R.; intr. 1971

'Sea Jack' HT, lp; flowers baby pink; vigorous growth; [sport of 'Confidence']

'Sea Mist' HT, w, 1962, Armbrust, F. J.; bud long, pointed; flowers cream, center golden, large, semi-dbl., high-centered, slight fragrance; foliage leathery; vigorous growth; ['Helen Traubel' × 'Golden Harvest']; intr. 1960

'Sea Nymph' Min, pb, 1986, McDaniel, Earl; flowers petals blush pink, edged coral, large, 48 petals, high-centered, borne singly; foliage medium size, medium green, semi-glossy; prickles medium, curved; upright, bushy growth; [seedling × seedling]

'Sea of Fire' -- See 'Feuermeer'

'Sea of Tranquility' HT, ab, 1991, Keene's Rose Nursery; bud classical, delicate light pink; flowers opening to apricot-pink blush, lighter reverse, holds color, 4¾ in., 40-45 petals, high-centered, borne singly, slight sweet fragrance; foliage light green, small, disease-resistant; upright (up to 5 ft.), non-spreading growth; [sport of 'Sylvia']

'Sea Pearl' ('Flower Girl') F, pb, 1964, Dickson, Patrick; bud long, pointed; flowers soft pink, reverse flushed peach and yellow, well-formed, 4½ in., 24 petals, borne in clusters; foliage dark; stems strong, straight; upright, bushy (4 ft.) growth; ['Kordes' Perfecta' × 'Montezuma']

'Sea Rodney' ('Admiral') Min, m, McCann, Sean; flowers mauve and white, intense fragrance; intr. 2001

'Sea Spray' HMsk, w, 1923, Pemberton; flowers stone-white, flushed pink, semi-dbl., borne in small clusters; non-recurrent; growth to 3-5 ft.

'Sea Spray' -- See 'Macnewing'

'Seaaffi' ('Cancan Swirl') F, m, 2003, McCann, Sean; flowers have lighter edges, large, full, flat, borne in large clusters, moderate fragrance; foliage medium size, medium green, semi-glossy; prickles moderate; growth upright, medium; garden decorative; ['Gentle Annie' × Charles de Gaulle®]; intr. 2003

'Seaanne' ('Anneli') MinFl, ob, 2004,

McCann, Sean; flowers bright orange, reverse yellow, 1½ in., semi-dbl., borne in small clusters, moderate fragrance; foliage medium size, medium green, semi-glossy; prickles small, straight, green, moderate; growth compact, garden variety; ['Kiss 'n' Tell' × 'Bloomsday']; intr. 2006

'Seabasket' ('Flower Basket') Min, rb, 1995, McCann, Sean; flowers handpainted carmine red with pink stripes, fades to white with dark red, dbl., borne mostly singly, moderate fragrance; foliage small, medium green, semi-glossy; numerous prickles; bushy, very low growth; [Rose Gilardi™ × 'Ain't Misbehavin'']; intr. 1996

'Seabet' ('Elizabeth Munn') Min, pb, 1993, McCann, Sean; flowers mainly pink with lighter reverse, dbl., flat, borne in small clusters; foliage medium size, medium green, semi-glossy; some prickles; medium, upright growth; intr. 1993

'Seabird' HT, my, 1913, Dickson, H.; flowers primrose-yellow, paling to creamy yellow, medium, dbl.; vigorous growth

'Seabla' ('Ain't Misbehavin'') Min, dr, 1990, McCann, Sean; flowers 5 petals; foliage small, green, semi-glossy; bushy growth; ['Oonagh' × ('Pot Black' × Black Jade™)]; intr. 1991

'Seabreeze' Min, mp, 1976, Lemrow, Dr. Maynard W.; bud short, pointed; flowers from dusty rose to lavender pink, cream shadings on reverse, 1 in., 25-35 petals, cupped, ruffled, borne in clusters of 7 - 12, slight fragrance; recurrent; foliage light to medium green; prickles very few, slight downward curve; very vigorous, upright (15-18 in.), bushy growth; hips globular, orange-red; PP4025; ['White Fairy' × seedling]

'Seabud' ('Bud Meyers') MinFl, ob, 2006, McCann, Sean; flowers orange, reverse lighter, 1½-2 in., single, borne mostly solitary; foliage small, dark green, semi-glossy; prickles small, hooked, tan, moderate; growth compact, short (3 ft.); ['Bloomsday' × seedling]; intr. 2006

'Seabutt' ('Buttermilk Sky') F, ab, 2002, McCann, Sean; flowers apricot cream with yellow hints, medium, full, borne in large clusters, intense fragrance; foliage medium size, dark green,; prickles moderate; growth upright, medium; garden decorative; ['Laura's Laughter' × 'Ulster Monarch']; intr. 2003

'Seacancan' ('Christine Marina') F, m, 2003, McCann, Sean; flowers edged lighter, large, full, flat, borne in large clusters, moderate fragrance; foliage medium size, medium green, semi-glossy; prickles moderate; growth upright, medium; garden decorative; ['Gentle Annie' × Charles de Gaulle®]; intr. 2003

'Seacap' ('Capricious') Min, lp, 2002, McCann, Sean; flowers medium, full, borne mostly solitary; foliage medium size, medium green, semi-glossy; few prickles; growth upright, medium; exhibition; ['Kiss 'n' Tell' × Kristin™]

'Seacaro' ('Caroline Louise') HT, mp, 2000, McCann, Sean; flowers large, full, borne mostly solitary, intense fragrance; foliage large, dark green, very matte; numerous prickles; growth spreading; ['Prima Ballerina' × 'Fragrant Cloud']

'Seacatch' ('Dreamcatcher') Cl Min, rb, 1995, McCann, Sean; flowers medium to dark red striped with white, 2-2½ in., 35-40 petals, borne singly, moderate damask fragrance; foliage medium size, medium green, glossy; tall, spreading growth; PPRR; ['Lady in Red' × ((Rose Gilardi™ × 'Wit's End') × (Remember Me® × 'Stars 'n' Stripes'))]; intr. 1995

'Seacaval' ('Laughing Cavalier') M, rb, 2001, McCann, Sean; flowers red with white stripes, large, semi-dbl., borne mostly solitary, slight fragrance; foliage medium size, dark green, glossy; numerous prickles; growth upright, medium; garden decorative; [(Rose Gilardi™ × 'Ferdinand Pichard') × (Rose Gilardi™ × 'William Lobb')]

'Seacharm' ('Different Charm') MinFl, or, 2004, McCann, Sean; flowers orange-red, reverse lighter red, 2½ in., very full, borne mostly solitary, slight fragrance; foliage medium size, medium green, semi-glossy; prickles small, straight; growth compact (2½ ft.); garden decoration; [unknown × unknown]; intr. 2004

'Seacia' ('Ciana Rose') Min, lp, 2002, McCann, Sean; flowers medium, dbl., borne in large clusters; foliage medium size, medium green, semi-glossy; few prickles; growth compact, medium; garden decorative; ['Kiss 'n' Tell' × Sexy Rexy®]

'Seacloak' ('Velvet Cloak') Min, dr, 1999, McCann, Sean; flowers burgundy red, very prominent yellow stamens, 2 in., dbl., borne mostly singly, slight fragrance; foliage medium size, medium green, semi-glossy; prickles moderate; bushy, medium (20-24 in.) growth; ['Lady in Red' × 'Ain't Misbehavin'']; intr. 1998

'Seacoat' ('Dreamcoat') Min, yb, 1996, McCann, Sean; flowers medium to dark yellow with scarlet accent, fades to reddish, 2½ in., dbl.; foliage large, dark green, semi-glossy; upright, tall (4-6 ft.) growth; PPRR; ['Lady in Red' × Joseph's Coat®]; intr. 1997

'Seacolette' ('Colette Pappin Glynn') Min, w, 2001, McCann, Sean; flowers white with yellow center, small, dbl., borne in small clusters; foliage small, medium green, semi-glossy; few prickles; growth compact, low; ['Someday Soon' × Kent™]

'Seacombe' w, Bates, Michael; intr. 2001

'Seadai' ('Daisy Lane') S, dr, 2000, McCann, Sean; flowers black-red, medium, semi-dbl., borne in small clusters, slight fragrance; foliage medium size, medium green, semi-glossy; some prickles; growth upright; garden decorative; ['Lady in Red' × 'Fountain']

'Seadarby' ('Darby O'Gill') Min, ob, 1996, McCann, Sean; flowers orange with creamy white striping, 1½ in., 18 petals, borne mostly singly, slight fragrance; foliage medium size, dark green, glossy; some prickles; upright, medium (24-26 in.) growth; PPAF; ['Tattooed Lady' × 'Lady in Red']; intr. 1996

'Seadark' ('Dark Mirage') Min, dr, 1996, McCann, Sean; flowers velvety dark red with very dark shading at tip, reverse dark shadows, 2 in., full, high-centered, borne mostly singly, intense fragrance; foliage medium size, dark green, glossy, highly serrated; stems long; medium (18-20 in.) growth; PPRR; ['Lady in Red' × 'Fountain']; intr. 1997

'Seadead' ('Tye-Dye') MinFl, rb, 2006, Sean McCann; flowers red striped with yellow, 1½-2 in., full, borne mostly solitary; foliage medium size, medium green, semi-glossy; prickles small, straight, pointed, light green, few; growth compact, bushy, medium (3 ft.); garden decorative; [seedling × seedling]

'Seadeep' ('Tattooed Lady') Min, rb, 1993, McCann, Sean; flowers red, yellow reverse, yellow stripes and veins, large, dbl., borne mostly singly, slight fragrance; foliage medium size, dark green, bronze, glossy; numerous prickles; medium (12-14 in.), upright growth; ['Siobhan' × ('Picasso' × 'Near You')]; intr. 1994

'Seadot' ('Crazy Dottie') Min, ob, 1988, McCann, Sean; flowers orange-red with star-shaped copper center, small, 5 petals; foliage small, medium green, semi-glossy; bushy growth; ['Rise 'n' Shine' × ('Sheri Anne' × 'Picasso')]

'Seadow' ('Margaret McDowell') HT, mr, 1992, McCann, Sean; flowers medium, full; foliage medium size, medium green, semi-glossy; some prickles; growth medium (36; [('Ruby Wedding' × (seedling × 'Oonagh')) × (seedling × 'Oonagh')]

'Seaeliz' ('Paddy 'n' Elizabeth') S, ob, 2006, McCann, Sean; flowers orange-yellow-pink blend, reverse orange fading to light green, 2 in., single, borne in small clusters; foliage medium green, matte; prickles medium, hooked, light, moderate; growth bushy (36 in.); garden; [Joseph's Coat® × 'Kiss 'n' Tell']; intr. 2007

'Seaeus' ('Eustacia') F, pb, 1999, McCann, Sean; flowers handpainted with patches of pink and red, yellow center, 3 in., dbl., borne in small clusters; foliage medium size, medium green, glossy; numerous prickles; upright, medium (30 in.) growth; [('Copper Pot' × 'Maxi') × 'Picasso']

'Seaeva' ('Fair Eva') Min, lp, 2003, McCann, Sean; flowers medium, semi-dbl., borne mostly solitary; foliage medium size, dark green, glossy; growth spreading, short; groundcover; ['Kiss 'n' Tell' ×

'New Dawn']; intr. 2003

'Seafair' HT, ab, 1960, Von Abrams; bud long, pointed; flowers deep apricot, large, 45 petals, high-centered; foliage glossy; vigorous, upright, symmetrical growth; RULED EXTINCT 4/86; ['Charlotte Armstrong' × 'Signora']; intr. 1959

'Seafarer' -- See 'Hartilion'

'Seafibs' ('Little White Lies') Min, w, 2000, McCann, Sean; flowers white with bright yellow stamens, 1¼ in., single, borne in small clusters, no fragrance; foliage small, medium green, semi-glossy; numerous prickles; growth spreading, low (8-10 in. × 2 ft.); [Kent™ × 'Cliffs of Dover']; intr. 2001

'Seafubar' ('Colin's Fubar') HT, lp, 2000, McCann, Sean; flowers soft pink, veined, medium, dbl., globular, borne mostly singly, moderate fragrance; foliage medium size, medium green, semi-glossy; few prickles; growth upright; ['Pink Favorite' × 'Fragrant Cloud']

'Seafun' ('Looks Like Fun') Min, pb, 1997, McCann, Sean; flowers medium, 41 petals, borne mostly singly, moderate fragrance; foliage medium size, medium green, semi-glossy; spreading, bushy, medium (16 in.)growth; ['Lady in Red' × (Rose Gilardi™ × seedling)]

'Seager Wheeler' HSpn, lp, 1947, Wheeler; flowers semi-dbl.; non-recurrent; growth to 6 ft.; hardy; [R. spinosissima altaica × unknown]

'Seaglad' ('Glad Eye') Min, rb, 2003, McCann, Sean; flowers red with bright yellow eye, medium, semi-dbl., borne in small clusters; foliage medium size, medium green, glossy; growth compact, low-growing,; ['Crazy Dottie' × seedling]

'Seagold' ('Gold Country') MinFl, my, 1986, McCann, Sean; flowers small, 20 petals, high-centered, borne singly, intense fragrance; foliage small, light green, semi-glossy; bushy growth; ['Rise 'n' Shine' × ('Rise 'n' Shine' × Casino®)]; intr. 1987

'Seagood' ('Lady Be Good') Min, mp, 1990, McCann, Sean; flowers dbl.; foliage small, medium green, semi-glossy; bushy growth; ['Kiss 'n' Tell' × ('Irish Mist' × Matangi®)]; intr. 1991

'Seagru' ('Blushing Groom') Min, w, 1982, McCann, Sean; flowers near white, small, 35 petals, slight fragrance; foliage small, dark, semi-glossy; upright growth; ['Rise 'n' Shine' × 'Karl Herbst']; intr. 1983

'Seagull' HMult, w, 1907, Pritchard; bud tinged pink; flowers pure white, stamens golden, 3 cm., single, borne in large clusters, moderate fragrance; non-remontant; foliage grey-green; prickles large; very vigorous growth; [R. multiflora × 'Général Jacqueminot']

'Seaheart' ('Irish Heartbreaker') Cl Min, rb, 1990, McCann, Sean; flowers small, full, slight fragrance; foliage medium size, medium green, semi-glossy; upright growth; ['Rise 'n' Shine' × ('Oonagh' × 'Siobhan')]; intr. 1989

'Seaheight' ('Height of Fashion') F, yb, 2003, McCann, Sean; flowers tan with apricot touches, medium, dbl., borne mostly solitary; foliage medium size, medium green; growth upright; [(Brandy™ × Royal Dane™) × 'Tantalizing Mary']

'Seairish' ('My Wild Irish Rose') S, pb, 2004, McCann, Sean; flowers pink, reverse apricot, 2 in., single, borne in small clusters, moderate fragrance; foliage medium size, dark green, glossy; prickles medium, hooked, red/brown, moderate; growth spreading, medium, lax (to 7 ft.); hedge; [seedling × seedling]; intr. 2004

'Seaisa' ('Isabella Cara') Min, w, 2003, McCann, Sean; flowers white with tones of light pink, medium, dbl., borne in small clusters; foliage medium size, dark green, glossy; growth spreading, low, some tall stems; ['Kiss 'n' Tell' × 'New Dawn']

'Seakiss' ('Kiss 'n' Tell') Min, ab, 1985, McCann, Sean; flowers small, 35 petals, flat, slight fragrance; foliage small, medium green, semi-glossy; bushy growth; ['Rise 'n' Shine' × ('Sally Mac' × 'New Penny')]; intr. 1989

'Seaknock' ('Knocktopher Lady') Min, pb, 2001, McCann, Sean; flowers striped peach/cream, fading to linen, small, semi-dbl., borne in small clusters, slight fragrance; foliage small, light green, matte; some prickles; growth upright; garden decorative; ['Dreamcoat' × 'Dreamcatcher']

'Sealady' ('Lady in Red') Min, rb, 1989, McCann, Sean; flowers red with touch of white at base of petals, small, dbl.; foliage small, medium green, semi-glossy; bushy growth; ['Rise 'n' Shine' × 'Siobhan']; intr. 1988

'Sealands' ('Highlands Rose') F, mp, 2000, McCann, Sean; flowers changing from rose pink to lilac with age, medium, semi-dbl., borne in small clusters, slight fragrance; foliage medium size, medium green (dark red when young), glossy; few prickles; growth upright; garden decorative; ['Gentle Annie' × 'Dainty Dora']

'Sealark' ('Big Jim Larkin') HT, rb, 1998, McCann, Sean; flowers red with silver reverse, silvers flecks on top surface, 4½-5 in., very dbl., borne in large clusters; foliage large, dark green, semi-glossy; free blooming, spreading, medium (4 ft.) growth; ['Lady in Red' × 'Old Master']; intr. 1999

'Sealaura' ('Laura's Laughter') Min, pb, 2000, McCann, Sean; flowers dusty pink, reverse silvery pink, 1½ in., full, borne mostly singly, slight fragrance; foliage medium size, medium green, semi-glossy; prickles moderate; growth bushy, medium (22-26 in.); ['Kiss Me Quick' × Kristin™]

'Seale Peach' Min, ab, Seale

'Sealife' ('High Life') Min, rb, 1996, McCann, Sean; flowers medium red with white at throat, reverse white with red, fading with age, 2½ in., full, high-centered; foliage large, medium green, dull; upright, tall (30 in.) growth; PPRR; ['Lady in Red' × 'Oriana']; intr. 1997

'Sealily' Min, pb, 1984, Lemrow, Dr. Maynard W.; flowers white, petals edged pink, small, 35 petals; foliage medium size, dark, semi-glossy; ['Max Colwell' × unknown]

'Sealing Wax' HMoy, mp, 1938, Royal Hort. Soc.; flowers large; hips abundant, brilliant red; [R. moyesii × unknown]

'Sealove' ('Lovers Only') Min, rb, 1990, McCann, Sean; sepals are fancy; flowers cherry red, with straw-yellow bicolor, reverse fades to cream, dbl.; foliage medium size, medium green, glossy; prickles pubescent on peduncle; upright, compact growth; ['Rise 'n' Shine' × 'Siobhan']; intr. 1989

'Sealure' ('Alluring') HT, pb, 2003, McCann, Sean; flowers veined pink and cream, medium, full, borne in small clusters, moderate fragrance; foliage large, medium green, semi-glossy; growth upright, medium; garden decorative; [seedling × seedling]

'Seamar' ('Martin Martin') HT, w, 1985, McCann, Sean; flowers cream, petals tipped red, large, high-centered; foliage large, dark, semi-glossy; upright growth; ['Jimmy Greaves' × 'Irish Gold']

'Seamary' ('Mary 'n' John') MinFl, my, 2000, McCann, Sean; flowers medium, dbl., borne in small clusters, slight fragrance; foliage medium size, medium green, semi-glossy; some prickles; growth bushy, medium; garden decorative; ['Rise 'n' Shine' × 'Amy Rebecca']

'Seamit' ('Misty Eyed') MinFl, w, 2003, McCann, Sean; flowers white with suggestions of gray, medium, dbl., borne in small clusters, slight fragrance; foliage medium size, medium green, semi-glossy; growth spreading, medium; garden decorative; ['Jennifer' × seedling]; intr. 2005

'Seamom' ('Stolen Moment') Min, m, 1990, McCann, Sean; flowers mauve blend, small, 6-14 petals; foliage small, medium green, semi-glossy; bushy growth; ['Kiss 'n' Tell' × ('Aunty Dora' × Charles de Gaulle®)]

'Seamood' ('In the Mood') Min, yb, 1989, McCann, Sean; flowers yellow streaked pink, small, 20 petals, slight fragrance; foliage small, medium green, semi-glossy; bushy growth; ['Rise 'n' Shine' × seedling]; intr. 1988

'Seamou' ('Mouse') Min, pb, 1999, McCann, Sean; flowers pink yellow at base, changes to red-pink, 1 in., dbl., borne in small clusters; foliage small, medium green, semi-glossy; few prickles; bushy, medium (18 in.) growth; ['Portland Dawn' × 'Siobhan']

'Seamurp' ('Murphy's Law') HT, mp, 1982,

McCann, Sean; flowers medium pink, lighter reverse, large, 35 petals; foliage medium size, dark, matte; bushy growth; ['Fragrant Cloud' × ('Prima Ballerina' × 'Gavotte')]; intr. 1983

'Sean' S, w, Sutherland, P; [sport of 'Mme Segond Weber']; intr. 2000

'Sean and Joan' -- See 'Bosrexhold'

'Seanear' ('Near You') Min, w, 1990, McCann, Sean; flowers medium, dbl.; foliage small, medium green, semi-glossy; spreading growth; ['Rise 'n' Shine' × (Elina® × 'Royal Gold')]

'Seaannie' ('Gentle Annie') F, m, 2000, McCann, Sean; flowers purple, bright yellow stamens, large, semi-dbl., borne in very large clusters; foliage medium size, medium green, glossy; some prickles; upright, medium growth; [(News® × International Herald Tribune®) × 'Stolen Moment']

'Seaodd' ('Alice Faye') Min, rb, 1992, McCann, Sean; flowers full circle of red with distinct yellow eye from the bottom view, 2½ in., 22-24 petals; foliage large, medium green, semi-glossy; upright, tall growth; [seedling × seedling]; intr. 1992

'Seaoodle' ('Canoodling') MinFl, ob, 2004, McCann, Sean; flowers deep orange with yellow markings, 1½ in., semi-dbl., borne in small clusters, no fragrance; foliage small, dark green, semi-glossy; prickles small, straight, brown, moderate; growth upright, medium; garden; ['San Francisco Sunset' × seedling]; intr. 2004

'Seaoona' ('Oonagh') HT, mr, 1990, McCann, Sean; flowers large, full; foliage medium size, medium green, semi-glossy; very spreading growth; [Matangi® × 'Gavotte']

'Seaquick' ('Kiss Me Quick') Min, lp, 2000, McCann, Sean; flowers light pink, reverse pink salmon, fades slowly, 2 in., full, borne mostly singly, slight fragrance; quick repeat; foliage medium size, medium green, semi-glossy; upright, medium (18-22 in.) growth; ['Kiss 'n' Tell' × 'Lady in Red']; intr. 2000

Search for Life™ -- See 'Wilsfol'

'Searich' ('Rich and Rare') Min, rb, 1986, McCann, Sean; flowers scarlet, reverse white veined red, small, 35 petals, high-centered, borne singly; foliage small, dark, semi-glossy; bushy growth; [('Rise 'n' Shine' × 'Siobhan') × 'Beauty Secret']; intr. 1987

'Searodney' ('Admirable') Min, w, 1991, McCann, Sean; bud ovoid, sharply pointed sepals; flowers soft pink with darker accent, reverse ivory with pink accent, 2½ in., 38 petals, high-centered, borne usually singly, intense fruity fragrance; foliage large, medium green, semi-glossy; long, straight stems; upright, tall growth; [seedling × 'Admiral Rodney']; intr. 1992

'Searonan' ('Street Wise') Min, op, 1996, McCann, Sean; flowers orange and pink, reverse yellow at throat, 60 petals, borne mostly singly; foliage medium size, medium green, semi-glossy; numerous prickles; upright, medium growth; PPAF; ['Rise 'n' Shine' × 'Siobhan']; intr. 1996

'Seaset' ('San Francisco Sunset') MinFl, or, 2004, McCann, Sean; flowers dbl., borne in small clusters, slight fragrance; foliage medium size, medium green, semi-glossy; prickles medium, straight; growth upright, medium (24 in.); garden decoration; ['Kiss'n'tell' × (Orangeade® × Alexander®)]; intr. 1997

'Seashell' HWich, mp, 1916, Dawson; flowers large, semi-dbl., borne in large clusters; foliage glossy

'Seashell' HT, op, Kordes, R.; bud short, pointed; flowers burnt-orange, imbricated, 3-4 in., 48 petals, slight fragrance; free-flowering; upright growth; PP3685; [seedling × 'Colour Wonder']; intr. 1976

'Seashore' HT, op, Williams, J. B.; intr. 1996

'Seasio' ('Siobhan') F, rb, 1985, McCann, Sean; flowers red, reverse yellow, medium, 20 petals, hybrid tea form, borne in small clusters, slight fragrance; recurrent; foliage medium size, dark bronze, semi-glossy; upright (3-5 ft.) growth; ['Maxi' × 'Copper Pot']; intr. 1984

'Seasol' ('Solitude') Min, pb, McCann, Sean

'Seasons' S, ob; flowers single; intr. 2003

'Seasoon' ('Someday Soon') Min, ly, 1992, McCann, Sean; flowers light yellow framed in creamy white outer petals, reverse cream, 1½ in., 52 petals, high-centered, borne singly, slight spicy fragrance; foliage medium size, light green, matte, highly serrated; upright, medium growth; ['Miniature seedling' × 'Antique Silk']; intr. 1993

'Seasop' ('Sophisticate') HT, pb, 2003, McCann, Sean; flowers pink, reverse silver, large, dbl., borne mostly solitary, moderate fragrance; foliage medium size, medium green, semi-glossy; bushy, medium growth: garden decorative; ['Sally Mac' × seedling]

'Seaspit' ('Spitfire Paddy') HT, ob, 2004, McCann, Sean; flowers orange-yellow, 4 in., full, borne mostly solitary, slight fragrance; foliage medium size, dark green, semi-glossy; prickles large, straight; growth upright, medium (36 in.); garden decoration; [Piccadilly® × seedling]; intr. 2004

'Seaspray' -- See 'Macnewing'

'Seaswan' ('Swansong') Min, w, 1988, McCann, Sean; flowers small, dbl., intense fragrance; foliage small, medium green, semi-glossy; bushy growth; [('Rise 'n' Shine' × Party Girl™) × Margaret Merril®]

'Seatant' ('Tantalizing Mary') MinFl, yb, 2000, McCann, Sean; flowers yellow, aging to apricot centers, medium, full, borne mostly solitary, intense fragrance; foliage medium size, medium green, glossy; some prickles; growth upright, medium; prickles garden decorative; ['Ladies View' × ('Someday Soon' × 'New Dawn')]

'Seatel' ('Margaret Telfer') Min, w, 1992, McCann, Sean; flowers large, dbl., borne in small clusters; foliage small, medium green, semi-glossy; some prickles; low (14 in.), upright growth; ['Kiss the Bride' × Margaret Merril®]

'Seatier' ('Tiernan's Gold') Min, my, 2001, McCann, Sean; flowers yellow fading to white, small, semi-dbl., borne in small clusters; foliage medium size, light green, semi-glossy; few prickles; compact, low growth; ['Rise 'n' Shine' × 'Amy Rebecca']

'Seatip' ('Portland Dawn') Min, pb, 1989, McCann, Sean; flowers veined pink and bronze, small, 20 petals; foliage small, medium green, semi-glossy; bushy growth; ['Rise 'n' Shine' × ('Copper Pot' × 'Maxi')]; intr. 1988

'Seatoff' ('Toffee') Min, ob, 1992, McCann, Sean; flowers bright orange, yellow eye, dark orange stamens, 1 in., 18 petals, urn-shaped, loose, borne singly, slight fruity fragrance; recurrent; foliage medium size, medium green, semi-glossy, disease-resistant; bushy, medium growth; ['Bloomsday' × 'miniature seedling']; intr. 1993

'Seatoo' ('Mary Toomey') Min, yb, 2001, McCann, Sean; flowers yellow-apricot, small, semi-dbl., borne in small clusters; foliage small, medium green, semi-glossy; growth compact, short; [seedling × 'You 'n' Me']

Seattle Scentsation™ -- See 'Savaseat'

Seattle Sunrise™ -- See 'Moeseattle'

'Seatwinkle' ('Jazz Dancer') Min, ob, 1999, McCann, Sean; flowers orange and yellow, reverse orange, 1¾ in., full, borne mostly singly; foliage medium size, dark green, glossy; prickles moderate; compact, medium (14-16 in.) growth; intr. 1999

'Seaurug' ('Rosario Algorta') HT, ly, 2006, McCann, Sean; flowers cream, 3 in., dbl., borne mostly solitary; foliage medium size, dark green, semi-glossy; prickles medium, straight, light brown, moderate; upright, 36 in. growth; [seedling × seedling]; intr. 2006

'Seaview' ('Ladies' View') Min, yb, 1991, McCann, Sean; flowers small, dbl., slight fragrance; foliage small, medium green, semi-glossy; bushy growth; ['You 'n' Me' × Amber Queen®]

'Seavin' ('True Vintage') Min, mr, 1999, McCann, Sean; flowers medium red to fuchsia, reverse silver/light red, medium, semi-dbl., borne mostly singly, slight fragrance; recurrent; foliage medium size, medium green, semi-glossy; numerous prickles; compact, medium (16-18 in.) growth; [Rose Gilardi™ × 'Stolen Moment']; intr. 1999

'Seavivial' ('Convivial') Cl Min, ab, 2003,

McCann, Sean; flowers light apricot, finishing white, small to medium, dbl., quartered, borne in small clusters, no fragrance; foliage medium size, dark green, semi-glossy; stems long; growth spreading, medium; [('S.W.A.L.K.' × 'Kiss 'n' Tell') × 'New Dawn']

'Seawalk' ('Love 'n' Kisses', 'S. W. A. L. K.') Cl Min, mr, 1999, McCann, Sean; flowers barn red, 2¼ in., full, high-centered, borne mostly singly, slight fragrance; recurrent; foliage medium size, dark green, glossy; prickles moderate; climbing (6-7 ft.) growth; trellis or fence for support; [seedling × seedling]; intr. 1998

'Seawhi' ('Kiss the Bride') Min, w, 1986, McCann, Sean; flowers small, 20 petals, borne singly and in clusters of 4 - 6, moderate spicy fragrance; foliage medium size, medium green, semi-glossy; bushy growth; ['Rise 'n' Shine' × 'White Bouquet']; intr. 1987

'Seawish' ('Wishful Thinking') Min, rb, 1996, McCann, Sean; flowers medium red light yellow eye, heavy mass of yellow stamens, 1½ in., dbl., petals very reflexed, intense fragrance; foliage medium size, dark green to light orange, glossy; upright, medium (16-20 in.) growth; PPRR; [seedling × 'Wit's End']; intr. 1997

'Seawit' ('Wit's End') Min, rb, 1989, McCann, Sean; flowers red with yellow reverse, small, 20 petals, borne in sprays of 3 - 5, slight fragrance; foliage small, medium green, semi-glossy; bushy growth; ['Rise 'n' Shine' × 'Siobhan']

'Seayou' ('You 'n' Me') Min, w, 1985, McCann, Sean; flowers white, light apricot center, small, dbl., high-centered; foliage small, medium green, semi-glossy; bushy growth; ['Avandel' × Party Girl™]

'Sebago' (Tyler™) HT, rb, 1988, Poor, Cuyler; bud ovoid; flowers medium to dark red, reverse lighter, 4¾ in., 30-35 petals, high-centered, borne singly, slight fragrance; recurrent; foliage medium size, dark green, matte; prickles some, medium length; upright (5 ft.), vigorous growth; hips globular, medium, orange-yellow; PP8076; [('Tamango' × 'Red Planet') × 'First Prize']; intr. 1988

Sebastian Kneipp® -- See 'Korpastato'

'Sebastian Schultheis' Gr, dp, Schultheis; flowers bright carmine pink, dbl., cupped, borne mostly in clusters, slight fragrance; free-flowering; stems long; upright, tall, bushy growth; [Queen Elizabeth® × unknown]; intr. 1979

'Sebastopol Queen' HMult, w; flowers white with blushed edges, single, borne in large clusters, slight fragrance; non-remontant; hips abundant, soft salmon-orange; chance seedling; may be from R. soulieana crossed with a multiflora rambler; intr. 2003

'Secco' HT, yb, Sasaki; intr. 1997

'Second Chance' HT, pb, 1989, Stoddard, Louis; bud ovoid; flowers coral-orange, tips orange-red, reverse deep pink, aging medium pink with red edges, 35 petals, high-centered, moderate damask fragrance; foliage medium size, medium green to maroon, semi-glossy, a bit rugose; bushy, slightly spreading growth; ['Carefree Beauty' × 'Sonia']; intr. 1991

Secret™ -- See 'Hilaroma'

'Secret Love' HT, dr, 1973, Armstrong, D.L.; bud ovoid; flowers deep red, large, dbl., high-centered, moderate fragrance; foliage leathery; moderate, upright, bushy growth; PP3584; [seedling × seedling]

'Secret Obsession' -- See 'Rensecobses'

'Secret Recipe' -- See 'Morwinst'

'Secrétaire Allard' HP, mr, 1869, David; flowers velvety scarlet-vermilion, large, full

'Secrétaire Belpaire' HT, op, 1934, Lens; flowers brilliant salmon-pink, large, dbl.; foliage bright bronze; vigorous growth; ['Angèle Pernet' × 'Mme Edouard Herriot']

'Secrétaire Général Delaire' HP, dr, 1899, Corboeuf; flowers very large, very full; ['Baronne Adolphe de Rothschild' × 'Alphonse Soupert']

'Secrétaire J. Nicolas' ('Secrétaire Jean Nicolas') HP, m, 1883, Schwartz; flowers dark red and velvety purple, reverse lighter, large, full, cupped, globular, borne mostly solitary; foliage light green, finely dentate; prickles thin, pointed, numerous; growth upright

'Secrétaire Jean Nicolas' -- See 'Secrétaire J. Nicolas'

'Secretaris Zwart' HT, dp, 1918, Van Rossem; flowers bright rose, reverse silvery rose, large, full, globular, moderate fragrance; recurrent; ['Gen. MacArthur' × 'Lyon Rose']

Sedana® ('Sedana Flower Carpet') S, ob, Noack; flowers cream-orange to apricot, some soft pink tones, 2 in., semi-dbl., shallow cup, borne in clusters; recurrent; foliage medium green, glossy, leathery; low (2 ft.), bushy growth; intr. 2006

'Sedana Flower Carpet' -- See 'Noa97400A'

'Sedgebrook' -- See 'Murse'

'Seduction' -- See 'Meivrita'

'Seduction, Climbing' -- See 'Nietar'

'Séduction' Pol, mp, 1927, Turbat; flowers peach-blossom-pink, large, dbl., borne in clusters of 50-60; few prickles; dwarf growth

'Seduction' -- See 'Meibeausai'

'Seefeld' F, rb, 1958, Delforge; bud oval; flowers red tinted lighter, open, medium, dbl., borne in large clusters; foliage glossy; very vigorous, bushy growth; ['Fashion' × Orange Triumph®]

'Seftopolis' Gr, dp, 1985, Staikov, Prof. Dr. V.; flowers deep pink, large, 36 petals; foliage glossy, leathery; vigorous growth; [Queen Elizabeth® × seedling]; intr. 1977

'Segmisty' (Misty Moonlight™) LCl, lp, 2004, Graham, Susan Brandt; flowers light pink fading to white, petals ruffled, 3 in., 50-80 petals, old-fashioned, borne in small and large clusters, slight fragrance; foliage large, medium green, semi-glossy; prickles medium, straight; growth spreading, climbs if trained, tall (10-12 ft.); pillar; [sport of Dream Weaver™]; intr. 2006

Segovia™ S, pb, Olesen; bud urceolate with pointed apex; flowers varying shades of light to medium pink, 5 cm., very full, globular, to rosette, borne singly and in small clusters, slight fragrance; recurrent; foliage dark green, glossy; prickles numerous, 4-5 mm., hooked downward; upright to bushy (60-100 cm.) growth; PP16961; [seedling × Bernstorff™]; intr. 2005

'Segovia' HT, Combe, M.; intr. 1964

'Segprize' ('What A Surprize') Min, op, 2004, Graham, Susan Brandt; flowers orange pink with yellow base, 2-2½ cm., dbl., borne mostly solitary; foliage medium size, dark green, semi-glossy; prickles moderate, medium, curved; growth upright, medium (24-30 in.); containers, borders, exhibition; [sport of Hot Tamale™]; intr. 2005

'Séguier' HGal, m, 1853, Robert; flowers purple/violet with white stripes, medium, dbl.

'Segyoyo' (Yoyo™) Min, rb, 2003, Graham, Susan Brandt; flowers deep red with orange markings, each different; white eye; golden stamens, 1½-2 in., single, borne mostly solitary, no fragrance; foliage medium size, medium green, semi-glossy; prickles medium, straight, green, moderate; growth compact, medium (16-20 in.); containers, borders; [sport of Gizmo™]; intr. 2003

Sehnsucht® F, dr

'Sei-Ka, Climbing' -- See 'Seika, Climbing'

'Sei-Ka' -- See 'Olympic Torch'

'Seigneur d'Harzelhaard' HGal, m, about 1845, Calvert; flowers dark violet-purple, center red, medium, full

'Seika' HT, ob, Teranishi; flowers single; intr. 1966

'Seika, Climbing' ('Olympic Torch, Climbing', 'Sei-Ka, Climbing') Cl HT, rb, Keisei; [sport of 'Olympic Torch']; intr. 1985

'Seika' -- See 'Olympic Torch'

'Seiko' HT, dy, 1977, Keisei Rose Nurseries; buds ovoid; flowers non-fading, deep lemon yellow, dbl, high-centered, borne in clusters; foliage large, semi-glossy; growth very vigorous; intr. 1975

'Seion' HT, my, 1988, Yokota, Kiyoshi; flowers large, 35-40 petals, high-centered, moderate fragrance; foliage light green; few prickles; upright, medium growth; hips medium, pale orange; ['Grandpa Dickson' × 'Sunblest']

'Seiryoden' HT, pb, Kuroda; intr. 1961

'Seiryu' HT, m, 2005, Kobayashi, Moriji; flowers 12 cm., dbl., borne mostly solitary, slight fragrance; foliage medium size, light green, matte; prickles medium; growth upright, 160 cm; cutting, garden; [('Ondina' × ('Madame Violet' × seedling)]

'Seisho' HT, pb, 1999, Ohkawara, Kiyoshi; flowers soft pink, deep pink petal edge, 5½ in., 30-35 petals, high-centered; foliage dark green; growth to 5 ft.; ['Michele Meilland' × 'Maria Teresa Bordas']; intr. 1992

'Seishun' ('Youth') HT, dp, Hiroshima; intr. 1996

'Sekel' S, yb, 1985, Lundstad, Arne; flowers light yellow with red spreading down from the petal edges, large, 11 petals, shallow cup, borne in large clusters of up to 21, slight fragrance; foliage dark, leathery, glossy; vigorous, upright growth; [Lichterloh® × 'Zitronenfalter']; intr. 1984

'Seki-Yoh' HT, or, 1986, Suzuki, Seizo; flowers large, 52 petals, high-centered; foliage dark, leathery, semi-glossy; upright, compact growth; ['Miss France' × 'Christian Dior']; intr. 1975

'Selandia' LCl, mp, 1913, Poulsen, D.T.; flowers medium pink, fading to light rose pink, reverse lighter, 4 cm., dbl., borne in medium to large clusters; foliage glossy; vigorous growth; ['Mme Norbert Levavasseur' × 'Dorothy Perkins']

'Selazteca' ('Red Azteca') HT, mr, 1990, Select Roses, B.V.; bud pointed, tapering, slender; flowers bright red, no fading, large, 30-35 petals, cupped, borne singly; foliage large, dark green, glossy; prickles reddish, with yellow tip; upright, tall growth; [seedling × seedling]

'Selbar 0152' (Firestar®) LCl, mr, Barni; intr. 1994

Selena™ HT, dr, deVor; intr. 1996

Selenia® F, w, J&P; flowers white with cream centers, large, dbl., high-centered; free-flowering; compact, low, well-branched growth; intr. 2002

'Selfridges' ('Berolina') HT, dy, 1984, Kordes, W.; bud large; flowers amber yellow, large, 35 petals, high-centered, borne mostly singly, moderate fragrance; foliage medium size, medium green, semi-glossy; upright growth; intr. 1984

'Sélima Dubos' -- See 'Célina Dubos'

'Selina' -- See 'Reysel'

'Selphosphor ' HT, mp, Select Roses BV; intr. 1999

'Selstar' ('Christina') HT, my, 1990, Select Roses, B.V.; bud pointed; flowers bright lemon-yellow, non-fading, medium to large, 43 petals, cupped, borne singly, no fragrance; foliage large, dark green, glossy; prickles declining, light red; upright, tall growth; ['Eliora' × seedling]; intr. 1990

Selvetta® HT, pb, 1983, Cazzaniga-Como; flowers light pink, petals edged salmon, large, 40 petals, high-centered, no fragrance; foliage medium size, dark, matte; upright growth; intr. 1982

'Selwyn Bird' HT, or, 1970, Cocker; flowers salmon-cerise, 35 petals, high-centered, moderate fragrance; foliage dark, glossy; vigorous growth; ['Fragrant Cloud' × 'Stella']; intr. 1969

'Selwyn Toogood' Min, mp, 1984, Eagle, Barry & Dawn; flowers small, 33 petals, high-centered; foliage small, light green; prickles light moss on stems; bushy, upright growth; ['Heidi' × unknown]; intr. 1983

'Sémèlé' T, w, about 1844, Guérin or Boyau; flowers flesh white, aging darker, medium, dbl.

'Semi' (R. laxa form), w, 1913; flowers small; blooms all summer; tall (8 ft.) growth; hips bright red; very hardy

'Semi-Double' M, dp, before 1826, Vibert; flowers large, semi-dbl.

'Semi-Double Marbled Rose' -- See 'Marmorea'

'Semi-Double Striped Moss' -- See 'Panachée'

'Semi-Plena' -- See 'Alba Semi-plena'

'Semillante' HT, Combe, M.; intr. 1976

'Seminole Wind' -- See 'Kortersen'

'Sémiramis' D, pb, 1841, Vibert; flowers salmon-rose, center fawn, large, dbl.

'Semiramis' HT, yb, 1957, Motose; bud pointed; flowers rose, center buff or amber, 5 in., 35-45 petals, high-centered, intense raspberry fragrance; foliage dark, glossy; vigorous growth; PP1552; [('Capistrano' × ('Peace' × 'Crimson Glory')]

'Sémonville' A, w, before 1815, Charpentier; flowers white with coppery yellow-pink, medium, semi-dbl.; foliage veined; prickles long, intermixed with glandular bristles; ['Evratina' × unknown]

'Sémonville à Fleurs Doubles' A, pb, 1823, Hardy; flowers pink tinted yellow-copper, large, dbl.

'Semperflorens' -- See 'Slater's Crimson China'

'Sempervirens Major' -- See 'Plena'

'Sempervirens Pleno' -- See 'Plena'

'Sénat Romain' -- See 'Duc de Guiche'

'Sénateur Amic' HG, mr, 1924, Nabonnand, P.; bud long, pointed; flowers brilliant carmine, large, semi-dbl., cupped; very vigorous growth; [R. gigantea × 'General MacArthur']

'Sénateur Belle' HT, op, 1900, Pernet-Ducher; flowers salmon pink, center dark golden, edges shaded carmine, medium, full, globular

'Sénateur Favre' -- See 'François Fontaine'

'Sénateur La Follette' -- See 'La Follette'

'Sénateur Laubet' -- See 'Sénateur Loubet'

'Sénateur Loubet' ('Sénateur Laubet') T, yb, 1891, Reboul; flowers delicate pink on a ground of metallic yellow, changing to poppy, large, very full; growth dwarf but vigorous

'Sénateur Mascuraud' HT, ly, 1909, Pernet-Ducher; flowers light yellow, center darker, dbl.

'Sénateur Potié' HT, ob, 1937, Dot, Pedro; flowers orange-yellow, large, semi-dbl., cupped; foliage glossy, bronze; vigorous growth; ['Mme Butterfly' × 'Carito MacMahon']

'Sénateur Réveil' HP, rb, 1863, Damaizin; flowers shining crimson, shaded dark purple, large, full

'Sénateur Saint-Romme' HT, op, 1904, Schwartz; bud light red; flowers salmon on a pink ground, large, full

'Sénateur Vaïsse' HP, rb, 1859, Guillot Père; flowers red, shaded darker, large, 32 petals; occasionally recurrent bloom; upright growth; ['Général Jacqueminot' × unknown]

'Senator' HT, mr, 1926, Florex Gardens; bud long, pointed; flowers brilliant scarlet, dbl.; ['Red Columbia' × 'Premier']

Senator Burda® -- See 'Meivestal'

'Senator Joe T. Robinson' HT, dr, 1938, Vestal; bud long, pointed; flowers dark crimson, semi-dbl., cupped; foliage leathery; vigorous growth; ['Harvard' × 'David O. Dodd']

'Senator McNaughton' T, w, 1895 or before, California Nursery Co.; flowers creamy white, large, full; foliage glossy; [sport of 'Perle des Jardins']

'Senbatsuru' ('A Thousand Cranes') HT, w, Hiroshima; intr. 1994

'Send in the Clowns' ('Circus Clown') HWich, mp, Clements, John; flowers candy pink, small to medium, dbl., borne in clusters; foliage dark green, glossy; vigorous (12 ft.) growth; intr. 1997

'Seneca Queen' HT, pb, 1965, Boerner; flowers apricot-pink, reverse darker, 6 in., 50 petals, high-centered, moderate fragrance; foliage leathery; vigorous growth; PP2629; [(('Serenade' × unknown) × 'Fashion') × 'Golden Masterpiece']

'Sénégal' Cl HT, dr, 1944, Mallerin, C.; flowers very dark crimson, aging to brown/black, 3 in., dbl., intense fragrance; recurrent; very vigorous growth; ['Guinée' × unknown]

'Senff' (strain of R. canina), lp; almost thornless; growth sometimes used as understock; similar to Kukolinsky, but somewhat more disease-resistant

'Sengodea' HT, pb; flowers white with lavender pink edges, dbl., high-centered; intr. 1995

'Senhora da Graça' HT, rb, Moreira da Silva; flowers red with carmine reflections

'Senior' HT, rb, 1932, Spanbauer; bud pointed; flowers scarlet-crimson, open, dbl., moderate fragrance; foliage thick; long stems; very vigorous growth; PP2; ['Richmond' × 'Général Jacqueminot']

'Senior Moment' HT, m?, Benardella, Frank; intr. 2007

'Senior Prom' HT, dp, 1964, Brownell, H.C.; bud long, pointed; flowers China rose pink, 4½ in., 35-40 petals, high-centered, borne singly and several together, slight fragrance; recurrent;

foliage abundant, dark green, glossy; prickles several, short, hooked slightly downward, red to brown; stems long, strong; vigorous, upright growth; hips short, globular, smooth, green; PP2521; ['Pink Princess' × Queen Elizabeth®]; intr. 1964

'Señor Philippe' LCl, m; flowers lilac-pink, center paler, dbl.; vigorous growth

'Señora de Bornas' HT, mr, 1958, Camprubi, C.; flowers vermilion-red, medium, very dbl., cupped, intense fragrance; foliage glossy; vigorous, upright growth; ['J.M. Lopez Pico' × 'Concerto']; intr. 1955

'Señora de Carulla' F, mr, 1961, Torre Blanca; flowers cerise-red

'Señora Gari' HT, yb, 1935, Dot, Pedro; bud long, pointed; flowers deep orange-yellow, very large, dbl., high-centered; sprawling growth; ['Mari Dot' × 'Constance']

'Señora Leon de Aujuria' HT, ob, 1935, La Florida; flowers orange; foliage glossy; vigorous growth

'Señorita' -- See 'Jacdor'

'Señorita Carmen Sert' HT, yb, 1917, Pernet-Ducher; flowers Indian yellow, shaded pale pink, edged bright carmine, dbl.; ['Marquise de Sinéty' × unknown]

'Señorita de Alvarez' HT, mp, 1931, Cant, B. R.; bud long, pointed; flowers glowing salmon, very large, single, cupped; foliage leathery, dark; vigorous growth

Sensass Delbard® -- See 'Delmoun'

'Sensation' HT, ob, Tracy, Sr.; Daniel L.; bud medium, ovoid; flowers orange blend with peach tones, 5½-6 in., 26-30 petals, high-centered, borne mostly singly, moderate fragrance; foliage large, medium green, leathery; prickles medium to large, thin, downward angle; growth vigorous, bushy, upright (24 in.); PP8355; ['Capella' × 'Golden Fantasie']; intr. 1992

'Sensation' HT, mr, 1922, Joseph H. Hill Co.; bud long, pointed; flowers scarlet-crimson, 5 in., 36 petals, open, moderate fragrance; foliage dark green; free, branching growth; ['Hoosier Beauty' × 'Premier']

'Sensucht' F, Noack, Werner; intr. 1978

Sensuous™ -- See 'Sensuous Parade'

'Sensuous Parade' (Carmen™, Sensuous™) Min, mr, Poulsen; flowers medium red, medium, dbl., no fragrance; growth bushy, 20-40 cm.; intr. 2000

'Senta Schmidt' Pol, ob, 1930, Schmidt, R.; flowers coppery orange, semi-dbl.; foliage small, soft, light; dwarf growth; [sport of 'Suzanne Turbat']

'Senteur des Iles' -- See 'Cocdana'

Senteur Royale® -- See 'Tanschaubud'

Senteur Royale® HT, m, Tantau; flowers violet-magenta, 12 cm., very full, cupped, intense fragrance; recurrent; foliage glossy, disease-resistant; compact, upright (60-80 cm.) growth; intr. 2005

Sentimental™ -- See 'Poultal'

'Sentinel' HT, pb, 1934, Clark, A.; flowers velvety cerise, reverse silvery cerise, large, dbl., cupped, intense fragrance; foliage glossy; vigorous growth

'Sentir' HT, rb, Christensen; intr. 1998

'Sentry' HT, dr, 1948, Fletcher; bud long, pointed; flowers clear crimson, 4-5 in., 25 petals; dwarf, compact growth

'Sentyana' Min, m; flowers purple, well-formed, full, high-centered; intr. 1994

Sentyna® -- See 'Intertyn'

'Seppenrade' S, ob, Scholle, E.; flowers salmon-orange, large, dbl.; intr. 1970

'Seppenrade Elfe' HKor, mr, Scholle, E.; flowers crimson, medium, dbl., borne in medium clusters; intr. 1975

'September Dawn' -- See 'Burseptdawn'

'September Days' Min, dy, 1978, Saville, F. Harmon; bud pointed; flowers reflexed, micro-mini, 1½ in., 40 petals, high-centered, moderate fragrance; foliage glossy; upright, compact growth; ['Rise 'n' Shine' × 'Yellow Jewel']; intr. 1976

'September Eighteenth' -- See 'Wilsept'

'September Morn' HT, pb, 1913, Dietrich & Turner; flowers flesh-pink, center deeper, large, full, flat, moderate fragrance; recurrent; vigorous growth; [sport of 'Mme Pierre Euler']

September Mourn™ -- See 'Meiwhiflo'

'September Song' Gr, ab, 1981, Buck, Dr. Griffith J.; bud ovoid; flowers apricot-pink, outer petals fading to blush, 28 petals, cupped, borne singly and in clusters of 5-8, moderate fruity fragrance; foliage dark, tinted with copper, semi-glossy, leathery; prickles thin, awl-like; erect, bushy growth; [('Vera Dalton' × 'Prairie Princess') × ('Apricot Nectar' × 'Prairie Princess')]

'September Wedding' HT, mp, 1964, Schloen, J.; bud ovoid; flowers deep pink, reverse darker, large, dbl., high-centered; foliage dark, glossy; vigorous, tall, compact growth; [sport of 'Montezuma']

'Septime' HGal, m, about 1845, Calvert; flowers light purple, center petals often white, medium, full

'Sequoia' HT, ob, 1939, Verschuren-Pechtold; flowers ripe pumpkin-flesh shaded apricot, dbl., globular; foliage leathery, bronze; vigorous growth

'Sequoia, Climbing' Cl HT, ob, 1940, Swim, H.C.; [sport of 'Sequoia']

'Sequoia Ballet' Gr, pb, Moore, Ralph; flowers blend of pink and white, 3 in., double, borne in clusters; recurrent; tall (6 ft.) growth; intr. 2007

Sequoia Gold™ -- See 'Morsegold'

'Sequoia Jewel' -- See 'Morsewel'

'Sequoia Ruby' -- See 'Mordora'

'Sequoia Twist' -- See 'Morsetwist'

'Serafina Longa' HT, dp, 1933, La Florida; flowers old-rose, heavily veined, well-formed, large; vigorous growth; ['Mme Butterfly' × 'Mme Abel Chatenay']

'Seraphim' -- See 'Seraphine'

'Seraphine' ('Seraphim') HSet, pb, 1840, Prince Nursery; flowers soft pink, center darker, very dbl.

'Serena' HT, Lens; intr. 1955

'Serena' S, mr, Mekdeci; flowers rose red, very full, intense fragrance; free-flowering; foliage glossy; few prickles; tolerates partial shade.; intr. 1996

'Serenade' HT, ob, 1949, Boerner; bud ovoid; flowers coral-orange, 4-4½ in., 28 petals, cupped, loose, slight fragrance; free-flowering; foliage glossy, leathery; vigorous, upright growth; PP852; ['Sonata' × R.M.S. Queen Mary]

Serenade™ LCl, lp, Poulsen; flowers light mauve-pink, 5-8 cm., 15-20 petals, cupped, borne in clusters, no fragrance; recurrent; foliage matte; growth bushy, 150-200 cm.; intr. 2004

'Serenade' F, m, Hiroshima; intr. 2005

'Serenata' -- See 'Barser'

'Serendipity' S, ob, 1978, Buck, Dr. Griffith J.; bud ovoid, pointed; flowers orange to buttercup-yellow, 4-5 in., 20-25 petals, cupped, borne in clusters, moderate fragrance; foliage dark green, glossy, leathery; vigorous, upright, spreading, bushy growth; winter hardy; [(Western Sun™ × 'Carefree Beauty') × ('Apricot Nectar' × 'Prairie Princess')]

'Serendipity' F, my, Harkness; flowers canary yellow, large, cupped, borne in clusters, moderate fragrance; recurrent; medium growth; intr. 2000

'Serene' HT, w, 1940, Mallerin, C.; bud long, pointed, light buff; flowers shining silvery white, open, very large, 30-40 petals; foliage sparse, soft; vigorous, upright growth

'Serene Bouquet' -- See 'Lavser'

'Serenella' HT, 1954, Cazzaniga, F. G.

'Serenella '99' Min, dy, Barni; flowers deep lemon yellow, 2 in., 35 petals, borne in clusters of 3 - 5, no fragrance; recurrent; foliage small; growth to 12-16 in.; intr. 2000

'Serenissima' -- See 'Jacshok'

'Serenissima' LCl, m, 1981, Takatori, Yoshiho; bud pointed; flowers light lilac, 38 petals, intense fragrance; recurrent bloom; foliage large, light green, matte; prickles straight, reddish-green; upright growth; intr. 1980

'Sérénité' HT, my, 1946, Gaujard; bud pointed; flowers chrome-yellow, large; foliage reddish; stiff stems; very vigorous growth; ruled extinct, 07/86

Sérénité® HT, my, 1987, Gaujard, Jean; flowers coppery-yellow, dbl., high-centered, borne singly, intense fragrance; foliage large, medium green; prickles large; tall growth; rounded fruit; ['John Armstrong' × Tanagra®]; intr. 1980

'Sérénité St. Michel' F, my, Adam; intr. 2000

'Serenity' -- See 'Broser'

'Serenity' F, lp, Snetsinger; [sport of Playgirl™]

'Serezo' F, lp, Kakujitsu; intr. 1997

'Serge Basset' HT, dr, 1918, Pernet-Ducher; flowers brilliant garnet-red, dbl.

'Sergeant Pepper' -- See 'Kortenses'

'Sergent Ulmann'   HT, dr, 1930, Mallerin, C.; bud long, pointed; flowers deep garnet, lightened with scarlet, open, very large, semi-dbl.; foliage leathery, bronze; vigorous growth; ['Grenoble' × 'Mme Van de Voorde']

'Serin' -- See 'Luteola'

Serpent Rose® -- See 'Lensnaba'

Serpent Vert® -- See 'Lenwich'

'Serratipetala' ('Fimbriata à Pétales Frangés', 'Œillet de Saint-Arquey', R. chinensis serratipetala, 'Rose Œillet de Saint-Arquey (Vilfroy)')   Ch, pb, 1831, Jacques; flowers medium, petals fringed, outer crimson, inner pink, full, flat, slight fragrance; recurrent; stems red-green, smooth; probably introduced by Jacques in 1831, but lost for many years and reintroduced by Vilfroy, 1912

'Seseragi' ('Brook')   HT, m, Hiroshima; intr. 1996

'Set of Gold'   HT, yb, Delbard; intr. 1994

'Setina' ('Cetina', 'Hermosa, Climbing')   Cl HCh, lp, 1879, Henderson; flowers silvery-rose, medium, full, globular, moderate fragrance; varies considerably; [sport of 'Hermosa']

'Setsuko'   HT, w, 1999, Sasaki, Keiji; flowers cream white, blended red in petal edge, 5 in., 37 petals; foliage dark green, half leathery; growth to 4½ ft.; ['Marchenkonigin' × 'Hakuchoh']; intr. 1996

'Seven Seas'   F, m, 1972, Harkness; flowers lilac, wavy, stamens powder yellow, 4 in., 26 petals, shallow cup, moderate Tea-Damask fragrance; recurrent; foliage large, glossy; ['Lilac Charm' × 'Sterling Silver']; intr. 1971

'777' -- See 'The 777 Rose'

'Seven Sisters' ('Grevillia Rose', 'Platyphylla', R. cathayensis platyphylla, R. multiflora platyphylla, R. platyphylla, R. thoryi, 'Seven Sisters Rose')   HMult, pb, 1815; flowers pale rose to mauve-purple, varying considerably in size and petalage, borne in clusters of 8-30, moderate fragrance; non-remontant; foliage somewhat rugose; vigorous, tall growth; possibly a natural cross of R. multiflora carnea and R. rugosa; sent from China to Charles Greville of London in 1815

'Seven Sisters Rose' -- See 'Seven Sisters'

'Seventeen'   F, pb, 1960, Boerner; bud ovoid; flowers pink-coral, large, 20-25 petals, cupped, borne in pyramidal clusters, intense fragrance; foliage dark, leathery; vigorous, upright growth; PP1765; [('Pinocchio' × unknown) × ('Fashion' × unknown)]; intr. 1959

'Seventh Heaven'   HT, dr, 1966, Armstrong, D.L. & Swim, H. C.; flowers large, dbl., high-centered; foliage glossy; upright, bushy growth; PP2832; [seedling × 'Chrysler Imperial']

'Seventh Heaven'   HT, ob, Fryer; flowers apricot orange, mid-sized, dbl., moderate fragrance; repeats well; foliage glossy, dark green; vigorous, bushy (3 ft. × 2 ft.) growth; intr. 2004

'Séverine'   HT, rb, 1918, Pernet-Ducher; flowers coral-red, passing to shrimp-red, semi-dbl.; foliage bronze; vigorous growth

'Severn Vale'   HT, ob, 1967, Sanday, John; flowers salmon, 4½ in., high-centered; free growth; [sport of 'Beauté']

'Sevillana' -- See 'Meigekanu'

'Sevilliana'   S, pb, 1976, Buck, Dr. Griffith J.; bud ovoid, pointed; flowers light claret-rose, stippled red, yellow from base, 3½-4 in., 15 petals, cupped, moderate spicy fragrance; recurrent; foliage tinted copper, leathery; upright, bushy growth; [('Vera Dalton' × 'Dornroschen') × (('World's Fair' × 'Floradora') × 'Applejack')]

Sexy Rexy® -- See 'Macrexy'

'Sfinge'   HT, rb, 1954, Aicardi, D.; flowers deep red edged rose; long stems; vigorous, upright growth; ['Julien Potin' × 'Sensation']

'Shabnam'   F, w, 1976, IARI; bud ovoid; flowers white, center pinkish, open, 2 in., 85 petals; foliage soft; upright, open growth; ['Baby Sylvia' × unknown]; intr. 1975

'Shades of Autumn'   HT, rb, 1943, Brownell; flowers red to pink with some yellow, center yellow, large, dbl., intense fragrance; free-flowering; foliage glossy, leathery; vigorous, compact, upright, bushy growth; PP542; ['Golden Glow' × 'Condesa de Sástago']

Shades of Pink™   F, pb, 1985, Mander, George; flowers pink with white eye, imbricated, large, 33 petals, borne in large clusters, no fragrance; foliage medium green, glossy; prickles curved, hooked; bushy, upright growth; ['Robin Hood' × Pascali®]

'Shadow'   HT, dr, Dawson; flowers black red, medium, dbl.; stems long; medium growth; intr. 1966

'Shadow Dance'   F, rb, 1969, Fankhauser; bud ovoid; flowers silver-pink edged red, small, 30-35 petals; foliage glossy, leathery; vigorous, low, compact growth; ['Pink Parfait' × 'Crimson Glory']

Shadow Dancer™ -- See 'Morstrort'

'Shadow Ninja' -- See 'Garninja'

'Shady Charmer' -- See 'Micshade'

'Shady Flame'   Min, or, 1981, Jolly, Betty J.; flowers 35 petals, high-centered, borne usually singly; foliage small, light green; prickles straight; compact, bushy growth; [Prominent® × 'Zinger']

'Shady Lady' -- See 'Meisecaso'

'Shady Lady'   Min, dy, 1981, Jolly, Betty J.; flowers yellow-orange, 35 petals, high-centered, borne mostly singly; foliage tiny, green; no prickles; upright, bushy growth; [(Prominent® × 'Zinger') × 'Puppy Love']

'Shady Lane'   HT, pb, 1990, Bridges, Dennis A.; bud ovoid; flowers deep pink to white base, aging deeper pink, large, 35 petals, high-centered, borne usually singly, intense damask fragrance; foliage medium size, dark green, semi-glossy; prickles medium, pointed downwards, light green; upright, medium growth; ['Thriller' × 'Just Lucky']

'Shafter' -- See 'Dr Huey'

'Shaida'   HT, or, 1979, Lens, Louis; bud long, pointed; flowers red-orange-salmon, 3½-4½ in., 28-32 petals, high-centered, borne 3 - 7 per cluster, slight fragrance; recurrent; foliage dark green, leathery; prickles triangular; vigorous, upright growth; [('Fandango' × 'Fillette') × 'Coloranja']; intr. 1976

'Shailer's Provence'   C, lp, before 1799, Shailer; flowers lilac-pink, base white, inner petals rolled and wrinkled, dbl., cupped, often borne in clusters of 2 or 3, moderate fragrance; foliage small; vigorous (4-5 ft.), branching growth; [R. centifolia × R. lheritieranea]

'Shailer's White Moss' ('Ancienne', 'Old White Moss', 'White Moss Rose', R. × centifolia albomuscosa, 'Mousseuse Blanche', 'Double White Moss', 'Blanche', 'Blanc Carné', R. muscosa alba)   M, w, 1788, Shailer; flowers flesh white, center darker, large, dbl., cupped; [sport of 'Common Moss']; very often confused with 'White Bath', and probably mixed in commerce

'Shakespeare' -- See 'Kean'

'Shakespeare Festival'   Min, my, 1979, Moore, Ralph S.; bud long, pointed; flowers clear yellow, 1½ in., 35-45 petals, high-centered, borne singly and several together, moderate tea fragrance; recurrent; foliage medium green, matte; prickles average, slender, hooked downward, brown; stems slender, wiry; bushy, compact (12-14 in.) growth; hips apple-shaped ; PP4656; ['Golden Angel' × 'Golden Angel']

'Shakespeare Garden Eglantine'   HEg, w; flowers white with yellow stamens, single, moderate fragrance; non-remontant; chance seedling found in the old Shakespeare Garden at the Huntington

'Shakira'   HT, dp, Meilland; flowers fuchsia-pink, full, high-centered, borne mostly singly, recurrent; cut flower rose.; intr. 2004

'Shaleen Surtie-Richards'   HT, op, Taschner, Ludwig; flowers coral-pink, large, dbl., borne mostly singly, intense fragrance; recurrent; medium growth; [sport of Electron®]; intr. 1996

'Shalimar'   HWich, yb, 1914, Burrell; flowers creamy blush, picotee edge of bright rose-pink, medium, dbl., borne in very large clusters; occasional autumn repeat; vigorous, climbing growth; [sport of 'Minnehaha']

'Shalimar'   HT, pb, Ghosh, Mr. & Mrs. S.; flowers large, dbl., high-centered; intr. 1998

Shalom™ ('Flammenmeer')   F, or, 1978, Poulsen, Niels D.; bud globular; flowers 3½-4 in., 23 petals, no fragrance; foliage dark green, glossy; vigorous, bushy, upright (150-200 cm.) growth; [('Korona' × unknown) × ('Korona' × unknown)]; intr. 1973

'Shameless' -- See 'Welsham 0600'

'Shandon' HT, dr, 1899, Dickson, A.; flowers deep carmine, center lighter, large, dbl., intense fragrance

'Shanghai Autumn' HT, yb; flowers medium yellow, edges shaded pink; free-flowering

'Shanghai Princess' HCh, lp, Clements, John; flowers soft pink, small; recurrent; foliage dark green; rounded, bushy (2½ ft.) growth; intr. 1993

'Shangri-La' HT, mp, 1945, Howard, F.H.; bud long, pointed; flowers silvery pink, open, 3½-4½ in., 35 petals, intense fragrance; foliage leathery; long stems; very vigorous, upright, bushy growth; PP665; ['Mrs J.D. Eisele' × 'Pres. Herbert Hoover']

'Shania' HT, dp, Delbard; flowers bright cerise pink, large, full, high-centered, borne mostly singly; recurrent; stems long; tall, strong growth; intr. 2005

'Shankar Jaikishan' HT, rb, 2005, Shastri, N.V.; flowers red, reverse light red turning silvery, 4½ in., very full, borne mostly solitary, no fragrance; foliage medium size, dark green, matte; prickles medium, crooked; upright, medium (40 in.) growth; garden decoration, exhibition; ['Captain Harry Stebbings' × 'Christian Dior']; intr. 1997

'Shannie' -- See 'Gelshan'

Shannon® HT, mp, 1965, McGredy, Sam IV; bud ovoid, pointed; flowers rosy-pink, reverse slightly darker, 5 in., 58 petals, high-centered, borne singly; recurrent; foliage large, dark green, semi-glossy, rounded; prickles large, slightly hooked, red to tan; stems stout, erect; vigorous, upright (4-5 ft.), spreading growth; PP2919; [Queen Elizabeth® × 'McGredy's Yellow']

'Shantaraj' HT, dr, K&S; flowers large, full, high-centered, intense tea fragrance; intr. 1998

'Shanthi Pal' HT, op, Pal, Dr. B.P.; flowers salmon, touched coral, large, dbl., high-centered; intr. 1989

Shanti® (Shanty®) HT, rb, Tantau; flowers bright red, white reverse, medium, dbl., high-centered, borne mostly singly; good repeat; stems medium to long; florist rose; intr. 2002

Shantung® -- See 'Delchine'

'Shantung Yellow' Ch, my, before 1867; virtually identical to Marechal Niel

Shanty® -- See 'Shanti'

'Sharada' -- See 'Saroda'

'Shari' HT, pb, 1992, Perry, Astor; flowers lighter than Swarthmore, petals do not burn, large, full, slight fragrance; foliage medium size, medium green, matte; upright (185 cm.) growth; [sport of 'Sweetie Pie']; flowers, growth and foliage same as Swarthmore, flower color lighter; intr. 1993

'Sharifa' -- See 'Ausreef'

'Sharifa Asma' -- See 'Ausreef'

'Sharon' HT, lp, 1962, Spandikow; bud long, pointed; flowers soft pink edged lighter, base light yellow, reverse darker pink, 5½ in., 35-40 petals, high-centered; foliage leathery, dull; vigorous, upright growth; PP2232; ['Golden Rapture' × 'Happiness']

'Sharon Anne' -- See 'Boslorvet'

'Sharon Frances' HT, pb, 1999, Poole, Lionel; flowers light pink blending to peach center, 5½-6 in., full, borne mostly singly, slight fragrance; foliage large, dark green, glossy; some prickles; upright, tall (3 ft.) growth; ['Tom Foster' × 'Ravenswood Village']

'Sharon Lorraine' F, rb, 1981, Bossom, W.E.; bud pointed; flowers ivory yellow, aging red, reverse red, full, borne 30-36 per cluster; foliage dark, semi-glossy; prickles long, red; medium, upright (2-2½ ft.) growth; [seedling × seedling]; intr. 1978

'Sharon Louise' HT, w, 1968, Parkes, Mrs M.H.; bud ovoid; flowers near white, center pale pink, medium, dbl., slight fragrance; foliage dark, leathery; vigorous, tall, bushy growth; [Queen Elizabeth® × 'Virgo']

'Sharon Marie' HT, rb, 2006, Saffell, Jack C.; flowers white edged magenta, reverse white, 5 in., full, borne mostly solitary; foliage large, dark green, semi-glossy; prickles 3/8, facing downward, copper-bronze, moderate; growth upright, medium (5 ft.); exhibition, garden decorative; ['Lynn Anderson' × Sheer Elegance™]; intr. 2006

'Sharon McKenna' Min, my; intr. 2007

'Sharon Muxlow' Min, op, 1980, Dobbs; bud globular; flowers bright coppery orange,, 1 in., 25 petals, flat; foliage leathery; upright growth; ['Anytime' × 'Persian Princess']

'Sharon's Delight' -- See 'Morsharon'

'Sharon's Love' -- See 'Lenruma'

'Sharron with Two R's' -- See 'Jaysharr'

'Shasta' F, w, 1962, Schwartz, Ernest W.; bud pointed; flowers 4 in., 20-25 petals, open, borne in clusters, moderate fragrance; free-flowering; foliage leathery; vigorous, bushy growth; ['Paul's Lemon Pillar' × 'Fashion']; intr. 1962

'Shatadhara' F, mp, Chiplunkar; flowers rose pink, yellow stamens, flat, borne in large clusters; intr. 1991

'Shayela' ("Swonderful") F, yb, 1999, Schakelford, Grace; flowers yellow-orange, reverse lighter, similar to Little Darling, 1½ in., full, high-centered, borne in small clusters, moderate fragrance; foliage small, dark green, glossy; prickles moderate; upright, medium (4 ft.); patio growth; ['Pink Petticoat' × 'Redgold']; intr. 1998

'She' F, or, 1962, Dickson, Patrick; flowers salmon-opal, base lemon, 2½ in., 19 petals, borne in clusters; moderate, bushy growth; [('Independence' × 'Fashion') × 'Brownie']; intr. 1962

'Shearer's Delight' HRg, m, Sutherland; intr. 2002

'Sheelagh Baird' Pol, pb, 1934, Cant, F.; flowers shell-pink, overlaid rich rose pink, base yellow, large, dbl., borne in large trusses; vigorous growth

'Sheena F. Gordon' -- See 'Rawblister'

'Sheena Louise' -- See 'Worcopper'

'Sheer Bliss' -- See 'Jactro'

'Sheer Delight' -- See 'Harwazzle'

'Sheer Elegance, Climbing' -- See 'Devbill'

Sheer Elegance™ -- See 'Twobe'

'Sheer Grace' HT, pb, Patil, B.K.; flowers pink with white stripes and streaks; [sport of 'Sheer Bliss']; intr. 1995

Sheer Magic™ -- See 'Jaceleco'

'Sheer Stripes' S, pb, 1999, Lowe, Malcolm; flowers dark pink and white stripes, 3 in., single, shallow cup to flat, borne in small clusters, slight fragrance; recurrent; foliage medium size, medium green, semi-glossy; few prickles; upright, tall (6 ft.) growth; ['Hurdy Gurdy' × Heritage®]

'Sheerwater' HT, ly, 1977, Plumpton, E.; flowers beige to cream, veined carmine, 5 in., 35 petals; foliage dark, matte green; free growth; ['My Choice' × 'Premier Bal']

'Sheffield Pride' -- See 'Webcyrene'

'Sheila' Pol, op, Walsh, J.; flowers orange-salmon; intr. 1930

'Sheila' HT, mp, 1895, Dickson, A.; flowers bright pink

'Sheila Bellair' HT, op, 1937, Clark, A.; bud long, pointed; flowers salmon-pink, large, semi-dbl., cupped, moderate fragrance; recurrent; foliage rich green, leathery; bushy (4 ft.) growth; ['Miss Mocatta' × unknown]

'Sheila Fleming' Gr, mp, 1995, Fleming, Joyce L.; flowers medium pink with darker edges, prominent stamens, medium, 5 petals, flat, borne 15 - 20 per cluster, moderate fragrance; recurrent; foliage medium size, medium green, matte; upright (120 cm.), bushy growth; ['Märchenland' × 'Montezuma']; intr. 1994

'Sheila MacQueen' F, lp, Harkness; flowers shell pink, fading to blush as petals open, dbl., cupped, borne in clusters, moderate fragrance; recurrent; moderate (2½-3 ft.) growth; often confused with Harwotnext, also named Sheila MacQueen; intr. 1994

'Sheila MacQueen' -- See 'Harwotnext'

'Sheila Mitchell' HT, yb, 1998, Mitchell, Harold V.; flowers yellow shading to pink, reverse lemon yellow, 5 in., 41 petals, high-centered, borne mostly singly; foliage large, medium green, semi-glossy; prickles moderate; compact, medium (3 ft.) growth; [Trumpeter® × 'Grandpa Dickson']; intr. 2000

'Sheila Sorensen' ('Lovace') HT, mp, 2005, Paul Chessum Roses; flowers 7 cm., full, borne mostly solitary, moderate fragrance; recurrent; foliage medium size, medium green, semi-glossy; prickles moderate, medium size; growth upright, medium (80 cm.); bedding, garden decorative; [seedling × seedling]; intr. 2004

'Sheila Wilson' HT, mr, 1910, Hall; flowers light scarlet; vigorous growth

'Sheila's Perfume' -- See 'Harsherry'

'Shekat' F, mp, Sherwood; intr. 1994

'Shelby Wallace' ('Souv de Shelby Wallace') Cl Pol, op, 1929, Moore, Ralph S.; flowers light salmon-pink, small, semi-dbl.; ['Cécile Brunner, Climbing' × unknown]

'Sheldon's Honor' -- See 'Reshonor'

'Shell Beach' -- See 'Trobeach'

'Shell-Pink Radiance' -- See 'Mrs Charles J. Bell'

'Shell Queen' Gr, lp, 1961, Allen, L.C.; flowers shell pink, fading white; [sport of Queen Elizabeth®]

'Shellbrook Pink' HRg, mp; intr. 2003

'Shellbrook Rose' (form of R. acicularis), dr; long, bottle-shaped fruit

'Shelley Higgins' -- See 'Reyshelley'

'Shelly' HT, pb, 1988, Melville Nurseries Pty., Ltd.; flowers pale pink with cyclamen-pink shading, reverse silver flecked and striped with pink-silver, large, 20-25 petals, decorative, borne in sprays of 5 - 6, slight sweet fragrance; foliage dark green, glossy, disease-resistant; prickles slightly hooked, beige-cream; medium growth; [sport of 'Francine']

Shelly Renee™ -- See 'Savashel'

Shenandoah™ -- See 'Poulege'

'Shenandoah' -- See 'Bridoah'

'Shenandoah' LCl, dr, 1935, Nicolas; bud long, pointed; flowers crimson, large, semi-dbl., high-centered, intense fragrance; foliage large, glossy; vigorous, climbing (10 ft.) growth; ['Étoile de Hollande' × 'Schoener's Nutkana']

'Shepherdess' F, yb, 1967, Mattock; flowers yellow flushed salmon, 3½-4 in., dbl., borne in clusters; foliage dark, glossy, leathery; vigorous growth; [Allgold® × 'Peace']

'Shepherd's Delight' F, rb, 1958, Dickson, A.; flowers flame and yellow, 3 in., 15 petals, borne in trusses, slight fragrance; foliage dark green; vigorous growth; [('Masquerade' × unknown) × 'Joanna Hill']; intr. 1957

'Shepherd's Oriole' -- See 'Golden Oriole'

'Sherbert Fizz' ('Sherbet Fizz') S, lp; flowers dbl., borne in clusters; foliage glossy; compact (2 ft.) growth; intr. 2003

'Sherbet Fizz' -- See 'Sherbert Fizz'

'Sheri Anne' Min, or, 1975, Moore, Ralph S.; bud long, pointed; flowers orange-red, base yellow, 1-1½ in., 17-20 petals, cupped, flowers borne singly or several together, moderate sweet fragrance; recurrent; foliage glossy, leathery; prickles few, medium, hooked slightly downward, brown; upright, bushy growth; hips numerous, fairly large ; PP3826; ['Little Darling' × 'New Penny']; intr. 1973

'Sherice' ('Jason') HT, mp, 1999, Sheridan, John; flowers deep pink, reverse paler, medium, dbl., borne mostly singly; foliage medium size, dark green, dull; few prickles; upright (4 ft.) growth; ['Silver Jubilee' × ('Redgold' × 'Golden Slippers')]

'Sheridan Pink' F, dp; intr. 1998

'Sherigrey' ('Dorothy Lloyd') HT, yb, 1998, Sheridan, John; flowers grey with brown center, reverse grey, 4 in., dbl., borne in small clusters; foliage medium size, medium green, semi-glossy; prickles few, medium, straight; bushy, medium (2½ ft.) growth; ['Cream Peach' × 'Paradise']

'Sherijill' ('Jill Carter') F, yb, 1993, Sheridan, John; flowers yellow edged red, small, dbl., borne in small clusters, moderate fragrance; foliage small, dark green, semi-glossy; few prickles; medium, upright growth; ['Sheila's Perfume' × 'Darling Flame']

'Sherijoe' ('Smokey Joe's Cafe') HT, dp, 1999, Sheridan, John; flowers 3½-4 in., dbl., borne in small clusters; foliage medium size, medium green, semi-glossy; few prickles; upright, medium (2½ ft.) growth; ['Red Planet' × 'Pretty Lady']

'Sherilip' ('Linda's Lipstick') F, mr, 1998, Sheridan, John; flowers scarlet red, white reverse, hand painted, 3 in., 8-14 petals, borne in large clusters; foliage medium size, dark green, semi-glossy; prickles moderated, pointed; upright, tall growth; [seedling × 'Picasso']

'Sherilowstri' ('Little Stripes') Min, yb, 1999, Sheridan, John; flowers yellow with orange stripes, reverse yellow, 2 in., dbl., borne in small clusters; foliage medium size, semi-glossy; few prickles; patio; compact, low (18 in.) growth; ['Summer Tan' × seedling]

'Sherimiky' ('Miky Tea') HT, pb, 1999, Sheridan, John; flowers pink blend, reverse cream, 4 in., 8-14 petals, borne in small clusters; foliage medium size, light green, semi-glossy; few prickles; upright, low (2 ft.) growth; ['Cream Peach' × Double Delight™ ®]

'Sherinigel' ('Nigel Quiney') F, w, 2001, Sheridan, John; flowers cream flushed deep pink with cream reverse, hand-painted, large, semi-dbl., borne in small clusters, moderate fragrance; foliage medium size, medium green, glossy; prickles small, pointed, moderate; growth compact, low (2 ft.); ['Little Darling' × 'Old Master']

'Sherired' ('Mike Thompson') HT, mr, 1997, Thompson, Mike; flowers large, full, borne mostly singly, slight fragrance; foliage large, dark green, semi-glossy; some prickles; medium, bushy growth; [('Silver Jubilee' × seedling) × ('Red Planet' × Pharaoh®)]

'Sheriscent' ('Betty Wilson') Min, rb, 1998, Sheridan, John; flowers red, reverse yellow, 2 in., dbl., borne in small clusters; foliage medium size, light green, glossy; prickles few, small, hooked; upright, medium (2 ft.) growth; patio; ['Sheila's Perfume' × ('Little Darling' × seedling)]

'Sherisilver' ('Emma May') HT, mp, 1999, Sheridan, John; flowers light pink, reverse deeper pink, 5-6 in., dbl., high-centered, borne mostly singly; foliage large, dark green, semi-glossy; prickles moderate, upright, medium (3½ ft.) growth; ['Silver Jubilee' × 'Dr A. J. Verhage']

'Sheriskep' ('Mary May') F, rb, 1999, Sheridan, John; flowers red on white, reverse white, 3 in., dbl., borne in small clusters; foliage small, dark green, semi-glossy; prickles moderate; bushy (2 ft.) growth; ['Daily Sketch' × ('Cream Peach' × unknown)]

'Sherlock Holmes' S, lp, Hortico; flowers soft lavender-pink, fading to white, semi-dbl. to dbl., open cup, slight fragrance; recurrent; moderate (3 ft.) growth; intr. 2006

'Sherlock Holmes' -- See 'St. Richard of Chichester'

'Sheroo' HT, mr, Shastri, Dr. N.V.; flowers flower bright, medium red, large, dbl., high-centered; [Pristine® × 'Swarthmore']; intr. 2002

Sherrill Anne™ -- See 'Byrsherrill'

'Sherry' F, r, 1960, McGredy, Sam IV; flowers dark sherry color, coppery-orange to terracotta, 2½ in., 14 petals, borne in clusters, slight fragrance; foliage dark green; vigorous growth; ['Independence' × 'Orange Sweetheart']; intr. 1960

'Sherry Parks Sunrise' -- See 'Jalpark'

'Sherwood' F, my, Harkness; flowers citron yellow, very dbl., moderate spicy fragrance; intr. 1999

'Shi Tz-mei' -- See 'Crimson Rambler'

'Shi-un' -- See 'Shiun'

'Shigyoku' HGal, m; intr. before 1883

'Shii Yan Fueh' HCh, mp

'Shikibu' HT, m, Hiroshima; intr. 1999

'Shiko' ('Purple Fragrance') HT, m, Keisei; intr. 1993

'Shiloh Hill Rose' -- See 'Jalshilo'

'Shimmering Dawn' F, mp, 1965, Verschuren; bud rose-pink; flowers blush-pink, 3 in., borne in clusters; foliage dark, glossy; very vigorous growth

'Shimmering Silk' HT, rb, 1968, Barter; flowers cerise tinted silvery pink, large, dbl.; foliage dark; vigorous, upright growth; ['Ena Harkness' × 'Molly Doyle']

'Shimsha' HT, pb, Kasturi; intr. 1976

'Shin-sei' -- See 'Shinsei

'Shin-Setsu' ('Fresh Snow', 'Sinsetu') LCl, w, 1974, Suzuki, Seizo; bud ovoid; flowers white, center soft cream, large, very dbl., high-centered, moderate fragrance; foliage glossy, dark; very vigorous, climbing growth; [('Blanche Mallerin' × 'Neige Parfum') × ('New Dawn' × unknown)]; intr. 1969

'Shine On'™ -- See 'Dictalent'
'Shiner'™ -- See 'Poulshine'
'Shining Coral' -- See 'Hadcoral'
'Shining Flare' -- See 'Hadflare'
'Shining Hope'™ -- See 'Jacveryp'
'Shining Hour'™ -- See 'Jacyef'
'Shining Light' -- See 'Cocshimmer'
'Shining Ruby' -- See 'Hadruby'
'Shining Star' -- See 'Tulsa'
'Shining Star' ('Mme P. Olivier', 'Trylon') HT, my, 1945, Mallerin, C.; bud long, pointed; flowers vivid chrome-yellow, large, dbl., moderate fruity fragrance; foliage dark, leathery; ['Soeur Thérèse' × 'Feu Pernet-Ducher']
'Shining Sun' HT, yb, 1932, Van Rossem; bud long, pointed, golden yellow splashed scarlet; flowers yellow deepening to reddish center, dbl.; foliage thick, bronze; vigorous growth; ['Charles P. Kilham' × 'Julien Potin']
'Shining Sun' -- See 'Mrs Paul Goudie'
'Shinju' HT, lp, 1986, Harada, Toshiyuki; bud large, ovoid; flowers light pink, paler at petal edges, large, 28 petals, high-centered, borne singly or in small clusters, moderate fragrance; foliage medium green, leathery; prickles numerous, medium, slanted downward; vigorous, upright growth; ['Royal Highness' × 'Garden Party']; intr. 1976
'Shinjugai' F, w; intr. 2004
'Shinoburedo' F, m, Keisei; intr. 2007
'Shinsei' ('Shin-sei') HT, dy, 1978, Suzuki, Seizo; bud pointed; flowers well-formed, large, 35-45 petals, high-centered, borne singly, moderate fragrance; recurrent; foliage medium large, medium green, glossy; prickles slanted downward; upright, bushy growth; [('Ethel Sanday' × 'Lydia') × 'Koto']; intr. 1979
'Shirakawa' ('White River') HT, w; intr. 1995
'Shiralee' HT, yb, 1965, Dickson, Patrick; flowers yellow flushed orange, 5½ in., 36 petals, high-centered, moderate fragrance; vigorous, tall growth; [seedling × 'Kordes' Perfecta']
'Shire County' -- See 'Harsamy'
'Shirley' HT, rb, 1933, Dickson, A.; bud shaded russet; flowers light prawn-red, base yellow; vigorous growth
'Shirley' HT, rb; flowers bright red with white reverse,, dbl., high-centered, star-shaped; stems long; narrow, upright, medium to tall growth; intr. 2003
'Shirley A. Ryals' -- See 'Gelryals'
'Shirley Hibberd' T, my, 1874, Levet, F.; flowers small; ['Mme Falcot' × unknown]
'Shirley Holmes' HT, ob, 1960, Mee; bud long, pointed; flowers golden orange, 4 in., 30 petals, intense fragrance; vigorous, bushy growth; ['McGredy's Yellow' × 'Ethel Sanday']; intr. 1958
'Shirley Laugharn' HT, yb, 1976, Swim, H.C.; bud ovoid; flowers creamy yellow, edged pink, 5 in., 35 petals, moderate fruity fragrance; foliage dark; very vigorous, upright, slightly spreading growth; ['Granada' × 'Garden Party']; intr. 1974
'Shirley Marie' -- See 'Dwashirley'
'Shirley Rose' HT, pb, 1966, Lawrence; flowers cream and carmine, loose,, 5 in.; foliage dark; upright growth; [sport of Eden Rose®]
'Shirley Spain' -- See 'Cocharod'
'Shirley Temple' HT, ly, 1936, Engle; flowers light yellow, edged lemon-yellow; [sport of 'Joanna Hill']
'Shiro Yametsu-Hime' Min, w; intr. after 1961
'Shirpa' LCl, op, Eve, A.; flowers dark coral pink, 3 in., loose; free-flowering; vigorous (10-13 ft.) growth; intr. 1976
'Shirynne Cowan' -- See 'Manian'
'Shiun' ('Shi-un') HT, m, 1985, Suzuki, Seizo; flowers deep lilac purple, reverse deeper, 30-35 petals, high-centered, borne usually singly, moderate sweet fragrance; foliage dark, leathery, semi-glossy; prickles slanted downward; vigorous, upright, bushy growth; [(Blue Moon® × 'Twilight') × ('Red American Beauty' × 'Happiness')]; intr. 1984
'Shizu no Mai' HT, lp, 1991, Ohtsuki, Hironaka; flowers light pastel pink, large, 32-35 petals, high-centered, borne usually singly, slight fragrance; foliage medium size, dark green, semi-glossy; sturdy, upright growth; ['Jana' × 'Madame Violet']
'Shleby Belogorsky' HMsk, w; intr. 1996
'Shobha' ('Beauty Show') HT, ob, Friends Rosery; flowers orange with broad white stripes, large, dbl.; [sport of 'Otohime']; intr. 1988
'Shocking' Pol, rb, 1967, Hémeray-Aubert; flowers dark red, reverse lighter, 3 in., high-centered, borne in clusters; foliage dark, glossy; very low, erect growth; ['Red Favorite' × 'Alain']
Shocking™ Min, m, Poulsen; intr. 2000
Shocking Blue® F, m, 1975, Kordes; bud very large, pointed; flowers lilac-mauve, 2½-3½ in., 28 petals, high-centered to cupped, borne in clusters, intense fragrance; recurrent; foliage large, dark green, glossy, leathery; prickles few, medium, hooked downward, brown; vigorous, upright, bushy growth; PP3846; [('Zorina' × seedling) × 'Silver Star']; intr. 1974
'Shocking Blue, Climbing' Cl F, m; [sport of Shocking Blue®]; intr. after 1974
'Shocking Pink' HT, mp, 1970, McCannon; flowers large, dbl., cupped, intense fragrance; foliage leathery; vigorous, upright growth; PP3072; [sport of 'Pink Sensation']; intr. 1968
'Shocking Sky' -- See 'Korgenda'
Shockwave™ -- See 'Wekgojolo'
'Shogun' ('Constanze') LCl, pb, Tantau; flowers deep pink, lighter reverse, 3-4 in., dbl., high-centered, borne usually in clusters, slight fragrance; recurrent; strong (10-13 ft.) growth; intr. 2000
'Shola' F, mr, 1971, IARI; bud pointed; flowers sparkling orient red, medium, dbl.; foliage leathery; vigorous, dwarf growth; ['Anna Wheatcroft' × unknown]; intr. 1969
'Shona' -- See 'Dicdrum'
'Shonoburedo' F, m, Keisei; intr. 2007
'Shooting Star' Min, yb, 1972, Meilland; bud ovoid; flowers yellow, tipped red, small, dbl., cupped, slight fragrance; foliage small, light, soft; vigorous, dwarf growth; ['Rumba' × ('Dany Robin' × 'Perla de Montserrat')]
'Shooting Star' F, yb, Diby's; flowers yellow, turning to pink, aging to crimson, borne in well-formed trusses; intr. 2005
'Shootout' Min, ab, 1981, Borst, Jim; bud ovoid; flowers apricot-orange, 28 petals, borne singly; foliage medium green; prickles long, triangular, light green; vigorous, bushy growth; ['Tiki' × 'Darling Flame']
'Short 'n' Sweet' -- See 'Tinshort'
Shortcake™ -- See 'Keibelmi'
'Shot Silk, Climbing' Cl HT, pb, 1931, Knight, G. (also Low, 1935); flowers pale-cerise with a golden glow and orange center, large, dbl., high-centered to loose; foliage large, dark green, glossy; growth to 10 ft.; [sport of 'Shot Silk']
'Shot Silk' HT, pb, 1924, Dickson, A.; flowers cherry-cerise, shading to golden yellow at base, medium, 27 petals, loose, intense tea fragrance; recurrent; foliage glossy, slightly curled; vigorous, compact (3 ft.) growth; [('Hugh Dickson' × unknown) × 'Sunstar']
'Show' HT, lp, RvS-Melle; ['Frederik Chopin' × 'Mme Butterfly']; intr. 1993
'Show 'n' Tell' -- See 'Foutell'
'Show Carpet' -- See 'Lavbric'
'Show Garden' ('Everblooming Pillar No. 82', 'Pink Arctic') LCl, mp, 1954, Brownell; bud medium, pointed; flowers crimson to rose-bengal, then magenta, 4-5 in., 40-45 petals, rounded, borne singly and in small clusters, slight tea fragrance; remontant; prickles several, ⅓ in., red to clear; stems long, stiff; growth like a hybrid tea, with additional canes going to 10 ft.; PP1295; [seedling × 'Queen o' the Lakes']
'Show Girl' HT, mp, 1946, Lammerts, Dr. Walter; bud long, pointed; flowers rose-pink, deepening to claret pink, 3½-4½ in., 15-20 petals, high-centered, moderate fragrance; foliage leathery; vigorous, upright, bushy growth; PP646; ['Joanna Hill' × 'Crimson Glory']
'Show Girl, Climbing' Cl HT, mp, 1949, Chaffin; PP892; [sport of 'Show Girl']
'Show Stopper' -- See 'Benseah'
'Showbiz, Climbing' Cl F, mr, Tejganga; flowers scarlet-red, borne in large clusters; [sport of 'Showbiz']; intr. 1995
'Showbiz' -- See 'Tanweieke'
'Showboat' F, yb, 1964, Patterson; bud ovoid; flowers deep yellow on pink to cream ground, 2½ in., 30 petals, moderate fragrance; foliage leathery; moderate, bushy growth; PP2661; ['Carrousel' × seedling]; intr. 1963
Showbound™ Min, op

'Showcase' Min, ab, 1984, Stoddard, Louis; flowers small, 35 petals; foliage small, light green, semi-glossy; bushy growth; ['Rise 'n' Shine' × 'Over the Rainbow']; intr. 1986

'Showdown' -- See 'Tanogrew'

'Showdown' -- See 'Minishow'

'Shower of Gold' HWich, my, 1910, Paul, G.; flowers golden yellow, rapidly fading to pale yellow, 7-8 cm., dbl., rosette, borne in clusters of 5-15, no fragrance; non-recurrent; foliage coppery green, glossy, fern-like; very vigorous, climbing growth; ['Jersey Beauty' × 'Instituteur Sirdey']

ShowMotion® S, yb; flowers light yellow with apricot-tan tones, full, cupped; intr. 2006

'Showoff' -- See 'Arowago'

'Showoff' LCl, mr, 1952, Moffet; flowers scarlet, medium to large, very dbl., cupped, borne in large clusters; profuse, repeated bloom; vigorous growth; [sport of 'Blaze']

'Showpiece' HT, mr, 1958, Ratcliffe; flowers bright scarlet

'Showqueen' HT, mp, Williams, J. Benjamin; flowers pink with lavender shading, dbl., high-centered, borne mostly singly; recurrent; stems long; intr. 1997

'Showstopper' HT, dr, 1981, Warriner, William A.; bud pointed; flowers deep red, spiral, 33 petals, borne singly or 3-4 per cluster, intense fragrance; foliage large; prickles long; strong, upright, bushy growth; PP4851; [seedling × 'Samantha']

Showstopper™ -- See 'Benseah'

'Showtime' -- See 'Noagut'

'Showtime' HT, mp, 1970, Lindquist; flowers large, dbl., high-centered, blooms in flushes, moderate fruity fragrance; foliage glossy, leathery; vigorous, bushy growth; PP3044; ['Kordes' Perfecta' × 'Granada']; intr. 1969

'Showtime' LCl, mr, Lim, Ping; flowers clear red, golden stamens, 3.5 in., 5 petals; recurrent; foliage dark green, glossy; strong (to 8 ft.) growth; PPAF; a climber in warm climates; intr. 2007

'Showy Gold' F, dy

'Showy Miss' HT, dp; flowers warm, unfading pink; free-flowering; short growth; flora-tea

'Showy Pavement' ('Passion', 'Rokoko') HRg, mp, Baum; flowers large, dbl., intense fragrance; low, arching, spreading (2 ft.) growth; intr. 1985

'Showy Pinocchio' Min, yb, Delbard; flowers golden yellow striped and splashed with deep tangerine, fading lighter, dbl., cupped, borne in small clusters; medium growth; intr. 2001

'Shree Dayananda' HT, dp, 1980, Hardikar, Dr. M.N.; bud ovoid; flowers deep pink, 90 petals, moderate fragrance; foliage small, green; prickles beak-shaped; bushy, dwarf growth; ['Scarlet Knight' × 'Festival Beauty']; intr. 1979

Shreveport™ Gr, ob, 1981, Kordes, R.; bud ovoid, pointed; flowers orange, 3½-4½ in., 50 petals, globular to cupped, borne 1-3 per cluster, slight tea fragrance; recurrent; foliage large; prickles small, hooked downward; stems medium, strong; tall, upright, vigorous growth; hips short, ovoid, smooth, yellow-green; PP5157; ['Zorina' × Uwe Seeler®]

'Shrewsbury Show' HT, dr, Fryer, Gareth; flowers crimson, unfading, spiral; intr. 1988

'Shreyasi' HT, m, IARI; flowers plum red with silvery grey reverse, petal base yellow, moderate fragrance; free-flowering; intr. 1992

'Shri Swamy Samarth' LCl, dp, Patil, B.K.; intr. 1992

Shrimp™ -- See 'Poulshrimp'

'Shrimp Hit' ('Birthday Wishes', Shrimp™) MinFl, or, Poulsen; bud broad ovate; flowers bright orange-red, 1½-2 in., 20-30 petals, flat, borne in small clusters, no fragrance; free-flowering; foliage dark; prickles few, concave to flat, yellow-green; bushy, compact (16-20 in.) growth; PP12987; ['Everglades' × 'Victory Parade']; intr. 2001

'Shrimp Pink Castle' -- See 'Poulmax'

'Shringar' F, dp, 1974, IARI; buds small, pointed, flowers deep camellia-rose with lighter reverse and base, medium, semi-dbl., open, borne singly and in small clusters; foliage medium size, glossy; growth vigorous, upright (90 cm.); ['Eiffel Tower' × 'Suryodaya']; intr. 1972

'Shropshire Lass' S, lp, 1970, Austin, David; flowers blush-pink, fading to white, golden stamens, 5 in., single to semi-dbl., flat, borne singly and in small clusters, moderate myrrh fragrance; summer bloom; robust, large (8 ft.) growth; ['Mme Butterfly' × 'Mme Legras de St. Germain']; intr. 1969

'Shrub Cecile Brunner' -- See 'Bloomfield Abundance'

'Shrubby Pink' -- See 'Sunday Times'

'Shu-getsu' -- See 'Shugetsu'

'Shu-oh' HT, or, 1986, Suzuki, Seizo; flowers medium, cupped, moderate fragrance; foliage dark, semi-glossy; prickles slanted downward; upright growth; ['San Francisco' × Pharaoh®]; intr. 1982

'Shugetsu' ('Autumn Moon', 'Shu-getsu') HT, dy, 1985, Suzuki, Seizo; flowers large, 38 petals, high-centered, moderate fragrance; foliage large, dark, glossy; prickles large, straight; upright, bushy growth; ['Seiko' × King's Ransom®]; intr. 1984

'Shunpo' ('Spring Fragrance') HT, lp, Suzuki, Seizo; intr. 1987

'Shunyo' HT, ob, 1985, Kono, Yoshito; flowers light yellow orange, large, 33 petals, high-centered; foliage glossy; prickles sickle-shaped; vigorous upright growth; [('Golden Sun' × Summer Holiday®) × ('Garden Party' × 'Narzisse')]; intr. 1984

'Shurpee' HT, mr

'Shuzao Red' S, mr; from China

'Shy Beauty' -- See 'Lyoshy'

'Shy Girl' -- See 'Jacwhim'

'Shy Maiden' -- See 'Andshy'

'Si' Min, w, Dot, Pedro; flowers rosy white, micro-mini, ¾-1 in., semi-dbl.; foliage dark green; dwarf growth; ['Perla de Montserrat' × ('Anny' × 'Tom Thumb')]; intr. 1957

Si Bemol® -- See 'Lenmol'

'Sibelius' -- See 'Lenbar'

'Sibelius' HT, mr, 1959, Verschuren; flowers velvety crimson, dbl., high-centered; vigorous growth; ['New Yorker' × 'Étoile de Hollande']; intr. 1958

Sibilla® -- See 'Barsib'

'Sibylle' F, op

'Siddartha' HT, rb, Kasturi; flowers red with stripes and splashes of white and green; [sport of 'Christian Dior']; intr. 1973

'Side Kick' -- See 'Pixkick'

'Sidi-Brahim' HT, dy, 1953, Robichon; flowers jonquil-yellow, dbl.; strong stems; ['Feu Pernet-Ducher' × 'Mme Rene Lefevre']

'Sidney Peabody' F, dp, 1956, deRuiter; flowers reddish-pink, well-formed, large, 36 petals, borne in clusters; foliage dark, leathery; very vigorous growth; ['Rome Glory' × 'floribunda seedling']; intr. 1955

'Sidonie' ('Sydonie') HP, mp, 1847, Dorisy; flowers rosy blush to salmon or flesh, medium, full, quartered, borne in small clusters, moderate damask fragrance; recurrent; ['Belle de Trianon' × unknown]; sometimes classed as either Damask Perpetual or Portland

'Siegeslied' -- See 'Bouquet'

'Siegesperle' Pol, ly, 1915, Kiese; flowers small, semi-dbl.; ['Tausendschön' × unknown]

'Siegfried' T, op, 1893, Drögemüller; flowers dark salmon pink, large, full, semi-globular; ['Gloire de Dijon' × unknown]

'Siegfried Sassoon' -- See 'Macjuliat'

'Sieguier' HGal, m, 1853, Robert

'Sielemon' ('Lemon Blush') A, ly, Sievers; intr. 1988

'Siena Vigorosa' -- See 'Korfeining'

'Sieroyal' ('Royal Blush') A, lp, Sievers; intr. 1988

'Sierra Dawn' HT, pb, 1967, Armstrong, D.L.; bud long, pointed; flowers bright pink blend, large, dbl., high-centered, moderate fragrance; foliage dark, bronze, leathery; vigorous, upright, bushy growth; PP2914; ['Helen Traubel' × 'Manitou']

'Sierra Glow' HT, pb, 1942, Lammerts, Dr. Walter; bud ovoid; flowers shrimp-pink, reverse strawberry-pink,, 3½-4½ in., 33 petals, high-centered, moderate fragrance; recurrent; foliage leathery; vigorous, bushy, spreading growth; PP521; ['Crimson Glory' × 'Soeur

Thérèse']

'Sierra Gold' HT, my, 1960, Lammerts, Dr. Walter; bud urn shaped; flowers Indian yellow, 4-4½ in., 45-55 petals, high-centered; foliage leathery, semi-glossy; upright, compact growth; PP2036; [Queen Elizabeth® × 'Tawny Gold']; intr. 1960

'Sierra Lynn' -- See 'Gellynn'

'Sierra Skye' ('Garden Jubilee Sierra Skye') HT, mr, Ping Lim; bud round to oval; flowers deep red with orange tones on petal edge, 2½-3 in., 30 petals, pompon, borne in clusters; recurrent; foliage medium green, satiny; growth shrub or climber, depending upon climate; hips 0.5; PP16661; ['Orange Fire' × 'seedling 5-180A']; intr. 2004

'Sierra Snowstorm' S, ly, 1936, Moore, Ralph S.; bud long, pointed, cream and yellow; flowers open, 2 in., single, borne in clusters; abundant, recurrent bloom; foliage large, leathery, glossy, light; vigorous (5-6 ft.), bushy, arching growth; ['Gloire des Rosomanes' × 'Dorothy Perkins']

'Sierra Sun' HT, rb

'Sierra Sunrise' -- See 'Morliyel'

'Sierra Sunset' LCl, yb, 1961, Morey, Dr. Dennison; bud pointed; flowers blend of yellow, peach, orange and red, 6 in., full, high-centered, borne in clusters; intense fruity fragrance; foliage glossy; vigorous (6-8 ft.) growth; PP2322; [('Capt. Thomas' × 'Joanna Hill') × 'Mme Kriloff']; intr. 1961

'Sierra's Smile' Min, ob, 2004, Wells, Verlie W.; flowers gray orange, 2 in., very full, borne mostly solitary, no fragrance; foliage medium size, dark green, semi-glossy; prickles ¼ in., straight; spreading, medium (2 ft.) growth; exhibition, garden decoration; [seedling × seedling]; intr. 2004

'Sieska Fervid' F, Klimenko, V. N.

'Sieson' ('Crimson Blush') A, dr, Sievers; intr. 1988

'Siesta' F, or, 1966, Meilland; flowers light vermilion on cream base, large, semi-dbl.; free-flowering; foliage glossy, leathery; very free growth; [Sarabande® × 'Dany Robin']

Siesta® S, pb, Meilland; flowers magenta pink with white eye, small, single, borne in large clusters; bushy (3-4 ft.) growth; intr. 2001

'Sif' LCl, ob, 1969, Lundstad; flowers tangerine-orange, large, 25 petals, cupped; foliage dark, glossy; vigorous, climbing growth; ['Traumland' × 'Royal Gold']

'Sight Saver' ('Sightsaver') HT, lp, Fryer, Gareth; flowers soft pink, 4 in., 30-35 petals, high-centered, borne singly and in small clusters, intense tea fragrance; recurrent; rounded, medium (3 ft.) growth; intr. 1997

'Sightsaver' -- See 'Sight Saver'

'Siglinde' F, Noack, Werner; intr. 1972

'Signal Red' Pol, mr, 1949, deRuiter; flowers scarlet, 2 in., rosette, borne in large trusses; foliage glossy, bronze; vigorous, bushy growth; ['DeRuiter's Herald' × 'polyantha seedling']

'Signal Rot' F, VEG; intr. 1982

Signalfeuer® ('Fire Signal') F, or, 1959, Tantau, Math.; flowers cinnabar to orange, dbl., borne in clusters; bushy growth; ['Lumina' × ('Cinnabar' × unknown)]

Signature® -- See 'Jacnor'

'Signe Relander' HRg, dr, 1928, Poulsen, D.; flowers bright dark red, small, fringed petals, dbl., borne in clusters, moderate fragrance; recurrent bloom; vigorous (6½ ft.) growth; [R. rugosa hybrid × 'Orléans Rose']; intr. 1928

'Signet' HT, dp, 1938, Montgomery Co.; bud long, pointed; flowers deep pure pink, large, dbl., high-centered, intense fragrance; foliage leathery; very vigorous growth; PP199; ['Premier' × 'Talisman']

'Signora' ('Signora Piero Puricelli') HT, ob, 1936, Aicardi, D.; bud long, pointed; flowers orange-apricot, suffused gold, outer petals magenta-pink, large, 27 petals, cupped, moderate fragrance; foliage glossy; vigorous growth; PP201; ['Julien Potin' × 'Sensation']

'Signora, Climbing' Cl HT, ob; flowers deep salmon, pink at center, darker edges, 6 in.; [sport of 'Signora']

'Signora Maria Sgaravatti' HT, Sgaravatti, A.

'Signora Piero Puricelli' -- See 'Signora'

'Sika' HT, op, Dorieux; flowers bright, dbl., high-centered; free-flowering; intr. 1974

'Sila' HT, op, Cocker; intr. 1983

'Silberlachs' ('Silver Salmon') F, op, 1944, Tantau; flowers pale salmon, 6-8 petals, borne in clusters of 3 - 10; foliage light green; upright, bushy growth; ['Rosenelfe' × 'Hamburg']

'Silberzauber' F, mp, GPG Bad Langensalza; flowers large, dbl.; intr. 1985

'Silbixlar' ('Georgie Bee') HT, rb, 2005, Smith, John T; flowers dark red with white reverse, petal edges darker, 6 in., very full, decorative, borne mostly solitary, no fragrance; foliage large, dark green, semi-glossy; prickles long, hooked downward, brown, moderate; growth upright (4-5 ft.); hedging; ['Gemini' × 'Donna Darling']

'Silbluebell' ('Mary C') HT, pb, 2005, Smith, John T; flowers medium pink, reverse white, 4½-5 in., full, high-centered, borne mostly solitary; foliage medium size, dark green, semi-glossy; prickles long, straight, light red, moderate; growth compact, medium (3½-4 ft.); hedging, exhibition; ['Gemini' × 'Donna Darling']; intr. 2007

'Silbyrun' ('Snuffy') HT, op, 2005, Smith, John T; flowers orange, reverse coral pink, 5-6 in, dbl., high-centered, borne mostly solitary; foliage large, dark green, semi-glossy; prickles large, straight, white, moderate; growth vigorous, branching, spreading, tall (48 in.); exhibition; [Gemini™ × Veterans' Honor™]; intr. 2007

'Silchester Sunset' HT, rb, 2004, Paul Chessum Roses; flowers small, dbl., borne in small clusters, slight fragrance; foliage medium size, medium green, semi-glossy; growth upright, medium (80 cm.); beds, borders; [seedling × seedling]; intr. 2004

'Silène' T, op, before 1866; flowers flesh pink, large, full, moderate fragrance

'Silent Night' HT, yb, 1969, McGredy, Sam IV; flowers creamy yellow suffused pink, well-formed; ['Daily Sketch' × 'Hassan']

'Silfairknerr' ('Bob & Linda') HT, pb, 2005, Smith, John T.; flowers dark pink with darker edges, reverse white, 4-4½ in., full, high-centered, borne mostly solitary, no fragrance; foliage medium size, dark green, semi-glossy; prickles medium, straight, red, moderate; growth compact, medium (3½-4 ft.) hedging, exhibition; [Gemini™ × 'Donna Darling']; intr. 2007

Silhouette® HT, w, 1981, Warriner, William A.; bud broad, oval, pointed; flowers creamy white, 5 in., 45-50 petals, high-centered, borne singly; free-flowering; foliage large, light green; prickles brown, hooked down; slightly angular growth; PP4813; ['Tonight' × 'Coral Satin']; intr. 1984

'Silhouette' HT, dp, Richardier; intr. 1999

'Silhouette' -- See 'Miss Harp'

'Silhouette' -- See 'Jacolite'

'Silitalia' ('Dina Gee') HT, rb, 2005, Smith, John T.; flowers red, reverse white, 4-5 in., full, high-centered, borne mostly solitary, no fragrance; foliage medium size, medium green, matte; prickles large, straight, light red, moderate; growth upright, tall (4½- 5 ft.) pillar; [Moonstone™ × Signature®]; intr. 2007

'Siljonscott' ('Randy Scott') HT, w, 2007, Smith, John T.; flowers have a slight yellow cast at center in autumn, 4½-5½ in., full, high-centered, borne mostly solitary; foliage medium, medium green, matte; prickles long, straight, white, moderate; growth upright, slightly spreading, tall (4½-5 ft.); hedging, exhibition; [Crystalline™ × Moonstone™]; intr. 2008

'Silk' HT, w; florist rose; intr. 2001

'Silk Butterflies' -- See 'Mateo's Silk Butterflies'

'Silk Button' -- See 'Korzeito'

Silk Cover™ -- See 'Poultc007'

Silk Hat™ -- See 'Arosilha'

'Silk 'n' Satin' -- See 'Judsilk'

'Silk Parasol' -- See 'Kinugasa'

'Silk Pierrine' Min, w, Taschner, Ludwig; bud pointed; flowers creamy white; vigorous growth; [sport of 'Pierrine']; intr. 2006

'Silk Road' Cl Min, w, 2003, Ishii, Tsuyashi; flowers single, borne in small clusters, slight fragrance; foliage small, medium green, glossy; prickles small, numerous; growth spreading, tall (200 cm.); ground cover, weeping standard; [*R. yakushimensis* × 'Snowball']

'Silk Sash' HT, pb, 1971, Fankhauser; flowers pastel pink, reverse silvery pink, very large, 85 petals, high-centered; foliage dark, leathery; vigorous, upright growth; ['Memoriam' × 'Elizabeth Fankhauser']

Silken Laumann® -- See 'Lavcom'

'Silky Mist' -- See 'Simsilko'

'Silky Petals' HT, dp, Ghosh, Mr. & Mrs. S.; flowers bright, clear, deep pink, dbl., high-centered; intr. 1998

'Silorbright' ('Autumn Spice') HT, ob, 2005, Smith, John T.; flowers brilliant orange, reverse yellow, 4½-5 in., full, high-centered, borne mostly solitary; foliage medium size, dark green, semi-glossy; prickles medium, straight slightly downward, red, moderate; growth compact, medium (3½-4 ft.); hedging; ['Gemini' × 'Donna Darling']; intr. 2007

'Silpinke' ('Pink Promises') HT, dp, 2005, Smith, John T; flowers deep pink, reverse lighter pink, 4-4½ in., dbl., borne mostly solitary, no fragrance; foliage large, medium green, semi-glossy, disease-resistant; prickles short, straight, brown, numerous; growth compact, medium (3-3½ ft.); landscape, garden decoration; [Crystalline™ × Veterans' Honor™]; intr. 2007

'Silsarjo' ('Howard and Sara') HT, mr, 2007, Smith, John T.; flowers medium red with lighter reverse, sometimes with darker edging on petals, 4½-6 in., very full, high-centered, borne mostly solitary; foliage medium, dark green, glossy; prickles medium, straight, light brown, moderate; growth spreading, medium (4-5 ft.); hedging, garden decoration; [Crystalline™ × 'Donna Darlin'']; intr. 2008

'Silsmilark' ('Soul Mate') HT, pb, 2005, Smith, John T.; flowers dark pink, reverse lighter, 4½-5 in., full, borne mostly solitary; foliage large, dark green, semi-glossy; prickles large, slightly downward, red, moderate; growth bushy, medium (3½-4½ ft.); hedging, exhibition; ['Gemini' × 'Donna Darling']; intr. 2007

'Silva' -- See 'Keiromo'

Silva® HT, pb, 1964, Meilland, Alain A.; bud long, pointed; flowers yellowish-salmon shaded bright rose, 5½ in., 38 petals, high-centered, borne mostly singly, slight fragrance; foliage dark, glossy, leathery; vigorous, upright growth; ['Peace' × 'Confidence']; intr. 1964

'Silva Graça' HT, ob, 1956, Moreira da Silva; flowers salmon and yellow shaded pink, well-shaped; ['Michèle Meilland' × 'Comtesse Vandal']

'Silvabella' HT, pb, 1967, Guiseppe, M.; flowers deep pink, reverse carmine-pink, large, dbl., cupped; foliage leathery; upright, bushy growth; ['Dr. Debat' × Eden Rose®]

'Silvana' HT, mp, Spek; flowers clear pink , 12 cm., 30-35 petals, high-centered, borne mostly singly; recurrent; few prickles; stems long; florist rose

'Silver Angel' -- See 'Gelangel'

'Silver Anniversary' -- See 'Meiborfil'

Silver Anniversary™ -- See 'Poulari'

Silver Anniversary™ -- See 'Jaclav'

'Silver Beauty' F, m, 1956, Verschuren; flowers silvery rose-madder; vigorous, bushy growth; ['La France' × unknown]

'Silver Bell' ('Gin no suzu') F, lp, 1976, Takatori, Yoshiho; bud ovoid; flowers soft light pink, 2 in., 35 petals, high-centered; foliage glossy; vigorous, upright growth; ['Gene Boerner' × seedling]

'Silver Celebration' Gr, w; flowers pure white, dbl., cupped, borne in clusters, moderate fragrance; good repeat; foliage semi-glossy; tall growth; intr. 1980

'Silver Chalice' F, lp, Williams, J.B.; flowers silvery pink., single, slight fragrance; foliage reddish; growth to 5 ft.; intr. 2004

'Silver Charm' F, m, 1968, LeGrice; flowers lavender-blue, large, semi-dbl., borne in large trusses; foliage dark; vigorous, low growth; ['Lilac Charm' × 'Sterling Silver']; intr. 1968

'Silver Cloud' F, r, Moore; flowers silver and coffee with cream, dbl., flat, borne in clusters, slight fragrance; free-flowering; sturdy, vigorous, medium growth; intr. 1990

'Silver Cloud' LCl, pb, Benny, David; flowers rich rose magenta, paling to silver tips at the petal margins, dbl, moderate rose/apple fragrance; intr. 2004

'Silver Columbia' HT, pb, 1924, Leonard; flowers clear silver-pink; [sport of 'Columbia']

Silver Dawn™ -- See 'Virmoon'

'Silver Dawn' LCl, w, 1942, Zombory; flowers creamy white, center deeper, stamens golden yellow, open, large, 90-100 petals; foliage large, leathery, glossy, dark; vigorous (10-12 ft.), compact, climbing growth; ['Silver Moon' × 'Silver Moon']

Silver Dream® -- See 'Intergri'

'Silver Enchantment' HT, rb, 1971, Gregory; flowers rich red, reverse silver, conical, large, 36 petals; foliage dark; very free growth; ['Tropicana' × unknown]

'Silver Fox' -- See 'Devspilio'

'Silver Gem' F, m, 1969, deRuiter; flowers silver-mauve, large, semi-dbl., borne in trusses; foliage dark, leathery; bushy growth

'Silver Ghost' ('Escimo') S, w, Kordes; flowers pure white, yellow stamens, 1½-2 in., single, shallow cup, borne in clusters, no fragrance; recurrent; foliage disease-resistant; upright (2 ft.), bushy growth; intr. 2004

Silver Jubilee® HT, pb, 1977, Cocker; bud long, pointed; flowers silvery pink, reverse darker, 5 in., 30-35 petals, high-centered, borne mostly singly, moderate fragrance; recurrent; foliage dark green, glossy; vigorous (5 ft.) growth; [(('Highlight' × 'Colour Wonder') × (Parkdirektor Riggers® × Piccadilly®)) × 'Mischief']; intr. 1978

'Silver Jubilee, Climbing' Cl HT, pb, 1983, Cocker; intr. 1985

'Silver Jubilee' HT, yb, 1937, Dickson, A.; flowers light golden yellow, base chrome, edged canary, very large, dbl., moderate fragrance; foliage very large, glossy; vigorous growth; ruled extinct 04/77

'Silver Lady' F, m, 1991, Taylor, Pete & Kay; flowers pale lavender, with a hint of darker lavender on edges of petals, large, dbl., borne singly and in small clusters, no fragrance; foliage medium size, medium green, semi-glossy; some prickles; medium (90 cm.), upright, bushy growth; ['Azure Sea' × seedling]; intr. 1993

'Silver Lining, Climbing' -- See 'Dicsilving'

'Silver Lining' HT, pb, 1960, Dickson, A.; flowers silvery rose, edges deeper, 5 in., 30 petals, high-centered, borne mostly singly, intense fragrance; recurrent; vigorous (4 ft.) growth; ['Karl Herbst' × (Eden Rose® × unknown)]; intr. 1959

'Silver Moon' HWich, w, 1910, Van Fleet; bud long, pointed; flowers creamy white, base amber, stamens darker, 8-11 cm., single to semi-dbl., borne mostly solitary; may show some repeat; foliage large, dark, leathery, glossy; very vigorous (to 20 ft or more) growth; [*R. wichurana* × 'Devoniensis']; DNA studies have proved that this is not a hybrid of *R. laevigata*

'Silver Peach' Min, ab, Hannemann, F.; ['Silver Jubilee' × 'Oz Gold']; intr. 1989

'Silver Peak' -- See 'Ginrei'

'Silver Phantom' -- See 'Renhom'

Silver Pink® -- See 'Lensilve'

'Silver Princess' HT, ob, 1934, Burbank; bud salmon-yellow to delicate pink; flowers almost ivory-white, tinged pink, very large, semi-dbl.; vigorous growth

'Silver Queen' HP, pb, 1887, Paul, W.; flowers silvery pink and red, shaded rose pink in center, large, full, cupped; [sport of 'Queen of Queens']

'Silver Queen' ('Barsilv') HT, w

Silver River® -- See 'Lensiver'

'Silver Salmon' -- See 'Silberlachs'

'Silver Shadows' HT, m, 1985, Buck, Dr. Griffith J.; flowers light blue-lavender, large, 33 petals, cupped, borne 3 - 5 per cluster, intense fragrance; repeat bloom; foliage large, dark, leathery; prickles awl-like, tan; upright, bushy growth; hardy; [((('Soir d'Automne × Music Maker') × 'Solitude') × (Blue Moon® × 'Tom Brown')) × 'Autumn Dusk']; intr. 1984

'Silver Slippers' -- See 'Pixislip'

'Silver Spoon' HT, m, 1985, Weeks, O.L.; bud large, long pointed; flowers silvery lavender, center and reverse appearing slightly darker, 4½-5 in., 25-35 petals,

The Official Registry and Checklist — Rosa 687

high-centered, borne singly, no fragrance; recurrent; foliage large, medium green, semi-glossy; prickles few, narrow, pointing downward, brownish; upright (4-5 ft.), bushy, spreading growth; PP5858; ['Louisiana' × seedling]

'Silver Star' HWich, w, 1918, Undritz, Frederick R. M.; flowers white with cream tints, large, dbl., moderate fragrance

'Silver Star' Gr, m, Weeks, O.L.; bud large, ovoid; flowers light to medium lavender, 4 in., 24-30 petals, cupped, borne in small clusters, slight fragrance; recurrent; foliage medium green, semi-glossy; prickles numerous, straight to slightly hooked downward; bushy (4-5 ft.) growth; PP14434; ['Sterling Silver' × 'Silver Spoon']; intr. 2001

Silver Star® -- See 'Kordes' Silver Star'

'Silver Tips' Min, pb, 1961, Moore, Ralph S.; bud pointed; flowers pink, reverse and tips silvery, becoming soft lavender, 1 in., 50 petals, slight fragrance; foliage leathery; vigorous, bushy (10-12 in.) growth; [(R. wichurana × 'Floradora') × 'Lilac Time']; intr. 1961

'Silver Wedding' HT, w, 1921, Amling Co.; flowers almost identical to parent; [sport of 'Ophelia']

'Silver Wedding' HT, w, Gregory; flowers white to cream, dbl., high-centered, borne mostly singly, slight fragrance; free-flowering; foliage dark green; bushy (2½ ft.) growth; intr. 1976

'Silver Wedding Celebration' F, w; flowers pure white, medium, full, cupped, borne in clusters; recurrent; foliage medium green; bushy (3 ft.), spreading growth

'Silver Wings' HT, w, 1943, McGredy; bud long, pointed; flowers ivory-white, large, dbl., high-centered; foliage glossy; vigorous, upright, bushy growth

'Silver Wishes' -- See 'Pink Hit'

'Silver World' -- See 'Ginseikei'

'Silverado' -- See 'Arogrewod'

'Silverelda' HT, pb, Riethmuller; flowers veined silvery buff-pink, edged lighter, base yellow, 35 petals; foliage glossy; vigorous, compact growth; ['Heinrich Wendland' × 'Nancy Wilson']

'Silverhill' -- See 'Talsilver'

'Silvery Moon' -- See 'Leosilmu'

Silvia™ ('Silvia Hit') S, dy, Poulsen; flowers deep yellow, 8-10 cm., dbl., no fragrance; foliage dark; growth bushy, 40-60 cm.; PP13104; intr. 2000

'Silvia' ('Sylvia') D, m, 1819, Vibert; flowers light rose-purple, large, dbl.; foliage oval, large

'Silvia' ('Yellow Ophelia') HT, yb, Pierson, F.R.; flowers sulfur-yellow shading to white; [sport of 'Ophelia']; intr. 1920

'Silvia Hit' -- See 'Silvia'

'Silvia Leyva' HT, mr, 1933, Dot, Pedro; flowers cardinal-red, large, dbl., cupped; foliage glossy; vigorous growth; ['Mrs C.W. Edwards' × 'Mari Dot']

Silvina Donvito® F, dy, Barni; flowers ochre-apricot, 6-7 cm., 30-35 petals, cupped, borne in clusters, moderate fragrance; free-flowering; foliage medium size, light green; compact (40-60 cm.), uniform growth; [seedling × Rita Levi Montalcini®]; intr. 2003

'Simmer' ('Mercy') HT, dr, Simpson; intr. 1997

'Simaramam' ('Marama') HT, w, 1980, Simpson, J.W.; bud pointed; flowers 45 petals, high-centered, intense fragrance; foliage large, medium green, semi-glossy; prickles dark brown; bushy, medium growth; ['Lady Helen' × seedling]

'Simba' -- See 'Korbelma'

'Simcho' F, r, Simpson; intr. 1986

'Simchoka' ('Chocolate Prince') HT, r, Simpson; intr. 2003

'Simerose' HT, rb, 1939, Meilland, F.; bud long; flowers nasturtium-red, reverse golden yellow; vigorous growth; ['Charles P. Kilham' × ('Charles P. Kilham' × 'Margaret McGredy')]

'Simetna' ('Tane') F, r, 1980, Simpson, J.W.; bud pointed; flowers 38 petals, high-centered, borne 4-10 per cluster, no fragrance; foliage small, dark, very glossy; prickles short, straight, dark brown; vigorous, upright growth; [(Orangeade® × 'Megiddo') × (seedling × 'Jocelyn')]

'Simfonia' HT, w, Wagner, S.; flowers 29 petals, high-centered, borne mostly singly or in clusters; foliage dark green, semi-glossy; growth vigorous upright; ['Mount Shasta' × Pascali®]; intr. 1977

'Simhaha' ('Hamish') HT, yb, 1980, Simpson, J.W.; bud ovoid; flowers 50 petals, high-centered; foliage medium green; prickles dark brown; vigorous, medium, upright to bushy growth; ['Fairy Dancers' × 'Diamond Jubilee']

'Simhina' Min, dy; intr. 2001

'Simhopan' ('Hot Pants') HT, or, 1980, Simpson, J.W.; bud high-pointed; flowers 48 petals, high-centered, borne usually 3 per cluster, no fragrance; foliage medium green; few prickles; spreading growth; ['Gypsy Moth' × 'Princesse']

'Similam' ('Ilam', 'Roseworld') HT, mr, 1994, Simpson, Nola; flowers 3-3½ in., full, borne mostly singly; foliage medium size, medium green, semi-glossy; few prickles; medium, upright growth; [Melina® × 'Mme G. Delbard']; intr. 1994

'Similor' N, pb, 1840, Boyau; flowers yellowish-carmine, center pink, fading white shaded pink, small, very full

'Simina' F, mp, Wagner, S.; flowers clear pink, 40 petals, cupped, borne in clusters, moderate fragrance; foliage large, dark green, glossy; growth vigorous tall upright; ['Vigorosa' × Allgold®]; intr. 1997

'Simjezbel' ('Anne Kercher') HT, dp, 1980, Simpson, J.W.; bud long, pointed; flowers deep pink, 30 petals, high-centered, borne singly or 3 per cluster; foliage large, dense, medium green; prickles straight; vigorous, very bushy, compact growth; ['First Prize' × seedling]

'Simkayjay' ('Kirsty Jane') F, or, 1980, Simpson, J.W.; bud ovoid; flowers fluted, 28 petals, borne 3-10 per cluster, no fragrance; foliage medium size, glossy; prickles straight brown; bushy, vigorous growth; [(Orangeade® × unknown) × 'Megiddo']

'Simon Bolivar' HT, or, 1966, Armstrong, D.L.; bud ovoid; flowers bright orange-red, 4-5 in., 30-40 petals, high-centered, borne singly and in small clusters, slight fragrance; good repeat; foliage dark, glossy, leathery; prickles numerous, medium, straight to hooked downward, reddish brown; stems medium, strong; vigorous, upright, bushy growth; PP2705; ['Roundelay' × 'El Capitan']

'Simon de St Jean' HP, m, 1861, Liabaud; flowers velvety purple, dbl.

'Simon Dot' -- See 'Dotsurodo'

'Simon Estes' ('Bucaroo', 'Buckaroo') S, mp, 2006, Buck, Dr. Griffith J.; flowers full, borne mostly solitary; foliage medium size, medium green, semi-glossy; prickles ½ in., awl, brownish-tan, moderate; growth upright, medium (3-4 ft.); garden decorative; ['Carefree Beauty' × ('The Yeoman' × 'Country Dancer')]; intr. 2003

'Simon Fraser' S, mp, 1992, Svejda, Felicitas, & Ogilvie, Ian S.; bud ovoid; flowers have 5 petals during intial bloom flush, subsequent cycles have 20+ petals, 2 in., single, then double, cupped, then flat, borne singly and in small clusters, slight fragrance; foliage dark green, semi-glossy; prickles some, slightly concave, brown; low (60 cm.), upright growth; extremely winter hardy; PP9178; [(('Bonanza' × 'Arthur Bell') × ('Red Dawn' × 'Suzanne')) × ((R. × kordesii × unknown) × Champlain)]; intr. 1992

'Simon Robinson' -- See 'Trobwich'

Simona® HT, lp, Tantau; flowers large, double, high-centered, borne mostly singly, moderate fragrance; recurrent; stems medium to long; florist rose; intr. 2006

'Simona' -- See 'Tanmosina'

'Simone' HT, w, 1924, Buatois; flowers flesh-white, center deeper pink, passing to creamy white, dbl., moderate fragrance; ['Mme Caroline Testout' × 'Paul Monnier']

'Simone' ('Mauve Mallerin', 'Parme') HT, m, Mallerin, C.; bud ovoid; flowers pastel lilac, 6 in., 50 petals, high-centered, moderate fragrance; foliage leathery, dark, glossy; vigorous growth; PP1847; [('Peace' × 'Independence') × 'Grey Pearl']; intr. 1957

'Simone Damaury' HT, dr, 1925, Soupert & Notting; bud long, pointed; flowers brilliant crimson, semi-dbl.; ['Liberty' × 'Gen. MacArthur']

'Simone de Chevigné' HT, pb, 1924, Pernet-Ducher; flowers flesh-pink, shaded yellow, dbl.

'Simone de Nanteuil' HT, pb, 1925, Schwartz, A.; bud long, pointed; flowers rosy white, tinted carmine-pink, reverse flesh, dbl.; ['Ophelia' × 'Mme Vittoria Gagniere']

'Simone Guérin' HT, my, 1929, Mallerin, C.; flowers coral-yellow, large, semi-dbl., high-centered, slight fragrance; foliage glossy, dark green; vigorous growth; ['Constance' × 'hybrid tea seedling']

'Simone Labbé' HT, ab, 1922, Ketten Bros.; bud long, pointed; flowers apricot-yellow, passing to clear saffron-yellow, dbl.; ['Le Progres' × 'Lady Greenall']

'Simone Mayery' HT, yb, 1937, Chambard, C.; bud long, pointed, cream-yellow, shaded carmine-pink; flowers cream, center dark yellow, very large, cupped; foliage bronze; vigorous growth

Simone Merieux® -- See 'Méduse'

'Simone Thomas' T, rb, before 1927; flowers carmine to coppery-red

'Simonet' -- See 'Metis'

'Simonet's Double Pink Rugosa' HRg, mp, Simonet; flowers pink, smaller than Hansa, very dbl.; non-recurrent; hardy; [R. macounii × 'Mme Georges Bruant' (?)]

'Simpalno' ('Happy Day', 'Velvet Lustre') HT, rb, 1980, Simpson, J.W.; bud pointed; flowers 30 petals, high-centered, borne singly, moderate fragrance; recurrent; foliage large, dark, semi-glossy; prickles brown; strong, upright, medium growth; ['First Prize' × 'Gypsy Moth']

'Simple' -- See 'Single'

'Simple Gifts' -- See 'Korbasren'

Simple Pleasures™ -- See 'Talsimple'

'Simple Simon' Min, mp, 1955, deVink; flowers carmine-rose, base yellow,, dbl.; [((R. multiflora nana × Mrs Pierre S. duPont) × (R. multiflora nana × Mrs Pierre S. duPont)) × 'Tom Thumb']

Simple Splendor™ -- See 'Crlsimple'

'Simplex' Min, w, 1961, Moore, Ralph S.; bud long, pointed, apricot; flowers 1½ in., single, flat, borne in small clusters, slight fragrance; recurrent; foliage leathery; vigorous, bushy (12-14 in.) growth; [(R. wichurana × 'Floradora') × seedling]; intr. 1961

'Simplex' A, w

'Simplex Multiflora' HMult, pb, 1905

'Simplicity' -- See 'LLX8161'

'Simplicity' ('Irish Simplicity') HT, w, 1909, Dickson, H.; bud cup-shaped; flowers pure white, large, single, open; foliage glossy, rich green; declared extinct, ARA 1979

Simplicity™ -- See 'Jacink'

'Simply' S, mp, Noack; flowers soft pink, 1½ in., dbl., cupped, borne in clusters; recurrent; upright (3 ft.), arching growth; intr. 2003

'Simply Beautiful' -- See 'Welodd'

'Simply Charming' F, op, Delbard; flowers soft pink with cream eye, intensifying to coral, prominent stamens, single, shallow cup to flat, borne in clusters, slight fragrance; recurrent; medium (5 ft.) growth; intr. 2005

'Simply Divine' F, rb, 1978, Anderson's Rose Nurseries; flowers large, 18 petals; foliage dark; [Elizabeth of Glamis® × 'Evelyn Fison']

'Simply Elegant' Gr, dy, Delbard; flowers full, cupped, moderate fragrance; medium growth; intr. 2001

'Simply Elegant' -- See 'Busimel'

'Simply Heaven' HT, ly, Dickson; flowers light lemon, tinted bronze, large, dbl., high-centered, borne mostly singly; foliage dark green, glossy; stems long; tall, healthy growth; intr. 2002

'Simply Irresistible' -- See 'Burbrahmvidya'

'Simply Magic' -- See 'Meitobla'

Simply Marvelous!™ -- See 'Jacideso'

'Simply Sunblaze' -- See 'Meidipser'

'Simply the Best' -- See 'Macamster'

'Simply the Best' F, pb, J&P; flowers pink with lighter tones, fades lighter with age, semi-dbl. to double, opens nearly flat, borne in clusters; recurrent; growth medium height

'Simpson's Red' HT, dr, 1977, Simpson, J.W.; flowers large, full; ['Red Lion' × 'Grande Amore']

'Simpson's Ruby' F, mr, Horner; intr. 2006

'Simref' F, mp, Simpson; intr. 2000

'Simsalabim' HT, yb, Kordes; flowers striped; intr. 2002

'Simsilko' ('Silky Mist') HT, lp, Simpson; bud long; intr. 1989

'Simteono' ('Te Moana') HT, pb, 1980, Simpson, J.W.; bud pointed; flowers 38 petals, high-centered, borne mostly singly, intense fragrance; foliage dark, semi-glossy; prickles brown; medium, bushy, upright growth; [('Gypsy Moth' × 'Percy Thrower') × 'First Prize']

'Simway' ('Jenny Charlton') HT, w, Simpson

'Sinbad' HT, op, 1964, Leenders, J.; flowers salmon-pink; ['Pink Lustre' × 'Circus']

'Sincera' -- See 'Amistad Sincera'

'Sincerely Mine' Min

'Sincerely Yours' -- See 'Mordort'

'Sincerity' HT, ob, 1940, LeGrice; bud long, pointed; flowers flesh, shaded amber and orange, large, dbl.; foliage dark, leathery; vigorous, compact growth; [('Comtesse Vandal' × unknown) × 'Mrs Sam McGredy']

'Sindoor' F, or, 1981, Division of Vegetable Crops and Floriculture; bud long, pointed; flowers 23 petals, borne singly or 15 per cluster, no fragrance; foliage large, glossy, coppery when young; prickles straight, bending downward; upright, tall growth; ['Sea Pearl' × 'Suryodaya']; intr. 1980

Sinea® F, mr, Noack; intr. 2007

'Singalong' -- See 'Macsingal'

'Singin' in the Rain' -- See 'Macivy'

'Single' ('Simple') M, lp, 1807, Wandes; flowers rose pink, medium, single; foliage unequally dentate; prickles numerous, straight, sharp

'Single Bliss' Min, pb, 1980, Saville, F. Harmon; bud short, pointed; flowers deep pink and white, 5 petals, flat, borne in clusters of 5 - 30; foliage very small, very glossy; prickles straight; very compact, bushy growth; ['Seabreeze' × 'Baby Betsy McCall']

'Single Charm' -- See 'Umscharm'

'Single Cherry' HSpn, pb; flowers cerise red, medium, single

'Single Crimson Moss Rose' -- See 'Rivers' Single Crimson Moss'

'Single Moss' -- See 'Centifolia Muscosa'

'Single Pink' HRg, mp, 1930, Smith; flowers medium, single

'Single Red' ('Red Nelly') HSpn, rb; flowers red, white at petal base, small, single

Single's Better™ -- See 'Savabet'

'Sinica Anemone' -- See 'Anemone'

'Sinjun' HT, w, Harada; flowers white with touch of pink in center, dbl., high-centered; free-flowering

'Sinoia' Pol, ob

'Sinsetu' -- See 'Shin-Setsu'

'Siobhan' -- See 'Seasio'

'Sioux' HT, op, Kordes ; bud slender, salmon-orange; flowers salmon pink, medium, dbl., high-centered, borne usually singly; good repeat; few prickles; stems long; florist rose; intr. 2001

'Sioux Beauty' S, rb, 1927, Hansen, N.E.; flowers bright rose, center dark crimson, 100 petals; non-recurrent bloom; hardy; ['Tetonkaha' × 'American Beauty']

'Sir' -- See 'Jolsir'

'Sir Alexander N. Rochfort' HT, ob, 1917, Le Cornu; flowers flesh, center darker; ['Lady Alice Stanley' × 'Marquise de Sinéty']

'Sir Arthur Streeton' HT, mp, 1940, Clark, A.; flowers pink, well-formed

'Sir Basil McFarland' HT, ob, 1931, McGredy; bud long, pointed; flowers orange-salmon-pink, flushed yellow, dbl., high-centered; foliage thick; vigorous growth

'Sir Billy Butlin' ('Sir William Butlin') HT, or, 1969, Gandy, Douglas L.; flowers red-orange, large, 30 petals, cupped, slight fragrance; foliage bronze; vigorous, upright growth; [Bettina® × 'Majorca']

'Sir C. V. Raman' HT, or, Pal, Dr. B.P.; flowers scarlet, large, dbl.; free-flowering; intr. 1989

'Sir Cedric Morris' LCl, w, 1980; bud small, globular; flowers small, 5 petals, borne 20-40 per cluster, slight fragrance; summer bloom only in large quantity; foliage elongated, large; prickles large; very vigorous growth; [R. rubrifolia × R. mulligani]; from the garden of Sir Cedric Morris, at Benton End, Hadleigh; intr. 1979

'Sir Cliff Richard' -- See 'Cliff Richard'

'Sir Clough' S, dp, Austin, David; flowers deep, brilliant pink, large, semi-dbl., shallow cup, moderate fragrance; good repeat; tall (5 ft.), strong, arching growth;

intr. 1983

'Sir Dallas Brooks'   HT, mr, 1963, Smith, R.W.; bud long, pointed; flowers large, dbl., high-centered, moderate fragrance; foliage leathery; vigorous, upright, open growth; ['Ena Harkness' × 'Charles Mallerin']; intr. 1962

'Sir David Davis'   HT, rb, 1926, McGredy; bud long, pointed; flowers deep glowing crimson, base light yellow, dbl., high-centered; foliage dark, leathery; vigorous growth

'Sir David Reid'   HT, mr, 1941, Dickson, A.; flowers crimson-red, large, 25 petals, flat

'Sir Donald Bradman' -- See 'Meiafone'

'Sir Edward Elgar' -- See 'Ausprima'

'Sir Edward's Rose'   HT, mp, Dawson; intr. 1998

'Sir Frederick Ashton'   HT, w, Beales, Peter; flowers white to cream, large, dbl., intense sweet fragrance; foliage dark green, leathery; stems strong; upright, vigorous growth; [sport of 'Anna Pavlova']; intr. 1987

'Sir Galahad' -- See 'Hareasy'

'Sir Galahad'   F, dp, 1967, Harkness; flowers deep pink, medium, dbl.; foliage glossy; ['Pink Parfait' × 'Highlight']

'Sir Garnet Wolseley'   HP, mr, 1875, Cranston; flowers rich vermilion shaded bright carmine, very large, full, borne mostly solitary; prickles coppery brown; ['Prince Camille de Rohan' × unknown]

Sir George Watt™ -- See 'Virwatt'

'Sir Harry'   HT, my, 1990, Bracegirdle, A.J.; bud ovoid; flowers medium, 30 petals, high-centered, borne usually singly, slight fruity fragrance; foliage medium size, dark green, glossy; prickles triangular, brown; bushy, medium growth; hips round, orange; ['Irish Gold' × ('Pink Favorite' × 'Golden Autumn')]; intr. 1989

'Sir Harry Pilkington' -- See 'Tanema'

Sir Henry® -- See 'Koropas'

'Sir Henry Collett™ -- See 'Vircollette'

'Sir Henry Seagrave'   HT, ly, 1932, Dickson, A.; bud long, pointed; flowers light primrose-yellow, large, dbl., high-centered, intense fragrance; good repeat; foliage leathery

'Sir J. C. Bose'   HT, dp, Ghosh, Mr. & Mrs. S.; flowers deep pink, reverse darker, dbl., high-centered; vigorous growth; intr. 2004

'Sir John A. Macdonald' -- See 'John A. Macdonald'

'Sir John Mills' -- See 'Beadaffy'

'Sir John Sebright'   Ayr, mp, before 1866; flowers bright carmine, small, dbl.

'Sir Joseph '   Min, pb, 2004, Smith, Joe and Landers, Brenda; flowers striped with deep pink, medium pink, and light pink, 1½ in., dbl., borne mostly solitary, no fragrance; foliage medium green, semi-glossy; upright, short growth; [sport of 'Aristocrat']; intr. 2005

'Sir Joseph Paxton' ('Paxton') B, dr, 1852, Laffay, M.; flowers deep red tinted violet, well-formed, medium, full, borne in small clusters, moderate fragrance; recurrent; foliage grey green; upright (6 ft.), narrow growth

'Sir Lancelot'   F, ab, 1967, Harkness; flowers apricot-yellow, 3-4 in., semi-dbl., cupped, slight fragrance; recurrent; foliage light green, glossy; upright growth; ['Vera Dalton' × 'Woburn Abbey']

'Sir Lancelot' ('Harglisser (withdrawn)') F, dp, Harkness; flowers dark rose pink, moderate fruity fragrance; large growth; original denomination of Harglisser was withdrawn at request of French authorities; intr. 1999

'Sir Matthew Nathan'   HT, dp, 1927, Harrison, A.; ['Rhea Reid' × 'Laurent Carle']

'Sir Neville Marriner' -- See 'Glanmusic'

'Sir Paul Smith' -- See 'Beapaul'

'Sir Robert Duff   Cl T, lp, 1893, Johnson; ['Gloire de Dijon' × unknown]

'Sir Rowland Hill'   HP, m, 1888, Mack; flowers dark purple/red, large, very dbl.; [sport of 'Charles Lefebvre']

'Sir Thomas Lipton'   HRg, w, 1900, Van Fleet; bud ovoid; flowers very white, medium, dbl., round and cupped, intense fragrance; recurrent; foliage dark, leathery, vigorous (6-8 ft.), bushy growth; [R. rugosa (alba?) × 'Clotilde Soupert']

'Sir Tristram'   F, mr, Attfield; flowers velvety red; medium growth; intr. 2003

Sir Walter Raleigh™ -- See 'Ausspry'

'Sir Walter Raleigh'   HT, ob, 1919, Le Cornu; bud long, pointed; flowers coppery reddish-salmon, reverse deep crimson, dbl.; ['Lady Pirrie' × seedling]

'Sir Walter Raleigh Mutant'   S, ob; flowers orange, moderate fragrance; growth to 1 m.; [sport of 'Sir Walter Raleigh']

Sir Wilfrid Laurier®   LCl, lp; flowers clear rosy pink, dbl., hybrid tea, moderate fragrance; pillar rose growth, remains upright with little support

'Sir William Butlin' -- See 'Sir Billy Butlin'

'Sir William Leech' -- See 'Hortropic'

'Sir Winston Churchill'   HT, op, 1956, Dickson, A.; flowers salmon-pink shaded orange, 5 in., 48 petals, high-centered, moderate fragrance; foliage dark green, glossy; very vigorous growth; [seedling × 'Souv. de Denier van der Gon']; intr. 1955

'Siren'   F, or, 1953, Kordes; bud ovoid; flowers bright scarlet-red, 3-3½ in., 18 petals, cupped, borne in clusters, moderate fragrance; foliage leathery; vigorous, compact growth; PP1197; [('Baby Chateau' × 'Else Poulsen') × 'Independence']

'Sirena' -- See 'Charlotte Klemm'

'Sirena'   HT, rb, 1941, Aicardi, D.; bud ovoid; flowers cardinal-red, center shaded yellow, very large, dbl., cupped; foliage leathery; very vigorous growth; ['Saturnia' × 'Anemone']

'Sirene' -- See 'Charlotte Klemm'

'Sirenella'   HT

Sirenetta®   Min, ab

'Sirius'   Cl HT, mr, 1939, Fitzhardinge; bud long, pointed; flowers cherry-red, center lighter, large, dbl.; intermittent bloom; vigorous, climbing (15 ft.), open habit growth; [seedling × 'Lubra']

'Sirocco'   F, or, 1971, Delforge; bud globular; flowers vermilion-red, large, very dbl., cupped; foliage dark, leathery; vigorous, bushy growth; ['Independence' × Orangeade®]

Sirocco+   HT, ob, Voom, Lex; flowers orange, salmon reverse , double, high-centered, borne mostly singly; recurrent; stems medium to long; florist rose

Sirohi Sunrise™ -- See 'Virgiant'

'Sis' -- See 'Brisis'

'Sisena' -- See 'Charlotte Klemm'

'Sisi Ketten'   Pol, dp, 1900, Gebrüder Ketten; flowers peach pink veined carmine, large, dbl.; ['Mignonette' × 'Safrano']

'Sisley'   HP, mr, 1835, Sisley; flowers rosy crimson, medium, full, flat

Sissel™ -- See 'Poulen012(N)'

'Sissel Renaissance' (Sissel™) S, lp, Olesen; bud pointed ovoid; flowers blush pink to creamy white, 4 in., 45-50 petals, deep cup, borne in clusters (usually of 3), moderate fragrance; recurrent; foliage dark green; prickles few, 7 mm., concave, dark brown; narrow, bushy (75 cm.) growth; PP15388; ['Clair Renaissance' × seedling]; intr. 2003

'Sissi' -- See 'Tannacht'

'Sissi, Climbing' -- See 'Blue Moon, Climbing'

'Sissinghurst Castle' -- See 'Rose des Maures'

'Sister Elizabeth' -- See 'Auspalette'

Sister Hellie™ -- See 'Jaysis'

'Sister Joan' -- See 'Kenmado'

'Sister Kenny'   F, mr, 1954, Joseph H. Hill, Co.; bud ovoid; flowers scarlet, medium, 10-12 petals, flat, borne in clusters; foliage leathery; very vigorous, upright growth; PP1146; ['Baby Chateau' × 'Red Delicious']

'Sister Susan'   HT, rb, Oliver, F.; bud ovoid, yellow stained crimson; flowers cream tinted flesh, center copper-orange, base yellow, medium, 48 petals, high-centered; foliage leathery, glossy, dark; vigorous, spreading growth; ['Mrs Sam McGredy' × 'Soeur Thérèse']

'Sister Thérèse' -- See 'Soeur Thérèse'

'Sisters at Heart'   F, ab, Zary, Keith; bud pointed ovoid; flowers light apricot, 4 in., 35-40 petals, hybrid tea, borne in clusters, moderate spicy fragrance; recurrent; foliage dark green, glossy; stems 14 - 16 in.; medium (3 ft.) growth; PPAF; intr. 2006

'Sister's Fairy Tale' -- See 'Korgrasotra'

'Sitpretty' ('Glenda Marie') F, w, 1999, Sitton, John; flowers white with shrimp pink edges, reverse darker, large, dbl., borne in small clusters, no fragrance; foliage medium dark green, glossy; prickles moderate; bushy, shrub-like, tall (5-6 ft.) growth; [sport of 'Hannah

Gordon']; intr. 2000

'Sitting Bull' HSet, dp, Horvath; flowers deep pink, semi-dbl.; non-recurrent; growth to 6-8 ft.; not hardy

'Sitting Pretty' -- See 'Tinsit'

'Siwa' S, mp, 1910, Geschwind; flowers medium, full, flat, no fragrance; once-blooming; upright (5 ft.) growth; hybrid canina

'Six Flags' ('Manja Mourier', 'Manja') Gr, mr, 1962, Swim, H.C.; flowers cherry-red, 3½-4 in., 25-30 petals, high-centered; foliage slender, leathery, semi-glossy; vigorous, upright, spreading growth; PP1835; ['First Love' × 'Roundelay']

'Six Fours Auri' Misc OGR, w

'Sixteen Candles' F, pb, Harkness; bud pointed ovoid; flowers blend of peach and pink, 4 in., 25 petals, cupped, borne in clusters, slight sweet fragrance; recurrent; foliage dark green, glossy; stems 10 - 16 in.; compact, upright (3-4 ft.) growth; PPAF; intr. 2006

'Sixth Sense' ('Grannie's Bonnet') F, pb, J&P; flowers cerise pink with silver-pink stripes and white eye, semi-dbl., flat, borne in clusters; free-flowering; foliage dark green; bushy, compact, short growth; intr. 1996

'65 Roses' ('Cystic Fibrosis') S, w, Thomson; flowers clear white with yellow stamens, single, flat, borne in clusters, intense sweet clove fragrance; stems long; medium to tall growth; named for Cystic Fibrosis research; intr. 2001

Sizzle Pink™ HT, dp, Marciel, Stanley G.; bud slender, tapering; flowers deep pink, sweetheart, large, 25 petals, cupped, borne singly; foliage large, dark green, matte; prickles declining, olive green; upright, tall growth; PP7562; [seedling × seedling]; intr. 1989

'Sizzler' Min, or, 1978, Saville, F. Harmon; flowers 1-1½ in., 28 petals, high-centered, moderate spicy fragrance; vigorous, upright, spreading growth; ['Sheri Anne' × Prominent®]; intr. 1975

'Sjoukji Dijkstra' Pol, mr, 1966, Buisman, G. A. H.; bud ovoid; flowers scarlet, medium, semi-dbl., borne in large clusters; compact growth; ['Chatter' × 'Paprika']

'Skaggarak' F, mr, 1970, Poulsen; flowers clear red, 3½-5 in., 18-20 petals, open, borne several together, slight fragrance; free-flowering; vigorous growth; hardy; ['Irish Wonder' × seedling]

'Skaidra' HRg, Rieksta, Dr. Dz.

'Skarlagen General MacArthur' HT, dr, 1985, Poulsen, S.; flowers scarlet, large, dbl.; foliage medium size, dark, semi-glossy; upright growth; ['General MacArthur' × seedling]; intr. 1930

'Skinner's Rambler' LCl, lp, 1956, Skinner; bud small, long, pointed; flowers pale pink, open, small, 5 petals, borne in clusters of 10-40; foliage soft green; very vigorous, climbing (20 ft. annually) growth; [R. maximowicziana × unknown]; intr. 1955

'Skinner's Red' S, mr, Skinner

'Skogul' F, dp, 1969, Lundstad; flowers rose-madder, open, 18 petals, borne in clusters; foliage dark, glossy; vigorous growth; [Lichterloh® × 'Lumina']

'Skvost' HT

'Sky High' -- See 'Franriser'

'Sky Tower' -- See 'Somskywer'

'Skylark' F, mp, 1959, deVor, Paul F.; bud urn shaped; flowers pink, reverse darker, 2½ in., 55-65 petals, high-centered, borne in clusters of 3-15; foliage glossy; very vigorous, upright growth; PP1678; [sport of 'Carol Amling']; intr. 1958

'Skylark' -- See 'Ausimple'

'Skyline' -- See 'Tanilyks'

'Skyliner' LCl, Delforge; intr. 1980

'Skylon' HT, rb, 1952, Lowe; bud very long, pointed; flowers orange shaded peach, veined red, 5½-6 in., 26 petals; foliage glossy; very free growth; [sport of 'Mme Henri Guillot']

'Skyrocket' ('Wilhelm') HMsk, dr, 1934, Kordes; bud long, pointed, black-red; flowers bright blood red, 2 in., semi-dbl., cupped to flat, borne in very large clusters, moderate fragrance; recurrent bloom; foliage large, glossy, leathery; vigorous, bushy (6-8 ft.) growth; ['Robin Hood (HMsk)' × 'J. C. Thornton']

Sky's the Limit™ -- See 'Wekprimsoul'

'Slater's Crimson China' ('Belfield (from Bermuda)', 'Old Crimson', 'Yueh Yueh Hong', 'Semperflorens', 'Rosier du Bengale', R. semperflorens, R. indica sertulata, R. indica semperflorens, R. diversifolia, R. chinensis semperflorens, 'Old Crimson China', 'Le Bengale à Bou) Ch, mr, 1790; flowers velvety red-crimson, 2½ in., dbl., borne usually solitary; foliage shows a tint of purple when young; slender stems; growth medium (3-4 ft.); hips round, scarlet; introduced by Slater

'Slats' HT, mp, 1999, Edwards, Eddie; flowers 6 in., full, borne mostly singly, moderate fragrance; foliage large, medium green, semi-glossy; prickles moderate; upright, tall (5-6 ft.) growth; ['Louise Estes' × 'Great Scott']; intr. 1999

Slava™ -- See 'Wilslav'

'Sláva Böhmova' HT, rb, 1930, Böhm, J.; bud long; flowers salmon-red, base golden yellow, large, dbl.; foliage blood-red, mahonia-like; ['Covent Garden' × 'Golden Emblem']

'Slavia' Cl Pol, w, 1934, Brada, Dr.; bud pink; flowers rosy white, 4 cm., dbl., borne in small clusters, intense fragrance; recurrent bloom; vigorous growth; ['Tausendschön' × unknown]

'Slávuse' HT, w, 1936, Brada, Dr.; flowers formed like a cactus dahlia

'Sleeping Beauty' -- See 'Dornröschen'

'Sleeping Beauty' -- See 'Savasleep'

'Sleeping Beauty' HT, w, 1968, Morey, Dr. Dennison; bud long, pointed; flowers large, dbl., high-centered, moderate fragrance; foliage leathery; vigorous, upright growth; [('Frau Karl Druschki' × 'Rex Anderson') × 'Virgo']

'Sleeping Beauty' HT, pb, Hiroshima; intr. 2004

'Sleepy' ('Balduin') Pol, mp, 1958, deRuiter; flowers very small, dbl., borne in trusses; [(Orange Triumph® × 'Golden Rapture') × 'polyantha seedling']; intr. 1955

'Sleepy Time' Min, op, 1974, Moore, Ralph S.; bud long, pointed; flowers soft peach to soft salmon-pink, small, dbl.; foliage small, light, leathery; vigorous, dwarf, upright, bushy growth; ['Ellen Poulsen' × 'Fairy Princess']; intr. 1973

'Sleigh Bells' HT, w, 1950, Howard, P.J.; bud ovoid, cream; flowers white, center creamy, open, large, 40 petals, cupped, intense fragrance; recurrent; foliage leathery, glossy; very vigorous, upright growth; PP1004; ['Capt. Thomas' × 'Eternal Youth']

'Sleigh Bells, Climbing' ('Miriam's White (found)') Cl HT, w, Wilkins; [sport of 'Sleigh Bells']; intr. 1995

'Slot van Laarne' S, lp, RvS-Melle; [R. fedtschenkoana × Pernille Poulsen™]; intr. 1992

'Sly Fox' S, mr, Kordes; flowers bright red, yellow stamens, dbl., cupped, borne in clusters; recurrent; foliage glossy; moderate (3-4 ft.), spreading growth; intr. 2003

'Small Fantasy' Min, lp, 1983, Dobbs, Annette E.; flowers small, dbl.; foliage small, light green, semi-glossy; bushy growth; ['Snow Magic' × 'Blue Mist']; intr. 1982

'Small Miracle' -- See 'Jacimin'

'Small Slam' -- See 'Lavlinc'

'Small Talk' F, my, 1963, Swim & Weeks; flowers 2½ in., 33 petals, high-centered, borne in large clusters; foliage leathery, glossy, dark; compact, low growth; PP2226; ['Yellow Pinocchio' × 'Circus']; intr. 1963

'Small Victories' F, mr, Drummond; intr. 1996

'Small Virtue' Min, w, 1986, Jolly, Marie; flowers small, 48 petals, high-centered, borne singly and in sprays of 2-7; foliage small, medium green, semi-glossy; prickles medium pink; low, bushy growth; fruit not observed; [Party Girl™ × 'Snow Bride']; intr. 1983

'Small Wonder' Min, pb, 1984, Hardgrove, Donald L.; flowers light pink, darker reverse, small, dbl., high-centered, borne singly, no fragrance; foliage small, medium green, semi-glossy; upright, bushy growth; ['Futura' × 'Orange Honey']; intr. 1983

'Small World' Min, or, 1975, Moore, Ralph S.; bud pointed; flowers rich orange-red, 2½ in., 21 petals, flat; foliage small, glossy, leathery; dwarf, compact growth; PP4027; ['Little Chief' × 'Fire Princess']

'Smart' F, op, Kordes; flowers salmon orange, medium, dbl., urn-shaped, borne mostly singly; recurrent; stems medium

(16 in.); florist rose; intr. 1999

Smart Kordana® Min, mp, Kordes; flowers dusky pink, full, high-centered to cupped, borne mostly singly; container plant

'Smart Roadrunner' HRg, dp, Uhl; flowers deep magenta pink, yellow stamens, 2 in., semi-dbl. to dbl., cupped, borne in trusses, moderate fragrance; recurrent; foliage dense, semi-glossy; bushy, upright (2 ft.) growth; groundcover; intr. 2004

Smarty® -- See 'Intersmart'

'Smell Me' HT, dp, Pearce; flowers deep magenta pink, large, dbl., high-centered, intense fragrance; recurrent; vigorous, tall growth; intr. 2005

'Smerisal' HT, op

'Smile' S, pb, Clements, John; flowers pink, edges tinged copper, white eye, golden stamens, 3½-4 in., 12 petals, flat, borne in clusters of 12 - 24, moderate fruity fragrance; free-flowering; upright (4½ ft.), arching growth; PPAF; intr. 2002

'Smile' -- See 'Sunrise Vigorosa'

'Smile' -- See 'Emi'

Smile Kordana® Min, my, Kordes; flowers dbl.

'Smiles' F, lp, 1937, Nicolas; flowers light salmon-pink, semi-dbl., borne in clusters, slight fragrance; recurrent; foliage leathery; compact, bushy growth; PP331; ['Echo' × 'Rev. F. Page-Roberts']

'Smiles' -- See 'Jacsmi'

'Smiley' F, ob, 1980, Murray, Nola; bud pointed; flowers orange, apricot, yellow, shapely, 2½ in., 21 petals; foliage matte green; tall, vigorous, upright growth; ['Arthur Bell' × 'Little Darling']

'Smiling Susan' S, op, Delbard; flowers blend of light peach to burnt orange, semi-dbl., cupped, open, borne in large clusters; vigorous, large, arching growth; large shrub or small climber; intr. 2001

'Smiling Through' F, or, 1976, Anderson's Rose Nurseries; flowers orange to red, 3 in., 27 petals; foliage glossy, light; [Orange Sensation® × 'Mme Louis Laperriere']

'Smiling Wings' F, dp

'Smitfirst' (Summer Serenade®) F, ab, 1987, Smith, Edward; flowers apricot to gold, fading to cream, medium, 25 petals, urn-shaped; foliage medium size, dark green, glossy; prickles medium, pointed, brown; upright, medium growth; hips round, small, orange; [(seedling × Zambra®) × 'Baby Bio']; intr. 1987

'Smithfield Rose' S, ob, Taschner, Ludwig; flowers blend of bright orange, apricot, peach and yellow, large, dbl., loose, borne in clusters; free-flowering; medium, broad growth; intr. 1999

'Smithii' -- See 'Smith's Yellow China'

'Smith's Parish' -- See 'Fortune's Five-colored Rose'

'Smith's Yellow China' ('Jaune of Smith', 'Noisette Jaune', 'Smithii') T, dy, 1834, Smith; flowers sulphur yellow, large, full, cupped; ['Blush Noisette' × 'Parks' Yellow Tea-Scented China']

'Smitling' ('Lady Taylor') F, or, 1982, Smith, Edward; flowers vermilion, medium, 35 petals; foliage medium size, medium green, matte; bushy growth; [Elizabeth of Glamis® × Topsi®]; intr. 1983

'Smits' Briar' HRg; [R. rugosa × R. canina]; used for understock

'Smitsblanc' ('Fragrant Mist') F, w, 1983, Smith, Edward; flowers well-formed, medium, 35 petals, intense fragrance; foliage medium size, medium green, matte; upright growth; [Elizabeth of Glamis® × 'Jubilee Celebration']; intr. 1984

'Smitshort' ('Richard Buckley') F, mp, 1994, Smith, Edward; flowers pale salmon pink, medium, dbl., borne in small clusters; foliage medium size, medium green, matte; some prickles; low (45-55 cm.), bushy, compact growth; ['Lady Taylor' × Regensberg®]; intr. 1992

'Smoke Screen' HT, or, Benardella, Frank; intr. 1997

Smoke Signals™ -- See 'Minaxco'

'Smoked Salmon' Min, pb, 2007, Chapman, Bruce; flowers 4-5 cm., dbl., blooms borne in small clusters; foliage small, dark green, glossy; prickles small, hooked, brown, few; growth upright, short; garden decoration; ['Rise 'n' Shine' × 'First Prize']; intr. 2007

'Smokey Joe' HT, ob, Williams, J. Benjamin; flowers orange, yellow base, smokey overlay, full, high-centered, slight fragrance; intr. 1998

'Smokey Joe' HT, or, Cocker; bud deep copper-orange; flowers burne orange-scarlet with a smokey edge, dbl., high-centered, slight fragrance; medium to tall growth; intr. 2003

'Smokey Joe's Cafe' -- See 'Sherijoe'

Smoking Gun™ -- See 'Moesmoke'

'Smoky' HT, rb, 1970, Combe; bud medium, ovoid; flowers smoky oxblood-red shaded burgundy, medium, dbl., open, borne mostly singly, slight fragrance; free-flowering; foliage medium size, medium green; stems medium; vigorous, upright growth; PP2981; intr. 1968

'Smoky Mountain' Min, m, 1988, Bridges, Dennis A.; bud pointed; flowers deep mauve, medium, 24 petals, high-centered, borne usually singly; foliage medium size, dark green, semi-glossy; prickles straight, pointed, small, tan; upright, medium growth; [Black Jade™ × seedling]; intr. 1989

'Smooth Angel' -- See 'Hadangel'

Smooth Ballerina™ -- See 'Hadbal'

'Smooth Buttercup' -- See 'Hadcup'

Smooth Delight™ -- See 'Haddel'

'Smooth Lady' -- See 'Hadlady'

'Smooth Melody' -- See 'Hadmelody'

Smooth Moonlight™ -- See 'Hadmoo'

'Smooth Perfume' -- See 'Hadperfume'

'Smooth Prince' -- See 'Hadprince'

'Smooth Princess' -- See 'Hadness'

Smooth Queen™ -- See 'Hadque'

Smooth Romance™ -- See 'Hadromance'

'Smooth Sailing' Gr, w, 1977, Davidson, Harvey D.; flowers cream color, 4 in., 30 petals, slight fragrance; foliage dark, glossy; tall growth; ['Little Darling' × 'Pink Favorite']

'Smooth Satin' -- See 'Hadsatin'

Smooth Snowflake™ -- See 'Hadsno'

'Smooth Talk' F, w, 1988, Weeks, O.L.; bud long, pointed ovoid; flowers ivory-white, aging bright white, abundant, 3 in., 25-35 petals, high-centered, borne in clusters of 3-7, slight anise fragrance; recurrent; foliage medium size, medium green, semi-glossy; prickles few, pointed, small, yellow-brown; upright, bushy, compact (3-3½ ft.) growth; exhibition; PP7156; [seedling × seedling]; intr. 1988

Smooth Touch™ -- See 'Hadcup'

'Smooth Velvet' -- See 'Hadvelvet'

'Smuts Memory' HT, dr, 1950, Leenders, M.; flowers brilliant deep crimson-red; ['Sensation' × 'World's Fair']

'Snappie' HT, rb, 1990, Bridges, Dennis A.; bud pointed; flowers medium red with yellow at base, reverse creamy-yellow, aging, 52 petals, high-centered; foliage medium size, dark green, semi-glossy; prickles curved slightly downward, medium, deep pink; upright, medium growth; ['Lady X' × 'Wini Edmunds']; intr. 1990

'Snazzy' F, my, Meilland; [sport of 'Tequila']

'Snedronningen' -- See 'Frau Karl Druschki'

'Sneezy' ('Bertram') Pol, dp, 1958, deRuiter; flowers Neyron rose, small, single, slight fragrance; free-flowering; foliage dark green, glossy; vigorous growth; intr. 1955

'Snehurka' Min, Vik

'Snehurka' Pol, w, 1937, Böhm, J.; flowers small, dbl.

'Snehurka' Min, w, Urban, J.

'Sneprincess' Pol, w, 1958, Bang; bud ovoid; flowers pure white, small, dbl., cupped, borne in clusters; foliage light green, glossy; moderate, upright, bushy growth; [sport of 'Mothersday']; intr. 1953

Sneprinsesse® ('Paree White', 'Snow White') Pol, w, 1946, Grootendorst, F.J.; flowers small, globular, borne in clusters; bushy growth; [sport of 'Dick Koster']

'Sniedze' HRg, Rieksta, Dr. Dz.

'Sniffer' -- See 'Bocrogosnif'

'Sno' Min, w, 1983, Meredith, E.A. & Rovinski, M.E.; flowers 48 petals, high-centered, borne in clusters of 1-3, intense fragrance; foliage narrow, light green, matte; sprawling growth; [seedling × 'Gold Pin']

'Sno Cone' -- See 'Pixsno'

'Snodoll' -- See 'Trasno'

'Snookie' -- See 'Tinsnook'

'Snoopy' HT, rb, 1973, Cadle's Roses; flowers carmine, reverse silver, very large, 28 petals, urn-shaped, moderate spicy fragrance; foliage large, glossy; ['Paddy McGredy' × Rose Gaujard®]

'Snövit' -- See 'Blanche Neige'

'Snövit' ('White Dick Koster') Pol, w, 1946, Grootendorst, F.J.; flowers pure white; [sport of 'Dick Koster']

Snow™ -- See 'Snow Hit'

Snow™ ('Snow Parade') Min, w, Poulsen; flowers white, medium, semi-dbl., slight wild rose fragrance; foliage dark; growth bushy, 20-40 cm.; PP10649; intr. 1998

'Snow Angel' -- See 'Jacwhip'

Snow Ballet® (Snowballet®) S, w, 1977, Clayworth; flowers pure white, 4-5 cm., 45 petals, cupped, slight fragrance; foliage small, dark green, glossy; growth to 16-20 in.; ['Sea Foam' × 'Iceberg']; intr. 1977

'Snow Bear' -- See 'Adasnow'

'Snow Beauty' -- See 'Morden Snowbeauty'

'Snow Bride' Min, w, 1982, Jolly, Betty J.; flowers medium, 20 petals, high-centered, borne mostly singly, slight fragrance; recurrent; foliage medium size, medium green, semi-glossy; bushy growth; PP5579; ['Avandel' × 'Zinger']

'Snow Bunny' -- See 'Moesnow'

'Snow Bunting' -- See 'Brobunt'

'Snow-Bush Rose' -- See 'Dupontii'

'Snow Cap' -- See 'Snowcap'

'Snow Carol' HT, w, Teranishi; intr. 1998

Snow Carpet® -- See 'Maccarpe'

'Snow Cloud' ('Le Plessis Robinson', 'Satina') S, w, Tantau; intr. 1993

Snow Cover™ -- See 'Niagara'

'Snow Cream' HT, w, 1986, Bridges, Dennis A.; flowers cream, yellow stamens, medium, single to semi-dbl., flat, borne singly and in clusters of 4 - 8; recurrent; foliage medium size, dark, glossy; prickles medium, red, hooked; medium, upright, vigorous growth; ['Garden Party' × 'Portrait']

'Snow Crystal' -- See 'Rawsolann'

'Snow Crystal' HT, w, 1982, Verschuren, Ted; flowers large, 20 petals; foliage large, light green, semi-glossy; ['Sonia' × Pascali®]; intr. 1978

'Snow Diamond' -- See 'Koise'

'Snow Dolphin' HT, w, Asami; intr. 1987

'Snow Drop' Min, w; intr. 1975

'Snow Drop' Min, w, Welsh; intr. 1996

'Snow Dwarf' -- See 'Schneezwerg'

'Snow Fairy' F, w, 1964, Camprubi, C.; bud pointed; flowers 18 petals, cupped, borne in clusters, moderate fragrance; foliage dark, glossy, leathery; vigorous, bushy growth; PP2376; ['Virgo' × 'Katharina Zeimet']; intr. 1963

'Snow Flurry' F, w, 1952, Moore, Ralph S.; bud small, long, pointed, tinted pink in cool weather; flowers open, semi-dbl., borne in clusters; foliage leathery, glossy, dark; vigorous, bushy growth; [seedling × 'Red Ripples']

'Snow Goose' -- See 'Auspom'

'Snow Gosling' F, w, Poulsen; flowers 3 in., dbl., cupped, borne in clusters, moderate fragrance; free-flowering; upright (3 ft.) growth; intr. 1982

'Snow Hedge' HRg, w, 1963, Nyveldt; flowers pure white, medium, single; hips red; [(R. rugosa rubra × R. cinnamomea) × R. nitida]

'Snow Hit' ('Pearl Wishes', Snow™) MinFl, w, Poulsen; flowers creamy white, 5-8 cm., full, cupped, borne in clusters, moderate fragrance; recurrent; foliage dark green, glossy; bushy (40-60 cm.) growth; intr. 2000

'Snow Infant' -- See 'Koyuki'

'Snow Kiss' (Schneeküsschen®) Min, w, Kordes; bud blush pink, high-centered; flowers blush white, yellow stamens, 3 cm., semi-double, shallow cup, borne in clusters, no fragrance; recurrent; foliage small, fresh green; upright (12 in.) growth; intr. 1993

'Snow Magic' Min, w, 1976, Moore, Ralph S.; bud short pointed, light pink; flowers medium, 40 petals, cupped, borne in clusters, slight fragrance; free-flowering; foliage small, soft, light to medium green; bushy, spreading growth; ['polyantha seedling' × unknown]

'Snow Maiden' -- See 'Jusmaiden'

Snow Meillandina® ('Snow Sunblaze') Min, w, Meilland; bud large, ovoid; flowers white with yellow tones in center, 2½ in., 85 -95 petals, cupped, borne singly and in small clusters, slight fragrance; free-flowering; foliage dark green, glossy; prickles normal, medium to large, greenish-pink to tan; bushy (12 in.) growth; PP8063; [sport of Lady Sunblaze™]; intr. 1991

'Snow on the Heather' -- See 'Korconta'

'Snow Owl' -- See 'White Pavement'

'Snow Parade' -- See 'Poulnou'

'Snow Pavement' -- See 'Schneekoppe'

'Snow Princess' -- See 'Lavpert'

'Snow Princess' -- See 'Yukihime'

'Snow Queen' -- See 'Frau Karl Druschki'

'Snow Queen, Climbing' -- See 'Frau Karl Druschki, Climbing'

'Snow Queen' HT, w, Taschner, Ludwig; flowers pure white, dbl., high-centered, borne mostly singly, moderate damask fragrance; recurrent; stems long; medium to tall growth; [sport of 'Bewitched']; intr. 2001

'Snow Queen' F, w; flowers double, globular, borne in clusters; recurrent; foliage glossy; intr. 2007

'Snow Rambler' HMult, w, Nieuwesteeg, J.; intr. 1995

'Snow Ruby' MinFl, rb, Clements, John; flowers velvety red, white reverse, dbl., cupped, spiral, borne mostly singly, slight fresh fragrance; medium growth; intr. 1996

'Snow Shower' -- See 'Jacwade'

'Snow Showers' Polyantha, w, 2004, Wilke, William; flowers pure white, reverse white, 1 in., dbl., borne in very large sprays on long stems, no fragrance; foliage medium size, medium green, semi-glossy; prickles 3/8 in., straight out; stems long; growth upright, medium (2½-3 ft.); garden, hedge; ['Sweet Afton' × unknown]

'Snow Spray' F, w, 1957, Riethmuller; flowers pure white, stamens yellow, dbl.; dwarf growth; ['Gartendirektor Otto Linne' × 'Gartendirektor Otto Linne']

'Snow Sunblaze' -- See 'Meigovin'

Snow Twinkle™ -- See 'Morsno'

'Snow Waltz' -- See 'Schneewalzer 87'

'Snow Waltz' HT, w

'Snow White' -- See 'Landisney'

'Snow White' HT, w, 1938, Dot, Pedro; flowers well-formed, large, intense fragrance; PP348; ['White Ophelia' × 'Nuria de Recolons']

'Snow White' HT, w, Joseph H. Hill Co.; bud long, pointed; flowers large, dbl., high-centered, moderate fragrance; foliage leathery, dark; vigorous, bushy, compact growth; ['Joanna Hill' × 'White Briarcliff']; intr. 1941

'Snow White' Min, w, Robinson, T.; flowers white tinted blush, 1 in., dbl., borne in clusters; low (3-6 in.), spreading growth; ['Little Princess (Pol)' × 'Baby Bunting']; micro-mini; intr. 1955

'Snow White, Climbing' Cl HT, w, Cant, F.; intr. before 1965

'Snow White' -- See 'Sneprinsesse'

'Snow Wonder' Min, w, 1980, Lyon; bud ovoid, pointed; flowers 48 petals, borne 3-5 per cluster; foliage tiny, medium green; prickles tiny, curved; vigorous, bushy growth; ['Red Can Can' × 'Baby Betsy McCall']; intr. 1978

'Snowball' -- See 'Boule de Neige'

'Snowball' -- See 'Macangel'

'Snowball' Pol, w, 1901, Walsh; flowers dbl.; ruled extinct ARA 1985

Snowballet® -- See 'Snow Ballet'

'Snowbank' F, w, 1937, Nicolas; flowers white tinted blush, changing to white, large, 30 petals, dbl.; foliage leathery, dark; dwarf growth; PP279; ['Mrs E.P. Thom' × 'Gloria Mundi']

'Snowbelt' ('Cassie') Pol, w, 1997, Jerabek, Paul E.; flowers medium, dbl., borne in large clusters; foliage medium size, light green turning medium green, semi-gloss; some prickles; medium, bushy growth; [seedling × seedling]

'Snowbird' HT, w, 1936, Hatton; bud long, pointed; flowers white, center creamy, very dbl., old-fashioned, intense sweet fragrance; recurrent; foliage leathery; vigorous, compact, bushy growth; ['Chastity' × 'Louise Crette']

'Snowbird, Climbing' Cl HT, w, 1949, Weeks; flowers white, tinged lemon-yellow, 4 in., very dbl.; recurrent; vigorous, tall (15 ft.) growth; [sport of 'Snowbird']

'Snowblush' -- See 'Clesnow'

'Snowbound' -- See 'Lavaway'

'Snowcap' ('Snow Cap') Min, w; flowers antique white, creamy center, very dbl., rosette, borne in dense clusters, slight fragrance; free-flowering; mounded (12-18 in.) growth; intr. 1999

Snowcone™ -- See 'Jacwipet'

'Snowdance' F, w, 1971, deRuiter; flowers 3 in., 36 petals, slight fragrance; moderate, bushy growth; [Orange Sensation® × 'Iceberg']

'Snowdon' HRg, w, Austin, David; flowers pure white, medium, dbl., flat, borne in clusters, slight fragrance; recurrent; large (7 × 7 ft.) growth; intr. 1989

'Snowdrift' HWich, w, 1913, Walsh; flowers pure white, small, dbl., borne in clusters of 20-30; foliage very large, light; vigorous (8-12 ft.) growth; ruled extinct ARA 1985, but is not

'Snowdrift' HWich, w, Smith, W. R.; flowers pure white, small, dbl., borne in clusters of 20-30; non-recurrent; foliage large; intr. 1914

'Snowdrift' S, w, Lim, Ping; flowers creamy white with hint of apricot in center , 2 in., 50 petals, cupped, borne in clusters; recurrent; upright (3 - 4 ft.), uniform growth ; PPAF; PPAF; intr. 2007

Snowdrift™ -- See 'Wilsnod'

'Snowdrop' -- See 'Amoru'

'Snowdwarf' -- See 'Schneezwerg'

Snowfall™ -- See 'Lemfall'

'Snowfire' HT, rb, 1973, Kordes, R.; bud large, pointed ovoid; flowers bright red, reverse white, 4-6 in., 25-35 petals, cupped, flat top, borne singly, slight fruity fragrance; recurrent; foliage large, dark, leathery; prickles numerous, long, hooked downward, brown; stems medium, strong; vigorous, medium growth; PP3014; ['Detroiter' × 'Liberty Bell']; intr. 1970

'Snowflake' -- See 'Flocon de Neige'

'Snowflake' -- See 'White Flower Carpet'

'Snowflake' -- See 'Sunsnofle'

'Snowflake' T, w, 1890, Strauss & Co.

'Snowflake' Min, w, Ludwig Roses; flowers white with faint pink center, dbl.; free-flowering; vigorous growth; [sport of 'Chipper']; intr. 1977

'Snowflake' HWich, w, Cant, F.; flowers pure white, 4 cm., dbl., globular, borne in small to medium clusters, intense fresh fragrance; non-recurrent; foliage dark green, glossy; vigorous, climbing growth; intr. 1922

'Snowflake' -- See 'Marie Lambert'

'Snowflakes' Min, w, 1954, Moore, Ralph S.; flowers small, dbl.; dwarf (6 in.) growth; [(*R. wichurana* × 'Floradora') × 'Zee']

'Snowgoose' -- See 'Barshiflo'

Snowline™ (Edelweiss™) F, w, 1971, Poulsen, Niels D.; flowers white with creamy center, 3-4 in., 31 petals, cupped, borne in clusters, slight wild rose fragrance; recurrent; foliage dark green, glossy; bushy (3-5 ft.) growth; intr. 1970

'Snowman' -- See 'Mattjo'

'Snowsong' HT, w, 1961, Jelly; bud long, pointed; flowers white, base yellow, 4½ in., 20 petals, slight sweetbriar fragrance; foliage dark, glossy; moderately vigorous, upright growth; PP2165; ['Snow White (HT, Hill)' × ('Snow White' × unknown)]; intr. 1961

'Snowsong Supreme' HT, w, 1969, Jelly; bud long, pointed; flowers white, base greenish, medium, high-centered, moderate fragrance; moderate growth; PP2624; ['Snowsong' × 'White Butterfly']; intr. 1965

'Snowstorm' HMsk, w, 1907, Paul; flowers pure white, small, semi-dbl., borne in clusters of 6-20; recurrent bloom; vigorous growth; [*R. moschata* × a climber]

'Snowwhite Climber' LCl, w, 1938, Burbank; flowers large, dbl.; long, strong stems; vigorous climbing growth; PP267

'Snowy Jewel' F, w; intr. 2001

'Snowy Summit' -- See 'Delblan'

'Snuffy' -- See 'Silbyrun'

'Snuggles' -- See 'Renuggle'

'So In Love' F, w, Umsawasdi, Dr. Theera; flowers near white, medium, full, borne mostly singly, moderate fragrance; foliage medium size, medium green, semi-glossy; few prickles; medium, bushy, spreading growth; ['Golden Wings' × unknown]; intr. 1996

'So Pretty' HT, mp, Meilland; flowers light, creamy pink, full, high-centered, borne mostly singly; good rebloom; florist rose; intr. 2004

'Soak Red' F, mr; flowers very full, intense fragrance; medium growth; intr. 2006

'Soaring Flight' HWich, pb, Clements, John K.; flowers salmon pink with gold and apricot centers, 3 in., 8-12 petals, cupped, borne in clusters, moderate sweet/honey fragrance; recurrent; foliage dark green; vigorous, tall (14 ft.) growth; intr. 1996

'Soaring Spirits' -- See 'Wekbecfoj'

'Soaring Wings' HT, ob, 1979, W. Kordes Söhne; bud ovoid; flowers deep dusky orange, golden base, large, 64 petals, high-centered, borne mostly singly, moderate fragrance; recurrent; foliage medium green, matte; numerous prickles; vigorous, upright, bushy growth; ['Colour Wonder' × unknown]

'Sobhag' ('Good Luck') F, ob, 1973, Bansal, O.P.; bud urn shaped; flowers orange, open, medium, semi-dbl., moderate fragrance; foliage glossy, dark, leathery; vigorous, bushy growth; [Orangeade® × unknown]; intr. 1972

'Socalp' ('Moonlight Lady') Min, w, 1985, Eagle, Barry & Dawn; flowers creamy white, center buff pink, small, 52 petals, high-centered, borne singly and in small clusters; foliage medium size, dark, semi-glossy; prickles narrow, red; upright growth; ['Pink Petticoat' × 'Pink Petticoat']; intr. 1986

'Socalt' Min, ob, Eagle; intr. 1998

'Socamp' ('Petticoat Lane') Min, pb, 1985, Eagle, Barry & Dawn; flowers medium pink, deeper in center, light pink reverse, small, 28 petals, high-centered; foliage small, dark, semi-glossy; upright, very small growth; ['Pink Petticoat' × 'Pink Petticoat']; intr. 1986

'Socapan' ('Calumet') Min, yb, 1985, Eagle, Barry & Dawn; flowers creamy yellow, petals edged with pink, 30 petals, high-centered, borne 1-3 per cluster; foliage medium green, semi-glossy; prickles very few, small, red; upright, bushy growth; ['Golden Angel' × 'Golden Angel']

'Socblue' ('Scentillating Blues') MinFl, m, 2003, Eagle, B & D; flowers dbl., borne mostly solitary, intense fragrance; foliage medium size, medium green, matte; prickles small, straight; growth upright, tall (65-70 cm.); garden, cutting, exhibition; [Winter Magic™ × Sachet™]; intr. 2000

'Socbob' ('Sarah Jayne') Min, ob, 2003, Eagle, B & D; flowers orange with yellow base, reverse orange, 3-3½ cm., dbl., borne mostly solitary, slight fragrance; foliage medium size, dark green, matte; prickles small, straight; growth upright, tall (50-60 cm.); garden, cutting; ['Patio Flame' × 'Golden Angel']; intr. 1996

'Socdoc' ('Southern Honey') Min, my, 2003, Eagle, B & D; flowers blushed pink on petal edges as flower ages, large, full, borne in small clusters, slight fragrance; foliage medium size, dark green, semi-glossy; prickles small, straight; growth bushy, medium (40 cm.); garden, cutting; ['Golden Angel' × 'San Jose Sunshine']; intr. 1998

'Social Climber' LCl, mp; bud pointed, ovoid; flowers 4 in., very full, cupped, moderate spicy fragrance; good repeat.; foliage glossy, dark green.; branching (6 ft.) growth; PPAF; [Seedling × Seedling]; intr. 2004

'Société d'Horticulture de Melun et Fontainebleau' HP, w, 1852, Cochet; flowers white, center creamy yellow, medium, full

'Society Belle' -- See 'Tomroz'

'Society Special' -- See 'Chewsos'

'Sockap' ('Southern Dawn') Min, lp, 2003, Eagle, B & D; flowers light pink, reverse deeper pink, with unusual fluting when open, 3½ cm., semi-dbl., borne in small clusters, no fragrance; very quick repeat; foliage small, dark green, semi-glossy, disease-resistant; prickles small, straight; growth bushy, medium (40-45 cm.); garden, containers, exhibition; ['Kapiti' × seedling]; intr. 2000

'Socluck' ('Lucky Me') MinFl, dp, 2003, Eagle, B & D; flowers reverse deep pink with white base, 5-5½ cm., full, borne in small clusters, no fragrance; good repeat; foliage dark green, semi-glossy, disease-resistant; prickles small, straight; growth bushy, medium (40-50 cm.); garden, cutting; ['Heidi' × seedling]; intr. 1993

'Socmagic' ('Bundle of Joy') Min, lp, 2003, Eagle, B & D; flowers light pink with slightly deeper pink in center, 5 cm., full, borne mostly solitary, no fragrance; foliage medium size, medium green, matte, disease-resistant; prickles small, slightly hooked; growth upright, tall (60 cm.); [Magic Carrousel® × unknown]; intr. 2000

'Socmount' ('Aoraki') Cl Min, w, 2003, Eagle, B & D; flowers white/pale pink, reverse white, sometimes darker pink on edges, 4 cm., semi-dbl., borne in small clusters, no fragrance; foliage medium size, medium green, matte; prickles slightly hooked; growth spreading, tall (300 cm.); garden, fences, pillars; ['Jeanne Lajoie' × seedling]; intr. 1994

'Socnoma' Min, ab, Eagle, Barry; intr. 1990

'Sococ' HT, ab; flowers dbl., moderate fragrance

'Socotra' ('Orange Spice') Min, ob, 1985, Eagle, Barry & Dawn; flowers orange, yellow reverse, small, 25 petals, borne singly and in small clusters; foliage small, medium green; prickles very few; short, compact, very bushy growth; ['Over the Rainbow' × 'Over the Rainbow']

'Socpan' ('Panache') Min, pb, 2003, Eagle, B & D; flowers pink/lavender/tan, prominent stamens, 5 cm., semi-dbl., borne mostly solitary, intense fragrance; foliage medium size, medium green, matte; prickles small, straight; growth bushy, medium (35-40 cm.); garden; [sport of Sachet™]; intr. 1995

'Socpeta' MinFl, ob, Eagle, Dawn; intr. 1999

'Socrate' ('Baronne G. Chandon', 'Princesse Marie Dagmar') T, pb, 1858, Moreau et Robert; flowers deep rose tinged fawn, large, dbl.

'Socred' ('Black Magic') Min, dr, 2003, Eagle, B & D; flowers dbl., borne in small clusters, slight fragrance; foliage medium size, dark green, glossy, disease-resistant; prickles small, straight; growth upright, medium (40-50 cm.); garden, exhibition; ['Patio Prince' × Black Jade™]; intr. 1997

'Socsis' ('My Sister') Min, w, 2003, Eagle, B & D; flowers very pure white, long-lasting when cut, 4-5 cm., full, borne in small clusters, intense fragrance; foliage medium size, medium green, semi-glossy; prickles small, straight; growth bushy, medium (40-50 cm.); garden, cutting; [Winter Magic™ × seedling]; intr. 1999

'Socsouth' ('Southern Alps') Min, w, 2003, Eagle, B & D; flowers have slightly pale pink center before flower opens fully, 3½ cm., very full, borne in small clusters, no fragrance; foliage small, dark green, matte; growth upright, tall (120 cm.); shrub or short climber, garden decoration; ['Jeanne Lajoie' × seedling]; intr. 1996

'Socspo' ('Apricot Mist') Min, ab, Eagle, Barry & Dawn

'Sodenia' HWich, rb, 1911, Weigand, C.; flowers bright carmine changing to deep pink, streaked with white to medium pink, 5 cm., dbl., borne in large clusters, no fragrance; good repeat; foliage small, glossy, climbing growth

'Sodori-Himé' ('La Blancheur') HT, w, 1979, Onodera, Toru F.; flowers 4½ in., 30 petals, high-centered, slight fragrance; foliage dark; bushy growth; ['White Knight' × 'White Prince']; intr. 1975

'Soestdijk' F, ob, 1949, Leenders, M.; flowers deep orange, base buttercup-yellow, medium, semi-dbl.; vigorous, compact growth; ['Vanessa' × seedling]

'Soeur Bernède de St Vincent de Paul' HP, dp, 1879, Bernède; flowers large, very full; ['Jules Margottin' × unknown]

'Soeur Emmanuelle' ('Towering Rose Magic') HT, m, Delbard; bud deep rosy mauve; flowers rose-lilac, large, very full, cupped, intense herbal, spicy fragrance; recurrent; foliage dark green, thick, leathery ; prickles reddish ; stems strong; vigorous, tall growth; intr. 2005

'Soeur Kristin' HKor, my, 1984, James, John; flowers large, 20 petals, borne singly; repeat bloom; foliage medium size, medium green, glossy; semi-spreading growth; ['Blanche Mallerin' × (R. × kordesii × (Van Bergen × Soeur Thérèse))]; intr. 1978

'Soeur Marie-Ange' F, w, 1957, Privat; flowers snow-white, very dbl.; bushy, dwarf growth

'Soeur Marthe' M, dp, 1848, Vibert; bud mossed; flowers light pink, darker at center, 7-8 cm., full, cupped, moderate fragrance; once-bloomer; stems mossed; upright (3-5 ft.) growth

'Soeur Thérèse' ('Sister Thérèse') HT, yb, 1931, Gillot, F.; bud long, pointed; flowers golden yellow flushed and edged carmine, large, 25 petals, cupped, slight fragrance; free-flowering; foliage leathery, bronze; vigorous, bushy growth; [('Général Jacqueminot' × 'Juliet') × 'Souv. de Claudius Pernet']

'Soeur Thérèse, Climbing' Cl HT, yb, 1953, Shira; [sport of 'Soeur Thérèse']

Sofiero™ F, mp, Poulsen; flowers medium pink, lightening as they open, 10-15 cm., full, cupped, borne in clusters, no fragrance; recurrent; foliage dark green, glossy; bushy, medium (60-100 cm.) growth; intr. 2000

'Soft Blush' F, lp; flowers soft pearly pink, dbl., rosette; foliage glossy; stems long; growth medium

Soft Cover™ -- See 'Poultc010'

'Soft Meidiland' S, pb, Meilland; flowers soft pink with showy white base, single, borne in large sprays, slight fragrance; recurrent; low (2 ft.), spreading growth; intr. 2005

Soft Morning™ -- See 'Rosoft'

'Soft Scent' F, pb, 1988, Rennie, Bruce F.; bud ovoid; flowers pink blend, reverse light pink, sweetheart, medium, 48 petals, high-centered, urn-shaped, borne usually singly, intense spicy fragrance; foliage medium size, dark green, semi-glossy; prickles straight, medium, red; bushy, medium growth; hips elongated, medium, orange; ['Paul Shirville' × 'California Girl']; intr. 1990

'Soft Steps' -- See 'Flosof'

'Soft Touch' -- See 'Jacouch'

'Softee, Climbing' Cl Min, w, Hannemann, F.; [sport of 'Softee']; intr. 1992

'Softee' -- See 'Morfree'

'Softee, Softee' Min, pb, 2008, Rupert, Kim L.; flowers 1 in., dbl., flat, borne in small clusters; foliage medium, dark green, semi-glossy; no prickles; growth spreading, short (2 × 2 ft.); groundcover, patio standard; ['Softee' × 'Softee']; intr. 2007

'Softly Softly' -- See 'Harkotur'

'Softy' -- See 'Tanpretty'

'Softy' Pol, lp, Tantau; flowers small, dbl.; intr. 1992

'Sogno' HT, mr, 1974, Calvino; bud ovoid, globular; flowers orient red to geranium-like, open, medium, dbl., cupped; foliage large, dark, leathery; vigorous, upright, bushy growth; PP2933

'Sogno Rosa' -- See 'Pink Traumland'

'Soir d'Automne' HT, m, 1966, Dot; bud long, pointed; flowers violet, medium, dbl., cupped; foliage light green, leathery; vigorous growth; [('Sterling Silver' × 'Intermezzo') × ('Sterling Silver' × 'Simone')]

'Soir de Fete' HT, my, Croix

'Soir d'Eté' F, mr, Croix; flowers rose red, slight fragrance; free-flowering; growth medium; intr. 1977

'Soiree' -- See 'Soiree de Bonheur'

'Soirèe' Min, ob, Teranishi; intr. 1997

'Soiree de Bonheur' ('Soiree') S, op, Croix; flowers salmon pink, semi-dbl., borne in clusters, slight fragrance; free-flowering; vigorous (8 ft.) growth; intr. 1993

'Solar Flair' -- See 'Benbaas'

'Solar Flair' Min, rb, 1996, Tucker, Robbie; flowers bright crimson with yellow reverse, small, 6-14 petals, borne mostly singly or in small clusters, no fragrance; foliage small, dark green, glossy; some prickles; compact, low growth; ['Rise 'n' Shine' × Captivation™]

'Solar Flare' -- See 'Capflare'

'Solar Flare' F, ob, Tolmasoff, Jan; flowers burnt orange with some gold on the reverse, 1½ in., no fragrance; blooms continuously; growth to 2½ ft.; [sport of 'Charisma']; intr. 2001

'Solar Flash' -- See 'Capflare'

'Solar Sensation' -- See 'Gelsol'

'Solarflare' -- See 'Capflare'

'Solarflash' -- See 'Capflare'

'Solaria' HT, or, 1979, W. Kordes Söhne; bud long, pointed; flowers dbl., cupped; foliage dark; upright growth; [(Anabell® × 'Zorina') × seedling]; intr. 1976

'Solarium' HWich, w, 1925, Turbat; flowers velvety vermilion-red, stamens yellow, 6 cm., single, borne in clusters of 15-20; foliage rich glossy green; very vigorous, climbing growth

'Soldier Boy' LCl, mr, 1953, LeGrice;

flowers scarlet, 4 in., single, borne in small clusters, slight fragrance; recurrent; vigorous, pillar growth; hips red; [seedling × 'Guinee']

'Soldier's Pride' HT, dr, 1987, MacLeod, Major C.A.; flowers medium, full; foliage medium size, dark green, semi-glossy; upright growth; ['Red Planet' × 'Clare']

'Sole di San Remo' S, Mansuino; intr. 1975

'Soleil Brillant' HGal, dp, before 1790; bud yellow-green; flowers medium, moderate fragrance; from Holland; Agathe group

'Soleil d'Angers' HFt, yb, 1910, Détriché; flowers orange-yellow, medium, very dbl., cupped to flat; [sport of 'Soleil d'Or']

'Soleil de France' HT, yb, 1931, Mermet; flowers sun-yellow, center reddish, large, dbl.; foliage thick; vigorous growth; ['Souv. de Claudius Pernet' × seedling]

'Soleil de Lyon' F, op, 1955, Robichon; flowers salmon-pink; vigorous growth

'Soleil de Minuit' HT, Delbard-Chabert

'Soleil de Rustica' LCl, dy, Cognet; flowers golden yellow, large

'Soleil d'Été' HT, my, Orard; intr. 2000

'Soleil d'Été' -- See 'Summer Sunshine'

'Soleil d'Or' HFt, yb, 1900, Pernet-Ducher; bud long, pointed; flowers orange-yellow to ruddy gold, shaded nasturtium-red, large, full, globular to flat, moderate citrus, orange fragrance; recurrent; foliage rich green, smooth; prickles thin, straight; vigorous, upright growth; ['Antoine Ducher' × *R. foetida persiana*]

'Soleil d'Orient' ClHT, rb, 1935, Croibier; bud long, pointed; flowers Indian red, shaded yellow, 4 in., dbl.; occasional repeat; foliage glossy; long stems; vigorous, climbing (6 ft.) growth; ['Frau Karl Druschki' × 'Mme Edouard Herriot']

'Soleil Levant' LCl, ob, 1956, Mondial Roses; flowers scarlet/orange, single; ['Spectacular' × unknown]

'Soleil Rouge' ('Janita Claassen') HT, rb, Dorieux; flowers bright red with yellow reverse , double, high-centered, borne mostly singly; recurrent; stems long; tall, vigorous, upright growth; intr. 2001

Soleillade® F, dy, Dorieux; flowers golden yellow, salmon edges as it ages , borne in clusters; recurrent; intr. 1996

Solero ® HT, dy, Kordes; flowers brass yellow, full, high-centered, borne mostly singly; recurrent; stems medium; intr. 2005

'Solette' HT, ab, Kordes; intr. 1999

'Solfatare' -- See 'Solfaterre'

'Solfaterre' ('Augusta', 'Solfatare') N, my, 1843, Boyau; flowers sulphur yellow, 9 cm., dbl., cupped, borne in clusters of 3-5; remontant; numerous prickles; vigorous growth; ['Lamarque' × unknown]

'Solid Gold' -- See 'Leonoro'

Solidor® -- See 'Meifarent'

Solidor® HT, dy, Meilland; flowers dbl.,
high-centered, borne mostly singly; PPAF; florist rose; intr. 1999

'Soliman' F, VEG; intr. 1975

'Solistka Baleta' ('Prima Ballerina') HT, yb, 1955, Klimenko, V. N.; flowers soft lemon-yellow edged pink, large; [('Peace' × 'Crimson Glory') × 'Poinsettia']

'Solitaire' F, mp, 1970, Cants of Colchester, Ltd.; flowers coral-pink, reverse silvery, 3 in., 25 petals; foliage glossy, dark; vigorous growth; [Queen Elizabeth® × Elysium®]

'Solitaire, Climbing' Cl F, yb, 1997, Earnshaw, Ronald; flowers medium, dbl., moderate fragrance; foliage medium size, medium green, semi-glossy; numerous prickles; upright (7ft.) growth; [sport of 'Solitaire']

'Solitaire' -- See 'Macyefre'

'Solitude' -- See 'Seasol'

Solitude™ -- See 'Poulbero'

'Soller' HT, my, 1949, Dot, Pedro; bud long, pointed; flowers overlarge, very dbl.; foliage glossy, bronze; bushy growth; ['Eduardo Toda' × 'Senateur Potie']

Solliden™ -- See 'Poulmax'

'Solliden' HT, rb, 1924, Leenders, M.; bud long, pointed; flowers carmine, reverse shaded ochre, open, large, semi-dbl.; foliage dark; vigorous growth; [('Mme Mélanie Soupert' × 'George C. Waud') × 'Mme Edouard Herriot']

Solo® LCl, mr, 1959, Tantau, Math.; flowers fiery crimson, large, dbl., borne in small clusters, slight fragrance; recurrent; foliage dark, leathery; vigorous growth; ['Crimson Glory' × unknown]; intr. 1956

'Solo' HT, rb, Tantau; intr. 2004

'Solo Mio' -- See 'Sophia Renaissance'

'Sologne' mr, Vire Aimery; intr. 1989

Solstice™ -- See 'Jaczeyel'

'Solus' S, or, 1967, Watkins Roses; flowers bright orange-scarlet,, 2½ in., 19 petals, borne in clusters; foliage dark, glossy, leathery; very vigorous growth; ['Kathleen Ferrier' × 'Dickson's Flame']

'Solvang' HT, dr, 1988, Olesen, Pernille & Mogens N.; flowers large, 6-14 petals; foliage large, dark green, glossy; prickles average; bushy, vigorous growth; ['Vision' × seedling]; intr. 1987

'Soma' HT, m, 1981, Division of Vegetable Crops and Floriculture; bud long, pointed; flowers mauve blend, 40 petals, borne 8 per cluster, no fragrance; foliage dark, leathery; prickles straight; bushy growth; ['Chandrama' × 'Surekha']; intr. 1980

'Somasila' -- See 'Virsila'

'Sombrero' F, pb, 1962, McGredy, Sam IV; flowers cream flushed pink, well-formed, 4 in., 25 petals; foliage light green; vigorous growth; ['Masquerade' × 'Rubaiyat']; intr. 1962

'Sombreuil' ('Colonial White') LCl, w, about 1880; flowers creamy white, 3 in., very dbl., flat, borne singly and in small clusters, slight fragrance; recurrent;
foliage large, medium green, semi-glossy; growth climbing, tall (8-12 ft.); not synonymous with Mlle de Sombreuil. Registered again in error in 1960 as Colonial White.

'Somcarflow' Min, dp, Sommerfield; intr. 2007

'Someday Soon' -- See 'Seasoon'

'Somersault' -- See 'Jacply'

Something Else™ -- See 'Savapie'

'Something for Judy' -- See 'Tinjudy'

'Something Special' HT, ly, McGredy; flowers pale yellow with hints of apricot and peach, dbl., high-centered, intense fragrance; recurrent; foliage dark green, glossy; upright (3-3½ ft.) growth; intr. 1999

'Something Special' F, pb, 2001, Hill, Ernest H.; flowers salmon peach, lighter reverse, 2½ in., dbl., high-centered, borne in large clusters, slight fragrance; foliage medium size, dark green (dark copper when young), glossy; numerous prickles; growth upright, medium (2-3 ft.)

'Sommerabend' ('Red Immensee', 'Summer Evening') S, dr, Kordes; flowers vivid dark red, 1½ in., single, cupped, borne in clusters, no fragrance; recurrent; foliage medium size, glossy; low (12 in.), bushy, spreading growth; groundcover; intr. 1995

Sommerduft® -- See 'Tanfudermos'

'Sommerfreude' F, lp, Noack; intr. 1988

Sommerfreude® F, pb, Noack; flowers pink with apricot shading , 6 cm., double, cupped, borne in clusters, slight fragrance; recurrent; foliage olive green, glossy; 60 - 70 cm. growth; intr. 2007

'Sommerlachen' F, ob, GPG Bad Langensalza; flowers coppery orange and dark golden yellow, large, dbl.; intr. 1972

'Sommerliebe' HT, or, Pörschmann; flowers large, dbl.; intr. 1975

'Sommerliebe' F, ob, GPG Bad Langensalza; flowers coppery-pink, large, dbl.; intr. 1986

Sommermärchen® -- See 'Korpinka'

'Sommermärchen' F, dp, 1945, Tantau; flowers dark rose, petals shell-shaped, large, single, borne in clusters of 12-18; foliage light green, leathery; upright, vigorous, bushy growth; ['Prof. Gnau' × 'Baby Chateau']

'Sommermelodie' -- See 'Noamel'

Sommermond® ('Country Gold') F, my, Kordes; flowers canary yellow, fading to cream; continuous bloom; growth medium and spreading; intr. 1991

'Sommermorgen' -- See 'Korfullwind'

'Sommernachtstraum' Pol, rb, 1944, Krause; flowers carmine-red with white, medium, single

'Sommerschirm' F, Tantau; intr. 1993

'Sommerschnee' F, w, VEG; flowers large, dbl.

'Sommerschnee' Min, w, Hetzel, Karl; intr. 1999

Sommerspiel® S, dp; intr. 2005

'Sommertag' -- See 'Summer Holiday'

'Sommertraum'   F, pb, 1965, van Engelen, A. J.; flowers pink, red and yellow, semi-dbl., borne in clusters; foliage dark; ['Masquerade' × seedling]; intr. 1962

'Sommerwind' -- See 'Korlanum'

'Sommerwind Fuchsia'   S, dp, Vidal; intr. after 1988

'Sommesson' ('Petite Agathe') HGal, mp, before 1820, Pelletier; flowers lilac pink, small, full; prickles numerous, strong, crooked; Agathe group

'Sommet'   LCl, or, 1960, Mallerin, C.; flowers well-formed, dbl.; foliage bright green; vigorous growth

'Somnip' ('Blackberry Nip') HT, m, 1996, Somerfield, Rob; flowers deep purple, very dbl., borne mostly singly, intense fragrance; foliage medium size, medium green, semi-glossy; some prickles; upright, medium growth; ['Deep Secret' × 'Old Port']

'Somskywer' ('Sky Tower') LCl, mp, 2004, Somerfield, Rob; flowers lighter pink, reverse bright pink, medium, dbl., borne in large clusters, no fragrance; foliage large, dark green, glossy; prickles medium, downward facing, numerous; stems long; growth bushy, tall (10 ft.), climbing; ['Strawberry Ice' × 'Hot Chocolate']; intr. 2004

'Somsmoko' ('Star Quality') F, mp, 2005, Somerfield, Rob; flowers smokey pink, 8 cm., semi-dbl., borne in large clusters, no fragrance; foliage medium size, light green, matte; prickles medium, moderate; bushy, medium (1 m.) growth; ['Hans Christian Andersen' × 'Class Act']; intr. 2006

'Somspice' ('Scent to Remember') F, ab, 2005, Somerfield, Rob; flowers peach/apricot, reverse dark apricot, 10 cm., full, borne in small clusters, moderate fragrance; foliage small, dark green, glossy; prickles medium, moderate; growth bushy, medium (1¼ m.); [Enchantment × 'Warm Wishes']; intr. 2006

'Somtabco' ('Kaimai Sunset') LCl, r, 2004, Somerfield, Rob; flowers light russet, reverse dark russet, medium, dbl., borne in small clusters, no fragrance; foliage medium size, dark green, glossy; prickles medium, slightly downfacing, few; growth bushy, tall (3 m.), climbing; ['School Girl' × 'Hot Chocolate']; intr. 2002

'S. A. R. Mme La Princesse de Hohenzollern, Infante de Portugal' -- See 'Princesse Hohenzollern'

'Sonata'   HT, pb, 1942, Van Rossem; bud long, pointed; flowers red becoming lively pink, reverse darker,, 4 in., 30 petals, high-centered, moderate fruity fragrance; foliage glossy; vigorous, bushy growth; PP732

'Sonata' -- See 'Zipson'

'Sonata in Pink' -- See 'Jolson'

'Sonatina'   F, lp, 1982, Sanday, John; flowers small, 35 petals; foliage medium size, dark, semi-glossy; ['Red Maid' × Sarabande®]

'Soncy'   T, ly; flowers lemon-ivory to ivory-white, large, high-centered, moderate tea fragrance; recurrent; foliage olive green; stems plum colored; discovered in Bermuda

'Sondermeldung' -- See 'Independence'

'Song and Dance'   HT, ob, Fryers; flowers bright coral-orange, dbl., urn-shaped, moderate fragrance; recurrent; foliage dark green, dense; vigorous (85 cm.) growth; intr. 2006

'Song Bird'   Gr, w, 1979, Ryan, C.; PP4419; [sport of 'Tammy']; intr. 1978

'Song of Paris' ('Saphir') HT, m, 1967, Delbard-Chabert; bud short, ovoid to globular; flowers silvery lavender, 4 in., 35-45 petals, high-centered, borne singly or in small clusters, moderate fragrance; recurrent; foliage leathery, glossy; prickles several, medium, almost straight, brown; stems medium, strong; upright growth; PP2669; [('Holstein' × 'Bayadere') × 'Prelude']; intr. 1964

'Song of Songs'   HT, dr, 1998, Poole, Lionel; flowers dark red, 5½ in., very dbl., high-centered, borne mostly singly; foliage medium size, dark green, semi-glossy; some prickles; upright, bushy, medium (3½ ft.) growth; ['Adrienne Berman' × ('Royal William' × 'Gabi')]

'Song of the Stars' -- See 'Ardmarbré'

'Songfest' -- See 'Zipson'

'Songs of Praise' -- See 'Red Abundance'

'Sonia'   HT, rb, 1938, Horvath; flowers cherry-red, center orange, semi-dbl., camellia-like; occasional repeat; foliage glossy, dark; short stems; vigorous, bushy growth; hardy; PP299; [(R. multiflora × R. canina) × 'Hortulanus Budde']

'Sonia, Climbing' ('Sonia Meilland, Climbing', 'Sweet Promise, Climbing', Grimpant Sonia Meilland®) Cl Gr, pb, 1979, Meilland, Mrs. Marie-Louise; bud coral pink; flowers dusky pink, quartered, flat, strong fruity fragrance; [sport of 'Sonia']; intr. 1976

'Sonia' -- See 'Meihelvet'

'Sonia Meilland, Climbing' -- See 'Sonia, Climbing'

'Sonia Meilland' -- See 'Meihelvet'

'Sonia Rykiel' -- See 'Masdogui'

Sonia Sunblaze® -- See 'Meijelior'

'Sonia Supreme'   Gr, ab, Williams, J. B.; flowers salmon-peach with yellow base, dbl., high-centered; spreading, upright growth; ['Sonia' × unknown]; intr. 1996

Sonja™ -- See 'Sonja Parade'

'Sonja 92'   Gr, mp

'Sonja Henie'   HT, pb, 1949, Hinner, P.; bud long, pointed to ovoid; flowers pink, reverse darker, very large, very dbl., high-centered; foliage leathery, dark; vigorous, upright growth; ['Briarcliff Supreme' × 'Rosemarie Hinner']

'Sonja Horstmann'   HT, mr

'Sonja Parade'   (Sonja™) MinFl, yb, Poulsen; bud pointed ovoid to globular; flowers yellow with red to pink edges, 2 in., 80-85 petals, high-centered, borne mostly singly, slight fragrance; recurrent; foliage dark; bushy, compact (20-40 cm.) growth; PP15120; [sport of 'Mistral Parade']; container rose; intr. 2003

'Sonne der Freundschaft'   F, dy, GPG Bad Langensalza; flowers golden yellow, medium, semi-dbl. to dbl., cupped, borne singly or several together, slight fragrance; foliage dark green, glossy; bushy, low growth; intr. 1978

'Sonne des Allgäus' -- See 'Korsoalgu'

'Sonnengold'   HT, dy, 1936, Kordes; bud long, pointed; flowers golden yellow, large, dbl., high-centered; foliage leathery, glossy, light; bushy growth; ['Lilian' × 'Sir Basil McFarland']

Sonnenkind® -- See 'Korhitom'

'Sonnenlicht'   HSpn, my, 1910, Krüger; flowers canary-yellow, semi-dbl., moderate fragrance; non-recurrent; vigorous growth; ['Lady Mary Fitzwilliam' × 'Harison's Yellow']

Sonnenröschen®   Min, w, Kordes; flowers ivory, conspicuous yellow stamens, 3 cm., single, shallow cup, borne in clusters of 3 - 6, moderate fragrance; recurrent; foliage small, dense, dark green, very glossy; upright, compact (12 in.), wide growth; intr. 2005

Sonnenröschen® -- See 'Korsonn'

Sonnenschirm® ('Broadlands', 'Canicule', 'Golden Touch') S, my, Tantau; flowers lemon yellow, 6-8 cm., 33 petals, cupped, borne in clusters; foliage dark green, glossy; low (2 ft.), spreading growth; intr. 1993

'Sonnenuntergang'   F, deRuiter; intr. 1970

'Sonnet'   HT, lp, 1961, Boerner; bud ovoid; flowers light salmon-pink,, 5 in., 58 petals, cupped, moderate fragrance; foliage leathery; vigorous, upright growth; PP2167; ['Golden Masterpiece' × 'Spartan']; intr. 1962

'Sonningdean'   HWich, 1916, Hicks, Elisha

'Sonny'   S, ab, Peden, G.H.; intr. 1995

'Sonnychild' ('Zonnekeild') HT, yb, 1949, Lowe; flowers yellow, reverse edged scarlet, 6 in., 20 petals; foliage glossy; vigorous growth

'Sonoma'   F, mp, 1971, Armstrong, D.L.; flowers medium salmon-pink, medium, dbl., high-centered, moderate fragrance; foliage leathery; vigorous, upright, bushy growth; PP3302; ['Sumatra' × 'Circus']; intr. 1973

'Sonora'   F, yb, 1962, Boerner; bud ovoid; flowers buff-yellow flushed to pink, 3½-4 in., 30 petals, cupped, borne several together, moderate tea fragrance; recurrent; foliage large, leathery, dark green; prickles numerous, medium, hooked downward; stems medium, strong; vigorous, upright growth; hips none ; PP2223; ['Orange Mist' × 'Mayday']; intr. 1962

'Sonora Sunset' -- See 'Devmauve'

'Sonrisa'   HT, dr, 1969, Swim & Weeks;

flowers deep crimson-red, medium-large, 48 petals, high-centered, intense damask fragrance; foliage dark, leathery; vigorous, upright growth; PP3007; [Mister Lincoln® × 'Night 'n' Day']
Sophia™ -- See 'Sophia Renaissance'
'Sophia'   HT, pb, 1988, Weddle, Von C.; flowers medium pink with persimmon-orange, large, 27 petals, high-centered, borne usually singly, moderate fruity fragrance; foliage large, dark green, glossy; no prickles; upright, tall growth; no fruit; ['First Prize' × Dolce Vita®]; intr. 1988
'Sophia'   HT, mp, Pekmez; intr. 2002
'Sophia Fleur'   F, ly, 1977, Timmerman's Roses; flowers creamy yellow; [sport of Elizabeth of Glamis®]; intr. 1978
Sophia Loren®   HT, mr, 1967, Tantau, Math.; flowers bright, velvety red, well-formed, large, 33 petals; foliage glossy; vigorous, upright growth
'Sophia Neate'   T, op, 1910, Bide; flowers bright salmon pink, reverse darker, large, full
'Sophia Renaissance' ('Solo Mio', Rita Barbera™, Sophia™) S, dy, Olesen; bud long, pointed; flowers deep amber yellow, 4-5 in., 70-90 petals, cupped, borne 1 - 3 per stem, moderate fruity, herbaceous fragrance; foliage large, matte; prickles many on older wood, few on newer, deeply concave; vigorous, upright to bushy (3-4 ft.) growth; PP12268; [seedling × seedling]; intr. 1999
'Sophia Smith'   HT, m, 1996, Linck, Robert G.; flowers pinkish-mauve with salmon center, reverse pinkish-mauve suffused on buff, to yellow at petal base, 8-10 cm., very dbl., borne mostly singly; foliage medium size, dark green; prickles moderate; upright, medium (5 ft.) growth; ['Lady X' × (Blue Moon® × 'Great News')]; intr. 1996
Sophia's Song™   HT, op, 1989, Marciel, Stanley G.; bud slender, tapering; flowers coral, large, 32 petals, high-centered, borne singly, slight fruity fragrance; foliage medium size, dark green, semi-glossy; prickles declining, copper brown with pea green tinges; upright, tall growth; PP7455; ['Emily Post' × Prominent®]
'Sophie'   F, lp, Eve, A.; bud long; flowers pale pink, 8 cm., semi-dbl., cupped, borne in clusters, intense fragrance; upright (3-4 ft.) growth; intr. 1972
'Sophie'   HT, lp, Tantau; intr. 2000
'Sophie Coquerel'   HP, mp, 1842, Coquerel; flowers very large, full
'Sophie de Bavière' ('Celamire') A, mp, before 1826, Cottin/Vibert; flowers clear pink, very regular, medium, dbl.
'Sophie de Marsilly'   M, pb, 1863, Moreau et Robert; flowers pink with light white stripes, dbl., globular; some repeat; vigorous, upright growth
'Sophie Deborah' -- See 'Kirstein'
'Sophie Ella Sloane Hicks'   F, pb, 2005, Paul Chessum Roses; flowers 6 cm.,

dbl., borne in small clusters; foliage small, light green, semi-glossy; growth compact, medium (60 cm.); containers, garden decorative; [seedling × seedling]; intr. 2004
'Sophie MacKinnon'   HT, dr, 1937, Clark, A.; flowers deep red, large, dbl.; vigorous growth; ['John Cromin' × unknown]
'Sophie Ortlieb'   HP, mp, 1933, Walter, L.; bud long, pointed; flowers silvery pink, very large, dbl.; foliage wrinkled; very vigorous, open growth; ['Georg Arends' × seedling]
'Sophie Scholl'   S, w, Schultheis/Scholl; flowers full , classic hybrid tea, moderate fragrance; recurrent; upright (1 - 1.5 m.) growth; intr. 2007
'Sophie Thomas' ('Bloomfield Loveliness') Cl HT, my, 1931, Thomas; flowers deep yellow, passing to lighter yellow but not cream, large, dbl.; foliage good; long, strong stems; vigorous growth; ['climbing seedling' × 'Los Angeles']
'Sophie's Perpetual'   Ch, pb, before 1905, Paul, W.; flowers pale pink, overlaid with deep pink and cerise red, globular; foliage dark green; growth to 8 ft.; sometimes classed as B; re-introduced by Humphrey Brooke, 1960
'Sophileo' -- See 'Machorowhen'
'Sophisticate' -- See 'Seasop'
'Sophisticated Lady' -- See 'Riplady'
'Sophisticated Lady'   Gr, lp, 1986, Epperson, Richard G.; flowers 25 petals, high-centered, borne usually singly, slight fruity fragrance; foliage medium size, medium green, semi-glossy; prickles medium, hooked, dull red; upright, tall growth; [Queen Elizabeth® × 'Arlene Francis']; intr. 1985
'Sophocle'   HT, m, 1978, Gaujard; flowers velvety purple-red, large; [Rose Gaujard® × 'Credo']; intr. 1974
'Sophy's Rose' -- See 'Auslot'
'Soprano'   F, or, 1961, Lens; flowers large, dbl.; vigorous growth; ['Mannequin' × 'Aztec']
Soraya™ -- See 'Soraya Hit'
Soraya, Climbing® (Grimpant Soraya®) Cl HT, or, 1960, Meilland; flowers orange vermilion, reverse darker, 5-6 in.; [sport of 'Soraya']; intr. 1960
Soraya®   HT, or, 1958, Meilland, F.; bud pointed; flowers orange-red, reverse crimson-red, large, 30 petals, cupped, slight fragrance; foliage glossy; vigorous, bushy growth; [('Peace' × 'Floradora') × 'Grand'mère Jenny]; intr. 1955
'Soraya Hit' (Soraya™) MinFl, mp, Poulsen; flowers medium pink, 5-8 cm., dbl., no fragrance; foliage dark; growth bushy, 40-60 cm.; intr. 2000
'Sorbet' -- See 'Meisinplox'
'Sorbet'   LCl, lp, Meilland; flowers light pink, reverse lighter, medium, semi-dbl. to dbl., borne singly or in small clusters; recurrent; foliage dark green; bushy (8 ft.) growth; intr. 1993
Sorbet Bouquet™ -- See 'Jaczotta'
Sorbet Framboise®   S, pb, Delbard;

flowers white with red and pink stripes, medium, semi-dbl., cupped, borne in clusters, slight fragrance; free-flowering; growth to 100 cm.; intr. 1994
'Sorbet Fruite, Cl.'   Cl F, yb, Meilland; flowers red and yellow blend, dbl.; growth to 2 m. plus; intr. 2002
Sorbet Pêche-Abricot®   S, yb, Delbard; intr. 2003
Sorcerer™ -- See 'Savasorc'
'Sorcier'   LCl, ob, 1958, Hémeray-Aubert; flowers bright orange; recurrent bloom; foliage bronze; vigorous growth; [seedling × 'Spectacular']
Søren Kanne™ -- See 'Poulege'
'Sorento'   S, mr, Noack; flowers bright red , 5 cm., semi-double, low (70 - 80 cm.), bushy growth; intr. 2006
'Soroptimist International' -- See 'Benstar'
'Soroptomist'   HT, dy, 1960, Verbeek; flowers orange-yellow, well-formed,, 4 in., full; foliage glossy; vigorous growth; ['Golden Scepter' × seedling]; intr. 1958
'Sorraya' ('Golden Starlite') HT, dy, Meilland; flowers dbl., high-centered, borne mostly singly; florist rose; intr. 2002
Sorrento® ('Scarlet Flower Carpet') S, mr, Noack; flowers bright red, 2 in., dbl., open cup, borne in clusters; recurrent; foliage dark green, glossy; bushy (70-80 cm.) growth; intr. 2006
'SOS Children's Rose'   F, ob, Delbard; bud long, pointed, apricot orange; flowers reddish-gold with irregular yellow stripes, aging to blend of pinks, dbl., cupped, borne singly and in clusters; recurrent; stems medium long, strong; vigorous, medium growth; intr. 2001
'Soshun' ('Early Spring') F, lp, Keisei; intr. 1991
'Souchet' -- See 'Des Peintres'
'Souchet'   B, m, 1842, Souchet; flowers purple/pink, large, dbl., intense fragrance; foliage glossy; prickles large, hooked, red
'Soufflé de Zéphire'   A, w, about 1815, Descemet
'Soukara-Ibara' -- See 'Crimson Rambler'
'Soul Mate' -- See 'Silsmilark'
'Soulmate' -- See 'Worant'
'Souma'   HT, mp, 1977, Souma Rose Soc.; flowers 6 in., 45 petals, high-centered; foliage glossy, dark; vigorous, upright growth
Soupert & Notting, Frères'   T, yb, 1871, Levet; flowers yellow-white, with pink and lilac reflections, edges crimson, medium, full
'Soupert et Notting'   M, dp, 1874, Pernet père; bud moderately mossy; flowers deep pink, very large, full, globular, then flat, borne in small clusters, intense fragrance; recurrent bloom; foliage 5 leaflets per leaf, small, greyish-green; dwarf (3 ft.) growth
'Source d'Or'   LCl, yb, 1913, Turbat; flowers amber-yellow, edged creamy

yellow, 5-6 cm., very dbl., borne in small clusters, intense fragrance; abundant, non-recurrent bloom; foliage glossy, dark; short stems; growth to 6-8 ft.

'Sourire d'Antan' -- See 'LLX8554'

'Sourire de France' HT, ob, 1940, Meilland, F.; bud oval; flowers orange, base ochre-yellow, open, medium, dbl.; foliage leathery, glossy; vigorous, bushy growth; ['Ampere' × ('Charles P. Kilham' × 'Capucine Chambard')]

Sourire d'Enfant® HT, ly, Orard; flowers pale yellow, dbl., moderate fragrance; intr. 1990

'Sourire d'Orchidée' S, lp, Croix; bud pink; flowers light mauve-pink fading to white, reverse darker, with yellow stamens, 1½-2 in., single, flat, borne in large clusters, slight fragrance; reliable repeat; foliage small, light green, matte; growth climbing, tall (to 15 ft.), as arching shrub (6-8 ft.); intr. 1983

'Sourire Rose' -- See 'LLX8869'

'Sousse' HT, lp, 1942, Meilland, F.; flowers large, dbl.

'Sousyun' F, w

'South Africa' Gr, dy, Kordes; flowers golden yellow, large, dbl., high-centered, borne in large clusters, moderate fragrance; free-flowering; foliage very disease-resistant; vigorous (5 ft.) growth; intr. 2001

'South Moon' -- See 'Gelmoon'

'South Orange Perfection' ('Perfection Orange') HWich, pb, 1899, Horvath; flowers blush-pink, turning white, 3 cm., dbl., rosette, borne in clusters of about 20, moderate fragrance; very hardy; [R. wichurana × 'Cramoisi Supérieur']

South Pacific™ F, dy, 1988, Christensen, Jack E.; flowers medium, hold color well, 26 petals, cupped, borne in sprays of 4-6; foliage medium size, medium green, glossy; prickles hooked slightly downward, medium, few,green to tan; bushy, medium growth; no fruit; ['Sunsprite' × seedling]; intr. 1988

'South Seas' ('Mers du Sud') HT, op, 1962, Morey, Dr. Dennison; bud large, ovoid; flowers coral-pink, 6-7 in., 45-50 petals, cupped to flat, borne singly and several together, moderate fragrance; recurrent; foliage large, dark green, leathery; prickles normal, medium, hooked downward; stems long, strong; vigorous, upright growth; hips none ; PP2184; ['Rapture' × 'climbing hybrid tea seedling']; intr. 1962

'Southampton' ('Susan Ann') F, ab, 1971, Harkness; bud pointed; flowers apricot-orange, flushed red on guard petals, 3 in., 28 petals, cupped, borne in clusters, moderate fragrance; free-flowering; foliage glossy; vigorous (3½ ft.) growth; [('Ann Elizabeth' × Allgold®) × 'Yellow Cushion']

'Southend Jubilee' F, dp, 1965, McCreadie; flowers deep pink, 2½ in., semi-dbl., flat, borne in clusters; very vigorous, bushy growth

'Southern Alps' -- See 'Socsouth'

'Southern Aurora' F, rb, 1999, Le Fevre, Ian; flowers red, reverse orange, 3 in., dbl.; foliage medium size, medium green, semi-glossy; few prickles; upright, medium (4½ ft.) growth; [sport of 'Redgold']

'Southern Beauty' HP, mp, 1888, Nanz & Neuner

'Southern Beauty' HT, Dingee & Conard; intr. 1897

'Southern Beauty' HT, pb, Rowe; flowers deep rose-pink, edged light pink; [sport of 'Columbia']; intr. 1926

'Southern Belle' HT, Perry, Anthony; PP2831

'Southern Belle' HT, pb, 1981, Swim, H.C. & Ellis, A.E.; bud ovoid, long, pointed; flowers deep pink, white reverse, spiraled, 28 petals, borne singly; foliage large, semi-glossy; prickles long, narrow; medium, upright, spreading growth; PP5077; ['Pink Parfait' × 'Phoenix']

'Southern Belle' Gr, ly, J&P; bud pointed; flowers soft, pastel yellow, outer petals fading as they open, 4-5 in., 40 petals, high-centered to cupped, moderate spicy, fruity fragrance; recurrent; foliage dark green ; stems medium to long; rounded (5 ft.) growth; PPAF; intr. 2008

'Southern Breeze' HT, m, 2004, Adlong, Paula; flowers full, borne in large clusters, slight fragrance; foliage medium size, medium green, matte; prickles average; upright, tall growth; [Crystalline™ × 'Louise Estes']; intr. 2004

'Southern Charm' -- See 'Bricharm'

'Southern Cross' HT, mp, 1931, Clark, A.; flowers pink, dbl., globular; bushy growth; ['Joseph Hill' × 'Gen. MacArthur']

'Southern Cross' F, dy, Jack; [sport of 'Redgold']; intr. 1977

'Southern Dawn' -- See 'Sockap'

'Southern Delight' -- See 'Mordashin'

'Southern Honey' -- See 'Socdoc'

'Southern Lady' HT, pb, 1989, Bridges, Dennis A.; bud pointed; flowers light pink, center flesh tones, reverse slightly darker pink, full, high-centered, moderate fragrance; foliage medium size, dark green, semi-glossy; prickles downward pointed, medium, tan; upright, medium growth; ['Lady X' × 'Flaming Beauty']; intr. 1989

'Southern Spring' Min, m, 1989, Bridges, Dennis A.; bud ovoid; flowers light mauve shaded pink, reverse lighter mauve edges, darker, 65 petals, moderate fragrance; foliage medium size, dark green, matte; prickles slightly downward pointed, medium, tan; bushy, low growth; [Twilight Trail™ × seedling]; intr. 1989

'Southern Sun' HT, ob, Herholdt; flowers blend of gold, orange and red, large, dbl., high-centered, borne singly and in clusters, moderate fragrance; recurrent; vigorous, medium growth; intr. 1986

'Southern Sunrise' MinFl, ob, Eagle, Dawn; flowers bright orange with yellow reverse, 40 petals; low growth; ['Orange Honey' × unknown]; intr. 1999

'Southern Sunset' ('Tamrabarani') HT, ob, 1997, Viraraghavan, M.S. Viru; flowers silky orange with yellow reverse and copper overtones, 4 in., full, borne mostly singly, slight fragrance; foliage large, dark green, glossy; numerous prickles; upright, compact, medium (2½ ft.) growth; intr. 1988

'Southport' HT, mr, 1933, McGredy; bud long, pointed; flowers bright scarlet, 18 petals, cupped; vigorous growth; [('George Dickson' × 'Crimson Queen') × 'Souv. de George Beckwith']

'Southport, Climbing' Cl HT, mr, 1946, Howard Rose Co.; [sport of 'Southport']

'Soutine' HT, rb; flowers white with crimson stripes that widen with age, dbl., globular, slight fragrance; recurrent; intr. 2000

'Souvenance' HT, m, 1979, Lens; bud very long, pointed; flowers deep lavender-lilac, 3½-4½ in., 25-30 petals, high-centered, intense fragrance; foliage dark; moderately vigorous growth; [seedling × 'Sterling Silver']; intr. 1965

'Souvenir' HT, dy, 1930, Pierson, A.N.; bud pointed; flowers golden yellow, 36-42 petals, moderate fragrance; foliage glossy; vigorous growth; PP25; [sport of 'Talisman']

'Souvenir' (Sunny Sky™) F, ob, Kordes/Grootendorst; bud pointed; flowers orange, medium, dbl., rosette, borne in large clusters; foliage fresh green, glossy; low, bushy, compact growth; intr. 1991

'Souv d'Adèle Launay' B, mr, 1872, Moreau et Robert; flowers bright rose pink, large, full, globular

'Souv d'Adolphe de Charvoik' HWich, lp, 1911; flowers bright pink, 4 cm., semi-dbl., borne in clusters of 5-15, slight fragrance; once-blooming; foliage light green, glossy; thornless; vigorous (5 m.) growth

'Souv d'Adolphe Thiers' HP, mr, 1877, Moreau et Robert; flowers red, tinged with vermilion, very large, dbl., moderate fragrance

'Souv d'Adolphe Turc' ('Souvenir de Adolphe Turc') Pol, op, 1924, Turc; flowers clear salmon-pink, 3 cm., semi-dbl. to dbl., cupped, borne in large clusters, slight fragrance; good repeat; low (2 ft.) growth

'Souv d'Adrien Bahivet' HP, dp, 1867, Cochet; flowers carmine, shaded violet-purple, large, full

'Souv d'Aimée Terrel des Chenes' Ch, op, 1897, Widow Schwartz; flowers coppery-pink, small, dbl.

'Souv d'Alexandre Bacot' HT, mr, 1958, Arles; flowers geranium-red, large, 50 petals; very vigorous growth; ['Crimson Glory' × 'Independence']

'Souv d'Alexandre Bernaix'   HT, dr, 1926, Bernaix, P.; flowers crimson-scarlet, shaded darker, very large, dbl., cupped; foliage purplish green; vigorous growth; ['Étoile de Hollande' × 'Gen. MacArthur']

'Souv d'Alexandre Hardy'   HP, mr, 1898, Lévêque; flowers maroon, tinted carmine and vermilion, large, dbl.

'Souv d'Aline Fontaine'   HP, lp, 1879, Fontaine; flowers flesh pink, aging lighter, very dbl.

'Souv d'Alma de l'Aigle' -- See 'Andenken an Alma de l'Aigle'

'Souv d'Alphonse Lavallée'   HP, dr, 1884, Verdier, C.; flowers dark velvety crimson to maroon, 8 cm., full, cupped, moderate fragrance; recurrent; few prickles; growth to 6 ft.

'Souv d'André Raffy'   HP, dr, 1899, Vigneron; flowers vermilion red, with velvety touches, large, dbl., globular, intense fragrance

'Souv d'Angèle Opdebeeck'   HT, my, 1926, Verschuren; bud golden yellow, long, pointed; flowers canary-yellow, large, dbl., moderate fragrance; ['Golden Ophelia' × 'Golden Emblem']

'Souv d'Angelique'   N, lp

'Souv d'Anne Frank' ('Anne no Omoide')   F, ob, 1960, Delforge; flowers orange tinted yellow and salmon, medium, 17 petals, cupped, borne in clusters; foliage glossy, dark; moderate, bushy growth; ['Reve de Capri' × 'Chanteclerc']

'Souv d'Anne-Marie'   HT, op, 1902, Gebrüder Ketten; flowers yellowish salmon-pink, large, dbl.; ['Safrano' × 'Mme Caroline Testout']

'Souv d'Anselme' ('Enfant d'Ajaccio')   B, dp; flowers bright cherry red, large, dbl., cupped

'Souv d'Antonin Poncet'   HT, dr, 1921, Schwartz, A.; bud long, pointed; flowers carmine, flecked paler, dbl.; ['Mme Maurice de Luze' × 'Lady Ashtown']

'Souv d'Arthur de Sansal'   HP, mp, 1876, Guénoux; flowers clear rose, large, dbl., intense fragrance; ['Jules Margottin' × unknown]

'Souv d'Auguste Legros'   T, mr, 1890, Bonnaire; flowers red-crimson, large

'Souv d'Auguste Métral'   HT, dr, 1895, Guillot, P.; flowers varying from purple red to crimson, large, full, moderate fragrance

'Souv d'Auguste Rivière' ('Auguste Rivière')   HP, rb, 1877, Verdier; flowers rich crimson red, purple and scarlet, large, full; foliage delicate green, irregularly toothed; prickles numerous, unequal, very sharp, reddish; growth upright

'Souvenir de Adolphe Turc' -- See 'Souv d'Adolphe Turc'

'Souv de Amand Opdebeeck'   HT, yb, 1936, Belge; bud long, pointed; flowers yellowish apricot-pink, edged pink, very large, dbl., high-centered; foliage leathery, bronze; very vigorous growth

'Souv de Bélicant-Gibey'   T, pb, 1902, Bonnaire; flowers fresh pink, center coppery, large, full

'Souv de Ben-Hur'   HT, mr, 1960, Verschuren; bud pointed; flowers crimson-scarlet, 5 in., dbl.; very vigorous growth; ['Ena Harkness' × 'Charles Mallerin']; intr. 1960

'Souv de Béranger'   HP, mp, 1857, Bruant; flowers rose, large, dbl.; moderate growth

'Souv de Bernardin de St. Pierre'   HP, dr, 1864, Guillot; flowers velvety dark crimson with slatey violet-red, large, full

'Souv de Bertrand Guinoisseau'   HP, m, 1895, Chédane-Guinoisseau; flowers purple red nuanced crimson, large, very dbl., moderate fragrance

'Souv de Brod' -- See 'Erinnerung an Brod'

'Souv de Caillat'   HP, rb, 1867, Verdier, E.; flowers purple and flame, large, full, borne in small clusters

'Souv de Catherine Fontaine'   HT, yb, 1934, Soupert, C.; bud long, pointed; flowers brownish yellow, center brick-red, reverse coral-red, very large; ['Souv. de Jean Soupert' × 'Mme Edouard Herriot']

'Souv de Catherine Guillot'   T, rb, 1895, Guillot, P.; bud long, nasturtium red; flowers coppery carmine, center shaded orange, large, dbl., intense fragrance; weak growth

'Souv de Charles Gouverneur'   HT, pb, 1927, Chambard, C.; bud long, pointed; flowers flesh-pink, center salmon-orange, very large

'Souv de Charles Laemmel'   HT, yb, 1919, Gillot, F.; bud very large, ovoid; flowers golden yellow, streaked orange and shaded pink, large, full, intense fragrance; foliage dark green, glossy; growth upright, vigorous; ['Frau Karl Druschki' × 'Soleil d'Or']

'Souv de Charles Montault'   HP, dr, 1862, Robert & Moreau; flowers velvety purple suffused with crimson, large, full, cupped

'Souv de Charles Verdier'   HP, dp, Lévêque; flowers dark carmine, shaded purple, large, full; intr. 1900

'Souv de Charles Verdier'   HP, m, 1894, Verdier, E.; flowers purple-violet, shaded crimson and slate-purple, medium to large, full

'Souv de Christophe Cochet'   HRg, mp, 1894, Cochet-Cochet; flowers bright flesh pink, flushed carmine, 6 cm., semi-dbl. to dbl., cupped, open, moderate fragrance; non-recurrent; foliage dark green, leathery; upright (5 ft.), bushy growth; hips large, bright red; ['Alba Simplex' × 'Comte d'Epremesnil']

'Souv de Clairvaux'   T, pb, 1890, Verdier, E.; flowers China pink, with apricot yellow at base, tinted carmine, medium to large, full, moderate fragrance; foliage glossy

'Souv de Claude Vially'   HT, rb, 1931, Reymond; bud long, pointed; flowers light red, tinted pink and aurora

'Souv de Claudius Denoyel' ('Denoyel')   Cl HT, dr, 1920, Chambard, C.; bud long, pointed; flowers rich crimson-red, tinted scarlet, large, dbl., cupped, moderate fragrance; sparse, recurrent bloom; vigorous, climbing growth; ['Château de Clos Vougeot' × 'Commandeur Jules Gravereaux']

'Souv de Claudius Pernet'   HT, my, 1920, Pernet-Ducher; bud long, pointed; flowers pure sunflower-yellow, center deeper, large, 28 petals, moderate fragrance; foliage large, glossy, rich green; long, strong stems; growth vigorous, branching; ['Constance' × seedling]; very susceptible to foliage diseases

'Souv de Claudius Pernet, Climbing'   Cl HT, my, 1925, Western Rose Co.; flowers sunflower yellow, 6 in., full, globular, moderate fragrance; [sport of 'Souv de Claudius Pernet']; (also Schmidt, 1932, Gaujard, 1933, Square, 1937)

'Souv de Clermonde'   HT, pb, 1925, Pernet-Ducher; flowers salmon-rose, center darker, shaded yellow, semi-dbl.

'Souv de Coulommiers' ('Triomphe de Coulommiers')   HP, dr, 1868, Desmazures; flowers dark scarlet with violet reflections, large, full

'Souv de David d'Angers'   T, dr, 1856, Moreau-Robert; flowers dark red, shaded maroon, very large, dbl.

'Souv de Denier van der Gon'   HT, yb, 1935, Verschuren-Pechtold; bud long, pointed; flowers reddish-yellow to golden yellow, large, dbl., moderate fragrance; very vigorous growth; ['Roselandia' × 'Souv. de Claudius Pernet']

'Souv de Ducher'   HP, m, 1874, Verdier, E.; flowers purple, center velvety dark violet, medium, full

'Souv de Ernest H. Morse' -- See 'Ernest H. Morse'

'Souv de F. Bohé'   HT, op, 1922, Chambard, C.; bud long, pointed; flowers orange-salmon, 35 petals; ['Willowmere' × seedling]

'Souv de Fernand Leroy'   HSpn, pb, Brochet-Lanvin; flowers striped, small, pompon; non-remontant

'Souv de Francis Borges'   HT, ob, 1932, Chambard, C.; flowers flesh, center orange, very large; vigorous growth; ['Mme Leon Pain' × seedling]

'Souv de François Gaulain'   T, rb, 1889, Guillot; flowers crimson and violet, moderate fragrance

'Souv de François Graindorge'   HT, yb, 1928, Grandes Roseraies; bud long, pointed; flowers ochre-yellow, base Indian yellow, dbl.; ['Benedicte Sequin' × 'Lady Hillingdon']

'Souv de François Mercier'   HT, ob, 1923, Laperrière; bud long, pointed; flowers light coppery rose, edged deeper, dbl.; [sport of 'Antoine Rivoire']

'Souv de François Richardier'   HT, rb, 1923, Richardier; flowers bright carmine-pink, tinted cherry

'Souv de Gabriel Luizet' HT, yb, 1922, Croibier; flowers sulfur-yellow tinted salmon, passing to deep rich yellow and later straw yellow, dbl.; [('Mme Mélanie Soupert' × unknown) × 'Lyon Rose']

'Souv de Gabrielle Drevet' T, op, 1884, Guillot et Fils; flowers salmon-pink, base coppery, large, well-formed, intense fragrance

'Souv de Gaston Commagères' HT, ob, 1954, Privat; flowers orange-ivory veined yellow, edge veined pink, very dbl.; vigorous, bushy growth

'Souv de Général Gange' B, dp, 1855, de Fauw; flowers lilac pink, aging to red, medium, full

'Souv de Geneviève Godard' T, mp, 1893, Godard

'Souv de George Beckwith' HT, pb, 1919, Pernet-Ducher; bud long, pointed; flowers shrimp-pink, tinted chrome-yellow, base deeper, very large, 55 petals, globular; foliage glossy; very vigorous growth; [seedling × 'Lyon Rose']

'Souv de George Knight' HT, my, 1926, Knight, J.; flowers nankeen yellow; [sport of 'Rayon d'Or']

'Souv de George Sand' T, yb, 1876, Widow Ducher; bud carmine; flowers salmony yellow, reverse ribboned lilac, very large, full

'Souv de Georges Pernet' HT, op, 1921, Pernet-Ducher; bud globular; flowers medium salmon-pink, large, 31 petals, rosette, borne in clusters, intense fragrance; foliage dark, bronze; vigorous growth; [seedling × 'Mme Edouard Herriot']

'Souv de Georges Pernet, Climbing' Cl HT, op, 1927, Pernet-Ducher; flowers red exterior, carmine interior, large, full; [sport of 'Souv de Georges Pernet']

'Souv de Germain de Saint-Pierre' T, dr, 1882, Nabonnand; flowers purple-red, large, full, borne in small clusters

'Souv de Gilbert Nabonnand' T, pb, 1920, Nabonnand, P.; flowers yellow base edged carmine-pink, dbl., intense fragrance; vigorous growth

'Souv de Giosue Carducci' -- See 'Ricordo di Giosue Carducci'

'Souv de Gonod' HP, mr, 1890, Gonod; flowers cherry red, very large, full; ['Baronne Adolphe de Rothschild' × unknown]

'Souv de Grégoire Bordillon' HP, mr, 1889, Moreau et Robert; flowers bright red nuanced vermilion, very large, full, globular; foliage dark green; prickles sharp, dense

'Souv de Greuville' S, m, Schultheis; flowers soft lilac-pink, fading to white, small, dbl., pompon, borne in clusters, slight fragrance; recurrent; foliage medium green; low (60-80 cm.), bushy growth; intr. 2004

'Souv de Gustave Prat' HT, ly, 1909, Pernet-Ducher; flowers pure light sulfur-yellow, large, dbl.

'Souv de Gustave Schickelé' HT, yb, 1927, Ketten Bros.; bud long, pointed; flowers chrome-yellow, reverse bright rosy scarlet, shaded apricot, dbl.; ['Mme Edouard Herriot' × 'Duchess of Wellington']

'Souv de H. A. Verschuren' HT, yb, 1922, Verschuren; bud long, pointed; flowers yellow to orange-yellow, pink tones on edges, large, 38 petals, high-centered, moderate fragrance; vigorous growth; [seedling × 'Golden Ophelia']

'Souv de H. A. Verschuren, Climbing' Cl HT, yb, 1927, H&S; [sport of 'Souv de H. A. Verschuren']

'Souv de Henri Faassen' HT, pb, 1929, Faassen-Hekkens; bud long, pointed; flowers deep pink, base orange-yellow, open, large, semi-dbl.; foliage bronze; very vigorous growth; ['Betty Uprichard' × ('Mrs George Shawyer' × 'Los Angeles')]

'Souv de Henri Lévêque de Vilmorin' HP, dr, 1899, Lévêque; flowers deep velvety crimson, large, full; foliage dark green

'Souv de Henri Venot' HT, mr, 1931, Lens; flowers brilliant red, very dbl.; foliage dark; vigorous growth; ['Lord Charlemont' × 'Red Star']

'Souv de Henry Clay' HSpn, lp, 1854, Boll; flowers light lilac pink, medium; some repeat in autumn

'Souv de Henry Graham' HT, yb, 1915, Dickson; flowers creamy yellow with carmine reflections, large, full, moderate fragrance

'Souv de J. B. Guillot' ('Rose d'Herbeys') T, or, 1897, Guillot; flowers bright coppery-red, shaded crimson, large, full; growth to 1 m.

'Souv de J. B. Weibel' HT, dr, 1930, Sauvageot, H.; flowers carmine, very large, dbl., cupped; foliage dark; very vigorous, bushy growth; [('Mrs Bullen' × unknown) × 'Edouard Mignot']; intr. 1930

'Souv de J. Chabert' ('Bobbie Robbie', 'Pépite') F, mr, 1956, Delbard-Chabert; flowers well-formed, large, dbl., borne in clusters of 3-6; foliage dark, bronze; vigorous, low growth; ['Francais' × seedling]

'Souv de J. Mermet' HWich, dr, 1934, Mermet; flowers silvery carmine, reverse lighter to medium, 4-5 cm., full, rosette, borne in small to medium clusters, slight fragrance; repeats in autumn; foliage bronze-green, glossy; very vigorous, tall growth

'Souv de J. Passinge' HT, op, 1912, Chambard; flowers coppery dawn pink, shaded carmine and dark yellow, large, full, moderate fragrance

'Souv de Jacques Verschuren' HT, op, 1950, Verschuren-Pechtold; bud long, pointed; flowers apricot-salmon, large, dbl.; foliage leathery, dark; vigorous, bushy growth; ['Katharine Pechtold' × 'Orange Delight']

'Souv de Jean Croibier' HT, pb, 1921, Croibier; flowers bright salmon-pink shaded chamois, center coral-red shaded yellow, dbl.; ['Mme Mélanie Soupert' × 'Lyon Rose']

'Souv de Jean Ginet' HT, mr, 1935, Brenier, E.C.; flowers scarlet-red, base coppery, reverse golden yellow

'Souv de Jean Sisley' HP, m, 1891, Dubreuil; flowers dark carmine-purple, shaded magenta and amaranth, large, full

'Souv de Jean Soupert' HT, my, 1929, Soupert & Notting; bud long, pointed; flowers golden yellow, very large, semi-dbl., cupped; foliage bronze; vigorous growth; ['Ophelia' × 'Feu Joseph Looymans']

'Souv de Jeanne Balandreau' -- See 'Souv de Mme Jeanne Balandreau'

'Souv de Jeanne Cabaud' T, yb, 1896, Guillot, P.; flowers coppery yellow, tinted with apricot and carmine, very large, full, moderate fragrance

'Souv de John E. Knight' HT, ob, 1928, Knight, J.; flowers terra-cotta, salmon-pink and flesh streaked yellow; foliage dark; vigorous growth

'Souv de John Gould Veitch' HP, dr, 1872, Verdier, E.; flowers deep crimson, shaded violet-purple, large, full

'Souv de Josefina Plà' HT, mr, 1929, Munné, B.; flowers bright red, large, semi-dbl.; vigorous growth; ['Étoile de Hollande' × 'Mme Butterfly']

'Souv de Joseph Besson' HT, rb, 1931, Brenier, E.C.; flowers reddish-orange, base yellow

'Souv de Jules Godard' T, w, 1894, Godard; flowers flesh white, medium, full, moderate fragrance

'Souv de Jules Nicolas Mathieu Lamarche' Pol, rb, 1934, Soupert, C.; flowers cardinal-red, base yellow, very small, single, borne in large panicles; ['Eblouissant' × 'Petit Constant']

'Souv de Julie Gonod' HP, mp, 1871, Gonod; flowers glowing silky pink, large, full

'Souv de la Bataille de Marengo' -- See 'Russelliana'

'Souv de la Comtesse de Roquette-Buisson' HT, lp, 1908, Ketten; flowers flesh pink, aging to flesh-white, tinted salmon, very large, very full, moderate fragrance; ['Laure Wattine' × 'William Askew']

'Souv de la Malmaison' ('Queen of Beauty and Fragrance') B, lp, 1843, Béluze; flowers creamy flesh, center rosy shaded, 4 in., dbl., quartered, flat, intense spicy fragrance; repeat bloom; dwarf, bushy (2 ft.) growth; ['Mme Desprez (B)' × a tea rose (possibly 'Devoniensis')]

'Souv de la Malmaison, Climbing' Cl B, lp, 1893, Bennett; flowers blush white, slightly darker at center, 10-12 cm., very full, flat, quartered, moderate fragrance; [sport of 'Souv de la Malmaison']

'Souv de la Malmaison Rose' -- See 'Leweson-Gower'

'Souv de la Malmaison Rouge' -- See 'Malmaison Rouge'

'Souv de la Princesse Amélie des Pays-Bas' HP, m, 1873, Liabaud; flowers grenadine red shaded purple, large, dbl., globular

'Souv de la Princesse de Lamballe' -- See 'Reine des Iles-Bourbons'

'Souv de la Reine d'Angleterre' HP, mp, 1855, Cochet Freres; flowers bright pink, large, dbl.; recurrent bloom; very vigorous growth; ['La Reine' × unknown]

'Souv de la Reine des Belges' ('Prince Albert') HP, pb, 1850, de Fauw; flowers fiery light carmine, edges bright carmine, medium

'Souv de la Reine des Pay-Bas' HP, m, 1876, Schwartz; flowers purple with darker reflections

'Souv de la Russie' HT, pb, 1905; flowers dark pink, marbled white

'Souv de Lady Ashburton' T, rb, 1890, Verdier, C.; flowers rich coppery red, suffused with pale orange yellow

'Souv de Laffay' HP, mr, 1878, Verdier, E.; flowers crimson-red, large, very full, borne in small clusters; foliage oblong, dark green, regularly toothed; prickles large, short, upright; growth upright, short

'Souv de l'Ami Labruyère' HP, mp, 1884, Gonod; flowers outer petals China pink, center darker; growth upright

'Souv de l'Amiral Courbet' T, mr, 1885, Pernet père; flowers bright fiery red, medium, dbl., globular, borne in large clusters; growth upright

'Souv de Laurent Guillot' T, pb, 1894, Bonnaire; flowers China pink with peach yellow center, edges carmine, large, full; foliage bronze-green

'Souv de l'Aviateur Métivier' HWich, ly, 1913, Tanne; flowers clear yellow, passing to white, dbl.; vigorous, climbing growth; [R. wichurana × 'Mme Ravary']

'Souv de l'Aviateur Olivier de Montalent' HWich, rb, 1913, Tanne; flowers dull rose, base salmon, dbl., borne in clusters; profuse bloom, rarely recurrent; foliage very glossy, dark; vigorous, climbing growth; [R. wichurana × 'Anna Olivier']

'Souv de Léon Gambetta' HP, pb, 1908, Vigneron; flowers flesh pink, nuanced carmine red, 5 in.; foliage bright green; prickles large recurved; ['Victor Verdier' × unknown]

'Souv de Léon Roudillon' HP, dr, 1908, Vigneron; flowers deep velvety red, fiery red center, large, full; foliage dark green; ['Général Appert' × 'Louis Van Houtte']

'Souv de Leveson Gower' HP, mr, 1852, Guillot père; flowers dark red, changing to ruby, very large, full

'Souv de l'Exposition de Bordeaux' HMult, lp, 1905, Puyravaud; flowers pale pink, lighter at center, 5-6 cm., dbl., globular, borne in clusters of more than 40; nonerecurrent; prickles close-set, straight, reddish; ['Turner's Crimson Rambler' × 'Simon de St Jean']

'Souv de l'Exposition de Brie' -- See 'Maurice Bernardin'

'Souv de l'Exposition de Londres' B, mr, 1851, Guillot père; flowers velvety poppy red, medium to large, full

'Souv de Lilette' HT, w, 1937, Chambard, C.; bud very long; flowers snow-white, large, foliage slightly bronze; compact, bushy growth

Souv de Louis Amade® S, mp, Delbard; flowers lilac pink, dbl., globular to cupped, moderate licorice fragrance; free-flowering; moderate (2-3 ft.) growth; intr. 1998

'Souv de Louis Bertrand' HWich, 1910, Béluze

'Souv de Louis Eugene Rantz' HT, Rantz, Louis M.; PP2828

'Souv de Louis Gaudin' B, dr, 1864, Trouillard; flowers reddish-purple, almost black, medium, full

'Souv de Louis Moreau' HP, mr, 1891, Moreau & Robert; flowers flame red, aging to dark crimson, large, full, globular

'Souv de Louis Simon' -- See 'Mrs Miniver'

'Souv de Louis Van Houtte' -- See 'Crimson Bedder'

'Souv de Lucie' N, dp, 1893, Schwartz; bud small, crimson; flowers cerise pink, lighter reverse to medium, 5 cm., dbl., flat, borne in small clusters; foliage small, glossy; ['Fellemberg' × 'Ernestine de Barante']

Souvenir de Lucien Massad® S, op, Massad/Ducher; flowers blend of pink, orange, salmon and yellow, large, double, cupped, moderate fruity fragrance; recurrent; strong (4 - 5 ft.) growth; intr. 2007

'Souv de Lucienne Valayer' HT, pb, 1938, Chambard, C.; bud long; flowers soft pink, shaded light salmon, very large, cupped; vigorous, bushy growth

'Souv de Ma Petite Andrée' T, w, 1901, Chauvry; flowers cream-white, edged pearly pink, large, very full, moderate fragrance; ['Mme Clément Massier' × unknown]

'Souv de Mme A. Henneveu' T, pb, 1892, Bernaix; flowers silky China pink, sometimes with coppery amaranthe, dbl.

'Souv de Mme A. Hess' HT, pb, 1936, Chambard, C.; bud long, pointed; flowers shrimp-pink, center deep coral, very large, cupped; foliage bronze; very vigorous, bushy growth; [seedling × 'Ami F. Mayery']

'Souv de Mme Achille van Herreweghe' HT, dr, 1936, Van Herreweghe-Coppitters; flowers carmine-red; vigorous growth

'Souv de Mme Alexandre Mathian' T, w, 1903, Bonnaire; flowers ivory white, base apricot-yellow, large, full, globular

'Souv de Mme Alfred Vy' HP, dr, 1880, Jamain; flowers deep currant red, large, full

'Souv de Mme Auguste Charles' B, mp, 1866, Moreau et Robert; flowers medium pink tinged salmon, outer petals fading quickly, medium, full, rounded, pompon, slight fruity fragrance; recurrent; angular (3-5 ft.) growth

'Souv de Mme Augustine Gillot' HT, op, 1920, Gillot, F.; bud long, pointed; flowers salmony flesh-pink, base salmon-yellow, reverse silvery flesh; ['Frau Karl Druschki' × 'Lyon Rose']

'Souv de Mme Berthier' HP, dr, 1881, Berthier/Liabaud; flowers velvety red, sometimes streaked white, large, very full; very remontant; growth to 5 ft.; ['Victor Verdier' × 'Jules Margottin']

'Souv de Mme Boll' HP, rb, Boyau; flowers rich red blend, full, cupped, moderate fragrance; recurrent; large (5 ft.) growth; intr. 1866

'Souv de Mme Boullet' HT, dy, 1921, Pernet-Ducher; bud long, pointed; flowers golden yellow with apricot tones, large, dbl., cupped, borne mostly singly, moderate tea fragrance; recurrent; foliage bronzy-purple; stems wiry; vigorous, spreading (4 ft.) growth; ['Sunburst' × seedling]

'Souv de Mme Boullet, Climbing' Cl HT, dy, 1930, H&S; [sport of 'Souv de Mme Boullet']

'Souv de Mme Breuil' B, dp; flowers deep cerise magenta, large, full, pompon, intense fragrance; recurrent; arching (2 m.) growth

'Souv de Mme Breul' ('Souv de Monsieur Bruel') B, mr, 1889, Levet; flowers light red, large, full; foliage dark green; prickles large

'Souv de Mme C. Chambard' HT, op, 1931, Chambard, C.; flowers coral-rose-pink, center flushed gold, large, semi-dbl., cupped; vigorous growth

'Souv de Mme C. Chambard, Climbing' Cl HT, op, 1935, Armstrong, J.A.; [sport of 'Mme C. Chambard']

'Souv de Mme Camusat' HT, lp, 1897, Bonnaire; flowers flesh pink, carmine at center, large, full

'Souv de Mme Canel' HT, rb, 1932, Gillot, F.; flowers carmine-orange, large, very dbl.; foliage pointed, bronze; robust, bushy growth

'Souv de Mme Chédane-Guinoisseau' HP, mr, 1900, Chédane-Guinoisseau; flowers bright geranium red, very large, dbl.

'Souv de Mme de Corval' HP, dp, 1867, Gonod; flowers dawn pink, medium, dbl.; recurrent

'Souv de Mme Durand' HT, yb, 1954, Privat; flowers naples yellow, base bright yellow, edges veined pink, dbl., globular; foliage glossy; strong stems

'Souv de Mme Dussordet' ('Souv de Monsieur Dussordet') HP, mp, 1860, Clément/Guillot

'Souv de Mme Ernest Cauvin' HT, pb, 1898, Pernet-Ducher; flowers flesh pink, bordered brighter pink, center light yellow to orange-yellow, large, very full; few prickles; growth upright

'Souv de Mme Ernest Oudin' HT, w,

1906, Bonnaire; flowers white, shaded bluish, large, full

'Souv de Mme Eugène Verdier' HP, pb, 1894, Jobert; flowers bright pink, reverse silver, full, globular

'Souv de Mme Eugène Verdier' HT, w, Pernet-Ducher; flowers white, base saffron-yellow, large, very full; foliage finely serrated; growth upright; ['Lady Mary Fitzwilliam' × 'Mme Chedane-Guinoisseau']; intr. 1895

'Souv de Mme F. Zurich' HT, mp, 1910, Puyravaud; flowers silvery pink, large, dbl.; ['Laure Wattinne' × 'Mme Bérard']

'Souv de Mme Faure' HP, dr, 1888, Bernaix; flowers dark, velvety carmine, shaded purple, very large, very full, globular

'Souv de Mme Fontaine' -- See 'Toujours Fleuri'

'Souv de Mme Frogère' HP, w, 1900, Chédane-Guinoisseau; flowers white, shaded pink, very large, full

'Souv de Mme Gauthier-Dumont' HT, mr, 1921, Guillot, P.; bud long, pointed; flowers scarlet

'Souv de Mme H. Thuret' HP, pb, 1922, Texier; flowers salmon-pink, center shrimp-red, edged chrome, well-formed, cupped; foliage rich green; very vigorous growth; ['Frau Karl Druschki' × 'Lyon Rose']

'Souv de Mme Hélène Lambert' T, pb, 1885, Gonod; flowers pink-yellow, reverse dark flesh pink, medium to large; ['Beauté de l'Europe' × unknown]

'Souv de Mme Hennecart' HP, mp, 1869, Carré/Cochet; flowers glossy pink fading to icy pink, large, dbl.

'Souv de Mme Jeanne Balandreau' ('Souv de Jeanne Balandreau') HP, mr, 1899, Vilin; flowers red, shaded vermilion, medium, full, globular to cupped; recurrent; foliage dark grey-green; upright (3-5 ft.) growth; [sport of 'Ulrich Brunner Fils']; intr. 1899

'Souv de Mme Joseph Métral' ('Mme Joseph Métral') Cl HT, mr, 1887, Bermaix; flowers bright cerise, illuminated with crimson and vermilion, 9-10 cm., very dbl.; ['Mme Bérard' × 'Eugene Fürst']

'Souv de Mme Jules Pages' HMult, pb, 1937, Reiter; flowers deep pink shaded orange and red, open, small, dbl.; free, intermittent bloom; vigorous, climbing or pillar growth; ['Phyllis Bide' × 'Eblouissant']

'Souv de Mme Krenger' HT, op, 1919, Chambard, C.; flowers pure salmon-orange, passing to coppery pink, dbl.; ['Mme Mélanie Soupert' × 'Willowmere']

'Souv de Mme l'Advocat' N, op, 1899, Veysset; flowers coppery pink, medium, dbl.; [sport of 'Duarte de Oliveira']

'Souv de Mme Lambard' T, yb, 1890, California Nursery Co.; flowers canary yellow, shaded and tinted with salmon rose, large

'Souv de Mme Lefèbvre' HT, rb, 1929, Richardier; flowers oriental red, passing to pink, golden yellow and red; vigorous growth

'Souv de Mme Léonie Viennot' Cl T, yb, 1898, Bernaix, A.; flowers deep peachy yellow-pink, aging to paler pink, reverse silvery, 10 cm., very dbl., intense tea fragrance; foliage dark green; vigorous (10-15 ft.) growth; ['Gloire de Dijon' × unknown]

'Souv de Mme Levet' T, ob, 1891, Levet, F.; flowers orange-yellow, large, full; foliage dark green; few prickles; growth vigorous; ['Mme Carot' × 'Mme Eugène Verdier']

'Souv de Mme Louise Cretté' HT, yb, 1924, Cretté; flowers golden yellow, shaded coral and red, dbl.; ['Mme Edouard Herriot' × unknown]

'Souv de Mme Morin-Latune' HT, dp, 1920, Bernaix, P.; bud long, pointed; flowers cream-rose, dbl.

'Souv de Mme Pidoux' HT, yb, 1926, Chambard, C.; bud long, pointed; flowers chrome-yellow, reverse pink, cupped; [seedling × 'Mrs Aaron Ward']

'Souv de Mme Robert' HP, lp, 1879, Moreau et Robert; flowers icy salmon-pink, center brighter, large, dbl.; ['Jules Margottin' × unknown]

'Souv de Mme Rousseau' -- See 'Souv de Monsieur Rousseau'

'Souv de Mme Sablayrolles' T, ab, 1891, Bonnaire; flowers apricot-pink edged with carmine, large, full, globular, borne mostly solitary; ['Devoniensis' × 'Souv d'Elise Vardon']

'Souv de Mme Sadi Carnot' HP, dr, 1898, Lévêque; flowers deep carmine red nuanced purple, very large; foliage glaucous green; ['Mme Victor Verdier' × unknown]

'Souv de Mme Salati-Mongellaz' HP, dp, 1937, Croibier; bud long, pointed; flowers satiny rose-pink, very large, dbl.; foliage dark; very vigorous growth; ['Frau Karl Druschki' × seedling]

'Souv de Mme Victor Verdier' HP, dp, 1883, Verdier, E.; flowers shining dark pink, reverse lighter, large, full

'Souv de Mme William Wood' HP, m, 1865, Verdier, E.; flowers purple; vigorous growth; ['Général Jacqueminot' × unknown]

'Souv de Madeleine Rouillon' HT, ob, 1929, Bernaix, P.; bud long, pointed; flowers orange, base yellow, dbl.; ['Manon' × 'Elvira Aramayo']

'Souv de Mlle Élise Châtelard' Pol, mr, 1891, Bernaix; flowers carmine red

'Souv de Mlle Juliet de Bricard' Pol, lp, 1934, Délépine; flowers pale rosy pink, 2 in., very dbl., globular, borne in clusters; recurrent; foliage glossy, dark; vigorous (2 ft.), bushy growth; ['Cécile Brunner' × 'Yvonne Rabier']

'Souv de Mlle Victor Caillet' T, w, 1892, Bernaix; flowers pure white, medium, full

'Souv de Malmedy' HGal, mp, Scarman; flowers clear pink, full, shallow cup; growth to 4 ft.; intr. 1996

'Souv de Maman Corboeuf' HP, mp, 1900, Corboeuf; flowers medium, dbl.

Souv de Marcel Proust® F, my, Delbard; flowers intense yellow, large, full, cupped, quartered, intense citronelle fragrance; free-flowering; foliage medium green; moderate, branching growth; intr. 1992

'Souv de Marcelle Balage' ('Marcella Baldge') HT, pb, 1930, Bernaix, P.; bud long, pointed; flowers satiny flesh-pink, center slightly tinted salmon, very large, dbl., cupped, intense fragrance; foliage dark; ['Willowmere' × 'Mme Pizay']

'Souv de Maria Clotilde' HT, ly, 1934, Carneiro; bud long; flowers amber-white, often passing to light yellow, center sometimes flesh-pink, large, dbl., moderate fragrance; vigorous growth; [sport of 'Mme Abel Chatenay']

'Souv de Maria de Zayas' HT, mr, 1906, Soupert & Notting; bud long, pointed; flowers carmine red veined deep red, very large, dbl., moderate fragrance; [seedling × 'Papa Gontier']

'Souv de Maria Zozaya' HT, or, 1903, Soupert & Notting; bud long; flowers coral-red, silvery center, very large, full; ['Souv de Wootton' × 'Mrs W. J. Grant']

'Souv de Marie Finon' HT, ab, 1924, Croibier; flowers apricot-yellow passing to clear yellow shaded salmon, dbl.

'Souv de Marie-Thérèse' HT, w, Chabanat; flowers ivory-white; low growth

'Souv de Marie Thérèse Privat' Pol, mr, 1935, Privat; flowers bright vermilion, well-formed, very dbl., borne in clusters of 40-50; foliage bright green; dwarf, good habit growth

'Souv de Marques Loureiro' HT, rb, 1912, Ketten Bros.; flowers light red shading to rose, tinted yellow and purple, dbl.; ['Mons. Paul Lédé' × 'Mme Hoste']

'Souv de Maurice Chevalier' -- See 'Delsouche'

'Souv de McKinley' HT, lp, 1902, Godard; flowers delicate pink, full, moderate fragrance; recurrent; ['Magna Charta' × 'Captain Christy']; sometimes classed as HP or P

'Souv de Mère Fontaine' HCh, mr, 1874, Fontaine; flowers bright red, nuanced carmine, very large, full

'Souv de Mon Ecole' S, dr

'Souv de Monsieur Boll' HP, mr, 1866, Boyau; flowers bright cherry red, very large, full

'Souv de Monsieur Bruel' -- See 'Souv de Mme Breul'

'Souv de Monsieur Claude Dupont' T, dp, 1893, Godard; flowers dark pink, shaded red, large, full; ['Souv de Victor Hugo' × unknown]

'Souv de Monsieur Droche' HP, mp, 1881, Pernet père; flowers carmine-rose, large, dbl., globular

'Souv de Monsieur Dussordet' -- See 'Souv de Mme Dussordet'

'Souv de Monsieur Faivre' HP, mr, 1879, Levet; flowers poppy red with slate reflections, very large, full

'Souv de Monsieur Frédéric Vercellone' HT, pb, 1906, Schwartz; flowers carmine pink, lightly coppery, nuanced blush white tinted bright carmine, large, full; ['Antoine Rivoire' × 'André Schwartz']

'Souv de Monsieur Poncet' P, lp, 1892, Pernet; flowers light pink, large, dbl

'Souv de Monsieur Rousseau' ('Souv de Mme Rousseau') HP, mr, 1861, Fargeton; flowers scarlet, changing to crimson, shaded maroon, velvety, large, dbl.

'Souv de Némours' B, mp, 1859, Hervé; flowers fresh rose, reverse darker, large, full, moderate fragrance; recurrent; medium growth

'Souv de Norah Lindsay' LCl, mp; flowers bright pink, stamens golden, very large, single; vigorous, pillar growth

'Souv de Nungesser' HT, dr, 1927, Croibier; flowers brilliant deep carmine-red, dbl.; ['Mme Maurice de Luze' × 'Laurent Carle']

'Souv de Papa Calame' HT, dp, 1922, Guillot; flowers large, dbl.

'Souv de Paul Grandclaude' HT, yb, 1923, Sauvageot, H.; bud large, long, pointed; flowers yellow, shaded pink and in autumn light brown, semi-dbl.; ['Mme Mélanie Soupert' × 'Beauté de Lyon']

'Souv de Paul Neyron' T, yb, 1871, Levet, A.; flowers salmon-yellow edged pink, semi-globular, large; very vigorous growth; [sport of 'Ophirie × unknown, or Devoniensis × Souv de la Malmaison']

'Souv de Paul Raudnitz' HWich, lp, 1910, Cochet-Cochet; flowers white tinged with salmon, 3-4 cm., very dbl., borne in clusters of 25-35; some autumn repeat; foliage elliptical, bright green, glossy; prickles strong, slightly hooked, sparse, gray; [R. wichurana × 'Turner's Crimson Rambler']

'Souv de Périgueux' HT, mr, 1913, Croibier; flowers bright, glossy carmine-red, large, full; ['Mme M. de Luze' × 'Liberty']

'Souv de Philémon Cochet' HRg, w, 1899, Cochet-Cochet; flowers white, center rose tinged salmon, 10-12 cm., very full, moderate fragrance; recurrent; medium growth; [sport of 'Blanc Double de Coubert']; same as Blanc Double de Coubert except for slight color difference

'Souv de Pierre Dupuy' B, dr, 1876, Levet; flowers deep velvety red, 3 in., full, globular, borne singly and in small clusters, moderate fragrance; some repeat; ['Général Jacqueminot' × unknown]

'Souv. de Pierre Guillot' HT, ob, 1928, Guillot, M.; bud long, pointed; flowers coral-orange-yellow blend, dbl.; ['Marie Adélaïde' × seedling]

'Souv de Pierre Ketten' HT, pb, 1928, Ketten Bros.; bud long, pointed; flowers bright rose, inside pink, base chrome-yellow, 30-35 petals, intense fragrance; ['Mme Mélanie Soupert' × 'Pilgrim']

'Souv de Pierre Leperdrieux' HRg, mr, 1895, Cochet-Cochet; flowers bright wine red, 9-10 cm., semi-dbl., borne in large clusters; large fruit

'Souv de Pierre Notting' T, yb, 1902, Soupert & Notting; bud long, pointed; flowers sunflower-yellow tinted apricot and coppery yellow, edged rose, very dbl., cupped, slight fragrance; free-flowering; foliage rich green, soft; ['Maréchal Niel' × 'Maman Cochet']

'Souv de Pierre Notting, Climbing' Cl T, ab, 1913, Cant, F.; flowers apricot yellow with hints of gold, fading to pink, edged carmine, 10 cm., very full, borne in small clusters; [sport of 'Souv de Pierre Notting']

'Souv de Pierre Sionville' HP, mr, 1906, Boutigny; flowers bright red, large, very full, cupped; sometimes classed as HT

'Souv de Pierre Vibert' M, dr, 1867, Moreau et Robert; flowers dark red, shaded carmine and violet, large, dbl., slight fragrance; sometimes recurrent bloom; moderate growth

'Souv de Poiteau' HP, op, 1868, Margottin; flowers bright salmon pink, large, full, cupped

'Souv de Prosper Fraissenon' HT, m, 1927, Richardier; bud long, pointed; flowers geranium-red tinted violet

'Souv de R. B. Ferguson' HT, pb, 1922, Ferguson, W.; flowers shell-pink and apricot, sometimes shaded rose-pink and cerise; [seedling × 'Constance']

'Souv de Raymond Gaujard' HT, yb, 1943, Gaujard; bud ovoid; flowers golden yellow, reverse often veined red, open, medium, dbl.; foliage dark, glossy; vigorous, upright growth

'Souv de René Bahaud' T, op, 1897, Bahaud; flowers salmon pink, opening golden yellow, aging to China pink, large, full

'Souv de René Grognet' HT, ob, 1921, Chambard, C.; bud long, pointed; flowers coppery orange-yellow, shaded carmine

Souv de Robert Schuman® S, ab, Guillot-Massad; flowers amber yellow, fading to white, semi-dbl., cupped to flat, borne in clusters; recurrent; foliage dark green, glossy; intr. 2006

'Souv de Romain Desprez' HP, lp, 1871, de Sansal; flowers flesh pink, shaded slate, center brighter, very large, full

'Souv de Rose Berkley' -- See 'Rose Berkley'

'Souv de Rose-Marie' -- See 'Lentrita'

'Souv de S. A. Prince' ('The Queen') T, w, 1889, Dingee & Conard; flowers pure white, large, full, globular; [sport of 'Souv. d'un Ami']

'Souv de St Anne's' B, lp, before 1916; flowers blush-pink, medium, semi-dbl., moderate fragrance; recurrent bloom; medium to tall growth; [sport of 'Souv. de la Malmaison']; from the garden of Lady Ardilaun, at Saint-Anne, near Dublin; intr. 1950

'Souv de Saintonge' N, w, 1904, Chauvry; flowers white, base canary yellow

'Souv de Shelby Wallace' -- See 'Shelby Wallace'

'Souv de Simon de St Jean' HP, mr

'Souv de Solférino' HP, dp, 1861, Margottin; flowers velvety carmine, shaded brown, large, full

'Souv de Spa' HP, dr, 1873, Gautreau; flowers deep red with scarlet reflex, large, full, globular; ['Mme Victor Verdier' × unknown]

'Souv de Thérèse Levet' T, dr, 1886, Levet, A.; flowers crimson, shaded pink at the center, large, full, globular to cupped, moderate sweet fragrance; foliage dark green; prickles large, hooked; compact (4 ft.), spreading growth; ['Adam' × unknown]

'Souv de Victoire Landeau' ('Souv de Victor Landeau') HP, pb, 1884, Moreau et Robert; flowers fresh pink to cherry red, center darker, large, dbl., globular

'Souv de Victor Hugo' HP, lp, 1885, Pernet père; flowers bright satiny pink, very large, very dbl., globular; foliage thick, light green; growth upright; ['Ambrogio Maggi' × unknown]

'Souv de Victor Hugo' T, pb, 1886, Bonnaire; flowers China-pink, center salmon-pink, large, dbl., intense fragrance; recurrent; stems purple-red; upright growth; ['Duchesse de Brabant' × 'Regulus']

'Souv de Victor Landeau' B, mr, 1890, Moreau et Robert; buds rose pink; flowers vivid red, shaded carmine, very large, full, cupped, borne in clusters, moderate fragrance; recurrent

'Souv de Victor Landeau' -- See 'Souv de Victoire Landeau'

'Souv de Victor Verdier' HP, rb, 1878, Verdier, E.; flowers scarlet poppy-red nuanced purple crimson, flame, and violet, large, full; very remontant; foliage oval, delicate green, regularly toothed; prickles numerous, recurved, sharp; growth upright

'Souv de William Robinson' T, op, 1899, Bernaix fils; bud ovoid; flowers peony-pink, with salmon, partly cream white and apricot yellow with violet veins

'Souv de William Wood' HP, dr, 1864, Verdier, E.; flowers dark blackish purple, centers flame red, large, full, semi-globular, moderate fragrance; ['General Jacqueminot' × unknown]

'Souv de Yeddo' HRg, mp, 1874, Morlet; flowers silky China pink, shaded white, large, dbl.; [R. rugosa × a tea]

'Souv d'E. Guillard' HT, rb, 1912, Chambard, C.; flowers reddish-yellow shaded coppery carmine, large, dbl.; very vigorous, branching growth; ['Beauté Inconstante' × 'Le Progres']

'Souv d'Elise Vardon' ('Xiang Fen Lian') T, w, 1855, Marest; flowers creamy white, center yellowish, very large, dbl., globular, moderate fragrance; recurrent;

foliage leathery, glossy; moderate (3-4 ft.) growth

'Souv d'Emile Mayrisch' HT, dr, 1932, Ketten Bros.; flowers dark crimson-garnet, well-formed, large, 35-40 petals; stiff stems; vigorous growth

'Souv d'Émile Peyrard' T, w, 1900, Bonnaire; flowers pearly white, edges tinted pink

'Souv d'Emile Zola' Cl HT, lp, 1907, Begault-Pigné; bud bright pink; flowers light silvery pink, very large, full; ['La France de '89' × unknown]

'Souv d'Emmanuel Buatois' HT, rb, 1932, Buatois; bud long, pointed; flowers coral-red shaded shrimp-red, reverse clear rose, base golden, dbl.; foliage leathery, bronze; vigorous growth; ['Mme Edouard Herriot' × 'Souv. de Claudius Pernet']

'Souv d'Enghien' M, mp, about 1830, Parmentier; flowers bright pink, medium, full

'Souv d'Ernest Thébault' HWich, dr, 1921, Thébault; flowers small, dbl., borne in clusters of 10-20; vigorous, climbing growth

'Souv d'Espagne' T, yb, 1888, Pries/Ketten Bros.; flowers coppery yellow and rose, edged with pinkish carmine, medium, dbl., cupped

'Souv d'Henri Puyravaud' HT, w, 1901, Puyravaud; flowers white, center tinted chrome yellow, large, full; ['Lady Mary Fitzwilliam' × 'Lady Emily Peel']

'Souv di Castagneto' HP, lp, Scarman; intr. 1988

'Souv du Baron de Rochetaillée' HP, m, 1888, Liabaud; flowers purple, large, full

'Souv du Baron de Rothschild' B, mp, 1868, Avoux / Crozy; flowers carmine pink, large, full

'Souv du Baron de Sémur' HP, m, 1874, Lacharme, F.; flowers deep purple-red shaded fiery red and black, large, dbl.; vigorous growth; ['Charles Lefebvre' × unknown]

'Souv du Capitaine Crémona' HT, rb, 1928, Bernaix, P.; flowers salmon-carmine over yellow ground, dbl.; ['Admiration' × 'Gorgeous']

'Souv du Capitaine Fernand Japy' HT, mr, 1922, Sauvageot, H.; flowers purple pink, large, dbl.; ['Le Progres' × 'Les Rosati']

'Souv du Capitaine Ferrand' HT, rb, 1939, Gaujard; bud long, well formed; flowers nasturtium-red, reverse golden yellow; erect, vigorous growth

'Souv du Comte Cavour' HP, dr, 1861, Robert & Moreau; flowers dark bluish-red

'Souv du Comte Cavour' HP, mr, Margottin; flowers velvety crimson shaded darker crimson, large, full; intr. 1861

'Souv du Docteur Albert Reverdin' HT, rb, 1930, Bernaix, P.; bud long, pointed; flowers brilliant carmine, shaded vermilion, large, very dbl.; foliage dark; strong stems; vigorous growth; ['George C. Waud' × 'Mrs Edward Powell']

'Souv du Docteur Jamain' HP, dr, 1865, Lacharme, F.; flowers plum shaded deep crimson, yellow stamens, small to medium, dbl., cupped, moderate old rose fragrance; recurrent; few prickles; growth arching, tall (5-9 ft.); ['Charles Lefebvre' × unknown]

'Souv du Dr Passot' T, mr, 1889, Godard; flowers velvety crimson red, fading lighter, large, full

'Souv du Dr Abel de Bouchard' T, w, 1900, Chauvry; flowers white, center greenish-yellow, coppery reflections, very large, moderate fragrance; ['Mme Eugene Verdier' × unknown]

'Souv du Lieutenant Bujon' B, mr, 1891, Moreau et Robert; flowers light red, aging to carmine, very large, dbl., moderate fragrance; foliage dark green

'Souv du Papa Calame' HT, pb, 1921, Gillot, F.; bud long, pointed; flowers carmine-pink, reverse silvery pink, stamens salmon, dbl.; [sport of 'Jonkheer J.L. Mock']

'Souv du Petit Roi de Rome' HP, lp, 1850, Béluze; flowers flesh pink, center darker

'Souv du Président Carnot' HT, lp, 1894, Pernet-Ducher; bud long, pointed; flowers flesh-pink, center shell-pink, full, moderate fragrance; recurrent; foliage medium green, matte; moderate growth; ['Lady Mary Fitzwilliam' × unknown]

'Souv du Président Carnot, Climbing' Cl HT, lp, 1926, Grandes Roseraies; [sport of 'Souv du Président Carnot']

'Souv du Président Daurel' HT, dp, 1906, Chauvry; flowers large, dbl.; [sport of 'Mme Caroline Testout']

'Souv du Président Lincoln' B, mr, 1865, Moreau et Robert; flowers crimson red, shaded black, medium, full, slight fragrance; some repeat; bushy (5 ft.) growth

'Souv du Président Plumecocq' HT, rb, 1958, Laperrière; flowers bright red, reverse marked silvery, large, dbl.; foliage bronze; very vigorous, well branched growth; [seedling × 'Peace']

'Souv du Président Porcher' HP, dp, 1880, Granger, T.; flowers dark pink, reverse lighter, large, full; foliage light green; few prickles; growth upright

'Souv du Prince Charles d'Arenberg' N, my, 1897, Soupert & Notting; flowers canary yellow, center darker, large, full, moderate fragrance; ['Rêve d'Or' × 'Duchesse d'Auerstädt']

'Souv du Reverend Père Planque' HT, ob, 1932, Bel; flowers orange-chrome-yellow, fading lighter, large, full; foliage very glossy; very vigorous growth; [seedling × 'Souv. de Georges Pernet']

'Souv du Rosiériste Gonod' HP, mr, 1889, Ducher fils; flowers cerise red, veined bright pink, very large, dbl., intense fragrance

'Souv du Rosiériste Rambaux' T, pb, 1883, Rambaux; bud ovoid; flowers straw yellow, heavily bordered with bright rose, cupped, intense tea fragrance; foliage medium size, glossy; ['Bon Silène' × unknown]

'Souv du Sénateur Bazire' HMult, m, 1918, Lottin; flowers violet, center violet-rose, semi-dbl., borne in clusters of 25-50; ['Veilchenblau' × 'Bordeaux']

'Souv du Sergent Cretté' HT, yb, 1921, Chambard, C.; bud long, pointed; flowers coppery golden yellow, shaded carmine, very large, cupped; foliage bronze; very vigorous growth; ['Mme Mélanie Soupert' × seedling]

'Souv d'un Ami' ('Mme Tixier', 'Queen Victoria') T, lp, 1846, Bélot-Défougère; flowers pale rose tinged salmon, very large, dbl., cupped, intense fragrance; recurrent; vigorous growth

'Souv d'un Frère' B, dr, 1850, Oger; flowers purple-red and carmine, medium, dbl.

'Souv of Miami' HT, dr, 1925, Cook, J.W.

'Souv of Portland' HT, m, 1910, Dickson, H.; flowers dark purple, large, full

'Souv of Stella Gray' T, ob, 1907, Dickson, A.; flowers deep orange splashed apricot, salmon and crimson, small to medium, semi-dbl.

'Souv of the Old Rose Garden' HT, pb, 1929, Cant, B. R.; flowers silvery pink, brighter inside, very large, dbl., globular; foliage glossy, light; strong stems; vigorous growth

'Souv of Wootton' HT, mr, 1888, Cook, J.W.; flowers rich velvety red, very large, dbl.; foliage dark, leathery; vigorous growth; ['Bon Silène' × 'Louis van Houtte']

'Souv of Wootton, Climbing' Cl HT, mr, 1899, Butler; flowers bright magenta red, large, full, cupped, borne singly and in small clusters; [sport of 'Souv of Wooton']

'Souvenire' -- See 'Wekjuvoo'

'Souviens-Toi' F, yb, 1986, Kriloff, Michel; flowers medium yellow, petals edged and washed carmine, large, 38 petals, moderate fragrance; foliage matte

'Sovereign' HT, dy, 1922, Cant, B. R.; flowers deep yellow and old-gold, open, cupped, intense fruity fragrance; foliage glossy, dark, bronze; vigorous growth; ['Queen Mary' × seedling]

'Sovrana' HT, ob, 1930, Aicardi, D.; flowers orange streaked yellow, well-formed, large; very vigorous, upright growth; ['Julien Potin' × ('Signora' × unknown)]

'Sowetan Peace' -- See 'Jacsowe'

'Sox' -- See 'Micsox'

'Soyécourt' HT, rb, 1921, Jersey Nursery; flowers blood-red, overlaid orange; ['Gen. MacArthur' × 'George C. Waud']

Soyeuse de Lyon® S, op, 2007, Ducher; flowers orange salmon, large, full, cupped; recurrent; strong (4 ft.) growth; intr. 2007

'Space Girl' LCl, dr, 1966, Barter; flowers dark crimson, very large, dbl.; foliage dark; vigorous, climbing growth; [Queen

Elizabeth® × 'Étoile de Hollande']
'Space Invader' -- See 'Dicrocky'
Space Odyssey™ -- See 'Weksnacare'
'Space Probe' -- See 'Minacon'
Space Walk™ -- See 'Minabcco'
'Spaethiana' (*R.* × *spaethiana*) S, m; flowers purple, large, single, borne in clusters; may possibly repeat; [*R. palustris* × *R. rugosa*]; possibly 1902 or earlier
'Spangled Red' HT, rb, 2007, Heath, William L.; flowers medium red, reverse red with white speckles and stripes, 3½ in., full, high-centered, borne mostly solitary; foliage medium, dark green, matte; prickles medium, triangular, straw-colored, moderate; growth upright, medium (3 ft.): exhibition, cutting, garden decoration; ['Gemma Louise' × 'Joyce Mary']; intr. 2007
'Spangles' -- See 'Ganspa'
'Spanish Beauty' -- See 'Mme Grégoire Staechelin'
'Spanish Dancer' HT, pb, Meilland; flowers cream, edged strong pink, full, pompon; intr. 2002
'Spanish Dancer' -- See 'Morliz'
'Spanish Enchantress' S, pb; intr. 1999
'Spanish Eyes' F, op, 1978, Takatori, Yoshiho; flowers orange-salmon, reverse yellow; [sport of Prominent®]; intr. 1981
'Spanish Fort' -- See 'Talspanish'
'Spanish Gold' HT, dy, 1960, Fletcher; flowers straw-yellow; tall, bushy growth
'Spanish Lady' HT, rb; flowers striped
'Spanish Main' -- See 'Marquesa del Vadillo'
'Spanish Musk Rose' ('Hispanica Moschata Simplex') HMsk, w, before 1629; flowers white, sometimes shade pink at center, medium, single
'Spanish Orange' F, ob, 1966, deRuiter; flowers orange, 1½ in., very dbl., borne in clusters; foliage dark, glossy; very free growth
'Spanish Rhapsody' S, pb, 1985, Buck, Dr. Griffith J.; flowers deep pink, tinted orange and freckled red, large, 30 petals, shallow cup, borne 1 - 8 per cluster, moderate raspberry fragrance; recurrent; foliage medium-large, leathery, dark olive green; prickles awl-like; upright, bushy, branching growth; hardy; ['Gingersnap' × 'Sevilliana']; intr. 1984
'Spanish Sun' F, dy, 1966, Boerner; bud large, ovoid; flowers imbricated, 3½-4½ in., 35-40 petals, borne singly and several together, intense russet apple fragrance; recurrent; foliage glossy, leathery; prickles normal, medium, some hooked downward and some upward; stems long, strong; vigorous, bushy growth; hips none ; PP2809; ['Golden Garnette' × 'Yellow Pinocchio climbing seedling']; intr. 1966
'Spanish Sunset' F, ob, Franko; flowers tropical orange, suffused with yellow, yellow center, 3.5-4 in., 10-12 petals, flat, borne in clusters, no fragrance; recurrent; foliage medium green, glossy; uniform, rounded (3 - 4 ft.) growth; PPAF; intr. 2008
'Spanky' Min, yb, 1986, Bridges, Dennis A.; flowers bright yellow, shaded pink to red, reverse yellow, aging pink, dbl., high-centered; foliage large, medium green, semi-glossy; prickles few, pink, small; medium, upright growth; ['Rise 'n' Shine' × unknown]
Spanky® -- See 'Bagspank'
'Sparkels' HT, rb, 1956, Webber; bud urn shaped; flowers red striped white, medium, 35-50 petals, high-centered, intense fragrance; foliage leathery; PP1464; [sport of 'Briarcliff']
'Sparkie' Min, mr, 1957, Moore, Ralph S.; flowers bright red, becoming darker, 6 petals, borne in clusters; foliage glossy; vigorous (12-16 in.) growth; [(*R. wichurana* × 'Floradora') × 'Little Buckaroo']
'Sparkle' HT, pb, 1949, Brownell; bud pointed, ovoid; flowers white turning cream, rose-pink and yellow toward center, large, dbl., high-centered, moderate fragrance; foliage glossy, light green; vigorous, upright, bushy growth; PP928; ['Pink Princess' × 'Shades of Autumn']
'Sparkle Berry' -- See 'Benfebu'
'Sparkle On' F, mr
'Sparkle Plenty' F, ob, 1976, Patterson; bud ovoid; flowers bright orange, to open, 3 in., 25 petals, high-centered; foliage dark, leathery, wrinkled; vigorous growth; ['Ma Perkins' × 'Engagement']
'Sparkler' Pol, mr, 1929, deRuiter; flowers clear red touched with scarlet, slight fragrance; recurrent; [sport of 'Golden Salmon']; intr. 1929
'Sparkler' -- See 'Poulcov'
'Sparkler' -- See 'Delecla'
'Sparkling Burgundy' F, dr, 1965, Williams, J. Benjamin; flowers burgundy-red, open, medium, dbl., borne in clusters; foliage dark, leathery, glossy; vigorous, upright growth; [Queen Elizabeth® × 'Carrousel']
'Sparkling Burgundy II' Gr, dr, Williams, J. Benjamin; flowers dark scarlet, prominent golden stamens, single; intr. 1996
Sparkling Cupido® Min, dp, deRuiter; intr. 2004
'Sparkling Fire' -- See 'Brospark'
Sparkling Orange™ -- See 'Devilk'
Sparkling Pink™ -- See 'Pouleas'
'Sparkling Rouge' Min, rb, Delbard; flowers deep red, heavily brushed with creamy white, full, cupped to flat; tall growth
'Sparkling Ruffle' S, rb
'Sparkling Scarlet' ('Iskara', 'Iskra') Cl F, mr, 1971, Meilland; flowers scarlet-red, 2½ in., 13 petals, borne in clusters, moderate fruity fragrance; recurrent; foliage large, semi-glossy; to 7-10 ft. growth; [Danse des Sylphes® × Zambra®]; intr. 1970
Sparkling White™ -- See 'Poulcov'
Sparkling Yellow™ -- See 'Poulgode'
Sparks™ -- See 'Savaspark'
'Sparrieshoop' S, lp, 1953, Kordes; bud long, pointed; flowers light salmon-pink, gold stamens, 4 in., single, borne in large sprays, intense fragrance; repeat bloom; foliage leathery; very vigorous (5 ft.), upright, bushy growth; [('Poulsen's Pink' × 'Siren') × ('Johannes Böttner' × *R. rubiginosa magnifica*)]
'Spartan' ('Aparte') F, or, 1956, Boerner; bud large, pointed ovoid; flowers orange-red to reddish-coral, 3-3½ in., 25-30 petals, high-centered, borne singly and in clusters, intense sweet briar/geranium fragrance; quick repeat; foliage dark, leathery, glossy; prickles normal, medium, straight or hooked downward; stems medium, strong; vigorous, bushy growth; hips none ; PP1357; ['Geranium Red' × 'Fashion']; intr. 1955
'Spartan, Climbing' Cl F, or, 1958, Martinez (also Kordes, 1960; Boerner, 1965); PP1616; [sport of 'Spartan']; same as bush form except for climbing habit; intr. 1964
'Spartan Blaze' Min, rb, 1991, Gruenbauer, Richard; bud ovoid; flowers red with yellow reverse, medium, dbl., high-centered, borne usually singly, slight fragrance; foliage medium size, medium green, semi-glossy; upright growth; ['Poker Chip' × 'Rise 'n' Shine']; intr. 1991
'Spartan Dawn' Min, yb, 1990, Gruenbauer, Richard; bud rounded; flowers yellow with orange edges, reverse yellow to cream to orange, 30 petals, no fragrance; foliage medium size, medium green, matte; few or no prickles; bushy, medium growth; hips round, flat on top, orange-red; ['Rise 'n' Shine' × 'Hokey Pokey']
'Spartan II' F, Moreira da Silva, A.
Späth 250® -- See 'Späth's Jubiläum'
'Späth's Jubiläum' (Späth 250®) F, or, 1976, Kordes; bud ovoid; flowers 2½ in., 22 petals, high-centered; foliage dark, soft; vigorous, upright, bushy growth; ['Castanet' × seedling]; intr. 1970
'Speaker Sam' HT, yb, 1962, Dean; flowers light yellow edged red; PP2053; [sport of 'Peace']; intr. 1962
'Spearmint' Min, w; bud pointed; flowers creamy white, dbl., cupped; recurrent; medium growth; [sport of Angela Rippon®]; intr. after 1977
Spebola HT, op, Spek; intr. 2002
'Spebrown' F, r, Spek; intr. 2005
'Spebruis' F, op, Spek; intr. 2005
'Spebutti' F, ly, Spek; intr. 2002
'Specawijk' ('Aruba') HT, mr, Spek; intr. 1996
'Special Angel' Min, m, 1992, Stoddard, Louis; flowers mauve, tipped in pink, 1½ in., dbl., high-centered, borne mostly singly; foliage medium size, dark green, semi-glossy; few prickles; tall (60-70 cm.), upright, bushy growth; [Jean

Kenneally™ × ('Rise 'n' Shine' × Acey Deucy™)]; intr. 1992

Special Anniversary™   HT, mp, Smith, Edward; flowers rose pink, dbl., globular, intense fragrance; foliage dark green, glossy; short (3 ft.), bushy growth; intr. 2003

'Special Bond'   S, mp, Bond; flowers medium pink in center, petals fade as they open, large, full, intense fragrance; prickles very few; medium growth; intr. 2002

Special Border™ -- See 'Santa Rosa'

'Special Child' -- See 'Taniripsa'

'Special Effects' -- See 'Desspecial'

'Special Event'   HT, m; intr. 2005

'Special Friend'   Min, lp, Kirkham; flowers blush pink with salmon heart, full, cupped, borne usually in clusters of 5 - 8, slight fragrance; recurrent; foliage pale green, glossy; dense (18 in.) growth; intr. 1999

'Special Guest'   HT, mr, 1992, Guest, M.M.; flowers crimson, 3-3½ in., very dbl., borne singly; foliage medium size, medium green, semi-glossy; numerous prickles; medium (70 cm.), bushy growth; [sport of 'Jan Guest']; intr. 1990

'Special Merit'   HT, mr, 1991, Wambach, Alex A.; bud medium, ovoid, pointed; flowers large, 30 petals, high-centered, borne singly, slight spicy fragrance; recurrent; foliage medium size, dark green, semi-glossy; prickles average, medium, curved downward; stems long (24 in.); medium (5 ft.), upright, bushy growth; hips globular ; PP9862; ['seedling 83-1' × 'First Prize']; intr. 1993

'Special Moment'   F, ab; intr. 2005

'Special Occasion' -- See 'Fryyoung'

'Special Reserve'   Pol, dp, diCillo; intr. 2002

'Special Son'   Min, mr; intr. 2005

'Special Wishes' -- See 'Poultop'

'Speckled Delight'   HT, rb, Patel

'Speclever'   HT, dy, Spek; intr. 2005

'Speclown'   HT, pb, Spek; intr. 2005

'Specoffie'   HT, r, Spek; intr. 2005

'Specoi'   HT, op, Spek; intr. 2005

'Speconan'   HT, pb, Spek; intr. 2003

'Specream'   HT, w, Spek; intr. 2005

'Spectabile' -- See 'Spectabilis'

'Spectabilis'   ('Ayez', 'Spectabile', 'Rose Ayez', 'Noisette Ayez') HSem, m, before 1832; bud dark crimson; flowers bright rosy lilac, fading to white, medium, dbl., cupped, borne in small, loose clusters, intense musky fragrance; occasionally repeats in autumn; vigorous, climbing growth; [possibly R. sempervirens' × Noisette hybrid]; possibly by Jacques; intr. 1832

Spectacular™ -- See 'Poulac013(N)'

'Spectacular' -- See 'Danse de Feu'

'Spectacular Palace'   (Spectacular™) MinFl, ab, Poulsen; flowers apricot blend, 5-8 cm., dbl., no fragrance; foliage dark; growth bushy, 40-60 cm.; PP15569; intr. 2003

'Spectra'   ('Banzai 83') LCl, yb, Meilland; flowers yellow suffused with red on upper surface, numerous short, irregular petals in center, 3-4 in., very full, borne singly or in small clusters of 2 or 3, slight fragrance; abundant in spring, sporadic thereafter; foliage large, deep green, glossy; few prickles; growth vigorous, well branched, long arching canes; PP5396; [('Kabuki' × Peer Gynt®) × ((Zambra® × 'Suspense') × King's Ransom®)]; intr. 1983

'Spectrum'   LCl, mr, Thomas

'Spedaba'   HT, or, Spek; intr. 2005

'Spedappy'   HT, mr, Spek; intr. 2004

'Spedelah'   HT, dp, Spek; intr. 2006

'Spedeni' -- See 'Denice'

'Spedilap'   HT, yb, Spek; intr. 2006

'Spedilla'   HT, lp, Spek; intr. 2005

'Spedish'   HT, yb, Spek; intr. 2006

'Spedole'   HT, pb, Spek; intr. 2006

'Spedonna'   F, mp, Spek; intr. 2005

'Spedoon'   F, pb, Spek; intr. 2005

'Speearring'   HT, ly, Spek; intr. 2006

Speechless™ -- See 'Kinspeech'

Speelwark® -- See 'Korwarpeel'

'Spefarine'   F, yb, Spek; intr. 2006

'Spefesco'   F, w, Spek; intr. 2006

'Spefeyes'   F, w, Spek; intr. 2006

'Spefido'   F, dr, Spek; intr. 2006

'Spefire'   HT, mr, Spek; intr. 2006

'Spefunky'   F, pb, Spek; intr. 2006

'Spegage'   HT, mr, Spek; intr. 2006

'Spegain'   HT, pb, Spek; intr. 2006

'Spegamo'   HT, dp, Spek; intr. 2006

'Spegana'   F, dy, Spek; intr. 2006

'Spegaris'   HT, ab, Spek; intr. 2006

'Spegemble'   HT, rb, Spek; intr. 2006

'Speging'   HT, mp, Spek; intr. 2006

'Spegyrthe'   HT, rb, Spek; intr. 2006

'Spehewe'   HT, dr, Spek; intr. 1996

'Spekes'   ('Our Sacha', 'Sacha') HT, mr, Spek; bud long, pointed ovoid; intr. 1996

'Spekren'   Pol, w, Spek; intr. 2001

'Spekrien'   ('The Fairy Queen') Pol, mr, Vurens; intr. 1998

'Spek's Centennial' -- See 'Macivy'

'Spek's Improved'   HRg

'Spek's Yellow, Climbing'   ('Golden Scepter, Climbing') Cl HT, dy, 1956, Walters; [sport of 'Golden Scepter']

'Spek's Yellow' -- See 'Golden Scepter'

'Spellbinder'   ('Oratorio') HT, pb, 1974, Warriner, William A.; bud ovoid; flowers ivory to crimson, large, dbl., high-centered; foliage large, dark, leathery; vigorous growth; PP3571; ['South Seas' × seedling]; intr. 1975

'Spellbound'   HT, dr, 1949, Sodano, J.; flowers deep velvety red, becoming darker, 5½-6 in., 25-30 petals, moderate fragrance; foliage dark; thornless; very vigorous, upright growth; PP840; [sport of 'Better Times']

Spellbound -- See 'Poulrim'

Spellbound™ -- See 'Jacpribe'

'Spellcaster' -- See 'Jacangel'

'Spencer' -- See 'Spenser'

'Spencer's Delight'   HT, ab, 1998, Spencer, Keith V.; flowers coral pink, reverse soft amber, 3½-4½ in., full, high-centered, borne mostly singly, moderate fragrance; foliage medium size, dark green, semi-glossy; prickles moderate; long, straight stems; vigorous, upright, tall (48-62 in.) growth; [sport of 'Maid of Honor']; intr. 2002

'Spenser'   ('Spencer') HP, lp, 1892, Paul, W.; flowers soft pink, moderate fragrance; [sport of 'Merveille de Lyon']

'Speragina'   T, dp, Hay

'Sperien'   ('The Fairy Queen') Pol, mr, Vurens; intr. 1998

'Speruge'   ('Red Dagmar') HRg, mr, Spek; intr. 1997

'Spes'   HT, mp, Urban, J.; flowers large, very dbl.; intr. 1970

'Spevu'   ('Lovely Fairy') Pol, dp, Spek, Hette; bud small; intr. 1990

'Sphinx'   HT, lp, 1970, Gaujard; flowers bright pink tinted lighter, very large, dbl., moderate fragrance; foliage leathery; vigorous, bushy growth; [Rose Gaujard® × 'Gail Borden']; intr. 1967

'Spice'   F, or, 1954, Boerner; bud globular; flowers scarlet-red, 3 in., 53 petals, cupped, borne in clusters, moderate fragrance; foliage glossy; vigorous, compact, upright growth; PP1396; [('Goldilocks' × 'Floradora') × floribunda seedling]; intr. 1954

'Spice 'n' Nice'   HT, lp, Twomey, Jerry

Spice Drop™ -- See 'Savasweet'

'Spice of Life'   F, ob, Dickson; bud reddish pink; flowers orange blend with scarlet edges, reverse suffused with lemon yellow, dbl., cupped, borne in large clusters, slight fragrance; recurrent; foliage dense, red when young; upright (3-4 ft.), bushy growth; intr. 2004

Spice So Nice™ -- See 'Wekwesflut'

Spice Trail™ -- See 'Virsila'

Spice Twice™ -- See 'Jacable'

'Spiced Coffee' -- See 'Macjuliat'

'Spicup'   Min, mp, 1981, Spies, Mark C.; bud ovoid

'Spicy'   Min, yb, Delbard; flowers blend of ochre and tan with splashes of cinnamon; medium growth

'Spicy'   HT, ob, Kordes; bud large, triangular; flowers bronze gold, reverse copper red, fading to rose pink, full, high-centered, star shape, borne singly and several together, moderate fragrance; recurrent; stems long, sturdy; vigorous, upright growth; florist rose; needs disbudding and spraying; intr. 1999

'Spicy Minijet' -- See 'Lavglo'

Spielplatz DRS®   HT, yb, Huber

'Spin Out'   F, ob

Spinning Wheel™   S, rb, 1991, Williams, J. Benjamin; flowers cherry red with ivory striping, large, full, borne in large clusters, slight fragrance; recurrent; foliage large, dark green, semi-glossy; tall, upright, spreading growth; [Handel® × 'Love']

'Spion-Kop'   F, mr, 1968, Ellick; flowers signal-red, 3-5 in., 30-35 petals; foliage light, bronze, matte green; vigorous

growth; ['Evelyn Fison' × Orange Sensation®]
'Spirit' HT, mr
'Spirit Abundance' -- See 'Spirit of Tollcross'
'Spirit of '76' Gr, or, 1971, Whisler, D.; bud ovoid; flowers medium, dbl., moderate fragrance; foliage large, glossy, dark; vigorous, upright growth; PP3820; [Queen Elizabeth® × 'San Francisco']
'Spirit of Canada' F, dr, 1995, Fleming Joyce; flowers dark red enriched with flashes of scarlet, prominent stamens, medium, 10 petals, flat, borne in small and large clusters, moderate fragrance; recurrent; foliage medium size, medium green, semi-glossy; numerous prickles; upright, bushy, tall growth; [Bambula® × 'Red Max Graf']; intr. 1995
'Spirit of Freedom' -- See 'Ausbite'
'Spirit of Glasnost' -- See 'Jacara'
'Spirit of Hope' -- See 'Machahei'
'Spirit of Ocean City' HT, rb, Williams, J. B.; flowers red with yellow reverse, large, dbl., borne mostly singly, moderate fragrance; foliage large, mahogany to dark green, glossy, disease-resistant; vigorous, tall (6 ft.), bushy growth; ['Oregold' × 'Tropicana']; intr. 1996
'Spirit of Peace' -- See 'Jacstine'
'Spirit of Peace' -- See 'Meinivoz'
'Spirit of Pentax' -- See 'Harwex'
'Spirit of SACS' -- See 'Pure Magic'
Spirit of Southland® F, ob, Attfield; flowers blend of orange, red and yellow, dbl., high-centered; tall growth; intr. 1999
'Spirit of the Heath' HT, mp, 2001, Poole, Lionel; flowers full, borne in small clusters, slight fragrance; foliage large, dark green, very glossy; prickles medium, triangular, few; growth upright, bushy, medium (1 m.), very vigorous & strong; garden, exhibit; ['Hazel Rose' × 'Silver Jubilee']; intr. 2002
'Spirit of Tollcross' ('Spirit Abundance') F, or, Harkness; flowers vermilion, often with white stripe in center of petals, dbl., cupped to flat, borne in clusters; recurrent; medium growth; intr. 1998
'Spirit of Youth' -- See 'Meivestal'
'Spitfire' HT, mr, 1943, Joseph H. Hill, Co.; bud oxblood-red; flowers carmine, open, 2-3 in., 25-30 petals, moderate fragrance; foliage dark, leathery; short stems; vigorous, upright, much branched growth; PP617; ruled extinct 06/86; ['Better Times' × 'Colleen Moore']
'Spitfire' Min, mr, 1986, McDaniel, Earl; flowers large, 38 petals, high-centered, borne singly; foliage medium size, medium green, matte; prickles thin, light green; upright, bushy growth; [seedling × seedling]
'Spitfire Improved' HT, dr, 1949, Joseph H. Hill, Co.; bud medium, short-pointed, ovoid; flowers velvety dark carmine, 4-5 in., semi-dbl., globular, intense fragrance; foliage leathery, dark; vigorous, upright, bushy growth; PP749; ruled extinct 06/86; [sport of 'Spitfire']
'Spitfire Paddy' -- See 'Seaspit'
'Spitzenschleier' S, lp, VEG; flowers small, single
Splash® HT, yb, Spek; flowers medium yellow, brushed pink , 10-11 cm., 40-45 petals, high-centered, borne mostly singly; recurrent; prickles moderate ; stems very long; florist rose; intr. 2006
'Splendens' ('Ayrshire Splendens', 'Myrrh-Scented Rose', 'Splendid Sweet-Brier', 'Repens', R. arvensis splendens) Ayr, w, about 1835, from England; bud crimson; flowers pale flesh to creamy blush, fading to white, 6-7 cm., semi-dbl. to dbl., globular, strong myrrh fragrance; pendulous growth
'Splendens' -- See 'Francofurtana'
'Splendid' F, w, Roman, G., and Wagner, S.; flowers cream-white, flushed pink, large, 30 petals, borne in clusters, slight fragrance; foliage large, dark green, glossy; ['Centennaire de Lourdes' × 'Cläre Grammerstorf']; intr. 1997
'Splendid Garland' HSem, lp, 1835, Wells; flowers medium, dbl.
'Splendid Garland' -- See 'The Garland'
Splendid Lady™ -- See 'Declady'
'Splendid Sweet-Brier' -- See 'Splendens'
'Splendid!' -- See 'Levsplen'
'Splendor' HT, or, 1933, Sauvageot, H.; bud long, pointed; flowers orange-carmine, dbl., cupped, moderate fragrance; foliage leathery, glossy; vigorous growth; ['La Marechale Petain' × 'Souv. de Claudius Pernet']
'Splendor' HT, mr, Abrams, Von; bud long; flowers rose-red, reverse slightly lighter, pointed, 4-5 in., dbl., intense fragrance; foliage dark; PP403; [sport of 'Better Times']; intr. 1940
'Splendora' -- See 'Pondora'
'Splish Splash' -- See 'Korfolga'
'Splish Splash' -- See 'Morgoldart'
'Spoboom' ('Boomerang') Min, rb, 1992, Spooner, Raymond A.; flowers red and white, large, full, borne in small clusters, no fragrance; foliage medium size, medium green, semi-glossy; some prickles; medium, bushy growth; [seedling × seedling]; intr. 1993
'Spochey' ('Cheyenne') Min, ab, 1985, Spooner, Raymond A.; flowers golden apricot, 20 petals, borne singly; foliage medium size, medium green, semi-glossy; upright growth; ['Rise 'n' Shine' × Center Gold™]; intr. 1984
'Spodarc' ('Darcelle') Min, w, 1991, Spooner, Raymond A.; flowers medium, single, borne in sprays of 3-5, slight fragrance; foliage small, medium green, semi-glossy; bushy, low (13 cm.), very compact growth; [('Whistle Stop' × 'Popcorn') × 'Nozomi']; intr. 1991
'Spodash' ('Dasher') Min, mr, 1993, Spooner, Raymond A.; flowers large, full, borne mostly singly, slight fragrance; foliage medium size, medium green, semi-glossy; some prickles; medium (40 cm.), upright, bushy growth; [Maurine Neuberger™ × seedling]; intr. 1994
'Spoday' ('Alisha') Min, pb, 1995, Spooner, Raymond A.; flowers soft pink with white margin on outer edge, medium, very dbl., borne mostly singly, no fragrance; foliage medium size, medium green, matte; few prickles; medium (20 in.), bushy growth; ['Marriotta' × seedling]; intr. 1995
'Spode' HT, ob, 1973, Fryers Nursery, Ltd.; flowers orange-scarlet, flushed cream, long, pointed, 6 in., 35 petals, intense fragrance; foliage glossy, dark; ['Diorama' × 'Fragrant Cloud']
'Spoglo' ('Superglo') Min, or, 1985, Spooner, Raymond A.; flowers small, semi-dbl.; foliage small, medium green, semi-glossy; bushy growth; [((Prominent® × 'Rise 'n' Shine') × Trumpeter®) × Chattem Centennial™]
'Spogret' ('Gretta') Min, dp, 1993, Spooner, Raymond A.; flowers deep pink, large, very dbl., borne mostly singly; foliage medium size, dark green, glossy; some prickles; bushy (44 cm.) growth
'Spohawk' ('Sadie Hawkins') Min, pb, 1990, Spooner, Raymond A.; bud globular; flowers medium pink with white stripes, reverse white, aging lighter, 16 petals, moderate fruity fragrance; foliage medium size, medium green, matte; no prickles; bushy, medium growth; hips globular, medium green; ['Roller Coaster' × seedling]; intr. 1990
'Spojean' (Jeanette™) Min, pb, 2001, Spooner, Ray; flowers 1¾ in., full, borne mostly solitary, no fragrance; foliage medium size, medium green, semi-glossy; prickles 1/16 in., few; growth bushy, compact, medium (14 in.); garden decorative; [Maurine Neuberger™ × seedling]; intr. 1997
'Spolar' ('Larado') Min, mr, 1991, Spooner, Raymond A.; flowers bright, clear red with small white eye in center, micro-mini, semi-dbl., borne singly, no fragrance; foliage small, medium green, semi-glossy; micro-mini; low (15 cm.), bushy growth; ['Tobo Yellow' × seedling]; intr. 1992
'Spolav' ('Lavender Spoon') Min, m, 1995, Spooner, Raymond A.; flowers large, 5 petals, borne in sprays of 3-7; foliage small, dark green, semi-glossy; some prickles; growth medium (12-14 in.), bushy; [(Black Jade™ × 'Blue Peter') × seedling]; intr. 1995
'Spomaur' (Maurine Neuberger™) Min, mr, 1989, Spooner, Raymond A.; bud pointed; flowers medium, 30 petals, high-centered, borne singly, moderate fragrance; foliage medium size, medium green, matte; prickles needle-like, light brown; upright, medium growth; hips ovoid, light green; PP7772; [(Prominent® × 'Zinger') × Centerpiece™]
'Spomeg' ('Little Meghan') Min, dy, 1993, Spooner, Raymond A.; flowers bright yellow, medium, dbl., borne mostly

singly; foliage small, light green, matte; no prickles; growth low, compact; [Good Morning America™ × seedling]; intr. 1994

'Spomerit' ('Merit') Min, ob, 1989, Spooner, Raymond A.; bud pointed; flowers brilliant orange, yellow base, reverse yellow, small, 17 petals, high-centered; foliage small, dark green, semi-glossy; prickles needle-like, brown; bushy, low growth; no fruit; [(Prominent® × 'Zinger') × 'miniature seedling']

'Spong' ('Pompon Spong', 'Provincialis Hybrida') C, mp, 1805, Spong; flowers rose-pink, richer in center, small, very dbl., cupped, borne in small clusters, slight to moderate fragrance; early bloom; foliage ovate-pointed, serrate, gray-green; branching, dwarf, compact (to 4 ft.) growth; intr. 1805

'Spooner' Min, ob, Spooner; intr. 2006

'Sporose' ('Rosetta') Min, rb, 1991, Spooner, Raymond A.; flowers white center, red on outer half of petals, medium, full, borne singly and in sprays, no fragrance; foliage small, medium green, semi-glossy, disease-resistant; bushy (34 cm.) growth; [Scamp™ × seedling]; intr. 1992

'Sporting Duo' -- See 'Harbar'

Spot Meillandina® -- See 'Meidipser'

'Spot Minijet' -- See 'Meizogrel'

'Spot o' Gold' -- See 'Weespot'

'Spotlight' HT, my, 1969, Dickson, A.; flowers peach and gold, globular; foliage dark; free growth; [seedling × Piccadilly®]

'Spotlight' -- See 'Morbrights'

'Spotted Gold' -- See 'Kortelin'

'Spovegas' ('Little Vegas') Min, mr, 1985, Spooner, Raymond A.; flowers small, 20 petals, high-centered; foliage small, medium green, semi-glossy; growth bushy; [('Rise 'n' Shine' × Prominent®) × 'red seedling']; intr. 1984

'Spowest' ('Dr Mark Weston') Min, mr, 2005, Spooner, Ray; flowers medium, full, borne mostly solitary, no fragrance; foliage medium size, medium green, semi-glossy; prickles few, 1/8 in., pointed; bushy, medium (14-18 in.) growth; garden decoration, exhibition; [seedling × seedling]; intr. 2005

'Spray Cécile Brünner' Pol, pb, 1941, Howard Rose Co.; bud long, pointed; flowers bright pink on yellow, edged clear pink, center yellowish, dbl., borne in large sprays, moderate fragrance; foliage sparse, soft, dark; compact, bushy growth; [sport of 'Mlle Cécile Brunner']

'Spray Wit' S, w, Yanagisawa

'Spreeathen' HT, mr, Rupprecht-Radke; flowers large, dbl.; intr. 1968

'Spreeglut' S, dr, Kopenick; flowers small to medium, semi-dbl., shallow cup, borne singly or several together; free-flowering; upright (4 ft.), branching growth; intr. 1985

Spring™ ('Spring Parade') Min, dy, Poulsen; flowers deep yellow, medium, dbl., slight wild rose fragrance; foliage dark; growth bushy, 20-40 cm.; PP10738; intr. 2000

'Spring' -- See 'Wesnianka'

Spring™ -- See 'Poulac010'

'Spring Beauty' -- See 'Mineco'

'Spring Beginning' -- See 'Frühlingsanfang'

'Spring Belle' Min, dp; flowers deep rose pink, large, hybrid tea; tall growth

'Spring Bouquet' -- See 'Tinspring'

'Spring Break' -- See 'Straheidi'

'Spring Bride' LCl, w; flowers blush white, slight fragrance; tall (12-15 ft.) growth; intr. 2003

'Spring Carnival' Min, r, Benardella, Frank; flowers deep tan and orange apricot tonings, well-formed; free-flowering; strong, tall growth

'Spring Charm' -- See 'Frühlingszauber'

'Spring Fever' S, lp, Takeuchi ; bud very long and slender; flowers cream pink to white, appleblossom-like, 2.5-3.5 cm., 5-7 petals, flat , borne in pyramidal clusters of 20 - 30, light fragrance; recurrent; foliage dark green, very glossy, disease-resistant; prickles numerous, 6-8 mm., hooked downward, tan ; stems 12 - 16 in. for cluster, 1 - 2 in. for bloom; low (16 in.), broad (4 ft.), flat growth ; PP14376; ['Korsami' × seedling]; intr. 2008

'Spring Fever' -- See 'Arocant'

Spring Fling™ -- See 'Wekmeymo'

'Spring Fragrance' -- See 'Shunpo'

'Spring Fragrance' -- See 'Vesenii Aromat'

'Spring Fragrance' -- See 'Frühlingsduft'

'Spring Frolic' Min, my, 1979, Williams, Ernest D.; bud ovoid; flowers dbl., 70 petals, pompon, intense fragrance; low, compact, spreading growth; [('Little Darling' × 'Gold Coin') × 'Golden Angel']; intr. 1978

'Spring Frost' Min, w, 1979, Schwartz, Ernest W.; flowers pure white, ruffled, 1 in., 17 petals; foliage small; low, very compact growth; intr. 1978

'Spring Gold' Min, dy

'Spring Gold' -- See 'Frühlingsgold'

'Spring Hill's Freedom' -- See 'Twofree'

'Spring Hill's Pink Freedom' S, mp; flowers salmon pink to rose pink, 3½ in., dbl., cupped, borne in clusters, slight fragrance; free-flowering; bushy (4-6 ft.) growth; intr. 1997

Spring Melody™ -- See 'Minmco'

'Spring Morning' -- See 'Frühlingsmorgen'

'Spring Palace' (Spring™) MinFl, mp, Olesen; bud pointed ovoid; flowers medium pink, aging lighter, 5 cm., 40-45 petals, rosette, borne in clusters, very slight fragrance; recurrent; foliage dark green, glossy; prickles numerous, 6 mm., concave, olive green; bushy, 40-60 cm. growth; PP15831; [Fredensborg™ × seedling]; intr. 2003

'Spring Parade' -- See 'Poulrato'

'Spring Snow' -- See 'Frühlingsschnee'

'Spring Song' S, dp, 1954, Riethmuller; flowers rich carmine-pink, semi-dbl., moderate fragrance; vigorous, tall growth; ['Gartendirektor Otto Linne' × unknown]

'Spring Song' Min, pb, Moore, Ralph S.; flowers pink tinted salmon, small, full, rosette, borne in clusters, no fragrance; recurrent; foliage medium green, glossy; bushy (18-24 in.), spreading growth; [(R. wichurana × 'Floradora') × 'Thumbelina']; intr. 1957

'Spring Time' HT, pb, Ghosh, Mr. & Mrs. S.; flowers blend of pink, orange and apricot, large, high-centered; free-flowering; intr. 2003

Spring Time™ -- See 'Wilspring'

'Springfields' -- See 'Dicband'

'Springhill Freedom' -- See 'Twofree'

'Springmoon' ('Full Moon') Min, ly, 1994, Sproul, James A.; flowers creamy light yellow, 1-1½ in., full, slight fragrance; foliage medium size, medium green, semi-glossy, disease-resistant; few prickles; medium (20 in.), spreading, rounded growth; ['Avandel' × 'Olympiad']

'Springpromise' ('Crimson Promise') Min, dr, 1994, Sproul, James A.; flowers antique, smoky dark red, 1¼-1¾ in., full, borne mostly singly, no fragrance; foliage medium size, dark green, semi-glossy, disease-resistant; few prickles; medium (20 in.), bushy growth; ['Avandel' × 'Chrysler Imperial']

Springs 75™ -- See 'Pouganda'

'Spring's A Comin'' -- See 'Welcom'

'Springtime' F, lp, 1935, Howard, F.H.; flowers wild-rose-pink, center white, semi-dbl., cupped, borne in clusters; foliage leathery; bushy growth; PP268; RULED EXTINCT 7/90; ['Miss Rowena Thom' × seedling]

Springtime® S, ly, Lens; flowers soft yellow, 4 cm., single, shallow cup; once-blooming; foliage light green; compact (4½-6 ft.) growth; intr. 1984

'Springtime' S, mp; intr. 2004

'Springvale' HT, w, 1976, Miller, J.; flowers white to pink, 4 in., 50 petals, high-centered; foliage dark; [sport of 'Mme A. Meilland']

Springwood Beauty™ -- See 'Lavnew'

Springwood Classic™ -- See 'Lavclass'

Springwood Coral™ -- See 'Lavscent'

Springwood Gold™ -- See 'Lavtynine'

Springwood Mauvette® -- See 'Lavisle'

Springwood Pink™ -- See 'Lavdusk'

Springwood Pink Satin® -- See 'Lavsat'

Springwood Purple™ -- See 'Lavpurr'

Springwood Red™ -- See 'Lavred'

Springwood Red Victor® -- See 'Lavbert'

'Springwood Ruby' -- See 'Lavaru'

Springwood White™ -- See 'Lavsnow'

'Sprint' F, mr, 1961, Gaujard; bud oval; flowers bright red, open, 2½ in., 12 petals, borne in clusters; foliage glossy, dark; vigorous growth; ['Jolie Princesse' × 'Chanteclerc']

Sprinter® HT, dy, Ilsink; flowers bright yellow, dbl., high-centered; free-flowering; short to medium growth; intr. 1989

'Sprite' F, lp, 1945, Armacost; flowers pale pink; PP649; [sport of 'Rosenelf']

'Sprobaby' Min, pb, 2001, Sproul, James A.; bud pointed; intr. 2001

'Sprobiolacentennial' ('Biola Centennial') Min, rb, 2007, Sproul, James A.; flowers red, reverse white, with good form, medium, 2 in., dbl., borne mostly solitary; foliage medium, medium green, matte; prickles small, curved downward, few; growth bushy, medium (24 in.); [(Stainless Steel™ × 'Singin' in the Rain') × Hot Tamale™]; intr. 2008

'Sprocarolyn' ('Carolyn Elizabeth') Min, m, 2003, Sproul, James A.; flowers 1½ in., dbl., borne in small clusters, intense fragrance; foliage large, medium green, matte; few prickles; growth bushy, 30-36 in; garden decoration; ['Chipmunk' × Stainless Steel™]; intr. 2002

'Sproday' (This Is The Day™) Min, r, 2003, Sproul, James A.; flowers red/orange, 1½ in., hybrid tea, borne mostly solitary, no fragrance; recurrent; foliage medium size, dark green, semi-glossy; prickles few, average, slightly hooked; growth bushy, medium (24 in.); garden, exhibition; PPAF; ['Chipmunk' × 'Michel Cholet']; intr. 2003

'Sprograce' ('Grace Amazing') Min, my, 2003, Sproul, James A.; flowers yellow, reverse yellow, 1½-2 in., dbl., borne mostly solitary; foliage medium size, medium green, semi-glossy; prickles few, small; upright, medium (24-30 in.) growth; ['Singin' in the Rain' × 'Fairhope']; intr. 2003

'Sprohass' ('Glorious Hass') HT, dp, 2008, Sproul, James A.; flowers deep pink, reverse lighter, 5 in., full, borne mostly solitary; foliage medium, medium green, semi-glossy; prickles medium, slightly curved, few; growth bushy to spreading, medium (40 in.); [(Sheer Bliss × Granada) × Seedling]; intr. 2008

'Sproheather' ('Heather Sproul') Min, mp, 2004, Sproul, James A.; buds long, tapered; flowers dbl., high-centered, borne in small clusters, slight fragrance; foliage medium size, dark green, semi-glossy, mildew-resistant; prickles medium; growth compact, medium (18 to 24 in.); borders, containers; [('Lynn Anderson' × 'Tournament of Roses') × Hot Tamale™]; intr. 2004

'Sprolake' (Mee Maw™) MinFl, pb, 2006, Sproul, James A.; flowers reverse lighter, 2 in., dbl., high-centered, borne in small clusters; foliage medium size, medium green, semi-glossy, resistant to powdery mildew; prickles medium, few; growth bushy, medium (24-36 in.); [('Lynn Anderson' × 'Tournament of Roses') × Hot Tamale™]; intr. 2006

'Sprolife' ('Life Lines') Cl Min, or, 2004, Sproul, James A.; flowers orange-red striped white, reverse lighter, 1½-2 in., semi-dbl., borne in large clusters, no fragrance; foliage medium size, medium green, semi-glossy, mildew-resistant; prickles medium, curved downward; growth upright, tall (60 to 72 in.); trellis, pillar; ['Roller Coaster' × Hot Tamale™]

'Spropearl' (Pearl Sanford™) Min, pb, 2007, Sproul, James A.; flowers creamy white with pink edging, 1½ in., dbl., high-centered, borne in small clusters; foliage medium size, dark green, semi-glossy; prickles small, few; growth compact, short (16-20 in.); borders, containers; hips numerous; [('Chipmunk' × 'Heather Sproul') × (('Singin' in the Rain' × 'Roller Coaster') × Tropical Twist™)]; intr. 2007

'Sprorebel' ('Lil' Rebel') Min, mr, 2003, Sproul, James A.; flowers red, reverse red, 1½-2 in., 5-7 petals, borne in small clusters, no fragrance; foliage small, medium green, matte; few prickles; growth upright, tall (30-36 in.); bedding; ['Anytime' × 'Santa Claus']; intr. 2003

'Sprose' ('Rose Country') Min, lp, 2001, Sproul, James; bud pointed; flowers medium, 25-35 petals, borne singly and in small clusters, slight fragrance; foliage medium size, dark green, semi-glossy; prickles medium, few; growth upright, bushy (30-36 in.); garden decorative; disease-resistant; [Sexy Rexy® × 'Michel Cholet']; intr. 2001

'Sprotri' ('Sam Trivitt') Min, ab, 2000, Sproul, James; bud pointed; flowers light golden apricot, 1½ in., full, high-centered, borne singly or in small clusters, slight fragrance; foliage medium size, dark green, semi-glossy; few prickles; growth upright, bushy, medium (3 ft.); ['Chipmunk' × ('San Jose Sunshine' × 'Prima Donna')]

'Spruce Up' Min, dp

'Spun Gold' HT, my, 1941, McGredy; flowers gold, 4½ in., 27 petals, high-centered; foliage glossy, leathery; vigorous, bushy, fairly compact growth; PP495; [seedling × 'Portadown Glory']

'Spunglass' HT, w, 1989, Marciel, Stanley G.; bud pointed; flowers very large, 50 petals, cupped, borne singly, slight spicy fragrance; foliage large, dark green, glossy; prickles declining, pea green; upright, tall growth; PP7613; [seedling × Angel™]

'Spunky' -- See 'Judspunk'

'Sputnik' F, or, 1958, Maarse, G.; flowers semi-dbl., borne in large trusses of 25-30; low, bushy growth; ['Jiminy Cricket' × 'Gloria Mundi']

'Square Dancer' S, dp, 1972, Buck, Dr. Griffith J.; bud ovoid; flowers deep pink, large, dbl., cupped, moderate fragrance; repeat bloom; foliage large, dark, leathery; vigorous, upright, bushy growth; ['Meisterstuck' × (('World's Fair' × 'Floradora') × 'Applejack')]; intr. 1973

'Squatter's Dream' S, my, 1923, Clark, A.; flowers medium yellow, becoming lighter, golden stamens, medium to large, single to semi-dbl., shallow cup, moderate fragrance; recurrent; foliage dark bronze-green; no prickles; dwarf (4 ft.), bushy growth; [(sport of R. gigantea × unknown)]

'Srdce Evropy' HWich, dp, 1937, Böhm, J.; flowers deep pink, white center, 4½-5 cm., single, borne in very large clusters, slight fragrance; numerous prickles

'Srebra' F, pb, 1985, Staikov, Prof. Dr. V.; flowers pink, shaded mauve, dbl., borne in clusters of 5-20, moderate tea fragrance; foliage dark, glossy; bushy growth; ['Highlight' × 'Masquerade']; intr. 1975

'Sri Chinmoy' F, my, 2005, Paul Chessum Roses; flowers medium yellow, 6 cm., dbl, borne in small clusters, moderate fragrance; foliage medium size, medium green, matte; growth compact, medium (75 cm.); beds, borders, containers; intr. 2004

'Sri Sri Paramananda Yogananda' HT, ab, Ghosh, Mr. & Mrs. S.; flowers apricot and pink blend, reverse medium yellow, high-centered; intr. 2006

'Srinivasa' HT, rb, Kasturi; flowers red with white reverse, full, high-centered; intr. 1969

'Staatspräsident Päts' ('President Pats') HT, my, 1937, Weigand, C.; bud long, pointed; flowers amber-yellow, very varying, very large, dbl.; foliage leathery, dark; vigorous growth; ['Ophelia' × 'Souv. de Claudius Pernet']

'Staccato' F, mr, 1965, van de Water; bud ovoid; flowers vermilion-red, open, medium, 14-20 petals; moderately vigorous, bushy growth; [sport of 'Cantate']; originally registered as Pol; intr. 1959

'Stacey' F, yb, 1965, Verschuren, A.; flowers maize-yellow tinted blush, 4-5 in., 25-30 petals, borne in clusters; foliage dark, glossy, leathery; vigorous growth

'Stacey Nicole' HT, pb, Lougheed, Larry; flowers large, 30-35 petals, borne mostly singly; recurrent; foliage dark burgundy, turning green as it matures; medium to tall, branching growth; intr. 2007

'Stacey Sue' Min, lp, 1976, Moore, Ralph S.; bud short, pointed; flowers soft pink, 1 in., 50-70 petals, rounded, borne usually in small clusters, slight sweet fragrance; recurrent; foliage small, medium green, glossy; prickles several, slender, slightly curved, inclined downward, brown; stems sturdy, wiry, short to medium; short (10-12 in.), bushy, rounded growth; hips few to none ; PP4158; ['Ellen Poulsen' × 'Fairy Princess']

'Stacey's Star' -- See 'Horstacey'

'Stad den Haag' F, mr, 1969, McGredy, Sam IV; flowers scarlet, open, large, 20 petals; foliage glossy; free growth; ['Evelyn Fison' × ('Spartan' × 'Red Favorite')]

'Stad Kortrijk' S, rb, Kordes; flowers creamy white with splotches of red and pink, dbl., cupped, borne in small clusters, slight fragrance; recurrent; foliage dark green, resistant; vigorous (4 ft.) growth; intr. 2003

'Stadt Basel' -- See 'Meivilanic'

'Stadt Darmstadt' Pol, mr, 1966, deRuiter; bud ovoid; flowers bright red, small, semi-dbl., borne in clusters; foliage dark; ['Red Favorite' × 'The Doctor']

'Stadt den Helder' -- See 'Interhel'

Stadt Eltville® ('Glowing Achievement') F, mr, Tantau; flowers bright red, 3-4 in., dbl., high-centered, borne in clusters, no fragrance; recurrent; foliage reddish when young, then dark green; medium growth; intr. 1990

'Stadt Essen' Pol, mr, 1937, Tantau, Math.; flowers medium, dbl.

'Stadt Ettelbrück' S, mr, Lens, Louis; flowers medium-large, semi-dbl.; intr. 1981

'Stadt Hildesheim' -- See 'Meipopul'

'Stadt Hockenheim' HMsk, ob, Weihrauch

Stadt Kiel® S, mr, 1964, Kordes, R.; flowers cinnabar-red, medium, 30 petals, borne in large clusters, slight fragrance; foliage dark green; very vigorous, bushy growth; intr. 1963

'Stadt Luzern' F, op, Huber; flowers bright salmon, borne singly and in clusters, slight fragrance; recurrent; foliage dark green; stems long, strong, strong, upright (80-100 cm.) growth; best in partial shade; intr. 1967

'Stadt Pilsen' -- See 'Plzen'

Stadt Potsdam® S, mr, Tantau; flowers blood-red; intr. 2003

'Stadt Pottrop' F, deRuiter; intr. 1961

Stadt Rosenheim® S, or, 1961, Kordes, R.; flowers dbl., borne in clusters (up to 10); foliage glossy, light green; vigorous, upright growth

'Stadt Wurzburg' -- See 'Korgust'

'Stadtholder' -- See 'Hybride Stadtholder'

'Stadtrat F. Köhler' HT, mr, 1906, Geduldig; bud pointed; flowers very large, very full, borne mostly solitary

'Stadtrat Glaser' HT, yb, 1910, Kiese; bud long; flowers sulfur-yellow edged soft red, large, full

'Stadtrat Meyn' Pol, mr, 1919, Tantau; flowers luminous brick-red, large, full, cupped, borne in pyramidal clusters, slight fragrance; recurrent; ['Orléans Rose' × unknown]

'Staffa' HSpn, w; flowers milk white shading to yellow at center, occasionally mottled pink, large, 20-40 petals, strong fragrance; growth moderate (90-120 cm.); very hardy; from Scotland, about 1832

Stagecoach™ -- See 'Kincoach'

'Stained Glass' Min, pb, 2003, Barnes, Karen W.; flowers 1½ in., full, borne mostly solitary, no fragrance; foliage medium size, medium green, semi-glossy; prickles ¼, slightly curved, brown, few; bushy (12 in.) growth; containers; [unknown × unknown]; intr. 2003

Stainless Steel™ -- See 'Wekblusi'

Stairway to Heaven™ -- See 'Jacetima'

'Stamela' F, (Holland)

'Stämmler' HP, mp, 1933, Tantau; flowers rose-pink, large, very dbl., cupped, intense fragrance; foliage glossy; vigorous (120-140 cm.) growth; ['Victor Verdier' × 'Arabella']

'Standard of Marengo' -- See 'Étendard de Marengo'

'Standing' Pol, dr, 1969, Delforge; flowers open, medium, dbl.; foliage dark, glossy; vigorous growth; [Atlantic® × seedling]

Standing Ovation™ -- See 'Tuckstand'

'Standout' HT, rb, 1978, Weeks; bud ovoid, pointed; flowers red, white reverse, 3-4 in., full, high-centered, slight tea fragrance; vigorous, upright growth; PP4583; ['Tiffany' × 'Suspense']; intr. 1977

'Stanislas Dubourg' B, dp, about 1850, Pradel; flowers medium, full

'Stanley Duncan' Min, ab

'Stanley Gibbons' HT, op, 1976, Gregory; flowers salmon-orange, pointed,, 4 in., 28 petals; foliage glossy, dark; ['Fragrant Cloud' × Papa Meilland®]

'Stanley Matthews' HT, dr, 1964, Latham; flowers crimson-scarlet, 4½-5 in., 26 petals; foliage glossy, light green; vigorous growth; [('Independence' × 'Crimson Glory') × 'Happiness']

'Stanwell Perpetual' HSpn, w, before 1836, Lee; flowers blush, medium, dbl., cupped, very early first bloom, moderate fragrance; recurrent; foliage very small; numerous prickles; moderate, spreading growth; ['Duchess of Portland' × R. spinosissima]; found in a garden at Stanwell

'Stanza' F, lp, 1971, Pal, Dr. B.P.; bud ovoid; flowers light pink, center darker, open, medium, semi-dbl.; foliage dark; very vigorous, bushy growth; intr. 1969

'Star Burst' S, Ilsink, Peter; intr. 1994

Star Child® -- See 'Dicmadder'

'Star Dance' F, w; intr. 2002

'Star Delight' -- See 'Morstar'

'Star Dust' -- See 'Morstardust'

'Star Dust' -- See 'Hoshikage'

'Star Gazer' HT, pb

'Star Magic' -- See 'Morsemuri'

'Star of Bethlehem' HWich, w, 1947, Fisher, R.C.; flowers with red stamens, 3-3½ in., 5 petals; moderate bloom; foliage glossy; ['Innocence' × 'Silver Moon']

'Star of Hurst' HWich, 1916, Hicks, Elisha

'Star of Persia' HFt, my, 1919, Pemberton; flowers bright yellow, stamens golden, 3-5 cm., semi-dbl., borne singly or in small clusters, slight fragrance; vigorous (8-10 ft.) growth; [R. foetida × Trier®]

'Star of Queensland' HT, w, 1909, Williams, A.; flowers creamy white, medium, full, high-centered; foliage grayish green; vigorous, bushy growth; ['Étoile de France' × 'Earl of Dufferin']

'Star of Thailand' HT, w, 1978, Chinprayoon; flowers creamy white, medium, full, high-centered; foliage grayish green; vigorous, bushy growth; ['Mount Shasta' × Pascali®]; intr. 1977

'Star of the Nile' S, dp, Clements, John; flowers intense pink, 4 in., 80 petals, moderate fruity/sweet myrrh fragrance; free-flowering; foliage bronzy red turning to dark green, matte; upright (4 ft.) growth; PPAF; intr. 2000

'Star of the Republic' S, ob, 2005, Shoup, George Michael; flowers peachy-apricot, center deeper, 3½ in., very full, cupped, quartered, borne mostly solitary, moderate fragrance; strong fall repeat; foliage large, dark green, semi-glossy; few prickles; growth spreading, tall (8 ft.); hedging; [Graham Thomas® × R. wichuraiana]; intr. 1998

'Star of Tokio' Min, Dot, Simon; intr. 1984

'Star of Waltham' ('Pickering Red HP (found)') HP, mr, 1875, Paul, W.; flowers carmine-crimson, mottled pink reverse, medium, dbl., semi-globular, moderate fragrance; recurrent; foliage very large; occasional red prickles; stems smooth, green; growth medium to tall

'Star Performer' -- See 'Chewpearl'

'Star Profusion' -- See 'Horcoexist'

'Star Quality' -- See 'Somsmoko'

'Star Rose' or, Pekmez; intr. 1988

'Star Trail' -- See 'Meidanover'

'Star Twinkle' Min, pb, 1978, Moore, Ralph S.; bud pointed; flowers pink, coral and orange, 1 in., 5 petals, star shaped; recurrent; foliage glossy; bushy, compact, low growth; ['Fairy Moss' × 'Fire Princess']

Star 2000® HT, or, Pekmez, Paul; flowers intense vermilion, large, 32-34 petals, high-centered, borne mostly singly, slight fragrance; good repeat; foliage medium size, medium green, semi-glossy; upright (60-80 cm.) growth; intr. 1992

'Star Wheel' F, rb, Zary, Keith; bud long, pointed ovoid; flowers white edged in red, 3½ in., 40-45 petals, high-centered, borne in flat clusters of 5 - 7, slight fragrance; good repeat; foliage large, leathery, glossy; prickles few, long, hooked slightly downward; stems strong, long (20 - 24 in.); vigorous, upright (6 ft) growth; PP11738; ['Princess' × 'Purple Tiger']; florist rose; intr. 1999

'Starbright' HT, w, 1962, Boerner; bud ovoid; flowers 4 in., 43 petals, high-centered, moderate fragrance; foliage glossy, dark; vigorous, upright growth; PP2128; ['Princess White' × 'hybrid tea seedling']; intr. 1962

'Starbright' -- See 'Lily White'

'Starburst' Gr, rb, 1969, Meilland, Mrs. Marie-Louise; bud ovoid; flowers red and yellow, medium, dbl., high-centered; foliage glossy; vigorous, bushy growth; PP2974; [Zambra® × 'Suspense']

'Starburst' S, my, Williams, J.B.; flowers bright yellow, dbl., high-centered, slight fragrance; foliage glossy, green; prickles quite thorny; growth to 4 ft.; intr. 2004

'Starburst' -- See 'Jachart'

Stardance™ -- See 'Wilblank'

'Stardust' F, m, Pearce; flowers lilac magenta, golden stamens, semi-dbl., shallow cup, borne in clusters, intense fragrance; recurrent; very few prickles; dwarf (18-24 in.) growth; intr. 1995

'Stardust' HT, w, 1939, Florex Gardens; flowers rose-red; PP330; RULED EXTINCT 5/92; [sport of 'Better Times']

'Stardust' -- See 'Interdust'

'Stardust' -- See 'Devstar'

'Stardust Memory' -- See 'Kenrhapso'

'Starfire' Gr, mr, 1959, Lammerts, Dr. Walter; bud short, pointed; flowers bright rose red, 4-5 in., 25-34 petals, high-centered to cupped, borne in clusters, moderate spicy fragrance; recurrent; foliage large, glossy; prickles numerous, long, straight; vigorous, tall, bushy growth; PP1742; ['Charlotte Armstrong' × ('Charlotte Armstrong' × 'Floradora')]; intr. 1959

'Starfire, Climbing' Cl F, mr, Jack, V.; [sport of 'Starfire']; intr. 1972

'Stargazer' F, ob, 1976, Harkness; flowers orange-red, yellow eye, small to medium, single, borne in large clusters, slight fragrance; free-flowering; foliage medium size, medium green, matte; medium, bushy growth; ['Marlena' × 'Kim']; intr. 1977

'Starglo' Min, w, 1974, Williams, Ernest D.; bud long, pointed; flowers creamy white with hint of pink, small, dbl., high-centered, slight fragrance; free-flowering; foliage small, leathery; vigorous, bushy growth; ['Little Darling' × 'Jet Trail']; intr. 1973

'Stargold' HT, my, 1936, Brownell; bud long, pointed; flowers yellow, often splashed red, 32 petals, high-centered, intense fragrance; foliage dark, glossy; long, strong stems; branching, upright growth; PP248; [('Mary Wallace' × 'Mary Wallace') × (seedling × seedling)]

Starina® Min, or, 1965, Meilland, Mrs. Marie-Louise; bud short, ovoid; flowers orange-scarlet, 1½ in., 23-28 petals, high-centered, borne singly and in small clusters, very slight fragrance; recurrent; foliage small, leathery, glossy; prickles several, brown; vigorous, dwarf growth; PP2646; [('Dany Robin' × 'Fire King') × 'Perla de Montserrat']

'Starina, Climbing' Cl Min, or, 1982, Asami, Hitoshi; [sport of Starina®]; intr. 1979

'Starion' HT, rb, NIRP; flowers shades of light red and medium to deep pink, 4 in., 40 petals, cupped, borne mostly singly, slight fragrance; recurrent; few prickles; stems long (50 - 70 cm); growth upright; florist rose; intr. 2007

Starion® HT, pb, Dorieux; flowers pale yellow and white, pink petal edges, dbl., high-centered, moderate fragrance; intr. 1987

'Stark Whitecap' F, w, 1959, Boerner; flowers pure white, 3 in., 30-35 petals, cupped, borne in clusters; foliage glossy; vigorous, upright growth; ['Glacier' × 'Garnette']

'Starkrimson' HT, dr, 1963, Morey, Dr. Dennison; flowers scarlet-red, 4½ in., 48 petals, cupped, intense fragrance; foliage leathery; vigorous, upright growth; PP1964; ['Happiness' × 'San Fernando']; intr. 1961

'Starla' -- See 'Pixarla'

'Starlet' F, my, 1957, Swim, H.C.; bud pointed; flowers 2½ in., 60 petals, high-centered, borne in clusters; foliage dark, leathery, glossy; vigorous, compact, upright growth; PP1694; ['Goldilocks' × seedling]

Starlet™ MinFl, w, Poulsen; flowers white, 5-8 cm., dbl., no fragrance; growth bushy, 20-40 cm.; intr. 2005

'Starlight' HMult, w, 1909, Paul, W.; flowers white, reverse tinted violet, medium, single

'Starlight' HT, ob, Wood & Ingram; flowers orange and buff, moderate fragrance; vigorous growth; ruled extinct 03/87; intr. 1934

'Starlight' HT, my, Guest, M.M.; flowers medium, full; foliage large, light green, matte; bushy growth; ['Devotion' × 'Benson & Hedges Gold']; intr. 1987

'Starlight' Min, ab, Coyier, Duane L.; flowers ¾ in., dbl., high-centered, pointed, borne in small clusters, no fragrance; good repeat; foliage small, medium green, matte; compact, low (12 in.) growth; containers, decorative; [sport of Rainbow Surprise™]; intr. 2003

Starlight™ -- See 'Poulstar'

'Starlight' -- See 'Arolaqueli'

'Starlight Express' LCl, dp, Robinson, T.; moderate (8 ft.) growth; intr. 1997

'Starlight Fantasy' F, w, Zary; bud long, pointed ovoid; flowers white with yellow tones in center, 3½ in., 25-30 petals, high-centered, flattens, borne in clusters of 4 - 7, no fragrance; good repeat; foliage large, leathery; prickles normal, medium size, hooked slightly downward; stems strong, 18 - 22 in. long; vigorous, upright (5½ ft.) growth; PP11841; ['Princess' × seedling]; florist rose; intr. 1999

'Starlight Parade' (Starlight™) Min, w; bud short, pointed ovoid; flowers white, 1 in., 25 petals, high-centered, then flat, borne singly and several together, no fragrance; recurrent; foliage dark green, glossy; prickles few, short, straight; stems short, strong; bushy, upright (16-18 in.) growth; PP9016; ['Evita' × seedling]; intr. 1991

'Starlina' Min, mp

'Starlite' F, ly, Meilland; bud conical; flowers lemon yellow, outer petals whiten, 4 in., 33 petals, cupped, borne mostly singly, slight anise fragrance; good repeat; foliage dark green, glossy; prickles numerous, small, light brown; erect (4 ft.) growth; PP9581; ['Golden Times' × ('Meitaranja' × 'Golden Garnette')]; florist rose; intr. 1995

'Starlite' HT, w, 1942, Nicolas; bud long, pointed; flowers clear white, center tinted cream, large, full, high-centered; foliage dark, soft; vigorous, upright, bushy growth; PP414; RULED EXTINCT 3/87; [seedling × 'White Briarcliff']

'Starlite' HT, my, Meilland; bud spherical; flowers sunny yellow, full, pompon, moderate fragrance; free-flowering; bushy, moderate (80 cm.) growth; intr. 1989

'Starqueli' ('Magic Lantern', 'Remy Martin') Gr, ob, 1995, Royon, René; flowers copper-orange-gold, large, full, borne in small clusters, slight fragrance; foliage medium green, semi-glossy; some prickles; upright, bushy (150 cm.) growth; PP8861; [sport of Gold Medal®]; intr. 1994

'Starry Bouquet' S, rb, Clements, John K.

'Starry Eyed' -- See 'Horcoexist'

'Starry Eyed' -- See 'Morstar'

'Starry Night' S, w, Orard; bud pointed, conspicuous neck; flowers white with bright yellow stamens, 2½ in., 5 petals, borne in clusters of 5 - 25, no fragrance; free-flowering; foliage small, dark green, glossy; prickles few, straight or hooked slightly downward; stems long, strong; low (18-24 in.), spreading (3-5 ft.) growth; hips none; PP14785; ['Anisley Dickson' × R. wichurana]; intr. 2002

'Stars 'n' Stripes' Min, rb, 1976, Moore, Ralph S.; bud long, pointed; flowers striped red and white, 1½ in., 18-23 petals, high-centered, soon flat, borne singly and in small clusters, moderate sweet fragrance; recurrent; foliage small, light to medium green, semi-glossy; prickles few, small, hooked slightly downward, brown; bushy, upright (16-20 in.) growth; hips few ; PP4029; ['Little Chief' × ('Little Darling' × 'Ferdinand Pichard')]; intr. 1976

'Stars and Stripes' S, pb, Williams, J.B.; flowers pink and white striped., semi-dbl., slight fragrance; recurrent; intr. 2004

'Stars 'n' Stripes Forever' S, rb, Clements, John; flowers pink with stripes of white and dark pink, 2½ in., 10-16 petals, cupped, moderate fragrance; recurrent; foliage glossy; tidy, even, bushy growth; intr. 2003

'Starscent' HT, pb, 1976, Parkes, Mrs M.H.; flowers rich pink, base yellow, 4½ in., 20 petals; foliage dull, blue-green; upright growth; ['Silver Star' × Peter Frankenfeld®]

'Starshine' HT, yb, 1972, Hamm; flowers pink and yellow blend, very large, dbl., globular; foliage glossy; vigorous, bushy growth; ['Peace' × 'Condesa de Sástago']; intr. 1971

'Starshine' -- See 'Tulsa'

'Starship' -- See 'Bristar'

'Starstruck' -- See 'Meirolour'

'Starstruck' -- See 'Tinstar'

'Start' F, or, VEG; flowers medium, semi-dbl.

Starting Over™ -- See 'Byrstarting'

'Startler' HT, or, 1955, Robinson, H.;

flowers orange-scarlet, base rich yellow, well-formed; vigorous growth; ['Hector Deane' × 'Mary Wheatcroft']

'State of Maine' HT, w, 1930, de Bree; flowers white, center slightly tinged greenish, large, very dbl., high-centered; [sport of 'Lady Ursula']

'Stately' HT, lp, 1930, Clark, A.; bud long, pointed; flowers pale flesh, center deeper, well-shaped, large, dbl., high-centered; vigorous growth; ['Souv. de Gustave Prat' × seedling]

'Statesman' HT, dr, 1991, Burks, Larry; flowers large, full, borne mostly singly, slight fragrance; foliage medium size, medium green, matte; medium, bushy growth; [seedling × seedling]; intr. 1991

'Steadfast' HT, ob, 1939, Clark, A.; flowers amber, flushed yellow and pink, semi-dbl.; vigorous growth; ['Mme Auguste Choutet' × unknown]

'Stebigpu' ('Big Purple', 'Nuit d'Orient', 'Stephens' Big Purple', 'Stephens' Rose Big Purple') HT, m, 1986, Stephens, Pat; bud large; flowers reddish-purple, 5 in., 35 petals, high-centered, borne mostly singly, intense fragrance; recurrent; foliage large, medium green, matte; prickles few, medium, recurved; stems long; upright (4-5 ft.) growth; PP6262; [seedling × 'Purple Splendour']; intr. 1986

'Steeple Rose' C, dp; bud full, globular, large; flowers rich rosy crimson with large green foliage; [perhaps a sport of Prolifera de Redoute]

'Steeple Rose' -- See 'Prolifera de Redouté'

'Stefanie Gachot' -- See 'Beni-Kanoko'

'Stefanovitch, Climbing' Cl HT, dr, 1943, Meilland, F.; flowers large, dbl.; recurrent bloom; vigorous growth; [sport of 'Lemania']

'Steffi Graf' HT, mp, Hetzel; flowers medium pink, reverse with brownish tones, large, full, high-centered, borne singly or in small clusters, intense fragrance; recurrent; bushy, moderate growth; intr. 1993

'Steiler Rambler' -- See 'Steyl Rambler'

'Steino' HT, my, 1965, Stein; bud ovoid; flowers dbl.; foliage dark; [sport of 'Golden Rapture']

'Stekelly-Leigh' ('Kelly-Leigh') Min, yb, 1984, Stephens, Paddy; flowers white and gold, medium, semi-dbl., no fragrance; foliage medium size, medium green, glossy; bushy growth; ['Ko's Yellow' × seedling]; intr. 1981

'Steliana' HT, mr, Roman, G., and Wagner, S.; flowers carmine-red, large, 50 petals, spiral-shaped, slight fragrance; foliage large, dark green, leathery, glossy; ['Romstar' × 'Peace']; intr. 2005

'Stella' HMult, rb, 1905, Soupert & Notting; flowers bright red, white center, 3-4 cm., single, borne in small clusters; ['Turner's Crimson Rambler' × seedling]

Stella® Gr, pb, Tantau, Math.; bud ovoid; flowers blush, edged deep pink on outer petals, 4-5 in., 36 petals, high-centered, borne in clusters; recurrent; foliage dark green, leathery; few prickles; vigorous, upright growth; [Horstmann's Jubilaumsrose × 'Peace']; intr. 1958

'Stella di Bologna' ('Étoile de Bologne') HT, m, 1909, Bonfiglio, A.; flowers violet pink, lighter at base, large, dbl., moderate fragrance; ['L'Innocence' × unknown]

'Stella Dorata' -- See 'Tantern'

'Stella Duce' F, dr, 1956, Leenders, M.; flowers dark crimson-red, stamens deep gold; vigorous growth

'Stella Elisabeth' Min, w, 1983, Moore, Ralph S.; flowers creamy white, petals edged light pink, small, 35 petals; foliage small, medium green, semi-glossy; bushy growth; [seedling × seedling]

'Stella Giles' ('The Soroptimist Rose') F, ab; intr. 1999

'Stella Mattutina' HT, lp, 1958, Giacomasso; flowers flesh-pink, well-formed, large, 35 petals; foliage glossy; vigorous growth; ['Numa Fay' × 'Asso Francesco Baracca']; intr. 1951

'Stella Pacis' HT, ob, 1946, Giacomasso; flowers combination of orange, salmon, red and yellow, large; vigorous growth; ['Julien Potin' × 'Mme G. Forest-Colcombet']

'Stella Polaris' HRg, w, 1890, Jensen; flowers silvery white, large, single; recurrent bloom; foliage dark; vigorous (4 ft.) growth

'Stellmacher' S, mr, 1937, Tantau; flowers bright red, full, borne in small clusters, moderate fragrance; abundant, recurrent; growth to 5 ft.; hardy; ['D.T. Poulsen' × 'Stammler']

'Stelvio Coggiatti' F, dy, Barni, V.; flowers deep, intense yellow, full, cupped, borne in clusters, moderate fragrance; free-flowering; foliage dark green, glossy; regular, compact (40-60 cm.) growth; intr. 1999

'Stephan' Pol, mp, 1967, Delforge; bud ovoid; flowers cyclamen-pink, large, dbl., borne in clusters; foliage glossy; vigorous, upright growth; ['Maria Delforge' × 'Arc-en-Ciel']

'Stephanie' Cl HT, lp, 1973, Gatty, Joseph; flowers open, large, semi-dbl.; profuse, repeated bloom; foliage glossy; vigorous, climbing growth; [Coral Dawn® × 'Titian']

'Stéphanie' -- See 'Aspasie'

'Stephanie Ann' Min, mp, 1979, Lyon; bud long, pointed; flowers Neyron rose, 1 in., 16 petals; foliage tiny; upright, bushy growth; intr. 1978

'Stephanie Ann' HT, rb, Edwards, Eddie, & Phelps, Ethan; flowers red and white, 4-5 in., full, borne mostly solitary, slight fragrance; foliage large, dark green, semi-glossy; prickles hooked; upright, medium growth; exhibition, garden decoration; [Veterans' Honor™ × 'White Success']; intr. 2005

'Stéphanie de Monaco' -- See 'Portrait'

'Stephanie Diane' HT, mr, 1980, Bees; flowers scarlet-red, paler center, 5 in., 50 petals, imbricated, borne singly and in clusters of 3, slight sweet fragrance; recurrent; foliage large, medium green, semi-glossy; prickles slightly hooked; moderately vigorous, upright growth; ['Fragrant Cloud' × 'Cassandra']; intr. 1971

'Stéphanie et Rodolphe' -- See 'Fiançailles de la Princesse Stéphanie et de l'Archiduc Rodolphe'

'Stephanie Jo' HT, w, Allender, Robert William; [sport of 'Sylvia']; intr. 1995

'Stephen F. Austin' S, yb, 2006, Shoup, George Micheal; flowers light yellow to cream, orange stamens, 3 in., semi-dbl., cupped, borne mostly solitary, moderate fragrance; recurrent; foliage large, dark green, semi-glossy; numerous prickles; upright, tall (6 ft.) growth; hedging; ['Carefree Beauty' × Graham Thomas®]; intr. 2000

'Stephen Foster' LCl, mp, 1950, Rosen, H.R.; bud ovoid; flowers pink, recurved, 3½-4 in., 20 petals; vigorous, upright growth, spreading to 15 ft. or more; [seedling × 'Black Knight']

'Stephen Langdon' F, dr, 1969, Sanday, John; flowers deep scarlet, large, semi-dbl., slight fragrance; foliage dark green; vigorous, compact growth; ['Karl Herbst' × Sarabande®]

'Stephen Rulo' Gr, r, 2007, Chaney, William; bud high-centered, beige, gold and lavender; flowers beige with gold base and lavender on petal edges, reverse beige and gold, developing tones of brown, lavender, and gray, large, full, borne in small clusters; foliage medium, medium green, glossy; prickles medium, downward pointed, beige, moderate; growth upright, tall; exhibition, garden decoration; ['Singin' in the Rain' × Stainless Steel™]; intr. 2008

'Stephens' Big Purple' -- See 'Stebigpu'

'Stephens' Rose Big Purple' -- See 'Stebigpu'

'Steppin' Out' -- See 'Bristep'

'Sterckmanns' -- See 'Triomphe de Sterckmanns'

'Stereo' F, or, 1979, Lens, Louis; bud long, pointed; flowers pure orange, open, 3-3½ in., 18-24 petals; foliage brownish, leathery; bushy growth; [Baccará® × ('Ole' × 'Independence')]; intr. 1972

'Sterkmanns' HGal, mr, 1847, Vibert; flowers large, dbl.

'Sterling' HT, mp, 1933, E.G. Hill, Co.; bud long, pointed; flowers brilliant pink, base yellow, large, 35 petals, moderate fragrance; foliage glossy; vigorous growth; PP21; ['Mme Butterfly' × seedling]

Sterling™ -- See 'Poulra016(N)'

'Sterling '95' -- See 'Jacnuel'

'Sterling Parade' (Sterling™) MinFl, mr, Poulsen; flowers medium red, 5-8 cm., dbl., no fragrance; foliage dark; growth bushy, 20-40 cm.; PP16077; intr. 2001

'Sterling Silver, Climbing' Cl HT, m, 1963, Miyawaki; seldom blooms on new wood; tall (8-10 ft.) growth; PP2473; [sport of 'Sterling Silver']

'Sterling Silver' HT, m, 1956, Fisher, E. G.; bud long, pointed; flowers lilac, becoming lighter, large, 30-35 petals, high-centered to cupped, borne singly, intense fragrance; recurrent; foliage large, dark green, glossy; very few prickles; stems strong, but not heavy; vigorous, upright (4 ft.) growth; PP1433; [seedling × 'Peace']; intr. 1956

Sterling Star™ -- See 'Ortsar'

'Stern von Prag' HRg, dr, 1924, Berger, V.; flowers dark blood-red, large, dbl.; foliage large, dark; very vigorous, bushy growth; [(*R. rugosa* × Edward Mawley) × unknown]

'Sternenflor' S, w, Schultheis; flowers small, single, flat, borne in large clusters, moderate fragrance; free-flowering; foliage dark green, glossy; low (30-40 cm.), spreading growth; hips round, small, red; intr. 1989

'Sternschnuppe' S, w, Schultheis; flowers semi-double to double, cupped to flat, borne in clusters, slight fragrance; recurrent; foliage small, glossy; low (60 cm.), spreading growth; ['Snowflake' × 'Sämling']; intr. 2007

Sterntaler® -- See 'Korquelda'

'Stesam' ('Sam') F, r, 1984, Stephens, Paddy; flowers russet, reverse cream, 20 petals; foliage medium size, dark, glossy; bushy growth; ['Brown Eye' × seedling]; intr. 1981

'Steteaw' ('Big John', 'Te Awamutu Centennial') HT, rb, 1985, Stephens, Pat; flowers white, edged medium red, 35 petals, slight fragrance; foliage dark, glossy; bushy growth; ['Strawberry Ice' × seedling]; intr. 1985

'Steve Chase' -- See 'Ripchase'

'Steve Clark' HT, ly, 2002, Poole, Lionel; flowers cream flushed pink, 4½-5 in., dbl., borne in small clusters; recurrent; foliage large, medium green, glossy; prickles medium, long, pointed, moderate; growth upright, medium (3 ft.); garden, beds, borders; ['Silver Jubilee' × 'Pedrus Aquarius']; intr. 2003

'Steve Redgrave' -- See 'Pure Gold'

'Steve Silverthorne' -- See 'Fulsteve'

'Stevens,Climbing' -- See 'Mrs Herbert Stevens, Climbing'

'Stevie' -- See 'Bustev'

'Steyl Rambler' ('Steiler Rambler') HMult, mr, 1915, Leenders, M.; flowers light geranium-red to medium, 3-4 cm., dbl., borne in large clusters; non-recurrent

'Stiedward' ('Hilton Edward') HT, mp, 1994, Stibbard, Robert H.; flowers lavender pink, 3-3½ in., dbl., borne mostly singly, intense fragrance; foliage large, dark green, semi-glossy; some prickles; tall, upright growth; ['Sweet Afton' × News®]; intr. 1995

'Stifontein Rose' -- See 'Tannietnof'

Stile '800® HT, ab, Barni, Enrico; flowers warm apricot and salmon, 9-11 cm., 40 petals, cupped, strong fragrance; recurrent; foliage large, deep green; vigorous (90 - 110 cm.) growth; [Antico Amore® × Louis de Funes®]; intr. 2000

'Sting' -- See 'Meimater'

'Stint' S, or, Williams, J. Benjamin; flowers more orange than red, single, flat, borne in clusters, slight fragrance; recurrent; growth to 3 ft.; intr. 2006

'Stirling Castle' F, mr, 1978, Cocker; flowers bright scarlet, 3 in., 18-20 petals; foliage matte; low, compact growth; [(Anne Cocker® × Elizabeth of Glamis®) × (Orange Sensation® × 'The Optimist')]

'Stockton Beauty' HT, pb, 1948, Raffel; bud long, pointed; flowers deep salmon-pink, base yellow, large, dbl., open, moderate fragrance; foliage soft; very vigorous, bushy growth; [sport of 'Banner']; much like Charlotte Armstrong except for color

'Stockton Red' Cl HT, mr, 1962, Raffel; flowers clear red, well-formed; very long stems, vigorous growth

'Stodels Beauty' -- See 'Jaczeman'

'Stokes' HT, op, 1982, Perry, Astor; flowers peach, reverse salmon, large, 35 petals, high-centered, slight fruity fragrance; foliage medium green, matte; prickles very few; medium-tall growth; ['Susan Massu' × 'yellow seedling']

'Stolen Dream' -- See 'Micsteal'

'Stolen Moment' -- See 'Seamom'

'Stonelea Rambler' HMsk, lp, Nieuwesteeg, J.; intr. 1994

'Stop Street' S, mr, Kordes; flowers bright red, semi-dbl., cupped, borne in large clusters; recurrent; vigorous, tall growth; intr. 2000

'Stoplite' Pol, mr, 1955, Jelly; flowers rose-red, medium, 45-55 petals, moderate fragrance; vigorous, upright growth; PP1315; ['Garnette' × seedling]; intr. 1955

'Stormly' HT, op, 1966, Caranta, M. & H.; flowers coral, reverse red-pink, oval, cupped; foliage dull; tall growth; [('Eclipse' × 'Michele Meilland') × Baccará®]

'Stormy Mountain' -- See 'Ranzan'

Stormy Weather™ -- See 'Ministorm'

'Straheidi' ('Spring Break') HT, dp, 1993, Strickland, Frank A.; flowers deep florescent pink, medium, dbl., high-centered, borne mostly singly, no fragrance; foliage medium size, medium green, matte; some prickles; medium, upright growth; ['Secret Love' × 'Kardinal']; intr. 1994

Straight Arrow™ -- See 'Rdsarrow'

'Strange Music' -- See 'Mormum'

'Stratford' HT, op, 1936, Nicolas; bud long-pointed, ovoid; flowers luminous pink tinted salmon, very dbl., intense fragrance; foliage leathery; long stems; very vigorous, bushy growth; PP160; [('Emile Charles' × 'La France') × 'Marechal Niel']

'Stratosféra' HSet, dp, 1934, Böhm, J.; flowers purple-red, 4-6 cm., semi-dbl., cupped, borne in small clusters, moderate fragrance; once-bloomer; upright, tall (2 m.) growth; ['Geschwind's Nordlandrose' × *R. centifolia*]

'Strauchmaskerade' S, yb

'Strawberries and Cream' -- See 'Geestraw'

'Strawberry' HT, mr, 1950, Fletcher; flowers strawberry, reverse deep flesh, 5½-6 in., 35-40 petals; foliage light green; vigorous, compact growth; ['McGredy's Pink' × 'Phyllis Gold']

'Strawberry Blonde' Gr, or, 1966, Armstrong, D.L.; bud urn-shaped; flowers light orange-red, medium, 25 petals, high-centered, moderate spicy fragrance; recurrent; foliage dark green, leathery; very vigorous, upright, bushy growth; PP2707; ['Ma Perkins' × 'Spartan']

'Strawberry Cream' F, pb, 1972, Ellick; flowers strawberry-pink, streaked cream, 3 in., 45 petals; foliage light; vigorous, low growth

'Strawberry Crush' F, mr, 1976, Dickson, A.; flowers unfading scarlet, 3 in., full, slight fragrance; foliage red when young, then rich green, glossy; [Bridal Pink™ × 'Franklin Engelmann']; intr. 1974

'Strawberry Crush' S, pb, Horner; flowers shades of strawberry pink with yellow eye, fading to creamy pink, large, double, shallow cup; recurrent; foliage dark green, glossy, disease-resistant; low, mounded growth; intr. 2008

'Strawberry Delight' -- See 'Renerry'

'Strawberry Fair' F, mr, 1966, Gregory; flowers scarlet, 2 in., dbl., borne in clusters; foliage dark; vigorous, bushy growth; [Orangeade® × unknown]

'Strawberry Fayre' -- See 'Arowillip'

'Strawberry Fields' -- See 'Rawbus'

'Strawberry Hill' -- See 'Ausrimini'

'Strawberry Ice' ('Delbara', Bordure Rose®, 'Happy Anniversary', 'Roslyne') F, w, 1976, Delbard, G.; flowers bordered cyclamen pink, center cream white, 3-3½ in., 22-25 petals, borne several together; foliage dark, slightly glossy; compact, bushy, low growth; [(('Goldilocks' × 'Virgo') × (Orange Triumph® × 'Yvonne Rabier')) × 'Fashion']; originally registered as Pol; re-registered as Bordure Rose, F, 1986; intr. 1975

'Strawberry Kiss' -- See 'Clekiss'

'Strawberry Parfait' -- See 'Delivour'

'Strawberry Romance' -- See 'Resstraw'

Strawberry Shake™ -- See 'Trsstshake'

'Strawberry Social' F, mr, 1980, Taylor, Thomas E.; bud ovoid; flowers 23 petals, high-centered, borne 3-7 per cluster; foliage medium green, semi-glossy; prickles hooked; upright to spreading, bushy growth; ['Pink Parfait' × 'Chrysler Imperial']

'Strawberry Sundae' -- See 'Leostra'

'Strawberry Swirl' Min, rb, 1978, Moore, Ralph S.; bud ovoid, pointed, lightly mossed; flowers red mixed with white,

1 in., 48 petals, high-centered, borne in clusters; recurrent; bushy, spreading growth; PP4495; ['Little Darling' × 'miniature seedling']

'Strawrose' Pol, mr, Schneider, S.; intr. 1998

'Streaker' -- See 'Bocrugostre'

'Stream' HT, lp, 2003, Yasuda, Yuji; flowers dbl., borne mostly solitary, slight fragrance; foliage medium size, dark green, matte; prickles medium, hooked; growth upright, medium (4 ft.); cutting, garden; ['Marchenkonigin' × 'Seisho']; intr. 2003

'Street Party' Min, ob; intr. 2001

'Street Wise' -- See 'Searonan'

'Stretch Johnson' -- See 'Macfirwal'

'Striata' ('Rouge Striée', 'Rubra Variegata') S, rb, before 1817, from England; flowers crimson, striped with white, large, full; foliage oval, finely toothed, pale green; prickles reddish, sparse

Strike It Rich™ -- See 'Wekbepmey'

'Strildew' ('Just For Fun') HT, lp, 1996, Strickland, Frank A.; flowers light pink, outer petals sometimes white with inner petals l, 6 in., very dbl.; foliage medium size, medium green, dull; prickles moderate; very long stems, upright, medium (4-5 ft.) growth; ['Secret Love' × 'First Prize']

'Strilli' F, my, Kordes; flowers clear, unfading yellow, medium, dbl., high-centered, borne singly and in clusters, slight fragrance; free flowering, prolific; medium growth; intr. 1993

'String of Pearls' S, w, Williams, J. Benjamin; flowers white, shaded pearl pink; vigorous, compact (3 ft.) growth; intr. 1981

'String of Pearls' F, w, 1985, Gandy's Roses, Ltd.; flowers near white, medium, semi-dbl.; foliage medium size, dark, semi-glossy; dwarf, bushy growth; ['Meg, Climbing' × 'Sunsprite']

'String of Pearls' Min, op, deRuiter; flowers coral pink, fading to pearl pink, narrow petals, small, dbl., pompon, moderate fragrance; recurrent; moderate growth; containers, borders; intr. 1991

'String of Rubies' Min, dp, Taschner, Ludwig; bud oval; flowers pleasing medium to deep pink, pompon, moderate fragrance; medium growth; containers, borders; [sport of 'String of Pearls']; intr. 2001

'Striped Crimson Perpetual' -- See 'Panachée de Lyon'

'Striped Fairy Rose' Min, rb

Striped Festival™ -- See 'Lavming'

'Striped La France' -- See 'Mme Angélique Veysset'

'Striped Meillandina' -- See 'Mormum'

'Striped Moss' -- See 'Panachée'

'Striped Moss' -- See 'Panachée Pleine a Petales Etroites'

'Striped Moss' -- See 'Œillet Panachée'

'Striped Pet' -- See 'Lavdance'

'Striped Radiance' HT, rb, 1919, Vestal; flowers red, distinctly striped white; [sport of 'Red Radiance']

'Striped Texas Centennial' HT, ob, 1950, Heckmann; flowers orange-red with dark yellow striping, large, dbl.

'Striped Unique' -- See 'Unique Panachée'

'Stripey Fred' Min, rb; flowers striped; intr. 2005

'Stripez' HT, pb, 1942, Janssen; flowers striped and variegated; PP550; [sport of 'Better Times']

'Strjillian' ('Sweet Cheeks') MinFl, yb, 2003, Strickland, Frank A.; flowers yellow blend, reverse yellow, 4 in., semi-dbl., high-centered, borne in small clusters, intense fragrance; foliage medium green, semi-glossy; prickles ¼ in., slight hook down, reddish brown; upright, medium (18 in.) growth; exhibition; ['Little Darling' × (Funkuhr® × Funkuhr®)]; intr. 2004

'Strody' HSpn, w, Strobelsingle; intr. 1999

'Stroke-o-Luck' F, yb

'Stroller' F, rb, 1970, Dickson, A.; bud loose; flowers cerise, reverse gold, dbl., borne in trusses; foliage matte; ['Manx Queen' × 'Happy Event']

'Strolon' ('Polar Sun') HRg, mp, Strobel; intr. 1991

'Strombergzauber' -- See 'Helkleger'

Stromboli™ ('Stromboli Palace') S, rb, Poulsen; flowers red with orange and yellow tones, 8-10 cm., full, slight wild rose fragrance; bushy, low (20-40 cm.) growth; hips none; intr. 2004

'Stromboli Palace' -- See 'Stromboli'

'Stryke Me Pink' S, mp, Tantau; flowers medium to porcelain pink; quick repeat; intr. 1998

'Stryker' HT, pb, 1994, Edwards, Eddie; flowers pink and white, veining in outer petals, 3 in., full, borne mostly singly, slight fragrance; foliage medium size, dark green, glossy; tall, bushy, upright growth; [Pristine® × 'Suffolk']

'Stuart's Quarry' HT, pb, 1977, Bailey; bud high centered; flowers pale bluish pink, reverse silver, 4 in., 30 petals; bloom repeats quickly; foliage small, glossy, dark; ['Silver Lining' × 'Anne Letts']

'Studienrat Schlenz' Cl HT, mp, 1926, Lambert, P.; flowers rose-pink, reverse darker, large, dbl., moderate fragrance; non-recurrent; growth to 6½-8 ft.; ['Mrs Aaron Ward' × 'Frau Karl Druschki']

Stunning™ HT, m, Olesen; bud globular; flowers light lavender, 8 cm., very full, globular, borne in large clusters, slight wild rose fragrance; recurrent; foliage dark green, glossy; prickles normal, deeply concave; narrow, bushy (60-100 cm.) growth; PP15406; [seedling × seedling]; intr. 2003

'Sturdy Gertie' HT, op, 1949, Taylor, C.A.; flowers coral-pink, medium, 30 petals, moderate raspberry fragrance; foliage small, dark, glossy, somewhat ribbed; ['Pink Princess' × 'Peace']

'Stuttaford Van Lines' HT, pb, Kordes; intr. 2008

'Stuttgart' HT, my, 1928, Berger, V.; bud long, pointed; flowers pure yellow, medium; ['Edith Cavell' × 'Mrs Franklin Dennison']

'STW-1' S, mr, Moore, Ralph; flowers light red, fading to pinkish-red, 8-12 petals, flat, borne in clusters, slight fragrance; blooms in large flushes; tall, V-shaped growth; ['Soeur Therese' × 'Wilhelm']; used primarily as breeding stock; never formally introduced.; intr. before 1951

'Stylish' HT, pb, 1953, Robinson, H.; flowers rose-pink, base yellow, 5-6 in., high-centered; foliage dark, glossy; vigorous growth

'Su Excelencia Señora de Franco' F, mr, 1958, Camprubi, C.; bud long, pointed; flowers medium, dbl., cupped; foliage dark, glossy; vigorous, upright growth; ['Cocorico' × 'Independence']; intr. 1956

'Su-Spantu' F, m, 1962, Borgatti, G.; flowers purplish pink, 25 petals, borne in clusters of 7-8; upright growth; ['Alain' × 'Independence']

'Suaveolens' -- See 'Alba Semi-plena'

'Subaru' F, mr, 1977, Kikuchi, Rikichi; bud pointed; flowers single, 5 petals; foliage dark; low growth; ['Masquerade' × 'Permanent Wave']

'Sublaevis' (R. × sublaevis) Ayr, op; flowers salmon pink, fading to rose pink, small, single, borne in small clusters; possibly R. arvensis × a gallica

'Sublime' HT, op, 1931, Amling Co.; bud long, pointed; flowers orange-salmon, suffused scarlet, semi-dbl.; long stems; very vigorous growth; [sport of 'Talisman']

'Sublime' S, dp, Tantau; groundcover; intr. 2002

Sublime™ -- See 'Tucsublime'

'Sublimely Single' -- See 'Delmur'

'Subnigra' ('Atropurpurea', 'Négretienne', 'Negrette', 'Nigrette', 'Noire de Holland', 'Subnigra Marron') HGal, m, before 1811; bud round, slightly pointed; flowers violet purple tending towards black, medium, semi-dbl.; possibly synonymous with either 'Cramoisie Éblouissante' or 'Superbe en Brun'

'Subnigra Marron' -- See 'Subnigra'

'Substitut Jacques Chapel' HT, pb, 1922, Bernaix, P.; flowers peach-blossom-pink, edged rose-pink, base shaded citron-yellow; ['Mme Mélanie Soupert' × 'Lyon Rose']

'Subviolacea' -- See 'Ternaux'

'Succes' S, lp, 1954, deRuiter; flowers pinkish white, single, borne in trusses; foliage dark, glossy; [R. canina × unknown]

'Succès Fou' HT, mr, 1963, Delbard-Chabert; bud long; flowers deep cherry-red, well-formed; vigorous growth; ['Walko' × 'Souv. de J. Chabert']

'Success Story' -- See 'Jacbitou'

'Suchitra' F, pb, 1974, IARI; buds large, long pointed; flowers Rhodaminepink with mimosa-yellow reverse and base, large, dbl, high-centered, borne in clusters; foliage large, dark green, soft; growth very vigorous, compact, bushy (90 cm.); ['Lady Frost' × 'Swati']; intr. 1972

'Sudha' HT, yb, Datta, Sekhar; flowers bright yellow with pink, dbl., moderate fragrance; [sport of 'Lido di Roma']; intr. 2005

'Sudhanshu' HT, lp, 2006, Jagtap, Ramrao S.; flowers light pink deepening at center, reverse light pink, 10-12 cm., high-centered, borne mostly solitary, strong fragrance; prickles 5 mm., cream, few; growth to 1-1½ m.; bedding; ['Lilac Airs' × 'Paradise']; intr. 2005

'Sue Belle' -- See 'Talsue'

'Sue Betts' -- See 'Betsue'

'Sue Earley' -- See 'Lovbed'

'Sue Hipkin' ('Chimène', 'Lady Jane Grey', 'Sweet Lady', 'Sweet Revelation') HT, ab, Harkness; flowers apricot, blushed pink, medium, dbl., imbricated, intense fragrance; recurrent; foliage dark green; vigorous, bushy (4 ft.) growth; intr. 1997

Sue Jo™ -- See 'Minavco'

'Sue Lawley' -- See 'Macspash'

'Sue Leat' HT, pb, 1984, Summerell, B.L.; flowers medium pink on outer half of petals, golden yellow on lower, 20 petals, moderate fragrance; prickles brown; upright growth; ['Golden Slippers' × 'Anne Letts']; intr. 1983

Sue Ryder® -- See 'Harlino'

'Sue Watkins' -- See 'Bosdonford'

Suela® HT, dy; flowers deep yellow, petal edges fading white, medium to large, dbl., blooms in flushes, no fragrance; recurrent; intr. 2002

'Suffolk' HT, w, 1984, Perry, Astor; flowers white with pink petal tips, large, very full, high-centered, borne mostly singly, slight fragrance; recurrent; foliage large, medium green, matte; upright growth; ['Garden Party' × yellow seedling]; intr. 1984

Suffolk™ -- See 'Poulgode'

'Suffolk' -- See 'Kormixal'

'Sugandha' HT, dr, P. Bhattacharjee & Sons; flowers crimson, large, slight fragrance; intr. 1963

'Sugandha Raj' HT, dr, Datt, Brahm; flowers non-fading crimson red, full, moderate fragrance; intr. 1992

'Sugandhini' HT, lp, 1971, IARI; bud pointed; flowers medium, dbl., intense fragrance; foliage glossy, light; bushy growth; ['Margaret Spaull' × unknown]; intr. 1969

'Sugar & Spice' Min, lp, Pearce; flowers soft pink, dbl., pompon, slight fragrance; free-flowering; foliage light green, disease-resistant; low (12 in.) growth; intr. 2000

'Sugar 'n' Spice' -- See 'Tinspice'

'Sugar Babe' Min, lp, 1979, Lyon; bud long, pointed; flowers 1 in., 16 petals; foliage bronze; compact growth; intr. 1978

'Sugar Baby' Min, dp, Tantau; flowers rich pink, small, dbl., cupped, borne in clusters, moderate fragrance; free-flowering; low (12 in.) growth; intr. 1997

'Sugar Bear' Min, w, 1987, Bridges, Dennis A.; flowers medium, 18 petals, high-centered, borne singly; foliage medium size, medium green, semi-glossy; prickles straight, pointed, medium, light green; upright, medium growth; [Heartland™ × seedling]

'Sugar Bells' HT, w; bud globular; flowers creamy white; medium growth; [sport of 'Joybells']; intr. 2003

'Sugar Candy' Pol, mp, 1951, Proctor; flowers pink, very small, dbl.; profuse, repeated bloom; compact growth

Sugar Cookie™ -- See 'Pixcook'

'Sugar Daddy' -- See 'Jaclorna'

'Sugar Elf' Min, pb, 1975, Moore, Ralph S.; bud long, pointed; flowers pink and gold blend, 1 in., 15 petals; foliage glossy, leathery; bushy, spreading growth; intr. 1974

Sugar Magnolia™ -- See 'Talsugar'

'Sugar Plum' HT, mp, 1954, Swim, H.C.; bud ovoid; flowers Tyrian rose, 4-5 in., 55 petals, high-centered, moderate spicy fragrance; foliage dark, glossy, leathery; vigorous, upright, bushy growth; PP1255; ['Crimson Glory' × 'Girona']; intr. 1954

'Sugar Plum' -- See 'Chewpope'

'Sugar Plum' -- See 'Morplum'

'Sugar Plum Fairy' Min, m, Hannemann, F.; ['Sweet Chariot' × seedling]

'Sugar Sweet' F, pb, 1973, Sanday, John; flowers soft pink, reverse yellow and pink, 3-4 in., 13 petals, high-centered; foliage green, matte; ['Wendy Cussons' × 'Prima Ballerina']

Sugarland Run™ (Golden Eye Cover™) S, my; flowers bright yellow, 5 cm., semi-dbl. to dbl., open cup, borne in clusters, very slight fragrance; recurrent; foliage dark green, glossy; growth bushy, 40-60 cm.; intr. 2005

'Suhasini' F, lp, 1974, Pal, Dr. B. P.; buds medium, pointed; flowers soft pink, medium, dbl, borne singly and several together; foliage medium size, glossy; growth vigorous, upright (105 cm.); [Queen Elizabeth® × unknown]; intr. 1972

'Suitor' Pol, lp, 1942, Clark, A.; flowers light pink; growth low; intr. 1942

'Sujata' HT, dr, 1973, IARI; buds very large, long pointed; flowers deep crimson red, large, dbl, high-centered, borne singly; foliage medium size, dark green, leathery; growth vigorous, bushy, compact; intr. 1971

'Sukumari' F, w, 1985, Gupta, Dr. M.N. & Datta, Dr. S.K.; flowers rosy white; [sport of 'America's Junior Miss']; intr. 1983

'Sulcova Kladenska' Pol, lp, 1936, Sulc; flowers bright pink; vigorous growth

Sullivan ™ -- See 'Sullivan Hit'

'Sullivan Hit' (Sullivan ™) MinFl, my, Poulsen; flowers medium yellow, 5-8 cm., dbl., no fragrance; growth bushy, 20-40 cm.; intr. 2005

'Sulphurea' ('Jaune Soufré', 'Lutea Plena') HSpn, ly, before 1838, Hardy; flowers pale straw yellow, large, semi-dbl., cupped, foliage small, almost round, finely toothed, yellowish-green; prickles very fine, uneven, rather crooked

'Sulphurea' T, ly, Paul, W.; flowers sulfur-yellow, large, full; intr. 1900

'Sulphurea' -- See 'Multiplex'

'Sulphurea Nana' -- See 'Pompone Jaune'

'Sulphureux' T, dy, Ducher; flowers sulphur-yellow

'Sultan of Zanzibar' HP, m, 1876, Paul & Son; flowers purplish maroon, medium, globular; ['Duke of Edinburgh' × unknown]

'Sultana' ('Maxima', 'Regina') C, mp, before 1829; flowers medium, very dbl., intense fragrance; prickles numerous, short, hooked, blackish green; stems strong; growth vigorous, tall

'Sultane' HT, rb, 1946, Meilland, F.; bud long, pointed; flowers vermilion, reverse gold, petals quilled, 5 in., 40 petals, slight fragrance; recurrent; foliage leathery, bronze; ['J.B. Meilland' × 'Orange Nassau']

'Sultane, Climbing' Cl HT, rb, after 1946; [sport of 'Sultane']

'Sultane Favorite' -- See 'Félicie'

Sultry™ -- See 'Jacyelap'

'Suma' ('Rosy Creeper') S, dp, Onodera, Toru F.; flowers rose-pink, 1 in., 12-18 petals, cupped, borne in clusters, slight fragrance; foliage small, dense; low (1-2 ft.), spreading (5-6 ft.) groundcover growth

'Suma no Ura' HT, mr, 1986, Teranishi, K.; flowers crimson, full, high-centered, borne singly, no fragrance; foliage small, medium green, semi-glossy; prickles large, reddish-brown; medium, bushy growth; [(Rob Roy® × 'Himatsuri') × seedling]; intr. 1980

'Suman' HT, lp, Ghosh, Mr. & Mrs. S.; flowers soft pink, broad petals, large, high-centered, moderate fragrance; intr. 1998

'Sumatra' F, or, 1957, Mallerin, C.; bud ovoid; flowers signal-red, 3 in., 26 petals, globular, borne in pyramidal clusters, moderate fragrance; foliage leathery; moderate, upright growth; PP1572; ['Olga' × 'Fashion']; intr. 1957

'Sumire-no-Oka' LCl, m, 2005, Kobayashi, Moriji; flowers dbl., borne in small clusters, intense fragrance; foliage medium size, medium green, matte; prickles medium; spreading (200 cm.) growth; containers; [seedling × seedling]; intr. 2005

Summer™ -- See 'Poulcape'

'Summer Beauty' -- See 'Kororbe'

Summer Beauty™ -- See 'Minahco'

'Summer Blossom' F, mp, 1971, deRuiter; flowers soft geranium-pink, open, 2-3 in.;

upright, bushy growth; PP3584; [Orange Sensation® × Kimono®]
'Summer Blush' A, dp, Sievers, Rolf; flowers deep pink to medium red, full, cupped, moderate fragrance; spring flowering; medium growth; intr. 1988
'Summer Breeze' F, mp, Meilland
'Summer Breeze' -- See 'Korelasting'
'Summer Breeze' -- See 'Talsum'
'Summer Breeze' -- See 'Korlanum'
'Summer Butter' Min, dy, 1979, Saville, F. Harmon; bud ovoid, pointed; flowers deep yellow, slightly fading as it ages, 1-1½ in., 20-25 petals, cupped, borne mostly singly, intense spicy-sweet fragrance; recurrent; foliage medium size, glossy; prickles moderate, straight, pointed; vigorous, compact growth; hips round ; PP4457; ['Arthur Bell' × 'Yellow Jewel']
'Summer Charm' S, pb, Williams, J.B.; flowers pink fading to white, borne in masses of blooms; recurrent; upright growth; intr. 2003
'Summer Cloud' -- See 'Zipcloud'
'Summer Crest' -- See 'Hercres'
'Summer Damask' ('Carthage Rose', R. belgica, 'Rose of Paestum', 'Rose of Castile', R. polyantha, 'The Pompeii Rose', R. gallica damascena, 'Damask Rose', 'Castilian Rose', R. × damascena, R. calendarum) D, lp, before 1600; sepals not persistent; flowers highly variable in color from almost white to dark pink, medium, semi-dbl. to dbl., loose, borne in small to medium clusters, intense fragrance; early summer; foliage oval acute, gray-green, reverse lighter, downy, usually with 5-7 leaflets; prickles moderate, short, hooked; stems long, arching, pale green; growth to 5-7 ft.; hips obovoid, bristly, about 1 in., bright red, (28, 35); referenced by Virgil about 50 B.C., and later by Pliny; probably introduced into Europe by the Romans, and reintroduced during the Crusades; recent research (Japan) indicates parentage is (R. moschata × R. gallica) × R. fedtschenkoana
'Summer Dawn' Min, op, Benardella, Frank; flowers deep coral pink with copper tonings, borne mostly singly, moderate fragrance; recurrent; medium growth
'Summer Dawn' Pol, mp, 1950, Proctor; flowers soft rose-pink, globular, moderate fragrance; recurrent; foliage small, dainty; [sport of 'Margo Koster']
'Summer Days' HT, ly, 1976, Bees; flowers pale yellow, large, 36 petals, high-centered; vigorous growth; ['Fragrant Cloud' × 'Dr. A. J. Verhage']
'Summer Dream' ('Beautiful Dreamer', 'Sweet Memories') F, ab, Fryer, Gareth; bud globular; flowers peachy-apricot, large, dbl., cupped, borne in clusters, moderate fragrance; free-flowering; foliage light green; vigorous, medium growth; [sport of 'Sweet Dream']; intr. 1990

'Summer Dream' -- See 'Jacshe'
'Summer Evening' Min, ob, 1999, Jolly, Betty J.; flowers orange and white, reverse white, 1¾ in., full, high-centered, borne mostly singly, no fragrance; foliage medium size, dark green, semi-glossy; few prickles; upright, medium (14 in.) growth; ['Tennessee' × Kristin™]; intr. 1998
'Summer Evening' -- See 'Sommerabend'
'Summer Fantasy' -- See 'Zipjul'
'Summer Fashion' -- See 'Jacale'
Summer Festival™ -- See 'Lavsum'
'Summer Fever' F, or, Mehring; flowers scarlet, medium, dbl., open cup; free-flowering; foliage large, glossy; neat, bushy (2 ft.) growth; intr. 2006
'Summer Fever' HT, my
'Summer Fields' F, dp, 1971, Mattock; flowers light scarlet, yellow eye, 5 in., 17 petals, moderate fragrance; recurrent; foliage red when young, then green, matte; hips large, orange; ['Tropicana' × 'Goldmarie']
'Summer Fragrance' -- See 'Tanfudermos'
'Summer Frost' F, w, 1962, Boerner; bud ovoid; flowers white with slight yellow tones in center early, 4½ in., 30-35 petals, cupped, borne singly and several together, moderate tea fragrance; recurrent; foliage medium size, leathery, dark green; prickles normal, medium length, straight; stems medium, strong; vigorous, bushy, compact growth; PP2115; ['Princess White' × 'Golden Masterpiece']; intr. 1962
'Summer Glory' HT, my, 1961, Leenders, J.; flowers lemon, well-formed, large; upright growth; ['Dr. van Rijn' × seedling]
'Summer Glow' HT, yb, Courage; flowers soft yellow, pink blush spreading with age, dbl., cupped, moderate sweet fragrance; recurrent; foliage dark green; medium (4-5 ft.) growth; intr. 2001
Summer Gold™ -- See 'Poulreb'
'Summer Gold' -- See 'Tanduft'
'Summer Harvest' -- See 'Pixhar'
Summer Holiday® ('Sommertag') HT, or, 1967, Gregory; flowers vermilion, 48 petals, high-centered, moderate fragrance; recurrent; foliage semi-glossy; very vigorous growth; ['Tropicana' × unknown]; intr. 1967
'Summer Joy' HWich, dp, 1911, Walsh; bud pure white; flowers dark rose-pink, dbl., cupped, borne in clusters, moderate fragrance; foliage large, glossy; vigorous, climbing (18-20 ft.) growth
'Summer Jubilee' S, rb, Williams, J.B.; flowers light red and ivory, borne in clusters; recurrent; foliage dark green, glossy; low, compact growth; intr. 2003
Summer Lady® ('Renown's Summer Lady') HT, pb, Tantau; bud long; flowers creamy pink overlaid with deeper salmon tones, dbl., high-centered, borne mostly singly, moderate fragrance; recurrent; foliage large, leathery; upright,

medium growth; intr. 1991
'Summer Love' -- See 'Franluv'
Summer Love™ -- See 'Wekhocamito'
Summer Madness™ -- See 'Foumad'
'Summer Magic' Min, op, 1990, Jolly, Marie; bud ovoid; flowers light pink blended apricot, reverse cream center, pink edging, 150 petals, high-centered, slight fruity fragrance; foliage small, medium green, matte; no prickles; bushy, spreading, medium growth; ['Fashion Flame' × Anita Charles™]; intr. 1991
'Summer Meeting' F, my, 1968, Harkness, R.; flowers large, 45 petals, borne in trusses; foliage glossy; compact, bushy growth; ['Selgold' × 'Circus']; intr. 1968
'Summer Memories' F, w, Kordes; flowers creamy white, large, full, cupped, slight fragrance; recurrent; foliage medium green; bushy, upright growth; intr. 2005
'Summer Morning' -- See 'Korfullwind'
'Summer Night' -- See 'Tuckpuzzle'
'Summer Pageant' F, yb
'Summer Palace' (Summer™) S, w, Olesen; bud pointed; flowers white with yellow tones in center, 3 in., 50-60 petals, cupped, borne in clusters, slight wild rose fragrance; recurrent; foliage medium size, dark green, glossy; prickles few, concave to linear; bushy, compact (40-60 cm.) growth; PP10730; [Sexy Rexy® × seedling]; intr. 1998
'Summer Perfume' LCl, mr, 1962, Leenders, J.; flowers vermilion-red, 19 petals; [Coral Dawn® × 'Cocorico']
'Summer Promise' HT, ly, 1971, Von Abrams; flowers very large, dbl., high-centered; foliage glossy; vigorous growth; intr. 1969
'Summer Queen' HT, w, 1966, Delforge; flowers ivory-white, center tinted pink; [sport of Queen Elizabeth®]
'Summer Rainbow' HT, pb, 1966, Jelly; bud medium, pointed ovoid; flowers pink, reverse yellow, 6 in., 45-50 petals, high-centered, borne singly, slight tea fragrance; free-flowering; foliage medium size, glossy, leathery; prickles several, reddish brown; stems medium to long; vigorous, bushy growth; PP2746; ['Peace' × 'Dawn']
Summer Samba™ -- See 'Jacsumre'
'Summer Scent' -- See 'Rensum'
Summer Serenade® -- See 'Smitfirst'
'Summer Snow' F, w, 1938, Perkins, C.H.; flowers large, cupped, borne in large clusters, slight fragrance; heavy, recurrent; foliage light green; bushy growth; PP416; [sport of 'Summer Snow, Climbing']
'Summer Snow, Climbing' Cl F, w, 1936, Couteau; flowers 2 in., semi-dbl., cupped, borne in large clusters; sparse recurrent bloom; foliage leathery; vigorous, pillar (8-10 ft.) growth; PP400; ['Tausendschön' × unknown]
'Summer Snow' -- See 'Weopop'
'Summer Snowflake' -- See 'Katharina Zeimet'

'Summer Snows' -- See 'Rigobec 2'
'Summer Song' ('Chanson d'Été') F, ob, 1962, Dickson, Patrick; flowers orange and yellow, large, 12 petals, borne in clusters; foliage glossy; low, bushy growth; [seedling × 'Masquerade']
'Summer Song' -- See 'Austango'
'Summer Spice' Min, ab, 1983, Bridges, Dennis A.; flowers light apricot, medium, 35 petals; foliage medium size, medium green, semi-glossy; spreading growth; ['Sheri Anne' × seedling]
Summer Splash™ -- See 'Pixsummer'
'Summer Sun' Min, my; bud ovoid; flowers bright yellow, 1 in., 28 petals; recurrent; foliage medium green, semi-glossy; vigorous, bushy (12 - 18 in.) growth
'Summer Sun' -- See 'Adasun'
'Summer Sun' -- See 'Morgogard'
'Summer Sunrise' S, lp, 2006, Beales, Amanda; flowers dbl., borne in small clusters, slight fragrance; foliage small, medium green, glossy; prickles moderate, 6-8 mm., deeply concave; growth spreading, bushy, short (40-60 cm.); groundcover, containers; ['Bonica' × 'New Dawn']; intr. 1994
'Summer Sunset' S, dp, 2006, Beales, Amanda; flowers deep pink, reverse deep pink, 4-6 cm, semi-dbl., borne in small clusters; foliage small, dark green, glossy; prickles 6-8 mm., concave, moderate; growth spreading, bushy, short (60 cm.); groundcover, containers; ['New Dawn' × 'Robin Redbreast']; intr. 1994
Summer Sunset® HT, ob; flowers orange and yellow blend, dbl., high-centered; foliage dark green
'Summer Sunset' -- See 'Brisun'
'Summer Sunshine' ('Soleil d'Été') HT, dy, 1962, Swim, H.C.; bud ovoid; flowers canary yellow, 3½-5 in., 22-28 petals, high-centered to cupped, borne usually singly, slight fragrance; recurrent; foliage leathery, dark green, semi-glossy; prickles few to several, medium, straight to hooked downward, brown; vigorous, upright, well-branched growth; PP2078; ['Buccaneer' × 'Lemon Chiffon']; intr. 1962
'Summer Sunshine, Climbing' Cl HT, dy
'Summer Surprise' Min, mp, 1991, Gruenbauer, Richard; bud rounded; flowers pink with yellow stamens, slightly darker reverse, aging light pink, medium, 60 petals, rosette, no fragrance; foliage small, medium green, matte; bushy, low growth; ['Libby' × seedling]; intr. 1990
'Summer Sweet' S, pb
'Summer Sweet' HT, ly, Bell, Laurie; flowers creamy pale primrose yellow, well-formed, moderate fragrance; free-flowering; medium growth
'Summer Symphony' Min, yb, 1985, Hardgrove, Donald & Mary; flowers large, dbl., high-centered, intense fragrance; foliage medium size, medium green, semi-glossy; bushy, spreading growth; ['Lady Eve' × 'Little Darling']; intr. 1984

'Summer Tan' F, lp, 1979, Sheridan, John; flowers flesh-pink; foliage medium green, semi-glossy; vigorous, compact growth; ['Golden Slippers' × 'Picasso']
'Summer Time' -- See 'Chewlarmoll'
'Summer Wedding' -- See 'Jalwed'
'Summer Wind' S, op, 1975, Buck, Dr. Griffith J.; bud ovoid, pointed; flowers orange-pink, aging to rose pink, 3½-4 in., single to semi-dbl., flat, borne singly and in clusters, moderate spicy clove fragrance; foliage dark green, leathery; prickles large; moderately vigorous, erect, bushy growth; [('Fandango' × 'Florence Mary Morse') × 'Applejack']
'Summer Wine' -- See 'Korizont'
'Summerdale' -- See 'Taldal'
'Summerfield' Min, dp, Sommerfield; intr. 2007
'Summerrose' -- See 'Intersum'
'Summer's Kiss' -- See 'Meinivoz'
'Summertime' HT, mp, 1957, Boerner; bud medium, ovoid; flowers cameo-pink overcast rose-pink, 4-4½ in., 65-70 petals, high-centered, borne in irregular clusters, intense Old Rose (centifolia) fragrance; free-flowering; foliage medium size, glossy, olive-green; prickles normal, medium, hooked downward; stems medium; vigorous, upright, bushy growth; PP1541; ['Diamond Jubilee' × 'Fashion']; intr. 1957
'Summertime' HT, ly, Meilland; flowers light yellow, out petals fading, dbl., high-centered, borne mostly singly; recurrent; florist rose; intr. 2004
'Summertime' -- See 'Chewlarmoll'
'Summertime Dream' S, ab, Sauer; intr. 2008
'Summerwind' -- See 'Korlanum'
'Summerwine' HT, mp, 1975, Warriner, William A.; bud ovoid, pointed; flowers 4-6 in., 45 petals; foliage leathery; PP3665; ['Tiffany' × 'South Seas']; intr. 1974
'Summit' LCl, mr, Williams, J. B.; flowers candy-apple red, dbl., moderate fragrance; foliage dark green; growth to 6 ft.; intr. 2005
Sun™ -- See 'Sun Hit'
'Sun Blush' HT, yb, 1981, Anderson's Rose Nurseries; flowers 37 petals, high-centered, borne singly or 4 per cluster; foliage mid-green; prickles broad based, dark red; upright growth; ['Circus' × 'Summer Sunshine']
'Sun Chariot' -- See 'Jalsun'
'Sun City ' -- See 'Korsun'
'Sun City 2' HT, yb, Kordes; flowers deep yellow with orange-red spreading down from petal edges, dbl., high-centered, moderate fragrance; stems strong; medium to tall growth
Sun Cover™ -- See 'Poulurt'
'Sun Drops' -- See 'Lyodro'
'Sun Dust' -- See 'Sundust'
Sun Flare, Climbing™ -- See 'Buryellow'
'Sun Flare, Climbing' -- See 'Jaclem'
'Sun Flare' -- See 'Jacjem'
'Sun Glory' -- See 'Jacmey'

'Sun Glow' HT, op, 1934, Florex Gardens; bud long, pointed; flowers dark coral-pink, large, dbl., high-centered, moderate fragrance; foliage glossy; long, strong stems; very vigorous growth; PP209; [sport of 'Talisman']
'Sun God' HT, pb, 1930, Klyn; flowers shrimp-pink, yellow, and orange-copper, very dbl.; foliage leathery, bronze; short stems; dwarf growth; [seedling × 'Mme Edouard Herriot']
'Sun Goddess' -- See 'Jacdash'
'Sun Gold' HT, my, 1935, Elmer's Nursery; flowers pure yellow, large, dbl.; foliage glossy, dark; very vigorous growth; RULED EXTINCT 3/83
'Sun Hit' ('Golden Wishes', Sun™) MinFl, my, Olesen; bud long, pointed ovoid; flowers medium to deep, bright yellow, 2½ in., 30-35 petals, cupped, borne singly and several together, slight fragrance; recurrent; foliage dark green, glossy; prickles normal, short, hooked downward; stems strong, short; upright, bushy (40-60 cm.) growth; PP9716; [seedling × 'Goldmarie 82']; intr. 1996
'Sun Honey' -- See 'Morhoney'
Sun King® HT, my, 1954, Meilland, F.; bud long, pointed ovoid with conspicuous neck; flowers bright lemon-yellow, large, 45 petals, high-centered, borne mostly singly, moderate fragrance; recurrent; foliage dark green, glossy, leathery; prickles several, medium, slighty hooked downward; stems medium; vigorous, upright, bushy growth; hips none ; PP1342; ['Peace' × 'Duchesse de Talleyrand']; intr. 1954
Sun King® HT, dy, Meilland; flowers bright, sunny, lemon yellow, dbl., high-centered, borne mostly singly; good repeat; florist rose; intr. 2004
'Sun King' -- See 'Meinarval'
'Sun King '74' -- See 'Meinarval'
'Sun Kissed' -- See 'Pixkiss'
Sun Princess® Min, lp, Laver, Keith G.; flowers light salmon-pink, small, 35 petals, slight fragrance; foliage small, medium green, semi-glossy; bushy, spreading growth; [('Dwarfking '78' × Starina®) × 'Lemon Delight']; intr. 1984
'Sun-Ray' HT, my, 1932, Bentall; flowers golden yellow, semi-dbl.; vigorous growth
'Sun Runner' -- See 'Interdust'
'Sun Sparkle' -- See 'Lyosun'
Sun Sprinkles™ -- See 'Jachal'
'Sun Up' HT, lp, 1951, Brownell; flowers China-pink, large, dbl., moderate fragrance; vigorous growth; PP1015; [sport of 'Break o' Day']
'Sun Valley' ('Yukon') HT, dy, 1952, Whisler; bud ovoid; flowers golden yellow, open, 4-5 in., 30-35 petals, intense spicy fragrance; foliage dark, leathery; vigorous, upright growth; PP1135; ['Soeur Thérèse' × 'Mark Sullivan']
'Sun Valley, Climbing' Cl HT, dy, Whisler; [sport of 'Sun Valley']
Sun Valley™ (Sunburst Border™) S, dy,

Poulsen; flowers deep yellow, 8-10 cm., semi-dbl., open cup, borne in clusters, slight wild rose fragrance; recurrent; foliage dark green, glossy; bushy (100-150 cm.) growth; intr. 2000

'Sunabro' -- See 'Sunambro'

'Sunalad' ('Aladdin') Min, op, 1999, Schuurman, Frank B.; flowers, 1¾-2 in., full, borne in large clusters, moderate fragrance; foliage large, dark green, glossy; prickles moderate; spreading, tall growth; ['Tinkerbell' × 'Texas']; intr. 1995

'Sunambro' ('Ambrosia', 'Sunabro') Gr, mp, 1999, Schuurman, Frank B.; flowers 2¾-3 in., full, borne in small clusters, moderate fragrance; foliage large, medium green, semi-glossy; prickles moderate; bushy, medium growth; [Sexy Rexy® × New Year®]; intr. 1996

'Sunanda' HT, pb, Ghosh, Mr. & Mrs. P.; flowers deep pink with purple shadings, lighter reverse, large, dbl., high-centered, moderate tea fragrance; intr. 1998

'Sunauck' ('Barossa Dream') HT, ab, 1999, Schuurman, Frank B.; flowers apricot, reverse light apricot, 4½-5 in., dbl., borne mostly singly; foliage large, medium green, semi-glossy; prickles moderate; bushy, tall (3-4 ft.) growth; ['City of Auckland' × New Year®]; intr. 1995

'Sunbeam' T, 1908, California Rose Co.; [sport of 'Golden Gate']

'Sunbeam' HT, yb, Cant; flowers dark golden yellow, shaded peach, aging to fawn, large, full; intr. 1912

'Sunbeam' HT, Le Cornu; intr. 1927

'Sunbeam' Min, my, Robinson, T.; flowers rich yellow, intense fragrance; free-flowering; dwarf (14-18 in.) growth; [('Tom Thumb' × 'Polly Flinders') × 'Golden Scepter']; intr. 1957

'Sunbeam' ('Sunbeam 2000') HT, ab, Kordes; flowers copper-yellow, medium, full, high-centered, borne mostly singly; recurrent; stems long; intr. 1999

Sunbeam® -- See 'Kordoselbla'

'Sunbeam' -- See 'Margo Koster'

'Sunbeam, Climbing' -- See 'Margo Koster, Climbing'

Sunbeam Kordana® Min, my, Kordes; flowers golden-yellow, full; container rose; intr. 2005

'Sunbeam 2000' -- See 'Sunbeam'

Sunbird™ -- See 'Poulnish'

'Sunbird' -- See 'Jacpoy'

'Sunblaze' -- See 'Meiponal'

'Sunblaze' -- See 'Meijikatar'

'Sunblest' ('Landora') HT, dy, 1971, Tantau, Math.; flowers 5 in., 38 petals; foliage glossy; [seedling × King's Ransom®]; intr. 1970

'Sunblest, Climbing' -- See 'Clinora'

'Sunbonnet' F, dy, 1969, Swim & Weeks; bud pointed; flowers bright greenish yellow, medium, 30-38 petals, high-centered, borne usually in clusters, moderate fragrance; recurrent; foliage dark green, leathery; prickles numerous, medium, straight to slightly hooked downward; vigorous, low, bushy growth; hips short, globular, yellow-russet; PP2815; ['Arlene Francis' × ('Circus' × 'Sweet Talk')]; intr. 1967

'Sunbonnet' Min, dy, Delbard; flowers golden-yellow; free-flowering; bushy, short growth

'Sunbonnet Sue' S, yb, 1985, Buck, Dr. Griffith J.; flowers yellow stippled with scarlet, large, 25 petals, high-centered, borne singly or in cluster up to 10, moderate sweet fragrance; repeat bloom; foliage large, leathery, semi-glossy, medium green; prickles small, awl-like, brown; upright, bushy growth; hardy; ['Gold Dot' × 'Malaguena']; intr. 1984

Sunbright® HT, my, 1978, Warriner, William A.; bud long, pointed ovoid; flowers chrome yellow, 4-5 in., 25-35 petals, high-centered, flattens, borne singly and several together, very slight fragrance; recurrent; foliage medium size, leathery; prickles numerous, long, straight; stems medium; vigorous, upright growth; PP4438; [seedling × 'New Day']; intr. 1984

'Sunburn' S, yb, Rupert, Kim; flowers open yellow and turn pink in the sun, single, borne singly and in clusters; bushy growth

'Sunburnt' -- See 'Gelburn'

'Sunburnt Country' -- See 'Korav'

'Sunburst' HT, yb, 1912, Pernet-Ducher; bud long, pointed; flowers variable yellow, toward orange,, dbl., cupped

'Sunburst, Climbing' Cl HT, dy, 1914, Howard Rose Co. (also Low, 1915); [sport of 'Sunburst']

Sunburst™ S, or, John Clements; flowers bright orange-red, 3½ in., 18 petals, shallow cup, moderate fragrance; free-flowering; foliage disease-resistant; bushy (4½-5 ft.) growth; intr. 2003

'Sunburst' HT, ob; intr. 2005

'Sunburst' -- See 'Mme Joseph Perraud'

Sunburst Border™ -- See 'Sun Valley'

'Sunburst Jewel' HT, rb, 1979, Herholdt, J.A.; bud pointed; flowers red, reverse pale gold, 35 petals; bushy growth; [Muchacha® × seedling]

'Suncharm' MinFl, dy, Harkness; flowers golden amber, dbl., cupped; foliage dark green, glossy; compact, bushy growth; intr. 1998

'Suncluster' -- See 'Korgrapet'

'Suncor' ('Coralitos') Min, op, 1999, Schuurman, Frank B.; flowers 1 in., dbl., borne in small clusters; foliage small, medium green, semi-glossy; prickles moderate; spreading, low (12-16 in.) growth; intr. 1996

'Suncral' ('Kia Ora') Gr, mp, 1999, Schuurman, Frank B.; flowers 4 in., borne in large clusters; foliage medium green, glossy; few prickles; bushy, medium growth; ['Innocenti' × 'Firefly']; intr. 1994

'Suncredel' ('Cream Delight', 'Darling') Gr, lp, 1983, Schuurman, Frank B.; flowers full; foliage medium size, medium green, glossy; upright growth; [sport of 'Sonia']

'Sundance' F, yb, 1957, Poulsen, S.; flowers orange-yellow changing to bright rose-pink, 2½ in., 22 petals, borne in trusses; foliage light green, matte, thin; vigorous, tall (4 ft.), upright, uneven growth; ['Poulsen's Supreme' × 'Eugene Furst']

'Sundance' -- See 'Sundance Palace'

Sundance™ -- See 'Jaczeman'

'Sundance' -- See 'Jacnel'

'Sundance Palace' ('Sundance') MinFl, dy, Olesen ; bud blunt to ovoid; flowers 6 cm., 15 -20 petals, borne singly and in small clusters, slight citrus fragrance; recurrent; foliage glossy; prickles moderate, straight; vigorous, compact (2 ft.), bushy growth; PP11611; [Fragrant Delight® × seedling]; intr. 1999

'Sundancer' HT, yb, deVor; flowers large, moderate fragrance; blooms in flushes; intr. 1995

'Sunday Best' Cl HP, rb, 1924, Clark, A.; bud long, pointed; flowers brilliant red, center white, single, borne in clusters; long seasonal bloom; foliage wrinkled; vigorous, climbing growth; ['Frau Karl Druschki' × unknown]

'Sunday Brunch' -- See 'Morday'

'Sunday China' -- See 'Gelday'

'Sunday Lemonade' -- See 'Molsunlem'

'Sunday Press' ('Minden') HT, mr, 1971, Kordes; flowers 4½ in., 53 petals, high-centered; intr. 1970

'Sunday Times' ('Shrubby Pink') F, dp, 1972, McGredy, Sam IV; flowers deep rosy pink, medium, dbl., globular; foliage light; moderate, dwarf growth

'Sundel' (Delilah®) HT, m, 1999, Schuurman, Frank B.; flowers 4 in., dbl., borne mostly singly, no fragrance; foliage large, medium green, glossy; few prickles; upright, tall (3-4 ft.) growth; PP10918; [seedling × 'Osiana']; intr. 1995

'Sunderland Supreme' -- See 'Nossun'

'Sundia' ('Little Diamond') Min, or, 1999, Schuurman, Frank B.; flowers 1 in., full, borne in small clusters, no fragrance; foliage medium size, dark green, glossy; few prickles; upright, medium (12-18 in.) growth; [Sexy Rexy® × 'Firefly']; intr. 1993

Sundial™ -- See 'Arolyme'

'Sundoha' ('Double Happy') HT, rb, 1999, Schuurman, Frank B.; flowers bi-color red and yellow, large, dbl., borne mostly singly; foliage medium size, dark green, semi-glossy; prickles moderate; upright, medium (30-36 in.) growth; ['Louise Gardner' × 'Goldmarie']; intr. 1999

'Sundown' HT, mp, 1934, Scittine; bud globular; flowers pink, large, 35-40 petals; foliage glossy; very vigorous growth; [sport of 'Talisman']

'Sundown' LCl, ob; flowers two-toned yellow and orange, moderate fragrance

'Sundowner' Gr, ab, 1978, McGredy,

Sam IV; flowers golden orange, fading to salmon orange, 4 in., 35-40 petals, classic, borne mostly singly, intense fruity fragrance; recurrent; foliage large, leathery; prickles medium, pointed; tall (5½ ft.), upright, vigorous growth; hips globular ; PP4309; ['Bond Street' × Peer Gynt®]

Sundra® F, dr, 1968, Gaujard; bud pointed; flowers large, semi-dbl., cupped; foliage glossy; vigorous, bushy growth; ['Club' × 'Lilli Marlene']

'Sundream' F, Leenders; intr. 1971

'Sundry' S, rb, Williams, J. Benjamin; flowers red with a few pink and white stripes, semi-dbl., flat, moderate fragrance; recurrent; growth to 4 ft.; intr. 2006

'Sundust' ('Sun Dust') Min, yb, 1977, Moore, Ralph S.; bud pointed; flowers yellow with apricot tones, more yellow in warm weather, 1½ in., 23 petals, borne singly and in clusters, moderate fruity fragrance; free-flowering; foliage small, light green; low, bushy, compact growth; ['Golden Glow' × 'Magic Wand']; intr. 1977

'Suneva' -- See 'Noalesa'

'Sunfire' F, or, 1974, Warriner, William A.; bud ovoid, blunt; flowers mandarin-red, 3½ in., 30 petals, high-centered, borne singly and in rounded clusters, slight fragrance; recurrent; foliage large, leathery; prickles ordinary, broad base, hooked downward; stems long, strong; vigorous, upright, bushy growth; PP3510; ['Tropicana' × 'Zorina']; intr. 1974

'Sunflare' -- See 'Jacjem'

'Sungirl' F, yb, 1981, Rose Barni-Pistoia; flowers deep yellow, light red on petal tips, 25 petals; foliage medium size, deep green, glossy; prickles reddish-green; upright growth; ['Charleston' × seedling]

'Sunglo' F, or, 1976, Kuramoto, H.; bud ovoid; flowers open, 3 in., 25 petals, flat, slight fruity fragrance; PP3725; [sport of 'Woburn Abbey']

Sunglow™ Min, my, Olesen; flowers dbl., 25-30 petals, moderate wild rose fragrance; foliage dark green, glossy; growth bushy, low (40-60 cm.); PP13493; intr. 2000

Sunglow™ -- See 'Poulpal026(N)'

'Sunglow' -- See 'McGredy's Orange'

'Sunglow' -- See 'Welglow 0232'

'Sunglow Palace' (Sunglow™) MinFl, my, Poulsen; flowers medium yellow, 5-8 cm., dbl., no fragrance; foliage dark; growth bushy, 40-60 cm.; intr. 2005

'Sungold' Cl HT, my, 1939, Thomas; bud long, pointed; flowers bright golden yellow, large, dbl., slight fragrance; foliage glossy, dark; vigorous (15-18 ft.) growth; ['Margaret Anderson'] × 'Souv. de Claudius Pernet, Climbing']

'Sungold' Min, my, Schuurman, Frank B.; intr. 1991

'Sungold' -- See 'Morlem'

'Sunhap' ('Happy Go Lucky') Gr, dr, 1999, Schuurman, Frank B.; flowers dark red, reverse medium red, 3 in., dbl., borne in large clusters; foliage medium size, medium green, semi-glossy; prickles moderate; spreading, medium (30-36 in.) growth; ['Happy Days' × 'Only Love']; intr. 1998

'Sunhifi' ('High Five') F, m, 1999, Schuurman, Frank B.; flowers 3¼ in., full, borne in large clusters, slight fragrance; foliage medium size, dark green, glossy; prickles moderate; spreading, medium (30-36 in.) growth; [Jacaranda® × 'French Lace']; intr. 1997

'Sunhino' ('Reddy Teddy') Min, ab, 1999, Schuurman, Frank B.; flowers 1½ in., dbl., borne mostly singly; foliage small, medium green, semi-glossy; prickles moderate; compact, low (8-12 in.) growth; [Sexy Rexy® × 'Firefly']; intr. 1996

Suni® F, pb, Barni, V.; flowers creamy white with carmine edges spreading down the petals, large, dbl., high-centered, moderate fragrance; recurrent; strong, robust (40-60 cm.) growth; intr. 1993

'Sunil Gavaskar' F, m, 1986, Hardikar, Dr. M.N.; flowers 3 in., 60 petals, cupped, borne in clusters of 7 or more, no fragrance; foliage large, dark, leathery; prickles light green, needle-like; dwarf, bushy growth; [('First Rose Convention' × 'Scarlet Knight') × 'Ena Harkness']; intr. 1985

Sunita™ S, ob, Clements, John; flowers soft golden orange, deep orange shaded light crimson on petal edges, 3 in., dbl., hybrid tea, moderate honey/spice fragrance; recurrent; growth to 3½ ft.; intr. 2006

'Sunjew' ('Little Jewel') Min, ob, 1999, Schuurman, Frank B.; flowers 1½-2 in., dbl., borne in small clusters, slight fragrance; foliage small, medium green, semi-glossy; prickles few, small; growth upright; ['Innocenti' × 'Firefly']; intr. 1991

Sunking™ F, dy

'Sunkissed' HT, yb, 1981, Tantau, Math.; bud ovoid, pointed; flowers yellow-orange, borne singly, no fragrance; foliage leathery; prickles long, light green, hooked down; upright growth; PP4799; ['Minigold' × 'Precilla']; intr. 1980

Sunkist™ HT, ob, 1932, E.G. Hill, Co.; flowers orange-copper; [sport of 'Joanna Hill']

'Sunkist' Min, my, Moore, Ralph; flowers bright yellow; medium growth; intr. 2001

'Sunlampo' (Bellisima®) F, ob, 1999, Schuurman, Frank B.; flowers 2½ in., full, borne mostly singly, slight fragrance; foliage medium size, dark green, glossy; few prickles; upright, medium growth; ['Lambada' × 'Pot O' Gold']; intr. 1998

'Sunlight, Climbing' ('Grisbi, Climbing') Cl HT, my, 1963, Meilland, Mrs. Marie-Louise; [sport of 'Sunlight']

Sunlight™ HT, dy, Meilland; flowers golden yellow, tinged with orange on reverse, full, high-centered, borne mostly singly; recurrent; florist rose; intr. 2004

'Sunlight' -- See 'Meisha'

Sunlight Romantica® S, my, Meilland; flowers bright golden-yellow, very full, cupped, moderate fragrance; recurrent; low to medium growth; intr. 2002

'Sunlit' HT, ab, 1937, Clark, A.; flowers rich apricot, medium, dbl., globular to cupped, intense fragrance; free-flowering; foliage dark green; compact growth

'Sunlock' ('Goldilocks') Min, my, 1999, Schuurman, Frank B.; flowers medium yellow, reverse light yellow, 1½ in., full, borne in large clusters, moderate fragrance; foliage large, medium green, glossy; prickles moderate; spreading, tall growth; ['Scentasia' × seedling]; intr. 1998

'Sunluck' (Gold Strike®) HT, dy, 1999, Schuurman, Frank B.; flowers 4½ in., full, borne in small clusters, slight fragrance; foliage large, dark green, glossy; prickles moderate; upright, tall growth; PP11752; [seedling × seedling]; intr. 1997

Sunmaid® Min, ob, Spek; flowers golden yellow with orange edges spreading down the petals, turning red with age, 40 petals, rosette, no fragrance; recurrent; foliage medium green; upright (18-24 in.) growth; intr. 1972

'Sunmani' ('Manaia', 'Oasis Sunset') HT, ob, 1999, Schuurman, Frank B.; flowers orange, reverse apricot, 4½-5 in., dbl., borne mostly singly; foliage large, medium green, semi-glossy; prickles moderate; bushy, tall (3½-4 ft.) growth; intr. 1994

'Sunmapa' Min, m, Schuurman; intr. 1999

'Sunmist' F, ly, 1940, Kordes; bud pointed; flowers clear light sulfur-yellow, open, semi-dbl.; foliage leathery; vigorous growth; [('Eva' × 'Golden Rapture') × 'Hede']

'Sunningdale' HT, mp, 1929, Hicks; bud long, pointed; flowers reddish-carmine passing to cherry-pink, dbl., high-centered

'Sunny' F, my, 1952, Moore, Ralph S.; bud pointed, yellow overlaid red; flowers lighter yellow, open, small, semi-dbl.; foliage leathery, glossy; vigorous, upright, bushy growth; [seedling × 'Goldilocks']

Sunny™ Min, my, Poulsen; intr. 2000

'Sunny Abundance' ('Peter Cottrell', 'Sunny Spring', 'Sunshine Abundance') F, yb; flowers yellow with pink blush on petal edges, medium, 30 petals, imbricated, borne in clusters, slight fruity fragrance; free-flowering; foliage dark green, glossy; upright (3 ft.) growth; intr. 1999

'Sunny Afternoon' -- See 'Talsun'

'Sunny Boy' HT, pb, 1961, Delforge; flowers buff-pink, tinted gold and lilac, center

darker, well-formed; foliage bronze; ['Mme Butterfly' × 'The Queen']
'Sunny Boy' F, my, J&P; intr. 2006
'Sunny California' HT, my, 1936, Hanshaw, E.; bud long, pointed; flowers yellow like Ville de Paris, very large, dbl., cupped; [sport of 'Feu Joseph Looymans']
Sunny Child® -- See 'Havychi'
Sunny Day™ -- See 'Savasun'
'Sunny Days' HT, my, 1939, Verschuren; bud long, pointed; flowers chrome-yellow at edges, large, dbl., high-centered; foliage leathery, dark; vigorous growth; RULED EXTINCT 11/86
'Sunny Daze' HT, my; flowers clear yellow, slight darkening on edges, dbl., high-centered, intense lemon fragrance; recurrent; foliage dark green, glossy, leathery; growth to 5 ft.
'Sunny Delight' HT, my; flowers bright yellow, dbl., high-centered, moderate fragrance; recurrent; foliage dark green, glossy; vigorous (4 ft.) growth; intr. 2005
'Sunny Dew' -- See 'Sunnydew'
Sunny Eudora® HT, dy, Interplant; intr. 2006
'Sunny Honey' F, yb, 1973, Dickson, Patrick; flowers yellow-pink blend, reverse red, 4 in., 20-25 petals, high-centered, moderate fragrance; recurrent; foliage large, dark; ['Happy Event' × Elizabeth of Glamis®]; intr. 1972
'Sunny Jean' HT, my, Zary, Keith; intr. 2000
'Sunny Jersey' HT, ab, 1928, Le Cornu; flowers bronze, apricot, salmon and orange; [sport of 'Mme Edouard Herriot']
'Sunny June' S, dy, 1952, Lammerts, Dr. Walter; bud long, pointed; flowers deep canary-yellow, 3-3½ in., 5 petals, cupped to flat, borne in large clusters, slight spicy fragrance; foliage large, dark green, glossy; prickles few, medium, hooked downward; stems strong, short; upright, compact, pillar or shrub (8 ft.) growth; hips none, cultivar sterile ; PP1239; ['Crimson Glory' × 'Captain Thomas']
Sunny Knock Out™ -- See 'Radsunny'
'Sunny Kordana' -- See 'Sunny Kordana Mini Brite'
'Sunny Kordana Mini Brite' ('Sunny Kordana') Min, my, Kordes; intr. 1998
Sunny Leonidas® HT, ob, Meilland; flowers orange with yellow reverse, dbl., high-centered, borne mostly singly; recurrent; intr. 2002
'Sunny Maid' F, my, 1949, Fletcher; flowers bright yellow, 4 in., 6-8 petals, borne in clusters; foliage glossy, light green; very vigorous, upright growth; [('Golden Rapture' × 'Fred Walker') × seedling]
Sunny Meillandina® -- See 'Meiponal'
'Sunny Milva' HT, yb, Tantau; intr. 2004
'Sunny Morning' Min, my, 1977, Moore, Ralph S.; bud medium long, pointed; flowers medium to creamy yellow, 1-1½ in., 30-35 petals, flat, borne singly or several together, moderate sweet fragrance; recurrent; foliage small, medium green, leathery; prickles normal, medium length, straight, inclined downward; stems strong, medium; bushy, upright (12-16 in.) growth; hips none ; PP3800; ['Golden Glow (LCl)' × 'Peachy White']; intr. 1974
'Sunny Prophyta' HT, dy, van der Hoorn; bud medium, ovate; flowers clear yellow, 3 in., 26 petals, high-centered, borne mostly singly, very slight fragrance; good repeat; foliage medium size, leathery, semi-glossy; prickles normal, hooked downward; stems 20 in.; narrow, vigorous, bushy growth; hips pitcher-shaped, large seed vessel at petal fall ; PP9391; [sport of 'Ruirovingt']; cut flower variety
Sunny Rose® -- See 'Korkilgwen'
'Sunny Royal 21st Century' Cl Min, dp, 2003, Ishii, Tsuyashi; flowers dbl., borne in small clusters, slight fragrance; foliage small, medium green, semi-glossy; prickles moderate; spreading, tall (10 ft.) growth; [R. wichurana × miniature seedling]
'Sunny Sam' -- See 'Noldanyu'
'Sunny San Joaquin' F, rb, 1962, Raffel; flowers cerise-red, reverse tinted ivory, well-shaped, borne in large clusters; tall growth; ['Little Darling' × 'Gertrude Raffel']
'Sunny Side Up' -- See 'Pixsun'
'Sunny Sky' HT, yb, Kordes; flowers copper-yellow, large, full, high-centered, borne mostly singly; good repeat; stems medium to long; florist rose; intr. 2000
Sunny Sky™ -- See 'Souvenir'
'Sunny South' HT, pb, 1918, Clark, A.; flowers soft pink flushed carmine, base yellow, large, semi-dbl., cupped, moderate fragrance; free-flowering; foliage rich green; stems long; very vigorous (5 ft.) growth; ['Gustav Grunerwald' × 'Betty Berkeley']
'Sunny Spring' -- See 'Sunny Abundance'
'Sunny Sunblaze' -- See 'Meiponal'
'Sunny Today' F, dy, 1971, Whisler, D.; flowers clear deep yellow, petals quilled, medium, dbl., high-centered, moderate fruity fragrance; recurrent; foliage glossy, dark green; moderate, bushy growth; [('Summer Sunshine' × 'Gold Cup') × 'Isobel Harkness']; intr. 1970
Sunny Waterfall™ -- See 'Meidrepil'
'Sunny Yellow' HT, dy; intr. 2004
Sunnybrook® HT, my; flowers creamy primrose yellow, dbl., high-centered
'Sunnydew' ('Sunny Dew') Min, dy, 1979, Schwartz, Ernest W.; bud ovoid; flowers clear yellow, 1 in., 18 petals, high-centered, slight fragrance; free-flowering; foliage small; bushy, well-branched, spreading growth; ['Yellow Doll' × seedling]; intr. 1978
'Sunnymount' HT, my, 1936, Grillo; bud sharp pointed but short; flowers buttercup-yellow, large, 50 petals, intense fragrance; foliage leathery; vigorous growth; PP334; [sport of 'Joanna Hill']
'Sunnyside' HT, op, 1949, Andre; bud pointed, orange; flowers pink shaded orange, 4½-5 in., 24-30 petals, high-centered; very vigorous growth; PP822; [sport of 'Yellow Gloria']
Sunnyside® Min, yb, Lens; flowers yellow, becoming pink and then red; vigorous growth; [('Purpurine' × 'miniature seedling') × 'Rosina']; intr. 1963
Sunnyside ™ -- See 'Niagara'
'Sunnyside '83' -- See 'Lensun'
'Sunpach' ('Pachinko') F, or, 1999, Schuurman, Frank B.; flowers 3 in., semi-dbl., borne in large clusters; foliage medium size, dark green, glossy; prickles moderate; spreading, medium (30-36 in.) growth; [Alexander® × 'Golden Emblem']; intr. 1997
'Sunpari' (La Parisienne®) HT, ab, 1999, Schuurman, Frank B.; flowers 4½ in., full, borne mostly singly; foliage large, dark green, glossy; prickles moderate; upright, tall growth; ['Kia Ora' × 'Texas']; intr. 1996
'Sunpaste' ('Pastelina') F, w, 1992, Schuurman, Frank B.; flowers near white, medium, full; foliage medium size, medium green, glossy; upright growth; [White Dream® × Freegold®]; intr. 1991
'Sunpat' ('Little Opal') Min, lp, 1992, Schuurman, Frank B.; flowers medium, dbl.; foliage small, medium green, glossy; upright growth; [White Dream® × 'Dicky Bird']; intr. 1991
'Sunpearl' ('Little Pearl') Min, lp, 1992, Schuurman, Frank B.; flowers medium, full; foliage small, medium green, glossy; few prickles; medium (50 cm.), upright growth; ['Innocent' × 'MACfrabro']
'Sunpete' ('Peter Pan') F, mr, 1999, Schuurman, Frank B.; flowers 2 in., full, borne in large clusters and sprays, no fragrance; foliage medium size, dark green, glossy; prickles moderate; upright, medium growth; PP10937; ['Pink Delight' × seedling]; intr. 1993
'Sunpino' ('Pinocchio') Min, m, 1999, Schuurman, Frank B.; flowers magenta, 2-2½ in., dbl., borne in large clusters, no fragrance; foliage large, dark green, semi-glossy; prickles moderate; upright, medium growth; patio; ['Tinkerbell' × Chess®]; intr. 1998
'Sunplay' ('Player') HT, pb, 1999, Schuurman, Frank B.; flowers 4½-5 in., dbl., borne mostly singly; foliage large, dark green, glossy; numerous prickles; upright, tall (4½-5 ft.) growth; ['Raspberry Ice' × 'Karen']; intr. 1993
'SunQueen' F, yb, 2005, Singer, Judith A.; flowers glowing yellow, fading to white, reverse white, 3½ in., very full, borne in small clusters, moderate fragrance; foliage small, dark green, glossy; prickles small, straight, beige to light brown, moderate; growth upright, medium; [Loving Touch™ × seedling]; intr. 2006
'Sunrise' T, op, 1899, Piper; bud long,

pointed, scarlet and yellow; flowers salmon-rose, center yellow, salmon and orange, medium, dbl.; foliage glossy; [sport of 'Sunset']

'Sunrise' HT, mp, Dot, Pedro; bud long, pointed; flowers salmon, open, large, dbl.; foliage glossy, bronze; vigorous, bushy growth; ['Pilarin Vilella' × 'Rosa Gallart']; intr. 1939

'Sunrise' HT, yb; flowers light golden yellow with pink edges on opened petals, medium, dbl., high-centered, slight fragrance; foliage glossy; bushy, medium growth; intr. 2003

'Sunrise' -- See 'Kormarter'

'Sunrise at Heirloom' S, ob, Clements, John; flowers firey orange, ruffled, 3 in., 15-20 petals, cupped to flat, no fragrance; profuse; foliage shiny green; bushy (3 ft.) growth; PPAF; intr. 2003

Sunrise Cupido® Min, ob, Pouw; bud pear-shaped; flowers orange, salmon pink and yellow, 4 cm., 25 petals, rosette, cupped, borne singly and in small clusters, no fragrance; recurrent; foliage dark green, leathery; prickles very few, short; compact, uniform growth; PP10685; [seedling × seedling]; container rose; intr. 2001

'Sunrise-Sunset' HT, pb, 1971, Swim & Weeks; bud pointed, with conspicuous neck; flowers blended pink, cream and lavender, 5 in., 46-52 petals, high-centered, borne mostly singly, slight fragrance; recurrent; foliage glossy, light to dark green, leathery; prickles numerous, medium, almost straight, brown to dull green; stems long, strong, vigorous, upright growth; PP3244; ['Tiffany' × (seedling × 'Happiness')]; intr. 1971

'Sunrise Sunset' ('Garden Path Sunrise Sunset') S, pb, Ping Lim; bud medium, pointed; flowers bright fuchsia-pink with apricot yellow centers, 2-2½ in., 13-19 petals, cupped, borne in clusters of about 5, slight fragrance; blooms constantly; foliage slightly blue-green, semi-glossy; dense, spreading (2-3 ft.) growth; PP16770; [seedling × seedling]; intr. 2004

'Sunrise Vigorosa' ('Smile') S, my, Kordes

'Sunsalm' ('Little Gem', 'Patio Gem') Min, op, 1992, Schuurman, Frank B.; flowers moderately patio, medium, dbl., moderate fragrance; foliage small, medium green, matte; spreading growth; [Sexy Rexy® × 'Firefly']; intr. 1991

'Sunsap' ('Little Sapphire') Min, mp, 1999, Schuurman, Frank B.; flowers medium pink, reverse light pink, 2½-3 in., dbl., borne in small clusters; foliage medium size, medium green, semi-glossy; prickles moderate; bushy, medium (16-20 in.) growth; [White Dream® × seedling]; intr. 1993

'Sunsation' -- See 'Korgust'
'Sunsation' -- See 'Wekcelpep'
'Sunsational' -- See 'Brysun'

'Sunscent' ('Scentasia') Min, ly, 1999, Schuurman, Frank B.; flowers creamy yellow, 1½-2 in., full, borne in large clusters, moderate fragrance; foliage large, medium green, semi-glossy; few prickles; spreading, tall (20-28 in.) growth; ['Tinkerbell' × 'Little Nugget']; intr. 1997

'Sunseeker' -- See 'Dicracer'

'Sunset' T, dy, 1883, Henderson, P.; flowers orange-yellow, medium, full, moderate tea-rose fragrance; recurrent; tall growth; [sport of 'Perle des Jardins']

'Sunset' Cl HT, yb, Marsh; flowers peach and apricot, reverse yellow,, 5 in., 45-60 petals, cupped, vigorous growth; PP1191; [sport of 'Faience']; intr. 1947

'Sunset' Min, yb, Benardella, Frank; flowers yellow, edged red, dbl., imbricated; free-flowering; intr. 1999

Sunset™ -- See 'Poulgelb'
'Sunset Beauty' -- See 'Websense'
'Sunset Boulevard' -- See 'Harbabble'
Sunset Celebration™ -- See 'Fryxotic'

Sunset Folies® F, rb, Meilland; florist rose; intr. 2004

'Sunset Glory' HT, ab, 1947, Boerner; bud ovoid; flowers golden yellow overlaid dusty rose-pink, 4-4½ in., 35-40 petals, cupped, moderate fruity fragrance; vigorous, upright, compact growth; PP738; [sport of 'McGredy's Sunset']

'Sunset Glow' -- See 'Canarienvogel'

'Sunset Jubilee' HT, pb, 1973, Boerner; bud ovoid; flowers medium pink, tinted lighter, large, dbl., high-centered; foliage large, light, leathery; vigorous, upright, bushy growth; PP2980; ['Kordes' Perfecta' × ('Pink Duchess' × unknown)]

'Sunset Memory' LCl, ab, Itami; intr. 2003

'Sunset Parade' (Sunset™) Min, dy, Poulsen; flowers deep yellow, medium, dbl., slight wild rose fragrance; bushy (20-40 cm.) growth; intr. 1996

'Sunset Party' Min, yb, Benardella, Frank; flowers two-tone yellow and red, intense fragrance; medium growth

'Sunset Song' -- See 'Cocason'

'Sunset Strip' Min, or; flowers orange red with yellow to white eye, double, high-centered; intr. 2007

'Sunset Strip' -- See 'Arocore'

'Sunshine' HT, yb, 1918, Chaplin Bros.; bud long, pointed; flowers golden yellow, shaded apricot, dbl., moderate fragrance

'Sunshine' Pol, ob, Robichon; bud ovoid; flowers golden orange, small, dbl., borne in clusters, moderate sweet fragrance; free-flowering; foliage glossy; dwarf growth; ['George Elger' × 'William Allen Richardson']; intr. 1927

'Sunshine' HT, my, Kordes; flowers pleasant yellow; free-flowering; [sport of 'Sunbeam 2000']; intr. 2002

'Sunshine Abundance' -- See 'Sunny Abundance'

'Sunshine Flower Carpet' -- See 'Noasun'

'Sunshine Girl' -- See 'Pixisun'

'Sunshine Girl' -- See 'Living Fire'
'Sunshine Princess' -- See 'Andsun'

'Sunshine Sally' S, my, Moore, Ralph; bud clear yellow; flowers soft yellow, 1½-2 in., dbl., borne in clusters and sprays; foliage glossy; growth shrub (5 × 5 ft.) or can be trained as a climber; intr. 2000

'Sunshower' F, my, 1975, Golik; bud ovoid; flowers bright yellow, ruffled, 2½ in., 16 petals, foliage glossy, light; moderate growth; [Golden Showers® × 'Prairie Fire']; intr. 1974

'Sunsien' (Citronella®) HT, ly, 1999, Schuurman, Frank B.; flowers 4½-5 in., full, borne mostly singly, slight fragrance; foliage large, medium green, glossy; prickles moderate; upright, tall growth; [sport of 'La Parisienne']; intr. 1998

'Sunsilk' F, my, 1976, Fryer, Gareth; flowers lemon-yellow, 5 in., 30 petals, cupped, slight fragrance; foliage dark; ['Pink Parfait' × 'Redgold seedling']; intr. 1974

Sunsmile™ -- See 'Jacmiy'

'Sunsnofle' ('Snowflake') Min, w, 1999, Schuurman, Frank B.; flowers 1 in., full, borne in small clusters, no fragrance; foliage small, light green, semi-glossy; prickles moderate; compact, low growth; intr. 1996

'Sunsong' Gr, ob, 1975, Poulsen; bud globular to urn-shaped; flowers opening pure strong orange, aging to coral blend, 3 in., 55-70 petals, informal, borne in clusters, slight tea/musk fragrance; foliage medium size, glossy, leathery; upright, bushy growth; PP3794; ['Folie d'Espagne' × (Zambra® × 'Danish Pink')]; patent issued to Olaf Soenderhousen; intr. 1976

'Sunsplash' -- See 'Cocweaver'
Sunsplash™ -- See 'Jacyim'

'Sunspot' F, my, 1965, Fisher, G.; flowers mimosa-yellow, large, dbl., cupped, borne in clusters; foliage leathery; vigorous, bushy growth; PP2576; ['Golden Anniversary' × 'Masquerade']

Sunspray™ -- See 'Arorasp'

'Sunsprite, Climbing' ('Friesia, Climbing') Cl F, dy, 1989, Kroeger, Henry; [sport of 'Sunsprite']

'Sunsprite' -- See 'Korresia'

'Sunstar' F, ly, Kordes; flowers soft to cream yellow , 7 cm., double, high-centered, then shallow cup, slight fragrance; recurrent; upright (80 cm.) growth; intr. 2007

'Sunstar' HT, or, 1921, Dickson, A.; bud long, pointed; flowers orange and red, medium, semi-dbl., intense fragrance; foliage light green; vigorous, bushy growth; ['Mrs C.V. Haworth' × 'Hugh Dickson']

'Sunstar, Climbing' Cl HT, or, 1925, Dickson, A.; [sport of 'Sunstar']

'Sunstone' HT, yb, 1959, Fletcher; bud long; flowers bright yellow splashed red, 6 in.; foliage glossy, bronze; strong stems; vigorous, tall growth; ['Bridget' ×

'Marcelle Gret']; intr. 1957

'Sunstrike' F, dy, 1974, Warriner, William A.; bud small, pointed, ovoid; flowers medium, dbl., high-centered; foliage large, light, leathery; very vigorous, bushy growth; PP3651; ['Spanish Sun' × ('Buccaneer' × 'Zorina')]

'Sunstruck' Min, yb, 1979, Lyon; bud long, pointed; flowers aureolin-yellow and signal-red, 2 in., 20 petals, intense fragrance; foliage dark; upright growth; ['Redgold' × unknown]; intr. 1978

Sunstruck™ -- See 'Weksunvoye'

Sunswept™ -- See 'Benbrett'

'Suntan' HT, dy, 1939, Hansen, N.J.; flowers deep orange-yellow, fading slowly, large, 35 petals; foliage leathery, dark, bronze; strong stems; ruled extinct 04/92; ['Nanjemoy' × 'Mrs Pierre S. duPont']

'Suntan' HT, op, 1940, Yoder; bud long, pointed; flowers buff-salmon, base yellow, reverse light coral-red, large, 25 petals, cupped, moderate fragrance; vigorous, upright growth; PP354; ruled extinct 04/92; [sport of 'Mrs Franklin D. Roosevelt']; never introduced

Suntan™ -- See 'Interbronzi'

Suntan Beauty™ -- See 'Minawco'

'Sunthumb' ('Thumbelina') Min, ly, 1999, Schuurman, Frank B.; flowers 1¾ in., dbl., borne in small clusters; foliage medium size, medium green, glossy; prickles moderate; patio; compact, medium growth; [Champagner® × 'Tinkerbell']; intr. 1998

'Suntick' ('People's Princess', 'Tickled Pink') HT, pb, 1999, Schuurman, Frank B.; bud large, pointed; flowers 5 in., 36-42 petals, imbricated, borne mostly singly, moderate old rose fragrance; recurrent; foliage large, medium green, glossy; prickles very few; upright, tall (4 ft.) growth; PP11400; [Jacaranda® × Gold Medal®]; intr. 1997

'Suntink' ('Tinkerbell') F, lp, 1999, Schuurman, Frank B.; bud small, pointed; flowers soft, light pink, 1½-2½ in., 26-30 petals, slightly cupped, borne in large clusters and sprays, moderate fruity fragrance; recurrent; foliage medium size, dark green, glossy; prickles moderate, 1 cm., thin, straight, brown with green tips; stems 16 - 20 in.; upright, medium (2 ft.) growth; PP10940; [White Dream® × 'Evelien']; intr. 1993

'Suntoto' ('Rangitoto') HT, m, 1992, Schuurman, Frank B.; flowers medium, very dbl.; foliage medium size, medium green, glossy; upright growth; ['Champagne' × 'Chantilly Lace']; intr. 1990

'Sunwend' ('Wendy') F, w, 1999, Schuurman, Frank B.; flowers 1½ in., full, borne in large sprays, no fragrance; foliage medium size, medium green, glossy; numerous prickles; upright, medium growth; intr. 1993

'Super Aribau' HT, dr, 1960, Dot, Pedro; flowers crimson-carmine, reverse silvery crimson, large, 24 petals; strong stems; upright, vigorous growth; ['Aribau' × 'Director Rubió']

'Super Bianca' -- See 'Heinrich Blanc'

'Super Bowl' -- See 'Macsupbow'

'Super Cascade Coral' -- See 'Jalcoral'

'Super Celeste' F, op; intr. 1999

'Super Chief' HT, mr, 1976, Patterson; bud globular; flowers bright red, aging darker, 5 in., 60-65 petals, high-centered; foliage dark; vigorous growth; [Queen Elizabeth® × 'Happiness']

'Super Congo' HT, dr, 1950, Meilland, F.; bud ovoid; flowers velvety dark blood-red, medium, 30 petals, slight fragrance; foliage dull green; upright growth; ['Congo' × 'Léonce Colombier']

'Super Delilah' HT, m, Scherman; flowers lavender, very large, dbl., high-centered; PPAF; intr. 2002

'Super Derby' -- See 'Easter Bonnet'

'Super Disco' ('Olytel') F, pb, Olij, Huibert W. ; bud small, conical; flowers light cardinal pink suffused red, reverse cream yellow suffused pink, 8 cm., 27-30 petals, cupped, borne mostly singly, slight fragrance; recurrent; foliage dark green, semi-glossy; prickles few, small, greenish-pink; upright, bushy growth; PP8862; ['Fantasia' × 'Vivaldi']; florist rose; intr. 1994

Super Dorothy® ('Dorothy Superior') HWich, mp, Hetzel; flowers medium to deep pink, fading to white, reverse lighter, 4-5 cm., semi-dbl., borne in large clusters, slight green apple fragrance; recurrent; foliage small, glossy; prickles moderate; vigorous (12 ft.) growth; intr. 1986

'Super-Dupont' -- See 'Dolly Madison'

'Super Elfin' -- See 'Helkleger'

Super Excelsa® ('Excelsa Superior') LCl, mr, Hetzel; flowers carmine-crimson, occasional white stripe, reverse lighter, 3½ cm., dbl., cupped, borne in very large clusters, slight fragrance; good repeat; vigorous (12 ft.) growth; [unknown × unknown]; intr. 1986

Super Fairy® -- See 'Helsufair'

'Super Gamusin' HT, m, 1962, Dot, Pedro; flowers chamois to mauve; ['Grey Pearl' × 'Tristesse']

Super Gold™ -- See 'Wingold'

'Super Green' HT, w; flowers greenish white, ruffled edges; foliage dark; intr. 2004

'Super Harrington' HT, dr, 1938, Brown, John; bud oval; flowers dark crimson, mottled scarlet, medium, dbl., loose, moderate fragrance; foliage leathery; vigorous, upright growth; ['Tassin' × 'Victoria Harrington']

'Super Hero' F, mr, Lim, Ping; bud medium, pointed; flowers medium red to fuchsia , 5.5 cm. , 13-19 petals, high-centered to open, borne in clusters, slight fragrance; recurrent; foliage medium to dark green, satiny; dense, spreading, low (60 - 90 cm.) growth ; PP16770; [seedling × seedling]; intr. 2008

'Super Iceberg' F, w, Hetzel; flowers pure white , double, cupped, borne in clusters; recurrent; tall growth; intr. 2008

'Super Jane' ('Limberlost PInk') HMsk, mp, 2008, Rupert, Kim L.; flowers 2 in., single, borne mostly solitary; foliage medium-size, medium green, semi-glossy, disease-resistant; no prickles; growth tall (12 ft. or more); climber, pillar, specimen; ['Renae' × unknown]; both heat and shade tolerant; intr. 2009

'Super Lass' LCl, pb, Hetzel; flowers lilac-pink with cream-white eye, flat, borne in large trusses, moderate fragrance; recurrent; vigorous (8-10 ft.) growth; intr. 1999

'Super Nova' -- See 'Jacsunov'

'Super Pink' -- See 'LLX8772'

'Super Prince Tango' F, Delbard; intr. 1971

'Super Rugostar' HRg, mr; flowers bright red, small, dbl., cupped to flat, borne in clusters; recurrent; intr. 1998

'Super Sparkle' -- See 'Helfels'

'Super Star' ('Tropicana') HT, or, 1960, Tantau, Math.; bud pointed; flowers coral-orange, well-formed, 5 in., 30-35 petals, high-centered, cupped, borne singly and in clusters, intense fruity fragrance; recurrent; foliage dark, glossy, leathery; prickles normal, medium, straight or hooked upward; stems long, strong; vigorous, upright growth; PP1969; [(seedling × 'Peace') × (seedling × 'Alpine Glow')]; original registration (1961 ARS Annual) is for Super Star; intr. 1960

'Super Star, Climbing' ('Tropicana, Climbing') Cl HT, or, 1966, Blaby; bud pointed; PP2701; [sport of 'Tropicana']; patent issued to Boerner; separate registration published in 1970

'Super Star Supreme' HT, or, 1982, U.S. Patent Sales, Inc.; flowers deeper color; [sport of 'Tropicana']

'Super Sun' HT, my, 1967, Bentley; flowers maize-yellow; [sport of Piccadilly®]

'Super Swany' -- See 'Meicoublan'

'Super Tabarin' F, ob, 1965, Gaujard; flowers coppery, reverse orange, semi-dbl.; vigorous growth; ['Faust' × 'Tabarin']

'Super Tan' Min, op, Interplant; flowers coppery orange, small to medium, semi-dbl.; intr. 1995

'Superb' HT, lp, 1924, Evans; flowers pale pink, tinted blush; ['Mme Caroline Testout' × 'Willowmere']

Superb, Climbing' Cl Pol, dr, 1933, Guillot, P.; [sport of 'Superb']

'Superb' -- See 'Superba'

'Superb Striped Unique' -- See 'Unique Panachée'

'Superb Tuscan' -- See 'Tuscany Superb'

'Superb Tuscany' -- See 'Tuscany Superb'

'Superba' HT, dp, Aicardi, L.; flowers intense rose with yellow reflections, overlarge, intense fragrance; long stems; ['Julien Potin' × seedling]; intr. 1940

'Superba' HMoy, dr; flowers dark crimson,

large, dbl.; no fruit; ['Charles P. Kilham' × *R. moyesii*]; intr. before 1958

'Superba' Misc OGR; selected Dutch strain of *R. multiflora* used as understock; intr. before 1965

'Superba' HSet, lp, 1843, Feast; flowers pale pink, varying to flesh and white, very dbl., borne in large clusters

'Superba' ('Superb') Pol, dr, de Ruiter; either a sport or seedling of Orléans Rose; intr. 1927

'Superba, Climbing' Cl Pol, mr, 1932, Guillot; flowers scarlet-crimson, large; [sport of 'Superba']

'Superbe' A, w, before 1846; flowers full

'Superbe' -- See 'Cramoisie Triomphante'

'Superbe Brune' -- See 'Achille'

'Superbe Cramoisie' ('Apollon') C, mr, about 1850, Robert; flowers crimson, very large, full

'Superbe du Bengale' -- See 'Louis-Philippe'

'Superbe en Brun' ('La Négresse', 'Nigritiana', 'Reine des Nègres') HGal, m, before 1810, Dupont; flowers deep velvety purple, 2 in., dbl., flat; prickles hooked, paired

'Superbissima' -- See 'Admirable'

'Supercandy' Gr, Mansuino; intr. 1967

'Superga' HT, lp, 1958, Giacomasso; flowers rose-pearl, high pointed; foliage dark, glossy; long stems; very vigorous growth; [sport of 'Savoia']; intr. 1956

'Superglo' -- See 'Spoglo'

'Superior' F, ab, 1968, LeGrice; flowers apricot-yellow, semi-dbl., borne in trusses; foliage dark, glossy; vigorous, low growth; ['Masquerade' × 'Amberlight']

Supernova® S, w, Barni; flowers pure white, dbl., pompon, borne in clusters, moderate fragrance; recurrent; low (2 ft.), arching, sprawling growth; groundcover; intr. 2003

'Superstition' HT, m; flowers deep lavender, some with reddish edges, dbl., high-centered, blooms in flushes; recurrent; foliage dark green, glossy.; intr. 2002

Suplesse™ HT, w, Tantau; florist rose

Supra™ -- See 'Meirobidor'

'Supravat' HT, mp, Ghosh, Mr. & Mrs. S.; flowers large, dbl., high-centered; intr. 1996

'Supreme' HT, my, 1963, LeGrice; flowers lemon-yellow, well-formed, 4½-5 in., 40-45 petals; foliage dark, leathery, glossy; vigorous, tall growth; ['Golden Masterpiece' × 'Ethel Sanday']

Supreme Cover™ -- See 'Poulor'

'Supreme Rendezvous' HT, pb, 1961, Langbecker; flowers cream to pale pink, edged carmine; [sport of 'Day of Triumph']

'Supreme's Sister' F, mp, 1965, Jones; bud red; flowers coppery salmon to salmon-pink, medium, 42 petals; foliage leathery, bronze; low, bushy growth; intr. 1960

'Supriya' HT, pb, Sen, Dr. N.C.; flowers pure pink with cream and white stripes and splashes, dbl., high-centered; [sport of 'Princess Margaret of England']; intr. 1982

'Surabhi' HT, mp, 1976, IARI; bud long, pointed; flowers phlox-pink, 80 petals, high-centered, intense fragrance; foliage glossy, dark; upright, compact growth; ['Oklahoma' × 'Delhi Princess']; intr. 1975

'Surain' HT, mp, 1985, Elliott, Charles P.; flowers large, 35 petals, high-centered; upright growth; [seedling × 'Forever Yours']

'Surbrunnsgatan' HP, mp; flowers strong pink, edges lighter, large, full, cupped, borne mostly singly, moderate fragrance; recurrent; upright (4 ft.) growth; from Sweden

'Surekha' HT, or, 1971, IARI; bud pointed; flowers coral-red, large, dbl.; foliage dark, leathery; very vigorous, upright growth; [Queen Elizabeth® × unknown]

'Surf' F, op, Laperrière; intr. 2000

'Surf Rider' S, w, 1970, Holmes, R.A.; flowers creamy white, medium, 25 petals, loose, borne in large trusses, moderate musk fragrance; recurrent; foliage bright, glossy; very vigorous, erect (6 ft.) growth; ['Ivory Fashion' × 'Ballerina']; intr. 1968

'Surfer Girl' -- See 'Renfer'

'Surf's Up' -- See 'Lemsur'

'Surfside' -- See 'Micsurf'

'Surkhab' HT, m, 1976, Pal, Dr. B.P.; bud globular; flowers Tyrian purple, reverse silvery amaranth,, 4 in., 76 petals, cupped, intense fragrance; foliage leathery; very vigorous, upright, compact growth; intr. 1975

'Surpasse Singleton' -- See 'Illustre'

'Surpasse Tout' ('Cérisette la Jolie', 'Junon') HGal, mr, before 1811; flowers rosy crimson, fading cerise-pink, medium, full, cupped to flat, moderate fragrance; once blooming; foliage large; upright (3 ft.) growth; probably from Holland

'Surprise' HT, mp, 1925, Van Rossem; flowers salmon-pink, dbl., cupped; ['Frau Karl Druschki' × 'Mme Edouard Herriot']

'Surprise!' S, w; flowers white with pink blush in center, dbl., globular, intense fragrance; medium growth; intr. 2004

'Surprise' -- See 'Kortikel'

'Surprise Party' -- See 'Jelroganor'

'Surprise Surprise' -- See 'Morlavmag'

'Surprise Treat' F, dr, Delbard; flowers deep red with prominent yellow stamens; intr. 2001

Surrey™ -- See 'Patio Princess'

'Surrey' -- See 'Korlanum'

'Surville' HT, mr, 1924, Croibier; bud fat, deep rose red; flowers Indian red, shaded cerise, golden stamens, dbl., globular, moderate fragrance; recurrent; ['Mme Edouard Herriot' × unknown]

'Survivor' HKor, dr, Svejda, Dr. Felicitas; flowers dark scarlet, large; bushy (5 ft.), arching growth; intr. 1975

'Surya Kiran' F, or, 1980, Pal, Dr. B.P.; bud pointed; flowers 19 petals, borne 2-14 per cluster; foliage large, glossy; prickles hooked; tall, upright, vigorous, open growth; ['Flamenco' × Orangeade®]; intr. 1979

'Surya Shikha' HT, pb, Diby; flowers striped and splashed pink and yellow, large, dbl.; free-flowering; [sport of 'Grand Opera']; intr. 1992

'Suryodaya' F, ob, 1968, IARI; bud ovoid; flowers bright orange, medium, semi-dbl.; foliage dark, leathery; very vigorous, upright growth; [Orangeade® × unknown]

Susan™ ('Susan Renaissance', Gettysburg™) S, w, Poulsen; flowers white with ivory tones in center, 10-15 cm., full, moderate fragrance; foliage dark green, glossy; bushy, tall (100-150 cm.) growth; intr. 2000

'Susan' F, mr, 1955, Robinson, H.; flowers crimson, well-formed, semi-dbl., borne in large clusters; foliage dark; bushy, compact growth; ['Donald Prior' × 'Our Princess']

'Susan' HT, lp, Kordes; flowers pale pink, sometimes deeper in center, dbl., high-centered, borne mostly singly, intense fragrance; recurrent; foliage leathery; robust growth; intr. 1996

'Susan Ann' -- See 'Southampton'

'Susan Barry' HT, rb, 2007, Edwards, Eddie and Phelps, Ethan; flowers 5 in., full, borne singly and in small clusters; foliage medium, dark green, glossy; few prickles; stems long; growth upright, tall (6 ft.); exhibition; ['Marilyn Wellan' × 'Hot Princess']; intr. 2007

'Susan Beckwith' HT, mp, 1998, Beckwith, R.; bud short, squat; flowers medium pink, apricot base, opens flat, 4-4½ in., very dbl., flat, borne in clusters; foliage medium size, medium green, semi-glossy; prickles moderate; bushy, medium (2½ ft.) growth; ['Dr. Sybil Johnston' × seedling]; intr. 1998

'Susan Blixen' -- See 'Poulari'

'Susan Daniel' -- See 'The English Lady'

'Susan Devoy' -- See 'Macreno'

'Susan Elizabeth' -- See 'Schuprak'

'Susan Hampshire' -- See 'Meinatac'

'Susan Hayward' Cl HT, lp, 1967, Hayward; flowers light pink, center and reverse darker, large, dbl., high-centered; foliage dark, glossy; vigorous, climbing, open habit growth; ['Fontanelle' × 'Gen. MacArthur']

'Susan Irvine' -- See 'Tomsue'

'Susan Jellicoe' -- See 'Horkeepog'

'Susan Louise' T, lp, 1929, Adams, Charles E.; bud very long, pointed, deep pink; flowers flesh-pink, reverse deeper, semi-dbl., loose, slight fragrance; recurrent; vigorous (4-5 ft.), bushy growth; ['Belle Portugaise' × unknown]; intr. 1929

'Susan Massu' HT, yb, 1973, Kordes, R.;

bud ovoid; flowers light yellow and salmon blend, large, dbl., cupped, moderate fragrance; foliage glossy, dark, leathery; vigorous, upright growth; ['Colour Wonder' × 'Liberty Bell']; intr. 1970

Susan Munro™ -- See 'Jaysus'

'Susan Noel' Min, ab, 1986, Jolly, Nelson F.; flowers light apricot, small, 80 petals, urn-shaped, borne usually singly; foliage small, medium green, semiglossy; prickles small, slightly hooked, gray-orange; medium, upright growth; small, globular fruit; ['Rise 'n' Shine' × 'Orange Honey']

'Susan Osborn Lloyd' -- See 'Jayllo'

'Susan Renaissance' -- See 'Poulen001'

'Susan Schneider' S, yb, 1999, Jerabek, Paul E.; flowers med. yellow, turning orange pink, then red, reverse med. yellow, 3 in., 8-14 petals, borne in small clusters, slight fragrance; foliage medium size, medium green, glossy; prickles moderate, tan; spreading, medium (5 ft.) growth; intr. 1998

'Susan Wilce' -- See 'Lioblanch'

'Susana Marchal' HT, or, 1958, Dot, Pedro; bud pointed; flowers coral-red, large, 18 petals, high-centered; foliage clear green; strong stems; upright growth; ['Cynthia' × 'Vive la France']; intr. 1953

'Susane Dot' Cl HT, dr, 1963, Dot, Simon; flowers crimson, large, 32 petals; vigorous growth; [Queen Elizabeth® × 'Peace, Climbing']

'Susanna' Pol, lp, 1914, Weigand, C.; flowers small, dbl.; [sport of 'Tausendschön']

'Susanna Tamaro' HT, op, Barni; flowers salmon-pink, full, borne mostly singly, intense fragrance; free-flowering; foliage deep green; vigorous (3-4 ft.), bushy growth; intr. 2004

Susanne® S, yb, Huber; flowers golden yellow in center, whitish on outer petals, full, slight fragrance; growth to 4-5 ft.; intr. 2006

'Susanne Marie' -- See 'Dwasusanne'

'Sushma' F, m, Kasturi; intr. 1975

'Susie' HT, mp, 1955, Spandikow; flowers pink, base yellow, 4-6 in., 45-50 petals, high-centered; foliage leathery; vigorous, bushy growth; PP1423; RULED EXTINCT 11/90; ['Mme Butterfly' × 'Sally']

'Suspense' HT, rb, 1960, Meilland, F.; bud ovoid; flowers turkey-red, reverse yellow-ochre, 4½-5 in., 58 petals, high-centered; foliage leathery, dark, glossy; vigorous, upright, bushy growth; PP1944; ['Henri Mallerin' × ('Happiness' × 'Floradora')]; intr. 1960

'Suspense, Climbing' Cl HT, rb; [sport of 'Suspense']

'Suspense' F, w, Asaoka, Keisuke; bud yellow; flowers greenish-white to white, petal tips very light pink; PP4660; [sport of 'Faberge']; same as Fabergé except for bud and bloom color

'Sussex' ('Apricot Cottage Rose') S, ab, Poulsen; flowers peachy-apricot, scalloped petals and amber stamens, 3 in., dbl., cupped, borne in large clusters, slight fragrance; free-flowering; foliage medium to dark green, glossy; compact (2-3 ft.), bushy growth; intr. 1991

'Sutter's Gold' HT, ob, 1950, Swim, H.C.; bud orange overlaid indian red; flowers golden orange, often with red on outer petals, 4-5 in., 33 petals, high-centered, borne usually singly, intense fragrance; recurrent; foliage dark, leathery; very vigorous, upright growth; PP885; ['Charlotte Armstrong' × 'Signora']

'Sutter's Gold, Climbing' ('Grimpant Sutter's Gold') Cl HT, ob, 1950, Weeks; bud vermilion; flowers golden yellow with ruddy guard petals, 5 in., borne mostly solitary, moderate fragrance; scattered repeat bloom; vigorous (10-14 ft.) growth; PP1185; [sport of 'Sutter's Gold']

Sutton Place™ ('5th Avenue') Gr, pb, 1991, Williams, J. Benjamin; flowers white with dark salmon-pink edge, aging to pink, single, borne singly and in clusters of 5-6, intense fragrance; foliage large, dark green, semi-glossy; tall, upright, bushy growth; [Queen Elizabeth® × ('Carla' × 'Command Performance')]; intr. 1996

'Suzaku' HT, ob, Keihan; intr. 1977

'Suzan Ball' F, ab, 1958, Warriner, William A.; bud conical; flowers salmon-coral, to loosely open, 2½-3½ in., 25 petals, high-centered, borne in clusters, moderate spicy fragrance; foliage dark; vigorous, upright growth; PP1588; ['Tom Breneman' × 'Fashion']; intr. 1956

'Suzanne' HSpn, op, 1950, Skinner, Dr. F. L.; flowers pale coral-pink, medium, dbl., cupped, moderate fragrance; occasional repeat; foliage small, dark, turning bronze purple and red in autumn; tall (4-5 ft.), arching growth; hips bright red, turning purple; cold hardy; [second generation R. laxa × R. spinosissima]; intr. 1949

'Suzanne Albrand' Pol, mr, 1930, Turbat; flowers bright red, large, borne in large clusters; foliage glossy; vigorous growth

'Suzanne Balitrand' HT, or, 1942, Mallerin, C.; flowers coral edged fiery red, stamens yellow

'Suzanne Bidard' Pol, mp, 1914, Vigneron; flowers small, dbl.

'Suzanne Blanchet' T, lp, 1885, Nabonnand, G.; flowers flesh-pink, large

'Suzanne Carrol of Carrolton' HP, mp, 1924, Nabonnand, P.; flowers light satiny rose and salmon, large, semi-dbl.; vigorous growth; ['Frau Karl Druschki' × 'Mme Gabriel Luizet']

'Suzanne Dolard' Pol, dr, Gaujard; flowers medium, semi-dbl.; intr. 1966

'Suzanne Étienne' HMult, w, 1909, Cochet

'Suzanne Finger' HT, 1908, Walter

'Suzanne Hester' Cl HT, w, 1950, Hester; bud ovoid; flowers white, base tinted yellow, 30 petals, high-centered; foliage glossy; vigorous growth; [sport of 'Marie Maass']

'Suzanne-Marie Rodocanachi' ('Mlle Suzanne-Marie Rodocanachi') HP, mp, 1883, Lévêque; flowers dark rosy cerise, shaded and bordered lighter, well-formed, 45 petals, globular; profuse bloom, somewhat recurrent; ['Victor Verdier' × unknown]

'Suzanne Meyer' Pol, w, 1926, Walter, L.; flowers white shaded soft pink, center bright rose-pink, medium; medium growth; ['Tausendschön' × 'Rosel Dach']

'Suzanne Michela' HT, my, 1932, Chambard, C.; bud long, pointed; flowers pure chrome-yellow, very large, dbl., cupped; very vigorous growth; ['Mme la Generale Ardouin' × seedling]

'Suzanne Miller' Pol, mr, 1927, Wezelenburg; flowers clear bright cherry-red, medium, dbl., borne in clusters; low, bushy growth

'Suzanne Turbat' Pol, ob, 1919, Turbat; flowers coral-red, shaded shrimp-pink, medium, dbl., cupped, borne in clusters of 10-20; dwarf growth; [('Petit Constant' × unknown) × seedling]

'Suzanne Villain' HT, pb, 1935, Ketten Bros.; flowers peach-blossom-pink suffused cherry-red, reverse salmon-pink, 60-65 petals; foliage rich green; vigorous, bushy growth; [('Rev. Williamson' × 'Gorgeous') × 'Mrs John Bell']

'Suzanne Wood' HP, mp, 1869, Verdier, E.; flowers large, dbl.

'Suzette' Misc OGR, w, Eve, Andre; intr. 2000

'Suzette van der Merwe' -- See 'Jachoc'

'Suzon' LCl, pb, Eve; flowers blend of pink, apricot and yellow, 8 cm., semi-dbl., cupped, borne in large clusters, moderate sweet, musky fragrance; vigorous, very tall (to 8 m.), fast growth; ['Kiftsgate' × Joseph's Coat®]; intr. 1994

'Suzon Lothé' HT, pb, 1951, Meilland, F.; bud peach; flowers pearl-pink, flushed deeper toward edge, 4-5 in., 60 petals, high-centered, borne mostly singly, intense damask fragrance; recurrent; foliage dark; few prickles; very vigorous growth; PP934; ['Peace' × ('Signora' × 'Mrs John Laing')]

'Suzon Lothé, Climbing' Cl HT, pb, 1964, Trimper, K.; vigorous (10 ft.) growth; [sport of 'Suzon Lothé']; intr. 1964

'Suzy' LCl, yb, Eve; flowers yellow to pale peach, 10 cm., dbl., cupped, quartered, borne in large clusters, moderate fruity fragrance; growth very tall (to 10 m.); intr. 1994

'Suzy' -- See 'Brisuzy'

Suzy Q™ -- See 'Jachill'

'Svatopluk Cech' LCl, dy, 1936, Brada, Dr.; bud buff; flowers orange-yellow, medium, full, intense fragrance; recurrent bloom; vigorous growth

'Svaty Václav' HT, w, 1936, Berger, A.; flowers white, center yellowish, large

'Sven' S, m, Zuzek; flowers range from violet to mauve to dark pink, double, cupped, intense fragrance; recurrent; foliage dark green; compact growth; intr. 2008

'Svensk Pimpinelle' HSpn, w

'Svetla Albena' F, yb, 1986, Staikov, Prof. Dr. V.; flowers opening yellow orange, aging red, 85 petals, borne in large clusters; foliage dark; vigorous, upright growth; ['Highlight' × 'Masquerade']; intr. 1974

'Svetlana' F, dy, Urban, J.

'Svitani' HT, my, Kavka

'Svornost' Pol, dr, 1935, Böhm, J.; flowers pure dark red, with fiery streaks, borne in large clusters; [sport of 'Orléans Rose']

'Swagatam' HT, ab, 1989, Patil, B.K.; flowers light pink, reverse apricot; [sport of 'Surkhab']; intr. 1987

'Swami' HT, lp, 1979, Hardikar, Dr. M.N.; bud long, pointed; flowers 5 in., 100 petals, high-centered, moderate fragrance; very vigorous, upright growth; ['Scarlet Knight' × 'Festival Beauty']; intr. 1973

'Swan' -- See 'Auswhite'

'Swan' -- See 'Hakucho'

'Swan Lake' (Schwanensee®) LCl, w, 1968, McGredy, Sam IV; flowers white, center tinged pinkish, large, 50 petals, inbricated, borne in small clusters, slight fragrance; free-flowering; foliage dark green; vigorous (8 ft.) growth; ['Memoriam' × 'Gruss an Heidelberg']

'Swansdown' HT, w, 1928, Dickson, A.; bud large, long, pointed; flowers creamy white, center deeper cream, dbl., spiral; foliage olive-green; fairly vigorous growth

'Swansong' -- See 'Seaswan'

'Swantje' F, w, 1936, Tantau; flowers snow-white, 3 in., dbl., borne in clusters, slight fragrance; recurrent; foliage glossy, deep green; very vigorous, bushy growth; ['Johanna Tantau' × ('Prof. Gnau' × 'Joanna Hill')]

Swany® -- See 'Meiburenac'

Swany Folies® F, w, Meilland; intr. 2004

Swany Mimi® HT, w, Meilland; flowers white with yellow tint in heart, dbl., high-centered, borne mostly singly; recurrent; intr. 2004

'Swany River' -- See 'Fredagh of Bellinchamp'

'Swarthmore' HT, pb, 1964, Meilland, Alain A.; bud pointed ovoid, with conspicuous neck; flowers blended shades of pink, petal edges will blacken in heat, 4 in., 45-55 petals, high-centered, borne mostly singly, slight tea fragrance; recurrent; foliage dark green, leathery; prickles several, reddish-brown; stems long, strong; vigorous, tall, bushy growth; PP2444; [('Independence' × 'Happiness') × 'Peace']; intr. 1964

'Swarthmore, Climbing' Cl HT, pb, 1976, Thomas, Dr. A.S.; [sport of 'Swarthmore']; intr. 1973

'Swashbuckle' HT, or, Dawson; intr. 1990

'Swati' Pol, w, 1968, IARI; bud pointed; flowers white, edged deep pink, open, small, semi-dbl.; foliage dark, leathery; moderate, bushy growth; ['Winifred Coulter' × unknown]

'Swedish Doll' Min, op, 1976, Moore, Ralph S.; bud long, pointed; flowers bright coral pink, 1½ in., 22-28 petals, high-centered, then open, borne singly or several together in loose cluster, very slight fragrance; recurrent; foliage small, medium green, glossy, leathery; prickles normal, large, straight, angled slightly downward, brown; stems medium, sturdy, wiry; vigorous, upright, branched growth; PP4160; ['Fire King' × 'Little Buckaroo']

'Sweepstakes' ('Margaret Trudeau') HT, op, 1977, McGredy, Sam IV; bud long, pointed; flowers coral-orange to salmon-pink, imbricated, 3½-5 in., 35 petals, high-centered, moderate fragrance; upright, spreading, bushy growth; PP4503; ['Prima Ballerina' × 'Ginger Rogers']; intr. 1978

'Sweet' Min, my, 1980, Lyon; bud long, pointed; flowers 50 petals, borne 1-3 per cluster; foliage tiny, glossy, deep green; prickles tiny, curved; compact, bushy growth; [seedling × seedling]; intr. 1979

Sweet™ ('Sweet Paillette') HT, ob, Poulsen; intr. 1997

Sweet™ ('Sweet Party') Min, mp, Poulsen; flowers medium pink, medium, dbl., no fragrance; foliage dark; growth bushy, 20-40 cm.; intr. 1999

'Sweet Adeline' HT, mp, 1929, Joseph H. Hill, Co.; bud long, pointed; flowers rose-pink, large, semi-dbl., moderate fragrance; PP6; ['Rapture' × 'Souv. de Claudius Pernet']

'Sweet Adeline' S, mp, Erskine, Robert; flowers soft pink, 20-40 petals, cupped, borne in clusters, moderate fragrance; non-remontant; durable (4-5 ft.) growth; winter hardy; ['Will Alderman' × 'Victory Year']

'Sweet Afton' HT, w, 1964, Armstrong, D.L. & Swim, H. C.; flowers near white, reverse pale pink, 4½-5 in., dbl., high-centered, intense sweet fragrance; recurrent; foliage dark green, leathery; tall (5 ft.), spreading, bushy growth; PP2654; [('Charlotte Armstrong' × 'Signora') × ('Alice Stern' × 'Ondine')]

'Sweet Akito' HT, mp, Tantau; flowers clean pink, slow opening, dbl., high-centered; [sport of 'Akito']; intr. 2004

'Sweet Allison' MinFl, rb, 1985, Jolly, Nelson F.; flowers orange-red shading to yellow or white, reverse cream, deeper, 35 petals; foliage medium size, medium green, semi-glossy; upright, bushy growth; ['Bonny' × ('Tiki' × seedling)]

'Sweet Amazone' HT, op

'Sweet Amy' HT, mp, 1999, Edwards, Eddie; flowers medium pink, reverse lighter, 4-5 in., full, borne mostly singly, intense fragrance; recurrent; foliage medium size, dark green, glossy; prickles moderate; upright, medium (5 ft.) growth; [Crystalline™ × Stainless Steel™]; intr. 1999

'Sweet and Low' F, pb, 1962, Schwartz, Ernest W.; bud globular; flowers salmon-pink, center lighter, small, 36 petals, borne in large clusters; foliage glossy, bronze; compact, low growth; ['Pinocchio' × 'Sweet Fairy']; intr. 1962

'Sweet 'n' Pink' HT, dp, 1976, Weeks; bud ovoid, pointed; flowers soft pink in heart, blending to deeper pink toward outer edges, 4-4½ in., 48 petals, high-centered, borne singly and in small clusters of 2 - 3, intense fragrance; free-flowering; foliage large, dark green, waxy; prickles numerous, medium, straight, brown; stems medium; upright, branching growth; PP4003; [(('Prima Ballerina' × seedling) × seedling]

'Sweet Anise Rose' -- See 'Narcisse'

'Sweet Arlene' -- See 'Tinarlene'

Sweet Avalanche+ HT, lp, Voom, Lex; flowers blush pink, double, high-centered, borne mostly singly; recurrent; stems medium to long; [sport of Avalanche+]; florist rose; intr. 2006

'Sweet Ballymaloe' S, mp; intr. 2001

'Sweet Bouquet' -- See 'SABchurchill'

'Sweet Bouquet' -- See 'Lenpac'

'Sweet Breeze' F, ly, Athy; flowers pale yellow, double, high-centered, intense fragrance; recurrent; medium growth; intr. 2006

'Sweet Briar Queen' F, mp, 1960, Schenkel; flowers rose-pink, 2 in., 45-50 petals, flat, borne in clusters, moderate fragrance; foliage maroon when young, leathery; vigorous, branching growth; PP2046; [sport of 'Rosemary']

'Sweet Butterfly' -- See 'Lavstar'

Sweet Candia® HT, pb, Meilland; flowers orchid pink, edged Neyron pink, dbl., cupped, borne mostly singly; recurrent; florist rose; intr. 1998

'Sweet Caress' F, mp, 1959, Boerner; bud ovoid; flowers rose-pink, large, 55-60 petals, moderate fragrance; foliage leathery, glossy; vigorous, upright growth; ['Pigmy Red' × 'Demure']; intr. 1959

'Sweet Caroline' -- See 'Micaroline'

'Sweet Cecilia' HRg, w, Johnston, Ronald; flowers pure white, yellow stamens, 3 in., double, shallow cup, intense fragrance; recurrent; foliage bright Rugosa green; branching (3 ft.) growth; [sport of Topaz Jewel™]; intr. 2007

Sweet Chariot™ -- See 'Poulac004(N)'

Sweet Chariot™ -- See 'Morchari'

'Sweet Charity' HT, w, 1969, Park, F.; flowers waxy white, sometimes marked pink, medium, semi-dbl., moderate fragrance; recurrent; foliage dark, glossy; vigorous, upright growth; intr. 1967

'Sweet Chateau' HT, lp, Teranishi; intr.

2002

'Sweet Cheeks' -- See 'Strjillian'

'Sweet Cherry' ('Cherry Glow') HT, mr, 1960, Dickson, A.; flowers cherry-red and yellow, large, high-centered; ['Margaret' × 'Karl Herbst']

Sweet Cover™ -- See 'Monticello'

'Sweet Diana' HT, lp; intr. 1999

'Sweet Diana' -- See 'Savadiana'

'Sweet Dream' -- See 'Fryminicot'

'Sweet Dreams' ('Kojo') HT, pb, 1976, Takatori, Yoshiho; bud long, pointed; flowers light pink, reverse deep pink, 6 in., 45-50 petals, high-centered, slight tea fragrance; foliage dark; vigorous, very upright growth; ['JRN. No. 8 seedling' × 'Royal Highness']; intr. 1977

'Sweet Dreams' -- See 'Jacams'

'Sweet Ecstasy' -- See 'Hinsweet'

'Sweet Fairy' Min, lp, 1946, deVink; flowers soft pink, 1 in., 57 petals, cupped to rosette, moderate sweet fragrance; foliage small, dark; vigorous, dwarf (6-8 in.) growth; PP748; ['Tom Thumb' × seedling]

'Sweet Fragrance' F, pb; intr. 1999

'Sweet Fragrance' Gr, ab, Lim, Ping; flowers apricot, maturing to salmon-pink, 3 -4 in., 35 petals, borne in clusters, moderate sweet fragrance; recurrent; vigorous, upright (2 - 4 ft.) growth ; PPAF; intr. 2007

'Sweet Frédérique' S, pb, Interplant; intr. 1997

'Sweet Freedom' HT, w, Zary, Keith; bud long, pointed; flowers ivory, hint of green on outer petals, 4 in., 25-30 petals, cupped, borne mostly singly, moderate honeysuckle fragrance; recurrent; foliage dark green, glossy; stems 16 - 20 in.; growth to 5 ft.; PPAF; intr. 2006

'Sweet Gesture' -- See 'Maccarlto'

'Sweet Hannah' Min, my, Moore; flowers light yellow, changing to deeper yellow as it ages, 1½ in., full, cupped to rosette, borne singly and in small clusters, moderate fragrance; recurrent; foliage dark green, glossy; growth to 12-18 in.; intr. 1998

'Sweet Harmony' F, pb, 1962, Gaujard; flowers canary-yellow edged crimson-pink, large, 36 petals, borne in clusters, moderate spicy fragrance; free-flowering; foliage glossy, light green; vigorous (3 ft.) growth; ['Peace' × 'Masquerade']; intr. 1962

Sweet Haze® S, lp, Tantau; flowers pale pink with red stamens, single, flat, borne in clusters; heavy spring bloom; foliage disease-resistant; intr. 2004

'Sweet Heart Shelley' -- See 'Lioshell'

'Sweet Home' ('Reginella') HT, dp, 1970, Meilland, Mrs. Marie-Louise; flowers carmine-lake with vermilion red reverse, large, 35 petals, high-centered to cupped, slight fruity fragrance; foliage large, leathery; vigorous growth; [('Jolie Madame' × Baccará®) × (Baccará® × 'Jolie Madame')]

'Sweet Home Alabama' -- See 'Talsweet'

'Sweet Honesty' Min, w

'Sweet Honey' HT, ly, Kordes; bud slender; flowers honey-cream, dbl., high-centered, moderate sweet fragrance; recurrent; prickles very few; medium to tall growth; intr. 1999

'Sweet India' HT, w, Tejganga; flowers creamy white, large, full, intense fragrance; free-flowering; [sport of 'Sweet Surrender']; intr. 1996

'Sweet Inspiration' -- See 'Jacsim'

'Sweet Interlude' HT, pb, 1990, Wambach, Alex A.; bud pointed; flowers white center with pink edging, large, slow opening, 32 petals, high-centered, borne singly, intense fragrance; foliage medium green, disease-resistant; prickles moderate, brown; upright, bushy, medium growth; [Pristine® × 'Olympiad']; intr. 1989

'Sweet Juliet' -- See 'Ausleap'

'Sweet Keri' HT, lp, 1988, Wilson, George D.; flowers light pale pink, large, 44 petals, high-centered, borne singly; foliage medium green, large; prickles triangular, red; medium, upright growth; ['Judith Marten' × Folklore®]

'Sweet Lady' -- See 'Meizeli'

'Sweet Lady' -- See 'Sue Hipkin'

'Sweet Lara' HT, m, 2004, Edwards, Eddie; flowers white to very pale lavender, deeper lavender highlights on petal edges, 5½ in., full, high-centered, borne mostly solitary, intense fragrance; recurrent; foliage medium size, dark green, semi-glossy; growth upright, medium (5 ft.); exhibition; [Crystalline™ × 'Barbra Streisand']

'Sweet Lavender' HMult, pb, 1912, Paul; flowers blush, edged mauve, single, borne in large clusters

'Sweet Lavinia' HT, my, 1967, McTeer, F.; flowers high-centered, high-centered; foliage glossy; ['Golden Scepter' × 'Peace']

'Sweet Lelanie' HT, lp, 1967, Duehrsen; flowers light pink, base yellow, large, dbl., globular; foliage wrinkled, bronze; vigorous, upright growth; ['Charlotte Armstrong' × seedling]

'Sweet Lemon Dream' Min, ly; intr. 2003

'Sweet Little Queen' -- See 'The Sweet Little Queen of Holland'

'Sweet Love' HT, mp, 1985, Rijksstation Voor Sierplantenteelt; flowers medium-large, 90 petals, flat, borne singly and in clusters of up to 7, no fragrance; foliage matte, dark; prickles red; upright growth; [Queen Elizabeth® × 'Duke of Windsor']; intr. 1980

'Sweet Magic' -- See 'Dicmagic'

'Sweet Maid' HT, lp, 1950, Moss; bud pointed; flowers porcelain-pink, semi-dbl.

'Sweet Mandarin' Min, ob, 1979, Schwartz, Ernest W.; bud pointed; flowers light orange, small, 16 petals, flat, moderate fragrance; foliage small, soft; compact growth; ['Sweet and Low' × ('Gypsy Moth' × unknown)]; intr. 1978

'Sweet Marie' Min, ob; flowers orange-yellow blend, semi-dbl.; free-flowering; foliage very glossy; low (10-14 in.) growth

'Sweet Marvel' Min, w, deRuiter

Sweet Meidiland® S, lp, Meilland; flowers soft pink, small, semi-dbl., globular, borne in clusters; free-flowering; compact (3 ft.) growth; intr. 2003

'Sweet Melina' HT, Tantau; intr. 2002

'Sweet Melody' F, Leenders

'Sweet Melody' Min, ab, Fischer; flowers almost white with touch of apricot; medium to tall growth; [sport of 'Pierrine']; intr. 1998

'Sweet Memorie' HT, mp, 1937, Hieatt; flowers pink, base yellow, reverse purplish, large, semi-dbl., cupped; foliage leathery; vigorous growth; ['Mrs C.W. Edwards' × 'Rose Marie']

'Sweet Memories' MinFl, my, Whartons Roses; flowers lemon yellow, medium, full, cupped, borne in clusters, slight fragrance; recurrent; foliage light green; bushy growth; [sport of 'Sweet Dream']; intr. 1995

'Sweet Memories' -- See 'Summer Dream'

'Sweet Memory' F, lp, 1991, Yasuda, Yuji; bud pointed; flowers 4 in., 30 petals, high-centered, moderate fragrance; foliage medium size, medium green, matte; bushy, medium growth; ['Hana-Gasumi' × ('Lady X' × 'Paradise')]

'Sweet Memory' -- See 'Koraburg'

Sweet Mimi® -- See 'Haumi'

Sweet Moments® HT, lp, Schreurs; intr. 2004

'Sweet Moon' F, m, Teranishi; intr. 2002

'Sweet Mystery' -- See 'Flomyst'

'Sweet Nell' -- See 'Cocavoter'

Sweet Nothings™ -- See 'Jacenram'

'Sweet Osmanthus' -- See 'Newxu'

'Sweet Paillette' -- See 'Poulpol'

'Sweet Party' -- See 'Poulset'

'Sweet Passion' -- See 'Jaswee'

'Sweet Pea' Pol, m, 2006, Shoup, George Michael; flowers lavender and mauve, bright yellow stamens, 1-1½ in., full, borne in large clusters, moderate fragrance; remontant; foliage small, medium green, semi-glossy; prickles moderate; compact, short (2-3 ft.) growth; ['Lavender Pink Parfait' × 'Lavender Pink Parfait']; intr. 1996

'Sweet Perfume' -- See 'Peaperfume'

'Sweet Perfumella' HT, op, Meilland; intr. 2004

'Sweet Petite' Min, mp, Fryer, Gareth; flowers salmon-pink; free-flowering; intr. 1994

'Sweet Pickins' -- See 'Tinsweet'

'Sweet Pretty' Pol, lp, Meilland; flowers light pink to white, purple stamens, single, flat, no fragrance; recurrent; foliage dark green; compact, bushy (60 - 80 cm.) growth; intr. 2005

'Sweet Prince' HT, pb, 1984, Stoddard, Louis; flowers deep pink, petals edged medium red, 3½ in., 20 petals, borne singly, intense fragrance; foliage large, dark, matte; heavily prickled; bushy growth; ['Honey Favorite' × 'Granada']; intr. 1987

'Sweet Promise' ('Sonia Meilland', 'Sonia') Gr, pb, 1971, Meilland; bud long, somewhat cylindrical; flowers pink suffused coral to yellow, 4-4½ in., 30 petals, high-centered, borne mostly singly, intense fruity fragrance; recurrent; foliage glossy, dark, leathery; prickles moderate, medium, straight to slightly hooked; upright growth; hips rounded, orange-yellow; PP3095; [Zambra® × (Baccará® × 'White Knight')]; originally registered as F; patent issued as Gr

'Sweet Promise' HT, op, Meilland; flowers deep salmon, medium , 45-50 petals, shallow cup, intense old rose fragrance; recurrent; foliage dark green, almost black when young; tall, bushy growth; [Unknown × Unknown]; intr. 2007

'Sweet Promise, Climbing' -- See 'Sonia, Climbing'

'Sweet Raspberry' Min, dp, 1984, Jolly, Nelson F.; flowers deep purplish pink, small, 28 petals, urn-shaped to flat, slight fragrance; free-flowering; foliage small, medium green, matte; bushy growth; ['Little Rascal' × 'Cinderella']

'Sweet Remembrance' HT, my, Kirkham; flowers bright yellow, fading to cream primrose, golden stamens, semi-dbl. to dbl., flat, opens quickly; foliage glossy; strong, upright, medium growth; intr. 2003

'Sweet Repose' ('The Optimist') F, yb, 1956, deRuiter; bud medium, ovoid, with conspicuous neck; flowers maize-yellow tinged carmine, becoming carmine, 3-4 in., 23-28 petals, high-centered, to cupped, borne in large clusters, moderate sweet fragrance; recurrent; foliage dense, leathery, parsley-green; prickles numerous, medium, hooked downward; vigorous, upright, bushy growth; hips short, globular, smooth, fern green; PP1533; ['Golden Rapture' × floribunda seedling']; intr. 1955

'Sweet Repose, Climbing' Cl F, yb

'Sweet Revelation' -- See 'Sue Hipkin'

'Sweet Revenge' -- See 'Tinrevenge'

'Sweet Rosamini' ('ruimarso') Min, lp, deRuiter; intr. 1987

'Sweet Saffron' -- See 'Densaf'

'Sweet Salmon' F, Leenders

'Sweet San Carlos' F, m, 2006, Coiner, Jim; flowers medium, semi-dbl., borne in small clusters; foliage small, dark green, glossy; prickles ¼ in., triangle, red, moderate; growth compact, medium (3½ ft.); garden decorative; [seedling × seedling]; intr. 2006

'Sweet Scent' -- See 'Rensweet'

'Sweet Sensation' -- See 'Liebeslied'

'Sweet Seventeen' HT, lp, 1923, Clark, A.; flowers semi-dbl., moderate fragrance; foliage light, wrinkled; bushy, dwarf growth; ['Frau Karl Druschki' × 'Bardou Job']

'Sweet Seventeen' Gr, mp, Leenders, J.; flowers pink, small; vigorous growth; ['Fred Howard' × 'Cocorico']; intr. 1960

'Sweet Shaddow' HT, mr, 1963, Barter; flowers scarlet, edged darker, 4½ in., 22 petals; foliage dark; vigorous growth; [Queen Elizabeth® × 'Étoile de Hollande']

'Sweet Shadow' HT, dr, 1965, Barter; flowers vivid scarlet, almost black edged, petals reflexed, borne mostly singly, moderate sweet fragrance; foliage large, dark green

'Sweet Shirley' -- See 'Cleshir'

'Sweet Shot' HT, mp, deRuiter; intr. 2001

'Sweet Sixteen' S, ab, Clements, John; flowers soft pink blended with soft peach, golden stamens, 4 in., 70 petals, borne in clusters, moderate peach fragrance; foliage crimson red when new, maturing to rich, leathery green; upright (4 × 3 ft.) growth; PPAF; intr. 2002

'Sweet Sixteen' F, mp, Johnson, T. H.; flowers clear Venetial pink; PP3585; [sport of 'Seventeen']; intr. before 1975

'Sweet Sixteen' HT, pb, 1943, Lammerts, Dr. Walter; bud long, pointed; flowers salmon-pink, base yellow, 4-5 in., 16-20 petals, intense fragrance; vigorous, upright, bushy growth; PP631; ['Mrs Sam McGredy' × 'Pres. Herbert Hoover']

'Sweet Sonata' -- See 'Meioffic'

'Sweet Song' F, mp, 1971, Meilland; flowers 4½ in., 35 petals, moderate fruity fragrance; bushy growth; ['Fidélio' × Bettina®]

'Sweet Success' Gr, lp, Pottschmidt

'Sweet Sue' HT, op, 1940, Lammerts, Dr. Walter; bud long, pointed, flame to blood-red; flowers coral-pink, stamens maroon, single, cupped, moderate spicy fragrance; vigorous growth; ['Joanna Hill' × 'Night']

'Sweet Sue' Min, lp, Bennett, Dee; bud ovoid; flowers very small, 13 petals, high-centered, borne in clusters of 10-25; foliage small, dark; bushy growth; ['Pink Ribbon' × 'Pink Ribbon']; intr. 1979

'Sweet Sultan' ('Swet Sultain') Cl HT, dr, 1959, Eacott; flowers crimson shaded maroon, 4 in., 5 petals, borne in trusses, intense fragrance; recurrent; vigorous, pillar growth; ['Independence' × 'Honour Bright']; intr. 1958

Sweet Sunblaze® -- See 'Meitonje'

'Sweet Sunsation' -- See 'Korfisro'

'Sweet Sunshine' -- See 'Morsun'

'Sweet Surrender' HT, mp, 1982, Weeks, O.L.; bud pointed; flowers medium silvery pink, large, 40 petals, cupped, borne usually singly, intense tea fragrance; recurrent; foliage dark green, leathery; stems long, strong; medium to tall growth; PP5130; [seedling × 'Tiffany']; intr. 1983

'Sweet Symphony' -- See 'Meibarke'

'Sweet Talk' F, ly, 1964, Swim & Weeks; flowers lemon to white,, dbl., borne in clusters, moderate fragrance; foliage light green, leathery; low, uniform., bushy growth; PP2542; ['Frolic' × 'Lavender Pinocchio']

'Sweet Tangela' MinFl, yb, 2002, Giles, Diann; flowers yellow/pink, medium, full, borne in large clusters, slight fragrance; foliage medium size, medium green, matte; growth upright, low, garden, exhibition; [seedling × seedling]; intr. 2001

'Sweet Thoughts' HT, lp, 1965, Cant, F.; flowers 5 in.; vigorous growth; ['Kordes' Perfecta' × 'Show Girl']

'Sweet Twilight' Cl HT, ly, 1954, Motose; flowers buff-yellow, center darker, 4-5½ in., 25 petals, high-centered, moderate fruity fragrance; abundant, recurrent bloom; vigorous (15-30 ft.) growth; PP1343; [sport of 'Tawny Gold']

'Sweet Unique' HT, pb, deRuiter; bud large, soft pink; flowers medium pink, edges darker, reverse lighter, dbl., high-centered, borne mustly singly; good repeat; stems long; florist rose

'Sweet Valentine' Min, dr, Benardella, Frank; flowers deep, velvety red, classic hybrid tea form; free-flowering; medium, bushy growth

'Sweet Valentine' -- See 'Jacbrant'

'Sweet Velvet' F, mr, 1969, Martin, J.; flowers velvety scarlet, large, dbl., hybrid tea, moderate sweet fragrance; foliage small, leathery, glossy; moderate growth; ['Leverkusen' × 'S'Agaro']

'Sweet Vibes' -- See 'Gelsweet'

'Sweet Vigorosa' -- See 'Kordatura'

'Sweet Vivid' Min, pb; flowers pink, yellow center, well-formed, dbl.; vigorous growth

'Sweet Vivien' F, pb, 1963, Raffel; bud ovoid; flowers pink, center white and light yellow, 3 in., 17 petals, shallow cup to flat, borne in clusters, slight honey/spice fragrance; recurrent; foliage small, dark, glossy; stems short; very compact, bushy growth; large, pear-shaped fruit; ['Little Darling' × 'Odorata (HT)']; intr. 1963

'Sweet Wishes' -- See 'Poulpah032(N)'

'Sweet Wonder' MinFl, ab; flowers apricot-orange-peachy-pink, full, pompon, borne in clusters, slight fragrance; good repeat; foliage glossy; upright (2 ft.) growth; intr. 1999

'Sweetcorn' Min, yb, Hannemann, F.; intr. 1991

'Sweetheart' HWich, w, 1901, Walsh; bud rose-pink; flowers white with faint blush to medium, 2½ in., very dbl., borne in clusters of 10-15, moderate fragrance; foliage small, glossy, dark; vigorous, climbing growth; [R. wichurana × 'Bridesmaid']

'Sweetheart' -- See 'Cocapeer'

'Sweetheart Rose' -- See 'Mlle Cécile Brünner'

'Sweetheart Rose,Climbing' -- See 'Mlle Cécile Brünner, Climbing'

'Sweetie' -- See 'Peach Clementine'

'Sweetie Pie'   HT, lp, 1970, Hyde; flowers light pink, outer edges darker; PP3055; [sport of 'Swarthmore']; intr. 1971

'Sweetie Pie'   Min, dp, Bell; flowers carmine pink with salmon tonings, full, flat; medium growth

'Sweetlips Minijet'   Min, mp, Meilland

'Sweetness'   HT, ab, Dickson, A.; bud long, pointed; flowers apricot-yellow shaded pink, spiral, reflexed petals, large, dbl., moderate fragrance; foliage glossy; very vigorous growth; intr. 1935

'Sweetness'   HT, mp, 1919, McGredy; flowers intense rose-pink, shaded scarlet, well-formed, moderate fragrance

Sweetness™ -- See 'Jacmearo'

'Sweetnesse'   HT, mp, Tantau; intr. 1995

'Sweetwaters' -- See 'Macsweetwa'

'Swet Sultain' -- See 'Sweet Sultan'

Swift™ -- See 'Poulnana'

Swing® -- See 'Intersiree'

'Swinger'   Min, my, 1984, Jolly, Nelson F.; flowers , 35 petals, high-centered, borne usually singly, slight fragrance; recurrent; foliage medium size, medium green, semi-glossy; prickles moderate, slightly hooked; spreading growth; hips globular ; PP6560; ['Rise 'n' Shine' × 'Puppy Love']

'Swinging Sixties'   F, yb; intr. 1995

'Swingtime'   F, rb, 1965, Morgan; bud pointed; flowers crimson, reverse buff-white, medium, full, cupped, moderate sweetbriar fragrance; vigorous, upright growth; PP2331; ['Little Darling' × ('Red Pinocchio' × 'Masquerade')]; intr. 1963

'Swisa' -- See 'White Satin'

'Swishrev'   (Revelry™) HT, dr, 1998, Swisher, Stan; flowers dark red to purple, 4 in., full, borne mostly singly, moderate fragrance; foliage medium size, dark green, semi-glossy; upright, tall growth; [Pristine® × National Velvet™]; intr. 1998

'Swiss Bliss'   Min, my, 1988, Lemrow, Dr. Maynard W.; flowers aging lighter, decorative, small, 45-50 petals, borne singly or in sprays of 3-5; foliage small, medium green, matte, serrated; prickles reddish-brown; upright, bushy, medium growth; ['Anytime' × seedling]

Swiss Fire®   HT, or, 1979, Huber; bud globular, flowers orange-red; flowers 4-4½ in., 50 petals; foliage dark; upright growth; ['Fragrant Cloud' × 'Ena Harkness']; intr. 1975

'Swiss Gold' -- See 'Schweizer Gold'

'Swiss Lass' -- See 'Lemswi'

"Swonderful" -- See 'Shayela'

'Sword of Hope'   HT, mr, 1964, Von Abrams; bud long, pointed; flowers 5-6 in., 45 petals, high-centered; foliage glossy; vigorous, upright growth

'Sybil'   HT, op, 1921, Bees; bud long, pointed; flowers silvery salmon-rose, center orange-salmon, very dbl., moderate fragrance; ['Sunburst' × 'Mary, Countess of Ilchester']

'Sybil Hipkin'   HT, dy, Dawson; flowers deep bright yellow, dbl., cupped, borne singly and in small clusters, moderate fragrance; recurrent; stems long; upright growth; intr. 1978

'Sybil Thorndike'   HT, mr, 1976, Kordes; flowers full, 5 in., 25 petals; foliage dark; ['Liebeszauber' × seedling]

'Sydney'   HCh, mp, Svedja, Felicitas; bud ovoid; flowers phlox-pink, 3-3½ in., 20 petals, cupped, intense fragrance; foliage rugose, yellow-green; bushy, spreading growth; ['Old Blush' × Dagmar Hastrup®]; intr. 1977

'Sydney'   HP, mp, 1908, Moore, A.K.; [sport of 'Prince Camille de Rohan']

'Sydney Mary' -- See 'Worchief'

'Sydonie' -- See 'Sidonie'

'Sydonie Dorizy'   B, op, 1846, Dorizy; flowers peach pink, aging to red, shaded lilac, medium

'Sylph'   T, w, 1895, Paul, W.; flowers white tinted with peach, large, high-centered

Sylphide®   F, dp

'Sylphide'   HGal, w; flowers white with pink edges; probably extinct

'Sylt' -- See 'Korylt'

'Sylvaine'   HT, lp

'Sylvan Sunset'   HT, pb, 1980, Taylor, Thomas E.; bud pointed; flowers 28 petals, high-centered; foliage medium green, semi-glossy; prickles hooked; vigorous, upright, tall, bushy growth; ['Swarthmore' × 'First Prize']

'Sylvana'   HT, w, Huber

'Sylvander'   S, my, Preston, Isabella; flowers clear yellow, large, single; dwarf (2-3 ft.) growth; [R. × harisonii × unknown]

'Sylvanus Thompson'   HT, mr, 2002, Poole, Lionel; flowers brilliant red, 5½ in., very full, high-centered, borne mostly solitary, slight fragrance; foliage large, dark green, semi-glossy; prickles large, slightly hooked down, moderate; growth upright, bushy, medium (3 ft.); garden decorative, exhibition, bedding; [('Gavotte' × 'Spirit of the Heath') × 'Mike Thompson']; intr. 2003

'Sylvia'   S, m, Geschwind; flowers purple-pink, edges lighter, large, very full; intr. 1895

'Sylvia'   HWich, ly, Paul, W.; flowers pale lemon-yellow, passing to white, dbl., moderate fragrance; moderate growth; intr. 1911

'Sylvia'   HT, my, Foster; flowers buttercup-yellow, 25 petals, moderate fruity fragrance; ruled extinct 01/79; [sport of 'Golden Gleam']; intr. 1949

'Sylvia' -- See 'Korlift'

'Sylvia' -- See 'Silvia'

'Sylvia Dot'   F, lp, 1970, Dot, Simon; bud pointed; flowers salmon, medium, 30 petals, high-centered; foliage glossy, bronze; upright, dense growth; [Queen Elizabeth® × 'Orient']; intr. 1965

'Sylvia Groen'   HT, pb, 1935, Groen; flowers coral-rose, shaded crimson; vigorous, upright growth; [sport of 'Pres. Herbert Hoover']

'Sylvia Louise'   HT, op, 1980, Shaw, H.C.W.; flowers pink and orange blend; foliage glossy; ['Ena Harkness, Climbing' × unknown]; intr. 1973

'Sylvie Briant'   HT, op

'Sylvie Leblanc'   F, w, Lens; intr. 1992

Sylvie Vartan®   Pol, mp, Eve; flowers bright pink, 8 cm., dbl., borne in clusters, slight fragrance; recurrent; foliage dark green, healthy; bushy (70-100 cm.) growth; intr. 1968

'Sylvor'   HT, Croix; intr. 1971

Symbol®   F, mr

'Symbol Miru'   HWich, w, 1937, Böhm, J.; flowers lemon yellow, fading to white, 6-8 cm., dbl., borne singly or in small clusters, moderate fragrance

'Symbole'   S, mr, 1945, Robichon; bud thick, pointed; flowers carmine, well-shaped, very large; long, strong stems; vigorous growth; ['Mev. G.A. van Rossem' × 'Roseraie de l'Hay']

'Symmetry'   HP, mr, 1910, Paul, G.; ['Mrs John Laing' × unknown]

Sympathie®   HKor, mr, 1964, Kordes, R.; flowers velvety dark red, opens quickly, 9 cm., dbl., high-centered, borne in small clusters, intense fragrance; some repeat; foliage glossy, dark; very vigorous (9-12 ft.) growth; ['Wilhelm Hansmann' × 'Don Juan']; intr. 1964

'Symphonette'   Min, pb, 1974, Morey, Dennison; bud ovoid; flowers light pink, reverse deep pink, small, dbl., moderate fragrance; foliage small, glossy, leathery; vigorous, dwarf, bushy growth; ['Cécile Brunner' × 'Cinderella']; intr. 1973

'Symphonie'   HT, pb, 1951, Meilland, F.; bud pointed, ovoid to globular; flowers shades of pink, broad petals, veined carmine-pink, 4½-5 in., 25 petals, high-centered, moderate fragrance; recurrent; foliage glossy, leathery; vigorous, upright, bushy growth; PP958; ['Peace' × ('Signora' × 'Mrs John Laing')]

'Symphonie, Climbing'   Cl HT, pb, Elmer's Nursery; [sport of 'Symphonie']

'Symphonie Lumiere' -- See 'Meitomkin'

'Symphonie No. 1'   Min, mp, Meilland

'Symphonie No. 3'   Min, ob, Meilland

'Symphonie No. 3' -- See 'Meidrepil'

'Symphony'   HP, lp, 1935, Weigand, C.; bud long, pointed; flowers large, dbl., cabbagy, moderate fragrance; recurrent; foliage leathery, dark; PP79; ['Frau Karl Druschki' × 'Souv. de Claudius Pernet']

'Symphony' -- See 'Auslett'

'Syr'   S, dr, 1978, Lundstad; bud pointed, ovoid; flowers 4 in., 23 petals, high-centered, borne in small clusters, slight fragrance; recurrent; foliage glossy, dark; very vigorous, upright (5-7 ft.) growth; [Stadt Rosenheim® × 'Sangerhausen']; intr. 1977

'Syracuse'   HT, mr, 1930, Mallerin, C.; bud crimson; flowers scarlet-crimson, large, dbl.; foliage dark, leathery; vigorous growth; ['Mme G. Forest-Colcombet' × 'Aspirant Maumejean']

'Syrikit'   HT, Mondial Roses; intr. 1969

'Syringa'   HWich, w, 1931, Browning; flowers medium to large, 4-5 cm., single,

The Official Registry and Checklist — Rosa

borne in clusters of 5-20

'Syris' HGal, mp, before 1836, Coquerel; flowers glossy carmine, large, full

'Syvdal' ('Rosa davidii 'Syvdal'') S, dp, Olsen, Aksel; hips large, bottle-shaped, orange-red; hybrid of *R. davidii*; intr. 1960

— T —

'T. B. McQuesten' F, ab

'T. F. Crozier' HT, dy, 1918, Dickson, H.; flowers deep canary-yellow, fading to white, dbl., high-centered

'T. V. Times' HT, dr, 1970, Dickson, A.; flowers crimson, ovate, 5½ in., 35 petals; foliage very large, dull; very free growth; ['Gallant' × ('Brilliant' × seedling)]

'T. W. Girdlestone' HP, mr, 1891, Dickson, A.; flowers glossy vermilion-red, shaded salmon red, very large, full

'Ta Nase Pisnicka Ceska' Pol, mp, 1938, Böhm, J.; flowers small, dbl.

'Ta Ta' -- See 'Minatco'

'Tabarin' F, pb, 1956, Gaujard; bud oval; flowers salmon-pink flushed yellow and copper-orange to red, 3-4 in., semi-dbl.; foliage light green; vigorous, bushy growth; ['Opera' × 'Masquerade']

'Tabatha' HT, pb, 2005, Edwards, Eddie & Phelps, Ethan; flowers blush pink with deeper pink edges, 5 in., very full, high-centered, borne mostly solitary; foliage medium size, dark green, glossy; prickles medium, hooked; growth upright, tall (5 ft.); exhibition; [Gemini™ × 'White Success']; intr. 2005

'Table Mountain' HT, pb; flowers white center, pink petal edges, and green on reverse, dbl., high-centered; recurrent; growth 5 × 4 ft.; intr. 1990

'Table Queen' HT, ob, Williams, J.B.; flowers deep orange, very dbl., high-centered; intr. 2003

'Tablers' Choice' F, rb, 1974, Harkness; flowers deep red, yellow reverse, 4 in., 38 petals; foliage glossy; [('Ann Elizabeth' × Allgold®) × ('Tropicana' × Piccadilly®)]

Taboo™ -- See 'Tanelorak'

'Tabris' -- See 'Korweiso'

'Tabriz' HT, lp, 1986, Kriloff, Michel; flowers soft pink, petals quill, large, dbl., high-centered; recurrent; few prickles; ['Belle Epoque' × seedling]

Tache de Beauté® -- See 'Lenpic'

'Tackholmii' (*R.* × *hibernica*, *R. balsamea*, *R.* × *tackholmii*) S, mp, before 1922; flowers pink, solitary or few; early flowering; vigorous, erect, shrub growth

'Tacoma' HT, ab, 1921, Chervenka; bud long, pointed; flowers flaming apricot, dbl.; ['Mme Butterfly' × 'Honeymoon']

Taconis® F, or, 1968, deRuiter; flowers orange-scarlet, borne in trusses; foliage glossy; vigorous growth; ['Ruth Leuwerik' × 'City of Nottingham']

'Taffeta' HT, pb, 1947, Lammerts, Dr. Walter; bud urn-shaped; flowers pink-yellow blend, 3-3½ in., 20 petals, moderate fragrance; foliage leathery, glossy, bronze-green; vigorous, upright growth; PP716; ['Mrs Sam McGredy' × 'Pres. Herbert Hoover']

'Taffeta, Climbing' Cl HT, pb, 1954, Armstrong, J.A.; PP1104

'Taffeta' Cl Min, w, Warner, Chris; flowers pure white, quartered, moderate fragrance; recurrent; intr. 1997

'Taffy' -- See 'Baktaf'

'Taft Rose' HT, op, before 1911; flowers salmon-pink, shaded with chrome-yellow; ['Kaiserin Auguste Viktoria' × 'Mme Cusin']

'Tag-a-long' -- See 'Morcoat'

'Tagore' F, my, 1955, Maarse, G.; flowers yellow-ochre, reverse shaded orange, borne in clusters; compact growth; ['Pinocchio' × unknown]

'Tahiti' HT, yb, 1947, Meilland, F.; flowers amber-yellow suffused carmine, 6 in.; foliage glossy, dark; ['Peace' × 'Signora']

'Tahiti' HT, ab, Interplant; intr. 2005

'Tahitian Moon' S, ly, Ping Lim; flowers soft, pale yellow, center darker, 2 in., very full, cupped, quartered, borne in clusters; foliage glossy, dark green; growth low in cool climates, 6 ft. and more in warm zones; PP16994; intr. 2004

Tahitian Sunset™ -- See 'Jacgodde'

'Tahore' HT, mp, 1958, Buyl Frères; flowers rose, large, 45-50 petals, high-centered; foliage glossy; strong stems; vigorous, upright growth; ['Peace' × seedling]

'Tai-Gong' ('Apachi') F, or, 1976, Kordes; bud long, pointed; flowers orange to red, large, 28 petals, high-centered; foliage glossy, dark; vigorous, upright growth; ['Klaus Stortebeker' × seedling]; intr. 1974

'Taïcoun' HRg, mp, before 1872

'Taifun' -- See 'Typhoon'

'Taifun' -- See 'Typhoon'

'Taiga' HT, rb, Tantau; intr. 2003

Taiga® -- See 'Tantaga'

'Taihape Sunset' HT, ob, Kordes; flowers orange, backed with yellow, dbl.; recurrent; medium to tall growth; intr. 1987

'T'Aime' HT, Shinoda, D. S. & Umeda, G. Y.; PP3960

'Taischa' HT, m, Robinson; flowers blend of various mauve shades, quilled, full, flat, moderate fragrance; recurrent; ['Rêve d'Or' × 'Lavender Pinocchio']; intr. 1989

'Taj Mahal' HT, dp, 1972, Armstrong, D.L.; bud medium, ovoid; flowers deep pink, 5-6 in., 45-50 petals, high-centered, cupped, borne mostly singly, moderate fragrance; recurrent; foliage large, leathery, olive green; prickles several, hooked slighty downward, reddish brown; vigorous, upright, bushy growth; hips globular, strong yellow; PP3314; ['Manitou' × 'Grand Slam']

'Takao' HT, yb, 1986, Okamoto, K.; flowers deep yellow, aging scarlet, medium, 33 petals, high-centered, borne usually singly, moderate damask fragrance; recurrent; foliage medium size, medium green; prickles deep brown; medium, bushy growth; [('Masquerade' × 'Lydia') × ('Montezuma' × 'Miss Ireland')]; intr. 1975

Takapuna® -- See 'Mactenni'

'Takatori Prominent' F, op, 1981, Takatori, Yoshiho; flowers orange-salmon; [sport of Prominent®]

'Taksun' ('Margaret Thatcher') F, rb, 1981, Takatori, Yoshiho & Sunao; flowers striped red and white; [sport of Bridal Pink™]; growth habit and other characteristics same as 'Bridal Pink'; intr. 1983

'Talalconbury' ('Alconbury') F, dp, 1996, Taylor, Franklin; flowers deep pink with touch of violet, medium, very dbl., high-centered, borne singly and in sprays; foliage medium size, dark green, semi-glossy; few prickles; tall (48 in.), upright, bushy growth; intr. 1997

'Talalf' ('Alfie Luv') Min, op, 1991, Taylor, Pete & Kay; flowers orange-pink with lavender hue, yellow base, large, dbl., borne mostly singly, slight fragrance; foliage medium size, medium green, semi-glossy; some prickles; upright, medium (60 cm.) growth; ['Azure Sea' × seedling]; intr. 1992

'Talali' ('Alice Lee') Min, pb, 1991, Taylor, Pete & Kay; bud pointed; flowers pink with color lighter towards edge of petals, giving a lavender cast. medium, 15-18 petals, high-centered, borne singly, slight fragrance; foliage medium size, medium green, semi-glossy; upright, bushy, medium growth; ['Azure Sea' × seedling]; intr. 1990

'Talbaby' ('Baby Cakes') Min, rb, 1995, Taylor, Pete & Kay; flowers white, edged red, opening to red and white appearance, small, dbl., borne mostly singly; foliage medium size, medium green, semi-glossy; few prickles; upright, bushy, medium (28 in.) growth; [Party Girl™ × 'Admiral Rodney']; intr. 1996

'Talber' ('Berry Berry Red') Min, mr, 1993, Taylor, Franklin; flowers medium red, large, dbl., borne mostly singly, slight fragrance; foliage medium size, medium green, semi-glossy; few prickles; medium (24 in.), upright, bushy growth; [Party Girl™ × Papa Meilland®]; intr. 1993

'Talblo' ('Bloomtown') Min, pb, 1993, Taylor, Franklin "Pete" & Kay; flowers pink petals with slightly darker edges, reverse cream, large, dbl., borne in small clusters; foliage medium size, medium green, semi-glossy; some prickles; medium (24 in.), upright, spreading growth; [Party Girl™ × 'Andrea']; intr. 1993

'Talbro' ('Brown Sugar') Min, ab, 1995, Taylor, Pete & Kay; flowers medium, dbl., borne mostly singly; foliage medium size, dark green, glossy; some prickles; upright, bushy, medium (30 in.) growth; [Party Girl™ × Julia's Rose®];

intr. 1996

'Talcaj' ('Cajun Dancer') Min, rb, 1993, Taylor, Franklin "Pete" & Kay; flowers red with white eye, light reverse, large, 6-14 petals, borne singly and in large clusters; foliage medium size, dark green, semi-glossy; some prickles; tall (36 in.), upright, bushy growth; [Party Girl™ × unknown]; intr. 1993

'Talcan' ('Candy Corn™) Min, ob, 1999, Taylor, Franklin "Pete" & Kay; flowers orange-yellow, 1¼ in., single, borne mostly singly; foliage medium size, medium green, semi-glossy; few prickles; upright, bushy, medium (18 in.) growth; intr. 1998

'Talchelsea' ('Chelsea Belle') Min, mr, 1991, Taylor, Pete & Kay; bud pointed; flowers medium red with white base, whitish reverse, aging lighter, medium, 28-30 petals, high-centered, borne mostly singly, moderate fragrance; foliage medium size, medium green, semi-glossy; upright, bushy, medium growth; ['Azure Sea' × Party Girl™]; intr. 1990

'Talchris' ('Father Christmas') Min, rb, 1996, Taylor, Franklin; flowers red with white base and white reverse, 1½ in., full, borne in small clusters; foliage small, dark green, semi-glossy; some prickles; low (18 in.), upright, bushy growth; [Party Girl™ × seedling]; intr. 1997

'Talclouseau' ('Clouseau') Min, mr, 1995, Taylor, Pete & Kay; flowers medium red, cream reverse, large, full, borne mostly singly; foliage medium size, dark green, semi-glossy; some prickles; upright, bushy, medium (48 in.) growth; ['Azure Sea' × 'Marijke Koopman']

'Taldal' ('Summerdale') Min, dy, 1991, Taylor, Pete & Kay; bud pointed; flowers deep yellow, aging lighter, medium, 30-35 petals, cupped, loose, borne usually singly and in sprays of 3 - 4, no fragrance; foliage small, medium green, matte; bushy, low growth; ['Rise 'n' Shine' × seedling]; intr. 1990

'Taldearpru' ('Dear Prudence') F, pb, 1995, Taylor, Franklin & Kay; flowers light pink blushing with darker pink edges, medium, dbl., borne in large clusters; foliage medium size, medium green, semi-glossy; some prickles; upright, bushy, medium (38 in.) growth; [seedling × seedling]; intr. 1996

'Taldon' ('Donna Jean') F, m, 1991, Taylor, Pete & Kay; flowers mauve with white eye, medium, semi-dbl., borne singly and in small clusters, no fragrance; foliage medium size, dark green, semi-glossy; medium, upright, bushy growth; ['Azure Sea' × Party Girl™]; intr. 1991

'Taldor' ('Dora Delle') Min, pb, 1991, Taylor, Pete & Kay; flowers light pink with lavender hue, lighter in center, reverse creamy white, medium, full, high-centered, borne usually singly, moderate fragrance; foliage medium size, medium green, semi-glossy; medium, upright growth; ['Azure Sea' × Jean Kenneally™]; intr. 1991

'Taldre' ('Dreamsicle') Min, ob, 1992, Taylor, Franklin "Pete" & Kay; flowers creamy white edged with orangish pink edges, reverse same, large, dbl.; foliage small, medium green, semi-glossy; some prickles; medium (36 cm.), compact growth; ['Poker Chip' × Party Girl™]; intr. 1993

Talea+ HT, lp, Voom, Lex; flowers pale, creamy pink , double, high-centered, borne mostly singly; recurrent; stems medium to long; florist rose; intr. 2004

'Talend' ('Endeavour') Min, ab, 1993, Taylor, Franklin; flowers apricot with yellow base, reverse slightly darker, color fading with age, large, full, slight fragrance; foliage medium size, medium green, semi-glossy; few prickles; medium, upright growth; [Party Girl™ × 'Azure Sea']; intr. 1993

'Talfairhope' ('Fairhope') Min, ly, 1989, Taylor, Franklin "Pete" & Kay; bud pointed; flowers soft, light pastel yellow, aging same, color holds well, 16-28 petals, high-centered; foliage medium size, medium green, semi-glossy; prickles straight, medium, red; upright, bushy, medium growth; hips round, small, green; ['Azure Sea' × seedling]

'Talfat' ('Fat Tuesday') Min, m, 1991, Taylor, Pete & Kay; flowers lavender with darker edges, blending to lighter center, reverse lighter, large, full, borne mostly singly, no fragrance; foliage medium size, medium green, semi-glossy; some prickles; tall (76 cm.), upright growth; ['Azure Sea' × 'Lavender Jewel']; intr. 1992

'Talflora' ('Flora Bama') Min, rb, 1996, Taylor, Franklin; flowers medium red blending to cream center, cream reverse, large, full, borne mostly singly; foliage medium size, dark green, semi-glossy; few prickles; medium (24 in.), upright, spreading growth; [Party Girl™ × 'Poker Chip']; intr. 1997

'Talgeorgia' ('Georgia Belle') MinFl, op, 2000, Taylor, Pete & Kay; flowers orange pink, reverse lighter, 2 in., very full, exhibition, borne mostly singly; foliage medium size, dark green, glossy; prickles moderate; upright, bushy, tall (30 in.) growth; [unknown × 'Gitte']; intr. 2000

'Talgoo' ('Good Day Sunshine') Min, dy, 1992, Taylor, Franklin "Pete" & Kay; flowers bright yellow, reverse same, large, very dbl., high-centered, borne mostly singly; foliage medium size, medium green, semi-glossy; few prickles; medium (60 cm.), upright, bushy, spreading growth; [Party Girl™ × Elina®]; intr. 1993

'Talgul' ('Gulf Breeze') Min, pb, 1991, Taylor, Pete & Kay; flowers creamy getting darker pink toward edges, yellow base, large, very full, borne mostly singly, slight fragrance; foliage medium size, medium green, semi-glossy; some prickles; upright, medium (35 cm.), bushy growth; [Baby Katie™ × 'Poker Chip']; intr. 1992

'Talheather' ('Heather Leigh') Min, mp, 1989, Taylor, Franklin "Pete" & Kay; bud pointed; flowers medium pink, reverse slightly darker, aging lighter, holds color well, 35-40 petals, high-centered, borne singly; foliage medium size, medium green, semi-glossy; prickles straight, small, reddish-brown; upright, bushy, medium growth; no fruit; ['Azure Sea' × 'miniature seedling']

'Talhon' ('Honky Tonk') Min, rb, 1996, Taylor, Franklin "Pete" & Kay; flowers red with darker edges, white reverse, large, dbl., borne mostly singly; foliage medium size, dark green, glossy; numerous prickles; medium (30 in.), upright, bushy growth; [Party Girl™ × seedling]; intr. 1997

'Talia' ('Barsin') S, Barni, V.; intr. 1990

'Talina' ('Ina') Min, w, 1994, Taylor, Franklin "Pete" & Kay; flowers white with pinkish edge, moderately good form, large, dbl., borne in clusters; foliage medium size, medium green, semi-glossy; few prickles; medium (30 in.), upright, bushy growth; [Party Girl™ × 'Fairhope']; intr. 1993

'Talisman' HT, yb, 1929, Montgomery Co.; bud pointed; flowers golden yellow and copper, medium, 25 petals, cupped to flat, moderate fruity, clove fragrance; recurrent; foliage light green, leathery, glossy; vigorous growth; ['Ophelia' × 'Souv. de Claudius Pernet']

'Talisman, Climbing' Cl HT, yb, 1930, Western Rose Co. (also Dixie, 1932); flowers scarlet red and golden yellow, medium, semi-dbl., very fragrance; [sport of 'Talisman']

'Talisman No. 5' HT, yb; flowers deeper color; free bloom

'Taljac' ('Jackson Square') Min, dr, 1995, Taylor, Pete & Kay; flowers dark red, medium, full, borne mostly singly; foliage medium size, medium green, semi-glossy; some prickles; upright, bushy, medium (30 in.) growth; [Jean Kenneally™ × Black Jade™]; intr. 1996

'Taljub' ('Jubilee Sunset') Min, ob, 1991, Taylor, Pete & Kay; flowers bright vivid orange, yellow eye, reverse creamy yellow, bright yellow stamens, large, dbl., borne mostly singly, slight fragrance; foliage medium size, medium green, semi-glossy; some prickles; low (40 cm.), upright, bushy growth; [Baby Katie™ × 'Poker Chip']; intr. 1992

'Taljum' ('Jumping Jack Flash') Min, yb, 1992, Taylor, Franklin "Pete" & Kay; flowers yellow edged with deep pink to red, cream reverse, tipped with deep pink, large, dbl., high-centered; foliage medium size, medium green, semi-glossy; few prickles; medium (42 cm.), upright, bushy growth; [Party Girl™ ×

'Poker Chip']; intr. 1993

'Talkat' ('Katy Lampkin') Min, mp, 1993, Taylor, Franklin; flowers medium pink, cream base, medium, dbl., borne singly and in small clusters, slight fragrance; foliage small, medium green, semi-glossy; few prickles; low (18 in.), compact growth; ['Winsome' × 'Admiral Rodney']; intr. 1993

'Talkev' ('K. T.', 'Kev') Min, dy, 1991, Taylor, Pete & Kay; flowers medium, full, borne mostly singly, no fragrance; foliage medium size, medium green, semi-glossy; medium, upright growth; ['Azure Sea' × Party Girl™]; intr. 1991

'Tall Poppy' -- See 'Morten'

Tall Story® -- See 'Dickooky'

'Tallaz' ('Lazy Daze') Min, m, 1991, Taylor, Pete & Kay; flowers light lavender, reverse slightly darker, white base, large, very full, bloom sometimes quarters, borne mostly singly; foliage small, medium green, semi-glossy; some prickles; low (30 cm.), compact growth; ['Azure Sea' × seedling]; intr. 1992

'Tallou' (Louisiana Lady™) Min, yb, 1997, Taylor, Franklin; flowers medium, full, borne mostly singly; foliage medium size, medium green, semi-glossy; upright, bushy, medium (24 in.) growth; [seedling × seedling]

'Tallulah' -- See 'Beelah'

'Tallyho' HT, dp, 1948, Swim, H.C.; bud urn-shaped; flowers deep pink, 3½-4 in., 35 petals, high-centered, intense spicy fragrance; recurrent; foliage leathery; vigorous, upright, bushy growth; PP828; ['Charlotte Armstrong' × seedling]

'Tallyho, Climbing' Cl HT, dp, 1952, Armstrong, J.A.; PP1087

'Talmag' ('Mary Margaret') Min, op, 1993, Taylor, Franklin; flowers coral pink, creamy yellow base, medium, full, borne mostly singly; foliage medium size, medium green, semi-glossy; few prickles; low (18 in.), spreading growth; [Party Girl™ × 'Watercolor']; intr. 1993

'Talmaid' ('Maids of Jubilee') Min, pb, 1989, Taylor, Franklin "Pete" & Kay; bud pointed; flowers bright deep pink with cream base in center, reverse cream and pink blend, 25-30 petals, high-centered; foliage medium size, dark green, semi-glossy; prickles yellowish-green; upright, bushy, medium growth; ['Azure Sea' × 'miniature seedling']

'Talmar' ('Mary Edith') Min, w, 1991, Taylor, Pete & Kay; flowers white, tipped with pink edges, flower turns darker pink tints with age, medium, full, borne mostly singly, moderate fragrance; foliage medium size, medium green, semi-glossy; low, upright, bushy growth; ['Azure Sea' × seedling]; intr. 1991

'Talmemo' ('Making Memories') Min, mp, 2003, Taylor, Franklin & Kay Taylor; flowers medium pink, reverse lighter, 2 in., dbl., borne mostly solitary; foliage medium size, dark green, Semi-glossy; prickles small, straight, brown, few; growth upright, medium (3 ft.); garden/decorative; ['Mobile Jubilee' × 'Gitte']; intr. 2003

'Talmid' ('Midnight Rambler') Cl Min, rb, 1993, Taylor, Franklin "Pete" & Kay; flowers red with white eye, large, 6-14 petals, borne in small clusters; foliage medium size, medium green, semi-glossy; some prickles; medium (30 in.), spreading growth; [Party Girl™ × 'Andrea']; intr. 1993

'Talmimosa' ('Mimosa Cocktail') HT, ob, 2003, Taylor, Pete & Kay Taylor; flowers soft tangerine with yellow base, ruffled, 4 in., full, decorative, borne mostly solitary, intense fragrance; foliage medium size, medium green, semi-glossy; prickles medium, slight hook, brown, moderate; upright, medium (4 ft.) growth, garden/decorative/cut blooms; [unknown × unknown]; intr. 2003

'Talming' ('Meringue Kisses') Min, ab, 2003, Taylor, Pete & Kay; flowers apricot with yellow base, 1½ in., full, borne in small clusters, slight fragrance; foliage small, dark green, semi-glossy; prickles small, straight, brown; growth compact, medium (2 ft.); garden decorative; [unknown × unknown]; intr. 2003

'Talmobile' ('Mobile Jubilee') Min, op, 1994, Taylor, Franklin; flowers light salmon blending to darker edges, yellow base, large, full; foliage medium size, medium green, semi-glossy; some prickles; tall (90 cm.), upright, bushy growth; [Party Girl™ × 'Gitte']; intr. 1994

'Talmoney' ('Money For Nothing') Min, ab, 2003, Taylor, Franklin (Pete) & Kay Taylor; flowers full, high-centered, borne mostly solitary, moderate fragrance; foliage medium size, medium green, semi-glossy; prickles small, slight hook, brown, few; growth bushy, medium (3 ft.); exhibition, garden decorative, cutting; [unknown × unknown]; intr. 2003

'Talmontrose' ('Montrose') Min, mp, 1994, Taylor, Franklin; flowers medium pink with bright yellow stamens, large, dbl., borne in large clusters, moderate fragrance; foliage medium size, dark green, semi-glossy; some prickles; medium (60 cm.), upright, bushy growth; [Party Girl™ × 'Andrea']; intr. 1994

'Talnola' ('New Orleans Lady') Min, mp, 2003, Taylor, Pete & Kay; flowers medium pink with yellow base, reverse lighter, 1½ in., full, borne mostly solitary, no fragrance; foliage medium size, medium green, semi-glossy; prickles medium, straight, brown, moderate; growth upright, medium (2 ft.); exhibition/garden/cut blooms; [unknown × unknown]; intr. 2003

'Talpen' ('Penny Lane') Min, lp, 1992, Taylor, Franklin; flowers cream base blending to light pink, medium, full, high-centered, no fragrance; foliage small, medium green, semi-glossy; few prickles; medium (38 cm.), upright, bushy growth; [Party Girl™ × 'Maids of Jubilee']; intr. 1993

'Talpin' ('Pink Bunting') Min, mp, 1993, Taylor, Franklin; flowers pink, creamy yellow base blending to pink edges around petals, medium, dbl., no fragrance; foliage small, dark green, semi-glossy; few prickles; low (12 in.), spreading, compact growth; intr. 1993

'Talpoi' ('Point Clear') Min, w, 1991, Taylor, Pete & Kay; flowers white, light yellow base, medium, full, borne mostly singly, slight fragrance; foliage small, medium green, semi-glossy; some prickles; low (40 cm.), upright growth; ['Azure Sea' × Party Girl™]; intr. 1992

'Talras' ('Raspberry Ruffles') F, dp, 1991, Taylor, Pete & Kay; bud pointed; flowers deep pink with white eye, deep pink reverse, aging lighter, medium, 18-20 petals, high-centered, opens flat, borne in sprays of 4 - 6, intense fragrance; foliage medium size, medium green, semi-glossy; upright, bushy, medium growth; ['Garnette' × seedling]; intr. 1990

'Talroad' ('Winding Road') Min, w, 2003, Taylor, Franklin & Kay; flowers white with red edges, 1½ in., full, borne in small clusters, no fragrance; foliage medium size, dark green, semi-glossy; prickles moderate, medium, straight, brown; growth climber, tall (6 to 7 ft.); pillar; ['Nicole' × 'Chelsea Belle']; intr. 2003

'Talrum' ('Rum Butter') Min, ab, 1991, Taylor, Pete & Kay; bud pointed; flowers apricot with yellow base, with a lavender cast blended with apricot, small, semi-dbl., high-centered, borne singly and in sprays of 4-5, no fragrance; foliage medium size, medium green, semi-glossy; upright, bushy, medium growth; ['Azure Sea' × seedling]; intr. 1990

'Talsilver' ('Silverhill') Min, pb, 1996, Taylor, Franklin; flowers pink with mauve tint, blending to cream center and cream reverse, large, full, high-centered; foliage medium size, medium green, semi-glossy; some prickles; medium (36 in.), upright, bushy growth; ['Azure Sea' × seedling]; intr. 1997

'Talsimple' (Simple Pleasures™) Min, rb, 1999, Taylor, Franklin "Pete" & Kay; flowers red petals, white eye, yellow stamens, 1¾ in., single, borne mostly singly; foliage medium size, medium green, semi-glossy; few prickles; upright, spreading, medium (18 in.) growth; intr. 1998

'Talspanish' ('Spanish Fort') Min, pb, 2003, Taylor, Franklin & Kay; flowers medium pink, yellow base, reverse lighter, 2 in., dbl., borne mostly solitary, slight fragrance; foliage medium size, medium green, semi-glossy; prickles medium, slight hook, brown, few; growth upright, medium (2 ft.); garden/decorative; [unknown × unknown]; intr. 2003

'Talspi' ('Cajun Spice') Min, ob, 1993, Taylor, Franklin; flowers bright orange, white eye, light reverse, large, semi-dbl., borne mostly singly, no fragrance;

foliage medium size, medium green, semi-glossy; some prickles; medium (24 in.), upright, bushy growth; [Party Girl™ × Baby Diana™]; intr. 1993

'Talsprings' (Magnolia Springs™) Min, w, 1999, Taylor, Franklin "Pete" & Kay; flowers white with pink edge, greenish guard petals, 2 in., 41 petals, borne in large clusters; foliage medium size, medium green, semi-glossy; few prickles; upright, bushy, medium (18 in.) growth; intr. 1998

'Talsue' ('Sue Belle') Min, ob, 1992, Taylor, Franklin "Pete" & Kay; flowers orange with yellow eye, yellow stamens, aging to pink, large, 6-14 petals; foliage small, medium green, semi-glossy; some prickles; medium (40 cm.), upright, bushy growth; [Party Girl™ × 'Poker Chip']; intr. 1993

'Talsugar' (Sugar Magnolia™) F, w, 1999, Taylor, Franklin "Pete" & Kay; flowers white, burgundy pistil and stamens, set against fleshtone petals, 2¾ in., dbl., borne in small clusters; foliage medium size, dark green, semi-glossy; few prickles; upright, bushy (3 ft.) growth; intr. 1998

'Talsum' ('Summer Breeze') Min, op, 1991, Taylor, Pete & Kay; flowers light orange-pink, ages lighter, yellow base, reverse slightly darker, medium, full, borne mostly singly or in small clusters, slight fragrance; foliage medium size, medium green, semi-glossy; some prickles; low (40 cm.), spreading growth; [Baby Katie™ × 'Poker Chip']; intr. 1992

'Talsun' ('Sunny Afternoon') Min, yb, 1995, Taylor, Franklin; flowers light yellow, outer edges pinkish/apricot tinge, 1½ in., dbl., borne mostly singly; foliage medium size, medium green, semi-glossy; some prickles; medium, upright, bushy growth; [Party Girl™ × Elina®]; intr. 1995

'Talsweet' ('Sweet Home Alabama') Min, pb, 1995, Taylor, Franklin; flowers magenta pink with white reverse, white eye, 1½ in., full, borne mostly singly; foliage medium size, medium green, semi-glossy; some prickles; upright, bushy, medium growth; [Party Girl™ × 'Azure Sea']; intr. 1996

'Taltrick' ('Trick Or Treat') Min, ob, 1996, Taylor, Franklin "Pete" & Kay; flowers orange blending to yellow base, 1½ in., 41 petals, flat, borne mostly singly; foliage small, medium green, semi-glossy; few prickles; medium (24 in.), upright, bushy growth; [seedling × seedling]; intr. 1997

'Taluptown' ('Uptown') Min, m, 1991, Taylor, Pete & Kay; flowers lavender, edges darker violet, reverse lighter, yellow base, medium, full, exhibition, borne mostly singly, no fragrance; foliage medium size, medium green, semi-glossy; some prickles; medium (46 cm.), upright, bushy growth; ['Azure Sea' × Party Girl™]; intr. 1992

'Talwil' ('Wildest Dreams') Min, yb, 1992, Taylor, Franklin "Pete" & Kay; flowers yellow blending to deep pink edges, aging lighter, reverse yellow, large, dbl.; foliage small, medium green, semi-glossy; few prickles; medium (40 cm.), upright, bushy growth; ['Poker Chip' × unknown]; intr. 1993

'Tam o'Shanter' F, yb, 1969, Cocker; flowers yellow and red, dbl., borne in clusters; low, compact growth; [Orange Sensation® × 'Circus']

'Tam Tam' F, my, 1961, Boerner; bud ovoid; flowers yellow flushed pink, 3 in., 35-40 petals, cupped, moderate fragrance; foliage glossy; vigorous, upright growth; PP2181; RULED EXTINCT 1/88; [('Goldilocks' × unknown) × ('Demure' × unknown)]; intr. 1961

'Tam-Tam' Min, lp, 1988, Onodera, Toru F.; flowers inner petals upright, 18-20 petals, flat, borne in large clusters; foliage small, light green; hips elongated, orange; [('Nozomi' × 'Nozomi') × 'Bo-Peep']

'Tama' HT, op, 1989, Sato, Kohi; bud pointed; flowers salmon-pink, fringed with pink, reverse creamy yellow, large, 35 petals, high-centered, urn-shaped, borne in sprays of 2 or 3, slight fragrance; foliage dark green; prickles small, lower part hollow; upright, tall growth; ['Red Lion' × 'Garden Party']

Tamango® F, dr, 1967, Meilland, Mrs. Marie-Louise; flowers rose red with crimson shading, large, 35 petals, cupped, borne in large clusters, slight fragrance; free-flowering; foliage clear green; vigorous, free growth; PP2857; [('Alain' × 'Mutabilis') × ('Radar' × 'Caprice')]

Tamango® ('Tamango Folies') F, dr, Olij; flowers full, cupped, borne in clusters; recurrent; intr. 1998

'Tamango Folies' -- See 'Tamango'

'Tamara' HT, mr, 1969, Mondial Roses; flowers geranium-red, dbl., high-centered; foliage dark; very vigorous growth; ['Parel van Aalsmeer' × 'Independence']; intr. 1966

'Tamara' F, ab, Kordes; flora-tea; intr. 1988

'Tamarisk' HT, mp, 1954, Ratcliffe, R. & E.; flowers clear rose-pink, camellia-like, intense fragrance; foliage leathery, dull green; very vigorous growth; ['Mme Butterfly' × 'Signora']

'Tamayuru' HT, ob, Hiroshima; intr. 2002

'Tambourine' F, rb, 1959, Dickson, A.; flowers cherry-red, base yellow, reverse light burnt-orange, large, 25 petals, borne in clusters, slight fragrance; foliage dark, veined; vigorous, tall, bushy growth; [('Independence' × unknown) × 'Karl Herbst']; intr. 1958

'Tambourine' -- See 'Hardolly'

'Tammy' Pol, lp, 1974, Byrum (possibly 'Sweet, Jack'); flowers medium, dbl., high-centered, moderate fragrance; foliage large, leathery; vigorous, upright, bushy growth; PP3094; ['Seventeen' × 'Jack Frost']; intr. 1972

Tammy Darlene™ -- See 'Rictammy'

'Tamora' -- See 'Austamora'

'Tamouree' F, Combe

Tampa Bay™ -- See 'Kinbay'

'Tampico' HT, or, 1974, Warriner, William A.; bud ovoid, long, pointed; flowers coral-pink, 4-5 in., 30-35 petals, high-centered, borne mostly singly, slight fragrance; recurrent; foliage large, leathery; prickles normal, long, hooked downward; stems long, strong; vigorous, upright growth; PP3677; ['South Seas' × 'Hawaii']; intr. 1976

'Tamrabarani' -- See 'Southern Sunset'

'Tan Cho' ('Crane', 'Tanche') HT, rb; intr. 1986

'Tan00107' HT, rb, Tantau; intr. 2003
'Tan00125' HT, yb, Tantau; intr. 2003
'Tan00146' ('Mary') HT, or, Tantau; intr. 2003
'Tan00151' HT, dy, Tantau; intr. 2003
'Tan00163' HT, lp, Tantau; intr. 2003
'Tan00370' HT, w, Tantau; intr. 2004
'Tan00641' HT, pb, Tantau; intr. 2007
'Tan00814' Min, dr, Tantau; intr. 2007
'Tan00942' HT, dp, Tantau; intr. 2007
'Tan01030' HT, rb, Tantau; intr. 2007
'Tan01220' Ht, dy, Tantau; intr. 2005
'Tan01221' HT, ob, Tantau; intr. 2005
'Tan01250' HT, ab, Tantau; intr. 2006
'Tan01441' HT, ob, Tantau; intr. 2004
'Tan01541' HT, dr, Tantau; intr. 2007
'Tan01549' HT, mr, Tantau; intr. 2004
'Tan01579' HT, w, Tantau; intr. 2004
'Tan01622' HT , op, Tantau; intr. 2005
'Tan01687' HT, pb, Tantau; intr. 2006
'Tan01693' HT, ab, Tantau; intr. 2004
'Tan01993' HT, w, Tantau; intr. 2005
'Tan01994' HT, rb, Tantau; intr. 2004
'Tan02056' HT, lp, Tantau; intr. 2006
'Tan02060' HT, rb, Tantau; intr. 2006
'Tan02066' HT, my, Tantau; intr. 2006
'Tan02360' HT, w, Tantau; intr. 2007
'Tan02474' HT, w, Tantau; intr. 2006
'Tan02522' HT, w, Tantau; intr. 2006
'Tan02525' HT, ly, Tantau; intr. 2006
'Tan02584' HT, ob, Tantau; intr. 2006
'Tan02997' HT, ob, Tantau; intr. 2006
'Tan02998' HT, dy, Tantau; intr. 2007
'Tan03244' HT, rb, Tantau; intr. 2007
'Tan03266' HT, mp, Tantau; intr. 2007
'Tan03384' HT, or, Tantau; intr. 2007
'Tan03388' HT, pb, Tantau; intr. 2007
'Tan03434' HT, op, Tantau; intr. 2007
'Tan04111' HT, lp, Tantau; intr. 2007
'Tan94448' HT, dy, Tantau; intr. 2003
'Tan94475' ('Sweetie') Min, ab, Tantau; intr. 2002
'Tan9576' Min, mr, Tantau; intr. 2004
'Tan96138' HT, m, Tantau; intr. 2004
'Tan96145' HT, ob, Tantau; intr. 2006
'Tan96205' ('Rick Stein') HT, ab, Tantau; intr. 2005
'Tan96295' HT, dp, Tantau; intr. 2003
'Tan97103' HT, mp, Tantau; intr. 2005
'Tan97150' S, m, Tantau; intr. 2005
'Tan97159' ('The Duchess of Cornwall') HT, op, Tantau; intr. 2006

'Tan97174' F, yb, Tantau; intr. 2002
'Tan97497' HT, ob, Tantau; intr. 2001
'Tan97607' F, m, Tantau; intr. 2005
'Tan98055' HT, dr, Tantau; intr. 2001
'Tan98106' S, mr, Tantau; intr. 2008
'Tan98145' Min, w, Tantau; intr. 2006
'Tan98145' Min, w, Tantau; intr. 2007
'Tan98264' ('Honeybun') Min, ab, Tantau; intr. 2006
'Tan98351' HT, pb, Tantau; intr. 2003
'Tan98356' HT, mr, Tantau; intr. 2004
'Tan98398' HT, pb, Tantau; intr. 2004
'Tan98399' (Shanty®) HT, rb, Tantau; intr. 2002
'Tan98485' HT, m; intr. 2002
'Tan99065' HT, rb, Tantau; bud pointed ovoid; intr. 2002
'Tan99317' HT, lp, Tantau; intr. 2003
'Tan99520' HT, ab, Tantau; intr. 2003
'Tanabamar' S, ob, Evers, Hans-Jurgen; bud rounded; intr. 2002
'Tanadac' ('Escada') F, mr, Tantau; intr. 1994
'Tanadeepdac' HT, dr, Tantau
'Tanafira' F, rb, Tantau
'Tanaggar' HT, ob, Tantau; intr. 1997
'Tanagnarat' (Taranga®) F, mr, 1983, Tantau, Math.; flowers medium, semi-dbl. to dbl., cupped, borne in large clusters, slight fragrance; free-flowering; foliage medium size, medium green, semi-glossy; bushy, upright (3 ft.) growth; intr. 1981
'Tanagosh' ('Constanze') LCl, pb, Tantau; intr. 2000
Tanagra® HT, or, 1969, Gaujard; bud long, pointed; flowers large, dbl.; foliage soft; vigorous, upright growth; [Queen Elizabeth® × 'Tropicana']
'Tanakinom' (Monika®) HT, pb, 1985, Tantau, Math.; flowers medium, 35 petals; foliage medium size, dark, glossy; upright growth
'Tanakni' HT, dy, Tantau; intr. 1993
'Tanal' F, or, 1959, Tantau, Math.; intr. 1958
'Tanalam' ('Unforgettable') HT, dr, Tantau
'Tanaledef' HT, w, Evers, Hans J.; bud long, pointed ovoid; intr. 1997
'Tanaledev' HT, w, Evers, Hans J.; bud long, pointed ovoid; intr. 1997
'Tanalednev' ('Velvet Star') HT, w, Tantau
'Tanalephar' HT, ob, Tantau; bud long pointed, ovoid; intr. 1994
'Tanallepa' ('Charlie Dimmock', 'Charlies Rose', Acapella®) HT, pb, 2000, Tantau, Math.; bud long, pointed; flowers pink, reverse silver pink, 14-15 cm., full, borne mostly singly, intense fragrance; foliage large, dark green, semi-glossy; numerous prickles; upright, vigorous growth, 100-120 cm; [seedling × seedling]; intr. 1998
'Tanallet' (Castella®) S, mr, 1985, Tantau, Math.; flowers medium, semi-dbl.; foliage large, dark, semi-glossy; upright growth; intr. 1984
'Tanaloap' ('Paola') HT, mr, 1983, Tantau, Math.; flowers large, 20 petals, high-centered, moderate fragrance; foliage large, dark, matte; intr. 1981
'Tanaluma' Min, pb, Tantau; intr. 1991
'Tanalzergo' ('Moonlight Serenade', Pfälzer Gold®) HT, dy, 1983, Tantau, Math.; flowers large, 20 petals, no fragrance; intr. 1981
'Tanamola' ('La Paloma 85', 'The Dove') F, w, 1985, Tantau, Math.; flowers medium, 20 petals, no fragrance; foliage medium size, light green, glossy; upright growth
'Tananaistrua' ('Austriana') F, mr, 2000, Tantau, Math.; flowers small, single, borne in large clusters, no fragrance; foliage medium size, dark green, glossy, disease-resistant; prickles moderate; growth compact, low; [seedling × seedling]; intr. 1996
'Tananilov' (Violina®) HT, pb, Tantau; bud long, pointed, dark pink; intr. 1997
'Tananim' ('Romina') HT, dp, Tantau; intr. 1994
'Tananitap' HT, w, Tantau; intr. 1997
'Tanaran' HT, ob, Tantau; intr. 1998
'Tanarasah' S, yb, Tantau; intr. 1996
'Tanaronam' (Manora®) HT, mr, Tantau; intr. 1992
'Tanarua' HT, ab, Tantau; intr. 1997
'Tanatesil' (Ilseta®) F, mp, 1985, Tantau, Math.; flowers medium, 35 petals; foliage medium size, medium green, matte; upright growth; PP5707; intr. 1983
'Tanatiram' (Marietta®) F, yb, 1985, Tantau, Math.; flowers gold, yellow and orange, medium, 20 petals, no fragrance; foliage medium green, glossy; upright growth
'Tanattenin' (Ninetta®) F, dp, 1985, Tantau, Math.; flowers deep pink, medium, 20 petals; foliage medium green, semi-glossy; upright growth
'Tanattigam' (Magitta®) HT, mr, 1983, Tantau, Math.; flowers large, 20 petals; foliage medium size, medium green, semi-glossy; upright growth; intr. 1981
'Tanatulp' F, mr, Tantau, Math.; intr. 1986
'Tanau' ('Pétillante') HT, dp, 1963, Tantau, Math.; bud pointed
'Tanavilo' ('Lola') HT, mr, Tantau
'Tanavit' F, ob, Tantau
'Tanavl' HT, ob, Tantau; intr. 1999
'Tanavlim' F, m, 1985, Tantau, Math.; flowers medium, 35 petals; foliage medium size, medium green, semi-glossy; upright growth; intr. 1983
'Tanba' ('Baby Carnaval', 'Baby Mascarade', 'Baby Maskarade', 'Baby Carnival', Baby Masquerade®) Min, rb, 1956, Tantau, Math.; bud ovoid; intr. 1956
'Tanbak' S, yb, Tantau; intr. 2000
'Tanbakede' ('Baby Carnaval', 'Baby Mascarade', 'Baby Maskarade', 'Baby Carnival', Baby Masquerade®) Min, rb, 1956, Tantau, Math.; bud ovoid; intr. 1956
'Tanbeedee' ('Belinda') F, ob, 1973, Tantau, Math.; bud ovoid; flowers copper to orange, medium, dbl., moderate fragrance; vigorous, upright, bushy growth; PP3382; [seedling × 'Zorina']; intr. 1971
'Tanblady' (Black Lady®) HT, dr, 1977, Tantau, Math.; bud globose; flowers blackish-red, medium, dbl., intense fragrance; foliage matte; bushy growth; intr. 1976
'Tanbror' HT, r, Tantau; intr. 1999
'Tanca' HT, rb, 1970, Tantau, Math.; bud pointed; intr. 1967
'Tancary' ('Canary') HT, yb, 1976, Tantau, Math.; flowers yellow, petals marked orange, well-formed, medium, dbl.; intr. 1972
'Tanceila' F, w, Tantau; intr. 1988
'Tancelia' F, w, Tantau; intr. 1988
'Tanche' -- See 'Tan Cho'
'Tancheab' HT, r, Tantau; intr. 2001
'Tancofeuma' (Cosima®) F, or, 1983, Tantau, Math.; flowers medium, 20 petals, no fragrance; foliage large, dark, glossy; intr. 1981
'Tancrède' HP, mr, 1876, Oger; flowers medium, full, globular
'Tancressor' (Celebrate America™) HT, mr, 1991, Rosen Tantau; flowers crimson red, 4-4¾ in., 45-55 petals, high-centered, borne usually singly; foliage large, medium green, semi-glossy; upright, spreading, medium growth; PP7333; [seedling × seedling]; intr. 1990
'Tandalaum' ('Dreamland') F, lp, 1959, Tantau, Math.; intr. 1958
'Tandelbel' ('Magenta Diadem') F, m, Tantau; intr. 1994
'Tandinadi' (Diana®) F, my, 1978, Tantau, Math.; bud globular; flowers medium, dbl., slight fragrance; foliage medium size, glossy; vigorous, upright growth
'Tandirpkrap' ('Parkstown's Pride') HT, pb, Tantau; intr. 1990
'Tandomo' ('Domino') Min, mr, Tantau; intr. 1994
'Tanduft' ('Duftgold', 'Fragrant Gold', 'Summer Gold') HT, dy, 1983, Tantau, Math.; intr. 1981
'Tandugoft' ('Duftgold', 'Fragrant Gold', 'Summer Gold') HT, dy, 1983, Tantau, Math.; flowers large, semi-dbl., moderate fragrance; foliage medium size, dark, glossy; upright growth; intr. 1981
'Tane' -- See 'Simetna'
'Tanecnice' F, mr, Strnad
'Tanedallab' ('Ballade') F, lp, Tantau; intr. 1991
'Tanefle' (Elfe®) HT, lp, 1985, Tantau, Math.; flowers medium, 20 petals; foliage medium size, medium green, matte; upright growth; intr. 1982
'Tanegnaro' ('Orange Baby', 'Orange Babyflor') Min, or, Tantau; intr. 1994
'Taneidol' ('Frank Michael', 'Majora') F, rb, Tantau
'Taneiglat' ('Antique Nostalgia', 'La Garçonne') HT, rb, Tantau; intr. 1995
'Taneitber' (Bernstein®) F, dy, Tantau; intr. 1987

'Taneivom' ('Movie Star') HT, op, Tantau; intr. 1995

'Tanekily' ('Ionian Rose') HT, pb, Tantau; intr. 1989

'Tanelaigib' F, pb, Tantau; intr. 1988

'Tanelfe' ('L'Alcazar') LCl, w, Tantau; intr. 2001

'Taneliet' ('African Queen') HT, dp, Tantau; intr. 1996

'Tanelleira' (Cosima®) HT, mp, Tantau; intr. 2001

'Tanellelog' ('Gold Fountain') F, dy, Tantau, Math.; intr. 1988

'Tanellis' ('Fragrant Cloud', 'Nuage Parfumé') HT, or, 1967, Tantau, Math.; bud ovoid; intr. 1968

'Tanelliv' ('Glowing Achievement') F, mr, Tantau; intr. 1990

'Tanellqua' HT, yb, Tantau; intr. 2002

'Tanelorak' ('Grand Château', Barkarole®, Taboo™) HT, dr, 1993, Evers, Hans & Rosen Tantau; bud pointed, ovoid, almost black; flowers deepest red, velvety, 4-5 in., 25-30 petals, high-centered, borne mostly singly, moderate sweet citrus fragrance; recurrent; foliage large, dark green, semi-glossy; prickles some, large, hooked downward; stems long, strong; tall (170 cm.), upright, bushy growth; PP7665; [seedling × seedling]; intr. 1994

'Tanema' ('Sir Harry Pilkington', Melina®) HT, mr, 1973, Tantau; flowers well-formed, 4-5 in., 30 petals, high-centered, borne mostly singly; foliage dark; [Inge Horstmann × Sophia Loren®]

'Tanemita' HT, ob, Tantau; intr. 1994

'Tanemrac' ('Carmen') HT, or, Tantau; intr. 1986

'Tanenimel' S, mp, Tantau; intr. 1998

'Tanensch' (Schneeweisschen®) Min, w, Tantau; intr. 1992

'Tanerised' (Desirée®) HT, lp, 1985, Tantau, Math.; flowers large, 35 petals; foliage large, dark, semi-glossy; upright growth; intr. 1985

'Tanerou' -- See 'Juwena'

'Taneselbon' HT, op, Tantau; intr. 1989

'Tanessenor' HT, or, Tantau; intr. 1989

'Tanetidor' ('Foundation') HT, ab, Tantau; intr. 2003

'Tanetorde' (Red Diadem®) F, dr, Tantau; intr. 1991

'Tanettola' ('Charlotte') HT, mr, Evers, Hans-Jurgen; bud long, pointed ovoid; intr. 1997

'Tanezamor' ('Romance', 'Romanze') S, mp, 1985, Tantau, Math.; flowers medium, petals ruffled, 9 cm., 20 petals, borne in clusters, slight fragrance; recurrent; foliage medium size, dark green, semi-glossy; bushy, upright (5 ft.) growth; intr. 1984

'Tanfifum' ('Blue Perfume', Blue Parfum®, 'Violette Parfum') HT, m, 1978, Tantau, Math.; bud ovoid; flowers mauve-blush, large, dbl.; foliage glossy; bushy, upright growth; intr. 1977

'Tanfudermos' ('Summer Fragrance', Sommerduft®) HT, dr, 1985, Tantau, Math.; flowers very dark red, medium-large, 20 petals, high-centered, borne mostly singly, moderate spicy fragrance; recurrent; foliage medium size, dark, semi-glossy; stems long, strong; upright growth; intr. 1986

'Tanfulltax' S, dp, Tantau; intr. 2002

'Tangeglow' -- See 'Dicmadder'

'Tanger' HT, rb, 1949, Dot, Pedro; bud ovoid; flowers crimson, reverse yellow, large, 60 petals; moderate, compact growth; ['Condesa de Sástago' × 'Peace']

'Tanger Folies' F, ob, Keisei; flowers orange, yellow reverse, dbl., cupped, borne in clusters; recurrent; intr. 2004

'Tangerina' HT, ob, Dickson; intr. 2004

'Tangerine' HT, op, 1942, Joseph H. Hill, Co.; bud globular, coral-red; flowers light salmon-orange,, 3½-4 in., 30-35 petals; foliage dark, leathery; strong stems; vigorous, very upright, well branched growth; PP566; ['Capt. Glisson' × R.M.S. Queen Mary]

'Tangerine' HT, ob, Dickson; intr. 2004

'Tangerine Contempo' F, ob, 1985, Gupta, Dr. M.N. & Datta, Dr. S.K.; flowers tangerine orange; [sport of 'Contempo']; intr. 1983

Tangerine Dream™ -- See 'Meimonblan'

'Tangerine Jewel' -- See 'Mortange'

'Tangerine Mist' -- See 'Renist'

'Tangerine Twist' -- See 'Mictwist'

'Tangier' HT, rb, 1955, Parmentier, J.; bud long, pointed; flowers peach-red to scarlet-copper, medium, 60 petals, high-centered; vigorous, bushy growth; PP1400; ['Katharine Pechtold' × R.M.S. Queen Mary]

'Tangiwdul' S, mp, Tantau; intr. 1994

Tangkul Treasure™ -- See 'Virtreasure'

'Tango' HT, mr, 1937, H&S; flowers scarlet, reverse bronze, base shaded old-gold; vigorous growth; [seedling × 'Talisman']

Tango™ LCl, lp, Poulsen; flowers light pink, 5-8 cm., dbl., no fragrance; foliage dark; growth bushy, 100-150 cm.; PP15956; intr. 2002

'Tango' HT, mr, Delforge; bud long; flowers tango-red, open, large, dbl., moderate fragrance; foliage dark, glossy; vigorous, bushy growth; ['The Doctor' × 'Karl Herbst']; intr. 1955

'Tango' -- See 'Jacboy'

'Tango' -- See 'Macfirwal'

'Tango Rose' -- See 'Deltanga'

'Tango Showground' S, ob; intr. 2006

'Tangolca' (Golden Monica®) HT, dy, Tantau; intr. 1988

'Tangonc' HT, my, Tantau; intr. 2000

'Tangostar' ('Tropicana, Climbing') Cl HT, or, 1966, Blaby; bud pointed

'Tangust' ('Fox-Trot', 'Hayley Westenra', 'Rachel') S, pb, Tantau; intr. 2000

'Tania' ('Landora') HT, dy, 1971, Tantau, Math.; intr. 1970

'Tania Verstak' HT, mr, 1964, Armbrust; flowers rich red, large, dbl.; foliage light green, soft; vigorous, upright growth; ['Charlotte Armstrong' × 'Happiness']; intr. 1962

'Tanibara' F, ob, Tantau; intr. 1986

'Tanigino' ('Neige d'Été', 'Schneekönigin', Magic Blanket™, 'Regina della Neve') S, w, 1999, Evers, Hans & Rosen Tantau; flowers creamy white, blushed light pink, 2½ in., 12-21 petals, flat, borne in large clusters, self cleaning, slight sweet fragrance; foliage medium size, dark green, glossy; prickles moderate; growth spreading, mounding, medium (to 3 ft.); groundcover; intr. 1992

'Tanija' (Janina®) HT, ob, Tantau; intr. 1974

'Tanilasor' (Rosali 83®, Rosali®) F, mp, 1985, Tantau, Math.; flowers apple blossom pink, medium, 20 petals, borne in clusters, no fragrance; free-flowering; foliage medium size, medium green, glossy; compact, bushy, low growth; winter hardy; intr. 1983

'Tanilknip' Gr, Tantau; intr. 1986

'Tanilsepo' (Perl-Ilseta®) F, w, 1985, Tantau, Math.; flowers pearly white; [sport of Ilseta®]; intr. 1984

'Tanilvoba' (Orange Ilseta®) F, ob, 1985, Tantau, Math.; flowers orange; [sport of Ilseta®]

'Tanilyks' ('Skyline') HT, my, Tantau; bud long, pointed ovoid; intr. 1991

'Tanimita' HT, m, Tantau; intr. 2001

'Taninaso' ('Le Plessis Robinson', 'Satina') S, w, Tantau; intr. 1993

'Taninat' ('Harewood') S, mp, Tantau; intr. 1992

'Tanipep' (Pepino®) F, lp, Tantau; intr. 1987

'Tanipilanmau' ('Sogno Rosa') F, mp, Tantau; intr. 1996

'Tanireb' ('Belle of Berlin') HT, mp, Tantau; bud long, slim; intr. 1994

'Taniripsa' ('Aspirin', 'Glacier Magic', 'Special Child', 'Aspirin-Rose') F, w, 2001, Rosen Tantau; flowers white, shadings of pink, 6 cm., dbl., cupped, borne in large clusters, slight fragrance; recurrent; foliage large, medium green, glossy; prickles medium, curved, moderate; compact, bushy, medium growth; garden, containers; [seedling × seedling]; intr. 1997

'Tanitef' (Konfetti®) HT, ob, Tantau; intr. 1991

'Tanito' F, w, 1973, Tantau, Math.; bud ovoid

'Tanjack' HT, dp, Tantau; intr. 2002

'Tanjeka' ('Jehoca', 'Jessica', Jessika®) HT, op, 1974, Tantau, Math.; bud long, pointed; flowers peach-salmon, medium, dbl., moderate fragrance; free-flowering; vigorous, upright growth; ['Colour Wonder' × Piccadilly®]; intr. 1971

'Tanjenju' (Jennie June™) HT, mr, 1990, Rosen Tantau; bud ovoid; flowers medium red, reverse lighter with some bluing, large, 50 petals, high-centered, borne usually singly, slight fragrance; foliage large, medium green, semi-glossy; prickles short, narrow, hooked down, red-green; upright, spreading, medium growth; [seedling × seedling]; intr. 1990

'Tanjuka' ('Juleschke') F, mr, 1974, Tantau, Math.; bud long, pointed

'Tanjuwe' F, dy, Tantau; intr. 2003

'Tankalcig' ('Black Magic') HT, dr, Tantau; bud almost black, pointed, ovoid buds; intr. 1997

'Tankanusch' (Anuschka®) F, or, 1978, Tantau, Math.; bud ovoid; flowers large, 23 petals; foliage large; bushy, upright growth

'Tankeijoli' (Majolika®) F, lp, Tantau; bud creamy ivory; intr. 1988

'Tankenfram' (Frankenland®) F, or, 1982, Tantau, Math.; bud medium, pointed; flowers brilliant scarlet, 23 petals, high-centered, borne in large clusters, no fragrance; foliage large, dark, semi-glossy; prickles straight, brown-red; bushy, low growth; intr. 1978

'Tanklesant' (Santana®) LCl, mr, 1985, Tantau, Math.; flowers vermilion-red, 4 in., 20 petals, borne in small clusters, no fragrance; foliage large, medium green, glossy; upright growth

'Tanklewi' ('Lavinia', Lawinia®) LCl, mp, 1983, Tantau, Math.; flowers translucent pink, darker at center, 4 in., 20 petals, cupped, moderate fragrance; foliage large, medium green, semi-glossy; spreading (to 8 ft.) growth; intr. 1980

'Tankobi' (Bubikopf®) MinFl, pb, Tantau, Math.; intr. 1986

'Tankorab' ('Barock') HT, my, Tantau; intr. 1990

'Tanky' ('Whisky') HT, yb, 1969, Tantau, Math.; bud ovoid; intr. 1967

'Tanlarpost' ('Evita', 'Polar Spire', 'Polar Star', Polarstern®) HT, w, 1983, Tantau, Math.; flowers pale yellow to white, medium, 35 petals, high-centered, slight fragrance; good repeat; foliage medium size, medium green, matte; bushy growth; intr. 1982

'Tanledolg' ('Bijou d'Or', 'Peter Mac Gold Jewel', Goldjuwel®) Min, dy, Tantau; intr. 1995

'Tanli' F, mp, 1973, Tantau, Math.; bud long, pointed; intr. 1971

'Tanlilida' (Dalli Dalli®) F, dr, 1979, Tantau, Math.; bud ovoid; flowers medium, dbl., cupped, slight fragrance; foliage very glossy; upright, bushy growth; intr. 1977

'Tanliram' ('Marlyn') HT, mp, Tantau; intr. 1977

'Tanlopo' ('A Royal Bride') HT, w, 2001, Rosen Tantau; flowers full, borne mostly solitary, slight fragrance; foliage medium size, medium green, glossy; prickles medium, straight, moderate; upright, tall (100 cm.) growth; garden, cut flower; [seedling × seedling]; intr. 2001

'Tanlorip' ('Pirol') Pol, dy, Tantau; intr. 1994

'Tanlypolo' (Polygold®) F, dy, 1983, Tantau, Math.; flowers medium, semi-dbl., no fragrance; foliage medium size, light green, glossy; bushy growth; intr. 1978

'Tanmaritan' ('Orchid Splendour') HT, m, Tantau

'Tanmarsa' ('Bora Bora', 'King David') HT, r, Tantau; intr. 1998

'Tanmauve' ('Cloud No. 9') HT, m, Tantau

'Tanmeda' ('Diadeem', 'Royal Bouquet') F, mp, Tantaudbl.; intr. 1986

'Tanmirsch' ('Broadlands', 'Canicule', 'Golden Touch') S, my, Tantau; intr. 1993

'Tanmixa' ('Joy of Life', 'Maxime') HT, rb, Tantau; intr. 1993

'Tanmop' F, mp, Tantau; intr. 1984

'Tanmosina' ('Simona') HT, ab, 1982, Tantau, Math.; flowers large, 20 petals, moderate fragrance; foliage large, medium green, matte; upright growth; intr. 1979

'Tanmurse' ('Blenheim') S, w, Tantau

'Tannacht' ('Blå Måndag', 'Blue Monday', 'Mainzer Fastnacht', 'Sissi') HT, m, 1965, Tantau, Math.; bud long, pointed; intr. 1964

'Tannali' F, dr, 1973, Tantau, Math.; bud ovoid

'Tanned Beauty' -- See 'Triolet'

'Tanned Toddler' F, ab; flowers buff apricot, medium, hybrid tea, moderate fragrance; free-flowering; stems short, firm; short, compact growth; intr. 2000

'Tannietnof' ('Stifontein Rose') HT, ob, Tantau

'Tannimoll' ('Mistigri') F, or, 1964, Tantau, Math.dbl.

'Tannipola' (Lapponia®) F, op, 1978, Tantau, Math.; bud broadly ovoid; flowers medium salmon-pink, 25 petals; bushy, upright growth

'Tannus' ('Capri Sun') HT, ob, Tantau; intr. 1991

'Tanob' F, op, 1959, Tantau, Math.; intr. 1955

'Tanobmam' F, ob, Tantau; intr. 1998

'Tanobmil' HT, dy; intr. 2002

'Tanodakim' F, mp, Tantau

'Tanogrew' ('Showdown') Min, ob, Tantau

'Tanokor' (Rokoko®) S, ly, Tantau; intr. 1987

'Tanolfeu' (Olympisches Feuer®) F, ob, 1973, Tantau, Math.; bud ovoid; flowers orange, medium, dbl.; upright growth; ['Ahoi' × Signalfeuer®]; intr. 1971

'Tanolfeu92' ('Olympic Fire') F, or, Tantau; intr. 1992

'Tanolg' ('Anneliesse Rothenberger', 'Silhouette', 'Oregold') HT, dy, 1970, Tantau, Math.; intr. 1970

'Tanolgnil' ('Barley Gold', 'Bowled Over', Goldelse®, 'Golden Fancy', 'Mulbry Rose') F, ab, 2001, Rosen Tantau; flowers amber yellow, reverse amber yellow, 5 cm., dbl., borne in small clusters; foliage small, medium green, glossy; prickles moderate; growth compact, medium; garden decoration, containers; [seedling × seedling]

'Tanollipa' ('Papillon') HT, my, Tantau; intr. 1997

'Tanolokip' (Piccolo®) F, or, 1985, Tantau, Math.; flowers medium, 20 petals, no fragrance; foliage large, dark green, glossy; upright growth; intr. 1983

'Tanolop' ('Polo') HT, w, Tantau; intr. 1997

'Tanonicca' HT, dy, Tantau; intr. 1999

'Tanope' F, op, Tantau, Math.; intr. 1964

'Tanopina' HT, mr, Tantau; intr. 1998

'Tanoras' ('Renown's Rosario') S, mp, Tantau; intr. 1993

'Tanorelav' ('Red Velvet') HT, dr, Tantau; intr. 1994

'Tanoronez' ('Chateau Merlot', 'Red Mirato') S, mr, Tantau; bud pointed ovoid; intr. 2002

'Tanorstar' ('Tropicana') HT, or, 1960, Tantau, Math.; bud pointed; intr. 1960

'Tanosyl' -- See 'Calypso'

'Tanotax' ('Chatsworth', 'Mirato', 'Footloose') S, dp, 1998, Evers, Hans; Tantau; bud pointed ovoid; flowers , 20-25 petals, high-centered, borne in large clusters, no fragrance; recurrent; foliage small, dark green, glossy; prickles moderate, straight; stems strong, 14 - 18 in.; growth spreading, bushy, medium (3½ ft.); PP11572; [seedling × Rosali 83®]; intr. 1990

'Tanotika' HT, w, Tantau; intr. 1998

'Tanpen' ('Penny Heyns') F, ly, Tantau; intr. 1997

'Tanpika' (Piroschka®) HT, mp, 1972, Tantau, Math.; bud long, pointed; flowers large, dbl.; moderate, upright growth; ['Fragrant Cloud' × 'Dr. A. J. Verhage']

'Tanpinaiso' ('Pink Osiana') HT, lp, Tantau; bud long, pointed ovoid; intr. 1997

'Tanpress' HT, mr, Tantau; intr. 2003

'Tanpretty' ('Softy') HT, lp, Tantau; intr. 1990

'Tanprik' F, or, 1959, Tantau, Math.; bud long, pointed; intr. 1958

'Tanpusbon' HT, w, Tantau

'Tanragus' Min, dp, Tantau; intr. 1997

'Tanrausch' F, mp, 1972, Tantau, Math.; bud globularsemi-dbl.

'Tanravens' ('Wild West') F, or, 1993, Evers, Hans & Rosen Tantau; three sepals very slightly bearded; flowers orange-red, medium, very dbl., borne in large clusters; foliage large, medium green, glossy, resistant to powdery mildew; prickles small, soft, glandular on peduncles; medium (85-95 cm.), bushy growth; ['Showbiz' × seedling]; intr. 1993

'Tanre' F, mr, Tantau

'Tanrecktor' (Rotelfe®) F, mr, 1985, Tantau, Math.; flowers medium, semi-dbl.; foliage small, medium green, semi-glossy; groundcover; spreading growth

'Tanrekta' ('Renica', Rebecca®) HT, rb, 1974, Tantau, Math.; bud ovoid; flowers red, yellow reverse, well-formed, large, dbl.; vigorous, upright growth; ['Konfetti' × Piccadilly®]; intr. 1970

'Tanreufis' S, mr, Tantau; intr. 1988

'Tanrezlaw' ('Snow Waltz', 'Valse des

Neiges') LCI, w, Tantau; intr. 1987

'Tanrif' ('First Lady') S, mp, Tantau; intr. 1997

'Tanrikas' ('Saphir') HT, m, Tantau; intr. 1989

'Tanrised' HT, mp, Tantau; intr. 1986

'Tanrolfy' (Babyflor®) Min, m, Tantaudbl.; intr. 1992

'Tanrosilb' ('Naas Botha') F, pb, Tantau; intr. 1990

'Tanrostax' ('Pearl Chatsworth') S, lp, Tantau; bud pointed ovoid; intr. 2002

'Tanrotreili' (Natali®) F, mp, 1985, Tantau, Math.; flowers large, 20 petals, high-centered; recurrent; foliage medium size, medium green, matte; intr. 1981

'Tanrowisa' (Wimi®) HT, pb, 1985, Tantau, Math.; flowers shiny pink, silver reverse, well-formed, large, 20 petals, intense fragrance; foliage large, dark, semi-glossy; bushy growth; intr. 1983

'Tanrupeza' ('Leeds Castle', 'Purple Haze') S, m, 1998, Tantau; flowers carmine purple, reverse medium pink, 1½ in., single, borne in large clusters, no fragrance; foliage medium size, dark green, glossy; prickles moderate; spreading, low (30-40 cm.) growth; groundcover; intr. 1998

'Tanryrandy' ('Cherry Brandy '85') HT, ob, 1985, Tantau, Math.; flowers orange, large, 35 petals, no fragrance; foliage large, medium green, glossy; upright growth

'Tansaras' ('Century Sunset', 'Herz Ass', 'Herz As') HT, dr, 1999, Tantau; flowers 4½-5 in., full, borne mostly singly, slight fragrance; foliage large, dark green, semi-glossy; prickles moderate; upright, medium (2-2½ ft.) growth; intr. 1998

'Tanschaubud' ('Olde Fragrance', Senteur Royale®, Duftrausch®) HT, mp, 1985, Tantau, Math.; flowers large, dbl.; foliage medium size, medium green, semi-glossy; upright growth; intr. 1986

'Tanschneewa' ('Schneewalzer') F, w, 1973, Tantau, Math.; bud ovoid; flowers large, dbl.; moderate, upright growth

'Tanschweigru' ('Holländerin', 'Schweizer Gruss', 'Salut à la Suisse', 'Red Favourite') F, mr, 1954, Tantau, Math.; bud ovoid; intr. 1951

'Tanselmi' HT, mp, Tantau; intr. 1995

'Tansenfrie' (Friesensöhne®) S, dy, 1983, Tantau, Math.; bud long, blunt top; flowers yellow-orange, 3½-4 in., 25-30 petals, high-centered, flattens, borne singly and in clusters, very slight fragrance; recurrent; foliage medium size, light, glossy; prickles numerous, long, straight, brown; stems short, strong; vigorous, upright growth; PP5706; [seedling × seedling]; intr. 1981

'Tanseus' ('The Robe') HT, dr, Tantau

'Tansimetra' HT, w, Tantau; intr. 2003

'Tansinnroh' ('Frohsinn 82', 'Peccato di Giola', 'Joyfulness') HT, ab, 1985, Tantau, Math.; flowers apricot and orange blend, large, 35 petals, borne singly and in clusters; foliage large, dark, glossy; intr. 1982

'Tansirk' ('Keith Kirsten') F, or, Tantau; intr. 1990

'Tanspolett' (Pink Diadem®) F, dp, Tantau; intr. 1994

'Tant Mieux' ('Saskabec') S, ob, 1983, Wright, Percy H.; flowers tangerine, yellow center, 5 petals, borne in clusters, no fragrance; foliage medium size, medium green, glossy; bushy growth; [R. gallica × 'Maria Stern']; intr. 1984

'Tanta' F, or, Tantau, Math.; bud long, pointed; intr. 1968

'Tantaatsyr' HT, ob, Tantau; intr. 1992

'Tantaga' (Taiga®) F, mp, 1972, Tantau, Math.; bud globular; flowers pink, medium, dbl.; vigorous, upright growth; ['Geisha' × 'Junior Miss']

'Tantaliser' F, ab

'Tantalizing Mary' -- See 'Seatant'

'Tantalizing Red' HT, m, 2001, Coiner, Jim; flowers large, 38 petals, high-centered, then flat, borne in small clusters, slight fragrance; recurrent; foliage large, dark green, matte; prickles average, 3/8 in.; stems long; growth upright, vigorous, tall (5 ft.); hips round, 1/2 in., olive green; PP16200; [seedling × seedling]

'Tantallon' HT, mp, 1934, Dobbie; flowers salmon-pink, base yellow, reverse cerise-red touched orange, dbl.; foliage glossy, dark; dwarf, stocky growth

'Tantanoras' S, lp, Tantau; intr. 2006

'Tantarra' HT, r, Gardner; flowers soft tan, toned pink and apricot, moderate fragrance; recurrent; bushy growth; intr. 1996

'Tantasch' ('Castle Howard Tercentenary', 'Goldschatz', 'Golden Jet') F, dy, 1998, Rosen Tantau; flowers deep yellow, 4 in., dbl., borne in small clusters, slight fragrance; foliage large, medium green, glossy; prickles moderate; bushy, medium (70 cm.) growth; [seedling × seedling]; intr. 1996

'Tantau's Delight' F, or, 1951, Tantau; bud long, pointed; flowers open, large, semi-dbl., borne in clusters; foliage dark, glossy; vigorous, bushy growth; ['Cinnabar' × 'Kathe Duvigneau']

'Tantau's Konfetti' (Konfetti®) HT, ob, Tantau; flowers orange blend, reverse yellow with orange edges, dbl., high-centered, borne mostly singly; recurrent; stems long; cut flower rose; intr. 1991

'Tantau's Surprise' ('Tantau's Ueberraschung') F, mr, 1951, Tantau; flowers blood-red, large, full, borne in clusters of 5-8; foliage dark, glossy; upright growth; ['Bouquet' × 'Hamburg']

'Tantau's Triumph, Climbing' Cl Pol, mr, Rosarium Sangerhausen; flowers medium, semi-dbl.; intr. 1957

'Tantau's Triumph' -- See 'Cinnabar'

'Tantau's Ueberraschung' -- See 'Tantau's Surprise'

'Tante Frieda' HT, mr, Michler, K. H.; flowers large, dbl.; intr. 1995

'Tantern' ('Gold Star', 'Golden Star', 'Stella Dorata') HKor, my, 1966, Tantau, Math.; bud long, pointed

'Tantharina' HT, lp, Tantau; intr. 2000

'Tantide' ('Glad Tidings', Lübecker Rotspon®, 'Peter Wessel', 'Victoria') F, dr, 1989, Tantau, R.; bud ovoid; flowers bright crimson, medium, 20 petals, cupped, borne in sprays, no fragrance; foliage medium size, medium green, semi-glossy; upright, medium (2 ft.) growth; [seedling × seedling]; intr. 1988

'Tantivvy' Pol, mr, 1954, Ratcliffe; flowers crimson-scarlet, semi-dbl., rosette; compact, bushy growth; [sport of 'Gloire du Midi']

'Tantocnirp' HT, dp; intr. 2000

'Tantoras' ('Happy Retirement') F, lp, 2000, Rosen Tantau; flowers soft pink, 5 in., dbl., borne in small clusters, slight fragrance; foliage large, medium green, glossy; prickles moderate; bushy, tall (3 ft.) growth; [seedling × seedling]; intr. 2000

'Tantreika' (Inka®) HT, op, 1978, Tantau, Math.; bud pointed; flowers salmon, large, dbl.; foliage large, glossy; upright, bushy growth

'Tanttelos' ('Violett Satina') S, dp, Tantau; intr. 1994

'Tantumleh' ('Red Nostalgie') HT, dr, Tantau, Math.; intr. 1996

'Tanvery' HT, ob, 1974, Tantau, Math.; bud ovoid; intr. 1972

'Tanweieke' ('Bernhard Daneke Rose', 'Ingrid Weibull', 'Showbiz') F, mr, 1983, Tantau, Math.; bud short, globular, blunt top; flowers bright medium red, 2½-3½ in., 20-30 petals, flat, borne in clusters, slight sweet fragrance; recurrent; foliage medium size, dark, semi-glossy; prickles normal, long, hooked downward; stems short; bushy, low (2-2½ ft.) growth; PP4844; ['Dream Waltz' × 'Marlena']; intr. 1981

'Tanya' ('Majeure') HT, ob, 1960, Combe; bud pointed; flowers deep orange to apricot-orange, 5 in., 48 petals, high-centered, moderate fragrance; foliage leathery, glossy; vigorous, upright growth; PP1712; ['Peace' × ('Peace' × 'Orange Nassau')]

'Tanya Kim' HT, my, 1976, Marks; flowers clear yellow, 4½ in., 24 petals, intense fragrance; foliage glossy; [sport of 'Whisky Mac']; intr. 1975

'Tanya Marie' Min, rb, 2002, Fletcher, Ira R.; flowers red with white center, 3½ cm., single, borne mostly solitary, no fragrance; foliage small, medium green, matte; prickles moderate, 6 mm., very fine, slightly curved; bushy, medium (60 cm.) growth; ['Grace Seward' × 'Hanini']

'Tanyab' ('Bavarian Gold', 'Baviera d'Oro', 'Goldbay') F, my, Tantau, intr. 1990

'Tanybab' ('Pink Babyflor') Min, dp, Tantau; intr. 1993

'Tanyboh' Min, dp, Tantau; intr. 2001

'Tanydal' ('Renown's Summer Lady') HT, pb, Tantau; bud long; intr. 1991

'Tanydor' ('Viking') S, mr, Tantau; intr. 1995

'Tanydrib' HT, rb, Tantau; intr. 1997

'Tanydu' ('Judy') HT, my, Tantau; intr. 1997

'Tanyellda' ('Yellow Belinda') F, dy, 1973, Tantau, Math.; bud long, pointed; flowers orange-yellow, medium, dbl.; [sport of 'Belinda']; intr. 1972

'Tanyssek' -- See 'Kessy'

'Tanzahde' ('Beaulieu', 'Red Haze') S, mr, 1998, Rosen Tantau; flowers medium red, 2½ in., single, borne in large clusters, no fragrance; foliage medium size, dark green, glossy; prickles moderate; low, spreading (30 cm.) growth; [seedling × seedling]; intr. 1998

'Tanzaja' HT, ob, Tantau

'Tanzecon' ('Constanze') HT, ob, Tantau; intr. 1992

'Tanziewsim' ('Miss Schweiz') HT, dr, Tantau; intr. 1996

'Tanzwol' ('Dukat') HT, my, Tantau; intr. 2005

Taora® F, or, Tantau, Math.; bud long, pointed; flowers large, dbl.; foliage glossy; very vigorous, bushy growth; ['Fragrant Cloud' × 'Schweizer Gruss']; intr. 1968

Taos™ -- See 'Poulbambe'

'Tapestry' HT, rb, 1959, Fisher, G.; bud pointed; flowers red, yellow and pink, 4½-6 in., 38 petals, high-centered, moderate spicy fragrance; foliage glossy; upright, bushy growth; PP1812; ['Peace' × 'Mission Bells']; intr. 1959

'Tapestry' -- See 'Tomtap'

'Tapis' -- See 'Tapis Rose'

'Tapis Afghan' -- See 'Pekinois'

'Tapis Blanc' Pol, w, 1927, Turbat; flowers pure white, center tinted cream, large, dbl., borne in clusters; bushy, dwarf growth

'Tapis de Soie' -- See 'Wee Man'

'Tapis d'Orient' -- See 'Yesterday'

'Tapis Jaune® -- See 'Rugul'

'Tapis Magique' -- See 'Magic Carpet'

'Tapis Persan' -- See 'Maceye'

'Tapis Rose' ('Tapis') F, mp, 1950, Meilland, F.; bud ovoid; flowers rose-pink, 2-2½ in., full, high-centered, borne in clusters, moderate fragrance; foliage leathery, dark; vigorous, upright, bushy growth; PP960; ['Pinocchio' × 'Mme Jules Gouchault']

'Tapis Rouge' -- See 'Interop'

'Tapis Rustic' S, mr

Tapis Volant® -- See 'Lenplat'

'Tapti' Gr, lp, Kasturi, G.; flowers delicate pink, large, moderate spicy fragrance; [sport of 'Camelot']; intr. 1978

'Tara' -- See 'Macwaiwer'

'Tara Allison' -- See 'Macwaiwer'

'Tara Red' HT, dr, 1975, Golik; bud ovoid; flowers carmine-red, becoming very dark,, 6 in., 38 petals, high-centered, moderate fragrance; foliage leathery; tall growth; ['Peace' × 'Charles Mallerin']; intr. 1974

'Taranaki Dawn' F, ab, 2001, Sherwood, George; flowers apricot/cream, apricot/pink reverse, 8 cm., dbl., borne in large clusters, slight fragrance; foliage medium size, medium green, semi-glossy; prickles moderate, 8 mm., slightly curved; growth upright, tall (1½ m.); garden decorative; ['Kate Sheppard' × 'Kate Sheppard']; intr. 2001

Taranga® -- See 'Tanagnarat'

Tarantella® HT, dy, 1936, Tantau; flowers deep golden yellow, large, dbl., cupped; foliage light, wrinkled; vigorous, bushy growth; ['Charles P. Kilham' × 'Pres. Herbert Hoover']

'Tarantella' HT, w, Spek; flowers white to blush pink; florist rose; intr. 2003

Tarantella® -- See 'Korantel'

'Tarantelle' -- See 'Tarentelle'

'Tarde Gris' ('Evening Light') HT, m, 1970, Dot, Simon; flowers soft lilac, large, 25 petals, moderate fragrance; foliage dark; upright growth; [('Sterling Silver' × 'Intermezzo') × ('Sterling Silver' × 'Simone')]; intr. 1966

'Tarentelle' ('Tarantelle') HT, op, 1965, Laperrière; flowers Orient red with reflections of rose salmon, full; foliage bronze; vigorous, bushy growth; [('Beauté × 'Ma Fille') × 'Magicienne']

'Target' -- See 'Jacrim'

'Taro' HT, my, 1977, Ota, Kaichiro; bud oval; flowers high pointed, 5½ in., 35 petals; foliage dark, leathery; vigorous, upright growth; ['Edith Krause' × 'Narzisse']

'Tarragona' HT, ab, 1945, Dot, Pedro; flowers apricot-yellow, open, 25-35 petals, high-centered; foliage glossy; upright growth; ['Duquesa de Peñaranda' × 'Federico Casas']

'Tarragona' -- See 'Diputacion de Tarragona'

'Tarrawarra' Pol, pb, Nieuwesteeg, J.; intr. 1992

'Tartarus' HP, m, 1887, Geschwind; flowers violet purple; ['Erinnerung an Brod' × 'Souv du Dr Jamain']

'Tartufe' F, mr, 1956, Buyl Frères; flowers dark geranium-red, 28 petals; moderate growth; ['Pompadour Red' × 'Independence']

'Taryn' Min, op

'Tarzan' LCl, mr, 1955, Delbard-Chabert; flowers coppery carmine, darker reverse, medium, dbl., moderate fragrance; free, recurrent bloom; foliage dark bronze-green, glossy; very vigorous growth

Tascaria® S, mr, Noack; flowers bright red, 2 in., semi-dbl., open cup, borne in clusters; recurrent; foliage medium to dark green, glossy; vigorous, broad (4 × 4 ft.) growth; intr. 2005

'Taser Bibi' ('Queen of Hearts') HT, mr, Ghosh, Mr. & Mrs. S.; flowers bright, velvet scarlet red, large, dbl., high-centered; intr. 2000

'Tasja' HT, w, RvS-Melle

'Tasman' -- See 'Murta'

'Tasman Bay' LCl, w, Pratt, Florence; flowers single, borne in large sprays; early flowering; vigorous (4 m.) growth; intr. 1994

'Tasman Venture' S, dr, 2004, Marriner, Max; flowers dark red, reverse darker, medium, single, borne in small clusters, slight fragrance; foliage medium size, medium green, matte; prickles 2 cm., average; growth spreading, tall (2 m.); garden decorative; [Altissimo® × 'Penelope']; intr. 2004

'Tasman's Pursuit' LCl, mr; intr. 2006

'Tasogare' ('Twilight') F, m, 1977, Kobayashi, Moriji; bud cupped; flowers 2½-4 in., 18 petals, flat; foliage glossy; vigorous, spreading growth; ['Gletscher' × ('Sterling Silver' × 'Gletscher')]; intr. 1977

'Tassie Corraline' HT, mr, 2007, Eiszele, L. H.; flowers 11 cm., dbl., borne mostly solitary; foliage medium size, medium green, matte; prickles small, hooked, red, moderate; growth upright, short (30 in.); [unknown × unknown]

'Tassie Diana' F, lp, 2007, Eiszele, L.H.; flowers medium, with a button eye, very full, borne in small clusters; foliage small, medium green, semi-glossy; prickles small, moderate; growth spreading, medium; ['Bonica 82' × unknown]; intr. 2007

'Tassie Laua-Maree' F, dp, 2007, Eiszele, L. H.; flowers deep pink, reverse pink blend, 9 cm., very full, borne in small clusters; foliage medium size, dark green, semi-glossy; prickles medium, regular, red, moderate; growth upright, medium (1½ m.); ['Pink Perpetue' × unknown]

'Tassie Mme Mariah' F, w, 2007, Eiszele, L. H.; flowers white blend, 9 cm., very full, borne in small clusters; foliage medium size, medium green, semi-glossy; few prickles; growth upright, medium (20 in.); borders; ['Iceberg' × unknown]

'Tassie Melanie' HT, lp, 2007, Eiszele, L. H.; flowers 10 cm., dbl., borne mostly solitary; foliage medium size, medium green, matte; prickles medium, regular, red, moderate; growth upright, medium (1½ m.); ['Proud Titania' × unknown]

'Tassie Miss Carolyn' F, mp, 2007, Eiszele, L.H.; flowers have quilled petals, 7 cm., very full, borne in small clusters; foliage small, medium green, semi-glossy; prickles small, green, few; growth upright, short; borders; ['Bonica 82' × unknown]; intr. 2007

'Tassie Princess' F, dp, 1999, Elszele, L. H.; flowers 2-2½ in., dbl., borne in small clusters; foliage small, medium green, semi-glossy; few prickles; bushy, low (36 in.) growth

'Tassili' -- See 'Oraju'

'Tassin, Climbing' Cl HT, mr, Moreira da Silva; [sport of 'Tassin']; intr. about 1950

'Tassin' HT, mr, 1942, Meilland, F.; bud ovoid; flowers large, dbl., urn-shaped, moderate fragrance; recurrent; foliage leathery; vigorous, upright (4 ft.) growth;

['National Flower Guild' × 'Lemania']
'Taste of Honey' F, ob, 1977, Young, S.A.; bud ovoid; flowers honey color, aging pink, open, large, dbl.; foliage leathery; vigorous, upright growth; [sport of Elizabeth of Glamis®]
'Tata Centenary' HT, rb, 1978, Pradhan, Rauf, Murmu, Ghosh; flowers deep carmine, striped pale yellow, reverse buff, large, dbl., high-centered, slight fragrance; recurrent; [sport of 'Pigalle']; intr. 1974
'Tata Centenary, Climbing' Cl HT, rb, K&S; [sport of 'Tata Centenary']; intr. 1995
'Tate's Multiflora' Sp, clone of *R. multiflora*; used for understock
'Tathgata' HT, w, Ghosh, Mr. & Mrs. S.; flowers white with slight pink blush, large, full, high-centered; intr. 1999
'Tatiana' S, op, Monteith, Joan; flowers apricot-orange, large, semi-dbl., shallow cup to flat, intense fragrance; recurrent; medium growth; [Heritage® × Westerland®]
'Tatik Brada' HP, op, 1933, Brada; flowers large, full
'Tatjana'® ('Rosenthal') HT, dr, 1973, Kordes, R.; bud long, pointed; flowers large, dbl., cupped, intense fragrance; foliage leathery, soft; vigorous, upright growth; ['Liebeszauber' × 'Prasident Dr. H.C. Schroder']; intr. 1970
'Tatoo'™ LCl, dr, Poulsen; flowers 2-3 in., dbl., cupped, borne in clusters, very slight fragrance; recurrent; foliage small, dark green, glossy; vigorous (5-7 ft.) growth; intr. 2002
'Tattletale' -- See 'Ziptale'
'Tatton' ('Casanova', Francois Mauriac®) F, ob, Fryer; flowers burnt orange, large, full, cupped, borne in clusters, moderate fruity fragrance; recurrent; foliage large, disease-resistant; vigorous, medium growth; intr. 2001
'Tattooed Lady' -- See 'Seadeep'
'Taubie Kushlik' HT, pb, Kordes; flowers silvery pink, deeper reverse, dbl., high-centered, borne mostly singly, slight fragrance; recurrent; vigorous, medium growth; intr. 1991
'Taunusblümchen' HMult, m, 1902, Weigand, C.; flowers violet-pink, 4-5 cm., semi-dbl., borne in clusters of 10-20; ['Turner's Crimson Rambler' × 'Mlle Blanche Rebatel']
Taupo® -- See 'Macmisech'
'Tauranga Centennial' F, or, 1983, Wareham, Phyllis E.; flowers orange-red, center yellow, large, 22 petals, borne in clusters of 3; prickles light brown; upright growth; ['Arthur Bell' × (Alexander® × 'Sympathy')]
'Taurinia' HT, mp, 1942, Aicardi; bud ovoid; flowers bright salmon-pink, large, very dbl., cupped; foliage leathery; very vigorous growth; ['Julien Potin' × 'Sensation']
'Tauro' F, dr, 1959, Bofill; bud globular; flowers oxblood-red, large, dbl., borne in clusters; foliage glossy; upright growth;

['Poinsettia' × 'Alain']; intr. 1958
'Taurus' Min, or, 1978, Ellick; bud pointed, ovoid; flowers vermilion, 2-3 in., 35-40 petals; foliage dark; compact, upright growth; [Baby Masquerade® × ('Spion-Kop' × 'Evelyn Fison')]
'Taurus' ('The Bull') F, ab; flowers salmon-pink, outer petals fading lighter, dbl., borne in clusters, slight fragrance; foliage medium green; to 75 cm. growth; intr. 2004
'Tausendschön' ('Merveille', 'Thousand Beauties', *R. banksiae rosea*, 'Pink Banksia Rose') HMult, pb, 1906, Kiese; flowers deep rose-pink, center white, fading lighter, 6 cm., dbl., cupped, borne in clusters of 20-40; foliage soft green; climbing (8-10 ft.) growth; ['Daniel Lacombe' × 'Weisser Herumstreicher']
'Tawny Gold' HT, dy, 1951, Leenders, M.; bud pointed; flowers tawny gold, well-shaped, 5 in., 25 petals, high-centered, intense fragrance; foliage leathery; bushy, compact growth; PP950; ['Vanessa' × 'Burgemeester van Oppen']
'Tawny Profusion' F, ly, Fryer; intr. 2007
'Tawny Superior' HT, my, 1958, Leenders, M.; flowers golden yellow
'Tawny Tiger' F, r, Fryer; flowers dark orange striped and rippled with terracotta and brown, semi-dbl., cupped, loose, borne in good-sized clusters, moderate fragrance; repeats well; foliage glossy; bushy (70 cm.) growth; intr. 2003
'Taxi' HT, dr, 1986, Poulsen, Niels D.; flowers large, 35 petals, exhibition, borne usually singly, intense fragrance; foliage large, dark, matte; vigorous, upright growth; ['Fragrant Cloud' × Gisselfeld®]; intr. 1977
'Taxi' F, rb, 1969, Trew, C.; flowers mandarin red, reverse soft rose, pointed, large, dbl.; foliage dark, matte; ruled extinct 12/85; ['Isabelle de France' × 'Basildon Belle']
'Tay Caitlin' Min, ab, 1997, Garrett, Troy O.; flowers dbl., borne mostly singly; foliage medium size, medium green, semi-glossy; some prickles; upright, medium (16-22in.) growth; [sport of 'Queen City']
'Taybird' ('Bird of Fire') HT, yb, 1992, Taylor, Thomas E.; flowers yellow blending to reddish edges, reverse yellow, aging lighter, 4-4¾ in., 25-30 petals, high-centered; foliage medium size, dark green, semi-glossy, leathery, reddish w; upright, bushy, medium growth; [Fragrant Delight® × 'Sunsilk']
'Taylors Gold' -- See 'Horbarjeff'
'Taymar' ('Mary Louise') HT, pb, 1996, Taylor, Thomas E.; flowers light pink, reverse medium pink, 5 in., dbl., form similar to First Prize, borne mostly singly; foliage medium size, medium green, glossy, similar to Honey Favorite; prickles moderate; compact, bushy, medium (3-4 ft.) growth; ['Honey Favorite' × 'First Prize']; intr. 2000
'Taymel' ('Melinda Claire') Min, m, 1990,

Taylor, Thomas E.; bud pointed; flowers reddish-magenta, yellow stamens, small to medium, 15 petals, high-centered, borne usually singly; foliage medium size, medium green, semi-glossy; prickles curved downward, small, widely spaced, brownish; hips globular, medium, orange; ['Charmglo' × 'Charmglo']; intr. 1990
'Tblbeta' HT, pb, 2007, Chapman, Bruce; intr. 2007
'Tblcoudith' HT, lp, 2007, Courage, Ray; intr. 2007
'Tblcourmagic' F, pb, 2007, Courage, Ray; intr. 2007
Tchaikovski™ -- See 'Meichibon'
'Tchin-Tchin, Climbing' Cl F, ob, Meilland; [sport of 'Tchin-Tchin']; intr. 1995
'Tchin-Tchin' -- See 'Meikinosi'
'Tchin-Tchin' -- See 'Meichanso'
'Te Awamutu Centennial' -- See 'Steteaw'
'Te Kawanata Hou' S, w, Nobbs
'Te Kowhai' F, dr, 1960, Bennett, H.; flowers dark velvety red, reverse white overlaid red; [('Florence Mary Morse' × 'Border Queen') × 'Confidence']
'Te Moana' -- See 'Simteono'
'Tea Clipper' -- See 'Ausrover'
'Tea Party' Min, ab, 1973, Moore, Ralph S.; flowers orange-apricot to pink, small, dbl.; foliage small, light; vigorous, dwarf, bushy growth; [(*R. wichurana* × 'Floradora') × 'Eleanor']; intr. 1972
'Tea Rambler' HMult, op, 1904, Paul, W.; bud pointed; flowers soft salmon-pink, 4-5 cm., dbl., flat, borne in clusters of 3-15, moderate fragrance; early; foliage dark green, edged red; vigorous, climbing growth; ['Turner's Crimson Rambler' × a climbing Tea (possibly 'Gloire de Dijon')]
'Tea Rose' -- See 'Hume's Blush Tea-Scented China'
'Tea-Scented Ayrshire' -- See 'Ruga'
'Tea-Scented Rose' -- See 'Hume's Blush Tea-Scented China'
'Tea Time' HT, ob, Tantau; flowers smoky orange with brown shades, petals ruffled, medium, dbl., rosette, borne singly and in clusters, slight fragrance; recurrent; upright (3 ft.) growth; intr. 1994
Tea Time® HT, ab, Tantau; flowers medium, double, high-centered, borne mostly singly; recurrent; stems short to medium; florist rose; intr. 2006
'Tea Time' F, mp, 1960, Boerner; bud ovoid; flowers clear pink, medium, 60-65 petals, high-centered, borne in clusters; foliage leathery; vigorous, bushy growth; ['floribunda seedling' × 'Demure']; intr. 1960
'Teacher's Pet' HT, ab, 1980, Taylor, Thomas E.; bud ovoid, pointed; flowers apricot, 30 petals, high-centered; foliage dark green with red mid-rib and edges; prickles straight; upright, bushy growth; ['First Prize' × 'Bonsoir']
'Tear Drop' -- See 'Dicomo'
'Tease' F, ob, 1967, Boerner; bud ovoid,

The Official Registry and Checklist — Rosa 739

coppery; flowers golden yellow, dbl., cupped; foliage leathery; vigorous, upright growth; ['Yellow Pinocchio' × ('Fashion' × unknown)]

'Teasing Georgia' -- See 'Ausbaker'

'Teatime' F, pb; flowers creamy white with heavy blush of soft pearly pink, slight fragrance; foliage disease-resistant; short growth

'Technikon Pretoria' HT, yb, Kordes; bud triangular, deep yellow; flowers deep yellow with bright orange-red edges growing as it opens, dbl., high-centered; recurrent; short growth; intr. 1993

'Ted Allen' -- See 'Guesgenus'

'Ted Carnac' LCl, 1968, Gowie; vigorous growth

'Ted Gore' -- See 'Hormislac'

'Ted Goves' -- See 'Kirpark'

'Tedcastle' HP, m, 1940, Tedcastle; flowers purple, open, very dbl., cupped; foliage glossy; upright, bushy growth; ['Ulrich Brunner Fils' × 'Paul Neyron']

'Teddy' HT, lp, Pratt, Florence; bud pink; flowers pale peach-pink, dbl.; medium growth; [Margaret Merril® × unknown]; intr. 1994

'Teddy Bear, Climbing' Cl Min, r, Saito; intr. 1997

Teddy Bear™ -- See 'Savabear'

'Teddy's Coat' F, dy

'Ted's Red' -- See 'Reyred'

'Teenager' HT, yb, 1960, Arnot; flowers yellow shaded pink and carmine, loosely formed, 4-5 in., 25 petals, intense fragrance; foliage dark, leathery; vigorous, upright growth; PP1783; ['Ena Harkness' × 'Sutter's Gold']; intr. 1958

'Teenager' F, pb, Boerner; bud ovoid; flowers La France pink, lightly overcast shrimp-pink, 3½ in., 55-60 petals, high-centered to cupped, intense fragrance; foliage leathery; strong stems; vigorous, upright growth; ['Demure' × 'Demure']; a greenhouse variety; intr. 1958

'Teeny Bopper' -- See 'Tinbopper'

Teeny Bopper™ -- See 'Wekiscorou'

Teeny WeenyN -- See 'Poulteeny'

'Tegala' S, dp, 1927, Hansen, N.E.; flowers deep pink, semi-dbl.; non-recurrent; growth to 5 ft.; very hardy; ['Tetonkaha' × 'Alika']

'Teide' LCl, mr, 1948, Dot, M.; flowers carmine, 3 in., full; foliage reddish; ['Texas Centennial' × 'Guinee']

'Tejas' -- See 'Pontejas'

'Téléthon' HT, ab, Delbard; flowers cream edges, apricot center, full, pointed to rosette, intense lilac and fruit fragrance; recurrent; foliage glossy; growth to 80 cm.; intr. 2005

'Telford's Promise' -- See 'Chewoz'

'Tell Belle' -- See 'Majtelbel'

Telluride™ -- See 'Poulbut'

'Telstar' F, ob, 1963, Gandy, Douglas L.; flowers orange to orange-buff, flushed scarlet, large, 14 petals, borne in clusters of up to 5, moderate fragrance; foliage dark; vigorous, upright growth; ['Flash (F)' × 'Masquerade']

'Temno' HT, m, 1936, Böhm, J.; flowers dark maroon, fairly large, dbl.; vigorous growth

'Temper Tantrum' Min, dr, 1987, Jolly, Marie; flowers white center, medium, 30 petals, high-centered, borne usually singly or in sprays of 2; foliage small, medium green, semi-glossy; no prickles; upright, medium growth; no fruit; ['Red Beauty' × 'Libby']; intr. 1988

'Temperament' ('Vivacity') F, mr, 1959, Tantau, Math.; flowers light scarlet, open, 2½ in., 24 petals, borne in clusters; foliage glossy, leathery; vigorous, upright growth; ['Fanal' × 'Karl Weinhausen']; intr. 1957

'Tempest, Climbing' LCl, rb, 1962, Verschuren; bud pointed; flowers yellow, pink and orange-red, 2½-3 in., 26 petals, borne in clusters; foliage dark, glossy; vigorous growth; ['Masquerade' × seedling]; intr. 1962

Tempi Moderni® F, ob, Barni, V.; bud golden yellow; flowers golden yellow, flushed with vermilion orange which spreads with age, dbl., cupped, borne in clusters, slight fragrance; recurrent; vigorous (60-80 cm.) growth; intr. 1996

'Tempie Lee' HT, pb, 1991, Whittington, Sr., J.O.; flowers medium, full, high-centered, borne mostly singly, slight fragrance; foliage medium size, medium green, semi-glossy; some prickles; stems long; vigorous, medium, spreading growth; [sport of 'Elizabeth Taylor']; intr. 1998

'Templar' HT, mr, 1924, Montgomery Co.; flowers bright red, dbl., globular; foliage dark, leathery; vigorous growth; ['Premier' × seedling]

'Temple Bells' Cl Min, w, 1972, Morey, Dennison; flowers single, 7 petals, slight fragrance; foliage small, glossy; growth tall; climber (if supported) or groundcover; [R. wichurana × 'Blushing Jewel']; intr. 1971

'Temple d'Apollon' ('Cramoisi Brillant', 'Pourpre Rouge', 'Vesta') HGal, dr, 1816, possibly Prévost; bud long, pointed; sepals short; flowers velvety violet-crimson, large, semi-dbl.

'Temple Flame' F, or, 1970, Pal, Dr. B.P.; flowers orange flushed red, open, medium, semi-dbl.; foliage leathery; very vigorous, upright, compact growth; [Orangeade® × unknown]; intr. 1965

'Tempo' LCl, dr, 1974, Warriner, William A.; bud ovoid; flowers deep red, large, very dbl., slight fragrance; recurrent; foliage large, glossy, dark; climbing growth; PP3652; ['Ena Harkness, Climbing' × unknown]; intr. 1975

'Tempo' -- See 'Meinececa'

'Temptation' LCl, mr, 1950, Jacobus; bud ovoid, carmine-red; flowers rose-red, open, large, 40 petals; free, recurrent boom; foliage large, glossy; vigorous, climbing growth; good pillar; very hardy; [('New Dawn' × 'Crimson Glory') × 'Dream Girl']

'Temptation' -- See 'Intertropa'

'Temptation' -- See 'Tropat'

'Temptress' HT, mr, 1948, Joseph H. Hill, Co.; bud long, pointed, crimson; flowers carmine, medium, 35-40 petals, cupped, moderate fragrance; foliage leathery, dark; vigorous, upright, bushy growth; PP864; [('Lucile Hill' × 'Chieftain') × seedling]

'Temptress' -- See 'Wamtress'

'Temptress' -- See 'Korromalu'

'Tempus-Fugit' HT, mr, 1976, Ellick; flowers cardinal-red, 3-4 in., 40-45 petals, moderate fragrance; foliage glossy, dark; very free growth; ['Chopin' × 'Heidelberg']; intr. 1977

'Ten Sisters' -- See 'Crimson Rambler'

'Ten Ten' -- See 'Ten Ten CFRB'

'Ten Ten CFRB' ('Ten Ten') HT, mr, McGredy; flowers striking, velvet red, dbl., cupped; recurrent; stems long; intr. 1987

'Ten Thousand Leaves' -- See 'Manyo'

'Tenacious' F, yb, McGredy; flowers striped cherry red, lemon, and yellow maturing to blush pink, loose, slight fragrance; foliage bright green, glossy; short to medium growth; intr. 2004

'Tenacity' S, mr, Williams, J. Benjamin; flowers semi-dbl., flat, borne in clusters, slight fragrance; recurrent; foliage reddish; stems reddish; growth to 2 ft.; intr. 2006

Tendence® F, dy, Noack; intr. 2002

Tender™ Min, mp, Olesen; PP11499; intr. 1998

'Tender Blush' A, lp, Sievers; flowers blush pink, 4½ in., very full, cupped; once blooming; tall (5-6 ft.), arching growth; [bred from 'Maiden's Blush']; intr. 1988

'Tender Love' Min, lp, 1980, Strawn, Leslie E.; bud slender, tapering; flowers 23 petals, borne mostly singly, sometimes 3-5 per cluster; foliage glossy, medium green; prickles dilated at base; tall, upright growth; ['Doris Ashwell' × 'Sheri Anne']

'Tender Love' HT, mp, Ghosh, Mr. & Mrs. S.; bud long, tapering; flowers rosy pink, broad petals; free-flowering; vigorous growth; intr. 2000

'Tender Love' F, mp; intr. 2006

'Tender Love' -- See 'Bosrexch'

'Tender Loving Care' -- See 'Bospeabay'

'Tender Mercy' -- See 'Renmercy'

'Tender Night' ('Florian') F, mr, 1971, Meilland; flowers 4 in., 25 petals, slight fruity fragrance; foliage matte, dark; upright growth; ['Tamango' × ('Fire King' × 'Banzai')]

'Tender Night, Climbing' -- See 'Meilaursar'

'Tender One' -- See 'Nejenka'

'Tender Spirit' S, op, Williams, J. Benjamin; flowers single; intr. 2005

'Tenderly' HT, Delforge; intr. 1984

'Tenderly Yours' -- See 'Renyours'

'Tenderness' HT, lp, Delbard; flowers pale pink, large, dbl., high-centered, borne mostly singly; recurrent; foliage light green; stems straight, rigid, medium to long; florist rose; intr. 2003

'Tendresse' -- See 'Deltendre'

'Tendresse' -- See 'Deljofem'

'Tendresse' -- See 'Sachsengruss'

'Tendresse Admirable' -- See 'Marie-Louise'

'Tendresse d'Apollon' HGal, m, before 1836, Prévost; flowers lilac pink, edges fading to white, medium, full

'Tenerezza' HT, rb, 1974, Calvino; bud ovoid, long, pointed; flowers spinel-rose to cherry-red, medium, dbl., cupped, moderate fragrance; foliage large, dark, leathery; vigorous, upright, bushy growth; PP2932; [seedling × 'Ninfa Rossa']

'Teneriffe' HT, op, 1973, Timmerman's Roses; flowers deep orange, yellowish reverse, pointed, 5 in., 45 petals, intense fragrance; foliage glossy, dark; ['Fragrant Cloud' × Piccadilly®]; intr. 1972

'Tennessee' HT, ob, Van de Meer, Peter; bud long, pointed; flowers orange with darker edges and yellow base, 9 cm., 30-40 petals, cupped, then flat, borne usually singly, very slight fragrance; recurrent; foliage dark green; upright (80 cm.) growth; hips round, orange; PP9170; ['Eliora' × Cocktail®]; intr. 1988

Tennessee™ -- See 'Kintenn'

'Tennessee Belle' HSet, mp, before 1898, from U.S.A.; flowers bright rosy blush, large, dbl., borne in clusters, moderate fragrance; vigorous, climbing growth

'Tennessee Sunrise' -- See 'Weltenn'

'Tennessee Sunset' -- See 'Welsun'

'Tennessee Waltz' -- See 'Welwalt'

'Ténor' LCl, mr, 1963, Delbard-Chabert; flowers velvety red, medium, semi-dbl., borne in small to medium clusters, no fragrance; early; very vigorous growth

'Tentation' -- See 'Dortem'

'Tenth Rose Convention' HT, dy, Patil, B.K.; flowers dbl., high-centered; intr. 1990

'Teodora' HT, mr, 1983, Stoddard, Louis; flowers large, 30 petals, cupped; foliage large, brownish-green, matte; prickles reddish-green; upright growth; ['Honey Favorite' × 'Command Performance']

Teodora® HT, mr, Barni; bud globular; flowers brilliant red, large, dbl., slight fragrance; medium (4 ft.) growth; intr. 2003

'Tequila' F, ob, Meilland; flowers orange with yellow tones, dbl., high-centered, borne mostly singly; recurrent; florist rose; intr. 1998

'Tequila' F, ob, Meilland; flowers bright orange, semi-dbl., cupped to flat, borne in clusters; growth to 70 cm.; intr. 2003

'Téquila' F, ab; bud conical; flowers 3-3½ in., 29 petals, cupped, borne in clusters of 2 - 5, no fragrance; free-flowering; foliage dark green, semi-glossy; growth bushy, 80-90 cm.; PP16342; [Golden Holstein® × 'Bonica']; intr. 2004

Tequila® -- See 'Meigavesol'

'Tequila Gold' F, my, Meilland; intr. 2008

'Tequila Sunrise' -- See 'Dicobey'

Tequila Sunset™ -- See 'Wilsun'

'Teresa Finotti-Masieri' HT, m, 1929, Ketten Bros.; bud long, pointed; flowers brilliant purple-rose, rosy scarlet reflexes, bordered yellow; ['George C. Waud' × 'Souv. de Gabriel Luizet']

'Teresa Ozores' Cl HT, lp, 1958, Camprubi, C.; bud ovoid; flowers soft pearly pink, large, dbl., cupped, intense fragrance; vigorous growth; ['Frau Karl Druschki' × 'Lady Sylvia']; intr. 1957

'Ternaux' ('Subviolacea') Ch, m, about 1830, Ternaux; flowers violet purple, medium, full

'Terra Cotta' -- See 'Terracotta'

'Terra Jubilee' F, ab, Zary, Dr. Keith W.; flowers soft apricot, fading to almost white, large, semi-dbl., flat, moderate fragrance; recurrent; intr. 1996

'Terracotta' ('Terra Cotta') HT, r; bud conical; flowers brick red, 12-14 cm., dbl., cupped, high-centered, borne mostly singly, no fragrance; recurrent; foliage medium green, semi-glossy; prickles numerous, medium, tan; upright (4-5 ft.) growth; PP10622; [sport of 'Leonidas']; florist rose; intr. 1999

'Terracotta, Climbing' Cl HT, r, Meilland; intr. 2001

'Terracotta' ('Chocolate Prince') HT, r, Simpson; flowers reddish-brown, dbl., high-centered, slight fragrance; growth medium to tall; many sources show code-form name as Simchoca, but NZ authority says it is Simchoka; intr. 2003

Terrazza Amore™ F, dr, de Ruiter; flowers dbl., borne in clusters; PPAF; intr. 2007

Terrazza Bella™ F, pb, de Ruiter; flowers blend of pink, yellow and white , dbl; intr. 2007

Terrazza Corazon™ F, mr, de Ruiter; flowers dbl.; intr. 2007

Terrazza Del Sol™ F, my, de Ruiter; flowers dbl; intr. 2007

Terrazza Rosa™ F, dp, de Ruiter; flowers hot pink, dbl.; intr. 2007

Terrazza Sunset™ F, ob, de Ruiter; flowers orange with apricot reverse, dbl.; intr. 2007

Terrazza Voila™ F, op, de Ruiter; flowers blend of orange and pink, dbl.; intr. 2007

'Terrell Anne' -- See 'Gretag'

'Terri King' -- See 'Moeterri'

'Terry Ann' -- See 'Rawgolface'

'Terry Edwards' -- See 'Websummer'

'Terry O'' F, rb, 1977, Hughes; flowers dark red, reverse copper yellow; [sport of 'Redgold']; intr. 1976

'Terry Wogan' F, dy

'Tersicore' ('Barzos') S, Barni, V.; intr. 1985

'Teschendorffs Jubiläumsrose' Pol, dr, 1928, Teschendorff; flowers vivid rosy crimson, darker than Orleans Rose and more brilliant; [sport of 'Orléans Rose']

'Teschendorffs Jubiläumsrose, Rankende' Cl F, dp, 1930, Teschendorff; flowers deep pink, fading to medium pink, small, dbl., borne in medium clusters

'Teschendorff's Unterlage' HMult, dp, about 1911

'Tesco Bernstein' F, dy, 1973, Haenchen, E.; bud ovoid; flowers brownish yellow, open, medium, semi-dbl., globular; foliage glossy, dark, leathery; vigorous, bushy growth; ['Cognac' × Allgold®]; intr. 1972

'Tesco Bernstein' -- See 'Bernstein'

'Tesco Blickfang' F, or, 1973, Haenchen, E.; bud ovoid; flowers dark vermilion-red, large, dbl.; foliage dark, soft; vigorous, upright, bushy growth; ['Dicksons Flame' × 'Circus']; intr. 1972

'Tesco Brennpunkt' F, or, 1973, Haenchen, E.; bud ovoid; flowers bright vermilion-red, open, medium, semi-dbl.; foliage dark, soft; vigorous, upright growth; ['Highlight' × 'Dickson's Flame']; intr. 1972

'Tesco Goldteppich' F, my, 1973, Haenchen, E.; bud ovoid; flowers medium, semi-dbl., cupped; foliage glossy, dark, leathery; vigorous, bushy growth; ['Cognac' × Allgold®]; intr. 1972

'Tesco Lichtblick' S, ob, 1973, Haenchen, E.; flowers pink and orange-pink on yellow ground, large, dbl., high-centered; abundant, continuous bloom; foliage glossy, leathery; vigorous, upright growth; ['Yellow Holstein' × 'Heidelberg']; intr. 1972

'Tesco Romanze' F, pb, 1973, Haenchen, E.; bud globular; flowers pink, center white, open, small, semi-dbl.; foliage small, glossy, dark, leathery; vigorous, dwarf, bushy growth; ['Marchenland' × unknown]; intr. 1972

Tesorino® Min, lp, 1983, Rose Barni-Pistoia; flowers fresh light pink, small, 20 petals, borne in clusters, no fragrance; free-flowering; foliage small, light green, matte; prickles light green; low (30-50 cm.), spreading growth; groundcover; [seedling × seedling]; intr. 1982

'Tess' HMult, mp, 1939, Beckwith; flowers Neyron pink, passing to deeper pink, center brighter, large, dbl.; foliage large, rich green; strong stems; very vigorous growth; RULED EXTINCT 11/91

'Tess' -- See 'Macramar'

'Tess' -- See 'Cletess'

'Tess of the d'Urbervilles' -- See 'Ausmove'

'Tessa ' F, mp, Gandy; flowers lilac-pink to rosey pink, slight fragrance; recurrent; foliage matte; compact, upright, medium growth; intr. 2003

'Tessa O'Keeffe' -- See 'Kenmoll'

'Testa Rossa' -- See 'Kordiam'

'Tête de Pavot' -- See 'Grosse Mohnkopfs Rose'

'Tête d'Or' F, my; flowers medium yellow, outer petals lighter, very dbl., shallow cup, borne usually in clusters, slight fragrance; big spring flush, recurrent;

low (50-60 cm.), compact growth; intr. 2005

'Teton Beauty' HRg, dp, 1927, Hansen, N.E.; flowers rich pink to crimson, dbl., cupped; recurrent bloom; foliage rugosa-like; very hardy; ['Tetonkaha' × 'American Beauty']

'Tetonkaha' HRg, dp, 1912, Hansen, N.E.; flowers deep rich pink, medium, semi-dbl.; profuse, non-recurrent bloom; vigorous (6 × 6 ft.) growth; hardy; [*R. macounii* × *R. rugosa* hybrid]

Teutonia® HT, dp, Noack, Werner

'Tewantin' Cl HT, dp, 1953, Ulrick, L.W.; bud globular; flowers deep pink, large, dbl.; long stems; vigorous (12 ft.) growth; ['Editor McFarland' × 'Editor McFarland']

'Texan' ('The Texan') Gr, mr, 1956, Lindquist; bud ovoid; flowers rose-red, 3½-4 in., 23 petals, high-centered, borne singly and in clusters, moderate fragrance; foliage dark, leathery; vigorous, upright growth; PP1471; ['Improved Lafayette' × 'Peace']

'Texas' HT, my, Kordes; bud long, pointed ovoid; flowers bright yellow, 4½-5 in., 35-40 petals, high-centered, borne singly, intense fruity fragrance; recurrent; foliage large, dark green, leathery, glossy; prickles average, short, hooked downward; stems long; vigorous, upright growth; PP8617; [seedling × 'Cocktail 80']; intr. 1993

Texas™ -- See 'Poultex'

'Texas Centennial, Climbing' Cl HT, rb, 1936, Dixie Rose Nursery (also Armstrong Roses, 1942); PP565; [sport of 'Texas Centennial']

'Texas Centennial' HT, rb, 1935, Watkins, A.F.; flowers vermilion-red with some gold, center lighter, dbl., intense fragrance; recurrent; tall growth; PP162; [sport of 'Pres. Herbert Hoover']

'Texas Centennial Panachée' HT, ob, 1939, Tantau, Math.; flowers light orange with white stripes, large, dbl.

Texas Girl™ -- See 'Meicijas'

'Texas Gold' HT, my, 1935, Wolfe; flowers golden yellow occasionally tinged pink, large, dbl., intense fragrance; PP135; [sport of 'Pres. Herbert Hoover']

'Texas Queen' HT, mp, 1965, Leidy; flowers base cream, shading to light and darker pink, large, 100 petals, intense fragrance; foliage light green, soft; almost thornless; vigorous growth; PP2565; [sport of 'Tip Toes']

'Texas Sunrise' -- See 'Umstex'

'Texas Wax' HMult, lp, before 1935; [sport of probably *R. multiflora* × *R. odorata*]

'Thaïs' -- See 'Memaj'

'Thalassa' HT, m, Dorieux; intr. 1978

'Thalia' ('White Rambler') HMult, w, 1895, Schmitt; bud pinkish; flowers very pure white, 3 cm., dbl., borne in large clusters, moderate fragrance; early, non-recurrent; few prickles; [*R. multiflora* × 'Paquerette']

'Thalia' -- See 'Thalie La Gentille'

'Thalia Remontant' ('Perpetual Thalia') HMult, w, 1903, Lambert, P.; flowers pure white, 2½-3 cm., semi-dbl. to dbl., borne in large clusters, strong musky fragrance; freely remontant; upright (8 ft.), branching growth; [('Thalia' × unknown) × 'Mme Laurette Messimy']

'Thalie La Gentille' ('Thalia') HGal, dp, before 1811, possibly Descemet; flowers deep rose, small, very full, cupped, moderate fragrance; sometimes classed as C

'Thandi' HT, dp; flowers deep petunia pink, dbl., high-centered; stems long; vigorous, tall growth; [sport of 'Mother's Value']; intr. 2000

'Thanet Ballerina' HT, w, 1974, Court; flowers pearl-white, blushed pink, moderate fragrance; foliage rich green; vigorous growth; [sport of 'Prima Ballerina']; intr. 1973

'Thank You' MinFl, pb, Chessum, Paul; flowers deep pink with shades of pink, yellow centers, semi-dbl., cupped, borne in clusters; foliage glossy; growth to 2 ft.; intr. 1996

'Thank You' -- See 'Tomteer'

Thanks To Sue™ -- See 'Morsalvatore'

'Thanksgiving' HT, ob, 1963, Warriner, William A.; bud ovoid; flowers bronze shades, reverse orange-red, 3½ in., 38 petals, high-centered; foliage dark, leathery; vigorous growth; ['Fred Howard' × seedling]; intr. 1962

'Thanksgiving' HT, pb, Howard, A. P.; buds medium, conical; flowers porcelain-rose with coppery tones, base of petals barium yellow, 4-4½ in., 35-45 petals, high-centered, borne mostly singly; foliage medium size, medium green; growth upright, branching, tall (5-7 ft.); hips ovoid, dark green; PP2524; ['Louis Philippe' × 'The Doctor']

'Thanx Mom' -- See 'Julesdear'

'Thanx Mum' -- See 'Julesdear'

Thari® S, dr

'That's Incredible' -- See 'Incredible'

'That's Jazz' ('Jazz', 'Naheglut') LCl, dr, Olesen; bud pointed ovoid; flowers intense dark red, 10 cm., 45-50 petals, flat, borne in small to medium clusters, moderate spicy, floral fragrance; recurrent; foliage large, dark green, glossy; prickles few, 6 mm., curved downward, light green; growth bushy, 200-300 cm.; PP12552; [seedling × Norita®]; intr. 1997

'Thé a Fleur Gigantesque' -- See 'Gigantesque'

'The Abbottsford Rose' -- See 'Wiljoeg'

'The Adjutant' HT, mr, 1922, Pemberton; bud long, pointed; flowers bright red, dbl.

'The Adjutant, Climbing' Cl HT, mr; flowers large, dbl.

'The Alamo' HT, mr, 1958, Meilland, F.; bud ovoid; flowers cardinal red, 3½-4½ in., 110 petals; foliage leathery; vigorous, upright, bushy growth; PP1689; ['Happiness' × 'Independence']; intr. 1957

'The Alexandra' -- See 'Alexandra'

'The Alexandra Rose' -- See 'Ausday'

'The Allies' Pol, w, 1930, Heers; flowers white suffused pale pink, small, dbl., open, borne in clusters, slight fragrance; foliage small, glossy; dwarf, bushy growth

'The Alnwick Rose' -- See 'Ausgrab'

'The Archbishop' -- See 'Tombaron'

'The Attenborough Rose' F, lp, Dickson; flowers delicate pink with green tinge on petal edges, large, dbl., cupped, borne in clusters of 4-17; recurrent; foliage medium green, glossy; few prickles; vigorous, upright to bushy growth; intr. 2005

'The Audrey Hepburn Rose' -- See 'UNICEF'

'The Auld Mug' HT, pb, Matthews; flowers antique pink, paling to beige, dbl., cupped; foliage medium green; upright, medium growth; intr. 2000

'The Australian Bicentennial' ('Bi-Centennial Rose') HT, mr, 1987, Bell, Ronald J.; flowers medium to deep red, well-formed, 30 petals, borne usually singly, intense fragrance; foliage medium size, medium green, glossy, disease-resistant; prickles curved, green; tall, branching, average growth; [('Daily Sketch' × unknown) × 'Red Planet']; named in commemoration of the Australian Bicentennial and the World Federation Rose Convention, 1988; intr. 1988

'The Backpackers Rose' -- See 'Horbondarc'

'The Bairn' HT, dy, 1977, Wood; flowers golden yellow, large, 40-50 petals; foliage dark, leathery; dwarf growth; ['Arthur Bell' × seedling]

'The Balvenie Rose' -- See 'Worcat'

'The Beacon' HWich, rb, 1922, Paul, W.; flowers bright fiery-red with white-eye (as in American Pillar), 5 cm., semi-dbl., cupped, borne in large clusters, no fragrance; foliage apple-green, glossy; numerous prickles; vigorous, climbing (to 8 ft.) growth

'The Belfast Operatic Company' -- See 'Worcalm'

The Belle Canadese™ HT, lp, 2006, Gareffa, N.; flowers delicate, creamy, light pink with a bit of yellow at the base, 3-4 in., full, borne mostly solitary, intense fragrance; continuous bloom; foliage medium size, medium green, semi-glossy; prickles small, slightly hooked, moderate; growth upright, short (about 2 ft.); ['Savoy Hotel' × seedling]

'The Bells of Hiroshima' -- See 'Hiroshima no Kane'

'The Beloved' -- See 'Priyatama'

'The Bishop' HT, dr, 1937, Dickson, A.; flowers bright crimson, large, dbl.; foliage dark; vigorous growth

'The Bishop' -- See 'Le Rosier Évêque'

'The Bishop of Bradford' S, dy, Pearce, J.; flowers deep old gold, moderate fragrance; foliage dark green, matte;

numerous prickles; growth to 12-15 in.; [sport of 'Maigold']; intr. 2006

'The Bourbon Jacques' -- See 'Bourbon Rose'

'The Braintree Rose' -- See 'Horlobrain'

'The Bride' T, w, 1885, May; flowers white tinged pink; [sport of 'Catherine Mermet']

'The Bride' HT, w, Herholdt, J.A.; bud pointed, ivory-white; flowers well-formed, 30 petals; foliage glossy; ['White Swan' × seedling]; intr. 1963

'The Brownie Rose' F, my, Harkness; flowers clear yellow, dbl., cupped, borne in clusters, moderate fragrance; recurrent; medium (1 m.) growth; intr. 2005

'The Bull' -- See 'Taurus'

'The Cambridge Rose' -- See 'Cantabrigiensis'

'The Care Rose' -- See 'Horapsunmolbabe'

'The Carer's Rose' -- See 'Tomcare'

'The Caron Keating Rose' F, ab, Harkness; flowers apricot in center, outer petals fading lighter, 4 in., dbl., high-centered, borne in trusses, slight fragrance; free-flowering; vigorous, bushy (80 cm.) growth; intr. 2006

'The Charlestonian' N, w, 2000, Patterson, William M.; flowers light pink, reverse white, 1 in., very full, borne in small clusters, slight fragrance; foliage medium size, medium green, semi-glossy; prickles moderate; growth spreading, medium (6 ft.); ['Champneys' Pink Cluster' × unknown]; intr. 2001

'The Cheshire Regiment' ('Good Morning') HT, ab, Fryer, Gareth; flowers apricot-salmon, high-centered; free-flowering; disease-resistant foliage; sturdy (3 ft.) growth; intr. 1995

'The Chief' ('Chief') HT, ob, 1940, Lammerts, Dr. Walter; bud long, pointed; flowers flame, coral and copper, 4-6 in., 35 petals, intense fragrance; vigorous, bushy, spreading growth; PP456; ['Charles P. Kilham' × 'Pres. Herbert Hoover']

'The Children's Rose' -- See 'Meitebros'

'The Children's Rose' -- See 'Meilivar'

'The Clerk' S, dr, Jerabek, Paul E.; intr. 1997

'The Colour Purple' -- See 'Jalpurple'

'The Colwyn Rose' F, m, Cowlishaw, Frank; flowers lavender to mauve, dbl., cupped to pompon, borne in clusters, slight fragrance; recurrent; intr. 1992

'The Commodore' -- See 'Kommodore'

'The Compass Rose' S, w, Kordes; flowers pure white with red stamens, semi-dbl., cupped, borne in clusters, intense fragrance; recurrent; foliage dark green, glossy; medium (3 ft.) growth; intr. 1997

'The Compassionate Friends' -- See 'Harzodiac'

'The Conductor' -- See 'Dirigent'

'The Constance Pink' -- See 'Rawgoldrog'

'The Cottage Rose' -- See 'Ausglisten'

The Countryman® -- See 'Ausman'

'The Coxswain' -- See 'Cocadilly'

'The Creakes Rose' -- See 'Woramble'

'The Crepe Rose' -- See 'Paul Perras'

'The Dahlia Rose' -- See 'Mordal'

'The Daldry Rose' -- See 'Horquandaldry'

'The Dandy' HT, dr, 1905, Paul, G.; flowers fiery maroon crimson, small; ['Bardou Job' × unknown]

The Daniel™ -- See 'Wildan'

'The Dark Lady' -- See 'Ausbloom'

'The Dawson Rose' -- See 'Dawson'

'The Dazzler' Cl HT, mr, 1955, Marsh's Nursery; flowers bright red, petals ruffled, single; profuse, repeated bloom; ['Dainty Bess, Climbing' × unknown]

'The Derby Rose' -- See 'Worabraham'

'The Didgemere Rose' -- See 'Fertry'

'The Dixon Rose' S, mp, Clements, John; flowers single; upright (4 ft.) growth; intr. 2004

'The Doctor' HT, mp, 1936, Howard, F.H.; flowers satiny pink, well-formed, 6 in., 25 petals; foliage soft, light; dwarf, bushy growth; ['Mrs J.D. Eisele' × 'Los Angeles']

'The Doctor, Climbing' Cl HT, mp, 1950, Dyess; flowers silky pink, 6 in., intense fragrance; [sport of 'The Doctor']

'The Doll's Festival' -- See 'Hinamatsuri'

'The Dove' -- See 'Ausdove'

'The Dove' -- See 'Tanamola'

'The Dowager Countess of Roden' HT, lp, 1919, Paul, W.; flowers bright silvery pink, dbl.; ['Viscountess Enfield' × 'George C. Waud']

'The Dragon's Eye' -- See 'Cledrag'

'The Duchess of Cornwall' -- See 'Tan97159'

'The Duke' HT, rb, 1956, Von Abrams; bud globular; flowers carmine-red, reverse gold, 5-6 in., 55 petals, high-centered, borne in clusters of 3 - 15, slight fragrance; foliage semi-glossy; vigorous, open growth; PP1522; ['Applause' × 'Peace']; intr. 1956

'The Ednaston Rose' LCl, w

'The Edwardian Lady' -- See 'Chewlegacy'

'The Endeavour' S, op, Austin, David; flowers salmon pink with yellow background, full, shallow cup, moderate spicy fragrance; free-flowering; foliage dark; growth to 4 ft.; favors hot weather

'The English Lady' ('Susan Daniel') F, ab, Harkness; flowers apricot-pink, fading lighter, 4 in., dbl., cupped, borne in clusters, moderate fruity fragrance; recurrent; medium (100 cm.), rounded growth; intr. 2005

'The Fairy' ('Dainty Double Pink Cushion Rose', 'Fairy', 'Fairy Rose', 'Féerie') Pol, lp, 1932, Bentall, Ann; flowers pink, small, dbl., rosette, borne in clusters, no fragrance; recurrent bloom; foliage glossy, small; compact, arching, spreading growth; hardy; ['Paul Crampel' × 'Lady Gay']

'The Fairy Queen' -- See 'Sperien'

'The Farmer's Wife' F, lp, 1962, Boerner; bud ovoid; flowers 4½ in., 38 petals, cupped, borne in clusters, intense fragrance; foliage leathery, glossy; upright, moderate growth; PP2196; [Queen Elizabeth® × 'Spartan']; intr. 1962

'The Farquhar Rose' -- See 'Farquhar'

The Faun™ -- See 'Pouloma'

'The Fisherman's Cot' -- See 'Harwicklow'

'The Flower Arranger' -- See 'Fryjam'

'The Fordham Rose' HT, rb, Williams, J. Benjamin; flowers medium red with plum edges, dbl., high-centered, moderate fragrance; foliage large, dark green, disease-resistant; intr. 1995

'The Freda Perry' -- See 'Worcycle'

'The French Strumpet' HGal, dp, 2006, Hulse, Merrill; flowers a mix of OGR and modern form, 1½ in., dbl., borne in small clusters, slight fragrance; once-blooming, in Spring; foliage medium green, typical Gallica; prickles moderate, 1/16 in., setaceous, brown; growth spreading, tall (6 ft.); specimen; [unknown × unknown]

'The Friar' S, lp, 1969, Austin, David; flowers blush, edged white, medium, 10 petals; repeat bloom; foliage dark; ['Ivory Fashion' × seedling]

The Garden Editor® -- See 'Minasco'

'The Gardener' -- See 'Jaczorba'

'The Garland' ('Splendid Garland', 'Wood's Garland', 'Wells's Garland') HMult, w, 1835, Wood or Wells; flowers faint yellow, pink, and white, semi-dbl., borne in corymbose clusters, moderate musk fragrance; late-season, not recurrent; prickles numerous, large; moderate climbing (8 ft.) growth; [probably R. moschata × R. multiflora]; sometimes classed as HMsk or Hsemp

'The Gathering' -- See 'Daniel Boon'

'The Gem' -- See 'Marie van Houtte'

'The General' HT, mr, 1920, Pemberton; flowers blood-red, flushed lighter, large, dbl., globular, moderate damask fragrance; foliage dark, bronze, leathery; vigorous, low growth

The Generous Gardener™ -- See 'Ausdrawn'

'The Gentleman' HT, yb, 1958, Hay; bud long; flowers creamy yellow flushed pink, semi-dbl.; [seedling × 'Irish Fireflame']

'The Gift' Pol, w, Demits; flowers pure white with yellow stamens, very small, single, flat, borne in long clusters, slight sweet fragrance; recurrent; foliage disease-resistant; vigorous, low growth; hips tiny, prolific, currant red; intr. 1981

The Gold Award Rose™ (Duke of Edinburgh™) F, dy, Olesen; flowers deep yellow, reverse lighter, 2½-3 in., very full, open cup, borne in large clusters, very slight fragrance; recurrent; foliage dark green, glossy; prickles some, 6 mm., linear to concave,; bushy (40-60 cm.) growth; PP15499; [seedling × 'Joey's Palace]; intr. 2003

The Official Registry and Checklist — Rosa 743

The Governator™ -- See 'Grenewgov'
'The Grace Land Rose' -- See 'Hordreamflight'
'The Great Showman' HT, dp, Shastri, Dr. N.V.; flowers deep, clear pink, large, dbl.; prickles very few; vigorous growth; intr. 2004
'The Green Rose' -- See 'Green Rose'
'The Guthrie Rose' -- See 'Welrose'
'The Halcyon Days Rose' -- See 'Kortersen'
The Herbalist™ -- See 'Aussemi'
'The Holt' -- See 'Mehsherry'
'The Hon Mrs Cat' D, mp, Scarman; non-remontant; growth to 4 ft.; intr. 1995
'The Hughes' -- See 'Bridesmaid'
'The Hunter' -- See 'Hunter'
'The Imposter' S, pb, 2007, Meilland International/ Star Roses; flowers with petals having a paint-splattered look, medium, single, clematis-like, borne mostly solitary; foliage medium green, semi-glossy; prickles moderate; growth compact, short (30 in.); R. laxa in background; intr. 2007
'The Impressionist' LCl, yb, Clements, John; flowers color varies from yellow to pumpkin orange, 4 in., 100 petals, moderate honey/peachy myrrh fragrance; recurrent; foliage dark green with slight blue cast; growth to 9-12 ft. high, 6-8 ft. wide; PPAF; intr. 2000
'The Indian' HT, dr, 1939, Clark, A.; flowers very dark red, large, semi-dbl.; vigorous growth; ['Sensation' × seedling]
The Ingenious Mr Fairchild™ -- See 'Austijus'
'The Ionian Rose' -- See 'Phyllis McDonald'
'The J. S. E. Rose' -- See 'Korgreyel'
'The Jacobite Rose' -- See 'Alba Maxima'
'The Jester' ('Leerder's Harlequin') Gr, yb, 1960, Leenders, J.; flowers yellow changing to red, compact, dbl., borne in clusters, slight fragrance; foliage dark; ['Masquerade' × 'High Noon']; intr. 1959
'The John Ray Trust Rose' -- See 'Horlobrain'
The Jubilee Rose™ -- See 'P. G. Wodehouse'
'The Karnival' -- See 'Meilasso'
'The King's Rubies' HMult, mr, Clements, John; flowers deep ruby red, 2 in., very full, cupped, borne in large clusters; once-blooming, long season; vigorous (15 ft.) growth; intr. 2000
'The Knight' S, dr, 1969, Austin, David; flowers crimson turning purple and mauve, petals soft, medium, 80 petals, flat, moderate Damask fragrance; recurrent; foliage dark green; ['Chianti' × seedling]
'The Ladakh Rose' -- See 'Ladakh Rose'
'The Lady' -- See 'Fryjingo'
'The Lady Scarman' HMsk, w, Scarman; flowers white; recurrent; growth to 5 ft.; there are reports of a version growing 12 ft. tall; intr. 1985

'The Lifeline Rose' -- See 'Walifeline'
'The Linda Smith Rose' -- See 'Websilver'
'The Lion' HMult, dp, 1901, Paul, G.; flowers bright crimson, white center, 7-10 cm., single, flat, borne in small clusters, no fragrance; ['Turner's Crimson Rambler' × 'Beauté Inconstante']
'The Lion' -- See 'Leo'
'The Little Mermaid' -- See 'Nolpeg'
The Magician™ S, yb, Clements, John; flowers open yellow, changing to orange, pink and red, 5 in., 10-12 petals, shallow cup, slight fragrance; recurrent; vigorous, medium to tall, bushy growth; intr. 2008
'Thé Maréchal' -- See 'Lamarque'
'The Marquess of Bristol' HT, yb, 1998, Webster, Robert; flowers yellow, pink edge, yellow reverse, 4-5 in., dbl., borne mostly singly, slight fragrance; foliage medium size, medium green, glossy; prickles moderate, medium, hooked; upright, medium growth; [Pristine® × Remember Me®]; intr. 1999
'The Master' HT, lp, Datta, Sekhar; bud pointed; flowers baby pink, well-formed; free-flowering; strong growth; intr. 2005
'The Master Cutler' HT, mr, 1954, Liberty Hill Nurs.; flowers cherry-red shaded rose, well-formed, very large, dbl.; vigorous growth; [sport of 'The Doctor']
'The Matsukawa Rose' -- See 'Horkedgeree'
The Matthew™ -- See 'Jaymatt'
'The Mayflower' -- See 'Austilly'
The McCartney Rose™ -- See 'Meizeli'
'The McClaren Rose' Min, dy, Jalbert; intr. 2000
'The Mencap Rose' -- See 'Brian Rix'
'The Merrion Rose' -- See 'Kensheco'
'The Meteor' HT, dr, 1887, Evans; bud large; flowers velvety crimson, large, semi-dbl., moderate fragrance
'The Meteor' ('Meteor') HT, mr, 1887, Evans/Bennett; flowers velvety crimson-carmine, open, medium, dbl., borne in clusters of 3-6; recurrent bloom; foliage small, soft; prickles few thorns; dwarf growth
'The Midlands Rose' -- See 'Delocabri'
'The Miller' S, mp, 1981, Austin, David; bud globular; flowers 40 petals, rosette, borne 1 - 4 per cluster, moderate fragrance; recurrent; foliage medium green; prickles hooked, red; upright, bushy growth; ['Baroness Rothschild' × Chaucer®]; intr. 1970
'The Moth' -- See 'Moth'
'The Mountie' F, mr, 1949, Eddie; flowers cherry-red, medium, 12-15 petals, borne in huge trusses; foliage leathery, glossy, light green; bushy growth; ['Springtime' × 'World's Fair']
'The Mouse' -- See 'Grey Pearl'
'The Nanango Rose' -- See 'Kathleen Kellehan'
'The New Century' -- See 'New Century'
'The New Dawn' -- See 'New Dawn'

'The New Riviera Rose' -- See 'Fortuna'
'The Nightwatch' S, rb, Williams, J.B.; flowers wine red and pink stripes, aging to purple-pink, borne in large clusters; foliage dark green; growth spreading; intr. 2003
'The Nun' S, w, Austin, David; flowers creamy white, semi-dbl., deeply cupped, borne in sprays, slight fragrance; free-flowering; stems slim, plentiful; upright (4 ft.) growth; intr. 1987
'The Nurse' S, w; intr. 2004
'The Observer' -- See 'Frytango'
'The Old Fashioned Rose' HT, 1930, Archer; flowers deep crimson, dbl.; very vigorous growth
'The Optimist' -- See 'Sweet Repose'
'The Painter' -- See 'Mactemaik'
'The Papworth Hospital Rose' -- See 'Lovatlas'
'The Pearl' -- See 'Purezza'
'The People' -- See 'People'
'The People's Princess' -- See 'Geepeop'
'The Phantom of the Opera Rose' -- See 'Worclerk'
The Physician™ -- See 'Matdoc'
The Pilgrim™ ('Gartenarchitekt Günther Schulze') S, my, Austin, David; bud globular, pointed ovoid; flowers yellow in center, fading to creamy white on outer petals, 2½-3¼ in., 170 petals, cupped, borne singly and in small clusters, intense tea and myrrh fragrance; recurrent; foliage bright green, leathery; prickles few, medium, hooked downward; stems medium to long; strong, upright (3-3½ ft.) growth; PP8678; [Graham Thomas® × Yellow Button®]; intr. 1993
'The Pink Professor' -- See 'Harforay'
'The Poet' S, dy, Clements, John; flowers deep primrose yellow, 3½ in., very full, cupped, intense fresh fragrance; recurrent; foliage deep green, glossy, holly-like; compact (3 ft.) growth; PPAF; intr. 2003
'The Polar Star' -- See 'Polstjärnan'
'The Pompeii Rose' -- See 'Summer Damask'
'The Portland from Glendora' -- See 'Johasine Hanet'
'The Portland Rose' -- See 'Duchess of Portland'
'The Prestbury Rose' -- See 'Worcoconut'
The Prince™ S, dr, Austin, David; bud long, globular, cuspidate apex; flowers dark magenta, 2¾ in., 125 petals, deeply cupped, flattens, borne singly and in clusters of up to 12, intense old rose fragrance; recurrent; foliage dark green, leathery; prickles numerous, straight, slanted downward; short (30-36 in.), upright, bushy growth; PP8813; [Lilian Austin® × The Squire®]; intr. 1990
'The Prince Imperial' F, dp, Delbard; bud globular; flowers deep pink with touch of orange, large, dbl., cupped, borne in clusters, slight fragrance; recurrent;

medium growth; intr. 1995

'The Prince's Trust' ('Prince's Trust') LCl, mr; flowers cherry red, 3½ in., dbl., borne in large clusters, from top to bottom, moderate sweet, spice fragrance; recurrent; foliage dark green; vigorous (10-12 ft.) growth; intr. 2002

'The Princess' -- See 'Mackinat'

'The Princess Elizabeth' HT, ob, 1927, Wheatcroft Bros.; flowers orange-yellow, edged deep cerise, large, dbl.; [sport of 'The Queen Alexandra Rose']

'The Princess of Wales' -- See 'Princess of Wales'

'The Prioress' S, lp, 1969, Austin, David; flowers blush to white, yellow stamens, medium, dbl., cupped, moderate fragrance; recurrent; vigorous, upright (4 ft.) growth; ['La Reine Victoria' × seedling]

'The PTA News Centenary' -- See 'Macgeorgi'

'The Puritan' HT, w, 1886, Bennett; flowers white, tinged light yellow at base, large, moderate fragrance; ['Mabel Morrison' × 'Devoniensis']

'The Queen' HT, ob, Lowe; bud pointed; flowers orange suffused salmon, medium, 26-30 petals, moderate fragrance; very free growth; intr. 1954

'The Queen' HMsk, dr, before 1936; flowers dark purple-crimson, large, semi-dbl.

'The Queen' -- See 'Souv de S. A. Prince'

'The Queen Alexandra Rose' ('Queen Alexandra') HT, rb, 1918, McGredy; bud old gold; flowers bright red, reverse shaded old-gold, base orange, 5 in., dbl., cupped, moderate fragrance; foliage glossy, dark; bushy growth

'The Queen Alexandra Rose, Climbing' Cl HT, rb, 1929, Lindecke (also Harkness, 1931); flowers light red, orange center, large, full, moderate fragrance; [sport of 'The Queen Alexandra Rose']

'The Queen Elizabeth Rose' -- See 'Queen Elizabeth'

'The Queen Elizabeth Rose, Climbing' -- See 'Queen Elizabeth, Climbing'

'The Queen Mother' F, mp, 1959, Stedman; flowers soft rosy pink, large, 45-50 petals, borne on large trusses; foliage glossy, light green; vigorous growth; [sport of 'Nymph']

'The Queen Mother' -- See 'August Seebauer'

'The Queen of Persia' HT, ob, 1940; flowers light orange-yellow, large, dbl.

'The Queen's London Child' -- See 'Happy Day'

'The Quest' -- See 'Harquince'

'The Rajah' HT, dr, 1937, Clark, A.; flowers deep red, dbl.; bushy growth; ['Red-Letter Day' × unknown]

The Reeve® S, dp, 1981, Austin, David; bud globular; flowers 58 petals, cupped, borne 1 - 5 per cluster, intense fragrance; repeat bloom; foliage red, turning to green; prickles hooked, red; spreading, shrubby growth; [Lilian Austin® × Chaucer®]; intr. 1973

'The Rhenish Rose' HT, lp, Kordes; flowers creamy pale pink, dbl., high-centered, borne mostly singly; recurrent; stems sturdy; medium growth; intr. 2000

'The Ribbon Rose' -- See 'Ribbon Rose'

'The Ridge School' -- See 'Pouldra'

'The Robe' -- See 'Tanseus'

'The Rose Tatoo' ('La Rose Tatouée') HT, m, 1958, Gaujard; flowers salmon-pink tipped and spotted lavender, large, semi-dbl.; foliage leathery; very vigorous, upright growth; [('Opera' × unknown) × ('Opera' × seedling)]

'The Roseville College' -- See 'The Roseville College Rose'

'The Roseville College Rose' ('Roseville College', 'The Roseville College') HT, yb; intr. 1990

'The Rotarian' -- See 'Rotary Sunrise'

'The Royal Brompton Rose' -- See 'Meivildo'

'The Royal Society of Organists Rose' F, lp, Tantau; intr. 2004

'The Rugby Rose' HT, ob, Gandy, Douglas; flowers apricot-orange, well-shaped, long-lasting, large, slight fragrance; foliage olive green, disease-resistant, commissioned by the Rugby Burough Council; intr. 2001

The St. Edmund's Rose™ -- See 'Poulen009(N)'

'The Sandylands Rose' -- See 'Evehorgold'

'Thé Sapho' -- See 'Mistress Bosanquet'

'The Schofield Rose' -- See 'Weksacsodor'

'The Scorpion' -- See 'Scorpio'

The Scotsman™ HT, m, Olesen; bud pointed ovoid; flowers lavender, 10-15 cm., 25-30 petals, high-centered, flattens, borne singly, slight spicy fragrance; recurrent; foliage dark green, glossy; prickles few, 5-8 mm., deeply concave; bushy, medium (2-3 ft.) growth; PP13293; [Karen Blixen™ × 'Mainzer Fastnacht']; intr. 2001

'The Seckford Rose' -- See 'Korpinrob'

'The Senator' HT, mr, 1981, Weeks, O.L.; bud ovoid, long; flowers bright medium red, petals loosely rolled outward, 46 petals, borne mostly singly, slight musk fragrance; foliage large, leathery, wrinkled, dark; prickles long, narrow-based, brown, curved down; tall, upright growth; PP4709; [seedling × 'Suspense']; intr. 1980

'The Service Rose' -- See 'Women in Military'

'The 777 Rose' ('777') HT, dr; flowers crimson to royal purple, velvety, large, double, cupped, moderate fragrance; recurrent; 4 - 6 ft. growth; Initial distributor described variously as ING or W.I.N. Inc.; intr. about 2001

'The Shepherdess' -- See 'Austwist'

'The Sir Steven Redgrave Rose' -- See 'Pure Gold'

'The Sobell Rose' F, dp, 2004, Paul Chessum Roses; flowers strong deep pink, 5 cm., full, borne in small clusters, slight fragrance; foliage medium size, medium green, semi-glossy; growth compact, medium (60 cm.); beds, borders, containers; intr. 2004

'The Soham Rose' ('Pearl Abundance') F, lp, Harkness; flowers pearl blush, dbl., high-centered, slight fragrance; recurrent; growth to 3 ft.; intr. 2004

'The Songbird Rose' -- See 'Lengra'

'The Soroptimist Rose' -- See 'Benstar'

'The Soroptimist Rose' -- See 'Stella Giles'

'The Spiedel Rose' -- See 'Jayspei'

The Squire® S, dr, 1981, Austin, David; bud globular; flowers very dark red, large, heavy, 120 petals, cupped, borne 1 - 3 per cluster, intense old rose fragrance; recurrent; foliage dark; prickles straight; open, bushy (3 ft.) growth; ['The Knight' × 'Château de Clos Vougeot']; intr. 1976

'The St Mark's Rose' -- See 'Rose d'Amour'

'The St Michael's Hospice Rose' -- See 'Liomich'

'The Stork' HT, mp, 1952, Whisler; bud long, pointed; flowers carmine-rose, 5-5½ in., 28 petals, high-centered; foliage leathery; bushy growth; PP1134; [seedling × 'The Doctor']

'The Sulgrave Rose' -- See 'Horsul'

'The Sun' F, op, 1974, McGredy, Sam IV; flowers salmon-orange, large, 15 petals; [('Little Darling' × 'Goldilocks') × 'Irish Mist']; intr. 1973

'The Sunflower' -- See 'Malso'

'The Surgeon' HT, mp, 1956, Verschuren; flowers darker rose-pink, more vigorous than the doctor, dbl.; ['The Doctor' × unknown]

'The Sweet Little Queen of Holland' ('Sweet Little Queen') T, yb, 1897, Soupert & Notting; bud long; flowers rich golden yellow, center shaded with orange and blush, large, dbl.; ['Céline Forestier' × 'Mme Hoste']

The Temptations™ -- See 'Wekaq'

'The Texan' -- See 'Texan'

'The Times Rose' -- See 'Korpeahn'

'The Twins' -- See 'Gemini'

'The Twins Rose' S, ob, Delbard; flowers bright orange, dbl., deep cup; recurrent; stems firm, medium-long; vigorous, medium growth; intr. 2001

'The Valois Rose' -- See 'Kordadel'

'The Venerable Bede' F, yb, 1973, Wood; flowers yellow to cherry, 3-3½ in., 20-30 petals; foliage small, glossy; moderate, free growth; ['John Church' × 'Bobby Shafto']

'The Wallflower' ('Wallflower') HMult, mr, 1901, Paul, G.; flowers bright red, 4-5 cm., semi-dbl., borne in medium clusters, moderate fragrance; late; prickles few, large; vigorous growth; ['Crimson Rambler' × 'Beauté Inconstante']

'The Wasa Star' -- See 'Polstjärnan'

'The Wedding Rose' -- See 'Geaaward'

'The Wendy Ackerman Rose' (Fire FoxTM) HT, ob; flowers orange, double, high-centered; growth medium height

'The Westbridge Rose' -- See 'Worcrazy'

'The Whitgift Rose' -- See 'Carwhit'

'The Widow of the South' -- See 'Ownwid'

'The Wife of Bath' ('Wife of Bath') S, pb, 1969, Austin, David; flowers deep rose-pink, reverse blush, outer petals fading blush, small to medium, very full, cupped, borne in clusters, intense myrrh fragrance; recurrent; foliage small, medium green; bushy, twiggy (3 ft.) growth; ['Mme Caroline Testout' × ('Ma Perkins' × Constance Spry®)]

'The Wild One' -- See 'Tomwild'

'The World' -- See 'Diekor'

'The Wright Brothers' HT, pb, 2005, Eddie Edwards & Ethan Phelps; flowers light to medium pink with shading on the petal edges, 4½ in., full, high-centered, borne mostly solitary, intense fragrance; recurrent; foliage medium size, dark green, glossy; prickles hooked, moderate; growth upright (5-6 ft.); exhibition; ['Hot Princess' × Signature®]; intr. 2005

'The Wyevale rose' -- See 'Meibalbika'

'The Yank' HT, mr, 1942, Joseph H. Hill, Co.; flowers rose-red, very large, 55-60 petals, intense fragrance; foliage leathery, dark; long, strong stems; very vigorous, upright, much branched growth; PP715; ['Chieftain' × 'Lucile Hill']

'The Yeoman' S, op, 1969, Austin, David; flowers salmon-pink, medium, 50 petals, cupped to flat, intense fragrance; recurrent bloom; moderate (100 cm.) growth; ['Ivory Fashion' × (Constance Spry® × 'Monique')]

'The Yvonne Arnaud Theatre Rose ' -- See 'Worartist'

'Thea Harrison' HT, lp, 1927, Harrison, A.

'Thea Russel' F, mr, 1954, Leenders, M.; flowers bright red; vigorous growth; ['Ambassadeur Nemry' × 'Cinnabar']

'Théagène' -- See 'Pucelle de Lille'

'Théano' HWich, lp, 1894, Geschwind, R.; flowers small, semi-dbl., cupped, borne in small clusters, no fragrance

'Theda Mansholt' Gr, my, 1966, Buisman, G. A. H.; bud ovoid; flowers medium, dbl.; foliage dark; upright growth; ['Peace' × 'Garden Party']

'Thelma' HWich, op, 1927, Easlea; flowers coral-pink, suffused carmine-red, center lighter, 3 in., semi-dbl., borne in clusters of 3-10; foliage light green, glossy; few prickles; vigorous, climbing growth; [R. wichurana × 'Paul's Scarlet Climber']

'Thelma Amling' Pol, w, 1942, Amling Bros.; bud globular; flowers small, semi-dbl.; foliage small, leathery; short stems; vigorous, bushy growth; [sport of 'Mrs R.M. Finch']

'Thelma Bader' HT, ob, 1958, Lathan; flowers orange-scarlet to salmon-pink, 3 in., 20 petals; foliage dark, glossy; moderately vigorous growth; [seedling × ('Independence' × 'Fashion')]; intr. 1957

'Thelma Barlow' HT, mp, Fryer; flowers porcelain pink, large, dbl., high-centered, moderate fragrance; good repeat; foliage dark green; upright (4 ft.) growth; intr. 2002

'Thelma Walton' HT, pb, 1974, Walton; flowers deep pink, lightly edged silver, very large, very dbl., high-centered; foliage glossy, dark; vigorous, upright growth; [sport of 'Red Devil']; intr. 1970

'Thelma's Glory' -- See 'Jalglory'

'Thémis' B, lp, about 1836, Bertin; flowers flesh pink, medium, semi-dbl.

'Themis' F, Gaujard; intr. 1984

Theodor Körner® S, mp, Lützow; flowers large, very full, shallow cup, moderate fruity fragrance; foliage red when young, matures to full green, large; upright (200 cm.), strong growth; intr. 1999

'Theodora' HT, dr, 1985, Staikov, Prof. Dr. V.; flowers large, 16 petals; ['Apricot Nectar' × 'Dame de Coeur']; intr. 1984

'Theodora Milch' HWich, mp, 1906, Weigand, C.; flowers very dbl., flat, borne in small to medium clusters, moderate fragrance; foliage small, glossy

'Théodore Liberton' HP, mr, 1887, Soupert & Notting; flowers carmine red nuanced madder pink, fading to deep pink, reverse light purple, large, dbl., moderate fragrance

'Theodore Roosevelt' -- See 'Burred'

'Theone' C, mp, before 1820, Noisette; flowers medium, very full; foliage oval, lightly dentate; prickles large and small, flattened and hooked

'Theresa' HT, ab, 1909, Dickson, A.; flowers dark orange-apricot, aging to pink, shaded carmine, dbl.

'Theresa Morley' HT, dp, 1928, H&S; flowers brilliant carmine-cerise, dbl.; ['Mme Segond Weber' × 'Lady Battersea']

'Theresa Scarman' HGal, lp, Scarman; flowers soft pink, full, cupped, non-remontant, intense fragrance; growth to 4 ft.; hardy; intr. 1996

'Therese Bauer' HSet, mp, 1963, Ludwig; flowers open, large, semi-dbl., borne in clusters; profuse, repeated bloom; very vigorous, upright growth; [('Hansa' × R. setigera) × R. setigera]

'Thérèse Bonnaviat' HT, lp, 1934, Chambard, C.; bud long, pointed; flowers clear pink, center coppery pink, very large; foliage purplish green; very vigorous growth; ['Mrs Arthur Robert Waddell' × seedling]

'Thérèse Bugnet' HRg, mp, 1950, Bugnet; bud conical but square-tipped; flowers rose aging pale pink, white center line on top of petals, 4 in., 35 petals, borne in small clusters, moderate spicy fragrance; repeat bloom; foliage quilted, grey-green; vigorous, 5-6 ft. growth; [((R. acicularis × R. rugosa kamtchatica) × (R. amblyotis × R. rugosa plena)) × 'Betty Bland']

Therese de Lisieux® HT, w, Orard; flowers pure white, dbl., high-centered, slight fragrance; foliage dark green, matte; growth to 80-100 cm.; intr. 1992

'Thérèse Lambert' T, pb, 1887, Soupert & Notting; flowers delicate rose, base of petals tinged with gold, center pale silvery salmon, very, full; ['Mme Lambard' × 'Socrate']

'Thérèse Margat' B, mp

'Thérèse Schopper' HT, mr, 1933, Kordes; bud long, pointed, blood-red; flowers nasturtium-red, reverse yellow, open, large, semi-dbl., high-centered; foliage leathery, dark; vigorous growth; [('Charles P. Kilham' × 'Mev. G.A. van Rossem') × 'Lady Forteviot']

'Therese Welter' -- See 'Baronne Henriette de Loew'

'Therese Zeimet-Lambert' HT, dp, 1922, Lambert, P.; bud long, pointed; flowers deep rose, yellow ground, base orange, large, dbl., high-centered; foliage glossy, bronze; vigorous growth; ['Richmond' × 'Mrs Aaron Ward']

'Theresette' S, mp, 1987, James, John; flowers deep soft pink edged white, carnation-like, medium, dbl., frilly, borne in clusters, moderate fragrance; foliage small, medium green, semi-glossy, disease-resistant; bushy, hardy, compact, dwarf growth; ['Arctic Glow' × 'Therese Bugnet']; intr. 1986

'Theresia' S, lp, 1925, Alfons; flowers small, single; hybrid canina

Theresie® F, ab, Noack; flowers salmon to apricot-pink, 4-5 cm., semi-dbl., shallow cup to flat, borne in clusters; recurrent if deadheaded; foliage dark green, glossy; low (50-70 cm.) growth; hips decorative; intr. 2004

'Thermidor' S, ly, 1909, Corboeuf-Marsault; flowers medium, dbl., moderate fragrance; ['Turner's Crimson Rambler' × 'Perle des Jardins']

'Thin Ink' -- See 'Usuzumi'

'Think Pink' -- See 'Tinthink'

'Thinking of You' HT, mr, Fryer; bud long, dark; flowers velvety, shaded blood red and deep crimson, dbl., high-centered, borne mostly singly, slight fruity fragrance; recurrent; foliage bright red when young, turning green with maturity; medium (85 cm.) growth

'Thirza' HT, or, 1932, Bentall; flowers orange-scarlet

This Is The Day™ -- See 'Sproday'

This Little Piggy™ -- See 'Moepiggy'

'Thisbé' ('À Odeur de Noisette') HCh, lp, about 1825, Noisette; flowers light flesh pink, medium, full, moderate hyacinth fragrance

'Thisbé' B, m, 1850, Robert

'Thisbe' HMsk, ly, 1918, Pemberton; flowers chamois-yellow, medium, dbl., rosette, borne in large clusters, intense musky fragrance; recurrent; vigorous, bushy (5 ft.) growth; [sport of 'Daphne']

'Thomas A. Edison' HT, pb, 1931,

Bernaix, P.; bud long, pointed; flowers two-toned pink, very large, dbl., cupped, moderate fragrance; recurrent; very vigorous growth

'Thomas Affleck' S, dp, 2005, Shoup, George Michael; flowers deep cerise pink, large, dbl., deeply cupped, borne mostly solitary, moderate fragrance; recurrent; foliage large, dark green, semi-glossy; few prickles; bushy, tall (6 ft.) growth; hedging; hips large; ['Carefree Beauty' × 'Basye's Blueberry']; intr. 1996

'Thomas Andrew Elliott' HT, yb, 1995, Thomas, D.; flowers golden yellow with yellow and pink reverse, 4 in., 41 petals, borne mostly singly; foliage medium size, medium green, semi-glossy; some prickles; medium (50-60 cm.), upright growth; ['Grandpa Dickson' × (('City of Gloucester' × seedling) × 'Polarstar')]

'Thomas Barton' -- See 'Meihirvin'

'Thomas Garces' HT, Dot, Simon; intr. 1986

'Thomas H. Elliott' HT, w; intr. 2002

'Thomas Methven' HP, dp, 1869, Verdier, E.; flowers bright carmine, large, full

'Thomas Mills' HP, dp, 1873, Verdier, E.; flowers rosy crimson, large, dbl., cupped; non-recurrent; vigorous growth

'Thomas Rivers' HP, m, 1857, Margottin; flowers lilac, large, full

'Thoom' ('Glamorgan') F, op, 1994, Thompson, M.L.; flowers coral-salmon, medium, 14 petals, borne in large clusters; foliage medium size, red when young turning to medium green, glos; some prickles; low to medium (2½ ft.), upright, compact growth; ['Old Master' × 'Red Splendor']; intr. 1995

'Thor' HSet, dr, 1940, Horvath; bud ovoid; flowers crimson-red, 4-5 in., 58 petals, slight damask fragrance; foliage large, leathery, dark; numerous prickles; vigorous, climbing (8-10 ft.) growth; PP387; [('Alpha' × R. xanthina) × 'Pres. Coolidge']

'Thor Supreme' LCl, dr, 1951, Horvath; flowers dark crimson edged deeper, 4 in., intense damask fragrance; foliage large, leathery, dark; vigorous, climbing growth

'Thora Hird' F, w, 1988, Bracegirdle, A.J.; flowers white deepen to cream in center with pink veins, loose, medium, 40 petals, moderate sweet fragrance; foliage medium size, dark green, semi-glossy; prickles straight, brown; bushy, medium growth; hips round, amber; [Chinatown® × 'Picasso']; intr. 1987

'Thora McCrea' HT, mr, 1987, Summerell, B.L.; flowers , 20-25 petals, high-centered; foliage dark green; prickles red-brown; well-shaped, upright, medium growth; ['Pink Parfait' × 'Crimson Glory']

'Thoresbyana' -- See 'Bennett's Seedling'

'Thorin' HP, mp, 1866, Lacharme; flowers brilliant carmine pink, large, dbl., widely cupped

'Thornbury Castle' -- See 'Harmusky'

'Thornfree Wonder' -- See 'Nobal'

'Thornhem' -- See 'Interway'

'Thornless Beauty' HT, dr, 1938, Grillo; bud long, pointed, dark crimson-red; flowers light crimson-red,, 4 in., 50 petals, moderate fragrance; foliage leathery; thornless; long, strong stems; vigorous growth; PP382; [sport of 'Better Times']

'Thornless Beauty' F, op, Patil, B.K.; flowers salmon-pink, large, semi-dbl.; medium growth; [sport of 'City of Lucknow']; intr. 1990

'Thornless Blush' HT, lp, 1954, Grillo; bud globular; flowers blush-pink, 4½ in., 70 petals, high-centered; foliage leathery; thornless; very vigorous, upright growth; [sport of 'Rosalind Russell']

'Thornless Fringedale' HT, lp, 1955, Grillo; flowers 4 in., 25 petals; thornless; [sport of 'Thornless Beauty']

'Thornless Glory' LCl, lp, 1935, Izzo; flowers clear pink, 3 in., 20 petals; early summer bloom; thornless; long stems; vigorous, climbing growth; PP236

'Thornless Mirage' HT, mr, 1955, Grillo; flowers red suffused blush-pink,, 5 in., 25 petals; thornless; [sport of 'Jewel']

'Thornless Premier' HT, mp, 1955, Grillo; bud globular, pointed; flowers rich pink, 4½ in., 75 petals, thornless; ['Victory Stripe' × 'Jewel']

'Thornless Victory Stripe' HT, rb, 1955, Grillo; bud long, pointed; flowers dark red and blush-pink, striped, 5 in., 50 petals; thornless; ['Victory Stripe' × 'Jewel']

'Thoughtful' -- See 'Resto'

'Thoughts Of Eileen' Min, ab, 2005, Paul Chessum Roses Ltd; flowers 3 cm., single, borne in small clusters, slight fragrance; foliage small, medium green, semi-glossy; prickles few, small, short, red; growth bushy, tall (24 in.); bedding, borders, containers; [seedling × seedling]; intr. 2005

Thoughts of Yesteryear™ -- See 'Byryesteryear'

'Thoughts of You' Min, dp; flowers pinky-red, cupped, borne in clusters, slight fragrance; free-flowering; foliage medium green; compact (18-24 in.) growth; intr. 1999

'Thousand Beauties' -- See 'Tausendschön'

'Thousand Kisses' F, mp, J&P; flowers age lighter , double , cupped, borne in clusters; recurrent; growth medium height

'Threads & Crafts' S, pb, Delbard; flowers silvery white with strong carmine flowing down from the petal edges, large , full, cupped, moderate fragrance; recurrent; moderate growth; intr. 2006

'Three Cheers' F, dp, Dickson; flowers cerise pink, fading with age, dbl., shallow cup, borne in clusters; free-flowering; foliage dense, medium green, glossy; rounded (85 cm.) growth; intr. 2005

'Three Weddings' ClMin, pb, Pallek; intr. 2004

'Thriller' HT, pb, 1987, Bridges, Dennis A.; flowers white center, pink edges, reverse slight pink edging, pink highlights with sun, large, 28-30 petals, high-centered, borne singly, moderate fruity fragrance; recurrent; foliage medium size, dark green, glossy; prickles medium, long, light green, pointed downwards; upright, medium, strong growth; ['Lady X' × 'Flaming Beauty']; intr. 1986

'Thumbelina' Min, rb, 1954, Moore, Ralph S.; flowers cherry-red, white eye, small, semi-dbl.; foliage dark, glossy; dwarf (6-8 in.), bushy growth; ['Eblouissant' × 'Zee']

'Thumbelina' -- See 'Sunthumb'

'Thumbs Up' -- See 'Hornothing'

'Thunder Bolt' HT, dr, Shastri, Dr. N.V.; bud long, tapered; flowers deep, sparkling red, large, broad; intr. 2002

'Thunder Cloud' Min, or, 1979, Moore, Ralph S.; bud ovoid; flowers currant red, showing more orange in bright sunlight, 1-1½ in., 70-80 petals, rounded, carnation-like, borne in tight clusters of 3-7, very slight fragrance; recurrent; foliage small, glossy, leathery, pointed; prickles average, slender, inclined downward, brown; stems slender, wiry; growth vigorous, bushy, upright (12-14 in.); hips none ; PP4624; ['Little Chief' × 'Fire Princess']

'Thunderbird' F, mr, 1959, deVor, Paul F.; bud urn-shaped; flowers rose-red, 2½ in., 48 petals, high-centered, borne in clusters of 3-8; vigorous, spreading growth; PP1677; [sport of 'Skylark']; intr. 1958

'Thunderbolt' -- See 'Bribolt'

'Thungabhadra' HT, ob, Kasturi; flowers coppery orange with carmine; intr. 1985

'Thusnelda' HRg, mp, 1886, Müller, Dr. F.; flowers soft rose pink, fading lighter, large, semi-dbl., cupped, moderate fragrance; non-recurrent; foliage rugose; vigorous, upright (100-150 cm.) growth; [R. rugosa alba × 'Gloire de Dijon']

'Thyra Hammerich' HP, lp, 1868, Hugues Vilin; flowers white slightly tinted flesh pink, more intense at base, large, very dbl., cupped, moderate sweet fragrance; repeats in late summer; foliage light violet; prickles few, small, hooked; growth to 5 ft.; ['Duchesse de Sutherland' × unknown]

'Thyrion' HT, McGredy, Sam IV; intr. 1969

'Tiamo' HT, dr, Spek; flowers brilliant dark red, medium, dbl.; strong, medium to tall growth; florist rose; intr. 1996

'Tiara' F, w, 1960, Boerner; bud ovoid, medium; flowers 3 in., 45-50 petals, cupped, borne in clusters, moderate tea fragrance; recurrent; foliage leathery; prickles average, medium, straight; stems long, strong; vigorous, bushy growth; hips none ; PP1981; ['Chic' × ('Demure' × unknown)]; florist rose; intr. 1960

'Tibeert' S, Delforge; intr. 1991

'Tibet' HT, w; flowers 30 petals; intr. 2008

'Tibet-Rose' S, my, Schultheis; flowers sunny yellow, wavy edges, red stamens, semi-double, cupped, slight tea rose fragrance; recurrent; broad, upright growth; ['Lichtkönigen Lucia' × 'Sämling']

'Ticino' F, mr, Huber; flowers vermilion red, large, dbl.; intr. 1979

'Tick-Tock' -- See 'Anytime'

'Ticker Tape' ClMin, op; intr. 2005

'Tickle Me Pink' -- See 'Pixink'

'Tickled Pink' HT, mp, 1963, Lammerts, Dr. Walter; bud long, pointed; flowers medium, dbl., high-centered, moderate spicy fragrance; upright, bushy growth; PP2369; [Queen Elizabeth® × 'Fashion']

'Tickled Pink' F, mp, Fryer; flowers large, full, hybrid tea, borne in clusters, slight fragrance; free-flowering; foliage very disease-resistant; vigorous, medium growth; intr. 2007

'Tickled Pink' -- See 'Suntick'

Tickles™ -- See 'Dyktick'

'Tidal Wave' -- See 'Browave'

'Tidbit Rose' -- See 'Conditorum'

Tiddly Winks™ -- See 'Wekglezno'

'Tidewater' -- See 'Britide'

'Tiecelijn' HT, Delforge; intr. 1990

'Tiergarten' HMult, dy, 1904, Lambert; flowers ochre-yellow, aging to white, small, full; ['Euphrosyne' × 'Safrano']

'Tiergartendirektor Timm' F, dp, 1944, Kordes; bud long, pointed; flowers carmine-pink, open, very large, semi-dbl., borne in clusters; foliage dark, glossy; very vigorous, upright growth; ['Sweetness' × 'Hamburg']

'Tiernan's Gold' -- See 'Seatier'

Tiffany™ ('Tiffany Hit') S, mp, Poulsen; flowers medium pink, 8-10 cm., dbl., moderate fragrance; foliage dark; growth bushy, 20-40 cm.; PP15722; intr. 2001

'Tiffany' HT, pb, 1954, Lindquist, R. V.; bud long, pointed ovoid; flowers pink-yellow blend, 4-5 in., 25-30 petals, high-centered, borne usually singly, intense tea fragrance; recurrent; foliage dark green, leathery, semi-glossy; prickles several, medium to long, almost straight, cinnamon; stems long, straight; vigorous, upright growth; hips turbinate, green; PP1304; ['Charlotte Armstrong' × 'Girona']; intr. 1954

'Tiffany, Climbing' ('Grimpant Tiffany') Cl HT, pb, 1958, Lindquist, R. V.; bud medium, pointed ovoid; flowers pink/yellow blend, 4-5 in., 25-30 petals, high-centered, borne usually singly, intense tea fragrance; recurrent; foliage dark green, leathery, semi-glossy; prickles several, medium to long, almost straight, cinnamon; stems medium; vigorous, upright, climbing growth; hips turbinate, green; PP1836; [sport of 'Tiffany']; like parent except for taller growth and shorter stems; intr. 1958

'Tiffany Hit' -- See 'Tiffany'

'Tiffany Lite' -- See 'Gellite'

'Tiffany Lynn' MinFl, pb, 1985, Jolly, Nelson F.; flowers light to medium pink at edges, blending to white in center, large, 21 petals, high-centered, borne singly and in small clusters, slight fragrance; recurrent; foliage medium size, medium green with red edges, semi-glossy; prickles slanted downward; stems long; upright, bushy growth; [('Tiki' × seedling) × Party Girl™]

'Tiffie' Min, lp, 1980, Bennett, Dee; bud long, pointed; flowers soft pink, sometimes apricot, 15-20 petals, high-centered, borne singly, moderate lilac fragrance; foliage medium green; prickles large, red; upright growth; PP5590; ['Little Darling' × 'Over the Rainbow']; intr. 1979

'Tifton' HT, yb, 1983, Perry, Astor; flowers brilliant yellow, petal tips red, red spreading with age, large, very full, high-centered, borne usually singly, moderate fragrance; recurrent; foliage large, medium size, semi-glossy; tall, bushy growth; ['Fire Magic' × 'Oregold']

'Tiger' ('Deborah Beggs Moncrief') HT, rb, McGredy, Sam IV; bud medium, ovoid; flowers orange-red, reverse yellow, 5-5½ in., 38-43 petals, high-centered, borne singly, slight sweet fragrance; foliage large, medium green, glossy, deeply dentate; prickles few, on main stalks and laterals; growth upright, vigorous, tall (5 ft.); ['Penthouse' × 'Macputar']; intr. 1990

'Tiger Belle' F, ob, 1962, Jelly; bud ovoid; flowers light signal-red, 2-2½ in., 25-35 petals, cupped; moderate growth; ['Orange Sweetheart' × 'Lovelight']; intr. 1962

'Tiger Butter' -- See 'Pixiter'

Tiger Cub™ -- See 'Poulcub'

'Tiger Eyes' S, yb, Warner; flowers yellow with red eye, single; recurrent; growth to 3-4 ft. high and twice as wide; bred from *R. persica*; intr. 2005

Tiger Paws™ -- See 'Lavtipaws'

'Tiger Stripes' -- See 'Cletig'

'Tiger Tail' -- See 'Jactiger'

'Tiglia' S, yb, 1962, Leenders, J.; flowers creamy yellow tinged pink, dbl.; recurrent bloom; ['Ma Perkins' × 'High Noon']

'Tigress' F, yb; intr. 2002

Tigress™ -- See 'Jacturpl'

'Tigris' -- See 'Harprier'

'Tiki' F, pb, 1964, McGredy, Sam IV; flowers light pink and white blend, well-formed, flora-tea, large, 30 petals; foliage dark; vigorous growth; ['Mme Léon Cuny' × 'Spartan']

'Tiki, Climbing' Cl F, pb

'Till Uhlenspiegel' HEg, rb, 1950, W. Kordes Söhne; bud pointed; flowers bright red, white eye, 5 petals, borne in clusters; non-recurrent; foliage large, glossy, dark reddish-green; tall (to 10 ft.), arching growth; ['Holstein' × 'Magnifica']

'Tillicum' HT, 1924, Wilber; flowers deep rose-pink shaded orange, dbl.; ['Général Jacqueminot' × 'Old Gold']

'Tilly Ashton' Gr, lp, Nieuwesteeg, J.; [sport of Queen Elizabeth®]; intr. 1996

Tilt Symphonie® Min, dr, Meilland; flowers bright red, dbl., borne in clusters; free-flowering; bushy (12-16 in.) growth; intr. 1994

'Tim Page' HT, 1920, Page; flowers rich daffodil yellow

'Timeless' ('White Timeless') HT, w, Pouw; bud ovate; flowers cream, fades quickly to white., 11 cm., 30 petals, high-centered, borne singly, very slight fragrance; recurrent; foliage dark green, leathery, semi-glossy; prickles normal, average size, concave, reddish-brown; vigorous, narrow, bushy growth; hips pitcher-shaped, large; PP9421; [seedling × seedling]; intr. 1995

Timeless™ -- See 'Jacecond'

'Timeless Beauty' -- See 'Korpeahn'

'Timeless Delight' -- See 'Rentdel'

'Times Past' ('Melba') LCl, mp; flowers shell pink, very dbl., cupped, moderate fruity fragrance; free-flowering; foliage matte, mid-green; growth climber to 8 ft.; intr. 2002

'Times Square' HT, ob, 1943, Lammerts, Dr. Walter; bud peach; flowers orange, center golden yellow, large; foliage leathery, glossy; vigorous growth; ['Mrs Sam McGredy' × 'Pres. Herbert Hoover']

'Timmie Arkles' F, lp, 1954, Boerner; flowers 3 in., dbl., flat, borne in clusters of 30-40, moderate fruity fragrance; vigorous growth; PP1320; ['Mrs R.M. Finch' × (('Improved Lafayette' × unknown) × ('Rochester' × unknown))]

'Timm's Jubilaümsrose' F, or, 1976, Kordes; bud globular; flowers 2 in., 27 petals, globular; foliage soft; vigorous, upright, bushy growth; ['Marlena' × Europeana®]; intr. 1975

'Timmy Williams' -- See 'Kentrib'

'Timothy Berlen' Min, ob, 1987, Jolly, Marie; flowers orange, yellow center, reverse yellow fading dark pink, medium, 20 petals, high-centered; foliage small, medium green, semi-glossy; prickles bayonet-shaped, light pink; upright, spreading, low growth; hips round, green-yellow-orange; [Anita Charles™ × 'Poker Chip']; intr. 1988

'Timothy Eaton' HT, op, 1968, McGredy, Sam IV; flowers salmon-pink, well-formed, dbl., slight fragrance; recurrent; ['Radar' × 'Mischief']

'Tina' F, ob, Tantau; florist rose

'Tina Marie' HP, w; flowers white touched with pink, moderate fragrance; recurrent; foliage large, drooping, grey-green; tall growth; [sport of 'Grandmother's Hat']

'Tina Turner' HT, ob, 1992, Thompson, Robert; flowers medium, full, borne mostly singly, moderate fragrance; foliage large, dark green, glossy; some prickles; bushy (60 cm.) growth; ['Silver Jubilee' × Doris Tysterman®]; intr. 1990

'Tinabler' ('Elizabeth Abler') Min, mr, 1991, Bennett, Dee; flowers medium red, opening to paler red at center, micro-mini, semi-dbl., high-centered, borne mostly singly, moderate fragrance; foliage small, medium green, semi-glossy; no prickles; low (20-30 cm.), bushy, compact growth; [('Christian Dior' × 'Brian Lee') × unknown]; intr. 1992

'Tinamigo' ('Little Amigo') Min, mr, 1983, Bennett, Dee; flowers small, 35 petals, high-centered, no fragrance; foliage small, medium green, semi-glossy; upright growth; PP5380; ['Futura' × 'Orange Honey']

'Tinarlene' ('Sweet Arlene') MinFl, m, 2001, Bennett, Dee; flowers very pale lavender, 2½-3 in., full, high-centered, borne in small clusters, intense fragrance; foliage medium size, medium green, semi-glossy; prickles moderate; growth upright, vigorous, medium (2½-3 ft.); garden, cutting, exhibition; [Lagerfeld™ × 'Ernie']; intr. 2002

'Tinbab' ('Big and Beautiful') Min, ab, 1999, Bennett, Dee; flowers deep apricot, 1-1½ in., full, borne mostly singly, slight fragrance; foliage medium size, medium green, semi-glossy; prickles moderate; upright, bushy, tall (5-6 ft.) growth; ['Futura' × Jean Kenneally™]; intr. 2000

'Tinbaby' ('Ooo! Baby!') Min, rb, 2000, Bennett, Dee; flowers full, high-centered, borne mostly singly, moderate fragrance; foliage medium size, medium green, matte; few prickles; growth bushy, medium (18-24 in.); [Shocking Blue® × Jean Kenneally™]; intr. 2001

'Tinbopper' ('Teeny Bopper') Min, rb, 1989, Bennett, Dee; bud ovoid; flowers white with red blush on outer petals, aging red with white, semi-dbl., cupped, slight damask fragrance; foliage small, medium green, semi-glossy; no prickles; micro-mini, bushy growth; hips globular, yellow-green-orange; PP7449; ['Little Squirt' × seedling]; intr. 1988

'Tinbuford' ('Linda Buford') Min, ly, 1993, Bennett, Dee; flowers soft light yellow, medium, full, borne mostly singly; foliage small, medium green, semi-glossy; some prickles; medium, bushy growth; ['Irish Gold' × Jean Kenneally™]; intr. 1994

'Tinbutt' ('Bread 'n' Butter') Min, ob, 1985, Bennett, Dee; flowers golden orange blended yellow, 5 cm., 28 petals, cupped, borne usually singly, some small clusters, moderate fragrance; recurrent; foliage medium size, medium green, semi-glossy; prickles moderate, slender, hooked slightly downward; stems long; upright, bushy growth; hips globular, orange; PP6135; ['Arizona' × 'Orange Honey']; intr. 1985

'Tincarol' ('Little Carol') Min, dp, 1990, Bennett, Dee; bud ovoid; flowers deep magenta-pink, reverse slightly lighter, medium, 38 petals, high-centered, borne singly, slight spicy fragrance; foliage medium size, dark green, semi-glossy, disease-resistant; prickles hooked slightly downward, red, few; upright, tall growth; hips globular, green-brown; PP7970; ['Sonia' × Jean Kenneally™]; intr. 1989

'Tinchan' ('Dr K. C. Chan') Min, my, 1987, Bennett, Dee; flowers medium yellow, fading pale yellow, medium, 25-30 petals, urn-shaped, borne usually singly, slight fragrance; foliage medium size, medium green, semi-glossy; prickles slender, straight, reddish; mini-flora; upright, bushy, medium growth; hips globular, medium, brown; ['Irish Gold' × 'Rise 'n' Shine']; intr. 1986

'Tincheer' ('Cheer Up') Min, ob, 1986, Bennett, Dee; flowers deep orange, 28 petals, high-centered, urn-shaped, borne usually singly and in small clusters, slight fragrance; foliage medium size, dark, semi-glossy; prickles small, red; medium, upright, bushy growth; hips globular, 1½ in., green and brown; PP6456; ['Futura' × 'Bread 'n' Butter']

'Tinchocolate' ('White Chocolate') Min, w, 2001, Bennett, Dee; flowers cream, dbl. to full, high-centered, borne mostly solitary, slight fragrance; recurrent; foliage medium size, medium green, semi-glossy; prickles moderate; stems long; growth upright, tall (2½-3 ft.); garden decorative, exhibition, cutting; [sport of Jean Kenneally™]; intr. 2001

'Tinchris' ('Christopher') Min, mr, 1988, Bennett, Dee; flowers medium red, medium, 30-35 petals, high-centered, borne usually singly or in sprays of 3-5; foliage medium size, medium green, semi-glossy; prickles hooked slightly downward, yellow-red; upright, medium growth; hips globular, green-brown; PP7191; ['Futura' × 'Big John']

'Tinchula' ('Chula Vista') Min, dr, 1992, Bennett, Dee; flowers medium, full, high-centered, borne mostly singly, slight fragrance; foliage small, medium green, semi-glossy, disease-resistant; some prickles; long stems; medium (60-80 cm.), bushy growth; ['Christian Dior' × 'Brian Lee']; intr. 1993

'Tincuddle' ('Cuddle Up') Min, yb, 1991, Bennett, Dee; bud ovoid; flowers creamy yellow with coral pink blush, medium, 25-30 petals, high-centered, moderate fruity fragrance; foliage medium size, medium green, semi-glossy; bushy, medium growth; [Lagerfeld™ × 'My Delight']; intr. 1990

'Tincupie' ('Cupie Doll') Min, lp, 1983, Bennett, Dee; flowers light pink with fine coral edging on petals, heavy substance, 25 petals, high-centered, slight fragrance; foliage small, medium green, semi-glossy; upright, bushy growth; PP5518; [seedling × 'Coral Treasure']

'Tindad' ('Love 'Ya Dad') Min, mr, 1996, Bennett, Dee; flowers do not fade, 1½ in., full, high-centered, borne mostly singly, intense fragrance; foliage medium size, dark green, semi-glossy, disease-resistant; prickles moderate; stems long; growth upright, bushy, tall (70-80 cm.), vigorous; ['Carrousel' × 'Big John']; intr. 1997

'Tindawn' Min, yb, 1982, Bennett, Dee; bud ovoid

'Tindeb' ('Debra Gaye') Min, op, 1985, Bennett, Dee; flowers orange-pink, soft yellow reverse, medium, 38 petals, high-centered; foliage medium size, medium green, semi-glossy; bushy, upright growth; PP6136; ['Futura' × 'Fairest of Fair']

'Tindel' ('Del Mar Fair') F, dp, 1993, Bennett, Dee; flowers deep pink, 3-3½ in., full, borne in large clusters, moderate fragrance; foliage medium size, medium green, semi-glossy; some prickles; medium, upright, bushy growth; ['Gene Boerner' × 'Pucker Up']; intr. 1994

'Tindick' ('High Cloud') Min, r, 1997, Bennett, Dee; flowers soft tan with yellow base, lighter reverse, 1½ in., full, borne singly or in small clusters, moderate fragrance; foliage medium size, medium green, glossy; bushy, tall (60-70 cm.) growth; [Lagerfeld™ × 'Ernie']

'Tindilly' ('Dilly Dilly') MinFl, m, 1985, Bennett, Dee; flowers lavender, medium, 35 petals, high-centered, moderate fragrance; foliage medium size, medium green, semi-glossy; upright growth; PP6141; ['Chrysler Imperial' × 'Plum Duffy']; intr. 1984

'Tindink' ('Fair Dinkum') Min, pb, 1983, Bennett, Dee; flowers soft pink, petal margins darker, small, 25 petals, high-centered, slight fragrance; foliage small, medium green, semi-glossy; upright, bushy growth; PP5564; [seedling × 'Coral Treasure']

'Tindonn' ('Brian Donn') Min, dr, 1991, Bennett, Dee; bud ovoid; flowers darkest ruby red to maroon, dark ruby red reverse, ages only slightly lighter, medium, 35-45 petals, high-centered, moderate damask fragrance; foliage medium size, medium green, semi-glossy; bushy, medium growth; ['Intrique' × 'Big John']; intr. 1990

'Tindream' ('Dreamy') Min, yb, 1987, Bennett, Dee; flowers cream, edges blushed pink, reverse cream with more intense blush, 20-25 petals; foliage medium size, medium green, semi-glossy; prickles slender, small, reddish, slanted downward; upright, medium growth; hips globular, medium, brown; ['Irish Gold' × Party Girl™]

'Tineally' (Jean Kenneally™) Min, ab, 1984, Bennett, Dee; flowers pale to medium apricot, small, 22 petals, high-centered, borne mostly singly;

foliage medium size, medium green, semi-glossy; long stems; upright, bushy, vigorous growth; PP5637; ['Futura' × Party Girl™]

'Tineke' HT, w, 1990, Select Roses, B.V.; bud pointed, ovoid; flowers creamy white, 4 in., 50-55 petals, cupped with high center, borne singly, very slight fragrance; recurrent; foliage large, dark green, semi-glossy; prickles yellow-green with reddish tip; stems strong, upright; upright, tall growth; hips pear-shaped ; PP8055; [seedling × seedling]; intr. 1990

Tineke van Heule® -- See 'Lentini'

'Tinernie' ('Ernie') Min, m, 1989, Bennett, Dee; bud ovoid; flowers light mauve, medium, 48 petals, urn-shaped, borne occasionally singly and in clusters of 6-12, moderate fruity fragrance; foliage medium size, medium green, semi-glossy; prickles hooked slightly downward, pale yellow-brown, few; upright, bushy, tall growth; hips globular, yellow-brown; [Blue Nile® × 'Blue Mist']

'Tingail' ('Gail') MinFl, yb, 1986, Bennett, Dee; flowers golden yellow with orange blush on petal tips, orange spreading with age, large, 38 petals, high-centered, borne singly, moderate fragrance; foliage large, medium green, semi-glossy; prickles small reddish; medium, bushy, spreading growth; hips globular, 5/8 in., light green; ['Arizona' × 'Orange Honey']; intr. 1986

'Tingirl' ('Bloomer Girl') Min, op, 1984, Bennett, Dee; flowers soft vermilion to medium pink, small, 35 petals, slight fragrance; foliage medium size, medium green, semi-glossy; upright, bushy growth; PP5523; ['Futura' × 'Pink Petticoat']; intr. 1983

'Tingrace' ('Grace Seward') Min, w, 1991, Bennett, Dee; bud ovoid; flowers medium, 5 petals, moderate damask fragrance; good repeat; foliage medium size, medium green, semi-glossy; bushy, tall growth; PP8899; ['Watercolor' × seedling]; intr. 1990

'Tinhat' ('G'Day', 'Madhatter') Min, my, 1988, Bennett, Dee; flowers medium yellow, aging paler, medium, 25-30 petals, high-centered, borne usually singly or in sprays of 3-5, moderate damask fragrance; foliage medium size, medium green, semi-glossy; prickles hooked slightly downward, reddish; bushy, medium growth; hips globular, green-brown; ['Autumn' × 'Avandel']

'Tinheart' ('California Heart') MinFl, or, 2004, Bennett, Dee; flowers orange-red, reverse orange, medium, dbl., high-centered, borne mostly solitary, slight fragrance; foliage medium size, medium green, semi-glossy, disease-resistant; stems long; growth bushy, medium (18-30 in.); garden, containers, exhibition; ['Futura' × Jean Kenneally™]; intr. 2003

'Tinhelen' ('Helen') Min, mr, 1991, Bennett, Dee; flowers medium, full, high-centered, borne mostly singly, moderate fruity fragrance; foliage small, medium green, semi-glossy, disease-resistant; some prickles; long cutting stems; tall (60-80 cm.), upright, bushy growth; ['Carrousel' × Starina®]; intr. 1992

'Tinherb' ('Herbie') Min, m, 1987, Bennett, Dee; flowers rich mauve, outer petals deep mauve at margins, 25-30 petals, urn-shaped, slight fragrance; foliage medium size, medium green, semi-glossy; prickles slender, straight, average, reddish; upright, bushy, medium growth; hips globular, medium size, brown; PP6787; ['Deep Purple' × 'Dilly Dilly']

'Tinhuzzy' ('Little Huzzy') Min, rb, 1991, Bennett, Dee; flowers white with striping of pink to medium red over most upper surfaces of petals, large, full, high-centered, borne mostly singly, moderate fragrance; foliage small, medium green, semi-glossy, disease-resistant; some prickles; stems long; growth tall (60-80 cm.), upright; ['Futura' × 'Pucker Up']; intr. 1992

'Tinjean' ('Jean Rose') Min, pb, 1987, Bennett, Dee; flowers peach-pink with yellow base, reverse soft yellow, fading lighter, 20-25 petals; foliage medium size, medium green, semi-glossy; prickles few, slender, small, reddish; upright, medium growth; hips globular, medium size, brown; [Electron® × 'Fairest of Fair']

'Tinjosh' ('Josh') Min, dy, 1999, Bennett, Dee; flowers 1-1½ in., full, borne singly and in small clusters, slight fragrance; foliage medium size, medium green, semi-glossy; prickles moderate; upright, bushy, medium (2-3 ft.) growth; ['Futura' × 'Rise 'n' Shine']; intr. 2000

'Tinjudy' ('Something for Judy') MinFl, pb, 1995, Bennett, Dee; flowers cream with deep pink blush, medium, dbl., borne mostly singly; foliage medium size, medium green, semi-glossy; tall (2-3 ft.), bushy growth; ['Angel Face' × 'Big John']; intr. 1995

'Tinkay' ('Kay Denise') Min, pb, 1995, Bennett, Dee; flowers soft creamy pink, pink blush margins, full, high-centered, borne mostly singly, moderate fragrance; foliage small, medium green, semi-glossy; some prickles; upright, bushy, tall growth; PP10946; ['Tiki' × 'My Delight']; intr. 1995

'Tinker Bell'   Min, mp, 1954, deVink; bud ovoid; flowers bright rose-pink, 1½ in., 60 petals, cupped, borne in irregular clusters, very slight fragrance; free-flowering; foliage small, leathery; prickles few, medium, straight; stems medium; dwarf (8 in.), bushy growth; no hips; PP1293; ['Ellen Poulsen' × 'Tom Thumb']

'Tinkerbell' -- See 'Suntink'

'Tinketeer' ('Roseketeer') Min, ob, 2001, Bennett, Dee; flowers soft orange with a bright white eye, 1-1½ in., single, borne mostly solitary, no fragrance; foliage medium size, medium green, semi-glossy; few prickles; growth compact, low (1-2 ft.); garden decorative, containers, exhibition; ['Angel Face' × seedling]; intr. 2001

'Tinkin' ('Punkin') Min, ob, 1983, Bennett, Dee; flowers orange with yellow eye, ages red, 5 petals, borne singly, no fragrance; foliage small, medium green, semi-glossy; upright growth; PP5522; ['Orange Honey' × 'Orange Honey']

'Tinlady' ('Always A Lady') Min, m, 1988, Bennett, Dee; flowers pale mauve to lavender, medium, 25-30 petals, high-centered, borne usually singly or in sprays of 3-5, moderate damask fragrance; foliage medium size, medium green, semi-glossy; prickles hooked slightly downward, pale yellow; bushy, medium growth; hips globular, green-brown; PP7187; ['Deep Purple' × 'Dilly Dilly']; intr. 1987

'Tinlee' ('Brian Lee') Min, m, 1986, Bennett, Dee; flowers dark red, aging mauve, 28 petals, high-centered, urn-shaped, borne in small clusters; foliage medium size, dark, semi-glossy; prickles small reddish; medium, upright, bushy growth; hips 5/8 in.; globular, brown-green; PP6789; ['Carrousel' × 'Plum Duffy']

'Tinleslie' ('Leslie') Min, mp, 1997, Bennett, Dee; flowers 1¼ in., dbl., borne in small clusters; foliage medium size, medium green, semi-glossy; bushy (40-50 cm.), tall growth; ['Deep Purple' × Jean Kenneally™]; intr. 1997

'Tinlips' ('Hot Lips') Min, op, 1988, Bennett, Dee; flowers deep coral to orange, aging paler, medium, 25-30 petals, high-centered, borne usually singly, slight fruity fragrance; foliage medium size, medium green, semi-glossy; prickles hooked slightly downward, reddish; upright, bushy, tall growth; hips globular, green to yellow-brown; ['Futura' × 'Why Not']

'Tinlois' ('Lois') Min, mp, 1985, Bennett, Dee; flowers medium lilac pink, medium, dbl., high-centered; foliage medium size, medium green, semi-glossy; upright, bushy growth; PP6140; ['Deep Purple' × 'Plum Duffy']

'Tinlove' ('Mother's Love') Min, pb, 1989, Bennett, Dee; bud ovoid; flowers pastel pink, blending to soft yellow at base, medium, 23 petals, high-centered, slight fruity fragrance; foliage medium size, medium green, semi-glossy; prickles straight, tapering, reddish; upright, bushy, medium growth; hips globular, green-yellow-brown; PP7484; ['Futura' × Party Girl™]; intr. 1988

'Tinluis' ('Luis Desamero') Min, ly, 1989, Bennett, Dee; bud ovoid; flowers pastel yellow, medium, 28 petals, high-centered, borne usually singly and in sprays of 3-5, slight fruity fragrance; foliage medium size, medium green, semi-glossy; prickles straight and tapering, pale yellow, reddish base; upright, bushy, tall growth; hips globular, green-yellow-orange; PP7496; ['Tiki' × Baby Katie™]; intr. 1988

'Tinmad' ('Madeline Spezzano') MinFl, mp, 1985, Bennett, Dee; flowers medium, 45 petals, high-centered; foliage large, medium green, semi-glossy; upright, bushy growth; PP6132; ['Sonia' × 'Beauty Secret']

'Tinmary' ('Ms Mary') Min, yb, 1999, Bennett, Dee; flowers pale yellow/apricot, reverse pale yellow, 1 in., full, borne mostly singly, moderate fragrance; foliage medium size, medium green, semi-glossy; prickles moderate; compact, bushy, low (18-24 in.) growth; ['Deep Purple' × 'Fairest of Fair']; intr. 1999

'Tinmere' ('Meredith Anne') Min, pb, 1984, Bennett, Dee; flowers salmon-pink, soft pink reverse, 23 petals, high-centered, borne in clusters; prickles brown to pale yellow; vigorous growth; PP5630; ['Sonia' × 'Tea Party']; intr. 1983

'Tinmurphy' ('Dr Murphy's Magic Touch') Min, m, 2000, Bennett, Dee; flowers mauve, 1½-2 in., full, exhibition, borne mostly singly; foliage medium size, medium green, dull; prickles moderate; growth bushy, tall (3 ft.); [Lagerfeld™ × 'Brian Lee']; intr. 2001

'Tinmyde' ('My Delight') Min, lp, 1984, Bennett, Dee; flowers small, 30 petals, high-centered; foliage medium size, medium green, semi-glossy; upright, spreading growth; PP5437; ['Futura' × 'Avandel']; intr. 1983

'Tinnaughty' ('Naughty But Nice') Min, ab, 1991, Bennett, Dee; bud ovoid; flowers soft apricot, medium, 20-25 petals, high-centered, slight damask fragrance; foliage medium size, medium green, semi-glossy; bushy, tall growth; ['Futura' × 'Why Not']; intr. 1990

Tino Rossi® ('Your Garden') HT, mp, Meilland; flowers soft rose pink, large, dbl., high-centered, borne mostly singly, intense fragrance; free-flowering; vigorous (90-100 cm) growth; intr. 1990

'Tinold' ('Old Fashioned Girl') Min, w, 1992, Bennett, Dee; flowers soft lavender to white, large, full, similar to OGRs, intense fragrance; foliage small, medium green, semi-glossy; some prickles; medium (60-80 cm.), bushy growth; ['Blue Ribbon' × 'miniature seedling']; intr. 1993

'Tinpanky' ('Hanky Panky') Min, ob, 1991, Bennett, Dee; flowers range from orange to golden peach as they open, large, full, borne mostly singly, moderate fruity fragrance; foliage small, medium green, semi-glossy, disease-resistant; some prickles; medium (40-60 cm.), bushy, spreading growth; ['Deep Purple' × Party Girl™]; intr. 1992

'Tinpat' ('Patty Sue') Min, mp, 1985, Bennett, Dee; flowers medium, 35 petals, high-centered; foliage medium size, medium green, matte; vigorous, upright growth; ['Little Darling' × 'Little Chief']

'Tinpauline' ('Pauline') Min, w, 2004, Fletcher, Ira; flowers pure white, 1-1½ in., dbl., high-centered, borne mostly solitary, slight fragrance; good repeat; foliage small, light green, semi-glossy; growth compact, short (12-18 in.); garden decoration, containers, exhibition; ['Fairhope' × June Laver™]; intr. 2004

'Tinpeaces' ('Little Peaces') Min, yb, 1985, Bennett, Dee; flowers yellow, edged pink, medium, 33 petals, high-centered; foliage medium size, medium green, semi-glossy; compact, bushy growth; [Electron® × 'Fairest of Fair']

'Tinpin' ('Hat Pin') Min, m, 1987, Bennett, Dee; flowers pale lavender, small, 12-15 petals, urn-shaped, borne usually singly, moderate fruity fragrance; foliage small, medium green, semi-glossy; prickles straight, extremely small, pale yellow; micro-mini upright,bushy, low growth; hips globular, small, brown; PP6790; ['Angel Face' × Angelglo™]; intr. 1986

'Tinpleasure' ('Ultimate Pleasure') Min, pb, 1999, Bennett, Dee; flowers light pink, reverse medium pink, 1-1½ in., 25-35 petals, high-centered, cupped, borne mostly singly or in small clusters, moderate fragrance; recurrent; foliage medium size, medium green, semi-glossy; prickles moderate, slender, hooked slightly downward, reddish; extremely vigorous, bushy, upright, tall (24-36 in.) growth; PP12179; ['Gene Boerner' × Jean Kenneally™]; intr. 1999

'Tinpops' ('Pops') Min, dp, 1984, Bennett, Dee; flowers deep pink, small, 20 petals, high-centered; foliage medium size, medium green, semi-glossy; bushy growth; PP5424; ['Sheri Anne' × 'Little Girl']; intr. 1983

'Tinporce' ('Pink Porcelain', 'Porcelain Pink') Min, lp, 1983, Bennett, Dee; flowers small, 23 petals, high-centered, borne singly and in clusters; foliage small, medium green, semi-glossy; upright growth; PP5470; ['Futura' × 'Avandel']

'Tinpuck' ('Pucker Up') Min, or, 1984, Bennett, Dee; bud small; flowers bright, velvety orient-red with some darker shadowing, 1-1½ in., 20-25 petals, urn-shaped, borne usually singly, slight fragrance; good repeat; foliage medium size, medium green, semi-glossy; prickles small, slender, straight, reddish; upright, bushy growth; PP5407; ['Futura' × 'Avandel']; intr. 1983

'Tinqueen' ('Bingo Queen') Min, pb, 1996, Bennett, Dee; flowers light pink with medium pink inner petals, 1½ in., full, high-centered; foliage medium size, medium green, semi-glossy; prickles moderate; bushy, medium (50-60 cm.) growth; [Brandy™ × Jean Kenneally™]; intr. 1997

'Tinquiet' ('Quiet Time') MinFl, m, 1995, Bennett, Dee; flowers lavender-pink with inner petals of soft tan, small, full, borne mostly singly; foliage medium size, medium green, semi-glossy; bushy growth; [Lagerfeld™ × 'Ernie']; intr. 1995

'Tinresist' (Irresistible™) Min, w, 1990, Bennett, Dee; bud ovoid; flowers white with pale pink center, medium, greenish in shade, 43 petals, high-centered, borne singly and in small clusters, moderate spicy fragrance; foliage medium size, medium green, semi-glossy; prickles straight, yellow with red; upright, tall growth; hips globular, green to yellow-brown; PP7971; ['Tiki' × 'Brian Lee']; intr. 1989

'Tinrevenge' ('Sweet Revenge') Min, ob, 1995, Bennett, Dee; flowers soft orange with blush of deep orange on outer petals, 2 in., 25 -35 petals, urn-shaped to cupped, borne mostly singly; recurrent; foliage medium size, dark green, semi-glossy; prickles moderate, slender, hooked slightly downward; tall (2-3 ft.), bushy growth; PP9776; ['Tony Jacklin' × 'Pucker Up']; intr. 1995

'Tinrita' ('Rita Applegate') MinFl, ly, 1996, Bennett, Dee; flowers light yellow to softest gold with heart of deeper yellow/gold, 2 in., full, high-centered, borne mostly singly, moderate fragrance; foliage medium size, medium green, semi-glossy; prickles moderate; long-stemmed; growth upright, bushy, tall (80-90 cm.); ['Pink Porcelain' × unknown]; intr. 1997

'Tinroy' ('Rowdy Roy') MinFl, rb, 2005, Bennett, Dee; flowers variable in color, from scarlet to deep burgundy with pink to white striping, 2½-3 in., full, borne mostly solitary, slight fragrance; foliage medium size, medium green, matte; prickles small, straight; growth compact, short (2-2½ ft.); garden, cut flower, exhibition; ['October' × 'Fool's Gold']; intr. 2005

'Tinruth' ('Ruthie') Min, w, 1988, Bennett, Dee; flowers cream-white with pink blush on outer petals, aging paler with deeper blush, 2 in., 25-30 petals, cupped, borne usually singly, moderate damask fragrance; recurrent; foliage medium size, medium green, semi-glossy, aging darker; prickles hooked slightly downward, yellow to reddish; upright, tall growth; hips globular, green-brown; PP7189; ['Sonia' × 'Little Melody']

'Tinsassy' ('Fat 'n' Sassy') Min, rb, 1986, Bennett, Dee; flowers white with a reddish border, reverse white, aging reddish blush, 28 petals, cupped, borne singly, slight fragrance; foliage medium size, medium green, semi-glossy; prickles small, reddish; medium, upright, bushy growth; hips globular, 5/8 in., green-brown; PP6455; ['Carrousel' × 'Sheri Anne']

'Tinseltown' HT, pb, Edwards, Eddie; intr. 1996

'Tinshine' ('My Sunshine') Min, my, 1986, Bennett, Dee; flowers medium yellow, aging soft orange, bright yellow stamens, single, flat, borne singly and in small clusters, moderate fragrance; foliage medium size, medium green, semi-glossy; prickles small, reddish-brown; medium, upright, bushy growth; hips globular, 1/2 in., green; PP6453; ['Sunsprite' × 'Fool's Gold']

'Tinshort' ('Short 'n' Sweet') Min, dp, 1984, Bennett, Dee; flowers deep pink, very small, 35 petals; foliage medium size, medium green, semi-glossy; bushy, spreading growth; ['Sheri Anne' × seedling]

'Tinshoultz' ('Bonnie Jack') F, ly, 2000, Bennett, Dee; flowers full, high-centered, borne in small clusters, slight fragrance; foliage medium size, medium green, matte; prickles moderate; growth upright, tall (4-5 ft.); ['Irish Gold' × Party Girl™]; intr. 2001

'Tinsit' ('Sitting Pretty') Min, pb, 1986, Bennett, Dee; bud ovoid; lacy sepals; flowers apricot-pink, yellow base, 35-40 petals, high-centered, borne usually singly, occasionally in small clusters, moderate damask fragrance; foliage medium size, medium green, semi-glossy; prickles small, straight, red; stems long, with long peduncle; medium (2-3 ft.), upright, bushy growth; hips globular, 1/2 in., yellowish-green; PP6454; ['Sonoma' × 'Mabel Dot']

'Tinsnook' ('Snookie') Min, ob, 1984, Bennett, Dee; flowers deep orange, blushing red with age, very small, 33 petals; foliage medium green, semi-glossy; bushy, tiny growth; ['Torchy' × 'Orange Honey']

'Tinspice' ('Sugar 'n' Spice') Min, lp, 1985, Bennett, Dee; flowers light peach-pink, medium, 28 petals, high-centered; foliage medium size, medium green, semi-glossy; upright, bushy growth; PP6139; ['Futura' × 'Avandel']

'Tinspring' ('Spring Bouquet') Min, pb, 1985, Bennett, Dee; flowers crimson pink, blended with yellow, medium, high-centered; foliage medium size, medium green, semi-glossy; upright, bushy growth; ['Portrait' × Party Girl™]

'Tinsquirt' ('Little Squirt') Min, dy, 1984, Bennett, Dee; flowers micro-mini, very small, 14 petals, high-centered; foliage small, medium green, semi-glossy; upright, compact growth; intr. 1983

'Tinstaley' ('Ruth Staley') Min, mp, 1990, Bennett, Dee; bud ovoid; flowers medium shell pink, reverse lighter, medium, 25 petals, high-centered, borne singly and occaisionally in clusters of 3-5, moderate fruity fragrance; foliage medium size, dark green, semi-glossy, disease-resistant; prickles slender, straight, red; upright, tall growth; hips globular, green-brown; [Electron® × 'Peachy Keen']; intr. 1989

'Tinstar' ('Starstruck') Min, ob, 1986, Bennett, Dee; flowers deep golden orange with petals edged red, reverse medium red, 32 petals; foliage medium size, medium green, semi-glossy; prickles small, thin, reddish; low, spreading growth; hips globular, 3/8 in., brownish; ['October' × 'Orange Honey']

'Tinsweet' ('Sweet Pickins') Min, lp, 1987, Bennett, Dee; flowers pale pink, medium, 35-40 petals, urn-shaped, borne usually singly, moderate fruity fragrance; foliage medium size, medium green, semi-glossy; prickles slender, straight, small, reddish; micro-mini upright, bushy, medium growth; hips globular, medium, brown; PP6788; ['Futura' × Party Girl™]

'Tintagel' LCl, w, McLeod, J.; [sport of R. brunonii seedling?]

'Tintai' ('Yantai') MinFl, yb, 1989, Bennett, Dee; bud ovoid; flowers pastel yellow, deeper yellow in center and pink blush on outer petals, 25-30 petals, high-centered, cupped, borne usually singly, moderate fruity fragrance; recurrent; foliage medium size, medium green, semi-glossy; prickles some, hooked downward, yellow to red; bushy, spreading, tall, vigorous growth; PP7962; ['Portrait' × Party Girl™]; intr. 1988

'Tintail' ('Cottontail') Min, w, 1983, Strawn, Leslie E.; flowers small, 33 petals, borne in large clusters; foliage medium size, medium green, semi-glossy; upright, bushy growth; PP5436; ['Pink Petticoat' × 'Pink Petticoat']

'Tinthink' ('Think Pink') Min, mp, 1983, Bennett, Dee; flowers soft pink, outer petals fade quickly, golden stamens, small, 28 petals, intense apple fragrance; foliage small, medium green, semi-glossy; bushy growth; PP5670; [Electron® × 'Little Chief']

'Tintin' F, or, 1964, Mondial Roses; flowers cinnabar-red, large, semi-dbl., cupped, borne in large clusters; moderate growth

Tintinara™ -- See 'Dicuptight'

'Tintwee' ('Tweedle Dee') Min, op, 1987, Bennett, Dee; flowers coral pink, reverse lighter, small, 35-40 petals, urn-shaped, borne usually singly, slight fragrance; recurrent; foliage small, medium size, semi-glossy; no prickles; micro-mini upright, bushy, low growth; hips globular, small, brown; ['Deep Purple' × Cupcake™]; intr. 1986

'Tinviolet' ('Lavender Mist', 'Violet Mist') MinFl, m, 1993, Bennett, Dee; flowers pale soft lavender, medium, full, borne mostly singly, slight fragrance; recurrent; foliage small, medium green, semi-glossy; some prickles; medium, bushy growth; [Lagerfeld™ × 'Ernie']; intr. 1994

'Tinwell Moss' ('Cramoisi', 'Damas Mousseux', 'Crimson Moss', 'Crimson Moos', 'Crimson') M, dp, before 1827, Tinwell/Lee; bud large, well mossed; flowers very dark rose pink, large, dbl.; foliage large

'Tinwild' ('Wild Thing') Min, ob, 1992, Bennett, Dee; flowers bright orange-yellow, large, dbl., borne mostly singly, moderate fruity fragrance; foliage small, medium green, semi-glossy, disease-resistant; some prickles; medium (60-80 cm.), bushy growth; ['Gingersnap' × Baby Katie™]; intr. 1993

'Tinx' ('X-Rated') Min, pb, 1993, Bennett, Dee; flowers creamy white, edges blush a soft coral to pink, medium, 4-5 cm., 25-35 petals, cupped, borne mostly singly, moderate fragrance; recurrent; foliage small, medium green, semi-glossy; prickles some, slender, hooked slightly downward, reddish; medium, bushy growth; PP9375; ['Tiki' × Baby Katie™]; intr. 1994

Tiny Bubbles™ -- See 'Jacbub'

Tiny Dancer™ -- See 'Wildance'

'Tiny Flame' Min, or, 1969, Moore, Ralph S.; flowers coral-orange-red, micro-mini, very small, dbl., rosette, borne in clusters; free-flowering; foliage very small; dwarf (6 in.), bushy growth; [(R. wichurana × 'Floradora') × 'New Penny']

'Tiny Grace' HT, pb, Teranishi; intr. 2005

'Tiny Jack' Min, mr, 1962, Moore, Ralph S.; bud pointed; flowers 1-1½ in., 28 petals, cupped; foliage leathery, dark; vigorous, bushy (12-14 in.)growth; PP2484; [(R. wichurana × 'Floradora') × ('Oakington Ruby' × 'Floradora')]; intr. 1962

'Tiny Jewel' S, lp, Williams, J.B.; flowers blush pink, golden stamens, single, borne in clusters; growth low; groundcover; intr. 2003

'Tiny Jill' Min, mp, 1962, Moore, Ralph S.; bud pointed; flowers dbl., 45 petals, high-centered, moderate fragrance; foliage glossy; vigorous, bushy (12-14 in.) growth; PP2483; [(R. wichurana × 'Floradora') × 'Little Buckaroo']; intr. 1962

'Tiny Love' Min, dr, 1981, Lyon; bud ovoid; flowers 11 petals, cupped, borne 1-3 per cluster, intense fragrance; foliage dark; prickles straight; open, bushy growth; [seedling × seedling]; intr. 1980

'Tiny Petals' -- See 'Tinypetals'

'Tiny Stars' -- See 'Trastar'

'Tiny Tears' Min, mp, 1979, Bennett, Dee; bud ovoid; flowers soft pink, fading lighter, yellow stamens, very small, 5 petals, borne in clusters of 10 - 25; foliage glossy, dark, small; trailing (12 in.) growth; ['Pink Ribbon' × 'Pink Ribbon']

'Tiny Tim' F, my, 1943, Brownell; bud long, pointed; flowers clear yellow, open, small, 23 petals, high-centered; foliage glossy; moderately vigorous, compact to open growth; ['Golden Glow' × 'Shades of Autumn']

'Tiny Tot' Min, mp, 1955, Robinson, T.; flowers deep cerise-pink; very dwarf growth

'Tiny Tot' -- See 'Bentintot'

'Tiny Visions' Min, rb, 1981, Lyon; bud long; flowers crimson with white center,

5 petals, cupped, borne mostly singly; foliage dark, apple-scented; prickles very tiny, hooked, brown; very tiny, bushy growth; [seedling × seedling]; intr. 1980

'Tiny Warrior' Min, rb, 1976, Williams, Ernest D.; bud ovoid; flowers 1 in., 34 petals, flat; foliage small, glossy, very dark, embossed; upright, bushy growth; ['Starburst' × 'Little Chief']; intr. 1975

'Tinypetals' ('Tiny Petals') Min, rb, 1992, Bennett, Dee; flowers geranium lake with cream reverse, 1½-2 in., 25-35 petals, high-centered, borne mostly singly, very slight fragrance; recurrent; foliage small, dark green, semi-glossy, disease-resistant; prickles some, average, slender, hooked slightly downward; stems long; medium (60-80 cm.), bushy growth; PP9319; ['San Antonio' × Jean Kenneally™]; intr. 1993

'Tinzel' ('Zelda Lloyd') Min, mp, 1988, Bennett, Dee; flowers medium pink, reverse deep pink, 2-3 cm., 5 petals, shallow cup to flat, borne usually singly, slight fruity fragrance; recurrent; foliage medium size, medium green, semi-glossy; prickles hooked slightly downward, reddish; bushy, medium growth; hips globular, green-yellow-brown; PP7190; ['Deep Purple' × 'Blue Mist']

'Tione Pietro' -- See 'Pietro Tione'

'Tip Toes' HT, op, 1948, Brownell; bud pointed; flowers salmon-pink, shading to yellow at base, large, semi-dbl., high-centered, moderate fragrance; foliage glossy; vigorous, upright growth; PP849; [(('Général Jacqueminot' × 'Dr. W. Van Fleet') × 'Anne Vanderbilt']

Tip-Top® ('Baby Doll') Pol, w, 1909, Lambert, P.; flowers white, tipped Tyrian rose, aging white and pale yellow, reverse white, dbl.; bushy, dwarf growth; [Trier® × (*R. foetida bicolor* × unknown)]

'Tip Top' F, op, Tantau, Math.; flowers salmon-pink, fading lighter, large, semi-dbl. to dbl., cupped, borne in clusters, moderate fragrance; free-flowering; foliage disease-resistant; short (2 ft.), vigorous growth; intr. 1964

'Tip Top, Climbing' Cl F, op

'Tipo Ideale' -- See 'Mutabilis'

Tipper™ Min, mp, 1988, Jolly, Marie; flowers medium pink, touch of coral early, aging lighter, 1½ in., 32-36 petals, high-centered, borne singly, slight fragrance; recurrent; foliage medium size, medium green, semi-glossy; prickles very few, medium, bayonet, light brown; stems long, straight; upright, medium growth; hips round, 1.4 cm., orange; PP7340; ['Chris Jolly' × Chattem Centennial™]; intr. 1988

'Tipperary' HT, my, 1917, McGredy; bud long, pointed; flowers golden yellow, semi-dbl.; ['Mrs Aaron Ward' × unknown]

'Tipsy' HT, dp, 1969, Trew, C.; flowers soft rose, reverse geranium-red, pointed, large, dbl.; foliage dark, dull; free growth; ['Basildon Belle' × seedling]

'Tipsy Imperial Concubine' T, pb; flowers soft pink with tones of lemon and red, large, full, globular, moderate fragrance; recurrent; moderate (2-3 ft.) growth; intr. 1989

Tipu's Flame™ -- See 'Virtipu'

'Tira-Mi-Su' HT, ab, 1999, Teranishi, K.; flowers pale copper and orange blend, 5 in., 28 petals, slight fragrance; growth to 4½ ft.; [('Julia' × seedling) × seedling]; intr. 1994

'Tirza' HT, mr, 2002, Poole, Lionel; flowers full, high-centered, borne mostly solitary, slight fragrance; foliage medium size, medium green, semi-glossy; prickles moderate, medium, slightly hooked; growth upright, bushy, medium (1 m.); garden decorative, exhibition; ['Adrienne Berman' × ('Royal William' × 'Gabi')]

'Titania' Ch, rb, 1915, Paul, W.; flowers deep salmon-red, shaded clear yellow at base, small, dbl.; dwarf, bushy growth

'Titania' Pol, lp, 1938, Leenders, M.; flowers salmon-flesh to rosy white, large, very dbl.; foliage leathery, dark; vigorous, bushy growth; ['Mev. Nathalie Nypels' × seedling]

'Titanic' F, w, McGredy; flowers creamy white edged with blush pink, 4 in., 20 petals, high-centered, moderate tea fragrance; recurrent; foliage shiny, dark green; sturdy (3½ × 3 ft.) growth; intr. 1999

'Titi Parisien' F, dr, 1959, Delbard-Chabert; flowers crimson, center lighter, stamens ivory, 3 in., 5 petals; bushy, low growth; [('Francais' × unknown) × ((Orange Triumph® × unknown) × 'Floradora')]

'Titian' F, dp, 1950, Riethmuller; flowers dusky cerise pink, large, dbl., rounded, then flat, borne in clusters, slight fragrance; recurrent; vigorous, tall growth

'Titian, Climbing' Cl F, dp, 1964, Kordes

'Tivoli' F, mp, 1955, Poulsen, S.; flowers warm rose-pink, center yellow, well-formed, 3 in., 24 petals, borne in clusters; foliage dark, glossy; very vigorous growth; ['Poulsen's Supreme' × ('Souv. de Claudius Denoyel' × 'Hvissinge-Rose')]; intr. 1954

'Tivoli' -- See 'Poulduce'

Tivoli 150™ -- See 'Poulduce'

'Tivoli Gardens' -- See 'Poulduce'

'Tiz' -- See 'Tzigane'

'Tiziana' F, op, 1969, Cazzaniga, F. G.; bud pointed; flowers copper-pink, large, semi-dbl.; foliage light green; vigorous, compact growth; ['Papillon Rose' × 'Gay Paris']

To Mummy™ -- See 'Dicwhynot'

Tobago® -- See 'Deltogo'

'Tobainoko' Min, lp

Tobo™ -- See 'Kinbo'

'Toboné' -- See 'Prima Donna'

'Toby Jo' Min, yb, 1997, Garrett, Troy O.; flowers yellow and orange, lighter reverse, pink tips, 1 in., dbl., borne singly, no fragrance; foliage medium size, medium green, semi glossy; few prickles; upright, medium (16-20 in.) growth; [sport of 'Old Glory']

'Toby Tristram' HMult, w; bud pink; flowers cream, fading to white, 3 cm., single, moderate musk fragrance; some repeat; foliage medium green, soft; vigorous, very tall growth; rediscovered by Mrs. Targett; intr. about 1970

Tocade® F, yb; flowers yellow, striped rose pink, dbl., cupped, borne in clusters; recurrent; foliage semi-glossy; vigorous (90-110 cm) growth; intr. 2000

'Tocade' -- See 'Werina'

'Toccata' F, or, 1959, Lens; flowers well-formed, borne in large clusters; low growth; ['Independence' × 'Cinnabar']

'Toccata' HT, mp, Sanday, John; flowers light rose edged darker, reverse silvery, becoming redder, 5 in., 27 petals, moderate fragrance; vigorous growth; ['Karl Herbst' × seedling]; intr. 1963

Today™ -- See 'Maccompu'

'Toddler' F, pb, 1976, LeGrice; flowers pink, reverse deeper,, 2 in., 19 petals; foliage small, dark; very low, bushy growth; [seedling × seedling]; intr. 1977

'Todoroki' HT, dr, 1977, Keisei Rose Nurseries, Inc.; bud pointed; flowers 6½ in., 33 petals, high-centered; foliage dark; vigorous growth; [('Pharaon' × 'Kagayaki') × 'Yu-Ai']

'Toffee' -- See 'Seatoff'

'Together For Ever' -- See 'Bosarthric'

'Together Forever' ('Forever Together') F, op, Dickson; flowers orange with yellow center, turning to pale peach-pink, 4 in., 23 petals, cupped, borne in clusters of 5 - 25; recurrent; foliage dense, light to medium green, semi-glossy; upright to bushy (95 cm.) growth; intr. 2006

'Togo' HT, Cazzaniga, F. G.; intr. 1959

'Tohbai-no-ko' -- See 'Fuyuume-no-ko'

'Toison d'Or' HT, ab, 1921, Pernet-Ducher; flowers apricot-yellow, shaded orange-red, dbl.

'Toison d'Or' -- See 'Golden Fleece'

Tojo® F, mr, McGredy, Sam IV; flowers dbl., cupped, borne in clusters; recurrent; intr. 1978

'Tokay' -- See 'Ziptok'

'Token' HT, yb, 1933, Montgomery Co.; bud ovoid; flowers glowing orange, open, large, dbl., moderate fragrance; foliage glossy; strong stems; vigorous growth; PP95; ['Mme Butterfly' × 'Premier Supreme']

'Token Glory' HT, or, 1959, Grillo; bud pointed; flowers orange, 4 in., 40 petals, moderate fragrance; foliage dark, leathery; long stems; very vigorous, upright, bushy growth; [sport of 'Token Supreme']; intr. 1957

'Token Supreme' HT, ob, 1940, Grillo; flowers deep orange, 5 in., 35 petals; [sport of 'Token']

'Tokimeki' F, dp, Ichibashi; intr. 1995

'Tokonatsu' ('Endless Summer') HT, ob,

Keisei; intr. 2005

'Tokyo' Cl F, my, 1972, Oliver, W.G.; flowers 3 in., 5 petals; profuse May-June bloom; foliage light; vigorous growth; ['Salute' × 'Canary Bird']

Toledo™ ('Toledo Hit') S, yb, Poulsen; flowers yellow blend, 8-10 cm., dbl., no fragrance; foliage matte; growth bushy, 20-40 cm.; PP15041; intr. 2003

'Toledo Gold' HT, my

'Toledo Hit' -- See 'Toledo'

Toliman® Min, m; intr. about 1992

'Tolstoï' HSet, mp, 1938, Böhm, J.; flowers pale pink, reverse slightly darker, 8-10 cm., dbl., globular, intense fragrance; non-remontant; tall (2 m.) growth

'Tom Barr' HT, op, 1932, McGredy; bud long, pointed; flowers salmon and scarlet, suffused yellow and orange, large, dbl., high-centered; vigorous growth

'Tom Breneman, Climbing' Cl HT, dp, 1954, H&S

'Tom Breneman' HT, dp, 1950, Howard, F.H.; bud ovoid; flowers rose-pink, red stamens, 4-4½ in., 30-40 petals, globular, intense fragrance; recurrent; foliage leathery, dark; very vigorous, upright growth; PP986; ['Mauna Loa' × R.M.S. Queen Mary]

'Tom Brown' F, r, 1964, LeGrice; flowers orangy-brown, reverse brownish-red, well-shaped, 3 in., 32 petals, borne singly and in clusters, intense fragrance; recurrent; foliage leathery, dark; vigorous, bushy growth; [seedling × 'Amberlight']

'Tom Delahanty' Min, pb, 2008, Delahanty, James; flowers pink/white, 2 in., single, borne mostly solitary; foliage medium-size, medium green, semi-glossy; prickles ¼ in., straight, brown, moderate; growth to 2 ft.; [sport of 'Hurdy Gurdy']; intr. 2008

'Tom Foster' HT, my, Poole, Lionel; flowers medium yellow, large, very dbl., borne mostly singly, moderate fragrance; foliage medium size, dark green, semi-glossy; some prickles; bushy, medium growth; ['Gertrude Shilling' × Helmut Schmidt®]; intr. 1996

'Tom Maney' LCl, mp, 1953, Maney; bud ovoid; flowers rose-pink, 4-5 in., 35-40 petals, cupped, borne in clusters of 3-4; non-recurrent; foliage leathery, dark; vigorous, climbing (15-20 ft.) growth; quite hardy; [R. maximowicziana pilosa × 'Kitchener of Khartoum']

'Tom Pilliby' F, or, 1963, Combe; flowers semi-dbl., borne in large clusters; vigorous growth

'Tom Thumb' ('Peon') Min, rb, 1936, deVink; flowers deep crimson, center white, ½-1 in., semi-dbl., shallow cup to flat, borne singly and in clusters, recurrent; foliage leathery, light green; very dwarf (8-12 in.) growth; PP169; ['Rouletii' × 'Gloria Mundi']

'Tom Tom' F, dp, 1958, Lindquist; bud ovoid; flowers Neyron rose, 3-3½ in., 25 petals, high-centered to flat, borne in clusters, slight spicy fragrance; recurrent bloom; foliage dark green, semi-glossy; prickles several, medium, hooked slightly downward, russet; vigorous, upright, bushy growth; hips none ; PP1671; ['Improved Lafayette' × 'Floradora']; intr. 1957

'Tom Tom, Climbing' Cl F, dp, 1962, Lindquist; PP2173

'Tom Wood' HP, mr, 1896, Dickson, A.; flowers cherry-red, 8 cm., dbl., cupped, borne in clusters, moderate fragrance; recurrent; compact (3-4 ft.) growth

'Tomabra' ('Lady Phelia') S, pb, 2004, Thomson, George L.; flowers copper pink, reverse lighter, 8-10 cm., very full, borne in small clusters; foliage small, light green, semi-glossy; prickles small, hooked,; growth bushy, medium (3-4½ ft.); garden decorative; [(Abraham Darby® × 'Anna Oliver') × 'Mrs Mary Thomson']; intr. 2004

'Tomaln' ('Alan Sandys') MinFl, mr, 2006, Thomson, George L.; flowers medium red, reverse lighter, 2 in., very full, borne in small clusters; foliage medium size, dark green, glossy; prickles medium, hooked, brown, moderate; growth compact, short (24 in.); garden decorative; [seedling × Europeana®]; intr. 2006

'Tomás Batâ' HP, dr, 1932, Böhm, J.; flowers shaded crimson, passing to maroon, large, dbl.; foliage leathery, glossy, dark; very vigorous growth; ['Fisher Holmes' × 'Prince Camille de Rohan']

'Tombaron' ('The Archbishop') HT, pb, 2004, Thomson, George L.; flowers smoky pink, reverse silver, medium, full, borne mostly solitary, moderate fragrance; foliage medium size, dark green, glossy; prickles medium, hooked; growth upright, medium to tall, (4½-5½ ft.); garden decorative; ['Baronne E. de Rothschild' × 'Granada']; intr. 2002

'Tombola' F, dp, 1967, deRuiter; flowers deep pink, 4 in.; foliage dark, glossy; vigorous, upright, bushy growth; ['Amor' × ('Ena Harkness' × 'Peace')]

'Tombola' HT, op, Spek; flowers pale salmon pink, 4½ in., 30-35 petals, high-centered, borne mostly singly; recurrent; foliage dark green; few prickles; stems long; florist rose; intr. 2002

'Tombosa' ('Australia Fair') F, pb, 2001, Thomson, George L.; flowers soft pink, slightly darker reverse, 1 in., dbl., borne in large clusters, moderate fragrance; foliage medium size, medium green, semi-glossy; prickles medium, hooked, moderate, brown; growth compact, low (1 m.); garden decorative; ['Tombot' × ('Madam President' × unknown)]; intr. 2001

'Tomboss' ('Deane Ross') S, pb, 2004, Thomson, George L.; flowers lavender pink, reverse darker, 10 cm., very full, borne in small to large clusters, intense fragrance; foliage medium size, dark green, matte; prickles small, hooked; growth spreading, short (3-4 ft.); garden decorative; [(Gertrude Jekyll® × 'Anna Oliver') × 'Tomone']; intr. 2002

'Tombot' ('Botanica') F, pb, 1998, Thomson, George L.; flowers pink with touch of lilac, 2 in., 26-41 petals, borne in large clusters; foliage medium size, medium green, dull; prickles moderate; bushy, medium (3-3½ ft.) growth; ['Avandel' × 'Madam President']

'Tomboy' -- See 'Zipboy'

'Tomcare' ('The Carer's Rose') HT, w, 2000, Thomson, George L.; flowers white with rose on outer petals, 5 in., dbl., borne mostly singly, moderate fragrance; foliage medium size, dark green, glossy; few prickles; growth upright, medium (4-5 ft.); ['Francis Phoebe' × 'Ophelia']; intr. 1999

'Tomdel' ('Adelaide Tonight') Min, mp, 1999, Thomson, George L.; flowers pink, reverse lighter, ½-¾ in., dbl., borne in large clusters; foliage medium size, medium green, semi-glossy; prickles moderate; spreading, medium (18-24 in.) growth; ['Avandel' × 'Little Mike']

'Tomfair' ('Flinders') S, pb, 2001, Thomson, George L.; flowers ruffled, mid-pink, small to medium, very full, borne in large clusters, moderate fragrance; foliage medium size, dark green, glossy; prickles medium, hooked, moderate, brown; growth prostrate, medium (½ × 2 m.); groundcover; ['Bonica' × 'The Fairy']; intr. 2001

'Tomfed' ('Canberra Rose') F, pb, 1999, Thomson, George L.; flowers medium pink, reverse darker, 3 in., 16-40 petals, borne in large clusters; foliage medium size, dark green, glossy; prickles moderate; upright, medium (3-4 ft.) growth; ['Watercolour' × 'Madam President']; intr. 2000

'Tomfib' ('Cystic Fibrosis') S, w, Thomson, intr. 2001

'Tomfire' ('Wildfire 2000') F, yb, 2000, Thomson, George L.; flowers yellow with blazing orange overtones, reverse lighter, 2 in., dbl., borne in small clusters, moderate fragrance; foliage medium size, medium green, glossy; prickles moderate; compact, medium (3-4 ft.) growth; [Remember Me® × 'Tequila Sunrise']; intr. 1999

'Tomflo' ('Howard Florey') F, ab, 1998, Thomson, George L.; flowers apricot, lighter reverse, 2 in., dbl., borne in small clusters; foliage medium size, medium green, semi-glossy; prickles moderate; bushy, medium (3½ - 4½ ft.) growth; ['Seduction' × 'Apricot Nectar']

'Tomgift' ('Love's Gift') S, rb, 2001, Thomson, George L.; flowers creamy yellow with cherry red edges, 3½-5 in., semi-dbl., borne in small clusters, slight fragrance; foliage medium size, dark green, glossy; prickles medium, hooked, numerous; growth upright, tall (5½-6.5 ft.); garden decorative; ['Hannah Gordon' × 'Tomone']; intr. 2001

'Tomgold' ('International Gold') Min, my,

2004, Thomson, George L.; flowers gold, 2-3 cm., full, borne in small to large clusters, no fragrance; foliage medium size, medium green, semi-glossy; prickles small, straight; growth bushy, medium (20-30 cm.); garden decorative, containers; ['Rise "n" Shine' × 'Peace']; intr. 2005

'Tomhope' ('Hope') S, w, 2001, Thomson, George L.; flowers cream to light pink, lighter reverse, medium, full, borne in small clusters, moderate fragrance; foliage medium size, medium green, semi-glossy; prickles medium, hooked, moderate; growth spreading, medium (4½-5½ ft.); garden decorative; [('Dove' × unknown) × 'Ophelia']; intr. 2001

'Tomkins Red' F, dr, 1943, Brownell; bud long, pointed; flowers deep velvety crimson turning maroon, open, 18 petals, borne in clusters, moderate fragrance; foliage dark, glossy; long stems; vigorous, compact, upright growth; [('Dr. W. Van Fleet' × 'Général Jacqueminot') × 'Nigrette']

'Tomkris' ('Lonesome Dove') HWich, w, 2006, Thomson, George L.; flowers 4 cm., very full, borne in small clusters; summer flowering, with some autumn repeat; foliage medium size, glossy, evergreen; prickles medium, hooked, brown, numerous; growth rambling, tall (20 m.) climber; [(seedling × 'May Queen') × seedling]

'Tommac' ('Philadelphia', 'Ronald McDonald') HT, yb, 2001, Thomson, George L.; flowers lemon yellow, 2 in., full, borne mostly solitary, moderate fragrance; foliage medium size, dark green, glossy; prickles medium, hooked; growth upright, medium (4½ - 5½ ft.); garden decorative; ['Francis Phoebe' × 'Ophelia']; intr. 2001

'Tommelise' -- See 'Kortenay'

'Tommop' ('Mary of Penola') HT, pb, 1999, Thomson, George L.; flowers dark pink, reverse darker, 6 in., 41 petals, borne mostly singly; foliage medium size, medium green, glossy; prickles moderate; upright, medium (3-3½ ft.) growth; ['Maria Callas' × Elina®]

'Tommops' S, m, Thomson; intr. 2002

'Tommount' ('Pride of Mountbarker') HT, ab, 1996, Thomson, George L.; flowers peach cream tinted rose edge, apricot center, lighter reverse, full, moderate fragrance; foliage small, medium green, semi-glossy; prickles moderate; upright, medium (5 × 2 ft.) growth; [Gold Medal® × 'Sylvia']

'Tommy' HT, pb, Schreurs; flowers pink with green tips, borne mostly singly; recurrent

'Tommy Bright' F, mr, 1961, Boerner; bud ovoid; flowers scarlet-red, large, 35-40 petals, cupped, moderate fragrance; foliage leathery; strong stems; very vigorous, upright growth; PP2129; [('Chatter' × unknown) × 'Garnette Supreme']; intr. 1961

'Tommy Thompson' HT, or, 1976, Golik; bud ovoid; flowers 5 in., 50 petals, high-centered, moderate spicy fragrance; foliage glossy, very dark; moderate growth; ['Queen o' the Lakes' × 'Tropicana']; intr. 1974

'Tommy Tucker' Min, lp, 1955, Robinson, T.; flowers silvery pink, 1 in., dbl., borne in clusters; ['Rouletti' × 'Tom Thumb']

'Tomone' ('Mrs Mary Thomson') S, pb, 1996, Thomson, George L.; flowers lilac pink, cream center, prominent gold stamens, reverse slightly lighter, 5½-6½ in., 8-14 petals, borne in large clusters, intense fragrance; foliage medium size, medium green, dull; few prickles; spreading, medium (5 × 4 ft.) growth; ['Dapple Dawn' × 'Ophelia']

'Tomonoura' HT, w, Hiroshima; intr. 2007

'Tomorrow' F, dy, Christensen; intr. 1989

'Tompal' Min, w, Thomsondouble; intr. 2002

'Tomring' ('Onkaparinga') S, ab, 1997, Thomson, George L.; flowers apricot-pink, reverse lighter, ages pink, 4-5 in., 41 petals, borne in small clusters, intense myrrh fragrance; foliage medium size, medium green, semi-glossy; spreading growth; ['Cymbaline' × 'Troilus']; intr. 1999

'Tomrom' ('Dame Roma') HT, op, 2004, Thomson, George L.; flowers salmon pink, reverse lighter, 15 cm., very full, borne mostly solitary; foliage large, medium green, glossy; prickles medium, hooked; growth upright, tall (5½-7 ft.); garden decorative; ['Sweetheart' × 'Kardinal 89']; intr. 2004

'Tomroyal' (Crown Princess Mary™) HT, w, 2006, Thomson, George L.; flowers varying from ivory and cream to light pink, reverse cream, 7-10 cm., very full, borne in small clusters; foliage medium size, glossy; prickles small, hooked, brown, few; growth bushy, (1¼-1½ m.); garden decorative; [('The Wild One' × 'Frances Phoebe') × 'Ophelia']

'Tomroz' ('Society Belle') HT, pb, 2008, Thompson, George L.; flowers lavender pink, reverse silver, 4½ in., very full, borne in small clusters; fast repeat; foliage medium, medium green, matte; prickles small, hooked, brown, few; growth upright, medium (5 ft.); garden decorative; [('Baronne de Rothschild' × Manou Meilland®) × Charles de Gaulle®]; intr. 2008

'Tom's Pink' Pol, mp, Horsfield; flowers 4 cm., moderate fragrance; compact (40 cm.) growth; intr. 1986

'Tomsal' ('Sally Jean') HT, ab, 2001, Thomson, George L.; flowers golden apricot, lighter reverse, 6 in., full, borne mostly solitary, intense fragrance; foliage large, medium green, semi-glossy; prickles large, hooked, few, brown; stems long; growth upright, tall (6-7 ft.); garden decorative; [King's Ransom® × Papa Meilland®]; intr. 2001

'Tomsave' ('Salvation') F, mr, 2001, Thomson, George L.; flowers velvet red, 2-2½ in., semi-dbl., borne in large clusters, slight fragrance; free-flowering; foliage medium size, dark green, glossy; prickles medium, hooked, brown, numerous; growth bushy, low (3-3½ ft.); garden decorative; [Trumpeter® × 'Showbiz']; intr. 2001

'Tomson' ('Mawson') F, w, 2001, Thomson, George L.; flowers medium, full, borne in large clusters, moderate fragrance; foliage medium size, dark gren, glossy; prickles medium, hooked; growth compact, medium (1 m.); garden decorative; [('Iceberg' × unknown) × ('Francis Phoebe' × unknown)]; intr. 2002

'Tomsue' ('Susan Irvine') HG, pb, 1997, Thomson, George L.; flowers rose pink, cream center, prominent gold stamens, 2½-3½ in., 8-14 petals, borne in large clusters, moderate fragrance; foliage medium size, medium green, semi glossy; bushy, medium (5 ft.) growth; ['Mrs. Mary Thomson' × (R. gigantea × unknown)]

'Tomtal' ('Laura Chantal') Min, pb, 1997, Thomson, George L.; flowers varying shades of pink, dark reverse, full, borne in small clusters, intense fragrance; foliage medium size, medium green, semi glossy; upright, medium (30 in.) growth; ['Avandel' × 'Madam President']

'Tomtap' ('Tapestry') S, ab, 2001, Thomson, George L.; flowers apricot to coppery-pink, lighter reverse, medium, very full, borne in small clusters, moderate fragrance; foliage medium size, dark green, glossy; prickles medium, hooked; growth spreading, medium (4½-5½ ft.); garden decorative; [(Rugelda® × unknown) × 'Howard Florey']; intr. 2001

'Tomteer' ('Thank You') HT, pb, 2004, Thomson, George L.; flowers dark pink, reverse lighter, 15 cm., full, borne mostly solitary, intense fragrance; foliage medium size, medium green, semi-glossy; prickles small, hooked,; growth upright, medium (4-5 ft.); garden decorative; ['Baronne E. de Rothschild' × 'Kordes' Perfecta']; intr. 2001

'Tomtwo' ('Linda Thomson') F, dp, 1996, Thomson, George L.; flowers dark dusky pink, ruffled edge, reverse darker, large, dbl., borne in large clusters, moderate fragrance; foliage medium size, dark green, glossy; bushy, medium growth; ['Fidelio' × 'Showbiz']

'Tomwest' ('Marnie Louise') HT, w, 2004, Thomson, George L.; flowers cream bordered red, reverse cream, 14 cm., full, borne mostly solitary, moderate fragrance; foliage medium size, dark green, glossy; prickles medium, hooked; growth compact, medium (4-5 ft.); garden decorative; ['Pascali × Frances Phoebe' × 'Ophelia']; intr. 2004

'Tomwild' ('The Wild One') S, w, 1998, Thomson, George L.; flowers cream with touch of rose, reverse lighter, stamens gold, 4½-5½ in., single, borne in small clusters; foliage large, light green, semi-glossy; numerous prickles; upright, medium (4 -5 ft.) growth; ['Wild Flower' × 'Ophelia']

'Tomxav' ('St Francis Xavier') T, dr, 2004, Thomson, George L.; flowers deep crimson, 4 in., very full, borne in small clusters, intense fragrance; foliage medium size, dark green, glossy; prickles medium, hooked; growth bushy, medium (3-4½ ft.); garden decorative; ['Francis Dubrieul' × 'Papa Gontier']; intr. 2004

'Tonehime' HT, w, 1985, Kikuchi, Rikichi; flowers white, creamy center, large, 30 petals, high-centered, borne mostly singly; foliage small, dark, glossy; few prickles; vigorous, slender, tall growth; ['Mizuho' × 'Sodori-Hime']; intr. 1984

'Tonga' HT, ob, 1955, Lowe; flowers deep golden orange, outer petals veined bronze and scarlet,, dbl.; foliage dark, leathery; vigorous, upright growth

'Toni Corsari' F, dr, 1961, Delforge; flowers velvety deep red, medium, semi-dbl., borne in large clusters; bushy, low growth; ['Red Favorite' × seedling]

'Toni Lander' F, ob, 1961, Poulsen, D. T.; flowers salmon-orange, 3 in., 22 petals, borne in large clusters; foliage dark; bushy growth; ['Independence' × 'Circus']

'Toni Thompson's Musk' HMsk, w, Thompson, T.; [*R. brunonii* × unknown]

'Tonia' -- See 'Francibel'

'Tonia's Friendship' HT, pb, 2004, Poole, Lionel; flowers ivory, edged pink, reverse ivory/pink, 5 in., full, borne in large clusters, intense fragrance; foliage medium size, medium green, semi-glossy; prickles moderate, medium size, slightly hooked; growth upright, bushy, medium (1 m.); garden decorative; [('Hazel Rose' × 'Cardiff Bay') × 'New Zealand']; intr. 2005

Tonic Meillandina® Min, mr, Meilland

'Tonight' HT, mr, 1973, Warriner, William A.; bud ovoid; flowers bright red, large, dbl., high-centered; foliage leathery; vigorous growth; PP3522; [seedling × 'Forever Yours']

'Tonimbuk' HT, pb, Dawson; flowers flower blush pink with tints of strong pink, dbl., high-centered, very slight fragrance; recurrent; foliage dark green; medium growth; intr. before 1990

'Toniro' ('Doktor Sieber') HT, yb, Hiroshima; intr. 1998

Tonnere® F, dr, 1956, Mallerin, C.; flowers deep velvety red, 3 in., 24 petals, borne in large clusters; foliage dark; vigorous, bushy growth; ['Holstein' × 'Francais']; intr. 1954

'Tonner's Fancy' HG, w, 1928, Clark, A.; flowers white, tinted pink, fading to cream, large, semi-dbl., globular, moderate fragrance; non-remontant; vigorous, climbing (15 ft.) growth; [(*R. gigantea* × unknown) × seedling]

'Tonsina' HT, ob
'Tonsina' -- See 'Korbasta'
'Tony Jacklin' F, op, 1974, McGredy, Sam IV; flowers orange-salmon, floratea, 4 in., 30 petals, hybrid tea, slight fragrance; foliage dark green, glossy; tall growth; intr. 1972

'Tony Peace' HT, ab, 1967, Brundrett; flowers buff-yellow to apricot; [sport of 'Peace']; intr. 1964

'Tony Spalding' HT, dr, 1933, McGredy; flowers brilliant crimson, semi-dbl., high-centered; foliage glossy; very vigorous growth

'Tonybrac' F, w, 1988, Bracegirdle, A.J.; intr. 1987

'Tony's Two Tone' -- See 'Majlybtwo'

'Too Cute' Pol, lp, Rupert; flowers light pink fading to white, 1½-2 in., very full, rosette, borne in large clusters, slight fragrance; recurrent; growth low, compact, bushy; intr. 2001

'Too Hot To Handle' -- See 'Macloupri'

'Toorenburg' HT, ab, Kordes; intr. 2008

'Tooth of Time' -- See 'Rentime'

'Tootie' Min, mp; flowers , 30-35 petals, slight fragrance; free-flowering; foliage small; compact (12-18 in.), rounded growth; intr. 2003

'Tootsie' -- See 'Gretoots'

'Top Billing' HT, dr, Ludwig; flowers crimson red, large, dbl., pointed, urn-shaped, borne mostly singly; recurrent; foliage dark green, glossy; stems sturdy, long; growth medium, rounded plant

'Top Brass' -- See 'Harxaglen'

'Top Choice' Min, op, 1985, Hardgrove, Donald L.; flowers medium salmon-pink, medium, 36 petals; foliage small, medium green, semi-glossy; dense, spreading, bushy growth; ['Gingersnap' × Baby Katie™]

'Top Contender' -- See 'Weltopcon'
'Top Gear' -- See 'Macmanly'
Top Gun™ -- See 'Kingun'

'Top Hat' F, ab, 1968, Fankhauser; bud ovoid; flowers apricot-blush, medium, dbl., high-centered; foliage small, dark, glossy; compact, low growth; ['Ma Perkins' × 'Garden Party']

Top Hit™ -- See 'Poultop'
'Top Marks' -- See 'Fryministar'
'Top Meillandina' -- See 'Meiferjac'
'Top Mode' HT, w, Hiroshima; intr. 1996
Top Notch™ -- See 'Macamster'

'Top of the Bill' ('Gensuar') Min, dp, Genesis; flowers fuchsia-pink, semi-dbl. to dbl., cupped, moderate fragrance; recurrent; foliage dark green, glossy; moderate (12-24 in.) growth; intr. 1996

'Top Rose' -- See 'Cocgold'

'Top Secret' Min, mr, 1971, Moore, Ralph S.; [sport of 'Beauty Secret']

'Top Secret' -- See 'Meibolnay'
Top Star® HT, ob, Noack, Werner
'Top Star' -- See 'Jactop'

'Top Symphonie' Min, ob, Meilland; intr. 2002

'Topaz' Pol, yb, 1937, Tantau; flowers lemon-yellow, petals edged cream, reverse lemon and cream, small, very dbl., high-centered, slight fragrance; foliage small, leathery; dwarf, spreading growth; PP300; ['Joanna Tantau' × ('Prof. Gnau' × 'Julien Potin')]

Topaz® HT, dp, Tantau; flowers very large , double, high-centered, borne mostly singly; recurrent; stems long; florist rose; intr. 2007

'Topaz' -- See 'Jacant'

Topaz Jewel™ ('Frau Dagmar Hastrup Geel', 'Rustica 91', 'Yellow Dagmar Hastrup', 'Yellow Fru Dagmar Hartopp', 'Gelbe Dagmar Hastrup', 'Gull Dagmar') HRg, my, 1987, Moore, Ralph S.; bud large, pointed; flowers medium yellow fading to cream, 3-3½ in., 20-30 petals, cupped, borne usually in sprays of 5-8, moderate fruity fragrance; repeat bloom; foliage large, medium green, rugose, matte; prickles numerous, hooked downward, brown, in variable sizes; upright, bushy, spreading, vigorous growth; no fruit; PP6793; ['Golden Angel' × 'Belle Poitevine']; intr. 1987

'Topaze' F, ab, Guillot-Massad; flowers apricot-pink, dbl., rosette, borne in clusters, moderate apple fragrance; recurrent; foliage bright, glossy; low (50 cm.) growth; intr. 1995

'Topaze Orientale' HT, yb, 1967, Delbard-Chabert; flowers maize-yellow to light pink, 5-6 in., dbl., high-centered, moderate fragrance; tall growth; ['Sultane' × Queen Elizabeth®]; intr. 1965

'Topeka' F, mr, 1978, Wisbech Plant Co.; bud long, pointed; flowers 3 in., 21 petals, flat; foliage glossy; vigorous, upright growth; ['Vera Dalton' × seedling]

Topkapi™ -- See 'Topkapi Palace'

'Topkapi Palace' (Topkapi™) S, dp, Olesen; bud ovoid; flowers deep pink to light red, 2-3 in., 55-60 petals, rounded, then flat, borne singly and in small clusters, slight wild rose fragrance; recurrent; foliage dark; prickles few, 5-7 mm, linear to concave, light pink; stems 14-18 in.; bushy (2-2½ ft.) growth; PP10883; [sport of Queen Margrethe™]; intr. 1996

'Topper' HT, mr, 1959, Joseph H. Hill, Co.; bud short, pointed; flowers signalred to crimson, 3-3½ in., 25-30 petals, high-centered to open; foliage dark, leathery; long, strong stems; vigorous, upright growth; PP1566; ['Pink Bountiful' × 'Sister Kenny']; for greenhouse use

'Toprose' -- See 'Cocgold'

Topsi® F, or, 1973, Tantau, Math.; bud ovoid; flowers orange-scarlet, medium, semi-dbl., spiral to open, slight fragrance; recurrent; moderate, dwarf growth; ['Fragrant Cloud' × Signalfeuer®]; intr. 1971

'Topsi's Friend' F, lp, 1981, Anderson's Rose Nurseries; flowers 15 petals, rosette, borne 5 per cluster; foliage light green, glossy; prickles green; upright growth; ['Dreamland' × Topsi®]

'Topsy' -- See 'Jacrove'

Topsy Turvy™ -- See 'Wekcocbeb'

'Toque Rouge' -- See 'Korred'

'Torch' Cl Pol, or, 1942, deRuiter; flowers scarlet-orange, white eye, 1½ in., 15 petals, borne in clusters; foliage glossy, dark; vigorous, climbing (6-8 ft.) growth; PP726; [climbing orange polyantha seedling]

Torch of Liberty™ -- See 'Mortorch'

'Torch Song' HT, or, 1959, Meilland, F.; bud ovoid; flowers vermilion, 5 in., 30-35 petals, high-centered; foliage dark, leathery; vigorous, upright, bushy growth; PP1760; [('Peace' × 'Floradora') × 'Grand'mère Jenny']; intr. 1959

Torche Rose® -- See 'Intertor'

'Torchlight' F, or, 1951, LeGrice; flowers brilliant orange-scarlet shaded deeper, large, 5-8 petals, borne in clusters of up to 30, moderate fragrance; foliage dark; vigorous growth; ['Dusky Maiden' × 'Holstein']

'Torchy' F, or, 1969, Armstrong, D.L.; bud pointed to urn-shaped; flowers brick-orange, medium, dbl., high-centered, moderate fragrance; foliage leathery; moderate, bushy growth; PP3016; ['Heat Wave' × 'Spartan']

'Toreador' HT, pb, 1919, Paul, W.; flowers rosy red, reverse golden yellow, medium, semi-dbl.

'Toresky, Climbing' Cl F, lp, 1958, Bofill, F.; intr. 1956

'Toresky' F, lp, 1931, Padrosa; flowers light pink with white eye, dbl., cupped, borne in large clusters; foliage wrinkled, light; dwarf growth; ['Perle d'Or' × 'Antoine Rivoire']

'Torino' F, mp, 1960, Mansuino, Q.; flowers spinel-rose, small to medium; vigorous growth; [seedling × 'Cocorico']

Tornado® -- See 'Kortor'

Tornado Kordana® Min, mr, Kordes; flowers dbl., high-centered

Tornella® S, dr, Noack; flowers velvety dark red, 8 cm., dbl., cupped, borne in clusters; recurrent; foliage dark green, glossy, leathery; upright (5 ft.), bushy growth; intr. 2006

'Tornerose' ('Lovely Fairy') F, mr, Roldskov; flowers small, 20-40 petals, cupped to flat, borne in clusters, no fragrance; recurrent; intr. 1995

'Toro' -- See 'Uncle Joe'

'Toro de Fuego' S, Delbard-Chabert; intr. 1970

'Torrero' F, ob, 1961, Leenders, J.; flowers pink-orange-red, 3 in., 18 petals, flat; ['Ma Perkins' × 'Cocorico']

'Torrida' HP, pb, 1839, Boyau; flowers velvety dark carmine-purple, streaked white, medium, dbl.

'Torvill & Dean' -- See 'Lantor'

'Tosca' ('Toscana') F, or, 1972, Warriner, William A.; bud long, pointed; flowers open, medium, dbl.; foliage large, leathery; very vigorous, upright growth; PP3347; [seedling × 'Ginger']

'Toscana' HT, dp, 1954, Cazzaniga, F. G.; flowers deep pink, dbl.; vigorous growth

'Toscana' F, mr, Kordes; flora-tea; intr. 1991

'Toscana' -- See 'Korstesgli'

'Toscana' -- See 'Tosca'

'Toscana Vigorosa' -- See 'Korstesgli'

'Toscanini' HT, lp, Olij ; bud large, ovoid; flowers light pink to cream, reverse darker, 12 cm., very full, high-centered, borne usually singly, slight woodsy fragrance; recurrent; foliage dark green, semi-glossy; prickles numerous, medium, tan; erect (5-6 ft.) growth; PP11494; [Prophyta™ × ('Meibrimel' × 'Super Disco')]; intr. 1999

Total Recall™ -- See 'Savacall'

'Totenviksrosen' HSpn

'Totote Gélos' HT, w, 1915, Pernet-Ducher; bud long, pointed; flowers flesh-white, center shaded chrome-yellow, dbl.

'Tottie' F, mr, 1961, Borgatti, G.; flowers purplish red, 3 in., 35-40 petals, borne in clusters of 6; vigorous, bushy growth; ['Alain' × 'Fashion']

'Totty's Red' HT, dr, 1926, Totty; flowers crimson-scarlet; [sport of 'Premier']

Touch of Class™® -- See 'Kricarlo'

'Touch o' Cloves' -- See 'Minitoc'

'Touch of Coral' -- See 'Jaceleco'

'Touch of Elegance' -- See 'Leotoelg'

'Touch of Fire' -- See 'Renfire'

'Touch of Glamour' Min, w; flowers delicate pink, full, shallow cup, rosette; recurrent; compact (20 in.) growth; intr. 2005

'Touch of Kiwi' HT, yb, 1989, Cattermole, R.F.; bud tapering; flowers creamy yellow, 1/4" wide orange margin on petals, dbl.; foliage medium green; prickles pointed, light brown, varying size; upright growth; ['Kiwi Queen' × 'Command Performance']

'Touch of Magic' HT, or, 1979, Patterson; bud globular; flowers 5 in., 40-45 petals, high-centered, intense fragrance; very vigorous growth; ['San Francisco' × 'Peace']; intr. 1977

Touch o' Midas™ -- See 'Minabco'

Touch of Raspberry™ -- See 'Devicio'

'Touch of Spring' ('Perfume Pleasure') HT, pb, J&P; flowers medium pink with lighter reverse , double, high-centered to flat; recurrent; growth medium height

'Touch of Velvet' -- See 'Leovelv'

'Touch of Venus' HT, w, 1970, Armstrong, D.L.; flowers near white, center shaded pink, large, dbl., high-centered, intense fragrance; foliage large, leathery; vigorous, upright growth; PP3131; ['Garden Party' × 'Sweet Afton']; intr. 1971

'Touch-Up' -- See 'Foutouch'

'Touchdown' Min, mr, 1989, Jolly, Nelson F.; bud ovoid; flowers reverse red with white center, aging bluish, small, 40 petals, urn-shaped, no fragrance; foliage small, medium green, matte; no prickles; low, upright growth; no fruit; ['Sheri Anne' × Anita Charles™]; intr. 1989

'Touché' HT, rb; intr. 2003

'Touché' -- See 'Lavont'

'Touching Lives' -- See 'Lovangle'

'Touggourt' F, or, 1963, Arles; bud globular; flowers orange-shrimp-pink, open, large, dbl.; foliage dark, leathery; vigorous, bushy growth; [('Gruss an Teplitz' × 'Independence') × ('Floradora' × 'Independence')]; intr. 1959

'Toujours Fleuri' ('Souv de Mme Fontaine') B, m, 1856, Cherpin; flowers dark violet, large

'Toujours Gai' Misc OGR, pb, 2008, Shimbo, Fara; flowers pink with light pink to white spots, crinkled petals, 3 in., full, borne mostly solitary; foliage small, grass-green to slightly bluish-green, rather hairy, matte; prickles very small, needle, slight hooked, beige, few; growth to about 1 m.; hedging; ['Fa's Marbled Moss' × unknown]; intr. 2008

Toulouse Lautrec® -- See 'Meirevolt'

'Tour de France' F, or, 1963, Mondial Roses; flowers deep orange-scarlet shaded blood-red, large to medium, semi-dbl.; vigorous, bushy growth; [('Alain' × Orange Triumph®) × seedling]

'Tour de Malakoff' C, m, 1856, Pastoret; flowers mauve-pink shaded purple, heavily veined, center green, large, dbl., deeply cupped, borne singly and in clusters of 2-3, moderate fragrance; non-remontant; foliage oblong, pointed, with 3-5 leaflets; prickles few, only on old wood; sprawling (7 ft.) growth

'Tour Eiffel' -- See 'Eiffel Tower'

'Tour Eiffel 2000' LCl, mr, Delbard; flowers semi-dbl., cupped, borne in clusters, slight fresh fragrance; recurrent; foliage disease-resistant; vigorous (8-10 ft.) growth; a rugosa included in parentage somewhere; intr. 1998

'Tour Malakoff' HGal, m, 1856, Robert; flowers lilac/flesh pink, 10-12 cm., full, globular

Touraine™ -- See 'Poulander'

'Tourbillon' ('French Cancan') F, rb, 1959, Delbard-Chabert; flowers red, reverse silvery pink, well-formed, 3-4 in., 30-35 petals, borne in clusters of 6-8; very vigorous, bushy growth; RULED EXTINCT 4/85; ['Michèle Meilland' × ('Incendie' × ('Floradora × Orange Triumph®))]

'Tourbillon' -- See 'Delnolli'

Tourmaline® HT, pb, 1970, Delbard-Chabert; flowers creamy white, widely edged carmine, large, 28 petals, high-centered, cupped, very slight fragrance; recurrent; foliage light green; moderate growth; ['Michèle Meilland' × 'Chic Parisien']; intr. 1965

'Tournament of Roses' -- See 'Jacient'

'Tournee' F, dy, VEG; flowers luminous golden yellow, medium, semi-dbl.

'Toussaint L'Ouverture' B, m, 1849, Miellez; flowers deep violet red, medium, full; sometimes classed as Ch

'Tove Pedersen' F, dr

'Tower Bridge' -- See 'Haravis'

'Towering Rose Magic' -- See 'Soeur Emmanuelle'

'Town Crier' HT, ly, 1960, Joseph H.

Hill, Co.; bud pointed ovoid; flowers straw-yellow, 5-6 in., 30-35 petals, high-centered, borne singly, moderate tea fragrance; recurrent; foliage large, dark green, glossy; prickles several, medium, hooked downward; stems long, strong; vigorous, upright, well-branched growth; PP1807; ['Peace' × 'Yellow Perfection']; intr. 1961

'Town Talk, Climbing' Cl F, or, 1976, Weeks, O. L.; PP3909; intr. 1975

'Town Talk' F, or, 1969, Swim & Weeks; bud ovoid; flowers small, dbl., cupped, foliage dark, leathery; moderate growth; PP2709; [('Circus' × 'Garnette') × 'Spartan']; originally registered as Pol; patent issued as Pol; intr. 1966

'Townsend' HSpn, mp, before 1885, from Scotland; flowers carmine striped with crimson, small, dbl.; non-recurrent; intr. before 1885

'Townswoman' HT, rb, 1973, Anderson's Rose Nurseries; flowers red-purple, reverse silver, 5 in., 35 petals, globular; foliage light; free growth; [seedling × Piccadilly®]

'Toy Balloon' Min, dr, 1979, Moore, Ralph S.; bud ovoid, pointed; flowers deep scarlet crimson, 1½ in., 45-50 petals, high-centered, slight fragrance; recurrent; foliage dark; bushy, spreading growth; PP4512; ['Fairy Moss' × 'Fire Princess']

'Toy Clown' Min, rb, 1966, Moore, Ralph S.; flowers white edged red, small, semi-dbl., borne mostly singly; recurrent; foliage small, leathery; bushy, dwarf growth; PP2909; ['Little Darling' × 'Magic Wand']

'Toy Soldier' -- See 'Curtoy'

'Toyland' Min, mr, 1978, Lyon; bud ovoid; flowers Indian red, 1 in., 10 petals; foliage tiny; compact, bushy growth; intr. 1977

'Toynbee Hall' -- See 'Korwonder'

'Tracait' ('Caitlin') Min, w, 1987, Travis, Louis R.; flowers flesh pink fading white, small, 12-15 petals, urn-shaped, borne in sprays, slight spicy fragrance; foliage small, medium green, semi-glossy; prickles straight, tan-brown; bushy, low growth; no fruit; ['Fairy Moss' × 'Fairy Moss']

'Tracey Wickham' Min, yb, 1984, Welsh, Eric; flowers bright yellow, petals edged bright red, small, 30 petals, hybrid tea, borne singly and in clusters, moderate fragrance; foliage medium size, medium green, semi-glossy; upright growth; ['Avandel' × 'Redgold']

'Traci' -- See 'Geltra'

'Tracla' ('Classy') Min, yb, 1987, Travis, Louis R.; flowers yellow with pink overlay, small, 13-18 petals, high-centered, borne singly, intense spicy fragrance; foliage small, medium green, semi-glossy; prickles straight, very few, tan-brown; bushy, low growth; hips round, green-orange; ['Yellow Jewel' × 'Yellow Jewel']

'Trade Wind' ('Trade Winds') HT, rb, 1964, Von Abrams; bud long, pointed; flowers dark red, reverse silver, 5 in., 55 petals, high-centered, intense fragrance; foliage glossy; vigorous, tall growth; PP2664; [('Multnomah' × seedling) × ('Carrousel' × seedling)]; intr. 1964

'Trade Winds' -- See 'Trade Wind'

'Tradescant' -- See 'Ausdir'

'Tradition' HT, mr, 1965, Kordes, R.; flowers scarlet-crimson, 4½ in., 35 petals; ['Detroiter' × 'Don Juan']

'Tradition® -- See 'Korkeltin'

'Tradition 95' -- See 'Korkeltin'

'Traditional Home® -- See 'Burwintradhom'

'Traditional Home Rose 2001' -- See 'Wekswetrup'

'Trafalgar' Cl HT, Fell, J.B.; ['Mons Desir' × 'Gruss an Teplitz']

'Trafalgar Square' F, mp, 1965, Van den Akker Bros.; flowers large, dbl.; vigorous growth

'Trailblazer' F, or, 1976, Harvey, R.E.; bud long, pointed; flowers 2½ in., 22 petals, high-centered, slight fragrance; foliage glossy; ['Albert' × Orange Sensation®]; intr. 1975

'Trailblazer' -- See 'Meifersi'

'Trakiika' HT, dr, 1985, Staikov, Prof. Dr. V.; flowers large, 25 petals, cupped, moderate fragrance; foliage dark; vigorous, upright, bushy growth; ['Tallyho' × 'Spartan']; intr. 1974

'Tramonto' HT, yb, 1943, Giacomasso; flowers yellow and orange, darker at edges, large, dbl., high-centered, borne mostly singly

'Tramonto Estivo' F, yb, Barni; flowers yellow shading to orange, turning bright red and carmine, single, shallow cup, borne in clusters, moderate fragrance; recurrent; foliage dark green; vigorous, bushy (2 - 3 ft.) growth; intr. 2004

'Tranquil' HT, dp, Dawson; intr. 1977

'Tranquility' Cl Pol, op, before 1952, Radmore; flowers coral-salmon, rosette form, small, borne in trusses; foliage light green; vigorous growth; RULED EXTINCT 11/82; [sport of 'Princess van Orange']

'Tranquility' S, lp, Clements, John; flowers delicate light pink shading to near white, 4 in., 60 petals, borne individually and in small clusters, intense myrrh fragrance; foliage bronzy red maturing to dark green; bushy, compact (3 × 3 ft.) growth; PPAF; intr. 2004

'Tranquility' -- See 'Barout'

'Transit' F, VEG; intr. 1984

'Transon-Goubault' HGal; flowers bright red, edges darker, large, full

'Transparente' -- See 'Vilmorin'

'Trapom' ('Fairy Pompons') Min, w, 1987, Travis, Louis R.; flowers flesh pink fading white, small, 45-60 petals, high-centered, borne usually singly, slight spicy fragrance; foliage small, medium green, matte; prickles straight, tan-brown; bushy, low growth; no fruit; ['Fairy Moss' × 'Fairy Moss']; intr. 1986

'Trasno' ('Snodoll') Min, w, 1987, Travis, Louis R.; flowers , 30-40 crinkled, translucent petals, borne singly, slight fruity fragrance; foliage small, medium green, semi-glossy; prickles bowed, white; upright growth; no fruit; ['Yellow Doll' × 'Yellow Doll']; intr. 1986

'Trastar' ('Tiny Stars') Min, rb, 1987, Travis, Louis R.; flowers white with red narrow edges, small, 12 petals, cupped, borne usually singly and in clusters of 3-4, no fragrance; foliage small, medium green, matte; almost thornless; micro-mini; bushy, low growth; no fruit; [Magic Carrousel® × Magic Carrousel®]; intr. 1986

'Trasuz' ('Crepe Suzette') Min, ob, 1987, Travis, Louis R.; flowers deep yellow with orange overlay, fading white with orange-red, 25-30 petals, high-centered, moderate fruity fragrance; foliage small, medium green, semi-glossy; prickles bowed, tan-brown; bushy, low growth; no fruit; ['Orange Honey' × 'Orange Honey']

'Trat' ('Little 't') Min, w, 1989, Travis, Louis R.; bud pointed; flowers white tinged pale pink, reverse white, small, dbl., cupped, borne in sprays; foliage small, medium green, matte; no prickles; growth bushy; no fruit; ['Cinderella' × seedling]

Träumerei® -- See 'Reikor'

'Traumland' ('Dreamland') F, lp, 1959, Tantau, Math.; flowers light peach-pink, well-formed, 20 petals, borne in clusters, slight fragrance; recurrent; foliage dark, leathery; upright, bushy growth; ['Cinnabar Improved' × 'Fashion']; intr. 1958

Travemünde® F, mr, 1970, Kordes; bud ovoid; flowers dbl., borne in large clusters, no fragrance; recurrent; foliage dark green, matte; bushy, compact (50 cm.), vigorous growth; [Lilli Marleen® × 'Ama']; originally registered as Pol; intr. 1968

'Traverser' HG, yb, 1928, Clark, A.; flowers yellow and cream, 11 cm., semi-dbl. to dbl., borne in clusters; vigorous, climbing growth

'Travesti' F, yb, 1965, deRuiter; flowers yellow to carmine-red, medium, 38 petals, cupped, borne in clusters, moderate fragrance; recurrent; foliage dark; vigorous, bushy growth; [Orange Sensation® × 'Circus']

'Traveston' Cl HT, dr, 1953, Ulrick, L.W.; bud long, pointed; flowers crimson, medium, semi-dbl.; vigorous growth; ['Black Boy' × 'Editor McFarland']

'Travesty' F, deRuiter; intr. 1965

Traviata™ -- See 'Meilavio'

Traviata™ HT, rb, 1964, Meilland, Alain A.; bud ovoid, pointed; flowers bright red blending to white base, 4½ in., 30-35 petals, high-centered, cupped, borne in clusters, moderate tea fragrance; free-flowering; foliage leathery; vigorous, bushy growth; PP2283; [Baccará® ×

('Independence' × 'Grand'mere Jenny')]; intr. 1962

'Treasure' HT, ab, 1929, Fletcher; bud pointed; flowers apricot-pink, 6 in., dbl.; foliage glossy, dark; very vigorous growth; ['Golden Rapture' × 'Fred Walker']

'Treasure Box' F, pb; flowers bright pink with silvery white reverse, borne in clusters, moderate sweet fragrance; free-flowering; strong, medium growth

'Treasure Chest' HT, my, 1968, Whisler, D.; bud ovoid; flowers large, dbl., high-centered; foliage glossy; vigorous, upright growth; PP2992; ['Charlotte Armstrong' × 'Fred Howard']

'Treasure Gold' HT, my, 1950, Brownell; bud ovoid, pointed; flowers yellow, some petals splashed red, 4 in., 38 petals, moderate fragrance; upright, branching growth; PP1111; ['Pink Princess' × 'Free Gold (HT)']

'Treasure Island' HT, op, 1938, Raffel; bud long, pointed; flowers light salmon, reverse flaming coppery pink, base orange, large, dbl., high-centered; foliage leathery, bronze; vigorous growth; ['Comtesse Vandal' × 'Mme Nicolas Aussel']

'Treasure Island, Climbing' Cl HT, op, 1941, Hennessey

'Treasure Isle' F, op, 1967, Raffel; bud slender, pointed; flowers salmon-pink, reverse coppery, small, dbl., moderate fragrance; recurrent; foliage glossy; vigorous, bushy growth; [seedling × 'Treasure Island']

'Treasure Trove' ('Treasure Trow') LCl, ab, 1977, Treasure; flowers apricot, mauve-pink and cream, 1½-2 in., 23 petals, cupped, borne in large clusters, intense fragrance; non-remontant; vigorous growth; hips numerous, red; ['Kiftsgate' × unknown]

'Treasure Trove' HT, my, Warriner, William A.; intr. 1991

'Treasure Trow' -- See 'Treasure Trove'

'Treasured Memories' -- See 'Kenesca'

'Treasured Memories' F, dr, Dickson; flowers dark red, bright yellow stamens, small, semi-dbl., shallow cup, borne in clusters; recurrent; foliage dense, small, glossy; bushy, spreading growth; intr. 2006

'Treasured Moments'

'Treasured Moments' -- See 'Kenrhapso'

Trelleborg™ (Acadia™) F, ab, Olesen; bud long; flowers orangy-apricot, 7-8 cm., full, cupped, borne in small clusters of 3 - 8, slight wild rose fragrance; recurrent; foliage dark green, glossy; prickles few, 8-10 mm, greyed-yellow; bushy, compact (60-100 cm) growth; [seedling × 'Avon']; intr. 2001

'Tremblevif' S, mr, Gilet; intr. 2005

'Trend' HT, op, VEG; flowers large, dbl.

'Très-Petite Fleur' (R. parvula) HMult, lp, 1866, Cochet; flowers pale pink, fading to pinky-white, ½ in., dbl., borne in large clusters; spring; foliage ovate, sharply pointed, finely toothed; prickles small, few, nearly straight

'Trésarin' HGal, m, about 1845, Calvert; flowers purple, medium, very full

'Tresor' -- See 'Krinico'

'Tresor' my, Pekmez; intr. 1989

'Tresor de Thorigny' S, w; flowers white with some blush pink tints, yellow stamens, 1½ in., dbl., cupped to flat, loose, borne in clusters, slight fragrance; recurrent; vigorous, arching growth; landscape shrub, climber

'Tressor' HT, ob; intr. 2002

'Trevi Fountain' LCl, ob

Trevor Griffiths™ -- See 'Ausold'

Triade® S, mr, Noack; flowers bright red, yellow stamens, 4 cm., semi-dbl. to dbl., shallow cup, borne in clusters; recurrent; foliage medium green, glossy; compact, bushy, upright (4 ft.) growth; intr. 2004

'Trianon' -- See 'LLX8736'

'Triathlon' S, pb; flowers shades of pink, yellow stamens, small, dbl., cupped, borne in clusters; recurrent; low, bushy growth; intr. 1998

'Tribute' -- See 'Jacrose'

'Tribute' HT, w, Chakraborty, Dr. K.; flowers cream white, gain red flush as they age, large, full, intense fragrance; free-flowering; upright growth; intr. 2000

'Tricentenaire' HT, mp, 1949, Lens; bud long, pointed; flowers pink, center deeper, medium, 25 petals, high-centered; foliage leathery, small; vigorous growth; ['Charles P. Kilham' × 'Neville Chamberlain']

'Tricia' -- See 'Jacwhy'

'Tricia' LCl, lp, 1942, O'Neal; bud long, pointed; flowers flesh-pink to ivory-pink, dbl., high-centered, intense fragrance; foliage dark, glossy; growth vigorous (about 8 ft.); hardy; ['New Dawn' × unknown]

'Tricia's Joy' LCl, op, 1986, McKirdy, J.M.; flowers deep coral pink, large, 35 petals, moderate fragrance; foliage medium size, dark, semi-glossy; vigorous growth (to 18 ft.); ['Mme Caroline Testout, Climbing' × Blessings®]; intr. 1973

'Trick Or Treat' -- See 'Taltrick'

'Trickster' -- See 'Britrick'

'Tricolore' ('Belle Alliance', 'Reine Marguerite', 'Rose Marguerite', 'Ruban Doré', 'Mexica Aurantia') HGal, rb, before 1821, Stegerhoek; flowers velvety crimson purple striped with yellowish-white, small, full; growth erect; possibly re-introduced by Vibert, about 1840, as 'Reine Marguerite'

'Tricolore' HWich, rb, Weigand, C.; flowers variegated red, white, and pink, 5-6 cm., dbl., flat, borne in medium clusters, slight fragrance; foliage small, dark green; intr. 1906

'Tricolore' HGal, pb, Lahaye père; flowers lilac-pink, fringed at edges, dotted and mottled white, small, dbl., moderate fragrance; non-remontant; thornless; sturdy, upright (4 ft.) growth; intr. 1827

'Tricolore' ('Multiflore Tricolore') HMult, pb, Robert et Moreau; flowers lilac-pink, toothed and deckled white, 7 cm., full, globular, borne in corymbs of 20-50; non-recurrent; growth more vigorous than Gallica of the same name; [R. multiflora × unknown]; intr. 1863

'Tricolore de Flandre' HGal, pb, 1846; flowers pale blush, striped bright pink, fading to mauve, with a small green eye, small, full, rosette, moderate fragrance; non-remontant; foliage dark green, oval; prickles very few; moderate (3 ft.) growth; possibly from Parmentier

'Tricolore d'Enghien' P, pb, about 1830, Parmentier; flowers carmine, shaded dark purple, striped white, small, full

'Tricolore d'Orléans' HGal, rb; flowers red, striped white, medium, full

Trier® HMult, w, 1904, Lambert, P.; bud salmony pink; flowers rosy white, base straw-yellow, small, semi-dbl., borne in clusters of 30-50, moderate fragrance; moderate repeat; foliage dark green, glossy; prickles few; growth to 6-8 ft.; probably an 'Aglaia' self-seedling, but 'Aglaia' × 'Mrs. R. G. Sharman-Crawford' has been noted

'Trier 2000' -- See 'Kormetter'

'Trieste' F, Mansuino; intr. 1960

'Trifling' MinFl, rb, Williams, J. Benjamin; flowers soft red with white tones and eye, single, shallow cup to flat, borne in large clusters, slight fragrance; recurrent; foliage medium green, matte; growth to 2 ft.; intr. 2006

'Trigintipetala' (R. × damascena trigintipetala, R. trigintipetala) D, mp, 1899; flowers bright pink, aging to white, medium, semi-dbl. to dbl.; non-recurrent; foliage clear green, oval, with 5-7 leaflets; prickles large, numerous; [R. gallica × R. damascena]; first described in 1689; often thought to be the same as 'Kazanlik', and possibly 'Prof. Émile Perrot'

'Trigo' HT, ab, 1931, Dickson, A.; bud long, pointed; flowers Indian yellow, reverse apricot, tinted cerise, large, dbl., high-centered; foliage thick, bronze, glossy; vigorous growth

'Trilby' HT, op, 1927, Dobbie; flowers rich salmon, dbl.

'Trinity' T, w; flowers pale pink to white, gold stamens, nodding, 4 in., semi-dbl., borne usually singly, moderate fragrance; free-flowering; foliage dark; vigorous, bushy, spreading growth; discovered in Bermuda

'Trinity' HT, pb, 1977, de Freitas; flowers variegated pink and yellow, medium, dbl., globular, intense fragrance; vigorous, upright, compact growth; ['Korovo' × unknown]; intr. 1976

'Trinity' -- See 'Macredparap'

'Trinity Rambler' LCl, dp

'Trinket' Min, mp, 1965, Moore, Ralph S.; flowers phlox-pink, micro-mini, small, dbl., cupped to rosette, borne in clusters; free-flowering; foliage glossy; vigorous, bushy, dwarf (10 in.) growth; [(R. wichurana × 'Floradora') × 'Magic

The Official Registry and Checklist — Rosa 759

Wand']
'Trintago' HT, mr, 1962, Leenders, J.; flowers cardinal-red, well-formed, dbl.; ['Souv. de Jacques Verschuren' × 'Charles Mallerin']
'Trio' F, pb, 1966, Dickson, A.; flowers gold and pink, well-formed, large; ['Kordes' Perfecta' × 'Shot Silk']
'Triodene' -- See 'Korituscha'
'Triolet' ('Tanned Beauty') HT, ab, Orard; flowers creamy apricot-salmon, darker reverse, dbl., borne mostly singly, moderate fragrance; recurrent; stems long; vigorous, medium growth
'Triomphe Angevin' Pol, mr, 1934, Délépine; flowers cerise-red, semi-dbl., cupped, borne in clusters, slight fragrance; recurrent; foliage glossy; very vigorous, bushy growth
'Triomphe Briard' F, op, 1958, Robichon; flowers coral, dbl., borne in clusters; foliage glossy; moderate growth; [seedling × 'Fashion']
'Triomphe d'Alencon' HP, dp, 1858; flowers intense red, very large, dbl.; usually attributed to Touvais, but may be from Chauvel and sold by Touvais
'Triomphe d'Amiens' -- See 'Général Jacqueminot'
'Triomphe d'Avranches' HP, mr, 1855, Baudry; flowers scarlet-amaranth, shaded velvety carmine, edged white, large, full
'Triomphe de Bollvillers' -- See 'Triomphe de Bolwyller'
'Triomphe de Bolwyller' (R. sempervirens odorata, 'Triomphe de Bollvillers') HSem, w, about 1860, Baumann; flowers white, center tinted yellow, large, globular, moderate fragrance; non-remontant; apparently a hybrid between R. sempervirens and a Tea
'Triomphe de Brabant' -- See 'Duchesse d'Angoulême'
'Triomphe de Caen' -- See 'Prince Arthur'
'Triomphe de Caen' HP, dr, 1861, Oger; flowers deep velvety grenadine, shaded with purple, large, full
'Triomphe de Coulommiers' -- See 'Souv. de Coulommiers'
'Triomphe de Flore' HGal, lp, before 1821; flowers delicate blush pink, medium, very dbl.; from Rouen
'Triomphe de France' HP, mp, 1875, Garçon; flowers bright carmine rose, very large, very dbl., moderate fragrance
'Triomphe de Guillot Fils' T, pb, 1861, Guillot fils; flowers apricot-pink at center, lighter edges, 9 cm., dbl.
'Triomphe de Guillotière' T, w, 1861, Guillot; flowers white, shaded cream, medium, dbl.
'Triomphe de Guillotière' S, w, Guillot et Fils; flowers white tinged pink; [probably R. roxburghii × R. odorata]; intr. 1863
'Triomphe de Jaussens' HGal, dp, before 1850; flowers bright carmine, shaded purple
'Triomphe de la Duchèr' B, lp, 1846, Béluze; flowers pale rose, medium, full, borne in large clusters
'Triomphe de la Malmaison' HT, dp, 1946, Gaujard; flowers dark satiny pink, very large, petals reflexed; foliage dark; vigorous growth
'Triomphe de la Terre des Roses' ('Henderson') HP, mp, 1864, Guillot père; flowers violaceous pink, large, dbl.; freely remontant; moderately vigorous growth
'Triomphe de Laffay' HCh, w, about 1830, Laffay; flowers delicate flesh, changing to white, expanded, large, very dbl.; recurrent; pendulous growth
'Triomphe de l'Exposition' HP, mr, 1855, Margottin; flowers cherry-red, 4-5 in., 55 petals, borne singly or in small clusters; recurrent bloom; foliage elongated oval, deeply serrate, dark green, glossy; prickles few, strong, very sharp, slightly curved; vigorous, bushy growth
'Triomphe de Lille' ('Bride of Lille', 'Pride of Lille') D, lp, before 1826, Vibert; flowers white, with a pink center, medium, full; foliage deeply serrate; prickles rare, slender, mixed with numerous glandular bristles
'Triomphe de Luxembourg' -- See 'Triomphe du Luxembourg'
'Triomphe de Lyon' HP, mr, 1859, Cordier; flowers velvety crimson, medium, semi-dbl.
'Triomphe de Milan' T, w, 1877, Widow Ducher; flowers white, with a deep yellow center, large, full, no fragrance; growth vigorous, upright
'Triomphe de Nancy' HP, dr, 1862, Crousse; flowers velvety dark crimson, large, full
'Triomphe de Paris' HP, dp, 1852, Margottin; flowers carmine, shaded velvety blackish-red, very large, very full
'Triomphe de Pernet Père' HT, m, 1890, Pernet; flowers reddish-violet, large, very dbl.; ['Monsieur Désir' × 'Général Jacqueminot']
'Triomphe de Plantier' B, pb, 1837, Plantier; flowers lilac pink, center carmine, large, very full
'Triomphe de Rennes' N, my, 1857, Panaget or Lancezeur; flowers canary yellow, center gold, very large, full; ['Lamarque' × unknown]
'Triomphe de Rennes' HGal, dr; flowers purple-red, shaded slate, very large, very full; intr. before 1936
'Triomphe de Rouen' D, mp, 1826, Lecomte; flowers soft pink, touched lilac, large, full
'Triomphe de Saintes' -- See 'Le Triomphe de Saintes'
'Triomphe de Sterckmanns' ('Sterckmanns') HGal, dp, 1847, Vibert; flowers large, full
'Triomphe de Toulouse' HP, rb, 1873, Brassac; flowers red, shaded with violet-crimson, large, full
'Triomphe de Valenciennes' ('Mme Campbell d'Islay') HP, lp, 1847, Schneider; flowers flesh pink shaded carmine, striped purple-violet, large, full; may have been re-introduced by Baudry in 1859
'Triomphe de Vibert' HGal, mr, about 1835, Vibert; flowers carmine-red, medium, full
'Triomphe des Beaux-Arts' HP, m, 1857, Fontaine; flowers velvety dark purple, large, full; ['Général Jacqueminot' × unknown]
'Triomphe des Noisettes' N, dp, 1887, Pernet père; flowers bright rose, fading lighter, 9-10 cm., full, often quartered, borne in small clusters; foliage very dark green; prickles numerous, protrusive; ['Général Jacqueminot' × 'Ophirie']
'Triomphe d'Orléans' HP, dr, 1902, Corboeuf; flowers red and deep violet; ['Général Jacqueminot' × 'Général de la Martinière']
'Triomphe du Luxembourg' ('Triomphe de Luxembourg') T, pb, 1835, Hardy; flowers salmon-buff shaded rose, full; recurrent; growth to 3 ft.
'Triomphe Orléanais' Pol, mr, 1912, Peauger; flowers cherry-red, 1½-2 in., semi-dbl., borne in large clusters; foliage leathery, glossy, bright; vigorous growth
'Triomphe Orléanais, Climbing' Cl Pol, mr, 1922, Turbat; flowers small, semi-dbl., borne in medium to large clusters; non-recurrent
'Triple Treat' -- See 'Rosenstadt Freising'
'Tristan' F, my, Lowe; flowers bright yellow, fading lighter, semi-double, flat, borne in large clusters, moderate fragrance; recurrent; tall (3 - 5 ft.) growth; intr. 2005
'Tristesse' ('Tristeza') HT, m, 1953, Camprubi, C.; flowers gray-mauve, medium, 30-40 petals, flat; foliage glossy; vigorous growth; ['Charles P. Kilham' × 'Betty Uprichard']
'Tristeza' -- See 'Tristesse'
'Triton' HT, yb, 1978, Dickson, Patrick; flowers white to light yellow, petals edged pink, large, 47 petals; upright growth; ['Colour Wonder' × 'Tzigane']
'Triumphant' HSet, mp, 1850, Pierce; flowers deep rose pink, aging to pale violet, medium, very dbl., borne in clusters of 20-30; foliage very large, undulated, deeply and sharply serrated; [R. setigera × unknown]
'Trix' Pol, or, VEG; flowers medium, dbl.
'Trixx!' HT, ob, Schreurs; greenhouse rose; intr. 2002
'Triyabell Trust' -- See 'Worcrust'
'Troball' ('Joan Ball') Min, mp, 1986, Robinson, Thomas, Ltd.; flowers small, 30 petals, high-centered, borne in sprays of 3-6, moderate fruity fragrance; foliage small, dark, glossy; prickles short, thin, red-brown; upright, bushy growth; [Orange Sensation® × seedling]
'Trobeach' ('Shell Beach') Min, w, 1983, Thomas Robinson, Ltd.; bud soft pink; flowers creamy white, 28 petals, borne

in clusters; foliage small, medium green, semi-glossy; bushy growth; ['Simon Robinson' × 'Simon Robinson']

'Trobee' ('Dollie B') Min, rb, 1982, Robinson, Thomas, Ltd.; flowers medium red, silver reverse, small, 35 petals; foliage small, dark green, red edges, glossy; bushy growth; [Parkdirektor Riggers® × 'Darling Flame']

'Trobelle' ('Calay') Min, my, 1982, Robinson, Thomas, Ltd.; flowers lemon yellow, small, semi-dbl.; foliage small, dark, glossy; upright, bushy growth; ['Rumba' × 'New Penny']

'Trobette' ('Jennie Robinson') Min, op, 1982, Robinson, Thomas, Ltd.; flowers orange flushed pink, patio, small, 35 petals, moderate fragrance; foliage small, dark, glossy; bushy growth; ['Rumba' × 'Darling Flame']

'Trobgina' ('Gina Louise') Min, op, 1987, Robinson, T.; flowers bright orange-pink, opening to bright yellow, gold anthers,, 35 petals, high-centered, intense damask, fruity fragrance; foliage small, dark green, semi-glossy; prickles thin, red pointed down; bushy, low growth; hips globular, large, orange; [Orange Sensation® × seedling]; intr. 1986

'Trobglow' ('Paint-Pot') Min, or, 1983, Robinson, Thomas, Ltd.; flowers medium, 24 petals, intense fragrance; foliage small, medium green, semi-glossy; bushy growth; [seedling × 'Darling Flame']

'Trobgold' ('Woodland Sunbeam') Min, my, 1984, Robinson, Thomas, Ltd.; flowers patio, medium, 23 petals; foliage small, dark, glossy, few prickles; vigorous, bushy growth; [Orange Sensation® × 'Calay']

'Trobguern' ('Guernsey Gold') Min, dy, 1992, Robinson, Thomas, Ltd.; flowers golden yellow, large, full, urn-shaped, borne in small clusters, slight fragrance; foliage small, medium green, semi-glossy; some prickles; low (30 cm.), upright, bushy growth; ['Rise 'n' Shine' × seedling]; intr. 1990

'Trobic' ('Just Magic') Min, pb, 1990, Robinson, Thomas, Ltd.; bud rounded; flowers cream to deep pink, reverse cream tinged pink, aging often strongly, 21 petals, cupped, moderate damask fragrance; foliage small, dark green, glossy; prickles very thin, pointed, red aging brown; upright, bushy, medium growth; hips spheroid, orange; [(Parkdirektor Riggers® × 'New Penny') × ((Parkdirektor Riggers® × 'New Penny') × seedling)]

'Trobina' ('Pink Secret') Min, mp, 1982, Robinson, Thomas, Ltd.; [sport of 'Beauty Secret']

'Trobinette' ('Sarah Robinson') Min, ab, 1982; flowers soft apricot, small, 20 petals, intense fragrance; foliage small, dark, glossy; compact, bushy growth; ['Rumba' × 'Darling Flame']

'Trobinka' ('Ginny-Lou') Min, mr, 1983, Robinson, Thomas, Ltd.; flowers bright medium red, dbl., borne in clusters; foliage small, dark, semi-glossy; bushy growth; ['Dollie B.' × seedling]; intr. 1984

'Troblove' ('Guernsey Love') Min, dr, 1986, Robinson, Thomas, Ltd.; flowers small, 35 petals, cupped, borne in sprays of 4-5, moderate fruity fragrance; foliage small, dark, glossy; prickles thin, red, curving downward; upright, bushy growth; hips globular, medium, orange-red; ['Dollie B.' × seedling]

'Trobric' ('Little Russel') Min, mr, 1982, Robinson, Thomas, Ltd.; flowers small, 20 petals; foliage small, dark, glossy; bushy growth; ['Marlena' × 'New Penny']; intr. 1983

'Trobroy' (Royal Worcester®) S, w, 1992, Robinson, Thomas, Ltd.; flowers peachy cream, large, semi-dbl., borne in large clusters, moderate fragrance; foliage medium size, dark green, very glossy; some prickles; low to medium (60 cm.), bushy, compact growth; ['Simon Robinson' × 'Gina Louise']; intr. 1991

'Trobsa' ('Woodlands Lady') Min, mp, 1982, Robinson, Thomas, Ltd.; flowers medium salmon-pink, small, 15 petals, borne in large clusters; foliage small, dark, glossy; compact, bushy growth; [seedling × 'New Penny']

'Trobspread' ('Unforgettable') S, yb, 1992, Robinson, Thomas, Ltd.; flowers amber, 3-3½ in., dbl., borne in large clusters; repeat bloom; foliage small to medium size, dark green, glossy; some prickles; medium (90 cm.), bushy, spreading (hemisphere shape) growth; [Snow Carpet® × 'Woodland Sunbeam']; intr. 1994

'Trobstar' LCl, dp, Robinson, T.; intr. 1997

'Trobsun' ('Woodlands Sunrise') Min, yb, 1982, Robinson, Thomas, Ltd.; flowers small, 35 petals; foliage small, dark, glossy; upright, bushy growth; ['Rumba' × 'Darling Flame']

'Trobwich' ('Simon Robinson') Min, mp, 1982, Thomas Robinson, Ltd.; flowers small, single, borne in large clusters, moderate fragrance; foliage small, dark green, glossy; compact, low, bushy growth; [R. wichurana × 'New Penny']

'Trocadero' HT, mr, 1964, Delforge; bud pointed, bright red; foliage bronze; vigorous growth; ['Karl Herbst' × seedling]

'Trocadero 'D'' HT, Delforge; intr. 1989

Troika™ -- See 'Poultroi'

'Troika, Climbing' Cl HT, ob, Thomas, Dr. A.S.

'Troilus' -- See 'Ausoil'

'Troja' HT, w, 1927, Mikes; bud long, pointed, cream-yellow; flowers creamy white, full, moderate fragrance; vigorous, bushy growth; [sport of 'Mrs Herbert Stevens']; intr. 1928

'Trojan' Gr, yb, 1961, Von Abrams; bud long, pointed; flowers pastel pink, reverse yellow,, 5 in., 40 petals, high-centered; foliage leathery; upright growth; ['Sutter's Gold' × ('Mme Henri Guillot' × seedling)]; intr. 1961

'Trojan Victory' -- See 'Korperki'

'Trollhattan' HRg, dp, Essunga Planteskole; flowers rosy lilac that blush irregularly to pale lavender pink, petals twisted, large, dbl.

'Trompeter von Säckingen' HMult, m, about 1890, Geschwind, R.; flowers purple red, aging to cerise and medium pink, lighter reverse, 5-6 cm., full, flat, borne in small clusters, moderate fragrance; non-remontant; strong, upright (5 ft.) growth

'Tropat' ('Temptation') F, or, 1992, Robinson, Thomas, Ltd.; flowers 3-3½ in., 5 petals, borne in small clusters; foliage medium size, medium green, semi-glossy; some prickles; low (70 cm.), dense, bushy, compact growth; [Orange Sensation® × seedling]

'Trophée' ('Trophy') LCl, mr, 1970, Robichon; flowers medium to large, 4 in., dbl., borne in clusters, no fragrance; recurrent; foliage glossy, vigorous, climbing growth; ['Valenciennes' × 'Etendard']; intr. 1968

'Trophy' -- See 'Trophée'

'Tropical' F, Cazzaniga, F. G.; intr. 1966

'Tropical Amazone' HT, ob, deRuiter; flowers soft orange, dbl., high-centered, borne mostly singly; recurrent

'Tropical Fragrance' S, mr, Clements, John; flowers crimson red, yellow stamens, 4 in., 18-24 petals, shallow cup to flat, borne in clusters of 5 to 10, moderate citrus/honey/spice fragrance; recurrent; foliage leathery, dark green; compact (3 × 2½ ft.) growth; PPAF; intr. 2002

'Tropical Oasis' F, r, 2004, Mueller, Joanna; flowers russet, reverse russet/orange, medium, full, borne mostly solitary, no fragrance; foliage semi-glossy, dense; growth upright, short; garden decoration; ['Tropicana' × Hot Cocoa™]

'Tropical Paradise' -- See 'Bursrtpara'

'Tropical Passion' -- See 'Carange'

'Tropical Sherbet' F, yb, Keihan; intr. 2003

'Tropical Skies' -- See 'Interdays'

'Tropical Sunrise' -- See 'Johillgold'

Tropical Sunset™ -- See 'Mactaurang'

Tropical Twist™ -- See 'Jacorca'

'Tropicana' -- See 'Tanorstar'

'Tropicana, Climbing' -- See 'Tangostar'

Tropicana® HT, rb, Tantau; flowers bright red with yellow base and reverse, large, double, high-centered, borne mostly singly; recurrent; stems long; florist rose; intr. 2006

'Tropico Sunblaze' Min, my, Meilland; intr. 1995

'Tropique' LCl, or, 1956, Delbard-Chabert; flowers velvety crimson, 3 in., dbl., borne singly or in small clusters; recurrent; foliage small, dark green, glossy, some bronze tones

'Troubadour' HWich, mr, 1911, Walsh;

flowers bright red, shaded maroon, sometimes streaked with white to medium pink, 5-6 cm., dbl., borne in clusters of 10-25; free seasonal bloom; foliage large, glossy, dark; vigorous, climbing growth

'Troubadour' HT, Buyl Frères; flowers rose-copper, large, dbl.; free bloom; strong stems; moderate growth; RULED EXTINCT; intr. 1956

'Troubadour of Love' HT, dr

'Trpaslik' Min, Strnad

'Trsmeera' (Meera™) Min, pb, 2001, Siddiqui, Tariq; flowers medium pink with darker edges, large, high-centered, borne mostly solitary, slight fragrance; foliage medium size, medium green, matte; prickles moderate; growth upright, tall (24 in.); garden decorative, exhibition; [Irresistible™ × unknown]

'Trsstshake' (Strawberry Shake™) Min, rb, 2001, Siddiqui, Tariq; flowers white with red edges, large, dbl., high-centered, borne mostly solitary, slight fragrance; foliage medium size, medium green, matte; prickles moderate; growth upright, tall (40 in.); garden decorative, exhibition; [Irresistible™ × unknown]

'Truby King' F, dp, 1965, Harris, L.M.; flowers carmine, open, large, semi-dbl., borne in large clusters; foliage leathery, glossy, bronze; vigorous, tall growth; ['Border Queen' × 'Helen Traubel']; intr. 1957

'Trudor' -- See 'Micaëla'

Trudy Mimi™ F, dp, Meilland

True™ Min, ob, Olesen; flowers dbl., 25-30 petals, borne mostly solitary, slight fragrance; foliage dark green, glossy; growth bushy, low (40-60 cm.); intr. 2000

'True Friend' T, ly, 1905, California Nursery Co.

True Gold™ -- See 'Lavtru'

'True Love' -- See 'Rutrulo'

True Love™ -- See 'P. G. Wodehouse'

'True Love' ('Grand Amour') HT, dr, 1971, Delbard; flowers deep red, 3½-4 in., 30 petals; foliage glossy; moderately vigorous growth; intr. 1970

'True Vintage' -- See 'Seavin'

'Truly Amazing' HT, ab, Athy; bud reddish apricot; flowers apricot-pink, red stamens, moderate fragrance; medium growth; intr. 2004

'Truly Fair' F, w, 1953, Ratcliffe; flowers cream, center apricot, small, semi-dbl., borne in sprays of 4-5; bushy growth

Truly Yours™ -- See 'Wekosunkora'

'Truly Yours' HT, ob, 1973, Robinson, H.; flowers coral-salmon to orange, 5 in., 44 petals, globular, intense fragrance; foliage large; vigorous, upright growth; ['Miss Ireland' × 'Stella']

'Trump' -- See 'Korionluck'

Trump Card™ HT, pb, 2007, Orent, Cliff; flowers pink, reverse yellow, 8½-11 cm., dbl., borne mostly solitary; prickles ¾-1 cm., almost straight, moderate, greyed orange; growth tall (120-140 cm.); garden decoration, cutting; [sport of 'Rosie O'Donnell']; intr. 2007

'Trumpet' F, my, 1963, Von Abrams; bud small, long-pointed; flowers medium yellow, 4 in., 15-22 petals, cupped, borne in clusters; foliage glossy; growth vigorous, upright (4 ft.); ['Goldilocks' × 'Captain Thomas']; intr. 1962

Trumpet® -- See 'Mactrum'

'Trumpeter, Climbing' Cl F, op; [sport of Trumpeter®]; intr. about 1997

'Truper' -- See 'Persepolis'

Tryfosa™ -- See 'Poultry'

'Trylon' -- See 'Shining Star'

'Tschaika' HT, lp, Klimenko, V. N.; flowers large, dbl.; intr. 1959

'Tschaka' HT, ab, Tschanz, E.; intr. 1989

'Tschernowa Ukrajina' HT, mr, 1940, Kosteckij; flowers large, semi-dbl.

'Tschin-Tschin' F, mr, Meilland; flowers luminous red, medium, dbl.; intr. 1973

'T-620038' Sp; clone of R. multiflora; used for understock

'Tsukiakari' ('Moonlight') HT, w, 1985, Ota, Kaichiro; flowers creamy white, large, 35 petals, high-centered, globular, borne singly or in small clusters, no fragrance; foliage medium green, semi-glossy; prickles medium; bushy growth; ['Utage' × 'Anne Letts']; intr. 1984

'Tsurumi 90' ('Crane Viewing') HT, ob, Keihan; intr. 1990

'Tsuzuki' F, pb; flowers soft pink with white tones and white eye, stamens yellow, semi-dbl., shallow cup; foliage bright green, disease-resistant; small, compact growth

'Tubantia' HT, op, Verbeek; flowers reddish-orange and pink, large, dbl.; intr. 1975

'Tuc30reunion' (Class of '73™) MinFl, pb, 2003, Tucker, Robbie; flowers light pink with dark edging, 1½ in., dbl., borne mostly solitary, no fragrance; foliage medium green, semi-glossy; thornless; growth upright, medium (to 24 in.); exhibition, cut flower, garden; ['Sam Trivitt' × Dancing Flame™]; intr. 2004

'Tucan' HT, yb, Tantau; flowers yellow with red-orange edges, suffused down petals as it opens, medium, dbl., high-centered, borne mostly singly; recurrent; stems medium to long; florist rose; intr. 2003

'Tuckaberlady' (Aberlady™) MinFl, dy, 2007, Tucker, Robbie; flowers 1¾ dbl., borne mostly solitary; foliage medium, dark green, glossy; prickles medium to large, straight, deep red on new growth, moderate; growth upright, tall (4-5 ft. for mature plant); exhibition, cut flower, garden; [seedling × seedling]; intr. 2008

'Tuckable' (Able™) Min, yb, 2006, Tucker, Robbie; flowers yellow with orange edge, ¾ in., dbl., borne mostly solitary; foliage dark green, glossy; prickles small, slightly curved downward, red to brown, moderate; growth compact, medium (to 30 in.); exhibition, cut flower, landscape; ['Cal Poly' × 'Soroptimist International']; intr. 2007

'Tuckach' (Cachet™) MinFl, w, 1997, Tucker, Robbie; flowers full, high-centered, borne mostly singly, no fragrance; foliage medium size, medium green, semi-glossy; upright, tall (3 ft.) growth; PP10828; [seedling × seedling]; intr. 1998

'Tuckaliena' (Aliena™) MinFl, yb, 2002, Tucker, Robbie; flowers deep yellow with red edging, reverse light yellow, 1½-2 in., dbl., borne mostly solitary, no fragrance; foliage dark green, matte; prickles small, straight, green to brown, few; growth bushy, tall (4 ft.); [seedling × seedling]; intr. 2002

'Tuckamy' (Amy Grant™) MinFl, lp, 1998, Tucker, Robbie; flowers light pink, varies by temperature, 1½-1¾ in., dbl., high-centered, borne mostly singly; foliage medium size, dark green, glossy; prickles few, small, slightly hooked downward; growth low (18-24 in.), upright; PP12270; [Loving Touch™ × 'White Masterpiece']; intr. 1999

'Tuckarc' ('Arcanum') Min, ab, 2000, Tucker, Robbie; flowers creamy apricot, 4-7 cm., dbl., high-centered, borne mostly singly, no fragrance; foliage medium size, medium size, very glossy; some prickles; growth bushy, medium (20 in.); [seedling × Kristin™]; intr. 2001

'Tucker's Folly' HT, pb, 1951, Fletcher; flowers glowing cerise overlaid orange, 6-7 in., 35-40 petals; foliage bronze; very vigorous growth

'Tucker's Yellow' HT, dy, Tucker; flowers deep golden yellow; [sport of 'Max Krause']

'Tuckfate' (Kismet™) MinFl, yb, 2005, Tucker, Robbie; flowers yellow with red edging, reverse yellow and red, up to 2 in., dbl., high-centered, borne in small clusters; foliage medium size, dark green, glossy; prickles few, ¼ to ½ in., slightly curved downward, brown; growth compact, medium (to 30 in.); exhibition, cut flower, garden; ['Cal Poly' × 'Soroptimist International']; intr. 2005

'Tuckferrin' ('Ferrin') MinFl, mp, 2000, Tucker, Robbie; flowers medium pink, 7 cm., dbl., high-centered, borne singly or in small clusters; foliage medium size, medium green, dull; numerous prickles; upright, medium (20-24 in.) growth; [seedling × Figurine']; intr. 2001

'Tuckflame' (Dancing Flame™) Min, yb, 2001, Tucker, Robbie; flowers yellow with red edges, 1½-2 in., dbl., borne mostly solitary, no fragrance; foliage medium size, medium green, glossy; prickles medium, hooked downward, light green to brown; growth upright, medium (24 in.); exhibition, garden decorative, cutting; [seedling × Kristin™]; intr. 2001

'Tuckflip' (Miss Flippins™) Min, mr, 1997, Tucker, Robbie; flowers medium red, deep pink reverse, 1½ in., dbl., high-centered, borne mostly singly or in small clusters of up to 4, no fragrance; foliage medium size, dark green, glossy; prickles moderate, hooked downward; stems strong; bushy, medium (2 ft.) growth; PP10601; ['Elizabeth Taylor' × Kristin™]; intr. 1997

'Tuckgrinnel' (Roxie™) MinFl, op, 2001, Tucker, Robbie; flowers light orange, 2 in., dbl., high-centered, borne in small clusters, no fragrance; foliage dark green, glossy; prickles 1 cm., straight to slightly downward, red on new growth; growth bushy, medium (to 30 in.); exhibition, cutting, garden decorative; ['Elsie Melton' × Kristin™]; intr. 2001

'Tuckjerry' (Jerry Lynn™) MinFl, ab, 2004, Tucker, Robbie; flowers light apricot, 2¼ in., full, borne mostly solitary, no fragrance; foliage medium green, semi-glossy; prickles no thorns on new growth, few on mature wood; growth bushy, medium (36 in.); exhibition, cutting, garden decoration; ['Sam Trivitt' × 'Memphis King']; intr. 2005

'Tuckjohnboy' (John Boy™) Min, yb, 2006, Tucker, Robbie; flowers yellow with light pink edge, ¾ in., full, borne in large clusters; foliage medium green, semi-glossy; prickles ¼-½ in., straight, pointed slightly down, green to brown; growth compact, medium (to 36 in.); exhibition, cut flower, landscape; ['Cal Poly' × Little Tommy Tucker™]; intr. 2007

'Tuckladye' ('Lady E'owyn') MinFl, pb, 2000, Tucker, Robbie; flowers white with crimson petal edges, sometimes green tinge on outer petals, full, high-centered, no fragrance; foliage medium size, medium green, matte; some prickles; growth bushy, medium (24 in.); [seedling × 'Lynn Anderson']; intr. 2001

'Tucklucy' (Luscious Lucy™) MinFl, m, 2004, Tucker, Robbie; flowers cream/yellow center reddish/mauve edges, reverse white and mauve, 2 in., dbl., borne mostly solitary, no fragrance; foliage dark green, semi-glossy; prickles few, tiny, straight; growth bushy, medium (30 in.); exhibition, cutting, garden; ['Sam Trivitt' × seedling]; intr. 2005

'Tuckmarie' (Dolores Marie™) MinFl, m, 2001, Tucker, Robbie; bud on very long peduncle; flowers mauve with dark edge, 2½-3 in., very full, old-fashioned, borne mostly solitary, intense fragrance; foliage medium green, matte; prickles very small, straight downward, reddish-brown; growth upright, medium (18 in.); exhibition, garden decorative, cutting; [seedling × Scentsational™]; intr. 2001

'Tuckmate' (Checkmate™) MinFl, rb, 2002, Tucker, Robbie; flowers orange-pink with white at base, reverse light orange-pink, 2½-3 in., full, borne mostly solitary, slight fragrance; foliage large, medium green, matte; prickles medium, straight, green to brown, moderate; growth bushy, tall (3½ ft.); garden decorative, exhibition; [seedling × seedling]; intr. 2002

'Tucknemesis' (Nemesis™) MinFl, rb, 2004, Tucker, Robbie; flowers red, reverse red with yellow tones, small, dbl., borne mostly solitary, no fragrance; foliage medium green, matte; prickles medium, straight; upright, medium growth; exhibition, cutting, garden; ['Proprietary Seedling' × 'Soroptimist International']; intr. 2005

'Tucknox' (Equinox™) MinFl, ob, 2005, Tucker, Robbie; flowers orange and white, reverse white, medium, full, borne mostly solitary, no fragrance; foliage medium size, medium green, matte; prickles moderate, ¼ to ½ in., slightly curved downward, light green to brown; growth upright, medium (30 in.); exhibition, cut flower, garden; [seedling × 'Memphis King']; intr. 2005

'Tuckpuzzle' ('Summer Night', Conundrum™) MinFl, yb, 2002, Tucker, Robbie; flowers yellow with red edging, deepening with age, 2-3 in., dbl., high-centered, borne mostly solitary, slight fragrance; foliage medium size, dark green, semi-glossy; prickles regular, few; growth upright, medium (2-2½ ft.); exhibition, cutting, garden decorative; ['Cal Poly' × Kristin™]; intr. 2002

'Tuckready' (Ready™) MinFl, yb, 2006, Tucker, Robbie; flowers yellow with red edging, 1½ in., full, borne mostly solitary; foliage dark green, glossy; prickles ¼ to ½ in., straight with point slightly down, reddish brown; growth bushy, medium (to 30 in.); landscape, exhibition; ['Cal Poly' × Little Tommy Tucker™]; intr. 2007

'Tuckrox' (Roxie Baby™) HT, op, 1998, Tucker, Robbie; flowers orange to pink, reverse lighter, 3-4 in., 65 petals, high-centered, borne mostly singly; foliage dark green, glossy; upright, medium (5 ft.) growth; ['Elizabeth Taylor' × 'Hoagy Carmichael']; intr. 1999

'Tuckscotland' (Caledonia™) MinFl, ly, 2007, Tucker, Robbie; flowers light yellow to almost white, 2 in., full, borne mostly solitary; foliage medium, dark green, semi-glossy; prickles medium to large, straight, light brown, numerous; growth upright, tall (4-5 ft. for mature plant); exhibition, cut flower, landscape; ['Cal Poly' × Cachet™]; intr. 2008

'Tucksky' (Bonnie Sky™) MinFl, pb, 2007, Tucker, Robbie; flowers medium pink, reverse light pink to white, 2 in., full, borne in small clusters; foliage small, dark green, matte; prickles small, straight with point slightly downward, light red, moderate; growth compact, short (24 in.); cutting; [seedling × Scentsational™]; intr. 2008

'Tuckstand' (Standing Ovation™) HT, rb, 1998, Tucker, Robbie; flowers white with red edge, 4½ in., very dbl., high-centered, borne singly or in small clusters, slight fragrance; recurrent; foliage medium size, dark green, semi-glossy; prickles moderate; upright, medium (4-5 ft.) growth; ['Elizabeth Taylor' × 'White Masterpiece']; intr. 1999

'Tucktommy' (Little Tommy Tucker™) Min, my, 1998, Tucker, Robbie; flowers medium yellow, reverse lighter, long-lasting, 1½-1¾ in., dbl., high-centered, borne in small clusters, no fragrance; foliage medium size, dark green, glossy; prickles few, small to medium, slightly hooked downward; upright, low (14-20 in.) growth; PP12360; ['Rise 'n' Shine' × Captivation™]; intr. 1999

'Tuckty' (Ty™) Min, dy, 2005, Tucker, Robbie; flowers non-fading yellow, 2 in., dbl., high-centered, borne mostly solitary, no fragrance; recurrent; foliage medium green, matte; prickles moderate, to ¼ in., straight with point slightly downward; growth upright, medium (to 36 in.); exhibition; ['Cal Poly' × 'Soroptimist International']; intr. 2006

'Tuckviceversa' (Vice Versa™) MinFl, rb, 2006, Tucker, Robbie; flowers red, reverse white, 1 in., dbl., borne mostly solitary; foliage medium size, medium green, glossy; prickles ½-¾ in., curving downward, red to brown, moderate; growth compact, medium (to 30 in.); exhibition, cut flower, landscape; [seedling × 'Soroptimist International']; intr. 2007

'Tuckwilling' (Willing™) Min, yb, 2006, Tucker, Robbie; flowers yellow and red, ¾ in., dbl., borne mostly solitary; foliage dark green, semi-glossy; prickles ¼ to ? in., straight, red to brown, moderate; growth upright, tall (to 48 in.); exhibition, cut flower, garden; ['Cal Poly' × Dancing Flame™]; intr. 2007

'Tuckzell' ('Zell') Min, pb, 2000, Tucker, Robbie; flowers dbl., high-centered, borne singly and in small clusters, no fragrance; foliage small, light green, matte; some prickles; growth bushy, compact, low (12-18 in.) groundcover; ['Chelsea Belle' × seedling]; intr. 2001

'Tucprov' (Providence™) MinFl, my, 2003, Tucker, Robbie; flowers non-fading, 1½-2¼ in., full, borne in small clusters, no fragrance; foliage medium green, glossy; prickles small ¼ in., straight to slightly turned, light red to brown,; growth bushy, medium (30 in.); exhibition, cut flower, garden decorative; ['Cal Poly' × Kristin™]; intr. 2003

'Tucsublime' (Sublime™) Min, rb, 2003, Tucker, Robbie; flowers white with red edging, reverse white, 2 in., dbl., borne mostly solitary, no fragrance; foliage medium size, light green, matte; prickles numerous, small, straight, light green; compact, short (to 18 in.) growth; [seedling × Dancing Flame™]; intr. 2004

Tudelum™ -- See 'Kinlum'

'Tudor' ('Pechtold's Flame') HT, mr, 1953, Verschuren-Pechtold; flowers spectrum-red overcast scarlet-red, 5 in., 20-25 petals, high-centered, moderate fragrance; long stems; vigorous growth; PP1223; ['Katharine Pechtold'

× 'Crimson Glory']

'Tudor Prince' ('Prince Philip') Gr, mr, 1960, Leenders, J.; bud long, pointed, chestnut; flowers bright red shaded geranium-red, large, 30-40 petals; foliage glossy, dark; vigorous, upright growth; ['Independence' × 'Buccaneer']; intr. 1959

'Tudor Rose' S, Porter, L.; [R. brunonii × unknown]; intr. 1989

'Tudor Sunsation' S, lp, Kordes; flowers lightly brushed pink, deep cup, borne in fan-like clusters; recurrent; compact, prostrate, groundcover growth; intr. 1997

'Tudor Victory' HT, dr, 1988, Bracegirdle, Derek T.; flowers dusky, dark red, reverse medium red, aging purple, medium, 27 petals, high-centered, born in sprays of 2-3, slight damask fragrance; foliage large, medium green, semi-glossy; prickles straight, large, red; upright, tall growth; [Queen Elizabeth® × John Waterer®]

'Tuff Stuff' -- See 'Meichonar'

'Tuhua' HMult, ab, 1980, Murray, Nola; bud small, pointed; flowers 11 petals, borne 3-5 per cluster, no fragrance; early bloomer with some repeat; foliage small, glossy; prickles small, red-brown; vigorous, lax, tall growth; ['Iceberg' × 'Tausendschon']

'Tulipe Paltot' -- See 'Unique Panachée'

'Tullamore' S, op

'Tulsa' ('Shining Star', 'Starshine') HT, yb, Perry, Astor; flowers yellow with red tones on petal edges, dbl., high-centered; recurrent; tall growth; intr. 1995

'Tulsa Town' -- See 'Weltown'

'Tumbarumba Schoolhouse' HMult, dp

Tumbling Waters™ -- See 'Poultumb'

'Tumulte' HT, Kordes, R.

'Tunusblumchen' LCl, m

'Tupa' HT, mr, Ghosh, Mr. & Mrs. S.; flowers non-fading; free-flowering; intr. 2003

'Tupperware' HT, pb, 1982, Williams, J. Benjamin; bud ovoid, pointed; flowers carmine pink, reverse silver, 65 petals, high-centered, borne singly or in cluster of up to 5, moderate fragrance; foliage large, dark, glossy; prickles medium; vigorous, upright growth; [(Pink Peace® × Queen Elizabeth®) × ('Kordes' Perfecta' × 'Peace')]

'Turbinata' -- See 'Venusta'

'Turbo' -- See 'Meirozrug'

Turbo Meidiland® -- See 'Meirozrug'

'Turbo Rugostar' -- See 'Meirozrug'

'Turbulance' -- See 'Gelance'

'Turduq' ('Duquesa') T, lp, 2005, Turner, James C.; flowers light pink with peach tones at center, medium, very full, borne in small clusters, intense fragrance; foliage medium size, medium green, semi-glossy; prickles moderate; ['Mons. Tillier' × 'Duchesse de Brabant']; intr. 2005

'Turenne' Ch, m, about 1835, Laffay; flowers dark violet, small to medium, full

'Turenne' HP, dr, Verdier, V.; flowers maroon, medium, full; vigorous growth; [sport of 'Général Jacqueminot']; intr. 1861

'Turenne' HGal, dp, Vibert (?); flowers rose-red, large, full, cupped to flat; growth to 4 ft.; intr. 1846

'Turenne' M, m, Robert & Moreau; flowers violet-amaranth; intr. 1858

'Turgida' -- See 'Turneps'

'Türke's Rugosa-Sämling' HRg, pb, 1923, Türke; bud long, pointed; flowers peach-pink on yellow ground, large, semi-dbl., intense fragrance; foliage dark, leathery; strong stems; vigorous (2½-3 ft.) growth; ['Conrad Ferdinand Meyer' × 'Mrs Aaron Ward']

'Turkish Delight' -- See 'Jacturpl'

'Turlock High' -- See 'Clelock'

'Turn of the Century' -- See 'Greeliz'

'Turneps' Bosc ('À Feuilles de Frêne', 'Turnip Rose', 'Fraxinifolia', R. fraxinifolia, R. × rapa, 'Turgida') Misc OGR, dp, before 1770; sepals very long, incised; flowers deep rose, medium to large, dbl., borne in small clusters; foliage ovoid-oblong, smooth, tinted purple beneath; prickles sparse, unequal, intermixed with crimson bristles; stems tinted red

'Turner's Crimson Damask' -- See 'Crimson Damask'

'Turner's Crimson Rambler' -- See 'Crimson Rambler'

'Turnip Rose' -- See 'Turneps'

'Turnvater Jahn' HP, pb, 1927, Müller, Dr. F.; flowers white with pink, very large, dbl.; ['Frau Karl Druschki' × ('Mme Abel Chatenay' × 'General MacArthur')]

'Tuscan Beauty' -- See 'Hintuscan'

'Tuscan Charm' F, dy, Benny, David; flowers dusky yellow, edges bronze, medium, dbl., borne in trusses; free-flowering; foliage medium green, glossy; medium growth

Tuscan Sun™ -- See 'Jacthain'

'Tuscany' ('Old Tuscan', 'Old Velvet Rose') HGal, m, before 1598; flowers velvety blackish-crimson to deep purple, sometimes touched with white lines, yellow stamens, large, semi-dbl., flat, borne singly or in clusters of 2-5; foliage medium green, small, rounded; numerous prickles; vigorous, upright growth

'Tuscany Superb' ('Rivers' Super Tuscan', 'Superb Tuscan', 'Superb Tuscany') HGal, m, before 1837, Rivers; flowers dark, velvety blackish-red, yellow stamens, large, semi-dbl. to dbl., borne singly or in clusters of 2-3; foliage light green, large, oval; ['Tuscany' × unknown]

Tuscia® HT, mr, Barni, V.; flowers cherry red, full, high-centered, no fragrance; growth to 80 cm.; intr. 1993

'Tut's Treasure' Min, dy

'Tutti-Frutti' -- See 'Jactutti'

'Tutti Frutti' -- See 'Meichonar'

'Tutu' Min, pb, 1979, Rovinski & Meredith; bud ovoid; flowers pink and rose, 1 in., 40 petals, high-centered, slight fragrance; upright, bushy growth; ['Over the Rainbow' × seedling]; intr. 1978

'Tutu Mauve' F, m, 1963, Delbard-Chabert; flowers magenta shaded mauve and rose, well-formed, 4 in., 30 petals; bushy, low growth

'Tutu Petite' F, pb, 1967, Samuels; flowers pink, reverse darker, semi-dbl., borne in clusters; foliage glossy, light; compact, bushy growth; ['Rudolph Timm' × unknown]

'Tuxedo' -- See 'Arobrisp'

'Tweedle Dee' -- See 'Tintwee'

'Tweetie' Min, lp, 1974, Moore, Ralph S.; bud ovoid, long, pointed; flowers soft pink, small, dbl.; foliage small, light, leathery; moderate, dwarf, bushy growth; ['Perle d'Or' × 'Fairy Princess']; intr. 1973

'Tweety' -- See 'Umsatweet'

'Twenty-Fifth' -- See 'Beatwe'

'Twenty First Century' -- See 'Pertwentyfirst'

'21st Century' -- See 'Pertwentyfirst'

'Twenty-First Century' HT, pb; flowers blend of pink and peach with yellow reverse, dbl., cupped, slight fragrance; low to medium growth; intr. 1999

'21 Again!' -- See 'Meinimo'

'Twice as Nice' HT, rb, 1985, Patterson, Randell E.; flowers white blending to red at edges, large, 40 petals, intense fragrance; foliage large, dark, semi-glossy; ['Peace' × 'Mirandy']; intr. 1984

'Twice in a Blue Moon' HT, m, Tantau; flowers silvery lilac, full, cupped, borne mostly singly, moderate to intense fragrance; recurrent; foliage medium green, glossy; upright growth; intr. 2004

'Twilight' -- See 'Tasogare'

'Twilight' HT, m, 1955, Boerner; bud pointed; flowers lavender-lilac, reverse silvery, 4½ in., 30-35 petals, high-centered, moderate fragrance; foliage dull green; bushy, upright growth; PP1434; ['Grey Pearl' × 'Lavender Pinocchio']; intr. 1955

'Twilight' S, dp, Noack, Werner; part of Flower Carpet series; intr. 1997

'Twilight' Min, rb, Bell; flowers red and yellow blend; free-flowering; bushy, medium growth

'Twilight Beauty' Min, m, 1978, Williams, Ernest D.; bud long, pointed; flowers red-purple, 1-1½ in., 40 petals, high-centered, moderate fragrance; bushy, spreading growth; ['Angel Face' × 'Over the Rainbow']; intr. 1978

'Twilight Dream' -- See 'Mindream'

'Twilight Glow' -- See 'Meitosier'

'Twilight Mist' -- See 'Yugiri'

'Twilight Mist' LCl, m, Robinson, P.; flowers soft lavender, large, semi-dbl., shallow cup, blooms in profusion, moderate fragrance; non-remontant; large growth; ['Montecito' × unknown]; intr. 1995

Twilight Secret™ -- See 'Viranil'

'Twilight Skies' -- See 'Morlight'

'Twilight Time' Min, m

Twilight Trail™ -- See 'Minxco'

Twilight Tryst™ -- See 'Virtryst'

'Twilight Zone' Min, mr, 1985, Hardgrove, Donald L.; flowers well-formed, medium, 60 petals; foliage small, dark, semi-glossy; bushy, dense growth; ['Scarlet Knight' × 'Big John']

'Twilight Zone' Gr, m, Williams, J. Benjamin; flowers lavender with yellow reverse, dbl., high-centered, slight fragrance; recurrent; low growth; intr. 1996

Twin® HT, w, Kordes; flowers wihte with green tint on outer petals and slight pink tone in center, medium, full, high-centered, borne mostly singly; recurrent; stems medium; ['Duett' × 'Not stated']; florist rose; intr. 2002

Twin Kordana® Min, pb, Kordes; flowers deep pink with cream stripes and splotches, lighter reverse, full, high-centered

'Twin Peaks' -- See 'Wekfrag'

'Twin Pinks' -- See 'Cletwin'

'Twin Sisters' S, mr, Williams, J.B.; flowers bright red, borne in masses of blooms; recurrent; spreading, groundcover growth; intr. 2003

'Twinkie' Min, lp, 1975, Moore, Ralph S.; bud pointed; flowers light clear pink, 1 in., 40 petals; foliage small, glossy; upright, very bushy growth; [(*R. wichurana* × 'Floradora') × 'Eleanor']; intr. 1974

'Twinkle' -- See 'Kirari'

Twinkle™ -- See 'Intertwik'

'Twinkle Bright' Min, yb; free-flowering; growth to 20-24 in.; intr. 1998

'Twinkle Charm' Min, mr; free-flowering; growth to 20-24 in.; intr. 1998

'Twinkle Eyes' Min, rb; free-flowering; growth to 20-24 in.; intr. 1998

'Twinkle Pink' Min, mp; free-flowering; growth to 20-24 in.; intr. 1998

'Twinkle Star' Min, w; free-flowering; growth to 20-24 in.; intr. 1998

'Twinkle Toes' -- See 'Lyoto'

'Twinkle Twinkle' Min, ab, 1981, Bennett, Dee; bud pointed; flowers white with apricot petal edges, aging dark pink, 23 petals, blooms borne singly, slight tea fragrance; foliage medium green, semi-glossy; prickles very fine, curved; slender, straight, upright growth; ['Contempo' × 'Sheri Anne']

'Twinkler' Min, pb, Datt, Braham

'Twinkles' Min, w, 1954, Spek; bud flesh; flowers small, 43 petals, moderate fragrance; compact, dwarf (8 in.) growth; PP1407; ['Perla de Montserrat' × 'polyantha seedling']; introduced as a miniature Hybrid China; intr. 1954

'Twins' -- See 'Lentrifel'

'Twirly Whirly' S, dr, Peden, R.

Twist™ LCl, pb, Poulsen; flowers striped pink, red and cream, 10-15 cm., dbl., borne usually in clusters, no fragrance; recurrent; foliage dark green, glossy; bushy (150-200 cm.) growth; intr. 2000

'Twist 'n' Twirl' Gr, or, Delbard; flowers orange-red, overlaid with stripes and splashes of silvery white, dbl., cupped, borne in clusters; recurrent; medium growth; intr. 2001

'Twister' -- See 'Mortwister'

Two Faces+ HT, m, Voom, Lex; flowers greyish-mauve, reverse brighter mauve , double, high-centered, borne mostly singly; recurrent; stems medium to long; florist rose

Two Sisters™ -- See 'Wiltwos'

'2004 Better Homes & Gardens Rose' -- See 'Weksunvoye'

'Two Thumbs Up' -- See 'Geltwo'

'Two-Timer' -- See 'Morswiss'

'Twoadmire' ('American Glory') HT, dr, 1991, Twomey, Jerry; bud ovoid, pointed; flowers cardinal red, large, 28 petals, cupped, borne usually singly, slight damask fragrance; foliage medium size, dark green, semi-glossy; upright, bushy, medium growth; PP7973; ['Portland Trailblazer' × 'Silver Jubilee']; intr. 1991

'Twoadore' ('Audrey Hepburn', 'Joan's Desire') HT, lp, 1991, Twomey, Jerry; bud pointed; flowers blush pink, fading to lighter pink, large, 30-32 petals, moderate fruity fragrance; foliage medium size, dark green, glossy; upright, bushy, medium growth; PP7980; ['Evening Star' × 'Silver Jubilee']; intr. 1991

'Twoadvance' (All That Jazz™) S, op, 1991, Twomey, Jerry; bud pointed; flowers coral salmon blend, loose, 4½ in., 10-15 petals, cupped, loose, borne in sprays of 3-5, moderate damask fragrance; foliage medium size, dark green, glossy; prickles moderate; upright, bushy, medium growth; PP7978; ['Gitte' × seedling]; intr. 1991

'Twoaebi' ('Acapulco Sunset', 'Dream Orange') HT, or, 1999, Twomey, Jerry; flowers large, full, borne in small clusters; foliage medium size, medium green, semi-glossy; prickles moderate; bushy, medium (5 ft.) growth; PP11525; ['Cherish' × ('Evening Star' × Trumpeter®)]; intr. 2000

'Twoagain' ('Dream Scarlet') HT, mr, 2002, Twomey, Jerry; flowers very full, borne in very large clusters, moderate fragrance; foliage large, medium green, matte; prickles 6-12 mm., slanting downward, numerous; growth upright (1½ m.); garden decorative; PP15396; ['Karma' × unknown]; intr. 2002

'Twoangel' ('Angela Lansbury') HT, pb, Twomey, Jerry; intr. 1995

'Twoat' ('Dream Blush') HT, lp, 1999, Twomey, Jerry; flowers 5 in., dbl., borne in small clusters, slight fragrance; foliage large, medium green, semi-glossy; few prickles; compact, medium (4 ft.) growth; PP11527; ['Evening Star' × 'Marijke Koopman']

'Twobe' (Sheer Elegance™) HT, op, 1990, Twomey, Jerry; bud pointed; flowers soft creamy pink with dark pink edges, 4½ in., 30-35 petals, high-centered, borne singly, moderate musk fragrance; good repeat; foliage large, dark green, glossy; prickles slightly curved, red with green; stems long; upright, tall (5 ft.) growth; hips pear-shaped, yellow-orange; PP7901; [Pristine® × 'Fortuna']; intr. 1990

'Twoblush' (Bridal Blush™) HT, w, 1990, Twomey; bud ovoid; flowers white with pink margins, petals imbricated, large, 75 petals, cupped, borne singly; foliage medium size, dark green, semi-glossy; prickles variable, green with brownish-orange; growth upright, medium; [Queen Elizabeth® × Helmut Schmidt®]; intr. 1990

'Twocherish' ('Color Burst') Gr, dp, Twomey, Jerry; intr. 1995

'Twodi' (Charming Diana™) HT, mp, 1998, Twomey, Jerry; flowers pink, reverse medium, 6 in., dbl., borne singly, very large; foliage large, dark green, glossy; numerous prickles; bushy, medium growth

'Twodream' (Endless Dream™) HT, mp, 1990, Twomey, Jerry; bud pointed; flowers medium, soft pink, large, 32 petals, cupped, borne singly, moderate musk fragrance; foliage large, dark green, semi-glossy; prickles declining, grayish-white with black spots; upright, medium growth; PP7561; ['Emily Post' × ('Sweepstakes' × 'Silver Jubilee')]; intr. 1990

'Twoetern' ('Eternity') Gr, rb, 1991, Twomey, Jerry; flowers red/cream bicolor, medium, full, borne in large clusters, moderate fragrance; foliage medium size, dark green; some prickles; tall (6 ft.), upright growth; PP8413; ['Gitte' × 'Silver Jubilee']; intr. 1991

'Twoex' (Our Diana™) HT, mp, 1998, Twomey, Jerry; flowers pink, reverse medium pink, 5 in., dbl., borne singly, drops clean; foliage medium size, medium green, semi-glossy; some prickles; bushy, medium growth

'Twofan' (American Fantasy™) HT, op, 1990, Twomey, Jerry; bud ovoid; flowers salmon pink, reverse lighter, large, 32 petals, cupped, borne singly, moderate fruity fragrance; foliage medium size, dark green, semi-glossy; prickles declining, yellow with red tinge; upright, medium growth; ['Sonia' × seedling]; intr. 1990

'Twofavor' ('Favorite Dream') HT, pb, Twomey, Jerry; intr. 1995

'Twofree' ('Freedom USA', 'Spring Hill's Freedom', 'Springhill Freedom') S, mr, 1990, Twomey, Jerry; bud ovoid, pointed; flowers scarlet red, 7 cm., 30-35 petals, cupped, borne singly, slight musk fragrance; free-flowering; foliage medium size, medium green, semi-glossy; prickles slightly curved, red-purple; stems strong, upright; vigorous, upright, medium growth; PP7868; ['Samantha' × seedling]; intr. 1990

'Twogreen' ('Lady Joan') HT, w, 2001, Twomey, Jerry; flowers 10 cm., very full, borne mostly solitary, moderate fragrance; foliage large, medium green, matte; prickles 6 mm., straight, moderate; growth upright, medium-tall (1¼ m.); garden decorative, greenhouse; ['Bahia' × Marina®]; intr. 2001

'Twohave' ('Proud Mary') Gr, or, 1991, Twomey, Jerry; bud pointed; flowers scarlet red, medium, 19-21 petals, moderate damask fragrance; foliage medium size, dark green, semi-glossy; upright, bushy, medium growth; PP7981; [(Sarabande® × Marina®) × 'Royalty']; intr. 1991

'Twohonor' ('American Honor') HT, mp, 1993, Twomey, Jerry; flowers very dbl., high-centered, borne mostly singly; foliage medium size, dark green, semi-glossy; few prickles; medium (110 cm.), upright growth; PP9443; [Sheer Elegance™ × 'Silver Jubilee']; intr. 1993

'Twojoan' ('Dream Pink', 'My Amore') HT, mp, 1999, Twomey, Jerry; flowers large, dbl., borne mostly singly, moderate fragrance; foliage large, medium green, glossy; prickles moderate; upright, medium (4 ft.) growth; PP11524; ['White Masterpiece' × 'Silver Jubilee']; intr. 2000

'Twolad' ('Aladdins Dream') HT, dp, Twomey, Jerry; intr. 1995

'Twoloy' ('Lloyd Center Supreme') Gr, pb, 1990, Twomey, Jerry; bud pointed; flowers light pink with yellow base, reverse dark pink blending to yellow, large, 25 petals, high-centered, borne in sprays of 4 - 7, moderate fruity fragrance; foliage medium size, dark green, glossy; upright, bushy, medium growth; PP7979; ['Brion' × seedling]; intr. 1990

'Twomin' ('Apache Princess') Min, or, 1990, Twomey, Jerry; bud ovoid; flowers bright orange-red, medium, 38 petals, cupped, borne singly, slight fruity fragrance; foliage medium size, medium green, semi-glossy; prickles declining, purple; upright, medium growth; PP8064; [(Cricket™ × 'Christ 78') × 'Fireburst']; intr. 1990

'Twopaul' ('Dream Red', 'Miss Salsa') HT, mr, 1999, Twomey, Jerry; flowers large, borne in small clusters; foliage medium size, dark green, glossy; prickles moderate; bushy, medium (5 ft.) growth; PP11503; ['Esmeralda' × 'Fireburst']; intr. 1999

'Tworight' ('Fireburst') F, or, 1993, Twomey, Jerry; flowers 3-3½ in., very dbl., borne mostly singly, slight fragrance; foliage medium size, medium green, semi-glossy; some prickles; medium (111 cm.), bushy growth; ['Evening Star' × seedling]; intr. 1993

'Twowin' (Winning Colors™) Gr, ob, 1990, Twomey, Jerry; bud ovoid; flowers yellow with deep orange margins, 4 in., 60 petals, cupped, borne mostly singly, moderate musk fragrance; recurrent; foliage medium size, dark green, glossy; prickles declining, yellow-green; stems long, sturdy; upright, medium (5 ft.) growth; PP7907; ['Gingersnap' × Marina®]; intr. 1990

'Twoyel' ('Dream Yellow', 'Our Anniversary') HT, my, 1999, Twomey, Jerry; flowers 5 in., dbl., borne mostly singly, intense fragrance; foliage medium size, medium green, semi-glossy; prickles moderate; upright, medium (3 ft.) growth; PP11528; [('Sonia' × Prominent®) × 'Whisky Mac']; intr. 1999

'Twyford' HT, op, 1939, Waterer; bud long; flowers bright salmon-pink, base gold, reverse deep salmon flushed orange; foliage dark, reddish; vigorous growth

Ty™ -- See 'Tuckty'

'Tycoon' -- See 'Brity'

'Tye-Dye' -- See 'Seadead'

'Tylea' S, dp; flowers dark pink; free-flowering; low (40 cm.), groundcover growth

Tyler™ -- See 'Sebago'

'Tynwald' -- See 'Mattwyt'

'Typ Kassel' ('Typ Kasselunk') C, mp; flowers full, globular, moderate sweet fragrance; recurrent; foliage large, bright green; growth to 5 ft.; possibly synonymous with 'Lippoldsburg'

'Typ Kasselunk' -- See 'Typ Kassel'

'Typhoo Tea' ('Doux Parfum', 'Été Parfumé') HT, rb, 1974, McGredy, Sam IV; bud medium, pointed; flowers medium red, silver reverse, 4-5 in., 50 petals, classic hybrid tea, borne mostly singly, moderate citrus fragrance; recurrent; foliage small, medium olive-green, glossy; prickles several, medium to long, hooked slightly downward, brown; bushy, upright (4-5 ft.) growth; hips very few; PP3845; ['Fragrant Cloud' × 'Arthur Bell']; intr. 1974

'Typhoon' ('Taifun') F, yb, Kordes; flowers yellow with red petal edges, 18 -20 petals, cupped, borne in large clusters; recurrent; growth to 5 ft.; intr. 2002

'Typhoon' ('Taifun') HT, op, 1972, Kordes, R.; flowers salmon, shaded yellow, 4 in., 35 petals, intense fragrance; recurrent; medium growth; ['Dr. A.J. Verhage' × 'Colour Wonder']

'Tyrelle' Cl Min, w, Staedler, Jan; flowers pure white , 1-1.5 in., double, cupped, borne in clusters, slight fragrance; recurrent; tall (6 - 10 ft.) growth; [sport of 'Jeanne Lajoie']; intr. 2008

'Tyriana' HT, dp, 1965, Meilland, Alain A.; bud pointed, ovoid; flowers rose-pink, well-formed, 4½-5 in., 40 petals, moderate fragrance; foliage leathery, dark; vigorous, upright growth; [('Happiness' × 'Independence') × 'Paris-Match']

'Tyrius' HT, m, 1973, Gandy, Douglas L.; flowers Tyrian purple, 5 in., 20 petals; foliage glossy, bronze; [Bettina® × 'Prima Ballerina']; intr. 1972

'Tzigane' ('Tiz') HT, rb, 1955, Meilland, F.; bud ovoid; flowers rose-red, reverse yellow, large, dbl., cupped to cactus-formed, moderate fragrance; foliage dark, glossy, leathery; upright, bushy, medium growth; PP1188; ['Peace' × 'J. B. Meilland']; intr. 1951

'Tzigane, Climbing' Cl HT, rb, 1958, Lagoona Nursery; [sport of 'Tzigane']; intr. 1958

— U —

'U. P. Hedrick' HSpn, mp, 1932, Central Exp. Farm; flowers pink, open, large, single; profuse, non-recurrent bloom; foliage soft, dark; vigorous (6 ft.), bushy, compact growth; [R. spinosissima altaica × 'Betty Bland' (probably)]

'Ubekomachi' LCl, mp

Ubuntu Panarosa™ S, yb, Delbard; flowers light yellow with apricot pink markings on the reverse , double, cupped, borne in clusters, no fragrance; recurrent; tall (2 - 3 m.), overhanging growth; intr. 2006

'Uetersen' -- See 'Kortersen'

Uetersen® ('Zenith') S, mr, 1939, Tantau; flowers glowing red, semi-dbl.; recurrent bloom; upright, bushy growth; ['Kitchener of Khartoum' × 'Stammler']

'Uetersener Klosterrose' LCl, w, Tantau; flowers creamy white with yellow stamens, double, cupped, slight fragrance; recurrent; rugged growth

'Ufhoven' HMult, op, Berger; flowers salmon pink, medium, full; intr. 1964

'Uhland' HMsk, yb, 1916, Lambert, P.; flowers reddish-yellow, petals fringed, borne in clusters of 3-15; foliage pointed, like Tip-Top; ['Geheimrat Dr. Mittweg' × Tip-Top®]

'Uhlarium' HRg, mp, Uhl; intr. 2003

'Uhlater' ('Pierette Pavement', 'Yankee Lady') HRg, dp, Uhl, J.semi-dbl. to dbl.; intr. 1987

'Uhlensch' ('Schnee-Eule', 'Snow Owl') HRg, w, Uhl, J.; bud pale pink, pointed; intr. 1989

'Uhlpurp' HRg, m, Uhl; intr. 2007

'Uhlrom' HRg, dp, Uhl; intr. 2004

'Uhlrutida' HRg, dp, Uhl; intr. 2004

'Uhlwe' ('Foxi Pavement', 'Foxi', 'Foxy Pavement', 'Luberon') HRg, dp, Uhl, J.; intr. 1989

'Ukigumo' ('Floating Cloud') F, w, Keisei; intr. 1998

'Ukrainian Dawn' -- See 'Ukrainskaia Zorka'

'Ukrainskaia Zorka' ('Ukrainian Dawn') F, mr, 1955, Klimenko, V. N.; flowers bright cinnamon-red, medium; ['Independence' × unknown]

'Ulla Land' Misc OGR, mr

Ulmer Münster® -- See 'Kortello'

'Ulrich Brunner fils' HP, dp, 1882, Levet; flowers geranium-red to carmine, tinted light purple, large, 30 petals, cupped; sparse repeat; foliage leathery; few prickles; stems upright; growth vigorous; some sources say it is a sport of 'Paul Neyron', others say seedling of 'Anna de Diesbach'

'Ulrick's Buttercup' F, ly, 1953, Ulrick, L.W.; bud ovoid; flowers medium, dbl., cupped, borne in clusters; foliage bronze; very vigorous, bushy growth;

['Yvonne Rabier' × 'Baby Alberic']
'Ulrick's Gem' F, pb, 1955, Ulrick, L.W.; flowers deep pink and white, very dbl., borne in clusters; foliage glossy; very vigorous, bushy growth; ['Mrs Tom Henderson' × 'Mrs Tom Henderson']
'Ulrick's Red' HT, mr, 1954, Ulrick, L.W.
'Ulrick's Smokie' F, m, 1953, Ulrick, L.W.; bud long, pointed; flowers smoky mauve, background white, large, very dbl., borne in clusters; foliage light green; bushy growth; ['Mrs Tom Henderson' × Tip-Top®]
'Ulrick's Yellow' HT, my, 1953, Ulrick, L.W.; bud globular; flowers yellow, center darker, medium, dbl., cupped; foliage light green; bushy growth; ['Mrs Pierre S. duPont' × 'Lady Hillingdon']
Ulrike® F, r
'Ulster' HP, mr, 1900, Dickson, A.; flowers salmon-red, large, dbl.
'Ulster Gem' HT, my, 1917, Dickson, H.; bud long, pointed; flowers canary-yellow, large, single
'Ulster Monarch' HT, r, 1951, McGredy, Sam IV; flowers apricot shaded buff, high-pointed, medium, 50 petals; foliage glossy, bright green; upright growth; ['Sam McGredy' × ('Mrs Sam McGredy' × unknown)]
'Ulster Queen' F, ob, 1960, McGredy, Sam IV; flowers salmon-orange, well-formed, 3 in., 25 petals, borne in clusters; vigorous growth; ['Cinnabar' × 'Independence']; intr. 1960
'Ulster Standard' HT, dr, 1917, Dickson, H.; flowers deep crimson, with prominent yellow stamens, large, single
'Ulster Volunteer' HT, mr, 1918, Dickson, H.; flowers brilliant cherry-red, base clear white, 5-6 in., single
Ultimate Pink™ -- See 'Jacval'
'Ultimate Pleasure' -- See 'Tinpleasure'
'Ulysees' HT, ab, Meilland; flowers creamy apricot, ruffled , borne mostly singly, intense fragrance; recurrent; stems long; 5 ft. growth; intr. 2006
'Ulysse' ('La Napolitaine') HGal, mr, before 1838, Crammwell; flowers velvety crimson
'Uma Rao' HT, pb, Pal, Dr. B.P.; flowers pink with cream reverse, dbl., high-centered, moderate fragrance; intr. 1989
Umberglo™ -- See 'Miniumber'
'Umbra' -- See 'Ardluna'
'Umilo' -- See 'Marie Curie'
'Umsafield' (Field of Dreams™) F, mp, 2003, Umsawasdi, Dr. Theera & Chantana; flowers pink with yellow eye, reverse pink, medium, semi-dbl., borne in small clusters; prickles average, curved; [Loving Touch™ × 'Peggy T']; intr. 2005
'Umsalllovu' ('Always Love You') F, dy, 2000, Umsawasdi, Dr. Theera; flowers medium, dbl., borne in small clusters, slight fragrance; foliage medium size, medium green, semi-glossy; prickles moderate; growth upright, bushy, medium; [Loving Touch™ × Lanvin™]; intr. 1999
'Umsapetite' ('La Petite') Min, lp, 2002, Umsawasdi, Dr. Theera & Chantana; flowers medium, full, borne in small clusters; foliage medium size, medium green, glossy; prickles average, curved, moderate; growth upright, medium; garden decorative; [Loving Touch™ × 'Hansa']; intr. 2002
'Umsasecret' ('Our Little Secret') Min, w, 2002, Umsawasdi, Dr. Theera & Chantana; flowers white with pink edge, medium, full, borne in small clusters, no fragrance; foliage medium size, dark green, glossy; prickles average, curved, moderate; growth upright, medium (24 in.); garden decorative; [Loving Touch™ × Rainbow's End™]; intr. 2002
'Umsatweet' ('Tweety') S, my, 2003, Umsawasdi, Dr. Theera & Chantana; flowers medium, dbl., borne in large clusters, slight fragrance; foliage medium size, medium green, semi-glossy; prickles small, curved; growth spreading, bushy, medium (4 ft.); [((Loving Touch™ × Rainbow's End™) × Summer Madness™]; intr. 2003
'Umschan' ('Chantana') HT, pb, Umsawasdi, Dr. Theera; intr. 1995
'Umscharm' ('Single Charm') Min, pb, 1991, Umsawasdi, Dr. Theera; flowers hand-painted white with pink edge, small, 5 petals, borne mostly singly, no fragrance; foliage small, medium green, matte; tall, upright, bushy growth; ['Jennifer' × seedling]
'Umsdad' ('Manit') HT, dr, 1991, Umsawasdi, Dr. Theera; flowers medium, semi-dbl., borne mostly singly, no fragrance; foliage medium size, medium green, matte; upright, bushy, tall (5-6 ft.) growth; [seedling × 'Olympiad']
'Umsfire' ('Fiery Star') F, rb, Umsawasdi, Dr. Theera; intr. 1995
'Umsflame' ('Flaming Heart') F, pb, Umsawasdi, Dr. Theera; intr. 1995
'Umskoochie' ('Hoochie Koochie') HT, m, 2000, Umsawasdi, Dr. Theera; flowers lavender, large, dbl., borne mostly singly, intense fragrance; foliage large, dark green, semi-glossy; few prickles; upright, tall growth; ['Azure Sea' × Mister Lincoln®]; intr. 2000
'Umslamoon' ('Lamoon') F, w, Umsawasdi, Dr. Theera; intr. 1995
'Umslove' F, w, Umsawasdi, Dr. Theera; intr. 1996
'Umsnira' ('Niramol') Min, ab, 1991, Umsawasdi, Dr. Theera; flowers medium, dbl., borne mostly singly, no fragrance; foliage medium size, medium green, semi-glossy; medium, bushy growth; [Loving Touch™ × seedling]
'Umspretty' ('Pretty 'n' Single') Min, dp, 1990, Umsawasdi, Dr. Theera; flowers deep pink, small, 5 petals; foliage medium size, dark green, semi-glossy; upright, bushy, tall growth; ['Nymphenburg' × 'Libby']; intr. 1986
'Umspriub' ('Priub') HT, ly, 1990, Umsawasdi, Dr. Theera; flowers yellowish-cream turning to pure white, large, 5 petals; foliage medium size, medium green, semi-glossy; numerous prickles; vigorous, upright, tall growth; [seedling × seedling]; intr. 1986
'Umsrum' ('Rum Candy') Min, r, 1990, Umsawasdi, Dr. Theera; flowers brownish apricot, light apricot shaded light pink when fully open, small, semi-dbl., borne mostly singly, slight fragrance; foliage small, light green, matte; upright, bushy, low (18 cm.) growth; [Twilight Trail™ × seedling]
'Umstar' ('Ruby Star') Min, dr, 1991, Umsawasdi, Dr. Theera; flowers small, 5 petals, borne mostly singly, no fragrance; foliage medium size, dark green, semi-glossy; upright, bushy, tall (24 cm.) growth; [High Spirits™ × seedling]
'Umstex' ('Texas Sunrise') Min, yb, 1991, Umsawasdi, Dr. Theera; flowers yellow at times with pinkish edge, small, dbl., borne mostly singly, no fragrance; foliage medium size, medium green, semi-glossy; upright, bushy growth; [sport of 'Arizona Sunset']
'Una' S, ly, 1900, Paul; bud sulphur yellow; flowers buff-yellow becoming creamy white, large, single to semi-dbl.; non-recurrent; vigorous growth; ['Gloire de Dijon' × R. canina]
'Una Hawken' F, ly, 1973, Murray, Nola; bud ovoid; flowers butter-yellow to cream, medium, dbl., cupped, moderate fragrance; foliage glossy, leathery; vigorous, upright, bushy growth; ['Arthur Bell' × 'Arthur Bell']; intr. 1972
'Una van der Spuy' HT, mp, Kordes; bud pointed; flowers silver pink , full, quartered, rosette, borne singly and in clusters; recurrent; medium growth; intr. 2006
'Una Wallace' HT, dp, 1921, McGredy; flowers soft, even-toned cherry-rose, well-formed, dbl., moderate fragrance; long, strong stems; vigorous, tall growth
Unbridled™ -- See 'Decbridled'
'Uncle Bill' HT, mp, Temple-Bourne, Rev. W.; flowers soft pink, moderate fragrance; free-flowering; [sport of Alec's Red®]; intr. 1984
'Uncle Joe' ('El Toro', 'Toro', 'Gladiator') HT, dr, 1973, Kern Rose Nursery; flowers very large, very dbl., high-centered, borne singly; recurrent; foliage large, dark green, leathery; very vigorous, upright, tall growth; [('Mirandy' × 'Charles Mallerin') × seedling]; registered as Toro, by Melvin Wyant, in 1973; parentage stated as Karl Herbst × Big Red; intr. 1971
'Uncle John' -- See 'Majlynlin'
'Uncle John' T, ly, 1904, Thorpe; flowers creamy yellow, large, full, moderate fragrance; [sport of 'Golden Gate']
'Uncle Lou' HT, dp, 1997, Roth, Louis A.; flowers deep pink, medium sized, full, borne singly; foliage medium size,

medium green, semi-glossy; upright, tall (4½ - 5 ft.) growth; [Queen Elizabeth® × 'Christian Dior']

'Uncle Sam'   HT, dp, 1965, Warriner, William A.; bud pointed, conical; flowers deep rose-pink, 5½-6 in., 30-35 petals, high-centered, moderate fragrance; recurrent; foliage dark, leathery, glossy; few prickles; vigorous, tall growth; PP2696; ['Charlotte Armstrong' × 'Heart's Desire']

'Uncle Steve' -- See 'Resunc'

'Uncle Walter'   HT, mr, 1963, McGredy, Sam IV; flowers crimson-scarlet, 5 in., 30 petals, high-centered, borne often in clusters, slight fragrance; recurrent; foliage leathery, coppery; vigorous, tall growth; ['Detroiter' × 'Heidelberg']

'Unconditional Love' -- See 'Ardwesternstar'

'Unconditional Love'   F, ab; flowers amber-yellow, full, cupped, borne mostly in clusters; free-flowering; foliage medium green, glossy; compact, bushy, medium growth; intr. 2004

'Uncut Gem' -- See 'Aratama'

'Undine'   HT, ob, 1901, Jacobs; flowers dark orange, medium; upright, bushy growth; ['L'Ideal' × 'Sunset']

'Unermüdliche' ('Geschwind's Unermüdliche') Ch, m, 1904, Geschwind; flowers maroon with white center, medium, semi-dbl.; introduced by either Lambert or Chotek in about 1930

'Unforgettable' -- See 'Jachyp'

'Unforgettable' -- See 'Tanalam'

'Unforgettable' -- See 'Trobspread'

'Unguiculata' -- See 'Œillet'

'Unica Alba' -- See 'White Provence'

'Unica Spectabilis' -- See 'Unique Admirable'

'UNICEF' ('The Audrey Hepburn Rose') F, ob, Cocker; intr. 1993

UNICEF-Rose®   F, mp, Kordes; flowers pink with touch of salmon, 2 in., semi-double, flat, borne in clusters, no fragrance; recurrent; bushy, wide, upright (70 cm.) growth; intr. 2006

Union-Rose St Helena® -- See 'Canlish'

'Unique' -- See 'White Provence'

'Unique' ('Unique Nouvelle') M, dr, Robert; flowers blackish crimson-purple, spotted and marbled with white and violet, medium, full; intr. 1852

'Unique'   LCl, op, Evans; flowers bright fawn-orange-salmon, 4-5 cm., full, borne in small clusters; recurrent bloom; vigorous growth; [Tip-Top® × 'hybrid perpetual']; sometimes classed as HMult; intr. 1928

'Unique'   T, pb, Guillot; flowers vivid pink, edged purple, base white, large, full; intr. 1869

'Unique'   Ch, w, Laffay, M.; flowers white edged pink, compact; intr. before 1836

'Unique'   HSpn, w, about 1825, Cartier; flowers medium to large, full

'Unique'   T, rb, Moreau & Robert; flowers red over yellow, medium; intr. 1872

'Unique Admirable' ('Unica Spectabilis') C, dp, before 1820, Descemet; flowers rose pink, medium, full; foliage widely spaced, simply serrate

'Unique Anglais' -- See 'Rubra'

'Unique Anglaise' -- See 'Unique Rose'

'Unique Blanche' -- See 'White Provence'

'Unique Blanche Panachée' -- See 'Unique Panachée'

'Unique Carnée' ('Belle de Vilmorin', 'Carnea', 'La Transparente', 'Rosalie', 'Vilmorin') C, lp, before 1811, Vilmorin; flowers blush pink, large, full, borne singly and in small clusters, moderate fragrance; foliage light green; prickles numerous, bristly

'Unique de Provence' -- See 'White Provence'

'Unique de Provence' -- See 'Unique Moss'

'Unique Moss' ('Provence Moss', 'Unique de Provence') M, w, 1844, Robert; flowers pure white, occasionally tinted pink, well-mossed, large, dbl.; prickles shoots very spiny; [sport of 'Unique Blanche']

'Unique Nouvelle' -- See 'Unique'

'Unique Panachée' -- See 'La Félicité'

'Unique Panachée' ('Maid of the Valley', 'Superb Striped Unique', 'Unique Blanche Panachée', 'Tulipe Paltot', 'Mutabilis Variegata', 'Mme d'Hébray', 'Striped Unique') C, w, Chaussée, Mme; flowers white, faintly striped rose and lilac, large, dbl., globular; vigorous growth; [sport of 'Unique Rouge']; the synonym Mme d'Hébray was applied by Pradel; intr. 1821

'Unique Rose' -- See 'Rubra'

'Unique Rose' ('Unique Anglaise') C, lp, before 1810, Cels; flowers light bright pink, medium to large, dbl., moderate fragrance; foliage edged pink; prickles small, ashen

'Unique Rouge' -- See 'Rubra'

'Unique Rouge'   C, mp, before 1824; flowers bright pink, medium, dbl.

'Unison'   HT, ob, Hiroshima; intr. 2004

'United Nations'   F, op, 1949, Leenders, M.; flowers salmon-pink, open, medium, 26 petals, borne in clusters; foliage glossy; very vigorous, bushy growth; ['Mev. Nathalie Nypels' × 'Rosamunde']

'United Nations Rose' -- See 'Harbella'

'United States'   HT, op, 1918, Verschuren; flowers yellowish-salmon pink, large, semi-dbl.

'Unity'   HT, dp, 1959, Sansam; flowers deep pink, reverse slightly darker, well-shaped, 5½ in., 45 petals, intense fragrance; foliage dark; vigorous, upright growth; [sport of 'Red Ensign']; intr. 1957

'Universal Favorite' ('Double Pink Memorial Rose') HWich, mp, 1898, Horvath; flowers soft rose, fading to white, 2½ cm., dbl., borne in large clusters, moderate fragrance; vigorous, climbing growth; [R. wichurana × 'Pâquerette']

'Université d'Orléans'   Pol, mr, 1966, Hémeray-Aubert; bud globular; flowers semi-dbl., cupped, borne in large clusters; vigorous growth; [unknown × 'Ronde Endiablee']

'Unn'   F, dp, 1972, Lundstad; bud ovoid; flowers deep pink, open, medium, semi-dbl.; foliage glossy; dwarf, moderate growth; ['Rimosa' × 'Fidélio']

'Unser Stolz'   HT, dr, 1965, Verschuren, A.; flowers bright crimson-scarlet, large, dbl.; foliage leathery, dark, glossy; upright growth; ['Ena Harkness' × seedling]; intr. 1961

'Unveiled' -- See 'Kejunvel'

Upper Alpine®   HT, w, Preesman; flowers double, high-centered, cupped

Upper Class®   HT, mr, Preesman

Upper Cloud®   HT, lp, Preesman; flowers soft pink with some greenish tints, double, high-centered

'Uppingham School' -- See 'Franburst'

'Upright Multiflora'   Sp; a clone of R. multiflora used for understock

'Upstart' -- See 'Jacup'

'Uptown' -- See 'Taluptown'

'Urania'   HP, dr, 1906, Walsh; flowers bright crimson, dbl.; recurrent bloom; ['American Beauty' × 'Suzanne-Marie Rodocanachi']

'Urara' -- See 'Keifupira'

'Urdh'   HP, mp, 1933, Tantau; bud long, pointed; flowers large, 45 petals, high-centered, intense fragrance; recurrent; vigorous growth; ['Victor Verdier' × 'Papa Lambert']; intr. 1930

'Urmibala'   HT, ob, Ghosh, Mr. & Mrs. S.; flowers blend of orange-yellow and pink; intr. 2004

'Ursel'   Pol, mr, 1938, Vogel, M.; flowers carmine red, medium, semi-dbl.

'Ursel Tgarth'   HFt, yb, 1938, Ketten, Gebrüder; flowers yellow and red, medium, dbl.

Ursula® -- See 'Lapon'

'Uschi'   F, dp, 1973, Tantau, Math.; flowers medium, dbl.; foliage glossy, dark; vigorous, bushy growth; [sport of Marimba®]

'Usha'   F, dr, 1976, IARI; bud ovoid; flowers deep red, open, 1½ in., 35-40 petals; foliage soft; compact, bushy growth; [Orangeade® × unknown]; intr. 1975

'Usmev'   HT, op, Strnad

'Usuzumi' ('Thin Ink') HT, r, Hiroshima; intr. 1995

'Usvit'   F, op, Urban, J.; flowers salmon-pink, medium, dbl.; intr. 1978

'UT Tyler Rose'   Gr, ob, 1984, Weeks, O.L.; flowers orange, medium, 35 petals; foliage large, medium green, matte; upright growth; [seedling × seedling]

'Uta Maro'   HT, mr; flowers red with silvery reverse, large, dbl.

'Utage'   HT, w, 1977, Ota, Kaichiro; bud pointed; flowers very large, 30-35 petals, high-centered; foliage leathery; vigorous, upright growth; ['Edith Krause' × 'Bridal Robe']

'Utage'   HT, dr, Keisei; intr. 1979

'Utano'   HT, w; flowers white with orange

tones; intr. 1985

'Utopia' HT, rb, Select; flowers creamy yellow base, edged and suffused red, 4 in., 35-45 petals, high-centered, borne mostly singly; recurrent; stems long; intr. 2003

'Utro Moskvy' ('Morning in Moscow', 'Moscow Morn') HT, mp, 1952, Shtanko, E.E.; flowers soft rose tinted carmine, large, 60 petals, slight fragrance; foliage leathery, grayish; spreading growth; ['Frau Karl Druschki' × 'Independence']

'Uttam' HT, lp, 1971, IARI; bud pointed; flowers pastel pink, large, dbl.; foliage glossy; vigorous, upright growth; ['Elite' × unknown]; intr. 1969

Uwe Seeler® -- See 'Korsee'

— V —

'V for Victory' HT, ly, 1941, Brownell; bud ovoid, long, pointed; flowers yellow faintly tinted orange, 45 petals, high-centered, intense fragrance; foliage glossy; vigorous, bushy, compact to open growth; PP543; ['Golden Glow' × 'Condesa de Sástago']

'V G Glowing HT' HT, rb

'V O N Canada' F, ob

'V Y F Rose' HT, mr

'V. Viviand-Morel' ('Mme V. Morrell') T, dr, 1887, Bernaix; bud long; flowers rich crimson shaded dark red and carmine, large, dbl.; foliage leathery, glossy; growth upright, robust; ['Red Safrano' × unknown]

'V. Vivo É Hijos' T, rb, 1894, Bernaix; flowers carmine pink, paler at center and base, tinted with yellow, salmon & apricot, med

'Vabene' -- See 'Meitrogana'

'Vagabonde' F, ob, 1966, Lens; bud long, pointed; flowers salmon-orange, 25 petals, high-centered, borne in clusters of 3 or more; foliage dark, glossy; vigorous, bushy growth; ['Mannequin' × 'Fashion']; intr. 1963

'Vahine' HT, or, 1964, Combe; flowers dark cardinal-red tinted orange; strong stems; vigorous, upright growth

'Vainqueur' HT, m, 1937, Heizmann, E.; bud ovoid, dark red; flowers velvety purple, reverse dark red, very large, very dbl.; foliage bright green; long, strong stems; very vigorous growth; ['Sensation' × unknown]

'Vainqueur de Goliath' HP, mr, 1862, Moreau, F.; flowers brilliant crimson-scarlet, very large, dbl.

'Vainqueur de Solférino' -- See 'Cardinal Patrizzi'

'Vaire' -- See 'Château de Vaire'

'Vaishnavi' HT, or, K&S; flowers vibrant vermilion, broad petals, dbl., high-centered; vigorous growth; intr. 1992

'Vajont' F, Galesso, G.; intr. 1966

'Val Boughey' -- See 'Valerie Boughey'

'Val d'Authion' HT, mp, Minier; flowers Neyron pink, undertones of bluish and silver, large, full, cupped, moderate fragrance; recurrent; foliage rich green, glossy; strong, bushy (1 m.) growth; intr. 1967

'Val De Mosa' HT, my, 1970, Ellick; flowers 70 petals, moderate fragrance; foliage dark, glossy; vigorous growth; ['La Jolla' × 'Cynthia Brooke']

'Val Johnston' S, mp, 2004, Johnston, Graeme; flowers full, cupped, opening flat, borne in large clusters, moderate fragrance; foliage medium size, semi-glossy; prickles medium, 1½-2 cm., straight; growth upright, tall (to 2 m); garden decorative; hips none; ['Frau Dagmar Hastrupp' × unknown]; intr. 1992

'Valdemar' HMult, mp, Back

'Valdemossa' HT, Dot, Simon; intr. 1991

'Vale of Clwyd' -- See 'Beeval'

'Valence Dubois' HGal, mp, 1880, Fontaine; flowers medium, dbl.

Valencia® -- See 'Koreklia'

'Valencia' HT, ab, 1967, Kordes, R.; bud large, pointed ovoid; flowers apricot-orange, 6 in., 40-45 petals, high-centered, borne singly and several together, moderate tea fragrance; recurrent; foliage large, glossy, leathery; prickles ordinary, medium, hooked downward; stems long, strong; vigorous, upright growth; hips none ; PP2651; ['Golden Sun' × 'Chantré']

Valencia® ('Oranje Meisieskool') HT, ab, Kordes; flowers apricot-gold, reverse adds copper tints, large , full, high-centered, borne mostly singly; recurrent; stems sturdy, medium long; medium, upright growth; florist rose; intr. 2003

'Valencia 89' -- See 'Koreklia'

'Valencia Kordana' Min, yb, Kordes; container rose

'Valenciennes' LCl, dr, 1960, Robichon; bud long, pointed; flowers crimson, fading to cherry red, 8 cm., semi-dbl., borne in clusters, slight fragrance; good repeat; foliage dark, glossy; very vigorous growth; ['Paul's Scarlet Climber' × seedling]

'Valentin Beaulieu' HWich, m, 1902, Barbier; flowers violet-pink, darker at center, aging lighter, 5-7 cm., dbl., borne in small clusters; foliage dark green; prickles fine, slightly curved, red; [R. wichurana × 'Souv de Catherine Guillot']

Valentina™ -- See 'Poulhi005(N)'

'Valentina Borgatti' HT, Borgatti, G.; intr. 1969

'Valentina Cortese' F, Cazzaniga, F. G.; intr. 1976

'Valentina Hit' (Valentina™) Min, mr, Poulsen; flowers medium red, 5-8 cm., 25-30 petals, borne mostly solitary, no fragrance; foliage dark green, glossy; growth bushy, low (40-60 cm.); PP14798; intr. 2001

'Valentine' F, mr, 1951, Swim, H.C.; flowers bright red, 2½-3 in., 18 petals, borne in large clusters, slight fragrance; free-flowering; foliage dark olive-green; spreading, bushy, compact growth; PP1029; ['China Doll' × 'World's Fair']

'Valentine Cupido' Min, mr, Pouw; bud ovoid; flowers 4 cm., 35 petals, rosette, borne in tight sprays, slight fragrance; free-flowering; foliage dark green, glossy; prickles few, 3 mm, linear; upright (12 in), spreading growth; PP12862; [seedling × seedling]; container rose; intr. 2003

'Valentine Heart' -- See 'Dicogle'

'Valentine Surprise Mini Brite' Min, rb, J&P; flowers striped; intr. 2000

Valentine's Day™ -- See 'Wekamrav'

'Valeria Sykes' -- See 'Horflashrob'

'Valerie' F, w, 1932, Chaplin Bros.; bud pointed, yellow; flowers cream, large, borne in large clusters; foliage glossy, dark; bushy growth

'Valerie' HT, mp, Select; florist rose; intr. 1994

'Valerie' -- See 'Kenyacker'

'Valerie Ann' -- See 'Woraddress'

'Valerie Boughey' ('Val Boughey') HT, op, 1960; flowers coppery salmon-pink, high pointed,, 6 in., 36 petals, moderate fragrance; foliage leathery, glossy; vigorous, upright growth; [sport of 'Tzigane']; intr. 1960

'Valerie Howard' ('Oreseed') HT, or, 2004, Bossum, Bill; flowers orange/red, reverse straw, 3 in., dbl., borne in small clusters, slight fragrance; foliage medium size, medium green, semi-glossy; prickles few, 3 mm.; growth upright, medium (3 ft.); garden; ['Oreana' × seedling]; intr. 2004

'Valerie Jeanne' Min, dp, 1981, Saville, F. Harmon; bud globular; flowers deep magenta pink, 1½-2 in., very full, high-centered, borne mostly singly, and in clusters of up to 20, slight fragrance; recurrent; foliage dark green, very glossy; prickles few, long, straight, thin; vigorous, upright growth; PP4811; ['Sheri Anne' × 'Tamango']

'Valerie June' HT, lp, Allender, Robert William; intr. 1982

'Valerie Kathleen' -- See 'Horvalkath'

'Valerie Purves' HT, mp, 1940, Clark, A.; flowers pink, well-formed; vigorous growth

'Valerie Swane' -- See 'Arobipy'

'Valeta' F, or, 1960, deRuiter; flowers red shaded vermilion, open, dbl., borne in clusters (up to 20); foliage dark; vigorous growth; ['Signal Red' × 'Fashion']

'Valette' -- See 'Lavalette'

'Valfleury' F, or, Croix; flowers geranium red, borne in clusters; free-flowering; vigorous, medium growth; intr. 1971

'Valia Balkanska' -- See 'Manclassic'

'Valiant' HT, mr, 1948, Boerner; bud long, pointed; flowers bright red, large, 30 petals, high-centered, moderate fragrance; foliage dark, leathery; vigorous, upright, branching growth; PP914; ['Poinsettia' × 'Satan']

Valiant Heart™ (Abendglut™) F, dr, Olesen; flowers deep red, dbl., cupped, borne in large trusses, very slight fragrance; free-flowering; foliage green,

The Official Registry and Checklist — Rosa   769

glossy; bushy, upright (60-100 cm.) growth; intr. 2000

'Validé' M, lp, 1857, Robert & Moreau; flowers light pink, shaded carmine, 2½-3 in., full, rosette; some repeat

'Valkita' ('Mariska') F, dr; intr. 1995

'Valldemose' F, mr, 1958, Dot, M.; flowers fiery red, large, 20 petals, globular; foliage glossy; vigorous, open growth; ['Magrana' × 'Radar']; intr. 1956

'Vallée de Chamonix' T, yb, 1872, Ducher; bud pink and orange-pink; flowers pinkish yellow, lightly coppery at center, medium, very dbl., flat

'Valour' HT, dr; flowers velvety dark red, dbl., cupped, borne mostly singly, intense fragrance; recurrent; stems long, strong; medium (4-5 ft.) growth

'Valrose' LCl, w, 1964, Mondial Roses; flowers white suffused pink at edges, medium, semi-dbl., borne in clusters of 3; recurrent bloom

'Valse des Neiges' -- See 'Schneewalzer 87'

'Valstar' HT, dp, 1962, Mondial Roses; flowers deep pink, well-formed, large, dbl.; foliage leathery; strong stems

'Vamp' Min, dr, 1980, Gatty, Joseph; flowers 5 petals, cupped, borne 3 per cluster, no fragrance; foliage dark; prickles pointed; angular growth habit; ['Fairy Moss' × 'Fairy Moss']; intr. 1981

'Van Artevelde' HGal, dp, before 1847, Parmentier; flowers deep pink, petals imbricated in whorls, large, very dbl.

'Van Bergen' S, ly, 1980, James, John; bud pointed; flowers light yellow fading to white, 48 petals, borne in clusters of 3, 5 or 7, slight fruity fragrance; repeat bloom; foliage small, glossy, dark; prickles hooked, red; vigorous, compact, bushy growth; [(R. wichurana × Baronne Prevost) × 'Fun Jwan Lo']

Van Gogh™ -- See 'Wilgogh'

'Van Huysum' -- See 'Belle Couronnée'

'Van Huysum' ('Vanhuisson') D, dr, before 1841, Parmentier; flowers violet pink, large, dbl.; occasionally recurrent; sometimes classed as HGal or HCh

'Van Nes' -- See 'Permanent Wave'

'Van Rossem's Jubilee' HT, op, 1937, Van Rossem; flowers bright carmine or coral; foliage glossy, bronze; vigorous growth

'Van Spaendonck' C, dp, 1821, Cartier; flowers medium to large, full

'Vanamali' HT, m, 1979, Viraraghavan, M.S. Viru; bud long, pointed; flowers orchid-mauve, 6 in., 35-40 petals, high-centered, moderate fragrance; foliage dark, leathery; tall, vigorous, bushy growth; ['Lady X' × (('Gruss an Teplitz' × unknown) × ('Lake Como' × 'Angel Face'))]; intr. 1978

'Vancouver' HT, pb, Twomey, Jerry

'Vancouver Belle' -- See 'Jalbelle'

'Vancouver Centennial' -- See 'Jan Wellum'

'Vanda Beauty' ('Golden Bouquet') HT, dy, 1971, Gregory, C.; flowers deep yellow, large, 28 petals, high-centered, borne several together; foliage dark green, glossy

'Vandael' M, m, 1850, Laffay, M.; bud well mossed; flowers rich purple, edged lilac, large, dbl.; vigorous growth

'Vanessa' HT, pb, 1946, Leenders, M.; bud ovoid; flowers coral, reverse yellow, 4½ in., 25 petals; foliage bright green; vigorous growth; ['Arch. Reventos' × 'Lord Baden-Powell']

'Vanessa' HT, mr, Taschner, Ludwig; flowers cherry red, medium, dbl., high-centered; free-flowering; stems long; vigorous, tall growth; [sport of 'Esther Geldenhuys']; intr. 1998

'Vanessa' HT, ob, Dräger; intr. 2000

'Vanessa Belinda' -- See 'Brandyglow'

Vanessa Campello® -- See 'Febesa'

'Vanguard' HRg, op, 1932, Stevens, G.A.; flowers bronze-orange-salmon, large, full, moderate fragrance; foliage light, very glossy, leathery; vigorous (to 10 ft.) growth; [(R. wichurana × R. rugosa alba) × 'Eldorado']

'Vanhuisson' -- See 'Van Huysum'

Vanilla® ('Emely Kordana', 'Our Vanilla') F, w, Kordes; flowers light yellow to ivory, outer petals have green tinge, medium, dbl., high-centered, borne mostly singly; recurrent; stems medium to long; florist rose, also has been sold as Emely Kordana as a pot rose when treated heavily with growth regulators; intr. 1994

'Vanilla Bonica'

'Vanilla Bonica' S, w, Meilland; intr. 2007

'Vanilla Cream' F, ly, Lens; flowers light, creamy yellow, dbl., cupped, borne in clusters, slight fragrance; recurrent; foliage clear green, glossy; moderate (2 ft.) growth; intr. 2000

Vanilla Kordana® ('Vanilla Kordana Mini Brite') Min, ly, Kordes; flowers light, creamy yellow, dbl.; intr. 2000

'Vanilla Kordana Mini Brite' -- See 'Vanilla Kordana'

'Vanilla Meidiland' S, w, Meilland; flowers vanilla white, dbl., cupped, borne in clusters; recurrent; low (2 ft.) growth; intr. 2005

Vanilla Perfume™ -- See 'Jacwotte'

Vanilla Sky® HT, w, Kordes; flowers cream, large, full, high-centered, borne mostly singly; recurrent; stems long; florist rose; intr. 2005

'Vanilla Twist' F, w, Dickson; bud white with pinkish-red flush; flowers pure white, full, rosette, borne in clusters; recurrent; foliage dense, medium green, glossy; upright (100 cm.), bushy growth; intr. 2007

'Vanille-Groseille' S, pb, Delbard; intr. 2001

'Vanity' T, my, 1911, Halstead; flowers canary yellow

'Vanity' HMsk, dp, 1920, Pemberton; flowers rose-pink, medium to large, single, borne in large, loose sprays, intense fragrance; recurrent bloom; foliage rich green, leathery; very vigorous (to 8 ft.), bushy growth; ['Château de Clos Vougeot' × seedling]

'Vanity' HT, mp, Select Roses BV; flowers , 30-35 petals, high-centered; intr. 1999

'Vanity Fair' HT, lp, 1942, Roberts; bud long, pointed; flowers cameo-pink, large, 19 petals, high-centered; foliage soft; long stems; very vigorous, upright growth; PP583; ['Better Times' × 'Golden Rapture']; intr. 1944

'Vannie' -- See 'Frevan'

'Van's Choice' F, ob, Williams, J. Benjamin; flowers light, soft orange, dbl., cupped; free-flowering; strong growth; intr. 1998

'Vanto' Pol, dr, 1955, Nanto, Mikko; flowers borne in clusters; very hardy; [sport of 'Dick Koster']

'Varbole' ('Caesar', 'Carambole') HT, mr, 1982, van Veen, Jan; bud ovoid; flowers cardinal red, 23 petals, high-centered, borne 2-3 per cluster, slight tea fragrance; foliage leathery, medium green, semi-glossy; prickles red; upright, branched growth; PP4992; ['Ilona' × seedling]

'Varelvi' ('Elvira') HT, ab, 1982, van Veen, Jan; flowers large, 35 petals, no fragrance; foliage medium size, medium green, semi-glossy; upright growth; ['Zorina' × 'Dr. A. J. Verhage']; intr. 1978

'Varenna Allen' F, ab, Harkness; flowers golden apricot, semi-dbl., cupped, borne in clusters, slight fragrance; recurrent; medium, robust growth; intr. 2006

'Variant' F, op, VEG; flowers medium, dbl.

'Variegata' -- See 'Panachée'

'Variegata' ('À Fleurs Panachées', 'Bunte Provinrose', 'Centifolia Variegata', R. centifolia variegata) C, pb, about 1845; flowers ivory white, striped rose pink, very dbl.; foliage ovate, pointed, toothed; there is much confusion about this rose, and there may be 2 or 3 cultivars under this name; the one in commerce today is probably that found about 1845, near Angers, France

'Variegata' HWich, w, about 1915, possibly Conard & Jones; foliage variegated green and white, occasionally tinted pink

Variegata di Barni® HT, yb, Barni; bud long, narrow; flowers yellow striped orange, double, pointed, moderate fragrance; foliage large; bushy (90 - 110 cm.) growth; intr. 2007

'Variegata di Bologna' B, rb, 1909, Bonfiglioli; flowers white, striped purplish red, large, dbl., globular, borne in clusters of 3 - 5, moderate fragrance; vigorous (6-8 ft.) growth

'Variegata di Bologna Rouge' B, dr, Lowe

'Variegated Damask' -- See 'Panachée'

'Varieté' F, m, VEG; flowers purple/pink with lighter shading, large, dbl.;

intr. 1987

'Variety Club' Min, or; flowers bright orange-vermilion, dbl., cupped, rosette; recurrent; vigorous (28 in.) growth; intr. 1999

'Variety Club' F, yb, 1965, McGredy, Sam IV; flowers yellow marked rose-red, well-formed, 48 petals, borne in clusters; foliage dark; ['Columbine' × 'Circus']

'Varin' -- See 'Sarah'

'Variora' ('Eloira') HT, my, 1982, van Veen, Jan; flowers large, 35 petals, no fragrance; foliage medium size, medium green, semi-glossy; upright growth; ['Elvira' × seedling]; intr. 1981

'Varlon' ('Ilona') HT, mr, 1974, Verbeek; flowers 4-4½ in., full; foliage glossy, leathery; bushy growth; PP3540; ['Miracle' × ('Romantica' × 'Edith Piaf')]; intr. 1973

'Varna' S, dy, GPG Bad Langensalza; flowers large, dbl.; intr. 1979

'Varo Iglo' HT, w, Verbeek; flowers medium, dbl.; intr. 1969

'Varo Rania' HT, Verbeek; intr. 1969

'Varsha' F, w, K&S; flowers pure white, margined rose pink; free-flowering; medium growth; ['Nicole' × 'Not stated']; intr. 1992

'Vasant' HT, yb, 1981, Division of Vegetable Crops and Floriculture; bud pointed; flowers yellow edged pink, high-centered, borne in clusters of 10, slight spicy fragrance; foliage dark; prickles straight, brown; upright, bushy growth; ['Sweet Afton' × 'Delhi Princess']; intr. 1980

'Vasavi' HT, dr, Kasturi; flowers deep blackish red, dbl., high-centered; intr. 1976

'Vasco da Gama' F, mr, Moreira da Silva; flowers velvety red; ['Pinocchio' × 'Alain']

'Vassar Centennial' HT, pb, 1961, Meilland, Mrs. Marie-Louise; flowers peach to shell-pink, 4½-5 in., 30 petals, high-centered, moderate fragrance; foliage dark, leathery; upright, branching growth; PP2031; ['Helene de Roumanie' × 'Confidence']; intr. 1961

'Vater Rhein' HT, dr, 1922, Kiese; flowers very dark red, dbl.; ['Kynast' × seedling]

'Vaterland' HT, dr, 1928, Berger, V.; flowers dark red with coppery reflexes, large, dbl.; foliage bronze, leathery; vigorous growth; ['National Emblem' × 'Earl Haig']

Vatertag® ('Father's Day', 'Paree Salmon', 'Fête des Pères', 'Jour des Pères') Pol, ob, 1959, Tantau, Math.; flowers salmon-orange, small, globular, borne in clusters; recurrent; bushy growth; [sport of 'Muttertag']; intr. 1959

'Vatertag, Climbing' ('Fête des Pères, Climbing') Cl Pol, ob; [sport of Vatertag®]; intr. after 1959

Vatican® -- See 'Delop'

'Vaucresson' A, lp, before 1885; flowers flesh pink, medium, full

Vavoom™ -- See 'Wekjutono'

'Vedette' HT, mr, 1951, Gaujard; flowers brilliant red, large, 28 petals; foliage leathery; [('Frau Karl Druschki' × 'George Dickson') × seedling]

'Vee Bryan' F, w, 1998, Jones, L.J.; flowers cream, edged pink maroon, 2 in., full, borne in large clusters, moderate fragrance; ['Solitaire' × 'Solitaire']; intr. 1997

'Vee Marie' -- See 'Judvee'

Vegesacker Charme® S, pb, Kordes; flowers pink with white eye, golden stamens, medium, single, shallow cup, borne in clusters, slight fragrance; foliage dark green, semi-glossy; strong, upright (4 ft.) growth; intr. 2003

'Veilchenblau' ('Blue Rambler', 'Blue Rosalie', 'Violet Blue') HMult, m, 1909, Schmidt, J.C.; bud purplish-pink; flowers violet, petals streaked with white, center white, yellow stamens, 1¼ in., semi-dbl., cupped, moderate fragrance; non-recurrent; foliage large, pointed, glossy, light; prickles very few; stems short; vigorous, climbing (10-15 ft.) growth; ['Crimson Rambler' × 'Erinnerung an Brod']

'Velay-Rose' LCl, op, Croix; flowers salmon-pink; free-flowering; intr. 1972

'Veldfire' -- See 'Korgust'

'Velhepi' HMsk, dp, Velle-Boudolf; intr. 2003

'Velindre' HT, mr, 1998, Poole, Lionel; flowers red-pink with peach reverse, high-centered, 5½ in., full, borne singly, moderate fragrance; foliage large, dark green, semi-glossy; some prickles; upright, bushy, medium growth; ['Solitaire' × seedling]

'Velingstorprosen' HGal, m

Velizy® -- See 'Delsamour'

'Velluto' HMoy, dr, 1934, San Remo Exp. Sta.; bud long, pointed; flowers velvety dark crimson, stamens red, medium, semi-dbl.; intermittent bloom; foliage dark; [R. moyesii × 'J. C. Thornton']

'Velour' F, mr, 1967, Boerner; bud ovoid; flowers dbl., flat; foliage glossy; vigorous, upright, bushy growth; [('Garnette' × unknown) × ('Hawaii' × unknown)]

'Velours Épiscopal' HCh, m, before 1908, Roseraie de l'Hay; flowers violet purple/pink, large, dbl., globular, moderate fragrance; non-remontant; some suggest it may have been introduced before 1863, but no other support found for that dating

'Velours Parfumé' -- See 'Fryperdee'

'Velours Pourpre' ('Cramoisi Incomparable') HGal, dr, before 1811, from Holland; flowers crimson, tending towards violet, lighter purple center, 1½-2 in., very dbl., pompon; foliage elongated; prickles numerous, small, brown

'Velours Pourpre' HP, m, Verdier; flowers velvety carmine with violet reflections, large, full; intr. 1866

'Velouté d'Orléans' B, m, 1852, Dauvesse; flowers light purple, large, full

'Velsheda' HT, lp, 1936, Cant, F.; flowers softest rose-pink, well-formed, large, dbl.; foliage dark; strong, erect stems; vigorous growth

'Velutina' HGal, m, 1810, Van Eeden; flowers velvety purple shaded violet, golden stamens, three rows of

'Veluwezoom' HT, dp, 1909, Pallandt; flowers brilliant carmine passing to deep rose, large, dbl., moderate fragrance; ['Mme Caroline Testout' × 'Soleil d'Or']

'Velvet Abundance' -- See 'Red Abundance'

Velvet Alibi® -- See 'Rouge Adam'

'Velvet Arrow' HT, dr

'Velvet Beauty' -- See 'Barkhatnaia Krasavitsa'

'Velvet Beauty, Climbing' Cl Min, dr, Bell; flowers very deep velvet red, hybrid tea; intr. 2003

'Velvet Beauty' HT, mr, Fisher, G.; bud high pointed; flowers currant-red, 5-5½ in., 40-55 petals, high-centered, moderate clove fragrance; vigorous, upright growth; PP2100; ['Happiness' × 'New Yorker']

'Velvet Cloak' -- See 'Seacloak'

Velvet Cover™ -- See 'Poulria'

'Velvet Dreams' -- See 'Lyoet'

'Velvet Flame' ('Joséphine Baker') HT, dr, 1974, Meilland; flowers 5-5½ in., 30 petals, slight fragrance; foliage dark; vigorous growth; ['Tropicana' × Papa Meilland®]; intr. 1972

'Velvet Flame, Climbing' Cl HT, Orard, Joseph; intr. 1981

'Velvet Flower Carpet' ('Red Velvet') S, mr, Noack; flowers velvety red, single, shallow cup, borne in clusters, no fragrance; low (2 ft.), spreading growth; intr. 2002

'Velvet Fragrance' -- See 'Fryperdee'

'Velvet Hour' HT, dr, 1978, LeGrice; flowers oxblood-red, 3 in., 44 petals, high-centered, quilled, moderate fragrance; recurrent; foliage dark; vigorous, upright growth

'Velvet Lady' -- See 'Hadprettie'

'Velvet Lustre' -- See 'Simpalno'

Velvet Mist™ ('Fragrant Lavendar') HT, m, 1990, Christensen, Jack E.; flowers deep lavender, medium, 25-35 petals, high-centered, borne usually singly, moderate fruity fragrance; foliage large, medium green, matte, disease-resistant; upright, bushy, medium to tall growth; ['Blue Ribbon' × Shocking Blue®]; intr. 1984

'Velvet Queen' HT, dr, 1965, Herholdt, J.A.; flowers blood-red, pointed, 4 in.; moderate growth; ['Fandango' × seedling]

'Velvet Robe' -- See 'Atombombe'

'Velvet Rose' -- See 'Holoserica'

'Velvet Ruby' -- See 'Machoro'

'Velvet Ruby' LCl, mr

'Velvet Soft Touch' HT, dr, 2001, Coiner, Jim; flowers 3½ in., semi-dbl., borne mostly solitary, no fragrance; recurrent; foliage medium size, medium green, semi-glossy; prickles numerous, small, fin-shaped; upright, vigorous, tall (5½ ft.)

The Official Registry and Checklist — Rosa 771

growth; intr. 2001
'Velvet Star' -- See 'Tanalednev'
'Velvet Star' LCl, mr, Barni, V.; flowers velvety red, dbl., high-centered, cupped, intense fragrance; vigorous, tall growth; intr. 1998
'Velvet Times' HT, dr, 1960, Peters, Lincoln & Norman; bud pointed; flowers rose-red, 4½-5 in., 40-50 petals, high-centered, intense fragrance; foliage leathery; vigorous, upright growth; PP1858; [sport of 'Better Times']; intr. 1959
'Velvet Touch' -- See 'Savavel'
'Velvet Treasure' -- See 'Jacvet'
'Velveteen' -- See 'Meisoyris'
'Velvetier' HT, dr, 1946, Brownell; bud long, pointed; flowers deep velvety red, 4-5 in., 28-35 petals, high-centered, moderate fragrance; foliage glossy; vigorous, upright growth; hardy for the class; PP843; ['Pink Princess' × 'Crimson Glory']
'Velvia' -- See 'Harxample'
Vendée Globe® HT, yb, Dorieux; flowers yellow with carmine tints, large, dbl., cupped, intense fragrance; recurrent; strong, medium growth; intr. 2000
'Vendée Globe, Climbing' (Grimpant Vendée Globe®) Cl HT, yb, Dorieux; flowers yellow with carmine tints, large, moderate fragrance; [sport of Vendée Globe®]; intr. 2005
Vendée Impériale® HT, ob, Adam; flowers buff-yellow with bright orange edges, suffused down the petals when opening, large, dbl., cupped, moderate fragrance; recurrent; moderate, compact growth
'Vendela' HT, w, Evers, Hans J.; bud long, pointed ovoid; flowers ivory white, 4-4½ in., 30-35 petals, high-centered, borne singly, slight fragrance; recurrent; foliage large, dark green; prickles normal, medium, hooked downward; stems long, strong; vigorous, upright (6 ft.) growth; PP10999; [seedling × 'Tanweisa']; florist rose; intr. 1997
'Vendôme' F, ob, Gaujard; bud long; flowers bright salmon, medium, dbl., moderate fragrance; foliage dark, glossy; bushy growth; ['Comtesse Vandal' × ('Fashion' × 'Vogue')]; intr. 1957
'Vendôme' HWich, mr, 1923, Mouillère; flowers 5 cm., dbl., borne in clusters of 5-15; foliage dark green, glossy
'Vendulka' F, mp, Vecera, L.; flowers large, dbl.; intr. 1974
Venere® F, mp, Delbard; flowers brilliant pink, dbl., borne in clusters of 5 - 7; recurrent; foliage glossy, new growth red; strong (1 m.) growth; intr. 1991
'Venerie' -- See 'Scouts Honor'
'Venezuela' F, op, 1959, Silva; flowers salmon, edged dull red; very vigorous growth; ['Joanna Hill' × 'Pinocchio']; intr. 1957
'Venice' S, w, Noack; bud soft salmon-pink; flowers white, stamens golden with red base, 6 cm., single, shallow cup, borne in clusters; recurrent; foliage dark green, glossy; bushy (80-100 cm.) growth; hips decorative; intr. 2004
'Venise' HT, rb, 1946, Meilland; flowers red with silvery white reverse flushed salmon-carmine, large, dbl.; spreading growth; ['Joanna Hill' × 'Margaret McGredy']
'Venise' Min, op, Adam; flowers orange-salmon, small, full, rosette, borne in clusters; recurrent; low (12-16 in.) growth; intr. 1997
'Venlo' F, or, 1960, Leenders, G.; bud pointed; flowers medium, semi-dbl., flat, borne in compact clusters; foliage dark; moderate, compact growth; ['Cinnabar' × 'Fashion']
'Venrosa' HT, mr, St Zila; flowers large, dbl.; intr. 1973
Vent des Indes® -- See 'Maukeole'
'Vent d'Été' -- See 'Korlanum'
'Venture' S, mp, 1984, James, John; flowers semi-dbl., borne in clusters, moderate fragrance; foliage medium size, light green, glossy; upright, slender growth; [('Charlotte Armstrong' × ('Cecilia' × 'China Belle')) × 'Prevue']; originally registered as Pol
'Venu-Vaishali' HT, pb, 1970, Deshpande; bud ovoid; flowers light pink, striped white, base yellow, large, dbl.; foliage large, soft; very vigorous, upright growth; [sport of 'Astree']
Venus™ -- See 'Fetino'
'Venus' -- See 'Jaceve'
'Venus' HGal, w, 1845, Vibert; flowers white with pink tints, medium to large, full
'Venus' F, w, Maarse, G.; flowers pure white, well-shaped, borne in large trusses; long stems; vigorous, bushy growth; ['Pinocchio' × unknown]; intr. 1955
'Venus' HT, dp, Bees; bud long, pointed; flowers carmine, edge flushed cream, very dbl., moderate fragrance; ['J. Barriot' × 'Sunburst']; intr. 1921
'Vénus' A, w; flowers pure white, medium, full, cupped; intr. before 1846
'Venus' HP, dr, Kiese; flowers purple-red, large, full; ['Général Jacqueminot' × 'Princesse de Béarn']; sometimes attributed to Schmidt; intr. 1895
'Venus' M, mr, Welter; flowers fiery red, large to very large, very full; occasional repeat; ['Mme Moreau' × 'Deuil de Paul Fontaine']; the rose in commerce today does not match older descriptions; intr. 1904
'Vénus Mère' -- See 'Bouquet Charmant'
Venusic® -- See 'Deldra'
'Venusta' P, lp, before 1814, Descemet; flowers delicate rosy pink, very dbl.
'Venusta' ('Turbinata') A, w; flowers flesh-white, becoming yellowish-white, medium, semi-dbl.
'Venusta Pendula' Ayr, w; bud pink; flowers blush white, fading to creamy white, 6-8 cm., semi-dbl., borne in clusters, no fragrance; early flowering; numerous prickles; vigorous (to 15 ft.) growth; origin unknown; reintroduced by Kordes in 1928
'Venustus' HGal, m, about 1835, Calvert; flowers dark purple, medium, full
'Vera' HT, op, 1922, Paul, W.; flowers deep salmon, shaded coral-red, dbl.
'Vera Allen' HT, op, 1939, Dickson, A.; flowers salmon-pink, well-formed, large, dbl.; compact growth
'Vera Brown' -- See 'Rawcleet'
'Vera Cruz' HT, pb, 1938, Moreira da Silva; bud long, pointed; flowers pink shaded mauve, flushed red and yellow, large, dbl., high-centered; foliage soft; vigorous growth; ['Frank Reader' × 'Johanniszauber']
'Vera Dalton' F, mp, 1961, Norman; bud pointed; flowers soft pink, 4 in., 24 petals, cupped, borne in clusters, moderate fragrance; foliage glossy, dark; vigorous, bushy growth; [('Paul's Scarlet Climber' × 'Paul's Scarlet Climber') × ('Mary' × Queen Elizabeth®)]
Vera Johns® Gr, or, 1978, Kordes, R.; bud ovoid, pointed; flowers large, 40 petals, high-centered, slight fragrance; recurrent; foliage glossy, dark, leathery; vigorous, upright growth; [unknown × Prominent®]; intr. 1977
'Vera Johns' F, ob, 1990, Kordes; buds pointed, salmon; flowers deepening to orange, dbl., high-centered, star-shaped, borne mostly singly, slight fragrance; recurrent; foliage glossy green; well-branched, medium to tall growth; intr. 1990
'Vera Parker' Min, mr, 2001, Parker, William David; flowers medium red, reverse lighter, 2 in., full, borne in large clusters, slight fragrance; foliage medium size, medium green, semi-glossy; prickles moderate, straight; growth bushy, medium (18-24 in.); garden decorative; [Sexy Rexy® × 'Winsome']
'Vera Roberta Carver' -- See 'Worarch'
'Vera Schwick' F, mp; intr. 2007
'Verano' HT, ob; flowers orange with red petal edges and lighter reverse, high-centered; intr. 2002
'Verastella' HT, mp, 1958, Giacomasso; flowers rose, center deeper; strong stems; vigorous growth; intr. 1954
'Verbeeka' F, ob
'Verbessert Mme Norbert Levavasseur' -- See 'Verdun'
'Verbesserte Tantau's Triumph' -- See 'Cinnabar Improved'
'Vercors' -- See 'Harvintage'
'Vercors' HT, or, 1946, Mallerin, C.; flowers brilliant orient red, large, dbl., globular; vigorous growth; [('Mme Arthaud' × 'Mme Henri Guillot') × ('Comtesse Vandal' × 'Brazier')]
'Verdi' -- See 'Lenbit'
'Verdi' ('Llorver') HT, rb; flowers white with burgundy red edges, dbl., high-centered, borne mostly singly; recurrent; stems long; florist rose
'Verdi' -- See 'Interpool'
'Verdun' ('Verbessert Mme Norbert Levavasseur') Pol, m, 1918, Barbier;

flowers vivid carmine-purple, large, dbl., globular, borne in clusters of 25 - 50; vigorous, dwarf growth
'Verdun Superior' Pol, m; flowers somewhat lighter than Verdun, and borne in larger clusters
'Verena' F, dr, 1975, Hetzel; bud ovoid; flowers dark velvety red, center lighter, medium, dbl., intense fragrance; foliage glossy, bluish green; upright, bushy growth; ['Lucy Cramphorn' × Inge Horstmann]; intr. 1973
'Vergenal' HP, w
'Verhaux' -- See 'Rose Verreux'
'VERjo' HT, dp, 1970, Verbeek
'Verlaine' HT, w; flowers white with greenish tint
'Vermilion Patio' Min, or
'Vermillon' HT, or, 1929, Barbier; flowers scarlet tinged orange, base yellow, semi-dbl.; ['Constance' × 'Paul's Scarlet Climber']
'Vermont' T, mp, about 1840, Béluze; flowers carmine pink, medium, full
'Vermont Vérité' S, mp, 2000, Cunningham, David F.; flowers dbl., borne in large clusters, slight fragrance; foliage medium size, purplish to dark green, glossy; numerous prickles; spreading, medium growth; very hardy; [R. macrantha × 'William Baffin']
'Verna Mackay' HT, ly, 1912, Dickson, A.; flowers buff to bright lemon-yellow, medium, dbl., borne mostly solitary
'Vernon Love' -- See 'Greluv'
'Verona' F, lp, 1963, Swim & Weeks; bud long, pointed, conspicuous neck; flowers 2½-3 in., 32-50 petals, high-centered, borne singly and in small clusters, slight tea fragrance; abundant bloom; foliage leathery, dark green; prickles very few, medium, straight, brown; stems long for the class; vigorous, bushy growth; PP2282; ['Spartan' × 'Garnette']; greenhouse rose
'Véronèse' ('Richdame', Koba®) HT, mp, Richardier; flowers full, cupped; moderate (80-100 cm) growth; intr. 2004
'Veronica' -- See 'Korflüg'
'Veronica' HT, w, 1950, Prosser; bud pale yellow; flowers snow-white, imbricated, 4½ in., 32 petals, intense fragrance; recurrent; vigorous growth
Veronica 92® F, mp, Noack, Werner
'Veronica Arnott' S, my, Harkness; flowers medium yellow, outer petals fading lighter, full, cupped, moderate fragrance; medium (1 m.) growth; intr. 2004
'Veronica Kay' Min, pb, Welsh, Eric
'Veronique' F, mr, 1961, Delforge; flowers bright raspberry-red, 4 in., 9 petals, borne in clusters; foliage dark, glossy; vigorous, bushy growth; ['Sumatra' × 'Philippe']
Véronique B.® S, op, Guillot-Masad; flowers salmon-pink in center, white outer petals, very full, cupped, intense fragrance; foliage disease-resistant; medium (80 cm.) growth; intr. 2002
'Verrystata' HT, ob, Kordes

Versailles® -- See 'Delset'
Versailles™ -- See 'Versailles Palace'
Versailles™ S, or, Poulsen; flowers orange-red, 8-10 cm., dbl., no fragrance; growth bushy, 40-60 cm.; intr. 2001
'Versailles Blanca' HT, w; intr. after 1967
'Versailles Palace' (Versailles™) F, or, Olesen; bud pointed ovoid; flowers more orange in greenhouse, more red outdoors, 3 in., 40-45 petals, cupped, borne in small clusters, no fragrance; recurrent; foliage large, dark green, glossy; prickles few, 5-7 mm, linear to curved; bushy (2 ft.) growth; PP11501; [('Gavno' × Red Minimo™) × (Red Minimo™ × 'Absolute Hit ')]; intr. 1999
'Verschuren' HT, lp, Verschuren; flowers clear light pink, cupped, moderate fragrance; recurrent; foliage variegated; strong growth; intr. 1904
'Verschuren's Glow' Pol, mr, 1939, Verschuren; flowers medium, semi-dbl.
'Verschuren's Pink' HT, op, 1950, Verschuren; flowers salmon-pink with darker reflections, reflexed, 3-4 in., 42 petals, high-centered; foliage glossy, dark; very vigorous growth; ['Mme Butterfly' × 'Pink Pearl']
'Versigny' S, ob, Guillot-Massad; flowers orange in center, orange pink outer petals, full, cupped, moderate fragrance; growth to 4 ft.; intr. 1998
'Versilia' HT, op; bud pointed, green tinted; flowers coral and apricot blend, outer petals tinted green, large, dbl., high-centered; recurrent; sturdy, medium growth; intr. 1996
'Very Busy' Min, pb, 1974, Moore, Ralph S.; bud long, pointed; flowers pink and yellow, small, dbl.; foliage small, leathery; dwarf, bushy growth; ['Perle d'Or' × 'Fairy Princess']; intr. 1973
Very Cherry™ -- See 'Jacrenew'
'Vesely' HT, pb
'Vesenii Aromat' ('Spring Fragrance') HT, or, 1955, Klimenko, V. N.; flowers red tinted orange, base lighter, medium, 73 petals; foliage dark, glossy; very vigorous, spreading growth; ['Crimson Glory' × 'Peace']
'Vesna' HT, mp, Vecera, L.
'Vesper' F, ob, 1966, LeGrice; flowers orange, reverse burnt orange, medium, dbl., scrolled, borne in clusters, slight fragrance; recurrent; foliage small, blue-gray; moderate growth
'Vesta' -- See 'Feu de Vesta'
'Vesta' -- See 'Temple d'Apollon'
'Vesta' F, mr, 1946, Leenders, M.; flowers currant-red, semi-dbl.; ['Irene' × 'Donald Prior']
'Vestal's Coral Gem' HT, op, 1939, Vestal; flowers soft salmon-pink, reverse glowing carmine with coppery sheen, dbl.; foliage leathery, light; vigorous growth; ['Betty Uprichard' × unknown]
'Vestal's Red' HT, mr, 1937, Vestal; flowers clear red, large, dbl., cupped; foliage leathery, light; vigorous growth

'Vestal's Torchlight' HT, rb, 1939, Vestal; bud long, pointed; flowers red and gold, open, large, dbl.; foliage leathery, bronze; vigorous growth; ['Pres. Herbert Hoover' × seedling]
'Vestey's Pink Tea' -- See 'Général Schablikine'
'Vesuv' F, mr, Vilmorin; flowers medium, dbl.; intr. 1963
'Vésuve' -- See 'Le Vésuve'
'Vesuvia' -- See 'Red Flower Carpet'
'Vesuvius' HT, dr, 1923, McGredy; bud long, pointed; flowers dark velvety crimson, golden stamens, large, 6 petals, cupped, moderate fragrance; recurrent; foliage light, leathery; vigorous growth
'Vesuvius' F, or, Vilmorin-Andrieux; flowers geranium-red, large, very vigorous growth; intr. 1963
Veterans' Honor™ -- See 'Jacopper'
'Véturie' ('Véturine') D, mp, 1842, Vibert; flowers rose pink, medium, full
'Véturine' -- See 'Véturie'
'Vevey' HT, my, 1953, Heizmann & Co.; flowers sun-yellow, large, dbl.
'Vi Ambler' HMult, m; intr. 1994
Via Mala® -- See 'Viakor'
'Via Romana' -- See 'Ljuba Rizzoli'
'Viakor' (Via Mala®) HT, w, 1977, W. Kordes Söhne; bud long, pointed; flowers creamy white, 4 in., 33 petals, high-centered, slight fragrance; foliage glossy, dark, leathery; vigorous, upright, bushy growth; ['Silver Star' × Peer Gynt®]
'Vianden' HT, pb, 1932, Ketten Bros.; flowers reddish old-rose and pink, reverse ochre-yellow and raw sienna, 90-100 petals; vigorous, bushy growth; ['George C. Waud' × 'Ruth']
Viborg™ (Gripsholm™) F, dy, Poulsen; flowers deep yellow, 8-10 cm., full, cupped, borne in clusters, slight wild rose fragrance; recurrent; foliage dark green, glossy; bushy, medium (60-100 cm.) growth; intr. 2000
'Vice-President Curtis' -- See 'Autumn Queen'
Vice Versa™ -- See 'Tuckviceversa'
'Viceroy' -- See 'Broroy'
'Vicki Buck' F, yb, Hiroshima; intr. 1996
'Vicki Kennedy' HT, pb, 1976, Murray & Hawken; bud globular; flowers deep rose-pink, center yellow, 4 in., 53 petals; foliage large, bronze, upright, bushy growth; [Queen Elizabeth® × 'Red Lion']
'Vickie Thorne' HT, lp, 1972, Thorne; flowers 4-4½ in., 25 petals; foliage dark; vigorous growth; [sport of 'Prima Ballerina']
'Vick's Caprice' HP, pb, 1891, Vick; flowers lilac-rose, striped white and carmine, large, dbl., cupped, moderate fragrance; repeat bloom; upright, medium growth; [sport of 'Archiduchesse Elisabeth d'Autriche']
'Vicky' HT, or, 1978, Gaujard; bud long, pointed; flowers orange-vermilion, moderate fragrance; ['Canasta' × 'Peace'];

intr. 1972

'Vicky' F, or, Noack, Werner; intr. 1994

'Vicky Brown' HT, rb; intr. 1994

'Vicky I' -- See 'Hormemory'

'Vicky Marfá' HT, mp, 1959, Dot, Simon; bud ovoid; flowers begonia-pink, center yellow, large, 32 petals, high-centered, moderate fragrance; strong stems; upright, compact growth; [('Soraya' × 'Ellinor LeGrice') × 'Henri Mallerin']; intr. 1958

'Vicomte de Lauzières' HP, m, 1889, Liabaud; flowers purplish red, very large, full, cupped; recurrent; foliage dark green; growth erect

'Vicomte Fritz de Cussy' B, me, 1845, Margottin; sepals narrow and long; flowers cherry red, tinged with purple, 7-8 cm., very dbl.; foliage dark green, deeply toothed; prickles large, slightly hooked, light red

'Vicomte Maison' HP, mr, 1868, Fontaine; flowers cherry-red, large, full

'Vicomte Maurice de Mellon' HT, ab, 1921, Ketten Bros.; flowers apricot and yellowish-salmon with coppery reflexes, washed pink, dbl.; ['Earl of Warwick' × 'Sunburst']

'Vicomte Vigier' HP, dr, 1861, Verdier, V.; flowers dark red, shaded violet, large, full

'Vicomtesse d'Avesne' N, mp, 1848, Roeser; flowers light salmon-rose, 3 cm., full, borne in clusters; recurrent; growth to 3-4 ft.

'Vicomtesse de Bernis' T, op, 1884, Nabonnand, G.; flowers coppery rose to fawn and deep salmon, large, dbl.

'Vicomtesse de Chabannes' HWich, rb, 1921, Buatois; flowers purplish crimson, center white, forming a distinct eye, 5-6 cm., semi-dbl., borne in small clusters, moderate fruity fragrance; foliage dark green, glossy; vigorous, climbing growth

'Vicomtesse de Grassin' T, pb, 1899, Levrard; flowers carmine, striped lighter pink

'Vicomtesse de Montesquieu' HP, op, 1861, Quétier

'Vicomtesse de Vautier' -- See 'Vicomtesse de Wauthier'

'Vicomtesse de Vezins' ('Comtesse de Vezins') HP, mp, 1867, Gautreau; flowers bright glossy pink, large, full

'Vicomtesse de Wauthier' ('Vicomtesse de Vautier') T, rb, 1886, Bernaix; bud long; flowers bright carmine red, center and reverse silver rose, large, full

'Vicomtesse d'Hautpoul' T, w, 1881, Brassac; flowers white with salmon, large, very full

'Vicomtesse Laure de Gironde' HP, mp, 1852, Pradel; flowers clear delicate pink, medium, full

'Vicomtesse Marie de Bourges' -- See 'Comtesse Marie de Bourges'

'Vicomtesse Pierre du Fou' Cl HT, op, 1923, Sauvageot, H.; flowers red aging to deep coral pink, 3-4 in., dbl., borne singly or in small clusters, intense fragrance; recurrent bloom; foliage large, glossy, bronze; vigorous, climbing growth; ['L'Ideal' × 'Joseph Hill']

'Vicomtesse R. de Savigny' T, pb, 1899, Guillot; flowers varying from dark China pink to deep dawn pink, base yellowish-white, large, full, moderate fragrance

'Vic's Refrain' Gr, w, 2008, Gleason, Michael T.; flowers 4 in., dbl., borne in large clusters; foliage medium, medium green, matte; few prickles; growth bushy, medium (4 ft.); [sport of 'Earth Song']; intr. 2008

'Victoire Fontaine' B, m, 1882, Fontaine; flowers satiny purple pink, medium to large, very full

'Victoire Modeste' HBc, pb, before 1835, Guérin; flowers yellowish-pink, large, full

'Victor' HT, dp, 1918, E.G. Hill, Co.; bud long, pointed; flowers deep rose, often red, semi-dbl.; [('Ophelia' × unknown) × 'Killarney Brilliant']

Victor Borge™ -- See 'Poulvue'

'Victor-Emmanuel' B, dr, 1859, Guillot père; flowers velvety black carmine, ruffled, large, dbl., rosette to quartered, intense fragrance; recurrent; growth to 130 cm.

'Victor Ferrant' HT, dp, 1933, Ketten Bros.; flowers carmine changing to purplish pink, base Indian yellow, very, 60-70 petals; vigorous growth; ['C.W. Cowan' × 'Pres. Cherioux']

Victor Hugo® -- See 'Meivestal'

'Victor Hugo' HCh, m, about 1840; flowers lilac-pink, very large, full, globular

'Victor Hugo' HP, dr, 1885, Schwartz, J.; flowers carmine-red shaded purple, medium, 30 petals, globular, moderate fragrance; recurrent; vigorous growth; ['Charles Lefebvre' × unknown]

'Victor le Bihan' HP, mp, 1868, Guillot père; flowers bright carmine pink, very large, full; recurrent; moderate growth

'Victor Lemoine' HP, dr, 1888, Lévêque; flowers dard red nuanced purple, brown, and violet, large, dbl.; foliage dark green

'Victor Magnin' Pol, mr, 1930, Van Gelderen; flowers bright red, dbl., borne in large clusters; vigorous growth

'Victor Mayer' HT, dr, 1921, Buatois; bud long, pointed; flowers blood-red, reflexes deeper

'Victor Morlot' HP, mr, 1906, Chauvry; flowers velvety scarlet, becoming poppy red, shaded darker red, very large, very full, moderate fragrance

'Victor Parmentier' HGal, mp, before 1847, Parmentier; flowers medium, dbl., cupped to flat, borne singly and in small clusters, moderate fragrance; non-remontant; upright (1 m.), arching growth

'Victor Pulliat' T, ly, 1870, Ducher; bud long; flowers pale yellow, medium, full, flat, borne in small clusters; ['Mme Mélanie Willermoz' × unknown]

'Victor Teschendorff' HT, w, 1920, Ebeling; flowers almost pure white on pale greenish yellow ground, very large, dbl., high-centered, foliage glossy, dark; long stems; vigorous growth; ['Frau Karl Druschki' × 'Mrs Aaron Ward']

'Victor Veladin' T, w; flowers lemon-white, large, with very large petals, somewhat nodding, moderate fragrance; recurrent

'Victor Verdier' B, mr, 1852, Dorisy

'Victor Verdier' ('Monsieur Victor Verdier') HP, dp, Lacharme, F.; flowers bright rose, center carmine, reverse lighter, large, 50 petals, globular, moderate fragrance; vigorous growth; ['Jules Margottin' × 'Safrano']; arguably the first Hybrid Tea; intr. 1859

'Victor Verdier, Climbing' Cl HP, mp, 1871, Paul, G.; [sport of 'Victor Verdier']

'Victor Verne' HP, mr, 1871, Damaizin; flowers currant red, large, full

'Victor Waddilove' HT, dp, 1923, McGredy; bud long, pointed; flowers bright carmine-pink, base yellow, large, very dbl.

'Victoria' -- See 'Victoria de los Angeles'

'Victoria' -- See 'Antoinette'

'Victoria' HT, dp, Prince; bud long, pointed; flowers deep rose-pink, center darker, dbl., intense fragrance; ['Isobel' × unknown]; intr. 1924

'Victoria' F, pb, Leenders, M.; flowers carmine, center white, large, semi-dbl., moderate fragrance; ['Irene' × 'Donald Prior']; intr. 1946

'Victoria' HT, ly, Robinson, H.; flowers pale lemon-yellow, large, moderate fragrance; foliage dark green; vigorous growth; ['Golden Dawn' × 'Phyllis Gold']; intr. 1947

'Victoria' HT, lp; intr. 2003

'Victoria' Cl F, or, Moreira da Silva; flowers clear geranium-red; [seedling × 'Alain']

'Victoria' HT, op; flowers peach pink, double, high-centered, borne mostly singly; recurrent; stems long; growth medium height

'Victoria' ('Carnée', 'Double Blush') HFt, yb, before 1846, Guérin; flowers salmon blush, buff center, large, semi-dbl., cupped

'Victoria' -- See 'Tantide'

'Victoria de los Angeles' ('Victoria') HT, or, 1952, Dot, Pedro; bud ovoid; flowers velvety geranium-red, medium, 35 petals; vigorous, compact growth; ['Cynthia' × 'Manuelita']

'Victoria Girls' S, my, Taschner, Ludwig; flowers clear yellow, dbl., globular, to shallow cup, borne mostly singly; recurrent; foliage glossy green, disease-resistant; vigorous, neat, medium growth; intr. 1997

'Victoria Gold' F, my, Welsh; bud deep golden yellow; flowers bright yellow, petals can be edged deeper, medium, dbl., shallow cup, borne in clusters, moderate fragrance; recurrent; foliage dark green, glossy; moderate (2-3 ft.)

growth; one report says Gold Bunny is one of parents; intr. 1999

'Victoria Harrington, Climbing' Cl HT, rb, 1938, Mordigan Evergreen Nursery

'Victoria Harrington' HT, rb, 1931, Thomas; flowers very dark red shaded orange-brown, center lighter, large, full, intense spicy fragrance; recurrent; foliage leathery, dark; vigorous growth; ['Diadem' × 'Hadley']

'Victoria Hyland' HT, op, 1976, Golik; bud ovoid; flowers red-pink to coral, 4 in., 34 petals, moderate fruity fragrance; foliage glossy; moderate, compact growth; [seedling × 'Colour Wonder']; intr. 1973

'Victoria Park' ('Quintet') HT, op, Pink; flowers salmon-pink, dbl., high-centered, borne singly; recurrent; intr. 1994

'Victoria Regina' HT, yb, 1938, Hillock; flowers golden yellow, reverse brownish yellow, sometimes blushed peach, 40 petals; vigorous, compact growth; ['Nellie E. Hillock' × 'Golden Dawn']

'Victorian Charm' S, lp, Clements, John; flowers 4 in., 50-60 petals, cupped to flat, borne in large clusters; recurrent; foliage glossy, oval shaped, dark green; stems long; vigorous (5 ft.) growth; PPAF; intr. 2000

'Victorian Gold' HMsk, my, Clements, John; flowers double; upright, spreading growth; intr. 2004

'Victorian Lace' -- See 'Devcal'

'Victorian Spice' -- See 'Harzola'

'Victoriana' F, ob, 1976, LeGrice; flowers orange, reverse silver, 5 in., 28 petals, slight anise fragrance; foliage dark green; compact, low to medium growth; intr. 1977

'Victoria's Pride' S, mp, Lassig, Rob; flowers medium pink, outer petals fade lighter, 4-5 cm., dbl., cupped to loose, borne in clusters of 5 - 15; recurrent; thornless; strong (4 ft.) growth; intr. 2004

'Victoria's Secret' HT, w, Martin; intr. 2003

Victoria's Song™ -- See 'Ortvic'

'Victorine' HT, w, 2002, McCall, Sharan; flowers cream with pink blush, white reverse, 5 in., dbl., borne mostly solitary, moderate fragrance; foliage medium size, medium green, semi-glossy; prickles moderate, ¼ in., slanting downwards; growth upright, tall (5 ft.); garden decorative, exhibition; ['Thriller' × 'Dorothy Anne']

'Victorine Helfenbein' HP, mp, 1850, Guillot; flowers bluish pink, medium, full

'Victorine la Couronnée' HGal, pb, before 1811; bud round; flowers light pink, striped red, medium, full, slight fragrance; foliage nearly round, deeply serrated; nearly thornless; Agathe group

'Victory' HT, dr, McGredy; flowers scarlet-crimson, dbl., moderate fragrance; intr. 1920

Victory™ ('Victory Parade') Min, mr; flowers medium red, medium, dbl., moderate fragrance; foliage dark; growth narrow, bushy, 20-40 cm.; intr. 1996

'Victory' HWich, dp, 1918, Undritz; flowers deep pink, center darker, 7-8 cm., dbl., borne in small clusters, moderate fragrance; foliage glossy; numerous prickles; vigorous, climbing growth; ['Dr. W. Van Fleet' × 'Mme Jules Grolez']

'Victory Parade' -- See 'Poulvic'

'Victory Red' HT, dp, 1939, Elliott; flowers rose-red; PP369; [sport of 'Pink Delight']

'Victory Rose' HP, mp, 1901, Dingee-Conard

'Victory Stripe' HT, rb, 1942, Grillo; flowers cerise-red variegated white and light pink, 5 in., 50 petals; [sport of 'Jewel']

'Victory Year' S, mp, 1951, Wright, Percy H.; bud ovoid; flowers clear pink, open, medium, semi-dbl.; profuse, non-recurrent bloom; foliage leathery; very vigorous, upright growth; ['Betty Bland' × unknown]

'Vida Beglan' F, ly, 1993, Beglan, M.; flowers lemon yellow with very small traces of salmon, medium, full, borne in small clusters, intense fragrance; foliage medium size, medium green, matte; numerous prickles; medium (90 cm.), upright growth; [sport of Elizabeth of Glamis®]; intr. 1992

'Vidal Sassoon' -- See 'Macjuliat'

'Vidiago' HT, mr, 1962, Dot, Simon; flowers currant-red, reverse geranium-red, large, 26 petals; very vigorous growth; [Baccará® × ('S'Agaro' × 'Peace')]

'Vidyut' F, dp, 1984, Yadava, U.N.; flowers deep pink; [sport of Europeana®]; intr. 1983

'Vie en Rose' -- See 'Rosy Life'

'Vie en Rose' ('La Vie en Rose') F, lp, 1994, Kameyama, Yasushi; flowers bright pink, white reverse, medium, semi-dbl., borne in large clusters, moderate fragrance; foliage medium size, medium green, semi-glossy; some prickles; medium, spreading growth; ['Charleston' × 'Friesia']; intr. 1991

'Vienna Charm' ('Charme de Vienne', 'Charming Vienna', Wiener Charme®) HT, ob, 1963, Kordes, R.; bud large, pointed; flowers coppery, orange, 6 in., 27-35 petals, high-centered, borne singly and several together, moderate tea fragrance; recurrent; foliage dark green, leathery; prickles ordinary, short, hooked downward; stems long, strong; vigorous, tall growth; PP2550; ['Chantré' × 'Golden Sun']; intr. 1963

'Vienna Charm, Climbing' Cl HT, ob, 1972, Gandy, Douglas L.

'Vienna Maid' F, my, 1958, deRuiter; flowers empire-yellow, 2½ in., 30 petals, borne in large clusters; foliage dark, glossy; moderately bushy growth; intr. 1957

'Vienna Woods' -- See 'Wienerwald'

'Vierge' -- See 'Alba Semi-plena'

'Vierge' -- See 'Des Peintres'

'Vierge' ('Vierge de Cléry') HSpn, w, 1820, Prévost

'Vierge de Cléry' -- See 'Vierge'

'Vierge de Cléry' C, w, 1888, Baron-Veillard; sepals long; flowers pure white, medium to large, full, cupped; foliage medium green, large; prickles moderate; sometimes thought to be synonymous with White Provence, but it is not

'Vierge Folle' -- See 'My Fifi'

'Vierge Ivryenne' HT, w, 1909, Lévêque; flowers pure white with yellow tints, large, full

'Vierlanden' -- See 'Pink Delight'

'Vierländerin' -- See 'Korvila'

'Vieux Chateau Certan' F, ab, Dorieux; flowers amber with pink tones; intr. 1994

View® -- See 'Lenvie'

'Vif Eclat' -- See 'LLX8764'

'Vigane' HT, rb, 1962, Buyl Frères; flowers red and light yellow bicolor, dbl.

Vigilance™ -- See 'Minivig'

'Vigilant' HT, dr, 1941, Clark, A.; flowers very dark red; ['Night' × unknown]

'Vigo' F, Moreira da Silva, A.

'Vigoro' HT, op, 1958, Dot, Pedro; flowers salmon-pink, large, 30 petals, high-centered, moderate fragrance; foliage clear green; very vigorous, upright, compact growth; ['Ophelia' × 'Federico Casas']; intr. 1953

'Vigorosa' S, pb, Wagner, S.; bud short; flowers medium sized, 12 petals, flat, moderate fragrance; foliage medium-large, dark green, semi-glossy; [('Frankfurt am Main' × 'Maria Callas') × 'Dr Faust']; intr. 1984

'Viking' -- See 'Rody'

'Viking' HT, dr, 1965, Moro; bud large, pointed ovoid; flowers crimson, 4½-5½ in., 45-50 petals, high-centered, becoming flat, borne singly, moderate fragrance; recurrent; foliage leathery, dark green; prickles numerous, medium, hooked downward; stems long, strong; vigorous, upright growth; hips globular, scarlet, with conspicuous neck; PP2333; ['Volcano' × 'Happiness']

'Viking Princess' -- See 'Pouldron'

'Viking Queen' LCl, mp, 1965, Phillips; flowers medium to deep pink, 3-4 in., 60 petals, globular, borne singly or in small clusters, intense fragrance; recurrent bloom; foliage dark, glossy, leathery; vigorous growth; [White Dawn® × 'L.E. Longley']; intr. 1963

'Viktoria Adelheid' HT, yb, 1932, Kordes; flowers golden yellow edged and shaded nasturtium-red, large, dbl.; foliage leathery, glossy; dwarf growth; ['Charles P. Kilham' × 'Mev. G.A. van Rossem']

'Vilia' F, op, 1960, Robinson, H.; flowers bright coral-pink, 2½ in., single, borne in large clusters; foliage dark, glossy; moderate growth

'Villa de Bilbao' HT, mr, 1933, La Florida; flowers cardinal-red, large, dbl., cupped; vigorous growth; ['O. Junyent' × 'Margaret McGredy']

'Villa de Madrid' HT, or, 1965, Dot, Pedro; flowers vermilion-red to poppy-red, large, 60 petals, moderate musk fragrance; strong stems; upright growth; PP2462; ['Baccará® × 'Peace']

'Villa de Sitges' HT, op, 1930, Munné, B.; flowers pink shaded salmon; very vigorous, spreading growth; ['Frau Karl Druschki' × 'Mme Edouard Herriot']

'Villa des Tybilles' HRg, mr, 1899, Gravereaux; flowers large, single

'Villa Pia' HT, dr, 1926, Leenders Bros.; bud long, pointed; flowers velvety deep red, almost black, dbl.; ['Pres. Vignet' × 'Château de Clos Vougeot']

'Villa Rosa' -- See 'Evepi'

'Villa Rosa' HT, op, Taschner, Ludwig; bud pointed, coral pink; flowers salmon-pink, large, dbl., high-centered, star-shaped, borne mostly singly; recurrent; stems strong; tall, sturdy growth; intr. 2005

'Village Charm' HMult, lp, McLeod, J.; intr. 1990

'Village de Taradeau' F, lp, RvS-Melle; ['Kanegem' × Sonja™]; intr. 1995

'Village Festival' -- See 'Fure-Daiko'

'Village Lass' Min, mr; flowers deep, rich cherry red, moderate fragrance; short growth

'Village Maid' -- See 'La Rubanée'

'Villandessa' HT, ob, 1978, W. Kordes Söhne; bud long, pointed; flowers orange-blend, 4½ in., 33 petals, high-centered; vigorous, upright, bushy growth; [Peer Gynt® × seedling]; intr. 1977

'Villaret de Joyeuse' HP, mp, 1874, Damaizin; flowers bright pink, shaded darker, very large, full, moderate fragrance

'Ville d'Angers' HT, mr, 1934, Delaunay; bud long, pointed; flowers pure currant-red, large, semi-dbl., cupped; foliage leathery, dark; vigorous, bushy growth; ['Souv. de Georges Pernet' × 'Souv. de Claudius Denoyel']

Ville d'Arcis sur Aube® HT, op, Vially

'Ville d'Asnières' S, ob, Croix; flowers orange-red with silvery cast to reverse, spiral; free-flowering; foliage disease-resistant; intr. 2000

'Ville de Backnang' S, pb, Croix, D.; flowers stippled and marbled tyrian and white, large, double, borne in clusters, slight fruity fragrance; recurrent; foliage glossy; 1 meter growth; Also exists in a taller, climbing version.; intr. 2006

'Ville de Bâle' -- See 'Meivilanic'

'Ville de Bar sur Seine' HT, my, Orard; intr. 1996

'Ville de Bordeaux' HT, dr, 1955, Privat; bud long; flowers dark scarlet-red, dbl.; very vigorous growth

'Ville de Brest' HT, or, 1942, Gaujard; flowers fiery orange veined reddish-copper, medium, semi-dbl., globular; foliage bronze, glossy; vigorous growth

'Ville de Bruxelles' -- See 'La Ville de Bruxelles'

Ville de Caen® HEg, mr, Adam; flowers single; intr. 2006

'Ville de Chalons' HT, or, 1938, Champion; flowers reddish-orange shaded darker, dbl.

'Ville de Chine' -- See 'Chinatown'

'Ville de Doué' F

'Ville de Gand' HT, op, 1951, Gaujard; flowers deep salmon, well-formed, large, 25 petals; foliage bronze; very vigorous, upright growth; [('Georges Chesnel' × unknown) × (('Mme Joseph Perraud' × unknown) × R. foetida bicolor)]

'Ville de Grace' mp, Requena; intr. 1976

'Ville de Grenoble' ('Grenoble') HT, mr, 1927, Mallerin, C.; flowers clear scarlet, large, 30-40 petals, high-centered, slight spicy fragrance; foliage thick; very vigorous growth; ['Capt. F. Bald' × 'Mme Van de Voorde']; intr. 1931

'Ville de Liffre' HT, dp, Adam; flowers clear, strong pink, large, dbl., high-centered, intense fragrance; vigorous (100-150 cm.) growth

'Ville de Londres' HGal, dp, 1850, Vibert or Robert

'Ville de Lorgues' F, pb, RvS-Melle; [seedling × Pernille Poulsen™]; intr. 1992

'Ville de Lyon' HP, mp, 1866, Ducher; flowers metallic rose and wilvery-white, large, full

'Ville de Malines' HT, yb, 1929, Lens; bud long, pointed, yellow shaded cherry-red; flowers orange to pink shaded yellow, large, full; vigorous growth

'Ville de Moulins' -- See 'Oralamar'

'Ville de Nancy' HT, pb, 1940, Gillot, F.; bud long, pointed, old-rose shaded gold; flowers buff-pink, edges penciled white, reverse light pink, base yellow, 50-55 petals, cupped; foliage leathery, dark; vigorous, upright growth; ['Souv. de Claudius Pernet' × 'Federico Casas']

'Ville de Paris' HT, my, 1925, Pernet-Ducher; flowers clear bright yellow, large, dbl., globular; foliage reddish green, glossy; vigorous, growth; ['Souv. de Claudius Pernet' × seedling]

'Ville de Paris, Climbing' Cl HT, my, 1935, Armstrong, J.A. (also Cognet)

'Ville de Prague' HT, or, 1940, Chambard, C.; bud long, bright coral-red; flowers scarlet and copper, very large; foliage bright green; bushy growth

'Ville de Roanne' HT, Dorieux; intr. 1966

'Ville de Romilly Sur Seine' HT, ob, Orard; intr. 1994

'Ville de Saint Denis' HP, mp, 1853, Thomas; flowers rosey carmine, large, full, globular; [sport or seedling of 'La Reine']

'Ville de St Maur' Ayr, w, 1909, Denis; flowers medium, borne in corymbs; stems very flexile

'Ville de Saverne' HT, or, 1937, Heizmann, E.; flowers orange-scarlet, tinted brownish red, reverse tinted yellow, dbl.

'Ville de Toulouse' HGal, pb, 1876, Brassac; flowers carmine pink, reverse near white, medium, full, loosely quartered, slight fragrance; non-remontant

Ville de Troyes® HT, dr

'Ville de Valenciennes' HT, or, 1954, Gaujard; flowers orange-copper, well-formed, very large, dbl.; vigorous growth; ['Peace' × seedling]

Ville de Villeurbanne® HT, op, Guillot; flowers strong pink with lemon-cream reverse, large, dbl., turbinate, moderate fragrance; moderate (4 ft.) growth; intr. 1984

Ville de Zurich® F, or, 1970, Gaujard; flowers well-formed, 25 petals, moderate fragrance; foliage bright green; vigorous, bushy growth; ['Miss France' × 'Nouvelle Europe']; intr. 1967

'Ville d'Ettelbruck' -- See 'Lenivill'

'Ville du Havre' HT, w, 1931, Cayeux, H.; flowers cream-white, washed rose-pink, base yellow, very dbl.; foliage dark; very vigorous growth; ['Kitchener of Khartoum' × 'Souv. de Claudius Pernet']

'Ville du Perreux' -- See 'Delrula'

'Ville du Roeulx' F, dp, RvS-Melle; flowers dark pink with lighter shadings, 6 cm., 19 petals, borne in clusters; strong (2.5 ft.) growth; ['Melflor' × 'Esperanza']; intr. 1990

'Vilmorin' -- See 'Unique Carnée'

'Vilmorin' ('Carné', 'Couleur de Chair', 'Flore Pallido', 'Incarnate', 'Pale-Flowered', 'Transparente') M, lp, about 1805, Vilmorin; flowers pale blush pink, medium to large, full, cupped

'Vim' HT, mp, 1963, Wyant; bud pointed; flowers pink, medium, single; moderate bloom; foliage soft; moderate, bushy growth; ['Charlotte Armstrong' × 'Applause']

'Vin Rosé' HT, mp, 1969, Boerner; bud long, pointed; flowers light coral-pink, large, 30-35 petals, high-centered; foliage glossy; vigorous, upright growth; PP3018; ['Revelry' × 'Hawaii']

'Vince Butterworth' -- See 'Rawdred'

'Vincent Godsiff' Ch, mr; flowers deep luminous rosy-red, yellow stamens, 2 in., 10 petals, cupped; foliage dark; compact, upright (to 3 ft.) growth; discovered in Bermuda.

'Vincent-Hippolyte Duval' HP, mp, 1879, Duval, H.; flowers bright carmine pink, large, full

'Vincent van Gogh' Pol, or, 1969, Buisman, G. A. H.; bud ovoid; flowers medium, dbl., cupped, borne in clusters; recurrent; foliage dark; [Allotria® × 'Hobby']

'Vincente Peluffo' HP, mr, 1902, Lévêque; flowers light cerise pink nuanced darker, very large, dbl.; very remontant

'Vincenz Bergers Weisse' ('Vinzens Berger's Weisse') HT, w, 1943, Berger, V.; bud long, pointed, sulphur; flowers open, very large, dbl., high-centered; foliage glossy, bronze; very vigorous, upright growth; ['Mrs Sam McGredy' × seedling]

Vindonissa® F, rb, Huber; flowers bright

cerise with yellow eye and reverse, 8 cm., 21-30 petals, cupped, borne singly and in clusters; recurrent; foliage green, matte; upright (2 ft.), bushy growth; intr. 1986

Vinesse® F, op, Noack; flowers pink with orange and apricot tones, fading to yellow-orange, 6 cm., dbl., cupped, borne in clusters; recurrent; foliage dark green, glossy; moderate (2 ft.) growth; intr. 2002

'Vineyard Song' -- See 'Morgrapes'

'Vino Delicado' ('Delicate Wine') HT, m, 1973, Raffel; bud long, pointed; flowers mauve, edged purple-red, well-formed, large, dbl., slight incense fragrance; recurrent; foliage large, leathery; upright, strong growth; [seedling × Mauve Melodee®]; intr. 1972

'Vino Rosso' HT, rb, Tantau; bud pointed ovoid; flowers bordeaux-red, reverse pink, slow opening, 4½ in., 29 petals, high-centered, globular, borne singly, slight red wine fragrance; recurrent; foliage large, dark green, leathery; prickles numerous on main canes, few on laterals, straight, brown; stems long, strong; upright (110 cm.), bushy growth; no hips; PP15628; [seedling × seedling]; intr. 2002

'Vinoca' HT, mp, 1906, Amaury-Fonseca

'Vintage Visalia' -- See 'Morlu'

'Vintage Wine' -- See 'Poullack'

'Vinzens Berger's Weisse' -- See 'Vincenz Bergers Weisse'

'Viola' HT, m, 1956, Gaujard; flowers lilac-pink, very large, dbl., intense fragrance; foliage leathery; vigorous, upright growth; [Orange Triumph® × ('Peace' × unknown)]

'Viola' HT, m, Ghosh, Mr. & Mrs. S.; flowers deep mauve with reddish petal edges, large, full, high-centered, borne mostly singly; recurrent; stems strong; intr. 1998

'Viola Lougheed' -- See 'Louviola'

'Violacea' -- See 'La Belle Sultane'

'Violacée' -- See 'Purpurea'

'Violacée' M, m, 1876, Soupert & Notting; flowers purple, shaded violet to grayish pink, large, dbl.

'Violaine' HT, m, 1968, Gaujard; bud long, pointed; flowers large, dbl., high-centered; foliage leathery; tall, vigorous growth; ['Eminence' × 'Simone']

'Violante' S, Michler, K. H.; intr. 1991

'Viola's Diamond'™ -- See 'Wilclde'

Violet™ -- See 'Violet Hit'

'Violet Bengal' -- See 'Reversa'

'Violet Bengal' -- See 'Purple Bengal'

'Violet Blue' -- See 'Veilchenblau'

'Violet Brillant' -- See 'Rouge Formidable'

'Violet Carson' F, op, 1964, McGredy, Sam IV; flowers peach-pink, reverse silvery, well-formed, 35 petals, borne in large clusters, moderate fragrance; foliage dark, glossy, compact, bushy growth; ['Mme Léon Cuny' × 'Spartan']

'Violet Dawson' -- See 'Resone'

'Violet Doly' Min, m, Asami; intr. 1983

'Violet Fontaine' S, m, 1972, Tantau, Math.; bud ovoid; flowers violet-purple, large, dbl.; abundant, continuous bloom; foliage large, soft; vigorous, upright, bushy growth; [unknown × unknown]

'Violet Hit' (Violet Paillette™, Violet™) MinFl, m; flowers 5-8 cm., no fragrance; foliage dark; growth bushy, 40-60 cm.; PP10164; intr. 1995

'Violet Hood' S, m, 1979, Lens, Louis; bud ovoid; flowers dark violet, 1 in., 18 petals, pompon, intense fragrance; recurrent; foliage ribbed, brownish; very vigorous, overhanging growth; ['Robin Hood' × 'Baby Faurax']; intr. 1976

'Violet Liddell' HT, pb, 1904, Schwartz, A.; flowers light pink to white, center and reverse coppery salmon

'Violet Messenger' LCl, lp, 1973, Cadle's Roses; flowers shell-pink, base yellow, reflexed, 6 in., 30 petals, intense fragrance; foliage large, matte green; ['Spek's Yellow, Climbing' × 'Masquerade']; intr. 1974

'Violet Mist' -- See 'Tinviolet'

Violet Paillette™ -- See 'Violet Hit'

'Violet Parncutt' HT, yb, 1923, Easlea; bud small, pointed; flowers brownish gold, semi-dbl.

'Violet Queen' HP, m, 1892, Paul, G.; flowers marbled crimson and violet

'Violet Queen' HT, m, Northfield; flowers deep violet-pink, pointed, 4 in., 35-40 petals, intense fragrance; foliage dark; upright, free growth; [seedling × 'Violette Dot']; intr. 1970

'Violet Ruffles' HT, m, Davidson; flowers violet with ruffled edges, semi-dbl.; intr. 1997

'Violet Simpson' HT, op, 1930, Simpson; flowers vivid prawn-pink, base yellow, dbl.; foliage purple

'Violet Wilton' HT, mp, 1930, Ketten Bros.; bud very long, pointed; flowers bright rose-pink on flesh-white ground, tinted yellow, large, 35-40 petals; vigorous growth; ['Gen. MacArthur' × 'Mme Charles Lutaud']

'Violetera' ('Embruixada') HT, m, 1981, Dot, Simon; bud ovoid; flowers reddish-mauve, 30 petals, shallow cupped, borne singly to 3 per cluster, intense fragrance; foliage medium size, light green, matte; prickles curved, reddish-green; bushy growth; intr. 1980

'Violett Satina' -- See 'Tanttelos'

'Violetta' -- See 'Violette'

'Violetta' Pol, m, Bruant; flowers dark, smoky magenta, small, 25 petals, flat, borne in clusters; recurrent; low, bushy growth; intr. 1924

'Violetta' HT, m, 1957, Croix, A.; foliage glossy; vigorous growth; ['Peace' × 'Guinee']

'Violetta' -- See 'Harquantum'

'Violette' ('Violetta') HMult, m, 1921, Turbat; flowers pure deep violet, 3 cm., very dbl., slightly cupped, borne in large clusters, slight fragrance; vigorous growth

'Violette Agréable' HGal, m, before 1815, Descemet

'Violette Bouyer' HP, w, 1881, Lacharme, F.; flowers pinkish white, large, cupped; ['Jules Margottin' × 'Mlle de Sombreuil']

'Violette Bronzée' -- See 'Busard Triomphant'

'Violette de Crémer' HGal, m, 1824, from Douai; flowers dark violet, large, very full

'Violette Dot' HT, m, 1960, Dot, Simon; flowers ageratum-blue, medium, 20 petals; strong stems; spreading growth; ['Rosa de Friera' × 'Prelude']

'Violette et Rouge' HGal, rb, before 1908; flowers violet over red

'Violette Fire' HMult, m; flowers violet-pink with white eye, moderate fragrance; very tall (10 m.) growth; intr. 1980

'Violette Niestlé' -- See 'Harvintage'

'Violette Parfum' -- See 'Tanfifum'

Violette Parfumée® -- See 'Dorient'

'Violette Parfumee, Climbing' -- See 'Melodie Parfumée, Climbing'

Violina® -- See 'Tananilov'

Violina® HT, w, Tantau; flowers cream, large, double, high-centered, borne mostly singly, moderate fragrance; recurrent; stems long; vigorous growth; florist rose; intr. 2004

'Violine' -- See 'Lendadi'

'Violinista Costa' HT, rb, 1936, Camprubi, C.; flowers red to deep purplish red, well-formed, large, full, moderate fragrance; foliage glossy; vigorous growth; ['Sensation' × 'Shot Silk']

'Violiniste Emile Lévêque' HT, lp, 1897, Pernet-Ducher; bud long; flowers bright flesh pink nuanced yellow with orange reflections, large, dbl.; foliage purplish green

Violon d'Ingres® HT, yb; bud large, globular; flowers clear yellow, nuanced salmon on petal edges, 5 in., very dbl., cupped, borne singly or in clusters of 3, no fragrance; recurrent; foliage dark green, matte; prickles numerous, large, curved slightly downward, tan; vigorous, bushy (70-90 cm) growth; hips round, 2 cm. ; PP12876; ['Pigalle' × ('Paloma Blanca' × 'Carefree Beauty')]; intr. 2003

'Violoncelliste Albert Fourès' HT, ab, 1920, Croibier; flowers orange-yellow, shaded buff-yellow, dbl.; ['Joseph Hill' × seedling]

Viorita® -- See 'Harquantum'

'Víra' HRg, mr, 1936, Böhm, J.; flowers bright red; very vigorous growth

'Virago' HSet, lp, 1887, Geschwind, R.; flowers deep flesh, 6 cm., semi-dbl., cupped, opening flat, borne in small clusters, no fragrance; foliage large

'Viralliance' (Ganges Mist™) S, w, 2005, Viraraghavan, M.S. Viru; flowers 3½-4 in., semi-dbl., borne in small clusters; foliage small, medium green, semi-glossy; prickles large, triangular pointing down, green, moderate; growth upright, medium (5 ft.); pillar; ['Alliance' × ('Arthur Bell' × ('Little Darling' × (*R. clinophylla* × *R. bracteata*)))]; intr. 2005

'Viramber' ('Nefertiti') HT, my, 1997, Viraraghavan, M.S. Viru; flowers amber yellow, 6 in., dbl., high-centered, borne mostly singly, slight fragrance; foliage large, medium green, semi glossy; upright, medium (3 ft.) growth; ['Julien Potin' × 'First Prize']; intr. 1985

'Viranil' ('Rose Anil', Twilight Secret™) Gr, m, 2005, Viraraghavan, M.S. Viru; flowers magenta pink, large, full, cupped, borne in small clusters; foliage medium size, dark green, semi-glossy; prickles ¼ in., pointed; bushy, medium growth; garden decorative; [('Vanamali' × seedling) × 'Deep Purple']; intr. 2000

'Viranvar' my, Vire Aimery

'Virapricot' (Krishna's Peach™) T, ab, 2006, Viraraghavan, M.S. Viru; flowers 4 in., full, high-centered, hybrid tea form, borne mostly solitary; foliage medium size, medium green, semi-glossy; prickles small, triangular, brown, few; growth spreading, medium (4 ft.); garden decorative; ['Safrano' × (mixed Tea × *R. gigantea*)]; intr. 2007

'Virblush' (New Blush™) HG, pb, 2005, Viraraghavan, M.S. Viru; flowers medium pink, deep pink in center, 3 in., full, borne mostly solitary; foliage medium size, medium green, semi-glossy; prickles few, slender, small, ¼ in., straight, light brown; growth spreading, short (1½ ft.); specimen; ['Old Blush' × ('Tea' × *R. gigantea*)]; intr. 2005

'Virbright' (Emina™) HT, rb, 2006, Viraraghavan, M.S. Viru; flowers claret red, reverse yellow, up to 4 in, dbl., borne mostly solitary; foliage large, dark green, semi-glossy; prickles small, long,slender, triangular base, dark brown, few; growth bushy, medium (4 ft.); [bicolor hybrid tea × Sirohi Sunrise™]; hybrid gigantea heritage; intr. 2006

'Virbrown' ('Coffee Country', 'Coorg') F, m, 1997, Viraraghavan, M.S. Viru; flowers russet and coffee brown, mauve suffusion, light yellow reverse, 4 in., dbl., borne in small clusters; foliage medium size, medium green, semi glossy; spreading, medium (3 ft.) growth; [(('Zorina' × 'Cecile Brunner') × ('The Fairy' × 'Nordia')]

'Vircarefree' (Naga Belle™) HT, dp, 2006, Viraraghavan, M.S. Viru; flowers 5 in., full, high-centered, hybrid tea form, borne mostly solitary; foliage large, blue-green, glossy; prickles medium, triangular, slender, pointed, dark brown, numerous; growth bushy, tall (5 ft.); garden decorative, hedge, exhibition; ['Carefree Beauty' × ('Carmosine' × *R. gigantea*)]; intr. 2006

'Vircloud' (Amber Cloud™) HG, dy, 2006, Viraraghavan, M.S. Viru; flowers deep yellow-apricot, reverse deep yellow, 5 in., single, borne mostly solitary; foliage large, medium green, glossy; prickles large, triangular, pointing downward, grey brown, numerous; growth spreading, climbing, tall (up to 20 ft.); ['Reve d'Or' × *R. gigantea*]; intr. 2006

'Vircollette' (Sir Henry Collett™) HG, w, 2008, Viraraghavan, M.S.; flowers cream, 4½ in., dbl., borne in small clusters; profuse winter/spring bloom and intermittent flowering there; foliage large, medium green, glossy; prickles large, sharp pointed with triangular , red edging to grey, numerous; growth vigorous, climbing, tall (20 ft. or more); arches, fences, pergolas; ['Reve d'Or' × *R. gigantea*]; intr. 2008

'Virdor' (Manipur Magic™) HG, ly, 2005, Viraraghavan, M.S. Viru; flowers up to 5 in., full, borne in small clusters; will repeat when established; foliage large, light green, semi-glossy; prickles small, triangular, down curving, grey, moderate; growth climbing, tall (to 20 ft); ['Reve d'Or' × *R. gigantea*]; intr. 2005

'Viredi' my, Vire Aimery

'Vireterna' (Pink Prelude™) HG, mp, 2005, Viraraghavan, M.S. Viru; flowers up to 5 in., full, camellia-like, borne mostly solitary; foliage large, medium green, glossy, disease-resistant; prickles large, triangular, grey brown, numerous; growth upright, tall; pillar or hedge; ['Eterna' × Sirohi Sunrise™]; intr. 2005

'Virgen de Farnés' HT, mp, 1960, Dot, M.; flowers bright rose, reverse lighter, well-formed, 26 petals; strong stems; vigorous growth; [Queen Elizabeth® × 'Virgo']

'Virgene' (Evergreen Gene™) HG, ly, 2006, Viraraghavan, M.S. Viru; flowers 5 in., full, high-centered, hybrid tea form, borne in small clusters; foliage large, medium green, semi-glossy; prickles large, pointing downward, grey, moderate; growth climbing, tall (12 ft.); ['Carmosine' × *R. gigantea*]; intr. 2007

'Virgiant' (Sirohi Sunrise™) HG, ob, 2005, Viraraghavan, M.S. Viru; flowers full, borne mostly solitary; foliage large, medium green, glossy; prickles large, triangular; growth pillar-like, tall (8 ft.); garden decorative; ['Brown Velvet' × ('Carmousine' × *R. gigantea*)]; intr. 2004

'Virgin' -- See 'Jeleit'

'Virgin' Min, w, Lens, Louis; flowers small, dbl.

'Virginal' -- See 'White Bath'

'Virginale' -- See 'Beauté Virginale'

'Virginale' HP, w, 1858, Lacharme, F.; flowers pearly white, with pale flesh center, medium, dbl.

'Virginale' C, w; flowers pure white, often touched pink on one petal, abundant bloom, moderate fragrance; non-remontant; arching growth

'Virginia' -- See 'Pekwhina'

'Virginia' T, dy, 1894, Dingee & Conard; ['Safrano' × 'Maréchal Niel']

'Virginia' LCl, ob, 1934, Nicolas; flowers brilliant flame, suffused gold, open, large, dbl., moderate fragrance; non-recurrent; foliage large, dark; vigorous, climbing (9 ft.) growth; ['Magnafrano' × 'Eldorado']; intr. 1934

'Virginia Baker' HT, mr, 2004, Baker, Larry Sr.; flowers medium red, reverse lighter, 2½-3 in., full, high-centered, borne mostly solitary, intense fragrance; good repeat bloom; foliage large, medium green, semi-glossy; growth bushy, tall (4 ft.); exhibition; [sport of 'Uncle Bill']

'Virginia Dare' -- See 'Cledare'

'Virginia Dare' HT, dp, 1934, Thompson's, J.H., Sons; bud long, pointed; flowers deep cerise-pink, large, dbl.; foliage leathery, dark; long stems; very vigorous growth; ['Joanna Hill' × 'dark red seedling']

'Virginia Lass' HSet, w, about 1846, Pierce; flowers blush white, medium, full

'Virginia Lee' -- See 'Miclee'

'Virginia R. Coxe' -- See 'Gruss an Teplitz'

'Virginia R. Coxe, Climbing' -- See 'Gruss an Teplitz, Climbing'

'Virginia Reel' S, dp, 1975, Buck, Dr. Griffith J.; bud ovoid, pointed; flowers light red, 4-4½ in., 35-45 petals, cupped, borne both singly and in clusters of 5 - 10, moderate sweet fragrance; recurrent; foliage large, dark green, leathery; erect, bushy growth; ['Tickled Pink' × 'Prairie Princess']

'Virginian Rambler' Ayr, lp, before 1855, from U.S.A.; flowers whitish pink, 6 cm., dbl.; nearly thornless

'Virginie' S, lp, Schultheis; flowers mother of pearl pink, fading quickly almost to white, medium, dbl., rosette, slight fragrance; free-flowering; robust (60-100 cm.) growth; ['Bonica' × unknown]; intr. 1999

'Virginie' HGal, mp, 1825, Vibert; flowers rose pink, large, full, cupped

'Virginie' Ch, pb, before 1866; flowers flesh pink, centers dawn-pink, large, very full

'Virginie Baltet' HP, dp, 1854, Baltet

'Virginie Demont-Breton' N, op, 1902, Cochet; flowers coppery pink; ['Isabella Gray' × unknown]

'Virgo' ('Virgo Liberationem') HT, w, 1947, Mallerin, C.; flowers white, sometimes blush-pink, 5 in., 30 petals, high-centered; foliage dark, leathery; vigorous growth; ['Blanche Mallerin' × 'Neige Parfum']

'Virgo, Climbing' Cl HT, w, 1957, Mondial Roses

'Virgo' F, my, Burston; flowers golden yellow, lightening to medium yellow, dbl., cupped, borne in large clusters; recurrent; foliage medium green; compact (80 cm) growth; intr. 2004

'Virgo Liberationem' -- See 'Virgo'

'Virhold' (Golden Threshold™) HG, dy, 2005, Viraraghavan, M.S. Viru; flowers have distinctive red pollen, 4 in., single, borne mostly solitary; foliage large, medium green, glossy; prickles large, triangular; growth upright, tall; pillars, pergolas; [Golden Showers® × 'Virgiant']; intr. 2004

'Virkanya' (Kanyakumari™) LCl, op, 2006, Viraraghavan, M.S. Viru; flowers orange salmon, reverse orange salmon, 20-25 cm., single, borne mostly solitary; prickles small, triangular, pointed downward, reddish brown, moderate; growth climbing (12 ft.); pillar, trellis. arch; ['Montezuma' × seedling]; intr. 1979

'Virmagenta' (Incense Indigo™) HT, m, 2005, Viraraghavan, M.S. Viru; flowers mauve, 5 in., full, borne mostly solitary, intense damask fragrance; foliage medium size, medium green, semi-glossy; prickles ¼ in., pointed; growth bushy, medium (3 ft.); garden decorative; [unknown × unknown]; intr. 2004

'Virmanipuri' ('Manipuri', Alister's Gift™) HG, lp, 2006, Viraraghavan, M.S. Viru; bud long, elegant; flowers light pink, reverse medium pink, 5 in., dbl., high-centered, borne in small clusters; foliage large, medium green, semi-glossy; prickles medium, pointing down, brown, moderate; growth bushy, tall (4 ft.); garden decorative, exhibition; [Naga Belle™ × 'Lady Mann']; intr. 2007

'Virmoon' ('Bonmoon', Silver Dawn™) S, w, 2005, Viraraghavan, M.S. Viru; flowers single, borne in small clusters; foliage large, medium green, glossy; prickles medium, pointed; growth bushy, tall (5 ft.); garden decorative; [('Bonica' × R. clinophylla) × 'Silver Moon']; hybrid clinophylla; intr. 2004

'Virolay' HT, ob, Camprubi, C.; flowers edges orange-red, base deep yellow, large, high-centered; vigorous growth

'Virpicotee' (Garnet Crest™) T, pb, 2006, Viraraghavan, M.S. Viru; flowers up to 3½ in., full, borne in small clusters; foliage large, medium green, semi-glossy; prickles small, slender, point down, grey, few; growth bushy, tall (4 ft.); garden decorative; [mixed tea × R. gigantea seedling × unknown]; intr. 2007

'Virred' (Out of India™) HG, mr, 2005, Viraraghavan, M.S. Viru; flowers medium red, changing to purple, 4 in., dbl., borne in small clusters; foliage large, semi-glossy; prickles few, small, straight, grey; growth bushy, medium (4 ft.); garden decorative; ['Carefree Beauty' × ('Bonica' × Sirohi Sunrise™)]; intr. 2006

'Virsila' ('Somasila', Spice Trail™) HT, pb, 2006, Viraraghavan, M.S. Viru; bud pointed; flowers soft pink edged darker, up to 5 in., dbl., borne mostly solitary, intense fragrance; foliage medium size, medium green, semi-glossy; prickles medium, pointed, grey, moderate; growth bushy, medium (3-4 ft.); garden decorative; [Pristine® × 'Orient Spice']; intr. 1984

'Virsilver' (Blushing Yuki™) HT, rb, 2006, Viraraghavan, M.S. Viru; flowers red and dark pink with white in center, reverse white, hand-painted, 4 in., dbl., borne mostly solitary; foliage large, medium green, semi-glossy; prickles medium, slender, pointing down, light brown, moderate; growth bushy, medium (3 ft.); garden decorative; ['Silver Jubilee' × 'Priyatama']; intr. 2006

'Virsolo' mr, Vire Aimery; intr. 1989

'Virsplash' ('Bodhisatva', 'Magic East') S, pb, 1998, Viraraghavan, M.S. Viru; flowers white with pink and white splashes, creamy yellow eye, 5 in., dbl., borne singly and in clusters, slight fragrance; foliage medium size, blue green, matte; prickles moderate, medium; bushy, medium growth; [Honor™ × 'Priyatama']; intr. 1995

'Virtipu' (Tipu's Flame™) S, rb, 2005, Viraraghavan, M.S. Viru; flowers bright red, reverse white, 4 in., full, borne in small clusters, slight fragrance; foliage medium size, dark green, semi-glossy, dense; prickles numerous, large, triangular pointing down, grey; growth bushy, shrubby, medium (3½ ft.); garden decoration; ['Alliance' × 'Priyatama']; intr. 1990

'Virtreasure' (Tangkul Treasure™) HG, w, 2008, Viraraghavan, M.S.; flowers cream, 4 in., very full, old-fashioned, borne mostly solitary; prickles medium, sharp, pointed, brown, moderate; growth vigorous, climbing (20 ft.); arches, pergolas, fences; ['Reve d'Or' × R. gigantea]; named in honor of the Tangkul Naga tribe; intr. 2008

'Virtryst' (Twilight Tryst™) HT, m, 2006, Viraraghavan, M.S. Viru; flowers rich, deep purple, up to 5 in, single, borne mostly solitary, intense fragrance; foliage large, medium green, semi-glossy; prickles small, downward pointing, grey, few; growth bushy, medium (to 4 ft.); garden decorative; [('Vanamali' × seedling) × 'Deep Purple']; intr. 2007

'Virwatt' (Sir George Watt™) HG, ly, 2008, Viraraghavan, M.S.; flowers cream with dark yellow base, reverse white, 4½ in., dbl., high-centered, borne in small clusters; profuse winter/spring blooms, thereafter intermittent; foliage large, medium green, glossy; prickles medium, sharp pointing down, dark brown edging, moderate; growth climbing, tall (20 ft.); arches, pergolas, fences; ['Reve d'Or' × R. gigantea]; intr. 2008

'Virwhite' ('Annapurna', Faith Whittlesey™) HG, w, 2005, Viraraghavan, M.S. Viru; flowers white, varying to blush pink in cool weather, blush center, reverse white, 3½ in., dbl., borne mostly solitary; foliage medium size, medium green, semi-glossy; prickles small, triangular downpointed, dark grey, few; growth bushy, medium (2½ ft.); bedding; ['Reve d'Or' × (('Echo' × R. gigantea) × 'Marie van Houtte')]; intr. 2005

'Vi's Violet' -- See 'Morvi'

'Visa' -- See 'Meired'

'Visalia Gold' S, ly, Moore, Ralph; flowers creamy yellow; low, groundcover growth

'Viscount Carlow' HT, mp, 1911, Dickson; flowers carmine pink, base cream, moderate fragrance

'Viscount Southwood' HT, pb, 1949, Cobley; flowers China-pink shaded creamy peach to copper, 4-5 in., 35-40 petals, high-centered; vigorous growth; ['Walter Bentley' × 'Aribau']

'Viscountess Charlemont' HT, mp, 1937, McGredy; bud salmon-rose; flowers satiny rose-pink, base deep buttercup-yellow, large, dbl.; foliage dark cedar green; branching growth

'Viscountess Devonport' HT, dy, 1923, Hicks; flowers rich Indian yellow, dbl.

'Viscountess Enfield' HT, pb, 1910, Pernet-Ducher; flowers coppery old-rose, shaded yellow; [unknown × ('Soleil d'Or' × unknown)]

'Viscountess Falmouth' HT, pb, 1879, Bennett; flowers deep pink, mottled, reverse silvery, very large, dbl., globular, moderate fragrance; numerous prickles; growth dwarf, slender; ['Adam' × 'Soupert et Notting's Perpetual Moss']

'Viscountess Folkestone' HT, pb, 1886, Bennett; flowers creamy silver-pink, center deep salmon-pink, dbl., moderate fragrance; recurrent

'Viscountesse Folkestone, Climbing' -- See 'Gainsborough'

Vision® -- See 'Poulonі'

Vision® HT, pb, 1967, Dickson, A.; flowers gold and pink, 5½ in., dbl.; foliage glossy; ['Kordes' Perfecta' × 'Peace']

'Vision Blanc, Climbing' -- See 'Ice White, Climbing'

Vision Blanc® -- See 'Ice White'

'Vision in Sight' HT, w, Dorieux; flowers white with subtle apricot tones in center, large, double, spiral, pointed, borne mostly singly; recurrent; stems sturdy, shortish; neat, medium growth; intr. 2006

'Visqueuse' -- See 'Bourbon'

'Visse' Min, op, Delbard; flowers pure salmon pink, hybrid tea; free-flowering; bushy, medium growth

Vista™ -- See 'Savalav'

Vital™ ('Vital Parade') Min, my, Olesen; bud long, pointed ovoid; flowers golden yellow, 4-5 cm., 25-30 petals, borne singly; recurrent; foliage dark green, glossy; prickles numerous, 3-5 mm, concave, grey-brown; upright, compact growth; PP13491; [seedling × Easter™]; intr. 2000

'Vital' ('Red Corvette') HT, dr, Kordes; flowers clear, deep red, dbl., high-centered, borne mostly singly; recurrent; foliage dark green; few prickles; stems long, strong; [sport of Corvette™]; intr. 1997

'Vital Parade' -- See 'Vital'

'Vital Spark' -- See 'Cocacert'

'Vitality' S, or, Williams, J. Benjamin; flowers bright orange-red, single to semi-dbl., shallow cup to flat, slight fragrance; recurrent; growth to 4 ft.; intr. 2006

'Vitex Spinosa' -- See 'Rouge de Belgique'

'Vittonville-Rose' HT, ob, 1945, Mallerin, C.; flowers orange, base yellow, reverse lighter; vigorous growth

'Viuda Verdaguer' HT, ob, 1934, Dot, Pedro; flowers orange, open, very large, dbl.; foliage glossy, dark; very vigorous growth; ['Shot Silk' × 'Mari Dot']

'Viva' F, dr, 1973, Warriner, William A.; bud ovoid; flowers medium, dbl., high-centered; foliage glossy, dark; vigorous, upright growth; PP3579; [seedling × seedling]; intr. 1974

Viva™ Min, my, Olesen; intr. 1999

'Viva Romana' HT, rb, Dot; flowers crimson red, slight fragrance

'Vivacé' F, or, 1974, Kordes; flowers large, dbl., high-centered; foliage large, leathery; very vigorous, upright growth; ['Klaus Stortebeker' × unknown]

'Vivacious' F, mp, 1971, Gregory; flowers phlox-pink, 4 in., 35 petals; very free growth; ['Tropicana' × unknown]

'Vivacious Dianne' -- See 'Chrisjevans'

'Vivacity' -- See 'Temperament'

'Vivaldi' -- See 'Lenmobar'

Vivaldi™ HT, lp; bud medium, pointed, ovate; flowers creamy light pink, 14 cm., 24-28 petals, cupped, becoming flat, borne singly, very slight fragrance; recurrent; foliage dark green, weakly glossy; prickles some, straight, slanted slightly downward; upright, bushy, vigorous growth; hips large, pitcher-shaped; PP7362; ['Flamingo (Korflug)' × 'Madelon']; greenhouse rose; intr. 1988

'Vivarose' HT, mr, Croix; flowers bright red; free-flowering; vigorous growth

'Vivastella' HT, dp, Aicardi, D.; flowers laque de Robbie color (possibly carmine), well-shaped; ['Julien Potin' × 'Sensation']

'Vive la France' HT, rb, 1944, Mallerin, C.; bud pointed, well formed; flowers purplish red, reverse yellow, large, dbl.; foliage glossy; vigorous growth; ['Shining Star' × 'Mme Arthaud']

'Vive La Suisse' F, Tschanz, E.

'Vivian Vivio Stolaruk' -- See 'Burstol'

'Viviand-Morel' T, mp, 1888, Bernaix; flowers carmine pink; ['Rote Safrano' × unknown]

'Vivid' ('Rosier de Normandie') B, m, 1853, Paul, A.; flowers brilliant magenta to magenta-pink, small to medium, dbl., moderate fragrance; foliage glossy; robust, prickly growth; growth to 6 ft.

'Vivid' F, or, 1951, LeGrice; flowers brilliant orange-scarlet, large, 5-7 petals, borne in huge clusters; compact growth

'Vivid Mason' HT, dp, 1934, Mason, J.A.; flowers vivid dark pink, base yellow, large, dbl.; foliage leathery, glossy; very vigorous growth; PP52; ['Premier' × 'Mme Alexandre Dreux']

'Vivien' HT, dp, 1922, Paul, W.; flowers deep rose-pink, dbl.

'Vivien Leigh' HT, mr, 1963, McGredy, Sam IV; flowers crimson, 5 in., 35 petals, high-centered; foliage dark; very free growth; [Queen Elizabeth® × 'Detroiter']

Vivienne Maire' D, mp

'Vivre' HT, mp, Delbard-Chabert; intr. 1974

'Vixen' -- See 'Jacormin'

'Vlam' HT, or, 1956, Leenders, M.; flowers fiery red, dbl.; vigorous growth; ['Tawny Gold' × 'Sarie Mareis']

'Vlammenspel' LCl, mr

'Vlasta Burian' Pol, m, 1937, Böhm, J.; flowers purple/pink, small, dbl.

'Vlatava' HMult, dr, 1936, Böhm; flowers violet red, medium, full

'Vltava' LCl, m, 1936, Böhm, J.; flowers violet, passing to purplish red, 4-5 cm., dbl., globular, borne in small clusters, no fragrance; foliage glossy; very vigorous, climbing growth; ['Veilchenblau' × unknown]

'Voeux de Bonheur' ('Bon Voyage') HT, pb, 1960, Delbard-Chabert; bud very large, long, pointed; flowers creamy white, petals edged cerise-pink, reverse white, large, 30-35 petals, high-centered, borne several together on long stem, moderate violet fragrance; foliage dark green, glossy, leathery; growth vigorous, bushy; ['Michèle Meilland' × 'Chic Parisien']; intr. 1969

'Voeux de Bonheur' -- See 'Rotary Sunrise'

'Vogelpark Walsrode' -- See 'Korlomet'

'Vogue' F, pb, 1951, Boerner; bud ovoid; flowers cherry-coral, 3½-4½ in., 25 petals, high-centered, borne in clusters, moderate fragrance; recurrent; foliage glossy; vigorous, upright, bushy, compact growth; PP926; ['Pinocchio' × 'Crimson Glory']

'Vogue' HT, pb, Pekmez, Paul; flowers light pink with darker pink edges, dbl., high-centered, borne mostly singly; recurrent; intr. 1997

'Voice of Thousands' -- See 'Horsunsmile'

'Voie Lactée' Cl HT, w, 1949, Robichon; bud globular, creamy white; flowers pure white, 8 cm., dbl., intense fragrance; foliage glossy; very vigorous, climbing (10 - 14 ft.) growth; ['Frau Karl Druschki' × 'Julien Potin']

'Voie Romaine' HT, Dot, Simon; intr. 1977

'Voila' F, or, Croix; flowers borne in clusters of 6 or 7; free-flowering; foliage green, disease-resistant; intr. 1969

'Voila' HT, op, Spek; florist rose; intr. 2005

'Vol de Nuit' -- See 'Delrio'

'Volare' HT, dr, 1977, McDaniel, Earl; bud ovoid; flowers bright red, large, 38-44 petals, high-centered; foliage leathery; bushy, upright growth; PP4172; intr. 1976

'Volare' -- See 'Macvolar'

'Volcano' HT, dp, 1950, Moro; bud long, pointed; flowers cherry-red, 6½ in., 25 petals, cupped, moderate fruity fragrance; foliage dark; vigorous, upright growth; PP951; ['Charles P. Kilham' × 'Rome Glory']

'Volcano' S, mr; intr. 2007

'Volki' -- See 'Angelika'

'Volumineuse' HGal, mp, before 1828; flowers large, full

'Volunteer' -- See 'Harquaker'

'Volunteer Spirit' S, rb, J. B. Williams; intr. 2005

'Volupté' -- See 'La Volupté'

Voluptuous!™ -- See 'Jactourn'

'Von Hötzendorf' HP, pb, 1916, Schmidt, J.C.; flowers golden rose-pink, richly tinted coppery red, dbl.; vigorous growth; ['Frau Karl Druschki' × 'Beauté de Lyon']

'Von Liliencron' HFt, pb, 1916, Lambert, P.; bud yellowish red; flowers yellowish light pink with white, reverse salmon-pink, dbl., high-centered, moderate fragrance; profuse bloom, sometimes recurrent; foliage glossy, dark, bronze; vigorous (6 ft.) growth; ['Geheimrat Dr. Mittweg' × 'Mrs Aaron Ward']

'Von Scharnhorst' S, ly, 1921, Lambert, P.; bud medium, ovoid; flowers yellow to yellowish-white, medium to large, semi-dbl., loose, open, borne in small clusters on short laterals, slight fragrance; occasional repeat; vigorous (6-8 ft.) growth; ['Frau Karl Druschki' × 'Gottfried Keller']

'Vonava Elysium' HT, Strnad

Voodoo™ -- See 'Aromiclea'

'Voodoo Charm' -- See 'Jacmouse'

'Voorburg' F, op, 1959, Buisman, G. A. H.; flowers salmon-pink, semi-dbl., borne in large clusters; foliage bronze to dark; vigorous growth; ['Sangerhausen' × 'Vogue']

'Vorace' B, mr, 1849, Lacharme (possibly Foulard); flowers bright crimson, medium, full

'Vobergii' (R. × harisonii vobergii, R. vobergii) HSpn, w, before 1902, Zabel; flowers creamy white with a faint tint of yellow, single; [R. foetida × R. spinosissima]

'Vox Populi' HT, dr, 1945, Mallerin, C.; flowers velvety dark red, semi-dbl.

'Voyage' HT, pb, Tantau; flowers medium pink, reverse lighter, medium to large, dbl., high-centered, borne mostly singly, slight fragrance; recurrent; prickles few to none; stems long; florist rose; intr. 2003

'Voyager' -- See 'Micvoyage'

'Vrouefederasie Roos' HT, pb, Taschner, Ludwig; flowers medium pink with cream reverse, full, high-centered, deep cup, moderate fragrance; recurrent; medium growth; intr. 2004

'Vrystaat' HT, ob, Tantau; flowers bright orange, dbl., high-centered; recurrent;

medium growth; intr. 1992

'Vulcain' HP, dr, 1861, Verdier, V.; flowers rich dark crimson, well-formed, dbl.

'Vulcain' Pol, mr, Turbat; flowers deep cherry-red, dbl.; vigorous growth; intr. 1921

'Vulcana' LCl, dr, 1964, Mondial Roses; flowers blood-red, semi-dbl., borne in clusters; vigorous growth

'Vulcania' HT, mr, 1948, Giacomasso; bud long; flowers purplish red, well-formed, overlarge; foliage dark; ['Matador' × 'Principe di Piemonte']

'Vulcanic' -- See 'Jacfrain'

'Vulcanie' B, mp, 1840, Bizard; flowers medium, full

'Vulgens' Pol, mr, 1942, Koster; flowers medium, semi-dbl.

'Vulkan' HT, dr, VEG; flowers large, dbl.

'Vuurbaak' F, or, 1946, Leenders, M.; flowers scarlet, open, 4 in., 15 petals, borne in clusters; foliage reddish green; vigorous, upright growth; ['Florentina' × 'World's Fair']

'Vydehi' F, ob, Datt, Braham

'Vyslanek Kalina' HP, mr, 1935, Böhm, J.; flowers large, dbl.

— W —

'W. A. Bilney' HT, ab, 1927, Easlea; flowers pale apricot suffused cerise, reverse yellow tinted pink, large; foliage dark, leathery; vigorous growth

'W. A. Willett' HT, op, 1960, Kernovske, V.R.; bud globular; flowers pink to salmon-pink, base coppery, large, dbl., moderate fragrance; foliage leathery; moderate, upright growth; ['Picture' × 'Tahiti']; intr. 1959

'W. C. Gaunt' HT, dr, 1916, Dickson, A.; bud long, pointed; flowers velvety crimson-scarlet, reflexed petals tipped scarlet, rev, dbl.

'W. E. Chaplin, Climbing' Cl HT, dr, 1936, Heizmann, E.

'W. E. Chaplin' HT, dr, 1929, Chaplin Bros.; flowers crimson, deepening to maroon, large, dbl., high-centered; vigorous growth

'W. E. Lippiat' HT, dr, 1907, Dickson, A.; flowers deep crimson shaded maroon, large, full

'W. E. Wallace' HT, dy, 1922, Dickson, H.; flowers deep golden yellow, well-formed, large, dbl.; [sport of 'Gorgeous']

'W. Freedland Kendrick' HT, pb, 1920, Thomas; flowers pink with peach tones, large, dbl.

'W. Freeland Kendrick' ('Bloomfield Endurance') LCl, lp, 1920, Thomas; flowers flesh, center peach, 8-9 cm., very dbl., borne in small clusters, moderate fragrance; some repeat; foliage dark, bronze, leathery, glossy; vigorous, semi-climbing growth; ['Aviateur Blériot' × 'Mme Caroline Testout']

'W. G. Pountney' F, or, 1964, Bennett, H.; flowers scarlet; tall growth; [Moulin Rouge® × 'Mrs Inge Poulsen']

'W. H. Cotton' HT, ab, 1946, Cobley; flowers orange shaded gold, large; foliage dark; vigorous, upright growth; ['Mrs Beatty' × 'Mrs Sam McGredy']

'W. H. Dunallan' HT, mr, 1939, Clark, A.; flowers very rich bright red, flushed darker, semi-dbl.; vigorous growth; ['Edith Clark' × unknown]

'W. H. Troy' HT, op, 1906, Dickson, A.; flowers salmon

'W. J. Matthews' T, mp, Matthews, W.J.

'W. R. Hawkins' HT, op, 1948, Toogood, F D; bud ovoid; flowers tango-pink, large, very dbl., high-centered, intense fragrance; foliage glossy; vigorous, upright growth; [('Crimson Glory' × unknown) × 'Silver Jubilee']

'Waanrode' -- See 'LLX7722'

'Waban' T, dp, 1891, Wood; flowers deep, bright pink; otherwise identical to its parent; [sport of 'Catherine Mermet']

'Wabash Dawn' S, op, 1978, Williams, J. Benjamin; bud tapered; flowers bright orange-pink, 4-4½ in., 34 petals, high-centered; repeat bloom; foliage large, glossy; vigorous, upright growth; [(Queen Elizabeth® × 'Gladiator') × ('Aztec' × 'Little Darling')]

'Wachhilde' Misc OGR, 1910, Geschwind; flowers large, full

'Wadeii' (R. × wadeii Hurran) HRg, op; flowers salmon-pink, 3 in., single; June; foliage rough, yellowish; growth low, sprawling; [R. rugosa × R. moyesii]; introduced in 1919

'Wagbi' -- See 'Blebar'

'Wageningen' Pol, my, 1970, Buisman, G. A. H.; bud ovoid; flowers medium, dbl.; foliage dark; [Golden Giant® × 'Peace']; intr. 1968

Wagtail™ -- See 'White Magic Carpet'

Wagtail Cover™ -- See 'White Magic Carpet'

Waiheke™ -- See 'Macwaihe'

'Waikato' -- See 'Machoro'

'Waikiki' -- See 'Macwaihe'

'Waikiki' -- See 'Los Angeles Beautiful'

'Waimarie' HT, m, Matthews; intr. 2001

'Waipounamu' HT, yb, 1983, Cattermole, R.F.; flowers creamy yellow, shaded mauve-pink on outer petals, 50 petals, high-centered, intense fragrance; foliage bronze green, glossy; upright growth; ['Peace' × Blue Moon®]

'Wait 'n' See' Min, ab, Geytenbeek

Waitemata® -- See 'Macweemat'

'Waitziana' (R. × waitziana) S, dp, before 1849; flowers deep rose, 2½ in., single, borne mostly solitary; growth tall (8 ft.); [R. canina × R. gallica]

'Walburga' S, m, Scholle; flowers magenta, large, full, cupped, to almost pompon, borne usually in clusters, slight fragrance; recurrent; foliage green, glossy; strong, upright (5 ft.), broad growth

'Walderfange' HMsk, pb, Lens; intr. 1992

'Waldfee' HP, mr, 1960, Kordes, R.; flowers blood-red, 4 in., dbl., camellia-shaped, borne in small clusters, moderate fragrance; recurrent bloom; foliage glossy; vigorous, tall (10 ft.), dense growth; ['Independence' × 'Mrs John Laing']

'Waldtraut Nielsen' ('Waltraud Nielsen') M, dp, 1932, Nielsen; flowers clear deep pink, large, full, globular, moderate fragrance; non-remontant; tall, arching growth; ['Cristata' × 'Arabella']

'Walferdange' -- See 'Lenwal'

'Walfriends' ('Compassionate Friends') Gr, ly, 2000, Walsh, Richard; flowers semi-dbl., 6-14 petals, borne in small clusters; foliage medium size, light green, semi-glossy; few prickles; upright, tall growth; [('Ginger Heggs' × 'City of Leeds') × Gold Medal®]

'Walifeline' ('The Lifeline Rose') F, rb, 2000, Walsh, Richard; flowers red, reverse white, large, full, borne in small clusters, slight fragrance; free-flowering; foliage medium size, dark green, semi-glossy; numerous prickles; compact, medium growth

'Walkiss' ('Autumn Kiss') Min, mp, 1994, Walsh, Richard Bruce; flowers medium salmon pink, medium, dbl., borne in small clusters, slight fragrance; foliage small, dark green, glossy; few prickles; medium, upright growth; ['Ginger Meggs' × 'Avandel']

'Walko' F, dr, 1957, Delbard-Chabert; flowers dark crimson, small, 23 petals, cupped to flat, borne in clusters of 6 - 8, moderate Damask fragrance; recurrent; [('Incendie' × 'Holstein') × 'Rouge Chabert']

'Walküre' S, lp, 1909, Geschwind, R.; flowers whitish pink, darker at center, 6 cm., full, quartered, flat, borne in small clusters, nodding, moderate fragrance; non-remontant; tall growth; [R. canina × a tea]

'Walküre' HT, w, Ebeling; bud long, pointed; flowers cream-white, center ochre-yellow, dbl.; ['Frau Karl Druschki' × 'Mme Jenny Gillemot']; intr. 1919

'Walkyrie' HT, dr, 1959, Moro, L.; bud urn shaped or ovoid; flowers low-centered, large; bushy growth; ['Happiness' × 'Volcano']

Wall Street® HT, op, Barni, V.; flowers orange pink, yellow reverse, large, dbl., classic hybrid tea, borne mostly singly, moderate fragrance; recurrent; foliage bright green; vigorous, medium growth

'Wallflower' -- See 'The Wallflower'

'Wallove' ('Love Me') Min, w, 1994, Walsh, Richard Bruce; flowers creamy white, pink edge, medium, dbl., borne in small clusters; foliage small, medium green, matte; few prickles; low, upright growth; [Magic Carrousel® × 'Old Master']; intr. 1992

'Walsham Gold' HT, my, 1965, LeGrice; flowers yellow with burnished gold and copper overtones in cool weather

'Walshine' ('Wollongong Gold') Gr, ly, 1997, Walsh, Richard Bruce; flowers light creamy yellow, flushed pink, 1½-3 in., full, borne in small clusters, slight fragrance; foliage medium size, light green, semi glossy; low (1 m.) bushy growth; ['Violet Carson' × 'Arizona']

'Walsh's Rambler' -- See 'America'

'Walter'   HT, dp, 1949, Lens; bud long, pointed; flowers pink, reverse vivid rosy red, open, very large, 20 petals; foliage bronze, leathery; very vigorous, bushy growth; ['Charles P. Kilham' × 'Comtesse Vandal']

'Walter Bentley'   HT, op, 1938, Robinson, H.; bud long, pointed; flowers coppery orange shaded pink, very large, dbl., high-centered; foliage leathery, glossy, dark, bronze; vigorous growth; ['Mrs Sam McGredy' × 'Dame Edith Helen']

'Walter Butt'   S, dp, 1905, Butt; hybrid microgusa; intr. 1905

'Walter C. Clark'   HT, dr, 1917, Paul, W.; bud long, pointed; flowers deep maroon-crimson, shaded black, large, dbl., high-centered; foliage dark, leathery; vigorous growth

'Walter Rieger'   S, dp, 1978, Hetzel; bud pointed; flowers pink to reddish, medium, dbl.; continuous bloom; foliage glossy; vigorous growth; [Carina® × Molde®]; intr. 1977

'Walter Ross'   HT, my, 1970, Morey, Dennison; bud ovoid; flowers large, dbl., high-centered, moderate fragrance; foliage large, glossy, dark, bronze, leathery; vigorous, upright, bushy growth; ['Mme Marie Curie' × King's Ransom®]

'Walter Sisulu' -- See 'Grande Amore'

'Walter Speed'   HT, dy, 1909, Dickson, A.; flowers deep lemon-yellow, passing to milk-white, dbl.

'Waltham Bride'   HMult, w, 1905, Paul, W.; flowers snow-white, 3-4 cm., semi-dbl., borne in small to medium clusters, moderate fragrance; virtually thornless; sometimes classed as HWich or LCl

'Waltham Climber No. 1'   Cl HT, mr, 1885, Paul, W.; flowers rosy crimson, imbricated, large, dbl., borne singly or in small clusters, intense fragrance; recurrent bloom; nearly thornless; vigorous, climbing growth; ['Gloire de Dijon' × unknown]

'Waltham Climber No. 2'   Cl HT, or, 1885, Paul, W.; flowers flame-red, tinted crimson, large, dbl., borne singly or in small clusters; recurrent bloom; nearly thornless

'Waltham Climber No. 3'   Cl HT, mr, 1885, Paul, W.; flowers deep rosy crimson, imbricated, large, dbl.; recurrent bloom; vigorous, climbing growth

'Waltham Crimson'   HT, dr, 1922, Chaplin Bros.; flowers deep crimson

'Waltham Cross'   HT, dr, 1927, Chaplin Bros.; flowers glowing crimson-scarlet, semi-dbl.

'Waltham Flame'   HT, 1921, Chaplin Bros.; flowers deep terra-cotta, shaded bronzy orange

'Waltham Rambler'   HMult, dp, 1903, Paul, W.; flowers deep rosy pink, center paler, stamens bright yellow, single; early; vigorous, climbing growth

'Waltham Scarlet'   HT, dr, 1914, Paul, W.; flowers crimson-scarlet, single

'Waltham Standard'   HP, dr, 1897, Paul, W.; flowers Rich carmine, shaded scarlet and violet, medium

'Waltrap' ('Bett's Little Rhapsody') Min, op, 1996, Walters, Betty & Richard; flowers orange-pink, medium, 76 petals, borne mostly singly; foliage medium size, dark green with pink edge, glossy; upright, very compact, medium (3-4 ft.) growth; ['Bett's White Delight' × seedling]

'Waltraud Nielsen' -- See 'Waldtraut Nielsen'

'Waltz'   Min, ob, Benardella, Frank; flowers orange with white eye and reverse, high-centered, moderate fragrance; recurrent; intr. 1999

Waltz™   LCl, w, Poulsen; flowers white with yellow tones in center, 5-8 cm., full, cupped, borne in clusters, slight rose fragrance; recurrent; foliage dark green, glossy; bushy (150-200 cm.) growth; intr. 2000

'Waltz Time' -- See 'Saint-Exupéry'

'Waltz Time'   Min, w, Benardella, Frank; flowers ivory white with tonings of shrimp pink along the outer edges; free-flowering; bushy growth

'Waltzing Calumet'   Min, yb; flowers light cream yellow, rich buttercup yellow along petal edges; bushy, medium growth

'Waltzing Matilda'   HT, rb, 1965, Jack, J.; flowers red splashed light to dark pink, well-shaped, large, dbl.; vigorous growth; [sport of 'Christian Dior']

'Walzertraum'   HT, mr, 1968, Tantau, Math.; flowers dbl.; foliage dark; intr. 1968

'Walzertraum'   HT, dp, Tantau; flowers strong, stable, deep pink, 4-5 in., very full, cupped, borne mostly singly, slight fragrance; recurrent; upright, strong growth; intr. 2004

'Wambeaird' ('Dr Charles T. Beaird') Gr, op, 1999, Wambach, Catherine; flowers coral, medium, dbl., borne mostly singly and in small clusters; foliage medium size, medium green, semi-glossy; prickles moderate; upright, spreading, medium growth; intr. 2000

'Wamhale' ('Denise Hale') HT, pb, 1996, Wambach, Catherine; flowers light cream pink, darker edge, lighter reverse, 4½ in., full, borne singly; foliage medium size, dark green, semi-glossy; prickles moderate; upright, medium growth; ['Elsie Melton' × seedling]; intr. 1996

'Wamhome' (1997 Traditional Home™) HT, pb, 1997, Wambach, Catherine; flowers light pale pink with ivory shading, full, slight fragrance; foliage medium size, dark green, dull; medium (5 ft) growth; ['Bobby Charlton' × Touch of Class™®]

'Wamlilsapol' ('Elisabeth Pollon') HT, ob, 2000, Wambach, Catherine; flowers orange blend, 4 in., full, borne mostly singly; foliage medium size, dark green, semi-glossy; few prickles; upright, medium growth; ['Elsie Melton' × 'King of Hearts']; intr. 2000

'Wammary' ('Mary Johnston') HT, lp, 1997, Wambach, Alex A.; flowers light pink, 4 in., full, borne mostly singly, slight fragrance; foliage medium size, dark green, semi glossy; medium (4½ ft.) growth; ['Elizabeth Taylor' × Touch of Class™®]

'Wamsper'   HT, mr, 1991, Wambach, Alex A.; bud medium, ovoid, pointed; intr. 1993

'Wamtress' ('Temptress') HT, w, 1998, Wambach, Catherine; flowers white, 4½-5 in., full, high-centered, borne singly, moderate fragrance; foliage medium size, medium green, semi-glossy; few prickles; upright, tall (5½ ft.) growth; ['Elsie Melton' × Elina®]; intr. 1999

Wanaka® -- See 'Macinca'

'Wanda'   HT, dr

'Wanda'   HT, mp, 1953, Joseph H. Hill, Co.; bud short, pointed; flowers rose, 3½-4½ in., 28-30 petals, high-centered, intense fragrance; foliage leathery, vigorous, upright growth; PP1227; ['Pink Bountiful' × 'Celebrity']

'Wanderer' -- See 'Horwander'

'Wanderin' Wind'   S, lp, 1972, Buck, Dr. Griffith J.; flowers two-toned light pink, medium, dbl., high-centered, intense fruity fragrance; free-flowering; foliage large, glossy, dark, leathery; very vigorous, upright, bushy growth; ['Dornroschen' × 'Andante']; intr. 1973

'Wandering Minstrel' -- See 'Harquince'

'Wang-Jang-Ve' -- See 'Fortune's Double Yellow'

'Wanguafong'   HT, m, Shanghai; sepals striped pale pink with purplish pink; [sport of 'Shi-un']; intr. 1993

Wanted®   HT, mr, Spek; flowers 11-12 cm., 40-45 petals, high-centered, borne mostly singly; recurrent; numerous prickles; stems long; intr. 2006

'Waon'   F, ly, Keisei; intr. 2005

'Wapex'   Pol, my, 1968, Buisman, G. A. H.; bud pointed; flowers medium, semi-dbl., borne in clusters; foliage dark; [Golden Showers® × 'Fata Morgana']

Wapiti® ('Dazzler', 'Laurence Olivier', Dazzla®) F, rb, Meilland; flowers medium red with silver reverse, small, dbl., cupped, borne in trusses, slight fragrance; free-flowering

'War Dance' -- See 'Macfirinlin'

'War Dance'   Gr, or, 1961, Swim & Weeks; bud ovoid; flowers dark orange-red, 4-4½ in., 34 petals, high-centered; foliage leathery; vigorous, bushy growth; PP2017; ['Roundelay' × 'Crimson Glory']; intr. 1962

'War Paint'   LCl, mr, 1930, Clark, A.; flowers large, dbl., globular; vigorous, pillar or climbing (8 ft.) growth; [('Rhea Reid' × unknown) × unknown]

'Warabeuta'   F, op, Keisei; intr. 1999

'Warana Festival' HT, mp, 1963, Jack, J.; flowers rich pink, base rich apricot, well-formed, dbl.; vigorous growth; [sport of 'Christian Dior']

Warbler™ ('Fairy Moon') S, my, Olesen; flowers medium yellow, small, dbl., slight wild rose fragrance; recurrent; foliage dark green, glossy; broad, bushy (60-100 cm.) growth

'Wardido' ('Oratorio') HT, pb, 1974, Warriner, William A.; bud ovoid; intr. 1975

'Wardlip' -- See 'Chewaze'

'Wardrosa' ('Chanterelle') HT, dp, Warriner, William A.; bud long; intr. 1976

'Warley Jubilee' F, mp, Warley Rose Gardens

'Warleyensis' (R. × warleyensis) S, mp; sepals persistent; flowers borne mostly solitary; numerous prickles; hips bright red, 1/2 in.; [R. blanda × R. rugosa]

Warm & Fuzzy™ -- See 'Wekhasamiro'

'Warm Rain' Min, mr, 1985, Hardgrove, Donald L.; flowers medium coral-red, medium, 70 petals, high-centered; foliage small, medium green, semi-glossy; vigorous, upright, bushy growth; ['Fragrant Cloud' × 'Orange Honey']

'Warm Welcome' -- See 'Chewizz'

'Warm Wishes' -- See 'Fryxotic'

'Waroujo' (Fulgurante®) HT, mr, J&P; intr. 1977

'Warpel' ('Pete Paul') HT, mp, 2000, Warner, A.J.; flowers very full, high-centered, borne mostly singly, slight fragrance; foliage dark green, glossy; prickles moderate; very vigorous, upright, bushy, tall (5-6 ft.) growth; [sport of 'Swarthmore']

'Warrawee' HT, mp, 1935, Fitzhardinge; bud long, pointed; flowers flesh-pink shaded rose-pink, large, 30 petals, high-centered, moderate fragrance; foliage glossy; vigorous growth; PP140; ['Padre' × 'Rev. F. Page-Roberts']

'Warrior' HT, mr, 1906, Paul, W.; flowers bright scarlet-vermilion, large, dbl., moderate fragrance

'Warrior' F, or, LeGrice; flowers scarlet-red, 3-4 in., 32 petals, cupped, borne in trusses, slight fragrance; recurrent; foliage light green, semi-glossy; [City of Belfast® × 'Ronde Endiablee']; intr. 1977

'Warszawa' HT, ob, 1957, Grabczewski; flowers bright orange, reverse golden yellow; foliage dark, glossy; [sport of 'Carioca']

'Wartburg' HMult, mp, 1910, Kiese; flowers pink to magenta, twisted and reflexed petals, 3-4 cm., dbl., cupped, borne in large, open clusters, moderate sweet fragrance; normally non-recurrent; foliage large, light green; thornless; strong stems; very vigorous, climbing (15-20 ft.) growth; ['Tausendschön' × unknown]

'Wartburg 77' S, my, Berger; flowers bright yellow, lightening to cream, large, dbl., borne mostly in clusters, slight fragrance; recurrent; stems long; upright, arching growth; intr. 1977

'Warwhoop' Min, or, 1974, Williams, Ernest D.; bud ovoid; flowers brilliant orange-red, small, very dbl.; foliage small, glossy, dark; vigorous, bushy growth; [Baccará® × 'Little Chief']; intr. 1973

Warwick Castle® -- See 'Auslian'

'Warwickshire' S, pb, Kordes; flowers white with rosy pink painted on the petals, single, flat, borne in clusters; recurrent; foliage dark green, glossy; short (30 in.), spreading growth; intr. 1991

'Wasagaming' HRg, mp, 1939, Skinner; flowers clear rose pink, dbl., moderate spicy fragrance; recurrent; vigorous growth; [(R. rugosa × R. acicularis) × 'Gruss an Teplitz']

'Wasastiernan' -- See 'Polstjärnan'

'Waskasoo' ('Red Deer') HRg, dr, 1963, Erskine; flowers dbl., high-centered, borne mostly singly, intense fragrance; recurrent; growth typical rugosa; ['Little Betty' × 'Hansa']

'Watarase' HT, m, 2005, Kobayashi, Moriji; flowers full, borne mostly solitary, moderate fragrance; foliage medium green, matte; prickles medium; growth upright, 160 cm.; cutting, garden; [seedling × seedling]; intr. 2005

'Watchfire' -- See 'Minfire'

'Watchung' HT, yb, 1932, Didato; flowers yellow tipped pink, large, 24-26 petals; PP50; [sport of 'Pres. Herbert Hoover']

'Water Lily' -- See 'Jalwater'

'Water Music' LCl, dp, 1983, Bell, Ronald J.; flowers deep pink, darker on petal edges, medium, 20 petals, slight fragrance; foliage dark, medium size, glossy; spreading, climbing growth; [Handel® × unknown]; intr. 1982

'Watercolor' ('Watercolour') Min, mp, 1976, Moore, Ralph S.; bud long, pointed; flowers bright pink, 1½ in., 22-26 petals, high-centered, borne singly and in small clusters, slight sweet fragrance; recurrent; foliage small, glossy, leathery; prickles few, small, straight, inclined downward, brown; stems sturdy, wiry, medium; vigorous, upright, bushy growth; PP4031; ['Rumba' × ('Little Darling' × 'Red Germain')]

Watercolors™ -- See 'Wekclaflobo'

'Watercolour' -- See 'Watercolor'

'Waterloo' HMsk, w, Lens, Louis; flowers creamy white, 2-3 cm., dbl., cupped, borne in clusters; recurrent; foliage dark green; upright (4-5 ft.), arching, rounded growth; intr. 1996

Watermelon Ice™ -- See 'Jacair'

'Waterwise Blush' S, w, Kordes; bud small, blush pink; flowers open white, yellow stamens, small, semi-dbl., cupped, borne in clusters; free-flowering; foliage hardy, disease-resistant; low, spreading growth; intr. 2002

'Watmill' ('Pink Millie') Min, mp, 2003, Wathen, E.N.; flowers full, high-centered, borne mostly solitary, slight fragrance; foliage medium size, medium green, semi-glossy; prickles moderate; growth medium (12-14 in.); exhibition; [sport of Millie Walters™]

'Wave of Flame' -- See 'Ho-No-o-no-nami'

Waverland® -- See 'Lenway'

'Waverley' F, dr, Norman; flowers crimson-scarlet, large, 22 petals, borne in trusses; foliage glossy, dark; vigorous, bushy, compact growth

'Waverley Garden Club' HT, pb, Dawson; intr. about 1983

'Waverley Triumph' Pol, mp, 1951, Poulter; flowers bright pink, base yellow, small, semi-dbl., cupped, borne in clusters; foliage glossy, light green; vigorous, bushy growth; [sport of Orange Triumph®]

'WAVES' ('Admiral') HT, mp, 1944, Dickson, A.; bud ovoid, pointed; flowers rose-pink, open, 4½ in., 35 petals, cupped, intense fragrance; recurrent; foliage dark, leathery, wrinkled; vigorous growth; PP638; ['deep salmon seedling' × 'Lucie Marie']

'Waves of Flame' -- See 'Ho-No-o-no-nami'

'Waves of Wisteria' -- See 'Fujinami'

'Wavria' F, or, 1979, Lens, Louis; flowers orange-crimson; [sport of Europeana®]; intr. 1973

'Waxwing' -- See 'Poulma'

'Wayside Garnet' Min, dr, 1956, Wayside Gardens Co.; flowers garnet-red, small, dbl.; dwarf, compact growth; [sport of 'Oakington Ruby']

We Salute You™ -- See 'Wekvoosun'

'We Zair' C, pb; flowers two-tone pink

'Webbread' ('Bob's Peach') Min, op, 1997, Webster, Robert; flowers medium, dbl., borne in large clusters; foliage large, medium green, glossy; numerous prickles; growth bushy, tall (28 in.); ['Robin Redbreast' × 'Pot O'Gold']; intr. 1998

'Webbrook' ('Jorja Julianna') HT, ob, 2003, Webster, Robert; flowers pale orange, 4 in., full, borne mostly solitary; foliage medium size, medium green, glossy; prickles 6 mm., slightly hooked,; growth bushy, medium (30 in.); bedding; [('Indian Summer' × ('Matangi × Memorium') × Gold Bunny®) × (('Daily Sketch' × 'Eye Paint') × 'Freedom')]; intr. 2004

'Webcoquette' ('Alwyn's Favourite') HT, my, 2007, Robert Webster; flowers full, borne in small clusters, moderate fragrance; foliage medium size, medium green, semi-glossy; prickles 6 mm., triangular, few; growth compact, short (24 in.); bedding, garden decorative; [(('Royal Volunteer' × Modern Art™) × 'The Marquess of Bristol') × 'Jorja Julianna']

'Webcrimson' ('Our Terry') MinFl, dr, 2001, Webster, Robert; flowers 3 in., full, borne mostly solitary; foliage medium size, dark green, glossy; prickles 10 mm., hooked, moderate; growth compact, medium (24 in.); bedding; ['Sealady' × 'Poulvue']; intr. 2003

'Webcyrene' ('Sheffield Pride') Min, mp, 1994, Webster, Robert; flowers medium, very dbl., borne in small clusters; foliage small, dark green, semi-glossy; some prickles; low, compact growth; ['Robin Red Breast' × Matangi®]; intr. 1995

'Webdance' ('Marlene Castronovo') HT, mp, 2000, Webster, Robert; flowers medium, very full, borne mostly singly, no fragrance; foliage medium size, medium green, glossy; prickles moderate; growth upright, medium (36 in.); [City of London® × 'Fragrant Hour']

'Webdesire' ('Foster's Ruby Glow') HT, pb, 2007, Webster, Robert; flowers dusky pink, reverse gold, 4-5 in., very full, borne mostly solitary; foliage medium, dark green, glossy; prickles 10 mm., slightly hooked, moderate; growth compact (36 in.); garden decoration; ['Samantha Barker' × 'National Trust']; intr. 2008

'Webelina' ('Emma Brady') F, yb, 2003, Webster, Robert; flowers yellow, pink stripes, reverse pale yellow, 2½ in., dbl., borne in large clusters; foliage medium size, medium green, glossy; prickles 10-12 mm., straight,; growth bushy, medium (30 in.); bedding; ['Fairhope' × 'Crazy for You']; intr. 2004

'Webeyam' ('Jeanette Talbot') F, op, 1998, Webster, Robert; flowers orange-pink, yellow at center, 2 in., dbl., borne in small clusters; foliage small, medium green, glossy; prickles moderate; compact, low (18 in.) growth; [('Robin Redbreast' × 'Typhoon') × 'The Lady']; intr. 1998

'Webfascin' ('Rose Myra Grimbley') HT, mp, 2002, Webster, Robert; flowers large, full, borne in small clusters, moderate fragrance; foliage medium size, medium green, semi-glossy; prickles moderate, 8 mm., triangular; bushy, medium (36 in.) growth; bedding; ['Dave Hessayon' × ((Matangi® × 'Memorium') × Gold Bunny®)]

'Webfree' ('Samantha Barker') HT, ly, 2001, Webster, Robert; flowers lemon yellow, changing to cream/lemon blend late in season, medium, full, borne in small clusters, intense fragrance; foliage medium size, medium green, glossy; prickles 8-10 mm., triangular, moderate; growth compact, low (30 in.); bedding; ['The Marquess of Bristol' × 'Indian Summer']; intr. 2003

'Webgold' ('Donna Rose') F, my, 2003, Webster, Robert; flowers large, dbl., borne in small clusters; foliage medium size, dark green, glossy; prickles 8 mm., slightly hooked,; growth bushy, medium (30 in.); bedding; [(('Robin Redbreast' × 'Typhoon') × 'The Lady') × 'Indian Summer']; intr. 2004

'Webheart' HT, op, 1998, Webster, Robert

'Weblady' HT, yb, 1998, Webster, Robert; intr. 1999

'Weblove' ('Frederick Keeling') HT, op, 2001, Webster, Robert; flowers salmon pink, 4-5 in., very full, borne mostly solitary, moderate fragrance; foliage medium size, dark green, glossy; prickles 8 mm., hooked, moderate; growth bushy, medium (36 in.); bedding; ['The Marquess of Bristol' × 'Indian Summer']

'Webmoment' ('Rainbows Heaven Scent') HT, ab, 2007, Webster, Robert; flowers peach and gold, medium, full, borne mostly solitary; foliage medium, dark green, glossy; prickles 6-8 mm., triangular, hooked, moderate; growth bushy, medium (36-42 in.); garden decoration; ['The Marquess of Bristol' × 'Indian Summer']; intr. 2007

'Webmorrow' ('My Mum') F, pb, 2000, Webster, Robert; flowers ivory, shaded red and pink, reverse ivory with red edge, medium, full, borne in large clusters; foliage medium size, dark green, glossy; prickles moderate; growth compact, low; ['Robin Red Breast' × Regensberg®]

'Webpass' ('Garry Woodward') HT, or, 2000, Webster, Robert; flowers orange-red, medium, full, borne in small clusters; foliage medium size, medium green, semi-glossy; prickles moderate; compact, low (30 in.) growth; ['Jeanette Talbot' × 'The Marquess of Bristol']; intr. 2001

'Webpriace' ('Distant Sounds') HT, pb, Webb; intr. 1996

'Webrhapsody' ('Maureen Elizabeth') HT, ab, 2005, Webster, Robert; flowers pale apricot, 5 in., full, borne in small clusters, moderate fragrance; foliage medium size, dark green, glossy; prickles moderate, 10 mm., triangular; growth upright, medium (42 in.); garden; ['Samantha Barker' × 'Golden Future']; intr. 2006

'Webrut' ('Dancing Dawn') F, lp, 2005, Webster, Robert; flowers peach, pronounced red stamens, 2½ in., semi-dbl., borne in small clusters, moderate fragrance; foliage small, dark green, semi-glossy; prickles 5 mm., slightly hooked, moderate; compact, short (30 in.) growth; bedding; ['Arizona Sunset' × ('Indian Summer' × ('Matangi × Memorium)' × Gold Bunny®))]; intr. 2004

'Websense' ('Sunset Beauty') LCl, op, 2006, Webster, Robert; flowers peach pink and gold, 2½ in., semi-dbl., borne in large clusters; foliage medium size, medium green, glossy; prickles 8 mm., triangular, numerous; growth upright, climbing, medium (12 ft.); [Western Sun™ × 'Sue Lawley']; intr. 2006

'Websilver' ('The Linda Smith Rose') HT, w, 2007, Webster, Robert; flowers white, with center petals flushed pink, 4 in., very full, borne mostly solitary; foliage medium, dark green, glossy; prickles 10 mm., slightly hooked, moderate; growth upright, medium (36 in.); garden decoration; ['Golden Future' × 'Perception']; intr. 2008

'Webspark' ('Heavens Above') MinFl, rb, 2003, Webster, Robert; flowers bright red, reverse pale red, 1½-2 in., full, borne in small clusters; foliage medium size, medium green, semi-glossy; prickles triangular; growth bushy, medium (24 in.); bedding, containers; [Little Jackie™ × ('Anytime' × Western Sun™)]; intr. 2004

'Websummer' ('Terry Edwards') F, my, 2001, Webster, Robert; flowers 3½-4 in., very full, borne in small clusters; foliage medium size, medium green, semi-glossy; prickles moderate, 15 mm., triangular; growth bushy, medium (36 in.); bedding; ['Arizona Sunset' × 'The Lady']; intr. 2003

'Websun' ('Sarah Penrose') HT, yb, 2005, Webster, Robert; flowers yellow, outer petals lemon, 5 in., very full, borne mostly solitary, slight fragrance; foliage medium size, light green, matte; prickles moderate, 8 mm., slightly hooked; growth compact, medium (30 in.); bedding; ['Golden Wedding' × Golden Giant®]

'Webten' ('Destiny's Dream') LCl, my, 2006, Webster, Robert; flowers straw yelllow, 2 in., very full, borne in large clusters, moderate fragrance; foliage small, medium green, semi-glossy; prickles 3 mm., needle, moderate; growth upright, short (6-8 ft.); pillar climber; [Laura Ford® × 'The Marques of Bristol']; intr. 2006

'Webtweed' ('Eric's Choice') Min, or, 2005, Webster, Robert; flowers semi-dbl., borne in large clusters, slight fragrance; foliage medium size, dark green, glossy; prickles moderate, 5 mm., slightly hooked; growth compact, short (12 in.); bedding; ['Pink Petticoat' × 'Darling Flame']

'Webwarm' ('Bob Thomas') HT, pb, 2000, Webster, Robert; flowers pale salmon pink shades, medium size, full, borne mostly singly, slight fragrance; foliage medium size, medium green, semi-glossy; prickles moderate; upright, medium (30 in.) growth; ['The Marquess of Bristol' × 'Warm Wishes']

'Webyoung' ('Pamela Jane Taylor') HT, w, 2004, Webster, Robert; flowers ivory, 4 in., very full, borne in small clusters, moderate fragrance; foliage medium size, dark green, glossy; prickles 10 mm., straight,; growth bushy, medium (30 in.); bedding; ['Samantha Barker' × 'Golden Future']; intr. 2004

Wedded Bliss™ -- See 'Savawed'

'Weddigen' ('Weddingen') HT, lp, 1916, Lambert, P.; flowers silver-pink, large, full, moderate fragrance; ['General MacArthur' × 'Goldelse']

'Wedding Bells' HMult, w, 1906, Walsh; flowers white, outer half of petals soft pink, 3 cm., dbl., cupped, opening flat, borne in clusters of 10-20, no fragrance; foliage light; short stems; very vigorous, climbing (12-15 ft.)growth; ['Crimson Rambler' × unknown]

'Wedding Cake' -- See 'Morcake'

'Wedding Celebration' -- See 'Poulht006'
'Wedding Day' ('English Wedding Day') LCl, w, 1950, Stern, Sir Frederich; bud pale apricot; flowers yellow to white, flushed pink, 3 cm., single, borne in large clusters, intense fruity fragrance; non-remontant; foliage pewter-green; growth to 20 ft.; hips round, orange; [*R. longicuspis* × *R. moyesii*]
'Wedding Garland' LCl, w, Taschner, Ludwig; flowers pure white, dbl., cupped, moderate fragrance; recurrent; tall, arching growth; Iceberg is one ancestor; intr. 2003
'Wedding Night' S, Ping Lim; intr. 2005
'Wedding Pink' -- See 'Jacbip'
'Wedding Ring' HT, my, 1958, Shepherd; bud long, pointed; flowers golden yellow, 4-4½ in., 25-35 petals, slight fragrance; foliage dark green, glossy, leathery; vigorous, upright, compact growth; ['Ville de Paris' × 'Mrs Sam McGredy']; intr. 1957
'Wedding Song' HT, w, 1972, Whisler, D.; upright growth; ['Virgo' × 'Ivory Fashion']; intr. 1971
'Weddingen' -- See 'Weddigen'
'Wee Ack' -- See 'Renack'
'Wee Barbie' -- See 'Jelbar'
'Wee Benny' Pol, mp, J. B. Williams; dwarf, polyantha-like growth; intr. 2005
'Wee Beth' Min, op, 1981, Cherry, R. & Welsh, E.; bud pointed, mossy; flowers salmon-pink, 11 petals, borne in clusters of 3 - 20, moderate sweetbriar fragrance; foliage small, dark, bristles on reverse; prickles red; bushy growth; ['Orange Silk' × 'Fairy Moss']
'Wee Butterflies' Pol, pb, 1990, Jerabek, Paul E.; bud pointed; flowers medium pink with white eye, small, single, borne in sprays of 3 - 35, slight fragrance; foliage medium size, light green, glossy; prickles straight, pink; bushy, low growth; hips round, small, red; ['The Fairy' × seedling]; intr. 1989
'Wee Cracker' -- See 'Cocmarris'
Wee Jock® -- See 'Cocabest'
'Wee Lass' Min, mr, 1975, Moore, Ralph S.; bud pointed; flowers blood-red, ½-1 in., 18 petals; foliage small, dark; upright, bushy growth; ['Persian Princess' × 'Persian Princess']; intr. 1974
'Wee Man' ('Tapis de Soie') Min, mr, 1975, McGredy, Sam IV; flowers scarlet, 2 in., 14 petals; foliage glossy, dark; ['Little Flirt' × 'Marlena']; intr. 1975
'Wee Matt' -- See 'Macweemat'
'Wee One' Min, mp, Tantau; intr. 1994
'Wee Snowflake' -- See 'Weesnowflake'
'Wee Topper' -- See 'Andwee'
'Weeblush' ('Blushing Dawn') Min, pb, 1985, Weeks, Michael W.J.; flowers creamy white, peach pink eye, yellow stamens, petals painted peach pink, 7-8 petals, moderate fragrance; foliage medium size, dark, matte; low, bushy growth; ['Jeanne Lajoie' × Eyepaint®]; intr. 1983
'Weegold' ('Fine Gold') HT, dy, 1982, Weeks, Michael W.J.; flowers deep golden yellow, 26 petals, high-centered, borne 1-3 per stem, moderate fragrance; foliage medium size, dark, glossy; branching, upright growth; [seedling × sport of Hawaii]
'Week End' HT, pb, Ghosh, Mr.&Mrs. S.; bud pointed; flowers light pink with apricot tones, reverse darker, petals prominently veined, large, dbl., high-centered, moderate sweet fragrance; recurrent; intr. 1998
'Week-End' S, dp
'Weemicrowhite' ('Micro White') Min, w, 2001, Weeks, Michael; flowers ½ in., semi-dbl., borne in small clusters, moderate fragrance; foliage small, medium green, semi-glossy; prickles small, pointed, few; growth bushy, low (5 in.); garden decorative, containers; ['Weesnowflake' × unknown]
'Weepaint' ('Open Secret') F, ab, 1987, Weeks, Michael W.J.; flowers peach to salmon-pink, sometimes flecked darker, shading to w, 5 petals; foliage medium size, medium green, semi-glossy; bushy, tall growth; [sport of Eyepaint®]
'Weeping China Doll' -- See 'China Doll, Climbing'
'Weeplumsncream' ('Plums 'n' Cream') F, rb, 2001, Weeks, Michael; flowers plum red, cream reverse, 2½ in., dbl., borne in small clusters, moderate fragrance; foliage large, dark green, glossy; prickles large, pointed, numerous; growth spreading, medium (3 ft.); garden decorative; ['Picasso' × unknown]
'Weepy' -- See 'Lenyak'
'Weequill' ('Pink Quill') Min, mp, 1992, Weeks, Michael W.J.; flowers medium bright pink, medium, semi-dbl., borne in large clusters, moderate fragrance; foliage medium size, dark green, bronze when young, semi-glossy; some prickles; tall (25 cm.), spreading growth; ['Mr Bluebird' × unknown]
'Weesnowflake' ('Wee Snowflake') S, w, 2001, Weeks, Michael; flowers dbl., borne in large clusters, intense fragrance; non-remontant; foliage medium size, medium green, semi-glossy; prickles moderate, medium, hooked; growth spreading, tall (20-25 ft.); climber; fences, walls, pergolas; ['Kiftsgate' × unknown]; once-blooming
'Weespot' ('Spot o' Gold') Min, my, 1992, Weeks, Michael W.J.; flowers yellow stamens, medium, single, borne in small clusters; foliage medium size, medium green, semi-glossy; some prickles; bushy (20 cm.) growth; ['Rise 'n' Shine' × unknown]
'Weetwood' HWich, lp, Bawden; flowers delicate rose pink, touched buff in heart, 4-5 in., full, rosette, borne in hanging clusters, slight fragrance; some repeat; foliage dark green; vigorous (20-25 ft.) growth; intr. 1983
'Weggis' HT, pb, Huber; intr. 2001
'Wehrinsel' S, dr, Berger, W.; flowers medium, semi-dbl., cupped, borne in clusters, slight fragrance; recurrent; strong, upright (2 m.) growth; intr. 1959
'Weidenia' S, lp, 1927, Alfons; flowers medium, single; hybrid canina
'Weigand's Crimson Rambler' -- See 'Non Plus Ultra'
'Weight Watcher Success' -- See 'Jacbitou'
'Weihenstephan' S, dp, 1964, Kordes; flowers rich pink, small, semi-dbl., borne in large clusters, slight fragrance; recurrent; vigorous (4½ ft.) growth
'Weisse aus Sparrieshoop' ('White Sparrieshoop') S, w, 1962, Kordes; flowers white, add pink tones in cool weather, 4 in., single, borne in large clusters, moderate fragrance; free-flowering; robust, tall growth; [sport of 'Sparrieshoop']
'Weisse Better Times' HT, w, 1940, Wirth; flowers large, dbl.
'Weisse Echo' Pol, w, 1925, Kiese; flowers medium, semi-dbl.
'Weisse Gruss an Aachen' ('White Gruss an Aachen') F, w, 1944, Vogel; bud ovoid; flowers snow-white, large, very dbl., borne in clusters, moderate fragrance; recurrent; upright, bushy growth; [sport of 'Gruss an Aachen']
Weisse Immensee® -- See 'Korweirim'
'Weisse Jacques Cartier' -- See 'White Jacques Cartier'
'Weisse Margo Koster' Pol, w, 1939, Teschendorff; flowers small to medium, dbl.
Weisse Max Graf® -- See 'Korgram'
'Weisse Nelkenrose' HRg, w, Münster; flowers white, petals frayed, medium, dbl., cupped, borne in large clusters, slight fragrance; recurrent; strong (1 m.) growth; [sport of 'F.J. Grootendorst']; intr. 1966
'Weisse New Dawn' ('Arcata Light Yellow Wichurana') LCl, w, Berger; bud crimson-tipped; flowers medium, full, moderate fragrance; [sport of 'New Dawn']; intr. 1959
Weisse Repandia® -- See 'Koriant'
'Weisse Seerose' -- See 'Nymphaea Alba'
'Weisse Tausendschön' HMult, w, 1909, Kiese; bud pale yellow; flowers pure white; [sport of 'Tausendschön']
'Weisse Woge' HSpn, w, Strobel; flowers single; intr. 1999
Weisse Wolke® ('Nuage Blanc', 'White Cloud') S, w, Kordes; flowers pure white, yellow stamens, semi-dbl. to double, cupped, borne in clusters, moderate fragrance; recurrent; foliage dark green, glossy; bushy (3 ft.) growth; intr. 1993
'Weisser Engel' F, w, Verschuren; flowers clean white, dbl., cupped, borne in clusters, slight fragrance; recurrent; bushy (2 ft.), broad growth; intr. 1966
'Weisser Herumstreicher' HMult, w, 1899, Kiese; flowers pure white, large, dbl., borne in clusters; vigorous, climbing growth; ['Daniel Lacombe' × 'Pâquer-

ette']

'Weisser Maréchal Niel' N, w, 1896, Deegan; flowers pure creamy-white, large, full, moderate tea fragrance

'Weisserote Mme de Sancy de Parabère' HSem, pb, Grimm, Wernt; flowers pink with a white center; intr. 1980

'Weisses Meer' F, w, VEG; flowers medium, semi-dbl.

'Wekairyven' (Wing-Ding™) Pol, mr, 2006, Carruth, Tom; flowers scarlet orange-red, 2-4 cm., single, shallow cup, borne in large clusters, very slight fragrance; foliage medium size, dark green, semi-glossy; prickles average, slightly hooked, brown, moderate; growth spreading, medium (45 to 60 cm.); garden decoration; ['Red Fairy' × Raven™; like The Fairy in habit, very large clusters, somewhat spreading, bright long lived color; intr. 2007

'Wekajazoul' (Long Tall Sally™) S, w, 1999, Carruth, Tom; flowers buff white, 3-3½ in., single, borne in large clusters, moderate fragrance; foliage large, dark green, semi-glossy; prickles moderate; upright, very vertical, tall (5-7 ft.) growth; PP14041; [All That Jazz™ × *R. soulieana* derivative]; intr. 1999

'Wekamanda' ('Irish Luck', 'Limelight', St Patrick™, 'Saint Patrick') HT, yb, 1999, Strickland, Frank A.; flowers yellow gold, shaded green in heat, 5 in., 30-35 petals, high-centered, borne mostly singly, slight fragrance; foliage large, medium green, matte; prickles moderate; upright, bushy, medium (3-4 ft.) growth; PP9591; [Brandy™ × Gold Medal®]; intr. 1996

'Wekamarsodo' (Reba K. Rowland™) LCl, dr, 2003, Carruth, Tom; flowers deep velvet red, reverse slightly lighter red, 6½-8½ cm., full, borne in small clusters, slight fragrance; foliage large, dark green, glossy; prickles few, average, hooked slightly downward, greenish tan; growth spreading, climbing (250-380 cm.); garden decorative; PP15089; [('America' × Marina®) × (*R. soulieana* derivative × Dortmund®)]; intr. 2003

'Wekamrav' (Valentine's Day™) Cl MinFl, dr, 2004, Carruth, Tom; flowers deep velvet red, 5-7 cm., 30 petals, cupped, borne in small clusters, slight fragrance; recurrent; foliage medium size, dark green, semi-glossy; prickles moderate, small, almost straight; growth spreading, climbing canes, tall, canes of 180 to 220 cm.; garden decoration; ['Amalia' × Raven™]; intr. 2006

'Wekanchaco' (Ann Cox Chambers™) F, w, 2003, Carruth, Tom; flowers very pastel apricot to near white, 9-11 cm., dbl., borne in small clusters, slight fragrance; foliage medium size, dark green, semi-glossy; prickles moderate, average, straight, greenish brown; growth bushy, rounded, medium (90-110 cm.); garden decoration; [Moonstone™ × Marilyn Monroe™]; intr. 2003

'Wekaq' (The Temptations™) HT, pb, 1990, Winchel, Joseph F.; bud pointed; flowers pink blend, medium pink reverse, aging slightly lighter, 4 in., 25-30 petals, high-centered, borne singly and in small clusters, moderate fruity fragrance; recurrent; foliage medium size, dark green, semi-glossy, disease-resistant; prickles slightly hooked, medium, green; upright, tall growth; hips oval, medium, orange; PP8516; ['Paradise' × 'Admiral Rodney']; intr. 1984

'Wekausboy' (Jacob's Robe™) LCl, yb, 2006, Carruth, Tom; flowers yellow, peach, pink stripe blushing all pink, reverse similar but with more yellow, 9-11 cm., dbl., borne in small clusters, moderate spice fragrance; foliage large, medium green, very glossy; prickles various, slightly hooked, brown, numerous; growth spreading, climbing, canes up to 250 cm. long, garden decoration; [Autumn Sunset™ × Playboy®]; intr. 2008

'Wekbecfoj' ('Soaring Spirits') LCl, pb, 2004, Carruth, Tom; flowers pastel pink, yellow & cream stripes, 10-13 cm., single, borne in large clusters, moderate apple fragrance; foliage large, light green, glossy; prickles mixed, almost straight; growth spreading, climbing, tall (210-250 cm.); garden decoration; [Berries 'n' Cream™ × Fourth of July™]; intr. 2005

'Wekbepmey' (Strike It Rich™) Gr, yb, 2005, Carruth, Tom; buds long; flowers yellow gold blended with orange-red, 9-11 cm., full, borne in large clusters, intense spice and fruit fragrance; recurrent; foliage medium size, medium green, semi-glossy; prickles moderate, average, pointed, brown; stems dark red; upright, vigorous, tall (175 to 200 cm.) growth; PPAF; ['Chriscinn' × 'Mellow Yellow']; intr. 2007

'Wekbiphitsou' F, m, Carruth, Tom; intr. 2004

'Wekbipuhit' ('New Age', Purple Heart™) F, m, 1999, Carruth, Tom; flowers magenta purple, 3½-4 in., 30-35 petals, cupped, borne in large clusters, intense clove and spice fragrance; foliage medium size, medium green, matte; prickles moderate; rounded, compact, bushy, medium (3½ ft.) growth; PP11513; ['Stephen's Big Purple' × International Herald Tribune®]; intr. 1999

'Wekblagab' ('Australia's Olympic Gold Rose Rose', Golden Eagle™) Gr, dy, 2005, Carruth, Tom; flowers deep golden yellow, 7-10 cm., full, borne mostly solitary, slight fragrance; foliage medium size, medium green, semi-glossy; prickles average, slightly hooked, beige, moderate; growth upright, medium (125 to 130 cm.); garden decoration; [Brite Lites® × 'Joshua Bradley']; intr. 1995

'Wekblunez' ('Heaven Scent', Memorial Day™, 'Parfum de Liberté') HT, mp, 2002, Carruth, Tom; bud globular to somewhat ovoid; flowers pink with orchid wash, reverse slightly darker, 12-14 cm., 28-52 petals, old-fashioned, borne mostly solitary, intense old rose fragrance; good repeat; foliage large, medium green, matte; prickles few, medium-small, slightly hooked, brownish-green; stems very well foliated, strong, medium to long; growth upright to somewhat spreading, medium (110-130 cm.); garden decorative; hips moderately obovate, somewhat flat at the top ; PP16572; [Blueberry Hill™ × 'New Zealand']; intr. 2002

'Wekblusi' (Stainless Steel™) HT, m, 1991, Carruth, Tom; bud pointed to ovoid; flowers clean, silvery gray lavender, 5-6 in., 22-28 petals, high-centered, borne mostly singly, with some clusters, intense sweet fragrance; recurrent; foliage large, medium green, semi-glossy; some prickles; stems long, strong; tall to medium (130-150 cm.), vigorous growth; PP10188; [Blue Nile® × 'Silverado']; intr. 1995

'Wekboroco' (Rockin' Robin™) S, rb, 1999, Carruth, Tom; bud short, pointed to globular; flowers red, white and pink stripes and splashes, ruffled, 1½-2½ in., 40-45 petals, cupped, borne in large clusters, slight apple fragrance; foliage medium size, dark green, glossy; prickles moderate; fountainous, rounded, bushy (4 ft.) growth; PP10070; ['Bonica' × 'Roller Coaster']; intr. 1997

'Wekcalroc' ('George Burns Centennial', George Burns™) F, yb, 1996, Carruth, Tom; flowers yellow striped irregularly with red, cream and pink, 3-3½ in., full, borne in small clusters, moderate fruit and citrus fragrance; foliage large, clean, dark green, glossy; numerous prickles; upright, compact, medium (3-3½ ft.) growth; PP10334; ['Calico' × 'Roller Coaster']; intr. 1997

'Wekcatlart' ('Orange P'ins', Gizmo™) Min, ob, 1998, Carruth, Tom; flowers scarlet orange with white eye, long lasting, 1½-3 in., single, borne in small clusters, slight apple fragrance; foliage medium size, dark green, semi-glossy; prickles moderate, small, rounded, compact, medium (18 in.) growth; PP12327; [Carrot Top™ × Little Artist®]; intr. 2000

'Wekcelpep' ('Sunsation') HT, pb, 1996, Carruth, Tom; flowers yellow striped pink, 5 in., full, borne mostly singly, intense fragrance; foliage large, light green, dull; some prickles; upright, bushy, medium growth; PPAF; ['Celebrity' × 'Peppermint Twist']; intr. 1996

'Wekchrisg' ('Crowd Pleaser') HT, dp, 2000, Greenwood, Chris; flowers cerise pink, brushed with cream on reverse, 9-11 cm., 25-30 petals, high-centered, borne mostly singly; upright, tall growth; PP14138; [sport of 'Lynn Anderson']; intr. 2001

'Wekcisbako' (Home Run™) S, mr, 2004, Carruth, Tom; flowers bright velvet red,

6-8 cm., single, borne in small clusters, slight fragrance; foliage medium size, dark green, matte, very disease-resistant; prickles slightly hooked; growth compact, rounded, medium (70-90 cm.); garden decoration; [(City of San Francisco™ × 'Baby Love') × Knock Out™]; intr. 2006

'Wekclaflobo' (Watercolors™) S, yb, 2006, Carruth, Tom; flowers yellow edged pink blushing all pink, reverse similar but with less blush color, 6-8 cm., single, shallow cup, borne in small clusters; recurrent; foliage medium size, dark green, semi-glossy; prickles average, slightly hooked, beige, moderate; growth bushy, to slightly spreading, medium (75-90 cm.); garden decoration; [('Santa Claus' × Flower Carpet™) × Betty Boop™]; intr. 2007

'Wekclauni' ('Harm Saville') MinFl, dr, 2004, Carruth, Tom & Bedard, Christian; flowers very deep red, 5-6 cm., dbl., borne mostly solitary; foliage medium size, dark green, semi-glossy; prickles small, almost straight; growth bushy, medium (60 to 80 cm.; garden decoration; ['Santa Claus' × Opening Night™]; intr. 2005

'Wekcobeju' (Cinco de Mayo™) F, r, 2007, Carruth, Tom; flowers multi-color, smoky lavender-orange, medium, 8-10 cm., dbl., borne in large clusters; nearly continuous bloom; foliage medium, dark green, semi-glossy; new growth dark red; prickles average, almost straight, light brown, moderate; growth bushy, rounded, medium (90-120 cm.); garden decoration; [Topsy Turvy™ × Julia Child™]; intr. 2009

'Wekcocbeb' (Topsy Turvy™) F, rb, 2005, Carruth, Tom; flowers scarlet red, reverse white, 8-10 cm., 10-15 petals, open pinwheel, borne in large clusters, slight apple fragrance; recurrent; foliage medium size, dark green, glossy, new shoots dark red; prickles numerous, average, almost straight, taupe; growth bushy, very rounded, medium (60 to 70 cm.); garden decoration; PPAF; [Countess Celeste™ × Betty Boop™]; intr. 2006

'Wekcrying' (Dolores Hope™) HT, dp, 2003, Carruth, Tom; flowers cerise pink, 12-14 cm., full, high-centered, borne mostly solitary, slight fragrance; foliage large, dark green, semi-glossy; prickles average, almost straight, brown, moderate; growth upright, to slightly spreading, tall (140-160 cm.); garden decoration; [Crystalline™ × 'Ingrid Bergman']; intr. 2004

'Wekcryland' ('Cadillac DeVille', 'Marguerite Bourgeoys', Moonstone™) HT, w, 1998, Carruth, Tom; flowers ivory white with a fine, delicate pink edging, 4½-5 in., full, high-centered, borne singly, slight fragrance; recurrent; foliage large, medium green, dull; prickles moderate; upright, medium (120-160 cm.) growth; PP11384; [Crystalline™ × 'Lynn Anderson']; intr. 1998

'Wekcryplag' (Blueberry Hill™) F, m, 1999, Carruth, Tom; bud plump, pointed, dark lilac; flowers clear lilac, curved petals, golden stamens, 4 in., single, high-centered, borne in small clusters, moderate apple fragrance; foliage very serrated, large, dark green, glossy; prickles moderate; upright, medium, rounded, bushy (3-4 ft.) growth; PP10072; [Crystalline™ × Playgirl™]; intr. 1997

'Wekcryreg' ('Gracie Allen') F, pb, 1999, Carruth, Tom; flowers white with a pink heart, 4½ in., 25-30 petals, borne in small clusters, slight apple fragrance; foliage medium size, dark green, glossy; prickles moderate; upright, bushy, medium (3-4 ft.) growth; PP11103; [Crystalline™ × Regensberg®]; intr. 1998

'Wekdesc' ('Descanso Dream') Min, w, 1995, Carruth, Tom; flowers white blend, small, dbl., no fragrance; foliage small, dark green, semi-glossy; few prickles; low (25-30 cm.), bushy, compact growth; [Origami™ × Little Artist®]; intr. 1994

'Wekdoclem' ('Atlanta') HT, dy, 1992, Lemrow, Dr. Maynard W.; flowers deep clear yellow, long-lasting color, 3-3½ in., dbl., borne mostly singly; foliage medium size, medium green, matte; some prickles; medium (90-120 cm.), upright, bushy, full growth; [Honor™ × 'Gingersnap']; intr. 1996

'Wekdocpot' (Dream Come True™) Gr, yb, 2006, Pottschmidt, Dr. John; flowers yellow edged with cerise pink, reverse similar but with more yellow, 10-12 cm., 40 petals, borne mostly solitary, slight tea fragrance; recurrent; foliage large, dark green, matte; prickles average, almost straight, beige, moderate; stems long; growth upright, tall (170 to 200 cm.); garden decoration; PPAF; [(Touch of Class® × unknown) × unknown]; intr. 2008

'Wekdoudou' (Coffee Bean™) Min, r, 2006, Bedard, Christian; flowers smoky chocolate-orange, reverse cinnamon-orange, 3-4 cm., dbl., borne mostly solitary; foliage medium size, dark green, very glossy; prickles small, sligtly hooked, beige-brown, few; growth compact, bushy, short (30-50 cm.); garden decoration, exhibition; ['Santa Claus' × Hot Cocoa™]; intr. 2008

'Wekdykstra' ('Heart of Gold', Heart O' Gold™, 'Rose of Narromine') Gr, yb, 1999, Dykstra, Dr. A. Michael; flowers deep gold surrounded by cerise pink, 4-4½ in., 35-40 petals, high-centered, borne in large clusters, intense fruit and rose fragrance; foliage large, medium green, semi-glossy; prickles moderate; upright, tall (5-6 ft.) growth; PP10713; ['Broadway' × Gold Medal®]; intr. 1997

'Wekearman' (Let Freedom Ring™) HT, mr, 2005, Earman, Ernest; flowers light strawberry red, 10-13 cm., dbl., high-centered, borne mostly solitary, no fragrance; foliage medium size, medium green, matte; prickles average, straight; stems long; growth upright, tall (160-190 cm.); garden decoration; ['Prima Donna' × Touch of Class®]; intr. 2006

'Wekemilcho' ('Neon Cowboy') Min, rb, 2001, Carruth, Tom; flowers red with yellow eye, 3-4 cm., single, borne in small clusters, slight fragrance; foliage small, dark green, glossy; prickles moderate, small, straight, light brown; growth compact, short (28-38 cm.); garden decoration; PP15256; ['Emily Louise' × (Playboy® × Little Artist®)]; intr. 2001

'Wekfabpur' (Midnight Blue™) S, m, 2003, Carruth, Tom; flowers deep velvety purple, reverse slightly lighter, 6-8 cm., dbl., borne in large clusters, intense clove fragrance; foliage medium size, light green, semi-glossy; prickles moderate, small, almost straight, light brown; growth compact, bushy, short (60-80 cm.); garden decoration; [(('Sweet Chariot' × Blue Nile®) × 'Stephen's Big Purple') × ((International Herald Tribune® × *R. soulieanna* derivative) × ('Sweet Chariot' × Blue Nile®))]; intr. 2004

'Wekfrag' ('Twin Peaks', Ain't She Sweet™) HT, or, 1993, Winchel, Joseph F.; flowers large, terra-cotta orange to deep orange-red, 3-3½ in., 30-35 petals, high-centered, borne mostly singly, intense spice and rose fragrance; foliage large, medium green, matte; some prickles; new stems dark red; medium, rounded, bushy growth; PP9071; [seedling × 'Dolly Parton']; intr. 1994

'Wekfrancoly' (In the Mood™) HT, mr, 2005, Carruth, Tom; flowers bright clear red, 12-14 cm., full, borne mostly solitary, slight fragrance; recurrent; foliage large, dark green, semi-glossy; prickles moderate, average, slightly hooked, beige; growth upright, medium (120 to 150 cm.); garden decoration; [City of San Francisco™ × 'Olympiad']; intr. 2007

'Wekgibotex' (John-John™) F, my, 1999, Carruth, Tom; flowers bright yellow, 3-3½ in., dbl., borne in small clusters; foliage medium size, light green, dull; prickles moderate; upright, bushy, medium (3-4 ft.) growth; PP13106; [(seedling × 'Sunsprite') × ('Old Master' × 'Texas')]; intr. 2000

'Wekglezno' (Tiddly Winks™) Min, yb, 2006, Carruth, Tom; flowers yellow with a broad cerise edging, reverse yellow, retaining color well, 3-5 cm., dbl., borne in small clusters; foliage small, medium green, semi-glossy; prickles small, straight, beige, moderate; growth compact, rounded, bushy, short (30-45 cm.); garden decoration; PPAF; [(Golden Holstein® × Easy Going™) × 'Neon Cowboy']; intr. 2008

'Wekgobnez' (Rock & Roll™) Gr, rb, 2007, Carruth, Tom; flowers upper dark & light red & white stripe, reverse mostly white, large, 11-13 cm., very full, borne mostly solitary; foliage abundant, large, dark green, semi-glossy; prickles average, almost straight, light brown, moderate; growth upright, bushy, medium (125-140 cm.); garden decoration; [George Burns™ × 'New Zealand']; intr. 2008

'Wekgojolo' (Shockwave™) F, my, 2007, Carruth, Tom; flowers deep intense bright yellow, fading very little, medium, 6-8 cm., full, borne in small clusters; foliage medium, bright, light green, glossy; prickles small, hooked, light green, few; growth compact, rounded, medium; garden decoration; PPAF; ['Gold Marie' × (seedling × 'Baby Love')]; intr. 2008

'Wekhasamiro' (Warm & Fuzzy™) Min, mr, 2007, Carruth, Tom; bud fragrant, mossy, well-shaped; flowers even medium red, 3-4 cm., dbl., borne in small clusters; foliage medium size, dark green, matte; prickles mixed, almost straight, tan, numerous; growth compact, short (40-50 cm.); garden decoration; [(seedling × 'Santa Claus') × 'Danny Boy']; intr. 2009

'Wekhelen' (Peach Fuzz™) Min, ab, 1990, Carruth, Tom; bud pointed, moss; flowers apricot blend fading to pastel, medium, 22 petals, high-centered, borne singly or in small clusters, intense moss fragrance; foliage medium size, dark green, glossy; prickles straight, yellow brown; bushy, rounded, full, medium growth; ['Fairy Moss' × New Year®]; intr. 1990

'Wekhilpurnil' ('Le Chainon', Neptune™) HT, m, 2003, Carruth, Tom; flowers blended lavender, reverse blended lavender sometimes edged purple, 11-14 cm., full, borne mostly solitary, intense fragrance; foliage large, medium green, semi-glossy; prickles average, almost straight, brown, none; growth upright, medium (90 to 120 cm.); garden decoration; [(Blueberry Hill™ × 'Stephen's Big Purple') × Blue Nile®]; intr. 2004

'Wekhocamito' (Summer Love™) HT, my, 2007, Carruth, Tom; flowers clear, soft, medium yellow, large, 11-13 cm., full, borne mostly solitary; foliage large, medium green, matte; prickles average, almost straight, greenish-beige, moderate; growth upright, bushy, medium (110-130 cm.); garden decoration; ['Hotel California' × Midas Touch™]; intr. 2009

'Wekibertaz' (Cancun™) HT, or, 1999, Carruth, Tom; flowers dark orange-red, 5-6 in., full, borne mostly singly, slight fragrance; foliage large, dark green, glossy; prickles moderate; upright, medium (3½-4 ft.) growth; ['Ingrid Bergman' × All That Jazz™]; intr. 1999

'Wekiscorou' (Teeny Bopper™) S, rb, 2007, Bedard, Christian; flowers scarlet red with a white eye, reverse mostly white, very long-lasting, small, 3-4 cm., dbl., borne in small clusters; foliage small, medium green, very glossy; prickles small, almost straight, brown, moderate; growth compact, short (30-45 cm.); garden decoration; [City of San Francisco™ × 'Rabble Rouser']; intr. 2009

'Wekisosblip' (Wild Blue Yonder™) Gr, m, 2004, Carruth, Tom; flowers lavender with a broad red--purple border, 9-11 cm., 25-30 petals, cupped, ruffled, borne in large clusters, intense spicy fragrance; recurrent; foliage large, dark green, semi-glossy; prickles almost straight; growth bushy, medium (100-130 cm.), upright; garden decoration; [((International Herald Tribune® × R. soulieana derivative) × ('Sweet Chariot' × Blue Nile®)) × (Blueberry Hill™ × 'Stephen's Big Purple')]; intr. 2006

'Wekjoe' ('Lynn Anderson', 'Oh My God') HT, pb, 1993, Winchel, Joseph F.; flowers white edged deep pink, 5-5½ in., full, high-centered, borne mostly singly; foliage very large, medium green, matte; few prickles; tall (170-180 cm.), upright, bushy growth; PP9389; [seedling × Gold Medal®]; intr. 1995

'Wekjojojap' ('Phyllis Diller') Gr, dy, 2005, Carruth, Tom; flowers very deep pure yellow, long lasting, 11-13 cm., dbl., borne in small clusters; foliage large, dark green, glossy; prickles average, straight; growth bushy, medium (100-130 cm.); garden decoration; [John-John™ × seedling]; intr. 2006

'Wekjutono' (Vavoom™) F, ob, 2005, Carruth, Tom; flowers bright orange yellow, ruffled, 7-9 cm., 35 petals, high-centered, borne mostly solitary, moderate fragrance; recurrent; foliage medium size, dark green, glossy; prickles moderate, average, almost straight, brown; compact, bushy, medium growth; PPAF; [Julie Newmar™ × Top Notch™]; intr. 2007

'Wekjuvoo' ('Raymond Kopa', Chris Evert™, 'Souvenire') HT, ob, 1996, Carruth, Tom; flowers clear orange-yellow blushing red, reverse with less blush, full, high-centered, borne singly, moderate fruity fragrance; foliage clean, medium size, dark green, semi-glossy; prickles moderate; upright, compact, medium (3-4 ft.) growth; PP10071; [Voodoo™ × ('Katherine Loker' × 'Gingersnap')]

'Weklappell' (Louis J. Appell, Jr.™) HT, w, 2003, Carruth, Tom; buds long, elegant; flowers pure white, 12-14 cm., full, borne in small clusters, slight fragrance; foliage large, dark green, semi-glossy; prickles moderate, average, almost straight, greenish brown; growth upright, compact (100-120 cm.); garden decoration; [Moonstone™ × Sunset Celebration™]; intr. 2004

'Weklezpat' (Jean Pierre Coffe®, Julie Newmar™) HT, yb, 2003, Carruth, Tom; flowers soft gold blushing deep pink, reverse soft gold, ruffled, 12-14 cm., full, borne mostly solitary, intense fragrance; foliage medium size, light green, matte; prickles moderate, average, almost straight, light greenish brown; growth upright, slightly spreading, medium (120-150 cm.); garden decoration; PP17175; [Livin' Easy™ × St Patrick™]; intr. 2004

'Weklips' (Little Paradise™) Min, m, 1988, Carruth, Tom; flowers deep lavender, blushing purple, reverse deep lavender, aging lighter, 20 petals, high-centered, slight fragrance; foliage small, dark green, semi-glossy, disease-resistant; prickles nearly straight, small, yellow-brown; upright, medium, vigorous, abundant growth; no fruit; PP7580; [Shocking Blue® × 'Helen Boehm']; intr. 1991

'Wekmar' ('Imagination') HT, ab, 1992, Winchel, Joseph F.; bud large, shapely; flowers apricot orange, yellow reverse, good distinct bicoloration,, 3-3½ in., 26-30 petals, borne mostly singly; foliage large, clean, medium green, semi-glossy; some prickles; medium (100-130 cm.), attractive, compact, upright, bushy growth; PP8414; ['Marmalade' × seedling]; intr. 1993

'Wekmeredoc' (Meredith™) HT, lp, 2002, Carruth, Tom; flowers very pastel pink, 10-12 cm., full, borne mostly solitary, intense fragrance; foliage large, dark green, glossy; prickles moderate, average, straight, light brown; growth upright, medium (90-110 cm.); garden decorative; [Karen Blixen™ × 'New Zealand']; intr. 2002

'Wekmeyer' (Pearly Gates™) LCl, mp, 1999, Meyer, Lawrence; flowers pastel pearl pink, 5 in., very dbl., borne in small clusters on old and new wood, intense spicy fragrance; foliage large, medium green, dull; few prickles; climbing, tall (9-12 ft.) growth; PP10640; [sport of 'America']; intr. 1999

'Wekmeymo' (Spring Fling™) Min, mr, 2006, Meyer, Lawrence; flowers bright clear red, 3-5 cm., single, borne mostly solitary; foliage small, dark green, glossy; prickles average, slightly hooked, beige, few; growth compact, short (30-45 cm.); garden decoration; [sport of Gizmo™]; intr. 2006

'Wekmoomar' (Falling in Love™) HT, pb, 2006, Carruth, Tom; flowers medium to soft pink, reverse creamy pink, long-lasting, 11-13 cm., full, high-centered, borne mostly solitary, moderate rose and fruit fragrance; recurrent; foliage large, dark green, semi-glossy; prickles medium large, slightly hooked, greenish beige, numerous; growth upright, and bushy, medium (125-140 cm.); garden decoration; [Moonstone™ × Marilyn Monroe™]; intr. 2007

'Wekmorfis' (Route 66™) S, m, 2001, Carruth, Tom; flowers velvet black/purple with white eye, 5-7 cm., single, borne in large clusters, Intense clove fragrance; foliage medium size, dark green, semi-glossy; prickles few, average, almost straight, light brown; growth bushy, medium (90-110 cm.); garden decorative; PP15374; [(('Sweet Chariot' × Blue Nile®) × 'Purple Splendor') × ((International Herald Tribune® × *R. soulieana* derivative) × ('Sweet Chariot' × Blue Nile®))]; intr. 2001

'Wekonine' (Cajun Moon™) HT, w, 2001, Carruth, Tom; flowers white edged pink, 11-13 cm., full, high-centered, borne mostly solitary, slight fragrance; foliage large, dark green, semi-glossy; prickles very few, average, straight; growth upright, tall (140 to 170 cm.); garden decoration, exhibition; [Crystalline™ × 'Lynn Anderson']; intr. 2001

'Wekosomit' ('Jean Pierre Ferland', 'Mellow Yellow') HT, dy, 2000, Carruth, Tom; bud pointed to slightly ovoid; flowers solid yellow, 10-12 cm., 39-44 petals, cupped, borne mostly singly or in clusters of 2 or 3, moderate fruity fragrance; good repeat; foliage medium size, dark green, semi-glossy; prickles moderate; growth upright, vigorous, bushy, medium (110-150 cm.); PP14401; [O Sole Mio® × Midas Touch™]; intr. 2002

'Wekosunkora' ('Fernand Gignac', Truly Yours™) HT, lp, 2004, Carruth, Tom; flowers light salmon pink, 10-13 cm., full, borne mostly solitary, slight fragrance; recurrent; foliage large, medium green, matte; prickles moderate, medium, almost straight; growth very compact, medium (60-90 cm.); garden decoration; [((O Sole Mio® × seedling) × unknown) × 'Koronam']; intr. 2006

'Wekosupalz' (About Face™) Gr, ob, 2003, Carruth, Tom; flowers deep orange gold, reverse burnished red, 9-12 cm., full, borne mostly solitary, no fragrance; foliage large, dark green, semi-glossy; prickles moderate, average, almost straight, brown; growth upright, very vigorous, tall (180-200 cm.); garden decoration; [((O Sole Mio® × seedling) × Midas Touch™) × Hot Cocoa™]; intr. 2005

'Wekpaltlez' ('Hot Chocolate', 'Nubia', 'Kiwi', Hot Cocoa™) F, r, 2001, Carruth, Tom; flowers smoky orange with deep rust reverse, 7-9 cm., full, cupped, borne in small clusters, moderate fragrance; foliage large, dark green, glossy; prickles numerous, assorted sizes, straight, light brown; growth bushy, rounded, medium (90-115 cm.); garden decoration; PP15155; [(Playboy® × Altissimo®) × Livin' Easy™]; intr. 2003

'Wekpascisou' (Paul Ecke, Jr.™) S, ob, 2004, Carruth, Tom; flowers bright orange with a broad smoky edge, reverse deep orange, 2-3 in., single, borne in large, showy clusters, no fragrance; foliage medium size, dark green, semi-glossy, disease-resistant; prickles average, straight; growth spreading, medium (130 to 150 cm.); garden decoration; PPAF; [(Playboy® × Altissimo®) × ('Santa Claus' × (International Herald Tribune® × *R. soulieana* derivative))]; intr. 2005

'Wekpearl' ('Pearl') HT, w, 1999, Winchel, Joseph F.; flowers pearl white, 4½-5 in., dbl., borne mostly singly, slight fragrance; foliage large, dark green, glossy; prickles moderate; upright, bushy, medium (4-5 ft.) growth; PP13115; [unknown × unknown]; intr. 1999

'Wekpegjuc' (Heather Lenkin™) F, ab, 2007, Carruth, Tom; flowers upper apricot-yellow, reverse yellow, , 8-10 cm., full, old-fashioned, borne in small clusters, moderate fruity fragrance; foliage medium, medium green, very glossy; prickles average, almost straight, brown, moderate; growth compact, medium (90-120 cm.); garden decoration; [seedling × Julia Child™]; intr. 2008

'Wekpipogop' (Pillow Fight™) S, w, 1999, Carruth, Tom; flowers bright white, 1½-2 in., dbl., rosette, borne in large clusters, intense honey and rose fragrance; floriferous; foliage medium size, dark green, glossy; few prickles; rounded, bushy, medium (30-36 in.) growth; PP13113; [Pink Pollyanna™ × 'Gourmet Popcorn']; intr. 2000

'Wekplagneze' ('Longueuil', Home and Family™) HT, w, 2002, Carruth, Tom; flowers pure white, 10-12 cm., full, borne mostly solitary, slight fragrance; foliage large, dark green, glossy; prickles few, average, pointed, brownish-green; stems long; very upright, medium (120-140 cm.) growth; PP14356; [(Playboy® × Lagerfeld™) × 'New Zealand']; intr. 2002

'Wekplapep' (Scentimental™) F, rb, 1999, Carruth, Tom; bud pointed to globular; flowers striped burgundy and white, or cream, or red, opening quickly, 4-4½ in., 25-30 petals, cupped, borne in small clusters, intense spicy & Damask fragrance; foliage large, quilted, medium green, semi-glossy; prickles moderate; compact, rounded, medium (3-4 ft.) growth; hips short, globular ; PP10126; [Playboy® × 'Peppermint Twist']; intr. 1997

'Wekplapic' ('Centenary of Federation', Betty Boop™) F, rb, 1999, Carruth, Tom; bud pointed; flowers rosy edged, yellow at base when fresh, fading to white; bright stamens, 4 in., 6-12 petals, borne in small cluster of 3 to 5, moderate fruity fragrance; floriferous; foliage medium size, dark green, glossy, dark red new growth; prickles moderate; rounded, bushy, medium (4 ft.) growth; PP11517; [Playboy® × 'Picasso']; intr. 1999

'Wekplasol' (Flutterbye™) S, yb, 1999, Carruth, Tom; flowers multicolor yellow, coral, orange, tangerine, pink, 1½-2 in., 5-9 petals, borne in large clusters, moderate spice fragrance; foliage medium size, dark green, glossy; prickles moderate; very large, rounded, fountainous growth; PP9715; [Playboy® × (*R. soulieana* derivative × Sunsprite); intr. 1996

'Wekpluroco' ('Purple Reign') S, m, 1997, Carruth, Tom; flowers irregularly striped magenta and white, 1½-2½ in., 8-14 petals, borne in large clusters; foliage large, dark green, glossy; spreading, medium (60-70 cm.)growth; ['Fragrant Plum' × 'Roller Coaster']; intr. 1997

'Wekprimsoul' (Sky's the Limit™) LCl, my, 2005, Carruth, Tom; flowers clear, pure yellow, ruffled, 8-10 cm., 20-25 petals, borne in large clusters, moderate fruity fragrance; free-flowering; foliage medium size, medium green, glossy; prickles moderate, average, almost straight, beige; climbing, tall (10-12 ft.) growth; garden decoration; PPAF; [Princess Marianna™ × *R. soulieana* derivative]; intr. 2007

'Wekpurosot' (Night Owl™) LCl, m, 2005, Carruth, Tom; flowers deep wine red, bright yellow stamens, 9-11 cm., single, borne in large clusters, moderate fragrance; foliage large, medium grayish-green, semi-glossy; prickles few, average, pointed, beige; growth spreading, long (to 200 cm.) climbing canes; garden decoration; PPAF; [((International Herald Tribune® × *R. soulieana* derivative) × ('Sweet Chariot' × Blue Nile®)) × 'Rosy Outlook']; intr. 2007

'Wekquahofa' (Ruffles & Flourishes™) HT, mp, 2007, Carruth, Tom; flowers pure even pink, 10-12 cm., very full, borne mostly solitary, very intense rose fragrance; foliage large, medium green, glossy; prickles below average, slightly hooked, beige, few; stems long, straight; growth upright, tall (130-150 cm.); garden decoration; [(Blue Nile® × ('Ivory Tower' × 'Angel Face')) × 'Home & Family']; intr. 2008

'Wekquaneze' ('Barbra Streisand') HT, m, 1999, Carruth, Tom; flowers lavender, blushing darker, slow opening, 3½-4 in., 25-30 petals, borne in small clusters, intense fragrance; foliage large, dark green, glossy; prickles moderate; upright, bushy, medium (3-4 ft.) growth; PP13120; [(Blue Nile® × ('Ivory Tower' × 'Angel Face')) × 'New Zealand']; intr. 2000

'Wekradler' (Lemon Meringue™) S, ly, 2003, Radler, William; flowers clear light yellow, 11-13 cm., dbl., borne in large clusters, intense spicy fragrance; foliage large, dark green, glossy, clean; prickles numerous, average, almost straight, brown; growth spreading, near climbing, tall (over 200 cm.); garden decoration; [sport of Autumn Sunset™]; intr. 2005

'Wekrera' ('City of San Diego') S, rb, 2000, Carruth, Tom; flowers cherry red, reverse lighter red, finishing purple-red, 2-3 in., dbl., borne in large clusters, slight fragrance; foliage medium size, medium green, glossy; spreading, bushy (5-6 ft.) growth; PP13511; ['Red Fairy' × Raven™]; intr. 2001

'Wekrigoyelo' (Gentle Giant™) HT, pb, 2005, Carruth, Tom; flowers cerise pink with a yellow base, 12-14 cm., 30 petals, borne mostly solitary, slight fragrance; foliage large, light green, matte; prickles few, average, slightly hooked, beige; stems very long; growth upright, medium (120 to 150 cm.); garden decoration; ['Rina Hugo' × seedling]; intr. 2006

'Wekroalt' ('Crazy For You', 'Hanabi', Fourth of July™) LCl, rb, 1999, Carruth, Tom; flowers velvety red and white striped, ruffled, 4-4½ in., 10-16 petals, borne in medium to large clusters, moderate apple fragrance; reliable repeat; foliage large, deep green, glossy; prickles moderate; climbing, tall (10 ft.) growth; PP11518; ['Roller Coaster' × Altissimo®]; intr. 1999

'Wekrorobluni' (Della Reese™) HT, m, 2003, Carruth, Tom; flowers magenta, 11-14 cm., full, borne mostly solitary, intense fragrance; foliage large, dark green, glossy; prickles moderate, medium, almost straight, light brown; growth upright, tall (120-140 cm.); garden decoration; PPAF; ['The Roseanne Rose' × Blue Nile®]; intr. 2005

'Wekrosopela' (Candy Land™) LCl, pb, 2006, Carruth, Tom; flowers rose pink with yellow-white stripes, 9-11 cm., dbl., hybrid tea form, borne in large clusters, recurrent; foliage large, bright medium green, glossy; prickles average, almost straight, brown, moderate; growth spreading, climbing, canes up to 200 cm. long; garden decoration; ['Rosy Outlook' × 'Pretty Lady']; intr. 2007

'Weksacquem' S, mr, Carruth, Tom; intr. 2006

'Weksacsodor' ('The Schofield Rose', Jacob's Ladder™) LCl, dr, 2003, Carruth, Tom; flowers clear red, 12-14 cm., 8-14 petals, borne in large clusters, slight fragrance; foliage extremely large, dark green, glossy; prickles moderate, large, almost straight, greenish brown; growth upright, free standing pillar, tall (170-200 cm.); garden decoration; PPAF; ['Santa Claus' × R. soulieana derivative]; intr. 2003

'Weksacsoul' (Be-Bop™) S, rb, 2003, Carruth, Tom; flowers light red with a large yellow eyezone, reverse yellow, 5½-7 cm., single, borne in large rounded clusters, slight fragrance; foliage medium size, medium green, semi-glossy; prickles moderate, average, almost straight, light tan; growth spreading, medium (80-100 cm.); garden decoration; ['Santa Claus' × R. soulieana derivative]; intr. 2003

'Weksactrumi' (Ruby Ruby™) Min, mr, 2003, Carruth, Tom; buds shapely; flowers stable cherry red, 3-4 cm., full, high-centered, borne in large clusters, slight fragrance; recurrent; foliage small, dark green, glossy; prickles average, almost straight; growth bushy, slightly spreading, medium (45-60 cm.); garden decoration; PP15066; ['Santa Claus' × (Trumpeter® × Red Minimo™)]; intr. 2004

'Weksamsou' (All Ablaze™) LCl, mr, 1999, Carruth, Tom; bud short, ovoid; flowers medium cherry red, ruffled, 4 in., 35 petals, borne in small clusters, slight spice fragrance; foliage medium size, dark green, semi-glossy; vigorous (12 ft.) growth; PP13107; ['Don Juan' × ((R. soulieana × unknown) × Trumpeter®)]; intr. 2000

'Weksanpoly' ('Red Rhapsody', City of San Francisco™) F, mr, 2000, Carruth, Tom; flowers clear, lasting, pure red, ruffled petals, 3-4 in., dbl., borne in small clusters; foliage medium size, dark green, semi-glossy; prickles moderate; compact (80-100 cm.), bushy growth; PP13513; ['Santa Claus' × (Playboy® × 'Olympiad')]

'Wekscemala' ('Anna Leese', Chihuly™) F, rb, 2003, Carruth, Tom; flowers yellow blushing to orange, sometimes with subtle striping, finishing red, reverse more yellow with less blue, 9-11 cm., dbl., borne in small clusters, slight fragrance; foliage medium size, dark green, glossy; prickles moderate, average, straight, brown; stems dark red when new; growth bushy, medium (100-120 cm.); garden decoration; PP15076; [Scentimental™ × 'Amalia']; intr. 2004

'Weksiamia' (Legends™) HT, mr, 2007, Carruth, Tom; flowers bright cherry red, very large, 14-18 cm., full, borne mostly solitary; foliage large, dark green, matte; prickles medium, angled downward, greenish-beige, few; growth upright, medium (110-130 cm.); garden decoration: [(City of San Francisco™ × 'Olympiad') × ('Amalia' × ('Ingrid Bergman' × All That Jazz™))]; good color stability, large foliage cups slightly downward; intr. 2009

'Wekslats' ('Pink Crystal') HT, m, Wathen; intr. 1998

'Weksmopur' (Ebb Tide™) F, m, 2004, Carruth, Tom; flowers deep smoky purple, 8-10 cm., full, old-fashioned, borne in small clusters, intense clove fragrance; foliage medium size, dark green, semi-glossy; prickles average, almost straight; growth upright, medium (60 to 80 cm.); garden decoration: [(('Sweet Chariot' × Blue Nile®) × 'Stephen's Big Purple') × ((International Herald Tribune® × R. soulieana derivative) × ('Sweet Chariot' × Blue Nile®))]; intr. 2006

'Weksnacare' (Space Odyssey™) Min, rb, 1999, Carruth, Tom; flowers red with white eye, reverse white, 1-1½ in., semi-dbl., shallow cup, borne in small clusters, slight fragrance; recurrent; foliage small, dark green, glossy; few prickles; compact, spreading, low (16-20 in.) growth; PP13514; ['Santa Claus' × 'Times Square']; intr. 2000

'Weksproulses' (Honey Dijon™) Gr, r, 2003, Sproul, James; flowers golden tan, 10-12 cm., full, classic, borne in small clusters, intense fragrance; foliage medium size, dark green, glossy; prickles moderate, average, almost straight, brown; growth upright, vigorous, medium (120-140 cm.); garden decoration; [Stainless Steel™ × 'Singin' In The Rain']; intr. 2005

'Wekstephitsu' ('Outta the Blue') S, m, 2000, Carruth, Tom; flowers magenta, reverse magenta and yellow, aging to blue lavender, 9-11 cm., full, old-fashioned, borne in small clusters; foliage medium size, medium green, matte; prickles moderate; upright, bushy, medium (120-140 cm.) growth; PP13449; ['Stephen's Big Purple' × (International Herald Tribune® × R. soulieana derivitive)]; intr. 2001

'Weksunspat' (Marilyn Monroe™) HT, ab, 2001, Carruth, Tom; bud greenish; flowers soft apricot, 10-12 cm., full, high-centered, borne mostly solitary, no fragrance; foliage medium size, medium green, semi-glossy; prickles moderate, assorted sizes, almost straight, light brown; growth upright to spreading, medium (110-125 cm.); garden decoration; PP14398; [Sunset Celebration™ × 'Saint Patrick']

'Weksunvoye' ('2004 Better Homes & Gardens Rose', Sunstruck™) HT, ab, 2004, Carruth, Tom; flowers apricot gold edged darker, reverse apricot gold with a yellow fan veination, 11-14 cm., full, high-centered, borne mostly solitary, slight fruity fragrance; recurrent; foliage large, dark green, semi-glossy; prickles medium, straight; stems long; growth upright, medium (140-160 cm.); garden decoration; [Sunset Celebration™ × (Voodoo™ × seedling)]; intr. 2005

'Wekswetrup' ('ITV 50th Anniversary Coronation Street Rose', Mary Adrienne™, 'Traditional Home Rose 2001') S, op, 2001, Carruth, Tom; flowers coral pink, deepening in cool weather, 5-7 cm., semi-dbl., borne in large clusters, somewhat pendulous, slight fragrance; foliage light green, matte; prickles moderate, small, nearly straight, light brown; growth bushy, medium (80-100 cm.); garden decorative; ['Sweet Chariot' × Trumpeter®]; intr. 2002

'Weksybil' ('Heartbreaker') Min, pb, 1989, Carruth, Tom; bud pointed; flowers deep pink with white base, small, dbl., high-centered, borne in sprays of 3 - 5; foliage small, dark green, glossy; prickles nearly straight, small, dark red-brown; upright, bushy, medium, vigorous growth; hips globular, small, dark orange; PP7588; [Crystalline™ × Magic Carrousel®]; intr. 1990

'Wektorcent' ('City of Carlsbad', 'Hanky Panky') F, ob, 2000, Carruth, Tom; flowers orange striped white, 9-11 cm., dbl., borne in small clusters, slight fragrance; foliage large, dark green, glossy; prickles moderate; upright, bushy (80-120 cm.) growth; PP13512; ['Rosy Outlook' × Scentimental™]; intr. 2001

'Wektorroc' ('Rosy Outlook') LCl, pb, 1999, Carruth, Tom; flowers deep pink striped white, large, dbl., borne in large clusters, slight fragrance; foliage large, dark, green, glossy; prickles moderate; spreading, climbing, tall (10-12 ft.) growth; hardy; ['Tournament of Roses' × 'Roller Coaster']; intr. 1999

'Wekuz' (Columbus™) F, dp, 1990, Carruth, Tom; bud ovoid, pointed; flowers deep rose pink, fading very little, large, 28-35 petals, high-centered, borne usually singly, slight fragrance; foliage large, medium green, dull; prickles almost straight, slightly hooked, medium, pinkish-brown; bushy, medium growth; PP8183; [seedling × Bridal Pink™]; intr. 1991

'Wekvoosun' (We Salute You™) HT, op, 2005, Carruth, Tom; buds long; flowers opening orange, aging to pink, 12-14 cm., 30-35 petals, high-centered, classic, borne mostly solitary, moderate fragrance; recurrent; foliage large, very dark green, glossy; prickles moderate, average, slightly hooked, beige; upright, medium (110 to 130 cm) growth; PPAF; [Voodoo™ × Sunset Celebration™]; intr. 2006

'Wekvossutono' (Julia Child™) F, my, 2005, Carruth, Tom; flowers butter gold, 8-10 cm., full, cupped, old-fashioned, borne in small clusters, intense sweet licorice fragrance; free-flowering; foliage medium size, medium green, very glossy; prickles medium, straight; growth compact, medium (65-80 cm.); garden decoration; [((Voodoo™ × *R. soulieanna* derivative) × 'Summerwine') × Top Notch™]; intr. 2006

'Wekvosuimp' ('Evelyn Lauder', Miami Moon™) F, op, 2000, Carruth, Tom; flowers shrimp or seashell pink, ruffled, 10-13 cm., 30-35 petals, borne in small clusters, slight spice fragrance; foliage large, medium green, semi-glossy, clean; prickles numerous, variable in length, straight; growth upright, compact, rounded, medium (80-110 cm.); garden decorative; PP13509; [(Voodoo™ × (*R. soulieana* × unknown)) × 'Impatient']; intr. 2002

'Wekwapunk' (Pennies from Heaven™) Cl Min, r, 2006, Carruth, Tom; flowers smoky lavender-brown and orange blend, reverse similar but slightly lighter, 3-5 cm., semi-dbl., borne in small clusters; foliage small, dark green, glossy; prickles moderate, small, straight, beige; growth spreading, climbing, canes up to 150 cm. long; garden decoration; PPAF; ['What a Peach' × Easy Going™]; intr. 2007

'Wekwesflut' (Spice So Nice™) LCl, ab, 2000, Carruth, Tom; bud mossed, pointed to somewhat ovoid; flowers ruffled petals of apricot orange with yellow reverse and eye, 3-4 in., 30 petals, cupped, borne in clusters on old and new wood.; recurrent; foliage large, dark green (dark red new growth), glossy, quilted; prickles moderate, medium-large, straight; stems strong, short to medium; growth spreading, tall (180-250 cm.); garden decorative, climber; hips rounded to globular ; PP16154; [Westerland® × Flutterbye™]; intr. 2002

'Wekwesytpla' (Louise Hay™) HT, ab, 2007, Carruth, Tom; bud very long, elegant; flowers upper even apricot, , large, 11-13 cm., dbl., borne mostly solitary; foliage large, dark green, semi-glossy, clean; prickles average, almost straight, yellow-brown, moderate; stems long; growth spreading, medium (130-150 cm.); garden decoration; [We Salute You™ × (Secret™ × 'Pretty Lady')]; intr. 2008

'Wekwinwin' ('Carnival', 'Ninety-Niner', 'Rosie O'Donnell', 'Win Win', 'Drama Queen', 'New Era', 'Cédrika Provencher') HT, rb, 1999, Winchel, Joseph F.; bud pointed to ovoid, long; flowers velvety scarlet red with creamy yellow reverse, 5-5½ in., 30-35 petals, high-centered, borne mostly singly, slight tea fragrance; recurrent; foliage large, dark green, matte to semi-glossy; prickles several, long, almost straight, angled downward; strong, long stems; medium, upright, slightly spreading growth; PP11382; [unknown × unknown]; intr. 1998

'Wekyegi' ('Lemon Drop') Min, my, 1999, Carruth, Tom; flowers clear yellow, 1-1½ in., full, borne in small clusters, slight fragrance; foliage medium size, light green, semi-glossy; few prickles; upright, compact, medium (20-24 in.) growth; PP14555; [Gingerbread Man™ × seedling]; intr. 1999

'Wekyosotono' (Carol Burnett™) F, ab, 2008, Carruth, Tom; bud long; flowers even apricot-yellow, retaining color well, 8-10 cm., full, high-centered, borne in small clusters; foliage medium, very dark green, glossy; prickles average, almost straight, greenish-beige, moderate; growth upright, medium (90-120 cm.); garden decoration; [(seedling × O Sole Mio®) × Top Notch™]; intr. 2006

'Welabb' ('Abby's Angel') MinFl, dy, 2007, Wells, Verlie W.; flowers deep yellow, red on edge on first few petals, reverse deep yellow, 3 in., full, borne mostly solitary; foliage medium size, dark green, semi-glossy; prickles hooked, few; growth upright, tall (3½-4 ft.); exhibition; [seedling × Bees Knees™]; intr. 2007

'WElan' HT, pb, 1973, Wyant

'Welangel' (Angelica Renae™) Min, pb, 1996, Wells, Verlie W.; flowers bright medium pink blend, full, high-centered, borne mostly singly, slight fragrance; foliage medium size, dark green, matte; some prickles; upright, bushy (24-30 in.) growth; [Anita Charles™ × seedling]; intr. 1996

'Welbell' ('Lovely Lynda') HT, my, 2005, Wells, Verlie W.; flowers light to medium yellow, 4½-5 in., full, borne mostly solitary; foliage medium size, dark green, semi-glossy; prickles moderate, ½ in., straight; growth upright, bushy, medium (4 ft.); garden decorative, exhibition; [seedling × seedling]; intr. 2005

'Welbest' ('Best of 04') Min, yb, 2005, Verlie W. Wells; flowers yellow orange blend, reverse orange edge to yellow, 1½-1¾ in., dbl., borne mostly solitary; foliage medium size, medium green, semi-glossy; prickles ¼ in., hooked; growth upright, slightly spreading, medium (2½ ft.); garden, exhibition; [seedling × seedling]; intr. 2004

'Welbliss' ('Autumn Bliss') MinFl, yb, 2005, Wells, Verlie, W.; flowers odd shade of yellow, 1 in., full, borne mostly solitary; foliage medium size, medium green, semi-glossy; prickles ¼ in., straight, few; growth upright, medium (2-3 ft.); exhibition, garden decorative; [seedling × seedling]; intr. 2005

'Welblue' ('Memphis Blues') MinFl, m, 2005, Wells, Verlie W.; flowers mauve to red, reverse light mauve, 1½ in., dbl., borne mostly solitary; foliage medium size, dark green, glossy; prickles few, 3/8 in., hooked; growth spreading, medium (2-3 ft.); exhibition, garden decorative; [seedling × 'Memphis Magic']; intr. 2005

'Welbud' ('Bosum Buddy') HT, op, 2003, Wells, Verlie W.; flowers full, borne mostly solitary; foliage medium size, dark green, semi-glossy; prickles ¼ in., hooked; growth upright, medium; garden, exhibition; ['Friendship' × 'Dolly Parton']; intr. 2003

'Welbyrd' ('Yellow Bird') MinFl, my, 2004, Verlie W. Wells; flowers medium yellow, reverse light yellow, 2-2½ in., full, high-centered, borne in small clusters, slight fragrance; foliage medium size, medium green, semi-glossy; prickles moderate, ¼ in., straight; bushy, medium growth; garden decoration, exhibition; [seedling × seedling]; intr. 2003

'Welcajun' ('Memphis Cajun') MinFl, m, 2006, Wells, Verlie W.; flowers light mauve, reverse darker, 1¾ in., full, borne in small clusters; foliage medium size, dark green, glossy; prickles 3/8 in., hooked, moderate; growth upright, medium (2½ ft.); garden, exhibition; [seedling × seedling]; intr. 2006

'Welcard' ('Brighton Cardinals') Min, rb, 2005, Wells, Verlie W.; flowers white with red edges, reverse white, ¾ in., full, high-centered, borne mostly solitary; foliage medium size, medium green, semi-glossy; prickles ¼ in., straight, moderate; growth upright, medium (2-3 ft.); exhibition, garden decorative; [seedling × seedling]; intr. 2005

'Welchoice 0377' ('First Choice') MinFl, w, 2007, Wells, Verlie W.; flowers white with a slight mauve pink edge, 2½ in., dbl., borne mostly solitary; foliage medium, medium green, semi-glossy;

prickles ½ in., straight, red, moderate; growth upright, medium (3 ft.); garden decoration, exhibition; ['Regina Lee' × seedling]; intr. 2008

'Welch's Multiflora' (strain of *R. multiflora*), w; thornless; sometimes used as understock;

'Welco' ('Ashgrove Jubilee') HT, pb, 1991, Welsh, Eric; flowers cream, shading to deep rose at edges, 30 petals, classic hybrid tea, borne singly, slight fragrance; foliage thick, shiny, dark green, obtuse at base; tall, upright growth; ['Mascot' × ((seedling × 'Red Lion') × 'Silver Lining')]; intr. 1990

'Welcom' ('Spring's A Comin'') MinFl, pb, 2001, Wells, Verlie; flowers white with pink edge, 2 in., dbl., high-centered, borne mostly solitary; foliage medium size, dark green, semi-glossy; prickles medium, hooked, few; growth upright, tall (3-4 ft.); garden decorative, exhibition; [seedling × seedling]; intr. 2002

'Welcome' HT, mp, 1948, Dickson, A.; bud ovoid; flowers glistening rose-pink, very large, 35 petals, high-centered; foliage leathery; vigorous, upright, bushy growth

'Welcome Guest' HT, ab, 1985, Cox, Arthur George; flowers apricot with a tinge of pink around edges of petals; [sport of 'Jan Guest']; intr. 1984

'Welcome Home' -- See 'Andwel'

'Welcome Home' LCl, pb, Kordes; intr. 2002

Welcome Home™ -- See 'Jacsumio'

'Welcome Stranger' F, my, 1968, Fankhauser; flowers large, single; foliage extra large, glossy, leathery; very vigorous, compact growth; ['Ophelia, Climbing' × Allgold®]

'Welcord' ('Cherry Cordial') Min, rb, 1997, Wells, Verlie W.; flowers medium, bright red with white reverse, very dbl., borne mostly singly; foliage medium size, dark green, semi-glossy; upright, medium growth; [Magic Carrousel® × seedling]; intr. 1997

'Weldream' ('Brandon's Dream') HT, pb, 2003, Wells, Verlie W.; flowers large, full, borne mostly solitary, intense fragrance; foliage large, medium green, semi-glossy; prickles 5/8 in., straight; growth upright, tall; garden decoration; [seedling × seedling]; intr. 2003

'Weldust' ('Dusty Red') Min, dr, 2003, Wells, Verlie W.; flowers full, borne mostly solitary; foliage medium size, dark green, semi-glossy; prickles ¼ in., hooked, moderate; growth upright, medium (18-24 in.); garden, exhibition; [seedling × seedling]; intr. 2002

'Welfreck' ('Freckle Face') Min, pb, 2003, Wells, Verlie W.; flowers pink with speckles, reverse white, 1-1½ in., full, borne mostly solitary, slight fragrance; foliage medium size, dark green, semi-glossy; prickles ¼ in., hooked, moderate; growth upright, medium (18-24 in.); garden, exhibition; [seedling × seedling]; intr. 2002

'Welfull' ('Wonderful') MinFl, pb, 2003, Wells, Verlie W.; flowers pink with yellow base, 3 in., full, borne mostly solitary, intense fragrance; foliage medium size, medium green, semi-glossy; prickles ¼ in., hooked; growth upright, tall (36 in.); garden, exhibition; [seedling × seedling]; intr. 2002

'Welgirl' ('Grandmaw's Girl') Min, mp, 2003, Wells, Verlie W.; flowers light pink, reverse light pink, 1¼ in., dbl., borne mostly solitary; foliage medium size, dark green, semi-glossy; prickles ¼ in., hooked, few; growth upright, tall (24-36 in.); garden, exhibition; [seedling × seedling]; intr. 2002

'Welglow 0232' ('Sunglow') MinFl, my, 2007, Wells, Verlie W.; flowers large, single, borne in small clusters; foliage large, medium green, semi-glossy; prickles 1 cm., straight, few; growth upright, medium (3 ft.); garden decoration, exhibition; [seedling × seedling]; intr. 2008

'Welgold' F, my, Welsh; bud deep golden yellow; intr. 1999

'Welgood' ('Looking Good') HT, pb, 2004, Wells, Verlie W.; flowers large, very full, borne in small clusters, slight fragrance; foliage medium size, medium green, semi-glossy; prickles ¼ in., hooked; growth upright, medium; exhibition; [seedling × 'mixed hybrid tea pollen']; intr. 2004

'Welgrace 0656' ('Emma Grace') Min, ob, 2007, Wells, Verlie W.; flowers yellow-orange, 1½ in., dbl., borne mostly solitary; foliage medium, medium green, semi-glossy; prickles ¼ in., hooked, few; growth upright, medium (3 ft.); garden decoration, exhibition; [Bees Knees™ × seedling]; intr. 2008

'Welharp 1999' ('Deford Bailey') F, mr, 2008, Wells, Verlie W.; flowers medium red, reverse lighter, 3½ in., full, high-centered, borne mostly solitary; foliage medium, medium green, matte; prickles ¼ in., slightly hooked, few; growth upright, medium (3 ft.); [seedling × seedling]; intr. 2008

'Welhigh' ('High Ambition') MinFl, ab, 2006, Wells, Verlie W.; flowers light apricot, reverse lighter apricot, 1¾ in., full, borne mostly solitary; foliage medium size, medium green, semi-glossy; prickles 5/8 in., straight, moderate; growth upright, medium (36-45 in.); garden decorative, exhibition; [seedling × seedling]; intr. 2006

'Welhis 0464' ('Memphis Bell') Min, rb, 2007, Wells, Verlie W.; flowers red, white at base, medium, dbl., blooms borne mostly solitary; foliage medium, dark green, glossy; prickles ½ in., straight, few; growth upright, medium (2½ ft.); exhibition, garden decoration; [seedling × seedling]; intr. 2008

'Welhonor' ('Ground Zero') HT, pb, 2002, Wells, Verlie W.; flowers white with pink edge, 3½-4½ in., full, borne mostly solitary, intense fragrance; foliage medium size, dark green, semi-glossy; prickles small, straight, moderate; growth upright, medium; garden decorative, exhibition; [seedling × 'Admiral Rodney']; intr. 2002

'Welhugh's' ('Fitzhugh's Diamond') MinFl, yb, 2005, Wells, Verlie W.; flowers yellow base with pink & white edge, 1½ in., full, borne mostly solitary, no fragrance; foliage medium size, dark green, semi-glossy; prickles 1/16 in., hooked; growth upright, medium (3½ ft.); garden and show; ['Wonderful' × seedling]; intr. 2005

'Welin' Min, dr, Wells, Whit; intr. 2005

'Welinspir' ('My Inspiration', 'Regina Lee's Sister') MinFl, w, 2007, Wells, Verlie W.; flowers white with pink edge, reverse creamy white, 2½-3 in., full, borne mostly solitary; foliage medium size, dark green, semi-glossy; prickles 3/8 in., hooked, few; growth upright, medium (3 ft.); exhibition; [seedling × 'Soroptimist International']; intr. 2007

'Welira' ('Woman's Day') F, pb, Welsh, Eric; intr. 1993

'Welivory' ('Wells' White Ivory', 'White Ivory') HT, w, 2003, Wells, Verlie W.; flowers ivory white, 4½ in., full, borne mostly solitary, intense fragrance; foliage medium size, dark green, semi-glossy; prickles 5/8 in., straight; growth upright, tall; garden, exhibition; [seedling × seedling]; intr. 2003

'Weliz' HT, mr, 1987, Welsh, Eric; intr. 1987

'Weljoy 0505' ('Joyful') MinFl, pb, 2007, Wells, Verlie W.; flowers pink and white, reverse creamy white, 3 in., dbl., borne mostly solitary; foliage medium, medium green, semi-glossy; prickles 1 cm., slightly hooked, few; growth upright, medium (3 ft.); garden decoration, exhibition; [seedling × seedling]; intr. 2008

'Welking' ('Memphis King') MinFl, dr, 2002, Wells, Verlie W.; flowers bright, dark red, reverse red with orange base, medium, full, high-centered, borne singly and in small clusters, slight fragrance; foliage medium size, medium green, semi-glossy; prickles moderate, ¼ to ½ in., hooked; growth upright, medium; exhibition; [seedling × seedling]; intr. 2003

'Well-Being' S, yb, Harkness; flowers yellow centers blushed orange towards the rim, 4 in., 30 petals, open, cupped, borne in clusters of about five blooms, intense citrus, licorice and cloves fragrance; growth upright, tall (4-5 ft.); PPAF; intr. 2004

'Well Done' Min, my; flowers magnolia yellow, full, cupped, borne in clusters, moderate fragrance; free-flowering; robust (24 in.) growth

'Wellady' ('Louisville Lady') MinFl, dp, 2003, Wells, Verlie W.; flowers deep pink, reverse lighter, long-lasting, 2 in., full, high-centered, borne mostly solitary, slight fragrance; foliage large, dark green, glossy; prickles ¼ in., hooked; growth spreading, bushy, tall (36 in.); garden, exhibition; [seedling × seedling]; intr. 2002

'Wellee' ('Regina Lee') MinFl, rb, 2005, Verlie W. Wells; intr. 2004

'Wellee' ('Dorris Lee') Min, ab, 1994, Wells, Verlie W.; flowers apricot blend, large, full, borne singly and in small clusters, moderate fragrance; foliage dark green, semi-glossy; some prickles; medium, upright growth; [seedling × Party Girl™]; intr. 1994

'Wellesley' HT, dp, 1905, Montgomery, A.; flowers dark rosy pink, large, dbl.; ['Bridesmaid' × 'Liberty']

'Wellington' C, m, 1832, Calvert; flowers crimson-rose, medium, full, cupped; growth branching; sometimes classed as HGal

'Well's Climber' ('Well's Pink and White Climber') LCl, pb, Wells; intr. 1994

'Wells' Mauve' HT, m, Wells; intr. 2007

'Well's Pink and White Climber' -- See 'Well's Climber'

'Wells' White Climber' -- See 'Mme d'Arblay'

'Wells' White Ivory' -- See 'Welivory'

'Wellsned' ('Lucille McWherter') Min, pb, 1997, Wells, Verlie W.; flowers medium, pink blend, 8-14 petals; foliage medium size, dark green, glossy; upright, medium (18-24in.) growth; [seedling × seedling]

'Wells's Garland' -- See 'The Garland'

'Wellworth' HT, pb, 1949, LeGrice; flowers peach shaded gold, pointed, 5 in., 40 petals; foliage grayish green; vigorous growth; ['Leontine Contenot' × 'Golden Dawn']

'Welmagic' ('Memphis Magic') MinFl, dr, 2005, Wells, Verlie W.; flowers dark red / almost black, reverse red, 2½ in., dbl., borne in small clusters; foliage medium size, medium green, semi-glossy; prickles ½ in., hooked; upright, medium growth; garden decorative, exhibition; [seedling × 'Black Magic']; intr. 2004

'Welmost' ('Almost Perfect') Min, dr, 2003, Wells, Verlie W.; flowers dark velvet red, reverse red with white base, 1 in., full, borne mostly solitary, slight fragrance; foliage small, dark green, semi-glossy; prickles 1/16 in., straight; growth upright, medium (18 in.); garden, exhibition; [seedling × seedling]; intr. 2002

'Welmusic' ('Memphis Music') MinFl, rb, 2006, Wells, Verlie W.; flowers dark red and yellow stripes, reverse yellow and red, 1½ in., dbl., borne mostly solitary; foliage medium size, medium green, semi-glossy; prickles few, 3/8 in., straight; growth upright, medium (24-30 in.); show and garden; [sport of 'Memphis Magic']; intr. 2006

'Welmy 0525' ('My Hometown') Min, rb, 2007, Wells, Verlie W.; flowers red with white eye, reverse red with white at base, 2 in., dbl., borne mostly solitary; foliage medium, dark green, semi-glossy; prickles ½ in., straight, moderate; growth upright, medium (2 ft.); garden decoration, exhibition; ['Cherry Cordial' × seedling]; intr. 2008

'Welnat' ('Nature's Wonder') MinFl, pb, 2007, Wells, Verlie W.; flowers deep pink, reverse creamy white, 1½ in., dbl., borne mostly solitary; foliage medium size, dark green, semi-glossy; prickles ¼ in., straight, few; growth upright, medium (3½ ft.); exhibition, garden decoration; [seedling × seedling]; intr. 2007

'Welnice 0501' ('White But Nice') Min, w, 2008, Wells, Verlie W.; flowers yellow with white base tinted pink, reverse yellow with white base, 2 in., full, borne mostly solitary; foliage medium, medium green, semi-glossy; prickles ¼ in., slightly hooked, red, moderate; growth bushy, medium (2 ft.); exhibition, garden decoration; [seedling × seedling]; intr. 2008

'Welodd' ('Simply Beautiful') MinFl, m, 2003, Wells, Verlie W.; flowers lavender blend, 2 in., dbl., borne mostly solitary, intense fragrance; foliage medium size, medium green, semi-glossy; prickles moderate, 3/16 in., straight; growth upright, medium (24 in.); garden, exhibition; ['Tom Brown' × seedling]; intr. 2002

'Welosb' ('Betty O') HT, pb, 2006, Wells, Verlie W.; flowers light to medium pink, reverse light pink, 3½ in., full, borne in small clusters; foliage medium size, dark green, semi-glossy; prickles 3/8 in., straight, moderate; growth upright, medium (4 ft.); garden, exhibition; ['Virginia' × unknown]; intr. 2006

'Welparty' ('Party Girl's Daughter') Min, pb, 2005, Wells, Verlie W.; flowers pink and yellow, reverse yellow, 1 in., dbl., borne in small clusters; foliage small, dark green, semi-glossy; prickles moderate, ¼ in., straight; growth compact, upright, medium (1½-2 ft.); garden decoration, exhibition; [Party Girl™ × unknown]; intr. 2005

'Welpin' ('Edmund Rice') HT, dp, 1992, Welsh, Eric; bud classic HT form; flowers light red, non-fading, petals pointed and reflexed, 5 in., 45-50 petals, high-centered, borne 5-7 per cluster and singly, moderate fragrance; repeats quickly; foliage very red when young, dark green, shiny, leathery; bushy, upright (4 ft.) growth; ['Red Lion' × 'Pink Silk']; intr. 1992

'Welpink' ('Peachy Pink') HT, pb, 2006, Wells, Verlie W.; flowers pink, reverse lighter, 4 in., dbl., borne mostly solitary; foliage medium size, medium green, semi-glossy; prickles 3/16 in., straight, moderate; growth upright, medium (4 ft.); garden decorative, exhibition; [seedling × seedling]; intr. 2006

'Welpretty' ('Pink-n-Pretty') Min, pb, 2007, Wells, Verlie W.; flowers medium pink, reverse dark pink, 2 in., dbl., borne mostly solitary or in sm; foliage medium size, medium green, semi-glossy; prickles ¼ in., straight, few; growth upright, medium (2½ ft.); exhibition, garden decorative; [seedling × seedling]; intr. 2007

'Welqueen' ('Memphis Queen') Min, w, 1997, Wells, Verlie W.; flowers medium, very full, borne mostly singly, slight fragrance; foliage medium size, dark green, glossy; upright, medium (60 cm.) growth; PP11645; [Miss Pearl™ × 'Pacesetter']; intr. 1997

'Welreg' ('Regina Lee') MinFl, rb, 2005, Verlie W. Wells; flowers white edged red, reverse creamy white, 1¾-2 in., full, borne mostly solitary, slight fragrance; foliage medium size, dark green, semi-glossy; prickles ¾ in., hooked; growth spreading, medium (2½ ft.); garden, exhibition; ['Soroptimist International' × seedling]; intr. 2004

'Welrose' ('The Guthrie Rose') MinFl, rb, 2006, Wells, Verlie W.; flowers red and yellow, reverse light red with white base, 1½ in, dbl., borne in small clusters; foliage medium size, dark green, semi-glossy; prickles 3/16 in., hooked, few; growth upright, bushy, medium (36-45 in.); garden decorative, exhibition; [seedling × 'Memphis King']; intr. 2006

'Welrum' ('Kathleen Rumble') Min, lp, 1994, Wells, Verlie W.; flowers pale pink, dbl., borne mostly singly, slight fragrance; foliage medium size, dark green, glossy; some prickles; medium (6 cm.), upright growth; [seedling × Miss Pearl™]; intr. 1994

'Welsam' ('Samantha Ruth') Min, yb, 1994, Wells, Verlie W.; flowers blend of cream, orange and pink, large, very full, high-centered, borne mostly singly, slight fragrance; foliage medium size, dark green, semi-glossy; some prickles; medium, upright growth; [(Party Girl™ × Magic Carrousel®) × seedling]; intr. 1994

'Welscot' ('Mr Lenard') MinFl, mp, 2007, Wells, Verlie W.; flowers reverse slightly lighter, 2¼ in., full, borne mostly solitary; foliage medium size, dark green, semi-glossy; prickles ¼ in., straight, brown, few; growth upright, medium (36-40 in.); exhibition; [seedling × seedling]; intr. 2007

Welsh Gold™ -- See 'Welwyn Garden Glory'

'Welsham 0600' ('Shameless') MinFl, rb, 2007, Wells, Verlie W.; flowers white at base, with red edge, reverse white with slight red edge, 2½ in., full, borne mostly solitary; foliage medium, dark green, semi-glossy; prickles 1 cm., slightly hooked, moderate; growth upright, medium (3½ ft.); exhibition, garden decoration; [seedling × seedling]; intr. 2008

'Welsun' ('Tennessee Sunset') MinFl, yb, 2002, Wells, Verlie W.; flowers pink with yellow base, medium, full, borne in small clusters, slight fragrance; foliage medium size, medium green, semi-glossy; prickles few, ¼ in., hooked; growth compact, medium; [seedling × seedling]; intr. 2002

'Weltenn' ('Tennessee Sunrise') MinFl, ob, 2001, Wells, Verlie; flowers 2½ in., full, borne mostly solitary, moderate fragrance; foliage medium size, dark green, semi-glossy; prickles moderate, short, straight; growth upright, medium (24-36 in.); garden decorative, exhibition; [seedling × seedling]; intr. 2002

'Weltmeister 90' HT, dp, Dräger; intr. 1990

'Welton' ('Ashton') MinFl, pb, 2005, Wells, Verlie W.; flowers light pink, reverse light pink edge, 1½-1¾ in., dbl., borne mostly solitary, no fragrance; foliage medium size, medium green, semi-glossy; prickles ¼ in., straight; growth compact, medium (2½ ft.); garden decorative, exhibition; [seedling × 'Louisville Lady']; intr. 2004

'Weltop' ('Rocky Top') MinFl, or, 2004, Verlie W. Wells; flowers orange, reverse lighter orange, 3 in., dbl., high-centered, borne mostly solitary, slight fragrance; foliage medium size, dark green, semi-glossy; prickles moderate, ¼ in., hooked; upright, medium growth; garden decoration, exhibition; [seedling × seedling]; intr. 2003

'Weltopcon' ('Top Contender') MinFl, dy, 2006, Wells, Verlie W.; flowers dbl., borne mostly solitary; foliage medium size, medium green, semi-glossy; prickles ¼ in., straight, few; growth upright, medium (36-40 in.); garden decorative, exhibition; [sport of 'Memphis Music']; intr. 2006

'Weltown' ('Tulsa Town') Min, ob, 2003, Wells, Verlie W.; flowers full, borne mostly solitary, intense fragrance; foliage medium size, dark green, semi-glossy; prickles ¼ in., straight; upright, medium growth; garden, exhibition; [seedling × seedling]; intr. 2003

'Weltroy' ('Dr Troy Garret') MinFl, mr, 2005, Wells, Verlie W.; flowers medium red, reverse light red, 2 in., full, high-centered, borne mostly solitary, moderate fragrance; foliage large, medium green, semi-glossy; prickles moderate, ¼ in., straight; growth upright, tall (3½ - 4 ft.); garden decorative, exhibition; [seedling × 'Memphis King']; intr. 2005

'Weltrue' ('Picture Perfect') MinFl, pb, 2007, Wells, Verlie W.; flowers medium pink with yellow base, reverse creamy white with yellow base, 3 in., full, borne mostly solitary; foliage medium size, dark green, semi-glossy; prickles ¼ in., straight, few; growth upright, medium (3 ft.); exhibition, garden decorative; [seedling × seedling]; intr. 2007

'Welvass' ('Loyal Vassal') MinFl, ob, 2007, Wells, Verlie W.; flowers medium orange, reverse yellow and darker orange, 1½-1¾ in., full, borne mostly solitary; foliage medium size, dark green, semi-glossy; prickles 3/8 in., straight, moderate; growth upright, tall; garden decoration, exhibition; [seedling × seedling]; intr. 2007

'Welwalt' ('Tennessee Waltz') Min, pb, 2005, Wells, Verlie W.; flowers white at base, pink edges, reverse white, 1½ in., semi-dbl., borne mostly solitary; foliage medium size, medium green, semi-glossy; prickles few, ¼ in., straight; growth upright, medium (2-3 ft.); garden decorative, exhibition; ['Figurine' × 'mixed pollen']; intr. 2005

'Welwife' ('My Wife Kathryn') HT, ob, 2005, Wells, Verlie W.; flowers orange blend, reverse yellow blend, 4½ in., full, borne in small clusters, moderate fragrance; foliage medium size, dark green, semi-glossy; prickles moderate, ½ in., hooked; growth upright, bushy, medium (4-5 ft.); garden decorative, exhibition; [seedling × 'Rosie O'Donnell']; intr. 2005

'Welwyn Garden Glory' ('Welsh Gold™') HT, ab, Harkness; bud short; flowers amber-apricot, large, dbl., cupped, flared, moderate fragrance; recurrent; upright growth; intr. 1996

'Welzero' ('Nine-Eleven') HT, mr, 2002, Wells, Verlie W.; flowers velvety dark red, 4 in., very full, borne mostly solitary, no fragrance; foliage medium size, dark green, semi-glossy; prickles few, hooked; growth upright, medium (4 ft.); exhibition, garden; [Alec's Red® × ('First Prize' × unknown)]; intr. 2002

'Wembley Stadium' F, dp

'Wemcor' ('Corinne's Choice') Min, w, 2004, Meagher, William E.; flowers 1¼ in., full, high-centered, star-shaped, borne mostly solitary; foliage medium size, dark green, matte; prickles 1/8 in., needle-like; growth bushy, medium (18 in.); garden decoration, exhibition; [Hot Tamale™ × 'Reiko']

'Wenche' HT, mr, 1997, Poole, Lionel; flowers large, very dbl., borne mostly singly; foliage medium size, dark green, semi-glossy; upright, medium growth; ['Silver Jubilee' × 'Loving Memory']

'Wenche' -- See 'Jakwen'

'Wendelien' F, mr, 1946, Leenders, M.; flowers cardinal-red, 4 in., 22 petals, globular, borne in clusters; foliage bright green; vigorous, branching growth; ['Donald Prior' × seedling]

'Wendy' -- See 'Zipwen'

'Wendy' -- See 'Sunwend'

'Wendy' -- See 'Para Ti'

'Wendy' Pol, mp, 1949, Heers; flowers pink, open, medium, dbl., borne in clusters; foliage soft, light green; moderately vigorous, upright growth; RULED EXTINCT 11/91; [Tip-Top® × 'Dorothy Perkins']

'Wendy' -- See 'Worcanter'

'Wendy Ackerman Rose' HT, ob; intr. 1998

'Wendy Barrie' Pol, op, 1936, Beckwith; flowers orange-salmon, well-formed, dbl.; vigorous, dwarf growth

'Wendy Cussons' HT, mr, 1960, Gregory; bud long, pointed; flowers rose-red, 5-6 in., 30 petals, high-centered, borne mostly singly, intense fragrance; recurrent; foliage leathery, glossy, dark; vigorous, well-branched growth; PP2104; believed to be Independence × Eden Rose; intr. 1960

'Wendy Cussons, Climbing' Cl HT, mr, 1967, Follen

'Wendy Duckett' F, mr, 1999, Jones, L.J.; flowers red cream, striking color, 1¼ in., full, borne in small clusters, slight fragrance; foliage small, medium green, glossy, impervious to rain; few prickles; upright, compact, medium growth; ['Sheri Anne' × ('Whippet' × 'Party Girl™')]

'Wendy Pease' -- See 'Debraf'

'Wendy van Wanten' F, ob, RvS-Melle; ['Madelon' × 'Patricia']; intr. 1994

Wenlock® -- See 'Auswen'

'Wenzel Geschwind, Climbing' Cl HT, m, 1940, Vogel, M.; flowers purple/pink, medium to large, dbl.; [sport of 'Wenzel Geschwind']

'Wenzel Geschwind' HT, m, 1902, Geschwind, R.; flowers purple/pink, medium to large, dbl., cupped, moderate fragrance; recurrent; upright (100 cm.), branching growth; ['Princesse de Sagan' × 'Comte de Bobrinsky']

'Weokay' ('Playmate') F, rb, 1987, Fonda, Henry; flowers vivid scarlet, yellow center, large, 5 petals, borne usually singly; foliage medium size, dark green, glossy; upright, bushy growth; [Playboy® × seedling]; intr. 1986

'Weopop' ('Gourmet Popcorn', 'Summer Snow') Min, w, 1987, Desamero, Luis; flowers pure white, medium, semi-dbl.; foliage large, dark green, glossy; upright, bushy growth; PP6809; [sport of 'Popcorn']; intr. 1986

'Werina' ('Tocade') Gr, ob, 1974, Weeks; bud urn-shaped; intr. 1975

'Werner Dirks' LCl, w, 1937, Kordes; bud long, pointed; flowers ivory-white, 4 in., dbl., high-centered, borne in clusters, moderate fragrance; foliage large, leathery, wrinkled; numerous prickles; long, strong stems; very vigorous, climbing growth; ['Mrs Pierre S. duPont' × 'Daisy Hill']

'Werner Otto' HT, my, 1995, Mungia, Larry; flowers medium yellow, 4-4½ in., 56 petals, borne mostly singly; foliage large, dark green, glossy; few prickles; medium, upright growth; [sport of 'Golden Fantasie']; intr. 1994

'Werner Teschendorff' F, op, 1949, Tantau; bud ovoid; flowers medium, dbl., cupped, borne in clusters; foliage glossy; vigorous, upright, bushy growth; ['Swantje' × 'Hamburg']

Werner von Blon® S, m, Hetzel; flowers bright lilac-pink, moderate fragrance; good repeat; intr. 1993

'Wesnianka' ('Spring') HT, w, 1941, Costetske; flowers white, base carmine-yellow; ['Mme Butterfly' × 'Mrs T. Hillas']

'Wessie Roos'   HT, mr, Kordes; bud pointed; flowers velvet red, brilliant red reverse, large, dbl., high-centered, slight fragrance; recurrent; foliage glossy; medium, rounded growth; intr. 1993

West Coast® -- See 'Macnauru'

'West Country'   F, rb, Gandy; flowers red and gold, borne in large trusses; recurrent; foliage light green; bushy, medium growth; intr. 2002

'West Grove'   HT, 1914, Dingee & Conard; ['Liberty' × 'Kaiserin Auguste Viktoria']

'Westbroekpark'   F, or, 1968, deRuiter; flowers medium, dbl., borne in clusters; foliage dark; [Orange Sensation® × Kimono®]

Westerland®   S, ab, 1976, Kordes; bud ovoid; flowers apricot-orange, 3-5 in., 20 petals, cupped, borne in clusters, intense rose, clove, spice fragrance; recurrent; foliage large, dark green, soft; vigorous, upright, climbing growth; ['Friedrich Worlein' × 'Circus']; intr. 1969

'Western Gold'   HT, my, 1932, Western Rose Co.; flowers clear yellow; [sport of 'Talisman']

Western Sun™   HT, dy, 1965, Poulsen, Niels D.; flowers deep yellow, 5 in., 40 petals, no fragrance; free-flowering; foliage dark green; moderate growth; [('Golden Scepter' × unknown) × 'Golden Sun']

'Western Sunlight' -- See 'Hadsun'

'Western Sunset'   F, yb, 1958, Silva; bud pointed; flowers yellow tipped pink, becoming pink and then mahogany-red, bor, 1½-2 in., 35 petals, cupped; foliage leathery; vigorous, upright growth; PP2191; ['Maxine' × 'Masquerade']

'Westfalen'   S, Scholle, E.; intr. 1969

'Westfalengold'   F, Noack, Werner; intr. 1979

'Westfalengruss'   F, mr, 1978, Hubner; bud ovoid; flowers fire-red, medium, dbl., foliage glossy; low, bushy growth

Westfalenpark® -- See 'Korplavi'

'Westfield Beauty'   HT, ab, 1923, Morse; bud long, pointed; flowers deep coppery apricot, tinted golden and salmon-pink, dbl.; ['Lady Pirrie' × 'Mme Edouard Herriot']

'Westfield Flame'   HT, or, 1925, Morse; bud long, pointed; flowers very deep flame, dbl.; ['Mme Edouard Herriot' × 'Diadem']

'Westfield Gem'   HT, dr, 1925, Morse; flowers dark maroon-crimson, dbl.; [sport of 'Col. Oswald Fitzgerald']

'Westfield Scarlet'   HT, mr, 1931, Morse; flowers clear scarlet, open, very large, dbl.; foliage leathery, dark; bushy growth; [sport of 'Lady Inchiquin']

'Westfield Star'   HT, w, 1922, Morse; bud sulphur yellow; flowers cream, fading white, flat, moderate fragrance; recurrent; strong, vigorous growth; [sport of 'Ophelia']

'Westfriesia'   F, dp, 1965, deVries; bud ovoid; flowers pink-red, small, very dbl., borne in clusters

'Westminster'   HT, rb, 1960, Robinson, H.; flowers red, gold base and reverse, large, 35 petals, loose, intense fragrance; recurrent; foliage dark; vigorous, tall growth; ['Gay Crusader' × 'Peace']

'Westminster 50th Anniversary' -- See 'Aguigolden'

'Westminster Pink'   HT, mp, Fryer, Gareth; flowers pink with touch of coral, large, dbl., high-centered, borne mostly singly, moderate fragrance; recurrent; foliage dark green, glossy; medium, rounded growth; intr. 1998

'Westmont'   Min, mr, 1959, Moore, Ralph S.; bud pointed; flowers bright red, 1½ in., semi-dbl.; foliage leathery, semi-glossy; small vigorous (12-18 in.), bushy growth; PP1950; [(R. wichurana × 'Floradora') × ('Oakington Ruby' × 'Floradora')]; intr. 1958

'Westward Ho!'   HT, rb, 1964, Allen, E.M.; flowers mahogany-red, reverse silver, 4½ in., 42 petals; foliage very dark; vigorous, upright, compact growth; ['Karl Herbst' × 'Pink Charming']

Westzeit®   F, ob, Noack; flowers orange with apricot and pink tones, 6 cm., dbl., cupped, borne in clusters; fast repeat; foliage dark green (new growth reddish), glossy; medium growth; intr. 2006

'Wetteriana'   F, or

'Wettra, Climbing'   Cl F, mr

'Wettra' ('Cherry Chinks')   F, mr, 1985, Rijksstation Voor Sierplantenteelt; flowers large, 20 petals, cupped, borne 4-15 per cluster, no fragrance; foliage dark, matte; prickles red; upright growth; ['Pink Puff' × 'Barcarolle']; intr. 1976

'Wezaprt' (Bronze Star™)   HT, ab, 2000, Weeks, O.L.; bud globular; flowers amber-apricot, reverse gold-apricot, petals scalloped, 4-5 in., 19-26 petals, cupped, borne mostly singly, intense spicy fragrance; recurrent; foliage large, medium green, semi-glossy; prickles numerous, 1 cm., hooked, brown; bushy, tall (4-5 ft.) growth; PP15020; ['Just Joey' × seedling]; intr. 2000

'Wezcanary' (Canary Diamond™)   HT, dy, 2002, Weeks, O.L.; flowers bright canary yellow, 4 in., dbl., borne mostly solitary, moderate fragrance; foliage large, dark green, semi-glossy; prickles few, average, curved; growth upright, medium (5 ft.); garden decorative; ['Summer Sunshine' × 'Georgia']; intr. 2002

'Wezeip' ('Burning Sky', Paradise™, 'Passion')   HT, m, 1979, Weeks; bud long, pointed; flowers silvery lavender shading to ruby-red at edge, well-formed, 3½-4½ in., 22-28 petals, high-centered, borne singly and in clusters, moderate rose with slight musk fragrance; recurrent; foliage large, glossy, dark green, waxy; prickles several, long, hooked downward, brown; upright growth; hips oblong, very smooth, yellow-green; PP4552; ['Swarthmore' × seedling]; intr. 1978

'Wezgrey' (World War II Memorial Rose™)   HT, m, 2000, Weeks, O.L.; bud large, pointed; flowers white with pinkish-lavender tones toward the petal edges, 4-5 in., 20-32 petals, high-centered, borne mostly singly; recurrent; foliage medium size, medium green, semi-glossy; prickles moderate, 5 mm., nearly straight, tan; upright (4 ft.) growth; PP14433; ['Silver Spoon' × 'Paradise']; intr. 2001

'Wezlavn'   Gr, m, Weeks, O.L.; bud large, ovoid; intr. 2001

'Weznov' (Novelty™)   HT, ob, 2002, Weeks, O.L.; flowers orange/yellow with gold, orange blend reverse, 4 in., full, borne mostly solitary, moderate fragrance; foliage medium size, medium green, matte; prickles average, curved, few; growth upright, medium (5 ft.); garden decorative; ['First Prize' × 'Arizona']; intr. 2002

'Wezsacheart' (Sacred Heart™)   HT, dr, 2002, Weeks, O.L.; flowers 4 in., full, high-centered, borne mostly solitary, moderate fragrance; foliage medium size, medium green, semi-glossy; prickles average, recurved, moderate; upright, medium (5 ft.) growth; garden decorative; ['Chrysler Imperial' × 'Happiness']; intr. 2002

'Whamemo'   MinFl, my, Whartons Roses; intr. 1995

'Whastiluc'   HT, mp, Smith, Edward; intr. 2003

'What a Peach' -- See 'Chewpeachdell'

'What A Surprize' -- See 'Segprize'

'Wheatcroft Giant'   HT, lp, 1962, Wheatcroft Bros.; flowers pearly pink, well-formed, large; vigorous growth

'Wheatcroft's Baby Crimson' -- See 'Perla de Alcañada'

'Wheatcroft's Golden Polyantha' -- See 'Goldene Johanna Tantau'

'Wheato'   F, dp, Rearsby Roses, Ltd.

'Wheaton's Red'   LCl, dr, Williams, J.B.; flowers dark red blend; good repeater; foliage disease-resistant; nearly thornless; intr. 2004

'Wheel Horse Classic' -- See 'Harelite'

'Where The Heart Is' -- See 'Cocoplan'

'Whicaw' ('Mr McCawber')   F, w, 1989, White, James J.; bud pointed, white flushed pink; flowers medium, 15-17 petals, high-centered, borne in sprays of 8-10; foliage medium size, medium green, semi-glossy, disease-resistant; prickles hooked, light brown; upright, bushy, tall, prolific growth; hips globular, orange; [('French Lace' × 'Simplex') × (Pristine® × 'White Angel')]; intr. 1988

'Whickham Highway' -- See 'Hormasbrick'

'Whimsical'   Min, pb, 1980, Strawn, Leslie E.; bud pointed; flowers either light pink or deeper peach-pink on same plant at same time, 48 petals, high-centered, borne singly, no fragrance; foliage medium green; upright, bushy growth;

PP4898; ['Tiki' × 'Baby Betsy McCall']

'Whipped Cream' Min, w, 1968, Moore, Ralph S.; bud pointed, ivory; flowers small, dbl.; foliage light green, leathery; vigorous, bushy, dwarf growth; [(*R. wichurana* × Carolyn Dean) × 'White King']

'Whippet' HT, pb, 1973; flowers salmon-pink, reverse lighter, 5 in., 35 petals, high-centered, ivory, slight fragrance; moderate growth; intr. 1972

Whirlaway™ -- See 'Decwhirl'

'Whirlygig' -- See 'Jusprop'

'Whisky' -- See 'Tanky'

'Whisky, Climbing' -- See 'Andmac'

'Whisky' F, yb, 1964, Delforge; flowers yellow shaded orange-bronze, open, large, dbl., borne in clusters; foliage glossy, light green; very vigorous, upright growth; ['Cognac' × 'Arc-en-Ciel']

'Whisky Gill' HT, ob, 1973, Colby; flowers burnt-orange to bright orange; [sport of 'Whisky Mac']; intr. 1972

'Whisky Mac, Climbing' -- See 'Andmac'

'Whisky Mac' ('Whisky') HT, yb, 1969, Tantau, Math.; bud ovoid; flowers bronze-yellow, well-formed, large, 30 petals, urn-shaped, borne mostly singly, intense sweet fragrance; free-flowering; foliage dark green, glossy; vigorous, upright, bushy growth; intr. 1967

'Whisper' HT, w, Dickson; bud pointed, ovoid; flowers ivory, 5 in., 30-35 petals, high-centered, borne singly, slight musk fragrance; recurrent; foliage semi-glossy, dark green; prickles some, 5-8 mm, straight, brown; stems strong; vigorous (5-6 ft.) growth; PP14596; ['Solitaire' × Elina®]; intr. 2003

'Whisper' F, lp, 1971, Cants of Colchester, Ltd.; flowers pale pink, 3-3½ in., 10 petals; foliage light; vigorous growth; [Queen Elizabeth® × 'Monique']

'Whisper' Pol, Jelly, R. G.; PP3402; intr. before 1975

'Whisper Louise' Pol, lp, Robinson; flowers soft clear pink, dbl., cupped, opening flat, moderate musk fragrance; recurrent; ['Kathleen' × Unknown]; intr. 1994

'Whistle Stop' -- See 'Macmosco'

'White Aachen' F, ly, 1937, Western Rose Co.; flowers buff-yellow to pure white; [sport of 'Gruss an Aachen']

'White Alaska' HT, w, 1960, Hartgerink; bud long, pointed; flowers pure white, 4½-5 in., 20 petals, high-centered; foliage leathery, dark; vigorous, upright growth; PP1862; ['White Ophelia' × seedling]

'White America' LCl, w

'White American Beauty, Climbing' -- See 'Freedom'

'White American Beauty' -- See 'Frau Karl Druschki'

'White Angel' Min, w, 1973, Moore, Ralph S.; bud long, pointed; flowers white, yellow tints in center, 1 in., 30 petals, high-centered, borne singly and several together, slight fragrance; recurrent; foliage small, light green, semi-glossy; prickles few, medium, hooked slightly downward; stems sturdy, wiry; vigorous, dwarf, bushy growth; hips none ; PP3538; [(*R. wichurana* × 'Floradora') × ('Little Darling' × red miniature seedling)]; intr. 1971

'White Arrow' F, ab, Teranishi; intr. 2005

'White Aster' Min, w, Moore; bud long-pointed, small, soft pink; flowers white, small, full, borne in small clusters; foliage foliate leathery, glossy, disease-resistant; growth vigorous, bushy dwarf (10 in.); PP1767; [(*R. wichurana* × 'Floradora') × ('Carolyn Dean' × 'Tom Thumb')]; intr. 1957

'White Avalanche' -- See 'Wilwavl'

'White Baby Rambler' -- See 'Katharina Zeimet'

'White Baby Star' Min, w, 1965, Spring Hill Nursery; [sport of 'Baby Gold Star']

'White Balconia' -- See 'Bristly Cushion'

'White Baroness' HP, w, Paul & Son; flowers pure white, large, full; [sport of 'Baroness Rothschild']

'White Bath' ('Blanche Anglaise', 'Virginal', 'New White Moss', 'Mousseuse Blanche Nouvelle', 'Clifton Moss', 'Blanche Nouvelle', 'Blanche de Bath', 'Blanche Mousseuse') M, w, 1817, Slater; flowers pure white, occasionally striped carmine, large, full, globular; [sport of 'Common Moss']

'White Beauty' -- See 'My Fifi'

'White Beauty' HT, w, 1965, Brooks, M.L.; bud large, pointed; flowers pure white, 4½-5½ in., 30-35 petals, high-centered, cupped, borne singly, moderate spicy fragrance; recurrent; foliage medium green, semi-glossy; prickles several, medium, straight; stems strong, medium; bushy growth; hips short, globular, green; PP1825; [sport of 'The Doctor']; intr. 1964

'White Bella Rosa' -- See 'Kortuel'

'White Belle of Portugal' LCl, w

White Bells™ -- See 'Poulwhite'

'White Bianca' -- See 'Ausca'

'White Blush' A, w, Sievers, Rolf; flowers cream white, full, cupped, moderate fragrance; non-remontant; medium growth; intr. 1988

'White Bon Silène' -- See 'Bon Silène Blanc'

'White Bonnet' F, w

'White Bougère' T, w, 1898, Dunlop; flowers pure white

'White Bouquet' F, w, 1957, Boerner; bud ovoid; flowers , 45 petals, gardenia-like, borne in irregular clusters, moderate spicy fragrance; foliage dark green, glossy; bushy growth; PP1415; ['Glacier' × ('Pinocchio' × unknown)]; intr. 1956

'White Boursault' -- See 'Calypso'

'White Briarcliff' HT, w, 1932, Lens; bud long, pointed; flowers pure white, large, dbl., high-centered, moderate fragrance; foliage leathery; vigorous growth; PP108; [('Briarcliff' × 'Kaiserin Auguste Viktoria') × ('Briarcliff' × 'Mrs Herbert Stevens')]

'White But Nice' -- See 'Welnice 0501'

'White Butterfly' HT, w, 1954, Spanbauer; bud long, pointed; flowers white, inner petals pale chartreuse, center, 3½-4½ in., 24 petals, cupped, moderate fragrance; foliage leathery; vigorous, compact growth; PP1337; ['Ophelia' × 'Curly White']

'White Cap' -- See 'Everblooming Pillar No. 3'

'White Captain' HRg, w, Spek/Captain

White Carpet™ -- See 'Poullen'

White Cascade™ -- See 'Carcade'

'White Castle' -- See 'Poulcs004(N)'

'White Cécile Brünner' Pol, w, 1909, Fauque; flowers white, sulfur yellow and buff; [sport of 'Mlle Cécile Brunner']

'White Chariot' Min, w, Williams, J. Benjamin; bud light apricot; flowers open to almost white, small, slight fragrance; recurrent; intr. 2005

White Charm™ -- See 'Minaqco'

'White Charm' F, w, 1959, Swim & Weeks; bud long, pointed; flowers white, base yellow-green, 2½-3 in., 17-22 petals, high-centered, moderate fragrance; foliage leathery; bushy, upright growth; PP1837; RULED EXTINCT 10/88; ['Pinocchio' × 'Virgo']; intr. 1958

'White Chateau' HT, w, 1999, Teranishi, K.; bud ivory; flowers pure white, 5 in., full, high-centered, slight fragrance; growth to 4½ ft.; ['Ophelia' × seedling]; intr. 1996

'White Chatillon' ('Chatillon White') Pol, w; bud pale pink, fading to white.; [probably a sport of 'Chatillon Rose']

'White Chipper' Min, w, Collazo, Ezequiel; flowers white, with an occasional pink tint, dbl.; PP5182; [sport of 'Chipper']; intr. about 1984

'White Chocolate' -- See 'Tinchocolate'

'White Christmas' HT, w, 1953, H&S; bud long, pointed; flowers pure white, medium, dbl., high-centered; foliage leathery, light green; moderate, upright growth; ['Sleigh Bells' × seedling]

'White Christmas, Climbing' Cl HT, w, Nakasuji; intr. 1968

'White Clair Matin' S, w; growth large shrub or low (2 m.) climber; [sport of Clair Matin®]; intr. 2004

'White Cloud' -- See 'Weisse Wolke'

White Cloud™ Min, w, 1988, Saville, F. Harmon; flowers white with pale pink; PP6876; [sport of Buttons 'n' Bows™]

'White Cloud' -- See 'Hakuun'

'White Clouds' Cl HT, w, 1953, Silva; bud long, pointed; flowers 4½ in., 50 petals; foliage leathery, dark; vigorous growth; RULED EXTINCT 8/88; ['Frau Karl Druschki' × 'Kaiserin Auguste Viktoria']

'White Cochet' -- See 'White Maman Cochet'

'White Cockade' LCl, w, 1969, Cocker; flowers 8 cm., dbl., borne in small clusters, moderate fragrance; foliage dark green, glossy; numerous prickles; vigorous, low, climbing growth; ['New

Dawn' × 'Circus']

'White Colorado'   F, w; intr. 1998

'White Columbia, Climbing'   Cl HT, w, 1934, Clark's Rose Nursery

'White Comet' -- See 'Deloblan'

White Cover™ -- See 'Poulcov'

'White Cross'   LCl, w, 1950, Hester; bud ovoid; flowers white, center tinted lemon, large, very dbl.; foliage leathery, glossy; very vigorous growth; [sport of 'Mrs Arthur Curtiss James']

'White Crystal' -- See 'LLX8797'

'White Cupido'   Min, w, deRuiter; intr. 2004

'White Daily Rose' -- See 'Indica Alba'

White Dawn® ('White New Dawn') LCl, w, 1949, Longley, L.E.; flowers pure white, 3-3½ in., 30-35 petals, gardenia-shaped, borne in small to medium clusters, moderate sweet fragrance; recurrent; foliage glossy, dark green; numerous prickles; very vigorous, climbing growth; ['New Dawn' × 'Lily Pons']; often thought to be the same as 'Weisse New Dawn', but the flowers of 'White Dawn' are pure white whereas those of 'Wiesse New Dawn' are tinted crimson

'White de Meaux' -- See 'Rose de Meaux White'

'White Decumba'   S, w; flowers pure white, yellow stamens, small, single, flat, borne in small clusters, moderate fragrance; recurrent; foliage glossy; low, spreading, groundcover growth; hips small; intr. 2003

'White Delight'   HT, w, 1989, Warriner, William A.; bud ovoid, pointed; flowers white with pink blush, 4½ in., 35-40 petals, high-centered, borne usually singly, slight fragrance; recurrent; foliage medium size, dark green, matte; prickles moderate, hooked, medium, brown; stems long, strong; upright, medium growth; PP6664; ['White Masterpiece' × 'Futura']; intr. 1990

'White Demure'   F, w, 1952, Boerner; bud ovoid; flowers 2-2½ in., 30-35 petals, flat; foliage leathery; vigorous, compact, bushy growth; PP1222; [sport of 'Demure']

White Diamond® -- See 'Interamon'

'White Dian'   Min, w, 1965, Moore, Ralph S.; flowers white, sometimes light pink; [sport of 'Dian']

'White Dick Koster' -- See 'Snövit'

'White Dog'   S, w

'White Dorothy' ('White Dorothy Perkins') HWich, w, 1908, Cant, B. R.; flowers creamy white, small, 30-40 petals, pompon, borne in large clusters, no fragrance; recurrent; [sport of 'Dorothy Perkins']

'White Dorothy Perkins' -- See 'White Dorothy'

White Dream® -- See 'Lenblank'

White Drift™   S, w, Meilland, Alain; bud small, ovoid; flowers bright white, 2-4.5 cm., 6 petals, flat, borne usually in clusters, moderate fragrance; free-flowering; foliage medium green, glossy; prickles several, small, hooked downward, green; low, spreading, mounded growth; PP15960; [(R. wichurana × The Fairy) × 'Iceberg']; intr. 2004

'White Duchess'   HT, w, 1964, Herholdt, J.A.; bud spiral, pointed; flowers snow-white, medium; foliage glossy; strong stems; vigorous growth

'White Duchesse de Brabant' -- See 'Mme Joseph Schwartz'

White Eden™ -- See 'Meiviowit'

'White Edge'   HRg, w; intr. 2003

'White Elegance'   HT, w, Hiroshima; intr. 1996

'White Elfe'   Pol, w, 1954, Holmes, V.E.; bud pointed; flowers white faintly tinted pink, 2-2½ in., 40-45 petals, high-centered, borne in clusters of 3-7; foliage dark, leathery; vigorous growth; PP1377; [sport of 'Rosenelfe']; intr. 1954

'White Ensign' ('Monty's White') HT, w, 1925, McGredy; flowers creamy white, large, very dbl., rosette, slight fragrance; free-flowering; foliage leathery, dark green, glossy; vigorous growth

'White Ensign'   F, w, J&P; flowers creamy white, double, high-centered, borne in clusters; medium growth; intr. 2005

'White Erfurt'   S, w; bud pointed, petals edged red; flowers white with a pink blush, semi-double, cupped, borne in clusters; recurrent; foliage dark green, glossy; 5 ft. × 4 ft. growth; [sport of 'Erfurt']

'White Esteem'   HT, w, K&S; flowers clear white, medium, double, high-centered, borne mostly singly; recurrent; intr. 2001

'White Euphoria'   S, w, Interplant; intr. 1999

'White Fairy'   Min, w, 1952, Moore, Ralph S.; flowers small, very dbl., borne in clusters

'White Fairy' ('Margina') Pol, w, Martin, John & Gina; flowers pure white, pompon, borne in large clusters; foliage dark green; low growth; intr. 1998

'White Feather' -- See 'Morfeat'

'White Festival' -- See 'Lavsnow'

'White Finch'   Pol, w, 1937, Stielow, F.C.; flowers white, tinted pink; PP277; [sport of 'Mrs R.M. Finch']

White Fleurette® ('Rosenzauber') S, w, Briant; flowers pure white, yellow stamens, medium, single, flat, borne in small clusters; recurrent; bushy growth; intr. 1989

'White Flight' -- See 'White Mrs Flight'

'White Floorshow'   S, w; flowers pure white, 3 in., 30 petals, slight fragrance; profuse; foliage mid-green; growth spreading, mounding, 2½ × 3½ ft.; intr. 2001

White Flower Carpet® ('Flower Carpet Blanc', 'Snowflake', Opalia®, Schneeflocke®) F, w, Noack, Werner; flowers clear white, yellow stamens, 6 cm., semi-double, shallow cup, borne in large clusters; recurrent; foliage medium to dark green, glossy; erect growth; intr. 1991

'White Forcer'   Pol, w, 1926, Spek; flowers larger and borne in larger trusses than parent; [sport of 'Jesse']

'White Four Seasons Rose' (R. bifera alba) D, w, before 1785; flowers very pale blush; not dependably remontant

'White Fragrant Mist'   HT, w, 1990, Oregon Roses, Inc.; bud pointed; flowers white with slight lavender tinge, large, dbl., cupped, borne mostly singly, heavy fruity fragrance; foliage medium size, dark green, glossy; growth upright, tall; [sport of 'Lavande']

'White Garnette'   F, w, 1952, Boerner; flowers white tinged cream, 2 in., 30-35 petals, borne in clusters; foliage rich green; bushy growth; PP1225; [('Pinocchio' × unknown) × 'Garnette']

White Gem®   Min, w, 1976, Meilland; bud long; flowers soft ivory, shaded pale tan, 1½ in., 90 petals, slight fragrance; foliage large, glossy, dark green; upright, bushy growth; ['Darling Flame' × 'Jack Frost']

'White Gene Boerner'   F, w, 1978, Takatori, Yoshiho; [sport of 'Gene Boerner']

'White Gold' -- See 'Cocquiriam'

'White Gold'   LCl, w, 1943, Brownell; bud long, pointed; flowers white, center yellow, petals reflexed, dbl., high-centered; foliage dark, glossy; vigorous, climbing (20 ft.) growth; ['Glenn Dale' × 'Mrs Arthur Curtiss James']

'White Gold 98' -- See 'Cocquiriam'

'White Golden Gate' -- See 'Ivory'

'White Grootendorst'   HRg, w, 1962, Eddy; flowers small, full, moderate fragrance; [sport of 'Pink Grootendorst']

'White Gruss an Aachen' -- See 'Weisse Gruss an Aachen'

White Haze®   S, w, Tantau; flowers shining white, guard petals may have violet-red stripe, yellow stamens, semi-double, shallow cup, borne in clusters; recurrent; foliage dark green, very glossy; compact, spreading, bushy growth; intr. 2006

'White Hedge'   HRg, w; flowers pure white, small yellow stamens, large, single, shallow cup, moderate fragrance; recurrent; foliage light green; upright, closely packed growth; possibly from Nyveldt, 1955

'White Heritage' -- See 'Ausome'

'White Hermosa' -- See 'Marie Lambert'

'White Hero'   S, w, Rex, Dr. Robert W.

'White House' -- See 'Resline'

'White House'   HT, w, 1951, Silva; bud high-centered to ovoid; flowers satiny white; foliage thick, light green; ['McGredy's Yellow' × 'Frau Karl Druschki']

'White Ivory' -- See 'Welivory'

'White Jacques Cartier' ('Weisse Jacques Cartier') P, w; flowers clean white, very full, intense fragrance; recurrent; strong (5 ft.) growth; [sport of 'Jacques Cartier']

'White Jewel'   F, w, 1960, Boerner; flowers 4 in., 33 petals, cupped, borne in clusters, moderate fragrance; vigorous, bushy growth; PP1628; [('Starlite' × unknown) × ('Glacier' × unknown)]; intr. 1957

'White Joy'   HT, w, 1952, Spanbauer; bud pointed; flowers pure white, 4-5 in., 55-65 petals, flat, moderate fragrance; foliage leathery; bushy, upright growth; PP1048

'White Junior Miss'   F, w; flowers dainty white

'White Killarney'   HT, w, 1909, Waban Conservatories; flowers snowy white, with enormous petals, large, semi-dbl., moderate fragrance; recurrent; [sport of 'Killarney']

'White Killarney, Climbing'   Cl HT, w, 1920, Conard & Jones; [sport of 'Killarney']

'White King'   Min, w, 1961, Moore, Ralph S.; bud pointed, ovoid; flowers cream-white, 1½ in., 45 petals, moderate fragrance; foliage leathery; bushy (12 in.) growth; PP2366; ['Golden Glow' × 'Zee']

'White Knight, Climbing' -- See 'Message, Climbing'

'White Knight' -- See 'Meban'

'White Knights' -- See 'Poulaps'

'White La France' -- See 'Augustine Guinoisseau'

'White La Vie en Rose'   F, w

'White Lace'   S, w; flowers creamy white, double, rosette, borne in clusters; recurrent; foliage glossy; compact (20 in.) growth

'White Lady' -- See 'Dame Blanche'

'White Lady'   HT, w, 1889, Paul; [sport of 'Lady Mary Fitzwilliam']

'White Lafayette' -- See 'Dagmar Späth'

White Lightnin'™ -- See 'Arowhif'

'White Linen'   HT, w, 2005, Adlong , Paula; flowers white with pale pink edges, reverse white, 4-4½ in., full, borne mostly solitary, intense fragrance; foliage medium size, medium green, matte; prickles moderate, average, straight, green; upright, tall (4-5 ft.) growth; ['Chrystalline' × 'Louise Estes']

'White Look'   HT, w

'White Love'   HT, w, 1978, Buisman, G. A. H.; bud long; flowers ivory-white, large, intense fragrance; foliage dark; bushy growth; ['Frau Karl Druschki' × ('Peace' × seedling)]; intr. 1973

'White Ma Perkins'   F, w, 1962, McDonald; bud long, pointed; flowers snow white, large, 20-40 petals, borne in clusters, intense fragrance; recurrent; foliage light green; very vigorous, upright growth; PP1965; [sport of 'Ma Perkins']; intr. 1962

'White Madonna'   Min, w, 1975, Moore, Ralph S.; bud long, pointed; flowers white to pale pink, 1 in., 33 petals, slight fragrance; foliage glossy, leathery; upright, bushy growth; PP3844; [(R. wichurana × 'Floradora') × ('Little Darling' × unnamed red miniature)]; intr. 1973

'White Magic' -- See 'LLX8751'

'White Magic' -- See 'Jacare'

'White Magic'   HT, w; intr. 1998

White Magic Carpet™ (Wagtail Cover™, Wagtail™) S, w; flowers white, less than 2 in., dbl., borne in clusters, slight wild rose fragrance; recurrent; foliage dark green, glossy; broad, bushy (40-60 cm.) growth; intr. 1994

'White Majesty'   HT, w, Meilland; flowers pure white, 15-20 petals, high-centered, borne mostly singly, no fragrance; recurrent; foliage dark green, glossy; stems long, strong; upright, medium growth; PPAF; [sport of 'Paris d'Yves St. Laurent']; intr. 2006

'White Majesty'   HT, w, Meilland

'White Maman Cochet, Climbing'   Cl T, w, 1907, Knight, G.; flowers white streaked pink, very large, dbl.; [sport of 'White Maman Cochet']; intr. 1911

'White Maman Cochet' ('White Cochet') T, w, 1896, Cook, J.W.; flowers white, often flushed pink; [sport of 'Maman Cochet']

'White Marie Curie'   F, w, Meilland; flowers white; free-flowering; intr. 2006

'White Masterpiece'   HT, w, 1969, Boerner; bud long, pointed; flowers satiny white, long peduncle, 5½-6 in., 50-60 petals, high-centered, borne mostly singly, slight tea fragrance; recurrent; foliage large, dark green, leathery; prickles some, angled downward; stems long, strong; upright, spreading growth; PP2998; [('Revelry' × 'Pink Masterpiece') × seedling]

'White Masterpiece, Climbing'   Cl HT, w, Sakagami; intr. 1982

'White Max Graf' -- See 'Korgram'

'White Meidiland' -- See 'Meicoublan'

'White Meillandina' -- See 'Meiblam'

'White Meilove'   F, w; intr. 2003

'White Merveille' -- See 'White Tausendschön'

'White Midinette'   Cl Min, w, Taschner, Ludwig; flowers white with yellow stamens , small, double, pompon, borne in clusters; free-flowering; tall (10 ft.), arching growth; intr. 2003

'White Mikado'   F, w, Tantau; florist rose

'White Mimollet'   F, w, 1985, Ota, Kaichiro; [sport of 'Mimollet']; intr. 1984

White Mini-Wonder™ -- See 'Meizogrel'

'White MiniJet' ('Meisogrel') Min, w, Meilland; flowers double, cupped; container rose

'White Minimo'   Min, w, Interplant; intr. 1989

'White Mite' -- See 'Fromite'

'White Moss' -- See 'Comtesse de Murinais'

'White Moss Rose' -- See 'Shailer's White Moss'

'White Mothersday' -- See 'Morsdag Alba'

'White Mountains'   LCl, w, 1960, Risley; bud globular; flowers white, becoming greenish, small, dbl., borne in clusters; profuse, intermittent bloom; foliage glossy; vigorous growth; quite hardy; ['Skinner's Rambler' × 'Skinner's Rambler']; intr. 1958

'White Mrs Flight' ('White Flight') HMult, w, 1916, Rockford; flowers bone white, medium, semi-dbl., cupped, open, borne in large clusters, slight fragrance; non-remontant; foliage small, medium green; tall, vigorous growth; [sport of 'Mrs F. W. Flight']

White Multirosa®   S, w, J&P; intr. 2007

'White Mystery' -- See 'Devabe'

'White Neverland'   S, w, Hiroshima; intr. 2005

'White New Dawn' -- See 'White Dawn'

'White Night' -- See 'Byakuya'

White Nights™ -- See 'Poulaps'

'White Noblesse'   HT, w, Tantau; florist rose; intr. 1998

'White Nun'   HT, w, 1970, Pal, Dr. B.P.; flowers open, medium, dbl.; foliage glossy; vigorous, upright growth; ['Virgo' × unknown]; intr. 1968

'White Ophelia'   HT, w, 1920, Cleveland Cut-Flower Co.; flowers white, center faintly tinted pink, becoming white, well-formed, semi-dbl.; [sport of 'Ophelia']

'White Orléans'   Pol, w, 1920, Van Eyk; [sport of 'Orléans Rose']

'White Pacific'   HT, w

White Pagode™   MinFl, w, Poulsen; flowers white, 5-8 cm., dbl., borne in clusters, no fragrance; foliage dark; cascading growth, hanging basket type; PP13453; intr. 2000

'White Patio Wonder' -- See 'Jalwhitepat'

'White Pavement' ('Schnee-Eule', 'Snow Owl') HRg, w, Uhl, J.; bud pale pink, pointed; flowers opening soft white, large, double, cupped, moderate fragrance; recurrent; foliage dark green, disease-resistant; moderate (2½ ft.), spreading growth; hips rose-red; intr. 1989

'White Peach Ovation'   Min, w, deRuiter

'White Pearl'   T, w, 1889, Ritter/Nanz & Neuner; foliage large; growth upright; [sport of 'Perle des Jardins']

'White Pearl'   HT, w, Totty; bud long, pointed; flowers glistening white, well-formed, large, 45-50 petals, open; foliage large, soft; very vigorous, upright growth; ruled extinct 04/85; intr. 1948

'White Pearl'   Min, w, Totty, Charles; [sport of Minnie Pearl™]; intr. 1993

'White Pearl in Red Dragon's Mouth' ('Chi Long Han Zhu') Ch, rb; flowers cerise to cherry red, white eye, semi-dbl. to double, cupped, slight spicy fragrance; recurrent; moderate (3-4 ft.) growth

'White Penthouse'   Gr, Fineschi, G.; intr. 1995

'White Perfection' -- See 'Pristine Pavement'

'White Pet' ('Little White Pet') Pol, w, 1879, Henderson, P.; flowers small, dbl., pompon, borne in large clusters, slight fragrance; recurrent; very dwarf, mounded growth; [sport of 'Félicité-Perpétue']

'White Pet, Climbing' ('Little White Pet, Climbing') Cl Pol, w, 1894, Corboeuf;

flowers snowy white, borne in large clusters; [sport of 'White Pet']; probably synonymous with 'Félicité-Perpétue'

'White Pillar'   LCl, w, 1958, Hay; flowers silvery white with button eye, large, very dbl., quartered rosette, borne in clusters, moderate fragrance; recurrent; pillar (8 ft.) growth; ['William F. Dreer' × unknown]

'White Pinocchio'   F, w, 1950, Boerner; bud ovoid; flowers 2½ in., 50 petals, globular, moderate fragrance; vigorous growth; PP1010; ['Mrs R.M. Finch' × 'Pinocchio']

'White Popcorn'   S, w, Williams, J. Benjamin; flowers small, double, cupped, borne in large clusters, slight fragrance; recurrent; foliage bluish-green; low (2 ft.), spreading growth; intr. 2005

'White Prince'   HT, w, 1961, Von Abrams; bud pointed; flowers creamy white, 5-6 in., 50-80 petals, globular, borne usually singly, slight fragrance; recurrent; foliage large, leathery, glossy; prickles numerous, medium, hooked downward, brown; stems long, strong; vigorous, upright growth; hips large, globose, variable orange; PP2246; [('Blanche Mallerin' × 'Peace') × ('Peace' × 'Frau Karl Druschki')]; intr. 1961

'White Provence'   ('Blanche Unique', R. centifolia nivea, 'Unique de Provence', 'Unique Blanche', 'Unique', 'Unica Alba', R. provincialis alba, R. centifolia mutabilis, 'Nivea', 'Neige', 'Mutabilis', 'Lacteola', 'Changeante', 'Rose Unique') C, w, 1775, Grimwood; bud rounded, deep pink; flowers white, sometimes tinged pink, green eye, large, dbl., cupped, incurved petals, moderate fragrance; foliage doubly serrated; erect, low (3 ft.) growth; [sport of R. × centifolia]

'White Queen'   HT, w, 1959, Boerner; bud long; flowers white, center creamy,, 5 in., 30 petals, cupped, borne singly and several together, moderate tea fragrance; recurrent; foliage large, leathery; prickles numerous, medium, straight or hooked downward; stems medium, strong; vigorous, upright growth; hips none ; PP1762; [('Starlite' × unknown) × ('Glacier' × unknown)]; intr. 1958

'White Queen Elizabeth'   ('Blanc Queen Elizabeth') F, w, 1965, Banner; flowers creamy white, 4 in., borne in clusters, moderate fragrance; recurrent; foliage light green, leathery; vigorous, tall growth; [sport of Queen Elizabeth®]

'White Quill'   MinFl, w, Williams, J.B.; flowers white with creamy center, double, globular to cupped; recurrent; intr. 2003

'White Radiance' -- See 'Mary Nish'

'White Radox Bouquet'   S, w, 1989, Melville Nurseries Pty., Ltd.; bud small, rounded; flowers white with pink tinge in center, large, 50 petals, borne in sprays of 5 or more, moderate fragrance; foliage dark green, leathery; prickles hooked, small, beige; tall, shrub to semi-climber growth; [sport of 'Radox Bouquet']

'White Rain' -- See 'Morcas'

'White Rambler' -- See 'Thalia'

'White River' -- See 'Shirakawa'

White Roadrunner®   S, w, Uhl; flowers pure white, 5 cm., semi-double, cupped, borne in clusters, intense fragrance; recurrent; foliage dark green, leathery, very disease-resistant; bushy, compact (2 ft.) growth; intr. 2003

'White Rock'   LCl, w, Barni, V.; flowers pure white, double, cupped, moderate fragrance; tall growth; intr. 1996

'White Rosamini'   Min, w

'White Rose de Meaux' -- See 'Rose de Meaux White'

'White Rose of Finland' -- See 'Polstjärnan'

'White Rose of York'   ('La Rose de York', R. × alba, R. usitatissima, R. procera, R. × collina) A, w, before 1600; sepals leafy; flowers white, medium, single to semi-dbl., borne usually several together, moderate hyacinth fragrance; summer bloom; foliage medium size, grayish, blunt, composed of 5-7 leaflets; prickles hooked, mixed with bristles, distributed irregularly; stems clear green; growth to 5 ft.; hips ovoid, large, scarlet; [R. gallica × R. canina]; probably known to the Romans (Pliny) before 77 A.D.

'White Rose of York' -- See 'Duc d'York'

'White Russian' -- See 'Gelrus'

'White Satin'   ('Swisa') HT, w, 1965, Swim & Weeks; bud short pointed, conspicuous neck; flowers white, center light greenish yellow on lower half of petals, 4-4½ in., 60-80 petals, high-centered, borne singly, moderate tea fragrance; recurrent; foliage upper dark green, under light gray-green, leathery; prickles some, medium, straight, brown; stems long; vigorous, tall, bushy growth; hips long, flat at top, yellow; PP2648; ['Mount Shasta' × 'White Butterfly']

'White Scotch'   HSpn, w, from Scotland; flowers pure white

'White Seduction'   Pol, w; [sport of 'Seduction']

'White Sheen'   F, w, 1960, Boerner; bud ovoid; flowers 2 in., 25-30 petals, borne in clusters, intense fragrance; foliage dark, glossy, upright growth; [('Ma Perkins' × unknown) × ('Demure' × unknown)]; intr. 1960

White Simplicity® -- See 'Jacsnow'

'White Skyliner'   LCl, w, Cowlishaw; flowers pure white with yellow stamens, small, semi-double, cupped, borne in clusters; recurrent; tall (6-8 ft.) growth; freestanding shrub or small climber; intr. 2003

'White Sparrieshoop' -- See 'Weisse aus Sparrieshoop'

'White Spire'   HT, w, Kordes; bud pointed; flowers double, high-centered, borne in small clusters, moderate fragrance; recurrent; upright, tall growth; intr. 1994

'White Spray'   F, w, 1968, LeGrice; bud creamy white; flowers pure white, well-formed, small, double, borne in clusters, moderate fragrance; recurrent; stems long; vigorous, compact growth; [seedling × 'Iceberg']

'White Spray' -- See 'Lenpli'

'White Star'   HWich, w, 1901, Manda; flowers 3 cm., borne in clusters of 20-30; ['Jersey Beauty' × 'Manda's Triumph']

'White Star'   HT, w, Morse; flowers ivory-white, base shaded lemon-yellow, intense fragrance; [sport of 'Ophelia']; intr. 1920

'White Star of Finland' -- See 'Polstjärnan'

'White Stream'   LCl, w, Teranishi; intr. 2003

'White Success' -- See 'Jelpirofor'

'White Sunsation' -- See 'Korgazell'

'White Sunshine' -- See 'Jonwhite'

'White Supreme'   HT, w, Williams, J.B.; flowers white, large, moderate fragrance; recurrent; growth to 5 ft.; intr. 2004

'White Surprise' -- See 'LLX8657'

'White Swan'   ('Cygne Blanc') HT, w, 1951, Verschuren-Pechtold; bud ovoid; flowers pure white, 4½-5 in., 30 petals, high-centered, moderate fragrance; foliage glossy, dark; vigorous, upright growth; PP1115; [('Kaiserin Auguste Viktoria' × unknown) × 'white seedling']

'White Sweetheart'   F, w, 1941, J&P; flowers white flushed blush-pink when half open, small, dbl., high-centered; foliage leathery; short, strong stems; vigorous, upright, bushy growth; [sport of 'Rosenelfe']

'White Symphonie'   HT, w, RvS-Melle; flowers 4 in., 59 petals; foliage matte; strong growth; intr. 1991

'White Tausendschön'   ('White Merveille') HMult, w, 1913, Paul, W. (also Roehrs, 1918); flowers white, sometimes flaked pink; [sport of 'Tausendschön']

'White Timeless' -- See 'Ruicrevi'

'White Timeless'   HT, w; flowers dbl.; [sport of 'Timeless']

'White Treasure' -- See 'Hadtreasure'

'White Valerie'   HT, w; intr. 1998

'White Wedding'   LCl, w, Scarman; flowers creamy white with yellow stamens, single, shallow cup, borne in large clusters; free-flowering; vigorous (8 ft.) growth; intr. 1995

White Wedding®   HT, w, Tantau; flowers creamy white, medium to large , double, high-centered, borne mostly singly; recurrent; stems medium to long; florist rose; intr. 2007

'White Week-end'   F, w

'White Wine' -- See 'Resine'

'White Wings'   HT, w, 1947, Krebs; bud long, pointed; flowers ivory white, wine colored stamens, anthers chocolate-colored, large, 5 petals, borne in large clusters, moderate fragrance; recurrent; foliage leathery, dark green; vigorous, upright, bushy growth; PP850; ['Dainty Bess' × seedling]

The Official Registry and Checklist — Rosa   799

'White Wings'   HT, w, Poulsen; flowers pure white with crimson stamens, single; growth to 2½ ft.; intr. 1979

'White Woge'   HSpn, w; flowers white, single; recurrent; low (50 cm.) growth; intr. 1997

'Whitecap'   F, w, 1960, Boerner, E. S.; bud medium; flowers pure white, medium, dbl., cupped; foliage medium size, abundant; growth vigorous, upright, bushy; PP1910; intr. 1959

'Whiteout' -- See 'Macwhitout'

'Whitfield Wonder'   LCl, mp, Scarman; flowers , old-fashioned, borne in clusters, slight fragrance; foliage disease-resistant; tall (8 ft.) growth; intr. 2001

'Whitley Bay' -- See 'Horharryplus'

'Whitney' -- See 'Briney'

'Whitston'   MinFl, lp, Chessum, Paul; intr. 1995

'Who Dat'   HT, pb, 2005, Edwards, Eddie & Phelps, Ethan; flowers striped, 4-5 in., full, high-centered, borne mostly solitary, slight fragrance; foliage dark green, glossy; prickles small, hooked; growth upright, medium (5-6 ft.); exhibition; intr. 2005

Whoop De Doo™ -- See 'Moewhoop'

Whoopi™ -- See 'Savawhoop'

'Why Not' -- See 'Morwhy'

'Why Not Cerise'   HT, dp, 2001, Coiner, Jim; flowers very showy, large, full, borne mostly solitary, no fragrance; foliage medium size, light green, matte; few prickles; growth compact, medium (48 in.); [seedling × seedling]; intr. 2001

'Whytewold'   S, w, 1961, Skinner; flowers dbl., cupped; non-recurrent; growth to 3 ft.

'Wichmoss'   HWich, lp, 1911, Barbier; bud long, pointed, mossed; flowers pale blush-pink fading to white, 2 in., semi-dbl., borne in clusters of 6-15; foliage dark, leathery; vigorous, climbing growth; [R. wichuraiana × 'Salet']

'Wichurana Grandiflora'   (R. wichurana grandiflora) S, w; flowers 2-2½ in.; assumed to be a tetraploid form; discovered in the fields of an English nursery

'Wicking'   HMlt, pb, 1909, Geschwind; flowers yellowish carmine-pink, center white, medium, full

'Wickwar'   S, w, Steadman; flowers creamy white, 5 cm., single, moderate musk fragrance; foliage grayish; hips small, red; probably R. soulieana × R. brunonii; intr. 1960

'Wiener Blut'   F, or, 1961, Horstmann, bud globular; flowers salmon-red, 30 petals, borne in clusters; vigorous, upright growth

Wiener Charme® -- See 'Vienna Charm'

'Wiener Donaupark'   F, lp

'Wiener Walzer'   ('Pur Sang') F, mr, 1965, Tantau, Math.; bud pointed; flowers velvety bright red, large, 25-30 petals; foliage glossy; very vigorous, upright growth

'Wienerwald'   ('Vienna Woods') HT, op, 1974, Kordes; bud long, pointed; flowers pink flushed with salmon, large, dbl., borne singly and several together, moderate fragrance; recurrent; foliage large, dark green, leathery; vigorous, upright, bushy growth; ['Colour Wonder' × seedling]

'Wieteke van Dordt' -- See 'Potifar'

'Wife of Bath' -- See 'The Wife of Bath'

'Wiggy' -- See 'Kendanqu'

'Wijhe'   F, or, 1961, Buisman, G. A. H.; flowers dbl., borne in clusters; foliage dark; moderate growth; [seedling × 'Alpine Glow']

'Wil Pink Supreme'   S, op

'Wilace'   (Peggy Rockefeller™) HT, dr, 1992, Williams, J. Benjamin; flowers bright crimson to cherry red with dark, smoky red on edge of petals, 40 petals, moderate spicy fragrance; foliage large, dark green, semi-glossy; few prickles; upright, bushy, medium growth; [Queen Elizabeth® × 'Swarthmore']; intr. 1991

'Wilalex'   ('Alexandria Rose', 'City of Alexandria') S, rb, 1988, Williams, J. Benjamin; flowers ivory to white with light red washing on petal edge, deeper yellow at base, large, dbl., pointed; free-flowering; foliage large, dark green, glossy, disease-resistant; upright, bushy, vigorous, strong, hardy growth; [(Queen Elizabeth® × 'Kordes' Perfecta') × 'Mount Shasta']

'Wilalno'   ('Robert Aliano') HT, dr, 1998, Williams, J. Benjamin; flowers deep velvet red, dull reverse, 4½-5 in., dbl., high-centered, borne mostly singly; foliage large, dark green, semi-glossy; few prickles; strong, upright, tall (4-5 ft.) growth; ['Chrysler Imperial' × Mister Lincoln®]; intr. 1999

'Wilangil'   ('Reynolda House') HT, pb, 1992, Williams, J. Benjamin; flowers light pink with ivory and coral blend, medium, full, borne mostly singly, intense fragrance; foliage medium size, dark green, semi-glossy, disease-resistant; few prickles; upright, bushy, medium (3-4 ft.) growth; winter hardy; ['Royal Highness' × 'Command Performance']

'Wilannb'   (Leonore Annenberg™) HT, pb, 2004, Williams, J. Benjamin; flowers medium pink, reverse deeper, 4½-5 in., full, borne mostly solitary, moderate fragrance; foliage large, dark green, semi-glossy; prickles medium, curved downward; growth upright, tall (3½ -4 ft.); garden, exhibition, cutting; ['First Prize' × 'Love']

'Wilbakd'   (Celine Dion™) S, ob, 2000, Williams, J. Benjamin; flowers bright orange with lighter reverse, 3-3½ in., single, borne in large clusters, moderate fragrance; foliage medium size, dark green, semi-glossy, disease-free; prickles few, very small, curved down; growth compact, bushy (2½-3 ft.); bedding, containers, cutting; hardy; ['Fifth Ave.' × 'Tropicana']; intr. 2000

'Wilbard'   (Barbie Dazzler™) HT, pb, 2004, Williams, J. Benjamin; flowers light pink blend, reverse deep pink, large, ruffled, 4½-5 in., dbl., borne mostly solitary, moderate fragrance; foliage large, dark green, glossy; prickles small-medium, curved down; vigorous, upright, tall, 3½-4 ft. growth; ['Sonia' × Boulie's Dream™]; intr. 2004

'Wilbentur'   (Pixie Delight™) Min, w, 1982, Williams, J. Benjamin; flowers dbl.; foliage small, dark, semi-glossy; upright growth; PP5270; ['Ma Perkins' × 'Easter Morning']; intr. 1981

'Wilberforce'   C, dr, about 1840; flowers dark crimson, large, dbl.; [probably R. centifolia × R. gallica]

'Wilblank'   (Stardance™) MinFl, w, 1982, Williams, J. Benjamin; bud broadly ovoid; flowers white, deep yellow stamens, 5-6 cm., 35 petals, cupped to flat, borne in small clusters, slight fragrance; good repeat; foliage small, medium green, semi-glossy; prickles few, medium, straight, straw; bushy, semi-erect (60-80 cm.) growth; PP5222; ['Ma Perkins' × ('Charlie McCarthy' × 'Easter Morning')]

'Wilbrid'   ('All-American Bride') HT, w, 2000, Williams, J. Benjamin; flowers white, delicate washed blush, reverse white, 4½-5 in., full, high-centered, borne mostly singly, moderate fragrance; foliage large, dark green, glossy, disease-resistant; few prickles; growth upright, bushy; very hardy; ['White Masterpiece' × 'Miss All-American Beauty']

'Wilcamp'   ('Campfire') Min, or, 1991, Williams, J. Benjamin; bud pointed; flowers fiery orange neon red, ages deeper, medium, 26 petals, high-centered, borne singly, moderate damask fragrance; foliage medium size, dark green, semi-glossy; upright, bushy growth; [Marina® × Starina®]; intr. 1990

'Wilcan'   ('Canadian Sunset') HT, rb, 1996, Williams, J. Benjamin; flowers red with yellow reverse, large, dbl., borne mostly singly, moderate fragrance; recurrent; foliage large, mahogany to dark green, glossy, disease-resistant; vigorous, upright (3½ - 4 ft.), bushy growth; ['Oregold' × 'Tropicana']

'Wilcans'   ('Magic Beauty') HT, yb, 2000, Williams, J. Benjamin; flowers bright golden yellow aging to blend of yellow and purple-red, 4½-5 in., dbl., borne mostly solitary, intense fragrance; foliage large, dark green, glossy; prickles medium, curved down, few; growth upright, tall (4½ - 5 ft.); PP12655; ['Love' × Gold Medal®]; intr. 2000

'Wilcapa'   (Carolyn's Passion™) MinFl, my, 2006, Williams, J. Benjamin; flowers yellow, petals quilling with age, 1-1½ in., dbl., high-centered, borne in small clusters, moderate fragrance; recurrent; foliage small, medium green, matte; prickles small, straight, light tan, moderate; growth compact, short (12 in.); containers, hedging; ['Hershey's Yellow' × 'Yellow Butterfly']; intr. 2005

'Wilcgir' ('Country Girl', 'Emsie Girl') HT, ob, 1999, Williams, J. Benjamin; bud pointed; flowers creamy white with bright orange edge, dbl.; ['Garden Party' × American Heritage®]

'Wilcher' (Cherry Pastel™) Min, mr, 1997, Williams, J. Benjamin; flowers bright cherry red, medium, dbl., borne mostly singly, moderate fragrance; [Red Sunblaze® × Pink Sweetheart™]; intr. 1997

'Wilcipks' ('Jamestown', Cicely Phippen Marks™) S, lp, 2007, Williams, J. Benjamin; flowers delicate peach/apricot/pink, with yellow stamens and yellow hue in center, medium, 2-3 in., dbl., borne in small clusters; foliage medium, dark green, semi-glossy; prickles ¼ in., moderate; growth compact, medium; massed plantings, borders,display; ['Rose Parade' × seedling]; intr. 1999

'Wilclde' (Viola's Diamond™) Gr, w, 2004, Williams, J. Benjamin; flowers white, reverse white, 3-3½ in., dbl., borne in small clusters, moderate fragrance; foliage medium size, medium green, semi-glossy, disease-resistant; prickles few, small, curved down, light tan; growth spreading, vigorous, medium; border, hedge, garden; ['Mount Shasta' × 'Sea Foam']; intr. 2004

'Wilcrest' ('Cedar Crest College') F, dy, 1992, Williams, J. Benjamin; flowers deep golden yellow, medium, 6-14 petals, borne in small clusters; foliage medium size, dark green, glossy; few prickles; medium (3-4 ft.), upright, bushy growth; ['Ivory Fashion' × 'Sunsprite']; intr. 1993

'Wilcrown' ('Copper Crown') S, op, 1992, Williams, J. Benjamin; flowers rusty copper with orange center, large, 5 petals, slight fragrance; foliage medium size, dark green, semi-glossy; upright (4 × 4 ft.), bushy growth; [Westerland® × 'Orange Velvet']; intr. 1992

'Wild Amazone' HT, dp

'Wild 'n' Rare' Min, m

'Wild at Heart' -- See 'Korades'

Wild Berry Breeze™ -- See 'Jacrulav'

Wild Blue Yonder™ -- See 'Wekisosblip'

'Wild Cherry' HT, mr, 1985, Bridges, Dennis A.; flowers large, dbl., moderate fragrance; foliage large, dark, glossy; bushy growth; ['King of Hearts' × 'Granada']; intr. 1985

'Wild Child' S, lp, 1980, Hall, William W.; bud small, pointed; flowers 5 petals, borne 3-15 per cluster, moderate tea fragrance; repeat bloom; foliage small, light green, 9 leaflet, slightly rugose; prickles curved, thin; vigorous, erect, some arching growth; [R. rugosa rubra × (Dortmund® × unknown)]; intr. 1982

Wild Dancer™ -- See 'Jacina'

'Wild Edric' -- See 'Aushedge'

'Wild Flame' HT, or, 1974, Meyer, C.; bud ovoid; flowers medium, dbl., moderate fragrance; foliage leathery; vigorous, upright growth; PP3668; ['Granada' × 'South Seas']; intr. 1973

'Wild Flower' HT, ob; intr. 2004

'Wild Flower' Min, rb; flowers white, heavily striped and splashed red, double, cupped, moderate fragrance; large growth

'Wild Flower' -- See 'Auswing'

'Wild Ginger' Gr, ob, 1976, Buck, Dr. Griffith J.; bud ovoid, pointed; flowers ginger, apricot orange, 4-4½ in., 30-35 petals, cupped, borne in clusters of 4 - 10, moderate fruity fragrance; recurrent; foliage dark green, leathery; upright, bushy growth; winter hardy; [(Queen Elizabeth® × 'Ruth Hewitt') × 'Lady Elgin']

'Wild Honey' HT, ab, 1978, Weeks; bud long, pointed; flowers coral and peach, 3-5 in., 40-50 petals, high-centered, cupped, borne singly and in small clusters, intense spicy fragrance; recurrent; foliage medium size, leathery, dark green; prickles some, short, hooked slightly downward; tall, vigorous growth; PP4357; intr. 1977

'Wild One' -- See 'Lyowe'

Wild Plum™ -- See 'Jacwig'

'Wild Rover' F, m, Dickson; recurrent; foliage large, light green, semi-glossy; 130 cm. growth; intr. 2007

'Wild Spice' -- See 'Jacruwhi'

'Wild Spirit' S, mr, 1985, James, John; flowers bright medium red, small, 5 petals; non-recurrent; foliage small, dark, matte; vigorous, upright, branched growth; ['Alika' × R. moyesii]

'Wild Thing' -- See 'Tinwild'

Wild Thing™ -- See 'Jactose'

'Wild West' -- See 'Tanravens'

'Wildac' (Dr Adam Christman™) Gr, dr, 1987, Williams, J. Benjamin; flowers dark crimson red to scarlet, large, full, borne in large sprays, slight fragrance; foliage large, dark green, semi-glossy; upright growth; [Queen Elizabeth® × 'Chrysler Imperial']

'Wildak' (Amber Flash™) MinFl, ob, 1982, Williams, J. Benjamin; flowers medium, dbl., moderate fragrance; foliage medium size, dark, semi-glossy; PP5271; ['Zorina' × Starina®]

'Wildan' (The Daniel™) HT, dr, 1990, Williams, J. Benjamin; bud ovoid; flowers dark velvety red, reverse burgundy, medium, 36 petals, high-centered, borne usually singly, no fragrance; foliage large, dark green, semi-glossy, few prickles; upright, medium growth; fruit not observed; ['Chrysler Imperial' × Queen Elizabeth®]; intr. 1990

'Wildance' (Tiny Dancer™) Min, lp, 1990, Williams, J. Benjamin; flowers bright, light coral pink, 34 petals, high-centered, borne usually singly, slight spicy fragrance; foliage small, dark green, dwarf; prickles very few; upright, low growth; [('Carla' × 'Sonia') × ('Circus' × 'Ma Perkins')]; intr. 1990

'Wildawn' (Dawn Creeper™) S, dp, 1995, Williams, J. Benjamin; flowers deep pink, small, semi-dbl., borne in small clusters; foliage small, dark green, glossy; some prickles; low (10-12 in.), spreading growth; ['The Fairy' × ('Sea Foam' × 'Sea Foam')]; intr. 1996

'Wildeb' ('Deborah Beggs Moncrief', Deborah Moncrief™) HT, pb, 1991, Williams, J. Benjamin; flowers pink with ivory blend, large, full, borne mostly singly, intense fragrance; foliage large, dark green, matte; few prickles; medium (3 ft.), bushy, spreading growth; ['Carla' × 'Sonia']; intr. 1991

'Wildels' (Delany Sisters™) Gr, pb, 1997, Williams, J. Benjamin; flowers white with orange-pink highlights on outer petal edges, large, dbl., cupped, ruffled, borne mostly singly and in large clusters, intense fragrance; foliage large, dark green, semi-glossy; upright, bushy, tall (4½-5 ft.) growth; ['Love' × Handel®]; intr. 1997

'Wildenfels Gelb' HFt, w, 1929, Dechant; flowers soft yellow, large, single, moderate Rosa foetida fragrance; recurrent; foliage basil-green; vigorous, strong growth

'Wildenfels Rosa' HFt, mp, 1928, Dechant; flowers rose pink, yellow stamens, medium, single, flat, slight fragrance; early, free flowering; upright, robust growth

'Wildest Dreams' -- See 'Talwil'

'Wildeve' -- See 'Ausbonny'

Wildfang® ('Noawild') S, mp, Noack, Werner; flowers intensive, clear pink, 5 cm., double, cupped, borne in clusters; recurrent; foliage medium to dark green, glossy; mounding growth; intr. 1991

'Wildfeuer' S, mr, 1953, Kordes; flowers fiery red, 4½ in., semi-dbl.; non-remontant; bushy, tall growth

'Wildfire' Min, ob, Fryer's; flowers flame orange, double, pointed, moderate fragrance; free-flowering; compact (2 ft.) growth; intr. 2005

'Wildfire' F, mr, 1956, Swim, H.C.; bud ovoid; flowers bright red, 3 in., 8-10 petals, borne in clusters; foliage leathery; vigorous, bushy, compact growth; PP1381; ['World's Fair' × 'Pinocchio']; intr. 1955

Wildfire™ -- See 'Jacdouce'

'Wildfire 2000' -- See 'Tomfire'

'Wildflower' -- See 'Auswing'

Wildlife® S, pb, Dickson, Patrick

'Wildrem' (Miss All-American Dream™) HT, dp, 1997, Williams, J. Benjamin; flowers large, deep pink, 5½-6 in., very dbl., borne mostly singly, intense fragrance; foliage large, dark green, semi-glossy; prickles moderate; upright, bushy, tall growth; ['Miss All-American Beauty' × 'Bride's Dream']; intr. 1996

'Wildwood' HT, op, 1937, H&S; bud long, pointed; flowers gold, salmon and bronze, semi-dbl.; foliage glossy, wrinkled; vigorous growth

'Wilf Taylor' HT, ab, 1982, Bracegirdle, A.J.; flowers large, 35 petals, high-centered; foliage large, dark, matte; upright growth; ['Gavotte' × 'Red Lion']; intr. 1981

'Wilfolk' ('Musketeer', Boulie's Dream™) S, ob, 1998, Williams, J. Benjamin; flowers orange-red inside, yellow reverse, 4½-5 in., full, borne singly and in large clusters, intense fragrance; foliage large, dark green, semi-glossy; few prickles; strong, vigorous, upright, climbing, arched growth; [Folklore® × 'self']; intr. 1999

'Wilford' (Fordham Rose™) HT, dr, 1990, Williams, J. Benjamin; bud pointed; flowers deep maroon-red with deep, black, velvety tones, dbl., urn-shaped, moderate fragrance; foliage large, dark green, semi-glossy, thick, disease-resistant; prickles few, ovoid, curved down, medium, tan; upright, medium growth; ['Chrysler Imperial' × 'Josephine Bruce']; intr. 1990

'Wilfred Dion ' HT, dr; intr. 2006

'Wilfred H. Perron' -- See 'Lavshrimp'

'Wilfred Norris' HT, op, 1973, Harkness; flowers medium salmon-pink, large, 23 petals; foliage matte; ['Tropicana' × Elizabeth of Glamis®]; intr. 1972

'Wilfred Pickles' HT, op, 1939, Mee; flowers peach shaded gold, well-formed, 6 in., 26 petals; foliage glossy, dark; stems red; very vigorous growth; ['Mrs Charles Lamplough' × 'Edith Mary Mee']

'Wilgene' ('Angel's Blush', 'Gene Jones') F, w, 2000, Williams, J. Benjamin; flowers ivory white, with pink washing, 2½-3 in., dbl., borne in small clusters; foliage medium size, medium green, semi-glossy, disease-resistant; few prickles; growth vigorous, bushy, medium (3½-4 ft.); [Handel® × Stardance™]

'Wilgmar' ('Maren') S, mr, 1988, Gimpel, W.F.; flowers deep scarlet red with velvet overtones, large, full; foliage large, dark green, semi-glossy, leathery; disease-resistant; growth upright, spreading, vigorous, free-standing; ['Red Fountain' × 'Red Fountain']; intr. 1989

'Wilgogh' (Van Gogh™) S, rb, 1996, Williams, J. Benjamin; flowers red and white striped, reverse pale whitish pink with stripes, 3½-4 in., dbl., high-centered, borne in large clusters; foliage large, dark green, semi-glossy; prickles moderate; bushy, medium (3-3½ ft.) growth; [Spinning Wheel™ × Handel®]; intr. 1997

'Wilgold' (Golden Earing™) Min, dy, 1997, Williams, J. Benjamin; flowers large, mini flora, dbl., borne singly and in clusters; ['Hershey Yellow' × 'Copper Kittel']

'Wilgosh' (Gold Sweetheart™) Min, my, 1985, Williams, J. Benjamin; flowers deep yellow, small, 35 petals, slight fragrance; foliage small, medium green, semi-glossy; upright, bushy growth; ['Sunsprite' × 'Rise 'n' Shine']

'Wilhelm' -- See 'Skyrocket'

'Wilhelm Breder' -- See 'Glowing Sunset'

'Wilhelm Hansmann' ('William Hansmann') HKor, dr, 1958, Kordes; bud ovoid; flowers deep crimson, 6-7 cm., dbl., high-centered, borne in large clusters, slight fragrance; recurrent; foliage dark green, leathery; very vigorous growth; [('Baby Château' × 'Else Poulsen') × R. × kordesii]; intr. 1955

'Wilhelm Hartmann' T, rb, 1902, Brauer; flowers shining red with fresh pink, base tinted yellow, full; ['Marie van Houtte' × 'Papa Gontier']

'Wilhelm Kauth' HT, ly, 1930, Kauth; flowers large, very dbl.

'Wilhelm Kordes' HT, op, 1922, Kordes, H.; bud long, pointed; flowers salmon, copper and golden blend, large, dbl., high-centered; foliage bronze, leathery, glossy; bushy growth; ['Gorgeous' × 'Adolf Koschel']

'Wilhelm Kordes, Climbing' Cl HT, op, 1927, Wood & Ingram; flowers salmon and copper yellow, large, full, moderate fragrance; [sport of 'Wilhelm Kordes']

'Wilhelm Marx' S, mr, 1939, Vogel, M.; flowers medium, dbl.

'Wilhelm May' HT, dr, Michler, K. H.; flowers velvety dark red, dbl.; intr. 1989

'Wilhelm Teetzmann' ('Advance Guard') F, mr, 1943, Kordes; flowers intense crimson, open, large, semi-dbl., borne in clusters; very vigorous, upright, bushy growth; ['Holstein' × 'Crimson Glory']

Wilhelm Tell® F, mr, Meilland

'Wilhelm III' -- See 'William III'

'Wilherb' ('Lady Harriet') HT, op, 1992, Williams, J. Benjamin; flowers coral and peach blend, deep orange washings on petals, long, 3-3½ in., full, intense fragrance; foliage large, dark green, semi-glossy; few prickles; tall (4-5 ft.), upright, bushy growth; ['Carla' × 'Sonia']; intr. 1993

'Wilhire Country' -- See 'Willhire Country'

'Wilhkpk' (Rittenhouse™) HT, ob, 1988, Williams, J. Benjamin; flowers fiery orange to copper blended, large, full, moderate fragrance; foliage large, dark green, glossy, disease-resistant; upright, vigorous, mass-blooming, winter hardy growth; [Queen Elizabeth® × 'Zorina']; intr. 1989

'Wilivory' (Ivory Carpet™) S, w, 1995, Williams, J. Benjamin; flowers pure white, ½-1 in., very dbl., borne in small clusters; foliage small, dark green, glossy; some prickles; growth low (10-12 in.), spreading; [('Sea Foam' × 'The Fairy') × 'Star Dance']; intr. 1996

'Wiljame' ('Burgundy Queen', 'James Biddle') HT, mr, 1998, Williams, J. Benjamin; flowers burgundy red, reverse medium red, light silver edges, 4½-5 in., very dbl., high-centered, borne mostly singly; few prickles; [Pink Peace® × Queen Elizabeth®]; intr. 1998

'Wiljoea' ('Lavender Lady', Just Joanna™) HT, m, 2000, Williams, J. Benjamin; flowers lavender pink & ivory blend, lavender pink with deep lavender reverse, 4½-5 in., very full, high-centered, borne mostly solitary, moderate fragrance; foliage large, dark green, glossy; prickles moderate; growth upright, medium (3½-4 ft.); garden, cutting, exhibition; ['Kordes' Perfecta' × 'Lady X']; intr. 1996

'Wiljoeg' ('The Abbottsford Rose', Joe Grey™) S, m, 2002, Williams, J. Ben; flowers lavender pink, reverse purplish pink, ½-1 in., single, borne in large clusters, slight fragrance; foliage small, medium green, matte; prickles small, curved down; stems arching, with numerous branches; growth bushy, medium (3-4 ft.); landscape, hedging; [R. chinensis × R. multiflora nana]; intr. 2003

'Wilkaya' ('Kay Ann', 'Pocahontas') HT, rb, 2000, Williams, J. Benjamin; flowers red and yellow blend, large, full, borne mostly singly or in small clusters, moderate fragrance; repeats well; foliage large, dark green, semi-glossy, disease-resistant; few prickles; strong, compact, upright (3½-4 ft.) growth; ['Peace' × 'Canadian Sunset']; intr. 2000

'Wilkbsp' (Brown County Splendor™) S, yb, 1985, Williams, J. Benjamin; flowers ivory to yellow blended with peach to orange-red, large, 35 petals; foliage large, dark, semi-glossy; upright, spreading growth; ['Paul's Lemon Pillar' × ('Garden Party' × 'Command Performance')]; intr. 1984

'Wilktwo' (Joan Longer™) S, w, 1991, Williams, J. Benjamin; bud pointed; flowers blush pink opening to ivory with a hint of coral pink in center, medium, semi-dbl., cupped, borne in sprays of 5 - 9, moderate damask fragrance; foliage large, dark green, semi-glossy; upright, bushy, tall growth; [Queen Elizabeth® × 'Ivory Fashion, Climbing']; intr. 1991

'Will Alderman' HRg, mp, 1954, Skinner; flowers clear rose-pink, well-shaped, large, dbl.; repeat bloom; erect (4 ft.), bushy growth; [(R. rugosa × R. acicularis) × unknown hybrid tea]

'Will-o'-the-Wisp' -- See 'Clemist'

'Will Rogers' HT, dr, 1936, Howard, F.H.; flowers velvety maroon-crimson, base almost black, burning in sun, 3 in., 65 petals, intense damask fragrance; recurrent; foliage leathery, light; vigorous, bushy, spreading growth; PP256; [seedling × ('Hadley' × 'Crimson Glory')]

'Will Rogers, Climbing' Cl HT, dr, 1940, H&S

'Will Scarlet' HMsk, mr, 1948, Hilling; flowers scarlet, golden stamens, medium, semi-dbl., cupped, ruffled, slight to moderate fragrance; recurrent; [sport of 'Skyrocket']; intr. 1956

'Willash' (Lavender Sweetheart™) Min, m, 1985, Williams, J. Benjamin; flowers deep blue lavender, small, 20 petals, high-centered, borne mostly singly, intense fragrance; foliage small, dark, semi-glossy; bushy growth; ['Double Feature' × 'miniature seedling']

'Willavq' (William Carroll™) Gr, m, 1995, Williams, J. Benjamin; flowers mauve, medium, full, borne mostly singly and in small clusters, slight fragrance; foliage large, dark green, semi-glossy; some prickles; tall (4-5 ft.), upright growth; [Queen Elizabeth® × 'Angel Face']

'Willea' ('Marylea Johnson Richards') HT, ab, 1992, Williams, J. Benjamin; flowers light pink with peach tones, medium, full, borne mostly singly and in small clusters, intense fragrance; foliage medium size, dark green, semi-glossy; few prickles; medium (3-4 ft.), upright, bushy growth; ['Royal Highness' × 'Command Performance']

'Willhire Country' ('Wilhire Country') F, ob, 1981, Beales, Peter; flowers flat-topped, 25 petals, borne 6-8 per cluster; foliage glossy, round, dark; prickles broad, hooked, brown; tall, upright growth; [Elizabeth of Glamis® × 'Arthur Bell']; intr. 1979

'Willi Maass' -- See 'Red Ripples'

'William A. Bilney' HT, pb, 1927, Easlea; flowers pink with light orange, large, very dbl.

'William Allen Richardson' N, yb, 1878, Ducher, Vve.; bud pointed; flowers orange-yellow, usually white at petal edges, medium to large, dbl., borne in small to medium clusters; early bloom, repeating; foliage dark green, glossy; very vigorous, climbing (12 ft.) growth; ['Reve d'Or' × unknown]

'William and Mary' S, rb, Beales, Peter; flowers deep silvery-pink with crimson and carmine highlights, large, double, cupped, borne singly and in clusters, slight fragrance; recurrent; foliage greyish-green, matte; bushy, upright (5-6 ft.) growth; intr. 1988

'William Baffin' HKor, dp, 1983, Svedja, Felicitas; bud ovoid; flowers deep strawberry-pink touched white near the center, 2½ in., 20 petals, flat, borne in clusters of up to 30, slight fragrance; free-flowering; foliage small, medium green, glossy; vigorous, climbing growth; [R. × kordesii × unknown]

'William-Booth' -- See 'AC William-Booth'

'William Booth' -- See 'AC William-Booth'

'William Bowyer' HT, mr, 1924, Chaplin Bros.; bud long, pointed; flowers velvety red; ['Hadley' × 'Hoosier Beauty']

'William C. Egan' HWich, lp, 1900, Dawson; flowers flesh-pink, 7-8 cm., very dbl., quartered, borne in large clusters, moderate fragrance; non-recurrent; foliage bright, glossy; prickles long; long stems; vigorous, semi-climbing growth; [R. wichurana × 'Général Jacqueminot']

William Carroll™ -- See 'Willavq'

'William Carter' HT, dp, 1957, Carter; flowers deep pink; very vigorous growth; [sport of 'Red Ensign']

William Christie® S, mp, Guillot-Massad; flowers rose pink, very full, cupped, borne in clusters, moderate fragrance; recurrent; vigorous (4-5 ft.) growth; intr. 2000

'William Cooper' HT, dr, 1914, Dickson, H.; flowers dark laquered red, very large, full

'William Corbett' F, dp, 1968, Seale Rose Gardens; flowers claret-rose, semi-dbl., borne in trusses, slight fragrance; vigorous growth; [sport of 'Dorothy Wheatcroft']

'William David' -- See 'Pearoyal'

'William E. Nickerson' HT, or, 1928, Easlea; flowers glowing orange-cerise, large, dbl.; foliage light; vigorous growth; ['Priscilla' × 'William F. Dreer']

'William F. Dreer' HT, lp, 1920, H&S; flowers shell-pink, base yellow, sometimes suffusing the entire flower, dbl., high-centered; ['Mme Segond Weber' × 'Lyon Rose']

'William F. Ekas' HT, op, 1935, Cremer; bud cupped; flowers salmon-orange, suffused pink,, 4 in., 45-50 petals, moderate fragrance; PP177; [sport of 'Souvenir']

'William Francis Bennett' HT, mr, 1886, Bennett; bud long; flowers crimson, large, dbl., moderate fragrance; foliage very dark; ['Adam' × 'Xavier Olibo']

'William Godfrey' S, lp, 1954, Skinner; bud white; flowers pale pink, well-shaped, large, very dbl.; intermittent bloom all season; moderately vigorous, erect growth; ['Altalaris' × 'hybrid perpetual']

'William Grant' HGal, dp

'William Griffith' HP, pb, 1850, Portemer; flowers glossy pink, changing to light satin-rose, medium, very full, cupped; foliage dark green, slightly rugose; prickles large, slightly hooked, reddish

'William Grow' M, dr, 1858, Laffay, M.; flowers velvety violet/red, medium, dbl., borne in clusters of 6-8; foliage dark green; numerous prickles

'William Hansmann' -- See 'Wilhelm Hansmann'

'William Harvey' HT, mr, 1948, Norman; flowers scarlet, 4-6 in., dbl., high-centered; vigorous, bushy growth; ['Crimson Glory' × 'Southport']

'William Jesse' HCh, mr, 1838, Laffay, M.; flowers red suffused violet, large, dbl., flat; unreliable repeat; growth erect; [probably 'Mme Desprez' × uncertain]; sometimes classed as B

'William K. Harris' HWich, lp, 1903, Hoopes & Thomas; flowers light flesh pink, large, dbl.; [R. wichurana × 'Bon Silène']

'William Leech' -- See 'Hortropic'

'William Lobb' ('Duchesse d'Istrie', 'Old Velvet Moss') M, m, 1855, Laffay, M.; bud heavily mossed; flowers dark crimson-purple, reverse lilac-pink, fading to grayish-lilac, large, semi-dbl., flat, moderate fragrance; non-remontant; foliage medium size, dark grey-green; extremely prickly; vigorous, tall, arching growth; sometimes attributed to Portemer

'William McGown' S, ob, Peden, G.H.

'William Moore' HT, mp, 1935, McGredy; bud long, pointed; flowers soft, even-toned pink, becoming deeper, large, dbl., cupped; foliage soft, light; bushy growth

'William Morris' -- See 'Auswill'

'William Notting' HT, rb, 1904, Soupert & Notting; bud long; flowers salmon-red, center brighter, large, dbl., moderate fragrance; foliage dark green; ['Mme Abel Chatenay' × 'Antoine Rivoire']

'William Orr' HT, mr, 1930, McGredy; bud long, pointed; flowers crimson-scarlet, large, 45 petals, high-centered, intense fragrance; recurrent; foliage light, glossy, leathery; vigorous growth

'William P.J. McCarthy' S, mp, Jalbert, Brad; intr. 2008

'William Paul' HP, mp, 1862, Guillot; flowers carmine, medium, full

'William Quarrier' -- See 'Coclager'

'William R. Smith' ('Blush Maman Cochet', 'President Wm. R. Smith', 'Charles Dingee', 'Jeanette Heller', 'Maiden's Blush', 'President Smith') T, pb, 1908, Bagg; bud pointed; flowers center pale pink, outer petals creamy flesh, base citron-yellow, large, dbl.; foliage rich green, leathery; vigorous growth; ['Maman Cochet' × 'Mme Hoste']

'William Rollison' HP, mr, 1865, Verdier, E.; flowers bright cherry-red, aging to scarlet, large, full, globular

'William Saunders' HT, 1918, Byrnes

William Shakespeare® -- See 'Ausroyal'

'William Shakespeare 2000' -- See 'Ausromeo'

'William Shean' HT, mp, 1906, Dickson, A.; bud long, tapering; flowers clear rose-pink, veined darker, very large, dbl.

'William Silva' HT, 1951, Silva; prickles few at base; vigorous growth; ['Étoile de Hollande' × 'Radiance']

'William Stubbs' -- See 'Bosneech'

'William IV' HSpn, w, before 1838, from England; flowers small to medium

'William III' ('Wilhelm III') HSpn, m, before 1910; flowers magenta-crimson, changing to rich plum, fading to dark lilac, reverse paler, small, single to semi-dbl., cupped, borne mostly singly, moderate spicy/sweet fragrance; non-remontant; foliage tiny, dark leaden green; modest, arching growth; hips round, shiny black

'William Thomson' Pol, pb, 1921, Leenders, M.; flowers salmon-carmine and bright rose, small, borne in clusters; compact, bushy growth; ['Maman Turbat' × 'Ellen Poulsen']

'William Tyndale' LCl, m, Marshall; intr. 1990s

'William Walker' -- See 'Debraro'

'William Warden' HP, op, 1878, Mitchell; flowers salmon-pink, very large, full, slight fragrance; recurrent; [sport of 'Mme Clémence Joigneaux']

'William Wright Walcott' HT, lp, 1921, McGorum; flowers outer petals darker, dbl.; ['Richmond' × 'Ophelia']

'Williams' Double Yellow' ('Double Yellow Scots Rose', 'Double Yellow', 'Jaune de William', 'Jaune Double', *R. spinosissima lutea plena*) HFt, my, before 1819, Williams, John; flowers pine-yellow with green carpels in center, 2 in., semi-dbl., borne mostly singly, intense sweet fragrance; very free blooming in spring; foliage tiny, dark green; growth free but spindly; often classed as a HSpn

'William's Evergreen' HSem, w, 1850, William; flowers white, center rosy flesh, borne in large clusters; possibly synonymous with 'Flore'

'Williamsburg' HT, lp, 1965, Howard, A.P.; bud long, pointed; flowers rose-pink, medium, dbl., cupped, moderate fragrance; foliage dark, glossy; vigorous, upright growth; PP2730; ['Contrast' × Queen Elizabeth®]

'Williamsburg Days' S, rb, Williams, J. Benjamin; flowers red with varying number of pink stripes, yellow stamens, semi-double, flat; recurrent; intr. 1998

'Williams's Sweetbriar' HEg, lp, about 1800, Williams of Turnham Green; flowers dbl.

'Willie Mae' Min, mr, 1966, Moore, Ralph S.; flowers small, dbl.; foliage dark, glossy, leathery; vigorous, bushy, dwarf growth; PP2834; [(*R. wichurana* × Carolyn Dean) × 'Little Buckaroo']

'Willie Winkie' Min, lp, 1955, deVink; flowers light rose-pink, small, dbl., globular; small, micro-mini growth; ['Katharina Ziemet' × 'Tom Thumb']

'Willildeb' ('Yvon Cléroux', Little Deb™) MinFl, or, 2002, Williams, J. Ben; flowers bright, velvety orange, reverse dull orange-red, 1-1½ in., semi-dbl., borne in small clusters; foliage small, dark green, semi-glossy; prickles insignificant; growth compact, short (12-14 in.); containers, edging, borders; [Scarlet Sunblaze™ × Orange Sunblaze™]; intr. 2003

Willing™ -- See 'Tuckwilling'

'Willits Crescendo' LCl, lp

'Williwaw' HT, m, 1978, R. v. S. Melle; bud pointed; flowers red-purple, yellow at base, 60 petals, cupped, moderate fragrance; foliage glossy, dark; prickles hooked; upright growth; ['Silver Lining' × 'Duke of Windsor']

'Willork' (Louise Park™) HT, mr, 2005, Williams, J. Benjamin; flowers bright red, 3 in., dbl., cupped, ruffled, borne mostly solitary, moderate fragrance; free-flowering; foliage small, medium green, glossy; prickles moderate, 1/8 in., downturned; growth upright, medium; garden decorative; winter hardy; ['Pete Musser' × 'Peggy Rockerfeller']; originally named Firefighter; intr. 2003

'Willowmere' HT, op, 1913, Pernet-Ducher; bud long, pointed, coral-red; flowers rich shrimp-pink, center yellow, large, dbl., cupped; foliage light green; prickles red, numerous, strong; medium, spreading growth; [seedling × 'Lyon Rose']

'Willowmere, Climbing' Cl HT, op, 1924, Mermet; flowers shrimp-red, shaded yellow at center, large, full; [sport of 'Willowmere']

'Willuce' (Luce di Todi™) HT, dr, 1998, Williams, J. Benjamin; flowers dark velvet red, 5 in.-5½ in., 26-41 petals, high-centered, borne singly, intense fragrance; foliage large, dark green, semi-glossy; few prickles; tall (4-5 ft.), upright, growth; [Mister Lincoln® × 'Miss All-American Beauty']; intr. 2000

'Willy Chapel' HT, yb, 1930, Delhaye; flowers coppery yellow, shaded salmon and shrimp-pink; vigorous growth

'Willy Den Ouden' Pol, or, 1938, Den Ouden; flowers intense orange, small, rosette, borne on trusses; dwarf, compact growth

'Wilmag' (Little Magician™) Min, yb, 1990, Williams, J. Benjamin; bud ovoid; flowers light yellow with orange-red blend, loose, small, 32 petals, high-centered, borne usually singly, slight damask fragrance; foliage small, medium green, semi-glossy; no prickles; growth low; winter hardy; ['Circus' × Magic Carrousel®]; intr. 1990

'Wilmnng' (Midnight Magic™) HT, dr, 1985, Williams, J. Benjamin; flowers large, 35 petals, high-centered; foliage large, dark, semi-glossy; [('Chrysler Imperial' × Mister Lincoln®) × ('Christian Dior' × 'Josephine Bruce')]; intr. 1986

'Wilmtho' (Mary Lyon™) Gr, w, 1988, Williams, J. Benjamin; flowers pure chalk white, medium, full, intense fragrance; foliage large, dark green, semi-glossy, thick; upright, hardy growth; [('Mount Shasta' × 'Sonia') × ('White Masterpiece' × 'Ivory Fashion')]

'Wilorpat' (Orange Pastel™) Min, ob, 1997, Williams, J. Benjamin; flowers medium, bright orange-red, reverse dull, 2½-3 in., dbl., borne in small clusters, slight fragrance; foliage medium size, dark green, semi-glossy; few prickles; growth compact, low (12-18in.); [Red Sunblaze® × Orange Sunblaze™]; intr. 1997

'Wilpada' (Patio Dance™) MinFl, rb, 1985, Williams, J. Benjamin; flowers medium red, white reverse, small, 20 petals, high-centered; foliage medium size, dark, glossy; strong, low, bushy growth; ['Winifred Coulter' × White Gem®]

'Wilpago' (Patio Gold™) MinFl, my, 1985, Williams, J. Benjamin; flowers small, dbl.; foliage medium size, dark, semi-glossy; low, compact, bushy growth; ['Patio Patty' × 'Rise 'n' Shine']

'Wilpasn' (Patio Snow™) MinFl, w, 1985, Williams, J. Benjamin; flowers small, 35 petals, moderate fragrance; foliage small, medium green, semi-glossy; groundcover; very compact, spreading growth; ['Sea Foam' × 'Charlie McCarthy']

'Wilpavl' ('Pink Avalanche') S, mp, 1988, Williams, J. Benjamin; flowers coral pink to medium red, small, dbl., borne in sprays of 20-30; foliage medium size, medium green, glossy; spreading, compact growth; ['Sea Foam' × 'The Fairy']; intr. 1989

'Wilpete' ('Liaison', 'Pete Musser') F, or, 2000, Williams, J. Benjamin; flowers orange-red, non-fading, large, full, high-centered, borne mostly singly, moderate fragrance; foliage large, dark green, glossy; few prickles; upright, tall (3½-4 ft.) growth; ['Olympiad' × Mister Lincoln®]; intr. 2000

'Wilpink' ('Hot Pink Pastel', Pink Sweetheart™) F, mp, 1985, Williams, J. Benjamin; intr. 1985

'Wilpksh' ('Hot Pink Pastel', Pink Sweetheart™) F, mp, 1985, Williams, J. Benjamin; flowers medium coral pink, well-formed, 2-2½ in., dbl., borne singly, moderate fragrance; foliage medium size, medium green, semi-glossy; prickles moderate; upright, dwarf growth; [('Carla' × 'Sonia') × ('Circus' × 'Ma Perkins')]; intr. 1985

'Wilplpd' (Plum Pudding™) Min, m, 1985, Williams, J. Benjamin; flowers blue-lavender washed red and purple, small, 35 petals, moderate fragrance; foliage small, dark, semi-glossy; upright, bushy growth; ['Angel Face' × 'lavender seedling']

'Wilpop' (Pink Popcorn™) S, lp, 1991, Williams, J. Benjamin; flowers light pink to coral, small, semi-dbl., borne in large clusters in small, grape-like sprays, slight fragrance; foliage small, medium green, matte, disease-resistant; few prickles; low (12-18 in.), compact, bushy growth; [*R. chinensis minima* × ('Sea Foam' × 'The Fairy')]

'Wilpurp' (Purple Popcorn™) S, m, 1991, Williams, J. Benjamin; flowers bluish purple, small, semi-dbl., borne in small, grape-like clusters, slight fragrance; foliage small, medium green, matte, disease-resistant; few prickles; low (12-18 in.), compact, bushy growth; [*R. chinensis minima* × ('Sea Foam' × 'The Fairy')]

'Wilrib' ('Red Pastel', Red Ribbon™, 'Red Riddle') F, mr, 1997, Williams, J. Benjamin; flowers medium, dbl., borne in small clusters, moderate fragrance; foliage medium size, medium green, semi-glossy; upright, compact, medium (14-18 in.)growth; [Red Sunblaze® × Pink Sweetheart™]

'Wilrss' ('Pat's Delight') S, mr, 1987, Williams, J. Benjamin; flowers crimson to light scarlet, loose, 16 petals, cupped, borne in sprays of 5-7; foliage large, dark green, glossy; prickles light green, curving downwards; upright, strong, good branching growth; [Queen Elizabeth® × 'Chrysler Imperial']

'Wilsab' ('Gabriela Sabatini') Min, or, 1992, Williams, J. Benjamin; flowers bright fire orange-red, medium, dbl., borne mostly singly, slight fragrance; foliage small, dark green, semi-glossy; few prickles; growth low (14-20 in.); [Marina® × Pink Sweetheart™]

'Wilscarlet' (Scarlet Spreader™) S, dr, 1995, Williams, J. Benjamin; flowers dark scarlet red, 1-1½ in., 6-14 petals, borne in small clusters; foliage small, dark green, glossy; some prickles; dwarf, spreading, low (10-12 in.) growth; [seedling × 'Red Fountain']; intr. 1996

'Wilscso' (Elizabeth Scholtz™) Gr, yb, 1988, Williams, J. Benjamin; flowers deep yellow with orange washing, reverse yellow with orange, full, high-centered, moderate damask fragrance; foliage large, plum-red to dark green, glossy; upright, bushy growth; [('Granada' × 'Oregold') × ('Arizona' × 'Sunblest')]

'Wilsent' (Charlotte Jan™) S, mp, 2005, Williams, J. Benjamin; flowers 3 in., dbl., old-fashioned, borne in small clusters, moderate fragrance; remontant; foliage medium size, medium green, semi-glossy; prickles medium, curved down, light green, few; growth compact, medium (3-3½ ft.); beds, hedging, landscaping; ['Rose Parade' × 'Jin Bowie']; intr. 1999

'Wilsept' ('September Eighteenth') HT, pb, 1991, Williams, J. Benjamin; bud ovoid; flowers shell pink, reverse deep coral pink, aging light pink, medium, dbl., high-centered, borne usually singly or in sprays of 3 - 4, intense damask fragrance; foliage large, light green, semi-glossy; medium, bushy growth; ['Carla' × Queen Elizabeth®]

'Wilsfol' (Search for Life™) HT, mr, 1988, Williams, J. Benjamin; flowers large, full, high-centered; foliage large, dark green, semi-glossy; vigorous, hardy, abundant growth; ['Miss All-American Beauty' × Mister Lincoln®]

'Wilshire'   HT, mp, 1991, Woodard, Joe M.; bud pointed; flowers medium, 25 petals, high-centered, moderate fragrance; foliage medium size, medium green, glossy; upright, tall growth; [sport of 'Don Juan']; intr. 1991

'Wilslav' (Slava™) HT, rb, 1987, Williams, J. Benjamin; flowers scarlet red, reverse ivory white, large, 34 petals, high-centered, borne singly, moderate damask fragrance; foliage large, dark green, glossy, disease-resistant; prickles medium, few, yellow-green, hooked downwards; upright, bushy, tall growth; hips rounded, medium, pumpkin-orange; ['Garden Party' × 'Love']; intr. 1988

'Wilsma' (Astra™) Min, mp, 1982, Williams, J. Benjamin; flowers pink, bright yellow stamens, small, 5 petals, borne singly and in small clusters; foliage small, medium green, semi-glossy; short, upright growth; PP5272; ['Pinafore' × ('Lilibet' × 'Fairy Queen')]

'Wilsnod' (Snowdrift™) S, w, 1985, Williams, J. Benjamin; flowers small, 35 petals, borne in large sprays, slight fragrance; repeat bloom; foliage medium size, dark, semi-glossy; low, spreading growth; ['Sea Foam' × 'The Fairy']; intr. 1986

'Wilspring' (Spring Time™) Min, w, 1991, Williams, J. Benjamin; bud pointed; flowers ivory white with light red edge, reverse ivory with light yellow base, small, 26 petals, high-centered, borne usually singly, intense damask fragrance; foliage small, dark green, semi-glossy; bushy, low growth; [('Easter Morning' × 'Easter Morning') × 'Toy Clown']; intr. 1990

'Wilstar' ('Scarlet Star') LCl, mr, 1999, Williams, J. Benjamin; bud pointed, small to medium; flowers smoky red, 2½-3 in., 20 -25 petals, informal, borne in large clusters, slight spicy fragrance; foliage large, medium green, semi-glossy; prickles numerous, curved and hooked; climbing, upright, bushy, tall (12-15 ft.) growth; PP11834; ['Red Fountain' × Mister Lincoln®]; intr. 1999

'Wilsue'   S, mr, William, J. Benjamin; intr. 2004

'Wilsun' (Tequila Sunset™) F, ob, 1991, Williams, J. Benjamin; bud ovoid; flowers brilliant orange and yellow blend, petals quilled, medium, 32 petals, urn-shaped, borne in sprays of 3-7, moderate fruity fragrance; foliage medium size, medium green, semi-glossy; growth upright, bushy, medium; ['Redgold' × 'Tropicana']; intr. 1992

'Wilton'   S, w, Tantau ?; groundcover?; intr. 2002

'Wiltshire' ('Beautiful Carpet', 'Elfrid') S, mp, Kordes; flowers bright rose pink, double, cupped, borne in clusters, slight fragrance; recurrent; foliage medium green, glossy; growth low, spreading plant; intr. 1993

'Wiltshire Pride' -- See 'Sanwife'

'Wiltwos' (Two Sisters™) S, w, 1993, Williams, J. Benjamin; flowers light pink to white, color variable, medium, full, borne in large clusters, slight fragrance; recurrent; foliage medium size, dark green, semi-glossy; some prickles; medium (3½-4 ft.), bushy, spreading growth; ['Sea Foam' × 'The Fairy']; intr. 1993

'Wilvang'   S, pb, Williams, J.B.; intr. 2004

'Wilwavl' ('White Avalanche') S, w, 1988, Williams, J. Benjamin; flowers cream, opening to pure white, small, dbl., borne in clusters; foliage medium size, medium green, glossy, disease-resistant; spreading, compact, uniform., winter hardy growth; ['Sea Foam' × 'The Fairy']

'Wilwind' ('Windmill') Gr, rb, 1992, Williams, J. Benjamin; flowers burgundy with ivory white on reverse, 3-3½ in., single, borne singly; foliage medium size, medium green, semi-glossy; few prickles; medium (3-5 ft.), bushy, spreading growth; [Handel® × ('Love' × 'Double Feature')]; originally registered as S; intr. 1994

'Wilyeld' (Ebby™) S, dy, 2005, Williams, Benjamin R.; flowers semi-dbl., high-centered, borne in small clusters, moderate fragrance; foliage medium size, dark green, semi-glossy; prickles moderate, straight; growth compact, medium (36 in.); garden decorative; ['Ben's Gold' × 'Eclipse']; intr. 2005

'Wilyelp' (Yellow Pastel™) Min, dy, 1997, Williams, J. Benjamin; flowers bright butter yellow, reverse slightly darker, medium, dbl., borne mostly singly, slight fragrance; foliage medium size, medium green, semi-glossy; upright, compact, medium (13-18in.) growth; ['Sunnydew' × 'Rise'n'Shine']

'Wim Oudshoorn'   F, pb; flowers soft, pastel pink, yellow stamens, semi-dbl. to double, high-centered, flattens, borne mostly in clusters; recurrent; foliage fresh green; low, broad growth

Wimi® -- See 'Tanrowisa'

'Win Win' -- See 'Wekwinwin'

'Winbilee' (Better Homes & Gardens Diamond Jubilee™) HT, rb, 1997, Winchel, Joseph F.; flowers ivory cream, silvery with raspberry edges, 3 in., full, slight fragrance; foliage medium size, medium green, semi-glossy; upright, medium (5ft.) growth; ['Lynn Anderson' × seedling]

'Winbob' ('Dr Bob Harvey') HT, lp, 1993, Winchel, Joseph F.; flowers soft pink, medium, full, no fragrance; foliage medium size, medium green, matte; bushy growth; [seedling × seedling]

'Winbur' (American Dream™) HT, dr, 1987, Winchel, Joseph F.; flowers deep red, large, 25 petals, high-centered, borne singly, slight damask fragrance; foliage medium size, medium green, semi-glossy; prickles average, dark brown, slightly recurved; upright, tall growth; hips round, average, medium size, medium orange; [('My Dream' × 'Charles Mallerin') × seedling]; intr. 1990

Winchester Cathedral® -- See 'Auscat'

'Wind Chimes' HMsk, mp, 1946; flowers rosy pink, 1 in., single, borne in large clusters, intense fragrance; recurrent; vigorous (15-20 ft.) growth; hips flattened, orange; intr. 1949

'Wind Rhythm'   MinFl, ob, Jalbert; flowers blend of oranges and yellows, large, full, hybrid tea; low (12-14 in.) growth

'Wind Song'   HT, ab, 1970, Morey, Dennison; flowers orange, large, dbl., moderate fragrance; foliage leathery; bushy growth; ['Royal Sunset' × 'Sierra Sunset']; intr. 1968

'Windekind'   F, mr, 1976, Institute of Ornamental Plant Growing; bud pointed; flowers 3 in., 34 petals, cupped; foliage matte, dark; upright growth; ['Colour Wonder' × 'Geisha']; intr. 1974

'Windermere'   HWich, dp, 1932, Chaplin

Bros.; flowers carmine-rose, 6-7 cm., semi-dbl., borne in small clusters, slight fragrance; foliage dark green, glossy; numerous prickles; vigorous growth

'Windermere' -- See 'Aushomer'

'Windflower' -- See 'Auscross'

'Winding Road' -- See 'Talroad'

'Windjammer' -- See 'Savswat'

'Windlass' HCh, m, Sutherland, P; [sport of 'Simon Robinson' seedling]; intr. 1995

'Windmill' -- See 'Wilwind'

'Windonna' ('Donna Darlin'') HT, rb, 1993, Winchel, Joseph F.; flowers yellow blending pink to bright red, medium, dbl., slight fragrance; foliage large, dark green, semi-glossy; some prickles; medium (4 ft.), bushy growth; PP10112; [seedling × Double Delight™ ®]; intr. 1994

Windrose® S, lp, Noack, Werner; flowers soft pink, yellow stamens, 4 cm., single, shallow cup, borne in clusters; recurrent; foliage dark green, glossy; upright, arching growth; intr. 1993

Windrush® -- See 'Ausrush'

'Windsor' HT, mr, 1929, Chaplin Bros.; flowers rich crimson-scarlet; vigorous growth

'Windsor Castle' -- See 'Constance Finn'

'Windsor Charm' HT, lp, 1978, LeMire, Walter; bud long, tulip shaped; flowers light pink to ivory,, 5-5½ in., 27-30 petals; foliage leathery; vigorous, bushy growth; [sport of 'First Prize']

'Windsounds' HT, lp, 1977, Scoggins; [sport of 'First Prize']; intr. 1976

'Windstar' -- See 'Pink Bowie'

'Windy City' Min, dp, 1974, Moore, Ralph S.; bud long, pointed; flowers deep pink, reverse lighter, small, 3-3½ cm., dbl., high-centered, borne singly and several together, slight sweet fragrance; recurrent; foliage small, bronze early, then medium green, semi-glossy; prickles few, medium, hooked downward, brown; stems strong, medium; upright, bushy growth; hips none ; PP3792; ['Little Darling' × ('Little Darling' × (R. wichurana × seedling))]

Wine and Dine™ -- See 'Dicuncle'

'Wine and Roses' HMsk, dr, Clements, John K.; flowers dark wine red, semi-double, borne in large trusses; foliage rich green, glossy, long, narrow; bushy (3½ ft.) growth; PPAF; intr. 1999

'Wine Buff' F, yb, Benny, David; flowers peach/chardonnay, dbl; foliage reddish green when young, aging to medium green, glossy

'Winefred Clarke' HT, my, 1964, Robinson, H.; flowers 5½ in., 34 petals, high-centered; foliage dark, glossy; ['Peace' × 'Lydia']

'Winfpage' (Front Page™) HT, rb, 2000, Winchel, Joseph F.; flowers red with pink reverse, 5 in., 27-28 petals, high-centered, borne mostly singly, slight fragrance; recurrent; foliage large, dark green, semi-glossy; prickles moderate, dorsal, light yellow; compact, low (2-3 ft.) growth; PP12609; [Blue Nile® × seedling]; intr. 2000

Wing-Ding™ -- See 'Wekairyven'

'Winged Fellowship' -- See 'Horwingfel'

'Wingold' (Super Gold™) HT, ly, 1999, Winchel, Joseph F.; flowers 2½ in., dbl., borne mostly singly, slight fragrance; foliage large, dark green, glossy; few prickles; upright, tall (36 in.) growth; PP12739; [Gold Medal® × seedling]; intr. 2000

'Wini Edmunds' HT, rb, 1974, McGredy, Sam IV; bud ovoid; flowers red, reverse blush white, 5½-6 in., 20-24 petals, high-centered, spiral, borne singly, slight sweet fragrance; recurrent; foliage large, dark green, leathery; prickles few, large, recurved; vigorous, upright (5 ft.) growth; hips round, flattened, yellow; PP3822; ['Red Lion' × 'Hanne']; intr. 1973

'Winifred' HT, yb, 1930, Chaplin Bros.; flowers deep yellow, shaded peach to old-gold, large, dbl.; vigorous growth; ruled extinct 04/81 but exists at Sangerhausen

'Winifred' Gr, mp, Jerabek, Paul E.; bud pointed; flowers bright medium pink, 23 petals, slight fragrance; foliage reddish when young; prickles slightly hooked, red; vigorous, tall growth; [Queen Elizabeth® × seedling]; intr. 1981

'Winifred Coulter' F, rb, 1962, Kemple; bud pointed; flowers vermilion-scarlet, reverse silvery, 2½-3½ in., 18-26 petals, flat, borne in clusters, intense fragrance; recurrent; foliage leathery, glossy, dark green; prickles several, hooked downward; vigorous, bushy growth; hips globular, orange-red; PP2219; ['Baby Chateau' × 'Contrast']; intr. 1962

'Winifred Coulter, Climbing' Cl F, rb, Jarvis; intr. about 1968

'Winkfield Crimson Emperor' LCl, dr, 1960, Combe; flowers dark crimson, large, 27 petals, borne in clusters; recurrent bloom; foliage leathery, vigorous, pillar growth; ['Red Empress' × 'Surprise']; intr. 1958

'Winmom' ('Mom's Rose') HT, pb, 2003, Winchel, Joe; flowers smoky pink with pastel shading, large, 35 petals, classic hybrid tea, borne mostly solitary, slight fruity fragrance; recurrent; foliage medium size, medium green, semi-glossy; prickles average, curved; growth upright, medium (5 ft.); exhibition, garden decoration; [seedling × seedling]; intr. 2003

'Winners All' HT, dp, 1990; bud ovoid; flowers carmine pink with a touch of orange in center, loose, large, dbl., cupped, slight fruity fragrance; foliage medium size, medium green, semi-glossy; bushy, medium growth; [sport of 'Cherry Brandy']; intr. 1986

'Winner's Choice' -- See 'Jacmad'

Winner's Circle™ -- See 'Radwin'

'Winnie Davis' T, mp, 1892, Little; bud long, pointed; flowers pink with lighter reflexes, semi-dbl., moderate fragrance; ['Devoniensis' × 'Mme de Watteville']

'Winnie Renshaw' -- See 'Renwinnie'

Winning Colors™ -- See 'Twowin'

'Winnipeg Parks' S, dp, 1991, Collicutt, Lynn M.; bud slender, pointed; flowers dark pink-red, 7-10 cm., 22 petals, cupped, borne singly or in sprays of 2 - 4, slight fragrance; repeat bloom; foliage medium size, medium green, matte; prickles some, 4-6 mm, linear, angled downward, reddish; medium (2-3 ft.), bushy growth; winter hardy ; PP9122; [('Prairie Princess' × 'Cuthbert Grant') × (seedling × 'Morden Cardinette')]; intr. 1990

'Winptig' (Perfume Tiger™) F, rb, 1999, Winchel, Joseph F.; flowers dark red and white striped, 1¾ in., 41 petals, borne in large clusters, intense fragrance; foliage medium size, medium green, semi-glossy; prickles moderate; spreading, medium (27 in.) growth; PP12630; ['Roller Coaster' × seedling]; intr. 2000

'Winschoten' -- See 'Winshoten'

'Winshoten' ('Winschoten') S, dr, Meilland; flowers large, red, full, intense fragrance; intr. 2000

Winsome™ -- See 'Savawin'

'Winsome' HT, dp, 1924, E.G. Hill, Co.; flowers cherry-rose, dbl.; ruled extinct 01/85; ['Premier' × 'Hoosier Beauty']

'Winsome' Cl HT, mr, 1931, Dobbie; bud long, pointed; flowers cherry-red, 3-3½ in., dbl., borne in small clusters, strong tea fragrance; foliage leathery; very vigorous growth; ruled extinct ARA 1985, but it is not (Sangerhausen)

'Winsome Native' S, w, 1980, Stoddard, Louis; bud ovoid, pointed; flowers 20 petals, cupped, borne singly, no fragrance; sparse, repeat bloom; foliage finely serrated, 5 leaflet; no prickles; rounded, medium growth; ['Gene Boerner' × R. suffulta]

'Winspit' LCl, w, Bates; intr. 2001

'Winter Cheer' HMsk, mr, 1914, Pemberton; flowers crimson, medium, semi-dbl.

'Winter Gem' T, lp, 1898, Childs; flowers creamy pink, large, dbl.

'Winter Haven' -- See 'Caswin'

'Winter King' S, dp, 1985, James, John; flowers bright deep pink, 11 petals, borne singly; repeat bloom; foliage medium size, dark, leathery, matte; compact, branching growth; hardy; [(('McGredy's Scarlet' × 'Polly') × 'Frau Karl Druschki' × 'Northlander']

Winter Magic™ -- See 'Foumagic'

'Winter Princess' -- See 'Gelwin'

'Winter Sunset' ('Fuzzy Navel') S, yb, 1997, Buck, Dr. Griffith J.; flowers amber-orange, 4 in., 30-40 petals, high-centered, borne in small clusters, moderate fruity fragrance; recurrent; foliage large, dark green, glossy; upright, bushy, medium growth; ['Serendipity' × ('Country Dancer' × 'Alexandra')]; intr. 1985

Winter Wheat™ -- See 'Miniwin'

'Wintonbury Parish' -- See 'Berpar'
'Wintoniensis' (R. × wintoniensis) HMoy, mp, 1935; sepals long, leafy; flowers rosy pink, single, shallow cup, borne in large clusters; foliage with sweetbriar (apple) fragrance; vigorous (2 m.) growth; hips bristly, flagon-shaped; [R. moyesii × R. setipoda]
'Wircurob' ('Lizabeth's Lullabye') HT, yb, 1991, Robbins, William C.; flowers yellow with pink tips, large, 35-40 petals, moderate fragrance; foliage large, dark green, glossy; upright, tall growth; [Queen Elizabeth® × 'Song of Paris']
'Wisbech Gold' HT, yb, 1964, McGredy, Sam IV; flowers golden yellow edged pinkish, well-formed,, 4 in., 35 petals, cupped; vigorous, compact growth; [Piccadilly® × 'Golden Star']
Wisbech Rose Fragrant Delight® -- See 'Fragrant Delight'
'Wisbril' ('Brilliant Betty') HT, pb, 2000, Singer, Steven J.; flowers bright pink, reverse light pink, 4-5 in., full, borne mostly singly; foliage medium size, medium green, semi-glossy; prickles moderate; upright growth to 4-6 ft.; ['Great Scott' × 'King of Hearts']; intr. 2001
'Wise Portia' -- See 'Ausport'
'Wishful Thinking' -- See 'Seawish'
'Wishing' -- See 'Dickerfuffle'
Wishing Well® HT, w, Zary, Keith; intr. 1999
'Wisida' ('Ida') HT, dp, 2003, Singer, Steve; flowers deep pink, reverse light pink, 12 cm., full, borne mostly solitary, moderate fragrance; foliage medium size, dark green, semi-glossy; prickles few, small; growth upright, medium (3-5 ft.); garden decorative; [Sheer Elegance™ × 'Great Scott']; intr. 2003
'Wisley' -- See 'Ausintense'
'Wisoks' ('Oksana') HT, pb, 2001, Singer, Steven; flowers yellow, color blends into base of petals, 4-5 in., full, borne mostly solitary, intense fragrance; foliage medium size, medium green, semi-glossy; prickles moderate, medium, slightly downturned; growth upright, medium (4-5 ft.); garden, cutting; ['Great Scott' × Lanvin™]; intr. 1995
'Wisteria Maiden' -- See 'Fujimusume'
'Wistful' -- See 'Savawist'
'Witchcraft' F, yb, 1961, Verschuren; bud ovoid; flowers yellow, reverse scarlet, 2-2½ in., 45-50 petals, borne in large clusters; foliage dark, glossy; vigorous growth; ['Masquerade' × seedling]; intr. 1961
'Witching Hour' F, dr, 1967, Morey, Dennison H., Jr.; bud ovoid; flowers dark red, almost black, medium, dbl.; vigorous, bushy, compact growth; ['Rapture' × ('F.W. Alesworth' × 'Charles Mallerin')]
'With All My Love' -- See 'Coczodiac'
'With Love' -- See 'Andwit'
'With Thanks' -- See 'Fransmoov'
'Withersfield' -- See 'Horcopbond'
'Wit's End' -- See 'Seawit'
'Wiwait' ('Playfair') F, w, 1991, Wilke, William; flowers medium, single, borne in small clusters, slight fragrance; foliage medium size, medium green, semi-glossy; medium growth; [Playgirl™ × seedling]
'Wiwancy' ('Nancy Shaw') HT, lp, 1992, Wilke, William; flowers medium, full, borne mostly singly; foliage medium size, medium green, semi-glossy; some prickles; upright, bushy, tall (4 ft.) growth; ['Peggy Lee' × unknown]
'Wizard' -- See 'Macleide'
Wizo® HT, ob, 1972, Kriloff, Michel; flowers salmon-red, reverse darker, 40 petals, high-centered; foliage reddish-green, matte; PP3139; ['Tropicana' × ('Gamine' × 'Romantica')]; intr. 1968
'Woburn Abbey, Climbing' Cl F, ob, Brundrett, S; intr. 1972
'Woburn Abbey' F, ob, 1962, Sidey & Cobley; bud ovoid; flowers orange, 3½ in., 25 petals, cupped, borne singly and in irregular clusters, moderate tea fragrance; recurrent; foliage medium size, dark green, leathery; prickles average, medium, hooked downward; stems medium, strong; moderate, upright growth; hips none ; PP2319; ['Masquerade' × 'Fashion']; intr. 1962
'Woburn Gold' F, dy, 1970, Robinson, H.; flowers soft golden yellow; modest growth; [sport of 'Woburn Abbey']
'Wodan' HMult, mr, 1890, Geschwind, R.; flowers carmine-red with white at petal base, lighter reverse, large, semi-dbl., cupped, borne in clusters of 5-10, slight fragrance; foliage rounded; numerous prickles; ['Gloire des Rosomanes' × possibly R. multiflora]
'Wolfe's Glorie' Pol, op, 1943, Wolf, Van der; flowers salmon-pink to deep orange; vigorous growth; [sport of 'Orléans Rose']
'Wolfgang von Goethe' HP, pb, Weigand, L.; bud very long; flowers delicate bright yellowish-pink, very large, dbl., high-centered; vigorous growth; ['Frau Karl Druschki' × 'Souv. de Claudius Pernet']
'Wolley-Dod's Rose' -- See 'Duplex'
'Wollongong Gold' -- See 'Walshine'
Woman® HT, w; flowers ivory white with pink flush towards the center, full, high-centered, moderate fragrance
'Woman and Home' HT, ob, 1976, Gregory; flowers orange, pointed, 5 in., 33 petals; foliage glossy, dark; ['Apricot Silk' × (Piccadilly® × unknown)]
'Woman O'th North' -- See 'Kirlon'
'Woman Pioneer' -- See 'Pionerka'
'Woman's Day' -- See 'Welira'
'Woman's Day' HT, or, 1970, Armbrust; bud ovoid; flowers scarlet-orange, medium, semi-dbl., high-centered; foliage leathery; vigorous, upright growth; [Queen Elizabeth® × 'Karl Herbst']; intr. 1966
'Woman's Hour' F, pb, Beales, Peter; flowers satin pink, large white eye, semi-double, shallow cup, borne in clusters; recurrent; foliage light green; compact, bushy growth; intr. 1997
Woman's Own® Min, mp, 1973, McGredy, Sam IV; flowers pink, 1½ in., 45 petals; foliage dark; ['New Penny' × Tip-Top®]
'Woman's Realm' HT, mr, 1966, Gregory; flowers scarlet, 3½-4 in.; foliage glossy; upright growth; ['Chrysler Imperial' × unknown]
'Woman's Value' -- See 'Korvalue'
'Women in Military' ('The Service Rose') S, mr, 1993, Jerabek, Paul F.; flowers bright red, large, 20-30 petals, borne in small clusters, moderate fragrance; foliage medium size, medium green, glossy; some prickles; medium (135 cm.), upright growth
'Women O'th North' -- See 'Kirlon'
'Women's Institute' ('Panthea') HT, pb, Kordes; flowers cream with outer petals bordered and suffused deep pink, 4 in., double, high-centered, borne mostly singly; recurrent; medium (4-5 ft.) growth; intr. 1991
'Won Fang Yon' -- See 'Ardfang'
Wonder™ -- See 'Wonder Parade'
'Wonder of Woolies' F, ab, 1978, Bees; flowers deep apricot, 4½ in., 30 petals; vigorous growth; ['Arthur Bell' × Elizabeth of Glamis®]
'Wonder Parade' (Wonder™) Min, pb, Poulsen; flowers pink blend, medium, dbl., no fragrance; foliage dark; growth bushy, 20-40 cm.; PP10934; intr. 1996
'Wonderful' -- See 'Welfull'
Wonderful™ HT, my, Poulsen; flowers yellow that lasts, 10-15 cm., full, borne one to a stem, slight fragrance; recurrent; foliage reddish green; bushy (60-100 cm.) growth; hips none; intr. 2005
'Wonderful News' Min, rb, Jones, Chris; flowers cherry red with white eye and creamy white reverse, double, slight fragrance; free-flowering; foliage small, medium green, glossy; compact (12 in.), rounded growth; intr. 2001
Wonderglo™ -- See 'Miniwon'
Wonderland® S, yb, Dickson, Patrick; intr. 1994
'Wonderstar' F, my, 1960, Mondial Roses; flowers bright yellow, large, semi-dbl.; low, bushy growth; ['Goldilocks' × seedling]
'Wonderstripe' S, pb, Clements, John K.; flowers deep, smoky pink striped with creamy yellow and white, 4 in., very dbl., cupped, moderate fruity myrrh fragrance; recurrent bloom; foliage dark green; compact (4 ft.) growth; intr. 1997
'Wood Lawn' -- See 'Fialawn'
'Woodland Sunbeam' -- See 'Trobgold'
'Woodlands Lady' -- See 'Trobsa'
'Woodlands Sunrise' -- See 'Trobsun'
'Woodrow' Sp, lp; flowers 60 petals; fall bloom; low growth; collected in Sask., Canada; a form of R. suffulta; intr. 1936
'Wood's Garland' -- See 'The Garland'
'Woods of Windsor' -- See 'Korhanbu'
'Woodstock' -- See 'Morstock'

'Woody' HMsk, mr, Lens

'Woraardvark' ('Paul Cottingham') S, dy, 2006, Paul Chessum Roses; flowers dbl., borne mostly solitary, intense fragrance; foliage medium size, light green, semi-glossy; prickles medium, thin, pink, few; growth upright, medium (36 in.); beds, borders, containers; [seedling × seedling]; intr. 2005

'Worable' ('Gladys Quine') F, ob, 2005, Paul Chessum Roses; flowers dbl., borne in small clusters, slight fragrance; foliage medium size, dark green, semi-glossy; prickles medium, long, pink, moderate; growth bushy, medium (2 ft.); bedding, containers; [seedling × seedling]; intr. 2005

'Worabraham' ('The Derby Rose') MinFl, w, 2007, Paul Chessum Roses; flowers 4 cm., dbl., borne in large clusters; foliage small, medium green, semi-glossy; prickles small, sharp, medium green, moderate; growth bushy, short (16 in.); [seedling × seedling]; intr. 2005

'Woraddress' ('Valerie Ann') F, dy, 2005, Paul Chessum Roses; flowers dbl., borne in large clusters, moderate fragrance; foliage medium size, dark green, matte; prickles medium, flat, red, moderate; growth upright, medium (36 in.); bedding, containers; [seedling × seedling]; intr. 2005

'Worahat' ('Clifford') HT, ly, 2007, Paul Chessum Roses; flowers 4 in., full, blooms borne mostly solitary; foliage large, medium green, semi-glossy; prickles large, sharp, red, numerous; growth bushy, medium (2½ ft.); bedding, borders, containers; [seedling × seedling]; intr. 2005

'Woralps' ('Lady Jennifer Green') MinFl, w, 2006, Paul Chessum Roses; flowers 4 cm., single, borne mostly solitary, no fragrance; prickles large, sharp, yellow, few; growth to 18 in; beds, borders, containers; [seedling × seedling]; intr. 2005

'Woraltitude' ('Jean Beeden') F, yb, 2005, Paul Chessum Roses; flowers cream/yellow, reverse cream, 3 cm., semi-dbl., borne in small clusters, moderate fragrance; foliage medium size, medium green, matte; prickles medium, brown, moderate; growth bushy, medium (30 in.); bedding, containers; [seedling × seedling]; intr. 2005

'Woramble' ('The Creakes Rose') MinFl, ab, 2006, Paul Chessum Roses; flowers 4 cm., dbl., borne in small clusters; foliage medium size, dark green, semi-glossy; prickles large, sharp, tan/pink, numerous; growth bushy, medium (30 in.); garden decoration, beds, borders; intr. 2005

'Woramy' ('Kenneth Vincent Orpe Taylor') F, ab, 2005, Paul Chessum Roses; flowers dbl., borne in small clusters, slight fragrance; foliage large, medium green, semi-glossy; prickles large, sharp, yellow, few; growth bushy, tall (36 in.); bedding, containers; [seedling × seedling]; intr. 2005

'Woranchor' ('Mrs Mavis Watson') MinFl, ly, 2005, Paul Chessum Roses; flowers dbl., borne in large clusters; foliage medium size, dark green, semi-glossy; prickles medium, medium, pink, moderate; growth bushy, medium (24 in.); bedding, containers; [seedling × seedling]; intr. 2005

'Worangle' ('Caroline Nicholson') Min, mp, 2006, Paul Chessum Roses; flowers dbl., borne in small clusters; foliage medium size, medium green, semi-glossy; prickles small, short, pink, few; growth bushy, tall (2 ft.); bedding, borders, containers; intr. 2005

'Worangry' ('Kim Peters') MinFl, mp, 2006, Paul Chessum Roses; flowers 4 cm., full, borne mostly solitary, intense fragrance; foliage medium size, dark green, semi-glossy; prickles large, sharp, yellow, moderate; growth bushy, medium (24 in.); bedding, containers; [seedling × seedling]; intr. 2005

'Worankle' ('Irene') F, ly, 2006, Paul Chessum Roses; flowers dbl., borne in small clusters; foliage medium size, dark green, semi-glossy; prickles large, sharp, pink, numerous; growth bushy, medium (24 in.); bedding, containers; [seedling × seedling]; intr. 2005

'Worant' ('Soulmate') Min, w, 2007, Paul Chessum Roses; flowers dbl., borne in small clusters; foliage large, medium green, semi-glossy; prickles medium, sharp, yellow, few; growth bushy, medium (24 in.); beds, borders, containers; [seedling × seedling]; intr. 2005

'Worantelope' ('Quite Unforgettable') Min, ob, 2005, Paul Chessum Roses; flowers semi-dbl., borne in small clusters, slight fragrance; foliage medium size, medium green, semi-glossy; prickles medium, sharp, pink, few; growth compact, medium (18 in.); bedding, containers; [seedling × seedling]; intr. 2005

'Worantler' ('Zest For Life') MinFl, ob, 2005, Paul Chessum Roses; flowers medium, dbl., borne in small clusters, moderate fragrance; foliage medium size, medium green, semi-glossy; prickles medium, sharp, pink, few; growth compact, medium (18 in.); bedding, containers; [seedling × seedling]; intr. 2005

'Worapple' ('Janet Greig') F, ab, 2005, Paul Chessum Roses; flowers White, reverse Apricot, 3 cm., dbl., borne in large clusters, moderate fragrance; foliage medium size, medium green, semi-glossy; prickles medium, brown, few; growth bushy, medium; bedding, containers; [seedling × seedling]; intr. 2005

'Worarch' ('Vera Roberta Carver') MinFl, mp, 2005, Paul Chessum Roses; flowers dbl., borne in small clusters; foliage medium size, dark green, semi-glossy; prickles large, sharp, red, numerous; growth compact, medium (24 in.); bedding, containers; [seedling × seedling]; intr. 2005

'Worarm' ('Billy Fury') Min, lp, 2005, Paul Chessum Roses; flowers single, borne in small clusters; foliage medium size, dark green, glossy; prickles large, long, pink, numerous; growth compact, medium (24 in.); bedding, containers; [seedling × seedling]; intr. 2005

'Worartist' ('The Yvonne Arnaud Theatre Rose ') F, mr, 2005, Paul Chessum Roses; flowers dbl., borne in small clusters, slight fragrance; foliage medium size, dark green, glossy; prickles large, sharp, red/pink, moderate; growth upright, medium (36 in.); bedding, containers; [seedling × seedling]; intr. 2005

'Woraston' ('David D. Bernstein') Cl Min, mr, 2006, Paul Chessum Roses; flowers dbl., borne mostly solitary; foliage medium size, dark green, semi-glossy; prickles large, sharp, pink, moderate; growth upright, medium (36 in.); [seedling × seedling]; intr. 2005

'Worattack' ('Rio Rita') MinFl, dy, 2005, Paul Chessum Roses; flowers dbl., borne in small clusters; foliage medium size, dark green, glossy; prickles large, long, yellow, few; growth bushy, medium (24 in.); bedding, containers; [seedling × seedling]; intr. 2005

'Woraugust' ('Mary's Pleasure - The Mary Woods Rose') MinFl, dp, 2006, Paul Chessum Roses; flowers 3 cm., dbl., borne in small clusters; foliage medium size, light green, semi-glossy; prickles small, sharp, pink, few; growth compact, medium (12 in.); garden decorative, containers; [seedling × seedling]; intr. 2005

'Worauntie' ('Fab at Fifty') F, dp, 2006, Paul Chessum Roses; flowers 4 cm., dbl., borne in small clusters, slight fragrance; foliage medium size, dark green, matte; prickles large, long, yellow/pink, numerous; growth bushy, medium (2 ft.); bedding, borders, containers; [seedling × seedling]; intr. 2005

'Worbloom' ('Golden Fanfare') S, my, 2007, Paul Chessum Roses; flowers single, borne mostly solitary; foliage medium size, medium green, semi-glossy; prickles small, sharp, green, moderate; growth bushy, medium (80 cm.); beds, borders, containers; [seedling × seedling]; intr. 2005

'Worcabbage' ('Doris Stanbridge') F, my, 2007, World of Roses; flowers 3 cm., semi-dbl., borne in small clusters; foliage medium, medium green, semi-glossy; prickles large, sharp, red, moderate; growth upright, medium (24 in.); intr. 2005

'Worcable' ('Samantha Jose Home') F, ab, 2008, World of Roses; flowers 3 in., dbl., borne in large clusters; foliage medium, medium green, semi-glossy; prickles small, sharp, pink, few; growth upright, medium (2½ ft.); [seedling ×

seedling]; intr. 2006

'Worcad' ('Carol McLure') F, w, 2008, World of Roses; flowers medium, dbl., borne in large clusters; foliage medium, dark green, semi-glossy; prickles large, sharp, red, moderate; growth upright, medium (2½ ft.); [seedling × seedling]; intr. 2006

'Worcaddie' ('Brenda's Cosmic Dancer') F, mp, 2007, World of Roses; flowers 2 in., semi-dbl., blooms borne in small clusters; foliage medium, dark green, semi-glossy; prickles medium, sharp, pink, few; growth bushy, medium (24 in.); intr. 2005

'Worcake' ('Help For Children') HT, mr, 2007, World of Roses; flowers 4 in., dbl., borne in small clusters; foliage medium, medium green, semi-glossy; prickles large, long, brown, numerous; growth bushy, medium (30 in.); intr. 2005

'Worcall' ('Samantha') F, dp, 2007, World of Roses; flowers 4 in., dbl., borne in small clusters; foliage medium, dark green, semi-glossy; prickles medium, sharp, red, moderate; growth bushy, medium (30 in.); intr. 2005

'Worcalm' ('The Belfast Operatic Company') HT, dr, 2007, World of Roses; flowers 5 in., full, borne mostly solitary; foliage medium, dark green, semi-glossy; prickles medium, sharp, pink, moderate; growth bushy, medium (30 in.); intr. 2005

'Worcalorie' ('A True Gentleman') F, mp, 2007, World of Roses; flowers 4 in., dbl., borne mostly solitary; foliage medium, medium green, semi-glossy; prickles small, short, pink, moderate; growth compact, medium (24 in.); intr. 2005

'Worcamp' ('Bobbie B') F, pb, 2007, World of Roses; flowers 4 in., dbl., borne in small clusters; foliage medium, medium green, semi-glossy; prickles medium, sharp, red/pink, moderate; growth bushy, medium (24 in.); intr. 2005

'Worcandle' ('Charlotte Rose Elson') MinFl, ob, 2007, World of Roses; flowers 3 in., dbl., borne in large clusters; foliage medium, dark green, semi-glossy; prickles large, sharp, light brown, moderate; growth bushy, tall (36 in.); intr. 2005

'Worcanter' ('Wendy') F, lp, 2007, World of Roses; flowers 3 in., semi-dbl., borne in large clusters; foliage medium, medium green, semi-glossy; prickles large, pointed, red, few; growth upright, medium (30 in.); intr. 2005

'Worcarbon' ('Peter Hood') F, ob, 2008, World of Roses; flowers 4 cm., dbl., borne in small clusters; foliage medium-size, semi-glossy; prickles medium, sharp, pink, few; growth bushy, medium (24 in.); [seedling × seedling]; intr. 2006

'Worcard' ('Katie Prior') F, w, 2007, World of Roses; flowers 3 in., dbl., borne in small clusters; foliage medium, matte; prickles small, sharp, red, moderate; growth compact, medium (18 in.); intr. 2005

'Worcarrot' ('Robert Snowden') Min, yb, 2007, World of Roses; flowers 3 cm., semi-dbl., borne in small clusters; foliage medium, medium green, glossy; prickles large, long, pink, moderate; growth bushy, medium (18 in.); intr. 2005

'Worcarry' ('Amy Elizabeth') HT, ob, 2007, World of Roses; flowers 4 in., dbl., blooms borne in small clusters; foliage medium, medium green, semi-glossy; prickles small, sharp, yellow, few; growth bushy, medium (24 in.); intr. 2005

'Worcars' ('Amanda Ivy') F, dr, 2008, World of Roses; flowers 3 in., dbl., borne mostly solitary; foliage medium, dark green, semi-glossy; prickles large, sharp, pink, moderate; growth bushy, medium (24 in.); [seedling × seedling]; intr. 2006

'Worcart' ('Rose Marie Gorst') F, dp, 2007, World of Roses; flowers 3 in., semi-dbl., borne in small clusters; foliage medium, medium green, matte; prickles small, pink, numerous; growth compact, medium (12 in.); intr. 2005

'Worcarter' ('Alec and Paul') F, dr, 2008, World of Roses; flowers medium, dbl., borne in small clusters; foliage medium, dark green, glossy; prickles medium, sharp, red, few; growth compact, medium (2 ft.); [seedling × seedling]; intr. 2006

'Worcastle' ('Sarah Hartas') F, or, 2007, World of Roses; flowers medium, dbl., borne in small clusters; foliage medium, semi-glossy; prickles medium, sharp, pink, few; growth bushy, medium (24 in.); intr. 2005

'Worcat' ('The Balvenie Rose') F, dr, 2007, World of Roses; flowers 3 in., semi-dbl., borne in small clusters; foliage medium, dark green, semi-glossy; prickles small, red, few; growth compact, medium (18 in.); intr. 2005

'Worcauliflower' ('John Macmillan Pearson') F, mr, 2007, World of Roses; flowers 4 cm., dbl., borne in small clusters; foliage medium, dark green, glossy; prickles large, long, pink, moderate; growth bushy, medium (30 in.); intr. 2005

'Worcavity' ('Emma Wallace O'Flaherty') F, lp, 2007, World of Roses; flowers 4 in., dbl., borne in small clusters; foliage large, medium green, semi-glossy; prickles large, sharp, red, moderate; growth bushy, medium (24 in.); intr. 2005

'Worcentigrade' ('Leah Alison') F, ob, 2007, World of Roses; flowers 4 cm., dbl., borne in small clusters; foliage medium, medium green, semi-glossy; prickles large, sharp, yellow, few; growth bushy, medium (24 in.); intr. 2005

'Worcentury' ('Louise L. Hay') F, ob, 2007, World of Roses; flowers 4 cm., dbl., borne in small clusters; foliage medium, medium green, semi-glossy; prickles medium, sharp, yellow, moderate; growth compact, medium (18 in.); intr. 2005

'Worcestershire' S, my, Kordes; flowers bright yellow, yellow stamens, semi-double, shallow cup, borne in clusters, no fragrance; recurrent; foliage glossy; low (2 ft.), spreading growth; intr. 2000

'Worchapter' ('Angels') HT, ab, 2007, World of Roses; flowers 5 in., dbl., borne mostly solitary; foliage medium, light green, semi-glossy; prickles medium, sharp, yellow/pink, moderate; growth compact, medium (24 in.); intr. 2005

'Worcharacter' ('Holiday Inn') Min, ly, 2008, World of Roses; flowers medium, 4 cm., semi-dbl, borne in small clusters; foliage medium, medium green, semi-glossy; prickles small, sharp, green, moderate; growth compact, short (60 cm.); [seedling × seedling]; intr. 2006

'Worcherry' ('Iris May') F, mp, 2007, World of Roses; flowers medium, full, borne in small clusters; foliage medium, glossy; prickles small, short, red, moderate; growth bushy, medium (24 in.); intr. 2005

'Worchicken' ('Catherine and Thomas') F, ob, 2007, World of Roses; flowers 3 cm., dbl., borne in small clusters; foliage medium, semi-glossy; prickles large, sharp, tan, moderate; growth bushy, medium (24 in.); intr. 2005

'Worchief' ('Sydney Mary') Min, or, 2007, World of Roses; flowers 3 cm., semi-dbl., borne in small clusters; foliage medium, dark green, semi-glossy; prickles small, short, pink, moderate; growth compact, medium (18 in.); intr. 2005

'Worchild' ('Evie') F, ly, 2007, World of Roses; flowers 3 cm., single, borne in small clusters; foliage medium, dark green, semi-glossy; prickles large, sharp, pink, few; growth upright, medium (30 in.); intr. 2005

'Worchina' ('Rustington Rose') F, ob, 2007, World of Roses; flowers 4 in., dbl., borne mostly solitary; foliage small, dark green, semi-glossy; prickles large, sharp, red, moderate; growth upright, medium (36 in.); intr. 2005

'Worchronicle' ('Yvette') F, pb, 2008, World of Roses; flowers 4 in., dbl., borne in small clusters; foliage medium, dark green, matte; prickles very large, long, yellow-pink, numerous; growth bushy, medium (2 ft.); [seedling × seedling]; intr. 2006

'Worchurch' ('McCarthy Rose') F, mr, 2007, World of Roses; flowers 3 in., single, borne mostly solitary; foliage medium, medium green, semi-glossy; prickles medium, sharp, red, few; growth to 30 in.; intr. 2005

'Worcity' ('Hayley Scott') F, dp, 2007, World of Roses; flowers 4 cm., dbl., borne in small clusters; foliage medium, medium green, semi-glossy; prickles medium, sharp, pink, moderate; growth compact, medium (24 in.); intr. 2005

'Worclementine' ('Florence Daley') Min, lp, 2007, World of Roses; flowers 3 cm., dbl., borne mostly solitary; foliage medium, medium green, semi-glossy; prickles small, short, red, few; growth compact, medium (18 in.); intr. 2005

'Worclerk' ('The Phantom of the Opera Rose') Min, dr, 2008, World of Roses; flowers 3 in., semi-dbl., borne in small clusters; foliage medium, glossy; prickles small, short, red, few; growth compact, medium (18 in.); [seedling × seedling]; intr. 2005

'Worclim' ('Dordie's Rose') F, ob, 2008, World of Roses; flowers 3 in., single, borne in small clusters; foliage medium-size, medium green, matte; prickles large, sharp, red, numerous; growth bushy, medium (30 in.); [seedling × seedling]; intr. 2006

'Worclimate' ('Frankish') F, dy, 2008, World of Roses; flowers 3 in., semi-dbl., borne in small clusters; foliage medium, medium green, glossy; prickles large, flat, red, moderate; growth bushy, medium (24 in.); [seedling × seedling]; intr. 2006

'Worcloud' ('Mary Hankins') HT, ob, 2007, World of Roses; flowers 5 in., full, borne mostly solitary; foliage medium, light green, semi-glossy; prickles large, sharp, red, numerous; growth compact, medium (36 in.); intr. 2005

'Worcoconut' ('The Prestbury Rose') F, ab, 2007, World of Roses; flowers 4 cm., dbl., borne in small clusters; foliage medium, medium green, matte; prickles small, sharp, pink, moderate; growth bushy, medium (24 in.); intr. 2005

'Worcola' ('Margaret Turnbull') F, op, 2008, World of Roses; flowers 4 in., dbl., borne in small clusters; foliage small, dark green, glossy; prickles large, very sharp, red/pink, numerous; growth bushy, medium (2½ ft.); [seedling × seedling]; intr. 2006

'Worcold' ('Derbyshire Dawn') F, lp, 2007, World of Roses; flowers 3 in., dbl., borne in small clusters; foliage medium, dark green, semi-glossy; prickles large, long, red, moderate; growth bushy, medium (24 in.); intr. 2005

'Worcollar' ('Janet's Passion') F, dp, 2007, World of Roses; flowers 4 cm., dbl., borne in small clusters; foliage large, medium green, semi-glossy; prickles medium, long, red, few; growth upright, medium (30 in.); intr. 2006

'Worcollege' ('Maria Kent') F, ob, 2007, World of Roses; flowers 4 cm., dbl., borne in small clusters; foliage medium, medium green, semi-glossy; prickles small, short, yellow, few; growth bushy, short (18 in.); intr. 2005

'Worcolourful' ('Imagine') MinFl, dp, 2007, World of Roses; flowers 3 in., semi-dbl., borne in small clusters; foliage medium, dark green, semi-glossy; prickles medium, sharp, pink, few; growth bushy, medium (12 in.); intr. 2005

'Worcomputer' ('Esmae Lilly') S, ly, 2007, World of Roses; flowers 2 in., dbl., borne in small clusters; foliage large, medium green, semi-glossy; prickles long, thin, red, moderate; growth upright, medium (42 in.); intr. 2006

'Worcontrast' ('Fay Euphemia Evelyn Benson Gibson Cullen') F, dr, 2008, World of Roses; flowers 4 in., dbl., borne in small clusters; foliage medium, medium green, semi-glossy; prickles large, long, tan/yellow, moderate; growth bushy, medium (30 in.); [seedling × seedling]; intr. 2006

'Worcookie' ('Dignity 2008') Min, yb, 2008, World of Roses; flowers 3 in., semi-dbl., borne in small clusters; foliage medium, medium green, semi-glossy; prickles large, sharp, red-yellow, numerous; growth compact, medium (18 in.); [seedling × seedling]; intr. 2006

'Worcopper' ('Sheena Louise') Min, dr, 2007, World of Roses; flowers 3 cm., semi-dbl., borne in small clusters; foliage medium, medium green, semi-glossy; prickles medium, medium, red, few; growth bushy, tall (30 in.); intr. 2005

'Worcorridor' ('Ask Maureen') F, mp, 2008, World of Roses; flowers 4 in., single, borne mostly solitary; foliage medium, medium green, glossy; prickles small, short, red, moderate; growth bushy, medium (2 ft.); [seedling × seedling]; intr. 2006

'Worcrab' ('Molly de Balkany') F, lp, 2008, World of Roses; flowers 5 in., full, borne in small clusters; foliage medium, dark green, semi-glossy; prickles sharp, red, moderate; growth upright, medium (24 in.); [seedling × seedling]; intr. 2006

'Worcrackle' ('Maisy Wakefield') Min, dp, 2008, World of Roses; flowers 3 cm., single, blooms borne in small clusters; foliage medium, medium green, semi-glossy; prickles medium, long, pink, moderate; growth compact, medium (18 in.); [seedling × seedling]; intr. 2006

'Worcradle' ('Patricia Mary') F, mr, 2007, World of Roses; flowers 4 in., single, borne in small clusters; foliage medium, dark green, semi-glossy; prickles large, sharp, brown, few; growth upright, medium (48 in.); intr. 2006

'Worcranberry' ('Debbie Trinder') F, my, 2007, World of Roses; flowers 3 in., dbl., borne mostly solitary; foliage medium, medium green, semi-glossy; prickles small, sharp, brown, numerous; growth compact, medium; intr. 2005

'Worcrane' ('Lana Jane') S, mp, 2007, World of Roses; flowers 3 cm., semi-dbl., borne in large clusters; foliage medium, medium green, glossy; prickles small, sharp, red, moderate; growth upright, medium (36 in.); intr. 2005

'Worcrank' ('Deana') S, yb, 2008, World of Roses; flowers 3 in., full, borne mostly solitary; foliage medium, medium green, matte; prickles small, sharp, pink, few; growth upright, medium (36 in.); [seedling × seedling]; intr. 2006

'Worcrazy' ('The Westbridge Rose') MinFl, my, 2008, World of Roses; flowers 3 cm., semi-dbl., borne in large clusters; foliage medium, medium green, semi-glossy; prickles medium, sharp, tan, few; growth spreading, medium (30 in.); [seedling × seedling]; intr. 2006

'Worcreate' ('Emilia Rose Burke') F, dp, 2007, World of Roses; flowers 4 in., dbl., borne in small clusters; foliage medium, dark green, semi-glossy; prickles medium, sharp, red, numerous; growth bushy, medium (24 in.); intr. 2005

'Worcreek' ('Pamela') F, lp, 2007, World of Roses; flowers 4 in., dbl., borne in small clusters; foliage medium, dark green, matte; prickles large, long, pink/red, moderate; growth bushy, medium (30 in.); intr. 2005

'Worcross' ('Hilda's Beauty') F, op, 2007, World of Roses; flowers 4 cm., single, borne in small clusters; foliage medium, medium green, semi-glossy; prickles large, sharp, yellow/tan, moderate; growth bushy, medium (24 in.); intr. 2005

'Worcrunch' ('Dear Kath') F, mp, 2008, World of Roses; flowers 3 in., semi-dbl., borne in small clusters; foliage large, dark green, semi-glossy; prickles large, sharp, red, few; growth upright, tall (42 in.); [seedling × seedling]; intr. 2006

'Worcrust' ('Triyabell Trust') F, or, 2007, World of Roses; flowers 4 in., dbl., borne in small clusters; foliage medium, dark green, semi-glossy; prickles medium, sharp, pink, numerous; growth bushy, medium (24 in.); intr. 2005

'Worcube' ('Loving Care') S, mr, 2007, World of Roses; flowers 3 cm., dbl., borne in small clusters; foliage medium, dark green, matte; prickles medium, sharp, red, moderate; growth compact, short (12 in.); intr. 2005

'Worcupboard' ('Florence Ethel Read') F, mp, 2008, World of Roses; flowers 4 in., semi-dbl., borne mostly solitary; foliage medium, dark green, semi-glossy; prickles medium, sharp, red, moderate; growth bushy, medium (2 ft.); [seedling × seedling]; intr. 2006

'Worcurrant' ('Little Alice') Min, mp, 2008, World of Roses; flowers 3 cm., single, borne in small clusters; foliage medium, medium green, semi-glossy; prickles large, long, pink, moderate; growth compact, medium (18 in.); [seedling × seedling]; intr. 2006

'Worcycle' ('The Freda Perry') F, lp, 2007, World of Roses; flowers 3 in., semi-dbl., borne in small clusters; foliage medium, dark green, semi-glossy; prickles small, sharp, red, moderate; growth compact, medium (24 in.); intr. 2005

'Worjackie' -- See 'Kirworjackie'
'Work of Art' -- See 'Morart'
'World Class' -- See 'Hardimple'
World Peace™ -- See 'Burworpe'
'World Peace 2000' HT, my, Pearce; intr. 2000
'World Rose' -- See 'Diekor'

World War II Memorial Rose™ -- See 'Wezgrey'

'World's Fair, Climbing' Cl F, dr, 1941, J&P; PP546

'World's Fair' ('Minna Kordes') F, dr, 1939, Kordes; flowers deep crimson fading to scarlet, 4 in., 19 petals, borne in clusters, moderate spicy fragrance; foliage leathery; vigorous, bushy growth; PP362; ['Dance of Joy' × 'Crimson Glory']

'World's Fair Salute' HT, mr, 1964, Morey, Dr. Dennison; bud ovoid; flowers crimson-red, 5½ in., 33 petals, high-centered, moderate fragrance; foliage leathery; vigorous, upright growth; PP2558; ['Mardi Gras' × 'New Yorker']

'Wörlitz' S, yb, Berger, W.; flowers coral-orange with cream yellow center, large, dbl., borne singly, slight fragrance; recurrent; stems strong; intr. 1962

'Worthington' (natural variation of *R. setigera*), lp; flowers clear pink

'Worthwhile' HT, ob, 1973, LeGrice; flowers orange, reverse lighter, pointed, 5-6 in., 33 petals, pointed, slight fragrance; foliage matte, olive-green; ['Gavotte' × 'Vienna Charm']

'Woschod' HT, w, Bülow; flowers large, dbl.; intr. 1973

'Wow!' -- See 'Pixiwow'

'Wow' HT, ob, deRuiter; flowers dusty orange, 11 cm., 30 petals, high-centered, borne mostly singly, no fragrance; recurrent; prickles moderate; stems long; intr. 2004

'Wretham Rose' C, dp, Hoellering; flowers cerise pink, very full, heavy early summer bloom, moderate clove fragrance; non-remontant; numerous prickles; sturdy, tall growth; chance seedling found in Mrs. Hoellering's garden; intr. 1997

'Wright's Salmon' HT, op, 1960, Wright & Son; flowers salmon, 5 in., 32 petals, high-centered; [sport of 'Opera']

'Wrimarlon' ('Marlon's Day') HT, w, 2005, Wright, Fred; flowers white with pink edge, white reverse, large, full, borne mostly solitary, no fragrance; foliage large, dark green, semi-glossy; prickles angled down; growth upright, medium; garden decorative, exhibition; [sport of Moonstone™]

'Wripic' ('Picaninni') Min, ob, Wright, intr. 1991

'Wurzburg' -- See 'Korgust'

WWF® F, rb, Dorieux; flowers bright red and straw yellow, double, cupped, borne in clusters; recurrent; strong growth; intr. 2006

'Wyanda' F, mp, 1968, Heidemy; bud ovoid; flowers pink, medium, dbl.; foliage dark; ['United Nations' × seedling]

'Wyrala' HT, dr, Heers, C W; ['Lemania' × 'Ami Guinard']

'Wyralla' HT, dr, 1949, Heers; bud ovoid; flowers large, semi-dbl., high-centered; vigorous, bushy growth; ['Lemania' × 'Ami Guinard']

--- X ---

'X-Rated' -- See 'Tinx'

'Xanadu' S, op, 2003, Manners, Malcolm M.; flowers 3½ in., dbl., borne mostly solitary, slight fragrance; foliage medium size, medium green, semi-glossy; prickles moderate; bushy, medium growth; ['Carefree Beauty' × unknown]; plant closely resembles Carefree Beauty but flower is much more double and deeper pink; intr. 2002

'Xanadu' F, pb, J&P; flowers light pink with deep pink brush strokes on outer portion of petals, double, high-centered, borne in clusters; recurrent; compact growth

'Xavier Olibo' HP, dr, 1865, Lacharme, F.; flowers velvety deep crimson shaded purplish; [sport of 'Général Jacqueminot']

'Xaviere' -- See 'Meilavio'

'Xénia' -- See 'Korpinka'

Xerius® S, mr, Tantau; flowers bright red, yellow stamens, cupped, borne in clusters; recurrent; foliage glossy, disease-resistant; low (60 - 70 cm.), spreading growth; intr. 2008

'Xerxes' -- See 'Harjames'

'Xiang Fen Lian' -- See 'Souv d'Elise Vardon'

'Xu Gui Hua' -- See 'Newxu'

'XXL' -- See 'Korbilant'

--- Y ---

'Y2K' -- See 'Savyk'

'Ya Ya's Girl' HT, pb, 2003, Sievers, Maryanne; flowers pink and cream with yellow base, 4 in., full, borne mostly solitary, slight fragrance; foliage medium size, medium green; prickles moderate, 16 mm., triangular; growth bushy, medium; garden decorative, exhibition; [sport of Mon Cheri™]

Yabadabadoo® -- See 'Macyaba'

Yabadabadoo® HT, or, Spek; flowers bright orange-red, 10-11 cm., 30-35 petals, high-centered, borne mostly singly; recurrent; few prickles; stems long; florist rose; intr. 2005

'Yabusame' HT, mr, 1999, Ohtsuki, Hironaka; flowers crimson, 6 in., 35 petals, high-centered; growth to 6 ft.; ['Big Chief × Papa Meilland®]; intr. 1998

'Yachiyo-Nishiki' F, ob, 1987, Suzuki, Seizo; flowers orange, reverse yellow, medium, 28 petals, borne 2-5 per stem, moderate fragrance; recurrent; foliage dark green, semi-glossy; prickles curved downwards; upright, compact growth; [('Maxim' × 'Myo-Joh') × 'Duftwolke']; intr. 1984

Yakiman® F, m, Adam; flowers fuchsia, full, moderate lemon fragrance; prickles very few; upright (2 ft.) growth; intr. before 1997

Yakimour® -- See 'Meipsilon'

'Yametsu-Hime' Min, pb, 1961, Hebaru; flowers white edged pink, small, semi-dbl.; foliage glossy, light; dwarf growth; ['Tom Thumb' × seedling]

'Yamini Krishnamurti' HT, m, 1971, Singh; flowers lilac, medium, dbl., high-centered; foliage glossy; moderate growth; ['Sterling Silver, Climbing' × unknown]; intr. 1969

'Yanina' F, op, 1964, Yeoman & Sons; flowers salmon-pink, large, 16 petals; foliage glossy; vigorous growth; ['Fashion' × Queen Elizabeth®]

'Yanka' S, mp, 1927, Hansen, N.E.; flowers semi-dbl., borne in clusters; non-recurrent; growth to 3-4 ft.; very hardy

Yankee Doodle® HT, yb, 1975, Kordes, R.; bud pointed ovoid; flowers apricot to peachy pink, with butter-yellow reverse, 4-5 in., 65-75 petals, high-centered, cupped, borne mostly singly, slight tea fragrance; recurrent; foliage glossy, dark olive green, leathery; prickles moderate, medium, hooked slightly downward, brown; stems strong, medium; upright, bushy growth; PP3957; ['Colour Wonder' × King's Ransom®]; intr. 1976

'Yankee Lady' -- See 'Pierette'

'Yankor' HT, yb, 1975, Kordes, R.; bud pointed ovoid; intr. 1976

Yann Arthus-Bertrand® ('Kampaÿ', Pretty Sunrise®) S, op, Meilland; flowers coppery pink with yellow stamens, single, shallow cup to flat, borne in clusters; recurrent; 2 - 3 ft. growth; intr. 2007

'Yantai' -- See 'Tintai'

'Yardley Baroque' -- See 'Beayar'

'Yardley English Rose' ('Jana') HT, mp, Kordes; flowers double, high-centered; recurrent; intr. 1990

'Yaroslavna' ('Famous Cliff') HT, mp, 1958, Sushkov & Besschetnova; flowers large, 60 petals; foliage dark; vigorous growth; ['La Parisienne' × 'Peace']

'Yasaka' HT, op, Keihan; intr. 1972

'Yasaka, Climbing' Cl HT, op, 1978; intr. 1978

'Yashwant' HT, rb, 1987, Patil, B.K.; flowers red, striped white and yellow, reverse yellow, striped red, 55-60 petals, high-centered; foliage glossy; prickles pale, green, curving downwards; vigorous, upright, bushy growth; [sport of 'Suspense']; intr. 1985

'Yasnaya Poliana' ('Bright Meadow') HT, op, 1958, Shtanko, I.; flowers salmon-pink, well-formed, large, 45-50 petals; foliage dark; vigorous, compact growth; ['Independence' × 'Luna']

'Yaswanth' HT, rb; flowers red with white reverse, double

'Yatkan' S, mp, 1927, Hansen, N.E.; flowers 2½ in., dbl.; non-recurrent; very hardy; [probably 'Gruss an Teplitz' × 'La Mélusine']

'Yawa' S, op, 1940, Hansen, N.E.; flowers light coral-pink, 2 in., 58 petals, borne in clusters of 4-12 on 8-12 in. stems; free, non-recurrent bloom; tall, wide spreading (pillar to 9 ft.) growth; very hardy; ['Anci Bohmova' × *R. blanda*]

'Yayoi' F, lp, Fujii

'Ye Hamstead' HT, dr, Drummond; intr. 1991

'Ye Primrose Dame' T, yb, 1886, Bennett;

flowers yellow with apricot-pink center, large, full, globular

'Year 2000' -- See 'Jalyear'

'Yeller Rose O'Texas' HT, dy, 1987, Wambach, Alex A.; flowers medium, full, intense fragrance; foliage medium size, medium green, semi-glossy; upright growth; [sport of 'Arizona']

'Yello Yo Yo' F, dy, 1980, Weeks; bud slender, long; flowers 2½-3 in., 20-25 petals, high-centered, becoming open, borne singly and in clusters, slight tea fragrance; recurrent; foliage medium green, semi-glossy, leathery; prickles numerous, long, angled slightly downward, brown; bushy, upright growth; PP4047; ['Arlene Francis' × seedling]

'Yello Yo Yo, Climbing' Cl F, dy, 1976, Weeks, O. L.; buds slender, medium, long, globular; flowers 20 petals, high-centered, borne singly and in small clusters, slight tea fragrance; foliage medium green; upright (6-8 ft.) growth; PP4048; [sport of 'Yello Yo Yo']

'YelloGlo' -- See 'Delbut'

Yellow™ -- See 'Poulsendo'

'Yellow Altai' HSpn, my, 1950, Wright, Percy H.; flowers bright yellow, becoming lighter, small, borne in clusters; profuse, non-recurrent bloom; foliage light green, soft; stems reddish-brown; vigorous (7 ft.), upright growth; hardy (to -60F); [*R. spinosissima altaica* × 'Persian Yellow']

'Yellow Amer' F, dy

'Yellow and Fragrant' HT, dy; intr. 2006

'Yellow Angel' -- See 'Korgosumo'

'Yellow Baby Rambler' -- See 'George Elger'

'Yellow Bantam' Min, ly, 1960, Moore, Ralph S.; bud pointed, yellow; flowers yellow to white, very small, ½ in., 25 petals; foliage glossy; bushy (10 in.) growth; [(*R. wichurana* × 'Floradora') × 'Fairy Princess']; intr. 1960

'Yellow Bantam, Climbing' Cl Min, ly, 1965, Rumsey, R.H.

'Yellow Beauty' HT, my, 1945, Ruzicka's; bud longer, more pointed, clear golden yellow; more uniform growth than its parent; [sport of 'Golden Rapture']

'Yellow Bedder' HT, ly, 1923, Van Rossem; flowers clear yellow to cream, dbl.; ['Mr Joh. M. Jolles' × 'Mme Edouard Herriot']

'Yellow Belinda' -- See 'Tanyellda'

'Yellow Belle' HT, dy, Bell; flowers unfading golden yellow, small to medium, moderate fragrance; foliage disease-resistant; short growth

'Yellow Bird' HT, dy, 1974, McGredy, Sam IV; bud ovoid; flowers large, 42 petals; upright growth; ['Sunlight' × 'Arthur Bell']; intr. 1973

'Yellow Bird' -- See 'Welbyrd'

'Yellow Blaze' -- See 'Buryellow'

'Yellow Blush' A, ly, Sievers; intr. 1988

'Yellow Bouquet' -- See 'Lavkin'

'Yellow Brick Road' S, dy, Lim, Ping; flowers lemon yellow, maturing to butter cream, 2 - 3 in., 38 petals, old-fashioned, borne in clusters; recurrent; neat, round, compact (2 - 3 ft.) growth ; PPAF; intr. 2007

'Yellow Butterfly' -- See 'Morwings'

'Yellow Butterfly' HT, ob, 1927, Scott, R.; flowers orange-yellow; RULED EXTINCT 1/89; [sport of 'Mme Butterfly']

Yellow Button® S, yb, 1981, Austin, David; bud globular; flowers medium yellow, deeper in center, rosette, 90 petals, flat, borne singly and in clusters of up to 15; repeat bloom; foliage dark; prickles straight, red; bushy growth; ['Wife of Bath' × Chinatown®]; intr. 1975

'Yellow Cécile Brünner' -- See 'Perle d'Or'

'Yellow Cécile Brünner, Climbing' -- See 'Perle d'Or, Climbing'

Yellow Charles Austin® ('Ausyel') S, ly, 1981, Austin, David; flowers lemon-yellow, very full, cupped, moderate fruity fragrance; recurrent; tall (5 ft.) growth; [sport of Charles Austin®]; intr. 1979

'Yellow Cluster' F, my, 1949, deRuiter; flowers mimosa-yellow; spreading growth; ['Golden Rapture' × 'polyantha seedling']

'Yellow Cochet' -- See 'Alexander Hill Gray'

'Yellow Colette' -- See 'Meijacolet'

'Yellow Condesa de Sástago' -- See 'Yellow Sástago'

'Yellow Condesa de Sastago' -- See 'Jean Bostick'

'Yellow Contempo' F, dy, 1985, Gupta, Dr. M.N., Datta, Dr. S.K. & Banerji, Shri B; [sport of 'Contempo']; intr. 1983

'Yellow Coral' ('Feloma') F, my; florist rose; intr. 2005

Yellow Cover™ -- See 'Poulgode'

'Yellow Creeping Everbloom' LCl, my, 1953, Brownell; recurrent bloom; growth very vigorous; pillar or groundcover; [(('Orange Everglow' × 'New Dawn') × seedling) × 'Free Gold']

'Yellow Curls' HT, my, 1947, Brownell; flowers open, dbl., moderate fragrance; foliage glossy; vigorous growth; ['Golden Glow' × 'Golden Glow']

'Yellow Cushion' F, my, 1966, Armstrong, D.L.; bud pointed ovoid; flowers light to medium yellow, paling with age, 3-4 in., 30-40 petals, high-centered, cupped, borne in small clusters, slight to moderate fragrance; recurrent; foliage medium size, glossy, leathery; prickles several, medium, hooked slightly downward, brown; stems strong, short to medium; vigorous, bushy growth; hips globular, rough, orange to brown; PP2849; ['Fandango' × 'Pinocchio']; intr. 1962

'Yellow Dagmar Hastrup' -- See 'Moryelrug'

'Yellow Dazzler' -- See 'Yellowhammer'

'Yellow Delight' -- See 'Mme Chiang Kai-shek'

'Yellow Doll' Min, ly, 1962, Moore, Ralph S.; bud pointed ovoid; flowers clear yellow to cream, 1½ in., 55-75 petals, high-centered, opening flat, borne singly and in small clusters, moderate tea rose fragrance; recurrent; foliage medium green, leathery, glossy; prickles several, medium, hooked slightly downward; vigorous, bushy (12 in.) growth; no hips; PP2450; ['Golden Glow' × 'Zee']; intr. 1962

'Yellow Doll, Climbing' Cl Min, ly, 1976, Kirk; [sport of 'Yellow Doll']

'Yellow Dot' -- See 'Interbab'

'Yellow Dot' HT, ob, 1938, Joseph H. Hill, Co.; bud short, pointed; flowers light orange-yellow, reverse coral-red, small, dbl.; foliage soft, dark; short stems; vigorous growth; PP312; ['Rapture' × 'Betsy Ross']

'Yellow Dream' Min, my; flowers dull medium yellow, outer petals fading lighter, double, globular, borne in clusters, slight fragrance; recurrent; foliage healthy green, glossy; low (12 in.), broad growth

Yellow Euphoria® S, my, Interplant; intr. 2006

'Yellow Faïence' HT, my, 1942, C-P; flowers lemon-yellow; [sport of 'Faience']

Yellow Fairy™ -- See 'Poulfair'

'Yellow Festival' -- See 'Lavlinger'

Yellow Fleurette® ('Golden Nuggets') S, ly; flowers yellow with yellow stamens, semi-dbl., borne in sprays, no fragrance; foliage medium size, dark green, glossy; strong, bushy (2½ ft.) growth; intr. 1992

'Yellow Floorshow' S, yb; flowers soft yellow with pink rim, fading to blush, semi-dbl. to double, cupped, slight to moderate fragrance; recurrent; erect, compact, wide growth; intr. 1999

'Yellow Flower Carpet' -- See 'Noasun'

Yellow Folies® F, my, Keisei; flowers bright yellow, medium, double, cupped; recurrent; florist rose; intr. 2005

'Yellow Fontaine' S, my, 1972, Tantau, Math.; bud ovoid; flowers large, dbl.; free, continuous bloom; foliage large, glossy; vigorous, upright growth; [unknown × unknown]

'Yellow Fru Dagmar Hartopp' -- See 'Moryelrug'

'Yellow Gamette' Pol, my

'Yellow Gloria' HT, my, 1936, Bertanzel; bud long, pointed; flowers golden yellow, base saffron, large, dbl., high-centered, moderate fragrance; foliage leathery; long, strong stems; vigorous growth; PP240; [sport of 'Talisman']

'Yellow Goddess' F, dy, Zary; PPAF

'Yellow Gold' HT, dy, 1957, Boerner; bud ovoid; flowers deep golden yellow, 5 in., 30-35 petals, cupped, intense fragrance; foliage leathery, glossy; strong stems; vigorous growth; PP1643

'Yellow Hammer' -- See 'Yellowhammer'

'Yellow Hammer, Climbing' -- See 'Yellowhammer, Climbing'

'Yellow Hammer, Climbing' Cl F, my, Dorieux; flowers bright yellow, small; intr. 1976

'Yellow Herriot' -- See 'Florence Chenoweth'

'Yellow Hit' -- See 'Poullow'

'Yellow Holstein' -- See 'Gelbe Holstein'

'Yellow Hoover' HT, my, 1933, Western Rose Co.; flowers pure yellow; [sport of 'President Herbert Hoover']

'Yellow Hybrid Musk' HMsk, my

'Yellow Island' HT, ly, Brill; flowers large, double, high-centered; stems long; florist rose; intr. 2002

'Yellow Jacket' -- See 'Jacyepat'

'Yellow Jewel' Min, my, 1973, Moore, Ralph S.; bud long, pointed; flowers clear yellow, red eye, 1¼ in., 10 petals, open, loose, borne singly and in small clusters, slight to moderate fragrance; recurrent; foliage small, dark green, glossy, leathery; prickles moderate, slender, hooked slightly downward, brown; compact, bushy growth; hips few, round, greenish to orange; PP3627; ['Golden Glow' × ('Little Darling' × seedling)]

'Yellow Joanna Hill' HT, my, 1932, White, C.N.; bud long, pointed; flowers well-formed, 28 petals; foliage light; long stems; vigorous growth; PP22; [sport of 'Joanna Hill']

'Yellow Kaiserin Auguste Viktoria' -- See 'Franz Deegen'

'Yellow Keops' Cl Min, my; flowers lemon yellow, double, borne in clusters; recurrent; flexible canes; 2.5 meter growth; intr. 2008

'Yellow Light' -- See 'LLX8877'

'Yellow Mme Albert Barbier' HP, my, 1937, Lens; flowers sunflower-yellow; [sport of 'Mme Albert Barbier']

'Yellow Magic' -- See 'Randilla Jaune'

'Yellow Magic' Min, my, 1970, Moore, Ralph S.; bud long, pointed; flowers small, semi-dbl.; foliage small, glossy, dark, leathery; vigorous, dwarf, upright, bushy growth; ['Golden Glow' × ('Little Darling' × seedling)]

'Yellow Maman Cochet' -- See 'Alexander Hill Gray'

'Yellow Maman Cochet' -- See 'Mme Derepas-Matrat'

'Yellow Meillandina' -- See 'Meitrisical'

'Yellow Mellow' Min, my, 1985, Bridges, Dennis A.; flowers small, 35 petals; foliage large, dark, glossy; bushy growth; ['Rise 'n' Shine' × unknown]; intr. 1985

'Yellow Mermet' -- See 'Muriel Grahame'

'Yellow Mikado' F, my, Tantau; florist rose

'Yellow Mini-Wonder' -- See 'Lavglo'

'Yellow Miniature' Min, my, Wayside Gardens Co.; flowers bright yellow, small; [sport of 'Rosina' seedling]; intr. 1961

'Yellow Minijet' -- See 'Lavglo'

'Yellow Minnehaha' HWich, w, before 1933, Cant, F.; flowers white with yellow centers

'Yellow Moss' M, dy, 1932, Walter, L.; bud ovoid, slightly mossed, deep yellow; flowers yellow, edges tinted pink, semi-dbl., cupped, moderate fragrance; intermittent bloom; foliage thick; vigorous growth; ['Old Moss' × 'Mme Edouard Herriot']

'Yellow Mozart' S, my, Kordes; flowers darker in center with pale, creamy yellow outer petals, double; foliage medium green; vigorous (4 ft.), bushy growth

Yellow Multirosa® S, my, J&P; flowers bright yellow, adding pink tones with age, golden stamens , single, flat, borne in clusters; recurrent; foliage glossy; low, spreading growth; intr. 2007

'Yellow Nature' S, my; recurrent; moderate (100 cm.) growth; intr. 1999

'Yellow Necklace' Min, ly, 1965, Moore, Ralph S.; bud pointed; flowers straw-yellow, small, dbl.; foliage leathery; vigorous, dwarf growth; ['Golden Glow (LCl)' × 'Magic Wand']

Yellow Nugget Mega Brite™ MinFl, dy, Walden; bud short, pointed ovoid; flowers pure deep yellow, 2½ in., 40-50 petals, quartered to cupped, borne singly and in clusters of 3-7, slight fragrance; recurrent; foliage dark green, glossy, leathery; prickles ordinary, long, straight, brown; stems short; upright (24 in.) growth; PP11143; ['Sunsplash' × 'Ferris Wheel']; intr. 1998

'Yellow Ocean' LCl, my

'Yellow Ophelia' -- See 'Silvia'

'Yellow Pages' HT, yb, 1973, McGredy, Sam IV; flowers dbl., 50 petals, high-centered, moderate fragrance; foliage small, glossy; ['Arthur Bell' × Peer Gynt®]; intr. 1972

Yellow Pagode™ MinFl, my, Poulsen; flowers medium yellow, 5-8 cm., borne in clusters, no fragrance; foliage dark; cascading growth, hanging basket type; PP13471; intr. 2000

'Yellow Paillette' (Yellow™) MinFl, my, Poulsen; flowers medium yellow, 5-8 cm., slight fragrance; foliage dark; growth narrow, bushy, 40-60 cm.; intr. 1998

'Yellow Panarosa' S, my, Kordes; intr. 2008

Yellow Parade™ -- See 'Poulwee'

Yellow Pastel™ -- See 'Wilyelp'

'Yellow Patio' Min, my; flowers golden yellow, double, cupped, very slight fragrance; vigorous (18 in.) growth

'Yellow Perfection' HT, ly, 1952, Joseph H. Hill, Co.; bud long, pointed, lemon-yellow; flowers canary-yellow, medium, 25-30 petals, high-centered; foliage leathery, dark; vigorous, upright growth; PP1083; ['Pearl Harbor' × 'Golden Rapture']

'Yellow Perle d'Or' -- See 'Ravensworth'

'Yellow Petals' HT, my, 1972, Robinson, H.; flowers 5½ in., 30 petals, high-centered, moderate fragrance; foliage large, light; [King's Ransom® × 'Dorothy Peach']; intr. 1971

'Yellow Pigmy' F, my, 1964, Moore, Ralph S.; flowers small, dbl.; foliage small, glossy; dwarf, spreading growth; containers; [seedling × ('Eblouissant' × 'Goldilocks')]

'Yellow Pinocchio' F, my, 1949, Boerner; bud ovoid; flowers apricot-yellow, fading to cream, 3 in., 45 petals, cupped, borne in clusters, moderate fragrance; recurrent; foliage dark green; vigorous, bushy growth; PP992; ['Goldilocks' × 'Marionette']

'Yellow Pinocchio, Climbing' Cl F, my, 1961, Palmer; intr. 1959

'Yellow Pompon' -- See 'Pompone Jaune'

'Yellow Président Carnot' HP, my, 1910, California Rose Co.; [sport of 'Président Carnot']

'Yellow Profusion' -- See 'Randilla Jaune'

'Yellow Queen Elizabeth' ('Queen Elizabeth Jaune') Gr, my, 1964, Vlaeminck; flowers orange-yellow, fading to primrose yellow, outer petals lighter; [sport of Queen Elizabeth®]

'Yellow Quill' MinFl, my, Williams, J. Benjamin; intr. 1998

'Yellow Rambler' -- See 'Brownell Yellow Rambler'

'Yellow Rambler' -- See 'Aglaia'

'Yellow Ribbon' -- See 'Dicalow'

'Yellow Ribbons' S, dy, Warner; bud pointed, ovoid; flowers light yellow to near white, 2 in., 20-25 petals, borne in clusters, slight fresh fragrance; recurrent; foliage glossy, dark green; growth speading, groundcover, 1-2 ft. tall, 2 ft. wide; PPAF; intr. 2005

'Yellow River' HT, my, 1972, Timmerman's Roses; flowers pointed, large, 30 petals; foliage glossy; vigorous growth; [sport of Bettina®]

'Yellow River' ('Olysko') F, my, Olij, H.W.; bud conical; flowers bright yellow, 8 cm., double, cupped, borne singly and in small clusters; recurrent; foliage dark green, glossy; prickles average, medium, light brown; erect, low (18 in.) growth; PP9512; [Frisco® × 'Vivaldi']

'Yellow Robusta' HRg, ly, Maarse, J.D.; bud medium yellow; flowers light yellow, fading as they open, large, flat, moderate fragrance; non-remontant; [sport of 'Robusta']; intr. 1992

Yellow Romantica™ -- See 'Meijacolet'

'Yellow Rose of Texas' LCl, yb, Thomson

'Yellow Rose of Texas' -- See 'Lemon Chiffon'

'Yellow Ruffles' HT, my, 1953, Brownell; flowers 4-5 in., 35-50 wavy petals, moderate fragrance; foliage dark, glossy; compact growth; PP1405; [sport of 'Orange Ruffels']

'Yellow Sástago' ('Yellow Condesa de Sástago') HT, my, 1939, Howard Rose Co.; [sport of 'Condesa de Sástago']

'Yellow Sea' LCl, my, 1978, Fong; bud long, pointed; flowers lemon-yellow, 6 in., 18-20 petals, high-centered, intense honey spice fragrance; [seedling × 'Ivory Fashion']; intr. 1977

'Yellow Shot Silk' HT, my, 1944, Beckwith; [sport of 'Shot Silk']

'Yellow Simplicity' -- See 'Jacyelsh'
'Yellow Splendor'   F, my; intr. 1998
'Yellow Springs'   HSpn, ly, Monteith; intr. 2006
'Yellow Star'   F, my, 1965, deRuiter; flowers well-shaped, medium; foliage glossy; moderate growth
'Yellow Submarine'   S, my, Lim, Ping; bud slender; flowers bright lemon yellow aging to pale yellow and white, 2 in., 32 petals, borne in clusters of about 5, moderate fragrance; recurrent; foliage medium green, semi-glossy; prickles several, long, triangular, slightly hooked; very upright (2-3½ ft.), bushy growth; hips ellipsoid, green with splotches of purple-brown; PP16659; ['Singin' in the Rain' × 'shrub rose']; intr. 2004
'Yellow Sunbeam'   Min, my
'Yellow Sunblaze' -- See 'Meitrisical'
Yellow Sunblaze™ -- See 'Meiskaille'
'Yellow Sunblaze 2004' -- See 'Meiskaille'
'Yellow Sunsation' -- See 'Kortisching'
'Yellow Sunset'   HT, my, Dawson, George; intr. 1997
'Yellow Sweet Dreams'   Mln, dy, Scott; flowers quite deep yellow, 1¼ in.; [sport of 'Sweet Dreams']; intr. 2000
'Yellow Sweet Magic'   Min, my, Dickson; [sport of 'Sweet Magic']; intr. 2004
'Yellow Sweetheart'   F, my, 1952, Boerner; bud pointed; flowers lemon-yellow, reverse sulfur-yellow, becoming, 3½-4 in., 35 petals, globular; foliage leathery; vigorous, branching growth; PP1011; ['Pinocchio' × seedling]
'Yellow Sweetheart, Climbing'   Cl F, ly, 1952, Moore, Ralph S.; flowers apricot-yellow to creamy -yellow, small, 26 petals, high-centered, moderate fragrance; foliage leathery, glossy; vigorous, climbing (12 ft.) growth; PP1235; [('Étoile Luisante' × unknown) × 'Goldilocks']
'Yellow Sweetheart' -- See 'Rosina'
Yellow Taifun® -- See 'Yellow Typhoon'
'Yellow Talisman'   HT, ly, 1929, Amling Co.; flowers bright, clear yellow, paling with age; [sport of 'Talisman']
'Yellow Talisman'   HT, ly, 1935, Eddie; flowers pale sulfur-yellow; [sport of 'Talisman']
'Yellow Talisman, Climbing'   Cl HT, ly, Stocking
'Yellow Tausendschön' -- See 'Madeleine Seltzer'
'Yellow Tiffany'   HT, yb, 1976, Floradale Nurs.; flowers yellow tinted pink; [sport of 'Tiffany']
'Yellow Timeless'   HT, yb, Ammerlaan; bud ovate; flowers bright yellow with orange tint, reverse lighter, 5 in., 25 petals, high-centered, spiral, borne singly, slight fruity fragrance; recurrent; foliage dark green, glossy; prickles ordinary, concave, cinnamon; stems long; vigorous, narrow (6 ft.), bushy growth; hips pitcher-shaped ; PP10890; [sport of 'Timeless']; florist rose; intr. 1999
Yellow Tombola®   HT, dy, Spek; flowers 11 cm., 30-35 petals, high-centered, borne mostly singly; recurrent; thornless; stems long; intr. 2005
'Yellow Treasure'   HT, dy; intr. 2001
'Yellow Triumph'   HT, Herholdt
Yellow Typhoon™ (Yellow Taifun®) F, my, Kordes; flowers double , cupped, borne in sprays of up to 20; recurrent; growth to 5 ft.; intr. 2006
Yellow Unique™   HT, dy, de Ruiter ; bud medium, ovate; flowers deep yellow, reverse lighter, 9 cm., 25 petals, pointed, spiral, borne singly, slight sweet, fruity fragrance; recurrent; foliage medium size, dark green, semi-glossy; prickles numerous, concave, red-brown; stems long; vigorous, narrow to bushy (6 ft.) growth; hips funnel-shaped, orange-yellow; PP10530; [seedling × seedling]; florist rose; intr. 1997
'Yellow Wings'   S, my, 1987, James, John; flowers light-medium yellow, fading to cream, large, 16 petals, borne in clusters, moderate fragrance; foliage medium size, light green, glossy, disease-resistant; prickles straight, brown; bushy growth; [(('Will Scarlet' × 'Sutter's Gold') × 'Paula') × 'Golden Wings']; intr. 1986
'Yellow Wonder' -- See 'Macbern'
'Yellowcrest'   HT, ly, 1935, LeGrice; bud small, pointed; flowers clear canary-yellow, dbl.; foliage light, glossy, small; vigorous growth
'Yellowhammer' ('Yellow Dazzler', 'Yellow Hammer')   F, my, 1956, McGredy, Sam IV; bud medium, pointed ovoid; flowers golden yellow to light yellow, 3-3½ in., 45-50 petals, open, flat, borne in clusters, moderate fruity (apple) fragrance; free-flowering; foliage large, dark green, glossy; prickles ordinary, medium, hooked downward; stems medium; vigorous, upright, bushy growth; no hips; PP1667; ['Poulsen's Yellow' × seedling]
'Yellowhammer, Climbing' ('Yellow Hammer, Climbing')   Cl F, my, Dorieux; intr. 1976
'Yellowstone'   HT, my, 1975, Weeks; bud pointed; flowers soft tawny yellow to lighter yellow, 3½-4 in., 38-44 petals, moderate tea fragrance; foliage glossy, dark, leathery; tall, upright growth; [seedling × seedling]
Yellowstone™ (Eurostar™, Marselisborg™, Schloss Neuschwanstein™, Summer Gold™) F, my, Olesen; bud short, globular; flowers medium yellow in center, lighter at outer edges, 7-10 cm., 60-75 petals, cupped, open, borne singly and in small clusters, moderate old rose fragrance; recurrent; foliage medium green, semi-glossy; prickles numerous, 8-12 mm., deeply concave, brown; vigorous, bushy (3-4 ft.) growth; PP12534; [seedling × seedling]; intr. 1996
Yesterday® ('Tapis d'Orient') Pol, mp, 1974, Harkness; flowers lilac pink, golden stamens, 1½ in., 13 petals, borne in trusses, slight fragrance; foliage small, glossy; bushy growth with polyantha characteristics; [('Phyllis Bide' × 'Shepherd's Delight') × 'Ballerina']
'Yesterday Reef'   HT, w, 1984, Stoddard, Louis; flowers white, faintly tinted pink and yellow, large, 35 petals, high-centered; foliage large, medium green, matte; narrowly upright growth; [('Tiffany' × 'Sunblest') × 'Irish Gold']
'Yesterday's Garden' -- See 'Morshakrug'
'Yesteryear'   HT, ab, Harkness; flowers soft peachy-apricot, large, full, cupped, borne singly, intense fragrance; quick repeat; foliage dark green, glossy; stems long, strong; vigorous (4 ft.) growth; ['Just Joey' × unknown]
'Yeswant'   HT, rb, Patil, B.K.
'Yi Bang Fen'   Ch, mp
'Yi-Hong Yuan'   HT, rb, 1995, Hong-Quan, Li; flowers yellow, edged salmon, reverse lighter, 4½ in., very dbl., borne mostly singly; foliage medium size, dark green, semi-glossy; some prickles; upright, medium growth; ['Osiria' × 'New Bal']
'YKH 501' -- See 'Arashiyama'
'Yoimatsuri'   F, ob, 1989, Kikuchi, Rikichi; bud ovoid; flowers orange and yellow tinged, medium, 5 petals, cupped, borne in large sprays; foliage small, light green, glossy; prickles ordinary; spreading, medium growth; ['Masquerade' × 'Subaru']; intr. 1990
'Yolande d'Aragon' ('Jolanda d'Aragon') P, m, 1843, Vibert; flowers purple-rose, tinted lilac, small eye at center, very large, very dbl., flat-cupped, quartered, borne in clusters, strong fragrance; foliage medium green, large, rounded; growth vigorous, tall (1½-2 m.), strongly branching; sometimes classed as HP; the cultivar currently in commerce under this name is probably not correct
'Yolande Fontaine'   B, m, 1840; flowers dark violet, medium, full
'Yongjoon'   S, lp, 2005, Ogawa, Hiroshi; flowers light pink, reverse silver pink, 7 cm., dbl., borne in small clusters, intense fragrance; foliage small, light green, matte; prickles thin; growth upright, medium (120 cm.); garden decoration, containers; ['Peach Blossom' × 'Pearl Ring']; intr. 2005
'Yoriko'   Pol, lp, 1997, Ohmori, Yoriko; flowers light pink, reverse white, 1½ in., single, slight fragrance; foliage small, light green, semi-glossy; few prickles; spreading (45 cm.) growth; hips oval, 6-7 mm, deep orange; [seedling × seedling]
'York and Lancaster' -- See *R.* × *damascena versicolor*
'York et Lancastre' -- See *R.* × *damascena versicolor*
'Yorkshire'   S, w, Kordes; flowers pure white, yellow stamens, semi-double, shallow cup, borne in small clusters, slight fragrance; recurrent; low (2 ft.), spreading growth; intr. 1998

'Yorkshire' -- See 'Korstarnow'

'Yorkshire Bank' -- See 'Rutrulo'

'Yorkshire Lady'   HT, ly, 1992, Thompson, Robert; flowers soft primrose yellow to linen white, medium, full, high-centered, borne mostly singly, moderate fragrance; foliage medium size, medium green, glossy; few prickles; upright (95-100 cm.) growth; [(('Red Lion' × 'Royal Highness') × 'Yellow Petals') × Piccadilly®]; intr. 1992

'Yorkshire Provence' ('Cricks') C, mp, before 1821; flowers bright rose pink

'Yorkshire Sunblaze' -- See 'Meiblam'

'Yorokobi' ('Joy') Pol, mp, Suzuki; intr. 1955

'Yosemite'   HT, ob, 1934, Nicolas; bud long, pointed; flowers scarlet-orange, reverse suffused carmine, dbl., cupped, moderate fragrance; foliage leathery; vigorous growth; PP109; ['Charles P. Kilham' × 'Mrs Pierre S. duPont']

'Yoshino'   HT, w, 1997, Ohtsuki, Hironami; flowers dbl.; foliage medium size, medium green, semi-glossy; some prickles; tall (200 cm.) growth; ['Confidence' × 'Garden Party']

'Yoshodama's Rose'   LCl, my; flowers clear pastel yellow, ruffled petals, 5-7 in., double; intr. 2007

'Yosooi'   Min, w, Keisei; intr. 1991

'You'   S, pb, Takatori

'You Are My Sunshine'   HT, dy, Fryer; flowers golden yellow, color holds, large, double, hybrid tea, borne singly and several together; recurrent; neat, bushy, medium growth; intr. 2007

'You 'n' Me' -- See 'Seayou'

Youki San® ('Mme Neige') HT, w, 1965, Meilland; flowers clear white, large, 40 petals, intense sweet fragrance; foliage light green; tall growth; ['Lady Sylvia' × 'White Knight']

'Youki San, Climbing'   Cl HT, w; intr. 1972

'Young America'   HT, dr, 1902, E.G. Hill, Co.; flowers medium, dbl.; ['Duke of Edinburgh' × 'The Meteor']

'Young at Heart' -- See 'Arocharm'

'Young Cale' -- See 'Macinca'

'Young France' ('Jeune France') HT, lp, 1945, Meilland, F.; bud long, pointed; flowers apple-blossom-pink, base flushed orange, tipped silvery pink, high-centered; foliage soft, dark; vigorous, upright growth; ['Joanna Hill' × 'Mme Joseph Perraud']

'Young Hearts' -- See 'Renheart'

'Young Love'   Min, ob, 1980, Lyon; bud medium-long, pointed; flowers orange, yellow-center, 18 petals, borne singly and in small clusters; foliage tiny, dark; prickles tiny, curved; compact, bushy growth; [seedling × seedling]; intr. 1979

'Young Love'   Min, rb, Williams, J. Benjamin; flowers red and white; intr. 1994

'Young Mistress'   Min, lp, Kordes; flowers bright pink, full, borne in clusters; intr. 1988

'Young Mistress' -- See 'Macyoumis'

'Young 'n' Innocent' -- See 'Renyoung'

Young Quinn® -- See 'Macbern'

'Young Venturer' -- See 'Mattsun'

'Young Venturer, Climbing'   Cl F, ab, Fineschi, Gianfranco

'Youpi'   Min, my, 1979, Lens; bud ovoid; flowers lemon-chrome, 1 in., 12-19 petals, cupped, moderate fruity fragrance; foliage light green; vigorous, compact growth; [*R. wichurana* × 'Pour Toi']; intr. 1966

'Your Family'   HT, pb, Taschner, Ludwig; bud pointed, urn-shaped; flowers mother of pearl, touched with more pink when touched by the sun, large, full, classic hybrid tea form, borne singly, moderate sweet fragrance; recurrent; vigorous, tall growth; intr. 2004

'Your Garden' -- See 'Meicelna'

'Your Smile'   HT, my, 1999, Ohata, Hatsuo; flowers 6 in., 35 petals, high-centered; foliage medium green; growth to 3 ft.; ['Miss Harp' × 'Golden Sun']; intr. 1997

'Yours Always'   HT, or, Delbard; flowers luminous orange-red, medium, full, high-centered; tall growth; intr. 2003

'Yours Truly'   HT, mp, 1945, Morris; bud long, pointed; flowers rose-pink, base golden yellow, open, 4½ in., 48 petals, intense spicy fragrance; foliage leathery; very vigorous, upright growth; PP697; [seedling × 'Texas Centennial']

'Youth'   HT, w, 1935, Cook, J.W.; bud ovoid; flowers creamy, suffused pink, very large, 60 petals, high-centered, moderate fragrance; foliage dark; long stems; PP192; ['Souv. de Claudius Pernet' × 'My Maryland']

'Youth' -- See 'Molodost'

'Youth' -- See 'Seishun'

'Youth of the World'   HT, mr; flowers large, dbl.

Yoyo™ -- See 'Segyoyo'

'Ypsilanté' -- See 'Ypsilanti'

'Ypsilanti' ('Ipsilanté', 'Ypsilanté') HGal, m, 1821, Vibert; flowers lilac pink, fading to violet, small eye at center, very large, dbl., quartered, borne singly or in clusters of 2-3; non-remontant; foliage light green, oval; few prickles; vigorous growth

'Yu-Ai' ('Fellowship') HT, rb, 1973, Suzuki, Seizo; bud ovoid; flowers bright red, base yellow, large, dbl., cupped; foliage dark, leathery; very vigorous, bushy growth; [(Sarabande® × unknown) × ('Peace' × unknown)]; intr. 1970

'Yueh Yueh Hong' -- See 'Slater's Crimson China'

'Yugiri' ('Twilight Mist') HT, pb, Suzuki, Seizo; intr. 1987

'Yuhla'   HSet, mr, 1927, Hansen, N.E.; flowers crimson, large, semi-dbl.; non-recurrent; very hardy; ['wild rose from Lake Oakwood (SD)' × 'Général Jacqueminot']; perhaps hybrid Macounii rather than hybrid Setigera

'Yuka'   F, lp, Keisei; intr. 2005

'Yuki Akari'   Cl Min, w, Komatsu; intr. 2004

'Yuki-Matsuri'   HT, w, 1989, Yokota, Kiyoshi; bud ovoid; flowers large, 42 petals, high-centered, urn-shaped, borne usually singly; foliage medium size, dark green, glossy; prickles sparse; medium growth; hips large, light orange; [(Dolce Vita® × 'Royal Highness') × 'Nobility']

'Yukihime' ('Snow Princess') Min, w, Kubota

'Yukon' -- See 'Sun Valley'

'Yuletide'   HT, mr, 1956, Joseph H. Hill, Co.; bud ovoid; flowers currant-red, 3½-4½ in., 43 petals, high-centered; foliage leathery, semi-glossy; vigorous, upright, bushy growth; PP1391; ['Hill Crest' × 'Silver Kenny']

'Yume'   HT, ab, Keisei; intr. 1994

'Yumeka' ('Fragrant Dream') F, pb, Keisei; intr. 2007

'Yumeotome'   Min, lp, 1989, Tokumatsu, Kazuhisa; bud ovoid; flowers pink changing to white, 38 petals, slight fragrance; foliage small, dark green; lower part of prickles hollow, about 15 on a stem; bushy growth; [sport of 'Miyagino']

'Yusai'   HT, yb, 1989, Ota, Kaichiro; bud ovoid; flowers bright yellow with reddish fringe, reverse changing to red, 30 petals, high-centered; foliage medium size, dark green with bronze tinge, slightly dentate; bushy, spreading growth; [((American Heritage® × unknown) × 'Christian Dior') × 'Miss Ireland']

'Yuubae'   HT, op, Hiroshima; intr. 1996

'Yuzen'   Gr, pb, 1986, Suzuki, Seizo; flowers pink, blending deeper at petal edges, urn-shaped, large, 50 petals, high-centered, moderate fragrance; foliage dark, glossy; prickles slanted downward; upright growth; [seedling × 'Confidence']; intr. 1982

'Yvan Meneve'   HT, dp; intr. 1998

'Yvan Mission'   Pol, mp, 1922, Soupert & Notting; flowers peach-blossom-pink, borne in large clusters; ['Jeanny Soupert' × 'Katharina Zeimet']

'Yves Druhen'   HT, dr, 1920, Buatois; flowers dark velvety red, dbl.; ['Gen. MacArthur' × 'Château de Clos Vougeot']

'Yves Latieule' -- See 'Mme Yves Latieule'

Yves Piaget® -- See 'Meivildo'

'Yves Piaget, Climbing'   Cl HT, mp, Meilland; intr. 2006

'Yvette'   HT, op, 1921, Buatois; flowers salmon-yellow; ['Mrs T. Hillas' × 'Mme Edouard Herriot']

'Yvette'   Pol, lp, Scarman; flowers pale pink; free-flowering; moderate (2 ft.) growth; ['Yvonne Rabier' × Unknown]; intr. 1996

'Yvette' -- See 'Worchronicle'

'Yvette Gayraud'   F, op; flowers orange salmon, small, semi-double, cupped; free-flowering; foliage medium green, glossy, disease-resistant; strong (3 ft.) growth; intr. 2004

'Yvette Horner'   HT, pb, Sauvageot;

intr. 2006

'Yvon Cléroux' -- See 'Willildeb'

'Yvonne' HWich, pb, 1921, Cant, F.; flowers blush-pink, base deep pink shaded yellow, 4 cm., dbl., borne in large clusters, moderate fragrance; foliage dark olive green, glossy; very vigorous growth

'Yvonne Alexander' F, rb, 2002, Fleming, Joyce L.; flowers medium red, reverse light red, 1¼-1½ in., single, borne in small clusters; foliage medium size, medium green, matte, disease-resistant; prickles 1/8 in., triangular; growth spreading, medium (12-15 in.); bedding, hanging baskets; hardy; ['Red Hot' × 'Lavender Friendship']; intr. 2002

'Yvonne Caret' HT, ob, 1965, Gaujard; flowers orange-red, reverse golden yellow, 4½ in., 25 petals; foliage bright green; intr. 1963

'Yvonne Corboeuf' HP, mr, 1900, Corboeuf; flowers cherry red; ['Mme Ferdinand Jamin' × 'John Hopper']

'Yvonne d'Huart' HT, rb, 1932, Ketten Bros.; bud long, pointed; flowers coral-red to Lincoln red, base chrome yellow, large, dbl.; very vigorous growth

'Yvonne Kenny' HT, pb; flowers soft pink, palest pink at outer edges, soft yellow at base, cup and saucer, ruffled petals; medium growth; intr. 2003

'Yvonne Millot' HT, ab, 1936, Mallerin, C.; bud pointed; flowers apricot-yellow, large, dbl., high-centered; foliage glossy; vigorous growth; [('Pharisaer' × 'Constance') × 'Feu Joseph Looymans']

'Yvonne Plassat' HT, or, 1941, Moulin-Epinay; flowers coppery orange to glowing red, dbl.

'Yvonne Printemps' HT, or, 1939, Gaujard; bud long, almost red; flowers orange, veined copper, reverse bright yellow

'Yvonne Rabier' Pol, w, 1910, Turbat; flowers pure white, center slightly tinted sulfur, dbl., borne in clusters; recurrent; foliage rich green, glossy; vigorous growth; [R. wichurana hybrid × unknown]

'Yvonne Vacherot' HT, w, 1905, Soupert & Notting; bud long, pointed; flowers porcelain-white, strongly flushed rose-pink, imbricated, large, dbl., high-centered; vigorous growth; ['Antoine Rivoire' × 'Souv. d'un Ami']

'Yvonne Virlet' HT, my, 1936, Walter, L.; flowers golden yellow, large, dbl.

— Z —

'Zabeth' ('Hessoise Anémone', 'Zabeth Bombifera') HEg, mp, before 1813, Dupont; flowers bright pink, medium, semi-dbl.; foliage oblong ovate, very fragrant; prickles long, recurved, almost absent from blooming shoots; growth small (2-3 ft.); hips globose, bright red

'Zabeth Bombifera' -- See 'Zabeth'

Zach™ -- See 'Riczach'

'Zacharley Rose' HT, pb, 1998, Poole, Lionel; flowers pink, shaded peach at base, 4½ in., very dbl., high-centered, borne mostly singly; foliage medium size, medium green, semi-glossy; few prickles; long stems; very floriferous, upright, tall (4½ ft.) growth; ['Hazel Rose' × 'Loving Memory']; intr. 1998

'Zachary' MinFl, op, 2008, Fletcher, Ira; flowers 3¼ in., dbl., borne mostly solitary; foliage medium, medium green, semi-glossy; prickles ½ in., slightly curved, red, moderate; growth compact, short; garden decoration; ['Pauline' × Seattle Scentsation™]; intr. 2008

'Zagreb' -- See 'Rogzag'

'Zahov Hatabor' F, yb, Fischel

'Zaïd' S, rb, 1937, Chambard, C.; bud bright yellow and copper-red; flowers coppery flame-red, semi-dbl.; non-recurrent; foliage glossy, bright green; vigorous growth; [R. foetida bicolor × (R. wichurana × unknown)]

'Zaida' HT, op, 1922, Lippiatt; flowers pale coral-pink, large, dbl.

'Zaiga' HRg, dp, Rieksta, Dr. Dz.; flowers bright pink to rose pink, fading after opening, large, semi-double to double, shallow cup to flat, slight fragrance; recurrent; foliage disease-resistant; bushy (4 ft.), arching growth; winter hardy; originated in Latvia; intr. 1967

'Zaïre' M, dp, 1849, Vibert; flowers 3 in., full, shallow cup to flat; non-remontant; growth to 4 ft.

Zambra, Climbing® -- See 'Meialfisar'

Zambra® F, ob, 1961, Meilland, Mrs. Marie-Louise; bud ovoid, pointed; flowers vermilion orange, reverse dark, 2½-3 in., 10-15 petals, high-centered early, then flat, borne in clusters, slight sweetbriar fragrance; recurrent; foliage leathery, glossy, light green; prickles several, reddish-brown; vigorous, well-branched, low to medium growth; hips globular, reddish; PP2140; [('Goldilocks' × 'Fashion') × ('Goldilocks' × 'Fashion')]; intr. 1961

'Zambra '80' -- See 'Meirilocra'

'Zambra 93' ('Magic Fire') F, op, Meilland, Alain A.; flowers coral pink, medium, dbl., high-centered; free-flowering; foliage dark green, semi-glossy; low (70 cm) growth; intr. 1993

'Zandrina' HT, Zandri, R.; intr. 1977

'Zani' S, mr, 1927, Hansen, N.E.; flowers dark crimson, with a white streak through center petals, semi-dbl.; non-recurrent; growth to 6-8 ft.; very hardy; [(R. rugosa × 'Anna de Diesbach') × 'Tetonkaha']

'Zansho' HT, rb, 1978, Takahashi, Takeshi; bud ovoid; flowers scarlet and yellow,, 6 in., 45 petals, high-centered; foliage dark, leathery; upright, bushy growth; ['Garden Party' × 'Christian Dior']; intr. 1975

'Zanta Hofmeyer' HT, pb, Laver; flowers porcelain pink, deeper pink in center, dbl., high-centered, borne mostly singly; recurrent; foliage dark green; medium growth; intr. 2003

'Zanzibar' F, mr, 1964, Leenders, J.; flowers bright red; ['Paradis' × 'Circus']

'Zara Hore-Ruthven' HT, mp, 1932, Clark, A.; flowers rich pink, large, dbl., cupped, slight fragrance; foliage medium green; ['Mme Abel Chatenay' × 'Scorcher']

Zaria™ HT, w, Meilland; flowers clear white, full, cupped, borne mostly singly; recurrent; foliage medium green, matte; florist rose; intr. 2004

'Zärtlichkeit' S, lp, Wänninger, Franz; flowers small, single; intr. 1992

'Zaryellow' HT, my, Zary, Dr. Keith; PP15955

'Zauberlehrling' F, op, 1963, Kordes, R.; flowers light salmon, well-formed, large, dbl.; strong stems; bushy, low growth

Zayed of Abu Dhabi® S, mr, Guillot-Massad; flowers bright red, full, cupped, borne in clusters, slight fragrance; recurrent; foliage dark green, glossy; 1 meter growth; intr. 2007

'Zborov' Pol, dr, 1935, Böhm, J.; flowers blood-red, very dbl., borne in large clusters; foliage glossy, dark; vigorous growth; [sport of 'Corrie Koster']

'Zburlici' F, dp, Wagner, S.; flowers 15 petals, rosette, slight fragrance; foliage medium large, light green, glossy; [Bonica '82® × La Sevillana®]; intr. 1995

'Zebra' HT, rb, Benardella, Frank A.; bud small, ovoid; flowers red with white stripes, fading to medium pink with yellowish-white, 9-11 cm., 43-46 petals, high-centered, borne singly, moderate fragrance; recurrent; foliage medium size, dark green, semi-glossy; prickles few, medium, slightly curved downward; stems long; upright, compact growth; PP10148; ['Picasso' × seedling]; intr. 1995

'Zee' Cl Min, mp, 1940, Moore, Ralph S.; flowers pink, very small; recurrent bloom; foliage very small; nearly thornless; growth to 30 in.; ['Carolyn Dean' × 'Tom Thumb']

'Zeiber House Red' -- See 'Laurent Carle'

'Zelda Lloyd' -- See 'Tinzel'

'Zélia Pradel' ('Zilia Pradel') T, w, 1861, Pradel; flowers pure white, center yellow, large, full, moderate fragrance; sometimes classed as N

'Zell' -- See 'Tuckzell'

'Zen' HT, w, 2004, Ohtsuki, Hironaka; flowers pure white, 15 cm., full, borne mostly solitary, intense fragrance; foliage large, dark green, semi-glossy; prickles moderate, medium, downward; growth upright, tall (120-180 cm.); cutting, exhibition; [Honor™ × 'Hoshizakuyo']; intr. 2004

'Zena' HT, dr, 1985, Plumpton, E.; flowers dark crimson, large, 25 petals, borne singly or several together; foliage medium size, medium green, semi-glossy; upright growth; [seedling × 'New Style']; intr. 1986

'Zena' -- See 'Lioblush'

'Zénaïre' HGal, m, before 1828, Dubourg; flowers speckled white

'Zenaitta' Pol, rb, 1991, Jerabek, Paul E.; bud ovoid; flowers bright medium red with small white area at petal base, small, dbl., cupped, borne in sprays of 3-65, no fragrance; foliage small, medium green, glossy; bushy, medium growth; [seedling × seedling]

'Zenith' -- See 'Uetersen'

'Zenith' -- See 'Delzen'

'Zenobia' M, mp, 1892, Paul, W.; bud well mossed; flowers satiny pink, 4 in., full, cupped, moderate Damask fragrance; non-remontant; foliage large; vigorous, tall,, slender growth

'Zénobie' A, lp, before 1844, Vibert; flowers pale rose, medium, full

'Zephelene' Min, w; flowers white, petal edges turning bright coral as they open, relatively large, double, cupped; recurrent; strong, rounded, medium growth; intr. 1994

'Zéphirine Drouhin' ('Belle Dijonnaise', 'Ingegnoli Prediletta', 'Mme Gustave Bonnet') B, mp, 1868, Bizot; bud long, pointed; flowers cerise pink, base white, 3 in., 25-30 petals, borne mostly singly, moderate damask fragrance; recurrent bloom; foliage soft, light; vigorous, semi-climbing growth

'Zephyr' F, yb, Verschuren; flowers yellow tipped pink, 2½-3 in., 64 petals, borne in clusters; foliage glossy, light; very vigorous growth; ['Goldilocks' × seedling]; intr. 1961

'Zephyr' T, yb, 1895, Paul, W.; flowers sulphur yellow with white reflections, large, full, cupped

'Zest For Life' -- See 'Worantler'

'Zesty' Min, ab, Benardella, Frank; flowers deep apricot with golden yellow blendings; medium growth

'Zeus' HSet, my, 1959, Kern, J. J.; bud long, pointed; flowers 4-6 cm., 25 petals, loose, slight fragrance; recurrent; foliage leathery, dark; vigorous (15-20 ft.) growth; ['Doubloons' × unknown]

'Zhang Zuo Shuang' ('China Sunrise') HT, ab, 2001, Newman, Laurie; flowers light apricot, darker reverse, 8 cm., 25-30 petals, borne mostly solitary, intense fragrance; foliage medium size, dark green, glossy; prickles moderate, medium, slightly curved; upright, medium (1½ m.) growth; ['Parador' × 'Jocelyn']; intr. 2001

'Zi Yan Fei Wu' Ch, mp

'Zig-Zag' -- See 'Pixzig'

'Zigeunerbaron' F, dr, 1954, Baron, W.; flowers large, dbl.

'Zigeunerblut' ('Gipsy Blood') Bslt, dr, 1889, Geschwind, R.; flowers purplered, large, full, cupped, moderate fragrance; [R. pendulina × a Bourbon]

'Zigeunerknabe' ('Gipsy Boy', 'Gypsy Boy') B, dr, 1909, Geschwind; flowers dark crimson-red shaded violet-purple, medium, moderate fragrance; non-recurrent; vigorous, angular (3-5 ft.) growth

'Ziggy Stardust' -- See 'Renzig'

'Zigri' LCl, m

'Zika' S, lp, 1927, Hansen, N.E.; flowers shell-pink, semi-dbl.; non-recurrent bloom; very hardy; [(R. rugosa × 'Anna de Diesbach') × 'Tetonkaha']

'Zilda Villaboin' Pol, 1910, Amaury Fonseca

'Zilia Pradel' -- See 'Zélia Pradel'

'Zingaro' F, mr, 1964, Sanday, John; flowers bright crimson, 2 in., 12 petals, borne in clusters; foliage dark; compact, low growth; ['Masquerade' × ('Independence' × unknown)]

'Zinger' Min, mr, 1978, Schwartz, Ernest W.; bud long, pointed; flowers crimson, shaded scarlet, yellow stamens, 1½ in., 11 petals, flat, moderate fragrance; recurrent; very vigorous, spreading growth; PP4293; ['Zorina' × Magic Carrousel®]

'Zipalm' ('Almond Glory') Min, ab, 1991, Zipper, Herbert; flowers deep apricot, small, full, high, borne in small clusters, moderate fragrance; foliage small, dark green, glossy; few prickles; medium (30 cm.), compact growth; ['Rise 'n' Shine' × High Spirits™]; intr. 1992

'Zipamb' ('Amber Ribbon') Min, ab, 1987, Zipper, Herbert; bud pointed; flowers deep apricot to deep yellow at base, aging butterscotch, 1½-2 in., 22 petals, high-centered, borne singly or in sprays of 2 - 5, slight fragrance; foliage medium size, dark green, semi-glossy; upright, tall growth; ['Rise 'n' Shine' × 'Pot 'o Gold']; intr. 1987

'Zipban' ('Banana Split') Min, yb, 1987, Zipper, Herbert; flowers creamy yellow blushed with pink, medium, dbl.; foliage medium size, medium green, semi-glossy; upright, bushy growth; ['Little Darling' × 'Poker Chip']

'Zipbell' ('Bellissima') MinFl, or, 1989, Zipper, Herbert; flowers orange-red, darker along edges, medium, dbl., high-centered, borne singly, no fragrance; foliage medium size, medium green, semi-glossy; upright growth; ['Pink Petticoat' × Lady Rose®]; intr. 1989

'Zipberry' ('Raspberry Ice') MinFl, rb, 1989, Zipper, Herbert; flowers white brushed with red, deeper red at petal edge, medium, 40 petals, no fragrance; foliage medium size, dark green, semi-glossy; mini-flora; upright growth; [High Spirits™ × 'Charmglo']; intr. 1989

'Zipboy' ('Tomboy') Min, mp, 1989, Zipper, Herbert; flowers small, 5 petals, no fragrance; foliage small, dark green, semi-glossy; upright, spreading growth; ['Maytime' × 'Poker Chip']; intr. 1989

'Zipbub' ('Bubbles') Min, yb, 1986, Zipper, H.; flowers medium yellow, shaded pink and coral, 35 petals, borne singly and in small clusters; foliage medium size, medium green, semi-glossy; upright, spreading growth; [('Little Darling' × ('Roundabout' × 'Redgold')) × 'Maytime' × 'Poker Chip')]

'Zipcan' ('Candice') Min, pb, 1987, Zipper, Herbert; flowers medium, dbl.; foliage medium size, medium green, semi-glossy; upright growth; ['Libby' × Queen Elizabeth®]

'Zipcha' ('Scott Chait') MinFl, ob, 2003, Zipper, Herbert; flowers orange, reverse cream, 1-1½ in., full, borne mostly solitary, slight fragrance; foliage medium size, medium green, matte; prickles few, 4 mm., hooked; growth bushy, medium (24-36 in.), very vigorous; exhibition, garden, cutting; ['Tiki' × 'Percussion']; intr. 2003

'Zipcloud' ('Summer Cloud') Min, w, 1990, Zipper, Herbert; bud ovoid; flowers white with hint of pink, large, 65 petals, high-centered, urn-shaped, borne singly and in sprays of 3-4; foliage medium size, medium green, semi-glossy; prickles straight, small, few, light brown; bushy, medium growth; hips globular, medium, brown-orange; ['Roundabout' × 'Erfurt']; intr. 1990

'Zipcool' ('Cool Wave') Min, w, 1987, Zipper, Herbert; flowers white with hints of yellow at petal base, medium, dbl., high-centered; foliage medium size, medium green, matte; ['Poker Chip' × 'Pink Parfait']

'Zipcork' ('Corky') F, rb, 1991, Zipper, Herbert; flowers white with red edges, white reverse, 3-3½ in., full, borne in small clusters, slight fragrance; foliage large, dark green, semi-glossy; few prickles; medium (100 cm.), bushy growth; ['Tamango' × seedling]; intr. 1992

'Zipcuss' ('Percussion') F, rb, 1990, Zipper, Herbert; bud ovoid; flowers dark red with touch of yellow at base, reverse white at base, 25 petals, high-centered, moderate sweet fragrance; foliage medium size, medium green, semi-glossy; prickles very small, tan; mini-flora; upright, tall growth; ['Sheri Anne' × 'Deep Purple']; intr. 1990

'Zipdew' ('Dew Drop') Min, rb, 1991, Zipper, Herbert; flowers red with white eye, medium, single, borne mostly singly, slight fragrance; foliage small, dark green, semi-glossy, very disease-resistant; few prickles; low (12 in.), compact growth; ['Sheri Anne' × Priscilla Burton®]; intr. 1992

'Zipeasy' ('Easy') Min, rb, 1992, Zipper, Herbert; flowers red and white, medium, very dbl., borne in small clusters, no fragrance; foliage small, dark green, glossy; few prickles; medium (35 cm.), bushy growth; ['Pink Petticoat' × 'Banana Split']

'Zipela' ('Elaina') Min, m, 1991, Zipper, Herbert; flowers medium, full, high-centered, borne in small clusters, moderate fragrance; foliage small, dark green, semi-glossy; few prickles; medium (35 cm.), bushy growth; [Blue Nile® × 'Big John']; intr. 1992

'Zipend' ('Endora') Min, pb, 1991, Zipper,

Herbert; flowers cream, edged deep pink, large, full, high-centered, borne mostly singly, slight fragrance; foliage small, medium green, semi-glossy; few prickles; medium (35 cm.), upright growth; [Pristine® × High Spirits™]; intr. 1992

'Zipest' ('Esther Jasik') MinFl, w, 1997, Zipper, Herbert; flowers large, 41 petals, borne mostly singly, slight fragrance; foliage medium size, dark green, dull; few prickles; upright, tall (3ft.) growth; [Shocking Blue® × 'Pink Petticoat']

'Zipfan' -- See 'Zipjul'

'Zipgold' ('Golden Coach') Min, dy, 1991, Zipper, Herbert; flowers medium, very full, no fragrance; borne mostly singly; foliage small, dark green, semi-glossy; few prickles; medium (40 cm.), upright, compact growth; ['Rise 'n' Shine' × 'Pot O'Gold']; intr. 1992

'Ziphigh' ('Highland Lass') Min, yb, 1991, Zipper, Herbert; flowers red and yellow with yellow reverse, medium, semi-dbl., borne in small clusters, no fragrance; foliage small, dark green, semi-glossy; few prickles; low (20 cm.), compact growth; ['Rise 'n' Shine' × High Spirits™]; intr. 1992

'Ziphill' ('Castle Hill') Min, dp, 1990, Zipper, Herbert; bud pointed; flowers deep pink with mauve undertones, shading lighter towards base, dbl., high-centered, no fragrance; foliage medium size, medium green, semi-glossy, highly mildew-resistant; prickles curved, small, tan; bushy, low growth; hips round, small, light orange; ['Sheri Anne' × 'Red Devil']; intr. 1990

'Zipjam' ('Jam Session') Min, op, 1986, Zipper, H.; flowers coral pink, yellow reverse, small, 20 petals, borne singly or in small clusters; foliage small, medium green, matte; upright growth; ['Poker Chip' × 'Anytime']

'Zipjeff' ('Jeff Chait') Min, rb, 2005, Zipper, Herbert; flowers velvety dark red, reverse silver, self-cleaning, 1-1½ in., very full, borne mostly solitary, no fragrance; foliage medium size, medium green, semi-glossy; prickles few, medium, downwards, green; growth bushy, medium (12-24 in.); garden decorative; ['Big John' × 'Charmglo']; intr. 2006

'Zipjul' ('Julie Lynne Zipper', 'Zipfan', 'Summer Fantasy') S, lp, 2003, Zipper, Herbert; flowers light pink, reverse dark pink, 2-2½ in., dbl., borne in small clusters, no fragrance; foliage small, dark green, semi-glossy, resistant to mildew; growth bushy, 3-4 ft.; ['Maytime' × 'Charmglo']; intr. 1999

'Ziplib' ('Liberty Miss') Min, pb, 1997, Zipper, Herbert; flowers medium, 8-14 petals, borne mostly singly; foliage medium size, medium green, semi-glossy; few prickles; bushy, medium (12-18 in.) growth; [seedling × Cupcake™]

'Ziplime' ('Limerick') MinFl, rb, 1991, Zipper, Herbert; flowers red with white reverse, medium, dbl., high-centered, borne in small clusters; foliage medium size, dark green, glossy; few prickles; medium (40 cm.), spreading growth; ['Tamango' × 'Jennifer']; intr. 1992

'Zipmia' ('Mama Mia') MinFl, mp, 1986, Zipper, H.; flowers mini-flora, dbl., high-centered, borne singly or in clusters of 3; foliage medium size, medium green, matte; growth upright, bushy; ['Sheri Anne' × 'Sparrieshoop']

'Zipmusic' ('Night Music') MinFl, mp, 1989, Zipper, Herbert; flowers deep pink, medium, dbl., borne singly and in sprays, intense fragrance; foliage large, medium green, semi-glossy; upright growth; ['Tamango' × 'Pink Petticoat']; intr. 1989

'Zipnic' ('Nicolina') Min, pb, 1991, Zipper, Herbert; bud ovoid; flowers coral pink shading to white, reverse pink edge, shading to creamy white, 1¼ in., 25 petals, cupped, borne usually singly, slight fragrance; foliage small, dark green, semi-glossy; upright, bushy, tall growth; [('Dandy Lyon' × 'Razzle Dazzle') × 'Pink Petticoat']; intr. 1992

'Zipnote' ('Love Note') MinFl, pb, 1990, Zipper, Herbert; flowers deep pink, light red going to cream at base, reverse deep pink, 35 petals, high-centered; foliage large, medium green, semi-glossy; prickles straight, small, light brown; bushy, tall growth; hips round, medium, orange; ['Tamango' × Cupcake™]; intr. 1991

'Zipoet' ('Poetry') Min, rb, 1991, Zipper, Herbert; bud pointed; flowers red with white at base, white reverse with some red at edges, medium, 30 petals, high-centered, borne usually singly, slight fragrance; foliage small, medium green, semi-glossy; bushy, low growth; ['Libby' × 'Deep Purple']; intr. 1991

'Zippink' ('Pink-a-ling') Min, w, 1989, Zipper, Herbert; flowers white edged deep pink, small, dbl., borne singly and in sprays; foliage medium size, dark green, glossy; upright growth; ['Tamango' × 'Avandel']; intr. 1989

'Zippro' ('Prom Night') MinFl, pb, 1987, Zipper, Herbert; flowers creamy yellow, shading to pink with deep pink flushing the edges, very dbl.; foliage large, medium green, matte; upright, bushy, candelabra-formed growth; ['Poker Chip' × 'Libby']

'Zipram' ('Ramapo') Min, mp, 1985, Zipper, Herbert; flowers small, 5 petals, borne singly; foliage small, medium green, matte; bushy growth; ['Maytime' × 'Libby']

'Ziproud' ('Roundabout') Min, mr, 1985, Zipper, Herbert; flowers small, 20 petals, borne mostly singly; foliage medium size, medium green, matte; bushy growth; ['Double Joy' × 'Libby']

'Zipson' ('Sonata', 'Songfest') Min, mp, 1987, Zipper, Herbert; flowers small, very dbl., high-centered, borne singly; foliage small, medium green, matte; bushy, compact growth; [Queen Elizabeth® × Baby Katie™]

'Ziptale' ('Tattletale') Min, mp, 1989, Zipper, Herbert; flowers deep pink, small, 33 petals, borne singly and in sprays, no fragrance; foliage small, dark green, semi-glossy; bushy, compact growth; [High Spirits™ × 'Charmglo']; intr. 1989

'Ziptease' ('Little Tease') Min, pb, 1989, Zipper, Herbert; flowers yellow to cream at base, suffused with clear pink, darker at edges, high-centered, no fragrance; foliage small, medium green, semi-glossy; bushy, compact growth; [High Spirits™ × 'Charmglo']; intr. 1989

'Ziptok' ('Tokay') F, ab, 1999, Zipper, Herbert; flowers apricot suffused with pink, reverse soft pink to apricot, 3 in., full, borne mostly singly, slight fragrance; foliage medium size, dark green, semi-glossy; prickles moderate; upright, tall (4-5 ft.) growth; ['Olympic Gold' × 'Spanish Sun']; intr. 1999

'Ziptown' ('Our Town') Min, mp, 1986, Zipper, H.; flowers small, semi-dbl., borne in small sprays; foliage small, medium green, semi-glossy; spreading growth; ['Maytime' × 'Sheri Anne']

'Zipvia' ('Bella Via') MinFl, w, 1991, Zipper, Herbert; flowers medium, full, high-centered, borne mostly singly, moderate fragrance; foliage medium size, dark green, matte; few prickles; medium (40 cm.), upright growth; ['Rise 'n' Shine' × 'Olympic Gold']; intr. 1992

'Zipvir' ('Irene Virag') F, rb, 1999, Zipper, Herbert; flowers red, white eye, reverse streaked red and white, 2-2½ in., single, borne in small clusters; small, medium green, semi-glossy, new foliage mahogany red; prickles moderate; bushy, tall (3-4 ft.) growth; [seedling × Playboy®]; intr. 1999

'Zipwen' ('Wendy') F, mp, 1991, Zipper, Herbert; flowers medium, dbl., exhibition, borne in small clusters, intense fragrance; foliage medium size, dark green, semi-glossy; few prickles; medium (75 cm.), upright growth; ['Wendy Cussons' × High Spirits™]; intr. 1992

'Zita' Pol, mr, 1965, Delforge; bud ovoid; flowers red shaded dark geranium, open, single; foliage dark, leathery; ['Amoureuse' × seedling]

'Zitkala' S, mr, 1942, Hansen, N.E.; flowers brilliant velvety red, 3 in., 25 petals, intense fragrance; non-recurrent; almost thornless; stems red; very hardy; [*R. blanda* × 'Amadis']

'Zitronenfalter' HSpn, ly, 1940, Berger, V.; flowers brimstone color; [(*R. spinosissima altaica* × Star of Persia) × 'Golden Ophelia']

Zitronenfalter® HMsk, my, Tantau, Math.; bud ovoid; flowers golden yellow, large, 20 petals, borne in clusters, moderate fruity fragrance; recurrent; foliage dark green, leathery; prickles few, curved;

upright, bushy growth; hips globular, slightly flattened on top; ['Marchenland' × 'Peace']; intr. 1956

Zitronenjette® -- See 'Korjoni'

'Zizi' F, dr, 1963, Delbard-Chabert; flowers garnet-red, medium, 15 petals, borne in clusters of 3-10, moderate fragrance; vigorous, bushy growth; ['Walko' × 'Souv. de J. Chabert']

'Zlata' F, dy, Vecera, L.

'Zlatá Praha' ('Das Goldene Prag') HT, my, 1931, Böhm, J.; flowers golden yellow; [sport of 'Kardinal Piffl']

'Zlaté Jubileum' HT, dy, 1938, Böhm, J.; flowers large, dbl.

'Zlaty Dech' HT, dy, 1936, Böhm, J.; flowers orange-yellow, large, semi-dbl.

'Zlecatherine' (Catherine Guelda™) S, m, 2006, Zlesak, David C.; flowers 2½ in., full, borne in small clusters; foliage medium size, medium green, matte; prickles moderate; growth upright, medium; ['Polyantha seedling' × 'Therese Bugnet']; intr. 2006

'Zlehanruby' (Hannah Ruby™) Min, rb, 2003, Zlesak, David C.; flowers dark red, reverse white blending to red edges, 1½ in., semi-dbl., borne in large clusters; foliage medium size, dark green, Semi-glossy; prickles moderate; growth spreading, medium; ['MORlavmag' × 'polyantha seedling']; intr. 2004

'Zlehoney' (Honeybee™) MinFl, ab, 2003, Zlesak, David C.; flowers very full, borne in small clusters, intense fragrance; foliage medium size, medium green, semi-glossy; prickles moderate; growth bushy, medium (28 in.); ['Rise 'N Shine' × 'induced tetraploid polyantha']; intr. 2004

'Zluta Zorina' HT, my, Strnad

'Zodiac' F, mr, 1961, Verschuren; flowers 2¼-3 in., 74 petals, camellia-like, borne in clusters; foliage leathery, light green; very vigorous growth; ['Red Favorite' × seedling]; intr. 1961

'Zodiac' F, pb, Kordes, R.; flowers begonia-pink, base yellow, dbl., borne in clusters of 25-30; low, bushy growth; ['Masquerade' × 'Karl Herbst']; intr. 1963

'Zoé' ('Moussue Partout', 'Zoé Barbet') M, lp, before 1829, Forest; sepals mossy, 3 foliaceous; flowers large, full, cupped, moderate fragrance; foliage ovoid, dentate at the tip; prickles numerous, long; all parts of plant are mossed

'Zoé' Ch, dp, Laffay; flowers dark pink to red, large, moderate violet fragrance; intr. about 1830

'Zoé' M, mp, Pradel; flowers large, full, moderate fragrance; intr. 1861

'Zoé' F, op, Spek; intr. 2005

'Zoé' HGal, mp, before 1826, Miellez; flowers bright pink at center, pale at edges, large, very dbl., moderate fragrance; extinct, according to La Rose de France, Joyaux, 1998, p. 303

'Zoé Barbet' -- See 'Zoé'

'Zoë Zorab' F, yb, Kordes; flowers blend of old gold and copper apricot, very full, cupped, borne in clusters, slight fragrance; recurrent; stems short; short growth; intr. 2001

'Zola' S, dy, 1979, Sanday, John; bud pointed; flowers golden yellow, 2½ in., 18 petals; foliage dark; vigorous, upright growth; ['Spek's Yellow' × 'Magenta']

'Zola Budd' -- See 'Korzola'

'Zoltan Kodaly' HT, my, Mark

'Zonnekeild' -- See 'Sonnychild'

'Zonnekind' HT, my, 1941, Leenders, M.; flowers buttercup-yellow, large, dbl.; ['Arch. Reventos' × 'Amalia Jung']

'Zonta Rose' -- See 'Hartanna'

'Zora' F, yb, 1985, Staikov, Prof. Dr. V.; flowers yellow, deep pink petal edges, aging deep pink, 18 petals, borne in clusters; foliage dark; vigorous growth; ['Masquerade' × 'Rumba']; intr. 1974

Zorba™ LCl, yb, Olesen; bud broad-based, pointed-ovoid; flowers yellow with orange reverse, 3½ cm., 25-30 petals, rosette, borne in large clusters, very slight fragrance; recurrent; foliage dark green, glossy; prickles moderate, 10 mm., deeply concave, dark reddish; vigorous, upright (5-7 ft.) growth; PP15771; [seedling × Aspen™]; intr. 2003

'Zorina' HT, my, Strnad

'Zorina' ('Rozorina') F, or, 1965, Boerner; bud ovoid; flowers 3 in., 25 petals, cupped, moderate fragrance; foliage glossy; vigorous, upright growth; PP2321; [('Pinocchio' × unknown) × 'Spartan']; intr. 1963

'Zorina, Climbing' Cl F, or

'Zorka' F, rb, Vecera, L.; flowers carmine-red with white,; intr. 1974

'Zublou' ('Louis Riel') S, w, 1996, Zubrowski, Stanley; flowers 5 petals; foliage medium size, purplish-green, dull; numerous prickles; bushy, tall growth; [R. rubrifolia × R. spinosissima altaica]

'Zuccariniana' -- See 'Kaiserin des Nordens'

'Zukunft' F, or, 1951, Verschuren; flowers scarlet-red; [sport of 'Lafayette']

'Zulu Queen' HT, dr, 1939, Kordes; bud long, pointed; flowers dark maroon, large, dbl., high-centered, moderate fragrance; recurrent; foliage leathery; short, bushy growth; PP363; [('Cathrine Kordes' × 'E.G. Hill') × 'Fritz Hoger']

'Zulu Queen, Climbing' Cl HT, dr, 1961, Moore

'Zulu Royal' -- See 'Dorient'

'Zulu Warrior' F, rb, 1980, Hawken, Una; flowers burgundy red, silver reverse, 9 petals, blooms borne 3-20 per cluster; foliage dark, tough; prickles large, reddish; medium growth; ['Arthur Bell' × 'Flaming Peace']

Zurella™ -- See 'Meivrofix'

'Zweibrücken' HKor, dr, 1958, Kordes; bud ovoid; flowers deep crimson, large, 5-6 cm., dbl., borne in large clusters, slight fragrance; recurrent; foliage dark green, leathery; very vigorous, climbing growth; [R. × kordesii × 'Independence']; intr. 1955

'Zwemania' Gr, or, 1976, Zwemstra; flowers light vermilion, 25-30 petals, high-centered, moderate fruity fragrance; foliage dark; very vigorous growth; PP4049; [sport of 'Sweet Promise']; intr. 1974

'Zwerg' -- See 'Rosa Zwerg'

'Zwerg-Rubin' Pol, mr, 1924, Schmidt, J.C.; flowers bright ruby-red, small, cupped, borne in clusters; dwarf growth; [('Rubin' × unknown) × 'Erna Teschendorff']

'Zwerg Teplitz' -- See 'Alsterufer'

'Zwergeliebe' Min, Delforge; intr. 1986

Zwergenfee® ('Dwarf Fairy') Min, or, 1979, Kordes, W.; bud globular; flowers 2 in., 29 petals, cupped, moderate fragrance; free-flowering; foliage small, glossy; dwarf, vigorous, upright growth; ['miniature seedling' × 'Traumerei']

'Zwergkönig' ('Dwarf King', 'Dwarfking') Min, mr, 1956, Kordes; flowers carmine, small, 25 petals, cupped, borne singly and in clusters, slight fragrance; foliage glossy; compact (8-10 in.) growth; PP1577; ['World's Fair' × 'Tom Thumb']

Zwergkönig 78® -- See 'Korkönig'

'Zwergkönigin' -- See 'Queen of the Dwarfs'

'Zwergkönigin '82' -- See 'Korwerk'